BOWHUNTING
Big Game Records of North America

Seventh Edition
2011

Pope & Young Club
BOWHUNTING
Big Game Records of North America

Seventh Edition
2011

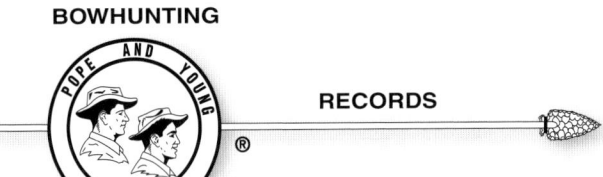

Book Editorial Committee

T. J. Conrads, Editor

Roger Atwood
Glenn Hisey
Mark Steffen
Kevin Hisey
Craig Oberle
M. R. James
Andy Carpenter
John D. "Jack" Frost
Doug Clayton
Tom Nelson
Mike Kistler
Ron Rockwell
Mike Schlegel

Jacket Design and Book Design by Steve Ashley

Copyright© 1975, 1981, 1987, 1993, 1999, 2005, 2011 by the Pope and Young Club. All rights reserved, including the right to reproduce the book or portions thereof in any form or by any means, electronic or mechanical, including photocopying, recording or by any information storage and retrieval system, without permission in writing from the Pope and Young Club.

Library of Congress Control Number: 2011922396
ISBN Number: 9780961796679
Published in April, 2011

All photographs by the authors and hunters except as noted.

Produced and Published in the United States of America by:
The Pope and Young Club
273 Mill Creek Road
PO Box 548
Chatfield, MN 55923

Dedication

This 50th Anniversary Pope and Young Record Book is dedicated to the memory of our founder, Mr. Glenn St. Charles. It is because of Glenn's vision that our Club has reached such a pinnacle in its history, and stands as the testimonial to ethical bowhunting of the finest species of game in North America. But the taking of such magnificent specimens is secondary to why we bowhunt. In Glenn's own words we find our code of ethics for this love we have in pursuing big game with the bow and arrow:

"I'd just like to remind everybody that it's about the hunting, not just the killing. In other words, it's about the total experience, the sport itself and the challenge involved. Bowhunting, done right, is a justifiable and honorable pursuit. Done for the wrong reasons, simply chalking ups kills and seeking personal glory, it's taking away rather than giving back to a principled way of life that has to be experienced to be understood."

Let us not forget Glenn's vision … let us proceed with honor, grace, humility, and this same ethical vision for the next 50 years.

Foreword

In your hands you hold history. This is not just a book of records of the finest North American big game animals taken with the bow and arrow, but also the cumulative contributions of bowhunters who have made this organization, the Pope and Young Club, one of the most esteemed bowhunting and conservation organizations in history.

Half a century ago the late Glenn St. Charles, along with a handful of trusted and determined bowhunters, founded the Pope and Young Club on January 27, 1961. From its humble beginnings in Glenn's modest home in a Seattle suburb the Club has grown to over 7,000 members. Within this book you hold, the Seventh Edition of the Pope & Young Club Bowhunting Big Game Records of North America, over 88,139 records of the biggest and most magnificent big game animals on this continent have been recorded. Sadly, Glenn could not be here to see this milestone of his dream; fifty years is, indeed, a grand achievement for any organization to obtain. But it is with much pride, honor, and respect that we can see the results of his dreams, ideals, and hunting ethics within these pages.

There comes a time in any organization's life where it must stop and look back, see where it has come from, take stock in its place in history, and look toward the future. With this in mind, the editorial content and direction of this book has been based on a theme of "Yesterday, Today, and Tomorrow: A Look at the History of the Pope and Young Club." One way to do this is go back and record the foundations of our organization. In this tome you will learn how the Club came into being, the history of our namesakes Saxton Pope and Art Young, how the recording system has evolved, history of our Conservation Program and Youth Programs, and a special section of testimonials from Club members — from 35 years of age to over 80, both men and women — who relate how the Pope and Young Club has shaped their bowhunting ethics, altered their beliefs in themselves and their abilities, created and melded friendships for a lifetime, and possibly shaped their entire life. Lastly, our president, Roger Atwood, leaves us with a challenge to not only remember our past and where we came from, but also to look to the future and where it will lead us.

Each and every line within these pages holds more than just a hunter and a score; they hold hundreds of stories afield of friendship and loneliness, success and defeat, sunny days and cold, damp nights, triumph and abject failure, personal sacrifice ... there is realness here. These things may not seem obvious to the casual observer, but there is far more here than simply dead animals and a bowhunter's name. The smell of wood smoke, the soft patter of rain upon a tent, the smell of bacon and eggs cooking over an open fire, the twang of a bowstring, the vision of the arrow in flight ... it's all here within the covers of this book, and if you really look close, you will find it.

T.J. Conrads
Mayfield, Idaho
January 7, 2011

Acknowledgments

The Pope and Young Club has achieved an historic milestone with this, the Seventh Edition of the Pope & Young Club Bowhunting Big Game Records of North America. Since its inception 50 years ago, the Club's membership has risen to more than 7,000, and entries have climbed from around 2,300 in the 1975 edition, to an astounding 88,139 with this edition. With each new book the Club publishes, the editorial content also increases to compliment the quantity, and quality, of the entries.

To create such a monumental undertaking as this book requires an immense amount of work, not the least of which is the editorial direction. Editor T.J. Conrads set the direction with the approval and assistance of the Editorial Committee consisting of Board Members Roger Atwood, Andy Carpenter, Doug Clayton, John D. "Jack" Frost, Glenn Hisey, M.R. James, Mike Kistler, Tom Nelson, Craig Oberle, Ron Rockwell, Mike Schlegel, and Mark Steffen.

Singular recognition goes to Executive Secretary Kevin Hisey for his behind-the-scenes coordination of all book production efforts. Not only did he maintain an open line of communications between Club headquarters, Board members, and the Editor, he also worked directly in securing printing production, paper and various book materials, researched and acquired many of the historical images published within the following pages, provided complete, correct, and up-to-date records for each species ... all the while effectively managing the day-to-day business of the Pope and Young Headquarters in Chatfield, Minnesota. His tireless efforts are reflected throughout this book.

Special thanks goes to members who have contributed to the editorial content of this book. Joe St. Charles, T.J. Conrads, Stan Rauch, Mike Schlegel, Glenn Hisey, Dirk Dieterich, Harv Ebers, and Roger Atwood provided the bulk of historical editorial content. Additional thanks goes to Nathan L. Andersohn, Connie Renfro, Jim Dougherty, Kathy Strecker, Scott Showalter, Stacee Frost, Tom Foss, Rit Heller, Pam M. Baird, M.R. James, Jack Frost, Marv Clyncke, Cindi Richardson, Charles Young, Andy Carpenter, Frank Noska, and Mike Schlegel for their contributions and testimonials on their relationship with the Pope and Young Club.

A special thanks is due the Pope and Young Club staff of Karla Hamersma and Julie Cordes, whose professional abilities allowed Kevin and Glenn Hisey the ability to maintain deadlines for book production. They are the true unsung heroes of our Club's home office.

Sincere thanks go to Steve Ashley for his many years of contributions to the Club as newsletter editor, but also for his dedicated and professional work on this, as well as several other, Pope and Young book productions. He is an invaluable asset to the Club, and the quality of the design and layout of this tome is a testament to his unique abilities.

Finally, a special thanks goes to the Boone and Crockett Club for allowing the Pope and Young Club to adapt, print, and use its scoring system and its record scoring forms for the last 50 years.

Table of Contents

Book One

The First 50 Years

- 14   The Beginnings of the Pope and Young Club — *By Joe St. Charles*
- 24   The Inspiration — *By T.J. Conrads*
- 32   Mentoring The Young Ones — *By Stan Rauch*
- 38   History and Overview of the Pope and Young Club Conservation Program — *By Mike Schlegel*
- 48   Evolution of the Pope & Young Club's Scoring System — *By Glenn Hisey*
- 60   Dreams Fulfilled — *As Told to Dirk Dieterich by Harv Ebers*

Personal Reflections

- 73   My Pope and Young Club Friends — *By Nathan L. Andersohn*
- 75   Why I Value the Pope and Young Club — *By Connie Renfro*
- 77   Looking Back — *By Jim Dougherty*
- 79   An Awesome Ride — *By Kathy Strecker*
- 81   My Fifteen Minutes — *By Scott Showalter*
- 83   What the Pope & Young Club has Meant to Me — *By Stacee Frost*
- 85   A Conversation with my Sons — *By Tom Foss*
- 87   We Were Not Disappointed — *By Rit Heller*
- 89   Friends and Experiences of a Lifetime — *By Pam M. Baird*
- 91   Last Minute Luck … Long Term Success — *By M. R. James*
- 93   The Pope and Young Club — My Perspective — *By Jack Frost*
- 95   The Pope and Young Club Influence — *By Marv Clyncke*
- 97   A Change of Perspectives — *By Cindi Richardson*
- 99   Pope and Young Reflections — *Charles Arthur Young, Jr.*
- 101   The Pope and Young Club and Me — *By Andy Carpenter*
- 103   Mesmerized — *By Frank Noska*
- 105   The Club and I — *By Mike Schlegel*
- 107   The Pope and Young Club and G. Fred Asbell

The Upshot

- 111   The Next 50 Years — *Roger Atwood*

Book Two

The Records

- 119 Notes and Explanations
- 120 Alaska Brown Bear
- 124 Black Bear
- 210 Grizzly Bear
- 214 Polar Bear
- 216 Bison
- 220 Barren Ground Caribou (including Velvet Entries)
- 228 Central Canada Caribou (including Velvet Entries)
- 234 Mountain Caribou (including Velvet Entries)
- 238 Quebec-Labrador Caribou (including Velvet Entries)
- 248 Woodland Caribou
- 252 Cougar (Mountain Lion)
- 274 Columbian Blacktail Deer (Typical including Velvet Entries)
- 286 Columbian Blacktail Deer (Non-Typical including Velvet Entries)
- 290 Sitka Blacktail Deer (including Velvet Entries)
- 296 Coues' Deer (Typical including Velvet Entries)
- 302 Coues' Deer (Non-Typical including Velvet Entries)
- 306 Mule Deer (Typical including Velvet Entries)
- 346 Mule Deer (Non-Typical including Velvet Entries)
- 354 Whitetail Deer (Typical including Velvet Entries)
- 634 Whitetail Deer (Non-Typical including Velvet Entries)
- 676 American Elk (Typical)
- 758 American Elk (Non-Typical)
- 764 Roosevelt's "Olympic" Elk
- 772 Tule Elk
- 776 Alaska-Yukon Moose (including Velvet Entries)
- 784 Canada Moose (including Velvet Entries)
- 794 Shiras' "Wyoming" Moose (including Velvet Entries)
- 800 Muskox
- 808 Pronghorn Antelope
- 874 Rocky Mountain Goat
- 884 Bighorn Sheep
- 890 Dall's Sheep
- 896 Desert Bighorn Sheep
- 900 Stone's Sheep

Appendix — CD only

Pope and Young Club Profile
Big Game Minimum Score Requirements
Official Scoring Charts of North American Big Game
Pope and Young Club History: Past and Present Club Officers
Past Award Recipients
Pope and Young Club Official Measurers

Book One

The First 50 Years

The Beginnings of the Pope and Young Club

By Joe St. Charles

The bow and arrow, a truly ancient weapon of mankind, was the world's most effective and efficient tool for hunting animals and waging war for thousands of years. With the advent of firearms, the use of the bow and arrow all but disappeared. With its decline as a survival and military tool, also went a lot of its respect. It would be a long uphill battle for the bow and arrow to gain new respect by sportsmen, as it was reborn into a tool of recreational bowhunting and game management.

As the use of the bow and arrow declined, it continued to be of interest to a few people, mainly as a target sport. By 1878, target archery became organized in the United States. During the 1870s and 1880s, Maurice Thompson wrote of his adventures while hunting with the bow and arrow with his brother Will in the southeastern United States. At that time, some gun hunters literally laughed at the idea of hunting with the bow and arrow, as documented from personal experience in some of Will's writings.

In 1911, when Ishi walked out of the California hills and into the care of Dr. Saxton Pope at the University of California at Berkley, a new chapter began in the interest of bowhunting. Ishi's abilities at hunting with the bow and arrow inspired Pope. Ishi's residence at the University drew many visitors and veteran bowhunter Will Compton came and learned of Pope's interest in Ishi and the bow and arrow. A short time later, Will brought Art Young to meet Ishi and Dr. Pope. This trio's adventures, recorded by the writings of Pope and Young as well as many newspaper reporters, inspired the growth of bowhunting in this country. Saxton Pope's book, Hunting with the Bow and Arrow, printed in 1923, became the bible of modern bowhunting. It provided the information needed to create effective bow equipment, and the philosophy behind hunting with the bow.

After the passing of Saxton Pope in 1926, Art Young continued to promote bowhunting by lecturing to dinner clubs, Boy Scout events, and even set up a booth at the Chicago World's Fair in 1934. He told of his adventures hunting with the bow, which included a slide show, and he demonstrated the effectiveness of his bows and arrows. His message was clean living, and the fair chase of bowhunting. His last effort was an article written for Sports Afield magazine printed in March of 1935, a month after his untimely death. The article, "Killing Power of the Feathered Shaft", discussed the difference between the effect of a rifle bullet and a broadhead arrow on big game animals, as well as his personal results of 16 years hunting with the bow. After Art Young's passing, a group led by Dr. Paul Klopsteg, C.J. Albrecht, and Leonard K. Osberg formed the Art Young Foundation in his honor. This organization created one of the first field archery rounds with unmarked distances.

The era of Compton, Pope, and Young faded, but they left behind well-documented adventures and experience that kindled the spark in others. From that time on, bowhunters everywhere struggled to gain recognition among the nation's fraternity of outdoorsmen to prove that their method was truly an efficient way of hunting. Progress was slow, though. Throughout the country many hunters, state conservation departments, and the general public had to be convinced bow and arrow hunting could be a good conservation practice as well as a factor in sound game management.

Many men played a major role in this struggle, some by their hunting exploits and others by their dedication and promotion. Individuals such as Roy Case, Aldo Leopold, and Carl Hulbert appeared on the scene in Wisconsin. In 1931, Wisconsin achieved the first major bowhunting breakthrough when the Wisconsin Game Commission revised their hunting laws to include the bow as a hunting weapon. In 1934, a bowhunting-only area was established thanks to the efforts of Case and his growing following of bowhunters. Much of this success spread to the neighboring states of Minnesota, Michigan, Indiana, and Illinois. Fred Bear and A.J. Michelson of Michigan were the driving forces in this Midwest effort.

Bowhunters everywhere became restless and were spurred on by these successes. In Washington State, the hunting archers looked to Kore Duryee for guidance. In 1935, John Cooter, Chet Stevenson, and Dr. George Cathey led bowhunters in Oregon in creating the first bowhunting area in that state. Dr. Cathey realized early on that bowhunter image was important. In the December 1935 issue of Ye Sylvan Archer he stated, *"The incentive, the objective, and the anticipation, as well as the outing, must be the archer's prime motive, rather than the kill."*

California bowhunters rallied around leaders John Yount and Earl Grubbs in the 1930s. By 1937 the Southern California Field Archers had organized. Hot shots Howard Hill and the Wilhelm brothers, Walt and Ken, participated at their field round events. These three were making headlines and archery history. Their remarkable feats with the longbow, which were on display in several shorts shown in movie theaters across the country, garnered considerable nationwide attention as well as interest in both field archery and bowhunting.

By 1939 the growth of bowhunting brought on the need for some other innovations, including practice for hunting. Local field archers had organized in some states, so a desire for a national organization grew. Rumblings within the National Archery Association (NAA) were heard. A splinter group wanted recognition for these field factions. The NAA had been under pressure for several years by this group. NAA Chairman Dr. Klopsteg and his successor, Henry Cummings, had tried to keep this new group under control and satisfy them with some various rounds. It was to no avail. Early in 1940, the NAA acknowledged the birth of the National Field Archery Association (NFAA) and four excellent NAA leaders and organizers went with it. They were William Folberth, A.J. Michelson, who eventually emerged as President, Paris B. Stockdale as Vice-President, and Karl Palmatier as Tournament Chairman. John Yount, the principal founder of the new movement, became Executive Secretary.

Waiting on the sidelines with support and much encouragement were such men as George Brommers, Kore Duryee, Fred Bear, W.B. Wescott, Forest Nagler, and many others, all eager to assist. The Field Archery Clubs of California, Oregon, Ohio, and Washington formed the nucleus of this fledgling organization.

Almost immediately there were troubles and misunderstandings between the two factions. One group was target oriented and concerned with tournaments. The hunting group maintained that since the NFAA was organized for hunters, practice rounds should be just that — practice for hunting with no standard distances or standard rounds. The tournament archers from the old NAA could not buy that philosophy. The wrangling went on for years and differences on how to shoot a bow still existed. It must be noted, however, that these factions did stay together and did try to work out their differences.

Also in 1940 the NFAA Art Young Big Game Award System came into being. This system was designed to embrace the aims and purposes of the Art Young Foundation formed earlier to perpetuate the name of the bowhunting pioneer.

About this same time, Glenn St. Charles, eventual Pope and Young Club founder, became involved in the NFAA cause. An ardent admirer of Kore Duryee of Seattle, St. Charles knew Duryee was keenly concerned with the NFAA and bowhunting in his home state. Soon the two men joined forces and, although neither knew it at the time, this association was to result in an event that was to determine the direction of bowhunting on a national scale. St. Charles recalls the occasion as follows: *"I accompanied Duryee to a two day Washington State Game Commission meeting in the spring of 1941. The Commission was in the process of setting the season dates and we had gone to present our proposals on behalf of the bowhunters. Washington had enjoyed three previous bowhunting seasons and we believed an annual archery season would continue. However, for no apparent reason the Commission suddenly decided to do away with this season. Of course, we were shocked and went away very disappointed. After talking it over, we decided to return the next day and try again. We were successful, but the humiliation of this second effort left me with a determination to commit myself to changing the bowhunter image."*

St. Charles soon became active with NFAA leaders at the national level. Working with Duryee, who had brought the Washington bowhunters into the NFAA fold, and A.T. Wallis, who became the NFAA Northwestern Representative in 1946, Glenn gained valuable experience. He also developed a deep understanding of the problems confronting bowhunters. This knowledge was to aid him considerably in facing the challenges to come.

In 1948 St. Charles was elected the NFAA Vice-President, serving under Dr. Arnold Haugen of Michigan. Haugen had been a Michigan Wildlife Researcher and was an avid bowhunter. This background enabled him to produce an excellent article entitled, "Bow and Arrow Hunting — Good Conservation." This material was used as a major aid in obtaining favorable bowhunting legislation. Haugen publicly delivered his article's message in St. Louis, Missouri, in an address to some one thousand game protectors and commissioners attending a Wildlife Conference. There was no question that these conservation officials left that meeting with more knowledgeable information about bowhunting than at any time in history.

At this point another influence on field archery and bowhunting must be noted. Roy Hoff of California, Editor of Archery Magazine, the written voice of the NFAA, played no small part in the advancement of bowhunting through his writings and promotional work. Hoff, along with William "Wild Bill" Childs and many others in their state's bowhunting fraternity, won a seesaw battle with a stubborn California legislature to bring bow and arrow hunting to that state. Public and governmental acceptance of bowhunting was growing.

Near the end of his term as Vice-President in 1950, St. Charles resigned to take over the position of Northwestern Representative of the NFAA so he could continue a more direct approach to the promotion of bowhunting. From 1950 through 1955, the NFAA had two more presidents, William Morrisey of Michigan and Jim Kinnee of Wisconsin. Kinnee made a real attempt to get the NFAA back to the basics of bowhunting with heavy tackle, and unmarked distances, but his efforts proved futile. Apparently, the light tackle, tournament-oriented field archers were too firmly entrenched.

Then, in 1956, Karl Palmatier became the NFAA President. Although he was truly tournament oriented, he saw the need to consolidate efforts of the states in their drive to gain recognition for bowhunters and to obtain archery seasons. He realized the NFAA must show that they were truly concerned with bowhunting and give bowhunters reason to belong. With this in mind, Palmatier established the Hunting Activities Committee with St. Charles as Chairman. The other active members were Paul Jeffries of Missouri, Nort Schensted of Minnesota, and Stuart Wilson, Jr. of New York. The leadership choice was a good one.

Past experiences had taught St. Charles that dealing with a far-flung national committee could be both time-consuming and difficult. Consequently, he took the initiative and organized a functional task force in Seattle comprised of Warren Berg, William Brown, Audrey Bryan, Wayne Hathaway, William Jardine, Dr. F. H. Kenagy, Jesse Rust, and Bill Soudan.

In the year that followed, questionnaires were developed by the St. Charles committee and sent to state associations, game departments, and other interested parties. By the returns it became apparent that bowhunters really needed to better their image. Despite the gains made by bowmen, the public and conservation departments needed additional proof that bowhunting was truly an efficient method of harvesting big game and that bowhunters were sincerely interested in the conservation policies that would ensure wildlife for future generations to enjoy.

Many answers from their questionnaires pointed to the need for a quality type club with which bowhunters could identify themselves. Thus, the Boone and Crockett Club idea came into focus. It was not a new idea, but one that had been kicked around as partial answer in the NFAA Price Buck Contest where one antler only is scored for winners.

St. Charles, a long time admirer of sportsman-conservationist Teddy Roosevelt, knew of the role played by the former President in founding the Boone and Crockett Club and the respected position that organization held in the eyes of the hunters. He reasoned if such an organization could work for one group, a similar one could work for bowhunters.

St. Charles and his inspired committee, along with the work of his personal secretary, Rosalyn Remick Malinoski, eagerly began to compile records of all bow and arrow animal trophies they could locate. Eventually rules were established, and a bowhunting program for trophy class animals was initiated. A percentage basis of Boone and Crockett minimums was used to establish the initial qualifying scores, the committee realizing full well that the minimums would have to be raised from time to time. As the true picture began to take shape, objectives and conditions were formulated that underscored the concern of the conservation of our nation's wildlife heritage.

At last, when the entire record keeping program appeared ready, it was presented to the NFAA Executive Committee for approval.

While waiting for an official okay, the Hunting Activities Committee upgraded the NFAA Art Young Award System to eliminate many lesser animals. This was an overt effort to change the image of participating bowmen to one of true big game hunters. Meanwhile, NFAA Secretary John Yount obtained permission from the Boone and Crockett Club to use their time-tested system in compiling a listing of bowhunting records.

Seven months after the record program was presented to the NFAA Executive Committee, approval was given. The new program was presented to bowhunters in the February issue of Archery in 1958. Response was immediate, positive, and gratifying. St. Charles sums it up with the comment,

"We knew we had a winner from the beginning."

In June of 1958, the first Awards Program was held in Grayling, Michigan in conjunction with the annual NFAA tournament. There were a total of 41 trophies in all categories. The top trophy of each species entered in this initial listing was recorded officially as a World Bowhunting Record for North American Big Game.

St. Charles and his committee members left Grayling fired up with a new enthusiasm, which was tempered only by the realization that certain refinements were necessary. Meanwhile, another NFAA election was held. Palmatier was re-elected and Glenn was elected Vice-President for a second time. He was asked to continue as head of the Hunting Activities Committee; however, at this point St. Charles decided that the workload needed to be separated. Much remained to be done in certain

NFAA bowhunting programs that would concern only the primary Hunting Activities Committee. At the same time the Seattle-based group, under Glenn's leadership, needed to concern itself with record keeping. The decision was made to form two distinct groups.

"The next two years were hectic," Glenn recalls. *"Measurers had to be trained and appointed in appropriate areas throughout the country. Up to this time we had been using very helpful Boone and Crockett measurers. The entries continued to pour in. Bowhunters everywhere seemed delighted to have something to relate to at last.*

"The conservation departments besieged us with requests for information concerning our records. Libraries were concerned about a future book that we might publish. It was difficult to keep up with the growing mountain of paperwork."

Early in 1960 preparations were made for another Awards Banquet in Grayling, again the site of the NFAA tournament. Tentative proposals were advanced so that the bowhunters who gathered there could discuss the possibility of a separate organization. By tourney time in late June, the 35 very interested bowhunters who attended the gathering in Michigan were in agreement. There was a need for a club similar to the Boone and Crockett Club, which would record North American big game animals harvested with a bow, a club dedicated to good conservation practices, quality hunting, and fair chase. It was determined that the club would be named after Dr. Saxton Pope and Arthur Young as a lasting tribute to these bowhunting pioneers. Recognizing the need for a good base, the group immediately sought to obtain the 1957-1960 records, which had been compiled by the NFAA Hunting Activities Committee. St. Charles, attending the NFAA Executive Committee meeting as Vice President, expressed the aims and desires of the Pope and Young group. After some debate, the NFAA reluctantly but graciously agreed to release these important records.

Six months and considerable correspondence later, the Pope and Young Club actually came into being on January 27th 1961. The first formal meeting of the Club was held in Seattle, which was to be the organization's headquarters for many years to come. Glenn St. Charles was elected Temporary Chairman, William Brown was elected Temporary Treasurer, and Rosalyn Remick Malinoski was appointed Temporary Recording Secretary. Glenn then appointed William Brown, Wayne Hathaway, William Jardine, G.H. Malinoski, and Jesse Rust as Temporary Directors.

Also established was a National Advisory Board designed to advise, approve, or disapprove action taken by the Club. Board members included Fred Bear, Michigan; Harvard Ebers, Missouri; Elisha Gray, Michigan; Martin Hanson, Wisconsin; Dr. Dean Henbest, New Mexico; K. K. Knickerbocker, Virginia; Robert Lee, Texas; Ben Pearson, Arkansas; Wayne Trimm, New York; and William Wright, California; and later, Rex Hancock, Arkansas.

It was determined that membership in the Club would be limited to 50 Regular Members. Regular Membership requirements were three big game animals, one of which qualified for the "book." Glenn, in a letter to the Advisory Board, comment-

ed on the strict requirements as follows: "*We must realize that perhaps our membership under this requirement will not fill up as fast and probably our objectives will not be reached as quickly, such as publishing a book. We can, however, begin work on a modest book and start small. I believe in the overall picture we will be glad that we maintained a high level for membership requirements. We aren't trying to fool anyone with the idea that we will hold the membership at 50. We all want to see it go to 100; however, it is important that we get this Club really off the ground before it gets too large. Keep in mind that what we are doing until June 1 will be only on a temporary basis. The Permanent By-Laws will not come into effect until we have 25 members or by June 1, whichever comes first. We will work on the Permanent By-Laws in the meantime and use the ideas of the Boone and Crockett Club By-Laws where possible or where they fit our purpose.*"

Four of the men in Seattle who helped organize the Club were qualified for Regular Membership. They included St. Charles, W.H. Peck, Wayne Hathaway, and William Brown. The others became Associate Members and were placed on a seniority list toward Regular Membership.

On January 21, 1962, the third meeting and Awards Banquet was held. There were 30 people in attendance at the Palmer House in Chicago, Illinois. Included in this group was Margaret Cooley of Illinois, the first woman to qualify for Regular Membership in the Club. Also worthy of note were two important changes that were proposed and accepted by the members. The first was a change of the competitions from an annual to biennial basis. The second change was raising minimum trophy requirements in six animal categories. At this time the total number of registered trophies in the records stood at 227. The Club had 25 Regular Members and 67 Associate Members. Also, there were 77 trained and registered measurers throughout the country.

In May of 1962, history was made with the first printing of the Club Records. It was a Pope and Young Records Pictorial, a 28.5″ by 22″ poster that included all records to the end of 1961. It was met with widespread success and several states made use of it in legislative programs for better understanding of bowhunting.

The Club's growth continued. By 1963 the number of Regular Members had climbed to 30, and the

Associate Members reached 80. The total number of trophies listed stood at 361. On June 5th, 1963, incorporation proceedings were completed in Seattle and the Club became an entirely independent entity.

On February 5th, 1964, some 75 Regular and Associate Members and their guests met at McCormick Place in Chicago for the third Pope and Young Club Awards Banquet. The Archery Institute donated booth space at the National Sporting Goods Association Show being held at the time and an impressive display of Pope and Young trophies was shown. A highlight of the meeting was the presentation of the first Ishi Award to Del Austin of Hastings, Nebraska, for his World Record Non-Typical Whitetail Deer. The number of registered trophies totaled 402 and by the end of the following competition period in 1965, nearly 700 trophy class animals were listed in the Pope and Young records. In June of the next year, the second Pictorial Records Poster was printed that contained the Records through to the end of the 1965 season.

In 1966, the Club's By-Laws were approved and adopted, making way for the first election of Pope and Young officers on November 20, 1967. To no one's surprise, Glenn St. Charles was elected at the Club's first President. His inspired leadership had carried the Club from its conception, through its formative years, and on into maturity. In August of 1975, after 14 years since its beginning, the Pope and Young Club printed its first Bowhunting Big Game Records of North America, a major milestone, and to this day, one of the Club's main purposes.

The Inspiration

By T.J. Conrads

It has been 50 years since Glenn St. Charles' vision of the Pope and Young Club came to fruition. Many hours of thought and time were spent in the formation of the Club, its recording system, and its goals. And when the time came to choose a name, Glenn and his able-bodied crew chose to use the namesakes of our forefathers: Saxton Pope and Arthur Young.

Like the Boone and Crockett Club, named after Daniel Boone and Davy Crockett, they sought to name the new organization after two influential bowhunters. They had to look no further than Saxton Pope and Art Young. Here were two individuals with whom the bowhunter could relate. But who were these two men, and how did they come to be such an inspiration to bowhunting in North America? To understand this, we need to look at the life of these two unique and adventurous bowmen.

Although Maurice Thompson ignited archers' interests in bowhunting through his classic work The Witchery of Archery, it wasn't until Saxton Pope published Hunting with the Bow & Arrow in 1923 that bowhunting started to gain widespread interest.

Saxton Temple Pope was born at Fort Stockton, Texas, September 4, 1875. His father, Benjamin Franklin Pope, was an army surgeon, a career that the younger Pope would follow later in life.

Saxton's elementary education was acquired haphazardly, as his early years were spent moving from one camp to another as his father's garrison constantly changed its duty station. His companions were a strange mix: Indians, half-breeds, cowboys, and others he met along the way. Because of his lifestyle, he developed an independent quality that would shape his entire life. He also loved to hunt, fish, swim, and shoot guns.

Even though he spent much of his youth constantly moving with his family, he eventually graduated in 1899 with honors, receiving a degree in medicine from the University of California. After his internship he moved to Watsonville, California south of San Francisco. There Dr. Pope established his practice and married another doctor, Emma Wightman. The Popes raised four children: Saxton Jr., Elizabeth, Virginia, and Willard Lee Pope.

Saxton spent about 12 years in Watsonville before he was offered a job as Instructor of Surgery at the Medical School of the University of California in 1912. Within a few years he was promoted to Assistant Professor, and then to Clinical Professor of Surgery. Even though Dr. Pope was active in the medical organization, and conducted intensive instruction for hospital units during the war, he still found time to publish over 32 scientific papers.

That same year he met Ishi, the last Yahi Indian, who was living next to the Medical School in the Museum. Ishi and Pope became close friends and Pope learned how to make and shoot Indian bows and arrows from Ishi, who called the doctor "Popey." In return, Pope saw to Ishi's needs, wheth-

er medical in nature or cultural. Many times Ishi had come to the Pope household for dinner and was always a man of good manners, never looking or speaking to Mrs. Pope, or any other woman, as that was considered rude in his culture.

Saxton Pope met William "Chief" Compton and Art Young in 1915. The three of them, along with Ishi, soon became good friends and spent their days making archery tackle, shooting at the range on the University grounds, and hunting both big and small game as far away as Humboldt County in northern California. In 1916, Ishi died from pulmonary tuberculosis, but the three remaining archers continued to pursue their love of bowhunting for many more years.

Describing his hunting with Ishi, Pope said, "Although Ishi took me on many deer hunts and we had several shots at deer, owing to the distance or the fall of the ground or obstructing trees, we registered nothing better than encouraging misses. He was undoubtedly hampered by the presence of a novice, and unduly hastened by the white man's lack of time. His early death prevented our ultimate achievement in this matter, so it was only after he had gone to the Happy Hunting Grounds that I, profited by his teachings, killed my first deer with a bow."

Saxton Pope and Art Young spent several years hunting northern California where they succeeded in taking deer, bear, cougar, and elk. Most notable was their trip into Yellowstone National Park. In the fall of 1919, after receiving a permit to enter Yellowstone in the attempt to secure several bears with their longbows for the California Academy of Sciences Museum, the two men started to organize their campaign for the following spring, with Ned Frost of Cody, Wyoming, as their guide. Frost was a man known to be the best grizzly hunter in America.

The following May, Pope, Young, and Frost, together with Pope's brother, G.D. Pope of Detroit, and Pope's friend, Judge Henry Hulbert, also of Detroit, entered the park on their quest for grizzly. The bowhunters had shipped their archery equipment ahead of time, which consisted of two bows apiece and " ... one hundred and forty-four broad-heads, the finest assembly of bows and arrows since the battle of Crecy." One of Young's

bows was 85 pounds, the other a proven veteran of many hunts, Old Grizzly, weighed in at 75 pounds. Both of Pope's bows were 75 pounds, one his favorite, Old Horrible, a bow that was sweet to shoot and hard hitting, as well as Bear Slayer, a fine-grained but crooked bow that was used to take the duo's first black bear in California.

Over the course of the spring the group looked for grizzlies, finding them scarce until the elk moved back into the park and began to calve. Their first encounter ended up with a ragged sow and a fine younger bear, although the latter too big for the museum's needs. As the days turned into weeks, the group began to dissipate as each member returned to work and civilization. In the end, Frost packed both Pope and Young to a new camp, stocked them with enough provisions for a few more weeks, and left to guide other hunters back in Wyoming.

For a over a week Pope and Young had been seeing a magnificent bear they called the Monarch of the Mountain, and finally decided to set an ambush in a perch of rocks above a trail the bear had been using. After several nights and close encounters, their opportunity came to fulfill the museum's request.

The two men headed to their blind about an hour before midnight, with the moon near full. A few hours later, a beautiful sow and three cubs made their way up the trail. When they were in range, Pope gave the signal and the two men loosed their shafts at the cubs, hitting one apiece. At the hits, the big sow roared and searched for the cause of the disturbance. She saw the two men and started to charge. At that very moment the big Monarch appeared; now there were five bears in front of the men.

Pope whispered to Young to shoot the big boar, while he sent an arrow deep into the sow as she charged. Pope's arrow turned the sow sideways where she roared, stumbled, and fell within sight. The old Monarch was growling and pacing back and forth not more than 65 yards away as Young sent three arrows his way, Pope getting off two arrows as well.

After the men had settled down, they began skinning the sow by flashlight. They recovered one of the cubs at daybreak. The other cub was not to be found. Retrieving their arrows, they found that one of Art's was missing. They followed the direction the boar had run and soon found blood. After an exhaustive search that took most of the day, they came upon the big bear where he had fallen and died. *"There lay the largest grizzly bear in Wyoming ... One great arrow had killed him,"* Pope later recounted.

Five years later the two men took the challenge of hunting Africa with the goal of securing the feared African lion by means of their primitive weapons. In February 1925 they set sail, arriving in Africa on April 6th. They spent the next four months traveling and hunting across what is now known as Kenya and Uganda, taking several specimens of African game including wildebeest, eland, waterbuck, kongoni, reedbuck, and Thompson's gazelle, as well as geese, rabbits, hyrax, and guinea hens, securing enough meat to feed the camp for the entire trip.

Pope and Young also shot several lions, but many had to be finished off with a gun at close quarters by a rifleman at the ready. This bothered the two bowhunters. *"No matter how many lions we shoot with the bow, somebody is always taking the joy out of the jungle by saying, 'Yes, but you couldn't do it*

without being backed up by the big boys with the guns!' " Pope wrote in The Adventurous Bowman. But this would soon change.

It was August 18th, 1925. Pope and Young had found an old boma, or blind, that had been built a year earlier by their professional hunter Leslie Simpson. A kongoni was shot and drug all over the country, finally being wired to a tree 15 yards in front of the boma. The first night the men stayed in camp while a lion had come and eaten part of the bait and left behind a large track. The following evening the two men sat in the blind, thinking of the absurdity of what they were doing, waiting for the lion to return. Pope later wrote, "*Sitting in a clump of thin, rotten thorns, waiting for a lion to come up and mess about you, is an emotional novelty act. You sit there, holding your breath, hoping that he does come, and fingering your arrow heads and bow string, wondering if you have done the right thing in leaving your nice warm bed and crawling into this miserable bunch of little sticks, so close to him.*"

The sun had set and a cool breeze blew as they lay back in the sweet jungle grass and waited. But the lion didn't wait long. A low grunt oozed in from the dark outside the boma, but the men could not hear any footsteps. The two bowhunters sat in the back of the boma, trying to arrest their heavy breathing, as the lion slowly made its way to the bait and finally, once it felt the situation safe, began licking and tearing at the kongoni. Art stole a glance from the blind, saw the lion lying broadside, and motioned Pope forward. They studied the beast, braced their bows, nocked arrows, and settled themselves to shoot. With a whispered count, they let their shafts fly.

"*There was a grunting roar and in one bound the lion stood before the aperture in our blind, his mane standing erect, glaring at us with green eyes like two X-ray tubes. He was so near I could have touched him with my bow. I saw the shadowed outline of a feathered shaft deep in his side,*" Pope later recounted. The lion took off into the night. They heard him stumble and fall, biting at the shaft protruding from his side. He gave a long, low moan, and then all was quiet.

The men stayed in the boma until daylight whereupon they found the lion, very much dead, facing toward them as if to defend himself. Young's arrow was buried to the feathers, through the chest above the heart. Death was quick. "*After being hit, he had not lived 15 seconds. One arrow had killed him ... There lay the finest maned lion in Africa killed with the bow and arrow. It was a wonderful sight!*" Pope wrote. The adventures of Saxton Pope and Art Young in Africa are well documented in Pope's book, The Adventurous Bowmen. The famed hunter and author Stewart Edward White also relates these stories from a different perspective in his book, Lions in the Path.

Unfortunately, the African safari was to be the last bowhunt Saxton Pope and Art Young would enjoy together. Soon after Pope returned to California he contracted pneumonia and passed away in 1926.

Arthur H. Young was born in Kelseyville, California, on August 17, 1883. His father, William Gaylord Young, was a Union Army veteran who had moved west in 1881 with his family. They settled in Kelseyville, in California's Lake County, and lived near Mt. Konocti, known as a home for Indian gods. William Young taught school in Kelseyville and owned the local general merchandise store as well.

Art had an older sister, Orrie, and three brothers: Willard, Charlie, and Roy. The kids all attended the local grade school in Kelseyville, and continued their high school education in San Francisco. After his father passed away, Art left San Francisco and returned to Kelseyville to run his father's business.

The country around Kelseyville held vast numbers of fish and game, and Art and his brothers spent considerable time hunting, fishing, and shooting, mastering the use of rifles and pistols. Art would later compete in both pistol and rifle matches for the Olympic Club in San Francisco.

During these young, formative years, Art was lessoned in the violin, of which he became expertly proficient at playing. This talent stayed with him, and when he and Saxton Pope would go hunting in the years to come Art would take his shortened violin, while Saxton packed his miniature guitar, and the two men would play and sing by the campfires in the evenings.

Art was an excellent athlete. His finely honed and handsome body allowed him to excel at any sport he undertook, and he became a tremendous swimmer. He played water polo and was a champion in the 220, 440 and 880 swimming events. It is reported he never lost an event during his swimming career.

Eventually, Art moved back to San Francisco after the family's business in Kelseyville had been stabilized. He was hired into the circulation department of the San Francisco Call newspaper where he worked 14 years.

While living in San Francisco, Art visited the Panama-Pacific Exposition in 1915. While viewing an exhibit of Japanese archery, he met a man who would later become his mentor, William "Chief" Compton. The two men became close friends and Compton taught Art how to shoot the bow and arrow. Chief Compton introduced Art to Ishi and Saxton Pope and the four men spent much time together building bows and hunting together for several years. The Chief taught Pope and Young how to make the English style longbow from Pa-

cific yew, the style of bow they used to take grizzly bear in Yellowstone National Park in Wyoming.

In the early 1920s, Art started making bows out of Osage orange, a bow wood he had picked up from E.F. Pope who lived in Woodville, Texas. Art liked Osage since it was much more durable than the yew he had been using for some years, a trait that proved handy since his hunting methods involved situations where his equipment received much abuse.

Between 1924 and 1925 Art and his friend, Jack Robertson, were financed to travel to Alaska to record on film that land's four seasons, especially the beauty of its summers, as well as birds, fish, small game, caribou, sheep, moose, and bear. More importantly, Art had planned to hunt several species of game while Jack was to be the cameraman for the journey. They spent almost two years traveling, filming, and bowhunting all across Alaska.

More than anything, Art wanted to prove to skeptics that the bow was a formidable weapon to be used on the great Kodiak bear. He and Jack eventu-

ally located the bear on Kodiak Island, where they were gorging themselves on salmon in the streams. Finding the situation unsportsmanlike, they resorted to simply filming the animals. One morning, Art spotted four bear making their way down to the river to feed. Finding the situation more to his liking of fair chase, he decided to attempt a shot in the open grass. Neither man carried a rifle or sidearm for protection while in Alaska; they relied on Art's longbow to keep trouble at bay.

Jack positioned himself on a tuft of high ground while Art made his way up a dry wash to cut off the bear. When he ran out of cover, he decided to attack the bruins head-on. Much later he related the event to Saxton Pope, " ... *I walked boldly out into the open to meet the bears. I practically invited them to charge since they were reputed to be so easily insulted. At first they paid little attention to me, then the two in advance sat up on their haunches in astonishment and curiosity. I approached to a distance of fifty yards, then the largest brownie began champing his jaws and growling; then he 'pinned back his ears' preparing to come at me. Just as he was about to lunge forward I shot him in the chest. The arrow went deep and stuck out a foot beyond his shoulder. He dropped on all fours and before he could make up his mind what hit him, I shot him again in the flank. This turned him and feeling himself badly wounded he wheeled about and ran. While this was going on an old female also stood in a menacing attitude, but as the wounded bear galloped past her, she came to the ground and ran diagonally from us. All of them*

followed suit, and as they swept out of the field of vision the wounded bear weakened and fell less than a hundred yards from the camera."

Many of these events were captured on film and made into a movie short called Alaskan Adventures. Besides the beautiful scenery of Alaska, this film shows Art shooting a Dall ram, Alaskan moose, and Kodiak bear, as well as several salmon with his bow.

For years, Art listened to skeptics who said the bow and arrow could not kill game. At first it was rabbits and squirrels, and then deer. As each of the animals fell to his and Saxton's bows, a new big game animal was named that surely could not be brought down with a bow. Soon moose, and then the great Kodiak bear, were added to the list. Eventually the topic of taking an African lion was brought up, so Art Young and Saxton Pope set their sights on the Dark Continent where Art Young became the first white man to kill an African lion with one arrow.

After returning from Africa, Art took an expedition to Greenland in 1926 with George P. Putnum on the ship Morrisey, piloted by Captain Bob Bartlett. On this expedition, Art harvested both a polar bear and a walrus, proving once again that the bow was a viable, efficient weapon for taking big and dangerous game. This trip was well documented in Putnum's book <u>David Goes to Greenland</u>.

In taking the walrus from a small skiff, Art had just placed the fourth arrow in the huge animal when it " ... *changed tactics and decided to become a boat-wrecker. I caught a quick glimpse of some blackish motion below me at the bow of our launch, and then the pop-eyed monster shot up out of the depths and snorted right in my face. Those white tusks looked mighty big.*

"*Savagely the walrus clinched the bow of our boat between his front flippers and with a decided snap of his head plunged those tusks through the side of our boat not very far from my shins. He quickly jerked his weapons out of the ragged holes and like a flash swung his head and tusks in a most dexterous manner to the right and crashed the two long ivories through the other side of our launch. I grabbed the lance and made a jab at the raging beast, but, as luck would have it, the cutting blade was on the other end of the handle! Not wishing to risk turning the lance around after having seen how fast the wrecker could work, I used all my strength to keep the weakening, fighting monster away from our craft."*

It has been said that Art Young was one of the finest gentlemen known. During his life he never smoked or drank, nor ever used a foul word. His ethics and morals were beyond reproach, his demeanor fit for a saint. He was an athlete and an archer of unsurpassed ability, and gave us a heritage to be proud of. He spent many years on the lecture circuit before being admitted to a hospital with a ruptured appendix. Arthur H. Young passed away from complications with peritonitis on February 26, 1935, at the young age of 51.

Saxton Pope was not only a pioneer in archery and bowhunting, he was also an excellent writer who left two exceptional volumes of his escapades with the bow and arrow, as well as several essays and a complete history of Ishi, the last truly wild American Indian. But without Art Young, Pope may have never tackled such feats at bowhunting grizzly bear and, eventually, African lions. Together, these two men set out to prove exactly what could be done with the bow and arrow, and how it could effectively and humanely take every big game animal in North America, as well as many species of African game.

In choosing Saxton Pope and Art Young as the namesakes for the Pope and Young Club, Glenn St. Charles launched a vision that has transcended the early opinions of bowhunters, and has stood the test of time. Today, the names of Pope and Young are synonymous with ethical, moral, and effective taking of big game with the bow and arrow. Pope's written accounts of bowhunting, and about the ethics of this endeavor we hold dear, can be summed up the following passage:

"Here is no common hunter, no insensate slayer of animals. Here we have the poet afoot, — the archaic adventurer in modern game fields; the champion of fair play and clean sport; all that is strong and manly. I take off my hat to Arthur Young."

Dr. Saxton Pope

Mentoring The Young Ones

By Stan Rauch

Throughout the existence of the Pope and Young Club there has been a strong desire to help youngsters become more familiar with the outdoor world and how it can become an intricate part of their lives. It was in the 1990s that the Club took the initiative to establish an organized program that would directly assist youngsters to become more aware of and take an active part in the outdoors and gain an appreciation for shooting the bow and arrow.

The endeavor became a reality by way of the Club's Discover The Outdoors Camp (DTOC), the first of which was held on July 4-6, 1996 near Jamestown, Colorado at the Calwood Environmental Center. Club members Judy Clyncke, Ken Kozar, and Gene Hopkins were the major players who brought the camp together and ran the programs. Judy and Ken were the coordinators and Gene was responsible for the curricula. Fred Asbell and Marv Clyncke were also vital keys to the success of that historic first camp as were Betty Gulman and Jay Verzuh. There were about 30 single-parent families that attended the inaugural camp and everyone loved it from the minute they arrived. It was apparent the Club had hit on something really big.

During the years the DTOC was held in Colorado many other Club member volunteers came to assist. There were also generous donations of money and equipment as well as take home items for the attendees.

You may ask: Why single-parent families at the camp? The life of a single-parent family is often tougher than we can imagine. Generally, it is the mother who is the head of the household. Time and money are often in short supply as the mother tries to work and keep the family functioning. There is not likely a stronger, more capable person in the world than the single-parent mother. However, there are barriers that can keep her and her children from finding and learning how to enjoy the wonders and benefits of the outdoor life.

For example, most single-parent mothers just don't have a background in hunting, fishing, or camping. Therefore, they have feelings of anxiety when faced with the possibility of taking the kids camping. What kind of problems will they face? Will there be any danger involved? Will they be comfortable or will this be a nightmare? That parent might also feel a lack of confidence that keeps her from taking a chance with this new activity.

Our challenge then, and now, is to help the parent break down these barriers and get the kids outdoors for some fun and excitement as well as education through participation. The Discover The Outdoors Camp program agenda was designed to teach the skills necessary to build the confidence levels of the youth and adult so that enjoying the outdoors would be a part of their lives in the future. The program agenda generally included activities such as team-building exercises, basic camping skills, orienteering, outdoor meals, safety and comfort in the outdoors, archery, fishing, wildlife identification, special presentations, and the medicine bag ceremony.

Archery was the activity the kids and parents enjoyed the most. Mothers, fathers, and kids were hitting balloons and aerial targets by the end of the camp. Most had never shot a bow and arrow before. They came away wanting to continue to shoot the bow in the future, own equipment, and know more about the sport.

It was always the intent that the Club's DTOC would serve as a model so other camps could be established around the country. Due to the success of the camp in the early years the wheels were put in motion to establish a guidebook so bowhunters and their organizations in individual states could establish their own Discover The Outdoors Camps. Prepared by Gene Hopkins and Fred Richter, a step-by-step DTOC coordinator's manual was published and it is available yet today from the Club's office.

Despite the Club's best efforts with the Discover The Outdoors Camp in Colorado the program was struggling, as it was difficult to get enough attendees to make it a worthwhile endeavor from an economic point of view. We certainly enjoyed putting it on but it was expensive and we were not getting enough "bang for our buck" as we hoped for. Basically, the various states and state organizations could send kids to camp in their own states for much, much less money. The Colorado high country was a great experience for the attendees, but it wasn't com-

peting well and the last DTOC conducted by the Club was in 2001.

Meanwhile, although participation by the states in the Discover The Outdoors Camp program was limited, Indiana and Montana instituted their own successful DTOCs. Gene Hopkins established the DTOC in Indiana and I had the pleasure of being the coordinator for the Montana Bowhunters Association establishing the camp in partnership with the Montana Department of Fish, Wildlife and Parks.

The Montana DTOC was held at the Fish, Wildlife and Parks' Beartooth Game Management Area near Holter Lake in central Montana. The attendees fished on the lake and received their own fishing gear to take home with them. There were evening boat tours through the Gates of the Mountains on the Missouri River where they saw mountain goats, bighorn sheep, mule deer, antelope, and bald eagles. They learned about camping — from backpacking to camping out of their car — and they discovered the wonders of Dutch oven cooking. They helped put up a tipi, made their own medicine bags, and placed mementos of the camp and some of their dreams of the future in them. They made new friends and there was an increased bonding between parent and child as a result of their participation together in the various outdoor activities. They were off and running with a new appreciation of how it was within their grasp to enjoy the great outdoors much more in the future.

The Club's current active involvement with introducing young persons to the outdoors, archery and bowhunting is the partnership with the Jack Creek Preserve Foundation (JCPF). The Jack Creek Preserve is a 5,000-acre ranch located east of Ennis, Montana, which is owned by Jon and Dottie Fossel. It consists of wild and scenic mountain country with diverse wildlife that has been set aside to conserve and protect wildlife and its habitat while also being developed into a Youth Education Center. The major focus of the Foundation's mission is to provide educational opportunities that give young people a deeper understanding and involvement with ecology and conservation, wildlife management, ethical hunting, hunter conservationists, and bowhunting. Since its inception in 2005, the Pope and Young Club has had a representative on the Jack Creek Preserve Foundation board of directors.

A major part of the JCPF's youth involvement centers on the annual youth camp, which has been an ongoing program since 2005. About 30 young people from throughout the United States come each year to learn a wide variety of outdoor skills. The number one favorite activity — no big surprise — is shooting the bow and arrow. In fact, it's often difficult to get them to stop when a particular session comes to the end of its scheduled time. The archery and bowhunting related portions of the camp continue to be conducted in large part by Pope and Young Club members.

The Club provided a $5,000 conservation grant to the JCPF in 2005 in direct support of its archery program, which were used to help construct a cabin on the archery range. The building is designed for hanging and/or working on bows, includes a storage area for archery equipment, plus it has a lounging area where archers can socialize. It serves as an excellent complement to the well laid out 3-D archery range that is available for use by the public by prior arrangement. Monetary support to the JCPF by the Club is provided on a continuing annual basis by way our Conservation Program, with the funds designated to support the youth camp by way of the promotion of the archery and bowhunting aspects of it.

The Jack Creek Preserve is rapidly developing into a Youth Conservation Center to be used for additional bowhunting, fishing, camping, hiking, educational field trips, cross country skiing, and other outdoor recreation, as well as year-round conservation activities.

"It's our sincere wish to ensure that there always will be an opportunity for America's youth to gain first-hand knowledge of wildlife conservation, habitat protection, ethical hunting, sustainable use of natural resources, and an understanding of how hunters, ranchers, loggers, and developers can work together to benefit people and wildlife," said Jon Fossel.

In addition to the annual youth camp and other youth oriented activities, the JCPF provides two scholarships annually for college students to study conservation or wildlife management. It also provides bowhunting opportunities by way of an annual free elk or bear hunt for a U.S veteran wounded and disabled as the result of serving in Iraq or Afghanistan. A dedicated bowhunter and Pope and Young Club member, JCPF co-chairman Jon Fossel has, since 2005, generously donated two elk bowhunts for our auctions and has also donated youth bear

hunts in support of the Club's conservation fundraising efforts.

In this day and age, kids seem to have high demands on their time due to being involved in so many activities. This situation often makes it even more difficult for them to branch out into an area that is previously unexplored, such as learning about and experiencing the outdoor world and how it can be an intricate, enriching part of their lives. This is especially the reality if they have no family member adult to introduce him or her to it. We can individually make a big difference with youngsters beyond our own immediate families if we just take the time to be mentors.

Simply introducing kids to archery is a good start and that activity can easily instill the desire in them to do much more in the outdoors. The National Archery in the Schools Program, which the Club has actively supported since its inception, is an outstanding example of how kids immensely enjoy shooting the bow and arrow and how it leads to bigger and better things on so many levels.

Invest some time to help a youngster become exposed to archery, hunting, fishing, camping and many other aspects of the great outdoors. You will be glad you did.

History and Overview of the Pope and Young Conservation Program

By Mike Schlegel

When the Pope and Young Club was conceived in 1961, its primary focus was demonstrating and documenting the bow and arrow as an efficient and effective hunting weapon to wildlife management agencies. As this goal gained fruition and the Club's reputation within the hunting community grew, Club leaders began to expand the goals of the Club. In 1975 the Board awarded its first conservation grant; $250 to a wildlife graduate student at the University of Idaho conducting a study to determine the effects of logging practices on elk habitat. Also, in 1975 the Club bestowed its first conservation award to William R. Wadsworth for "*his outstanding work in scouting and as a member of the Conservation Council of the State of New York.*" During fiscal year 2010, $117,500 was approved for conservation projects.

Initially, the President assigned the responsibility of soliciting projects and making recommendations to the Board to a Board member. Initially this duty was assigned to Dr. Lowell Eddy and Wayne Trimm.

In 1977 the Board, with membership approval officially created the Conservation Committee through an addition to the bylaws. Specifically Article II, Section 4 of the Bylaws reads: "*The objectives and purposes of the Club shall be to promote the welfare and conservation of North American big game and their habitats.*"

Glenn St Charles, in 1981, declared, "*We have reached our initial goal of proving the bow and arrow is effective in the harvesting of big game animals. Bowhunters are now respected; surely the Pope and Young Club's conservation program and its impressive record lists of trophy animals have been factors.*" He also stated "*As the balance of nature becomes increasingly fragile, there will be extreme environmental concern. We share in this concern and, wherever possible, provide help through our conservation program.*"

Conservation Committee Chairman Charlie Kroll, also in 1981, wrote: "*Many, however, are unaware of that our organization works behind the scenes, actively supporting various field research and game management programs with moral and financial support.*"

Conservation Committee Chairman and Committee Member Selection. The chairman of the conservation committee is a non-elected Board position. The President nominates the chairman. Appointment is contingent upon Board approval. The tenure of the chairman is tied to the President's term, two years. Upon appointment the chairman then selects a slate of committee members for Board approval. The committee members also serve a two-year tenure. There is no set number of committee members; it is left to the discretion of the chairman. During the past several years there have been 12 members, plus the chairman. Members of the conservation committee are selected to obtain a geographic representation, a representation from the various membership levels within the Club, an interest in conservation and from a volunteer pool. Two Board members and the President also have committee membership status. A list of Club Conservation Committee Chairmen is found

on accompaning CD in the *Past and Present Club Officers* section of its Appendix.

Conservation Grant Selection. Grant applications received by the Club are funneled to the chairman of the conservation committee. Prior to the annual Board meeting, usually in March, the chairman will send a copy of all applications to each committee member for their review and ranking of the proposals. The committee members rank each application on a scale of 0-5. The chairman then assimilates the rankings, prioritizes the applications based upon the cumulative ranking, assigns a monetary amount and submits a proposal to the Board during its annual April meeting. Following Board review and discussion, the Board then selects and approves funding to conservation grants for the upcoming fiscal year. The Board goal is to select a cross section of grants consisting of field projects (management and research), educational, youth oriented, professional associations, memberships, sponsorships, plus earmarking projects that benefit the Club directly, for example a conservation section in the museum and the Club's joint television program with the Boone and Crockett Club.

Conservation Funding. Funding for the conservation program is derived from several sources; record book sales, record book entries, commissioned wildlife prints, raffles, auctions, and donations. The vast majority of the monies are generated from the conservation raffle and the auction during the Club's biennial convention. However the backbone of the financial base for the conservation program can be attributed to the generosity of the donors and the memberships support through the purchase of raffle ticket and lively bidding during the auction.

Conservation Program Planning. In April of 1991 a Club member with a passion for conservation donated $10,000 to the Club specifically earmarked for the conservation program with a promise of another $10,000 in 1992. This member's goal was to elevate the Club's conservation program to a higher level. In order to fulfill this goal a plan was needed. In June 1991 the Conservation Committee met in Colorado and drafted a Conservation Plan for the Pope and Young Club. This plan would provide a basis for future conservation activities and donations for the Club. A conservation program mission statement was crafted during this meeting and revisited during a subsequent conservation program-planning meeting in 2001. The Club's conservation effort was greatly accelerated as a result of these meeting. The following is the Club's Conservation Mission Statement and the goals identified by which to achieve the mission:

Mission Statement: To protect the future of our bowhunting heritage and promote the conservation and welfare of habitat and wildlife.

Goal 1. To support educational and conservation activities that communicate the benefits of proper wildlife management.

Goal 2. To foster the collection and dissemination of information on the beneficial role of bowhunting in wildlife management.

Goal 3. To continue to create and enhance networks and partnership activities with individuals, agencies, and organizations leading to positive exposure for bowhunting and the Pope and Young Club.

Goal 4. To suggest methods of funding to support bowhunting, conservation, education and related activities.

Goal 5. To foster quality bowhunting and other outdoor experiences from recreational use and enjoyment of sustained, healthy wildlife populations.

Strategic Plan Goals and Objectives. In 2003 the Club began developing Strategic Goal Management Plans to address each of the goals developed for the Club's Mission Statement: *"To ensure bowhunting for future generations by preserving and promoting its heritage and values."* Specifically the goal for the Club's conservation activity is *"To have an effective conservation program."* The following is the Strategic Plan, Goals and Objectives developed for the Club's conservation program:

Strategic Goal for the Pope and Young Club Conservation Program Mission Statement: Promote the Conservation and Scientific Management of Wildlife and Their Habitats and To Sustain and Protect Our Bowhunting Heritage

Goal 1. To Support Education and Conservation Activities that Adhere to the Principles of Scientific Wildlife Management.

Objective A: To contribute funds, support and expertise to educational programs, wildlife management programs, conferences, and symposiums.

The Club will provide financial assistance, technical expertise, materials and supplies and physical support on an "as requested/approved" basis to educational programs, wildlife management programs, conferences and symposiums. Authorization for Club support is dependent upon Board review and approval and/or authorization by the Club Executive Secretary, President and Conservation Committee Chairman. To this end the Club will maintain an active and involved relationship with groups and organizations that promote scientific wildlife management and ethical, fair-chase hunting; e.g. the American Wildlife Conservation Partners (AWCP), the Wildlife Management Institute, the Association of Fish and Wildlife Agencies, U.S. Sportsmen's Alliance, the North American Bowhunting Coalition, the Interna-

tional Bowhunter Education Foundation, Congressional Sportsmen's Foundation, the Boone and Crockett Club, etc.

Objective B: To enhance the Clubs conservation award program.

Currently the Club has three conservation achievement awards:

The Pope and Young Club Conservation Award, established in 1993 to recognize achievement by a person or organization in the promotion of the future of bowhunting and hunting, and the conservation and wise use of our natural resources.

The Stewardship Award, established in 1995 to recognize a Bowhunter or bowhunting organization that, by their actions, has conveyed a positive, good-citizen image to the hunting and non-hunting public.

The Lee Gladfelter Memorial Award, created in 1995 to recognize a wildlife professional who, through their efforts, has made a significant contribution to bowhunting and wildlife conservation.

The Club will continue to promote these awards by soliciting nominees from its general membership, plus other wildlife conservation and wildlife management organizations to identify a pool of worthy recipients.

The Club will enhance the prestige of the awards and promote the recognition of the recipients of these awards through its newsletter

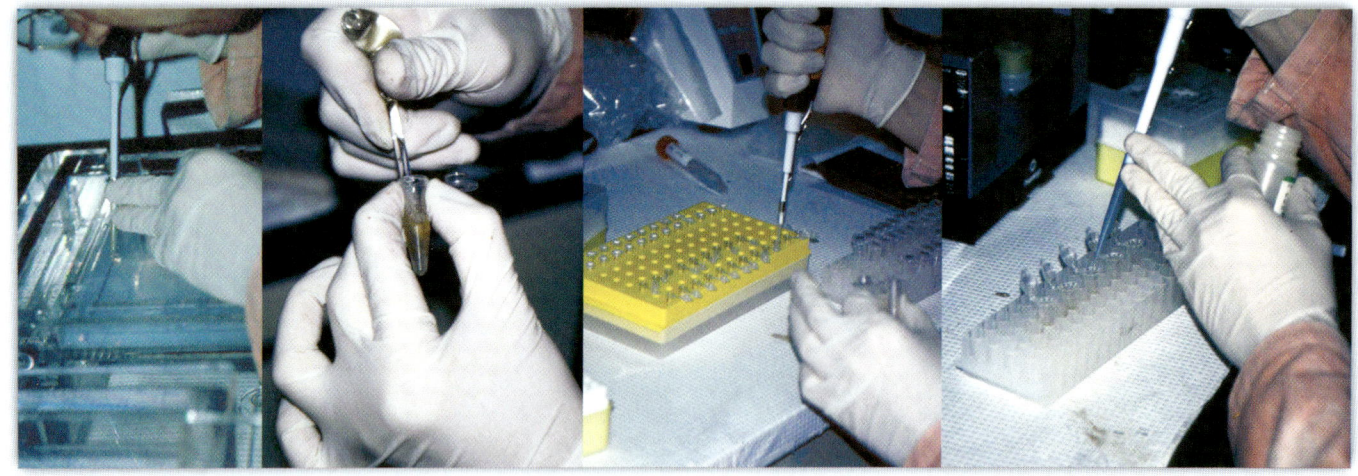

as well as media news releases to the appropriate sources

In addition, opportunities to create new awards will be evaluated, specifically, a Scholarship program, a Conservation Officer of the Year Award, and a Volunteer of the Year Award.

Goal 2. **To Promote the Collection and Dissemination of Information on the Beneficial Role of Bowhunting in Wildlife Management.**

Objective A: To network with, and provide information, expertise and funding to federal and state wildlife management agencies, and private wildlife conservation organizations.

The Club shall establish and promote itself as an authority regarding the role of bowhunting in wildlife management, the focus of which is bowhunter ethics, fair chase, and equipment technology as they relate to bowhunting.

Complimentary copies of the Club newsletter will be distributed to appropriate state and federal wildlife management agencies, plus selected national wildlife conservation organizations.

The Club will explore establishing a direct one-on-one relationship with all state wildlife management agencies, national wildlife organizations and state bowhunting organizations. This will involve Regular and Senior membership involvement.

Professional wildlife management publications will be reviewed annually for materials relating to bowhunting and wildlife management. A database will be developed and maintained by the Club Conservation Committee. This database will be available through the Club website.

The Club will be proactive and responsive to anti-bowhunting, anti-hunting, and anti-wildlife management publicity and campaigns. This will include dispensing information to its membership as well as local and national news media outlets as needed and/or necessary.

Objective B: To represent and advocate bowhunting to federal and state wildlife management agencies and non-government wildlife conservation organizations.

The Club will provide information and expertise to federal and state entities regarding the utilization of conventional bowhunting equipment to address modern-day wildlife management problems, e.g. the management of white-tailed deer in urban areas.

Goal 3. **To Create and Enhance Network and Partnership Activities with State and Federal Agencies, National Conservation Organizations and Individuals, Leading to Positive Exposure of Bowhunting and the Pope and Young Club.**

Objective A: To communicate the virtues of bowhunting to the general public and wildlife professionals through education, communication, and public meeting forums.

Promoting a positive image of bowhunting and fair chase to the general public and the wildlife management and conservation community is a priority for the Club. Developing and maintaining a proactive public relations program which disseminates the positive attributes of bow hunting is paramount to achieving this objective. Specifically, development of educational information programs that inform the general public, as well as the hunting public of the Club's commitment to fair chase and ethical hunting techniques and to maintaining the heritage of bowhunting equipment.

The Club shall be in the forefront to denounce activities, programs and/or hunting activities and equipment the Club deems detrimental to the future of bowhunting, bowhunting opportunity, hunting in general and wildlife management.

Included in this objective will be the promotion and communication of the Club's Conservation Program Mission Statement: *"Promote the Conservation and Scientific Management of Wildlife and Their Habitats and To Sustain and Protect Our Bowhunting Heritage."*

The Club will design and manage its museum as a showcase of the history and evolution of bowhunting, bowhunting equipment and wildlife conservation in North America.

Objective B: Engage in wildlife management programs and wildlife conservation issues throughout North America.

The Club shall network and partner with private, state, federal, national and international bowhunting, wildlife conservation and wildlife management entities to foster bowhunting and professional scientific wildlife management programs. This will necessitate a Club presence at local, state, national, and occasionally international events of Club appointed representation. A requirement of the individual(s) representing the Club shall be a written report and/or oral presentation to the Board outlining the highlights and benefits/impacts to the Club. Additionally, the Club will provide active participation and involvement where appropriate. This will include serving on committees, making presentations, providing assistance with the planning and/or organization of events.

Objective C: To partner with wildlife management and wildlife conservation organizations.

The Club will sustain, and when possible enhance its involvement with wildlife, conservation, bowhunting, general hunting, and educational groups to promote and campaign for bowhunters and bowhunting. The degree of Club involvement and/or activity relative to specific groups will be determined by the Board and shall include providing information, expertise, manpower and/or financial support.

Goal 4. **Explore Opportunities to Fund and Support Bowhunting, Wildlife Conservation, Education and Wildlife Conservation Related Activities.**

Objective A: To enhance Club fund-raising activities.

The Conservation Committee and the Board shall continue to explore and utilize opportunities to enhance financial support and growth of the Club's conservation program. Currently the major source of revenue is through the biennial convention auction and raffle. A major goal is to identify a consistent source of revenue. Potential funding sources include a "round-up" program in cooperation with participating. Bowhunting equipment retailers on bowhunting related equipment and clothing. Specifically, a buyer would have the opportunity to round up the price of his purchase to the next whole dollar amount. That amount would be earmarked for the Club's conservation program.

Another option is to increase the fee for entering animals into the Clubs record program with a portion of the increase dedicated to the conservation program.

Objective B: To cultivate benefactor, donor and patron programs dedicated to the Conservation Program.

The Club will identify and promote programs whereby members can include the Club as a benefactor of their estate.

Tax-deductible incentive programs will be explored.

The Club will research grant application opportunities, including matching grants, as a source of funding for specific programs and projects.

Goal 5. **To Promote Bowhunting and Other Outdoor Experiences from the Recreational Use and Enjoyment of Sustained, Scientifically Managed Wildlife Populations.**

Objective A: The Club will encourage bowhunting opportunities through participating in hunter recruitment and retention programs, youth mentoring programs.

Objective B: The Club will promote the philosophy and concept of fair chase and ethical hunting while simultaneously advocating and promoting the principles of professional scientific wildlife management and the significance of the North American Model of Wildlife Conservation to the hunting and non-hunt-

ing public throughout North America.

The following Conservation Committee members were involved in developing the Strategic plan for the Club's conservation program:

Mike Schlegel, Chairman	Tom Nelson
Jim Akenson	Bob Speegle
Keith Dana	Rick Stowell
Dave Doran	M.R James, President
Tom Foss	Susan Barrett, Board Member
Chase Fulcher	Doug Clayton, Board Member
Gary Williams	

Pope and Young Club Conservation Achievement Awards

The Pope and Young Club has three conservation awards: the Conservation Award; the Stewardship Award; and the Lee Gladfelter Memorial Award. All three are currently awarded during the Club's biennial conference.

Conservation Award: *"To be given to the person or organization that has promoted the future of bowhunting and hunting, the image of bowhunting and hunting, and the conservation and wise use of our natural resources."* The Board established this award in 1992 and it was first awarded in 1993. The following is a list of the recipients for this award:

1993 Recipient
  Archery Manufacturers Organization: "Save Our Heritage" Program
1995 Recipient
  Wildlife Legislative Fund of America

45

1997 Recipient
   Becoming An Outdoors Woman Program
1999 Recipient
   National Bowhunter Education Foundation
2001 Recipient
   Congressional Sportsmen's Foundation
2003 Recipient
   Boone and Crockett Club
2005 Recipient
   National Archery in the Schools Program
2007 Recipient
   Dennis Ballard
2009 Recipient
   Kelly Semple, Hunting for the Future Foundation

Stewardship Award: *"to be given to the bowhunter or bowhunting organization that by their actions has conveyed a positive, good-citizen image, to the hunting and non-hunting public."* Award created in 1994, initiated in 1995.

1995 Recipient
   Indiana Bowhunters Assoc. (For donations to Children's Hospital, Indianapolis, over $100,000 in 4 years)
1997 Recipient
   United Bowhunters of Connecticut (For donations to St. Jude's Children's Hospital, over $96,000 1994-1996)
1999 Recipient
   Cheff Center Charity Bowhunters Tournament (For donations of over $100,000 to Cheff Center in past 10 years)
2001 Recipient
   Hunt For A Cure Cancer Fund Raiser, Rob Evans and Dr. Arnold S. Leonard
2003 Recipient
   Farmers and Hunters Feeding the Hungry; An outreach program obtaining venison and distributing it to the hungry, over 12,000,000 servings in the past six years.
2005 Recipient
   Camp Compass Academy; a nonprofit organization targeting urban middle and high school disadvantaged youth created by John Annoni. John and his volunteer staff mentor youth, providing hunting, fishing, archery, tutoring, social guidance, plus other outdoor youth activities. Camp Compass has been featured in USA Today, The New York Times, Breakthrough Magazine, plus the Mossy Oaks TNN show.
2007 Recipient
   Ray Howell's Kicking Bear Foundation; founded by Ray Howell as a nationwide mentoring program dedicated to enriching the lives of troubled and at-risk young people through outdoor experiences. The Foundation has 501 C-3 non-profit tax status and its goals are: 1. Raise the awareness of the significant number of young people who need a mentor; 2. Train those that want to become a mentor; 3. Provide contact for mentors and youth seeking a mentor; 4. Organize free public events for mentors and youth. *"We are a National Not-For-Profit organization promoting adult mentorship, making the world a better place, one kid at a time."*
2009 Recipient
   New York Bowhunters Inc. Since its inception in 1991 the New York Bowhunters have added several programs which enrich the lives of its members and the lives of the individuals that live within New York State and to others outside of NY. These programs include; Youth Archery Camps, Youth Archery Hunts, Physically Challenged Committee, Physically Challenged Archery Hunts, Physically Challenged Adaptive Equipment, Urban Deer Committee, Town Of Irondequoit Bowhunting Success, Town Of Erwin Bowhunting Success, NYB Scholarship, and the Doug Kerr Scholarship Fund

Lee Gladfelter Memorial Award: *"to the wildlife professional, who, through their efforts, has made a significant contribution to bowhunting and wildlife conservation."* The recipient receives $1,000, plus $500 expenses for travel to receive the award. The recipient may select the location to receive the award from the following three options; 1) at a national wildlife conference; 2) at the Pope and Young convention or 3) at a suitable time and place mutually agreed upon by the recipient and the Club. This award was created in 1994 and first awarded in 1995.

1995 Recipient
   Jay McAninch, Wildlife Biologist, MN Dept. Natural Resources

1997 Recipient
   Robert McDowell, Director, New Jersey Dept. Inland Fish & Game
1999 Recipient
   Dr. R. Ben Peyton, Wildlife Professor, Michigan State University
2001 Recipient
   Eric Kurzejeski, Director of Research, Missouri Dept Conservation
2003 Recipient
   Dr. Dave Samuel, Wildlife Professor, West Virginia University
2005 Recipient
   Gary Alt, Wildlife Biologist (retired), PA Game Commission
2007 Recipient
   Frank H. Rice (Posthumously), Wildlife Biologist, PA Game Comm.
2009 Recipient
   Kenneth Mayer, Director, Nevada Department of Wildlife

During the past decade the Club has been very involved in national wildlife conservation and bowhunting issues. Most notably through its affiliation with the American Wildlife Conservation Partners (AWCP), and the Congressional Sportsmen's Foundation Congressional Caucus program, plus its financial and professional expertise contributions to various entities nationwide.

The Club is also regularly represented at the following annual meetings: the North American Wildlife and Natural Resources Conference; the Association of Fish and Wildlife Agencies of which the Club has representation on two committees, the Hunting and Shooting Sports Participation and the Sustainable Use of Wildlife; the American Wildlife Conservation Partners and the National Assembly of Sportsmen's Caucuses Sportsman-Legislator Summit.

Sponsorships have been another activity in which the Club has excelled. Sponsorship highlights include the CWD Alliance, National Hunting and Fishing Day, the Sportsman-Legislator Summit, the White House Conference on North American Wildlife Policy, Wildlife For the 21st Century and the Hunting Heritage Trust documentary "Democracy of the Wild — A Triumph of Sportsman-Supported Conservation in America".

Programs the Club has supported throughout the history of its conservation program are too numerous to mention, however recent highlights include the National Bowhunter Education Foundation, Conservation Leaders for Tomorrow, National Conservation Leadership Institute, Orion — The Hunters Institute, Alaska Wood Bison Restoration, National Archery in the Schools Program, Jack Creek Preserve Foundation, and the North American Bowhunting Coalition.

Recently, money generated for the conservation program has been dedicated to Club programs, for example, the conservation section of the museum and our partnership with the Boone and Crockett Club.

The Club's conservation program has grown, both monetarily and in scope. This growth has occurred primarily from the contributions of donors and support of the membership. As the objectives and goals of the conservation strategic plan are implemented, and with continued support of the membership, the conservation program will continue to grow.

Charlie Kroll's writing in the Second Edition of Bowhunting Big Game Records of North America eloquently portrays the Club's philosophy regarding its conservation program. "*We of the Pope and Young Club are as actively committed to the perpetuation of suitable habitat and other beneficial wildlife management practices as we are to the Rules of Fair Chase and the recording of trophies. This motivation is, and will continue to be, expressed through the activities of our Conservation Committee.*"

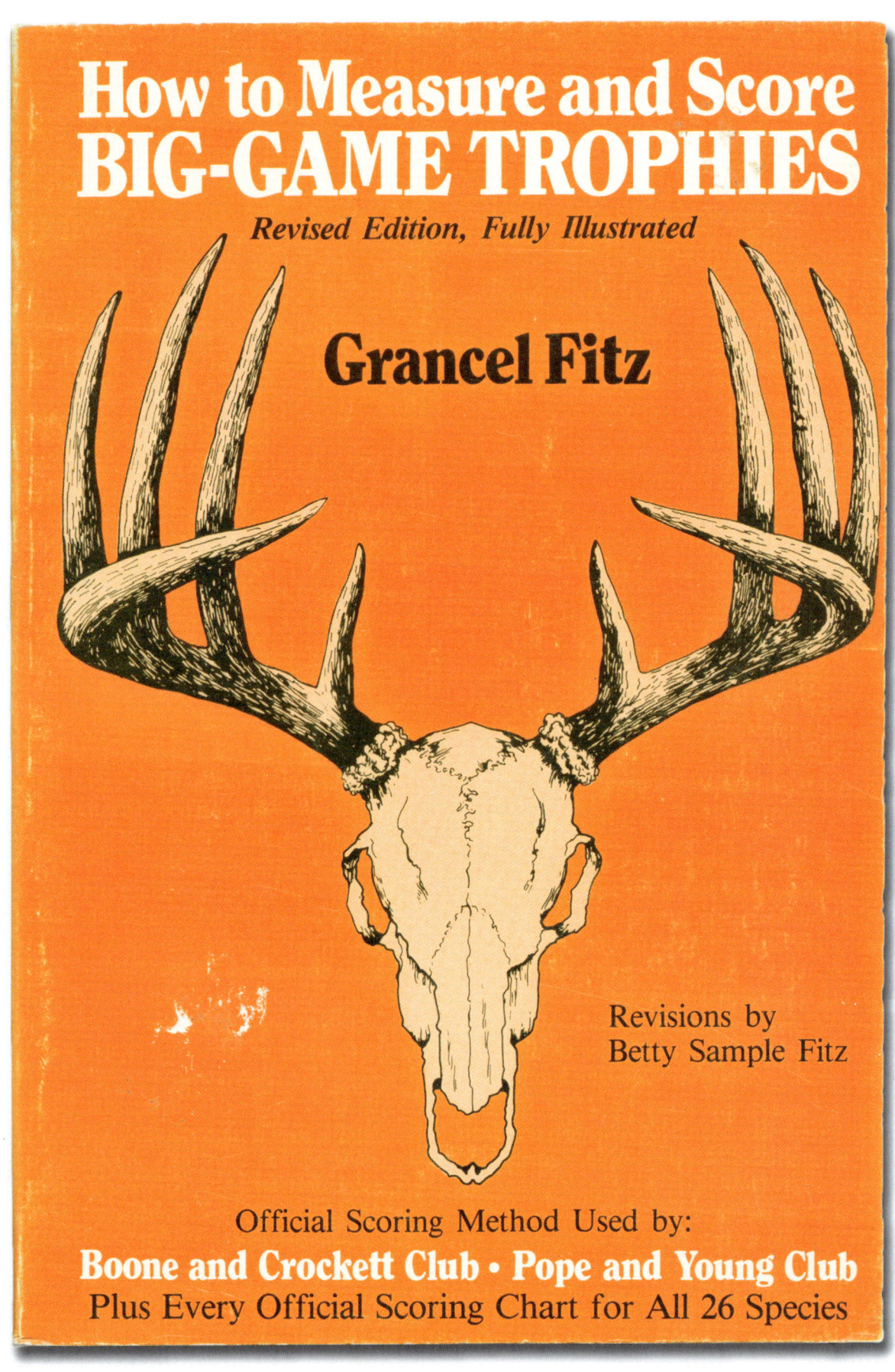

Evolution of the Pope & Young Club's Scoring System

By Glenn Hisey

Historical Perspective

Man's interest in records and statistics is everywhere. In sports, man keeps track of the number of home runs, who can run the four-minute mile, the number of TKOs, or 3-pointers in basketball. In other areas of life, man keeps track of the number of inches of rainfall or the coldest day on record in July. The list goes on and on.

Man has always been interested in comparisons. Back to early man, relative size of animals was apparent on pre-historic cave paintings and in Egyptian hieroglyphics. Harvesting large specimens brought fame and a certain amount of glory to early hunters; it was a badge of courage.

In the present day, fresh water fishing has its own Hall of Fame, and wild turkeys are measured by weight and beard length. These examples, and many others, all have their means of comparison.

Big game is certainly no exception. Various ways of comparison have come and gone over the years, and some still remain. In the late 1800s, Theodore Roosevelt was concerned about the demise of North American big game animals and lack of conserving our natural resources. That is the underlining reason Roosevelt and a few of his influential friends started the Boone and Crockett Club. One time he was asked to judge a display of big game animals and did so by trying to rank the animals by size of the antlers and horns.

During the latter part of Roosevelt's presidency, bison had dwindled down to a few hundred head. Whitetails and other big game species were mostly gone from the eastern states. Many people felt that due to the expansion of America to the west, all big game species in North America would become extinct. Due to this dire expectation, William T. Hornaday and Madison Grant, members of the Boone & Crockett Club, worked from 1906 to 1922 to put together the National Collection of Heads and Horns at the Bronx Zoo in New York City. This collection was to serve as a reminder of what North America once had in abundance with its big game. Thankfully, the presence of the National Collection started an interest in conservation of North America's big game species and in the recording of measurements of our big game animals.

In 1932, Prentiss Gray authored Records of North American Big Game, the first record book of the Boone & Crockett Club. There were only 500 copies made and it soon became a collector's item. It was ranked by a single measurement, but also listed the number of points. Gray recognized at that time *"no one dimension is the controlling factor, and we hope that eventually some fair scoring method may be devised which is acceptable."*

This book only listed four categories of deer: mule deer, whitetail deer, blacktail deer and Arizona whitetail deer. It only had one category listing for elk — wapiti. It only had one category for each species of antlered game — typical, with no reference to non-typical. It had only three categories of caribou: barren ground, woodland and mountain. All of the other categories were similar to today's

Boone and Crockett record books.

Dr. James L. Clark, the director of the American Museum of Natural History, was asked to devise an equitable scoring system. 1935 saw the 1st North American Big Game Competition for the Boone and Crockett Club. There were some flaws, but it was a step in the right direction. In 1939, the Boone & Crockett Club published the 2nd Edition of North American Big Game Records. This book gave more information than the 1932 book did, but still ranked animals on a single measurement. The only change in categories was changing the name of Arizona whitetail to Coues' deer. It also did not have any non-typical categories. Of special note, is a chapter written by Grancel Fitz, titled "Rating of Trophies." In that chapter, he outlines a system he designed for scoring and judging North American big game animals. His supporting score charts printed in that chapter are very similar to present day forms. The accepted viewpoint at that time was that all abnormal points were freak points and not desirable. Grancel Fitz questioned that, if there were an abundance of freak points, shouldn't that be desirable? The big question was what amount would it take to tip the scale and be enough to list separately.

World War II interrupted the process of making improvements to the scoring system. Things were put on hold until after the war ended and things got back to normal.

In 1949, the Boone & Crockett Club developed a records system committee. The committee consisted of Dr. James L. Clark, Grancel Fitz, Dr. Harold Anthony, Frederick Barbour, Milford Baker, and Samuel Webb as the chairman. Within two years, they hammered out 15 scoring charts covering all North American big game, accurately evaluating the trophy, but keeping it simple at the same time.

The year 1952 saw the publishing of Records of North American Big Game, 3rd Edition Boone and Crockett record book. This was the first published record book using the current scoring system. It was greeted with popular appeal.

Today, this system is universally accepted as the official comparison of North American big game. The general principles were, and are, designed to represent mass and symmetry. The system functionally works in terms of comparison, as the calculated final score is just a meaningless number without the longterm consistency in terms and means of comparison. Each final score is meaningful only in terms of the baseline comparison to the ideal for that particular species and with/against all others judged equivocally to it.

As the B&C scoring system was coming into being, so too was modern-day bowhunting in its infancy. In the early to mid-twentieth century, there were few bowhunters. Game agencies and others did not recognize bowhunting in the hunting community as a viable means of harvesting big game. There were poor (if any) bow seasons throughout the country.

The Hunting Activities Committee of the National Field Archery Association was formed in 1956. Headed by Glenn St. Charles, this committee was put together out of the need to better the image of bowhunting. The idea of using a method similar to the prestigious Boone and Crockett Club was deemed to be the best way to accomplish this goal. The NFAA gained permission to use the Boone & Crockett Club's scoring system to establish a records program hopefully to provide tangible proof of the effectiveness of the bow and arrow as a hunting weapon.

Because of the limitations of the bow and arrow, when compared to a firearm, lower minimum scores were necessary for determining what a record class animal is. The initial minimum scores were established by using a percentage of the Boone and Crockett Club's minimums. The committee agreed that minimums would have to be raised from time to time to reflect what was deemed a record class animal. There were 26 categories listed initially.

As soon as the NFAA directors gave their final approval to the project, the Committee presented the recording program to the bowhunters of America in the February 1958 issue of Archery magazine. The response was great and by June of 1958, there were already 41 entries in all categories. The need for an individual organization, separate from NFAA, became apparent because of the different goals of the two groups. Through surveys and much discussion, the idea of a prestigious type club similar to the Boone & Crockett Club was formulated.

On January 27, 1961, the Pope and Young Club came into being. Glenn St. Charles was chosen as the first president. The NFAA transferred all of the big game records that they had to-date over to the new organization.

Changes in Categories and Minimum Entry Scores

The accompanying chart depicts how minimum entry score requirements have evolved over our first 50 years. The changes come not by happenstance, but after thoughtful and thorough consideration. The overall trend has been an increase in minimum scores—a result of several factors, including the initial "feeling out" of appropriate minimums, increasing bowhunting numbers, increasing species population health, increasing bowhunting opportunity, changing attitudes to trophy quality and the affects of advancing bowhunting methods and equipment.

Through our first fifty years, one species category has been terminated and six have been added. In some cases, these were driven by biological matters, in some by new or increasing bowhunting opportunity, and in some cases by Records Program management decisions. In 1969, a category for non-typical Coues' deer was established. The year 1975 saw the bison category introduced. Three new categories were created in 1981: Quebec/Labrador caribou, Sitka blacktail deer and muskox.

	1957	1962	1969	1975	1981	1983	1985	1987	1988	1990	1993	1995	1999	2000	2008	2011
Alaska Brown Bear	20															20
Black Bear	17			18												18
Grizzly Bear	17	18		19												19
Polar Bear	15	17		20												20
Bison	****	****	****	80							100					100
*Barren Ground Caribou	265			300							325*					325*
*Central Canada Barren Ground	****	****	****	****	****	****	****	****	****	****	300*					300*
*Mountain Caribou	265										300*					300*
*Quebec/Labrador Caribou	****	****	****	****	300						325*					325*
*Woodland Caribou	220										220*					220*
Cougar	10	12	13					138/16								13 8/16
Jaguar	9	12		14				****	****	****	****	****	****	****	****	****
*Columbian Blacktail Deer, typical	75		90								90*					95*
*Columbian Blacktail Deer, non-typical	****	****	****	****	****	****	****	****	****	110 (9)	110*(9)	125*				115* (10)
*Sitka Blacktail Deer	****	****	****	****	65						75*					75*
*Coues' Deer, typical	68				60		65				65*					70*
*Coues' Deer, non-typical	****	****	78		66						75* (7)	95*		80*		80* (5)
*Mule Deer, typical	125	135	140	145				145*								145*
*Mule Deer, non-typical	125(20)		150(20)	160(16)							160*(16)		170*			170*(124/8)
*Whitetail Deer, typical	115			125							125*					125*
*Whitetail Deer, non-typical	105(15)		135(15)	150(15)							150*(15)	155*				155* (15)
*Roosevelt's Elk	210										225*					225*
*Tule Elk	****	****	****	****	****	****	****	****	****	****	****	****	****	****	225*	225*
*American Elk, typical	250	225		240			260				260*					260*
*American Elk, non-typical	****	****	****	****	****	****	****	****	300(20)			335*				300* (20)
Rocky Mountain Goat	35			40												40
*Alaska/Yukon Moose	150			170							170*					170*
*Canada Moose	135										135*					135*
*Shiras' Moose	115										115*		125*			125*
Muskox	****	****	****	****	65			90								90
Pronghorn Antelope	57					64							67			67
Bighorn Sheep	130						140									140
Dall's (White) Sheep	120															120
Desert Bighorn Sheep	115						140							120		120
Stone's Sheep	120															120

*Velvet entries are accepted. The same minimums apply as for the corresponding hard-horned category.

51

In 1985, the jaguar category was dropped from the listing of the records. Actually, another category, the one for polar bear, was suspended at that time as well, but was later reintroduced due to changes in government importation laws. The non-typical Yellowstone (American) elk category was created in 1988. In 1990, the Records Program gained the non-typical Columbian blacktail deer category. Central Canada barren ground caribou were separated into a category in 1993. Lastly, Tule elk were separated into a category in 2008.

Policy Changes, Developments and Clarifications

The scoring system is based in science and statistical analysis. It requires consistency of application as well as historical consistency. The Pope and Young Club has worked with the Boone and Crockett Club throughout the years to protect and maintain the system. It has evolved over time as we've dealt with situations or procedures that require new interpretation or improvement in rulings. It pays to consider that we are dealing with a phenomenon of nature…antler and horn growth. Over the years, we've encountered never-before-seen antler configurations that have required new interpretations and procedures. Some of the more interesting procedural changes and interpretations in the history of our Records Program are addressed here.

Starting in 1979, the use of a plastic-coated steel cable was allowed for measuring beam length and point lengths on deer, elk and caribou measurements. Prior to that time, all measurements had to be taken with a ¼ inch steel tape.

The muskox horn length measurement, when taken over the outer curvature of the horn, was variable, depending upon the path of the measurement over the curve. In 1981, a method was developed whereby the measurement starts in the center of the boss and then follows the same lateral groove all the way to the tip. This was the only measurement on the horned animals that a cable was allowed to be used due to the ease in running the cable in the lateral groove.

A change in the ruling on determining common base points went into effect in 1982. From that time forward, in order to be treated as common base points (with both points being measured all the way to the parent structure), there must be a distinct groove between the points (a "figure 8" or peanut-shaped cross-sectional view) going all the way to the base line on both the inside and the outside of the points. Prior to that time, the groove only needed to be present on one side.

A rule implemented in the 1980s stated that, if a completely separate third main beam were present, then it, and all points coming off of it, would be treated as abnormal points.

Another change in the early 1980s allowed the measurer the option of choosing which point would be G-4 on mule deer/blacktail deer if there were two front fork points. This option would be available only if both points were forward facing. If the middle point comes straight upward off the main beam, it must be treated as an abnormal point.

In April 1986, the Club eliminated the "double penalty" on all antlered game. The new ruling stated "the inside spread may equal but not exceed the length of the longest antler." There no longer will be a deduction in the difference column for the excess.

A change on Roosevelt's elk allowed any abnormal point on or above G-4 to be treated as a crown point. At this time (considering that the typical and desired presence of crown points often results in apparent mismatch of growth in normal points) the required symmetry for normal points G-5 and beyond, as well as for crown points, was eliminated.

With antlered animals the main beam lengths were measured at the center of the antler over the outer curve to the tip. The starting point was generally over the eye socket. The starting point using this method was somewhat arbitrary. When Randy Byers was Records Chairman, he initiated a rule whereby the measurer lines up the two burrs of the main beams and then determines the center of the nearest burr. That spot is the starting point for the main beam length.

In 1987, a special rule was put in effect on measuring moose palm length if only a spike is present as a frontal palm. A normal moose frontal palm has two or more points and the length of palm measurement is taken to a dip between two of these points. However, a spike palm (especially common on Shiras' moose) has no obvious ending location. The new rule provided a definitive location by stating that the palm length measurement could not cross open "space" between the upper palm and the frontal palm spike (while still maintaining the palm length criteria of being parallel to the inside edge of the main palm).

Also in 1987, a rule was made requiring that the D-2 measurement on antelope is always taken below the prong and D-3 is always taken above the prong. If the location for these measurements falls on the swelling of the prong, the measurements are adjusted up or down so that the swelling does not inflate the score.

Record book entries of antlered animals shot "in velvet" for which the velvet was maintained on the antlers had never been accepted. Beginning as a trial category for mule deer, progressing to the establishment of a "category" for mule deer in 1988, and later expanding to all antlered big game species in 1993, we began recognizing "velvet" entries. This occurred after numerous years and much debate. We recognized that more animals were being shot and left "in velvet," due in part to earlier bowhunting seasons and in part due to advancements in taxidermy practices of successfully preserving the velvet. There were problems that needed to be addressed, though. It was recognized that "velvet" antlers could not be measured as accurately as "hard-horned" antlers. There was also the issue of our desire not to have competing "world's records" for the same species. Those issues, and others, led us to several stipulations for the acceptance of velvet entries:

1) Velvet entries will appear in their own separate, unranked listing in the record books at the end of the "hard-horned" category. A velvet entry will be listed in one, and only one, edition of the all-time record book.

2) No penalty for velvet will be assessed, since the velvet-antlered specimen appears in a separate listing. They will be entered with the actual score arrived at in the measuring process.

3) The same minimum score requirement applies to the velvet listing as that of the respective "hard-horned" category.

4) Such specimens are not eligible for the numerical awards recognition at the biennial conventions. They will not be requested to be submitted for panel judging verification. The Records Chairman may request that top quality specimen be sent in to the convention for display purposes only.

5) A velvet entry cannot receive recognition as a World's Record. Hence, if a specimen were to be recognized as a World's Record, it would need to be entered into the regular "hard-horned" category. This ruling was passed to eliminate the confusion that would be present in having, for example, two "World's Record" typical mule deer.

6) A specimen can only exist in one category. A particular entry cannot be entered first in the velvet listing and then stripped and entered a second time in the regular category, unless it is first removed from the velvet listing.

Up until 1993, the center of the boss on muskox was found by laying a tape measure from the edge on the front side of the boss up over the top of the boss to the edge of the boss on the backside. That measurement was divided in two to find the center of boss starting point for length of horn measurement.

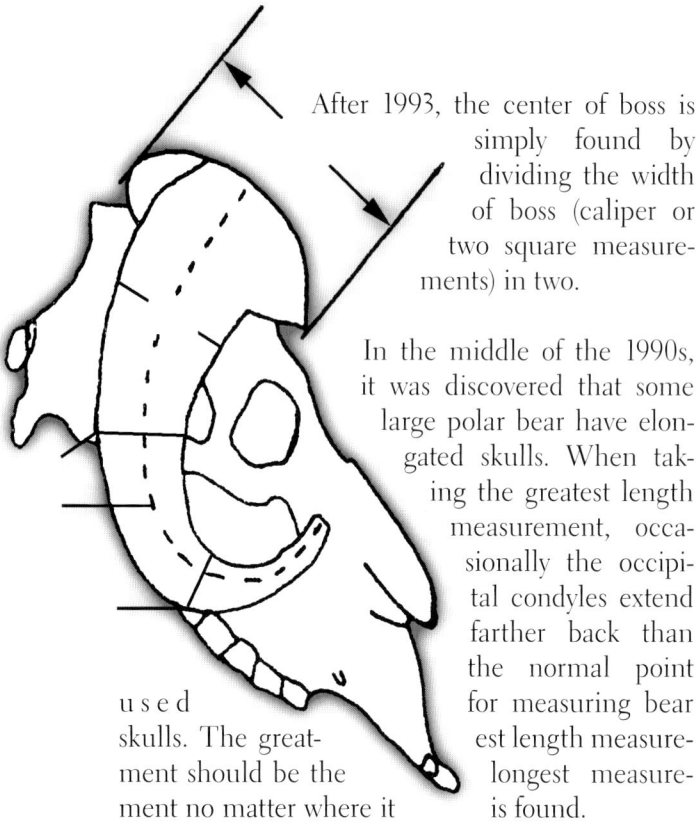

After 1993, the center of boss is simply found by dividing the width of boss (caliper or two square measurements) in two.

In the middle of the 1990s, it was discovered that some large polar bear have elongated skulls. When taking the greatest length measurement, occasionally the occipital condyles extend farther back than the normal point for measuring bear used skulls. The greatest length measurement should be the longest measurement no matter where it is found.

The requirements for an animal to be eligible to be entered into the non-typical categories have evolved over the history of the Records Program. From the Program's advent until 1995, a set minimum amount of total abnormal point length was required (shown in parenthesis on the minimum score chart). In 1995, the length of abnormal point requirements to be entered into a non-typical category was dropped. Instead, hunters were given the choice of which category (typical or non-typical) to enter an animal (provided it had at least one score-able abnormal point). They were encouraged to enter the animal in the category for which it scored higher over the respective minimum score (typical versus non-typical). In 2006, that procedure was adjusted to actually require that it be entered into the category for which it scored higher over the respective minimum score. Now, at the beginning of the 28th Recording Period (January 1, 2011), the requirement of meeting or exceeding a set minimum amount of total abnormal point length has been reestablished. While varying in terminology, these definitions have mostly remained philosophically consistent, with the guiding principle being to honor the animal in the category that best represents it.

Because there is no credit given for spread on pronghorn and wide pronghorn may be more desirable to many hunters, in 1995, the spread penalty on pronghorn antelope was eliminated. The Records Chairman was given discretion to reject "freak" heads, though.

A new interpretation of non-symmetry points was implemented in the late 1990s, which states that any point (long or short) that is an extra unmatched point, not at the end of the main beam, is a non-symmetry point. Prior to that time, the rule was any point that upsets the balance of the rack would be ruled as non-symmetry.

On September 1, 1999, the following rule for pronghorn went into effect: If a filler substance has been used to attach the horn sheaths to the horn cores at the time before the official measurements are taken, then the D-1 (basal circumference) measurement can not exceed the D-2 (1st quarter circumference) measurement. This procedure was put into place to address the concern over an observed pattern of individuals purposefully expanding the bases of pronghorn horns to enhance the score.

In April of 2004, the name of Yellowstone elk was changed to American elk.

As you can see, the scoring methods have changed from time to time to reflect more accurate methods and/or more consistent application of the program. When asked whether measuring is a science or an art, one has to admit it is an art, as there are still judgment calls on the part of the measurer, due to the fact antlers and horns are unique.

Acceptability and Fair Chase

To be entered into the Pope & Young Club Records, the animal must meet the minimum scoring requirements, and must be taken in complete compliance with the controlling game laws and the Rules of Fair Chase. The basic premise of the Rules of Fair Chase is that the hunter does not have an undo advantage over the animal being hunted. The term "Fair Chase" shall not include the taking of animals under the following conditions:

> Helpless in a trap, deep snow or water, or on ice.
>
> From any power vehicle or powerboat.
>
> While inside escape-proof fenced enclosures.
>
> By "Jacklighting" or shining at night.
>
> By the use of any tranquilizers or poisons.
>
> By the use of any power vehicles or power boat for herding or driving animals, including use of aircraft to land alongside or to communicate with or direct a hunter on the ground.
>
> By the use of electronic devices for attracting, locating, or pursuing game, or guiding the hunter to such game, or by the use of a bow or arrow to which any electronic device is attached.
>
> Any other condition considered by the Board of Directors as unacceptable.

The Rules of Fair Chase, as listed above, are the result of modifications to the original rules. Significant position developments have included:

In 1988, the Club resolved deliberations on the growing concerns about technological advancements in bowhunting equipment, and its possible negative impacts on bowhunting's future. A Rule of Fair Chase was amended to disallow the "use of a bow or arrow to which an electronic device is attached."

In March of 1992, for bear and cougar, the dog statement was added. In many states and provinces it is legal and common practice to hunt cougar or bear with the use of dogs. Special fair chase concerns involved with the use of dogs in hunting cougar and bear have prompted the inclusion of the DOG STATEMENT on the front side of the scoring form. This question must be answered and signed on all bear and cougar entries. This addresses two rulings established by the Club. First, the hunter must be present at the time the dogs were initially released to pursue the animal. Secondly, if electronic collars were on the dogs, then the receivers can not have been used at any time during the pursuit and harvest of the animal.

In April 2001, the Fair Chase Rules were changed to reject all entries taken behind high fences of any kind. Prior to that time, we had specifically excluded game farms and any commercial hunting operation enclosures.

Some changes to the Club's definitions of acceptable bowhunting equipment have occurred as well:

In 1988, at the same time we were addressing the electronics issue mentioned above, the established definition of a hunting bow was amended to establish a limit on compound bow let-off of 65%.

In 2003, the definition of the eligibility of compound bows was changed to allow for animals taken with compound bows possessing let-off greater than 65% (AMO standard), provided such were legal in the appropriate state/province. Animals taken with bows having let-off greater than 65% (the previous rule), will be acknowledged with an asterisk.

The following documents are required when submitting the measurements of a big game animal for entry into the Clubs records:

1) An official scoring form, completed by an official measurer of the Pope and Young Club or the Boone and Crockett Club.
2) A completed Fair Chase Affidavit, including the Hunt Information form on the backside.
3) Three (3) or more photos of the antlers, horns or skull showing a view from the front side, a view from the left side and a view from the right side. A field photo, at the site of kill, is also requested, if possible.
4) A recording fee, which is currently $35.00, is required for each animal submitted for the Records.
5) A copy of the hunting license is also required for wild sheep entries. It is not required for other entries, but is beneficial to include if readily available.

The hunter information form on the backside of the Fair Chase Affidavit was added in 1985 to provide useful information and statistics.

A sixty- (60) day "drying period" from date of harvest is required before an entry can be officially measured. For the sixty day "drying period" to be legitimate, the trophy must have been stored at room temperature and room humidity without any modifications and without any attempt to prevent normal drying. The basic purpose of the drying period is to bring all specimen into a more-consistent and equal state, no matter what time of the year they are harvested.

Initially the signature of the guide or outfitter was required for all trophies taken on a guided hunt; however, this requirement was eliminated in 1987. The guide or outfitter's name and address is still required on the scoring form, but the guide's signature on the Fair Chase Affidavit is no longer required.

It is the responsibility of all hunters to give total effort to recover a game animal by track and trail until every reasonable possibility has been exhausted. This is a fundamental principle well taught in our heritage and in hunter education. This ethic, coupled with the fact that the Club's Records Program records only bow-harvested animals, translates into a policy stating that an animal for which the search was abandoned and the animal later recovered will not be eligible for entry. Any time an entry is received for which the recovery was not immediate (within a day), a wide range of circumstances surrounding the recovery process is reviewed on a case-by-case basis to determine the eligibility of the individual entry.

Entries are occasionally dropped if an entry is found to be illegal or does not meet our fair chase rules. If an entry has already been accepted and later found to have been taken illegally or not meeting Club criteria, the Board of Directors may remove the entry. Depending on the severity of the infraction, either that one animal will be dropped or that animal plus all past entries will be dropped and that individual will be barred from any future entries.

Official Measurers

A dedicated crew of over 900 certified measurers provide the backbone of the Records Program. The overwhelming success of our Records Program is directly attributable to the efforts of these men and women. Not only do these dedicated and tireless volunteers provide the public service of measuring antlers, horns and skulls for hunters wishing to honor these animals with a listing in the Records Program, but they are also "field ambassadors" of the Pope and Young Club, providing a crucial direct contact with the bowhunting public. With these duties comes a great deal of responsibility. As volunteers, official measurers cannot receive payment for providing this service.

In the early days of the Club, the need for additional measurers scattered throughout the country precluded the need for formal training. Initial prospective measurers were asked if they had the Grancel Fitz book <u>How To Measure and Score Big Game Trophies</u>. If the answer was "yes", they were appointed as Official Measurers.

Then in November of 1977, Scott Showalter, Records Chairman at the time, on behalf of the Pope & Young Club, obtained the copyright to the Grancel Fitz book from 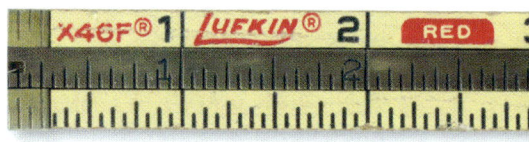 Fitz's widow, Betty Fitz Dingwall. The plan was to edit this book to fit the special situations encountered with bow-harvested animals due to our lower minimums. It was soon decided to abandon the idea of editing the old book, and instead put together a completely new Measurer's Manual. This project took a lot longer than anticipated, but was finally completed in 1989 by C. Randall Byers, the Pope & Young Club's Records Chairman at that time. It was done in a three-ring binder, loose-leaf concept. Since then it has been revised in 1995, 1996, 2002 and 2008 and is used as a guide to aid in measuring decisions.

Official measurers serve at the discretion of the Records Committee Chairman and are appointed for periods of three years. Now all official measurers must first attend a training workshop, which are periodically conducted by the Club. The first Measurer Training class was conducted at the convention in Bismarck, North Dakota, in 1985. Since then, classes have been held every year. Most years, three different workshops are held with their locations moved around the country. Several classes have been conducted in Canada as well. Normally class size is limited to around 20 individuals so as to do more hands-on teaching in lieu of just lecture.

At the end of each three-year period, the measurers are reviewed/re-appointed. Official measurers can be removed for actions that are detrimental to the goals of the Pope and Young Club and the Records Program, as well as for other reasons. Conduct of official measurers reflects positively or negatively on the Club and, as such, their conduct and allegiance to the organization is important to the long-

term health of the program. To that end, we do address certain situations as needed. For instance, we have a policy that tries to dis-associate official measurers from horn-buyers and that activity.

We continue our long-standing policy to accept entries measured by Boone and Crockett Club Official Measurers, as long as they follow our guidelines, policies, and entry procedures. Measurers are required to be members of the Pope and Young Club.

Records Committee

The first Records Committee was formed in 1980 by the Records Chairman Scott Showalter. The Records Committee is an advisory committee, advising the Records Committee Chairman. The Records Chairman provides oversight of all aspects of the Records Program, and can use the Records Committee for review of procedures, minimum score requirements, general regulations concerning the entry of trophies, and so forth. Major changes to the Records Program must then be approved by the Board of Directors.

Biennial Panel Judging Sessions and Biennium Awards

The Pope and Young Club archives trophies in biennial recording periods ending on December 31st of even-numbered years. Shortly after the end of each two-year period, the Club requests that several of the largest trophies in every species category be sent to a specific location for judging and panel measuring. Panel measuring is mainly a means of verifying the final score for the top trophies taken during that two-year period and provides an additional level of scrutiny aiding in the longterm consistency of the Program.

Starting in 1994, it was determined that if the panel arrives at a score that is within normal shrinkage, then the original measurer's score will remain. If the panel arrives at a larger score than the original measurer's, the animal is given the larger score. The only way the score will go down is if it was originally mis-measured or has had excessive shrinkage.

Any trophy that ranks in the all time top five for

that category is required to be sent to panel judging, else it will be removed from the records. This step is necessary to ensure that top records shown in the book have all been measured under the same standards. The panel judging is the final step in the chain of events designed to keep the Club's recording system as accurate as possible.

Awards are presented during each biennial program to the top three trophies in each category, plus honorable mentions to those that the panel judges deem worthy. During the biennial Conventions, new World's Records are recognized. While it is not mandatory for the hunter to be present at the banquet, the trophy must be in order for award recognition to be given. New World's Records are only recognized at this time; until such trophies have been panel measured and presented at the awards banquet, it is only proper to refer to them as pending World's Records.

The Ishi Award, named in honor of the man who was widely considered the last truly primitive Indian in North America and who befriended Saxton Pope and spurred the revolution of hunting with the bow and arrow, is the highest honor that can be bestowed by the Pope and Young Club. It is given in recognition of a truly outstanding example of a North American big game animal. The Ishi Award may be awarded only once during a biennium, and may not always be awarded. Seventeen Ishi Awards have been presented in the history of the Club (list found in the Appendix).

Evolution of Entry Fees

In the beginning, trophy fees were not charged for entries because the Pope & Young Club was anxious to receive entries in order to prove hunting big game with a bow was viable. The Board established the first entry fee ($10) in August of 1969. This fee was increased to $20 in 1976. The entry fee was raised to $25 in 1981. Twenty-seven years later, in 2008, the entry fee was raised to $35. The entry fee does not constitute a membership in the Pope

1961 - Poster		244
1963-65 Poster		402
1975 - 1st Edition Record Book		2,372
1977 – 10th Recording Period	516	
1979 – 11th Recording Period	624	
1981 – 12th Recording Period	1,065	
1981 – 2nd Edition Record Book		4,202
1983 – 13th Recording Period	1,437	
1985 – 14th Recording Period	1,933	
1987 – 15th Recording Period	2,699	
1987 – 3rd Edition Record Book		9,278
1989 – 16th Recording Period	2,941	
1991 – 17th Recording Period	4,105	
1993 – 18th Recording Period	5,696	
1993 – 4th Edition Record Book		22,020
1995 – 19th Recording Period	5,325	
1997 – 20th Recording Period	6,658	
1999 – 21st Recording Period	7,384	
1999 – 5th Edition Record Book		41,387
2001 – 22nd Recording Period	6,352	
2003 – 23rd Recording Period	6,884	
2005 – 24th Recording Period	8,071	
2005 – 6th Edition Record Book		62,694
2007 – 25th Recording Period	8,354	
2009 – 26th Recording Period	8,368	
2011 – 27th Recording Period	8,723	
2011 – 7th Edition Record Book		88,139

and Young Club. Instead, it is simply a one-time, per animal, processing fee for accepting the animal into the Records Program.

Publications and Posters

In 1961, history was made when the first pictorial poster of the records of Pope and Young trophies was published. The pictorial met with widespread success and several states made use of it in legislative programs for better understanding of bowhunting. This poster had pictures of the World's Records for each species and listed in print, all of the 244 entries into the Pope & Young Club's Records program. In 1965, the Pope & Young Club published another poster with 402 entries.

1975, history was made once again when the first Pope & Young Club's Bowhunting Big Game Records of North America, 1st Edition, was published. It was available in a hardbound format, and listed 2,372 entries. From that time on, the Pope & Young

Club has published their Bowhunting Big Game Records of North America every six years.

Since 1977, (the 10th Recording Period), at the end of each Recording Period, the Pope & Young Club publishes a paperback Recording Period Booklet. This booklet contains the trophy listings entered into the Pope & Young Club's Records Program during that Recording Period. This booklet also has statistical information garnered from the Hunt Information Sheet located on the back of the Fair Chase Affidavit that each hunter fills out at the time of entry.

The Pope & Young Club published its first specialty book in 1997, with the creation of Bowhunting Records of North American Whitetail Deer, 1st Edition. This book contains all listings of whitetail deer, both typical and non-typical and Coues' deer, both typical and non-typical. State and provincial listings are separated and ranked in numerical order by final score. After each state/province listing, there is a density map broken down by county or area. Bowhunting Records of North American Whitetail Deer, 2nd Edition was published in 2003, and the 3rd Edition was published in 2009. This book will continue on the same schedule of every six years.

In 2007, a landmark examination of the spirit, heart and soul of hunting with the bow and arrow was undertaken in the publishing of A Traditional Journey. This very special book contains five generations of story telling, including original texts by Saxton Pope, Fred Bear and Glenn St. Charles. How-to chapters discuss the finer aspects of the art and craft of bowhunting. This book includes all traditional-equipment entries in the Records Program.

Summary

The Pope & Young Club's early goals and principles were to record for posterity, and disseminate information on the finest trophies of North American big game harvested legally and ethically with the bow and arrow. The Pope & Young Club's archive is the official repository of information on bowhunting records. The Pope & Young Club encourages quality hunting by awakening interest in outstanding examples of this continent's big game animals. The Club was formed to promote and protect our bowhunting heritage and its future. It promotes sound wildlife conservation and management practices. These goals and principles were sound ones, and they have not altered over the last 50 years. The Club's reach and programs have broadened, while maintaining the intent of the original founders. Sound guidance throughout the years has seen these principles and goals work for our organization, and for bowhunting as a whole. The Records Program remains our best avenue for perpetuating and elevating fair chase standards and hunting ethics of the bowhunting community.

Dreams Fulfilled

As Told to Dirk Dieterich by Harv Ebers

The year was 1958. Elvis Presley had been drafted into the Army in the spring. Then, in the early fall, President Dwight D. Eisenhower signed the Alaska Statehood Act into law allowing Alaska to become the 49th state.

About the same time a young man fresh out of the University of Missouri, with a degree in engineering in hand and a promising baseball career laid to rest due to a shoulder injury, set his sights on the last frontier: Alaska.

Driven by a childhood passion borne from the exploits of Jack O'Connor written so eloquently in the pages of Outdoor Life, Sports Afield, and Field & Stream, Harvard Ebers knew at an early age that his life would never be complete until he could experience first hand the wonders of the Alaskan frontier.

A couple of years earlier, the National Field Archery Association (NFAA), in response to rumblings within their ranks, formed the Hunting Activities Committee and appointed a young, aggressive fella named Glenn St. Charles to chair the effort. Their task was to form an alliance with the various state associations and game departments to prove to the hunting public that bowhunting was an efficient means of harvesting big game animals and that bowhunters, as a group, were sincerely interested in the conservation policies that would insure that wildlife resources would be available for future generations. Furthermore, it was their desire to establish bowhunting seasons in all states and Canadian provinces as well as to form a designated record keeping organization for bowhunting fashioned after the Boone & Crockett Club, which was founded by Teddy Roosevelt.

NFAA Secretary John Yount obtained permission from the Boone & Crockett Club for the use of their big game scoring system on bowhunting trophies. In February of 1958 the NFAA Executive Committee approved the record-keeping program. This then led to the first awards program held in Grayling, Michigan, home of Bear Archery, in June 1958.

Harv Ebers had caught the archery bug while in college. Tutored by well-known Quincy, Illinois, bowyer Gordon Botuck, Harv had fabricated a couple of dozen longbows by 1958. He had also become quite skilled at building arrows of red cedar that he typically tipped with Hilbre broadheads. To date, however, he had no big game harvests to his credit.

The fall of 1958 was a busy time for this Midwest farm boy. He had married and accepted a job with the engineering firm Gardner-Denver in Seattle, Washington. Soon after graduation the Ebers packed their bags and moved to the Pacific Northwest. Once in Seattle, Harv spent considerable time frequenting the Jonas Brothers taxidermy studio. There he was lured by stories of vast herds of caribou accessible by car near the small Eskimo village of Glennallen some 183 miles east of Anchorage and located at the intersection of the Glenn Highway and the Richardson Highway. With a month or so before he was to start his career with Gardner-Denver, he quizzed the Jonas Brothers' manager, Bert Kleinberger, about the area. Bert told Harv of an old gas station/café owned by Bruno Zimbecke and his wife located at the intersection of the Richardson Highway and the Mount McKinley cutoff that could serve as his base. With fuel available and a café, Harv would have all that he needed. All that was left was to convince his new bride that he should head north to Alaska to fulfill his lifelong dream.

Luckily for Harv, that task proved easy. Soon, he was boarding a plane for Anchorage with a newly acquired Standard Oil credit card, a couple of hundred dollars, his favorite homemade longbow, a dozen arrows, a change of clothes, and a heavy canvas overcoat that would have to double for the sleeping bag that he couldn't afford.

Anchorage at that time was a small frontier town of some 50,000 residents, with one paved street and one rental car agency. Upon landing, Harv located the Hertz car rental agency and was able to secure a 1958 Chevy with two-wheel drive. He then stopped by the local fish and game office and bought a $25 caribou license. Then he went to the local grocery store where he picked up a large bag of Hershey chocolates, after which he steered the car east down the graveled Glenn Highway and toward the adventure of a lifetime.

Night one in the tundra left Harv with vivid memories that have stayed with him for over a half of a century. Parking the Chevy shortly before dusk, he was overwhelmed with the vastness of the rolling tundra-crested landscape, dotted with the occasional stand of black spruce trees — their growth stunted by the short growing seasons of the extreme northerly latitude — and interrupted by hundreds of ponds and streams with waters as pure as the freshly fallen snow.

To the northwest he was blessed with the rare clear view of Mount McKinley, or Denali (the high one) to the native people. Rising from 2,000 feet above sea level to 20,320 feet, it is the tallest landmass in the world from base to summit. It dominated the landscape like nothing this young man had ever dreamed. The massive snowcapped peak lined with streamers of cold blue ice was a spectacular backdrop for the well-deserved slumber overtaking him. With the sun setting in the west the horizon was ablaze with a kaleidoscope of bright colors exaggerated by the pureness of the Alaskan air and framing the majesty of Mt. McKinley.

While certainly no competition for a 4-Star hotel, the Chevy was acceptable for lodging in this forbidding land. Tall and lanky, Harv curled up in the back seat, protected from the sub-zero cold of the twilight only by the trench coat that would have to suffice in the absence of a sleeping bag. A couple of hours into the long Alaskan night he awoke shivering to a sight that frightened the young man to the core. The northern sky was on fire, not unlike the great grass fires of his youth in the plains of Missouri. The lower sky was rimmed with dancing spires of amber reds and greenish glows. What was this? Was the world coming to an end? Should he crank the Chevy's engine and head south as fast as he possibly could? Needless to say this scene jolted him from his deep sleep to an enhanced state of awareness. He tightly gripped the Rosary that held a permanent place deep within his right pocket. As his brain raced, he seemed to recall O'Connor writing of the brilliance of the northern lights (aurora borealis), which could explain the phenomenon that was currently rocking his world. His nerves settled as his heart rate decreased. Wow! Welcome to Alaska, the land of the midnight sun!

The first few days of hunting were largely uneventful. Harv mostly cruised up and down the graveled Denali Highway in search of caribou as they aimlessly wandered through the tundra along the path of their seasonal migration. Midday on the fourth day he finally spotted movement in the form of two distant animals. Grabbing his bow and strapping on his King back quiver, he began his initial stalk. Early on he was frustrated by the challenges of the terrain. Rolling hillsides were separated by gentle valleys carved by centuries of cascading streams fueled by gravity. Each and every one gave homage to the local beaver populations and, therefore, deep ice lined ponds causing Harv to have to zig-zag around them on his quest. Furthermore, each step through the tundra, comprised of lichen's and mosses some twelve inches thick, was akin to hiking through a blanket of sponges similar in texture to those of the kitchen variety. It wasn't long before he made the decision, due to the fading light, to simply wade through the numerous beaver ponds rather than navigate them. In the bitter cold inherent to the Alaskan fall, his pants rapidly froze solid between each pond, making the simple chore of hiking difficult at best. After an hour or so of this he was close enough to make the determination that the objects of his considerable effort were in fact a cow moose and calf, and not the caribou that he was licensed to hunt. Arriving back at the Chevy well after dark he was afraid that he would have to cut off his frozen trousers. After careful consideration, however, he determined that he could crank the Chevy, turning the heat on full blast and eventually thaw the pants.

A couple of days later the quietness of the Alaskan day was disturbed as Harv heard the familiar whine of a small aircraft in the distance. The pilot guided the plane over by Harv and passed close enough that it was obvious he was interested in the nature of Harv's intrusion. The next day a three-quarter-ton pickup with a Department of the Interior sign on it pulls up and out steps a federal game warden with a cigarette hanging out of his parched mouth. The polite man introduces himself as Ivan L. Marks and explains to Harv that they always travel in pairs, one on the ground and one in the air, and that they communicated via WWII vintage base radios to protect each other.

Ivan told Harv that the pilot, Mel Zahn, spotted Harv the previous day and directed Ivan to his whereabouts, figuring that he was poaching moose since he was hunting the creek bottoms and valleys frequented by the largest member of the deer family. Harv replied that that wasn't the case, but rather that he was just a dumb young coon hunter from Missouri with a dream of killing a caribou with his bow. That was all it took for the seeds of a lifelong friendship to be planted. It turned out that Ivan was himself one hell of a hound man and had spent a lifetime in pursuit of lions, bear, and bobcats. The afternoon was filled with lies and exaggerations of blue tick and red bone hound escapades.

Ivan explained to Harv that the caribou migration was nowhere near this area. Mel and Ivan were staying in a government shack near the small Eskimo village of Glennallen some 150 miles to the north. He invited Harv to join them and offered Mel's services to locate the nomadic Nelchina herd and then Ivan's help to get Harv in on

63

the herd. Ivan felt sure that with their assistance Harv's dream was obtainable.

For the first time in Harv's brief life he felt like a rich man! Here he was in the vast wilds of Alaska, too poor to afford the luxury of a sleeping bag, but invited to stay in a heated lodge with a pilot to locate the migrating caribou herds, and the services of a local guide to direct him to his quarry. Jack O'Connor beware — there was a new legend in the making!

Harv and his new friend Ivan arrived at the cabin a little before dusk, followed shortly by Mel in the float plane, which gently settled in on the rippling surface of the small lake bordering the cabin and taxied to the pebble strewn shoreline. Mel cut the engine and jumped out of the plane onto the left pontoon as it glided toward shore, pitching the tie down rope to the occupants on shore. Mel was every bit the gentleman that Ivan was and Harv immediately felt that he had known him for years. The men proceeded into the warmth of the shack and hot food. Mel assured Harv that he would fly out in the morning and locate the 5,000 or so animals in the Nelchina herd. He felt sure that they were currently located south of Mt. McKinley near the Glenn Highway. As soon as he located them he would radio their location to Ivan. In spite of the fact that Harv was tired to the bone, he still wrestled with a virtually sleepless night, short in duration and filled with anticipation greater than any Harv had ever experienced.

The next morning the men were up well before daybreak. They slammed down a quick breakfast as they headed out the door. Mel untied the plane from its mooring, pushed it out into the lake, pulled himself up on the float, and was airborne in the matter of a few scant minutes. Harv gathered up his hunting gear and followed Ivan to the truck, which he had heading down the road toward Denali as the sun broke the confines of the eastern horizon. They hadn't gone far before the men heard Mel chime in on the radio, *"Tell Harv the herd is between mile markers 112 and 115 and 12 miles or so west of the road. Tell him to go get him one."*

Ivan drove Harv down to mile marker 112, which was nothing more than a wooden stake, painted white and driven into the ground along the road. Arriving in the late morning, they hiked toward the west as quickly as they possibly could, covering mile after mile, stopping occasionally to look for caribou and the grizzly bears known to inhabit the area.

Three to four hours into the excursion they topped a hill and were greeted with a scene known to Harv only through the printed words of Jack O'Connor. There were caribou everywhere they looked. As far as they could see — north, west, south … it didn't matter which direction they looked — hundreds, if not thousands, of them dotting the landscape like sheep in the old western movies Harv had seen at the local movie theater in Missouri as a kid. It was the most overwhelming sight the young country boy had ever witnessed. More than he could ever have dreamed, the ground seemed alive with caribou moving in small bands in all directions. It was, however, apparent that there was a definite southerly flow to the masses.

By this time the sun was hanging low in the western sky and Ivan reminded Harv that they were in grizzly country and that they best get out of there before dark. Ivan promised Harv that he would have him back to the let-off spot in the morning well before daybreak and that would give Harv a full day of sunlight to fulfill his dream. The hike back to the truck was an easy one, fueled by the strength of youth and the passion burning in Harv's soul.

The next morning Ivan dropped Harv off at mile marker 112 around 4 a.m. and loaned him his government issued binoculars. Harv didn't even know what binoculars were but welcomed the addition with Ivan's encouragement.

There was no concern of getting lost. The agreement between the men was that Harv would hunt until late afternoon, then put the sight of the Talkeetna mountains to his backside as he headed east until he reached the Richardson Highway, which generally ran north and south. At that point he was to follow the road back to mile marker 112 where Ivan would be waiting in the truck. Ivan told Harv that he would wait there for up to two days and if Harv hadn't shown up by then, he would call in Mel and the plane to locate him.

Harv covered the twelve miles to the hillside he had regrettably vacated the previous afternoon like an Olympic marathon runner in quest of gold, accompanied only by the bow he had fashioned with his own hands and a quiver full of a dozen arrows.

In no time it seemed he was within the boundaries of the massive herd, a lone predator in a virtual sea of caribou, surrounded only by the incessant sound of clacking hooves. He would concentrate on a single band of caribou and work as best he could at getting himself within bow range. Several times over the next couple of hours Harv positioned himself for a shot at the herd bull, which never seemed closer than 50 yards. He watched helplessly, time after time, as the snow-covered tundra swallowed up his errant arrows as the caribou disappeared as quickly as they had appeared.

It wasn't long before Harv was down to only four arrows in his back quiver. It was obvious that he was badly in need of a new strategy. Accustomed to retrieving his spent arrows, he never dreamed that the ground would swallow up his limited supply of arrows like a rainbow trout does a well-cast dry fly. He opted to take a rest on the highest point that he could find, allowing him to quietly observe the wanderings of the herd. After a short period of time it became apparent that even though the caribou initially seemed to wander aimlessly in this rolling terrain, they obviously preferred to follow the contours of the narrow valleys, traveling in small bands usually comprised of fifteen to twenty cows and one large herd bull trailed by a small group of satellite bulls.

Armed with his newfound knowledge, Harv set up an ambush in a well-traveled valley. It wasn't long before he observed a small band of caribou working toward him with a large bull in the middle of the group. The lead cow turned as she passed him at forty yards exposing her vitals as she scurried off kicking up small patches of muskeg laced with snow. Soon, three or four more cows passed similarly as the bull approached. The old bull turned as the cows had at forty yards, Harv locked his predatory stare behind the bull's left shoulder, drew back the bowstring, and released sending the arrow on its way. The arrow flew true, seemingly in slow motion, and made a loud KWACK! as it entered the bull's formidable shoulder, knocking the bull briefly to the ground. As quickly as he fell to the ground, the bull was up and raced down the valley to rejoin his herd with a significant crimson patch visible on his left shoulder.

Not knowing whether to rejoice or cry, Harv scurried up the nearest hillside in order to gain a vantage point. With literally thousands of caribou still within eyesight, he was relieved to discover that with the considerable aide of the binoculars it wasn't difficult to pick the injured bull out of the herd. Furthermore, there was a considerable blood trail, amplified by the thin crust of snow, lying in patches upon the tundra.

It was at this point that the young man hailing from the Show Me State showed his resolve. He promised himself that the bull can run all the way to the North Pole if he liked, but Harv was going to "dog his ass" all the way. No way was he leaving without recovering his caribou! So he began the arduous task of doing just that — dogging it ... pushing the caribou just as a grizzly bear digs up a marmot in its den. It wasn't long before it became apparent to Harv that the old bull was indeed slowing down. He was using his left front leg less and less. Finally, after some three to four intense hours, sweat streaming down Harv's face, he observed the bull lying down, the fight playing out of him. Harv crawled in on the bull, close enough to see the bull's chest heave as he labored for every breath, and slipped two more arrows into the fallen monarch's chest. It was over. The bull was dead.

Harv was overjoyed, but for the first time all day felt worn out and hungry, not having eaten anything since before he left the warmth of Ivan's truck in the moonlight. To further dampen his spirits he noted that the sun was beginning to fade and he realized that he had no idea where he was. He pulled his last arrow out of his quiver, removed the red bandana that he had kept tied around his neck, secured it to the arrow and stuck the arrow in the ground next to his caribou. Then in one movement he picked up his bow and turned his back on the view of the Talkeetna's in the distance and began the long journey back to the Richardson Highway, a successful bow hunter with his first big game bow kill under his belt.

He reached the road near mile marker 115 around 1 a.m. and headed toward mile marker 112 and the rendezvous point Ivan had noted. He was more than relieved to find Ivan's truck parked as promised with the occupant sound asleep inside. A sharp rap on the window and Harv observed movement from within as Ivan scrambled to life. *"Did you get a caribou?"* Ivan hollered as he came to his senses.

"I did ... you got any food?" Harv responded as he rapidly changed the subject as by now he was starved. Ivan dug around behind the seat and held up a can of sardines.

"Will this do?" Ivan retorted.

"Hell, yes, and I will whip any grizzly's ass that tries to take it from me." Harv said smiling widely.

Ivan turned the key and fired up the truck's engine. Harv relayed to him the adventure of the past day as they headed toward the shack, arriving as the first rays of sunlight peeked over the eastern horizon. Ivan said that they would head back to recover the caribou early the next morning. In the meantime he would check with Father Joe, the local Jesuit priest, and see if he might be willing to help recover the caribou, provided that Harv would donate the meat to the children of the local school. It seems Father Joe had a Deuce and a half with a weasel ... in other words, a six-ton truck with a half-track and winch.

Father Joe was glad to pitch in and they loaded up the equipment and headed back to mile marker 115 early the next morning. After unloading the equipment, Father Joe, Ivan, and Harv jumped on board and headed west with Harv feeling every bit the newly crowned king of this great land. Two or three hours later Ivan spotted the red bandana with his binoculars. Much to Harv's relief there was no grizzly on the carcass. In no time at all they

had the caribou cut up and loaded in the weasel for the trip back to the truck and ultimately the shack.

By this time Harv was beginning to come back down to earth and the realities of life. He had been gone from his new home and wife for nearly three weeks with no contact. He had no idea if he would still have a job when he returned, and more importantly his wife had no idea if he was dead or alive. He only knew that he needed to head home as soon as possible. Not having any idea how to cape an animal out, Ivan gladly offered to take care of the task for Harv. Harv packed what little gear he had into the Chevy, then tied the caribou head and cape in the trunk, thanked Ivan, placed the key in the ignition, rotated it and to his surprise the engine failed to even turn over. Further investigation revealed that the frigid Alaska cold had frozen the block that had subsequently broken.

"Not a problem" said Ivan. *"I will contact the fish and game office in Anchorage and have them contact Hertz and send someone up here to get you and the car."*

Two days later, up drove a car occupied by two obviously intoxicated natives accompanied by two women of ill repute and trailed by a welcomed tow bar. Harv greeted the unlikely crew with skepticism and noticed immediately that the car was laced with the stench of cheap whiskey from the day's journey from Anchorage. The natives hooked Harv's car up to the tow bar while Harv informed them that he would be riding in the Chevy with his caribou so that he would be able to steer it while in tow. What he didn't consider was that with the temperature hovering near 0°F, he would nearly freeze to death during the miserable journey back to Anchorage.

The natives pulled up to the Hertz rental office well before daylight, unhooked the car and disappeared rapidly into the darkness engulfing the town, no doubt in search of additional libations funded by the labors of the past day.

Harv was freezing, shaking uncontrollably, but still totally unwilling to separate from his trophy. With his caribou in tow he began walking up 4th Street in search of warmth. Not far up the road he happened upon a taxicab dispatch, which was open 24/7. He asked ... no, pleaded with the lady in the office to allow him to come in, with his caribou of course, and sit in warmth until the city came to life and he could deliver the caribou to the Jonas Brothers receiving office his friends in Seattle had told him about. No doubt probably more through fear than reason, she agreed to his request.

As soon as morning broke Harv thanked the lady and carried his prized possession down to Jonas Brothers, settled up with Hertz, grabbed his gear, and headed to the airport and back to Seattle ... back to the civilized world and, hopefully, back to his wife and job.

Arriving back in his new abode in Seattle, Harv's wife was thrilled to greet her emaciated husband. He intrigued and frightened her with his stories of the great journey. He was relieved as well to discover that he did, in fact, have a job, which he started soon after returning to Seattle.

A couple of weeks later Harv received a call from Bert Kleinberger with Jonas Brothers letting him know that they had his caribou and would be working on the mount. About that same time he got a call from Glenn St. Charles who owned Northwest Archery and also frequented Jonas Brothers. St. Charles let Harv know that they were going to measure Harv's bull and that they believed that it would be a new world record.

Records at that time were kept by the NFAA in their big game section. St. Charles was working on getting a new record-keeping club going that would eventually be called the Pope & Young Club. He had gotten the NFAA to release all bowhunting records to him for the new club. By the fall of 1959 St. Charles was heading up meetings held at Northwest Archery dedicated to the formation of the new club. Harv was invited to participate, partially because his caribou had put him on the bowhunting roadmap and partially because they needed a representative from the Midwest.

A few months later, the Ebers moved back to Missouri.

The Pope & Young Club was formally established on January 27, 1961. The first formal meeting of the new Club was held in Seattle, which would serve as the Club's headquarters' for many years to come. At the meeting Glenn St. Charles would be elected Temporary Chairman, William Brown was elected Temporary Treasurer and Roselyn Remick was appointed Temporary Recording Secretary. St. Charles then appointed William Brown, Wayne Hathaway, William Jardine, G.H. Malinoski and Jesse Rust as Temporary Directors.

Lastly, there was also established a National Advisory Board which was designed to advise, approve or disapprove action taken by the new club. The membership included Fred Bear from Michigan, Harv Ebers from Missouri, Elisha Gray also from Michigan, Martin Hanson from Wisconsin, Dr. Dean Henbest from New Mexico, K.K. Knickerbocker from Virginia, Robert Lee from Texas, Ben Pearson from Arkansas, Wayne Trimm from New York, William Wright from California, and later Dr. Rex Hancock from Arkansas.

Harv's well-earned caribou trophy was actually measured by an official measurer soon after Glenn St. Charles' call. It actually came in as the number two barren ground caribou in the world being barely nosed out by a caribou killed by an up and coming young bowhunter rapidly gaining fame named Fred Bear at the Little Delta River a couple of weeks prior. It is still listed as the 26th largest barren ground caribou ever taken with a bow some 50+ years later.

Harv remained on the Board of Directors of the Pope & Young Club for over 30 years serving in various capacities and retiring at the April, 2007 meeting, which coincidentally was the first Board meeting attended by the author in his capacity as Treasurer of the Club and the start of a very special friendship.

Personal Reflections

What is it that draws bowhunters to the Pope and Young Club? To some, it may be the fact that they have finally taken an animal that is worthy of entry into the Record Book; however, for most members the Club has far more influential value. Is it the heritage, the history that lures them, or is it the networking of friends? The list is as endless as the number of members.

More than just a record keeping organization, the Pope and Young Club has become a place to hang one's hat, a place to share and enjoy outdoor experiences with other like-minded bowhunters. For many, it is way of life … it is what makes us who we are as ethical, moral, and concerned outdoorsmen and outdoorswomen.

The following are personal testimonials from a wide spectrum of Pope and Young members on how the Club has influenced their lives, and their strong connection to the Club and its members. The sampling is not haphazard; the authors were carefully chosen to represent the entire spectrum of Club members. They encompass both men and women, young and old … from 35-years of age to 80 … from all walks of life. They represent members from every fold of our society, and they have something to share. For those who are longtime, active members of the Pope and Young Club, you will find similar ideals of how the Club has changed our lives. For those who have yet to become active members, these personal reflections may open their eyes to the wonderful opportunities the Club offers.

My Pope and Young Club Friends

By Nathan L. Andersohn

To me, the Pope and Young Club has meant camaraderie with like-minded bowhunters for most of my adult life. It has been an honor to associate and build friendships with serious bowhunters from throughout North America.

There have been several defining moments for me in the Club. I can vividly remember sitting at my first Board meeting giving legal advice on several issues. As I looked around the table at Fred Asbell, Jim Dougherty, Harv Ebers, Randy Byers, M.R. James, George Moerlein, Ron Sherer, Glenn Hisey, and Billy Ellis, it was a dream come true, sitting with the who's who of bowhunting. That evening I ended up at a social hour talking to Glenn St. Charles for a half hour … it was memorable.

A few years later, I was invited by Billy Ellis to hunt Central Barren Ground caribou in the Northwest Territories. The hunt included Pope and Young members Jay St. Charles, Joe St. Charles, Dale Holpainen, Russ Tye, Dick and Carol Mauch, Jack Joseph, Max Thomas, T.J. Conrads, Larry Fischer, John Evans, and Glenn St. Charles.

We traveled to Yellowknife, and then by floatplane to camp, and proceeded to share countless hours fishing for lake trout and stalking caribou. There were campfires, happy hours, and daily meals where we would talk and relive our days afield … great adventures with good people in the North Country in the tradition of our bowhunting forefathers. The experience of hunting and fishing with so many dedicated bowhunters and the resulting life long friendships couldn't have been better.

Had I never joined and become active in Pope and Young, I would have still spent a good part of my life bowhunting; however, it would have been different. The concepts of ethical hunting, conservation, and promoting bowhunting to other hunters and non-hunters would not have become such refined principals of the sport for me.

I would not have reached as far nor attempted as much with my bow had I not met so many individuals with insatiable desires to accomplish so much with the stick and string. It would have seemed impossible to take all four species of sheep with a bow had I not met bowhunters who had done just that.

Talking to bowhunters who had hunted Australia and Africa led me to stalk water buffalo in the Northern Territory of Australia and wait for a fine kudu bull at a water hole in South Africa.

It's been great to have a network of friends to discuss gear and clothing requirements for everything from jungle adventures to the ice and snow of the Arctic Circle. Those friendships have made the preparation and anticipation of the unknown a reality.

Having friends from both coasts of North America stop me at conventions and inquire about the successes and hardships of a hunting trip allow me to reminisce. Pope and Young members listen to your adventures and pay attention to advice on the hunts, as many of them may be contemplating the same hunt someday.

Pope and Young Conventions are like class reunions; they are full of old friends who have shared fires with you in the mountains or on the tundra. It never gets old sitting down in a corner somewhere and reliving the highlights of a special hunt. Plus, there are new faces and young up-and-coming hunters to mingle with. Just as many of the old-timers took me under their wing, I find myself doing the same.

It has been good to grow with the Club. Many things have changed, and the members of Pope and Young have struggled with some challenges, but as a fraternity of hunters we have evolved. Some things have changed while many things have remained the same. There is room in the Club for many ideals, and it's not hard to find a group of bowhunters within the Club who share common philosophies. The Club has a purpose — actually many purposes — and there is room for growth in ideas as the Club progresses. The foundation of the organization has been the strength of its members from many varied backgrounds. It's easy to feel a little isolated at home and work when I have little contact with people who live and breathe bowhunting, but when I walk into a Pope and Young Convention I'm immediately immersed with brothers of the bow who live like I do.

Watching so many men and women give so much personal time and effort to bowhunting is an inspiration for many to do the same. Whether it is at the local archery club, making donations, writing, or giving speeches at events, it is not hard to get caught up in the flow of things. Our members are a solid group of hunters who are willing to give to something they believe in without any tangible rewards.

I haven't missed a convention since 1989 and I get an email from Pope and Young members daily. I guess I'm hooked.

Over twenty years ago, I sewed a Pope and Young patch on a wool hunting jacket and wore it with pride. I suppose when I walk that last ridge, old and frail, and carry my longbow for the final time, I will still have a Pope and Young patch on my shoulder and know in my heart that I was part of something good.

Why I Value the Pope and Young Club

By Connie Renfro

I was a latecomer to the world of bowhunting, seeing my first season come and go in 1987-1988. With so much to learn on so many levels, after my first season ended I began to delve into the "modern" history of our sport. Opening the pages of Maurice Thompson's The Witchery of Archery, I entered a door into an enchanting adventure laced with sadness and triumph, grace and humility. Soon I was racing through the excitement of Hunting with the Bow and Arrow by Saxton Pope, Ishi, by Theodora Kroeber, Wild Adventure and Hunting the Hard Way by Howard Hill and, later on, Trailing a Bear by Robert Munger, Bows on the Little Delta by Glenn St. Charles, and so many more.

I began to realize the importance of the Pope and Young Club through the historical perspective of bowhunting. The Pope and Young Club, founded under the leadership of Glenn St. Charles, created a means of archiving a small part of our history, while also providing legitimacy to bowhunting. The Club laid the foundation for bowhunting ethics, fair chase, shot placement, and animal recovery. As our society and culture changed, bowhunters throughout the country had to adapt and adjust to ensure the non-hunting public still accepted our means and methods of hunting. No longer were bowhunting "shorts" played at the local theatres to the delight of the audiences; we were being relegated to the role of defending bowhunting as a viable and humane method of taking game. The days of Saxton and Art's 85-155 yard shots with, at times, doubtful results have long since passed.

As my knowledge and passion for bowhunting continued to grow, I reveled in the times spent wandering the wild country with a simple stick and string and a quiver full of homemade arrows. The simplicity and grace of the sport is not lost on me, and my love for the bow and arrow has continued unabated. I smile as I read a quote from Saxton Pope's The Adventurous Bowman; it captures the true essence of archery for so many of us. *"The bow becomes part of his mood; member of his faculties, yielding service and direct action in proportion to the throbbing life placed in it. The very sinews of the huntsman are implicated in his weapon. The poise and nicety of his mental state is made manifest in the flight of his arrow. The serenity and steadfast nature of his nerves are registered in its true flight."*

While it is true that some of my best trophies will never be a part of the Pope and Young Records, animals like my first elk — a spike taken after many years of effort — I still carry in my mind the purpose and objectives as put forth by the Pope and Young Club. I strive to remember the importance of leading by example, with unquestionable ethics, integrity, and honor even with no one around to judge my actions. For me, bowhunting has captured my heart and soul and I am honor-bound to do my absolute best by the animals I hunt. I am knowledgeable and confident with my equipment, I work to maintain my skills, limit my shot distances, follow every blood trail, respect my quarry and their wild homes, and carry myself at all times as if the eyes of the world were watching.

Armed with the knowledge of our proud heritage, I continue learning the sport of archery and bowhunting to this day. I now leaf through the pages of the Pope and Young Record Books with a great deal of nostalgia. Names and animals that grace the pages fire off memories of people long since passed, and wild places that remain untouched to this day. I see the names of friends and recall stories around a shared campfire, reliving the adventures of the hunt. I wonder about new names that I read, hoping that they, too, have been caught up in the love of the sport.

The Pope and Young Club continues its important role in documenting our history and it provides a means of reflection on our past. As with every aspect of mankind and our history, we would do well to remember our heritage and proceed forth with humility, honor, and integrity.

Looking Back
By Jim Dougherty

Back in the late 1950s, as a starry-eyed, young bowhunter who dreamed of taking moose, elk, bear, and other animals armed with my bow and arrows, I was content just to get a cottontail or an occasional ground squirrel. Still, I kept to my dreams.

Somewhere around the late 1950s into the 1960s I kept hearing about an organization that, under the auspices of Glenn St. Charles, wanted to take the big game records away from the National Field Archery Association (NFAA) and put them in his new organization. As a member of the NFAA, I was aware of his efforts and, on the surface, without any true knowledge of what it truly meant at that time, was slightly opposed to this new venture. I got over it!

As time went on I began to understand what was going on, and the more I learned the more I became interested. Shortly thereafter I joined as an Associate Member having been encouraged by my friend Doug Walker, the representative for Bear Archery on the West Coast who was also very involved with California archery politics. Doug was also a good friend with Fred Bear and Glenn St. Charles, the latter principle and a major player in this new organization.

By that time I had shot a few deer, a bear, and needed a record-class third species to qualify for Regular Membership. I achieved that with a rather smallish cougar from New Mexico that both Glenn St. Charles and Doug Walker measured at my home one evening. With that I became one of the first 100 Regular Members.

While acquiring Regular Membership seemed a personal ego building experience, and I suppose to some extent it was, it was not the reason I sought Regular Membership. Slowly but surely the Club's objective was reaching game departments, wildlife and conservation agencies, the general public, and bowhunters with its message that hunting with bow and arrow was a valid, effective, and humane hunting method, something I strongly supported and sincerely believed in.

Over time, especially every two years when the Club's Biennial Conventions roll around, it was always interesting and a very real pleasure to meet and share this time with both old and new friends and debate the pros and cons affecting bowhunting and our Club, which has struggled on occasion but, in every case, those struggles have only proved to make it a stronger more volatile organization. No entity pleases every member all the time.

In later years, I somehow became president of the Pope and Young Club and served two terms. Those were rather tumultuous times in the Club's history that took a great deal of patience to straighten out. Those four years rank in my mind as the finest opportunity any president could have had, working with the finest board and officers, people whose dedication to our tasks was unparalleled. It was hard work at times, and took a great deal of our personal time, sometimes away from family and bowhunting where we would much rather have been I'm sure, but it was one of the most rewarding of times too.

I have often been told, and I must honestly agree, that our group did a pretty good job in straightening out the Club's issues and personalities, and that every other new regime has done an even better job in overseeing the Clubs' well being.

Saying the Pope and Young Club is important to me would be a gross understatement; more to the point, it has become a way of life ... my life. Since those long ago days when a cottontail brought on shaking knees and trembling fingers, through all the years of bigger game, and my life in the archery industry and other organizations, the Club has always been and will continue to be first.

I am ever thankful in what the Pope and Young Club has accomplished, what it stands for, how it has brought bowhunting to the spotlight and how it continues to be a leader in hunting ethics. May it continue to be so.

An Awesome Ride …

By Kathy Strecker

To say that the Pope and Young Club and bowhunting have helped shape the person that I have become would be an understatement. Bowhunting has given me opportunities to bowhunt all over North America and Africa. I owe a debt of gratitude to the Pope and Young Club for making it possible for all bowhunters to pursue the passion that I love. One way I feel I can give back is by being a Bowhunter Education Instructor.

I went to my first convention in Minneapolis in 1993 and walked around in awe as I saw people I had previously only read about. I looked at the animal displays and never in my wildest dreams did I even think about shooting a record book animal. I just wanted to go hunting and be good enough to harvest an animal every now and then.

My husband and I have not missed a convention since the first one in Minneapolis. At each convention I sit and listen to the accomplishments of the Club and have been impressed. The commitment and the dedication of the Club members are second to none. I remember visiting with Glenn and Margaret St. Charles and how friendly and open they were. I have the picture Margaret took of me, my husband Doug, and Glenn. Margaret enclosed a little note with the picture and it still amazes me how she would remember everyone. The photo is one of my prized possessions.

Doug was the one who got me started in bowhunting and was the one who kept telling me I should join the Pope and Young Club. My response was, *"This is way out of my league."* He would remind me I had the animal needed to be an Associate

Member and that the Club was not just for people who have shot record book animals.

That first convention got me hooked. As the years went by, I got to that stage where I was okay with going home without a tag filled. To get a mature animal was more important than filling a tag. You all know the stage that I'm talking about. When I shot my first book animal, an antelope in Wyoming, I was so excited to get my certificate in the mail.

I finally got tired of not being able to go to the membership meetings due to the fact I still wasn't a member. I wanted to be part of this group that was so committed to conservation and the future of bowhunting. I became an Associate Member in 1996 and a Regular Member in 2007. I am now serving on the Membership Committee, and was involved when the by-laws were changed. I feel that it is very important to earn each one of the membership steps. Advancement should not just be obtained by shooting the required animals. Each of us must give back to the sport of bowhunting that has given so much to us.

In 1996 I went on a caribou hunt to the Northwest Territories with my husband and some of his hunting buddies. It was my first big hunt with "the guys" and it was with some pretty experienced hunters, like Randy Doyle, Glenn and Kevin Hisey, Larry Streiff, and Jay and Karen Deones. It was a great experience and I harvested a record book caribou. At the end of the trip the camp manager ask if I thought I could get a group of ladies together for a bowhunt for caribou. I thought, what a perfect opportunity to share a trip most of my friends might not ever get a chance to go on! I contacted all my lady hunting friends and came up with a group of women who were very interested. Most of the ladies had only hunted whitetails, so this was a big trip for them. I knew this would be a great experience just seeing the animals and I had no idea how successful we would be, filling 16 of the 20 tags. Nine of those caribou are now listed in the Pope and Young Record Book. When you get a chance to share and give back, you should do it. It made me understand why my husband has a smile on his face that is as big as mine when I harvest an animal.

I harvested a Pope and Young whitetail in Kansas in 2007 on a hunt that I purchased at the 2007 Pope and Young Convention. I know that being a member of the Pope and Young Club comes with big responsibilities and in 2015, when I'm able to apply for Senior Membership status, I will have worked very hard to meet all the necessary criteria.

Being involved with the Pope and Young Club has been an awesome ride up to this point, and I'm looking forward to many more days in the field. I also look forward to future conventions, meeting old friends and making new ones.

My Fifteen Minutes

By Scott Showalter

I first heard of the Pope and Young Club from Al Dawson, one of the first members and a sales representative of Bear Archery. The possibility of joining a trophy hunting organization was fascinating and I set out determined to meet the requirements to be a Regular Member. It took a few years, but a Yellowstone elk met the minimum score in place at that time and allowed me to apply for Regular Membership.

Dr. Lowell Eddy and I attended the Pope and Young Club banquet at the Brown Palace Hotel in Denver. We were the final two Regular Members allowed in, bringing the total membership to 100.

Like most bowhunters attending their first convention, I was thrilled to see all the trophies on display, and to see and listen to all the stories told by the famous bowhunters in attendance. I asked permission and followed Glenn St. Charles and Dick Mauch into a room at the hotel to watch them check the score of a big non-typical Kansas whitetail. I decided then and there I wanted to become an Official Measurer. After months of very persistent pestering of Dick Mauch with phone calls, requests, and offers of assistance, he finally sold me a copy of Grancel Fitz's How to Measure and Score Big-Game Trophies and appointed me an Official Measurer.

The Club was growing from infancy to adolescence and money was more than short. The Club structure as we know it now did not exist. Glenn and Dick were overloaded with responsibility. Being a newcomer at that time, I volunteered for anything and everything and I am sure they gave me things to do to get me out from under their feet.

Glenn was the anchor holding everything together. The lack of structure was itself an obstacle. When a problem did arise, Glenn would call a group of officials and members together and those who could afford to travel would meet and try to work out a solution. One of these meetings was held in Denver in 1972 to discuss the transfer of the trophy records from Dick Mauch to Doug Walker. It was at this meeting that I got to know George Moerlein and Dr. James Scott. We became hunting companions and lifelong friends. We spent many hours on hunting trips discussing the Club and where we each felt it should go. Needless to say, we did not always agree.

Sometime between 1972 and 1974, I was appointed temporary Membership Chairman. The Associate ranks were around 200 people at that time. Letters were sent to all members, Regular and Associate alike, requesting that everyone get out and actively try to enroll as many new Associates as possible. The response was terrific, especially around Chicago and in the state of Minnesota. The Associate Membership rose to 2000 and remained around that number for decades. The Membership Chairman was not originally a voting member of the board but that was changed during my tenure.

In July 1974, I was appointed temporary Executive Secretary and Records Chairman. This was changed to a permanent appointment in November of 1974. Carl Hurlbert took over the Executive Secretary position in January of 1975 and the Records Chairman job remained in my hands.

My tenure as Records Chairman was the high point in my association with the Pope and Young Club. It was the most rewarding job I have ever had.

The early 1970s were tumultuous and exceedingly stressful. We were short of money and we were trying to publish our first record book. As a book editorial committee, we were long on opinions and short on experience. We did trample on each other's toes at times, but the lack of money was the major source of stress. Old timers will remember passing the hat to get enough money to cover convention expenses. Every officer paid their own way to the meetings and chipped in to help others to make the trip. Fred Bear was very generous with multiple contributions during this period.

As an organization, we survived the 1970s. We established Senior Membership to allow the Club to grow. We, through the efforts of George Moerlein and Billy Ellis, established a trust fund. We published our first book, which was the magic bullet to improving our financial situation. Getting that first record book published was the turning point in putting the Club on firm financial footing. From that point forward we have become bigger and better.

Glenn St. Charles was the guiding light of the Pope and Young Club. It was his support that allowed me to serve in the positions that I have held in the club. He was my role model, my mentor, a great hunting companion and, best of all, my friend.

My opinion of the Pope and Young Club was published on the last page of the 10th recording period booklet. The Club structure has changed some since then but my feelings for the Club and what it stands for have never changed.

It has always been a privilege to serve the Pope and Young Club.

What the Pope and Young Club has Meant to Me

By Stacee Frost

The Pope and Young Club has been a solid base, a grounding of values and ideals for me. The members of the Club are like my family. The hunter I am today is but for their shaping me along the way.

Through the Conventions I have attended over the years, I have been fortunate in creating and cultivating friendships and memories — a network and support system of friendships has been forged over the years the strength of which is stronger than any other I know.

From my first Convention (at the time I was merely a trailing family member — Dad was a member and the Convention also afforded an opportunity for our family to get together), I was making fast friends. I knew very few people at that first convention; however, that feeling of singularity was never to be felt again. Everyone was friendly and genuine and I have very close friends today whom I know I met at my very first Convention.

Eventually I was able to join as an Associate Member, attended conventions in my own capacity, and later became an Official Measurer, all the while continuously making friends along the way. The scope and focus of friendships forged through Pope and Young Club connections is not limited to hunting; they are friends in all aspects of my life. They have watched me through undergraduate and grad school and job interviews. They have served as mentors and sounding boards in starting my own business. They have poured out their hearts to me in prayer and sympathy lifting me up to help me through the care and later loss of my husband after his brave battle with cancer.

The value of a network of friends across the country and beyond is immeasurable. My Pope and Young Club friends have been there to share time afield and have been there to share a cup of coffee and stories. They have been there to fish me out of jams (central Wyoming with a newly expired driver's license and thus no ability to rent a car), and they can be relied upon for sage referrals and advice on where and with whom to hunt. They are mentors-become-friends and friends-become-mentors. From the sharing and cheering to the shoring-up and support provided through life's roller coaster, I have been so blessed to have friends from the Pope and Young Club.

A Conversation with my Sons

By Tom Foss

Climbing up the last pitch to our lookout point, I looked up at the two figures powering up the rugged slope in front of me. My sons were older and stronger now, and it was they who were now waiting on me. It was only a few years earlier when I purposely set a slower pace and carried the majority of the gear, but now the tables had turned. They were in great shape, practiced, trained, and were veterans of many trips into the mountains. They were happy to be out together again for another one of our annual backpack sheep hunts. With two days before the season opener, we were hoping to find rams in the basin.

Suddenly it was raining, and as it started to intensify we hunkered down under a light tarp, taking the downpour in stride. We had been in this situation before, and were reminiscing about the journey that had brought us to this part of the mountain … the years of shooting, past hunts, the training, the hiking, and the good fortune that we had enjoyed … the good times that we had spent together on other mountains, together and with friends.

Almost on cue they both asked me, *"Dad, I know why you love this sheep hunting, but tell me why you belong to Pope and Young?"* Well, we had time so I started.

"You boys know my old friend, David Richardson? He is a wonderful gentleman and has hunted with many of the early members of the Club. He spent many nights at the archery range introducing me to the longbow, and then later to the benefits of being a supporter of the Club. You remember when I went to the Convention in Edmonton? It was the only place outside of the United States to host the Biennial Convention. You guys also know that Alberta Bowhunters support the Club at one of the highest per capita rates. There may be more measurers, Senior

Members, and past directors per capita here than any other state or province.

"One day Dave pushed a nice mulie past me and 60 days later we spent an evening measuring my first Pope and Young animal. He was as proud of it as I was and explained that I should enter it to recognize the animal, but also to help with the record keeping and confirmation of bowhunting as an effective management tool."

"I know the Pope and Young records the entries and establishes the minimums, but what else do they do?" Adam asked.

Before I could reply, Cameron replied, *"They also set out the Rules of Fair Chase and do a lot of work promoting bowhunting and the image of the bowhunter. It's more than just entering a head!"*

I had to agree, as my involvement had grown from just entering an animal to attending a Convention. Later, it was Ryk Vischer who challenged me to get involved as the Regulations Chairman for the Alberta Bowhunters Association. After that, Mike Schlegel asked me to be a part of the Pope and Young Conservation Committee.

"You boys know that I believe every bowhunter should be a member of their local archery club, their provincial or state association, and then a larger organization. If they have a specific interest, then one or more specialty conservation organization might be added.

"To me, belonging to a bigger group does so much for the archer, and also for the organization as well as the resource. We all know how much these associations do for the animals we are so fortunate to hunt. Belonging makes me a better hunter, a better person, and a stronger advocate. The collective voice of the bowhunters is amplified and being a member gives us the strength of numbers and our concerns are heard."

Adam nodded in appreciation and understanding, turned to me and said, *"As a Foss, we have grown up learning from you and being part of a bowhunting family. We followed you on your chase and love for mountain sheep. It's that challenge, the remoteness and the beauty of the mountains they inhabit that keeps me coming back. I am lucky to have you and Cameron, but to others they might get some of that feeling by belonging to the Pope and Young family."* I felt a feeling of pride as the tears were welling up in my eyes. I couldn't have said it any better!

"Yeah Dad, I know for us we have learned so much from you, but now I know that you have learned your ethics, your commitment to bowhunting, conservation, and the promotion of bowhunting from others," Cameron said. *"We are lucky that you shared that with us, but you are lucky all those other Pope and Young guys have shared stuff with you. Those of us who hunt with stick and string are in a class of our own. Those who do so with the collective strength of a wonderful group of friends family and members who are committed to an organization like the Pope and Young Club are really in the rare air as those rams we chase."*

"I will chase after you boys and hunt with my bow until it becomes physically impossible," I replied. *"Then I will still try to help out by cooking, tending camp, and sharing my knowledge. Through all of this, I will always be a member of the Pope and Young Club and will have the comfort of knowing the benefits of belonging."*

Hunting with my boys is special. The pride of seeing them take to the field, with me, and on their own, is special. These hunts that we share together are an extension of the Club. I can't imagine a world where I cannot bowhunt, or share days in the field with my friends and family. For those without a hunting family, being part of the Club brings that same sense of satisfaction and joy as well as the sharing that comes with it.

When the fury of the rain had stopped, we shook off the last water drops and suddenly sheep appeared in the saddle below us. It was a great start to our hunt and confirmation that we were in the right place. I knew right then and there, although I had seen hundreds of examples prior, that bowhunting, and the Club, were in the good and kind hands of hunters like my sons. With the next generation of bowhunters, and with the Pope and Young Club leading the way promoting ethical bowhunting, there will be bowhunting opportunities for the generations that follow. I can only imagine my grandchildren sharing this same conversation with their fathers many years from now. The pride of ownership, the confirmation of morals and ethics, and the satisfaction of sharing are only enhanced by those of us who have been truly touched by the Club.

We Were Not Disappointed

By Rit Heller

My first real connection to the Pope and Young Club began on a hunting trip in late August 1972 with Rolland Esterline and Dutch Wambold. We had flown in from Pennsylvania to Denver for two weeks of hunting, planning to spend a week in Colorado bowhunting for mule deer and elk, and then a week in Wyoming chasing pronghorn.

Dutch was the one who insisted we arrive a few days early for the Colorado hunt so we could attend the Pope and Young meetings and Banquet that were being held in Denver. During these early years, the Pope and Young gatherings were held in the fall instead of the spring so the hunters could more easily tie in a hunt with our meetings.

Dutch was already a Regular Member of the Club as well as an Official Measurer. He had also been writing a monthly column for <u>Archery World</u> magazine for some years. Dutch was the one who realized almost from the beginning what the Club was attempting to do, and what the organization could really become, and make a difference for the bowhunter. He had been tracking the progress of the Club through various sources, letters, and phone calls with some of the main people involved. He told us he would introduce us to them. Dutch was a funny guy and liked to kid around so you never knew with him. For all we knew, he may not have known anyone!

I, too, was a Regular Member at this time, having being accepted in August 1969 and, by sheer coincidence, became the 100th original member of the Club. Rolland had not yet joined the Club but had mentioned he wanted to do so on this trip.

I was looking forward to the meetings over the next two days. Hearing first hand what was happening and how far along the Club was progressing with all the different things we were hearing about, and what they were trying to do over the years was exciting to me. Even though I was a member, I wanted to better understand what I had become a part of.

The timing for the Club to "spread its wings" was now. Bowhunting had really caught on, and it seemed the hunters were looking for something real to be able to identify with. The Club would do that.

During those years prior to the Denver gathering it seemed as though we ordinary hunters in the bowhunting world were only getting bits and pieces of information on what the Club was about or what it actually was trying to do. There was often reference to "The Book," but at this time there was no actual book.

The reality was the records were nothing more than loose score sheets and pieces of paper recording hunt information and stored in metal filing cabinets. All this was kept with whoever the Records Committee Chairman happened to be, and there were four different members who did this until the first book came out in 1975.

The first morning of the meeting Rolland and I walked in and saw Dutch talking to someone. He called us over and said, "*Hey, I want you to meet someone.*" That person happened to be Fred Bear. He introduced us and we shook hands and just stood there.

A few seconds later another guy came over and said, "*Come on, Fred. They are holding our table for breakfast.*" That person was Glenn St. Charles, and both he and Fred invited us to join them for breakfast. Rolland and I just sat and listened to the men at the table talk. It turned out to be a very interesting conversation for me. Most of the men had been working to keep the Club going, hoping to have it accepted. As we sat with them I started to recognize some of the names from magazine articles I had read, and began to realize with whom we were sitting with. These men were some of the organizers who originally dreamed about starting the Pope and Young Club.

The two days of meetings were very interesting and informative, and very busy with plenty of different opinions from members who wanted to help. At times the meetings got very heated. Let me tell you, the room was full of energy! I could just feel the positive things that were going to be accomplished. As a new person to this sort of thing, I knew in my heart that I wanted to become more involved. I was definitely impressed with the emotions of some of the people involved with the Club.

Two years later, I was accepted as an Official Measurer and I remain one to this day. I have found measuring to be very worthwhile, have met some interesting people, and truly enjoy it.

Early in 1978 Glenn St. Charles asked me to run for directorship on the board, which I did, and served for three terms from 1978 to 1990. In doing this we had some eastern representation for the Club.

Many of the friends that I made during those early meetings have remained lifelong friends that I have either hunted or fished with somewhere or sometime over the years. We often shared our views on the Club and a lot of things that needed to be discussed were cleared up. These times remain special to me, as many of these friendships were firmed up. It made our working relationships easier.

Many of us realized we needed a well-organized club such as ours is today, to have a record book that all bowhunters, whether they are members or not, could relate to, and provide all the other things the Club offers … to define our rules of fair chase and our code of ethics so everyone would know exactly what we expect from the bowhunting fraternity. With all the talk about trophies and trophy hunting, the upcoming book, etc., we must have gotten caught up in the whole thing. The three of us left Denver thinking somehow we were now real trophy hunters.

Some Thoughts …

A lot of people worked very hard for a long time to get the Pope and Young Club to where it is today. My hope is that more good people will continue to come along and keep it going and growing. I also hope every bowhunter has the chance to come and visit the museum, to see our history, and better understand our heritage.

Friends and Experiences of a Lifetime

By Pam M. Baird

My story of respect and passion for the Pope and Young Club begins in the spring of 1989. I was fortunate to harvest a record class black bear in Ontario in 1982 and an antelope in my home state of North Dakota in 1988. I had known about the Pope and Young Club for some years through good friends like Warren Buss, Scott Lang, and Craig Richardson — to mention a few — all who have been official scorers for many years. I decided to have my antelope scored that fall by Warren Buss while we were at our annual fall bow shoot our local club puts on to kick off the new bow season. Warren had heard my husband and I were going to try our hand at elk hunting in Idaho in the fall of 1989. He asked if we would be interested in attending a Pope and Young Convention where a seminar on elk densities in Idaho was to be put on by members of the Idaho Fish & Game.

In the spring of 1989 we made our first appearance at the 16th Biennial Convention in Boise, Idaho. It was impressive to see all the outstanding animals taken during the previous two-year Recording Period. Warren had taken us under his wing during the day and wee hours of the night to introduce us to friends he knew, like Ron and Suzy Sherer, Mike Traub, Stan and Carolyn Godfrey, and many others. At the Saturday night Awards Banquet, we sat down to our pre-assigned table with fellow bowhunters. A fellow bowhunter named Elmer (Al) Luce, from St Francis, Wisconsin, was at the table that night. It was the start of a 21-year friendship. Al had given my husband and me an unlimited amount of information on backpack hunting in wilderness areas for elk and many other species. We were fortunate to share many campfires with him until he passed of bone cancer in August of 2010.

89

Attending our first Convention led us to countless new friends throughout North America. We gained more knowledge of the Pope and Young Club's goals, intentions, and bowhunting heritage that our founders intended for the respect of animals taken with archery equipment, as well as the high recognition of animals harvested by others

I am entering my 36th year as an avid bowhunter and continue to meet new bowhunters with the same passion at every Pope and Young Convention I attend. My intention is to try to pass on the good values the Pope and Young Club promotes for all responsible hunters trying to harvest animals with their bows. I have always said it is not the harvest that counts, but the experience of the hunt and friendships maintained. My son Dustin, as well as one of his best friends, is so enthused with bowhunting and the Pope and Young Club that they have chosen to use the bow and arrow exclusively for hunting big game. If we can get younger generations to understand the true value and respect of hunting animals with a bow, we can say we have all accomplished the plan for the future of the bowhunting heritage that our founders intended.

I hope to have several more campfires like the last one in British Columbia, in the beautiful Pink Mountains, with my best friend (my husband John) and my new friends, Rorie Hoyt, Shane Hoyt, and William Newman.

Last Minute Luck ... Long Term Success

By M. R. James

Blind luck blessed me with my first whitetail in November of 1963. It was the final day of Indiana's archery season, and hunting had been downright tough. For one thing, Hoosier deer were few and far between back then (I'd seen exactly one doe since early October). For another, I was a whitetail novice who bowhunted bucks the same way I hunted bunnies, picking my way slowly through hardwood jungles and zigzagging across brush-choked weed fields. My hope was to see a deer before it saw me or maybe jump a buck and get off a shot before my quarry bounced out of range.

Very little did I know.

Not surprisingly, when I bumped into several does late that final afternoon and watched their snowy tails waving goodbye, I immediately trailed after them. And why not? The clock was ticking with only a couple of hours of daylight remaining. What was there to lose, really? I quickly dropped into a dry creek bed and moved off in the general direction those spooked deer had run.

The rut-goofy buck I bumped into moments later was so busy dogging a hot doe that I was almost in bow range when I first spotted him. He was grunting audibly while walking through waist-high underbrush, pausing occasionally to glance my way as if to display his wide, heavy rack. There was no doubt he knew I was there, but it appeared he had more pressing business on his mind. And each time he'd turn to take up the doe's trail, I'd edge closer, arrow nocked, heart thudding, looking for a shooting lane in the tangled honeysuckle jungle.

When my shot finally came, the buck was standing maybe 25 yards away. He ran another three times that far with my cedar arrow in his ribs before folding with his left antler snugged against a small sapling. I was the proudest and most surprised deer hunter in Hoosierland.

"Are you going to enter him in the record book?" a friend asked the following day as we stood together admiring that big old deer.

"Never thought about it," I admitted.

"You should," he urged. *"That's a nice buck."*

He was nice and later I had him officially scored. Although I didn't know it at the time, entering that eleventh hour '63 whitetail in the Pope and Young records launched a half-century association between a beginning bowhunter and a fledgling record-keeping organization. I joined the Pope and Young Club as an Associate in January of 1971 after arrowing a record book Utah cougar, attended my first P&Y convention in Denver in 1972, and became a Regular Member in 1975. I was named an official measurer in 1978 and qualified for Senior membership in 1980, six years before being elected to the P&Y Board of Directors for the first time.

Looking back over my decades with Pope and Young, I recall with special fondness editing the Club's first record book in 1975 (and working with Glenn St. Charles, Fred Bear, Larry Bamford, Harv Ebers, Carl Hulbert, Chuck Young, Dick Mauch, Norm Goodwin, George Moerlein, Scott Showalter, Wayne Trimm, and Dr. Lowell Eddy to accomplish that memorable milestone). I also remember President Jim Dougherty inviting me to be the featured speaker at the Club's 1983 Milwaukee convention and editing two more P&Y record books in the 1990s while serving with President Fred Asbell and his Board as First Vice President. Finally, I can never forget the humbling honor of being elected P&Y President and serving our Club in that leadership capacity from 2006 to 2010. The meaningful friendships made and unforgettable hunts shared with other P&Y members are too numerous to mention.

Today, whenever I'm asked why I've supported the Pope and Young Club for so long, I simply point to the organization's impressive track record of positive pro-hunting, pro-conservation efforts that benefit wildlife, hunters, and non-hunters alike. I'll cite the hundreds of thousands of dollars raised and donated to benefit wildlife research, game management, and habitat improvement. I'll note the Club's growing repository of scientific information gleaned and recorded from documenting the largest North American big game animals taken with the bow and arrow. I'll bring up the Club's educational efforts to inform the public of the role that selective hunting plays in the twenty-first century. I'll mention with special fraternal pride how Pope and Young members strive to lead by example in practicing ethical, responsible, and safe fair chase hunting.

Finally, I'll sometimes quote Club founder Glenn St. Charles, who perfectly summed up the essence of bowhunting and the Pope and Young philosophy, when he said:

"I'd just like to remind everybody that it's about the hunting, not just the killing. In other words, it's about the total experience, the sport itself and the challenge involved. Bowhunting, done right, is a justifiable and honorable pursuit. Done for the wrong reasons, simply chalking up kills and seeking personal glory, it's taking from rather than giving back to a principled way of life that has to be experienced to be fully understood."

I know that I have matured considerably since 1963 as the Club itself grew to maturity over the past half century. Admittedly, the Pope and Young Club and its strict standards are not for every bowhunter. But for those who eagerly embrace our challenging sport and believe that hunting the hard way means hunting the right way, our respected organization will mean as much to you as it means to me.

The Pope and Young Club, My Perspective

Jack Frost

1961, the year the Pope and Young Club was founded, happens to be the year of my first bow harvest of a whitetail deer. I was aware of the Club from early on because of my involvement with the NFAA through a local archery club in Pennsylvania. I had no concept then of how important bowhunting and the Pope and Young Club would become in my life.

Growing up in north-central Pennsylvania, I struggled to just take any deer with my Bear recurve bow in the days before treestands. I never expected to actually kill a record book animal.

In 1973 I moved to Anchorage, Alaska, courtesy of the United States Air Force. I took my archery gear along but did very little bowhunting until I met Curt Lynn.

Curt Lynn was a Senior Member of the Pope and Young Club who ignited my long smoldering love of bowhunting. I first met Curt in 1978 through mutual hunting friends. He was intense, focused on ethical trophy bowhunting, and a proud, strong supporter of the Pope and Young Club. He liked mentoring new bowhunters. It only took him about a year to get me to totally give up hunting big game with a firearm.

In the next few years I harvested several animals in Alaska with my bow. At Curt's urging, I attended my first Pope and Young Convention in Spokane, Washington in 1981. There, I met Glenn St Charles, Fred Bear, Judd Cooney, Jim Dougherty, and many other serious big time bowhunters. They were approachable, friendly, and encouraging. I was hooked! I became an Associate Member and have not missed a convention since. It took me 18 years to become a Regular Member. I have been privileged to serve on the Board of Directors for the last six years as an elected director.

The Pope and Young Club is much more than just a simple record keeping organization. Its records are certainly the foundation that gives the Club strength. They are the Gold Standard for bowhunting records of North American big game. They demand adherence to not only the law, but also to fair chase ethics in our modern world. Our measurers are carefully trained and recertified on a regular basis. In spite of that, we do not accept a single measurer's score for truly outstanding records but demand that the top entered specimens be sent to a panel measuring where a team of our very best measurers re-measures these great specimens.

The records program initially was developed to show that bowhunting was a legitimate pursuit, and that bowhunters could harvest mature big game animals. It was also intended to provide a repository of data that could be used by hunters and game agencies for scientific study of trends in animal populations and harvest success.

The Records Program is the foundation of our Club. Our Museum and Conservation programs are also very important parts of our Club. Perhaps they represent the castle and the roof of the Pope and Young Club. The most important part of the Club to me is the individuals who live in and around that Castle. Our Club is formed by a group of dedicated bowhunters. You only really begin to realize this by attending conventions and getting to know the individuals who make up the Club.

Some of the friendships established by attending the Pope and Young Conventions will last for a lifetime. The networking with other successful bowhunters will lead to hunting opportunities of which you might have never dreamed. I have been encouraged by my bowhunting friends to accept new challenges and set new goals. That results in my accomplishing things that I might have otherwise never tried. As an example, I live in Alaska and can hunt caribou every year. I never thought that I would have any desire to hunt the five different species of caribou. Two of my Pope and Young friends, Tom Hoffman and Bob Speegle, invited me to join them on a hunt for Central Canada barren ground caribou. I did so simply to share a hunt with them, but after taking that species I began to think it would be fun to hunt all of the caribou species. I eventually did just that but it would have never happened without the encouragement of good friends. As we age we learn that it is our memories and our friends that are most important to us.

I would encourage anyone who loves to bowhunt to join the Pope and Young Club. Get active, come to conventions, make new friends, and become involved. You will be amazed at where you can go and what you can do. Most of all, keep making good bowhunting memories.

The Pope and Young Club Influence
By Marv Clyncke

It was 1960. I had just read where a new organization was being formed to keep track of big game animals taken with the bow and arrow. I thought that was a great idea as I had just decided to hunt exclusively with my bow. I hadn't been very successful with my bow, but I had read articles by Glenn St. Charles, Fred Bear, Howard Hill, Ben Pearson, Harv Ebers, and other bowhunters who had taken many different species with archery equipment.

In those days most hunters didn't think you could kill big game animals other than deer with an arrow. I decided that Glenn and the others knew what they were doing and so I went after elk here in my home state of Colorado in 1960. I was successful taking a cow on that hunt, only the second elk killed with bow and arrow in Colorado. I knew then that these ole boys knew what they were talking about. The next year, 1961, was when the Pope and Young Club officially started. I sent for information and a poster that showed the entries and the world records in each big game category. I was amazed at the size of some of these great trophies that had been taken with archery equipment. Right then and there I became hooked on going after other species of animals besides mule deer and elk.

Fast-forward to 1969, the Brown Palace Hotel in Denver. When Judy and I walked in the door at the hotel, there stood a huge, life-sized mounted grizzly taken by Rex Hancock. There were many more mounted specimens of all different species of big game. But way more important than the trophies was the fact that all the folks from the world of bowhunting were there, and we got to shake hands and talk with these bowhunters who had started the

Pope and Young Club. I immediately joined as an Associate Member, as I had already taken mulies, elk, and antelope with my bow. Because of that first influence from the Pope and Young Club and its beliefs, I also helped start the Colorado Bowhunters Association (CBA) so we could retain our bow season and open other species up for archery hunting. I had been the Records Chairman for the Colorado State Archery Association for two years before we stated the CBA, so was familiar with scoring big game antlers and horns. I had corresponded with the Pope and Young Club Records Chairman during this time and was really becoming enthused with the Club. I looked forward to becoming a Regular Member of the Club and did so in 1971.

Judy and I chaired the biennial banquet and awards program at the Harvest House Hotel in Boulder in 1973. I was hooked on the Pope and Young Club for sure by then. I could see that the Club was the leader in bowhunting in North America … and still is to this day.

Because of that influence, I started hunting the more difficult animals in Colorado, namely bighorn sheep and mountain goats. I had run into Fred Bear and Jim Dougherty on a late-season hunt on the Blue River in central Colorado and again peppered Fred with questions about his hunting for Dall's rams in Alaska and Stone's sheep in British Columbia. I probably asked him the same questions at the Pope and Young banquet in Denver, but he was always anxious to talk sheep hunting as there were very few bowhunters who had stalked the elusive rams. After his encouragement and helpful knowledge, I knew I wanted to someday hunt those faraway rams. I did get to Alaska shortly after that and was unsuccessful in arrowing a Dall's sheep, but it was an unforgettable hunt. I knew I would go back until I got one, and eventually I did.

Just seeing the great entries in the Pope and Young Record Book was enough to keep me going after many different species of big game with my bow. I also wanted to help the Club in any way I could, so ran for the Board of Directors and was elected as a Director in the 1980s, and then later as Vice-President. I always felt that the Pope and Young Club and the great members helped me so much in my bowhunting that I wanted to give back and help other bowhunters as well. After I had become an Official Measurer, I got to see and score a lot of the qualified animals taken in Colorado and other states. In the process, I learned to judge the size of animals that I hunted. I would guess what the animal scored before I measured it, and then compare it to the actual score when I was done measuring. Not only did this help in my own hunting, but it also made it fun to have a friendly competition with my hunting buddies of guessing how big an animal was in the field or on the ground.

Many times I've heard bowhunters say that "record books" cause unethical hunting and poaching, and the measuring of heads and horns should be kept out of hunting. That's like saying guns kill people! It's not the gun: it's the person holding the gun, and it's not the record book — it's the hunter who abuses the record book. The Pope and Young records are a great reference source to compare the quality and the size of animals from one area to the other, and the quantity of animals in different areas. I love to go through them from time to time to see the trends of quality and quantity of large, recordable heads, horns, and antlers. There simply is no better way to pick a hunting area, especially if traveling to another state, and no better way to show non-bowhunters the lethality of the bow and arrow.

I'm not the only bowhunter who was — and is — heavily influenced by the Pope and Young Club, as evidenced by the longevity of the members, and the growing number of bowhunters who belong and volunteer for what the Club is and stands for. I firmly believe that without those old boys starting this organization in 1960, we would not have the great bowhunting opportunities we have today.

Change of Perspectives

By Cindi Richardson

My love of the outdoors and hunting with the family was instilled in me as a young girl while accompanying my dad and grandfather on the annual rifle deer hunt in southern Arizona; however, it wasn't until I met and married my high school sweetheart that I was introduced to a whole new world of hunting. This is when my passion for hunting big game with a bow and arrow began to blossom.

Early on in our marriage, my husband Corky was fortunate enough to harvest a trophy mule deer in northern Arizona. It was large enough to be invited for panel scoring for the 16th Recording Period. Understanding what an honor this was, we decided that not only should we send the deer to be scored, but try to also attend the Convention. With three young kids and a single income this would be difficult but, as usual, God provided. With a little help thrown in from our parents on the babysitting front, we booked our flights, room, and tickets to attend the Convention in Boise, Idaho.

The convention surpassed our expectations. To be amongst fellow hunters is one thing, but to be in a place where everyone was a bowhunter was amazing in itself. We had so much fun, and friendships were formed that we still value to this day. I personally had a unique experience of meeting another female hunter, Pam Baird, who shared my love for bowhunting. Pam and I, along with our husbands, sat up late every night talking about our passions of hunting with our families. Wow, another gal who loved to bowhunt as much as I did, regardless of the conditions … rain, snow, wind, mud, or dirt, it didn't matter. We loved spending time in God's creation, the challenge of bowhunting and, frankly, we enjoyed being with our husbands and kids in the wild. From that point on we vowed to attend every Convention we could. Secretly, I personally made a vow to myself to harvest a qualifying species, as I had not yet harvested a book animal. I wanted to attend the next Convention with an entry and as a member myself, not just the wife of a member.

Thanks to a great hunting partner, my husband Corky, coupled with my slightly competitive nature, I was able to harvest a book mountain lion and attend the next Convention with an entry and as a member of the Club! I have a number of book animals to this date, but that first entry is special to me.

As time went on, and we attended more Conventions, I began to understand that just hunting was not enough. I began to see the Pope and Young Club focus on important issues such as conservation, education of the next generations, preserving the heritage of those bowhunters before us, and becoming more and more involved in federal legislation to help protect the right and privilege of hunting in this great country. The Pope and Young Club encourages everyone to contribute in their respective home states, so we became involved with our state bowhunting organizations, taught hunter education classes, and most importantly learned to set an example to the non-hunting world of what it means to be an ethical, responsible, proud, and honorable sportsman.

Now, I also have to chuckle at some of the member meetings we have attended: the disagreements over Regular Member numbers versus Associate, the number of Senior Members we should carry, the sometimes heated debates over recurve versus compound, and, gasp, … 65% let-off! Yet, in the end we are able to set aside the differences and come together for the good of our sport. After the meetings we go out and fellowship with those same fellow bowhunters we debated with just minutes ago, and enjoy each other's fireside stories and hunting tales.

Looking back, it is funny how my perspective has changed. I am still as competitive as it gets, but I would much rather see my ten-year-old son harvest a huge elk, see my daughter take her first archery species (a Desert sheep, no less), sit around the campfire with my family and friends, stop at the edge of the Grand Canyon in a snowstorm to marvel at God's magnificent creation, stand in triumph at the top of a mountain in Alaska that I fought hard to reach only to be awed by the splendor that few see, or sit in a treestand all day praying and reading my Bible only to be perfectly content whether a shot presented itself or not. I love it all!

I thank God for a husband who encouraged me, treated me as an equal, and to this day would rather hunt with me than most men. I thank God for the success he has granted me, both measurable and immeasurable.

Thank you, Pope and Young Club, for helping my family and me to become fair and ethical hunters, for providing us with a platform to make a difference, for honoring the founders of our sport, and for striving to provide a future for our generations to come.

Pope and Young Reflections

Charles Arthur Young, Jr.

Art Young had one son, Charles Arthur Young, born December 15, 1907, in San Francisco. The family home was at 1520 Masonic Avenue. Young Art was raised by his aunt, Art's sister Orrie who never married. When he was eight-years old, he met Ishi. But bowhunting did not take hold of young Art, and his father traveled a great deal during his formative years. He married at 26 to Helen Thomson from Harlowton, Montana, and they took up residence in San Francisco just half a block from 1520 Masonic Avenue.

Art Young died in 1935. I was born in 1936, a junior. They called me Chuck to distinguish from the two Arts. My dad told me about how he has met Ishi and Dr. Pope, but it took many years for me to realize the significance of the names. I played on the black bear rug — the first one Pope and Young shot about 1918. I practiced throwing the African spear Art brought back in 1925 … there were mounted heads in the dining room, and a cheetah skin on Aunt Orrie's grand piano. My dad taught me to camp, fish, and observe wildlife. A trip to Yellowstone in 1945 was most memorable.

A lot of Art Young's trophies, heads, and bows and arrows were displayed at Viking Archery on Market Street in San Francisco. Bill Wright, an original member of the Pope and Young Club, managed Viking Archery. Bill made me a lemonwood bow at about age 12. I was bored with target shooting so I took to shooting at neighborhood cats. Soon after, the bow was taken from me.

Fast forward to 1969. One day I was in a drug store looking at magazines. I saw a winter issue of Archery World. Thumbing through it, I found a book review, Ishi in Two Worlds, by Theodora Kroeber. I also read an article about a bowhunter who shot a large animal with a "Pope & Young" score of ... something. Coincidence? I wrote the editor and he gave me the name of Richard (Dick) Mauch in Bassett, Nebraska, secretary of the Pope and Young Club. I wrote Dick and he told me that Art Young's personal scrapbook was in Illinois with Dr Paul Klopsteg. That June, I was driving my family to Yellowstone so I stopped at Dr Klopsteg's and he gave me the scrapbook. I then stopped at Dick Mauch's and showed it to him. Living in Pennsylvania, he suggested I meet Al Dawson, the Bear Archery rep for the state. In August the world championships were held in Valley Forge, just a few miles from my home. I met Al there plus Fred Bear and Len Cardinale. Al gave me a Bear Grizzly bow and I started shooting carp with it. Later in August, the Pope and Young Convention was in Denver, Colorado. My dad and I attended and it was very memorable. We were visiting with the first 100 Regular Members. I believe there were at that time only 68 Associate Members. Larry Bamford suggested I join and run for office as their representative. I wrote 68 letters and won and held the position of Third Vice President for ten years.

During the 1970s, Len Cardinale had big game contests for his archery shop hunters. He had a Pope and Young-style contest for the locals: carp, groundhog, and whitetail deer. An annual dinner recognized the winners. I used to go to these with Rit Heller, Dutch Wambold, Harold Hill, Dick Sage, Walt Saville, and a number of other old timers. I hunted deer with Len and Jim Dougherty in northern Pennsylvania, eventually taking three deer with my bow.

During my terms as Vice President, we began holding Associate's meetings. These were at first mostly educational events. As we got more Associate Members and a waiting list for Regular Membership that began at a year and stretched to five to six years, more calls for opening the 100 Regular Member limitation were heard. And there was the issue of whether or not animals treed by dogs was considered fair chase. The Board of Directors over the years has addressed many issues and today's Club is a far cry and infinitely more complex than when I served. We were very conservative back then compared to now.

I have enjoyed my association with the Club and have tried to contribute as I'm able. I have donated nearly all my Art Young things to the museum, and have found and had measured a number of bear skulls taken by both Pope and Young from 1920-1926. I was able to locate the Pope family in Connecticut and have them donate many of Pope's personal things and an Ishi flint broadhead. T.J. Conrads approached me one year and asked if he could refurbish Art's African lion skin for the museum. Today, it is on display in Chatfield, Minnesota. I presently serve on the museum committee and consider preserving the past's things most important. I look forward to each Pope and Young convention ... friends meeting and making friends, and living a life of fair chase and good sportsmanship.

The Pope & Young Club and Me

By Andy Carpenter

I have had the desire to hunt as far back as I can remember. As a child, I was fascinated with stories of hunting big game in faraway places. I spent hours reading <u>Outdoor Life</u> and other magazines and books, dreaming of being at Fred Bear's side as he stalked big game on some remote piece of ground. I imagined being with Jack O'Conner on sheep hunts. I kept up with Howard Hill's pursuits and read everything Peter Capstick wrote. My first hunting trips were with my dad as he pursued whitetails in the Mississippi Delta.

When I was twelve-years-old, Dad bought me a left-handed Shakespeare target bow and some arrows. That summer, I scared the life out of every small critter around our house. During my teenage and college years I didn't hunt as much but was still drawn to the idea of the hunt. At some point shortly after that time, I started hunting again and killed my first big game animal with a bow and arrow. It wasn't long before I became a serious bowhunter and hunted with a bow as often as family and work would allow. I have not looked back.

I suspect your desire to bowhunt started in a similar fashion. If you are reading this, I also suspect you are a serious bowhunter and consider yourself different than other hunters. When I refer to a serious bowhunter, I am not referring to those among us who only bowhunt during archery season, then use the appropriate weapon allowed in other seasons. And of course there is nothing wrong with that, as I believe the more of us out there hunting is a good thing. But we serious bowhunters ARE different. We think bowhunting all year long. We never stop shooting our bows. We talk bowhunting to anyone who will listen. I know; I've seen me do it!

I mention this to you because there is a strong group of men and women within that group of serious bowhunters who are even more different and even more serious, and those are the active members of the Pope and Young Club. I believe this group to be exclusive. I believe this group to be elite among other bowhunters not because they are a better shot or kill more trophy animals, but because they choose to play an active role in Pope and Young. They serve on committees. They serve on the Board. They volunteer and attend the Conventions. They regularly contribute to the Trust Fund, the Museum Fund, and other projects. They enter their animals in the record book. Many are measurers. They are the lifeblood of the Club. Many of them happen to be my closest friends.

I became a part of this group in 1992. My good friend Billy Ellis encouraged me to join Pope and Young after several years of bowhunting whitetails with him on his property. He also dragged me to my first Convention in Traverse City, Michigan, where I became hooked on the history, the ethics, and ideals of the Club. During that wonderful weekend, I rubbed shoulders and shook hands with many of my bowhunting heroes. While there, I discovered that most of these men and women, who I had considered larger than life, were actually very approachable. They were from all walks of life who, like me, loved the sport of hunting big game with a bow and arrow. I had a wonderful and memorable time at that Convention. I developed lasting friendships with many of them and hunt and communicate with them today. I have been fortunate to hunt in many places, all with hunting buddies I met through Pope and Young.

I started out helping the Club by being on a few of the committees. This helped me understand the workings of the Club. I liked the structure. I liked the fact you cannot buy your way in to the Club — you must earn your position. During my years as an Associate, I was not treated any differently than I am now. There was no class separation. I liked that.

I like our record book and record keeping system. I believe it to be the gold standard in big game record keeping. Our measurers are the backbone of the Club, and the failsafe methods we use to check and double check measurements insure our book to be as accurate as possible. Is the system fool proof? Of course not, but I would put the integrity of our record book against any other.

Because we want our record book to be beyond reproach, we have rules, regulations, and equipment limitations that must be followed before an animal can be entered. I like that. Sometimes the industry and newcomers to the sport frown upon these rules, regulations, and limitations as new products are constantly being introduced making shooting a bow easier. Many consider Pope and Young anti-industry, but that couldn't be further from the truth. Some of our most active members are in the archery and hunting industry full time, many of them having celebrity status. The Club really doesn't care what accessory you add to you bowhunting arsenal, but if you want to enter an animal in the records, it must be taken a certain way with certain equipment limitations making the playing field equal for all, and that's a good thing.

The Pope and Young Club has a fantastic museum named after our founder, the late, great Glenn St. Charles. I love walking through that museum! Besides the virtual dioramas featuring Glenn in his workshop, Saxton Pope, Art Young, and Ishi in hunting scenes, the collection of old bows, arrows, arrowheads, and taxidermy from many of our members' hunts, there are many other things any bowhunter can appreciate. At the grand opening of the museum, I had the opportunity to push Glenn St. Charles in his wheelchair through the maze of displays. When we stopped at his diorama, he gazed up at his likeness and said, *"He looks more like me than I do!"* If you are a serious bowhunter, you should visit the museum at every opportunity as the Club is constantly updating and adding things.

The record book, the museum, the ethics and fair chase mentality of the Pope and Young Club, and the thousands of dollars spent on conservation projects are all things I love about our Club. I look forward to the Conventions every other year, to hang out with my best friends, and to celebrate the most fantastic display of trophy big game animals killed with a bow and arrow. I will play an active role in Pope and Young as long as it will let me. It is a part of me.

Mesmerized

By Frank Noska

What does archery, bowhunting, and the Pope and Young Club mean to me? First, a short explanation of how I started bowhunting is necessary.

As a young kid, I was naturally interested in and fascinated about the bow and arrow. Born and raised in north Texas, I was fortunate to meet an accomplished bowhunter while I was in high school. John Cambis, my first archery teacher and mentor, taught me about archery and bowhunting basics. He and I shot many an arrow after school and shared lots of whitetail deer camps in Texas.

As time went by, my archery knowledge increased and as I gained bowhunting experience. I sent my first arrow through a big game animal, a "trophy" button buck whitetail deer in 1984, while perched in a big live oak tree in Marble Falls, Texas. A gentleman named Don Graham took me on this first bowhunt.

I had several consecutive days off in a row one particular month in 1991 and had planned a trip to visit Alaska. While reading one of my bowhunting magazines, I learned that the Pope and Young Club Convention was being held in Seattle, Washington. At the time I was not a member of the Club, nor did I know much about the Club; however, I did know they scored and recorded trophy sized North American animals harvested with a bow and arrow. I also knew the Club represented bowhunters and consisted of members who were serious about bowhunting. This was all the information I needed, and decided to attend the Seattle Convention.

At 24-years-old and absolutely obsessed with bow-

103

hunting, my first Convention had a lasting effect on me. Never before had I seen so many accomplished, serious bowhunters gathered in one place. All the knowledge and information was overwhelming. The passion these bowhunters had for their sport was obvious. Even as a young bowhunter, I shared the same intense interest and felt comfortable amongst them. I saw legends and heroes of mine whom I had read about and saw in videos walking around visiting with other hunters.

The animals on display at the Convention were impressive. I had never seen such great trophies and wandered from species to species, animal to animal, absorbing the vastness of exceptional animals. At the time of my first convention in 1991, I had not arrowed my first Pope and Young animal. After witnessing the caliber of animals and the exceptional displays, I decided to endeavor to harvest an animal that would make the record book. I set a goal for myself, which was accomplished in 1994, when I arrowed my first Pope and Young animal, a 64 inch Pronghorn in Wyoming.

After the Convention, I traveled a short distance to Northwest Archery and met Glenn St. Charles for the first time. I vividly remember him giving me a tour of his archery shop and museum. His wife Margaret took a picture of Glenn and me and promised to mail a copy after it was developed. I provided her with my contact information and she made note of the exposure number. Time passed and I received an envelope containing the photo. On the back Margaret wrote, *"During Pope and Young Convention in Seattle, 4-13-91, Glenn St. Charles, Frank Noska, at museum in Northwest Archery building. PS. If I goofed and this picture isn't you Frank, please let me know in the endorsed stamped self addressed envelope."* This picture is special to me and I have cherished it for all these years.

It was only natural that I joined the Pope and Young Club while I was there at my first Convention in Seattle in 1991. I have remained a proud member since, eventually advancing to a Senior Member. Bowhunting is not a hobby to me; it is my life as I moved to Alaska for more opportunities. Being involved and immersed in bowhunting, I find that most of my closest friends are also passionate bowhunters and members of the Pope and Young Club. It is a big family enjoying themselves while taking pride and supporting the unique sport. The Pope and Young Club mission statement says it all: *"To ensure bowhunting for future generations by preserving its heritage and values."*

The Club and I

By Mike Schlegel

As with most hunters, I am intrigued with "trophy" caliber animals. I fantasize about shooting trophy class animals as well as enjoy looking at them in the field and trophy rooms alike. A trophy blacktail buck dominated my mind's eye when I purchased my first deer tag in 1953. This affinity still affects me 57 years later regardless of the critter hunted. Thus it was natural to be attracted to the Boone and Crockett Club and later the Pope and Young Club. I began hunting with a bow in 1953. However, I did not become a "bowhunter" until many years later, joining the Pope and Young Club in 1981.

After becoming a certified measurer, achieving membership, and attending conventions I began to learn more about the Pope and Young Club. In addition my hunting partner Ron Sherer was a Director for the Club. Both he and his wife Suzy were Regular and Senior Members, respectively.

The Club's first mission was to document to state wildlife management agencies that the bow and arrow were efficient and legitimate hunting weapons. However, it was soon apparent to me the Pope and Young Club encompassed more than merely being a records keeping organization. In addition to recording and archiving bowhunting records, the Club emphasizes fair chase, the cultural and traditional values of bowhunting, plus wildlife conservation. Beginning with its inception, leaders of the Club recognized and actively promoted the role hunters and hunting have had in molding wildlife management and conservation in North America. Thus the guiding principles of the Pope and Young Club mirrored my personal philosophy regarding fair chase, hunter ethics, and conservation. The Club was a natural fit for me!

While working in the wildlife profession as a Conservation Officer and wildlife research biologist/manager I saw the good, the bad, and the ugly within the hunting community. There were times when I was truly embarrassed and/or angry regarding the way "hunters" conducted themselves. Fortunately there were also many times it was very rewarding to be associated and affiliated with hunters and hunting. Obviously one's motivation to hunt and one's conduct while hunting are highly personal. It has been my observation that many of today's hunters have developed an "instant, self gratification" attitude toward hunting. Unfortunately using all the latest and greatest gadgets, plus getting a "trophy" animal is often their primary motivation.

My association and involvement with the Pope and Young Club has made a definite impact on my attitude regarding bowhunting. Yes, I would like to get a "book" animal on every hunt as well as one for all 29 species recognized by the Club. However, I realize and accept the fallacy of that attitude — the hunt is more than about getting a "book" animal. It is commendable the Club holds steadfast to fair chase and a high standard of ethics as the cornerstones of their records keeping program. My personal philosophy is that ALL animals killed with a bow and arrow while abiding to fair chase are trophies — some are just bigger than others. Also, a successful hunt, in my opinion, includes the following three ingredients: 1) the esthetics of the area hunted; 2) the interaction with the species hunted, plus non-target species; and 3) the camaraderie of the hunting party. A kill is not necessary for a successful hunt —–the kill is additive to a successful hunt!

Too often hunters believe they have to prove themselves by killing an animal every year. And you are a better "hunter" if you get a book animal every year. I have to admit I got caught up in this game. In my case I was a professional wildlife biologist. More specifically I was an elk research biologist. Therefore I reasoned I should get an elk every year. I did for 20 years. The pressure was tremendous and hunting was no longer enjoyable — I HAD to kill an elk every year! After much soul searching I realized I was no less a hunter, nor did I lose my professional creditability if I did not kill an elk every year. And, most importantly, elk hunting was again enjoyable!

The keeping and publishing of harvest (trophy) records is double edged. The validity of the bow and arrow as a hunting tool has been documented. Unfortunately, it also provided a mechanism for some to abuse the system for personal and/or monetary gain, often at the expense of what is in the best interest of bowhunters and bowhunting.

Hunting is a grand activity and hunters are the heart of the wildlife conservation movement in North America. However, as the demographics of our society have changed from rural to urban the attitude toward hunting is changing. People, especially youth, are spending less time in pursuit of outdoor activities related to nature. The proportion of hunters in our society, nationwide, is dwindling. The anti-hunting movement seems to be gaining momentum. It is the non-hunting segment of our society that allows us to hunt — provided they do not perceive the hunter as having an unfair advantage over the hunted. Hunter behavior has a great impact on how hunting is perceived by the general public. It takes only one irresponsible act to create a negative and lasting impression about hunters and hunting. In addition to hunter behavior, "gadgets" and hunting techniques available to and used by hunters have a definite influence within our society regarding hunting and hunters. For example: is 1,000+ yard shooting really hunting; is a "canned" hunt really a hunt; what impression does the assault rifle look to the modern hunting rifle have on the non-hunter?

The founding principles and philosophy of the Pope and Young Club, my experiences as a wildlife professional, and my passion for bowhunting have instilled a deep sense of responsibility within me to maintain and perpetuate the cultural and traditional values of bowhunting and bowhunting equipment. Please understand I am not anti-compound bow. However, I am deeply concerned about the effect technological advancement in bowhunting equipment will have on the future of bowhunting opportunity, especially in the western states. Bowhunting, by its very nature, is a close range, challenging activity requiring skill and commitment. As technology continues to make bowhunting "easier" the value and appreciation of the challenge and commitment diminish. I applaud and support the Pope and Young Club in their quest to maintain and preserve bowhunting as the "King of Sports" for present and future generations to enjoy, appreciate and participate. Please help keep the spirit alive!

Pope & Young Club and G. Fred Asbell

My beginnings with the bow and arrow, bowhunting, and the Pope and Young Club are so mixed together that it's difficult for me to separate them or consider them as anything but one and the same. And that's because they all blew into my life on almost the same gust of wind.

I was totally consumed with shooting the bow and arrow when I saw a film of Fred Bear bowhunting, which pulled me off the range and put me into the woods, and in almost the same moment the Pope and Young Club came on the scene talking about bowhunting for big animals. Even then the concept of pursuit of the most difficult animals with the most difficult weapon seemed so very honorable, and I took to it like a quest for the Holy Grail. I shot a mule deer and a black bear and then an Indiana whitetail that was big enough and was on the phone calling Glenn St. Charles about Pope and Young membership before my application had probably cleared the local post office. I'd shot the animal and applied in 1966. In 1969, after at least 100 telephone calls, Glenn finally got around to telling me I was a member. He wasn't nearly as excited about it as I was, and to my great disappointment almost no one else was either. It was a good life lesson. I knew what a great honor it was, but I saw that this Pope and Young thing was a personal achievement, not something to be run up a flagpole for recognition, and I saw that very thing when I attended my first Pope and Young banquet that year in Denver.

Athletic heroes, and the winning competitive archers I'd met, mostly seemed full of exaggerated egos and did a lot of strutting and posturing, and here I saw a completely different attitude with a humble acceptance of honor by the hunter, but also a deep respect for the animal, and an understanding that this was a time and place thing and that the hunter was fortunate to have been in the loop. That attitude impressed me immensely and I suspect I hitched my wagon to the Pope and Young star for that reason more than any other.

After 40+ years of membership, 24 of them on the Board of Directors, I'm still sold on pursuit of the finest and the Pope and Young ethic of fair chase bowhunting.

The Upshot

The Next 50 Years

By Roger Atwood

As the Pope and Young Club transformed from dream to reality, the vision of our founder included the necessity to defend the bow and arrow as a legitimate hunting tool. The very purpose of the Records Program was to prove the effectiveness of the bow and arrow and the hunting archer. As the program evolved, the records were sought after and provided to state and provincial agencies involved in the establishment of hunting seasons. Big game managers throughout North America soon learned bowhunting was a valid tool in their wildlife conservation model. The Records Program also proved to be effective in diminishing the skepticism surrounding bowhunting seasons, and bowhunting in general.

The Pope and Young Club in its first 50 years has successfully accomplished the task our early founders set out to complete. No other segment of the hunting interest has grown as fast or as large as the bowhunting community. Special archery-only seasons exist throughout North America. Bowhunters today enjoy liberal seasons, abundant big game populations, and tremendous success compared to our forefathers.

Glenn St Charles, our founder, proclaimed in 1981, *"The uphill struggle for bowhunters from the era of Saxton Pope and Art Young has been difficult. We have come a long way. We have reached our initial goal of proving that the bow and arrow is effective in the harvesting of big game animals. Bowhunters are now respected. Surely the Pope and Young Club's conservation program and its impressive record lists of trophy animals have been factors.*

"We must consolidate our position and that of all bowhunters by treating our success with reserve and humility. There is much more to do. As the balance of nature becomes increasingly fragile, there will be extreme environmental concern. We share in this concern and, wherever possible, provide help through our conservation program.

"It appears that bowhunting has a bright future; however, it is not an unclouded future. As the human population increases, animal habitat decreases. Western states also have the added factor of many diverse groups, all concerned over the available land. Timber, cattle, and other interests have to be served.

"The time has come when states must face up to the fact that big game herds in some parts of the continent can withstand, little, if any, increased pressure. There is much pushing and pulling between various hunting groups, all vying for the same hunting times and places. Some things will change. States will take longer looks at hunting methods and styles, taking into consideration their impacts on animal resources.

"Bowhunters could play a larger role in big game hunting as long as our success ratio remains relatively low and bowhunting equipment remains reasonably primitive. We must continue to seek ways to educate the non-hunting public in the importance of game and habitat preservation and the vital role the hunter plays in game management and conservation. The future of big game hunting lies in our ability to persuade the non-hunting public."

Even though the future looks bright, as Glenn St. Charles stated in 1981, *"It is not an unclouded future."* The hunting world is a minority compared to the non-hunting public. Yet we depend on the public to support our cause in the voting booth. I would like to refer to research completed by Mark Damian Duda and Martin Jones on Public Opinion on and Attitudes Toward Hunting.

Research indicates that most Americans support hunting in general; however, support for and opposition to hunting can vary dramatically based on numerous factors, including personal values and characteristics, attitudes toward hunters, attitudes toward animal welfare, the motivation for participating, and the species involved, to name a few.

Attitudes toward hunting are not fixed. Public opinion changes based on the amount and type of information that people receive on the issues, and it changes based on circumstances within wildlife populations ... particularly when the populations of certain species greatly increase.

About three-quarters of Americans support hunting. One nationwide survey found that 77% of adult Americans approve of legal hunting, while 16% disapprove. Another nationwide study found that 75% of adults approve, while 17% disapprove. There is a multitude of reasons that people oppose hunting. Some of the prominent ones include the following: moral opposition to hunting, feelings regarding animal pain and suffering, hunter behavior, safety issues, and perceived damage to wildlife populations and ecosystems. The perception among some that many hunters are unskilled creates public concern. One study examined numerous reasons that may fuel anti-hunting sentiment and found that there was much concern about wounding an animal and about the animals' suffering, rather than the killing of an animal. In short, the public does not express concern for quick kills by skilled hunters as much as for slow, lingering kills (and wounding) by unskilled hunters. Related to this, Americans are more willing to accept wildlife population reductions to benefit wildlife, habitat, or the environment than to benefit people.

Another common reason that people oppose hunting is poor behavior of the hunters themselves. Researchers found the major problems perceived by the public were hunters' failing to track wounded animals, hunters shooting animals that they are not allowed to shoot, hunters ignoring safety regulations, hunter trespassing, hunters shooting too close to highways, and hunters not knowing what they are shooting at.

American hunters, not anti-hunters, hold the key to public opinion on hunting. The American public supports hunting and that support appears to be increasing; however, there also appears to be a discrepancy between the public's opinion on hunting and the public's opinion of the hunter. The perception of hunting can be threatened by poor hunter behavior. Some negative public attitudes toward and opinions on hunting appear to be more a result of damage from the "inside out" rather than from the "outside in." Efforts to further enhance public perceptions and attitudes toward hunting must begin with hunter behavior. Any money spent on hunter ethics or hunter education programs is money spent on increasing the overall perceptions of hunters, and ultimately, hunting itself. Good behavior in the field is imperative.

"Voluntary adherence to an ethical code elevates the self-respect of the sportsman, but it should not be forgotten that voluntary disregard of the code degenerates and depraves him." Aldo Leopold

Lasting Impressions

During my early years, I was fascinated with pocketknives. Consequently, at the ripe old age of five or six, I was overtaken by desire and while visiting the local drug store I helped myself to a beautiful folding knife. When I returned home my mother noticed my new prized possession. As any good mother would do, she quizzed me about where I got it. Of course she knew I had no money. This same wonderful mother had taught me the importance of honesty, so I grudgingly admitted I had taken it without paying for it. She instructed me to return to the store, give back the knife and tell Mr. Hill I was sorry. That was the most difficult thing I have ever had to do. It left a "lasting impression." I haven't taken anything that didn't belong to me since. I was so overwhelmed by that experience, that I am one of the most honest people you will ever meet. Bowhunters need to leave positive "lasting impressions."

What does the next 50 years hold for the Pope and Young Club?

As previously mentioned, bowhunting has experienced exceptional growth. Attracted by early and liberal seasons, and occasionally by new challenges, a person merely needs to buy a bow and a hunting license to become a bowhunter. As they enter the bowhunting scene, they have very little knowledge or experience. Selection of equipment, hunting methods, and animal species to be hunted, are influenced by a myriad of sources. Friends, television, and advertising are most likely the leading influences as newcomers make choices. The Pope and Young Club needs to play a major role in the development of bowhunters.

Education is vitally important as we protect the sport we so dearly love. We must reach out to bowhunters of all ages, levels of experience, and interests with the important message of fair chase hunting, ethical behavior, challenge, heritage, and sportsmanship. We must reach out to the non-hunting public and enhance perceptions and attitudes toward hunting. In other words, the Pope and Young Club needs to increase communication and be more active in defending bowhunting as we continue to meet the challenges of the future.

The Pope and Young Club is currently expanding its communication efforts. We have formed a committee of communication experts to enable us to be more effective in our outreach efforts and the promotion of bowhunting. We have partnered with the Boone and Crockett Club in the production of an ethical and fair chase hunting show for television. We are partnering with the Boy Scouts of America to develop archery on the national level through scout jamborees that will touch the lives of thousands of young men. We are actively involved with the National Archery in Schools Program (NASP) and plan to get more involved. Our intent is to influence young people to ensure a secure future for archery and bowhunting.

There is nationwide concern that hunter numbers are on the decline. Young people are faced with more and more electronic gadgetry and less and less outdoor opportunity. When I was young, it was common practice to grab a gun after school (or a fishing pole) and tramp across the countryside. We were always careful in our conduct and as a result we were recognized and welcomed by the landowners. Those opportunities seldom exist in today's society. As hunting access disappears, coupled with higher hunting fees and lease costs, we see increased dropout rates with the older bowhunter as well as young hunters. The Pope and Young Club needs to assume a bigger role in hunter recruitment and retention.

As noted in the research data above, the non-hunting public has concerns on several hunting-related issues. Interestingly enough, fair chase is a major concern. As hunters, are we allowing our quarry equal opportunity to escape? Do we seek the animal on his terms, in his house, with the opportunity to outsmart us? The movement to raise and hunt penned animals cannot be tolerated. This alone will turn the public against our opportunity to hunt. The Pope and Young Club opposes such practices and takes precaution to prevent pen-raised animals from being entered into the Book. The credibility of the Record System is at stake.

The non-hunting public will not tolerate taking unfair advantage of wildlife in our hunting quest. What falls under the umbrella of "unfair advantage"? Often times, legal does not mean fair or ethical. A one hundred yard shot is legal, but is it ethical? Where do trail cameras with monitors in the treestand fit in? How much ATV use should be allowed and at what point does it take away fair chase? Electronics and their use is becoming an issue not only with the public, but also with many game departments. Here in the western states, limited wildlife populations receive heavy hunting pressure. Game departments are concerned about equipment efficiency. As technological advancements continue to develop, harvest figures increase, placing more pressure on declining wildlife populations. In the near future, officials will be required to react to rising harvest figures, either by reducing season lengths, or equipment limitations. Idaho has already given consideration to more lengthy traditional seasons verses shorter modern equipment seasons. The Pope and Young Club will continue to be proactive in equipment definition and use.

Each individual must decide what constitutes unfairness and what is ethical. A hunter who takes time to ponder his or her personal feelings and ethical preferences will be prepared to make the correct choice when a quick decision is required. The decisions we make as hunters will determine our future. If we voluntarily restrict our hunting methods to include fairness, challenge, and ethical practices, and we continue to educate the non-hunting public about the value hunting provides to healthy wildlife populations, hunting will have a bright future. If, however, we fail to impose limitations on ourselves and our equipment and show disregard for public sentiment, we will most likely lose.

In the 1940s Aldo Leopold wrote, *"There is value in any experience that exercises those ethical restraints collectively called 'sportsmanship.' Our tools for the pursuit of wildlife improve faster than we do, and sportsmanship is a voluntary limitation in the use of these armaments. It is aimed to augment the role of skill and shrink the role of gadgets in the pursuit of wild things."*

As bowhunters, we have the responsibility to practice, prepare, and develop the skills necessary to make quick, humane kills. Included is the development of skill necessary to close enough distance to prevent old "buck fever" from fouling up the shot. As bowhunters, our conduct must be impeccable ... conduct that leaves positive "lasting impressions" on the public. Leave an impression that leaves no room for question in one's mind. Be a bowhunter who has high ethical standards, is a great representative of the bowhunting fraternity, and deserves to be afield.

Book 2

Notes:

Velvet Entries
Beginning in 1995, the Club began accepting entries into the Records for which the velvet remained on the antlers. This occurred for all antlered species categories. Some stipulations were placed on their acceptance. First, "velvet" entries are listed in only one all-time record book. They remain in the Records archives permanently, but are simply listed in the first published all-time record book after their acceptance. Secondly, the "velvet" entries are listed at the conclusion of their respective "hard-horned" category and are unranked. Finally, there is no designation of "world record" status for an animal with velvet remaining on its antlers.

CD of Records
Included with this publication (inside the back cover) is a compact disc. The CD contains a digital version of the record book in its entirety, in .pdf format. Additionally, the CD includes the Records archives information in database format (Microsoft Excel, Microsoft Access and comma delimited files). Popularly sought-after and requested, this format allows users to personally sort the data fields at their choosing. The CD contains a wealth of additional information, including: a list of Ishi Award winners, a list of Past and Present Board of Directors members, current list of Official Measurers, all of the scoring forms and more.

Copyright restrictions do not allow for the reproduction or dissemination of this information.

Typical Whitetail Deer Listing
Due to the tremendous size of the whitetail deer listing, readers will notice a break in the listing that occurs on page 531. In a necessary effort to control the physical size of the record book itself, a portion of this listing was selected. This particular book edition, itself, lists the top 16,682 typical whitetail deer entries plus all that have been accepted into the Records Program since the previous edition of the all-time record book (Bowhunting Big Game Records of North America, 6th Edition, 2005). The full and complete typical whitetail deer listing is included in each of the formats on the CD. Additionally, the Pope and Young Club produces an exclusive whitetail deer record book series that began in 1997 and is published on a six-year cycle.

Percent of Let-off
An asterisk (in front of the score) designates an entry that was taken with a compound bow possessing let-off greater than 65 percent. Effective January 1, 2004, the Club began accepting entries taken with compound bows having more than 65 percent of let-off. The previous rule had established 65 percent as the limit.

"Let-off" is the characteristic of a bow that results in a reduction of the force necessary to increase the draw length after the highest level of draw force has been reached. It is a characteristic generally associated with compound bows. In simple terms, the percent of let-off is calculated as follows: (peak draw force) minus (minimum holding force) divided by (peak draw force) multiplied by 100.

Pope & Young Club

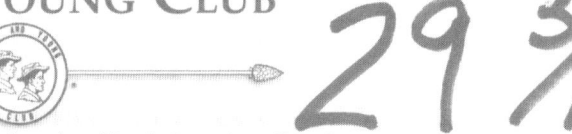

PANEL MEASURED

Official Scoring System for Bowhunting North American Big Game

MINIMUM SCORE	
black bear	18
grizzly bear	19
Alaska brown bear	20
polar bear	20

BEAR

24TH RECORDING PERIOD 2003-04

SEX
☒ Male
☐ Female

KIND OF BEAR (check one)
☐ black bear
☐ grizzly
☒ Alaska brown bear
☐ polar

	MEASUREMENTS
A. Greatest Length With...	18 2/16
B. Greatest Width	11 1/16
	29 3/16

Location of Kill:
Date Killed:
Owner:
Owner's Address:
Guide's Name an...

Were dogs used in conjunction w...

WORLD RECORD ALASKAN BROWN BEAR
Score: 29 3/16
Location: Lake Iliamna, Alaska
Date: 2004
Hunter: Jack Brittingham

Alaskan Brown Bear

by Jack Brittingham

Suddenly, out of nowhere, the monstrous animal appeared in the marsh about 250 yards ahead! As I watched his huge body moving along, the thought occurred that this may actually be the same bear from two years before. With a tail end as big as a Volkswagen, I thought it unlikely that there would be two bears of such size in the same location.

We were able to close the distance to less than 140 yards as the bear edged close to the timber. He then did something that would prove to be a fatal mistake. The giant beast had found a location suitable for his afternoon nap! Down he went like an oversized dog, first on his stomach, and then over on his back. Obviously the dominant bear in the area, he had very little to fear. Occasionally, he would raise his huge head and look around for any sign of danger, but it was a half-hearted effort.

Erin, Bill, and I wasted no time lining up the small dead spruce trees between us and the bear and began carefully making our way to within bow range of the bear. As we did so, the animal's immense size became more apparent. Not wanting to rush the stalk and make a mistake, I forced myself to slowly move forward towards the small dead spruce. I almost decided to take the shot at his vitals, but the massive forearm was too close to the area where I wanted the arrow to penetrate. Switching positions, the bear then rolled onto his side with his back facing us. Once again, I evaluated the shot opportunity and quickly eliminated it because the chance of only hitting one lung was too great.

More time passed, and the huge animal rolled onto his stomach with his forelegs stretched out in front of him exposing the heart and lung area completely. No shot opportunity could have been better! It was a shot that I could tell the instant it left my bowstring would fly true! It struck the resting bear in the intended location just behind his left shoulder. He was on his feet in a flash. I was amazed at how fast he moved. He spun around looking for his assailant. Not seeing anything behind him, he was immediately back facing the other direction. The arrow had buried up to the fletching in the bear's side. Still intent upon locating his attacker, he came up on his hind legs and scanned the area. It was at this moment the immensity of his true size became apparent. He reminded me of Godzilla in the old black and white movie swatting down helicopters as they flew by! He sat down briefly on his haunches, then got up and walked slowly into the edge of the timber where he went down and quickly expired. All of the events described above took place in less than two minutes, but it was an adrenaline-packed two minutes, to say the least!

His size was unbelievable. His hide was in perfect condition. His teeth showed great wear, indicating a bear in excess of twenty years. His claws were white and very long, and his head was immense! After an extremely long, exciting, and arduous day, we made our way back to our camp very tired but extremely happy!

ALASKAN BROWN BEAR

Minimum Score 20

Ursus arctos middendorffi and certain related subspecies

SCORE	GREATEST LENGTH	GREATEST WIDTH	SEX	AREA	STATE/ PROVINCE	HUNTER'S NAME	DATE	RANK
29 3/16	18 2/16	11 1/16	M	Iliamna Lake	AK	Jack Brittingham	2004	1
28 7/16	17 11/16	10 12/16	M	Unimak Island	AK	John D. 'Jack' Frost	1985	2
28 7/16	18 0/16	10 7/16	M	Ursus Cove	AK	Monty Browning	1995	2
28 6/16	16 13/16	11 9/16	M	Sturgeon River	AK	James R. Gabrick	2007	4
28 3/16	17 6/16	10 13/16	M	Kodiak Island	AK	Jim Horneck	2009	5
28 0/16	17 15/16	10 1/16	M	Wide Bay	AK	Fred Bear	1960	6
*27 13/16	16 8/16	11 5/16	M	Deadman Bay	AK	Jimmie R. Ryan	2005	7
27 12/16	16 12/16	11 0/16	M	Kodiak Island	AK	Arthur Heinze	1993	8
27 8/16	16 6/16	11 2/16	M	Grayback Mtn.	AK	Scott Mileur	1997	9
27 5/16	16 10/16	10 11/16	M	Kodiak Island	AK	Bob Ameen	1994	10
27 5/16	17 1/16	10 4/16	M	Stroganof Point	AK	Kyle Koschmeder	2003	10
27 5/16	16 10/16	10 11/16	M	Afognak Island	AK	Julian D. Salutregui	2008	10
27 1/16	16 15/16	10 2/16	M	Bear Bay	AK	Fred Bear	1962	13
27 1/16	17 2/16	9 15/16	M	Dog Salmon River	AK	Chuck Adams	1989	13
27 1/16	16 7/16	10 10/16	M	Deadman Bay	AK	Jimmie R. Ryan	1995	13
27 1/16	16 5/16	10 12/16	M	Kodiak Island	AK	Eugene Arndt	2004	13
*27 1/16	16 13/16	10 4/16	M	Cold Bay	AK	Gary Joseph	2007	13
27 1/16	16 13/16	10 4/16	M	Deadman Bay	AK	Scott Dulin	2008	13
27 1/16	17 4/16	9 13/16	M	False Pass	AK	Randy Ulmer	2009	13
26 13/16	17 0/16	9 13/16	M	Wide Bay	AK	Archie Nesbitt	1991	20
26 13/16	16 3/16	10 10/16	M	Kodiak Island	AK	James Hens	2007	20
*26 10/16	16 6/16	10 4/16	M	Iliamna Lake	AK	Joe Thomas	2008	22
26 10/16	16 4/16	10 6/16	M	Deadman Bay	AK	Matthew Liljenquist	2009	22
26 7/16	16 7/16	10 0/16	M	Sparrevohn Lake	AK	John Shaffer, Jr.	2005	23
26 6/16	16 12/16	9 10/16	M	Wide Bay	AK	David E. Snowden, Jr.	1997	24
26 4/16	16 14/16	9 6/16	M	Naknek River	AK	Gary M. Martin	1997	26
26 2/16	16 7/16	9 11/16	M	Killey River	AK	Frank Sanders	2004	27
26 1/16	15 14/16	10 3/16	M	Deadman Bay	AK	Randy Liljenquist	1998	28
*26 1/16	15 12/16	10 5/16	M	Kodiak Island	AK	Joe Ciottariello	2009	28
25 13/16	16 2/16	9 11/16	M	Meshik River	AK	Robert Speegle, MD	1997	30
25 12/16	16 4/16	9 8/16	M	Afognak Island	AK	Bradley W. Mongold	2007	31
25 11/16	16 6/16	9 5/16	M	Yakutat	AK	George Harms	2006	32
25 11/16	15 9/16	10 2/16	M	Deadman Bay	AK	Hunter P. Moates	2009	32
*25 9/16	16 2/16	9 7/16	M	Afognak Island	AK	Mark "Gutz" Gutsmiedl	2008	34
25 8/16	16 5/16	9 3/16	M	Kodiak Island	AK	Tim R. Dawson	1998	35
25 6/16	16 1/16	9 5/16	M	S. Auckland Mtns.	AK	Ron Murphy	2005	36
25 6/16	15 12/16	9 10/16	M	Stepovak Bay	AK	Robert D. Hancock, Jr.	2008	36
25 5/16	15 14/16	9 7/16	M	Lake Clark	AK	Richard L. Busk	1991	38
25 4/16	15 12/16	9 8/16	M	Fraser Lake	AK	Howard Young	2001	39
25 2/16	16 2/16	9 0/16	M	Chichagof Island	AK	Kenneth T. Wotring	1982	40
25 1/16	16 0/16	9 1/16	M	Unimak Island	AK	Tony Casagrande	2007	41
25 0/16	15 14/16	9 2/16	M	Kodiak Island	AK	Lloyd L. Garrels	1993	42
25 0/16	15 11/16	9 5/16	M	Bachatna Creek	AK	Bernie Weisgerber	2010	42
24 15/16	15 5/16	9 10/16	M	Zachar Bay	AK	Bill Hartman	2003	44
24 14/16	15 10/16	9 4/16	M	Naknek River	AK	Joseph D. Maddock	1998	45
24 14/16	15 9/16	9 5/16	M	Aliulik Peninsula	AK	John D. "Jack" Frost, MD	2006	45
24 13/16	16 3/16	8 10/16	M	Deer Creek	AK	Roy L. Walk	2007	47
24 13/16	15 6/16	9 7/16	M	Gull Cove	AK	Don R. Russell	2008	47
24 12/16	16 3/16	8 9/16	M	Port Heiden	AK	Gardner Rowell	1995	49
24 12/16	15 14/16	8 14/16	M	Tsiu River	AK	Gary F. Bogner	1998	49
24 11/16	15 2/16	9 9/16	M	Dillingham	AK	Clint Hukill	2007	51
24 10/16	15 4/16	9 6/16	M	Kodiak Island	AK	Dean Stebner	1991	52
24 8/16	15 12/16	8 12/16	M	Port Heiden	AK	Stephen Kotz	1999	53
24 8/16	15 7/16	9 1/16	F	Herendeen Bay	AK	John Paul Schaffer	2007	53
24 6/16	16 0/16	8 6/16	M	Wide Bay	AK	Tim Walters	2005	55
*24 5/16	15 1/16	9 4/16	M	Chichagof Island	AK	Jonathon Geary	2008	56
24 3/16	15 7/16	8 12/16	M	Cold Bay	AK	Frank S. Noska IV	2009	57
24 2/16	15 3/16	8 15/16	M	Admiralty Island	AK	Rick Kinmon	1992	58
24 2/16	15 11/16	8 7/16	M	Cold Bay	AK	George Krasinski	1997	58
24 1/16	14 12/16	9 5/16	M	Admiralty Island	AK	Richard J. Callahan	1991	60
24 1/16	15 7/16	8 10/16	M	Admiralty Island	AK	David Benitz	2002	60
23 14/16	15 11/16	8 3/16	M	Port Heiden	AK	H. Gale McKnight	1995	62
23 14/16	15 4/16	8 10/16	M	Talkeetna Mtns.	AK	Braun Kopsack	2005	62
23 13/16	15 3/16	8 10/16	M	Deadman Bay	AK	Dwight S. Wolf	2002	64
23 11/16	14 11/16	9 0/16	F	Olga Bay	AK	Richard E. Boggio	1993	65
23 11/16	15 10/16	8 1/16	M	Admiralty Island	AK	Matt Hentrick	2001	65
23 11/16	14 12/16	8 15/16	F	O'Malley Lake	AK	Anthony Del Mastro	2002	65
23 11/16	15 7/16	8 4/16	M	Crooked Creek	AK	Roy M. Goodwin	2003	65
23 10/16	15 2/16	8 8/16	F	Port Heiden	AK	George P. Mann	1989	69
23 10/16	15 3/16	8 7/16	M	Kayak Island	AK	Forest Keith	2010	69
23 9/16	14 15/16	8 10/16	M	Kodiak Island	AK	Angie Ryan	2003	71
23 8/16	14 14/16	8 10/16	M	Kaskanak Creek	AK	Richie Bland	2002	72
23 7/16	15 1/16	8 6/16	M	Aniak River	AK	Dennis Doherty	2006	73
23 6/16	14 6/16	9 0/16	M	Kodiak Island	AK	Gordon Longville	1961	74
23 6/16	15 1/16	8 5/16	M	Afognak Island	AK	Bruce Morrison	2006	74
23 5/16	15 5/16	8 0/16	M	Admiralty Island	AK	Frank S. Noska IV	2004	76
23 4/16	14 11/16	8 9/16	M	Admiralty Island	AK	John R. Thiele	1984	77
23 4/16	15 3/16	8 1/16	F	Joshua Green River	AK	John Koldeway	1985	77
23 4/16	15 8/16	7 12/16	M	False Bay	AK	Lon Hadfield	1999	77
23 4/16	14 9/16	8 11/16	M	Old Harbor	AK	Ken Vorisek	2002	77
23 4/16	14 10/16	8 10/16	M	Admiralty Island	AK	M. Robert DeLaney	2004	77
23 3/16	15 5/16	7 14/16	M	Seal Islands	AK	John Koschmeder	2003	82
23 3/16	14 11/16	8 8/16	M	Admiralty Island	AK	Ken Vorisek	2010	82
23 2/16	15 2/16	8 0/16	M	Sunflower Creek	AK	Bruce S. Richardson	1996	84
23 2/16	15 5/16	7 13/16	M	Yantarni Bay	AK	Mark "Gutz" Gutsmiedl	1999	84
23 0/16	15 3/16	7 13/16	M	Wide Bay	AK	Lou Kindred	2003	86
22 15/16	14 2/16	8 13/16	F	Sheepcreek-Valdez	AK	Gerald R. Gold	1966	87
*22 15/16	14 11/16	8 4/16	M	Afognak Island	AK	Roy K. Keefer	2006	87
22 13/16	15 0/16	7 13/16	M	Port Heiden	AK	Ed De Young	2003	89
22 11/16	14 12/16	7 15/16	M	Lake Nerka	AK	Scott Whitlock	2000	90
22 11/16	14 9/16	8 2/16	M	Cordova	AK	Rob Swanson	2002	90
22 11/16	14 13/16	7 14/16	M	Yakutat	AK	Rob Harms	2006	90
22 9/16	14 6/16	8 3/16	F	Yakutat	AK	George R. Harms	2002	93
22 9/16	14 12/16	7 13/16	M	Doame River	AK	Tom Taylor	2004	93
22 8/16	15 1/16	7 7/16	M	Cinder River	AK	Ken Grosslight	1997	95

122

ALASKAN BROWN BEAR

Minimum Score 20   Continued

SCORE	GREATEST LENGTH	GREATEST WIDTH	SEX	AREA	STATE/ PROVINCE	HUNTER'S NAME	DATE	RANK
22 8/16	14 5/16	8 3/16	F	Cordova	AK	Robin Lee Radach	2005	95
22 7/16	14 2/16	8 5/16	F	Merrill Pass	AK	Ralph Ertz	1975	97
22 7/16	14 10/16	7 13/16	M	Baranof Island	AK	Ivan Muzljakovich	2006	97
22 6/16	14 4/16	8 2/16	M	Kodiak Island	AK	Buddy Watson	1965	99
22 6/16	13 15/16	8 7/16	F	Iliamna Lake	AK	Terry Grimes	1998	99
22 5/16	14 9/16	7 12/16	M	Portage Creek	AK	John C. Culpepper III	1991	101
22 5/16	14 3/16	8 2/16	M	Dice Bay	AK	Thomas M. Basch	2005	101
22 3/16	14 0/16	8 3/16	M	Chichagof Island	AK	David Heller	1995	103
22 3/16	14 15/16	7 4/16	M	East Alsek River	AK	Michael Wolff	2003	103
22 2/16	14 8/16	7 10/16	M	Chichagof Island	AK	John Gary Price	1995	105
22 2/16	13 10/16	8 8/16	F	Eyak Lake	AK	Kenneth D. Carvajal	1999	105
22 2/16	14 0/16	8 2/16	F	Sandy River	AK	Aaron Armstrong	2005	105
22 0/16	14 8/16	7 8/16	M	Wide Bay	AK	Randy Lee Waddell	1995	108
22 0/16	14 5/16	7 11/16	M	Cooper Landing	AK	Kenneth D. Carvajal	1998	108
21 15/16	14 7/16	7 8/16	M	Kajulik Bay	AK	Thomas J. Hoffman	1983	110
21 15/16	13 11/16	8 4/16	F	Talkeetna Mtns.	AK	Robert Wickler	2004	110
*21 14/16	14 5/16	7 9/16	M	Lake Beverley	AK	Trent Penrod	2003	112
21 13/16	13 15/16	7 14/16	F	Merrill Pass	AK	Dan Hollingsworth	1975	113
21 13/16	13 4/16	8 9/16	F	Dana Glacier	AK	Dan W. Morrison	1975	113
21 13/16	14 2/16	7 11/16	M	Baranof Island	AK	Dennis Dunn	2004	113
21 12/16	14 0/16	7 12/16	M	Afognak Island	AK	Dr. Chuck Leidheiser	1996	116
21 12/16	13 10/16	8 2/16	F	Chilakot River	AK	Glenn Klomsten	2002	116
21 11/16	13 14/16	7 13/16	M	Chilkat River	AK	Richard LaCrone	2005	118
*21 11/16	13 15/16	7 12/16	F	Sheep River	AK	Keith Redding	2005	118
21 10/16	13 14/16	7 12/16	F	Alaska Peninsula	AK	Bill Van Houten	1961	120
21 10/16	13 9/16	8 1/16	F	Alphabet Hills	AK	Braun Kopsack	1996	120
21 9/16	14 4/16	7 5/16	M	Alaska Peninsula	AK	Kurt Lepping	1989	122
21 9/16	14 4/16	7 5/16	M	Ramsey Bay	AK	Michael A. Wilson	2007	122
21 8/16	13 9/16	7 15/16	M	Hoonah	AK	Len Cardinale	1979	124
21 8/16	14 0/16	7 8/16	M	Wide Bay	AK	John Ribic	1993	124
21 8/16	13 9/16	7 15/16	M	Deadman Bay	AK	Walter Palmer	1994	124
21 7/16	13 8/16	7 15/16	F	Fidalgo Bay	AK	Joseph West	1966	127
21 7/16	14 1/16	7 6/16	M	Chichagof Island	AK	Ray Keenan	1984	127
21 7/16	13 11/16	7 12/16	M	Clear Creek	AK	Eric Colledge	1992	127
21 7/16	13 15/16	7 8/16	M	Lynn Canal	AK	Scott J. Leslie	2001	127
21 6/16	13 13/16	7 9/16	F	Imuya Bay	AK	J. Dale Hale	1991	131
21 6/16	13 12/16	7 10/16	F	Wide Bay	AK	Lucien Rouse	1999	131
21 4/16	13 10/16	7 10/16	M	Chichagof Island	AK	Darren Baucom	2000	133
21 2/16	13 14/16	7 4/16	M	Anaktuvuk River	AK	Martin Hanson	1958	134
21 2/16	13 12/16	7 6/16	M	Iliamna Lake	AK	Thomas J. Edgington	2005	134
21 1/16	13 12/16	7 5/16	F	Mat-Su Borough	AK	Rickie D. Snell	1985	136
21 1/16	13 6/16	7 11/16	F	Kodiak Island	AK	Bob Ameen	2006	136
21 0/16	13 13/16	7 3/16	M	Karluk Lake	AK	Gary G. Wall	2003	138
*21 0/16	13 4/16	7 12/16	F	Clear Creek	AK	Alan Harris	2008	138
21 0/16	13 15/16	7 1/16	F	Kitty Lake	AK	Steve Edwards	2008	138
20 15/16	13 4/16	7 11/16	M	Admiralty Island	AK	Allen L. Grierson	1985	141
20 15/16	12 14/16	8 1/16	F	Iliamna Lake	AK	Mark Buehrer	2001	141
20 14/16	13 10/16	7 4/16	M	Chulitna River	AK	Rick D. Snell	1997	143
20 12/16	13 8/16	7 4/16	F	King Salmon	AK	Rhonda Baker	1977	144
20 12/16	13 14/16	6 14/16	M	Iliamna River	AK	Mark Calkins	2001	144
20 11/16	13 9/16	7 2/16	M	Talkeetna Mtns.	AK	L.M. Peppers	1983	146
20 11/16	13 5/16	7 6/16	F	Becharof Lake	AK	Lon E. Lauber	1999	146
20 11/16	13 8/16	7 3/16	M	Yakutat	AK	Chris Parrino	2004	146
20 10/16	13 7/16	7 3/16	M	Cottonwood Bay	AK	R. Todd Beckman	2001	149
20 8/16	13 3/16	7 5/16	M	Kichatna River	AK	Douglas W. Hill	1994	150
20 8/16	13 8/16	7 0/16	F	Ugashik Lake	AK	Gus Congemi	2007	150
20 7/16	13 4/16	7 3/16	M	Wide Bay	AK	Keith Appel	1994	152
20 7/16	13 8/16	6 15/16	F	Wide Bay	AK	William Welton	1995	152
20 7/16	13 4/16	7 3/16	M	Misty Fiords	AK	Michael R. Deschamps	2001	152
20 7/16	13 2/16	7 5/16	M	Talkeetna River	AK	Michael R. Traub	2004	152
20 4/16	12 14/16	7 6/16	F	Funnel Creek	AK	Stacee Frost	2007	156
20 4/16	13 3/16	7 1/16	M	Iliamna River	AK	Gary Gapp	2009	156
20 3/16	12 3/16	8 0/16	M	Sunday Creek	AK	Bob Ehle	1998	158
20 3/16	13 3/16	7 0/16	F	Port Heiden	AK	Rick Duggan	2001	158
20 2/16	13 6/16	6 12/16	F	Cold Bay	AK	Paul E. Korn	2003	160
20 1/16	12 14/16	7 3/16	M	Fog Lakes	AK	Dennis L. Lattery	1984	161
20 0/16	13 6/16	6 10/16	M	Bering River	AK	Tom Miranda	1999	162

123

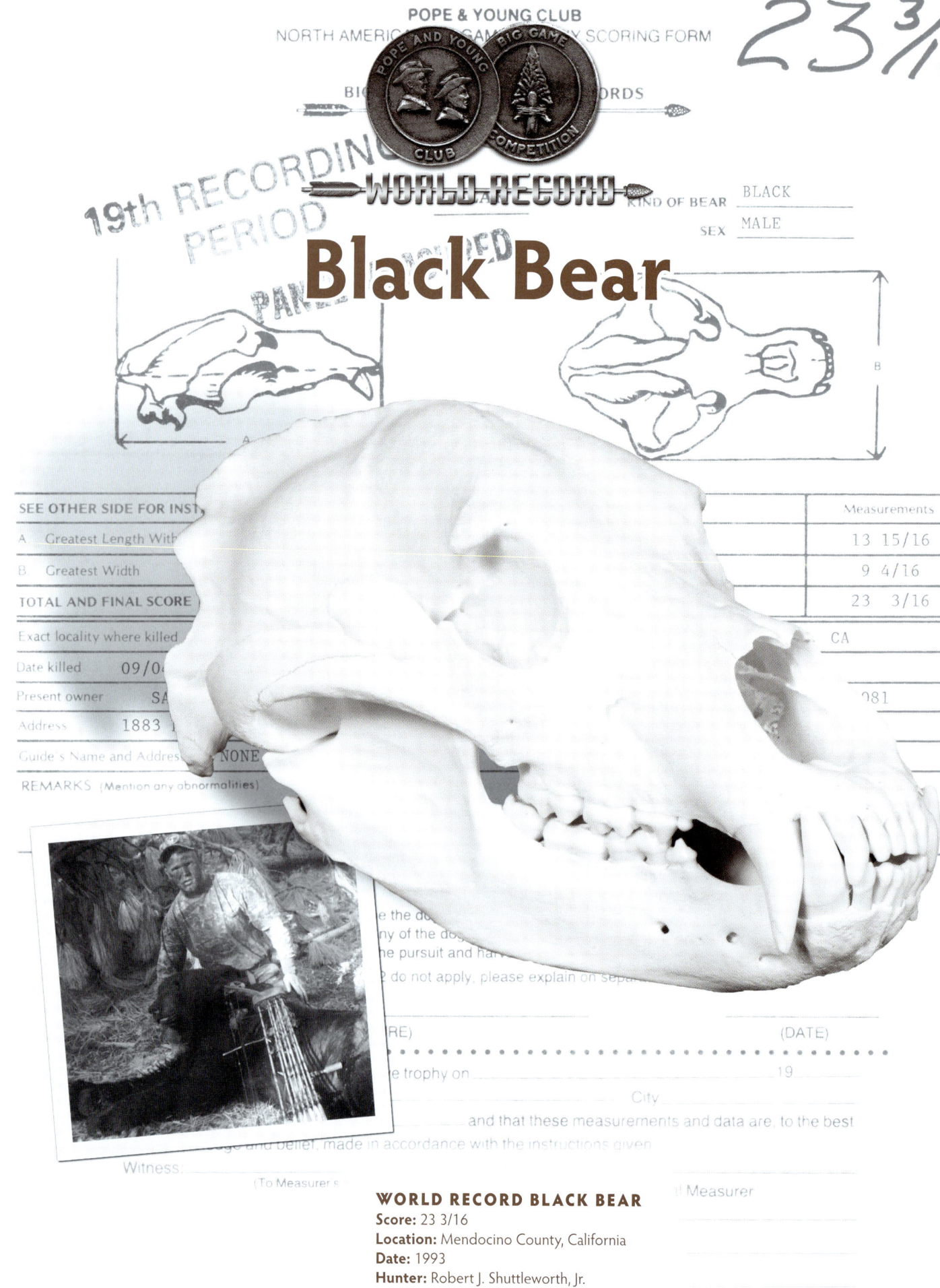

WORLD RECORD BLACK BEAR
Score: 23 3/16
Location: Mendocino County, California
Date: 1993
Hunter: Robert J. Shuttleworth, Jr.

BLACK BEAR

Minimum Score 18 *Ursus americanus americanus* and certain related subspecies

SCORE	GREATEST LENGTH	GREATEST WIDTH	SEX	AREA	STATE/ PROVINCE	HUNTER'S NAME	DATE	RANK
23 3/16	13 15/16	9 4/16	M	Mendocino County	CA	Robert J. Shuttleworth, Jr.	1993	1
22 13/16	14 1/16	8 12/16	M	Olha	MAN	Robert "Rob" Evans	2008	2
22 11/16	14 3/16	8 8/16	M	Chippewa County	WI	Duane Helland	2003	3
22 8/16	14 1/16	8 7/16	M	Kanawha County	WV	G. Murphy / V. Ryan	1991	4
*22 8/16	13 15/16	8 9/16	M	Haywood County	NC	Thad Surrett	2008	4
*22 7/16	14 1/16	8 6/16	M	Chippewa County	WI	Jason Wunderlich	2009	5
22 6/16	13 12/16	8 10/16	M	Gronlid	SAS	Floyd Forster	1992	6
*22 6/16	13 13/16	8 9/16	M	Sullivan County	NY	Michael R. Mangano	2009	6
22 4/16	13 7/16	8 13/16	M	Sinbad Ridge	CO	Ray Cox	1978	9
22 4/16	14 1/16	8 3/16	M	Woodridge	MAN	Peter U. Funk	2000	9
22 3/16	14 2/16	8 1/16	M	Grahamdale	MAN	Collin P. Stone	1996	11
22 2/16	14 0/16	8 2/16	M	Olha	MAN	Carl Farler	1992	12
22 2/16	13 15/16	8 3/16	M	Rusk County	WI	Dean R. Ecker	2001	12
22 2/16	14 1/16	8 1/16	M	St. Croix County	WI	Gary L. Kurtz	2002	12
22 2/16	13 14/16	8 4/16	M	Richer	MAN	Ryan Eckert	2004	12
22 2/16	13 15/16	8 3/16	M	Yavapai County	AZ	Edward F. Balmes	2004	12
22 1/16	13 15/16	8 2/16	M	Orange County	NY	Mike Maillet	2006	17
*22 1/16	13 13/16	8 4/16	M	Rapid View	SAS	Darcy Fehr	2008	17
22 0/16	13 11/16	8 5/16	M	Lincoln County	WI	Bob Faufau	1981	20
22 0/16	13 12/16	8 4/16	M	Prince of Wales Island	AK	George P. Mann	1991	20
22 0/16	13 10/16	8 6/16	M	Bronson Lake	SAS	Roger Fournier	1992	20
22 0/16	13 11/16	8 5/16	M	Graham County	AZ	Mark D. Morris	1995	20
22 0/16	13 11/16	8 5/16	M	Pine County	MN	Darrin Stream	1995	20
*22 0/16	14 2/16	7 14/16	M	Livingston County	NY	Ronald Perham	2008	20
*22 0/16	13 10/16	8 6/16	M	Sioux Lookout	ONT	Aaron Augedahl	2010	20
21 15/16	13 13/16	8 2/16	M	Prince of Wales Island	AK	Stanley L. Parkerson	1991	27
21 15/16	13 9/16	8 6/16	M	Poplarfield	MAN	Samuel Amodeo	1995	27
21 15/16	13 13/16	8 2/16	M	Olha	MAN	Rob Evans	2006	27
*21 15/16	13 7/16	8 8/16	M	Clark County	WI	Frederick Moen	2006	27
21 14/16	13 7/16	8 7/16	M	Prince of Wales Island	AK	Jim Ponciano	1990	31
21 14/16	13 14/16	8 0/16	M	Weldon	SAS	Ron S. Bodnarchuk	1998	31
21 14/16	13 8/16	8 6/16	M	Flood Lake	ALB	Steve Ecklund	2009	31
21 13/16	13 9/16	8 4/16	M	Idaho County	ID	Harold Boyack	1976	34
21 13/16	13 1/16	8 12/16	M	Dog Lake	ONT	Larry Murray	1990	34
21 13/16	14 4/16	7 9/16	M	Rossburn	MAN	Barry Minshull	1990	34
21 13/16	13 12/16	8 1/16	M	White County	GA	John Wood	1995	34
21 13/16	13 5/16	8 8/16	M	Prince of Wales Island	AK	Dyrk Eddie	1996	34
21 13/16	13 5/16	8 8/16	M	Choiceland	SAS	John Foster	1998	34
21 13/16	13 8/16	8 5/16	M	Rusk County	WI	Bob Brunkow	2000	34
21 13/16	13 9/16	8 4/16	M	Sevier County	UT	Todd Newby	2003	34
*21 13/16	13 8/16	8 5/16	M	Fremont County	WY	Herky Clark	2007	34
21 13/16	13 12/16	8 1/16	M	St. Walberg	SAS	Gary Johnston	2009	34
21 12/16	13 5/16	8 7/16	M	Price County	WI	Robert Brotske	1981	44
21 12/16	13 6/16	8 6/16	M	Big River	SAS	Bill Dear	1985	44
21 12/16	13 3/16	8 9/16	M	Prince of Wales Island	AK	Mark Robecker	1991	44
21 12/16	13 10/16	8 2/16	M	Alonsa	MAN	Cory Mozdzen	1991	44
21 12/16	13 6/16	8 6/16	M	Peace River	ALB	Mike Scott	1992	44
21 12/16	13 0/16	8 12/16	M	Greene County	NY	Edward Rivenburg, Jr.	1997	44
21 12/16	13 10/16	8 2/16	M	Riding Mtn.	MAN	Mike Minshull	1998	44
21 12/16	13 14/16	7 14/16	M	Montrose County	CO	Donald E. Tunget	1998	44
21 12/16	13 14/16	7 14/16	M	Loon Lake	SAS	Jarred Lee Faust	2004	44
21 12/16	13 10/16	8 2/16	M	Menominee County	MI	Jason Welch	2004	44
21 12/16	12 15/16	8 13/16	M	Slave Lake	ALB	Gregory S. Spitzley	2006	44
21 12/16	13 11/16	8 1/16	M	Assiniboine River	MAN	Barry Minshull	2008	44
21 12/16	13 10/16	8 2/16	M	Jackson County	OR	John Souza	2008	44
21 12/16	13 5/16	8 7/16	M	Mesa County	CO	John Bailey	2009	44
21 12/16	13 9/16	8 3/16	M	Rusk County	WI	Robert H. Breed	2009	44
*21 12/16	13 10/16	8 2/16	M	French River	ONT	Art B. Blanchard	2010	44
21 11/16	13 9/16	8 2/16	M	Nipawin	SAS	Ray Mastel	1974	60
21 11/16	13 7/16	8 4/16	M	Sevier County	UT	Robert F. Fitzgerald	1984	60
21 11/16	13 9/16	8 2/16	M	Chelan	SAS	Ray Svennes	1995	60
21 11/16	13 13/16	7 14/16	M	Rusk County	WI	Gregory Baneck	1995	60
21 11/16	13 4/16	8 7/16	M	Olha	MAN	Gary G. Lex	1996	60
21 11/16	13 7/16	8 4/16	M	Prince of Wales Island	AK	Chad Berry	2003	60
21 11/16	13 11/16	8 0/16	M	Utah County	UT	Ben Lowder	2004	60
21 11/16	13 9/16	8 2/16	M	Menominee County	MI	Peter Granquist	2004	60
21 10/16	13 6/16	8 4/16	M	Hudson Bay	SAS	Craig Richardson	1985	68
21 10/16	13 5/16	8 5/16	M	Grande Prairie	ALB	Blair Trout	1989	68
21 10/16	13 10/16	8 0/16	M	Prince of Wales Island	AK	James E. Hodson	1991	68
21 10/16	13 4/16	8 6/16	M	North Battleford	SAS	John Leite	1993	68
21 10/16	13 8/16	8 2/16	M	Grant County	WV	Carnie Carr, Jr.	1993	68
21 10/16	13 6/16	8 4/16	M	Prince of Wales Island	AK	Kelly King	2001	68
21 10/16	13 9/16	8 1/16	M	Peace River	ALB	Randy Stadler	2002	68
21 10/16	13 8/16	8 2/16	M	Raleigh County	WV	Harold Williams, Jr.	2003	68
21 10/16	13 10/16	8 0/16	M	Cass County	MN	Terry Petersen	2004	68
21 10/16	13 4/16	8 6/16	M	Townsend Lake	SAS	Mitch Bilokreli	2005	68
21 10/16	13 7/16	8 3/16	M	Manaki	ONT	Nicholas M. Farr	2005	68
21 10/16	13 4/16	8 6/16	M	Bayfield County	WI	Dennis E. Krueger	2006	68
21 10/16	13 2/16	8 8/16	M	Ulster County	NY	Kenny Lord	2007	68
21 10/16	13 7/16	8 3/16	M	Polk County	WI	Dani Backes	2009	68
21 10/16	13 11/16	7 15/16	M	Los Angeles County	CA	Jim Riner	2009	68
21 10/16	13 5/16	8 5/16	M	Rennie	MAN	Gus Congemi	2010	68
21 9/16	13 5/16	8 4/16	M	Iron County	WI	Gary Johnson	1982	83
21 9/16	13 9/16	8 0/16	M	Bay Tree	ALB	David E. Samuel	1990	83
21 9/16	13 5/16	8 4/16	M	Duck Mtns.	MAN	Mark Braun	1997	83
21 9/16	13 5/16	8 4/16	M	Mantagao Lake	MAN	Bruce V. Huewan	2001	83
21 9/16	13 5/16	8 4/16	M	Saddle Hills	ALB	David W. Watson	2003	83
21 9/16	13 7/16	8 2/16	M	Hamilton County	NY	James B. Cook, Sr.	2003	83
21 9/16	13 10/16	7 15/16	M	Goochland County	VA	Stacy L. McLeod	2003	83
*21 9/16	13 9/16	8 0/16	M	Olha	MAN	Gil Gilbertson	2005	83
*21 9/16	13 7/16	8 2/16	M	Forest County	WI	Thomas Karl	2009	83
21 8/16	13 6/16	8 2/16	M	Hudson Bay	SAS	Garry Benson	1976	92
21 8/16	13 2/16	8 6/16	M	Kern County	CA	Dean M. Lutge	1981	92
21 8/16	13 2/16	8 6/16	M	Shasta County	CA	Ed Woodring	1996	92
21 8/16	13 10/16	7 14/16	M	Sawyer County	WI	James M. Slepicka, Sr.	2000	92

125

BLACK BEAR

Minimum Score 18 — Continued

SCORE	GREATEST LENGTH	GREATEST WIDTH	SEX	AREA	STATE/ PROVINCE	HUNTER'S NAME	DATE	RANK
21 8/16	13 8/16	8 0/16	M	Minitonas	MAN	Jeff Lute	2001	92
21 8/16	13 8/16	8 0/16	M	Bayfield County	WI	Jerry Waara	2004	92
*21 8/16	13 7/16	8 1/16	M	Preston County	WV	Nicholas Allen Loughry	2004	92
21 8/16	13 8/16	8 0/16	M	Barron County	WI	Racheal Gifford	2008	92
21 7/16	13 7/16	8 0/16	M	Nipawin	SAS	Don Adams	1975	100
21 7/16	13 7/16	8 0/16	M	Mendocino County	CA	Jim Oliver	1984	100
21 7/16	13 0/16	8 7/16	M	Garfield County	CO	Norman J. O'Bryan	1985	100
21 7/16	13 11/16	7 12/16	M	Gordondale	ALB	Zig Kertenis, Jr.	1993	100
21 7/16	13 2/16	8 5/16	M	Ellice	MAN	Jamie Poole	1994	100
21 7/16	13 8/16	7 15/16	M	Clinch County	GA	Danny Hinson	1997	100
21 7/16	13 2/16	8 5/16	M	Garfield County	CO	Kurt A. Grimm	1999	100
21 7/16	13 6/16	8 1/16	M	Becker County	MN	Mike Honek	2001	100
21 7/16	13 10/16	7 13/16	M	Sullivan County	NY	Edward T. Murran	2003	100
21 7/16	12 15/16	8 8/16	M	George Lake	SAS	Gordon J. Wilson	2004	100
21 7/16	13 5/16	8 2/16	M	Yorkton	SAS	Kevin R. Williams	2004	100
21 7/16	13 5/16	8 2/16	M	Barron County	WI	Jeffery Tomesh	2005	100
21 7/16	13 6/16	8 1/16	M	Wollaston Lake	SAS	Vance Edward Grimes	2006	100
21 7/16	13 6/16	8 1/16	M	Lac La Biche	ALB	Stephane Titley	2007	100
21 7/16	13 7/16	8 0/16	M	Saline County	AR	Don Barnett	2008	100
21 7/16	13 2/16	8 5/16	M	Chilliwack Valley	BC	Terry Riffin	2009	100
21 7/16	13 9/16	7 14/16	M	Utah County	UT	Ryan Gasser	2010	100
21 6/16	13 6/16	8 0/16	M	Bayfield County	WI	Larry L. Frye	1975	117
21 6/16	13 6/16	8 0/16	M	Grant County	WV	Carnie Carr, Sr.	1988	117
21 6/16	13 4/16	8 2/16	M	North Hudson Bay	SAS	Malcolm Garratt	1991	117
21 6/16	13 2/16	8 4/16	M	York County	NBW	Kenneth J. Fluck	1991	117
21 6/16	12 15/16	8 7/16	M	Girouxville	ALB	Ed Spruyt	1996	117
21 6/16	13 15/16	7 7/16	M	Sawyer County	WI	Rolland Manthei	1998	117
21 6/16	13 8/16	7 14/16	M	Rio Blanco County	CO	Sonny Busch	2000	117
21 6/16	13 10/16	7 12/16	M	Lac du Bonnet	MAN	Jason M. Singbeil	2002	117
21 6/16	12 14/16	8 8/16	M	Hodgson	MAN	Michael D. Rutten	2004	117
21 6/16	13 14/16	7 8/16	M	Preston County	WV	T. J. Teter	2005	117
21 6/16	13 4/16	8 2/16	M	Chautauqua County	NY	Dan Beres	2005	117
21 6/16	13 13/16	7 9/16	M	Pierceland	SAS	Mike DeVore, Sr.	2006	117
*21 6/16	13 2/16	8 4/16	M	Qu'Appelle River	SAS	Mike Eckersley	2007	117
21 6/16	13 4/16	8 2/16	M	Fannin County	GA	Stephan Patton	2009	117
21 5/16	13 5/16	8 0/16	M	Ministikwan	SAS	Gary Mutter	1985	131
21 5/16	13 0/16	8 5/16	M	Kenora	ONT	Robert Svoboda	1986	131
21 5/16	13 2/16	8 3/16	M	Swan River	MAN	Richard C. Weber	1991	131
21 5/16	12 14/16	8 7/16	M	Sawyer County	WI	Mark Heath	1991	131
21 5/16	13 4/16	8 1/16	M	Prince of Wales Island	AK	Rick Schikora	1992	131
21 5/16	12 12/16	8 9/16	M	Terrace	BC	Wayne Topolewski	1992	131
21 5/16	13 8/16	7 13/16	M	Sawyer County	WI	Steve Bouton	1992	131
21 5/16	13 4/16	8 1/16	M	Round Lake	SAS	Floyd Forster	1994	131
21 5/16	13 10/16	7 11/16	M	Bay Tree	ALB	Zig Kertenis, Jr.	1995	131
21 5/16	13 6/16	7 15/16	M	Horseshoe Lake	ALB	Darren Daniel	1995	131
21 5/16	13 5/16	8 0/16	M	Shawano County	WI	Scott Johnson	1995	131
21 5/16	13 2/16	8 3/16	M	Falher	ALB	Stephen L. Collins	1996	131
21 5/16	13 15/16	7 6/16	M	Usherville	SAS	John Stephen Williams	1997	131
21 5/16	13 2/16	8 3/16	M	Prince of Wales Island	AK	Steven R. Martin	1998	131
21 5/16	13 6/16	7 15/16	M	Wolf Lake	ALB	Thomas G. Lester III	1998	131
21 5/16	13 3/16	8 2/16	M	Mono County	CA	Greg Brackett	1999	131
21 5/16	13 12/16	7 9/16	M	Grafton County	NH	Jeffrey D. Stout	2000	131
21 5/16	13 2/16	8 3/16	M	Peace River	ALB	Gino Giannetti	2001	131
21 5/16	13 7/16	7 14/16	M	Olha	MAN	Bill Clink	2001	131
21 5/16	13 3/16	8 2/16	M	Bronson Lake	SAS	Lynn Drechsel	2004	131
21 5/16	13 9/16	7 12/16	M	Broome County	NY	Kimberly Knapp Moravcik	2005	131
21 5/16	13 1/16	8 4/16	M	Kipahigan Lake	MAN	Scott Hettinger	2007	131
21 5/16	13 7/16	7 14/16	M	Manitoba Lake Narrows	MAN	Raymond Reading	2009	131
21 4/16	13 7/16	7 13/16	M	Tehama County	CA	Jim Cox	1980	154
21 4/16	13 5/16	7 15/16	M	Cass County	MN	Myles Keller	1980	154
21 4/16	13 4/16	8 0/16	M	Duck Mtn.	MAN	Dave Cordes	1984	154
21 4/16	13 8/16	7 12/16	M	Spiritwood	SAS	Ron Schira	1985	154
21 4/16	13 4/16	8 0/16	M	Mille Lacs County	MN	Timothy J. Dusbabek	1987	154
21 4/16	13 1/16	8 3/16	M	Catron County	NM	Gary L. Raney	1988	154
21 4/16	13 0/16	8 4/16	M	Ketchikan	AK	Doug Miller	1989	154
21 4/16	13 5/16	7 15/16	M	Flatbush	ALB	Dave Falls	1990	154
21 4/16	13 4/16	8 0/16	M	Flotten Lake	SAS	Michael S. Meier	1991	154
21 4/16	13 4/16	8 0/16	M	Prince of Wales Island	AK	George P. Mann	1993	154
21 4/16	13 4/16	8 0/16	M	Prince of Wales Island	AK	Eric Lance Whary	1995	154
21 4/16	13 0/16	8 4/16	M	St. Louis County	MN	Glen J. Tischler	1998	154
21 4/16	13 5/16	7 15/16	M	Hampshire County	WV	Craig S. Brinker	1999	154
21 4/16	13 6/16	7 14/16	M	Richards Lake	SAS	M. R. James	2001	154
21 4/16	13 4/16	8 0/16	M	Price County	WI	Tim Gehrke	2002	154
21 4/16	13 3/16	8 1/16	M	Gunnison County	CO	Brandon J. Hockenberry	2003	154
21 4/16	13 1/16	8 3/16	M	Ulster County	NY	Steven Witte	2003	154
21 4/16	13 4/16	8 0/16	M	Grand Bay	NBW	Elio Spadafora	2006	154
21 4/16	13 7/16	7 13/16	M	Polk County	WI	Mitchell J. Gebheim	2008	154
*21 4/16	13 8/16	7 12/16	M	Yorkton	SAS	Dean Schill	2010	154
21 3/16	13 0/16	8 3/16	M	Eaglehead Lake	ONT	Ty Sweeney	1986	174
21 3/16	12 15/16	8 4/16	M	Lane County	OR	Ray Cross	1989	174
21 3/16	13 3/16	8 0/16	M	Prince of Wales Island	AK	George P. Mann	1990	174
21 3/16	13 3/16	7 12/16	M	Assiniboine River	SAS	Rodney S. Petrychyn	1991	174
21 3/16	13 1/16	8 2/16	M	Catron County	NM	John M. Burton, Jr.	1991	174
21 3/16	13 3/16	8 0/16	M	Prince of Wales Island	AK	Darren Emery	1993	174
21 3/16	12 12/16	8 7/16	M	Ulster County	NY	David Bell	1993	174
21 3/16	13 3/16	8 0/16	M	Kashabowie	ONT	Kevin Wagner	1994	174
21 3/16	13 1/16	8 2/16	M	Sawyer County	WI	Robert Bernard Stushek	1996	174
21 3/16	13 1/16	8 2/16	M	Beltrami County	MN	Tim Good	1996	174
21 3/16	12 12/16	8 7/16	M	Orange County	NY	David Bell	1997	174
21 3/16	12 14/16	8 5/16	M	Thunder Bay	ONT	Reg Begin, Jr.	1998	174
21 3/16	12 13/16	8 6/16	M	Big River	SAS	Warren Dugan	2000	174
21 3/16	12 12/16	8 7/16	M	Marathon County	WI	Ron Roth	2005	174
21 3/16	12 15/16	8 4/16	M	Orange County	NY	Paul Gale	2005	174
21 3/16	13 6/16	7 13/16	M	Vanderhoof	BC	Chris Davidson	2008	174
21 3/16	12 12/16	8 7/16	M	Clark County	WI	Roy Lato	2008	174

BLACK BEAR

Minimum Score 18   Continued

SCORE	GREATEST LENGTH	GREATEST WIDTH	SEX	AREA	STATE/ PROVINCE	HUNTER'S NAME	DATE	RANK
*21 3/16	13 4/16	7 15/16	M	Boulder County	CO	Edward Ivkov	2009	174
21 2/16	13 2/16	8 0/16	M	Madera County	CA	Clarke Merrill	1963	192
21 2/16	13 6/16	7 12/16	M	Hubbard County	MN	Dean Como	1974	192
21 2/16	13 4/16	7 14/16	M	Hudson Bay	SAS	Sam Qualls	1981	192
21 2/16	13 10/16	7 8/16	M	Langlade County	WI	Mike Steliga	1981	192
21 2/16	13 1/16	8 1/16	M	Caribou County	ID	Ronald J. Thompson	1986	192
21 2/16	12 14/16	8 4/16	M	Herkimer County	NY	John Palmer	1986	192
21 2/16	13 4/16	7 14/16	M	Glaslyn	SAS	Tony L. Johnson	1989	192
21 2/16	13 0/16	8 2/16	M	Jackson County	OR	Brian Day	1989	192
21 2/16	13 9/16	7 9/16	M	Prairie River	SAS	Tom White	1991	192
21 2/16	13 3/16	7 15/16	M	Fort a la Corne	SAS	Gerald Gilmore	1994	192
21 2/16	13 10/16	7 8/16	M	Coos County	NH	Gary J. Russell	1996	192
21 2/16	13 5/16	7 13/16	M	St. Louis County	MN	Dale Long	1997	192
21 2/16	13 1/16	8 1/16	M	Choiceland	SAS	James Foster	1998	192
21 2/16	13 0/16	8 2/16	M	Aroostook County	ME	Linda Harlow	1998	192
21 2/16	13 4/16	7 14/16	M	Wexford County	MI	Mike D. Horton	1999	192
21 2/16	13 0/16	8 2/16	M	Burnett County	WI	Don S. Karastes	2000	192
21 2/16	13 0/16	8 2/16	M	Irondale	ONT	Al Cavers	2000	192
21 2/16	13 2/16	8 0/16	M	Langlade County	WI	Harvey R. Roth	2001	192
21 2/16	13 6/16	7 12/16	M	Athabasca River	ALB	Walter Krom	2002	192
21 2/16	13 2/16	8 0/16	M	Gimli	MAN	Dave Bryce	2002	192
21 2/16	13 3/16	7 15/16	M	Sullivan County	NY	Charles Hahl	2002	192
21 2/16	13 4/16	7 14/16	M	Fond du Lac River	SAS	Andy Carpenter	2003	192
21 2/16	13 1/16	8 1/16	M	Suwannee River	MAN	Becky Johnston	2003	192
21 2/16	12 15/16	8 3/16	M	Rocky Mountain House	ALB	Rob Hutton	2005	192
21 2/16	13 5/16	7 13/16	M	Steuben County	NY	William A. Coates	2005	192
21 2/16	12 15/16	8 3/16	M	Alstead Lake	SAS	Nelson J. Capestany	2008	192
21 2/16	13 1/16	8 1/16	M	Saddle Hills	ALB	Mike Ukrainetz	2008	192
*21 2/16	12 13/16	8 5/16	M	Glenn County	CA	Roy R. Ellis	2008	192
21 2/16	13 5/16	7 13/16	M	Carlton County	MN	Debra K. Zime	2008	192
21 2/16	13 8/16	7 10/16	M	Union County	OR	Jarom Hibbert	2008	192
21 1/16	13 1/16	8 0/16	M	Hubbard County	MN	Darrell Magnussen	1974	222
21 1/16	13 2/16	7 15/16	M	Quetico Provincial Park	ONT	Robert Filbrandt	1981	222
21 1/16	13 1/16	8 0/16	M	Cass County	MN	John Hughes	1987	222
21 1/16	13 1/16	8 0/16	M	Lincoln County	WI	Daniel Lemke	1987	222
21 1/16	12 13/16	8 4/16	M	Siskiyou County	CA	Jules Pacheco	1987	222
21 1/16	13 1/16	8 0/16	M	Charlevoix County	MI	Gerald L. Fuller	1988	222
21 1/16	13 0/16	8 1/16	M	Kanawha County	WV	Brian Petty	1991	222
21 1/16	13 4/16	7 13/16	M	Oconto County	WI	Patrick J. Gauthier	1995	222
21 1/16	13 1/16	8 0/16	M	Prince of Wales Island	AK	Shawn Price	1996	222
21 1/16	13 5/16	7 12/16	M	Hudson Bay	SAS	Arlan Dowiasch	1996	222
21 1/16	13 3/16	7 14/16	M	Round Lake	SAS	Floyd Forster	1997	222
21 1/16	13 2/16	7 15/16	M	Lincoln County	WI	Kraig M. See	1997	222
21 1/16	13 1/16	8 0/16	M	Polk County	AR	Donald Cost	1997	222
21 1/16	13 0/16	8 1/16	M	Swan River	MAN	Richard Barrett	1998	222
21 1/16	13 9/16	7 8/16	M	Washburn County	WI	Chris McDonald	1999	222
21 1/16	13 7/16	7 10/16	M	Douglas County	WI	Larry Selzler	1999	222
21 1/16	13 2/16	7 15/16	M	Prince of Wales Island	AK	Chad Doell	2000	222
21 1/16	13 7/16	7 10/16	M	Saddle Hills	ALB	Terry Hagman	2000	222
21 1/16	13 6/16	7 11/16	M	Rocanville	SAS	Luc M. Syrenne	2001	222
21 1/16	13 4/16	7 13/16	M	Geikie River	SAS	Dan Evans	2003	222
21 1/16	13 1/16	8 0/16	M	Wasco County	OR	Chris Phillips	2003	222
21 1/16	13 7/16	7 10/16	M	Juneau County	WI	Dennis E. Dodge	2003	222
21 1/16	12 13/16	8 4/16	M	Lincoln County	WI	Timothy J. Grzesiak	2003	222
21 1/16	13 2/16	7 15/16	M	Frederick County	VA	David Iser	2003	222
21 1/16	13 5/16	7 12/16	M	Olha	MAN	Kevin Harmon	2004	222
21 1/16	13 5/16	7 12/16	M	Ochre River	MAN	Doug Bobick	2005	222
21 1/16	13 2/16	7 15/16	M	Spirit River	ALB	Michael Siegler	2007	222
*21 1/16	12 13/16	8 4/16	M	Lac du Bonnet	MAN	Ed Parker	2008	222
*21 1/16	12 13/16	8 4/16	M	Garfield County	CO	Josh Gustad	2008	222
*21 1/16	13 6/16	7 11/16	M	Fairview	ALB	Troy Dzioba	2009	222
*21 1/16	12 13/16	8 4/16	M	Delta County	MI	Stephen E. Rucinski	2009	222
21 1/16	12 14/16	8 3/16	M	Sherridon	MAN	Shannon Nielsen	2010	222
*21 1/16	13 4/16	7 13/16	M	Mariposa County	CA	Gareth Chin	2010	222
21 0/16	12 13/16	8 3/16	M	Sioux Narrows	ONT	R. B. Cooley	1960	255
21 0/16	13 3/16	7 13/16	M	Shasta County	CA	Norman Mallonee	1974	255
21 0/16	12 14/16	8 2/16	M	Uncompahgre N.F.	CO	Dr. James Emerson	1974	255
21 0/16	13 3/16	7 13/16	M	Ashland County	WI	Bryan C. Anderson	1980	255
21 0/16	13 2/16	7 14/16	M	Yavapai County	AZ	Mike Whelan	1981	255
21 0/16	13 2/16	7 14/16	M	Riding Mtn.	MAN	James A. Carson	1982	255
21 0/16	13 2/16	7 14/16	M	Sawyer County	WI	John G. Bohmann	1982	255
21 0/16	13 3/16	7 13/16	M	Langlade County	WI	Michael Steliga	1982	255
21 0/16	12 15/16	8 1/16	M	Kosciusko Island	AK	Michael C. Fezatte	1982	255
21 0/16	13 4/16	7 12/16	M	Hudson Bay	SAS	Archie Lovelace	1983	255
21 0/16	12 10/16	8 6/16	M	Echouani Lake	QUE	Collins F. Kellogg	1985	255
21 0/16	13 3/16	7 13/16	M	Debden	SAS	Allan Sykes	1986	255
21 0/16	13 1/16	7 15/16	M	Carrot River	SAS	Demetry Procyk	1987	255
21 0/16	13 0/16	8 0/16	M	Carbon County	UT	Lonnie K. Bell	1989	255
21 0/16	12 13/16	8 3/16	M	Iron County	WI	Todd J. Braver	1989	255
21 0/16	13 0/16	8 0/16	M	Le Domaine	QUE	Tony Beceiro	1990	255
21 0/16	12 14/16	8 2/16	M	Lake County	MT	Colin L. Andrews	1990	255
21 0/16	12 12/16	8 4/16	M	Herkimer County	NY	Glen Stedman	1990	255
21 0/16	13 0/16	8 0/16	M	Ventura County	CA	Jeff Prentice	1991	255
21 0/16	13 1/16	7 15/16	M	Peace River	ALB	Doug Walker	1991	255
21 0/16	13 1/16	7 15/16	M	Prince of Wales Island	AK	Rick M. Young	1992	255
21 0/16	12 14/16	8 2/16	M	Bay Tree	ALB	Sedgwick Bryant Loyd II	1994	255
21 0/16	12 13/16	8 3/16	M	Delay River	QUE	Brian Dayett	1994	255
21 0/16	12 14/16	8 2/16	M	Washburn County	WI	Sonjonae Setser	1995	255
21 0/16	13 3/16	7 13/16	M	Barron County	WI	Jeffrey P. Tomesh	1995	255
21 0/16	12 10/16	8 6/16	M	Ulster County	NY	Thomas Nolan	1995	255
21 0/16	12 14/16	8 2/16	M	Marathon County	WI	Orville Sazama	1996	255
21 0/16	13 3/16	7 13/16	M	Mineral County	WV	Rex D. Miller	1996	255
21 0/16	13 5/16	7 11/16	M	Crooked Creek	ALB	Ryan Poland	1997	255
21 0/16	13 13/16	7 3/16	M	Sidney Lake	SAS	Donald Wright	1998	255
21 0/16	13 2/16	7 14/16	M	Shasta County	CA	Randy Burger	1999	255

127

BLACK BEAR

Minimum Score 18   Continued

SCORE	GREATEST LENGTH	GREATEST WIDTH	SEX	AREA	STATE/ PROVINCE	HUNTER'S NAME	DATE	RANK
21 0/16	12 11/16	8 5/16	M	Onion Lake	SAS	Lannon Nault	2000	255
21 0/16	12 14/16	8 2/16	M	Mono County	CA	Mark Cordeiro	2000	255
21 0/16	13 2/16	7 14/16	M	Sawyer County	WI	Shane Loveland	2000	255
21 0/16	13 2/16	7 14/16	M	Duck Mtns.	MAN	Wayne R. Schatzman	2000	255
21 0/16	12 15/16	8 1/16	M	Olha	MAN	Duane Seiler II	2001	255
21 0/16	13 2/16	7 14/16	M	Cold Lake	ALB	James E. Jones, Jr.	2002	255
21 0/16	13 2/16	7 14/16	M	Sawyer County	WI	Robin R. Zillmer	2002	255
21 0/16	12 13/16	8 3/16	M	Sprague	MAN	Merle D. Lohse	2003	255
21 0/16	13 2/16	7 14/16	M	Morgan County	WV	Edmund T. Powers	2003	255
21 0/16	12 15/16	8 1/16	M	Turnor Lake	SAS	Bill Bishman	2004	255
21 0/16	13 6/16	7 10/16	M	Clear Lake	MAN	Gene Welle	2005	255
21 0/16	12 8/16	8 8/16	M	Marinette County	WI	Scott Dyer	2006	255
*21 0/16	13 8/16	7 8/16	M	Schoharie County	NY	Patrick S. Irwin	2006	255
*21 0/16	13 2/16	7 14/16	M	Roblin	MAN	Justin R. Brown	2007	255
21 0/16	12 14/16	8 2/16	M	Prince of Wales Island	AK	Bill Potts	2007	255
*21 0/16	13 4/16	7 12/16	M	Delta County	MI	Brandon J. Podolak	2008	255
*21 0/16	12 15/16	8 1/16	M	Navajo County	AZ	Chris Wade	2009	255
20 15/16	13 4/16	7 11/16	M	Sequoia National Forest	CA	Robert Shilling	1971	303
20 15/16	12 12/16	8 3/16	M	Lincoln County	WI	Jay Manthei	1980	303
20 15/16	13 1/16	7 14/16	M	Nipawin	SAS	Glen Sellsted	1981	303
20 15/16	12 14/16	8 1/16	M	Goodsoil	SAS	Ralph Clarke	1982	303
20 15/16	12 11/16	8 4/16	M	Routt County	CO	Mark A. Chapman	1982	303
20 15/16	13 0/16	7 15/16	M	Monominto	MAN	Erik Thienpondt	1983	303
20 15/16	12 15/16	8 0/16	M	Meadow Lake	SAS	Bruce Stieber	1986	303
20 15/16	12 11/16	8 4/16	M	Washago	ONT	Chris Marsh	1992	303
20 15/16	12 15/16	8 0/16	M	Makwa	SAS	Raymond Schediny	1995	303
20 15/16	13 0/16	7 15/16	M	Carswell Lake	SAS	Steve Rucinski	1995	303
20 15/16	13 3/16	7 12/16	M	Delta County	MI	Joseph E. Glencer	1999	303
20 15/16	12 14/16	8 1/16	M	Fond du Lac River	SAS	Tom Nelson	2004	303
20 15/16	12 14/16	8 1/16	M	Saskatchewan River	SAS	Chad Rohel	2005	303
*20 15/16	13 2/16	7 13/16	M	Wild Rose	MAN	William Craig Holt	2005	303
20 14/16	12 8/16	8 6/16	M	Mesa County	CO	Richard A. Schreiber	1973	317
20 14/16	13 0/16	7 14/16	M	Prince of Wales Island	AK	Gary G. Smith	1978	317
20 14/16	12 8/16	8 6/16	M	Red Lake	ONT	George Law	1981	317
20 14/16	13 2/16	7 12/16	M	Cass County	MN	Craig Enervold	1982	317
20 14/16	13 6/16	7 8/16	M	Duck Mtn.	MAN	John "Jack" Cordes	1984	317
20 14/16	12 9/16	8 5/16	M	Routt County	CO	Lonny Vanatta	1984	317
20 14/16	12 12/16	8 2/16	M	Thunder Bay	ONT	Tim Walters	1985	317
20 14/16	12 15/16	7 15/16	M	Camas County	ID	Ed Cushman	1986	317
20 14/16	12 13/16	8 1/16	M	Prince of Wales Island	AK	Kevin Robinson	1988	317
20 14/16	13 2/16	7 12/16	M	Edmonton	ALB	Bruce Nederveld	1990	317
20 14/16	13 0/16	7 14/16	M	Prince of Wales Island	AK	Thomas Chadwick	1991	317
20 14/16	12 11/16	8 3/16	M	Prince of Wales Island	AK	Robert A. Meister	1992	317
20 14/16	13 2/16	7 12/16	M	Ministikwan Lake	SAS	Brent Maxwell	1992	317
20 14/16	13 0/16	7 14/16	M	Venango County	PA	Larry Rossman	1992	317
20 14/16	12 8/16	8 6/16	M	Kamloops	BC	Mark Guglielmini	1995	317
20 14/16	12 14/16	8 0/16	M	Riding Mtn.	MAN	Dale E. Shoemaker	1995	317
20 14/16	12 14/16	8 0/16	M	Ministikwan Lake	SAS	Bud Nugent	1995	317
20 14/16	13 2/16	7 12/16	M	Missaukee County	MI	Larry Ritchie	1995	317
20 14/16	13 4/16	7 10/16	M	Pine County	MN	Kevin Kubat	1996	317
20 14/16	13 2/16	7 12/16	M	Bayfield County	WI	William R. See	1996	317
20 14/16	13 2/16	7 12/16	M	Prince of Wales Island	AK	Larry Daly	1997	317
20 14/16	12 13/16	8 1/16	M	St. Louis County	MN	David McKenzie	1997	317
20 14/16	13 4/16	7 10/16	M	Gila County	AZ	Thomas J. Hoffman	1998	317
20 14/16	13 1/16	7 13/16	M	Grande Prairie	ALB	Buck Horn	1998	317
20 14/16	12 13/16	8 1/16	M	New Fish Creek	ALB	Michael Rogers	1999	317
20 14/16	13 2/16	7 12/16	M	Carlton County	MN	Tim Jestus	1999	317
20 14/16	12 14/16	8 0/16	M	Vilas County	WI	Troy A. Martinez	2000	317
20 14/16	12 14/16	8 0/16	M	Navajo County	AZ	Lance Liljenquist	2000	317
20 14/16	13 3/16	7 11/16	M	Gaff Topsails	NFL	Lee Sisson	2001	317
20 14/16	12 10/16	8 4/16	M	Leaf Rapids	MAN	Jim Hamblin	2001	317
20 14/16	13 0/16	7 14/16	M	Frog Lake	ALB	Tracy Allen	2002	317
20 14/16	13 0/16	7 14/16	M	Olha	MAN	Myles Keller	2002	317
20 14/16	12 13/16	8 1/16	M	Beardmore	ONT	Corey Hopkins	2003	317
20 14/16	12 13/16	8 1/16	M	Hawkrock River	SAS	Raymond R. Jackson, Jr.	2004	317
20 14/16	13 2/16	7 12/16	M	Laurier	MAN	Dale E. Shoemaker	2005	317
*20 14/16	13 0/16	7 14/16	M	Fremont County	WY	Jake Green	2005	317
20 14/16	13 2/16	7 12/16	M	Weyakwin Lake	SAS	Stephen A. Dougherty	2005	317
20 14/16	13 1/16	7 13/16	M	McDowell County	WV	Brian Janutolo	2005	317
20 14/16	12 15/16	8 1/16	M	Kern County	CA	Jimmie Fox	2007	317
20 14/16	13 4/16	7 10/16	M	Chippewa County	WI	Travis Machler	2008	317
20 13/16	12 12/16	8 1/16	M	Marrns Creek	ID	Joe Schreideler	1977	357
20 13/16	12 11/16	8 2/16	M	Langlade County	WI	Eugene Strong	1978	357
20 13/16	12 14/16	7 15/16	M	Humboldt County	CA	Calvin Farner	1983	357
20 13/16	13 4/16	7 9/16	M	Meadow Lake	SAS	D. Mitch Kottas	1988	357
20 13/16	12 15/16	7 14/16	M	Carrot River	SAS	Mike Palmer	1989	357
20 13/16	12 14/16	7 15/16	M	Pine County	MN	Steven J. Gardas	1989	357
20 13/16	12 15/16	7 14/16	M	Prince of Wales Island	AK	George P. Mann	1992	357
20 13/16	12 13/16	8 0/16	M	Davidson	QUE	Jack Satterfield, Jr.	1992	357
20 13/16	13 2/16	7 11/16	M	Prince of Wales Island	AK	Lon E. Lauber	1993	357
20 13/16	12 14/16	7 15/16	M	Prince of Wales Island	AK	Kirk Westervelt	1993	357
20 13/16	12 15/16	7 14/16	M	Gila County	AZ	Tracy Gene Hardy	1994	357
20 13/16	13 2/16	7 11/16	M	Spiritwood	SAS	Dewayne Mullins	1995	357
20 13/16	12 12/16	8 1/16	M	Kiui Island	AK	Joel J. Bickler, DDS	1995	357
20 13/16	12 14/16	7 15/16	M	Buffalo Narrows	SAS	Roland J. Quick	1997	357
20 13/16	12 14/16	7 15/16	M	Bernalillo County	NM	Chris Zamora	1997	357
20 13/16	13 1/16	7 12/16	M	Caribou County	ID	Eldon Richter	1998	357
20 13/16	12 12/16	8 1/16	M	Guthrie Lake	MAN	Kevin Disney	1999	357
20 13/16	13 1/16	7 12/16	M	Orange County	NY	Joseph Hoehmann, Sr.	1999	357
20 13/16	13 0/16	7 13/16	M	Koochiching County	MN	Scott Schultz	2000	357
20 13/16	12 11/16	8 2/16	M	Arran	SAS	Jeff Lescalleet	2001	357
20 13/16	13 1/16	7 12/16	M	Kanabec County	MN	Jonathan A. Vander Vegt	2001	357
20 13/16	13 3/16	7 10/16	M	Chippewa County	WI	Timothy J. Kohls	2001	357
20 13/16	13 1/16	7 12/16	M	Pine County	MN	Daniel J. Fischer	2002	357
20 13/16	12 11/16	8 2/16	M	Gunnison County	CO	Robert F. McWilliams	2002	357

128

BLACK BEAR

Minimum Score 18 — Continued

SCORE	GREATEST LENGTH	GREATEST WIDTH	SEX	AREA	STATE/PROVINCE	HUNTER'S NAME	DATE	RANK
20 13/16	12 15/16	7 14/16	M	Hudson Bay	SAS	Rodman Lowe	2003	357
20 13/16	12 6/16	8 7/16	M	Mendocino County	CA	Dave Bruegeman	2003	357
20 13/16	13 5/16	7 8/16	M	Price County	WI	Dennis L. Jones	2003	357
20 13/16	12 15/16	7 14/16	M	Tulare County	CA	Vincent Torrente, Sr.	2003	357
20 13/16	13 1/16	7 12/16	M	Prince of Wales Island	AK	Kelly King	2004	357
*20 13/16	12 15/16	7 14/16	M	Dryden	ONT	Shawn M. Martin	2004	357
20 13/16	13 0/16	7 13/16	M	Laurier	MAN	Robert Tastsides	2004	357
20 13/16	12 12/16	8 1/16	M	Oconto County	WI	Ron Thomson	2004	357
20 13/16	13 3/16	7 10/16	M	Saskatchewan River	SAS	Floyd Forster	2005	357
20 13/16	13 1/16	7 12/16	M	Beltrami County	MN	Max Roszkowski	2005	357
20 13/16	13 2/16	7 11/16	M	Wicked Point	MAN	Wendell "Butch" Howes	2007	357
20 13/16	12 13/16	8 0/16	M	Meadow Lake	SAS	Rob Lavallee	2007	357
20 13/16	12 15/16	7 14/16	M	Weyakwin	SAS	Andy Milam	2009	357
20 12/16	12 12/16	8 0/16	M	Apache County	AZ	Dr. C. G. Clare	1967	394
20 12/16	12 5/16	8 7/16	M	Emmet County	MI	Hawley H. Rhew	1974	394
20 12/16	12 12/16	8 0/16	M	Douglas County	WI	Robert J. Schmidt	1975	394
20 12/16	12 15/16	7 13/16	M	Armstrong	ONT	Paul Mahaney	1977	394
20 12/16	13 0/16	7 12/16	M	San Miguel County	CO	John W. Rowe	1978	394
20 12/16	12 15/16	7 13/16	M	Bonneville County	ID	John Hill	1983	394
20 12/16	12 11/16	8 1/16	M	Prince of Wales Island	AK	Jack Williams	1985	394
20 12/16	12 12/16	8 0/16	M	Carbon County	WY	Steve Powell	1985	394
20 12/16	12 11/16	8 1/16	M	Plumas County	CA	Kevin Hull	1986	394
20 12/16	13 0/16	7 12/16	M	Aitkin County	MN	Merrill D. Holm	1986	394
20 12/16	12 14/16	7 14/16	M	Prince of Wales Island	AK	Kevin Robinson	1988	394
20 12/16	13 0/16	7 12/16	M	Douglas County	WI	Harold Halverson	1990	394
20 12/16	12 11/16	8 1/16	M	Ketchikan	AK	Greg Munther	1991	394
20 12/16	12 12/16	8 0/16	M	Lloydminster	SAS	Steve Preziosi	1991	394
20 12/16	13 0/16	7 12/16	M	Athabasca River	ALB	Larry Oppe	1992	394
20 12/16	12 14/16	7 14/16	M	Carswell Lake	SAS	Steven Rucinski	1992	394
20 12/16	12 7/16	8 5/16	M	Fort McMurray	ALB	Darrin West	1992	394
20 12/16	12 11/16	8 1/16	M	Torrance County	NM	Steve Alderete	1992	394
20 12/16	12 14/16	7 14/16	M	Preeceville	SAS	James D. Guess	1993	394
20 12/16	12 12/16	8 0/16	M	Hudson Bay	SAS	Paul Chinski	1994	394
20 12/16	12 13/16	7 15/16	M	Marquette County	MI	Darryl D. Ansel	1994	394
20 12/16	13 3/16	7 9/16	M	Slave Lake	ALB	Kay Shipley	1995	394
20 12/16	13 0/16	7 12/16	M	Darwell	ALB	John Saddoris	1995	394
20 12/16	12 13/16	7 15/16	M	Buffalo Narrows	SAS	Kenneth M. Asboth	1995	394
20 12/16	13 2/16	7 10/16	M	Apache County	AZ	Edward A. Petersen	1997	394
20 12/16	13 4/16	7 8/16	M	Steuben County	NY	Daniel Stambaugh	1997	394
20 12/16	12 14/16	7 14/16	M	Dipper Lake	SAS	Bryce Dillabough	1998	394
20 12/16	13 6/16	7 6/16	M	Peace River	ALB	Joe Coleman	1998	394
20 12/16	12 9/16	8 3/16	M	Taylor County	WI	Duane A. Wallner	1998	394
20 12/16	13 3/16	7 9/16	M	Polk County	WI	Joshua F. Schindeldecker	1998	394
20 12/16	13 5/16	7 7/16	M	Rossburn	MAN	Adam Bartsch	1999	394
20 12/16	12 12/16	8 0/16	M	Sawyer County	WI	Allen Nerby	2000	394
20 12/16	13 1/16	7 11/16	M	Prince of Wales Island	AK	Jon Vanderhoef	2002	394
20 12/16	13 3/16	7 9/16	M	Kipahigan Lake	MAN	Cameron Hayden	2002	394
20 12/16	13 0/16	7 12/16	M	Churchill Lake	SAS	Terry M. Dennis	2002	394
20 12/16	13 0/16	7 12/16	M	Prince of Wales Island	AK	Matt Meneghel	2003	394
20 12/16	12 14/16	7 14/16	M	St. Marc-des-Carrier	QUE	Sam Warrender, Jr.	2003	394
20 12/16	12 14/16	7 14/16	M	Prince of Wales Island	AK	Glen Berry	2003	394
20 12/16	12 7/16	8 5/16	M	Vilas County	WI	Marty Macco	2003	394
20 12/16	13 0/16	7 12/16	M	Bronson Lake	SAS	W. T. Garry Drummond	2004	394
20 12/16	13 0/16	7 12/16	F	Donnelly	ALB	Craig Holt	2004	394
20 12/16	12 9/16	8 3/16	M	Mistatim	SAS	Scott L. Koelzer	2005	394
20 12/16	12 11/16	8 1/16	M	Paradise Hill	SAS	Chad Gessner	2005	394
20 12/16	12 10/16	8 2/16	M	Price County	WI	Jeremy Bolton	2005	394
20 12/16	12 14/16	7 14/16	M	Allegany County	NY	Bruce M. Stevens	2006	394
*20 12/16	12 14/16	7 14/16	M	Delta County	CO	Jon G. Rapp	2007	394
20 12/16	13 6/16	7 6/16	M	Saskatchewan River	SAS	Robert Brion	2008	394
20 12/16	13 2/16	7 10/16	M	Beaver River	SAS	Jason Toews	2008	394
20 12/16	13 2/16	7 10/16	M	Coconino County	AZ	Jon R. Waggoner	2008	394
*20 12/16	13 3/16	7 9/16	M	Jackson County	WI	Mike Janicki, Jr.	2009	394
20 11/16	12 13/16	7 14/16	M	Thunder Bay	ONT	Mel Johnson	1974	444
20 11/16	12 14/16	7 13/16	M	Pitkin County	CO	Dale W. Gray	1975	444
20 11/16	13 2/16	7 9/16	M	Rio Blanco County	CO	Walter Krom	1976	444
20 11/16	13 2/16	7 9/16	M	Quesnel	BC	Russell Thornberry	1987	444
20 11/16	12 10/16	8 1/16	M	Sunbury County	NBW	Raymond Faulknor	1987	444
20 11/16	12 14/16	7 13/16	M	Chuit River	AK	George P. Mann	1987	444
20 11/16	13 3/16	7 8/16	M	Rappahannock County	VA	Jeff S. Good	1987	444
20 11/16	13 2/16	7 9/16	M	Prince of Wales Island	AK	Tracy Lucas	1989	444
20 11/16	12 11/16	8 0/16	M	Prince of Wales Island	AK	Glen Berry	1990	444
20 11/16	13 0/16	7 11/16	M	Douglas County	WI	Roger W. Hansen	1990	444
20 11/16	13 2/16	7 9/16	M	Prince of Wales Island	AK	Ken A. Vorisek	1991	444
20 11/16	12 15/16	7 12/16	M	Douglas County	WI	Steve Wittke	1992	444
20 11/16	12 13/16	7 14/16	M	Thorne Bay	AK	Steve McCoy	1993	444
20 11/16	12 11/16	8 0/16	M	Prince of Wales Island	AK	Miles A. Tanner	1994	444
20 11/16	12 11/16	8 0/16	M	Swan River	SAS	Donald L. Sagner	1994	444
20 11/16	12 10/16	8 1/16	M	Nipigon	ONT	Scott Beurkens	1995	444
20 11/16	12 14/16	7 13/16	M	Williams Lake	ONT	Cathy Barnowsky	1995	444
20 11/16	12 13/16	7 14/16	M	Piney	MAN	Russell K. Mehling	1995	444
20 11/16	12 14/16	7 13/16	M	DeBolt	ALB	Dave Jeffers	1996	444
20 11/16	13 3/16	7 8/16	M	Porcupine Plain	SAS	Dana Morezak	1996	444
20 11/16	13 0/16	7 11/16	M	Bayfield County	WI	Steven Henthorn	1997	444
20 11/16	12 14/16	7 13/16	M	Navajo County	AZ	Budd Ferre	1999	444
20 11/16	12 15/16	7 12/16	M	Prince of Wales Island	AK	Greg Megargel	2001	444
20 11/16	13 0/16	7 11/16	M	Olha	MAN	Steven L. Tebay	2001	444
20 11/16	12 13/16	7 14/16	M	Gunnison County	CO	Christian T. Johnson	2002	444
20 11/16	12 10/16	8 1/16	M	Gypsumville	MAN	David Waldschmidt	2003	444
20 11/16	12 13/16	7 14/16	M	Aroostook County	ME	Mike Smith	2003	444
20 11/16	13 5/16	7 6/16	M	Pine County	MN	David W. Miller	2003	444
20 11/16	12 13/16	7 14/16	M	Prince of Wales Island	AK	Kenton D. Miller	2004	444
20 11/16	12 11/16	8 0/16	M	Dog Lake	ONT	Dale Long	2004	444
*20 11/16	13 4/16	7 7/16	M	Oconto County	WI	Joseph Kanack	2004	444
20 11/16	13 2/16	7 9/16	M	Newdale	MAN	Don Baker	2005	444

129

BLACK BEAR

Minimum Score 18 — Continued

SCORE	GREATEST LENGTH	GREATEST WIDTH	SEX	AREA	STATE/PROVINCE	HUNTER'S NAME	DATE	RANK
20 11/16	12 15/16	7 12/16	M	Carrot River	SAS	Robert C. Farthing	2005	444
*20 11/16	12 14/16	7 13/16	M	Marinette County	WI	Chuck Gerbenskey	2006	444
20 11/16	13 0/16	7 11/16	M	Vilas County	WI	Robert B. Nadler	2006	444
*20 11/16	13 1/16	7 10/16	M	Scott County	AR	Adam Beason	2006	444
*20 11/16	12 8/16	8 3/16	M	Hadashville	MAN	Chad E. Baerwald	2007	444
20 11/16	12 13/16	7 14/16	M	Catron County	NM	John Liner	2007	444
20 11/16	12 13/16	7 14/16	M	Prince of Wales Island	AK	William H. Welton	2009	444
*20 11/16	12 14/16	7 13/16	M	Catron County	NM	Mike Bordovsky	2009	444
20 10/16	13 1/16	7 9/16	M	Rio Blanco County	CO	Frank 'Rit' Heller	1969	484
20 10/16	12 10/16	8 0/16	M	Sierra County	CA	Ervin K. McMakin	1971	484
20 10/16	12 14/16	7 12/16	M	Fort Frances	ONT	George Geisert	1973	484
20 10/16	12 10/16	8 0/16	M	Crawford Park	MAN	Brent Mills	1981	484
20 10/16	12 10/16	8 0/16	M	Tweed	ONT	John E. Lawson	1983	484
20 10/16	12 12/16	7 14/16	M	Lac La Ronge	SAS	Steve Hammond	1985	484
20 10/16	12 14/16	7 12/16	M	Cass County	MN	James D. Zahalka	1987	484
20 10/16	12 12/16	7 14/16	M	Prince of Wales Island	AK	Danny Moore	1990	484
20 10/16	12 8/16	8 2/16	M	Ravalli County	MT	John C. Locke	1990	484
20 10/16	12 11/16	7 15/16	M	Nairn Township	ONT	Ron Hergott	1990	484
20 10/16	12 13/16	7 13/16	M	Iron County	WI	Jeff Ott	1990	484
20 10/16	13 0/16	7 10/16	M	Stone Lake	ONT	Jack A. Vos	1991	484
20 10/16	12 15/16	7 11/16	M	Pine County	MN	Thomas Behrends	1991	484
20 10/16	12 15/16	7 11/16	M	Winefred Lake	ALB	Cornel Yarmoloy	1992	484
20 10/16	12 12/16	7 14/16	M	Green Lake	SAS	Randy K. McBroom	1995	484
20 10/16	13 2/16	7 8/16	M	Kirkland Lake	ONT	Jason Mazzocato	1995	484
20 10/16	13 0/16	7 10/16	M	Lake County	CA	Matt Schuler	1996	484
20 10/16	12 12/16	7 14/16	M	Kern County	CA	Gilbert R. Garcia	1996	484
20 10/16	12 12/16	7 14/16	M	Lewisporte	NFL	Francis Ogden	1996	484
20 10/16	12 9/16	8 1/16	M	Delta County	MI	Scott B. Merchant	1996	484
20 10/16	13 3/16	7 7/16	M	Reita Lake	ALB	Arliss McNalley	1997	484
20 10/16	13 6/16	7 4/16	M	Hudson Bay	SAS	Dairl Hicks	1997	484
20 10/16	12 14/16	7 12/16	M	Iron River	ALB	Michael K. Frank	1997	484
20 10/16	12 12/16	7 14/16	M	Dorion	ONT	Larry Paulsen	1997	484
20 10/16	12 10/16	8 0/16	M	Raleigh County	WV	Harold D. Williams, Jr.	1997	484
20 10/16	12 10/16	8 0/16	M	Green Lake	SAS	Randy Zion	1998	484
20 10/16	12 12/16	7 14/16	M	Thunder Hills	SAS	Nathan Jones	1998	484
20 10/16	12 12/16	7 14/16	M	Oconto County	WI	Ronald Thomson	1998	484
20 10/16	13 2/16	7 8/16	M	Warren County	VA	Brian Dolly	1998	484
20 10/16	13 2/16	7 8/16	M	White County	GA	Duane Truslow	1999	484
20 10/16	12 12/16	7 14/16	M	Augusta County	VA	W. A. Koontz	1999	484
20 10/16	12 12/16	7 14/16	M	Beaver County	UT	David Edwards	2000	484
20 10/16	13 0/16	7 10/16	M	Prince of Wales Island	AK	Chad Doell	2001	484
20 10/16	12 15/16	7 11/16	M	Engler Lake	SAS	M. R. James	2002	484
20 10/16	13 5/16	7 5/16	M	Shawano County	WI	Scott Zoromski	2002	484
20 10/16	12 10/16	8 0/16	M	Buffalo Narrows	SAS	Duyane Tucker	2003	484
20 10/16	12 14/16	7 12/16	M	Peace River	ALB	Chester Dodgson	2004	484
20 10/16	13 2/16	7 8/16	M	Yavapai County	AZ	William Gilbert	2004	484
*20 10/16	13 1/16	7 9/16	M	Kane Lake	SAS	Richard Crawford	2005	484
20 10/16	12 14/16	7 12/16	M	Saddle Hills	ALB	Brent Watson	2005	484
20 10/16	12 13/16	7 13/16	M	Nestor Falls	ONT	Steven S. Olmstead	2005	484
20 10/16	13 1/16	7 9/16	M	Porcupine Plain	SAS	Craig S. Lemon	2005	484
20 10/16	13 0/16	7 10/16	M	Camden County	NC	Timothy Leary	2005	484
20 10/16	12 15/16	7 11/16	M	Green Lake	SAS	Leads M. DuBois	2006	484
*20 10/16	12 11/16	7 15/16	M	Atikokan	ONT	Rickey L. Ashman	2007	484
*20 10/16	12 12/16	7 14/16	M	Fairview	ALB	Troy Dzioba	2008	484
*20 10/16	12 15/16	7 11/16	M	Hocking Lake	SAS	Lorraine McGown	2008	484
20 10/16	12 14/16	7 12/16	M	Tangleflags	SAS	Dustin Blondeau	2010	484
20 9/16	12 12/16	7 13/16	M	Lake County	MN	Art A. Heinze	1970	532
20 9/16	12 12/16	7 13/16	M	Prince of Wales Island	AK	Roy C. Ewen	1973	532
20 9/16	12 7/16	8 2/16	M	Grand County	CO	Curt Lynn	1973	532
20 9/16	12 12/16	7 13/16	M	Wawa	ONT	Robert C. McGuire	1975	532
20 9/16	12 11/16	7 14/16	M	Aitkin County	MN	Myles Keller	1977	532
20 9/16	13 1/16	7 8/16	M	Thunder Bay	ONT	Lester W. Jass	1979	532
20 9/16	12 13/16	7 12/16	M	Delta County	CO	Steve McCarthy	1982	532
20 9/16	12 9/16	8 0/16	M	Franklin County	NY	Edward M. Odell	1982	532
20 9/16	12 11/16	7 14/16	M	Missaukee County	MI	Gregory Korkoske	1983	532
20 9/16	12 10/16	7 15/16	M	Dryden	ONT	Larry Bauman	1984	532
20 9/16	13 1/16	7 8/16	M	Durban	MAN	David H. Boland	1985	532
20 9/16	12 7/16	8 2/16	M	Thunder Bay	ONT	Daniel Schuttler	1985	532
20 9/16	13 1/16	7 8/16	M	Florence County	WI	Daniel G. Villenauve	1986	532
20 9/16	12 9/16	8 0/16	M	Custer County	ID	Doug Burkman	1987	532
20 9/16	12 13/16	7 12/16	M	Prince of Wales Island	AK	Glen Berry	1988	532
20 9/16	12 10/16	7 15/16	M	Prince of Wales Island	AK	Richard L. Westervelt	1988	532
20 9/16	12 15/16	7 10/16	M	McAdam	NBW	David F. Baldwin	1988	532
20 9/16	12 13/16	7 12/16	M	Aroostook County	ME	Danny Corey	1988	532
20 9/16	13 3/16	7 6/16	M	Douglas County	WI	Steve Peterson	1988	532
20 9/16	12 10/16	7 15/16	M	Marinette County	WI	Perry Kosek	1988	532
20 9/16	13 1/16	7 8/16	M	Poplarfield	MAN	John C. Collins	1991	532
20 9/16	13 0/16	7 9/16	M	Catron County	NM	Patty Foley	1991	532
20 9/16	13 1/16	7 8/16	M	Summit County	UT	Maury Butterfield	1992	532
20 9/16	12 12/16	7 13/16	M	Ft. McMurray	ALB	Sammy J. Schrimsher	1992	532
20 9/16	13 6/16	7 3/16	M	Sudbury	ONT	Vinnie Pisani	1992	532
20 9/16	12 14/16	7 11/16	M	Smoky Lake	ALB	Cheryl Lane	1993	532
20 9/16	13 0/16	7 9/16	M	Arran	SAS	David G. Harmon	1994	532
20 9/16	12 10/16	7 15/16	M	Prince of Wales Island	AK	Michael Davis	1994	532
20 9/16	12 12/16	7 13/16	M	Catron County	NM	Robert W. Ricke	1994	532
20 9/16	12 10/16	7 15/16	M	Athabasca River	ALB	Steve Barnhill	1995	532
20 9/16	12 9/16	8 0/16	M	Besnard Lake	SAS	Carol Macaulay	1995	532
20 9/16	12 12/16	7 13/16	M	Mulchatna River	AK	Howard Olson	1996	532
20 9/16	12 13/16	7 12/16	M	Parry Sound	ONT	Jim C. DeHoey	1997	532
20 9/16	13 1/16	7 8/16	M	La Crete	ALB	Stanley Russell	1997	532
20 9/16	12 14/16	7 11/16	M	Peace River	ALB	Mitch Scott	1998	532
20 9/16	13 0/16	7 9/16	M	Preeceville	SAS	Howard J. Metts, Jr.	1998	532
20 9/16	13 5/16	7 4/16	M	Pine County	MN	Henry Vernon	1998	532
20 9/16	12 12/16	7 13/16	M	Cold Lake	ALB	Rick Hamm	2000	532
20 9/16	12 5/16	8 4/16	M	Millertown	NFL	David G. Payton	2000	532

BLACK BEAR

Minimum Score 18   Continued

SCORE	GREATEST LENGTH	GREATEST WIDTH	SEX	AREA	STATE/ PROVINCE	HUNTER'S NAME	DATE	RANK
20 9/16	13 0/16	7 9/16	M	Riding Mtn.	MAN	Rod McGrath	2002	532
20 9/16	12 11/16	7 14/16	M	Gronlid	SAS	Chad Rohel	2002	532
20 9/16	12 13/16	7 12/16	M	Mesa County	CO	Travis Stamper	2002	532
20 9/16	13 3/16	7 6/16	M	Burnett County	WI	Scott Jensen	2005	532
20 9/16	12 14/16	7 11/16	M	Cass County	MN	Shea Lange	2006	532
20 9/16	12 12/16	7 13/16	M	Iron County	MI	Paul Baumann	2006	532
20 9/16	12 10/16	7 15/16	M	Ashe County	NC	Billy Blevins	2006	532
*20 9/16	12 9/16	8 0/16	M	Wrangell	AK	Tom Butler, Sr.	2007	532
20 9/16	12 12/16	7 13/16	M	La Loche	SAS	Chris G. Sanford	2007	532
20 9/16	12 10/16	7 15/16	M	Porcupine Plain	SAS	Andrew Blake	2007	532
20 8/16	12 13/16	7 11/16	M	Queen Charlotte Island	BC	Peter Halbig	1960	581
20 8/16	12 14/16	7 10/16	M	Shawano County	WI	Bud Wiesman	1974	581
20 8/16	12 14/16	7 10/16	M	Kamsack	SAS	Steve Boychuk	1977	581
20 8/16	12 14/16	7 10/16	M	Tehama County	CA	Anthony P. Davi	1980	581
20 8/16	12 11/16	7 13/16	M	Strathnaver	BC	Dan Wicks	1981	581
20 8/16	12 13/16	7 11/16	M	Valley County	ID	Dave Scott	1982	581
20 8/16	12 1/16	8 7/16	M	Ignace	ONT	Jerry Klinesmith	1983	581
20 8/16	13 2/16	7 6/16	M	Cass County	MN	Anne M. Zahalka	1988	581
20 8/16	12 15/16	7 9/16	M	Dryden	ONT	Robert J. Crane	1990	581
20 8/16	12 15/16	7 9/16	M	Nolalu	ONT	Billy Roy Leach	1991	581
20 8/16	12 8/16	8 0/16	M	Tehama County	CA	Kim Cooper	1991	581
20 8/16	12 11/16	7 13/16	M	Pitkin County	CO	Stanley E. Lauriski	1992	581
20 8/16	12 12/16	7 12/16	M	Prince of Wales Island	AK	Glen Berry	1992	581
20 8/16	12 10/16	7 14/16	M	Mendocino County	CA	James W. Rutledge	1992	581
20 8/16	12 8/16	8 0/16	M	Plumas County	CA	Mike Ellena	1993	581
20 8/16	12 7/16	8 1/16	M	Klamath County	OR	Kelly D. Carson	1993	581
20 8/16	13 0/16	7 8/16	M	Sherwood Park	ALB	Pat Morphy	1994	581
20 8/16	12 13/16	7 11/16	M	Endeavour	SAS	Wayne Arnson	1994	581
20 8/16	12 14/16	7 10/16	M	Peace River	ALB	Tom Lester	1994	581
20 8/16	12 10/16	7 14/16	M	Vermilion Bay	ONT	Larry Saunders	1995	581
20 8/16	12 9/16	7 15/16	M	Athabasca River	ALB	John Visscher	1995	581
20 8/16	12 10/16	7 14/16	M	File Lake	MAN	Robert Schulz	1995	581
20 8/16	12 15/16	7 9/16	M	Beltrami County	MN	Steve Young	1995	581
20 8/16	13 1/16	7 7/16	M	Pineshill Forest Reserve	SAS	Kenneth D. Wiers	1996	581
20 8/16	12 12/16	7 12/16	M	Langlade County	WI	Charles W. Drexler, Sr.	1996	581
20 8/16	12 12/16	7 12/16	M	Marinette County	WI	Andrew Semrad	1997	581
20 8/16	12 15/16	7 9/16	M	Mistatim	SAS	Scott L. Koelzer	1998	581
20 8/16	12 14/16	7 10/16	M	Lac La Biche	ALB	Jeffrey S. Weisswasser	1998	581
20 8/16	12 10/16	7 14/16	M	Kississing Lake	MAN	Jonathan White	1998	581
20 8/16	12 13/16	7 11/16	M	Orange County	NY	Donald Bierstine	1998	581
20 8/16	12 11/16	7 13/16	M	Pilot Mtn.	BC	R. Newnham/L. Arnold-Smith	1999	581
20 8/16	12 15/16	7 9/16	M	Allegany County	NY	Heath A. Wedge	1999	581
20 8/16	12 11/16	7 13/16	M	Prince of Wales Island	AK	Kent Johns	2000	581
20 8/16	12 12/16	7 12/16	M	Prince of Wales Island	AK	Bob Ameen	2001	581
20 8/16	12 6/16	8 2/16	M	White River	ONT	Alfred D. Waterson	2001	581
20 8/16	12 10/16	7 14/16	M	Ashland County	WI	Leon Klueckman	2001	581
20 8/16	12 14/16	7 10/16	M	Prince of Wales Island	AK	Kelly King	2003	581
20 8/16	13 1/16	7 7/16	M	Nestor Falls	ONT	David S. Olmstead	2003	581
20 8/16	12 4/16	8 4/16	M	La Plata County	CO	Steve Vittetow	2003	581
20 8/16	13 0/16	7 8/16	M	Iron County	WI	Jere Hamel	2003	581
20 8/16	12 14/16	7 10/16	M	Sevier County	UT	Heather Newby	2003	581
*20 8/16	12 6/16	8 2/16	M	Ulster County	NY	Carlo Ferraiolo	2003	581
20 8/16	12 15/16	7 9/16	M	Kuiu Island	AK	Frank S. Noska IV	2004	581
20 8/16	13 0/16	7 8/16	M	Van Buren County	AR	Jason L. Vaughn	2004	581
20 8/16	12 11/16	7 13/16	M	Kern County	CA	Richard Krug	2004	581
20 8/16	13 2/16	7 6/16	M	Shawano County	WI	Allan Dorn	2005	581
20 8/16	12 11/16	7 13/16	M	Carrot River	SAS	Stoney Lee Grayson	2006	581
*20 8/16	12 13/16	7 11/16	M	Crow Wing County	MN	Nathan J. Van Risseghem	2007	581
*20 8/16	12 6/16	8 2/16	M	Gunnison County	CO	Charles Bolen	2008	581
*20 8/16	13 4/16	7 4/16	M	Marathon County	WI	Burton L. Willes	2008	581
20 8/16	12 13/16	7 11/16	M	Delaware County	NY	Giovanni B. DiMaggio	2008	581
20 8/16	12 11/16	7 13/16	M	Taylor County	WI	Richard Rosemeyer	2009	581
20 8/16	12 7/16	8 1/16	M	Routt County	CO	Keith Liefer	2009	581
*20 8/16	13 2/16	7 6/16	M	Scott County	AR	Adam Beason	2010	581
20 7/16	13 9/16	6 14/16	M	Nenana	AK	Robert Dunn	1968	635
20 7/16	12 14/16	7 9/16	M	Montezuma County	CO	Bryan C. Neeley	1974	635
20 7/16	12 10/16	7 13/16	M	Price County	WI	Bob Eckarot	1974	635
20 7/16	12 7/16	8 0/16	M	Whiteshell	MAN	Ken Warkentin	1978	635
20 7/16	12 11/16	7 12/16	M	Mille Lacs County	MN	Milt Zernechel	1980	635
20 7/16	12 6/16	8 1/16	M	Marquette County	MI	Thomas Benak	1982	635
20 7/16	12 11/16	7 12/16	M	Mat-Su Borough	AK	Jack V. Rouse	1983	635
20 7/16	12 10/16	7 13/16	M	St. Louis County	MN	Ken Lenk	1983	635
20 7/16	12 12/16	7 11/16	M	Garfield County	CO	Roger Bolander	1985	635
20 7/16	12 14/16	7 9/16	M	Arran	SAS	Bill Clink	1986	635
20 7/16	12 14/16	7 9/16	M	Valleyview	ALB	Stan Walchuk, Jr.	1986	635
20 7/16	12 11/16	7 12/16	M	Routt County	CO	Bill Grammer	1987	635
20 7/16	12 4/16	8 3/16	M	Atikokan	ONT	Kenny Stoner	1988	635
20 7/16	12 11/16	7 12/16	M	Prince of Wales Island	AK	Gary Roney	1988	635
20 7/16	12 12/16	7 11/16	M	Iron County	WI	Brian Tessmann	1989	635
20 7/16	12 7/16	8 0/16	M	Rappahannock County	VA	Collis W. Dodson, Jr.	1989	635
20 7/16	12 11/16	7 12/16	M	Prince of Wales Island	AK	Dennis Brieske	1990	635
20 7/16	12 12/16	7 11/16	M	Madera County	CA	James Joseph Doherty, Jr.	1991	635
20 7/16	12 5/16	8 2/16	M	St. Louis County	MN	Jim Ceglar	1991	635
20 7/16	12 12/16	7 11/16	M	Spirit River	ALB	Jim Stinson	1992	635
20 7/16	12 11/16	7 12/16	M	Fort McMurray	ALB	James Pike	1992	635
20 7/16	12 7/16	8 0/16	M	San Bernardino County	CA	Allen Davis	1992	635
20 7/16	13 0/16	7 7/16	M	Douglas County	WI	Mark P. Haan	1992	635
20 7/16	13 0/16	7 7/16	M	Rockingham County	VA	Donald Bare	1992	635
20 7/16	12 12/16	7 11/16	M	Perrault Falls	ONT	Patrick D. Gaffney	1993	635
20 7/16	12 8/16	7 15/16	M	Becker County	MN	Joe Caron	1993	635
20 7/16	12 12/16	7 11/16	M	Bayfield County	WI	Edwin A. Koenigs	1993	635
20 7/16	12 15/16	7 8/16	M	Pine River	MAN	Peter McGillivray	1994	635
20 7/16	12 9/16	7 14/16	M	Graham County	AZ	Warren Strickland	1994	635
20 7/16	12 11/16	7 12/16	M	Minto	NBW	Joseph Maringo	1994	635
20 7/16	12 13/16	7 10/16	M	Utterson	ONT	Jeff Coleman	1996	635

131

BLACK BEAR

Minimum Score 18   Continued

SCORE	GREATEST LENGTH	GREATEST WIDTH	SEX	AREA	STATE/ PROVINCE	HUNTER'S NAME	DATE	RANK
20 7/16	12 10/16	7 13/16	M	Wawa	ONT	Brett Grams	1996	635
20 7/16	12 15/16	7 8/16	M	Bayfield County	WI	Glenn A. Klomsten	1996	635
20 7/16	12 13/16	7 10/16	M	Trinity County	CA	Bart Pontoni	1996	635
20 7/16	12 6/16	8 1/16	M	Whiteswan Lake	SAS	Terry Krahn	1997	635
20 7/16	12 15/16	7 8/16	M	Kelwood	MAN	Doug J. Herman	1997	635
20 7/16	12 11/16	7 12/16	M	Ft. McMurray	ALB	Rhonda Hunter	1997	635
20 7/16	13 0/16	7 7/16	M	Olha	MAN	Dana M. Draper	1997	635
20 7/16	12 9/16	7 14/16	M	Carswell Lake	SAS	Christopher J. Leitzke	1998	635
20 7/16	12 8/16	7 15/16	M	Peace River	ALB	Jerry W. Laton	1998	635
20 7/16	12 8/16	7 15/16	M	Dipper Lake	SAS	Henry Chidgey	2000	635
20 7/16	13 1/16	7 6/16	M	Conklin	ALB	Neil Hamerlinck	2000	635
20 7/16	12 5/16	8 2/16	M	Christopher Lake	SAS	Velma L. Smith	2000	635
20 7/16	12 14/16	7 9/16	M	Clearwater County	MN	Dave Kyllo	2000	635
20 7/16	12 8/16	7 15/16	M	Mesa County	CO	Mike A. Rogers	2000	635
20 7/16	12 14/16	7 9/16	M	Tulare County	CA	Chris Gierlich	2001	635
20 7/16	12 12/16	7 11/16	M	Kitimat	BC	Harvey J. Surina	2002	635
20 7/16	12 10/16	7 13/16	M	Donnelly	ALB	Douglas Kirby Evert	2002	635
20 7/16	12 11/16	7 12/16	M	Navajo County	AZ	Jim Willems	2002	635
*20 7/16	12 7/16	8 0/16	M	Pine Falls	MAN	Bill MacFarland, Jr.	2005	635
20 7/16	12 14/16	7 9/16	M	Kosciusko Island	AK	M. Blake Patton	2005	635
20 7/16	12 13/16	7 10/16	M	Duck Mtn.	MAN	Daniel J. Harty	2005	635
20 7/16	12 4/16	8 3/16	M	El Dorado County	CA	Douglas L. Teakell	2005	635
20 7/16	12 9/16	7 14/16	M	Aroostook County	ME	Paul H. Demerchant	2005	635
*20 7/16	12 10/16	7 13/16	M	Fair Harbour	BC	Adam Bartsch	2006	635
20 7/16	12 8/16	7 15/16	M	Thorne Bay	AK	P. R. Potts	2006	635
20 7/16	13 4/16	7 3/16	M	Chippewa County	WI	Jon D. Schroeder	2006	635
20 7/16	13 2/16	7 5/16	M	Marinette County	WI	James Liska	2006	635
20 7/16	13 2/16	7 5/16	M	Dufferin Lake	SAS	John C. Casner	2008	635
20 7/16	12 14/16	7 9/16	M	Sublette County	WY	Jessica Edd	2008	635
20 7/16	13 1/16	7 6/16	M	Scott County	AR	Will Beason	2008	635
*20 7/16	12 15/16	7 8/16	M	Olha	MAN	Bill Clink	2009	635
20 7/16	12 15/16	7 8/16	M	Sandilands	MAN	Rorke Christiuk	2009	635
20 7/16	12 12/16	7 11/16	M	Aroostook County	ME	David L. Weaver	2009	635
*20 7/16	12 12/16	7 11/16	M	Cass County	MN	Jeremy Espelund	2009	635
20 7/16	13 1/16	7 6/16	M	Meadow Lake	SAS	Jason Toews	2009	635
20 7/16	12 10/16	7 13/16	M	Smoky River	ALB	Greg Wadsworth	2010	635
20 6/16	12 11/16	7 11/16	M	Tulare County	CA	Quentin M. Boutch	1967	702
20 6/16	12 11/16	7 11/16	M	Garfield County	CO	Steve Bergman	1970	702
20 6/16	12 15/16	7 7/16	M	Kern County	CA	Leo Farley	1973	702
20 6/16	12 8/16	7 14/16	M	Shasta County	CA	Susan Mallonee	1974	702
20 6/16	12 6/16	8 0/16	M	Saguache County	CO	Ed Wiseman	1975	702
20 6/16	12 11/16	7 11/16	M	Reindeer Lake	SAS	James Buchanan	1976	702
20 6/16	12 12/16	7 10/16	M	Flower Station	ONT	Richard H. Shoup	1977	702
20 6/16	12 9/16	7 13/16	M	Ear Falls	ONT	Terry R. Fletcher	1978	702
20 6/16	12 11/16	7 11/16	M	St. Louis County	MN	Russell Wimberly	1979	702
20 6/16	12 11/16	7 11/16	M	Reserve	SAS	Richard Loffler	1984	702
20 6/16	12 14/16	7 8/16	M	Bayfield County	WI	Paul Deckert	1984	702
20 6/16	12 9/16	7 13/16	M	Ignace	ONT	Randy J. Tylke	1985	702
20 6/16	13 2/16	7 4/16	M	Meadow Lake	SAS	Craig Larson	1986	702
20 6/16	12 5/16	8 1/16	M	Spiritwood	SAS	Robert W. Peet	1987	702
20 6/16	12 8/16	7 14/16	M	Wrangell Island	AK	Bob Smith	1987	702
20 6/16	12 13/16	7 9/16	M	Athabasca	ALB	John Visscher	1988	702
20 6/16	12 14/16	7 8/16	M	Hudson Bay	SAS	Kendall Haberstroh	1988	702
20 6/16	12 8/16	7 14/16	M	Rochester	ALB	Dave Gerber	1988	702
20 6/16	12 13/16	7 9/16	M	Wandering River	ALB	Warren Witherspoon	1988	702
20 6/16	12 10/16	7 12/16	M	Wallowa County	OR	Russell McCall	1989	702
20 6/16	12 15/16	7 7/16	M	Pine County	MN	Thomas Behrends	1989	702
20 6/16	12 14/16	7 8/16	M	Ashland County	WI	James A. Liermann	1989	702
20 6/16	12 9/16	7 13/16	M	Lac Forant	QUE	Harold Shepard	1990	702
20 6/16	12 10/16	7 12/16	M	La Plata County	CO	Paul Nichols	1991	702
20 6/16	12 10/16	7 12/16	M	Clearwater County	ID	Steve Stajkowski	1991	702
20 6/16	12 7/16	7 15/16	M	Missoula County	MT	Rick L. Stone	1991	702
20 6/16	12 11/16	7 11/16	M	Iron County	MI	Jeff Fontecchio	1991	702
20 6/16	12 6/16	8 0/16	M	Plumas County	CA	Bill Graves	1991	702
20 6/16	13 0/16	7 6/16	M	Hubbard County	MN	Hal Dickelman	1992	702
20 6/16	12 9/16	7 13/16	M	Wolf Lake	ALB	Tim Pardely	1993	702
20 6/16	13 0/16	7 6/16	M	Rio Arriba County	NM	Larson Panzy	1993	702
20 6/16	12 7/16	7 15/16	M	Clark County	WA	Michael T. Davis	1993	702
20 6/16	12 10/16	7 12/16	M	Fort Chimo	QUE	Jerry McNeal	1994	702
20 6/16	12 12/16	7 10/16	M	Orange County	NY	Richard Berger	1994	702
20 6/16	12 10/16	7 12/16	M	McKinley County	NM	Timothy T. Dwyer	1995	702
20 6/16	13 1/16	7 5/16	M	Mineral County	WV	Gary Wayne Evans	1995	702
20 6/16	12 8/16	7 14/16	M	Los Angeles County	CA	Jerry Maytum	1995	702
20 6/16	12 13/16	7 9/16	M	Qu'Appelle	SAS	Brad Thompson	1996	702
20 6/16	12 12/16	7 10/16	M	High Level	ALB	Charles H. Thatcher	1996	702
20 6/16	12 9/16	7 13/16	M	Sheridan County	WY	Dan Brockman	1996	702
20 6/16	12 12/16	7 10/16	M	Fort McMurray	ALB	Bob Ehle	1996	702
20 6/16	12 4/16	8 2/16	M	Falher	ALB	Vicki Cianciarulo	1996	702
20 6/16	13 1/16	7 5/16	M	Burnett County	WI	Jerry Strese	1996	702
20 6/16	12 1/16	8 5/16	M	Bobcaygeon	ONT	Giulio Calvelli	1997	702
20 6/16	12 10/16	7 12/16	M	Madison County	MT	Darryle "Pete" Otto	1997	702
20 6/16	13 2/16	7 4/16	M	Price County	WI	Douglas Erickson	1997	702
20 6/16	12 8/16	7 14/16	M	Tingley Creek	BC	Dave Schwemler	1998	702
20 6/16	12 10/16	7 12/16	M	McKnalley Lake	ALB	Donnie Covey	1998	702
20 6/16	12 11/16	7 11/16	M	Fahler	ALB	Michael Rabbe	1999	702
20 6/16	12 13/16	7 9/16	M	Prince of Wales Island	AK	Joey Buchanan	1999	702
20 6/16	13 1/16	7 5/16	M	Trocadero Bay	AK	John S. Borg	1999	702
20 6/16	12 10/16	7 12/16	M	Lac La Biche	ALB	Thomas Frank Vanecek	1999	702
20 6/16	12 12/16	7 10/16	M	McBride Lake	SAS	Carl Jeffries	1999	702
20 6/16	12 10/16	7 12/16	M	Lake of the Woods Cty	MN	Shannon E. Thomas	1999	702
20 6/16	13 0/16	7 6/16	M	Rio Blanco County	CO	James R. Fitzhugh	1999	702
20 6/16	12 2/16	8 4/16	M	Alpine County	CA	Ed Austin	2000	702
20 6/16	13 3/16	7 3/16	M	Washburn County	WI	James J. Johnson	2000	702
20 6/16	12 12/16	7 10/16	M	Prince of Wales Island	AK	Bruce Bartenfelder	2001	702
20 6/16	12 11/16	7 11/16	M	Clearwater County	ID	Dennis Michael	2001	702

BLACK BEAR

Minimum Score 18 Continued

SCORE	GREATEST LENGTH	GREATEST WIDTH	SEX	AREA	STATE/ PROVINCE	HUNTER'S NAME	DATE	RANK
20 6/16	12 10/16	7 12/16	M	Routt County	CO	Cedar Beauregard	2001	702
20 6/16	12 14/16	7 8/16	M	Swan River	MAN	Chet Hassemer	2001	702
20 6/16	12 9/16	7 13/16	M	Prince of Wales Island	AK	Craig Nordstrom	2002	702
20 6/16	12 14/16	7 8/16	M	Quesnel	BC	Barry Mueller	2002	702
20 6/16	13 1/16	7 5/16	M	Marshall County	MN	Troy Edberg	2003	702
*20 6/16	13 0/16	7 6/16	M	Sullivan County	NY	Steven Pecora	2003	702
20 6/16	12 10/16	7 12/16	M	Rio Arriba County	NM	Jim Willems	2004	702
20 6/16	12 10/16	7 12/16	M	Eau Claire County	WI	James Wilbur	2004	702
20 6/16	12 10/16	7 12/16	M	Bayfield County	WI	Gordon Gibbons	2004	702
20 6/16	12 8/16	7 14/16	M	Bayfield County	WI	Gary L. Shruck	2004	702
20 6/16	12 11/16	7 11/16	M	Buffalo Narrows	SAS	James W. Casto III	2005	702
20 6/16	12 11/16	7 11/16	M	Chippewa County	WI	Jeff Anderson	2005	702
20 6/16	12 7/16	7 15/16	M	Beltrami County	MN	Jayson Deziel	2005	702
20 6/16	12 8/16	7 14/16	M	Caribou County	ID	Joe L. Hyde	2007	702
20 6/16	12 13/16	7 9/16	M	Taylor County	WI	Raymond Rosemeyer	2007	702
20 6/16	12 11/16	7 10/16	M	Pine County	MN	Matthew Matson	2007	702
20 6/16	12 9/16	7 13/16	M	Albany County	WY	Steven Perkins	2008	702
20 6/16	12 10/16	7 12/16	M	Prince of Wales Island	AK	Bob Ameen	2008	702
20 6/16	13 3/16	7 3/16	M	Burnett County	WI	Jerry Strese	2008	702
*20 6/16	12 11/16	7 11/16	M	Oconto County	WI	Levi R. Missall	2008	702
*20 6/16	12 13/16	7 9/16	M	Van Buren County	AR	Jerry Snowden	2008	702
*20 6/16	12 13/16	7 9/16	M	Tyrrell County	NC	Ronnie E. Bruce	2008	702
*20 6/16	12 12/16	7 10/16	M	Frenchman Butte	SAS	Dana Gross	2009	702
*20 6/16	12 12/16	7 10/16	M	Florence County	WI	Anthony S. Weigert	2009	702
*20 6/16	13 0/16	7 6/16	M	Indiana County	PA	Bryon Whipkey	2009	702
*20 6/16	12 15/16	7 7/16	M	Gila County	AZ	George Harms	2010	702
20 5/16	12 14/16	7 7/16	M	Shasta County	CA	Harv Ebers	1964	787
20 5/16	12 11/16	7 9/16	M	St. Louis County	MN	Jay Deones	1970	787
20 5/16	12 13/16	7 8/16	M	Buncombe County	NC	Robert T. Austin	1971	787
20 5/16	13 0/16	7 5/16	M	Emma Lake	SAS	Ernie Johnston	1972	787
20 5/16	12 4/16	8 1/16	M	Montezuma County	CO	Stanley A. Coval	1975	787
20 5/16	12 11/16	7 10/16	M	Montrose County	CO	Jack Cassidy	1976	787
20 5/16	12 11/16	7 10/16	M	Lemhi County	ID	Richard R. Smith	1977	787
20 5/16	12 10/16	7 11/16	M	Lincoln County	NM	Tom Mitchell	1978	787
20 5/16	12 12/16	7 9/16	M	Marquette County	MI	Bernard E. Stiritz	1980	787
20 5/16	12 9/16	7 12/16	M	Hudson Bay	SAS	Sam Qualls	1981	787
20 5/16	12 13/16	7 8/16	M	Bonneville County	ID	Michael Ferraro	1981	787
20 5/16	12 3/16	8 2/16	M	Presque Isle County	MI	William C. Green III	1981	787
20 5/16	12 9/16	7 12/16	M	Devlin Lake	ONT	J. E. Abhold	1982	787
20 5/16	12 5/16	8 0/16	M	Meagher County	MT	Richard M. Campbell	1982	787
20 5/16	12 12/16	7 9/16	M	Otero County	NM	Michael Crabb	1984	787
20 5/16	12 7/16	7 14/16	M	Atikokan	ONT	Greg Morehead	1985	787
20 5/16	12 8/16	7 13/16	M	Archuleta County	CO	Ronald J. Murphy	1985	787
20 5/16	12 6/16	7 15/16	M	Jackson County	OR	David Greisen, Jr.	1985	787
20 5/16	12 10/16	7 11/16	M	Ontonagon County	MI	Dale W. Gray	1986	787
20 5/16	12 9/16	7 12/16	M	Siskiyou County	CA	Bob Jensen	1986	787
20 5/16	12 7/16	7 14/16	M	Gila County	AZ	Eric Pierce	1987	787
20 5/16	12 10/16	7 11/16	M	Douglas County	WI	William T. Solie	1987	787
20 5/16	12 12/16	7 9/16	M	Prince of Wales Island	AK	Mike Taylor	1989	787
20 5/16	12 4/16	8 1/16	M	Okanogan County	WA	D. Kirk Sapp	1989	787
20 5/16	12 10/16	7 11/16	M	Lincoln County	WI	Gerald O. Arndt	1989	787
20 5/16	13 0/16	7 5/16	M	Mesa County	CO	Paul Alan Seidelman	1989	787
20 5/16	12 14/16	7 7/16	M	Prince of Wales Island	AK	Glen Berry	1990	787
20 5/16	12 12/16	7 9/16	M	Lac La Biche	ALB	Ronald H. Haver	1990	787
20 5/16	12 9/16	7 12/16	M	Prince of Wales Island	AK	Timothy Putnam	1991	787
20 5/16	12 6/16	7 15/16	M	Shasta County	CA	Douglas Trouette	1991	787
20 5/16	12 7/16	7 14/16	M	Skownan	MAN	Walt Krom	1992	787
20 5/16	12 7/16	7 14/16	M	Wanless	MAN	Arley Paul Heer	1993	787
20 5/16	12 9/16	7 12/16	M	Stone Creek	BC	Joe Tschampa	1993	787
20 5/16	12 10/16	7 11/16	M	Fort Vermilion	ALB	Brian Burnstad	1993	787
20 5/16	12 10/16	7 11/16	M	Prince of Wales Island	AK	Larry D. Jones	1993	787
20 5/16	12 12/16	7 9/16	M	Wallowa County	OR	Stephen Herrera	1994	787
20 5/16	12 12/16	7 9/16	M	Bissett	MAN	Richard Nevels	1994	787
20 5/16	12 5/16	8 0/16	M	Athabasca River	ALB	Billy Tillotson	1994	787
20 5/16	12 6/16	7 15/16	M	Smeaton	SAS	Don G. Scofield	1994	787
20 5/16	12 6/16	7 15/16	M	Calling Lake	ALB	Rich McGowan	1994	787
20 5/16	12 10/16	7 11/16	M	Pine County	MN	John Cardinal	1994	787
20 5/16	12 10/16	7 11/16	M	Bayfield County	WI	Douglas E. Callies	1994	787
20 5/16	13 1/16	7 4/16	M	Burnett County	WI	Steven Constant	1994	787
20 5/16	13 1/16	7 4/16	M	Beltrami County	MN	Gregory T. Ose	1994	787
20 5/16	12 13/16	7 8/16	M	Rio Arriba County	NM	Robert John Seeds	1994	787
20 5/16	12 7/16	7 14/16	M	Chibougamau	QUE	Brian Brochu	1995	787
20 5/16	12 10/16	7 11/16	M	Cadillac	QUE	Ron Miller	1995	787
20 5/16	12 8/16	7 13/16	M	Plumas County	CA	Mark Nelson	1995	787
20 5/16	12 9/16	7 12/16	M	Hudson Bay	SAS	Glen Gulka	1995	787
20 5/16	12 6/16	7 15/16	M	St. Louis County	MN	Bill G. Koenig	1995	787
20 5/16	12 14/16	7 7/16	M	McDowell County	WV	Kevin P. Kelley	1995	787
20 5/16	12 11/16	7 10/16	M	Prince of Wales Island	AK	Jim Bauers	1996	787
20 5/16	12 12/16	7 9/16	M	Marathon County	WI	Dan Infalt	1997	787
20 5/16	12 11/16	7 10/16	M	Raleigh County	WV	Larry Murphy	1997	787
20 5/16	12 11/16	7 10/16	M	Spirit River	ALB	Michael Ambur	1998	787
20 5/16	12 9/16	7 12/16	M	Two Forks River	SAS	Don Mason	1998	787
20 5/16	12 12/16	7 9/16	M	Cibola County	NM	Michael A. Rendon	1998	787
20 5/16	12 11/16	7 10/16	M	Rio Arriba County	NM	Robert J. Seeds	1998	787
20 5/16	12 7/16	7 14/16	M	Prince of Wales Island	AK	Chad Doell	1999	787
20 5/16	12 11/16	7 10/16	M	Staney Creek	AK	Kelly King	1999	787
20 5/16	12 13/16	7 8/16	M	Whiteshell	MAN	Robert S. Kubicek	1999	787
20 5/16	12 15/16	7 6/16	M	Dolores County	CO	Jerry Parker	1999	787
20 5/16	12 12/16	7 9/16	M	Swan River	SAS	Randy Wahler	2000	787
20 5/16	12 7/16	7 14/16	M	Valleyview	ALB	Keith D. Levendorf	2000	787
20 5/16	12 14/16	7 7/16	M	Koochiching County	MN	Steve Schultz	2000	787
20 5/16	12 10/16	7 11/16	M	Prince of Wales Island	AK	Ricky Brown	2000	787
20 5/16	13 0/16	7 5/16	M	Lincoln County	WI	Mark Van Veghel	2000	787
20 5/16	12 14/16	7 7/16	M	Las Animas County	CO	Fred Eichler	2000	787
20 5/16	13 1/16	7 4/16	M	Sundown	MAN	Dennis Dalan	2001	787

133

BLACK BEAR

Minimum Score 18   Continued

SCORE	GREATEST LENGTH	GREATEST WIDTH	SEX	AREA	STATE/ PROVINCE	HUNTER'S NAME	DATE	RANK
20 5/16	12 9/16	7 12/16	M	Lebel-sur-Quevillon	QUE	Stephane Roberge	2001	787
20 5/16	12 10/16	7 11/16	M	Mesa County	CO	Cory A. Lindbo	2001	787
20 5/16	13 1/16	7 4/16	M	St. Louis County	MN	Kevin Dreier	2002	787
20 5/16	12 7/16	7 14/16	M	Marinette County	WI	Robert G. Cormier	2002	787
20 5/16	12 5/16	8 0/16	M	Berkshire County	MA	Joseph Brighenti	2002	787
20 5/16	12 10/16	7 11/16	M	Kosciusko Island	AK	Bob Ameen	2003	787
20 5/16	12 11/16	7 10/16	M	Wabigoon Lake	ONT	James Morrison	2003	787
20 5/16	12 8/16	7 13/16	M	Hodgson	MAN	Stacy Morton	2004	787
20 5/16	12 13/16	7 8/16	M	Churchill Lake	SAS	Terry M. Dennis	2004	787
20 5/16	12 5/16	8 0/16	M	Coos County	NH	Robert Lafrance	2005	787
20 5/16	12 4/16	8 1/16	M	Delta County	MI	Raymond G. Hagman	2005	787
20 5/16	12 13/16	7 8/16	M	Kupreanof Island	AK	Darryl Amason	2006	787
20 5/16	12 8/16	7 13/16	M	Thaddeus Lake	ONT	Karl J. Levisay	2006	787
*20 5/16	12 12/16	7 9/16	M	La Loche	SAS	Mar Miles	2007	787
20 5/16	12 15/16	7 6/16	M	Pine County	MN	Randy E. Broz	2007	787
*20 5/16	13 2/16	7 3/16	M	Johnson County	AR	Austin Brown	2007	787
*20 5/16	12 15/16	7 6/16	M	Swan River	MAN	Dan Jost	2008	787
20 5/16	12 9/16	7 12/16	M	Little Fishing Lake	SAS	Christopher Jensen	2008	787
20 5/16	12 10/16	7 11/16	M	De la Griffe d'Ours	QUE	Kevin Pugh	2009	787
*20 5/16	12 5/16	8 0/16	M	Hampshire County	WV	Andy Stotler	2009	787
*20 5/16	12 6/16	7 15/16	M	Grande Prairie	ALB	Chester Rudolf	2010	787
20 5/16	12 12/16	7 9/16	M	Houghton County	MI	Troy Sheats	2010	787
20 4/16	12 6/16	7 14/16	M	Oceana County	MI	William Benson	1967	878
20 4/16	12 11/16	7 9/16	M	Somerset County	ME	Felix Nosewicz	1968	878
20 4/16	12 10/16	7 10/16	M	Mesa County	CO	M. R. James	1971	878
20 4/16	12 12/16	7 8/16	M	Los Alamos County	NM	Kenneth A. Meyer	1971	878
20 4/16	12 12/16	7 8/16	M	Sawyer County	WI	George Geisert	1972	878
20 4/16	12 7/16	7 13/16	M	Madison County	MT	Bob Savage	1977	878
20 4/16	12 5/16	7 15/16	M	Kashabowie	ONT	Hans C. Forssell	1978	878
20 4/16	12 8/16	7 12/16	M	Siskiyou County	CA	Bill Waters	1981	878
20 4/16	12 7/16	7 13/16	M	Valora	ONT	Elmer R. Luce, Jr.	1981	878
20 4/16	12 8/16	7 12/16	M	Mesa County	CO	Larry A. McIntosh	1982	878
20 4/16	12 5/16	7 15/16	M	Nez Perce County	ID	Hubert M. Sims, Jr.	1982	878
20 4/16	12 7/16	7 13/16	M	Trinity County	CA	Rodney A. York	1983	878
20 4/16	12 8/16	7 12/16	M	Rockingham County	VA	Charles Larry Danner	1984	878
20 4/16	12 12/16	7 8/16	M	Carrot River	SAS	William Jorgensen	1985	878
20 4/16	12 8/16	7 12/16	M	Swan River	MAN	Marc N. Shaft	1985	878
20 4/16	12 11/16	7 9/16	M	Waterhen River	SAS	Pink Atkins	1986	878
20 4/16	12 10/16	7 10/16	M	Mat-Su Valley	AK	Bill Parker	1987	878
20 4/16	12 6/16	7 14/16	M	Wrangell Island	AK	Bob Smith	1987	878
20 4/16	12 10/16	7 10/16	M	Canoe Lake	SAS	Richard Robert Ritzel	1988	878
20 4/16	12 7/16	7 13/16	M	Ft. McMurray	ALB	Tom C. Johnson	1988	878
20 4/16	12 10/16	7 10/16	M	Prince of Wales Island	AK	Danny Moore	1989	878
20 4/16	12 5/16	7 15/16	M	Cranberry Portage	MAN	Dean K. Reidt	1989	878
20 4/16	12 14/16	7 6/16	M	King County	WA	Greg Winters	1989	878
20 4/16	12 12/16	7 8/16	M	Olha	MAN	Tim Stahman	1990	878
20 4/16	12 12/16	7 8/16	M	Lanark	ONT	Ben Graham	1990	878
20 4/16	12 7/16	7 13/16	M	Caramat	ONT	Rick Stump	1990	878
20 4/16	12 4/16	8 0/16	M	Dorion	ONT	Bruce Hudalla	1991	878
20 4/16	12 8/16	7 12/16	M	Ignace	ONT	Thomas C. Klinesmith	1991	878
20 4/16	12 10/16	7 10/16	M	Howley	NFL	Roger Lewis	1991	878
20 4/16	12 9/16	7 11/16	M	Lewis County	WA	Kevin R. Amos	1991	878
20 4/16	12 11/16	7 9/16	M	Lane County	OR	Dave Smith	1991	878
20 4/16	12 9/16	7 11/16	M	Camas County	ID	Archie Malone	1992	878
20 4/16	12 13/16	7 7/16	M	Dubreuilville	ONT	Terry J. DeBlaay	1992	878
20 4/16	12 4/16	8 0/16	M	Ear Falls	ONT	Larry Foreman	1992	878
20 4/16	12 7/16	7 13/16	M	Madison County	MT	Larry Stackhouse	1992	878
20 4/16	12 11/16	7 9/16	M	Beauval	SAS	Alan Sims	1993	878
20 4/16	12 8/16	7 12/16	M	Rocky Lake	MAN	Tim Finley	1993	878
20 4/16	12 9/16	7 11/16	M	Wabigoon	ONT	Kermit L. Johnson	1993	878
20 4/16	12 11/16	7 9/16	M	Jackson County	OR	Mark G. Nouguier	1993	878
20 4/16	12 14/16	7 6/16	M	Price County	WI	William Peterson	1993	878
20 4/16	12 14/16	7 6/16	M	Essex County	NY	Paul Durling	1993	878
20 4/16	12 6/16	7 14/16	M	Clarke Lake	SAS	Steve Byerly	1994	878
20 4/16	12 7/16	7 13/16	M	Snow Lake	MAN	Craig Warren Barrows	1994	878
20 4/16	12 9/16	7 11/16	M	Christopher Lake	SAS	Scott G. Yeomans	1994	878
20 4/16	12 8/16	7 12/16	M	Prince of Wales Island	AK	Fred C. Church	1995	878
20 4/16	12 10/16	7 10/16	M	Carswell Lake	SAS	Dave Donahue	1995	878
20 4/16	12 10/16	7 10/16	M	Alpine County	CA	John H. Wiegel	1995	878
20 4/16	12 7/16	7 13/16	M	Union County	OR	Frank Sanders	1995	878
20 4/16	12 12/16	7 8/16	M	Thunder Bay	ONT	Marc Hellinghausen	1996	878
20 4/16	12 11/16	7 9/16	M	Tulare County	CA	Dennis Crew	1996	878
20 4/16	12 15/16	7 5/16	M	Orange County	NY	George E. Decker	1996	878
20 4/16	12 10/16	7 10/16	M	Farwell Canyon	BC	Daryl Buchholtz	1997	878
20 4/16	13 6/16	6 14/16	M	Athabasca River	ALB	Roger Wintle	1997	878
20 4/16	12 11/16	7 9/16	M	Prince of Wales Island	AK	E. Lance Whary	1997	878
20 4/16	12 12/16	7 8/16	M	Brunswick Lake	ONT	Jerome L. Schellinger	1997	878
20 4/16	13 4/16	7 0/16	M	Clearwater County	MN	Donnie Hutson	1997	878
20 4/16	12 10/16	7 10/16	M	Apache County	AZ	Clyde H. Gavin	1997	878
20 4/16	12 8/16	7 12/16	M	Carrot River	SAS	Mike Polich	1998	878
20 4/16	12 6/16	7 14/16	M	Ile-a-La-Crosse	SAS	Dennis Wademan	1998	878
20 4/16	12 8/16	7 12/16	M	Spirit River	ALB	Joseph E. Barno	1998	878
20 4/16	12 9/16	7 11/16	M	Prince of Wales Island	AK	Robert Hewitt	1998	878
20 4/16	12 9/16	7 11/16	M	Cold Lake	ALB	Tom Rooney	1999	878
20 4/16	12 6/16	7 14/16	M	Grand Rapids	MAN	James K. Knoke	1999	878
20 4/16	12 14/16	7 6/16	M	Hubbard County	MN	Casey A. Blum	1999	878
20 4/16	12 11/16	7 9/16	M	Dunn County	WI	Lou Milanesi	1999	878
20 4/16	12 5/16	7 15/16	M	Orange County	NY	Daniel J. Schweikart	1999	878
20 4/16	12 10/16	7 10/16	M	Duck Mtns.	MAN	Ronnie Mason	2000	878
20 4/16	12 4/16	8 0/16	M	Lac La Pause	QUE	Michel Vezina	2000	878
20 4/16	12 3/16	8 1/16	M	Aitkin County	MN	Steven Shade	2000	878
20 4/16	12 8/16	7 12/16	M	Carswell Lake	SAS	Neil Demant	2001	878
20 4/16	12 12/16	7 8/16	M	Carswell Lake	SAS	Thomas Conrardy	2001	878
20 4/16	12 4/16	8 0/16	M	Koochiching County	MN	Larry M. Looman	2001	878
20 4/16	12 7/16	7 13/16	M	La Plata County	CO	Randall Shepard	2001	878

134

BLACK BEAR

Minimum Score 18   Continued

SCORE	GREATEST LENGTH	GREATEST WIDTH	SEX	AREA	STATE/ PROVINCE	HUNTER'S NAME	DATE	RANK
20 4/16	12 10/16	7 10/16	M	Shoshone County	ID	John Neal	2002	878
20 4/16	12 7/16	7 13/16	M	Rimouski	QUE	Robert O'Connell	2002	878
20 4/16	12 9/16	7 11/16	M	Kuiu Island	AK	Nathan L. Andersohn	2002	878
20 4/16	12 15/16	7 5/16	M	Dolores County	CO	James Geraghty	2002	878
20 4/16	12 12/16	7 8/16	M	Florence County	WI	Lee N. Hennes	2002	878
20 4/16	12 14/16	7 6/16	M	Gem County	ID	Forest Hunt	2002	878
20 4/16	12 2/16	8 2/16	M	Churchill Lake	SAS	Eric F. Efird	2003	878
20 4/16	12 7/16	7 13/16	M	Thunder Bay	ONT	Micheal Brozek	2003	878
20 4/16	12 6/16	7 14/16	M	Washington County	ME	Chad Thompson	2003	878
20 4/16	13 0/16	7 4/16	M	Clark County	WI	Mike Oberle	2003	878
20 4/16	12 10/16	7 10/16	M	Carrot River	SAS	Jim Horneck	2004	878
20 4/16	12 6/16	7 14/16	M	Sprott Lake	MAN	Bob MacDonald	2004	878
20 4/16	12 10/16	7 10/16	M	Apache County	AZ	Richard J. Stewart II	2004	878
20 4/16	13 1/16	7 3/16	M	Grandview	MAN	Ricky Suire	2005	878
20 4/16	13 0/16	7 4/16	M	Santa Cruz County	AZ	Miguel F. Morales	2005	878
20 4/16	12 14/16	7 6/16	M	Kern County	CA	Reed Prosser	2005	878
20 4/16	12 8/16	7 12/16	M	Sawyer County	WI	Jamie L. Back	2005	878
20 4/16	12 11/16	7 9/16	M	Fergus County	MT	Dylen Knerr	2006	878
20 4/16	12 14/16	7 6/16	M	Josephine Creek	ALB	Katie Popson	2006	878
20 4/16	12 1/16	8 3/16	M	Thunder Bay	ONT	Robert Loftus	2006	878
20 4/16	12 9/16	7 11/16	M	Carleton	NBW	Paul St. John	2007	878
20 4/16	13 0/16	7 4/16	M	Peace River	ALB	Craig R. Warmington	2007	878
20 4/16	12 15/16	7 5/16	M	St-Janvier de Chazel	QUE	Marcel Charrois	2007	878
*20 4/16	12 12/16	7 8/16	M	McDowell County	WV	Ricky Short	2007	878
20 4/16	12 14/16	7 6/16	M	Peace River	ALB	Kevin Young	2008	878
20 4/16	12 15/16	7 5/16	M	Gila County	AZ	Rodney L. Ronnebaum	2008	878
20 4/16	13 2/16	7 2/16	M	Warren County	PA	Brian E. Ristau	2008	878
20 4/16	12 10/16	7 10/16	M	Coconino County	AZ	Ryan Nogosek	2009	878
20 4/16	12 14/16	7 6/16	M	Lunenburg County	VA	Dale L. Sturdifen	2009	878
20 3/16	12 13/16	7 6/16	M	Prince Rupert	BC	Frank Huneck	1960	980
20 3/16	12 6/16	7 13/16	M	Ignace	ONT	Jerry Ulrich	1968	980
20 3/16	12 8/16	7 11/16	M	Coos County	OR	Robert L. Wegand	1971	980
20 3/16	12 4/16	7 15/16	M	Adams County	ID	Joe Adams	1971	980
20 3/16	12 12/16	7 7/16	M	Smoke Lake	ALB	Kenneth Szgatti	1975	980
20 3/16	12 3/16	8 0/16	M	Boise County	ID	Mark W. Powell	1975	980
20 3/16	12 5/16	7 14/16	M	Dolores County	CO	Marvin Reichenau	1979	980
20 3/16	12 6/16	7 13/16	M	Dolores County	CO	Randy E. Dossey	1979	980
20 3/16	12 10/16	7 9/16	M	Itasca County	MN	Gerald N. Rivetts, Jr.	1980	980
20 3/16	12 12/16	7 7/16	M	Burnett County	WI	Dan McElfresh	1982	980
20 3/16	12 8/16	7 11/16	M	Foxford	SAS	Brian Acton	1982	980
20 3/16	12 14/16	7 5/16	M	Loon Lake	SAS	Dennis Meyer	1984	980
20 3/16	12 13/16	7 6/16	M	Catron County	NM	John R. Caminiti	1984	980
20 3/16	12 3/16	8 0/16	M	Marquette County	MI	Kurt Funk	1985	980
20 3/16	12 13/16	7 6/16	M	Red Lake	ONT	Gerald Dykin	1986	980
20 3/16	12 12/16	7 7/16	M	Sioux Lookout	ONT	Tom Rosenthal	1986	980
20 3/16	12 12/16	7 7/16	M	McMunn	MAN	Rod Black	1987	980
20 3/16	12 11/16	7 8/16	M	Canterbury	NBW	David G. Cote	1987	980
20 3/16	12 4/16	7 15/16	M	Schefferville	QUE	Charles L. Buechel, Jr.	1987	980
20 3/16	12 7/16	7 12/16	M	Iron County	WI	Mike Lutz	1987	980
20 3/16	12 13/16	7 6/16	M	Fort Assiniboine	ALB	Wes Skakun	1988	980
20 3/16	12 8/16	7 11/16	M	Pine County	MN	Ed Nielsen	1989	980
20 3/16	12 8/16	7 11/16	M	Houghton County	MI	Loren G. Baker	1989	980
20 3/16	13 2/16	7 1/16	M	Chisago County	MN	Dennis Jaworski	1989	980
20 3/16	12 8/16	7 11/16	M	Coconino County	AZ	William Bedlion	1989	980
20 3/16	12 10/16	7 9/16	M	Goodsoil	SAS	Larry H. Hoyt	1990	980
20 3/16	12 5/16	7 14/16	M	Lac La Biche	ALB	Jesse Meyer	1991	980
20 3/16	12 10/16	7 9/16	M	La Loche	SAS	Robert Bramlett	1992	980
20 3/16	12 11/16	7 8/16	M	Wabasca River	ALB	Greg Duncan	1992	980
20 3/16	12 4/16	7 15/16	M	Chapleau	ONT	J. R. Mester	1992	980
20 3/16	12 9/16	7 10/16	M	Smoky Lake	ALB	Randy Ewen	1993	980
20 3/16	12 6/16	7 13/16	M	Ft. McMurray	ALB	David E. Stepp	1993	980
20 3/16	12 9/16	7 10/16	M	Hudson Bay	SAS	Dennis M. Dalan	1993	980
20 3/16	12 9/16	7 10/16	M	Cook County	MN	Rodney L. Tryon	1993	980
20 3/16	12 7/16	7 12/16	M	Rocky Mountain House	ALB	Steve Ouwerkerk	1994	980
20 3/16	12 10/16	7 9/16	M	Riding Mtn.	MAN	Gary L. Christensen	1994	980
20 3/16	12 10/16	7 9/16	M	Peace River	ALB	Zig Kertenis, Jr.	1994	980
20 3/16	12 6/16	7 13/16	M	Savant Lake	ONT	Brian Mark Winter	1994	980
20 3/16	13 3/16	7 0/16	M	Hudson Bay	SAS	Scott McCay	1994	980
20 3/16	12 10/16	7 9/16	M	Silver Lake	ONT	Walter Wright	1994	980
20 3/16	13 0/16	7 3/16	M	Timmins	ONT	Tony Muhich	1994	980
20 3/16	12 6/16	7 13/16	M	Catron County	NM	William F. Kern	1994	980
20 3/16	12 12/16	7 7/16	M	Clearwater County	ID	Dana L. Lott	1995	980
20 3/16	13 0/16	7 3/16	M	Mafeking	MAN	Kimberly J. Schwierking	1995	980
20 3/16	12 12/16	7 7/16	M	Nevada County	CA	Edward L. Tillotson	1995	980
20 3/16	12 5/16	7 14/16	M	Chinchaga	ALB	Dwayne Huggins	1996	980
20 3/16	12 12/16	7 7/16	M	Athabasca River	ALB	John Visscher	1996	980
20 3/16	12 15/16	7 4/16	M	Burnett County	WI	Ronald Peterson	1996	980
20 3/16	12 9/16	7 10/16	M	Athabasca River	ALB	Ronald T. Morgan	1997	980
20 3/16	12 9/16	7 10/16	M	Kane Lake	SAS	Tim Lupia	1997	980
20 3/16	12 14/16	7 5/16	M	Aitkin County	MN	Keith Van Hale	1997	980
20 3/16	12 10/16	7 9/16	M	Peace River	ALB	Gary Day	1998	980
20 3/16	12 14/16	7 5/16	M	Duck Mtn.	SAS	Ron Vandermeulen	1998	980
20 3/16	12 7/16	7 12/16	M	St. Louis County	MN	David Steven Sobczak	1998	980
20 3/16	12 5/16	7 14/16	M	Beltrami County	MN	David Janssen	1998	980
20 3/16	12 12/16	7 7/16	M	Pow Island	AK	Bob Ameen	1999	980
20 3/16	12 1/16	8 2/16	M	Egenolf Lake	MAN	Buzz Marvin	1999	980
20 3/16	12 15/16	7 4/16	M	Baker County	OR	Michael S. Chandler	1999	980
20 3/16	12 12/16	7 7/16	M	Price County	WI	Daniel R. Kluck	1999	980
20 3/16	12 13/16	7 6/16	M	Hardy County	WV	Mark Murphy	1999	980
20 3/16	12 14/16	7 5/16	M	Wrangell Island	AK	Dave Brown	2000	980
20 3/16	12 6/16	7 13/16	M	Fort Chip	ALB	William R. Dzyak	2000	980
20 3/16	12 15/16	7 4/16	M	Bear Canyon	ALB	Geordie Lund	2000	980
20 3/16	12 13/16	7 6/16	M	Manitouwadge	ONT	Edward A. Neering	2000	980
20 3/16	13 0/16	7 3/16	M	Beltrami County	MN	Caio Cesolini	2000	980
20 3/16	12 7/16	7 12/16	M	Hubbard County	MN	Jeff Goebel	2000	980

135

BLACK BEAR

Minimum Score 18

Continued

SCORE	GREATEST LENGTH	GREATEST WIDTH	SEX	AREA	STATE/ PROVINCE	HUNTER'S NAME	DATE	RANK
20 3/16	12 15/16	7 4/16	M	Oconto County	WI	Gerard J. Baugnet	2000	980
20 3/16	12 5/16	7 14/16	M	Ulster County	NY	Anthony J. Lamonaca	2000	980
20 3/16	12 14/16	7 5/16	M	Gronlid	SAS	Chad Rohel	2001	980
20 3/16	12 10/16	7 9/16	M	Kississing Lake	MAN	Monte Hoggarth	2001	980
20 3/16	12 8/16	7 11/16	M	Tulare County	CA	Kyle Narasky	2001	980
20 3/16	12 11/16	7 8/16	M	Douglas County	WI	John Parker	2001	980
20 3/16	12 9/16	7 10/16	M	Price County	WI	Paul S. Zondlo	2001	980
20 3/16	12 12/16	7 7/16	M	Bronson Lake	SAS	Lynn Drechsel	2002	980
20 3/16	12 13/16	7 6/16	M	Deer Hill	ALB	Bradley Baird	2002	980
20 3/16	12 10/16	7 9/16	M	Catron County	NM	Alex Ternes	2003	980
20 3/16	12 11/16	7 8/16	M	Iron County	WI	Mark J. Henry	2003	980
20 3/16	12 6/16	7 13/16	M	Carswell Lake	SAS	Dan Dowling	2006	980
20 3/16	12 9/16	7 10/16	M	Elma	MAN	Joseph F. Schrader III	2006	980
20 3/16	12 9/16	7 10/16	M	Hampden County	MA	Phil Sulewski	2006	980
20 3/16	12 8/16	7 11/16	M	Lincoln County	WI	Ryan Domaszek	2006	980
20 3/16	12 8/16	7 11/16	M	Kosciusko Island	AK	Tyler E. Lauber	2007	980
*20 3/16	12 11/16	7 8/16	M	Kesoh Lake	MAN	Jacki Moellenberndt	2007	980
*20 3/16	12 13/16	7 6/16	M	Prince Albert	SAS	Lou Evans	2007	980
20 3/16	12 8/16	7 11/16	M	Polk County	MN	Jared L. Call	2007	980
20 3/16	12 10/16	7 9/16	M	Oconto County	WI	Dale Missall	2007	980
20 3/16	12 11/16	7 8/16	M	Oconto County	WI	Leighton J. Trice	2007	980
20 3/16	12 7/16	7 12/16	M	Grandview	MAN	Harold Opheim	2008	980
20 3/16	12 10/16	7 9/16	M	Sawyer County	WI	Mark Beise	2008	980
20 3/16	12 12/16	7 7/16	M	Hardy County	WV	Korey Foltz	2008	980
*20 3/16	12 11/16	7 8/16	M	Tulare County	CA	Nate Treadwell	2008	980
*20 3/16	12 9/16	7 10/16	M	Placer County	CA	Ed Chavez	2008	980
20 3/16	12 8/16	7 11/16	M	Laurier	MAN	Dave McLaughlin	2009	980
20 3/16	12 6/16	7 13/16	M	Buffalo Narrows	SAS	Terry Jackson	2009	980
*20 3/16	12 7/16	7 12/16	M	San Bernardino County	CA	Craig Davis	2009	980
20 3/16	12 12/16	7 7/16	M	Augusta County	VA	Sam Lyon	2009	980
20 3/16	12 7/16	7 12/16	M	Lake Wasekamio	SAS	Richard B. Dyer	2010	980
20 2/16	12 9/16	7 9/16	M	St. Louis County	MN	James Harwood	1966	1077
20 2/16	12 9/16	7 9/16	M	St. Louis County	MN	Ron Johnson	1968	1077
20 2/16	12 6/16	7 12/16	M	Bayfield County	WI	Clarence J. Biddle	1973	1077
20 2/16	12 6/16	7 12/16	M	Iron County	WI	Chuck Ramsay	1973	1077
20 2/16	12 9/16	7 9/16	M	Delta County	CO	Bill Izon	1976	1077
20 2/16	12 10/16	7 8/16	M	Montrose County	CO	John Brandt	1978	1077
20 2/16	12 12/16	7 6/16	M	Montezuma County	CO	Floyd H. Hicks	1978	1077
20 2/16	12 1/16	8 1/16	M	Del Norte County	CA	Fred D. Davis, Jr.	1978	1077
20 2/16	12 8/16	7 10/16	M	Mesa County	CO	Dennis Behn	1979	1077
20 2/16	12 6/16	7 12/16	M	Mendocino County	CA	Kenneth Marquardt	1981	1077
20 2/16	12 12/16	7 6/16	M	Tehama County	CA	Randy Rehse	1981	1077
20 2/16	12 9/16	7 9/16	M	Delta County	CO	Scott Dillon	1981	1077
20 2/16	12 12/16	7 6/16	M	Hudson Bay	SAS	Randy Lorenz	1982	1077
20 2/16	12 7/16	7 11/16	M	Iron County	MI	George J. Hronkin III	1982	1077
20 2/16	12 10/16	7 8/16	M	Douglas County	WI	Ron Ekstrand	1983	1077
20 2/16	12 6/16	7 12/16	M	Kuiu Island	AK	William F. Burgess	1984	1077
20 2/16	12 7/16	7 11/16	M	Meadow Lake	SAS	Richard W. Theurer	1984	1077
20 2/16	12 8/16	7 10/16	M	Nipigon	ONT	Richard Scorzafava	1985	1077
20 2/16	12 4/16	7 14/16	M	Sudbury	ONT	Ben L. Staponski	1986	1077
20 2/16	13 1/16	7 1/16	M	Sudbury	ONT	Frank Calabro	1986	1077
20 2/16	12 13/16	7 5/16	M	Chisago County	MN	Mark Piel	1986	1077
20 2/16	12 6/16	7 12/16	M	Mendocino County	CA	Patrick M. Griffin	1986	1077
20 2/16	12 8/16	7 10/16	M	Lake of the Woods	ONT	Karen Raasch	1987	1077
20 2/16	12 8/16	7 10/16	M	Duchesne County	UT	Kenneth M. Labrum	1988	1077
20 2/16	12 6/16	7 12/16	M	El Paso County	CO	Russ Nily	1988	1077
20 2/16	12 14/16	7 4/16	M	Pine County	MN	Brian D. Scarnegie	1988	1077
20 2/16	12 7/16	7 11/16	M	Crawford County	MI	Jerry D. Pratt	1988	1077
20 2/16	12 8/16	7 10/16	M	Meadow Lake	SAS	Ian Twidale	1989	1077
20 2/16	13 0/16	7 2/16	M	Beltrami County	MN	James Luverne Johnson	1989	1077
20 2/16	12 7/16	7 11/16	M	Marathon County	WI	Daniel Auner	1989	1077
20 2/16	12 9/16	7 9/16	M	Sullivan County	NY	John P. Dise	1989	1077
20 2/16	12 8/16	7 10/16	M	Rabun County	GA	Terry Tyler	1989	1077
20 2/16	12 8/16	7 10/16	M	Catron County	NM	Larry Joe Cearley	1990	1077
20 2/16	12 10/16	7 8/16	M	Latah County	ID	Mick McCullough	1990	1077
20 2/16	12 7/16	7 11/16	M	Fort McMurray	ALB	Ron LeBreton	1990	1077
20 2/16	12 11/16	7 7/16	M	Kuiu Island	AK	Joe Miguel	1991	1077
20 2/16	12 8/16	7 10/16	M	Fort McMurray	ALB	Fred Joseph	1991	1077
20 2/16	12 8/16	7 10/16	M	Fort McMurray	ALB	Margaret Whittle Hice	1991	1077
20 2/16	12 8/16	7 10/16	M	Rabun County	GA	Chuck Conner	1991	1077
20 2/16	12 10/16	7 8/16	M	Otero County	NM	Beto Gutierrez	1991	1077
20 2/16	12 4/16	7 14/16	M	Square Lake	ALB	Dave Stull	1992	1077
20 2/16	12 12/16	7 6/16	M	Monds Township	ONT	Jeff Standafer	1992	1077
20 2/16	12 6/16	7 12/16	M	Peace River	ALB	John Lindell	1992	1077
20 2/16	12 10/16	7 8/16	M	Sussex	NBW	Kamel K. Wozniak, Jr.	1993	1077
20 2/16	12 7/16	7 11/16	M	Green Lake	SAS	Pat DeMeglio	1993	1077
20 2/16	12 11/16	7 7/16	M	Emo	ONT	James R. Gabrick	1993	1077
20 2/16	12 7/16	7 11/16	M	Lincoln County	NM	Dennis Holt	1993	1077
20 2/16	12 4/16	7 14/16	M	Green Lake	SAS	John C."Jack" Culpepper III	1994	1077
20 2/16	12 6/16	7 12/16	M	Lac Ile-a-la-Crosse	SAS	Dr. D. Kirk Brown, MD	1994	1077
20 2/16	12 10/16	7 8/16	M	Cranberry Portage	MAN	B. Duane Kropf	1994	1077
20 2/16	12 6/16	7 12/16	M	Crow Wing County	MN	Tom Neu	1994	1077
20 2/16	12 13/16	7 5/16	M	Otero County	NM	Earl McClaflin	1994	1077
20 2/16	12 8/16	7 10/16	M	Red Lake	ONT	Arden L. Straw	1994	1077
20 2/16	12 9/16	7 9/16	M	Usherville	SAS	James Scott Todd	1995	1077
20 2/16	12 10/16	7 8/16	M	McNalley Lake	ALB	Donald A. Carpenter	1995	1077
20 2/16	12 12/16	7 6/16	M	Rainbow Lake	ALB	Edward J. Roskopf	1995	1077
20 2/16	12 2/16	8 0/16	M	Thunder Bay	ONT	Ian Robinson	1995	1077
20 2/16	12 6/16	7 12/16	M	Besnard Lake	SAS	Andy Milam	1995	1077
20 2/16	12 13/16	7 5/16	M	Marathon County	WI	David C. Arndt	1995	1077
20 2/16	12 7/16	7 11/16	M	Alma	NBW	Ed Kiker, Jr.	1995	1077
20 2/16	12 12/16	7 6/16	M	Kane Lake	SAS	Peeler G. Lacey, MD	1996	1077
20 2/16	12 11/16	7 7/16	M	Iron River	ALB	Michael J. Madaj	1996	1077
20 2/16	12 5/16	7 13/16	M	Mattawa	ONT	Brian Lafreniere	1996	1077
20 2/16	12 4/16	7 14/16	F	Taylor Mtn.	AK	Terry Joe Day	1996	1077

136

BLACK BEAR

Minimum Score 18 — Continued

SCORE	GREATEST LENGTH	GREATEST WIDTH	SEX	AREA	STATE/PROVINCE	HUNTER'S NAME	DATE	RANK
20 2/16	12 8/16	7 10/16	M	Burnett County	WI	Dan Muchow	1996	1077
20 2/16	12 12/16	7 6/16	M	McNalley Lake	ALB	Donnie Covey	1997	1077
20 2/16	12 7/16	7 11/16	M	Peace River	ALB	Cordie Schlomer	1997	1077
20 2/16	12 6/16	7 12/16	M	Chibougamau	QUE	Seth Stevens	1997	1077
20 2/16	12 8/16	7 10/16	M	Temiscaming	QUE	H. James Blamy	1997	1077
20 2/16	12 6/16	7 12/16	M	Prince of Wales Island	AK	Scott Ballem	1998	1077
20 2/16	12 8/16	7 10/16	M	Smooth Rock Falls	ONT	Matthew S. Emkow	1998	1077
20 2/16	12 10/16	7 8/16	M	Snow Lake	MAN	Charles R. Neuman	1999	1077
20 2/16	12 12/16	7 6/16	M	Dolores County	CO	Arthur E. Johnson	1999	1077
20 2/16	12 9/16	7 9/16	M	Gogebic County	MI	Michael A. Zacharias	1999	1077
20 2/16	11 15/16	8 3/16	M	Polk County	WI	Chad Alden	1999	1077
20 2/16	12 11/16	7 7/16	M	Hodgson	MAN	Carl Pugliese	2000	1077
20 2/16	12 11/16	7 7/16	M	Chitek Lake	SAS	Wayne B. Six	2000	1077
20 2/16	12 8/16	7 10/16	M	Dolores County	CO	Russ Hasler	2000	1077
20 2/16	12 13/16	7 5/16	F	Yorkton	SAS	Shawn Frankfurt	2001	1077
20 2/16	12 8/16	7 10/16	M	Victoria	NBW	Antonio Ercolano	2001	1077
20 2/16	12 6/16	7 12/16	M	Turnor Lake	SAS	Peter L. Bucklin	2002	1077
20 2/16	12 6/16	7 12/16	M	Kuiu Island	AK	Dirk Dieterich	2002	1077
20 2/16	12 3/16	7 15/16	M	Turnor Lake	SAS	Ralph Van Soest	2002	1077
20 2/16	12 13/16	7 5/16	M	Koochiching County	MN	Tom Wanke	2002	1077
20 2/16	12 12/16	7 6/16	M	Riding Mtn.	MAN	Michael L. Baker	2003	1077
20 2/16	12 7/16	7 11/16	M	Tulare County	CA	Allen O. Anderson	2003	1077
20 2/16	12 9/16	7 9/16	M	Flatbush	ALB	Keith Dvoroznak	2004	1077
20 2/16	12 10/16	7 8/16	M	Fair Harbour	BC	Adam Bartsch	2004	1077
*20 2/16	12 9/16	7 9/16	M	Prince of Wales Island	AK	Earl Chauvin	2004	1077
20 2/16	12 4/16	7 14/16	M	Carswell Lake	SAS	Stephen Kotz	2004	1077
20 2/16	12 11/16	7 7/16	M	Ashland County	WI	Darrell "Skip" Peterson	2004	1077
20 2/16	12 13/16	7 5/16	M	Delta County	MI	Wayne Umlor	2004	1077
20 2/16	12 11/16	7 7/16	M	Meander River	ALB	Dennis B. Hansen	2005	1077
20 2/16	12 5/16	7 13/16	M	Sandy Lake	MAN	Richard Service	2005	1077
20 2/16	12 7/16	7 11/16	M	Larimer County	CO	Robert Devore	2005	1077
20 2/16	12 7/16	7 11/16	M	Colfax County	NM	Bob Ameen	2005	1077
20 2/16	12 9/16	7 9/16	M	Mesa County	CO	Travis Crowley	2005	1077
*20 2/16	12 10/16	7 8/16	M	Kelvington	SAS	Steve German	2006	1077
20 2/16	12 6/16	7 12/16	M	White Swan Lake	SAS	Mark L. Stambaugh	2006	1077
20 2/16	12 3/16	7 15/16	M	La Tuque	QUE	Cindy Rothrock	2006	1077
20 2/16	12 8/16	7 10/16	M	Clisby Lake	MAN	James O. Moermond	2006	1077
*20 2/16	12 5/16	7 13/16	M	Rio Arriba County	NM	Glenn A. Brungardt	2006	1077
20 2/16	12 4/16	7 14/16	M	Kosciusko Island	AK	Lon E. Lauber	2007	1077
20 2/16	12 13/16	7 5/16	M	Itasca County	MN	Timothy P. Elich	2007	1077
20 2/16	12 13/16	7 5/16	M	Round Lake	SAS	Floyd Forster	2007	1077
*20 2/16	13 12/16	6 6/16	M	Grayson County	VA	Allen S. Jones	2008	1077
20 2/16	12 10/16	7 8/16	M	Pima County	AZ	Phillip C. Dalrymple	2009	1077
*20 2/16	12 10/16	7 8/16	M	Dubreuilville	ONT	Michael J. Weber	2009	1077
*20 2/16	12 11/16	7 7/16	M	Hawk Junction	ONT	Daniel P. Miller	2009	1077
20 2/16	12 5/16	7 13/16	M	Kuiu Island	AK	Frank S. Noska IV	2010	1077
20 1/16	12 9/16	7 8/16	M	Shasta County	CA	Robert G. Sinclair	1967	1187
20 1/16	12 5/16	7 12/16	M	Nipigon	ONT	Wilfred J. Ritchie, Jr.	1968	1187
20 1/16	12 6/16	7 11/16	M	Vilas County	WI	Ben Jones	1972	1187
20 1/16	11 15/16	8 2/16	M	Deep Creek, Ruby	AK	Harry Copeland	1976	1187
20 1/16	12 10/16	7 7/16	M	Cowlitz County	WA	Smokey Crews	1976	1187
20 1/16	12 10/16	7 7/16	M	Kitsap County	WA	Bud Jones	1977	1187
20 1/16	12 4/16	7 13/16	M	Montrose County	CO	Mike Barber	1978	1187
20 1/16	12 10/16	7 7/16	M	Grand County	UT	Thomas W. Newman	1979	1187
20 1/16	12 0/16	8 1/16	M	Vilas County	WI	Peter J. Leder	1979	1187
20 1/16	12 10/16	7 7/16	M	E. Braintree	MAN	Ed Beamish	1979	1187
20 1/16	12 4/16	7 13/16	M	Archuleta County	CO	Len Cardinale	1980	1187
20 1/16	12 3/16	7 14/16	M	Archuleta County	CO	Judd Cooney	1980	1187
20 1/16	12 10/16	7 7/16	M	Mistatim	SAS	Gregory Simoneau	1980	1187
20 1/16	12 6/16	7 11/16	M	Clark County	ID	Garry James Kite	1981	1187
20 1/16	12 5/16	7 12/16	M	Fremont County	ID	Nancy Atwood	1981	1187
20 1/16	12 6/16	7 11/16	M	Hudson Bay	SAS	Jerry Bien	1982	1187
20 1/16	12 6/16	7 11/16	M	Hudson Bay	SAS	Craig Richardson	1982	1187
20 1/16	12 9/16	7 8/16	M	Glenn County	CA	Ron Fonseca	1982	1187
20 1/16	13 0/16	7 1/16	M	Bladen County	NC	R. G. Harris	1983	1187
20 1/16	12 8/16	7 9/16	M	Fergus County	MT	Tom Storm	1984	1187
20 1/16	12 1/16	8 0/16	M	Powell County	MT	Gene Coughlin	1984	1187
20 1/16	12 4/16	7 13/16	M	Lost Lake	ONT	Gunter Lemke	1985	1187
20 1/16	12 7/16	7 10/16	M	Lewis County	WA	Keith Heldreth	1985	1187
20 1/16	12 5/16	7 12/16	M	Siskiyou County	CA	Stan Allison	1985	1187
20 1/16	12 10/16	7 7/16	M	Hudson Bay	SAS	Bill Zahradka	1987	1187
20 1/16	12 5/16	7 12/16	M	Ft. McMurray	ALB	Reg Adair	1987	1187
20 1/16	12 4/16	7 13/16	M	Sevier County	UT	Tom Dale Harrison	1988	1187
20 1/16	12 7/16	7 10/16	M	Carbon County	WY	Bill McEwen	1988	1187
20 1/16	12 8/16	7 9/16	M	Ft. McMurray	ALB	Darrin West	1989	1187
20 1/16	12 3/16	7 14/16	M	Williams Lake	BC	Don Davidson	1989	1187
20 1/16	12 8/16	7 9/16	M	Sioux Lookout	ONT	Jim Graf	1989	1187
20 1/16	12 8/16	7 9/16	M	Dryden	ONT	Alan E. Forbes	1989	1187
20 1/16	12 11/16	7 6/16	M	Clatsop County	OR	David Soyars	1989	1187
20 1/16	12 11/16	7 6/16	M	Keweenaw County	MI	Fred Embry Pickett	1989	1187
20 1/16	12 11/16	7 6/16	M	Flatbush	ALB	Steve Neuberger	1990	1187
20 1/16	12 8/16	7 9/16	M	Glenfell	ONT	Lucien Fecteau	1990	1187
20 1/16	12 9/16	7 8/16	M	Prince of Wales Island	AK	Dennis Sturgis, Jr.	1990	1187
20 1/16	12 6/16	7 11/16	M	Aitkin County	MN	William Gene Kuhlman	1990	1187
20 1/16	12 2/16	7 15/16	M	Bathurst	NBW	Norbert Legacy	1991	1187
20 1/16	12 10/16	7 7/16	M	Tulare County	CA	Dean Grommet	1991	1187
20 1/16	12 9/16	7 8/16	M	Union County	OR	Gregg Hargett	1991	1187
20 1/16	12 2/16	7 15/16	M	Prince of Wales Island	AK	Don Davidson	1991	1187
20 1/16	12 7/16	7 10/16	M	Harney County	OR	Marti Boatman	1991	1187
20 1/16	12 15/16	7 2/16	M	Whitemouth Lake	MAN	Serge L. Proulx	1991	1187
20 1/16	12 5/16	7 12/16	M	Dolores County	CO	Scott Williams	1992	1187
20 1/16	12 8/16	7 9/16	M	Lynn Lake	MAN	Bill Lilly, Jr.	1993	1187
20 1/16	12 5/16	7 12/16	M	Zec Dumoine	QUE	John Ross	1993	1187
20 1/16	12 10/16	7 7/16	M	Douglas County	WI	Bob Kaszynski	1993	1187
20 1/16	12 6/16	7 11/16	M	Rock Island Lake	ALB	Gilles A. Blouin	1994	1187

137

BLACK BEAR

Minimum Score 18 — Continued

SCORE	GREATEST LENGTH	GREATEST WIDTH	SEX	AREA	STATE/PROVINCE	HUNTER'S NAME	DATE	RANK
20 1/16	12 2/16	7 15/16	M	Nestor Falls	ONT	Mark S. Gerstein	1994	1187
20 1/16	12 9/16	7 8/16	M	Echo Bay	ONT	William McDonald	1994	1187
20 1/16	12 6/16	7 11/16	M	Price County	WI	Dale S. Karch	1994	1187
20 1/16	12 8/16	7 9/16	M	Prince of Wales Island	AK	Craig D. Morrow	1995	1187
20 1/16	12 8/16	7 9/16	M	Valleyview	ALB	Mark Kobe	1995	1187
20 1/16	12 1/16	8 0/16	M	El Dorado County	CA	Michael Davis	1995	1187
20 1/16	12 12/16	7 5/16	M	Oxford County	ME	Gary J. Russell	1997	1187
20 1/16	12 3/16	7 14/16	M	Buffalo Narrows	SAS	Corey T. Williams	1998	1187
20 1/16	12 5/16	7 12/16	M	Prince of Wales Island	AK	Bob Ameen	1998	1187
20 1/16	12 14/16	7 3/16	M	Wabasca River	ALB	Mark Kronyak	1998	1187
20 1/16	12 4/16	7 13/16	M	Sioux Narrows	ONT	Clint Arndt	1998	1187
20 1/16	12 5/16	7 12/16	M	Wingdam Lake	BC	Robert A. Veitch	1999	1187
20 1/16	12 4/16	7 13/16	M	St. George	NBW	James E. Beard	1999	1187
20 1/16	12 10/16	7 7/16	M	Tulare County	CA	John Campos	1999	1187
20 1/16	12 14/16	7 3/16	M	Burnett County	WI	Brad Alden	1999	1187
20 1/16	12 15/16	7 2/16	M	Webster County	WV	Johnny Robinson	1999	1187
20 1/16	12 7/16	7 10/16	M	Carrot River	SAS	Steve Lowdermilk	2000	1187
20 1/16	12 5/16	7 12/16	M	Amos	QUE	Timothy L. Ross	2000	1187
20 1/16	12 6/16	7 11/16	M	Douglas County	WI	Gary M. Bay	2000	1187
20 1/16	12 9/16	7 8/16	M	Cumberland House	SAS	William P. Gangel, Jr.	2001	1187
20 1/16	12 9/16	7 8/16	M	Missipuskiow River	SAS	Dennis J. Francais	2001	1187
20 1/16	12 13/16	7 4/16	M	Prince of Wales Island	AK	Ty A. Mocabee	2002	1187
20 1/16	12 6/16	7 11/16	M	Black Bear Island	SAS	Gary L. Mucilli	2002	1187
20 1/16	12 9/16	7 8/16	M	Aroostook County	ME	James M. Cooper	2002	1187
20 1/16	12 9/16	7 8/16	M	Bayfield County	WI	Jeff Adank	2002	1187
20 1/16	12 7/16	7 10/16	M	George Lake	SAS	Thomas E. Frisk	2003	1187
20 1/16	12 8/16	7 9/16	M	Britt	ONT	Ken Sloetjes	2003	1187
20 1/16	12 9/16	7 8/16	M	Olha	MAN	John Wooldridge	2003	1187
20 1/16	12 7/16	7 10/16	M	Aitkin County	MN	Gary Vetsch	2003	1187
20 1/16	12 9/16	7 8/16	M	Juneau County	WI	Jerry D. Bowen	2003	1187
20 1/16	12 15/16	7 2/16	M	Brandon	MAN	Anthony Janecek	2004	1187
20 1/16	12 6/16	7 11/16	M	Catron County	NM	Ken Castaneda	2004	1187
20 1/16	12 8/16	7 9/16	M	Kenora	ONT	Todd Christian	2004	1187
20 1/16	12 14/16	7 3/16	M	Steuben County	NY	Tim Rumsey	2004	1187
*20 1/16	12 11/16	7 6/16	M	Olha	MAN	Bill Clink	2005	1187
20 1/16	12 8/16	7 9/16	M	Prince of Wales Island	AK	Danny Moore	2005	1187
*20 1/16	12 4/16	7 13/16	M	Churchill River	SAS	Jim Leqve	2005	1187
20 1/16	12 8/16	7 9/16	M	Hudson Bay	SAS	Monte Reid	2005	1187
20 1/16	12 7/16	7 10/16	M	Armstrong	ONT	Frederic F. Nowak	2005	1187
20 1/16	12 9/16	7 8/16	M	Gogebic County	MI	Andrew Curtiss	2005	1187
20 1/16	12 5/16	7 12/16	M	Big River	SAS	Tyson Craney	2006	1187
*20 1/16	12 4/16	7 13/16	M	Jackson County	OR	Michael Jahnke	2006	1187
20 1/16	12 4/16	7 13/16	M	Sioux Lookout	ONT	Brad Guentzel	2006	1187
*20 1/16	12 8/16	7 9/16	F	Berkshire County	MA	Robert A. Arcott	2006	1187
20 1/16	12 7/16	7 10/16	M	Uintah County	UT	Thomas R. Day	2007	1187
*20 1/16	12 8/16	7 9/16	M	Grande Prairie	ALB	Michael Reel	2007	1187
*20 1/16	12 9/16	7 8/16	M	Rusk County	WI	Donn W. Kubnick	2007	1187
*20 1/16	12 11/16	7 6/16	M	Prince Edward County	VA	James L. Gridley	2007	1187
20 1/16	12 6/16	7 11/16	M	Reindeer Lake	SAS	Jesse R. Baldwin, Jr.	2008	1187
*20 1/16	12 2/16	7 15/16	M	Ignace	ONT	Jessie Lynn Sobczak	2008	1187
20 1/16	12 9/16	7 8/16	M	Langlade County	WI	Brian M. Wolfe	2008	1187
20 1/16	12 5/16	7 12/16	M	El Dorado County	CA	Michael J. McEntee	2008	1187
*20 1/16	12 11/16	7 6/16	M	Lane County	OR	James Laird	2008	1187
20 1/16	12 2/16	7 15/16	M	Skead	ONT	James M. Deckler	2008	1187
20 1/16	13 0/16	7 1/16	M	Mesa County	CO	David T. Pinnt	2008	1187
20 1/16	12 10/16	7 7/16	M	Olha	MAN	Bryan Klein	2009	1187
*20 1/16	12 14/16	7 3/16	M	Grandview	MAN	Patrick Earl Voss	2009	1187
20 1/16	12 8/16	7 9/16	M	Becker County	MN	Bruce Anderson	2009	1187
20 1/16	13 0/16	7 1/16	M	Sawyer County	WI	Glenn Mentink	2010	1187
20 0/16	12 10/16	7 6/16	M	Oneida County	WI	Fred Felbab	1964	1295
20 0/16	13 4/16	6 12/16	M	Cumberland County	TN	Louis Wix	1970	1295
20 0/16	12 4/16	7 12/16	M	Shasta County	CA	Jim Dougherty	1970	1295
20 0/16	12 11/16	7 5/16	M	Fremont County	ID	Earl Peterson	1978	1295
20 0/16	12 4/16	7 12/16	M	Kalkaska County	MI	Doug Daniels	1978	1295
20 0/16	12 9/16	7 7/16	M	Adams County	ID	Jack Arbaugh	1979	1295
20 0/16	12 10/16	7 6/16	M	Tehama County	CA	Jim Dueval	1980	1295
20 0/16	12 7/16	7 9/16	M	Prince George	BC	Ron F. McKay	1980	1295
20 0/16	12 10/16	7 6/16	M	Ear Falls	ONT	Richard Eldridge	1981	1295
20 0/16	12 5/16	7 11/16	M	Grand County	CO	Randy O. Vineyard	1981	1295
20 0/16	12 6/16	7 10/16	M	Red Lake	ONT	Donald Schram	1981	1295
20 0/16	12 6/16	7 10/16	M	Bobcaygeon	ONT	Arthur H. Whitney	1982	1295
20 0/16	12 7/16	7 9/16	M	Sierra County	NM	Ray Hatfield	1983	1295
20 0/16	12 5/16	7 11/16	M	Otter Lake	QUE	C. Roger Jerzerick	1983	1295
20 0/16	12 3/16	7 13/16	M	Wallowa County	OR	Bill Lancaster	1983	1295
20 0/16	12 7/16	7 9/16	M	Itasca County	MN	Roger Millard	1984	1295
20 0/16	12 6/16	7 10/16	M	Apache County	AZ	Robert E. David	1984	1295
20 0/16	12 8/16	7 8/16	M	Langlade County	WI	Jeff Traska	1984	1295
20 0/16	12 2/16	7 14/16	M	Cowlitz County	WA	Annette Crews	1985	1295
20 0/16	12 12/16	7 4/16	M	Meadow Lake	SAS	Robert Bain	1986	1295
20 0/16	12 3/16	7 13/16	M	Thunder Bay	ONT	Bob Vrbsky	1986	1295
20 0/16	12 8/16	7 8/16	M	Caribou County	ID	Coby Tigert	1986	1295
20 0/16	12 15/16	7 1/16	M	Aitkin County	MN	Scott H. Mogen	1986	1295
20 0/16	12 8/16	7 8/16	M	Cold Lake	ALB	Glenn Moir	1987	1295
20 0/16	12 6/16	7 10/16	M	Pinehurst Lake	ALB	Jay Stewart	1988	1295
20 0/16	12 11/16	7 5/16	M	King County	WA	Brent R. Perschon	1988	1295
20 0/16	12 11/16	7 5/16	M	Lake of the Woods Cty	MN	Dallas Vanden Einde	1988	1295
20 0/16	12 5/16	7 11/16	M	Gogebic County	MI	Ted Nugent	1988	1295
20 0/16	12 6/16	7 10/16	M	Elmore County	ID	Mark E. Zastrow	1989	1295
20 0/16	12 5/16	7 11/16	M	Graham	ONT	Ian Robinson	1989	1295
20 0/16	12 5/16	7 11/16	M	Carbon County	UT	Dave Scott	1989	1295
20 0/16	12 4/16	7 12/16	M	Sudbury	ONT	Ray Hatfield	1989	1295
20 0/16	12 8/16	7 8/16	M	High Prairie	ALB	Thomas Hlinka	1989	1295
20 0/16	12 8/16	7 8/16	M	Wallowa County	OR	Terry Garbacik	1989	1295
20 0/16	12 5/16	7 11/16	M	Iron County	WI	R. Joe Maciejewski	1989	1295
20 0/16	12 9/16	7 7/16	M	Crawford County	MI	Jerry D. Pratt	1989	1295

BLACK BEAR

Minimum Score 18   Continued

SCORE	GREATEST LENGTH	GREATEST WIDTH	SEX	AREA	STATE/ PROVINCE	HUNTER'S NAME	DATE	RANK
20 0/16	12 8/16	7 8/16	M	Catron County	NM	Dr. Dale Mansfield	1989	1295
20 0/16	12 10/16	7 6/16	M	Ile-a-La-Crosse	SAS	Michael D Tofte	1990	1295
20 0/16	12 6/16	7 10/16	M	Kenora	ONT	Steven G. Dennis	1990	1295
20 0/16	12 0/16	8 0/16	M	Seibert Lake	ALB	Keith Dana	1990	1295
20 0/16	12 6/16	7 10/16	M	Garfield County	CO	Gus Sexauer	1990	1295
20 0/16	12 12/16	7 4/16	M	Fraser River	BC	Dave Hannas	1990	1295
20 0/16	12 3/16	7 13/16	M	Cowlitz County	WA	Edward H. Soyars	1991	1295
20 0/16	12 10/16	7 6/16	M	Pine County	MN	Tom Katt	1991	1295
20 0/16	12 6/16	7 10/16	M	Catron County	NM	Bruce Carlisle	1991	1295
20 0/16	12 12/16	7 4/16	M	Douglas County	WI	Philip Stener	1991	1295
20 0/16	12 7/16	7 9/16	M	Bissett	MAN	David Harris	1992	1295
20 0/16	12 12/16	7 4/16	M	Red Earth	ALB	Dave Bathke	1992	1295
20 0/16	12 8/16	7 8/16	M	Thompson	MAN	Jack Baltz	1992	1295
20 0/16	12 4/16	7 12/16	M	Robinson Township	ONT	Tom Harper	1992	1295
20 0/16	12 9/16	7 7/16	M	Hudson Bay	SAS	Lawrence Gulka	1992	1295
20 0/16	12 3/16	7 13/16	M	St. Calixte	QUE	Brian D. Hurd	1992	1295
20 0/16	12 8/16	7 8/16	M	Dryden	ONT	Bryan Moorefield	1993	1295
20 0/16	12 11/16	7 5/16	M	Itasca County	MN	Douglas Anderson	1993	1295
20 0/16	12 8/16	7 8/16	M	Pine County	MN	Dean K. Reidt	1993	1295
20 0/16	12 7/16	7 9/16	M	High Level	ALB	Keith Corporon	1994	1295
20 0/16	12 9/16	7 7/16	M	Fort McMurray	ALB	David W. Stuhr	1994	1295
20 0/16	12 7/16	7 9/16	M	Williamson Township	ONT	Maurice Benoit	1994	1295
20 0/16	12 2/16	7 14/16	M	Lac Seul	ONT	James Kurth	1994	1295
20 0/16	12 6/16	7 10/16	M	Crooked Creek	ALB	Rick Martin	1994	1295
20 0/16	12 3/16	7 13/16	M	Carlton County	MN	Tom King	1994	1295
20 0/16	12 0/16	8 0/16	M	Oneida County	WI	Chad Leal	1994	1295
20 0/16	12 4/16	7 12/16	M	Hornepayne	ONT	Jeff Holland	1995	1295
20 0/16	12 8/16	7 8/16	M	Vancouver Island	BC	Bruce Kuykendall	1995	1295
20 0/16	12 0/16	8 0/16	M	Poplarfield	MAN	Edwin J. Smith	1995	1295
20 0/16	12 9/16	7 7/16	M	Kahiltna River	AK	Danny J. Germany	1995	1295
20 0/16	12 10/16	7 6/16	M	Laurier	MAN	Bobby Joe Furlow	1995	1295
20 0/16	12 2/16	7 14/16	M	Rio Arriba County	NM	James Goss, Jr.	1995	1295
20 0/16	12 4/16	7 12/16	M	Perrault Falls	ONT	Scott A. Cisewski	1995	1295
20 0/16	12 11/16	7 5/16	M	Marquette County	MI	Gary Corlew	1995	1295
20 0/16	12 9/16	7 7/16	M	Ranger Lake	ONT	Bill McDonald	1995	1295
20 0/16	12 9/16	7 7/16	F	Price County	WI	David Pepper	1995	1295
20 0/16	12 5/16	7 11/16	M	Fresno County	CA	Alfredo Flores	1995	1295
20 0/16	12 14/16	7 2/16	M	Besnard Lake	SAS	Scotty Reynolds	1996	1295
20 0/16	12 7/16	7 9/16	M	Swan River	MAN	David A. Little	1996	1295
20 0/16	12 10/16	7 6/16	M	Bayfield County	WI	Blaine Wollin	1996	1295
20 0/16	12 15/16	7 1/16	M	Sawyer County	WI	Anthony R. Aaron	1996	1295
20 0/16	12 10/16	7 6/16	M	Vermette Lake	SAS	Ronald F. Lax	1997	1295
20 0/16	12 9/16	7 7/16	M	Kane Lake	SAS	Richard A. Jacobs	1997	1295
20 0/16	12 8/16	7 8/16	M	Tulare County	CA	Frank Birtcher	1997	1295
20 0/16	12 10/16	7 6/16	M	Barron County	WI	Kevin M. Gilles	1997	1295
20 0/16	12 11/16	7 5/16	M	Park County	MT	Larry Schwend	1997	1295
20 0/16	12 4/16	7 12/16	M	Snow Lake	MAN	Mike J. Sutter	1998	1295
20 0/16	12 11/16	7 5/16	M	Kenora	ONT	Dick Schwab	1998	1295
20 0/16	12 7/16	7 9/16	M	Dauphin River	MAN	Reginald Robillard	1998	1295
20 0/16	12 10/16	7 6/16	M	Greenlee County	AZ	Michael Wayne Spivey	1998	1295
20 0/16	12 9/16	7 7/16	M	Cumberland House	SAS	Mark Mazar	1999	1295
20 0/16	11 13/16	8 3/16	M	St. Paul	NBW	Algurt G. Cudney	1999	1295
20 0/16	12 9/16	7 7/16	M	Sawyer County	WI	Tony Aaron	1999	1295
20 0/16	12 4/16	7 12/16	M	High Level	ALB	Brian R. Butkiewicz	2000	1295
20 0/16	12 14/16	7 2/16	M	Livingston	SAS	Michael J. Wachowski	2000	1295
20 0/16	12 3/16	7 13/16	M	Kittitas County	WA	Nick Mayer	2000	1295
20 0/16	12 6/16	7 10/16	M	Prince of Wales Island	AK	Connie Renfro	2001	1295
20 0/16	12 11/16	7 5/16	M	Meadow Lake	SAS	Henri Lazar	2001	1295
20 0/16	12 6/16	7 10/16	M	Meadow Lake	SAS	Josh Hansen	2001	1295
20 0/16	12 2/16	7 14/16	M	Wolf Lake	ALB	Kevin Pardely	2001	1295
20 0/16	12 15/16	7 1/16	M	Wawa	ONT	Jay J. Kaster	2001	1295
20 0/16	12 5/16	7 11/16	M	Dog Lake	ONT	Dave McKenzie	2001	1295
20 0/16	12 0/16	8 0/16	M	Cass County	MN	Randy Schultz	2001	1295
20 0/16	12 10/16	7 6/16	M	Sawyer County	WI	Kirk L. Haugestuen	2001	1295
20 0/16	12 5/16	7 11/16	M	Catron County	NM	Gary Swinson	2001	1295
20 0/16	12 6/16	7 10/16	M	Laurier	MAN	Joseph M. Malloch	2002	1295
20 0/16	12 7/16	7 9/16	M	Wollaston Lake	SAS	Paul Czekuc	2002	1295
20 0/16	12 6/16	7 10/16	M	Redditt	ONT	Jeffery J. Coates	2002	1295
20 0/16	12 6/16	7 10/16	M	Cold Lake	SAS	Jeffrey M. Lade	2003	1295
20 0/16	12 12/16	7 4/16	M	Carrot River	SAS	Cal Weber	2003	1295
20 0/16	12 6/16	7 10/16	M	File Lake	MAN	Tim Doner	2003	1295
*20 0/16	12 7/16	7 9/16	M	Pima County	AZ	Chip Beiner	2003	1295
20 0/16	12 9/16	7 7/16	M	Routt County	CO	Gary Wissmueller	2003	1295
20 0/16	12 2/16	7 14/16	M	Oconto County	WI	Perry O. Kepler	2003	1295
20 0/16	12 14/16	7 2/16	M	Saskatchewan River	SAS	Gary Fidyk	2004	1295
20 0/16	11 7/16	8 9/16	M	Namur Lake	ALB	Stephen R. Haufsk	2004	1295
20 0/16	12 9/16	7 7/16	M	Caribou County	ID	Gregory Ryan Pimentel	2004	1295
20 0/16	12 8/16	7 8/16	M	Canoe Lake	SAS	Arnold DeCastro	2004	1295
20 0/16	12 7/16	7 9/16	M	Lincoln County	WI	Ken Alft	2004	1295
20 0/16	12 3/16	7 13/16	M	Prince of Wales Island	AK	Tracy Hicks	2004	1295
20 0/16	12 9/16	7 7/16	M	Port Alberni	BC	Carroll Moran	2005	1295
20 0/16	12 8/16	7 8/16	M	Saddle Hills	ALB	Terry Hagman	2005	1295
20 0/16	12 10/16	7 6/16	M	Madison County	ID	Sarah Perry	2005	1295
20 0/16	12 6/16	7 10/16	M	Whiteshell	MAN	Ron Kehler	2005	1295
20 0/16	12 11/16	7 5/16	M	Eriksdale	MAN	Mark R. Popp	2006	1295
20 0/16	12 4/16	7 12/16	M	San Juan County	UT	Mark Turner	2006	1295
*20 0/16	12 9/16	7 7/16	M	Caramat	ONT	Dennis J. Sumbera	2006	1295
20 0/16	12 3/16	7 13/16	M	Rappahannock County	VA	Thomas Walton Mansmann	2006	1295
20 0/16	12 8/16	7 8/16	M	Hardy County	WV	Noah Long	2006	1295
20 0/16	12 11/16	7 5/16	M	Jim Lake	SAS	Michael D. Tofte	2007	1295
20 0/16	12 2/16	7 14/16	M	La Ronge	SAS	Wade Schwake	2007	1295
*20 0/16	12 7/16	7 9/16	M	Taylor County	WI	Jeremy Shramek	2007	1295
20 0/16	12 13/16	7 3/16	M	Rossburn	MAN	Tim Yaremchuk	2008	1295
20 0/16	12 0/16	8 0/16	M	Las Animas County	CO	Eric Coe	2008	1295
20 0/16	12 6/16	7 10/16	M	Scott County	AR	Dawaine Nix	2008	1295

BLACK BEAR

Minimum Score 18   Continued

SCORE	GREATEST LENGTH	GREATEST WIDTH	SEX	AREA	STATE/ PROVINCE	HUNTER'S NAME	DATE	RANK
20 0/16	12 6/16	7 10/16	M	Woman River	ONT	Jon Clark	2008	1295
20 0/16	12 8/16	7 8/16	M	Alpine County	CA	James R. Jarvis	2008	1295
20 0/16	12 6/16	7 10/16	M	Carleton	NBW	Salvatore La Russo	2009	1295
*20 0/16	12 4/16	7 12/16	M	Sublette County	WY	Karen J. Clause	2010	1295
19 15/16	11 15/16	8 0/16	F	Iron County	WI	Robert W. Blair	1967	1430
19 15/16	12 7/16	7 8/16	M	Blind River	ONT	John Lee	1973	1430
19 15/16	12 0/16	7 15/16	M	Bayfield County	WI	Gary P. Kalal	1973	1430
19 15/16	12 8/16	7 7/16	M	Dryden	ONT	Robert C. Kirschner	1974	1430
19 15/16	12 3/16	7 12/16	M	Conejos County	CO	Joseph Strasser, Jr.	1978	1430
19 15/16	12 4/16	7 11/16	M	Grande Prairie	ALB	Wolf Hoffman	1979	1430
19 15/16	12 1/16	7 14/16	M	Gunnison County	CO	Arthur Pace	1980	1430
19 15/16	12 8/16	7 7/16	M	Florence County	WI	Peter H. Kortenhorn	1981	1430
19 15/16	12 7/16	7 8/16	M	Dolores County	CO	Stanley A. Coval	1981	1430
19 15/16	12 2/16	7 13/16	M	Ear Falls	ONT	Mike Woolman	1981	1430
19 15/16	11 14/16	8 1/16	M	Penobscot County	ME	Henry C. Williams III	1983	1430
19 15/16	12 3/16	7 12/16	M	Sandoval County	NM	James M. Finn	1984	1430
19 15/16	12 9/16	7 6/16	M	Burnett County	WI	Jerry Strese	1984	1430
19 15/16	12 8/16	7 7/16	M	Baker County	OR	Steven E. Lewis	1986	1430
19 15/16	12 0/16	7 15/16	M	Dryden	ONT	Lane Foshee	1987	1430
19 15/16	12 4/16	7 11/16	M	Pine County	MN	Randy Broz	1987	1430
19 15/16	12 7/16	7 8/16	M	Carrot River	SAS	Ron Gunwall	1988	1430
19 15/16	12 1/16	7 14/16	M	Pickerel River	ONT	Walter L. Douglas	1988	1430
19 15/16	12 10/16	7 5/16	M	Garfield County	CO	James Bowerman	1988	1430
19 15/16	12 13/16	7 2/16	M	Douglas County	WI	Timothy E. Freid	1988	1430
19 15/16	12 9/16	7 6/16	M	Chippewa County	MI	Edwin A. Armentrout	1988	1430
19 15/16	12 5/16	7 10/16	M	Clearwater County	ID	John H. Dyche	1989	1430
19 15/16	12 4/16	7 11/16	M	Grande Prairie	ALB	Ron Jungwirth	1990	1430
19 15/16	12 9/16	7 6/16	M	Wahkiakum County	WA	Brandon Casey	1990	1430
19 15/16	12 9/16	7 6/16	M	Jackson County	OR	Joe Holland	1990	1430
19 15/16	12 9/16	7 6/16	M	Bayfield County	WI	Jeffrey Tuescher	1990	1430
19 15/16	12 4/16	7 11/16	M	Torrance County	NM	Eric Montoya	1990	1430
19 15/16	12 7/16	7 8/16	M	Prince of Wales Island	AK	Chuck Lynde	1991	1430
19 15/16	12 5/16	7 10/16	M	Kenora	ONT	Gary Liebsch	1991	1430
19 15/16	12 3/16	7 12/16	M	La Ronge	SAS	James E. Hummel	1992	1430
19 15/16	12 7/16	7 8/16	M	Prince of Wales Island	AK	Don Vernay	1992	1430
19 15/16	12 2/16	7 13/16	M	Matagami	QUE	Jacques Harvey	1992	1430
19 15/16	12 8/16	7 7/16	M	Riding Mtn.	MAN	Robert J. Wech	1992	1430
19 15/16	12 5/16	7 10/16	M	Ear Falls	ONT	Fay Williams, Jr.	1992	1430
19 15/16	12 8/16	7 7/16	M	Price County	WI	Gary L. Hintz	1992	1430
19 15/16	12 3/16	7 12/16	M	Missaukee County	MI	Owen Anderson	1992	1430
19 15/16	12 7/16	7 8/16	M	Wapawekka Lake	SAS	Douglas R. Peterson	1993	1430
19 15/16	12 5/16	7 10/16	M	Price County	WI	Les Strunk	1993	1430
19 15/16	12 2/16	7 13/16	M	Tulare County	CA	Gary W. Thurow	1993	1430
19 15/16	12 7/16	7 8/16	M	Entwhistle	ALB	Andre Titley	1994	1430
19 15/16	12 8/16	7 7/16	M	McNalley Lake	ALB	Jody Davis	1994	1430
19 15/16	12 12/16	7 3/16	M	Carrot River	SAS	Craig Kaczmarek	1994	1430
19 15/16	12 4/16	7 11/16	M	Aitkin County	MN	Dennis Winzenburg	1994	1430
19 15/16	12 6/16	7 9/16	M	Crawford County	MI	Terry Bart Paladino	1994	1430
19 15/16	12 3/16	7 12/16	M	Prince of Wales Island	AK	Bob Ameen	1995	1430
19 15/16	12 10/16	7 5/16	M	Trapper Creek	AK	William Simmang	1995	1430
19 15/16	12 14/16	7 1/16	M	Frenchman Butte	SAS	Donald Wayne Wright	1996	1430
19 15/16	12 5/16	7 10/16	M	Sioux Lookout	ONT	Scott A. Johnson	1996	1430
19 15/16	12 8/16	7 7/16	M	Hearst	ONT	Kenneth Neal Onken	1996	1430
19 15/16	12 8/16	7 7/16	M	Atikokan	ONT	Lynn Reese	1996	1430
19 15/16	12 6/16	7 9/16	M	Chilako River	BC	Emile Matte	1997	1430
19 15/16	12 8/16	7 7/16	M	Navajo County	AZ	Alfred J. Gemrich	1997	1430
19 15/16	12 4/16	7 11/16	M	Redditt	ONT	Don K. Petersen	1997	1430
19 15/16	12 9/16	7 6/16	M	Lake Nipigon	ONT	Andrew Van Timmeren	1997	1430
19 15/16	12 6/16	7 9/16	M	Parry Sound	ONT	Greg Peters	1997	1430
19 15/16	12 6/16	7 9/16	M	Biscotasing	ONT	Thomas Hlinka	1997	1430
19 15/16	12 14/16	7 1/16	M	Grant County	NM	Mike Scarsella	1997	1430
19 15/16	12 7/16	7 8/16	M	Elmore County	ID	Bill Magnusson	1997	1430
19 15/16	12 8/16	7 7/16	M	Douglas County	WI	David Hudacek	1997	1430
19 15/16	12 3/16	7 12/16	M	Missaukee County	MI	Dawn M. Adlen	1997	1430
19 15/16	12 5/16	7 10/16	M	Athabasca River	ALB	Leonard Anglewitz	1998	1430
19 15/16	12 5/16	7 10/16	M	High Level	ALB	Ray Farley	1998	1430
19 15/16	12 5/16	7 10/16	M	Kelvington	SAS	Cameron Hayden	1998	1430
19 15/16	12 12/16	7 3/16	M	Cass County	MN	Ron Patterson	1998	1430
19 15/16	12 10/16	7 5/16	M	Owl River	ALB	Dennis Dunkle	1999	1430
19 15/16	12 8/16	7 7/16	M	Dolores County	CO	Jeremy Roetz	1999	1430
19 15/16	12 9/16	7 6/16	M	Montezuma County	CO	Craig N. Johnson	1999	1430
19 15/16	12 10/16	7 5/16	M	Bayfield County	WI	Rick Ruetten	1999	1430
19 15/16	12 5/16	7 10/16	M	Buffalo Narrows	SAS	Steve Koskela	2000	1430
19 15/16	11 15/16	8 0/16	M	Dipper Lake	SAS	Mark McQueen	2000	1430
19 15/16	12 1/16	7 14/16	M	Snow Lake	MAN	Dan R. Worthington	2000	1430
19 15/16	12 2/16	7 13/16	M	Val-d'Or	QUE	Bryant Shermoe	2000	1430
19 15/16	12 7/16	7 8/16	M	Blueberry Hill	ALB	Bert Harlow	2000	1430
19 15/16	12 2/16	7 13/16	M	Douglas County	WI	Jeffrey C. Vian	2000	1430
19 15/16	12 2/16	7 13/16	M	Gillam	MAN	Bob Temple	2001	1430
19 15/16	12 7/16	7 8/16	M	La Plata County	CO	Samuel H. Stites	2001	1430
19 15/16	12 4/16	7 11/16	M	Prince of Wales Island	AK	Kelly J. King	2002	1430
19 15/16	12 0/16	7 15/16	M	Chilanko Forks	BC	Allan Tew	2002	1430
19 15/16	12 8/16	7 7/16	M	Grew Lake	ALB	Lowell T. Driver	2002	1430
19 15/16	12 13/16	7 2/16	M	Forest County	WI	Thomas R. Walters	2002	1430
19 15/16	12 7/16	7 8/16	M	Windham County	VT	Michael Budrewicz, Jr.	2002	1430
19 15/16	12 5/16	7 10/16	M	Ulster County	NY	Richard Soehngen	2002	1430
*19 15/16	12 13/16	7 2/16	M	Gilmer County	GA	Richard Esparza	2003	1430
19 15/16	12 6/16	7 9/16	M	Maple Lake	NS	Marc J. Ruyak	2004	1430
19 15/16	12 3/16	7 12/16	M	Jackson County	OR	James Dyer	2005	1430
19 15/16	12 7/16	7 8/16	M	Big Salt Lake	AK	Roy N. Leach	2006	1430
*19 15/16	12 1/16	7 14/16	M	Piscataquis County	ME	Lawrence S. Pyne	2006	1430
*19 15/16	12 1/16	7 14/16	M	Bancroft	ONT	Earl W. Edwards III	2006	1430
19 15/16	12 3/16	7 12/16	M	Alpine County	CA	Casey J. Nelson	2006	1430
*19 15/16	12 11/16	7 4/16	M	Westlock	ALB	Ronald Johnson	2007	1430
19 15/16	12 5/16	7 10/16	M	Wanless	MAN	Scott Rehak	2007	1430

140

BLACK BEAR

Minimum Score 18   Continued

SCORE	GREATEST LENGTH	GREATEST WIDTH	SEX	AREA	STATE/ PROVINCE	HUNTER'S NAME	DATE	RANK
*19 15/16	12 8/16	7 7/16	M	Gila County	AZ	Shawn Kaul	2008	1430
19 15/16	12 8/16	7 7/16	M	Eureka	AK	Charles W. Mahlen, Jr.	2009	1430
19 15/16	12 7/16	7 8/16	M	Mons Lake	ONT	Michael D. Saam	2009	1430
19 15/16	12 7/16	7 8/16	M	Kuiu Island	AK	Frank S. Noska IV	2010	1430
*19 15/16	12 9/16	7 6/16	M	Porcupine Hills	MAN	M. Blake Patton	2010	1430
19 14/16	12 2/16	7 12/16	M	Routt County	CO	Ronald C. Gravenkemper	1962	1526
19 14/16	12 2/16	7 12/16	M	Colcord Mtn.	AZ	Hugh Pearson	1963	1526
19 14/16	12 5/16	7 9/16	M	Rio Blanco County	CO	H. R. 'Dutch' Wambold	1969	1526
19 14/16	12 4/16	7 10/16	M	La Plata County	CO	Wayne E. Knisley	1971	1526
19 14/16	12 12/16	7 2/16	M	Tulare County	CA	Ronald J. Wade	1972	1526
19 14/16	12 0/16	7 14/16	M	Mesa County	CO	Clint Johnston	1973	1526
19 14/16	12 4/16	7 10/16	M	Ignace	ONT	Thomas Tietz	1977	1526
19 14/16	12 3/16	7 11/16	M	Thunder Bay	ONT	Lester W. Jass	1978	1526
19 14/16	12 2/16	7 12/16	M	Gunnison County	CO	Robert Feller	1979	1526
19 14/16	12 5/16	7 9/16	M	Marinette County	WI	Paul B. Pelzek	1979	1526
19 14/16	12 4/16	7 10/16	M	Routt County	CO	Mark Chapman	1979	1526
19 14/16	12 7/16	7 7/16	M	Sandoval County	NM	Mark Johnson	1980	1526
19 14/16	12 12/16	7 2/16	M	Hudson Bay	SAS	Jerry Bien	1980	1526
19 14/16	12 6/16	7 8/16	M	Baraga County	MI	Thomas G. Young	1981	1526
19 14/16	12 6/16	7 8/16	M	Glenn County	CA	Guy W. Foster	1982	1526
19 14/16	12 8/16	7 6/16	M	Duck Mtn.	MAN	John "Jack" Cordes	1983	1526
19 14/16	12 5/16	7 9/16	M	Mesa County	CO	Raymond Roussett, Jr.	1983	1526
19 14/16	12 5/16	7 9/16	M	Ear Falls	ONT	Brent Allen Poindexter	1985	1526
19 14/16	12 11/16	7 3/16	M	Kootenai County	ID	John S. Thomson, Jr.	1986	1526
19 14/16	12 4/16	7 10/16	M	Boise County	ID	Scott Privette	1986	1526
19 14/16	12 8/16	7 6/16	M	Little Susitna River	AK	Brett Blessing	1986	1526
19 14/16	12 5/16	7 9/16	M	Elmore County	ID	Ed Sweet	1988	1526
19 14/16	12 3/16	7 11/16	M	Dolores County	CO	Bill Corley	1988	1526
19 14/16	12 5/16	7 9/16	M	Warren	ONT	Gary Lawrence Harding	1988	1526
19 14/16	12 14/16	7 0/16	M	Douglas County	WI	Dale Jaworski	1988	1526
19 14/16	12 4/16	7 10/16	M	Delta County	CO	Rick L. Gillenwater	1989	1526
19 14/16	12 7/16	7 7/16	M	Dryden	ONT	Jeffrey R. Beilke	1989	1526
19 14/16	12 4/16	7 10/16	M	Green Lake	SAS	Fortunato Cuevas	1989	1526
19 14/16	12 7/16	7 7/16	M	Fredericton	NBW	Edward J. Bleau	1989	1526
19 14/16	12 4/16	7 10/16	M	Deep River	ONT	Rand J. Moore	1989	1526
19 14/16	12 1/16	7 13/16	M	Luce County	MI	Terry L. Cook	1989	1526
19 14/16	12 10/16	7 4/16	M	Clearwater County	ID	John M. Ramsey	1990	1526
19 14/16	12 7/16	7 7/16	M	Cumberland House	SAS	Jim Jarvis	1991	1526
19 14/16	12 5/16	7 9/16	M	Ile-a-La-Crosse	SAS	Gary Schwieters	1991	1526
19 14/16	12 4/16	7 10/16	M	Grand County	UT	Royce Carroll	1991	1526
19 14/16	12 7/16	7 7/16	M	Dryden	ONT	Bruce E. Crocker	1991	1526
19 14/16	12 8/16	7 6/16	M	Peace River	ALB	Cal Clevenger	1992	1526
19 14/16	12 7/16	7 7/16	M	Frog Lake	ALB	Mark Stevens	1992	1526
19 14/16	12 9/16	7 5/16	M	Pine County	MN	Kirk D. Grupa	1992	1526
19 14/16	12 10/16	7 4/16	M	Kitsap County	WA	Kenneth W. Holmes	1992	1526
19 14/16	12 8/16	7 6/16	M	Sawyer County	WI	Daniel T. Seibert	1992	1526
19 14/16	12 4/16	7 10/16	M	Zionville	NBW	Anthony "Del" DelMastro	1992	1526
19 14/16	12 4/16	7 10/16	M	Red Lake	ONT	John W. Flies	1993	1526
19 14/16	12 5/16	7 9/16	M	Christopher Lake	SAS	Richie Bland	1994	1526
19 14/16	12 10/16	7 4/16	M	St. Isadore	ALB	Charles R. Leidheiser	1994	1526
19 14/16	12 8/16	7 6/16	M	St. Louis County	MN	Mark J. Haus	1994	1526
19 14/16	12 6/16	7 8/16	M	Marshall County	MN	Tony Hoglo	1994	1526
19 14/16	12 10/16	7 4/16	M	Riding Mtn.	MAN	Mike T. Berceau	1994	1526
19 14/16	12 11/16	7 3/16	M	Creighton	SAS	Aaron Abaurrea	1995	1526
19 14/16	12 12/16	7 2/16	M	Ear Falls	ONT	John W. Flies	1996	1526
19 14/16	12 7/16	7 7/16	M	Carrot River	SAS	Kevin Kaczmarek	1996	1526
19 14/16	12 7/16	7 7/16	M	Duck Mtns.	MAN	Al Kuntz	1996	1526
19 14/16	12 6/16	7 8/16	M	Price County	WI	William T. Zeman	1996	1526
19 14/16	12 12/16	7 2/16	M	Washburn County	WI	Jerre Lerum	1996	1526
19 14/16	12 7/16	7 7/16	M	Mackinac County	MI	Wade Nixon	1996	1526
19 14/16	12 2/16	7 12/16	M	Sioux Lookout	ONT	Randall McPherson	1997	1526
19 14/16	12 6/16	7 8/16	M	Kenora	ONT	Dick Schwab	1997	1526
19 14/16	12 2/16	7 12/16	M	Falher	ALB	Jody Kellnhofer	1997	1526
19 14/16	12 4/16	7 10/16	M	San Juan County	NM	Jim Willems	1997	1526
19 14/16	12 9/16	7 5/16	M	Boone County	WV	Earl Albu	1997	1526
19 14/16	12 5/16	7 9/16	M	Seamore Canal	AK	Jerry Karsky	1998	1526
19 14/16	12 8/16	7 6/16	M	Grande Prairie	ALB	Jeff Davis	1998	1526
19 14/16	12 10/16	7 4/16	M	Navajo County	AZ	V. Randy Liljenquist	1998	1526
19 14/16	12 9/16	7 5/16	M	Kanabec County	MN	Michael F. Hertenstein	1998	1526
19 14/16	12 7/16	7 7/16	M	Kenora	ONT	Brad Hering	1998	1526
19 14/16	12 8/16	7 6/16	M	Archuleta County	CO	Don J. Papczynski	1998	1526
19 14/16	12 9/16	7 5/16	M	Shawano County	WI	Brett A. Olson	1998	1526
19 14/16	12 10/16	7 4/16	M	Pierceland	SAS	Kay C. Kimmich	1999	1526
19 14/16	12 6/16	7 8/16	M	Peace River	ALB	Rodney Alexander	1999	1526
19 14/16	12 4/16	7 10/16	M	Green Hill	NBW	Richard A. Hutchins, Jr.	1999	1526
19 14/16	12 7/16	7 7/16	M	Barron County	WI	Gerald L. Weinert	1999	1526
19 14/16	12 7/16	7 7/16	M	North Seal River	MAN	John McCurry	2000	1526
19 14/16	12 10/16	7 4/16	M	Sawyer County	WI	Roger P. Rucinski	2000	1526
19 14/16	12 9/16	7 5/16	M	Wawa	ONT	Danl Kissinger	2000	1526
19 14/16	12 2/16	7 12/16	M	Churchill Lake	SAS	Terry M. Dennis	2001	1526
19 14/16	12 5/16	7 9/16	M	Kississing Lake	MAN	Scott G. Hettinger	2001	1526
19 14/16	12 3/16	7 11/16	M	Pine Falls	MAN	Ed Parker	2001	1526
19 14/16	12 1/16	7 13/16	M	Koochiching County	MN	Timothy Kampa	2001	1526
19 14/16	12 9/16	7 5/16	M	Green Lake	SAS	Brian S. Lawler	2001	1526
19 14/16	12 1/16	7 13/16	M	Yakima County	WA	Dale Olson	2001	1526
19 14/16	12 11/16	7 3/16	M	Chip Lake	ALB	David Daniel, Sr.	2002	1526
19 14/16	12 6/16	7 8/16	M	Seal River	MAN	Keith Redding	2002	1526
19 14/16	12 2/16	7 12/16	M	Delta County	CO	A. Lenard Wagganer	2002	1526
19 14/16	12 0/16	7 14/16	M	Oxford County	ME	Roger Alves	2002	1526
19 14/16	12 6/16	7 8/16	M	Carrot River	SAS	Teejay Lansin	2003	1526
19 14/16	12 13/16	7 1/16	M	Lac Roger	QUE	Robert R. Agnew, Jr.	2003	1526
19 14/16	12 5/16	7 9/16	M	Mendocino County	CA	Greg Morris	2003	1526
19 14/16	12 2/16	7 12/16	M	Wabigoon	ONT	Carl Seek	2003	1526
19 14/16	12 8/16	7 6/16	M	Sawyer County	WI	Daniel N. Johnson	2003	1526
19 14/16	12 5/16	7 9/16	M	Alcona County	MI	Pete Revard	2003	1526

141

BLACK BEAR

Minimum Score 18
Continued

SCORE	GREATEST LENGTH	GREATEST WIDTH	SEX	AREA	STATE/PROVINCE	HUNTER'S NAME	DATE	RANK
19 14/16	12 1/16	7 13/16	M	Berens River	MAN	Matthew Schrum	2004	1526
19 14/16	12 7/16	7 7/16	M	Whatcom County	WA	Juan Lopez	2004	1526
19 14/16	12 10/16	7 4/16	M	Searcy County	AR	Chris Youngblood	2004	1526
19 14/16	12 5/16	7 9/16	M	White Shell	MAN	Richard Effaidana	2005	1526
19 14/16	12 10/16	7 4/16	M	Amos	QUE	Jerry May	2005	1526
19 14/16	12 6/16	7 8/16	M	Prince of Wales Island	AK	Glen Berry	2005	1526
19 14/16	12 12/16	7 2/16	M	Douglas County	WI	Charles Austin Pattee	2005	1526
19 14/16	12 9/16	7 5/16	M	Chemung County	NY	Greg A. Vaughn	2005	1526
*19 14/16	12 9/16	7 5/16	M	Kupreanof Island	AK	Rich Snapper	2006	1526
19 14/16	12 10/16	7 4/16	M	Saddle Hills	ALB	Mike Slocum	2006	1526
*19 14/16	12 8/16	7 6/16	M	Carrot River	SAS	Charles Heuring	2006	1526
*19 14/16	12 7/16	7 7/16	M	Forest County	WI	Ron Vander Kelen	2006	1526
19 14/16	12 4/16	7 10/16	M	Routt County	CO	Thane Anderson	2006	1526
19 14/16	12 10/16	7 4/16	M	Carrot River	SAS	Jim Horneck	2007	1526
19 14/16	12 7/16	7 7/16	M	Saddle Hills	ALB	David Watson	2007	1526
19 14/16	12 12/16	7 2/16	M	Oconto County	WI	Jerry Coy	2007	1526
19 14/16	12 6/16	7 8/16	M	Carswell Lake	SAS	Scott McKenzie	2008	1526
19 14/16	12 10/16	7 4/16	M	Gypsumville	MAN	Thomas Ward	2008	1526
*19 14/16	12 2/16	7 12/16	M	Nipigon	ONT	Bradley M. Good	2008	1526
19 14/16	12 6/16	7 8/16	M	Presque Isle County	MI	Curtis Lanxton	2008	1526
19 14/16	12 8/16	7 6/16	M	Carswell Lake	SAS	Duane Alexander	2009	1526
19 14/16	12 7/16	7 7/16	M	Spirit River	ALB	Jeff Jones	2009	1526
*19 14/16	12 11/16	7 3/16	M	Beaver Creek	MAN	David Lauer	2009	1526
*19 14/16	12 2/16	7 12/16	M	Matheson	ONT	Ryan Harris	2009	1526
19 14/16	12 12/16	7 2/16	M	Perry County	AR	Robert Stout	2009	1526
19 13/16	12 7/16	7 6/16	M	Shasta County	CA	Stan L. McIntyre	1968	1641
19 13/16	12 4/16	7 9/16	M	Dolores County	CO	Daryl Tieben	1976	1641
19 13/16	12 11/16	7 2/16	M	Wawa	ONT	Robert C. McGuire	1977	1641
19 13/16	12 7/16	7 6/16	M	Estaire	ONT	David L. Roose	1980	1641
19 13/16	12 5/16	7 8/16	M	Bonneville County	ID	Tom Edwards	1981	1641
19 13/16	12 6/16	7 7/16	M	Humboldt County	CA	Bill Hofferber	1981	1641
19 13/16	12 7/16	7 6/16	M	Douglas County	WI	Richard Peterson	1982	1641
19 13/16	12 9/16	7 4/16	M	Tucker County	WV	Robert B. Golightly	1982	1641
19 13/16	12 2/16	7 11/16	M	Beardmore	ONT	Mike Mooney	1984	1641
19 13/16	12 11/16	7 2/16	M	Hudson Bay	SAS	Craig Richardson	1985	1641
19 13/16	12 4/16	7 9/16	M	Graham	ONT	Todd Henck	1985	1641
19 13/16	12 5/16	7 8/16	M	Gallatin County	MT	LaVern Rucker	1985	1641
19 13/16	12 6/16	7 7/16	M	Calvin Township	ONT	Bob Foulkrod	1986	1641
19 13/16	12 3/16	7 10/16	M	Snohomish County	WA	Greg Winters	1986	1641
19 13/16	12 8/16	7 5/16	M	Revillagigedo Island	AK	Michael Edwards	1987	1641
19 13/16	12 0/16	7 13/16	M	Adies Pond	NFL	Ernest Libby	1988	1641
19 13/16	12 4/16	7 9/16	M	Ear Falls	ONT	Rickey L. Morley	1988	1641
19 13/16	12 3/16	7 10/16	M	Sexsmith	ALB	Oral Murphy	1989	1641
19 13/16	12 5/16	7 8/16	M	Cranberry Portage	MAN	Ron Rogers	1989	1641
19 13/16	12 1/16	7 12/16	M	Caramat	ONT	Steven Fowler	1990	1641
19 13/16	12 5/16	7 8/16	M	Rio Arriba County	NM	Dwayne Sargent	1990	1641
19 13/16	12 9/16	7 4/16	M	Prince of Wales Island	AK	Steve Hemrich	1991	1641
19 13/16	12 8/16	7 5/16	M	Frog Lake	ALB	Darrell Pinske	1991	1641
19 13/16	12 13/16	7 0/16	M	Riding Mtn.	MAN	Dean A. Toth	1991	1641
19 13/16	12 9/16	7 4/16	M	Sioux Lookout	ONT	Wayne D. Kluver	1992	1641
19 13/16	12 5/16	7 8/16	M	Utikamu	ALB	Donald L. DeLong	1992	1641
19 13/16	11 15/16	7 14/16	M	Brace Bridge	ONT	David D. Williams	1992	1641
19 13/16	12 8/16	7 5/16	M	Spokane County	WA	Rob Culp	1992	1641
19 13/16	12 5/16	7 8/16	M	Fergus County	MT	Stephen G. Gilpatrick	1992	1641
19 13/16	12 8/16	7 5/16	M	Ashland County	WI	Steven D. Pfaff	1992	1641
19 13/16	12 6/16	7 7/16	M	Marinette County	WI	Rick Semrad	1992	1641
19 13/16	12 5/16	7 8/16	M	Nakina	ONT	Harry Walker	1992	1641
19 13/16	12 9/16	7 4/16	M	Caramat	ONT	John E. Hartwig	1993	1641
19 13/16	12 2/16	7 11/16	M	Howley	NFL	Bill Vaznis	1993	1641
19 13/16	12 0/16	7 13/16	M	Koochiching County	MN	Jeremy Scott Kalisch	1993	1641
19 13/16	12 5/16	7 8/16	M	Green Lake	SAS	Robert B.J. Small	1994	1641
19 13/16	12 4/16	7 9/16	M	Madera County	CA	James J. Doherty, Jr.	1994	1641
19 13/16	12 5/16	7 8/16	M	Prince of Wales Island	AK	Randall F. Cooley	1994	1641
19 13/16	12 1/16	7 12/16	M	The Pas	MAN	Joseph P. Oreskovich	1995	1641
19 13/16	12 8/16	7 5/16	M	Sturgeon Landing	SAS	Corey Hugelen	1995	1641
19 13/16	12 5/16	7 8/16	M	Snow Lake	MAN	Thomas S. Pierce	1995	1641
19 13/16	12 4/16	7 9/16	M	Graham County	AZ	David Wolf	1995	1641
19 13/16	12 2/16	7 11/16	M	Missanabie	ONT	Alan J. Shier	1995	1641
19 13/16	12 8/16	7 5/16	M	Douglas County	WI	Michael Olsen	1995	1641
19 13/16	11 15/16	7 14/16	M	Schoolcraft County	MI	Scott Butler	1995	1641
19 13/16	12 7/16	7 6/16	M	Williams Lake	BC	Christopher R. Paquette	1996	1641
19 13/16	12 10/16	7 3/16	M	Endeavour	SAS	Lynn R. Jerome	1996	1641
19 13/16	12 1/16	7 12/16	M	Buffalo Narrows	SAS	Roland J. Quick	1996	1641
19 13/16	12 7/16	7 6/16	M	Athabasca River	ALB	Doy Curtis	1996	1641
19 13/16	12 9/16	7 4/16	M	Kearney	ONT	David W. Norton	1996	1641
19 13/16	12 8/16	7 5/16	M	Loon Lake	SAS	Philip Muller	1996	1641
19 13/16	12 5/16	7 8/16	M	Gander	NFL	John W. Shields	1996	1641
19 13/16	12 2/16	7 11/16	M	Rainbow Lake	ALB	R. Lee Williams, MD	1996	1641
19 13/16	12 4/16	7 9/16	M	Tulare County	CA	Bill Sweetser	1996	1641
19 13/16	12 14/16	6 15/16	M	Price County	WI	Fred Grambort	1996	1641
19 13/16	12 12/16	7 1/16	M	Ashland County	WI	Chris Gonyo	1996	1641
19 13/16	12 5/16	7 8/16	M	Santa Barbara County	CA	Robert D. Snyder	1996	1641
19 13/16	12 3/16	7 10/16	M	Bruce	ONT	Bob Phair	1997	1641
19 13/16	12 5/16	7 8/16	M	Prince of Wales Island	AK	Dyrk Eddie	1997	1641
19 13/16	12 3/16	7 10/16	M	Sioux Narrows	ONT	Phil Perry	1997	1641
19 13/16	12 1/16	7 12/16	M	Saddle Hills	ALB	Brad Stewart	1997	1641
19 13/16	12 7/16	7 6/16	M	Aroostook County	ME	Rocco Antonelli	1997	1641
19 13/16	12 1/16	7 12/16	M	Thurston	ALB	Douglas M. Schalla	1997	1641
19 13/16	12 4/16	7 9/16	M	Jackson County	CO	Thomas G. Kelley	1997	1641
19 13/16	12 7/16	7 6/16	M	Otero County	NM	Dale E. Guseman	1997	1641
19 13/16	12 7/16	7 6/16	M	Prince of Wales Island	AK	Lon E. Lauber	1998	1641
19 13/16	12 5/16	7 8/16	M	Bissett	MAN	Michael A. Toncevich	1998	1641
19 13/16	12 8/16	7 5/16	M	Weyakwin Lake	SAS	Neil R. Leidheiser	1998	1641
19 13/16	12 5/16	7 8/16	M	Madera County	CA	Keith Van Gilder	1998	1641
19 13/16	12 9/16	7 4/16	M	Crow Wing County	MN	Kevin P. Kozel	1998	1641

BLACK BEAR

Minimum Score 18   Continued

SCORE	GREATEST LENGTH	GREATEST WIDTH	SEX	AREA	STATE/ PROVINCE	HUNTER'S NAME	DATE	RANK
19 13/16	12 7/16	7 6/16	M	Prince of Wales Island	AK	Bob Fisher	1998	1641
19 13/16	12 7/16	7 6/16	M	Washburn County	WI	Christopher Zylka	1998	1641
19 13/16	12 11/16	7 2/16	M	Olha	MAN	Bill Clink	1999	1641
19 13/16	12 4/16	7 9/16	M	Fisher Branch	MAN	Dean Kuehl	1999	1641
19 13/16	12 3/16	7 10/16	M	Bonneville County	ID	Travis Heyrend	2000	1641
19 13/16	12 5/16	7 8/16	M	Prince of Wales Island	AK	Geoffrey Louis Blumenthal	2000	1641
19 13/16	12 9/16	7 4/16	M	Leland Lake	ALB	Chris Bayduza	2000	1641
19 13/16	12 4/16	7 9/16	M	Wawa	ONT	Michael E. Willbur	2000	1641
19 13/16	12 2/16	7 11/16	M	Chippewa County	WI	Joel Dupey	2000	1641
19 13/16	12 5/16	7 8/16	M	Harrop Lake	MAN	Bruce J. Campbell	2001	1641
19 13/16	12 1/16	7 12/16	M	Nestor Falls	ONT	Mark Kawolsky	2001	1641
19 13/16	12 12/16	7 1/16	M	Gunnison County	CO	Johnny Martin	2001	1641
19 13/16	12 9/16	7 4/16	M	Van Buren County	AR	William R. Ticer	2001	1641
19 13/16	12 4/16	7 9/16	M	La Ronge	SAS	Brian Hafkey	2002	1641
19 13/16	12 1/16	7 12/16	M	Hancock County	ME	Elaine Wardwell	2002	1641
*19 13/16	12 5/16	7 8/16	M	Annapolis County	NS	Scot A. Hearn	2002	1641
19 13/16	12 9/16	7 4/16	M	Longlac	ONT	Ronald Rezmer	2002	1641
19 13/16	12 11/16	7 2/16	M	Olha	MAN	Bill Clink	2002	1641
19 13/16	12 5/16	7 8/16	M	Frenchman Butte	SAS	Dowain Whitlaw	2003	1641
19 13/16	12 10/16	7 3/16	M	Fort a la Corne	SAS	Floyd Forster	2003	1641
19 13/16	12 5/16	7 8/16	M	Pine Falls	MAN	Russell K. Mehling	2003	1641
*19 13/16	12 8/16	7 5/16	M	Shawano County	WI	Douglas S. Johnson	2003	1641
19 13/16	12 7/16	7 6/16	M	Aitkin County	MN	Larry Luke	2003	1641
19 13/16	12 10/16	7 3/16	M	Lake of the Woods Cty	MN	Shannon Thomas	2003	1641
19 13/16	12 6/16	7 7/16	M	Slave Lake	ALB	Malcolm Keith Fearing III	2004	1641
19 13/16	12 8/16	7 5/16	M	Fort a la Corne	SAS	Floyd Forster	2004	1641
19 13/16	12 4/16	7 9/16	M	Vermilion Bay	ONT	Daniel S. Smith	2004	1641
19 13/16	12 5/16	7 8/16	M	Pine County	MN	David Cedarblade	2004	1641
19 13/16	12 14/16	6 15/16	M	Olha	MAN	Christopher J. Cordes	2004	1641
19 13/16	12 5/16	7 8/16	M	Lincoln County	WI	Timlin S. Groves	2004	1641
19 13/16	12 9/16	7 4/16	M	Laurier	MAN	Jon Lueck	2004	1641
*19 13/16	12 3/16	7 10/16	M	Churchill River	SAS	Michele Leqve	2005	1641
*19 13/16	12 7/16	7 6/16	M	Prince of Wales Island	AK	Earl Chauvin	2005	1641
19 13/16	12 8/16	7 5/16	M	Allegany County	NY	Joe Frair	2005	1641
19 13/16	12 12/16	7 1/16	M	Rossburn	MAN	Bryan Klein	2006	1641
19 13/16	12 10/16	7 3/16	M	Grandview	MAN	Michael E. Stark	2006	1641
19 13/16	12 4/16	7 9/16	M	Cook County	MN	Shawn Clough	2006	1641
*19 13/16	12 8/16	7 5/16	M	Barron County	WI	Nate Place	2006	1641
19 13/16	12 4/16	7 9/16	M	Prince of Wales Island	AK	M. Blake Patton	2007	1641
*19 13/16	11 14/16	7 15/16	M	Cumberland House	SAS	Judy L. Black	2007	1641
19 13/16	12 8/16	7 5/16	M	Hudson Bay	SAS	William Kelly Barlow	2008	1641
19 13/16	12 7/16	7 6/16	M	Carrot River	SAS	Patrick Pelikan	2008	1641
19 13/16	12 4/16	7 9/16	M	Sandoval County	NM	Lloyd Wood	2008	1641
19 13/16	12 6/16	7 7/16	M	Juniper	NBW	Kerry "Bama" Fann	2008	1641
*19 13/16	12 5/16	7 8/16	M	Cochise County	AZ	Brian Rimsza	2009	1641
19 13/16	12 1/16	7 12/16	M	Cree Lake	ONT	Trent Priest	2009	1641
19 13/16	12 12/16	7 1/16	M	Onanole	MAN	Dan Stillwell	2009	1641
*19 13/16	12 5/16	7 8/16	M	Neekik Lake	MAN	William R. Brown	2010	1641
19 12/16	11 14/16	7 14/16	M	Lake County	MT	Joe Lawrence	1966	1759
19 12/16	12 2/16	7 10/16	M	Chapleau	ONT	Lawrence Gallagher	1966	1759
19 12/16	12 7/16	7 5/16	M	Grand County	UT	Edmund H. Auffhammer	1968	1759
19 12/16	12 3/16	7 9/16	M	Chapleau	ONT	Anne M. Fiaschetti	1971	1759
19 12/16	12 7/16	7 5/16	M	Catron County	NM	Joe E. Stroube	1971	1759
19 12/16	12 4/16	7 8/16	F	Colfax County	NM	Bill Conn, Jr.	1973	1759
19 12/16	12 4/16	7 8/16	M	Itasca County	MN	James R. Kroupa	1973	1759
19 12/16	12 2/16	7 10/16	M	Conejos County	CO	Michael Miller	1974	1759
19 12/16	12 3/16	7 9/16	M	Siskiyou County	CA	Wayne Haley	1975	1759
19 12/16	12 6/16	7 6/16	M	Garfield County	CO	David Freeman	1976	1759
19 12/16	12 1/16	7 11/16	M	Killarney	ONT	Ken Barnhart	1979	1759
19 12/16	12 13/16	6 15/16	M	Crow Wing County	MN	Dave A. Engholm	1980	1759
19 12/16	12 8/16	7 4/16	M	Riding Mtn.	MAN	James Carson	1980	1759
19 12/16	12 0/16	7 12/16	M	North Bay	ONT	Ronald Gerrits	1980	1759
19 12/16	12 8/16	7 4/16	M	Beluga	AK	John Moline	1980	1759
19 12/16	12 5/16	7 7/16	M	Lewis & Clark County	MT	James L. Marlen	1980	1759
19 12/16	12 4/16	7 8/16	M	Caribou County	ID	Alan G. Smith	1981	1759
19 12/16	11 14/16	7 14/16	M	San Juan County	UT	Rick Collard	1982	1759
19 12/16	12 7/16	7 5/16	M	The Pas	MAN	Ken Evenson	1983	1759
19 12/16	12 3/16	7 9/16	M	Koochiching County	MN	Mike Little	1983	1759
19 12/16	12 8/16	7 4/16	M	Gogebic County	MI	Steven D. Baker	1983	1759
19 12/16	12 4/16	7 8/16	M	Madison County	MT	John Lantow	1984	1759
19 12/16	12 10/16	7 2/16	M	Game Area #23	MAN	Gary Kaluzniak	1984	1759
19 12/16	12 1/16	7 11/16	M	St. Louis County	MN	Clancy Lindvall	1984	1759
19 12/16	12 8/16	7 4/16	M	Union County	OR	Brad Hathaway	1984	1759
19 12/16	12 3/16	7 9/16	M	Roseau County	MN	Gregg L. Dirks	1985	1759
19 12/16	12 5/16	7 7/16	M	Ignace	ONT	Raymond Nowak, Jr.	1986	1759
19 12/16	12 5/16	7 7/16	M	Cass County	MN	Lauren Brorby	1986	1759
19 12/16	12 4/16	7 8/16	M	Mesa County	CO	Larry Shoop	1987	1759
19 12/16	12 6/16	7 6/16	M	Mesa County	CO	Stephen K. Meredith	1987	1759
19 12/16	12 10/16	7 2/16	M	Swan River	MAN	Harrey Bergen	1987	1759
19 12/16	12 4/16	7 8/16	M	Westbank	BC	Robert McCulley	1987	1759
19 12/16	12 8/16	7 4/16	M	Tucker County	WV	Russell L. James	1987	1759
19 12/16	12 8/16	7 4/16	M	Prince of Wales Island	AK	Glen Berry	1988	1759
19 12/16	12 6/16	7 6/16	M	Chaffee County	CO	Bob Merciez	1988	1759
19 12/16	12 6/16	7 6/16	M	Miles Bay	ONT	Kenneth Rader	1988	1759
19 12/16	12 6/16	7 6/16	M	Bear Paw Landing	QUE	Lonnie Rumley	1988	1759
19 12/16	12 5/16	7 7/16	M	St. Louis County	MN	Scott Gruhlke	1988	1759
19 12/16	12 0/16	7 12/16	M	Amos	QUE	Simon Harvey	1989	1759
19 12/16	12 0/16	7 12/16	M	Aitkin County	MN	Scott Dirkes	1989	1759
19 12/16	12 1/16	7 11/16	M	Sioux Lookout	ONT	Daniel J. Riegelman	1989	1759
19 12/16	12 10/16	7 2/16	M	St. Louis County	MN	Dr Eugene T. Altiere	1989	1759
19 12/16	12 4/16	7 8/16	M	Coos County	OR	Russell McCall	1989	1759
19 12/16	11 13/16	7 15/16	M	Vilas County	WI	Gary F. Robinson	1989	1759
19 12/16	12 11/16	7 1/16	M	Langlade County	WI	Stanley William Janusiewicz	1989	1759
19 12/16	12 9/16	7 3/16	M	Prince of Wales Island	AK	Dyrk Eddie	1990	1759
19 12/16	12 6/16	7 6/16	M	Athabasca	ALB	Ryk Visscher	1990	1759

143

BLACK BEAR

Minimum Score 18   Continued

SCORE	GREATEST LENGTH	GREATEST WIDTH	SEX	AREA	STATE/ PROVINCE	HUNTER'S NAME	DATE	RANK
19 12/16	12 6/16	7 6/16	M	Columbia County	WA	Kenneth Fuller	1990	1759
19 12/16	12 4/16	7 8/16	M	Atikokan	ONT	Rick Grooms	1991	1759
19 12/16	12 11/16	7 1/16	M	Iron County	MI	Michael A. Samuels	1991	1759
19 12/16	12 10/16	7 2/16	M	Newton County	AR	Joel Phillips	1991	1759
19 12/16	12 0/16	7 12/16	M	Harcourt Park	ONT	Henry Quittard	1991	1759
19 12/16	12 1/16	7 11/16	M	Las Animas County	CO	Garry Woodman	1992	1759
19 12/16	12 7/16	7 5/16	M	Prince of Wales Island	AK	Sheldon Doughty	1992	1759
19 12/16	12 8/16	7 4/16	M	La Plata County	CO	John L. Gardner	1992	1759
19 12/16	12 8/16	7 4/16	M	Vermette Lake	SAS	Eric Erickson	1992	1759
19 12/16	12 3/16	7 9/16	M	Lac Kipawa	QUE	Ken H. Taylor	1992	1759
19 12/16	12 6/16	7 6/16	M	Manitouwadge	ONT	Dolan D. Waters	1992	1759
19 12/16	12 11/16	7 1/16	M	Sawyer County	WI	Rodney Pearson	1992	1759
19 12/16	11 15/16	7 13/16	M	Clinton County	NY	Mark Wood	1992	1759
19 12/16	12 10/16	7 2/16	M	Prince of Wales Island	AK	George E. Mann	1993	1759
19 12/16	12 4/16	7 8/16	M	Prince of Wales Island	AK	Danny Moore	1994	1759
19 12/16	12 6/16	7 6/16	M	Peace River	ALB	Peter F. Woeck II	1994	1759
19 12/16	12 5/16	7 7/16	M	Lynn Lake	MAN	Ernest Gilbert	1994	1759
19 12/16	12 8/16	7 4/16	M	Keeley Lake	SAS	Paul J. Sisz	1994	1759
19 12/16	12 4/16	7 8/16	M	Umatilla County	OR	Tom Huebner	1994	1759
19 12/16	12 6/16	7 6/16	M	Roseau County	MN	Donald Roseen	1994	1759
19 12/16	12 5/16	7 7/16	M	St. Louis County	MN	Richard Cross	1994	1759
19 12/16	12 4/16	7 8/16	M	Bissett	MAN	Keith L. Mark	1994	1759
19 12/16	12 7/16	7 5/16	M	Brookfield	NS	Jeffrey H. Batula	1994	1759
19 12/16	12 8/16	7 4/16	M	Falher	ALB	Stephen L. Collins	1995	1759
19 12/16	12 11/16	7 1/16	M	Emo	ONT	Randy Loken	1995	1759
19 12/16	12 8/16	7 4/16	M	Bissett	MAN	Mitchell D. Storm	1995	1759
19 12/16	11 15/16	7 13/16	M	Bellecombe	QUE	Guy Roy	1995	1759
19 12/16	12 7/16	7 5/16	M	Courtenay	BC	Derek R. Nichols	1995	1759
19 12/16	12 9/16	7 3/16	M	Olha	MAN	Mike Lenz	1995	1759
19 12/16	12 9/16	7 3/16	M	Peace River	ALB	Robert S. Miller	1995	1759
19 12/16	12 6/16	7 6/16	M	Athabasca River	ALB	Gerald Cavaliere, Jr.	1995	1759
19 12/16	12 8/16	7 4/16	M	Catron County	NM	Lew Webb, Jr.	1995	1759
19 12/16	12 4/16	7 8/16	M	Kinwow Bay	MAN	Baird R. Booth	1996	1759
19 12/16	12 8/16	7 4/16	M	May Lake	ALB	Terry Ermel	1996	1759
19 12/16	12 2/16	7 10/16	M	Longlac	ONT	Harley Krauss	1996	1759
19 12/16	12 3/16	7 9/16	M	Dubreuilville	ONT	Randal L. Zorn	1996	1759
19 12/16	12 4/16	7 8/16	M	Ranger Lake	ONT	Bill McDonald	1996	1759
19 12/16	12 14/16	6 14/16	M	Swan River	MAN	Archie J. Nesbitt	1996	1759
19 12/16	12 11/16	7 1/16	M	Thurston County	WA	Mark Mager	1996	1759
19 12/16	12 7/16	7 5/16	M	King County	WA	Brad Thomsen	1996	1759
19 12/16	12 6/16	7 6/16	M	Koochiching County	MN	Jesse Turck	1996	1759
19 12/16	12 8/16	7 4/16	M	Nakina	ONT	Bob Wind	1996	1759
19 12/16	12 1/16	7 11/16	M	Franklin County	NY	Walter Tanzini	1996	1759
19 12/16	12 13/16	6 15/16	M	Douglas County	WI	Ken Bjorge	1996	1759
19 12/16	12 9/16	7 3/16	M	Polk County	AR	Keith W. Brown	1996	1759
19 12/16	12 8/16	7 4/16	M	Athabasca River	ALB	Robert B. Stryker	1997	1759
19 12/16	12 9/16	7 3/16	M	Saddle Hills	ALB	Allen Avery	1997	1759
19 12/16	12 6/16	7 6/16	M	Marathon County	WI	Jeff Wendt	1997	1759
19 12/16	12 5/16	7 7/16	M	Nicholas County	WV	Robert Trygstad	1997	1759
19 12/16	11 14/16	7 14/16	M	Beaver River	SAS	Jason Toews	1998	1759
19 12/16	12 7/16	7 5/16	M	Prince of Wales Island	AK	E. Lance Whary	1998	1759
19 12/16	11 15/16	7 13/16	M	Pakwash Lake	ONT	Charles Dunn	1998	1759
19 12/16	12 10/16	7 2/16	M	Wanless	MAN	Travis Tharp	1998	1759
19 12/16	12 10/16	7 2/16	M	Saddle Hills	ALB	Dale Hannas	1998	1759
19 12/16	12 7/16	7 5/16	M	Bayfield County	WI	Daniel Brandenburg	1998	1759
19 12/16	12 2/16	7 10/16	M	Smoky River	ALB	Craig Stokke	1999	1759
19 12/16	12 9/16	7 3/16	M	Lake of the Woods Cty	MN	Jon P. Smythe	1999	1759
19 12/16	12 10/16	7 2/16	M	Bayfield County	WI	Adam J. Jarozewski	1999	1759
19 12/16	12 5/16	7 7/16	M	Ile-a-La-Crosse	SAS	David Skiff	2000	1759
19 12/16	12 3/16	7 9/16	M	Minto Flats	AK	Michael C. Maddox, Sr.	2000	1759
19 12/16	12 4/16	7 8/16	M	Nipawin	SAS	Louis H. Birkholz	2000	1759
19 12/16	12 10/16	7 2/16	M	Pennington County	MN	Dale R. Gunufson	2000	1759
19 12/16	12 1/16	7 11/16	M	Aitkin County	MN	Ed Wojcik	2000	1759
19 12/16	12 6/16	7 6/16	M	Alexander Archipelago	AK	Steve Hohensee	2000	1759
19 12/16	12 0/16	7 12/16	M	Carbon County	UT	Kenny E. Leo	2000	1759
19 12/16	12 8/16	7 4/16	M	Hawks Creek	BC	Alan Cunningham	2001	1759
19 12/16	12 13/16	6 15/16	M	Swan River	MAN	Joseph T. Barnebee	2001	1759
19 12/16	12 8/16	7 4/16	M	Dipper Lake	SAS	Steve Dunn	2002	1759
19 12/16	12 1/16	7 11/16	M	Torch River	SAS	Kirt Hoffmann	2002	1759
19 12/16	12 7/16	7 5/16	M	Halliday Lake	SAS	R. W. Corpe	2002	1759
19 12/16	12 6/16	7 6/16	M	Oconto County	WI	Larry E. Glander	2002	1759
19 12/16	12 5/16	7 7/16	M	Montezuma County	CO	Rusty Pollard	2002	1759
19 12/16	11 12/16	8 0/16	M	Dryden	ONT	Niles K. "Nick" Gross	2002	1759
19 12/16	12 6/16	7 6/16	M	Prince of Wales Island	AK	Tony Russ	2003	1759
19 12/16	12 6/16	7 6/16	M	Kuiu Island	AK	Patrick K. Bolte	2003	1759
19 12/16	12 2/16	7 10/16	M	Reservoir Gouin	QUE	Donald H. Corey	2003	1759
19 12/16	12 7/16	7 5/16	M	Carswell Lake	SAS	Tom L. Sovereign	2003	1759
19 12/16	12 5/16	7 7/16	M	Clearwater County	ID	Richard M. Newell	2003	1759
19 12/16	12 4/16	7 8/16	M	Somerset County	ME	Reginald F. Rouse	2003	1759
19 12/16	12 4/16	7 8/16	M	Ulster County	NY	Matthew Koehler	2003	1759
19 12/16	12 2/16	7 10/16	M	Flatbush	ALB	Steve Kerr	2004	1759
*19 12/16	12 5/16	7 7/16	M	Kupreanof Island	AK	Rich Snapper	2004	1759
19 12/16	12 4/16	7 8/16	M	Ft. McMurray	ALB	Neil Berthume	2004	1759
19 12/16	12 12/16	7 0/16	M	Duck Mtns.	MAN	Jared Hook	2004	1759
19 12/16	12 4/16	7 8/16	M	San Juan County	UT	Don Mecham	2004	1759
19 12/16	12 8/16	7 4/16	M	Los Angeles County	CA	Jim Belleville	2004	1759
*19 12/16	12 4/16	7 8/16	M	Steuben County	NY	Terry L. Gunn	2004	1759
19 12/16	12 7/16	7 5/16	M	Olha	MAN	Louis C. Milanesi	2005	1759
19 12/16	12 8/16	7 4/16	M	Carswell Lake	SAS	Stephen Kotz	2005	1759
19 12/16	12 3/16	7 9/16	M	Raleigh County	WV	Sidney Layne	2005	1759
19 12/16	12 10/16	7 2/16	M	Cold Lake	ALB	Gary L. Boomsma	2006	1759
19 12/16	12 7/16	7 5/16	M	Hudson Bay	SAS	Ed Daniel	2006	1759
19 12/16	12 4/16	7 8/16	M	Press Lake	ONT	Charles G. Arnold	2006	1759
*19 12/16	12 8/16	7 4/16	M	Rainy Lake	ONT	Brian Spreuer	2006	1759
*19 12/16	12 4/16	7 8/16	M	Franklin County	ME	Robert J. Accettullo	2006	1759

BLACK BEAR

Minimum Score 18   Continued

SCORE	GREATEST LENGTH	GREATEST WIDTH	SEX	AREA	STATE/ PROVINCE	HUNTER'S NAME	DATE	RANK
*19 12/16	12 2/16	7 10/16	M	Lake Else River	BC	Jeffrey R. Lee	2006	1759
19 12/16	12 6/16	7 6/16	M	Marinette County	WI	Richard Klatkiewicz	2006	1759
19 12/16	12 6/16	7 6/16	M	Fort McMurray	ALB	Rodney Sampson	2007	1759
19 12/16	12 5/16	7 7/16	M	Leaf Rapids	MAN	Sherwin Van Kooten	2007	1759
*19 12/16	12 4/16	7 8/16	M	Jackson County	OR	David E. Evanow	2007	1759
19 12/16	12 3/16	7 9/16	M	Port Houton Bay	AK	Joe Williams	2008	1759
19 12/16	12 7/16	7 5/16	M	Cold Lake	ALB	Doug Cannons	2008	1759
*19 12/16	12 1/16	7 11/16	M	Reserve La Verendrye	QUE	Raynald Groleau	2008	1759
19 12/16	12 6/16	7 6/16	M	White Fox	SAS	Wallace Krull	2008	1759
*19 12/16	11 14/16	7 14/16	M	Summit County	CO	Mark Helton	2008	1759
*19 12/16	12 4/16	7 8/16	M	Price County	WI	Fred A. Richter, Sr.	2008	1759
19 12/16	12 10/16	7 2/16	M	Pope County	AR	Mitchell Price	2008	1759
19 12/16	12 9/16	7 3/16	M	Harvey	NBW	Kyle Murray	2009	1759
19 12/16	12 7/16	7 5/16	M	Santa Cruz County	AZ	Robert Forrest	2010	1759
19 12/16	12 8/16	7 4/16	M	Koochiching County	MN	Charles W. Schultz	2010	1759
19 11/16	12 3/16	7 8/16	M	Atikokan	ONT	Dennis Gregory	1967	1916
19 11/16	12 2/16	7 9/16	M	Montezuma County	CO	Marvin Reichenau	1972	1916
19 11/16	12 3/16	7 8/16	M	La Plata County	CO	Robert L. Everett	1973	1916
19 11/16	12 4/16	7 7/16	M	Larimer County	CO	Lee Kline	1974	1916
19 11/16	11 15/16	7 12/16	M	Chapleau	ONT	Donald E. Meushaw	1975	1916
19 11/16	12 11/16	7 0/16	M	Garfield County	CO	C. David Wix	1976	1916
19 11/16	12 9/16	7 2/16	M	Montezuma County	CO	Marvin Reichenau	1976	1916
19 11/16	12 4/16	7 7/16	M	Somerset County	ME	Anthony Carratura	1977	1916
19 11/16	12 4/16	7 7/16	M	Washington County	ME	Charles Hardish	1977	1916
19 11/16	12 0/16	7 11/16	M	Ignace	ONT	John Dmytryka	1978	1916
19 11/16	12 6/16	7 5/16	M	Itasca County	MN	Daniel "Boone" Bell	1979	1916
19 11/16	11 11/16	8 0/16	M	Washington County	ME	Gary Farquhar	1979	1916
19 11/16	12 1/16	7 10/16	M	Boise County	ID	Michael Sherer	1981	1916
19 11/16	11 14/16	7 13/16	M	Essex County	NY	Paul Durling	1981	1916
19 11/16	12 5/16	7 6/16	M	Prince of Wales Island	AK	Doug Miller	1982	1916
19 11/16	12 3/16	7 8/16	M	Gunflint Lake	ONT	Kelly Wilhelmi	1982	1916
19 11/16	12 1/16	7 10/16	M	Routt County	CO	Guenter Hackl	1983	1916
19 11/16	12 11/16	7 0/16	M	Boise County	ID	L. Dean Goodner	1983	1916
19 11/16	12 5/16	7 6/16	M	Dickinson County	MI	Mike Vandeven	1983	1916
19 11/16	12 0/16	7 11/16	M	Archuleta County	CO	Britton F. Kelley, Jr.	1984	1916
19 11/16	12 0/16	7 11/16	M	Sioux Lookout	ONT	James E. Tiefenthaler	1984	1916
19 11/16	11 7/16	8 4/16	M	Gogama	ONT	Frank E. Brinton IV	1985	1916
19 11/16	11 15/16	7 12/16	M	Cascaden	ONT	Ronnie Long	1985	1916
19 11/16	12 6/16	7 5/16	M	Garfield County	CO	Paul B. Walker	1986	1916
19 11/16	12 0/16	7 11/16	M	Sudbury	ONT	Wendell L. DeWitt	1987	1916
19 11/16	12 7/16	7 4/16	M	Nestor Falls	ONT	Martin J. Weber	1987	1916
19 11/16	12 3/16	7 8/16	M	Valley County	ID	Jon Vanderhoef	1987	1916
19 11/16	12 7/16	7 4/16	M	Marinette County	WI	Tim H. Boucher	1988	1916
19 11/16	12 3/16	7 8/16	M	Forest County	WI	Tim B. Olk	1988	1916
19 11/16	12 5/16	7 6/16	M	Carbon County	UT	Bill Mamales	1989	1916
19 11/16	12 8/16	7 3/16	M	Ester Passage	AK	Don Williams	1989	1916
19 11/16	12 6/16	7 5/16	M	Grand County	UT	Paul Ensz	1989	1916
19 11/16	12 5/16	7 6/16	M	Dryden	ONT	Jack T. Wolf	1989	1916
19 11/16	12 5/16	7 6/16	M	Blair	ONT	Douglass J. Street	1989	1916
19 11/16	12 6/16	7 5/16	M	Alcona County	MI	Fred Eugene Upperstrom	1989	1916
19 11/16	12 7/16	7 4/16	M	Cynthia	ALB	Bert Skulmoski	1990	1916
19 11/16	12 1/16	7 10/16	M	Thaddeus Lake	ONT	Gary R. Ziesmer	1990	1916
19 11/16	12 12/16	6 15/16	M	Green Lake	SAS	Richard P. Smith	1991	1916
19 11/16	12 2/16	7 9/16	M	Fort McMurray	ALB	Edward Smith	1991	1916
19 11/16	11 15/16	7 12/16	M	Madison County	MT	Larry Rather	1991	1916
19 11/16	12 4/16	7 7/16	M	Prince of Wales Island	AK	Don Youngblood	1992	1916
19 11/16	12 8/16	7 3/16	M	Lake of the Woods	ONT	Earl Fulkerson	1992	1916
19 11/16	11 14/16	7 13/16	M	Vancouver Island	BC	Richard P. Smith	1992	1916
19 11/16	12 7/16	7 4/16	M	Fort McMurray	ALB	Steve Swinhoe	1992	1916
19 11/16	12 1/16	7 10/16	M	Harvey Station	NBW	Dennis Hayden	1992	1916
19 11/16	12 2/16	7 9/16	M	Sideburn Lake	ONT	David Jerome Miller	1992	1916
19 11/16	12 4/16	7 7/16	M	Lincoln County	MT	Gary C. Cargill	1992	1916
19 11/16	12 5/16	7 6/16	M	Prince of Wales Island	AK	Joe K. Lilley	1993	1916
19 11/16	12 9/16	7 2/16	M	Torch River	SAS	Floyd Forster	1993	1916
19 11/16	12 2/16	7 9/16	M	McNulty Lake	ONT	Alexander MacPherson	1993	1916
19 11/16	12 12/16	6 15/16	M	Pine County	MN	Roger Glenn Rarick	1993	1916
19 11/16	12 11/16	7 0/16	M	Florence County	WI	William Schommer	1993	1916
19 11/16	12 1/16	7 10/16	M	Carroll County	NH	Jack Smith	1993	1916
19 11/16	12 8/16	7 3/16	M	Wood County	WI	Jack Rueth	1993	1916
19 11/16	12 4/16	7 7/16	M	Shole Cove	AK	Jeffrey C. Kinney	1994	1916
19 11/16	12 0/16	7 11/16	M	Hallam Township	ONT	Barry Vondette	1994	1916
19 11/16	12 7/16	7 4/16	M	File Lake	MAN	Bobby Harrell	1994	1916
19 11/16	12 0/16	7 11/16	M	Forestville	QUE	Marty Adams	1994	1916
19 11/16	12 8/16	7 3/16	M	Waldo County	ME	Robert J. Amaral	1994	1916
19 11/16	12 6/16	7 5/16	M	Polk County	MN	Dana C. Klos	1994	1916
19 11/16	12 3/16	7 8/16	M	Chalk River	ONT	Kirk McCutcheon	1995	1916
19 11/16	12 1/16	7 10/16	M	Weyakwin	SAS	Joseph L. Wright	1995	1916
19 11/16	12 6/16	7 5/16	M	Oak Lake	ONT	Mike Guenther	1995	1916
19 11/16	12 1/16	7 10/16	M	Smoothstone Lake	SAS	Vance A. Fairhurst	1995	1916
19 11/16	12 12/16	6 15/16	M	Rossburn	MAN	Barry Minshull	1995	1916
19 11/16	12 5/16	7 6/16	M	Bayfield County	WI	Arthur E. Hyde	1995	1916
19 11/16	12 10/16	7 1/16	M	Beaverdam	ALB	Randy Babey	1996	1916
19 11/16	12 3/16	7 8/16	M	Wrangell	AK	Chris Staniar	1996	1916
19 11/16	12 11/16	7 0/16	M	Olha	MAN	Thomas Blanchard	1996	1916
19 11/16	12 2/16	7 9/16	M	Umatilla County	OR	Randall F. Hoeft	1996	1916
19 11/16	12 9/16	7 2/16	M	Price County	WI	Scott Lewandowski	1996	1916
19 11/16	12 6/16	7 5/16	M	Meagher County	MT	Billy Howard	1996	1916
19 11/16	12 11/16	7 0/16	M	Bowron River	BC	John H. Ames	1997	1916
19 11/16	12 0/16	7 11/16	M	Iron County	WI	Tom Brewczynski	1997	1916
19 11/16	12 5/16	7 6/16	M	Crawford County	MI	Christopher J. Scott	1997	1916
19 11/16	12 9/16	7 2/16	M	Price County	WI	Mike Jacobs	1997	1916
19 11/16	12 5/16	7 6/16	M	Meadow Lake	SAS	Lyle Sheppard	1998	1916
19 11/16	12 7/16	7 4/16	M	Fort McMurray	ALB	Terry C. Parkinson	1998	1916
19 11/16	12 10/16	7 1/16	M	Stenen	SAS	David B. Cull	1998	1916
19 11/16	12 4/16	7 7/16	M	Lakeville	NBW	Kevin Gallagher	1998	1916

BLACK BEAR

Minimum Score 18 — Continued

SCORE	GREATEST LENGTH	GREATEST WIDTH	SEX	AREA	STATE/ PROVINCE	HUNTER'S NAME	DATE	RANK
19 11/16	12 9/16	7 2/16	M	Fremont County	ID	Aaron Bateman	1998	1916
19 11/16	12 6/16	7 5/16	M	Savant Lake	ONT	Ken Nelms	1998	1916
19 11/16	12 8/16	7 3/16	M	Rossburn	MAN	Adam Bartsch	1998	1916
19 11/16	12 9/16	7 2/16	M	Page County	VA	Rodney L. Atkins	1998	1916
19 11/16	12 5/16	7 6/16	M	Carrot River	SAS	Mark P. Wagner	1999	1916
19 11/16	12 4/16	7 7/16	M	Spirit River	ALB	Stephen R. Boster	1999	1916
19 11/16	12 3/16	7 8/16	M	Kississing Lake	MAN	Scott G. Hettinger	1999	1916
19 11/16	11 15/16	7 12/16	M	Lac Farrington	QUE	John T. Faulkner	1999	1916
19 11/16	12 4/16	7 7/16	M	Aroostook County	ME	Ernest A. LaFazia	1999	1916
19 11/16	12 3/16	7 8/16	M	Eau Claire County	WI	Richard Price	1999	1916
19 11/16	12 1/16	7 10/16	M	Herkimer County	NY	Anthony Paparella	1999	1916
19 11/16	12 14/16	6 13/16	M	Meadow Lake	SAS	Tom Schultz	2000	1916
19 11/16	12 1/16	7 10/16	M	Grahamdale	MAN	Tracey Casey	2000	1916
19 11/16	12 3/16	7 8/16	M	Pointe du Bois	MAN	Joshua Morrow	2000	1916
19 11/16	12 2/16	7 9/16	M	Nipissing	ONT	Michael A. Frey	2000	1916
19 11/16	12 8/16	7 3/16	M	Grande Prairie	ALB	Mike Slocum	2001	1916
19 11/16	12 7/16	7 4/16	M	Hudson Bay	SAS	Michael S. Stammen	2001	1916
19 11/16	12 1/16	7 10/16	M	Evain	QUE	Jacques Robichaud	2001	1916
19 11/16	12 6/16	7 5/16	M	Forest County	WI	Dennis D. Klemick	2001	1916
19 11/16	12 9/16	7 2/16	M	Eau Claire County	WI	Shaun Koenig	2001	1916
19 11/16	12 3/16	7 8/16	M	Garfield County	CO	Eric H. Wolff	2001	1916
19 11/16	12 2/16	7 9/16	M	Huerfano County	CO	Bruce A. Rheuff	2002	1916
19 11/16	12 7/16	7 4/16	M	Webster County	WV	Robert Schmidt	2002	1916
19 11/16	12 8/16	7 3/16	M	Lac La Hache	BC	Allan Tew	2003	1916
19 11/16	12 7/16	7 4/16	M	Churchill River	SAS	Jim Leqve	2003	1916
19 11/16	11 14/16	7 13/16	M	Churchill River	SAS	Mike Felderman	2003	1916
19 11/16	12 6/16	7 5/16	M	Ignace	ONT	William Wissestad	2003	1916
19 11/16	12 5/16	7 6/16	M	Grand Rapids	MAN	Brad Davis	2003	1916
19 11/16	12 4/16	7 7/16	M	Vilas County	WI	William Winch	2003	1916
19 11/16	12 5/16	7 6/16	M	Grand Rapids	MAN	Robert Gagnon	2004	1916
*19 11/16	12 3/16	7 8/16	M	Reserve Chic-Chocs	QUE	Ernest J. Gove III	2004	1916
*19 11/16	12 12/16	6 15/16	M	Geraldton	ONT	Jay M. Wilczak	2004	1916
19 11/16	11 15/16	7 12/16	M	Carrot River	SAS	Jay Trudell	2004	1916
19 11/16	12 12/16	6 15/16	M	Olha	MAN	John "Jack" Cordes	2004	1916
19 11/16	12 13/16	6 14/16	M	Clark County	WI	Duane Dubiel	2004	1916
19 11/16	12 4/16	7 7/16	M	Tazewell County	VA	Kevin White	2004	1916
19 11/16	12 6/16	7 5/16	M	Kern County	CA	Noel Carter	2004	1916
19 11/16	12 4/16	7 7/16	M	Cold Lake	ALB	Doug Cannons	2005	1916
19 11/16	12 6/16	7 5/16	M	Prince of Wales Island	AK	Kelly King	2005	1916
19 11/16	12 7/16	7 4/16	M	High Level	ALB	William Kelly Barlow	2005	1916
19 11/16	12 1/16	7 10/16	M	Ponton	MAN	James Ekern	2005	1916
19 11/16	12 6/16	7 5/16	M	Stoney Rapids	SAS	Ron R. Maguire	2005	1916
*19 11/16	12 9/16	7 2/16	M	Oak Lake	ONT	Nick L. Matthews	2005	1916
19 11/16	12 1/16	7 10/16	M	Montezuma County	CO	Bryon D. Long	2005	1916
*19 11/16	12 12/16	6 15/16	M	Botetourt County	VA	Wendell K. Lackey	2005	1916
*19 11/16	12 2/16	7 9/16	M	Big Horn County	MT	Doyle Moss	2006	1916
19 11/16	12 7/16	7 4/16	M	Garfield County	CO	Adrian Hesterman	2006	1916
*19 11/16	12 6/16	7 5/16	M	Lac Minto	QUE	Dennis Duckert	2006	1916
19 11/16	12 4/16	7 7/16	M	Bayfield County	WI	Dan Keppen	2006	1916
19 11/16	12 4/16	7 7/16	M	Greenlee County	AZ	William D. Wright	2006	1916
*19 11/16	12 3/16	7 8/16	M	Vancouver Island	BC	George Richison	2007	1916
19 11/16	12 8/16	7 3/16	M	Prairie River	SAS	Ken H. Taylor	2007	1916
*19 11/16	12 4/16	7 7/16	M	Christopher Lake	SAS	Gary L. Temple	2008	1916
19 11/16	12 7/16	7 4/16	M	Dufferin Lake	SAS	Jack Walker	2008	1916
19 11/16	12 4/16	7 7/16	M	Fort McMurray	ALB	Curt Dinges	2008	1916
19 11/16	12 9/16	7 2/16	M	Rusk County	WI	Ben Manor	2008	1916
19 11/16	12 8/16	7 3/16	M	Saline County	AR	Eric M. Eckert	2008	1916
19 11/16	12 14/16	6 13/16	M	Peace River	ALB	Rodney J. Kelly	2009	1916
19 11/16	12 3/16	7 8/16	M	Bayfield County	WI	Linda G. Fischer	2009	1916
*19 11/16	12 7/16	7 4/16	M	Powhatan County	VA	Robert Phillip Fore	2009	1916
19 11/16	12 3/16	7 8/16	M	Marinette County	WI	Gary J. Gruszynski	2009	1916
*19 11/16	11 15/16	7 12/16	M	La Ronge	SAS	Van Wall	2010	1916
19 10/16	12 0/16	7 10/16	M	Lincoln County	NM	David B. Terk	1964	2058
19 10/16	12 6/16	7 4/16	M	Iron County	WI	William Tutt	1966	2058
19 10/16	12 10/16	7 0/16	M	Madera County	CA	John D. Faulconer	1971	2058
19 10/16	12 4/16	7 6/16	M	Forest County	WI	James L. Rablin	1972	2058
19 10/16	12 2/16	7 8/16	M	Nez Perce County	ID	Bob Gulman	1972	2058
19 10/16	12 7/16	7 3/16	M	Boise County	ID	Jimmie DeSaro, Jr.	1975	2058
19 10/16	11 13/16	7 13/16	M	El Paso County	CO	Billy Mulholland	1976	2058
19 10/16	12 4/16	7 6/16	M	La Ronge	SAS	David L. Miller	1976	2058
19 10/16	12 6/16	7 4/16	M	Sandilands	MAN	Jerry Parizek	1976	2058
19 10/16	12 4/16	7 6/16	M	Gunnison County	CO	Travis L. Wakefield	1977	2058
19 10/16	12 6/16	7 4/16	M	Grand County	UT	Sam Nesi, Jr.	1979	2058
19 10/16	12 12/16	6 14/16	M	Itasca County	MN	Gordon Steffen	1979	2058
19 2/16	12 2/16	7 8/16	M	St. Louis County	MN	Richard G. Butters	1979	2058
19 10/16	12 3/16	7 7/16	M	Trinity County	CA	Willis Duhon	1981	2058
19 10/16	11 12/16	7 14/16	M	Fort Frances	ONT	Ron Carlson	1982	2058
19 10/16	12 2/16	7 8/16	M	Vermilion Bay	ONT	Dean Hamilton	1983	2058
19 10/16	12 2/16	7 8/16	M	Siskiyou County	CA	Jerry Martinez	1983	2058
19 10/16	12 11/16	6 15/16	M	Iron County	MI	Leslie Vorpahl	1983	2058
19 10/16	12 9/16	7 1/16	M	Sioux Lookout	ONT	Larry J. Selzler	1984	2058
19 10/16	12 6/16	7 4/16	M	Langlade County	WI	Thomas Radtke	1984	2058
19 10/16	12 5/16	7 5/16	M	Archuleta County	CO	Joel L. Duncan	1986	2058
19 10/16	12 1/16	7 9/16	M	Lanark	ONT	Elmer M. Hagood, Jr.	1986	2058
19 10/16	12 4/16	7 6/16	M	Sudbury	ONT	Richard W. Dohm	1987	2058
19 10/16	12 3/16	7 7/16	M	Woody Lake	SAS	L. 'Andy' Anderson	1987	2058
19 10/16	12 2/16	7 8/16	M	Gallatin County	MT	Frank W. Holland	1987	2058
19 10/16	12 4/16	7 6/16	M	Siskiyou County	CA	Jeff Buck	1987	2058
19 10/16	13 1/16	6 9/16	M	Limestone Lake	ONT	Steve Schwarzkopf	1988	2058
19 10/16	12 5/16	7 5/16	M	Squaw Rapids	SAS	Phillip M. Revering	1988	2058
19 10/16	12 8/16	7 2/16	M	Oxford County	ME	Richard Grannis	1988	2058
19 10/16	12 5/16	7 5/16	M	Clearwater River	BC	Michael H. Ritcey	1988	2058
19 10/16	11 14/16	7 12/16	M	Marquette County	MI	John Spanel	1988	2058
19 10/16	12 4/16	7 6/16	M	Valley County	ID	Robert Dowen	1989	2058
19 10/16	12 9/16	7 1/16	M	Archuleta County	CO	Ron R. Maez	1989	2058

BLACK BEAR

Minimum Score 18   Continued

SCORE	GREATEST LENGTH	GREATEST WIDTH	SEX	AREA	STATE/ PROVINCE	HUNTER'S NAME	DATE	RANK
19 10/16	12 4/16	7 6/16	M	Smeaton	SAS	Gene A. Welle	1990	2058
19 10/16	12 2/16	7 8/16	M	Vivian	MAN	Erik Thienpondt	1990	2058
19 10/16	12 4/16	7 6/16	M	Grande Prairie	ALB	Tom Zimmerman	1990	2058
19 10/16	12 2/16	7 8/16	M	Wawa	ONT	Edwin L. DeYoung	1990	2058
19 10/16	12 2/16	7 8/16	M	Troy Lake	MAN	Derek McCarthy	1990	2058
19 10/16	12 5/16	7 5/16	M	Canterbury	NBW	Don Rahe	1990	2058
19 10/16	12 2/16	7 8/16	M	Gila County	AZ	Amos Culbert	1990	2058
19 10/16	12 2/16	7 8/16	M	La Plata County	CO	John L. Gardner	1990	2058
19 10/16	12 6/16	7 4/16	M	Gila County	AZ	Warren Mark Smith	1990	2058
19 10/16	12 8/16	7 2/16	M	Cordova	AK	Tony Casagrande	1990	2058
19 10/16	12 2/16	7 8/16	M	Kosciusko Island	AK	Rob Seelye	1991	2058
19 10/16	12 7/16	7 3/16	M	The Pas	MAN	Marvin Weible	1991	2058
19 10/16	12 5/16	7 5/16	M	Thompson	MAN	Thomas P. Rabette	1991	2058
19 10/16	12 1/16	7 9/16	M	Athabasca River	ALB	Bruce R. Schoeneweis	1991	2058
19 10/16	12 3/16	7 7/16	M	Taylors Brook	NFL	Thomas Spero	1991	2058
19 10/16	12 8/16	7 2/16	M	Clinton County	NY	Jim Provost	1991	2058
19 10/16	12 5/16	7 5/16	M	Sechelt	BC	Ken Davidson	1992	2058
19 10/16	12 8/16	7 2/16	M	Beluga River	AK	James R. Bussell	1992	2058
19 10/16	12 6/16	7 4/16	M	Thurston County	WA	Curt L. Lake	1992	2058
19 10/16	12 1/16	7 9/16	M	Ear Falls	ONT	Robert J. Skorupski	1992	2058
19 10/16	12 8/16	7 2/16	M	Coos County	NH	Paul Michaud	1992	2058
19 10/16	12 2/16	7 8/16	M	Dryden	ONT	Mike Barkac	1992	2058
19 10/16	12 4/16	7 6/16	M	Swan River	MAN	Jeff Glaser	1992	2058
19 10/16	12 2/16	7 8/16	M	St. Louis County	MN	Kenneth G. Larsen	1992	2058
19 10/16	12 2/16	7 8/16	M	Las Animas County	CO	Lonny Stuht	1992	2058
19 10/16	12 3/16	7 7/16	M	Delta County	MI	Ronald J. Sharkey	1992	2058
19 10/16	12 2/16	7 8/16	M	Nestor Falls	ONT	Roy R. Loomis	1993	2058
19 10/16	11 12/16	7 14/16	M	Wabowden	MAN	Ken Whitney	1993	2058
19 10/16	12 0/16	7 10/16	M	Besnard Lake	SAS	Travis Todd	1993	2058
19 10/16	11 15/16	7 11/16	M	Green Lake	SAS	Ray Murphy	1993	2058
19 10/16	11 14/16	7 12/16	M	Hastings	ONT	Robert L. Moon, Jr.	1993	2058
19 10/16	12 2/16	7 8/16	M	Thunder Bay	ONT	Joseph Scott Mandel	1993	2058
19 10/16	12 5/16	7 5/16	M	Catron County	NM	Mark Rucker	1993	2058
19 10/16	12 6/16	7 4/16	M	Sullivan County	NY	Theresa Henriksen	1993	2058
19 10/16	11 9/16	8 1/16	M	Buffalo Narrows	SAS	Bill Rethage	1994	2058
19 10/16	12 8/16	7 2/16	M	Sturgeon Landing	SAS	Ryan Hugelen	1994	2058
19 10/16	12 1/16	7 9/16	M	Silver Valley	ALB	Walter Krom	1994	2058
19 10/16	12 3/16	7 7/16	M	Lemhi County	ID	Michael Judas	1995	2058
19 10/16	12 3/16	7 7/16	M	La Ronge	SAS	Steve Hammond	1995	2058
19 10/16	12 5/16	7 5/16	M	Carrot River	SAS	Ronald Gullickson	1995	2058
19 10/16	12 7/16	7 3/16	M	Tuolumne County	CA	David R. Krawchuk	1995	2058
19 10/16	11 12/16	7 14/16	M	El Dorado County	CA	Rick L. Self	1995	2058
19 10/16	12 4/16	7 6/16	M	Atikokan	ONT	Ted Bower	1995	2058
19 10/16	12 8/16	7 2/16	M	Sioux Narrows	ONT	Gary W. Bishop	1995	2058
19 10/16	12 2/16	7 8/16	M	Madera County	CA	Jim Doherty, Jr.	1995	2058
19 10/16	12 4/16	7 6/16	M	Prince of Wales Island	AK	Danny Moore	1996	2058
19 10/16	12 0/16	7 10/16	M	Birch Mtns.	ALB	John "Jack" Nothardt	1996	2058
19 10/16	11 14/16	7 12/16	M	Jellicoe	ONT	Dale Long	1996	2058
19 10/16	12 7/16	7 3/16	M	Sawyer County	WI	David Fetting	1996	2058
19 10/16	12 8/16	7 2/16	M	Bayfield County	WI	Jerald Smith	1996	2058
19 10/16	12 2/16	7 8/16	M	Los Angeles County	CA	David Whiteman	1996	2058
19 10/16	12 3/16	7 7/16	M	Clarke Lake	SAS	Robert C. Braun	1997	2058
19 10/16	12 15/16	6 11/16	M	Kelvington	SAS	Leamon Ferrell	1997	2058
19 10/16	12 5/16	7 5/16	M	Woodcamp Creek	AK	George Grovhoug	1997	2058
19 10/16	12 4/16	7 6/16	M	Peace River	ALB	Zig Kertenis, Jr.	1997	2058
19 10/16	12 3/16	7 7/16	M	Peace River	ALB	Cordie Schlomer	1997	2058
19 10/16	11 11/16	7 15/16	M	Wabigoon	ONT	Enoch S. Studley, Jr.	1997	2058
19 10/16	12 0/16	7 10/16	M	Cochrane	ONT	Tim Guminski	1997	2058
19 10/16	12 11/16	6 15/16	M	Menominee County	MI	Dean R. Heath	1997	2058
19 10/16	12 3/16	7 7/16	M	Vilas County	WI	Robin Kendler	1997	2058
19 10/16	12 7/16	7 3/16	M	Pope County	AR	Stephen Lynn	1997	2058
19 10/16	12 5/16	7 5/16	M	Lac Ile-a-la-Crosse	SAS	Jerry Bodar	1998	2058
19 10/16	12 5/16	7 5/16	M	Clearwater County	ID	Kevin Schmid	1998	2058
19 10/16	11 15/16	7 11/16	M	Black River	ONT	Jack Leggo	1998	2058
19 10/16	12 2/16	7 8/16	M	Wawa	ONT	Tad H. Ralston	1998	2058
19 10/16	12 3/16	7 7/16	M	Cook County	MN	Gregory T. Bolf	1998	2058
19 10/16	12 4/16	7 6/16	M	Elmore County	ID	David Kelm	1999	2058
19 10/16	12 0/16	7 10/16	M	Wapawekka Lake	SAS	Randall Otwell	1999	2058
19 10/16	12 3/16	7 7/16	M	Fairbanks	AK	Bart Colledge	1999	2058
19 10/16	12 0/16	7 10/16	M	Sussex	NBW	Richard Johns	1999	2058
19 10/16	12 0/16	7 10/16	M	Kanawha County	WV	Ronzel Moss	1999	2058
19 10/16	12 7/16	7 3/16	M	McDowell County	WV	Paul Delida, Jr.	1999	2058
19 10/16	12 5/16	7 5/16	M	Prince of Wales Island	AK	Jack M. Heil	2000	2058
19 10/16	12 5/16	7 5/16	M	Dolores County	CO	Mike Schwartz	2000	2058
19 10/16	12 5/16	7 5/16	M	Eagle County	CO	Dale L. Toltzmann	2000	2058
19 10/16	12 2/16	7 8/16	M	Orange County	NY	Rich McCoy	2000	2058
19 10/16	12 8/16	7 2/16	M	Duck Mtn.	SAS	Scott M. Gauthier	2001	2058
19 10/16	12 4/16	7 6/16	M	Wanless	MAN	Scotty A. Rehak	2001	2058
19 10/16	12 8/16	7 2/16	M	Olha	MAN	John Wooldridge	2001	2058
19 10/16	12 13/16	6 13/16	F	St. Louis County	MN	David Nordberg	2001	2058
19 10/16	12 10/16	7 0/16	M	Delta County	CO	Nate Hawkins	2001	2058
19 10/16	12 4/16	7 6/16	M	Bonneville County	ID	Brian McKinney	2002	2058
19 10/16	12 4/16	7 6/16	M	Wabasca River	ALB	Mike Hauser	2002	2058
19 10/16	12 6/16	7 4/16	M	La Ronge	SAS	Mark F. Willms	2002	2058
19 10/16	11 15/16	7 11/16	M	Thunder Hills	SAS	Nathan Jones	2002	2058
19 10/16	12 0/16	7 10/16	M	Lake Richards	SAS	Owen Keeton, Jr.	2002	2058
19 10/16	12 7/16	7 3/16	M	Ashland County	WI	Randy King	2002	2058
19 10/16	12 3/16	7 7/16	M	Mesa County	CO	Richard Schroder	2002	2058
19 10/16	12 2/16	7 8/16	M	Roddickton	NFL	Mark J. Yurchisin, MD	2002	2058
19 10/16	12 7/16	7 3/16	M	Orange County	NY	Dean O'Hanlon	2002	2058
19 10/16	12 1/16	7 9/16	M	McCreary	MAN	Lonnie Hamil	2003	2058
19 10/16	12 3/16	7 7/16	M	Centerville	NBW	Nathan Fenderson	2003	2058
19 10/16	12 6/16	7 4/16	M	Dorion	ONT	Tom J. Joy	2003	2058
19 10/16	12 6/16	7 4/16	M	Aitkin County	MN	Dustin Brodina	2003	2058
*19 10/16	12 7/16	7 3/16	M	Preston County	WV	Skip V. Greathouse	2003	2058

147

BLACK BEAR

Minimum Score 18 — Continued

SCORE	GREATEST LENGTH	GREATEST WIDTH	SEX	AREA	STATE/ PROVINCE	HUNTER'S NAME	DATE	RANK
19 10/16	12 4/16	7 6/16	M	Churchill River	SAS	Jim Leqve	2004	2058
19 10/16	12 8/16	7 2/16	M	Fort McMurray	ALB	Steve Dultz	2004	2058
19 10/16	12 6/16	7 4/16	M	Churchill Lake	SAS	Eric F. Efird	2004	2058
19 10/16	12 8/16	7 2/16	M	Lake County	MN	Cory Hendricks	2004	2058
19 10/16	12 14/16	6 12/16	M	Forest County	WI	Eugene J. Wagner	2004	2058
19 10/16	12 6/16	7 4/16	M	Florence County	WI	Eric Burling	2004	2058
19 10/16	12 8/16	7 2/16	M	Burnett County	WI	Janet Ann Renfrow	2004	2058
*19 10/16	12 7/16	7 3/16	M	Red Lake	ONT	Les Traub	2004	2058
19 10/16	11 14/16	7 12/16	M	Aroostook County	ME	Marco A. Sierra	2004	2058
*19 10/16	12 10/16	7 0/16	M	Logan County	AR	Ken Panther	2004	2058
19 10/16	12 3/16	7 7/16	M	Frobisher Lake	SAS	Richard B. Dyer	2005	2058
19 10/16	12 0/16	7 10/16	M	Cadogan	ALB	Michael S. Elson	2005	2058
*19 10/16	12 4/16	7 6/16	M	La Loche	SAS	Joe Schaffer	2005	2058
*19 10/16	11 15/16	7 11/16	M	Redditt	ONT	James Kingsley	2005	2058
19 10/16	12 10/16	7 0/16	M	Kittson County	MN	Doug Strecker	2005	2058
*19 10/16	12 10/16	7 0/16	M	Kittson County	MN	Thad Nelson	2005	2058
19 10/16	12 4/16	7 6/16	M	Alpena County	MI	Chad Smith	2005	2058
19 10/16	11 13/16	7 13/16	M	Bearhead Lake	MAN	Alvin Haugen	2005	2058
19 10/16	12 6/16	7 4/16	M	Tulare County	CA	LaRon Storck	2005	2058
19 10/16	12 5/16	7 5/16	M	Blaine County	ID	Andrew Beck	2006	2058
19 10/16	12 1/16	7 9/16	M	Jellicoe	ONT	Kory Lang	2006	2058
19 10/16	12 5/16	7 5/16	M	El Dorado County	CA	Randy Long	2006	2058
19 10/16	12 7/16	7 3/16	M	McWatters	QUE	Ronald Guertin	2007	2058
19 10/16	12 5/16	7 5/16	M	Kuiu Island	AK	Frank S. Noska IV	2007	2058
*19 10/16	12 4/16	7 6/16	M	Willow Creek	ONT	Ronald F. Lax	2007	2058
19 10/16	12 6/16	7 4/16	M	Perrault Falls	ONT	Ted J. Wolf	2007	2058
*19 10/16	12 6/16	7 4/16	M	Hornepayne	ONT	Joel Van Lannen	2007	2058
19 10/16	11 10/16	8 0/16	M	Eriksdale	MAN	Todd Yoder	2007	2058
19 10/16	13 1/16	6 9/16	M	Sawyer County	WI	Thomas Granica	2007	2058
*19 10/16	12 9/16	7 1/16	M	Alma	NBW	Michael Benbrook	2008	2058
19 10/16	12 5/16	7 5/16	M	Grande Prairie	ALB	David J. Nicolai	2008	2058
*19 10/16	12 5/16	7 5/16	M	Donnelly	ALB	William Craig Holt	2008	2058
19 10/16	12 12/16	6 14/16	M	The Pas	MAN	William Peterson	2008	2058
19 10/16	12 3/16	7 7/16	M	Clearwater County	ID	Cliff Campbell	2008	2058
*19 10/16	11 12/16	7 14/16	M	Thunder Bay	ONT	Tom Schettling	2008	2058
19 10/16	12 12/16	6 14/16	M	Rusk County	WI	Kevin J. Lockwood	2008	2058
*19 10/16	12 3/16	7 7/16	M	Biscotasing	ONT	Brett Ridgway	2009	2058
19 10/16	11 15/16	7 11/16	M	Cook County	MN	David D. Schwantz	2009	2058
19 10/16	12 4/16	7 6/16	M	High Level	ALB	Von L. Evans	2010	2058
19 9/16	12 10/16	6 15/16	M	Douglas County	WI	Edwin Fitzgerald	1966	2225
19 9/16	12 6/16	7 3/16	M	Grand County	CO	Judd Cooney	1967	2225
19 9/16	12 0/16	7 9/16	M	Ignace	ONT	Gordon Bentley	1968	2225
19 9/16	11 15/16	7 10/16	M	Idaho County	ID	Kenneth Wallenberg	1970	2225
19 9/16	11 9/16	8 0/16	M	Boise County	ID	Ronald L. Sherer	1971	2225
19 9/16	12 1/16	7 8/16	M	Blount County	TN	Gary Jordan	1973	2225
19 9/16	12 5/16	7 4/16	M	Franklin County	ME	Ralph Pfister	1977	2225
19 9/16	11 9/16	8 0/16	M	Boise County	ID	Susan D. Sherer	1978	2225
19 9/16	12 4/16	7 5/16	M	Idaho County	ID	Bob Jacobsen	1979	2225
19 9/16	12 4/16	7 5/16	M	Valley County	ID	L. Dean Goodner	1979	2225
19 9/16	11 11/16	7 14/16	M	Sandilands	MAN	Ron Derlago	1979	2225
19 9/16	12 4/16	7 5/16	M	Grand County	CO	Leonard L. Kohan	1980	2225
19 9/16	12 0/16	7 9/16	M	Pitkin County	CO	Judy Nielsen	1981	2225
19 9/16	11 11/16	7 14/16	M	Bobcaygeon	ONT	Dale W. Gray	1982	2225
19 9/16	12 4/16	7 5/16	M	Ear Falls	ONT	Grant A. Poindexter	1982	2225
19 9/16	12 0/16	7 9/16	M	Fort Wainwright	AK	Gregory Dean Royse	1983	2225
19 9/16	12 4/16	7 5/16	M	Coconino County	AZ	Dale H. Long	1983	2225
19 9/16	12 5/16	7 4/16	M	Sawyer County	WI	Richard Carolfi	1983	2225
19 9/16	12 3/16	7 6/16	M	Mesa County	CO	Jeff Tedore	1984	2225
19 9/16	12 8/16	7 1/16	M	Beluga River	AK	Chad Burris	1984	2225
19 9/16	12 5/16	7 4/16	M	Itasca County	MN	Dennis K. Fideldy	1984	2225
19 9/16	12 6/16	7 3/16	M	Uintah County	UT	John C. Matejov	1985	2225
19 9/16	12 6/16	7 3/16	M	La Tuque	QUE	John C. Hutchinson	1986	2225
19 9/16	12 5/16	7 4/16	M	Bonneville County	ID	Larry Cross	1986	2225
19 9/16	12 7/16	7 2/16	M	Washington County	ME	Cliff Wiseman	1986	2225
19 9/16	12 7/16	7 2/16	M	Hudson Bay	SAS	Bill Zahradka	1987	2225
19 9/16	12 1/16	7 8/16	M	Kenora	ONT	Scott A. Lamphier	1987	2225
19 9/16	12 5/16	7 4/16	M	Atikokan	ONT	Lawrence A. Meyers	1987	2225
19 9/16	12 5/16	7 4/16	M	Fort Coulonge	QUE	Harvey D. Garrett	1988	2225
19 9/16	12 1/16	7 8/16	M	Barron County	WI	Dennis O. Freid	1988	2225
19 9/16	12 10/16	6 15/16	M	Taylor County	WI	Rick Smith	1988	2225
19 9/16	12 4/16	7 5/16	M	Emmet County	MI	Randall J. McCune	1988	2225
19 9/16	12 2/16	7 7/16	M	Madison County	MT	Gary R. Petty	1988	2225
19 9/16	12 1/16	7 8/16	M	Prince of Wales Island	AK	Carl E. Brent	1989	2225
19 9/16	11 11/16	7 14/16	M	Las Animas County	CO	R. L. Erdmann	1989	2225
19 9/16	12 4/16	7 5/16	M	Killala Lake	ONT	Orrin Malick	1989	2225
19 9/16	12 9/16	7 0/16	M	Saint John	NBW	Mike L. LaVan	1989	2225
19 9/16	11 15/16	7 10/16	M	Fort Coulonge	QUE	J. J. Fegan	1989	2225
19 9/16	12 1/16	7 8/16	M	Carrot River	SAS	Quince Hale	1989	2225
19 9/16	12 7/16	7 2/16	M	Prince of Wales Island	AK	Dan E. Hiltz	1989	2225
19 9/16	12 11/16	6 14/16	M	Messines	QUE	Charles L. Hart III	1989	2225
19 9/16	12 6/16	7 3/16	M	Kings County	NBW	Ernest Sperl	1989	2225
19 9/16	12 5/16	7 4/16	M	Mowat Township	ONT	Ricky McDaniel	1990	2225
19 9/16	12 1/16	7 8/16	M	Boise County	ID	James L. Sullivan	1990	2225
19 9/16	12 5/16	7 4/16	M	Madison County	ID	Rita Harris	1990	2225
19 9/16	11 15/16	7 10/16	M	Lac Flavrian	QUE	Eric Grandbois	1990	2225
19 9/16	12 5/16	7 4/16	M	Somerset County	ME	Gregory A. Bonecutter, Sr.	1990	2225
19 9/16	12 1/16	7 8/16	M	Lake of the Woods Cty	MN	Brian McGregor	1990	2225
19 9/16	12 0/16	7 9/16	M	Sudbury	ONT	Jim Bratton	1991	2225
19 9/16	12 0/16	7 9/16	M	High Level	ALB	R. E. Smith	1991	2225
19 9/16	11 13/16	7 12/16	M	Leaf River	QUE	Gary Kjellander	1991	2225
19 9/16	12 4/16	7 5/16	M	St. Louis County	MN	Edwin John Durushia	1991	2225
19 9/16	12 4/16	7 5/16	M	Dolores County	CO	Jay Jaburg	1991	2225
19 9/16	12 2/16	7 7/16	M	Routt County	CO	Bob Sanders	1991	2225
19 9/16	12 9/16	7 0/16	M	Logan Lake	BC	Abe Dougan	1992	2225
19 9/16	12 5/16	7 4/16	M	Remigny	QUE	Steve Reedy	1992	2225

BLACK BEAR

Minimum Score 18   Continued

SCORE	GREATEST LENGTH	GREATEST WIDTH	SEX	AREA	STATE/ PROVINCE	HUNTER'S NAME	DATE	RANK
19 9/16	12 0/16	7 9/16	M	Lynn Lake	MAN	Ernest B. Gilbert	1993	2225
19 9/16	12 3/16	7 6/16	M	Kipawa	QUE	John Mascellino	1993	2225
19 9/16	12 6/16	7 3/16	M	Hector Lake	ONT	Dick Clark	1994	2225
19 9/16	11 15/16	7 10/16	M	Ena Lake	SAS	John R. Burgher	1994	2225
19 9/16	12 4/16	7 5/16	M	Holinshead Lake	ONT	Michael Kemp	1995	2225
19 9/16	12 2/16	7 7/16	M	Lake Nameigos	ONT	Jeffrey T. Schwartz	1995	2225
19 9/16	11 15/16	7 10/16	M	Mendocino County	CA	Michael J. Camp	1995	2225
19 9/16	12 7/16	7 2/16	M	Bayfield County	WI	Roger Lemler	1995	2225
19 9/16	12 6/16	7 3/16	M	Rio Arriba County	NM	Rick Thaden	1995	2225
19 9/16	12 6/16	7 3/16	M	Slave Lake	ALB	Terry C. Parkinson	1996	2225
19 9/16	12 5/16	7 4/16	M	Conklin	ALB	Tom Nelson	1996	2225
19 9/16	12 1/16	7 8/16	M	Wawang Lake	ONT	Jeffrey J. Rhinehart	1996	2225
19 9/16	12 2/16	7 7/16	M	Poplarfield	MAN	Jim Jepson	1996	2225
19 9/16	12 6/16	7 3/16	M	Indian River	AK	Rick Schikora	1996	2225
19 9/16	12 4/16	7 5/16	M	Aroostook County	ME	Mike Bacher	1996	2225
19 9/16	12 4/16	7 5/16	M	Chippewa County	WI	Matthew T. Hussin	1996	2225
19 9/16	12 1/16	7 8/16	M	Grande Prairie	ALB	Daniel R. Strickland	1996	2225
19 9/16	12 4/16	7 5/16	M	Iron County	WI	Dennis J. Kaderavek	1996	2225
19 9/16	12 3/16	7 6/16	M	Weymouth	NS	Paul I. Scott	1996	2225
19 9/16	12 7/16	7 2/16	M	Burnett County	WI	Scott J. Strese	1996	2225
19 9/16	12 5/16	7 4/16	M	Athabasca River	ALB	Russell Thornberry	1997	2225
19 9/16	12 3/16	7 6/16	M	Jogues	ONT	Dennis L. Fulcer	1997	2225
19 9/16	12 0/16	7 9/16	M	Lemhi County	ID	Brian Oestreich	1997	2225
19 9/16	11 12/16	7 13/16	M	Preissac	QUE	Paul Sedera	1997	2225
19 9/16	12 10/16	6 15/16	M	Kittitas County	WA	Dave Boothman	1997	2225
19 9/16	11 15/16	7 10/16	M	Greenlee County	AZ	Woody Kazlo	1997	2225
19 9/16	12 7/16	7 2/16	M	Bissett	MAN	Robert W. Harris	1998	2225
19 9/16	12 8/16	7 1/16	M	Duck Mtn.	MAN	Robert J. Fox	1998	2225
19 9/16	12 2/16	7 7/16	M	Nestor Falls	ONT	Marty Landreth	1998	2225
19 9/16	12 3/16	7 6/16	M	Ft. McMurray	ALB	Michael Frellsen	1998	2225
19 9/16	11 15/16	7 10/16	M	Chipewyan Lake	ALB	David D. Manuszak	1998	2225
19 9/16	12 4/16	7 5/16	M	Sussex	NBW	Harold Croteau	1998	2225
19 9/16	12 9/16	7 0/16	M	Pennington County	MN	Dana C. Klos	1998	2225
19 9/16	12 2/16	7 7/16	M	Athabasca River	ALB	Ronald T. Morgan	1999	2225
19 9/16	12 2/16	7 7/16	M	Athabasca River	ALB	James E. Schmid	1999	2225
19 9/16	12 2/16	7 7/16	M	Fergus County	MT	Donny Roy	1999	2225
19 9/16	12 9/16	7 0/16	M	Elk Point	ALB	Andy P. Charchun	1999	2225
19 9/16	11 15/16	7 10/16	M	Nipawin	SAS	Mark Balzer	1999	2225
19 9/16	12 3/16	7 6/16	M	Alexander Archipelago	AK	Steve Hohensee	1999	2225
19 9/16	12 9/16	7 0/16	M	Smoothstone Lake	SAS	Gregory Hoffmeister	2000	2225
19 9/16	11 14/16	7 11/16	M	Pikwitonei	MAN	Kenneth Brown	2000	2225
19 9/16	12 5/16	7 4/16	M	Mistatim	SAS	William Prunty	2000	2225
19 9/16	12 0/16	7 9/16	M	Matachewan	ONT	Thomas E. Hain	2000	2225
19 9/16	12 9/16	7 0/16	M	Olha	MAN	Bill Clink	2000	2225
19 9/16	12 4/16	7 5/16	M	Utah County	UT	Reid Hendrickson	2000	2225
*19 9/16	12 4/16	7 5/16	M	Tucker County	WV	Wayne E. McKenzie	2001	2225
19 9/16	12 0/16	7 9/16	M	Ft. McMurray	ALB	Jeffery G. Woodlee	2002	2225
19 9/16	11 15/16	7 10/16	M	Nevada County	CA	Richard Gonzales	2002	2225
19 9/16	12 5/16	7 4/16	M	Marathon County	WI	David Falkowski	2002	2225
19 9/16	12 2/16	7 7/16	M	Prince of Wales Island	AK	Stephen D. Carver	2002	2225
19 9/16	12 0/16	7 9/16	M	Routt County	CO	Cedar Beauregard	2002	2225
19 9/16	12 4/16	7 5/16	M	Kanawha County	WV	Clinton Mullins	2002	2225
19 9/16	12 7/16	7 2/16	M	Fort McMurray	ALB	Steve P. Dultz	2003	2225
19 9/16	12 7/16	7 2/16	M	Grandview	MAN	Todd Standke	2003	2225
19 9/16	11 11/16	7 14/16	M	Prince of Wales Island	AK	Cameron R. Hanes	2003	2225
19 9/16	12 3/16	7 6/16	M	Albaa Creek	BC	Rick Davis	2003	2225
19 9/16	12 4/16	7 5/16	M	High Level	ALB	Richard M. Penn	2003	2225
19 9/16	11 13/16	7 12/16	M	Buffalo Narrows	SAS	Billy Sherwood	2003	2225
19 9/16	12 2/16	7 7/16	M	Lake Egenolf	MAN	John A. Laitinen, Jr.	2003	2225
19 9/16	11 14/16	7 11/16	M	Amos	QUE	Sam Moss	2003	2225
19 9/16	12 3/16	7 6/16	M	Zec Capitachouane	QUE	Ken H. Taylor	2003	2225
19 9/16	12 4/16	7 5/16	M	Emo	ONT	Kevin Hungerford	2003	2225
*19 9/16	12 11/16	6 14/16	M	Marshall County	MN	Nathan Blakesley	2003	2225
19 9/16	12 3/16	7 6/16	M	Ontonagon County	MI	John R. Reck	2003	2225
19 9/16	12 12/16	6 13/16	M	Athabasca	ALB	Doug Long	2004	2225
19 9/16	11 10/16	7 15/16	M	Salmond River	NBW	Gary Dennis	2004	2225
19 9/16	12 7/16	7 2/16	M	Prince of Wales Island	AK	Ronnie Moore	2004	2225
19 9/16	12 6/16	7 3/16	M	Stephenville	NFL	Lloyd Smith	2004	2225
19 9/16	12 6/16	7 3/16	M	Cree River	SAS	Owen Keeton, Jr.	2004	2225
19 9/16	12 3/16	7 6/16	M	Ignace	ONT	Bradford Pittman	2004	2225
19 9/16	12 10/16	6 15/16	M	Marinette County	WI	David D. Waldschmidt	2004	2225
*19 9/16	12 6/16	7 3/16	M	Chippewa County	MI	John D. Yezbak	2004	2225
19 9/16	12 13/16	6 12/16	M	Arkansas County	AR	Don Barnett	2004	2225
*19 9/16	12 5/16	7 4/16	M	Frenchman Butte	SAS	Gregory Stewart	2005	2225
*19 9/16	12 7/16	7 2/16	M	Pierceland	SAS	John E. Taylor	2005	2225
19 9/16	11 13/16	7 12/16	M	Thompson Lake	SAS	R. Charles Suttles	2005	2225
19 9/16	12 5/16	7 4/16	M	Ignace	ONT	Ryan J. Smith	2005	2225
19 9/16	12 3/16	7 6/16	M	Oconto County	WI	Michael J. Molitor	2005	2225
19 9/16	12 4/16	7 5/16	M	King County	WA	Patrick T. Balzer	2005	2225
19 9/16	12 7/16	7 2/16	M	Grayson County	VA	John Hauser	2005	2225
*19 9/16	12 8/16	7 1/16	M	Carrot River	SAS	Casey Hande	2006	2225
*19 9/16	12 3/16	7 6/16	M	Rice River	SAS	Corbin Gallmeier	2006	2225
19 9/16	12 5/16	7 4/16	M	Zeballos River	BC	Adam Bartsch	2006	2225
*19 9/16	12 8/16	7 1/16	M	Fond du Lac River	SAS	Robert G. Barden	2006	2225
*19 9/16	12 7/16	7 2/16	M	Waupaca County	WI	Jenny Koerner	2006	2225
19 9/16	12 2/16	7 7/16	M	Baraga County	MI	Thomas Hlinka	2006	2225
19 9/16	12 9/16	7 0/16	M	Bird River	MAN	Matt Parr	2007	2225
19 9/16	11 11/16	7 14/16	M	Chapleau	QUE	Danny Torboli	2007	2225
19 9/16	11 9/16	8 0/16	M	Bissett	MAN	Michael Clark	2007	2225
19 9/16	12 3/16	7 6/16	M	Matagami	QUE	Ken H. Taylor	2007	2225
*19 9/16	12 3/16	7 6/16	M	Zec Dumoine	QUE	Jeff C. Stimpson	2007	2225
19 9/16	12 5/16	7 4/16	M	Oba	ONT	Neil R. Leonard	2007	2225
19 9/16	12 4/16	7 5/16	M	Clearwater Lake	QUE	Walter J. Palmer	2007	2225
19 9/16	12 2/16	7 7/16	M	Kuiu Island	AK	Allyn Ladd	2008	2225
19 9/16	12 1/16	7 8/16	M	Utah County	UT	Shaun Evans	2008	2225

149

BLACK BEAR

Minimum Score 18   Continued

SCORE	GREATEST LENGTH	GREATEST WIDTH	SEX	AREA	STATE/ PROVINCE	HUNTER'S NAME	DATE	RANK
19 9/16	12 9/16	7 0/16	M	Tanana Flats	AK	Bert E. Thomas, Jr.	2008	2225
19 9/16	12 0/16	7 9/16	M	Lake St. Patrice	QUE	John P. O'Meara	2008	2225
*19 9/16	12 6/16	7 3/16	M	Price County	WI	William Poole	2008	2225
*19 9/16	12 8/16	7 1/16	M	Ashland County	WI	Joey Kranz	2008	2225
19 9/16	11 11/16	7 14/16	M	Las Animas County	CO	Scott Nelson	2008	2225
19 9/16	12 2/16	7 7/16	M	Athabasca River	ALB	Steff Stefanovich	2009	2225
*19 9/16	12 0/16	7 9/16	M	Biscotasing	ONT	Christopher F. Schoenherr	2010	2225
19 9/16	12 1/16	7 8/16	M	French River	ONT	Robert E. Kearney	2010	2225
19 8/16	12 3/16	7 5/16	M	Chapleau	ONT	Bob Sharpe	1959	2384
19 8/16	12 4/16	7 4/16	M	Presque Isle County	MI	Eugene W. McKechnie	1964	2384
19 8/16	12 6/16	7 2/16	M	Forest County	WI	Jerad Dittrich	1965	2384
19 8/16	12 1/16	7 7/16	M	Piscataquis County	ME	James Matulis	1967	2384
19 8/16	12 6/16	7 2/16	M	Crow Wing County	MN	James L. Beard	1975	2384
19 8/16	11 12/16	7 12/16	M	Boise County	ID	Jack Arbaugh	1976	2384
19 8/16	12 2/16	7 6/16	M	Ear Falls	ONT	Grant Poindexter	1978	2384
19 8/16	11 11/16	7 13/16	M	Atikokan	ONT	David Graves	1978	2384
19 8/16	12 5/16	7 3/16	M	Archuleta County	CO	Robert Hoague	1981	2384
19 8/16	12 3/16	7 5/16	M	Broadwater County	MT	Jan Hamer	1982	2384
19 8/16	12 3/16	7 5/16	M	Remigny	QUE	Joe Hopwood	1982	2384
19 8/16	11 15/16	7 9/16	M	Madison County	MT	Shep Lantow	1982	2384
19 8/16	12 7/16	7 1/16	M	Loon Lake	SAS	Brian Acton	1984	2384
19 8/16	11 15/16	7 9/16	M	Fergus County	MT	Jim Nette	1984	2384
19 8/16	12 6/16	7 2/16	M	Hudson Bay	SAS	Bill Zahradka	1984	2384
19 8/16	12 0/16	7 8/16	M	Las Animas County	CO	Sam Durham	1984	2384
19 8/16	11 11/16	7 13/16	M	Converse County	WY	Neil Hymas	1984	2384
19 8/16	12 8/16	7 0/16	M	Sioux Narrows	ONT	Kenneth E. Krahn	1985	2384
19 8/16	12 2/16	7 6/16	M	Grant County	OR	Mike E. Billman	1985	2384
19 8/16	11 14/16	7 10/16	M	Siskiyou County	CA	Richard L. Westervelt	1985	2384
19 8/16	12 6/16	7 2/16	M	One Portage Lake	MAN	Paolo Strapazzon	1986	2384
19 8/16	12 4/16	7 4/16	M	Minden	ONT	William J. Davi	1986	2384
19 8/16	12 8/16	7 0/16	M	Lincoln County	MT	Jim Eff	1986	2384
19 8/16	12 4/16	7 4/16	M	Custer County	ID	Richard D. Stocking	1986	2384
19 8/16	12 5/16	7 3/16	M	Huerfano County	CO	Randy Wright	1987	2384
19 8/16	11 13/16	7 11/16	M	Essex County	NY	Paul Durling	1987	2384
19 8/16	12 5/16	7 3/16	M	Hancock County	ME	John R. Mitchell	1987	2384
19 8/16	12 4/16	7 4/16	M	Bonneville County	ID	Larry Cross	1988	2384
19 8/16	12 0/16	7 8/16	M	Maniwaki	QUE	Aldo Bonacasta, Jr.	1989	2384
19 8/16	12 10/16	6 14/16	M	Duchesne County	UT	Jerry B. Reynolds	1989	2384
19 8/16	11 15/16	7 9/16	M	La Ronge	SAS	Robert D. Lingo	1989	2384
19 8/16	12 1/16	7 7/16	M	San Fernando Island	AK	Kurt Goesch	1989	2384
19 8/16	12 0/16	7 8/16	M	Zec Maganasipi	QUE	Stephen Kotz	1989	2384
19 8/16	12 2/16	7 6/16	M	Bigoray River	ALB	Gunter Lemke	1990	2384
19 8/16	12 11/16	6 13/16	M	Fort McMurray	ALB	Mike Menke	1990	2384
19 8/16	12 5/16	7 3/16	M	Archuleta County	CO	Roger DeGroat	1990	2384
19 8/16	12 4/16	7 4/16	M	Clackamas County	OR	Ben R. Cook	1990	2384
19 8/16	11 14/16	7 10/16	M	Custer County	ID	David J. McPherson	1990	2384
19 8/16	12 5/16	7 3/16	M	Forest County	WI	Mark Gaffke	1990	2384
19 8/16	12 3/16	7 5/16	M	Rio Arriba County	NM	Robert J. Seeds	1990	2384
19 8/16	12 7/16	7 1/16	M	Mons Township	ONT	Russell Trusty	1991	2384
19 8/16	12 1/16	7 7/16	M	Atikokan	ONT	Jim Aebel	1991	2384
19 8/16	11 14/16	7 10/16	M	Thunder Bay	ONT	Dave McKenzie	1991	2384
19 8/16	12 4/16	7 4/16	M	Zec Dumoine	QUE	John K. Deveney	1991	2384
19 8/16	12 0/16	7 8/16	M	Routt County	CO	Joel Anderson	1992	2384
19 8/16	12 4/16	7 4/16	M	Fort McMurray	ALB	Mark A. Balavender	1992	2384
19 8/16	12 0/16	7 8/16	M	Fort McMurray	ALB	Jim Trafford	1992	2384
19 8/16	12 5/16	7 3/16	M	Zec St. Patrice	QUE	Ted Brilhart	1992	2384
19 8/16	11 15/16	7 9/16	M	Snow Lake	MAN	Thomas C. Schnarre	1992	2384
19 8/16	11 15/16	7 9/16	M	Lake Preissac	QUE	Bob Sands	1992	2384
19 8/16	11 14/16	7 10/16	M	Obatogamau Lake	QUE	Zig Kertenis, Jr.	1992	2384
19 8/16	12 2/16	7 6/16	M	Athabasca River	ALB	Dean Bromberger	1993	2384
19 8/16	12 1/16	7 7/16	M	Lac La Biche	ALB	Tom Nelson	1993	2384
19 8/16	11 13/16	7 11/16	M	Besnard Lake	SAS	Tommy Mackey	1993	2384
19 8/16	12 0/16	7 8/16	M	Matagami	QUE	Jacques Harvey	1993	2384
19 8/16	12 8/16	7 0/16	M	Clearwater County	MN	Jon Drechsel	1993	2384
19 8/16	12 1/16	7 7/16	M	Butte County	CA	Dr. Douglas R. Hahn	1993	2384
19 8/16	12 4/16	7 4/16	M	Buffalo Narrows	SAS	Paul Kamenar, Jr.	1994	2384
19 8/16	11 12/16	7 12/16	M	Hearst	ONT	Tom Schoenike	1994	2384
19 8/16	12 3/16	7 5/16	M	Koochiching County	MN	Kenneth S. Turck	1994	2384
19 8/16	12 2/16	7 6/16	M	Atikokan	ONT	Dr. John R. Thodos	1994	2384
19 8/16	12 4/16	7 4/16	M	O'Sullivan Lake	ONT	Michael W. Ziembo	1994	2384
19 8/16	12 2/16	7 6/16	M	Sandoval County	NM	Phillip K. Whatley	1994	2384
19 8/16	11 14/16	7 10/16	M	Valley County	ID	Robert Staudt, Jr.	1994	2384
19 8/16	12 2/16	7 6/16	M	Boise County	ID	Scott Carlson	1995	2384
19 8/16	11 14/16	7 10/16	M	Smoky Lake	ALB	Mark Johnson	1995	2384
19 8/16	12 2/16	7 6/16	M	Athabasca River	ALB	Vince Migliorato	1995	2384
19 8/16	12 4/16	7 4/16	M	Hudson Bay	SAS	Tawnya M. Lee	1995	2384
19 8/16	12 2/16	7 6/16	M	Temiscaming	QUE	Tim Burris	1995	2384
19 8/16	12 4/16	7 4/16	M	St. Louis County	MN	Craig Mitchell Robarge	1995	2384
19 8/16	12 4/16	7 4/16	M	Grand Rapids	MAN	Dale Shove	1995	2384
19 8/16	12 0/16	7 8/16	M	Wawa	ONT	Joe Arbic, Jr.	1995	2384
19 8/16	12 8/16	7 0/16	M	Carrot River	SAS	Christopher Germain	1995	2384
19 8/16	12 6/16	7 2/16	M	Herkimer County	NY	Fran Madore	1995	2384
19 8/16	12 1/16	7 7/16	M	Oxford County	ME	Gary J. Russell	1995	2384
19 8/16	12 0/16	7 8/16	M	Anama Bay	MAN	Charles W. Haase	1995	2384
19 8/16	12 4/16	7 4/16	M	Lassen County	CA	Thomas Devlin	1995	2384
19 8/16	12 5/16	7 3/16	M	Kinwow Bay	MAN	Richard R. Sherman	1996	2384
19 8/16	12 7/16	7 1/16	M	Steepbank River	ALB	Don Budd	1996	2384
19 8/16	12 0/16	7 8/16	M	Fort McMurray	ALB	Joe Del Vecchio	1996	2384
19 8/16	12 4/16	7 4/16	M	Long Lake	ONT	John Nordrum	1996	2384
19 8/16	12 2/16	7 6/16	M	Candle Lake	SAS	David Clardy	1996	2384
19 8/16	12 2/16	7 6/16	M	High Level	ALB	John T. Harrison	1996	2384
19 8/16	12 5/16	7 3/16	M	Dorion	ONT	Bruce Hudalla	1996	2384
19 8/16	12 2/16	7 6/16	M	Madison County	ID	Donald M. Sherick	1996	2384
19 8/16	12 3/16	7 5/16	M	Big Sandy Lake	SAS	Renee Welle	1996	2384
19 8/16	12 7/16	7 1/16	M	Hawkrock	SAS	Jacob Kuntz	1996	2384

BLACK BEAR

Minimum Score 18   Continued

SCORE	GREATEST LENGTH	GREATEST WIDTH	SEX	AREA	STATE/ PROVINCE	HUNTER'S NAME	DATE	RANK
19 8/16	12 4/16	7 4/16	M	Menominee County	MI	Niles H. Amundsen	1996	2384
19 8/16	12 4/16	7 4/16	M	Douglas County	WI	Gary M. Bay	1996	2384
19 8/16	12 2/16	7 6/16	M	Iron County	WI	John R. Guillen	1996	2384
19 8/16	12 4/16	7 4/16	M	Crooked Creek	ALB	Brent Watson	1997	2384
19 8/16	12 4/16	7 4/16	M	Dryden	ONT	Penny J. Bowser	1997	2384
19 8/16	11 12/16	7 12/16	M	Fort Vermilion	ALB	W. C. MacCarty III, MD	1997	2384
19 8/16	11 13/16	7 11/16	M	Lake Manitowik	ONT	Chuck Webb	1997	2384
19 8/16	12 5/16	7 3/16	M	English River	ONT	Lou Milanesi	1997	2384
19 8/16	12 8/16	7 0/16	M	Peace River	ALB	Mark Titus	1997	2384
19 8/16	12 1/16	7 7/16	M	Chelmsford	ONT	Kyle Geremesz	1997	2384
19 8/16	12 1/16	7 7/16	M	Grand Lake	NFL	William L. Switzer	1997	2384
19 8/16	11 12/16	7 12/16	M	Dryden	ONT	John R. Gegner	1997	2384
19 8/16	12 0/16	7 8/16	M	Howell	ONT	Bryan Cripe	1997	2384
19 8/16	12 1/16	7 7/16	M	Dryden	ONT	Marvin D. Dennison, Sr.	1997	2384
19 8/16	12 3/16	7 5/16	M	Addison County	VT	Alan Rixon	1997	2384
19 8/16	11 15/16	7 9/16	M	Grant County	WV	Terrence Weidman	1997	2384
19 8/16	12 4/16	7 4/16	M	Athabasca River	ALB	Leonard Anglewitz	1998	2384
19 8/16	12 1/16	7 7/16	M	Thunder Bay	ONT	Johnny Prewett	1998	2384
19 8/16	11 13/16	7 11/16	M	Manitouwadge	ONT	Jim Dunigan	1998	2384
19 8/16	11 15/16	7 9/16	M	Harvey Station	NBW	John D. Thomas, Jr.	1998	2384
19 8/16	12 3/16	7 5/16	M	Buffalo Narrows	SAS	Linda Carol Graham	1998	2384
19 8/16	12 10/16	6 14/16	M	Minnedosa	MAN	David M. Brush	1998	2384
19 8/16	12 3/16	7 5/16	F	Bayfield County	WI	Teresa Fredrickson	1998	2384
19 8/16	12 2/16	7 6/16	M	Riou Lake	SAS	Ken Witt	1999	2384
19 8/16	11 13/16	7 11/16	M	San Miguel County	CO	Scott Nelson	1999	2384
19 8/16	11 14/16	7 10/16	M	Red Lake	ONT	Jim Popp	1999	2384
19 8/16	11 15/16	7 9/16	M	Valley County	ID	Vernon Hickman	1999	2384
19 8/16	11 14/16	7 10/16	M	Elmore County	ID	David Kelm	2000	2384
19 8/16	12 5/16	7 3/16	M	Madison County	ID	Mark Wayne Griffin	2000	2384
19 8/16	12 8/16	7 0/16	M	Sturgeon Lake	ALB	Greg Sutley	2000	2384
19 8/16	12 2/16	7 6/16	M	Chibougamau	QUE	Brian R. Brochu	2000	2384
19 8/16	11 15/16	7 9/16	M	Navajo County	AZ	Larry A. Watkins	2001	2384
19 8/16	11 15/16	7 9/16	M	Prince of Wales Island	AK	Jeff Falkner	2001	2384
19 8/16	12 6/16	7 2/16	M	Lake of the Woods	MAN	Todd Miller	2001	2384
19 8/16	12 0/16	7 8/16	M	Carswell Lake	SAS	Matt Conrardy	2001	2384
19 8/16	11 10/16	7 14/16	M	Bathurst	NBW	Robert E. Smith	2001	2384
19 8/16	12 6/16	7 2/16	M	Smoothstone Lake	SAS	Bill Magaziner	2001	2384
19 8/16	12 0/16	7 8/16	M	Iron County	WI	Pat Kranz	2001	2384
19 8/16	12 3/16	7 5/16	M	Redditt	ONT	Jonathan Kjendle	2002	2384
19 8/16	12 0/16	7 8/16	M	Dog Lake	ONT	Dale Long	2002	2384
19 8/16	12 12/16	6 12/16	M	Barron County	WI	David R. Lois	2002	2384
19 8/16	12 5/16	7 3/16	M	Olha	MAN	Brad Madigan	2003	2384
19 8/16	11 14/16	7 10/16	M	Boise County	ID	William E. Dean	2003	2384
19 8/16	12 6/16	7 2/16	M	McDougall River	BC	Jiri Hlavacek	2003	2384
19 8/16	12 4/16	7 4/16	M	Coconino County	AZ	Rodney L. Ronnebaum	2003	2384
19 8/16	12 3/16	7 5/16	M	Somerset County	ME	Brad Rattigan	2003	2384
19 8/16	12 5/16	7 3/16	M	Conklin	ALB	Jason Trick	2003	2384
19 8/16	11 15/16	7 9/16	M	Jackson County	CO	Marty Forster	2003	2384
19 8/16	12 3/16	7 5/16	M	Emo	ONT	Jared Mertes	2003	2384
19 8/16	12 3/16	7 5/16	M	Scott County	VA	Terry Begley	2003	2384
19 8/16	12 8/16	7 0/16	M	Pocahontas County	WV	Walter M. Frazier	2003	2384
19 8/16	12 4/16	7 4/16	M	Alpine County	CA	Jeremy Austin	2004	2384
19 8/16	12 1/16	7 7/16	M	Laurier	MAN	Marvin W. Eisenhauer	2004	2384
19 8/16	12 4/16	7 4/16	M	Greene County	NY	James B. Cook, Sr.	2004	2384
19 8/16	12 4/16	7 4/16	M	Steamboat Lake	BC	Allan Tew	2005	2384
19 8/16	12 4/16	7 4/16	M	100 Mile House	BC	Ron Klassen	2005	2384
19 8/16	12 4/16	7 4/16	M	Smeaton	SAS	Clyde Erhardt	2005	2384
19 8/16	12 4/16	7 4/16	M	Saddle Hills	ALB	Brandon Brown	2005	2384
19 8/16	11 15/16	7 9/16	M	Ft. McMurray	ALB	Fred Eichler	2005	2384
*19 8/16	12 5/16	7 3/16	M	St. Louis County	MN	Michael Hoffmann	2005	2384
*19 8/16	12 4/16	7 4/16	M	Franklin County	ME	M. Jerome Richard	2005	2384
19 8/16	12 2/16	7 6/16	M	Lincoln County	WI	Randy Culpitt	2005	2384
19 8/16	12 4/16	7 4/16	M	Lac du Bonnet	MAN	Douglas C. Fink	2005	2384
19 8/16	12 1/16	7 7/16	M	Nungesser Lake	ONT	J. Scott Strickland	2005	2384
*19 8/16	12 4/16	7 4/16	M	Olha	MAN	Bill Clink	2006	2384
19 8/16	11 15/16	7 9/16	M	Prince of Wales Island	AK	Bob Ameen	2006	2384
19 8/16	12 5/16	7 3/16	M	Prince of Wales Island	AK	M. Blake Patton	2006	2384
19 8/16	12 6/16	7 2/16	M	Redditt	ONT	Cody Stamm	2006	2384
*19 8/16	12 0/16	7 8/16	M	Siskiyou County	CA	Kirk Edgerton	2006	2384
19 8/16	12 4/16	7 4/16	M	Mille Lacs County	MN	Tony Zens	2006	2384
19 8/16	12 7/16	7 1/16	M	Bayfield County	WI	Marcus P. Allard	2006	2384
*19 8/16	12 0/16	7 8/16	M	Dog Lake	ONT	Blair E. Konczal	2006	2384
*19 8/16	12 7/16	7 1/16	M	Wythe County	VA	Ricky Lee Shelton	2006	2384
*19 8/16	12 6/16	7 2/16	M	Fairview	ALB	Troy Dzioba	2007	2384
19 8/16	12 0/16	7 8/16	M	Josephine Creek	ALB	Kaitlyn Popson	2007	2384
19 8/16	12 3/16	7 5/16	M	Gunnison County	CO	Roger A. Draper	2007	2384
*19 8/16	12 5/16	7 3/16	M	Montrose County	CO	Larry G. Phillips	2007	2384
*19 8/16	12 0/16	7 8/16	M	Vancouver Island	BC	Chantelle Bartsch	2008	2384
*19 8/16	12 0/16	7 8/16	M	Madawaska	NBW	Simon Levesque	2008	2384
*19 8/16	12 2/16	7 6/16	M	Pacific County	WA	Kelly S. Barnum	2008	2384
19 8/16	12 3/16	7 5/16	M	Fresno County	CA	Jeff Balch	2008	2384
19 8/16	12 7/16	7 1/16	M	Round Lake	SAS	Floyd Forster	2008	2384
*19 8/16	12 7/16	7 1/16	M	Kanawha County	WV	Dennis Young	2008	2384
*19 8/16	12 8/16	7 0/16	M	Carrot River	SAS	Doug Miller	2009	2384
19 8/16	12 6/16	7 2/16	M	Kuiu Island	AK	Frank S. Noska IV	2009	2384
*19 8/16	12 5/16	7 3/16	M	La Corey	ALB	Harrison Emigh	2009	2384
19 8/16	12 7/16	7 1/16	M	Lake Wasekamio	SAS	Ramon Neil Bell	2009	2384
19 8/16	12 9/16	6 15/16	M	Prince of Wales Island	AK	Bob Ameen	2009	2384
19 8/16	12 5/16	7 3/16	M	Dryden	ONT	Jeff Kramer	2009	2384
19 8/16	12 5/16	7 3/16	M	Koochiching County	MN	Charles W. Schultz	2009	2384
19 8/16	12 11/16	6 13/16	M	Barron County	WI	Timothy W. Walker	2009	2384
19 8/16	11 14/16	7 10/16	M	Thunder Bay	ONT	Miles Weaver	2009	2384
*19 8/16	12 0/16	7 8/16	M	Sandoval County	NM	Frank Hinkle, Jr.	2009	2384
*19 8/16	12 2/16	6 12/16	M	Lake Manitoba Narrows	MAN	Randy Wold	2010	2384
19 8/16	12 3/16	7 5/16	M	Place Lake	BC	Allan Tew	2010	2384

151

BLACK BEAR

Minimum Score 18   Continued

SCORE	GREATEST LENGTH	GREATEST WIDTH	SEX	AREA	STATE/ PROVINCE	HUNTER'S NAME	DATE	RANK
*19 8/16	12 9/16	6 15/16	M	Beaverhead County	MT	Reese A. Hadley	2010	2384
19 7/16	12 3/16	7 4/16	M	Kenora	ONT	Norman Pint	1964	2567
19 7/16	12 5/16	7 2/16	M	Caribou County	ID	Ronald S. Curtis	1969	2567
19 7/16	11 10/16	7 13/16	M	St. Louis County	MN	Don Dvoroznak	1970	2567
19 7/16	11 15/16	7 8/16	M	Moffat County	CO	Louis Preba	1972	2567
19 7/16	12 0/16	7 7/16	M	Haddo Township	ONT	Paul Sorke	1974	2567
19 7/16	12 0/16	7 7/16	M	Nestor Falls	ONT	Dennis Bartness	1974	2567
19 7/16	12 7/16	7 0/16	M	La Plata County	CO	Mike Dunaway	1975	2567
19 7/16	12 7/16	7 0/16	M	Somme	SAS	Phil Patchin	1975	2567
19 7/16	12 3/16	7 4/16	M	Garfield County	UT	Lee G. Stoddard	1975	2567
19 7/16	12 1/16	7 6/16	M	Roscommon County	MI	Roger Maeder	1976	2567
19 7/16	12 7/16	7 0/16	M	Snohomish County	WA	Charles J. Bartlett	1976	2567
19 7/16	12 0/16	7 7/16	M	Larimer County	CO	Ron Breitsprecher	1977	2567
19 7/16	12 2/16	7 5/16	M	Costilla County	CO	Dr. Thomas I. LaValle	1978	2567
19 7/16	11 11/16	7 12/16	M	Fremont County	CO	Ronald E. Sniff	1978	2567
19 7/16	12 5/16	7 2/16	M	Byers Lake	AK	Eugene Smith, Jr.	1978	2567
19 7/16	12 4/16	7 3/16	M	Idaho County	ID	Ray Koenig	1979	2567
19 7/16	12 11/16	6 12/16	M	Tehama County	CA	Roy B. Cartwright	1980	2567
19 7/16	12 2/16	7 5/16	M	Starkey Unit	OR	Bill Lancaster	1980	2567
19 7/16	12 7/16	7 0/16	M	Cass County	MN	Wayne Enger	1980	2567
19 7/16	11 15/16	7 8/16	M	Wolf Lake	ONT	Gary Johnston	1981	2567
19 7/16	12 0/16	7 7/16	M	Huerfano County	CO	Kent Connally	1983	2567
19 7/16	11 14/16	7 9/16	M	Bayfield County	WI	Steve Finn	1983	2567
19 7/16	12 0/16	7 7/16	M	Dryden	ONT	Alan Koester	1984	2567
19 7/16	11 8/16	7 15/16	M	Caramat	ONT	Robert D. DuBois	1984	2567
19 7/16	12 3/16	7 4/16	M	Hudson Bay	SAS	Bill Zahradka	1986	2567
19 7/16	12 3/16	7 4/16	M	Archuleta County	CO	Richard M. Young, Jr.	1986	2567
19 7/16	11 8/16	7 15/16	M	Sioux Narrows	ONT	Richard Sapp	1986	2567
19 7/16	11 15/16	7 8/16	M	Mine Centre	ONT	Lonnie Johnson	1987	2567
19 7/16	12 3/16	7 4/16	M	Siskiyou County	CA	John E. Koblos	1987	2567
19 7/16	12 5/16	7 2/16	M	Lac La Biche	ALB	Daniel J. Hungle	1988	2567
19 7/16	11 13/16	7 10/16	M	Vermilion Bay	ONT	John Gritmacker	1988	2567
19 7/16	12 4/16	7 3/16	M	Marathon County	WI	Stanley J. Budleski	1988	2567
19 7/16	12 3/16	7 4/16	M	Catron County	NM	Parris Nottingham	1988	2567
19 7/16	12 0/16	7 7/16	M	Mayerthorpe	ALB	Dan Perez	1989	2567
19 7/16	12 5/16	7 2/16	M	Kimowin Lake	ALB	Thomas Schneider	1989	2567
19 7/16	12 4/16	7 3/16	M	Buffalo Narrows	SAS	Matt Curry	1990	2567
19 7/16	12 3/16	7 4/16	M	Cadillac	QUE	Bob Drumm	1990	2567
19 7/16	12 8/16	6 15/16	M	Prince of Wales Island	AK	Doy Curtis	1990	2567
19 7/16	12 8/16	6 15/16	M	Bayfield County	WI	George Herold	1990	2567
19 7/16	12 5/16	7 2/16	M	Baraga County	MI	Mark Savic	1990	2567
19 7/16	12 3/16	7 4/16	M	Otter Creek	SAS	Les King	1991	2567
19 7/16	12 1/16	7 6/16	M	Ear Falls	ONT	Joseph E. Church	1991	2567
19 7/16	12 6/16	7 1/16	M	Goodsoil	SAS	Charles Ranua	1991	2567
19 7/16	11 10/16	7 13/16	M	Apisko Lake	MAN	Karl Teitt	1991	2567
19 7/16	12 5/16	7 2/16	M	Boise County	ID	Russ Meyer	1991	2567
19 7/16	12 4/16	7 3/16	M	Menominee County	WI	Kurt L. Goodwill	1991	2567
19 7/16	12 0/16	7 7/16	M	Roseau County	MN	Rick Hill	1991	2567
19 7/16	12 1/16	7 6/16	M	Elk River	BC	Alan Williams	1991	2567
19 7/16	12 0/16	7 7/16	M	Garfield County	CO	Stace Strouse	1991	2567
19 7/16	12 5/16	7 2/16	M	Wallowa County	OR	Tony Piper	1991	2567
19 7/16	12 6/16	7 1/16	M	Peace River	ALB	Kevin A. Hayden	1992	2567
19 7/16	12 4/16	7 3/16	M	Meadow Lake	SAS	Matthew Curry	1992	2567
19 7/16	11 11/16	7 12/16	M	Williams Lake	ONT	Eric Matheson	1992	2567
19 7/16	11 9/16	7 14/16	M	Alpine County	CA	Kevin L. Hall	1992	2567
19 7/16	12 0/16	7 7/16	M	Florence County	WI	Steven J. Woulf	1992	2567
19 7/16	12 0/16	7 7/16	M	Houghton County	MI	Gary Lubinski	1992	2567
19 7/16	12 3/16	7 4/16	M	Orange County	NY	Eric Puletti	1992	2567
19 7/16	12 0/16	7 7/16	M	Clahome River	BC	Wayne L. Meyers	1993	2567
19 7/16	12 5/16	7 2/16	M	Bissett	MAN	David Harris	1993	2567
19 7/16	12 4/16	7 3/16	M	Wandering River	ALB	Chris Boscamp	1993	2567
19 7/16	11 14/16	7 9/16	M	Christopher Lake	SAS	Watson T. Jackson	1993	2567
19 7/16	12 5/16	7 2/16	M	Laurie Lake	SAS	Rene Suda	1993	2567
19 7/16	11 14/16	7 9/16	M	Oxford County	ME	Mark Kronyak	1993	2567
19 7/16	12 8/16	6 15/16	M	Augusta County	VA	Michael J. Sandy	1993	2567
19 7/16	12 5/16	7 2/16	M	Randolph County	WV	James Rowan	1993	2567
19 7/16	12 2/16	7 5/16	M	Athabasca River	ALB	George "Matt" Potts	1994	2567
19 7/16	12 2/16	7 5/16	M	Carrot River	SAS	Ronny Stoy	1994	2567
19 7/16	12 3/16	7 4/16	M	Livengood	AK	Ricky R. Janssen	1994	2567
19 7/16	12 6/16	7 1/16	M	Minto Flats	AK	Harry M. Ronsman	1994	2567
19 7/16	12 4/16	7 3/16	M	Oxford County	ME	Craig S. Anderson	1994	2567
19 7/16	12 4/16	7 3/16	M	Atikokan	ONT	Dr. John R. Thodos	1994	2567
19 7/16	12 2/16	7 5/16	M	Grafton County	NH	Darren Lee	1994	2567
19 7/16	11 14/16	7 9/16	M	Mesomikenda Lake	ONT	William H. Osborne	1994	2567
19 7/16	12 6/16	7 1/16	M	Bayfield County	WI	Jim Horneck	1994	2567
19 7/16	12 5/16	7 2/16	M	Orange County	NY	Joseph W. Talasco	1994	2567
19 7/16	12 5/16	7 2/16	M	Centre County	PA	Eric Anton Derugen	1994	2567
19 7/16	11 8/16	7 15/16	M	Waweig	NBW	Joseph E. White, Jr.	1995	2567
19 7/16	11 13/16	7 10/16	M	Lemhi County	ID	Bruce Carlisle	1995	2567
19 7/16	12 0/16	7 7/16	M	Upshur County	WV	Walter K. Depoy	1995	2567
19 7/16	12 5/16	7 2/16	M	Swastika	ONT	Mike Darlak	1996	2567
19 7/16	12 5/16	7 2/16	M	Waterhen	MAN	Ken Vettel	1996	2567
19 7/16	12 3/16	7 4/16	M	Camperville	MAN	Mark Vink	1996	2567
19 7/16	12 0/16	7 7/16	M	Evain	QUE	Jacques Robichaud	1996	2567
19 7/16	11 15/16	7 8/16	M	Ear Falls	ONT	Elmer Van Gheem	1996	2567
19 7/16	12 7/16	7 0/16	M	Mesa County	CO	Eric A. Sawyer	1996	2567
19 7/16	12 2/16	7 5/16	M	Summit County	CO	Kevin Brothers	1996	2567
19 7/16	12 2/16	7 5/16	M	Clearwater County	ID	Charles J. Kager	1997	2567
19 7/16	12 2/16	7 5/16	M	Carrot River	SAS	Mark P. Wagner	1997	2567
19 7/16	12 2/16	7 5/16	M	Clarke Lake	SAS	Robert Wood	1997	2567
19 7/16	12 7/16	7 0/16	M	Woodridge	MAN	Peter U. Funk	1997	2567
19 7/16	12 0/16	7 7/16	M	Lac des Mille Lacs	ONT	John Glick	1997	2567
19 7/16	12 3/16	7 4/16	M	Kaladar	ONT	James Deyo	1997	2567
19 7/16	11 14/16	7 9/16	M	Carlton County	MN	Walter W. Trader	1997	2567
19 7/16	12 1/16	7 6/16	M	Lake County	MN	Kevin Schmieg	1997	2567

BLACK BEAR

Minimum Score 18 Continued

SCORE	GREATEST LENGTH	GREATEST WIDTH	SEX	AREA	STATE/ PROVINCE	HUNTER'S NAME	DATE	RANK
19 7/16	12 2/16	7 5/16	M	White County	GA	Jim Collins	1997	2567
19 7/16	12 3/16	7 4/16	M	Riske Creek	BC	Daryl Buchholtz	1998	2567
19 7/16	12 2/16	7 5/16	M	Wabasca River	ALB	Warren Erickson	1998	2567
19 7/16	12 1/16	7 6/16	M	Wandering River	ALB	Doug McWilliams	1998	2567
19 7/16	12 3/16	7 4/16	M	Athabasca River	ALB	Johnny Watson	1998	2567
19 7/16	12 8/16	6 15/16	M	Trapper Creek	AK	Robert John Bruni	1998	2567
19 7/16	12 0/16	7 7/16	M	Siskiyou County	CA	Dan Kothgassner	1998	2567
19 7/16	12 4/16	7 3/16	M	Price County	WI	William Connelly	1998	2567
19 7/16	12 1/16	7 6/16	M	Ashland County	WI	Jeffrey L. Stezenski	1998	2567
19 7/16	11 15/16	7 8/16	M	Taylor County	WI	Ronald Stahmann	1998	2567
19 7/16	11 14/16	7 9/16	M	Bonner County	ID	Harlow McConnaughey	1998	2567
19 7/16	12 0/16	7 7/16	M	Mistatim	SAS	Bob Morton	1999	2567
19 7/16	12 8/16	6 15/16	M	Spirit River	ALB	Michael Ambur	1999	2567
19 7/16	12 7/16	7 0/16	M	Koochiching County	MN	Brian D. Scarnegie	1999	2567
19 7/16	12 2/16	7 5/16	M	Pendleton County	WV	Shawn McGann	1999	2567
19 7/16	11 15/16	7 8/16	M	Carrot River	SAS	Larry T. Fischer	2000	2567
19 7/16	12 3/16	7 4/16	M	Sandilands	MAN	Shelley A. Mehling	2000	2567
19 7/16	12 9/16	6 14/16	M	Fort MacKay	ALB	Thomas L. McNeil	2000	2567
19 7/16	12 2/16	7 5/16	M	Family Lake	MAN	John Trombley	2000	2567
19 7/16	12 13/16	6 10/16	M	Endeavour	SAS	Charles Sagner	2000	2567
19 7/16	12 3/16	7 4/16	M	Cass County	MN	Matthew C. Reineke	2000	2567
19 7/16	12 4/16	7 3/16	M	Marinette County	WI	Mike D. Schenian	2000	2567
19 7/16	12 7/16	7 0/16	M	Nicholas County	WV	Francis T. Johnson	2000	2567
19 7/16	12 7/16	7 0/16	M	Whitemouth Lake	MAN	Derek Rothwell	2001	2567
19 7/16	11 10/16	7 13/16	M	Koochiching County	MN	Timothy Kampa	2001	2567
19 7/16	12 3/16	7 4/16	M	Montezuma County	CO	John Gross	2001	2567
19 7/16	12 6/16	7 1/16	M	Andrew Lake	ALB	Kevin A. Speicher	2002	2567
19 7/16	12 0/16	7 7/16	M	Lake Athabasca	SAS	Andrew Stanco	2002	2567
19 7/16	12 2/16	7 5/16	M	Savant Lake	ONT	Neil Hamerlinck	2002	2567
19 7/16	11 15/16	7 8/16	M	La Plata County	CO	Terry Grimes	2002	2567
19 7/16	12 7/16	7 0/16	M	Rusk County	WI	Michael Cornelissen	2002	2567
19 7/16	12 11/16	6 12/16	M	Scott County	AR	Adam Beason	2002	2567
19 7/16	12 5/16	7 2/16	M	Greenbrier County	WV	Jeffrey Perdue	2002	2567
19 7/16	12 5/16	7 2/16	M	Peace River	ALB	Wayne Rogers	2003	2567
19 7/16	12 10/16	6 13/16	M	Saddle Hills	ALB	Duane Hagman	2003	2567
19 7/16	11 15/16	7 8/16	M	Black Bear Island	SAS	Gary Mucilli	2003	2567
19 7/16	12 3/16	7 4/16	M	George Lake	SAS	Brian Stoner	2003	2567
19 7/16	12 8/16	6 15/16	M	Carrot River	SAS	Bobby Robinson	2003	2567
19 7/16	12 5/16	7 2/16	M	Fredericton	NBW	Joseph Enders	2003	2567
19 7/16	12 8/16	6 15/16	M	Fayette County	WV	Daniel Fitzwater	2003	2567
19 7/16	12 3/16	7 4/16	M	Prince of Wales Island	AK	Chad Berry	2004	2567
19 7/16	12 2/16	7 5/16	M	Prince of Wales Island	AK	Glen Berry	2004	2567
19 7/16	12 1/16	7 6/16	M	Lake Apisko	MAN	Mike Morrow	2004	2567
19 7/16	12 3/16	7 4/16	M	Fond du Lac River	SAS	Joel M. Riotto	2004	2567
19 7/16	11 10/16	7 13/16	M	Papineau Labelle	QUE	Rickey Lane Lawrence	2004	2567
19 7/16	12 6/16	7 1/16	M	Ethelbert	MAN	Edward Oliver	2004	2567
19 7/16	12 3/16	7 4/16	M	Bayfield County	WI	Michael J. Faskell	2004	2567
19 7/16	11 14/16	7 9/16	M	Churchill Lake	SAS	Terry M. Dennis	2005	2567
*19 7/16	12 2/16	7 5/16	M	Maniwaki	QUE	Robert L. Kohl	2005	2567
19 7/16	12 2/16	7 5/16	M	Lac du Bonnet	MAN	Edward J. Chodyniecki	2005	2567
19 7/16	12 1/16	7 6/16	M	Grand Rapids	MAN	Rick Pegg	2005	2567
*19 7/16	12 2/16	7 5/16	M	Vilas County	WI	Roger Brunner	2005	2567
19 7/16	12 5/16	7 2/16	M	Gila County	AZ	Doug Strecker	2005	2567
*19 7/16	12 2/16	7 5/16	M	White Bear Lake	SAS	Charles Weiser	2006	2567
19 7/16	11 14/16	7 9/16	M	Chibougamau	QUE	Michael Walters	2006	2567
19 7/16	12 5/16	7 2/16	M	Churchill Lake	SAS	Terry M. Dennis	2006	2567
19 7/16	12 6/16	7 1/16	M	Ferrie	ONT	Jason DeMeester	2006	2567
19 7/16	11 15/16	7 8/16	M	Rusk County	WI	Greg Wallace	2006	2567
19 7/16	12 6/16	7 1/16	M	Marathon County	WI	Scott Selting	2006	2567
*19 7/16	12 3/16	7 4/16	M	Northumberland	NBW	Scott MacFarlane	2006	2567
19 7/16	11 15/16	7 8/16	M	Navajo County	AZ	Lee Sorcinelli	2007	2567
19 7/16	12 1/16	7 6/16	M	Stoney Rapids	SAS	Tom Nelson	2007	2567
*19 7/16	12 8/16	6 15/16	M	Puntledge River	BC	Adam Bartsch	2007	2567
*19 7/16	11 15/16	7 8/16	M	Terrace Bay	ONT	Dwayne Berggren	2007	2567
19 7/16	11 14/16	7 9/16	M	Ignace	ONT	Elliot Heath	2007	2567
19 7/16	12 3/16	7 4/16	M	Terrace	BC	Rick Duggan	2008	2567
19 7/16	11 12/16	7 11/16	M	Wintering Lake	ONT	Mark Mollen	2008	2567
19 7/16	12 5/16	7 2/16	M	Upsala Township	ONT	Alan J. Rhinerson	2008	2567
*19 7/16	12 8/16	6 15/16	M	Chesterfield County	VA	Adam Creswell	2008	2567
19 7/16	12 4/16	7 3/16	M	Carbon County	UT	Dave Hansen	2009	2567
19 7/16	12 1/16	7 6/16	M	Flin Flon	MAN	Jeffrey L. Nettleton	2009	2567
19 7/16	12 9/16	6 14/16	M	Graham County	AZ	Matthew Liljenquist	2009	2567
*19 7/16	12 4/16	7 3/16	M	Bayfield County	WI	Barry Truog	2009	2567
19 7/16	12 2/16	7 5/16	M	Ritchie County	WV	Lyle Moore	2009	2567
*19 7/16	12 3/16	7 4/16	M	La Loche	SAS	George Gallini	2010	2567
19 7/16	12 2/16	7 5/16	M	Las Animas County	CO	John Sakariason	2010	2567
19 6/16	12 7/16	6 15/16	M	Shasta County	CA	L. Dale Towery	1965	2737
19 6/16	11 14/16	7 8/16	M	Atikokan	ONT	Dennis Gregory	1969	2737
19 6/16	12 2/16	7 4/16	M	Franklin County	ME	Walter Seville	1971	2737
19 6/16	11 14/16	7 8/16	M	Mesa County	CO	Charles Leidheiser	1971	2737
19 6/16	12 6/16	7 0/16	F	Sawyer County	WI	Ronald Curry, Jr.	1972	2737
19 6/16	12 3/16	7 3/16	M	Uncompahgre N.F.	CO	Thomas J. Hentrick	1975	2737
19 6/16	12 2/16	7 4/16	M	Ashland County	WI	Jim Keim	1977	2737
19 6/16	12 2/16	7 4/16	M	Atikokan	ONT	Earle K. Gray	1979	2737
19 6/16	11 14/16	7 8/16	M	Wabigoon Lake	ONT	Gary W. Shaffer	1979	2737
19 6/16	11 13/16	7 9/16	M	Cascade County	MT	H. Richard Long	1981	2737
19 6/16	12 4/16	7 2/16	M	Lewis & Clark County	MT	Donald K. MacCallum	1982	2737
19 6/16	12 0/16	7 6/16	M	Aroostook County	ME	Frank 'Rit' Heller	1982	2737
19 6/16	12 2/16	7 4/16	M	Hampshire County	MA	James 'Boomer' Hayden	1982	2737
19 6/16	12 4/16	7 2/16	M	Hudson Bay	SAS	David Tofte	1983	2737
19 6/16	12 4/16	7 2/16	M	Sioux Lookout	ONT	Ray Ryan	1983	2737
19 6/16	12 2/16	7 4/16	M	Beluga River	AK	Christine Koldeway	1984	2737
19 6/16	12 9/16	6 13/16	M	Kitsap County	WA	Betty Jones	1984	2737
19 6/16	11 15/16	7 7/16	M	Lemhi County	ID	Ron Scherer	1985	2737
19 6/16	11 14/16	7 8/16	M	Drury Township	ONT	John Wyszynski	1985	2737

153

BLACK BEAR

Minimum Score 18 — Continued

SCORE	GREATEST LENGTH	GREATEST WIDTH	SEX	AREA	STATE/PROVINCE	HUNTER'S NAME	DATE	RANK
19 6/16	11 14/16	7 8/16	M	Heathcote	ONT	Joseph A. Lasch	1985	2737
19 6/16	11 10/16	7 12/16	M	Kenora	ONT	Mark D. Moss	1985	2737
19 6/16	12 1/16	7 5/16	M	Big Horn County	WY	Joel D. Prickett	1985	2737
19 6/16	12 0/16	7 6/16	M	Shasta County	CA	Larry Mork	1985	2737
19 6/16	12 1/16	7 5/16	M	Teton County	ID	Marc S. Johnson	1986	2737
19 6/16	11 12/16	7 10/16	M	Herkimer County	NY	Patrick Niznik	1986	2737
19 6/16	12 0/16	7 6/16	M	Trinity County	CA	Robert Pearce	1986	2737
19 6/16	12 0/16	7 6/16	M	Washago	ONT	James E. Doberstein	1987	2737
19 6/16	12 0/16	7 6/16	M	Clearwater County	ID	Dennis Blackford	1987	2737
19 6/16	12 2/16	7 4/16	M	Graham County	AZ	Jeffrey Keith Volk	1987	2737
19 6/16	12 3/16	7 3/16	M	Oneida County	WI	James J. Wallack	1987	2737
19 6/16	11 14/16	7 8/16	M	Hillsport	ONT	Richard Shive	1988	2737
19 6/16	11 15/16	7 7/16	M	Valley County	ID	William R. Vanderhoef	1988	2737
19 6/16	12 4/16	7 2/16	M	Madera County	CA	Ken Woolsey	1988	2737
19 6/16	11 14/16	7 8/16	M	Union County	OR	Jerry Cnossen	1988	2737
19 6/16	12 8/16	6 14/16	M	Prince of Wales Island	AK	Gary Roney	1988	2737
19 6/16	12 4/16	7 2/16	M	Fresno County	CA	DeeAnn Robinson	1988	2737
19 6/16	12 3/16	7 3/16	M	Bayfield County	WI	Daniel L Snider	1989	2737
19 6/16	12 3/16	7 3/16	M	Colfax County	NM	Steven A. Leyh	1990	2737
19 6/16	12 2/16	7 4/16	M	Fraser Lake	BC	Stanley D. Moore	1990	2737
19 6/16	11 14/16	7 8/16	M	Aulneau Peninsula	ONT	Mike Koska	1990	2737
19 6/16	12 3/16	7 3/16	M	Peace River	ALB	Mike Conroy	1990	2737
19 6/16	11 12/16	7 10/16	M	Franklin County	ME	Peter L. Shippee	1990	2737
19 6/16	12 1/16	7 5/16	M	Colfax County	NM	Daniel Hurd	1990	2737
19 6/16	11 14/16	7 8/16	M	Prince of Wales Island	AK	Mark Robecker	1990	2737
19 6/16	12 5/16	7 1/16	M	Prince of Wales Island	AK	David Rue	1991	2737
19 6/16	12 2/16	7 4/16	F	Lac La Biche	ALB	Bruce Nederveld	1991	2737
19 6/16	12 0/16	7 6/16	M	Fort McMurray	ALB	Galen F. Shinkle	1991	2737
19 6/16	12 6/16	7 0/16	M	Bruce County	ONT	Dean Adams	1991	2737
19 6/16	12 4/16	7 2/16	M	Minto Flats	AK	James Wayne Dillard	1991	2737
19 6/16	11 15/16	7 7/16	M	Falconbridge	ONT	Daniel Ralich	1991	2737
19 6/16	12 4/16	7 2/16	M	Darlens	QUE	Dennis L. Blankenship	1991	2737
19 6/16	12 7/16	6 15/16	M	Leaf River	QUE	Joseph Testerman	1991	2737
19 6/16	11 14/16	7 8/16	M	Lake County	MN	David Ruzek	1991	2737
19 6/16	12 1/16	7 5/16	M	Bancroft	ONT	Jeffrey C. Fretz	1991	2737
19 6/16	11 13/16	7 9/16	M	Iron County	MI	Craig A. Murdock	1991	2737
19 6/16	12 2/16	7 4/16	M	Hood River County	OR	Michael L. Tollen	1991	2737
19 6/16	12 1/16	7 5/16	M	Marathon County	WI	John J. Fischer	1991	2737
19 6/16	12 3/16	7 3/16	M	Hearst	ONT	Russell V. Riese	1992	2737
19 6/16	11 15/16	7 7/16	M	Sheridan County	WY	Lee Jernigan	1992	2737
19 6/16	11 14/16	7 8/16	M	Koochiching County	MN	Doug Streit	1992	2737
19 6/16	12 2/16	7 4/16	M	Rutland County	VT	Lawrence St. Pierre	1992	2737
19 6/16	12 5/16	7 1/16	M	Hudson Bay	SAS	Mark K. Swallow	1993	2737
19 6/16	11 12/16	7 10/16	M	Wanless	MAN	Leonard Rock	1993	2737
19 6/16	12 3/16	7 3/16	M	Clearwater County	ID	Kevin Schmid	1993	2737
19 6/16	12 2/16	7 4/16	M	Dryden	ONT	Ted Anderson	1993	2737
19 6/16	11 12/16	7 10/16	M	Canterbury	NBW	Tom Taylor	1993	2737
19 6/16	12 3/16	7 3/16	M	St. Louis County	MN	Vern Blonigen	1993	2737
19 6/16	12 0/16	7 6/16	M	Mora County	NM	Glen A. Fuller	1993	2737
19 6/16	12 0/16	7 6/16	M	Catron County	NM	Abe Dimas, Jr.	1993	2737
19 6/16	12 5/16	7 1/16	M	Oxford County	ME	Daniel J. Smith	1993	2737
19 6/16	12 0/16	7 6/16	M	Peace River	ALB	Peter C. Swenson	1994	2737
19 6/16	12 3/16	7 3/16	M	McNalley Lake	ALB	Jody Davis	1994	2737
19 6/16	12 9/16	6 13/16	M	Fisher Branch	MAN	James R. Weir	1994	2737
19 6/16	12 1/16	7 5/16	M	Lynn Lake	MAN	G. Fred Asbell	1994	2737
19 6/16	12 2/16	7 4/16	M	Larder Lake	ONT	Thomas R. Johnson	1994	2737
19 6/16	12 2/16	7 4/16	M	Atikokan	ONT	David N. Andersen	1994	2737
19 6/16	11 15/16	7 7/16	M	Washington County	ME	Perry L. Perkins	1994	2737
19 6/16	11 14/16	7 8/16	M	Sudbury	ONT	Carl L. Ledford	1995	2737
19 6/16	11 14/16	7 8/16	M	Thunder Hills	SAS	John J. Sestak	1995	2737
19 6/16	12 1/16	7 5/16	M	Atikokan	ONT	Todd Schumacher	1995	2737
19 6/16	12 5/16	7 1/16	M	North Bay	ONT	Marty Klemm	1995	2737
19 6/16	12 0/16	7 6/16	M	Wawa	ONT	Richard L. Warren	1995	2737
19 6/16	11 14/16	7 8/16	M	Holinshead Lake	ONT	Kenneth Beckel	1995	2737
19 6/16	12 4/16	7 2/16	M	Lake of the Woods Cty	MN	Chad D. Hagen	1995	2737
19 6/16	12 6/16	7 0/16	M	Klickitat County	WA	Gary Holwegner	1995	2737
19 6/16	12 2/16	7 4/16	M	Idaho County	ID	Pat Hylton	1996	2737
19 6/16	12 2/16	7 4/16	M	Ignace	ONT	Richard Schroeder	1996	2737
19 6/16	12 8/16	6 14/16	M	Bluffly Lake	ONT	Robb S. Thompson	1996	2737
19 6/16	12 4/16	7 2/16	M	Woodridge	MAN	Peter U. Funk	1996	2737
19 6/16	12 2/16	7 4/16	M	Raith	ONT	Paul E. Moore	1996	2737
19 6/16	11 14/16	7 8/16	M	King County	WA	Ken Melton	1996	2737
19 6/16	12 0/16	7 6/16	M	Somerset County	ME	Matthew Adamou	1996	2737
19 6/16	12 8/16	6 14/16	M	Chisago County	MN	Richard Owen	1996	2737
19 6/16	12 8/16	6 14/16	M	Douglas County	WI	James Wanner	1996	2737
19 6/16	12 2/16	7 4/16	M	Mariposa County	CA	Arthur M. Cain	1996	2737
19 6/16	12 4/16	7 2/16	M	Big Horn County	WY	Roger Coguill	1997	2737
19 6/16	12 4/16	7 2/16	M	Prince of Wales Island	AK	Danny Moore	1997	2737
19 6/16	12 0/16	7 6/16	M	Ranger Lake	ONT	Bill McDonald	1997	2737
19 6/16	12 3/16	7 3/16	M	Meadow Lake	SAS	Thomas Pigeon	1997	2737
19 6/16	12 4/16	7 2/16	M	Peace River	ALB	Robert S. Miller	1997	2737
19 6/16	12 3/16	7 3/16	M	Lake Wabigoon	ONT	Dwayne H. Cushman	1997	2737
19 6/16	11 14/16	7 8/16	M	Idaho County	ID	Don Polanski	1997	2737
19 6/16	11 13/16	7 9/16	M	King County	WA	Walt Treptow	1997	2737
19 6/16	12 3/16	7 3/16	M	Gila County	AZ	Gary Mehaffey	1997	2737
19 6/16	11 13/16	7 9/16	M	Rio Arriba County	NM	Zac Bryant	1997	2737
19 6/16	12 2/16	7 4/16	M	Holinshead Lake	ONT	Kenneth A. Shattuck, Jr.	1998	2737
19 6/16	12 5/16	7 1/16	F	Lynn Lake	MAN	William H. Peterson	1998	2737
19 6/16	11 14/16	7 8/16	M	Ignace	ONT	Wilmer Garlick	1998	2737
19 6/16	12 4/16	7 2/16	M	Saddle Hills	ALB	David Watson	1998	2737
19 6/16	12 7/16	6 15/16	M	Price County	WI	Kevin L. Kreuziger	1998	2737
19 6/16	12 1/16	7 5/16	M	Harney County	OR	Bill Andersen	1998	2737
19 6/16	12 4/16	7 2/16	M	Lake Enid	BC	Martin Gottinger	1998	2737
19 6/16	12 3/16	7 3/16	M	Revillagigedo Island	AK	Jason L. Pinsky	1999	2737
19 6/16	12 6/16	7 0/16	M	Christopher Lake	SAS	Earl R. Smith	1999	2737

BLACK BEAR

Minimum Score 18   Continued

SCORE	GREATEST LENGTH	GREATEST WIDTH	SEX	AREA	STATE/ PROVINCE	HUNTER'S NAME	DATE	RANK
19 6/16	12 1/16	7 5/16	M	Andrew Lake	ALB	Desmond Quinn	1999	2737
19 6/16	12 4/16	7 2/16	M	Lower Foster Lake	SAS	Jonathan Gonitzke	1999	2737
19 6/16	12 0/16	7 6/16	M	Lac Brush	QUE	William J. Hamilton	1999	2737
19 6/16	11 11/16	7 11/16	M	Lake County	MN	Kirk D. Grupa	1999	2737
19 6/16	12 5/16	7 1/16	M	Bayfield County	WI	Matthew J. Ostricki	1999	2737
19 6/16	12 3/16	7 3/16	M	Ashland County	WI	James C. Snortum	1999	2737
19 6/16	12 1/16	7 5/16	M	Boise County	ID	Anthony L. Mudd	2000	2737
19 6/16	12 0/16	7 6/16	M	Grand Rapids	MAN	Ray L. Paulsen	2000	2737
19 6/16	11 14/16	7 8/16	M	Dore Lake	SAS	Garry W. Harner	2001	2737
19 6/16	12 0/16	7 6/16	M	Prince of Wales Island	AK	Cole Eddie	2001	2737
19 6/16	12 2/16	7 4/16	M	Saint-Charles-Garnier	QUE	Gary R. Stutz	2001	2737
19 6/16	11 13/16	7 9/16	M	Redditt	ONT	Bruce Tatera	2001	2737
19 6/16	11 10/16	7 12/16	M	Foleyet	ONT	Wayne Mueller	2001	2737
19 6/16	11 14/16	7 8/16	M	Madison County	MT	Randy Sayre	2001	2737
19 6/16	12 6/16	7 0/16	M	Logan County	WV	Timmy Justice	2001	2737
19 6/16	12 5/16	7 1/16	M	Athabasca River	ALB	Jack A. Berry	2002	2737
19 6/16	12 6/16	7 0/16	M	Olha	MAN	Wayne Michael Goulet	2002	2737
19 6/16	12 4/16	7 2/16	M	Pinawa	MAN	Thomas K. Hagen	2002	2737
19 6/16	12 5/16	7 1/16	M	Conklin	ALB	Stephane Titley	2002	2737
19 6/16	12 0/16	7 6/16	M	Churchill Lake	SAS	Eric F. Efird	2002	2737
*19 6/16	12 3/16	7 3/16	M	Preissac	QUE	Tom Smith	2002	2737
19 6/16	12 0/16	7 6/16	M	Comox Lake	BC	Chantelle Bartsch	2002	2737
19 6/16	12 0/16	7 6/16	M	Price County	WI	Herman Pockelwald	2002	2737
19 6/16	11 10/16	7 12/16	M	Forestville	QUE	William J. Igo	2003	2737
*19 6/16	12 1/16	7 5/16	M	Conne River	NFL	Brian James Carpenter	2003	2737
19 6/16	12 1/16	7 5/16	M	Lake County	MN	Troy M. Hawkshead	2003	2737
19 6/16	12 7/16	6 15/16	M	Rusk County	WI	Doug Lodahl	2003	2737
*19 6/16	12 11/16	6 11/16	M	Dunn County	WI	Leigh Bryan	2003	2737
19 6/16	12 4/16	7 2/16	M	Trinity County	CA	Mike Walker	2003	2737
19 6/16	12 1/16	7 5/16	M	Kuiu Island	AK	Stephen Tyrrell	2004	2737
19 6/16	12 2/16	7 4/16	M	Outer Banks	QUE	Douglas Knaub	2004	2737
19 6/16	11 15/16	7 7/16	M	North Vancouver Island	BC	Alexander Z. Gaal	2004	2737
19 6/16	11 12/16	7 10/16	M	Plamondon River	QUE	Jerry May	2004	2737
19 6/16	12 1/16	7 5/16	M	Cree River	SAS	Jade Keeton	2004	2737
19 6/16	12 5/16	7 1/16	M	Franklin County	VA	Wanda L. Peeples	2004	2737
19 6/16	12 4/16	7 2/16	M	Peter Pond Lake	SAS	Ben Wallace, Jr.	2005	2737
19 6/16	12 4/16	7 2/16	M	Besnard Lake	SAS	Johnny Bragg	2005	2737
19 6/16	12 3/16	7 3/16	M	Prince of Wales Island	AK	Chad Berry	2005	2737
19 6/16	12 4/16	7 2/16	M	Tanana River	AK	Stan Parkerson	2005	2737
19 6/16	12 3/16	7 3/16	M	Evain	QUE	Jacques Robichaud	2005	2737
19 6/16	12 2/16	7 4/16	M	Caramat	ONT	George A. Archibald	2005	2737
19 6/16	12 9/16	6 13/16	M	Marinette County	WI	Keith LeMahieu	2005	2737
19 6/16	12 5/16	7 1/16	M	Florence County	WI	Jon Walber	2005	2737
19 6/16	12 3/16	7 3/16	M	Forest County	WI	David Cathey	2005	2737
19 6/16	12 3/16	7 3/16	M	Baraga County	MI	Ryan Aper	2005	2737
19 6/16	12 4/16	7 2/16	M	Latah County	ID	Nathan Dean Tumelson	2006	2737
*19 6/16	12 5/16	7 1/16	M	Cumberland House	SAS	Josiah Johnson	2006	2737
19 6/16	11 12/16	7 10/16	M	Redditt	ONT	Mark Jacobson	2006	2737
19 6/16	12 7/16	6 15/16	M	Lincoln County	WI	Michael J. Honerlaw	2006	2737
19 6/16	12 6/16	7 0/16	M	Bayfield County	WI	Teeger Seifert	2006	2737
19 6/16	11 13/16	7 9/16	M	Grafton County	NH	Charles L. Palmer	2006	2737
19 6/16	11 11/16	7 11/16	M	Thunder Bay	ONT	Trevor Hasenjager	2006	2737
19 6/16	12 9/16	6 13/16	M	Alcona County	MI	Kevin Black	2006	2737
*19 6/16	12 4/16	7 2/16	M	Johnson County	AR	W. Bruce Brown	2006	2737
*19 6/16	12 3/16	7 3/16	M	Poplarfield	MAN	Lori Mizwicki	2007	2737
*19 6/16	12 6/16	7 0/16	M	Almond	QUE	Don Cote	2007	2737
19 6/16	12 2/16	7 4/16	M	Summit County	UT	Shane Bushell	2007	2737
*19 6/16	11 14/16	7 8/16	M	Lac Denain	QUE	Bruce John Bedard	2007	2737
*19 6/16	12 2/16	7 4/16	M	Sickle Lake	MAN	Daniel C. Sheridan	2007	2737
19 6/16	12 2/16	7 4/16	M	Wapawekka Lake	SAS	Mitchell A. Goza	2007	2737
*19 6/16	11 12/16	7 10/16	M	Boise County	ID	Brian Stroschein	2007	2737
19 6/16	12 6/16	7 0/16	M	Koochiching County	MN	Larry M. Looman	2007	2737
19 6/16	12 9/16	6 13/16	M	Taylor County	WI	Todd Brinker	2007	2737
19 6/16	12 11/16	6 11/16	M	Gilmer County	GA	Galen Shinkle	2007	2737
19 6/16	12 0/16	7 6/16	M	Dipper Lake	SAS	Greg Dearth	2008	2737
*19 6/16	11 14/16	7 8/16	M	Vermilion Bay	ONT	Bryce Hanson	2008	2737
19 6/16	12 3/16	7 3/16	M	White County	GA	Henry Johnson	2008	2737
19 6/16	12 7/16	6 15/16	M	Ste. Rose du Lac	MAN	Mark F. Pedo	2009	2737
19 6/16	12 0/16	7 6/16	M	Elmore County	ID	Mont Richter	2010	2737
*19 6/16	12 7/16	6 15/16	M	Archuleta County	CO	Bruce W. Hoch	2010	2737
19 5/16	11 13/16	7 8/16	M	Clearwater County	ID	William R. Vanderhoef	1959	2921
19 5/16	11 12/16	7 9/16	M	Upper Peninsula	MI	Donald Schram	1961	2921
19 5/16	12 5/16	7 5/16	M	Gunnison County	CO	James Jarvis	1976	2921
19 5/16	11 12/16	7 9/16	M	Las Animas County	CO	Barry Powell	1976	2921
19 5/16	12 3/16	7 2/16	M	Raith	ONT	Jon K. Young	1976	2921
19 5/16	12 4/16	7 4/16	M	Mesa County	CO	T. J. Colburn	1977	2921
19 5/16	12 0/16	7 5/16	M	Washington County	ME	Dan Paugh	1978	2921
19 5/16	11 11/16	7 10/16	M	Ear Falls	ONT	Michael Mealey	1978	2921
19 5/16	11 11/16	7 10/16	M	Franklin County	ME	Al Del Greco	1978	2921
19 5/16	12 6/16	6 15/16	M	Dolores County	CO	Marv Reichenau	1979	2921
19 5/16	12 1/16	7 4/16	M	Oneida County	NY	Ronald J. Beerhalter	1980	2921
19 5/16	12 2/16	7 3/16	M	Tulare County	CA	Fred R. Cisneros	1981	2921
19 5/16	11 14/16	7 7/16	M	White Lake	ONT	Daniel B. Johnson	1981	2921
19 5/16	11 15/16	7 6/16	M	Bonneville County	ID	Richard K. Russell	1981	2921
19 5/16	12 2/16	7 3/16	M	Dryden	ONT	Craig A. Swenson	1982	2921
19 5/16	12 1/16	7 4/16	M	Sudbury County	ONT	William Doczy	1983	2921
19 5/16	12 4/16	7 1/16	M	St. Louis County	MN	Kimberley Anne McGurren	1983	2921
19 5/16	12 1/16	7 4/16	M	King County	WA	Larry Jensen	1983	2921
19 5/16	11 13/16	7 8/16	M	Smeaton	SAS	Gene Welle	1984	2921
19 5/16	11 14/16	7 7/16	M	Caribou County	ID	Coby Tigert	1984	2921
19 5/16	12 1/16	7 4/16	M	Snohomish County	WA	Mathew Hayvaz	1984	2921
19 5/16	12 1/16	7 4/16	M	Plumas County	CA	Dr. Ronald H. Thole	1984	2921
19 5/16	12 1/16	7 4/16	M	Parry Sound	ONT	Ronald D. Lundy	1985	2921
19 5/16	12 4/16	7 1/16	M	Cass County	MN	Brad Blanchard	1985	2921
19 5/16	12 8/16	6 13/16	M	Caldwell County	NC	Danny K. Adams	1986	2921

155

BLACK BEAR

Minimum Score 18 — Continued

SCORE	GREATEST LENGTH	GREATEST WIDTH	SEX	AREA	STATE/PROVINCE	HUNTER'S NAME	DATE	RANK
19 5/16	12 8/16	6 13/16	M	Grand County	UT	David Snyder	1986	2921
19 5/16	12 5/16	7 0/16	M	Valley County	ID	Brian Hunter Heck	1986	2921
19 5/16	11 9/16	7 12/16	M	Flathead County	MT	Jay Vojta, Jr.	1987	2921
19 5/16	12 1/16	7 4/16	M	Garfield County	WA	David Jansen	1987	2921
19 5/16	12 3/16	7 2/16	M	Catron County	NM	Stan Rauch	1988	2921
19 5/16	12 0/16	7 5/16	M	Rocky Lake	MAN	Cecil Tharp	1988	2921
19 5/16	12 3/16	7 2/16	M	Rocky Lake	MAN	Tim Finley	1988	2921
19 5/16	11 11/16	7 10/16	M	Fort Coulonge	QUE	David Keith Burchette	1988	2921
19 5/16	11 14/16	7 7/16	M	North Bay	QUE	Jeff Anderson	1988	2921
19 5/16	12 1/16	7 4/16	M	High Prairie	ALB	Joseph F. Petti	1989	2921
19 5/16	12 4/16	7 1/16	M	Montrose County	CO	Clint Hovey	1989	2921
19 5/16	11 15/16	7 6/16	M	Sioux Lookout	ONT	Stan Godfrey	1989	2921
19 5/16	12 1/16	7 4/16	M	Zec Maganasipi	QUE	F.Edward Campbell	1989	2921
19 5/16	11 14/16	7 7/16	M	Cold Lake	ALB	Glenn Moir	1989	2921
19 5/16	12 3/16	7 2/16	M	Fawcett	ALB	Garfield Vikse	1990	2921
19 5/16	11 10/16	7 11/16	M	Las Animas County	CO	David Brooks	1990	2921
19 5/16	11 15/16	7 6/16	M	Stranger Lake	ONT	Mitchell S. Thorpe	1990	2921
19 5/16	12 1/16	7 4/16	M	Oconto County	WI	James A. Krouse	1990	2921
19 5/16	11 15/16	7 6/16	M	MacNeil Township	ONT	Ted Whittle	1990	2921
19 5/16	12 9/16	6 12/16	M	Utah County	UT	Kevin D. Hatfield	1991	2921
19 5/16	11 15/16	7 6/16	M	High Level	ALB	Bobby G. Williams	1991	2921
19 5/16	12 1/16	7 4/16	M	Rio Arriba County	NM	Tim J. Mariner	1991	2921
19 5/16	12 6/16	6 15/16	F	Boise County	ID	Scott T. Doxey	1991	2921
19 5/16	12 2/16	7 3/16	M	Idaho County	ID	Charles R. Whitfield	1991	2921
19 5/16	12 3/16	7 2/16	M	Pitkin County	CO	James P. Krasinski, Sr.	1991	2921
19 5/16	12 0/16	7 5/16	M	Colfax County	NM	Stephen W. Long	1991	2921
19 5/16	12 1/16	7 4/16	M	Athabasca River	ALB	Casmir S. Domurat, Jr.	1991	2921
19 5/16	12 5/16	7 0/16	M	Wallowa County	OR	Rick Leach	1992	2921
19 5/16	12 7/16	6 14/16	M	Cranberry Portage	MAN	John Beardslee	1992	2921
19 5/16	11 12/16	7 9/16	M	Saguache County	CO	Dennis Reid	1992	2921
19 5/16	11 12/16	7 9/16	M	Tanana Flats	AK	Tommy L. Ramsey	1992	2921
19 5/16	11 15/16	7 6/16	M	Skagit County	WA	Rick W. Giles	1992	2921
19 5/16	12 7/16	6 14/16	M	Rusk County	WI	James R. Williams	1992	2921
19 5/16	12 5/16	7 0/16	M	Catron County	NM	David H. Boland	1992	2921
19 5/16	12 0/16	7 5/16	M	Oxford County	ME	Lance A. Tyler	1992	2921
19 5/16	12 5/16	7 0/16	M	Grande Prairie	ALB	Charles Markwood	1993	2921
19 5/16	12 2/16	7 3/16	M	Webbwood	ONT	Michael J. Perry	1993	2921
19 5/16	12 1/16	7 4/16	M	North Bay	ONT	Russell E. Steele	1993	2921
19 5/16	12 5/16	7 0/16	M	Lac Ile-a-la-Crosse	SAS	Dewayne Mullins	1993	2921
19 5/16	12 2/16	7 3/16	M	Nolalu	ONT	John E. Sliger	1993	2921
19 5/16	12 2/16	7 3/16	M	Kings County	NBW	Amedeo Guglielmo	1993	2921
19 5/16	12 0/16	7 5/16	M	Aulneau Peninsula	ONT	Michael Koska	1993	2921
19 5/16	11 15/16	7 6/16	M	Bayfield County	WI	Richard S. Nemitz	1993	2921
19 5/16	11 13/16	7 8/16	M	Athabasca River	ALB	Allen J. Miraglia	1994	2921
19 5/16	12 5/16	7 0/16	M	Carrot River	SAS	Andrew D. Pearson	1994	2921
19 5/16	12 3/16	7 2/16	M	Bonanza	ALB	Kirk Rawnsley	1994	2921
19 5/16	12 2/16	7 3/16	M	Sioux Narrows	ONT	Michael J. Goza	1994	2921
19 5/16	11 15/16	7 6/16	M	Slave Lake	ALB	Greg Ogle	1994	2921
19 5/16	12 6/16	6 15/16	M	Fort McMurray	ALB	Darlene J. Stansfield	1994	2921
19 5/16	12 8/16	6 13/16	M	Hudson Bay	SAS	James D. Ray	1994	2921
19 5/16	12 5/16	7 0/16	M	Carrot River	SAS	Larry T. Fischer	1994	2921
19 5/16	12 0/16	7 5/16	M	Idaho County	ID	Timothy R. McGuffin	1994	2921
19 5/16	12 3/16	7 2/16	M	Laurier	MAN	Clay Childress	1994	2921
19 5/16	12 6/16	6 15/16	M	Aulneau Peninsula	ONT	Michael Koska	1994	2921
19 5/16	11 9/16	7 12/16	M	McKinley County	NM	James Baumgardner	1994	2921
19 5/16	11 13/16	7 8/16	M	Plumas County	CA	Robert Trujillo	1994	2921
19 5/16	12 2/16	7 3/16	M	Nicholas County	WV	Harold Davis	1994	2921
19 5/16	12 2/16	7 3/16	M	High Level	ALB	David Westmoreland	1995	2921
19 5/16	11 13/16	7 8/16	M	Kenora	ONT	Howard Gibbs	1995	2921
19 5/16	12 1/16	7 4/16	M	Hearst	ONT	Thomas H. Meszler	1995	2921
19 5/16	12 4/16	7 1/16	M	High Level	ALB	Thomas L. Klug	1995	2921
19 5/16	11 10/16	7 11/16	M	Hornepayne	ONT	Mitchell J. Genz	1995	2921
19 5/16	11 10/16	7 11/16	M	Longlac	ONT	Thomas M. Stieg	1995	2921
19 5/16	11 11/16	7 10/16	M	Missanabie	ONT	Todd D. Armstrong	1995	2921
19 5/16	11 15/16	7 6/16	M	Clova	QUE	Nicolas Chrisovergis	1995	2921
19 5/16	12 4/16	7 1/16	M	Chapleau	ONT	Gregory James Bishop	1995	2921
19 5/16	11 15/16	7 6/16	M	Carroll County	NH	John Bassi	1995	2921
19 5/16	12 2/16	7 3/16	M	Holinshead Lake	ONT	Jeffery R. Bloniarz	1996	2921
19 5/16	11 9/16	7 12/16	M	Cook County	MN	Mike Redig	1996	2921
19 5/16	11 15/16	7 6/16	M	Chelsea Township	ONT	Marty W. Atkinson	1996	2921
19 5/16	12 5/16	7 0/16	M	Douglas County	WI	Tom Vengrin	1996	2921
19 5/16	12 8/16	6 13/16	M	San Jose Creek	BC	Allan Tew	1997	2921
19 5/16	12 1/16	7 4/16	M	Whiteswan Lake	SAS	Eugene Arndt	1997	2921
19 5/16	12 3/16	7 2/16	M	Bissett	MAN	Curtis A. Summer	1997	2921
19 5/16	12 2/16	7 3/16	M	Rosenberry	MAN	George Martinez	1997	2921
19 5/16	11 15/16	7 6/16	M	Carswell Lake	SAS	Dennis R. Allman	1997	2921
19 5/16	11 11/16	7 10/16	M	Wawa	ONT	Eric Adams	1997	2921
19 5/16	11 13/16	7 8/16	M	Lynn Lake	MAN	Don Barry	1997	2921
19 5/16	12 4/16	7 1/16	M	Vogar	MAN	Edward Antonacci	1997	2921
19 5/16	12 4/16	7 1/16	M	Nenana River	AK	Brock E. Graziadei	1997	2921
19 5/16	11 12/16	7 9/16	M	Bear Lake	BC	Lorenzo Bortolotto	1997	2921
19 5/16	11 13/16	7 8/16	M	Pueblo County	CO	David L. Montano	1997	2921
19 5/16	12 7/16	6 14/16	M	Prince of Wales Island	AK	Stephen Herrera	1998	2921
19 5/16	12 6/16	6 15/16	M	Athabasca River	ALB	Frank S. Noska IV	1998	2921
19 5/16	12 6/16	6 15/16	M	Dore Lake	SAS	Randy Rice	1998	2921
19 5/16	11 12/16	7 9/16	M	Guthrie Lake	MAN	John Beardslee	1998	2921
19 5/16	12 1/16	7 4/16	M	Chapleau	ONT	Jeff Fether	1998	2921
19 5/16	12 1/16	7 4/16	M	Fort Coulonge	QUE	James McCarthy	1998	2921
19 5/16	11 15/16	7 6/16	M	Zec Capitachouane	QUE	Ken H. Taylor	1998	2921
19 5/16	11 15/16	7 6/16	M	Wawa	ONT	Joe Arbic, Jr.	1998	2921
19 5/16	12 9/16	6 12/16	M	Kanabec County	MN	Dale Kane	1998	2921
19 5/16	12 4/16	7 1/16	M	Peace River	ALB	Doug Brummett	1999	2921
19 5/16	12 0/16	7 5/16	M	Reindeer Lake	SAS	Stuart Hagen	1999	2921
19 5/16	11 11/16	7 10/16	M	Fort Coulonge	QUE	Stanley Chafin	1999	2921
19 5/16	12 2/16	7 3/16	M	Coos County	NH	Robert Lafrance	1999	2921

BLACK BEAR

Minimum Score 18   Continued

SCORE	GREATEST LENGTH	GREATEST WIDTH	SEX	AREA	STATE/ PROVINCE	HUNTER'S NAME	DATE	RANK
19 5/16	12 6/16	6 15/16	M	Lake Athabasca	ALB	Glenn Helgeland	2000	2921
19 5/16	12 0/16	7 5/16	M	St. Louis County	MN	Chad A. Gill	2000	2921
19 5/16	11 15/16	7 6/16	M	McAdam	NBW	Ronald E. Carreau	2000	2921
19 5/16	12 0/16	7 5/16	M	Bissett	MAN	Stanley Meyers	2001	2921
19 5/16	12 5/16	7 0/16	M	Wolf Lake	ALB	Walter Krom	2001	2921
19 5/16	12 0/16	7 5/16	M	Chilako River	BC	Gordon Roy	2001	2921
19 5/16	11 13/16	7 8/16	M	Kupreanof Island	AK	David Benitz	2001	2921
19 5/16	12 0/16	7 5/16	M	St. Louis County	MN	D. Johnson	2001	2921
19 5/16	12 3/16	7 2/16	M	Dorion	ONT	Ken Ganter	2001	2921
19 5/16	11 11/16	7 10/16	M	Prince of Wales Island	AK	Dirk Dieterich	2001	2921
19 5/16	12 6/16	6 15/16	M	Douglas County	WI	Michael J. Jaszczak	2001	2921
19 5/16	12 2/16	7 3/16	M	Kanawha County	WV	Ronzel G. Moss	2001	2921
19 5/16	12 6/16	6 15/16	M	Bronson Lake	SAS	W. T. Garry Drummond	2002	2921
*19 5/16	12 4/16	7 1/16	M	Bay Tree	ALB	John Marcheso	2002	2921
19 5/16	11 15/16	7 6/16	M	Mirond Lake	SAS	W. Barry Byje Martin	2002	2921
19 5/16	12 2/16	7 3/16	M	High Level	ALB	Jay Kurelich	2002	2921
19 5/16	11 15/16	7 6/16	M	Espanola	ONT	Martin R. Obetts	2002	2921
19 5/16	11 14/16	7 7/16	M	Caramat	ONT	Steven A. Abbee	2002	2921
19 5/16	11 14/16	7 7/16	M	Aroostook County	ME	Normand D. Poitras	2002	2921
19 5/16	12 5/16	7 0/16	M	Athabasca	ALB	Jay Downes, Jr.	2003	2921
19 5/16	12 3/16	7 2/16	M	Peace River	ALB	Christopher G. Jones	2003	2921
19 5/16	12 0/16	7 5/16	M	Fort Coulouge	QUE	Robert E. Weibley	2003	2921
19 5/16	12 2/16	7 3/16	M	DeBolt	ALB	Tom Lester	2003	2921
19 5/16	11 13/16	7 8/16	M	Gypsumville	MAN	Tim Hockers	2003	2921
19 5/16	11 11/16	7 10/16	M	Black Bay Lake	SAS	Elizabeth M. Buxton	2003	2921
19 5/16	12 1/16	7 4/16	M	Cook County	MN	George Ostgarden	2003	2921
19 5/16	12 3/16	7 2/16	M	Hearst	ONT	Danny Ray Gushard	2003	2921
19 5/16	12 4/16	7 1/16	M	Shoshone County	ID	Ken Snyder	2004	2921
*19 5/16	12 3/16	7 2/16	M	La Loche	SAS	Harold Smith	2004	2921
19 5/16	12 6/16	6 15/16	M	Ft. McMurray	ALB	Chris Parrino	2004	2921
19 5/16	12 1/16	7 4/16	M	Amos	QUE	Leroy Hamilton	2004	2921
19 5/16	12 1/16	7 4/16	M	Hillsport	ONT	Gary L. Mayle, Jr.	2004	2921
19 5/16	12 1/16	7 4/16	M	Aroostook County	ME	Mark Robertson	2004	2921
*19 5/16	12 1/16	7 4/16	M	Sudbury	ONT	Timothy R. Frecka	2004	2921
19 5/16	12 0/16	7 5/16	M	Terrace	BC	Mark Vogt	2005	2921
19 5/16	11 15/16	7 6/16	M	High Level	ALB	Joseph M. Brown	2005	2921
19 5/16	11 14/16	7 7/16	M	Forestville	QUE	Andre Huard	2005	2921
19 5/16	12 1/16	7 4/16	M	Trapper Creek	AK	Robert L. Shafer	2005	2921
19 5/16	12 0/16	7 5/16	M	Redditt	ONT	Mike Churchill	2005	2921
*19 5/16	12 9/16	6 12/16	M	Grand County	CO	Wayne E. Thurston	2005	2921
19 5/16	12 4/16	7 1/16	M	Oconto County	WI	Jay Gilligan	2005	2921
19 5/16	12 1/16	7 4/16	M	Skilak Glacier	AK	Frank S. Noska IV	2005	2921
19 5/16	12 5/16	7 0/16	M	Dease Lake	BC	Al Campsall	2006	2921
19 5/16	12 0/16	7 5/16	M	Fond du Lac River	SAS	David Schrody	2006	2921
*19 5/16	12 2/16	7 3/16	M	Nipigon	ONT	Wade Musick	2006	2921
19 5/16	11 10/16	7 11/16	M	Plumas County	CA	Ryan Wright	2006	2921
*19 5/16	11 9/16	7 12/16	M	Vilas County	WI	Eric "Shoob" Schumacher	2006	2921
19 5/16	12 4/16	7 1/16	M	Price County	WI	Scott A. Swan	2006	2921
*19 5/16	11 15/16	7 6/16	M	Rio Arriba County	NM	Larry D. Sylvester	2006	2921
19 5/16	12 5/16	7 0/16	M	Iron County	WI	John T. Quade	2006	2921
*19 5/16	11 13/16	7 8/16	M	Pocahontas County	WV	Joseph P. Payne	2006	2921
*19 5/16	12 3/16	7 2/16	M	Berkshire County	MA	Edward H. Armstrong	2006	2921
19 5/16	12 1/16	7 4/16	M	Wabasca	ALB	Tom Nelson	2007	2921
19 5/16	12 2/16	7 3/16	M	Lake Wasekamio	SAS	Robert D. Brewer	2007	2921
*19 5/16	11 15/16	7 6/16	M	Lloyd Lake	SAS	Ronnie Diedrich	2007	2921
19 5/16	12 6/16	6 15/16	M	Deschambault Lake	SAS	Matt Griswold	2007	2921
*19 5/16	11 13/16	7 8/16	M	Reserve Faunique	QUE	Matt Lamp	2007	2921
19 5/16	12 7/16	6 14/16	M	Umatilla County	OR	Doug Radke	2007	2921
19 5/16	11 13/16	7 8/16	M	Tuolumne County	CA	Tim Craft	2007	2921
*19 5/16	12 4/16	7 1/16	M	Nampa	ALB	Gary Edwin Purcell	2008	2921
19 5/16	12 1/16	7 4/16	M	Livelong	SAS	William D. Eshee, Jr.	2008	2921
19 5/16	12 5/16	7 0/16	M	Sawyer County	WI	David Lane	2008	2921
*19 5/16	12 8/16	6 13/16	M	Montmorency County	MI	Robert Pizzuti	2008	2921
19 5/16	12 1/16	7 4/16	M	Gypsumville	MAN	Jim DeCicco	2009	2921
19 5/16	12 0/16	7 5/16	M	Ray River	AK	Tom Chadwick	2009	2921
19 5/16	12 2/16	7 3/16	M	Hodgson	MAN	Kim Engelbert	2009	2921
*19 5/16	12 3/16	7 2/16	M	Washburn County	WI	Tim Magnus	2009	2921
19 5/16	12 2/16	7 3/16	M	Allegany County	NY	Richard Wilkins	2009	2921
19 5/16	12 4/16	7 1/16	M	Cumberland House	SAS	Robert Brion	2010	2921
19 5/16	12 0/16	7 5/16	M	Cole Bay	SAS	Robert J. Sheehan	2010	2921
19 5/16	12 5/16	7 0/16	M	Saddle Hills	ALB	Steve Rogers	2010	2921
19 4/16	12 4/16	7 0/16	M	Ashland County	WI	Herbert H. Lange	1961	3112
19 4/16	12 4/16	7 0/16	M	Murphy Dome	AK	Thomas Clark	1963	3112
19 4/16	11 15/16	7 5/16	M	Jackson County	OR	Bob Jacobs	1964	3112
19 4/16	12 0/16	7 4/16	M	Idaho County	ID	Dick Gulman	1967	3112
19 4/16	12 3/16	7 1/16	M	L'Ascension	QUE	Michael L. Kaluszka	1971	3112
19 4/16	11 8/16	7 12/16	M	Idaho County	ID	Harold Boyack	1973	3112
19 4/16	11 12/16	7 8/16	M	Wasco County	OR	John Higgins	1974	3112
19 4/16	11 11/16	7 9/16	M	Gunnison County	CO	Roger Reinbold	1976	3112
19 4/16	11 11/16	7 9/16	M	Wanapitei River	ONT	Ken Barnhart	1976	3112
19 4/16	11 14/16	7 6/16	M	Pigeon Mtn.	ALB	David R. Coupland	1977	3112
19 4/16	12 4/16	7 0/16	M	Bayfield County	WI	Bruce Eggenberger	1977	3112
19 4/16	12 1/16	7 3/16	M	Saguache County	CO	Richard Baumfalk	1977	3112
19 4/16	12 0/16	7 4/16	M	Franklin County	ME	Harry Feaster	1978	3112
19 4/16	11 15/16	7 5/16	M	Capreol	ONT	Bobby Clenney	1978	3112
19 4/16	11 12/16	7 8/16	M	Bayfield County	WI	Dave Tabbert	1979	3112
19 4/16	11 13/16	7 7/16	M	Thessalon	ONT	Robert R. Rider	1979	3112
19 4/16	12 4/16	7 0/16	M	Ontonagon County	MI	Daniel F. Stiltner	1979	3112
19 4/16	12 1/16	7 3/16	M	Price County	WI	Glenn E. Gaulke	1980	3112
19 4/16	11 12/16	7 8/16	M	Shoshone County	ID	Bill Hoffman, Sr.	1980	3112
19 4/16	12 2/16	7 2/16	M	Archuleta County	CO	Denny Lane Williamson	1981	3112
19 4/16	11 14/16	7 6/16	M	Dryden	ONT	Gerald T. Flynn	1981	3112
19 4/16	11 12/16	7 8/16	M	Idaho County	ID	Ray Koenig	1981	3112
19 4/16	11 14/16	7 6/16	M	St. Lawrence County	NY	Henry P. Bouchard	1982	3112
19 4/16	12 1/16	7 3/16	M	Park County	MT	Gary Hartman	1982	3112

157

BLACK BEAR

Minimum Score 18 — Continued

SCORE	GREATEST LENGTH	GREATEST WIDTH	SEX	AREA	STATE/PROVINCE	HUNTER'S NAME	DATE	RANK
19 4/16	12 8/16	6 12/16	M	Burnett County	WI	David Hess	1982	3112
19 4/16	12 4/16	7 0/16	M	Mackinac County	MI	Dale H. Betcher	1983	3112
19 4/16	11 14/16	7 6/16	M	Emo	ONT	Hal McClelland	1983	3112
19 4/16	12 5/16	6 15/16	M	Game Area #23	MAN	Gary Kaluzniak	1984	3112
19 4/16	12 0/16	7 4/16	M	Susitna River	AK	Patricia A. Stewart	1984	3112
19 4/16	11 14/16	7 6/16	M	Touchwood Lake	ALB	Warren Witherspoon	1984	3112
19 4/16	12 0/16	7 4/16	M	Game Area #23	MAN	Gary Kaluzniak	1984	3112
19 4/16	11 12/16	7 8/16	M	Rollet	QUE	George Ollert	1984	3112
19 4/16	11 11/16	7 9/16	M	Siskiyou County	CA	Greg Nichols	1984	3112
19 4/16	11 14/16	7 6/16	M	Wawa	ONT	James C. Hicks	1984	3112
19 4/16	12 1/16	7 3/16	M	Archuleta County	CO	Lisa Cooney	1985	3112
19 4/16	12 2/16	7 2/16	M	Cheboygan County	MI	Steve E. Hutchinson	1985	3112
19 4/16	12 4/16	7 0/16	M	Madison County	MT	John Ralph	1985	3112
19 4/16	12 2/16	7 2/16	M	Siskiyou County	CA	Bruce Kipley	1985	3112
19 4/16	12 6/16	6 14/16	M	Turtle River	ONT	Al Haines	1986	3112
19 4/16	12 2/16	7 2/16	M	Archuleta County	CO	David Swanson	1986	3112
19 4/16	12 1/16	7 3/16	M	Keeley Lake	SAS	Bruce E. Menz	1986	3112
19 4/16	12 0/16	7 4/16	M	Delay River	QUE	Benjamin O. Brookhart III	1986	3112
19 4/16	12 3/16	7 1/16	M	Fort Coulonge	QUE	David W. Wachter	1987	3112
19 4/16	11 13/16	7 7/16	M	La Plata County	CO	Karen Stevens	1987	3112
19 4/16	12 0/16	7 4/16	M	Wawa	ONT	Bruce Waterman	1987	3112
19 4/16	12 0/16	7 4/16	M	Shining Tree	ONT	Alan J. Skowron	1988	3112
19 4/16	11 11/16	7 9/16	M	Canterbury	NBW	David G. Cote	1988	3112
19 4/16	12 2/16	7 2/16	M	Iron County	MI	Douglas Wagner	1988	3112
19 4/16	11 14/16	7 6/16	M	Iron County	WI	Roger Adamavich	1988	3112
19 4/16	11 15/16	7 5/16	M	Herkimer County	NY	Paul Tomeo	1988	3112
19 4/16	12 1/16	7 3/16	M	Grand County	UT	Jay Wick	1989	3112
19 4/16	11 15/16	7 5/16	M	High Level	ALB	Stuart Sinclair-Smith	1989	3112
19 4/16	12 0/16	7 4/16	M	Mitehell	QUE	Bruce D. Trapp	1989	3112
19 4/16	11 14/16	7 6/16	M	San Fernando Island	AK	Kurt Goesch	1989	3112
19 4/16	12 0/16	7 4/16	M	Dryden	ONT	Kreg A. Elmer	1989	3112
19 4/16	12 2/16	7 2/16	M	Douglas County	WI	Dennis Nicholson	1989	3112
19 4/16	11 14/16	7 6/16	M	Ravalli County	MT	Travis E. Proctor	1989	3112
19 4/16	12 2/16	7 2/16	M	Sandoval County	NM	James O. Marquis	1989	3112
19 4/16	12 0/16	7 4/16	M	Snow Lake	MAN	Jerry D. Heistan	1990	3112
19 4/16	11 11/16	7 9/16	M	River Valley	ONT	Jim D. Mullins	1990	3112
19 4/16	12 2/16	7 2/16	M	East Bull Lake	ONT	Gerald A. Dick II	1990	3112
19 4/16	12 1/16	7 3/16	M	Sheridan County	WY	Dennis F. Craft	1990	3112
19 4/16	12 2/16	7 2/16	M	Delta County	MI	Bob Bouck	1990	3112
19 4/16	12 7/16	6 13/16	M	Schoolcraft County	MI	Dennis W. Kleeman	1990	3112
19 4/16	11 12/16	7 8/16	M	Archuleta County	CO	Grant Adkisson	1991	3112
19 4/16	12 0/16	7 4/16	M	Lincoln County	OR	Chad Fletcher	1991	3112
19 4/16	11 11/16	7 9/16	M	Waldie Township	ONT	Richard C. Witt	1991	3112
19 4/16	12 5/16	6 15/16	M	Chippewa County	WI	William E. Gladitsch	1991	3112
19 4/16	12 0/16	7 4/16	M	Longlac	ONT	Steven R. Anderson	1992	3112
19 4/16	12 0/16	7 4/16	M	Yukon River	AK	Bruce A. Haas	1992	3112
19 4/16	12 2/16	7 2/16	M	Davidson	QUE	Brian I. King	1992	3112
19 4/16	11 14/16	7 6/16	M	Merrimack County	NH	Thomas Thayer	1992	3112
19 4/16	11 13/16	7 7/16	M	Bennington County	VT	Robert Marceau	1992	3112
19 4/16	12 4/16	7 0/16	M	Pocahontas County	WV	David N. Herndon	1992	3112
19 4/16	12 2/16	7 2/16	M	Blackhawk	ONT	Greg Wallace	1993	3112
19 4/16	12 4/16	7 0/16	M	Prince of Wales Island	AK	James D. Cruz	1993	3112
19 4/16	11 14/16	7 6/16	M	Kenora	ONT	Steven L. Ketelboeter	1993	3112
19 4/16	11 14/16	7 6/16	M	La Ronge	SAS	Mark C. Petersen	1993	3112
19 4/16	11 14/16	7 6/16	M	Ft. McMurray	ALB	Billy Tillotson	1993	3112
19 4/16	11 3/16	8 1/16	M	Cochrane	ONT	James De Luca, Jr.	1993	3112
19 4/16	12 0/16	7 4/16	M	Armstrong	ONT	Kenneth C. Schroeder	1993	3112
19 4/16	11 14/16	7 6/16	M	Fredericton	NBW	John Zilinski	1993	3112
19 4/16	12 3/16	7 1/16	M	Ft. McMurray	ALB	Richard R. Strelow	1993	3112
19 4/16	11 6/16	7 14/16	M	Siskiyou County	CA	Roy E. Grace	1993	3112
19 4/16	12 0/16	7 4/16	M	Webster	ONT	Kent Hare	1993	3112
19 4/16	12 0/16	7 4/16	M	Carrot River	SAS	Udo Kerber	1993	3112
19 4/16	11 15/16	7 5/16	M	Cleveland Peninsula	AK	William H. Welton	1994	3112
19 4/16	12 4/16	7 0/16	M	Peace River	ALB	Roy D. Baird	1994	3112
19 4/16	12 4/16	7 0/16	M	Wolf Lake	ALB	Greg Lumley	1994	3112
19 4/16	12 2/16	7 2/16	M	Carrot River	SAS	Gary Wissmueller	1994	3112
19 4/16	12 3/16	7 1/16	M	Buffalo Head Prairie	ALB	E. Josh Isbell	1994	3112
19 4/16	11 14/16	7 6/16	M	Baie Comeau	QUE	Trevor W.G. McEntyre	1994	3112
19 4/16	12 3/16	7 1/16	M	Fresno County	CA	Tony Williams	1994	3112
19 4/16	12 6/16	6 14/16	M	Ontonagon County	MI	Gregory Schleusner	1994	3112
19 4/16	11 10/16	7 10/16	M	Beaverhead County	MT	Kevin Hadley	1994	3112
19 4/16	11 13/16	7 7/16	M	Carroll County	NH	Richard N. Kimball	1994	3112
19 4/16	12 0/16	7 4/16	M	Kapuskasing	ONT	Floyd S. Kines	1995	3112
19 4/16	12 2/16	7 2/16	M	Yaughn Lake	ONT	Dewayne Leming	1995	3112
19 4/16	12 1/16	7 3/16	M	Chibougamau	QUE	Seth Stevens	1995	3112
19 4/16	12 2/16	7 2/16	M	Horsefly	BC	Allan Tew	1995	3112
19 4/16	11 15/16	7 5/16	M	Lake Besnard	SAS	Eric J. Collier	1995	3112
19 4/16	11 9/16	7 11/16	M	Mono County	CA	John H. Klaasen	1995	3112
19 4/16	12 2/16	7 2/16	M	Bissett	MAN	Glenn R. Daily	1995	3112
19 4/16	11 10/16	7 10/16	M	Wawa	ONT	Tad H. Ralston	1995	3112
19 4/16	11 13/16	7 7/16	M	Mendocino County	CA	Gerald E. Boelens	1995	3112
19 4/16	12 3/16	7 1/16	M	Kittitas County	WA	James O. Whitlatch, Jr.	1995	3112
19 4/16	11 14/16	7 6/16	M	Otero County	NM	Gene Foster	1995	3112
19 4/16	12 11/16	6 9/16	M	Burnett County	WI	Chad A. Olson	1995	3112
19 4/16	12 2/16	7 2/16	M	Snow Lake	MAN	Christopher Kaforski	1996	3112
19 4/16	12 5/16	6 15/16	M	Rossburn	MAN	Barry Minshull	1996	3112
19 4/16	12 1/16	7 3/16	M	Minaki	ONT	Brian L. Grimes	1996	3112
19 4/16	12 1/16	7 3/16	M	Hawkrock	SAS	Al Kuntz	1996	3112
19 4/16	11 15/16	7 5/16	M	Oxford County	ME	John R. Willhoyte	1996	3112
19 4/16	12 2/16	7 2/16	M	Florence County	WI	Peter Meeuwsen	1996	3112
19 4/16	11 12/16	7 8/16	M	Tulare County	CA	Clebio Leal Santos	1996	3112
19 4/16	11 14/16	7 6/16	M	Athabasca River	ALB	Robert B. Stryker	1997	3112
19 4/16	12 6/16	6 14/16	M	Meadow Lake	SAS	Tom Younger	1997	3112
19 4/16	12 0/16	7 4/16	M	Shining Tree	ONT	John F. Belha, Jr.	1997	3112
19 4/16	12 2/16	7 2/16	M	Kapuskasing	ONT	James E. Titchenell	1997	3112

BLACK BEAR

Minimum Score 18   Continued

SCORE	GREATEST LENGTH	GREATEST WIDTH	SEX	AREA	STATE/PROVINCE	HUNTER'S NAME	DATE	RANK
19 4/16	12 0/16	7 4/16	M	Lac des Mille Lacs	ONT	Doug Vislisel	1997	3112
19 4/16	12 5/16	6 15/16	M	Crow Wing County	MN	Dan Berger	1997	3112
19 4/16	11 15/16	7 5/16	M	Herkimer County	NY	Steve Balyszak	1997	3112
19 4/16	12 3/16	7 1/16	M	Rio Arriba County	NM	Richard A. Smith	1998	3112
19 4/16	11 13/16	7 7/16	M	Ear Falls	ONT	Walter J. Palmer	1998	3112
19 4/16	12 1/16	7 3/16	M	Black Bay	SAS	Bill Vaznis	1998	3112
19 4/16	11 14/16	7 6/16	M	Brunswick Lake	ONT	Thomas J. Kuehl	1998	3112
19 4/16	12 0/16	7 4/16	M	Athabasca	ALB	Steve Grue	1998	3112
19 4/16	12 6/16	6 14/16	M	Marchand	MAN	Don Reimer	1998	3112
19 4/16	11 12/16	7 8/16	M	Kississing Lake	MAN	Matthew White	1998	3112
19 4/16	11 15/16	7 5/16	M	Essex County	NY	Paul Durling	1998	3112
19 4/16	12 2/16	7 2/16	M	Otter Lake	QUE	Eric Ramble	1999	3112
19 4/16	12 2/16	7 2/16	M	Bronson Lake	SAS	Dale Lawrence	1999	3112
19 4/16	12 1/16	7 3/16	M	Bronson Lake	SAS	Lynn Drechsel	1999	3112
19 4/16	12 4/16	7 0/16	M	Sundown	MAN	Randell M. Livingston	1999	3112
19 4/16	11 12/16	7 8/16	M	Kings County	NBW	Alan Cunningham	1999	3112
19 4/16	12 4/16	7 0/16	M	Manigotagan	MAN	Richard Masling	1999	3112
19 4/16	12 4/16	7 0/16	M	Washburn County	WI	Ed Staedter	1999	3112
19 4/16	11 12/16	7 8/16	M	Price County	WI	Jason A. Steliga	1999	3112
19 4/16	12 2/16	7 2/16	M	Warren County	VA	Robert W. Henry	1999	3112
19 4/16	12 2/16	7 2/16	M	Christopher Lake	SAS	Tolbert C. Tichenor	2000	3112
19 4/16	12 2/16	7 2/16	M	Saddle Hills	ALB	Kurt Lund	2000	3112
19 4/16	11 12/16	7 8/16	M	Dipper Lake	SAS	Steve Dunn	2000	3112
19 4/16	12 8/16	6 12/16	M	Big River	SAS	Charley Beka	2000	3112
19 4/16	12 0/16	7 4/16	M	Prince of Wales Island	AK	Dyrk Eddie	2000	3112
19 4/16	12 0/16	7 4/16	M	Cockburn Island	ONT	Lonnie E. Avra	2000	3112
19 4/16	11 11/16	7 9/16	M	Brunswick Lake	ONT	Russell V. Riese	2000	3112
19 4/16	11 13/16	7 7/16	M	Maskwa River	MAN	John M. Love	2000	3112
19 4/16	11 15/16	7 5/16	M	Rio Arriba County	NM	Brian Hemphill	2000	3112
19 4/16	12 0/16	7 4/16	M	Carswell Lake	SAS	Art Haws	2001	3112
19 4/16	12 6/16	6 14/16	M	Olha	MAN	Greg Lompart	2001	3112
19 4/16	12 0/16	7 4/16	M	Spirit River	ALB	Michael Ambur	2001	3112
19 4/16	12 4/16	7 0/16	M	Green Lake	SAS	Mike Bruce	2001	3112
19 4/16	12 0/16	7 4/16	M	Big Sandy Lake	SAS	Kent Reierson	2001	3112
19 4/16	12 4/16	7 0/16	M	Churchill River	SAS	Glenn Lloyd	2001	3112
19 4/16	12 4/16	7 0/16	M	Dog Lake	ONT	Jeffery A. Grider	2001	3112
19 4/16	11 12/16	7 8/16	M	Montezuma County	CO	Toby Bauer	2001	3112
19 4/16	12 6/16	6 14/16	M	Polk County	WI	Michael K. Paulcheck	2001	3112
19 4/16	12 2/16	7 2/16	M	Herkimer County	NY	Justin Gitsis	2001	3112
19 4/16	11 9/16	7 11/16	M	Gold Bridge	BC	Leo P. Caito, Jr.	2002	3112
19 4/16	12 3/16	7 1/16	M	Frobisher Lake	SAS	Ramon Neil Bell	2002	3112
19 4/16	12 2/16	7 2/16	M	Sublette County	WY	Todd Plowman	2002	3112
19 4/16	12 4/16	7 0/16	M	File Lake	MAN	Mike Wendel	2002	3112
19 4/16	12 1/16	7 3/16	M	Lonesand	MAN	Shelley A. Mehling	2002	3112
19 4/16	11 12/16	7 8/16	M	Lake Tasiataq	QUE	Paul J. Harris	2002	3112
19 4/16	12 0/16	7 4/16	M	Carlton County	MN	Clyde Anderson	2002	3112
19 4/16	12 4/16	7 0/16	M	Randolph County	WV	James W. Hall	2002	3112
19 4/16	12 3/16	7 1/16	M	Teton County	WY	Deon Heiner	2003	3112
19 4/16	12 6/16	6 14/16	M	Gronlid	SAS	Clayton Myhre	2003	3112
19 4/16	11 14/16	7 6/16	M	Ignace	ONT	Richard Schroeder	2003	3112
19 4/16	11 12/16	7 8/16	M	St. Louis County	MN	Randy Bowe	2003	3112
19 4/16	12 2/16	7 2/16	M	Ashland County	WI	Matthew A. Kannenberg	2003	3112
19 4/16	12 6/16	6 14/16	M	Pierceland	SAS	Eric Farr	2004	3112
19 4/16	12 2/16	7 2/16	M	Ste. Rose du Lac	MAN	Chuck Webb	2004	3112
*19 4/16	12 2/16	7 2/16	M	Lac La Biche	ALB	Richard W. Wahl	2004	3112
19 4/16	11 12/16	7 8/16	M	Redditt	ONT	Ronald Pohlman, Jr.	2004	3112
19 4/16	12 6/16	6 14/16	M	High Level	ALB	Joseph M. Brown	2005	3112
*19 4/16	12 7/16	6 13/16	M	Glaslyn	SAS	J. R. Whitman	2005	3112
19 4/16	11 10/16	7 10/16	M	Buffalo Narrows	SAS	Philip Grady	2005	3112
19 4/16	12 0/16	7 4/16	M	Black Bear Island Lake	SAS	Curtis Grigonis	2005	3112
19 4/16	12 3/16	7 1/16	M	Riou Lake	SAS	M. Robert DeLaney	2005	3112
19 4/16	12 3/16	7 1/16	M	Aberdeen	ONT	Gerald L. Barefield	2005	3112
19 4/16	11 13/16	7 7/16	M	Hornepayne	ONT	Coby Smith	2005	3112
19 4/16	12 3/16	7 1/16	M	Itasca County	MN	Christopher J. Vouk	2005	3112
19 4/16	12 0/16	7 4/16	M	Granum	ALB	Donald Travis Peters	2005	3112
19 4/16	12 1/16	7 3/16	M	Ashland County	WI	Craig Raschein	2005	3112
19 4/16	12 2/16	7 2/16	M	Jellicoe	ONT	Kory Lang	2005	3112
19 4/16	11 15/16	7 5/16	M	Campbell River	BC	Mike Redman	2006	3112
19 4/16	12 4/16	7 0/16	M	Otter Creek	SAS	Joe Conard	2006	3112
19 4/16	12 3/16	7 1/16	M	Flatbush	ALB	Donald Dvoroznak	2006	3112
*19 4/16	12 4/16	7 0/16	M	Upsala	ONT	Floyd Gasser	2006	3112
19 4/16	12 0/16	7 4/16	M	Vaughn Lake	ONT	Jeff Rice	2006	3112
*19 4/16	12 4/16	7 0/16	M	Smoky River	ALB	John Biro	2007	3112
*19 4/16	11 12/16	7 8/16	M	Smooth Rock Falls	ONT	James Kochanski	2007	3112
19 4/16	12 3/16	7 1/16	M	Coos County	OR	Chris Metzgus	2007	3112
19 4/16	12 1/16	7 3/16	M	Lewis & Clark County	MT	Les Hicks	2007	3112
*19 4/16	12 7/16	6 13/16	M	Greenlee County	AZ	David Meicke	2007	3112
19 4/16	12 3/16	7 1/16	M	Oconto County	WI	Michael A. Burnside	2007	3112
19 4/16	12 9/16	6 11/16	M	Lincoln County	WI	John Nowak	2007	3112
*19 4/16	12 4/16	7 0/16	M	Lac Dix Milles	QUE	Farley B. Tucker	2008	3112
*19 4/16	12 0/16	7 4/16	M	Geikie River	SAS	Joel L. Unsworth	2008	3112
*19 4/16	11 14/16	7 6/16	M	Alice Arm	BC	Don Erbert	2008	3112
19 4/16	12 0/16	7 4/16	M	Indian Lake	MAN	Scott D. Scharf	2008	3112
*19 4/16	12 2/16	7 2/16	M	Converse County	WY	Matt Futter	2008	3112
19 4/16	11 14/16	7 6/16	M	La Plata County	CO	Larry D. Burcz	2008	3112
19 4/16	11 15/16	7 5/16	M	Aroostook County	ME	Glenn Raymond	2008	3112
*19 4/16	12 8/16	6 12/16	M	Yell County	AR	Bentley A. Smith	2008	3112
*19 4/16	12 0/16	7 4/16	M	East Selkirk	MAN	Dirk Schmidt	2009	3112
19 4/16	12 9/16	6 11/16	M	Carrot River	SAS	Joe Furlong	2009	3112
19 4/16	11 15/16	7 5/16	M	Temiscaming	QUE	Nathan Novak	2009	3112
19 4/16	11 15/16	7 5/16	M	Smoky River	ALB	Dallas Kaiser	2009	3112
*19 4/16	12 1/16	7 3/16	M	Vermilion Bay	ONT	Chris Luetkeman	2009	3112
19 4/16	12 3/16	7 1/16	M	Armstrong	ONT	Mike VanKeuren	2009	3112
19 4/16	11 12/16	7 8/16	M	Garfield County	CO	Mike Miller	2009	3112
*19 4/16	12 4/16	7 0/16	M	Hornepayne	ONT	Coby Smith	2009	3112

159

BLACK BEAR

Minimum Score 18   Continued

SCORE	GREATEST LENGTH	GREATEST WIDTH	SEX	AREA	STATE/ PROVINCE	HUNTER'S NAME	DATE	RANK
*19 4/16	12 4/16	7 0/16	M	Itasca County	MN	Gary Eichelberger	2009	3112
19 4/16	11 15/16	7 5/16	M	Powell County	MT	David E. Nolan	2009	3112
19 4/16	12 2/16	7 2/16	M	Madison County	AR	Bob Bruder	2009	3112
19 4/16	12 2/16	7 2/16	M	Rocky Mountain House	ALB	Cameron Cook	2010	3112
19 4/16	11 15/16	7 5/16	M	Grand Rapids	MAN	Harold Opheim	2010	3112
19 4/16	11 8/16	7 12/16	M	Lake Farrant	QUE	Richard L. Grams	2010	3112
*19 4/16	12 3/16	7 1/16	M	Pine County	MN	Zach Bernier	2010	3112
19 4/16	11 12/16	7 8/16	M	Chilanko River	BC	Leonard Scarborough	2010	3112
19 3/16	11 12/16	7 7/16	M	Mineral County	CO	Edward Wintz	1960	3334
19 3/16	12 2/16	7 1/16	M	Rio Arriba County	NM	Dan Ward	1964	3334
19 3/16	11 13/16	7 6/16	M	Iron Bridge	ONT	Philip L. Hawkins	1965	3334
19 3/16	11 12/16	7 7/16	M	Shasta County	CA	Michael D. Combs	1967	3334
19 3/16	11 11/16	7 8/16	M	Sudbury District	ONT	Floyd Eccleston	1970	3334
19 3/16	11 13/16	7 6/16	M	Uncompahgre N.F.	CO	Charles Bojarski	1971	3334
19 3/16	11 14/16	7 5/16	M	Sequoia National Forest	CA	Martin Szekeresh, Jr.	1973	3334
19 3/16	11 11/16	7 8/16	M	Powell County	MT	Gary L. Wilson	1975	3334
19 3/16	11 13/16	7 6/16	M	Fremont County	ID	Roger Atwood	1977	3334
19 3/16	12 3/16	7 0/16	M	Dryden	ONT	Bill Rose	1978	3334
19 3/16	11 13/16	7 6/16	M	Roscommon County	MI	Roger J. Maeder	1979	3334
19 3/16	11 14/16	7 5/16	M	Saguache County	CO	Ross M. Clark	1979	3334
19 3/16	11 14/16	7 5/16	M	Conejos County	CO	Frank Scott	1980	3334
19 3/16	11 15/16	7 4/16	M	Bonneville County	ID	Fred Huffman	1980	3334
19 3/16	12 1/16	7 2/16	M	Iron County	WI	Frank Rasch	1982	3334
19 3/16	11 15/16	7 4/16	M	Las Animas County	CO	Tom Nelson	1983	3334
19 3/16	12 1/16	7 2/16	M	Delta County	CO	Doug McCauley	1983	3334
19 3/16	12 1/16	7 2/16	M	Graham	ONT	Michael Perrott	1983	3334
19 3/16	11 12/16	7 7/16	M	Grand County	CO	Jim Williams	1983	3334
19 3/16	11 14/16	7 5/16	M	Kenora	ONT	Kenneth Gilb	1983	3334
19 3/16	12 3/16	7 0/16	M	Madison County	ID	Garry L. Bolinder	1983	3334
19 3/16	12 2/16	7 1/16	M	Hubbard County	MN	Omar Maggard	1984	3334
19 3/16	11 13/16	7 6/16	M	Black Sturgeon Lake	ONT	Clarence 'Bud' Mrozek	1985	3334
19 3/16	12 2/16	7 1/16	M	Durban	MAN	Bill Clink	1985	3334
19 3/16	12 6/16	6 13/16	M	Aitkin County	MN	Timothy J. Duffney	1985	3334
19 3/16	12 2/16	7 1/16	M	Whitemud Creek	ALB	Paul St. Laurent	1986	3334
19 3/16	11 11/16	7 8/16	M	Caramat	ONT	Burley Hall	1986	3334
19 3/16	11 15/16	7 4/16	M	Thunder Bay	ONT	Ron K. Serwa	1986	3334
19 3/16	11 15/16	7 4/16	M	Bending Lake	ONT	John Lamp	1986	3334
19 3/16	11 12/16	7 7/16	M	Park County	CO	Robert Wright	1987	3334
19 3/16	11 12/16	7 7/16	M	Sussex	NBW	Roger W. Kerry	1987	3334
19 3/16	11 15/16	7 4/16	M	Clearwater County	ID	Don Larson	1987	3334
19 3/16	11 11/16	7 8/16	M	Sioux Narrows	ONT	Todd Gebert	1987	3334
19 3/16	12 2/16	7 1/16	M	Custer County	CO	Rod Niles	1987	3334
19 3/16	11 15/16	7 4/16	M	Boise County	ID	Curtis B. Wiker	1987	3334
19 3/16	11 12/16	7 7/16	M	Franklin County	ME	Jim Roy	1987	3334
19 3/16	12 4/16	6 15/16	M	Itasca County	MN	Cary Dalton	1987	3334
19 3/16	12 1/16	7 2/16	M	Durban	MAN	Mike Delfino, Jr.	1987	3334
19 3/16	12 3/16	7 0/16	M	Siskiyou County	CA	Clifford Mosley	1987	3334
19 3/16	11 14/16	7 5/16	M	Boise County	ID	Dave Scott	1988	3334
19 3/16	11 9/16	7 10/16	M	Siskiyou County	CA	William Payne	1988	3334
19 3/16	11 15/16	7 4/16	M	High Prairie	ALB	Stephen Ebel	1989	3334
19 3/16	12 0/16	7 3/16	M	Latah County	ID	Steve Krier	1989	3334
19 3/16	11 11/16	7 8/16	M	Carbon County	UT	Hugh H. Hogle	1989	3334
19 3/16	11 10/16	7 9/16	M	Lac Le Truite Territory	QUE	Brian Hendricks	1989	3334
19 3/16	12 8/16	6 11/16	M	Extall River	BC	Larry H. Hill	1990	3334
19 3/16	12 4/16	6 15/16	M	Wawang Lake	ONT	Todd A. Sturgul	1990	3334
19 3/16	11 15/16	7 4/16	M	Manigotagan	MAN	Bruce Huewan	1990	3334
19 3/16	12 2/16	7 1/16	M	High Level	ALB	David Petet	1990	3334
19 3/16	11 12/16	7 7/16	M	Lane County	OR	Dave Elliott	1990	3334
19 3/16	11 15/16	7 4/16	M	Prince of Wales Island	AK	Glen Berry	1991	3334
19 3/16	12 2/16	7 1/16	M	Fort Chipwan	ALB	Patrick H. Aucoin	1991	3334
19 3/16	12 6/16	6 13/16	M	Nancy Lake	AK	Mark R. Daum	1991	3334
19 3/16	12 4/16	6 15/16	M	Beluga River	AK	Dr. Robert Edward Speegle	1991	3334
19 3/16	12 2/16	7 1/16	M	High Level	ALB	Gino Giannetti	1991	3334
19 3/16	12 4/16	6 15/16	M	Sheridan County	WY	Scott Runde	1991	3112
19 3/16	12 5/16	6 14/16	M	La Tuque	QUE	Bernard E. Beaudin	1991	3334
19 3/16	12 1/16	7 2/16	M	Grand Rapids	MAN	James R. Kramp	1991	3334
19 3/16	12 2/16	7 1/16	M	St. Louis County	MN	John Cardinal	1991	3334
19 3/16	12 3/16	7 0/16	M	Montezuma County	CO	Paula R. Morton	1992	3334
19 3/16	11 12/16	7 7/16	M	Edmonton	ALB	Keith Morris	1992	3334
19 3/16	12 2/16	7 1/16	M	Idaho County	ID	Charles R. Whitfield	1992	3334
19 3/16	12 3/16	7 0/16	M	Duchesne County	UT	Hal R. Stauff	1992	3334
19 3/16	11 13/16	7 6/16	M	Raleigh Lake	ONT	Jeffrey Rueth	1992	3334
19 3/16	11 15/16	7 4/16	M	Lemhi County	ID	Gary Sims	1992	3334
19 3/16	12 4/16	6 15/16	M	Apache County	AZ	James S. Nelson IV	1993	3334
19 3/16	12 3/16	7 0/16	M	Highland Valley	BC	Kenneth Arthur Brown	1993	3334
19 3/16	12 0/16	7 3/16	M	Monds Township	ONT	John Standafer	1993	3334
19 3/16	11 11/16	7 8/16	M	Atikokan	ONT	Darrell J. Langan	1993	3334
19 3/16	11 15/16	7 4/16	M	Archuleta County	CO	Tonnie Elwood Davis	1993	3334
19 3/16	12 0/16	7 3/16	M	McBride	BC	Reg Meisner	1993	3334
19 3/16	12 6/16	6 13/16	M	Oneida County	WI	Shawn Umland	1993	3334
19 3/16	11 14/16	7 5/16	M	Wapawekka Lake	SAS	Gary Schwieters	1993	3334
19 3/16	12 2/16	7 1/16	M	Kelowna	BC	Chris Partridge	1994	3334
19 3/16	12 6/16	6 13/16	M	White Fox	SAS	Edward Toelken	1994	3334
19 3/16	11 14/16	7 5/16	M	Fort McMurray	ALB	Mike Walker	1994	3334
19 3/16	12 10/16	6 9/16	M	Fort Frances	ONT	Greg Wallace	1994	3334
19 3/16	12 3/16	7 0/16	M	Prince of Wales Island	AK	Rick Schikora	1994	3334
19 3/16	12 0/16	7 3/16	M	Wabasca River	ALB	Dave Holt	1994	3334
19 3/16	11 15/16	7 4/16	M	Tucker County	WV	Charles R. Burks	1994	3334
19 3/16	11 13/16	7 6/16	M	Tulare County	CA	Herb DeLong	1994	3334
19 3/16	12 5/16	6 14/16	M	Olha	MAN	Bill Clink	1995	3334
19 3/16	11 12/16	7 7/16	M	Boise County	ID	Bruce A. Capes	1995	3334
19 3/16	12 4/16	6 15/16	M	Spiritwood	SAS	Frank Jones	1995	3334
19 3/16	12 1/16	7 2/16	M	Minaki	ONT	John W. Jansen	1995	3334
19 3/16	11 13/16	7 6/16	M	La Ronge	SAS	Patrick Young	1995	3334
19 3/16	12 0/16	7 3/16	M	Kapuskasing	ONT	Lester W. Fraser	1995	3334

BLACK BEAR

Minimum Score 18 — Continued

SCORE	GREATEST LENGTH	GREATEST WIDTH	SEX	AREA	STATE/ PROVINCE	HUNTER'S NAME	DATE	RANK
19 3/16	12 4/16	6 15/16	M	Lodge Pole	ALB	Steve MacKenzie	1995	3334
19 3/16	12 8/16	6 11/16	M	Cranberry Portage	MAN	Joseph F. Blazevich	1995	3334
19 3/16	12 0/16	7 3/16	M	Vermilion Bay	ONT	Roy Legler	1995	3334
19 3/16	12 0/16	7 3/16	M	Algoma	ONT	Todd Howard Parker	1995	3334
19 3/16	11 13/16	7 6/16	M	Fort McMurray	ALB	J. A. Tyburczy	1996	3334
19 3/16	12 0/16	7 3/16	M	Hudson	ONT	Steve Lehner	1996	3334
19 3/16	12 1/16	7 2/16	M	Usherville	SAS	Jeff Stephenson	1996	3334
19 3/16	11 12/16	7 7/16	M	Chibougamau	QUE	David Kretschmar	1996	3334
19 3/16	12 6/16	6 13/16	M	Pine County	MN	Mike Sannan	1996	3334
19 3/16	11 13/16	7 6/16	M	Aroostook County	ME	Daniel J. Dyer	1996	3334
19 3/16	11 13/16	7 6/16	M	Sturgeon Lake	ONT	Steven A. Page	1996	3334
19 3/16	11 14/16	7 5/16	M	Sawyer County	WI	Timothy Kelley	1996	3334
19 3/16	12 7/16	6 12/16	M	Carrot River	SAS	Brad Hedke	1997	3334
19 3/16	11 11/16	7 8/16	M	Athabasca	ALB	Grant Adkisson	1997	3334
19 3/16	12 7/16	6 12/16	M	Green Lake	SAS	Pink Atkins	1997	3334
19 3/16	11 13/16	7 6/16	M	Howell	ONT	Donnie Hamby	1997	3334
19 3/16	12 4/16	6 15/16	M	Whiteshell Provincial Park	MAN	Wendell Schatkowsky	1998	3334
19 3/16	12 5/16	6 14/16	M	Prince of Wales Island	AK	Danny Moore	1998	3334
19 3/16	12 1/16	7 2/16	M	Aubrey Falls	ONT	Donald Roy Bell	1998	3334
19 3/16	12 2/16	7 1/16	M	Calabogie	ONT	Randy R. Martin	1998	3334
19 3/16	12 1/16	7 2/16	M	High Level	ALB	Bruce "Bucky" Butkiewicz	1998	3334
19 3/16	12 3/16	7 0/16	M	St. Louis County	MN	Kenneth McLellan	1998	3334
19 3/16	12 5/16	6 14/16	M	Langlade County	WI	Daniel Rine	1998	3334
19 3/16	11 13/16	7 6/16	M	Ft. McMurray	ALB	Ronald Hallstrom	1999	3334
19 3/16	12 3/16	7 0/16	M	Peace River	ALB	Doug Brummett	1999	3334
19 3/16	11 14/16	7 5/16	M	Buffalo Narrows	SAS	Dennis A. Demsky	1999	3334
19 3/16	11 14/16	7 5/16	M	Howard Bay	AK	Forrest Bolles	1999	3334
19 3/16	12 2/16	7 1/16	M	Olha	MAN	Thomas Heideman	1999	3334
19 3/16	11 15/16	7 4/16	M	Athabasca River	ALB	Raymond Howell	1999	3334
19 3/16	12 0/16	7 3/16	M	Lemhi County	ID	Michael Judas	1999	3334
19 3/16	12 1/16	7 2/16	M	Brownvale	ALB	Gerald L. Miller	1999	3334
19 3/16	11 15/16	7 4/16	M	Harvey	NBW	Edward F. Klosowski	1999	3334
19 3/16	12 1/16	7 2/16	M	Koochiching County	MN	Michael G. Ohmann	1999	3334
19 3/16	12 6/16	6 13/16	M	Lincoln County	WI	David Martino	1999	3334
19 3/16	12 4/16	6 15/16	M	Bayfield County	WI	Dan Creviston	1999	3334
19 3/16	12 1/16	7 2/16	M	Ashland County	WI	Kurt R. Bollig	1999	3334
19 3/16	12 2/16	7 1/16	M	Gunnison County	CO	R. Louis Thomas	1999	3334
19 3/16	12 5/16	6 14/16	M	Kanawha County	WV	Dana B. Fisher	1999	3334
19 3/16	12 0/16	7 3/16	M	Flathead County	MT	Neil L. Jacobson	2000	3334
19 3/16	11 15/16	7 4/16	M	Gem County	ID	Phillip E. Jayo	2000	3334
19 3/16	12 3/16	7 0/16	M	Steuben County	NY	Michael Allen	2000	3334
19 3/16	11 13/16	7 6/16	M	Wolf Lake	ALB	Scott Clark	2001	3334
19 3/16	12 3/16	7 0/16	M	Prince of Wales Island	AK	David J. Sherman II	2001	3334
19 3/16	12 3/16	7 0/16	M	Prince of Wales Island	AK	Shawn P. Price	2001	3334
19 3/16	11 15/16	7 4/16	M	Iroquois Lake	SAS	Frank J. Bush III	2001	3334
19 3/16	12 0/16	7 3/16	M	Place Lake	BC	Allan Tew	2001	3334
19 3/16	12 0/16	7 3/16	M	Union County	OR	Dan R. Kloer	2001	3334
19 3/16	12 4/16	6 15/16	M	St. Louis County	MN	Keith Meinholz	2001	3334
19 3/16	12 5/16	6 14/16	M	Cass County	MN	Gene F. Mather, Jr.	2001	3334
19 3/16	11 13/16	7 6/16	M	Sawyer County	WI	Steve Schroeder	2001	3334
19 3/16	12 3/16	7 0/16	M	Chippewa County	WI	Larry Paulsen	2001	3334
19 3/16	12 3/16	7 0/16	M	Flatbush	ALB	Kirk Clark	2002	3334
19 3/16	12 2/16	7 1/16	M	Carswell Lake	SAS	Bob Gilbert	2002	3334
19 3/16	12 2/16	7 1/16	M	High Level	ALB	Bruce MacDonald	2002	3334
19 3/16	12 3/16	7 0/16	M	Mafeking	MAN	James R. Rubel	2002	3334
19 3/16	12 1/16	7 2/16	M	High Level	ALB	Tim Cotton	2002	3334
19 3/16	11 15/16	7 4/16	M	Dryden	ONT	Ron Duncan	2002	3334
19 3/16	12 3/16	7 0/16	M	Round Lake	SAS	Floyd Forster	2002	3334
19 3/16	11 12/16	7 7/16	M	Prince of Wales Island	AK	Kelly King	2003	3334
19 3/16	12 0/16	7 3/16	M	Boundary County	ID	Rick Ruzzamenti	2003	3334
19 3/16	12 3/16	7 0/16	M	Preeceville	SAS	Bob L. Walker	2003	3334
19 3/16	12 0/16	7 3/16	M	East Trout Lake	SAS	Ed Dickman	2003	3334
19 3/16	11 15/16	7 4/16	M	Lac Dasserat	QUE	Pierre Gendron	2003	3334
*19 3/16	11 15/16	7 4/16	M	Chelmsford	ONT	Bryan DeWine	2003	3334
19 3/16	12 1/16	7 2/16	M	McAdam	NBW	Steve Senderovitz	2003	3334
19 3/16	11 11/16	7 8/16	M	Cheshire County	NH	Vernon Hamlett	2003	3334
19 3/16	11 11/16	7 8/16	M	Val-d'Or	QUE	Robert Amaral	2004	3334
19 3/16	12 2/16	7 1/16	M	Kipawa	QUE	Daniel M. Klawender	2004	3334
19 3/16	11 15/16	7 4/16	M	Gunnison County	CO	Matt Reilly	2004	3334
*19 3/16	12 8/16	6 11/16	M	Warren County	VA	Gary A. Hepner, Sr.	2004	3334
*19 3/16	12 1/16	7 2/16	M	Goodsoil	SAS	Ray Roberts	2005	3334
*19 3/16	12 1/16	7 2/16	M	100 Mile House	BC	Dan Real	2005	3334
*19 3/16	11 15/16	7 4/16	M	Gogama	ONT	Dwayne A. Gay	2005	3334
19 3/16	12 0/16	7 3/16	M	Thaddeus Lake	ONT	Adam F. Frandrup	2005	3334
19 3/16	11 15/16	7 4/16	M	Hearst	ONT	Ronnie J. Rogers	2005	3334
19 3/16	12 0/16	7 3/16	M	Itasca County	MN	Tony Lee Scheldrup	2005	3334
*19 3/16	11 14/16	7 5/16	M	Ignace	ONT	Eddie J. Heath	2005	3334
19 3/16	12 2/16	7 1/16	M	Saskatchewan River	SAS	Chad Rohel	2006	3334
19 3/16	12 7/16	6 12/16	M	Loon Lake	SAS	Lanny Nault	2006	3334
*19 3/16	12 2/16	7 1/16	M	Carbon County	WY	Eugene Ray, Sr.	2006	3334
*19 3/16	11 8/16	7 11/16	M	Chibougamau	QUE	Brian Brochu	2006	3334
19 3/16	11 8/16	7 11/16	M	Polk County	OR	Micheal Dean Hudson	2006	3334
19 3/16	12 4/16	6 15/16	M	Wolf River	ONT	Patrick Vaughn	2006	3334
*19 3/16	11 12/16	7 7/16	M	Lac Seul	ONT	Chris J. Clark	2006	3334
19 3/16	11 10/16	7 9/16	M	Chippewa County	WI	Jamey Bowe	2006	3334
*19 3/16	12 6/16	6 13/16	M	La Loche	SAS	Harold Smith	2007	3334
19 3/16	11 12/16	7 7/16	M	Two Brooks	NBW	Mike Chirico	2007	3334
19 3/16	12 1/16	7 2/16	M	Bissett	MAN	Jeff Shull	2007	3334
19 3/16	11 10/16	7 9/16	M	Beltrami County	MN	Gordon W. Ledioyt	2007	3334
*19 3/16	12 4/16	6 15/16	M	Langlade County	WI	David L. Sipple	2007	3334
19 3/16	12 6/16	6 13/16	M	Pine County	MN	Randy E. Broz	2007	3334
*19 3/16	12 2/16	7 1/16	M	Skeena	BC	Jason Moore	2008	3334
19 3/16	12 3/16	7 0/16	M	Josephine Creek	ALB	Kaitlyn Popson	2008	3334
19 3/16	12 1/16	7 2/16	M	Multnomah County	OR	Keith Iles	2008	3334
19 3/16	12 3/16	7 0/16	M	Indian River	AK	Garry Thoms	2008	3334

BLACK BEAR

Minimum Score 18 Continued

SCORE	GREATEST LENGTH	GREATEST WIDTH	SEX	AREA	STATE/PROVINCE	HUNTER'S NAME	DATE	RANK
19 3/16	12 3/16	7 0/16	M	Upsala Township	ONT	Dale L. Toltzmann	2008	3334
19 3/16	12 1/16	7 2/16	M	Bayfield County	WI	Dennis Klapoetke	2008	3334
19 3/16	12 5/16	6 14/16	M	Garfield County	CO	Jack T. Evans, Jr.	2008	3334
*19 3/16	12 4/16	6 15/16	M	Steuben County	NY	Scott Leeds	2008	3334
19 3/16	11 10/16	7 9/16	M	Asotin County	WA	Kenneth Anderson	2009	3334
19 3/16	12 1/16	7 2/16	M	Canoe Lake	SAS	William Bowen Slade	2009	3334
*19 3/16	11 15/16	7 4/16	M	Waskwei Lake	SAS	Darren Van Essen	2009	3334
*19 3/16	12 0/16	7 3/16	M	Cook County	MN	Matt Schwinghammer	2009	3334
*19 3/16	11 12/16	7 7/16	M	Cook County	MN	Anthony A. Aukes	2009	3334
*19 3/16	11 13/16	7 6/16	M	Custer County	ID	Joe Kaul	2010	3334
19 3/16	12 0/16	7 3/16	M	Kosciusko Island	AK	Bob Ameen	2010	3334
19 3/16	12 3/16	7 0/16	M	Lake Wasekamio	SAS	Bobby W. Hooven	2010	3334
19 3/16	12 9/16	6 10/16	M	Portage County	WI	Al Hottenstine	2010	3334
19 2/16	11 9/16	7 9/16	M	Sudbury	ONT	Clarence Grandt	1963	3529
19 2/16	11 13/16	7 5/16	M	Chapleau	ONT	Gerald E. Taft	1968	3529
19 2/16	11 12/16	7 6/16	M	Blount County	TN	Don Dvoroznak	1968	3529
19 2/16	11 12/16	7 6/16	M	Trinity County	CA	Fred M. Frakes	1970	3529
19 2/16	12 3/16	6 15/16	M	Shasta County	CA	Gerald P. Doyle	1971	3529
19 2/16	11 14/16	7 4/16	M	Vilas County	WI	William L. Yessa	1971	3529
19 2/16	11 11/16	7 7/16	M	Kormak	ONT	Marvin E. Davis	1972	3529
19 2/16	12 0/16	7 2/16	M	Dolores County	CO	Marvin Reichenau	1973	3529
19 2/16	11 13/16	7 5/16	M	Lemhi County	ID	Curley Keadle	1973	3529
19 2/16	11 15/16	7 3/16	M	Uncompahgre N.F.	CO	Ed Bonardi	1973	3529
19 2/16	11 14/16	7 4/16	M	Archuleta County	CO	Judd Cooney	1974	3529
19 2/16	11 13/16	7 5/16	M	Vancouver Island	BC	F. Guillon/A. Klopfenstein	1974	3529
19 2/16	12 1/16	7 1/16	M	Dryden	ONT	Ken Horton	1977	3529
19 2/16	12 4/16	6 14/16	M	Vilas County	WI	Michael Gapa	1979	3529
19 2/16	11 14/16	7 4/16	M	Skamania County	WA	John H. Wahl	1979	3529
19 2/16	11 14/16	7 4/16	M	Douglas County	CO	Thomas P. Grainger	1980	3529
19 2/16	12 1/16	7 1/16	M	Chetwynd	BC	Ron F. McKay	1980	3529
19 2/16	12 0/16	7 2/16	M	Bayfield County	WI	William F. Schutte	1980	3529
19 2/16	11 11/16	7 7/16	M	Shasta County	CA	Mark David Broadhead	1980	3529
19 2/16	12 4/16	6 14/16	M	St. Louis County	MN	Charlie Paine	1981	3529
19 2/16	11 15/16	7 3/16	M	Las Animas County	CO	David S. Bunce	1981	3529
19 2/16	12 2/16	7 0/16	M	Flathead County	MT	Owen Weaver	1981	3529
19 2/16	12 4/16	6 14/16	M	Whitecourt	ALB	Wade Johnson	1981	3529
19 2/16	12 0/16	7 2/16	M	Boise County	ID	Larry Hoff	1982	3529
19 2/16	11 12/16	7 6/16	M	Las Animas County	CO	Bill R. Lopatta	1982	3529
19 2/16	12 0/16	7 2/16	M	Moose Creek	AK	Robert T. Thomason, Jr.	1983	3529
19 2/16	11 10/16	7 8/16	M	Gallatin County	MT	Pat Sinclair	1983	3529
19 2/16	11 14/16	7 4/16	M	Savant Lake	ONT	Mark Milford	1983	3529
19 2/16	12 4/16	6 14/16	M	Grassy Narrows	ONT	Mike Jacobs	1983	3529
19 2/16	11 12/16	7 6/16	M	Caramat	ONT	Thomas Hlinka	1983	3529
19 2/16	12 3/16	6 15/16	M	Aulneau Peninsula	ONT	Mike Koska	1984	3529
19 2/16	11 14/16	7 4/16	M	Atikokan	ONT	Roger L. Hensley	1984	3529
19 2/16	11 12/16	7 6/16	M	Mackinac County	MI	Carson D. McMullen	1984	3529
19 2/16	12 2/16	7 0/16	M	Grand County	UT	Diane Snyder	1985	3529
19 2/16	11 11/16	7 7/16	M	Valley County	ID	Kenneth A. Hyde	1985	3529
19 2/16	12 5/16	6 13/16	M	Hudson Bay	SAS	Floyd Forster	1985	3529
19 2/16	12 3/16	6 15/16	M	Sanpete County	UT	Terry Casper	1986	3529
19 2/16	12 1/16	7 1/16	M	Rocky Lake	MAN	Dennis Jacobson	1986	3529
19 2/16	12 0/16	7 2/16	M	French River	ONT	Mike Bishop	1986	3529
19 2/16	11 14/16	7 4/16	M	Boise County	ID	Gary Titus	1986	3529
19 2/16	12 0/16	7 2/16	M	Durban	MAN	David H. Boland	1986	3529
19 2/16	12 2/16	7 0/16	M	Duck Mtn.	MAN	Chris Switzer	1987	3529
19 2/16	12 0/16	7 2/16	M	Hearst	ONT	Paul David Forquer	1987	3529
19 2/16	12 0/16	7 2/16	M	King County	WA	Irvin E. Harris, Jr.	1987	3529
19 2/16	12 0/16	7 2/16	M	Catron County	NM	Perry D. Harper	1987	3529
19 2/16	12 7/16	6 11/16	M	Cass County	MN	Philip M. Scott	1987	3529
19 2/16	12 2/16	7 0/16	M	Haywood County	NC	Michael Treadway	1987	3529
19 2/16	11 15/16	7 3/16	M	Greenbrier County	WV	Billy J. Hutchinson	1987	3529
19 2/16	12 6/16	6 12/16	M	Taylor County	WI	Allen K. Beard	1988	3529
19 2/16	12 4/16	6 14/16	M	Price County	WI	Randall J. Johnson	1988	3529
19 2/16	11 8/16	7 10/16	M	Revillagigedo Island	AK	Nathan Wood	1988	3529
19 2/16	11 13/16	7 5/16	M	Rio Arriba County	NM	James H. Miller	1989	3529
19 2/16	12 2/16	7 0/16	M	Knouff Lake	BC	Steve Zelisko	1989	3529
19 2/16	11 10/16	7 8/16	M	Caramat	ONT	Chris Hile	1989	3529
19 2/16	12 1/16	7 1/16	M	Starr Lake	MAN	Brian Gross	1989	3529
19 2/16	11 14/16	7 4/16	M	Thunder Bay	ONT	E. Alex Gouthro	1989	3529
19 2/16	11 15/16	7 3/16	M	Jim Lake	AK	Tom Hocking	1989	3529
19 2/16	11 13/16	7 5/16	M	La Tuque	QUE	Ronald T. Kinnas	1989	3529
19 2/16	11 12/16	7 6/16	M	Prince of Wales Island	AK	Steve Martin	1989	3529
19 2/16	11 14/16	7 4/16	M	Thunder Bay	ONT	Dale Miller	1990	3529
19 2/16	12 2/16	7 0/16	M	Christopher Lake	SAS	Lance W. McCrary	1990	3529
19 2/16	11 15/16	7 3/16	M	Kenora	ONT	Jeffrey C. Dais	1991	3529
19 2/16	11 13/16	7 5/16	M	High Level	ALB	R. E. Smith	1991	3529
19 2/16	12 0/16	7 2/16	M	Longlac	ONT	Steven R. Anderson	1991	3529
19 2/16	12 1/16	7 1/16	M	Bear Paw Landing	ONT	Paul Keil, Jr.	1991	3529
19 2/16	11 12/16	7 6/16	M	Le Domaine	QUE	Steven J. Niedzielski	1991	3529
19 2/16	12 2/16	7 0/16	M	Pine County	MN	Joseph M. Butler	1991	3529
19 2/16	12 0/16	7 2/16	M	Cook County	MN	John Truebenbach	1991	3529
19 2/16	11 14/16	7 4/16	M	Sullivan County	NY	Larry Micera	1991	3529
19 2/16	12 0/16	7 2/16	M	Beauval	SAS	Don Lindsay	1992	3529
19 2/16	12 2/16	7 0/16	M	Cranberry Lake	ALB	Terry C. Parkinson	1992	3529
19 2/16	11 15/16	7 3/16	M	La Loche	SAS	Troy D. Huffman	1992	3529
19 2/16	11 12/16	7 6/16	M	Oxford County	ME	Gary J. Russell	1992	3529
19 2/16	11 15/16	7 3/16	M	Greene County	NY	Dean Close	1992	3529
19 2/16	12 4/16	6 14/16	M	Emo	ONT	Paul Kolbeck	1993	3529
19 2/16	11 12/16	7 6/16	M	Coal Creek	BC	Jim Helinger, Jr.	1993	3529
19 2/16	11 13/16	7 5/16	M	Kelvington	SAS	Milan R. Liesener	1993	3529
19 2/16	12 3/16	6 15/16	M	Susitna River	AK	Brian D. McJunkin	1993	3529
19 2/16	12 4/16	6 14/16	M	San Juan County	NM	Perry Harper	1993	3529
19 2/16	12 0/16	7 2/16	M	Bissett	MAN	Richard P. Smith	1993	3529
19 2/16	12 2/16	7 0/16	M	Bissett	MAN	Dennis Wylie	1993	3529
19 2/16	11 15/16	7 3/16	M	Remigny	QUE	Michael Bolin	1993	3529

BLACK BEAR

Minimum Score 18   Continued

SCORE	GREATEST LENGTH	GREATEST WIDTH	SEX	AREA	STATE/ PROVINCE	HUNTER'S NAME	DATE	RANK
19 2/16	11 14/16	7 4/16	M	Beauval	SAS	M. R. James	1993	3529
19 2/16	12 2/16	7 0/16	M	Marshall County	MN	Al Hugg	1993	3529
19 2/16	12 1/16	7 1/16	M	Grays Harbor County	WA	Tom McManus	1993	3529
19 2/16	12 0/16	7 2/16	M	French River	ONT	John Fredrick Orr	1994	3529
19 2/16	12 1/16	7 1/16	M	Besnard Lake	SAS	Ronald J. Collier	1994	3529
19 2/16	11 13/16	7 5/16	M	Evain	QUE	Jacques Robichaud	1994	3529
19 2/16	11 15/16	7 3/16	M	St. Louis County	MN	Jim Leqve	1994	3529
19 2/16	11 13/16	7 5/16	M	Penobscot County	ME	Norman Bisson	1994	3529
19 2/16	11 11/16	7 7/16	M	Aroostook County	ME	Richard W. Higgins	1994	3529
19 2/16	12 1/16	7 1/16	M	Steuben County	NY	Philip J. Pomeroy	1994	3529
19 2/16	12 1/16	7 1/16	M	Tulare County	CA	John Garr	1994	3529
19 2/16	12 3/16	6 15/16	M	Green Lake	SAS	Jeff Rouse	1995	3529
19 2/16	12 2/16	7 0/16	M	Sioux Narrows	ONT	Jeff Ramthun	1995	3529
19 2/16	12 0/16	7 2/16	M	High Level	ALB	Tracy Roy	1995	3529
19 2/16	11 9/16	7 9/16	M	Adair Township	ONT	David G. Bockheim	1995	3529
19 2/16	12 2/16	7 0/16	M	Mendocino County	CA	David W. Rickert II	1995	3529
19 2/16	11 1/16	8 1/16	M	Pine County	MN	Jeff Lengsfeld	1995	3529
19 2/16	12 0/16	7 2/16	M	Aroostook County	ME	Rudy Conley	1995	3529
19 2/16	12 4/16	6 14/16	M	Green Lake	SAS	David L. Miller	1996	3529
19 2/16	11 9/16	7 9/16	M	Mine Centre	ONT	Mike Wissink	1996	3529
19 2/16	11 13/16	7 5/16	M	Bonanza	ALB	John L. Nelson, Sr.	1996	3529
19 2/16	12 0/16	7 2/16	M	Snow Lake	MAN	Toby J. Williams	1996	3529
19 2/16	11 15/16	7 3/16	M	Riding Mtn.	MAN	Eric E. Hansen	1996	3529
19 2/16	12 4/16	6 14/16	M	Carrot River	SAS	Gary Greene	1996	3529
19 2/16	11 14/16	7 4/16	M	Hearst	ONT	Bernie Kibbe	1996	3529
19 2/16	12 2/16	7 0/16	M	Dryden	ONT	Dean Bergman	1996	3529
19 2/16	11 9/16	7 9/16	M	Washago	ONT	David A. Hammer	1996	3529
19 2/16	12 1/16	7 1/16	M	Algoma	ONT	Milford Cross	1996	3529
19 2/16	12 6/16	6 12/16	M	Remigny	QUE	Raymonde Paquin	1996	3529
19 2/16	11 14/16	7 4/16	M	Thompson	MAN	Chris Yaritz	1996	3529
19 2/16	12 3/16	6 15/16	M	Sawyer County	WI	Roger Nelson	1996	3529
19 2/16	12 8/16	6 10/16	M	Newton County	AR	Eric R. Duncan	1996	3529
19 2/16	12 1/16	7 1/16	M	Revillagigedo Island	AK	Roy L. Redifer	1997	3529
19 2/16	12 0/16	7 2/16	M	Mossy River	SAS	Troy S. Johnson	1997	3529
19 2/16	12 4/16	6 14/16	M	Athabasca River	ALB	Henry F. Trotter III	1997	3529
19 2/16	12 4/16	6 14/16	M	Leoville	SAS	Compton Owens	1997	3529
19 2/16	12 4/16	6 14/16	M	Clark County	ID	Aaron Bateman	1997	3529
19 2/16	11 12/16	7 6/16	M	Falher	ALB	Jody Kellnhofer	1997	3529
19 2/16	12 2/16	7 0/16	M	Carroll County	NH	Matt Troiano	1997	3529
19 2/16	12 2/16	7 0/16	M	Delta County	CO	Kelly Brooks	1997	3529
19 2/16	12 8/16	6 10/16	M	Ferry County	WA	Doug Kikendall	1997	3529
19 2/16	12 2/16	7 0/16	M	San Jose Creek	BC	Allan Tew	1998	3529
19 2/16	12 2/16	7 0/16	M	Barrhead	ALB	Edwin E. Orr	1998	3529
19 2/16	12 5/16	6 13/16	M	Olha	MAN	Bill Clink	1998	3529
19 2/16	11 14/16	7 4/16	M	Lac La Biche	ALB	Patrick J. Rankin	1998	3529
19 2/16	11 15/16	7 3/16	M	Tanana Flats	AK	Tommy L. Ramsey	1998	3529
19 2/16	12 1/16	7 1/16	M	Moyie River	BC	Bob Faiers	1998	3529
19 2/16	12 2/16	7 0/16	M	Madoc	ONT	Barry T. Ritter	1998	3529
19 2/16	12 0/16	7 2/16	M	Chilkat Valley	AK	Andrew Friske	1998	3529
19 2/16	12 1/16	7 1/16	M	Deschambault Lake	SAS	Glenn D. Fields	1998	3529
19 2/16	12 2/16	7 0/16	M	Nipawin	SAS	Jim Horneck	1998	3529
19 2/16	11 11/16	7 7/16	M	Yakima County	WA	Isaac Conrad	1998	3529
19 2/16	12 0/16	7 2/16	M	Olha	MAN	Thomas Heideman	1998	3529
19 2/16	12 5/16	6 13/16	M	Ashland County	WI	Marlin L. Wavra	1998	3529
19 2/16	12 4/16	6 14/16	M	Missoula County	MT	Vinnie Pisani	1998	3529
19 2/16	12 4/16	6 14/16	M	Athabasca River	ALB	Michael Sulish	1999	3529
19 2/16	12 2/16	7 0/16	M	Ethelbert	MAN	Hubert A. Sexton	1999	3529
19 2/16	12 2/16	7 0/16	M	Clearwater County	ID	Kent Russell	1999	3529
19 2/16	11 15/16	7 3/16	M	Grand Rapids	MAN	Harold J. Palmer	1999	3529
19 2/16	11 12/16	7 6/16	M	Gunnison County	CO	Tate Endersby	1999	3529
19 2/16	12 5/16	6 13/16	M	Lloydminster	ALB	Danny Fisher	2000	3529
19 2/16	11 15/16	7 3/16	M	Frobisher Lake	SAS	Ron Ward	2000	3529
19 2/16	12 5/16	6 13/16	M	Wapawekka Lake	SAS	Larry H. Aarsby	2000	3529
19 2/16	12 0/16	7 2/16	M	Carrot River	SAS	Joseph P. Furlong	2000	3529
19 2/16	12 4/16	6 14/16	M	Beltrami County	MN	Brent A. Kaiser	2000	3529
19 2/16	12 0/16	7 2/16	M	Koochiching County	MN	Timothy L. Kampa	2000	3529
19 2/16	11 14/16	7 4/16	M	Piscataquis County	ME	Scot J. Sioch	2000	3529
19 2/16	11 12/16	7 6/16	M	Grand Rapids	MAN	Glen A. Paulsen	2000	3529
19 2/16	12 2/16	7 0/16	M	Missaukee County	MI	Robert E. Colby	2000	3529
19 2/16	12 3/16	6 15/16	M	Swan River	MAN	Mark Sterk	2001	3529
19 2/16	12 1/16	7 1/16	M	Dipper Lake	SAS	Gilbert Gresham	2001	3529
19 2/16	12 1/16	7 1/16	M	Koochiching County	MN	Steve Ruchti	2001	3529
19 2/16	11 13/16	7 5/16	M	Fremont County	ID	Travis Allen	2001	3529
19 2/16	12 1/16	7 1/16	M	Custer County	CO	Richard A. Madison	2001	3529
19 2/16	11 13/16	7 5/16	M	Penobscot County	ME	Michael S. Larrabee	2001	3529
19 2/16	11 12/16	7 6/16	M	Cartier	ONT	Brian Ross	2001	3529
19 2/16	12 1/16	7 1/16	M	York	NBW	Joseph P. Renik, Jr.	2001	3529
19 2/16	11 14/16	7 4/16	M	Iron County	WI	Ryan Murphy	2001	3529
19 2/16	12 9/16	6 9/16	M	Warren County	VA	Mark J. Basalyga	2001	3529
19 2/16	12 5/16	6 13/16	M	Allegany County	NY	Colin M. Bailey	2001	3529
19 2/16	12 2/16	7 0/16	M	Mendocino County	CA	Brian Lane	2001	3529
19 2/16	11 13/16	7 5/16	M	Vancouver Island	BC	Adam Bartsch	2002	3529
19 2/16	12 6/16	6 12/16	M	Rossburn	MAN	Barry Minshull	2002	3529
19 2/16	11 15/16	7 3/16	M	Redditt	ONT	Mark Jacobson	2002	3529
19 2/16	12 3/16	6 15/16	M	Upsala	ONT	Dale Toltzmann	2002	3529
19 2/16	12 0/16	7 2/16	M	Klickitat County	WA	Michael A. Wilcox	2002	3529
19 2/16	11 12/16	7 6/16	M	Grand Forks	BC	Tom Anzalone	2002	3529
19 2/16	11 14/16	7 4/16	M	Grant County	OR	John B. DeVorss	2002	3529
19 2/16	12 1/16	7 1/16	M	Luce County	MI	Robert D. Hall	2002	3529
19 2/16	11 14/16	7 4/16	M	Towns County	GA	Hollis Crocker	2002	3529
19 2/16	12 1/16	7 1/16	M	Olha	MAN	Bill Clink	2003	3529
19 2/16	12 2/16	7 0/16	M	Fraser River	BC	Charles M. Frick	2003	3529
19 2/16	11 15/16	7 3/16	M	Bathurst	NBW	Anthony Lopez	2003	3529
19 2/16	12 2/16	7 0/16	M	Cash Lake	MAN	John J. Miklos	2003	3529
19 2/16	11 8/16	7 10/16	M	Idaho County	ID	Ernesto M. Santana	2003	3529

BLACK BEAR

Minimum Score 18 — Continued

SCORE	GREATEST LENGTH	GREATEST WIDTH	SEX	AREA	STATE/ PROVINCE	HUNTER'S NAME	DATE	RANK
19 2/16	11 12/16	7 6/16	M	Nerepis	NBW	Dennis Gittins	2003	3529
19 2/16	11 15/16	7 3/16	M	Iron County	WI	Gary Goland	2003	3529
19 2/16	12 0/16	7 2/16	M	The Pas	MAN	J. Alex Wick	2004	3529
19 2/16	12 5/16	6 13/16	M	Flatbush	ALB	Kirk Clark	2004	3529
19 2/16	12 0/16	7 2/16	M	Lesser Slave Lake	ALB	Gene A. Welle	2004	3529
19 2/16	11 13/16	7 5/16	M	Idaho County	ID	Ray N. Andersen	2004	3529
19 2/16	12 2/16	7 0/16	M	Frobisher Lake	SAS	O. T. Fowler, Jr.	2004	3529
*19 2/16	11 10/16	7 8/16	M	Lynn Lake	MAN	Jeff Furstenau	2004	3529
19 2/16	11 13/16	7 5/16	M	Red Bank	NBW	Rick Todd Fleming	2004	3529
19 2/16	11 15/16	7 3/16	M	Charlotte	NBW	Shawn L. Radis	2004	3529
19 2/16	12 1/16	7 1/16	M	Gila County	AZ	Kathy Trimble	2004	3529
19 2/16	12 1/16	7 1/16	M	Harriot Lake	SAS	Scott Decker	2005	3529
19 2/16	11 11/16	7 7/16	M	Sullivan County	NY	Kenneth Malone	2005	3529
19 2/16	12 0/16	7 2/16	M	La Loche	SAS	Chris G. Sanford	2006	3529
19 2/16	12 1/16	7 1/16	M	Red Rose	MAN	Michael E. Hartigan	2006	3529
19 2/16	11 13/16	7 5/16	M	Cook County	MN	Kelly R. Alexander	2006	3529
19 2/16	11 13/16	7 5/16	M	Stevens County	WA	David V. Burdge, Jr.	2006	3529
19 2/16	12 2/16	7 0/16	M	Root Lake	MAN	K. Joel Kayer	2007	3529
19 2/16	11 13/16	7 5/16	M	Ile-a-La-Crosse	SAS	Thomas "Hap" Roberts	2007	3529
*19 2/16	11 14/16	7 4/16	M	Espinosa Inlet	BC	Adam Bartsch	2007	3529
*19 2/16	11 14/16	7 4/16	M	Preissac	QUE	Gary Alvis	2007	3529
*19 2/16	11 9/16	7 9/16	M	Chibougamau	QUE	Jon Massie	2007	3529
*19 2/16	11 12/16	7 6/16	M	Redditt	ONT	Harvey Horel	2007	3529
*19 2/16	12 3/16	6 15/16	M	Hornepayne	ONT	Tom Mozena	2007	3529
*19 2/16	12 2/16	7 0/16	M	Redditt	ONT	Charles G. Denton	2007	3529
19 2/16	12 0/16	7 2/16	M	Baraga County	MI	Kevin E. Bastian	2007	3529
19 2/16	12 1/16	7 1/16	M	Cumberlain Lake	SAS	Tony Nogy	2007	3529
*19 2/16	11 12/16	7 6/16	M	Vancouver Island	BC	Adam Bartsch	2008	3529
*19 2/16	12 1/16	7 1/16	M	Ft. McMurray	ALB	Todd Beckgerd	2008	3529
19 2/16	12 0/16	7 2/16	M	High Level	ALB	Bill Hartman	2008	3529
*19 2/16	12 2/16	7 0/16	M	La Ronge	SAS	Manny Santos	2008	3529
*19 2/16	11 15/16	7 3/16	M	Flotten Lake	SAS	Mark Sergi	2008	3529
19 2/16	11 13/16	7 5/16	M	Matagami	QUE	Ken H. Taylor	2008	3529
19 2/16	12 0/16	7 2/16	M	Ignace	ONT	Ryan Martinovici	2008	3529
*19 2/16	11 13/16	7 5/16	M	Wawa	ONT	Travis J. Tourjee	2008	3529
19 2/16	12 0/16	7 2/16	M	Crook County	OR	Michael J. Medina	2008	3529
19 2/16	12 9/16	6 9/16	M	Perry County	AR	Michael Smith	2008	3529
19 2/16	12 6/16	6 12/16	M	Somerset County	PA	Jonathan M. Lori	2008	3529
*19 2/16	12 4/16	6 14/16	M	Loon Lake	SAS	Tom Yanchuk	2009	3529
19 2/16	12 4/16	6 14/16	M	Kittitas County	WA	Robert Hambrick	2009	3529
*19 2/16	11 13/16	7 5/16	M	Schreiber	ONT	Chad Denike	2009	3529
*19 2/16	12 1/16	7 1/16	M	Longlac	ONT	Chris Kershaw	2009	3529
*19 2/16	12 3/16	6 15/16	M	Greenlee County	AZ	Larry Marin	2009	3529
*19 2/16	12 2/16	7 0/16	M	Ashland County	WI	Matthew Bruckner	2009	3529
*19 2/16	12 0/16	7 2/16	M	Barrows	MAN	Michael A. Zeringue	2009	3529
19 2/16	11 15/16	7 3/16	M	Washington County	ME	George Baggitt	2009	3529
*19 2/16	12 7/16	6 11/16	M	Sawyer County	WI	Mark Sobotta	2009	3529
19 2/16	11 11/16	7 7/16	M	Sanders County	MT	James V. Day	2009	3529
*19 2/16	11 9/16	7 9/16	M	High Rock Lake	SAS	Reginald E. Faber, Jr.	2010	3529
*19 2/16	12 0/16	7 2/16	M	Rio Blanco County	CO	Peter John Tait	2010	3529
19 1/16	11 12/16	7 5/16	M	Mineral County	CO	Ed Wintz	1959	3756
19 1/16	11 1/16	8 0/16	M	Jackson County	OR	Leander Lowel	1959	3756
19 1/16	11 15/16	7 2/16	M	Gogebic County	MI	Margaret R. Cooley	1961	3756
19 1/16	11 15/16	7 12/16	M	Upper Peninsula	MI	Jerry D. Anderson	1967	3756
19 1/16	12 1/16	7 0/16	M	Red Lake	ONT	Don Ellett	1969	3756
19 1/16	11 15/16	7 2/16	M	Langlade County	WI	Roland Mantzke	1969	3756
19 1/16	11 14/16	7 3/16	M	Archuleta County	CO	Maurice Chambers	1973	3756
19 1/16	11 15/16	7 2/16	M	Marquette County	MI	Pete Hillesheim	1974	3756
19 1/16	11 4/16	7 13/16	M	Vancouver Island	BC	Klaus Schultz	1974	3756
19 1/16	12 1/16	7 0/16	M	Itasca County	MN	William Biggs	1976	3756
19 1/16	12 3/16	6 14/16	M	Garfield County	CO	Michael D. Dickess	1976	3756
19 1/16	12 0/16	7 2/16	M	Kitsap County	WA	Larry A. Martin	1977	3756
19 1/16	11 11/16	7 6/16	M	St. Louis County	MN	Gerry Benson	1977	3756
19 1/16	11 10/16	7 7/16	M	Oxford County	ME	James P. Wellever	1978	3756
19 1/16	12 1/16	7 0/16	M	Lincoln County	WY	Ronell Skinner	1979	3756
19 1/16	12 2/16	6 15/16	M	Oneida County	WI	Douglas A. Severson	1979	3756
19 1/16	11 12/16	7 5/16	M	Marquette County	MI	Jeff Apel	1980	3756
19 1/16	11 13/16	7 4/16	M	Coos County	NH	James 'Boomer' Hayden	1980	3756
19 1/16	12 2/16	6 15/16	M	Cass County	MN	Robert M. Burtch	1980	3756
19 1/16	12 0/16	7 1/16	M	Terrace	BC	Bill Coburn	1981	3756
19 1/16	11 12/16	7 5/16	M	Caribou Snare Creek	AK	Bill Krenz	1981	3756
19 1/16	11 14/16	7 3/16	M	Franklin County	ME	Albert J. Kolatac	1982	3756
19 1/16	11 14/16	7 3/16	M	Nestor Falls	ONT	Larry Streiff	1982	3756
19 1/16	11 12/16	7 5/16	M	Espanola	ONT	Donald W. Taylor	1982	3756
19 1/16	12 2/16	6 15/16	M	Bayfield County	WI	Larry Frye	1982	3756
19 1/16	11 15/16	7 2/16	M	Kenora	ONT	Ray Hawver	1982	3756
19 1/16	11 15/16	7 2/16	M	Bonneville County	ID	Ronnel J. Stacey	1983	3756
19 1/16	11 15/16	7 2/16	M	Jellicoe	ONT	Ed Herzog	1983	3756
19 1/16	12 1/16	7 0/16	M	Pitkin County	CO	Perry Smith	1983	3756
19 1/16	12 3/16	6 14/16	M	Hudson Bay	SAS	Warren Buss	1984	3756
19 1/16	12 0/16	7 1/16	M	Essex County	NY	Paul Durling	1984	3756
19 1/16	11 15/16	7 2/16	M	Plumas County	CA	Mike Holley	1984	3756
19 1/16	12 1/16	7 0/16	M	Coos County	OR	Rick Gabbard	1984	3756
19 1/16	11 14/16	7 3/16	M	Redditt	ONT	Jim Christman	1985	3756
19 1/16	11 15/16	7 2/16	M	Little Bear Lake	SAS	Michael J. Ward	1986	3756
19 1/16	12 2/16	6 15/16	M	Terrance Lake	ONT	Jerry Krolik	1986	3756
19 1/16	12 6/16	6 11/16	M	Nez Perce County	ID	Steve Marcell	1986	3756
19 1/16	11 15/16	7 2/16	F	Sanpete County	UT	Judy Hallman	1986	3756
19 1/16	12 2/16	6 15/16	M	Plumas County	CA	Mike Holley	1986	3756
19 1/16	12 3/16	6 14/16	M	Alpine County	CA	Rick Lund	1986	3756
19 1/16	12 2/16	6 15/16	M	Carbon County	UT	Hugh Hogle	1987	3756
19 1/16	11 13/16	7 4/16	M	Fremont County	CO	Cheryl Ray	1987	3756
19 1/16	11 15/16	7 2/16	M	Atikokan	ONT	Paul Maas	1987	3756
19 1/16	11 15/16	7 2/16	M	Grand County	UT	O. Clair Adams	1988	3756
19 1/16	11 15/16	7 2/16	M	Zone 67	SAS	Ivan Buss	1988	3756

164

BLACK BEAR

Minimum Score 18   Continued

SCORE	GREATEST LENGTH	GREATEST WIDTH	SEX	AREA	STATE/ PROVINCE	HUNTER'S NAME	DATE	RANK
19 1/16	12 0/16	7 1/16	M	Dryden	ONT	Terry C. Arndt	1988	3756
19 1/16	11 14/16	7 3/16	M	Bryson Lake	QUE	Stephen P. Pointer	1988	3756
19 1/16	11 10/16	7 7/16	M	Inyo County	CA	Jim Voges	1988	3756
19 1/16	11 15/16	7 2/16	M	Millville	NBW	Lamar M. Shafer	1988	3756
19 1/16	12 0/16	7 1/16	M	Smoky Lake	ALB	Greg Reynolds	1989	3756
19 1/16	11 14/16	7 3/16	M	Hornepayne	ONT	Paul R. Chaffee	1989	3756
19 1/16	11 14/16	7 3/16	M	Larimer County	CO	Ed Bennett	1989	3756
19 1/16	11 6/16	7 11/16	M	Dryden	ONT	Troy S. Lowrey	1989	3756
19 1/16	12 2/16	6 15/16	M	Porcupine Mtns.	SAS	Dave McKenzie	1989	3756
19 1/16	11 10/16	7 7/16	M	Warren	ONT	Gary Lawrence Harding	1989	3756
19 1/16	11 13/16	7 4/16	M	Kenora	ONT	Chuck Harris	1989	3756
19 1/16	11 15/16	7 2/16	M	Sudbury	ONT	Randolph J. Hempton	1989	3756
19 1/16	11 14/16	7 3/16	M	Fort McMurray	ALB	Jim Trafford	1990	3756
19 1/16	11 14/16	7 3/16	M	Kenora	ONT	Shawn A. Wahl	1990	3756
19 1/16	12 1/16	7 0/16	M	Duchesne County	UT	Roger Cyfers	1990	3756
19 1/16	11 15/16	7 2/16	M	Marathon	ONT	David Weerstra	1990	3756
19 1/16	11 12/16	7 5/16	M	Stevens County	WA	Robert M. Larson	1990	3756
19 1/16	12 1/16	7 0/16	M	Prince of Wales Island	AK	Bernie Weisgerber	1990	3756
19 1/16	11 11/16	7 6/16	M	Wallowa County	OR	Dick Dohm	1990	3756
19 1/16	12 1/16	7 0/16	M	Prince of Wales Island	AK	Dan Moore	1991	3756
19 1/16	12 3/16	6 14/16	M	Lincoln County	OR	Richard S. Gaebel	1991	3756
19 1/16	11 9/16	7 8/16	M	Prince of Wales Island	AK	Frank Sanders	1991	3756
19 1/16	11 3/16	7 14/16	F	Riding Mtn.	MAN	Cory A. Pardon	1991	3756
19 1/16	12 4/16	6 13/16	M	High Level	ALB	Gino Giannetti	1991	3756
19 1/16	11 12/16	7 5/16	M	Sandoval County	NM	Wayne C. Wendel	1991	3756
19 1/16	12 1/16	7 0/16	M	Beltrami County	MN	Charles W. Gahagan	1991	3756
19 1/16	12 3/16	6 14/16	M	Smoky Lake	ALB	Andy Melnychuk	1991	3756
19 1/16	12 0/16	7 1/16	M	Preston County	WV	Robert Peddicord	1991	3756
19 1/16	11 15/16	7 2/16	M	Grand County	CO	Cary Laman	1992	3756
19 1/16	12 0/16	7 1/16	M	Montrose County	CO	Johnnie R. Walters	1992	3756
19 1/16	11 15/16	7 2/16	M	Trinity County	CA	Edward Bianchi	1992	3756
19 1/16	12 2/16	6 15/16	M	Prince of Wales Island	AK	Kelly Norskog	1992	3756
19 1/16	11 13/16	7 4/16	M	Sioux Narrows	ONT	Steve Young	1992	3756
19 1/16	11 15/16	7 2/16	M	Prince of Wales Island	AK	Monty Moravec	1993	3756
19 1/16	12 1/16	7 0/16	M	Prince of Wales Island	AK	Danny Moore	1993	3756
19 1/16	12 1/16	7 0/16	M	Fisher Branch	MAN	Michael Delfino, Sr.	1993	3756
19 1/16	11 12/16	7 5/16	M	Kashabowie	ONT	Andrew Schweitzer	1993	3756
19 1/16	11 15/16	7 2/16	M	Redditt	ONT	Gary Niesen	1993	3756
19 1/16	12 0/16	7 1/16	M	Le Domaine	QUE	Nicholas J. Barone, Jr.	1993	3756
19 1/16	12 5/16	6 12/16	M	Beltrami County	MN	Keith Dahl	1993	3756
19 1/16	12 3/16	6 14/16	M	Atikokan	ONT	Mark A. Stephens	1993	3756
19 1/16	12 4/16	6 13/16	M	Isanti County	MN	Bryan Becklin	1993	3756
19 1/16	11 15/16	7 2/16	M	Alsek River	BC	Randy R. McGregor	1994	3756
19 1/16	11 12/16	7 5/16	M	Blind River	ONT	Eugene Morgan	1994	3756
19 1/16	12 3/16	6 14/16	M	Lake Brunswick	ONT	Kevin J. Benzschawel	1994	3756
19 1/16	11 10/16	7 7/16	M	Stenen	SAS	Tim R. Dawson	1994	3756
19 1/16	11 9/16	7 8/16	M	Thunder Bay	ONT	Skip Simpson	1994	3756
19 1/16	12 1/16	7 0/16	M	Saddle Hills	ALB	Dale Collins	1994	3756
19 1/16	12 2/16	6 15/16	M	Iron County	WI	Richard M. Kanzelberger	1994	3756
19 1/16	12 1/16	7 0/16	M	Gogebic County	MI	Brian R. Hewitt	1994	3756
19 1/16	12 3/16	6 14/16	M	Albemarle County	VA	John Patterson	1994	3756
19 1/16	12 0/16	7 1/16	M	Tehama County	CA	Greg Carr	1994	3756
19 1/16	11 11/16	7 6/16	M	La Ronge	SAS	Paul Wolf	1995	3756
19 1/16	11 11/16	7 6/16	M	Ghost River	ONT	Roy L. Walk	1995	3756
19 1/16	11 15/16	7 2/16	M	Elsas	ONT	William R. Hecker, Jr.	1995	3756
19 1/16	12 5/16	6 12/16	M	Porcupine Hills	SAS	Wayne R. Schatzman	1995	3756
19 1/16	12 1/16	7 0/16	M	Koochiching County	MN	Arnie Streit	1995	3756
19 1/16	11 12/16	7 5/16	M	Sawyer County	WI	Bill Yoakum	1995	3756
19 1/16	11 9/16	7 8/16	M	Sipiwesk Lake	MAN	Jeffrey Williams	1996	3756
19 1/16	12 6/16	6 11/16	M	Nipawin	SAS	Gregory Bokash	1996	3756
19 1/16	11 13/16	7 4/16	M	Candle Lake	SAS	Ed Anderson	1996	3756
19 1/16	12 5/16	6 12/16	M	Beltrami County	MN	Brian Aune	1996	3756
19 1/16	11 11/16	7 6/16	M	Swan River	MAN	Daniel M. Permanian	1996	3756
19 1/16	12 2/16	6 15/16	M	Vermilion Bay	ONT	Sandy Schulz	1996	3756
19 1/16	12 0/16	7 1/16	M	Fremont County	ID	Rod L. Perkins	1997	3756
19 1/16	11 14/16	7 3/16	M	Blaine County	ID	Larry R. Newton	1997	3756
19 1/16	11 15/16	7 2/16	M	Buffalo Narrows	SAS	Arnt A. Fossum	1997	3756
19 1/16	11 12/16	7 5/16	M	Wawa	ONT	Wendall Matson	1997	3756
19 1/16	12 1/16	7 0/16	M	Coconino County	AZ	Lynn E. DeSpain	1997	3756
19 1/16	11 15/16	7 2/16	M	Dorion	ONT	Bruce Hudalla	1998	3756
19 1/16	11 13/16	7 4/16	M	Fort McMurray	ALB	Mark Kuhn	1998	3756
19 1/16	11 13/16	7 4/16	M	Chimney Lake	BC	Daryl Buchholtz	1998	3756
19 1/16	12 0/16	7 1/16	M	Wabasca River	ALB	William T. Nuttle	1998	3756
19 1/16	12 5/16	6 12/16	M	Lewis Lake	MAN	Jeff Celletti	1998	3756
19 1/16	12 1/16	7 0/16	M	Lynn Lake	MAN	Terry Coward	1998	3756
19 1/16	11 13/16	7 4/16	M	Wabigoon	ONT	Carl Seek	1998	3756
19 1/16	11 8/16	7 9/16	M	Skamania County	WA	Annette Crews	1998	3756
19 1/16	12 2/16	6 15/16	M	Firebag River	ALB	Richard Hal Otte	1999	3756
19 1/16	12 2/16	6 15/16	M	Alexander Archipelago	AK	Steve Hohensee	1999	3756
19 1/16	12 5/16	6 12/16	M	Barrhead	ALB	Drew Chalifoux	1999	3756
19 1/16	12 2/16	6 15/16	M	Buffalo Narrows	SAS	David Wayne Jolley	1999	3756
19 1/16	12 4/16	6 13/16	M	Des Ruisseaux	QUE	Johanne Perron	1999	3756
19 1/16	11 15/16	7 2/16	M	Lac Aveluy	QUE	Duane Watlington	1999	3756
19 1/16	12 0/16	7 1/16	M	Thunder Hills	SAS	Nathan Jones	1999	3756
19 1/16	11 10/16	7 7/16	M	Leaf Rapids	MAN	Don Gentry	2000	3756
19 1/16	12 0/16	7 1/16	M	Mono County	CA	Richard Bronson	2000	3756
19 1/16	11 15/16	7 2/16	M	Kirkland Lake	ONT	Mark Mayberry	2000	3756
19 1/16	11 12/16	7 5/16	M	Missoula County	MT	James R. O'Neill	2001	3756
19 1/16	12 0/16	7 1/16	M	Lewis Lake	MAN	Ivica Hrdjun	2001	3756
19 1/16	11 14/16	7 3/16	M	Clearwater County	ID	Jo Dee Martin	2001	3756
19 1/16	11 14/16	7 3/16	M	St. Louis County	MN	Mark Anderson	2001	3756
19 1/16	12 3/16	6 14/16	M	Kapuskasing	ONT	Willard Zook	2001	3756
19 1/16	12 2/16	6 15/16	M	Dryden	ONT	Joseph G. Daube	2001	3756
19 1/16	12 5/16	6 12/16	M	Itasca County	MN	James L. Carlson	2001	3756
19 1/16	12 2/16	6 15/16	M	Iron County	MI	Matthew Geurts	2001	3756

BLACK BEAR

Minimum Score 18 — Continued

SCORE	GREATEST LENGTH	GREATEST WIDTH	SEX	AREA	STATE/ PROVINCE	HUNTER'S NAME	DATE	RANK
19 1/16	11 13/16	7 4/16	M	Sheridan County	WY	Randy Burtis	2002	3756
19 1/16	12 1/16	7 0/16	M	Little Bear Lake	SAS	Rick Stockburger	2002	3756
19 1/16	11 7/16	7 10/16	M	Waskesiu Lake	SAS	Andy Russell	2002	3756
19 1/16	11 12/16	7 5/16	M	Engler Lake	SAS	Dyrk Eddie	2002	3756
19 1/16	11 11/16	7 6/16	M	Dorion	ONT	Kenneth Ganter	2002	3756
19 1/16	11 8/16	7 9/16	M	Powassan	ONT	Rodney Shepley	2002	3756
19 1/16	12 1/16	7 0/16	M	Rusk County	WI	Lawrence R. Hermanson	2002	3756
19 1/16	12 1/16	7 0/16	M	Price County	WI	Timothy John Biewer	2002	3756
*19 1/16	12 1/16	7 0/16	M	Rappahannock County	VA	Jason A. Foster	2002	3756
19 1/16	12 3/16	6 14/16	M	Peace River	ALB	Steven Derkson	2003	3756
19 1/16	11 15/16	7 2/16	M	Chippewa Lake	ALB	Kevin B. Shively	2003	3756
19 1/16	11 12/16	7 5/16	M	Reserve Rouge Matawin	QUE	Robert Lockhart	2003	3756
19 1/16	11 9/16	7 8/16	M	Armstrong	ONT	Kyle Harpham	2003	3756
19 1/16	12 6/16	6 11/16	M	Olha	MAN	Richard Jerome	2003	3756
19 1/16	12 2/16	6 15/16	M	Bayfield County	WI	Timothy D. Mattson	2003	3756
*19 1/16	11 12/16	7 5/16	M	Dolores County	CO	Barry Estes	2003	3756
19 1/16	12 0/16	7 1/16	M	Mason County	WA	Glen Davis	2003	3756
19 1/16	11 15/16	7 2/16	M	Ft. McMurray	ALB	Chris Parrino	2004	3756
*19 1/16	11 12/16	7 5/16	M	Deer Lake	NFL	Mark H. Hayes	2004	3756
19 1/16	12 0/16	7 1/16	M	Carswell Lake	SAS	Fred Johnston III	2004	3756
19 1/16	11 14/16	7 3/16	M	Raleigh Lake	ONT	William Wissestad	2004	3756
19 1/16	11 15/16	7 2/16	M	Piscataquis County	ME	Scott H. Pelletier	2004	3756
19 1/16	11 14/16	7 3/16	M	Matheson	ONT	Timothy J. Dillinger	2004	3756
19 1/16	11 15/16	7 2/16	M	Brookfield	NS	Mark Goodwin	2004	3756
19 1/16	11 13/16	7 4/16	M	Redditt	ONT	Gary D. Clark	2004	3756
19 1/16	11 15/16	7 2/16	M	Shoshone County	ID	Steve Bromley	2005	3756
19 1/16	11 15/16	7 2/16	M	Kuiu Island	AK	Frank S. Noska IV	2005	3756
19 1/16	11 10/16	7 7/16	M	Pinawa	MAN	Matthew P. Jensen	2005	3756
19 1/16	12 0/16	7 1/16	M	Churchill River	SAS	Mike Feldermann	2005	3756
*19 1/16	12 4/16	6 13/16	M	St. Martin	MAN	John B. Gutz	2005	3756
19 1/16	12 1/16	7 0/16	M	Deschambault Lake	SAS	Mike Grundmann	2005	3756
19 1/16	11 14/16	7 3/16	M	White River	ONT	Daniel E. Abbott	2005	3756
19 1/16	11 13/16	7 4/16	M	Kenora	ONT	Jerry Burgett	2005	3756
19 1/16	12 2/16	6 15/16	M	Langlade County	WI	Gary G. Neubert	2005	3756
*19 1/16	11 15/16	7 2/16	M	Tsolum River	BC	Adam Bartsch	2005	3756
19 1/16	11 15/16	7 2/16	M	Lake Wasekamio	SAS	Pink Atkins	2006	3756
*19 1/16	12 1/16	7 0/16	M	Frobisher Lake	SAS	O. T. Fowler, Jr.	2006	3756
*19 1/16	11 15/16	7 2/16	M	Oba	ONT	Richard McConnell	2006	3756
*19 1/16	12 2/16	6 15/16	M	Mono County	CA	Jerry Hinton	2006	3756
19 1/16	12 0/16	7 1/16	M	Kenora	ONT	Troy E. Brant	2006	3756
19 1/16	12 3/16	6 14/16	M	Attiti Lake	SAS	Jason S. Levy	2007	3756
19 1/16	11 15/16	7 2/16	M	Bathurst Mines	NBW	Stephen P. McLaughlin	2007	3756
*19 1/16	12 0/16	7 1/16	M	Abitibi	QUE	Jerry Goings II	2007	3756
19 1/16	11 15/16	7 2/16	M	Ignace	ONT	Joseph E. Reindl	2007	3756
*19 1/16	11 9/16	7 8/16	M	Madison County	MT	Kirk Clark	2007	3756
19 1/16	12 7/16	6 10/16	M	Plumas County	CA	Jay Yokomizo	2007	3756
19 1/16	12 0/16	7 1/16	M	Elmore County	ID	Andrew Drewiske	2008	3756
19 1/16	12 2/16	6 15/16	M	Shakeen Creek	AK	C. Michael Betts	2008	3756
19 1/16	11 15/16	7 2/16	M	Matheson	ONT	Chad Vaughn	2008	3756
19 1/16	12 1/16	7 0/16	M	Oneida County	WI	Brian Houp	2008	3756
*19 1/16	11 11/16	7 6/16	M	La Plata County	CO	Matthew L. Burcz	2008	3756
*19 1/16	12 0/16	7 1/16	M	Ray River	AK	Kevin Schaus	2009	3756
19 1/16	12 3/16	6 14/16	M	Kuiu Island	AK	David Duthie, Jr.	2009	3756
19 1/16	12 3/16	6 14/16	M	Little Smoky	ALB	Remington Dietzen	2009	3756
*19 1/16	11 15/16	7 2/16	M	Forestville	QUE	Kevin T. Krauss	2009	3756
*19 1/16	12 1/16	7 0/16	M	Forestville	QUE	Tyler Baechtle	2009	3756
*19 1/16	12 3/16	6 14/16	M	Birnie	MAN	Thomas M. Young	2009	3756
19 1/16	11 15/16	7 2/16	M	Alstead Lake	SAS	Michael J. Windemuller	2009	3756
19 1/16	12 4/16	6 13/16	M	Athabasca River	ALB	Joel M. Riotto	2009	3756
19 1/16	11 14/16	7 3/16	M	Renous	NBW	Jody Biesenkamp	2009	3756
19 1/16	12 4/16	6 13/16	M	Atikokan	ONT	Steve Mathy	2009	3756
*19 1/16	12 5/16	6 12/16	M	Logan County	AR	Glen Sturgeon	2009	3756
*19 1/16	12 3/16	6 14/16	M	Ashland County	WI	Jeffery Ernest	2009	3756
19 1/16	11 15/16	7 2/16	M	Lake Manitoba Narrows	MAN	Alisa Wold	2010	3756
*19 1/16	11 15/16	7 2/16	M	Chilcolth Mtns.	BC	Donald Bradford Schofield	2010	3756
*19 1/16	12 0/16	7 1/16	M	Olha	MAN	Bill Clink	2010	3756
19 0/16	12 6/16	6 10/16	M	Iron County	WI	Charles Kroll	1966	3962
19 0/16	11 9/16	7 7/16	M	Sioux Narrows	ONT	Walter J. Sawicki	1967	3962
19 0/16	11 12/16	7 3/16	M	Kamloops	BC	Terry J. Haines	1968	3962
19 0/16	11 12/16	7 4/16	M	Chapleau	ONT	Kenneth R. Larson	1968	3962
19 0/16	11 15/16	7 1/16	M	Ignace	ONT	Stanley Olson	1968	3962
19 0/16	11 10/16	7 6/16	M	Kenora	ONT	Barry Englehardt	1969	3962
19 0/16	11 8/16	7 8/16	M	Shasta County	CA	Patrick J. Marley	1969	3962
19 0/16	11 12/16	7 4/16	M	Armstrong	ONT	James Mahoney	1969	3962
19 0/16	11 11/16	7 5/16	M	Skamania County	WA	Dennis E. DesJardins	1970	3962
19 0/16	11 7/16	7 9/16	M	Grand County	UT	C. Donald Lechner	1970	3962
19 0/16	11 9/16	7 7/16	M	Lemhi County	ID	Douglas Kittredge	1971	3962
19 0/16	11 11/16	7 5/16	M	Saguache County	CO	Gary Ginther	1973	3962
19 0/16	11 14/16	7 2/16	M	Cloyne	ONT	Tom Erkinger	1976	3962
19 0/16	11 14/16	7 2/16	M	Lanark	ONT	Guy Pointer	1977	3962
19 0/16	11 14/16	7 2/16	M	St. Louis County	MN	Jimmy F. Rogers	1978	3962
19 0/16	11 8/16	7 8/16	M	Wawa	ONT	Don LaDuke	1980	3962
19 0/16	12 5/16	6 11/16	M	Sullivan County	NY	John Nasuta	1980	3962
19 0/16	11 9/16	7 7/16	M	Boise County	ID	Richard C. Nichols	1981	3962
19 0/16	12 1/16	6 15/16	M	Fort St. John	BC	Duane Hicks	1981	3962
19 0/16	11 8/16	7 8/16	M	Coos County	NH	Edward Silva	1981	3962
19 0/16	11 14/16	7 2/16	M	North Bay	ONT	Grant R. Beattie	1981	3962
19 0/16	11 11/16	7 5/16	M	Ravalli County	MT	Rod Osburn	1981	3962
19 0/16	11 14/16	7 2/16	F	San Juan County	UT	Sheldon Anderson	1982	3962
19 0/16	12 1/16	6 15/16	M	Las Animas County	CO	Bob Lopatta	1982	3962
19 0/16	11 14/16	7 2/16	M	Pacific County	WA	Annette Crews	1983	3962
19 0/16	11 13/16	7 3/16	M	Siskiyou County	CA	Fred Searle	1983	3962
19 0/16	11 14/16	7 2/16	M	Fort Frances	ONT	Kerry Ella	1984	3962
19 0/16	11 9/16	7 7/16	M	Chapleau	QUE	Joseph D. Maddock	1984	3962
19 0/16	11 13/16	7 3/16	M	Meadow Lake	SAS	Gary Bauer	1984	3962

166

BLACK BEAR

Minimum Score 18   Continued

SCORE	GREATEST LENGTH	GREATEST WIDTH	SEX	AREA	STATE/ PROVINCE	HUNTER'S NAME	DATE	RANK
19 0/16	12 1/16	6 15/16	M	Fremont County	ID	Joe Bronson	1984	3962
19 0/16	11 15/16	7 1/16	M	York County	NBW	Daniel L. Shaffer	1984	3962
19 0/16	11 13/16	7 3/16	M	Bingham County	ID	Mike Lee Wohlschlegel	1984	3962
19 0/16	12 1/16	6 15/16	M	Lincoln County	WI	Jim Wurster	1984	3962
19 0/16	11 14/16	7 2/16	M	Vilas County	WI	Mike Eidson	1984	3962
19 0/16	11 13/16	7 3/16	M	Mine Centre	ONT	Bob Roulet	1985	3962
19 0/16	12 2/16	6 14/16	M	Ear Falls	ONT	Brent Allen Poindexter	1985	3962
19 0/16	11 8/16	7 8/16	M	Chelan County	WA	Leroy E. House	1986	3962
19 0/16	11 14/16	7 2/16	M	Ravalli County	MT	John Locke	1987	3962
19 0/16	11 14/16	7 2/16	M	Grays Harbor County	WA	Mark Tupper	1987	3962
19 0/16	12 0/16	7 0/16	M	Tulare County	CA	Don Reid	1987	3962
19 0/16	11 14/16	7 2/16	M	Snohomish County	WA	Colin MacRae	1987	3962
19 0/16	12 0/16	7 0/16	M	Smeaton	SAS	Gene Welle	1988	3962
19 0/16	12 7/16	6 9/16	M	Cranbrook	BC	Jasper Kenneth White, Jr.	1988	3962
19 0/16	11 10/16	7 6/16	M	Sioux Lookout	ONT	Steve Schmidt	1988	3962
19 0/16	12 4/16	6 12/16	M	Langlade County	WI	Jeff Traska	1988	3962
19 0/16	11 13/16	7 3/16	M	Carroll County	NH	Brian Libby	1988	3962
19 0/16	12 0/16	7 0/16	M	Hardy County	WV	Clarence W. Houck	1988	3962
19 0/16	11 12/16	7 4/16	M	Cold Lake	ALB	Ron R. Dixon	1989	3962
19 0/16	11 9/16	7 7/16	M	Cochrane	ONT	Ed Rogalski	1989	3962
19 0/16	12 2/16	6 14/16	M	Ft. McMurray	ALB	James Pike	1989	3962
19 0/16	12 0/16	7 0/16	M	Chapleau	ONT	Dennis D. Wentz	1989	3962
19 0/16	11 13/16	7 3/16	M	Foleyet	ONT	Mike Schmidt	1989	3962
19 0/16	11 14/16	7 2/16	M	Drury Township	ONT	Marty Masek	1989	3962
19 0/16	11 10/16	7 6/16	M	Sandoval County	NM	Noble Sinclair	1989	3962
19 0/16	11 12/16	7 4/16	M	Kitsap County	WA	Gary A. Bell	1989	3962
19 0/16	11 11/16	7 5/16	M	Pierce County	WA	Warren L. Byrd	1989	3962
19 0/16	11 15/16	7 1/16	M	Aroostook County	ME	Louis J. Lorenzo	1989	3962
19 0/16	12 1/16	6 15/16	M	Langlade County	WI	Glen A. Rutten	1989	3962
19 0/16	11 11/16	7 5/16	M	Bella Coola	BC	J. Dale Hale	1989	3962
19 0/16	12 0/16	7 0/16	M	Sheridan County	WY	Larry O. Burtis	1990	3962
19 0/16	11 8/16	7 8/16	M	Chelmsford	ONT	Timothy C. Shock	1990	3962
19 0/16	11 13/16	7 3/16	M	Chapleau	ONT	Dennis Dawson	1990	3962
19 0/16	12 2/16	6 14/16	M	Minaki	ONT	Carroll Cunningham	1990	3962
19 0/16	11 12/16	7 4/16	M	Wallowa County	OR	Eugene Smith, Jr.	1990	3962
19 0/16	12 1/16	6 15/16	M	Bayfield County	WI	Randall O. Nash	1990	3962
19 0/16	12 0/16	7 0/16	M	Sawyer County	WI	Kim Lemke	1990	3962
19 0/16	11 9/16	7 7/16	M	Manitouwadge	ONT	Rick Buchanan	1991	3962
19 0/16	11 15/16	7 1/16	M	Remigny	QUE	Max Reagin	1991	3962
19 0/16	11 14/16	7 2/16	M	Hearst	ONT	Steven B. Karel	1991	3962
19 0/16	11 10/16	7 6/16	M	Matagami	QUE	Jacques Harvey	1991	3962
19 0/16	12 5/16	6 11/16	M	Sevier County	UT	Dennis Nielsen	1991	3962
19 0/16	12 4/16	6 12/16	M	Ft. McMurray	ALB	Floyd Forster	1991	3962
19 0/16	12 0/16	7 0/16	M	Ontonagon County	MI	Carl R. Birely	1991	3962
19 0/16	11 12/16	7 4/16	M	Oxford County	ME	Gary J. Russell	1991	3962
19 0/16	12 0/16	7 0/16	M	Custer County	ID	Pascal Perrin	1992	3962
19 0/16	11 14/16	7 2/16	M	Hudson Bay	SAS	Sheldon Poss	1992	3962
19 0/16	11 9/16	7 7/16	M	Holinshead Lake	ONT	John E. Larsen	1992	3962
19 0/16	11 10/16	7 6/16	M	Thompson	MAN	Jack Baltz	1992	3962
19 0/16	11 9/16	7 7/16	M	Grande Prairie	ALB	Les Baird	1992	3962
19 0/16	11 4/16	7 12/16	M	Wanless	MAN	Tim Finley	1992	3962
19 0/16	11 9/16	7 7/16	M	Mammeville	QUE	George A. Kearns	1992	3962
19 0/16	12 0/16	7 0/16	M	Goodsoil	SAS	Carol Hathaway	1992	3962
19 0/16	12 2/16	6 14/16	M	Koochiching County	MN	Arnie Streit	1992	3962
19 0/16	11 14/16	7 2/16	M	Houghton County	MI	Jeffrey D. Emanuel	1992	3962
19 0/16	11 10/16	7 6/16	M	Zec Rapides des Joachims	QUE	Arthur E. Thibodeau, Jr.	1992	3962
19 0/16	12 2/16	6 14/16	M	Blackhawk	ONT	Gary Marion	1993	3962
19 0/16	11 11/16	7 5/16	M	White River	ONT	David A. Dusthimer	1993	3962
19 0/16	11 14/16	7 2/16	M	Lac Ile-a-la-Crosse	SAS	Rocky Drake	1993	3962
19 0/16	11 11/16	7 5/16	M	Lake County	MN	Donald Van Meveren	1993	3962
19 0/16	12 5/16	6 11/16	M	Aitkin County	MN	Pete Peterson	1993	3962
19 0/16	11 9/16	7 7/16	M	Powell County	MT	Scott C. Godown	1993	3962
19 0/16	11 12/16	7 4/16	M	Alpena County	MI	Brett Anderson	1993	3962
19 0/16	11 14/16	7 2/16	M	Elmore County	ID	Kirk W. Reese	1994	3962
19 0/16	12 3/16	6 13/16	M	Hudson Bay	SAS	Mike Adkins	1994	3962
19 0/16	11 14/16	7 2/16	M	Slave Lake	ALB	Greg Ogle	1994	3962
19 0/16	11 10/16	7 6/16	M	Nipawin	SAS	Robert H. Torstenson	1994	3962
19 0/16	11 10/16	7 6/16	M	Baie Comeau	QUE	Louis J. Lorenzo	1994	3962
19 0/16	12 0/16	7 0/16	M	Emo	ONT	Randy Loken	1994	3962
19 0/16	12 2/16	6 14/16	M	Woman River	ONT	Paul Borden	1994	3962
19 0/16	11 13/16	7 3/16	M	Grand Falls	NFL	Dean Coppolella	1994	3962
19 0/16	12 6/16	6 10/16	M	Aitkin County	MN	Michael Thorp	1994	3962
19 0/16	11 11/16	7 5/16	M	Dog Lake	ONT	Keith Goodrow	1994	3962
19 0/16	11 12/16	7 4/16	M	Marinette County	WI	Kevin Sommers	1994	3962
19 0/16	11 12/16	7 4/16	M	Clark County	WI	Richard Rinehart	1994	3962
19 0/16	12 1/16	6 15/16	M	Lane County	OR	Rick Wayne Miller	1994	3962
19 0/16	12 4/16	6 12/16	M	Spirit River	ALB	James R. Stinson	1995	3962
19 0/16	12 4/16	6 12/16	M	Dryden	ONT	Richard J. Kain	1995	3962
19 0/16	12 4/16	6 12/16	M	Creighton	SAS	Cory Smith	1995	3962
19 0/16	12 0/16	7 0/16	M	Vancouver Island	BC	Guy Davis	1995	3962
19 0/16	12 2/16	6 14/16	M	Wabigoon	ONT	Anita D. Daggett	1995	3962
19 0/16	12 2/16	6 14/16	M	Northmark	ALB	Phil Neiser	1995	3962
19 0/16	12 6/16	6 10/16	M	Otero County	NM	George W. Semple	1995	3962
19 0/16	11 13/16	7 3/16	M	Campbell River	BC	Gary F. Bogner	1996	3962
19 0/16	11 15/16	7 1/16	M	Lynn Lake	MAN	Jeff Welhouse	1996	3962
19 0/16	12 8/16	6 8/16	M	Dryden	ONT	Christopher J. Dean	1996	3962
19 0/16	11 11/16	7 5/16	M	Cadillac	QUE	John McDonald	1996	3962
19 0/16	11 14/16	7 2/16	M	Oba	ONT	William E. Haynes	1996	3962
19 0/16	11 15/16	7 1/16	M	Beluga	AK	Ryan Garet Rechner	1996	3962
19 0/16	11 14/16	7 2/16	M	Greenlee County	AZ	Rick Forrest	1996	3962
19 0/16	11 14/16	7 2/16	M	Baraga County	MI	Mike Holy	1996	3962
19 0/16	11 15/16	7 1/16	M	Coos County	NH	Mark P. Lachapelle	1996	3962
19 0/16	11 15/16	7 1/16	M	Athabasca River	ALB	Sonny Evans	1997	3962
19 0/16	11 14/16	7 2/16	M	Bissett	MAN	David Harris	1997	3962
19 0/16	12 4/16	6 12/16	M	Carrot River	SAS	Larry Peterson	1997	3962

BLACK BEAR

Minimum Score 18   Continued

SCORE	GREATEST LENGTH	GREATEST WIDTH	SEX	AREA	STATE/ PROVINCE	HUNTER'S NAME	DATE	RANK
19 0/16	12 2/16	6 14/16	M	Theodore River	AK	H. Gale McKnight	1997	3962
19 0/16	11 12/16	7 4/16	M	Woodstock	NBW	Frederick Winkelmann	1997	3962
19 0/16	12 0/16	7 0/16	M	Cabonga Reservoir	QUE	Vincent Grasso	1997	3962
19 0/16	12 3/16	6 13/16	M	Chibougamau	QUE	Brian Brochu	1997	3962
19 0/16	11 7/16	7 9/16	M	Ignace	ONT	Chuck Harris	1997	3962
19 0/16	11 11/16	7 5/16	M	Pinard	ONT	Gerald L. Cripe	1997	3962
19 0/16	12 4/16	6 12/16	M	Price County	WI	Dennis L. Lemke	1997	3962
19 0/16	11 12/16	7 4/16	M	Chilliwack Valley	BC	Robert Zseder	1998	3962
19 0/16	11 14/16	7 2/16	M	Zama	ALB	Tom Jordan	1998	3962
19 0/16	11 15/16	7 1/16	M	Nusatsum River	BC	Rick Paquette	1998	3962
19 0/16	12 0/16	7 0/16	M	Oak Lake	ONT	Ronald A. Hall	1998	3962
19 0/16	11 15/16	7 1/16	M	Shining Tree	ONT	J. T. Kreager	1998	3962
19 0/16	12 2/16	6 14/16	M	Theodore River	AK	H. Gale McKnight	1998	3962
19 0/16	11 10/16	7 6/16	M	Belleterre	QUE	Robert Amaral	1998	3962
19 0/16	11 14/16	7 2/16	M	Red Lake County	MN	Robert Wagoner	1998	3962
19 0/16	11 13/16	7 3/16	M	Siskiyou County	CA	James Brent Kincaid	1998	3962
19 0/16	12 0/16	7 0/16	M	Aroostook County	ME	Ken Lamb	1998	3962
19 0/16	11 12/16	7 4/16	M	Savant Lake	ONT	Dean E. Fidler	1998	3962
19 0/16	11 12/16	7 4/16	M	Hoyt	NBW	Joe Lorenti	1998	3962
19 0/16	11 13/16	7 3/16	M	Keg River	ALB	Robert E. Fyock	1998	3962
19 0/16	12 0/16	7 0/16	M	La Ronge	SAS	Roger Bell	1999	3962
19 0/16	11 8/16	7 8/16	M	Cold Lake	ALB	Nicholas M. Trotta	1999	3962
19 0/16	11 12/16	7 4/16	M	Chibougamau	QUE	Michael M. Walter	1999	3962
19 0/16	11 8/16	7 8/16	M	Thompson	MAN	William F. Curlis II	1999	3962
19 0/16	11 13/16	7 3/16	M	Riviere Dore	QUE	Ken H. Taylor	1999	3962
19 0/16	12 1/16	6 15/16	M	Siskiyou County	CA	John C. Shuping	1999	3962
19 0/16	11 12/16	7 4/16	M	Piscataquis County	ME	John B. Ward, Jr.	1999	3962
19 0/16	11 13/16	7 3/16	M	Ashland County	WI	Dan Ferch	1999	3962
19 0/16	11 8/16	7 8/16	M	Herkimer County	NY	Stan Rozyla	1999	3962
19 0/16	12 0/16	7 0/16	M	Iron County	WI	John Quade	1999	3962
19 0/16	12 0/16	7 0/16	M	Frobisher Lake	SAS	David E. Stepp	2000	3962
19 0/16	11 15/16	7 1/16	M	Long Lake	MAN	Chris Murphy	2000	3962
19 0/16	11 13/16	7 3/16	M	Lac Brush	QUE	Stephen Kotz	2000	3962
19 0/16	11 14/16	7 2/16	M	Hudson Bay	SAS	Tony Willwerth	2000	3962
19 0/16	11 13/16	7 3/16	M	Rossburn	MAN	David Capestany	2000	3962
19 0/16	11 15/16	7 1/16	M	Zitziana River	AK	James Jones	2000	3962
19 0/16	12 2/16	6 14/16	M	Oneida County	WI	Kenneth Wollermann	2000	3962
19 0/16	12 0/16	7 0/16	M	Towns County	GA	Terry Owenby	2000	3962
19 0/16	11 13/16	7 3/16	M	Idaho County	ID	Marlon J. Clapham	2001	3962
19 0/16	11 15/16	7 1/16	M	Wandering River	ALB	Ed Hendricks	2001	3962
19 0/16	11 11/16	7 5/16	M	Thompson	MAN	Daniel R. Wendling	2001	3962
19 0/16	11 11/16	7 5/16	M	Blaine County	ID	Brian Brockette	2002	3962
19 0/16	12 0/16	7 0/16	M	Big River	SAS	Marc N. Shaft	2002	3962
19 0/16	12 0/16	7 0/16	M	High Level	ALB	John F. Harding	2002	3962
19 0/16	11 11/16	7 5/16	M	Kamloops Lake	BC	A. E. "Gene" Tisdale	2002	3962
19 0/16	12 3/16	6 13/16	M	Arran	SAS	Keith Headley	2002	3962
19 0/16	11 11/16	7 5/16	M	Washington County	ME	Michael Lazarz	2002	3962
19 0/16	12 0/16	7 0/16	M	Baker County	OR	Eric J. Magidson	2002	3962
19 0/16	11 13/16	7 3/16	M	Conejos County	CO	Shawn Wilson	2002	3962
19 0/16	11 13/16	7 3/16	M	Ontonagon County	MI	David Alan Bell	2002	3962
19 0/16	12 1/16	6 15/16	M	Big River	SAS	James Gordon Morris	2003	3962
*19 0/16	12 1/16	6 15/16	M	Fairview	ALB	Steve Bugbee	2003	3962
19 0/16	12 4/16	6 12/16	M	Carswell Lake	SAS	Bob Gilbert	2003	3962
19 0/16	11 13/16	7 3/16	M	Vermette Lake	SAS	Josh Hansen	2003	3962
19 0/16	12 0/16	7 0/16	M	Churchill River	SAS	Michele Leqve	2003	3962
19 0/16	12 0/16	7 0/16	M	Riou Lake	SAS	Robert D. Hancock, Jr.	2003	3962
19 0/16	11 14/16	7 2/16	M	Amos	QUE	Josh Dearth	2003	3962
19 0/16	11 12/16	7 4/16	M	Grand Rapids	MAN	Jason Lowe	2003	3962
19 0/16	11 15/16	7 1/16	M	Thaddeus Lake	ONT	Adam Carlson	2003	3962
19 0/16	11 13/16	7 3/16	M	Simcoe	ONT	John Orr	2003	3962
19 0/16	12 7/16	6 9/16	M	Ashland County	WI	Mike Richards	2003	3962
19 0/16	12 3/16	6 13/16	M	Luce County	MI	Terry L. Cook	2003	3962
19 0/16	12 5/16	6 11/16	M	Pennington County	MN	Alan W. Smith	2003	3962
19 0/16	12 0/16	7 0/16	M	Chapleau	ONT	Troy White	2003	3962
19 0/16	11 15/16	7 1/16	M	Tsolum River	BC	Adam Bartsch	2003	3962
19 0/16	12 3/16	6 13/16	M	Douglas County	WI	Rick Polson	2003	3962
19 0/16	11 15/16	7 1/16	M	Tulare County	CA	John Garr	2003	3962
19 0/16	12 0/16	7 0/16	M	Olha	MAN	Bill Clink	2004	3962
19 0/16	12 0/16	7 0/16	M	Dorintosh	SAS	Chris Dorris	2004	3962
19 0/16	12 0/16	7 0/16	M	Prince of Wales Island	AK	Kaye Rue	2004	3962
19 0/16	11 11/16	7 5/16	M	Kipahigan Lake	MAN	Scott G. Hettinger	2004	3962
*19 0/16	12 0/16	7 0/16	M	Carlisle	NBW	Cliff B. Beaver	2004	3962
19 0/16	12 0/16	7 0/16	M	Carrot River	SAS	Justin Ryan Falatok	2004	3962
*19 0/16	11 14/16	7 2/16	M	Caramat	ONT	Judd E. Stead	2004	3962
19 0/16	11 14/16	7 2/16	M	Atikokan	ONT	Jim Saunoris, Jr.	2004	3962
19 0/16	12 0/16	7 0/16	M	Wheeler County	OR	Joe Pastor	2004	3962
19 0/16	12 0/16	7 0/16	M	Price County	WI	Gary T. Sotak	2004	3962
19 0/16	11 14/16	7 2/16	M	Chilkat Peninsula	AK	Mark Wayne Smith	2005	3962
19 0/16	12 5/16	6 11/16	M	Endeavour	SAS	Keith Goodrow	2005	3962
19 0/16	12 2/16	6 14/16	M	Carrot River	SAS	Patrick W. Shiroda	2005	3962
19 0/16	11 12/16	7 4/16	M	Besnard Lake	SAS	Bruce Carroll	2005	3962
19 0/16	12 1/16	6 15/16	M	Leaf Rapids	MAN	Shawn Sand	2005	3962
19 0/16	11 15/16	7 1/16	M	Upsala	ONT	Linda Gasser	2005	3962
19 0/16	11 13/16	7 3/16	M	Thunder Bay	ONT	Marlene Odahlen-Hinz	2005	3962
19 0/16	12 0/16	7 0/16	M	Horwood Lake	ONT	Bobby Bumgardner	2005	3962
19 0/16	11 14/16	7 2/16	M	Lake County	MN	Robert Johnson, Jr.	2005	3962
19 0/16	12 3/16	6 13/16	M	Bayfield County	WI	Kelly Klesmith-Ostricki	2005	3962
19 0/16	11 14/16	7 2/16	M	Torch River	SAS	Wayne Vertein	2006	3962
19 0/16	11 12/16	7 4/16	M	Carswell Lake	SAS	Stephen Kotz	2006	3962
*19 0/16	11 15/16	7 1/16	M	Weyakwin Lake	SAS	Michael L. Ritter, Jr.	2006	3962
19 0/16	12 4/16	6 12/16	M	Boise County	ID	John F. Burke	2006	3962
19 0/16	12 3/16	6 13/16	M	Matagami	QUE	Ken H. Taylor	2006	3962
*19 0/16	12 2/16	6 14/16	M	Emo	ONT	Donald Hunt	2006	3962
*19 0/16	11 12/16	7 4/16	M	Vaughn Lake	ONT	Dick Rice	2006	3962
19 0/16	12 4/16	6 12/16	M	Marinette County	WI	Garrick Loberger	2006	3962

BLACK BEAR

Minimum Score 18   Continued

SCORE	GREATEST LENGTH	GREATEST WIDTH	SEX	AREA	STATE/ PROVINCE	HUNTER'S NAME	DATE	RANK
*19 0/16	12 0/16	7 0/16	M	San Bernardino County	CA	Michael P. Anglin	2006	3962
19 0/16	11 12/16	7 4/16	M	Big River	SAS	Cecil R. Castle	2007	3962
19 0/16	12 5/16	6 11/16	M	Oconto County	WI	Patrick T. Gauthier	2007	3962
*19 0/16	11 8/16	7 8/16	M	Vancouver Island	BC	Adam Bartsch	2008	3962
*19 0/16	11 10/16	7 6/16	M	Vancouver Island	BC	Chantelle Bartsch	2008	3962
19 0/16	11 10/16	7 6/16	M	Adams County	ID	Michael S. Moore	2008	3962
*19 0/16	12 2/16	6 14/16	M	Athabasca River	ALB	John W. Ellas	2008	3962
19 0/16	11 13/16	7 3/16	M	Grave Lake	BC	Andrew S. MacIntyre	2008	3962
*19 0/16	11 15/16	7 1/16	M	Cedar Lake	MAN	John Terhark	2008	3962
19 0/16	11 15/16	7 1/16	M	Carroll County	NH	James Stockman	2008	3962
19 0/16	12 0/16	7 0/16	M	Smyth County	VA	Dana Dove	2008	3962
19 0/16	11 15/16	7 1/16	M	Hudson Bay	SAS	Doug Zastrow	2009	3962
19 0/16	11 14/16	7 2/16	M	Black River	QUE	Joe Ravak	2009	3962
19 0/16	11 15/16	7 1/16	M	Churchill River	SAS	Shay McGowan	2009	3962
*19 0/16	12 0/16	7 0/16	F	Poplarfield	MAN	Janice R. Crook	2009	3962
19 0/16	11 14/16	7 2/16	M	Desha County	AR	Chris Patton	2009	3962
19 0/16	11 12/16	7 4/16	M	Westmorland	NBW	Dale Doiron	2010	3962
18 15/16	11 9/16	7 6/16	M	King George IV Lake	NFL	Frank M. Davis	1958	4198
18 15/16	11 15/16	7 0/16	M	Flathead County	MT	Danny Moore	1976	4198
18 15/16	12 1/16	6 14/16	M	Pitkin County	CO	Sharon Payne	1976	4198
18 15/16	12 2/16	6 13/16	M	Hubbard County	MN	Dr. James Schubert	1978	4198
18 15/16	12 0/16	6 15/16	M	St. Louis County	MN	Roy Kahabka	1978	4198
18 15/16	11 14/16	7 1/16	M	Delta County	CO	Bob Gulman, Jr.	1979	4198
18 15/16	12 0/16	6 15/16	M	Pough Lake	ONT	Jozset Vass	1979	4198
18 15/16	11 4/16	7 11/16	M	Kalkaska County	MI	Gregory Korkoske	1979	4198
18 15/16	11 11/16	7 4/16	M	Roscommon County	MI	Lloyd B. Beebe	1980	4198
18 15/16	11 15/16	7 0/16	M	Sandilands	MAN	Fred Hay	1981	4198
18 15/16	12 1/16	6 14/16	M	Boise County	ID	Jack Arbaugh	1981	4198
18 15/16	12 0/16	6 15/16	M	San Miguel County	NM	Dick McClain	1981	4198
18 15/16	12 1/16	6 14/16	M	Espanola	ONT	Martin Masek	1982	4198
18 15/16	12 0/16	6 15/16	M	Valley County	ID	Bob Dawson	1982	4198
18 15/16	11 15/16	7 0/16	M	Larimer County	CO	Douglas Beck	1982	4198
18 15/16	11 9/16	7 6/16	M	Pontiac	QUE	Chuck Wade	1983	4198
18 15/16	11 10/16	7 5/16	M	Warren	ONT	Clarence Keaton	1983	4198
18 15/16	11 14/16	7 1/16	M	Coos County	NH	Greg White	1984	4198
18 15/16	12 2/16	6 13/16	M	Little Sturge Lake	ONT	David F. Martinek	1985	4198
18 15/16	11 15/16	7 0/16	M	Delta County	CO	Terry Bridgman	1985	4198
18 15/16	11 9/16	7 6/16	M	Renfrew	ONT	Jeffrey Tucker	1985	4198
18 15/16	11 14/16	7 1/16	M	Temiscaming	ONT	Gary F. Greene	1985	4198
18 15/16	11 8/16	7 7/16	M	Poitras	ONT	Robert H. Pavlovic	1985	4198
18 15/16	12 2/16	6 13/16	M	Mine Centre	ONT	Larry Looman	1986	4198
18 15/16	11 12/16	7 3/16	M	Hudson Bay	SAS	Bruce Balerud	1986	4198
18 15/16	12 4/16	6 11/16	M	Espanola	ONT	Terry J. Gerber	1986	4198
18 15/16	11 14/16	7 1/16	M	Cygnet Lake	ONT	Greg Roufs	1986	4198
18 15/16	12 0/16	6 15/16	M	Sioux Lookout	ONT	Dr. Joe Nilsson	1986	4198
18 15/16	11 12/16	7 3/16	M	Findlay Lake	QUE	Paul Bertrand	1986	4198
18 15/16	11 13/16	7 2/16	M	King County	WA	Steven Jackl	1986	4198
18 15/16	11 11/16	7 4/16	M	Lincoln County	WY	Vaughn Ballard	1987	4198
18 15/16	11 14/16	7 1/16	M	Coos County	OR	G. Julie Woodman	1987	4198
18 15/16	11 7/16	7 8/16	M	Herkimer County	NY	Daniel R. Walters	1987	4198
18 15/16	12 1/16	6 14/16	M	Rockingham County	VA	Donald G. Hodges	1987	4198
18 15/16	11 12/16	7 3/16	M	Cold Lake	ALB	Joseph R. Weber	1988	4198
18 15/16	11 12/16	7 3/16	M	Latah County	ID	David B. Silcock	1988	4198
18 15/16	11 14/16	7 1/16	M	Iron County	WI	Henry J. Lindberg	1988	4198
18 15/16	11 14/16	7 1/16	M	Lemhi County	ID	Randy Lee Davison	1988	4198
18 15/16	11 6/16	7 9/16	M	Elmore County	ID	John Turner	1989	4198
18 15/16	11 10/16	7 5/16	M	Caramat	ONT	Charles P. Morgan, Jr.	1989	4198
18 15/16	11 8/16	7 7/16	M	Boise County	ID	Julian Salutregui	1989	4198
18 15/16	11 7/16	7 8/16	M	Zec Restigo	QUE	Clade St. Amour	1989	4198
18 15/16	12 1/16	6 14/16	M	Fayette County	WV	Michael D. King	1989	4198
18 15/16	11 10/16	7 5/16	M	Tucker County	WV	Robert McGee	1989	4198
18 15/16	12 6/16	6 9/16	M	Beltrami County	MN	Ronald Alan Lemire	1990	4198
18 15/16	12 1/16	6 14/16	M	Otero County	NM	John F. Schultz	1990	4198
18 15/16	11 14/16	7 1/16	M	Tucker County	WV	Randall Lee Marsh	1990	4198
18 15/16	12 1/16	6 14/16	M	Lincoln County	NM	Jack Berger	1990	4198
18 15/16	12 1/16	6 14/16	M	Kenora	ONT	David Johnson	1991	4198
18 15/16	11 12/16	7 3/16	M	Valley County	ID	David R. Heck	1991	4198
18 15/16	11 11/16	7 4/16	M	Fort McMurray	ALB	Wes Whenham	1992	4198
18 15/16	11 13/16	7 2/16	M	Siebert Lake	ALB	Orest Popil	1992	4198
18 15/16	11 13/16	7 2/16	M	Aroostook County	ME	Richard C. Tucker	1992	4198
18 15/16	11 14/16	7 1/16	M	St. Louis County	MN	Clarence A. Plansky	1992	4198
18 15/16	11 12/16	7 3/16	M	Baie Comeau	QUE	Richard J. Bombard	1993	4198
18 15/16	12 1/16	6 14/16	M	Swan River	MAN	Jim Horneck	1993	4198
18 15/16	11 14/16	7 1/16	M	Kenora	ONT	Dale R. Perreault	1993	4198
18 15/16	11 15/16	7 0/16	M	High Level	ALB	Dean Yardley	1993	4198
18 15/16	11 12/16	7 3/16	M	Thompson	MAN	Ralph Pfister	1993	4198
18 15/16	11 11/16	7 4/16	M	Zec Dumoine	QUE	Richard Deveney	1993	4198
18 15/16	11 13/16	7 3/16	M	Flathead County	MT	James Hershberger	1993	4198
18 15/16	12 0/16	6 15/16	M	Fayette County	WV	Gordon L. Pugh	1993	4198
18 15/16	11 15/16	7 0/16	M	Alsek River	BC	Randy R. McGregor	1994	4198
18 15/16	11 12/16	7 3/16	M	Alsek River	BC	Scott Ebert	1994	4198
18 15/16	12 1/16	6 14/16	M	Carswell Lake	SAS	Patrick C. Resch	1994	4198
18 15/16	11 13/16	7 2/16	M	Green River	NBW	Larry E. Gardiner	1994	4198
18 15/16	11 13/16	7 2/16	M	Cranberry Portage	MAN	Lee A. Hofer	1994	4198
18 15/16	11 10/16	7 5/16	M	Thompson	MAN	Jeff Danielson	1994	4198
18 15/16	11 15/16	7 0/16	M	Mono County	CA	Guy Taylor	1994	4198
18 15/16	11 13/16	7 2/16	M	St. Louis County	MN	Kevin Murphy	1994	4198
18 15/16	12 1/16	6 14/16	M	Catron County	NM	Jeffrey N. Engleberth	1994	4198
18 15/16	12 1/16	6 14/16	M	Houghton County	MI	Don Bell	1994	4198
18 15/16	12 2/16	6 13/16	M	Mackinac County	MI	Jerry D. Pratt	1994	4198
18 15/16	12 0/16	6 15/16	M	Richer	MAN	David A. Goertzen	1995	4198
18 15/16	12 0/16	6 15/16	M	Prince of Wales Island	AK	Justin Westervelt	1995	4198
18 15/16	11 15/16	7 0/16	M	Lesser Slave Lake	ALB	Robert "Grub" Matthews	1995	4198
18 15/16	11 6/16	7 9/16	M	Marathon	ONT	Arnita Finch	1995	4198
18 15/16	11 14/16	7 1/16	M	Cranberry Portage	MAN	Kevin Reid	1995	4198

169

BLACK BEAR

Minimum Score 18   Continued

SCORE	GREATEST LENGTH	GREATEST WIDTH	SEX	AREA	STATE/ PROVINCE	HUNTER'S NAME	DATE	RANK
18 15/16	12 0/16	6 15/16	M	Prince of Wales Island	AK	Jerome J. Krier, Jr.	1995	4198
18 15/16	11 12/16	7 3/16	M	Nipigon	ONT	Tim Walters	1995	4198
18 15/16	11 11/16	7 4/16	M	Dryden	ONT	Al Smith	1995	4198
18 15/16	11 14/16	7 1/16	M	Dryden	ONT	Kevin Bradley Mills	1995	4198
18 15/16	12 6/16	6 9/16	M	Pine County	MN	John Cardinal	1995	4198
18 15/16	12 2/16	6 13/16	M	Sublette County	WY	John Gedroez	1995	4198
18 15/16	12 1/16	6 14/16	M	Price County	WI	Dale Grant	1995	4198
18 15/16	11 12/16	7 3/16	M	Nestor Falls	ONT	Larry Burman	1996	4198
18 15/16	11 13/16	7 2/16	M	Seibert Lake	ALB	Orest Popil	1996	4198
18 15/16	11 9/16	7 6/16	M	Limestone Siding	NBW	Daniel Dyer	1996	4198
18 15/16	11 15/16	7 0/16	M	Rocky Mountain House	ALB	Vern McPherson	1996	4198
18 15/16	11 15/16	7 0/16	M	Mine Centre	ONT	Richard D. Friedrichsen	1996	4198
18 15/16	11 10/16	7 5/16	M	Senneterre	QUE	Scott Schulze	1996	4198
18 15/16	12 2/16	6 13/16	M	Wabigoon	ONT	Robert Barrie	1996	4198
18 15/16	12 0/16	6 15/16	M	Koochiching County	MN	Charles Oslund	1996	4198
18 15/16	11 10/16	7 5/16	M	Ashland County	WI	Greg Tarlton	1996	4198
18 15/16	12 1/16	6 14/16	M	Athabasca River	ALB	M. R. James	1997	4198
18 15/16	12 3/16	6 12/16	M	Olha	MAN	Paul K. Koslowski	1997	4198
18 15/16	11 11/16	7 4/16	M	Clarke Lake	SAS	Gordon Braun	1997	4198
18 15/16	12 0/16	6 15/16	M	Ear Falls	ONT	Randy Neukirch	1997	4198
18 15/16	12 3/16	6 12/16	M	Bradbury River	MAN	Larry G. Lottman	1997	4198
18 15/16	11 12/16	7 3/16	M	Prince William	NBW	Jeffrey Durham Thomas	1997	4198
18 15/16	12 2/16	6 13/16	M	Skamania County	WA	Kevin Schmid	1997	4198
18 15/16	11 8/16	7 7/16	M	Lewis County	NY	Ben Nellenback	1997	4198
18 15/16	11 14/16	7 1/16	M	Sheridan County	WY	Chris Boll	1998	4198
18 15/16	12 1/16	6 14/16	M	Beluga	AK	Lewis Ledlow	1998	4198
18 15/16	11 8/16	7 7/16	M	Plaster Rock	NBW	Stephen Brecq	1998	4198
18 15/16	11 14/16	7 1/16	M	Maraiche Lake	SAS	Russell Thornberry	1998	4198
18 15/16	11 15/16	7 0/16	M	Black Sturgeon Lake	ONT	Jim Case	1998	4198
18 15/16	12 0/16	6 15/16	M	Teton County	ID	Rick Goodliffe	1998	4198
18 15/16	11 14/16	7 1/16	M	Indian River	AK	Kristen Thomas	1998	4198
18 15/16	11 15/16	7 0/16	M	Cranberry Portage	MAN	Gregory W. Palmer	1998	4198
18 15/16	11 13/16	7 2/16	M	Lynn Lake	MAN	Kenneth M. Thompson	1998	4198
18 15/16	12 3/16	6 12/16	M	Sawyer County	WI	Todd Zeuske	1998	4198
18 15/16	11 15/16	7 0/16	M	Washburn County	WI	Rand "Joe" Kramer	1998	4198
18 15/16	12 1/16	6 14/16	M	Kanawha County	WV	Sidney L. Mullins	1998	4198
18 15/16	12 1/16	6 14/16	M	Pierceland	SAS	Allen E. Cobane	1999	4198
18 15/16	11 15/16	7 0/16	M	Kootenai County	ID	Casey Freise	1999	4198
18 15/16	11 14/16	7 1/16	M	Cluff Lake	SAS	Tom Conrardy	1999	4198
18 15/16	12 0/16	6 15/16	M	Prince of Wales Island	AK	Louis Strahler	1999	4198
18 15/16	12 0/16	6 15/16	M	Aitkin County	MN	Gary Kroells	1999	4198
18 15/16	11 12/16	7 3/16	M	Grand Rapids	MAN	Walter J. Palmer	1999	4198
18 15/16	11 15/16	7 0/16	M	Aerobus Lake	ONT	Barry M. Ver Meer	1999	4198
18 15/16	12 1/16	6 14/16	M	Eagle County	CO	Steven E. Ator	1999	4198
18 15/16	11 13/16	7 2/16	M	Skead	ONT	Kirk A. Sherwood	1999	4198
18 15/16	11 12/16	7 3/16	M	Greenbrier County	WV	Bryan Richard Shires	1999	4198
18 15/16	12 0/16	6 15/16	M	Fit Lake	BC	Allan Tew	2000	4198
18 15/16	12 0/16	6 15/16	M	Pierceland	SAS	Don M. Broom	2000	4198
18 15/16	11 14/16	7 1/16	M	Pearl Lake	MAN	Gary Dahl	2000	4198
18 15/16	12 6/16	6 9/16	M	Fort Vermilion	ALB	Jim Clifford	2000	4198
18 15/16	12 4/16	6 11/16	M	Fort Nelson	BC	Chris Partridge	2000	4198
18 15/16	11 15/16	7 0/16	M	Belair	MAN	Matt Epp	2000	4198
18 15/16	12 0/16	6 15/16	M	Boise County	ID	Jake Stevens	2000	4198
18 15/16	11 14/16	7 1/16	M	Delaronde Lake	SAS	Barrie A. Hendrickson	2000	4198
18 15/16	12 2/16	6 13/16	M	Pierceland	SAS	Ray Wix	2000	4198
18 15/16	12 0/16	6 15/16	M	Buffalo Narrows	SAS	Terry M. Dennis	2000	4198
18 15/16	11 13/16	7 2/16	M	Shining Tree	ONT	Gary L. Nostrant	2000	4198
18 15/16	12 1/16	6 14/16	M	Ashland County	WI	Rick Oldenburg	2000	4198
18 15/16	12 2/16	6 13/16	M	Orange County	NY	Frank Devaney	2000	4198
18 15/16	11 12/16	7 3/16	M	Haines	AK	Dewain Campbell	2001	4198
18 15/16	12 1/16	6 14/16	M	Whittier	AK	Ken Radach	2001	4198
18 15/16	12 3/16	6 12/16	M	Saddle Hills	ALB	Duane Hagman	2001	4198
18 15/16	11 12/16	7 3/16	M	Athabasca River	ALB	Jan Whately	2001	4198
18 15/16	11 9/16	7 6/16	M	St. John	NBW	Michael P. Mongelli	2001	4198
18 15/16	11 10/16	7 5/16	M	Cook County	MN	Mark R. Batterson	2001	4198
18 15/16	12 0/16	6 15/16	M	Otero County	NM	Gene Dobbs	2001	4198
18 15/16	11 15/16	7 0/16	M	Chelan County	WA	Michael Blaylock	2002	4198
18 15/16	12 2/16	6 13/16	M	Price County	WI	Vicki Lemke	2002	4198
18 15/16	11 8/16	7 7/16	M	Millville	NBW	Ed Engels	2002	4198
18 15/16	11 14/16	7 1/16	M	Orange County	NY	Michael Endrizzi	2002	4198
18 15/16	11 10/16	7 5/16	M	Wolf Lake	ALB	Christine P. Williamson	2003	4198
18 15/16	11 12/16	7 3/16	M	Prince of Wales Island	AK	Earl Chauvin	2003	4198
18 15/16	11 11/16	7 4/16	M	Riou Lake	SAS	Steve Card	2003	4198
18 15/16	11 11/16	7 4/16	M	Montbray	QUE	Normand Grenier	2003	4198
*18 15/16	12 0/16	6 15/16	M	Thaddeus Lake	ONT	Brad Kocian	2003	4198
18 15/16	11 12/16	7 3/16	M	Terrace Bay	ONT	Brad Brown	2003	4198
18 15/16	12 0/16	6 15/16	M	Clearwater County	MN	Scott Anderson	2003	4198
18 15/16	11 13/16	7 2/16	M	Marquette County	MI	Jeffrey A. Martin	2003	4198
18 15/16	12 3/16	6 12/16	M	Grayson County	VA	Franklin McDonald	2003	4198
18 15/16	12 0/16	6 15/16	M	Chemung County	NY	Chad M. McDonald	2003	4198
18 15/16	11 15/16	7 0/16	M	Ft. McMurray	ALB	Chris Barton	2004	4198
18 15/16	12 1/16	6 14/16	M	Athabasca River	ALB	Steve Mount	2004	4198
18 15/16	11 12/16	7 3/16	M	Whiteswan Lake	SAS	Derik Ford	2004	4198
18 15/16	12 3/16	6 12/16	M	Smoothstone Lake	SAS	Velma L. Smith	2004	4198
18 15/16	11 11/16	7 4/16	M	Lac Marcelle	QUE	Peter W. Page	2004	4198
18 15/16	11 13/16	7 2/16	M	Clemenseau	SAS	Wayne Rogers	2004	4198
18 15/16	12 2/16	6 13/16	M	Carrot River	SAS	Greg Toogood	2004	4198
*18 15/16	11 14/16	7 1/16	M	Chelmsford	ONT	Ryan Annesser	2004	4198
*18 15/16	11 15/16	7 0/16	M	Smoky River	ALB	John Biro	2005	4198
18 15/16	11 8/16	7 7/16	M	Dipper Lake	SAS	Jeff Johnson	2005	4198
18 15/16	11 9/16	7 6/16	M	Athabasca	ALB	Michael Harvey	2005	4198
18 15/16	11 12/16	7 3/16	M	Berens River	MAN	Lynn Schrum	2005	4198
18 15/16	12 6/16	6 9/16	M	Sundown	MAN	Dave Anderson	2005	4198
18 15/16	11 15/16	7 0/16	M	Prince of Wales Island	AK	Alan Harris	2005	4198
18 15/16	11 15/16	7 0/16	M	Ray River	AK	Thomas Chadwick	2005	4198

170

BLACK BEAR

Minimum Score 18   Continued

SCORE	GREATEST LENGTH	GREATEST WIDTH	SEX	AREA	STATE/ PROVINCE	HUNTER'S NAME	DATE	RANK
18 15/16	12 0/16	6 15/16	M	Fort McMurray	ALB	Steve C. Crooks	2005	4198
18 15/16	11 13/16	7 2/16	M	Sandy Lake	MAN	Robert Vogel	2005	4198
*18 15/16	11 13/16	7 2/16	M	Abitibi	QUE	Alvin Hager	2005	4198
18 15/16	11 10/16	7 5/16	M	Piscataquis County	ME	Roy G. Claar, Jr.	2005	4198
18 15/16	11 14/16	7 1/16	M	Dolland Pond	NFL	Roy M. Goodwin	2005	4198
18 15/16	11 15/16	7 0/16	M	Prince William Sound	AK	David Chilcote	2006	4198
18 15/16	11 11/16	7 4/16	M	Clearwater County	ID	Tyler A. VanOpdorp	2006	4198
18 15/16	12 2/16	6 13/16	M	Black Lake	SAS	Troy Sprenger	2006	4198
18 15/16	12 2/16	6 13/16	M	Montreal River	ONT	Gar Nelson	2006	4198
18 15/16	11 10/16	7 5/16	M	Oskondaga River	ONT	Brett Olson	2006	4198
*18 15/16	11 12/16	7 3/16	M	Nipigon	ONT	Roger Holland	2006	4198
18 15/16	11 8/16	7 7/16	M	Grant County	OR	Peter Shetler	2006	4198
*18 15/16	11 15/16	7 0/16	M	Fayette County	WV	James Wolfe	2006	4198
18 15/16	12 2/16	6 13/16	M	Spirit River	ALB	Jason Siegler	2007	4198
*18 15/16	12 3/16	6 12/16	M	Athabasca River	ALB	Keith Bach	2007	4198
18 15/16	12 2/16	6 13/16	M	Lebel-sur-Quevillon	QUE	Butch Augustine	2007	4198
18 15/16	11 12/16	7 3/16	M	Ste-Anne du Lac	QUE	Patrick Frechette	2007	4198
*18 15/16	11 12/16	7 3/16	M	Abitibi	QUE	Gary Richardson	2007	4198
18 15/16	11 6/16	7 9/16	M	Somerset County	ME	Christopher A. Stover	2007	4198
18 15/16	11 12/16	7 3/16	M	Missoula County	MT	Brian E. Poling	2007	4198
18 15/16	11 14/16	7 1/16	M	Fulton County	NY	Scott L. Hughes	2007	4198
*18 15/16	11 15/16	7 0/16	M	Dipper Lake	SAS	Michele Leqve	2008	4198
*18 15/16	11 15/16	7 0/16	M	Dowel Bay	AK	Bruce Teel	2008	4198
18 15/16	11 15/16	7 0/16	M	Kosciusko Island	AK	Bob Ameen	2008	4198
18 15/16	11 13/16	7 2/16	M	Cochise County	AZ	Robert Rimsza	2008	4198
*18 15/16	12 5/16	6 10/16	M	Sawyer County	WI	Tim Seidl	2008	4198
18 15/16	12 2/16	6 13/16	M	Grandview	MAN	Denny Graham	2008	4198
*18 15/16	12 0/16	6 15/16	M	Mesa County	CO	M. Scott Ghan	2008	4198
*18 15/16	11 12/16	7 3/16	M	Pope County	AR	John VanLandingham	2008	4198
*18 15/16	11 10/16	7 5/16	M	Preamu Lake	SAS	Michele Leqve	2009	4198
*18 15/16	11 9/16	7 6/16	M	Sioux Lookout	ONT	Mark A. Hess	2009	4198
18 15/16	11 11/16	7 4/16	M	Armstrong	ONT	Justin Ray Lynton	2009	4198
18 15/16	11 9/16	7 6/16	M	Union County	OR	Clifford M. Wolbert	2009	4198
*18 15/16	12 2/16	6 13/16	M	Clearwater County	MN	Devin Krinke	2009	4198
18 15/16	12 1/16	6 14/16	M	Bayfield County	WI	Steven Henthorn	2009	4198
18 15/16	12 0/16	6 15/16	M	Wyoming County	WV	Lula McKinney	2009	4198
*18 15/16	11 12/16	7 3/16	M	Wawa	ONT	Mary M. Johnson	2010	4198
*18 15/16	11 11/16	7 4/16	M	Wawa	ONT	Chris TerBush	2010	4198
*18 15/16	11 11/16	7 4/16	M	Fremont County	ID	Rashelle Schneiter	2010	4198
18 14/16	11 6/16	7 8/16	M	Vermilion Bay	ONT	Wayne I. Munkel	1966	4410
18 14/16	12 7/16	6 7/16	M	Vanderhoof	BC	Cecil Raphael	1967	4410
18 14/16	11 2/16	7 12/16	M	Cranberry Portage	MAN	Carl Anderson	1968	4410
18 14/16	11 11/16	7 2/16	M	Orleans County	VT	James Gilman	1969	4410
18 14/16	11 12/16	7 2/16	M	Idaho County	ID	Peter Eremo	1970	4410
18 14/16	12 2/16	6 12/16	M	Mesa County	CO	Jerry Cunningham	1972	4410
18 14/16	12 3/16	6 11/16	M	Madera County	CA	Duane A. Whittle	1973	4410
18 14/16	11 13/16	7 1/16	M	Lincoln County	OR	Stanley D. Miles	1974	4410
18 14/16	11 12/16	7 2/16	M	Lake County	MN	Art Heinze	1974	4410
18 14/16	12 2/16	6 12/16	M	Vermilion Bay	ONT	Myles Keller	1974	4410
18 14/16	11 14/16	7 0/16	M	Minaki	ONT	Greg Stezenski	1975	4410
18 14/16	12 0/16	6 14/16	M	Wabigoon	ONT	Keith Olson	1975	4410
18 14/16	11 14/16	7 0/16	M	Somerset County	ME	John J. Sweeney	1976	4410
18 14/16	11 10/16	7 4/16	M	Nipigon	ONT	Vickery Frederick	1976	4410
18 14/16	11 13/16	7 1/16	M	Prince George	BC	Jim Jackson	1976	4410
18 14/16	11 12/16	7 2/16	M	Big Horn Mtns.	WY	David M. Nahrgang	1978	4410
18 14/16	11 13/16	7 1/16	M	Custer County	CO	William Henderson	1978	4410
18 14/16	12 0/16	6 14/16	M	Washington County	ME	Raymond Olson	1979	4410
18 14/16	11 10/16	7 4/16	M	Sandilands	MAN	Larry Kraynyk	1980	4410
18 14/16	11 14/16	7 0/16	M	Bob Marshall Wilderness	MT	James Dean	1980	4410
18 14/16	11 14/16	7 0/16	M	Dryden	ONT	Gary J. O'Donnell	1981	4410
18 14/16	11 11/16	7 3/16	M	Marquette County	MI	William Robert Baltrip	1981	4410
18 14/16	12 0/16	6 14/16	M	Ignace	ONT	Robert I. Mussey	1981	4410
18 14/16	11 9/16	7 5/16	M	Grant County	NM	Ross Johnson	1981	4410
18 14/16	11 9/16	7 5/16	M	Kootenai County	ID	Stanley Leake	1982	4410
18 14/16	11 12/16	7 2/16	M	Chapleau	ONT	Robert J. Davis	1982	4410
18 14/16	11 15/16	6 15/16	M	Sioux Lookout	ONT	Michael R. Traub	1982	4410
18 14/16	11 14/16	7 0/16	M	Montezuma County	CO	William C. Shuster	1983	4410
18 14/16	11 9/16	7 5/16	M	Aulneau Peninsula	ONT	Michael F. Koska	1983	4410
18 14/16	11 13/16	7 1/16	M	Thunder Bay	ONT	Todd Gilb	1983	4410
18 14/16	11 13/16	7 1/16	M	Park County	MT	Cecil Hendricks	1983	4410
18 14/16	11 12/16	7 2/16	M	Mine Centre	ONT	Al Haines	1984	4410
18 14/16	11 9/16	7 5/16	M	Jackson County	CO	Kurt Keskimaki	1984	4410
18 14/16	11 12/16	7 2/16	M	Tatalina River	AK	Timothy J. Barber	1984	4410
18 14/16	11 6/16	7 8/16	M	Fort Frances	ONT	Lloyd R. Branchcomb	1984	4410
18 14/16	11 13/16	7 1/16	M	Wallowa County	OR	Jerry Jensen	1984	4410
18 14/16	11 12/16	7 2/16	M	Scoop Lake	BC	Ronald Montross	1984	4410
18 14/16	11 8/16	7 6/16	M	Mine Centre	ONT	Gary Schuler	1985	4410
18 14/16	11 12/16	7 2/16	M	Fremont County	CO	Leroy Miller	1985	4410
18 14/16	12 1/16	6 13/16	M	Ignace	ONT	Ken Terry	1985	4410
18 14/16	11 10/16	7 4/16	M	Atikokan	ONT	Eugene Francisco	1985	4410
18 14/16	11 12/16	7 2/16	M	San Miguel County	NM	Dick McClain	1986	4410
18 14/16	12 0/16	6 14/16	M	Grant County	OR	Don D. Litts	1986	4410
18 14/16	11 15/16	6 15/16	M	Coos County	OR	Bruce B. Stamp	1986	4410
18 14/16	11 10/16	7 4/16	M	Park County	CO	Mike Boland	1987	4410
18 14/16	11 8/16	7 6/16	M	Ignace	ONT	Robert James Lewis	1987	4410
18 14/16	12 2/16	6 12/16	M	Archuleta County	CO	H. Kitchener Layland, Jr.	1987	4410
18 14/16	11 9/16	7 5/16	M	Ear Falls	ONT	Daniel J. Mercer	1988	4410
18 14/16	11 11/16	7 3/16	M	Green Lake	SAS	Steven Kent Camburn	1988	4410
18 14/16	12 0/16	6 14/16	M	Winefred Lake	ALB	Danny Moore	1988	4410
18 14/16	11 11/16	7 3/16	M	Fort Coulonge	QUE	Hubert L. Norfleet, Jr.	1988	4410
18 14/16	11 9/16	7 5/16	M	Idaho County	ID	Ron Smith	1988	4410
18 14/16	11 13/16	7 1/16	M	Saddle Hills	ALB	Ben White	1988	4410
18 14/16	11 12/16	7 2/16	M	Waterhen River	SAS	Pink Atkins	1988	4410
18 14/16	12 0/16	6 14/16	M	Koochiching County	MN	Matt Barry	1988	4410
18 14/16	12 1/16	6 13/16	M	Luce County	MI	Terry L. Cook	1988	4410

171

BLACK BEAR

Minimum Score 18   Continued

SCORE	GREATEST LENGTH	GREATEST WIDTH	SEX	AREA	STATE/ PROVINCE	HUNTER'S NAME	DATE	RANK
18 14/16	11 12/16	7 2/16	M	Mann River	SAS	David P. Heinselman II	1989	4410
18 14/16	11 10/16	7 4/16	M	Prince William Sound	AK	Richard Moran	1989	4410
18 14/16	12 2/16	6 12/16	M	Espanola	ONT	Leonard Rock	1989	4410
18 14/16	11 15/16	6 15/16	M	Sioux Lookout	ONT	Tom Nebbs	1989	4410
18 14/16	11 13/16	7 1/16	M	Pelican Narrows	SAS	Doug Otte	1989	4410
18 14/16	12 4/16	6 10/16	M	Rocky Lake	MAN	Cecil Tharp	1989	4410
18 14/16	11 12/16	7 2/16	M	Fort Coulonge	QUE	Barry J. Horton	1989	4410
18 14/16	11 8/16	7 6/16	M	Coos County	NH	Mark Milne	1989	4410
18 14/16	11 15/16	6 15/16	M	Sanders County	MT	Greg L. Munther	1989	4410
18 14/16	11 10/16	7 4/16	M	Le Club Trout Lake	QUE	Kenneth Augsburger	1990	4410
18 14/16	11 15/16	6 15/16	M	Trois Rivers	QUE	Lee Libbey	1990	4410
18 14/16	11 8/16	7 6/16	M	Boise County	ID	Julian Salutrequi	1990	4410
18 14/16	11 11/16	7 3/16	M	Minaki	ONT	Joe Devlin	1990	4410
18 14/16	11 5/16	7 9/16	M	Elmore County	ID	John Turner	1990	4410
18 14/16	11 15/16	6 15/16	M	Forest County	WI	Douglas R. Oswald	1990	4410
18 14/16	12 2/16	6 12/16	M	Chippewa County	WI	Donald J. Lunemann	1990	4410
18 14/16	12 0/16	6 14/16	M	Lincoln County	NM	Rocky Drake	1991	4410
18 14/16	11 7/16	7 7/16	M	Lynn Lake	MAN	Steve Gorr	1991	4410
18 14/16	11 14/16	7 0/16	M	Grays Harbor County	WA	Alex Langbell	1991	4410
18 14/16	11 12/16	7 2/16	M	Creston	BC	Robert Kuny	1991	4410
18 14/16	12 0/16	6 14/16	M	Beltrami County	MN	Brian Aune	1991	4410
18 14/16	11 14/16	7 0/16	M	Stevens County	WA	Michael R. Brunson	1991	4410
18 14/16	11 12/16	7 2/16	M	Monds Township	ONT	Phillip H. Fisher	1992	4410
18 14/16	11 12/16	7 2/16	M	Ignace	ONT	Tony Dickerson	1992	4410
18 14/16	12 5/16	6 9/16	M	Linn County	OR	Alec Hansen	1992	4410
18 14/16	11 12/16	7 2/16	M	Juniper	NBW	Ray Busch	1992	4410
18 14/16	11 14/16	7 0/16	M	Randolph County	WV	Daniel R. Gillenwater	1992	4410
18 14/16	11 11/16	7 3/16	M	Vancouver Island	BC	Ben Gibson	1993	4410
18 14/16	11 9/16	7 5/16	M	Dryden	ONT	Dennis Hudek	1993	4410
18 14/16	11 12/16	7 2/16	M	Dryden	ONT	Al Forbes	1993	4410
18 14/16	12 1/16	6 13/16	M	Christopher Lake	SAS	Foster V. Yancey, Jr.	1993	4410
18 14/16	11 13/16	7 1/16	M	Snow Lake	MAN	Dan Pitts	1993	4410
18 14/16	12 0/16	6 14/16	M	Bayfield County	WI	Russ Fritsch	1993	4410
18 14/16	12 1/16	6 13/16	M	Eau Claire County	WI	Mark R. Scholze	1993	4410
18 14/16	11 15/16	6 15/16	M	Rabun County	GA	Kirk Perteet	1993	4410
18 14/16	11 7/16	7 7/16	M	Beaver Creek	BC	Gordon Morrison	1993	4410
18 14/16	11 15/16	6 15/16	M	Athabasca River	ALB	William Wuerthele	1994	4410
18 14/16	12 1/16	6 13/16	M	White River	ONT	Dennis J. Arnold	1994	4410
18 14/16	11 14/16	7 0/16	M	Athabasca River	ALB	Billy Tillotson	1994	4410
18 14/16	11 12/16	7 2/16	M	High Level	ALB	Todd Veal	1994	4410
18 14/16	11 12/16	7 2/16	M	Armstrong	ONT	Kevin Daniels	1994	4410
18 14/16	12 1/16	6 13/16	M	Ear Falls	ONT	Robert L. Bara	1994	4410
18 14/16	11 12/16	7 2/16	M	Aroostook County	ME	Mike Collins	1994	4410
18 14/16	11 10/16	7 4/16	M	Woodstock	NBW	Tom Smith	1994	4410
18 14/16	12 0/16	6 14/16	M	Kapuskasing	ONT	Vaughn Wright	1995	4410
18 14/16	12 0/16	6 14/16	M	High Level	ALB	Kevin Rousseau	1995	4410
18 14/16	12 0/16	6 14/16	M	Oba	ONT	Robert J. Dunne, Jr.	1995	4410
18 14/16	12 6/16	6 8/16	M	Aitkin County	MN	James Henriksen	1995	4410
18 14/16	12 1/16	6 13/16	M	Oconto County	WI	Gregory A. Stingle	1995	4410
18 14/16	11 12/16	7 2/16	M	Minaki	ONT	Joe Crnkovich	1995	4410
18 14/16	11 14/16	7 0/16	M	Idaho County	ID	W. J. Lucas III	1995	4410
18 14/16	12 0/16	6 14/16	M	Torch River	SAS	William S. Garner	1996	4410
18 14/16	11 14/16	7 0/16	M	Sturgeon Landing	SAS	Joe Ness	1996	4410
18 14/16	12 4/16	6 10/16	M	Athabasca River	ALB	Jewell Leadford	1996	4410
18 14/16	12 1/16	6 13/16	M	Coconino County	AZ	John David Willis	1996	4410
18 14/16	11 14/16	7 0/16	M	Page County	VA	Robert L. Cave	1996	4410
18 14/16	11 14/16	7 0/16	M	Athabasca River	ALB	Roger Wintle	1997	4410
18 14/16	12 0/16	6 14/16	M	Sturgeon Landing	SAS	Ryan Hugelen	1997	4410
18 14/16	11 15/16	6 15/16	M	Wawa	ONT	Joe Arbic, Jr.	1997	4410
18 14/16	12 2/16	6 12/16	M	Garnier Lake	ALB	Greg Lumley	1997	4410
18 14/16	12 0/16	6 14/16	M	Brunswick Lake	ONT	Mark H. Kulke	1997	4410
18 14/16	11 14/16	7 0/16	M	Riou Lake	SAS	Chuck Moughler	1997	4410
18 14/16	12 1/16	6 13/16	M	Cass County	MN	Bill Blevins	1997	4410
18 14/16	11 11/16	7 3/16	M	Rio Arriba County	NM	Mike Whatley	1997	4410
18 14/16	11 10/16	7 4/16	M	Oneida County	NY	Ed Rosenburgh	1997	4410
18 14/16	11 12/16	7 2/16	M	Missoula County	MT	Vinnie Pisani	1997	4410
18 14/16	12 0/16	6 14/16	M	Carrot River	SAS	Larry T. Fischer	1998	4410
18 14/16	11 12/16	7 2/16	M	Fort McMurray	ALB	Mark Kuhn	1998	4410
18 14/16	12 0/16	6 14/16	M	Smeaton	SAS	Gene A. Welle	1998	4410
18 14/16	11 9/16	7 5/16	M	Dryden	ONT	Robert A. Cuff	1998	4410
18 14/16	11 14/16	7 0/16	M	Manitoulin Island	ONT	Warren T. Stewart	1998	4410
18 14/16	11 12/16	7 2/16	M	Lac Maxwell	QUE	Vincent P. Yarmlak	1998	4410
18 14/16	12 0/16	6 14/16	M	Joutel	QUE	Anthony Moles	1998	4410
18 14/16	12 1/16	6 13/16	M	Trinity County	CA	Terry J. Hunter	1998	4410
18 14/16	11 14/16	7 0/16	M	Price County	WI	Gary L. Hintz	1998	4410
18 14/16	12 2/16	6 12/16	M	Athabasca River	ALB	Ron Adamson	1999	4410
18 14/16	11 14/16	7 0/16	M	Hepburn Lake	SAS	Jennifer Hanson	1999	4410
18 14/16	12 2/16	6 12/16	M	Frobisher Lake	SAS	Thomas V. Bell	1999	4410
18 14/16	11 11/16	7 3/16	M	Long Lake	MAN	Gerald Allen	1999	4410
18 14/16	11 10/16	7 4/16	M	Keeley Lake	SAS	Ronald E. Wohlschlegel	1999	4410
18 14/16	11 11/16	7 3/16	M	Lynn Lake	MAN	Kip Padgelek	1999	4410
18 14/16	11 11/16	7 3/16	M	Ft. McMurray	ALB	Will McNeil	1999	4410
18 14/16	11 10/16	7 4/16	M	Lake County	MN	Steven Klein	1999	4410
18 14/16	12 0/16	6 14/16	M	Grant County	OR	Nate Simmons	1999	4410
18 14/16	11 14/16	7 0/16	M	Grand County	UT	Carl Gramlich	1999	4410
18 14/16	11 11/16	7 3/16	M	Willow Mtn.	AK	Frankie Kish	2000	4410
18 14/16	11 13/16	7 1/16	M	Gut Lake	SAS	Steve Hammond	2000	4410
18 14/16	12 2/16	6 12/16	M	Fort McMurray	ALB	Scott Lysenko	2000	4410
18 14/16	12 0/16	6 14/16	M	Togo	SAS	Ron Hannant	2000	4410
18 14/16	11 8/16	7 6/16	M	Cook County	MN	Scott R. Klose	2000	4410
18 14/16	11 12/16	7 2/16	M	Shenandoah County	VA	Terrence F. Burke	2000	4410
18 14/16	12 2/16	6 12/16	M	Flatbush	ALB	Wayne J. Hood, Jr.	2001	4410
18 14/16	11 8/16	7 6/16	M	Lac Bonnet	MAN	David Campbell	2001	4410
18 14/16	11 14/16	7 0/16	M	Fort Coulonge	QUE	Mark Sullivan	2001	4410
18 14/16	11 12/16	7 2/16	M	Churchill Lake	SAS	Eric F. Efird	2001	4410

BLACK BEAR

Minimum Score 18 — Continued

SCORE	GREATEST LENGTH	GREATEST WIDTH	SEX	AREA	STATE/ PROVINCE	HUNTER'S NAME	DATE	RANK
18 14/16	11 12/16	7 2/16	M	Lumberton	BC	Bob Smith	2001	4410
18 14/16	11 8/16	7 6/16	M	Val-d'Or	QUE	Peter Grimard	2001	4410
18 14/16	11 10/16	7 4/16	M	Atikokan	ONT	Kenneth R. Heitz	2001	4410
18 14/16	11 8/16	7 6/16	M	St. Louis County	MN	Brad Brockhouse	2001	4410
18 14/16	11 13/16	7 1/16	M	Yarmouth	NS	Daniel Beyer	2001	4410
18 14/16	12 0/16	6 14/16	M	Moncton	NBW	Michael R. Fox	2001	4410
18 14/16	11 9/16	7 5/16	M	Chibougamau	QUE	Brian R. Brochu	2002	4410
18 14/16	11 15/16	6 15/16	M	Bay d'Espoir	NFL	Charles W. Rehor	2002	4410
18 14/16	11 11/16	7 3/16	M	Algar Lake	ALB	Tommy D. Langston	2002	4410
18 14/16	11 10/16	7 4/16	M	St. John	NBW	Alan Heritage	2002	4410
18 14/16	11 7/16	7 7/16	M	La-Dora	QUE	Michael R. McMillan	2002	4410
18 14/16	11 14/16	7 0/16	M	Idaho County	ID	Sam Wells	2002	4410
18 14/16	12 2/16	6 12/16	M	Dryden	ONT	James M. Teal	2002	4410
18 14/16	12 2/16	6 12/16	M	Aroostook County	ME	Theodore W. Cooper	2002	4410
18 14/16	12 0/16	6 14/16	M	Moffat County	CO	Gary L. Nichols	2002	4410
18 14/16	11 11/16	7 3/16	M	Jellicoe	ONT	Tim Egnoski	2002	4410
18 14/16	12 0/16	6 14/16	M	Peace River	ALB	Robert E. Carmack	2003	4410
18 14/16	12 1/16	6 13/16	M	Prince of Wales Island	AK	Danny Moore	2003	4410
18 14/16	11 15/16	6 15/16	M	Prince of Wales Island	AK	Bob Ameen	2003	4410
18 14/16	12 5/16	6 9/16	M	Olha	MAN	Christopher J. Cordes	2003	4410
18 14/16	11 12/16	7 2/16	M	Colfax County	NM	Steve E. Fegley	2003	4410
18 14/16	11 8/16	7 6/16	M	Montezuma County	CO	Bryon D. Long	2003	4410
18 14/16	12 4/16	6 10/16	M	Chippewa County	WI	Brian R. Jiskra	2003	4410
18 14/16	12 0/16	6 14/16	M	Alma	NBW	Daniel Bolduc	2004	4410
18 14/16	11 9/16	7 5/16	M	Cree River	SAS	Matthew Reilly	2004	4410
18 14/16	12 4/16	6 10/16	M	Fond du Lac River	SAS	Mark Bertram	2004	4410
*18 14/16	11 8/16	7 6/16	M	Laurentides Mtns.	QUE	Rick L. Shelton	2004	4410
18 14/16	11 11/16	7 3/16	M	Yakima County	WA	Steven L. Epperson	2004	4410
*18 14/16	11 13/16	7 1/16	M	Shawano County	WI	Thomas Kestly	2004	4410
18 14/16	11 15/16	6 15/16	M	Loring	ONT	Jim Cramer	2004	4410
*18 14/16	12 3/16	6 11/16	M	McDowell County	WV	Michael East, Jr.	2004	4410
*18 14/16	11 5/16	7 9/16	M	White Bear Lake	SAS	Charles Weiser	2005	4410
18 14/16	11 12/16	7 2/16	M	Frazier River	BC	Ken Sorg	2005	4410
18 14/16	11 6/16	7 8/16	M	Fremont County	ID	Mark D. Morris	2005	4410
18 14/16	11 10/16	7 4/16	M	Besnard Lake	SAS	Ronald Webb	2005	4410
18 14/16	11 11/16	7 3/16	M	Lynn Lake	MAN	Stephen C. Roehm	2005	4410
18 14/16	11 13/16	7 1/16	M	Thompson Lake	MAN	Sam Durham	2005	4410
18 14/16	12 0/16	6 14/16	M	Vermilion Bay	ONT	Steve Frank	2005	4410
*18 14/16	11 14/16	7 0/16	M	Gallatin County	MT	Tim Vicars	2005	4410
18 14/16	11 11/16	7 3/16	M	Alstead Lake	SAS	Tim Bradley	2006	4410
18 14/16	11 8/16	7 6/16	M	Elk Lake	ONT	Martin R. Obetts	2006	4410
18 14/16	11 15/16	6 15/16	M	Fisher Branch	MAN	Gregory Horrocks	2006	4410
18 14/16	11 12/16	7 2/16	M	Thunder Bay	ONT	Randy K. Thompson	2006	4410
18 14/16	11 13/16	7 1/16	M	Skamania County	WA	John P. Howley	2006	4410
*18 14/16	11 15/16	6 15/16	M	Churchill River	SAS	Michele Leqve	2007	4410
18 14/16	12 3/16	6 11/16	M	Dorintosh	SAS	Thomas Olszewski	2007	4410
18 14/16	12 5/16	6 9/16	M	Carrot River	SAS	Mike Honerlaw	2007	4410
18 14/16	11 10/16	7 4/16	M	Lemhi County	ID	Brandon Fahnholz	2007	4410
18 14/16	11 14/16	7 0/16	M	Timmins	ONT	Carl Bosch	2007	4410
*18 14/16	11 14/16	7 0/16	M	Ignace	ONT	William J. Stahl	2007	4410
*18 14/16	12 0/16	6 14/16	M	Rusk County	WI	Matt Schmidt	2007	4410
18 14/16	12 4/16	6 10/16	M	Sawyer County	WI	Michael Siegler	2007	4410
*18 14/16	12 0/16	6 14/16	M	Athabasca River	ALB	Richard L. Drewry	2008	4410
18 14/16	12 0/16	6 14/16	M	Teton County	WY	Ronell Skinner	2008	4410
18 14/16	11 8/16	7 6/16	M	Evain	QUE	Jacques Robichaud	2008	4410
*18 14/16	11 9/16	7 5/16	M	Hillsport	ONT	Michael Vermeesch	2008	4410
*18 14/16	12 0/16	6 14/16	M	Piscataquis County	ME	Scot John Sioch	2008	4410
18 14/16	11 15/16	6 15/16	M	Price County	WI	David Guerard	2008	4410
18 14/16	11 15/16	6 15/16	M	Marquette County	MI	Glen E. Martin	2008	4410
18 14/16	12 4/16	6 10/16	M	Highland County	VA	Keith T. Weaver	2008	4410
18 14/16	11 14/16	7 0/16	M	Alstead Lake	SAS	Edward Pylman	2009	4410
18 14/16	11 12/16	7 2/16	M	Lac du Bonnet	MAN	Kevin Brown	2009	4410
18 14/16	11 8/16	7 6/16	M	Evain	QUE	Jacques Robichaud	2009	4410
18 14/16	12 0/16	6 14/16	M	Geraldton	ONT	Matt Bilow	2009	4410
*18 14/16	11 15/16	6 15/16	M	Sioux Lookout	ONT	Shane Ruckle	2009	4410
*18 14/16	11 14/16	7 0/16	M	Cook County	MN	Joel Goodman	2009	4410
*18 14/16	12 3/16	6 11/16	M	Beltrami County	MN	Casey Badger	2009	4410
18 14/16	11 15/16	6 15/16	M	Bayfield County	WI	Rob M. Rueth	2009	4410
18 14/16	12 2/16	6 12/16	M	Togo	SAS	Robbie McDougall	2010	4410
18 14/16	11 6/16	7 8/16	M	Grand County	UT	Thomas Cox	2010	4410
*18 14/16	11 14/16	7 0/16	M	Sheridan County	WY	Ellen Allemand	2010	4410
18 13/16	11 11/16	7 2/16	M	Iron County	MI	John E. Lawson	1971	4632
18 13/16	11 8/16	7 5/16	M	Washington County	ME	Norman Jolliffe	1973	4632
18 13/16	11 11/16	7 2/16	M	Colfax County	NM	Jerry R. Wood	1974	4632
18 13/16	11 6/16	7 7/16	M	Jefferson County	CO	Chuck Hutton	1974	4632
18 13/16	11 10/16	7 3/16	M		ONT	Lee Murphy	1975	4632
18 13/16	11 8/16	7 5/16	M	Pemberton	BC	Dr. Michael R. Cummings	1976	4632
18 13/16	11 8/16	7 5/16	M	Sanders County	MT	Jay Gunter	1976	4632
18 13/16	11 12/16	7 1/16	M	Dryden	ONT	Dr. Bill Young	1977	4632
18 13/16	11 7/16	7 6/16	M	Messines	QUE	Larry R. Scott, Sr.	1977	4632
18 13/16	11 14/16	6 15/16	M	Chapleau	ONT	Maurice Perrault	1978	4632
18 13/16	11 10/16	7 3/16	M	Somerset County	ME	Ray King	1978	4632
18 13/16	12 0/16	6 13/16	M	Gem County	ID	DeLoy Desaro	1978	4632
18 13/16	11 12/16	7 1/16	M	Wawa	ONT	Robert C. McGuire	1979	4632
18 13/16	11 11/16	7 2/16	M	Smoky Mtn.	WA	Ronald D. Hopkins	1979	4632
18 13/16	11 13/16	7 0/16	M	Koochiching County	MN	Mark A. Andrist	1979	4632
18 13/16	11 11/16	7 2/16	M	Thunder Bay	ONT	David Manthei	1980	4632
18 13/16	12 4/16	6 9/16	M	Lincoln County	WI	Bob Faufau	1980	4632
18 13/16	11 14/16	6 15/16	M	Armistice Lake	ONT	Cliff Buland, Jr.	1982	4632
18 13/16	12 4/16	6 9/16	M	Price County	WI	Gary Berg	1982	4632
18 13/16	12 3/16	6 10/16	M	Tulare County	CA	Bill Sweetser	1982	4632
18 13/16	12 1/16	6 12/16	M	Hudson Bay	SAS	Mark Hughes	1982	4632
18 13/16	11 15/16	6 14/16	M	Kenora	ONT	John L. Angel	1982	4632
18 13/16	12 0/16	6 13/16	M	The Pas	MAN	Scott Lang	1983	4632
18 13/16	11 12/16	7 1/16	M	Iron County	MI	John O. Cowell	1983	4632

173

BLACK BEAR

Minimum Score 18
Continued

SCORE	GREATEST LENGTH	GREATEST WIDTH	SEX	AREA	STATE/ PROVINCE	HUNTER'S NAME	DATE	RANK
18 13/16	11 5/16	7 8/16	M	Caramat	ONT	Robert A. Boyer	1984	4632
18 13/16	12 1/16	6 12/16	M	Sunbury County	NBW	Burchel Blevins	1984	4632
18 13/16	12 1/16	6 12/16	M	Dist. 21	ONT	Ron Harger	1985	4632
18 13/16	11 7/16	7 6/16	M	Otter Lake	QUE	Dana P. Calhoun	1985	4632
18 13/16	12 2/16	6 11/16	M	St. James Bay	AK	John Gary Price	1985	4632
18 13/16	11 11/16	7 2/16	M	Thunder Bay	ONT	Howard Leopold	1985	4632
18 13/16	12 0/16	6 13/16	M	Sierra County	NM	Kendall Doyle	1985	4632
18 13/16	11 14/16	6 15/16	M	Kenora	ONT	Ron Books	1986	4632
18 13/16	11 8/16	7 5/16	M	Gallatin County	MT	Stephen Lockington	1986	4632
18 13/16	11 12/16	7 1/16	M	Nakina	ONT	Ronald Mifflin	1986	4632
18 13/16	11 11/16	7 2/16	M	Archuleta County	CO	Lonnie Draper	1986	4632
18 13/16	12 3/16	6 10/16	M	Wasilla	AK	Ted Grover	1986	4632
18 13/16	12 0/16	6 13/16	M	Atikokan	ONT	Steve Weekly	1987	4632
18 13/16	11 10/16	7 3/16	M	Sundridge	ONT	Abby Lape	1987	4632
18 13/16	11 8/16	7 5/16	M	Archuleta County	CO	Mark Charles Petersen	1987	4632
18 13/16	12 2/16	6 11/16	M	Fox Creek	ALB	Ryk Visscher	1987	4632
18 13/16	11 14/16	6 15/16	M	Crook County	OR	Jeff Carver	1987	4632
18 13/16	11 12/16	7 1/16	M	Teton County	MT	Ron Carpenter	1987	4632
18 13/16	11 7/16	7 6/16	M	Hampshire County	MA	Raymond H. Moulton, Jr.	1987	4632
18 13/16	11 14/16	6 15/16	M	Wawa	ONT	Dale Rohrbeck	1988	4632
18 13/16	12 1/16	6 12/16	M	Pine County	MN	Arnold F. Ostgarden	1988	4632
18 13/16	11 15/16	6 14/16	M	Bayfield County	WI	William F. Schutte	1988	4632
18 13/16	12 0/16	6 13/16	M	Iron County	WI	Gary G. Johnson	1988	4632
18 13/16	12 0/16	6 13/16	M	Las Animas County	CO	Richard J. Racioppi	1989	4632
18 13/16	11 7/16	7 6/16	M	Mine Centre	ONT	Willard L. Voight	1989	4632
18 13/16	11 12/16	7 1/16	M	Cowan	MAN	Vito Benedetto	1989	4632
18 13/16	11 9/16	7 4/16	M	Nestor Falls	ONT	Robert E. Grainger	1989	4632
18 13/16	11 10/16	7 3/16	M	La Tuque	QUE	Bernard E. Beaudin, Jr.	1989	4632
18 13/16	11 12/16	7 1/16	M	Cadillac	QUE	Jerry Woodrum	1989	4632
18 13/16	12 2/16	6 11/16	M	Aitkin County	MN	David Emmen	1989	4632
18 13/16	11 10/16	7 3/16	M	Fayette County	WV	James E. Grey	1989	4632
18 13/16	11 10/16	7 3/16	M	Grafton County	NH	Donald O. Goodwin	1989	4632
18 13/16	11 14/16	6 15/16	M	Fawcett	ALB	Troy Dzioba	1990	4632
18 13/16	11 14/16	6 15/16	M	Gowganda	ONT	Bob E. Collins	1990	4632
18 13/16	11 11/16	7 2/16	M	Wawa	ONT	Pauly Paul	1990	4632
18 13/16	11 15/16	6 14/16	M	Augusta County	VA	Raymond Leverock	1990	4632
18 13/16	12 4/16	6 9/16	M	Apache County	AZ	Stephen D. Hornady	1991	4632
18 13/16	12 0/16	6 13/16	M	Creston	BC	Robert Kuny	1991	4632
18 13/16	11 9/16	7 4/16	M	Fauquier	ONT	Bradley I. Anderson	1991	4632
18 13/16	12 0/16	6 13/16	M	Hubbard County	MN	Loren Schoewe	1991	4632
18 13/16	11 15/16	6 14/16	M	Asotin County	WA	Brady Olson	1991	4632
18 13/16	11 11/16	7 2/16	M	St. Louis County	MN	Jeffrey C. Minske	1991	4632
18 13/16	11 13/16	7 0/16	M	Baker County	OR	Tom Christakos	1991	4632
18 13/16	10 14/16	7 15/16	M	Madison County	MT	Tom L. Miller	1991	4632
18 13/16	12 0/16	6 13/16	M	Montezuma County	CO	Jerry Rush	1992	4632
18 13/16	11 14/16	6 15/16	M	Camas County	ID	Dallas Smith	1992	4632
18 13/16	11 10/16	7 3/16	M	Grand County	CO	Terry Sleppy	1992	4632
18 13/16	12 0/16	6 13/16	M	Red Lake	ONT	Jeff Basco	1992	4632
18 13/16	11 10/16	7 3/16	M	Kenora	ONT	Jerry Lee Andrews	1992	4632
18 13/16	11 12/16	7 1/16	M	Kuiu Island	AK	Michael Speigle	1992	4632
18 13/16	11 10/16	7 3/16	M	Schoolcraft County	MI	Delbert Franklin Steward	1992	4632
18 13/16	12 0/16	6 13/16	M	Moffat County	CO	Rodney Lee Wilt	1992	4632
18 13/16	11 15/16	6 14/16	M	Caribou County	ID	Russell Clark	1992	4632
18 13/16	11 12/16	7 1/16	M	Fannin County	GA	Mac Gignilliat	1992	4632
18 13/16	11 10/16	7 3/16	M	Lane County	OR	Vernon E. King, Jr.	1993	4632
18 13/16	11 5/16	7 8/16	M	Loring	ONT	Douglas L. Buchler	1993	4632
18 13/16	11 15/16	6 14/16	M	Minitonas	MAN	Gregory B. McPhillips	1993	4632
18 13/16	11 15/16	6 14/16	M	Clam Lake	ONT	Dick Byers	1993	4632
18 13/16	12 1/16	6 12/16	M	Milner Ridge	MAN	Daniel Chartrand	1993	4632
18 13/16	11 10/16	7 3/16	M	Sublette County	WY	Justin J. Shirley	1993	4632
18 13/16	11 14/16	6 15/16	M	Belleterre	QUE	Jerry Ashley	1993	4632
18 13/16	12 3/16	6 10/16	M	Josephine County	OR	Steven Mazzola	1993	4632
18 13/16	11 15/16	6 14/16	M	Koochiching County	MN	Scott Schultz	1993	4632
18 13/16	12 1/16	6 12/16	M	Aitkin County	MN	Mike Smieja	1993	4632
18 13/16	11 15/16	6 14/16	M	Itasca County	MN	Donald J. Bergstrom	1993	4632
18 13/16	12 6/16	6 7/16	M	Alpena County	MI	Alan Dale Shepherd	1993	4632
18 13/16	12 0/16	6 13/16	M	Pacific County	WA	Ricky Ray Foster	1993	4632
18 13/16	11 9/16	7 4/16	M	Canterbury	NBW	Arthur W. Little	1994	4632
18 13/16	12 3/16	6 10/16	M	Camas County	ID	David Sass	1994	4632
18 13/16	11 13/16	7 0/16	M	Wabigoon Township	ONT	Ronnie Blewer	1994	4632
18 13/16	12 1/16	6 12/16	M	High Level	ALB	Kenneth Kovar	1995	4632
18 13/16	11 9/16	7 4/16	M	Minaki	ONT	Joe Krejci	1995	4632
18 13/16	12 1/16	6 12/16	M	Prince of Wales Island	AK	Danny Moore	1995	4632
18 13/16	12 5/16	6 8/16	M	Carrot River	SAS	Mark A. Johnson	1995	4632
18 13/16	12 0/16	6 13/16	M	Red Earth	ALB	John Clark Fisher	1995	4632
18 13/16	11 13/16	7 0/16	M	Prince of Wales Island	AK	Dyrk Eddie	1995	4632
18 13/16	11 10/16	7 3/16	M	High Level	ALB	Earnie Banks	1995	4632
18 13/16	11 11/16	7 2/16	M	Finleson Lake	ONT	Kevin Van Arsdale	1995	4632
18 13/16	12 5/16	6 8/16	M	Ignace	ONT	Ray Redlin, Jr.	1995	4632
18 13/16	11 13/16	7 0/16	M	Fort McMurray	ALB	Tom Bridenstine	1995	4632
18 13/16	11 12/16	7 1/16	M	Larder Lake	ONT	Karl W. Lockwood	1995	4632
18 13/16	11 14/16	6 15/16	M	Wawa	ONT	Mitchell R. Sitterding	1995	4632
18 13/16	11 9/16	7 4/16	M	Wawa	ONT	William D. Brooks	1995	4632
18 13/16	11 10/16	7 3/16	M	Tulare County	CA	Frank Steven Birtcher	1995	4632
18 13/16	11 15/16	6 14/16	M	Kenora	ONT	Jeff Pals	1995	4632
18 13/16	11 9/16	7 4/16	M	Missanabie	ONT	Robert L. Busch	1995	4632
18 13/16	11 13/16	7 0/16	M	Keg River	ALB	Eric Rauhanen	1995	4632
18 13/16	11 14/16	6 15/16	M	Fort a la Corne	SAS	Kevin Sean Schauenberg	1996	4632
18 13/16	12 1/16	6 12/16	M	Big Sandy Lake	SAS	Brian Richard Trachsel	1996	4632
18 13/16	11 13/16	7 0/16	M	Sioux Lookout	ONT	Jim Witkowski	1996	4632
18 13/16	11 7/16	7 6/16	M	Kirkland Lake	ONT	Shawn Rothrock	1996	4632
18 13/16	11 11/16	7 2/16	M	Spring Creek	ALB	Douglas E. Erickson	1996	4632
18 13/16	11 5/16	7 8/16	M	Snohomish County	WA	Christopher C. Hill	1996	4632
18 13/16	11 11/16	7 2/16	M	Atikokan	ONT	Jim Saunoris, Jr.	1996	4632
18 13/16	12 3/16	6 10/16	M	Itasca County	MN	Mark A. Slinger	1996	4632

BLACK BEAR

Minimum Score 18   Continued

SCORE	GREATEST LENGTH	GREATEST WIDTH	SEX	AREA	STATE/ PROVINCE	HUNTER'S NAME	DATE	RANK
18 13/16	11 13/16	7 0/16	M	Douglas County	WI	Todd D. Sorenson	1996	4632
18 13/16	12 0/16	6 13/16	M	Moffat County	CO	Scott Brasfield	1996	4632
18 13/16	11 12/16	7 1/16	M	Red Lake	ONT	Janet M. King	1997	4632
18 13/16	11 12/16	7 1/16	M	Kipawa	QUE	Bill Griffin	1997	4632
18 13/16	12 0/16	6 13/16	M	The Pas	MAN	Bill Prigge	1997	4632
18 13/16	11 6/16	7 7/16	M	Armstrong	ONT	Jim Patterson	1997	4632
18 13/16	11 14/16	6 15/16	M	Livengood	AK	Tom Everett	1997	4632
18 13/16	11 9/16	7 4/16	M	Thompson	MAN	Chris Yaritz	1997	4632
18 13/16	11 7/16	7 6/16	M	Hawk River	SAS	Ricky Bullington	1997	4632
18 13/16	12 0/16	6 13/16	M	Coconino County	AZ	Dave R. Goitia, Jr.	1997	4632
18 13/16	12 0/16	6 13/16	M	Green Lake	SAS	John B. Mesics, Sr.	1998	4632
18 13/16	11 9/16	7 4/16	M	Fredericton	NBW	Terry M. Phelps	1998	4632
18 13/16	11 6/16	7 7/16	M	Hillsport	ONT	Andrew Rushing, Jr.	1998	4632
18 13/16	11 7/16	7 6/16	M	Lytton	QUE	John D. Boulter	1999	4632
18 13/16	12 0/16	6 13/16	M	Swan River	MAN	Morgan E. Lambert	1999	4632
18 13/16	12 6/16	6 7/16	M	Buffalo Narrows	SAS	Michael Wolff	1999	4632
18 13/16	11 13/16	7 0/16	M	Redditt	ONT	Matt Kooiman	1999	4632
18 13/16	12 2/16	6 11/16	M	Penobscot County	ME	Daniel L. Boisvert	1999	4632
18 13/16	11 13/16	7 0/16	M	Alban	ONT	Don Pedo	1999	4632
18 13/16	11 7/16	7 6/16	M	Sevier County	TN	Mark Trentham	1999	4632
18 13/16	11 15/16	6 14/16	M	House River	ALB	Tom Hentrick	2000	4632
18 13/16	11 15/16	6 14/16	M	McCreary	MAN	Randall B. Jones	2000	4632
18 13/16	12 0/16	6 13/16	M	Duck Mtn.	MAN	Dan Leonard, Sr.	2000	4632
18 13/16	11 13/16	7 0/16	M	Thompson	MAN	Ronald C. Scray	2000	4632
18 13/16	11 11/16	7 2/16	M	Markstay	ONT	Jerry Sell	2000	4632
18 13/16	11 9/16	7 4/16	M	Grafton County	NH	Kevin Cook	2000	4632
18 13/16	11 14/16	6 15/16	M	Bocquene Lake	ALB	John F. Levicke	2001	4632
18 13/16	12 1/16	6 12/16	M	Laurier	MAN	John Leno	2001	4632
18 13/16	12 1/16	6 12/16	M	Waskesiu Lake	SAS	Michael L. Ritter, Jr.	2001	4632
18 13/16	11 15/16	6 14/16	M	Whale Passage	AK	David Rue	2002	4632
18 13/16	11 12/16	7 1/16	M	Prince of Wales Island	AK	Bob Ameen	2002	4632
18 13/16	11 13/16	7 0/16	M	Lewis Lake	MAN	Jerry Thomas	2002	4632
18 13/16	11 9/16	7 4/16	M	Grand-Remous	QUE	Herbert Duane Ross, Sr.	2002	4632
18 13/16	12 2/16	6 11/16	M	Rossburn	MAN	Monty McKenzie	2002	4632
18 13/16	11 15/16	6 14/16	M	Wallowa County	OR	Roy Jackson	2002	4632
18 13/16	11 9/16	7 4/16	M	Herkimer County	NY	John Dreimiller	2002	4632
18 13/16	11 14/16	6 15/16	M	Athabasca River	ALB	Ron Maguire	2003	4632
18 13/16	11 13/16	7 0/16	M	Kipahigan Lake	MAN	Cameron Hayden	2003	4632
18 13/16	11 10/16	7 3/16	M	Dorion	ONT	John R. Patterson	2003	4632
18 13/16	12 4/16	6 9/16	M	Carrot River	SAS	Brian Ratayczak	2003	4632
18 13/16	11 13/16	7 0/16	M	Towns County	GA	Hollis Crocker	2003	4632
18 13/16	11 8/16	7 5/16	M	Cariboo Lake	BC	Kevin Kansky	2004	4632
18 13/16	11 15/16	6 14/16	M	Prince William Sound	AK	Ken Radach	2004	4632
18 13/16	12 2/16	6 11/16	M	Skeena River	BC	Richie Bland	2004	4632
18 13/16	11 10/16	7 3/16	M	Gogama	ONT	Daniel Kelly	2004	4632
18 13/16	11 14/16	6 15/16	M	Stevens County	WA	Jeff Lathrop	2004	4632
18 13/16	11 13/16	7 0/16	M	Utah County	UT	Mitchell Curtis	2004	4632
18 13/16	12 2/16	6 11/16	M	Peace River	ALB	Daniel R. Green	2005	4632
18 13/16	12 1/16	6 12/16	M	La Ronge	SAS	Brian L. Cameron	2005	4632
18 13/16	11 13/16	7 0/16	M	Geikie River	SAS	Walter Chewning	2005	4632
18 13/16	11 15/16	6 14/16	M	Kenora	QUE	Jim Waggoner	2005	4632
18 13/16	12 0/16	6 13/16	M	Kittson County	MN	Darren Szczepanski	2005	4632
18 13/16	11 9/16	7 4/16	M	Union County	OR	Ty Callicotte	2005	4632
18 13/16	12 0/16	6 13/16	F	Rusk County	WI	Allen L. Pfeiffer	2005	4632
18 13/16	12 3/16	6 10/16	M	Albany County	WY	Robert J. Bustos	2006	4632
*18 13/16	12 4/16	6 9/16	M	Polk County	AR	Nathan Fowler	2006	4632
*18 13/16	11 10/16	7 3/16	M	Bear Lake	ONT	Andrew R. Wright	2006	4632
18 13/16	12 2/16	6 11/16	M	Fort Frances	ONT	Brent Berning	2006	4632
18 13/16	11 9/16	7 4/16	M	Douglas County	OR	Cody Rice	2006	4632
18 13/16	11 9/16	7 4/16	M	Red Lake	ONT	Andrew C. Bair	2006	4632
*18 13/16	12 0/16	6 13/16	M	Fort McMurray	ALB	Mike Wall	2007	4632
18 13/16	11 14/16	6 15/16	M	Natrona County	WY	Randy Conner	2007	4632
18 13/16	12 2/16	6 11/16	M	Mendocino County	CA	Butch Carley	2007	4632
18 13/16	11 13/16	7 0/16	M	Price County	WI	Dan W. Fehling	2007	4632
*18 13/16	11 14/16	6 15/16	M	Larimer County	CO	R. Scott Reach	2007	4632
18 13/16	12 2/16	6 11/16	M	Calling Lake	ALB	Cory Svenson	2008	4632
18 13/16	11 10/16	7 3/16	M	Grande Prairie	ALB	Steve Smith	2008	4632
*18 13/16	11 13/16	7 0/16	M	Hastings Arm	BC	Don Erbert	2008	4632
18 13/16	11 15/16	6 14/16	M	The Pas	MAN	Michael Sanger	2008	4632
18 13/16	12 1/16	6 12/16	M	Hunta	ONT	Joseph D. Fornaro	2008	4632
*18 13/16	12 2/16	6 11/16	M	Vilas County	WI	Lori Schumacher	2008	4632
*18 13/16	11 12/16	7 1/16	M	Bayfield County	WI	Jeffrey J. Blatz	2008	4632
18 13/16	11 11/16	7 2/16	M	Kingston	ONT	William R. Boyd	2008	4632
18 13/16	11 14/16	6 15/16	M	Summit County	UT	Glen O. Hallows	2009	4632
*18 13/16	11 12/16	7 1/16	M	Sherridon	MAN	Steve Finegan	2010	4632
*18 13/16	12 0/16	6 13/16	M	Cold Lake	ALB	Connor Emigh	2010	4632
*18 13/16	12 0/16	6 13/16	M	Whitmore Lake	MAN	Shannon Salyer	2010	4632
18 12/16	12 1/16	6 11/16	M	Shasta County	CA	Harv Ebers	1964	4828
18 12/16	11 11/16	7 1/16	M	Carbon County	UT	Marvin Tye	1965	4828
18 12/16	11 9/16	7 3/16	M	Manowam Lake	QUE	Dennis H. Driscoll	1969	4828
18 12/16	11 5/16	7 7/16	M	Siskiyou County	CA	W. E. Cates	1972	4828
18 12/16	11 13/16	6 15/16	M	Franklin County	ME	Bob Kuhar	1973	4828
18 12/16	11 14/16	6 14/16	M	Trinity County	CA	Daniel Higuera	1974	4828
18 12/16	11 13/16	6 15/16	M	Uncompahgre N.F.	CO	Anthony Keeling	1975	4828
18 12/16	12 1/16	6 11/16	M	Hubbard County	MN	Jack Smythe	1977	4828
18 12/16	12 2/16	6 10/16	M	Lesser Slave Lake	ALB	Gene Solyntjes	1978	4828
18 12/16	11 14/16	6 14/16	M	Fremont County	ID	Dennis L. Shirley	1979	4828
18 12/16	11 3/16	7 9/16	M	Franklin County	ME	John Janelli	1980	4828
18 12/16	11 10/16	7 2/16	M	Franklin County	ME	Len Cardinale	1980	4828
18 12/16	12 2/16	6 10/16	M	Gunnison County	CO	James F. Dougherty	1980	4828
18 12/16	11 14/16	6 14/16	M	Lake County	MN	Herbert O. Lundberg	1980	4828
18 12/16	12 0/16	6 12/16	M	Lemhi County	ID	Bob Ulshafer	1981	4828
18 12/16	11 12/16	7 0/16	M	Clear Creek County	CO	David L. Skiff	1981	4828
18 12/16	11 15/16	6 13/16	M	Sandy Bar Creek	CA	Dale H. Bracken	1981	4828
18 12/16	11 12/16	7 0/16	M	Warren County	VA	Joseph A. Ramey	1981	4828

175

BLACK BEAR

Minimum Score 18 — Continued

SCORE	GREATEST LENGTH	GREATEST WIDTH	SEX	AREA	STATE/PROVINCE	HUNTER'S NAME	DATE	RANK
18 12/16	11 14/16	6 14/16	M	Remigny	QUE	Richard L. Jackson	1982	4828
18 12/16	12 1/16	6 11/16	M	Idaho County	ID	Robert Dale Evans	1982	4828
18 12/16	11 14/16	6 14/16	M	Madoc	ONT	Mel Johnson	1982	4828
18 12/16	11 6/16	7 6/16	M	Archuleta County	CO	Steve Vittetow	1982	4828
18 12/16	12 0/16	6 12/16	M	Kenmount	ONT	James D. Murray	1983	4828
18 12/16	11 8/16	7 4/16	M	McAdam	NBW	David W. Peltier	1983	4828
18 12/16	12 3/16	6 9/16	M	Langlade County	WI	Michael Steliga	1983	4828
18 12/16	12 2/16	6 10/16	M	Langlade County	WI	Larry Petts	1983	4828
18 12/16	11 13/16	6 15/16	M	Graham	ONT	Joe Neal Walters	1984	4828
18 12/16	11 6/16	7 6/16	M	Boise County	ID	Gary Kinney	1984	4828
18 12/16	11 14/16	6 14/16	M	Koochiching County	MN	Daniel Krasean	1984	4828
18 12/16	11 12/16	7 0/16	M	Koochiching County	MN	Larry Hillman	1984	4828
18 12/16	12 0/16	6 12/16	M	Dryden	ONT	Mark Guelzow	1985	4828
18 12/16	12 0/16	6 12/16	M	Riverside County	CA	Paul Persano	1985	4828
18 12/16	11 11/16	7 1/16	M	Capreol	ONT	Lawrence M. Sowders	1986	4828
18 12/16	11 9/16	7 3/16	M	Pitkin County	CO	Gary B. McClure	1986	4828
18 12/16	11 12/16	7 0/16	M	Wawa	ONT	Thomas May	1986	4828
18 12/16	11 14/16	6 14/16	M	Savant Lake	ONT	Marlo G. Sloan	1987	4828
18 12/16	11 14/16	6 14/16	M	Thunder Bay	ONT	Eugene M. Tonk II	1987	4828
18 12/16	12 0/16	6 12/16	M	Cumberland House	SAS	Dave Kapanke	1987	4828
18 12/16	11 6/16	7 6/16	M	Killaloe Station	ONT	Norman J. Roy	1987	4828
18 12/16	12 1/16	6 11/16	M	Ft. McMurray	ALB	James Pike	1987	4828
18 12/16	12 6/16	6 6/16	M	Otero County	NM	Ronnie B. Hall	1987	4828
18 12/16	11 10/16	7 2/16	M	King County	WA	Curtis A. Geise	1987	4828
18 12/16	11 5/16	7 7/16	M	Marquette County	MI	Alvin Meadows	1987	4828
18 12/16	11 10/16	7 2/16	M	Spokane County	WA	Tracy Kenworthy	1987	4828
18 12/16	11 15/16	6 13/16	M	Peers	ALB	Kevin Hehn	1988	4828
18 12/16	11 13/16	6 15/16	M	Yaremko Township	ONT	Ed Oplinger	1988	4828
18 12/16	11 13/16	6 15/16	M	Oxford County	ME	Robert Grannis	1988	4828
18 12/16	11 10/16	7 2/16	M	Marquette County	MI	Dale B. Parish	1988	4828
18 12/16	11 8/16	7 4/16	M	Gunnison County	CO	Michael K. Ward	1989	4828
18 12/16	12 1/16	6 11/16	F	Rio Arriba County	NM	Kelley B. Ward	1989	4828
18 12/16	11 10/16	7 2/16	M	Snow Lake	MAN	Dick Pugh	1989	4828
18 12/16	11 9/16	7 3/16	M	Eagle Lake	ONT	Allan Marohn	1989	4828
18 12/16	11 10/16	7 2/16	M	Rapide-des-Joachims	QUE	Ron Bice	1989	4828
18 12/16	11 8/16	7 4/16	M	Zec Dumoine	QUE	Paul J. Sisz	1989	4828
18 12/16	11 8/16	7 4/16	M	Aitkin County	MN	Dr. Ken Nordberg	1989	4828
18 12/16	11 10/16	7 2/16	M	Shoshone County	ID	Randy Huber	1989	4828
18 12/16	11 14/16	6 14/16	M	Ferry County	WA	Bob Conyers	1989	4828
18 12/16	11 8/16	7 4/16	M	Mesa County	CO	Ricky R. Lowery	1990	4828
18 12/16	11 9/16	7 3/16	M	Highwinds Lake	ONT	John E. Larsen	1990	4828
18 12/16	11 15/16	6 13/16	M	Black River	ONT	James S. Nowakowski	1990	4828
18 12/16	11 14/16	6 14/16	M	Lac La Ronge	SAS	Randy G. Cook	1990	4828
18 12/16	11 11/16	7 1/16	M	Clearwater County	ID	Stan Bocian	1990	4828
18 12/16	11 7/16	7 5/16	M	Atikokan	ONT	Roger Carpenter	1990	4828
18 12/16	11 12/16	7 0/16	M	Mystery Lake	MAN	Lois Monteath	1991	4828
18 12/16	11 11/16	7 1/16	M	Idaho County	ID	Dr. Andrew F. Jones	1991	4828
18 12/16	11 9/16	7 3/16	M	Kapuskasing	ONT	Harold A. Eichorn	1991	4828
18 12/16	11 10/16	7 2/16	M	Caramat	ONT	Rick Stump	1991	4828
18 12/16	11 15/16	6 13/16	M	Wasilla	AK	Sam J. Smith	1991	4828
18 12/16	11 4/16	7 8/16	M	Fredericton	NBW	Mark Clerici	1991	4828
18 12/16	11 6/16	7 6/16	M	Bayfield County	WI	Cynthia G. Sotona	1991	4828
18 12/16	12 0/16	6 12/16	M	Kootenai County	ID	Mark Jones	1992	4828
18 12/16	12 0/16	6 12/16	M	Prince of Wales Island	AK	Dave Rue	1992	4828
18 12/16	12 1/16	6 11/16	M	Shoshone County	ID	Craig R. Anderson	1992	4828
18 12/16	11 15/16	6 13/16	M	Fort Assiniboine	ALB	Brian R. Burrows	1992	4828
18 12/16	11 13/16	6 15/16	M	Flatbush	ALB	Kevin Wilson	1992	4828
18 12/16	11 10/16	7 2/16	M	Riverton	MAN	Richard D. Riesberg	1992	4828
18 12/16	11 8/16	7 4/16	M	Butler	ONT	Robert H. Pavlovic	1992	4828
18 12/16	11 9/16	7 3/16	M	Kashabowie	ONT	Chris Neumann	1992	4828
18 12/16	11 9/16	7 3/16	M	Terrace Bay	ONT	Alvin Anderson	1992	4828
18 12/16	11 11/16	7 1/16	M	Temiscaming	ONT	Jerry Boudreault	1992	4828
18 12/16	11 7/16	7 5/16	M	Skamania County	WA	Larry E. Sides, Jr.	1992	4828
18 12/16	11 12/16	7 0/16	M	Coconino County	AZ	James Q. Anderson	1992	4828
18 12/16	11 10/16	7 2/16	M	Wawa	ONT	Peter G. Dykstra	1992	4828
18 12/16	11 8/16	7 4/16	M	Cook County	MN	Arthur Heinze	1992	4828
18 12/16	11 12/16	7 0/16	M	Stevens County	WA	Dan L. Moultrie	1992	4828
18 12/16	11 13/16	6 15/16	M	Iron County	WI	Keith Skadahl	1992	4828
18 12/16	11 9/16	7 3/16	M	Crooked Lake	ONT	Robert Hagan	1993	4828
18 12/16	12 0/16	6 12/16	M	May Lake	ALB	Terry Ermel	1994	4828
18 12/16	11 5/16	7 7/16	M	Athabasca River	ALB	William Wuerthele	1994	4828
18 12/16	11 11/16	7 1/16	M	Peace River	ALB	Mark Zimmermann	1994	4828
18 12/16	12 0/16	6 12/16	M	Thompson	MAN	C. M. "Lucky" Lentz	1994	4828
18 12/16	12 2/16	6 10/16	M	Prince of Wales Island	AK	Garry A. Thoms	1994	4828
18 12/16	11 10/16	7 2/16	M	Athabasca River	ALB	Chris Davis	1994	4828
18 12/16	11 7/16	7 5/16	M	Rio Arriba County	NM	Michael A. Sisneros	1994	4828
18 12/16	11 7/16	7 5/16	M	White River	ONT	Dave Slager	1994	4828
18 12/16	12 1/16	6 11/16	M	Anglin Lake	SAS	Alan Bzdel	1994	4828
18 12/16	11 15/16	6 13/16	M	West Tree	ONT	Frances Higley	1994	4828
18 12/16	11 7/16	7 5/16	M	Dryden	ONT	Paul Tuscher	1994	4828
18 12/16	12 0/16	6 12/16	M	Notre-Dame	QUE	Richard J. Hale	1994	4828
18 12/16	11 13/16	6 15/16	M	Lane County	OR	Rick DeAlba	1994	4828
18 12/16	11 14/16	6 14/16	M	Mahnomen County	MN	Mike Ahles	1994	4828
18 12/16	11 14/16	6 14/16	M	High Level	ALB	Ben Catriz	1995	4828
18 12/16	12 3/16	6 9/16	M	Prince Albert	SAS	Eldon Richter	1995	4828
18 12/16	11 7/16	7 5/16	M	Baie Comeau	QUE	Stan Andriski, Jr.	1995	4828
18 12/16	11 10/16	7 2/16	M	Baie Comeau	QUE	Michael Heywood	1995	4828
18 12/16	11 10/16	7 2/16	M	Siskiyou County	CA	Lon E. Lauber	1995	4828
18 12/16	11 10/16	7 2/16	M	Franklin County	ME	Jeffery S. Pillsbury	1995	4828
18 12/16	11 12/16	7 0/16	M	Luce County	MI	Mark Alan Boulton	1995	4828
18 12/16	12 1/16	6 11/16	M	Sublette County	WY	Ron Gunyan, Jr.	1995	4828
18 12/16	11 12/16	7 0/16	M	Essex County	NY	Paul Durling	1995	4828
18 12/16	11 9/16	7 3/16	M	Bathurst	NBW	Bill LaHue	1996	4828
18 12/16	12 4/16	6 8/16	M	Swan River	MAN	Patrick Reeve	1996	4828
18 12/16	11 14/16	6 14/16	M	Oak Lake	ONT	Thomas G. Vils	1996	4828

BLACK BEAR

Minimum Score 18   Continued

SCORE	GREATEST LENGTH	GREATEST WIDTH	SEX	AREA	STATE/ PROVINCE	HUNTER'S NAME	DATE	RANK
18 12/16	11 11/16	7 1/16	M	Slave River	ALB	N. Carlton Baker, Jr.	1996	4828
18 12/16	12 0/16	6 12/16	M	Clarke Lake	SAS	Tony Chirles	1996	4828
18 12/16	11 8/16	7 4/16	M	Thaddeus Lake	ONT	Nick Martin	1996	4828
18 12/16	11 15/16	6 13/16	M	Fort McMurray	ALB	Erik Danielsen	1996	4828
18 12/16	11 10/16	7 2/16	M	La Tuque	QUE	T. Scott McKnight	1996	4828
18 12/16	11 15/16	6 13/16	M	Prince of Wales Island	AK	Charles Wagner	1996	4828
18 12/16	11 10/16	7 2/16	M	Sawtooth Mtns.	AK	Pete Buist	1996	4828
18 12/16	11 12/16	7 0/16	M	Rusk County	WI	Duane Coates	1996	4828
18 12/16	12 0/16	6 12/16	M	Sawyer County	WI	Timothy Schneider	1996	4828
18 12/16	11 10/16	7 2/16	M	Rio Arriba County	NM	Mike Whatley	1996	4828
18 12/16	11 13/16	6 15/16	M	Rio Arriba County	NM	James E. Vance	1997	4828
18 12/16	12 1/16	6 11/16	M	Buffalo Narrows	SAS	Christopher R. Beck	1997	4828
18 12/16	11 8/16	7 4/16	M	Sioux Lookout	ONT	John G. Nelson	1997	4828
18 12/16	12 0/16	6 12/16	M	La Crete	ALB	Ronald D. Rod	1997	4828
18 12/16	11 10/16	7 2/16	M	Slave River	ALB	Owen Keeton, Jr.	1997	4828
18 12/16	11 15/16	6 13/16	M	Bradbury River	MAN	Steven W. Hartley	1997	4828
18 12/16	11 13/16	6 15/16	M	Thaddeus Lake	ONT	Nick Martin	1997	4828
18 12/16	11 15/16	6 13/16	M	Hazel Dell	SAS	Ron Luthi	1998	4828
18 12/16	11 14/16	6 14/16	M	Olha	MAN	Marty Stubstad	1998	4828
18 12/16	11 12/16	7 0/16	M	Mattice	ONT	Ed Pollock	1998	4828
18 12/16	11 12/16	7 0/16	M	Brunswick Lake	ONT	Thomas E. Schoenike	1998	4828
18 12/16	11 9/16	7 3/16	M	Idaho County	ID	James R. Ball	1998	4828
18 12/16	11 15/16	6 13/16	M	Oak Lake	ONT	Ole Braaten	1998	4828
18 12/16	11 14/16	6 14/16	M	Christopher Lake	SAS	Ben W. Fitzgerald	1998	4828
18 12/16	12 2/16	6 10/16	M	Athabasca River	ALB	Jason Adamson	1998	4828
18 12/16	11 13/16	6 15/16	M	Chipewyan Lake	ALB	David D. Manuszak	1998	4828
18 12/16	11 8/16	7 4/16	M	Clearwater County	ID	R. M. "Dick" Newell	1998	4828
18 12/16	11 15/16	6 13/16	M	Alcurve	SAS	Carl Furman	1999	4828
18 12/16	11 14/16	6 14/16	M	Point Howard	AK	Don Martin	1999	4828
18 12/16	11 15/16	6 13/16	M	Indian River	AK	Mark Berrie	1999	4828
18 12/16	12 0/16	6 12/16	M	Meadow Lake	SAS	Robert H. Torstenson	1999	4828
18 12/16	11 14/16	6 14/16	M	Bissett	MAN	Joe Lovoi	1999	4828
18 12/16	11 14/16	6 14/16	M	Rossburn	MAN	Barry Minshull	1999	4828
18 12/16	12 2/16	6 10/16	M	Snipe Creek	ALB	David J. Barrow	1999	4828
18 12/16	11 10/16	7 2/16	M	Redditt	ONT	Larry Braatz	1999	4828
18 12/16	11 10/16	7 2/16	M	Vermilion Bay	ONT	Ronnie Hicks	1999	4828
18 12/16	11 6/16	7 6/16	M	Siskiyou County	CA	Wayne Raupe	1999	4828
18 12/16	11 8/16	7 4/16	M	Blind River	ONT	Todd Mrowca	1999	4828
18 12/16	12 4/16	6 8/16	M	Menominee County	MI	Gene Thoney	1999	4828
18 12/16	11 13/16	6 15/16	M	San Juan County	UT	Mario R. Richardson	1999	4828
18 12/16	11 15/16	6 13/16	M	Bronson Lake	SAS	Kevin Maloney	2000	4828
18 12/16	11 10/16	7 2/16	M	Grand Rapids	MAN	James Knoke	2000	4828
18 12/16	11 8/16	7 4/16	M	Moose Pass	AK	Marty Sada	2000	4828
18 12/16	12 0/16	6 12/16	M	Itasca County	MN	Dan Blegen	2000	4828
18 12/16	11 9/16	7 3/16	M	Custer County	ID	Darrell Nunez	2001	4828
18 12/16	11 14/16	6 14/16	M	St. George	NBW	David M. Krampitz	2001	4828
18 12/16	12 1/16	6 11/16	M	Ignace	ONT	Tim Johnston	2001	4828
18 12/16	12 0/16	6 12/16	M	Cook County	MN	Marcus Nettz	2001	4828
18 12/16	11 12/16	7 0/16	M	Ear Falls	ONT	Randy D. Oleson	2001	4828
18 12/16	12 2/16	6 10/16	M	Fort a la Corne	SAS	Travis Teiber	2002	4828
18 12/16	12 0/16	6 12/16	M	Sturgeon Landing	SAS	Jay Haverluk	2002	4828
18 12/16	11 14/16	6 14/16	M	Carrot River	SAS	Leo J. George	2002	4828
18 12/16	11 14/16	6 14/16	M	Wells	BC	Bill Barton	2002	4828
18 12/16	11 14/16	6 14/16	M	Lynn Lake	MAN	Tim Dreier	2002	4828
18 12/16	11 11/16	7 1/16	M	Aroostook County	ME	Gene P. Miller, Jr.	2002	4828
18 12/16	11 10/16	7 2/16	M	Oneida County	WI	Gregory Reed	2002	4828
18 12/16	12 1/16	6 11/16	M	Rossburn	MAN	John Derr	2003	4828
18 12/16	12 0/16	6 12/16	M	Glendon	ALB	Mike Siegler	2003	4828
18 12/16	11 13/16	6 15/16	M	Snohomish County	WA	Kenneth Dean Ramey	2003	4828
18 12/16	12 0/16	6 12/16	M	Olha	MAN	Dennis R. Allen	2003	4828
18 12/16	11 7/16	7 5/16	M	Nestor Falls	ONT	Steven S. Olmstead	2003	4828
18 12/16	11 10/16	7 2/16	M	Hodgson	MAN	William H. Gross, Jr.	2003	4828
18 12/16	11 15/16	6 13/16	M	Chippewa County	WI	Ryan Boettcher	2003	4828
18 12/16	12 0/16	6 12/16	M	Iron County	MI	Jeff Joseph	2003	4828
*18 12/16	11 12/16	7 0/16	M	Petersville	NBW	George Allwes	2003	4828
18 12/16	11 12/16	7 0/16	M	Tulare County	CA	Richard Flynn	2003	4828
18 12/16	11 8/16	7 4/16	M	Custer County	ID	Darrell Nunez	2004	4828
18 12/16	11 13/16	6 15/16	M	Pemberton	BC	Chad Harrison	2004	4828
*18 12/16	12 1/16	6 11/16	M	Ponton	MAN	Rob Myers	2004	4828
18 12/16	12 3/16	6 9/16	M	St. John	NBW	Laurie A. Fitzgerald	2004	4828
18 12/16	11 10/16	7 2/16	M	Prince of Wales Island	AK	Keith Treece	2005	4828
*18 12/16	11 7/16	7 5/16	M	Val-d'Or	QUE	Brian J. Belair	2005	4828
18 12/16	11 9/16	7 3/16	M	Wawa	ONT	James C. Hicks	2005	4828
18 12/16	11 12/16	7 0/16	M	Raleigh Lake	ONT	William Wissestad	2005	4828
18 12/16	11 11/16	7 1/16	M	Redditt	ONT	Bill Leighty	2005	4828
18 12/16	11 6/16	7 6/16	M	Vermilion Bay	ONT	Chris Smith	2005	4828
18 12/16	11 11/16	7 1/16	M	Douglas County	OR	Curt Crook	2005	4828
18 12/16	12 1/16	6 11/16	M	Barron County	WI	Ryan Ebner	2005	4828
*18 12/16	11 13/16	6 15/16	M	Millarville	ALB	Sean Border	2005	4828
*18 12/16	11 12/16	7 0/16	M	Catron County	NM	Paul Badgett	2005	4828
18 12/16	12 5/16	6 7/16	M	Bonneville County	ID	Alan L. Hall	2005	4828
*18 12/16	12 0/16	6 12/16	M	Spirit River	ALB	John Albrecht	2006	4828
18 12/16	11 13/16	6 15/16	M	Baranof Island	AK	Ivan Muzljakovich	2006	4828
*18 12/16	12 0/16	6 12/16	M	Harcourt	NBW	Daniel J. Provenzano	2006	4828
18 12/16	11 12/16	7 0/16	M	Leaf Rapids	MAN	Christopher Fuller	2006	4828
18 12/16	11 7/16	7 5/16	M	Saskatchewan River	SAS	Floyd Forster	2006	4828
*18 12/16	11 15/16	6 13/16	M	English River	ONT	Wayne E. Thurston	2006	4828
18 12/16	11 12/16	7 0/16	M	Cook County	MN	Dave Vomela	2006	4828
18 12/16	12 1/16	6 11/16	M	Madison County	MT	Shane Zettle	2006	4828
18 12/16	11 9/16	7 3/16	M	Navajo County	AZ	Bryan Ledbetter	2006	4828
18 12/16	11 8/16	7 4/16	M	Terrace	BC	Jim Carlson	2007	4828
18 12/16	11 4/16	7 8/16	M	Zec Collin	QUE	Larry G. Evans	2007	4828
18 12/16	11 14/16	6 14/16	M	Susitna River	AK	Bryon Woytek	2007	4828
18 12/16	11 8/16	7 4/16	M	Brown Mtn.	AK	Mike L. Yonker	2007	4828
18 12/16	11 12/16	7 0/16	M	Kenora	ONT	Kurt Klemp	2007	4828

BLACK BEAR

Minimum Score 18   Continued

SCORE	GREATEST LENGTH	GREATEST WIDTH	SEX	AREA	STATE/ PROVINCE	HUNTER'S NAME	DATE	RANK
18 12/16	11 12/16	7 0/16	M	Hornepayne	ONT	Coby Smith	2007	4828
*18 12/16	11 11/16	7 1/16	M	Lac Seul	ONT	Mike Cherner	2007	4828
*18 12/16	11 8/16	7 4/16	M	Somerset County	ME	Mark T. Luzier	2007	4828
18 12/16	11 8/16	7 4/16	M	Tranquil Island	AK	William R. Hintz	2008	4828
18 12/16	11 15/16	6 13/16	M	Firebag River	ALB	Tim L. Donnelly	2008	4828
18 12/16	11 14/16	6 14/16	M	Minitonas	MAN	Eric J. Parthenay	2008	4828
18 12/16	11 13/16	6 15/16	M	Kosciusko Island	AK	Earl Chauvin	2008	4828
*18 12/16	12 0/16	6 12/16	M	Oneida County	WI	Brian Henn	2008	4828
18 12/16	12 0/16	6 12/16	M	Huerfano County	CO	David Betts, Jr.	2008	4828
*18 12/16	11 14/16	6 14/16	M	Houghton County	MI	Kevin Deacons	2008	4828
18 12/16	12 0/16	6 12/16	M	Iron County	WI	Robert E. Quade	2008	4828
18 12/16	11 12/16	7 0/16	M	McNalley Lake	ALB	Tamera Lundin	2009	4828
18 12/16	11 12/16	7 0/16	M	Custer County	ID	Boone Petersen	2009	4828
*18 12/16	12 0/16	6 12/16	M	Perry County	AR	James R. Fitzhugh	2009	4828
18 12/16	11 14/16	6 14/16	M	Kosciusko Island	AK	Bob Ameen	2010	4828
*18 12/16	11 7/16	7 5/16	M	White River	ONT	Ben Hershberger	2010	4828
18 12/16	11 15/16	6 13/16	M	Pend Oreille County	WA	Quenten J. Cole	2010	4828
18 11/16	11 12/16	6 15/16	M	Presque Isle County	MI	Herbert Miller	1957	5053
18 11/16	11 8/16	7 3/16	M	Chirvakum Creek	WA	Joe Zuend	1962	5053
18 11/16	11 13/16	6 14/16	M	Iron County	MI	Donald Schram	1965	5053
18 11/16	11 7/16	7 4/16	M	Shawano County	WI	Kenneth Karbon	1970	5053
18 11/16	11 10/16	7 1/16	M	Lac Cayamant	QUE	Charles Shaffner	1971	5053
18 11/16	11 9/16	7 2/16	M	Grand County	UT	Dennis Schoenick	1972	5053
18 11/16	11 7/16	7 4/16	M	San Miguel County	NM	Dr. Rick H. Jackson	1975	5053
18 11/16	11 12/16	6 15/16	M	Nestor Falls	ONT	Greg Roach	1977	5053
18 11/16	11 7/16	7 4/16	M	Clearwater County	ID	John Wagner	1978	5053
18 11/16	11 10/16	7 1/16	M	Lake Nipigon	ONT	Gary L. Smith	1978	5053
18 11/16	11 11/16	7 0/16	M	Estaire	ONT	Donnie Evans	1978	5053
18 11/16	11 15/16	6 12/16	M	Itasca County	MN	Harold Whitt	1979	5053
18 11/16	11 10/16	7 1/16	M	Franklin County	ME	Jeff Roberts	1980	5053
18 11/16	11 9/16	7 2/16	M	Huerfano County	CO	Patricia J. Matarazzo	1980	5053
18 11/16	11 11/16	7 0/16	M	Gogebic County	MI	Edward Burley	1981	5053
18 11/16	11 10/16	7 1/16	M	Itasca County	MN	Tom Brudeli	1981	5053
18 11/16	11 11/16	7 0/16	M	Iron County	MI	Tom A. Longnecker	1981	5053
18 11/16	11 12/16	6 15/16	M	Washington County	ME	Lincoln Michaud	1981	5053
18 11/16	11 11/16	7 0/16	M	Dryden	ONT	Harry L. Stalter	1981	5053
18 11/16	11 8/16	7 3/16	M	Franklin County	MA	George Holmes, Jr.	1982	5053
18 11/16	11 9/16	7 2/16	M	Chapleau	ONT	Jim Grooters	1982	5053
18 11/16	11 11/16	7 0/16	M	Atikokan	ONT	Al Taylor	1983	5053
18 11/16	11 15/16	6 12/16	M	Dorset	ONT	Daryll E. Smith	1983	5053
18 11/16	11 5/16	7 6/16	M	Lynn Lake	MAN	Gord Monteath	1983	5053
18 11/16	11 12/16	6 15/16	M	Valley County	ID	George Wadsworth	1983	5053
18 11/16	11 6/16	7 5/16	M	Klamath County	OR	Jeffery K. Russell	1983	5053
18 11/16	11 13/16	6 14/16	M	Rio Arriba County	NM	William Rule	1983	5053
18 11/16	11 10/16	7 1/16	M	Fort Frances	ONT	Kerry Ella	1984	5053
18 11/16	11 7/16	7 4/16	M	Muskoka	ONT	Alexander Button	1984	5053
18 11/16	11 9/16	7 2/16	M	Bonner County	ID	Brian T. Farley	1984	5053
18 11/16	11 14/16	6 13/16	M	Franklin County	ME	Harold Osborne	1984	5053
18 11/16	11 15/16	6 12/16	M	Spokane County	WA	David Lossett, Sr.	1984	5053
18 11/16	11 11/16	7 0/16	M	Smeaton	SAS	Randy Modin	1985	5053
18 11/16	11 9/16	7 2/16	M	Opasatika	ONT	Rob J. Smith	1985	5053
18 11/16	11 12/16	6 15/16	M	Huerfano County	CO	Jerry Barth	1985	5053
18 11/16	11 13/16	6 14/16	M	Sioux Lookout	ONT	Todd Koelzer	1986	5053
18 11/16	11 15/16	6 12/16	M	Lost Lake	ONT	Richard Martin	1986	5053
18 11/16	11 10/16	7 1/16	M	Fort Coulonge	QUE	Kevin Ball	1986	5053
18 11/16	12 2/16	6 9/16	M	Duck Mtns.	MAN	Terry Schar	1986	5053
18 11/16	12 0/16	6 11/16	M	Aroostook County	ME	Gilbert P. Verwey	1986	5053
18 11/16	11 14/16	6 13/16	M	Oconto County	WI	James S. Nowakowski	1986	5053
18 11/16	11 10/16	7 1/16	M	Routt County	CO	Lonny Vanatta	1987	5053
18 11/16	11 12/16	6 15/16	M	Ear Falls	ONT	Jeff Knights	1987	5053
18 11/16	11 5/16	7 6/16	M	Fremont County	WY	Pat Eastes	1987	5053
18 11/16	11 12/16	6 15/16	M	Delay River	QUE	W. R. "Tony" Dukes	1987	5053
18 11/16	11 14/16	6 13/16	M	Ashland County	WI	Joe VyVyan	1987	5053
18 11/16	12 1/16	6 10/16	M	Catron County	NM	Nick Arnett	1987	5053
18 11/16	11 12/16	6 15/16	M	Gila County	AZ	Paul Neill	1987	5053
18 11/16	11 9/16	7 2/16	M	Boise County	ID	Troy M. Miller	1988	5053
18 11/16	11 10/16	7 1/16	M	Zec Maganasipi	QUE	Shawn P. Harrington	1988	5053
18 11/16	11 12/16	6 15/16	M	Valley County	ID	Jim Wilson	1988	5053
18 11/16	11 9/16	7 2/16	M	Coos County	NH	Gerard D. Theriault	1988	5053
18 11/16	11 7/16	7 4/16	M	Franklin County	ME	Jim Roy	1988	5053
18 11/16	11 10/16	7 1/16	M	Madison County	MT	Ricky Huffstetler	1988	5053
18 11/16	12 3/16	6 8/16	M	Carrot River	SAS	Kurt Schroeder	1988	5053
18 11/16	11 15/16	6 12/16	M	Larimer County	CO	James Little	1989	5053
18 11/16	11 11/16	7 0/16	M	Idaho County	ID	Ronald Smith	1989	5053
18 11/16	11 7/16	7 4/16	M	McAdam	NBW	Joseph Khan	1989	5053
18 11/16	11 11/16	7 0/16	M	Coos County	NH	David G. Cote	1989	5053
18 11/16	11 5/16	7 6/16	M	Manitouwadge	ONT	Charles W. Haertel	1990	5053
18 11/16	11 11/16	7 0/16	M	Owl River	ALB	Thomas J. Papoutsis	1990	5053
18 11/16	11 15/16	6 12/16	M	Mesa County	CO	Ron A. Stover	1990	5053
18 11/16	12 2/16	6 9/16	M	Coos County	NH	Gary J. Russell	1990	5053
18 11/16	12 0/16	6 11/16	M	Luce County	MI	Owen Anderson	1990	5053
18 11/16	11 12/16	6 15/16	M	Rocky Mountain House	ALB	Randy Bernier	1991	5053
18 11/16	11 15/16	6 12/16	M	Remigny	QUE	Steve Reedy	1991	5053
18 11/16	11 15/16	6 12/16	M	Wanless	MAN	Louis Raimondi	1991	5053
18 11/16	11 15/16	6 12/16	M	Thompson	MAN	Richard E. Davis	1991	5053
18 11/16	11 14/16	6 13/16	M	Chulitna River	AK	Karen L. Schwanke	1991	5053
18 11/16	11 9/16	7 2/16	M	Essex County	NY	Paul Durling	1991	5053
18 11/16	11 13/16	6 14/16	M	Maple Leaf	ONT	Kurt M. Zurawski	1992	5053
18 11/16	11 8/16	7 3/16	M	Wabigoon	ONT	John H. Rosenstock	1992	5053
18 11/16	11 10/16	7 1/16	M	Wanless	MAN	Damon Finley	1992	5053
18 11/16	11 9/16	7 2/16	M	Nenana	AK	David E. Rankin	1992	5053
18 11/16	11 6/16	7 5/16	M	Thunder Bay	ONT	Randy Adkins	1992	5053
18 11/16	11 7/16	7 4/16	M	McNeil Township	ONT	Archie Mackinnon	1992	5053
18 11/16	11 11/16	7 0/16	M	Zec Maganasipi	QUE	Thaddeus A. Tykarsky	1992	5053
18 11/16	11 12/16	6 15/16	M	Carroll County	NH	Arthur E. Thibodeau, Jr.	1992	5053

178

BLACK BEAR

Minimum Score 18   Continued

SCORE	GREATEST LENGTH	GREATEST WIDTH	SEX	AREA	STATE/ PROVINCE	HUNTER'S NAME	DATE	RANK
18 11/16	12 0/16	6 11/16	M	Rusk County	WI	Douglas Bleecker	1992	5053
18 11/16	11 10/16	7 1/16	M	Houghton County	MI	Mitchell Bellamy	1992	5053
18 11/16	12 4/16	6 7/16	M	Sawyer County	WI	Steve Johnson	1992	5053
18 11/16	11 14/16	6 13/16	M	Charlevoix County	MI	Ronald E. Olund	1992	5053
18 11/16	11 5/16	7 6/16	M	Cadotte Lake	ALB	Mitchell Morra	1993	5053
18 11/16	11 13/16	6 14/16	M	Ravalli County	MT	Robert A. Bourne	1993	5053
18 11/16	11 15/16	6 12/16	M	McBride Lake	SAS	Howard Beeson	1993	5053
18 11/16	11 4/16	7 7/16	M	Terrace Bay	ONT	Larry L. Huffman	1993	5053
18 11/16	11 6/16	7 5/16	M	Idaho County	ID	Michael G. Teff	1993	5053
18 11/16	11 13/16	6 14/16	M	Itasca County	MN	Peter Q. Hill	1993	5053
18 11/16	11 5/16	7 6/16	M	Nakina	ONT	Darren W. Wilson	1993	5053
18 11/16	11 13/16	6 14/16	M	Fort St. John	BC	Scott Ebert	1994	5053
18 11/16	11 8/16	7 3/16	M	Vasiloff Township	ONT	Michael L. Ritter	1994	5053
18 11/16	11 14/16	6 13/16	M	Carlton County	MN	Donald Schleicher	1994	5053
18 11/16	11 15/16	6 12/16	M	Lake of the Woods Cty	MN	Bob Rippel	1994	5053
18 11/16	11 10/16	7 1/16	M	Umatilla County	OR	Jim Dunigan	1994	5053
18 11/16	11 10/16	7 1/16	M	Ontonagon County	MI	Terry Riley	1994	5053
18 11/16	11 15/16	6 12/16	M	Plumas County	CA	W. Kent Brown	1994	5053
18 11/16	12 2/16	6 9/16	M	Icy Bay	AK	Wade Keatts	1995	5053
18 11/16	11 13/16	6 14/16	M	Millville	NBW	Edward A. Hornberger	1995	5053
18 11/16	11 6/16	7 5/16	M	Bryce Township	ONT	Joe Hassinger	1995	5053
18 11/16	11 4/16	7 7/16	M	Penobscot County	ME	Robert Shannon Brewer	1995	5053
18 11/16	11 9/16	7 2/16	M	St. Louis County	MN	Dave Cerise	1995	5053
18 11/16	11 11/16	7 0/16	M	Aitkin County	MN	Bill Gratz	1995	5053
18 11/16	11 6/16	7 5/16	M	Juniper	NBW	Frederick Donarummo	1995	5053
18 11/16	11 10/16	7 1/16	M	Rio Arriba County	NM	Paul Voshell	1995	5053
18 11/16	11 12/16	6 15/16	M	Worthington	ONT	Jack A. Wilson	1996	5053
18 11/16	11 15/16	6 12/16	M	High Level	ALB	Bob Hudson, Jr.	1996	5053
18 11/16	12 3/16	6 8/16	M	High Prairie	ALB	David Wesley Dickson	1996	5053
18 11/16	11 13/16	6 14/16	M	Pierceland	SAS	Pat R. Potts	1996	5053
18 11/16	11 14/16	6 13/16	M	Slave River	ALB	N. Carlton Baker, Jr.	1996	5053
18 11/16	12 5/16	6 6/16	M	Carrot River	SAS	Marvin Pinkowski	1996	5053
18 11/16	11 9/16	7 2/16	M	Atikokan	ONT	David Wolf	1996	5053
18 11/16	12 0/16	6 11/16	M	Red Lake	ONT	Mike Koback	1996	5053
18 11/16	11 11/16	7 0/16	M	Lake of the Woods	ONT	Jack Kelley	1996	5053
18 11/16	11 11/16	7 0/16	M	Carrot River	SAS	Greg Hunter	1996	5053
18 11/16	11 9/16	7 2/16	M	Bathurst	NBW	Bruce A. Grant	1996	5053
18 11/16	11 11/16	7 0/16	M	St. Louis County	MN	Bruce Christopherson	1996	5053
18 11/16	12 0/16	6 11/16	M	Beltrami County	MN	Todd Hannon	1996	5053
18 11/16	12 1/16	6 10/16	M	Forest County	WI	Steve Daebler	1996	5053
18 11/16	11 13/16	6 14/16	M	Forest County	WI	Alfred J. Keyser	1996	5053
18 11/16	11 14/16	6 13/16	M	Calaveras County	CA	Darrel Sudduth	1996	5053
18 11/16	11 14/16	6 13/16	M	Skownan	MAN	Nick Wegner	1997	5053
18 11/16	11 10/16	7 1/16	M	Falher	ALB	Stephen L. Collins	1997	5053
18 11/16	11 9/16	7 2/16	M	Sudbury	ONT	William J. Igo	1997	5053
18 11/16	11 7/16	7 4/16	M	Fort Coulonge	QUE	Terry Lee Worley	1997	5053
18 11/16	11 10/16	7 1/16	M	Rapide-des-Joachims	QUE	Don Delabbio	1997	5053
18 11/16	11 6/16	7 5/16	M	Turtle Lake	QUE	Ricky D. McKinney	1997	5053
18 11/16	12 0/16	6 11/16	M	Taylor County	WI	Scott C. Sedivy	1997	5053
18 11/16	11 8/16	7 3/16	M	Grafton County	NH	Dr. Michael G. Tveraas	1997	5053
18 11/16	12 0/16	6 11/16	M	Eureka Peak Mtn.	BC	Byron LaFollette	1997	5053
18 11/16	12 1/16	6 10/16	M	Fisher Branch	MAN	T. Noble II	1998	5053
18 11/16	11 13/16	6 14/16	M	Gordondale	ALB	Zig Kertenis, Jr.	1998	5053
18 11/16	11 11/16	7 0/16	M	Maynard Falls	ONT	Scott G. Hettinger	1998	5053
18 11/16	11 11/16	7 0/16	M	Red Earth	ALB	Tim Dennis	1998	5053
18 11/16	11 9/16	7 2/16	M	Athabasca River	ALB	Joseph Seagle	1998	5053
18 11/16	11 14/16	6 13/16	M	West Prairie River	ALB	Don Lind	1998	5053
18 11/16	11 9/16	7 2/16	M	Harvey Station	NBW	Edward F. Klosowski, Jr.	1998	5053
18 11/16	11 11/16	7 0/16	M	Forest County	WI	Al Breit	1998	5053
18 11/16	11 12/16	6 15/16	M	Westfield	NBW	David M. Smith	1998	5053
18 11/16	11 6/16	7 5/16	M	San Juan County	UT	David R. Lundberg	1998	5053
18 11/16	12 1/16	6 10/16	M	Bayfield County	WI	Joseph C. Hinderman	1998	5053
18 11/16	11 13/16	6 14/16	M	Coos County	NH	Brian J. Emerson	1998	5053
18 11/16	11 8/16	7 3/16	M	Piscataquis County	ME	Heath King	1998	5053
18 11/16	11 13/16	6 14/16	M	Peace River	ALB	Leon Hill	1999	5053
18 11/16	12 2/16	6 9/16	M	Bronson Lake	SAS	Michael Scagnelli	1999	5053
18 11/16	11 13/16	6 14/16	M	Mossy River	SAS	Donald Roy Fellows, Jr.	1999	5053
18 11/16	11 15/16	6 12/16	M	Athabasca River	ALB	J. P. McLaughlin	1999	5053
18 11/16	11 6/16	7 5/16	M	Amos	QUE	Jerry May	1999	5053
18 11/16	11 8/16	7 3/16	M	Forestville	QUE	Jeff Baechtle	1999	5053
18 11/16	11 15/16	6 12/16	M	Aroostook County	ME	Robert A. Eisenhart	1999	5053
18 11/16	11 12/16	6 15/16	M	Quesnel Lake	BC	Randy Liljenquist	2000	5053
18 11/16	11 7/16	7 4/16	M	Hudson Bay	SAS	Max E. Hatfield	2000	5053
18 11/16	11 11/16	7 0/16	M	Tolovana River	AK	Holland K. Sands	2000	5053
18 11/16	11 15/16	6 12/16	M	St. Louis County	MN	Shane Bruning	2000	5053
18 11/16	11 14/16	6 13/16	M	La Plata County	CO	Larry D. Burcz	2000	5053
*18 11/16	12 1/16	6 10/16	M	Pope County	AR	Darren Murphy	2000	5053
18 11/16	11 10/16	7 1/16	M	Fisher Branch	MAN	Rick Dunn	2001	5053
18 11/16	11 8/16	7 3/16	M	Ville-Marie	QUE	Larry R. Faught	2001	5053
18 11/16	11 11/16	7 0/16	M	High Level	ALB	Tom Foss	2001	5053
18 11/16	11 8/16	7 3/16	M	La-Pouruoirie-Du-Barrage	QUE	Terry Putman	2001	5053
*18 11/16	11 15/16	6 12/16	M	Atikokan	ONT	Bryan VanRyn	2001	5053
18 11/16	11 13/16	6 14/16	M	Clearwater County	ID	Karl Krill	2001	5053
18 11/16	12 4/16	6 7/16	M	Onanole	MAN	Jerry Shavrnoch	2002	5053
18 11/16	12 1/16	6 10/16	M	Fort Coulonge	QUE	Robert E. Weibley	2002	5053
18 11/16	12 0/16	6 11/16	M	Sandilands	MAN	Russell K. Mehling	2002	5053
18 11/16	12 1/16	6 10/16	M	Whiteshell	MAN	Layton Brown	2002	5053
18 11/16	11 8/16	7 3/16	M	Ray River	AK	Thomas Chadwick	2002	5053
18 11/16	11 11/16	7 0/16	M	Kupreanof Island	AK	David Benitz	2002	5053
18 11/16	11 13/16	6 14/16	M	White Mtns.	AK	Douglas W. Merritt	2002	5053
18 11/16	11 6/16	7 5/16	M	Koochiching County	MN	Mark Evans	2002	5053
18 11/16	11 13/16	6 14/16	M	Summerberry River	MAN	Steve Seibold	2003	5053
18 11/16	11 13/16	6 14/16	M	Chinchaga River	ALB	James Anderson	2003	5053
18 11/16	11 15/16	6 12/16	M	McNalley Lake	ALB	John Lundin	2003	5053
18 11/16	11 11/16	7 0/16	M	Ft. McMurray	ALB	Doug Clayton	2003	5053

BLACK BEAR

Minimum Score 18 — Continued

SCORE	GREATEST LENGTH	GREATEST WIDTH	SEX	AREA	STATE/ PROVINCE	HUNTER'S NAME	DATE	RANK
18 11/16	11 14/16	6 13/16	M	Otero County	NM	Austin Terry	2003	5053
18 11/16	11 15/16	6 12/16	M	Price County	WI	Mark D. Pauli	2003	5053
18 11/16	12 1/16	6 10/16	M	Loring	ONT	Edward Hatcher	2003	5053
18 11/16	11 15/16	6 12/16	M	Peace River	ALB	Ken Farmer	2004	5053
18 11/16	11 12/16	6 15/16	M	Fish Creek	AK	Tony Dawson	2004	5053
18 11/16	11 10/16	7 1/16	M	Kosciusko Island	AK	Bob Ameen	2004	5053
18 11/16	11 15/16	6 12/16	M	File Lake	MAN	Jeff Menchhofer	2004	5053
*18 11/16	11 8/16	7 3/16	M	Preissac	QUE	Gary Alvis	2004	5053
18 11/16	11 12/16	6 15/16	M	Oconto County	WI	Lee Brockman	2004	5053
*18 11/16	11 11/16	7 0/16	M	Cheshire County	NH	Vernon R. Hamlett	2004	5053
18 11/16	11 14/16	6 13/16	M	Ethelbert	MAN	Kenneth A. Leimone	2005	5053
18 11/16	11 10/16	7 1/16	M	Stoney Rapids	SAS	Tom Nelson	2005	5053
18 11/16	11 6/16	7 5/16	M	Gaspereau Forks	NBW	Kenneth M. Mills	2005	5053
*18 11/16	11 11/16	7 0/16	M	White River	ONT	Dr. Dawn A. Merritt	2005	5053
*18 11/16	11 8/16	7 3/16	M	Terrace Bay	ONT	Bill Bourke	2005	5053
18 11/16	11 7/16	7 4/16	M	Lake County	MN	Troy M. Hawkshead	2005	5053
*18 11/16	11 10/16	7 1/16	M	Penobscot County	ME	Steven L. Van Blair	2005	5053
18 11/16	11 12/16	6 15/16	M	Tobin Lake	SAS	Dean Lindaman	2006	5053
*18 11/16	11 11/16	7 0/16	M	Thompson	MAN	H. Wayne Pyle	2006	5053
*18 11/16	11 9/16	7 2/16	M	Lake County	MN	David Shockman	2006	5053
18 11/16	11 10/16	7 1/16	M	Thunder Bay	ONT	Miles Weaver	2006	5053
18 11/16	12 1/16	6 10/16	M	Green Lake	ONT	Rick Horwath	2006	5053
18 11/16	11 14/16	6 13/16	M	Alstead Lake	SAS	Joe Bradley	2007	5053
18 11/16	12 1/16	6 10/16	M	Douglas County	OR	Christopher Tipton	2007	5053
18 11/16	12 2/16	6 9/16	M	Cumberland House	SAS	Scott Homrich	2007	5053
*18 11/16	11 6/16	7 5/16	M	Gunnison County	CO	Todd Ronk	2007	5053
18 11/16	11 6/16	7 5/16	M	Thunder Bay	ONT	Connie Sue Clark	2008	5053
*18 11/16	12 0/16	6 11/16	M	Manitowik Lake	ONT	Randy Lemke	2008	5053
18 11/16	11 11/16	7 0/16	M	Las Animas County	CO	Mark Turner	2008	5053
*18 11/16	11 13/16	6 14/16	M	Ashe County	NC	Chris Lucas	2008	5053
18 11/16	12 2/16	6 9/16	M	Cold Lake	ALB	Richard T. Joseph Holder	2009	5053
*18 11/16	11 11/16	7 0/16	M	Conklin	ALB	Andre Titley	2009	5053
18 11/16	11 12/16	6 15/16	M	Wasatch County	UT	Stephen Davis	2009	5053
*18 11/16	11 9/16	7 2/16	M	Lac Dasserat	QUE	Brook L. Pari	2009	5053
18 11/16	12 1/16	6 10/16	M	Clark County	ID	Rosston Nielson	2009	5053
*18 11/16	11 12/16	6 15/16	M	Endeavour	SAS	Mike Davenport	2009	5053
*18 11/16	11 8/16	7 3/16	M	Ashland County	WI	Gary Pavloski	2009	5053
18 11/16	12 0/16	6 11/16	M	Athabaska River	ALB	R. Kirk Sharp	2010	5053
*18 11/16	12 0/16	6 11/16	M	Loon Lake	SAS	Shawn Nault	2010	5053
18 10/16	11 8/16	7 2/16	M	Iron County	WI	Carl Hulbert	1963	5265
18 10/16	11 8/16	7 2/16	M	Montreal River	ONT	S. Robinson/J. Beach	1966	5265
18 10/16	11 7/16	7 3/16	M	Rio Grande County	CO	Rod Wintz	1967	5265
18 10/16	11 11/16	6 15/16	M	Vermilion Bay	ONT	Thomas L. A. Pucci	1968	5265
18 10/16	11 12/16	6 14/16	M	Idaho County	ID	Randolph Coleman	1970	5265
18 10/16	12 2/16	6 8/16	M	McLeod Lake	BC	Ron McKay	1973	5265
18 10/16	11 5/16	7 5/16	M	Madison County	ID	Bruce W. Baird	1974	5265
18 10/16	11 0/16	7 10/16	M	Marinette County	WI	Dan Stencel	1974	5265
18 10/16	11 8/16	7 2/16	M	Las Animas County	CO	Dr. John Adams	1974	5265
18 10/16	11 8/16	7 2/16	M	Franklin County	ME	Mark Checki	1976	5265
18 10/16	11 13/16	6 13/16	M	Starkey Unit	OR	Timothy D. Palmore	1976	5265
18 10/16	11 5/16	7 5/16	M	Grand County	CO	Lyle Willmarth	1976	5265
18 10/16	11 11/16	6 15/16	M	Lewis & Clark County	MT	Scott Koelzer	1977	5265
18 10/16	12 1/16	6 9/16	M	Palmer	AK	John F. Sumrall	1977	5265
18 10/16	11 10/16	7 0/16	M	Clearwater County	ID	Tom Cummings	1977	5265
18 10/16	11 10/16	7 0/16	M	Chaffee County	CO	Frank A. Morminello	1978	5265
18 10/16	11 8/16	7 2/16	M	Uncompahgre N.F.	CO	William Hendricks	1978	5265
18 10/16	11 12/16	6 14/16	M	Stone Creek	BC	Larry McKay	1978	5265
18 10/16	11 10/16	7 0/16	M	Mendocino County	CA	Russell L. Browning	1979	5265
18 10/16	11 14/16	6 12/16	M	Dolores County	CO	Stanley A. Coval	1979	5265
18 10/16	11 14/16	6 12/16	M	Pipe Lake	ONT	Richard Colby	1980	5265
18 10/16	11 5/16	7 5/16	M	Boise County	ID	Richard C. Nichols	1981	5265
18 10/16	11 2/16	7 8/16	M	Judith Basin County	MT	Don Davidson	1981	5265
18 10/16	11 7/16	7 3/16	M	Thunder Bay	ONT	Roberta Byerly	1982	5265
18 10/16	11 7/16	7 3/16	M	Warren County	NY	Ernie Ahr	1982	5265
18 10/16	12 0/16	6 10/16	M	Susitna River	AK	Matt Jones	1982	5265
18 10/16	11 12/16	6 14/16	M	Gunnison County	CO	Mike Miller	1982	5265
18 10/16	11 10/16	7 0/16	M	Meagher County	MT	John Levison	1983	5265
18 10/16	11 14/16	6 12/16	M	Clearwater County	ID	Tim Newbold	1983	5265
18 10/16	11 9/16	7 1/16	M	Ear Falls	ONT	Ron Marion	1983	5265
18 10/16	11 14/16	6 12/16	M	Douglas County	OR	Ralph Burt	1983	5265
18 10/16	11 2/16	7 8/16	M	Rouyn-Noranda	QUE	Claude St. Amour	1983	5265
18 10/16	12 0/16	6 10/16	M	Mine Centre	ONT	Edwin John Durushia	1984	5265
18 10/16	11 13/16	6 13/16	M	Lemhi County	ID	Clint Bevins	1984	5265
18 10/16	11 13/16	6 13/16	M	Beluga River	AK	Dennis Redden	1984	5265
18 10/16	12 2/16	6 8/16	M	Fremont County	WY	Jerry Bodar	1984	5265
18 10/16	12 1/16	6 9/16	M	Valley County	ID	Gary Angell	1985	5265
18 10/16	11 11/16	6 15/16	M	Hudson Bay	SAS	Warren Buss	1985	5265
18 10/16	11 6/16	7 4/16	M	Huerfano County	CO	Michael Beckwith	1985	5265
18 10/16	11 7/16	7 3/16	M	Jellicoe	ONT	John Paul McKown	1985	5265
18 10/16	11 13/16	6 13/16	M	Las Animas County	CO	Tom Storr	1985	5265
18 10/16	11 10/16	7 0/16	F	Sanpete County	UT	C. Danny Butler	1986	5265
18 10/16	11 14/16	6 12/16	M	Nestor Falls	ONT	Byron Korby	1986	5265
18 10/16	11 12/16	6 14/16	M	Fort Coulonge	QUE	Glenn R Noel	1986	5265
18 10/16	11 4/16	7 6/16	M	Papineau Township	ONT	Fred Law	1986	5265
18 10/16	11 10/16	7 0/16	M	Fort Coulonge	QUE	F. Edward Campbell	1986	5265
18 10/16	11 6/16	7 4/16	M	Carlton County	MN	Donald Schleicher	1986	5265
18 10/16	11 14/16	6 12/16	M	Long Lake	ALB	Dave Gerber	1987	5265
18 10/16	11 14/16	6 12/16	M	Sturgeon Landing	SAS	Jeff Scherr	1987	5265
18 10/16	11 13/16	6 13/16	M	Black River	QUE	Robert L. Brilhart	1987	5265
18 10/16	12 0/16	6 10/16	M	Price Creek	ONT	Rick Candos	1987	5265
18 10/16	11 10/16	7 0/16	M	Sudbury	ONT	William F. Boggess	1987	5265
18 10/16	12 3/16	6 7/16	M	Ignace	ONT	Donald W. Goers	1987	5265
18 10/16	11 13/16	6 13/16	M	Sioux Lookout	ONT	Mike Prokop	1987	5265
18 10/16	11 11/16	6 15/16	M	Fort Coulonge	QUE	James E. Turner, Jr.	1987	5265
18 10/16	11 12/16	6 14/16	M	Lemhi County	ID	Art C. Hrabec	1988	5265

BLACK BEAR

Minimum Score 18 Continued

SCORE	GREATEST LENGTH	GREATEST WIDTH	SEX	AREA	STATE/ PROVINCE	HUNTER'S NAME	DATE	RANK
18 10/16	11 10/16	7 0/16	M	Dryden	ONT	Tony Mollus	1988	5265
18 10/16	11 10/16	7 0/16	M	Perrault Falls	ONT	Ronald R. Mower	1988	5265
18 10/16	11 12/16	6 14/16	M	Black River	QUE	Ronald E. Whitfield	1988	5265
18 10/16	11 8/16	7 2/16	M	Bathurst	NBW	Thomas J. Liguori	1988	5265
18 10/16	12 2/16	6 8/16	M	Tulare County	CA	Bill Sweetser	1988	5265
18 10/16	11 12/16	6 14/16	M	Florence County	WI	Richard J. Gohr	1988	5265
18 10/16	11 13/16	6 13/16	M	Coos County	OR	Rick Gabbard	1988	5265
18 10/16	11 10/16	7 0/16	M	Bathurst	NBW	Larry D. Benedict	1989	5265
18 10/16	11 15/16	6 11/16	M	King County	WA	David B. Young	1989	5265
18 10/16	11 13/16	6 13/16	M	Ashland County	WI	Wilbur C. Kuecker	1989	5265
18 10/16	11 6/16	7 4/16	M	Catron County	NM	Tracy G. Hardy	1989	5265
18 10/16	11 12/16	6 14/16	M	Poplarfield	MAN	Karl Dunich	1990	5265
18 10/16	11 12/16	6 14/16	M	Smoky River	ALB	Chris G. Sanford	1990	5265
18 10/16	11 2/16	7 8/16	M	Boise County	ID	Gary C. Gapp	1990	5265
18 10/16	11 9/16	7 1/16	M	Chibougamau	QUE	Brian R. Brochu	1990	5265
18 10/16	11 12/16	6 14/16	M	King County	WA	Donald H. Hubble	1990	5265
18 10/16	11 10/16	7 0/16	M	Blind River	ONT	Thomas M. Losiewski	1990	5265
18 10/16	11 15/16	6 11/16	M	Perry Sound	ONT	Robert Hill, Jr.	1990	5265
18 10/16	11 10/16	7 0/16	M	Page County	VA	Charles F. Cave	1990	5265
18 10/16	12 1/16	6 9/16	M	Prince of Wales Island	AK	Ken A. Vorisek	1991	5265
18 10/16	11 11/16	6 15/16	M	Zec Capitachouane	QUE	Jay A. Mengel	1991	5265
18 10/16	11 11/16	6 15/16	M	Idaho County	ID	Stephan S. Jones	1991	5265
18 10/16	11 11/16	6 15/16	M	Chapleau	ONT	Linda S. Schwochert	1991	5265
18 10/16	11 6/16	7 4/16	M	Los Alamos County	NM	David R. Aikin	1991	5265
18 10/16	11 13/16	6 13/16	M	Barrier Lake	SAS	Ray Fredin	1991	5265
18 10/16	11 12/16	6 14/16	M	Coos County	NH	Harry Bodenrader	1991	5265
18 10/16	11 11/16	6 15/16	M	Wallowa County	OR	Brett Duane Monaghan	1991	5265
18 10/16	11 10/16	7 0/16	M	Millville	NBW	Stephen Buck	1991	5265
18 10/16	11 12/16	6 14/16	M	Ontonagon County	MI	Bruce R. Bell	1991	5265
18 10/16	11 6/16	7 4/16	M	French River	ONT	Kenneth E. Briggs	1992	5265
18 10/16	11 11/16	6 15/16	M	Zec Maganasipi	QUE	Frank Luksa	1992	5265
18 10/16	11 12/16	6 14/16	M	Terrace Bay	ONT	Paul J. Paiser	1992	5265
18 10/16	11 11/16	6 15/16	M	Sandilands	MAN	Jac D. Hiebert	1992	5265
18 10/16	11 10/16	7 0/16	M	Yukon River	AK	Timothy J. Barber	1992	5265
18 10/16	11 14/16	6 12/16	M	Price County	WI	Daniel E. Kester	1992	5265
18 10/16	11 13/16	6 13/16	M	Aitkin County	MN	Donald K. Olson	1992	5265
18 10/16	11 11/16	6 15/16	M	Wallowa County	OR	Jeff Matson	1992	5265
18 10/16	11 15/16	6 11/16	M	Grand Rapids	MAN	Robert L. Loveall	1993	5265
18 10/16	11 12/16	6 14/16	M	Sioux Lookout	ONT	Marlene Odahlen-Hinz	1993	5265
18 10/16	11 10/16	7 0/16	M	Lake Preissac	QUE	Brian Sands	1993	5265
18 10/16	11 9/16	7 1/16	M	Kipawa	QUE	Carol Ference	1993	5265
18 10/16	11 10/16	7 0/16	M	Houghton County	MI	Robert K. Benson	1993	5265
18 10/16	11 11/16	6 15/16	M	La Loche	SAS	Brian E. Ronneberg	1994	5265
18 10/16	11 12/16	6 14/16	M	Bonneville County	ID	Spencer P. Barnard	1994	5265
18 10/16	11 14/16	6 12/16	M	Keeley Lake	SAS	Charles Niessner	1994	5265
18 10/16	11 11/16	6 15/16	M	Armstrong	ONT	Scott J. Teigen	1994	5265
18 10/16	11 15/16	6 11/16	M	Carrot River	SAS	Christopher Germain	1994	5265
18 10/16	12 2/16	6 8/16	M	Coconino County	AZ	Donald Kenneth Baker	1994	5265
18 10/16	11 14/16	6 12/16	M	Pakwash Lake	ONT	Lou Edelis	1995	5265
18 10/16	11 5/16	7 5/16	M	Boise County	ID	Terry Bennett	1995	5265
18 10/16	11 14/16	6 12/16	M	Clarke Lake	SAS	Ron Tandy	1995	5265
18 10/16	11 11/16	6 15/16	M	Lake Winnipegosis	MAN	Gerald Catterfeld	1995	5265
18 10/16	11 12/16	6 14/16	M	Wabigoon	ONT	Allen S. Kenyon	1995	5265
18 10/16	11 11/16	6 15/16	M	Blueberry River	ONT	Conway Marvin	1995	5265
18 10/16	11 12/16	6 14/16	M	Lake Cowen	SAS	Richard A. Pippenger	1995	5265
18 10/16	11 8/16	7 2/16	M	Fort Coulonge	QUE	Quinton E. Johnston	1995	5265
18 10/16	11 6/16	7 4/16	M	Armstrong	ONT	Robert Terrance Hurley	1995	5265
18 10/16	11 14/16	6 12/16	M	Iron County	WI	Christopher Gorenc	1995	5265
18 10/16	11 14/16	6 12/16	M	Athabasca River	ALB	William Riley	1996	5265
18 10/16	11 12/16	6 14/16	M	Kootenai County	ID	Shane Moyer	1996	5265
18 10/16	11 10/16	7 0/16	M	Hearst	ONT	Kenyon W. Woods	1996	5265
18 10/16	11 12/16	6 14/16	M	Hudson Bay	SAS	Gary Jensen	1996	5265
18 10/16	11 10/16	7 0/16	M	Peace River	ALB	Daniel A. Kasprzyk	1996	5265
18 10/16	11 12/16	6 14/16	M	High Level	ALB	Ken Whitney	1996	5265
18 10/16	11 10/16	7 0/16	M	Lynn Lake	MAN	Dave Canfield	1996	5265
18 10/16	11 11/16	6 15/16	M	Lemhi County	ID	Russell D. Kennedy	1996	5265
18 10/16	11 7/16	7 3/16	M	Cook County	MN	Earl Lowell Goodman	1996	5265
18 10/16	11 5/16	7 5/16	M	Coos County	NH	Mark Hakansson	1996	5265
18 10/16	11 11/16	6 15/16	M	Boise County	ID	John F. Thomas	1997	5265
18 10/16	11 13/16	6 13/16	M	Fairview	ALB	Richard Tucker	1997	5265
18 10/16	11 7/16	7 3/16	M	Sheridan County	WY	Andrew D. Weisgerber	1997	5265
18 10/16	11 14/16	6 12/16	M	Domaine Preissac	QUE	Jeanne Hughes	1997	5265
18 10/16	11 14/16	6 12/16	M	Clearwater River	ALB	Darryl Quidort	1997	5265
18 10/16	12 0/16	6 10/16	M	Lac des Mille Lacs	ONT	Thomas E. Rothrock	1997	5265
18 10/16	11 10/16	7 0/16	M	Lynn Lake	MAN	Sean T. Barry	1997	5265
18 10/16	11 9/16	7 1/16	M	Riou Lake	SAS	Pat Reilly	1997	5265
18 10/16	11 9/16	7 1/16	M	Ear Falls	ONT	Don Noonan	1997	5265
18 10/16	11 10/16	7 0/16	M	Jackson County	OR	G. Pat Crisler	1997	5265
18 10/16	11 14/16	6 12/16	M	Sawyer County	WI	Scott Tenold	1997	5265
18 10/16	12 0/16	6 10/16	M	Oconto County	WI	Ronald F. Lax	1997	5265
18 10/16	12 1/16	6 9/16	M	Webster County	WV	Scott Cochran	1997	5265
18 10/16	11 12/16	6 14/16	M	Navajo County	AZ	Steve D. Munier	1997	5265
18 10/16	11 6/16	7 4/16	M	Yuba County	CA	Scott Walker	1997	5265
18 10/16	11 9/16	7 1/16	M	La Ronge	SAS	Mike Maser	1998	5265
18 10/16	11 14/16	6 12/16	M	Lost Lake	SAS	Scott Basler	1998	5265
18 10/16	11 13/16	6 13/16	M	Brunswick Lake	ONT	Mark H. Kulke	1998	5265
18 10/16	11 12/16	6 14/16	M	Amisk Lake	SAS	Lee Wahlund	1998	5265
18 10/16	11 12/16	6 14/16	M	Red Lake	ONT	Jon Lozzio	1998	5265
18 10/16	11 8/16	7 2/16	M	Ear Falls	ONT	Dwight Hearing	1998	5265
18 10/16	11 6/16	7 4/16	M	Cadillac	QUE	Andrew E. Sands	1998	5265
18 10/16	12 1/16	6 9/16	M	Arborg	MAN	James H. Fogt	1998	5265
18 10/16	11 12/16	6 14/16	M	High Prairie	ALB	Bill Vaznis	1998	5265
18 10/16	11 9/16	7 1/16	M	Aroostook County	ME	James D. Lunemann	1998	5265
18 10/16	11 13/16	6 13/16	M	Marinette County	WI	Scott Dyer	1998	5265
18 10/16	11 10/16	7 0/16	M	Kootenai County	ID	Ron Hise	1999	5265

BLACK BEAR

Minimum Score 18 — Continued

SCORE	GREATEST LENGTH	GREATEST WIDTH	SEX	AREA	STATE/PROVINCE	HUNTER'S NAME	DATE	RANK
18 10/16	11 10/16	7 0/16	M	Tanana	AK	Ralph L. Moore	1999	5265
18 10/16	12 0/16	6 10/16	M	Doig River	ALB	Doyle Markham	1999	5265
18 10/16	11 8/16	7 2/16	M	Dipper Lake	SAS	Steve Dunn	1999	5265
18 10/16	11 10/16	7 0/16	M	The Pas	MAN	Scott Lang	1999	5265
18 10/16	11 12/16	6 14/16	M	St. Louis County	MN	Martin Bollum	1999	5265
18 10/16	11 9/16	7 1/16	M	Kuskokwim Mtns.	AK	Scott Jankowski	1999	5265
18 10/16	12 1/16	6 9/16	M	Marinette County	WI	Scott Bystol	1999	5265
18 10/16	11 12/16	6 14/16	M	Itasca County	MN	Scott Elich	1999	5265
18 10/16	11 13/16	6 13/16	M	Peers	ALB	Kevin Weeks	2000	5265
18 10/16	11 14/16	6 12/16	M	Laurier	MAN	Norbert Martin	2000	5265
18 10/16	11 14/16	6 12/16	M	High Level	ALB	Charles M. Frick	2000	5265
18 10/16	11 11/16	6 15/16	M	Zitziana River	AK	Anna Whitehead	2000	5265
18 10/16	11 12/16	6 14/16	M	Onanole	MAN	Adam Bartsch	2000	5265
18 10/16	11 12/16	6 14/16	M	Evain	QUE	Nathalie Robert	2000	5265
18 10/16	11 8/16	7 2/16	M	Caramat	ONT	Willie Runnels	2000	5265
18 10/16	11 8/16	7 2/16	M	Piscataquis County	ME	Henry G. Tuttle	2000	5265
18 10/16	11 9/16	7 1/16	M	Rio Arriba County	NM	Robert E. Cyrier	2000	5265
18 10/16	11 8/16	7 2/16	M	Greene County	NY	James P. Antippas	2000	5265
18 10/16	11 10/16	7 0/16	M	Bissett	MAN	Kenneth Jordan	2001	5265
18 10/16	11 6/16	7 4/16	M	Frobisher Lake	SAS	David E. Stepp	2001	5265
18 10/16	12 0/16	6 10/16	M	Ministikwan Lake	SAS	Michael S. Jackson	2001	5265
18 10/16	11 11/16	6 15/16	M	San Josef River	BC	Jason Bowman	2001	5265
18 10/16	11 11/16	6 15/16	M	Cook County	MN	Kirk A. Schnitker	2001	5265
18 10/16	11 11/16	6 15/16	M	Dog Lake	ONT	Dale Long	2001	5265
18 10/16	11 8/16	7 2/16	M	Hancock County	ME	Mark A. Rohrback, Sr.	2001	5265
18 10/16	12 4/16	6 6/16	M	Olha	MAN	Adam Bartsch	2001	5265
18 10/16	11 14/16	6 12/16	M	Price County	WI	Daniel D. Miracle	2001	5265
18 10/16	11 9/16	7 1/16	M	Kindiogami Lake	ONT	Kevin W. Black	2001	5265
18 10/16	11 15/16	6 11/16	M	Glaslyn	SAS	Matt Rosensweet	2001	5265
18 10/16	12 2/16	6 8/16	M	Izard County	AR	Greg Manry	2001	5265
18 10/16	11 14/16	6 12/16	M	Orange County	NY	James L. Campbell	2001	5265
18 10/16	11 11/16	6 15/16	M	Athabasca River	ALB	Matt Liljenquist	2002	5265
18 10/16	11 11/16	6 15/16	M	Meadow Lake	SAS	Wayne Muth	2002	5265
18 10/16	11 12/16	6 14/16	M	Paradise Hill	SAS	Will Chistenson	2002	5265
18 10/16	11 0/16	7 10/16	M	Maniwaki	QUE	John J. Mascellino, Sr.	2002	5265
18 10/16	11 11/16	6 15/16	M	Amos	QUE	Carl Straight	2002	5265
18 10/16	11 15/16	6 11/16	M	Atikokan	ONT	Jim Saunoris, Jr.	2002	5265
18 10/16	11 10/16	7 0/16	M	Atikokan	ONT	Blair E. Konczal	2002	5265
18 10/16	12 0/16	6 10/16	M	Itasca County	MN	Alan Muyres	2002	5265
18 10/16	12 2/16	6 8/16	M	Carrot River	SAS	Brian Ratayczak	2002	5265
18 10/16	12 0/16	6 10/16	M	Iron County	WI	Mike DeLaney	2002	5265
18 10/16	12 0/16	6 10/16	M	Ontonagon County	MI	Keith Brooks	2002	5265
18 10/16	11 8/16	7 2/16	M	Dryden	ONT	Dionne Shepley	2002	5265
18 10/16	11 11/16	6 15/16	M	Iron County	WI	Paul Korn	2002	5265
18 10/16	11 10/16	7 0/16	M	Fort McMurray	ALB	Steven L. Lysenko	2003	5265
18 10/16	11 7/16	7 3/16	M	Chimney Lake	BC	David Tew	2003	5265
18 10/16	11 8/16	7 2/16	M	Val-d'Or	QUE	Joseph E. Defibaugh	2003	5265
18 10/16	11 8/16	7 2/16	M	Kississing Lake	MAN	Scott G. Hettinger	2003	5265
18 10/16	11 12/16	6 14/16	M	Boise County	ID	Bill Watts, Jr.	2003	5265
18 10/16	11 7/16	7 3/16	M	Ignace	ONT	Bob Miller	2003	5265
18 10/16	12 4/16	6 6/16	M	St. Louis County	MN	Steve Fondie	2003	5265
18 10/16	11 10/16	7 0/16	M	Itasca County	MN	Scott Elich	2003	5265
18 10/16	11 9/16	7 1/16	M	Marty Lake	ONT	Larry D. Carter	2003	5265
18 10/16	12 1/16	6 9/16	M	Douglas County	WI	Jim Finn	2003	5265
18 10/16	12 3/16	6 7/16	M	Coconino County	AZ	Mike Ornoski, Jr.	2003	5265
18 10/16	11 13/16	6 13/16	M	Valleyview	ALB	Derek Daniel Pearson	2004	5265
18 10/16	11 12/16	6 14/16	M	Idaho County	ID	Matt R. Andersen	2004	5265
18 10/16	12 1/16	6 9/16	M	Onanole	MAN	Don Soltys	2004	5265
*18 10/16	11 14/16	6 12/16	M	DeBolt	ALB	Wade Soderberg	2004	5265
18 10/16	11 11/16	6 15/16	M	Mombray	QUE	Normand Grenier	2004	5265
18 10/16	11 6/16	7 4/16	M	Lake of the Woods	ONT	Michael Millard	2004	5265
*18 10/16	11 14/16	6 12/16	M	Churchill River	SAS	Randy Steverson	2005	5265
18 10/16	11 11/16	6 15/16	M	Yakutat	AK	Stacee Frost	2005	5265
18 10/16	11 11/16	6 15/16	M	Egenolf Lake	MAN	Bruce Grant	2005	5265
18 10/16	11 10/16	7 0/16	M	Emo	ONT	Chad Bierman	2005	5265
18 10/16	12 0/16	6 10/16	M	East Trout Lake	SAS	Aaron Wolf	2006	5265
*18 10/16	12 2/16	6 8/16	M	Armit	SAS	Thomas Scott Meyer	2006	5265
18 10/16	11 12/16	6 14/16	M	Valley County	ID	David Priest	2006	5265
*18 10/16	11 8/16	7 2/16	M	Churchill River	SAS	Michele Leqve	2006	5265
18 10/16	11 9/16	7 1/16	M	Haines	AK	Joshua B. LaCrone	2006	5265
18 10/16	11 11/16	6 15/16	M	Prince of Wales Island	AK	Thomas Enewold	2006	5265
18 10/16	11 12/16	6 14/16	M	Custer County	ID	Darrell Nunez	2006	5265
18 10/16	11 8/16	7 2/16	M	Besnard Lake	SAS	Bob Henry	2006	5265
18 10/16	11 5/16	7 5/16	M	Valley County	ID	Hunter Reichert	2006	5265
18 10/16	11 10/16	7 0/16	M	Calm Lake	ONT	Dennis R. Nicholson	2006	5265
18 10/16	11 13/16	6 13/16	M	Ear Falls	ONT	Robert J. Pierson	2006	5265
*18 10/16	11 7/16	7 3/16	M	Nipigon	ONT	Anthony S. Appleton	2006	5265
18 10/16	12 0/16	6 10/16	M	Fort McMurray	ALB	Jason E. Wiest	2007	5265
18 10/16	11 13/16	6 13/16	M	Fort McMurray	ALB	Mike Brinkerhoff	2007	5265
*18 10/16	11 12/16	6 14/16	M	Saw Mill Bay	AK	Dustin Kelone	2007	5265
18 10/16	12 0/16	6 10/16	M	Fishing Lake	ALB	Scott Silverness	2007	5265
18 10/16	11 14/16	6 12/16	M	Tiekel River	AK	Mike Falkner	2007	5265
18 10/16	12 2/16	6 8/16	M	Riding Mtn.	MAN	Ray Groshong	2007	5265
18 10/16	11 15/16	6 11/16	M	Rusk County	WI	Charles Wyatt	2007	5265
*18 10/16	11 7/16	7 3/16	M	Rio Arriba County	NM	Don Erbert	2007	5265
18 10/16	11 8/16	7 2/16	M	Kootenai County	ID	Richard M. Penn	2007	5265
*18 10/16	12 1/16	6 9/16	M	Mercer County	WV	Gary Lusk	2007	5265
18 10/16	12 0/16	6 10/16	M	Peace River	ALB	Ken Creek	2008	5265
18 10/16	11 10/16	7 0/16	M	Kipahigan Lake	MAN	Brandon Zinne	2008	5265
18 10/16	11 5/16	7 5/16	M	Stevens County	WA	Raymond Johnson	2008	5265
*18 10/16	11 7/16	7 3/16	M	Searchmont	ONT	Andy Gross	2008	5265
18 10/16	11 8/16	7 2/16	M	Kenora	ONT	Monte W. Reid	2008	5265
18 10/16	11 12/16	6 14/16	M	Perrault Falls	ONT	Dean Reiter	2008	5265
*18 10/16	12 2/16	6 8/16	M	Johnson County	AR	Joshua C. Kyles	2008	5265
*18 10/16	11 10/16	7 0/16	M	Keirstead	NBW	Gordon Hunting, Jr.	2009	5265

BLACK BEAR

Minimum Score 18   Continued

SCORE	GREATEST LENGTH	GREATEST WIDTH	SEX	AREA	STATE/ PROVINCE	HUNTER'S NAME	DATE	RANK
18 10/16	11 13/16	6 13/16	M	Manitoba Lake Narrows	MAN	Randy Wold	2009	5265
*18 10/16	12 1/16	6 9/16	M	Ochre River	MAN	Nick J. Wegner	2009	5265
18 10/16	11 11/16	6 15/16	M	Athabasca River	ALB	Steff Stefanovich	2009	5265
18 10/16	11 9/16	7 1/16	M	Clark County	ID	Johnny Watson	2009	5265
18 10/16	11 12/16	6 14/16	M	Zec de Kipawa	QUE	Harold H. Halfmann	2009	5265
18 10/16	11 12/16	6 14/16	M	St. Louis County	MN	Timothy J. Cardinal	2009	5265
*18 10/16	11 9/16	7 1/16	M	Ignace	ONT	Todd C. Thome	2009	5265
18 10/16	12 1/16	6 9/16	M	Fresno County	CA	Ken Dias	2009	5265
18 10/16	11 12/16	6 14/16	M	Bowsman	MAN	Shawn Vachal	2009	5265
18 10/16	11 13/16	6 13/16	M	Stone County	AR	James Roper Blackwell	2009	5265
18 10/16	11 10/16	7 0/16	M	Flin Flon	MAN	Dean Conrad	2010	5265
*18 10/16	11 13/16	6 13/16	M	Blueberry	ALB	Thanos Natras	2010	5265
18 10/16	11 11/16	6 15/16	M	Rio Arriba County	NM	Garrett Chavez	2010	5265
18 9/16	11 5/16	7 4/16	M	Chelan County	WA	Wayne Hathaway	1960	5524
18 9/16	11 6/16	7 3/16	M	Olsen Bay	AK	Don Daniels	1963	5524
18 9/16	11 10/16	6 15/16	M	Iron County	MI	Don Schram	1964	5524
18 9/16	11 10/16	6 15/16	M	Mattawa	ONT	Dr. Max G. Menefee	1966	5524
18 9/16	11 5/16	7 4/16	M	St. Louis County	MN	Ron Johnson	1967	5524
18 9/16	11 6/16	7 3/16	M	Nez Perce County	ID	Betty Gulman	1972	5524
18 9/16	11 5/16	7 4/16	M	Blue Jay Ridge	CA	Delbert Allmon	1972	5524
18 9/16	11 12/16	6 13/16	M	Rio Arriba County	NM	Curtis W. McClahan	1973	5524
18 9/16	12 0/16	6 9/16	M	Swan Hills	ALB	Gerald L. Egbert	1976	5524
18 9/16	11 7/16	7 2/16	M	Franklin County	ME	John G. Morningstar	1977	5524
18 9/16	11 9/16	7 0/16	M	Ottawa River	QUE	Roger D. Davis	1978	5524
18 9/16	11 12/16	6 13/16	M	Fremont County	ID	Tom Savage	1979	5524
18 9/16	11 13/16	6 12/16	M	Wabigoon	ONT	Jon Helgason	1979	5524
18 9/16	11 4/16	7 5/16	M	Caramat	ONT	John LaForge	1979	5524
18 9/16	11 5/16	7 4/16	M	Idaho County	ID	Darrel Howard	1980	5524
18 9/16	11 13/16	6 12/16	M	Sawyer County	WI	Joe Gohres	1980	5524
18 9/16	11 6/16	7 3/16	M	Catron County	NM	Cornie P. Intveld	1980	5524
18 9/16	11 11/16	6 14/16	M	Ravalli County	MT	Mike F. Bartz	1981	5524
18 9/16	11 9/16	7 0/16	M	Marquette County	MI	Gary Lohman	1981	5524
18 9/16	11 7/16	7 2/16	M	Idaho County	ID	Darrell Howard	1982	5524
18 9/16	11 11/16	6 14/16	M	Marquette County	MI	Keith B. Putnam	1982	5524
18 9/16	11 7/16	7 2/16	M	Nipigon	ONT	James P. Kina	1982	5524
18 9/16	11 13/16	6 12/16	M	Dryden	ONT	Dennis L. Havey	1982	5524
18 9/16	11 8/16	7 1/16	M	Susitna River	AK	Patrick McKay	1982	5524
18 9/16	12 3/16	6 6/16	M	Game Area #23	MAN	Gary Kaluzniak	1983	5524
18 9/16	12 5/16	6 4/16	M	Carlton County	MN	Larry H. Hoyt	1983	5524
18 9/16	11 10/16	6 15/16	M	Ear Falls	ONT	Scott J. Strook	1984	5524
18 9/16	11 9/16	7 0/16	M	Cedar Lake	ONT	Brad Wiehr	1984	5524
18 9/16	11 8/16	7 1/16	M	Temiscaming	QUE	Joe G. Hopwood	1984	5524
18 9/16	11 9/16	7 0/16	M	Idaho County	ID	Ronald J. Larson	1984	5524
18 9/16	11 9/16	7 0/16	M	Shasta County	CA	Peter Esposito	1984	5524
18 9/16	11 8/16	7 1/16	M	Sudbury	ONT	Vinnie Pisani	1985	5524
18 9/16	11 9/16	7 0/16	M	Dryden	ONT	James F. Hendricks	1985	5524
18 9/16	11 10/16	6 15/16	M	Pancake Bay	ONT	Brad L. Rogers	1985	5524
18 9/16	11 10/16	6 15/16	M	Mendocino County	CA	Charles Verne	1985	5524
18 9/16	11 7/16	7 2/16	M	Lemhi County	ID	Thomas Fuller	1985	5524
18 9/16	11 12/16	6 13/16	M	Cass County	MN	Larry Fischer	1985	5524
18 9/16	11 6/16	7 3/16	M	Missoula County	MT	Terry See	1985	5524
18 9/16	11 12/16	6 13/16	M	Sudbury	ONT	David L. Willis	1986	5524
18 9/16	11 11/16	6 14/16	M	Boundary County	ID	Walt Dinning	1986	5524
18 9/16	11 11/16	6 14/16	M	Clearwater County	ID	Ronnie Larson	1986	5524
18 9/16	11 2/16	7 7/16	M	Caramat	ONT	Scott A. Atton	1986	5524
18 9/16	11 9/16	7 0/16	M	Fort Coulonge	QUE	Westley Keller	1986	5524
18 9/16	11 10/16	6 15/16	M	Washington County	ME	Marty Kane	1986	5524
18 9/16	12 2/16	6 7/16	M	Burnett County	WI	Duane Hoefs	1986	5524
18 9/16	11 9/16	7 0/16	M	Mine Centre	ONT	Stan H. Myers	1987	5524
18 9/16	11 13/16	6 12/16	M	Monominto	MAN	Erik Thienpondt	1987	5524
18 9/16	11 10/16	6 15/16	M	Montreal River	ONT	Thomas Hlinka	1987	5524
18 9/16	12 1/16	6 8/16	M	Clearwater County	MN	Kevin Anderson	1987	5524
18 9/16	11 5/16	7 4/16	M	Puperville	ONT	John DeWyse	1987	5524
18 9/16	11 8/16	7 1/16	M	Los Alamos County	NM	Robert Hand	1987	5524
18 9/16	11 9/16	7 0/16	M	Jackson County	OR	Jeff S. Cleveland	1987	5524
18 9/16	11 10/16	6 15/16	M	Kenora	ONT	James G. Aldrich	1988	5524
18 9/16	11 10/16	6 15/16	M	Wanless	MAN	Jon P. Thomas	1988	5524
18 9/16	11 9/16	7 0/16	M	Kenora	ONT	John E. Larsen	1988	5524
18 9/16	11 6/16	7 3/16	M	Clearwater County	ID	Gregg Tanner	1988	5524
18 9/16	11 8/16	7 1/16	M	Temiscaming	QUE	Daniel E. Wallace	1988	5524
18 9/16	11 13/16	6 12/16	M	Oneida County	WI	Tim Johnson	1988	5524
18 9/16	11 14/16	6 11/16	M	Oneida County	WI	Greg L. Reed	1988	5524
18 9/16	11 14/16	6 11/16	M	Prince of Wales Island	AK	Dyrk Eddie	1989	5524
18 9/16	11 12/16	6 13/16	M	Lane County	OR	Steven T Jones	1989	5524
18 9/16	11 6/16	7 3/16	M	Clericy	QUE	Roger Stricklen	1989	5524
18 9/16	11 10/16	6 15/16	M	Swift Creek	BC	Dan Yalowega	1989	5524
18 9/16	11 11/16	6 14/16	M	Waterhen Lake	MAN	Walt Krom	1989	5524
18 9/16	11 8/16	7 1/16	M	San Miguel County	NM	Harold Wallace	1989	5524
18 9/16	11 10/16	6 15/16	M	Idaho County	ID	Monty Moravec	1990	5524
18 9/16	11 8/16	7 1/16	M	Campbell River	BC	Don Quackenbush	1990	5524
18 9/16	11 9/16	7 0/16	M	Pluto Lake	ONT	John D. Schmidt	1990	5524
18 9/16	11 7/16	7 2/16	M	Whitefish Lake	ONT	Kevin Peterson	1990	5524
18 9/16	11 10/16	6 15/16	M	King County	WA	G. Dan Feighner	1990	5524
18 9/16	11 11/16	6 14/16	M	Lincoln County	NM	Charlie C. Bing	1990	5524
18 9/16	11 15/16	6 10/16	M	Marinette County	WI	Jeffrey J. Zepnick	1990	5524
18 9/16	11 12/16	6 13/16	M	Holinshead Lake	ONT	Jack Leschner	1991	5524
18 9/16	11 5/16	7 4/16	M	Clearwater County	ID	Johnny Watson	1991	5524
18 9/16	11 6/16	7 3/16	M	County #1	ALB	Douglas E. Erickson	1991	5524
18 9/16	11 12/16	6 13/16	M	Grand County	UT	Kim Tatman	1991	5524
18 9/16	11 3/16	7 6/16	M	Haileybury	ONT	Dean G. Bartolomucci	1991	5524
18 9/16	11 13/16	6 12/16	M	Idaho County	ID	Monty Moravec	1991	5524
18 9/16	12 2/16	6 7/16	M	Lewis County	WA	Ronald D. Amrine	1991	5524
18 9/16	11 11/16	6 14/16	M	Somerset County	ME	Corey Sibbio	1991	5524
18 9/16	11 13/16	6 12/16	M	Gallatin County	MT	Bruce A. Porisch	1991	5524
18 9/16	11 12/16	6 13/16	M	Slave Lake	ALB	Bill Vaznis	1991	5524

BLACK BEAR

Minimum Score 18 Continued

SCORE	GREATEST LENGTH	GREATEST WIDTH	SEX	AREA	STATE/ PROVINCE	HUNTER'S NAME	DATE	RANK
18 9/16	11 15/16	6 10/16	M	Roscommon County	MI	Elmer E. Clemson	1991	5524
18 9/16	11 12/16	6 13/16	M	Gila County	AZ	Mark Ovitt	1991	5524
18 9/16	12 2/16	6 7/16	M	Warren County	VA	John B. Stewart	1991	5524
18 9/16	10 14/16	7 11/16	M	Nicholas County	WV	Steve A. Antoline	1991	5524
18 9/16	11 13/16	6 12/16	M	Erickson	MAN	Glen Newton	1992	5524
18 9/16	11 13/16	6 12/16	M	Emo	ONT	Steven J. Snyder	1992	5524
18 9/16	11 12/16	6 13/16	M	Snohomish County	WA	John P. Hennessy	1992	5524
18 9/16	12 1/16	6 8/16	M	Rock Island Lake	ALB	Dean Bromberger	1993	5524
18 9/16	11 13/16	6 12/16	M	Dalton Highway	AK	Ronald W. Lang, Jr.	1993	5524
18 9/16	11 11/16	6 14/16	M	Prince of Wales Island	AK	Jim Young	1993	5524
18 9/16	11 9/16	7 0/16	M	McBride	BC	Richard Kopp	1993	5524
18 9/16	11 10/16	6 15/16	M	Highwinds Lake	ONT	Robert G. Carter	1993	5524
18 9/16	12 1/16	6 8/16	M	Upper Skeena River	BC	Kristen J. Mustad	1993	5524
18 9/16	11 10/16	6 15/16	M	Stenen	SAS	Tom Langford	1993	5524
18 9/16	11 7/16	7 2/16	M	Ft. McMurray	ALB	Jim Miller, Jr.	1993	5524
18 9/16	11 9/16	7 0/16	M	Idaho County	ID	K-Tal Johnson	1993	5524
18 9/16	11 9/16	7 0/16	M	Baie Comeau	QUE	Trevor W.G. McEntyre	1993	5524
18 9/16	11 6/16	7 3/16	M	La Tuque	QUE	Daniel F. Walsh	1993	5524
18 9/16	11 11/16	6 14/16	M	Bella Coola	BC	Lawrence Michalchuk	1993	5524
18 9/16	11 9/16	7 0/16	M	Iron County	WI	Paul Jaeger	1993	5524
18 9/16	12 0/16	6 9/16	M	Jackson County	OR	Brian Day	1993	5524
18 9/16	11 12/16	6 13/16	M	Lemhi County	ID	Mark A. Mathews	1994	5524
18 9/16	12 2/16	6 7/16	M	Duck Mtns.	SAS	Jeff Jacob	1994	5524
18 9/16	11 11/16	6 14/16	M	Timmins	ONT	James F. Blanton	1994	5524
18 9/16	11 5/16	7 4/16	M	Atikokan	ONT	Mark "Root" Gies	1994	5524
18 9/16	11 10/16	6 15/16	M	Sioux Lookout	ONT	John P. Liska	1994	5524
18 9/16	11 8/16	7 1/16	M	Zec Dumoine	QUE	Frederick Hendrickson	1994	5524
18 9/16	12 1/16	6 8/16	M	Cass County	MN	Dorian Cornelius	1994	5524
18 9/16	11 11/16	6 14/16	M	Union County	OR	Dave M. Seida	1994	5524
18 9/16	11 7/16	7 2/16	M	Ravalli County	MT	Scott Lindsey	1994	5524
18 9/16	12 0/16	6 9/16	M	Latah County	ID	Nicholas Orth	1994	5524
18 9/16	11 10/16	6 15/16	M	Hudson Bay	SAS	Tag Reed	1995	5524
18 9/16	11 9/16	7 0/16	M	Slave Lake	ALB	Gregory Noble Spickler	1995	5524
18 9/16	11 11/16	6 14/16	M	Cabonga	QUE	Len Cardinale	1995	5524
18 9/16	11 12/16	6 13/16	M	Upsala	ONT	Dale L. Toltzmann	1995	5524
18 9/16	11 7/16	7 2/16	M	Washington County	ME	Brian D. Smith	1995	5524
18 9/16	11 6/16	7 3/16	M	Kirkland Lake	ONT	Howard L. Nester	1995	5524
18 9/16	11 12/16	6 13/16	M	Ignace	ONT	Kevin Linton	1995	5524
18 9/16	12 3/16	6 6/16	M	Ontonagon County	MI	Troy A. Martinez	1995	5524
18 9/16	11 15/16	6 10/16	M	Greenbrier County	WV	Donald Dorsey	1995	5524
18 9/16	11 14/16	6 11/16	M	Lincoln County	WI	James H. Dimpfl	1995	5524
18 9/16	11 15/16	6 10/16	M	Kootenai County	ID	Cristina Lafrenz	1996	5524
18 9/16	11 14/16	6 11/16	M	La Corey	ALB	Dawn Ollenberger	1996	5524
18 9/16	11 11/16	6 14/16	M	Athabasca River	ALB	Doy Curtis	1996	5524
18 9/16	11 14/16	6 11/16	M	Shoshone County	ID	Roger Stewart	1996	5524
18 9/16	11 15/16	6 10/16	M	Atikokan	ONT	Hugh McWane	1996	5524
18 9/16	11 8/16	7 1/16	M	Wawang Lake	ONT	Frank Frye	1996	5524
18 9/16	11 14/16	6 11/16	M	Franklin County	ME	Thomas R. Umlauf	1996	5524
18 9/16	11 10/16	6 15/16	M	Grafton County	NH	Jeffrey D. Stout	1996	5524
18 9/16	11 14/16	6 11/16	M	Sawyer County	WI	Gene Dehnhoff	1996	5524
18 9/16	11 13/16	6 12/16	M	Orange County	NY	Joseph W. Talasco	1996	5524
18 9/16	11 11/16	6 14/16	M	Tuolumne County	CA	Jef Lindenmayer	1996	5524
18 9/16	12 0/16	6 9/16	M	High Level	ALB	Tom Russom	1997	5524
18 9/16	11 14/16	6 11/16	M	High Level	ALB	Kevin Drysdale	1997	5524
18 9/16	11 10/16	6 15/16	M	Lac La Ronge	SAS	Steve Hammond	1997	5524
18 9/16	11 13/16	6 12/16	M	Big Sandy Lake	SAS	Duane Reitmeier	1997	5524
18 9/16	11 13/16	6 12/16	M	Montreal River Harbour	ONT	Thomas J. Liguori	1997	5524
18 9/16	11 13/16	6 12/16	M	Yavapai County	AZ	Chris J. Dunn	1997	5524
18 9/16	11 12/16	6 13/16	M	Sandilands	MAN	Russell K. Mehling	1998	5524
18 9/16	11 6/16	7 3/16	M	Carroll Inlet	AK	Larry Daly	1998	5524
18 9/16	11 8/16	7 1/16	M	Ray River	AK	Michael Chadwick	1998	5524
18 9/16	11 15/16	6 10/16	M	Valleyview	ALB	Dale E. Harkins	1998	5524
18 9/16	11 8/16	7 1/16	M	Wawa	ONT	Lynn A. Reed, Jr.	1998	5524
18 9/16	11 8/16	7 1/16	M	Swan Lake	ALB	Derrill Herman	1998	5524
18 9/16	11 7/16	7 2/16	M	Cooper Landing	AK	David Robert Wickline	1998	5524
18 9/16	11 15/16	6 10/16	M	Wabigoon	ONT	Leon R. Meidam	1998	5524
18 9/16	11 11/16	6 14/16	M	Nipawin	SAS	Michael E. Puhl	1998	5524
18 9/16	11 12/16	6 13/16	M	St. Louis County	MN	Ronald Schmidt	1998	5524
18 9/16	11 14/16	6 11/16	M	Carrot River	SAS	Charles M. Heuring	1999	5524
18 9/16	11 14/16	6 11/16	M	Indian River	AK	Kristen Thomas	1999	5524
18 9/16	11 10/16	6 15/16	M	Lampugh	ONT	Gary L. Nunn	1999	5524
18 9/16	11 14/16	6 11/16	M	Oconto County	WI	Patrick J. Gauthier	1999	5524
18 9/16	12 3/16	6 6/16	M	Rappahannock County	VA	Paul Ey	1999	5524
18 9/16	11 12/16	6 13/16	M	Camas County	ID	Hoyt Michener	2000	5524
18 9/16	11 14/16	6 11/16	M	Mattawin	QUE	Jeffrey L. Scott	2000	5524
18 9/16	11 5/16	7 4/16	M	Koochiching County	MN	Jay Taylor	2000	5524
18 9/16	12 6/16	6 3/16	M	Carlton County	MN	Dean Crawford	2000	5524
18 9/16	11 13/16	6 12/16	M	Aitkin County	MN	Rick Stidger	2000	5524
18 9/16	11 15/16	6 10/16	M	Ashland County	WI	Randy D. Oleson	2000	5524
18 9/16	11 6/16	7 3/16	M	Terrace	BC	Bob Ehle	2000	5524
18 9/16	12 3/16	6 6/16	M	Chippewa County	WI	Donald J. Sorensen	2000	5524
18 9/16	11 8/16	7 1/16	M	Vancouver Island	BC	Lou Kindred	2001	5524
18 9/16	11 3/16	7 6/16	M	Moffet	QUE	Robert E. Coyle	2001	5524
18 9/16	11 6/16	7 3/16	M	Clearwater County	ID	R. M. (Dick) Newell	2001	5524
18 9/16	11 13/16	6 12/16	M	Ashland County	WI	Stan W. Janusiewicz	2001	5524
18 9/16	11 13/16	6 12/16	M	Ripple	NBW	Russell Perry	2002	5524
18 9/16	11 11/16	6 14/16	M	High Level	ALB	Mark Murphy	2002	5524
18 9/16	11 6/16	7 3/16	M	Lemhi County	ID	Dan Hooper	2002	5524
18 9/16	11 7/16	7 2/16	M	Kipawa	QUE	John R. Goble	2002	5524
18 9/16	11 11/16	6 14/16	M	Thunder Bay	ONT	Paul E. Korn	2002	5524
18 9/16	12 1/16	6 8/16	M	Pima County	AZ	Rick Forrest	2002	5524
18 9/16	11 8/16	7 1/16	M	Hearst	ONT	Chris Klettke	2002	5524
18 9/16	11 11/16	6 14/16	M	Wild Goose Lake	ONT	Sam M. Derugen, Jr.	2002	5524
18 9/16	12 0/16	6 9/16	M	Gilmer County	GA	Christopher Mazza	2002	5524
18 9/16	12 0/16	6 9/16	M	Missoula County	MT	Aaron Hardy	2002	5524

BLACK BEAR

Minimum Score 18 Continued

SCORE	GREATEST LENGTH	GREATEST WIDTH	SEX	AREA	STATE/ PROVINCE	HUNTER'S NAME	DATE	RANK
18 9/16	11 11/16	6 14/16	M	Plumas County	CA	Sidney D. Kelly	2002	5524
18 9/16	12 2/16	6 7/16	M	Matanuska	AK	Philip C. VanDongen, MD	2003	5524
18 9/16	11 12/16	6 13/16	M	Rollet	QUE	Kevin J. Close	2003	5524
18 9/16	11 9/16	7 0/16	M	Red Lake	ONT	Kenny Storie	2003	5524
18 9/16	11 9/16	7 0/16	M	Rio Arriba County	NM	Mark C. Brown	2003	5524
18 9/16	12 0/16	6 9/16	M	Douglas County	WI	Michael H. Smith	2003	5524
*18 9/16	11 12/16	6 13/16	M	Windsor County	VT	Christopher Perrino	2003	5524
18 9/16	11 13/16	6 12/16	M	Barrhead	ALB	Drew Chalifoux	2004	5524
*18 9/16	11 9/16	7 0/16	M	Fraser River	BC	Teddy J. Roberts	2004	5524
18 9/16	11 14/16	6 11/16	M	Leaf Rapids	MAN	Michael R. Rigazio	2004	5524
18 9/16	11 4/16	7 5/16	M	Long Lake	ALB	J. Michael Wilder	2004	5524
18 9/16	11 6/16	7 3/16	M	Gogama	ONT	Greg LeVan	2004	5524
*18 9/16	11 8/16	7 1/16	M	Webster	ONT	Christopher W. Hare	2004	5524
18 9/16	11 10/16	6 15/16	M	Kake	AK	Mike Gudenschwager	2004	5524
18 9/16	11 12/16	6 13/16	M	San Juan County	UT	Darrin M. Hurdsman	2004	5524
18 9/16	11 12/16	6 13/16	M	Florence County	WI	Peter Hennes	2004	5524
18 9/16	11 7/16	7 2/16	M	Columbia County	WA	Christopher Artz	2004	5524
18 9/16	12 2/16	6 7/16	M	Bissett	MAN	Drew Doornbos	2005	5524
18 9/16	12 0/16	6 9/16	M	Soda Bay	AK	Cameron R. Hanes	2005	5524
18 9/16	12 1/16	6 8/16	M	Olha	MAN	Steve Bryant	2005	5524
18 9/16	11 12/16	6 13/16	M	Leaf Rapids	MAN	Mike Weaver	2005	5524
18 9/16	12 1/16	6 8/16	M	Cordova	AK	Ken Radach	2005	5524
18 9/16	12 0/16	6 9/16	M	Carrot River	SAS	Bruce Shine	2005	5524
18 9/16	11 7/16	7 2/16	M	Piscataquis County	ME	D. Kenneth Kain	2005	5524
18 9/16	11 8/16	7 1/16	M	Rio Arriba County	NM	Gerald T. Dowell	2005	5524
*18 9/16	11 10/16	6 15/16	M	Thessalon	ONT	Joe Weber	2005	5524
18 9/16	11 14/16	6 11/16	M	Clearwater County	ID	Larry A. Welchlen	2006	5524
18 9/16	11 12/16	6 13/16	M	Missinipe	SAS	Keith Lantta	2006	5524
18 9/16	11 12/16	6 13/16	M	Clisby Lake	MAN	Kim B. Engelbert	2006	5524
18 9/16	12 0/16	6 9/16	M	Scott County	AR	Will Beason	2006	5524
18 9/16	12 3/16	6 6/16	M	Swan Plain	SAS	Ralph Alspach	2007	5524
*18 9/16	11 14/16	6 11/16	M	Riding Mtn.	MAN	Gary Howey	2007	5524
*18 9/16	11 7/16	7 2/16	M	La Ronge	SAS	Karey Kroells	2007	5524
*18 9/16	11 11/16	6 14/16	M	Hornepayne	ONT	Michael Budrecki	2007	5524
18 9/16	11 10/16	6 15/16	M	Gathto Creek	BC	Ernie Santana	2007	5524
18 9/16	11 11/16	6 14/16	M	Taylor County	WI	Joseph N. Brenner	2007	5524
18 9/16	11 4/16	7 5/16	M	Boise County	ID	Jeffrey Stevens	2007	5524
18 9/16	11 8/16	7 1/16	M	Berkshire County	MA	Edward Elias	2007	5524
*18 9/16	11 13/16	6 12/16	M	Hard Luck Creek	ALB	Dean Kirkeby	2008	5524
18 9/16	11 7/16	7 2/16	M	Mt. Freemantle	AK	Rick Parish	2008	5524
*18 9/16	11 6/16	7 3/16	M	Washington County	ME	Brian Smith	2008	5524
18 9/16	11 11/16	6 14/16	M	Thompson	MAN	Wade Patrick Wolkart	2008	5524
*18 9/16	11 12/16	6 13/16	M	Pendleton County	WV	Christopher Eric Armentrout	2008	5524
*18 9/16	11 13/16	6 12/16	M	Peace River Breaks	ALB	Dennis Stiklestad	2009	5524
18 9/16	11 9/16	7 0/16	M	McNalley Lake	ALB	Mark Buehrer	2009	5524
*18 9/16	11 6/16	7 3/16	M	Chibougamau	QUE	Russel Howard, Jr.	2009	5524
18 9/16	11 8/16	7 1/16	M	Carleton	NBW	David Adams	2009	5524
18 9/16	11 2/16	7 7/16	M	Baie Comeau	QUE	Paul D'Auteuil	2009	5524
18 9/16	11 12/16	6 13/16	M	Lemhi County	ID	R. Craig Oberle	2010	5524
18 8/16	11 8/16	7 0/16	M	Whatcom County	WA	Jack Fish	1961	5750
18 8/16	11 13/16	6 11/16	M	Prince William Sound	AK	Bob Snelson	1962	5750
18 8/16	11 8/16	7 0/16	M	Iron County	WI	Maynard Peck	1963	5750
18 8/16	11 6/16	7 2/16	M	Clearwater County	ID	Robert J. Kreisher	1965	5750
18 8/16	11 11/16	6 13/16	M	Sapawe	ONT	Dennis Gregory	1967	5750
18 8/16	11 4/16	7 4/16	M	Mineral County	CO	Rod Wintz	1967	5750
18 8/16	11 12/16	6 12/16	M	Siskiyou County	CA	Lyle L. Stroble	1968	5750
18 8/16	11 7/16	7 1/16	M	Franklin County	ME	John Miterko	1970	5750
18 8/16	12 0/16	6 8/16	M	Forest County	WI	Vilas Backhaus	1972	5750
18 8/16	11 4/16	7 4/16	M	Messines	QUE	John W. Redmond	1973	5750
18 8/16	11 10/16	6 14/16	M	Somerset County	ME	John D. Bonargo	1974	5750
18 8/16	11 0/16	7 8/16	M	Messines	QUE	Arthur R. Litschewski	1975	5750
18 8/16	11 7/16	7 1/16	M	La Plata County	CO	Ronald C. Gaines	1975	5750
18 8/16	11 7/16	7 1/16	M	Hopetown	ONT	Dale Bailey	1976	5750
18 8/16	11 6/16	7 2/16	M	Dryden	ONT	Jim Dyer	1977	5750
18 8/16	11 6/16	7 2/16	M	Sioux Narrows	ONT	David Bailey	1978	5750
18 8/16	11 6/16	7 2/16	M	Sandoval County	NM	Johnny R. Trujillo	1978	5750
18 8/16	11 8/16	7 0/16	M	Cook County	MN	Paul Smith	1978	5750
18 8/16	11 4/16	7 4/16	M	Franklin County	ME	John Janelli	1979	5750
18 8/16	11 13/16	6 11/16	M	Lincoln County	WI	James Lechleitner	1981	5750
18 8/16	12 0/16	6 8/16	M	Burnett County	WI	Gary K. Roholt	1981	5750
18 8/16	11 6/16	7 2/16	M	Atikokan	ONT	Larry Stewart	1982	5750
18 8/16	11 12/16	6 12/16	M	Kanabec County	MN	Raymond J. Altman	1982	5750
18 8/16	11 3/16	7 5/16	M	Love	SAS	David M. Tofte	1982	5750
18 8/16	11 10/16	6 14/16	M	Bancroft	ONT	Dean J. Farkas	1982	5750
18 8/16	11 7/16	7 1/16	M	Terrace Bay	ONT	William J. Ernst	1983	5750
18 8/16	11 7/16	7 1/16	M	McAdam	NBW	David Baldwin	1983	5750
18 8/16	12 1/16	6 7/16	M	Ear Falls	ONT	Ernest C. Boser	1983	5750
18 8/16	11 12/16	6 12/16	M	Langlade County	WI	Raymond Juedes	1983	5750
18 8/16	11 11/16	6 13/16	M	Vilas County	WI	Alan L. Black	1983	5750
18 8/16	11 8/16	7 0/16	M	Park County	CO	Larry A. Welchlen	1984	5750
18 8/16	11 2/16	7 6/16	M	Carbon County	WY	Vaughn Cross	1984	5750
18 8/16	11 10/16	6 14/16	M	Swan River	MAN	Kevin Hisey	1984	5750
18 8/16	11 6/16	7 2/16	M	Spokane County	WA	Kenneth R. Wengert	1984	5750
18 8/16	11 11/16	6 13/16	M	Iron County	WI	Gary Johnson	1984	5750
18 8/16	11 9/16	6 15/16	M	Ft. McMurray	ALB	Darrin West	1985	5750
18 8/16	11 12/16	6 12/16	M	Kootenai County	ID	Kenneth R. Wengert	1985	5750
18 8/16	11 7/16	7 1/16	M	Trout Creek	ONT	Gary R. Leonard	1985	5750
18 8/16	11 10/16	6 14/16	M	Susitna River	AK	Roger Stewart	1985	5750
18 8/16	11 9/16	6 15/16	M	Fremont County	ID	Doug Burkman	1985	5750
18 8/16	11 10/16	6 14/16	M	Penobscot County	ME	G. Kent Tableman	1985	5750
18 8/16	11 14/16	6 10/16	M	Shasta County	CA	Larry Walkley	1985	5750
18 8/16	11 6/16	7 2/16	M	Pitkin County	CO	Richard E. Davis	1986	5750
18 8/16	11 4/16	7 4/16	M	Lemhi County	ID	Art Hrabec	1986	5750
18 8/16	11 6/16	7 2/16	M	White River	ONT	Daniel B. Meece	1986	5750
18 8/16	11 11/16	6 13/16	M	St. James Bay	AK	Ronald Callahan	1986	5750

185

BLACK BEAR

Minimum Score 18   Continued

SCORE	GREATEST LENGTH	GREATEST WIDTH	SEX	AREA	STATE/ PROVINCE	HUNTER'S NAME	DATE	RANK
18 8/16	11 5/16	7 3/16	M	Palfrey Lake	NBW	Lou Probo	1986	5750
18 8/16	11 7/16	7 1/16	M	Jones	ONT	Hank Denowski	1986	5750
18 8/16	11 8/16	7 0/16	M	Cook County	MN	Kevin Cook	1986	5750
18 8/16	11 10/16	6 14/16	M	Augusta County	VA	W. Thurman Hensley	1986	5750
18 8/16	12 0/16	6 8/16	M	Siskiyou County	CA	Larry Holmes	1986	5750
18 8/16	11 10/16	6 14/16	M	Rusagonis	NBW	Stephen Buckingham	1987	5750
18 8/16	11 13/16	6 11/16	M	Savant Lake	ONT	Rod Brasel	1987	5750
18 8/16	11 12/16	6 12/16	M	Atikokan	ONT	Dean M. Westby	1987	5750
18 8/16	11 12/16	6 12/16	M	Mine Centre	ONT	Terry Hadd	1987	5750
18 8/16	11 12/16	6 12/16	M	Hartland	NBW	Frank Cinquemani	1987	5750
18 8/16	11 5/16	7 3/16	M	Oliver	BC	A. R. Bryant	1987	5750
18 8/16	11 6/16	7 2/16	M	Caramat	ONT	William M. Long	1987	5750
18 8/16	11 4/16	7 4/16	F	Grassy Narrows	ONT	Mike Jacobs	1987	5750
18 8/16	11 9/16	6 15/16	M	Pennhorwood Township	ONT	Harry A. Weishaar	1987	5750
18 8/16	12 4/16	6 4/16	M	National Mills	MAN	T. J. Kearns	1987	5750
18 8/16	11 9/16	6 15/16	M	Lincoln County	NM	Jon R. Reid	1987	5750
18 8/16	11 13/16	6 11/16	M	Iron County	MI	Andy Holinga	1987	5750
18 8/16	11 11/16	6 13/16	M	Unit 66	SAS	Donald Goracke	1987	5750
18 8/16	11 8/16	7 0/16	M	Dryden	ONT	Tommy M. Brown	1988	5750
18 8/16	12 0/16	6 8/16	M	Wallowa County	OR	William Kevin McCadden	1988	5750
18 8/16	11 14/16	6 10/16	M	Mesa County	CO	Ron A. Stover	1988	5750
18 8/16	11 13/16	6 11/16	M	Houghton County	MI	Daniel Glinn	1988	5750
18 8/16	11 6/16	7 2/16	M	Ravalli County	MT	John Locke	1988	5750
18 8/16	11 6/16	7 2/16	M	Douglas County	OR	Tom E. Tipton	1988	5750
18 8/16	11 11/16	6 13/16	M	Rocky Mountain House	ALB	Andrew Wiese	1989	5750
18 8/16	11 13/16	6 11/16	M	Wapawekka Hills	SAS	Ronald J. Collier	1989	5750
18 8/16	11 12/16	6 12/16	M	Archuleta County	CO	Michael G. Morton	1989	5750
18 8/16	11 1/16	7 7/16	M	Webbwood	ONT	Jim Norris	1989	5750
18 8/16	11 11/16	6 13/16	M	Red Lake	ONT	Donald Tjader	1989	5750
18 8/16	11 14/16	6 10/16	M	Felix	ONT	Scott Trelstad	1989	5750
18 8/16	11 10/16	6 14/16	M	Shining Tree	ONT	Bernard J. Higley	1989	5750
18 8/16	11 10/16	6 14/16	M	Las Animas County	CO	Joe Johnston	1989	5750
18 8/16	11 9/16	6 15/16	M	Baraga County	MI	Randy I Lee	1989	5750
18 8/16	11 12/16	6 12/16	M	Douglas County	OR	Stephen Herrera	1989	5750
18 8/16	11 6/16	7 2/16	M	Atikokan	ONT	Robert M. Jurica	1990	5750
18 8/16	11 8/16	7 0/16	M	Ft. McMurray	ALB	James Pike	1990	5750
18 8/16	11 12/16	6 12/16	M	Peace River	ALB	Roy M. Goodwin	1990	5750
18 8/16	11 9/16	6 15/16	M	Rocky Lake	MAN	Morris McManus	1990	5750
18 8/16	11 9/16	6 15/16	M	Highland Grove	ONT	Bob Capece	1990	5750
18 8/16	11 14/16	6 10/16	M	Doaktown	NBW	Scott E. Komaridis	1990	5750
18 8/16	11 10/16	6 14/16	M	St. Alexis Des Monts	QUE	Mike Hammond	1990	5750
18 8/16	11 15/16	6 9/16	M	Swan River	MAN	Joseph S. Holiday	1990	5750
18 8/16	11 2/16	7 6/16	M	Somerset County	ME	Bob Eisele	1990	5750
18 8/16	11 9/16	6 15/16	M	Shawano County	WI	Ricky R. Kauffman	1990	5750
18 8/16	11 6/16	7 2/16	M	Zec Rapides des Joachins	QUE	Ken Dwyer	1990	5750
18 8/16	11 10/16	6 14/16	M	Graham County	AZ	Dave Bushell	1991	5750
18 8/16	11 14/16	6 10/16	M	Peace River	ALB	Bruce McRae	1991	5750
18 8/16	11 13/16	6 11/16	M	Fawcett	ALB	James W. Thomson	1991	5750
18 8/16	11 8/16	7 0/16	M	Braice Township	ONT	Timothy A. Salisbury	1991	5750
18 8/16	11 10/16	6 14/16	M	Hythe	ALB	Rex Dacus	1991	5750
18 8/16	11 9/16	6 15/16	M	Brown Bear Lake	ONT	Mark Kayser	1991	5750
18 8/16	11 15/16	6 9/16	M	Lewis County	WA	Wayne A. Grasseth	1991	5750
18 8/16	11 10/16	6 14/16	M	Grand County	UT	Pat Snyder	1991	5750
18 8/16	11 14/16	6 10/16	M	Sioux Lookout	ONT	John Shields	1991	5750
18 8/16	11 14/16	6 10/16	M	Doaktown	NBW	George Louis	1991	5750
18 8/16	11 14/16	6 10/16	M	Remigny	QUE	Tom Mundy	1991	5750
18 8/16	11 4/16	7 4/16	M	Ear Falls	ONT	Steve Jancar	1991	5750
18 8/16	11 12/16	6 12/16	M	Pine County	MN	Brandon R. Johnson	1991	5750
18 8/16	11 6/16	7 2/16	M	Forest County	WI	Steven W. Kluth	1991	5750
18 8/16	11 8/16	7 0/16	M	Linn County	OR	Rick Kopf	1991	5750
18 8/16	11 5/16	7 3/16	M	Pelican Lake	MAN	Douglas R. Buchler	1992	5750
18 8/16	11 14/16	6 10/16	M	Cold Lake	ALB	Ron Dixon	1992	5750
18 8/16	11 12/16	6 12/16	M	Barrier Lake	SAS	Ray Fredin	1992	5750
18 8/16	11 12/16	6 12/16	M	Tanana Flats	AK	Tommy L. Ramsey	1992	5750
18 8/16	11 14/16	6 10/16	M	Fisher Branch	MAN	Fred W. Lambley	1992	5750
18 8/16	11 9/16	6 15/16	M	Wabigoon	ONT	Charles Drerup	1992	5750
18 8/16	11 8/16	7 0/16	M	Cochrane	ONT	Stephen Ferris	1992	5750
18 8/16	11 4/16	7 4/16	M	Blind River	ONT	Argene Miracle, Jr.	1992	5750
18 8/16	11 9/16	6 15/16	M	Klamath County	OR	Ronald Aubry	1992	5750
18 8/16	11 5/16	7 3/16	M	Custer County	ID	Darrell Nunez	1993	5750
18 8/16	11 6/16	7 2/16	M	Aulneau Peninsula	ONT	Michael Koska	1993	5750
18 8/16	11 10/16	7 8/16	M	Christopher Lake	SAS	Harold Alka	1993	5750
18 8/16	11 10/16	6 14/16	M	Armstrong	ONT	Jerome D. Larson	1993	5750
18 8/16	12 0/16	6 8/16	M	Arntfield	QUE	Ken H. Taylor	1993	5750
18 8/16	12 2/16	6 6/16	M	Pine County	MN	Adam Flod	1993	5750
18 8/16	11 14/16	6 10/16	M	Baraga County	MI	Pat Barnett	1993	5750
18 8/16	11 11/16	6 13/16	M	Trinity County	CA	Michael R. Geller	1993	5750
18 8/16	12 0/16	6 8/16	M	Carrot River	SAS	Luke M. Fischer	1994	5750
18 8/16	11 5/16	7 3/16	M	Wapawekka Lake	SAS	Jerry Bowen	1994	5750
18 8/16	11 9/16	6 15/16	M	Patuanak	SAS	M. Robert DeLaney	1994	5750
18 8/16	11 10/16	6 14/16	M	Sioux Lookout	ONT	Gregory G. Henan	1994	5750
18 8/16	11 12/16	6 12/16	M	Rossburn	MAN	Barry Minshull	1994	5750
18 8/16	11 10/16	6 14/16	M	Dryden	ONT	Mark Kendrick Williams	1994	5750
18 8/16	11 12/16	6 12/16	M	Sawyer County	WI	Jay Girard	1994	5750
18 8/16	11 12/16	6 12/16	M	Ontonagon County	MI	David A. Kasten	1994	5750
18 8/16	11 13/16	6 11/16	M	Burnett County	WI	Tom McAlpine	1994	5750
18 8/16	11 8/16	7 0/16	M	Fredericton	NBW	Tony DeMase	1994	5750
18 8/16	12 0/16	6 8/16	M	Lane County	OR	Gary Nyden	1994	5750
18 8/16	11 6/16	7 2/16	M	Mac Millan River	YUK	Ed DeYoung	1995	5750
18 8/16	11 6/16	7 2/16	M	Poplarfield	MAN	Larry L. Helgerson	1995	5750
18 8/16	11 6/16	7 2/16	M	Prince of Wales Island	AK	Garry A. Thoms	1995	5750
18 8/16	11 15/16	6 9/16	M	Mistatim	SAS	John David Bryant	1995	5750
18 8/16	11 5/16	7 3/16	M	Kearl Lake	ALB	Kenneth Hinke	1995	5750
18 8/16	11 8/16	7 0/16	M	Thessalon	ONT	William Fry	1995	5750
18 8/16	11 1/16	7 7/16	M	Searchmont	ONT	Edward Pylman	1995	5750

BLACK BEAR

Minimum Score 18   Continued

SCORE	GREATEST LENGTH	GREATEST WIDTH	SEX	AREA	STATE/ PROVINCE	HUNTER'S NAME	DATE	RANK
18 8/16	11 14/16	6 10/16	M	Wawa	ONT	James J. Borg	1995	5750
18 8/16	11 6/16	7 2/16	M	Kitsap County	WA	Roy L. Schultz	1995	5750
18 8/16	11 8/16	7 0/16	M	Somerset County	ME	David Bilotti	1995	5750
18 8/16	12 0/16	6 8/16	M	Pine County	MN	Scott Ketchmark	1995	5750
18 8/16	11 9/16	6 15/16	M	Dryden	ONT	Brian Kendall	1995	5750
18 8/16	12 0/16	6 8/16	M	Crook County	OR	Jim Merrill	1995	5750
18 8/16	11 8/16	7 0/16	M	Oneida County	WI	Richard A. Klassa	1995	5750
18 8/16	11 14/16	6 10/16	M	Big Sandy Lake	SAS	Gale Olsen	1996	5750
18 8/16	11 8/16	7 0/16	M	English River	ONT	Paul Cox	1996	5750
18 8/16	11 4/16	7 4/16	M	Matheson	ONT	Dr. Anthony Marrara	1996	5750
18 8/16	11 10/16	6 14/16	M	Indian River	AK	Rick Schikora	1996	5750
18 8/16	11 8/16	7 0/16	M	Rimouski	QUE	Chris Noack	1996	5750
18 8/16	11 14/16	6 10/16	M	Mistinibi Lake	QUE	Bruno Martel	1996	5750
18 8/16	12 0/16	6 8/16	M	Polk County	WI	William Didlo	1996	5750
18 8/16	11 13/16	6 11/16	M	Price County	WI	David J. Kerkove	1996	5750
18 8/16	11 14/16	6 10/16	M	Buffalo Narrows	SAS	Randy A. Shobe	1997	5750
18 8/16	11 11/16	6 13/16	M	Pelican Lake	MAN	Kent George	1997	5750
18 8/16	11 13/16	6 11/16	M	Love	SAS	Bruce Ott	1997	5750
18 8/16	11 14/16	6 10/16	M	Chapleau	ONT	Thomas LaCombe	1997	5750
18 8/16	11 11/16	6 13/16	M	St. Mary's River	BC	Robert Faiers	1997	5750
18 8/16	11 12/16	6 12/16	M	Shoshone County	ID	Roger Stewart	1997	5750
18 8/16	11 8/16	7 0/16	M	Mattice	ONT	Myron E. Jochmann	1997	5750
18 8/16	11 12/16	6 12/16	M	Teton County	ID	Thomas Thiel	1997	5750
18 8/16	11 10/16	6 14/16	M	Doaktown	NBW	Morris W. Shreves	1997	5750
18 8/16	11 3/16	7 5/16	M	Cartier	ONT	Vernon Sowers	1997	5750
18 8/16	11 8/16	7 0/16	M	La Tuque	QUE	John Mange, Jr.	1997	5750
18 8/16	11 13/16	6 11/16	M	Lenswood	MAN	Darren Diederich	1997	5750
18 8/16	11 10/16	6 14/16	M	Grant County	WV	Jimmy Lucas, Jr.	1997	5750
18 8/16	11 9/16	6 15/16	M	Athabasca River	ALB	Gene Mathias	1998	5750
18 8/16	11 11/16	6 13/16	M	Hornepayne	ONT	Brian Stiglich	1998	5750
18 8/16	11 12/16	6 12/16	M	Tulliby Lake	ALB	Larry Flaata	1998	5750
18 8/16	11 9/16	6 15/16	M	Ile-a-La-Crosse	SAS	Drew McCartney	1998	5750
18 8/16	11 12/16	6 12/16	F	Calling Lake	ALB	Robert L. Read	1998	5750
18 8/16	11 9/16	6 15/16	M	Marathon	ONT	Robert Zabavski	1998	5750
18 8/16	11 8/16	7 0/16	M	Savant Lake	ONT	Lee Nelms	1998	5750
18 8/16	11 5/16	7 3/16	M	Lac Barriere	QUE	Dan Lindsey	1998	5750
18 8/16	11 4/16	7 4/16	M	Tulare County	CA	James A. Jacoby	1998	5750
18 8/16	11 9/16	6 15/16	M	St. Louis County	MN	Keith McCarty	1998	5750
18 8/16	11 11/16	6 13/16	M	Itasca County	MN	Kory Michalke	1998	5750
18 8/16	11 10/16	6 14/16	M	Piscataquis County	ME	Steven C. Gatling	1998	5750
18 8/16	11 15/16	6 9/16	M	Bayfield County	WI	Bob Ross	1998	5750
18 8/16	11 15/16	6 9/16	M	Bayfield County	WI	Bruce Zuehlke	1998	5750
18 8/16	11 7/16	7 1/16	M	Montreal Lake	SAS	Edward X. Thompson	1999	5750
18 8/16	11 10/16	6 14/16	M	Black Current Lake	MAN	Paul Davidson	1999	5750
18 8/16	11 5/16	7 3/16	M	Lynn Lake	MAN	James Thomas Schmitz	1999	5750
18 8/16	11 7/16	7 1/16	M	Val-d'Or	QUE	William Medeiros, Jr.	1999	5750
18 8/16	11 12/16	6 12/16	M	Duck Mtn.	SAS	Ron Vandermeulen	1999	5750
18 8/16	11 8/16	7 0/16	M	Idaho County	ID	K-Tal Johnson	1999	5750
18 8/16	11 5/16	7 3/16	M	St-Michel-des-Saints	QUE	Walt Guthrie	1999	5750
18 8/16	11 4/16	7 4/16	M	Aroostook County	ME	Thomas J. Dussault	1999	5750
18 8/16	11 13/16	6 11/16	M	Gunnison County	CO	Rex Droessler	1999	5750
18 8/16	11 7/16	7 1/16	M	Hornepayne	ONT	Dan DelBarba	1999	5750
18 8/16	11 12/16	6 12/16	M	Price County	WI	Troy Tiber	1999	5750
18 8/16	11 14/16	6 10/16	M	Fishing Lake	ALB	Marc Johnson	2000	5750
18 8/16	11 13/16	6 11/16	M	Bronson Lake	SAS	Frank Czyzewski	2000	5750
18 8/16	11 13/16	6 11/16	M	Carrot River	SAS	Gregory White	2000	5750
18 8/16	11 9/16	6 15/16	M	Christopher Lake	SAS	T. Keith Lamar	2000	5750
18 8/16	11 15/16	6 9/16	M	Buffalo Narrows	SAS	Eric F. Efird	2000	5750
18 8/16	11 13/16	6 11/16	M	Elbow Lake	MAN	Frank A. Stringer	2000	5750
18 8/16	11 5/16	7 3/16	M	Franklin County	ME	James Martin	2000	5750
18 8/16	11 14/16	6 10/16	M	Chippewa County	WI	Thomas R. Budick	2000	5750
18 8/16	11 10/16	6 14/16	M	Idaho County	ID	Michael Schnider	2000	5750
18 8/16	11 6/16	7 2/16	M	Chittenden County	VT	Ray Ingham	2000	5750
18 8/16	11 10/16	6 14/16	M	Slave River	ALB	John MacPeak	2001	5750
18 8/16	11 0/16	7 8/16	M	Beluga	AK	Gene Hopkins	2001	5750
18 8/16	11 8/16	7 0/16	M	Forestville	QUE	Timothy A. Mitchell	2001	5750
18 8/16	11 8/16	7 0/16	M	Otter Lake	QUE	Matt E. Swain	2001	5750
18 8/16	11 12/16	6 12/16	M	Elk Lake	ONT	John Henrich	2001	5750
18 8/16	11 10/16	6 14/16	M	Redditt	ONT	Ronald M. Pohlman, Jr.	2001	5750
18 8/16	11 5/16	7 3/16	M	Herkimer County	NY	Jeff Nadeau	2001	5750
18 8/16	11 10/16	6 14/16	M	Carrot River	SAS	Kenneth Musgrove	2002	5750
18 8/16	11 12/16	6 12/16	M	Athabasca River	ALB	Paul Esch	2002	5750
18 8/16	11 13/16	6 11/16	M	Lost Dog Creek	BC	Allan Atwood	2002	5750
18 8/16	11 11/16	6 13/16	M	Andrew Lake	ALB	Kevin A. Speicher	2002	5750
18 8/16	11 10/16	6 14/16	M	Athabasca River	ALB	Ron Maguire	2002	5750
18 8/16	11 11/16	6 13/16	M	Smeaton	SAS	Gene A. Welle	2002	5750
18 8/16	11 10/16	6 14/16	M	Gander	NFL	Paul D. Clayton II	2002	5750
18 8/16	11 14/16	6 10/16	M	Idaho County	ID	Sam Wells	2002	5750
18 8/16	12 1/16	6 7/16	M	Beltrami County	MN	Robert Heimer	2002	5750
18 8/16	11 8/16	7 0/16	M	Piscataquis County	ME	Daniel E. Geibel	2002	5750
18 8/16	11 13/16	6 11/16	M	Cormorant Lake	MAN	Jeremy Graber	2002	5750
18 8/16	11 4/16	7 4/16	M	Perry County	AR	Jeffrey J. Kaluza	2002	5750
18 8/16	11 14/16	6 10/16	M	Benewah County	ID	Brian Woster	2003	5750
18 8/16	11 10/16	6 14/16	M	Snow Lake	MAN	Bob Naumann	2003	5750
18 8/16	11 14/16	6 10/16	M	Piney	MAN	Dale L. Stiebs	2003	5750
18 8/16	11 12/16	6 12/16	M	St. Isadore	ALB	Peter F. Woeck II	2003	5750
18 8/16	12 2/16	6 6/16	M	Frazier River	BC	David Mitchell	2003	5750
18 8/16	11 3/16	7 5/16	M	Lac Rock	QUE	Richard Healey	2003	5750
18 8/16	11 8/16	7 0/16	M	Costigan Lake	SAS	Reginald E. Faber, Jr.	2003	5750
18 8/16	11 10/16	6 14/16	M	Eagle Lake	CO	Tony W. Cleveland	2003	5750
18 8/16	11 12/16	6 12/16	M	Marathon County	WI	James D. Churchill	2003	5750
18 8/16	11 12/16	6 12/16	M	Marinette County	WI	James R. Vickman	2003	5750
18 8/16	11 7/16	7 1/16	F	Bayfield County	WI	Dale Krajenka, Jr.	2003	5750
18 8/16	11 13/16	6 11/16	M	Ashland County	WI	Todd C. Koelzer	2003	5750
18 8/16	11 10/16	6 14/16	M	La Corey	ALB	Matthew G. Strueby	2004	5750

187

BLACK BEAR

Minimum Score 18 — Continued

SCORE	GREATEST LENGTH	GREATEST WIDTH	SEX	AREA	STATE/ PROVINCE	HUNTER'S NAME	DATE	RANK
18 8/16	11 5/16	7 3/16	M	Vancouver Island	BC	Derek Gentile	2004	5750
*18 8/16	11 9/16	6 15/16	M	Reserve Rimouski	QUE	Raynald Groleau	2004	5750
18 8/16	11 12/16	6 12/16	M	Aroostook County	ME	William J. Langer	2004	5750
18 8/16	12 1/16	6 7/16	M	Orange County	NY	Richard Powles	2004	5750
18 8/16	11 9/16	6 15/16	M	Flatbush	ALB	Don Dvoroznak	2005	5750
18 8/16	11 12/16	6 12/16	M	Valley County	ID	Chris Reichert	2005	5750
18 8/16	12 0/16	6 8/16	M	Lesser Slave Lake	ALB	Gene Welle	2005	5750
18 8/16	11 12/16	6 12/16	M	Teton County	WY	Ronell Skinner	2005	5750
18 8/16	11 5/16	7 3/16	M	Clearwater County	ID	Richard M. Newell	2005	5750
18 8/16	12 0/16	6 8/16	M	Stevens County	WA	James P. Morgan	2005	5750
18 8/16	11 11/16	6 13/16	M	Kenora	ONT	Roger Hoefs	2005	5750
*18 8/16	11 14/16	6 10/16	M	St. Louis County	MN	Jeremiah S. Dietrich	2005	5750
18 8/16	12 2/16	6 6/16	M	Clearwater County	MN	Josh Mendenhall	2005	5750
18 8/16	11 13/16	6 11/16	M	Logan County	AR	James Waid	2005	5750
18 8/16	12 1/16	6 7/16	M	Cass County	MN	Bill Blevins	2005	5750
18 8/16	12 0/16	6 8/16	M	Ashland County	WI	James Hoppe	2005	5750
18 8/16	11 12/16	6 12/16	M	Wythe County	VA	Eldridge G. Delby, Jr.	2005	5750
18 8/16	11 10/16	6 14/16	M	Campbell River	BC	John Duggan	2006	5750
*18 8/16	11 14/16	6 10/16	M	Deschambault Lake	SAS	Svein Hostad	2006	5750
*18 8/16	12 0/16	6 8/16	M	Saddle Hills	ALB	Dale M. Tarleton	2006	5750
18 8/16	11 10/16	6 14/16	M	Lake Wasekamio	SAS	Ramon Neil Bell	2006	5750
18 8/16	11 8/16	7 0/16	M	Christopher Lake	SAS	Sam Brandriet	2006	5750
*18 8/16	11 7/16	7 1/16	M	Prince of Wales Island	AK	Tom Alvin	2006	5750
18 8/16	11 10/16	6 14/16	M	Sioux Lookout	ONT	Mark J. McCartney	2006	5750
18 8/16	11 9/16	6 15/16	M	Jellicoe	ONT	Bob Kostecki	2006	5750
*18 8/16	11 12/16	6 12/16	M	Florence County	WI	Tal Goodchild	2006	5750
18 8/16	11 12/16	6 12/16	M	Kenora	ONT	Thomas Filipiak	2006	5750
18 8/16	12 1/16	6 7/16	M	Pelly	SAS	Matt Guedes	2006	5750
*18 8/16	11 6/16	7 2/16	M	Seward	AK	James A. Thiel	2007	5750
18 8/16	11 13/16	6 11/16	M	West Hawk Lake	MAN	Shawn Domaszek	2007	5750
18 8/16	11 11/16	6 13/16	M	Buffalo Narrows	SAS	T. Brent Conner	2007	5750
18 8/16	11 9/16	6 15/16	M	Place Lake	BC	Allan Tew	2007	5750
18 8/16	11 12/16	6 12/16	M	La Plata County	CO	Steven J. Vittetow	2007	5750
18 8/16	11 15/16	6 9/16	M	Menominee County	MI	Anthony Newlin	2007	5750
18 8/16	11 8/16	7 0/16	M	Lake County	MT	Steve Bradstreet	2007	5750
18 8/16	11 13/16	6 11/16	M	Winnipegosis	MAN	Rohn Jack Findlay	2008	5750
18 8/16	11 8/16	7 0/16	M	File Lake	MAN	Randy E. Doyle	2008	5750
*18 8/16	11 12/16	6 12/16	M	Spirit River	ALB	Jordan R. Hach	2008	5750
18 8/16	11 9/16	6 15/16	M	Barry's Bay	ONT	Bill Barling	2008	5750
18 8/16	11 11/16	6 13/16	M	Chugiak	AK	Rick Helton	2009	5750
18 8/16	12 0/16	6 8/16	F	Hudson Bay	SAS	R. C. Peters	2009	5750
*18 8/16	11 8/16	7 0/16	M	Val-d'Or	QUE	James Stockweather	2009	5750
18 8/16	11 9/16	6 15/16	M	La Tuque	QUE	Jeff Springer	2009	5750
*18 8/16	11 12/16	6 12/16	M	Baie Comeau	QUE	Tim O'Leary	2009	5750
18 8/16	11 15/16	6 9/16	M	Nictau	NBW	Debra L. Sidwell	2009	5750
18 8/16	11 14/16	6 10/16	M	Josephine Creek	ALB	Helen Popson	2010	5750
18 8/16	11 15/16	6 9/16	M	Sandilands	MAN	Murray Penner	2010	5750
*18 8/16	11 13/16	6 11/16	F	Kelvington	SAS	Tom Mooi	2010	5750
18 8/16	11 5/16	7 3/16	M	Teton County	WY	Ronell Skinner	2010	5750
18 7/16	11 11/16	6 12/16	M	Oneida County	WI	Tim Johnson	1967	6035
18 7/16	11 5/16	7 2/16	M	Franklin County	ME	Ed Hall	1968	6035
18 7/16	11 8/16	6 15/16	M	Piscataquis County	ME	John Kuhar	1975	6035
18 7/16	11 11/16	6 12/16	M	Larimer County	CO	Ronald M. Breitsprecher	1975	6035
18 7/16	11 9/16	6 14/16	M	Clearwater County	ID	Edward Russell	1976	6035
18 7/16	11 13/16	6 10/16	M	Albemarle County	VA	J. C. Locke	1976	6035
18 7/16	11 12/16	6 11/16	M	Cass County	MN	Walter L. Lash	1976	6035
18 7/16	11 11/16	6 12/16	M	Atikokan	ONT	John Carlson	1977	6035
18 7/16	11 9/16	6 14/16	M	Lake County	MN	W. Dan Williams, Jr.	1977	6035
18 7/16	11 7/16	7 0/16	M	English Bay	AK	Roger Stewart	1978	6035
18 7/16	12 1/16	6 6/16	M	Iron County	WI	Douglas R. Parrott	1979	6035
18 7/16	11 1/16	7 6/16	M	Phelps Township	ONT	Robert C. Precious	1979	6035
18 7/16	11 6/16	7 1/16	M	Meagher County	MT	Gary H. Thompson	1980	6035
18 7/16	11 9/16	6 14/16	M	Franklin County	ME	Bob Spano	1980	6035
18 7/16	11 10/16	6 13/16	M	Almonte	ONT	Thomas S. Gerstner	1980	6035
18 7/16	11 12/16	6 11/16	M	Beluga	AK	Tom Atkins	1981	6035
18 7/16	11 4/16	7 3/16	M	El Paso County	CO	Max Tallent	1981	6035
18 7/16	11 15/16	6 8/16	M	Archuleta County	CO	James P. Mitchell	1982	6035
18 7/16	11 8/16	6 15/16	M	Kenora	ONT	Floyd McDanell	1982	6035
18 7/16	11 10/16	6 13/16	M		ONT	Bill Stonebraker	1982	6035
18 7/16	11 12/16	6 11/16	M	Sierra County	NM	James N. Amlong, Jr.	1983	6035
18 7/16	11 10/16	6 13/16	M	Kirkland Lake	ONT	Michael Hogan	1983	6035
18 7/16	11 7/16	7 0/16	M	Nipigon	ONT	Wayne Beltz, Jr.	1983	6035
18 7/16	11 9/16	6 14/16	M	Timmins	ONT	Paul Eldridge	1983	6035
18 7/16	11 10/16	6 13/16	M	Tatalina River	AK	Timothy J. Barber	1983	6035
18 7/16	11 6/16	7 1/16	M	Clackamas County	OR	Robert L. Smitherman	1983	6035
18 7/16	11 14/16	6 9/16	M	Pine County	MN	Alan C. Porter	1983	6035
18 7/16	11 9/16	6 14/16	M	Sudbury	ONT	Terry William Polkinghorne	1984	6035
18 7/16	11 1/16	7 6/16	M	Sioux Lookout	ONT	Steve Sherry	1984	6035
18 7/16	11 9/16	6 14/16	M	Skeleton Lake	ALB	Dwayne Alton	1984	6035
18 7/16	11 8/16	6 15/16	M	Devlin	ONT	Jim Leqve	1984	6035
18 7/16	11 11/16	6 12/16	M	Luce County	MI	Terry L. Cook	1984	6035
18 7/16	11 13/16	6 10/16	M	Marquette County	MI	Randy Clark	1984	6035
18 7/16	11 2/16	7 5/16	M	Lemhi County	ID	Dennis Derrer	1985	6035
18 7/16	11 7/16	7 0/16	M	Kenora	ONT	Steven Duerksen	1985	6035
18 7/16	11 2/16	7 5/16	M	Adams County	ID	Rick Clinton	1985	6035
18 7/16	11 13/16	6 10/16	M	Las Animas County	CO	Kelly Williams	1985	6035
18 7/16	11 9/16	6 14/16	M	Douglas County	OR	Jim Nielsen	1985	6035
18 7/16	11 7/16	7 0/16	M	Gallatin County	MT	Terry L. Anderson	1985	6035
18 7/16	11 9/16	6 14/16	M	Mine Centre	ONT	Bob Roulet	1986	6035
18 7/16	11 10/16	6 13/16	M	Emo	ONT	Bruce Eggenberger	1986	6035
18 7/16	11 12/16	6 11/16	M	Savant Lake	ONT	Daniel J. Gartner	1986	6035
18 7/16	11 9/16	6 14/16	F	Smith	ALB	Dave Gerber	1986	6035
18 7/16	12 0/16	6 7/16	M	Porcupine Plain	SAS	Peter Reimer	1987	6035
18 7/16	11 5/16	7 2/16	M	Perrault Falls	ONT	Larry Gohlke	1987	6035
18 7/16	11 7/16	7 0/16	M	Thunder Bay	ONT	Larry H. Hoyt	1987	6035

188

BLACK BEAR

Minimum Score 18 — Continued

SCORE	GREATEST LENGTH	GREATEST WIDTH	SEX	AREA	STATE/PROVINCE	HUNTER'S NAME	DATE	RANK
18 7/16	11 11/16	6 12/16	M	Victoria County	ONT	William H. Guile	1987	6035
18 7/16	11 9/16	6 14/16	M	Dryden	ONT	Richard E. Kohles	1987	6035
18 7/16	11 8/16	6 15/16	M	Halfway River	BC	Dave Hannas	1987	6035
18 7/16	11 7/16	7 0/16	M	Highland Valley	BC	Kenneth A. Brown	1987	6035
18 7/16	11 9/16	6 14/16	M	Chelmsford	ONT	Bernard Langhorne	1987	6035
18 7/16	11 7/16	7 0/16	M	Manitouwadge	ONT	Robert Mitchell	1988	6035
18 7/16	11 13/16	6 10/16	M	Ft. McMurray	ALB	James Pike	1988	6035
18 7/16	11 7/16	7 0/16	M	Geraldton	ONT	Gary E. Mayle	1988	6035
18 7/16	11 10/16	6 13/16	M	Kootenai County	ID	Linda Leake	1988	6035
18 7/16	11 11/16	6 12/16	M	Sublette County	WY	Keith Dana	1988	6035
18 7/16	11 11/16	6 12/16	M	Susitna River	AK	Dave Hyrb	1988	6035
18 7/16	11 12/16	6 11/16	M	King County	WA	David A. Emery	1988	6035
18 7/16	11 10/16	6 13/16	M	Somerset County	ME	David James Obuchowski	1988	6035
18 7/16	11 10/16	6 13/16	M	Kenora	ONT	Joe Devlin	1989	6035
18 7/16	11 15/16	6 8/16	M	Zec Restigo	QUE	Joseph Sabo	1989	6035
18 7/16	11 13/16	6 10/16	M	King County	WA	Clint W. Powell	1989	6035
18 7/16	11 4/16	7 3/16	M	Wawa	ONT	Michael J. Klaeser	1989	6035
18 7/16	11 9/16	6 14/16	M	Esther Island	AK	Tim Fritzler	1989	6035
18 7/16	11 10/16	6 13/16	M	Jefferson County	WA	Wayne Haag	1989	6035
18 7/16	12 1/16	6 6/16	M	Sawyer County	WI	John H. Henriksen	1989	6035
18 7/16	11 11/16	6 12/16	M	Belleterre	QUE	Terry Gaudlip	1990	6035
18 7/16	11 9/16	6 14/16	M	Ft. McMurray	ALB	Floyd Forster	1990	6035
18 7/16	11 11/16	6 12/16	M	Lincoln County	WY	John Trout, Jr.	1990	6035
18 7/16	11 4/16	7 3/16	M	Rollet	QUE	Claude St' Amour	1990	6035
18 7/16	11 12/16	6 11/16	M	Cumberland House	SAS	Mike Lewandowski	1991	6035
18 7/16	11 6/16	7 1/16	M	Latah County	ID	Daniel D. Davenport	1991	6035
18 7/16	11 10/16	6 13/16	M	La Ronge	SAS	Brian Hummel	1991	6035
18 7/16	11 6/16	7 1/16	M	Caramat	ONT	Kelly Russell	1991	6035
18 7/16	11 8/16	6 15/16	M	Moon Beam	ONT	John Meyers	1991	6035
18 7/16	11 11/16	6 12/16	M	Terrace Bay	ONT	Greg Huffman	1991	6035
18 7/16	11 3/16	7 4/16	M	Zec Dumoine	QUE	Joseph Arkuszeski	1991	6035
18 7/16	11 13/16	6 10/16	M	Lake of the Woods	ONT	Bob Wickler	1991	6035
18 7/16	11 11/16	6 12/16	M	Livengood	AK	Todd A. Wolf	1991	6035
18 7/16	11 12/16	6 11/16	M	Idaho County	ID	Dan Hiltz	1991	6035
18 7/16	11 13/16	6 10/16	M	Carbon County	WY	Damon Handley	1991	6035
18 7/16	11 9/16	6 14/16	M	Temiscaming	QUE	Louis Seville	1991	6035
18 7/16	11 9/16	6 14/16	M	Delta County	MI	James S. Stankowski	1991	6035
18 7/16	11 12/16	6 11/16	M	Houghton County	MI	Tony E. La Pratt	1991	6035
18 7/16	11 8/16	6 15/16	M	Spirit River	ALB	Paul Deme	1992	6035
18 7/16	11 2/16	7 5/16	M	Sudbury	ONT	Phillip Wilkinson	1992	6035
18 7/16	11 10/16	6 13/16	M	Fort McMurray	ALB	Jon P. Thomas	1992	6035
18 7/16	11 6/16	7 1/16	M	Lane County	OR	Charles A. Noe	1992	6035
18 7/16	11 8/16	6 15/16	M	Piscataquis County	ME	Robert G. Poth	1992	6035
18 7/16	11 8/16	6 15/16	M	Nemegauche	ONT	Lawrence Lee Wilbur	1992	6035
18 7/16	11 6/16	7 1/16	M	Wallowa County	OR	Thompson Holmes	1992	6035
18 7/16	11 12/16	6 11/16	M	Thunder Bay	ONT	Harry Domask	1993	6035
18 7/16	11 11/16	6 12/16	M	Chinchaga River	ALB	Patrick R. Cahill	1993	6035
18 7/16	11 11/16	6 12/16	M	Shorty Creek	AK	Roy Bartlett	1993	6035
18 7/16	11 5/16	7 2/16	M	Armstrong	ONT	Dianne Daniels	1993	6035
18 7/16	11 12/16	6 11/16	M	King County	WA	Garn J. Kennedy	1993	6035
18 7/16	11 10/16	6 13/16	M	St. Louis County	MN	Jeff P. Peterson	1993	6035
18 7/16	11 10/16	6 13/16	M	Caribou County	ID	Greg Blotter	1993	6035
18 7/16	11 9/16	6 14/16	M	Nevada County	CA	Gerald E. Boelens	1993	6035
18 7/16	11 10/16	6 13/16	M	Emo	ONT	Paul Kolbeck	1994	6035
18 7/16	11 14/16	6 9/16	M	Carrot River	SAS	Mark P. Wagner	1994	6035
18 7/16	11 9/16	6 14/16	M	Lac Ile-a-la-Crosse	SAS	Dewayne Mullins	1994	6035
18 7/16	11 10/16	6 13/16	M	Nestor Falls	ONT	Mark D. Bonneville	1994	6035
18 7/16	11 10/16	6 13/16	M	Carrot River	SAS	Jan P. Herzfeldt	1994	6035
18 7/16	11 15/16	6 8/16	M	Wabigoon	ONT	Sean M. Sarge	1994	6035
18 7/16	11 10/16	6 13/16	M	Zec Labrieville	QUE	Ken H. Taylor	1994	6035
18 7/16	11 11/16	6 12/16	M	Carlton County	MN	Eric Halverson	1994	6035
18 7/16	11 13/16	6 10/16	M	Cook County	MN	Dale R. Goodman	1994	6035
18 7/16	11 9/16	6 14/16	M	St. Louis County	MN	Daniel J. Weiss	1994	6035
18 7/16	11 14/16	6 9/16	M	Catron County	NM	Adrian P. Lucero	1994	6035
18 7/16	12 0/16	6 7/16	M	Rio Arriba County	NM	Nick Seifert	1994	6035
18 7/16	11 13/16	6 10/16	M	Carroll County	NH	Billy Jack Smith	1994	6035
18 7/16	11 5/16	7 2/16	M	Carroll County	NH	Paul Keyes	1994	6035
18 7/16	11 15/16	6 8/16	M	Goat River	BC	Ken Taylor	1995	6035
18 7/16	11 3/16	7 4/16	M	Mountainview	ALB	Bill Van Buskirk	1995	6035
18 7/16	12 1/16	6 6/16	M	Hudson Bay	SAS	Norma J. Weikert	1995	6035
18 7/16	11 8/16	6 15/16	M	Gowganda	ONT	Bruce Fair	1995	6035
18 7/16	11 12/16	6 11/16	M	Fredericton	NBW	Ronald Larsen	1995	6035
18 7/16	11 6/16	7 1/16	M	Dryden	ONT	Michael A. Lago	1995	6035
18 7/16	11 15/16	6 8/16	M	Lanark	ONT	Dave Glithero	1995	6035
18 7/16	11 5/16	7 2/16	M	Zec Capitachouane	QUE	Ken H. Taylor	1995	6035
18 7/16	11 9/16	6 14/16	M	Redditt	ONT	Bret A. Mattice	1995	6035
18 7/16	11 12/16	6 11/16	M	Kern County	CA	Larry Quary	1995	6035
18 7/16	11 8/16	6 15/16	M	Muldrew Lake	ONT	Jim Latour	1995	6035
18 7/16	12 0/16	6 7/16	M	San Juan County	UT	Kurt Wood	1995	6035
18 7/16	11 10/16	6 13/16	M	Chilako River	BC	Geoff Will	1996	6035
18 7/16	11 10/16	6 13/16	M	Kaministiquia	ONT	La Moine Dohms	1996	6035
18 7/16	11 7/16	7 0/16	M	Lac Leivesque	QUE	Laurier Therrien	1996	6035
18 7/16	11 9/16	6 14/16	M	Swan River	MAN	Russell A. Nichols	1996	6035
18 7/16	11 7/16	7 0/16	M	Thompson	MAN	Carm Bongiovanni	1996	6035
18 7/16	11 6/16	7 1/16	M	Dinorwic	ONT	Dick Schuette	1996	6035
18 7/16	11 5/16	7 2/16	M	Stewiacke	NS	Jason M. Van Hillo	1996	6035
18 7/16	11 14/16	6 9/16	M	Ranger Lake	ONT	Gene Gagne	1997	6035
18 7/16	12 4/16	6 3/16	M	Lac La Biche	ALB	John Alan Dormire	1997	6035
18 7/16	12 1/16	6 6/16	M	Bissett	MAN	Paul D. Redden	1997	6035
18 7/16	11 5/16	7 2/16	M	Ray River	AK	Amy Bothman	1997	6035
18 7/16	11 12/16	6 11/16	M	Oliver Lake	ONT	John M. Knight	1997	6035
18 7/16	11 7/16	7 0/16	M	Bathurst	NBW	Rodger Adydan	1997	6035
18 7/16	11 9/16	6 14/16	M	Carswell Lake	SAS	Vance Henry	1997	6035
18 7/16	11 6/16	7 1/16	M	Kane Lake	SAS	Dennis Dunn	1997	6035
18 7/16	11 4/16	7 3/16	M	Cranberry Portage	MAN	John Emerson Stelmok	1997	6035

189

BLACK BEAR

Minimum Score 18 — Continued

SCORE	GREATEST LENGTH	GREATEST WIDTH	SEX	AREA	STATE/PROVINCE	HUNTER'S NAME	DATE	RANK
18 7/16	11 6/16	7 1/16	M	Mendocino County	CA	Bart Pontoni	1997	6035
18 7/16	12 3/16	6 4/16	M	Missipuskiow River	SAS	Dennis J. Francais	1998	6035
18 7/16	11 8/16	6 15/16	M	Ignace	ONT	Paul Wenninger	1998	6035
18 7/16	11 11/16	6 12/16	M	Vickers Lake	MAN	Mike Wendel	1998	6035
18 7/16	11 13/16	6 10/16	M	Ray River	AK	Tom Chadwick	1998	6035
18 7/16	11 13/16	6 10/16	M	Delta Junction	AK	Jared Cummings	1998	6035
18 7/16	11 4/16	7 3/16	M	Nipigon River	ONT	Michael L. Whitaker	1998	6035
18 7/16	12 0/16	6 7/16	F	St. Louis County	MN	Randy D. Oleson	1998	6035
18 7/16	11 14/16	6 9/16	M	Lake of the Woods	ONT	Robert Carlson	1998	6035
18 7/16	12 2/16	6 5/16	M	Douglas County	WI	Richard L. Smith	1998	6035
18 7/16	11 9/16	6 14/16	M	Madison County	VA	Bryan A. Roach	1998	6035
18 7/16	11 13/16	6 10/16	M	High Level	ALB	Mark Kronyak	1999	6035
18 7/16	11 13/16	6 10/16	M	House River	ALB	Paul Maples	1999	6035
18 7/16	11 5/16	7 2/16	M	Lewis Lake	MAN	Duane McCan	1999	6035
18 7/16	11 9/16	6 14/16	M	Plaster Rock	NBW	Bradley Marley	1999	6035
18 7/16	11 9/16	6 14/16	M	Zama	ALB	Gary Durfee	1999	6035
18 7/16	11 9/16	6 14/16	M	Chipewyan Lake	ALB	Grant Russell	1999	6035
18 7/16	11 7/16	7 0/16	M	Siskiyou County	CA	James Brent Kincaid	1999	6035
18 7/16	11 13/16	6 10/16	M	St. Louis County	MN	Larry King	1999	6035
18 7/16	11 14/16	6 9/16	M	Skamania County	WA	Lane S. Stettler	1999	6035
18 7/16	11 11/16	6 12/16	M	Iron County	WI	Dale Blackwell	1999	6035
18 7/16	11 11/16	6 12/16	M	Schneider Lake	AK	Paul Gray	2000	6035
18 7/16	11 12/16	6 11/16	M	Seven Sisters	MAN	Dale Selby	2000	6035
18 7/16	11 8/16	6 15/16	M	Prince of Wales Island	AK	Cameron R. Hanes	2000	6035
18 7/16	11 12/16	6 11/16	M	Bathurst	NBW	Robert W. Allen	2000	6035
18 7/16	11 14/16	6 9/16	M	Washburn County	WI	Roger R. Resch	2000	6035
18 7/16	11 15/16	6 8/16	M	Ft. McMurray	ALB	Vincent Paul Pollock	2001	6035
18 7/16	11 9/16	6 14/16	M	Bourque Lake	ALB	Beverly Emigh	2001	6035
18 7/16	11 11/16	6 12/16	M	Turnor Lake	SAS	John A. Mortimer	2001	6035
18 7/16	11 6/16	7 1/16	M	El Dorado County	CA	Brian H. Kirksey	2001	6035
18 7/16	11 8/16	6 15/16	M	Powassan	ONT	Rod Shepley	2001	6035
18 7/16	12 0/16	6 7/16	M	San Miguel County	CO	Nels F. Nelson	2001	6035
18 7/16	11 9/16	6 14/16	M	Knight Inlet	BC	Erik Watts	2002	6035
18 7/16	11 15/16	6 8/16	M	Pine River	MAN	Dale Truna	2002	6035
18 7/16	11 11/16	6 12/16	M	Long Lake	MAN	Emile P. LeBlanc	2002	6035
18 7/16	11 7/16	7 0/16	M	Oxford County	ME	Mike Petruk	2002	6035
18 7/16	11 9/16	6 14/16	M	Caramat	ONT	Randel R. Neuman	2002	6035
18 7/16	11 10/16	6 13/16	M	Delta County	CO	Rick Curtis	2002	6035
18 7/16	11 10/16	6 13/16	M	Ashland County	WI	Brian G. Campbell	2002	6035
18 7/16	11 12/16	6 11/16	M	Highland County	VA	Wesley T. Blank	2002	6035
18 7/16	11 13/16	6 10/16	M	Fort McMurray	ALB	Steven L. Lysenko	2003	6035
18 7/16	11 5/16	7 2/16	M	Latah County	ID	Rick Lohman	2003	6035
18 7/16	11 11/16	6 12/16	M	Saddle Hills	ALB	Craig Stokke	2003	6035
*18 7/16	11 12/16	6 11/16	M	Edmonston	NBW	Stephen Samluk	2003	6035
18 7/16	11 8/16	6 15/16	M	Frobisher Lake	SAS	Ramon Neil Bell	2003	6035
18 7/16	11 7/16	7 0/16	M	Swan River	MAN	Douglas G. Middle	2003	6035
18 7/16	11 6/16	7 1/16	M	Lac St-Paul	QUE	Alin De Pierre	2003	6035
18 7/16	11 1/16	7 6/16	F	Fredericton	NBW	Brian Leitzel	2003	6035
18 7/16	11 11/16	6 12/16	M	Lewis County	NY	Tony Dicob	2003	6035
18 7/16	11 14/16	6 9/16	M	Kuiu Island	AK	Frank S. Noska IV	2004	6035
*18 7/16	11 8/16	6 15/16	M	Fort McMurray	ALB	Larry W. Richard	2004	6035
18 7/16	11 7/16	7 0/16	M	Plaster Rock	NBW	Chuck Adams	2004	6035
18 7/16	11 2/16	7 5/16	M	Fairview	ALB	Troy Dzioba	2004	6035
18 7/16	11 8/16	6 15/16	M	LaCroche	QUE	Val J. Antonio	2004	6035
18 7/16	11 3/16	7 4/16	M	Lemhi County	ID	Timothy A. Hyde	2004	6035
18 7/16	11 13/16	6 10/16	M	St. Louis County	MN	Todd Mullenbach	2004	6035
18 7/16	11 12/16	6 11/16	M	Piscataquis County	ME	Bruce Guyan	2004	6035
18 7/16	11 7/16	7 0/16	M	Orange County	VT	David Turner	2004	6035
18 7/16	11 9/16	6 14/16	M	Meadow Lake	SAS	Patrick Hanlon	2005	6035
18 7/16	12 1/16	6 6/16	F	Yorkton	SAS	Colin Laird	2005	6035
*18 7/16	11 6/16	7 1/16	M	Ponton	MAN	Jeff Nelson	2005	6035
18 7/16	11 10/16	6 13/16	M	Emo	ONT	Scott L. Gilbertson	2005	6035
18 7/16	11 7/16	7 0/16	M	Cochrane	ONT	Frederick Bickel	2005	6035
18 7/16	11 15/16	6 8/16	M	Cumberland House	SAS	Brent Navin	2006	6035
18 7/16	11 10/16	6 13/16	M	Boise County	ID	Roger E. Belau	2006	6035
18 7/16	11 12/16	6 11/16	M	Lake Weyakwin	SAS	Timothy J. Bruner	2006	6035
*18 7/16	11 6/16	7 1/16	M	Prince of Wales Island	AK	Richard Eckles	2006	6035
18 7/16	11 6/16	7 1/16	M	St-Emile	QUE	William M. Roach	2006	6035
18 7/16	11 12/16	6 11/16	M	Frobisher Lake	SAS	Kevin Dancy	2006	6035
18 7/16	12 1/16	6 6/16	M	Itasca County	MN	Jacob Gerber	2006	6035
18 7/16	12 0/16	6 7/16	M	Sawyer County	WI	Brian Gustke	2006	6035
18 7/16	11 8/16	6 15/16	M	Puntzi Lake	BC	Cheryl Earhart	2007	6035
18 7/16	11 8/16	6 15/16	M	Andygood Creek	BC	Richard Podrasky	2007	6035
*18 7/16	11 9/16	6 14/16	M	Sussex	NBW	Steve Ruhnke	2007	6035
*18 7/16	12 1/16	6 6/16	M	Christopher Lake	SAS	Mark Thiemann	2007	6035
*18 7/16	11 6/16	7 1/16	M	Sioux Lookout	ONT	Tom Hessler	2007	6035
18 7/16	11 14/16	6 9/16	M	Taylor County	WI	Chris Breu	2007	6035
18 7/16	11 15/16	6 8/16	F	Meadow Lake	SAS	Justin Paramzchuk	2008	6035
18 7/16	11 3/16	7 4/16	M	Wawa	ONT	Cory Franceus	2008	6035
18 7/16	11 5/16	7 2/16	M	San Miguel County	NM	Rick Varela	2008	6035
18 7/16	11 12/16	6 11/16	M	Firebag River	ALB	Spencer Snodsmith	2009	6035
*18 7/16	11 7/16	7 0/16	M	Lake Lareau	QUE	Paul Coulombe	2009	6035
18 7/16	11 13/16	6 10/16	M	Elmore County	ID	Gary Hubbard, Jr.	2009	6035
18 7/16	11 15/16	6 8/16	F	Lincoln County	MT	R. C. Peters	2009	6035
*18 7/16	11 11/16	6 12/16	M	Coos County	NH	Nicholas Verdura, MD	2009	6035
*18 7/16	11 5/16	7 2/16	M	Ignace	ONT	James R. Taylor	2009	6035
18 7/16	11 11/16	6 12/16	M	Bonneville County	ID	Adrienne Hayes	2010	6035
18 7/16	11 11/16	6 12/16	M	Red Earth	ALB	Tom Nelson	2010	6035
18 7/16	11 7/16	7 0/16	M	Chimney Lake	BC	Allan Tew	2010	6035
18 7/16	11 9/16	6 14/16	M	Hadashville	MAN	Ken Langlois	2010	6035
*18 7/16	11 11/16	6 12/16	M	Redditt	ONT	Bret A. Mattice	2010	6035
18 6/16	11 9/16	6 13/16	M	Mariposa County	CA	Douglas Walker	1965	6267
18 6/16	11 8/16	6 14/16	M	Fulton County	NY	Peter Mertens	1966	6267
18 6/16	11 10/16	6 12/16	M	Yancey County	NC	Jerry Rushing	1970	6267
18 6/16	11 8/16	6 14/16	M	Clear Creek County	CO	Jim Dougherty	1970	6267

BLACK BEAR

Minimum Score 18   Continued

SCORE	GREATEST LENGTH	GREATEST WIDTH	SEX	AREA	STATE/ PROVINCE	HUNTER'S NAME	DATE	RANK
18 6/16	11 12/16	6 10/16	M	Franklin County	ME	Joe Melchiore	1970	6267
18 6/16	11 8/16	6 14/16	M	Becker County	MN	Gordon Swenson	1973	6267
18 6/16	11 4/16	7 2/16	M	Valley County	ID	Charles F. Maloney	1973	6267
18 6/16	11 2/16	7 4/16	M	Chetwynd	BC	Lee E. Hansel	1973	6267
18 6/16	11 6/16	7 0/16	M	Dryden	ONT	John L. Dykes	1974	6267
18 6/16	11 12/16	6 10/16	M	Flathead County	MT	Dr. Barry Wensel	1974	6267
18 6/16	12 0/16	6 6/16	M	Snohomish County	WA	Jim Gregory	1975	6267
18 6/16	11 10/16	6 12/16	M	Saguache County	CO	Sandra Scheid	1975	6267
18 6/16	11 8/16	6 14/16	M	Archuleta County	CO	Judd Cooney	1975	6267
18 6/16	11 0/16	7 6/16	M	Larimer County	CO	Michael Lewis	1975	6267
18 6/16	11 6/16	7 0/16	M	Somerset County	ME	Anthony Ciletti	1976	6267
18 6/16	11 12/16	6 10/16	M	Rio Blanco County	CO	Brad Cook	1978	6267
18 6/16	11 5/16	7 1/16	M	Lemhi County	ID	Roy Auwen	1979	6267
18 6/16	11 8/16	6 14/16	M	Marinette County	WI	William Brunette	1979	6267
18 6/16	11 14/16	6 8/16	M	Thunder Bay	ONT	Neil E. Gilles	1980	6267
18 6/16	11 10/16	6 12/16	M	Red Lake	ONT	Leon L. Miller	1981	6267
18 6/16	11 4/16	7 2/16	M	Espanola	ONT	Ronald E. Hergott	1982	6267
18 6/16	11 5/16	7 1/16	M	Siskiyou County	CA	Dave S. Semple	1982	6267
18 6/16	11 7/16	6 15/16	M	Uintah County	UT	Bill Dunstan IV	1982	6267
18 6/16	11 14/16	6 8/16	M	Game Area #23	MAN	Gary Kaluzniak	1983	6267
18 6/16	11 8/16	6 14/16	M	McAdam	NBW	Donald R. Shipley	1983	6267
18 6/16	11 5/16	7 1/16	M	Ramsey Township	ONT	Robert H. Pavlovic	1983	6267
18 6/16	11 8/16	6 14/16	M	Montrose County	CO	Wayne Willis	1983	6267
18 6/16	11 12/16	6 10/16	M	Cheboygan County	MI	Roger A. Greve	1983	6267
18 6/16	11 15/16	6 7/16	M	Sawyer County	WI	Kevin Capelle	1983	6267
18 6/16	11 8/16	6 14/16	M	Chelan County	WA	Edward M. Beitner	1983	6267
18 6/16	11 15/16	6 7/16	M	Greene County	NY	Bob Spina	1983	6267
18 6/16	11 4/16	7 2/16	M	Douglas County	OR	Tim O'Kelly	1984	6267
18 6/16	11 15/16	6 7/16	M	Cass County	MN	James D. Zahalka	1984	6267
18 6/16	11 8/16	6 14/16	M	Marquette County	MI	George M. Barosko	1984	6267
18 6/16	11 10/16	6 12/16	M	Luce County	MI	Norman E. Bell	1984	6267
18 6/16	11 2/16	7 4/16	M	Bathurst	NBW	Daryl Labarron	1985	6267
18 6/16	11 4/16	7 2/16	M	Pontiac	QUE	Loren L. Fish	1985	6267
18 6/16	11 3/16	7 3/16	M	Carroll County	NH	Donald W. Murdock	1985	6267
18 6/16	11 8/16	6 14/16	F	Spiritwood	SAS	Kent W. Brigham	1986	6267
18 6/16	11 10/16	6 12/16	M	Rio Arriba County	NM	Terry Sanders	1986	6267
18 6/16	11 8/16	6 14/16	M	Thunder Bay	ONT	Gene Anderson	1986	6267
18 6/16	11 3/16	7 3/16	M	Valley County	ID	Larry Hoff	1986	6267
18 6/16	10 15/16	7 7/16	M	Fremont County	ID	Blair R. Jones	1986	6267
18 6/16	11 14/16	6 8/16	M	Hudson Bay	SAS	C. Randall Byers	1987	6267
18 6/16	11 3/16	7 3/16	M	Wabigoon	ONT	Robert Barrie	1987	6267
18 6/16	11 10/16	6 12/16	M	St. Louis County	MN	Loren Slette	1987	6267
18 6/16	11 9/16	6 13/16	M	Oxford County	ME	Patrick Ferrie	1987	6267
18 6/16	11 15/16	6 7/16	M	Lincoln County	WI	James G. Gouger	1987	6267
18 6/16	11 10/16	6 12/16	M	Wolf Lake	ALB	Keith Baker	1988	6267
18 6/16	11 15/16	6 7/16	M	Hudson Bay	SAS	Kent Brandt	1988	6267
18 6/16	11 15/16	6 7/16	M	Emo	ONT	Robert John Brown	1988	6267
18 6/16	11 6/16	7 0/16	M	Gull River	ONT	Larry R. Brosamle	1988	6267
18 6/16	11 7/16	6 15/16	M	Kenora	ONT	Dean M. Westby	1988	6267
18 6/16	11 11/16	6 11/16	M	Chelsea	QUE	Jim Ray	1988	6267
18 6/16	11 1/16	7 5/16	M	Jocko River	ONT	Gary Boals	1988	6267
18 6/16	12 1/16	6 5/16	M	Susitna River	AK	Richmon R. Schumann	1988	6267
18 6/16	11 8/16	6 14/16	M	La Plata County	CO	Dale Sunblom	1988	6267
18 6/16	11 6/16	7 0/16	M	Chibougamau	QUE	Dale R. Walburger	1988	6267
18 6/16	11 1/16	7 5/16	M	Okanogan County	WA	Duane N. Fink	1988	6267
18 6/16	11 4/16	7 2/16	M	Delay River	QUE	Dennis N. Ballweg	1988	6267
18 6/16	11 6/16	7 0/16	M	Ashland County	WI	Thomas J. Mischo	1988	6267
18 6/16	11 12/16	6 10/16	M	Coconino County	AZ	Richard Dawe, Jr.	1988	6267
18 6/16	11 11/16	6 11/16	M	Saguache County	CO	Sid Strzok	1989	6267
18 6/16	11 10/16	6 12/16	M	Mens Township	ONT	Jon T. Wente	1989	6267
18 6/16	11 7/16	6 15/16	M	Emo	ONT	Leo Hazelton	1989	6267
18 6/16	11 7/16	6 15/16	M	Peace River	ALB	John Peruchini	1990	6267
18 6/16	11 10/16	6 12/16	M	Dolores County	CO	Duain Morton	1990	6267
18 6/16	12 0/16	6 6/16	M	Buffalo Narrows	SAS	David M Tofte	1990	6267
18 6/16	11 4/16	7 2/16	M	Messines	QUE	Charles L. Hart III	1990	6267
18 6/16	11 7/16	6 15/16	M	Meadow Lake	SAS	Tonnie Elwood Davis	1990	6267
18 6/16	11 13/16	6 9/16	M	Bayfield County	WI	Gary J. Ader	1990	6267
18 6/16	11 14/16	6 8/16	M	Iron County	WI	Thomas R. Hujet	1990	6267
18 6/16	11 6/16	7 0/16	M	Clatsup County	OR	William H. Stevens	1991	6267
18 6/16	11 13/16	6 9/16	F	Rainy River	ONT	Michael Judas	1991	6267
18 6/16	11 12/16	6 10/16	M	Plevna	ONT	Brant Bergstrome	1991	6267
18 6/16	11 12/16	6 10/16	M	Itasca County	MN	Shawn E. Eyre	1991	6267
18 6/16	11 4/16	7 2/16	M	Colfax County	NM	Rodrigo Cruz	1991	6267
18 6/16	11 12/16	6 10/16	M	Caribou County	ID	Trent McBride	1991	6267
18 6/16	11 10/16	6 12/16	M	Savant Lake	ONT	Dean Wells	1992	6267
18 6/16	11 6/16	7 0/16	M	Elma	MAN	David A. Goertzen	1992	6267
18 6/16	11 12/16	6 10/16	M	Thunder Bay	ONT	Michael Kemp	1992	6267
18 6/16	11 7/16	6 15/16	M	Vermilion Bay	ONT	Dennis Forstner	1992	6267
18 6/16	11 12/16	6 10/16	M	Chippewa County	MI	William Pettett, Jr.	1992	6267
18 6/16	11 8/16	6 14/16	M	Lake Besnard	SAS	Roger Brock	1992	6267
18 6/16	11 9/16	6 13/16	M	Cascade County	MT	Mark Seabaugh	1992	6267
18 6/16	11 10/16	6 12/16	M	Sioux Narrows	ONT	Fay Lloyd	1992	6267
18 6/16	12 0/16	6 6/16	M	Fisher Branch	MAN	Robert G. Olafson	1993	6267
18 6/16	11 12/16	6 10/16	M	La Ronge	SAS	Trent Findley	1993	6267
18 6/16	11 15/16	6 7/16	M	Snohomish County	WA	John L. Campbell	1993	6267
18 6/16	11 10/16	6 12/16	M	Houghton County	MI	Rick W. DeMarr	1993	6267
18 6/16	11 12/16	6 10/16	M	Lewis & Clark County	MT	Gerald Biresch	1993	6267
18 6/16	11 9/16	6 13/16	M	Prince of Wales Island	AK	Dyrk Eddie	1994	6267
18 6/16	11 11/16	6 11/16	M	Cadillac	QUE	Edward M. Wojtys	1994	6267
18 6/16	11 6/16	7 0/16	M	Manitouwadge	ONT	Mike Losee	1994	6267
18 6/16	11 9/16	6 13/16	M	Umatilla County	OR	Javier Garcia	1994	6267
18 6/16	11 11/16	6 11/16	M	Aitkin County	MN	Brad Blanchard	1994	6267
18 6/16	11 11/16	6 11/16	M	McMeekin Township	ONT	Roger Thompson	1994	6267
18 6/16	11 4/16	7 2/16	M	Boarder Lake	BC	Tim R. Dawson	1994	6267
18 6/16	11 15/16	6 7/16	M	Riding Mtn.	MAN	Steven M. Bins	1994	6267

191

BLACK BEAR

Minimum Score 18   Continued

SCORE	GREATEST LENGTH	GREATEST WIDTH	SEX	AREA	STATE/ PROVINCE	HUNTER'S NAME	DATE	RANK
18 6/16	10 13/16	7 9/16	M	Beaverhead County	MT	Frank Russell	1994	6267
18 6/16	11 9/16	6 13/16	M	Shoshone County	ID	Roger Stewart	1995	6267
18 6/16	11 15/16	6 7/16	M	Aulneau Peninsula	ONT	Michael Koska	1995	6267
18 6/16	11 12/16	6 10/16	M	Prince Albert	ALB	Dave MacKenzie	1995	6267
18 6/16	11 12/16	6 10/16	M	Dryden	ONT	Rick Kroll	1995	6267
18 6/16	11 11/16	6 11/16	M	Alford Lake	ALB	Derrill Herman	1995	6267
18 6/16	11 7/16	6 15/16	M	Nestor Falls	ONT	Dale E. Springer	1995	6267
18 6/16	11 9/16	6 13/16	M	Cygnet Lake	ONT	Kelvin W. Lancaster	1995	6267
18 6/16	11 14/16	6 8/16	M	Red Lake	ONT	Doug Johnson	1995	6267
18 6/16	11 7/16	6 15/16	M	Oba	ONT	Robert J. Guarnaccio	1995	6267
18 6/16	11 13/16	6 9/16	M	Catron County	NM	Jason Ashcroft	1995	6267
18 6/16	11 13/16	6 9/16	M	Savante	ONT	Martin Hug	1995	6267
18 6/16	11 13/16	6 9/16	M	Uintah County	UT	Rick Copeland	1995	6267
18 6/16	11 10/16	6 12/16	M	Falcon Lake	MAN	D. P. Domaszek	1996	6267
18 6/16	11 7/16	6 15/16	M	Kenora	ONT	Dick Melka	1996	6267
18 6/16	11 8/16	6 14/16	M	Red Lake	ONT	Rocky A. King	1996	6267
18 6/16	11 14/16	6 8/16	M	Meadow Lake	SAS	Jerry W. Laton	1996	6267
18 6/16	11 6/16	7 0/16	M	Kirkland Lake	ONT	Roy L. Walk	1996	6267
18 6/16	11 9/16	6 13/16	M	Dryden	ONT	Richard Rogers	1996	6267
18 6/16	11 6/16	7 0/16	M	Ear Falls	ONT	Duane R. Hearing	1996	6267
18 6/16	11 8/16	6 14/16	M	Holinshead Lake	ONT	Don Davidson	1996	6267
18 6/16	11 13/16	6 9/16	M	Calling Lake	ALB	Robert Bartoshesky	1996	6267
18 6/16	11 6/16	7 0/16	M	Siskiyou County	CA	Fred V. Smith	1996	6267
18 6/16	11 11/16	6 11/16	M	Ontonagon County	MI	Paul Ranft	1996	6267
18 6/16	11 9/16	6 13/16	M	Red Lake	ONT	Daniel G. Prusik	1996	6267
18 6/16	11 10/16	6 12/16	M	Oconto County	WI	Richard Liebl	1996	6267
18 6/16	11 10/16	6 12/16	M	Washburn County	WI	Michael Prehn	1996	6267
18 6/16	11 12/16	6 10/16	M	Holokuk Mtns.	AK	Tom Crabill	1996	6267
18 6/16	11 9/16	6 13/16	M	Grouard	ALB	Greg Ogle	1997	6267
18 6/16	11 9/16	6 13/16	M	Woosey Lake	MAN	John Janke	1997	6267
18 6/16	11 12/16	6 10/16	M	Aerobus Lake	ONT	Kirt Hoffmann	1997	6267
18 6/16	11 8/16	6 14/16	M	French River	ONT	John Orr	1997	6267
18 6/16	11 12/16	6 10/16	M	Shikag Lake	ONT	Robert L. Gardner	1997	6267
18 6/16	11 8/16	6 14/16	M	Thessalon	ONT	Larry Cornett	1997	6267
18 6/16	11 5/16	7 1/16	M	Dog Lake	ONT	Wayne S. Walden	1997	6267
18 6/16	11 14/16	6 8/16	M	Ministikwan	SAS	Larry Hillis	1997	6267
18 6/16	11 2/16	7 4/16	M	Siskiyou County	CA	Fred V. Smith	1997	6267
18 6/16	11 5/16	7 1/16	M	Clackamas County	OR	Dan Ellis	1997	6267
18 6/16	11 10/16	6 12/16	M	Essex County	NY	Paul Durling	1997	6267
18 6/16	11 7/16	6 15/16	F	Prince of Wales Island	AK	Peggy "Bailey" Whary	1998	6267
18 6/16	11 11/16	6 11/16	M	Indian River	AK	Rick Schikora	1998	6267
18 6/16	11 12/16	6 10/16	M	Apache County	AZ	Robert G. Petersen	1998	6267
18 6/16	11 8/16	6 14/16	M	Dryden	ONT	Alan E. Forbes	1998	6267
18 6/16	11 10/16	6 12/16	M	Apache County	AZ	Robert G. Petersen	1998	6267
18 6/16	12 0/16	6 6/16	M	Sturgeon Landing	SAS	Ryan Hugelen	1998	6267
18 6/16	11 5/16	7 1/16	M	Marathon	ONT	Michael L. Ritter	1998	6267
18 6/16	11 12/16	6 10/16	M	Kenora	ONT	Alan Schwab	1998	6267
18 6/16	11 10/16	6 12/16	M	Missinipe	SAS	Robert E. Lillis	1999	6267
18 6/16	11 14/16	6 8/16	M	Tatla Lake	BC	Moe Monita	1999	6267
18 6/16	11 12/16	6 10/16	M	Athabasca River	ALB	Michael Travis	1999	6267
18 6/16	11 6/16	7 0/16	M	Fort a la Corne	SAS	Harlin Munro	1999	6267
18 6/16	12 1/16	6 5/16	M	Olha	MAN	Mike Windemuller	1999	6267
18 6/16	11 12/16	6 10/16	F	Fisher Branch	MAN	Joe T. Soto, Jr.	1999	6267
18 6/16	11 12/16	6 10/16	M	Conklin	ALB	Barron Naar	1999	6267
18 6/16	11 14/16	6 8/16	M	Carrot River	SAS	Phil Harris	1999	6267
18 6/16	11 12/16	6 10/16	M	Bayfield County	WI	Todd Standke	1999	6267
18 6/16	11 9/16	6 13/16	M	Fort Nelson	BC	Chris Partridge	2000	6267
18 6/16	11 8/16	6 14/16	M	Piscataquis County	ME	Norman Cognetto	2000	6267
18 6/16	11 10/16	6 12/16	M	Ft. McMurray	ALB	Kevin D. Springman	2001	6267
18 6/16	11 14/16	6 8/16	M	Blueberry Mtn.	ALB	Gary Gillett	2001	6267
18 6/16	11 5/16	7 1/16	M	Thompson	MAN	Chet Hayes	2001	6267
18 6/16	11 12/16	6 10/16	M	Zec Capitachouane	QUE	Bryan Hynicka	2001	6267
18 6/16	11 15/16	6 7/16	M	Duck Mtn.	SAS	Ron Vandermeulen	2001	6267
18 6/16	11 6/16	7 0/16	M	Sasagiu Rapids	MAN	Lawrence J. Finnegan, Jr.	2001	6267
18 6/16	11 11/16	6 11/16	M	Ste. Rose du Lac	MAN	Jeffrey D. Folsom	2001	6267
18 6/16	11 10/16	6 12/16	M	Tabusintac River	NBW	Ronald M. Tussel, Jr.	2001	6267
18 6/16	11 11/16	6 11/16	M	Kamsack	SAS	Ron R. Vandermeulen	2002	6267
18 6/16	11 8/16	6 14/16	M	Moose Lake	MAN	Warren W. Johnson	2002	6267
18 6/16	11 9/16	6 13/16	M	Zama	ALB	Grant M. Winn II	2002	6267
18 6/16	11 6/16	7 0/16	M	Bissett	MAN	James Collins	2002	6267
18 6/16	11 6/16	7 0/16	M	Anderson	AK	Harold Lloyd Donahue II	2002	6267
18 6/16	11 13/16	6 9/16	M	Taylor County	WI	Raymond R. Rosemeyer	2002	6267
18 6/16	11 6/16	7 0/16	M	Hancock County	ME	Vincent Gilbert	2002	6267
18 6/16	12 0/16	6 6/16	M	South Mtn.	NS	Ray Tobin	2002	6267
18 6/16	11 12/16	6 10/16	M	Cold Lake	SAS	Eddie J. Heath	2003	6267
18 6/16	11 12/16	6 10/16	M	Peace River	ALB	Ron Stover	2003	6267
18 6/16	11 8/16	6 14/16	M	Worsley	ALB	Jason Sturgill	2003	6267
18 6/16	11 10/16	6 12/16	M	Peace River	ALB	Ted K. Jaycox	2003	6267
18 6/16	11 12/16	6 10/16	M	Fraser River	BC	Scott Jankowski	2003	6267
18 6/16	11 9/16	6 13/16	M	Buffalo Narrows	SAS	Jeff Worman	2003	6267
18 6/16	11 14/16	6 8/16	M	Lac La Ronge	SAS	James E. Hummel	2003	6267
18 6/16	11 6/16	7 0/16	M	Cabonga Reservoir	QUE	Mark Kronyak	2003	6267
18 6/16	11 11/16	6 11/16	M	La Tuque	QUE	Thomas M. Phillips	2003	6267
18 6/16	11 8/16	6 14/16	M	Pontiac	QUE	Robert L. Wittman	2003	6267
18 6/16	11 10/16	6 12/16	M	Aroostook County	ME	Kenneth J. Knies	2003	6267
*18 6/16	11 5/16	7 1/16	M	Aroostook County	ME	Jeffrey S. Mangold	2003	6267
18 6/16	11 14/16	6 8/16	M	Marinette County	WI	William T. Koch	2003	6267
18 6/16	11 9/16	6 13/16	M	Langlade County	WI	Robert S. Popelka	2003	6267
*18 6/16	11 11/16	6 11/16	M	Thaddeus Lake	ONT	Todd Thorn	2003	6267
18 6/16	11 6/16	7 0/16	M	Price County	WI	Craig Smith	2003	6267
18 6/16	11 10/16	6 12/16	M	Langlade County	WI	Brent M. Kadubek	2003	6267
*18 6/16	11 11/16	6 11/16	M	Luce County	MI	Jerry M. Banaszak	2003	6267
18 6/16	11 3/16	7 3/16	M	Watabeag Lake	ONT	Stephen L. Wert	2003	6267
18 6/16	11 5/16	7 1/16	M	Trinity County	CA	Scott Walker	2003	6267
18 6/16	11 9/16	6 13/16	M	Peace River	ALB	Dave Browne	2004	6267

BLACK BEAR

Minimum Score 18
Continued

SCORE	GREATEST LENGTH	GREATEST WIDTH	SEX	AREA	STATE/ PROVINCE	HUNTER'S NAME	DATE	RANK
18 6/16	11 4/16	7 2/16	M	Carswell Lake	SAS	Steff Stefanovich	2004	6267
18 6/16	11 6/16	7 0/16	M	Josyln River	ALB	Walter Krom	2004	6267
18 6/16	11 6/16	7 0/16	M	Smoothstone Lake	SAS	Martin T. Greeley	2004	6267
18 6/16	11 4/16	7 2/16	M	Calling Lake	ALB	Jeffery Dale Ehlers	2004	6267
*18 6/16	11 8/16	6 14/16	M	Preissac	QUE	Richard J. Prine	2004	6267
18 6/16	11 8/16	6 14/16	M	Clearwater County	ID	R. M. "Dick" Newell	2004	6267
18 6/16	11 10/16	6 12/16	F	Clark County	WI	Richard Crabtree	2004	6267
18 6/16	11 5/16	7 1/16	M	Prince George	BC	Richard Krug	2005	6267
18 6/16	11 8/16	6 14/16	M	Shoshone County	ID	Roger Stewart	2005	6267
18 6/16	11 8/16	6 14/16	M	Chilkat River	AK	Richard LaCrone	2005	6267
18 6/16	11 14/16	6 8/16	M	Onanole	MAN	Mike Broadley	2005	6267
18 6/16	11 10/16	6 12/16	M	Valleyview	ALB	Raymond P. Mozes	2005	6267
18 6/16	11 5/16	7 1/16	M	Johnstone Bay	AK	Daniel R. Carey	2005	6267
18 6/16	11 11/16	6 11/16	M	Rimouski	QUE	Michael J. Chiricos	2005	6267
18 6/16	11 8/16	6 14/16	M	Sioux Lookout	ONT	Tyler Stanley	2005	6267
18 6/16	11 11/16	6 11/16	M	Ignace	ONT	Steven Krueger	2005	6267
18 6/16	12 2/16	6 4/16	M	Laurier	MAN	Robert Tastsides	2006	6267
18 6/16	11 9/16	6 13/16	M	Pabineau Falls	NBW	Kevin G. Pero	2006	6267
18 6/16	11 13/16	6 9/16	M	Tulare County	CA	Cliff Dupee	2006	6267
*18 6/16	11 10/16	6 12/16	M	Jellicoe	ONT	Scott Wahl	2006	6267
18 6/16	11 8/16	6 14/16	M	Plumas County	CA	Jerry Dollard	2006	6267
18 6/16	11 11/16	6 11/16	M	Lac du Bonnet	MAN	Josh Burkholder	2006	6267
*18 6/16	12 0/16	6 6/16	M	Grande Prairie	ALB	David J. Nicolai	2007	6267
18 6/16	11 9/16	6 13/16	M	High Level	ALB	Roman Cirignani	2007	6267
18 6/16	11 12/16	6 10/16	M	Cranberry Portage	MAN	Scott Lang	2007	6267
18 6/16	11 10/16	6 12/16	M	High Level	ALB	Robert L. Estes	2007	6267
*18 6/16	11 14/16	6 8/16	M	The Pas	MAN	Bruce Knuckles	2007	6267
18 6/16	11 13/16	6 9/16	M	Custer County	ID	Rob Silva	2007	6267
18 6/16	11 9/16	6 13/16	M	Timmins	ONT	Steven J. Hessel	2007	6267
*18 6/16	11 7/16	6 15/16	M	Ignace	ONT	David Sobczak	2007	6267
18 6/16	11 13/16	6 9/16	M	Prince Albert	SAS	Bailey Simpson	2008	6267
18 6/16	11 10/16	6 12/16	M	Rennie	MAN	Mark Dumansky	2008	6267
*18 6/16	11 12/16	6 10/16	M	Togo	SAS	Dave McPhee	2008	6267
*18 6/16	11 7/16	6 15/16	M	McAdam	NBW	Ryan Sullivan	2008	6267
*18 6/16	11 12/16	6 10/16	M	Athabasca River	ALB	John W. Ellas	2008	6267
18 6/16	11 15/16	6 7/16	M	Big River	SAS	Gary D. Amos	2008	6267
18 6/16	11 8/16	6 14/16	M	Spirit River	ALB	Mike Slocum	2008	6267
*18 6/16	11 12/16	6 10/16	M	Lac du Bonnet	MAN	Janice Parker	2008	6267
*18 6/16	10 13/16	7 9/16	M	Reindeer Lake	SAS	Jeff Hintze	2008	6267
18 6/16	11 10/16	6 12/16	M	Ignace	ONT	Joel Brophy	2008	6267
*18 6/16	11 15/16	6 7/16	M	Searchmont	ONT	Brad Beard	2008	6267
18 6/16	12 0/16	6 6/16	M	Arborg	MAN	Jason Van Kooten	2008	6267
*18 6/16	11 13/16	6 9/16	M	El Paso County	CO	Scott W. Meszaros	2008	6267
18 6/16	11 7/16	6 15/16	M	Las Animas County	CO	David L. Skiff	2008	6267
18 6/16	11 8/16	6 14/16	M	Sayward	BC	Timothy B. Fisk	2009	6267
*18 6/16	12 0/16	6 6/16	M	Spirit River	ALB	John Albrecht	2009	6267
18 6/16	11 6/16	7 0/16	M	La Tuque	QUE	Tom Phillips	2009	6267
18 6/16	11 10/16	6 12/16	M	Conmee	ONT	Dan Fadyshen	2009	6267
18 6/16	11 6/16	7 0/16	M	Skamania County	WA	Lane Stettler	2009	6267
18 6/16	11 10/16	6 12/16	M	Flathead County	MT	Charles C. Stafford	2009	6267
*18 6/16	11 8/16	6 14/16	M	Hudson Bay	SAS	Ryan Onufreychuk	2010	6267
*18 6/16	11 9/16	6 13/16	M	Dipper Lake	SAS	Michele Leqve	2010	6267
18 5/16	11 3/16	7 2/16	M	Iron Bridge	ONT	Philip L. Hawkins	1965	6513
18 5/16	11 6/16	6 15/16	M	St. Louis County	MN	Kay A. Schuver	1969	6513
18 5/16	11 9/16	6 12/16	M	Gogebic County	MI	LaVern Miller	1971	6513
18 5/16	11 6/16	6 15/16	M	Florence County	WI	Jim Thimmig	1971	6513
18 5/16	11 3/16	7 2/16	M	Forest County	WI	Ernie V. Hutchinson	1972	6513
18 5/16	11 4/16	7 1/16	M	St. Louis County	MN	Art Heinze	1973	6513
18 5/16	11 9/16	6 12/16	M	Coconino County	AZ	Stan Nordell	1975	6513
18 5/16	11 7/16	6 14/16	M	Gunnison County	CO	Rick Hunckler	1976	6513
18 5/16	11 7/16	6 14/16	M	Montezuma County	CO	Stanley A. Coval	1977	6513
18 5/16	11 9/16	6 12/16	M	Park County	MT	Charles Burdette	1980	6513
18 5/16	11 2/16	7 3/16	M	Douglas County	OR	Dan Viles	1980	6513
18 5/16	11 3/16	7 2/16	M	E. Braintree	MAN	Chester Surma	1980	6513
18 5/16	11 7/16	6 14/16	M	Ear Falls	ONT	John Brandt	1980	6513
18 5/16	11 5/16	7 0/16	M	Gogebic County	MI	Donald E. Thompson, Jr.	1981	6513
18 5/16	11 7/16	6 14/16	M	Blind River	ONT	Cleve Roush	1982	6513
18 5/16	11 11/16	6 10/16	M	Iron County	WI	Keith Kaat	1982	6513
18 5/16	11 11/16	6 10/16	M	Alatna River	AK	John D. 'Jack' Frost	1982	6513
18 5/16	11 4/16	7 1/16	M	Missoula County	MT	Tom Storm	1983	6513
18 5/16	11 9/16	6 12/16	M	Sundridge	ONT	Abby Lape	1983	6513
18 5/16	11 9/16	6 12/16	M	Kootenai County	ID	Larry M. Leake	1985	6513
18 5/16	11 8/16	6 13/16	M	Thunder Bay	ONT	Bob Kraus	1985	6513
18 5/16	11 11/16	6 10/16	M	Hudson Bay	SAS	Clark Jenner	1985	6513
18 5/16	11 8/16	6 13/16	M	Cold Lake	ALB	Orest Popil	1985	6513
18 5/16	11 6/16	6 15/16	M	Atikokan	ONT	Bruce Wynn	1985	6513
18 5/16	11 14/16	6 7/16	M	Grand County	CO	Lyle Willmarth	1986	6513
18 5/16	11 12/16	6 9/16	M	Lake County	MT	Don Davidson	1986	6513
18 5/16	11 8/16	6 13/16	M	Massey	ONT	Jim Hunsaker	1986	6513
18 5/16	11 11/16	6 10/16	M	Sudbury	ONT	Richard Dohm	1986	6513
18 5/16	11 4/16	7 1/16	M	Park County	CO	Gary Christoffersen	1986	6513
18 5/16	11 13/16	6 8/16	M	Rocky Lake	MAN	Tim Finley	1986	6513
18 5/16	11 5/16	7 0/16	M	Blaine County	ID	Larry R. Newton	1986	6513
18 5/16	11 11/16	6 10/16	M	Iron County	MI	Richard Seasword	1986	6513
18 5/16	11 5/16	7 0/16	M	Kootenai County	ID	Linda Leake	1987	6513
18 5/16	11 8/16	6 13/16	M	Algonquin	ONT	Stephen Michael Carroll	1987	6513
18 5/16	11 11/16	6 10/16	M	Saint James Bay	AK	Richard J. Callahan	1987	6513
18 5/16	11 7/16	6 14/16	M	Lemhi County	ID	Mike Lyons	1987	6513
18 5/16	11 2/16	7 3/16	M	Plumas County	CA	Steven Demello	1987	6513
18 5/16	11 5/16	7 0/16	M	Somerset County	ME	Al Cresci	1987	6513
18 5/16	11 10/16	6 11/16	M	Placer County	CA	Kenneth Braden	1987	6513
18 5/16	11 13/16	6 8/16	M	Athabasca River	ALB	Archie J. Nesbitt	1988	6513
18 5/16	11 11/16	6 10/16	M	Sundre	ALB	David R. Coupland	1988	6513
18 5/16	11 9/16	6 12/16	M	Ignace	ONT	Joel Breitung	1988	6513
18 5/16	11 9/16	6 12/16	M	Bonneville County	ID	Terri L. Stephens	1988	6513

BLACK BEAR

Minimum Score 18   Continued

SCORE	GREATEST LENGTH	GREATEST WIDTH	SEX	AREA	STATE/ PROVINCE	HUNTER'S NAME	DATE	RANK
18 5/16	11 12/16	6 9/16	M	San Miguel County	CO	LaJuan Hare	1989	6513
18 5/16	11 11/16	6 10/16	M	Grand County	UT	Troy Olson	1989	6513
18 5/16	11 10/16	6 11/16	M	Manitouwadge	ONT	Stuart Hazard III	1989	6513
18 5/16	11 8/16	6 13/16	M	Boise Franc Rd.	QUE	August S. Gray	1989	6513
18 5/16	11 6/16	6 15/16	M	Pierce County	WA	Howard L. Harding	1989	6513
18 5/16	11 7/16	6 14/16	M	Aroostook County	ME	Tad David Proudlove	1989	6513
18 5/16	11 3/16	7 2/16	M	Powell Lake	ONT	Michael J. Goza	1989	6513
18 5/16	11 4/16	7 1/16	M	MacNeil Township	ONT	Ted Whittle	1989	6513
18 5/16	11 14/16	6 7/16	M	Lemhi County	ID	Al Youman	1990	6513
18 5/16	11 1/16	7 4/16	M	Gravel Lake	ONT	James D. Smith	1990	6513
18 5/16	11 3/16	7 2/16	M	Prince of Wales Island	AK	Gordon Diehl	1990	6513
18 5/16	11 10/16	6 11/16	M	Ashland County	WI	Kenneth A. Johnson	1990	6513
18 5/16	11 11/16	6 10/16	M	Oconto County	WI	Chuck D. Peterson	1990	6513
18 5/16	11 12/16	6 9/16	M	Telegraph Creek	BC	Rick Simonson	1990	6513
18 5/16	11 6/16	6 15/16	M	Crimson Lake	ALB	Dale Peters	1991	6513
18 5/16	11 2/16	7 3/16	M	Chipmunk Creek	BC	Ken Scheer	1991	6513
18 5/16	11 8/16	6 13/16	M	Atikokan	ONT	Judy Grooms	1991	6513
18 5/16	11 1/16	7 4/16	M	Clearwater County	ID	Gary L. Haynes	1991	6513
18 5/16	11 6/16	6 15/16	M	Las Animas County	CO	H. Brian Jackson	1991	6513
18 5/16	11 12/16	6 9/16	M	Poplarfield	MAN	Jim McHale	1991	6513
18 5/16	11 6/16	6 15/16	M	Sandoval County	NM	Noble Sinclair	1992	6513
18 5/16	11 10/16	6 11/16	M	Laurier	MAN	Ted Hysell	1992	6513
18 5/16	11 4/16	7 1/16	M	Idaho County	ID	Rex Summerfield	1992	6513
18 5/16	11 5/16	7 0/16	M	Grafton County	NH	Dana E. Plourde	1992	6513
18 5/16	11 8/16	6 13/16	M	Swan River	MAN	Richard C. Weber	1992	6513
18 5/16	11 12/16	6 9/16	M	Chippewa County	WI	Anthony F. Grimme	1992	6513
18 5/16	11 10/16	6 11/16	M	Clark County	WI	Dennis M. Oczachowski	1992	6513
18 5/16	11 12/16	6 9/16	M	Towns County	GA	Willis Dyer	1992	6513
18 5/16	11 7/16	6 14/16	M	Lac La Biche	ALB	Lewis Coker	1993	6513
18 5/16	11 8/16	6 13/16	M	Bonneville County	ID	Ken Lumpkin	1993	6513
18 5/16	11 9/16	6 12/16	M	Fort Coulonge	QUE	Russ Kay	1993	6513
18 5/16	11 14/16	6 7/16	M	Longlac	ONT	Terry J. Smith	1993	6513
18 5/16	11 6/16	6 15/16	M	Madison County	MT	David Moris	1993	6513
18 5/16	11 9/16	6 12/16	M	Beaverhead County	MT	Lee Murphree	1993	6513
18 5/16	11 5/16	7 0/16	M	Washington County	ME	Del Dinsmore	1993	6513
18 5/16	11 8/16	6 13/16	M	Sup Lake	ONT	Scott Ellery	1993	6513
18 5/16	12 4/16	6 1/16	M	La Corey	ALB	Dewain Ollenberger	1994	6513
18 5/16	11 11/16	6 10/16	M	Slave Lake	ALB	Carl H. Breidegam	1994	6513
18 5/16	11 9/16	6 12/16	M	Smeaton	SAS	Gene A. Welle	1994	6513
18 5/16	11 9/16	6 12/16	M	High Level	ALB	Donny Roy	1994	6513
18 5/16	11 8/16	6 13/16	M	High Level	ALB	Kenneth T. Blount	1994	6513
18 5/16	11 5/16	7 0/16	M	Foleyet	ONT	James Twork	1994	6513
18 5/16	11 5/16	7 0/16	M	Benton County	OR	Gary Champion	1994	6513
18 5/16	11 11/16	6 10/16	F	Olha	MAN	Mike W. Lenz	1994	6513
18 5/16	11 3/16	7 2/16	M	Thunder Bay	ONT	James Sturz	1994	6513
18 5/16	11 12/16	6 9/16	M	Itasca County	MN	John E. Tasker	1994	6513
18 5/16	11 12/16	6 9/16	M	Prince of Wales Island	AK	Kirk Westervelt	1994	6513
18 5/16	11 11/16	6 10/16	M	San Miguel County	CO	Anthony Scott Wagner	1994	6513
18 5/16	11 6/16	6 15/16	M	Bridgeville	NS	Christopher M.W. Tobin	1994	6513
18 5/16	11 13/16	6 8/16	M	Kootenai County	ID	D. V. Moyer	1995	6513
18 5/16	11 7/16	6 14/16	M	Dryden	ONT	Paul Tuscher	1995	6513
18 5/16	11 6/16	6 15/16	M	Elmore County	ID	Anthony L. Mudd	1995	6513
18 5/16	11 10/16	6 11/16	M	Nipawin	SAS	Thomas J. Beissel	1995	6513
18 5/16	11 11/16	6 10/16	M	Smeaton	SAS	Gene Welle	1995	6513
18 5/16	11 7/16	6 14/16	M	Fort McMurray	ALB	Wayne Palinckx	1995	6513
18 5/16	11 5/16	7 0/16	M	Kenora	ONT	Matt Schwab	1995	6513
18 5/16	11 6/16	6 15/16	M	Lake Manitowik	ONT	Chuck Webb	1995	6513
18 5/16	11 15/16	6 6/16	M	St. George	NBW	Mike Steever	1995	6513
18 5/16	11 11/16	6 10/16	M	Forest County	WI	Steven W. Jackson	1995	6513
18 5/16	11 7/16	6 14/16	M	Snow Lake	MAN	George Massie	1996	6513
18 5/16	11 8/16	6 13/16	M	Deux Rivers	QUE	Albert Gawet	1996	6513
18 5/16	11 10/16	6 11/16	M	Caramat	ONT	A. Will Vander Ende	1996	6513
18 5/16	11 6/16	6 15/16	M	High Level	ALB	Landon Koteskey	1996	6513
18 5/16	11 11/16	6 10/16	M	Piscataquis County	ME	Thomas Giambrone	1996	6513
18 5/16	11 10/16	6 11/16	M	Athabasca River	ALB	Michael Hilley	1997	6513
18 5/16	11 5/16	7 0/16	M	High Level	ALB	Del Karnuth	1997	6513
18 5/16	11 5/16	7 0/16	M	Marathon	ONT	Michael L. Ritter	1997	6513
18 5/16	11 14/16	6 7/16	M	Tanana River	AK	George W. Pearson	1997	6513
18 5/16	11 12/16	6 9/16	M	Beltrami County	MN	Todd Hannon	1997	6513
18 5/16	11 13/16	6 8/16	M	Orange County	NY	Mark Gentile	1997	6513
18 5/16	11 10/16	6 11/16	M	Swan Lake	ALB	Derrill Herman	1998	6513
18 5/16	11 11/16	6 10/16	M	Clarke Lake	SAS	Lori Goldade	1998	6513
18 5/16	11 10/16	6 11/16	M	Smeaton	SAS	Nathan V. Schwartz	1998	6513
18 5/16	11 11/16	6 10/16	M	Wabasca River	ALB	Bradley G. Davidson	1998	6513
18 5/16	11 10/16	6 11/16	M	Oak Lake	ONT	Daniel J. Gartner	1998	6513
18 5/16	11 12/16	6 9/16	M	Beluga	AK	Terry L. Kolich	1998	6513
18 5/16	11 8/16	6 13/16	M	Apache County	AZ	Michael J. Windemuller	1998	6513
18 5/16	11 12/16	6 9/16	M	Lake County	MN	Steven S. Bruggeman	1998	6513
18 5/16	11 11/16	6 10/16	M	Pine County	MN	Charles R. Keller	1998	6513
18 5/16	11 12/16	6 9/16	M	Pierceland	SAS	Bruce A. Hatch	1999	6513
18 5/16	11 5/16	7 0/16	M	St. Mary's River	BC	Bob Wright	1999	6513
18 5/16	12 0/16	6 5/16	M	Athabasca River	ALB	Ron Adamson	1999	6513
18 5/16	11 0/16	7 5/16	M	Idaho County	ID	John Albrecht	1999	6513
18 5/16	11 9/16	6 12/16	M	Slave River	ALB	Henry Loving	1999	6513
18 5/16	11 4/16	7 1/16	M	Luce County	MI	Thomas J. Carpenter	1999	6513
18 5/16	11 12/16	6 9/16	M	Ashland County	WI	Allan Guth	1999	6513
18 5/16	11 10/16	6 11/16	M	Botetourt County	VA	John B. Hall	1999	6513
18 5/16	11 9/16	6 12/16	M	Curry County	OR	Matthew C. Gerlach	2000	6513
18 5/16	11 9/16	6 12/16	M	Marchand	MAN	Murray Penner	2000	6513
18 5/16	11 15/16	6 6/16	M	Duck Mtn.	SAS	Ron Vandermeulen	2000	6513
18 5/16	11 11/16	6 10/16	M	Laurier Lake	ALB	Kerwin Laumbach	2000	6513
18 5/16	11 6/16	6 15/16	M	Cranberry Portage	MAN	Joe Ness	2000	6513
18 5/16	11 12/16	6 9/16	M	Fort Smith	ALB	Frank T. Roberts	2000	6513
18 5/16	11 11/16	6 10/16	M	St. Louis County	MN	Kenneth J. Bellin	2000	6513
18 5/16	11 8/16	6 13/16	F	Hubbard County	MN	Gerald R. Schwartz	2000	6513

BLACK BEAR

Minimum Score 18 Continued

SCORE	GREATEST LENGTH	GREATEST WIDTH	SEX	AREA	STATE/PROVINCE	HUNTER'S NAME	DATE	RANK
18 5/16	11 1/16	7 4/16	M	Nestor Falls	ONT	Mark Kawolsky	2000	6513
18 5/16	11 11/16	6 10/16	M	Penobsquis	NBW	Keith Dibble	2000	6513
18 5/16	12 1/16	6 4/16	M	Barron County	WI	Travis Ebner	2000	6513
18 5/16	11 8/16	6 13/16	M	Wapawekka Lake	SAS	Gary L. Stefanovsky	2001	6513
18 5/16	11 11/16	6 10/16	M	Zec Capitachouane	QUE	Daryl Mull	2001	6513
18 5/16	11 12/16	6 9/16	M	Misty Fiords	AK	Michael R. Deschamps	2001	6513
18 5/16	11 4/16	7 1/16	M	Val-d'Or	QUE	Ronald Zajac	2001	6513
18 5/16	11 12/16	6 9/16	M	Thunder Hills	SAS	Nathan Jones	2001	6513
18 5/16	11 9/16	6 12/16	M	Lemhi County	ID	Phillip Forbord	2001	6513
18 5/16	11 4/16	7 1/16	M	Penobscot County	ME	Galen J. Wertz	2001	6513
18 5/16	11 11/16	6 10/16	M	Itasca County	MN	Thomas C. Davis	2001	6513
18 5/16	11 12/16	6 9/16	M	Oconto County	WI	Dave Janssen	2001	6513
18 5/16	11 11/16	6 10/16	M	Price County	WI	Tony S. Cacciotti	2001	6513
18 5/16	11 12/16	6 9/16	F	Clark County	WI	Mark S. Biddle	2001	6513
18 5/16	11 8/16	6 13/16	M	La Plata County	CO	Joseph Alan Bradley	2001	6513
18 5/16	11 9/16	6 12/16	M	MacKay	ALB	David Threadgold	2002	6513
18 5/16	11 9/16	6 12/16	M	Prince of Wales Island	AK	Brad Dorsing	2002	6513
18 5/16	11 9/16	6 12/16	M	Peace River	ALB	Dave Browne	2002	6513
18 5/16	11 11/16	6 10/16	M	Sheridan County	WY	Kerry Johnson	2002	6513
18 5/16	11 3/16	7 2/16	M	Siskiyou County	CA	Jeff Stoddard	2002	6513
18 5/16	11 13/16	6 8/16	M	Smeaton	SAS	John R. Long	2003	6513
18 5/16	11 9/16	6 12/16	M	Valley County	ID	Tyler Pinon	2003	6513
18 5/16	11 10/16	6 11/16	M	Buffalo Narrows	SAS	Rich Haak	2003	6513
18 5/16	11 10/16	6 11/16	M	Bowron River	BC	Steve Edwards	2003	6513
18 5/16	11 4/16	7 1/16	M	Quesnel Lake	BC	Robert J. Gibson	2003	6513
18 5/16	11 8/16	6 13/16	M	Piscataquis County	ME	D. Kenneth Kain	2003	6513
18 5/16	11 3/16	7 2/16	M	Houghton County	MI	Donald J. Wenzlick	2003	6513
18 5/16	11 7/16	6 14/16	M	Idaho County	ID	Kent Rotchy	2003	6513
18 5/16	11 11/16	6 10/16	M	Nicholas County	WV	Homer "Smokey" Clay	2003	6513
18 5/16	11 11/16	6 10/16	M	Smoothstone Lake	SAS	Earl R. Smith	2004	6513
18 5/16	11 7/16	6 14/16	M	Lemhi County	ID	Devlin G. Griebeler	2004	6513
18 5/16	11 13/16	6 8/16	M	Carrot River	SAS	Kenneth Musgrove	2004	6513
18 5/16	11 5/16	7 0/16	M	Pabineau Falls	NBW	Kyle P. Konecny	2004	6513
18 5/16	11 9/16	6 12/16	M	Zec Captitachione	QUE	Paul Fenwick	2004	6513
18 5/16	11 5/16	7 0/16	M	Redditt	ONT	Chris Kingsley	2004	6513
18 5/16	11 5/16	7 0/16	M	Ignace	ONT	William J. Stahl	2004	6513
*18 5/16	11 13/16	6 8/16	M	Peace River	ALB	James C. Kelly	2004	6513
18 5/16	11 5/16	7 0/16	M	Ignace	ONT	Tyler S. Streit	2004	6513
18 5/16	12 1/16	6 4/16	M	Churchill River	SAS	Bill Salzmann	2005	6513
18 5/16	12 1/16	6 4/16	M	Duck Mtn.	MAN	Mike Dunnaway	2005	6513
18 5/16	11 8/16	6 13/16	M	Kipahigan Lake	MAN	Scott G. Hettinger	2005	6513
18 5/16	11 13/16	6 8/16	M	Choiceland	SAS	Eric Kuhlman	2005	6513
18 5/16	11 13/16	6 8/16	M	Stoney Rapids	SAS	Chris Whytock	2005	6513
18 5/16	11 11/16	6 10/16	M	Fresno County	CA	Robert West	2005	6513
18 5/16	11 11/16	6 10/16	M	Orange County	NY	Matthew P. Brocker	2005	6513
18 5/16	11 8/16	6 13/16	M	Seyward	BC	Lorne D. Rinkel	2006	6513
*18 5/16	11 13/16	6 8/16	M	Grande Prairie	ALB	John Mayer	2006	6513
18 5/16	11 11/16	6 10/16	M	Alstead Lake	SAS	Jeff Gourley	2006	6513
*18 5/16	11 4/16	7 1/16	M	Frazen	ONT	Carl Phipps	2006	6513
18 5/16	11 9/16	6 12/16	M	Cook County	MN	Jeff A. Lissick	2006	6513
18 5/16	11 9/16	6 12/16	M	Douglas County	WI	Charles J. Ajer, Sr.	2006	6513
18 5/16	11 3/16	7 2/16	M	Hearst	ONT	David S. Balowski	2006	6513
18 5/16	11 11/16	6 10/16	M	Susitna River	AK	Jeffrey R. Hanson	2006	6513
18 5/16	12 1/16	6 4/16	M	Searcy County	AR	Bobby Boswell	2006	6513
18 5/16	11 8/16	6 13/16	M	Carbon County	WY	T. J. Thrasher	2007	6513
18 5/16	11 6/16	6 15/16	M	Ile-a-La-Crosse	SAS	Dayner Roberts	2007	6513
18 5/16	11 7/16	6 14/16	M	High Mountain Ridge	MAN	Ronald Brunink	2007	6513
18 5/16	11 5/16	7 0/16	M	Gallatin County	MT	Justin Sabol	2007	6513
18 5/16	11 9/16	6 12/16	M	Athabasca River	ALB	Chad Lenz	2008	6513
*18 5/16	11 10/16	6 11/16	M	Geraldton	ONT	Kyle M. Matusinec	2009	6513
18 5/16	11 2/16	7 3/16	M	Boise County	ID	Alan Brock	2009	6513
*18 5/16	12 0/16	6 5/16	M	Lake Manitoba Narrows	MAN	Andrew Vigen	2009	6513
*18 5/16	11 5/16	7 0/16	M	Bissett	MAN	Tyler Triepke	2009	6513
*18 5/16	11 13/16	6 8/16	M	Dolores County	CO	Mike Loyd	2009	6513
*18 5/16	11 15/16	6 6/16	M	Olha	MAN	Dave McFarlin	2010	6513
*18 5/16	11 9/16	6 12/16	M	Snow Lake	MAN	Lloyd Taylor	2010	6513
18 5/16	11 11/16	6 10/16	M	Caswell	AK	Jeremy R. Allegrucci	2010	6513
*18 5/16	11 8/16	6 13/16	M	Chipewyan Lake	ALB	Tad A. Yetter, MD	2010	6513
18 4/16	10 14/16	7 6/16	M	Latah County	ID	Don Lawrence	1962	6719
18 4/16	11 7/16	6 13/16	M	Curry County	OR	Gerald Rimbey	1962	6719
18 4/16	11 4/16	7 0/16	M	Shawano County	WI	Peter Erickson	1967	6719
18 4/16	11 12/16	6 8/16	M	Fort Frances	ONT	Wayne Keefer	1968	6719
18 4/16	11 6/16	6 14/16	M	Idaho County	ID	Larry W. Gehre	1972	6719
18 4/16	11 12/16	6 8/16	M	Itasca County	MN	Lonny Herrick	1973	6719
18 4/16	11 7/16	6 13/16	M	Tuolumne County	CA	Willis Chapman	1974	6719
18 4/16	11 10/16	6 10/16	M	La Plata County	CO	Kenneth L. Biegel	1974	6719
18 4/16	11 6/16	6 14/16	M	Harcourt	ONT	Robert M. Sweisthal	1977	6719
18 4/16	11 7/16	6 13/16	M	Boise County	ID	Richard C. Nichols	1978	6719
18 4/16	11 12/16	6 8/16	M	Caribou County	ID	Randy J. Stephens	1978	6719
18 4/16	11 7/16	6 13/16	M	Piscataquis County	ME	Mark Sutherly	1979	6719
18 4/16	11 8/16	6 12/16	M	Mesa County	CO	David E. Samuel	1979	6719
18 4/16	11 9/16	6 11/16	M	Beltrami County	MN	Greg Siekaniec	1979	6719
18 4/16	11 7/16	6 13/16	M	Vermilion Bay	ONT	Daniel D. Carlson	1979	6719
18 4/16	11 6/16	6 14/16	M	Lily Lake	BC	Stanley Moore	1979	6719
18 4/16	11 7/16	6 13/16	M	Essex County	VT	James 'Boomer' Hayden	1980	6719
18 4/16	11 12/16	6 8/16	M	Tehama County	CA	Gerald McKenzie	1980	6719
18 4/16	11 7/16	6 13/16	M	St. Louis County	MN	Mike Schullo	1981	6719
18 4/16	11 8/16	6 12/16	M	Dryden	ONT	Alan E. Forbes	1982	6719
18 4/16	11 12/16	6 8/16	M	Saginaw Lake	SAS	Don G. Scofield	1982	6719
18 4/16	11 12/16	6 8/16	M	Susitna River	AK	Mel Hein	1983	6719
18 4/16	11 6/16	6 14/16	M	Seine River	ONT	George David Shelton	1983	6719
18 4/16	11 4/16	7 0/16	M	Cloud Bay	ONT	Ronald C. Maikranz	1983	6719
18 4/16	11 10/16	6 10/16	M	Iron County	MI	Jim Johnson	1983	6719
18 4/16	11 10/16	6 10/16	M	Mistatim	SAS	Jeff Grewe	1984	6719
18 4/16	11 8/16	6 12/16	M	Saguache County	CO	Jerry Barth	1984	6719

BLACK BEAR

Minimum Score 18   Continued

SCORE	GREATEST LENGTH	GREATEST WIDTH	SEX	AREA	STATE/ PROVINCE	HUNTER'S NAME	DATE	RANK
18 4/16	10 14/16	7 6/16	M	Idaho County	ID	James Jay Hill	1984	6719
18 4/16	11 4/16	7 0/16	M	Langlade County	WI	Edward R. Jenelewicz	1984	6719
18 4/16	11 8/16	6 12/16	M	Oxford County	ME	Gary Russell	1984	6719
18 4/16	11 12/16	6 8/16	M	Sudbury	ONT	Nancy A. Guisbert	1985	6719
18 4/16	11 10/16	6 10/16	M	Fawcett Lake	ALB	David R. Coupland	1985	6719
18 4/16	11 8/16	6 12/16	M	Bell Lake	ONT	Dale D. Conley	1985	6719
18 4/16	11 8/16	6 12/16	M	Jellicoe	ONT	Mike Mooney	1985	6719
18 4/16	11 0/16	7 4/16	M	Oxford County	ME	Allen Baker	1985	6719
18 4/16	11 6/16	6 14/16	M	Lemhi County	ID	Mark Neer	1985	6719
18 4/16	12 0/16	6 4/16	M	Fort Assiniboine	ALB	Jim Dahlberg	1985	6719
18 4/16	11 10/16	6 10/16	M	Siskiyou County	CA	Arthur M. Cain	1985	6719
18 4/16	11 5/16	6 15/16	M	Smeaton	SAS	Renee Welle	1986	6719
18 4/16	11 8/16	6 12/16	M	Standard Creek	AK	William B. Childress	1986	6719
18 4/16	11 10/16	6 10/16	M	Fort Coulonge	QUE	Anthony G. Horrell	1986	6719
18 4/16	11 2/16	7 2/16	M	Dryden	ONT	Gene Rokus	1986	6719
18 4/16	11 10/16	6 10/16	M	Beaconsfield	NBW	William Clark	1986	6719
18 4/16	11 8/16	6 12/16	M	Fergus	ONT	David L. Reeves	1986	6719
18 4/16	11 11/16	6 9/16	M	Lac du Bonnet	MAN	Russell R. Popp	1987	6719
18 4/16	11 3/16	7 1/16	M	Grand County	CO	Jerry L. Novak	1987	6719
18 4/16	11 5/16	6 15/16	M	Boise County	ID	Jim Wilson	1987	6719
18 4/16	11 15/16	6 5/16	M	Canoe Lake	SAS	Kim Steven Hussong	1988	6719
18 4/16	11 12/16	6 8/16	M	Slave Lake	ALB	Kevin Hehn	1988	6719
18 4/16	11 4/16	7 0/16	M	Felix	ONT	Bradley C. Chamberlain	1988	6719
18 4/16	11 5/16	6 15/16	M	Kenora	ONT	Greg Zirbel	1988	6719
18 4/16	11 14/16	6 6/16	M	Jackson County	OR	Jim Turcke	1988	6719
18 4/16	11 7/16	6 13/16	M	Duchesne County	UT	Dirk B. Watrous	1989	6719
18 4/16	11 11/16	6 9/16	M	Sioux Lookout	ONT	Manfred Gehrlein	1989	6719
18 4/16	11 8/16	6 12/16	M	Lake Manitou	QUE	Keith Mitchell	1989	6719
18 4/16	11 5/16	6 15/16	M	Lincoln County	MT	Robert W. "Bill" Armstrong, Jr.	1989	6719
18 4/16	11 2/16	7 2/16	M	Ravalli County	MT	James Patenaude	1989	6719
18 4/16	11 4/16	7 0/16	M	Gallatin County	MT	Andy Locker	1989	6719
18 4/16	11 10/16	6 10/16	M	Conejos County	CO	Rick Ivers	1990	6719
18 4/16	11 7/16	6 13/16	M	Unit 9A	ONT	Dave Steinhorst	1990	6719
18 4/16	11 12/16	6 8/16	M	Rainy River	ONT	Michael Judas	1990	6719
18 4/16	11 7/16	6 13/16	M	Green Lake	SAS	Herb B. Merkert, Jr.	1990	6719
18 4/16	11 2/16	7 2/16	M	Biscotasing	ONT	Thomas Hlinka	1990	6719
18 4/16	11 8/16	6 12/16	M	Sultan	ONT	Daniel A. Phillips	1990	6719
18 4/16	11 8/16	6 12/16	M	Chibougamau	QUE	Alfred Bergeron	1990	6719
18 4/16	11 7/16	6 13/16	M	Wawa	ONT	Mark R. Sherman	1990	6719
18 4/16	11 6/16	6 14/16	M	Border Lake	BC	Dean Stebner	1990	6719
18 4/16	11 5/16	6 15/16	M	Moon Beam	ONT	Dick Clark	1991	6719
18 4/16	11 6/16	6 14/16	M	Boise County	ID	Richard R. Larrivee	1991	6719
18 4/16	11 10/16	6 10/16	M	Buffalo Narrows	SAS	Bernard J. Garcarz	1991	6719
18 4/16	11 2/16	7 2/16	M	Kapuskasing	ONT	Jim Melton	1991	6719
18 4/16	11 9/16	6 11/16	M	Longlac	ONT	Douglas C. Arnold	1991	6719
18 4/16	11 6/16	6 14/16	M	Temiscaming	QUE	Fred Wallace	1991	6719
18 4/16	11 5/16	6 15/16	M	La Plata County	CO	Perry Howell	1991	6719
18 4/16	11 8/16	6 12/16	M	Kalkaska County	MI	David L. Roose	1991	6719
18 4/16	11 5/16	6 15/16	M	Mink Lake	ONT	David Kennedy	1992	6719
18 4/16	11 9/16	6 11/16	M	Saddle Hills	ALB	Ken Baker	1992	6719
18 4/16	11 4/16	7 0/16	M	Rouyn-Noranda	QUE	Daniel K. Shivery	1992	6719
18 4/16	11 11/16	6 9/16	M	Manitouwadge	ONT	Douglas E. McGuire	1992	6719
18 4/16	11 8/16	6 12/16	M	Lac La Biche	ALB	Tom L. Nelson	1992	6719
18 4/16	11 8/16	6 12/16	M	Fort McMurray	ALB	Bill Thompson	1992	6719
18 4/16	11 10/16	6 10/16	M	Bird River	MAN	William Patrick McQuillen	1992	6719
18 4/16	11 5/16	6 15/16	M	Mine Centre	ONT	David Wolf	1992	6719
18 4/16	11 12/16	6 8/16	M	Boise County	ID	Bruce Capes	1992	6719
18 4/16	11 2/16	7 2/16	M	Wawa	ONT	Sam J. Salem, DDS	1992	6719
18 4/16	11 8/16	6 12/16	M	Kenora	ONT	Dick Schwab	1992	6719
18 4/16	11 8/16	6 12/16	M	Hearst	ONT	David L. Gubine	1992	6719
18 4/16	11 4/16	7 0/16	M	Valmont	QUE	Karlton Pinnix	1992	6719
18 4/16	11 5/16	6 15/16	M	Clearwater County	ID	Jim Bradford	1992	6719
18 4/16	11 4/16	7 0/16	M	Saguenay	QUE	Stan M. Hepler	1992	6719
18 4/16	11 10/16	6 10/16	M	Zec Restigo	QUE	William E. Lockwood, Jr.	1992	6719
18 4/16	11 11/16	6 9/16	M	Gogebic County	MI	Daniel Holtrop	1992	6719
18 4/16	11 8/16	6 12/16	M	Sawyer County	WI	Paul Strong	1992	6719
18 4/16	11 10/16	6 10/16	M	Valleyview	ALB	Bill Vaznis	1993	6719
18 4/16	11 9/16	6 11/16	M	Pelly River	YUK	Steve Byerly	1993	6719
18 4/16	11 6/16	6 14/16	M	Hastings	ONT	Donnie Covey	1993	6719
18 4/16	11 11/16	6 9/16	M	Campbell River	BC	Gary F. Bogner	1993	6719
18 4/16	11 5/16	6 15/16	M	King County	WA	Eric C. Laugen	1993	6719
18 4/16	11 2/16	7 2/16	M	Thunder Bay	ONT	Mark E. Lindgren	1993	6719
18 4/16	11 10/16	6 10/16	M	Boise County	ID	Tom D'Aquino	1993	6719
18 4/16	11 10/16	6 10/16	M	Preston County	WV	Rob Peddicord	1993	6719
18 4/16	11 6/16	6 14/16	M	East Bull Lake	ONT	Steven M. Best	1994	6719
18 4/16	11 8/16	6 12/16	M	Kenora	ONT	David E. Johnson	1994	6719
18 4/16	11 8/16	6 12/16	M	Carswell Lake	SAS	Steve Rucinski	1994	6719
18 4/16	11 12/16	6 8/16	M	Fort Vermilion	ALB	Johnnie R. Walters	1994	6719
18 4/16	11 1/16	7 3/16	M	Sioux Narrows	ONT	Lincoln O. Stafslien	1994	6719
18 4/16	11 8/16	6 12/16	M	Atikokan	ONT	Lynn Reese	1994	6719
18 4/16	11 7/16	6 13/16	M	Chisholm Township	ONT	Dennis Durocher	1994	6719
18 4/16	11 12/16	6 8/16	M	Koochiching County	MN	Gerald J. Gohman	1994	6719
18 4/16	11 10/16	6 10/16	M	Koochiching County	MN	Howard L. Turck	1994	6719
18 4/16	12 1/16	6 3/16	M	Craven County	NC	Tonnie Elwood Davis	1994	6719
18 4/16	11 8/16	6 12/16	M	White Fox	SAS	Jeffrey J. Tobin	1995	6719
18 4/16	11 13/16	6 7/16	M	Athabasca River	ALB	Steve Barnhill	1995	6719
18 4/16	11 10/16	6 10/16	M	Beauval	SAS	Mark Childers	1995	6719
18 4/16	11 12/16	6 8/16	M	Egg Lake	MAN	Jack Evans	1995	6719
18 4/16	11 14/16	6 6/16	M	Dryden	ONT	Dean Bergman	1995	6719
18 4/16	11 9/16	6 11/16	M	Thunder Bay	ONT	Dan Nagel	1995	6719
18 4/16	11 10/16	6 10/16	M	Fort McMurray	ALB	Wayne Palinckx	1995	6719
18 4/16	11 3/16	7 1/16	M	Bissett	MAN	J. Greg Keck	1995	6719
18 4/16	11 13/16	6 7/16	M	Atikokan	ONT	Travis Graves	1995	6719
18 4/16	11 8/16	6 12/16	M	Lemon Lake	BC	Joe Webster	1995	6719
18 4/16	11 10/16	6 10/16	M	St. Louis County	MN	Gregory Gall	1995	6719

BLACK BEAR

Minimum Score 18 Continued

SCORE	GREATEST LENGTH	GREATEST WIDTH	SEX	AREA	STATE/ PROVINCE	HUNTER'S NAME	DATE	RANK
18 4/16	11 8/16	6 12/16	M	La Plata County	CO	Dennis L. Howell	1995	6719
18 4/16	12 0/16	6 4/16	M	Carlton County	MN	Brent Larson	1995	6719
18 4/16	11 4/16	7 0/16	M	Gilmer County	GA	Billy J. Wilson, Jr.	1995	6719
18 4/16	11 2/16	7 2/16	M	Cold Lake	ALB	Glenn E. Moir	1996	6719
18 4/16	11 6/16	6 14/16	M	Dryden	ONT	Paul Martin Zizelman	1996	6719
18 4/16	11 7/16	6 13/16	M	Fort Vermilion	ALB	Stephen A. Hrycko	1996	6719
18 4/16	11 5/16	6 15/16	M	Meadow Lake	SAS	David L. Duncan	1996	6719
18 4/16	11 12/16	6 8/16	M	Bonanza	ALB	John L. Nelson, Sr.	1996	6719
18 4/16	11 3/16	7 1/16	M	Manitouwadge	ONT	Joe Herold	1996	6719
18 4/16	11 9/16	6 11/16	M	Ear Falls	ONT	Dwight Hearing	1996	6719
18 4/16	11 6/16	6 14/16	M	Bissett	MAN	Wayne Nicholson	1996	6719
18 4/16	11 8/16	6 12/16	M	Forest County	WI	Jackie Cook	1996	6719
18 4/16	11 12/16	6 8/16	M	Bayfield County	WI	K-Tal Johnson	1996	6719
18 4/16	11 8/16	6 12/16	M	Spirit River	ALB	Jim Stinson	1997	6719
18 4/16	11 10/16	6 10/16	M	Perth	NBW	Michael E. Breedlove	1997	6719
18 4/16	11 11/16	6 9/16	M	Prince of Wales Island	AK	Rick Tobalsky	1997	6719
18 4/16	11 12/16	6 8/16	M	Hudson Bay	SAS	Dale E. Mateer, DDS	1997	6719
18 4/16	11 9/16	6 11/16	M	Nipawin	SAS	Jim Horneck	1997	6719
18 4/16	11 12/16	6 8/16	M	Sheridan County	WY	Robert A. Austin	1997	6719
18 4/16	11 11/16	6 9/16	M	Indian River	AK	Rick Schikora	1997	6719
18 4/16	11 8/16	6 12/16	M	Nolalu	ONT	Heath Hagner	1997	6719
18 4/16	11 7/16	6 13/16	M	Dryden	ONT	Mark A. Ascheman	1997	6719
18 4/16	11 9/16	6 11/16	M	Itasca County	MN	Ken Thorson	1997	6719
18 4/16	11 8/16	6 12/16	M	Carroll Inlet	AK	Larry Daly	1998	6719
18 4/16	11 8/16	6 12/16	M	McNalley Lake	ALB	Dallas Smith	1998	6719
18 4/16	11 12/16	6 8/16	M	Slave River	ALB	William P. Woller	1998	6719
18 4/16	11 8/16	6 12/16	M	Fort Vermilion	ALB	Carl F. Marquardt	1998	6719
18 4/16	11 13/16	6 7/16	M	Bissett	MAN	Glen P. Mertens	1998	6719
18 4/16	11 4/16	7 0/16	M	White River	ONT	Stuart Wright, Jr.	1998	6719
18 4/16	11 8/16	6 12/16	M	Nestor Falls	ONT	Nicholas Vezzi	1998	6719
18 4/16	11 4/16	7 0/16	M	La Plata County	CO	Garth Schultheis	1998	6719
18 4/16	11 10/16	6 10/16	M	Price County	WI	David Woyak	1998	6719
18 4/16	11 15/16	6 5/16	M	Langlade County	WI	Mark A. Lehrer	1998	6719
18 4/16	11 12/16	6 8/16	M	Hubbard County	MN	Richard M. Olson	1999	6719
18 4/16	11 8/16	6 12/16	M	Coos County	NH	Paul Piwarunas	1999	6719
18 4/16	11 8/16	6 12/16	M	Boise County	ID	Curt L. Giese	2000	6719
18 4/16	11 7/16	6 13/16	M	Prince of Wales Island	AK	Danny Moore	2000	6719
18 4/16	11 9/16	6 11/16	M	Red Earth Creek	ALB	Quentin Falgoust	2000	6719
18 4/16	11 13/16	6 7/16	M	Cascade County	MT	Stephen Tylinski	2000	6719
18 4/16	11 11/16	6 9/16	M	Bissett	MAN	Joe M. Lovoi	2000	6719
18 4/16	11 7/16	6 13/16	M	Mirond Lake	SAS	Scott B. Schelm	2000	6719
18 4/16	11 10/16	6 10/16	F	Carrot River	SAS	Dennis Filipiak	2000	6719
18 4/16	11 10/16	6 10/16	M	Fort McMurray	ALB	H. Mike Palmer	2000	6719
18 4/16	11 8/16	6 12/16	M	Elk Point	ALB	Andy Viel	2001	6719
18 4/16	11 5/16	6 15/16	M	Big Sandy Lake	SAS	John Holt	2001	6719
18 4/16	11 14/16	6 6/16	M	Spruce Home	SAS	Roger Sokolosky	2001	6719
18 4/16	11 13/16	6 7/16	M	Rusk County	WI	Steve Fleck	2001	6719
18 4/16	11 13/16	6 7/16	M	Cold Lake	ALB	John Burke	2002	6719
18 4/16	11 9/16	6 11/16	M	Olha	MAN	Annette L. Gates	2002	6719
18 4/16	11 8/16	6 12/16	M	Penny	BC	Mark Christofferson	2002	6719
18 4/16	11 10/16	6 10/16	M	High Level	ALB	Robert J. Castle	2002	6719
18 4/16	11 6/16	6 14/16	M	Bonnyville	ALB	James A. Henderson	2002	6719
18 4/16	11 8/16	6 12/16	M	Lac Nilgaut	QUE	Robert R. Chappell	2002	6719
18 4/16	11 8/16	6 12/16	M	Matanuska River	AK	Walter J. Roth	2002	6719
18 4/16	11 5/16	6 15/16	M	Howley	NFL	Marc L. Meisel	2002	6719
18 4/16	11 9/16	6 11/16	M	Sublette County	WY	Gil Winters	2002	6719
18 4/16	11 8/16	6 12/16	M	Conejos County	CO	Tyler Smith	2002	6719
18 4/16	11 4/16	7 0/16	M	Jefferson County	CO	Daniel J. Lee	2002	6719
18 4/16	11 13/16	6 7/16	M	Warren County	VA	James Haffer, Jr.	2002	6719
18 4/16	11 12/16	6 8/16	M	Rappahannock County	VA	Marvin T. Breeden	2002	6719
18 4/16	11 12/16	6 8/16	M	Rossburn	MAN	Bryan Todd Klein	2003	6719
18 4/16	11 9/16	6 11/16	M	Kootenai County	ID	David Duthie, Jr.	2003	6719
18 4/16	11 12/16	6 8/16	M	Winnipeg River	MAN	Bill Otis	2003	6719
18 4/16	11 11/16	6 9/16	M	Hudson Bay	SAS	John David Hill	2003	6719
18 4/16	11 6/16	6 14/16	M	Quesnel	BC	Dawna Barton	2003	6719
18 4/16	11 9/16	6 11/16	M	Frobisher Lake	SAS	Richard B. Dyer	2003	6719
18 4/16	11 5/16	6 15/16	M	Idaho County	ID	Tony Jones	2003	6719
18 4/16	11 2/16	7 2/16	M	Idaho County	ID	Johnny Redmon	2003	6719
*18 4/16	11 9/16	6 11/16	M	Ignace	ONT	Joe Michalke	2003	6719
*18 4/16	10 14/16	7 6/16	M	Aroostook County	ME	David Kitchin	2003	6719
18 4/16	11 10/16	6 10/16	M	Clark County	WI	David L. Steiger	2003	6719
*18 4/16	11 14/16	6 6/16	M	Athabasca River	ALB	Neil Triplett	2004	6719
18 4/16	11 13/16	6 7/16	M	Carrot River	SAS	Mark Alexander	2004	6719
18 4/16	11 2/16	7 2/16	M	Churchill River	SAS	Michele Leqve	2004	6719
18 4/16	11 5/16	6 15/16	M	Peace River	ALB	J. P. McDonald	2004	6719
18 4/16	11 14/16	6 6/16	M	Gila County	AZ	Ray Baker	2004	6719
18 4/16	11 8/16	6 12/16	M	Washington County	AR	Ben Moffitt	2004	6719
18 4/16	11 10/16	6 10/16	M	Marinette County	WI	Alex Burnside	2004	6719
*18 4/16	12 0/16	6 4/16	M	Fauquier County	VA	Scott D. Smayda	2004	6719
18 4/16	11 10/16	6 10/16	M	Alstead Lake	SAS	Joseph Bradley	2005	6719
18 4/16	11 8/16	6 12/16	M	Peter Pond Lake	SAS	Ben B. Wallace	2005	6719
18 4/16	11 7/16	6 13/16	M	Churchill Lake	SAS	Eric F. Efird	2005	6719
18 4/16	11 8/16	6 12/16	M	Thompson Lake	SAS	David L. Butler	2005	6719
18 4/16	11 10/16	6 10/16	M	Cree Lake	ONT	James Seals	2005	6719
18 4/16	11 2/16	7 2/16	M	Elk Lake	ONT	Douglas Waite	2005	6719
18 4/16	11 10/16	6 10/16	M	St. Louis County	MN	Tim Stahman	2005	6719
18 4/16	11 10/16	6 10/16	M	Peace River	ALB	Bonnie Giannetti	2006	6719
18 4/16	11 6/16	6 14/16	M	Idaho County	ID	Gary Gapp	2006	6719
18 4/16	11 7/16	6 13/16	M	Ray River	AK	Thomas Chadwick	2006	6719
*18 4/16	11 11/16	6 9/16	M	Prince of Wales Island	AK	Pete Wilcox	2006	6719
*18 4/16	11 11/16	6 9/16	M	Wollaston Lake	SAS	Neil Hamm	2006	6719
18 4/16	11 6/16	6 14/16	M	St- Remi	QUE	Frank Reid	2006	6719
18 4/16	11 11/16	6 9/16	M	Holinshead Lake	ONT	Dennis J. Kohlmeyer	2006	6719
18 4/16	11 8/16	6 12/16	M	Buffalo Narrows	SAS	Dr. Dave Samuel	2007	6719
18 4/16	11 9/16	6 11/16	M	Dover River	ALB	Gunther Tondeleir	2007	6719

197

BLACK BEAR

Minimum Score 18   Continued

SCORE	GREATEST LENGTH	GREATEST WIDTH	SEX	AREA	STATE/PROVINCE	HUNTER'S NAME	DATE	RANK
18 4/16	11 1/16	7 3/16	M	Chilliwack Valley	BC	Robert Zseder	2007	6719
*18 4/16	11 6/16	6 14/16	M	Lloyd Lake	SAS	Kevin Diedrich	2007	6719
18 4/16	11 6/16	6 14/16	M	Val-d'Or	QUE	Robert Amaral	2007	6719
*18 4/16	11 4/16	7 0/16	M	English River	ONT	Rich Morrow	2007	6719
*18 4/16	11 13/16	6 7/16	M	Bear Lake	ONT	Kenny P. Clark	2007	6719
18 4/16	11 9/16	6 11/16	M	Mesa County	CO	Ken Karbon	2007	6719
18 4/16	11 3/16	7 1/16	M	Terrace Bay	ONT	Jason Hettler	2007	6719
18 4/16	11 12/16	6 8/16	M	Dunn County	WI	Frank Fetzer	2007	6719
18 4/16	11 9/16	6 11/16	M	Kuiu Island	AK	Allyn Ladd	2008	6719
*18 4/16	11 12/16	6 8/16	M	Dorintosh	SAS	Bobby Perry	2008	6719
*18 4/16	11 6/16	6 14/16	M	Val-d'Or	QUE	Tom M. Young	2008	6719
18 4/16	11 4/16	7 0/16	M	Aroostook County	ME	Dennis J. Zacholl	2008	6719
*18 4/16	11 8/16	6 12/16	M	Cook County	MN	Matt Dykes	2008	6719
*18 4/16	11 12/16	6 8/16	M	Barron County	WI	Sonja Diedrich	2008	6719
*18 4/16	11 6/16	6 14/16	M	St. James Bay	AK	Jonathan Geary	2009	6719
18 4/16	11 8/16	6 12/16	M	Coldfoot	AK	Johnny Blizzard	2009	6719
18 4/16	11 12/16	6 8/16	M	Prince of Wales Island	AK	Dale Drilling	2009	6719
*18 4/16	11 10/16	6 10/16	M	Bayfield County	WI	Daryl Jensen	2009	6719
*18 4/16	11 13/16	6 7/16	M	Spiritwood	SAS	Jeremiah Roberson	2010	6719
18 4/16	11 8/16	6 12/16	F	Duck Mtn.	SAS	Jeff Jacob	2010	6719
*18 4/16	11 8/16	6 12/16	M	Preissac	QUE	Charles F. Hughes, Jr.	2010	6719
18 3/16	11 1/16	7 2/16	M	Penobscot County	ME	Charles A. Kronyak	1965	6957
18 3/16	11 0/16	7 3/16	M	Custer County	ID	C. Randall Byers	1966	6957
18 3/16	11 15/16	6 4/16	M	Garfield County	CO	Bob Swinehart	1967	6957
18 3/16	11 6/16	6 13/16	M	Florence County	WI	Elaine S. Peck	1967	6957
18 3/16	11 4/16	6 15/16	M	Franklin County	ME	Philip Copp	1967	6957
18 3/16	11 3/16	7 0/16	M	Douglas County	CO	Larry Baker	1975	6957
18 3/16	11 8/16	6 11/16	M	Penobscot County	ME	Neil Zullo	1975	6957
18 3/16	11 6/16	6 13/16	M	Slave Lake	ALB	Gordon Roline	1976	6957
18 3/16	11 8/16	6 11/16	M	Targhee National Forest	ID	Thomas Pinkston	1978	6957
18 3/16	11 3/16	7 0/16	M	Sudbury	ONT	Alvin Lybarger	1979	6957
18 3/16	10 15/16	7 4/16	M	St. Louis County	MN	George Sheets	1979	6957
18 3/16	11 9/16	6 10/16	M	Anchorage	AK	Ronald Arch	1980	6957
18 3/16	11 10/16	6 9/16	M	Renfrew	ONT	Walter Cymbal	1980	6957
18 3/16	11 11/16	6 8/16	M	Fremont County	ID	Doug M. Chase	1981	6957
18 3/16	11 6/16	6 13/16	M	Thunder Bay	ONT	Sharon Larsen	1981	6957
18 3/16	11 7/16	6 12/16	M	Fort Frances	ONT	Pam Baird	1982	6957
18 3/16	11 3/16	7 0/16	M	Baraga County	MI	Jim Humber III	1982	6957
18 3/16	11 2/16	7 1/16	M	Meagher County	MT	Chuck Adams	1982	6957
18 3/16	11 6/16	6 13/16	M	Sierra County	CA	Robert Smith	1982	6957
18 3/16	11 8/16	6 11/16	M	Dryden	ONT	Richard Stock	1983	6957
18 3/16	11 6/16	6 13/16	M	Fremont County	CO	Al Weaver	1983	6957
18 3/16	11 1/16	7 2/16	M	Echouani Lake	QUE	Collins F. Kellogg	1983	6957
18 3/16	11 12/16	6 7/16	M	Burnett County	WI	Daniel D. Clayton	1983	6957
18 3/16	11 10/16	6 9/16	M	Otter Lake	QUE	Dana P. Calhoun	1984	6957
18 3/16	11 10/16	6 9/16	M	Moose River	ONT	Bob Duncan	1984	6957
18 3/16	11 5/16	6 14/16	M	Standard Creek	AK	James A. Jones	1984	6957
18 3/16	11 2/16	7 1/16	M	Idaho County	ID	David Gename	1984	6957
18 3/16	11 11/16	6 8/16	M	Langlade County	WI	Dan Buss	1984	6957
18 3/16	11 2/16	7 1/16	M	Wallowa County	OR	Mike Tyrholm	1984	6957
18 3/16	11 3/16	7 0/16	M	Valley County	ID	Douglas Bunch	1984	6957
18 3/16	11 6/16	6 13/16	M	Douglas County	WI	Dennis Plantenberg	1984	6957
18 3/16	11 10/16	6 9/16	F	Augusta County	VA	W. Thurman Hensley	1984	6957
18 3/16	11 6/16	6 13/16	M	Bear Paw Landing	ONT	Gordan Rabetski	1985	6957
18 3/16	11 3/16	7 0/16	M	Larimer County	CO	Doug O'Herron	1985	6957
18 3/16	11 7/16	6 12/16	M	English River	ONT	Richard Nielsen	1985	6957
18 3/16	11 3/16	7 0/16	M	Ignace	ONT	Walter E. Hammerling	1985	6957
18 3/16	12 1/16	6 2/16	M	Durban	MAN	Bill Wright, Jr.	1985	6957
18 3/16	11 6/16	6 13/16	M	Ear Falls	ONT	James C. Gates	1986	6957
18 3/16	11 15/16	6 4/16	M	Loon Lake	SAS	Harvey McNalley	1986	6957
18 3/16	11 4/16	6 15/16	M	Idaho County	ID	David Gename	1986	6957
18 3/16	11 6/16	6 13/16	M	King County	WA	Charles D. Singh	1986	6957
18 3/16	11 12/16	6 7/16	M	Catron County	NM	Stan Rauch	1987	6957
18 3/16	11 9/16	6 10/16	M	Minaki	ONT	Donald Schram	1987	6957
18 3/16	11 9/16	6 10/16	M	Webbwood	ONT	Stephen P. Turay	1987	6957
18 3/16	11 6/16	6 13/16	M	Gogama	ONT	Tom P. Kidwell	1987	6957
18 3/16	11 6/16	6 13/16	M	Jims Lake	QUE	David A. Shepard	1987	6957
18 3/16	11 5/16	6 14/16	M	Bonneville County	ID	Ron Stacey	1987	6957
18 3/16	11 2/16	7 1/16	M	Washington County	ME	Norman R. Gulbransen	1987	6957
18 3/16	11 11/16	6 8/16	M	Goodsoil	SAS	John Kalbfleisch	1987	6957
18 3/16	11 3/16	7 0/16	M	Oxford County	ME	Patrick Abalsamo	1987	6957
18 3/16	11 3/16	7 0/16	M	Ravalli County	MT	Shaun Twardoski	1987	6957
18 3/16	11 6/16	6 13/16	M	Chippewa Falls	ONT	Christopher J. Hodyna	1988	6957
18 3/16	11 13/16	6 6/16	M	Cordova	AK	Jack E. Lape	1988	6957
18 3/16	11 6/16	6 13/16	M	Sled Lake	SAS	Thomas C. Phillips	1988	6957
18 3/16	11 8/16	6 11/16	M	Dryden	ONT	Stanley M. Eddy	1988	6957
18 3/16	11 8/16	6 11/16	M	Idaho County	ID	Howard Holmes	1988	6957
18 3/16	11 1/16	7 2/16	M	Oxford County	ME	Jack Smith	1988	6957
18 3/16	11 12/16	6 7/16	M	Washburn County	WI	Edward Peterson	1988	6957
18 3/16	11 3/16	7 0/16	M	Lemhi County	ID	Dennis N. Minnich	1989	6957
18 3/16	11 7/16	6 12/16	M	Keg River	ALB	David W. Williams	1989	6957
18 3/16	11 5/16	6 14/16	M	Boise County	ID	Robert Barrow	1989	6957
18 3/16	11 8/16	6 11/16	M	Cass County	MN	Mike Honek	1989	6957
18 3/16	11 2/16	7 1/16	F	Prince of Wales Island	AK	Rickie D. Snell	1990	6957
18 3/16	11 10/16	6 9/16	M	Elk Point	ALB	C. B. Farnsworth	1990	6957
18 3/16	11 7/16	6 12/16	M	Longlac	ONT	David L. Fuller	1990	6957
18 3/16	11 11/16	6 8/16	M	Kenora	ONT	Wayne D. May	1990	6957
18 3/16	12 2/16	6 1/16	M	Beltrami County	MN	Evelyn Johnson	1990	6957
18 3/16	11 12/16	6 7/16	M	Bonnyville	ALB	Glen Garton	1991	6957
18 3/16	11 13/16	6 6/16	F	Camas County	ID	Archie Malone	1991	6957
18 3/16	11 2/16	7 1/16	M	Algoma	ONT	Patrick W. Farrow	1991	6957
18 3/16	11 13/16	6 6/16	M	Peace River	ALB	James D. Caldwell	1991	6957
18 3/16	11 6/16	6 13/16	M	Fairbanks	AK	Randolph M.S. Galloway	1991	6957
18 3/16	11 10/16	6 9/16	M	Grand County	UT	Dave Justmann	1991	6957
18 3/16	11 0/16	7 3/16	M	Dowling	ONT	Lawrence Fillhard	1991	6957

BLACK BEAR

Minimum Score 18 Continued

SCORE	GREATEST LENGTH	GREATEST WIDTH	SEX	AREA	STATE/ PROVINCE	HUNTER'S NAME	DATE	RANK
18 3/16	11 10/16	6 9/16	M	La Ronge	SAS	Roger Wintle	1991	6957
18 3/16	11 10/16	6 9/16	M	Fort McMurray	ALB	Len Cardinale	1991	6957
18 3/16	11 5/16	6 14/16	M	La Tuque	QUE	William R. Lewis	1991	6957
18 3/16	11 10/16	6 9/16	M	Grand Rapids	MAN	Billy J. Waddell	1992	6957
18 3/16	11 6/16	6 13/16	M	Conejos County	CO	Steve Brock	1992	6957
18 3/16	11 5/16	6 14/16	M	Zec Rapides des Joachims	QUE	John Neal, Jr.	1992	6957
18 3/16	11 7/16	6 12/16	M	Saddle Hills	ALB	Wilf Lehners	1992	6957
18 3/16	11 10/16	6 9/16	M	Lake Besnard	SAS	Roger Wintle	1992	6957
18 3/16	11 13/16	6 6/16	M	Zec Dumoine	QUE	James R. Battreall	1992	6957
18 3/16	12 0/16	6 3/16	M	Bayfield County	WI	Gile Gibbons	1992	6957
18 3/16	11 12/16	6 7/16	F	Forest County	WI	Scott P. Allen	1992	6957
18 3/16	11 12/16	6 7/16	M	Lac La Biche	ALB	Russell Bertch	1993	6957
18 3/16	11 8/16	6 11/16	M	Atikokan	ONT	Jim Kirkendall	1993	6957
18 3/16	11 11/16	6 8/16	M	Bissett	MAN	Robert Harris	1993	6957
18 3/16	11 11/16	6 8/16	M	Smeaton	SAS	Gene A. Welle	1993	6957
18 3/16	11 10/16	6 9/16	M	Thunder Bay	ONT	Michael J. Kemp	1993	6957
18 3/16	11 12/16	6 7/16	M	Lac La Biche	ALB	Bruce Nederveld	1993	6957
18 3/16	11 13/16	6 6/16	M	Pine County	MN	Jeff Zormeier	1993	6957
18 3/16	11 12/16	6 7/16	M	Itasca County	MN	Bob Stafford	1993	6957
18 3/16	11 6/16	6 13/16	M	Thunder Bay	ONT	Mike Hudalla	1994	6957
18 3/16	11 11/16	6 8/16	M	Exshaw	ALB	Mark Wuerthele	1994	6957
18 3/16	11 10/16	6 9/16	M	Prince of Wales Island	AK	Robert N. Titus	1994	6957
18 3/16	11 3/16	7 0/16	M	Strong Township	ONT	Roy A. Kelly	1994	6957
18 3/16	11 8/16	6 11/16	M	Cold Lake	ALB	Eric Rauhanen	1994	6957
18 3/16	11 9/16	6 10/16	M	Prince of Wales Island	AK	Gerald L. Egbert	1994	6957
18 3/16	11 7/16	6 12/16	M	Webbwood	ONT	William A. Dickerson	1994	6957
18 3/16	11 14/16	6 5/16	M	Hudson Bay	SAS	William E. Lee, Jr.	1994	6957
18 3/16	11 8/16	6 11/16	M	Forest Area	SAS	Ginger Fausel	1994	6957
18 3/16	11 12/16	6 7/16	M	Kelvington	SAS	Martin A. White	1994	6957
18 3/16	11 10/16	6 9/16	M	Penobscot County	ME	Wade A. Paradis	1994	6957
18 3/16	11 10/16	6 9/16	M	Otero County	NM	Kirk M. Folsom	1994	6957
18 3/16	11 1/16	7 2/16	M	Missoula County	MT	Johnnie Wisnewski	1994	6957
18 3/16	11 8/16	6 11/16	M	Lincoln County	NM	Chris Barrilleaux	1994	6957
18 3/16	11 5/16	6 14/16	M	Yarmouth County	NS	Bill Terry, Sr.	1994	6957
18 3/16	11 9/16	6 10/16	M	Red Earth	ALB	Philip Coulson	1995	6957
18 3/16	11 8/16	6 11/16	M	Shining Tree	ONT	John F. Belha, Jr.	1995	6957
18 3/16	11 7/16	6 12/16	M	Swanson River	AK	Keith Appel	1995	6957
18 3/16	11 6/16	6 13/16	M	Smoky Lake	ALB	Mark Johnson	1995	6957
18 3/16	11 5/16	6 14/16	M	Sioux Lookout	ONT	John Shields	1995	6957
18 3/16	11 5/16	6 14/16	M	Lynn Lake	MAN	Sam J. Valore	1995	6957
18 3/16	11 8/16	6 11/16	M	Ignace	ONT	Gaylord Winterberg	1995	6957
18 3/16	11 8/16	6 11/16	M	Oak Lake	ONT	Ronald A. Hall	1995	6957
18 3/16	11 7/16	6 12/16	M	Hearst	ONT	Russ Riese	1995	6957
18 3/16	11 4/16	6 15/16	M	Dorion	ONT	Larry Paulsen	1995	6957
18 3/16	10 15/16	7 4/16	M	Algoma	ONT	Robert V. Haley, Jr.	1995	6957
18 3/16	11 8/16	6 11/16	M	Lynn Lake	MAN	Andrew W. Szczesniak	1995	6957
18 3/16	11 14/16	6 5/16	M	Becker County	MN	Wayne Enger	1995	6957
18 3/16	11 10/16	6 9/16	M	Douglas County	WI	Lane M. Henck	1995	6957
18 3/16	11 11/16	6 8/16	M	Atikokan	ONT	Ted Kaczmarek	1996	6957
18 3/16	11 3/16	7 0/16	M	Valley County	ID	Jason L. Angell	1996	6957
18 3/16	11 12/16	6 7/16	M	Canton Township	ONT	Jeffery C. Weber	1996	6957
18 3/16	11 11/16	6 8/16	M	Emo	ONT	Robert Kopp	1996	6957
18 3/16	11 8/16	6 11/16	M	Wabigoon	ONT	Jay Peake	1996	6957
18 3/16	11 11/16	6 8/16	M	Marathon	ONT	Michael L. Ritter, Jr.	1996	6957
18 3/16	11 12/16	6 7/16	M	Fairbanks	AK	Robert G. Brown	1996	6957
18 3/16	11 9/16	6 10/16	M	Bayfield County	WI	Craig Stinebrink	1996	6957
18 3/16	11 8/16	6 11/16	M	Ellershouse	NS	Brian W. MacKenzie	1996	6957
18 3/16	11 7/16	6 12/16	M	Saddle Hills	ALB	Dustin Brown	1997	6957
18 3/16	11 7/16	6 12/16	M	Hawkrock River	SAS	Paul Rankin	1997	6957
18 3/16	11 9/16	6 10/16	M	Marshall County	MN	Bret R. Pederson	1997	6957
18 3/16	11 6/16	6 13/16	M	Chippewa County	WI	Brian R. Jiskra	1997	6957
18 3/16	11 2/16	7 1/16	M	Fulton County	NY	Paul W. Graham	1997	6957
18 3/16	11 11/16	6 8/16	M	Athabasca River	ALB	Steve Haufsk	1998	6957
18 3/16	11 8/16	6 11/16	M	Idaho County	ID	Marlon J. Clapham	1998	6957
18 3/16	11 6/16	6 13/16	M	Teton County	ID	Thomas Thiel	1998	6957
18 3/16	11 11/16	6 8/16	M	Gullrock Lake	ONT	Bruce Brinkman	1998	6957
18 3/16	11 10/16	6 9/16	M	Lincoln County	MT	Jay R. Anderson	1998	6957
18 3/16	11 10/16	6 9/16	M	Iron County	WI	William J. Niehaus	1998	6957
18 3/16	11 2/16	7 1/16	M	Sawyer County	WI	Michael Gerner	1998	6957
18 3/16	11 7/16	6 12/16	M	Oxford County	ME	Roger M. Tyler	1998	6957
18 3/16	11 14/16	6 5/16	M	Carrot River	SAS	Derek Revering	1999	6957
18 3/16	11 8/16	6 11/16	M	Quesnel	BC	Steven A. Sarbak	1999	6957
18 3/16	11 9/16	6 10/16	M	Lawrence Lake	ALB	Darrell DuFresne	1999	6957
18 3/16	11 6/16	6 13/16	M	Caribou County	ID	Mont Richter	1999	6957
18 3/16	11 4/16	6 15/16	M	Cadillac	QUE	Michael D. Murray	1999	6957
18 3/16	11 5/16	6 14/16	M	Fish Pott Lake	BC	Rod Stamps	1999	6957
18 3/16	11 8/16	6 11/16	M	Juneau	AK	Elgie Friesen	1999	6957
18 3/16	11 3/16	7 0/16	M	Chibougamau	QUE	Brian R. Brochu	1999	6957
18 3/16	11 10/16	6 9/16	M	Lac Rock	QUE	Paul R. Fenwick	1999	6957
18 3/16	11 8/16	6 11/16	M	Franklin County	ME	Leroy D. Robinson, Jr.	1999	6957
18 3/16	11 8/16	6 11/16	M	Orange County	NY	Darin Opel	1999	6957
18 3/16	11 12/16	6 7/16	M	McDowell County	WV	Barnard Gene Kennedy	1999	6957
18 3/16	11 5/16	6 14/16	F	Carrot River	SAS	Keith Oesterreich	2000	6957
18 3/16	11 9/16	6 10/16	M	Boise County	ID	Scott McGann	2000	6957
18 3/16	11 12/16	6 7/16	M	Berens River	MAN	Dr. Larry Menning	2000	6957
18 3/16	11 5/16	6 14/16	M	Frobisher Lake	SAS	Thomas V. Bell	2000	6957
18 3/16	11 9/16	6 10/16	M	Sandilands	MAN	Russell K. Mehling	2000	6957
18 3/16	11 4/16	6 15/16	M	Clearwater County	ID	Dave R. Burget	2000	6957
18 3/16	11 8/16	6 11/16	M	Bathurst	NBW	Daryl LaBarron	2000	6957
18 3/16	11 6/16	6 13/16	M	Sprott Lake	MAN	Randall F. Summers	2000	6957
18 3/16	11 3/16	7 0/16	M	Piscataquis County	ME	Mark L. Dorty	2000	6957
18 3/16	11 10/16	6 9/16	M	Sawyer County	WI	Mike Kistler	2000	6957
18 3/16	11 11/16	6 8/16	M	Laurier	MAN	Steven J. Malloch	2001	6957
18 3/16	11 7/16	6 12/16	M	Bellecombe	QUE	Richard Cote	2001	6957
18 3/16	11 8/16	6 11/16	M	Kipawa	QUE	Joseph L. Vincent	2001	6957

BLACK BEAR

Minimum Score 18 — Continued

SCORE	GREATEST LENGTH	GREATEST WIDTH	SEX	AREA	STATE/ PROVINCE	HUNTER'S NAME	DATE	RANK
18 3/16	11 10/16	6 9/16	M	Bissett	MAN	John Burgess	2001	6957
18 3/16	11 8/16	6 11/16	M	Round Lake	SAS	Floyd Forster	2001	6957
18 3/16	11 10/16	6 9/16	M	Wawa	ONT	Joe P. Arbic	2001	6957
18 3/16	11 12/16	6 7/16	M	Oconto County	WI	Perry Bertoni	2001	6957
18 3/16	11 9/16	6 10/16	M	Lake of the Woods	MAN	Todd Miller	2002	6957
18 3/16	11 3/16	7 0/16	M	Fort Coulonge	QUE	Rodney A. Cook	2002	6957
18 3/16	11 6/16	6 13/16	M	Murphy Lake	QUE	W. Dennis Showalter	2002	6957
18 3/16	11 10/16	6 9/16	M	Lac La Biche	ALB	Randy Mockerman	2003	6957
18 3/16	11 6/16	6 13/16	M	Val-d'Or	QUE	Bryant Shermoe	2003	6957
18 3/16	11 10/16	6 9/16	M	Idaho County	ID	Mike Moore	2003	6957
18 3/16	11 6/16	6 13/16	M	Redditt	ONT	Timothy Silha	2003	6957
18 3/16	11 7/16	6 12/16	M	Havlin Bay	ONT	Jason Lutter	2003	6957
18 3/16	11 5/16	6 14/16	M	Pemberton	BC	John Paul Schaffer	2004	6957
18 3/16	11 9/16	6 10/16	M	High Level	ALB	Jeff Ensor	2004	6957
18 3/16	11 7/16	6 12/16	M	Tulare County	CA	Clifford Dupee	2004	6957
18 3/16	11 4/16	6 15/16	M	St. Louis County	MN	Christopher D. Federman	2004	6957
18 3/16	11 10/16	6 9/16	M	Greenbrier County	WV	Dwayne R. O'Dell	2004	6957
*18 3/16	11 9/16	6 10/16	M	Vancouver Island	BC	Brandon Ray	2005	6957
*18 3/16	11 12/16	6 7/16	M	Olha	MAN	Stephan Sandness	2005	6957
18 3/16	12 0/16	6 3/16	M	Duck Mtns.	MAN	Royce DeCook	2005	6957
18 3/16	11 10/16	6 9/16	M	East Trout Lake	SAS	Dennis M. Filipiak	2005	6957
*18 3/16	11 12/16	6 7/16	M	Billings Creek	AK	Michelle Williamson	2005	6957
*18 3/16	11 8/16	6 11/16	M	Juniper	NBW	Charles Call	2005	6957
18 3/16	11 2/16	7 1/16	M	Siskiyou County	CA	Mike Walker	2005	6957
*18 3/16	11 11/16	6 8/16	M	Ignace	ONT	Tim R. Johnston	2005	6957
18 3/16	11 6/16	6 13/16	M	Wawa	ONT	James Robert Adkison	2005	6957
18 3/16	11 8/16	6 11/16	M	Fort McMurray	ALB	Kyle R. Hamilton	2006	6957
18 3/16	11 11/16	6 8/16	M	Yorkton	SAS	Colin Laird	2006	6957
18 3/16	11 10/16	6 9/16	M	Prince of Wales Island	AK	Danny Moore	2006	6957
*18 3/16	11 15/16	6 4/16	M	Fort McMurry	ALB	Michael Kevin Bell	2006	6957
18 3/16	11 9/16	6 10/16	M	Tiekel River	AK	Jonah M. Stewart	2006	6957
*18 3/16	11 8/16	6 11/16	M	Forestville	QUE	James Wilhelm	2006	6957
18 3/16	11 2/16	7 1/16	M	Mattice	ONT	Timothy M. Schlaegel	2006	6957
18 3/16	11 6/16	6 13/16	M	St. Louis County	MN	Donald Selby	2006	6957
*18 3/16	11 8/16	6 11/16	M	Eva Lake	ONT	Meegan W. Turnbeaugh	2006	6957
*18 3/16	11 10/16	6 9/16	M	Iron County	MI	James Kory	2006	6957
18 3/16	11 14/16	6 5/16	M	Ontonagon County	MI	Terry Lynn Sheats	2006	6957
18 3/16	11 10/16	6 9/16	M	Sheridan	MAN	Don Lentz	2007	6957
18 3/16	11 10/16	6 9/16	M	Prince of Wales Island	AK	Gary M. Martin	2007	6957
18 3/16	11 9/16	6 10/16	M	Lake Wasekamio	SAS	Richard B. Dyer	2007	6957
18 3/16	11 7/16	6 12/16	M	Perrault Falls	ONT	David G. Casady	2007	6957
18 3/16	11 11/16	6 8/16	M	Peace River	ALB	Timothy Peloso	2008	6957
*18 3/16	11 9/16	6 10/16	M	Athabasca River	ALB	Richard L. Drewry	2008	6957
*18 3/16	11 12/16	6 7/16	M	Minitonas	MAN	Marc Bestvater	2008	6957
*18 3/16	11 8/16	6 11/16	M	Abitibi	QUE	Clarence D. Richardson	2008	6957
18 3/16	11 7/16	6 12/16	M	Dorion	ONT	Dana Smith	2008	6957
18 3/16	11 11/16	6 8/16	M	Marinette County	WI	Donald C. Doolittle	2008	6957
18 3/16	11 11/16	6 8/16	M	Saddle Hills	ALB	Steve Rogers	2009	6957
18 3/16	11 10/16	6 9/16	M	Prince of Wales Island	AK	Don Davidson, Jr.	2009	6957
*18 3/16	11 3/16	7 0/16	M	Lake St. Jean	QUE	James A. Battersby	2009	6957
*18 3/16	11 2/16	7 1/16	M	Dubreuilville	ONT	Bruce Thompson	2009	6957
18 3/16	11 9/16	6 10/16	M	Florence County	WI	Anthony E. Walber	2009	6957
*18 3/16	11 9/16	6 10/16	F	Carrot River	SAS	Ryan Ladner	2010	6957
18 3/16	11 0/16	7 3/16	M	High Rock Lake	SAS	Ron Schauer	2010	6957
18 3/16	11 8/16	6 11/16	M	Pemberton	BC	John Paul Schaffer	2010	6957
*18 3/16	11 11/16	6 8/16	M	Cold Lake	ALB	Chad Emigh	2010	6957
*18 3/16	11 8/16	6 11/16	M	Wollaston Lake	SAS	Donald Hamm	2010	6957
*18 3/16	11 9/16	6 10/16	M	Meagher County	MT	Michael D. Anderson	2010	6957
18 2/16	11 8/16	6 10/16	M	Murphy Dome	AK	Richard Cooper	1955	7184
18 2/16	11 2/16	7 0/16	M	Sudbury	ONT	Floyd Eccleston	1961	7184
18 2/16	11 4/16	6 14/16	M	Penobscot County	ME	Bill L. Carlos	1963	7184
18 2/16	11 8/16	6 10/16	M	Penobscot County	ME	Dennis H. Driscoll	1967	7184
18 2/16	11 8/16	6 10/16	M	Franklin County	ME	Kenneth Rapp	1969	7184
18 2/16	11 5/16	6 13/16	M	Chapleau	ONT	Ed Helgason	1970	7184
18 2/16	11 6/16	6 12/16	M	Chetwynd	BC	Lee E. Hansel	1973	7184
18 2/16	11 9/16	6 9/16	M	La Plata County	CO	Rose Neeley	1975	7184
18 2/16	11 6/16	6 12/16	M	Waupaca County	WI	Neil Pietenpol	1975	7184
18 2/16	11 10/16	6 8/16	M	Marinette County	WI	Jack Baxter	1976	7184
18 2/16	11 12/16	6 6/16	M	Iron County	MI	Harry W. Squibb	1976	7184
18 2/16	10 14/16	7 4/16	M	Flathead County	MT	Paul P. Schafer	1976	7184
18 2/16	11 6/16	6 12/16	M	Madison County	ID	Paul Beesley	1977	7184
18 2/16	11 10/16	6 8/16	M	King County	WA	Stephen C. Zabransky	1978	7184
18 2/16	11 7/16	6 11/16	M	Kootenai County	ID	Stanley Leake	1979	7184
18 2/16	11 8/16	6 10/16	M	Powell County	MT	Paul Brunner	1979	7184
18 2/16	11 4/16	6 14/16	M	Whitney	ONT	Doug Merkel	1979	7184
18 2/16	11 11/16	6 7/16	F	Fremont County	ID	Paul Phillips	1979	7184
18 2/16	11 9/16	6 9/16	M	St. Louis County	MN	James D. Coakley	1979	7184
18 2/16	11 7/16	6 11/16	M	Boise County	ID	Larry Spiva	1979	7184
18 2/16	11 14/16	6 4/16	M	Boise County	ID	Larry Hoff	1980	7184
18 2/16	11 10/16	6 8/16	M	Gunnison County	CO	Holt Dougherty	1980	7184
18 2/16	11 4/16	6 14/16	M	Ear Falls	ONT	Robert J. Roach	1981	7184
18 2/16	10 15/16	7 3/16	M	Coos County	NH	Phillip E. Williams	1981	7184
18 2/16	11 11/16	6 7/16	M	Chichester	QUE	Don Marin	1981	7184
18 2/16	11 4/16	6 14/16	M	Piscataquis County	ME	Daniel E. Reznik	1981	7184
18 2/16	11 8/16	6 10/16	M	Ignace	ONT	Elmer R. Luce, Jr.	1982	7184
18 2/16	11 4/16	6 14/16	M	Washington County	ME	Richard Manchur	1982	7184
18 2/16	11 10/16	6 8/16	M	Clearwater County	ID	Dan J. Martin	1983	7184
18 2/16	11 4/16	6 14/16	M	Longlac	ONT	Bill Zaepfel	1983	7184
18 2/16	11 10/16	6 8/16	M	Algonquin	ONT	Walter F. Dotson, Jr.	1983	7184
18 2/16	11 8/16	6 10/16	M	Dwight	ONT	Walt Krom	1983	7184
18 2/16	11 5/16	6 13/16	M	Sundridge	ONT	Jack Lape	1983	7184
18 2/16	11 2/16	7 0/16	M	Haliburton	ONT	John Dawson	1983	7184
18 2/16	11 1/16	7 1/16	M	Boise County	ID	Larry Spiva	1983	7184
18 2/16	11 8/16	6 10/16	M	Oneida County	WI	Don Ries	1983	7184
18 2/16	11 7/16	6 11/16	M	Ontonagon County	MI	Greg M. Ebel	1983	7184

BLACK BEAR

Minimum Score 18   Continued

SCORE	GREATEST LENGTH	GREATEST WIDTH	SEX	AREA	STATE/ PROVINCE	HUNTER'S NAME	DATE	RANK
18 2/16	11 4/16	6 14/16	M	Latah County	ID	Marcus B. Caudill	1984	7184
18 2/16	11 2/16	7 0/16	M	Cumberland House	SAS	Wayne Muth	1984	7184
18 2/16	11 6/16	6 12/16	M	Latah County	ID	Robert Walter Brooks	1984	7184
18 2/16	11 10/16	6 8/16	M	Clearwater County	ID	Mark McMurray	1984	7184
18 2/16	11 6/16	6 12/16	M	Pontiac	QUE	Russ Kay	1984	7184
18 2/16	11 8/16	6 10/16	M	Fiddler Township	ONT	Mike Johnson	1984	7184
18 2/16	11 9/16	6 9/16	M	Valley County	ID	Kenneth Hyde	1984	7184
18 2/16	11 7/16	6 11/16	M	Sunbury County	NBW	Mike Lamade	1985	7184
18 2/16	11 4/16	6 14/16	M	Fort Coulonge	QUE	Wm. Fred Stone	1985	7184
18 2/16	11 6/16	6 12/16	M	Penobscot County	ME	Gary Thorne	1985	7184
18 2/16	11 6/16	6 12/16	M	Riverside County	CA	Jim Wagner	1985	7184
18 2/16	11 6/16	6 12/16	M	Jackson County	OR	Lou Probo	1985	7184
18 2/16	11 8/16	6 10/16	M	Eagle Lake	ONT	Paul Sieg	1986	7184
18 2/16	11 7/16	6 11/16	M	Fort Frances	ONT	Randy Durushia	1986	7184
18 2/16	11 9/16	6 9/16	M	Wabigoon	ONT	Robert Barrie	1986	7184
18 2/16	11 8/16	6 10/16	F	Hudson Bay	SAS	Floyd Forster	1986	7184
18 2/16	11 15/16	6 3/16	M	Duck Mtn.	MAN	Bill Clink	1986	7184
18 2/16	10 10/16	7 8/16	M	Thaddeus Lake	ONT	Robert Brodhagen	1986	7184
18 2/16	11 10/16	6 8/16	M	Grant County	NM	Dr. Douglas R. Hahn	1986	7184
18 2/16	11 1/16	7 1/16	M	Siskiyou County	CA	Kirk Westervelt	1986	7184
18 2/16	11 6/16	6 12/16	M	Atikokan	ONT	Jim Holdenried	1987	7184
18 2/16	11 12/16	6 6/16	M	Hudson Bay	SAS	Billy Ellis III	1987	7184
18 2/16	11 5/16	6 13/16	M	Ignace	ONT	Richard Nielsen	1987	7184
18 2/16	11 4/16	6 14/16	M	Clearwater County	ID	Timothy A. King	1987	7184
18 2/16	11 7/16	6 11/16	M	Teton County	ID	Frank W. Sparkman	1987	7184
18 2/16	11 6/16	6 12/16	M	Graham County	AZ	Michael E. Duperret	1987	7184
18 2/16	11 11/16	6 7/16	F	Duck Mtn.	MAN	Richard W. Sage	1987	7184
18 2/16	11 4/16	6 14/16	M	Marathon	ONT	Robert W. Russell	1987	7184
18 2/16	11 2/16	7 0/16	M	Essex County	NY	John Douglas Durling	1987	7184
18 2/16	11 15/16	6 3/16	M	King County	WA	Mark A. Graham	1987	7184
18 2/16	11 2/16	7 0/16	M	Baker County	OR	Scott Reed	1988	7184
18 2/16	11 7/16	6 11/16	M	Latah County	ID	Kirk T. Byers	1988	7184
18 2/16	11 6/16	6 12/16	M	Wabigoon	ONT	Albert J. Smith	1988	7184
18 2/16	11 6/16	6 12/16	M	Bear Lake County	ID	Rick Bergholm	1988	7184
18 2/16	11 7/16	6 11/16	M	La Tuque	QUE	Tracey S. Goodrich	1988	7184
18 2/16	11 6/16	6 12/16	M	Wawa	ONT	Donald L. Cox	1988	7184
18 2/16	11 8/16	6 10/16	M	Valley County	ID	Phil Barton	1988	7184
18 2/16	11 1/16	7 1/16	M	Sandoval County	NM	Derek A. Tierney	1988	7184
18 2/16	11 5/16	6 13/16	M	Atikokan	ONT	Marc Headington	1988	7184
18 2/16	11 13/16	6 5/16	M	Loon Lake	SAS	Daniel J. Robertson	1988	7184
18 2/16	11 8/16	6 10/16	M	Whitefish Bay	ONT	Walter Skic	1989	7184
18 2/16	11 7/16	6 11/16	M	Caviar Lake	ONT	Glen Bohl	1989	7184
18 2/16	11 2/16	7 0/16	M	Clearwater County	ID	Dr. Christopher L. Allen	1989	7184
18 2/16	11 8/16	6 10/16	M	Bernalillo County	NM	Joseph Strasser, Jr.	1989	7184
18 2/16	11 8/16	6 10/16	M	King County	WA	Kenneth Bean	1989	7184
18 2/16	11 12/16	6 6/16	M	Valley County	ID	Larry Hoff	1989	7184
18 2/16	11 10/16	6 8/16	M	Lincoln County	WI	William J. Niehaus	1989	7184
18 2/16	11 6/16	6 12/16	M	San Miguel County	NM	Dick McClain	1989	7184
18 2/16	11 6/16	6 12/16	M	Lane County	OR	Jay P. Marcott	1989	7184
18 2/16	11 8/16	6 10/16	M	Longlac	ONT	Steven R. Anderson	1990	7184
18 2/16	11 8/16	6 10/16	M	Cumberland House	SAS	Denny Raper	1990	7184
18 2/16	11 2/16	7 0/16	M	Lake Ascension	QUE	Michael Stone	1990	7184
18 2/16	11 2/16	7 0/16	M	Dryden	ONT	Robert J. Crane	1990	7184
18 2/16	11 4/16	6 14/16	M	Foleyet	ONT	Richard A. Bugher	1990	7184
18 2/16	11 2/16	7 0/16	M	Zec Restigo	QUE	Michael P. Murphy	1990	7184
18 2/16	11 8/16	6 10/16	M	Stevens County	WA	Allen J. Thrush	1990	7184
18 2/16	11 15/16	6 3/16	M	Polk County	AR	Don Cost	1990	7184
18 2/16	11 2/16	7 0/16	M	Lake Kipawa	QUE	Billy Feltman	1991	7184
18 2/16	11 8/16	6 10/16	M	Holinshead Lake	ONT	Linda Turek	1991	7184
18 2/16	11 8/16	6 10/16	M	Lebel Township	ONT	Mike Hartling	1991	7184
18 2/16	11 2/16	7 0/16	M	Aroostook County	ME	Charles Stulz	1991	7184
18 2/16	11 4/16	6 14/16	M	Gift Lake	ALB	Ronald C. Putzler	1992	7184
18 2/16	11 8/16	6 10/16	M	Winefred Lake	ALB	Billy Tillotson	1992	7184
18 2/16	11 11/16	6 7/16	M	Grand County	CO	Barry J. Smith	1992	7184
18 2/16	11 9/16	6 9/16	M	Tyson's Lake	ONT	Gary L. Seabright	1992	7184
18 2/16	11 9/16	6 9/16	M	Savant Lake	ONT	Jerry G. Marchant	1992	7184
18 2/16	11 10/16	6 8/16	M	Spiritwood	SAS	Nick A. Mathews	1992	7184
18 2/16	11 6/16	6 12/16	M	Margo Lake	ONT	Dean V. Ashton	1992	7184
18 2/16	11 12/16	6 6/16	M	Huerfano County	CO	Ronny Stephens	1992	7184
18 2/16	11 8/16	6 10/16	M	Archuleta County	CO	Kevin J. Fuksa	1992	7184
18 2/16	11 7/16	6 11/16	M	Porcupine Mtns.	MAN	John Paul Schaffer	1992	7184
18 2/16	11 4/16	6 14/16	M	Jogues	ONT	Robert J. Rinderknecht	1992	7184
18 2/16	11 10/16	6 8/16	F	Aaron	SAS	Troy Cooper	1993	7184
18 2/16	11 10/16	6 8/16	M	Tulliby Lake	ALB	Cliff Lovelace	1993	7184
18 2/16	11 2/16	7 0/16	M	La Ronge	SAS	James Hummel	1993	7184
18 2/16	11 8/16	6 10/16	M	Monds Township	ONT	Tim Standafer	1993	7184
18 2/16	11 7/16	6 11/16	M	Porcupine Plain	SAS	Ross D. Meyer	1993	7184
18 2/16	11 9/16	6 9/16	M	Candle Lake	SAS	Larry Kerschner	1993	7184
18 2/16	11 4/16	6 14/16	M	Clearwater County	ID	Loy Dean Peters	1993	7184
18 2/16	11 6/16	6 12/16	M	Sioux Lookout	ONT	Gary R. Shields	1993	7184
18 2/16	11 12/16	6 6/16	M	Swan River	MAN	Robert Burdick	1993	7184
18 2/16	11 4/16	6 14/16	M	Vermilion Bay	ONT	Dennis W. Tabor	1993	7184
18 2/16	11 2/16	7 0/16	M	Sussex	NBW	Rene Arsenault	1993	7184
18 2/16	11 9/16	6 9/16	M	Ile-a-La-Crosse	SAS	Dennis M. Filipiak	1993	7184
18 2/16	11 7/16	6 11/16	M	Zec Restigo	QUE	Frank J. Martin	1993	7184
18 2/16	11 9/16	6 9/16	M	Iron County	WI	Ron Macak	1993	7184
18 2/16	11 9/16	6 9/16	M	Sawyer County	WI	Dale A. Williquette	1993	7184
18 2/16	11 12/16	6 6/16	M	Bayfield County	WI	Todd W. Henck	1993	7184
18 2/16	11 8/16	6 10/16	M	Chisholm	ALB	Rob Kubicek	1994	7184
18 2/16	11 10/16	6 8/16	M	Rocky Mountain House	ALB	Darrell Peters	1994	7184
18 2/16	11 7/16	6 11/16	M	Canoe Lake	SAS	Stephen S. King	1994	7184
18 2/16	11 4/16	6 14/16	M	Fort McMurray	ALB	Robert L. Stansfield	1994	7184
18 2/16	11 14/16	6 4/16	M	Manitouwadge	ONT	Daniel Hoogerhyde	1994	7184
18 2/16	11 8/16	6 10/16	M	Barclay	ONT	Thomas B. Reinke	1994	7184
18 2/16	11 10/16	6 8/16	M	Lac Seul	ONT	Manfred Gehrlein	1994	7184

201

BLACK BEAR

Minimum Score 18   Continued

SCORE	GREATEST LENGTH	GREATEST WIDTH	SEX	AREA	STATE/ PROVINCE	HUNTER'S NAME	DATE	RANK
18 2/16	11 9/16	6 9/16	M	Sheridan County	WY	Lyle R. Prell	1994	7184
18 2/16	11 8/16	6 10/16	M	Fort Coulonge	QUE	Terry Lee Summey	1994	7184
18 2/16	11 2/16	7 0/16	M	Washington County	ME	Dennis De Marco	1994	7184
18 2/16	11 9/16	6 9/16	M	Harney County	OR	Brian K. Arndt	1994	7184
18 2/16	11 10/16	6 8/16	M	Marathon County	WI	James D. Churchill	1994	7184
18 2/16	11 0/16	7 2/16	M	Somerset County	ME	David W. Stanley	1994	7184
18 2/16	11 10/16	6 8/16	M	Caramat	ONT	Daniel E. Tyburski	1995	7184
18 2/16	11 6/16	6 12/16	M	Nobel	ONT	Peter N. Synyard	1995	7184
18 2/16	11 2/16	7 0/16	M	Ear Falls	ONT	Thomas R. Walters	1995	7184
18 2/16	11 5/16	6 13/16	M	Foleyet	ONT	Dennis R. Eynon	1995	7184
18 2/16	11 12/16	6 6/16	M	Duck Mtns.	MAN	Sam Y. Perone	1995	7184
18 2/16	11 5/16	6 13/16	M	Cowlitz County	WA	David H. Soyars	1995	7184
18 2/16	12 0/16	6 2/16	M	Sturgeon Lake	ONT	Mike Prokop	1995	7184
18 2/16	11 6/16	6 12/16	M	Lake of the Woods	ONT	Bradley Hering	1995	7184
18 2/16	11 12/16	6 6/16	M	Tehama County	CA	Doug Burgard	1995	7184
18 2/16	11 7/16	6 11/16	M	Tehama County	CA	Scott Vick	1995	7184
18 2/16	11 12/16	6 6/16	M	Garnier Lake	ALB	Vernon Goad	1996	7184
18 2/16	11 9/16	6 9/16	M	Byne Township	ONT	Gerald F. Maas	1996	7184
18 2/16	11 4/16	6 14/16	M	Rainbow Lake	ALB	Lorenzo Dow Utterback	1996	7184
18 2/16	11 6/16	6 12/16	M	St. Louis County	MN	Michael Loesch	1996	7184
18 2/16	11 4/16	6 14/16	M	Red Earth	ALB	Kevin Lamb	1997	7184
18 2/16	11 6/16	6 12/16	M	Ft. McMurray	ALB	Jeffrey L. Thacker	1997	7184
18 2/16	11 7/16	6 11/16	M	Rossburn	MAN	Barry Minshull	1997	7184
18 2/16	10 15/16	7 3/16	M	Terrace Bay	ONT	Jim Peterleus	1997	7184
18 2/16	11 7/16	6 11/16	M	Domaine Preissac	QUE	Joe Jackson	1997	7184
18 2/16	11 5/16	6 13/16	M	Navajo County	AZ	Douglas McEvers	1997	7184
18 2/16	11 8/16	6 10/16	M	St. Louis County	MN	Daniel Kleiber	1997	7184
18 2/16	11 5/16	6 13/16	M	Franklin County	MA	Vincent Paniczko	1997	7184
18 2/16	10 14/16	7 4/16	M	Cheboygan County	MI	Joe A. La Haie	1997	7184
18 2/16	11 11/16	6 7/16	M	Bayfield County	WI	Michael K. Paulcheck	1997	7184
18 2/16	11 8/16	6 10/16	M	Timmins	ONT	Rick Steep	1998	7184
18 2/16	11 2/16	7 0/16	M	Cleveland Peninsula	AK	William H. Welton	1998	7184
18 2/16	11 8/16	6 10/16	M	Sioux Lookout	ONT	John Shields	1998	7184
18 2/16	11 8/16	6 10/16	M	Ray River	ALB	Tom Chadwick	1998	7184
18 2/16	11 9/16	6 9/16	M	Poorman	AK	Jerry L. Cole	1998	7184
18 2/16	11 7/16	6 11/16	M	Cadillac	QUE	Mike Stover	1998	7184
18 2/16	11 9/16	6 9/16	M	Green Lake	SAS	Frank C. Barker, Jr.	1998	7184
18 2/16	11 14/16	6 4/16	M	Langlade County	WI	Terry Hanson	1998	7184
18 2/16	11 7/16	6 11/16	M	Dolores County	CO	Gary Hilbert	1998	7184
18 2/16	11 2/16	7 0/16	M	Chinchaga River	ALB	Gary R. Frost	1999	7184
18 2/16	11 6/16	6 12/16	M	Bathurst	NBW	Charles Dunning	1999	7184
18 2/16	11 2/16	7 0/16	M	Winnipeg	MAN	Chad L. Schmidt	1999	7184
18 2/16	11 11/16	6 7/16	M	Remigny	QUE	Charles Spivey	1999	7184
18 2/16	11 7/16	6 11/16	M	Docktown	NBW	Garry Wright	1999	7184
18 2/16	11 9/16	6 9/16	M	Christopher Lake	SAS	Ivan Muzljakovich	1999	7184
18 2/16	11 9/16	6 9/16	F	Fisher Branch	MAN	Dale Bruckner	1999	7184
18 2/16	11 9/16	6 9/16	M	Gunnison County	CO	Wendy L. Grumbling	1999	7184
18 2/16	11 12/16	6 6/16	M	Swan River	MAN	Mark Kayser	1999	7184
18 2/16	11 8/16	6 10/16	M	La Plata County	CO	Terry Grimes	1999	7184
18 2/16	11 6/16	6 12/16	M	Swallow Lake	ONT	Jayson Brendel	1999	7184
18 2/16	11 2/16	7 0/16	M	Fredericton	NBW	Louis Miranda III	2000	7184
18 2/16	11 10/16	6 8/16	M	William Henry Bay	AK	Matt Friesen	2000	7184
18 2/16	11 10/16	6 8/16	M	Chilkat Range	AK	Darren Baucom	2000	7184
18 2/16	11 10/16	6 8/16	M	Fisher Branch	MAN	Benjamin J. Schnerre	2000	7184
18 2/16	11 2/16	7 0/16	M	Ray River	AK	Thomas Chadwick	2000	7184
18 2/16	11 7/16	6 11/16	M	Saddle Hills	ALB	Terry Hagman	2000	7184
18 2/16	11 4/16	6 14/16	M	Val-d'Or	QUE	William Medeiros, Jr.	2000	7184
18 2/16	11 8/16	6 10/16	M	Chibougamau	QUE	Michael P. Kissel	2000	7184
18 2/16	11 4/16	6 14/16	M	Thunder Bay	ONT	Richard Cobb	2000	7184
18 2/16	11 7/16	6 11/16	M	Fisher Branch	MAN	Tim Mann	2000	7184
18 2/16	11 5/16	6 13/16	M	Nuka Bay	AK	Val M. Koeberlein	2001	7184
18 2/16	11 7/16	6 11/16	M	Pelican Portage	ALB	Wayne A. Carter	2001	7184
18 2/16	11 11/16	6 7/16	M	Rocky Lake	MAN	Bob Smith	2001	7184
18 2/16	11 6/16	6 12/16	M	Chibougamau	QUE	Brian R. Brochu	2001	7184
18 2/16	11 10/16	6 8/16	M	Gillam	MAN	Robert F. Scutt	2001	7184
18 2/16	11 8/16	6 10/16	M	Lac Brush	QUE	Gus Burmeister	2001	7184
18 2/16	11 10/16	6 8/16	M	Wawa	ONT	Thomas E. Hansen II	2001	7184
18 2/16	11 10/16	6 8/16	M	Redditt	ONT	Mark Jacobson	2001	7184
18 2/16	11 14/16	6 4/16	M	Bayfield County	WI	Floyd "Skip" Harvey	2001	7184
18 2/16	11 12/16	6 6/16	M	Pope County	AR	Ted Shinn	2001	7184
18 2/16	11 13/16	6 5/16	M	Meadow Lake	SAS	Bruce J. Church	2002	7184
18 2/16	11 11/16	6 7/16	M	Bathurst	NBW	Daryl A. Labarron	2002	7184
18 2/16	11 14/16	6 4/16	M	Weyakwin	SAS	Andy Milam	2002	7184
*18 2/16	11 12/16	6 6/16	M	Ear Falls	ONT	Tim R. Verhaagh	2002	7184
18 2/16	11 6/16	6 12/16	M	Rabun County	GA	Scott Moore	2002	7184
18 2/16	11 8/16	6 10/16	M	Fort Assiniboine	ALB	Tommy Johnson, Jr.	2003	7184
18 2/16	11 4/16	6 14/16	M	Fairview	ALB	James Collins	2003	7184
18 2/16	11 9/16	6 9/16	M	Frazier River	BC	Richard Combs	2003	7184
*18 2/16	11 10/16	6 8/16	M	Fairview	ALB	Steve Bugbee	2003	7184
18 2/16	11 9/16	6 9/16	M	Geikie River	SAS	Donald S. Dvoroznak	2003	7184
18 2/16	11 4/16	6 14/16	F	Bonneville County	ID	Trisha Hall	2003	7184
18 2/16	11 6/16	6 12/16	F	Buffalo Narrows	SAS	Ken Pettifor	2003	7184
18 2/16	11 12/16	6 6/16	M	Olha	MAN	Lou Milanesi	2003	7184
18 2/16	11 10/16	6 8/16	M	Bonneville County	ID	Wade Hall	2003	7184
18 2/16	11 8/16	6 10/16	M	File Lake	MAN	Mike Wendel	2003	7184
18 2/16	11 3/16	6 15/16	M	Reservoir Cabonga	QUE	Rob Grannis	2003	7184
18 2/16	11 8/16	6 10/16	M	La Tuque	QUE	Leonard Billings	2003	7184
18 2/16	11 0/16	7 2/16	M	Somerset County	ME	Leon C. Franken	2003	7184
18 2/16	11 9/16	6 9/16	M	Marathon County	WI	Jesse J. Arndt	2003	7184
18 2/16	11 4/16	6 14/16	M	Big River	SAS	Doug Sparling	2004	7184
18 2/16	11 8/16	6 10/16	M	Moose Lake	MAN	Warren W. Johnson	2004	7184
18 2/16	11 2/16	7 0/16	M	Frobisher Lake	SAS	S. Stone, Jr.	2004	7184
18 2/16	11 10/16	6 8/16	M	Fort McMurray	ALB	H. Mike Palmer	2004	7184
18 2/16	11 11/16	6 7/16	M	The Pas	MAN	Kelly Altendorf	2004	7184
18 2/16	11 8/16	6 10/16	F	Carrot River	SAS	John Smart	2004	7184

BLACK BEAR

Minimum Score 18   Continued

SCORE	GREATEST LENGTH	GREATEST WIDTH	SEX	AREA	STATE/ PROVINCE	HUNTER'S NAME	DATE	RANK
18 2/16	11 10/16	6 8/16	M	Fond du Lac River	SAS	David L. Butler	2004	7184
18 2/16	11 4/16	6 14/16	M	Redditt	ONT	James Kingsley	2004	7184
*18 2/16	11 10/16	6 8/16	M	Caribou Lake	ONT	Ronald F. Lax	2004	7184
18 2/16	11 12/16	6 6/16	M	Bayfield County	WI	James J. Hort	2004	7184
18 2/16	11 11/16	6 7/16	M	Winnipegosis	MAN	Christopher Vinton	2005	7184
18 2/16	11 8/16	6 10/16	M	Carrot River	SAS	Charles Druecke	2005	7184
18 2/16	11 6/16	6 12/16	M	Besnard Lake	SAS	Ronald Witcher	2005	7184
*18 2/16	11 4/16	6 14/16	M	La Tuque	QUE	Janine Hartman	2005	7184
18 2/16	11 11/16	6 7/16	M	Redditt	ONT	Adam Bauer	2005	7184
18 2/16	11 8/16	6 10/16	M	Ignace	ONT	Bruce Stremcha	2005	7184
*18 2/16	11 0/16	7 2/16	M	Gillies Township	ONT	Mark Foroscij	2005	7184
18 2/16	11 8/16	6 10/16	M	Grand Rapids	MAN	Jon L. Bronnenberg, Jr.	2005	7184
18 2/16	11 12/16	6 6/16	M	Houghton County	MI	Kenneth H. Rogers, Jr.	2005	7184
18 2/16	11 8/16	6 10/16	M	Rusk County	WI	Kurt A. Pike	2005	7184
18 2/16	11 6/16	6 12/16	M	Maple Lake	NS	Marc J. Ruyak	2005	7184
*18 2/16	11 11/16	6 7/16	M	Grande Prairie	ALB	John Mayer	2006	7184
18 2/16	11 6/16	6 12/16	M	Shoshone County	ID	William Freytag	2006	7184
18 2/16	11 7/16	6 11/16	M	Lemhi County	ID	Ben L. Fahnholz	2006	7184
18 2/16	11 12/16	6 6/16	M	Wabigoon	ONT	Alfred Boyer	2006	7184
18 2/16	11 12/16	6 6/16	M	Swan River	MAN	Jon L. Bronnenberg, Jr.	2006	7184
18 2/16	11 9/16	6 9/16	M	St. Louis County	MN	Nick Bistodeau	2006	7184
18 2/16	11 12/16	6 6/16	M	Perrault Falls	ONT	David Winkel	2006	7184
*18 2/16	11 4/16	6 14/16	M	Bathurst	NBW	Allen McNeal	2006	7184
18 2/16	11 8/16	6 10/16	M	Lincoln County	MT	Jeff Carmelt	2006	7184
18 2/16	11 11/16	6 7/16	M	Hay River	ALB	Robert G. Korman, Jr.	2007	7184
18 2/16	11 13/16	6 5/16	M	Puntzi Lake	BC	Tim L. Donnelly	2007	7184
*18 2/16	11 4/16	6 14/16	M	Churchill River	SAS	Jim Leqve	2007	7184
18 2/16	11 3/16	6 15/16	M	Amos	QUE	Jerry May	2007	7184
18 2/16	11 2/16	7 0/16	M	Lemhi County	ID	Shayne J. Hilton	2007	7184
18 2/16	11 4/16	6 14/16	M	Blind River	ONT	Peter M. Kasten	2007	7184
18 2/16	11 3/16	6 15/16	M	Zama	ALB	Ron Morgan	2007	7184
18 2/16	11 7/16	6 11/16	M	Siskiyou County	CA	Matt Petrini	2007	7184
*18 2/16	11 3/16	6 15/16	M	Skeena	BC	David Wildenstein	2008	7184
18 2/16	11 8/16	6 10/16	M	Prince of Wales Island	AK	Joseph M. Roath	2008	7184
18 2/16	11 6/16	6 12/16	M	Grizzly Mtn.	BC	Ken W. Scheer	2008	7184
18 2/16	11 13/16	6 5/16	M	Arborg	MAN	Sherwin Van Kooten	2008	7184
18 2/16	11 10/16	6 8/16	M	Boise County	ID	William E. Dean	2008	7184
18 2/16	11 8/16	6 10/16	M	Hoyt	NBW	John W. Connolly	2008	7184
18 2/16	11 8/16	6 10/16	M	Chitina	AK	Jonah Stewart	2008	7184
18 2/16	11 8/16	6 10/16	M	Wawa	ONT	Travis Siddall	2008	7184
18 2/16	11 8/16	6 10/16	M	Thompson	MAN	Ross Mathew Wolkart	2008	7184
*18 2/16	11 4/16	6 14/16	M	Caramat	ONT	Mark Larner	2008	7184
18 2/16	11 7/16	6 11/16	M	Las Animas County	CO	Ronald Rockwell	2008	7184
*18 2/16	11 5/16	6 13/16	M	Carswell Lake	SAS	Ryan L. Cramer	2009	7184
18 2/16	11 9/16	6 9/16	M	Gypsumville	MAN	Pat Thelen	2009	7184
18 2/16	11 9/16	6 9/16	M	Clark County	ID	Joseph E. Watson	2009	7184
18 2/16	10 14/16	7 4/16	M	El Paso County	CO	Harry J. Riemer II	2009	7184
18 2/16	11 4/16	6 14/16	M	Idaho County	ID	Spike R. Kennedy	2009	7184
18 2/16	11 10/16	6 8/16	M	Bland County	VA	Timothy Ray Compton	2009	7184
18 2/16	11 11/16	6 7/16	M	Athabasca River	ALB	R. Kirk Sharp	2010	7184
*18 2/16	11 1/16	7 1/16	M	Flathead County	MT	Norman B. Larsen	2010	7184
18 1/16	11 8/16	6 9/16	M	Chelan County	WA	Dick Smethurst	1965	7462
18 1/16	11 4/16	6 13/16	M	Clearwater County	ID	Jess Stinichcome	1965	7462
18 1/16	11 0/16	7 1/16	M	Somerset County	ME	Raymond Benedetto	1970	7462
18 1/16	11 7/16	6 10/16	M	Archuleta County	CO	A. H. Gutierrez, Jr.	1971	7462
18 1/16	11 7/16	6 10/16	M	Franklin County	ME	Walter Krom	1972	7462
18 1/16	11 3/16	6 14/16	M	Blackwater River	BC	Ron McKay	1974	7462
18 1/16	10 15/16	7 2/16	M	Chapleau	ONT	Kevin E. Murphy	1975	7462
18 1/16	11 3/16	6 14/16	M	Delta County	MI	Rick Moudry	1975	7462
18 1/16	11 12/16	6 5/16	M	Itasca County	MN	Chuck Schultz	1976	7462
18 1/16	11 4/16	6 13/16	M	Franklin County	ME	Bernard Caruso	1977	7462
18 1/16	11 1/16	7 0/16	M	Saguache County	CO	Robert Faris II	1977	7462
18 1/16	11 8/16	6 9/16	M	Kalkaska County	MI	Jerome H. Lubbers	1978	7462
18 1/16	11 3/16	6 14/16	M	Fremont County	CO	Robert Andrew	1978	7462
18 1/16	11 9/16	6 8/16	M	Cooper Landing	AK	Richard A. Hoag	1979	7462
18 1/16	11 10/16	6 7/16	M	Kenora	ONT	Ervin Wagner	1980	7462
18 1/16	11 6/16	6 11/16	M	Clearwater County	ID	George P. Mann	1980	7462
18 1/16	11 0/16	7 1/16	M	Oxford County	ME	Michael Matoushek	1980	7462
18 1/16	11 8/16	6 9/16	M	Iron County	MI	George Hronkin III	1981	7462
18 1/16	11 8/16	6 9/16	M	Mineral County	MT	Greg L. Munther	1982	7462
18 1/16	11 5/16	6 12/16	M	Idaho County	ID	Brad L. Johnson	1982	7462
18 1/16	11 9/16	6 8/16	M	Archuleta County	CO	Stephen E. Kennedy	1982	7462
18 1/16	11 9/16	6 8/16	M	Dryden	ONT	Anne M. Fancher	1982	7462
18 1/16	11 8/16	6 9/16	M	Dwight	ONT	Michael D. Moore	1983	7462
18 1/16	10 10/16	7 7/16	M	Fort Coulonge	QUE	Curtis A. Feterman	1983	7462
18 1/16	11 5/16	6 12/16	M	Park County	CO	Dan Tekavec	1983	7462
18 1/16	11 2/16	6 15/16	M	Colfax County	NM	Dean Oatman	1983	7462
18 1/16	11 10/16	6 7/16	M	Ignace	ONT	Kenneth C. Kaufmann	1984	7462
18 1/16	11 5/16	6 12/16	M	Clackamas County	OR	Bob Smitherman	1984	7462
18 1/16	11 13/16	6 4/16	M	Price County	WI	Tom Gouger	1984	7462
18 1/16	11 8/16	6 9/16	M	Marinette County	WI	James L. Behn	1984	7462
18 1/16	11 3/16	6 14/16	M	Ashland County	WI	Tony D. Snow	1984	7462
18 1/16	11 9/16	6 8/16	M	McBride Lake	SAS	John Rook	1985	7462
18 1/16	11 3/16	6 14/16	M	Clearwater County	ID	Gene Kiele	1985	7462
18 1/16	11 11/16	6 6/16	M	Nass River	BC	John Jones	1985	7462
18 1/16	11 9/16	6 8/16	M	King County	WA	Greg Winters	1985	7462
18 1/16	11 6/16	6 11/16	M	Payette County	ID	Gary Kinney	1986	7462
18 1/16	11 6/16	6 11/16	M	Lemhi County	ID	Anthony S. Winterer	1986	7462
18 1/16	11 5/16	6 12/16	M	Bird River	MAN	Dale Selby	1986	7462
18 1/16	11 2/16	6 15/16	M	Lemhi County	ID	Cathy Lee Jordan	1986	7462
18 1/16	11 5/16	6 12/16	M	Josephine County	OR	Terry Garbacik	1986	7462
18 1/16	11 8/16	6 8/16	M	Becker County	MN	Richard Erger	1986	7462
18 1/16	11 9/16	6 8/16	M	Wallowa County	OR	Michael Crawford	1986	7462
18 1/16	11 11/16	6 6/16	M	Delta County	CO	Jon P. Thomas	1986	7462
18 1/16	10 13/16	7 4/16	M	Pitkin County	CO	T. Michael Casey	1987	7462

203

BLACK BEAR

Minimum Score 18 — Continued

SCORE	GREATEST LENGTH	GREATEST WIDTH	SEX	AREA	STATE/ PROVINCE	HUNTER'S NAME	DATE	RANK
18 1/16	11 6/16	6 11/16	M	Natal Township	ONT	Terry D. Colescott	1988	7462
18 1/16	11 6/16	6 11/16	M	Maganasipi Lake	QUE	Gerard Mascellino	1988	7462
18 1/16	11 3/16	6 14/16	M	Timmins	ONT	Allen G. Hughes	1988	7462
18 1/16	11 4/16	6 13/16	M	Idaho County	ID	John Zawaski	1988	7462
18 1/16	11 9/16	6 8/16	M	Lemhi County	ID	Tim Kanapeckas	1988	7462
18 1/16	11 12/16	6 5/16	M	Houghton County	MI	John Knieper	1988	7462
18 1/16	11 7/16	6 10/16	M	Skamania County	WA	Annette Crews	1988	7462
18 1/16	11 11/16	6 6/16	M	Huerfano County	CO	Jim Witcombe	1989	7462
18 1/16	11 11/16	6 6/16	M	Mayerthorpe	ALB	Rudy Wilkison	1989	7462
18 1/16	11 7/16	6 10/16	M	Ignace	ONT	Gordan A. Etris	1989	7462
18 1/16	11 7/16	6 10/16	M	Ear Falls	ONT	Larry Sparks	1989	7462
18 1/16	11 1/16	7 0/16	M	Idaho County	ID	Monty Moravec	1989	7462
18 1/16	11 8/16	6 9/16	M	Terrace Bay	ONT	Troy D. Huffman	1989	7462
18 1/16	11 4/16	6 13/16	M	Rapide-des-Joachims	QUE	Pete Karels	1989	7462
18 1/16	11 8/16	6 9/16	M	McKerrow	ONT	Terry Walton	1989	7462
18 1/16	11 1/16	7 0/16	M	Dorion	ONT	Larry Paulsen	1989	7462
18 1/16	11 0/16	7 1/16	M	Custer County	ID	Patrick Patterson	1989	7462
18 1/16	11 3/16	6 14/16	M	Zec Dumoine	QUE	Richard E. Lockwood, Sr.	1989	7462
18 1/16	11 3/16	6 14/16	M	Lewis & Clark County	MT	Ronald Parker	1989	7462
18 1/16	11 9/16	6 8/16	M	Houston	BC	Michael Whited	1990	7462
18 1/16	11 5/16	6 12/16	M	Ear Falls	ONT	Mark Zink	1990	7462
18 1/16	11 3/16	6 14/16	M	Apisko Lake	MAN	Jerry Stroot	1990	7462
18 1/16	11 7/16	6 10/16	M	Nipigon	ONT	Fred W. Achilles	1990	7462
18 1/16	11 8/16	6 9/16	M	Green Lake	SAS	William Smith	1990	7462
18 1/16	11 7/16	6 10/16	M	Huerfano County	CO	Robert L. Beckwith	1990	7462
18 1/16	11 9/16	6 8/16	M	Lake of the Woods	ONT	Scott J. Simons	1991	7462
18 1/16	11 9/16	6 8/16	M	Geraldton	ONT	Clark M. Vickers	1991	7462
18 1/16	11 1/16	7 0/16	M	Pacific County	WA	Brandy Knight	1991	7462
18 1/16	11 8/16	6 9/16	M	Riding Mtn.	MAN	Ryan J. Dorak	1991	7462
18 1/16	11 6/16	6 11/16	M	Kelvington	SAS	Ross Meyer	1992	7462
18 1/16	11 10/16	6 7/16	M	Poplarfield	MAN	Dan Dietrich	1992	7462
18 1/16	11 9/16	6 8/16	M	Kelvington	SAS	Robert C. McCardell	1992	7462
18 1/16	11 3/16	6 14/16	M	Hornepayne	ONT	David M. Lakich	1992	7462
18 1/16	11 11/16	6 6/16	M	Buffalo Narrows	SAS	Dan Phenix	1992	7462
18 1/16	11 8/16	6 9/16	M	Dalton Highway	AK	Thomas Chadwick	1992	7462
18 1/16	11 5/16	6 12/16	M	Atikokan	ONT	Ron Smith	1992	7462
18 1/16	11 2/16	6 15/16	M	Whatcom County	WA	Marc Walker	1992	7462
18 1/16	11 12/16	6 5/16	M	Baraga County	MI	Roger Crosthwaite	1992	7462
18 1/16	11 11/16	6 6/16	M	Pine County	MN	Greg Gulden	1992	7462
18 1/16	11 7/16	6 10/16	M	Sawyer County	WI	Jeff Priest	1992	7462
18 1/16	11 6/16	6 11/16	M	DeBolt	ALB	Jim Hillstead	1993	7462
18 1/16	11 11/16	6 6/16	F	Apache County	AZ	Gregory A. Nixon	1993	7462
18 1/16	11 8/16	6 9/16	M	Thaddeus Lake	ONT	Mel Gilbertson	1993	7462
18 1/16	11 2/16	6 15/16	M	Whitefish Lake	ONT	John Matteson	1993	7462
18 1/16	11 7/16	6 10/16	M	Meadow Lake	SAS	Jim Richards	1993	7462
18 1/16	11 3/16	6 14/16	M	Bathurst	NBW	William LaHue	1993	7462
18 1/16	11 5/16	6 12/16	M	Aroostook County	ME	Joe Layton	1993	7462
18 1/16	11 4/16	6 13/16	M	Grant County	OR	Mike Slinkard	1993	7462
18 1/16	11 1/16	7 0/16	F	Duck Mtns.	SAS	Kurt Heffel	1993	7462
18 1/16	11 9/16	6 8/16	M	Candle Lake	SAS	Larry D. Kerschner	1994	7462
18 1/16	11 1/16	7 0/16	M	Radisson	ONT	Rodney Carpenter	1994	7462
18 1/16	11 4/16	6 13/16	M	Woodlands	MAN	Angelo Novelli	1994	7462
18 1/16	11 8/16	6 9/16	M	Wabigoon	ONT	Charles Drerup	1994	7462
18 1/16	11 8/16	6 9/16	M	Marathon County	WI	Jesse J. Arndt	1994	7462
18 1/16	11 13/16	6 4/16	M	Catron County	NM	Brad Miller	1994	7462
18 1/16	11 6/16	6 11/16	M	Halifax County	NS	Richard D. Russell	1994	7462
18 1/16	11 12/16	6 5/16	M	Polk County	AR	Don Cost	1994	7462
18 1/16	11 9/16	6 8/16	M	Poplarfield	MAN	Keith Boesel	1995	7462
18 1/16	11 6/16	6 11/16	M	Dryden	ONT	Jerry Carr	1995	7462
18 1/16	11 5/16	6 12/16	M	Copperfield	ONT	Thomas Lane	1995	7462
18 1/16	11 12/16	6 5/16	M	Besnard Lake	SAS	Stephen McCarty	1995	7462
18 1/16	11 8/16	6 9/16	M	San Juan County	UT	Gary A. Clum	1995	7462
18 1/16	11 9/16	6 8/16	M	Sandilands	MAN	Lynn Plett	1995	7462
18 1/16	11 0/16	7 1/16	F	Rio Arriba County	NM	Michael K. Fuller	1996	7462
18 1/16	11 4/16	6 13/16	M	Juniper	NBW	Joseph Bartlette	1996	7462
18 1/16	11 4/16	6 13/16	M	Searchmont	ONT	Michael J. Windemuller	1996	7462
18 1/16	11 7/16	6 10/16	M	Piscataquis County	ME	James E. Favreau	1996	7462
18 1/16	11 9/16	6 8/16	M	St. Louis County	MN	Kevin J. Westerberg	1996	7462
18 1/16	11 15/16	6 2/16	M	Polk County	WI	Craig Hedke	1996	7462
18 1/16	11 9/16	6 8/16	M	Langlade County	WI	Joel Taylor	1996	7462
18 1/16	11 10/16	6 7/16	M	Pacific County	WA	Dan Heasley	1996	7462
18 1/16	11 13/16	6 4/16	M	Tuolumne County	CA	Ron Jarvis	1996	7462
18 1/16	11 9/16	6 8/16	M	Carrot River	SAS	Chuck Riggenbach	1997	7462
18 1/16	11 9/16	6 8/16	M	Hudson Bay	SAS	Max E. Hatfield	1997	7462
18 1/16	11 4/16	6 13/16	M	Domaine Preissac	QUE	Clark M. Vickers	1997	7462
18 1/16	11 8/16	6 9/16	M	Lac Obalski	QUE	Max A. Landers	1997	7462
18 1/16	11 3/16	6 14/16	M	Elk Lake	ONT	Chuck J. Chirrup, Jr.	1998	7462
18 1/16	11 7/16	6 10/16	M	Athabasca River	ALB	John MacPeak	1998	7462
18 1/16	11 10/16	6 7/16	M	Sturgeon Landing	SAS	Nathaniel Schroeder	1998	7462
18 1/16	11 5/16	6 12/16	M	Sioux Lookout	ONT	Allen E. Borgeson	1998	7462
18 1/16	11 10/16	6 7/16	M	Threemile Creek	AK	Doug Ferry	1998	7462
18 1/16	11 5/16	6 12/16	M	Lower Ohio	NS	Matthew Marulli	1998	7462
18 1/16	11 6/16	6 11/16	F	Sandilands	MAN	Shelley A. Mehling	1998	7462
18 1/16	11 11/16	6 6/16	M	Dorintosh	SAS	Troy Eberle	1999	7462
18 1/16	11 1/16	7 0/16	M	Lower Chitanana River	AK	Ed Peddicord	1999	7462
18 1/16	11 0/16	7 1/16	M	Plaster Rock	NBW	Ron Krajcsovics	1999	7462
18 1/16	11 6/16	6 11/16	M	Place Lake	BC	Allan Tew	1999	7462
18 1/16	11 10/16	6 7/16	M	Aroostook County	ME	Mark J. Yost	1999	7462
18 1/16	11 7/16	6 10/16	M	Markstay	ONT	Christopher Allen Ewald	1999	7462
18 1/16	11 11/16	6 6/16	M	Madison County	VA	Stephen K. Weeks	1999	7462
18 1/16	11 12/16	6 5/16	M	Valleyview	ALB	Dr. David McNeill	2000	7462
18 1/16	11 3/16	6 14/16	M	Wood River	AK	Jason Manuell	2000	7462
18 1/16	11 8/16	6 9/16	M	Carrot River	SAS	Mark E. Taylor	2000	7462
18 1/16	11 12/16	6 0/16	M	Kanabec County	MN	Ryan Overson	2000	7462
18 1/16	11 3/16	6 14/16	M	Oneida County	NY	Patrick Walters	2000	7462

BLACK BEAR

Minimum Score 18
Continued

SCORE	GREATEST LENGTH	GREATEST WIDTH	SEX	AREA	STATE/ PROVINCE	HUNTER'S NAME	DATE	RANK
18 1/16	11 9/16	6 8/16	M	Rusk County	WI	Scott E. Cichacki	2000	7462
18 1/16	11 4/16	6 13/16	F	Wood River	AK	Dennis Manuell	2001	7462
18 1/16	11 0/16	7 1/16	M	The Pas	MAN	Jack D. Lambert	2001	7462
18 1/16	11 13/16	6 4/16	M	Loon Lake	SAS	Chad Ramsey	2001	7462
18 1/16	11 8/16	6 9/16	M	Smeaton	SAS	John R. Long	2001	7462
18 1/16	11 8/16	6 9/16	M	Fishing Lake	MAN	Mike Lamade	2001	7462
18 1/16	11 4/16	6 13/16	M	Lac Roger	QUE	Robert R. Agnew, Jr.	2001	7462
18 1/16	11 5/16	6 12/16	M	Val-Paradis	QUE	Bryan Burkhardt	2001	7462
18 1/16	11 9/16	6 8/16	M	Domaine Preissac	QUE	James O. Blevins, Jr.	2001	7462
18 1/16	11 6/16	6 11/16	M	Whittier	AK	Kenneth Carvajal	2001	7462
18 1/16	11 10/16	6 7/16	M	Oxford County	ME	Paul Piwarunas	2001	7462
18 1/16	11 9/16	6 8/16	M	Towns County	GA	Tom Winn	2001	7462
18 1/16	11 12/16	6 5/16	M	Buffalo Narrows	SAS	Michael Summers	2002	7462
18 1/16	11 6/16	6 11/16	M	Saddle Hills	ALB	David Watson	2002	7462
18 1/16	11 12/16	6 5/16	M	Smoothstone Lake	SAS	Gregory Hoffmeister	2002	7462
18 1/16	11 9/16	6 8/16	M	Sheridan County	WY	Kristopher Powers	2002	7462
18 1/16	11 9/16	6 8/16	M	Shining Tree	ONT	Mark W. Albaugh	2002	7462
18 1/16	11 5/16	6 12/16	M	Wawa	ONT	William Tennyson Krugh	2002	7462
18 1/16	11 9/16	6 8/16	M	Dryden	ONT	Tim Strobel	2002	7462
18 1/16	11 9/16	6 8/16	M	Poplarfield	MAN	Dale A. Yohe	2003	7462
18 1/16	11 9/16	6 8/16	M	Rossburn	MAN	Michael Smith	2003	7462
18 1/16	11 10/16	6 7/16	M	Athabasca River	ALB	Gary Forte	2003	7462
18 1/16	11 3/16	6 14/16	M	Buffalo Narrows	SAS	Jerry Rakes	2003	7462
18 1/16	11 6/16	6 11/16	M	Zec Captitachione	QUE	Joseph Russo	2003	7462
18 1/16	11 9/16	6 8/16	M	Dog Lake	ONT	Randy K. Thompson	2003	7462
18 1/16	11 9/16	6 8/16	M	Olha	MAN	Cory Wooldridge	2003	7462
18 1/16	11 7/16	6 10/16	M	Fisher Branch	MAN	Josh DePatie	2003	7462
18 1/16	11 8/16	6 9/16	M	Ignace	ONT	David Heath	2003	7462
18 1/16	11 10/16	6 7/16	M	Peace River	ALB	Edward C. Evans	2004	7462
18 1/16	11 9/16	6 8/16	M	Hornepayne	ONT	Coby Smith	2004	7462
18 1/16	11 8/16	6 9/16	M	Ear Falls	ONT	Lance John Pearce	2004	7462
18 1/16	11 12/16	6 5/16	M	Nerepis	NBW	Lloyd C. Jenkins	2004	7462
18 1/16	11 15/16	6 2/16	M	Paradise Hill	SAS	Leads M. DuBois	2005	7462
*18 1/16	11 10/16	6 7/16	M	Hudson Bay	SAS	Jeff Oliphant	2005	7462
*18 1/16	11 10/16	6 7/16	M	Birch	ALB	John Albrecht	2005	7462
18 1/16	11 0/16	7 1/16	M	Flathead County	MT	Shawn Price	2005	7462
*18 1/16	11 6/16	6 11/16	M	Weyakwin Lake	SAS	Jim Weison	2005	7462
18 1/16	11 5/16	6 12/16	M	Oromocto	NBW	Russ Williams	2005	7462
18 1/16	10 15/16	7 2/16	M	Val-d'Or	QUE	Robert Amaral	2005	7462
18 1/16	11 0/16	7 1/16	M	Reservoir Cabonga	QUE	Tom Lagatol III	2005	7462
18 1/16	11 3/16	6 14/16	M	Parkinson Township	ONT	David Rivers	2005	7462
18 1/16	11 8/16	6 9/16	M	Forrest	ONT	Christine Bouford	2005	7462
18 1/16	11 5/16	6 12/16	M	Fayette County	WV	Dwayne F. Hicks	2005	7462
*18 1/16	11 6/16	6 11/16	M	Timmins	ONT	Kirk Short	2006	7462
18 1/16	11 11/16	6 6/16	M	Swan River	MAN	Jon J. Heugel	2006	7462
18 1/16	11 9/16	6 8/16	M	Roscommon County	MI	Troy Spooner	2006	7462
18 1/16	11 13/16	6 4/16	M	Rossburn	MAN	Bryan Klein	2007	7462
*18 1/16	11 9/16	6 8/16	M	Hope	BC	Keith Holdsworth	2007	7462
18 1/16	11 10/16	6 7/16	M	Flatbush	ALB	Kirk Clark	2007	7462
18 1/16	11 8/16	6 9/16	M	Alstead Lake	SAS	Tim Bradley	2007	7462
18 1/16	11 5/16	6 12/16	F	Smeaton	SAS	Michael J. Weber	2007	7462
18 1/16	10 15/16	7 2/16	M	Fort Coulonge	QUE	Walter Dixon	2007	7462
18 1/16	11 3/16	6 14/16	M	Et Coucoushee	QUE	Bob Staniszewski	2007	7462
18 1/16	11 11/16	6 6/16	M	Kamkota	SAS	H. Mike Palmer	2007	7462
*18 1/16	11 8/16	6 9/16	M	Aroostook County	ME	Ronnie "Steve" Hall	2007	7462
18 1/16	11 8/16	6 9/16	M	Bayfield County	WI	Jerry Lunde	2007	7462
18 1/16	11 5/16	6 12/16	M	Boise County	ID	Larry Peplow	2008	7462
18 1/16	11 5/16	6 12/16	M	Gronlid	SAS	Ron Folk	2008	7462
18 1/16	11 5/16	6 12/16	M	Talkeetna River	AK	Matthew Van Dongen	2008	7462
18 1/16	11 2/16	6 15/16	M	Colester Lake	MAN	Bud Sidwell	2008	7462
18 1/16	11 4/16	6 13/16	M	Clearwater Lake	ONT	Dennis J. Kohlmeyer	2008	7462
18 1/16	11 9/16	6 8/16	M	Price County	WI	Brian S. Allison	2008	7462
18 1/16	11 1/16	7 0/16	M	Lemhi County	ID	Ben L. Fahnholz	2009	7462
18 1/16	11 1/16	7 0/16	M	La Tuque	QUE	John Ferris	2009	7462
18 1/16	11 7/16	6 10/16	M	Timmins	ONT	Lawrence W. Merlau	2009	7462
*18 1/16	11 9/16	6 8/16	M	Horsethief Creek	BC	Kent G. Kebe	2009	7462
18 1/16	11 12/16	6 5/16	M	Meadow Lake	SAS	Corey Toews	2009	7462
18 1/16	11 10/16	6 7/16	M	Buffalo Narrows	SAS	Scott Kirsch	2010	7462
18 1/16	11 9/16	6 8/16	M	Lemhi County	ID	Jeffrey Eder	2010	7462
*18 1/16	11 8/16	6 9/16	M	Dubreuilville	ONT	Michael J. Weber	2010	7462
18 0/16	11 0/16	7 0/16	M	Polk County	OR	H. Dale Overholser	1959	7671
18 0/16	11 9/16	6 7/16	M	Prince William Sound	AK	Bob Snelson	1962	7671
18 0/16	11 12/16	6 4/16	M	Franklin County	ME	John Iannuzzo	1966	7671
18 0/16	11 6/16	6 10/16	M	Jackson County	OR	Pat Mastan	1970	7671
18 0/16	11 2/16	6 14/16	M	Franklin County	ME	Donald R. Pyne	1970	7671
18 0/16	11 10/16	7 0/16	M	Franklin County	ME	John Fedor	1973	7671
18 0/16	11 8/16	6 8/16	M	Igitna River	AK	George Faerber	1974	7671
18 0/16	11 10/16	6 6/16	M	Franklin County	ME	Michael P. Murphy	1974	7671
18 0/16	11 4/16	6 12/16	M		ONT	Larry Kuskie	1974	7671
18 0/16	11 6/16	6 10/16	F	Taylor County	WI	Christopher A. Jeffords	1976	7671
18 0/16	11 9/16	6 7/16	M	Marathon County	WI	Jay Schultz	1977	7671
18 0/16	11 12/16	6 4/16	M	Boise County	ID	Clae Kress	1978	7671
18 0/16	11 6/16	6 10/16	M	Franklin County	ME	James E. Roy	1978	7671
18 0/16	11 6/16	6 10/16	M	Siskiyou County	CA	John Grochowski, Jr.	1979	7671
18 0/16	11 8/16	6 8/16	F	Hubbard County	MN	George Arimond	1979	7671
18 0/16	11 10/16	6 6/16	M	Bonneville County	ID	Paul M. Kniss	1980	7671
18 0/16	11 1/16	6 15/16	M	Somerset County	ME	Albert Buonanno	1980	7671
18 0/16	11 3/16	6 13/16	M	Almonte	ONT	Stephen Van Zile	1981	7671
18 0/16	11 8/16	6 8/16	M	Red Lake	ONT	Bernie Pawlaser	1981	7671
18 0/16	11 5/16	6 11/16	M	St. Lawrence County	NY	Richard Hurteau	1981	7671
18 0/16	11 4/16	6 12/16	M	Custer County	CO	Leonard Moore	1981	7671
18 0/16	11 8/16	6 8/16	M	Hatcher Pass	AK	Roger Stewart	1981	7671
18 0/16	11 7/16	6 9/16	M	Thunder Bay	ONT	Rob J. Smith	1981	7671
18 0/16	11 6/16	6 10/16	M	Susitna River	AK	Roger G. Stewart	1984	7671
18 0/16	11 7/16	6 9/16	M	Archuleta County	CO	Roy S. Marlow III	1984	7671

205

BLACK BEAR

Minimum Score 18   Continued

SCORE	GREATEST LENGTH	GREATEST WIDTH	SEX	AREA	STATE/ PROVINCE	HUNTER'S NAME	DATE	RANK
18 0/16	11 10/16	6 6/16	M	Little Susitna River	AK	Gary G. Wall	1984	7671
18 0/16	11 5/16	6 11/16	M	Beluga Mtn.	AK	Dick Carlson	1984	7671
18 0/16	11 6/16	6 10/16	M	Sublette County	WY	Randy Erye	1984	7671
18 0/16	11 1/16	6 15/16	M	North Bay	ONT	John R. Rexroad	1984	7671
18 0/16	11 6/16	6 10/16	M	Messines	QUE	Howard 'Butch' Malone	1984	7671
18 0/16	11 2/16	6 14/16	M	Kechika Range	BC	Wade L. Carstens	1984	7671
18 0/16	11 7/16	6 9/16	M	Iron County	WI	Floyd J. Vancil	1984	7671
18 0/16	11 7/16	6 9/16	M	Gilpin County	CO	Bryon Scott Johnson	1985	7671
18 0/16	11 3/16	6 13/16	M	Anchorage	AK	Ronald D. Mills	1985	7671
18 0/16	11 5/16	6 11/16	M	Idaho County	ID	Ed Vallee	1985	7671
18 0/16	11 9/16	6 7/16	M	Clearwater County	MN	Kyle Bauman	1985	7671
18 0/16	11 7/16	6 9/16	M	Wayne County	PA	Mike B. Lamade	1985	7671
18 0/16	11 10/16	6 6/16	M	Brandon	MAN	Gary Kaluzniak	1986	7671
18 0/16	11 6/16	6 10/16	M	Pasguia Hills	SAS	Marcus Vogel	1986	7671
18 0/16	11 1/16	6 15/16	M	Missoula County	MT	John L. Wozniak	1986	7671
18 0/16	11 6/16	6 10/16	F	Rouyn-Noranda	QUE	Roy Cucuzza	1986	7671
18 0/16	11 2/16	6 14/16	M	Breckenridge Township	ONT	John A. Bogucki	1986	7671
18 0/16	11 8/16	6 8/16	F	Duck Mtn.	MAN	Marty Stubstad	1986	7671
18 0/16	11 5/16	6 11/16	M	Idaho County	ID	Jay J. Bowman	1986	7671
18 0/16	11 8/16	6 8/16	M	Durban	MAN	Jerry V. Finley	1986	7671
18 0/16	11 5/16	6 11/16	M	Oxford County	ME	Christopher Scott Harriman	1986	7671
18 0/16	11 7/16	6 9/16	M	Cook County	MN	Richard P. Smith	1986	7671
18 0/16	11 9/16	6 7/16	M	Dryden	ONT	Jeff Duhrkopf	1986	7671
18 0/16	11 4/16	6 12/16	M	Clearwater County	ID	Christopher B. Holmes	1987	7671
18 0/16	11 8/16	6 8/16	M	Vermilion Bay	ONT	Jerry Podratz	1987	7671
18 0/16	11 5/16	6 11/16	M	Dryden	ONT	Kevin Smaby	1987	7671
18 0/16	11 10/16	6 6/16	M	Capreol	ONT	Tony Willwerth	1987	7671
18 0/16	11 8/16	6 8/16	M	Cowlitz County	WA	David Soyars	1987	7671
18 0/16	11 4/16	6 12/16	M	Muldrew Township	ONT	Daniel P. Wieske	1987	7671
18 0/16	11 11/16	6 5/16	M	Crow Wing County	MN	Ron Snyder	1987	7671
18 0/16	11 5/16	6 11/16	M	Conejos County	CO	Joseph E. Marrinan, Jr.	1988	7671
18 0/16	11 0/16	7 0/16	M	Dorion	ONT	Larry D. Paulsen	1988	7671
18 0/16	11 12/16	6 4/16	M	Talkeetna	AK	Beverly Hajenga	1988	7671
18 0/16	11 4/16	6 12/16	M	Fort Coulonge	QUE	Terry Lee Summey	1988	7671
18 0/16	11 9/16	6 7/16	M	Susitna River	AK	Tom Orbison	1988	7671
18 0/16	11 6/16	6 10/16	M	Valley County	ID	Julie E. Johnston	1988	7671
18 0/16	10 14/16	7 2/16	M	Atikokan	ONT	Matthew Andersen	1988	7671
18 0/16	11 11/16	6 5/16	M	Athabasca River	ALB	Grant Adkisson	1989	7671
18 0/16	11 4/16	6 12/16	M	Algoma	ONT	Denis Belcourt	1989	7671
18 0/16	11 6/16	6 10/16	M	Sexsmith	ALB	Ted Brown	1989	7671
18 0/16	11 9/16	6 7/16	M	Dryden	ONT	Albert J. Smith	1989	7671
18 0/16	11 8/16	6 8/16	M	Flotten Lake	SAS	Paul Prochaska	1989	7671
18 0/16	11 6/16	6 10/16	M	Lac Nilgaut	QUE	John S. Ashe	1989	7671
18 0/16	11 2/16	6 14/16	M	Rollet	QUE	Douglas E. Ott	1989	7671
18 0/16	11 9/16	6 7/16	M	Zec Restigo	QUE	David Dibblee	1989	7671
18 0/16	11 4/16	6 12/16	M	Beurling River	QUE	Philippe Galley	1989	7671
18 0/16	11 7/16	6 9/16	M	Saddle Hills	ALB	Dr. Michael D. Pickering, OD	1990	7671
18 0/16	11 5/16	6 11/16	M	Sturgeon Landing	SAS	Kay Lang	1990	7671
18 0/16	11 4/16	6 12/16	M	Cranberry Portage	MAN	Bob Beardsley	1990	7671
18 0/16	11 6/16	6 10/16	M	Red Lake	ONT	Fred Sprague	1990	7671
18 0/16	11 4/16	6 12/16	M	Echo Bay	ONT	Ralph W. Fairbanks	1990	7671
18 0/16	11 10/16	6 6/16	M	La Tuque	QUE	Ronald T. Kinnas	1990	7671
18 0/16	11 12/16	6 4/16	M	Lake County	MN	John Koschmeder	1990	7671
18 0/16	11 6/16	6 10/16	M	Delta County	MI	Rob Horwitz	1990	7671
18 0/16	11 6/16	6 10/16	M	Caldwell County	NC	Teddy Adams	1990	7671
18 0/16	11 6/16	6 10/16	M	Vermette Lake	SAS	Thomas Faulkner	1991	7671
18 0/16	11 9/16	6 7/16	M	The Pas	MAN	George G. Wilson, Jr.	1991	7671
18 0/16	11 10/16	6 6/16	M	Biscotasing	ONT	Everett W. Ayers	1991	7671
18 0/16	11 2/16	6 14/16	M	Norman Wells	NWT	Lyndon Walker	1991	7671
18 0/16	11 8/16	6 8/16	M	Minitonas	MAN	Mark C. Dale	1991	7671
18 0/16	11 11/16	6 5/16	M	Gunnison County	CO	Robert Kuntz	1991	7671
18 0/16	11 10/16	6 6/16	M	Tobin Lake	SAS	Kirk Winters	1991	7671
18 0/16	11 1/16	6 15/16	M	Chippewa County	WI	Larry Paulsen	1991	7671
18 0/16	11 5/16	6 11/16	M	Ravalli County	MT	David H. Stalling	1991	7671
18 0/16	11 9/16	6 7/16	M	Mesa County	CO	Steven R. Hickok	1992	7671
18 0/16	11 5/16	6 11/16	M	Lake Caviar	ONT	Roger E. Wendorf	1992	7671
18 0/16	11 9/16	6 7/16	M	Lincoln County	WY	Jim Fowler	1992	7671
18 0/16	11 0/16	7 0/16	M	Idaho County	ID	T. J. Conrads	1992	7671
18 0/16	10 14/16	7 2/16	M	Widdifield Township	ONT	Cliff O'Donnell	1992	7671
18 0/16	11 6/16	6 10/16	M	Dryden	ONT	Ollie Crow	1992	7671
18 0/16	11 8/16	6 8/16	M	La Plata County	CO	Dennis L. Howell	1992	7671
18 0/16	11 8/16	6 8/16	M	Swan River	MAN	Mark Barbee	1993	7671
18 0/16	11 6/16	6 10/16	M	Mariana Lakes	ALB	Ryk Visscher	1993	7671
18 0/16	11 14/16	6 2/16	M	Pine River	MAN	Jim Snyder	1993	7671
18 0/16	11 3/16	6 13/16	M	Caramat	ONT	Donald J. Stratton	1993	7671
18 0/16	11 3/16	6 13/16	M	Savant Lake	ONT	Brian Kent Foltz	1993	7671
18 0/16	11 7/16	6 9/16	M	Baraga County	MI	Dean A. Pode	1993	7671
18 0/16	11 4/16	6 12/16	M	Mackinac County	MI	David M. Cole	1993	7671
18 0/16	11 7/16	6 9/16	M	Athabasca River	ALB	Witt Stephens	1994	7671
18 0/16	11 5/16	6 11/16	M	Hillsport	ONT	Andrew V. Rushing, Sr.	1994	7671
18 0/16	11 11/16	6 5/16	M	Ile-a-La-Crosse	SAS	Michael Turner	1994	7671
18 0/16	11 5/16	6 11/16	F	Clearwater County	ID	Cory Schmid	1994	7671
18 0/16	11 6/16	6 10/16	M	Marathon	ONT	Dennis S. Kelly	1994	7671
18 0/16	11 8/16	6 8/16	M	Aitkin County	MN	Jason Bruestle	1994	7671
18 0/16	11 9/16	6 7/16	M	Oconto County	WI	Gary Sigl	1994	7671
18 0/16	11 13/16	6 3/16	M	Sawyer County	WI	William D. Baker	1994	7671
18 0/16	11 10/16	6 6/16	M	Cass County	MN	Bill Krout	1994	7671
18 0/16	11 7/16	6 9/16	M	Kirkland Lake	ONT	Nathan M. Lipsen	1995	7671
18 0/16	11 5/16	6 11/16	M	Monds Township	ONT	Bob Coyle	1995	7671
18 0/16	11 11/16	6 5/16	M	Rocky Lake	MAN	Scott D. Schmidt	1995	7671
18 0/16	11 7/16	6 9/16	M	Prince of Wales Island	AK	Gerald L. Egbert	1995	7671
18 0/16	11 8/16	6 8/16	M	Porcupine Hills	SAS	John Moorhouse	1995	7671
18 0/16	11 5/16	6 11/16	M	Ignace	ONT	Perry D. Larson	1995	7671
18 0/16	11 5/16	6 11/16	M	Lake Wabigoon	ONT	Lowell L. Dupee	1995	7671
18 0/16	11 3/16	6 13/16	M	Go Home Lake	ONT	Vito Palazzolo	1995	7671

BLACK BEAR

Minimum Score 18   Continued

SCORE	GREATEST LENGTH	GREATEST WIDTH	SEX	AREA	STATE/ PROVINCE	HUNTER'S NAME	DATE	RANK
18 0/16	11 9/16	6 7/16	M	Lake Wabigoon	ONT	Gary M. Glunn	1995	7671
18 0/16	11 6/16	6 10/16	M	La Tuque	QUE	Edward P. Bushey, Jr.	1995	7671
18 0/16	11 14/16	6 2/16	M	Wallowa County	OR	Pat Niemi	1995	7671
18 0/16	11 3/16	6 13/16	M	Colfax County	NM	Kim Sevitts	1995	7671
18 0/16	11 5/16	6 11/16	M	Brazeau Dam	ALB	Wayne Depperschmidt	1996	7671
18 0/16	11 4/16	6 12/16	M	Smeaton	SAS	James M. Augustine	1996	7671
18 0/16	11 6/16	6 10/16	M	Hearst	ONT	Jeff Phillips	1996	7671
18 0/16	11 7/16	6 9/16	M	Dorion	ONT	Casey A. Blum	1996	7671
18 0/16	11 13/16	6 3/16	M	High Level	ALB	Ronald R. Grenadier	1996	7671
18 0/16	11 7/16	6 9/16	M	Hearst	ONT	Gregory D. Keeton	1996	7671
18 0/16	11 0/16	7 0/16	M	Little Tomako Lake	ONT	Jeffrey Eddy	1996	7671
18 0/16	11 8/16	6 8/16	M	San Juan County	UT	David B. Nielsen	1996	7671
18 0/16	11 8/16	6 8/16	F	Apache County	AZ	Glen Johnson	1996	7671
18 0/16	11 9/16	6 7/16	M	Swan River	MAN	John P. "Jack" Verwey, Jr.	1996	7671
18 0/16	11 6/16	6 10/16	M	Rio Arriba County	NM	Blaine Underwood	1996	7671
18 0/16	11 5/16	6 11/16	M	Douglas County	WI	Robert M. Zembo	1996	7671
18 0/16	11 4/16	6 12/16	M	Athabasca River	ALB	Mark Calkins	1997	7671
18 0/16	11 9/16	6 7/16	M	Candle Lake	SAS	Carl L. Biscontini	1997	7671
18 0/16	10 12/16	7 4/16	M	Anishinabi Lake	ONT	Kim Knuti	1997	7671
18 0/16	11 7/16	6 9/16	M	Dorion	ONT	Bruce Hudalla	1997	7671
18 0/16	11 10/16	6 6/16	M	Cranberry Portage	MAN	Richard E. Christian	1997	7671
18 0/16	11 12/16	6 4/16	M	Ear Falls	ONT	Randy LeRoy Strong	1997	7671
18 0/16	11 10/16	6 6/16	M	Prince Albert	SAS	Nathan Jones	1997	7671
18 0/16	11 2/16	6 14/16	M	Kapuskasing	ONT	Mike Wiseman	1997	7671
18 0/16	11 12/16	6 4/16	M	Valley County	ID	Larry Hoff	1997	7671
18 0/16	11 11/16	6 5/16	M	Madera County	CA	Sandy Verlench	1997	7671
18 0/16	11 6/16	6 10/16	M	Aroostook County	ME	Robert J. Murowsky	1997	7671
18 0/16	11 11/16	6 5/16	M	Asotin County	WA	Gary Sciuchetti	1997	7671
18 0/16	11 9/16	6 7/16	M	Jackson County	WI	Stewart B. Gilbertson	1997	7671
18 0/16	11 8/16	6 8/16	M	Kitsap County	WA	Steve Simpson	1997	7671
18 0/16	11 12/16	6 4/16	M	Burnett County	WI	Janet Ann Renfrow	1997	7671
18 0/16	11 8/16	6 8/16	M	Hoyt	NBW	Nelson Graham	1997	7671
18 0/16	11 8/16	6 8/16	M	Nicholas County	WV	Joseph Miller	1997	7671
18 0/16	11 6/16	6 10/16	M	Helene Lake	SAS	Rick Stewart	1998	7671
18 0/16	11 7/16	6 9/16	M	Carrot River	SAS	Joseph P. Furlong	1998	7671
18 0/16	11 6/16	6 10/16	M	Cranberry Portage	MAN	David R. Rogers	1998	7671
18 0/16	11 2/16	6 14/16	M	Mattice	ONT	Martin Larson	1998	7671
18 0/16	11 7/16	6 9/16	M	Athabasca River	ALB	John MacPeak	1998	7671
18 0/16	11 6/16	6 10/16	M	Lac Kanasuta	QUE	Al Ferris	1998	7671
18 0/16	11 9/16	6 7/16	M	Lake County	MN	Jeff J. MacDonald	1998	7671
18 0/16	11 8/16	6 8/16	M	Iron Bridge	ALB	William G. Mason	1998	7671
18 0/16	11 4/16	6 12/16	M	Price County	WI	Matt Drossel	1998	7671
18 0/16	11 8/16	6 8/16	M	Salt Prairie	ALB	John Tillotson	1998	7671
18 0/16	11 6/16	6 10/16	M	Ft. McMurray	ALB	Charles L. Palmer	1999	7671
18 0/16	11 10/16	6 6/16	M	Peace River	ALB	Rodney Alexander	1999	7671
18 0/16	11 5/16	6 11/16	M	Elma	MAN	Joel Ross Webster	1999	7671
18 0/16	11 6/16	6 10/16	M	High Level	ALB	John F. Bender	1999	7671
18 0/16	11 10/16	6 6/16	M	Smoothstone River	SAS	Stan Thain	1999	7671
18 0/16	11 6/16	6 10/16	F	Taylor Lake	SAS	John P. Renwick	1999	7671
18 0/16	11 6/16	6 10/16	M	Fort Coulonge	QUE	Michael E. Wolpert	1999	7671
18 0/16	11 14/16	6 2/16	M	Sprague	MAN	Dean T. Thurston	1999	7671
18 0/16	11 11/16	6 5/16	M	Swan River	MAN	Stephen M. Talbott	1999	7671
18 0/16	11 8/16	6 8/16	M	St. George	NBW	Bruce Barrie	2000	7671
18 0/16	11 6/16	6 10/16	M	Idaho County	ID	John Albrecht	2000	7671
18 0/16	11 3/16	6 13/16	M	Custer County	ID	Trent R. Creger	2000	7671
18 0/16	11 3/16	6 13/16	M	Prince of Wales Island	AK	Tom Hoffman	2000	7671
18 0/16	11 7/16	6 9/16	M	Granada	QUE	Gaston Beaudoin	2000	7671
18 0/16	11 6/16	6 10/16	F	Hubbard County	MN	Michael J. Hetland	2000	7671
18 0/16	11 4/16	6 12/16	M	Aroostook County	ME	William S. O'Hearn, Jr.	2000	7671
18 0/16	11 5/16	6 11/16	M	Dorion	ONT	Bruce Hudalla	2000	7671
18 0/16	11 10/16	6 6/16	M	High Level	ALB	Robert Migliore	2001	7671
18 0/16	11 0/16	7 0/16	M	Cranberry Portage	MAN	Michael Wilson	2001	7671
18 0/16	11 5/16	6 11/16	M	Lac La Pause	QUE	Jeannine Vezina	2001	7671
18 0/16	11 8/16	6 8/16	M	Lac Brush	QUE	Stanley McGuigan	2001	7671
18 0/16	11 7/16	6 9/16	M	Sudbury	ONT	Pasquale Mastroianni	2001	7671
18 0/16	11 4/16	6 12/16	M	Chapleau	ONT	Gary Bouts	2001	7671
18 0/16	11 3/16	6 13/16	M	Aroostook County	ME	Daniel Dyer	2001	7671
18 0/16	11 9/16	6 7/16	M	Pikitigushi River	ONT	Scott Liebenguth	2001	7671
*18 0/16	10 14/16	7 2/16	M	Gowganda	ONT	Ronald Brogan, Jr.	2001	7671
18 0/16	11 10/16	6 6/16	M	Custer County	CO	William R. Hull	2001	7671
18 0/16	11 7/16	6 9/16	F	Rusk County	WI	James Zbigniewicz	2001	7671
18 0/16	11 7/16	6 9/16	M	Navajo County	AZ	Charles F. Dick	2002	7671
18 0/16	11 2/16	6 14/16	M	Maniwaki	QUE	Joe Cucuzza	2002	7671
18 0/16	11 8/16	6 8/16	M	Boise County	ID	Jeff Johnson	2002	7671
18 0/16	11 9/16	6 7/16	M	Shoshone County	ID	Kevin Auch	2002	7671
18 0/16	11 8/16	6 8/16	M	Clearwater County	MN	Eric G. Radcliffe	2002	7671
18 0/16	11 8/16	6 8/16	M	Poplarfield	MAN	Jim Caspers	2003	7671
18 0/16	11 6/16	6 10/16	M	Tatlanika Creek	AK	Jason Landing	2003	7671
18 0/16	11 9/16	6 7/16	M	Hudson Bay	SAS	Steve McCluskey	2003	7671
18 0/16	11 9/16	6 7/16	M	Schoolcraft County	MI	Dean W. Shippey	2003	7671
18 0/16	11 3/16	6 13/16	M	Routt County	CO	Newell Ficker	2003	7671
18 0/16	11 6/16	6 10/16	M	Prince of Wales Island	AK	Joe Keathley	2004	7671
18 0/16	11 11/16	6 5/16	M	Clear Lake	MAN	Gene A. Welle	2004	7671
18 0/16	11 6/16	6 10/16	M	Plaster Rock	NBW	David A. Lindsey	2004	7671
18 0/16	11 3/16	6 13/16	M	Idaho County	ID	Gene Hopkins	2004	7671
18 0/16	11 3/16	6 13/16	M	Redditt	ONT	Mark Jacobson	2004	7671
*18 0/16	11 6/16	6 10/16	M	Geraldton	ONT	Floyd Gasser	2004	7671
18 0/16	11 0/16	7 0/16	M	Aroostook County	ME	Shane Meenan	2004	7671
18 0/16	11 10/16	6 6/16	M	Ashland County	WI	David E. Nolan	2004	7671
*18 0/16	11 8/16	6 8/16	M	Florence County	WI	Bill Buechel	2004	7671
18 0/16	11 8/16	6 8/16	M	Redditt	ONT	Jim Meyer	2004	7671
*18 0/16	11 10/16	6 6/16	M	Missoula County	MT	Cy Hanson	2004	7671
18 0/16	11 8/16	6 8/16	M	Madison County	VA	Billy Handle	2004	7671
18 0/16	11 10/16	6 6/16	M	Rice Lake	SAS	James Frank	2005	7671
18 0/16	11 4/16	6 12/16	F	Whitewood	SAS	Kirby Fitch	2005	7671

207

BLACK BEAR

Minimum Score 18   Continued

SCORE	GREATEST LENGTH	GREATEST WIDTH	SEX	AREA	STATE/ PROVINCE	HUNTER'S NAME	DATE	RANK
18 0/16	11 7/16	6 9/16	M	Wapawekka Lake	SAS	Mike Goza	2005	7671
18 0/16	11 3/16	6 13/16	M	Redditt	ONT	Aaron Kingsley	2005	7671
18 0/16	11 6/16	6 10/16	M	Atikokan	ONT	James Misiukiewicz	2005	7671
*18 0/16	11 10/16	6 6/16	M	Lake Cignet	ONT	Bob Spitz	2005	7671
*18 0/16	11 3/16	6 13/16	M	Jellicoe	ONT	David Swiercz	2005	7671
18 0/16	11 8/16	6 8/16	M	Gallatin County	MT	William Elfland	2005	7671
*18 0/16	11 9/16	6 7/16	M	Carbon County	WY	Cedar Beauregard	2006	7671
18 0/16	11 10/16	6 6/16	M	Kuiu Island	AK	Frank S. Noska IV	2006	7671
*18 0/16	11 3/16	6 13/16	F	Carswell Lake	SAS	Todd Delaney	2006	7671
18 0/16	11 9/16	6 7/16	M	Alstead Lake	SAS	Joseph Bradley	2006	7671
18 0/16	11 10/16	6 6/16	M	Athabasca River	ALB	Ronald Rockwell	2006	7671
18 0/16	11 8/16	6 8/16	M	Lynn Lake	MAN	Pat Ronspies	2006	7671
18 0/16	11 4/16	6 12/16	M	Swanson River	AK	Michael Scott Overton	2006	7671
*18 0/16	11 6/16	6 10/16	M	Hartland	NBW	Richard A. Blair	2006	7671
18 0/16	11 11/16	6 5/16	M	Bayfield County	WI	Lawrence D. Yaap	2006	7671
18 0/16	11 10/16	6 6/16	M	Oromocto	NBW	Darrell Williams	2006	7671
18 0/16	11 4/16	6 12/16	M	Ft. McMurray	ALB	Gene Milton	2007	7671
18 0/16	11 11/16	6 5/16	M	Carrot River	SAS	Randy Templeton	2007	7671
*18 0/16	11 8/16	6 8/16	M	Whiteshell Provincial Park	MAN	Tim Graveline	2007	7671
18 0/16	11 8/16	6 8/16	M	Boise County	ID	Matthew Franks	2007	7671
*18 0/16	11 10/16	6 6/16	M	Nipawin	SAS	Phil Jane	2007	7671
*18 0/16	11 0/16	7 0/16	M	Terrace	BC	Chris Laris	2008	7671
18 0/16	11 7/16	6 9/16	M	Alstead Lake	SAS	Tim Bradley	2008	7671
*18 0/16	11 3/16	6 13/16	F	Prince of Wales Island	AK	M. Blake Patton	2008	7671
18 0/16	11 12/16	6 4/16	M	Lincoln County	NM	Brandon Ray	2008	7671
18 0/16	11 7/16	6 9/16	M	Redditt	ONT	Bret A. Mattice	2008	7671
18 0/16	11 7/16	6 9/16	M	Bonner County	ID	George L. Diffey	2008	7671
18 0/16	11 7/16	6 9/16	M	Koochiching County	MN	Charles W. Schultz	2008	7671
18 0/16	11 8/16	6 8/16	M	Big River	SAS	Woodrow Sullivan III	2009	7671
*18 0/16	11 8/16	6 8/16	M	Terrace	BC	Allen Bolen	2009	7671
18 0/16	11 11/16	6 5/16	M	Gila County	AZ	Jon R. Waggoner	2009	7671
*18 0/16	11 1/16	6 15/16	M	Kootenai County	ID	Jack Rinallo, Jr.	2009	7671
*18 0/16	11 3/16	6 13/16	M	Lincoln County	MT	Timothy J. Doll	2009	7671
*18 0/16	11 14/16	6 2/16	M	Sheridan County	WY	Lance Baker	2010	7671
*18 0/16	11 1/16	6 15/16	M	Sevier County	TN	Robert M. (Mike) Young	2010	7671

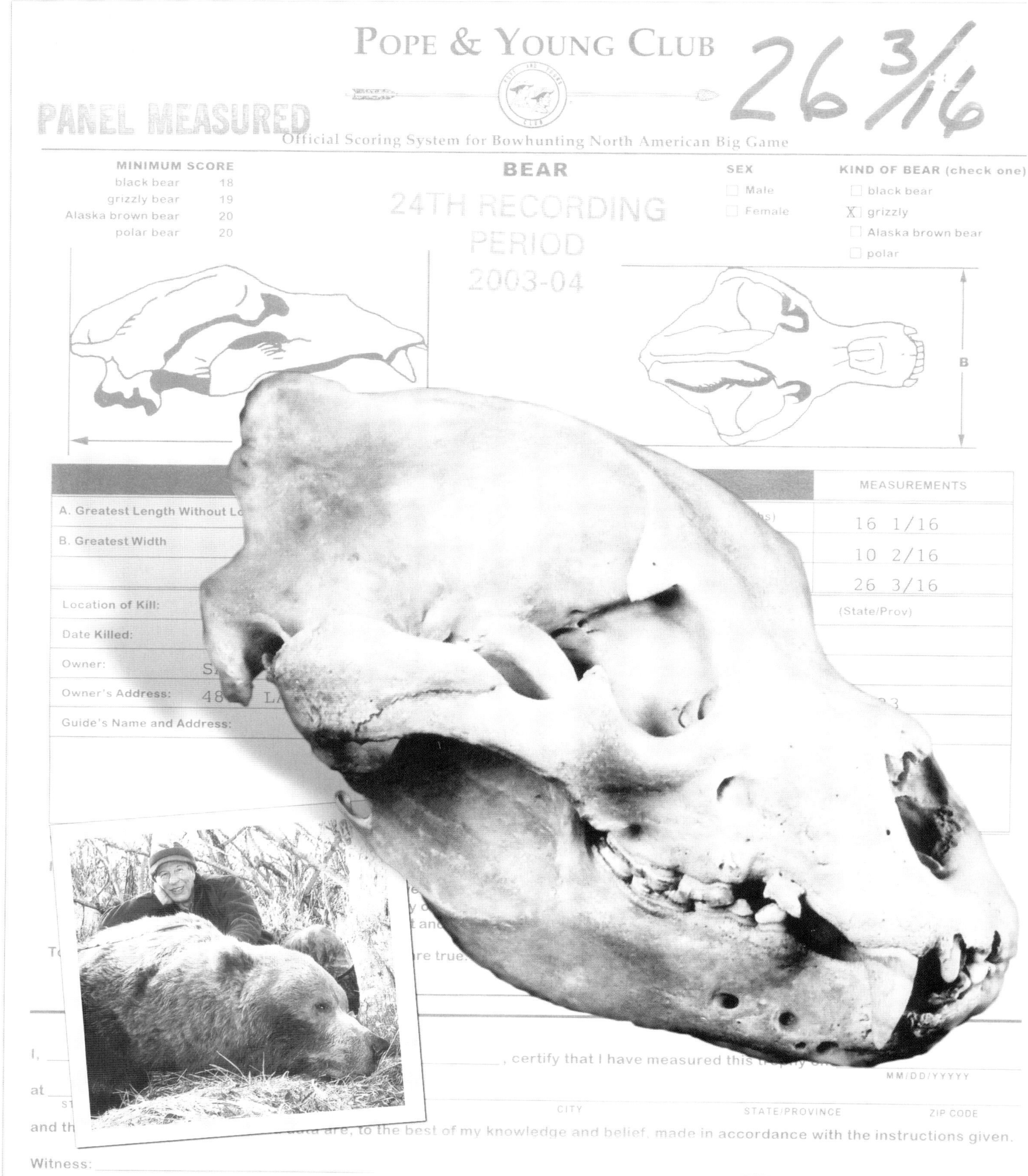

26 3/16
POPE & YOUNG CLUB
PANEL MEASURED
Official Scoring System for Bowhunting North American Big Game
MINIMUM SCORE
black bear 18
grizzly bear 19
Alaska brown bear 20
polar bear 20
BEAR
24TH RECORDING PERIOD 2003-04
SEX
Male
Female
KIND OF BEAR (check one)
black bear
X grizzly
Alaska brown bear
polar
B
MEASUREMENTS
A. Greatest Length Without Lo
B. Greatest Width
16 1/16
10 2/16
26 3/16
Location of Kill:
(State/Prov)
Date Killed:
Owner:
Owner's Address:
Guide's Name and Address:
, certify that I have measured this
MM/DD/YYYY
CITY
STATE/PROVINCE
ZIP CODE
data are, to the best of my knowledge and belief, made in accordance with the instructions given.
Witness:
TO MEASURER'S SIGNATU
P&Y OFFICIAL MEASURER
ADDRESS
STATE/PROVINCE
ZIP

WORLD RECORD GRIZZLY BEAR
Score: 26 3/16
Location: Unalakleet, Alaska
Date: 2004
Hunter: Dennis Dunn

WORLD RECORD
Grizzly Bear

by Dennis Dunn

Thanks to a miserable miscreant named "Murphy," who declared war on me way back in 1978, the previous several years had been an exercise in intense frustration. Any bowhunter knows that our beloved sport is often ruled by Murphy's Law, but I can assure you that Mr. Murphy moved me to the very top of his "hit list" in May of 2003.

When I arrived in hunting camp that May, it was my sixth attempt to take a grizzly in the space of just 31 months. I had hunted grizzly in both British Columbia and the Yukon, but this time I decided to try my luck in Alaska with outfitter Virgil Umphenour. His camp was situated on the shore of Norton Sound, not far south of the Seward Peninsula.

This particular hunt is designed to take advantage of a special situation that occurs every year. As soon as the shore is free of ice, herring by the millions arrive to deposit their spawn on the seaweed clinging to the rocks along the beaches. There are many big boulders there that give a bowhunter excellent cover for either a stalk or an ambush.

For eons the interior mountain grizzlies have undoubtedly known about this phenomenon and come down to the coast during the two weeks of the herring spawn to spend the nights feeding on the many herring that die after procreation. You learn quickly how to sleep during the day, so you can hunt by night. Well…it's not really night. That area is so far north that, during the second half of May, the sun barely dips below the horizon and the regulations allow you to hunt 24/7 during open seasons.

My first grizzly hunt with Virgil and his son, Eric, proved to be the most exciting, action-packed hunt I had ever experienced. Suffice it to say that within one 72-hour period, I had a close encounter with a large boar at four yards and then with a second one at under three yards. The miracle of it all was that, despite my best efforts, everybody (including both bruins) escaped essentially unscathed!

Not surprisingly, I could not wait to return to that same stretch of coastline the following year for one more attempt. I was convinced my luck would turn. On Tuesday morning, May 18, 2004, just after midnight, we spotted a real beast two miles south. He was moving north along the water's edge scavenging for herring.

When we had closed to within 400 yards, I chose a five-foot-high boulder right on the water's edge to crouch behind. The waves lapped around my calves. As "Brutus" stepped up onto the big flat rock next to me, I came to full draw and waited about ten seconds until he finally gave me the broadside opportunity I wanted. In the half-light of the arctic spring morning, I released an arrow from eight yards. On the way to the bear, the arrow skewered "Murphy's" ghost, then passed through both the bruin's lungs and sailed twenty-five yards beyond.

Persistence and determination had finally paid off! I am still in shock and awe that my old monarch of a griz—with virtually no teeth left in his mouth—has turned out to be the new World's Record with a bow! The Alaska Fish and Game tooth study reported that the bear's age was 28 years. Even though the hide only squared eight feet, the monster's skull turned out to be immense!

211

GRIZZLY BEAR

Minimum Score 19   *Ursus arctos horribilis*

SCORE	GREATEST LENGTH	GREATEST WIDTH	SEX	AREA	STATE/ PROVINCE	HUNTER'S NAME	DATE	RANK
26 3/16	16 1/16	10 2/16	M	Unalakleet	AK	Dennis Dunn	2004	1
25 13/16	16 1/16	9 12/16	M	Moose Lake	BC	Derril Lamb	1987	2
25 13/16	16 0/16	9 13/16	M	Gathto Creek	BC	Jim Boyer	1997	2
25 6/16	16 0/16	9 6/16	M	Anzac River	BC	Harley Tison	1972	4
25 6/16	15 12/16	9 10/16	M	Unalakleet River	AK	Mark Beeler	2001	4
25 3/16	15 13/16	9 6/16	M	Stevens Lakes	BC	Dr. Rex Hancock	1968	6
25 3/16	15 4/16	9 15/16	M	Unalakleet	AK	Jim Horneck	2010	6
25 2/16	16 0/16	9 2/16	M	Windy	AK	Rick D. Snell	1997	8
25 0/16	15 11/16	9 5/16	M	Klinaklini River	BC	George P. Mann	1999	9
24 15/16	15 8/16	9 7/16	M	Unalakleet	AK	Fred Eichler	2005	10
24 15/16	15 15/16	9 0/16	M	Norton Sound	AK	Frank S. Noska IV	2009	10
24 14/16	15 10/16	9 4/16	M	Yellowstone National Park	WY	Art Young	1920	12
24 13/16	15 6/16	9 7/16	M	Moose Lake	BC	Tony Di Giovanni	1993	13
24 12/16	15 15/16	8 13/16	M	Bella Coola	BC	Lawrence Michalchuk	2000	14
24 11/16	15 2/16	9 9/16	M	Stevens Lakes	BC	Dr. R. L. Hambrick	1965	15
24 11/16	15 5/16	9 6/16	M	Unalakleet River	AK	Anthony L. Mudd	2002	15
24 11/16	15 11/16	9 0/16	M	Alice Arm	BC	Tod Graham	2007	15
24 9/16	15 13/16	8 12/16	M	Bella Coola	BC	William P. Mastrangel	1956	18
24 8/16	15 4/16	9 4/16	M	Halfway River	BC	Dean Roe	2007	19
24 8/16	15 5/16	9 3/16	M	Sikanni Chief River	BC	Eric Kuhlman	2009	19
24 6/16	15 14/16	8 8/16	M	Unalakleet River	AK	Ted K. Jaycox	2000	21
24 6/16	15 0/16	9 6/16	M	Bear Creek	AK	J. R. Pederson	2009	21
24 5/16	14 13/16	9 8/16	M	Unalakleet River	AK	Thomas J. Hoffman	1993	23
24 5/16	15 14/16	8 7/16	M	Aniak	AK	Walter J. Palmer	2000	23
24 4/16	14 10/16	9 10/16	M	Unalakleet River	AK	Stan Godfrey	1997	25
24 0/16	15 0/16	9 0/16	M	Joe Poole Creek	BC	Scott L. Koelzer	2001	26
23 13/16	15 6/16	8 7/16	M	Gulkana River	AK	Art Kragness	1973	27
23 12/16	14 15/16	8 13/16	M	Kotzebue	AK	James P. Jacobson	1981	28
23 7/16	14 14/16	8 9/16	M	Kakwa River	ALB	Rick Michalski	1981	29
23 5/16	15 0/16	8 5/16	M	Fraser River	BC	James F. Watson	2004	30
23 4/16	14 14/16	8 6/16	M	Quesnel Lake	BC	Bob Fromme	2000	31
23 3/16	14 5/16	8 14/16	M	Bathurst Inlet	NUN	Michael R. Deschamps	2002	32
23 3/16	15 0/16	8 3/16	M	Quesnel Lake	BC	Robert J. Gibson	2003	32
23 2/16	15 1/16	8 1/16	M	Unalakleet	AK	Allyn Ladd	2007	34
23 1/16	14 11/16	8 6/16	M	Dietrich Camp	AK	Bart Colledge	2002	35
23 0/16	14 8/16	8 8/16	M	Tagagawik River	AK	Ronell Skinner	2001	36
22 14/16	14 4/16	8 10/16	M	Cassiar Mtns.	BC	John Paul Schaffer	2003	37
22 13/16	14 3/16	8 10/16	M	Kingcome Inlet	BC	Peter Halbig	1982	38
22 12/16	14 6/16	8 6/16	M	Brazeua River	ALB	Curt Lynn	1973	39
22 7/16	13 15/16	8 8/16	M	Earn Lake	YUK	Dr. R. D. Keeler	1986	40
22 6/16	14 2/16	8 4/16	M	Dietrich River	AK	Bart Colledge	2003	41
22 6/16	14 1/16	8 5/16	M	Joe Poole Creek	BC	Chris Parrino	2003	41
22 2/16	13 13/16	8 5/16	M	Blackstone River	YUK	Rick Duggan	2004	43
22 2/16	13 15/16	8 3/16	M	Anaktuvuk River	AK	Frank S. Noska IV	2008	43
22 1/16	14 0/16	8 1/16	M	Galena	AK	Larry Spiva	1992	45
22 1/16	13 14/16	8 3/16	M	Dalton Highway	AK	Bruce Hakel	1996	45
22 0/16	13 14/16	8 2/16	F	Kamano Bay	BC	Randy Liljenquist	2007	47
21 14/16	14 6/16	7 8/16	M	Norton Sound	AK	Neil Summers	2008	48
*21 13/16	14 1/16	7 12/16	M	Nome	AK	Jim Wondzell	2009	49
21 11/16	14 2/16	7 9/16	M	Unalakleet River	AK	George P. Mann	1996	50
21 11/16	14 3/16	7 8/16	M	Taku River	BC	Mark C. Booth	2000	50
21 10/16	13 9/16	8 1/16	F	Council	AK	Mark Wayne Smith	1996	52
21 10/16	13 9/16	8 1/16	M	Dietrich River	AK	Eric Colledge	2001	52
21 10/16	13 11/16	7 15/16	F	Unalakleet	AK	Joel A. Johnson	2005	52
21 8/16	13 15/16	7 9/16	F	Bella Coola	BC	J. Dale Hale	1989	55
21 6/16	13 1/16	8 5/16	M	Bear Creek	AK	J. R. Pederson	2008	56
21 4/16	13 2/16	8 2/16	F	White River	YUK	Ray F. Daniels	1994	57
21 3/16	13 13/16	7 6/16	M	East Fork Jack River	AK	Rick Hayley	1997	58
21 3/16	12 8/16	8 11/16	M	Whitehorse	YUK	George Harms	2003	58
21 2/16	13 10/16	7 8/16	F	Nome River	AK	Mark Wayne Smith	2004	60
21 2/16	13 15/16	7 3/16	M	Taku River	BC	Richard A. Smith	2006	60
21 1/16	13 3/16	7 14/16	F	Tolovana	AK	Larry Edward Townsend	1990	62
21 1/16	13 5/16	7 12/16	M	Atigun Pass	AK	J. R. Pederson	1996	62
21 0/16	13 11/16	7 5/16	M	Little Tok River	AK	Don Davidson, Jr.	1987	64
21 0/16	13 6/16	7 10/16	M	Bonnet Plume Range	YUK	Tim Good	1995	64
21 0/16	13 11/16	7 5/16	F	Klikitarik	AK	John MacPeak	2006	64
21 0/16	12 13/16	8 3/16	F	Crater Creek	AK	Bob Ameen	2009	64
20 13/16	13 2/16	7 11/16	F	Chicken	AK	Larry Daly	1997	68
20 13/16	13 5/16	7 8/16	F	Unalakleet River	AK	Raymond L. Howell, Sr.	1999	68
20 11/16	13 8/16	7 3/16	M	Knight Inlet	BC	Gary F. Bogner	1995	70
20 11/16	13 6/16	7 5/16	M	Taku River	BC	Roy L. Walk	2006	70
*20 11/16	13 5/16	7 6/16	M	Alice Arm	BC	Don Erbert	2008	70
20 10/16	13 3/16	7 7/16	F	Rivers Inlet	BC	Chuck Adams	1988	73
20 10/16	12 13/16	7 13/16	F	Kuparuk River	AK	Steven M. Stroka	1996	73
20 9/16	13 1/16	7 8/16	F	Meziadin Lake	BC	Glenn Hisey	1992	75
20 8/16	13 6/16	7 2/16	F	Nome	AK	Mark Wayne Smith	2002	76
20 7/16	13 0/16	7 7/16	F	Kispiox River	BC	Dr. Rex Hancock	1965	77
20 6/16	12 14/16	7 8/16	F	Scoop Lake	BC	Ronald Montross	1984	78
20 3/16	13 2/16	7 1/16	M	Galbraith Lake	AK	Maxallen D. Jackson	1981	79
20 2/16	13 0/16	7 2/16	F	Unalakleet River	AK	Chris Parrino	2006	80
20 2/16	12 11/16	7 7/16	F	St. Michael	AK	Mark Buehrer	2008	80
20 1/16	13 1/16	7 0/16	M	Stevens Lakes	BC	Fred Bear	1961	82
20 1/16	12 15/16	7 2/16	F	Kakwa River	ALB	Herb Schmidt	1983	82
20 1/16	12 12/16	7 5/16	M	Finlay River	BC	Tom Miranda	2009	82
20 0/16	12 14/16	7 2/16	F	Yellowstone National Park	WY	Saxton T. Pope	1920	85
20 0/16	12 13/16	7 3/16	M	Ivishak River	AK	Jeff Lindeman	1988	85
19 15/16	12 11/16	7 4/16	M	Dalton Highway	AK	Thomas Chadwick	1984	87
19 15/16	12 10/16	7 5/16	M	Dutch River	AK	Gary M. Martin	2005	87
19 14/16	12 8/16	7 6/16	F	Ptarmigan Creek	AK	Donald O. Smith	1964	89
19 14/16	13 0/16	6 14/16	M	Atigun Pass	AK	Alan Richey	1984	89
19 14/16	12 13/16	7 1/16	M	Caribou Mtn.	AK	Kenneth N. Liddle	1994	89
19 14/16	12 11/16	7 3/16	F	Ivishak River	AK	Frank Sanders	2000	89
19 13/16	12 13/16	7 0/16	M	Unalakleet River	AK	Steve Card	2003	93
19 12/16	12 12/16	7 0/16	F	Morkill River	BC	Archie Nesbitt	1993	94
19 12/16	12 8/16	7 4/16	F	Caribou Mtn.	AK	M. Steven Steel	2004	94

GRIZZLY BEAR

Minimum Score 19   Continued

SCORE	GREATEST LENGTH	GREATEST WIDTH	SEX	AREA	STATE/ PROVINCE	HUNTER'S NAME	DATE	RANK
19 12/16	12 6/16	7 6/16	F	Unalakleet	AK	Chris Parrino	2008	94
19 10/16	12 5/16	7 5/16	F	Stevens Lakes	BC	G. Fred Asbell	1969	97
19 9/16	12 14/16	6 11/16	F	Chetwynd	BC	Timothy B. Fisk	2002	98
19 8/16	12 8/16	7 0/16	M	Tangle Lakes	AK	John Musacchia	1972	99
19 8/16	12 10/16	6 14/16	M	Whitehorse	YUK	Scott Koelzer	1977	99
19 8/16	12 10/16	6 14/16	F	Golsovia River	AK	Mike Zacharies	2008	99
19 6/16	12 10/16	6 12/16	M	Unalakleet	AK	Allyn Ladd	2007	102
19 5/16	11 15/16	7 6/16	F	Stevens Lakes	BC	Walter Krom	1968	103
19 5/16	12 11/16	6 10/16	M	Pingston River	AK	John D. "Jack" Frost	1993	103
19 3/16	12 9/16	6 10/16	M	Taku Plateau	BC	Walter J. Palmer	1996	105
19 3/16	12 7/16	6 12/16	M	Coleen River	AK	Stacee Meyer	2002	105
19 3/16	12 9/16	6 10/16	M	Unalakleet	AK	Allyn Ladd	2005	105
19 2/16	12 12/16	6 6/16	F	Nenana River	AK	Rick D. Snell	1993	108
19 1/16	12 0/16	7 1/16	F	Obey Lake	BC	Greg Ogle	2000	109
19 1/16	12 1/16	7 0/16	F	Atigun Pass	AK	Frank S. Noska IV	2004	109
19 0/16	12 10/16	6 6/16	M	Kispiox River	BC	Charles Kroll	1960	111
19 0/16	12 8/16	6 8/16	M	Brooks Range	AK	Ronald W. Lang, Jr.	1992	111
19 0/16	12 0/16	7 0/16	M	Logan Mtns.	YUK	Jon P. Thomas	1993	111
19 0/16	12 4/16	6 12/16	F	Sagavanirktok River	AK	Garry A. Thoms	1995	111

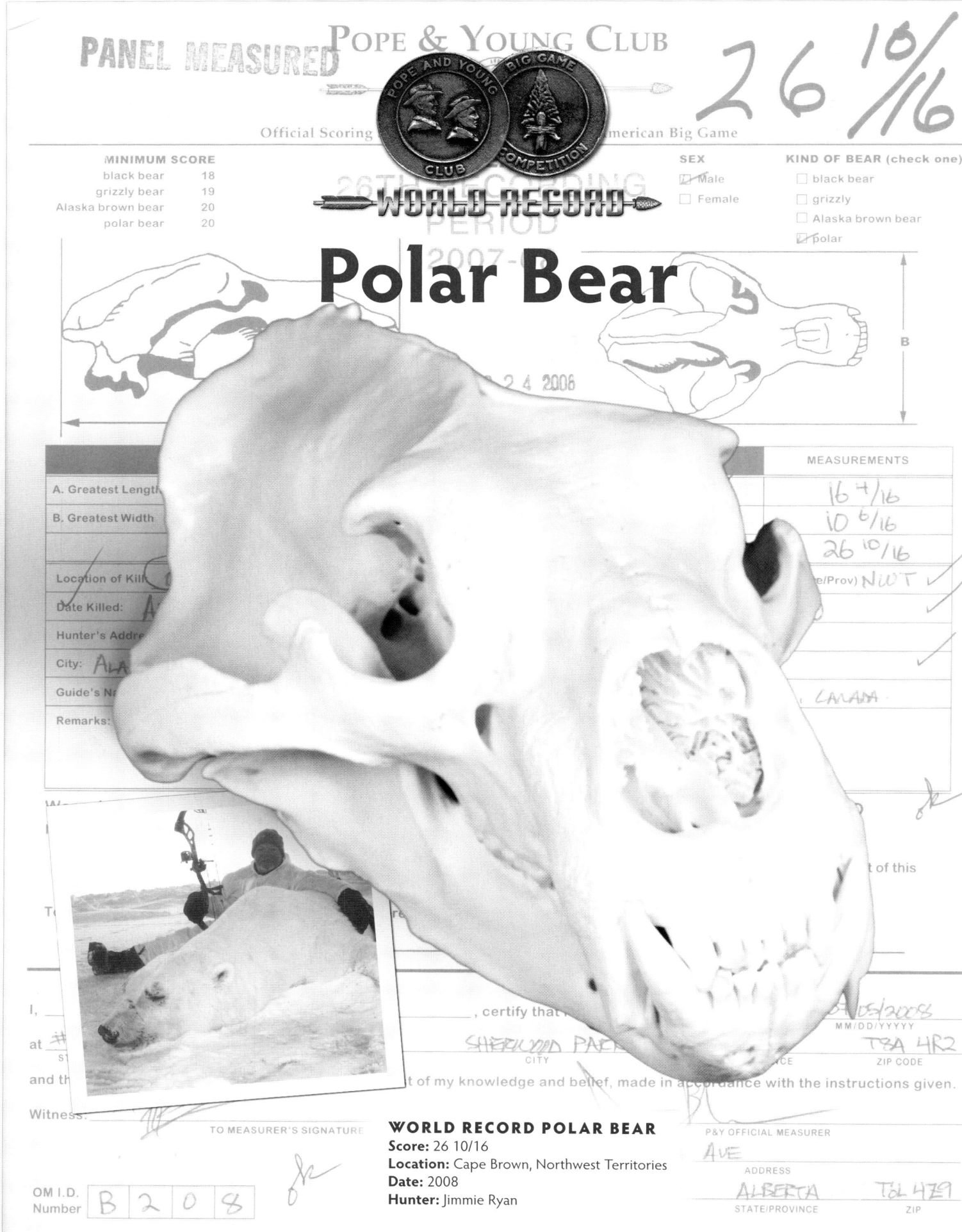

WORLD RECORD POLAR BEAR
Score: 26 10/16
Location: Cape Brown, Northwest Territories
Date: 2008
Hunter: Jimmie Ryan

POLAR BEAR

Ursus maritimus

Minimum Score 20

SCORE	GREATEST LENGTH	GREATEST WIDTH	SEX	AREA	STATE/PROVINCE	HUNTER'S NAME	DATE	RANK
26 10/16	16 4/16	10 6/16	M	Cape Brown	NWT	Jimmie R. Ryan	2008	1
26 6/16	16 4/16	10 2/16	M	Cape Lisburne	AK	Richard McIntyre	1958	2
26 6/16	16 13/16	9 9/16	M	Hanley Bay	NUN	Edwin DeYoung	2002	2
26 0/16	16 2/16	9 14/16	M	Resolute Bay	NUN	Gary F. Bogner	1989	4
26 0/16	16 1/16	9 15/16	M	Resolute Bay	NUN	M. Robert DeLaney	2007	4
25 14/16	16 3/16	9 11/16	M	Chukchi Sea	AK	Larry Jones	1965	6
25 11/16	15 15/16	9 12/16	M	Holman	NWT	David L. Duncan	2007	7
25 10/16	16 6/16	9 4/16	M	South Hampton Island	NUN	Gary M. Martin	2004	8
25 9/16	16 0/16	9 9/16	M	Lancaster Sound	NUN	Rick Duggan	2004	9
25 8/16	16 6/16	9 2/16	M	Norwegian Bay	NUN	Albert Hankins	2008	10
25 4/16	16 3/16	9 1/16	M	Baffin Island	NWT	George P. Mann	1994	11
*25 2/16	15 10/16	9 8/16	M	Baffin Island	NUN	Wayne F. Farnsworth, Jr.	2004	12
*25 2/16	15 10/16	9 8/16	M	Resolute Bay	NUN	Mark "Gutz" Gutsmiedl	2006	12
25 2/16	15 10/16	9 8/16	M	Resolute Bay	NUN	Tom Miranda	2007	12
25 2/16	15 11/16	9 7/16	M	Resolute Bay	NUN	Tim Walters	2008	12
25 1/16	15 5/16	9 12/16	F	Baffin Island	NWT	Arthur Young	1926	16
25 0/16	15 12/16	9 4/16	M	Resolute Bay	NUN	George P. Mann	1991	17
25 0/16	15 15/16	9 1/16	M	Resolute Bay	NUN	Frank S. Noska IV	2006	17
25 0/16	15 12/16	9 4/16	M	Pond Inlet	NUN	Bryce Olson	2009	17
24 15/16	15 3/16	9 12/16	M	Taloyoak	NUN	Ricardo Longoria	1998	20
24 14/16	15 11/16	9 3/16	M	Victoria Island	NWT	Archie Nesbitt	1993	21
24 11/16	15 7/16	9 4/16	M	Lancaster Sound	NUN	Michael R. Traub	2004	22
24 10/16	15 12/16	8 14/16	M	Resolute Bay	NUN	George Harms	2005	23
24 10/16	15 9/16	9 1/16	M	Resolute Bay	NUN	Stacee Frost	2006	23
24 10/16	15 8/16	9 2/16	M	Resolute Bay	NUN	Allyn Ladd	2008	23
24 9/16	15 7/16	9 2/16	M	Resolute Bay	NUN	Rob Harms	2005	26
24 9/16	16 7/16	8 2/16	M	Holman	NWT	Scott L. Koelzer	2005	26
*24 9/16	15 14/16	8 11/16	M	Resolute Bay	NUN	John MacPeak	2007	26
24 7/16	14 15/16	9 8/16	M	Resolute Bay	NUN	George R. Harms	2002	29
24 7/16	15 10/16	8 13/16	M	Resolute Bay	NUN	James Hens	2006	29
24 6/16	15 4/16	9 2/16	M	Resolute Bay	NUN	Tom Hoffman	2004	31
24 5/16	15 5/16	9 0/16	M	Wynniatt Bay	NWT	V. Randy Liljenquist	2001	32
24 5/16	15 13/16	8 8/16	M	Resolute Bay	NUN	Thomas M. Taylor	2003	32
24 4/16	15 5/16	8 15/16	F	Baffin Island	NWT	Arthur Young	1926	34
24 3/16	15 8/16	8 11/16	M	Lancaster Sound	NUN	Robert E. Speegle, MD	2003	35
24 3/16	15 5/16	8 14/16	M	Resolute Bay	NUN	Kevin Harms	2005	35
*24 2/16	15 6/16	8 12/16	M	Resolute Bay	NUN	Mark Beeler	2008	37
24 1/16	15 10/16	8 7/16	M	Resolute Bay	NUN	Camp Newton	2005	38
23 15/16	15 4/16	8 11/16	M	Resolute Bay	NUN	Gary F. Bogner	1989	39
23 13/16	14 15/16	8 14/16	M	Bathurst Island	NWT	Archie Nesbitt	1989	40
23 13/16	14 15/16	8 14/16	M	Resolute Bay	NUN	Kevin Dahm	2007	40
23 13/16	14 13/16	9 0/16	M	Resolute Bay	NUN	Donill Kenney	2007	40
23 10/16	15 5/16	8 5/16	M	Resolute Bay	NUN	Robert M. Daggett	2003	43
23 10/16	15 2/16	8 8/16	M	Ulukhaktok	NUN	Al Baldwin	2006	43
23 9/16	15 5/16	8 4/16	M	Pelly Bay	NUN	Dennis Dunn	1999	45
23 8/16	14 15/16	8 9/16	M	Gjoa Haven	NWT	Mark Connor	1998	46
23 8/16	15 6/16	8 2/16	M	Holman	NWT	Jim Wondzell	2007	46
*23 2/16	14 15/16	8 3/16	M	Baffin Bay	NUN	Michele Leqve	2006	48
23 0/16	14 12/16	8 4/16	M	Allan Island	NWT	Thomas J. Hoffman	1990	49
22 14/16	14 10/16	8 4/16	M	Resolute Bay	NUN	Roy M. Goodwin	2006	50
22 4/16	14 8/16	7 12/16	M	Coronation Gulf	NUN	Bob Ehle	2003	51
22 3/16	14 3/16	8 0/16	F	Resolute Bay	NUN	Rodney M. Brush	2005	52
21 15/16	14 6/16	7 9/16	M	Banks Island	NWT	Joel A. Johnson	2004	53
21 14/16	14 3/16	7 11/16	M	Cape Doroset	NWT	Philip J. Guarino, Jr.	1995	54
21 8/16	14 4/16	7 4/16	F	Holman	NWT	Walter J. Palmer	1998	55
21 6/16	13 7/16	7 15/16	F	Holman	NWT	Ken Vorisek	2002	56
21 3/16	13 11/16	7 8/16	F	Astronomical Society Island	NUN	Chris Parrino	2005	57
20 11/16	13 11/16	7 0/16	M	Agu Bay	NWT	Adrian L. Erickson	1994	58
20 11/16	13 10/16	7 1/16	F	Beaufort Sea	NWT	John D. "Jack" Frost	2002	58
20 10/16	13 6/16	7 4/16	M	Boothia Peninsula	NWT	Bruce R. Schoeneweis	1995	60
20 4/16	13 6/16	6 14/16	M	Gjoa Haven	NUN	Michael R. Deschamps	2000	61
20 4/16	13 4/16	7 0/16	F	Gjoa Haven	NUN	Robert S. Miller	2000	61

215

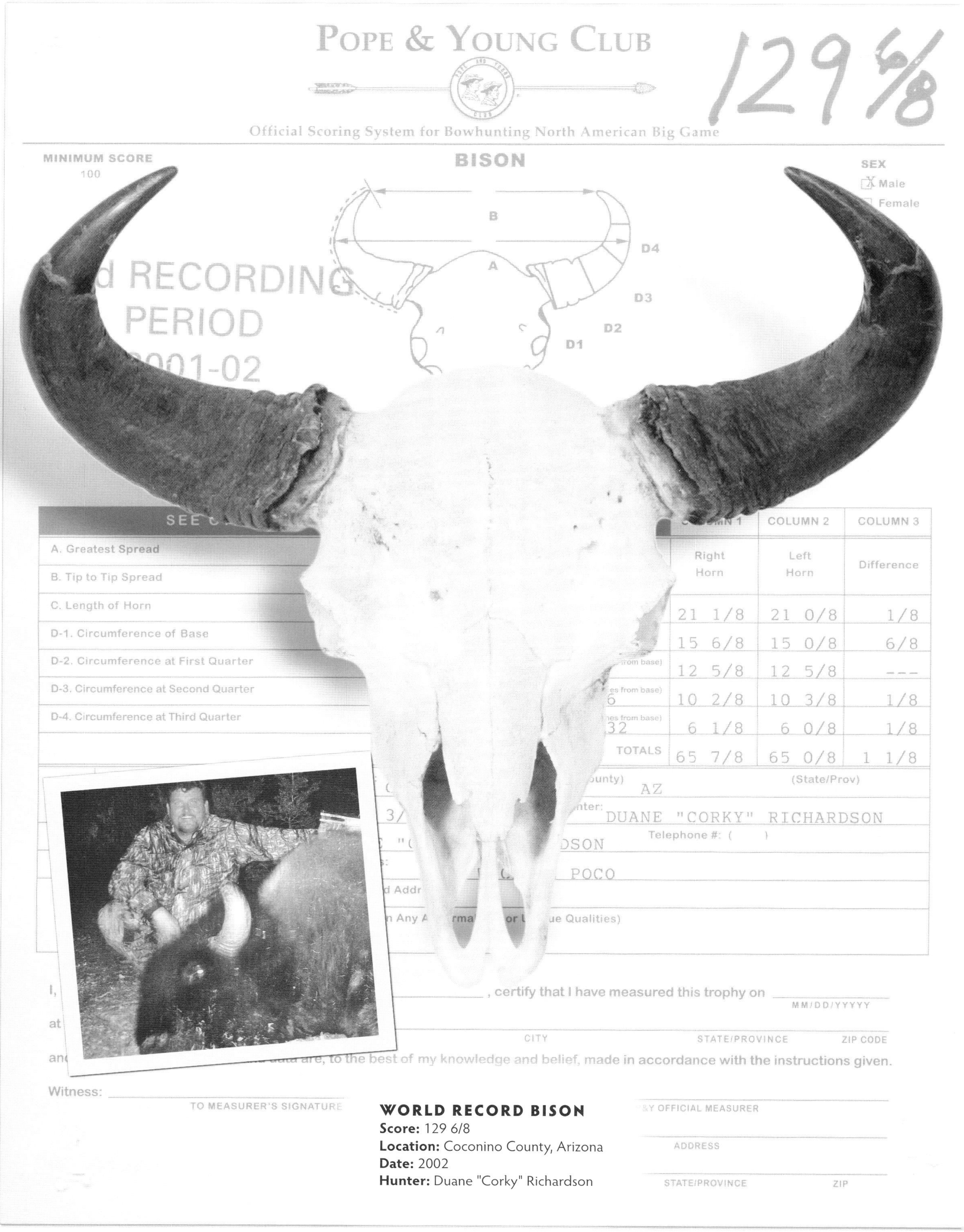

Pope & Young Club

Official Scoring System for Bowhunting North American Big Game

MINIMUM SCORE 100

BISON

SEX: ☒ Male ☐ Female

129 6/8

	COLUMN 1 Right Horn	COLUMN 2 Left Horn	COLUMN 3 Difference
A. Greatest Spread			
B. Tip to Tip Spread			
C. Length of Horn	21 1/8	21 0/8	1/8
D-1. Circumference of Base	15 6/8	15 0/8	6/8
D-2. Circumference at First Quarter	12 5/8	12 5/8	---
D-3. Circumference at Second Quarter	10 2/8	10 3/8	1/8
D-4. Circumference at Third Quarter	6 1/8	6 0/8	1/8
TOTALS	65 7/8	65 0/8	1 1/8

AZ (State/Prov)

Hunter: DUANE "CORKY" RICHARDSON

POCO

WORLD RECORD BISON
Score: 129 6/8
Location: Coconino County, Arizona
Date: 2002
Hunter: Duane "Corky" Richardson

Bison

by Duane "Corky" Richardson

I had drawn 1 of 4 bison tags for the House Rock Ranch hunt in northern Arizona. My father was the first archer to take a bison on the North Kiabab and I was excited to make that attempt. Scouting started in January with an aerial view of the land and building a team to help me. The Ranch manager had not seen nor heard of any buffalo since the first part of September, so we really had our work cut out for us.

When the hunt began, we had fresh snow that was helpful for locating tracks and sign. At the end of day one my Dad, George, and Bill Bolt were able to come up with some three-day-old sign. My uncle Bob and Craig Thornton and Phil Dalrymple and I checked other areas.

Five more days provided only old sign, no buffalo sightings, cold wet feet and sore leg muscles. We did track a rogue "moo" cow over ten miles. We moved camp a hundred miles on the sixth day and began again. While looking for an access point across a huge canyon, we found two very large sets of tracks. The tracks headed down a pi?on-juniper point. I circled around and found two fresh beds, still warm. I knocked an arrow. All of a sudden, the ground began to shake as two bulls came running from the south. The wind was perfect and I knew they had not heard me. But, something or someone had spooked them.

After seven days I was thankful to have finally seen buffalo. I hurried over to the edge of the draw where they had disappeared, to find the biggest one had stopped. On cue, the bull turned and headed back up the hill. I hurriedly took off my boots and ran quartering towards the bull in order to get a lane where I could get a good shot. He stopped in an opening thirty five yards away, with only his head entering the opening. I could see his right side and knew he was something special. I was at full draw when he finally stepped forward and I released the arrow. The arrow got there faster that I anticipated and hit him square in the front shoulder. I immediately followed, uncertain of how much penetration there was. To my amazement, he had already begun to weave and was having a hard time standing up. The arrow had penetrated to the opposite shoulder and only my fletch remained visible. I followed him for 150 yards before he stopped for the first time and was able to get another shot. As I continued on, I bumped into Dad and Craig, standing on a small rim above where the bull had just stopped. They explained how they had found these two bulls in the feeding area and had spooked them. They were following the tracks when one came towards them. Unbeknownst to me, the bull had stopped no further than ten yards below them. When, all of the sudden, they heard the sound of an arrow, and then saw an arrow sticking out of the bull.

I drove down to the game manager's house to confirm the bow kill before any field dressing took place. He couldn't believe that I had actually killed one with a bow on one of Arizona's most difficult hunts. He believes he had never seen this bull and aged it at more than sixteen years.

BISON

Minimum Score 100

Bison, bison, bison and *Bison bison athabascae*

SCORE	LENGTH OF R HORN L	CIRCUMFERENCE R OF BASE L	GREATEST SPREAD	AREA	STATE/ PROVINCE	HUNTER'S NAME	DATE	RANK
129 6/8	21 1/8 21 0/8	15 6/8 15 0/8	30 0/8	Coconino County	AZ	Duane "Corky" Richardson	2002	1
119 4/8	19 6/8 19 2/8	14 3/8 14 2/8	27 6/8	Pink Mtn.	BC	Camp Newton	2009	2
118 2/8	19 6/8 19 6/8	14 6/8 14 0/8	26 6/8	Coconino County	AZ	Russell Richardson	2005	3
118 0/8	18 4/8 18 1/8	14 3/8 14 3/8	30 0/8	Coconino County	AZ	Chuck Adams	2000	4
117 4/8	18 6/8 18 6/8	14 3/8 14 3/8	27 6/8	Coconino County	AZ	Chuck Adams	2002	5
116 5/8	15 5/8 16 5/8	14 0/8 14 2/8	29 5/8	Teton County	WY	Rick Parish	2010	6
115 6/8	16 4/8 17 7/8	13 2/8 14 0/8	29 0/8	Garfield County	UT	Pete Shepley	1991	7
115 6/8	18 0/8 15 5/8	14 1/8 14 2/8	30 2/8	Chitina River	AK	Lloyd Z. Crow	2008	7
115 2/8	18 2/8 18 2/8	13 6/8 13 6/8	28 1/8	Pink Mtn.	BC	Walter J. Palmer	2002	9
115 0/8	18 7/8 19 7/8	14 0/8 14 1/8	30 4/8	Coconino County	AZ	William B. Bedlion	1998	10
114 4/8	18 2/8 17 3/8	14 1/8 14 1/8	29 4/8	Sikanni River	BC	Darlene J. Stansfield	2005	11
114 4/8	18 2/8 18 1/8	13 7/8 14 2/8	29 2/8	Halfway River	BC	Ron Rockwell	2007	11
113 6/8	19 6/8 19 7/8	13 5/8 13 5/8	29 0/8	Coconino County	AZ	Phillip C. Dalrymple	2004	13
113 4/8	19 3/8 19 0/8	13 5/8 13 1/8	32 4/8	Coconino County	AZ	George Richardson	1996	14
112 2/8	18 4/8 18 0/8	14 1/8 14 1/8	29 6/8	Farewell Lake	AK	George A. Moerlein	1972	15
112 0/8	18 1/8 17 7/8	13 4/8 13 6/8	27 1/8	Halfway River	BC	Tom Taylor	2002	16
111 4/8	18 4/8 18 2/8	13 2/8 13 3/8	27 3/8	Wayne County	UT	Richie Bland	1996	17
111 4/8	17 6/8 17 7/8	14 0/8 14 0/8	27 6/8	Coconino County	AZ	Richard D. Tone	2008	17
111 0/8	18 0/8 17 6/8	13 3/8 13 4/8	27 2/8	Garfield County	UT	Craig Bonham	1983	19
111 0/8	17 0/8 18 1/8	14 3/8 13 0/8	28 1/8	Teton County	WY	Luke Roush	2009	19
110 6/8	19 0/8 18 7/8	12 7/8 12 6/8	27 2/8	Garfield County	UT	Jim Ryan	1989	20
110 6/8	17 4/8 17 2/8	13 5/8 13 4/8	26 4/8	Garfield County	UT	Archie J. Nesbitt	1996	20
110 4/8	16 2/8 15 2/8	14 1/8 14 1/8	26 7/8	Garfield County	UT	Paul B. Brunner	1979	23
110 2/8	14 4/8 14 5/8	13 4/8 13 4/8	23 7/8	Davis County	UT	Mike Ellena	1987	24
110 2/8	18 2/8 17 7/8	13 1/8 13 1/8	26 3/8	Garfield County	UT	Dallas Smith	2006	24
*110 0/8	17 4/8 17 2/8	13 4/8 13 5/8	26 2/8	Coconino County	AZ	Jim Machac	2008	26
109 6/8	18 3/8 18 5/8	13 1/8 13 2/8	25 4/8	Pink Mtn.	BC	Edwin L. DeYoung	2009	27
109 4/8	17 0/8 17 0/8	13 7/8 13 7/8	26 3/8	Coconino County	AZ	Brian Ham	2003	28
109 4/8	17 0/8 17 5/8	12 6/8 12 6/8	27 0/8	Teton County	WY	Tracy Villwok	2010	28
108 6/8	18 5/8 18 7/8	12 2/8 12 2/8	26 2/8	Garfield County	UT	Mike Poynor	1987	30
108 6/8	17 4/8 17 2/8	12 7/8 12 7/8	26 3/8	Pink Mtn.	BC	Jim Wondzell	2003	30
108 6/8	17 3/8 17 6/8	13 2/8 13 2/8	26 6/8	Coconino County	AZ	Randy Liljenquist	2007	30
108 4/8	16 3/8 17 7/8	12 6/8 12 7/8	30 0/8	Davis County	UT	Troy M. Miller	1991	33
107 6/8	15 7/8 16 5/8	13 5/8 13 6/8	26 0/8	Pink Mtn.	BC	Dyrk Eddie	2001	34
107 2/8	16 6/8 16 6/8	13 0/8 13 2/8	26 3/8	Pink Mtn.	BC	Fred Eichler	2003	35
107 0/8	17 2/8 17 2/8	12 7/8 13 0/8	24 3/8	Coconino County	AZ	George Harms	2008	36
106 6/8	17 2/8 16 4/8	13 0/8 12 7/8	25 0/8	Garfield County	UT	Chuck Adams	1986	37
*106 4/8	16 3/8 16 3/8	13 7/8 13 7/8	25 2/8	Pink Mtn.	BC	Mark "Gutz" Gutsmiedl	2009	38
106 2/8	16 3/8 16 3/8	12 7/8 12 4/8	25 7/8	Pink Mtn.	BC	Bob Ameen	2010	39
*106 0/8	16 2/8 16 7/8	12 1/8 12 4/8	28 1/8	Teton County	WY	Adam Todd	2009	40
105 6/8	18 0/8 18 2/8	12 6/8 12 7/8	28 5/8	Delta Junction	AK	David Ray Western	1990	41
105 6/8	19 0/8 17 7/8	12 5/8 12 7/8	27 7/8	Farewell	AK	John D. "Jack" Frost	2000	41
105 6/8	16 5/8 16 3/8	13 1/8 13 0/8	26 3/8	Pink Mtn.	BC	John P. Schaffer	2006	41
105 4/8	17 3/8 18 2/8	12 2/8 12 2/8	25 5/8	Pink Mtn.	BC	Gary M. Martin	2002	44
105 2/8	16 2/8 16 3/8	13 0/8 12 7/8	27 4/8	Delta Junction	AK	Scott Schultz	1986	45
105 0/8	17 4/8 17 4/8	12 2/8 12 3/8	23 0/8	Delta Junction	AK	Tony Russ	1992	46
104 6/8	17 3/8 17 4/8	12 1/8 12 0/8	25 5/8	Pink Mtn.	BC	Brandon Powell	2010	47
104 4/8	17 2/8 17 7/8	13 1/8 12 4/8	24 4/8	Withrow Mtn.	BC	George P. Mann	1992	48
104 4/8	17 1/8 13 4/8	13 4/8 13 2/8	26 4/8	Pink Mtn.	BC	M. R. James	2001	48
104 4/8	16 2/8 15 7/8	12 2/8 12 2/8	28 0/8	Coconino County	AZ	Chuck Adams	2002	48
*104 4/8	17 1/8 17 2/8	11 0/8 11 1/8	27 3/8	Pink Mtn.	BC	Mark Beeler	2007	48
104 0/8	16 2/8 16 1/8	12 3/8 12 4/8	25 4/8	Pink Mtn.	BC	Mark E. Zastrow	2009	52
103 6/8	17 4/8 17 7/8	11 6/8 12 0/8	25 2/8	Garfield County	UT	Thomas J. Hoffman	1990	53
103 6/8	15 7/8 15 7/8	13 0/8 12 7/8	25 2/8	Garfield County	UT	Eldon Richter	1996	53
103 6/8	18 5/8 17 6/8	11 7/8 12 0/8	26 6/8	Pink Mtn.	BC	M. Robert DeLaney	2001	53
103 4/8	18 3/8 18 1/8	12 1/8 12 4/8	26 7/8	Farewell	AK	Carl E. Brent	1996	56
103 4/8	17 4/8 17 3/8	13 0/8 12 5/8	24 6/8	Garfield County	UT	Don G. Scofield	1998	56
103 4/8	15 6/8 14 4/8	12 6/8 12 5/8	23 4/8	Pink Mtn.	BC	Thomas J. Hoffman	2003	56
*103 4/8	15 6/8 15 7/8	13 0/8 13 0/8	25 5/8	Pink Mtn.	BC	M. Blake Patton	2009	56
103 0/8	15 2/8 16 3/8	13 1/8 12 7/8	24 1/8	Garfield County	UT	Craig P. Mitton	2006	60
102 4/8	15 3/8 15 3/8	12 6/8 12 6/8	24 2/8	Garfield County	UT	Dale Drilling	1991	61
102 4/8	17 1/8 16 7/8	12 2/8 12 0/8	24 2/8	Pink Mtn.	BC	Glenn E. Hisey	2000	61
102 2/8	15 6/8 15 5/8	12 4/8 12 4/8	23 5/8	Garfield County	UT	Hugh H. Hogle	1992	63
102 2/8	16 2/8 16 2/8	12 2/8 12 0/8	25 1/8	Coconino County	AZ	Chuck Adams	2000	63
101 4/8	16 7/8 16 6/8	12 4/8 12 4/8	25 0/8	Delta Junction	AK	John Sarvis	1991	65
101 0/8	16 7/8 16 7/8	11 6/8 11 6/8	24 5/8	Farewell Lake	AK	Frank S. Noska IV	2005	66
100 6/8	16 1/8 16 1/8	12 1/8 12 0/8	24 1/8	Garfield County	UT	Max Park	1989	67
100 6/8	15 2/8 15 2/8	12 2/8 12 2/8	24 6/8	Pink Mtn.	BC	Mark Calkins	2009	67

WORLD RECORD BARREN GROUND CARIBOU
Score: 448 6/8
Location: Lake Clark, Alaska
Date: 1984
Hunter: Dennis Burdick

Barren Ground Caribou

by Dennis Burdick

My first trip to Alaska (September of 1981) was a cold snowy ordeal. I sighted only one caribou in a two-week period and he was not close enough for a shot. Harvesting a caribou with my bow has been a lifelong dream, so I returned to Alaska in August of 1984.

Keith Hymas and his sons, Neil and Troy, went with me. Keith and I have hunted with a bow since 1958. His sons had hunted for several years, as well. We had trained, ran, back-packed and worked hard to get ready for the trip. We studied books, magazine articles, documentaries and Fred Bear films. We wanted to hunt with our own experience and not use a guide. We decided to drop-camp on a small lake, then hunt above the timber line on a group of high rocky ridges. We carried side arms as a bear deterrent, but had committed ourselves to take the game with our bows or go home empty handed.

It was about 10am when we spotted this large caribou grazing across an open area about 400 yards below us. His antlers looked massive through the binoculars. Keith and I decided to try a stalk. We carefully descended a steep draw of slide-rock, trying very hard not to dislodge loose rock and spook the animal.

He was grazing at a fast walk and we had to make a fast stalk to intercept him. As we worked our way closer, there was a patch of bushes about 30 yards in diameter between us and the caribou. We paused for a moment, then decided that Keith would circle the lower side while I took the upper. As I crept along the edge of the bushes, my heart began to pound and I began to shake, realizing that at any second I might get a shot at my first caribou. As I reached the far end, my heart began to sink as there was nothing in sight. I thought, "oh, no, he has given us the slip." All at once, the caribou trotted to within 50 yards and stood quartering toward me. I drew and shot, and he went down.

I have always been a do-it-myself hunter, and I feel very fortunate to have taken such an outstanding trophy animal.

BARREN GROUND CARIBOU

Minimum Score 325

Rangifer tarandus granti, Rangifer tarandus stonei and *Rangifer tarandus arcticus*

SCORE	LENGTH OF R MAIN BEAM L	INSIDE SPREAD	NUMBER OF R POINTS L	AREA	STATE/ PROVINCE	HUNTER'S NAME	DATE	RANK
448 6/8	48 4/8 48 5/8	40 3/8	17 20	Lake Clark	AK	Dennis Burdick	1984	1
446 6/8	55 0/8 55 6/8	40 5/8	23 19	Meshik River	AK	Art Kragness	1970	2
424 6/8	50 1/8 49 7/8	45 2/8	15 13	Naknek River	AK	Jack Wood	1990	3
424 0/8	52 7/8 51 1/8	41 0/8	21 12	Delta River	AK	Bill Brown	1960	4
419 6/8	51 1/8 49 0/8	35 0/8	15 15	Pilot Point	AK	Scott Atton	1987	5
417 2/8	60 2/8 60 2/8	39 0/8	11 11	Dog Salmon River	AK	John S. Alley	1987	6
417 0/8	50 5/8 52 3/8	33 6/8	13 17	Little Delta River	AK	Fred Bear	1959	7
416 1/8	53 5/8 53 2/8	44 2/8	14 18	Kipchuk River	AK	Roy Humphires	1986	8
415 3/8	45 0/8 46 0/8	31 1/8	17 18	Ugashik River	AK	Ron Madsen	1987	9
414 6/8	48 3/8 47 1/8	39 7/8	13 12	Aleutian Range	AK	Robert Smith	1983	10
414 5/8	51 7/8 51 7/8	35 1/8	12 12	Shotgun Hills	AK	Doug Aikin	1995	11
414 3/8	62 1/8 63 6/8	51 7/8	14 10	King Salmon	AK	Larry Spiva	1983	12
414 1/8	50 5/8 50 0/8	46 7/8	12 12	Kenai Mtns.	AK	Craig E. Scarbrough	1998	13
412 5/8	53 3/8 54 3/8	37 3/8	15 21	Lake Iliamna	AK	Don Wells	1982	14
407 4/8	54 3/8 55 3/8	51 4/8	20 14	Lake Becharof	AK	Larry Jones	1969	15
407 4/8	57 3/8 52 6/8	29 3/8	10 15	Whitefish Lake	AK	Ron Lehmann	1984	15
407 2/8	51 7/8 53 0/8	34 3/8	14 11	Squirrel River	AK	George A. Moerlein	1993	17
406 7/8	50 3/8 49 7/8	49 3/8	12 12	Salmon River	AK	Gary R. Haske	1987	18
406 4/8	52 0/8 53 2/8	36 7/8	9 7	Lake Iliamna	AK	Wright W. Allen	1993	19
406 2/8	56 5/8 58 2/8	37 3/8	11 23	Port Heiden	AK	Art Heinze	1973	20
405 2/8	40 5/8 43 6/8	38 1/8	16 14	Iqiuqiq	AK	Ray Capp	1996	21
405 0/8	61 4/8 62 5/8	47 0/8	13 13	Bonanza Hills	AK	Dan Hollingsworth	1982	22
404 7/8	51 2/8 50 6/8	40 0/8	15 14	Franklin Bluffs	AK	Rickie D. Snell	1989	23
404 2/8	46 6/8 47 7/8	34 0/8	18 16	Mulchatna River	AK	Steven B Novy	1987	24
402 0/8	44 4/8 45 0/8	46 0/8	14 14	Kodiak Island	AK	Jerry Russell	2006	25
401 6/8	57 7/8 56 7/8	45 3/8	13 14	Purcell Mtn.	AK	Chris G. Sanford	1998	26
401 3/8	53 4/8 52 6/8	42 0/8	14 16	Glenn Highway	AK	Harv Ebers	1959	27
401 2/8	50 3/8 50 2/8	37 7/8	13 13	Lake Clark	AK	Pat Breen	1986	28
400 4/8	52 1/8 51 7/8	40 4/8	14 11	Otter Lake	AK	Jim Wondzell	1995	29
400 2/8	51 6/8 51 6/8	43 2/8	14 14	Upper Noatak River	AK	Patrick Campanella	1989	30
400 0/8	53 1/8 53 1/8	37 0/8	9 19	Lake Louise	AK	George Moerlein	1962	31
399 5/8	55 3/8 57 6/8	46 6/8	12 8	Swan River	AK	Dr. Steven G. Hammons	1992	32
399 2/8	51 2/8 51 5/8	41 6/8	15 14	Pilot Point	AK	Michael O'Brien	1996	33
399 0/8	50 5/8 51 2/8	40 2/8	16 14	Clemmons	AK	Bob Lee	1960	34
397 4/8	46 4/8 46 3/8	34 2/8	15 15	Telaquana Lake	AK	John Moline	1971	35
397 1/8	55 0/8 55 4/8	42 7/8	15 16	Ugashik River	AK	Jim McCain	1986	36
396 6/8	50 1/8 49 5/8	49 1/8	12 15	Aleutian Range	AK	Chuck Adams	1984	37
396 6/8	52 4/8 50 4/8	42 4/8	9 11	Fishtrap Lake	AK	Allen L. Dougal	1986	37
396 5/8	57 7/8 55 1/8	49 4/8	13 11	Tyone Lake	AK	James Moline	1961	39
396 5/8	50 0/8 46 6/8	40 5/8	13 16	Telaquana Lake	AK	Eldon W. Zeller	1972	39
396 2/8	55 3/8 53 0/8	33 3/8	18 19	Little Delta River	AK	Keith R. Clemmons	1958	41
*396 1/8	49 4/8 47 4/8	33 2/8	15 16	Upper Kuskokwim River	AK	Butch Carley	2009	42
395 7/8	41 7/8 44 0/8	34 6/8	15 14	Lake Clark	AK	Robert McCrum	1995	43
394 5/8	51 0/8 48 7/8	27 6/8	13 19	Susitna	AK	Ron Mason	1980	44
394 0/8	53 6/8 53 7/8	36 2/8	8 9	Port Alsworth	AK	Vince Shepherd	1989	45
393 7/8	51 0/8 49 5/8	36 6/8	12 13	Kenai Peninsula	AK	Earl Chauvin	2002	46
392 2/8	51 3/8 55 4/8	32 6/8	13 15	Aleutian Range	AK	Chuck Adams	1983	47
391 7/8	53 6/8 50 5/8	45 6/8	11 14	Glenn Highway	AK	Joe West	1965	48
391 7/8	57 0/8 56 3/8	31 4/8	11 14	Lake Clark	AK	Jim Jarvis	1982	48
391 7/8	53 6/8 54 1/8	40 6/8	9 9	Nushagak Hills	AK	James C. Kelly	1995	48
391 0/8	49 3/8 53 0/8	41 6/8	11 13	Ugashik River	AK	Dr. Robert Roland-Smith	1986	51
391 0/8	56 0/8 53 7/8	53 0/8	12 10	Kenai	AK	David L. Hawkins	1988	51
390 5/8	53 2/8 52 7/8	42 0/8	11 10	Hook River	AK	William Elfland	1990	53
390 1/8	43 5/8 41 1/8	37 7/8	12 15	Lake Iliamna	AK	Kevin Anderson	1992	54
390 0/8	58 7/8 57 1/8	37 5/8	15 16	Whitefish Lake	AK	Charles C. Smith	1988	55
389 7/8	47 3/8 49 1/8	40 7/8	16 14	Mulchatna River	AK	Greg L. Munther	1987	56
389 4/8	48 0/8 49 2/8	34 0/8	22 19	Mother Goose Lake	AK	Dennis L. Smythe	1975	57
389 3/8	44 0/8 45 1/8	35 3/8	16 15	Galena	AK	Lon E. Lauber	1993	58
388 5/8	52 0/8 53 2/8	32 6/8	18 18	Delta River	AK	Dick Bolding	1957	59
388 2/8	56 5/8 57 1/8	47 2/8	18 16	Ugashik River	AK	George Moerlein	1972	60
388 2/8	50 7/8 55 7/8	30 5/8	14 15	Atigun Pass	AK	Alan Richey	1984	60
388 2/8	46 1/8 45 0/8	36 2/8	18 19	Mulchatna River	AK	John Joseph Carvajal	1994	60
387 7/8	42 0/8 40 6/8	31 5/8	23 25	McGrath	AK	Robert Barrie	1975	63
387 5/8	60 2/8 59 1/8	45 4/8	8 10	Atigun Pass	AK	David E. Rankin	1989	64
387 3/8	54 5/8 55 0/8	33 3/8	19 17	Kogoluktuk River	AK	Tony Casagrande	2005	65
387 0/8	52 2/8 62 4/8	51 3/8	10 10	Lake Iliamna	AK	Jon Vanderhoef	1983	66
387 0/8	54 5/8 51 0/8	41 4/8	13 13	Becharof Lake	AK	Doug Fisher	1997	66
386 7/8	48 5/8 44 5/8	43 4/8	19 18	Little Delta	AK	Dale K. Marcy	1964	68
386 6/8	50 2/8 52 0/8	32 3/8	12 12	Nushagak River	AK	Richard Mazol	1991	69
385 5/8	51 2/8 53 5/8	40 0/8	13 11	King Salmon	AK	Tom Daley	1984	70
385 2/8	58 5/8 57 0/8	38 0/8	14 17	Talkeetna Mtns.	AK	Harvey Matz	1959	71
384 6/8	40 1/8 37 5/8	41 2/8	19 21	Yanert River	AK	E. Donnall Thomas, Jr.	1984	72
384 6/8	58 0/8 60 0/8	40 5/8	12 9	Cinder River	AK	Dean Stebner	1995	72
384 5/8	47 5/8 47 5/8	37 5/8	16 15	Talkeetna Mtns.	AK	Dr. Rex Hancock	1962	74
384 3/8	49 2/8 49 1/8	34 6/8	15 18	Alaska Peninsula	AK	Betty Gulman	1968	75
384 0/8	55 3/8 57 3/8	40 6/8	12 9	Mulchatna River	AK	Carl E. Brent	1990	76
384 0/8	60 0/8 56 0/8	45 0/8	7 6	Tidy Mtn.	AK	John (Jack) C. Culpepper III	1993	76
382 5/8	46 2/8 44 5/8	33 7/8	22 17	Wide Bay	AK	Archie Nesbitt	1991	78
382 4/8	50 2/8 51 3/8	39 2/8	17 27	King Salmon River	AK	Eugene Smith, Jr.	1978	79
382 3/8	57 6/8 58 6/8	41 7/8	11 12	Mulchatna River	AK	William C. Shuster	1993	80
381 6/8	41 7/8 40 7/8	31 4/8	12 11	Kuskokwim Mtns.	AK	Ted K. Jaycox	1995	81
381 5/8	51 1/8 47 1/8	39 1/8	14 19	Ugashik River	AK	Stanley J. Rogers, Jr.	1974	82
381 2/8	51 4/8 53 2/8	41 1/8	11 13	Ugashik River	AK	Craig Richardson	1988	83
381 1/8	52 4/8 50 7/8	43 2/8	12 17	Galbraith Lake	AK	Edward L. Russell	1981	84
381 1/8	52 6/8 57 5/8	36 5/8	13 11	Lyme Village	AK	Don Nettum	1993	84
380 7/8	46 1/8 47 7/8	36 7/8	13 15	Delta Creek	AK	Wayne Trimm	1960	86
380 5/8	61 0/8 62 2/8	36 5/8	8 9	King Salmon	AK	Glenn Hisey	1984	87
380 4/8	52 4/8 50 0/8	44 4/8	17 16	Upper Ugashik Lake	AK	Kim Hussong	1992	88
380 0/8	48 0/8 49 1/8	30 2/8	14 18	Cutler River	AK	Jay Deones	1990	89
380 0/8	48 1/8 46 4/8	37 7/8	13 14	Mulchatna River	AK	Michael J. Spence	1998	89
380 0/8	57 3/8 57 4/8	34 1/8	13 13	Lake Clark	AK	Eric J. Josey	2000	89
379 6/8	49 5/8 53 0/8	39 1/8	13 12	Shotgun Hills	AK	Joe Ellithorpe	1987	92
379 6/8	57 4/8 59 0/8	45 3/8	10 11	Kotzebue	AK	Bill Barkley	1993	92
379 6/8	53 0/8 53 0/8	36 7/8	12 10	Cinder River	AK	D. Kevin Moore, DDS	1994	92
379 5/8	46 2/8 48 4/8	33 2/8	20 19	Alatna River	AK	Don D. Seward	1975	95

BARREN GROUND CARIBOU

Minimum Score 325   Continued

SCORE	LENGTH OF MAIN BEAM R	LENGTH OF MAIN BEAM L	INSIDE SPREAD	NUMBER OF POINTS R	NUMBER OF POINTS L	AREA	STATE/PROVINCE	HUNTER'S NAME	DATE	RANK
379 4/8	51 0/8	49 0/8	37 7/8	14	12	Grayling Creek	AK	Carl H. Spaeth	2002	96
378 7/8	45 5/8	45 0/8	36 7/8	12	11	Moose Creek	AK	Richard Moran	1989	97
378 6/8	48 2/8	52 6/8	39 5/8	10	11	Killey River	AK	Ken Wolter	2003	98
378 4/8	46 2/8	48 2/8	45 6/8	14	18	Adak Island	AK	Tom Taylor	2006	99
378 3/8	55 2/8	55 1/8	49 2/8	13	15	Taylor Mtns.	AK	George P. Mann	1997	100
378 1/8	47 3/8	47 3/8	40 4/8	10	10	Lake Clark	AK	Neil K. Hymas	1984	101
377 7/8	55 7/8	57 0/8	40 0/8	11	11	Ugashik River	AK	Douglas A. Smythe	1986	102
377 7/8	47 4/8	46 6/8	37 0/8	14	15	Sagavanirktok River	AK	Jason Hutchins	2009	102
377 6/8	52 0/8	51 4/8	35 6/8	13	19	Dawn Lake	AK	Bob Kroll	1963	104
377 4/8	50 2/8	50 2/8	33 0/8	15	23	Kobuk River	AK	Mark Keiser	1994	105
377 3/8	51 6/8	51 6/8	39 1/8	13	13	Cutler River	AK	Tom Kothenbeutel	1999	106
376 7/8	50 2/8	45 4/8	40 2/8	14	13	Alaska Peninsula	AK	Bob Gulman	1968	107
376 7/8	52 6/8	50 5/8	49 4/8	16	14	Alaska Peninsula	AK	Roger O. Iveson	1976	107
376 6/8	63 5/8	63 7/8	44 6/8	11	10	Mulchatna River	AK	Nicholas Testi	1997	109
376 4/8	51 6/8	53 7/8	38 6/8	12	15	Little Underhill Creek	AK	Gary L. Stephens	1992	110
376 2/8	53 5/8	54 6/8	40 1/8	14	11	Sagavanirktok River	AK	Darin Patrick	2009	111
376 0/8	58 3/8	52 3/8	44 0/8	9	10	Lake Clark	AK	Joe Ball	1986	112
375 7/8	50 6/8	50 1/8	32 3/8	14	14	Cutler River	AK	Jay Deones	1997	113
375 5/8	54 0/8	56 1/8	39 3/8	14	13	Lake Iliamna	AK	Dr. Dale Schlehuber	1992	114
374 7/8	50 0/8	55 4/8	45 4/8	12	10	Nushagak Hills	AK	Steven J. Niedzielski	1995	115
374 4/8	51 2/8	50 4/8	38 3/8	13	11	Taylor Mtns.	AK	Bob Ehle	1998	116
374 3/8	57 2/8	51 4/8	33 4/8	11	12	Hohlitna River	AK	Rick Tollison	1978	117
374 3/8	51 0/8	50 5/8	37 5/8	9	11	Kobuk River	AK	David Rue	2000	117
374 1/8	46 6/8	45 2/8	43 6/8	13	13	Kodiak Island	AK	Randy Liljenquist	2006	119
374 0/8	48 0/8	49 7/8	40 5/8	10	8	Dog Salmon River	AK	Bob Holzberger	1991	120
373 6/8	47 5/8	47 5/8	40 2/8	11	17	Delta Creek	AK	Dwight Guynn	1980	121
373 5/8	46 6/8	46 7/8	39 5/8	18	15	Devil Creek	AK	Douglas Walker	1966	122
373 2/8	57 2/8	57 0/8	34 7/8	9	8	Kilbuck Mtns.	AK	Greg Munther	1998	123
372 5/8	44 6/8	44 6/8	25 5/8	11	11	Atigun River	AK	James W. Black, Jr.	1988	124
372 4/8	43 0/8	42 0/8	35 1/8	16	17	Franklin Bluffs	AK	Jason S. Moorman	2006	125
372 0/8	56 7/8	58 5/8	38 6/8	9	11	Lake Iliamna	AK	Gary Wright	1991	126
371 7/8	47 4/8	49 1/8	46 1/8	16	17	Prudhoe Bay	AK	Randy Richardson	1986	127
371 6/8	46 4/8	48 6/8	33 0/8	12	13	Cutler River	AK	Randy E. Doyle	1985	128
371 5/8	40 1/8	40 1/8	34 1/8	17	28	Maclaren River	AK	Dick Cooley	1962	129
371 5/8	48 5/8	49 1/8	41 6/8	20	15	Port Heiden	AK	Jim Dougherty	1968	129
371 5/8	57 1/8	58 5/8	33 3/8	12	11	Kobuk River	AK	David Rue	2000	129
371 4/8	46 4/8	45 2/8	31 2/8	11	13	Grayling Creek	AK	Carl H. Spaeth	1997	132
*371 4/8	54 2/8	47 4/8	35 4/8	9	12	Adak Island	AK	Mark "Gutz" Gutsmiedl	2004	132
371 3/8	51 5/8	51 6/8	39 5/8	11	17	Cinder River	AK	Keith Pilz	1976	134
370 7/8	56 5/8	56 1/8	42 6/8	11	12	Arctic Coastal Plain	AK	Robin D. Johnson	1987	135
370 6/8	53 3/8	55 5/8	37 1/8	10	10	King Salmon River	AK	Ed Evans	1990	136
370 6/8	58 4/8	60 0/8	39 1/8	12	12	Lake Iliamna	AK	Glen Berry	1993	136
370 5/8	45 3/8	48 3/8	39 2/8	11	15	Lake Iliamna	AK	John Meschko	1981	138
370 4/8	46 4/8	47 7/8	34 5/8	12	11	Dog Salmon River	AK	Gary Thompson	1991	139
370 3/8	48 7/8	49 7/8	32 3/8	10	12	Shenjek Lake	AK	J. Keith Chastain	1984	140
370 2/8	55 3/8	54 5/8	38 5/8	9	9	Mulchatna River	AK	William A. Sheka, Jr.	1984	141
370 2/8	52 3/8	51 3/8	41 7/8	13	12	Mulchatna River	AK	Matt Wood	1992	141
370 1/8	54 0/8	52 6/8	34 5/8	10	13	North Slope	AK	Ronald L. Sherer	1983	143
370 1/8	49 6/8	49 6/8	43 4/8	9	11	Lake Clark	AK	Ron Crouch	1989	143
370 1/8	50 0/8	50 2/8	38 5/8	12	14	Keefer Creek	AK	Mark Hockenberry	1994	143
370 0/8	54 0/8	51 6/8	42 1/8	12	12	Becharof Lake	AK	Bill B. Hobbins	1997	146
369 6/8	42 4/8	42 0/8	46 5/8	13	15	Lake Iliamna	AK	David L. Wolf	1988	147
369 5/8	44 0/8	44 4/8	34 4/8	13	14	Ugashik River	AK	William J. Stonebraker	1987	148
369 3/8	47 7/8	49 4/8	40 1/8	12	12	Mulchatna River	AK	Jeffrey L. Rentzel	1990	149
369 3/8	55 4/8	53 1/8	38 5/8	11	9	Wolf Lake	AK	Tim Cuthriell	1996	149
369 1/8	52 0/8	51 4/8	34 1/8	12	9	Fairbanks	AK	Keith Jensen	1986	151
368 7/8	52 1/8	46 3/8	36 2/8	10	10	Cheeneetnuk River	AK	Kim Wintz	1983	152
368 7/8	46 6/8	47 1/8	40 7/8	16	17	Prudhoe Bay	AK	Calvin Farner	1985	152
368 5/8	43 5/8	45 4/8	30 1/8	16	14	Lower Talarik Creek	AK	John D. "Jack" Frost	1994	154
368 4/8	58 2/8	55 6/8	40 4/8	12	11	Ambler	AK	Rick Kinmon	1983	155
368 2/8	51 1/8	53 6/8	44 1/8	12	12	Swift River	AK	Rolf J. Sandberg	1986	156
368 2/8	49 7/8	49 7/8	41 1/8	10	12	King Salmon	AK	David Isom	1987	156
368 2/8	48 2/8	48 5/8	40 0/8	10	10	Mulchatna River	AK	Rick Albers	1994	156
*368 1/8	52 0/8	50 1/8	35 4/8	12	12	Adak Island	AK	Mark "Gutz" Gutsmiedl	2006	159
*368 1/8	44 4/8	45 5/8	39 6/8	12	16	Kuskokwim River	AK	David Benitz	2010	159
368 0/8	51 5/8	46 4/8	36 3/8	14	19	Port Heiden	AK	John E. Lawson	1970	161
368 0/8	55 1/8	54 5/8	38 3/8	14	10	King Salmon River	AK	Rick Grooms	1979	161
367 4/8	50 2/8	52 1/8	49 7/8	12	13	Lake Iliamna	AK	David Niehaus	1991	163
367 4/8	47 1/8	47 1/8	35 0/8	12	12	Lake Iliamna	AK	Larry E. Sides, Jr.	1994	163
367 3/8	49 4/8	50 4/8	35 4/8	8	10	Sagavanirktok River	AK	Lee S. Peterson	2006	165
367 2/8	55 0/8	57 5/8	41 5/8	12	12	Tundra Lake	AK	Jim Garant	1988	166
367 1/8	51 1/8	54 6/8	39 4/8	14	11	Shungnak	AK	Eric F. Efird	2003	167
366 5/8	53 7/8	53 7/8	50 3/8	8	9	Franklin Bluffs	AK	Dick Carlson	1983	168
366 5/8	49 5/8	48 0/8	28 7/8	13	14	Carlos Creek	AK	Braun Kopsack	1989	168
366 4/8	48 1/8	52 4/8	47 0/8	13	13	Chicken Ridge	AK	Larry Daly	2002	170
366 3/8	45 0/8	47 7/8	41 6/8	12	10	Hohlitna River	AK	Vance Henry	1988	171
366 2/8	47 6/8	47 3/8	35 3/8	12	17	Stoney River	AK	Craig E. Thomas	1989	172
366 1/8	45 4/8	45 7/8	37 1/8	12	13	Iliamna	AK	Grady A. Shelton	1994	173
366 1/8	48 5/8	48 7/8	42 4/8	11	11	Shungnak	AK	Eric F. Efird	2003	173
366 0/8	54 1/8	53 5/8	47 7/8	10	12	Upper Stuyahok River	AK	Jim Bradford	1989	175
365 6/8	48 7/8	50 4/8	38 6/8	14	12	Shotgun Hills	AK	John L. Chase	1997	176
365 4/8	47 3/8	45 7/8	27 0/8	12	12	Cutler River	AK	Larry Streiff	1990	177
365 3/8	51 6/8	53 6/8	40 7/8	9	8	Naknek	AK	Joe Keathley	1996	178
365 3/8	47 6/8	43 1/8	32 4/8	17	18	Nuna River	AK	David Rue	2009	178
365 2/8	42 7/8	43 6/8	40 1/8	10	11	Ptarmigan Lake	AK	Dan Wolf	1997	180
*365 2/8	45 4/8	46 6/8	32 2/8	14	14	Ogilvie Mtns.	YUK	Logan Fink	2009	180
365 1/8	43 4/8	47 0/8	37 3/8	15	13	Iliamna	AK	Cory Hugelen	2000	182
364 7/8	45 6/8	45 3/8	32 3/8	12	14	Sagavanirktok River	AK	Gustav Daniel Wittenberg	1999	183
364 6/8	53 6/8	51 5/8	26 3/8	12	19	Sagavanirktok River	AK	Judd Cooney	1982	184
364 5/8	45 6/8	45 5/8	32 7/8	14	11	Cantwell	AK	Rick D. Snell	1991	185
364 4/8	54 1/8	54 7/8	37 0/8	11	13	Deadhorse	AK	David Carlson	2006	186
364 2/8	48 3/8	48 0/8	30 6/8	11	11	Cinder River	AK	Jack Dykstra	1991	187
363 6/8	52 0/8	53 4/8	39 3/8	13	14	Dillingham	AK	Glen Shatzer	1992	188
363 5/8	43 6/8	43 0/8	32 1/8	18	19	Toolik River	AK	Scottie A. Bagi	2001	189
363 2/8	52 5/8	50 4/8	35 2/8	13	15	Squirrel River	AK	John J. Boland	1995	190

223

BARREN GROUND CARIBOU

Minimum Score 325   Continued

SCORE	LENGTH OF R MAIN BEAM L	INSIDE SPREAD	NUMBER OF R POINTS L	AREA	STATE/PROVINCE	HUNTER'S NAME	DATE	RANK
363 2/8	53 4/8 51 7/8	36 3/8	15 13	Lake Iliamna	AK	Richard S. Kinas	1997	190
363 1/8	46 0/8 46 3/8	36 2/8	11 14	Council	AK	Mark Wayne Smith	2002	192
363 0/8	53 4/8 52 6/8	37 5/8	10 9	King Salmon	AK	Kent D. Keenlyne	1982	193
363 0/8	47 0/8 47 0/8	39 5/8	8 10	Aleutian Range	AK	H. Richard Long	1984	193
362 7/8	50 6/8 49 6/8	42 4/8	10 12	Happy Valley	AK	Jeff Krienke	1995	195
362 7/8	49 0/8 50 3/8	43 7/8	14 12	Kodiak Island	AK	William Newman	2008	195
362 6/8	54 3/8 52 0/8	37 6/8	7 9	Lake Clark	AK	John Thomas Cruger	1987	197
362 6/8	49 3/8 48 6/8	36 2/8	10 11	Ugashik Lake	AK	Kyle Culver	1989	197
362 4/8	44 3/8 47 2/8	34 4/8	17 18	Egegik River	AK	Walter Eslinger	1970	199
362 4/8	45 7/8 46 7/8	28 3/8	18 19	Healy River	AK	Ricky L. Mitchell	1988	199
362 3/8	44 0/8 47 2/8	35 2/8	10 9	Mulchatna River	AK	Ken Conley	1994	201
362 2/8	51 1/8 51 1/8	36 0/8	14 11	Sourdough	AK	Dan Jordan	1965	202
362 0/8	46 1/8 47 4/8	33 5/8	13 10	Swan River	AK	William C. Shuster	1993	203
361 7/8	57 4/8 57 0/8	34 1/8	13 13	White Hills	AK	Dick Carlson	1984	204
361 5/8	54 0/8 50 4/8	34 5/8	9 11	Blackstone River	YUK	Nathan L. Andersohn	2009	205
361 3/8	54 4/8 54 0/8	46 1/8	9 10	Kajulik Bay	AK	Thomas J. Hoffman	1983	206
361 3/8	51 6/8 52 5/8	44 2/8	13 12	Brooks Range	AK	John Ribic	1986	206
361 1/8	54 3/8 52 3/8	40 7/8	9 11	Sagavanirktok River	AK	Christopher B. Stone	2003	208
361 0/8	49 2/8 48 4/8	41 2/8	11 11	Mulchatna River	AK	James W. Southworth	1983	209
360 7/8	51 7/8 50 2/8	41 2/8	14 16	Iliamna	AK	Scott Halbert	1992	210
360 6/8	52 7/8 52 3/8	36 4/8	10 8	Lake Clark	AK	John W. Rose	1986	211
360 6/8	57 4/8 53 1/8	36 1/8	12 14	Cinnabar Creek	AK	James C. Davis	1994	211
360 5/8	52 6/8 54 4/8	36 1/8	10 14	Mulchatna River	AK	Donald C. Martin	1998	213
360 4/8	56 3/8 53 4/8	41 1/8	12 14	Ugashik Lake	AK	Bruce B. Stamp	1992	214
360 2/8	54 7/8 53 6/8	41 2/8	10 11	Ptarmigan Lake	AK	Paul D. Wolf	1997	215
360 2/8	50 2/8 50 2/8	39 6/8	13 10	Shungnak	AK	Christofer Schultz	1998	215
360 0/8	52 3/8 52 2/8	32 6/8	8 8	Maclaren River	AK	Rick D. Snell	1994	217
359 6/8	45 5/8 46 3/8	43 7/8	17 16	Mulchatna River	AK	Ralph Ertz	1982	218
359 6/8	51 3/8 51 1/8	40 1/8	15 14	Kujulik Bay	AK	Norman Stahlman	1987	218
359 6/8	53 5/8 52 5/8	37 7/8	15 13	Coleen River	AK	John D. "Jack" Frost	2002	218
359 3/8	52 7/8 53 4/8	29 7/8	10 9	Lake Clark	AK	Mark Buehrer	1985	221
358 6/8	41 4/8 45 4/8	39 0/8	11 10	Aniakchak River	AK	Gary N. Moore, DDS	1994	222
358 6/8	55 6/8 53 6/8	31 5/8	8 9	Taylor Mtns.	AK	Rick A. Albers	1996	222
358 6/8	47 4/8 47 7/8	35 6/8	12 12	Nushagak River	AK	Jerry Nied	1998	222
358 5/8	49 2/8 34 4/8	40 5/8	13 14	Becharof Lake	AK	Joseph O. Fogleman	1986	225
358 4/8	50 0/8 51 0/8	34 1/8	13 12	Alaska Peninsula	AK	Chris Cassidy	1982	226
358 2/8	54 7/8 57 1/8	35 5/8	13 10	Tyone Lake	AK	Jake Sonnentag	1961	227
358 2/8	53 5/8 54 5/8	41 0/8	13 13	Maclaren River	AK	George Moerlein	1963	227
358 0/8	48 4/8 49 3/8	36 5/8	9 11	King Salmon	AK	Norm Epperson	1983	229
358 0/8	46 1/8 45 6/8	35 3/8	14 13	Aniak Lake	AK	Kevin L. Hall	1998	229
358 0/8	46 0/8 45 3/8	36 4/8	10 11	Mulchatna River	AK	Dallas Smith	2000	229
357 7/8	48 4/8 48 4/8	39 4/8	17 13	Cutler River	AK	Tim Stahman	2001	232
357 7/8	59 6/8 61 4/8	41 4/8	8 10	Grayling Creek	AK	David L. Regel	2001	232
357 5/8	48 6/8 49 0/8	45 3/8	11 12	Deadhorse	AK	George P. Mann	1986	234
357 5/8	53 2/8 52 0/8	38 5/8	8 8	Maclaren River	AK	Debra A. Schaugaard	1994	234
357 5/8	42 0/8 45 3/8	37 7/8	11 14	Shungnak	AK	Eric F. Efird	2000	234
357 5/8	53 6/8 46 6/8	37 3/8	13 16	Grayling Creek	AK	Carl Spaeth	2001	234
357 4/8	57 0/8 57 5/8	35 5/8	11 10	Iliamna	AK	Mark Jensen	1994	238
357 3/8	48 0/8 48 3/8	39 7/8	11 13	King Salmon	AK	Gerry C. Stinski	1986	239
356 7/8	52 4/8 52 4/8	37 0/8	10 12	Toolik Lake	AK	Jacob Garon	2007	240
356 6/8	44 4/8 44 2/8	31 7/8	12 15	Dillingham	AK	Kurt M. Spencer	1996	241
356 6/8	52 1/8 52 4/8	38 0/8	10 9	Lake Selby	AK	Ricky Smith	1996	241
356 5/8	47 1/8 46 2/8	40 2/8	13 13	Unimak Island	AK	John D. "Jack" Frost	2001	243
356 4/8	49 7/8 49 6/8	38 1/8	12 12	Mulchatna River	AK	Scott McDowell	1994	244
356 3/8	46 4/8 48 1/8	35 7/8	12 9	Kotzebue	AK	Gary Gapp	2003	245
355 7/8	54 7/8 53 7/8	26 7/8	10 10	Mulchatna River	AK	Dan L. Carroll	1987	246
355 6/8	43 5/8 42 4/8	28 2/8	12 14	Deadhorse	AK	Jim Hodson	1985	247
355 6/8	49 3/8 50 0/8	33 3/8	14 14	Noatak River	AK	Roger A. Rasmussen	1990	247
355 5/8	57 0/8 56 0/8	44 0/8	15 16	Sagavanirktok River	AK	David D. Bestul	1986	249
355 4/8	48 5/8 48 2/8	32 4/8	14 11	Sagavanirktok River	AK	George Kamps	2005	250
355 1/8	50 1/8 50 2/8	41 5/8	11 8	Lake Iliamna	AK	Gardner Rowell	1995	251
354 7/8	46 0/8 46 0/8	36 0/8	10 10	Sagavanirktok River	AK	Kevin R. Wiley	1986	252
354 6/8	49 4/8 51 4/8	44 6/8	10 14	Kuktuli River	AK	Neil Summers	1982	253
354 6/8	47 1/8 45 0/8	44 1/8	12 13	Mulchatna River	AK	Richard LeBlond	1985	253
354 6/8	51 7/8 51 1/8	33 4/8	10 12	King Salmon	AK	Bruce A. Bouley	1987	253
354 4/8	49 0/8 47 1/8	42 4/8	13 13	Upnuk Lake	AK	Carl E. Garner	1997	256
354 1/8	49 0/8 50 6/8	39 1/8	10 9	Alaska Range	AK	Roger Wintle	1985	257
354 0/8	44 2/8 44 3/8	34 1/8	9 8	Lime Hills	AK	Bernard G. Norton	1990	258
353 6/8	52 5/8 52 4/8	47 1/8	12 10	Ugashik Lake	AK	Scott Lang	1988	259
353 5/8	48 1/8 46 7/8	37 4/8	14 12	Kotzebue	AK	Larry Welchlen	1988	260
353 3/8	48 2/8 46 6/8	36 7/8	17 13	Caribou Creek	AK	H. R. 'Dutch' Wambold	1964	261
353 3/8	54 4/8 53 7/8	43 2/8	11 12	Telaquana Lake	AK	Jake Sonnentag	1971	261
353 3/8	48 4/8 48 1/8	34 7/8	15 13	Galena	AK	Kenneth V. Butler	1995	261
353 1/8	45 4/8 46 2/8	37 4/8	13 14	Richardson Highway	AK	Donald O. Smith	1963	264
352 5/8	46 5/8 48 5/8	39 1/8	11 10	Carin Mtns.	AK	Wayne Haag	1997	265
352 4/8	49 2/8 45 4/8	31 6/8	8 10	Nushagak River	AK	Dwight Schuh	1993	266
352 3/8	48 2/8 46 5/8	30 1/8	14 14	Lacabana Lake	AK	O. Dale Porter	1986	267
352 2/8	54 1/8 54 0/8	45 1/8	9 10	Pilot Point	AK	John D. 'Jack' Frost	1980	268
352 1/8	53 2/8 55 2/8	33 4/8	11 9	Adak Island	AK	Steve Hohensee	2005	269
351 5/8	48 4/8 52 6/8	38 5/8	10 11	Ugashik Lake	AK	Diane Snyder	1984	270
*351 3/8	44 2/8 45 2/8	40 4/8	13 15	Galbraith Lake	AK	Chad Kinsley	2004	271
351 2/8	62 4/8 59 5/8	36 2/8	13 12	Ugashik Lake	AK	John Amundson	1986	272
351 2/8	46 1/8 48 6/8	38 1/8	14 12	Prudhoe Bay	AK	James R. Sanders, Jr.	1988	272
351 2/8	50 0/8 50 6/8	36 4/8	12 8	Ugashik River	AK	David A. Widby	1988	272
351 2/8	49 3/8 48 5/8	40 4/8	12 12	Port Heiden	AK	Mike Traub	1989	272
351 2/8	46 2/8 46 3/8	40 2/8	10 12	Kilbuck Mtns.	AK	Don G. Scofield	2002	272
351 1/8	50 6/8 49 6/8	40 2/8	13 11	Lake Clark	AK	Bob Schwanke	1988	277
351 1/8	44 5/8 45 1/8	40 2/8	13 14	Ugashik River	AK	Joe P. Twitchell, Jr.	1988	277
350 7/8	51 3/8 49 0/8	27 2/8	20 21	Big Delta	AK	Bill Brown	1958	279
350 6/8	55 1/8 56 0/8	31 4/8	9 8	Lake Clark	AK	Stacy M. Tompkinson	1986	280
350 6/8	46 7/8 47 1/8	37 2/8	9 10	Lime Hills	AK	John Crum	1988	280
350 5/8	51 1/8 47 6/8	43 4/8	9 11	Selawik River	AK	Kirk Westervelt	1985	282
350 3/8	51 3/8 44 0/8	41 3/8	11 14	Meshik River	AK	Art Kragness	1970	283
350 3/8	47 5/8 47 1/8	25 5/8	12 12	40 Mile River	AK	Stan Parkerson	1984	283
350 3/8	42 0/8 45 6/8	38 6/8	9 11	Fish Lake	AK	Vikki Gross	1991	283

224

BARREN GROUND CARIBOU

Minimum Score 325   Continued

SCORE	LENGTH OF R MAIN BEAM L	INSIDE SPREAD	NUMBER OF R POINTS L		AREA	STATE/ PROVINCE	HUNTER'S NAME	DATE	RANK
350 3/8	59 2/8	58 3/8	41 3/8	12	10	Selawik River	AK	Brian D. Gronski	1997	283
350 3/8	53 4/8	54 5/8	43 3/8	9	9	Franklin Bluffs	AK	Matthew Dickson	1998	283
350 2/8	50 3/8	48 4/8	33 6/8	10	10	Tidy Mtn.	AK	John (Jack) C. Culpepper III	1993	288
350 2/8	46 0/8	46 4/8	36 6/8	13	12	Kobuk River	AK	Bill Connors	1995	288
350 1/8	58 6/8	57 2/8	31 0/8	9	9	Mulchatna River	AK	Daniel P. Fleming	1994	290
350 0/8	50 2/8	48 0/8	36 1/8	13	10	Sagavanirktok River	AK	Guy Doyle	1991	291
349 7/8	52 2/8	45 3/8	35 1/8	15	11	Pilot Point	AK	Rolf J. Sandberg	1976	292
349 7/8	48 1/8	49 3/8	28 7/8	10	12	Franklin Bluffs	AK	Craig Kulchak	1982	292
349 6/8	51 2/8	53 0/8	43 5/8	9	10	Koktuli River	AK	Kristine Staffeldt	1992	294
349 5/8	47 7/8	47 3/8	44 6/8	11	8	Alaska Peninsula	AK	Vee F. Hanks	1990	295
349 5/8	50 0/8	50 0/8	46 6/8	11	8	Cutler River	AK	Jerry Notch	1997	295
349 4/8	55 7/8	57 3/8	39 2/8	9	11	Prudhoe Bay	AK	Rick Grooms	1986	297
349 4/8	46 2/8	48 0/8	34 5/8	12	13	Grayling Creek	AK	James C. Carlson	1997	297
349 4/8	52 7/8	53 2/8	41 2/8	10	11	Kogoluktuk River	AK	Steve Hohensee	1999	297
349 4/8	42 0/8	43 1/8	46 6/8	11	14	Ayakulik	AK	Jeffrey C. Utter	2008	297
349 2/8	52 4/8	51 5/8	36 4/8	13	8	Kobuk River	AK	Rick Kinmon	1986	301
349 2/8	49 7/8	48 7/8	41 1/8	8	10	Taylor Mtn.	AK	Mark A. McGillivray	1994	301
349 2/8	49 2/8	49 3/8	32 3/8	12	13	Galbraith Lake	AK	Thomas F. Johnson	2001	301
349 1/8	47 2/8	50 4/8	34 1/8	11	9	Deadhorse	AK	James M. Young	1980	304
348 3/8	43 6/8	44 6/8	42 0/8	13	14	Putilick Mtn.	AK	Gary B. Gingerich	1986	305
348 2/8	50 2/8	48 3/8	42 4/8	10	11	Lower Mulchatna River	AK	Robert L. Atchley	1993	306
348 2/8	48 5/8	48 4/8	34 4/8	13	11	Franklin Bluffs	AK	Eric Colledge	1996	306
348 1/8	49 0/8	49 6/8	39 2/8	7	8	Mulchatna River	AK	Leroy Hansen	1994	308
348 0/8	51 1/8	49 2/8	37 3/8	10	13	Alaska Range	AK	Salvatore J. Scaltrito	1983	309
348 0/8	48 5/8	49 2/8	43 7/8	10	8	Kaskanac Foothills	AK	Jeffrey S. Stevens	1988	309
348 0/8	50 4/8	50 0/8	29 0/8	13	12	Galbraith Lake	AK	Stan Parkerson	1990	309
348 0/8	47 4/8	46 0/8	32 7/8	16	18	Kotzebue	AK	Carl H. Spaeth	1991	309
348 0/8	51 1/8	53 0/8	34 4/8	12	13	Taylor Mtn.	AK	Edward A. Conkell	1994	309
347 7/8	48 1/8	48 7/8	30 4/8	9	7	Lake Iliamna	AK	Steve Bellis	1992	314
347 6/8	55 6/8	59 0/8	42 0/8	10	10	Stuyahok River	AK	Marlon Clapham	1989	315
347 5/8	46 4/8	47 5/8	37 6/8	20	16	Colville River	AK	John D. 'Jack' Frost	1982	316
347 4/8	46 2/8	45 2/8	41 7/8	12	14	Ogilvie Mtns.	YUK	Emile Gele	1965	317
347 4/8	51 4/8	48 1/8	34 0/8	11	13	Ivishak River	AK	Daniel Pine	1997	317
347 3/8	46 7/8	52 4/8	37 0/8	9	9	Mulchatna River	AK	Ray Roussett, Jr.	1986	319
347 1/8	52 0/8	50 1/8	39 0/8	14	13	Dog Salmon River	AK	Gary H. Thompson	1989	320
347 1/8	45 4/8	47 2/8	33 0/8	12	10	King Salmon River	AK	John "Rosey" Roseland	1991	320
346 7/8	50 4/8	50 2/8	32 0/8	10	19	Telaquana Lake	AK	Gary Wall	1974	322
346 5/8	50 0/8	48 6/8	36 5/8	10	12	Little Delta	AK	Herb Lindsay	1964	323
346 5/8	49 1/8	48 2/8	35 2/8	17	17	Sagavanirktok River	AK	Judd Cooney	1982	323
346 5/8	48 0/8	47 4/8	35 7/8	10	12	Porcupine River	AK	Mike Cummings	1994	323
346 4/8	48 6/8	48 6/8	37 5/8	11	9	Nigu River	AK	Lowell Thomas	2003	326
346 1/8	43 6/8	45 0/8	35 0/8	18	13	Shotgun Hills	AK	Doug Aikin	1995	327
346 0/8	56 0/8	55 3/8	30 3/8	16	12	Franklin Bluffs	AK	Pete Trottier	1994	328
345 7/8	49 3/8	50 7/8	36 0/8	10	11	Mulchatna River	AK	Michael J. Spence	1998	329
345 6/8	47 5/8	49 0/8	35 2/8	9	10	Prudhoe Bay	AK	Gary Keller	2003	330
345 5/8	49 5/8	49 5/8	35 6/8	12	12	Alaska Range	AK	Lon E. Lauber	1988	331
345 4/8	43 3/8	45 5/8	34 6/8	13	13	Toolik Lake	AK	Robbin L. Hams	2001	332
345 4/8	45 5/8	43 5/8	34 3/8	11	11	Kotzebue	AK	Alan Douglas Boehne	2004	332
345 3/8	47 5/8	49 0/8	37 4/8	16	22	Kuskokwim Mtns.	AK	Robert K. Paulson	1977	334
345 3/8	54 0/8	48 1/8	36 5/8	12	14	Cutler River	AK	Doug Strecker	1985	334
345 3/8	51 0/8	50 4/8	41 2/8	8	8	Wood-Tikchik	AK	Richard Van Valkenburg	1994	334
345 3/8	46 5/8	46 6/8	30 4/8	13	11	Becharof Lake	AK	Gary Tudor	1996	334
345 2/8	47 3/8	48 2/8	32 4/8	11	10	Port Heiden	AK	Dennis G. Goldbach	1979	338
345 2/8	46 4/8	48 7/8	34 4/8	10	11	Alaska Peninsula	AK	Calvin Farner	1987	338
345 2/8	56 3/8	57 0/8	37 7/8	9	9	Lake Clark	AK	Mel Tenneson	1988	338
345 2/8	45 5/8	46 4/8	28 6/8	12	12	Koksetna River	AK	Steve Brockmann	1994	338
345 1/8	51 4/8	53 4/8	43 1/8	9	8	Lake Lach Buna	AK	Bob Ebert	1983	342
345 1/8	47 2/8	45 5/8	42 1/8	10	12	Mulchatna River	AK	E. Donnall Thomas, Jr.	1985	342
345 0/8	56 0/8	52 1/8	39 2/8	14	9	Wrench Creek	AK	Richard L. Westervelt	1991	344
345 0/8	44 6/8	45 4/8	35 6/8	13	11	Ivishak River	AK	Frank S. Noska IV	2010	344
344 7/8	51 4/8	50 4/8	34 0/8	13	12	Lake Clark	AK	Troy Hymas	1984	346
344 7/8	49 1/8	48 1/8	37 2/8	10	14	Mulchatna River	AK	Dwight S. Wolf	1999	346
344 7/8	45 6/8	50 0/8	26 4/8	12	12	Squirrel River	AK	Ron Hise	2006	346
344 6/8	52 5/8	51 1/8	29 4/8	15	11	Susitna Valley	AK	Ronald D. Hopkins	1974	349
344 6/8	49 3/8	48 4/8	34 2/8	9	10	Sagavanirktok River	AK	Edwin A. Churchill, Jr.	2008	349
344 5/8	52 1/8	53 0/8	34 1/8	16	15	Squirrel River	AK	Gary Renfro	1998	351
344 4/8	49 7/8	51 6/8	38 6/8	13	16	Mirror Lake	AK	Robert E. Speegle, MD	1990	352
344 4/8	51 6/8	51 0/8	37 2/8	8	8	Ketok Mtn.	AK	Bob Koepsell	1992	352
344 2/8	46 1/8	43 6/8	27 7/8	11	13	Franklin Bluffs	AK	Matthew A. Jones	1987	354
344 2/8	49 1/8	49 2/8	34 2/8	11	12	Kiana	AK	Frank A. Johnson	1995	354
344 2/8	57 0/8	54 7/8	34 7/8	10	10	Galbraith Lake	AK	Frank S. Noska IV	2004	354
344 2/8	53 7/8	52 5/8	32 7/8	11	11	Deadhorse	AK	Terry Hudzinski	2010	354
344 1/8	49 2/8	50 0/8	33 2/8	11	10	Happy Valley	AK	Tim J. Mariner	1991	358
344 1/8	50 7/8	50 4/8	43 1/8	10	11	Tagagawik River	AK	Doug Larsen	1993	358
344 1/8	52 1/8	52 0/8	30 6/8	8	8	Sagavanirktok River	AK	Wayne R. Oman	2004	358
344 0/8	51 0/8	48 0/8	37 5/8	13	11	Toolik Lake	AK	Charles Mahlen	2009	361
*343 7/8	43 0/8	45 1/8	33 6/8	13	15	Adak Island	AK	Mark "Gutz" Gutsmiedl	2006	362
343 6/8	45 2/8	46 3/8	30 6/8	14	14	Mulchatna River	AK	Christopher G. Hixson	1990	363
343 6/8	53 0/8	51 7/8	33 1/8	13	11	Tagagawik River	AK	Gayland Jones	1991	363
343 6/8	52 6/8	54 1/8	30 3/8	10	9	Coleen River	AK	Marvin Whitehead	1997	363
343 5/8	50 6/8	53 6/8	41 0/8	8	12	Little Delta River	AK	Herman J. Griese	1980	366
343 4/8	48 0/8	50 1/8	28 6/8	16	13	Grayling Creek	AK	Carl G. Handyside	1997	367
343 3/8	54 6/8	52 7/8	46 4/8	9	10	Mulchatna River	AK	Donald Wagner	1993	368
343 2/8	45 4/8	47 7/8	35 6/8	9	8	Prudhoe Bay	AK	Victor Lee Littleton	1989	369
343 1/8	51 6/8	53 2/8	38 6/8	8	13	Taylor Highway	AK	Jae Beardon	1961	370
343 1/8	52 2/8	51 2/8	34 4/8	10	9	333 Dalton Highway	AK	Robert A. Chadwick	1987	370
343 0/8	49 4/8	48 2/8	40 7/8	9	14	Wrench Creek	AK	Kirk Westervelt	1991	372
343 0/8	54 7/8	55 4/8	33 6/8	13	16	Prudhoe Bay	AK	David E. Pawlak	2003	372
343 0/8	48 3/8	46 7/8	43 0/8	12	12	Shungnak	AK	Terry M. Dennis	2004	372
342 5/8	44 0/8	45 1/8	32 0/8	11	12	Toolik Lake	AK	Blaine L. Thompson	1995	375
342 5/8	47 2/8	47 1/8	38 1/8	6	9	Purcell Mtn.	AK	Chris G. Sanford	1998	375
342 5/8	47 4/8	48 4/8	30 7/8	13	10	Squirrel River	AK	Mike Brezonick	1998	375
342 4/8	50 7/8	53 2/8	38 0/8	9	10	Dalton Highway	AK	Tom Chadwick	1991	378
342 4/8	47 2/8	46 2/8	34 0/8	12	12	Mulchatna River	AK	Duane Burgess	1998	378
342 3/8	44 3/8	44 5/8	26 4/8	17	17	Tagagawik River	AK	Kim S. Brockhoff	2000	380

225

BARREN GROUND CARIBOU

Minimum Score 325 — Continued

SCORE	LENGTH OF MAIN BEAM R	L	INSIDE SPREAD	NUMBER OF POINTS R	L	AREA	STATE/PROVINCE	HUNTER'S NAME	DATE	RANK
342 3/8	51 7/8	52 1/8	34 2/8	11	12	Grayling Creek	AK	Carl H. Spaeth	2008	380
342 0/8	45 7/8	49 3/8	40 7/8	13	16	Imuya Bay	AK	Archie Nesbitt	1989	382
341 6/8	58 2/8	56 3/8	39 6/8	11	14	McGrath	AK	Jim Holdenried	1982	383
341 6/8	50 1/8	50 3/8	34 3/8	14	13	Grayling Creek	AK	Daniel K. Carlson	1997	383
341 5/8	48 5/8	47 6/8	33 4/8	12	13	Alaska Peninsula	AK	Edward L. Russell	1980	385
341 4/8	53 3/8	52 2/8	43 4/8	14	12	Franklin Bluffs	AK	Dr. Jack Harvey	1984	386
341 4/8	43 3/8	45 0/8	30 4/8	14	11	Brooks Range	AK	Jeff Lindeman	1988	386
341 2/8	49 2/8	49 7/8	29 1/8	9	8	Toolik Lake	AK	Judy Watson	1988	388
341 1/8	46 6/8	48 1/8	41 0/8	9	9	Axburgh Lake	AK	Ryan J. Dorak	1994	389
341 1/8	45 4/8	45 6/8	31 7/8	14	12	Nuna River	AK	Kaye Rue	2005	389
341 0/8	49 2/8	49 0/8	37 2/8	14	13	King Salmon	AK	Reggie Callender	1971	391
341 0/8	47 6/8	44 3/8	33 7/8	12	10	Toolik River	AK	Larry Daly	1999	391
340 7/8	46 1/8	46 7/8	30 6/8	8	8	Wolf Lake	AK	Tracy G. Hardy	1990	393
340 6/8	49 2/8	49 3/8	27 1/8	12	13	Brooks Range	AK	Roger G. Stewart	1983	394
340 5/8	46 2/8	50 2/8	38 3/8	11	11	Mulchatna River	AK	Dwight S. Wolf	1999	395
340 4/8	52 4/8	51 2/8	34 5/8	12	11	Sheenjek River	AK	Curtis Adams	1995	396
340 3/8	46 4/8	45 7/8	39 3/8	9	12	Mulchatna River	AK	Dr. Steven G. Hammons	1993	397
340 3/8	47 5/8	44 0/8	33 1/8	11	10	Kuparuk River	AK	Jeff Barnes, Sr.	1995	397
340 3/8	46 6/8	49 4/8	40 4/8	11	11	Lake Iliamna	AK	Dyrk Eddie	1995	397
340 2/8	44 4/8	42 2/8	37 0/8	12	12	Cutler River	AK	Ed Branchaw	2000	400
*340 2/8	60 5/8	60 0/8	38 7/8	14	13	Squirrel River	AK	Paul D. Atkins	2008	400
340 0/8	49 0/8	51 0/8	36 2/8	14	14	Franklin Bluffs	AK	John T. Toenes	1985	402
340 0/8	54 3/8	54 3/8	27 1/8	15	13	Ambler River	AK	Alvin L. Brandenberg	2000	402
*340 0/8	48 2/8	48 4/8	43 3/8	10	8	Franklin Bluffs	AK	Andy Andersen	2009	402
339 7/8	48 3/8	43 4/8	36 3/8	14	12	Prudhoe Bay	AK	John Bilek	1986	405
339 7/8	51 4/8	52 0/8	32 4/8	15	12	Sagavanirktok River	AK	Ron Serwa	1987	405
339 7/8	50 0/8	48 5/8	40 4/8	9	14	Branch River	AK	Dale E. Christiansen	1995	405
339 7/8	50 7/8	49 3/8	41 5/8	9	14	Dawson	YUK	George Harms	2008	405
339 6/8	44 4/8	47 5/8	32 4/8	12	9	Prudhoe Bay	AK	Wayne Piersol	1987	409
339 6/8	44 4/8	47 6/8	35 7/8	14	11	Mulchatna River	AK	Barbara Helm	1998	409
339 5/8	46 3/8	46 2/8	40 5/8	13	9	Becharof Lake	AK	Doug Fisher	1995	411
339 5/8	46 5/8	50 1/8	37 4/8	11	10	Mulchatna River	AK	Doug Aikin	1997	411
339 4/8	46 0/8	45 0/8	29 0/8	12	13	Port Heiden	AK	Dennis G. Goldbach	1980	413
339 4/8	49 5/8	51 7/8	41 0/8	12	10	Franklin Bluffs	AK	Roger E. Wheelock	1982	413
339 3/8	48 3/8	47 4/8	35 5/8	9	10	Sparvon Lake	AK	Brad Ham	1997	415
339 2/8	44 4/8	44 6/8	29 2/8	11	11	Mulchatna River	AK	Paul Voshell	1994	416
339 2/8	49 6/8	47 3/8	39 0/8	10	12	Grayling Creek	AK	Carl H. Spaeth	1997	416
339 1/8	52 5/8	53 4/8	38 4/8	10	12	Little Delta	AK	Dr. Judd Grindell	1959	418
339 0/8	45 3/8	51 5/8	34 4/8	18	13	Tyone Lake	AK	Jake Sonnentag	1963	419
338 7/8	47 2/8	48 1/8	29 6/8	8	9	Mulchatna River	AK	Brad C. Bryant	1993	420
338 6/8	52 6/8	49 0/8	31 6/8	13	10	Grayling Creek	AK	Carl H. Spaeth	1992	421
338 6/8	49 2/8	51 7/8	37 4/8	10	9	Nimiuktuk River	AK	Walter J. Palmer	2010	421
338 5/8	47 7/8	47 5/8	32 4/8	14	15	Taylor Mtns.	AK	Mike Kistler	1999	423
*338 5/8	50 3/8	48 3/8	34 2/8	13	12	Gulch Creek	AK	Jason Perez	2010	423
338 4/8	49 4/8	47 7/8	35 1/8	11	16	Bonanza Hills	AK	Larry Langston	1974	425
338 4/8	46 6/8	47 2/8	30 7/8	14	12	Brooks Range	AK	Lyle Willmarth	1984	425
338 3/8	52 4/8	49 1/8	29 3/8	9	10	Tundra Lake	AK	Carl Handyside	1991	427
338 3/8	44 7/8	41 1/8	32 4/8	7	7	Deadman Lake	AK	Larry Daly	1996	427
338 1/8	46 6/8	48 3/8	38 0/8	10	9	Ogilvie River	YUK	Terry W. Brew	2005	429
338 0/8	53 3/8	55 4/8	40 0/8	12	10	Adak Island	AK	Lon E. Lauber	1984	430
338 0/8	48 7/8	48 7/8	38 6/8	13	14	Ugashik Lake	AK	Dave Scott	1989	430
337 7/8	50 7/8	51 7/8	39 6/8	16	11	Cold Bay	AK	John Sarvis	1985	432
337 5/8	49 7/8	49 1/8	41 6/8	12	14	Cinder River	AK	Francis Hosch	1966	433
337 3/8	47 4/8	47 3/8	32 2/8	13	14	Maclaren River	AK	George Moerlein	1963	434
337 1/8	50 6/8	51 2/8	29 1/8	19	18	Dry Creek	AK	Russell Kucinski	1983	435
337 1/8	49 3/8	50 7/8	37 7/8	9	9	Lime Hills	AK	Clifford R. Neville, Sr.	1990	435
337 1/8	49 0/8	51 6/8	32 6/8	10	11	Mulchatna River	AK	Kent Reierson	1996	435
337 1/8	45 4/8	43 1/8	37 7/8	8	10	Nishlik Lake	AK	Robert Bartoshesky	1996	435
336 7/8	48 3/8	48 2/8	39 2/8	11	9	Tagagawik River	AK	Louis Strahler	1997	439
336 6/8	55 2/8	51 1/8	42 0/8	12	14	Featherly Pass	AK	Dale DeBoer	1987	440
336 4/8	47 4/8	48 6/8	31 6/8	14	12	Nimiuktuk River	AK	Walter J. Palmer	2010	441
336 2/8	43 3/8	45 1/8	36 5/8	13	15	Shungnak	AK	Eric F. Efird	2003	442
336 0/8	42 7/8	45 2/8	35 0/8	13	9	Lake Iliamna	AK	Todd F. Lewis	1988	443
336 0/8	46 3/8	48 5/8	36 4/8	10	10	Mulchatna River	AK	Stan Rauch	1994	443
336 0/8	42 0/8	44 5/8	36 2/8	16	11	Whitefish Lake	AK	Paul St. John	1997	443
335 5/8	52 4/8	55 2/8	25 4/8	10	6	Chilikadrotna River	AK	Charles W. Rehor	1993	446
335 4/8	43 6/8	45 5/8	36 4/8	15	12	Sagavanirktok River	AK	Stan Parkerson	1986	447
335 3/8	48 0/8	50 6/8	38 4/8	10	9	Lake Iliamna	AK	Steve Welch	1996	448
335 3/8	40 2/8	44 5/8	30 4/8	11	13	Godge Creek	AK	Steve Dollar	2004	448
335 2/8	50 0/8	49 1/8	24 6/8	10	10	Nushagak River	AK	Bob Ameen	1998	450
335 1/8	47 3/8	48 3/8	22 5/8	9	10	Colville River	AK	Bob Gulman	1984	451
335 0/8	45 1/8	45 0/8	28 1/8	13	15	Cutler River	AK	Jay Riewestahl	2000	452
334 7/8	52 7/8	54 1/8	34 0/8	14	10	Squirrel River	AK	James Borron	1992	453
334 5/8	43 6/8	42 3/8	33 0/8	15	11	Carlos Creek	AK	Braun Kopsack	1988	454
334 5/8	51 1/8	50 1/8	32 7/8	12	14	Wrench Creek	AK	Kirk Westervelt	1991	454
334 4/8	43 1/8	45 2/8	33 6/8	13	9	Franklin Bluffs	AK	John F. Gilmore	1991	456
334 4/8	50 2/8	51 7/8	36 2/8	8	9	Kotzebue	AK	Don Farbotnik	2000	456
334 1/8	45 7/8	50 0/8	35 1/8	7	10	Nikabuna Lake	AK	Timothy J. Conrads	1988	458
334 1/8	43 0/8	41 4/8	35 6/8	14	12	Pilot Point	AK	Joe W. Wright	1995	458
334 0/8	45 3/8	45 5/8	30 0/8	15	13	Happy Valley	AK	Michael Chadwick	1992	460
334 0/8	51 1/8	51 0/8	39 7/8	12	11	Kvnchak River	AK	Russell Hadley	1994	460
334 0/8	52 7/8	51 2/8	39 0/8	11	8	Wulik River	AK	Guy Leibenguth	2000	460
333 7/8	54 4/8	56 0/8	47 2/8	10	8	Selawik River	AK	Kirk Westervelt	1985	463
333 7/8	53 5/8	53 5/8	30 2/8	9	8	Nushagak River	AK	Bob Ameen	1998	463
333 5/8	47 2/8	47 2/8	32 5/8	15	11	Ugashik	AK	Stanley Winslow	1973	465
333 5/8	47 7/8	48 4/8	32 0/8	12	17	Happy Valley	AK	Troy Graziadei	1984	465
333 3/8	52 3/8	50 2/8	38 5/8	12	13	Nushagak River	AK	John M. Carbine	1998	467
333 1/8	44 0/8	44 6/8	35 0/8	12	12	Sagavanirktok River	AK	Steven M. Stroka	1991	468
333 0/8	44 6/8	44 7/8	35 4/8	11	13	Nicuhuna Lake	AK	Robert L. Atchley	1993	469
332 7/8	53 0/8	54 3/8	36 2/8	18	15	Denali Hwy.	AK	Junie Moll	1961	470
332 7/8	54 0/8	53 2/8	40 5/8	14	9	Mulchatna River	AK	Dan S. Frandsen	1993	470
332 7/8	49 4/8	49 5/8	39 1/8	9	7	Lime Village	AK	Kevin B. Calongne	2001	470
332 6/8	49 5/8	50 7/8	30 4/8	12	9	Squirrel River	AK	Charles Kuss	1992	473
332 6/8	49 0/8	46 7/8	30 3/8	7	9	Mulchatna River	AK	Jeff DeCavitch	1997	473
332 6/8	53 5/8	53 5/8	33 6/8	11	8	Dillon	YUK	Derek Duggan	2004	473

BARREN GROUND CARIBOU

Minimum Score 325   Continued

SCORE	LENGTH OF R MAIN BEAM L	INSIDE SPREAD	NUMBER OF R POINTS L	AREA	STATE/ PROVINCE	HUNTER'S NAME	DATE	RANK
332 5/8	48 1/8 47 2/8	35 7/8	18 13	Caribou River Drainage	AK	Al Reay	1981	476
332 4/8	47 2/8 47 3/8	40 3/8	10 11	Mulchatna River	AK	Skip Koske	1986	477
332 3/8	45 3/8 46 1/8	29 1/8	9 10	Mulchatna River	AK	Mike Barrett	1987	478
332 2/8	52 5/8 53 0/8	26 1/8	9 9	Kukaklek Lake	AK	Jay Kuhre	1989	479
332 2/8	42 0/8 46 1/8	34 7/8	9 9	Mulchatna River	AK	Rick Schack	1996	479
332 1/8	43 7/8 41 1/8	33 6/8	12 15	Iowa Creek	AK	Bart Colledge	1989	481
332 1/8	44 6/8 43 7/8	33 2/8	13 15	Mulchatna River	AK	Richard R. Schnell	1990	481
332 1/8	44 7/8 46 1/8	41 0/8	10 10	Non Dalton	AK	Gary L. Wilford	1992	481
332 1/8	46 2/8 46 3/8	35 5/8	12 10	Mulchatna River	AK	Rick Albers	1994	481
332 1/8	42 1/8 44 6/8	36 5/8	10 10	Kilbuck Mtns.	AK	Greg Munther	1998	481
332 1/8	47 0/8 44 3/8	37 4/8	14 15	Kotzebue	AK	Roger Gurley	2001	481
331 7/8	54 3/8 55 0/8	35 6/8	9 16	Port Heiden	AK	John E. Lawson	1970	487
331 7/8	52 6/8 54 0/8	39 3/8	7 9	Mulchatna River	AK	Ray Heal	1997	487
331 6/8	51 4/8 47 2/8	31 1/8	9 10	Cinnabar Creek	AK	Fred McCullar	2001	489
331 5/8	45 5/8 48 1/8	35 6/8	12 11	High Lakes	AK	Doug Walker	1970	490
331 5/8	50 3/8 50 5/8	39 3/8	12 11	Ugashik River	AK	Terry Sanders	1988	490
331 5/8	48 1/8 47 6/8	37 1/8	14 16	Brooks Range	AK	James L. Behn	1991	490
331 5/8	52 6/8 52 3/8	44 4/8	10 10	Dillon	YUK	Dustan Duggan	2004	490
331 1/8	47 6/8 46 1/8	28 7/8	12 14	Bonanza Hills	AK	Dan Klebenow	1990	494
330 7/8	40 4/8 41 1/8	30 5/8	13 11	Mulchatna River	AK	Timm W. Raddatz	2000	495
330 5/8	51 1/8 51 5/8	35 6/8	15 10	Tangle Lakes	AK	R. Glen Williams	1966	496
330 4/8	50 2/8 49 3/8	26 7/8	12 10	Atigun Pass	AK	Tom Payer	1994	497
330 2/8	47 7/8 49 7/8	34 3/8	13 10	Franklin Bluffs	AK	Eudane Vicenti	1991	498
330 2/8	41 4/8 40 4/8	29 4/8	11 10	Dillingham	AK	John Holt	1997	498
330 0/8	54 2/8 55 0/8	37 7/8	13 12	Atigun Pass	AK	Keith K. Appel	1984	500
329 7/8	47 4/8 47 3/8	31 0/8	10 15	Dawn Lake	AK	Chuck Kroll	1963	501
329 7/8	56 4/8 53 7/8	40 3/8	9 12	Little Delta	AK	Bill Tutt	1964	501
329 7/8	52 7/8 53 6/8	32 3/8	11 13	Nuna River	AK	David Rue	2005	501
329 6/8	49 6/8 49 4/8	33 1/8	6 8	Sagavanirktok River	AK	Patricia A. Stewart	1983	504
329 5/8	44 4/8 45 4/8	31 0/8	10 11	Alaska Peninsula	AK	Dave Neel	1980	505
329 4/8	57 6/8 53 2/8	41 3/8	8 9	Chandler River	AK	Chuck Roady	1986	506
329 4/8	46 0/8 46 1/8	37 7/8	15 12	Ugashik River	AK	Stan Rauch	1988	506
329 1/8	49 0/8 48 4/8	40 2/8	11 8	Ambler	AK	Dean Bergman	1986	508
329 0/8	46 4/8 46 4/8	40 4/8	9 6	Denali Hwy.	AK	Gordon Spidle	1988	509
328 7/8	49 3/8 48 7/8	37 6/8	10 7	Tutna Lake	AK	Gene Clark	1987	510
328 5/8	56 5/8 53 7/8	36 3/8	10 7	Selawik River	AK	Mike McCabe	1998	511
328 4/8	42 6/8 44 3/8	31 5/8	18 12	Little Delta	AK	Roy Bryan	1964	512
328 4/8	47 6/8 47 7/8	35 3/8	11 13	Sagavanirktok River	AK	Paul G. Barclay	1981	512
328 3/8	50 2/8 49 1/8	30 3/8	9 9	Prudhoe Bay	AK	Denver Perry	1981	514
328 2/8	42 0/8 39 7/8	27 2/8	8 9	Prudhoe Bay	AK	Gene Barcak	1985	515
328 1/8	47 0/8 47 5/8	32 7/8	7 10	Mulchatna River	AK	Joaquin Macias	1992	516
327 7/8	45 4/8 43 5/8	36 2/8	8 11	Mulchatna River	AK	Barbara Helm	1998	517
327 7/8	47 1/8 49 0/8	25 5/8	13 11	Green Lake	AK	Troy McGinnis	1998	517
327 6/8	40 7/8 41 3/8	36 7/8	15 12	Galbraith Lake	AK	G. Stevens Abdoe	1983	519
327 6/8	39 7/8 40 0/8	37 3/8	12 11	Sagavanirktok River	AK	Roger Stewart	1989	519
*327 6/8	54 6/8 51 1/8	28 4/8	9 10	Noatak River	AK	Randy Goza	2005	519
327 5/8	47 3/8 49 3/8	40 0/8	13 13	North Slope	AK	Susan D. Sherer	1983	522
327 5/8	45 5/8 46 4/8	36 1/8	11 10	Prudhoe Bay	AK	Dennis Redden	1992	522
327 3/8	46 1/8 47 0/8	40 0/8	8 9	Selawik River	AK	Richard L. Westervelt	1985	524
327 3/8	51 2/8 51 2/8	32 6/8	13 12	Prudhoe Bay	AK	Rocky Wilson	2003	524
327 2/8	45 6/8 48 5/8	35 6/8	12 12	Noatak River	AK	Donald R. Powers	1987	526
327 2/8	48 6/8 47 3/8	30 6/8	11 11	Kobuk River	AK	Niels Knudsen	1990	526
327 2/8	51 3/8 51 0/8	29 4/8	10 11	Dillingham	AK	John Holt	1997	526
326 7/8	47 5/8 51 2/8	27 3/8	15 13	Dago Creek	AK	Don Davidson	1980	529
326 7/8	48 0/8 49 4/8	40 7/8	11 10	Dillingham	AK	Mike McCormick	1998	529
326 7/8	49 3/8 52 3/8	30 2/8	11 10	Old Man Creek	AK	Todd A. Brickel	2002	529
326 6/8	49 1/8 47 3/8	41 0/8	12 18	Anchorage	AK	Roy Bryan	1964	532
326 6/8	48 1/8 47 4/8	31 0/8	11 10	Lake Tulik	AK	Craig Olthoff	2003	532
326 5/8	43 0/8 45 0/8	38 3/8	12 12	Galena	AK	Larry Spiva	1992	534
326 5/8	52 5/8 52 3/8	47 2/8	9 8	Nuna River	AK	David Rue	1998	534
326 4/8	47 7/8 49 7/8	31 7/8	10 11	Brooks Range	AK	Roger Stewart	1985	536
326 4/8	54 7/8 54 0/8	39 0/8	8 7	Iliamna	AK	David Wolf	1994	536
326 4/8	48 6/8 47 0/8	33 3/8	9 8	Lake Iliamna	AK	Mike Craig	1997	536
326 3/8	47 6/8 49 0/8	39 0/8	11 13	King Salmon	AK	Glenn Hisey	1983	539
326 3/8	51 0/8 53 1/8	41 1/8	11 10	Yellow Creek Hill	AK	Don Poole	1992	539
326 3/8	52 4/8 54 5/8	41 4/8	12 14	Ice Cut	AK	Kevin T. Schaus, Jr.	2005	539
326 0/8	54 5/8 52 6/8	19 0/8	11 12	Squirrel River	AK	Connie Renfro	1998	542
325 6/8	49 0/8 46 1/8	21 1/8	14 13	Atigun Pass	AK	Maxallen D. Jackson	1980	543
325 4/8	52 4/8 52 3/8	31 0/8	13 15	Galbraith Lake	AK	Maxallen D. Jackson	1981	544
325 3/8	45 5/8 48 1/8	33 0/8	15 16	Cerban Lake	AK	James F. Watson	1997	545
325 3/8	46 4/8 46 5/8	34 1/8	9 10	Grayling Creek	AK	Bill Cmiel	1997	545
325 1/8	55 7/8 55 6/8	32 3/8	8 9	Prudhoe Bay	AK	Garry A. Thoms	1986	547
325 0/8	46 6/8 48 5/8	30 5/8	8 9	Ugashik River	AK	Bob "Jake" Jacobsen	1988	548
325 0/8	46 6/8 42 0/8	35 6/8	9 10	Kodiak Island	AK	Bob Ameen	2002	548

BARREN GROUND CARIBOU (VELVET ANTLERS)

Minimum Score 325

SCORE	LENGTH OF R MAIN BEAM L	INSIDE SPREAD	NUMBER OF R POINTS L	AREA	STATE/ PROVINCE	HUNTER'S NAME	DATE	RANK
380 6/8	49 7/8 48 6/8	37 1/8	14 12	Echooka River	AK	Thomas J. Jashinsky	2010	*
374 3/8	50 6/8 49 0/8	32 3/8	10 10	Windy Creek	AK	Kyle Moffat	2005	*
373 0/8	50 7/8 49 6/8	34 7/8	11 10	Sagwon	AK	Michell Kay Anderson	2004	*
354 6/8	48 4/8 45 3/8	32 6/8	9 11	Sagavanirktok River	AK	Jason E. Nixon	2005	*
*343 6/8	51 0/8 48 3/8	38 4/8	14 12	Deadhorse	AK	Brent Peterson	2006	*
329 7/8	47 5/8 47 3/8	25 4/8	11 12	Cutler River	AK	Tom Kothenbeutel	1999	*

227

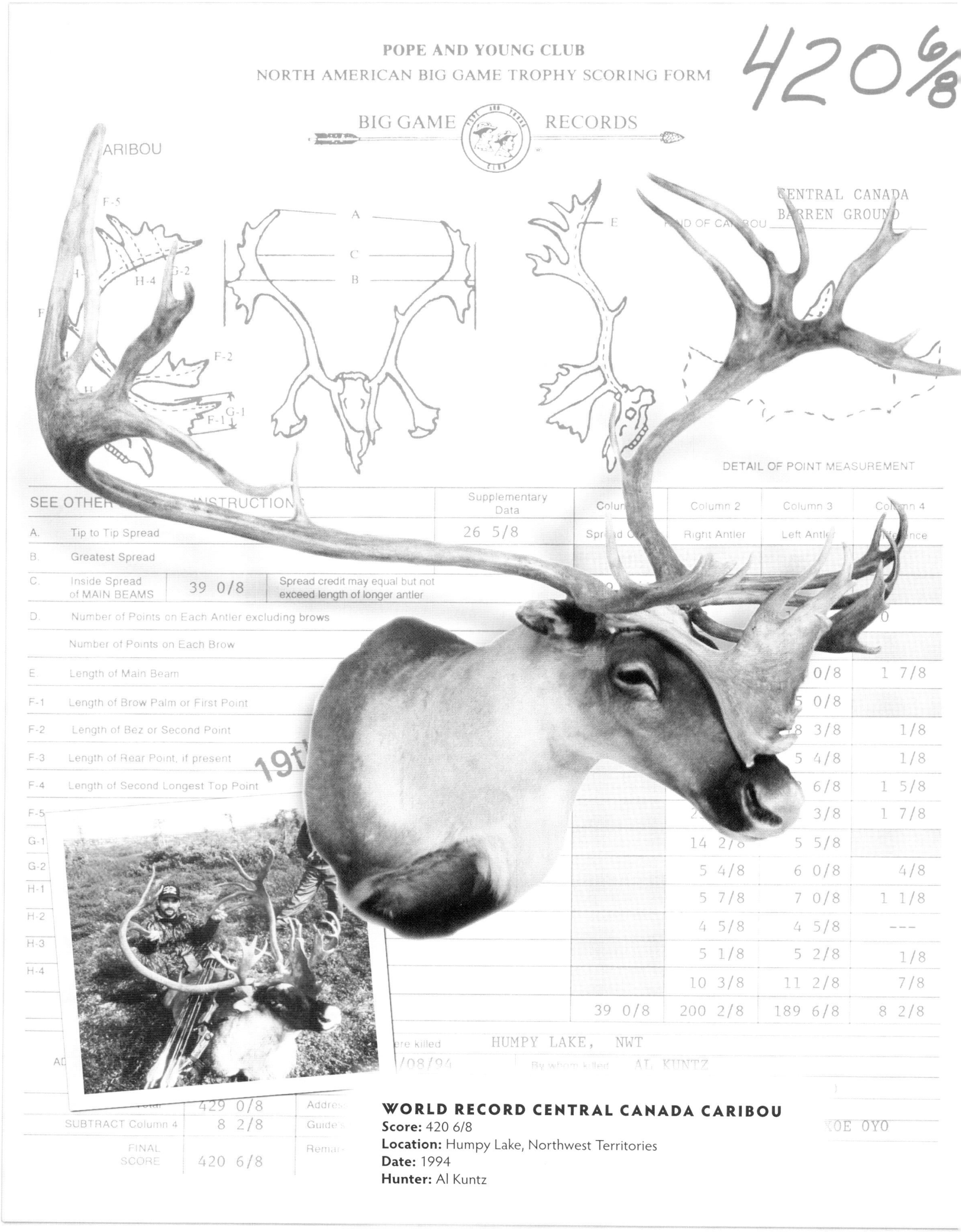

420 6/8

POPE AND YOUNG CLUB
NORTH AMERICAN BIG GAME TROPHY SCORING FORM

BIG GAME RECORDS

CARIBOU — CENTRAL CANADA BARREN GROUND

KIND OF CARIBOU

DETAIL OF POINT MEASUREMENT

		Supplementary Data	Column 1 Spread	Column 2 Right Antler	Column 3 Left Antler	Column 4 Difference
A.	Tip to Tip Spread	26 5/8				
B.	Greatest Spread					
C.	Inside Spread of MAIN BEAMS	39 0/8 — Spread credit may equal but not exceed length of longer antler				0
D.	Number of Points on Each Antler excluding brows					
	Number of Points on Each Brow					
E.	Length of Main Beam				0/8	1 7/8
F-1	Length of Brow Palm or First Point				5 0/8	
F-2	Length of Bez or Second Point				8 3/8	1/8
F-3	Length of Rear Point, if present				5 4/8	1/8
F-4	Length of Second Longest Top Point				6/8	1 5/8
F-5					3/8	1 7/8
G-1				14 2/8	5 5/8	
G-2				5 4/8	6 0/8	4/8
H-1				5 7/8	7 0/8	1 1/8
H-2				4 5/8	4 5/8	---
H-3				5 1/8	5 2/8	1/8
H-4				10 3/8	11 2/8	7/8
			39 0/8	200 2/8	189 6/8	8 2/8

Where killed: HUMPY LAKE, NWT
Date: /08/94 By whom killed: AL KUNTZ

Total: 429 0/8
SUBTRACT Column 4: 8 2/8
FINAL SCORE: 420 6/8

WORLD RECORD CENTRAL CANADA CARIBOU
Score: 420 6/8
Location: Humpy Lake, Northwest Territories
Date: 1994
Hunter: Al Kuntz

Central Canada Caribou

by Al Kuntz

Upon arrival in camp we sighted in, viewed hundreds of bulls and went fishing---there is no hunting on the same day as you fly. The following morning I paired off with my guide and we proceeded across the lake to a known funnel/crossing that was perfect for archery hunting. As we topped a small hill, it was evident that there were caribou in every direction. By 10:00 am the first day I had my first bull on the ground, a 60 yard shot to a well palmated bull took a lot of pressure off. Even as we took the photos, much larger bulls passed behind us within archery range. I swore at that point, I would not fill my second tag unless it was a real dandy.

The next two days provided many opportunities at 350" plus class bulls, but I chose to videotape instead. On the second morning, 16 bulls, all within 60 yards, fed and bedded down in front of me. At least five or six of these bulls would go 370". Thank goodness I had all of this on video…no one would ever believe this!

On the fourth day, I awoke to a clear crisp morning. I had an extremely good feeling about this day. We returned to the same knob as the first day for a vantage point. As I was glassing a herd of bulls, I noticed some movement directly behind me. Less than 80 yards away was the largest caribou I had ever seen in my life. The visual of well over 400 inches of antler, not to mention at least that much loose velvet blowing in the wind, kicked my adrenaline into high gear. My heart sank as I watched the trophy of a lifetime trot away with his head high. The guide's rifle never looked so inviting.

Once the bull made it past us, we decided to try to circle around him. We scurried to the top of a nearby hill to hopefully gain a better vantage point. The guide was still sure that this lone bull would pass through the funnel below us that was approximately 100 yards wide. I dropped into the cover below and the guide stayed up above to watch for the elusive trophy.

Within 20 minutes the bull appeared, just as we had hoped. When he zigged, I zagged, playing "cat and mouse" as he approached closer to my position. Due to the cover and the fact that I was hiding behind a bush on my knees, I could not see the bull…only the tops of his antlers from time to time. As my heartbeat quickened, the majestic trophy closed the gap. Perfectly broadside, but at 70 yards, I prayed for a break. I will never know if my prayers were answered or did the bull get curious with my movement. I was already at full draw when the bull turned in my direction and walked straight at me until he got to the 45-yard mark. When he turned broadside again the arrow was on its way.

What a feeling walking up to such a magnificent animal! We knew he was a dandy but never dreamed in a million years that he would be the New World Record. I can honestly say that this was one of the most enjoyable hunts that I have ever been on. Taking a world record was merely icing on the cake.

CENTRAL CANADA CARIBOU

Minimum Score 300   *Rangifer tarandus articus*

SCORE	LENGTH OF MAIN BEAM R / L	INSIDE SPREAD	NUMBER OF POINTS R / L		AREA	STATE/PROVINCE	HUNTER'S NAME	DATE	RANK
420 6/8	55 1/8 / 57 0/8	39 0/8	12	12	Humpy Lake	NWT	Al Kuntz	1994	1
405 3/8	55 5/8 / 53 7/8	34 5/8	16	17	MacKay Lake	NWT	Dan Gartner	1997	2
388 4/8	42 3/8 / 43 2/8	29 7/8	20	19	Little Marten Lake	NWT	Adrian L. Erickson	1990	3
387 3/8	55 4/8 / 52 2/8	31 0/8	14	11	Little Marten Lake	NWT	James Gopffarth	1996	4
387 1/8	53 2/8 / 55 6/8	36 3/8	13	13	Baffin Island	NWT	Randall J. Kiessel	1986	5
385 5/8	52 7/8 / 51 3/8	36 7/8	14	18	Munroe Lake	MAN	Thomas A. Koepke, MD	1997	6
382 3/8	52 3/8 / 53 0/8	41 6/8	10	10	Point Lake	NWT	N. Guy Eastman	2002	7
381 6/8	46 2/8 / 46 5/8	29 1/8	13	20	MacKay Lake	NWT	Tom Taylor	1995	8
374 3/8	51 1/8 / 51 1/8	32 6/8	15	13	Warburton Bay	NWT	Duane Hicks	1987	9
373 7/8	62 1/8 / 61 4/8	36 1/8	13	8	MacKay Lake	NWT	Ron K. Serwa	1999	10
373 2/8	45 2/8 / 47 4/8	23 4/8	8	10	Granite Lake	NWT	George R. Breiwa II	2000	11
373 1/8	48 4/8 / 49 7/8	40 3/8	11	13	MacKay Lake	NWT	Richard Martin	1990	12
372 2/8	46 0/8 / 48 4/8	30 0/8	14	14	Nejanilini Lake	MAN	Don McCrea	1992	13
372 1/8	47 4/8 / 52 5/8	31 3/8	14	11	MacKay Lake	NWT	John Sebert	1998	14
371 6/8	47 7/8 / 46 5/8	30 2/8	12	12	MacKay Lake	NWT	Greg Leroux	1990	15
371 1/8	50 3/8 / 48 4/8	44 0/8	13	13	MacKay Lake	NWT	Dan Brockman	1990	16
370 7/8	53 0/8 / 51 3/8	32 4/8	10	13	Warburton Bay	NWT	John Campbell	1995	17
370 7/8	50 4/8 / 51 0/8	33 6/8	13	13	MacKay Lake	NWT	James D. Powless	1997	17
370 2/8	49 4/8 / 49 5/8	33 6/8	13	12	Point Lake	NWT	John W. Dickenson	1997	19
369 2/8	53 5/8 / 54 3/8	37 5/8	11	9	White Island	NWT	Curt Wells	1996	20
368 2/8	51 7/8 / 51 7/8	31 7/8	11	11	Warburton Bay	NWT	Patrick M. Condie	1995	21
366 6/8	47 1/8 / 48 7/8	26 2/8	11	14	MacKay Lake	NWT	Thomas R. Ferris	2002	22
366 0/8	53 0/8 / 53 0/8	31 7/8	14	12	MacKay Lake	NWT	John D. Totemeier	1990	23
365 7/8	45 4/8 / 46 6/8	40 0/8	11	10	Desteffany Lake	NWT	Doug Strecker	1996	24
365 3/8	49 4/8 / 50 6/8	30 5/8	14	13	Courageous Lake	NWT	Thomas J. Hoffman	1994	25
365 1/8	47 2/8 / 47 1/8	31 0/8	14	13	Artillery Lake	NWT	Kenneth A. Heinrichs	1997	26
364 6/8	46 3/8 / 47 2/8	28 2/8	11	8	Courageous Lake	NWT	Steve Crooks	1990	27
364 6/8	55 0/8 / 54 6/8	36 1/8	12	12	MacKay Lake	NWT	Michael J. Spence	1995	27
364 5/8	53 5/8 / 54 6/8	36 1/8	10	9	Warburton Bay	NWT	Lyle Sheppard	1997	29
364 3/8	49 7/8 / 51 4/8	24 6/8	12	12	Baffin Island	NWT	John C. Gall	1992	30
364 0/8	52 6/8 / 52 0/8	36 7/8	11	11	MacKay Lake	NWT	T. J. Conrads	1997	31
362 3/8	53 0/8 / 51 0/8	40 3/8	15	10	MacKay Lake	NWT	William A. Dreyer III	1995	32
360 7/8	55 0/8 / 54 2/8	39 4/8	13	14	Courageous Lake	NWT	Ron Hise	1997	33
360 5/8	50 3/8 / 51 5/8	39 7/8	10	13	Humpy Lake	NWT	Bill Vaznis	1994	34
360 3/8	43 3/8 / 42 7/8	30 2/8	14	14	Courageous Lake	NWT	William Bishop	2002	35
359 7/8	47 2/8 / 47 6/8	32 1/8	13	9	Point Lake	NWT	James A. Brown	1990	36
359 6/8	53 6/8 / 54 4/8	33 3/8	8	9	MacKay Lake	NWT	Tom Taylor	1995	37
359 6/8	53 5/8 / 54 5/8	44 6/8	10	10	MacKay Lake	NWT	Scott R. Barefoot	1997	37
359 1/8	48 1/8 / 48 4/8	35 0/8	14	14	Courageous Lake	NWT	John D. "Jack" Frost	1994	39
358 6/8	49 1/8 / 49 3/8	37 1/8	12	12	Little Marten Lake	NWT	Chuck Adams	2000	40
358 3/8	54 4/8 / 51 2/8	36 7/8	12	14	Little Marten Lake	NWT	Mark Buehrer	1999	41
358 2/8	50 4/8 / 53 6/8	30 0/8	13	10	Artillery Lake	NWT	Brian T. Butts	1998	42
358 1/8	51 6/8 / 51 7/8	34 2/8	9	11	Lake Providence	NWT	Gerry Backhaus	1988	43
358 0/8	46 4/8 / 46 5/8	34 6/8	14	13	MacKay Lake	NWT	Mike Wheeler	1991	44
357 4/8	51 5/8 / 50 5/8	30 2/8	12	12	MacKay Lake	NWT	Glenn Hisey	1997	45
357 1/8	43 3/8 / 45 1/8	34 1/8	11	15	Desteffany Lake	NWT	Kathy Strecker	1996	46
356 4/8	47 0/8 / 44 7/8	29 6/8	15	15	Warburton Bay	NWT	Patrick M. Condie	1995	47
356 0/8	53 0/8 / 50 2/8	33 1/8	12	10	Courageous Lake	NWT	Bob Dawson	1988	48
356 0/8	55 1/8 / 55 2/8	39 4/8	14	9	Munroe Lake	MAN	Tim R. Reed	1998	48
356 0/8	15 0/8 / 13 0/8	32 4/8	51	52	White Wolf Lake	NWT	Ricardo Longoria	2009	48
355 6/8	47 0/8 / 48 6/8	40 3/8	15	14	MacKay Lake	NWT	Stan Godfrey	1988	51
355 6/8	50 5/8 / 49 5/8	31 6/8	12	14	Artillery Lake	NWT	Dave Popp	1997	51
355 3/8	41 0/8 / 44 0/8	33 0/8	21	22	MacKay Lake	NWT	William E. Gerhardt	1997	53
353 3/8	56 3/8 / 54 4/8	29 2/8	10	11	Schmock Lake	MAN	Quentin R. Plett	2001	54
353 2/8	55 7/8 / 56 6/8	39 5/8	13	12	MacKay Lake	NWT	Tom Taylor	1995	55
352 7/8	55 0/8 / 52 4/8	33 2/8	11	8	MacKay Lake	NWT	Fred Johnston III	2001	56
*352 3/8	54 6/8 / 54 3/8	39 2/8	9	9	MacKay Lake	NWT	Chad Dillabough	2001	57
351 7/8	50 3/8 / 49 5/8	35 7/8	14	13	Warburton Bay	NWT	Reagan Dunn	1997	58
351 5/8	46 6/8 / 46 6/8	33 2/8	8	8	Nejanilini Lake	MAN	Lon E. Lauber	2000	59
349 2/8	48 5/8 / 47 2/8	26 0/8	13	18	Lake No Name	MAN	Phil Orf	2007	60
348 5/8	45 6/8 / 44 4/8	30 3/8	14	17	Desteffany Lake	NWT	Jay Deones	1996	61
348 4/8	48 3/8 / 46 2/8	35 6/8	14	14	Artillery Lake	NWT	John Duggan	1999	62
348 1/8	44 0/8 / 44 0/8	39 1/8	16	15	Warburton Bay	NWT	David R. Coupland	1992	63
348 1/8	54 5/8 / 51 3/8	31 1/8	13	11	Warburton Bay	NWT	Tom Foss	1993	63
348 0/8	46 0/8 / 47 6/8	36 6/8	14	14	Lake Providence	NWT	Ron Books	1991	65
347 2/8	48 3/8 / 47 2/8	26 0/8	12	8	Aylmer Lake	NWT	Dennis A. Brown	2000	66
347 0/8	47 2/8 / 47 6/8	30 6/8	11	12	MacKay Lake	NWT	Stephen Kotz	2001	67
346 6/8	50 6/8 / 54 1/8	37 3/8	10	11	MacKay Lake	NWT	James D. Powless	1997	68
346 5/8	51 3/8 / 53 6/8	34 0/8	10	10	Glover Lake	MAN	Rick Hogg	1995	69
346 0/8	49 3/8 / 47 6/8	31 3/8	10	13	MacKay Lake	NWT	Stephen J. McCoy	1999	70
345 2/8	56 7/8 / 52 2/8	31 3/8	12	10	Yellowknife	NWT	Gil Gilbertson	1990	71
*344 0/8	48 7/8 / 46 6/8	29 3/8	11	9	Nejanilini Lake	MAN	Al Parent	2004	72
343 6/8	48 6/8 / 48 4/8	38 1/8	11	10	MacKay Lake	NWT	Christian Fourquet	1995	73
343 5/8	45 2/8 / 44 4/8	39 4/8	15	14	Desteffany Lake	NWT	Larry D. Jones	1994	74
343 3/8	53 2/8 / 52 0/8	37 5/8	9	10	MacKay Lake	NWT	Carolyn Godfrey	1990	75
343 3/8	44 0/8 / 44 3/8	35 4/8	16	13	Courageous Lake	NWT	Robert Edward Speegle, MD	1994	75
343 1/8	47 4/8 / 48 5/8	37 5/8	12	12	Lake Providence	NWT	Ron Books	1991	77
343 0/8	47 7/8 / 50 2/8	32 7/8	8	9	Nodinka Narrows	NWT	Gunter Lemke	1991	78
342 7/8	48 1/8 / 48 5/8	36 3/8	13	11	Humpy Lake	NWT	John Mathews	2000	79
342 6/8	44 6/8 / 43 7/8	24 2/8	14	12	MacKay Lake	NWT	Chuck Kronenwetter	1994	80
342 6/8	44 4/8 / 44 6/8	27 6/8	11	11	Desteffany Lake	NWT	David Harris	1998	80
342 4/8	50 4/8 / 51 1/8	26 5/8	11	15	MacKay Lake	NWT	Gerry Gwaltney	1999	82
341 4/8	52 2/8 / 51 7/8	31 5/8	10	10	Desteffany Lake	NWT	Kevin Hisey	1996	83
341 1/8	50 2/8 / 51 2/8	29 2/8	8	8	Courageous Lake	NWT	Rick C. Wilson	2000	84
341 0/8	53 4/8 / 50 6/8	27 5/8	11	10	Warburton Bay	NWT	Richard E. LaCrone	1997	85
340 2/8	48 2/8 / 46 4/8	30 4/8	14	14	Lake Providence	NWT	Doug Walker	1988	86
340 2/8	49 6/8 / 45 1/8	28 0/8	14	14	Lake Providence	NWT	Doug Walker	1988	86
340 1/8	45 1/8 / 45 6/8	23 5/8	13	11	Obstruction Rapids	NWT	Scott Walker	1990	88
340 0/8	45 0/8 / 44 6/8	32 6/8	13	14	Rendezvous Lake	NWT	Richard A. Hjort	1989	89
339 7/8	44 4/8 / 43 4/8	32 5/8	18	16	MacKay Lake	NWT	Ted Judson	2001	90
339 6/8	49 6/8 / 49 3/8	29 4/8	9	13	MacKay Lake	NWT	Mike Edwards	1999	91
339 5/8	50 6/8 / 48 4/8	34 5/8	10	10	Humpy Lake	NWT	Johnnie R. Walters	1992	92
339 4/8	51 0/8 / 51 0/8	27 4/8	11	10	MacKay Lake	NWT	Steve Tice	1994	93
338 7/8	44 7/8 / 41 3/8	22 2/8	12	9	MacKay Lake	NWT	Brian R. Brochu	2000	94
338 6/8	58 5/8 / 61 0/8	39 1/8	10	9	MacKay Lake	NWT	Stan Godfrey	1990	95

CENTRAL CANADA CARIBOU

Minimum Score 300   Continued

SCORE	LENGTH OF MAIN BEAM R	L	INSIDE SPREAD	NUMBER OF POINTS R	L	AREA	STATE/PROVINCE	HUNTER'S NAME	DATE	RANK
338 3/8	44 2/8	44 1/8	31 0/8	15	19	Humpy Lake	NWT	Tracy L. Epping	1999	96
337 6/8	50 3/8	48 2/8	34 5/8	12	13	MacKay Lake	NWT	Michael J. Spence	1995	97
337 2/8	39 7/8	40 7/8	23 6/8	18	17	Baker Lake	NUN	Jeff Herman	2003	98
336 7/8	46 1/8	46 2/8	28 4/8	14	13	MacKay Lake	NWT	Mark Wuerthele	1995	99
336 4/8	46 4/8	52 6/8	24 7/8	8	7	Humpy Lake	NWT	Dennis Bradley	1998	100
336 3/8	47 0/8	48 2/8	31 7/8	12	11	Little Duck Lake	MAN	Rick Hogg	1993	101
336 2/8	45 5/8	47 1/8	27 3/8	13	9	MacKay Lake	NWT	Stan Godfrey	1990	102
336 0/8	50 0/8	49 4/8	31 0/8	11	11	MacKay Lake	NWT	William E. Terry, Sr.	1995	103
336 0/8	47 0/8	49 2/8	37 3/8	14	10	Baker Lake	NUN	Mark C. Booth	2002	103
335 6/8	49 6/8	49 2/8	37 0/8	7	7	Nodinka Narrows	NWT	Marc Nyrose	1991	105
335 4/8	49 1/8	44 3/8	32 0/8	12	14	MacKay Lake	NWT	Dan Gartner	1997	106
335 2/8	42 3/8	43 4/8	27 3/8	14	17	MacKay Lake	NWT	R. E. Smith	1992	107
335 2/8	51 3/8	50 3/8	30 3/8	14	12	MacKay Lake	NWT	Mark Wuerthele	1995	107
335 2/8	45 2/8	46 5/8	22 5/8	16	15	Warburton Bay	NWT	Michael R. Westvang	1995	107
334 6/8	46 2/8	48 4/8	31 2/8	12	13	MacKay Lake	NWT	Fred Johnston III	2001	110
334 4/8	52 6/8	51 5/8	43 6/8	9	8	Jolly Lake	NWT	Mark Mathieson	1997	111
334 2/8	45 2/8	43 6/8	31 6/8	10	12	MacKay Lake	NWT	Michael J. Underhill	1990	112
333 7/8	46 2/8	45 6/8	35 1/8	14	12	MacKay Lake	NWT	John Sebert	1998	113
333 3/8	41 0/8	41 4/8	27 0/8	13	10	Granet Lake	NWT	Richie Bland	2002	114
333 0/8	41 5/8	43 1/8	22 1/8	13	13	MacKay Lake	NWT	Jay St. Charles	1992	115
332 5/8	42 5/8	42 0/8	27 3/8	10	8	Rendezvous Lake	NWT	Dan Ermatinger	1999	116
332 4/8	51 7/8	51 1/8	36 0/8	11	10	Lake Providence	NWT	Jeff Fitts	1993	117
332 3/8	46 4/8	47 4/8	26 7/8	13	11	Yellowknife	NWT	Bruce R. Schoeneweis	1990	118
332 3/8	42 0/8	42 0/8	39 0/8	16	19	Caribou Bay	NWT	Richard A. Case	1994	118
331 6/8	50 7/8	50 1/8	40 3/8	9	6	MacKay Lake	NWT	Kip Padgelek	1999	120
331 5/8	50 1/8	50 0/8	26 1/8	12	13	Desteffany Lake	NWT	Annette L. Gates	1999	121
331 4/8	53 2/8	54 0/8	29 0/8	11	11	Point Lake	NWT	Cam Wilson	1987	122
331 2/8	44 6/8	46 1/8	28 6/8	14	15	MacKay Lake	NWT	David Emken	1990	123
331 2/8	47 1/8	47 1/8	28 1/8	13	10	Rendezvous Lake	NWT	Lucas Osellame	1996	123
331 2/8	55 2/8	52 4/8	33 6/8	11	10	MacKay Lake	NWT	Robert Priem	1997	123
331 0/8	49 2/8	49 3/8	29 4/8	14	11	MacKay Lake	NWT	Charles L. Hunt	1990	126
330 7/8	47 5/8	46 7/8	33 5/8	11	11	Artillery Lake	NWT	Tyson Heiner	2003	127
330 7/8	46 5/8	45 4/8	28 4/8	9	11	MacKay Lake	NWT	Mark Calkins	2005	127
330 6/8	45 2/8	43 0/8	27 4/8	10	13	MacKay Lake	NWT	Archie J. Nesbitt	2000	129
330 3/8	46 6/8	47 0/8	32 0/8	11	11	MacKay Lake	NWT	Glenn Hisey	1997	130
330 0/8	52 0/8	50 6/8	31 6/8	9	9	MacKay Lake	NWT	Manfred Gehrlein	1990	131
329 7/8	52 2/8	50 0/8	35 0/8	9	11	Jolly River	NWT	Jay St. Charles	1987	132
329 7/8	47 4/8	49 4/8	32 0/8	12	11	Pellatt Lake	NWT	Nathan Jones	2004	132
329 6/8	45 1/8	48 4/8	35 2/8	15	16	Humpy Lake	NWT	Randy Kottke	1997	134
329 6/8	51 0/8	51 4/8	38 4/8	7	11	Courageous Lake	NWT	Dennis McCoy	2007	134
329 4/8	49 3/8	50 2/8	36 0/8	17	14	MacKay Lake	NWT	Terry Tabor	1990	136
329 4/8	46 0/8	47 0/8	25 6/8	16	12	MacKay Lake	NWT	Nick Mathews	2001	136
329 0/8	46 1/8	45 2/8	24 7/8	14	17	Humpy Lake	NWT	Rick Davis	2000	138
328 5/8	50 6/8	49 7/8	28 6/8	20	15	Little Marten Lake	NWT	Marc N. Shaft	1997	139
328 4/8	49 7/8	49 0/8	39 2/8	12	9	MacKay Lake	NWT	Ryk Visscher	1991	140
328 3/8	50 2/8	51 6/8	34 2/8	13	10	MacKay Lake	NWT	Tom Vanasche	1995	141
327 7/8	47 0/8	45 1/8	29 0/8	11	11	MacKay Lake	NWT	Charles L. Hunt	1990	142
327 7/8	49 0/8	46 5/8	30 2/8	18	14	MacKay Lake	NWT	Sheldon Showalter	1995	142
327 4/8	49 7/8	48 7/8	31 0/8	9	9	Warburton Bay	NWT	Dennis Dunn	1997	144
327 4/8	46 5/8	46 3/8	28 6/8	6	6	Artillery Lake	NWT	Ronell Skinner	2003	144
327 3/8	49 6/8	48 7/8	35 7/8	11	10	MacKay Lake	NWT	Archie J. Nesbitt	2000	146
327 2/8	45 0/8	47 4/8	33 7/8	9	11	Schmock Lake	MAN	Tom Nebbs	2000	147
327 1/8	46 2/8	46 3/8	23 0/8	15	15	MacKay Lake	NWT	Don Owen	1999	148
327 0/8	45 6/8	47 2/8	32 0/8	12	11	Desteffany Lake	NWT	Karen J. Deones	1999	149
326 7/8	49 1/8	47 1/8	30 7/8	11	10	MacKay Lake	NWT	Tom Taylor	1992	150
326 6/8	50 7/8	50 5/8	35 1/8	8	11	Artillery Lake	NWT	Brian T. Butts	1998	151
326 2/8	50 1/8	51 7/8	30 0/8	5	8	MacKay Lake	NWT	Ryk Visscher	2002	152
325 7/8	48 4/8	49 3/8	31 7/8	9	8	Nicholson Lake	MAN	Warren W. Johnson	2003	153
325 7/8	51 4/8	51 6/8	36 0/8	8	9	Warburton Bay	NWT	Mike Schueller	2004	153
325 6/8	44 3/8	45 6/8	29 0/8	6	9	Humpy Lake	NWT	Rick Davis	2000	155
325 6/8	48 6/8	49 0/8	19 0/8	11	11	MacKay Lake	NWT	Kevin Lyons	1997	156
*325 4/8	45 0/8	43 2/8	26 0/8	11	10	Point Lake	NWT	Stephen Klappenbach	2009	157
324 6/8	45 0/8	42 1/8	30 4/8	13	12	Glover Lake	MAN	Rick Hogg	1998	158
324 6/8	44 7/8	45 5/8	23 7/8	10	9	Humpy Lake	NWT	Dewayne Mullins	1998	158
324 2/8	49 4/8	49 7/8	34 5/8	8	8	Courageous Lake	NWT	Larry Fenton	1999	160
324 2/8	47 3/8	47 5/8	34 0/8	13	15	Little Forehead Lake	NWT	Skip Valentine	2001	160
323 7/8	39 7/8	46 2/8	29 1/8	11	13	Desteffany Lake	NWT	Jay Deones	1996	162
323 6/8	49 3/8	46 4/8	31 2/8	12	10	MacKay Lake	NWT	Scott R. Barefoot	1997	163
323 5/8	44 4/8	45 0/8	26 4/8	12	16	Wejalini Lake	MAN	Gord Monteath	1991	164
323 4/8	44 4/8	41 5/8	30 7/8	14	13	MacKay Lake	NWT	Jeff R. Lange	2002	165
322 4/8	44 6/8	43 5/8	26 4/8	13	12	MacKay Lake	NWT	Tom Taylor	1995	166
322 4/8	50 2/8	48 7/8	32 3/8	8	9	Little Marten Lake	NWT	Joe Coleman	1999	166
322 4/8	48 0/8	48 6/8	30 1/8	12	9	Artillery Lake	NWT	Edd Clack	2005	166
322 1/8	46 6/8	47 0/8	23 2/8	11	14	Desteffany Lake	NWT	Robert Harris	2002	169
322 0/8	51 4/8	51 6/8	36 2/8	8	10	MacKay Lake	NWT	Mike Connett	2004	170
321 7/8	51 7/8	52 2/8	36 1/8	9	11	Warburton Bay	NWT	Brian Tessmann	2002	171
320 5/8	50 7/8	50 5/8	27 6/8	12	11	Humpy Lake	NWT	Steve Boster	2005	172
320 4/8	53 4/8	54 4/8	30 3/8	7	7	MacKay Lake	NWT	Ryk Visscher	1991	173
320 2/8	52 2/8	54 2/8	35 2/8	8	11	MacKay Lake	NWT	Manfred Gehrlein	1990	174
320 1/8	53 0/8	48 6/8	24 4/8	7	2	MacKay Lake	NWT	Nick Mathews	2001	175
319 7/8	49 0/8	48 1/8	29 2/8	11	10	MacKay Lake	NWT	Larry Oppe	1999	176
319 5/8	48 2/8	47 5/8	27 0/8	10	11	Desteffany Lake	NWT	Robert Harris	1998	177
319 5/8	53 2/8	52 4/8	26 0/8	8	7	Little Forehead Lake	NWT	Steve Edwards	2003	177
319 4/8	47 6/8	47 0/8	35 6/8	13	9	MacKay Lake	NWT	Larry Oppe	1999	179
319 3/8	48 6/8	48 7/8	29 2/8	9	9	No Name Lake	MAN	Rod McGrath	2002	180
319 2/8	47 6/8	46 3/8	23 6/8	12	11	MacKay Lake	NWT	Sheldon Showalter	1995	181
319 1/8	43 1/8	44 1/8	28 0/8	14	12	Little Marten Lake	NWT	Mark Buehrer	1999	182
*319 1/8	47 6/8	47 4/8	23 3/8	13	16	Contwoyto Lake	NWT	Erik Watts	2007	182
318 2/8	49 2/8	48 2/8	37 2/8	7	7	Little Marten Lake	NWT	Richard M. Penn	2003	184
318 2/8	49 0/8	48 0/8	31 2/8	10	9	Little Marten Lake	NWT	John Stone	2003	184
318 0/8	45 6/8	46 2/8	28 2/8	12	10	Humpy Lake	NWT	Johnnie R. Walters	1992	186
318 0/8	52 1/8	52 3/8	35 1/8	7	9	Humpy Lake	NWT	Kenneth D. Musgrove	1998	186
318 0/8	46 6/8	45 6/8	31 4/8	9	11	Humpy Lake	NWT	Edward J. Roskopf	2000	186
318 0/8	46 4/8	47 0/8	23 6/8	12	11	MacKay Lake	NWT	Doug Clayton	2001	186
317 5/8	40 3/8	39 2/8	24 5/8	14	13	MacKay Lake	NWT	Darryl Kublik	2002	190

231

CENTRAL CANADA CARIBOU

Minimum Score 300 Continued

SCORE	LENGTH OF MAIN BEAM R	L	INSIDE SPREAD	NUMBER OF POINTS R	L	AREA	STATE/PROVINCE	HUNTER'S NAME	DATE	RANK
317 1/8	45 5/8	45 3/8	30 2/8	11	9	Artillery Lake	NWT	Perry Oates	1999	191
316 5/8	46 6/8	48 6/8	37 0/8	7	7	MacKay Lake	NWT	Howard L. Harding	1992	192
316 5/8	47 6/8	44 7/8	22 7/8	14	14	MacKay Lake	NWT	Robert Norotzky	2004	192
316 4/8	52 4/8	52 6/8	28 1/8	10	9	MacKay Lake	NWT	Robert G. Barden	1996	194
316 0/8	51 2/8	48 3/8	27 0/8	10	10	Humpy Lake	NWT	Joe Bell	2000	195
316 0/8	44 6/8	43 5/8	28 1/8	10	9	Point Lake	NWT	Reggie Spiegelberg	2001	195
315 6/8	46 6/8	50 0/8	28 4/8	11	11	MacKay Lake	NWT	Jim Visscher	1990	197
315 6/8	43 2/8	46 5/8	35 1/8	9	8	Warburton Bay	NWT	David R. Coupland	1992	197
315 6/8	52 0/8	51 3/8	35 4/8	9	6	MacKay Lake	NWT	Mike Miller	2004	197
315 5/8	49 7/8	48 6/8	29 7/8	13	8	Nejanilini Lake	MAN	Jeffrey Schwartz	1996	200
315 5/8	50 0/8	49 4/8	28 1/8	12	11	MacKay Lake	NWT	Don Owen	1999	200
315 4/8	38 2/8	40 0/8	28 6/8	12	13	Humpy Lake	NWT	Al Kuntz	1994	202
315 3/8	44 6/8	44 7/8	31 5/8	9	9	Nejanilini Lake	MAN	Russell K. Mehling	1994	203
315 3/8	46 6/8	45 1/8	21 0/8	15	15	MacKay Lake	NWT	Steve Hohensee	1994	203
315 0/8	43 3/8	42 5/8	27 5/8	13	17	Courageous Lake	NWT	Brad White	1997	205
313 7/8	49 2/8	50 5/8	31 6/8	6	8	MacKay Lake	NWT	Wade Carstens	1993	206
313 6/8	47 2/8	49 5/8	26 0/8	11	10	Jolly River	NWT	Ty Martin	1987	207
313 6/8	51 5/8	49 6/8	25 6/8	11	10	MacKay Lake	NWT	James Kelter	1992	207
313 5/8	45 6/8	47 0/8	23 6/8	14	11	Warburton Bay	NWT	Michael R. Westvang	1995	209
313 5/8	49 0/8	49 1/8	29 4/8	12	11	MacKay Lake	NWT	Stephen C. Roehm	2003	209
313 2/8	44 6/8	47 7/8	24 6/8	9	8	Desteffany Lake	NWT	Robert Harris	1998	211
313 2/8	48 7/8	53 4/8	27 3/8	13	10	Angelique Lake	NWT	John R. Simpson	2000	211
312 7/8	40 6/8	43 6/8	36 2/8	17	15	Baker Lake	NUN	Brad Wiehr	2005	213
312 6/8	50 0/8	50 4/8	30 4/8	13	11	MacKay Lake	NWT	Bret Estes	1996	214
312 3/8	44 2/8	45 0/8	31 3/8	13	11	Combo Lake	NWT	Thomas J. Hoffman	1997	215
312 2/8	47 0/8	46 0/8	38 6/8	10	10	MacKay Lake	NWT	Dennis G. Hicks	1990	216
312 2/8	41 7/8	45 0/8	29 0/8	13	11	Commonwealth Lake	MAN	Dennis Doherty	2006	216
312 0/8	51 4/8	44 5/8	24 4/8	14	17	MacKay Lake	NWT	Duane Hicks	1988	218
312 0/8	48 5/8	51 5/8	28 5/8	15	12	Rendezvous Lake	NWT	Albert Osellame	1996	218
312 0/8	43 2/8	43 0/8	32 4/8	13	12	Pellatt Lake	NWT	V. Randy Liljenquist	1997	218
311 6/8	51 7/8	50 3/8	35 4/8	8	9	Humpy Lake	NWT	Gary Martin	2003	221
311 4/8	50 1/8	48 3/8	28 0/8	8	11	MacKay Lake	NWT	Marc Nyrose	1991	222
311 4/8	52 5/8	50 6/8	25 6/8	12	8	Desteffany Lake	NWT	Linda B. Blanchard	1999	222
311 3/8	43 7/8	43 1/8	27 3/8	10	10	MacKay Lake	NWT	Andy Carpenter	1997	224
*311 2/8	43 4/8	48 0/8	33 1/8	11	9	Contwoyto Lake	NWT	Erik Watts	2007	225
311 0/8	48 2/8	47 4/8	40 7/8	10	10	MacKay Lake	NWT	John Visscher	1991	226
311 0/8	49 7/8	51 2/8	32 5/8	13	11	MacKay Lake	NWT	Todd Szmania	2000	226
310 7/8	51 0/8	52 2/8	25 1/8	13	8	MacKay Lake	NWT	Ryk Visscher	1990	228
310 4/8	44 7/8	45 3/8	40 3/8	9	12	Courageous Lake	NWT	James Gabrick	2000	229
310 3/8	47 3/8	47 1/8	30 5/8	9	9	Humpy Lake	NWT	Kenneth D. Musgrove	1998	230
310 3/8	49 5/8	53 0/8	31 4/8	14	12	Jolly Lake	NWT	Jeremiah Roberson	2002	230
310 1/8	47 6/8	47 5/8	23 6/8	14	12	Warburton Bay	NWT	Richard E. LaCrone	1997	232
310 0/8	42 2/8	45 6/8	21 4/8	9	11	MacKay Lake	NWT	John Visscher	1990	233
310 0/8	48 3/8	48 5/8	24 4/8	8	8	Desteffany Lake	NWT	Doug Strecker	1999	233
309 7/8	47 6/8	48 1/8	31 1/8	15	12	Little Marten Lake	NWT	Joel A. Johnson	2004	235
309 5/8	44 4/8	45 4/8	14 7/8	12	12	MacKay Lake	NWT	Steve Tice	1994	236
309 2/8	45 7/8	46 6/8	32 2/8	11	12	Little Marten Lake	NWT	Drew Mouton	1992	237
309 2/8	46 6/8	47 3/8	32 2/8	5	6	MacKay Lake	NWT	Kelly Semple	2002	237
309 1/8	45 6/8	47 1/8	31 4/8	7	6	MacKay Lake	NWT	Chuck Kronenwetter	1994	239
308 5/8	51 1/8	50 0/8	34 1/8	6	7	MacKay Lake	NWT	Greg Schleusner	1998	240
308 3/8	47 6/8	49 6/8	24 7/8	9	10	MacKay Lake	NWT	Roy Goodwin	1995	241
308 3/8	44 5/8	44 6/8	26 7/8	14	13	Artillery Lake	NWT	Michael Siegler	1999	241
308 0/8	42 4/8	45 5/8	30 5/8	10	11	White Island	NWT	Kendall Bauer	1996	243
307 7/8	47 0/8	48 4/8	30 6/8	10	10	MacKay Lake	NWT	Tom Taylor	1994	244
307 7/8	40 6/8	41 5/8	27 7/8	8	10	Cambridge Bay	NUN	Archie J. Nesbitt	2002	244
307 6/8	43 5/8	43 5/8	35 0/8	7	8	Yellowknife	NWT	Jim Wondzell	1994	246
307 3/8	50 6/8	48 4/8	31 3/8	14	11	MacKay Lake	NWT	Warren Witherspoon	1993	247
307 2/8	48 6/8	48 6/8	35 0/8	8	9	MacKay Lake	NWT	Joseph R. St. Charles	1993	248
307 1/8	48 6/8	51 6/8	34 7/8	10	11	Humpy Lake	NWT	Chester Kottke, Jr.	1997	249
307 1/8	46 0/8	46 2/8	22 2/8	12	14	Artillery Lake	NWT	Rick Duggan	1999	249
306 7/8	41 6/8	41 2/8	22 6/8	8	13	Desteffany Lake	NWT	Randy D. Doyle	1996	251
306 2/8	44 2/8	44 2/8	30 0/8	8	6	Nejanilini Lake	MAN	Don Reimer	2004	252
305 4/8	50 5/8	50 2/8	28 0/8	8	8	MacKay Lake	NWT	Dan Brockman	1990	253
305 1/8	48 4/8	48 0/8	22 1/8	11	11	Baker Lake	NUN	Stephen Carver	2003	254
305 0/8	52 5/8	53 2/8	33 6/8	6	5	Thonokied Lake	NWT	Chuck Adams	2002	255
*305 0/8	50 1/8	50 2/8	29 3/8	6	7	Humpy Lake	NWT	R. Kirk Sharp	2004	255
304 7/8	48 1/8	48 3/8	29 7/8	9	8	MacKay Lake	NWT	David R. Coupland	1991	257
304 7/8	39 4/8	38 6/8	31 2/8	11	16	MacKay Lake	NWT	Richard King	2001	257
304 6/8	45 3/8	46 0/8	25 2/8	13	11	MacKay Lake	NWT	Howard L. Harding	1992	259
304 4/8	53 6/8	54 3/8	33 2/8	7	7	Humpy Lake	NWT	Dr. Chuck Leidheiser	1997	260
304 3/8	44 2/8	44 5/8	20 3/8	10	11	MacKay Lake	NWT	Mitchel Arnold	1997	261
303 5/8	48 5/8	47 7/8	35 5/8	8	10	Desteffany Lake	NWT	Larry Streiff	1996	262
303 3/8	48 1/8	45 7/8	23 6/8	9	9	MacKay Lake	NWT	Matt Verhoff	2003	263
303 2/8	45 6/8	48 0/8	26 0/8	11	8	Jolly Lake	NWT	Greg Wadsworth	1996	264
303 2/8	47 7/8	44 6/8	30 1/8	13	13	MacKay Lake	NWT	Brian R. Brochu	2000	264
302 6/8	44 6/8	44 2/8	29 0/8	11	9	MacKay Lake	NWT	Les Malsch	1990	266
302 5/8	43 4/8	43 4/8	32 6/8	10	8	Providence Lake	NWT	Ted K. Jaycox	2001	267
302 4/8	46 2/8	46 2/8	33 5/8	9	14	Courageous Lake	NWT	Wm. R. Vanderhoef	1987	268
302 2/8	44 1/8	44 0/8	29 1/8	12	11	Jolly Lake	NWT	Jeremiah Roberson	2002	269
302 1/8	50 7/8	50 7/8	30 2/8	7	10	MacKay Lake	NWT	Russ Tye	1992	270
302 0/8	43 2/8	46 3/8	25 6/8	12	11	Jolly Lake	NWT	John Cogswell	2002	271
301 7/8	46 1/8	45 2/8	32 6/8	9	10	Little Marten Lake	NWT	Pat Lefemine	2005	272
301 6/8	47 4/8	48 3/8	27 4/8	13	9	Desteffany Lake	NWT	Debbie Holm	1999	273
*301 5/8	48 6/8	46 1/8	25 1/8	10	10	Robert's River	MAN	Ed Parker	2010	274
301 4/8	43 5/8	42 7/8	28 0/8	9	9	Little Marten Lake	NWT	Jerry Rush	1993	275
301 4/8	46 6/8	49 0/8	43 5/8	9	8	Little Marten Lake	NWT	Joel A. Johnson	2004	275
301 3/8	50 0/8	50 0/8	27 1/8	15	13	Little Marten Lake	NWT	Joe Coleman	1999	277
301 0/8	43 2/8	43 4/8	30 3/8	9	6	Jolly Lake	NWT	Greg Wadsworth	1996	278
300 6/8	40 4/8	39 7/8	30 4/8	10	15	MacKay Lake	NWT	Dale Holpainen	1992	279
300 6/8	45 1/8	45 1/8	37 2/8	11	11	Desteffany Lake	NWT	Dianna Beardsley	1999	279
300 2/8	43 5/8	48 3/8	27 2/8	11	11	Glover Lake	MAN	Russell K. Mehling	1999	281
300 1/8	43 6/8	39 3/8	30 0/8	10	9	MacKay Lake	NWT	Stacy Hoeme	2000	282

CENTRAL CANADA CARIBOU (VELVET ANTLERS)
Minimum Score 300

SCORE	LENGTH OF R MAIN BEAM L	INSIDE SPREAD	NUMBER OF R POINTS L		AREA	STATE/ PROVINCE	HUNTER'S NAME	DATE	RANK
384 4/8	55 6/8 54 1/8	39 7/8	8	11	Humpy Lake	NWT	Rodney Cockeram	2005	*
383 5/8	48 1/8 47 1/8	27 4/8	12	14	Point Lake	NWT	Tyler Allred	2008	*
370 5/8	47 6/8 46 4/8	30 6/8	16	15	MacKay Lake	NWT	Hoyt Michener	2007	*
*356 7/8	56 1/8 55 7/8	33 6/8	8	8	Point Lake	NWT	Wendy Klappenbach	2009	*
*355 4/8	51 4/8 51 2/8	28 4/8	9	10	Desteffany Lake	NWT	Tony A. Mahaffey	2004	*
351 6/8	49 1/8 48 4/8	33 1/8	9	9	Little Marten Lake	NWT	Walter Palmer	2006	*
346 2/8	48 0/8 48 1/8	37 0/8	12	16	Humpy Lake	NWT	John R. Simpson	2004	*
346 2/8	43 6/8 45 5/8	28 7/8	15	16	Artillery Lake	NWT	Edd Clack	2005	*
*338 5/8	49 0/8 46 0/8	27 3/8	9	13	Point Lake	NWT	Cameron R. Hanes	2005	*
335 0/8	47 2/8 48 5/8	31 0/8	14	13	Little Marten Lake	NWT	Nathan Jones	1999	*
334 6/8	43 3/8 44 7/8	24 1/8	11	12	Pellatt Lake	NWT	Nathan Jones	2004	*
332 2/8	46 7/8 49 4/8	27 2/8	12	15	Point Lake	NWT	Douglas W. Gill	2004	*
325 2/8	49 0/8 48 2/8	26 1/8	9	8	Pellatt Lake	NUN	Erik Watts	2005	*
324 6/8	47 0/8 47 0/8	34 2/8	11	12	Little Marten Lake	NWT	Jeff Carlson	2004	*
321 6/8	45 5/8 43 3/8	23 3/8	12	12	MacKay Lake	NWT	Steven J. Vittetow	2006	*
318 2/8	48 1/8 47 0/8	25 7/8	7	8	Desteffany Lake	NWT	Jesse Meyer	2009	*
315 3/8	51 7/8 50 5/8	32 7/8	12	13	Pellatt Lake	NWT	Jim Dougherty	2007	*
306 5/8	44 7/8 46 2/8	26 7/8	10	10	MacKay Lake	NWT	Renny R. Wylie	2007	*
305 7/8	43 0/8 43 6/8	29 2/8	7	8	Lake Providence	NWT	Michael Wolff	2007	*
302 2/8	49 6/8 50 5/8	31 6/8	9	9	Little Forehead Lake	NWT	George Harms	2008	*

WORLD RECORD MOUNTAIN CARIBOU
Score: 416 4/8
Location: Fire Lake, Yukon Territory
Date: 2004
Hunter: Pete Cintorino

Mountain Caribou

by Pete Cintorino

The Yukon during the last two weeks of September can be miserable with daily rain and snow, but here we were, my hunting partner Julian and I, packing out his moose horns. We had just finished dealing with a nasty grizzly that had claimed Julian's moose meat from the day before. Both of us had harvested two great moose the previous day and were finishing the packing out of his moose. After clearing the head high willows and getting control of seven nervous horses, we were on our seven mile journey back to our spike camp. We had only traveled about a half mile and were very close to where I had shot my moose the day before, when we both spotted this herd of about 20 mountain caribou crossing the flat valley floor from one mountain range to another.

Instantly both Julian and I realized the lead bull was huge. I grabbed my bow out of its scabbard, hunkered over and covered that quarter mile faster than I can remember. My heart was racing, yet I knew I had to get close and have the wind in my favor. While the caribou were pretty much focused on my hunting partner, guide and horses, the big bull managed to catch some movement from me in the low willows. At 50 yards I put my ranger finder on him. I was shaking so badly I could hardly hold the range finder still to get an accurate reading. Still I needed to narrow the distance more. So, on all fours in the wet moss, I crept to within 40 yards. At that moment, as might be expected, Murphy's Law jumped out of nowhere and the caribou started moving away. I stood up and ran forward and got up on a hummock of moss. Luckily for me the mountain caribou made his final mistake and looked back. At what appeared to be about 45 yards the arrow flew true, a perfect heart shot. He went only about 40 yards and fell over.

I couldn't believe it. After over 40 years of exclusively bow hunting I knew I had a world record contender. In all my years of bow hunting I am sure I have seen world records before and believe I even missed a couple. However, this is my greatest trophy ever and will be high lighted in my trophy room.

MOUNTAIN CARIBOU

Minimum Score 300

Rangifer tarandus osborni, *Rangifer tarandus fortidens* and *Rangifer tarandus montanus*

SCORE	LENGTH OF MAIN BEAM R	L	INSIDE SPREAD	NUMBER OF POINTS R	L	AREA	STATE/ PROVINCE	HUNTER'S NAME	DATE	RANK
416 4/8	41 1/8	41 1/8	39 7/8	20	24	Fire Lake	YUK	Pete Cintorino	2004	1
413 6/8	47 2/8	46 0/8	39 1/8	14	12	Divide Lake	NWT	Chuck Adams	1995	2
410 2/8	54 0/8	55 6/8	46 0/8	15	12	Cassiar Mtns.	BC	Thomas B. Frye	1978	3
399 0/8	49 7/8	51 5/8	40 2/8	8	11	Cassiar Mtns.	BC	Joseph Hinderman	1997	4
396 4/8	44 0/8	45 1/8	42 4/8	18	15	Divide Lake	NWT	John E. Anderson	1995	5
393 2/8	50 5/8	53 2/8	41 1/8	14	10	Tuya River	BC	T. J. Conrads	2006	6
391 3/8	53 3/8	54 1/8	36 6/8	13	15	Tuya Lake	BC	John D. "Jack" Frost	1995	7
390 4/8	48 3/8	48 1/8	25 5/8	10	17	O'Grady Lake	NWT	Kelly Joe Liljenquist	1999	8
390 1/8	55 2/8	51 6/8	34 1/8	15	11	Firesteel River	BC	Melvin K. Wolf	1970	9
387 6/8	44 3/8	42 7/8	36 0/8	15	14	Cold Fish Lake	BC	Steve Gorr	1976	10
*385 2/8	45 7/8	45 6/8	35 0/8	11	10	Klaza	YUK	Timothy B. Fisk	2008	11
*380 0/8	47 5/8	48 0/8	31 1/8	13	16	Stikine River	BC	David R. Hall	2005	12
378 2/8	49 3/8	47 4/8	37 0/8	11	10	O'Grady Lake	NWT	C. Randall Byers	1988	13
378 0/8	42 1/8	44 1/8	31 7/8	12	11	Tahltan River	BC	Arthur Harlow	1988	14
374 6/8	55 4/8	55 6/8	40 2/8	10	8	Thutade Lake	BC	Edward C. Pawinski	1984	15
374 1/8	43 6/8	47 1/8	35 0/8	16	16	Duti River	BC	Dr. Lowell Eddy	1967	16
373 3/8	45 5/8	43 7/8	31 0/8	13	17	June Lake	NWT	Dennis Palmer	1988	17
373 3/8	47 7/8	47 3/8	30 7/8	18	15	O'Grady Lake	NWT	Randall R. Giesey	1993	17
373 2/8	45 4/8	44 7/8	37 7/8	10	13	Natla River	NWT	Chuck Adams	1990	19
371 7/8	48 1/8	47 1/8	39 1/8	15	13	Tatlatui Lake	BC	Larry Alma	1979	20
371 7/8	46 0/8	46 0/8	36 4/8	14	12	Divide Lake	NWT	Mike Parsons	1988	20
371 3/8	38 7/8	39 3/8	30 3/8	16	15	Thutade Lake	BC	Bob Brill	1980	22
370 5/8	45 1/8	45 2/8	29 6/8	12	16	Cassiar Mtns.	BC	Ray Wilson	1988	23
370 1/8	45 5/8	48 4/8	40 6/8	8	10	Russell Lake	YUK	Bob Fromme	1990	23
370 0/8	46 4/8	44 5/8	30 4/8	14	14	Natla River	NWT	Janice J. Traub	1985	25
368 0/8	43 1/8	45 0/8	30 0/8	13	13	Keele River	NWT	Jay Brown	1991	26
367 4/8	47 0/8	45 4/8	29 7/8	17	13	June Lake	NWT	Nathan L. Andersohn	1995	27
366 5/8	46 2/8	46 0/8	24 6/8	14	18	O'Grady Lake	NWT	John MacPeak	2002	28
365 7/8	49 0/8	49 6/8	34 0/8	12	12	O'Grady Lake	NWT	R. Brian Oates	1990	29
365 2/8	47 4/8	48 5/8	32 1/8	14	13	Horseshoe Lake	NWT	Mike Parsons	1989	30
364 7/8	47 2/8	43 6/8	29 3/8	13	12	Cassiar Mtns.	BC	Donald Thompson	2003	31
364 2/8	42 2/8	41 0/8	29 3/8	13	11	Mackenzie Mtns.	NWT	Randy Liljenquist	2009	32
361 5/8	41 4/8	41 6/8	31 7/8	10	10	Mountain River	NWT	Rick Duggan	2003	33
361 3/8	49 4/8	53 2/8	31 7/8	12	10	O'Grady Lake	NWT	G. Fred Asbell	1988	34
359 5/8	47 0/8	48 0/8	35 3/8	14	12	Nahanni Buttes	NWT	Aaron Barsamian	2005	35
357 6/8	39 2/8	38 5/8	27 4/8	12	12	McNeil Lake	YUK	Todd Zeuske	1994	36
357 5/8	46 0/8	45 2/8	31 6/8	11	11	Caribou Pass	NWT	Duane Hicks	1996	37
356 5/8	38 7/8	40 5/8	32 0/8	15	16	Horseshoe Lake	NWT	Don Davidson	1989	38
356 0/8	49 0/8	49 0/8	30 4/8	12	14	Johiah Lake	BC	Poncho McCoy	2001	39
355 4/8	48 3/8	49 2/8	29 0/8	12	10	Johiah Lake	BC	Rick Wilson	2001	40
355 1/8	57 2/8	55 7/8	43 2/8	9	11	Kawdy Plateau	BC	Harvey J. Surina	1999	41
354 3/8	41 3/8	42 4/8	28 6/8	10	10	O'Grady Lake	NWT	C. Randall Byers	1991	42
353 5/8	42 5/8	41 0/8	29 2/8	14	12	O'Grady Lake	NWT	Randy Liljenquist	1999	43
352 1/8	44 7/8	43 7/8	36 5/8	13	15	June Lake	NWT	Garry Bolinder	1996	44
351 6/8	46 4/8	45 0/8	37 4/8	11	11	Watson Lake	YUK	Pete Shepley	1985	45
350 6/8	41 0/8	42 2/8	30 1/8	8	8	Caribou Lake	NWT	John W. Borlang	1989	46
350 5/8	46 7/8	46 5/8	33 7/8	12	13	Mountain River	NWT	Tom D. Slusser	1991	47
350 5/8	44 6/8	44 7/8	34 6/8	11	10	June Lake	NWT	Archie J. Nesbitt	1999	47
350 1/8	42 3/8	40 6/8	29 4/8	10	11	Liard River	BC	Richie Bland	2005	49
349 2/8	47 0/8	45 5/8	34 4/8	11	10	Nahanni Butte	NWT	William E. Terry, Sr.	1994	50
348 6/8	51 2/8	49 5/8	44 5/8	10	11	Ragged Range	NWT	Tom Taylor	1993	51
348 3/8	52 4/8	55 3/8	48 5/8	12	9	O'Grady Lake	NWT	Marc N. Shaft	1988	52
347 5/8	33 4/8	32 5/8	31 4/8	14	11	O'Grady Lake	NWT	Don Davidson	1991	53
347 1/8	44 4/8	46 4/8	37 6/8	14	12	Stikine River	BC	Claudio Canonica	1988	54
347 1/8	43 7/8	40 5/8	34 4/8	15	15	Divide Lake	NWT	Chuck Adams	1993	54
*345 7/8	48 1/8	44 3/8	41 4/8	9	8	Tuya Lake	BC	Dan Real	2006	56
345 3/8	51 3/8	49 5/8	33 3/8	13	11	Divide Lake	NWT	Al Reay	1982	57
344 4/8	57 3/8	56 2/8	38 6/8	10	9	O'Grady Lake	NWT	Steven R. Hohensee	1992	58
343 3/8	48 2/8	50 6/8	35 4/8	15	11	Serpentine Mtn.	BC	Randolph P. Wilson	1976	59
*343 3/8	47 0/8	47 3/8	38 5/8	12	13	Nahanni Butte	NWT	Michele Leqve	2008	59
342 5/8	48 1/8	48 0/8	20 1/8	12	15	Arctic Red River	NWT	Rocky Chisholm	2001	61
342 2/8	47 6/8	47 1/8	34 4/8	10	9	Divide Lake	NWT	Stanley Walchuk, Jr.	1984	62
342 0/8	40 6/8	36 4/8	32 0/8	18	17	Caribou Pass	NWT	Ryk Visscher	1996	63
340 7/8	46 4/8	45 3/8	37 3/8	9	12	Horseshoe Lake	NWT	Jerry Keller	1990	64
339 6/8	42 7/8	44 6/8	20 0/8	20	18	Tatlatui Lake	BC	G. Fred Asbell	1975	65
339 5/8	44 6/8	44 5/8	24 5/8	15	13	O'Grady Lake	NWT	Mark Wuerthele	1993	66
339 4/8	47 1/8	48 6/8	37 0/8	10	11	Divide Lake	NWT	Dan Brockman	1991	67
337 0/8	40 1/8	42 0/8	37 1/8	10	10	Cassiar Mtns.	BC	John Paul Schaffer	2004	68
336 7/8	45 1/8	47 4/8	29 2/8	8	10	June Lake	NWT	Mike Zech	1989	69
336 3/8	45 4/8	45 0/8	31 7/8	12	9	Divide Lake	NWT	Paul Anderson	1995	70
336 1/8	46 5/8	47 2/8	36 3/8	7	9	Summit Lake	YUK	Gregory White	1989	71
336 1/8	42 7/8	40 5/8	36 6/8	12	15	Nacha Creek	BC	Scott L. Koelzer	1994	71
335 4/8	43 7/8	43 7/8	32 0/8	13	10	Divide Lake	NWT	Mark Zastrow	1991	73
334 7/8	45 3/8	43 7/8	30 2/8	12	14	Mountain River	NWT	Dale Selby	2002	74
334 2/8	40 7/8	40 0/8	36 5/8	15	11	Wolverine Creek	NWT	Stan Godfrey	1988	75
334 1/8	40 4/8	41 1/8	33 7/8	13	17	Firesteel River	BC	Walter Krom	1971	76
333 5/8	45 1/8	47 2/8	31 0/8	12	11	Firesteel River	BC	Jay Deones	1978	77
332 1/8	40 0/8	40 4/8	32 5/8	10	12	Firesteel River	BC	Larry Alma	1984	79
332 0/8	49 2/8	50 2/8	38 0/8	12	10	O'Grady Lake	NWT	Frank S. Noska IV	2002	80
331 5/8	47 6/8	49 1/8	29 6/8	11	9	June Lake	NWT	Fred Eichler	2005	81
*330 6/8	38 2/8	39 0/8	34 2/8	11	10	Godlin River	NWT	M. Blake Patton	2010	82
330 5/8	44 0/8	44 7/8	39 0/8	13	12	Mountain River	NWT	Dewayne Mullins	1999	83
329 4/8	48 6/8	44 4/8	35 5/8	8	7	Southfork River	YUK	Kevin Harms	2003	84
329 1/8	44 6/8	44 5/8	29 4/8	12	15	Mayo	YUK	Derek Gentile	2006	85
328 5/8	51 4/8	50 5/8	40 4/8	9	12	Kilgore Lake	BC	Mike Parsons	1998	86
328 3/8	41 2/8	40 6/8	26 5/8	12	10	Divide Lake	NWT	Chuck Adams	1992	87
327 1/8	39 1/8	39 2/8	31 5/8	11	12	Toad River	BC	Richard Kirkland	2004	88
327 0/8	41 2/8	40 1/8	31 4/8	15	15	Mountain River	NWT	Mike Barrett	1990	89
326 7/8	46 2/8	47 4/8	34 4/8	10	8	Tae Mtn.	YUK	Edwin L. DeYoung	1996	90
326 3/8	53 2/8	52 2/8	26 5/8	9	8	Tay Mtn.	YUK	Don Lind	1997	91
326 2/8	37 7/8	41 1/8	27 7/8	15	14	Divide Lake	NWT	John Baird	1994	92
324 1/8	35 3/8	36 3/8	32 1/8	15	18	Cassiar Mtns.	BC	Mike Parsons	1994	93
324 1/8	38 5/8	40 4/8	31 5/8	10	10	Ludwig Lake	BC	Guy Leibenguth	1997	93
323 5/8	42 3/8	44 2/8	36 2/8	11	9	O'Grady Lake	NWT	J. Dale Hale	1998	95
322 1/8	35 6/8	38 4/8	27 4/8	14	13	June Lake	NWT	Dennis Dunn	2005	96

MOUNTAIN CARIBOU

Minimum Score 300 — Continued

SCORE	LENGTH OF MAIN BEAM R	L	INSIDE SPREAD	NUMBER OF POINTS R	L	AREA	STATE/PROVINCE	HUNTER'S NAME	DATE	RANK
321 7/8	48 4/8	47 3/8	32 4/8	13	14	Kitchener Lake	BC	Stephen E. Mitchell	1970	97
321 7/8	36 5/8	35 1/8	31 6/8	10	12	Rupert Lake	BC	John J.J. Rybinski	2001	97
320 6/8	43 6/8	44 4/8	31 7/8	11	12	Thutade Lake	BC	Jack W. Kriener	1974	99
*320 0/8	42 2/8	42 6/8	31 0/8	11	11	Nahanni Buttes	NWT	Blayne St. James	2008	100
319 3/8	45 0/8	45 2/8	40 5/8	10	12	Kitchener Lake	BC	Doug Strecker	1979	101
319 1/8	44 3/8	48 5/8	24 7/8	13	10	Cold Fish Lake	BC	Steve Gorr	1975	102
318 7/8	38 2/8	40 0/8	35 4/8	9	9	Mackenzie Mtns.	NWT	Steven Weekly	1987	103
318 5/8	41 4/8	43 5/8	39 6/8	10	12	Dease Lake	BC	James Gabrick	2002	104
318 4/8	40 4/8	38 0/8	36 3/8	10	10	Jennings Lake	BC	Gene A. Welle	2001	105
317 4/8	43 1/8	42 6/8	34 4/8	10	8	Divide Lake	NWT	Jim Wondzell	1993	106
317 3/8	43 1/8	45 5/8	29 0/8	11	11	Keele River	NWT	Ron Serwa	1988	107
316 3/8	42 6/8	43 2/8	30 6/8	11	11	Divide Lake	NWT	Neil Summers	2002	108
315 5/8	43 3/8	44 3/8	29 1/8	11	12	Kitchener Lake	BC	Dick Crowder	1976	109
314 7/8	42 6/8	46 0/8	33 5/8	10	10	Divide Lake	NWT	Dale Drilling	1989	110
314 5/8	44 7/8	47 6/8	32 7/8	10	9	Ittlemit Lake	YUK	Chuck Buchanan	1979	111
314 3/8	43 7/8	43 3/8	30 7/8	9	12	Divide Lake	NWT	Duane Zemliska	1991	112
314 2/8	42 7/8	44 0/8	28 3/8	10	10	O'Grady Lake	NWT	Don Davidson, Jr.	1988	113
*314 0/8	46 0/8	44 6/8	38 5/8	10	9	June Lake	NWT	John Stone	2007	114
313 4/8	40 2/8	45 1/8	32 7/8	10	8	Mackenzie Mtns.	NWT	John "Jack" Cordes	1985	115
*312 7/8	44 2/8	44 7/8	28 4/8	8	9	Whitehorse	YUK	Beard Hobbs	2006	116
309 2/8	43 3/8	41 2/8	27 2/8	10	13	Thutade Lake	BC	Harold H. VanderHorst	1974	117
307 7/8	46 6/8	47 4/8	29 7/8	9	9	Thutade Lake	BC	Kim S. Ades	1984	118
307 5/8	42 3/8	40 3/8	31 3/8	9	11	Norman Wells	NWT	Gary Martin	2000	119
306 6/8	40 0/8	40 4/8	30 1/8	11	9	Chapel Lake	BC	Scott L. Koelzer	2009	120
306 2/8	43 4/8	43 2/8	29 2/8	11	10	Tatlatui Lake	BC	Robert Pitt	1975	121
304 2/8	37 2/8	40 7/8	27 1/8	10	10	O'Grady Lake	NWT	P. Tod Byers	1991	122
303 6/8	42 4/8	42 4/8	25 2/8	9	12	Tatlatui Lake	BC	Rick Gilley	1983	123
301 7/8	41 2/8	43 1/8	36 4/8	10	11	Dease Lake	BC	Ron Klassen	2004	124

MOUNTAIN CARIBOU (VELVET ANTLERS)

Minimum Score 300

SCORE	LENGTH OF MAIN BEAM R	L	INSIDE SPREAD	NUMBER OF POINTS R	L	AREA	STATE/PROVINCE	HUNTER'S NAME	DATE	RANK
410 7/8	48 7/8	50 2/8	49 3/8	16	16	Arctic Red River	NWT	Rick Stockburger	2009	*
388 3/8	46 5/8	46 4/8	46 5/8	17	16	Arctic Red River	NWT	Jim L. Horneck	2006	*
*372 1/8	48 7/8	49 7/8	39 1/8	9	7	Arctic Red River	NWT	Randy Carey	2006	*
357 1/8	41 5/8	44 5/8	30 6/8	11	11	Gawa River	NWT	Adam Foss	2010	*
352 3/8	50 2/8	49 6/8	38 0/8	13	9	Godlin Lake	NWT	Bailey Simpson	2008	*
341 3/8	40 1/8	38 6/8	28 7/8	13	12	Gana River	NWT	Tom Foss	2009	*
*326 2/8	44 6/8	43 2/8	26 2/8	8	8	Keele River	NWT	Mark Beeler	2007	*
325 2/8	47 4/8	49 0/8	30 0/8	7	9	Norman Wells	NWT	George Harms	2008	*
319 1/8	41 6/8	44 1/8	24 0/8	12	11	Natla River	NWT	Lee Jernigan	2005	*
318 5/8	37 3/8	38 6/8	28 7/8	12	16	Natla River	NWT	Bob Ameen	2005	*
314 4/8	37 2/8	38 3/8	33 5/8	13	13	June Lake	NWT	Walt Palmer	2004	*
314 3/8	44 6/8	47 1/8	30 0/8	10	12	Nahanni River	NWT	Tom Miranda	2008	*
304 3/8	46 6/8	45 6/8	40 6/8	7	6	Timbered Ridge	NWT	Richard A. Smith	2007	*
300 0/8	43 6/8	44 5/8	38 6/8	11	11	June Lake	NWT	Joe Coleman	2004	*

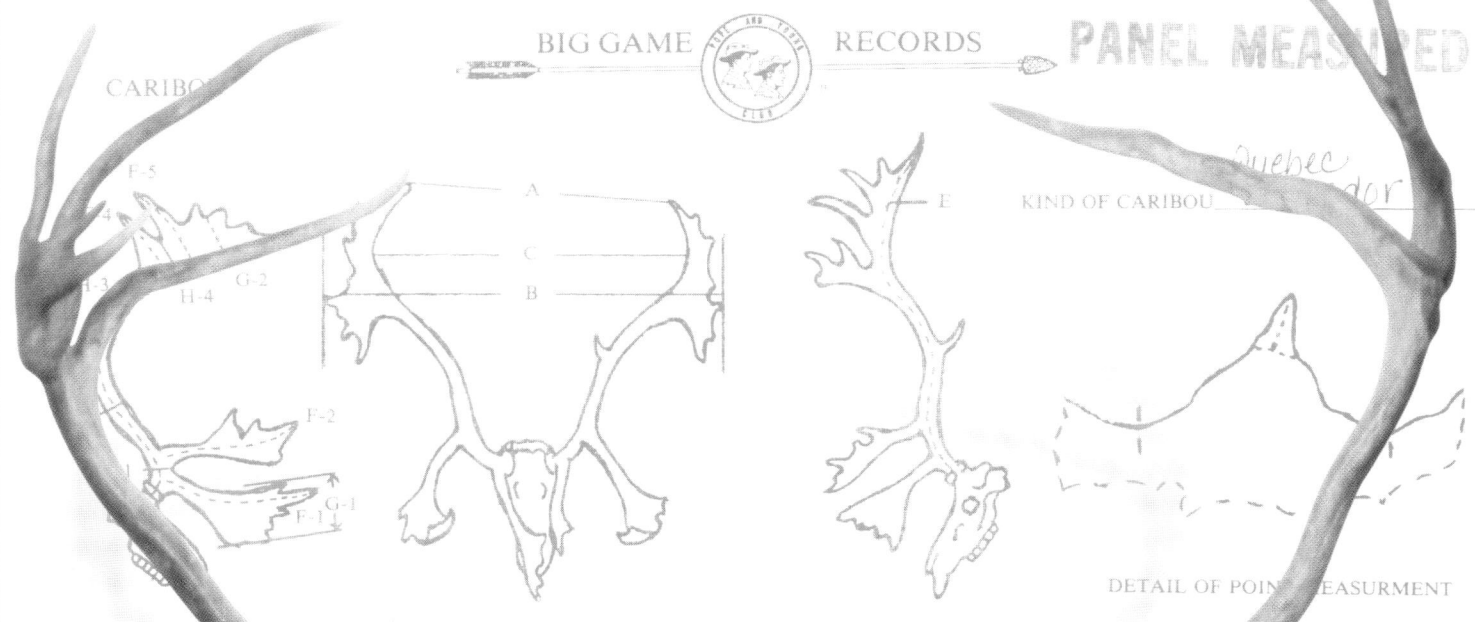

WORLD RECORD QUEBEC-LABRADOR CARIBOU
Score: 434 0/8
Location: Tunulik River, Quebec
Date: 1984
Hunter: Carol Ann Mauch

Quebec-Labrador Caribou

by Carol Ann Mauch

My husband, Dick, and I had enjoyed such a good time and successful hunt with Bobby Snowball on the Tunulik River in 1982, that we had returned for a second hunt in 1984.

Dick had chosen the area we were hunting because of the way the ridges worked to funnel a series of worn and rutted trails into a single "caribou highway" to a river crossing area. It was the second day of the hunt and Dick had gone upstream to glass for moving animals. Elijah, my guide, had taken me to a high point overlooking the river.

The crossing site was a mile or more wide at this spot. There was a long, narrow and rocky island about a third of the way out from the far shore. From our vantage point, Elijah soon spotted three bulls headed for the crossing and motioned for me to get in the boat. He took me to the far end of the rough island and out of sight of the caribou that were now in the water.

I was able to situate myself amidst the brush and rocks in the middle of the island. I could shoot either to the right or left without moving from my hiding place, should the bulls come ashore at my end of the island. Just as I had hoped, they came ambling down the beach to my left. I was excited, but ready. The two smaller bulls came by first with the big herd-master trailing behind. I waited until he was nearly broadside and passing before I drew my bow and let fly.

All the caribou broke into a run and I lost sight of them quickly in the rough and rocky terrain. I followed the tracks and the blood trail down the beach until I could see the end of the island, but no caribou. I ran back toward my hiding spot because the wind was now at my back and I didn't want to alert the caribou to my position. Climbing to the crest and crossing over, I saw the big bull facing me. I shot another arrow that went straight into his chest. I knew then that he was mine.

QUEBEC-LABRADOR CARIBOU

Minimum Score 325

Rangifer tarandus caboti from Quebec and Labrador

SCORE	LENGTH OF R MAIN BEAM L	INSIDE SPREAD	NUMBER OF R POINTS L		AREA	STATE/ PROVINCE	HUNTER'S NAME	DATE	RANK
434 0/8	53 6/8 56 1/8	46 1/8	17	12	Tunulik River	QUE	Carol Ann Mauch	1984	1
429 1/8	52 2/8 52 2/8	45 1/8	15	17	Delay River	QUE	Bob Foulkrod	1985	2
419 4/8	50 0/8 50 6/8	40 2/8	12	11	Natuak Lake	QUE	Patricio Sada Muguerza	1993	3
416 6/8	51 2/8 49 6/8	50 0/8	13	14	Lake Consigny	QUE	Ricardo L. Garza	1989	4
416 5/8	45 3/8 47 7/8	47 4/8	28	27	George River	QUE	Collins F. Kellogg	1978	5
415 7/8	51 5/8 55 3/8	53 0/8	16	16	Ungava Bay	QUE	Dr. Woodallen G. Snyder	1984	6
412 7/8	52 7/8 53 0/8	49 3/8	17	18	LG 4	QUE	Gary Robbins	1990	7
412 2/8	50 2/8 53 1/8	43 0/8	18	19	Delay River	QUE	Leonard L. Campbell	1995	8
411 4/8	56 4/8 57 0/8	52 0/8	16	14	Ungava Region	QUE	Richard S. Neely	1977	9
410 2/8	52 4/8 51 6/8	48 4/8	15	16	Pons Island	QUE	Don Young	1988	10
410 0/8	56 0/8 55 6/8	52 1/8	13	11	Schefferville	QUE	Charles L. Buechel, Jr.	1987	11
410 0/8	52 7/8 53 7/8	48 4/8	17	19	Kuujjuaq	QUE	Robert Harris	2005	11
408 4/8	50 1/8 49 5/8	40 4/8	14	20	Caniapiscau River	QUE	Fred B. Davis	2005	13
407 5/8	50 3/8 50 0/8	45 3/8	13	15	Delay River	QUE	Jeff Baker	1988	14
403 7/8	51 3/8 50 3/8	43 5/8	14	16	Delay River	QUE	Dr. James J. Barnes	1987	15
403 2/8	48 2/8 47 2/8	35 2/8	16	16	Lac Droilland	QUE	Tom Johnson	1991	16
402 3/8	59 4/8 57 7/8	56 6/8	13	14	Ungava Bay	QUE	Leonard J. Letendre	1989	17
401 3/8	49 4/8 49 0/8	51 1/8	14	14	Lac Pons	QUE	Gordon Demeritt	1988	18
399 7/8	52 3/8 53 1/8	49 6/8	12	12	Whiskey Lake	QUE	D.F.Baldwin & T. Barta	1985	19
399 0/8	51 4/8 49 1/8	53 0/8	11	17	Andrea Lac	LAB	Daniel R. Green	2008	20
398 5/8	52 2/8 54 2/8	51 1/8	20	17	George River	QUE	Richard Mielke	1981	21
398 5/8	54 4/8 54 5/8	52 4/8	10	11	Caniapiscau River	QUE	Henry O. Fromm	1987	21
398 1/8	51 4/8 52 2/8	48 3/8	11	11	Lac Otelnuk	QUE	Rudy Tremain	1989	23
396 3/8	55 0/8 51 6/8	42 7/8	12	12	Lake Mollett	QUE	Tim North	2001	24
396 1/8	51 6/8 51 2/8	48 1/8	14	15	Weymouth Inlet	QUE	Tink Nathan	1986	25
395 6/8	59 4/8 55 4/8	47 7/8	18	16	George River	QUE	Paul Brunner	1980	26
394 5/8	54 3/8 53 3/8	49 1/8	14	11	Deception Bay	QUE	Leo Neuls, Jr.	1998	27
393 4/8	48 4/8 49 6/8	44 0/8	19	16	Lac Chabanel	QUE	Jeff D. Stout	1998	28
392 4/8	52 4/8 53 4/8	44 7/8	15	13	Caniapiscau River	QUE	Mike Ingold	1988	29
392 2/8	53 4/8 59 2/8	42 2/8	13	11	Potier River	QUE	Donald L. Sagner	1995	30
392 2/8	41 6/8 43 4/8	35 5/8	17	22	Melezes River	QUE	Dennis Doherty	2005	30
392 0/8	51 4/8 50 6/8	48 2/8	18	27	Lac Cananee	QUE	Brad L. Johnson	1981	32
391 6/8	55 6/8 56 2/8	39 4/8	17	15	George River	QUE	Jim McCrory	1980	33
389 5/8	50 4/8 49 6/8	42 1/8	16	13	Ronalds Lake	QUE	Chris Kantianis	1993	34
388 3/8	49 2/8 51 6/8	40 5/8	12	12	Delay River	QUE	Richard E. Davis	1987	35
388 2/8	46 0/8 45 4/8	42 6/8	11	11	Delay River	QUE	William G. Mason	1988	36
387 6/8	62 1/8 60 7/8	53 7/8	12	11	Delay River	QUE	Roy M. Goodwin	1987	37
387 6/8	50 1/8 49 4/8	45 6/8	12	14	Pons River	QUE	Louis J. Lorenzo	1991	37
387 4/8	42 2/8 39 5/8	47 7/8	24	16	Delay River	QUE	Larry Smith	1987	39
387 4/8	43 5/8 46 2/8	51 2/8	16	13	Lake Mollett	QUE	Ronald C. Miller	2005	39
387 1/8	52 0/8 53 5/8	48 4/8	9	12	Schefferville	QUE	Tom Kayser	1986	41
387 1/8	47 0/8 44 5/8	46 6/8	14	13	Weeks Lake	QUE	Donald L. Stout	1990	41
*387 0/8	51 2/8 50 3/8	40 6/8	17	11	Lac Minto	QUE	Duane Armitage	2002	43
386 4/8	56 2/8 54 4/8	57 7/8	15	20	George River	QUE	John Kuhar	1972	44
385 5/8	50 2/8 52 2/8	50 7/8	16	18	Pons Island	QUE	James C. Walters	1987	45
*385 2/8	54 7/8 49 3/8	51 0/8	16	16	Lac Minto	QUE	Robert Carnahan	2005	46
385 1/8	47 0/8 49 2/8	43 3/8	12	15	Saglek Bay	LAB	Zig Kertenis, Jr.	1988	47
384 7/8	50 6/8 50 0/8	50 0/8	15	18	Whale River	QUE	David L. Willis	1986	48
384 7/8	46 1/8 45 7/8	57 6/8	12	11	Pons Lake	QUE	George P. Mann	1994	48
384 4/8	46 4/8 46 6/8	42 4/8	15	16	Schefferville	QUE	Elmer R. Luce, Jr.	1987	50
384 2/8	45 2/8 46 6/8	49 0/8	19	19	Schefferville	QUE	Elmer R. Luce, Jr.	1987	51
384 1/8	46 1/8 45 6/8	45 7/8	14	12	Caniapiscau River	QUE	Shaun R. Murphy	1994	52
384 0/8	46 0/8 44 3/8	43 0/8	17	17	Weymouth Inlet	QUE	Jules Pacheco	1986	53
383 7/8	47 3/8 49 5/8	46 7/8	14	17	Lake Loudin	QUE	Roger M. Schmitt	1988	54
383 6/8	49 6/8 48 3/8	46 1/8	26	18	Wayne Lake	QUE	Brian Preston	1993	55
383 4/8	49 6/8 50 0/8	46 0/8	14	12	Schefferville	QUE	Robert B. Stryker	1994	56
382 6/8	49 2/8 48 6/8	43 0/8	17	13	Lac Chabanel	QUE	Thomas Olszewski	2005	57
381 6/8	50 4/8 52 0/8	50 2/8	13	13	Delay River	QUE	Robert G. McCulley	1988	58
381 4/8	50 0/8 51 6/8	41 2/8	17	19	Wedge Hill Lodge	QUE	John Janelli	1980	59
381 3/8	52 0/8 49 2/8	48 0/8	13	14	Ungava Region	QUE	Wayne A. Vanstratten	1986	60
381 2/8	48 3/8 50 4/8	39 1/8	13	14	Caniapiscau River	QUE	David C. Arndt	1986	61
381 0/8	51 0/8 52 1/8	44 3/8	14	13	LG 4	QUE	Stephen Kotz	1990	62
380 6/8	56 0/8 52 1/8	40 4/8	12	12	Oltanook Lake	QUE	Ken Mowerson	1986	63
380 6/8	53 5/8 54 0/8	46 7/8	12	13	Kuujjuaq	QUE	Steven L. Fair	1993	63
380 6/8	49 4/8 49 6/8	44 4/8	12	12	Andrea Lac	LAB	Daniel R. Green	2008	63
380 5/8	57 6/8 53 5/8	56 7/8	11	16	Ungava Region	QUE	Donald Schram	1982	66
379 7/8	49 0/8 50 2/8	51 2/8	15	13	Schefferville	QUE	Michael C. Dysh	1990	67
379 6/8	49 4/8 49 0/8	42 5/8	11	12	Schefferville	QUE	Ted Jaycox	1986	68
379 6/8	45 7/8 50 1/8	48 2/8	16	16	Pons River	QUE	Chris Cass	1993	68
379 5/8	43 4/8 43 3/8	43 1/8	10	11	Clearwater Lake	QUE	Tyler Henriksen	2008	69
379 4/8	45 0/8 47 3/8	46 0/8	17	14	Alubiack Fiord	QUE	Tim Finley	1994	70
379 0/8	55 6/8 55 4/8	48 2/8	12	13	Delay River	QUE	Paul Rigsby	1988	71
378 7/8	54 2/8 54 2/8	54 3/8	11	12	Tunulik River	QUE	Jay G. St. Charles	1986	72
378 4/8	49 5/8 49 0/8	44 3/8	14	15	Fort Chimo	QUE	Robert Pyne	1989	73
*378 4/8	49 0/8 50 6/8	36 7/8	17	13	Leaf River	QUE	Gary L. Hilliard	2005	73
378 3/8	50 0/8 50 7/8	40 6/8	13	14	Fort Chimo	QUE	Nickoles J. Giannetti	1993	75
377 6/8	50 1/8 50 0/8	37 0/8	16	15	Clearwater Lake	QUE	Greg Abbas	2001	76
377 3/8	51 6/8 55 2/8	52 4/8	12	13	Schefferville	QUE	Frank 'Rit' Heller	1978	77
377 3/8	49 2/8 49 7/8	36 2/8	19	17	Lac Minto	QUE	Charles Nopper	1997	77
377 0/8	53 6/8 55 7/8	36 7/8	15	15	Delay River	QUE	Dale Underwood	1990	79
376 7/8	48 1/8 49 6/8	51 0/8	17	13	Lake Lac Hine	QUE	Edward A. Mertins	1990	80
376 7/8	43 5/8 44 1/8	44 0/8	14	14	Deception Bay	QUE	Leo Neuls, Sr.	1998	80
376 5/8	50 4/8 50 4/8	57 0/8	13	11	Ungava Bay	QUE	Ed Riley	1985	82
376 5/8	49 2/8 50 4/8	37 3/8	17	16	Lac Minto	QUE	Gene Vining	2001	82
376 2/8	49 2/8 48 2/8	49 4/8	17	18	Fort Chimo	QUE	David Bailey	1985	84
376 2/8	51 7/8 54 1/8	44 1/8	16	17	Boland Lake	QUE	John "Chip" Klass	1995	84
376 1/8	47 1/8 47 2/8	36 4/8	14	14	Deception Bay	QUE	Leo Neuls, Sr.	1998	87
376 0/8	51 0/8 50 4/8	42 0/8	11	13	Lac Bienville	QUE	L. Reed Breight	1997	88
375 7/8	46 2/8 47 6/8	37 2/8	24	25	Ungava Region	QUE	Jose Rivero	1979	89
375 5/8	51 4/8 52 2/8	50 2/8	14	16	Lac Minto	QUE	Jason D. Cook	1997	90
375 1/8	60 3/8 59 6/8	42 0/8	15	16	George River	QUE	Robert M. Sweisthal, Jr.	1980	91
*375 0/8	52 7/8 51 1/8	49 4/8	12	11	Nastapoka Lake	QUE	Brian D. Campbell, Jr.	2006	92
374 7/8	49 5/8 52 1/8	59 2/8	11	15	Ungava Region	QUE	Bob Frank	1979	93
374 6/8	47 5/8 48 7/8	43 6/8	13	12	Weeks Lake	QUE	Raymond Villeneuve	1990	94
374 4/8	54 0/8 59 2/8	34 7/8	9	12	Schefferville	QUE	Brian L. Johnson	1988	95

QUEBEC-LABRADOR CARIBOU

Minimum Score 325
Continued

SCORE	LENGTH OF R MAIN BEAM L	INSIDE SPREAD	NUMBER OF R POINTS L	AREA	STATE/ PROVINCE	HUNTER'S NAME	DATE	RANK
374 4/8	51 0/8 47 4/8	39 1/8	14 13	George River	QUE	David A. Spacek	1990	95
374 3/8	60 2/8 59 0/8	52 5/8	14 13	Schefferville	QUE	Bill Heather	1979	97
374 3/8	49 1/8 46 6/8	32 4/8	20 22	Bird Lake	QUE	David Steger	1993	97
374 2/8	49 6/8 50 6/8	49 5/8	17 11	Lake Craamolet	QUE	Roland L. Kauffman	2006	99
374 0/8	44 3/8 45 6/8	40 3/8	11 14	Clearwater Lake	QUE	Pat Powell	2007	100
373 6/8	48 1/8 47 0/8	36 3/8	6 6	Lippe Lake	QUE	Robert L. Goldsberry	1994	101
373 6/8	48 5/8 45 2/8	36 5/8	13 14	Pons River	QUE	Louis Kitcoff	1996	101
373 3/8	53 2/8 51 1/8	40 0/8	15 13	Fort Chimo	QUE	Scott M. Showalter	1982	103
373 2/8	49 2/8 44 4/8	43 0/8	15 13	LG 4	QUE	Christopher Germain	1992	104
373 0/8	45 3/8 44 2/8	39 2/8	20 10	Wolf Lake	QUE	Bruce A. Hopkins	1993	105
372 7/8	44 2/8 45 2/8	37 7/8	17 17	Delay River	QUE	Ray Moulton	1986	106
372 7/8	46 6/8 47 4/8	47 6/8	15 13	Henrys Lake	QUE	Kip Boten	1990	106
372 5/8	46 3/8 43 2/8	37 6/8	15 20	Ungava Bay	QUE	Si Pellow	1988	108
372 4/8	55 7/8 53 1/8	43 2/8	13 13	Ungava Bay	QUE	David Dunnigan	1984	109
372 4/8	53 0/8 58 7/8	43 4/8	11 10	Lac Lefrancois	QUE	Raymond W. Murray III	1990	109
372 4/8	45 6/8 45 5/8	41 1/8	16 16	LG 4	QUE	Paul J. Sisz	1991	109
372 1/8	52 6/8 53 2/8	52 4/8	17 15	Ungava Bay	QUE	Roy M. Goodwin	1989	112
371 6/8	48 7/8 50 1/8	42 6/8	17 16	Fort Chimo	QUE	Robert Pyne	1989	113
371 5/8	48 6/8 47 3/8	42 4/8	16 13	Maricourt Lake	QUE	James Kingsley	1992	114
371 2/8	46 5/8 49 5/8	38 6/8	12 10	Lac Kakiattuoluk	QUE	Ronald Rockwell	2001	115
371 1/8	48 5/8 49 1/8	46 4/8	12 12	Lac Minto	QUE	Kevin Kaczmarek	2006	116
370 7/8	46 6/8 44 5/8	41 2/8	5 6	Schefferville	QUE	Elmer R. Luce, Jr.	1986	117
370 5/8	45 0/8 48 0/8	37 5/8	20 14	Caniapiscau River	QUE	Gregory White	1987	118
370 5/8	47 6/8 47 7/8	49 6/8	12 11	Clearwater Lake	QUE	Greg Abbas	2001	118
370 3/8	53 0/8 52 1/8	42 7/8	14 15	Lake Mollett	QUE	Tim Lockner	1999	120
*370 3/8	49 2/8 47 4/8	42 3/8	11 11	Louis Lake	QUE	Mark Zebley	2007	120
370 2/8	46 0/8 46 7/8	55 1/8	12 13	Delay River	QUE	Mike Iuzzolino	1991	122
370 2/8	51 6/8 51 4/8	44 7/8	15 12	Lac Minto	QUE	Carl Spaeth	1999	122
370 1/8	50 3/8 49 6/8	38 3/8	11 11	Lac Merrville	QUE	Jack A. Smith	1998	124
369 4/8	47 2/8 44 7/8	40 2/8	18 19	Nautapoka River	QUE	Robert DeVlieger II	2002	125
369 1/8	53 6/8 52 4/8	50 5/8	14 12	Jack's Lake	QUE	Denis Weisensel	1989	126
369 1/8	48 0/8 51 3/8	40 5/8	13 13	Lake Mollett	QUE	Ken Stieh	2001	126
369 1/8	52 6/8 50 0/8	41 6/8	10 11	Lac DeGrais	QUE	Justin Rouillard	2005	126
368 6/8	51 3/8 52 6/8	51 7/8	11 14	Kuujjuak River	QUE	Glen Ogle	1988	129
368 5/8	52 0/8 46 1/8	44 4/8	21 15	Fort Chimo	QUE	Joseph A. Borgna	1989	130
368 5/8	47 2/8 46 2/8	46 0/8	15 16	LG 4	QUE	Claude St' Amour	1990	130
368 4/8	53 0/8 51 4/8	43 4/8	13 12	Fort Chimo	QUE	Jerry Schauer	1990	132
368 0/8	46 0/8 47 6/8	44 2/8	15 15	Caniapiscau River	QUE	Gary Weckwerth	1994	133
367 4/8	54 7/8 52 0/8	43 3/8	11 14	George River	QUE	Lee Kline	1980	134
367 1/8	50 6/8 51 5/8	39 7/8	13 11	Schefferville	QUE	Raymond A. Guay	1988	135
367 1/8	46 6/8 48 3/8	37 0/8	13 15	Lake Messin	QUE	Jonathan S. Becker	2005	135
367 0/8	47 0/8 48 0/8	44 7/8	12 12	Fort Chimo	QUE	James E. Doberstein	1989	137
367 0/8	55 3/8 53 4/8	47 4/8	11 15	LG 4	QUE	Anthony Pennimpede	1993	137
366 4/8	53 1/8 55 5/8	44 6/8	15 14	Fort Chimo	QUE	Larry DeVormer, Sr.	1988	139
366 2/8	54 7/8 52 3/8	55 0/8	20 16	Ungava Region	QUE	Joe Caruso	1979	140
366 1/8	48 0/8 48 2/8	38 2/8	21 14	Mistinibi Lake	QUE	Dieter Foerst	1981	141
365 7/8	53 5/8 53 1/8	46 4/8	16 14	Lac Minto	QUE	Greg Bonecutter, Sr.	1998	142
365 7/8	49 4/8 51 6/8	34 7/8	13 14	Deception Bay	QUE	Steve Calton	2000	142
365 6/8	49 0/8 49 3/8	39 5/8	20 17	Pons River	QUE	Thomas Mathews	1988	144
364 4/8	49 0/8 51 0/8	34 4/8	13 11	George River	QUE	Gary L. Fritzler	1983	145
364 4/8	54 6/8 54 1/8	53 6/8	10 9	Delay River	QUE	W. R. "Tony" Dukes	1987	146
364 3/8	53 4/8 53 1/8	48 0/8	12 10	George River	QUE	Billy Ellis	1980	147
364 3/8	50 5/8 50 6/8	41 5/8	11 17	Ungava Bay	QUE	Stephen Michael Carroll	1988	147
364 2/8	49 5/8 47 3/8	41 0/8	16 16	Big Island Lake	QUE	Jim Ponciano	1985	149
364 2/8	57 7/8 58 5/8	55 2/8	13 14	Delay River	QUE	Bob Watkins	1987	149
364 2/8	51 6/8 51 4/8	44 7/8	15 12	Lac Minto	QUE	Carl Spaeth	1999	149
363 7/8	50 3/8 50 1/8	49 1/8	12 11	Delay River	QUE	Robert Bain	1987	152
363 7/8	50 6/8 54 3/8	39 1/8	13 15	Lac Tasiataq	QUE	William J. Gleeson	1998	152
363 7/8	49 4/8 49 5/8	37 4/8	9 11	Pons Island	QUE	Dennis Dunn	2006	152
363 6/8	48 0/8 49 3/8	46 7/8	12 13	Fort Chimo	QUE	Chuck Adams	1996	155
363 4/8	52 6/8 52 2/8	34 2/8	14 15	Ungava Bay	QUE	Steve Bruggeman	1990	156
363 4/8	46 3/8 47 0/8	44 2/8	15 16	Caribou Lake	LAB	Michael R. Doane	1999	156
363 2/8	48 3/8 47 6/8	40 7/8	19 19	Tunulik River	QUE	Randal S. Maday	1992	158
363 0/8	48 6/8 47 5/8	48 6/8	13 14	Tunulik River	QUE	Rick Morgan	1986	159
363 0/8	45 5/8 48 0/8	44 3/8	10 14	Ungava Bay	QUE	James Norvell	1989	159
363 0/8	46 4/8 48 3/8	49 0/8	14 19	Clearwater Lake	QUE	Chad P. Brandel	2005	159
362 4/8	53 7/8 47 1/8	53 1/8	10 16	River De Paz	QUE	David F. Baldwin	1981	162
362 4/8	55 7/8 53 6/8	45 5/8	12 11	Fort Chimo	QUE	William H. Moyer	1988	162
362 4/8	51 0/8 49 2/8	41 4/8	16 11	Lac Minto	QUE	Martin E. Cain	2004	162
362 3/8	47 6/8 48 3/8	41 4/8	13 12	Tunulik River	QUE	David J. Hell	1986	165
362 2/8	53 0/8 52 1/8	47 6/8	11 12	Saglek Bay	LAB	Charles Allen Poole	1990	166
362 2/8	53 1/8 56 2/8	44 0/8	11 13	LG 4	QUE	Kurt M. Zurawski	1994	166
362 0/8	60 2/8 57 5/8	49 4/8	11 14	Delay River	QUE	Richard V. McKeown	1990	168
361 7/8	45 4/8 47 4/8	36 6/8	16 15	Musset Lake	QUE	Herman W. Kovar, Sr.	2001	169
361 4/8	48 2/8 47 2/8	40 4/8	11 14	Fort Chimo	QUE	Dave Seidelman	1985	170
361 4/8	54 6/8 55 0/8	53 4/8	11 11	Akuliak	QUE	Perry Merkes	1988	170
361 3/8	54 4/8 55 6/8	42 0/8	12 11	Schefferville	QUE	Elmer R. Luce, Jr.	1986	172
361 3/8	47 7/8 48 6/8	41 5/8	14 14	Delay River	QUE	John Akkerman	1990	172
361 0/8	52 2/8 51 1/8	36 5/8	15 12	Delay River	QUE	Jerry Costanza	1991	174
*361 0/8	49 7/8 49 4/8	40 6/8	19 14	Leaf River	QUE	Bernard Murphy	2005	174
360 3/8	50 0/8 51 0/8	42 1/8	14 12	Schefferville	QUE	Robert M. Burtch	1988	176
360 1/8	46 3/8 48 4/8	53 0/8	14 11	Schefferville	QUE	Steven H. Byerly	1989	177
360 0/8	57 2/8 58 4/8	43 6/8	10 10	Fort Chimo	QUE	Linda Berkompas	1989	178
360 0/8	55 2/8 52 7/8	42 0/8	12 10	Lac Minto	QUE	Reginald Rouse	2005	178
359 7/8	50 4/8 51 2/8	47 0/8	15 17	George River	QUE	Cecil Tharp	1982	180
359 7/8	50 0/8 50 1/8	42 2/8	11 11	Ribero Lake	QUE	Rick Bolin	1986	180
359 7/8	51 3/8 52 2/8	42 1/8	13 14	Delay River	QUE	Edward G. Gilkes	1988	180
359 7/8	53 6/8 53 6/8	40 7/8	13 20	Ungava Bay	QUE	Greg Strait	1989	180
359 6/8	49 6/8 50 5/8	35 4/8	13 12	Schefferville	QUE	Steven P. Salmieri	1989	184
359 4/8	53 7/8 54 0/8	42 0/8	13 17	Weymouth Inlet	QUE	David C. Smart	1988	185
359 4/8	48 2/8 52 2/8	50 7/8	12 14	Pons River	QUE	Mark J. Hendrickson	1997	185
359 3/8	44 7/8 46 1/8	37 1/8	18 15	Fort Chimo	QUE	Roger Schwarz	1988	187
359 3/8	49 1/8 47 5/8	51 6/8	9 11	Lake Sammy	QUE	Chuck Adams	1989	187
359 1/8	54 4/8 55 6/8	49 6/8	10 11	Lake Mollett	QUE	John W. Ellas	2002	189
359 1/8	56 6/8 55 2/8	41 4/8	15 15	Larch River	QUE	Jeff D. Fraka	2006	189

241

QUEBEC-LABRADOR CARIBOU

Minimum Score 325 — Continued

SCORE	LENGTH OF R MAIN BEAM L	INSIDE SPREAD	NUMBER OF R POINTS L	AREA	STATE/PROVINCE	HUNTER'S NAME	DATE	RANK
359 0/8	47 4/8 51 3/8	42 4/8	9 10	Maricourt River	QUE	Evan Steinhorst	1990	191
*358 7/8	49 4/8 50 4/8	41 2/8	15 13	Lac Droilland	QUE	Larry E. Havard	2006	192
358 6/8	50 6/8 53 1/8	42 2/8	18 23	George River	QUE	Dale Selby	1980	193
358 5/8	54 3/8 53 3/8	41 2/8	16 15	Lac Minto	QUE	David Broyles	2006	194
358 4/8	47 7/8 48 1/8	39 6/8	13 15	Iron Arm Lake	LAB	Greg Mathy	1999	195
358 4/8	46 5/8 46 5/8	39 0/8	13 13	Lac Minto Island	QUE	Ben Allen Graham	2000	195
358 3/8	50 0/8 48 4/8	45 6/8	13 15	Lac AuClear	QUE	John Scranton	2003	197
358 2/8	41 5/8 42 1/8	34 7/8	15 18	Delay River	QUE	Ray Moulton	1986	198
358 1/8	52 1/8 50 4/8	48 0/8	14 17	Pons Island	QUE	Harold B. "Pat" Clark	1987	199
358 1/8	49 2/8 54 0/8	51 2/8	16 12	Jack's Lake	QUE	Raymond A. Luce	1989	199
358 0/8	52 4/8 52 0/8	41 7/8	15 17	Ungava Region	QUE	Carl G. Esterly	1983	201
358 0/8	45 2/8 44 4/8	43 6/8	14 16	Delay River	QUE	Joel Adam	1992	201
357 7/8	49 0/8 50 5/8	42 1/8	12 11	Caniapiscau River	QUE	Alexander C. Maven	1994	203
357 7/8	45 7/8 43 5/8	41 2/8	15 15	Lac Minto	QUE	Michael Turner	2000	203
357 6/8	44 1/8 43 2/8	36 1/8	13 15	Kuujjuaq	QUE	Matthew Green	2001	205
357 5/8	56 1/8 52 4/8	43 3/8	17 15	Delay River	QUE	Steve Beilgard	1989	206
357 4/8	47 3/8 49 2/8	41 5/8	17 13	Sand Lake	QUE	Dale E. Parish	2001	206
357 2/8	50 3/8 50 5/8	47 5/8	15 14	Pons Lake	QUE	George P. Mann	1994	208
357 0/8	48 2/8 50 4/8	42 2/8	17 13	Lake Narcy	QUE	Roy Hampton	1988	209
356 6/8	49 1/8 49 3/8	41 6/8	13 13	Fort Chimo	QUE	Chris W. Taylor	1989	210
356 5/8	50 2/8 52 1/8	47 2/8	9 8	River aux Feuilles	QUE	Fred Krueger	1998	211
356 5/8	51 0/8 53 6/8	36 4/8	10 13	Lac Kaliattuoluk	QUE	Ivan C. James II	2001	211
356 4/8	51 5/8 53 3/8	44 6/8	11 10	Ungava Bay	QUE	Larry Nirk	1983	213
356 4/8	46 0/8 47 5/8	42 0/8	17 20	Schefferville	QUE	William A.S. Heuer, Jr.	1987	213
356 4/8	54 2/8 53 2/8	38 6/8	9 12	Fort Chimo	QUE	Roy Javenkowski	1989	213
356 4/8	48 7/8 46 1/8	50 2/8	15 13	Jack's Lake	QUE	William F. Jackson	1989	213
356 2/8	47 7/8 47 3/8	43 0/8	15 17	George River	QUE	Joseph Chapdelaine	1999	217
356 1/8	47 3/8 47 2/8	45 0/8	16 12	Lake Cambrian	QUE	Clyde Doolittle	1988	218
356 1/8	56 0/8 55 3/8	52 2/8	6 11	George River	QUE	Royce DeCook	2002	218
*356 1/8	58 2/8 58 3/8	40 5/8	11 10	Clearwater Lake	QUE	Colby Moellerberndt	2006	218
356 0/8	55 4/8 56 4/8	49 4/8	17 23	Schefferville	QUE	Gregory G. Justus	1980	221
356 0/8	54 3/8 54 0/8	45 6/8	10 8	Schefferville	QUE	Dr. Nicholas J. Gray	1981	221
355 5/8	55 6/8 58 0/8	50 4/8	10 14	George River	QUE	Charles E. Spreeman	1985	223
355 5/8	44 7/8 47 4/8	41 0/8	15 13	Delay River	QUE	Robert Hoague	1993	223
355 4/8	47 0/8 47 2/8	36 3/8	17 18	Sixteen Island Lake	QUE	W. Bruce Nicolls	1987	225
355 4/8	50 4/8 52 3/8	40 3/8	20 16	Ungava Bay	QUE	Marc Augustin	1992	225
355 4/8	45 3/8 47 5/8	37 6/8	17 16	Pixie Lake	QUE	Richard L. Warren	1999	225
355 2/8	46 0/8 48 3/8	41 2/8	15 13	Schefferville	QUE	Robert Migliore	2004	228
355 1/8	55 7/8 56 0/8	48 0/8	10 13	Tunulik River	QUE	Tom Paluso	1988	229
355 1/8	49 6/8 50 2/8	39 7/8	9 9	Schefferville	QUE	Jerry Keller	1991	229
355 0/8	58 3/8 54 1/8	35 4/8	9 10	Fort Chimo	QUE	Lewis Miller	1990	231
354 7/8	53 7/8 55 2/8	55 3/8	10 10	Bird Lake	QUE	Steve Draisey	1994	232
354 6/8	48 4/8 48 7/8	49 6/8	13 14	Schefferville	QUE	Tom Hlinka	1990	233
354 6/8	47 0/8 46 6/8	30 1/8	11 12	Lac Fremin	QUE	Richard G. Marshall	1995	233
354 5/8	56 2/8 55 7/8	40 2/8	13 13	Lac Minto	QUE	Charles Grubbs	1997	235
354 4/8	47 5/8 48 0/8	48 0/8	15 12	Lake Otelnuk	QUE	Steve Vanzile	1986	236
354 4/8	48 1/8 43 5/8	45 3/8	10 9	Doreen Lake	QUE	Eugene Arndt	1990	236
354 4/8	43 2/8 44 1/8	30 4/8	12 12	Lake Mollett	QUE	Steven S. Bruggeman	2002	236
354 3/8	49 2/8 45 1/8	47 5/8	14 13	Lac Lefrancois	QUE	Larry Cannata	2005	239
354 2/8	50 2/8 50 1/8	41 5/8	9 10	Big Island	QUE	Fred C. Church	1985	240
354 1/8	59 2/8 61 5/8	51 4/8	13 7	Ungava Bay	QUE	Joe Prinzi	1985	241
354 1/8	44 3/8 45 2/8	40 1/8	10 12	Schefferville	QUE	Robert Pyne	1985	241
354 0/8	50 3/8 50 1/8	48 2/8	13 13	Lake Des Bergere	QUE	Ronald L. Musser	1988	243
*354 0/8	49 5/8 51 4/8	37 6/8	12 13	Clate Auguay	QUE	Clarence Richardson	2005	243
353 7/8	57 0/8 53 6/8	45 0/8	12 14	Fort Chimo	QUE	David Samuel	1991	245
353 6/8	46 3/8 46 1/8	38 6/8	15 13	George River	QUE	James Bailey	2003	246
353 4/8	52 7/8 51 2/8	39 6/8	14 12	Schefferville	QUE	Robert J. Lewis	1986	247
353 3/8	47 0/8 48 4/8	46 1/8	10 14	Lac Minto	QUE	David Broyles	2006	248
*353 3/8	52 2/8 53 6/8	41 5/8	12 12	Ruisseau Lies	QUE	Alan Harris	2006	248
353 2/8	61 5/8 58 2/8	47 5/8	12 10	Tunulik River	QUE	Jon Vanderhoef	1984	250
353 1/8	54 2/8 54 1/8	44 4/8	11 12	Lake Mollett	QUE	John W. Ellas	2002	251
353 1/8	47 1/8 47 3/8	39 2/8	14 11	Lac Minto	QUE	Dan Novotny	2006	251
353 0/8	50 4/8 49 2/8	46 2/8	13 9	Ungava Region	QUE	Casimir Leknius	1977	253
353 0/8	45 4/8 45 3/8	30 1/8	15 18	Lac Minto	QUE	Mike Britton	2001	253
352 7/8	50 2/8 50 2/8	45 5/8	11 10	LG 4	QUE	Fred Stempky	2004	255
352 6/8	44 2/8 48 0/8	38 5/8	16 15	Delay River	QUE	Val S. Schmaus, Jr.	1989	256
352 4/8	50 2/8 47 1/8	48 4/8	11 11	Bear Lake	QUE	Glenn Schrempf	1994	257
352 3/8	51 1/8 48 2/8	40 4/8	11 12	Caniapiscau River	QUE	Jimmy J. Meadows	1990	258
352 0/8	55 4/8 54 6/8	44 3/8	11 11	Ungava Bay	QUE	Tink Nathan	1984	259
352 0/8	48 1/8 47 7/8	41 7/8	12 12	Mistinibi Lake	QUE	John Anthony Jerome	1987	259
351 6/8	44 0/8 43 5/8	35 1/8	20 20	Schefferville	QUE	Steven P. Salmieri	1989	261
351 6/8	48 3/8 48 0/8	36 2/8	14 10	Barrel Lake	QUE	Thomas Egnew	1994	261
351 5/8	51 4/8 49 1/8	48 1/8	15 14	George River	QUE	Frank Charette	1982	263
351 5/8	50 3/8 51 0/8	41 1/8	11 12	Lake Loudin	QUE	Steven J. Lepic	1988	263
351 4/8	52 0/8 55 1/8	43 7/8	9 10	Lac Minto Island	QUE	James Carlson	1999	265
351 4/8	44 2/8 41 5/8	39 3/8	15 16	Ricky Lake	QUE	William A.S. Heuer, Jr.	1987	266
351 3/8	49 7/8 50 0/8	40 1/8	10 10	Lac Minto	QUE	Robert Harris	2007	266
351 2/8	48 5/8 48 3/8	42 2/8	10 10	Delay River	QUE	Fred J. Ward	1988	268
351 1/8	44 0/8 48 1/8	43 6/8	14 16	Lake Mollett	QUE	Thomas J. Pluhar	2001	269
351 1/8	58 2/8 57 4/8	41 6/8	11 9	Lac Minto	QUE	Tim Wolford	2001	269
351 0/8	53 2/8 52 7/8	36 6/8	20 15	Dihourse Lake	QUE	Kenneth W. Lohr	1982	271
351 0/8	48 0/8 51 2/8	48 0/8	12 12	Delay River	QUE	Robert Bain	1987	271
350 7/8	49 7/8 50 2/8	39 3/8	14 15	Leaf River	QUE	Bill Hensley	2001	273
350 7/8	47 7/8 50 2/8	51 0/8	13 12	Lac Minto	QUE	Mike Bauer	2002	273
350 6/8	55 5/8 56 2/8	45 3/8	14 12	Tunulik River	QUE	Henry F. Rauch	1982	275
350 6/8	38 3/8 38 2/8	31 7/8	12 13	Jack's Lake	QUE	Tony Odhner	1989	275
350 6/8	56 7/8 55 5/8	35 5/8	16 14	Schefferville	QUE	John W. Offord	1990	275
350 6/8	50 2/8 51 6/8	39 0/8	18 16	De Pas River	QUE	John Daughetry	1998	275
350 5/8	46 2/8 46 6/8	38 7/8	12 13	Schefferville	QUE	Greg Seymour	1986	279
350 5/8	43 6/8 46 6/8	44 6/8	14 12	Ungava Bay	QUE	Alan Niemeyer	1989	279
350 3/8	49 5/8 49 6/8	46 0/8	16 14	Desbergere	QUE	Lee Burnett	1989	281
350 3/8	51 1/8 50 5/8	42 3/8	12 11	Lake Mollett	QUE	Steven S. Bruggeman	2002	281
350 2/8	55 7/8 52 0/8	46 6/8	13 14	Weymouth Inlet	QUE	Tom Taylor	1991	283
350 1/8	42 6/8 42 2/8	43 4/8	14 13	Ungava Bay	QUE	Jeff Bogart	1999	284
350 1/8	51 3/8 54 3/8	36 7/8	10 11	Lac Minto	QUE	Matt Curry	2006	284

QUEBEC-LABRADOR CARIBOU

Minimum Score 325 — Continued

SCORE	LENGTH OF MAIN BEAM R	L	INSIDE SPREAD	NUMBER OF POINTS R	L	AREA	STATE/ PROVINCE	HUNTER'S NAME	DATE	RANK
349 7/8	43 5/8	41 5/8	34 3/8	13	14	Kenny Lake	QUE	Ross Trujillo, Jr.	1991	286
349 6/8	47 0/8	44 1/8	37 4/8	20	15	George River	QUE	Charlie Kroll	1980	287
349 6/8	45 7/8	49 5/8	44 7/8	16	15	Ungava Peninsula	QUE	Bill VyVyan	1988	287
349 6/8	51 1/8	51 5/8	48 5/8	10	11	Lac Minto	QUE	Jack L. "Jackson" Ward	1997	287
349 6/8	53 0/8	52 7/8	46 5/8	10	10	George River	QUE	John Guillen	2004	287
349 4/8	51 0/8	51 3/8	37 0/8	12	13	Caniapiscau River	QUE	Henry O. Fromm	1987	291
349 4/8	46 5/8	46 2/8	43 2/8	17	13	Harold Lake	QUE	Don Davidson	1990	291
349 4/8	51 3/8	50 3/8	48 4/8	11	9	Delay River	QUE	Bob Mussey	1990	291
349 4/8	49 1/8	43 6/8	42 6/8	16	12	Ungava Bay	QUE	Steve Bruggeman	1990	291
349 3/8	48 6/8	52 4/8	44 0/8	8	11	Delay River	QUE	Roger Gipple	1988	295
349 3/8	49 2/8	53 2/8	45 6/8	17	16	Harold Lake	QUE	Craig Ambos	1992	295
349 2/8	49 5/8	49 0/8	37 5/8	10	11	Fort Chimo	QUE	James E. Doberstein	1989	297
349 1/8	50 5/8	51 0/8	42 4/8	13	13	River aux Melezes	QUE	Michael Minnick	2001	298
349 0/8	49 3/8	49 1/8	35 7/8	12	9	Tunulik River	QUE	Ty Martin	1986	299
349 0/8	46 7/8	45 6/8	45 4/8	10	13	Pons River	QUE	Wayne A. Lamoreux	1991	299
349 0/8	51 4/8	51 5/8	35 6/8	10	10	Drummondville	QUE	Jim Gabrick	1994	299
348 7/8	46 6/8	49 4/8	31 4/8	17	20	Mulay River	QUE	Don Keady	1987	302
348 7/8	50 2/8	52 1/8	39 2/8	12	14	Boland Lake	QUE	Robert J. Pastor	1995	302
348 6/8	48 1/8	51 6/8	40 7/8	10	12	Clearwater Lake	QUE	Walter J. Palmer	2007	304
348 5/8	52 0/8	51 7/8	45 0/8	9	10	Lac Coulounge	QUE	John W. Borlang	1987	305
348 5/8	49 6/8	52 2/8	48 3/8	11	14	LG 4	QUE	Donald W. Hoffman	1991	305
*348 5/8	47 3/8	47 4/8	43 3/8	14	13	Lac Minto	QUE	Randall L. Head	2006	305
348 3/8	53 0/8	49 7/8	40 4/8	11	14	Jack's Lake	QUE	William F. Jackson	1989	308
348 3/8	41 6/8	44 5/8	46 1/8	12	16	Kuujjuaq	QUE	Al Potter	1996	308
348 3/8	51 1/8	52 7/8	44 3/8	9	12	Lac Minto	QUE	Brad Simpson	2008	308
348 2/8	53 6/8	52 4/8	42 4/8	11	11	Little Whale River	QUE	Tricia Eichler	2000	311
348 2/8	37 0/8	33 7/8	35 7/8	17	16	Clearwater Lake	QUE	Frank Frost	2006	311
348 1/8	52 4/8	55 3/8	28 7/8	18	14	George River	QUE	Bob Goodall	1980	313
348 1/8	49 0/8	50 2/8	44 2/8	14	9	George River	QUE	Phillip J. Taylor	1984	313
348 0/8	47 5/8	49 0/8	38 1/8	14	17	Caniapiscau River	QUE	Rodney Fitzgerald	2000	315
347 7/8	53 1/8	54 1/8	49 6/8	15	14	Wayne Lake	QUE	Jay J. Kaster	1988	316
347 7/8	45 5/8	49 3/8	42 0/8	13	13	Radisson	QUE	Ken Wiersma	1999	316
347 5/8	52 3/8	52 2/8	49 0/8	12	12	Ungava Region	QUE	Charles R. Leidheiser	1977	318
347 5/8	44 6/8	45 3/8	41 7/8	13	12	Kenny Lake	QUE	Matt Lamoreux	1991	318
347 5/8	37 5/8	38 4/8	35 3/8	17	16	Caniapiscau River	QUE	James D. Bradley	2001	318
347 4/8	44 3/8	45 7/8	39 3/8	13	11	Delay River	QUE	Candace H. Roberts	1993	321
347 4/8	55 5/8	56 5/8	47 0/8	13	17	George River	QUE	Mark D. Thomson	1993	321
347 1/8	51 4/8	53 6/8	47 1/8	11	11	Schefferville	QUE	Ronnie Everett	1986	323
346 7/8	54 4/8	58 4/8	41 0/8	10	11	Akuliak	QUE	Lauri Johnson	1985	324
346 6/8	48 2/8	47 2/8	49 2/8	9	12	Delay River	QUE	Gregory J. Fries	1987	325
346 6/8	55 1/8	56 4/8	43 7/8	13	11	Delay River	QUE	Robert Pastor	1988	325
346 6/8	46 7/8	47 5/8	41 5/8	12	10	Jack's Lake	QUE	Curt Christensen	1989	325
346 6/8	41 4/8	43 3/8	40 6/8	18	17	Delay River	QUE	Michael L. Ritter	1994	325
346 6/8	50 2/8	47 5/8	43 4/8	14	10	Deception Bay	QUE	Tulsa Green	1998	325
346 6/8	46 6/8	48 6/8	46 5/8	15	15	Ungava Bay	QUE	Larry Comer	1999	325
346 3/8	47 5/8	47 3/8	40 6/8	11	10	Maricourt Lake	QUE	Jerry W. Huffaker	1990	331
346 2/8	50 5/8	49 1/8	44 3/8	11	13	Ungava Bay	QUE	Lou Kindred	1986	332
346 2/8	46 3/8	43 5/8	38 6/8	14	14	Lake Otelnuk	QUE	Eddie Cooper	1988	332
346 1/8	55 0/8	55 0/8	37 3/8	12	17	River Lac Cambrien	QUE	Kent W. Brigham	1987	334
346 1/8	41 0/8	42 5/8	39 5/8	17	15	Schefferville	QUE	Edward Faucher	1990	334
346 1/8	42 4/8	46 2/8	40 4/8	13	13	LG 4	QUE	Mark D. Mishinski	1991	334
346 1/8	45 2/8	49 0/8	50 4/8	7	8	Lake Ikirtuuq	QUE	Dallas Smith	1996	334
346 0/8	48 6/8	50 6/8	45 7/8	13	14	George River	QUE	William E. Bullock	1982	338
346 0/8	51 6/8	52 4/8	43 2/8	12	10	Delay River	QUE	Dennis N. Ballweg	1988	338
346 0/8	47 3/8	48 0/8	43 6/8	13	9	Camp Victoria	QUE	John D. "Jack" Frost	2006	338
345 7/8	52 6/8	54 1/8	45 2/8	11	13	Ungava Bay	QUE	John Musacchia	1978	341
345 7/8	52 3/8	51 7/8	44 2/8	13	17	Schefferville	QUE	Barry J. Smith	1988	341
345 7/8	52 2/8	52 3/8	57 2/8	12	12	Lake Mollett	QUE	Raymond L. Howell, Sr.	1999	341
345 7/8	44 6/8	43 4/8	36 0/8	17	17	Caniapiscau Lake	QUE	Walter E. Dixon	2005	341
345 6/8	49 6/8	43 6/8	48 0/8	12	17	Lake Ikirtuuq	QUE	Nicholas Barone, Jr.	1992	345
345 6/8	52 0/8	50 2/8	33 4/8	17	14	Delay River	QUE	William Elfland	1994	345
345 6/8	49 6/8	50 3/8	43 3/8	10	10	Ungava Bay	QUE	Bruce H. Sabaini	1996	345
345 6/8	43 5/8	45 5/8	36 5/8	13	13	Lac Minto	QUE	David M. Chauvet	1998	345
345 5/8	48 5/8	48 4/8	35 4/8	15	18	Marylin Lake	QUE	Neil Summers	2003	349
345 4/8	48 0/8	47 1/8	37 4/8	15	13	Lac Minto	QUE	Henry Bishop	1997	350
345 4/8	42 2/8	44 7/8	48 6/8	12	13	Leaf River	QUE	Robert E. Quillen	2002	350
345 4/8	40 5/8	42 3/8	42 3/8	15	14	Lac Minto	QUE	S. Ray White	2006	350
345 3/8	51 4/8	53 5/8	36 1/8	14	11	Maricourt River	QUE	Michael J. Churchill	1990	353
345 3/8	53 0/8	50 2/8	40 3/8	11	11	LG 4	QUE	Todd Fugate	1993	353
345 2/8	47 2/8	48 7/8	41 5/8	11	18	Fort Chimo	QUE	Bob Jensen	1982	355
345 2/8	43 2/8	48 0/8	48 0/8	10	12	Delay River	QUE	William "Ted" Bennett	1988	355
345 1/8	56 5/8	52 5/8	42 3/8	11	10	Ungava Bay	QUE	Richard Gamache	1988	357
345 1/8	50 3/8	53 1/8	41 4/8	16	14	Delay River	QUE	Steve Waible	1994	357
344 7/8	45 0/8	48 7/8	37 7/8	16	14	Mulay River	QUE	Don Keady	1987	359
344 6/8	51 0/8	50 5/8	38 6/8	10	11	Schefferville	QUE	Gregg Tanner	1985	360
344 6/8	53 6/8	55 3/8	41 5/8	15	18	16 Islands	QUE	Chris McDonnell	1990	360
344 5/8	46 5/8	46 1/8	41 4/8	12	12	Lac Minto	QUE	Joe P. Furlong	2001	362
344 4/8	45 6/8	46 7/8	45 0/8	12	10	Ungava Bay	QUE	David Baldwin	1986	363
344 4/8	44 4/8	47 6/8	41 4/8	14	12	Ungava Bay	QUE	James Norvell	1989	363
344 4/8	50 3/8	48 1/8	40 3/8	14	15	Lac Minto	QUE	Greg Bonecutter, Sr.	2003	363
344 2/8	43 2/8	43 0/8	43 2/8	13	13	Melezes River	QUE	G. Fred Asbell	1990	366
343 7/8	54 2/8	51 1/8	39 3/8	13	13	Lake Nullualuk	QUE	Clifford White	1992	367
343 7/8	44 1/8	46 3/8	34 3/8	13	13	Delay River	QUE	Michael L. Ritter	1993	367
343 6/8	48 0/8	48 0/8	38 4/8	11	14	Akuliak	QUE	Barry Dyar	1985	369
343 6/8	52 2/8	51 1/8	48 3/8	12	12	Schefferville	QUE	Gregory V. Pilot	1992	369
343 6/8	43 6/8	44 6/8	48 7/8	11	9	Caniapiscau River	QUE	Gary Weckwerth	1994	369
343 6/8	52 3/8	49 3/8	46 6/8	10	10	Kakiattukallak Lake	QUE	Daniel A. Scott	2005	369
343 3/8	48 0/8	47 0/8	44 7/8	14	12	George River	QUE	Leonard L. Kohan	1981	373
343 3/8	49 2/8	50 1/8	43 5/8	9	10	Ungava Bay	QUE	L. Dan Neebe	1988	373
343 3/8	47 0/8	45 5/8	40 5/8	8	11	Pons River	QUE	Martin R. Walls	1993	373
*343 3/8	45 5/8	46 0/8	43 0/8	11	15	Feuilles River	QUE	Gary J. Socola	2005	373
343 2/8	47 0/8	43 7/8	36 1/8	17	17	Delay River	QUE	Eric A. Voss	1993	377
343 2/8	45 0/8	46 1/8	43 3/8	13	13	Fort Chimo	QUE	Chuck Adams	1996	377
343 1/8	51 3/8	48 5/8	48 4/8	13	18	Kuujjuak River	QUE	Arthur J. Pelon	1985	379
343 1/8	51 3/8	50 0/8	54 2/8	15	14	Lake Mollett	QUE	Ken Stieh	2001	379

243

QUEBEC-LABRADOR CARIBOU

Minimum Score 325   Continued

SCORE	LENGTH OF R MAIN BEAM L	INSIDE SPREAD	NUMBER OF R POINTS L	AREA	STATE/ PROVINCE	HUNTER'S NAME	DATE	RANK
343 0/8	43 7/8 44 1/8	29 7/8	12 16	Lake Gomez	QUE	Jack D. Fields II	2006	381
342 7/8	53 4/8 52 6/8	39 5/8	14 14	George River	QUE	Frank Hogan	1980	382
342 7/8	54 4/8 54 2/8	41 4/8	11 10	Lac Minto Island	QUE	Greg Bonecutter, Sr.	1997	382
342 7/8	48 5/8 48 6/8	42 1/8	16 13	Deception Bay	QUE	Al Ferris	1997	382
342 6/8	43 3/8 47 1/8	40 7/8	17 17	Kuujjuak River	QUE	Steven Sendek	1985	385
342 5/8	47 4/8 50 3/8	46 1/8	15 10	Tuktu Camp	QUE	Martin G. Billeri	1977	386
342 5/8	50 5/8 51 0/8	46 4/8	14 14	LG 4	QUE	Gregory A. Bonecutter, Sr.	1991	386
342 4/8	43 1/8 45 4/8	44 0/8	11 13	Delay River	QUE	William Bos	1990	388
342 2/8	47 5/8 50 3/8	42 0/8	13 10	Ungava Bay	QUE	Rayot A. DiFate	1988	389
342 1/8	48 4/8 51 2/8	34 6/8	9 11	Lac Minto	QUE	Kirk Munger	1998	390
342 1/8	47 7/8 51 0/8	38 6/8	13 14	Wyske Lake	QUE	Bill Kotarski	2000	390
342 1/8	51 4/8 50 4/8	38 5/8	13 14	Lac Minto	QUE	Phil Potvin	2006	390
342 0/8	47 4/8 46 1/8	31 0/8	8 8	LG 4	QUE	Fred Stempky	2004	393
*342 0/8	53 6/8 54 6/8	45 6/8	14 12	Lac Minto	QUE	Robert Baker	2007	393
341 7/8	48 0/8 49 1/8	37 1/8	14 15	Lac Minto	QUE	John Koschmeder	1997	395
341 7/8	44 1/8 45 2/8	40 0/8	17 14	Lac Minto	QUE	Mark E. Havemann	2006	395
*341 7/8	47 7/8 48 5/8	44 2/8	10 10	Polaris River	QUE	Justin Brown	2007	395
341 6/8	47 4/8 47 5/8	44 1/8	10 13	Ungava Bay	QUE	Steve Crooks	1988	398
341 6/8	46 1/8 45 0/8	52 0/8	12 18	Delay River	QUE	Jim E. Roe	1988	398
341 6/8	52 4/8 52 1/8	56 7/8	9 9	Kuujjuaq	QUE	Dyrk Eddie	1999	398
341 6/8	53 6/8 55 5/8	52 4/8	11 11	Deception Bay	QUE	Viron Barbay	1999	398
341 5/8	53 7/8 53 5/8	41 6/8	7 11	Barrel Lake	QUE	John Hale	1994	402
341 5/8	48 2/8 46 5/8	35 2/8	13 14	Lac Minto	QUE	James H. Radford	2001	402
341 5/8	48 0/8 46 2/8	43 4/8	14 13	Lac Minto	QUE	Reginald Rouse	2005	402
341 4/8	43 1/8 44 4/8	38 0/8	14 15	Lake Tassey	QUE	C. Michael Betts	1999	405
341 4/8	45 2/8 45 7/8	35 7/8	10 11	Muttet Lake	QUE	David S. Hodnett	1999	405
341 3/8	48 5/8 48 2/8	47 4/8	14 15	George River	QUE	William B. Bullock, Jr.	1982	407
341 2/8	50 4/8 49 6/8	50 2/8	15 12	Pons River	QUE	Walter F. Dotson, Jr.	1987	408
341 2/8	49 3/8 44 6/8	48 6/8	13 11	Schefferville	QUE	Robert J. Lewis	1987	408
341 2/8	43 4/8 43 5/8	32 4/8	16 16	Caniapiscau River	QUE	Mike Klaeser	1994	408
341 1/8	49 4/8 46 3/8	39 0/8	12 14	Whiskey Lake	QUE	Matthew J. Niehaus	2001	411
341 1/8	49 5/8 47 5/8	42 1/8	15 13	Lac Minto	QUE	Matt Curry	2006	411
341 0/8	51 3/8 45 7/8	44 4/8	14 12	Ungava Region	QUE	Glenn Reno	1980	413
341 0/8	45 0/8 43 5/8	35 0/8	14 16	May Lake	QUE	Larry N. Peterson	1990	413
340 7/8	49 7/8 50 0/8	45 5/8	16 12	Lac Minto Island	QUE	Clark M. Vickers	1999	415
340 7/8	47 5/8 47 5/8	35 7/8	17 15	Lac Kakiattuoluk	QUE	Larry Newton	2001	415
*340 7/8	50 2/8 50 3/8	38 0/8	12 13	Nastapoka Lake	QUE	Brian D. Campbell	2006	415
340 6/8	46 3/8 47 4/8	35 1/8	12 10	Lac Minto	QUE	Aaron "Slim" Hamersma	2005	418
340 5/8	54 7/8 57 7/8	51 0/8	14 13	Tunulik River	QUE	Jean-Claude Duff	1985	419
340 5/8	46 4/8 46 1/8	34 0/8	17 14	Schefferville	QUE	Pat Vincenti	1990	419
340 4/8	50 5/8 49 7/8	36 6/8	14 13	Lac D'Iberville	QUE	Stephen M. Kenworthy	1997	421
340 3/8	39 2/8 48 7/8	31 5/8	18 15	George River	QUE	Craig Richardson	1982	422
340 3/8	45 7/8 47 2/8	41 0/8	12 12	Lac Minto	QUE	Jeffrey G. Starcher	1997	422
340 2/8	41 6/8 44 6/8	46 7/8	16 12	Shirley Lake	QUE	Duane Zemliska	1990	424
340 2/8	53 4/8 52 2/8	43 6/8	12 12	Lake Mollett	QUE	Raymond L. Howell, Sr.	1999	424
340 1/8	46 4/8 47 3/8	37 7/8	17 13	LG 4	QUE	Fred Johnston III	1991	426
340 1/8	43 7/8 41 7/8	37 0/8	17 14	Lac Minto	QUE	John Taylor Barnard II	2006	426
340 0/8	46 7/8 50 0/8	40 3/8	10 11	Lac Minto	QUE	Mark E. Havemann	2006	428
339 7/8	49 1/8 49 0/8	44 1/8	17 15	Weymouth Inlet	QUE	Chuck Adams	1991	429
339 7/8	47 4/8 47 4/8	37 7/8	13 11	Lac Minto	QUE	Kenneth Wade Anderson	1997	429
339 6/8	45 4/8 47 3/8	43 3/8	15 13	Ungava Bay	QUE	Dean M. Westby	1986	431
339 6/8	50 3/8 49 5/8	42 5/8	12 12	Ungava Peninsula	QUE	Bill Vyvyan	1988	431
339 6/8	42 2/8 41 5/8	51 1/8	13 13	Delay River	QUE	Robert Hermann	1989	431
339 6/8	48 1/8 48 3/8	46 0/8	11 11	Martha Lake	QUE	Mark Zastrow	1992	431
*339 6/8	46 4/8 47 2/8	41 6/8	15 16	Riviera de la Mort	QUE	Randy Petersburg	2004	431
339 4/8	47 7/8 48 2/8	44 6/8	13 15	Audiepure Lake	QUE	Stan Godfrey	1983	436
339 3/8	46 0/8 46 1/8	44 2/8	14 16	Tunulik River	QUE	David Quong	1992	437
339 3/8	45 5/8 45 7/8	45 6/8	11 13	Lac Minto	QUE	David M. Chauvet/Jeff Scott	1998	437
339 1/8	41 0/8 45 0/8	33 1/8	10 16	Lake Gordon	QUE	Lee Jernigan	1995	439
339 0/8	56 4/8 55 0/8	45 5/8	12 11	Tuktu Camp	QUE	John C. Mitchell	1984	440
339 0/8	47 6/8 47 6/8	51 3/8	12 10	Long Lake	QUE	Mark Gerhard	1990	440
338 7/8	47 2/8 46 4/8	36 3/8	13 14	Kuujjuaq	QUE	Stephen Teague	2008	442
338 6/8	55 4/8 55 0/8	36 2/8	13 12	Maricourt River	QUE	Ronald S. Pulcine	1989	443
338 6/8	48 7/8 51 0/8	37 4/8	9 8	Ungava Bay	QUE	Michael R. Knight	1991	443
338 5/8	46 3/8 48 2/8	47 1/8	10 12	Kuujjuaq	QUE	Stephen M. Gillis	2001	445
338 5/8	41 1/8 48 0/8	38 3/8	13 12	Riviere Serigny	QUE	William Snodgrass	2002	445
338 5/8	44 2/8 48 0/8	39 2/8	12 13	George River	QUE	Leslie Potts	2003	445
338 4/8	54 4/8 56 3/8	36 4/8	15 12	Potier River	QUE	Lawrence R. Gibbons	1990	448
338 4/8	45 6/8 47 1/8	39 6/8	16 15	Lac Minto	QUE	Gerald Greenleaf	2002	448
338 3/8	47 1/8 46 1/8	38 0/8	19 20	George River	QUE	Len Cardinale	1971	450
338 3/8	54 0/8 53 3/8	32 0/8	13 16	Schefferville	QUE	Kenneth C. Kaufmann	1987	450
338 3/8	51 2/8 53 4/8	41 1/8	11 15	Leaf River	QUE	Randy Liljenquist	2003	450
338 2/8	44 2/8 42 5/8	39 2/8	18 22	Lac Fremin	QUE	Edwin W. Hoffacker	1995	453
338 1/8	48 0/8 47 4/8	40 6/8	17 13	Ungava Bay	QUE	Alan Niemeyer	1989	454
338 1/8	42 4/8 42 6/8	43 3/8	12 15	Leaf River	QUE	Denny Campbell	1997	454
338 1/8	49 4/8 51 0/8	30 3/8	12 12	Serigny River	QUE	Steve Lamp	1999	454
338 0/8	40 3/8 45 0/8	34 7/8	15 16	Echo Lake	QUE	Matthew J. Luxem	1989	457
338 0/8	46 7/8 44 1/8	31 4/8	11 12	LG 4	QUE	Bryant Shermoe	1995	457
338 0/8	46 4/8 46 4/8	44 0/8	16 13	Lac Coursolles	QUE	Ed Hendricks	2005	457
338 0/8	42 0/8 43 1/8	41 1/8	14 14	Guenyveau Lake	QUE	Ben B. Wallace	2007	457
337 7/8	48 3/8 47 2/8	45 5/8	14 12	De Pas & George River	QUE	Fred F. Potts	1974	461
337 7/8	44 0/8 45 3/8	42 3/8	13 11	Schefferville	QUE	Dale Drilling	1987	461
337 7/8	52 3/8 53 1/8	41 6/8	13 14	Whiskey Lake	QUE	Thomas Ippolito	1987	461
337 7/8	51 1/8 52 4/8	43 6/8	10 9	Lac Minto	QUE	John Lincoln	2001	461
337 7/8	45 2/8 43 5/8	37 5/8	11 11	Lac Omalac	QUE	E. Fred Richter, Jr.	2005	461
337 6/8	52 0/8 51 7/8	45 4/8	9 10	Tunulik River	QUE	Jay E. Johnson	1985	466
337 6/8	51 0/8 51 5/8	48 4/8	8 9	Pons River	QUE	Bradford Higson	1986	466
337 5/8	47 4/8 46 2/8	36 1/8	15 10	Lac Minto	QUE	William Gaunt	2005	468
337 4/8	46 4/8 46 5/8	45 1/8	15 12	Wayne Lake	QUE	Randall L. Schoenly	1987	469
337 3/8	54 7/8 55 7/8	38 4/8	16 16	Whale River	QUE	Michael J. Vanden Heuvel, Sr.	2000	470
337 0/8	52 5/8 52 2/8	39 7/8	13 12	Jack's Lake	QUE	Greg Odhner	1989	471
337 0/8	49 6/8 50 2/8	45 5/8	12 14	Melezes River	QUE	Donald L. Clark	1993	471
336 7/8	45 5/8 45 2/8	42 5/8	16 15	Lake Nastapoka	QUE	Gerry R. Long, Jr.	2002	473
336 7/8	43 0/8 46 1/8	50 5/8	12 10	Kuujjuaq	QUE	Phillip C. Dalrymple	2005	473
336 6/8	48 2/8 46 5/8	34 7/8	17 16	Delay River	QUE	W.R. "Tony" Dukes	1987	475

244

QUEBEC-LABRADOR CARIBOU

Minimum Score 325   Continued

SCORE	LENGTH OF R MAIN BEAM L	INSIDE SPREAD	NUMBER OF R POINTS L	AREA	STATE/ PROVINCE	HUNTER'S NAME	DATE	RANK
336 6/8	48 0/8 47 3/8	38 5/8	10 9	George River	QUE	Pat Reilly	1993	475
336 6/8	45 4/8 44 7/8	44 5/8	12 11	Lac Minto	QUE	J. Ken Martin	1995	475
336 6/8	48 0/8 47 7/8	37 4/8	11 10	Caniapiscau River	QUE	Scott B. Longe	2003	475
336 4/8	53 4/8 52 2/8	41 0/8	10 10	George River	QUE	David Tofte	1982	479
336 4/8	51 3/8 52 4/8	38 6/8	10 10	Schefferville	QUE	William L. Hall	1994	479
336 1/8	53 0/8 52 0/8	51 0/8	15 19	Twin Lake	QUE	Jon P. Thomas	1982	481
336 0/8	42 3/8 41 7/8	45 3/8	13 13	Lake Leopard	QUE	Robert B. Seger II	1989	482
336 0/8	47 3/8 47 4/8	48 4/8	13 14	Lac Minto	QUE	John Kurkowski	1999	482
336 0/8	45 0/8 48 0/8	36 2/8	11 10	Lac Minto	QUE	Richie Bland	2000	482
335 6/8	44 4/8 44 4/8	37 0/8	15 16	Lake Helluva	QUE	Larry E. Flowers	1999	485
335 5/8	51 7/8 52 1/8	41 3/8	10 12	Tunulik River	QUE	DeeAnn Robinson	1992	486
335 5/8	47 3/8 46 4/8	43 6/8	14 14	Lac Boismenu	QUE	Ken H. Taylor	2007	486
335 4/8	48 1/8 50 0/8	40 2/8	10 14	Pons River	QUE	Thomas Hopkins	1987	488
335 4/8	50 4/8 45 6/8	44 5/8	11 10	Ungava Bay	QUE	Poncho McCoy	1999	488
335 3/8	49 1/8 46 2/8	49 1/8	16 17	Ungava Peninsula	QUE	Tony Snow	1988	490
335 3/8	50 3/8 53 0/8	39 7/8	12 12	Caniapiscau River	QUE	Robert H. Van Alstyne	1992	490
335 3/8	53 4/8 53 1/8	39 0/8	14 13	Delay River	QUE	Ryk Visscher	1995	490
335 3/8	44 0/8 45 2/8	47 0/8	13 10	Lac Minto	QUE	Art Fink	2006	490
*335 3/8	48 1/8 44 6/8	38 6/8	13 11	Gordon Lake	QUE	Daniel M. Stucky	2007	490
335 2/8	44 0/8 45 6/8	47 7/8	19 12	Lake Otelnuk	QUE	John L. Wagner	1989	495
335 0/8	51 2/8 50 2/8	42 4/8	9 12	Tunulik River	QUE	Robert A. Shank	1988	496
334 7/8	44 5/8 44 0/8	40 0/8	14 18	Pons River	QUE	Joe Hoffman	1991	497
334 7/8	53 4/8 51 3/8	47 5/8	14 11	Lac Minto	QUE	Dale Arner	2001	497
334 6/8	49 5/8 47 7/8	41 4/8	13 14	Shirley Lake	QUE	Jerry E. Burt	1990	499
334 4/8	53 4/8 50 6/8	49 0/8	14 9	Lac Minto	QUE	John R. Rolison	2007	500
334 2/8	48 7/8 46 7/8	34 3/8	13 14	Dugue River	QUE	Lee A. Heath	1990	501
334 2/8	43 6/8 44 6/8	43 4/8	14 14	Ungava Bay	QUE	David Gillette	1992	501
334 2/8	42 4/8 43 4/8	47 0/8	16 11	Lac Minto Island	QUE	Clark M. Vickers	1999	501
334 2/8	48 2/8 47 2/8	44 4/8	12 14	Lac Minto	QUE	Terry Joe Day	1999	501
334 1/8	40 5/8 43 3/8	38 4/8	17 13	Serigny River	QUE	Howard T. Isenberg, Jr.	1990	505
334 1/8	47 5/8 47 6/8	38 0/8	17 13	Lake Anonyme	QUE	Dennis Hayden	1992	505
334 1/8	50 6/8 49 5/8	51 0/8	10 15	Lac Minto	QUE	James H. Radford	2001	505
334 1/8	48 6/8 49 4/8	39 7/8	16 14	Lac Minto	QUE	Ken Sloetjes	2006	505
334 0/8	51 0/8 49 0/8	47 7/8	16 16	Lac Minto	QUE	Kenyon W. Woods	2001	509
333 7/8	44 0/8 41 7/8	47 2/8	13 12	Lake Gerido	QUE	Larry C. Reese	1996	510
333 6/8	47 1/8 45 4/8	43 6/8	10 11	Delay River	QUE	Steven Pfaff	1994	511
333 5/8	53 4/8 52 7/8	41 6/8	12 13	Tunulik River	QUE	Gregory G. Kilby	1985	512
333 5/8	43 2/8 45 0/8	48 6/8	8 8	Boland Lake	QUE	Rick L. Morley	1996	512
333 4/8	51 3/8 53 0/8	45 1/8	7 7	Delay River	QUE	Robert H. Pavlovic	1988	514
333 3/8	45 3/8 48 2/8	45 3/8	12 13	Lake Loudin	QUE	Jim Gompf	1990	515
333 2/8	55 4/8 52 6/8	47 5/8	13 15	Schefferville	QUE	Al Reay	1978	516
333 2/8	51 6/8 53 0/8	46 1/8	11 10	Whiskey Lake	QUE	Glenn R. Kuklick	1986	516
333 2/8	45 6/8 44 6/8	37 4/8	13 15	Lac Minto	QUE	Jamie Jones	2007	516
333 1/8	51 3/8 52 5/8	49 7/8	5 8	Schefferville	QUE	Robert James Lewis	1987	519
333 0/8	48 3/8 48 1/8	38 7/8	10 13	Lake Maricourt	QUE	Dale L. Hughes	1990	520
332 7/8	47 6/8 48 4/8	48 6/8	11 8	Schefferville	QUE	Darwin L. Damp	1988	521
332 6/8	49 1/8 46 2/8	40 4/8	10 12	Agnew Lake	QUE	James P Loughran	1989	522
332 6/8	48 6/8 53 5/8	34 7/8	14 14	George River	QUE	George H. Bock	2005	522
332 5/8	45 1/8 45 4/8	46 7/8	16 14	Lac Minto	QUE	Terry Heckert	1997	524
332 4/8	51 6/8 51 1/8	36 3/8	10 11	Tunulik River	QUE	Glenn St. Charles	1984	525
332 4/8	46 0/8 44 5/8	36 3/8	14 13	Lake Mollett	QUE	William E. Lee, Jr.	2002	525
332 3/8	56 2/8 51 2/8	39 6/8	9 12	Kuujjuak River	QUE	Mark Thompson	1987	527
332 3/8	48 3/8 48 4/8	43 4/8	12 12	Riviere aux Melezes	QUE	David R. Rogers	1987	527
332 3/8	45 1/8 41 6/8	38 4/8	16 16	Lac de Grasse	QUE	Dwaine S. Starr	1994	527
332 3/8	47 1/8 46 7/8	34 7/8	13 11	Lac Kakkakia	QUE	Eugene R. Thorn	2001	527
332 3/8	48 2/8 48 3/8	45 4/8	12 12	Lake Mollett	QUE	John North	2001	527
332 2/8	46 1/8 45 4/8	39 6/8	12 16	Tunulik River	QUE	Gail Martin	1982	532
332 2/8	46 6/8 46 6/8	40 6/8	14 11	LG 4	QUE	Gregory Dodson	1993	532
332 2/8	46 7/8 46 4/8	43 0/8	11 14	Lac Minto	QUE	Millard Glen Starcher	1997	532
332 1/8	47 7/8 45 6/8	26 5/8	8 10	Lake Martine	QUE	Glenn A. Wotring	2005	535
332 0/8	53 4/8 48 5/8	52 2/8	8 10	Ungava Bay	QUE	Richard J. Chobot, Jr.	1986	536
332 0/8	50 4/8 50 2/8	43 2/8	12 11	Weymouth Inlet	QUE	Kenneth M. Beno	1988	536
331 7/8	46 0/8 42 6/8	43 7/8	14 12	Fort Chimo	QUE	Harold Halverson	1991	538
331 7/8	46 0/8 45 0/8	48 5/8	13 14	Deception Bay	QUE	Marvin Stried	2000	538
331 6/8	52 0/8 52 6/8	45 4/8	15 14	Schefferville	QUE	Thomas E. Smith	1981	540
331 6/8	46 7/8 47 3/8	38 0/8	14 13	Cedar Lake	QUE	Anders J. Meyer	1989	540
331 6/8	47 3/8 47 1/8	43 0/8	11 11	Ungava Bay	QUE	Gary D. Bills	2000	540
331 6/8	47 5/8 49 1/8	44 2/8	9 12	Leaf River	QUE	Tim Otis	2000	540
331 5/8	55 5/8 55 4/8	39 1/8	14 9	Pons River	QUE	Robert Amaral	1986	544
331 5/8	46 1/8 48 2/8	45 3/8	10 11	Lake Ikirtuuq	QUE	Thomas Devlin	1999	544
331 5/8	47 7/8 46 2/8	38 4/8	10 10	George River	QUE	Dean Aggson	2003	544
331 3/8	47 0/8 47 1/8	47 1/8	9 9	Whiskey Lake	QUE	Peter L. Halbig	1986	547
331 3/8	45 3/8 47 1/8	35 4/8	14 16	Fort Chimo	QUE	Gene Culver	1989	547
331 3/8	45 7/8 48 0/8	50 4/8	10 9	Fort Chimo	QUE	John Leo Hojan	1990	547
331 2/8	36 6/8 34 7/8	33 5/8	13 14	Riviere Lefebvre	QUE	John Powell	2005	550
331 0/8	56 3/8 58 5/8	47 5/8	9 7	Waymouth Inlet	QUE	Edwin DeYoung	1989	551
331 0/8	43 4/8 45 2/8	35 0/8	11 14	Lac Minto	QUE	J. Ken Martin	1995	551
331 0/8	49 5/8 48 7/8	46 3/8	9 8	Lac Omarolluk	QUE	Ken Dobbins, Jr.	2008	551
330 7/8	49 4/8 48 0/8	42 4/8	12 10	LG 4	QUE	Frank Kozielec, Jr.	1992	554
330 7/8	48 7/8 50 4/8	47 6/8	10 11	Lac Minto	QUE	Billie Grogg	1997	554
330 7/8	45 3/8 46 4/8	36 1/8	15 12	Lac Tasiataq	QUE	Gilbert Hernandez	1998	554
*330 7/8	44 3/8 45 3/8	43 6/8	10 11	Wendell Lake	QUE	Carl Morrison	2003	554
330 6/8	45 5/8 47 1/8	36 0/8	13 14	Pons Island	QUE	Lou Edelis	1987	558
330 6/8	46 7/8 48 6/8	41 6/8	11 7	Caniapiscau River	QUE	John L. Gardner	1994	558
330 6/8	56 2/8 58 3/8	37 6/8	9 11	Schefferville	QUE	Len Rinke	2001	558
330 5/8	49 4/8 48 6/8	36 6/8	14 15	LG 4	QUE	Charles Moore	1991	561
330 5/8	41 1/8 42 4/8	37 0/8	16 15	Delay River	QUE	William E. Terry, Sr.	1992	561
330 5/8	42 3/8 45 7/8	42 2/8	16 13	Lac Chabanel	QUE	Thomas Olszewski	2005	561
330 3/8	42 5/8 45 0/8	36 5/8	9 6	Lake Mollett	QUE	Jim Griffin	2001	564
330 2/8	49 3/8 49 4/8	37 5/8	16 16	Delay River	QUE	Roy Goodwin	1986	565
330 2/8	46 0/8 48 7/8	37 0/8	14 11	Delay River	QUE	James Kingsley	1990	565
*330 2/8	45 2/8 45 2/8	37 6/8	11 12	Lac Minto	QUE	Cindy Rothrock	2006	565
330 0/8	49 5/8 45 6/8	31 0/8	12 10	Fort Chimo	QUE	Larry Hayes	1986	568
330 0/8	48 3/8 49 4/8	39 5/8	13 12	Caniapiscau River	QUE	Ken Bruckner	1992	568
330 0/8	50 2/8 49 4/8	43 0/8	11 8	Harold Lake	QUE	Ron Haver	1992	568

245

QUEBEC-LABRADOR CARIBOU

Minimum Score 325   Continued

SCORE	LENGTH OF MAIN BEAM R	LENGTH OF MAIN BEAM L	INSIDE SPREAD	NUMBER OF POINTS R	NUMBER OF POINTS L	AREA	STATE/PROVINCE	HUNTER'S NAME	DATE	RANK
330 0/8	51 7/8	50 7/8	47 5/8	12	12	Lake Mollett	QUE	Ira Horn	2002	568
329 7/8	42 2/8	43 0/8	41 3/8	13	17	Victoria Lake	QUE	Audrey Chislett	1997	572
329 7/8	43 4/8	44 0/8	42 3/8	11	11	Simone Lake	QUE	Jerry L. Martin	2002	572
329 4/8	44 2/8	47 2/8	39 2/8	12	10	Lac Minto	QUE	Gary W. Kelley	1997	574
329 4/8	49 4/8	49 3/8	44 0/8	14	15	Lac Minto Island	QUE	John D. Edman	1999	574
329 4/8	58 6/8	65 0/8	41 1/8	10	11	Lac Minto	QUE	Jack Hasse	2006	574
329 3/8	43 0/8	43 6/8	45 6/8	7	12	Lake Napier	QUE	Jim Leqve	2003	577
329 2/8	47 0/8	48 0/8	42 3/8	14	10	Schefferville	QUE	Jerry W. Robertson	1988	578
329 2/8	49 5/8	48 3/8	40 4/8	12	14	Lac Minto	QUE	Kurt Keskimaki	2000	578
329 1/8	52 5/8	48 7/8	43 7/8	16	13	George River	QUE	Jerry V. Finley	1981	580
329 0/8	42 6/8	39 5/8	40 2/8	13	15	Rogers Lake	QUE	Joe Powroznik	1988	581
329 0/8	51 5/8	55 2/8	37 7/8	8	7	Melezes River	QUE	A. Owen Shifflett	1989	581
328 7/8	43 3/8	47 6/8	40 4/8	16	14	Lac Minto	QUE	Greg Bonecutter, Sr.	1998	583
328 7/8	41 3/8	41 1/8	38 1/8	11	14	Lake Ikirtuuq	QUE	Caryn Maier	2000	583
328 6/8	55 4/8	56 7/8	42 3/8	9	11	Ungava Region	QUE	David L. Cook	1982	585
328 6/8	43 0/8	42 4/8	38 5/8	17	13	Schefferville	QUE	Michael J. Kennedy	1992	585
328 5/8	49 1/8	52 4/8	45 2/8	13	12	Pons River	QUE	Jim Ellis	1986	587
328 5/8	44 5/8	44 3/8	33 0/8	16	14	Schefferville	QUE	Kenneth C. Kaufmann	1987	587
328 5/8	44 3/8	44 1/8	39 4/8	10	10	Lac Pons	QUE	Mark C. Schwei	2003	587
328 4/8	44 6/8	43 0/8	39 0/8	16	16	Long Lake	QUE	David J. Stanislawski	1990	590
328 4/8	44 0/8	47 0/8	38 2/8	15	14	Lake Mollett	QUE	Jeff Jorgensen	1999	590
328 2/8	49 6/8	49 1/8	48 1/8	8	9	Pons Island	QUE	Gary Reich	1987	592
328 2/8	42 2/8	43 3/8	49 5/8	13	8	Delay River	QUE	August S. Gray	1988	592
328 2/8	45 2/8	50 2/8	40 6/8	14	15	Lac Minto	QUE	Jason Weimer	2000	592
328 0/8	47 6/8	47 1/8	41 5/8	11	10	Big Island	QUE	Ralph Willits	1989	595
328 0/8	51 6/8	48 7/8	44 6/8	12	8	Melezes River	QUE	Peter L. Bucklin	1990	595
328 0/8	54 4/8	56 0/8	44 7/8	12	15	Maricourt Lake	QUE	Doug Kerska	1990	595
327 7/8	47 1/8	48 0/8	40 7/8	12	12	Lac Minto Island	QUE	Patrick Farrow	1997	598
327 6/8	52 0/8	53 0/8	45 3/8	15	19	Schefferville	QUE	Irv Plotz	1981	599
327 6/8	49 3/8	48 5/8	48 6/8	14	17	Weymouth Inlet	QUE	David L. Stull	1989	599
327 5/8	43 0/8	44 4/8	45 3/8	11	18	LG 4	QUE	Stephen Kotz	1992	601
327 5/8	41 4/8	40 7/8	35 5/8	11	9	Lac Minto	QUE	Thomas Bahosh	2000	601
327 4/8	51 5/8	50 4/8	33 6/8	8	7	Sir James Lake	QUE	Bryan Lee White	1993	603
327 4/8	47 7/8	49 4/8	37 4/8	13	16	Lac Minto	QUE	Homer R. Kincaid	1997	603
327 4/8	48 5/8	49 0/8	37 6/8	8	9	Lac Minto	QUE	Gene Wilson	1997	603
327 4/8	51 6/8	50 4/8	40 7/8	14	11	Deception Bay	QUE	Viron Barbay	1999	603
327 4/8	45 0/8	44 5/8	40 4/8	10	8	Polaris River	QUE	Dusty Loveland	2005	603
*327 1/8	48 3/8	43 3/8	38 7/8	14	11	Lac Coursolles	QUE	Robert J. Accettullo	2006	608
327 0/8	47 3/8	47 0/8	44 3/8	12	15	Lake Martine	QUE	Tom Nelson	1990	609
326 7/8	45 3/8	45 6/8	50 2/8	11	6	Schefferville	QUE	Joseph Strasser, Jr.	1988	610
326 7/8	50 3/8	48 6/8	45 1/8	11	13	Deception Bay	QUE	Homer Kincaid	1999	610
326 7/8	46 4/8	44 3/8	42 6/8	14	13	Fort Chimo	QUE	Chuck Adams	1999	610
326 6/8	53 2/8	54 3/8	44 0/8	8	10	Tunulik River	QUE	Ty Martin	1986	613
326 6/8	44 0/8	47 0/8	34 1/8	12	13	Delay River	QUE	Douglas Kerska	1988	613
326 6/8	46 4/8	46 1/8	35 4/8	12	11	Pons Lake	QUE	George E. Mann	1995	613
326 6/8	50 3/8	50 2/8	39 4/8	12	11	Lac Minto Island	QUE	Greg Bonecutter, Sr.	1997	613
326 6/8	40 2/8	40 6/8	32 6/8	14	14	Laforge Reservoir	QUE	Robert L. Wickman	2003	613
326 5/8	48 7/8	50 1/8	48 7/8	10	11	Deception Bay	QUE	Gip Friesen	1999	618
326 5/8	48 5/8	48 4/8	45 0/8	8	10	Lac Minto	QUE	Steven W. Lachenmayr	2006	618
326 3/8	49 4/8	52 0/8	39 2/8	12	11	Drummondville	QUE	Leo Hazelton	1994	620
326 2/8	46 1/8	45 2/8	32 7/8	13	15	Lake Leopard	QUE	Wes Seaver	1989	621
326 2/8	45 0/8	46 6/8	47 7/8	7	7	Schefferville	QUE	Jerry Parsons	1990	621
326 2/8	48 2/8	46 3/8	45 5/8	6	5	Lac Fremin	QUE	Richard F. Wamboldt	1995	621
326 2/8	45 3/8	45 2/8	44 7/8	12	14	Serigny River	QUE	Greg Dearth	1999	621
326 2/8	52 0/8	50 3/8	33 6/8	10	9	Clearwater Lake	QUE	Walter L. Palmer	2007	621
326 1/8	59 3/8	57 0/8	43 6/8	10	17	Ungava Region	QUE	Gary L. Snyder	1977	626
326 1/8	48 0/8	49 2/8	46 7/8	8	8	Delay River	QUE	Roger Gipple	1988	626
326 1/8	48 2/8	49 4/8	58 6/8	9	11	Lake Sabrina	QUE	David C. Anderson	1993	626
326 0/8	45 6/8	45 5/8	45 0/8	12	14	Delay River	QUE	Warren Strickland	1989	629
326 0/8	52 5/8	53 7/8	43 5/8	9	12	Lac Chabanel	QUE	Thomas Olszewski	2007	629
325 7/8	50 6/8	50 2/8	35 0/8	12	8	Lac Minto	QUE	Kenneth Wade Anderson	1997	631
325 7/8	49 7/8	49 4/8	35 1/8	15	14	Clearwater Lake	QUE	Kevin Griffin	2006	631
325 6/8	54 1/8	54 0/8	48 7/8	11	12	Lac Minto	QUE	Kenneth E. Briggs	2001	633
325 6/8	43 0/8	43 1/8	43 5/8	14	15	Whiskey Lake	QUE	Bill Kotarski	2002	633
325 5/8	49 4/8	48 3/8	53 0/8	8	9	Delay River	QUE	Paul Converse	1991	635
325 5/8	49 1/8	49 2/8	37 6/8	12	10	Gordon Lake	QUE	Bobby J. Jones	1995	635
325 4/8	46 7/8	50 4/8	41 2/8	8	9	Lake Riqouville	QUE	Paul M. Kniss	1990	637
325 3/8	45 3/8	47 5/8	48 4/8	9	7	Lac Louis	QUE	Alan J. Rhinerson	1991	638
325 3/8	39 4/8	42 3/8	36 1/8	15	12	Kuujjuaq	QUE	Joseph S. Duarte, Jr.	1996	638
325 3/8	53 5/8	52 3/8	43 0/8	10	11	Lac Aigneau	QUE	Ken Miller	1998	638
325 2/8	51 5/8	52 7/8	43 1/8	9	14	Lac Minto	QUE	Tim L. Donnelly	2002	641
325 1/8	60 1/8	60 5/8	49 3/8	7	4	Tunulik River	QUE	Ron Carpenter	1982	642
325 1/8	42 0/8	46 4/8	40 4/8	11	11	Lake Narcy	QUE	Kenny E. Leo	1988	642
325 1/8	49 5/8	49 7/8	51 1/8	16	13	LG 4	QUE	Bryant Shermoe	1995	642
325 1/8	51 4/8	52 4/8	49 7/8	14	9	Deception Bay	QUE	James M. Tully	1999	642
325 1/8	49 5/8	49 4/8	45 6/8	14	7	Clearwater Lake	QUE	Seth Frost	2006	642

QUEBEC-LABRADOR CARIBOU (VELVET ANTLERS)

Minimum Score 325

SCORE	LENGTH OF R MAIN BEAM L	INSIDE SPREAD	NUMBER OF R POINTS L		AREA	STATE/ PROVINCE	HUNTER'S NAME	DATE	RANK
*371 1/8	51 2/8 50 2/8	52 6/8	12	12	Caniapiscau River	QUE	Cameron Hanes	2006	*
362 4/8	59 0/8 57 4/8	44 6/8	14	10	Lake McCabe	QUE	Abraham Garcia III	2007	*
355 3/8	45 3/8 46 5/8	50 6/8	11	10	Lake McCabe	QUE	Francisco Noriega, Jr.	2007	*
354 7/8	49 5/8 47 5/8	41 4/8	15	12	Leif River	QUE	Smokey Crews	2005	*
344 7/8	53 0/8 50 1/8	40 1/8	12	11	Leaf River	QUE	Chad Nelson	2006	*
343 7/8	51 7/8 51 5/8	46 2/8	9	11	Kuujjuaq	QUE	George Harms	2005	*
341 4/8	49 3/8 50 1/8	34 2/8	10	11	Leaf River	QUE	Steve Wilson	2004	*
339 3/8	45 2/8 46 2/8	37 2/8	16	15	Arbic Lake	QUE	Raymond G. Mankowski	2002	*
335 0/8	43 5/8 42 0/8	40 7/8	16	19	Lac Lefrancois	QUE	Earl O. Woods	2005	*
325 5/8	44 4/8 42 6/8	35 0/8	11	11	Lac Minto	QUE	Steven Bostic	2006	*

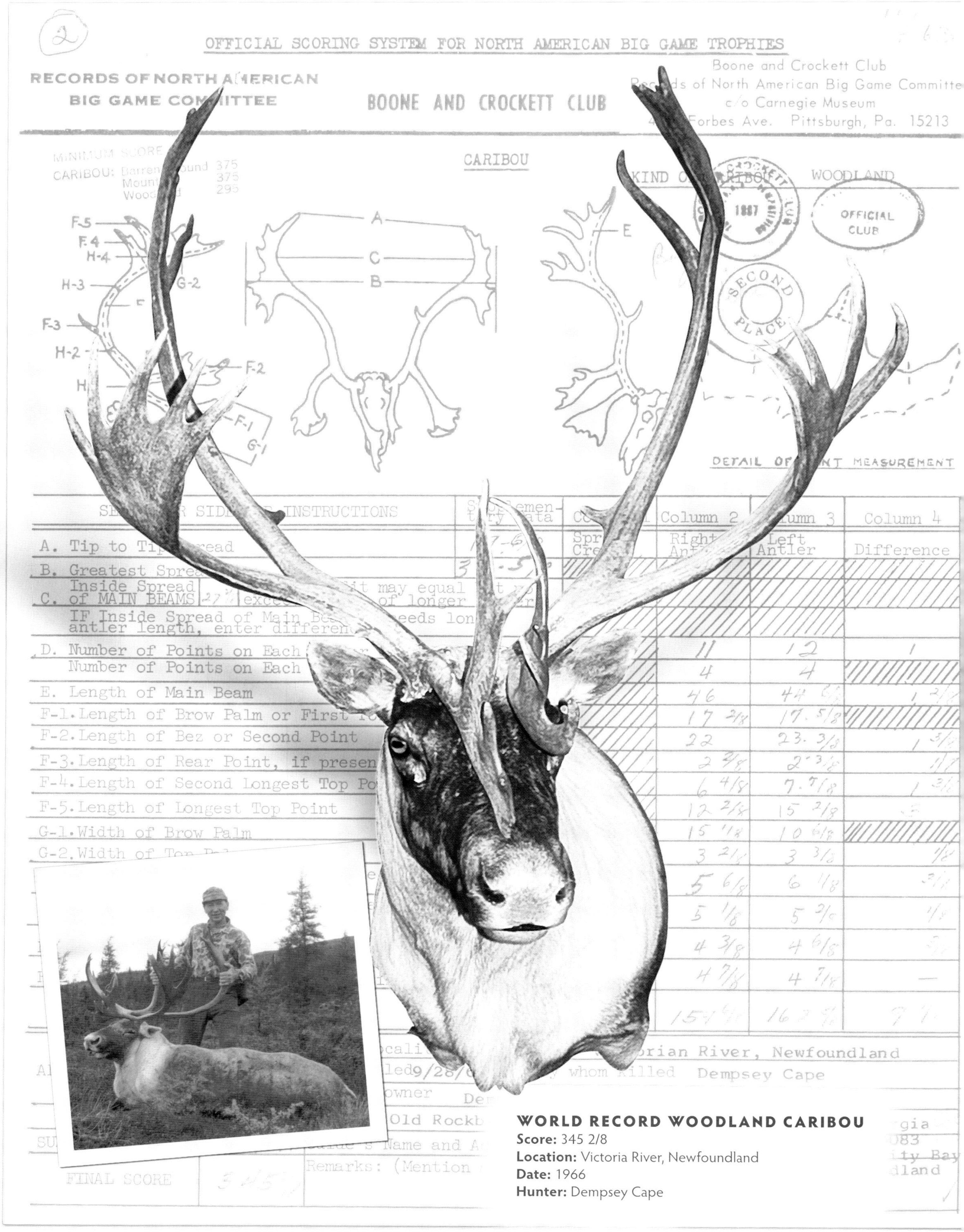

WORLD RECORD WOODLAND CARIBOU
Score: 345 2/8
Location: Victoria River, Newfoundland
Date: 1966
Hunter: Dempsey Cape

Woodland Caribou

by Dempsey Cape

My hunt took place in 1966 in the Millertown region about 50 miles into the Newfoundland wilderness. It was September and guide, John Newhook, and I had backpacked six miles to a spike camp.

Early in the hunt, I stalked a big bull caribou for four hours, only to miss a shot at 30 yards during a sudden downpour. Talk about disappointment!

The next morning we were glassing for another bull when a caribou even bigger than the one I'd missed was sighted. He was about a mile and a half across a flat valley floor, moving fast. The only hope we had was to run and try to head him off before he reached the safety of open country. This is where my training for the hunt paid off. I had walked or ran five miles every day for a month and was in good shape. We covered the distance in short order and I made my way onto a rocky terrace above and 40 yards away from the passing bull. My arrow hit him and he went down quickly.

I did not realize just how large the rack was until I reached the airport and compared it with the smaller racks brought in by gun hunters. As I stood there, an indescribable feeling welled up inside me and I knew the full meaning of a bowhunter's pride.

WOODLAND CARIBOU

Minimum Score 220

Rangifer tarandus caribou from Nova Scotia, New Brunswick, and Newfoundland

SCORE	LENGTH OF MAIN BEAM R	L	INSIDE SPREAD	NUMBER OF POINTS R	L	AREA	STATE/PROVINCE	HUNTER'S NAME	DATE	RANK
345 2/8	46 6/8	46 4/8	27 3/8	11	12	Victoria River	NFL	Dempsey Cape	1966	1
335 5/8	37 5/8	40 5/8	33 6/8	14	11	Dolland Pond	NFL	Larry Welchlen	2005	2
331 5/8	37 4/8	37 0/8	29 0/8	12	12	Gander River	NFL	David W. Schrody	2000	3
324 7/8	40 2/8	42 3/8	36 0/8	11	10	Deer Pond	NFL	Frank M. Monberger	1993	4
324 0/8	42 7/8	42 3/8	26 6/8	10	11	Sitdown Pond	NFL	Ed J. Bowser	1966	5
320 4/8	43 4/8	43 3/8	31 2/8	12	12	Middle Ridge	NFL	M. R. James	1999	6
316 3/8	37 0/8	36 7/8	21 5/8	13	12	Island Pond	NFL	Clinton Welding	2006	7
310 1/8	41 0/8	41 0/8	29 2/8	10	12	Millertown	NFL	Gerhart Huber	1966	8
310 0/8	40 5/8	40 2/8	37 0/8	13	15	Buchans Plateau	NFL	David Weber	1999	9
309 7/8	37 2/8	35 3/8	33 7/8	12	14	Taylers Brook	NFL	David Bosscher	2001	10
309 3/8	46 1/8	49 1/8	38 4/8	9	12	St. Anthony	NFL	Stuart G. Hazard III	1998	11
307 1/8	37 5/8	40 4/8	30 2/8	10	12	Gaff Topsails	NFL	Edward X. Thompson	2004	12
303 2/8	35 6/8	36 4/8	30 7/8	7	9	Deer Pond Lake	NFL	George S. Walker III	1998	13
301 4/8	38 5/8	36 3/8	30 0/8	7	9	Parsons Pond	NFL	Jeff Wingard	1997	14
299 4/8	33 3/8	38 7/8	29 4/8	8	9	Dolland Pond	NFL	Mark Turner	2006	15
298 5/8	38 2/8	42 1/8	35 0/8	14	11	Mitchell's Pond	NFL	Randy Cloak	1999	16
298 1/8	42 5/8	43 0/8	30 6/8	11	12	Hare Bay	NFL	Dan Mitchell	1998	17
297 2/8	40 5/8	43 4/8	29 6/8	8	8	Great Gull Lake	NFL	Alan Anglyn	2010	18
296 5/8	39 4/8	37 5/8	33 4/8	11	10	Gander River	NFL	Jack Griesinger	1999	19
291 6/8	41 6/8	40 1/8	42 2/8	9	7	Goose Pond	NFL	Bob Wrenn	2000	20
288 4/8	35 5/8	35 6/8	22 7/8	11	11	Dolland Pond	NFL	Larry Welchlen	2005	21
287 4/8	35 0/8	34 1/8	27 6/8	9	9	Dashwood Pond	NFL	Kerry K. Kammer	1990	22
286 4/8	37 0/8	37 0/8	29 5/8	9	11	Rocky Pond	NFL	Chuck Adams	1988	23
285 0/8	34 7/8	35 2/8	27 7/8	10	10	Dolland Pond	NFL	Roy Goodwin	2000	24
285 0/8	39 7/8	40 7/8	31 6/8	10	7	Grey River	NFL	Anthony D. Mazzarella	2007	24
284 5/8	39 0/8	41 1/8	37 0/8	14	10	Gander	NFL	Ron Timm	1997	26
284 2/8	37 3/8	35 7/8	28 4/8	11	11	Howley	NFL	Ken Adamson	1999	27
284 0/8	38 5/8	34 6/8	24 2/8	12	9	Bishop's Falls	NFL	Michael E. Petkwitz	1997	28
280 7/8	34 2/8	33 7/8	28 0/8	7	8	Gander River	NFL	Ron Dunne	1997	29
280 6/8	32 6/8	34 7/8	30 6/8	8	11	Dolland Pond	NFL	Roy M. Goodwin	2006	30
280 4/8	37 5/8	34 6/8	28 7/8	11	12	Buchans Plateau	NFL	Gary Martin	1996	31
279 2/8	36 6/8	34 5/8	25 3/8	16	11	Stag Lake	NFL	Mike Traub	1993	32
279 0/8	34 3/8	34 7/8	35 1/8	8	8	Grey River	NFL	Tim W. Schenk	2003	33
277 3/8	31 4/8	35 3/8	37 0/8	7	10	Middle Ridge	NFL	Richard Flynn	2006	34
277 1/8	36 0/8	36 6/8	24 2/8	9	10	Parsons Pond	NFL	Buck Herhei	2003	35
276 7/8	42 3/8	43 0/8	25 2/8	10	9	King George IV Lake	NFL	Mark McCarty	1966	36
276 3/8	33 3/8	32 7/8	26 2/8	11	11	Moss Pond	NFL	Robert McKay	1999	37
275 6/8	35 4/8	33 4/8	25 6/8	10	9	Alex Pond	NFL	Paul Locey	1988	38
275 6/8	31 6/8	30 7/8	28 6/8	8	12	Middle Ridge	NFL	Michael Hyland	1999	38
*275 6/8	33 4/8	32 5/8	27 6/8	9	10	Dolland Pond	NFL	Steve Finegan	2004	38
275 3/8	36 5/8	35 2/8	37 0/8	12	10	Deer Pond	NFL	John J.J. Rybinski	1998	41
275 1/8	34 7/8	34 7/8	21 3/8	14	11	Buchans Plateau	NFL	Thomas J. Pluhar	2006	42
274 7/8	38 5/8	39 4/8	29 0/8	8	8	Caribou Creek	NFL	Dan Bertalan	1992	43
274 5/8	36 5/8	37 1/8	22 3/8	9	9	Dolland Pond	NFL	Roy M. Goodwin	2005	44
272 4/8	41 0/8	45 0/8	30 4/8	7	7	Cross Pond	NFL	Thomas J. Hoffman	1993	45
272 1/8	33 2/8	33 0/8	25 2/8	13	10	Buchans Plateau	NFL	Eddie Smith	1988	46
272 1/8	40 4/8	42 3/8	27 7/8	7	8	Portland Creek	NFL	Jeff Herman	2004	46
270 6/8	33 5/8	33 6/8	34 2/8	9	10	Atikonak Lake	NFL	Dr. James L. Emerson	1973	48
270 5/8	35 1/8	35 6/8	37 0/8	7	8	Daniel's Harbour	NFL	Peter L. Bucklin	1998	49
*269 7/8	39 7/8	39 5/8	25 1/8	9	8	Dolland Pond	NFL	Mike Oldenburger	2004	50
269 1/8	37 1/8	37 4/8	23 4/8	15	13	Corner Brook	NFL	Al Reay	1980	51
267 7/8	29 3/8	31 4/8	27 4/8	12	11	Stag Lake	NFL	Richard A. Case	1993	52
267 6/8	40 6/8	42 1/8	32 1/8	10	8	Gaff Topsails	NFL	John D. "Jack" Frost	1997	53
267 5/8	34 6/8	35 5/8	27 3/8	7	7	Island Pond	NFL	Michael R. Harris	2001	54
267 4/8	37 1/8	35 2/8	23 2/8	8	10	Deer Pond	NFL	Neil Summers	1996	55
267 0/8	35 4/8	34 2/8	22 7/8	8	7	Alex Pond	NFL	James Pike	1991	56
266 4/8	31 6/8	29 0/8	30 0/8	9	9	Blue Pond	NFL	Jim Horneck	2008	57
265 7/8	39 1/8	38 5/8	32 0/8	9	11	Deer Pond	NFL	Dr. David Samuel	1998	58
265 4/8	41 2/8	40 0/8	22 5/8	6	8	Bishop's Falls	NFL	Jack Griesinger	1998	59
265 1/8	36 2/8	36 0/8	28 3/8	8	9	Deer Pond	NFL	Tom D. Slusser	1993	60
264 6/8	37 5/8	37 7/8	28 3/8	9	13	Ocean Pond	NFL	Dennis Hayden	1998	61
264 0/8	36 7/8	33 7/8	26 7/8	10	9	Grey River	NFL	James Gabrick	2005	62
263 2/8	35 5/8	35 3/8	34 5/8	7	9	Terra Nova	NFL	Glen Mertens	1995	63
*263 2/8	32 6/8	32 6/8	29 7/8	9	7	Island Pond	NFL	Patrick Murray	2003	63
262 6/8	39 4/8	41 2/8	34 4/8	6	7	Buchans Plateau	NFL	Fred A. Turner	1984	65
262 5/8	34 5/8	37 3/8	30 6/8	9	8	Gaff Topsails	NFL	Tom Vanasche	2002	66
262 0/8	28 5/8	30 5/8	29 5/8	12	11	Grey River	NFL	Jack Dawe	1998	67
262 0/8	39 7/8	39 6/8	28 1/8	8	9	Dolland Pond	NFL	Roy M. Goodwin	2001	67
261 3/8	41 6/8	42 3/8	31 0/8	8	8	Sam's Pond	NFL	Allyn Ladd	2010	68
261 2/8	34 3/8	34 6/8	20 3/8	9	9	Cross Pond	NFL	Duane D. Zemliska	1994	69
261 0/8	29 4/8	31 4/8	29 6/8	11	12	Koskaecodde Lake	NFL	Bill Kotarski	1997	70
260 6/8	31 7/8	29 7/8	23 1/8	10	12	Old Country Pond	NFL	Robert Swierczynski	2000	71
260 3/8	35 2/8	35 3/8	27 5/8	9	11	Buchans Plateau	NFL	William R. Vanderhoef	1986	72
260 1/8	35 5/8	35 3/8	25 0/8	7	8	Roddickton	NFL	Craig Roth	1999	73
260 0/8	33 2/8	32 6/8	22 6/8	8	12	Rocky Pond	NFL	Bill Kotarski	1999	74
259 5/8	37 6/8	32 2/8	34 7/8	10	11	Buchans Plateau	NFL	John "Jack" Cordes	1982	75
259 2/8	36 0/8	35 6/8	25 4/8	6	5	Main Brook	NFL	Robert S. Fruda	2000	76
259 0/8	31 1/8	27 4/8	27 0/8	12	16	Saddler Pond	NFL	Stan Godfrey	1989	77
259 0/8	37 0/8	37 6/8	29 6/8	8	8	Victoria River	NFL	J. D. Thomas	1996	77
258 7/8	40 4/8	37 6/8	33 1/8	6	7	Lloyds River	NFL	Harold A. Hill	1964	79
258 6/8	37 6/8	38 3/8	26 7/8	7	8	Stag Lake	NFL	R. Brian Oates	1993	80
258 5/8	33 6/8	33 0/8	25 6/8	10	9	Howley	NFL	Ken Mowerson	1989	81
258 5/8	37 1/8	38 4/8	26 7/8	9	9	Lapoile	NFL	Nicholas Misciagna	1992	81
258 3/8	36 5/8	34 4/8	24 5/8	7	6	Dolland Pond	NFL	Charles W. Rehor	2003	83
258 1/8	36 7/8	33 6/8	25 4/8	10	11	Atikonak Lake	NFL	Bill L. Carlos	1972	84
257 0/8	33 7/8	35 2/8	32 0/8	8	9	Buchans Plateau	NFL	Walter J. Palmer	1993	85
256 5/8	31 5/8	36 0/8	15 7/8	8	9	Alex Pond	NFL	Jay Deones	1993	87
256 3/8	31 7/8	33 4/8	24 4/8	8	9	Dolland Pond	NFL	Rick Duggan	2006	88
256 2/8	32 4/8	34 4/8	27 0/8	11	12	Alex Pond	NFL	Gary F. Bogner	1996	89
256 1/8	35 2/8	35 1/8	27 6/8	9	8	Dolland Pond	NFL	Roy M. Goodwin	2007	90
254 5/8	31 5/8	30 7/8	27 7/8	12	10	Parsons Pond	NFL	Bruce R. Schoeneweis	2007	91
254 2/8	35 3/8	38 6/8	36 4/8	9	7	Dolland Pond	NFL	Charles W. Rehor	2007	92
*254 1/8	32 7/8	36 2/8	23 2/8	8	9	Dolland Pond	NFL	Jim Leqve	2007	93
253 7/8	37 4/8	35 5/8	32 1/8	10	8	Buchans Plateau	NFL	Steve D. Munier	1990	94
253 6/8	38 6/8	43 5/8	27 1/8	6	7	Rocky Ridge Pond	NFL	Tim Burres	2001	95

250

WOODLAND CARIBOU

Minimum Score 220   Continued

SCORE	LENGTH OF MAIN BEAM R / L	INSIDE SPREAD	NUMBER OF POINTS R / L	AREA	STATE/ PROVINCE	HUNTER'S NAME	DATE	RANK
253 2/8	39 1/8 / 38 4/8	30 7/8	7 / 9	Alex Pond	NFL	Michael J. Spence	1993	96
253 1/8	33 6/8 / 33 4/8	24 0/8	10 / 9	Buchans Plateau	NFL	Mark Zastrow	1995	97
*252 7/8	38 1/8 / 36 5/8	31 4/8	7 / 9	Gander	NFL	Ray Kimmell	2002	98
252 4/8	35 7/8 / 36 5/8	34 0/8	9 / 7	Hampton Downs	NFL	Steff Stefanovich	2009	99
252 3/8	31 3/8 / 31 3/8	30 0/8	11 / 13	Grey River	NFL	Tyler A. Borth	2006	100
252 2/8	36 1/8 / 33 1/8	24 7/8	7 / 9	Alex Pond	NFL	Karen J. Deones	1993	101
252 0/8	35 4/8 / 38 0/8	29 3/8	12 / 10	Portland Creek	NFL	Clarence Bowers	1998	102
252 0/8	32 0/8 / 32 7/8	22 6/8	9 / 8	Grey River	NFL	Carl John Pieper	2003	102
*252 0/8	29 3/8 / 32 1/8	27 2/8	12 / 12	Dolland Pond	NFL	Amy L. Goodwin	2006	102
251 5/8	30 7/8 / 31 2/8	22 6/8	12 / 10	True Hill Pond	NFL	Roy M. Goodwin	2002	105
251 0/8	30 6/8 / 31 6/8	22 4/8	10 / 10	Island Pond	NFL	Joe Bell	2000	106
250 2/8	30 5/8 / 32 5/8	21 6/8	6 / 10	La Poile	NFL	Dyrk Eddie	1999	107
250 1/8	33 0/8 / 32 1/8	26 4/8	10 / 12	Deer Pond	NFL	Warren Strickland	1994	108
*250 0/8	35 2/8 / 35 1/8	28 3/8	7 / 8	Dolland Pond	NFL	Raymond Heal	2003	108
249 4/8	37 6/8 / 33 4/8	31 0/8	9 / 11	13 Mile Bog	NFL	John D. Thomas, Jr.	1998	110
249 3/8	36 5/8 / 37 2/8	26 4/8	9 / 9	Millertown	NFL	Cliff Wiseman	1962	111
248 5/8	32 3/8 / 30 1/8	27 2/8	6 / 8	Dolland Pond	NFL	Kevin Martin	2006	112
248 0/8	40 7/8 / 36 7/8	34 0/8	7 / 7	Sitdown Pond	NFL	Dr. Ed Bowser	1965	113
247 7/8	36 3/8 / 40 3/8	22 1/8	7 / 8	Deer Pond	NFL	John M. Cogswell	2008	114
247 6/8	33 2/8 / 33 7/8	33 7/8	8 / 7	Deer Pond	NFL	Joel A. Johnson	2000	115
247 3/8	34 5/8 / 37 4/8	28 4/8	7 / 7	King George IV Lake	NFL	Bill Hirst	1966	116
247 2/8	33 3/8 / 30 5/8	29 0/8	7 / 7	Millertown	NFL	J. D. Thomas	2000	117
246 3/8	35 6/8 / 35 7/8	21 0/8	9 / 8	Stag Lake	NFL	Susan D. Sherer	1996	118
246 2/8	32 4/8 / 29 0/8	27 0/8	10 / 9	Alex Pond	NFL	Darrin West	1991	119
245 4/8	33 2/8 / 35 5/8	29 1/8	8 / 8	Rogers River	NFL	Randy Petersburg	1998	120
245 4/8	33 4/8 / 32 6/8	25 5/8	9 / 7	Deer Lake	NFL	Dennis Doherty	2003	120
245 2/8	30 4/8 / 31 1/8	26 6/8	8 / 9	Mitchell's Pond	NFL	Wallace Walrath	2002	122
245 0/8	33 2/8 / 31 6/8	28 1/8	8 / 8	Dolland Pond	NFL	Dennis Dunn	2007	123
244 5/8	31 3/8 / 33 0/8	26 7/8	7 / 7	Gander River	NFL	David A. Widby	2004	124
243 6/8	34 6/8 / 34 6/8	27 7/8	7 / 6	Greys Island	NFL	Terry Krahn	1991	125
*243 2/8	33 0/8 / 34 2/8	28 1/8	9 / 8	Dolland Pond	NFL	Corey M. Goodwin	2006	126
242 6/8	36 2/8 / 33 2/8	22 4/8	8 / 8	Buchans Plateau	NFL	Willard F. Collins	2000	127
242 5/8	35 4/8 / 33 4/8	22 4/8	7 / 7	Dolland Pond	NFL	Marlin Harding	2004	128
242 1/8	36 1/8 / 36 5/8	30 5/8	7 / 8	Moon Lake	NFL	Michael R. Deschamps	1996	129
242 0/8	37 1/8 / 36 6/8	25 7/8	8 / 8	Dolland Pond	NFL	Ronald Rockwell	2005	130
241 6/8	33 2/8 / 30 6/8	29 2/8	9 / 11	Buchans Plateau	NFL	Glenn Hisey	1982	131
241 4/8	30 6/8 / 33 4/8	22 4/8	7 / 10	Daniel's Harbour	NFL	John M. Jennings	2000	132
241 3/8	34 0/8 / 34 4/8	31 4/8	7 / 6	Buchans Plateau	NFL	Jim Wondzell	2000	133
241 2/8	33 2/8 / 34 6/8	25 1/8	11 / 11	Interior District	NFL	Bill Goff	1965	134
241 0/8	31 6/8 / 34 3/8	18 4/8	11 / 10	Gander	NFL	John Stone	2000	135
240 4/8	36 2/8 / 37 6/8	31 1/8	8 / 6	Soufflets River	NFL	Kris Albaugh	1999	136
239 6/8	33 6/8 / 36 7/8	31 6/8	9 / 11	Main Brook	NFL	David Samuel	2001	137
239 1/8	35 3/8 / 34 0/8	26 6/8	10 / 12	Buchans Plateau	NFL	Mark Buehrer	1997	138
239 1/8	32 5/8 / 30 0/8	25 7/8	9 / 7	Middle Ridge	NFL	Richard Flynn	2006	138
238 7/8	19 1/8 / 27 2/8	26 7/8	9 / 8	Stag Lake	NFL	G. Fred Asbell	1996	140
237 4/8	35 4/8 / 35 6/8	27 5/8	7 / 6	Stag Lake	NFL	Ron Sherer	1996	141
237 2/8	35 0/8 / 36 2/8	29 7/8	7 / 8	Saddler Pond	NFL	Carolyn Godfrey	1989	142
237 1/8	35 1/8 / 35 2/8	24 6/8	10 / 7	Buchans Plateau	NFL	Doug Strecker	1990	143
236 5/8	30 0/8 / 34 7/8	29 4/8	9 / 9	Deer Lake	NFL	Randy Brandt	2001	144
236 3/8	36 0/8 / 35 0/8	25 3/8	12 / 9	Princess Lake	NFL	John Musacchia	1967	145
*236 3/8	36 4/8 / 36 0/8	24 7/8	7 / 7	Wolf Lake	NFL	John M. Carbine	2005	145
236 3/8	35 3/8 / 35 5/8	29 7/8	6 / 9	Dolland Pond	NFL	Roy "Butch" Goodwin, Jr.	2006	145
235 5/8	34 0/8 / 32 7/8	31 3/8	10 / 5	Springdale	NFL	Vito Palazzolo	1998	148
235 2/8	32 3/8 / 34 2/8	24 4/8	8 / 8	Buchans Plateau	NFL	John Neal	1998	149
235 1/8	35 2/8 / 37 3/8	23 1/8	8 / 10	Alex Pond	NFL	Dr. Eugene T. Altiere	1999	150
233 2/8	38 0/8 / 37 0/8	27 5/8	7 / 4	Gull Lake	NFL	M. W. Bowser	1958	151
232 6/8	34 2/8 / 31 2/8	32 2/8	7 / 5	Millertown	NFL	Tom Taylor	1992	152
232 5/8	33 3/8 / 35 0/8	24 5/8	6 / 7	Deer Lake	NFL	Douglas L. Buchler	1984	153
232 4/8	35 5/8 / 34 7/8	26 7/8	6 / 6	Buchans Plateau	NFL	Terrence H. Estes	1984	154
232 1/8	30 3/8 / 30 7/8	25 3/8	10 / 8	Victoria Lake	NFL	Robert Bartoshesky	1998	155
231 0/8	32 0/8 / 31 7/8	22 6/8	9 / 7	Grey River	NFL	Lou Kindred	1996	156
229 1/8	34 2/8 / 34 3/8	27 4/8	6 / 6	Cat Arm River	NFL	Michael J. Kennedy	1998	157
228 7/8	31 4/8 / 28 3/8	25 2/8	8 / 8	Buchans Plateau	NFL	Walter J. Palmer	1993	158
228 5/8	30 1/8 / 28 4/8	21 6/8	8 / 7	Stag Lake	NFL	Dr. Charles Leidheiser	1995	159
228 3/8	28 4/8 / 29 4/8	18 2/8	10 / 8	Loon Lake	NFL	Gerald J. Cavaliere, Jr.	1998	160
228 1/8	33 1/8 / 33 0/8	27 3/8	6 / 8	Ocean Pond	NFL	David J. Lamoreaux	1998	161
227 7/8	36 1/8 / 33 0/8	27 1/8	10 / 9	Princess Lake	NFL	Ken Rapp	1966	162
227 7/8	32 2/8 / 33 0/8	26 0/8	8 / 7	Indian Lake	NFL	James R. Welch	2004	162
227 1/8	30 7/8 / 33 4/8	26 6/8	6 / 6	Conne River	NFL	Alan H. Anglyn	2005	164
226 6/8	29 6/8 / 30 6/8	28 3/8	6 / 8	Buchans Plateau	NFL	Robert J. McCarthy	1997	165
*226 2/8	31 5/8 / 32 2/8	23 7/8	6 / 6	Buchans Plateau	NFL	David Wildenstein	2005	166
225 4/8	34 2/8 / 34 5/8	27 6/8	7 / 8	Bruce's Pond	NFL	Randy E. Doyle	1990	167
225 0/8	38 0/8 / 40 3/8	25 1/8	5 / 8	Victoria River	NFL	Clarence Bowers, Jr.	1966	168
224 4/8	32 2/8 / 31 1/8	28 0/8	7 / 8	Rogers River	NFL	Duane C. Baumler	1998	169
224 1/8	36 0/8 / 35 0/8	27 4/8	8 / 9	Lloyds River	NFL	Harold A. Hill	1965	170
223 4/8	36 6/8 / 37 5/8	28 0/8	5 / 9	Andrews Pond	NFL	Gregory White	1993	171
223 4/8	32 6/8 / 31 3/8	21 4/8	8 / 8	Howley	NFL	Bryan Smith	2007	171
222 1/8	31 2/8 / 30 4/8	29 7/8	7 / 7	Greys Island	NFL	William E. Terry, Sr.	1993	173
222 0/8	32 3/8 / 33 1/8	30 1/8	7 / 8	Buchans Plateau	NFL	Mark Connor	1998	174
221 0/8	32 6/8 / 30 2/8	27 2/8	11 / 8	Saddler Pond	NFL	Paul Locey	1982	175
220 2/8	37 6/8 / 40 7/8	24 0/8	7 / 14	Alex Pond	NFL	Dr. James J. Schubert	1980	176
220 1/8	33 6/8 / 31 3/8	24 2/8	8 / 8	Stony Lake	NFL	Larry Streiff	1995	177
220 1/8	27 6/8 / 28 4/8	25 2/8	8 / 6	Dolland Pond	NFL	Roy M. Goodwin	2001	177

WOODLAND CARIBOU (VELVET ANTLERS)

Minimum Score 220

SCORE	LENGTH OF MAIN BEAM R / L	INSIDE SPREAD	NUMBER OF POINTS R / L	AREA	STATE/ PROVINCE	HUNTER'S NAME	DATE	RANK
*254 2/8	34 4/8 / 34 5/8	26 0/8	7 / 9	Deer Lake	NFL	George Harms	2009	*

POPE & YOUNG CLUB
NORTH AMERICAN BIG GAME TROPHY SCORING FORM
BOWHUNTING
BIG GAME  RECORDS

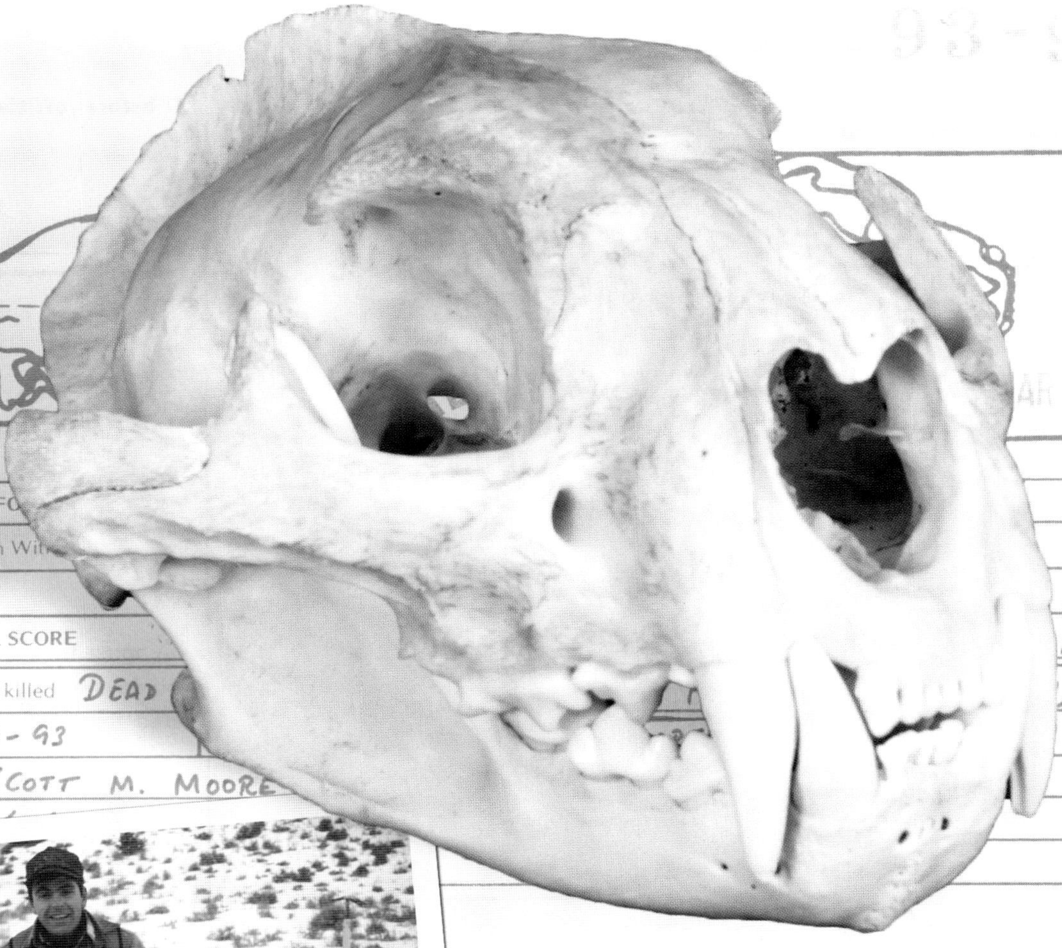

16 1/16

COUGAR   SEX **MALE**

	Measurements
A. Greatest Length	9-7/16
B. Greatest Width	6-10/16
TOTAL AND FINAL SCORE	16-1/16

Exact locality where killed: DEAD ... WYOMING
Date killed: 1-10-93
Present owner: SCOTT M. MOORE

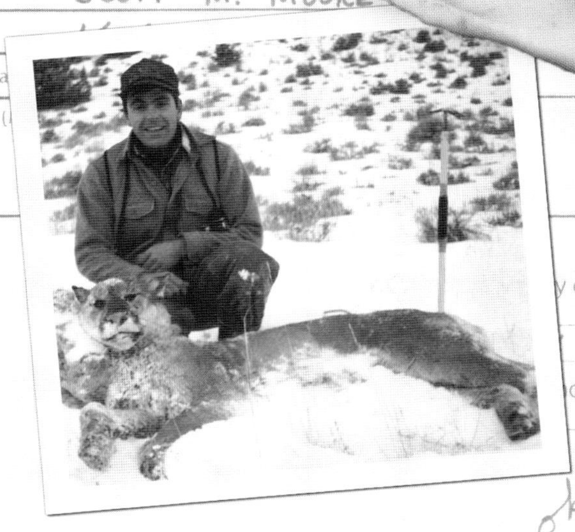

...on MARCH 12, 19 93
AVENUE   City CODY

Signature: Robert H. ...

WORLD RECORD COUGAR
Score: 16 1/16
Location: Park County, Wyoming
Date: 1993
Hunter: Scott M. Moore

82414 ZIP

Cougar

by Scott M. Moore

Finally, Scottie called and said we were to go again the next morning. Scottie, and his dogs, picked me up well before daylight and we headed for the mountains. As we drove in the dark we talked about past hunting trips and passed the time until daylight. There had been a great amount of snow and the arctic cold was entrenched upon us. The elk and deer were on their wintering grounds and we assumed the lions would be close by.

Soon, we cut a track. Scottie was excited because he knew it was a nice lion. With packs on, we crossed a creek and hoped to again find the fresh tracks. Instead, what we found was fresh lion tracks with a drag mark from a kill. Backtracking, we found that the lion had worked his way up the creek and happened on to a mule deer doe and fawn drinking at the creek. We figured this happened during the night. After trailing the drag for a while and finding the fawn carcass, we let the dogs go. The going was tough through the underbrush and downfalls of the canyon. Finally, Scottie turned to me and told me the dogs were barking treed.

As we approached, I tried to take a few camera shots, but my camera wasn't working…it was frozen. The lion was almost hidden in the pine branches and we couldn't see much of him at first. I was thinking he or she was not quite big enough---this was my first close up encounter with a lion! Scottie assured me I should take the shot and he then restrained the dogs (Ginger, Cleo and Mickey), since he has seen many dogs hurt by lions shot out of trees.

As I shot, I heard a distinctive "thunk" and was sure I hit him. However, Scottie told me that I had missed and the arrow had penetrated the branch he was laying on. Still, the lion didn't move. The second arrow soon followed and it hit perfectly in the chest. But, again, the lion acted like he was unscathed. A third arrow was right behind and on target.

COUGAR (MOUNTAIN LION)

Minimum Score 13 8/16
Felis concolor hippolestes

SCORE	GREATEST LENGTH	GREATEST WIDTH	SEX	AREA	STATE/PROVINCE	HUNTER'S NAME	DATE	RANK
16 1/16	9 7/16	6 10/16	M	Park County	WY	Scott M. Moore	1993	1
15 13/16	9 5/16	6 9/16	M	Brazeau	ALB	Glen Roberts	2007	2
15 11/16	9 2/16	6 9/16	M	Idaho County	ID	Jerry J. James	1982	3
15 11/16	9 4/16	6 7/16	M	Idaho County	ID	Mike McCall	1985	3
15 11/16	9 7/16	6 4/16	M	Ferry County	WA	Bill Buckingham	1986	3
15 11/16	9 3/16	6 8/16	M	Montrose County	CO	Randell Thompson	1992	3
15 11/16	9 3/16	6 8/16	M	Elmore County	ID	Susan Sherer	2003	3
15 10/16	9 0/16	6 10/16	M	Unit 5-5	BC	Harold J. Coult	1986	8
15 10/16	9 5/16	6 5/16	M	Kootenai County	ID	Thomas E. Bangs	1993	8
15 10/16	9 2/16	6 8/16	M	San Miguel County	CO	Robert D. Parker	1994	8
15 10/16	9 3/16	6 7/16	M	Sibbald Flats	ALB	Richard J. Howden	2002	8
*15 10/16	9 6/16	6 4/16	M	Rio Blanco County	CO	Greg Wisener	2008	8
15 9/16	9 3/16	6 6/16	M	Rio Arriba County	NM	Robert John Seeds	1995	13
15 9/16	9 3/16	6 6/16	M	Pembina River	ALB	Robert Sydenham	2007	13
15 8/16	9 1/16	6 7/16	M	Lemhi County	ID	Doug Kittredge	1971	15
15 8/16	8 15/16	6 9/16	M	Clearwater County	ID	John R. Bridwell	1988	15
15 8/16	8 15/16	6 9/16	M	Gila County	AZ	Stephen D. Hornady	1991	15
15 8/16	9 0/16	6 8/16	M	Sanders County	MT	Wayne M. Foley	1993	15
15 8/16	9 2/16	6 6/16	M	Lemhi County	ID	Ray F. Doskus	1994	15
15 8/16	9 3/16	6 5/16	M	Lemhi County	ID	Michael Judas	1995	15
15 8/16	9 4/16	6 4/16	M	Skinner Mtn.	BC	Jeff Ashe	1997	15
15 8/16	9 2/16	6 6/16	M	Garfield County	CO	Richard A. Mowles	1997	15
15 8/16	9 3/16	6 5/16	M	Flat Creek	ALB	A. Paul Kroshko	1998	15
15 8/16	9 2/16	6 6/16	M	Rio Arriba County	NM	Robert J. Seeds	1999	15
15 7/16	9 2/16	6 5/16	M	Huerfano County	CO	J. D. Dodge	1971	25
15 7/16	9 0/16	6 7/16	M	Idaho County	ID	William Egner	1972	25
15 7/16	9 4/16	6 3/16	M	Sandoval County	NM	Tom David	1980	25
15 7/16	9 2/16	6 5/16	M	Rio Arriba County	NM	Dick Ray	1985	25
15 7/16	9 2/16	6 5/16	M	Uintah County	UT	John M Mc Ateer	1985	25
15 7/16	9 0/16	6 7/16	M	Idaho County	ID	Steven Anderson	1986	25
15 7/16	8 15/16	6 8/16	M	Ferry County	WA	John Peruchini	1989	25
15 7/16	8 14/16	6 9/16	M	Shoshone County	ID	Eugene L. Lewis	1991	25
15 7/16	9 0/16	6 7/16	M	Clearwater County	ID	Dennis L. Butler	1992	25
15 7/16	9 3/16	6 4/16	M	Colfax County	NM	Donald Travis	1994	25
15 7/16	9 1/16	6 6/16	M	Clearwater County	ID	Mike Lewis	1997	25
15 7/16	9 2/16	6 5/16	M	Nordegg River	ALB	Kelly Hall	1998	25
15 7/16	9 0/16	6 7/16	M	Lewis & Clark County	MT	Matt Enrooth	2009	25
15 6/16	9 4/16	6 2/16	M	Grand County	UT	Art Kragness	1969	39
15 6/16	8 11/16	6 11/16	M	Taos County	NM	George P. Mann	1981	39
15 6/16	9 2/16	6 4/16	M	Water Valley	ALB	Don Ferguson	1983	39
15 6/16	9 0/16	6 6/16	M	Idaho County	ID	Ralph L. Hatter	1987	39
15 6/16	8 14/16	6 8/16	M	Lavington	BC	Chris Barker	1992	39
15 6/16	9 0/16	6 6/16	M	Elmore County	ID	Kelly Dougherty	1993	39
15 6/16	8 14/16	6 8/16	M	Dolores County	CO	Thadius Countess	1998	39
15 6/16	9 0/16	6 6/16	M	Idaho County	ID	James R. Ciardelli	2000	39
15 6/16	9 1/16	6 5/16	M	Nordegg	ALB	Darryl Kublik	2003	39
15 5/16	8 15/16	6 6/16	M	Mesa County	CO	John Lamicq, Jr.	1969	48
15 5/16	8 15/16	6 6/16	M	Larimer County	CO	Glenn Schmidt	1976	48
15 5/16	8 15/16	6 6/16	M	Mineral County	MT	Dennis Moos	1976	48
15 5/16	8 13/16	6 8/16	M	Madison County	MT	Don Schaufler	1982	48
15 5/16	9 0/16	6 5/16	M	Idaho County	ID	A. M. Oakes, Jr.	1985	48
15 5/16	9 2/16	6 3/16	M	Rio Blanco County	CO	Rob Raley	1985	48
15 5/16	9 0/16	6 5/16	M	Clearwater County	ID	Daniel J. Greve	1985	48
15 5/16	9 0/16	6 5/16	M	Idaho County	ID	Drexel Schilling	1987	48
15 5/16	9 1/16	6 4/16	M	Clearwater County	ID	Rudy Marmelo, Jr.	1990	48
15 5/16	9 0/16	6 5/16	M	Lindsey Lake	BC	Harvey J. Surina	1991	48
15 5/16	9 3/16	6 2/16	M	Rio Arriba County	NM	Robert John Seeds	1992	48
15 5/16	9 0/16	6 5/16	M	Delta County	CO	William E. Kallister	1995	48
15 5/16	9 1/16	6 4/16	M	Custer County	ID	Mike Woltering	1995	48
15 5/16	9 0/16	6 5/16	M	Clearwater County	ID	Bob Bosshardt	1997	48
15 5/16	8 15/16	6 6/16	M	Mesa County	CO	Darryl Powell	1997	48
15 5/16	8 13/16	6 8/16	M	Benchlands	ALB	John P. Lacroix	1998	48
15 5/16	9 0/16	6 5/16	M	Ravalli County	MT	James Behling	2005	48
15 4/16	9 0/16	6 4/16	M	Gila County	AZ	Dr. James L. Smith	1958	65
15 4/16	8 15/16	6 5/16	M	Ogden County	UT	Royce Ross	1971	65
15 4/16	9 0/16	6 4/16	M	Uintah County	UT	Albert L. Farace	1986	65
15 4/16	9 2/16	6 2/16	M	San Juan County	UT	Diane Snyder	1986	65
15 4/16	9 0/16	6 4/16	M	Madison County	MT	Pat Connell	1986	65
15 4/16	8 14/16	6 6/16	M	Clearwater County	ID	Elwood Schultz	1986	65
15 4/16	9 1/16	6 3/16	M	San Miguel County	CO	G. Merrill Jones	1987	65
15 4/16	9 0/16	6 4/16	M	Porcupine Hills	ALB	John Visscher	1990	65
15 4/16	8 15/16	6 5/16	M	Carbon County	UT	Kenny E. Leo	1993	65
15 4/16	8 13/16	6 7/16	M	Lewis & Clark County	MT	Lee D. Laeupple	1993	65
15 4/16	9 0/16	6 4/16	M	Shoshone County	ID	Paul Schaumburg	1993	65
15 4/16	9 2/16	6 2/16	M	Rio Arriba County	NM	Robert John Seeds	1994	65
15 4/16	9 0/16	6 4/16	M	Beaver Valley	BC	Jim Dunigan	1996	65
15 4/16	8 14/16	6 6/16	M	Moyie Lake	BC	Robert Faiers	1997	65
15 4/16	9 1/16	6 3/16	M	Broadwater County	MT	Kevin Harms	1998	65
15 4/16	9 1/16	6 3/16	M	Fremont County	ID	John Roseborough	2003	65
15 4/16	9 1/16	6 3/16	M	Rio Blanco County	CO	Jeff J. Thomas	2003	65
15 4/16	9 0/16	6 4/16	M	Whitecourt	ALB	Dale Fournier	2004	65
15 4/16	9 0/16	6 4/16	M	Jefferson County	CO	Calvin T. Behunin	2005	65
15 4/16	9 0/16	6 4/16	M	Brazeau	ALB	Troy Dzioba	2006	65
*15 4/16	8 14/16	6 6/16	M	Cynthia	ALB	Dean Kirkeby	2007	65
15 3/16	8 13/16	6 6/16	M	Ventura County	CA	Warren C. Johnston	1953	86
15 3/16	9 0/16	6 3/16	M	Fremont County	CO	Art Heinze	1976	86
15 3/16	8 14/16	6 5/16	M	Douglas County	CO	Donald R. Looper	1977	86
15 3/16	8 13/16	6 6/16	M	Rio Arriba County	NM	Anderson Bakewell, S.J.	1978	86
15 3/16	8 4/16	6 15/16	M	Cassia County	ID	Ronald C. Ward	1984	86
15 3/16	8 13/16	6 6/16	M	Clallam County	WA	Ron W. Cram	1984	86
15 3/16	8 14/16	6 5/16	M	Huerfano County	CO	Bob Sigman	1987	86
15 3/16	8 14/16	6 5/16	M	Clearwater County	ID	Mike T. McCain	1988	86
15 3/16	8 14/16	6 5/16	M	Lincoln County	MT	Jon Greeno Clark	1989	86
15 3/16	9 1/16	6 2/16	M	Ravalli County	MT	Mario Locatelli	1990	86
15 3/16	9 2/16	6 1/16	M	Archuleta County	CO	Charles T. Ames	1991	86

254

COUGAR (MOUNTAIN LION)

Minimum Score 13 8/16 — Continued

SCORE	GREATEST LENGTH	GREATEST WIDTH	SEX	AREA	STATE/PROVINCE	HUNTER'S NAME	DATE	RANK
15 3/16	8 15/16	6 4/16	M	Idaho County	ID	Steve B. Schilling	1992	86
15 3/16	8 15/16	6 4/16	M	Daggett County	UT	John Richardson	1992	86
15 3/16	8 13/16	6 6/16	M	Bannock County	ID	Brad Hough	1992	86
15 3/16	8 14/16	6 5/16	M	Lincoln County	MT	Terry Krogstad	1993	86
15 3/16	9 0/16	6 3/16	M	Clear Creek County	CO	Mark Turner	1995	86
15 3/16	8 15/16	6 4/16	M	Judith Basin County	MT	John "Rosey" Roseland	1997	86
15 3/16	8 15/16	6 4/16	M	Idaho County	ID	Jesse Higgins	1998	86
15 3/16	8 15/16	6 4/16	M	Rio Arriba County	NM	Robert J. Seeds	1998	86
15 3/16	8 14/16	6 5/16	M	McLean Creek	ALB	Neil G. Johnson	1999	86
15 3/16	8 15/16	6 4/16	M	Frazier River	BC	Gene A. Welle	2000	86
15 3/16	8 15/16	6 4/16	M	Golden	BC	Gilles Rondeau	2000	86
15 3/16	9 1/16	6 2/16	M	Clark County	ID	Cameron Ballard	2003	86
15 3/16	8 14/16	6 5/16	M	Cynthia	ALB	Chad Lenz	2003	86
15 3/16	8 14/16	6 5/16	M	Camas County	ID	Mark Kyle	2004	86
15 3/16	8 12/16	6 7/16	M	Elk River	BC	Kent Fraser	2006	86
15 3/16	9 0/16	6 3/16	M	Medicine Lake	ALB	Stephane Titley	2006	86
15 3/16	8 15/16	6 4/16	M	Grant County	OR	Richard Newton	2009	86
*15 3/16	9 0/16	6 3/16	M	Rio Blanco County	CO	Larry W. Flamisch, Jr.	2009	86
15 3/16	9 0/16	6 3/16	M	Black Creek	BC	Russell Zuffa	2009	86
15 2/16	8 15/16	6 3/16	M	Rio Blanco County	CO	Leonard Cardinale	1963	115
15 2/16	9 0/16	6 2/16	M	Grand County	UT	Richard Oakleaf	1967	115
15 2/16	8 12/16	6 6/16	M	Flathead County	MT	Jerry Almos	1971	115
15 2/16	8 14/16	6 4/16	M	Wallowa County	OR	Terrell Buchanan	1973	115
15 2/16	9 0/16	6 2/16	M	Utah County	UT	Max F. Park	1975	115
15 2/16	8 14/16	6 4/16	M	Sanders County	MT	Conrad Anderson	1984	115
15 2/16	8 14/16	6 4/16	M	Meagher County	MT	Gene Clark	1985	115
15 2/16	8 12/16	6 6/16	M	Teton County	WY	Craig Richardson	1986	115
15 2/16	8 14/16	6 4/16	M	Wallowa County	OR	Thomas C. Ashcroft	1986	115
15 2/16	8 14/16	6 4/16	M	Daggett County	UT	Franco DiPietro	1987	115
15 2/16	8 14/16	6 4/16	M	Conejos County	CO	Wayne Miller	1987	115
15 2/16	9 0/16	6 2/16	M	Mesa County	CO	Frank P. Alameno	1987	115
15 2/16	8 15/16	6 3/16	M	Clearwater County	ID	Michael J. Kennedy	1987	115
15 2/16	8 13/16	6 5/16	M	Pincher Creek	ALB	Duane B. Schultz	1988	115
15 2/16	8 12/16	6 6/16	M	Iron County	UT	Bob Spina	1989	115
15 2/16	8 15/16	6 3/16	M	Park County	CO	Jack P. Van Vianen	1990	115
15 2/16	8 13/16	6 5/16	M	Shoshone County	ID	Pat D. Jerald	1991	115
15 2/16	8 15/16	6 3/16	M	Rio Arriba County	NM	Robert John Seeds	1991	115
15 2/16	8 9/16	6 9/16	M	Lincoln County	MT	Jim Eff	1992	115
15 2/16	8 11/16	6 7/16	M	Kootenay Lake	BC	Robert Kuny	1993	115
15 2/16	8 12/16	6 6/16	M	Park County	MT	Primo Scapin	1993	115
15 2/16	8 15/16	6 3/16	M	Kootenay River	BC	Brian Schuck	1993	115
15 2/16	9 0/16	6 2/16	M	Larimer County	CO	Don Watowa	1994	115
15 2/16	8 13/16	6 5/16	M	Porcupine Hills	ALB	Dan Croy	1995	115
15 2/16	9 1/16	6 1/16	M	Mesa County	CO	M. David Bennett, Jr.	1996	115
15 2/16	8 15/16	6 3/16	M	Delta County	CO	Ray Kennedy	1996	115
15 2/16	8 12/16	6 6/16	M	Rio Arriba County	NM	Robert John Seeds	1996	115
15 2/16	8 14/16	6 4/16	M	Madison County	MT	Cody Stemler	1996	115
15 2/16	8 14/16	6 4/16	M	Rocky Mountain House	ALB	Dennis Tucker	1997	115
15 2/16	8 14/16	6 4/16	M	Chain Lakes	ALB	Tom Foss	1998	115
15 2/16	8 15/16	6 3/16	M	Missoula County	MT	Sam Anderson	2000	115
15 2/16	8 14/16	6 4/16	M	Skamania County	WA	Owen Sarkinen	2001	115
15 2/16	8 15/16	6 3/16	M	Cowlitz County	WA	Kip Burns	2005	115
15 2/16	8 13/16	6 5/16	M	Cochrane	ALB	Matthew Serwa	2006	115
15 1/16	8 13/16	6 4/16	M	Iron County	UT	William P. Mastrangel	1964	149
15 1/16	8 12/16	6 5/16	M	Nez Perce County	ID	Pete Baughman, Jr.	1979	149
15 1/16	8 15/16	6 2/16	M	Rio Arriba County	NM	Joe Strasser, Jr.	1980	149
15 1/16	8 14/16	6 3/16	M	San Juan County	UT	Shad D. Schmidt	1981	149
15 1/16	8 13/16	6 4/16	M	Archuleta County	CO	Judd Cooney	1982	149
15 1/16	9 1/16	6 0/16	M	Lincoln County	MT	Gary C. Cargill	1986	149
15 1/16	8 15/16	6 2/16	M	Clearwater County	ID	Charles "Smitty" Smith	1987	149
15 1/16	8 11/16	6 6/16	M	Sundre	ALB	Fred Houtstra	1987	149
15 1/16	9 1/16	6 0/16	M	Valley County	ID	Douglas L. Petty	1987	149
15 1/16	8 14/16	6 3/16	M	Ouray County	CO	Steven A. Rider	1989	149
15 1/16	9 0/16	6 1/16	M	Millard County	UT	Edwin A. Lewis	1990	149
15 1/16	8 14/16	6 3/16	M	Rio Blanco County	CO	Dr. Gerald L. Dowling	1990	149
15 1/16	9 0/16	6 1/16	M	Taos County	NM	Bill Porteous	1990	149
15 1/16	8 15/16	6 2/16	M	Mineral County	MT	Gerg Balzum	1990	149
15 1/16	8 12/16	6 5/16	M	Eagle County	CO	Richard E. Davis	1990	149
15 1/16	9 0/16	6 1/16	M	Sanders County	MT	Phillip J. Taylor	1992	149
15 1/16	8 10/16	6 7/16	M	Lincoln County	MT	William R. Vyvvan	1992	149
15 1/16	9 0/16	6 1/16	M	Carbon County	UT	Ray T. Bridge	1993	149
15 1/16	8 14/16	6 3/16	M	Sanders County	MT	Dennis Gripp	1994	149
15 1/16	8 11/16	6 6/16	M	Boundary County	ID	Ron Frederickson	1994	149
15 1/16	8 14/16	6 3/16	M	Flathead County	MT	Shawn P. Price	1994	149
15 1/16	8 14/16	6 3/16	M	Rio Blanco County	CO	Bruce R. Schoeneweis	1994	149
15 1/16	8 15/16	6 2/16	M	Grand County	CO	Rick Karbowski	1997	149
15 1/16	9 0/16	6 1/16	M	Eagle County	CO	David TerMaat	1997	149
15 1/16	9 0/16	6 1/16	M	Bear Lake County	ID	Quinn Erickson	1997	149
15 1/16	8 12/16	6 5/16	M	Park County	MT	Michael R. Deschamps	1997	149
15 1/16	8 13/16	6 4/16	M	Rocky Mountain House	ALB	Gary Hamilton	1998	149
15 1/16	8 10/16	6 7/16	M	Grand County	CO	Paul Tudor Jones	1999	149
15 1/16	8 15/16	6 2/16	M	Rio Arriba County	NM	James Vance	1999	149
15 1/16	9 0/16	6 1/16	M	Montrose County	CO	Steven R. Hickok	2000	149
15 1/16	8 15/16	6 2/16	M	Elmore County	ID	Kim Womer	2001	149
15 1/16	8 12/16	6 5/16	M	Castle River	ALB	Flint Simpson	2003	149
15 1/16	8 14/16	6 3/16	M	Sanders County	MT	Terry K. Turner	2003	149
15 1/16	9 0/16	6 1/16	M	Mesa County	CO	Randy St. Ores	2004	149
15 1/16	8 12/16	6 5/16	M	Ravalli County	MT	Robert S. Wood	2005	149
*15 1/16	8 14/16	6 3/16	M	Grand County	CO	Richard Morrow	2008	149
15 0/16	8 11/16	6 5/16	M	Elko County	NV	Earl Dudley	1959	185
15 0/16	8 13/16	6 3/16	M	Utah County	UT	Richard C. Smith	1968	185
15 0/16	8 11/16	6 5/16	M	Mizzezula Mtns.	BC	Bengt G. Bjalme	1969	185
15 0/16	8 12/16	6 4/16	M	Columbia Lake	BC	Ray Lundstrom	1979	185
15 0/16	8 14/16	6 2/16	M	Madison County	MT	George A. Dieruf	1980	185
15 0/16	8 11/16	6 5/16	M	Sandoval County	NM	Ernest C. Torres	1981	185

255

COUGAR (MOUNTAIN LION)

Minimum Score 13 8/16   Continued

SCORE	GREATEST LENGTH	GREATEST WIDTH	SEX	AREA	STATE/ PROVINCE	HUNTER'S NAME	DATE	RANK
15 0/16	8 12/16	6 4/16	M	Lemhi County	ID	Roy Auwen	1981	185
15 0/16	8 11/16	6 5/16	M	Rio Arriba County	NM	Mike Ray	1982	185
15 0/16	8 11/16	6 5/16	M	Mineral County	MT	Grover L. Hedrick	1983	185
15 0/16	8 10/16	6 6/16	M	Sanders County	MT	Joe Schaefer	1984	185
15 0/16	8 10/16	6 6/16	M	Wallowa County	OR	Chuck Warner	1985	185
15 0/16	9 0/16	6 0/16	M	Rio Grande County	CO	Richard J. Dugas	1986	185
15 0/16	8 12/16	6 4/16	M	San Juan County	NM	Richard M. Young, Jr.	1987	185
15 0/16	8 10/16	6 6/16	M	Sanpete County	UT	Craig Adams	1988	185
15 0/16	9 0/16	6 0/16	M	Elmore County	ID	Ed Strayhorn	1989	185
15 0/16	8 14/16	6 2/16	M	Rio Arriba County	NM	Robert J. Seeds	1989	185
15 0/16	8 13/16	6 3/16	M	Pillar Lake	BC	Kent Michie/Terry Wasylyszyn	1989	185
15 0/16	8 12/16	6 4/16	M	Cache County	UT	Gino Giannetti	1990	185
15 0/16	8 14/16	6 2/16	M	Carbon County	UT	Roy Wheeler, Jr.	1990	185
15 0/16	8 12/16	6 4/16	M	Camas County	ID	Andy Moore	1990	185
15 0/16	8 12/16	6 4/16	M	Shoshone County	ID	Buster Karrer	1991	185
15 0/16	8 11/16	6 5/16	M	Fergus County	MT	Chuck Taylor	1991	185
15 0/16	8 12/16	6 4/16	M	Spokane County	WA	Colin McRae	1991	185
15 0/16	8 14/16	6 2/16	M	Garfield County	UT	Gregory Nixon	1992	185
15 0/16	8 13/16	6 3/16	M	Gallatin County	MT	Darrell Otteson	1992	185
15 0/16	8 14/16	6 2/16	M	Lemhi County	ID	Daniel R. Darrah	1992	185
15 0/16	8 13/16	6 3/16	M	Montezuma County	CO	John L. Gardner	1993	185
15 0/16	8 12/16	6 4/16	M	Montrose County	CO	Corey W. Murray	1993	185
15 0/16	8 15/16	6 1/16	M	Montezuma County	CO	Robert D. Crask	1993	185
15 0/16	8 15/16	6 1/16	M	Boise County	ID	Mark W. Rose	1995	185
15 0/16	8 11/16	6 5/16	M	Battle Creek	BC	Glenn Dreger	1995	185
15 0/16	8 15/16	6 1/16	M	Valley County	ID	John Pyle	1995	185
15 0/16	9 0/16	6 0/16	M	Rio Arriba County	NM	K-Tal Johnson	1995	185
15 0/16	8 14/16	6 2/16	M	San Juan County	UT	David A. Bronson	1997	185
15 0/16	8 12/16	6 4/16	M	Bonner County	ID	Shawn Frederickson	1997	185
15 0/16	8 13/16	6 3/16	M	Benewah County	ID	Don Houk	1998	185
15 0/16	8 12/16	6 4/16	M	South Willow Creek	ALB	Paul S. Unger	1998	185
15 0/16	8 13/16	6 3/16	M	Humboldt County	NV	Ronald C. Miller, Jr.	1999	185
15 0/16	8 15/16	6 1/16	M	Canim Lake	BC	Peter L. McKeen	2000	185
15 0/16	8 10/16	6 6/16	M	Moffat County	CO	Aaron W. Tuck	2000	185
15 0/16	9 0/16	6 0/16	M	Utah County	UT	Dustin L. Mitchell	2001	185
15 0/16	8 9/16	6 7/16	M	Gallatin County	MT	Brian Koelzer	2001	185
15 0/16	9 0/16	6 0/16	M	Bull River	BC	Joseph Allan Borgna	2002	185
15 0/16	8 13/16	6 3/16	M	Fremont County	WY	Jim Parkins	2003	185
15 0/16	8 14/16	6 2/16	M	Clatsop County	OR	Clarence F. Lamping	2004	185
*15 0/16	8 14/16	6 2/16	M	Davis County	UT	Kelly Moore	2010	185
15 0/16	9 1/16	5 15/16	M	Idaho County	ID	Leslie K. Workman	2010	185
14 15/16	8 12/16	6 3/16	M	Lincoln County	MT	Allen Apling	1959	232
14 15/16	8 11/16	6 4/16	M	Boundary County	ID	Rick Furniss	1968	232
14 15/16	8 13/16	6 2/16	M	Rio Blanco County	CO	Stanley R. Winslow	1971	232
14 15/16	8 14/16	6 1/16	M	Rio Blanco County	CO	Jack Pawlak	1971	232
14 15/16	8 14/16	6 1/16	M	Carbon County	UT	Larry Wright	1975	232
14 15/16	8 11/16	6 4/16	M	Idaho County	ID	Dick Gulman	1976	232
14 15/16	8 12/16	6 3/16	M	Piute County	UT	Douglas Wagner	1976	232
14 15/16	8 11/16	6 4/16	M	Deer Lodge County	MT	Scott Koelzer	1979	232
14 15/16	8 15/16	6 0/16	M	Montezuma County	CO	Roy Keefer	1984	232
14 15/16	8 14/16	6 1/16	M	Cascade County	MT	Charles A. Vande Hei	1984	232
14 15/16	8 13/16	6 2/16	M	Sevier County	UT	Chuck Morger	1988	232
14 15/16	8 11/16	6 4/16	M	Park County	MT	Patrick Gilligan	1988	232
14 15/16	8 13/16	6 2/16	M	Ouray County	CO	Doug McCauley	1988	232
14 15/16	8 14/16	6 1/16	M	Garfield County	CO	Bruce R. Schoeneweis	1989	232
14 15/16	8 13/16	6 2/16	M	Bear Lake County	ID	Rick Berghelm	1990	232
14 15/16	8 12/16	6 3/16	M	Missoula County	MT	Mike Miller	1990	232
14 15/16	8 12/16	6 3/16	M	San Miguel County	CO	Monroe A. Hare	1991	232
14 15/16	8 12/16	6 3/16	M	Idaho County	ID	Mark Jacobson	1991	232
14 15/16	8 12/16	6 3/16	M	Missoula County	MT	Kenneth B. Scobie	1991	232
14 15/16	8 12/16	6 3/16	M	Ravalli County	MT	James A. Haase	1993	232
14 15/16	8 10/16	6 5/16	M	Kananaskis	ALB	Harry Schilling	1993	232
14 15/16	8 13/16	6 2/16	M	Elmore County	ID	Tony Mudd	1993	232
14 15/16	8 12/16	6 3/16	M	Sandoval County	NM	Rett Kelly	1993	232
14 15/16	8 15/16	6 0/16	M	Tatlayoka Lake	BC	Glenn Dreger	1994	232
14 15/16	8 13/16	6 2/16	M	Morgan County	UT	Claude Archuleta	1994	232
14 15/16	8 13/16	6 2/16	M	La Plata County	CO	Valerie Gardner	1994	232
14 15/16	8 13/16	6 2/16	M	Moffat County	CO	Rob Bathurst	1995	232
14 15/16	9 1/16	5 14/16	M	Crook County	OR	Trent Ough	1996	232
14 15/16	8 13/16	6 2/16	M	Caven Creek	BC	Brian Chittim	1996	232
14 15/16	8 11/16	6 4/16	M	Rio Blanco County	CO	Clare Streeter	1998	232
14 15/16	8 12/16	6 3/16	M	Kelowna	BC	Rick Pasutto	1998	232
14 15/16	8 12/16	6 3/16	M	Idaho County	ID	Ryan Lowery	1998	232
14 15/16	8 15/16	6 0/16	M	Caroline	ALB	Derrill Herman	1999	232
14 15/16	8 11/16	6 4/16	M	Corbin	BC	Scott Holberton	2005	232
14 15/16	8 12/16	6 3/16	M	Iron County	UT	David R. Spellman	2006	232
14 15/16	8 11/16	6 4/16	M	Missoula County	MT	Brennan W. Nelson	2008	232
14 14/16	8 14/16	6 0/16	M	Lincoln County	MT	Dr. B. L. Lundberg	1958	268
14 14/16	8 11/16	6 3/16	M	Flathead County	MT	Jack Whitney	1967	268
14 14/16	8 10/16	6 4/16	M	Lemhi County	ID	Ray Torrey	1969	268
14 14/16	8 10/16	6 4/16	M	Granite County	MT	John Lawler	1972	268
14 14/16	8 13/16	6 1/16	M	Elmore County	ID	Dan F. Hackney	1973	268
14 14/16	8 15/16	5 15/16	M	Lemhi County	ID	Jim Dougherty	1980	268
14 14/16	8 11/16	6 3/16	M	Utah County	UT	Kelly R. Clements	1981	268
14 14/16	8 12/16	6 2/16	M	Lemhi County	ID	Jay Meyers	1982	268
14 14/16	8 12/16	6 2/16	M	Iron County	UT	Craig R. White	1983	268
14 14/16	8 12/16	6 2/16	M	Montezuma County	CO	Ms. Charlie White	1983	268
14 14/16	8 12/16	6 2/16	M	Madison County	MT	Cecil I. Tharp	1984	268
14 14/16	8 14/16	6 0/16	M	Rio Blanco County	CO	Calvin Farner	1986	268
14 14/16	8 10/16	6 4/16	M	Flathead County	MT	Bruce Whitaker	1988	268
14 14/16	8 13/16	6 1/16	M	Utah County	UT	Daniel M. Taylor	1989	268
14 14/16	8 13/16	6 1/16	M	Clearwater County	ID	Reva Anne Hyde	1990	268
14 14/16	8 11/16	6 3/16	M	Grand County	UT	Joseph A. Segaria	1991	268
14 14/16	8 10/16	6 4/16	M	Fergus County	MT	Allen Fritz	1991	268
14 14/16	8 13/16	6 1/16	M	North Fork	ALB	Victor Lawson	1991	268

256

COUGAR (MOUNTAIN LION)

Minimum Score 13 8/16   Continued

SCORE	GREATEST LENGTH	GREATEST WIDTH	SEX	AREA	STATE/ PROVINCE	HUNTER'S NAME	DATE	RANK
14 14/16	8 12/16	6 2/16	M	Moffat County	CO	Mike Camilletti, Sr.	1993	268
14 14/16	8 11/16	6 3/16	M	Bonner County	ID	Timothy J. Duffney	1993	268
14 14/16	8 11/16	6 3/16	M	Stevens County	WA	Thomas Patterson	1993	268
14 14/16	8 13/16	6 1/16	M	Millard County	UT	David Edwards	1994	268
14 14/16	8 12/16	6 2/16	M	Rio Blanco County	CO	Frank L. Fackovec	1994	268
14 14/16	8 12/16	6 2/16	M	Whatshau River	BC	Gary Atkins	1994	268
14 14/16	8 12/16	6 2/16	M	Ravalli County	MT	Anthony "Del" DelMastro	1994	268
14 14/16	8 12/16	6 2/16	M	Lincoln County	MT	James Hershberger	1994	268
14 14/16	9 0/16	5 14/16	F	San Miguel County	CO	Wyatt C. Watson	1995	268
14 14/16	8 11/16	6 3/16	M	Toby Creek	BC	Kent G. Kebe	1995	268
14 14/16	8 12/16	6 2/16	M	Vaseux Creek	BC	Terry L. Bixler	1995	268
14 14/16	8 10/16	6 4/16	M	Teton County	WY	Craig A. Germond	1996	268
14 14/16	8 13/16	6 1/16	M	Montezuma County	CO	Ronald R. Grenadier	1998	268
14 14/16	8 10/16	6 4/16	M	Bonneville County	ID	Thomas N. Thiel	1999	268
14 14/16	8 14/16	6 0/16	M	Lemhi County	ID	Bernard H. Weisgerber	2001	268
14 14/16	8 14/16	6 0/16	M	Rio Arriba County	NM	Robert S. Miller	2001	268
14 14/16	8 13/16	6 1/16	M	Cowlitz County	WA	Robert Ferry	2004	268
14 14/16	8 12/16	6 2/16	M	Lincoln County	MT	Kevin Neidigh	2007	268
14 14/16	8 12/16	6 2/16	M	Saguache County	CO	R. Kirk Sharp	2009	268
14 13/16	8 11/16	6 2/16	M	Chelan County	WA	Dr. R. Congdon	1951	305
14 13/16	8 11/16	6 2/16	M	Ferry County	WA	R. O. Hilderbrant	1965	305
14 13/16	8 12/16	6 1/16	F	Duchesne County	UT	Larry Jones	1967	305
14 13/16	8 13/16	6 0/16	M	Garfield County	CO	Albert L. Heise	1971	305
14 13/16	8 13/16	6 0/16	M	Chaffee County	CO	Phillip B. Grable	1973	305
14 13/16	8 10/16	6 3/16	M	Huerfano County	CO	William F. Eikleberry	1974	305
14 13/16	8 12/16	6 1/16	M	Emery County	UT	Rex Peterson	1975	305
14 13/16	8 11/16	6 2/16	M	Uintah County	UT	Ronald D. Shank	1976	305
14 13/16	8 12/16	6 1/16	M	Warner	BC	John "Jack" Cordes	1977	305
14 13/16	8 10/16	6 3/16	M	Elmore County	ID	Dr. Robert T. Laughery	1979	305
14 13/16	8 10/16	6 3/16	M	Stevens County	WA	Tim C. Boyd	1979	305
14 13/16	8 14/16	5 15/16	M	Mesa County	CO	Jim R. Lewis	1981	305
14 13/16	8 13/16	6 0/16	M	Idaho County	ID	Ray Keenan	1982	305
14 13/16	8 12/16	6 1/16	M	Moffat County	CO	John A. Lee	1982	305
14 13/16	8 11/16	6 2/16	M	McGuire Creek	BC	William Morley	1983	305
14 13/16	8 12/16	6 1/16	M	Sanders County	MT	Gil Gilbertson	1984	305
14 13/16	8 11/16	6 2/16	M	San Miguel County	CO	David E. Smith	1985	305
14 13/16	8 12/16	6 1/16	M	Albany County	WY	R.D. Keeler, D.C.	1985	305
14 13/16	8 13/16	6 0/16	M	Camas County	ID	Larry R. Newton	1987	305
14 13/16	8 11/16	6 2/16	M	Fish Creek	ALB	Ken Maier	1987	305
14 13/16	8 9/16	6 4/16	M	Montezuma County	CO	Richard Kimball	1987	305
14 13/16	8 11/16	6 2/16	M	Clearwater County	ID	Thomas A. Kayser	1988	305
14 13/16	8 11/16	6 2/16	M	Clearwater County	ID	Ralph Albright	1989	305
14 13/16	8 12/16	6 1/16	M	Emery County	UT	Sam Raby	1989	305
14 13/16	8 12/16	6 1/16	M	Dolores County	CO	Robert R. Hoffa, Jr.	1990	305
14 13/16	8 10/16	6 3/16	M	Black Mtn.	ALB	Udo Kerber	1991	305
14 13/16	8 14/16	5 15/16	M	Powell County	MT	Todd Johnson	1991	305
14 13/16	8 10/16	6 3/16	M	Elko	BC	Gordon Mailey	1991	305
14 13/16	8 11/16	6 2/16	M	Carbon County	UT	Tracy Jacobsen	1992	305
14 13/16	8 13/16	6 0/16	M	Archuleta County	CO	Sam B. Ray	1992	305
14 13/16	8 12/16	6 1/16	M	Fremont County	CO	Robert W. Allen	1992	305
14 13/16	8 11/16	6 2/16	M	Sanders County	MT	Tony Naismith	1992	305
14 13/16	8 13/16	6 0/16	M	Shoshone County	ID	Kenneth L. Way	1992	305
14 13/16	8 11/16	6 2/16	M	Delta County	CO	Dennis Hayden	1993	305
14 13/16	8 9/16	6 4/16	M	Kittitas County	WA	Scott Kieser	1993	305
14 13/16	8 11/16	6 2/16	M	Gallatin County	MT	John Berger	1993	305
14 13/16	8 9/16	6 4/16	M	Sanders County	MT	Don E. Smith	1993	305
14 13/16	8 11/16	6 2/16	M	Boise County	ID	August S. Gray	1993	305
14 13/16	8 11/16	6 2/16	M	Las Animas County	CO	Richie Bland	1994	305
14 13/16	8 12/16	6 1/16	M	Granite County	MT	Mickey E. Lotz	1994	305
14 13/16	8 10/16	6 3/16	M	Madison County	MT	Robert Maier	1994	305
14 13/16	8 10/16	6 3/16	M	Saguache County	CO	Mike Haynes	1995	305
14 13/16	8 13/16	6 0/16	M	Boise County	ID	Barry Gwin	1996	305
14 13/16	8 12/16	6 1/16	M	Sanders County	MT	Judy Kovar	1996	305
14 13/16	8 11/16	6 2/16	M	Rio Blanco County	CO	Roger C. Trout	1997	305
14 13/16	8 11/16	6 2/16	M	Cache County	UT	Monte Green	1997	305
14 13/16	8 13/16	6 0/16	M	Latah County	ID	Ike Carpenter	1998	305
14 13/16	8 15/16	5 14/16	M	Rio Blanco County	CO	Steve Chin	1999	305
14 13/16	8 12/16	6 1/16	M	Socorro County	NM	Joseph Seagle	1999	305
14 13/16	8 11/16	6 2/16	M	Fording Mtn.	BC	Devon Musil	1999	305
14 13/16	8 12/16	6 1/16	M	Buckskin Lake	BC	Kenneth R. Sardegna	2001	305
14 13/16	8 11/16	6 2/16	M	Moffat County	CO	Dave Keller	2002	305
14 13/16	8 9/16	6 4/16	M	Rocky Mountain House	ALB	Mark Bold	2002	305
*14 13/16	8 13/16	6 0/16	M	Gila County	AZ	Russell Hunter	2005	305
14 13/16	8 12/16	6 1/16	M	Morgan County	UT	Glen O. Hallows	2005	305
14 13/16	8 10/16	6 3/16	M	Okanogan County	WA	Brad Harden	2006	305
14 13/16	8 9/16	6 4/16	M	Sanpete County	UT	Tom Miranda	2006	305
*14 13/16	8 14/16	5 15/16	M	Lincoln County	MT	Jesse Short	2007	305
14 13/16	8 11/16	6 2/16	M	Yavapai County	AZ	Steven M. Berry	2009	305
14 12/16	8 14/16	5 14/16	M	Chelan County	WA	Dr. R. Congdon	1952	364
14 12/16	8 12/16	6 0/16	M	Clallam County	WA	Lloyd Beebe	1953	364
14 12/16	8 9/16	6 3/16	M	Rio Blanco County	CO	LeRoy Wood	1965	364
14 12/16	8 12/16	6 0/16	M		CO	Clyde Hector	1967	364
14 12/16	8 13/16	5 15/16	M	Garfield County	UT	Harold Boyack	1968	364
14 12/16	8 11/16	6 1/16	M	Valley County	ID	John Buford Reese	1976	364
14 12/16	8 10/16	6 2/16	M	Maguire Creek	BC	William Morley	1979	364
14 12/16	8 10/16	6 2/16	M	Boulder County	CO	Doug Beck	1984	364
14 12/16	8 10/16	6 2/16	M	Larimer County	CO	Jim Johnson	1985	364
14 12/16	8 14/16	5 14/16	M	Moffat County	CO	Michael B. Moline	1985	364
14 12/16	8 11/16	6 1/16	M	Cache County	UT	Ed Lawlor	1985	364
14 12/16	8 9/16	6 3/16	M	Madison County	MT	Ken Hoehn	1985	364
14 12/16	9 0/16	5 12/16	M	Custer County	CO	David Waldrop	1986	364
14 12/16	8 12/16	6 0/16	M	Emery County	UT	Ricky Schroder	1986	364
14 12/16	8 11/16	6 1/16	M	Rio Arriba County	NM	Robert John Seeds	1988	364
14 12/16	8 11/16	6 1/16	M	Utah County	UT	Blake A. Ryan	1988	364
14 12/16	8 12/16	6 0/16	M	Saguache County	CO	Mark Wuerthle	1988	364

257

COUGAR (MOUNTAIN LION)

Minimum Score 13 8/16   Continued

SCORE	GREATEST LENGTH	GREATEST WIDTH	SEX	AREA	STATE/ PROVINCE	HUNTER'S NAME	DATE	RANK
14 12/16	8 9/16	6 3/16	M	Archuleta County	CO	Leo F. Neuls	1988	364
14 12/16	8 10/16	6 2/16	M	Wallowa County	OR	Paul Turcke	1988	364
14 12/16	8 10/16	6 2/16	M	Saguache County	CO	Roger Maurice Tyler	1989	364
14 12/16	8 8/16	6 4/16	M	San Juan County	UT	Henry Gilbertson	1989	364
14 12/16	8 11/16	6 1/16	M	Flathead County	MT	Gary A. Crowe	1989	364
14 12/16	8 10/16	6 2/16	M	Mesa County	CO	Kerry Kammer	1990	364
14 12/16	8 10/16	6 2/16	M	Sevier County	UT	James Schade	1991	364
14 12/16	8 13/16	5 15/16	M	Rio Blanco County	CO	Ross L. Talbott	1991	364
14 12/16	8 13/16	5 15/16	M	Elk River	BC	Doug Scott	1991	364
14 12/16	8 11/16	6 1/16	M	Duchesne County	UT	Kent E. Smith	1992	364
14 12/16	8 9/16	6 3/16	M	Lewis & Clark County	MT	Mike Knapstad	1992	364
14 12/16	8 10/16	6 2/16	M	Nakusp	BC	Edwin L. DeYoung	1992	364
14 12/16	8 11/16	6 1/16	M	Kootenay River	BC	Brian Schuck	1992	364
14 12/16	8 11/16	6 1/16	M	Lincoln County	NV	Stephen L. Geller	1992	364
14 12/16	8 8/16	6 4/16	M	Flathead County	MT	Ira S. Uradomo	1992	364
14 12/16	8 10/16	6 2/16	M	Princeton	BC	Dr. Peeler Grayson Lacey	1992	364
14 12/16	8 13/16	5 15/16	M	Carbon County	MT	Thomas E. Hart, Jr.	1993	364
14 12/16	8 12/16	6 0/16	M	Garfield County	CO	Jay R. Rasch	1993	364
14 12/16	8 11/16	6 1/16	M	La Plata County	CO	Michael Falcone	1993	364
14 12/16	8 14/16	5 14/16	M	Carbon County	UT	Hugh H. Hogle	1993	364
14 12/16	8 10/16	6 2/16	M	Ravalli County	MT	Mark Hoselton	1994	364
14 12/16	8 10/16	6 2/16	M	Huerfano County	CO	David Hinton	1994	364
14 12/16	8 13/16	5 15/16	M	Rio Blanco County	CO	Stephen W. Greer	1994	364
14 12/16	8 14/16	5 14/16	M	Wayne County	UT	Robert M. Daggett	1995	364
14 12/16	8 10/16	6 2/16	M	Madison County	MT	Mark Kronyak	1995	364
14 12/16	8 10/16	6 2/16	M	Lemhi County	ID	Dick Wenger	1995	364
14 12/16	8 12/16	6 0/16	M	San Miguel County	CO	Fritz A. Brennecke	1995	364
14 12/16	8 9/16	6 3/16	M	Jefferson County	CO	Dan Eaton	1995	364
14 12/16	8 9/16	6 3/16	M	Robb	ALB	Dwayne Huggins	1996	364
14 12/16	8 9/16	6 3/16	M	Clark County	ID	Aaron Bateman	1997	364
14 12/16	8 12/16	6 0/16	M	Rio Grande County	CO	Tobias Dellamano	1997	364
14 12/16	8 12/16	6 0/16	M	Clearwater County	ID	Larry Davis	1997	364
14 12/16	8 10/16	6 2/16	M	Lewis & Clark County	MT	Grant M. Winn II	1998	364
14 12/16	8 11/16	6 1/16	M	Missoula County	MT	Rory Indreland	1998	364
14 12/16	8 10/16	6 2/16	M	Kootenai County	ID	Marty J. Adams	1998	364
14 12/16	8 10/16	6 2/16	M	Lincoln County	MT	Kevin L. Kendrick	1998	364
14 12/16	8 12/16	6 0/16	M	Sandoval County	NM	Roy Weir	1998	364
14 12/16	8 10/16	6 2/16	M	Jefferson County	CO	Troy Cunningham	1999	364
14 12/16	8 10/16	6 2/16	M	Sanders County	MT	Wayne J. Hood, Jr.	1999	364
14 12/16	8 11/16	6 1/16	M	Lac La Hache	BC	Jerry Aiken, Jr.	1999	364
14 12/16	8 9/16	6 3/16	M	Powell County	MT	Marlon J. Clapham	2001	364
14 12/16	8 12/16	6 0/16	M	Archuleta County	CO	Daniel F. Sehr	2002	364
14 12/16	8 12/16	6 0/16	M	Deschutes County	OR	Brian Wilber	2003	364
14 12/16	8 13/16	5 15/16	M	Gunnison County	CO	James J. Ayer	2003	364
14 12/16	8 12/16	6 0/16	M	Elmore County	ID	Dale Karch	2003	364
14 12/16	8 13/16	5 15/16	M	Clear Creek County	CO	Matt Archuleta	2004	364
14 12/16	8 12/16	6 0/16	M	Delta County	CO	Joe L. Williams	2005	364
14 12/16	8 11/16	6 1/16	M	Valley County	ID	Jon Vanderhoef	2006	364
14 12/16	8 7/16	6 5/16	M	Sanders County	MT	Jesse Newman	2006	364
14 12/16	8 9/16	6 3/16	M	Garfield County	CO	Thomas Gore	2006	364
14 12/16	8 6/16	6 6/16	M	Edson River	ALB	Kaitlyn Popson	2009	364
*14 12/16	8 12/16	6 0/16	M	Silver Bow County	MT	Chad Duane Gochanour	2009	364
14 12/16	8 13/16	5 15/16	M	Eagle County	CO	Lance C. Nichols	2009	364
14 12/16	8 13/16	5 15/16	M	Sublette County	WY	Ronnie Hall	2009	364
*14 12/16	8 8/16	6 4/16	M	Jumping Pond	ALB	Cory Smith	2010	364
14 11/16	8 10/16	6 1/16	M	Sundre	ALB	Tom Decker	1966	436
14 11/16	8 8/16	6 3/16	M	Custer County	ID	Ralph V. Pehrson	1969	436
14 11/16	8 9/16	6 2/16	M	Boise County	ID	Harlow D. Austad	1971	436
14 11/16	8 8/16	6 3/16	M	Kettle River	BC	Irvin Plotz	1976	436
14 11/16	8 12/16	5 15/16	M	Lincoln County	MT	Ronald J. Wade	1976	436
14 11/16	8 10/16	6 1/16	M	Garfield County	UT	Bradford L. Sheltrown	1977	436
14 11/16	8 10/16	6 1/16	M	Middle Fork	ID	Robert Frank	1978	436
14 11/16	8 10/16	6 1/16	M	Flathead County	MT	Dr. James J. Shubert	1978	436
14 11/16	8 12/16	5 15/16	M	Columbia County	WA	John Wahl	1979	436
14 11/16	8 14/16	5 13/16	M	Custer County	CO	Philip Stegenga	1979	436
14 11/16	8 9/16	6 2/16	M	Ravalli County	MT	Bill Mitchell	1980	436
14 11/16	8 10/16	6 1/16	M	San Miguel County	CO	Judd Cooney	1981	436
14 11/16	8 12/16	5 15/16	M	Utah County	UT	Fred Tarran	1982	436
14 11/16	8 8/16	6 3/16	M	Chaffee County	CO	Reggie Spiegelberg	1983	436
14 11/16	8 11/16	6 0/16	M	Lemhi County	ID	Stewart P. Fitzgerald	1985	436
14 11/16	8 10/16	6 1/16	M	Washakie County	WY	Nelson Scherrer	1986	436
14 11/16	8 7/16	6 4/16	M	Socorro County	NM	Chuck Sherwin	1986	436
14 11/16	8 11/16	6 0/16	M	Montezuma County	CO	Carla D. Coval	1987	436
14 11/16	8 7/16	6 4/16	M	Elko County	NV	Robert Pyne	1987	436
14 11/16	8 12/16	5 15/16	M	Owyhee County	ID	Gladwin F. Mills	1988	436
14 11/16	8 11/16	6 0/16	M	Valley County	ID	Tom Augustine	1988	436
14 11/16	8 10/16	6 1/16	M	Washakie County	WY	Ron Books	1989	436
14 11/16	8 12/16	5 15/16	M	Teton County	WY	Joseph P. Furlong	1989	436
14 11/16	8 10/16	6 1/16	M	Park County	MT	Patrick Gilligan	1989	436
14 11/16	8 12/16	5 15/16	M	Lemhi County	ID	Randy Lee Cooley	1989	436
14 11/16	8 8/16	6 3/16	M	Clallam County	WA	Frank J. Knowles III	1989	436
14 11/16	8 12/16	5 15/16	M	Montezuma County	CO	Phil M. Elmore	1990	436
14 11/16	8 12/16	5 15/16	M	Humboldt County	NV	Dean Knoles	1990	436
14 11/16	8 8/16	6 3/16	M	Clearwater County	ID	Thomas Storr	1990	436
14 11/16	8 12/16	5 15/16	M	Lemhi County	ID	Bill Connors	1990	436
14 11/16	8 10/16	6 1/16	M	San Juan County	UT	Aaron Bronson	1991	436
14 11/16	8 12/16	5 15/16	M	Coconino County	AZ	George N. Davies	1991	436
14 11/16	8 12/16	5 15/16	M	Albany County	WY	Steven Perkins	1992	436
14 11/16	8 11/16	6 0/16	M	Lewis & Clark County	MT	Sonny Templeton	1993	436
14 11/16	8 8/16	6 3/16	M	Bragg Creek	ALB	Wayne Greene	1993	436
14 11/16	8 12/16	5 15/16	M	Montezuma County	CO	Russ Dufva	1994	436
14 11/16	8 2/16	6 9/16	M	Shoshone County	ID	Scott Trelstad	1995	436
14 11/16	8 12/16	5 15/16	M	Uintah County	UT	Scott Anspaugh	1995	436
14 11/16	8 11/16	6 0/16	M	Wayne County	UT	Jerry J. Gilbertson	1996	436
14 11/16	8 9/16	6 2/16	M	Redburn Creek	BC	Gilles Rondeau	1996	436

258

COUGAR (MOUNTAIN LION)

Minimum Score 13 8/16   Continued

SCORE	GREATEST LENGTH	GREATEST WIDTH	SEX	AREA	STATE/ PROVINCE	HUNTER'S NAME	DATE	RANK
14 11/16	8 11/16	6 0/16	M	Kane County	UT	Sean Crosby	1997	436
14 11/16	8 8/16	6 3/16	M	Wigwam River	BC	Tony Zielinski	1997	436
14 11/16	8 10/16	6 1/16	M	Carbon County	UT	Karen K. Jacobsen	1997	436
14 11/16	8 12/16	5 15/16	M	Corbin	BC	William T. Carroll, Jr.	1997	436
14 11/16	8 9/16	6 2/16	M	Custer County	ID	Scott C. Quinn	1998	436
14 11/16	8 12/16	5 15/16	M	Washington County	UT	Steve Letcher	1998	436
14 11/16	8 10/16	6 1/16	M	Wasatch County	UT	Ed Bitterman	1998	436
14 11/16	8 10/16	6 1/16	M	Nye County	NV	Ricardo Longoria	1998	436
14 11/16	8 12/16	5 15/16	M	San Juan County	UT	Nate Jacobson	2000	436
14 11/16	8 9/16	6 2/16	M	Johnson County	WY	Brad Vargo	2001	436
14 11/16	8 9/16	6 2/16	M	Blairmore	ALB	Dave Browne	2002	436
14 11/16	8 12/16	5 15/16	M	Graham County	AZ	Randy Liljenquist	2004	436
14 11/16	8 10/16	6 1/16	M	Priddis	ALB	Ken Maier	2004	436
14 11/16	8 8/16	6 3/16	M	Grand County	CO	Randy J. Kendrick	2005	436
14 11/16	8 14/16	5 13/16	M	Coconino County	AZ	Tim Wolford	2006	436
*14 11/16	8 11/16	6 0/16	M	Nordegg	ALB	Rod Tetreault	2007	436
14 11/16	8 11/16	6 0/16	M	Chaffee County	CO	Dale D. Blodgett	2007	436
14 11/16	8 12/16	5 15/16	M	Carbon County	WY	Jack L. Morey, Jr.	2008	436
14 11/16	8 11/16	6 0/16	M	Chaffee County	CO	Tom Ferguson	2009	436
14 11/16	8 11/16	6 0/16	M	Sundre	ALB	Gunther Tondeleir	2009	436
14 11/16	8 11/16	6 0/16	M	Larimer County	CO	Demetrios Mellos	2009	436
14 10/16	8 10/16	6 0/16	M	Lincoln County	MT	Dr. Lowell L. Eddy	1967	497
14 10/16	8 10/16	6 0/16	M	Idaho County	ID	C. Bruce Peeples, Jr.	1970	497
14 10/16	8 9/16	6 1/16	M	Carbon County	UT	Paul E. Nottingham	1972	497
14 10/16	8 10/16	6 0/16	M	Flathead County	MT	Jerry Karsky	1976	497
14 10/16	8 8/16	6 2/16	M	Rio Blanco County	CO	Paul Janke	1976	497
14 10/16	8 10/16	6 0/16	M	Pincher Creek	ALB	Theo Mitchell	1977	497
14 10/16	8 8/16	6 2/16	M	Madison County	MT	Don Schaufler	1977	497
14 10/16	8 10/16	6 0/16	M	Sevier County	UT	Harold Hugelen	1979	497
14 10/16	8 10/16	6 0/16	M	Fremont County	CO	Pete J. Santi	1979	497
14 10/16	8 11/16	5 15/16	M	Las Animas County	CO	Glenn R. Kuklick	1980	497
14 10/16	8 9/16	6 1/16	M	Elmore County	ID	L. Dean Goodner	1981	497
14 10/16	8 13/16	5 13/16	M	Fremont County	CO	Carolyn E. Lama	1981	497
14 10/16	8 10/16	6 0/16	M	Fremont County	CO	Johnny J. Lama	1981	497
14 10/16	8 10/16	6 0/16	M	Carbon County	UT	Claude A. Flippin	1982	497
14 10/16	8 8/16	6 2/16	M	Sanders County	MT	Scott Lennard	1982	497
14 10/16	8 13/16	5 13/16	M	San Miguel County	CO	James Yuds	1982	497
14 10/16	8 9/16	6 1/16	M	Box Elder County	UT	Jerry Mason	1982	497
14 10/16	8 10/16	6 0/16	M	Montezuma County	CO	Mike Morgan	1983	497
14 10/16	8 10/16	6 0/16	M	Piute County	UT	James C. Hicks	1983	497
14 10/16	8 15/16	5 11/16	M	Chaffee County	CO	Tom Bowman	1983	497
14 10/16	8 9/16	6 1/16	M	San Juan County	NM	Gary Weber	1984	497
14 10/16	8 9/16	6 1/16	M	Douglas County	NV	Kirk Westervelt	1986	497
14 10/16	8 8/16	6 2/16	M	Flathead County	MT	Dyrk Eddie	1986	497
14 10/16	8 9/16	6 1/16	M	Montrose County	CO	David Ernest Nesler	1987	497
14 10/16	8 11/16	5 15/16	M	Sevier County	UT	Kelly Poulsen	1987	497
14 10/16	8 13/16	5 13/16	M	Alamosa County	CO	Tim Walters	1987	497
14 10/16	8 10/16	6 0/16	M	Owyhee County	ID	Richard Fritz	1988	497
14 10/16	8 10/16	6 0/16	M	Carbon County	UT	Dennis G. McElvain	1988	497
14 10/16	8 9/16	6 1/16	M	Nye County	NV	Arrah C. Curry	1988	497
14 10/16	8 9/16	6 1/16	M	Gilpin County	CO	Garry V. Woodman	1988	497
14 10/16	8 12/16	5 14/16	M	Montezuma County	CO	Steven J. Vittetow	1989	497
14 10/16	8 9/16	6 1/16	M	Wheatland County	MT	Albert W. Winter	1989	497
14 10/16	8 10/16	6 0/16	M	Umatilla County	OR	Javier Garcia	1989	497
14 10/16	8 10/16	6 0/16	M	Judith Basin County	MT	John Rosey Roseland	1989	497
14 10/16	8 11/16	5 15/16	M	Clearwater County	ID	Bill Trescott	1989	497
14 10/16	8 7/16	6 3/16	M	Lander County	NV	Jack Dykstra	1990	497
14 10/16	8 11/16	5 15/16	M	Swan Lake	ALB	Dave Gerber	1990	497
14 10/16	8 10/16	6 0/16	M	Arrow Lake	BC	Jim Ryan	1990	497
14 10/16	8 10/16	6 0/16	M	Missoula County	MT	Monty Moravec	1990	497
14 10/16	8 12/16	5 14/16	M	Carbon County	UT	Paul Martinez	1991	497
14 10/16	8 12/16	5 14/16	M	Kane County	UT	Glen C. Ames	1991	497
14 10/16	8 10/16	6 0/16	M	Elko County	NV	Mike Stewart	1992	497
14 10/16	8 9/16	6 1/16	M	Morgan County	UT	Brian Dam	1992	497
14 10/16	8 7/16	6 3/16	M	Lincoln County	MT	Tony Snow	1992	497
14 10/16	8 8/16	6 2/16	M	Missoula County	MT	Max G. Bauer, Jr.	1992	497
14 10/16	8 8/16	6 2/16	M	Gila County	AZ	John Novak	1993	497
14 10/16	8 8/16	6 2/16	M	La Plata County	CO	Edward A. Petersen	1993	497
14 10/16	8 11/16	5 15/16	M	Lewis & Clark County	MT	Carl A. Templeton	1993	497
14 10/16	8 10/16	6 0/16	M	Phillips County	MT	Alan Fedorenko	1993	497
14 10/16	8 10/16	6 0/16	M	Powder River County	MT	Jim Wilkins	1994	497
14 10/16	8 8/16	6 2/16	M	Clear Creek County	CO	Connie Renfro	1994	497
14 10/16	8 12/16	5 14/16	M	Sanpete County	UT	Bobby Olsen	1994	497
14 10/16	8 11/16	5 15/16	M	Pueblo County	CO	Tommy Chambliss	1994	497
14 10/16	8 11/16	5 15/16	M	Elmore County	ID	Robert E. Speegle, MD	1994	497
14 10/16	8 13/16	5 13/16	M	Moffat County	CO	Dave Burke	1995	497
14 10/16	8 10/16	6 0/16	M	West Kettle	BC	James Harold Simonds, Jr.	1995	497
14 10/16	8 9/16	6 1/16	M	Boise County	ID	Norman Henderson	1995	497
14 10/16	8 10/16	6 0/16	M	Larimer County	CO	Thomas H. Harris	1995	497
14 10/16	8 10/16	6 0/16	M	Moyie	BC	Phil Renney	1995	497
14 10/16	8 9/16	6 1/16	M	Madison County	MT	Mark E. Steingruber	1996	497
14 10/16	8 11/16	5 15/16	M	Montrose County	CO	Lisa A. West	1996	497
14 10/16	8 9/16	6 1/16	M	Clearwater County	ID	Eugene Lewis	1996	497
14 10/16	8 7/16	6 3/16	M	Boise County	ID	Rick Tribby	1996	497
14 10/16	8 12/16	5 14/16	M	Sullivan Creek	ALB	David A. Little	1997	497
14 10/16	8 8/16	6 2/16	M	Clear Creek County	CO	David L. Skiff	1997	497
14 10/16	8 7/16	6 3/16	M	Las Animas County	CO	Pat Powell	1998	497
14 10/16	8 10/16	6 0/16	M	Harold Creek	ALB	Terry Hagman	1998	497
14 10/16	8 9/16	6 1/16	M	Iron County	UT	Randy D. Oleson	1999	497
14 10/16	8 9/16	6 1/16	M	Gila County	AZ	Michael Hunter McCarey	1999	497
14 10/16	8 12/16	5 14/16	M	Uintah County	UT	Kolby Kay	2000	497
14 10/16	8 12/16	5 14/16	M	Piute County	UT	Louis Strahler	2001	497
14 10/16	8 9/16	6 1/16	M	Grand County	CO	Alicia Viskoe	2001	497
14 10/16	8 10/16	6 0/16	M	Grand County	CO	Rick Duggan	2002	497
14 10/16	8 10/16	6 0/16	M	Mineral County	MT	Randy Firestone	2004	497

259

COUGAR (MOUNTAIN LION)

Minimum Score 13 8/16   Continued

SCORE	GREATEST LENGTH	GREATEST WIDTH	SEX	AREA	STATE/ PROVINCE	HUNTER'S NAME	DATE	RANK
14 10/16	8 8/16	6 2/16	M	Sevier County	UT	Al Schroeder	2004	497
14 10/16	8 8/16	6 2/16	M	Gunnison County	CO	Matthew Reilly	2004	497
14 10/16	8 12/16	5 14/16	M	Grant County	OR	Dan Stoneberg	2005	497
14 10/16	8 10/16	6 0/16	M	Montezuma County	CO	Sean Tennis	2008	497
14 10/16	8 10/16	6 0/16	M	Jackson County	CO	Thomas A. Cox, Jr.	2009	497
*14 10/16	8 8/16	6 2/16	M	Sweet Grass County	MT	Eric Jandro	2009	497
*14 10/16	8 10/16	6 0/16	M	Garfield County	CO	Richard Crawford	2010	497
14 9/16	8 5/16	6 4/16	M	Gila County	AZ	Ben Pearson	1958	578
14 9/16	8 10/16	5 15/16	M	Idaho County	ID	Keith N. Johnson	1966	578
14 9/16	8 8/16	6 1/16	M	Lemhi County	ID	Richard E. Vail	1974	578
14 9/16	8 8/16	6 1/16	M	Grand County	UT	Henry 'Hank' Frey	1974	578
14 9/16	8 11/16	5 14/16	M	Garfield County	UT	Al Schweitzer	1979	578
14 9/16	8 8/16	6 1/16	M	Sandoval County	NM	John W. Rose	1979	578
14 9/16	8 8/16	6 1/16	M	San Miguel County	NM	Richard McClain	1980	578
14 9/16	8 9/16	6 0/16	M	Jefferson County	CO	Lee Veldhouse	1984	578
14 9/16	8 6/16	6 3/16	M	Idaho County	ID	LeRoy West	1984	578
14 9/16	8 7/16	6 2/16	M	Elmore County	ID	Susan D. Sherer	1984	578
14 9/16	8 10/16	5 15/16	M	Rio Blanco County	CO	Don Waechtler	1984	578
14 9/16	8 9/16	6 0/16	M	Cherryville	BC	Al Breitkreutz	1985	578
14 9/16	8 9/16	6 0/16	M	Douglas County	CO	Wayne Kraft	1986	578
14 9/16	8 9/16	6 0/16	F	Wheatland County	MT	Jim Bouchard	1986	578
14 9/16	8 10/16	5 15/16	M	Fremont County	CO	Bill Goodspeed	1986	578
14 9/16	8 10/16	5 15/16	M	Clearwater County	ID	Jeffrey S. Stevens	1986	578
14 9/16	8 9/16	6 0/16	M	Asotin County	WA	Bill Meyers, Jr.	1987	578
14 9/16	8 9/16	6 0/16	M	Grand County	UT	Wes Walton	1987	578
14 9/16	8 10/16	5 15/16	M	Barnes Lake	BC	Kenneth Arthur Brown	1988	578
14 9/16	8 11/16	5 14/16	M	Chaffee County	CO	David Douty	1988	578
14 9/16	8 8/16	6 1/16	M	Jefferson County	CO	Steve Fausel	1989	578
14 9/16	8 10/16	5 15/16	M	Kane County	UT	Jeff Buck	1989	578
14 9/16	8 9/16	6 0/16	M	Owyhee County	ID	Bernard Langhorne	1990	578
14 9/16	8 10/16	5 15/16	M	Sanpete County	UT	Larry Mathis	1990	578
14 9/16	8 9/16	6 0/16	M	Duchesne County	UT	Don Keady	1991	578
14 9/16	8 8/16	6 1/16	M	Madison County	MT	Fred Richter	1991	578
14 9/16	8 9/16	6 0/16	M	Sanders County	MT	William A. Kaminski	1991	578
14 9/16	8 10/16	5 15/16	M	Valley County	ID	Bob Dawson	1991	578
14 9/16	8 9/16	6 0/16	M	Catron County	NM	Dwight E. Moser	1992	578
14 9/16	8 10/16	5 15/16	M	Water Valley	ALB	Steve Ouwerkerk	1992	578
14 9/16	8 9/16	6 0/16	M	Lemhi County	ID	Marc Williams	1992	578
14 9/16	8 11/16	5 14/16	M	Duchesne County	UT	Bruce J. Smith	1993	578
14 9/16	8 8/16	6 1/16	M	Clay Creek	BC	Glenn Dreger	1993	578
14 9/16	8 10/16	5 15/16	M	Hood River County	OR	Timothy R. McGuffin	1993	578
14 9/16	8 9/16	6 0/16	M	Grand County	CO	Barry J. Smith	1993	578
14 9/16	8 11/16	5 14/16	M	Kootenai County	ID	Michael Christoforo	1993	578
14 9/16	8 12/16	5 13/16	M	Larimer County	CO	Jay Ervin	1994	578
14 9/16	8 11/16	5 14/16	M	Granite County	MT	Douglas P. Stein	1994	578
14 9/16	8 10/16	5 15/16	M	Uintah County	UT	Steven E. Sheehy	1995	578
14 9/16	8 9/16	6 0/16	M	Montezuma County	CO	Robert Hermann	1995	578
14 9/16	8 10/16	5 15/16	M	Uintah County	UT	Scott Kunz	1995	578
14 9/16	8 9/16	6 0/16	M	Chaffen Creek	ALB	James Pike	1995	578
14 9/16	8 9/16	6 0/16	M	Ravalli County	MT	Larry Dominquez	1995	578
14 9/16	8 11/16	5 14/16	M	Adams County	ID	Blake Owen Fischer	1995	578
14 9/16	8 10/16	5 15/16	M	Laird Lake	BC	Ryan J. Dorak	1996	578
14 9/16	8 11/16	5 14/16	M	Madison County	MT	Todd Hanson	1996	578
14 9/16	8 11/16	5 14/16	M	Lemhi County	ID	Michael Judas	1996	578
14 9/16	8 12/16	5 13/16	M	Custer County	ID	Steve Farrell	1996	578
14 9/16	8 11/16	5 14/16	M	Lemhi County	ID	John R. Koschmeder	1997	578
14 9/16	8 9/16	6 0/16	M	Fremont County	WY	Jeff Strangfeld	1997	578
14 9/16	8 10/16	5 15/16	M	Sevier County	UT	Daniel P. Kelly	1997	578
14 9/16	8 10/16	5 15/16	M	Delta County	CO	Scott Hargrove	1998	578
14 9/16	8 12/16	5 13/16	M	Moffat County	CO	Mike E. Neilson	1998	578
14 9/16	8 11/16	5 14/16	M	Grand County	CO	Cary Laman	1999	578
14 9/16	8 8/16	6 1/16	M	Graham County	AZ	Mark Worischeck	1999	578
14 9/16	8 10/16	5 15/16	M	Rio Blanco County	CO	Jay A. Keeler	1999	578
14 9/16	8 6/16	6 3/16	M	Park County	WY	David Serbonich	2000	578
14 9/16	8 9/16	6 0/16	M	Douglas County	CO	Turk Wendell	2000	578
14 9/16	8 8/16	6 1/16	M	Horsefly	BC	Rick Young	2000	578
14 9/16	8 8/16	6 1/16	M	Humboldt County	NV	Rodger Gorham	2001	578
14 9/16	8 10/16	5 15/16	M	Garfield County	UT	Skip Valentine	2001	578
14 9/16	8 11/16	5 14/16	M	Juab County	UT	David B. Nielsen	2002	578
14 9/16	8 10/16	5 15/16	M	Vancouver Island	BC	David Owel	2002	578
14 9/16	8 10/16	5 15/16	M	East Trout Creek	ALB	Tim Sailer	2003	578
14 9/16	8 10/16	5 15/16	M	Grand County	CO	Riley K. McDonough	2004	578
14 9/16	8 10/16	5 15/16	M	Larimer County	CO	Barry L. Stafford	2005	578
14 9/16	8 10/16	5 15/16	M	Colfax County	NM	M. Blake Patton	2005	578
14 9/16	8 10/16	5 15/16	M	Duchesne County	UT	Jeremy Starr	2005	578
*14 9/16	8 11/16	5 14/16	M	Hood River County	OR	James Drennen	2007	578
14 9/16	8 9/16	6 0/16	M	Valley County	ID	Kevin Primrose	2007	578
14 9/16	8 10/16	5 15/16	M	Huerfano County	CO	Michael W. Stanley	2009	578
14 8/16	8 9/16	5 15/16	F	Latah County	ID	Charles Kelso	1965	649
14 8/16	8 8/16	6 0/16	M	Ventura County	CA	Betty Gulman	1967	649
14 8/16	8 10/16	5 14/16	M	Catron County	NM	Ed Schaub	1970	649
14 8/16	8 8/16	6 0/16	M	Weber County	UT	Norm Goodwin	1971	649
14 8/16	8 9/16	5 15/16	M	Lemhi County	ID	Dr. Henry C. McDonald	1971	649
14 8/16	8 9/16	5 15/16	M	Emery County	UT	Terry Molneux	1972	649
14 8/16	8 9/16	5 15/16	M	Kane County	UT	Charles F. Maloney, Jr.	1973	649
14 8/16	8 6/16	6 2/16	M	Lincoln County	MT	Jerry Brown	1975	649
14 8/16	8 6/16	6 2/16	M	Duchesne County	UT	Roland Mantzke	1976	649
14 8/16	8 10/16	5 14/16	M	Elmore County	ID	Ronald L. Sherer	1979	649
14 8/16	8 9/16	5 15/16	M	Boise County	ID	Richard C. Nichols	1981	649
14 8/16	8 12/16	5 12/16	M	Saguache County	CO	J. Keith Chastain	1982	649
14 8/16	8 7/16	6 1/16	M	Utah County	UT	Dell J. Christensen	1982	649
14 8/16	8 8/16	6 0/16	M	Eagle County	CO	Stephen W. Nottingham	1982	649
14 8/16	8 8/16	6 0/16	M	Sheep River	ALB	Bob Toothill	1984	649
14 8/16	8 10/16	5 14/16	M	Grand County	UT	Harold Lee Schuerman	1984	649
14 8/16	8 10/16	5 14/16	M	Washoe County	NV	Jerry Pennington	1984	649

260

COUGAR (MOUNTAIN LION)

Minimum Score 13 8/16   Continued

SCORE	GREATEST LENGTH	GREATEST WIDTH	SEX	AREA	STATE/ PROVINCE	HUNTER'S NAME	DATE	RANK
14 8/16	8 8/16	6 0/16	M	Garfield County	CO	Douglas Starks	1984	649
14 8/16	8 10/16	5 14/16	M	Union County	OR	Ken Richter	1984	649
14 8/16	8 9/16	5 15/16	M	Archuleta County	CO	Howard Payne	1985	649
14 8/16	8 7/16	6 1/16	M	Idaho County	ID	William A.S. Hever, Sr.	1985	649
14 8/16	8 9/16	5 15/16	M	Fremont County	CO	Oney Cole	1985	649
14 8/16	8 9/16	5 15/16	M	Iron County	UT	Patrick Barwick	1985	649
14 8/16	8 7/16	6 1/16	M	Elmore County	ID	Chris Koldeway	1985	649
14 8/16	8 10/16	5 14/16	M	Larimer County	CO	David Skiff	1987	649
14 8/16	8 9/16	5 15/16	M	Sweet Grass County	MT	Dwight Wagner	1987	649
14 8/16	8 7/16	6 1/16	M	Flathead County	MT	Chris Switzer	1987	649
14 8/16	8 8/16	6 0/16	M	Lane County	OR	Larry D. Jones	1987	649
14 8/16	8 5/16	6 3/16	M	Caribou County	ID	Eric De Clark	1987	649
14 8/16	8 8/16	6 0/16	M	Chaffee County	CO	Scott Pelino	1987	649
14 8/16	8 8/16	6 0/16	M	Saguache County	CO	William Larry Wray	1987	649
14 8/16	8 9/16	5 15/16	M	Garfield County	CO	Roy M. Goodwin	1988	649
14 8/16	8 12/16	5 12/16	M	Webb County	TX	Daniel Juarez, Jr.	1988	649
14 8/16	8 7/16	6 1/16	M	Sheridan County	WY	Bill Roberts	1988	649
14 8/16	8 9/16	5 15/16	M	Elko County	NV	Donald Thompson	1988	649
14 8/16	8 9/16	5 15/16	M	Missoula County	MT	Bob Lussier	1988	649
14 8/16	8 10/16	5 14/16	M	Custer County	ID	Chip Palmer	1989	649
14 8/16	8 8/16	6 0/16	M	Boise County	ID	Curtis Wiker	1989	649
14 8/16	8 8/16	6 0/16	M	Larimer County	CO	John D. Lindell	1989	649
14 8/16	8 9/16	5 15/16	M	Montrose County	CO	Jimmy C. Garner	1990	649
14 8/16	8 6/16	6 2/16	M	Linn County	OR	Wayne Mathews	1990	649
14 8/16	8 11/16	5 13/16	M	Judith Basin County	MT	Kelly Norskog	1990	649
14 8/16	8 10/16	5 14/16	M	Montezuma County	CO	Mark D. Thomson	1991	649
14 8/16	8 9/16	5 15/16	M	Sevier County	UT	Mayben Crane	1991	649
14 8/16	8 9/16	5 15/16	M	San Miguel County	CO	Dewayne Mullins	1992	649
14 8/16	8 10/16	5 14/16	M	Garfield County	CO	Carroll Thomas Roach	1992	649
14 8/16	8 8/16	6 0/16	M	Eagle County	CO	Ron Janicki	1992	649
14 8/16	8 6/16	6 2/16	M	Idaho County	ID	Rick A. Albers	1992	649
14 8/16	8 7/16	6 1/16	M	Nakusp	BC	Dave Richardson	1992	649
14 8/16	8 9/16	5 15/16	M	Gallatin County	MT	Kevin Conners	1992	649
14 8/16	8 10/16	5 14/16	M	Terrell County	TX	E. Josh Isbell	1992	649
14 8/16	8 12/16	5 12/16	M	San Miguel County	CO	Steve Mazur	1993	649
14 8/16	8 11/16	5 13/16	M	Chaffee County	CO	Terry J. Krause	1993	649
14 8/16	8 8/16	6 0/16	M	Valley County	ID	Rick Addison	1994	649
14 8/16	8 6/16	6 2/16	M	Lemhi County	ID	Bob Johnson	1994	649
14 8/16	8 8/16	6 0/16	M	Ravalli County	MT	Scott L. Henriques	1994	649
14 8/16	8 8/16	6 0/16	M	Los Alamos County	NM	Kevin Reid	1995	649
14 8/16	8 6/16	6 2/16	M	Coconino County	AZ	Casey Robinson	1995	649
14 8/16	8 9/16	5 15/16	M	Albany County	WY	Tom Pindell	1995	649
14 8/16	8 9/16	5 15/16	M	Mesa County	CO	Mark Richards	1995	649
14 8/16	8 10/16	5 14/16	M	Jefferson County	WA	Larry Keith Stauffer	1996	649
14 8/16	8 9/16	5 15/16	M	Moffat County	CO	Russell S. Overton	1996	649
14 8/16	8 8/16	6 0/16	M	Lemhi County	ID	William C. Shuster	1996	649
14 8/16	8 8/16	6 0/16	M	Sanders County	MT	Robert J. Kain	1996	649
14 8/16	8 8/16	6 0/16	M	Rio Blanco County	CO	Paul Chackan	1997	649
14 8/16	8 9/16	5 15/16	M	Owyhee County	ID	Bob Amaral	1997	649
14 8/16	8 11/16	5 13/16	M	Garfield County	UT	Randy Forsythe	1997	649
14 8/16	8 9/16	5 15/16	M	Juab County	UT	Jeremy Harness	1998	649
14 8/16	8 10/16	5 14/16	M	Garfield County	UT	Tom Hunt	1998	649
14 8/16	8 10/16	5 14/16	M	Boise County	ID	Jim Wilson	1998	649
14 8/16	8 8/16	6 0/16	M	Lincoln County	NV	Dale Cooley	1998	649
14 8/16	8 11/16	5 13/16	M	Montezuma County	CO	Scott Jankowski	1998	649
14 8/16	8 8/16	6 0/16	M	Fremont County	WY	Jerry Bodar	1999	649
14 8/16	8 11/16	5 13/16	M	Rio Blanco County	CO	Dennis Roehl	1999	649
14 8/16	8 12/16	5 12/16	M	Rio Blanco County	CO	Darrell Aplanalp	1999	649
14 8/16	8 8/16	6 0/16	M	Jefferson County	MT	Michael G. Ida	1999	649
14 8/16	8 8/16	6 0/16	M	Lemhi County	ID	Dave Erway, Jr.	2000	649
14 8/16	8 9/16	5 15/16	M	Madison County	MT	Ron D. Hinds	2000	649
14 8/16	8 8/16	6 0/16	M	Garfield County	CO	Cory Collins	2001	649
14 8/16	8 11/16	5 13/16	M	Stillwater County	MT	Dr. Dale W. Schlehuber	2002	649
14 8/16	8 9/16	5 15/16	M	Dolores County	CO	Jason Henry Pieper	2002	649
14 8/16	8 10/16	5 14/16	M	Rio Arriba County	NM	Ryan Panzy	2002	649
14 8/16	8 11/16	5 13/16	M	Granite County	MT	Jay Peake	2003	649
14 8/16	8 8/16	6 0/16	M	Garfield County	UT	Dan Staller	2004	649
14 8/16	8 2/16	6 6/16	M	Rosebud County	MT	Shawn Hayes	2005	649
14 8/16	8 7/16	6 1/16	M	Ravalli County	MT	Dean A. Klakken, Jr.	2006	649
14 8/16	8 8/16	6 0/16	M	Fergus County	MT	Kennie Williams	2007	649
14 8/16	8 8/16	6 0/16	M	Hill County	MT	Tony Ballard	2008	649
*14 8/16	8 9/16	5 15/16	M	Gunnison County	CO	Brian Meilinger	2009	649
*14 8/16	8 10/16	5 14/16	M	Moffat County	CO	Casey Smith	2009	649
*14 8/16	8 8/16	6 0/16	M	Navajo County	AZ	Gary L. Wilford	2009	649
*14 8/16	8 7/16	6 1/16	M	Caroline	ALB	Mark "Gutz" Gutsmiedl	2009	649
14 8/16	8 6/16	6 2/16	M	Flathead County	MT	John Z. Attebury	2009	649
14 8/16	8 7/16	6 1/16	M	Madison County	MT	Gunnar Smith	2009	649
*14 8/16	8 8/16	6 0/16	M	Catron County	NM	Arthur Brandt	2010	649
14 7/16	8 9/16	5 14/16	M	Elmore County	ID	William R. Vanderhoef	1966	744
14 7/16	8 11/16	5 12/16	M	Range Creek	UT	Gordy J. Longville	1967	744
14 7/16	8 8/16	5 15/16	M	Lemhi County	ID	Wally Rueger	1975	744
14 7/16	8 6/16	6 1/16	M	White Pine County	NV	Barry L. May	1975	744
14 7/16	8 9/16	5 14/16	M	Duffy Lake	BC	Wilfred Klingsat	1977	744
14 7/16	8 9/16	5 14/16	M	Carbon County	UT	Rick Hunckler	1977	744
14 7/16	8 6/16	6 1/16	M	Custer County	ID	Jim L. McCrory	1978	744
14 7/16	8 9/16	5 14/16	M	Ravalli County	MT	Kim Engelbert	1978	744
14 7/16	8 7/16	6 0/16	M	San Miguel County	CO	Bob Mays, Sr.	1979	744
14 7/16	8 6/16	6 1/16	M	Sevier County	UT	Lee Jernigan	1980	744
14 7/16	8 10/16	5 13/16	M	Lemhi County	ID	Daniel M. Alegre	1983	744
14 7/16	8 9/16	5 14/16	M	Sanders County	MT	Jerry V. Finley	1983	744
14 7/16	8 8/16	5 15/16	M	Franklin County	ID	Clair J. Buxton	1983	744
14 7/16	8 9/16	5 14/16	M	Judith Basin County	MT	Kay Davidson	1984	744
14 7/16	8 9/16	5 14/16	M	Duchesne County	UT	Jerry Ippolito	1984	744
14 7/16	8 8/16	5 15/16	M	Lemhi County	ID	Dennis N. Minnich	1984	744
14 7/16	8 6/16	6 1/16	M	Dolores County	CO	Ms. Charlie White	1984	744

261

COUGAR (MOUNTAIN LION)

Minimum Score 13 8/16   Continued

SCORE	GREATEST LENGTH	GREATEST WIDTH	SEX	AREA	STATE/ PROVINCE	HUNTER'S NAME	DATE	RANK
14 7/16	8 8/16	5 15/16	M	Lander County	NV	David P. Lindman	1985	744
14 7/16	8 9/16	5 14/16	M	Catron County	NM	Stan Rauch	1986	744
14 7/16	8 8/16	5 15/16	M	Mesa County	CO	Sandy Vancourt	1987	744
14 7/16	8 7/16	6 0/16	M	Emery County	UT	Clark James Stokes	1987	744
14 7/16	8 8/16	5 15/16	M	Skagit County	WA	Jerry Solie	1987	744
14 7/16	8 8/16	5 15/16	M	Meagher County	MT	Sandra L. Gratz	1987	744
14 7/16	8 9/16	5 14/16	M	Sanpete County	UT	Don M. Markus	1988	744
14 7/16	8 6/16	6 1/16	M	Garfield County	CO	Doug Starks	1988	744
14 7/16	8 9/16	5 14/16	M	San Miguel County	CO	Robert Bain	1989	744
14 7/16	8 6/16	6 1/16	M	Cascade County	MT	Gene Henck	1989	744
14 7/16	8 12/16	5 11/16	M	Carbon County	UT	Stanley W. Biltz	1989	744
14 7/16	8 7/16	6 0/16	M	Lemhi County	ID	John Henry Smith	1989	744
14 7/16	8 4/16	6 3/16	M	Madison County	MT	Stephen P. (Pat) Connell	1990	744
14 7/16	8 9/16	5 14/16	M	Wasatch County	UT	E. Duane Park	1990	744
14 7/16	8 9/16	5 14/16	M	Rio Arriba County	NM	Jim Marquis	1990	744
14 7/16	8 6/16	6 1/16	M	Wallowa County	OR	William K. McCadden	1990	744
14 7/16	8 8/16	5 15/16	M	Fremont County	CO	Steve Sylvia	1991	744
14 7/16	8 9/16	5 14/16	M	Rio Arriba County	NM	Vito Benedetto	1991	744
14 7/16	8 7/16	6 0/16	M	Millard County	UT	Phillip R. Brown	1992	744
14 7/16	8 6/16	6 1/16	M	Idaho County	ID	Fred H. Simonton III	1992	744
14 7/16	8 9/16	5 14/16	M	Rio Blanco County	CO	Tim Cuthriell	1992	744
14 7/16	8 8/16	5 15/16	M	Valley County	ID	Jeffrey Winters	1992	744
14 7/16	8 8/16	5 15/16	M	Churchill County	NV	Dan Klebenow	1992	744
14 7/16	8 11/16	5 12/16	M	Sanpete County	UT	J. Seth Kunz	1992	744
14 7/16	8 6/16	6 1/16	M	Rio Grande County	CO	John Olson	1992	744
14 7/16	8 9/16	5 14/16	M	Gilpin County	CO	Steve Barnhill	1992	744
14 7/16	8 9/16	5 14/16	M	Granite County	MT	William J. Siebeneck	1992	744
14 7/16	8 9/16	5 14/16	M	Utah County	UT	Britton Ercanbrack	1993	744
14 7/16	8 9/16	5 14/16	M	Duchesne County	UT	Jason Williams	1993	744
14 7/16	8 9/16	5 14/16	M	White Pine County	NV	Wayne Long	1993	744
14 7/16	8 10/16	5 13/16	M	Montezuma County	CO	Doug Aiken	1993	744
14 7/16	8 10/16	5 13/16	M	Park County	CO	Ron Adamson	1993	744
14 7/16	8 9/16	5 14/16	M	Douglas County	CO	Duffy Daugherty	1993	744
14 7/16	8 6/16	6 1/16	M	Montezuma County	CO	David R. Hall	1993	744
14 7/16	8 10/16	5 13/16	M	Elmore County	ID	Richard Nemitz	1993	744
14 7/16	8 8/16	5 15/16	M	Valley County	ID	Randy A. Reeves	1994	744
14 7/16	8 10/16	5 13/16	M	Lemhi County	ID	Jason F. Lambley	1994	744
14 7/16	8 6/16	6 1/16	M	Rosebud County	MT	Jae Notti	1994	744
14 7/16	8 10/16	5 13/16	M	Duchesne County	UT	Tim R. Dawson	1994	744
14 7/16	8 8/16	5 15/16	M	Nye County	NV	Wayne Piersol	1994	744
14 7/16	8 9/16	5 14/16	M	San Juan County	UT	Brad D. Bunker	1994	744
14 7/16	8 8/16	5 15/16	M	Boise County	ID	Angus M. Brown	1994	744
14 7/16	8 7/16	6 0/16	M	Porcupine Hills	ALB	Nick Frederick	1995	744
14 7/16	8 10/16	5 13/16	M	Deer Lodge County	MT	John M. Rokisky	1995	744
14 7/16	8 7/16	6 0/16	M	Grand County	CO	Paul M. Martin	1995	744
14 7/16	8 7/16	6 0/16	M	Powell County	MT	Cody Pallister	1996	744
14 7/16	8 7/16	6 0/16	M	Rio Blanco County	CO	Bob Black	1996	744
14 7/16	8 7/16	6 0/16	M	Box Elder County	UT	Craig P. Mitton	1996	744
14 7/16	8 9/16	5 14/16	M	Morgan County	UT	Tim J. Misewicz	1996	744
14 7/16	8 9/16	5 14/16	M	Ravalli County	MT	Jack E. Williams	1996	744
14 7/16	8 9/16	5 14/16	M	Mohave County	AZ	John Garr	1996	744
14 7/16	8 8/16	5 15/16	M	Boise County	ID	Daniel J. Smith	1996	744
14 7/16	8 8/16	5 15/16	M	Conejos County	CO	Jerry Lees	1997	744
14 7/16	8 9/16	5 14/16	M	Graham County	AZ	Joseph Barraza	1997	744
14 7/16	8 10/16	5 13/16	M	Millard County	UT	Kurt Wood	1997	744
14 7/16	8 9/16	5 14/16	M	Cochise County	AZ	Jame L. Todd	1998	744
14 7/16	8 5/16	6 2/16	M	Sugar Lake	BC	William T. Bos	1998	744
14 7/16	8 9/16	5 14/16	M	Flathead County	MT	Gregory D. Pisk	1998	744
14 7/16	8 7/16	6 0/16	M	Emery County	UT	Stewart B. Jones	1998	744
14 7/16	8 11/16	5 12/16	M	Camas County	ID	Brian Brockette	1999	744
14 7/16	8 11/16	5 12/16	M	Sundre	ALB	Jerry Oldfield	1999	744
14 7/16	8 9/16	5 14/16	M	Duchesne County	UT	Rodney Elder	1999	744
14 7/16	8 9/16	5 14/16	M	Mesa County	CO	Albert Lee Sargent	1999	744
14 7/16	8 9/16	5 14/16	M	Catron County	NM	Wess Ferris	1999	744
14 7/16	8 8/16	5 15/16	M	Utah County	UT	Andy Rymer	1999	744
14 7/16	8 9/16	5 14/16	M	San Juan County	UT	Raymond L. Howell, Sr.	2000	744
14 7/16	8 6/16	6 1/16	M	Fremont County	CO	Robert Snell	2000	744
14 7/16	8 9/16	5 14/16	M	Fremont County	CO	Jerry Woodland	2000	744
14 7/16	8 11/16	5 12/16	M	Harney County	OR	Patrick E. Wheeler	2001	744
14 7/16	8 9/16	5 14/16	M	Claresholm	ALB	Darrin West	2002	744
14 7/16	8 4/16	6 3/16	M	Coconino County	AZ	Ernest Oliviero	2003	744
14 7/16	8 9/16	5 14/16	M	White Pine County	NV	Scott Anderson	2003	744
14 7/16	8 7/16	6 0/16	M	Bonneville County	ID	Lyle A. Hall	2004	744
14 7/16	8 9/16	5 14/16	M	Kamloops	BC	John Paul Schaffer	2006	744
*14 7/16	8 9/16	5 14/16	M	Costilla County	CO	Tom Handy	2006	744
14 7/16	8 7/16	6 0/16	M	Carbon County	UT	Scott Dyer	2009	744
14 7/16	8 10/16	5 13/16	M	Moffat County	CO	Jerry William Culbertson	2009	744
14 7/16	8 7/16	6 0/16	M	Gallatin County	MT	Andy Cox	2010	744
14 6/16	8 7/16	5 15/16	M	Sequoia National Forest	CA	Douglas Walker	1960	839
14 6/16	8 7/16	5 15/16	M	Elmore County	ID	C. Randall Byers	1966	839
14 6/16	8 8/16	5 14/16	M	Missoula County	MT	John Hershey	1969	839
14 6/16	8 7/16	5 15/16	M	Lemhi County	ID	Ray Torrey	1971	839
14 6/16	8 7/16	5 15/16	M	Colfax County	NM	Richard A. Meyer	1974	839
14 6/16	8 8/16	5 14/16	M	Huerfano County	CO	Douglas E. Miller	1974	839
14 6/16	8 6/16	6 0/16	M	Falkland	BC	W. Klingsat	1974	839
14 6/16	8 7/16	5 15/16	M	Clearwater County	ID	Oscar Levingston	1975	839
14 6/16	8 7/16	5 15/16	M	Carbon County	UT	Thomas W. Pinkston	1977	839
14 6/16	8 8/16	5 14/16	M	Uintah County	UT	Donald Redfox	1978	839
14 6/16	8 5/16	6 1/16	M	Fremont County	CO	Russell Hull	1979	839
14 6/16	8 6/16	6 0/16	M	Chaffee County	CO	Judy Clyncke	1981	839
14 6/16	8 9/16	5 13/16	M	Dry Wash Creek	UT	Mark J. Checki	1981	839
14 6/16	8 8/16	5 14/16	M	Ravalli County	MT	Dean Irwin	1982	839
14 6/16	8 6/16	6 0/16	M	Colfax County	NM	Joseph Wambach	1982	839
14 6/16	8 8/16	5 14/16	M	San Juan County	NM	Mike Ray	1983	839
14 6/16	8 8/16	5 14/16	M	Wasatch County	UT	Kendall Julander	1983	839

262

COUGAR (MOUNTAIN LION)

Minimum Score 13 8/16   Continued

SCORE	GREATEST LENGTH	GREATEST WIDTH	SEX	AREA	STATE/PROVINCE	HUNTER'S NAME	DATE	RANK
14 6/16	8 7/16	5 15/16	M	Clearwater County	ID	Tim Newbold	1983	839
14 6/16	8 9/16	5 13/16	M	Walla Walla County	WA	Winford Bradford	1983	839
14 6/16	8 3/16	6 3/16	M	Caribou County	ID	Rhett Bradford	1984	839
14 6/16	8 6/16	6 0/16	M	Lemhi County	ID	Donald L. Minnich	1984	839
14 6/16	8 8/16	5 14/16	M	Lemhi County	ID	Phil R. Ginochio	1985	839
14 6/16	8 5/16	6 1/16	M	Boise County	ID	David W. Peltier	1985	839
14 6/16	8 8/16	5 14/16	M	Cochise County	AZ	John Holcomb	1985	839
14 6/16	8 6/16	6 0/16	M	Flathead County	MT	Earl W. Weaver	1986	839
14 6/16	8 8/16	5 14/16	M	Missoula County	MT	Vinnie Pisani	1987	839
14 6/16	8 8/16	5 14/16	M	Summit County	UT	Jeffrey W. Potter	1988	839
14 6/16	8 10/16	5 12/16	M	Fremont County	CO	Daniel Daly	1988	839
14 6/16	8 7/16	5 15/16	M	Sanders County	MT	Harold R. Anderson	1988	839
14 6/16	8 6/16	6 0/16	M	Lincoln County	MT	Rich Hjort	1989	839
14 6/16	8 11/16	5 11/16	M	Josephine County	OR	Brian Day	1990	839
14 6/16	8 9/16	5 13/16	M	Garfield County	CO	Johnnie R. Walters	1991	839
14 6/16	8 6/16	6 0/16	M	Oldman River	ALB	Tom Foss	1991	839
14 6/16	8 10/16	5 12/16	M	Beaver County	UT	Robert Barrie	1991	839
14 6/16	8 7/16	5 15/16	M	Elmore County	ID	William "Bill" MacCarty III	1991	839
14 6/16	8 6/16	6 0/16	M	Mesa County	CO	James Bornman	1992	839
14 6/16	8 8/16	5 14/16	M	Flathead County	MT	M. R. James	1992	839
14 6/16	8 6/16	6 0/16	M	Greenlee County	AZ	Tom Taylor	1993	839
14 6/16	8 10/16	5 12/16	M	Carbon County	UT	Dina Wise	1993	839
14 6/16	8 7/16	5 15/16	M	Chaffee County	CO	Al Miller	1993	839
14 6/16	8 8/16	5 14/16	M	Rio Arriba County	NM	Marvin M. Maestas	1994	839
14 6/16	8 8/16	5 14/16	M	Montrose County	CO	Ron Baldwin	1994	839
14 6/16	8 6/16	6 0/16	M	Nakusp	BC	Gary J. Burns	1994	839
14 6/16	8 7/16	5 15/16	M	Silver Bow County	MT	Mike Perala	1994	839
14 6/16	8 8/16	5 14/16	M	Duchesne County	UT	Thomas Ostrander	1994	839
14 6/16	8 8/16	5 14/16	M	Sanpete County	UT	Burke Lyon	1995	839
14 6/16	8 8/16	5 14/16	M	Porcupine Hills	ALB	Warren Witherspoon	1995	839
14 6/16	8 9/16	5 13/16	F	Ferry County	WA	Joe Arcieri	1995	839
14 6/16	8 9/16	5 13/16	M	Fergus County	MT	Donny Roy	1996	839
14 6/16	8 7/16	5 15/16	M	Steamboat Mtn.	BC	Kent G. Kebe	1996	839
14 6/16	8 7/16	5 15/16	M	Nakusp	BC	John Mastroianni	1996	839
14 6/16	8 9/16	5 13/16	M	Madison County	MT	Scott Dell	1996	839
14 6/16	8 9/16	5 13/16	M	Boise County	ID	Todd Felt	1996	839
14 6/16	8 11/16	5 11/16	M	San Juan County	UT	Melinda K. Schmidt	1997	839
14 6/16	8 9/16	5 13/16	M	Garfield County	UT	Henry Joseph Lohmeier	1997	839
14 6/16	8 6/16	6 0/16	M	Rio Blanco County	CO	Roger Becker	1997	839
14 6/16	8 9/16	5 13/16	M	Clearwater County	ID	Eugene Lewis	1997	839
14 6/16	8 11/16	5 11/16	M	Garfield County	CO	Terry J. Gerber	1998	839
14 6/16	8 7/16	5 15/16	M	Ravalli County	MT	Jack Edward Stanford	1999	839
14 6/16	8 6/16	6 0/16	M	Wasatch County	UT	Ted E. Smith	1999	839
14 6/16	8 5/16	6 1/16	M	Ravalli County	MT	Scott Lang	1999	839
14 6/16	8 7/16	5 15/16	M	Twin Falls County	ID	Darrell F. Nunez	2001	839
14 6/16	8 9/16	5 13/16	M	Carbon County	UT	Travis Bennett	2001	839
14 6/16	8 8/16	5 14/16	M	Grand County	UT	Jon D. Jenkins	2001	839
14 6/16	8 6/16	6 0/16	M	Moyie River	BC	Bob Smith	2001	839
14 6/16	8 6/16	6 0/16	M	Park County	MT	Leo P. Caito, Jr.	2002	839
14 6/16	8 9/16	5 13/16	M	Carbon County	UT	Buck Siler	2002	839
14 6/16	8 6/16	6 0/16	M	Fremont County	WY	Craig Overman	2002	839
14 6/16	8 8/16	5 14/16	M	Rio Blanco County	CO	Chad P. Birrenkott	2002	839
14 6/16	8 9/16	5 13/16	M	Emery County	UT	Robin Rudman	2002	839
14 6/16	8 7/16	5 15/16	M	Summit County	UT	Dennis L. Ingram	2002	839
14 6/16	8 7/16	5 15/16	M	Valley County	ID	Kevin Gaither	2005	839
14 6/16	8 8/16	5 14/16	M	Red Deer River	ALB	Dallas Kaiser	2005	839
14 6/16	8 8/16	5 14/16	M	Sevier County	UT	Scott A. Huebner	2006	839
14 6/16	8 9/16	5 13/16	M	Park County	MT	Alan McCollim	2006	839
14 6/16	8 8/16	5 14/16	M	Lemhi County	ID	Jason Seitz	2007	839
14 6/16	8 8/16	5 14/16	M	Cache County	UT	Pete LoPiccolo	2007	839
14 6/16	8 7/16	5 15/16	M	Shoshone County	ID	Ernest W. Clanton	2007	839
14 6/16	8 5/16	6 1/16	M	Lemhi County	ID	Jeffrey A. Eder	2008	839
14 6/16	8 8/16	5 14/16	M	Okanogan County	WA	Matt Marsh	2009	839
*14 6/16	8 6/16	6 0/16	M	Eagle County	CO	Cody Doig	2009	839
*14 6/16	8 12/16	5 10/16	M	Eagle County	CO	Brian Sewell	2010	839
14 5/16	8 6/16	5 15/16	M	Esmeralda County	NV	Don Schram	1965	921
14 5/16	8 8/16	5 13/16	M	Garfield County	UT	H. R. 'Dutch' Wambold	1966	921
14 5/16	8 9/16	5 12/16	M	Tatla Lake	BC	William L. Nickerson	1966	921
14 5/16	8 8/16	5 13/16	M	Garfield County	UT	Robert K. Paulson	1968	921
14 5/16	8 10/16	5 11/16	M	Carbon County	UT	M. R. James	1970	921
14 5/16	8 8/16	5 13/16	M	Chaffee County	CO	Michael Ballard	1975	921
14 5/16	8 8/16	5 13/16	M	Beaver County	UT	Bruce Post	1975	921
14 5/16	8 7/16	5 14/16	M	Las Animas County	CO	Barry L. Powell	1975	921
14 5/16	8 7/16	5 14/16	M	White Pine County	NV	James L. Beard	1975	921
14 5/16	8 8/16	5 13/16	M	Daggett County	UT	Bob Butler	1976	921
14 5/16	8 9/16	5 12/16	M	Elmore County	ID	L. Dean Goodner	1978	921
14 5/16	8 9/16	5 12/16	M	Fire Mtn.	BC	John "Jack" Cordes	1978	921
14 5/16	8 10/16	5 11/16	M	Grand County	UT	Terry L. Benzine	1978	921
14 5/16	8 7/16	5 14/16	M	Custer County	CO	William Henderson	1979	921
14 5/16	8 7/16	5 14/16	M	Montezuma County	CO	Marvin Reichenau	1981	921
14 5/16	8 7/16	5 14/16	M	Judith Basin County	MT	Don Davidson	1981	921
14 5/16	8 10/16	5 11/16	M	Dolores County	CO	Mike Gleason	1982	921
14 5/16	8 6/16	5 15/16	M	Lemhi County	ID	Stephen N. Bean	1983	921
14 5/16	8 8/16	5 13/16	M	Custer County	ID	Robert L. Hudman	1984	921
14 5/16	8 5/16	6 0/16	M	Jefferson County	CO	Jeff Fulkner	1984	921
14 5/16	8 8/16	5 13/16	M	Rio Blanco County	CO	Michael Ingold	1984	921
14 5/16	8 7/16	5 14/16	M	Sanders County	MT	Alan Gaston	1984	921
14 5/16	8 8/16	5 13/16	M	Sanpete County	UT	Judy Hallman	1985	921
14 5/16	8 5/16	6 0/16	M	Colfax County	NM	Jim Stauft	1985	921
14 5/16	8 7/16	5 14/16	M	Idaho County	ID	Jay D. Stringer	1985	921
14 5/16	8 8/16	5 13/16	M	Judith Basin County	MT	Joseph R. "Bob" Fabian	1986	921
14 5/16	8 9/16	5 12/16	M	Dona Ana County	NM	Larry M. Sellers	1986	921
14 5/16	8 9/16	5 12/16	M	Kane County	UT	Allan Dangerfield	1986	921
14 5/16	8 5/16	6 0/16	M	Sanders County	MT	Byron E. Wates, Jr.	1986	921
14 5/16	8 10/16	5 11/16	M	Pend Oreille County	WA	Leonard F. Rock	1986	921

263

COUGAR (MOUNTAIN LION)

Minimum Score 13 8/16 — Continued

SCORE	GREATEST LENGTH	GREATEST WIDTH	SEX	AREA	STATE/PROVINCE	HUNTER'S NAME	DATE	RANK
14 5/16	8 8/16	5 13/16	M	Daggett County	UT	Jeff Schneider	1987	921
14 5/16	8 9/16	5 12/16	M	Grand County	UT	James S. Saunoris	1987	921
14 5/16	8 7/16	5 14/16	M	Elmore County	ID	Alfred John Gemrich	1988	921
14 5/16	8 5/16	6 0/16	M	Idaho County	ID	Daniel R. Hooper	1988	921
14 5/16	8 6/16	5 15/16	M	Lane County	OR	John Stone	1988	921
14 5/16	8 6/16	5 15/16	M	Madison County	MT	Scott T. Smolen	1988	921
14 5/16	8 8/16	5 13/16	M	Mesa County	CO	Richard Gerhart	1988	921
14 5/16	8 7/16	5 14/16	M	Idaho County	ID	Doug Hawkins	1989	921
14 5/16	8 8/16	5 13/16	M	Sanders County	MT	Charles R. Gallo	1990	921
14 5/16	8 8/16	5 13/16	M	Broadwater County	MT	Mike Parsons	1990	921
14 5/16	8 7/16	5 14/16	M	West Kettle River	BC	Lyndon Walker	1990	921
14 5/16	8 5/16	6 0/16	M	San Miguel County	CO	Roger Degroat	1991	921
14 5/16	8 6/16	5 15/16	M	Fisher Creek	ALB	Robin Arthurs	1991	921
14 5/16	8 7/16	5 14/16	M	Montezuma County	CO	Jerry Rush	1991	921
14 5/16	8 7/16	5 14/16	M	Garfield County	CO	Marvin Weible	1991	921
14 5/16	8 7/16	5 14/16	M	Garfield County	CO	Terry C. Parkinson	1992	921
14 5/16	8 5/16	6 0/16	M	Lake County	MT	Dave R. Daubenberger	1992	921
14 5/16	8 6/16	5 15/16	M	Clear Creek County	CO	Mark Turner	1993	921
14 5/16	8 5/16	6 0/16	M	Edgewood	BC	Gerald V. Shields	1993	921
14 5/16	8 4/16	6 1/16	M	Sublette County	WY	Ron Couture	1993	921
14 5/16	8 8/16	5 13/16	M	Porcupine Hills	ALB	Ryk Visscher	1993	921
14 5/16	8 9/16	5 12/16	M	Duchesne County	UT	James L. Kelly III	1994	921
14 5/16	8 9/16	5 12/16	M	Grand County	CO	Dave Parri	1994	921
14 5/16	8 9/16	5 12/16	M	Custer County	ID	Scott Brower	1994	921
14 5/16	8 10/16	5 11/16	M	Sevier County	UT	Casey J. Cardwell	1994	921
14 5/16	8 10/16	5 11/16	M	Elko County	NV	Vincent D'Ascoli	1995	921
14 5/16	8 7/16	5 14/16	M	Lemhi County	ID	Mark A. Mathews	1995	921
14 5/16	8 7/16	5 14/16	M	Stevens County	WA	Avery L. Hansen	1995	921
14 5/16	8 6/16	5 15/16	M	Powell County	MT	Gene Meyer	1995	921
14 5/16	8 5/16	6 0/16	M	Madison County	MT	Ivan J. Muzljakovich	1995	921
14 5/16	8 8/16	5 13/16	M	Idaho County	ID	Matt March	1996	921
14 5/16	8 5/16	6 0/16	M	Larimer County	CO	Emilio Bonetti	1996	921
14 5/16	8 11/16	5 10/16	M	Elko County	NV	Wayne E. Testolin	1996	921
14 5/16	8 9/16	5 12/16	M	Moffat County	CO	Daniel L. Wells	1997	921
14 5/16	8 8/16	5 13/16	M	Park County	MT	Jon Drechsel	1997	921
14 5/16	8 6/16	5 15/16	M	Cascade County	MT	Jim Winjum	1997	921
14 5/16	8 6/16	5 15/16	M	Albany County	WY	Jerry Bowen	1997	921
14 5/16	8 7/16	5 14/16	M	Idaho County	ID	Larry E. Sholly, Jr.	1997	921
14 5/16	8 5/16	6 0/16	M	Ravalli County	MT	Mike Coutu	1997	921
14 5/16	8 7/16	5 14/16	M	Fergus County	MT	D. Mitch Kottas	1997	921
14 5/16	8 5/16	6 0/16	M	Utah County	UT	Scott Keetch	1998	921
14 5/16	8 6/16	5 15/16	M	Fergus County	MT	Kenneth Roy	1998	921
14 5/16	8 9/16	5 12/16	M	Wasatch County	UT	Larry Knight	1998	921
14 5/16	8 6/16	5 15/16	M	Sublette County	WY	Ray Alexander	1998	921
14 5/16	8 6/16	5 15/16	M	Fergus County	MT	Kristi Machler	1998	921
14 5/16	8 8/16	5 13/16	M	Graham County	AZ	David Kimbell, Jr.	1999	921
14 5/16	8 8/16	5 13/16	M	Fremont County	WY	Jack Wilson	1999	921
14 5/16	8 7/16	5 14/16	M	Elko County	NV	Mutt Wilson	2000	921
14 5/16	8 8/16	5 13/16	M	Idaho County	ID	John Albrecht	2000	921
14 5/16	8 6/16	5 15/16	M	Jefferson County	OR	Jon Cox	2001	921
14 5/16	8 6/16	5 15/16	M	Beaverhead County	MT	Monty Hankinson	2002	921
14 5/16	8 8/16	5 13/16	M	Flathead County	MT	Shaine Reece	2003	921
14 5/16	8 7/16	5 14/16	M	Elkford	BC	Frank Tuma	2004	921
14 5/16	8 6/16	5 15/16	M	Teton County	WY	Steven D. Larson	2004	921
14 5/16	8 8/16	5 13/16	M	Gila County	AZ	Joseph N. Denardo	2004	921
14 5/16	8 7/16	5 14/16	M	Mesa County	CO	Scot L. Hamilton	2005	921
*14 5/16	8 7/16	5 14/16	M	Rio Blanco County	CO	Terrance S. Marcum	2006	921
*14 5/16	8 7/16	5 14/16	M	Sanpete County	UT	Allen Bolen	2008	921
14 5/16	8 6/16	5 15/16	M	Garfield County	CO	Kent Hyrup	2009	921
*14 5/16	8 9/16	5 12/16	M	Cibola County	NM	M. Blake Patton	2010	921
14 4/16	8 8/16	5 12/16	M	Stoneman Lake	AZ	Dr. C. L. Clare	1962	1011
14 4/16	8 8/16	5 12/16	M	Lincoln County	MT	Dale McNutt	1964	1011
14 4/16	8 10/16	5 10/16	M	Elmore County	ID	Don Bennett	1968	1011
14 4/16	8 4/16	6 0/16	M	Missoula County	MT	Tony Dumay	1968	1011
14 4/16	8 6/16	5 14/16	M	Elmore County	ID	John E. Anderson	1972	1011
14 4/16	8 6/16	5 14/16	M	Lemhi County	ID	Kenneth Anselmi	1972	1011
14 4/16	8 6/16	5 14/16	M	Nye County	NV	Ken Viles	1972	1011
14 4/16	8 4/16	6 0/16	M	Salmon River	ID	Bob Tucker	1974	1011
14 4/16	8 4/16	6 0/16	M	Mesa County	CO	Robert Tobias	1975	1011
14 4/16	8 6/16	5 14/16	M	Lemhi County	ID	H. R. 'Rusty' Neely	1975	1011
14 4/16	8 6/16	5 14/16	M	Custer County	ID	Gerald Conway	1978	1011
14 4/16	8 8/16	5 12/16	M	McMullen County	TX	James E. Jordan	1978	1011
14 4/16	8 4/16	6 0/16	M	Washington County	UT	Richard L. Mobilio	1979	1011
14 4/16	8 8/16	5 12/16	M	Garfield County	UT	George Holfeltz	1980	1011
14 4/16	8 3/16	6 1/16	M	Colfax County	NM	Stephen 'Don' Hornady	1980	1011
14 4/16	8 6/16	5 14/16	M	Salt Lake County	UT	William L. Randles	1982	1011
14 4/16	8 4/16	6 0/16	M	Garfield County	CO	T. Michael Casey	1982	1011
14 4/16	8 8/16	5 12/16	M	Lincoln County	NV	David A. Widby	1982	1011
14 4/16	8 6/16	5 14/16	M	Clearwater County	ID	Ralph Ertz	1983	1011
14 4/16	8 5/16	5 15/16	M	Elmore County	ID	Brad L. Johnson	1983	1011
14 4/16	8 6/16	5 14/16	M	Lemhi County	ID	Bob Hudson	1984	1011
14 4/16	8 6/16	5 14/16	M	Spokane County	WA	Kenneth R. Wengert	1984	1011
14 4/16	8 7/16	5 13/16	M	Lander County	NV	Peter Esposito	1984	1011
14 4/16	8 8/16	5 12/16	M	Sanpete County	UT	C. Danny Butler	1985	1011
14 4/16	8 7/16	5 13/16	M	Lander County	NV	Leonard Ruimveld	1985	1011
14 4/16	8 5/16	5 15/16	M	Montrose County	CO	Tony Hoza	1986	1011
14 4/16	8 6/16	5 14/16	M	Colfax County	NM	John L. Chapman	1986	1011
14 4/16	8 8/16	5 12/16	M	Eureka County	NV	Marty Pawelek	1986	1011
14 4/16	8 6/16	5 14/16	M	Jackson County	OR	Jon Updegraff	1986	1011
14 4/16	8 6/16	5 14/16	M	Coconino County	AZ	Todd Rice	1986	1011
14 4/16	8 4/16	6 0/16	M	Nakusp	BC	Len Surina	1987	1011
14 4/16	8 5/16	5 15/16	M	Benewah County	ID	William N. Latshaw	1988	1011
14 4/16	8 8/16	5 12/16	M	Colfax County	NM	Robert L. Pagel	1988	1011
14 4/16	8 6/16	5 14/16	M	Ravalli County	MT	Erik "Rick" Aslesen	1988	1011
14 4/16	8 8/16	5 12/16	M	White Pine County	NV	Archie Nesbitt	1988	1011

COUGAR (MOUNTAIN LION)

Minimum Score 13 8/16   Continued

SCORE	GREATEST LENGTH	GREATEST WIDTH	SEX	AREA	STATE/ PROVINCE	HUNTER'S NAME	DATE	RANK
14 4/16	8 8/16	5 12/16	M	Iron County	UT	Bernie E. Belfrage	1988	1011
14 4/16	8 5/16	5 15/16	M	Douglas County	OR	Stanley Myers	1988	1011
14 4/16	8 7/16	5 13/16	M	Yavapai County	AZ	Roy Ruiz	1989	1011
14 4/16	8 7/16	5 13/16	M	Carbon County	UT	Mike Hillis	1990	1011
14 4/16	8 8/16	5 12/16	M	Converse County	WY	James P. Smith	1990	1011
14 4/16	8 8/16	5 12/16	M	Sweet Grass County	MT	Roger A. Greve, Jr.	1990	1011
14 4/16	8 5/16	5 15/16	M	Coconino County	AZ	H. Gordon Purl	1990	1011
14 4/16	8 6/16	5 14/16	M	Rio Blanco County	CO	Kenton Meyers	1990	1011
14 4/16	8 7/16	5 13/16	M	Ouray County	CO	Randy Caspersen	1991	1011
14 4/16	8 9/16	5 11/16	M	Fremont County	CO	Bill Hartman	1991	1011
14 4/16	8 4/16	6 0/16	M	Wasatch County	UT	Karl Hirst	1991	1011
14 4/16	8 8/16	5 12/16	M	Boise County	ID	Larry Hoff	1991	1011
14 4/16	8 7/16	5 13/16	M	Boise County	ID	William James Tuffield II	1991	1011
14 4/16	8 8/16	5 12/16	M	Clearwater County	ID	Patrick L. Hovey	1992	1011
14 4/16	8 9/16	5 11/16	M	Mesa County	CO	Alan Parkerson	1992	1011
14 4/16	8 4/16	6 0/16	M	Judith Basin County	MT	Don Davidson	1992	1011
14 4/16	8 6/16	5 14/16	M	Lake County	MT	Ken Vorisek	1992	1011
14 4/16	8 7/16	5 13/16	M	Carbon County	WY	Robert E. Bergquist	1992	1011
14 4/16	8 8/16	5 12/16	M	Ram Creek	BC	Tom Marshall	1993	1011
14 4/16	8 6/16	5 14/16	M	Utah County	UT	Dusty Mitchell	1993	1011
14 4/16	8 10/16	5 10/16	M	Rio Arriba County	NM	Nelson G. Martinez, Jr.	1993	1011
14 4/16	8 5/16	5 15/16	M	Coconino County	AZ	Blaine "Bub" Mathews	1993	1011
14 4/16	8 5/16	5 15/16	M	Meagher County	MT	Ed Rogalski	1993	1011
14 4/16	8 8/16	5 12/16	M	Lemhi County	ID	John Shaffer, Jr.	1993	1011
14 4/16	8 8/16	5 12/16	M	Washington County	UT	Pat Abalsamo	1994	1011
14 4/16	8 8/16	5 12/16	M	Lincoln County	NV	Tom Carter	1994	1011
14 4/16	8 8/16	5 12/16	M	Garfield County	CO	Robert L. Moon, Jr.	1994	1011
14 4/16	8 9/16	5 11/16	M	Idaho County	ID	Kevin Schmid	1994	1011
14 4/16	8 7/16	5 13/16	M	Valley County	ID	Lewis Zane Abbott	1994	1011
14 4/16	8 6/16	5 14/16	M	Archuleta County	CO	Dewey J. Mast	1995	1011
14 4/16	8 6/16	5 14/16	M	San Juan County	UT	Adam Bronson	1995	1011
14 4/16	8 6/16	5 14/16	M	Mohave County	AZ	Ward Villamor	1995	1011
14 4/16	8 7/16	5 13/16	M	Emery County	UT	Richard A. Smith	1996	1011
14 4/16	8 9/16	5 11/16	M	Fremont County	CO	Dave Vomela	1996	1011
14 4/16	8 5/16	5 15/16	M	Fergus County	MT	Brad Johnson	1996	1011
14 4/16	8 5/16	5 15/16	M	Platte County	WY	Mike Boughton	1996	1011
14 4/16	8 8/16	5 12/16	M	Okanagan Valley	BC	James Schomberg	1997	1011
14 4/16	8 7/16	5 13/16	M	Juab County	UT	Danny Yoder	1997	1011
14 4/16	8 4/16	6 0/16	M	Gunnison County	CO	Joe D. Belas	1998	1011
14 4/16	8 8/16	5 12/16	M	Meagher County	MT	Kevin Biegel	1998	1011
14 4/16	8 7/16	5 13/16	M	Idaho County	ID	Dan Drover	1998	1011
14 4/16	8 7/16	5 13/16	M	Mineral County	MT	Jon Burgdorf	1998	1011
14 4/16	8 8/16	5 12/16	M	Boise County	ID	Pat Lefemine	1998	1011
14 4/16	8 6/16	5 14/16	M	Elmore County	ID	Joe St. Charles	1999	1011
14 4/16	8 7/16	5 13/16	M	Apache County	AZ	Aimee Frost	1999	1011
14 4/16	8 8/16	5 12/16	M	Garfield County	CO	Gary W. Smith	1999	1011
14 4/16	8 6/16	5 14/16	M	Rocky Mountain House	ALB	Randy Bernier	1999	1011
14 4/16	8 8/16	5 12/16	M	Boise County	ID	Robert P. Hudson, Jr.	1999	1011
14 4/16	8 6/16	5 14/16	M	Carbon County	UT	Casey Mills	1999	1011
14 4/16	8 8/16	5 12/16	M	Mesa County	CO	Jamie Dahm	2000	1011
14 4/16	8 5/16	5 15/16	M	Jefferson County	CO	Jeff Samona	2000	1011
14 4/16	8 6/16	5 14/16	M	Lyon County	NV	Jon A. Hill	2001	1011
14 4/16	8 5/16	5 15/16	M	Garfield County	CO	Larry Thrun	2002	1011
14 4/16	8 7/16	5 13/16	M	Sevier County	UT	Jeremy Stevens	2004	1011
14 4/16	8 7/16	5 13/16	M	Lemhi County	ID	Brandon Fahnholz	2004	1011
*14 4/16	8 8/16	5 12/16	M	Rio Blanco County	CO	Kenneth W. Gamble	2005	1011
14 4/16	8 6/16	5 14/16	M	Lemhi County	ID	Todd G. Wendel	2005	1011
*14 4/16	8 5/16	5 15/16	M	Park County	WY	Dr. Larry Menning	2005	1011
*14 4/16	8 7/16	5 13/16	M	Cranbrook	BC	Robert A. Wilson	2005	1011
14 4/16	8 6/16	5 14/16	M	Lincoln County	NV	Pauly J. Paul	2006	1011
*14 4/16	8 9/16	5 11/16	M	Huerfano County	CO	Paul Rodriguez	2008	1011
*14 4/16	8 6/16	5 14/16	M	Larimer County	CO	Randy Carey	2009	1011
*14 4/16	8 8/16	5 12/16	M	San Juan County	UT	Douglas Stramel	2009	1011
14 4/16	8 8/16	5 12/16	M	Park County	WY	Jonathan E. Rhodes	2009	1011
14 4/16	8 8/16	5 12/16	M	Grand County	CO	Chance Martin	2009	1011
14 4/16	8 4/16	6 0/16	M	Albany County	WY	Austin Guerin	2010	1011
14 4/16	8 6/16	5 14/16	M	Cranbrook	BC	Eric Kuhlman	2010	1011
14 3/16	8 7/16	5 12/16	M	Ferry County	WA	Tom Smith	1968	1113
14 3/16	8 6/16	5 13/16	M	Nye County	NV	Dick Gulman	1968	1113
14 3/16	8 5/16	5 14/16	M	Grand County	UT	John B. Baughman	1969	1113
14 3/16	8 6/16	5 13/16	M	Douglas County	NV	Bill Fuller	1972	1113
14 3/16	8 7/16	5 12/16	M	Huerfano County	CO	Marvin C. Clyncke	1973	1113
14 3/16	8 9/16	5 10/16	M	Juab County	UT	Samuel McCarty	1975	1113
14 3/16	8 7/16	5 12/16	M	Stevens County	WA	Ronald A. Carpenter	1977	1113
14 3/16	8 8/16	5 11/16	M	Chaffee County	CO	John C. Dekker	1977	1113
14 3/16	8 8/16	5 11/16	M	Sevier County	UT	Claude Flippin	1980	1113
14 3/16	8 7/16	5 12/16	M	Adams County	ID	Rube Powell	1982	1113
14 3/16	8 4/16	5 15/16	M	Mesa County	CO	William G. Padilla	1982	1113
14 3/16	8 6/16	5 13/16	M	Judith Basin County	MT	Stan Colton	1983	1113
14 3/16	8 5/16	5 14/16	M	Madison County	MT	Tony Schaufler	1983	1113
14 3/16	8 4/16	5 15/16	M	Flathead County	MT	Gary A. Crowe	1983	1113
14 3/16	8 6/16	5 13/16	M	Sierra County	NM	Kendall Doyle	1985	1113
14 3/16	8 4/16	5 15/16	M	Montezuma County	CO	Duain Morton	1985	1113
14 3/16	8 5/16	5 14/16	F	Shuswap River	BC	Mark Siegmueller	1985	1113
14 3/16	8 5/16	5 14/16	M	Sanders County	MT	Jim Clark	1985	1113
14 3/16	8 4/16	5 15/16	M	Clearwater County	ID	Dexter Siler	1986	1113
14 3/16	8 7/16	5 12/16	M	Idaho County	ID	Tony E. Hyde	1986	1113
14 3/16	8 5/16	5 14/16	M	Lemhi County	ID	Ben L. Fahnolz	1987	1113
14 3/16	8 6/16	5 13/16	M	Idaho County	ID	G. Sam Cloninger	1987	1113
14 3/16	8 8/16	5 11/16	M	Elko County	NV	Charles Lee Pemble	1989	1113
14 3/16	8 8/16	5 11/16	M	Tooele County	UT	Dale G. Kelson	1989	1113
14 3/16	8 6/16	5 13/16	M	Fremont County	CO	R. E. Smith	1989	1113
14 3/16	8 5/16	5 14/16	M	Lemhi County	ID	Richard Smith	1990	1113
14 3/16	8 7/16	5 12/16	M	Ravalli County	MT	Jim Loughran	1990	1113
14 3/16	8 14/16	5 5/16	M	Grand County	CO	Cary Laman	1991	1113

265

COUGAR (MOUNTAIN LION)

Minimum Score 13 8/16   Continued

SCORE	GREATEST LENGTH	GREATEST WIDTH	SEX	AREA	STATE/ PROVINCE	HUNTER'S NAME	DATE	RANK
14 3/16	8 5/16	5 14/16	M	Sheridan County	WY	Tom Hlinka	1992	1113
14 3/16	8 4/16	5 15/16	M	Duchesne County	UT	M. Tim McIntyre	1994	1113
14 3/16	8 5/16	5 14/16	M	Fergus County	MT	Dan Gill	1994	1113
14 3/16	8 6/16	5 13/16	M	Lemhi County	ID	Dale F. Slama	1994	1113
14 3/16	8 7/16	5 12/16	M	Duchesne County	UT	William C. Bolt, Jr.	1994	1113
14 3/16	8 8/16	5 11/16	M	Garfield County	WA	Rick Leach	1994	1113
14 3/16	8 7/16	5 12/16	M	Dolores County	CO	David M. Richards	1995	1113
14 3/16	8 5/16	5 14/16	M	Uintah County	UT	Dennis Lee Ingram	1995	1113
14 3/16	8 5/16	5 14/16	M	Moffat County	CO	Kenny E. Leo	1996	1113
14 3/16	8 8/16	5 11/16	M	Unitah County	UT	Al Del Greco	1996	1113
14 3/16	8 8/16	5 11/16	M	Las Animas County	CO	Rick East	1997	1113
14 3/16	8 7/16	5 12/16	M	Moffat County	CO	Donald H. Corey	1997	1113
14 3/16	8 7/16	5 12/16	M	Washington County	UT	Rick Sarkisian	1997	1113
14 3/16	8 8/16	5 11/16	M	Piute County	UT	Robert Staudt, Jr.	1998	1113
14 3/16	8 6/16	5 13/16	M	Black Cat Hills	ALB	Brent Watson	1998	1113
14 3/16	8 4/16	5 15/16	M	Madison County	MT	Brian Koelzer	1998	1113
14 3/16	8 4/16	5 15/16	M	Yavapai County	AZ	Wayne Smith	1998	1113
14 3/16	8 6/16	5 13/16	M	Sanders County	MT	Garry Seaman	2000	1113
14 3/16	8 5/16	5 14/16	M	Boise County	ID	Ross M. Clark	2001	1113
14 3/16	8 5/16	5 14/16	M	Idaho County	ID	David Andersen	2001	1113
14 3/16	8 8/16	5 11/16	M	Rio Blanco County	CO	Chris W. Whytock	2003	1113
14 3/16	8 5/16	5 14/16	M	Sublette County	WY	Randy Spenner	2003	1113
14 3/16	8 5/16	5 14/16	M	Bonneville County	ID	Rodney Diemer	2003	1113
14 3/16	8 5/16	5 14/16	M	Yavapai County	AZ	Brian Anton Rimsza	2005	1113
*14 3/16	8 6/16	5 13/16	M	Brazeau River	ALB	Rod Tetreault	2005	1113
14 3/16	8 4/16	5 15/16	M	Pinal County	AZ	Richard J. Stewart II	2005	1113
*14 3/16	8 5/16	5 14/16	M	Larimer County	CO	Roger L. Young	2005	1113
*14 3/16	8 7/16	5 12/16	M	Gallatin County	MT	Ryan Richards	2006	1113
14 3/16	8 6/16	5 13/16	M	Beaver County	UT	Ted Carlson	2007	1113
14 3/16	8 4/16	5 15/16	M	Kananaskis	ALB	Shane Mascarin	2007	1113
14 3/16	8 5/16	5 14/16	M	Valley County	ID	Kevin Primrose	2009	1113
14 3/16	8 5/16	5 14/16	M	Idaho County	ID	Lee Wolford	2009	1113
14 3/16	8 7/16	5 12/16	M	Montrose County	CO	Michael D. Lichtenwalner	2009	1113
14 2/16	8 6/16	5 12/16	M	Okanogan County	WA	Dr. Russell Congdon	1950	1174
14 2/16	8 6/16	5 12/16	M	Kane County	UT	William P. Mastrangel	1957	1174
14 2/16	8 4/16	5 14/16	M	Fresno County	CA	John Faulconer	1964	1174
14 2/16	8 6/16	5 12/16	M	Garfield County	CO	Phillip C. Durr	1970	1174
14 2/16	8 4/16	5 14/16	M	Uintah County	UT	Larry Jones	1970	1174
14 2/16	8 6/16	5 12/16	M	Rio Blanco County	CO	James L. Emerson	1976	1174
14 2/16	8 4/16	5 14/16	M	Lane County	OR	Eugene W. Gramzow	1978	1174
14 2/16	8 5/16	5 13/16	M	Saguache County	CO	John T. Rauch	1979	1174
14 2/16	8 4/16	5 14/16	M	Ravalli County	MT	Dean Irwin	1980	1174
14 2/16	8 3/16	5 15/16	M	Montrose County	CO	Hoyte Driggers	1981	1174
14 2/16	8 4/16	5 14/16	M	Greenlee County	AZ	Fred L. Smith	1982	1174
14 2/16	8 8/16	5 10/16	M	Duchesne County	UT	Bill Painter	1982	1174
14 2/16	8 9/16	5 9/16	M	Duchesne County	UT	Michael Wieck	1983	1174
14 2/16	8 6/16	5 12/16	M	Garfield County	UT	Carl D. Winton	1984	1174
14 2/16	8 4/16	5 14/16	M	Sweet Grass County	MT	David W. Sorensen	1984	1174
14 2/16	8 2/16	6 0/16	M	Catron County	NM	Dean Hamilton	1985	1174
14 2/16	8 8/16	5 10/16	M	Ravalli County	MT	John L Wozniak	1985	1174
14 2/16	8 3/16	5 15/16	M	Mesa County	CO	David A. Schroeder	1986	1174
14 2/16	8 6/16	5 12/16	M	Sanpete County	UT	Joe Johnston	1986	1174
14 2/16	8 5/16	5 13/16	M	Larimer County	CO	Jerry L. Novak	1987	1174
14 2/16	8 6/16	5 12/16	M	Mesa County	CO	Norm Stahlman	1987	1174
14 2/16	8 6/16	5 12/16	M	Grand County	UT	J. Dale Hale	1988	1174
14 2/16	8 4/16	5 14/16	M	Lemhi County	ID	Kent Brandt	1988	1174
14 2/16	8 7/16	5 11/16	M	Dolores County	CO	Ernest N. Schroch	1988	1174
14 2/16	8 6/16	5 12/16	M	Garfield County	CO	James "Boomer" Hayden	1988	1174
14 2/16	8 4/16	5 14/16	M	Cranbrook	BC	Paul Deme	1989	1174
14 2/16	8 6/16	5 12/16	M	Mesa County	CO	Tom Nelson	1989	1174
14 2/16	8 9/16	5 9/16	M	Nye County	NV	Jesse Andrew Westby	1989	1174
14 2/16	8 4/16	5 14/16	M	Greenlee County	AZ	Brian Davis	1989	1174
14 2/16	8 1/16	6 1/16	M	Box Elder County	UT	Ellis Wall	1990	1174
14 2/16	8 6/16	5 12/16	M	Mesa County	CO	Don Marascalco	1990	1174
14 2/16	8 7/16	5 11/16	M	Custer County	ID	Trent Haberstroh	1990	1174
14 2/16	8 6/16	5 12/16	M	Park County	CO	Bryon Scott Johnson	1991	1174
14 2/16	8 6/16	5 12/16	M	Arrow Lakes	BC	Glenn Dreger	1991	1174
14 2/16	8 11/16	5 7/16	M	Wayne County	UT	Charles M. Moore	1991	1174
14 2/16	8 7/16	5 11/16	M	Sevier County	UT	Jack W. Powell	1991	1174
14 2/16	8 4/16	5 14/16	M	Elmore County	ID	Jon Brockfeld	1992	1174
14 2/16	8 8/16	5 10/16	M	Garfield County	UT	Steven R. Farr	1992	1174
14 2/16	8 8/16	5 10/16	M	Beaver County	UT	Glen L. Mahlum	1993	1174
14 2/16	8 5/16	5 13/16	M	Nye County	NV	Dave Steger	1993	1174
14 2/16	8 4/16	5 14/16	M	Archuleta County	CO	Lester D. Hawkins, Jr.	1993	1174
14 2/16	8 5/16	5 13/16	M	Lemhi County	ID	Rob Valnoski	1993	1174
14 2/16	8 5/16	5 13/16	M	Mesa County	CO	Paul Kamps	1994	1174
14 2/16	8 8/16	5 10/16	M	Wasatch County	UT	Dallas Smith	1994	1174
14 2/16	8 5/16	5 13/16	M	Duchesne County	UT	Steve Statler	1995	1174
14 2/16	8 5/16	5 13/16	M	Grand County	CO	Daniel Thomas Cresci	1995	1174
14 2/16	8 7/16	5 11/16	M	Moffat County	CO	John T. Johnson	1996	1174
14 2/16	8 6/16	5 12/16	M	Clearwater County	ID	Rod Simmer	1996	1174
14 2/16	8 5/16	5 13/16	M	Mora County	NM	Wes McAdams	1997	1174
14 2/16	8 4/16	5 14/16	M	Catron County	NM	William E. Webb	1997	1174
14 2/16	8 4/16	5 14/16	M	Fremont County	CO	Fred Eichler	1997	1174
14 2/16	8 2/16	6 0/16	M	Lincoln County	MT	Theodore J. Burbules	1997	1174
14 2/16	8 4/16	5 14/16	M	Idaho County	ID	Glenn Burney	1997	1174
14 2/16	8 4/16	5 14/16	M	Carbon County	MT	Mike O'Connor	1998	1174
14 2/16	8 4/16	5 14/16	M	Judith Basin County	MT	Bob S. Barber	1998	1174
14 2/16	8 6/16	5 12/16	M	Bonner County	ID	Mark Sterk	2000	1174
14 2/16	8 7/16	5 11/16	M	Las Animas County	CO	Fred Eichler	2000	1174
14 2/16	8 4/16	5 14/16	M	Graham County	AZ	Wayne Minde	2001	1174
14 2/16	8 7/16	5 11/16	M	Jeff Davis County	TX	Ronnie Whitt	2001	1174
14 2/16	8 4/16	5 14/16	M	Frazier River	BC	Camp Newton	2001	1174
14 2/16	8 4/16	5 14/16	M	Granby River	BC	Tom Anzalone	2002	1174
14 2/16	8 5/16	5 13/16	M	Frazier River	BC	John D. "Jack" Frost	2003	1174

COUGAR (MOUNTAIN LION)

Minimum Score 13 8/16   Continued

SCORE	GREATEST LENGTH	GREATEST WIDTH	SEX	AREA	STATE/ PROVINCE	HUNTER'S NAME	DATE	RANK
14 2/16	8 6/16	5 12/16	M	Shoshone County	ID	Joe Hassinger	2003	1174
14 2/16	8 4/16	5 14/16	M	Broadwater County	MT	Anthony D. Mazzarella	2003	1174
14 2/16	8 8/16	5 10/16	M	Cross River	BC	Gerard Devine	2005	1174
14 2/16	8 4/16	5 14/16	M	Idaho County	ID	Jeffrey D. Husted	2005	1174
*14 2/16	8 5/16	5 13/16	M	Grand County	CO	Wayne Thurston	2006	1174
14 2/16	8 3/16	5 15/16	M	Gila County	AZ	Todd Chapman	2007	1174
*14 2/16	8 9/16	5 9/16	M	Beaverhead County	MT	Chad Anderson	2007	1174
14 2/16	8 7/16	5 11/16	M	East Kootenay	BC	Andy MacIntyre	2008	1174
*14 2/16	8 6/16	5 12/16	M	Lewis & Clark County	MT	Eric Steingraber	2008	1174
14 2/16	8 6/16	5 12/16	M	Grand County	CO	Karen Johnson	2009	1174
*14 2/16	7 13/16	6 5/16	M	Box Elder County	UT	Justin Smith	2009	1174
14 1/16	8 14/16	5 3/16	M	Garfield County	CO	Jack Peters	1964	1247
14 1/16	8 7/16	5 10/16	M	Rio Blanco County	CO	Charles Kohler	1969	1247
14 1/16	8 7/16	5 10/16	M	Chaffee County	CO	Frank B. Parrish	1969	1247
14 1/16	8 6/16	5 11/16	M	Elmore County	ID	Jerry E. Burt	1971	1247
14 1/16	8 3/16	5 14/16	M	Mesa County	CO	Cary E. Weldon	1972	1247
14 1/16	8 5/16	5 12/16	M	Carbon County	UT	David K. Elliot	1973	1247
14 1/16	8 5/16	5 12/16	M	Butte County	ID	Ken Anselmi	1975	1247
14 1/16	8 5/16	5 12/16	M	Rio Blanco County	CO	Chris Christian	1976	1247
14 1/16	8 5/16	5 12/16	M	Wayne County	UT	C. Duane Kerr	1979	1247
14 1/16	8 5/16	5 12/16	M	Cache County	UT	Val D. Larsen	1980	1247
14 1/16	8 5/16	5 12/16	M	Coconino County	AZ	Fred McDonald	1980	1247
14 1/16	8 5/16	5 12/16	M	Elko County	NV	Don Tripp	1980	1247
14 1/16	8 5/16	5 12/16	M	Lemhi County	ID	Jim Jungk	1981	1247
14 1/16	8 4/16	5 13/16	M	Adams County	ID	Dennis Atwater	1982	1247
14 1/16	8 9/16	5 8/16	M	Coconino County	AZ	Dale Tasa	1982	1247
14 1/16	8 5/16	5 12/16	M	Douglas County	CO	Gary James Morrow	1982	1247
14 1/16	8 4/16	5 13/16	M	Madison County	MT	Dick Curtis	1983	1247
14 1/16	8 6/16	5 11/16	M	Madison County	MT	John E. Larsen	1984	1247
14 1/16	8 5/16	5 12/16	M	Tooele County	UT	Dennis L. Shirley	1984	1247
14 1/16	8 6/16	5 11/16	M	Flathead County	MT	Dean F. Bergman	1984	1247
14 1/16	8 5/16	5 12/16	M	Lander County	NV	Louis Probo	1984	1247
14 1/16	8 4/16	5 13/16	M	Gilpin County	CO	Kurt W. Keskimaki	1985	1247
14 1/16	8 4/16	5 13/16	M	Idaho County	ID	William J. Bowen	1986	1247
14 1/16	8 5/16	5 12/16	M	Lincoln County	MT	Ben Rossetto	1986	1247
14 1/16	8 8/16	5 9/16	M	Millard County	UT	Dave Scott	1987	1247
14 1/16	8 5/16	5 12/16	M	Lemhi County	ID	Bobby A. Berg	1987	1247
14 1/16	8 2/16	5 15/16	M	White Pine County	NV	Perry W. Greene, Jr.	1987	1247
14 1/16	8 5/16	5 12/16	M	Conejos County	CO	Mike Boland	1987	1247
14 1/16	8 5/16	5 12/16	M	Elmore County	ID	Mark Zastrow	1988	1247
14 1/16	8 5/16	5 12/16	M	Coconino County	AZ	Don Flagel	1988	1247
14 1/16	8 6/16	5 11/16	M	Montrose County	CO	Joe Garvey	1988	1247
14 1/16	8 5/16	5 12/16	M	Alamosa County	CO	Dan Call	1989	1247
14 1/16	8 6/16	5 11/16	M	Sevier County	UT	William G. Cummard II	1989	1247
14 1/16	8 5/16	5 12/16	M	Meagher County	MT	Michael A. Blase, Jr.	1990	1247
14 1/16	8 4/16	5 13/16	M	Custer County	ID	David Hotten	1991	1247
14 1/16	8 5/16	5 12/16	M	Eureka County	NV	Gilbert Hernandez	1991	1247
14 1/16	8 4/16	5 13/16	M	Garfield County	CO	Roger Wintle	1992	1247
14 1/16	8 4/16	5 13/16	M	Pueblo County	CO	Tim Rose	1992	1247
14 1/16	8 6/16	5 11/16	M	Park County	CO	Jack P. Van Vianen	1992	1247
14 1/16	8 6/16	5 11/16	M	Boise County	ID	Nelson Beane	1992	1247
14 1/16	8 5/16	5 12/16	M	Lemhi County	ID	Charles R. Setter	1992	1247
14 1/16	8 6/16	5 11/16	M	Custer County	ID	Charles G. Schibler	1993	1247
14 1/16	8 7/16	5 10/16	M	Porcupine Hills	ALB	David R. Coupland	1993	1247
14 1/16	8 6/16	5 11/16	M	Park County	MT	William R. Brown	1994	1247
14 1/16	8 5/16	5 12/16	M	Boise County	ID	Mike Carfello	1994	1247
14 1/16	8 7/16	5 10/16	M	Colfax County	NM	Jack Dell	1994	1247
14 1/16	8 4/16	5 13/16	M	Little Jumpingpound Creek	ALB	Michael F. Rijavec	1995	1247
14 1/16	8 3/16	5 14/16	M	Mesa County	CO	David F. Tess	1995	1247
14 1/16	8 7/16	5 10/16	M	Gila County	AZ	Thomas J. Hoffman	1995	1247
14 1/16	8 6/16	5 11/16	M	Boise County	ID	Mark Reimels	1995	1247
14 1/16	8 5/16	5 12/16	M	Boundary County	ID	John Thomas	1995	1247
14 1/16	8 5/16	5 12/16	M	Lemhi County	ID	L. Scot Jenkins	1995	1247
14 1/16	8 2/16	5 15/16	M	Madison County	MT	D. Mitch Kottas	1995	1247
14 1/16	8 8/16	5 9/16	M	White Pine County	NV	Marcos D. Alfaro	1996	1247
14 1/16	8 7/16	5 10/16	M	Rio Arriba County	NM	Joe Silva, Sr.	1997	1247
14 1/16	8 7/16	5 10/16	M	Sevier County	UT	Baird R. Booth	1997	1247
14 1/16	8 5/16	5 12/16	M	Garfield County	CO	Rob Crawford	1997	1247
14 1/16	8 5/16	5 12/16	M	Sanders County	MT	Ron Ruberstell	1997	1247
14 1/16	8 3/16	5 14/16	M	Madison County	MT	Carl Hanson	1997	1247
14 1/16	8 2/16	5 15/16	M	Sweet Grass County	MT	Bill Bryce	1998	1247
14 1/16	8 5/16	5 12/16	M	Elko County	NV	Dick Alverson	1998	1247
14 1/16	8 6/16	5 11/16	M	Porcupine Hills	ALB	Michael Heuving	1999	1247
14 1/16	8 5/16	5 12/16	M	Eagle County	CO	Ron Hagen	1999	1247
14 1/16	8 4/16	5 13/16	M	Missoula County	MT	Tim Dreier	1999	1247
14 1/16	8 7/16	5 10/16	M	Box Elder County	UT	Scott Barrus	2000	1247
14 1/16	8 4/16	5 13/16	M	Moffat County	CO	Tim M. Webster	2000	1247
14 1/16	8 7/16	5 10/16	M	Lemhi County	ID	Dean J. Hamontree	2001	1247
14 1/16	8 5/16	5 12/16	M	Grand Forks	BC	Steven L. Tebay	2001	1247
14 1/16	8 7/16	5 10/16	M	Dolores County	CO	Judy Grooms	2002	1247
14 1/16	8 5/16	5 12/16	M	Lemhi County	ID	Benjamin Fahnholz	2002	1247
14 1/16	8 4/16	5 13/16	M	Fremont County	CO	Mike Mattera	2002	1247
14 1/16	8 4/16	5 13/16	M	Madison County	MT	Michael F. Terry	2003	1247
14 1/16	8 3/16	5 14/16	M	Madison County	MT	Michael Beutel	2003	1247
14 1/16	8 5/16	5 12/16	M	Las Animas County	CO	Daniel D. Stonebarger	2003	1247
14 1/16	8 9/16	5 8/16	M	Delta County	CO	Steve McCoy	2004	1247
14 1/16	8 5/16	5 12/16	M	Drayton Valley	ALB	Clint Howard	2004	1247
14 1/16	8 4/16	5 13/16	M	Coconino County	AZ	Russ Richardson	2006	1247
14 1/16	8 5/16	5 12/16	M	Fremont County	CO	Rick Hayley	2006	1247
14 1/16	8 2/16	5 15/16	M	Clear Creek County	CO	Scott A. Gillespie	2006	1247
14 1/16	8 5/16	5 12/16	M	Judith Basin County	MT	John "Rosey" Roseland	2007	1247
14 1/16	8 6/16	5 11/16	M	Carbon County	WY	Dr. Michael Novak	2007	1247
14 1/16	8 7/16	5 10/16	M	Grand County	CO	Judy M. Thurston	2007	1247
14 1/16	8 3/16	5 14/16	M	Jefferson County	MT	Timothy E. Conway	2008	1247
14 1/16	8 3/16	5 14/16	M	Lemhi County	ID	Jason Kristbaum	2010	1247

267

COUGAR (MOUNTAIN LION)

Minimum Score 13 8/16   Continued

SCORE	GREATEST LENGTH	GREATEST WIDTH	SEX	AREA	STATE/ PROVINCE	HUNTER'S NAME	DATE	RANK
14 1/16	8 5/16	5 12/16	M	Garfield County	CO	Forest Keith	2010	1247
14 0/16	8 4/16	5 12/16	M	Uintah County	UT	Dr. Quentin F. Mangion	1962	1332
14 0/16	8 4/16	5 12/16	M	Gila County	AZ	Hugh Pearson	1963	1332
14 0/16	8 4/16	5 12/16	M	Flathead County	MT	Dorn L. Brinker	1969	1332
14 0/16	8 3/16	5 13/16	M	Valley County	ID	Ronald N. Kolpin	1972	1332
14 0/16	8 1/16	5 15/16	M	Yavapai County	AZ	Louis A. Vohs	1973	1332
14 0/16	8 5/16	5 11/16	M	Lemhi County	ID	T. A. Low IV	1977	1332
14 0/16	8 2/16	5 14/16	M	Duchesne County	UT	James Sot	1977	1332
14 0/16	8 4/16	5 12/16	M	Blacktail Mtn.	UT	Jerry Dittrich	1978	1332
14 0/16	8 4/16	5 12/16	M	San Juan County	UT	Gary Paluszcyk	1979	1332
14 0/16	8 5/16	5 11/16	M	Fremont County	CO	Gary Fisher	1979	1332
14 0/16	8 4/16	5 12/16	M	Boise County	ID	Paul Anderson	1980	1332
14 0/16	8 3/16	5 13/16	M	Coconino County	AZ	Larry Almaraz	1981	1332
14 0/16	8 3/16	5 13/16	M	San Miguel County	CO	Robert Finelli	1981	1332
14 0/16	8 5/16	5 11/16	M	Madison County	MT	Leland S. Speakes, Jr.	1984	1332
14 0/16	8 4/16	5 12/16	M	Wasatch County	UT	Vicki Mamales	1985	1332
14 0/16	8 2/16	5 14/16	M	Madison County	MT	Pat Sinclair	1985	1332
14 0/16	8 8/16	5 8/16	M	Rio Grande County	CO	Tom Tietz	1985	1332
14 0/16	8 2/16	5 14/16	M	Madison County	MT	Carl Spaeth	1986	1332
14 0/16	8 3/16	5 13/16	M	Coconino County	AZ	George Richardson	1987	1332
14 0/16	8 2/16	5 14/16	M	San Juan County	NM	Keith Hardy	1987	1332
14 0/16	8 6/16	5 10/16	M	Judith Basin County	MT	Noel J. Poux	1988	1332
14 0/16	8 4/16	5 12/16	M	San Miguel County	CO	Jack Downing	1988	1332
14 0/16	8 4/16	5 12/16	M	Idaho County	ID	David A. Shupp	1989	1332
14 0/16	8 7/16	5 9/16	M	Millard County	UT	Norman Bradley	1990	1332
14 0/16	8 4/16	5 12/16	M	Tooele County	UT	Merrill Clarke	1990	1332
14 0/16	8 6/16	5 10/16	M	Elmore County	ID	Julian Salutrequi	1990	1332
14 0/16	8 7/16	5 9/16	M	Iron County	UT	Ken Wilson	1990	1332
14 0/16	8 4/16	5 12/16	M	Lemhi County	ID	Larry Dockery	1990	1332
14 0/16	8 6/16	5 10/16	M	Union County	OR	Jeff Carver	1990	1332
14 0/16	8 5/16	5 11/16	M	Coconino County	AZ	Kenneth Meadors	1991	1332
14 0/16	8 3/16	5 13/16	M	Stoney Lake	BC	Gregory White	1991	1332
14 0/16	8 5/16	5 11/16	M	Carbon County	UT	Ty Jensen	1992	1332
14 0/16	8 2/16	5 14/16	M	Granite County	MT	Richard E. LaCrone	1992	1332
14 0/16	8 6/16	5 10/16	M	Routt County	CO	Gary F. Bogner	1992	1332
14 0/16	8 3/16	5 13/16	M	Lewis & Clark County	MT	Jay Roberson	1992	1332
14 0/16	8 6/16	5 10/16	M	Archuleta County	CO	Tony R. Stephens	1993	1332
14 0/16	8 4/16	5 12/16	M	Carbon County	WY	Craig Boheler	1993	1332
14 0/16	8 5/16	5 11/16	M	Routt County	CO	Glen Merica	1993	1332
14 0/16	8 4/16	5 12/16	M	Custer County	ID	Dan Strohecker	1993	1332
14 0/16	8 6/16	5 10/16	M	Wager Coulee	ALB	Archie Nesbitt	1993	1332
14 0/16	8 8/16	5 8/16	M	Montezuma County	CO	Brian T. Myers	1993	1332
14 0/16	8 4/16	5 12/16	M	Garfield County	CO	Michael Pratt	1994	1332
14 0/16	8 4/16	5 12/16	M	Valley County	ID	Kenneth Hyde	1994	1332
14 0/16	8 5/16	5 11/16	M	Jefferson County	CO	Jason Adamson	1994	1332
14 0/16	8 7/16	5 9/16	M	Chaffee County	CO	Ray Woods	1994	1332
14 0/16	8 6/16	5 10/16	M	Longview	ALB	Lauren Hoover	1996	1332
14 0/16	8 3/16	5 13/16	M	Powell County	MT	Michael A. Dunwell	1996	1332
14 0/16	8 4/16	5 12/16	M	Fremont County	CO	Rick Wilson	1997	1332
14 0/16	8 4/16	5 12/16	M	Moffat County	CO	Joe George	1997	1332
14 0/16	8 2/16	5 14/16	M	Maricopa County	AZ	Ronald R. Lacy	1997	1332
14 0/16	8 4/16	5 12/16	M	Mesa County	CO	Kerry N. Koning	1997	1332
14 0/16	8 3/16	5 13/16	M	Grand County	CO	Bob Bodemann	1998	1332
14 0/16	8 6/16	5 10/16	F	Salt Lake County	UT	Richard Carter	1998	1332
14 0/16	8 5/16	5 11/16	M	Humboldt County	NV	Mark Connor	1998	1332
14 0/16	8 7/16	5 9/16	M	Lemhi County	ID	Duane Seiler II	1999	1332
14 0/16	8 5/16	5 11/16	M	Washington County	UT	Rodney Sassaman	1999	1332
14 0/16	8 6/16	5 10/16	M	Clear Creek County	CO	Ron Rockwell	1999	1332
14 0/16	8 5/16	5 11/16	M	Clark County	ID	Jason J. McConeghy	2000	1332
14 0/16	8 4/16	5 12/16	M	Flathead County	MT	Danny Moore	2000	1332
14 0/16	8 7/16	5 9/16	M	Beaver County	UT	David N. Wildenstein	2001	1332
14 0/16	8 3/16	5 13/16	M	Johnson County	WY	David S. Harness	2001	1332
14 0/16	8 4/16	5 12/16	M	Tee Pee	BC	Lawrence St. John	2001	1332
*14 0/16	8 3/16	5 13/16	M	Granite County	MT	Steve Hough	2001	1332
14 0/16	8 4/16	5 12/16	M	Salmo River	BC	Chris Partridge	2001	1332
14 0/16	8 5/16	5 11/16	M	Elko County	NV	Bob Ehle	2002	1332
14 0/16	8 3/16	5 13/16	M	Flathead County	MT	Joseph F. Petti	2002	1332
14 0/16	8 3/16	5 13/16	M	Lake County	CO	Kevin Brothers	2004	1332
14 0/16	8 6/16	5 10/16	M	Montezuma County	CO	Steve Franchini	2005	1332
14 0/16	8 4/16	5 12/16	M	Pueblo County	CO	Enzo Gerardi	2007	1332
14 0/16	8 4/16	5 12/16	M	Lillooet	BC	John F. Cedarberg IV	2007	1332
14 0/16	8 4/16	5 12/16	M	Cochrane	ALB	Dan J. Ryle, Jr.	2007	1332
14 0/16	8 6/16	5 10/16	M	San Juan County	UT	Mark T. Cosiano	2007	1332
14 0/16	8 7/16	5 9/16	M	Kane County	UT	Shawn Friedbacher	2007	1332
*14 0/16	8 4/16	5 12/16	M	Longview	ALB	Gary Gillett	2008	1332
*14 0/16	8 3/16	5 13/16	M	Lunbrick	ALB	Darran Hollihan	2009	1332
14 0/16	8 6/16	5 10/16	M	Uintah County	UT	Joel Biltz	2010	1332
13 15/16	8 3/16	5 12/16	M	Gila County	AZ	Hugh Pearson	1963	1408
13 15/16	8 5/16	5 10/16	M	Rio Blanco County	CO	Joel Hogan	1967	1408
13 15/16	8 6/16	5 9/16	M	Okanogan County	WA	Stuart Irwin	1971	1408
13 15/16	8 5/16	5 10/16	M	Lemhi County	ID	John Mascellino	1972	1408
13 15/16	8 3/16	5 12/16	M	San Miguel County	CO	Ken Grandow	1979	1408
13 15/16	8 6/16	5 9/16	M	Elmore County	ID	Richard C. Nichols	1980	1408
13 15/16	8 3/16	5 12/16	M	Judith Basin County	MT	Ed Evans	1981	1408
13 15/16	8 5/16	5 10/16	M	Las Animas County	CO	David S. Bunce	1982	1408
13 15/16	8 5/16	5 10/16	M	Piute County	UT	Lynn Kuhlmann	1984	1408
13 15/16	8 3/16	5 12/16	M	Boise County	ID	William Atkinson, Jr.	1985	1408
13 15/16	8 4/16	5 11/16	M	Lemhi County	ID	James S. Disalvo	1985	1408
13 15/16	8 2/16	5 13/16	M	Elko County	NV	Donald Pyne	1987	1408
13 15/16	8 3/16	5 12/16	M	Elmore County	ID	Carolyn Godfrey	1987	1408
13 15/16	8 5/16	5 10/16	M	Sevier County	UT	Philippe Lantagne	1988	1408
13 15/16	8 6/16	5 9/16	M	Washington County	UT	Gerald Laurino	1988	1408
13 15/16	8 2/16	5 13/16	M	Carbon County	UT	Gail B. Raby	1989	1408
13 15/16	8 4/16	5 11/16	M	Nye County	NV	Charles Pat Walker, Jr.	1990	1408
13 15/16	8 4/16	5 11/16	M	Carbon County	UT	Roger Cyfers	1990	1408

268

COUGAR (MOUNTAIN LION)

Minimum Score 13 8/16   Continued

SCORE	GREATEST LENGTH	GREATEST WIDTH	SEX	AREA	STATE/ PROVINCE	HUNTER'S NAME	DATE	RANK
13 15/16	8 5/16	5 10/16	M	Chaffee County	CO	Scott Pelino	1990	1408
13 15/16	8 5/16	5 10/16	M	Beaverhead County	MT	Lynn Lamphiear	1991	1408
13 15/16	8 4/16	5 11/16	M	Lincoln County	MT	Dennis L. Kari	1991	1408
13 15/16	8 2/16	5 13/16	M	Flathead County	MT	David D. Johnston	1992	1408
13 15/16	8 4/16	5 11/16	M	Washington County	UT	Henry C. Williams, Jr.	1993	1408
13 15/16	8 6/16	5 9/16	M	Coconino County	AZ	Robert Y. Childers	1993	1408
13 15/16	8 5/16	5 10/16	M	Routt County	CO	Mike E. Neilson	1993	1408
13 15/16	8 6/16	5 9/16	M	San Miguel County	CO	Pat Snyder	1994	1408
13 15/16	8 0/16	5 15/16	M	Catron County	NM	Gary L. Robertson	1994	1408
13 15/16	8 6/16	5 9/16	M	Rio Arriba County	NM	Vince Podnar	1994	1408
13 15/16	8 5/16	5 10/16	M	Porcupine Hills	ALB	Pete Dohrs	1994	1408
13 15/16	8 3/16	5 12/16	M	Lemhi County	ID	Jay Parke	1994	1408
13 15/16	8 4/16	5 11/16	M	Shoshone County	ID	David J. Crownhart	1994	1408
13 15/16	8 2/16	5 13/16	M	Boise County	ID	Gene Hopkins	1995	1408
13 15/16	8 7/16	5 8/16	M	150 Mile House	BC	Daniel Kelly	1997	1408
13 15/16	8 3/16	5 12/16	M	Sanders County	MT	Kenneth Scott Gifford	1997	1408
13 15/16	8 4/16	5 11/16	M	Rio Blanco County	CO	James E. Corby	1998	1408
13 15/16	8 2/16	5 13/16	M	Coconino County	AZ	Phillip C. Dalrymple	1998	1408
13 15/16	8 4/16	5 11/16	M	Yavapai County	AZ	Josh Epperson	1998	1408
13 15/16	8 3/16	5 12/16	M	Wasatch County	UT	Melanie Knight	1998	1408
13 15/16	8 2/16	5 13/16	M	Iron County	UT	Brent Hoeverman	1999	1408
13 15/16	8 3/16	5 12/16	M	Garfield County	CO	Ivan Block	1999	1408
13 15/16	8 4/16	5 11/16	M	Valley County	ID	Kelly King	1999	1408
13 15/16	8 3/16	5 12/16	M	Nakusp	BC	Dave Croft	2000	1408
13 15/16	8 5/16	5 10/16	M	Elko County	NV	Brandt Halling	2000	1408
13 15/16	8 4/16	5 11/16	M	Mohave County	AZ	George Hunter Sensabough	2001	1408
13 15/16	8 5/16	5 10/16	M	Idaho County	ID	William H. Welton	2001	1408
13 15/16	8 4/16	5 11/16	M	San Juan County	UT	A. Jay Porter	2002	1408
13 15/16	8 4/16	5 11/16	M	Garfield County	UT	James Lopez	2002	1408
13 15/16	8 3/16	5 12/16	M	Garfield County	CO	Jerome P. McCauley, Sr.	2003	1408
13 15/16	8 3/16	5 12/16	M	Larimer County	CO	Brad Ham	2004	1408
*13 15/16	8 2/16	5 13/16	M	Las Animas County	CO	Thomas Ruggles	2005	1408
13 15/16	8 5/16	5 10/16	M	Washington County	UT	Douglas E. Callies	2006	1408
*13 15/16	8 2/16	5 13/16	M	Madison County	MT	Bill McGrath	2007	1408
13 15/16	8 3/16	5 12/16	M	San Miguel County	CO	Mike Hamberg	2008	1408
13 15/16	8 0/16	5 15/16	M	Garfield County	CO	Dollie Prather	2009	1408
13 14/16	8 4/16	5 10/16	M	Flathead County	MT	Jerry Almos	1970	1462
13 14/16	8 6/16	5 8/16	F	Coconino County	AZ	Midge Dandridge	1972	1462
13 14/16	8 1/16	5 13/16	M	Mesa County	CO	Stan Bocian	1974	1462
13 14/16	8 5/16	5 9/16	M	Chaffee County	CO	Ben Cuadra	1975	1462
13 14/16	8 2/16	5 12/16	M	Boise County	ID	Robert L. Bevan	1976	1462
13 14/16	8 6/16	5 8/16	M	Lemhi County	ID	James C. Costopoulos	1976	1462
13 14/16	8 1/16	5 13/16	M	Garfield County	CO	Lou Kindred	1977	1462
13 14/16	8 4/16	5 10/16	M	Lemhi County	ID	Dan E. Hershberger	1979	1462
13 14/16	8 4/16	5 10/16	M	Rio Blanco County	CO	Wayne Watson, Sr.	1979	1462
13 14/16	8 3/16	5 11/16	M	Uintah County	UT	Dan Darrell Boy	1980	1462
13 14/16	8 9/16	5 5/16	M	Washington County	UT	Scott Petersen	1982	1462
13 14/16	8 3/16	5 11/16	M	Grand County	UT	Henry 'Hank' Frey	1982	1462
13 14/16	8 3/16	5 11/16	M	Archuleta County	CO	Ronald Murphy	1983	1462
13 14/16	8 1/16	5 13/16	M	Lemhi County	ID	Wendell L. Seelig	1983	1462
13 14/16	8 2/16	5 12/16	M	Sevier County	UT	John Alden Brown, Jr.	1984	1462
13 14/16	8 3/16	5 11/16	M	Sanpete County	UT	Bob Fitzgerald	1984	1462
13 14/16	8 5/16	5 9/16	M	Chaffee County	CO	Raymond Roussett, Jr.	1985	1462
13 14/16	8 5/16	5 9/16	M	Elmore County	ID	John Koldeway	1985	1462
13 14/16	8 2/16	5 12/16	M	Gilpin County	CO	Lyle Willmarth	1986	1462
13 14/16	8 6/16	5 8/16	M	San Miguel County	CO	Ronald J. Collier	1986	1462
13 14/16	8 2/16	5 12/16	M	Sheridan County	WY	Mike Pilch	1987	1462
13 14/16	8 4/16	5 10/16	M	Coconino County	AZ	Cindi Richardson	1987	1462
13 14/16	8 5/16	5 9/16	M	Lincoln County	MT	Kenneth Mamatz	1988	1462
13 14/16	7 15/16	5 15/16	M	Sheridan County	WY	Harold Carnell	1988	1462
13 14/16	8 4/16	5 10/16	M	White Pine County	NV	Randy Bennett	1989	1462
13 14/16	8 4/16	5 10/16	M	Idaho County	ID	Kenny Holliday	1990	1462
13 14/16	8 3/16	5 11/16	M	Elmore County	ID	Stan Godfrey	1991	1462
13 14/16	8 2/16	5 12/16	M	Grand County	UT	Dale Bigger	1991	1462
13 14/16	8 3/16	5 11/16	F	Clearwater County	ID	Russ A. Van Rite	1991	1462
13 14/16	8 3/16	5 11/16	M	Madison County	MT	Randall Brown	1991	1462
13 14/16	8 5/16	5 9/16	M	Elmore County	ID	Richard A. Schreiber	1991	1462
13 14/16	8 4/16	5 10/16	M	Tooele County	UT	Anthony E. Martinez II	1992	1462
13 14/16	8 3/16	5 11/16	M	Catron County	NM	G. David Moser	1992	1462
13 14/16	8 7/16	5 7/16	M	Washington County	UT	Edward X. Thompson	1992	1462
13 14/16	8 2/16	5 12/16	M	Judith Basin County	MT	John "Rosey" Roseland	1993	1462
13 14/16	8 4/16	5 10/16	M	Sevier County	UT	Randy P. Forsythe	1994	1462
13 14/16	8 3/16	5 11/16	M	Lemhi County	ID	Stewart P. Fitzgerald	1995	1462
13 14/16	8 2/16	5 12/16	M	White Pine County	NV	W. Scott Perry	1996	1462
13 14/16	8 3/16	5 11/16	M	Montrose County	CO	Richard Weaver	1997	1462
13 14/16	8 2/16	5 12/16	M	Broadwater County	MT	Guy Jette	1997	1462
13 14/16	8 2/16	5 12/16	M	Madison County	MT	Ken Southworth	1998	1462
13 14/16	8 4/16	5 10/16	M	Larimer County	CO	K. C. Heinrich	1998	1462
13 14/16	8 2/16	5 12/16	M	Summit County	CO	Bob Reedy	1998	1462
13 14/16	8 5/16	5 9/16	M	Cochise County	AZ	Scott G. Hettinger	1998	1462
13 14/16	8 3/16	5 11/16	M	Ravalli County	MT	Wendy Decker	1999	1462
13 14/16	8 2/16	5 12/16	M	Sanders County	MT	Bret Van Vranken	1999	1462
13 14/16	8 2/16	5 12/16	M	Morgan County	UT	Rick Phillippie	2000	1462
13 14/16	8 2/16	5 12/16	M	Ravalli County	MT	James E. Beasley	2000	1462
13 14/16	8 5/16	5 9/16	M	Mora County	NM	Mike Powers	2003	1462
13 14/16	8 5/16	5 9/16	M	Las Animas County	CO	David B. Cull	2004	1462
13 14/16	8 5/16	5 9/16	M	Wasatch County	UT	Bob Ameen	2005	1462
13 14/16	8 2/16	5 12/16	M	Lemhi County	ID	Robert W. Miller	2006	1462
13 14/16	8 4/16	5 10/16	M	Sweetwater County	WY	Tommy Harrington	2006	1462
13 14/16	8 4/16	5 10/16	M	Grant County	OR	Devon M. Brown	2007	1462
13 14/16	8 1/16	5 13/16	M	Mesa County	CO	Alfred C. Faber	2007	1462
13 14/16	8 4/16	5 10/16	M	Elko County	NV	Shaundi L. Neal	2007	1462
13 14/16	8 0/16	5 14/16	M	Cache County	UT	Steve Smith	2008	1462
13 14/16	8 2/16	5 12/16	M	Sweet Grass County	MT	C. Scott Forst	2009	1462
13 14/16	8 3/16	5 11/16	M	Sevier County	UT	Kelly Bingham	2009	1462

COUGAR (MOUNTAIN LION)

Minimum Score 13 8/16 — Continued

SCORE	GREATEST LENGTH	GREATEST WIDTH	SEX	AREA	STATE/ PROVINCE	HUNTER'S NAME	DATE	RANK
13 14/16	8 4/16	5 10/16	M	Tooele County	UT	Bryan Durfee	2009	1462
13 14/16	8 5/16	5 9/16	M	Powder River County	MT	Shawn Wahl	2010	1462
13 13/16	8 2/16	5 11/16	M	Esmeralda County	NV	George Hooker	1961	1523
13 13/16	7 15/16	5 14/16	M	Lemhi County	ID	Vern Herman	1969	1523
13 13/16	8 2/16	5 11/16	M	EL Paso County	CO	L. Clark Kiser	1984	1523
13 13/16	8 4/16	5 9/16	M	Mesa County	CO	Edgar Bobo	1984	1523
13 13/16	8 1/16	5 12/16	M	Sandoval County	NM	David Taylor	1985	1523
13 13/16	8 1/16	5 12/16	M	San Juan County	UT	David Snyder	1985	1523
13 13/16	8 3/16	5 10/16	M	Johnson County	WY	Terry Krahn	1986	1523
13 13/16	8 3/16	5 10/16	M	Cochise County	AZ	Randy Hall	1987	1523
13 13/16	8 5/16	5 8/16	M	Boulder County	CO	Jerry Souders	1987	1523
13 13/16	8 0/16	5 13/16	M	Greenlee County	AZ	Eugene Fritsky	1989	1523
13 13/16	8 2/16	5 11/16	M	San Juan County	UT	Ronald D. Kirk	1990	1523
13 13/16	8 5/16	5 8/16	M	Garfield County	CO	Neil Smith	1990	1523
13 13/16	8 3/16	5 10/16	M	Chaffee County	CO	David Spacek	1990	1523
13 13/16	8 5/16	5 8/16	M	San Miguel County	CO	Evans V. Brewster	1991	1523
13 13/16	8 4/16	5 9/16	M	Coconino County	AZ	Stephen A. Kotz	1991	1523
13 13/16	8 1/16	5 12/16	M	San Juan County	UT	Daniel Willems	1992	1523
13 13/16	8 6/16	5 7/16	M	Chaffee County	CO	A. M. Salazar	1992	1523
13 13/16	8 2/16	5 11/16	M	Granite County	MT	Richard E. LaCrone	1994	1523
13 13/16	8 4/16	5 9/16	M	Archuleta County	CO	Grant Adkisson	1994	1523
13 13/16	8 5/16	5 8/16	M	White Pine County	NV	Mark Shrewsbury	1994	1523
13 13/16	8 8/16	5 5/16	M	Ferry County	WA	Michael R. Land	1994	1523
13 13/16	8 4/16	5 9/16	M	Chaffee County	CO	Paul Bohochik	1994	1523
13 13/16	8 3/16	5 10/16	M	Box Elder County	UT	H. Douglas Herold	1994	1523
13 13/16	8 3/16	5 10/16	M	San Juan County	UT	Michael C. Parkinson	1995	1523
13 13/16	8 1/16	5 12/16	M	Montezuma County	CO	Dennis L. Howell	1996	1523
13 13/16	8 1/16	5 12/16	M	Park County	CO	John Colby	1996	1523
13 13/16	8 3/16	5 10/16	M	Elmore County	ID	Dawn Traub	1996	1523
13 13/16	8 3/16	5 10/16	M	Broadwater County	MT	Marc Brittain	1996	1523
13 13/16	8 5/16	5 8/16	M	Boundary County	ID	Rich Wynn	1996	1523
13 13/16	8 1/16	5 12/16	M	Coconino County	AZ	Lon Hadfield	1997	1523
13 13/16	8 2/16	5 11/16	M	Montezuma County	CO	Dean Brown	1997	1523
13 13/16	8 4/16	5 9/16	M	Carbon County	UT	Bruce J. Rogers	1999	1523
13 13/16	8 5/16	5 8/16	M	Johnson County	WY	James Gabrick	2000	1523
13 13/16	8 2/16	5 11/16	M	Madison County	MT	Gary Dudden	2000	1523
13 13/16	8 0/16	5 13/16	M	Montrose County	CO	Rick Schrecengost	2001	1523
13 13/16	8 1/16	5 12/16	M	Blaine County	ID	John DeLorenzo	2001	1523
13 13/16	8 3/16	5 10/16	M	Sanders County	MT	Wes Brogan	2001	1523
13 13/16	8 4/16	5 9/16	M	Eagle County	CO	Frank S. Noska IV	2002	1523
13 13/16	8 2/16	5 11/16	M	Sibbald Flats	ALB	Gary Gillett	2002	1523
13 13/16	8 3/16	5 10/16	M	Bonneville County	ID	Wade R. Hall	2003	1523
13 13/16	8 4/16	5 9/16	M	Juab County	UT	Tom Straka	2004	1523
13 13/16	8 5/16	5 8/16	M	Valley County	ID	Kenneth Musgrove	2005	1523
13 13/16	8 3/16	5 10/16	M	Boundary County	ID	Stacee Frost	2005	1523
13 13/16	8 4/16	5 9/16	M	Laramie County	WY	Jim Carlson	2006	1523
13 13/16	8 4/16	5 9/16	M	Sublette County	WY	Gil Winters	2007	1523
13 13/16	8 0/16	5 13/16	M	Yavapai County	AZ	Bryan Nolte	2007	1523
13 13/16	8 2/16	5 11/16	M	Madison County	MT	Tom Morton	2007	1523
13 13/16	8 5/16	5 8/16	M	Chilcotin Mtns.	BC	Joseph Liska	2007	1523
13 13/16	8 3/16	5 10/16	M	Carbon County	WY	Michael Casey	2010	1523
13 13/16	8 4/16	5 9/16	M	Washoe County	NV	Jack Spencer, Jr.	2010	1523
13 12/16	8 4/16	5 8/16	M	Shasta National Forest	CA	Harv Ebers	1963	1573
13 12/16	8 0/16	5 12/16	M	Ravalli County	MT	Joe Lawrence	1965	1573
13 12/16	7 11/16	6 1/16	M	Garfield County	UT	Robert E. Todd	1969	1573
13 12/16	8 2/16	5 10/16	M	Pima County	AZ	Sherwin Lipsitz	1976	1573
13 12/16	8 3/16	5 9/16	M	Lemhi County	ID	Ray Torrey	1978	1573
13 12/16	8 3/16	5 9/16	M	Custer County	ID	Larry Bonetti	1979	1573
13 12/16	8 4/16	5 8/16	M	Lemhi County	ID	Buck Farni	1979	1573
13 12/16	8 3/16	5 9/16	M	Carbon County	UT	Claude Flippin	1981	1573
13 12/16	8 4/16	5 8/16	M	Uintah County	UT	Ken Labrum	1985	1573
13 12/16	8 2/16	5 10/16	M	Grand County	UT	Robert Jacobsen	1986	1573
13 12/16	8 4/16	5 8/16	M	Clearwater County	ID	George J. McCuster	1986	1573
13 12/16	8 0/16	5 12/16	M	Gallatin County	MT	Carmine Agostinelli	1986	1573
13 12/16	8 2/16	5 10/16	M	San Miguel County	CO	Joe Wright	1987	1573
13 12/16	8 2/16	5 10/16	M	Powell County	MT	Thomas W. Moore	1987	1573
13 12/16	8 3/16	5 9/16	M	Carbon County	UT	Jim Saunoris, Jr.	1987	1573
13 12/16	8 3/16	5 9/16	M	Lemhi County	ID	Dan L. Moultrie	1988	1573
13 12/16	8 2/16	5 10/16	M	Douglas County	OR	Rick Gabbard	1988	1573
13 12/16	8 4/16	5 8/16	M	Garfield County	CO	Warren Strickland	1989	1573
13 12/16	8 3/16	5 9/16	M	Rio Blanco County	CO	Tom Brakke	1990	1573
13 12/16	8 3/16	5 9/16	M	Beaverhead County	MT	Jeff D. Wingard	1991	1573
13 12/16	8 3/16	5 9/16	M	St. Mary's River	BC	Richard Kirkvold	1991	1573
13 12/16	8 6/16	5 6/16	M	Sandoval County	NM	Thomas W. Dunn	1991	1573
13 12/16	8 3/16	5 9/16	M	Montrose County	CO	Gregory Hise	1992	1573
13 12/16	8 4/16	5 8/16	M	Summit County	UT	Tony Park	1992	1573
13 12/16	8 4/16	5 8/16	M	Washington County	UT	Norman J. Roy	1993	1573
13 12/16	8 2/16	5 10/16	M	Boundary County	ID	Dustin Myers	1993	1573
13 12/16	8 0/16	5 12/16	M	Natrona County	WY	Miles Bundy	1994	1573
13 12/16	8 1/16	5 11/16	M	Lemhi County	ID	Michael Judas	1994	1573
13 12/16	8 2/16	5 10/16	M	Wasatch County	UT	Will Stump	1995	1573
13 12/16	8 0/16	5 12/16	M	Grand County	UT	Daniel Day	1995	1573
13 12/16	8 3/16	5 9/16	M	Carbon County	UT	Michael J. DeCaro	1995	1573
13 12/16	8 6/16	5 6/16	M	Garfield County	CO	Paul R. Esch	1996	1573
13 12/16	8 5/16	5 7/16	M	Catron County	NM	Robert A. Dale	1996	1573
13 12/16	8 3/16	5 9/16	M	Elko County	NV	Aaron T. Hughes	1997	1573
13 12/16	8 2/16	5 10/16	M	Boundary County	ID	Richard M. Penn	1997	1573
13 12/16	8 1/16	5 11/16	M	Shoshone County	ID	William N. Latshaw	1997	1573
13 12/16	8 3/16	5 9/16	M	Fremont County	CO	Ben L. Nelson	1997	1573
13 12/16	8 4/16	5 8/16	M	Flathead County	MT	Shawn Price	1997	1573
13 12/16	8 2/16	5 10/16	M	Washington County	UT	Dustin Oleson	1999	1573
13 12/16	8 1/16	5 11/16	M	Catron County	NM	Raymond Francingues, Jr.	1999	1573
13 12/16	8 3/16	5 9/16	M	Sweet Grass County	MT	Kevin W. Schweder	1999	1573
13 12/16	8 2/16	5 10/16	M	Fergus County	MT	Josef K. Rud	2000	1573
13 12/16	8 0/16	5 12/16	M	Las Animas County	CO	Stephen Haufsk	2001	1573

COUGAR (MOUNTAIN LION)

Minimum Score 13 8/16   Continued

SCORE	GREATEST LENGTH	GREATEST WIDTH	SEX	AREA	STATE/ PROVINCE	HUNTER'S NAME	DATE	RANK
13 12/16	8 0/16	5 12/16	M	Duchesne County	UT	Troy Bennett	2002	1573
13 12/16	8 3/16	5 9/16	M	Lincoln County	WY	Tyson Heiner	2002	1573
*13 12/16	8 4/16	5 8/16	M	Lemhi County	ID	Cliff Ritenour	2003	1573
13 12/16	8 4/16	5 8/16	M	Coconino County	AZ	John P. Zeman	2004	1573
13 12/16	8 0/16	5 12/16	M	Coconino County	AZ	Mark L. Teegarden, Sr.	2004	1573
13 12/16	8 0/16	5 12/16	M	Clear Creek County	CO	Larry A. Welchlen	2005	1573
*13 12/16	8 1/16	5 11/16	M	Bull River	BC	Gary Joseph	2006	1573
13 12/16	8 3/16	5 9/16	M	Jackson County	CO	Craig Thrasher	2007	1573
13 12/16	8 4/16	5 8/16	M	Wasatch County	UT	Sean P. Davis	2008	1573
13 12/16	8 1/16	5 11/16	M	Lemhi County	ID	David Gebo	2008	1573
*13 12/16	8 4/16	5 8/16	M	Washington County	UT	Cheryl Paul	2008	1573
13 12/16	8 0/16	5 12/16	M	Lincoln County	WY	David R. Ellis	2008	1573
13 11/16	8 3/16	5 8/16	M	Valley County	ID	Clarence Grandt	1972	1628
13 11/16	8 3/16	5 8/16	M	Mesa County	CO	William J. Vincent	1972	1628
13 11/16	7 15/16	5 12/16	M	Grand County	UT	David Seidelman	1975	1628
13 11/16	8 6/16	5 5/16	M	San Juan County	UT	James Karlovec	1975	1628
13 11/16	8 2/16	5 9/16	M	Carbon County	UT	Bernard R. Giacoletto	1975	1628
13 11/16	8 0/16	5 11/16	M	Garfield County	CO	Darlene Frye	1976	1628
13 11/16	8 4/16	5 7/16	M	Boise County	ID	Fred Sanders	1981	1628
13 11/16	7 15/16	5 12/16	M	Missoula County	MT	Blair Hamer	1983	1628
13 11/16	8 3/16	5 8/16	M	Gilpin County	CO	John Rhine	1984	1628
13 11/16	8 3/16	5 8/16	M	Clearwater County	ID	Mike I. Powers	1984	1628
13 11/16	8 3/16	5 8/16	F	Socorro County	NM	Paul Persano	1986	1628
13 11/16	8 3/16	5 8/16	M	Pima County	AZ	Ernest R. Allen	1987	1628
13 11/16	8 4/16	5 7/16	M	Boise County	ID	Raymond A. Guay	1987	1628
13 11/16	8 1/16	5 10/16	M	Nye County	NV	Ronald W. Lindquist	1987	1628
13 11/16	8 2/16	5 9/16	M	Elmore County	ID	Nancy Atwood	1988	1628
13 11/16	8 4/16	5 7/16	M	Washington County	UT	Jules Pacheco	1989	1628
13 11/16	8 0/16	5 11/16	F	Clearwater County	ID	Colin G. Crook	1989	1628
13 11/16	8 1/16	5 10/16	M	Asotin County	WA	Mark Kolowith	1990	1628
13 11/16	8 3/16	5 8/16	M	Fremont County	CO	Travis Todd	1990	1628
13 11/16	8 3/16	5 8/16	M	Jackson County	OR	Florian Davis	1990	1628
13 11/16	8 5/16	5 6/16	M	Uintah County	UT	Robert G. Petersen	1991	1628
13 11/16	8 4/16	5 7/16	M	Saguache County	CO	Roger M. Tyler	1992	1628
13 11/16	8 3/16	5 8/16	M	Fergus County	MT	Mike Bentler	1992	1628
13 11/16	8 2/16	5 9/16	M	Park County	WY	Rene Suda	1993	1628
13 11/16	8 3/16	5 8/16	M	Garfield County	CO	William Rasch	1993	1628
13 11/16	8 5/16	5 6/16	M	Garfield County	CO	Lee Bange	1993	1628
13 11/16	8 3/16	5 8/16	M	Los Alamos County	NM	Timothy F.H. Smith	1995	1628
13 11/16	8 1/16	5 10/16	M	White Pine County	NV	Thomas W. Fuller	1996	1628
13 11/16	8 2/16	5 9/16	M	Park County	MT	Mike O'Connor	1996	1628
13 11/16	8 1/16	5 10/16	M	Montrose County	CO	David C. Gordon, Jr.	1997	1628
13 11/16	8 5/16	5 6/16	M	Fremont County	CO	Stacy Hoeme	1997	1628
13 11/16	8 0/16	5 11/16	M	Elmore County	ID	George E. Mann	1997	1628
13 11/16	8 3/16	5 8/16	M	Sanpete County	UT	Don Noonan	1997	1628
13 11/16	8 1/16	5 10/16	F	Moffat County	CO	Wendell "Butch" Howes, Jr.	1998	1628
13 11/16	8 3/16	5 8/16	M	Humboldt County	NV	Donald Draper	1998	1628
13 11/16	8 3/16	5 8/16	M	Princeton	BC	Mark A. Jackson	1998	1628
13 11/16	8 2/16	5 9/16	M	Clearwater	BC	Bruce Knolmayer	1998	1628
13 11/16	8 2/16	5 9/16	M	Custer County	ID	Jim Riner	1998	1628
13 11/16	8 2/16	5 9/16	M	Elmore County	ID	Tom Vanasche	1999	1628
13 11/16	8 3/16	5 8/16	M	Nye County	NV	Roy L. Walk	2001	1628
13 11/16	8 1/16	5 10/16	M	Boise County	ID	Phillip E. Jayo	2001	1628
13 11/16	8 2/16	5 9/16	M	Custer County	ID	Gary M. Sheruda	2004	1628
*13 11/16	7 15/16	5 12/16	M	Comox Lake	BC	Adam Bartsch	2005	1628
13 11/16	8 3/16	5 8/16	M	Baca County	CO	Gary Zimmerer	2005	1628
13 11/16	8 3/16	5 8/16	M	Powell County	MT	Kenneth "Gus" Senst	2005	1628
13 11/16	8 3/16	5 8/16	M	Carbon County	WY	Clay J. Evans	2006	1628
13 10/16	8 2/16	5 8/16	F	Moffat County	CO	Roland C. Gravenkemper	1959	1674
13 10/16	8 0/16	5 10/16	F	Sana Arroya Canyon	UT	Edward Collins	1967	1674
13 10/16	7 14/16	5 12/16	M	Fremont County	CO	Jeffrey D. McKnight	1970	1674
13 10/16	7 15/16	5 11/16	M	Boise County	ID	Robert B. Braswell	1971	1674
13 10/16	7 12/16	5 14/16	M	Lemhi County	ID	Richard R. Smith	1976	1674
13 10/16	8 2/16	5 8/16	M	Grand County	UT	Karen Jacobsen	1980	1674
13 10/16	8 3/16	5 7/16	M	Sevier County	UT	Robert C. McGuire	1980	1674
13 10/16	8 0/16	5 10/16	M	Coconino County	AZ	Les Shelton	1981	1674
13 10/16	8 2/16	5 8/16	M	Garfield County	UT	William B. McGuire, Jr.	1983	1674
13 10/16	8 2/16	5 8/16	M	Sevier County	UT	Kenneth L. Jackson	1984	1674
13 10/16	8 0/16	5 10/16	M	Flathead County	MT	Charles J. Williams	1986	1674
13 10/16	8 4/16	5 6/16	M	Colfax County	NM	I. Lionel Kelley	1986	1674
13 10/16	7 15/16	5 11/16	M	Beaver County	UT	David L. Welch	1987	1674
13 10/16	8 2/16	5 8/16	M	Fergus County	MT	John "Rosey" Roseland	1987	1674
13 10/16	8 1/16	5 9/16	M	Millard County	UT	Roy Evans	1988	1674
13 10/16	8 1/16	5 9/16	M	Washington County	UT	Ken Mowerson	1988	1674
13 10/16	8 1/16	5 9/16	M	Lincoln County	NV	Glen R. Cousins	1988	1674
13 10/16	8 3/16	5 7/16	M	Blairmore	ALB	Larry Vayro	1990	1674
13 10/16	8 2/16	5 8/16	M	Elmore County	ID	Mike Ambur	1990	1674
13 10/16	8 1/16	5 9/16	M	Jackson County	OR	Randy D. Peyton	1990	1674
13 10/16	7 15/16	5 11/16	M	Iron County	UT	Jeryl F. Williams	1991	1674
13 10/16	8 1/16	5 9/16	M	Teller County	CO	Dennis R. Bader	1991	1674
13 10/16	8 0/16	5 10/16	M	Custer County	ID	Phil Sullivan	1991	1674
13 10/16	7 14/16	5 12/16	F	Montrose County	CO	Dale Laird	1992	1674
13 10/16	8 0/16	5 10/16	M	Taos County	NM	Robert L. Pagel	1992	1674
13 10/16	8 1/16	5 9/16	M	Washakie County	WY	Warren Warmbold	1993	1674
13 10/16	8 3/16	5 7/16	M	Granite County	MT	Mike Boyd	1993	1674
13 10/16	8 3/16	5 7/16	M	Grand County	CO	Andrew C. Bair	1994	1674
13 10/16	8 4/16	5 6/16	M	Rio Arriba County	NM	Joe Cordonier	1994	1674
13 10/16	8 1/16	5 9/16	M	Eagle County	CO	Sheldon S. Showalter	1994	1674
13 10/16	8 0/16	5 10/16	M	Catron County	NM	Jorge Garcia-Segovia	1995	1674
13 10/16	8 1/16	5 9/16	M	Kootenay River	BC	Gilles Rondeau	1995	1674
13 10/16	8 2/16	5 8/16	M	Idaho County	ID	W. J. Lucas III	1995	1674
13 10/16	7 14/16	5 12/16	M	Larimer County	CO	John E. Hostetler	1995	1674
13 10/16	8 3/16	5 7/16	M	Granite County	MT	Mike H. Boyd	1995	1674
13 10/16	8 0/16	5 10/16	M	Yavapai County	AZ	Al Kuntz	1996	1674
13 10/16	8 1/16	5 9/16	M	Coconino County	AZ	Joe Miguel	1996	1674

271

COUGAR (MOUNTAIN LION)

Minimum Score 13 8/16   Continued

SCORE	GREATEST LENGTH	GREATEST WIDTH	SEX	AREA	STATE/ PROVINCE	HUNTER'S NAME	DATE	RANK
13 10/16	8 2/16	5 8/16	M	Iron County	UT	Cindy L. Brush	1997	1674
13 10/16	8 0/16	5 10/16	M	White Pine County	NV	William C. Brewer	1997	1674
13 10/16	8 0/16	5 10/16	M	Carbon County	UT	Tommy D. Langston	1998	1674
13 10/16	8 3/16	5 7/16	M	Cow Lake	ALB	Jason J. Brown	1998	1674
13 10/16	7 15/16	5 11/16	M	Fir Mtn.	BC	Sharon Potter	1999	1674
13 10/16	7 14/16	5 12/16	M	Park County	MT	Ray N. Andersen	2000	1674
13 10/16	8 3/16	5 7/16	M	Albany County	WY	Mark E. Farrell	2000	1674
13 10/16	8 2/16	5 8/16	M	Lemhi County	ID	Gary C. Gapp	2000	1674
13 10/16	8 2/16	5 8/16	M	Sevier County	UT	Thomas Edgington	2000	1674
13 10/16	8 2/16	5 8/16	M	Boise County	ID	Bob Hopkins	2000	1674
13 10/16	8 1/16	5 9/16	M	Lincoln County	NM	Larry D. Napier	2001	1674
13 10/16	8 0/16	5 10/16	M	Coconino County	AZ	Eugene T. Fleming	2001	1674
13 10/16	8 3/16	5 7/16	M	Fremont County	CO	Keith Goodrow	2001	1674
13 10/16	8 2/16	5 8/16	M	Fergus County	MT	Pete Gierke	2002	1674
13 10/16	8 2/16	5 8/16	M	Coconino County	AZ	Tony White	2003	1674
13 10/16	8 1/16	5 9/16	M	Fremont County	CO	Mike A. Janicki, Jr.	2003	1674
13 10/16	8 8/16	5 2/16	M	Garfield County	UT	Arnold DeCastro	2003	1674
13 10/16	8 4/16	5 6/16	M	Washington County	UT	Keith Parrish	2004	1674
13 10/16	7 14/16	5 12/16	M	Coconino County	AZ	Michael D. Wall	2004	1674
13 10/16	8 0/16	5 10/16	M	Lemhi County	ID	Michael Brown	2004	1674
13 10/16	8 3/16	5 7/16	M	Montezuma County	CO	David Tullos	2006	1674
13 10/16	8 2/16	5 8/16	M	Utah County	UT	Jason Yates	2007	1674
13 10/16	8 1/16	5 9/16	M	Garfield County	CO	Shilo Holbrook	2009	1674
*13 10/16	8 1/16	5 9/16	M	Clearwater	ALB	Marco Pilon	2009	1674
13 9/16	8 0/16	5 9/16	M	Carbon County	UT	Tom Kludy	1965	1735
13 9/16	8 1/16	5 8/16	M	Elmore County	ID	Larry Bergmann	1972	1735
13 9/16	8 0/16	5 9/16	F	Custer County	ID	John Kuhar	1975	1735
13 9/16	8 1/16	5 8/16	M	Carbon County	UT	Michael Judas	1977	1735
13 9/16	7 15/16	5 10/16	M	Rio Blanco County	CO	John Horstman	1977	1735
13 9/16	8 0/16	5 9/16	M	Saguache County	CO	Ed R. Wiseman	1977	1735
13 9/16	8 3/16	5 6/16	M	Peachland	BC	Roger Gipple	1983	1735
13 9/16	7 15/16	5 10/16	M	Hot Springs County	WY	John Backs	1983	1735
13 9/16	8 5/16	5 4/16	M	Monroe County	UT	Peter Esposito	1984	1735
13 9/16	7 14/16	5 11/16	M	Sanders County	MT	Fred J. Hoppe	1984	1735
13 9/16	8 3/16	5 6/16	M	Beaver County	UT	Joseph Drover	1985	1735
13 9/16	8 2/16	5 7/16	M	San Juan County	UT	Charles R. Horvath	1985	1735
13 9/16	8 0/16	5 9/16	M	Lemhi County	ID	Ed Montouri	1985	1735
13 9/16	8 0/16	5 9/16	M	Sanders County	MT	Dr. Eugene T. Altiere	1985	1735
13 9/16	8 1/16	5 8/16	M	Juab County	UT	Kirt Prestwich	1986	1735
13 9/16	8 2/16	5 7/16	M	Clearwater County	ID	Terry L. Sochor	1987	1735
13 9/16	8 1/16	5 8/16	M	Garfield County	UT	George E. Wright	1987	1735
13 9/16	8 0/16	5 9/16	M	White Pine County	NV	Robert S. Price	1987	1735
13 9/16	8 3/16	5 6/16	M	Rio Blanco County	CO	Steven J. Lepic	1987	1735
13 9/16	8 0/16	5 9/16	M	Fremont County	CO	Chuck Anderson, Jr.	1987	1735
13 9/16	8 1/16	5 8/16	M	Garfield County	CO	Steven W. Kluth	1988	1735
13 9/16	8 2/16	5 7/16	M	Granite County	MT	Rocky Drake	1989	1735
13 9/16	8 4/16	5 5/16	M	Mesa County	CO	Steve Haberland	1990	1735
13 9/16	8 2/16	5 7/16	M	Mesa County	CO	Troy James	1991	1735
13 9/16	8 0/16	5 9/16	M	Duchesne County	UT	Roy Hampton	1992	1735
13 9/16	7 15/16	5 10/16	F	Chaffee County	CO	Dave Luko	1992	1735
13 9/16	8 4/16	5 5/16	F	Park County	CO	Howard D. Drummond	1992	1735
13 9/16	8 3/16	5 6/16	M	Elko County	NV	John F. Amerson	1993	1735
13 9/16	8 1/16	5 8/16	M	La Plata County	CO	Dr. S. Mark Rayburg	1994	1735
13 9/16	8 1/16	5 8/16	M	Fergus County	MT	D. Mitch Kottas	1994	1735
13 9/16	8 1/16	5 8/16	M	Carbon County	UT	David R. Scott	1995	1735
13 9/16	8 2/16	5 7/16	M	Sandoval County	NM	Robert Smith	1996	1735
13 9/16	8 1/16	5 8/16	M	Duchesne County	UT	Don R. Gifford	1996	1735
13 9/16	8 2/16	5 7/16	M	Montrose County	CO	Rod Van Sickle	1997	1735
13 9/16	8 0/16	5 9/16	M	Fremont County	CO	Brian Brochu	1998	1735
13 9/16	8 2/16	5 7/16	M	Socorro County	NM	Mark Yurchisin, MD	1999	1735
13 9/16	8 2/16	5 7/16	F	Umatilla County	OR	Kerry A. Fann	1999	1735
13 9/16	7 15/16	5 10/16	M	Larimer County	CO	Shawn A. Greathouse	2000	1735
13 9/16	7 13/16	5 12/16	M	Montezuma County	CO	Ronald G. Ralston	2001	1735
13 9/16	8 4/16	5 5/16	M	Hinton	ALB	Russell K. Mehling	2003	1735
13 9/16	8 1/16	5 8/16	M	Chaffee County	CO	Peter J. Selinski	2004	1735
13 9/16	8 2/16	5 7/16	M	Lincoln County	NV	Keith Wilds	2005	1735
13 9/16	8 6/16	5 3/16	M	Fremont County	WY	Marshall Balzly	2008	1735
13 9/16	8 0/16	5 9/16	M	Lincoln County	WY	Gary Hornberger	2009	1735
13 8/16	8 0/16	5 8/16	M	Uintah County	UT	Creetie Kerr	1964	1779
13 8/16	8 2/16	5 6/16	M	Uintah County	UT	Dr. George A. Waldriff	1965	1779
13 8/16	7 12/16	5 12/16	F	Lincoln County	MT	G. H. Malinoski	1967	1779
13 8/16	8 8/16	5 0/16	F	Churchill County	NV	Quentin P. Nightingale	1971	1779
13 8/16	8 1/16	5 7/16	M	Coconino County	AZ	Tim Kennedy	1974	1779
13 8/16	8 2/16	5 6/16	M	Coconino County	AZ	Robert West	1974	1779
13 8/16	8 0/16	5 8/16	M	Cassia County	ID	Leon Peterson	1978	1779
13 8/16	8 0/16	5 8/16	M	Carbon County	UT	John Brandt	1978	1779
13 8/16	8 2/16	5 6/16	M	Penticton	BC	Dale W. Gray	1979	1779
13 8/16	8 0/16	5 8/16	M	Lemhi County	ID	John A. McCarthy	1979	1779
13 8/16	8 1/16	5 7/16	M	Fremont County	CO	Steve Byerly	1981	1779
13 8/16	8 2/16	5 6/16	M	Clearwater County	ID	Donita K. Powers	1982	1779
13 8/16	7 10/16	5 14/16	M	Park County	WY	David C. Gordon, Sr.	1983	1779
13 8/16	8 1/16	5 7/16	F	Wallowa County	OR	Jim Turcke	1983	1779
13 8/16	8 1/16	5 7/16	M	Washington County	UT	Nic Blake	1984	1779
13 8/16	8 1/16	5 7/16	M	Alamosa County	CO	Barry J. Smith	1985	1779
13 8/16	7 13/16	5 11/16	M	Madison County	MT	Jim Ellis	1985	1779
13 8/16	8 3/16	5 5/16	M	Sevier County	UT	Greg Strait	1986	1779
13 8/16	8 0/16	5 8/16	M	Coconino County	AZ	Mike T. Miller	1988	1779
13 8/16	7 15/16	5 9/16	M	Fergus County	MT	Lisa Roseland	1988	1779
13 8/16	8 0/16	5 8/16	M	Fergus County	MT	John Fleharty	1988	1779
13 8/16	8 0/16	5 8/16	M	Montrose County	CO	Gene Mathias	1988	1779
13 8/16	8 0/16	5 8/16	M	Graham County	AZ	Tracy G. Hardy	1989	1779
13 8/16	8 3/16	5 5/16	M	Boise County	ID	Gerard J. Gareri	1990	1779
13 8/16	8 0/16	5 8/16	M	Lincoln County	MT	Jon Clark	1991	1779
13 8/16	8 2/16	5 6/16	M	Sevier County	UT	Raymond J. Francingues, Jr.	1992	1779
13 8/16	8 1/16	5 7/16	M	Fremont County	CO	Tommy M. Brown	1992	1779

272

COUGAR (MOUNTAIN LION)

Minimum Score 13 8/16   Continued

SCORE	GREATEST LENGTH	GREATEST WIDTH	SEX	AREA	STATE/ PROVINCE	HUNTER'S NAME	DATE	RANK
13 8/16	8 0/16	5 8/16	M	Idaho County	ID	Larry Campbell	1994	1779
13 8/16	8 3/16	5 5/16	M	Custer County	ID	Walter Palmer	1994	1779
13 8/16	8 1/16	5 7/16	M	Saguache County	CO	Michael C. Dysh	1994	1779
13 8/16	7 15/16	5 9/16	M	Coconino County	AZ	Tom Egnew	1994	1779
13 8/16	8 0/16	5 8/16	M	Wasatch County	UT	Timothy A. Presnell	1995	1779
13 8/16	8 0/16	5 8/16	M	Jefferson County	MT	Joseph R. Balyeat	1995	1779
13 8/16	8 0/16	5 8/16	M	Madison County	MT	Bob Morton	1995	1779
13 8/16	8 0/16	5 8/16	M	Custer County	ID	Brian Brockette	1996	1779
13 8/16	8 1/16	5 7/16	F	Delta County	CO	John "Jack" Nothardt	1997	1779
13 8/16	8 0/16	5 8/16	M	Garfield County	UT	Alan Scano	1997	1779
13 8/16	8 0/16	5 8/16	M	Montrose County	CO	Harry Seifred	1997	1779
13 8/16	8 1/16	5 7/16	M	Missoula County	MT	Rudy Lupp	1997	1779
13 8/16	8 0/16	5 8/16	M	Carbon County	UT	George Brandon Farish	1998	1779
13 8/16	8 0/16	5 8/16	M	White Pine County	NV	P. J. Londo	1998	1779
13 8/16	7 15/16	5 9/16	M	Ravalli County	MT	Bob Fisher	1998	1779
13 8/16	8 1/16	5 7/16	M	Montrose County	CO	Michael J. Schneider	1998	1779
13 8/16	8 0/16	5 8/16	M	Fergus County	MT	Larry Jensen	1998	1779
13 8/16	7 15/16	5 9/16	M	Gallatin County	MT	Eric Christophersen	1998	1779
13 8/16	8 0/16	5 8/16	M	Bear Lake County	ID	Chad Stearns	1998	1779
13 8/16	8 0/16	5 8/16	M	Ravalli County	MT	Corey Hugelen	1999	1779
13 8/16	8 1/16	5 7/16	M	Rio Arriba County	NM	William A. Sheka, Jr.	1999	1779
13 8/16	8 0/16	5 8/16	M	Bergen	ALB	Dallas Kaiser	1999	1779
13 8/16	7 15/16	5 9/16	F	Quesnel	BC	Joleen A. Mero	2000	1779
13 8/16	7 15/16	5 9/16	M	Cascade County	MT	Brandon C. Johns	2000	1779
13 8/16	8 1/16	5 7/16	M	Wallace Creek	BC	Thomas Anzalone	2000	1779
13 8/16	7 13/16	5 11/16	F	Saguache County	CO	Ron Charity	2001	1779
13 8/16	8 1/16	5 7/16	M	Chaffee County	CO	Nathan L. Andersohn	2001	1779
13 8/16	7 14/16	5 10/16	F	Costilla County	CO	Gary Oberer	2002	1779
13 8/16	8 3/16	5 5/16	M	Flathead County	MT	Logan O'Neil	2002	1779
13 8/16	8 0/16	5 8/16	M	Clearwater River	ALB	Dallas Kaiser	2003	1779
13 8/16	8 0/16	5 8/16	M	Montrose County	CO	Heather L. Knott	2004	1779
13 8/16	8 2/16	5 6/16	M	Rio Blanco County	CO	Aaron Jones	2004	1779
*13 8/16	8 2/16	5 6/16	M	Custer County	ID	Dan King	2007	1779
*13 8/16	7 15/16	5 9/16	M	Lincoln County	WY	Brett I. Ritter	2007	1779
13 8/16	8 2/16	5 6/16	M	Ouray County	CO	Neil V. Fino, Jr.	2008	1779
13 8/16	7 14/16	5 10/16	M	Elko County	NV	Toby Parker	2010	1779

273

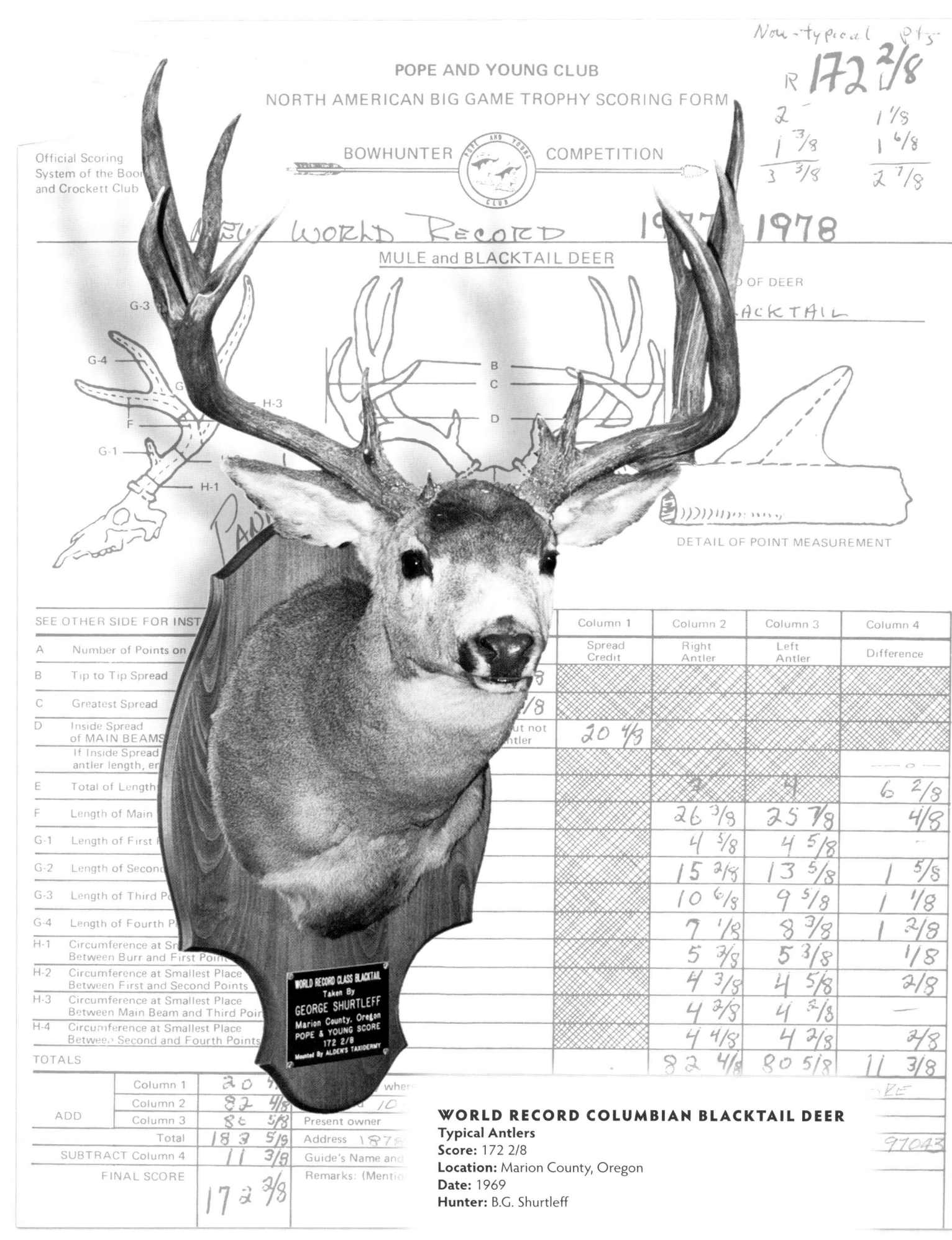

WORLD RECORD COLUMBIAN BLACKTAIL DEER
Typical Antlers
Score: 172 2/8
Location: Marion County, Oregon
Date: 1969
Hunter: B.G. Shurtleff

Typical Columbian Blacktail Deer

by B.G. Shurtleff

In 1960 I bought a bow, a bow reel and a fish arrow to shoot carp. The bow was heavy enough for deer hunting, so I bought some arrows and broadheads. With a lot of practice, I thought I was ready to try the September season in eastern Oregon. I did not take a deer on that hunt, but one part of that hunt probably did more to make me a bowhunter than taking a blacktail in the late season did.

One morning I took my eight-year-old son with me. We were just starting up the mountain when a large buck and a doe crossed the road. It was more like a skid trail that, with a lot of luck, you could get a pickup truck over. I stopped, got out and slipped down a dry wash to a place where I could cross to the other side to sneak on the deer.

It worked! At about 30 yards I was about to draw, when "honk honk" went the horn of the pickup and away went the deer. Delbert, my son, was very relieved when I came back to the pickup laughing. He had been so intent watching me sneak he had bumped the horn. The thrill of this, and the laughs we had about it, hooked us both on bowhunting.

A couple of years later I knocked a large trout off Delbert's hook with a landing net. He laughed and said, "Remember when I honked the horn at your deer? We're even now." Delbert became a good archer and took several deer before his death in 1971.

My best trophy was taken on October 2, 1969, on a one-day hunt near home. I drove a short distance into the hills on the east side of the Willamette valley. The brush in this area is so thick you can hardly get through it, so trail watching is the only answer. I had found a good trail near the creek under a rock bluff, and this was where I planned to sit. I was on my stand by daylight.

After what seemed like a very long time I was tempted to leave, quite sure nothing was going to come this way. Then I saw movement in the brush and all thoughts of leaving were gone! Then I saw antlers…and what a set of antlers! He was coming my way.

I was so excited I had to tell myself, "Cool it. Let him walk past before you move." As he walked past I drew, aimed and released all in one motion. It was a good hit. Talk about buck fever! I really had it now.

After working my way down off the bluff to where I had last seen the deer, I found blood and the deer was a short distance from there. Getting him out was an ordeal, but by cutting him up and making several trips, I was able to do so. Even this hard work did not dampen the thrill of taking one of the largest deer I have ever seen.

Years later, my brother-in-law talked me into having the rack measured for the Pope and Young Club.

COLUMBIAN BLACKTAIL DEER (TYPICAL ANTLERS)

Minimum Score 95   *Odocoileus hemionus columnianus*

SCORE	LENGTH OF R MAIN BEAM L	INSIDE SPREAD	NUMBER OF R POINTS L	AREA	STATE/PROVINCE	HUNTER'S NAME	DATE	RANK
172 2/8	26 3/8 25 7/8	20 4/8	7 7	Marion County	OR	B. G. Shurtleff	1969	1
172 0/8	26 4/8 25 5/8	22 6/8	4 4	Multnomah County	OR	Dave Brill	1985	2
169 5/8	25 6/8 26 2/8	19 7/8	9 8	Jackson County	OR	Randy Allen	1995	3
164 7/8	23 6/8 23 3/8	19 7/8	5 5	Marion County	OR	B. G. Shurtleff	1977	4
160 7/8	23 0/8 23 4/8	19 4/8	6 5	Jackson County	OR	Dr. G. Scott Jennings	1972	5
160 7/8	23 4/8 24 0/8	17 3/8	5 5	Jackson County	OR	David B. Baird	1991	5
158 5/8	21 2/8 21 6/8	17 3/8	5 5	Clark County	WA	Johnny Alderman	2003	7
156 7/8	23 5/8 24 1/8	23 1/8	5 5	Trinity County	CA	Steve Bradford	1986	8
154 5/8	24 6/8 26 2/8	20 7/8	5 5	Jackson County	OR	Bill Stiefel	2008	9
152 6/8	22 2/8 22 2/8	18 0/8	5 5	Clackamas County	OR	Phillip L. Severson	1991	10
151 5/8	22 1/8 25 0/8	21 3/8	5 4	Lake County	CA	Art Young	1921	11
151 3/8	21 3/8 22 4/8	18 0/8	5 6	Jackson County	OR	Mark A. Shanklin	1987	12
151 2/8	23 2/8 21 4/8	18 0/8	6 5	Siskiyou County	CA	Wally Schwartz	2004	13
150 6/8	23 3/8 23 5/8	18 2/8	5 5	Jackson County	OR	Ted Perreard	1999	14
150 4/8	23 4/8 23 1/8	20 2/8	5 5	Jackson County	OR	E. C. Brittsan	1976	15
148 1/8	21 4/8 22 0/8	14 3/8	5 6	Jackson County	OR	Brian Wolfer	2000	16
148 0/8	20 2/8 19 2/8	17 2/8	5 5	Benton County	OR	Richard Heeter	2005	17
147 3/8	22 5/8 23 3/8	17 4/8	5 6	Jackson County	OR	Sam Burton	1996	18
146 6/8	20 0/8 20 0/8	17 6/8	5 5	Marion County	OR	Jim Brackenbury	1990	19
146 6/8	22 3/8 24 2/8	15 0/8	5 5	Lane County	OR	Bryan P. Kamahoahoa	1993	19
146 2/8	21 4/8 22 4/8	17 2/8	5 5	Lane County	OR	Robert Martell	1988	21
145 5/8	20 7/8 19 0/8	14 7/8	5 5	Jackson County	OR	Steve Holte	2000	22
145 4/8	20 2/8 19 6/8	16 4/8	5 5	Whatcom County	WA	LeRoy Harkness	2005	23
145 1/8	21 1/8 22 6/8	20 1/8	5 5	Jackson County	OR	James Reeves	2002	25
144 5/8	21 2/8 20 3/8	16 6/8	6 7	Jackson County	OR	Leroy Bedingfield	1970	26
144 5/8	21 6/8 22 7/8	21 7/8	5 5	Contra Costa County	CA	Wayne Ortland	1993	26
144 2/8	21 1/8 21 3/8	16 5/8	6 5	Jackson County	OR	Cliff Skaggs	2007	28
143 7/8	21 0/8 20 6/8	21 0/8	5 5	Shasta County	CA	Dave Swenson	1968	29
143 7/8	22 4/8 21 5/8	19 5/8	5 6	Jackson County	OR	Todd Wolgamot	2003	29
143 6/8	21 2/8 21 3/8	17 0/8	5 5	Trinity County	CA	Chet Donato	2004	31
143 1/8	20 5/8 19 4/8	20 1/8	5 5	Josephine County	OR	David L. Hall	1979	32
142 4/8	21 4/8 21 5/8	17 4/8	5 5	Lane County	OR	Vernon King, Sr.	1988	33
142 2/8	19 1/8 19 7/8	19 0/8	5 5	Lake County	OR	Don Chandler	1968	34
141 7/8	20 7/8 21 0/8	17 3/8	5 5	Jackson County	OR	Chester Stevenson	1917	35
141 6/8	22 1/8 23 0/8	20 6/8	4 4	Trinity County	CA	Tod Hawkins	1993	36
* 141 4/8	21 2/8 20 4/8	18 0/8	5 5	Mendocino County	CA	Brett Gomes	2003	37
141 2/8	20 2/8 21 3/8	18 6/8	5 5	Jackson County	OR	Robert L. Freeman	1991	38
140 6/8	21 3/8 20 4/8	16 2/8	3 3	Jackson County	OR	Art W. Lee	1965	39
140 6/8	22 6/8 22 5/8	15 4/8	4 5	Jackson County	OR	Dr. G. Scott Jennings	1973	39
140 6/8	21 2/8 20 7/8	17 6/8	5 5	Jackson County	OR	Les Higinbotham	1992	39
140 3/8	19 6/8 21 0/8	16 7/8	5 6	Lewis County	WA	Nate Hamilton	1993	42
139 6/8	21 4/8 20 6/8	17 4/8	5 5	Whatcom County	WA	Juan Martinez	2006	43
138 5/8	22 3/8 21 1/8	17 7/8	5 6	Linn County	OR	John J. Sevc	2006	44
138 4/8	22 5/8 22 4/8	18 5/8	5 5	Siskiyou County	CA	John Bridgewater	1980	45
138 4/8	22 6/8 23 1/8	20 6/8	4 4	Tehama County	CA	Dean Chambers	2002	45
138 1/8	21 3/8 20 5/8	15 3/8	5 5	Glenn County	CA	Bret Cleland	2006	47
137 7/8	21 7/8 21 3/8	14 1/8	5 5	Clallam County	WA	Steve Anders, Jr.	2007	48
137 6/8	22 4/8 23 3/8	26 1/8	4 4	Jackson County	OR	David Shanklin	1982	49
137 6/8	20 3/8 22 0/8	15 6/8	5 5	Jackson County	OR	John Schauble	1986	49
137 2/8	20 2/8 19 7/8	16 1/8	6 5	Jackson County	OR	Steve Wirth	1983	51
137 2/8	20 7/8 22 0/8	17 6/8	6 6	Jackson County	OR	Dusty McGrorty	2003	51
137 1/8	21 2/8 20 1/8	16 1/8	4 6	Linn County	OR	Scot E. Lafond	1991	53
137 0/8	20 3/8 20 1/8	14 5/8	4 4	Mendocino County	CA	Russell L. Browning	1980	54
137 0/8	21 1/8 21 2/8	15 7/8	4 5	Linn County	OR	Charlie Endicott	1985	54
136 7/8	21 0/8 20 7/8	15 3/8	6 6	Skamania County	WA	Melvin W. Berry	1991	56
136 6/8	21 0/8 21 1/8	18 2/8	5 5	Linn County	OR	Tom Nichols	1985	57
136 6/8	21 2/8 21 2/8	14 6/8	4 4	Jackson County	OR	Ted Perreard	1995	57
136 5/8	21 1/8 22 1/8	17 1/8	4 5	Linn County	OR	Rebecca Saunders	1986	59
136 4/8	21 4/8 21 6/8	16 4/8	4 6	Clackamas County	OR	Craig Hyatt	1990	60
136 1/8	21 0/8 20 2/8	17 7/8	5 5	Jackson County	OR	Dave Hall	1991	61
135 7/8	21 3/8 21 4/8	20 3/8	5 5	San Mateo County	CA	Robert Caughey	2002	62
135 7/8	19 3/8 19 2/8	15 1/8	5 5	Lewis County	WA	Brett Doyle	2009	62
135 6/8	20 3/8 20 4/8	15 4/8	5 5	Benton County	OR	Mike Galloway	2002	64
135 2/8	19 5/8 20 1/8	16 0/8	6 5	Linn County	OR	Dave Evans	1995	65
135 2/8	21 0/8 20 6/8	17 2/8	4 4	Linn County	OR	Dennis R. Middleton	2000	65
135 2/8	19 1/8 19 2/8	15 0/8	5 5	Jackson County	OR	Kevin D. Ruf	2002	65
135 2/8	20 6/8 21 1/8	15 4/8	5 5	Douglas County	OR	Roger Fielding	2005	65
135 0/8	22 0/8 21 2/8	18 7/8	6 4	Jackson County	OR	Bob Staten	1964	69
135 0/8	21 7/8 22 3/8	17 0/8	6 5	Lane County	OR	Walt Metcalfe	2002	69
135 0/8	20 0/8 19 2/8	15 2/8	4 5	Jackson County	OR	Dusty McGrorty	2004	69
134 6/8	21 0/8 21 2/8	17 7/8	6 4	Benton County	OR	Richard G. Heeter	2009	71
134 5/8	21 0/8 16 0/8	16 2/8	5 4	Jackson County	OR	Milton L. Cady	1968	72
134 5/8	21 7/8 21 7/8	17 0/8	7 5	Trinity County	CA	Bob Auser	1981	72
134 5/8	18 3/8 19 2/8	15 3/8	5 5	Jackson County	OR	Dave Hall	2004	72
134 4/8	22 5/8 21 4/8	15 6/8	4 4	Glenn County	CA	Steve Bashaw	1989	75
134 1/8	20 4/8 20 5/8	13 7/8	5 5	Benton County	OR	Stanley Miles	2006	77
134 1/8	22 2/8 22 4/8	19 0/8	5 5	Napa County	CA	Michael Ratto	2009	77
134 0/8	20 3/8 20 4/8	16 4/8	5 5	Humboldt County	CA	David E. Evanow	2006	78
133 7/8	20 6/8 20 6/8	18 7/8	4 4	Jackson County	OR	Donald R. Pritchett	1966	79
133 7/8	19 4/8 21 6/8	13 7/8	7 7	Linn County	OR	J. C. James	1984	79
133 6/8	20 0/8 21 1/8	16 6/8	5 5	Polk County	OR	Carl E. Garner	1999	81
* 133 6/8	20 0/8 19 5/8	16 4/8	5 5	Trinity County	CA	Kevin Erwin	2008	81
133 4/8	20 0/8 20 3/8	16 2/8	4 4	Pierce County	WA	Ted J. Eidsmoe	1999	83
133 3/8	20 4/8 21 0/8	19 5/8	5 5	Trinity County	CA	Mike McCormick	1999	84
133 2/8	20 1/8 20 2/8	17 0/8	5 5	Jackson County	OR	Chester Stevenson	1921	85
133 1/8	18 7/8 17 6/8	15 3/8	5 5	Lane County	OR	Matt Dodson	1990	86
133 0/8	20 5/8 21 0/8	14 6/8	5 5	Benton County	OR	Robert W. Worthean	1982	87
133 0/8	20 6/8 20 0/8	17 3/8	5 7	Humboldt County	CA	Bradford C. Floyd	2001	87
133 0/8	18 3/8 18 6/8	19 0/8	5 5	Napa County	CA	Robert Covey	2001	87
132 7/8	20 0/8 20 0/8	14 7/8	5 5	Lane County	OR	Clyde Romero, Jr.	1991	90
132 7/8	22 1/8 22 2/8	15 5/8	6 7	Pierce County	WA	Jon Klosner	2005	90
132 6/8	20 1/8 20 6/8	18 0/8	4 5	Jackson County	OR	Stanley Moore	1962	92
132 6/8	19 2/8 18 7/8	17 4/8	4 4	Jackson County	OR	David Shanklin	1987	92
132 5/8	22 0/8 21 0/8	16 1/8	7 7	Clackamas County	OR	Charlie Medlicott	1983	94
132 4/8	21 0/8 21 2/8	16 5/8	6 5	Siskiyou County	CA	Kasey Rowland	2004	95

276

COLUMBIAN BLACKTAIL DEER (TYPICAL ANTLERS)

Minimum Score 95 Continued

SCORE	LENGTH OF R MAIN BEAM L	INSIDE SPREAD	NUMBER OF R POINTS L	AREA	STATE/ PROVINCE	HUNTER'S NAME	DATE	RANK
132 4/8	19 4/8 19 2/8	14 5/8	5 6	Mendocino County	CA	D. J. Wood	2004	95
132 3/8	18 6/8 19 4/8	16 7/8	5 5	Jackson County	OR	Donald R. Pritchett	1966	97
* 132 2/8	20 4/8 20 5/8	15 4/8	5 5	Linn County	OR	John Stone	2007	98
132 2/8	21 0/8 22 0/8	17 4/8	5 5	Linn County	OR	Jonathan Milani	2008	98
132 1/8	20 2/8 19 6/8	18 4/8	5 7	Jackson County	OR	John Schauble	1985	100
132 0/8	20 0/8 20 1/8	16 4/8	5 5	Jackson County	OR	Dustin S. McGrorty	2001	101
131 7/8	22 0/8 21 6/8	16 7/8	4 4	Douglas County	OR	Jim Hodson	1987	102
131 7/8	19 1/8 18 0/8	18 5/8	5 5	Josephine County	OR	Richard J. Darner	1993	102
131 6/8	18 0/8 18 6/8	16 6/8	5 5	Clackamas County	OR	Ray Kelton	2002	104
131 5/8	19 3/8 19 1/8	15 3/8	5 5	Del Norte County	CA	Steve Bigham	2003	105
131 5/8	21 6/8 20 5/8	14 7/8	5 5	Lane County	OR	Kevin Ford	2004	105
131 4/8	21 5/8 22 0/8	17 3/8	6 4	Multnomah County	OR	Dennis Thorud	1985	107
131 3/8	20 0/8 20 0/8	15 5/8	5 5	Jackson County	OR	Joe Williamson	1965	108
131 3/8	20 1/8 20 2/8	17 3/8	5 5	Douglas County	OR	Ken French	1988	108
131 3/8	20 4/8 20 6/8	17 3/8	5 5	Jackson County	OR	Leonard Scharf	1993	108
131 2/8	19 6/8 19 3/8	22 2/8	5 5	Linn County	OR	David F. Scheid	1968	111
131 2/8	19 2/8 18 3/8	18 0/8	5 5	Jackson County	OR	David Shanklin	1978	111
131 2/8	21 2/8 21 4/8	18 2/8	5 4	Clatsop County	OR	B. G. Shurtleff	1979	111
131 1/8	19 4/8 19 4/8	14 5/8	5 5	Kitsap County	WA	Dale Axtman	1983	114
130 7/8	22 2/8 21 4/8	15 2/8	6 7	Benton County	OR	Chuck Warner	1991	115
130 7/8	21 0/8 19 0/8	17 1/8	5 6	Marion County	OR	Loren A. McLaughlin	1993	115
130 7/8	18 7/8 18 5/8	14 1/8	5 5	Linn County	OR	Smokey Crews	1996	115
130 6/8	19 4/8 19 2/8	14 4/8	5 5	Linn County	OR	Daniel L. Sommers	2002	118
130 6/8	20 3/8 19 6/8	18 2/8	5 5	Chilliwack Valley	BC	Robert Zseder	2003	118
130 5/8	20 1/8 21 3/8	18 5/8	4 4	Mendocino County	CA	Carl Musto	1994	120
130 4/8	19 0/8 19 2/8	19 5/8	5 5	Humboldt County	CA	Jim Dervin	1992	121
130 4/8	19 2/8 20 7/8	18 3/8	5 6	Jackson County	OR	Dave Hall	2008	121
130 3/8	21 4/8 22 2/8	17 6/8	5 5	Glenn County	CA	Buck Devlin	1993	123
130 3/8	20 2/8 21 6/8	17 7/8	4 4	Mendocino County	CA	Brenda Carley	2005	123
130 3/8	22 0/8 22 5/8	20 3/8	4 4	Mendocino County	CA	Gary Island	2007	123
130 2/8	19 6/8 19 4/8	14 6/8	5 5	Lane County	OR	Steve Rogers	1992	126
130 1/8	19 0/8 18 7/8	15 1/8	5 5	Linn County	OR	Duane Etherington	1983	127
130 1/8	22 1/8 21 4/8	20 5/8	5 4	Santa Clara County	CA	Joel G. Sakamoto	2001	127
130 1/8	20 7/8 20 6/8	15 5/8	5 5	Jefferson County	WA	John Coon	2009	127
130 0/8	18 3/8 18 0/8	12 6/8	4 5	Skagit County	WA	Craig Meyer	2003	130
130 0/8	19 4/8 19 3/8	17 2/8	5 5	Clackamas County	OR	Neil M. Olsen	2007	130
130 0/8	19 3/8 19 5/8	18 0/8	5 5	King County	WA	Lance W. Axtell	2008	130
129 5/8	18 7/8 18 5/8	17 7/8	5 5	Colusa County	CA	Jay Overholtzer	1988	133
129 4/8	19 0/8 18 3/8	19 5/8	4 4	Jackson County	OR	Bruce B. Stamp	1988	134
129 3/8	26 1/8 25 3/8	19 2/8	5 3	Klamath County	OR	Troy Fennel	1964	135
129 3/8	21 4/8 21 1/8	16 3/8	5 5	Siskiyou County	CA	Daniel Franks	1991	135
* 129 2/8	18 5/8 17 7/8	14 2/8	6 5	Linn County	OR	John J. Sevc	2008	137
129 1/8	20 4/8 20 4/8	16 3/8	4 4	Douglas County	OR	Tom E. Tipton	1988	138
129 0/8	21 1/8 20 4/8	16 4/8	4 4	Lane County	OR	Scott P. Lawson	1994	139
129 0/8	20 4/8 20 3/8	17 0/8	5 5	Kitsap County	WA	John P. Perrenoud	1999	139
129 0/8	18 6/8 18 6/8	20 5/8	5 5	Mendocino County	CA	Brent Painter	2001	139
128 7/8	18 2/8 18 2/8	16 3/8	5 5	Lane County	OR	Dave E. Jarrett	1982	142
128 5/8	19 1/8 18 7/8	15 7/8	5 5	Lake County	CA	Joe Emmons	1989	143
128 5/8	19 6/8 19 7/8	16 5/8	5 5	Mendocino County	CA	Butch E. Carley	1993	143
128 5/8	23 1/8 23 4/8	17 7/8	4 4	Josephine County	OR	Lee Darrow	1995	143
128 5/8	21 7/8 21 4/8	19 7/8	4 4	Mendocino County	CA	Brenda Carley	2009	143
128 4/8	19 4/8 19 6/8	17 6/8	5 5	Fraser Valley	BC	Bill Pastorek	2007	147
128 3/8	19 3/8 19 7/8	14 5/8	4 5	Benton County	OR	Ray G. Kelton	1993	148
128 3/8	20 3/8 19 7/8	15 1/8	6 5	Humboldt County	CA	Dan Noga	1994	148
* 128 3/8	19 3/8 19 3/8	13 7/8	5 4	Island County	WA	Chris Hallberg	2008	148
128 2/8	19 3/8 19 4/8	14 4/8	8 5	Clackamas County	OR	John Christiansen	1981	151
128 2/8	20 1/8 20 3/8	15 2/8	6 5	Linn County	OR	Steve Richards	1983	151
128 2/8	20 3/8 20 6/8	21 6/8	5 4	Trinity County	CA	Seth Sanders	1997	151
128 1/8	20 6/8 20 7/8	17 1/8	5 5	Mendocino County	CA	Charles C. Pacheco	1993	154
128 1/8	20 4/8 20 1/8	15 3/8	5 5	Jackson County	OR	Dave Hall	2005	154
127 7/8	19 2/8 20 3/8	18 7/8	5 5	Linn County	OR	Chuck Warner	1987	156
127 6/8	18 1/8 17 0/8	13 2/8	5 5	Linn County	OR	Thomas K. Powell	2004	157
127 5/8	22 0/8 22 1/8	16 3/8	6 5	Josephine County	OR	Frank Sanders	1991	158
127 5/8	21 1/8 20 1/8	16 1/8	5 5	Douglas County	OR	Joe Hulburt	1991	158
127 5/8	21 1/8 20 3/8	17 3/8	6 5	Jackson County	OR	Dave Hall	1998	158
127 5/8	21 4/8 20 6/8	19 1/8	4 4	Glenn County	CA	Jim McDonald	2004	158
127 4/8	21 3/8 21 1/8	19 6/8	5 5	Linn County	OR	John Stone	1981	162
127 3/8	21 4/8 20 2/8	19 7/8	4 4	Mendocino County	CA	Lawrence Christensen	1991	163
127 2/8	20 2/8 19 6/8	14 6/8	5 5	Trinity County	CA	George Flournoy, Jr.	1986	164
127 1/8	18 7/8 19 5/8	16 1/8	6 5	Mendocino County	CA	James Buffum	1965	165
126 7/8	19 6/8 20 2/8	17 7/8	5 4	Snohomish County	WA	David Randolph	1997	166
126 7/8	21 0/8 19 5/8	16 5/8	5 5	King County	WA	Jeffrey Enera	1998	166
126 5/8	18 2/8 17 4/8	13 7/8	5 5	Douglas County	OR	Kenneth A. French	1989	168
126 5/8	24 4/8 23 1/8	19 5/8	3 3	Jefferson County	WA	Carter Tjemsland	2010	168
126 4/8	17 1/8 18 5/8	14 6/8	5 5	Linn County	OR	Dennis H. Wessels	1985	170
126 2/8	17 1/8 18 0/8	16 0/8	6 6	Skamania County	WA	Corbett D. McMaster	1990	171
126 1/8	19 7/8 19 5/8	18 1/8	4 4	Alameda County	CA	Robert Shuttleworth, Jr.	1998	172
126 1/8	19 7/8 20 1/8	17 3/8	5 5	King County	WA	Drew Heimbigner	2001	172
125 7/8	19 1/8 19 4/8	13 7/8	5 5	Marion County	OR	Doug Harris	1985	174
125 7/8	21 6/8 21 3/8	13 6/8	6 5	Jackson County	OR	Dave Hall	2000	174
125 6/8	19 3/8 18 5/8	14 2/8	4 4	Siskiyou County	CA	Cliff Dewell	1969	176
125 4/8	19 7/8 21 6/8	19 6/8	6 6	Josephine County	OR	Dave Hall	1983	177
125 4/8	19 5/8 19 7/8	14 2/8	5 5	Lane County	OR	Cameron R. Hanes	2000	177
125 3/8	18 1/8 18 6/8	16 1/8	5 5	Josephine County	OR	Lee Darrow	1973	179
125 3/8	22 0/8 23 4/8	19 3/8	5 4	Lane County	OR	Joe Lilley	1992	179
125 2/8	19 6/8 19 0/8	11 6/8	5 5	Douglas County	OR	Bruce B. Stamp	1990	181
125 1/8	18 5/8 18 4/8	15 3/8	5 5	Lane County	OR	Gary Johnston	2001	182
125 0/8	18 5/8 17 2/8	14 4/8	4 4	Jackson County	OR	Robert J. Jensen	1994	183
124 7/8	19 2/8 19 2/8	14 1/8	4 4	Humboldt County	CA	Mike Taylor	1987	184
124 7/8	18 0/8 19 0/8	15 3/8	4 4	Alameda County	CA	Eugene Damron	1988	184
124 7/8	20 0/8 20 2/8	14 3/8	5 4	Jackson County	OR	Robert L. Freeman	1994	184
124 7/8	18 6/8 19 4/8	16 1/8	5 5	Jackson County	OR	Dave Hall	2007	184
124 6/8	18 5/8 17 7/8	15 0/8	5 5	Clackamas County	OR	Rick M. Young	1982	188
124 6/8	20 7/8 19 0/8	16 6/8	4 5	Clackamas County	OR	Joseph Suire	1983	188
124 6/8	20 2/8 19 6/8	14 4/8	5 5	Jefferson County	WA	Jeffrey D. Husted	2006	188

277

COLUMBIAN BLACKTAIL DEER (TYPICAL ANTLERS)

Minimum Score 95   Continued

SCORE	LENGTH OF R MAIN BEAM L	INSIDE SPREAD	NUMBER OF R POINTS L	AREA	STATE/ PROVINCE	HUNTER'S NAME	DATE	RANK
124 4/8	22 4/8 22 3/8	20 0/8	5 3	Clackamas County	OR	Glen Berry	1995	191
124 2/8	20 0/8 20 6/8	16 4/8	4 5	Lewis County	WA	Sandy Tyler	1957	192
124 2/8	19 0/8 19 5/8	17 2/8	4 5	Lane County	OR	David Wright Bucknum	1989	192
124 1/8	19 2/8 17 5/8	14 7/8	5 5	San Mateo County	CA	Erik Markegard	2007	194
124 0/8	19 0/8 19 2/8	19 7/8	4 4	Kitsap County	WA	Boyd Edward Shelby, Jr.	1995	195
* 124 0/8	19 7/8 20 5/8	14 4/8	5 5	Lake County	CA	Rich Krug	2007	195
123 7/8	17 3/8 17 4/8	15 1/8	5 5	Siskiyou County	CA	Bill Collinsworth	1983	197
123 7/8	19 0/8 19 5/8	14 3/8	5 5	Marion County	OR	Mike Miller	1996	197
123 6/8	19 5/8 20 0/8	16 2/8	5 5	Lane County	OR	Steve Rogers	1990	199
123 6/8	20 3/8 21 0/8	19 6/8	4 4	Lane County	OR	Bruce Stevens	2007	199
123 5/8	19 0/8 19 0/8	15 1/8	5 5	Lewis County	WA	Bob Eisele	1991	201
123 5/8	21 6/8 22 1/8	18 1/8	5 4	King County	WA	Kelly McGuinness	1992	201
123 5/8	19 7/8 20 4/8	16 5/8	4 4	Jackson County	OR	Dave Cox	2004	201
123 5/8	20 4/8 20 1/8	15 3/8	4 4	Linn County	OR	Betty Weidenhaft	2005	201
123 5/8	20 6/8 20 6/8	17 3/8	5 5	Clackamas County	OR	Jordon Frost	2006	201
123 5/8	21 1/8 20 7/8	15 5/8	4 4	Humboldt County	CA	Jared Schmidt	2008	201
123 4/8	21 3/8 21 7/8	16 2/8	4 4	Thurston County	WA	Al Kowalski	1978	207
123 4/8	19 0/8 20 0/8	14 4/8	4 5	Lewis County	WA	Randal E. White	1990	207
123 4/8	19 0/8 19 6/8	15 2/8	6 4	Linn County	OR	Tad Jones	1993	207
123 3/8	18 6/8 19 1/8	17 3/8	5 5	Trinity County	CA	Glen S. Ceccon	1987	210
123 3/8	18 7/8 18 6/8	15 3/8	5 4	Humboldt County	CA	Lou Kindred	2000	210
123 2/8	21 4/8 21 3/8	16 6/8	4 5	Linn County	OR	Daniel L. Sommers	1999	212
123 1/8	20 0/8 20 3/8	16 1/8	5 6	Trinity County	CA	Gary Mayberry	1968	213
123 1/8	18 1/8 18 5/8	18 6/8	5 4	Lake County	CA	Will Willis	1983	213
* 123 1/8	20 0/8 19 1/8	16 2/8	5 7	Mendocino County	CA	Butch Carley	2009	213
123 0/8	20 0/8 21 0/8	14 4/8	6 5	Klickitat County	WA	Larry Ramsey	1977	216
123 0/8	18 6/8 18 7/8	14 6/8	6 6	Jackson County	OR	Larry Frost	1984	216
123 0/8	21 0/8 20 6/8	15 0/8	5 5	Clackamas County	OR	Alan M. Taylor	1991	216
123 0/8	19 1/8 19 2/8	14 0/8	5 5	Jefferson County	WA	David Neault	1996	216
123 0/8	18 5/8 18 4/8	14 4/8	4 5	Humboldt County	CA	Matthew McBride	2007	216
122 7/8	19 1/8 20 4/8	16 1/8	4 4	Trinity County	CA	Loran G. August	1981	221
122 7/8	19 5/8 19 4/8	17 1/8	4 4	Clackamas County	OR	Ryan Farner	2004	221
122 7/8	19 4/8 19 5/8	16 1/8	4 5	Skamania County	WA	Adam Burhop	2005	221
122 6/8	16 7/8 17 5/8	12 4/8	5 5	Lane County	OR	Bob Hayes	2007	224
122 5/8	17 7/8 18 1/8	15 3/8	5 4	Trinity County	CA	Ted Lohse	1985	225
122 5/8	19 0/8 19 1/8	15 1/8	5 4	Mendocino County	CA	Mark Masamori	1992	225
122 5/8	19 2/8 19 5/8	15 1/8	4 4	Linn County	OR	Mark Penninger	1993	225
122 3/8	19 1/8 18 6/8	17 1/8	6 6	Josephine County	OR	Grant McCarty	1994	228
122 1/8	19 5/8 19 5/8	17 4/8	5 6	Jackson County	OR	Richard G. Speer	1965	229
122 0/8	19 7/8 20 4/8	15 6/8	4 4	Contra Costa County	CA	Donald M. Graves	1990	230
122 0/8	18 6/8 18 5/8	14 2/8	5 5	Alameda County	CA	Jeff A. Dolin	1997	230
122 0/8	17 3/8 19 1/8	14 6/8	5 5	Linn County	OR	Lark Weidenhaft	2004	230
122 0/8	19 1/8 19 3/8	15 7/8	5 6	Benton County	OR	Mike Joos	2004	230
122 0/8	20 2/8 20 3/8	18 4/8	4 4	Grays Harbor County	WA	Mike Adkins	2004	230
121 7/8	18 7/8 19 7/8	13 7/8	5 6	Yamhill County	OR	David Foster	1983	235
121 7/8	20 5/8 20 6/8	15 7/8	5 5	Lewis County	WA	Robert E. Hill	1988	235
121 7/8	18 2/8 19 2/8	14 3/8	5 6	Linn County	OR	Daniel L. Sommers	2000	235
121 6/8	20 4/8 20 1/8	20 0/8	4 5	Glenn County	CA	Neil R. Cotter	2004	238
121 5/8	19 3/8 19 4/8	15 2/8	6 6	Josephine County	OR	Robert Lee Welch	2007	239
121 4/8	20 6/8 20 5/8	17 4/8	5 4	Lane County	OR	Bradley M. Dorsing	1991	240
121 4/8	17 7/8 16 5/8	15 0/8	4 4	Linn County	OR	Richard L. Rounds	1991	240
121 4/8	19 4/8 19 2/8	16 0/8	5 5	Douglas County	OR	James B. Howell	2007	240
121 3/8	15 5/8 15 2/8	14 0/8	5 5	Humboldt County	CA	Doug Walker	1965	243
121 2/8	22 4/8 22 4/8	22 2/8	4 4	Humboldt County	CA	Arthur Cain	1991	244
121 1/8	20 3/8 20 6/8	18 2/8	4 3	Yamhill County	OR	Ray Kelton	1981	245
121 0/8	18 0/8 17 0/8	14 4/8	5 5	Benton County	OR	Larry D. Jones	1966	246
121 0/8	19 0/8 19 2/8	16 0/8	5 5	Clackamas County	OR	Larry Bowman	1987	246
121 0/8	21 0/8 20 6/8	14 4/8	5 4	Glenn County	CA	David W. Rickert II	2002	246
121 0/8	19 3/8 19 0/8	14 6/8	4 6	Jackson County	OR	Dave Hall	2006	246
120 7/8	21 3/8 22 3/8	16 0/8	4 4	King County	WA	Russell Bogart	2005	250
120 6/8	18 5/8 19 0/8	15 4/8	5 5	Humboldt County	CA	Joe Henry	1980	251
120 6/8	20 0/8 19 0/8	18 2/8	5 3	Linn County	OR	Jim R. Brown	1987	251
120 6/8	22 0/8 20 7/8	16 2/8	4 4	Lane County	OR	T. J. Thrasher	2009	251
120 5/8	22 1/8 22 4/8	18 7/8	4 3	Glenn County	CA	Neil Cotter	2007	254
120 4/8	20 1/8 19 4/8	17 0/8	4 4	Mendocino County	CA	Brenda Carley	2008	255
120 3/8	17 1/8 18 1/8	12 7/8	5 5	Santa Cruz County	CA	Douglas G. Bonetti	1987	256
120 3/8	19 2/8 18 7/8	18 1/8	6 6	Glenn County	CA	Jim Alves	1987	256
120 3/8	20 5/8 21 1/8	14 2/8	5 6	Linn County	OR	Bob Sartini	1997	256
120 2/8	21 2/8 20 3/8	17 1/8	5 5	Linn County	OR	Steve L. Winterstein	1991	259
120 2/8	18 5/8 18 2/8	14 4/8	4 4	Lane County	OR	Roberta F. Tucker	2000	259
120 1/8	18 3/8 18 4/8	15 5/8	5 5	Lane County	OR	Dale Drilling	1990	261
120 0/8	21 4/8 22 0/8	19 6/8	4 4	Marion County	OR	Norman D. Arnold	1992	262
120 0/8	20 5/8 20 4/8	19 4/8	4 4	Lane County	OR	Keith Julien	1996	262
119 7/8	21 5/8 21 4/8	15 3/8	3 4	Shasta County	CA	G. Fred Asbell	2002	264
119 7/8	18 6/8 19 6/8	15 3/8	4 5	Skagit County	WA	Brant Hunger	2003	264
119 6/8	20 0/8 20 3/8	16 2/8	4 4	Pacific County	WA	John Higgins	1973	266
119 5/8	20 2/8 20 0/8	16 1/8	5 5	Marion County	OR	Ronald A. Bersin	1994	267
119 4/8	20 5/8 20 4/8	16 2/8	5 4	Mendocino County	CA	Edward W. Moore	1989	268
119 4/8	21 0/8 20 1/8	17 4/8	4 4	Chilliwack	BC	Terry Riffin	2008	268
119 3/8	20 4/8 20 2/8	16 1/8	5 6	Mount Washington	BC	Harald Dittkowski	2008	270
119 2/8	17 5/8 17 7/8	16 7/8	5 6	Snohomish County	WA	John Thomas	2006	271
119 0/8	20 6/8 19 2/8	15 6/8	5 5	Kitsap County	WA	Bob Devine	1986	272
119 0/8	20 3/8 19 5/8	19 0/8	5 4	Mendocino County	CA	Matt Burke	1996	272
119 0/8	20 0/8 18 2/8	13 6/8	4 5	King County	WA	Wade Bogart, Jr.	2005	272
118 7/8	18 2/8 17 7/8	16 4/8	7 6	Mendocino County	CA	Butch Carley	2008	275
118 6/8	20 4/8 20 2/8	14 6/8	4 5	Skamania County	WA	Frank Adkins	1967	276
118 6/8	18 4/8 17 7/8	14 4/8	4 4	Santa Clara County	CA	Eugene Damron	1987	276
* 118 6/8	21 0/8 20 5/8	18 6/8	4 3	King County	WA	Wade Bogart, Jr.	2006	276
118 5/8	19 0/8 19 5/8	19 5/8	4 4	Sonoma County	CA	Paul Fiedorek	1987	279
118 4/8	20 3/8 19 7/8	19 2/8	4 4	Slesse Creek	BC	Ken Davidson	1987	280
118 4/8	20 0/8 20 3/8	14 4/8	4 4	Lincoln County	OR	Terry Smith	1992	280
118 4/8	20 6/8 19 4/8	14 0/8	5 5	Lane County	OR	Cameron Hanes	1994	280
118 4/8	18 1/8 18 2/8	17 0/8	5 5	Kitsap County	WA	Boyd E. Shelby, Jr.	1997	280
118 4/8	19 4/8 18 7/8	16 4/8	5 5	Mendocino County	CA	Gary Island	2003	280
118 2/8	18 2/8 18 7/8	14 2/8	5 5	Linn County	OR	Kevin Christopher	1994	285

278

COLUMBIAN BLACKTAIL DEER (TYPICAL ANTLERS)

Minimum Score 95 Continued

SCORE	LENGTH OF R MAIN BEAM L	INSIDE SPREAD	NUMBER OF R POINTS L	AREA	STATE/PROVINCE	HUNTER'S NAME	DATE	RANK
118 2/8	21 6/8 20 2/8	19 6/8	4 4	Skamania County	WA	Kenneth R. Arveson, Jr.	2005	285
118 1/8	17 3/8 17 6/8	13 7/8	5 4	Lane County	OR	Ron Hartman	2003	287
118 0/8	18 3/8 19 2/8	15 4/8	4 4	Pierce County	WA	Danny Law	2007	288
117 7/8	18 0/8 18 1/8	15 7/8	5 4	Benton County	OR	Chuck Warner	1992	289
117 6/8	19 4/8 18 4/8	14 2/8	4 5	Island County	WA	Robin Brigge	1996	290
117 5/8	18 3/8 18 4/8	17 1/8	5 5	Jackson County	OR	Dan Thoren	2001	291
117 5/8	18 5/8 19 1/8	15 5/8	4 4	Linn County	OR	Robert G. Irving	2002	291
117 4/8	18 0/8 18 2/8	14 1/8	5 4	Benton County	OR	Chris Reed	1970	293
117 4/8	16 5/8 16 5/8	15 2/8	5 5	Lincoln County	OR	Bruce G. Wales	1992	293
117 4/8	18 4/8 18 4/8	15 6/8	4 4	Sonoma County	CA	Jerry Maytum	1994	293
117 3/8	18 5/8 19 4/8	15 1/8	4 4	Jackson County	OR	Duane A. Brentano	1972	296
117 3/8	18 1/8 18 3/8	16 3/8	4 4	Humboldt County	CA	Dennis A. McClelland	1989	296
117 3/8	18 3/8 19 7/8	16 3/8	4 4	Lincoln County	OR	Dianna Rorie	1991	296
117 2/8	18 3/8 18 6/8	13 2/8	5 4	Clackamas County	OR	Dan Sandberg	1992	299
* 117 2/8	19 3/8 18 6/8	17 4/8	4 5	Trinity County	CA	Joseph Templeton	2009	299
117 1/8	20 1/8 19 1/8	18 5/8	4 4	Polk County	OR	Eric Haines	2003	301
117 0/8	17 0/8 17 4/8	16 4/8	5 5	Lane County	OR	Brad Dorsing	1992	302
117 0/8	18 3/8 18 4/8	18 4/8	5 5	Mendocino County	CA	Darin Lake	2001	302
117 0/8	19 3/8 18 6/8	15 6/8	4 4	Benton County	OR	Jim Nielsen	2004	302
116 7/8	18 7/8 18 4/8	14 5/8	5 5	Jackson County	OR	David Shanklin	1985	305
116 7/8	18 6/8 18 2/8	13 7/8	5 5	Kitsap County	WA	Don D. Axtman	1990	305
116 7/8	20 7/8 20 1/8	18 7/8	5 5	Mendocino County	CA	Butch Carley	2005	305
116 5/8	19 5/8 20 3/8	12 5/8	4 5	Pacific County	WA	Smokey Crews	1969	308
116 5/8	20 1/8 20 7/8	17 3/8	4 4	Lincoln County	OR	Fred Rorie	1990	308
116 5/8	20 4/8 21 2/8	19 1/8	4 4	Snohomish County	WA	Jerry Solie	1995	308
116 4/8	17 2/8 18 2/8	16 0/8	5 5	Douglas County	OR	Dean A. Bright	2006	311
116 4/8	18 3/8 17 2/8	13 6/8	5 5	Black Creek	BC	Chantelle Bartsch	2007	311
116 3/8	16 4/8 16 4/8	14 5/8	5 5	Mission	BC	Albert Klimmer	1994	313
116 3/8	20 0/8 20 1/8	18 6/8	5 4	Humboldt County	CA	Robert C. Gregory	1996	313
116 2/8	18 7/8 19 7/8	19 0/8	4 4	Jackson County	OR	Ray Gibson	1962	315
116 2/8	18 6/8 18 4/8	16 6/8	5 5	Trinity County	CA	Mike Lindley	1983	315
116 2/8	17 4/8 17 2/8	14 0/8	5 4	Clackamas County	OR	W. Troy Stevens	1988	315
116 1/8	19 0/8 19 4/8	15 3/8	5 4	King County	WA	John Martin	1983	318
116 0/8	18 1/8 16 7/8	17 6/8	5 5	Jackson County	OR	Billy Mathews	1996	319
116 0/8	19 0/8 19 1/8	17 0/8	5 5	Kitsap County	WA	Neal Knudson	2000	319
115 6/8	19 6/8 19 6/8	16 6/8	5 5	Clackamas County	OR	Jack Smith	1981	321
115 6/8	19 2/8 18 2/8	18 0/8	5 5	Siskiyou County	CA	Fred Searle	1983	321
115 6/8	22 0/8 22 3/8	15 0/8	4 5	Benton County	OR	Richard Rowen	1994	321
* 115 6/8	19 4/8 19 5/8	14 0/8	5 4	Benton County	OR	Brian Donne	2009	321
115 5/8	17 0/8 17 1/8	14 5/8	5 5	Polk County	OR	Randy Gunn	1981	325
115 5/8	17 4/8 17 4/8	13 7/8	5 5	Siskiyou County	CA	Mike Garretson	1981	325
115 4/8	22 2/8 21 7/8	19 2/8	5 3	Lane County	OR	Ken Holland	1988	327
115 4/8	18 5/8 16 7/8	14 4/8	6 4	Mendocino County	CA	Butch Carley	2008	327
* 115 3/8	19 7/8 20 0/8	14 1/8	5 4	Mason County	WA	Corey L. McCullough	2008	329
115 2/8	19 4/8 19 4/8	16 2/8	4 4	Humboldt County	CA	J. E. Grundman	1963	330
115 2/8	16 6/8 16 4/8	15 4/8	5 5	Douglas County	OR	Kevin Dicke	1989	330
115 1/8	16 6/8 16 3/8	15 7/8	5 5	Sumas Mtn.	BC	Peter L. Halbig	1985	332
115 1/8	17 4/8 18 0/8	14 3/8	5 4	Marion County	OR	Ronald J. Miller	1989	332
115 1/8	18 7/8 18 5/8	18 5/8	4 5	Sonoma County	CA	Steve Wines	2001	332
115 1/8	18 7/8 18 4/8	15 2/8	4 5	Coos County	OR	Steve Wilson	2004	332
115 0/8	21 2/8 21 0/8	17 1/8	6 4	Marion County	OR	Chuck Lynde	1989	336
115 0/8	20 6/8 21 5/8	20 4/8	4 4	Mendocino County	CA	Doug Burgard	1995	336
114 7/8	20 6/8 20 4/8	18 7/8	4 4	Trinity County	CA	David E. Evanow	2004	338
114 7/8	18 4/8 18 4/8	14 7/8	4 4	Clackamas County	OR	Dan Ellis	2006	338
* 114 6/8	18 2/8 17 4/8	15 0/8	5 5	Lane County	OR	Debra A. Warren	2007	340
114 4/8	17 1/8 17 6/8	19 4/8	4 4	Clackamas County	OR	Darrell J. Scheffer	1995	341
114 4/8	18 2/8 18 2/8	17 6/8	4 4	Jackson County	OR	Jason Harvey	2000	341
114 4/8	18 2/8 18 7/8	12 2/8	4 4	Alameda County	CA	Peter S. Wilcox	2003	341
114 3/8	22 4/8 21 3/8	19 1/8	3 3	Pierce County	WA	Erik Ecklund	2002	344
114 3/8	18 0/8 17 7/8	14 7/8	5 5	Mendocino County	CA	Jamie Scotto	2009	344
114 2/8	20 5/8 20 3/8	13 2/8	4 3	Mendocino County	CA	Robert E. Chapman	2002	346
114 1/8	20 1/8 19 3/8	15 5/8	5 5	Kitsap County	WA	Boyd Shelby	1989	347
114 1/8	19 7/8 19 2/8	16 5/8	6 4	Clackamas County	OR	Jim E. Bolender	2005	347
114 0/8	17 3/8 16 6/8	16 0/8	5 4	Clackamas County	OR	Dave Showerman	1982	349
113 7/8	18 3/8 19 3/8	11 0/8	4 6	Siskiyou County	CA	William J. Bagdasarian	1993	350
113 7/8	17 6/8 17 2/8	14 3/8	6 4	Lane County	OR	Cameron Hanes	1994	350
113 6/8	17 3/8 15 6/8	15 0/8	5 5	Benton County	OR	Gregory M. McHuron	1966	352
113 5/8	18 7/8 19 1/8	18 3/8	4 4	Columbia County	OR	Cory Miller	1995	353
113 5/8	18 3/8 19 1/8	14 7/8	4 5	Mission	BC	Sheldon Danyliuk	2007	353
113 4/8	18 1/8 17 5/8	15 2/8	4 4	Mendocino County	CA	Jeff S. Spangler	1982	355
113 4/8	19 2/8 19 2/8	19 0/8	4 5	Linn County	OR	John Stone	1986	355
113 4/8	19 0/8 19 3/8	20 3/8	5 5	Sonoma County	CA	Jerry Giovannoni	1994	355
113 4/8	16 6/8 17 1/8	14 2/8	5 5	Linn County	OR	Felix Aaron Lafond	2006	355
113 3/8	19 2/8 18 1/8	17 1/8	4 4	Whatcom County	WA	Chad Brisky	2007	359
113 3/8	19 6/8 19 0/8	16 7/8	4 4	Glenn County	CA	Matt Battiato	2009	359
113 2/8	18 2/8 17 5/8	16 0/8	4 4	King County	WA	Vick Stevens	1984	361
113 2/8	17 0/8 16 7/8	12 2/8	4 4	Lane County	OR	Neil Summers	1991	361
113 0/8	17 2/8 17 3/8	13 4/8	5 5	Lewis County	WA	Don Kennedy	1989	363
113 0/8	19 5/8 20 1/8	17 0/8	4 4	Trinity County	CA	Dennis Dunn	2001	363
112 7/8	19 1/8 17 6/8	14 1/8	4 5	Skagit County	WA	J. B. Bright	1986	365
112 7/8	18 3/8 19 1/8	21 2/8	4 3	King County	WA	Darin Evans Brandt	1995	365
112 7/8	18 4/8 18 4/8	14 1/8	5 5	Lewis County	WA	Matt Turner	2006	365
112 7/8	17 3/8 16 7/8	12 1/8	5 5	Benton County	OR	Stanley Miles	2007	365
112 6/8	18 1/8 16 6/8	16 0/8	4 4	Mendocino County	CA	George Eichman	2007	369
112 5/8	21 2/8 20 4/8	14 1/8	5 5	King County	WA	Greg Tedlund	1984	370
112 5/8	18 2/8 18 5/8	13 5/8	5 5	Yamhill County	OR	Dean A. McMullen	1992	370
112 5/8	21 0/8 20 2/8	16 7/8	3 4	Pierce County	WA	Brandon J. White	1997	370
112 4/8	16 0/8 15 1/8	13 4/8	5 5	Trinity County	CA	Dennis Schroer	1982	373
112 4/8	18 6/8 17 6/8	14 2/8	5 5	Lane County	OR	Steve Rogers	1989	373
112 4/8	21 7/8 21 2/8	21 0/8	4 3	Contra Costa County	CA	John Howard	2008	373
112 3/8	16 7/8 16 3/8	13 7/8	5 5	Snohomish County	WA	Jack Davis	1975	376
112 3/8	17 4/8 19 2/8	13 6/8	4 5	Douglas County	OR	Ken French	1980	376
112 3/8	20 5/8 15 7/8	18 1/8	5 5	Lane County	OR	Chad T. Montgomery	1994	376
112 3/8	19 1/8 20 1/8	13 7/8	8 4	Trinity County	CA	Vince Elliott	2002	376
112 2/8	18 5/8 19 1/8	15 2/8	4 4	Pacific County	WA	Leon Poindexter	1968	380

COLUMBIAN BLACKTAIL DEER (TYPICAL ANTLERS)

Minimum Score 95 Continued

SCORE	LENGTH OF R MAIN BEAM L		INSIDE SPREAD	NUMBER OF R POINTS L		AREA	STATE/ PROVINCE	HUNTER'S NAME	DATE	RANK
112 2/8	19 2/8	19 1/8	18 0/8	4	4	Sonoma County	CA	William P. Morehead	2000	380
112 1/8	17 1/8	17 4/8	13 3/8	5	5	Benton County	OR	Gary Nyden	1986	382
112 0/8	18 4/8	19 2/8	16 4/8	4	4	Lane County	OR	Ken Kalinowski	1988	383
112 0/8	17 7/8	16 4/8	15 7/8	6	5	Island County	WA	Adam Caba	2003	383
112 0/8	19 3/8	19 4/8	12 2/8	4	4	Linn County	OR	Daniel L. Sommers	2004	383
111 7/8	17 7/8	17 0/8	14 5/8	4	4	Pacific County	WA	Smokey Crews	1967	386
111 7/8	17 7/8	19 1/8	13 1/8	4	4	Lane County	OR	Jonathan Dale Armstrong	2001	386
111 5/8	20 0/8	19 4/8	15 5/8	5	5	Pierce County	WA	Randy Cole	1989	388
111 5/8	16 4/8	15 5/8	12 3/8	5	5	Lincoln County	OR	Jeffrey D. Messmer	1989	388
111 5/8	17 7/8	18 4/8	14 1/8	5	5	Lane County	OR	Gary D. Nyden	1994	388
111 3/8	16 0/8	17 3/8	17 4/8	5	4	Linn County	OR	Chuck Warner	1985	391
111 3/8	19 5/8	19 6/8	16 3/8	5	4	Lane County	OR	David Chapman	1986	391
111 2/8	21 1/8	20 5/8	15 6/8	3	6	Lane County	OR	Brad Dorsing	1994	393
111 2/8	17 6/8	18 2/8	14 0/8	4	5	Abbotsford	BC	Brad Siemens	1998	393
* 111 2/8	15 5/8	17 6/8	17 2/8	4	3	Sonoma County	CA	Mike Hattam	2009	393
111 0/8	19 2/8	18 4/8	14 4/8	4	3	Skagit County	WA	Sam Ingram	1988	396
111 0/8	19 7/8	19 6/8	15 2/8	3	3	King County	WA	Clint W. Powell	1989	396
111 0/8	18 3/8	18 2/8	14 7/8	5	5	Lane County	OR	Stuart Johnson	1994	396
111 0/8	21 0/8	20 6/8	17 6/8	4	5	Mendocino County	CA	Mark Masamori	1997	396
110 7/8	18 3/8	17 0/8	16 3/8	4	4	Jackson County	OR	Dale K. Marcy	1966	400
110 7/8	17 5/8	18 3/8	14 5/8	4	5	Marion County	OR	David Conway	1991	400
110 6/8	18 4/8	17 7/8	17 0/8	4	4	Del Norte County	CA	Michael Penn	1979	402
110 6/8	20 6/8	21 5/8	19 4/8	3	3	Contra Costa County	CA	Richard L. Westervelt	1987	402
110 6/8	21 1/8	21 4/8	22 0/8	2	2	Mendocino County	CA	Ken Bilstein	1995	402
110 5/8	19 7/8	20 3/8	13 4/8	4	6	Jackson County	OR	Dr. G. Scott Jennings	1979	405
110 4/8	17 1/8	17 3/8	13 6/8	4	4	Clark County	WA	Larry D. Nahrstedt	1968	406
110 4/8	17 0/8	18 7/8	17 4/8	4	4	Marin County	CA	Howard C. Gold	1976	406
110 4/8	18 4/8	18 4/8	15 6/8	4	4	Pierce County	WA	Greg Paige	1990	406
110 4/8	19 1/8	19 3/8	14 4/8	5	4	Linn County	OR	Thomas K. Powell	2003	406
110 3/8	16 1/8	15 1/8	15 7/8	5	5	Wild Deer Lake	BC	Guy Anttila	1970	410
110 3/8	19 3/8	20 0/8	13 6/8	6	5	North Vancouver	BC	Fred Day	1970	410
110 3/8	17 7/8	17 3/8	14 7/8	4	4	Mendocino County	CA	Wayne Wood	2008	410
110 2/8	19 6/8	20 0/8	17 4/8	5	5	Lane County	OR	Richard M. Cook	1982	413
110 2/8	21 0/8	21 0/8	16 2/8	3	3	Humboldt County	CA	John D. "Jack" Frost	2002	413
110 2/8	19 4/8	19 1/8	18 0/8	3	3	Lane County	OR	Steve Osterholzer	2003	413
110 1/8	21 4/8	21 0/8	14 7/8	4	3	Linn County	OR	Dennis Bernard	1999	416
110 0/8	17 3/8	18 1/8	17 2/8	3	4	Sonoma County	CA	Ken Cook	1998	417
109 7/8	22 0/8	21 3/8	14 5/8	5	5	Linn County	OR	Steve Gilbert	1982	418
109 6/8	21 1/8	20 7/8	16 4/8	3	4	Lewis County	WA	Barney Johnson	1974	419
109 6/8	17 4/8	18 2/8	18 2/8	4	4	Santa Cruz County	CA	Robert Alan Nottingham	1992	419
109 6/8	18 0/8	19 2/8	14 4/8	4	4	King County	WA	Robert W. Beckham, Jr.	2007	419
109 5/8	20 4/8	19 4/8	15 3/8	5	4	Douglas County	OR	Teddy Rainville	1980	422
109 5/8	19 1/8	21 0/8	14 5/8	3	3	Lake County	CA	Paul W. Farina	1983	422
109 5/8	16 2/8	16 2/8	14 5/8	4	4	Siskiyou County	CA	Ralph Atkinson	1984	422
109 5/8	17 1/8	17 2/8	15 7/8	4	4	Clackamas County	OR	Randy Teeney	1985	422
109 5/8	18 4/8	18 6/8	15 5/8	4	4	Lane County	OR	Wm E. Sweetland	1985	422
109 5/8	21 4/8	19 7/8	19 5/8	3	3	Santa Clara County	CA	Eugene Damron	1991	422
109 5/8	19 3/8	19 6/8	13 3/8	5	5	Trinity County	CA	Michael Chiera	1995	422
109 5/8	19 1/8	18 6/8	18 5/8	4	4	Mendocino County	CA	Gary N. Island	2003	422
109 5/8	17 7/8	17 6/8	13 7/8	4	4	Lake County	CA	Phil Phillips	2006	422
109 4/8	19 6/8	19 7/8	14 2/8	6	5	Pierce County	WA	Don Axtman	1989	431
109 4/8	16 5/8	16 4/8	12 6/8	5	5	Clackamas County	OR	Nick G. Kathrein	1991	431
109 3/8	17 0/8	17 5/8	14 4/8	6	4	Lane County	OR	Mark Klein	1982	433
109 3/8	18 3/8	17 2/8	16 7/8	4	4	Clackamas County	OR	Stanley P. Stagl	1989	433
109 3/8	17 0/8	17 7/8	17 5/8	4	4	Cowlitz County	WA	Tom Heltemes	1990	433
109 3/8	18 3/8	17 0/8	15 1/8	4	3	Alameda County	CA	William Young, Jr. DVM	1991	433
109 3/8	16 2/8	16 2/8	15 1/8	5	5	Siskiyou County	CA	Fred V. Smith	2001	433
109 3/8	19 2/8	20 4/8	19 0/8	5	5	Sonoma County	CA	Mark Bonales	2002	433
109 2/8	17 5/8	16 5/8	14 2/8	5	5	Lane County	OR	Brandy Knight	1991	439
* 109 2/8	20 0/8	19 6/8	17 2/8	4	4	Clackamas County	OR	Dennis P. Turin	2008	439
109 1/8	19 7/8	19 7/8	14 1/8	5	4	Lewis County	WA	Glen Marquis	1990	441
109 1/8	19 0/8	19 0/8	15 3/8	4	4	Tehama County	CA	Tom Devlin	2002	441
109 0/8	20 0/8	20 0/8	15 6/8	4	3	Josephine County	OR	Sam Burten	1987	443
109 0/8	18 0/8	18 4/8	15 4/8	4	4	Humboldt County	CA	John Roley	1996	443
109 0/8	19 2/8	19 1/8	17 0/8	4	4	Alameda County	CA	Michael McCall	2007	443
108 7/8	17 6/8	19 1/8	13 7/8	5	5	Jackson County	OR	Joe Williamson	1963	446
108 7/8	16 7/8	17 0/8	13 5/8	5	5	Josephine County	OR	Michael Penn	1983	446
108 7/8	21 0/8	19 2/8	11 5/8	5	4	Pierce County	WA	Daniel Hoaas	2006	446
108 6/8	20 2/8	20 0/8	20 4/8	3	3	Linn County	OR	Gary S. Solberg	1994	449
108 5/8	19 2/8	18 4/8	16 3/8	3	3	Douglas County	OR	Rick Gabbard	1984	450
108 5/8	17 7/8	17 7/8	14 5/8	5	5	Lewis County	WA	Heath Hansen	2004	450
108 5/8	18 5/8	18 7/8	13 7/8	4	4	Lane County	OR	Paul M. Burrell	2004	450
108 4/8	16 1/8	16 2/8	11 6/8	5	5	Clackamas County	OR	Ed Franzen	1985	453
108 4/8	18 0/8	17 7/8	16 2/8	5	4	Lane County	OR	Jim Howell	1988	453
108 3/8	19 1/8	19 2/8	13 1/8	4	3	Mendocino County	CA	Gaylen Kessel	1988	455
108 3/8	18 3/8	18 4/8	17 3/8	5	3	Cowlitz County	WA	Daren Dahlman	2004	455
108 3/8	15 2/8	16 2/8	14 1/8	5	5	Benton County	OR	Steve Clark	2007	455
108 1/8	19 1/8	18 4/8	15 2/8	6	6	Skagit County	WA	Charles Kager	1988	458
108 1/8	18 0/8	17 5/8	17 5/8	4	4	Sonoma County	CA	Robert Larson	1992	458
108 1/8	21 2/8	19 2/8	12 6/8	5	5	King County	WA	Thomas E. Pugmire	1992	458
* 108 1/8	19 0/8	20 0/8	15 5/8	5	4	Trinity County	CA	Roy K. Keefer	2006	458
108 0/8	18 3/8	19 5/8	16 0/8	4	4	Trinity County	CA	Michael Hopper	1989	462
108 0/8	18 0/8	17 2/8	16 4/8	4	5	Lane County	OR	Dwight Schuh	1989	462
108 0/8	16 6/8	18 4/8	12 7/8	6	4	Douglas County	OR	Bruce B. Stamp	1994	462
108 0/8	16 4/8	17 0/8	12 4/8	5	5	Mendocino County	CA	Gary N. Island	2002	462
108 0/8	18 6/8	18 6/8	16 0/8	5	4	Jackson County	OR	David E. Evanow	2002	462
107 7/8	17 2/8	17 7/8	16 1/8	4	4	Tehama County	CA	Ernie Owen	1992	467
107 7/8	20 6/8	20 7/8	19 7/8	3	3	Sonoma County	CA	Michael Bradeen	1992	467
107 7/8	17 2/8	17 5/8	17 3/8	4	4	Skamania County	WA	Larry Bryan Skaar	2006	467
107 6/8	18 3/8	18 4/8	19 3/8	3	4	Trinity County	CA	Dennis Alan Betts	1980	470
107 6/8	17 2/8	17 4/8	13 0/8	4	3	Lane County	OR	James A. Conway	1988	470
107 6/8	18 1/8	18 0/8	15 4/8	4	4	Douglas County	OR	Joe Cordonier	1989	470
107 5/8	19 2/8	18 5/8	14 1/8	5	4	Clackamas County	OR	Bob Manley	1982	473
107 5/8	21 2/8	20 2/8	16 7/8	3	3	Lane County	OR	Rick Willhite	1993	473
107 5/8	16 6/8	17 3/8	13 3/8	5	4	Chilliwack	BC	Terrance Riffin	2009	473

280

COLUMBIAN BLACKTAIL DEER (TYPICAL ANTLERS)

Minimum Score 95   Continued

SCORE	LENGTH OF R MAIN BEAM L	INSIDE SPREAD	NUMBER OF R POINTS L	AREA	STATE/ PROVINCE	HUNTER'S NAME	DATE	RANK
107 4/8	21 4/8 22 3/8	19 4/8	2 2	Trinity County	CA	John R. Sample	1989	476
107 4/8	17 7/8 18 6/8	14 1/8	5 5	Lane County	OR	Tad Jones	1995	476
107 4/8	17 0/8 17 4/8	14 4/8	5 5	Sooke	BC	Scott Eddy	2004	476
107 3/8	18 2/8 19 0/8	17 5/8	4 4	Lane County	OR	Cameron Hanes	1993	479
107 3/8	18 2/8 19 2/8	12 3/8	5 5	Lewis County	WA	Michael E. Croft	1997	479
107 2/8	17 5/8 17 5/8	16 0/8	4 4	Mendocino County	CA	Edwin Thomas	1997	481
107 2/8	16 4/8 17 7/8	13 6/8	5 5	Douglas County	OR	Jason Saylor	2001	481
107 2/8	18 2/8 19 0/8	13 0/8	4 4	Humboldt County	CA	David E. Evanow	2005	481
107 1/8	15 7/8 15 4/8	13 7/8	4 4	Lincoln County	OR	Ray Kelton	1982	484
107 1/8	19 3/8 19 3/8	17 5/8	3 4	Clackamas County	OR	Guy P. Hurlbert	1995	484
107 0/8	17 5/8 16 7/8	12 4/8	5 5	Lane County	OR	Neil Summers	1990	486
107 0/8	17 6/8 17 0/8	16 2/8	4 5	Douglas County	OR	Charles Hunt	2005	486
106 7/8	18 3/8 18 2/8	16 3/8	4 3	Skamania County	WA	Steve Shipp	1984	488
106 7/8	18 3/8 19 1/8	13 3/8	4 4	King County	WA	Mike Adkins	1995	488
106 7/8	18 0/8 18 4/8	14 7/8	5 4	Saltspring Island	BC	Greg Knoblauch	2000	488
106 6/8	19 3/8 20 0/8	19 6/8	4 3	Contra Costa County	CA	Frank Sanders	1990	491
106 6/8	17 6/8 17 4/8	16 4/8	4 4	Mendocino County	CA	Joseph N. Fowles	1995	491
106 6/8	18 1/8 19 4/8	15 0/8	5 5	Lane County	OR	Jesse Lee Cannon	2001	491
106 6/8	19 0/8 18 4/8	15 2/8	4 4	Trinity County	CA	Allyn Ladd	2010	491
106 5/8	18 2/8 18 7/8	18 1/8	4 4	Pierce County	WA	Kenneth Villines	1996	495
106 5/8	15 1/8 15 0/8	15 7/8	5 5	Sonoma County	CA	Mike Camp	2002	495
106 4/8	19 3/8 19 6/8	14 6/8	4 5	Clackamas County	OR	Brandon C. Ek	2000	497
106 4/8	17 1/8 18 2/8	12 4/8	5 5	Lane County	OR	Bob Amos	2007	497
* 106 4/8	18 3/8 17 3/8	14 4/8	3 3	Mendocino County	CA	Nicholas Scotto	2009	497
106 3/8	17 6/8 17 0/8	14 1/8	4 5	Pierce County	WA	Kenneth D. Villines	1995	500
106 2/8	17 1/8 16 3/8	13 6/8	5 4	Lewis County	WA	Mike Mussman	1984	501
106 1/8	19 4/8 19 0/8	12 7/8	3 4	Trinity County	CA	Mike Lindley	1981	502
106 1/8	19 5/8 20 0/8	18 5/8	4 3	Jackson County	OR	Michael Moore	2007	502
106 0/8	17 4/8 17 6/8	17 7/8	4 5	Trinity County	CA	Chuck Adams	1982	504
106 0/8	17 5/8 17 5/8	14 2/8	4 4	Skamania County	WA	Jeffrey L. Kujala	1984	504
106 0/8	17 6/8 17 7/8	14 6/8	5 5	Lane County	OR	Dan Rogers	1989	504
105 7/8	17 7/8 17 3/8	14 7/8	4 5	Mendocino County	CA	Michael Christensen	1995	507
105 7/8	19 5/8 19 5/8	16 1/8	3 4	Clackamas County	OR	Tim Brown	1999	507
105 7/8	15 2/8 15 0/8	13 5/8	5 5	Sumas Mtn.	BC	Robert Zseder/Alden Abraham	2002	507
105 6/8	19 1/8 19 6/8	19 0/8	5 3	Clackamas County	OR	Dan Ellis	2003	510
105 6/8	17 4/8 18 2/8	16 4/8	4 4	Humboldt County	CA	Edwin L. DeYoung	2007	510
105 5/8	17 5/8 18 5/8	15 7/8	5 5	Cowlitz County	WA	Jay Wall	1994	512
105 5/8	18 5/8 18 4/8	19 6/8	5 5	Trinity County	CA	John R. Sample	1996	512
105 4/8	16 6/8 15 4/8	14 6/8	4 4	Mendocino County	CA	Serge Engurasoff	1998	514
105 4/8	16 6/8 16 0/8	14 6/8	4 4	Sonoma County	CA	Patrick J. Dunlop	1998	514
105 4/8	18 3/8 18 5/8	13 6/8	4 4	Clackamas County	OR	Daniel T. Ellis	2007	514
105 3/8	17 3/8 17 3/8	15 5/8	3 4	Coos County	OR	Gary Scorby	1971	517
105 3/8	19 3/8 19 2/8	15 6/8	7 5	Columbia County	OR	Leo E. Eickhoff	1995	517
105 2/8	15 2/8 14 4/8	11 0/8	5 5	Gambier Island	BC	Scott Spain	1997	519
105 1/8	18 6/8 19 2/8	15 7/8	3 3	Stanislaus County	CA	Harold Arnold	1970	520
105 1/8	18 1/8 18 1/8	18 4/8	3 3	San Mateo County	CA	John Grochowski	1985	520
105 1/8	18 1/8 17 6/8	14 1/8	4 4	Lane County	OR	Dan Schnell	2003	520
105 1/8	20 3/8 19 0/8	16 3/8	4 5	Whatcom County	WA	Aspen Crouter	2006	520
105 0/8	20 1/8 17 4/8	19 4/8	4 3	Mendocino County	CA	Matt Seever	2000	524
104 7/8	18 3/8 19 0/8	13 3/8	3 3	Douglas County	OR	Richard Baumgartner	1994	525
104 6/8	17 3/8 17 2/8	13 6/8	5 4	Coos County	OR	Darryl S. Herndon	1989	526
104 6/8	18 1/8 19 3/8	16 4/8	4 4	Napa County	CA	Glenn R. Elliott	2001	526
104 5/8	16 2/8 16 2/8	12 7/8	4 4	King County	WA	Ken Gettman	1987	528
104 5/8	17 3/8 18 0/8	15 5/8	4 4	Jackson County	OR	Robon Evans	1992	528
104 5/8	16 5/8 17 3/8	11 5/8	4 4	Linn County	OR	Gary Johnston	1992	528
104 5/8	17 4/8 17 0/8	13 1/8	5 5	Clackamas County	OR	Paul Askew	2006	528
104 4/8	16 3/8 17 7/8	15 0/8	4 3	Solano County	CA	Thomas D. Bors	2001	532
104 4/8	16 5/8 16 2/8	13 4/8	4 4	Linn County	OR	Lark Weidenhaft	2001	532
104 3/8	18 5/8 18 3/8	15 3/8	4 4	Polk County	OR	Tim Nolan	1987	534
104 3/8	17 4/8 18 2/8	16 5/8	4 4	Lane County	OR	Cameron Hanes	1990	534
104 3/8	19 7/8 20 0/8	12 1/8	4 4	Alameda County	CA	Wayne Piersol	1993	534
104 2/8	16 4/8 17 0/8	16 2/8	4 4	Lake County	CA	Phil Phillips	1991	537
104 2/8	17 2/8 17 4/8	16 2/8	5 4	Mendocino County	CA	Michael Christensen	1991	537
104 2/8	18 2/8 18 3/8	16 2/8	4 4	Humboldt County	CA	Ricardo Longoria	2008	537
104 1/8	15 4/8 15 6/8	13 3/8	5 5	Clackamas County	OR	Ben Cook	1988	540
104 1/8	21 4/8 21 4/8	18 7/8	5 6	Clackamas County	OR	Jake M. Willer	2001	540
104 1/8	18 2/8 18 4/8	15 7/8	5 3	Trinity County	CA	Carol Kindred	2010	540
104 0/8	18 6/8 21 6/8	15 1/8	5 5	Trinity County	CA	Chuck Adams	1982	543
104 0/8	18 0/8 17 5/8	17 2/8	4 4	Tehama County	CA	Robert Stockton	1993	543
104 0/8	17 3/8 17 4/8	13 0/8	5 5	Benton County	OR	Jeremy French	2001	543
104 0/8	22 4/8 21 6/8	17 6/8	2 2	Mendocino County	CA	Butch E. Carley	2003	543
104 0/8	16 6/8 16 7/8	16 2/8	4 4	Skagit County	WA	Andy Del Nagro	2003	543
104 0/8	17 1/8 17 2/8	13 6/8	4 3	Whatcom County	WA	James Branham	2003	543
103 7/8	18 6/8 19 7/8	16 1/8	3 3	Mendocino County	CA	Archie J. Nesbitt	2003	549
103 7/8	21 4/8 20 6/8	16 5/8	5 3	Mendocino County	CA	J. Dale Main	2006	549
103 6/8	15 7/8 16 4/8	12 2/8	5 5	Linn County	OR	Doug Bashor	1986	551
103 6/8	18 1/8 17 4/8	17 4/8	4 4	Sonoma County	CA	Charles Dunlop	2001	551
103 5/8	17 7/8 18 3/8	15 5/8	3 3	Linn County	OR	Gary Burns	1981	553
103 5/8	17 6/8 18 1/8	14 1/8	4 4	Linn County	OR	Delbert Kurtz	1996	553
103 5/8	18 2/8 17 2/8	12 3/8	4 4	Snohomish County	WA	Jim Frese	2002	553
103 4/8	19 0/8 19 5/8	13 2/8	3 3	Lane County	OR	Randy Cook	1988	556
103 4/8	16 6/8 17 1/8	13 7/8	5 4	Lane County	OR	Neil Summers	1989	556
103 4/8	15 4/8 15 4/8	14 6/8	4 5	Humboldt County	CA	Richie Bland	2001	556
103 3/8	16 7/8 16 6/8	17 0/8	3 4	Sonoma County	CA	Arnie Dado	1986	559
103 3/8	18 6/8 19 3/8	14 5/8	3 5	Trinity County	CA	Rick Duggan	2002	559
103 2/8	17 7/8 17 7/8	15 0/8	4 4	Lewis County	WA	Charles L. Hunt	1990	561
103 2/8	15 7/8 16 0/8	16 3/8	4 4	Polk County	OR	Jon Simonson	1995	561
103 2/8	16 2/8 16 5/8	13 6/8	4 4	Linn County	OR	Daniel L. Sommers	1997	561
103 1/8	18 5/8 18 5/8	18 1/8	3 3	Lake County	CA	Arnie Dado	1992	564
103 0/8	15 5/8 15 0/8	14 0/8	5 5	Mendocino County	CA	Gregg L. Welch	1982	565
103 0/8	19 2/8 19 0/8	14 4/8	5 3	Clark County	WA	W. R. "Rick" Hassler	1988	565
103 0/8	20 1/8 20 0/8	15 6/8	3 2	Tehama County	CA	Gary Shinn	1989	565
103 0/8	16 6/8 17 2/8	12 4/8	4 4	Santa Clara County	CA	Thomas L. Liston	1990	565
103 0/8	18 6/8 18 7/8	16 6/8	3 4	Josephine County	OR	Brain Day	1994	565
103 0/8	17 1/8 18 3/8	13 6/8	4 3	Douglas County	OR	Richard Baumgartner	1995	565

281

COLUMBIAN BLACKTAIL DEER (TYPICAL ANTLERS)

Minimum Score 95   Continued

SCORE	LENGTH OF R MAIN BEAM L	INSIDE SPREAD	NUMBER OF R POINTS L	AREA	STATE/ PROVINCE	HUNTER'S NAME	DATE	RANK
103 0/8	18 4/8 · 18 6/8	15 6/8	5 · 3	Mendocino County	CA	Wil Willis	2001	565
103 0/8	19 7/8 · 19 2/8	18 2/8	3 · 4	Snohomish County	WA	Curtis F. Rutkowski	2002	565
102 7/8	18 5/8 · 18 0/8	14 2/8	4 · 5	Lane County	OR	Larry D. Jones	1997	573
102 7/8	16 7/8 · 17 4/8	13 7/8	4 · 4	Thurston County	WA	Troy E. Gose	2003	573
102 6/8	17 4/8 · 17 4/8	17 4/8	3 · 3	Polk County	OR	Robert L. Ball	1975	575
102 5/8	16 7/8 · 16 6/8	14 5/8	4 · 4	Deschutes County	OR	Steve L. Stilwell	1976	576
102 4/8	18 0/8 · 18 0/8	14 4/8	4 · 3	Mendocino County	CA	Doug Burgard	1995	577
102 4/8	18 1/8 · 19 5/8	16 6/8	4 · 4	Lane County	OR	Bruce Stevens	2005	577
102 4/8	17 5/8 · 17 1/8	16 0/8	5 · 5	Mendocino County	CA	Brenda Carley	2008	577
102 3/8	18 4/8 · 19 1/8	16 5/8	4 · 4	Siskiyou County	CA	Terry Proctor	1988	580
102 3/8	19 4/8 · 18 5/8	17 3/8	5 · 5	Trinity County	CA	Jim Wondzell	2003	580
102 3/8	16 6/8 · 18 6/8	16 3/8	4 · 4	Jackson County	OR	Jim Winjum	2009	580
102 2/8	17 7/8 · 16 5/8	12 0/8	3 · 4	Clackamas County	OR	A. Corey Heath	1980	583
102 2/8	19 7/8 · 19 5/8	15 0/8	3 · 3	Mendocino County	CA	Walter Palmer	2007	583
* 102 2/8	18 6/8 · 17 5/8	14 0/8	4 · 5	Pierce County	WA	Chris Keithley	2010	583
102 0/8	17 2/8 · 17 0/8	13 6/8	4 · 4	Jackson County	OR	George Miller	1966	586
102 0/8	17 3/8 · 16 6/8	13 0/8	5 · 3	Lane County	OR	Bruce Stevens	1995	586
102 0/8	20 4/8 · 18 6/8	15 2/8	4 · 4	Linn County	OR	Lark A. Weidenhaft	2005	586
101 7/8	18 6/8 · 18 4/8	12 1/8	5 · 5	Lane County	OR	Ronald Gardner	2001	589
101 7/8	18 3/8 · 17 3/8	15 3/8	4 · 4	Sonoma County	CA	Jan Perry	2002	589
101 6/8	19 1/8 · 18 4/8	13 6/8	3 · 3	Pierce County	WA	James Tullis	1993	591
101 6/8	18 2/8 · 18 6/8	14 6/8	4 · 3	Josephine County	OR	Thomas J. Hoffman	1994	591
101 6/8	18 3/8 · 19 6/8	15 3/8	5 · 4	Josephine County	OR	Sam Burton	1995	591
101 5/8	17 3/8 · 16 7/8	15 1/8	4 · 4	Siskiyou County	CA	Brent Miller	1998	594
101 5/8	18 5/8 · 17 3/8	15 1/8	3 · 4	Humboldt County	CA	John Garr	2000	594
101 5/8	17 1/8 · 17 2/8	13 1/8	5 · 3	King County	WA	Mike Adkins	2003	594
101 5/8	19 2/8 · 18 2/8	17 7/8	3 · 3	Sonoma County	CA	John C. Martin	2005	594
101 4/8	18 5/8 · 17 5/8	15 1/8	5 · 5	King County	WA	Mike D. Dunham	1987	598
101 4/8	18 5/8 · 19 0/8	15 4/8	3 · 3	Clackamas County	OR	Dennis L. Brown	2005	598
101 3/8	17 0/8 · 17 4/8	15 3/8	4 · 3	Jackson County	OR	Dr. G. Scott Jennings	1959	600
101 3/8	18 7/8 · 18 5/8	18 7/8	2 · 4	Alameda County	CA	Robert Shuttleworth, Jr.	1999	600
101 3/8	15 4/8 · 15 2/8	12 3/8	5 · 3	Tillamook County	OR	Randy Stockwell	2002	600
101 2/8	17 1/8 · 18 2/8	13 4/8	4 · 3	Lane County	OR	Michael J. Fuller	1996	603
101 1/8	18 6/8 · 18 2/8	15 7/8	4 · 4	Skamania County	WA	Lyle Boschee	1998	604
* 101 1/8	19 3/8 · 19 6/8	17 1/8	3 · 3	Sonoma County	CA	Kirk Edgerton	2006	604
101 0/8	13 3/8 · 17 1/8	15 0/8	4 · 5	Lincoln County	OR	Terry W. Smith	1996	606
101 0/8	18 2/8 · 17 0/8	17 6/8	3 · 3	Lane County	OR	Bob Ameen	2004	606
100 7/8	17 1/8 · 17 2/8	14 7/8	4 · 4	Marshall Creek	BC	Ken Scheer	1988	608
100 7/8	17 0/8 · 18 1/8	14 5/8	4 · 4	Island County	WA	Ken Smiley	1998	608
100 6/8	15 6/8 · 15 5/8	15 4/8	4 · 5	Klamath County	OR	Dr. George Miller	1964	610
100 6/8	18 1/8 · 18 0/8	16 2/8	3 · 3	Humboldt County	CA	Steven Tisdale	1993	610
100 6/8	16 2/8 · 16 7/8	12 6/8	4 · 4	Jackson County	OR	Hank Baxter	2006	610
100 5/8	17 0/8 · 17 4/8	13 7/8	5 · 4	Clackamas County	OR	Stanley P. Stagl	1990	613
100 4/8	18 7/8 · 18 3/8	15 4/8	3 · 4	Washington County	OR	Everett A. Proctor	1992	614
100 4/8	17 7/8 · 17 6/8	17 0/8	4 · 4	Sonoma County	CA	Wilfred P. Willis	2000	614
100 4/8	18 0/8 · 18 0/8	16 4/8	2 · 2	Lake County	CA	Phil Phillips	2002	614
100 3/8	17 5/8 · 18 0/8	15 7/8	4 · 4	Sonoma County	CA	Bill Payne	2000	617
100 1/8	16 7/8 · 16 6/8	13 7/8	4 · 4	Douglas County	OR	James F. Rayner	1988	618
100 1/8	18 4/8 · 18 5/8	11 5/8	4 · 5	Lane County	OR	Cameron Hanes	1992	618
100 1/8	16 7/8 · 16 7/8	13 3/8	4 · 4	Lincoln County	OR	Terry W. Smith	1994	618
100 1/8	19 0/8 · 18 5/8	11 5/8	3 · 3	Multnomah County	OR	Marc B. Caldwell	1996	618
100 1/8	17 2/8 · 19 3/8	17 1/8	3 · 3	Mendocino County	CA	Zack Walton	2010	618
100 0/8	18 2/8 · 18 5/8	14 2/8	3 · 4	Kitsap County	WA	Boyd E. Shelby, Jr.	1990	623
99 6/8	20 6/8 · 20 0/8	14 0/8	2 · 2	Pacific County	WA	Robert A. Brown	1965	624
99 6/8	17 1/8 · 17 2/8	14 6/8	5 · 4	Humboldt County	CA	Greg Gottschalk	1990	624
99 6/8	18 3/8 · 18 3/8	16 4/8	4 · 3	Linn County	OR	Keith Julien	1994	624
99 6/8	17 4/8 · 18 1/8	15 0/8	3 · 3	Sonoma County	CA	Ed Fanchin	1998	624
99 5/8	17 3/8 · 18 1/8	12 7/8	4 · 4	Lewis County	WA	Eric H. Ames	1989	628
99 5/8	16 5/8 · 17 0/8	13 7/8	5 · 4	Clackamas County	OR	Tim Streight	1990	628
99 5/8	16 3/8 · 15 0/8	12 1/8	5 · 5	Linn County	OR	Mark A. Schneider	2001	628
99 4/8	19 4/8 · 18 7/8	17 0/8	3 · 2	Solano County	CA	Brian J. Morris	2000	631
99 4/8	19 3/8 · 19 0/8	17 2/8	4 · 4	Trinity County	CA	George Harms	2003	631
* 99 4/8	16 1/8 · 15 4/8	14 2/8	5 · 4	Whatcom County	WA	James L. Branham	2009	631
99 3/8	17 5/8 · 18 0/8	15 1/8	3 · 3	Siskiyou County	CA	Dave S. Semple	1984	634
99 3/8	16 2/8 · 16 0/8	15 1/8	4 · 4	Clark County	WA	Jerry K. Wake	1992	634
99 3/8	17 4/8 · 17 5/8	14 3/8	3 · 4	Comox Lake	BC	Adam Bartsch	2002	634
99 3/8	16 2/8 · 17 5/8	12 5/8	4 · 4	Pierce County	WA	Danny Law	2006	634
99 1/8	19 2/8 · 18 5/8	11 3/8	4 · 3	Lincoln County	OR	Fred Rorie	1988	638
99 1/8	16 1/8 · 14 2/8	10 7/8	5 · 6	Durrance Lake	BC	Klaus Wolff	1996	638
99 1/8	17 7/8 · 18 3/8	13 1/8	3 · 3	King County	WA	Todd Bosnick	1997	638
99 0/8	16 3/8 · 16 5/8	14 0/8	5 · 5	Lincoln County	OR	Charles M. Roeser	1974	641
99 0/8	21 2/8 · 19 7/8	15 6/8	4 · 5	Santa Clara County	CA	Mike Walker	1979	641
99 0/8	16 6/8 · 16 6/8	12 6/8	4 · 4	Mendocino County	CA	Russell L. Browning	1983	641
99 0/8	17 0/8 · 16 3/8	13 2/8	4 · 4	Contra Costa County	CA	Richard L. Westervelt	1985	641
99 0/8	16 2/8 · 16 5/8	14 6/8	4 · 5	Kitsap County	WA	Cecil McConnell	1986	641
99 0/8	16 7/8 · 15 7/8	15 4/8	4 · 4	Clackamas County	OR	Darrell Scheffer	1991	641
99 0/8	17 0/8 · 17 1/8	16 6/8	4 · 4	Trinity County	CA	George Harms	2003	641
98 7/8	20 2/8 · 19 4/8	14 1/8	3 · 2	Pacific County	WA	William V. Mishler	1968	648
98 7/8	16 1/8 · 16 5/8	12 5/8	4 · 3	Cowlitz County	WA	Neal Amos	1997	648
98 7/8	17 0/8 · 17 2/8	13 2/8	4 · 6	Mt. Elphinstone	BC	Ian F. Gazeley	2002	648
98 7/8	18 0/8 · 18 1/8	14 7/8	5 · 3	Skamania County	WA	Scott Dean Stettler	2004	648
98 6/8	17 5/8 · 18 0/8	16 0/8	4 · 3	Skagit County	WA	Eric Olson	1994	652
98 6/8	17 4/8 · 18 1/8	14 2/8	4 · 3	Mendocino County	CA	Jerry Boelens	1996	652
98 6/8	17 3/8 · 18 0/8	16 6/8	4 · 3	Linn County	OR	Lark Weidenhaft	2000	652
98 6/8	16 7/8 · 16 3/8	13 2/8	4 · 4	Whatcom County	WA	Paul A. Lehman	2004	652
98 6/8	18 5/8 · 18 6/8	18 4/8	3 · 3	Humboldt County	CA	Tim A. Nickols	2009	652
98 5/8	19 2/8 · 19 2/8	14 5/8	4 · 3	Mendocino County	CA	Joseph A. Wyman	1990	657
98 5/8	18 4/8 · 19 5/8	15 7/8	4 · 3	Lewis County	WA	Rich Anderson	2003	657
98 5/8	18 4/8 · 17 1/8	14 3/8	4 · 4	King County	WA	Rusty Bogart	2006	657
98 5/8	19 6/8 · 20 1/8	20 7/8	2 · 2	Mendocino County	CA	Butch Carley	2006	657
98 3/8	16 1/8 · 16 3/8	14 4/8	4 · 4	Sonoma County	CA	Ray Torrey	1967	661
98 3/8	16 3/8 · 16 4/8	17 0/8	4 · 2	Lane County	OR	Gary R. Swan	1990	661
98 1/8	16 0/8 · 16 3/8	12 7/8	4 · 4	Rogue Unit	OR	Barbara Richardson	1964	663
98 1/8	17 3/8 · 17 1/8	17 1/8	4 · 4	Clackamas County	OR	Blake M. Bartley	1988	663
98 1/8	17 6/8 · 17 6/8	14 5/8	3 · 4	Humboldt County	CA	Gary Martin	2001	663

COLUMBIAN BLACKTAIL DEER (TYPICAL ANTLERS)

Minimum Score 95   Continued

SCORE	LENGTH OF R MAIN BEAM L	INSIDE SPREAD	NUMBER OF R POINTS L	AREA	STATE/PROVINCE	HUNTER'S NAME	DATE	RANK
98 1/8	17 5/8 17 5/8	15 7/8	3 4	Thurston County	WA	Tom Ryle	2009	663
98 0/8	19 7/8 19 6/8	14 6/8	4 2	Pacific County	WA	Morris Wolters	1967	667
98 0/8	18 5/8 19 0/8	15 6/8	3 3	Sonoma County	CA	Mark Bonales	1996	667
98 0/8	15 6/8 15 0/8	11 7/8	4 5	Thurston County	WA	Isaac W. Garza	2001	667
98 0/8	16 7/8 17 4/8	15 4/8	4 5	Polk County	OR	Bryon Davidson	2006	667
97 7/8	16 3/8 15 5/8	16 1/8	5 5	Benton County	OR	Harold Stice	1957	671
97 6/8	16 2/8 16 2/8	14 2/8	4 4	Clallam County	WA	Joel Peterson	1996	672
97 5/8	20 2/8 19 7/8	16 7/8	3 3	Marin County	CA	Mike Taylor	1985	673
97 5/8	17 4/8 17 6/8	13 5/8	3 3	Siskiyou County	CA	Randy Root	1987	673
97 5/8	16 4/8 16 0/8	14 3/8	3 3	Lane County	OR	Riley Savage	2007	673
97 4/8	18 6/8 18 2/8	18 6/8	3 3	Whatcom County	WA	Steve Holland	1963	676
97 4/8	18 1/8 18 4/8	15 6/8	3 3	Marion County	OR	Ken Kalinowski	1981	676
97 4/8	20 3/8 19 7/8	15 4/8	4 3	Trinity County	CA	Rodney A. York	1987	676
97 4/8	17 2/8 18 0/8	17 0/8	3 3	Siskiyou County	CA	John Shuping	1994	676
97 4/8	17 5/8 17 6/8	15 2/8	5 3	Sumas Mtn.	BC	Robert Zseder	1998	676
97 4/8	17 4/8 15 5/8	13 0/8	4 4	Mendocino County	CA	Gary N. Island	2001	676
97 4/8	16 4/8 15 5/8	10 3/8	6 7	Lincoln County	OR	Brandon Goodwin	2002	676
97 3/8	19 1/8 18 4/8	20 0/8	3 3	Marin County	CA	Joe Checchio	1985	683
97 3/8	17 2/8 18 0/8	14 5/8	3 3	Linn County	OR	Michael A. Cramblit	1989	683
97 3/8	16 1/8 17 5/8	15 3/8	4 5	Marion County	OR	Craig Germond	1997	683
97 3/8	17 3/8 18 2/8	15 5/8	4 4	Clallam County	WA	Raymond L. Broderson	2003	683
97 2/8	16 7/8 17 0/8	12 2/8	4 3	Pacific County	WA	Todd Hubble	1980	687
97 2/8	17 4/8 17 4/8	13 4/8	4 4	King County	WA	Jay E. Tinker	1986	687
97 2/8	12 0/8 13 0/8	12 2/8	5 5	Skagit County	WA	Donald Dick	1999	687
97 2/8	16 6/8 17 3/8	13 2/8	5 5	Linn County	OR	Luke Bergey	2004	687
97 1/8	16 5/8 16 7/8	13 7/8	3 3	Cowlitz County	WA	Jerry W. Adams	1994	691
97 0/8	16 7/8 16 4/8	12 0/8	4 4	Pacific County	WA	Lawrence Rogers	1972	692
97 0/8	18 0/8 18 3/8	14 4/8	3 2	Mendocino County	CA	Wayne Piersol	1991	692
97 0/8	18 1/8 16 5/8	18 0/8	4 4	Jackson County	OR	Tony Snow	1992	692
97 0/8	17 3/8 17 5/8	17 0/8	3 3	Linn County	OR	William M. Dupee, Jr.	1995	692
97 0/8	15 7/8 16 1/8	12 2/8	4 3	Island County	WA	Adam Caba	2001	692
97 0/8	19 1/8 15 0/8	12 6/8	5 4	Jackson County	OR	Dennis C. Kerr	2005	692
96 7/8	17 2/8 17 2/8	14 7/8	4 4	Glenn County	CA	Joe Williams	1977	698
96 7/8	16 2/8 16 6/8	14 5/8	3 3	Kitsap County	WA	Boyd E. Shelby, Jr.	1991	698
96 7/8	16 7/8 17 3/8	13 3/8	5 3	Lane County	OR	John Scott	1993	698
96 7/8	18 0/8 18 5/8	15 3/8	3 3	Clackamas County	OR	Alan D. Eubanks	2000	698
96 6/8	16 5/8 16 3/8	12 0/8	4 4	Benton County	OR	John W. Shipley	1991	702
96 6/8	17 1/8 17 0/8	13 0/8	3 3	Linn County	OR	Tom Vanasche	1994	702
96 6/8	17 6/8 17 6/8	16 6/8	3 2	King County	WA	Tim Gordan Wallis	1995	702
96 6/8	16 1/8 15 3/8	15 6/8	5 4	Lane County	OR	Gary Johnston	1999	702
96 5/8	17 6/8 17 6/8	11 5/8	4 5	Clark County	WA	Lorie Lehman	1994	706
96 5/8	18 3/8 18 1/8	17 1/8	4 3	Douglas County	OR	Steve Hohensee	2007	706
96 4/8	18 2/8 17 4/8	12 4/8	4 3	Benton County	OR	Jim Nielsen	1997	708
96 4/8	17 1/8 17 2/8	13 0/8	4 5	Lewis County	WA	Jon P. Jones	2003	708
96 2/8	15 5/8 16 1/8	12 0/8	4 4	Marion County	OR	Roger W. Atwood	2002	710
96 1/8	15 4/8 15 0/8	13 3/8	4 4	Pacific County	WA	Lynne Sharp	1965	711
96 0/8	16 0/8 15 7/8	12 6/8	4 4	Soda Springs	OR	Harold Benson	1961	712
96 0/8	15 5/8 16 2/8	13 6/8	4 5	Clackamas County	OR	Robert Oxley	1989	712
95 7/8	16 6/8 17 4/8	14 5/8	4 4	Lewis County	WA	Lyle Boschee	2004	714
95 6/8	17 0/8 16 7/8	15 6/8	4 4	Mendocino County	CA	Gerald Boelens	1997	715
95 5/8	17 5/8 15 2/8	14 3/8	5 5	Siskiyou County	CA	Thomas V. Sieverding	1971	716
95 5/8	16 1/8 17 2/8	12 1/8	4 4	Humboldt County	CA	Calvin Farner	1983	716
95 5/8	16 7/8 17 2/8	12 3/8	6 4	Benton County	OR	Mike McGrath	2001	716
95 4/8	14 0/8 16 6/8	16 0/8	4 4	Josephine County	OR	Lee Darrow	1997	719
95 4/8	16 7/8 17 0/8	17 0/8	4 4	Mendocino County	CA	Gary Island	2000	719
95 3/8	17 1/8 18 1/8	13 3/8	4 4	Josephine County	OR	Sam Burton	1994	721
95 2/8	16 6/8 16 2/8	12 4/8	3 3	Trinity County	CA	Tim P. Kanapeckas	1995	722
94 7/8	17 7/8 18 2/8	16 3/8	2 2	Santa Cruz County	CA	Robert Alan Nottingham	1984	723
94 7/8	15 7/8 16 1/8	14 1/8	4 4	Shasta County	CA	Danny R. Shurtleff	1987	723
94 7/8	18 4/8 18 2/8	16 3/8	2 2	Sonoma County	CA	Wayne Piersol	1992	723
* 94 7/8	16 2/8 16 5/8	13 3/8	4 3	Puntledge River	BC	Adam Bartsch	2007	723
94 6/8	16 3/8 17 1/8	14 2/8	5 4	Lewis County	WA	Daniel A. Yirka	1987	727
94 6/8	18 7/8 19 3/8	17 2/8	3 2	Sonoma County	CA	Mike Taylor	1989	727
94 6/8	19 6/8 18 3/8	16 6/8	3 3	San Juan County	WA	Scott L. Buck	1998	727
94 5/8	15 6/8 15 3/8	10 7/8	4 4	Benton County	OR	Raymond E. Root	1970	730
94 5/8	15 7/8 15 5/8	16 1/8	4 4	Sonoma County	CA	Russell L. Browning	1980	730
94 5/8	15 3/8 15 2/8	12 5/8	4 4	Sonoma County	CA	Thomas K. Powell	1988	730
94 5/8	17 2/8 17 3/8	14 5/8	4 4	Sonoma County	CA	Mark Bonales	1995	730
94 5/8	17 2/8 17 0/8	13 7/8	5 3	Clackamas County	OR	Christian Kopp	2006	730
* 94 5/8	18 0/8 16 6/8	14 1/8	3 4	Douglas County	OR	Ruth Payne	2007	730
94 4/8	18 0/8 17 5/8	13 2/8	4 3	Mendocino County	CA	Chuck Adams	1983	736
94 4/8	15 4/8 15 4/8	16 4/8	4 4	Lake County	CA	Phil Phillips	2001	736
94 3/8	18 0/8 16 2/8	16 5/8	2 4	Klamath County	OR	Don Pritchett	1964	738
94 3/8	17 1/8 17 0/8	15 5/8	3 3	Siskiyou County	CA	William J. Bagdasarian	1993	738
94 2/8	15 4/8 16 0/8	14 0/8	5 4	Douglas County	OR	Kody Kellom	2004	740
94 0/8	16 7/8 18 4/8	12 0/8	4 4	Capitol Forest	WA	C. N. Pickle	1960	741
94 0/8	17 6/8 17 5/8	11 4/8	3 4	Benton County	OR	Edward U. Tobler	1970	741
94 0/8	16 6/8 16 5/8	18 0/8	3 3	Humboldt County	CA	Craig Coolahan	1989	741
93 7/8	18 2/8 16 4/8	16 5/8	4 5	Sonoma County	CA	Sean Dunn	1992	744
93 7/8	16 2/8 15 7/8	12 7/8	4 5	Douglas County	OR	Walter Phillips	1992	744
93 7/8	15 3/8 15 7/8	12 1/8	4 5	Humboldt County	CA	Steve Barnhill	2001	744
93 6/8	18 3/8 18 5/8	13 6/8	2 4	Lewis County	WA	Floyd Gregg	1962	747
93 6/8	15 6/8 15 5/8	12 6/8	4 4	Mendocino County	CA	Chuck Adams	1979	747
93 6/8	17 6/8 17 4/8	13 4/8	4 4	Washington County	OR	Joe Klink	2003	747
93 5/8	15 1/8 14 7/8	15 1/8	4 5	Jackson County	OR	Rodney Ness	1995	750
93 5/8	18 5/8 18 1/8	18 3/8	3 3	Alameda County	CA	Rodger M. Benadom	1996	750
93 4/8	17 3/8 18 3/8	17 2/8	2 3	Mendocino County	CA	Gary N. Island	2007	752
93 3/8	16 4/8 15 6/8	15 3/8	3 3	Coos County	OR	Steve Simpson	1985	753
93 3/8	18 5/8 18 5/8	15 6/8	5 5	Clackamas County	OR	Randy Teeney	1987	753
93 2/8	17 0/8 16 7/8	12 4/8	4 3	Linn County	OR	Joe Mengore	1983	755
93 2/8	16 2/8 17 2/8	17 3/8	3 3	Humboldt County	CA	Monty Clemmer	1986	755
93 2/8	14 3/8 14 1/8	12 6/8	4 3	Lane County	OR	Allan Sanford	2005	755
* 93 1/8	14 5/8 14 5/8	13 5/8	4 5	Mendocino County	CA	Douglas Rosin	2006	758
93 0/8	17 3/8 17 6/8	14 0/8	4 3	Clallam County	WA	Wayne Haag	1987	759
93 0/8	16 3/8 17 5/8	15 6/8	5 4	King County	WA	Steve Kempf	2002	759

283

COLUMBIAN BLACKTAIL DEER (TYPICAL ANTLERS)

Minimum Score 95   Continued

SCORE	LENGTH OF R MAIN BEAM L	INSIDE SPREAD	NUMBER OF R POINTS L	AREA	STATE/ PROVINCE	HUNTER'S NAME	DATE	RANK
93 0/8	15 3/8 16 3/8	11 0/8	4 4	Trinity County	CA	M. Robert DeLaney	2004	759
92 6/8	16 0/8 16 3/8	13 4/8	5 5	Marion County	OR	Larry Jones	1986	762
92 6/8	16 5/8 16 5/8	14 0/8	4 3	King County	WA	Randy L. Collecchi	1997	762
* 92 4/8	17 1/8 17 5/8	15 1/8	6 5	Sonoma County	CA	Tim Neil	2007	764
92 3/8	18 0/8 18 2/8	15 1/8	3 2	Mendocino County	CA	Wilfred Willis	1982	765
92 0/8	18 4/8 18 4/8	19 2/8	2 2	Josephine County	OR	Joe White	1986	766
92 0/8	16 4/8 16 5/8	16 0/8	3 3	Santa Cruz County	CA	H. Brian Malsbury	1987	766
92 0/8	17 0/8 17 2/8	14 6/8	3 3	Mendocino County	CA	Jamie Carley	2007	766
91 7/8	14 4/8 14 7/8	12 5/8	4 4	Pierce County	WA	Raymond Cooksey	1998	769
91 5/8	15 1/8 15 2/8	13 1/8	5 5	King County	WA	Vic Stevens	1986	770
91 5/8	17 6/8 17 7/8	18 0/8	3 3	Mendocino County	CA	Matt Seever	1999	770
91 3/8	17 3/8 17 0/8	16 3/8	2 2	Mendocino County	CA	Joseph Wyman	1991	772
91 3/8	17 5/8 16 6/8	12 3/8	3 3	Pierce County	WA	Boyd Edward Shelby, Jr.	1996	772
* 91 3/8	18 0/8 19 4/8	16 7/8	3 4	Trinity County	CA	John MacPeak	2008	772
* 91 3/8	18 2/8 18 0/8	15 7/8	2 2	Humboldt County	CA	Ryan Baker	2009	772
91 2/8	18 0/8 17 4/8	13 4/8	5 3	Yamhill County	OR	R. Keith Potter	1990	776
91 2/8	16 1/8 16 1/8	15 2/8	4 4	Sooke	BC	Scott Eddy	2002	776
* 91 2/8	15 4/8 15 4/8	12 6/8	4 5	Sonoma County	CA	Earl C. Farnsworth, Jr.	2005	776
91 1/8	17 1/8 18 0/8	13 1/8	3 3	Benton County	OR	Jim Nielsen	1981	779
91 1/8	15 3/8 16 5/8	13 1/8	3 4	Lane County	OR	Ken Kalinowski	1986	779
91 1/8	15 4/8 16 1/8	16 3/8	3 3	Sonoma County	CA	Ernie Fechter	1990	779
91 1/8	16 6/8 16 4/8	12 3/8	3 3	Lewis County	WA	Daren Dahlman	2000	779
91 1/8	15 5/8 15 6/8	13 5/8	4 4	Lane County	OR	Riley Timmins	2007	779
90 7/8	15 5/8 15 1/8	12 3/8	3 3	Clallam County	WA	Renny Mason	1989	784
90 6/8	14 7/8 15 2/8	14 0/8	3 3	Chilliwack Valley	BC	Robert Zseder	1999	785
90 5/8	16 7/8 17 1/8	15 1/8	2 2	Santa Clara County	CA	Sandee Cox	1989	786
90 5/8	19 5/8 17 3/8	14 7/8	3 2	Kitsap County	WA	Terry Ray Chapman	1992	786
90 5/8	15 4/8 16 1/8	9 7/8	4 4	Cowlitz County	WA	Ryan Davenport	1998	786
90 4/8	14 6/8 14 3/8	12 3/8	4 4	Whatcom County	WA	Jack Fish	1956	789
90 4/8	16 4/8 16 7/8	15 0/8	2 2	Merced County	CA	Jim Walton	1980	789
90 4/8	14 6/8 14 6/8	13 4/8	4 4	King County	WA	Mike Adkins	2001	789
90 3/8	16 6/8 15 6/8	14 3/8	4 5	Mendocino County	CA	Chuck Adams	1977	792
90 2/8	14 5/8 15 1/8	12 0/8	4 4	Pacific County	WA	Leonard Bray	1965	793
90 1/8	19 4/8 18 6/8	15 3/8	3 3	Saltspring Island	BC	Greg Knoblauch	1994	794
90 1/8	16 5/8 15 6/8	11 5/8	3 3	King County	WA	Don D. Axtman	1997	794
90 1/8	16 0/8 15 6/8	13 5/8	3 3	Saltspring Island	BC	Greg Knoblauch	1998	794
90 1/8	18 0/8 19 2/8	10 4/8	4 3	Douglas County	OR	Jason Hardesty	2002	794
90 1/8	18 4/8 17 7/8	15 1/8	2 2	San Juan County	WA	Danny Law	2007	794
90 1/8	17 2/8 17 3/8	14 7/8	4 3	Marion County	OR	Chris Dunlap	2010	794
90 0/8	15 0/8 14 6/8	12 6/8	4 4	Benton County	OR	Tom Ronchetti	1990	800
90 0/8	15 1/8 15 6/8	12 6/8	5 4	Douglas County	OR	Steve Hohensee	2009	800

COLUMBIAN BLACKTAIL DEER (TYPICAL VELVET ANTLERS)

Minimum Score 95

SCORE	LENGTH OF R MAIN BEAM L		INSIDE SPREAD	NUMBER OF R POINTS L		AREA	STATE/ PROVINCE	HUNTER'S NAME	DATE	RANK
157 0/8	23 0/8	22 7/8	21 4/8	5	5	Shasta County	CA	Anthony Wysock	2006	*
* 145 7/8	24 0/8	26 1/8	17 0/8	5	5	Siskiyou County	CA	Kirk Edgerton	2007	*
145 4/8	21 7/8	22 5/8	19 2/8	5	5	Mendocino County	CA	Dustin Robben	2007	*
143 4/8	21 5/8	20 7/8	19 4/8	5	5	Shasta County	CA	Austin Taff	2009	*
143 2/8	21 0/8	21 0/8	15 2/8	4	4	Trinity County	CA	Josh Martin	2008	*
142 4/8	22 0/8	22 0/8	18 6/8	5	5	Trinity County	CA	Jason Stanley	2005	*
* 137 5/8	21 0/8	21 3/8	15 5/8	5	5	Linn County	OR	Alan May	2008	*
* 134 3/8	20 2/8	20 5/8	22 6/8	5	4	Mendocino County	CA	Joe Policarpo	2008	*
133 1/8	23 2/8	21 4/8	20 3/8	4	5	Mendocino County	CA	Butch Carley	2004	*
133 0/8	22 0/8	20 7/8	18 6/8	4	4	Tehama County	CA	James Clemons	2005	*
* 130 3/8	21 1/8	21 1/8	16 5/8	5	5	Trinity County	CA	Anthony John Palermo	2009	*
123 5/8	21 6/8	20 2/8	17 7/8	4	5	Humboldt County	CA	Sean Campbell	2006	*
121 2/8	17 6/8	17 7/8	13 4/8	5	5	Siskiyou County	CA	Fred V. Smith	2003	*
120 3/8	19 3/8	18 2/8	16 5/8	4	4	Trinity County	CA	Brian Olson	2006	*
120 2/8	19 5/8	19 3/8	17 4/8	4	4	Lake County	CA	Phil Phillips	2009	*
119 7/8	22 0/8	21 1/8	15 5/8	3	4	Siskiyou County	CA	Fred V. Smith	1996	*
* 117 5/8	18 2/8	19 2/8	12 7/8	4	4	Siskiyou County	CA	Travis Schwartz	2006	*
114 4/8	18 3/8	19 6/8	16 6/8	4	5	Trinity County	CA	Mark Greving	1997	*
113 2/8	16 2/8	16 5/8	14 0/8	4	4	Humboldt County	CA	Steven R. Davis	2005	*
112 2/8	19 2/8	20 0/8	17 0/8	4	4	Mendocino County	CA	Michael R. Traub	2004	*
111 7/8	17 2/8	18 1/8	17 5/8	5	4	Mendocino County	CA	Michael J. Schneider	2007	*
110 6/8	22 0/8	21 0/8	13 6/8	3	4	Mendocino County	CA	Mark Zastrow	2005	*
109 4/8	19 6/8	18 2/8	17 0/8	4	4	Mendocino County	CA	Matt Petrini	2007	*
109 0/8	17 1/8	17 1/8	13 6/8	5	5	Humboldt County	CA	Craig P. Mitton	2010	*
107 0/8	18 6/8	17 3/8	17 4/8	4	4	Mendocino County	CA	Lon E. Lauber	2006	*
106 2/8	16 3/8	17 2/8	12 4/8	5	5	Humboldt County	CA	Paul E. Korn	2004	*
105 6/8	16 1/8	16 7/8	12 6/8	4	5	Humboldt County	CA	Donald P. Travis	2008	*
105 1/8	18 1/8	18 5/8	17 5/8	4	4	Humboldt County	CA	Charles E. Nichol	2005	*
104 2/8	17 6/8	17 2/8	16 2/8	4	4	Mendocino County	CA	Zack Walton	2008	*
103 0/8	19 3/8	19 2/8	15 0/8	4	4	Humboldt County	CA	Randy Cooling	2006	*
101 0/8	15 3/8	14 4/8	14 4/8	4	4	Lake County	CA	Phil Phillips	2008	*
100 4/8	15 7/8	16 0/8	13 4/8	4	4	Siskiyou County	CA	Fred V. Smith	2000	*
* 99 6/8	19 7/8	18 7/8	14 2/8	4	3	Humboldt County	CA	Earl Chauvin	2009	*
97 5/8	16 6/8	16 7/8	12 5/8	4	4	Siskiyou County	CA	Fred V. Smith	1997	*
96 5/8	18 2/8	18 0/8	13 3/8	3	3	Trinity County	CA	William J. Langer	2004	*
96 3/8	19 4/8	18 0/8	16 5/8	3	2	Humboldt County	CA	Cory McKee	2009	*
96 2/8	16 4/8	15 6/8	16 6/8	4	5	Napa County	CA	Matt Petrini	2006	*
94 7/8	18 0/8	18 7/8	15 5/8	2	2	Humboldt County	CA	Tim Walters	2010	*

WORLD RECORD COLUMBIAN BLACKTAIL DEER
Non-Typical Antlers
Score: 194 4/8
Location: Jackson County, Oregon
Date: 1988
Hunter: James Decker

Non-Typical Columbian Blacktail Deer

by James Decker

The 1988 season started off with me hunting the high Cascades for Roosevelt's elk. I've always been a meat hunter and I shot a nice five-pointer that provided 375 pounds of meat for the freezer. Now, I could be a little picky on the size of the deer I would tag this year.

When late season came, I was ready. This was a good year for rattling. Lots of bucks came in and it was hard to pass up a big buck at 15 yards, but I was waiting for a monster.

On the last evening of the season, I saw a nice four-by-four some 70 yards away. He had two does with him. I rattled and raked the ground. He'd look my way but wouldn't come any closer. Finally, the does came within 20 yards, but soon grazed back to the buck.

I grew tired of messing with the buck so I slipped away without spooking the deer. I hunted up to a strip of pines surrounded by oaks. Suddenly, I focused on a big buck standing down the hill. He was looking right at me, so I kept on walking, acting like I'd not seen him. When I passed behind the next big tree, I nocked an arrow, drew my bow and eased into view. I let go of the string. The arrow struck. He bucked and ran off.

I sat down and waited for a while before walking down to where he'd been standing. I didn't really need to blood trail him because he left tracks anyone could have followed—and he went down only 75 yards away. When I walked up, my eyes nearly popped out of my head. I could not believe the size of the rack. It had 12 points on each side and bits of bark clung to its burrs. My arrow had penetrated both lungs.

Being in the right place at the right time made it all possible.

COLUMBIAN BLACKTAIL DEER (NON-TYPICAL ANTLERS)

Minimum Score 115 — *Odocoileus hemionus columnianus*

SCORE	LENGTH OF R MAIN BEAM	L	INSIDE SPREAD	NUMBER OF R POINTS	L	AREA	STATE/ PROVINCE	HUNTER'S NAME	DATE	RANK
194 4/8	23 3/8	23 4/8	19 1/8	8	10	Jackson County	OR	James Decker	1988	1
174 1/8	25 0/8	23 7/8	19 1/8	6	5	Jackson County	OR	Norman J. Shanklin	1979	2
168 1/8	21 5/8	21 3/8	15 3/8	8	7	Jackson County	OR	Chuck Woolley	1991	3
168 0/8	22 7/8	22 2/8	19 1/8	6	8	Mendocino County	CA	Kevin Byler	2005	4
166 4/8	22 3/8	23 0/8	19 4/8	6	8	Marion County	OR	Chad A. Richardson	1997	5
165 0/8	24 0/8	24 6/8	24 6/8	8	6	Clatsop County	OR	Gerald E. Ryon	1972	6
162 5/8	23 5/8	22 2/8	21 0/8	7	7	Jackson County	OR	David Shanklin	1984	7
154 3/8	23 3/8	22 4/8	18 2/8	5	7	Jackson County	OR	David Shanklin	1983	8
152 1/8	20 2/8	19 3/8	20 1/8	5	6	Jackson County	OR	David Shanklin	1977	9
151 1/8	21 1/8	21 2/8	16 6/8	9	9	Lane County	OR	Chad Wilson	2006	10
147 2/8	21 1/8	21 3/8	17 7/8	6	7	Kitsap County	WA	Kirk Parker	2006	11
146 0/8	19 2/8	19 0/8	15 7/8	7	7	San Mateo County	CA	John Grochowski	1984	12
141 3/8	21 0/8	21 4/8	15 4/8	6	7	King County	WA	Jim L. Krieg	2001	13
141 0/8	24 0/8	23 7/8	22 2/8	5	7	Tehama County	CA	Richard C. Bendix	2002	14
139 5/8	18 6/8	18 6/8	15 7/8	5	8	Siskiyou County	CA	Kurt Case	1980	15
139 1/8	19 7/8	18 7/8	16 4/8	7	5	Trinity County	CA	Mark Greving	1982	16
137 7/8	19 5/8	20 0/8	14 0/8	6	6	Clackamas County	OR	David W. Nelson	1999	17
136 3/8	20 6/8	20 2/8	13 5/8	7	5	King County	WA	Cody Dean Davis	2001	18
134 4/8	20 1/8	18 4/8	13 5/8	4	7	Douglas County	OR	Fabian Carr	2009	19
133 4/8	18 0/8	18 4/8	13 2/8	6	6	Josephine County	OR	Robert K. Wood	1994	20
* 132 4/8	19 6/8	16 5/8	17 3/8	4	7	Island County	WA	Eric Nicholson	2005	21
132 3/8	18 0/8	18 4/8	18 6/8	6	6	Trinity County	CA	Jim Schaafsma	1991	22
132 1/8	18 7/8	20 5/8	16 6/8	5	4	Snohomish County	WA	Allan Lyndsay Moro	1992	23
131 6/8	22 7/8	22 6/8	18 3/8	7	4	Douglas County	OR	Jerry R. De Loach	1975	24
131 1/8	20 6/8	20 2/8	21 0/8	6	6	Clackamas County	OR	Dan Sandberg	2002	25
130 4/8	18 5/8	17 2/8	12 1/8	6	5	Trinity County	CA	Bob Ameen	2005	26
129 3/8	15 6/8	17 1/8	12 6/8	7	5	Benton County	OR	Thomas K. Powell	2001	27

COLUMBIAN BLACKTAIL DEER (NON-TYPICAL VELVET ANTLERS)

Minimum Score 95

SCORE	LENGTH OF R MAIN BEAM	L	INSIDE SPREAD	NUMBER OF R POINTS	L	AREA	STATE/ PROVINCE	HUNTER'S NAME	DATE	RANK
157 3/8	24 7/8	24 2/8	23 1/8	4	5	Sonoma County	CA	Angelo Nogara	2005	*
126 7/8	21 5/8	19 7/8	17 4/8	6	4	Tehama County	CA	Terry A. Cobb	2003	*

Sitka Blacktail Deer

116 3/8

KIND OF DEER: Sitka

	Supplementary Data R / L	Column 1 Spread Credit	Column 2 Right Antler	Column 3 Left Antler	Column 4 Difference
A. Number of Points each Antler	5 / 5				
B. Tip to Tip	5 0/8				
C. Greatest Spread	14 6/8				
D. Inside Spread of MAIN BEAMS		13 1/8			
E. Total of Lengths of all Abnormal Points					
F. Length of Main Beam			18 4/8	18 2/8	2/8
G-1. Length of First Point			2 6/8	2 4/8	2/8
G-2. Length of Second Point			9 1/8	7 4/8	1 5/8
G-3. Length of Third Point			5 3/8	3 2/8	2 1/8
G-4. Length of Fourth Point			6 5/8	6 3/8	2/8
H-1. Circumference Between Burr and First Point			3 7/8	3 7/8	—
H-2. Circumference Between First and Second Points			3 5/8	3 4/8	1/8
H-3. Circumference Between Main Beam and Third Points			3 0/8	3 0/8	—
H-4. Circumference Between Second Point and Beam tip			3 4/8	3 3/8	1/8
TOTALS			56 3/8	51 5/8	4 6/8

ADD	Column 1	13 1/8
	Column 2	56 3/8
	Column 3	51 5/8
	Total	121 1/8
SUBTRACT Column 4		4 6/8
FINAL SCORE		116 3/8

Present owner: Charles R.
Address: P.O. Box 6783

WORLD RECORD SITKA BLACKTAIL DEER
Score: 116 3/8
Location: Prince of Wales Island, Alaska
Date: 1987
Hunter: Charles Hakari

SITKA BLACKTAIL DEER

Minimum Score 75　　*Odocoileus hemionus sitkensis*

SCORE	LENGTH OF MAIN BEAM R / L	INSIDE SPREAD	NUMBER OF POINTS R / L	AREA	STATE/PROVINCE	HUNTER'S NAME	DATE	RANK
116 3/8	18 4/8 / 18 2/8	13 1/8	5 / 5	Prince of Wales Island	AK	Charles Hakari	1987	1
115 6/8	17 1/8 / 16 3/8	14 6/8	5 / 5	Prince of Wales Island	AK	Kirt O. Marsh	1988	2
114 3/8	18 5/8 / 18 7/8	18 1/8	5 / 5	Kodiak Island	AK	Jim Ryan	1986	3
112 2/8	19 0/8 / 19 2/8	16 4/8	4 / 4	Kodiak Island	AK	John D. "Jack" Frost	1987	4
110 7/8	17 5/8 / 18 5/8	14 5/8	5 / 5	Prince of Wales Island	AK	William H. Welton	2006	5
110 5/8	17 3/8 / 17 1/8	15 5/8	6 / 5	Kodiak Island	AK	Bill Krenz	1988	6
110 1/8	17 2/8 / 16 4/8	13 7/8	5 / 5	Kosciusko Island	AK	Bob Ameen	2003	7
108 4/8	16 4/8 / 15 6/8	15 0/8	5 / 5	Kodiak Island	AK	Chuck Adams	1986	8
107 6/8	17 2/8 / 16 2/8	14 2/8	5 / 5	Kodiak Island	AK	Chuck Adams	1986	9
107 4/8	17 3/8 / 17 4/8	14 4/8	5 / 5	Kodiak Island	AK	Chuck Adams	1987	10
107 4/8	17 3/8 / 17 1/8	14 4/8	5 / 5	Prince of Wales Island	AK	Danny Moore	1988	10
107 2/8	15 3/8 / 15 1/8	13 6/8	5 / 5	Kodiak Island	AK	Chris Dau	1986	12
106 6/8	17 0/8 / 16 6/8	15 6/8	4 / 4	Kosciusko Island	AK	Bob Ameen	2004	13
106 4/8	17 3/8 / 16 6/8	16 5/8	5 / 6	Kodiak Island	AK	Douglas G. Bonetti	1985	14
106 3/8	17 1/8 / 16 6/8	13 3/8	5 / 5	Deadman Bay	AK	Leon R. Meidam	1995	15
105 3/8	16 3/8 / 16 4/8	15 1/8	5 / 6	Kodiak Island	AK	John T. Toenes	1988	16
104 6/8	18 4/8 / 19 1/8	16 4/8	4 / 4	Kodiak Island	AK	Pat McCollum	1994	17
104 5/8	18 0/8 / 17 5/8	17 7/8	4 / 5	Kodiak Island	AK	Richard L. Westervelt	1987	18
103 5/8	18 4/8 / 17 2/8	15 7/8	4 / 5	Kodiak Island	AK	Chuck Adams	1987	19
103 2/8	18 3/8 / 17 5/8	17 4/8	4 / 5	Amook Island	AK	Garry A. Thoms	1989	20
103 1/8	17 2/8 / 17 3/8	15 5/8	4 / 4	Kodiak Island	AK	Tom Kothenbeutel	2005	21
103 0/8	17 7/8 / 17 1/8	12 6/8	5 / 4	Olga Bay	AK	John D. "Jack" Frost	1998	22
102 7/8	16 4/8 / 16 0/8	14 2/8	6 / 5	Kodiak Island	AK	John D. "Jack" Frost	1994	23
102 2/8	18 4/8 / 16 6/8	13 4/8	5 / 5	Kodiak Island	AK	Brad H. Parker	1989	24
102 1/8	15 4/8 / 15 4/8	13 5/8	5 / 5	Kodiak Island	AK	Chuck Adams	1996	25
102 0/8	18 0/8 / 18 0/8	16 2/8	5 / 4	Kodiak Island	AK	John D. 'Jack' Frost	1986	26
102 0/8	18 2/8 / 17 2/8	15 0/8	4 / 5	Sitkalidak Island	AK	Walter J. Palmer	2009	26
101 6/8	15 4/8 / 16 2/8	13 6/8	5 / 5	Kodiak Island	Ak	Gary G. Wall	1986	28
101 5/8	16 6/8 / 15 6/8	14 1/8	5 / 5	Kodiak Island	AK	John D. "Jack" Frost	1997	29
101 3/8	15 6/8 / 16 3/8	14 3/8	5 / 5	Kodiak Island	AK	Lon E. Lauber	1991	30
101 3/8	16 5/8 / 16 3/8	14 1/8	5 / 5	Kodiak Island	AK	V. Randy Liljenquist	1993	30
101 3/8	16 3/8 / 16 4/8	14 3/8	5 / 5	Etolin Island	AK	Dave Brown	1997	30
101 0/8	19 0/8 / 19 0/8	17 0/8	5 / 5	Kodiak Island	AK	Gene Coughlin	1984	33
101 0/8	18 1/8 / 17 7/8	16 4/8	5 / 4	Kodiak Island	AK	Danny Moore	1986	33
100 5/8	17 7/8 / 17 0/8	16 3/8	4 / 5	Ugak Bay	AK	Thomas Chadwick	1987	35
100 4/8	16 5/8 / 17 0/8	14 6/8	5 / 4	Kosciusko Island	AK	Bob Ameen	2005	36
100 3/8	17 4/8 / 17 5/8	13 7/8	4 / 4	Kodiak Island	AK	John D. "Jack" Frost	2002	37
100 0/8	12 7/8 / 14 0/8	12 0/8	5 / 5	Kosciusko Island	AK	Spencer Richter	2005	38
99 4/8	17 4/8 / 17 7/8	16 0/8	4 / 5	Kodiak Island	AK	Danny Moore	1984	39
99 4/8	16 0/8 / 15 6/8	13 2/8	5 / 5	Kodiak Island	AK	E. Lance Whary	1998	39
99 3/8	15 4/8 / 16 2/8	15 1/8	4 / 5	Kodiak Island	AK	Thomas J. Hoffman	1988	41
99 3/8	16 5/8 / 16 6/8	16 1/8	4 / 4	Kodiak Island	AK	Todd Zeuske	1998	41
99 3/8	16 4/8 / 16 3/8	14 1/8	4 / 4	Kodiak Island	AK	Lon E. Lauber	2002	41
99 2/8	16 6/8 / 16 2/8	13 6/8	4 / 5	Kodiak Island	AK	Chuck Adams	1995	44
99 0/8	14 1/8 / 15 5/8	13 4/8	5 / 5	Kodiak Island	AK	Al Besch	1984	45
98 7/8	16 6/8 / 16 6/8	14 5/8	5 / 4	Kodiak Island	AK	Danny Moore	1986	46
98 5/8	16 6/8 / 16 2/8	16 5/8	4 / 4	Kodiak Island	AK	Craig D. Morrow	1987	47
98 5/8	15 7/8 / 16 0/8	13 1/8	5 / 5	Kodiak Island	AK	Tim Moerlein	1992	47
98 5/8	16 6/8 / 16 1/8	13 7/8	5 / 5	Kodiak Island	AK	Chuck Adams	1998	47
98 4/8	16 4/8 / 14 2/8	14 0/8	4 / 5	Kodiak Island	AK	Michael L. Nunn	1984	50
98 4/8	14 4/8 / 17 0/8	17 1/8	5 / 4	Kodiak Island	AK	Tom Chadwick	1985	50
98 4/8	15 6/8 / 16 0/8	14 2/8	5 / 5	Prince of Wales Island	AK	Danny Moore	1993	50
98 2/8	14 7/8 / 14 7/8	13 4/8	5 / 5	Kodiak Island	AK	Philip F. Nuechterlein	1985	53
98 2/8	15 0/8 / 14 7/8	13 2/8	5 / 5	Kodiak Island	AK	Glenn Vandergaw	1988	53
98 0/8	17 0/8 / 16 6/8	15 4/8	4 / 4	Prince of Wales Island	AK	Donald R. Pritchett	2004	55
97 7/8	18 2/8 / 18 4/8	14 1/8	4 / 4	Larson Bay	AK	Carol Kindred	1989	56
97 6/8	18 1/8 / 18 0/8	18 0/8	4 / 3	Kodiak Island	AK	Patricia A. Stewart	1983	57
97 5/8	16 4/8 / 17 4/8	16 7/8	4 / 5	Prince of Wales Island	AK	Marvin H. Walter	1987	58
97 5/8	16 7/8 / 17 2/8	16 3/8	4 / 4	Kodiak Island	AK	Roger Stewart	1988	59
97 2/8	15 0/8 / 13 6/8	13 0/8	5 / 5	Kodiak Island	AK	Chuck Adams	1986	60
97 2/8	15 7/8 / 14 6/8	14 6/8	4 / 4	Kodiak Island	AK	Michael Dziekan	2008	60
* 97 2/8	15 6/8 / 15 7/8	13 3/8	5 / 4	Kodiak Island	AK	Ed Fanchin	2009	60
96 7/8	16 4/8 / 17 1/8	16 5/8	4 / 4	Kodiak Island	AK	William J. Gartland	1999	63
96 6/8	15 4/8 / 15 1/8	14 0/8	4 / 5	Kodiak Island	AK	Bob Ameen	1983	64
96 4/8	18 1/8 / 18 2/8	15 6/8	4 / 5	Prince of Wales Island	AK	Glen R. Shepard	1987	65
96 3/8	16 1/8 / 16 6/8	15 5/8	4 / 4	Kodiak Island	AK	Gary G. Wall	1986	66
96 2/8	17 5/8 / 17 0/8	15 6/8	3 / 4	Kodiak Island	AK	Dick McClain	1990	67
* 96 2/8	17 2/8 / 17 6/8	13 2/8	6 / 5	Kupreanof Island	AK	Ryan Marsh	2006	67
96 1/8	17 1/8 / 16 3/8	13 7/8	4 / 4	Kodiak Island	AK	Don Rossiter	1985	69
95 6/8	17 5/8 / 17 4/8	17 0/8	3 / 3	Kodiak Island	AK	Paul Persano	1986	70
95 6/8	17 3/8 / 17 2/8	14 4/8	5 / 4	Kodiak Island	AK	Terry Krahn	1995	70
95 5/8	16 7/8 / 16 2/8	16 7/8	4 / 4	Kodiak Island	AK	Carl E. Brent	1998	72
95 4/8	17 4/8 / 17 3/8	15 5/8	4 / 4	Kodiak Island	AK	John D. "Jack" Frost	1990	73
95 3/8	15 4/8 / 16 0/8	15 1/8	4 / 4	Kodiak Island	AK	Mike Traub	1992	73
95 3/8	16 1/8 / 15 7/8	14 5/8	4 / 4	Kodiak Island	AK	Bob Ameen	1995	73
95 1/8	18 0/8 / 17 6/8	16 4/8	4 / 5	Kodiak Island	AK	Thomas E. Rothrock	1997	76
95 1/8	14 4/8 / 14 0/8	12 3/8	5 / 5	Kosciusko Island	AK	Bob Ameen	2006	76
95 0/8	15 4/8 / 15 5/8	14 0/8	4 / 4	Kodiak Island	AK	Tony Dawson	2004	78
94 7/8	16 7/8 / 16 7/8	13 1/8	5 / 6	Kodiak Island	AK	Chuck Adams	1984	79
94 7/8	14 5/8 / 13 7/8	13 3/8	5 / 5	Olga Bay	AK	Dennis L. Howell	2007	79
94 6/8	16 0/8 / 15 2/8	13 6/8	4 / 4	Kodiak Island	AK	Bob Ameen	1993	81
94 6/8	18 2/8 / 17 7/8	14 7/8	4 / 4	Kodiak Island	AK	V. Randy Liljenquist	1993	82
94 3/8	16 1/8 / 15 5/8	16 1/8	4 / 4	Kodiak Island	AK	Dyrk Eddie	1986	83
94 3/8	16 4/8 / 16 1/8	15 5/8	4 / 4	Kodiak Island	AK	Doug Keller	1988	83
94 2/8	15 0/8 / 15 1/8	14 4/8	4 / 4	Kodiak Island	AK	F. Dan Dinelli	1996	85
94 2/8	15 3/8 / 15 6/8	14 4/8	4 / 5	Kodiak Island	AK	John D. "Jack" Frost	1997	85
94 1/8	16 5/8 / 17 2/8	14 5/8	4 / 4	Kodiak Island	AK	Chuck Adams	1997	87
94 1/8	16 4/8 / 16 7/8	13 5/8	6 / 4	Old Harbor	AK	Garry A. Thoms	1997	87
93 7/8	15 0/8 / 15 5/8	15 1/8	5 / 4	Kosciusko Island	AK	Bob Ameen	2006	89
93 5/8	17 3/8 / 17 2/8	15 7/8	4 / 4	Afognak Island	AK	Gregory White	2003	90
93 5/8	15 6/8 / 15 1/8	13 7/8	4 / 4	Kodiak Island	AK	John Sarvis	2009	90
93 4/8	15 2/8 / 15 4/8	15 4/8	5 / 4	Kodiak Island	AK	Paul Persano	1986	92
93 4/8	15 7/8 / 15 0/8	14 0/8	4 / 4	Kodiak Island	AK	David A. Widby	1996	92
93 4/8	16 2/8 / 16 1/8	17 0/8	4 / 4	Trinity Islands	AK	John Paul Schaffer	2002	92
93 4/8	17 2/8 / 17 0/8	12 2/8	5 / 4	Kodiak Island	AK	Bob Ameen	2004	92

291

SITKA BLACKTAIL DEER

Minimum Score 75 — Continued

SCORE	LENGTH OF R MAIN BEAM L	INSIDE SPREAD	NUMBER OF R POINTS L	AREA	STATE/ PROVINCE	HUNTER'S NAME	DATE	RANK
93 3/8	15 2/8 15 4/8	13 3/8	5 5	Kodiak Island	AK	Herman J. Griese	1982	96
93 3/8	17 4/8 15 4/8	13 5/8	4 4	Kodiak Island	AK	Chuck Adams	1987	96
93 3/8	17 3/8 16 7/8	13 5/8	3 3	Kodiak Island	AK	Bob Ameen	2006	96
93 2/8	16 0/8 15 6/8	15 0/8	4 4	Kodiak Island	AK	John Toenes	1987	99
93 2/8	18 0/8 17 1/8	14 0/8	4 4	Kodiak Island	AK	Russell M. Kucinski	1989	99
93 2/8	16 1/8 15 6/8	14 4/8	3 4	Kodiak Island	AK	Bob Ameen	1995	99
93 2/8	16 1/8 16 2/8	13 4/8	4 4	Kodiak Island	AK	Chuck Adams	1997	99
93 1/8	15 6/8 15 1/8	15 5/8	5 4	Kodiak Island	AK	Lon E. Lauber	1994	103
93 1/8	17 5/8 16 6/8	15 1/8	3 3	Kodiak Island	AK	Mark Penninger	2006	103
* 93 0/8	14 7/8 15 2/8	13 2/8	5 5	Kodiak Island	AK	Jarrett Finley	2007	105
92 7/8	16 3/8 15 6/8	15 1/8	4 4	Kodiak Island	AK	John Sarvis	1987	106
92 7/8	15 3/8 14 5/8	16 3/8	5 4	Prince of Wales Island	AK	William H. Welton	1993	106
92 7/8	16 0/8 16 0/8	14 1/8	4 4	Kodiak Island	AK	Lon E. Lauber	1994	106
92 7/8	16 6/8 16 2/8	14 1/8	3 3	Kodiak Island	AK	Roy Whitford	1994	106
92 4/8	16 2/8 15 5/8	13 3/8	4 5	Zarembo Island	AK	Dave Brown	2000	110
92 4/8	16 2/8 15 5/8	14 2/8	4 4	Kodiak Island	AK	Bob Ameen	2009	110
92 3/8	17 7/8 17 1/8	16 1/8	3 3	Kodiak Island	AK	William C. Shuster	1992	112
92 2/8	14 5/8 14 3/8	13 2/8	5 5	Kodiak Island	AK	Lon E. Lauber	1994	113
92 2/8	15 1/8 14 6/8	13 4/8	4 4	Kodiak Island	AK	Bob Ameen	2008	113
92 2/8	14 1/8 16 4/8	13 2/8	4 4	Kodiak Island	AK	John Sarvis	2009	113
92 1/8	14 7/8 14 0/8	15 0/8	4 4	Kodiak Island	AK	Richard Moran	1988	116
92 0/8	16 5/8 16 0/8	13 4/8	4 4	Kodiak Island	AK	Chuck Adams	1986	117
92 0/8	15 2/8 16 2/8	13 4/8	6 5	Larson Bay	AK	Lou Kindred	1989	117
91 7/8	16 1/8 16 5/8	14 7/8	4 4	Afognak Island	AK	Edward L. Russell	1980	119
91 7/8	14 4/8 15 0/8	12 3/8	4 4	Queen Charlotte Islands	BC	Grant Janczyn	1991	119
91 6/8	15 1/8 14 7/8	13 2/8	4 4	Kodiak Island	AK	Michael J. Schneider	2004	121
91 5/8	14 2/8 14 2/8	14 5/8	4 4	Afognak Island	AK	Ray Ryan	1984	122
91 5/8	14 4/8 15 1/8	12 7/8	5 5	Kodiak Island	AK	Danny Moore	1986	122
91 5/8	15 3/8 14 7/8	16 7/8	4 4	Kodiak Island	AK	John D. "Jack" Frost	2005	122
91 5/8	15 6/8 15 2/8	13 5/8	3 4	Kodiak Island	AK	Rodney B. Davis	2008	122
91 4/8	14 6/8 14 4/8	13 0/8	5 5	Kodiak Island	AK	Chuck Adams	1986	126
91 2/8	12 4/8 16 2/8	13 2/8	5 4	Kodiak Island	AK	Randy Mannix	1984	127
91 2/8	15 2/8 16 0/8	14 4/8	4 4	Kodiak Island	AK	Tim Stelzer	1988	127
91 1/8	15 4/8 14 4/8	15 1/8	4 4	Kodiak Island	AK	Bob Ameen	2009	129
91 0/8	17 4/8 16 2/8	16 6/8	4 3	Hawkins Island	AK	Ken Radach	2003	130
91 0/8	16 0/8 15 0/8	16 7/8	4 5	Kodiak Island	AK	Tom Vanasche	2006	130
90 7/8	15 4/8 15 3/8	15 1/8	4 4	Kodiak Island	AK	Kirk Westervelt	1987	132
90 7/8	15 6/8 15 4/8	13 1/8	4 4	Kodiak Island	AK	John Sarvis	1987	132
90 7/8	15 5/8 15 6/8	14 3/8	4 4	Kodiak Island	AK	Jon Vanderhoef	1989	132
90 7/8	15 5/8 15 7/8	13 5/8	4 4	Kodiak Island	AK	John R. Hughes	1994	132
90 7/8	16 4/8 15 2/8	13 1/8	4 5	Kodiak Island	AK	Chris Reynolds	1996	132
90 7/8	16 5/8 15 6/8	16 3/8	4 4	Kodiak Island	AK	John Sarvis	2010	132
90 6/8	18 2/8 16 6/8	16 4/8	3 3	Kodiak Island	AK	Lon E. Lauber	1993	138
90 6/8	14 3/8 14 0/8	12 2/8	5 5	Prince of Wales Island	AK	William H. Welton	1995	138
90 6/8	16 5/8 15 4/8	13 4/8	4 4	Kodiak Island	AK	Wil L. Milam	2000	138
90 6/8	16 0/8 15 5/8	15 0/8	3 4	Sitkinak Island	AK	Billy Jack Elbert	2004	138
90 5/8	16 0/8 16 0/8	12 3/8	3 3	Kodiak Island	AK	Bob Ameen	2002	142
90 4/8	15 3/8 15 3/8	13 3/8	5 5	Kodiak Island	AK	Reggie Spiegelberg	1986	143
90 4/8	15 3/8 14 6/8	14 0/8	4 4	Kodiak Island	AK	Stan Parkerson	1992	143
90 2/8	16 4/8 16 5/8	15 6/8	5 3	Kodiak Island	AK	Mike Fenton	1988	145
90 2/8	14 2/8 15 2/8	12 2/8	4 5	Sturgeon Bay	AK	Richard A. Williams	1997	145
90 2/8	17 3/8 17 6/8	17 0/8	5 3	Kodiak Island	AK	Gary M. Martin	2005	145
90 2/8	16 4/8 16 4/8	15 4/8	3 4	Kodiak Island	AK	John Sarvis	2005	145
90 0/8	14 2/8 14 2/8	14 0/8	4 4	Kodiak Island	AK	Patricia Stewart	1989	149
89 7/8	17 1/8 16 7/8	15 7/8	4 3	Kodiak Island	AK	John Sarvis	1991	150
89 6/8	15 1/8 14 3/8	12 4/8	5 4	Kodiak Island	AK	John Sarvis	1984	151
89 6/8	16 0/8 15 4/8	14 2/8	4 5	Kodiak Island	AK	Lon E. Lauber	1993	151
89 6/8	18 4/8 17 6/8	15 2/8	3 4	Kodiak Island	AK	E. Lance Whary	1997	151
89 5/8	16 1/8 17 0/8	16 5/8	3 4	Kodiak Island	AK	Tony Russ	1992	154
89 4/8	16 0/8 15 2/8	14 6/8	3 4	Kodiak Island	AK	Bennett L. McMillian	1997	155
89 4/8	15 4/8 15 5/8	15 2/8	4 5	Kodiak Island	AK	Chuck Adams	1998	155
89 3/8	17 7/8 17 1/8	15 3/8	3 3	Kodiak Island	AK	Chuck Adams	1994	157
89 3/8	15 6/8 15 3/8	12 7/8	5 3	Kodiak Island	AK	Chuck Adams	1997	157
89 3/8	16 3/8 16 4/8	13 7/8	4 4	Sitkalidak Island	AK	Bill Payton	2008	157
89 2/8	16 0/8 15 5/8	14 2/8	4 4	Kodiak Island	AK	Chuck Adams	1994	160
89 2/8	14 7/8 15 0/8	12 6/8	4 3	Kodiak Island	AK	Chuck Adams	1998	160
89 2/8	15 4/8 15 2/8	12 6/8	5 4	Kosciusko Island	AK	Bob Ameen	2010	160
89 1/8	17 2/8 16 4/8	16 3/8	3 2	Kiliuda Bay	AK	Rick Tollison	1978	163
89 1/8	13 3/8 12 4/8	12 1/8	4 4	Kodiak Island	AK	Loren Flagg	1997	163
89 0/8	16 3/8 16 4/8	18 3/8	4 3	Kodiak Island	AK	Roger Stewart	1987	165
89 0/8	15 7/8 15 0/8	13 2/8	4 4	Kodiak Island	AK	George A. Moerlein	1990	165
89 0/8	15 5/8 13 0/8	11 6/8	4 4	Kodiak Island	AK	Bob Ameen	1994	165
89 0/8	16 1/8 15 6/8	14 6/8	5 4	Kodiak Island	AK	Chuck Adams	1996	165
89 0/8	15 4/8 15 3/8	12 6/8	5 3	Kodiak Island	AK	Chuck Adams	1996	165
88 7/8	15 7/8 15 5/8	16 4/8	3 4	Kodiak Island	AK	Kirk Westervelt	1987	170
88 6/8	14 7/8 15 0/8	12 6/8	5 4	Kodiak Island	Ak	John Sarvis	1986	171
88 5/8	14 5/8 15 2/8	12 7/8	4 4	Queen Charlotte Islands	BC	Atley Lovelace	1984	172
88 5/8	17 0/8 16 4/8	15 5/8	3 4	Kodiak Island	AK	Larry Spiva	1986	172
88 5/8	14 1/8 14 2/8	13 3/8	5 4	Prince of Wales Island	AK	William H. Welton	1994	172
88 5/8	16 0/8 16 1/8	15 1/8	3 3	Kodiak Island	AK	Bob Ameen	2008	172
88 4/8	14 3/8 14 0/8	14 2/8	5 4	Afognak Island	AK	Edward L. Russell	1983	176
88 3/8	16 2/8 15 4/8	14 1/8	3 3	Kodiak Island	AK	Bob Ameen	1996	177
88 3/8	14 7/8 14 4/8	13 3/8	4 4	Kodiak Island	AK	John D. "Jack" Frost	1999	177
88 3/8	14 6/8 15 4/8	13 3/8	4 4	Kodiak Island	AK	James L. Anderson	2007	177
88 2/8	16 0/8 15 4/8	14 2/8	4 4	Kodiak Island	AK	Michael Menke	1986	180
88 2/8	16 0/8 16 0/8	15 2/8	3 3	Kodiak Island	AK	Reggie Spiegelberg	1986	180
88 1/8	16 0/8 15 5/8	12 7/8	4 4	Kodiak Island	AK	Nathan L. Andersohn	1998	182
88 1/8	15 7/8 15 3/8	12 3/8	4 4	Kodiak Island	AK	Bob Ameen	2007	182
88 0/8	16 7/8 16 0/8	15 0/8	3 4	Kodiak Island	AK	Richard L. Westervelt	1987	184
88 0/8	15 3/8 15 6/8	13 6/8	4 4	Kodiak Island	AK	Tony Russ	1992	184
88 0/8	16 0/8 15 5/8	15 4/8	4 4	Kodiak Island	AK	Neil J. Russell	1993	184
* 88 0/8	15 0/8 14 4/8	14 6/8	4 4	Kodiak Island	AK	George Harms	2009	184
87 7/8	16 5/8 17 3/8	15 0/8	5 3	Prince of Wales Island	AK	Donald R. Pritchett	2005	188
87 6/8	14 5/8 14 6/8	15 3/8	4 4	Kodiak Island	AK	Bob Ameen	1998	189
87 5/8	14 2/8 14 5/8	13 7/8	5 4	Kodiak Island	AK	Terry Proctor	2004	190

292

SITKA BLACKTAIL DEER

Minimum Score 75 Continued

SCORE	LENGTH OF R MAIN BEAM L	INSIDE SPREAD	NUMBER OF R POINTS L	AREA	STATE/ PROVINCE	HUNTER'S NAME	DATE	RANK
* 87 5/8	16 7/8 16 6/8	15 5/8	4 3	Kodiak Island	AK	M. Blake Patton	2008	190
87 4/8	15 7/8 15 5/8	12 6/8	4 4	Kodiak Island	AK	Wil Milam	2005	192
87 3/8	16 3/8 17 3/8	14 3/8	4 3	Kodiak Island	AK	Tom Payer	1988	193
87 2/8	16 6/8 16 5/8	17 1/8	4 2	Kodiak Island	AK	Lon E. Lauber	1990	194
87 2/8	16 0/8 16 4/8	16 0/8	4 3	Deadman Bay	AK	Leon R. Meidam	1995	194
87 2/8	16 2/8 17 0/8	15 0/8	4 4	Kodiak Island	AK	Neil Russell	1996	194
87 2/8	15 0/8 15 1/8	12 4/8	4 3	Kodiak Island	AK	Bob Ameen	2004	194
86 7/8	15 0/8 14 4/8	14 3/8	4 4	Kodiak Island	AK	Jim Hodson	1985	198
86 7/8	15 1/8 15 2/8	14 3/8	4 4	Kodiak Island	AK	Stan Parkerson	1990	198
86 7/8	14 5/8 14 7/8	12 3/8	4 4	Kodiak Island	AK	Chuck Adams	1998	198
86 6/8	16 2/8 14 7/8	14 2/8	4 4	Kodiak Island	AK	Matt Jones	1985	201
86 6/8	15 5/8 15 2/8	15 4/8	4 4	Kodiak Island	AK	Bob Ameen	1991	201
86 5/8	16 1/8 15 5/8	16 3/8	4 3	Admiralty Island	AK	Charles R. Hakari	1983	203
86 5/8	15 7/8 16 2/8	14 7/8	3 4	Kodiak Island	AK	Gary M. Martin	2005	203
86 4/8	13 7/8 15 0/8	14 0/8	5 5	Kodiak Island	AK	Emron A. Yancey	1986	205
86 4/8	15 2/8 14 4/8	15 2/8	4 4	Kodiak Island	AK	Bob Ameen	1995	205
86 4/8	15 2/8 15 5/8	14 6/8	4 3	Old Harbor	AK	David Rue	1997	205
* 86 4/8	15 4/8 16 1/8	15 4/8	4 4	Afognak Island	AK	Paul E. Korn	2005	205
* 86 3/8	15 5/8 15 6/8	15 1/8	3 3	Kodiak Island	AK	Jarrett Finley	2006	209
86 2/8	16 0/8 15 1/8	14 0/8	4 4	Kodiak Island	AK	Troy Graziadei	1989	210
86 2/8	12 7/8 12 7/8	12 0/8	4 5	Kodiak Island	AK	Frank S. Noska IV	2005	210
86 2/8	15 5/8 14 6/8	13 2/8	4 3	Deadman Bay	AK	Mark Turner	2009	210
86 1/8	15 0/8 13 7/8	12 7/8	4 4	Kodiak Island	AK	John Toenes	1987	213
86 1/8	14 6/8 15 5/8	12 5/8	3 3	Kodiak Island	AK	Elmer R. Luce, Jr.	1994	213
86 1/8	15 1/8 14 5/8	11 5/8	4 4	Kodiak Island	AK	Chuck Adams	1997	213
86 0/8	15 3/8 15 1/8	13 0/8	3 4	Kodiak Island	AK	Tom Foss	2009	216
85 6/8	15 6/8 15 2/8	13 6/8	4 3	Kodiak Island	Ak	Bob Hayes	1986	217
85 4/8	15 2/8 15 2/8	14 2/8	4 4	Kodiak Island	AK	Matthew Reetz	2002	218
85 3/8	16 3/8 16 0/8	15 5/8	3 3	Afognak Island	AK	Roger Stewart	1980	219
85 2/8	15 4/8 15 0/8	14 0/8	3 3	Afognak Island	AK	Ralph Ertz	1983	220
85 2/8	15 7/8 14 6/8	13 4/8	4 4	Kodiak Island	AK	Marv Walter	1989	220
85 1/8	16 0/8 15 4/8	15 7/8	4 3	Kodiak Island	AK	Nathan L. Andersohn	1996	222
* 85 1/8	14 5/8 15 3/8	17 2/8	4 4	Sitkinak Island	AK	John Stone	2004	222
85 0/8	14 6/8 14 5/8	15 7/8	4 4	Kodiak Island	AK	John Sarvis	1985	224
85 0/8	13 1/8 14 4/8	15 1/8	4 4	Kodiak Island	AK	Roger Stewart	1987	224
85 0/8	14 6/8 16 2/8	14 0/8	3 5	Kosciusko Island	AK	Danny Moore	1992	224
84 7/8	14 3/8 16 1/8	16 1/8	3 4	Kodiak Island	AK	George P. Mann	1996	227
84 7/8	15 2/8 14 6/8	13 1/8	4 4	Kodiak Island	AK	Tony Russ	1996	227
84 7/8	16 3/8 16 1/8	15 1/8	4 5	Kodiak Island	AK	Troy A. Cunningham	2002	227
84 5/8	14 1/8 13 5/8	13 3/8	4 4	Kodiak Island	AK	Lon E. Lauber	1992	230
84 5/8	14 6/8 14 2/8	12 3/8	4 4	Kodiak Island	AK	Dawn Traub	1992	230
84 5/8	16 2/8 15 4/8	15 0/8	5 5	Kodiak Island	AK	Kelly J. Campise	1998	230
84 5/8	16 5/8 16 0/8	13 7/8	3 4	Sitkalidak Island	AK	Mark Berrie	1998	230
84 2/8	14 6/8 14 1/8	14 7/8	4 3	Kodiak Island	AK	Bill Krenz	1988	234
84 1/8	16 2/8 16 6/8	15 1/8	4 3	Kodiak Island	AK	Ralph Ertz	1984	235
84 1/8	14 4/8 14 6/8	13 1/8	3 4	Kodiak Island	AK	Elmer R. Luce, Jr.	1994	235
84 0/8	16 0/8 16 1/8	15 2/8	3 3	Kodiak Island	AK	Lon E. Lauber	1990	237
83 6/8	14 1/8 14 4/8	11 6/8	4 4	Kodiak Island	AK	Russell M. Kucinski	1989	238
83 6/8	15 4/8 15 0/8	15 2/8	4 3	Kodiak Island	AK	Elmer R. Luce, Jr.	1997	238
83 6/8	14 0/8 13 7/8	14 1/8	3 4	Kodiak Island	AK	Troy A. Cunningham	2004	238
83 5/8	15 3/8 15 6/8	13 7/8	2 3	Kodiak Island	AK	Bob Ameen	1994	241
83 4/8	15 5/8 15 3/8	13 4/8	3 4	Kodiak Island	AK	Dale Holpainen	1997	242
83 4/8	16 0/8 16 0/8	14 2/8	3 3	Kodiak Island	AK	Frank S. Noska IV	2006	242
83 3/8	14 6/8 14 4/8	12 5/8	4 3	Prince of Wales Island	AK	Danny Moore	1994	244
83 3/8	15 0/8 14 2/8	14 1/8	4 4	Kodiak Island	AK	John Sarvis	1996	244
83 2/8	15 4/8 15 2/8	15 4/8	3 3	Montague Island	AK	Ray Uhl	1978	246
83 2/8	14 4/8 14 0/8	13 2/8	6 6	Afognak Island	AK	Ralph Ertz	1981	246
83 2/8	15 0/8 14 3/8	13 4/8	4 4	Kodiak Island	AK	David A. Widby	1996	246
83 2/8	15 2/8 16 1/8	15 2/8	5 3	Kodiak Island	AK	Lee Jernigan	2006	246
* 83 2/8	16 4/8 15 6/8	15 4/8	3 2	Kodiak Island	AK	M. Blake Patton	2009	246
83 1/8	15 1/8 14 1/8	13 7/8	4 3	Sitkinak Island	AK	Allen Karl	2004	251
83 0/8	14 3/8 13 3/8	12 4/8	4 4	Kodiak Island	AK	Rich Biehl	1992	252
82 7/8	15 3/8 15 1/8	14 5/8	4 3	Kodiak Island	AK	John Sarvis	1991	253
82 7/8	13 2/8 16 1/8	14 3/8	4 3	Kodiak Island	AK	Bob Ameen	2009	253
82 6/8	15 0/8 14 4/8	13 2/8	5 4	Kodiak Island	AK	Bob Ameen	1997	255
82 6/8	14 6/8 15 0/8	15 1/8	4 3	Kodiak Island	AK	Bob Ameen	1998	255
82 6/8	15 3/8 14 0/8	12 4/8	4 4	Kodiak Island	AK	Guy Leibenguth	1998	255
82 6/8	14 4/8 14 2/8	15 5/8	4 4	Kodiak Island	AK	Bob Ameen	2008	255
82 5/8	17 0/8 15 4/8	13 1/8	3 4	Sitkalidak Island	AK	Tom Chadwick	1998	259
82 5/8	15 1/8 14 4/8	13 5/8	4 3	Kodiak Island	AK	Greg Munther	1998	259
82 4/8	12 6/8 14 0/8	12 6/8	5 5	Afognak Island	AK	Ralph Ertz	1980	261
82 4/8	14 4/8 13 7/8	14 5/8	4 4	Kodiak Island	AK	Richard L. Westervelt	1986	261
82 4/8	14 4/8 15 4/8	14 6/8	3 3	Kodiak Island	AK	Kirk Westervelt	1986	261
82 4/8	14 4/8 14 1/8	14 0/8	4 3	Kodiak Island	AK	Ken Vorisek	1996	261
82 4/8	12 6/8 13 0/8	13 0/8	5 5	Kodiak Island	AK	Cameron R. Hanes	1997	261
82 4/8	13 7/8 14 5/8	12 2/8	4 4	Kodiak Island	AK	James J. Akenson	1998	261
* 82 4/8	13 6/8 14 0/8	14 4/8	4 4	Kodiak Island	AK	Jarrett Finley	2006	261
82 3/8	16 0/8 15 1/8	14 7/8	3 3	Kodiak Island	AK	Tony Russ	1992	268
82 3/8	14 0/8 14 5/8	13 1/8	4 3	Kodiak Island	AK	John Sarvis	1997	268
82 2/8	14 3/8 14 2/8	12 4/8	4 4	Kodiak Island	AK	Kurt Keskimaki	1986	270
82 2/8	15 7/8 14 5/8	15 2/8	3 4	Kodiak Island	AK	Barry J. Smith	1996	270
82 2/8	16 1/8 15 1/8	14 2/8	3 4	Kodiak Island	AK	Greg Munther	1998	270
82 1/8	15 6/8 14 7/8	13 7/8	3 4	Kodiak Island	AK	Kevin Hisey	1993	273
82 0/8	15 4/8 15 7/8	15 0/8	3 3	Kodiak Island	AK	Bob Ameen	1993	274
82 0/8	15 2/8 14 7/8	13 6/8	3 3	Kodiak Island	AK	Stephen Kotz	1996	274
82 0/8	16 6/8 16 6/8	20 4/8	3 3	Deadman Bay	AK	Larry E. Sides, Jr.	2003	274
82 0/8	15 1/8 15 1/8	14 0/8	3 3	Kodiak Island	AK	John D. "Jack" Frost, MD	2006	274
81 7/8	15 4/8 14 2/8	13 7/8	3 3	Kodiak Island	Ak	Dyrk Eddie	1986	278
81 7/8	15 2/8 14 4/8	11 7/8	4 4	Kodiak Island	AK	E. Lance Whary	1997	278
81 7/8	15 1/8 15 3/8	12 5/8	4 3	Kodiak Island	AK	Bob Ameen	2004	278
81 7/8	15 0/8 15 3/8	13 7/8	4 3	Kodiak Island	AK	Greg Bokash	2005	278
81 6/8	14 4/8 14 5/8	13 4/8	4 4	Kodiak Island	AK	Roger Stewart	1988	282
81 6/8	14 1/8 13 3/8	13 2/8	4 4	Kodiak Island	AK	George P. Mann	1996	282
81 5/8	16 3/8 15 6/8	15 7/8	2 2	Kodiak Island	AK	Thomas Chadwick	1997	284
81 5/8	16 0/8 16 1/8	13 7/8	2 2	Kodiak Island	AK	Cameron R. Hanes	2002	284

SITKA BLACKTAIL DEER

Minimum Score 75 — Continued

SCORE	LENGTH OF R MAIN BEAM L	INSIDE SPREAD	NUMBER OF R POINTS L	AREA	STATE/PROVINCE	HUNTER'S NAME	DATE	RANK
81 5/8	15 0/8 15 1/8	14 1/8	4 3	Kodiak Island	AK	John Sarvis	2006	284
81 5/8	14 2/8 14 3/8	14 7/8	4 4	Kodiak Island	AK	Tom Foss	2009	284
81 4/8	14 5/8 15 4/8	13 2/8	4 3	Kodiak Island	AK	Ron Faust	1995	288
81 4/8	13 3/8 13 3/8	12 6/8	3 3	Kodiak Island	AK	Bob Ameen	1996	288
81 3/8	12 7/8 13 3/8	13 6/8	4 3	Kodiak Island	AK	Lon E. Lauber	1991	290
81 3/8	14 6/8 14 4/8	13 7/8	4 3	Kodiak Island	AK	Craig P. Mitton	2007	290
81 3/8	15 1/8 15 7/8	14 3/8	3 5	Kodiak Island	AK	William Newman	2008	290
81 2/8	15 0/8 11 7/8	13 4/8	4 4	Kodiak Island	AK	Richard L. Westervelt	1986	293
81 2/8	14 2/8 14 2/8	15 5/8	2 2	Uyak Bay	AK	Herman Griese	1987	293
81 2/8	16 0/8 15 5/8	14 4/8	4 3	Amook Island	AK	Garry A. Thoms	1989	293
81 2/8	13 6/8 14 3/8	14 2/8	4 4	Kodiak Island	AK	T. J. Conrads	1996	293
81 2/8	14 0/8 15 0/8	16 0/8	3 4	Kodiak Island	AK	Bob Ameen	1997	293
81 2/8	14 5/8 14 1/8	14 2/8	4 4	Kodiak Island	AK	John Sarvis	1999	293
81 2/8	15 1/8 16 1/8	14 0/8	4 4	Trinity Islands	AK	John Paul Schaffer	2002	293
81 1/8	15 3/8 15 3/8	12 1/8	3 3	Sturgeon Bay	AK	Richard A. Williams	1997	300
81 1/8	14 0/8 14 6/8	13 5/8	5 4	Kodiak Island	AK	Bob Ameen	1997	300
81 0/8	14 7/8 15 1/8	13 6/8	3 4	Kodiak Island	AK	James J. Akenson	1998	302
80 7/8	14 4/8 14 5/8	12 1/8	4 4	Kodiak Island	AK	Chuck Adams	1996	303
80 7/8	16 0/8 15 7/8	12 3/8	3 3	Kodiak Island	AK	Bruce Bartenfelder	1997	303
80 6/8	14 2/8 13 0/8	13 0/8	4 4	Kodiak Island	AK	Roger Stewart	1988	305
80 5/8	16 2/8 15 5/8	14 1/8	3 2	Kodiak Island	AK	Bob Ameen	1994	306
80 5/8	14 5/8 14 4/8	10 3/8	4 5	Graham Island	BC	Skip Valentine	2000	306
80 5/8	15 0/8 15 3/8	16 5/8	3 3	Kodiak Island	AK	Brady Bradford	2005	306
80 4/8	14 2/8 15 7/8	13 2/8	4 3	Kodiak Island	AK	Steve Gorr	1989	309
* 80 3/8	14 2/8 15 3/8	14 1/8	2 3	Sitkinak Island	AK	John Stone	2004	310
80 2/8	15 1/8 14 6/8	14 2/8	4 4	Kodiak Island	AK	E. Lance Whary	1997	311
80 2/8	14 1/8 13 6/8	12 2/8	4 4	Kodiak Island	AK	William L. Snelgrove	1997	311
80 1/8	13 2/8 13 1/8	13 1/8	4 4	Kodiak Island	AK	Jim Hodson	1985	313
80 1/8	13 4/8 13 5/8	14 7/8	4 4	Kodiak Island	AK	Ron Rockwell	2004	313
80 1/8	12 7/8 13 5/8	13 1/8	3 3	Kodiak Island	AK	Greg Bokash	2005	313
80 0/8	15 6/8 14 5/8	14 2/8	3 4	Afognak Island	AK	Charlie Kroll	1984	316
80 0/8	13 4/8 13 6/8	13 0/8	4 4	Kodiak Island	AK	Tony Russ	1990	316
79 7/8	15 0/8 12 6/8	13 7/8	4 4	Ugak Bay	AK	Carl E. Brent	1988	318
79 7/8	15 0/8 14 7/8	14 3/8	3 3	Baranof Island	AK	Clay J. Evans	2009	318
79 6/8	13 1/8 13 3/8	13 0/8	4 4	Kodiak Island	AK	Bob Ameen	2003	320
79 6/8	13 4/8 13 7/8	11 4/8	4 4	Kodiak Island	AK	Ken Radach	2005	320
79 5/8	14 5/8 15 0/8	12 7/8	4 3	Kodiak Island	AK	Richard L. Westervelt	1988	322
79 5/8	13 3/8 13 5/8	12 3/8	4 3	Sitkinak Island	AK	Billy Jack Elbert	2002	322
79 4/8	15 0/8 13 5/8	14 0/8	3 3	Kodiak Island	AK	Jim Hodson	1986	324
79 4/8	13 7/8 14 0/8	15 4/8	3 3	Kodiak Island	AK	Richard Gibson	1988	324
79 4/8	13 6/8 13 7/8	13 6/8	4 4	Kodiak Island	AK	John Sarvis	1992	324
79 4/8	15 0/8 15 0/8	15 1/8	3 3	Kodiak Island	AK	Bob Ameen	1993	324
79 4/8	13 6/8 14 1/8	13 6/8	4 4	Kodiak Island	AK	Jim Hayes	1994	324
79 4/8	14 0/8 13 7/8	14 5/8	4 4	Kodiak Island	AK	Dean Stebner	1994	324
79 3/8	16 1/8 16 1/8	17 0/8	4 3	Kodiak Island	AK	Chad Doell	1991	330
79 3/8	14 0/8 13 7/8	12 3/8	4 4	Kodiak Island	AK	Louis Strahler	1995	330
79 2/8	14 7/8 15 1/8	14 4/8	4 3	Kodiak Island	AK	Lon E. Lauber	1990	332
79 2/8	15 0/8 14 4/8	12 2/8	3 4	Kodiak Island	AK	John Sarvis	1990	332
79 2/8	13 2/8 13 2/8	11 6/8	4 4	Afognak Island	AK	Tom Miranda	2009	332
79 0/8	14 7/8 14 0/8	13 4/8	3 3	Kodiak Island	AK	Jim Hodson	1987	335
78 6/8	13 7/8 14 3/8	13 0/8	4 4	Kodiak Island	AK	John Sarvis	1990	336
78 6/8	14 1/8 15 1/8	11 2/8	4 3	Kodiak Island	AK	Shawn McCrosky	1991	336
78 6/8	14 6/8 14 6/8	16 1/8	3 3	Glass Peninsula	AK	Marvin H. Walter	1992	336
78 6/8	13 5/8 13 0/8	13 4/8	4 4	Kodiak Island	AK	John Sarvis	2004	336
78 5/8	15 7/8 15 7/8	19 0/8	2 3	Kodiak Island	AK	Roger Stewart	1987	340
78 5/8	14 5/8 14 2/8	13 7/8	3 4	Kodiak Island	AK	Tim Moerlein	1988	340
78 5/8	14 2/8 13 2/8	13 5/8	3 3	Kodiak Island	AK	Bob Ameen	1997	340
78 4/8	14 2/8 13 4/8	13 0/8	3 4	Prince of Wales Island	AK	Danny Moore	1993	343
78 4/8	13 2/8 14 3/8	12 6/8	4 3	Kodiak Island	AK	Pete Wilcox	2005	343
78 2/8	14 2/8 13 2/8	14 4/8	3 3	Kodiak Island	AK	Lon E. Lauber	2001	345
78 2/8	14 0/8 14 2/8	14 4/8	3 4	Sitkinak Island	AK	Allen Clark	2004	345
* 78 2/8	13 0/8 13 2/8	11 4/8	3 3	Kodiak Island	AK	David Mitchell	2004	345
78 2/8	14 1/8 14 4/8	15 5/8	3 4	Kodiak Island	AK	Jeff Cumberworth	2006	345
78 1/8	14 3/8 15 1/8	12 3/8	3 3	Kodiak Island	AK	Danny Moore	1984	349
78 1/8	14 4/8 14 7/8	13 5/8	4 4	Kodiak Island	AK	Len Cardinale	1986	349
78 1/8	14 3/8 13 4/8	13 7/8	4 4	Kodiak Island	AK	Michael V. Frost	1990	349
78 1/8	14 1/8 14 0/8	11 3/8	3 3	Kodiak Island	AK	Alan Harris	1995	349
78 1/8	12 2/8 12 1/8	12 1/8	4 4	Kodiak Island	AK	Tom Vanasche	2005	349
78 0/8	13 1/8 12 6/8	12 6/8	3 3	Kodiak Island	AK	David A. Widby	1988	354
78 0/8	16 3/8 15 3/8	16 4/8	4 4	Kodiak Island	AK	Lon E. Lauber	1992	354
78 0/8	14 7/8 15 3/8	13 2/8	2 4	Kodiak Island	AK	Joseph D. Pault	1992	354
* 78 0/8	14 6/8 13 3/8	14 6/8	3 3	Kodiak Island	AK	Jarrett Finley	2006	354
78 0/8	15 6/8 14 4/8	10 6/8	4 4	Kodiak Island	AK	Bob Ameen	2007	354
77 7/8	14 4/8 14 0/8	14 3/8	3 3	Kodiak Island	AK	Stan Parkerson	1991	359
* 77 6/8	14 2/8 14 1/8	14 4/8	4 3	Kodiak Island	AK	Jarrett Finley	2007	360
77 5/8	14 3/8 14 2/8	15 1/8	3 4	Kodiak Island	AK	Bob Ameen	1986	361
77 4/8	14 6/8 15 3/8	15 0/8	4 3	Kodiak Island	AK	David A. Widby	1990	362
77 4/8	14 3/8 14 2/8	13 0/8	4 3	Kodiak Island	AK	Craig E. Scarbrough	1990	362
77 4/8	15 0/8 13 6/8	13 2/8	4 2	Kodiak Island	AK	Bob Ameen	1994	362
77 3/8	13 4/8 13 0/8	12 1/8	4 4	Kodiak Island	AK	John Sarvis	1990	365
77 3/8	15 1/8 14 7/8	15 1/8	2 2	Prince of Wales Island	AK	Don Davidson	1991	365
77 2/8	15 2/8 15 2/8	13 2/8	3 3	Kodiak Island	AK	Chuck Adams	1984	367
77 2/8	13 3/8 14 2/8	16 3/8	4 3	Kodiak Island	AK	Neil Russell	1996	367
77 2/8	12 1/8 12 3/8	11 6/8	4 4	Kodiak Island	AK	John Sarvis	1996	367
77 2/8	14 7/8 14 6/8	12 6/8	3 3	Kodiak Island	AK	William C. Shuster	1997	367
* 77 1/8	14 7/8 14 1/8	14 3/8	3 4	Kodiak Island	AK	M. Blake Patton	2008	371
77 0/8	14 3/8 14 4/8	15 7/8	3 3	Chichagof Island	AK	Chris Reynolds	2000	372
76 7/8	14 0/8 13 3/8	10 7/8	4 4	Kodiak Island	AK	John Sarvis	1987	373
76 7/8	14 0/8 13 7/8	13 7/8	4 3	Kodiak Island	AK	Chuck Adams	1994	373
76 7/8	14 0/8 13 3/8	13 3/8	3 3	Kodiak Island	AK	Lee Jernigan	2006	373
76 6/8	13 6/8 13 6/8	14 7/8	3 3	Kodiak Island	AK	Patricia Stewart	1988	376
76 6/8	13 6/8 14 0/8	13 2/8	3 3	Kodiak Island	AK	John Amerson	1994	376
76 6/8	13 4/8 13 7/8	13 0/8	3 3	Kodiak Island	AK	Bob Ameen	2007	376
76 6/8	13 0/8 13 7/8	10 4/8	5 4	Kodiak Island	AK	John Sarvis	2007	376
76 6/8	13 2/8 12 7/8	12 4/8	4 4	Kodiak Island	AK	John Sarvis	2008	376

294

SITKA BLACKTAIL DEER

Minimum Score 75   Continued

SCORE	LENGTH OF R MAIN BEAM L		INSIDE SPREAD	NUMBER OF R POINTS L		AREA	STATE/ PROVINCE	HUNTER'S NAME	DATE	RANK
76 5/8	12 7/8	13 1/8	13 5/8	4	3	Kodiak Island	AK	Tony Russ	1990	381
76 5/8	12 5/8	12 4/8	12 3/8	4	4	Kodiak Island	AK	John Sarvis	1998	381
76 5/8	14 2/8	14 7/8	15 7/8	3	3	Kodiak Island	AK	David Rue	2009	381
76 4/8	14 6/8	14 2/8	12 6/8	4	4	Sturgeon Bay	AK	Richard A. Williams	1997	384
76 2/8	14 7/8	13 7/8	14 4/8	2	2	Kodiak Island	AK	Bob Ameen	1996	385
76 2/8	14 2/8	14 2/8	13 4/8	2	2	Kodiak Island	AK	Bob Ameen	2002	385
76 1/8	15 3/8	14 6/8	13 3/8	3	3	Kodiak Island	AK	M. Blake Patton	2006	387
76 0/8	15 4/8	14 6/8	14 2/8	3	3	Kodiak Island	AK	Lyle Willmarth	1986	388
76 0/8	14 0/8	14 4/8	14 7/8	2	3	Old Harbor	AK	Garry A. Thoms	1997	388
76 0/8	12 6/8	12 7/8	11 6/8	4	5	Prince of Wales Island	AK	David A. Widby	2000	388
75 7/8	12 7/8	12 1/8	11 5/8	4	4	Kodiak Island	AK	Frank S. Noska IV	2003	391
75 6/8	13 5/8	13 7/8	12 0/8	3	4	Afognak Island	AK	H. Richard Long	1984	392
75 6/8	14 2/8	14 3/8	11 6/8	4	3	Kodiak Island	AK	Rick A. Albers	1997	392
75 4/8	12 4/8	12 2/8	11 4/8	4	4	Kodiak Island	AK	John Sarvis	1987	394
75 4/8	13 0/8	12 5/8	12 4/8	4	4	Kodiak Island	AK	John Sarvis	1988	394
75 4/8	13 1/8	12 3/8	12 0/8	3	3	Kodiak Island	AK	Mark F. Vancas	1994	394
75 3/8	12 4/8	12 1/8	11 5/8	4	4	Kodiak Island	AK	John Sarvis	1994	397
75 3/8	12 3/8	13 1/8	14 0/8	4	4	Kodiak Island	AK	Bob Ameen	1996	397
75 2/8	13 5/8	13 1/8	12 6/8	3	4	Kodiak Island	AK	Gary G. Wall	1985	399
75 2/8	13 4/8	13 0/8	13 7/8	3	4	Kodiak Island	AK	Lon E. Lauber	1991	399
75 1/8	14 3/8	14 0/8	14 1/8	3	3	Kodiak Island	AK	M. Blake Patton	2004	401
75 1/8	14 7/8	14 6/8	11 7/8	2	2	Kodiak Island	AK	Dave R. Burget	2008	401
75 0/8	14 2/8	14 2/8	12 2/8	4	3	Kodiak Island	AK	Richard Moran	1988	403
75 0/8	14 0/8	14 0/8	15 1/8	4	3	Old Harbor	AK	Garry A. Thoms	1997	403
75 0/8	14 0/8	13 3/8	13 6/8	2	3	Sitkalidak Island	AK	Bill Payton	2008	403

SITKA BLACKTAIL DEER (VELVET ANTLERS)

Minimum Score 75

SCORE	LENGTH OF R MAIN BEAM L		INSIDE SPREAD	NUMBER OF R POINTS L		AREA	STATE/ PROVINCE	HUNTER'S NAME	DATE	RANK
91 7/8	16 2/8	16 2/8	14 3/8	4	4	Prince of Wales Island	AK	Jammin Krebs	2009	*
86 3/8	14 6/8	14 4/8	13 7/8	3	3	Olga Bay	AK	Randy Ries	2008	*
* 81 0/8	13 0/8	13 4/8	12 6/8	4	3	Olga Bay	AK	Ed Fanchin	2008	*
* 78 5/8	12 7/8	12 5/8	14 0/8	3	3	Olga Bay	AK	Ed Fanchin	2008	*

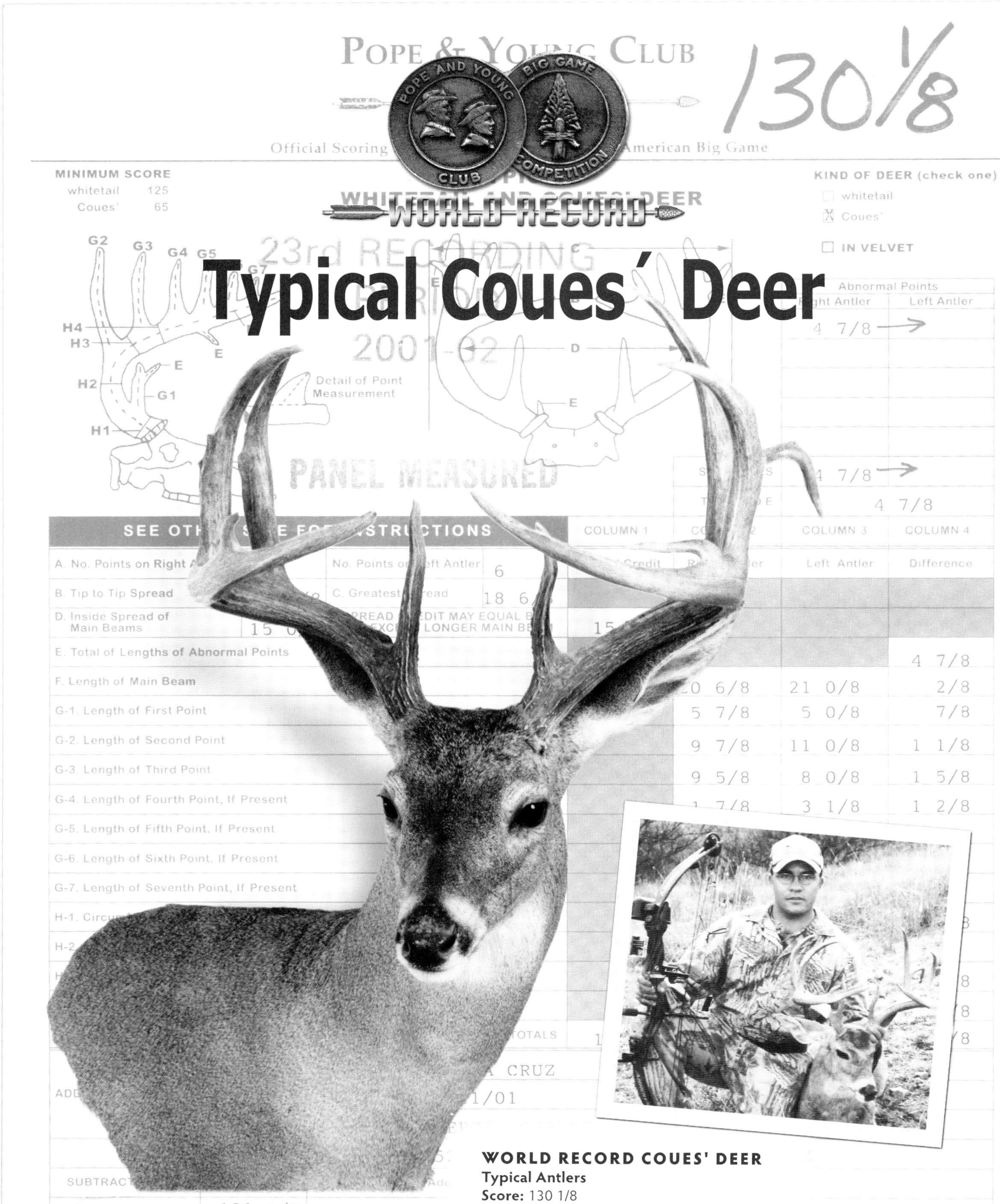

WORLD RECORD COUES' DEER
Typical Antlers
Score: 130 1/8
Location: Santa Cruz County, Arizona
Date: 2001
Hunter: Sergio Orozco

COUES' DEER (TYPICAL ANTLERS)

Minimum Score 70   *Odocoileus virginianus couesi*

SCORE	LENGTH OF R MAIN BEAM L	INSIDE SPREAD	NUMBER OF R POINTS L	AREA	STATE/ PROVINCE	HUNTER'S NAME	DATE	RANK
130 1/8	20 6/8 21 0/8	15 0/8	5 6	Santa Cruz County	AZ	Sergio Orozco	2001	1
*120 2/8	18 3/8 18 0/8	15 2/8	4 4	Pima County	AZ	Eric C. Rhicard	2006	2
120 1/8	18 4/8 18 7/8	17 3/8	4 5	Pima County	AZ	Bill P. Mattausch, Jr.	2006	3
119 7/8	19 3/8 18 3/8	14 5/8	5 5	Sonora	MEX	Jim Ryan	1999	4
119 0/8	18 1/8 18 2/8	14 6/8	4 4	Yavapai County	AZ	Randy Liljenquist	2010	5
116 0/8	17 3/8 18 2/8	12 0/8	6 6	Grant County	NM	Edward J. Holguin	1997	6
*114 0/8	19 1/8 19 6/8	14 2/8	4 4	Hidalgo County	NM	Roger A. Roan	2007	7
113 5/8	19 0/8 19 0/8	14 7/8	4 4	Socorro County	NM	Gerad Montoya	1999	8
113 2/8	19 0/8 18 6/8	16 0/8	4 5	Sonora	MEX	Randy Ulmer	2006	9
113 0/8	19 2/8 19 2/8	15 6/8	4 4	Cochise County	AZ	Dennis Eaton	1991	10
112 4/8	17 4/8 18 0/8	17 4/8	4 4	Gila County	AZ	Gary Iles	2006	11
112 2/8	19 4/8 19 6/8	18 4/8	4 5	Pima County	AZ	Kent J. Waller	2007	11
110 6/8	18 4/8 17 6/8	16 1/8	7 4	Gila County	AZ	Brian Rimsza	2009	14
110 5/8	19 5/8 19 2/8	16 1/8	4 4	Pinal County	AZ	Chuck Adams	1989	15
110 4/8	19 0/8 19 2/8	13 4/8	4 5	Pima County	AZ	Mike J. Frey	1991	16
109 1/8	17 5/8 17 3/8	12 7/8	6 7	Gila County	AZ	Dennis J. Montes	2006	17
108 0/8	17 0/8 17 7/8	13 6/8	4 4	Pima County	AZ	Michael "John" Bylina	2009	18
107 1/8	17 3/8 17 3/8	16 1/8	5 4	Gila County	AZ	Paul J. Koren	1996	19
107 0/8	16 7/8 16 6/8	14 0/8	5 4	Greenlee County	AZ	Todd Smith	2009	20
*106 7/8	17 5/8 16 6/8	13 5/8	4 5	Cochise County	AZ	Farrell Todd Poer	2009	21
106 6/8	20 3/8 20 0/8	17 2/8	4 4	Gila County	AZ	Jason Scarbrough	2007	22
106 4/8	16 0/8 16 4/8	12 6/8	4 4	Greenlee County	AZ	Eddie Claypool	1994	23
106 1/8	17 5/8 18 5/8	14 3/8	5 5	Cochise County	AZ	Harlon Wilson	1982	24
106 0/8	16 6/8 17 2/8	13 4/8	4 4	Sonora	MEX	Bruce Wilson	2009	25
105 7/8	17 5/8 17 2/8	11 7/8	4 6	Pima County	AZ	Harold Boyack	1985	26
105 6/8	16 2/8 16 6/8	14 4/8	5 4	Grant County	NM	Elmer R. Luce, Jr.	1998	27
105 3/8	15 5/8 14 7/8	14 3/8	4 4	Cochise County	AZ	Dagen Haymore	2009	28
104 6/8	16 2/8 16 5/8	13 5/8	6 7	Greenlee County	AZ	Bill Bishop, Sr.	2009	29
104 6/8	17 4/8 18 1/8	12 6/8	5 4	Sonora	MEX	Frank S. Noska IV	2010	29
104 2/8	18 2/8 17 7/8	15 0/8	4 4	Gila County	AZ	Larry Peterson	1978	31
103 5/8	17 7/8 17 5/8	16 1/8	5 5	Sonora	MEX	Jim Velazquez	1991	32
103 4/8	16 4/8 16 6/8	12 6/8	4 4	Pima County	AZ	Barry Sopher	1994	33
103 4/8	17 6/8 18 0/8	13 6/8	4 4	Sierra County	NM	David A. Widby	2005	33
103 2/8	16 7/8 17 2/8	14 4/8	4 4	Grant County	NM	Daryl Tow	1990	35
103 2/8	18 1/8 19 3/8	17 2/8	4 4	Gila County	AZ	Michael P. Wanat	1997	35
102 7/8	17 1/8 15 5/8	13 3/8	5 5	Grant County	NM	Daniel Morningstar	1988	37
102 5/8	16 6/8 17 1/8	13 7/8	4 4	Graham County	AZ	Kirk Westervelt	1996	38
102 4/8	16 4/8 16 7/8	15 2/8	4 4	Maricopa County	AZ	Dirk Van Dyke	2007	39
102 4/8	17 4/8 17 6/8	12 6/8	5 4	Sonora	MEX	Frank S. Noska IV	2009	39
102 2/8	17 2/8 17 3/8	15 7/8	5 4	Coconino County	AZ	Michael Wanat	1996	41
101 7/8	15 6/8 17 0/8	15 6/8	5 4	Grant County	NM	Peter LaScala	1989	42
101 6/8	16 4/8 19 6/8	15 4/8	4 4	Sonora	MEX	Dwight S. Wolf	2001	43
101 5/8	16 4/8 18 0/8	12 5/8	5 6	Sonora	MEX	Allyn Ladd	2009	44
101 4/8	16 2/8 15 4/8	13 2/8	4 4	Pima County	AZ	Heath Hibbard	1997	45
101 4/8	17 3/8 17 3/8	13 6/8	4 4	Pima County	AZ	Barry R. Sopher	2001	45
101 4/8	16 2/8 16 0/8	14 2/8	4 4	Pima County	AZ	Joe Ramos	2006	45
101 3/8	17 0/8 18 3/8	14 3/8	4 4	Sierra County	NM	John D. "Jack" Frost	1994	48
*100 7/8	17 0/8 16 2/8	14 1/8	5 5	Gila County	AZ	Mark Lucas	2004	49
100 6/8	16 6/8 16 3/8	12 6/8	4 4	Graham County	AZ	Hugh H. Hamman	1966	50
100 6/8	15 6/8 16 0/8	14 0/8	4 4	Cochise County	AZ	Joe Diedrich	2002	50
100 5/8	17 4/8 17 3/8	11 5/8	4 4	Cochise County	AZ	Mark Heller	1995	52
100 4/8	17 5/8 16 5/8	12 4/8	4 5	Cochise County	AZ	Dallas Scherck	1971	53
100 2/8	17 0/8 16 0/8	14 5/8	4 5	Cochise County	AZ	Ray Edwards	1984	54
100 1/8	16 6/8 17 7/8	14 1/8	4 5	Pima County	AZ	John D. "Jack" Frost	1993	55
100 1/8	16 7/8 17 2/8	15 3/8	4 4	Graham County	AZ	Mitch S. McInelly	2000	55
100 0/8	16 2/8 17 2/8	12 2/8	4 4	Hidalgo County	NM	Eddie Claypool	1997	57
100 0/8	16 2/8 16 2/8	14 0/8	4 4	Grant County	NM	Daryl Tow	2002	57
99 6/8	16 6/8 17 0/8	14 0/8	4 4	Pima County	AZ	Tracy Gene Hardy	1982	59
99 6/8	17 1/8 16 1/8	13 2/8	4 5	Cochise County	AZ	Milo Durfee	1997	59
99 6/8	17 3/8 15 3/8	12 2/8	4 4	Cochise County	AZ	Johnny Watson	2009	59
99 5/8	15 5/8 15 1/8	11 7/8	4 4	Greenlee County	AZ	Bill Bishop, Sr.	2007	62
99 4/8	16 7/8 16 4/8	13 0/8	5 4	Sierra County	NM	Bob Ameen	2002	63
99 3/8	16 7/8 16 0/8	13 3/8	4 4	Gila County	AZ	David B. Hatch	1988	64
99 2/8	17 4/8 17 6/8	15 7/8	7 4	Cochise County	AZ	Dagen Haymore	2000	65
* 99 2/8	16 0/8 15 3/8	12 2/8	4 4	Santa Cruz County	AZ	David Scott	2008	65
99 1/8	16 3/8 16 2/8	13 5/8	4 4	Pima County	AZ	Jim Walton	1992	67
99 1/8	17 5/8 17 7/8	14 7/8	4 4	Gila County	AZ	David R. Goitia, Jr.	2005	67
98 7/8	15 7/8 15 5/8	14 5/8	4 5	Gila County	AZ	Darryl Kessler	1978	69
98 5/8	13 0/8 13 4/8	12 3/8	6 4	Graham County	AZ	John A. Holcomb	1983	70
98 5/8	16 6/8 16 2/8	14 3/8	4 5	Pima County	AZ	George G. Alcorta	1989	70
98 5/8	17 2/8 16 1/8	12 1/8	4 4	Sonora	MEX	Frank S. Noska IV	2009	70
98 4/8	16 5/8 16 7/8	12 2/8	4 4	Santa Cruz County	AZ	Thomas J. Hoffman	1993	73
98 4/8	17 5/8 18 6/8	14 5/8	4 5	Gila County	AZ	William C. Bolt, Jr.	2007	73
98 3/8	17 1/8 17 0/8	13 7/8	4 4	Cochise County	AZ	David Schied	1973	75
98 3/8	18 2/8 18 0/8	15 1/8	4 4	Grant County	NM	Duane Beenblossom	1993	75
98 2/8	16 5/8 16 5/8	14 0/8	4 4	Grant County	NM	Larry M. Looman	1991	77
98 0/8	17 0/8 16 7/8	15 0/8	4 4	Cochise County	AZ	Brian Palmer	1990	78
97 7/8	16 0/8 16 3/8	12 3/8	4 4	Cochise County	AZ	Randy Breland	1989	79
97 6/8	16 2/8 16 2/8	11 4/8	4 4	Santa Cruz County	AZ	Brian Ham	1992	80
97 6/8	16 3/8 15 2/8	13 2/8	4 4	Sonora	MEX	Chuck Adams	2000	80
97 6/8	15 6/8 15 6/8	10 6/8	4 4	Sonora	MEX	Dr. David Samuel	2006	80
97 5/8	16 7/8 16 2/8	12 3/8	5 4	Gila County	AZ	Bill Longenbaugh	1999	83
97 4/8	16 0/8 15 0/8	14 1/8	4 5	Pima County	AZ	Steve Fossman	1989	84
97 4/8	16 2/8 16 0/8	13 6/8	4 4	Pima County	AZ	Robert D. Gallagher	1998	84
97 2/8	16 5/8 16 5/8	13 4/8	4 4	Cochise County	AZ	Dave Burdick	1994	86
* 97 2/8	15 2/8 15 4/8	13 2/8	4 4	Graham County	AZ	Robert Gray	2004	86
* 96 6/8	14 7/8 15 5/8	12 2/8	4 4	Grant County	NM	Doug Aikin	2010	88
96 5/8	16 0/8 16 0/8	13 7/8	4 4	Pima County	AZ	Jay Black	1993	89
96 5/8	16 0/8 16 5/8	13 5/8	4 4	Grant County	NM	Michael W. McKenna	2000	89
96 4/8	16 0/8 16 2/8	13 6/8	4 4	Pima County	AZ	Robert Forrest	2006	91
96 3/8	16 6/8 17 0/8	15 6/8	6 5	Graham County	AZ	Maurice Holthaus	1984	92
96 3/8	16 3/8 16 6/8	12 7/8	5 4	Grant County	NM	Duane Beenblossom	1992	92
96 2/8	16 5/8 17 1/8	12 0/8	4 4	Hermosillo	MEX	George Harms	2006	94
96 2/8	17 7/8 17 5/8	12 7/8	4 5	Sonora	MEX	Joel A. Johnson	2008	94
96 1/8	15 7/8 16 5/8	12 1/8	4 4	Greenlee County	AZ	Jim Van Norman	1998	96

COUES' DEER (TYPICAL ANTLERS)

Minimum Score 70 | | | | | | | | | Continued

SCORE	LENGTH OF R MAIN BEAM L	INSIDE SPREAD	NUMBER OF R POINTS L		AREA	STATE/ PROVINCE	HUNTER'S NAME	DATE	RANK
* 96 0/8	16 5/8 17 7/8	13 4/8	4	5	Santa Cruz County	AZ	Norman L. Bennett	2007	97
95 7/8	17 2/8 16 2/8	16 1/8	4	5	Gila County	AZ	Gary H. Mehaffey	2007	98
* 95 6/8	16 2/8 16 4/8	15 0/8	4	5	Gila County	AZ	Matt Reetz	2009	99
95 5/8	15 7/8 16 2/8	13 5/8	4	4	Santa Cruz County	AZ	Bill Krenz	1984	100
95 4/8	15 0/8 14 5/8	14 4/8	4	4	Cochise County	AZ	Charles W. Rehor	2010	101
95 3/8	17 2/8 17 6/8	15 3/8	5	4	Maricopa County	AZ	Bob Fromme	1986	102
95 3/8	17 4/8 17 5/8	13 7/8	5	4	Grant County	NM	Michael W. McKenna	2003	102
95 0/8	14 6/8 14 7/8	10 6/8	4	4	Santa Cruz County	AZ	Ted N. McMillion	1996	104
94 7/8	16 1/8 16 3/8	14 1/8	4	4	Sonora	MEX	Frank J. Benes III	2005	105
94 7/8	16 5/8 17 0/8	14 3/8	4	4	Sonora	MEX	Mike Brinkerhoff	2006	105
94 7/8	17 5/8 17 5/8	12 7/8	4	4	Sonora	MEX	William J. Langer	2006	105
94 5/8	15 5/8 14 7/8	12 3/8	5	5	Sonora	MEX	Dyrk Eddie	2005	108
94 5/8	17 5/8 18 1/8	14 4/8	4	4	Cochise County	AZ	Russ Richardson	2008	108
94 3/8	15 6/8 15 4/8	12 3/8	4	4	Cochise County	AZ	Randy Breland	1987	110
94 1/8	15 0/8 16 0/8	13 6/8	5	4	Greenlee County	AZ	John T. Skeen	1975	111
94 1/8	14 3/8 15 2/8	13 3/8	4	4	Cochise County	AZ	Daniel Staples	1981	111
94 0/8	16 6/8 16 1/8	14 0/8	4	4	Greenlee County	AZ	Jack Sartain	1983	113
94 0/8	16 4/8 16 6/8	12 6/8	4	5	Graham County	AZ	Dagen Haymore	2003	113
93 7/8	18 1/8 16 7/8	12 1/8	4	4	Gila County	AZ	Paula M. Koren	2005	115
93 6/8	17 1/8 17 1/8	13 2/8	4	4	Pima County	AZ	John DePonte III	1999	116
93 2/8	16 0/8 15 5/8	14 0/8	4	4	Sonora	MEX	Bob Ehle	2003	117
93 2/8	17 2/8 17 5/8	12 2/8	4	4	Santa Cruz County	AZ	Jonah M. Stewart	2006	117
93 1/8	14 3/8 15 0/8	14 3/8	4	4	Pima County	AZ	Jerry Muir	1982	119
92 6/8	16 0/8 17 0/8	13 4/8	4	4	Pima County	AZ	Peter C. Knagge	1986	120
92 6/8	15 7/8 16 0/8	13 0/8	4	4	Sonora	MEX	Allyn Ladd	2009	120
92 4/8	15 6/8 16 1/8	13 2/8	4	5	Pima County	AZ	Rick Forrest	1991	122
92 4/8	18 0/8 17 3/8	12 2/8	4	4	Sonora	MEX	Russ Richardson	2007	122
92 3/8	15 4/8 15 4/8	11 3/8	4	4	Santa Cruz County	AZ	Eugene A. Damron	1999	124
92 2/8	16 1/8 16 2/8	14 2/8	4	5	Santa Cruz County	AZ	Rowland J. Robinson	1985	125
92 2/8	17 5/8 17 4/8	12 6/8	4	5	Greenlee County	AZ	Tom Taylor	1993	125
92 1/8	15 4/8 16 2/8	13 5/8	4	4	Pima County	AZ	Rick Forrest	2005	127
* 92 1/8	15 4/8 15 6/8	14 1/8	4	4	Graham County	AZ	Ryan J. Baker	2006	127
92 1/8	16 0/8 16 2/8	12 7/8	4	4	Cochise County	AZ	Roger L. Bonesteel, Jr.	2008	127
92 1/8	15 6/8 16 0/8	14 1/8	3	3	Pima County	AZ	Barry R. Sopher	2009	127
91 7/8	18 4/8 17 7/8	14 1/8	4	4	Cochise County	AZ	Richard S. Barkley	1995	131
91 7/8	17 0/8 16 5/8	12 7/8	4	4	Grant County	NM	Jeff Campbell	1997	131
91 7/8	15 6/8 16 2/8	12 7/8	4	4	Cochise County	AZ	Dagen Haymore	2005	131
91 7/8	16 3/8 16 0/8	14 1/8	4	4	Santa Cruz County	AZ	Miguel F. Morales	2005	131
91 6/8	15 1/8 15 4/8	14 4/8	4	4	Cochise County	AZ	Randy Breland	1981	135
91 5/8	17 0/8 18 1/8	14 5/8	4	4	Pima County	AZ	Edward A. Chavez	1997	136
91 4/8	15 6/8 15 5/8	14 1/8	6	4	Gila County	AZ	Paul Koren	2000	137
91 4/8	15 0/8 15 3/8	12 0/8	4	4	Pima County	AZ	Patrick T. Lioy	2000	137
91 4/8	16 1/8 15 5/8	12 0/8	4	4	Gila County	AZ	Gary Mehaffey	2001	137
91 3/8	15 1/8 14 7/8	12 5/8	4	4	Pima County	AZ	Robert Forrest	2005	140
91 2/8	15 2/8 14 6/8	12 2/8	4	4	Santa Cruz County	AZ	Perry Schaal	1983	141
91 1/8	14 5/8 14 4/8	14 6/8	4	5	Yavapai County	AZ	Kyle Brock	1986	142
91 0/8	16 2/8 15 5/8	12 6/8	4	4	Gila County	AZ	John Radford	1972	143
90 6/8	17 0/8 17 5/8	14 6/8	4	4	Cochise County	AZ	Richard E. 'Dick' Johnson	1986	144
90 6/8	15 5/8 15 6/8	15 2/8	4	4	Gila County	AZ	Johnny D. Kemp, Sr.	2003	144
90 5/8	16 0/8 16 4/8	12 5/8	4	4	Cochise County	AZ	Gregory White	2005	146
90 5/8	16 0/8 15 0/8	13 1/8	4	4	Gila County	AZ	Bob Zavecz	2005	146
90 5/8	16 0/8 15 0/8	12 5/8	4	4	Sonora	MEX	Frank S. Noska IV	2010	146
90 2/8	15 5/8 16 6/8	12 6/8	4	4	Cochise County	AZ	Kim Wintz	1999	149
90 1/8	15 4/8 15 3/8	11 5/8	4	4	Pima County	AZ	Patrick L. Holehan	1999	150
90 1/8	15 5/8 16 2/8	13 1/8	4	4	Cochise County	AZ	Steve Crooks	2007	150
90 1/8	15 4/8 15 7/8	14 7/8	4	4	Greenlee County	AZ	Michael J. Larson	2009	150
90 0/8	15 5/8 14 6/8	10 4/8	4	4	Cochise County	AZ	Bob Ramirez	1990	153
90 0/8	16 2/8 17 1/8	14 2/8	4	4	Catron County	NM	Eddie Claypool	1998	153
90 0/8	15 5/8 14 7/8	14 6/8	4	4	Gila County	AZ	Eugene F. Wullkotte	2004	153
89 5/8	14 0/8 14 7/8	12 3/8	4	4	Pima County	AZ	Rick Forrest	1999	156
89 4/8	15 7/8 15 0/8	12 4/8	4	4	Pima County	AZ	Dwight Schuh	1997	157
89 3/8	14 6/8 14 6/8	10 3/8	4	4	Grant County	NM	John L. Gardner	2005	158
89 1/8	14 6/8 15 2/8	14 3/8	4	4	Gila County	AZ	Mark Ovitt	1994	159
89 1/8	14 1/8 14 3/8	14 1/8	4	4	Cochise County	AZ	Dagen Haymore	2004	159
89 0/8	15 3/8 16 5/8	13 2/8	4	4	Sierra County	NM	Perry Harper	1989	161
88 6/8	15 1/8 14 0/8	13 0/8	4	4	Graham County	AZ	Jack Smith	2004	162
88 6/8	15 2/8 15 0/8	13 6/8	4	5	Sonora	MEX	Stacee Frost	2010	162
88 5/8	14 2/8 15 1/8	11 3/8	4	4	Gila County	AZ	Michael P. Wanat	1995	164
88 5/8	15 6/8 16 0/8	14 3/8	4	4	Gila County	AZ	Kathy Trimble	2003	164
88 4/8	15 6/8 17 1/8	11 6/8	4	5	Cochise County	AZ	R. Ertz	1991	166
88 4/8	16 2/8 15 5/8	12 0/8	4	4	Cochise County	AZ	Walt Costello	1997	166
88 4/8	17 0/8 15 7/8	13 3/8	4	4	Grant County	NM	Michael W. McKenna	2007	166
88 2/8	16 4/8 15 4/8	13 1/8	4	5	Sonora	MEX	Jim Ryan	1999	169
88 1/8	14 2/8 14 2/8	9 7/8	4	4	Sonora	MEX	Archie J. Nesbitt	1999	170
88 1/8	16 4/8 15 3/8	14 1/8	4	4	Sonora	MEX	Adam Foss	2006	170
* 88 1/8	16 1/8 16 2/8	13 5/8	4	4	Hermosillo	MEX	Richard Davis	2010	170
88 0/8	13 7/8 13 4/8	11 2/8	4	4	Grant County	NM	Al Haines	1991	173
87 7/8	15 4/8 13 1/8	12 7/8	4	4	Cochise County	AZ	Dan Gwaltwey	1989	174
87 7/8	12 7/8 13 6/8	10 5/8	4	4	Apache County	AZ	Shaun Finch	1995	174
87 7/8	15 2/8 15 2/8	14 7/8	4	4	Sonora	MEX	Dennis Dunn	2006	174
87 6/8	13 7/8 14 6/8	13 6/8	3	4	Pima County	AZ	Patrick L. Holehan	1997	177
87 6/8	15 5/8 15 4/8	12 6/8	4	4	Sonora	MEX	Mark Zastrow	2003	177
87 5/8	16 2/8 15 5/8	9 5/8	5	4	Pima County	AZ	Joshua Forrest	2008	179
87 5/8	14 5/8 15 7/8	10 5/8	4	4	Pima County	AZ	Michael J. Bylina	2008	179
87 5/8	15 6/8 16 3/8	12 3/8	4	4	Sonora	MEX	Frank S. Noska IV	2009	179
87 3/8	15 6/8 15 6/8	13 7/8	4	4	Gila County	AZ	V. Randy Liljenquist	1996	182
87 3/8	16 2/8 15 6/8	13 5/8	4	3	Greenlee County	AZ	Bill Bishop, Sr.	2000	182
87 3/8	14 3/8 14 5/8	11 7/8	4	4	Santa Cruz County	AZ	Miguel Morales	2003	182
87 2/8	12 4/8 12 2/8	10 6/8	4	4	Sonora	MEX	Tom Foss	2007	185
87 1/8	14 1/8 13 6/8	10 3/8	4	4	Grant County	NM	Stan Godfrey	1993	186
87 1/8	15 4/8 15 2/8	11 1/8	4	4	Santa Cruz County	AZ	Michael "John" Bylina	1998	186
87 0/8	15 2/8 15 4/8	12 0/8	4	4	Santa Cruz County	AZ	Chris Warren	1998	188
87 0/8	16 7/8 17 4/8	11 6/8	4	4	Gila County	AZ	Brandt M. Lewis	2004	188
86 6/8	14 3/8 15 3/8	13 4/8	5	4	Santa Cruz County	AZ	William Rigas	2010	190
86 5/8	14 5/8 14 3/8	8 5/8	4	4	Santa Cruz County	AZ	Richard D. Amado	1994	191

298

COUES' DEER (TYPICAL ANTLERS)

Minimum Score 70   Continued

SCORE	LENGTH OF R MAIN BEAM L	INSIDE SPREAD	NUMBER OF R POINTS L		AREA	STATE/ PROVINCE	HUNTER'S NAME	DATE	RANK
86 5/8	15 5/8 15 1/8	12 3/8	4	4	Santa Cruz County	AZ	David Rue	2005	191
86 5/8	17 6/8 17 1/8	10 7/8	4	4	Sonora	MEX	Dennis Dunn	2010	191
* 86 4/8	16 7/8 16 2/8	13 0/8	4	4	Hermosillo	MEX	Angela K. Walk	2010	194
86 2/8	15 1/8 16 3/8	14 4/8	4	4	Grant County	NM	Bill Elmer	1992	195
86 2/8	15 5/8 16 3/8	12 0/8	4	4	Grant County	NM	Mike W. Leonard	1997	195
86 2/8	15 6/8 15 7/8	13 0/8	3	4	Grant County	NM	Patrick O. Finch	1999	195
86 1/8	14 7/8 15 6/8	14 3/8	4	3	Pinal County	AZ	Steve E. Allen	1979	198
86 1/8	14 5/8 15 1/8	13 5/8	4	3	Grant County	NM	Mike W. Leonard	2000	198
86 1/8	15 3/8 14 3/8	10 3/8	4	4	Cochise County	AZ	Dennis Doherty	2007	198
86 0/8	15 0/8 14 5/8	12 0/8	4	4	Cananea Aria	MEX	Edwin L. DeYoung	2002	201
85 7/8	17 4/8 16 6/8	15 1/8	5	4	Pima County	AZ	Reid Rutherford	1997	202
85 7/8	16 1/8 15 5/8	11 5/8	3	3	Santa Cruz County	AZ	Elmer R. Luce, Jr.	2010	202
85 6/8	14 2/8 14 7/8	14 0/8	4	4	Pima County	AZ	Brett D. Harris	2006	204
85 5/8	13 4/8 13 3/8	12 7/8	4	4	Hidalgo County	NM	John D. "Jack" Frost	1992	205
85 5/8	15 7/8 16 7/8	14 3/8	4	4	Grant County	NM	Steve T. Cecil	1996	205
85 5/8	14 2/8 14 7/8	15 7/8	4	4	Gila County	AZ	Terry Diedrick	2002	205
85 4/8	13 6/8 16 0/8	12 2/8	5	4	Santa Cruz County	AZ	Brad Wedding	1990	208
85 4/8	16 7/8 14 5/8	10 6/8	4	4	Santa Cruz County	AZ	Adam Blankenbaker	2002	208
85 2/8	15 2/8 16 2/8	11 4/8	3	4	Grant County	NM	Al Haines	2001	210
85 2/8	16 1/8 16 2/8	13 4/8	3	3	Cochise County	AZ	Eric Jensen	2007	210
85 2/8	14 4/8 14 5/8	10 4/8	4	4	Sonora	MEX	Carol Kindred	2008	210
85 1/8	14 7/8 14 7/8	11 3/8	4	4	Cochise County	AZ	Mark Escapule	1993	213
85 1/8	15 6/8 16 0/8	13 2/8	4	5	Gila County	AZ	Tom Johnson	2009	213
85 0/8	15 0/8 14 6/8	12 0/8	5	5	Graham County	AZ	Dennis L. Shirley	1991	215
85 0/8	13 6/8 14 7/8	11 4/8	4	4	Hermosillo	MEX	M. Robert DeLaney	2007	215
85 0/8	17 4/8 18 0/8	14 0/8	4	3	Sonora	MEX	Emma Narotzky	2009	215
84 7/8	13 0/8 12 2/8	10 3/8	4	4	Cochise County	AZ	Dave Rhodes	1976	218
84 7/8	15 5/8 15 6/8	11 5/8	4	4	Santa Cruz County	AZ	Dean Derby	2008	218
84 6/8	14 4/8 14 5/8	12 6/8	4	4	Pima County	AZ	Bill Thompkins	1988	220
84 6/8	15 6/8 15 4/8	13 4/8	3	3	Sonora	MEX	Dennis Dunn	2003	220
84 6/8	15 2/8 15 6/8	13 3/8	3	5	Santa Cruz County	AZ	Paul Navarre	2009	220
84 5/8	15 1/8 16 1/8	12 3/8	4	4	Graham County	AZ	Reggie Spiegelberg	2000	223
84 5/8	15 3/8 15 2/8	8 4/8	6	5	Sonora	MEX	Donald J. Aycock	2010	223
84 4/8	15 3/8 15 6/8	13 2/8	4	4	Pima County	AZ	Brandon Ray	2009	225
* 84 3/8	17 0/8 16 7/8	12 3/8	4	4	Sonora	MEX	Thomas J. Edgington	2008	226
84 2/8	15 0/8 13 4/8	13 2/8	4	4	Pima County	AZ	Robert W. Ledbetter	1989	227
84 2/8	15 4/8 15 0/8	15 2/8	4	4	Greenlee County	AZ	Donald P. Travis	1998	227
84 2/8	16 0/8 15 6/8	9 6/8	4	5	Cochise County	AZ	Dan Bonesteel	2006	227
* 84 2/8	14 4/8 14 2/8	12 2/8	4	4	Gila County	AZ	Joe Thomas	2006	227
84 1/8	13 4/8 13 7/8	12 5/8	4	4	Maricopa County	AZ	Ed Matteson	1963	231
84 1/8	14 6/8 15 2/8	11 7/8	4	4	Pima County	AZ	Robert B. Elam	1998	231
83 7/8	14 4/8 14 0/8	12 5/8	4	4	Gila County	AZ	Lee Hop III	2004	233
83 7/8	14 2/8 14 5/8	11 3/8	4	4	Cochise County	AZ	Duane "Corky" Richardson	2008	233
83 4/8	15 5/8 15 2/8	13 2/8	4	4	Sonora	MEX	Carol Kindred	2009	235
83 3/8	12 5/8 13 1/8	12 3/8	4	4	Cochise County	AZ	Danny Moore	2009	236
83 1/8	14 4/8 13 6/8	11 7/8	4	4	Santa Cruz County	AZ	Kurt W. Keskimaki	1995	237
* 83 0/8	15 5/8 15 5/8	13 6/8	3	4	Cochise County	AZ	Alan Harris	2007	238
83 0/8	13 3/8 14 1/8	9 4/8	4	4	Santa Cruz County	AZ	Phillip Rigas	2008	238
83 0/8	14 3/8 13 5/8	12 6/8	4	4	Coconino County	AZ	Elmer R. Luce, Jr.	2009	238
82 7/8	14 6/8 14 4/8	14 0/8	5	4	Grant County	NM	Michael W. McKenna	2006	241
82 6/8	15 3/8 15 7/8	13 3/8	4	4	Coconino County	AZ	Carl Vance	1973	242
82 6/8	14 7/8 14 2/8	10 2/8	4	4	Santa Cruz County	AZ	Thomas L. Wright	1993	242
* 82 6/8	14 2/8 14 6/8	12 6/8	4	4	Santa Cruz County	AZ	Donny D. Nash	2008	242
82 5/8	14 3/8 15 2/8	13 1/8	4	4	Gila County	AZ	Mike Mahoney	1976	245
82 4/8	14 4/8 14 1/8	12 0/8	4	5	Sonora	MEX	James Gabrick	2006	246
82 3/8	13 6/8 13 2/8	12 7/8	4	4	Apache County	AZ	Bill Bishop, Sr.	1999	247
82 3/8	14 0/8 14 5/8	13 1/8	4	4	Hermosillo	MEX	Gary Martin	2002	247
82 2/8	14 4/8 14 0/8	11 4/8	4	4	Sonora	MEX	Chuck Adams	2000	249
* 82 1/8	13 3/8 13 0/8	11 5/8	4	4	Grant County	NM	Andrew T. Dement	2007	250
81 7/8	15 7/8 9 1/8	14 3/8	4	4	Sonora	MEX	Eric Kolstad	2010	251
81 6/8	13 1/8 13 1/8	12 0/8	4	4	Pima County	AZ	Jack R. Frazier	1984	252
81 5/8	13 4/8 14 4/8	12 3/8	4	4	Greenlee County	AZ	David L. Willis	1992	253
81 2/8	12 4/8 12 1/8	13 0/8	4	4	Graham County	AZ	Bill Cross	1967	254
81 1/8	16 1/8 14 7/8	12 3/8	4	4	Pima County	AZ	Robert Forrest	1991	255
81 0/8	14 2/8 14 3/8	14 3/8	4	4	Grant County	NM	Bob J. Brown	1960	256
80 7/8	13 7/8 13 7/8	11 7/8	4	4	Gila County	AZ	Gary H. Mehaffey	1989	257
80 7/8	15 2/8 15 5/8	14 6/8	3	4	Pima County	AZ	Rick Goksel	2004	257
80 6/8	13 4/8 13 1/8	12 0/8	4	5	Grant County	NM	George M. Ratliff	1992	259
80 6/8	14 6/8 14 7/8	11 5/8	4	4	Cochise County	AZ	Brent McFarland	2009	259
80 5/8	14 5/8 14 0/8	13 3/8	3	3	Greenlee County	AZ	Glenn W. Isler	1993	261
80 5/8	14 2/8 14 7/8	12 7/8	4	4	Gila County	AZ	Ronald Nuss, Jr.	1994	261
80 5/8	15 0/8 15 6/8	12 7/8	4	4	Gila County	AZ	Justin Gabler	2003	261
80 4/8	16 1/8 15 2/8	12 7/8	3	4	Santa Cruz County	AZ	Thomas Chadwick	2005	261
80 4/8	13 7/8 14 5/8	14 4/8	5	4	Grant County	NM	Mike Burroughs	1993	265
80 2/8	14 7/8 14 4/8	11 0/8	4	4	Pinal County	AZ	Kenny Guyton	1999	265
80 2/8	16 4/8 15 2/8	14 6/8	3	4	Cochise County	AZ	Michael L. Holm	1968	267
80 1/8	14 4/8 13 4/8	10 3/8	4	4	Gila County	AZ	Randy L. Hill	1996	267
80 1/8	14 4/8 13 5/8	11 7/8	4	4	Pima County	AZ	Dave Snyder	1983	269
79 7/8	13 5/8 13 7/8	11 3/8	4	4	Grant County	NM	H. Glen Dodd	2006	269
79 6/8	13 3/8 13 5/8	11 2/8	4	4	Cochise County	AZ	Elmer R. Luce, Jr.	1996	271
79 6/8	16 2/8 15 6/8	12 6/8	4	4	Greenlee County	AZ	Ken Radach	2006	272
79 6/8	15 5/8 15 5/8	12 6/8	4	3	Cochise County	AZ	Todd Smith	2007	272
79 5/8	14 2/8 13 6/8	9 2/8	5	4	Sonora	MEX	Shawn Watts	2008	272
79 5/8	12 7/8 13 7/8	10 7/8	4	4	Grant County	NM	Walter Palmer	2009	272
79 3/8	16 2/8 15 7/8	13 3/8	3	3	Pima County	AZ	Mike Burroughs	1995	276
79 2/8	14 4/8 13 7/8	11 7/8	4	4	Sonora	MEX	Kevin P. Holt	2000	276
79 2/8	16 0/8 13 7/8	13 5/8	4	4	Pima County	AZ	Bailey Simpson	2007	278
79 0/8	14 2/8 13 7/8	13 2/8	4	4	Gila County	AZ	David C. Durkee	1987	279
79 0/8	15 6/8 14 2/8	14 4/8	3	4	Santa Cruz County	AZ	Colton Boulanger	2001	280
* 79 0/8	17 2/8 17 0/8	12 4/8	4	4	Sonora	MEX	Thomas Chadwick	2006	280
78 7/8	14 3/8 13 6/8	12 3/8	4	4	Sonora	MEX	Doug Harris	2010	280
78 6/8	13 3/8 13 3/8	10 0/8	4	4	Santa Cruz County	AZ	G. Lowe Morrison	2008	283
78 5/8	13 7/8 14 4/8	9 3/8	4	4	Grant County	NM	Eric A. Sawyer	2008	284
78 5/8	13 4/8 13 2/8	9 5/8	4	4	Sonora	MEX	Mike W. Leonard	1999	285
							Dan Brockman	2010	285

COUES' DEER (TYPICAL ANTLERS)

Minimum Score 70   Continued

Score	Length of Main Beam R	L	Inside Spread	Number of Points R	L	Area	State/Province	Hunter's Name	Date	Rank
78 4/8	13 1/8	14 0/8	11 0/8	4	4	Grant County	NM	David H. Boland	2006	287
* 78 4/8	14 3/8	13 7/8	10 6/8	4	4	Pima County	AZ	Gary E. Mitchell	2010	287
78 3/8	12 6/8	13 6/8	11 5/8	4	4	Pima County	AZ	Zach Nicholson	2008	289
78 2/8	14 0/8	14 1/8	12 4/8	4	4	Pima County	AZ	Jim Walton	1990	290
78 2/8	13 4/8	14 6/8	11 2/8	4	4	Santa Cruz County	AZ	Casey A. Blum	2002	290
78 2/8	12 6/8	12 5/8	10 0/8	4	4	Greenlee County	AZ	Bill Bishop, Sr.	2005	290
78 1/8	15 0/8	14 6/8	12 5/8	4	4	Santa Cruz County	AZ	Matt Mueller	1994	293
* 78 1/8	14 4/8	13 6/8	11 1/8	4	4	Cochise County	AZ	Conrad Sheley	2007	293
78 0/8	12 3/8	12 5/8	10 2/8	4	4	Gila County	AZ	Gary Mehaffey	1992	295
77 7/8	15 3/8	14 7/8	12 5/8	3	3	Gila County	AZ	Tom Hashem	1964	296
77 7/8	16 3/8	16 3/8	14 7/8	3	3	Sonora	MEX	Dwight S. Wolf	2003	296
77 7/8	13 2/8	15 7/8	12 3/8	4	4	Santa Cruz County	AZ	Karl Hirst	2006	296
77 6/8	14 2/8	14 1/8	9 6/8	5	5	Pima County	AZ	Richard Dawe, Jr.	1964	299
77 5/8	12 4/8	14 1/8	11 1/8	4	4	Cochise County	AZ	Dagen Haymore	2002	300
77 4/8	14 4/8	13 7/8	10 4/8	4	5	Sierra County	NM	Charles E. Franzoy	1972	301
77 3/8	14 1/8	14 0/8	11 5/8	4	4	Sonora	MEX	Rick Duggan	2003	302
77 2/8	13 4/8	13 4/8	10 2/8	4	4	Sonora	MEX	John M. Cogswell	2008	303
77 1/8	13 1/8	13 5/8	12 1/8	4	4	Gila County	AZ	Thomas J. Hoffman	1995	304
77 1/8	13 4/8	13 3/8	11 7/8	4	4	Sonora	MEX	Frank S. Noska IV	2006	304
77 0/8	14 1/8	14 2/8	10 6/8	4	4	Sonora	MEX	Ginger Brockman	2010	306
76 7/8	13 1/8	13 3/8	10 3/8	4	4	Cochise County	AZ	Rex B. Smith	1999	307
76 7/8	14 4/8	14 4/8	12 3/8	4	4	Greenlee County	AZ	Michael J. Larson	2007	307
76 7/8	12 1/8	12 4/8	11 3/8	4	5	Cochise County	AZ	Cindi Richardson	2008	307
76 6/8	12 7/8	13 3/8	12 0/8	4	3	Cochise County	AZ	Robert G. Ables	1989	310
76 6/8	12 7/8	12 6/8	12 2/8	4	4	Santa Cruz County	AZ	Kurt W. Keskimaki	1994	310
76 6/8	13 2/8	13 1/8	10 4/8	4	4	Gila County	AZ	Michael R. Fischer	2004	310
* 76 5/8	13 4/8	14 0/8	11 1/8	3	3	Cochise County	AZ	David Wildenstein	2008	313
76 5/8	13 2/8	12 7/8	12 2/8	4	5	Gila County	AZ	Gary H. Mehaffey	2008	313
76 4/8	14 7/8	14 3/8	12 0/8	3	4	Gila County	AZ	Monty Dyke	1989	315
76 2/8	12 2/8	12 7/8	10 2/8	4	4	Cochise County	AZ	Bob Bonesteel	2000	316
* 76 2/8	14 0/8	13 6/8	9 2/8	4	3	Sonora	MEX	Lou Kindred	2006	316
76 0/8	14 3/8	14 1/8	11 2/8	4	4	Cochise County	AZ	Phillip C. Dalrymple	2009	318
* 75 7/8	14 1/8	14 1/8	9 7/8	4	4	Cochise County	AZ	Conrad Sheley	2008	319
75 6/8	14 6/8	14 4/8	11 6/8	3	4	Pima County	AZ	Dalton Fisher, Jr.	2000	320
75 5/8	13 1/8	13 2/8	10 3/8	4	4	Cochise County	AZ	Daniel L. Sommer	2003	321
75 5/8	16 1/8	10 3/8	13 1/8	3	3	Cochise County	AZ	Richard D. Tone	2009	321
75 4/8	13 1/8	12 7/8	12 0/8	4	4	Coconino County	AZ	Les Shelton	1987	323
75 4/8	14 6/8	14 6/8	11 6/8	4	3	Pima County	AZ	Blair Sandberg	2006	323
75 4/8	13 1/8	12 5/8	10 4/8	4	4	Pima County	AZ	David Huba	2010	323
75 3/8	15 1/8	15 3/8	11 5/8	4	4	Sonora	MEX	Tim Walters	2006	326
75 3/8	13 3/8	14 0/8	9 7/8	3	4	Sonora	MEX	Tom Dyk	2010	326
75 3/8	14 1/8	14 2/8	11 7/8	4	3	Cochise County	AZ	Jim Dougherty	2010	326
75 2/8	13 2/8	13 7/8	10 2/8	4	4	Cochise County	AZ	Russell L. Gann	1987	329
75 2/8	14 4/8	14 6/8	12 0/8	4	4	Graham County	AZ	Chuck Adams	1989	329
75 2/8	12 7/8	13 0/8	10 6/8	4	4	Cochise County	AZ	R. Ertz	1990	329
75 2/8	13 4/8	13 5/8	11 6/8	4	3	Pima County	AZ	Tony Otte	1993	329
75 2/8	14 0/8	13 6/8	13 6/8	4	4	Cochise County	AZ	Stan Parkerson	1995	329
75 2/8	13 6/8	13 1/8	11 4/8	4	4	Sonora	MEX	Dale Karch	2005	329
75 1/8	11 3/8	11 3/8	12 0/8	4	4	Gila County	AZ	Brandt M. Lewis	2005	335
75 0/8	15 0/8	15 7/8	14 6/8	3	3	Grant County	NM	David H. Boland	1994	336
75 0/8	14 1/8	14 3/8	12 0/8	3	4	Sonora	MEX	Gregory White	2007	336
75 0/8	14 0/8	14 2/8	12 2/8	4	4	Santa Cruz County	AZ	Thomas Chadwick	2007	336
74 7/8	12 7/8	13 1/8	11 3/8	4	4	Arizbe	MEX	Matt Liljenquist	2001	339
74 7/8	13 1/8	14 4/8	10 7/8	4	4	Greenlee County	AZ	Bill Bishop, Sr.	2003	339
* 74 7/8	11 5/8	13 0/8	10 5/8	4	4	Sierra County	NM	Lisa Ameen	2005	339
74 6/8	13 0/8	13 2/8	12 0/8	4	4	Sonora	MEX	Charles E. Nichol	2008	342
74 5/8	14 5/8	14 6/8	10 5/8	3	4	Sierra County	NM	Jim Ryan	1988	343
74 4/8	12 4/8	12 5/8	12 4/8	4	4	Santa Cruz County	AZ	Jonah M. Stewart	2009	344
74 3/8	13 6/8	13 3/8	11 1/8	3	4	Greenlee County	AZ	Richard E. Bickley	1998	345
74 3/8	13 5/8	13 7/8	9 7/8	4	4	Sonora	MEX	Dennis C. Kerr	2001	345
74 2/8	12 6/8	12 1/8	9 4/8	4	4	Grant County	NM	Mike W. Leonard	1992	347
74 2/8	12 5/8	12 5/8	9 4/8	4	4	Hermosillo	MEX	Bryce H. Olson	2010	347
74 1/8	13 4/8	13 4/8	10 7/8	4	4	Sonora	MEX	Joe Keathley	2003	349
74 1/8	13 1/8	13 6/8	10 7/8	4	4	Santa Cruz County	AZ	Phillip Rigas	2010	349
73 6/8	12 6/8	13 1/8	10 4/8	4	4	Pima County	AZ	Howard Cooper	1980	351
73 6/8	12 2/8	13 5/8	11 2/8	4	3	Pima County	AZ	William E. Dickinson	1982	351
* 73 6/8	12 1/8	12 3/8	11 0/8	4	4	Pima County	AZ	Ian W. Cassidy	2009	351
73 5/8	12 2/8	12 7/8	13 4/8	5	4	Hidalgo County	NM	Larry Behrends	1969	354
73 4/8	15 0/8	14 4/8	13 2/8	2	4	Pima County	AZ	Michael L. Henrikson	1979	355
73 4/8	9 2/8	13 3/8	11 0/8	4	4	Pima County	AZ	Dave Rue	1994	355
73 4/8	15 3/8	14 1/8	10 2/8	3	3	Sonora	MEX	Steve Miller	2009	355
73 4/8	13 6/8	13 4/8	12 4/8	4	3	Graham County	AZ	Nolan Reid	2009	355
73 3/8	13 2/8	13 2/8	11 5/8	4	4	Cochise County	AZ	Beard Hobbs	2009	359
73 2/8	13 0/8	13 0/8	10 6/8	4	4	Gila County	AZ	Jim Mercer	1958	360
72 7/8	13 3/8	13 2/8	11 3/8	4	4	Pima County	AZ	Zack Walton	2009	361
72 6/8	13 2/8	13 4/8	12 4/8	4	3	Sierra County	NM	Thomas J. Hoffman	1994	362
72 6/8	13 5/8	13 2/8	11 4/8	3	4	Graham County	AZ	Jack Smith	2002	362
72 6/8	13 4/8	13 3/8	10 6/8	4	4	Sonora	MEX	Mark Buehrer	2008	362
72 5/8	13 7/8	14 2/8	11 1/8	4	4	Grant County	NM	Bill L. Marek	1997	365
72 5/8	13 2/8	13 4/8	10 1/8	4	5	Cochise County	AZ	Thomas L. Egnew	2007	365
72 5/8	13 3/8	13 1/8	10 5/8	4	4	Santa Cruz County	AZ	Jonah M. Stewart	2008	365
72 4/8	11 6/8	11 6/8	11 4/8	4	4	Gila County	AZ	Gary H. Behrends	1969	368
* 72 4/8	14 1/8	14 1/8	12 0/8	3	3	Sonora	MEX	Roy K. Keefer	2009	368
72 3/8	13 6/8	13 4/8	12 1/8	4	4	Hermosillo	MEX	Dr. Robert Narotzky	2006	370
72 2/8	12 5/8	13 0/8	9 6/8	4	4	Pima County	AZ	James Fenstermacher	2007	371
* 72 2/8	12 2/8	11 4/8	12 2/8	4	4	Santa Cruz County	AZ	Dave Spacek	2007	371
72 1/8	12 3/8	12 7/8	12 5/8	4	4	Gila County	AZ	Milo Durfee	2004	373
72 0/8	13 1/8	12 6/8	10 2/8	4	4	Greenlee County	AZ	Tom Taylor	1995	374
71 7/8	13 5/8	11 0/8	13 3/8	3	4	Gila County	AZ	Paula Koren	2002	375
71 5/8	12 5/8	12 3/8	11 3/8	4	4	Gila County	AZ	Arthur R. Baribault	1995	376
71 5/8	13 1/8	13 0/8	12 3/8	3	3	Santa Cruz County	AZ	Andrew J. Long	1996	376
71 4/8	15 1/8	14 7/8	14 0/8	3	2	Gila County	AZ	Gilbert Wiley	1996	378
71 2/8	12 7/8	12 7/8	13 2/8	4	3	Pima County	AZ	Stephen E. Johnson	1979	379
71 2/8	12 2/8	11 7/8	11 4/8	4	4	Hidalgo County	NM	Eddie Claypool	1999	379
71 2/8	13 6/8	14 4/8	9 2/8	4	4	Sonora	MEX	Paul E. Korn	2007	379

COUES' DEER (TYPICAL ANTLERS)

Minimum Score 70   Continued

SCORE	LENGTH OF R MAIN BEAM L	INSIDE SPREAD	NUMBER OF R POINTS L	AREA	STATE/ PROVINCE	HUNTER'S NAME	DATE	RANK
* 71 2/8	14 2/8 15 4/8	13 4/8	4 3	Maricopa County	AZ	Robert J. Dias	2009	379
70 7/8	13 3/8 15 0/8	12 5/8	4 4	Grant County	NM	David H. Boland	1996	383
70 7/8	13 4/8 14 6/8	13 1/8	3 3	Cochise County	AZ	Thomas Chadwick	1996	383
70 7/8	13 7/8 10 3/8	11 3/8	3 3	Cochise County	AZ	Barry Sopher	2003	383
70 7/8	11 7/8 12 3/8	10 3/8	4 4	Grant County	NM	Thomas E. Rothrock	2004	383
70 5/8	12 4/8 14 3/8	12 1/8	5 4	Santa Cruz County	AZ	Edwin John Conrath III	2005	387
70 5/8	13 1/8 14 0/8	13 3/8	4 4	Pima County	AZ	Bob Rimzsa	2006	387
70 3/8	15 0/8 13 4/8	10 1/8	5 4	Sonora	MEX	Richard J. Langer	2006	389
70 2/8	12 0/8 12 5/8	11 2/8	4 4	Cananea Aria	MEX	Edwin L. DeYoung	2002	390
70 1/8	12 0/8 12 6/8	8 7/8	3 3	Grant County	NM	Mike Leonard	2001	391
70 0/8	13 5/8 13 5/8	11 0/8	4 4	Sonora	MEX	Duane "Corky" Richardson	2007	392
69 7/8	15 5/8 11 4/8	10 7/8	4 4	Sonora	MEX	Craig P. Mitton	2009	393
69 2/8	12 6/8 13 2/8	9 6/8	4 4	Sonora	MEX	Michael Traub	2003	394
69 2/8	12 1/8 12 3/8	10 2/8	4 4	Gila County	AZ	Tim C. Smith	2004	394
* 69 2/8	13 0/8 12 0/8	8 6/8	3 3	Cochise County	AZ	Tod Graham	2008	394
69 1/8	10 7/8 11 6/8	11 3/8	4 4	Pima County	AZ	Anthony Bemer	1999	397
69 1/8	15 5/8 14 6/8	11 5/8	4 2	Santa Cruz County	AZ	Scott Hargrove	2008	397
* 69 1/8	13 4/8 13 5/8	10 3/8	4 4	Sierra County	NM	Doug Aikin	2009	397
68 6/8	13 2/8 12 7/8	10 0/8	3 4	Atasco Mtns.	AZ	Peter C. Knagge	1978	400
68 6/8	12 5/8 12 7/8	12 0/8	4 4	Cochise County	AZ	Daniel Staples	1980	400
68 5/8	12 0/8 12 2/8	11 7/8	3 3	Graham County	AZ	Matthew Liljenquist	1995	402
68 5/8	9 7/8 13 1/8	12 5/8	4 4	Grant County	NM	Mark A. McKenna	2009	402
68 1/8	11 3/8 12 3/8	9 7/8	4 4	Sonora	MEX	L. Grant Foster	2007	404
67 6/8	12 6/8 12 7/8	11 0/8	3 4	Gila County	AZ	Danny Dryden	1998	405
67 4/8	13 0/8 13 3/8	13 0/8	4 3	Graham County	AZ	Chuck Adams	1988	406
67 4/8	14 2/8 14 1/8	11 6/8	3 3	Greenlee County	AZ	Bill Bishop, Sr.	2001	406
67 1/8	14 3/8 14 3/8	11 5/8	3 2	Sonora	MEX	Frank S. Noska IV	2006	408
67 0/8	13 5/8 12 6/8	11 0/8	3 4	Graham County	AZ	Reggie Spiegelberg	2006	409
66 6/8	12 1/8 11 7/8	10 6/8	4 4	Pima County	AZ	Steve Neuberger	1989	410
66 5/8	11 5/8 11 6/8	10 3/8	4 4	Cochise County	AZ	Brian Bonesteel	2002	411
66 5/8	12 5/8 12 3/8	14 1/8	4 3	Coconino County	AZ	D. J. Wood	2002	411
66 4/8	12 3/8 12 4/8	8 6/8	3 3	Pima County	AZ	Larry Rogge	1984	413
66 3/8	12 1/8 12 5/8	9 7/8	4 4	Grant County	NM	Don Guber	1996	414
66 3/8	11 7/8 11 7/8	11 7/8	3 3	Cochise County	AZ	Joe Diedrich	1997	414
66 2/8	12 3/8 12 5/8	10 0/8	3 3	Grant County	NM	Chuck Schultz	1991	416
66 1/8	11 5/8 12 2/8	11 1/8	4 4	Graham County	AZ	Anna C. Ward	1997	417
65 2/8	13 3/8 13 3/8	12 6/8	2 3	Cochise County	AZ	Phillip C. Dalrymple	2005	418
65 0/8	14 3/8 11 0/8	7 2/8	4 3	Grant County	NM	Dr. Eugene T. Altiere	1998	419
65 0/8	12 7/8 12 5/8	9 4/8	4 4	Grant County	NM	Mike W. Leonard	2003	419

COUES' DEER (TYPICAL VELVET ANTLERS)

Minimum Score 70

SCORE	LENGTH OF R MAIN BEAM L	INSIDE SPREAD	NUMBER OF R POINTS L	AREA	STATE/ PROVINCE	HUNTER'S NAME	DATE	RANK
110 4/8	17 6/8 16 3/8	13 2/8	4 6	Cochise County	AZ	Jim Machac	2003	*
110 4/8	18 1/8 18 0/8	13 2/8	5 4	Gila County	AZ	Chris Carrera	2007	*
*109 7/8	18 6/8 18 5/8	13 7/8	4 4	Catron County	NM	Steve Nave	2009	*
*109 4/8	16 5/8 16 1/8	10 4/8	4 4	Gila County	AZ	Broc W. Brimhall	2009	*
*108 6/8	17 3/8 16 1/8	13 2/8	5 5	Gila County	AZ	Wallace Shane Church	2005	*
*107 0/8	17 2/8 17 5/8	17 2/8	5 5	Greenlee County	AZ	Kevin Scott	2007	*
*100 0/8	16 6/8 17 2/8	14 2/8	4 5	Gila County	AZ	Jimmy W. Toon, Sr.	2006	*
98 2/8	15 7/8 16 3/8	13 6/8	4 4	Greenlee County	AZ	Roy Jimenez	2005	*
98 0/8	17 5/8 17 4/8	17 4/8	3 4	Coconino County	AZ	Jeff Falls	2004	*
* 98 0/8	14 7/8 15 3/8	15 0/8	4 4	Gila County	AZ	Eric Kelsh	2007	*
96 7/8	15 7/8 15 7/8	14 3/8	4 5	Gila County	AZ	Carl Guilliams	2005	*
93 1/8	15 3/8 15 4/8	13 5/8	3 4	Gila County	AZ	Perry Vance Dunn	2007	*
93 0/8	15 0/8 15 2/8	11 0/8	4 4	Pinal County	AZ	Colton James Bagnoli	2002	*
92 5/8	14 6/8 14 6/8	13 7/8	4 4	Pima County	AZ	Bob Rimzsa	2009	*
91 1/8	15 5/8 16 0/8	15 5/8	5 5	Gila County	AZ	Mark Ovitt	2010	*
* 90 0/8	14 5/8 14 6/8	13 6/8	4 4	Gila County	AZ	Johnny Burris	2008	*
89 3/8	15 2/8 15 2/8	12 4/8	4 5	Pinal County	AZ	Craig Germond	2006	*
89 2/8	14 1/8 15 0/8	13 4/8	4 4	Yavapai County	AZ	Blake Lanoue	2009	*
89 0/8	14 3/8 14 5/8	11 4/8	4 5	Gila County	AZ	Rodney Ronnebaum	2008	*
88 7/8	15 1/8 16 1/8	13 7/8	4 4	Gila County	AZ	Mark Lucas	2006	*
* 88 2/8	15 5/8 14 6/8	11 6/8	4 4	Greenlee County	AZ	Doug Milam	2007	*
84 4/8	13 6/8 14 4/8	11 2/8	3 4	Greenlee County	AZ	Aliza Stephens	2007	*
* 84 4/8	14 2/8 14 4/8	11 0/8	4 4	Gila County	AZ	Randall Wesley Carroll	2010	*
82 7/8	16 5/8 17 5/8	13 5/8	4 4	Graham County	AZ	Cameron Broniarczyk	2006	*
* 82 6/8	16 2/8 15 6/8	15 2/8	3 4	Gila County	AZ	Jeremiah Devree	2006	*
* 81 6/8	13 7/8 13 7/8	10 0/8	4 4	Gila County	AZ	Gary Blaustein, Jr.	2007	*
* 80 4/8	13 3/8 14 6/8	10 4/8	4 4	Gila County	AZ	Richard H. Fraser, Jr.	2006	*
79 0/8	14 0/8 14 1/8	11 2/8	3 4	Pinal County	AZ	Thomas W. DeLeon	2008	*
78 5/8	13 5/8 14 2/8	12 5/8	4 4	Gila County	AZ	Stephan Waltz	2003	*
74 4/8	12 5/8 12 0/8	11 2/8	4 4	Gila County	AZ	Mark Ovitt	2008	*
73 5/8	13 6/8 13 6/8	10 1/8	4 3	Gila County	AZ	Mike Ornoski	2006	*
* 66 0/8	11 3/8 11 4/8	8 6/8	4 3	Pinal County	AZ	Ed Fanchin	2007	*

POPE & YOUNG CLUB

Official Scoring System for Bowhunting North American Big Game

NON-TYPICAL WHITETAIL AND COUES' DEER

127 1/8

PANEL MEASURED

MINIMUM SCORE
whitetail 155 (15)
Coues' 80 (5)

KIND OF DEER (check one)
☐ whitetail ☒ Coues'
☐ IN VELVET

Abnormal Points	Right Antler	Left Antler
	3/8	1 2/8
	6/8	
	/8	
TOTALS	9 5/8	1 2/8
E. TOTAL	10 7/8	

	COLUMN 2	COLUMN 3	COLUMN 4
	Right Antler	Left Antler	Difference
A. No. Points on Right Antler			
B. Tip to Tip Spread	13		
D. Inside Spread of Main Beams	17 0/8		
F. Length of Main Beam	18 2/8	17 5/8	5/8
G-1. Length of First Point	4 2/8	4 7/8	5/8
G-2. Length of Second Point	7 6/8	7 7/8	1/8
G-3. Length of Third Point	1/8	4 5/8	4/8
G-4. Length of Fourth Point, If Present	---	---	
G-5. Length of Fifth Point, If Present	---	---	
	/8	4 5/8	1/8
	/8	3 6/8	---
	/8	4 4/8	1/8
	/8	3 1/8	1/8
	/8	51 0/8	2 2/8

SUBTRACT Column 4	2 2/8
Subtotal	116 2/8
ADD Line E Total	10 7/8
FINAL SCORE	127 1/8

WORLD RECORD COUES' DEER
Non-Typical Antlers
Score: 127 1/8
Location: Gila County, Arizona
Date: 2008
Hunter: Nathan LaCost

Non-Typical Coues' Deer

by Nathan LaCost

The dull thump of the arrow string stopping, followed by the gut wrenching "clankety clank" as my arrow sailed harmlessly over the back of a dandy 100" Coues' buck…at what I thought was sixty yards…was the start of my December 2008 season. As it turned out, I would follow that buck through the snow for potentially another shot a half hour later. I drew back, but the shot, though broadside and clear of obstructions, didn't seem right. I pondered the shot only for a moment and that little voice telling me it didn't FEEL right, so I let my bow down. I continued following that buck until I came to a saddle and a spring. It was perfect: multiple runways, scrapes, rubs, and the only trees in the vicinity were 12 feet tall junipers. I quickly summed up the best scenario tree and wanted to come back later and put up my stand.

My hunting partner, Roger Frost, came with me to set up my chosen tree stand. He pointed out some larger trees a few yards away, but I was more than happy with the stand only 8 feet off the ground in the perfect location. We set up Roger down where I first encountered the other buck. I could tell by the scrapes and rubs there was a monster cruising the area. Due to work schedule I had to wait until the following weekend.

We found ourselves in bitter cold temperatures, hovering around zero degrees, with treacherous roads. I had to end up walking an extra mile just to avoid getting stuck. I knew due to the delay I had to get hurrying up. I finally snuck into my stand and settled in for a cold sit. At straight up 8 o'clock, I saw the socks of a deer coming up the trail. I shifted my weight on my stand so as get the shot sitting (I knew I wasn't going to have time to stand). I saw the glimpse of brow tines and knew he was a shooter.

The trail the buck was using actually went directly under my stand. He started walking, nose to the ground, closing in to 25 yards...clearing a low hanging oak branch at 15 yards his antlers looked huge. I kept telling myself "focus," "pick a spot," "you can't eat antlers." At 10 yards he stopped. I had my pin perfectly set on the sweet spot..."RELEASE!" The arrow hit perfect and he spun and darted 35 yards. Then there was silence.

Adrenaline was soaking me through. I managed calmed down with deep breaths. I actually took in a few minutes to look at the mountains, talk to the trees and hear the birds, which I hadn't noticed before. I approached my deer and was shocked when he had droptines on the right antler and lots of mass. I could barely fit my hands around the bases. I looked up and thanked the hunting gods for a perfect morning.

I can't begin telling Thank You to enough people that have come and gone in my life. I have been successful because they were successful as teachers and mentors for me. I remember looking through all my stepdad's hunting magazines and reading about Fred Bear, Chuck Adams, and Wayne Carlton, and the list goes on. I have learned first hand from my own dad, and my stepdad who kept his patience with me even when he was the one hanging my stand for me because I was too young. For the guys at the local archery shops for keeping me in arrows from customers' broken second hand stuff when I was a kid…..ThankYou. And for all the hunts in between, with old friends and family, swapping stories from the good ole days……ThankYou.

COUES' DEER (NON-TYPICAL ANTLERS)

Minimum Score 80   *Odocoileus virginianus couesi*

SCORE	LENGTH OF MAIN BEAM R	LENGTH OF MAIN BEAM L	INSIDE SPREAD	NUMBER OF POINTS R	NUMBER OF POINTS L	AREA	STATE/ PROVINCE	HUNTER'S NAME	DATE	RANK
127 1/8	18 2/8	17 5/8	17 0/8	7	5	Gila County	AZ	Nathan LaCost	2008	1
124 0/8	17 7/8	17 0/8	16 3/8	5	6	Coconino County	AZ	John George Evans	1987	2
*123 6/8	19 3/8	19 5/8	14 4/8	6	7	Gila County	AZ	Dale Gonzalez	2010	3
120 0/8	18 5/8	18 6/8	17 0/8	5	6	Gila County	AZ	Jeremy Ulmer	2008	4
119 5/8	19 3/8	18 6/8	13 0/8	6	6	Pima County	AZ	Art Gonzales	1987	5
*119 1/8	19 2/8	18 3/8	13 6/8	5	5	Gila County	AZ	Dennis R. Foster, Jr.	2008	6
118 4/8	11 7/8	13 7/8	13 4/8	8	9	Pima County	AZ	Michael C. Dysh	2007	7
116 7/8	16 7/8	17 0/8	11 5/8	6	8	Santa Cruz County	AZ	John F. May	1991	8
112 4/8	18 4/8	18 6/8	13 2/8	5	5	Pima County	AZ	David G. Snyder	1984	9
110 5/8	18 1/8	18 5/8	14 1/8	5	5	Greenlee County	AZ	Roy Jimenez	1998	10
107 1/8	16 0/8	17 5/8	15 3/8	6	4	Pima County	AZ	Michael J. Bylina	2007	11
104 7/8	16 1/8	16 2/8	11 6/8	7	5	Pima County	AZ	Patrick L. Holehan	2002	12
104 5/8	16 4/8	16 6/8	12 0/8	4	4	Sonora	MEX	Joe Keathley	2009	13
103 7/8	14 5/8	14 7/8	13 0/8	5	5	Gila County	AZ	Eugene Wullkotte	2006	14
103 0/8	15 6/8	16 7/8	13 4/8	5	5	Sonora	MEX	John C. "Jack" Culpepper III	2002	15
101 4/8	17 1/8	16 0/8	13 4/8	4	6	Grant County	NM	Daryl Tow	1993	16
100 6/8	16 4/8	16 4/8	14 4/8	5	5	Pima County	AZ	Michael John Bylina	2004	17
96 4/8	15 4/8	13 2/8	15 5/8	6	7	Gila County	AZ	Larry Behrends	1989	18
95 7/8	14 5/8	15 0/8	13 1/8	5	4	Grant County	NM	Steve T. Cecil	1997	19
95 4/8	16 4/8	15 2/8	12 5/8	5	5	Gila County	AZ	Brandt M. Lewis	2002	20
94 4/8	15 1/8	14 7/8	14 3/8	5	5	Gila County	AZ	Mark Ovitt	2004	21
93 2/8	16 4/8	16 1/8	13 3/8	6	5	Sonora	MEX	Butch E. Carley	2004	22
92 2/8	15 0/8	15 3/8	13 1/8	5	4	Pima County	AZ	T. J. Thrasher	2010	23
90 5/8	14 7/8	13 4/8	10 7/8	4	5	Grant County	NM	Daryl L. Tow	2001	24

COUES' DEER (NON-TYPICAL VELVET ANTLERS)

Minimum Score 80

SCORE	LENGTH OF R MAIN BEAM L	INSIDE SPREAD	NUMBER OF R POINTS L	AREA	STATE/ PROVINCE	HUNTER'S NAME	DATE	RANK
97 5/8	15 4/8 15 0/8	14 5/8	6 5	Gila County	AZ	Randy Springborn	2009	*

WORLD RECORD MULE DEER
Typical Antlers
Score: 205 0/8
Location: Hermosillo, Mexico
Date: 2009
Hunter: George Harms

Typical Mule Deer

by George Harms

Mule Deer, Hermosillo Mexico, December 2009

I hunted for mule deer with Jim Schaafsma and Nayo Balderama on a ranch in Mexico just outside Hermosillo. This was my second time here. My first trip was unsuccessful.

December 9, 2009, I first saw a beautiful deer at about 50 yards. My heart was pounding so hard I thought it was going to come out of my chest! As he got closer, at about 20 yards, I took the shot. I hit him a little back. We had decided not to pursue the deer that night. Instead, we came back at the first good light in the morning, trailed him and then found him.

This was an unbelievable hunt. Many thanks to Jim and TinaMarie Schaafsma and Nayo and Silvia Balderama.

What an unbelievable trophy!!!

MULE DEER (TYPICAL ANTLERS)

Minimum Score 145

Odocoileus hemionus and certain related subspecies

SCORE	LENGTH OF R MAIN BEAM L	INSIDE SPREAD	NUMBER OF R POINTS L	AREA	STATE/ PROVINCE	HUNTER'S NAME	DATE	RANK
*205 0/8	26 5/8 29 0/8	31 0/8	5 4	Hermosillo	MEX	George Harms	2009	1
203 1/8	28 5/8 27 6/8	30 2/8	7 7	White River N.F.	CO	Bill Barcus	1979	2
202 6/8	26 7/8 26 2/8	26 7/8	7 6	Gove County	KS	Carl Ghan, Jr.	1992	3
202 3/8	28 2/8 27 4/8	23 7/8	5 5	Montrose County	CO	Leland J. Cox	2004	4
202 0/8	29 1/8 28 2/8	25 0/8	5 6	Franklin County	WA	Thomas E. Adrian	2004	5
200 6/8	27 7/8 25 3/8	25 0/8	5 7	Eagle Creek	SAS	Ron Cordes	1998	6
200 0/8	24 7/8 26 2/8	25 1/8	6 5	Coconino County	AZ	Adam R. Kowalski, Jr.	1995	7
199 6/8	25 1/8 24 6/8	22 6/8	7 5	Billings County	ND	John F. Stuchlik, Jr.	2004	8
199 4/8	25 0/8 24 7/8	22 1/8	7 6	Logan County	KS	Stacy Hoeme	2001	9
198 4/8	28 0/8 26 0/8	32 2/8	7 7	Apache County	AZ	William T. Rose	1985	10
197 6/8	24 1/8 24 7/8	23 3/8	5 6	Dolores County	CO	Jim Horneck	1988	11
197 1/8	24 2/8 22 4/8	21 4/8	6 6	Beaver County	UT	David Snyder	1982	12
197 0/8	24 6/8 27 7/8	23 6/8	5 5	Park County	CO	Ronald E. Sniff	1969	13
196 7/8	25 4/8 25 1/8	24 1/8	5 5	Platte County	WY	Jerry Bowen	1999	14
196 6/8	25 1/8 23 5/8	23 4/8	5 5	Coconino County	AZ	Duane "Corky" Richardson	1988	15
196 5/8	25 0/8 25 6/8	23 4/8	5 6	Coconino County	AZ	Jim Wagner	1986	16
196 3/8	25 0/8 27 5/8	28 1/8	5 5	Gunnison County	CO	Leland J. Cox	2003	17
196 1/8	25 5/8 27 3/8	23 5/8	6 6	Calgary	ALB	Peter Tsoulamanis	2007	18
195 7/8	29 7/8 29 7/8	30 2/8	6 7	Crook County	OR	Gidion "Hop" Jackson	1990	19
195 6/8	28 0/8 29 4/8	28 4/8	5 7	San Juan County	NM	David A. Brooks	1995	20
195 4/8	26 1/8 24 4/8	24 0/8	5 7	Cereal	ALB	Steve Alderman	2007	21
194 7/8	25 1/8 24 3/8	22 7/8	5 5	Sublette County	WY	Gil Winters	1998	22
194 4/8	30 2/8 29 1/8	29 2/8	6 7	Coconino County	AZ	Matthew Liljenquist	2010	23
194 3/8	27 0/8 27 1/8	21 7/8	6 5	Arrowwood	ALB	Neil W. Friesen	2008	24
194 1/8	22 6/8 22 4/8	19 1/8	5 5	Elmore County	ID	Roger W. Taylor	1994	25
194 1/8	25 2/8 25 0/8	26 7/8	5 6	Coconino County	AZ	George R. Richardson, Jr.	2008	25
193 6/8	26 2/8 26 0/8	24 2/8	5 5	Sonora	MEX	Lou Kindred	2007	27
193 5/8	27 0/8 30 1/8	23 1/8	6 5	Cibola County	NM	Kenny R. Bruton	1987	28
193 3/8	28 2/8 28 0/8	24 7/8	6 5	Baker County	OR	Anthony A. Myers	1996	29
193 1/8	25 2/8 25 6/8	23 5/8	6 7	Rawlins County	KS	Matt Park	1997	30
193 0/8	28 1/8 28 5/8	31 0/8	5 6	Weld County	CO	Lance Hockett	1996	31
192 7/8	24 6/8 23 3/8	23 0/8	6 5	San Isabel National Forest	CO	Donald D. Garrison	1972	32
192 4/8	24 5/8 25 1/8	22 2/8	5 5	Salt Lake County	UT	Bryan W. Grant	2004	33
*192 4/8	27 3/8 26 0/8	27 1/8	5 7	Great Sandhills	SAS	Jim Clary	2007	33
192 1/8	25 3/8 26 2/8	23 0/8	6 5	Lemhi County	ID	Mike Nelson	1978	35
192 0/8	25 6/8 26 4/8	22 0/8	7 5	Uncompahgre Plateau	CO	Donald Click	1973	36
191 3/8	23 5/8 25 1/8	24 3/8	5 5	Rio Arriba County	NM	Ryan Turner	1995	37
191 2/8	24 6/8 22 4/8	26 1/8	5 5	Mohave County	AZ	Roy E. Grace	2008	38
190 6/8	27 4/8 27 4/8	25 7/8	9 8	Mesa County	CO	Allen Personious	1976	39
190 5/8	26 2/8 26 2/8	22 4/8	7 8	Teller County	CO	Dan Mersman	1982	40
190 4/8	26 0/8 25 4/8	25 6/8	6 6	Sandhills	SAS	Jim Clary	2004	41
190 3/8	26 2/8 26 7/8	23 1/8	7 7	Elbert County	CO	Kirk Mulkin	2004	42
190 2/8	21 3/8 23 3/8	21 7/8	6 5	Boise County	ID	Ricky D. Addison	1984	43
190 1/8	25 3/8 24 6/8	25 3/8	6 5	Moffat County	CO	Glenn Pritchard	1990	44
190 0/8	25 1/8 23 4/8	24 4/8	5 5	Utah County	UT	John Edwards	1967	45
190 0/8	24 6/8 27 2/8	25 2/8	6 5	Baker County	OR	Mike Raney	1996	45
190 0/8	26 4/8 26 7/8	24 0/8	5 5	Cheyenne County	KS	Kendall Helton	2000	45
*189 7/8	27 7/8 25 6/8	26 6/8	7 7	Rio Blanco County	CO	Sam Baca	2004	48
189 6/8	24 6/8 24 5/8	23 7/8	6 5	Montrose County	CO	LeRoy J. Gutierrez	2004	49
189 5/8	22 5/8 23 1/8	23 4/8	5 5	Rosebud River	ALB	Douglas R. Lowen	1994	50
189 5/8	22 7/8 23 2/8	21 1/8	5 5	Biggers	SAS	William J. Harris, Jr.	1997	50
189 3/8	27 0/8 27 0/8	24 1/8	6 5	Iron County	UT	Ken Davis	1963	52
189 2/8	26 4/8 26 0/8	26 6/8	5 5	Crook County	OR	John Nelson	1992	53
189 1/8	23 6/8 23 7/8	23 6/8	5 8	Chelan County	WA	R. Early/D. Davies, Jr.	1983	54
189 0/8	24 4/8 23 5/8	25 6/8	5 6	Montezuma County	CO	Al Newkirk	1983	55
188 7/8	25 2/8 26 3/8	21 1/8	6 6	Settlement Canyon	UT	Derald R. Evans	1965	56
188 6/8	24 5/8 24 6/8	21 2/8	5 5	Mesa County	CO	Bob Jensen	1974	57
188 6/8	24 0/8 23 1/8	23 0/8	7 5	Garfield County	UT	Cory Carlson	2009	57
188 4/8	25 6/8 26 6/8	24 3/8	6 5	Abbey	SAS	Barry Minor	1979	59
188 3/8	25 0/8 23 6/8	24 1/8	5 5	Lincoln County	CO	Windell Penton	1997	60
188 3/8	24 4/8 23 7/8	24 2/8	7 7	La Plata County	CO	John Sebert	2004	60
188 2/8	24 3/8 24 4/8	23 2/8	6 6	Mesa County	CO	John Lamicq, Jr.	1967	62
188 2/8	24 6/8 24 4/8	21 2/8	5 5	Montrose County	CO	Jim Holdenried	2002	62
*188 2/8	24 7/8 26 0/8	25 2/8	6 6	Meade County	SD	Gary Finn	2004	62
188 0/8	24 6/8 23 2/8	26 5/8	4 4	Saddle Hills	ALB	Dustin Brown	2005	65
187 7/8	23 7/8 24 7/8	22 5/8	5 6	Duck Creek	UT	Gerald Clark	1966	66
187 6/8	28 3/8 28 1/8	32 3/8	6 6	Weld County	CO	Randy Henderson	1993	67
187 6/8	24 0/8 24 0/8	26 3/8	5 5	Salt Lake County	UT	Dave Anderson	2003	67
187 5/8	23 2/8 22 5/8	18 3/8	5 5	Moffat County	CO	Leonard Jefferson	1971	69
187 5/8	25 0/8 25 1/8	28 3/8	8 5	Boulder County	CO	Jeff Biemiller	1991	69
187 5/8	24 4/8 25 7/8	25 1/8	5 5	Billings County	ND	Dan Simerson	1995	69
187 5/8	27 5/8 28 4/8	23 2/8	6 6	Rio Arriba County	NM	Pat Lovato	1998	69
187 4/8	26 3/8 25 0/8	25 6/8	5 5	El Rancho Carriva	MEX	Walter J. Palmer	2009	73
187 2/8	24 3/8 22 3/8	22 2/8	5 5	Dawes County	NE	Kirk Peters	1989	74
187 2/8	23 3/8 22 7/8	23 2/8	5 5	Mohave County	AZ	Kyle Bundy	1992	74
187 2/8	25 4/8 25 4/8	22 0/8	7 6	Teton County	WY	Don Hoard	1995	74
187 1/8	26 3/8 28 1/8	28 1/8	4 4	Elmore County	ID	James H. Rainey, Sr.	1960	77
187 1/8	23 6/8 25 6/8	25 2/8	7 7	Milk River	ALB	Robin Tremblay	1992	77
187 1/8	26 0/8 26 5/8	27 2/8	5 5	Ravalli County	MT	Larry D. Reynolds	2009	77
187 0/8	24 6/8 23 4/8	23 6/8	6 5	Rio Arriba County	NM	Doug Aikin	1995	80
187 0/8	26 7/8 26 2/8	24 4/8	5 5	Cochise County	AZ	Bradley D. Grap	2003	80
186 7/8	25 3/8 25 0/8	20 1/8	5 6	Eagle County	CO	Dr. J. D. Jones	1963	82
186 7/8	26 3/8 26 0/8	22 0/8	6 8	Uncompahgre Plateau	CO	Jerry Click	1973	82
186 7/8	25 2/8 25 3/8	21 7/8	4 4	Piegan Creek	ALB	Dave Moore	1993	82
186 7/8	26 0/8 25 2/8	25 7/8	5 6	Gove County	KS	Dean Hamilton	2001	82
186 7/8	22 4/8 25 2/8	24 5/8	5 6	Chaffee County	CO	Gary M. Babl	2002	82
*186 7/8	23 4/8 22 6/8	20 3/8	6 7	San Miguel County	CO	Anthony Pierino	2009	82
186 6/8	24 5/8 25 2/8	24 2/8	5 5	Cassia County	ID	Pat Miller	1965	88
186 5/8	25 1/8 25 6/8	19 2/8	5 6	Elbert County	CO	Loren Dellinger	1984	89
186 5/8	24 7/8 26 3/8	22 2/8	5 5	Douglas County	CO	Matt Hamilton	2003	89
186 4/8	24 2/8 23 1/8	24 4/8	5 5	White River N.F.	CO	Walt Seville	1977	91
186 3/8	23 5/8 23 5/8	21 7/8	5 5	Graham County	KS	Randy Wilson	2000	92
186 2/8	26 4/8 26 0/8	27 4/8	6 9	Gunnison County	CO	Don E. Lampert	1973	93
186 2/8	25 3/8 23 3/8	23 3/8	5 5	Baker County	OR	William D. Ross	1995	93
186 2/8	24 7/8 24 6/8	24 0/8	5 5	Bad Lake	SAS	Duane Hogan	2000	93

MULE DEER (TYPICAL ANTLERS)

Minimum Score 145 — Continued

SCORE	R MAIN BEAM L	INSIDE SPREAD	R POINTS L	AREA	STATE/ PROVINCE	HUNTER'S NAME	DATE	RANK
*186 2/8	27 5/8 26 2/8	23 0/8	5 5	Las Animas County	CO	Fred Eichler	2005	93
186 1/8	24 1/8 24 0/8	21 3/8	5 5	Cassia County	ID	Bill Shockey	1965	97
186 1/8	25 3/8 24 0/8	25 4/8	5 5	Humboldt County	NV	Tim Bray	1984	97
186 1/8	24 0/8 22 0/8	23 5/8	5 5	Mohave County	AZ	Kyle Bundy	1999	97
*186 1/8	24 3/8 24 5/8	22 3/8	5 5	Coconino County	AZ	Jeremy Bohn	2007	97
186 0/8	23 3/8 24 4/8	18 4/8	5 5	Jefferson County	CO	Jerry Grueneburg	2007	101
185 7/8	22 4/8 22 5/8	22 5/8	5 5	Cottle County	TX	Johnathan Burpo	2004	102
185 6/8	24 1/8 24 4/8	24 0/8	5 5	Imperial County	CA	Gilbert Clement	1982	103
185 6/8	23 6/8 24 6/8	22 4/8	5 5	Park County	MT	Tom Daley	2005	103
185 5/8	24 2/8 25 4/8	27 0/8	7 6	Mesa County	CO	Art Cook	1962	105
*185 5/8	23 2/8 26 0/8	25 2/8	5 7	Bow River	ALB	Blake Howland	2009	105
185 4/8	22 0/8 22 3/8	20 4/8	5 5	Coconino County	AZ	Ronald Hollamon	1978	107
185 4/8	23 7/8 24 6/8	24 4/8	5 5	El Paso County	CO	Greg Walters	2004	107
185 1/8	24 5/8 23 7/8	22 3/8	5 5	Larimer County	CO	Randy Ries	2004	109
185 0/8	26 0/8 26 2/8	26 3/8	5 6	Larimer County	CO	Don Lampert	1969	110
185 0/8	26 1/8 25 1/8	24 0/8	5 5	Montrose County	CO	Darryl L. Coe	1988	110
185 0/8	23 5/8 25 0/8	21 0/8	5 4	Norton County	KS	Pete Killman	1993	110
185 0/8	24 0/8 24 3/8	23 2/8	5 5	Clear Creek County	CO	Bradley John Kuhn	1996	110
185 0/8	25 0/8 23 0/8	23 6/8	5 5	Lincoln County	NV	Nick Gulli, Jr.	2005	110
184 7/8	25 7/8 25 4/8	21 7/8	5 5	Mesa County	CO	James L. Peterson	1983	115
184 7/8	24 2/8 24 4/8	25 1/8	6 5	Maricopa County	AZ	Timothy Gibson	1987	115
184 6/8	23 0/8 23 2/8	23 3/8	5 5	Mesa County	CO	David L. Myers	1976	117
184 3/8	24 4/8 23 3/8	28 4/8	6 6	Caribou County	ID	Coby Tigert	1983	118
184 3/8	25 1/8 26 4/8	23 0/8	6 6	Teton County	WY	Kevin D. Marshall	1995	118
*184 3/8	23 4/8 24 1/8	25 3/8	4 4	Teton County	WY	Donald R. Hoard	2001	118
184 2/8	25 2/8 24 3/8	22 7/8	5 6	Teton County	WY	Donald R. Williamson	1991	121
184 2/8	26 4/8 25 2/8	21 2/8	5 5	Coconino County	AZ	Wally Schwartz	1998	121
184 1/8	24 3/8 24 6/8	24 6/8	5 4	Delta County	CO	Scott Kolb	1963	123
184 1/8	27 5/8 27 0/8	25 3/8	5 4	Bernalillo County	NM	Gregory A. Gwash	1970	123
184 1/8	24 6/8 25 2/8	24 2/8	6 5	Ravalli County	MT	Brett Neal	1994	123
184 1/8	23 3/8 24 0/8	22 0/8	6 6	Garfield County	CO	Jeff Hoover	2005	123
184 0/8	24 1/8 25 1/8	24 2/8	6 6	Boise County	ID	Joseph Greenley	1984	127
184 0/8	25 2/8 25 6/8	25 0/8	6 5	Tooele County	UT	Jerry Reynolds	2001	127
184 0/8	22 2/8 22 0/8	23 5/8	5 5	Larimer County	CO	Charlie Hicks	2005	127
183 7/8	25 0/8 24 3/8	23 7/8	5 5	Moffat County	CO	Joel Hogan	1966	130
183 7/8	24 2/8 24 4/8	23 1/8	6 5	Pima County	AZ	Jimmy Marsh	1994	130
*183 7/8	26 7/8 27 5/8	22 1/8	5 7	Delta County	CO	Ron McCoy	2008	130
183 6/8	26 4/8 27 3/8	27 0/8	5 4	Iron County	UT	Ted Garrett	1963	133
183 6/8	23 4/8 23 2/8	24 2/8	5 5	Billings County	ND	Daniel J. Erickstad	1992	133
183 5/8	26 6/8 25 7/8	25 5/8	5 5	Sanpete County	UT	Weldon Noland	1965	135
183 5/8	20 2/8 19 3/8	20 2/8	6 6	Rio Arriba County	NM	Billy Terrazas	1985	135
183 5/8	24 1/8 23 7/8	24 3/8	5 5	Boise County	ID	Jerry W. Simmons	2002	135
183 4/8	29 0/8 26 5/8	23 6/8	5 4	Kiowa County	CO	Dave Moyer	1988	138
183 4/8	25 3/8 26 0/8	20 7/8	6 5	Duchesne County	UT	Kevin Richens	2004	138
183 3/8	25 7/8 26 1/8	22 4/8	7 5	Sevier County	UT	Kyle Johnson	1970	140
183 2/8	25 5/8 26 5/8	22 7/8	6 9	Wasatch County	UT	Blake Spencer	1963	141
183 1/8	25 0/8 25 1/8	24 5/8	5 6	White Pine County	NV	Robert Price	1986	142
*183 1/8	26 7/8 26 5/8	23 5/8	5 5	Cochrane	ALB	Doug Murray	2006	142
183 0/8	25 1/8 25 5/8	25 2/8	5 6	Lincoln County	MT	John C. Bartlett	1982	144
182 7/8	23 3/8 22 0/8	21 7/8	5 5	Caribou County	ID	Neil Dursteler	1967	145
182 7/8	24 4/8 25 1/8	24 1/8	5 5	Cache County	UT	Robert Bronson	1985	145
182 6/8	22 0/8 22 2/8	20 2/8	5 7	Chelan County	WA	Glenn St. Charles	1959	147
182 6/8	23 3/8 23 4/8	20 3/8	7 5	Moffat County	CO	Glenn Pritchard	1987	147
182 6/8	23 4/8 23 6/8	23 7/8	5 5	Elkwater	ALB	Aaron Arnell	2001	147
182 5/8	26 4/8 25 4/8	21 5/8	5 5	Lincoln County	WY	Lael Eddins	1978	150
182 5/8	24 7/8 25 2/8	21 5/8	5 5	Elbert County	CO	Donald L. Stiles	2009	150
182 4/8	25 2/8 24 2/8	25 0/8	5 5	Humboldt County	NV	George Rajnus	1985	152
182 4/8	24 5/8 24 3/8	21 4/8	5 5	Mesa County	CO	Charles C. Perry	1985	152
182 4/8	25 0/8 25 5/8	21 2/8	5 5	Mesa County	CO	David M. Gant	1986	152
182 4/8	23 5/8 25 4/8	20 4/8	5 5	Cypress	ALB	James Drader	1992	152
182 4/8	19 2/8 20 2/8	20 5/8	5 5	San Juan County	NM	Steven Vittetow	2004	152
182 4/8	22 7/8 23 2/8	19 6/8	5 5	Milk River	ALB	John Fletcher	2004	152
182 4/8	26 1/8 26 7/8	21 6/8	5 5	Lincoln County	WY	Matthew Asay	2007	152
182 2/8	25 6/8 24 2/8	25 2/8	6 5	Mesa County	CO	Robert C. Dawson	1974	159
182 2/8	25 1/8 25 2/8	24 0/8	6 5	Caribou County	ID	Eric Bowman	1983	159
182 2/8	25 4/8 26 1/8	23 6/8	7 9	Graham County	KS	Phillip L. Kirkland	1988	159
182 2/8	26 1/8 26 5/8	24 1/8	9 5	Morgan County	UT	Justin Smith	2009	159
182 1/8	25 1/8 24 1/8	22 5/8	6 6	Young	SAS	Dion Dieno	1999	163
182 0/8	23 5/8 23 3/8	20 6/8	5 5	Elmore County	ID	Dallas R. Doty, Jr.	1992	164
182 0/8	24 5/8 25 4/8	25 4/8	6 5	Natrona County	WY	Brent Stalkup	2003	164
181 7/8	21 7/8 21 1/8	22 6/8	5 5	Power County	ID	Austin Cummins	1970	166
181 7/8	25 6/8 24 6/8	22 5/8	7 7	Boulder County	CO	Leonard P. Quercioli	2002	166
181 7/8	24 4/8 25 7/8	23 5/8	5 6	Lake County	OR	Robert Havely	2003	166
181 6/8	25 5/8 25 3/8	22 2/8	5 5	Pasgua Lake	SAS	Jeremy McNaughton	2010	169
181 5/8	24 3/8 24 0/8	21 5/8	5 5	Wakely	CO	Lynn Grace	1964	170
181 5/8	26 2/8 25 7/8	21 6/8	5 6	Cabri	SAS	Glen A. Miller	2004	170
181 5/8	23 4/8 22 5/8	18 7/8	5 5	Garfield County	CO	Scott J. Bunney	2007	170
181 4/8	24 4/8 23 2/8	25 6/8	5 5	Garfield County	CO	Henry Wichers	1967	173
181 4/8	23 6/8 23 3/8	24 7/8	5 5	Butte County	ID	Richard A. Southwell	1980	173
181 4/8	23 0/8 23 1/8	23 7/8	6 5	El Paso County	CO	Craig E. Kimball	1998	173
181 4/8	27 3/8 27 5/8	23 7/8	7 6	Buffalo Crossing	ALB	Lou Vasseur	2000	173
181 4/8	22 4/8 22 6/8	23 1/8	5 5	Harding County	NM	Bucky Powell	2003	173
*181 4/8	24 5/8 24 3/8	24 0/8	5 5	San Juan County	NM	Benjamin Black	2009	173
181 3/8	26 0/8 26 5/8	26 3/8	5 5	Montrose County	CO	John Lamb	1981	179
*181 3/8	25 3/8 25 4/8	20 0/8	7 6	Ravalli County	MT	Remi J. Warren	2009	179
181 2/8	22 1/8 22 6/8	20 5/8	5 6	Larimer County	CO	Wayne Eberhard	1972	181
181 1/8	24 3/8 25 4/8	19 3/8	5 5	Union County	OR	Thomas Mussatto	1968	182
181 1/8	23 6/8 24 3/8	26 6/8	5 5	Rosebud County	MT	Art Hayes III	2005	182
181 1/8	21 6/8 23 5/8	21 1/8	5 5	Boise County	ID	Lee Blankenship	2005	182
181 1/8	23 0/8 22 0/8	20 4/8	5 7	Dungre	SAS	Sam Peterson	2009	182
181 0/8	24 7/8 22 7/8	23 0/8	6 6	Rio Arriba County	NM	Charles Tapia	1965	186
181 0/8	26 0/8 25 5/8	24 4/8	5 5	Boise County	ID	Tom D'Aquino	1991	186
181 0/8	25 5/8 26 2/8	24 6/8	5 7	San Juan County	NM	Steven J. Vittetow	2007	186
180 7/8	25 2/8 24 7/8	22 7/8	5 5	Washoe County	NV	Donald E. Callen	1984	189
180 7/8	26 0/8 25 3/8	23 4/8	7 6	Brooks	ALB	Randy Weidner	2002	189

MULE DEER (TYPICAL ANTLERS)

Minimum Score 145　　　Continued

SCORE	LENGTH OF R MAIN BEAM L	INSIDE SPREAD	NUMBER OF R POINTS L	AREA	STATE/ PROVINCE	HUNTER'S NAME	DATE	RANK
*180 7/8	24 0/8　25 0/8	21 5/8	6　6	Cheyenne County	KS	Rodney Lindsten	2008	189
180 6/8	23 6/8　24 6/8	20 4/8	5　5	La Plata County	CO	Ralph RePola	1988	192
180 6/8	23 0/8　23 7/8	24 4/8	6　6	Harney County	OR	John F. Nelson	1997	192
180 6/8	23 1/8　24 2/8	21 2/8	5　5	Pima County	AZ	Johnny Ray Estrada	2006	192
180 5/8	24 2/8　23 3/8	23 5/8	5　5	Cochise County	AZ	Wendell Miles	1992	195
180 5/8	25 6/8　26 2/8	23 1/8	7　5	Wheeler County	OR	Michael Hargrave	2006	195
180 4/8	24 1/8　25 1/8	21 6/8	4　4	Mesa County	CO	Jack Kruckenburg	1958	197
180 4/8	24 0/8　24 7/8	21 0/8	6　6	Fremont County	ID	Steven M. Jones	1979	197
180 4/8	24 6/8　25 3/8	24 0/8	6　6	Ravalli County	MT	Gary Habeck	1984	197
180 4/8	22 6/8　22 2/8	21 7/8	7　6	Montezuma County	CO	Marvin Reichenau	1987	197
*180 4/8	24 2/8　24 0/8	26 2/8	5　5	Hartley County	TX	Bucky Powell	2009	197
180 3/8	24 0/8　25 5/8	27 5/8	5　5	Boise County	ID	Benton K. Wetzel	1970	202
180 3/8	25 1/8　25 2/8	23 5/8	5　5	Kiowa County	CO	Jeff Barber	1994	202
180 3/8	26 2/8　25 7/8	24 7/8	6　5	Millarville	ALB	Gary Duet	1995	202
180 3/8	22 4/8　23 0/8	19 7/8	5　5	Fergus County	MT	Jimmy Graham	2004	202
180 2/8	24 5/8　24 7/8	25 7/8	8　5	Garfield County	CO	Michael R. Allen	1967	206
180 2/8	23 1/8　24 0/8	23 2/8	5　5	Lincoln County	NV	Fred B. Allen III	1974	206
180 2/8	23 2/8　24 2/8	24 0/8	5　5	Humboldt County	NV	Robert A. Ashby	1980	206
180 2/8	24 0/8　24 5/8	21 2/8	5　5	San Juan County	NM	Harry J. Dalton	1996	206
180 2/8	24 4/8　26 1/8	22 0/8	5　5	Deschutes County	OR	Travis E. Fields	2000	206
*180 2/8	25 2/8　24 5/8	22 6/8	5　5	Ponteix	SAS	Ken Chipley	2009	206
180 1/8	22 0/8　22 4/8	19 3/8	5　5	Dawson County	MT	Gordon M. Quilling	1957	212
180 1/8	24 6/8　24 4/8	21 5/8	5　5	Grant County	OR	Kim C. Thiele	1989	212
180 1/8	25 2/8　25 7/8	23 3/8	6　5	Cibola County	NM	Gary Patterson	1995	212
180 1/8	23 5/8　22 1/8	19 3/8	6　6	Natrona County	WY	Tom Carpenter	1999	212
180 0/8	25 5/8　25 4/8	22 2/8	5　5	Souris River	SAS	Marty Jordens	2007	216
179 7/8	23 7/8　22 5/8	23 7/8	5　5	Yuma County	CO	Michael Trujillo	1997	217
179 7/8	23 2/8　23 4/8	26 1/8	6　6	Jefferson County	CO	Matt Graham	2002	217
179 7/8	25 2/8　24 5/8	23 3/8	5　5	Crook County	OR	Virgil Lee	2009	217
179 6/8	25 0/8　25 7/8	20 0/8	5　5	Umatilla County	OR	Dannie W. Crawley	1991	220
179 6/8	25 2/8　25 3/8	22 2/8	5　5	Whiskey Gap	ALB	Don B. Yuill	1991	220
179 6/8	22 7/8　24 5/8	21 1/8	6　6	Okotoks	ALB	Harvey Paddock	1991	220
179 6/8	24 4/8　24 6/8	26 0/8	5　5	Montrose County	CO	J. T. Kreager	2009	220
179 5/8	26 4/8　27 1/8	27 2/8	5　7	Union County	NM	Ronnie Williams	1984	224
179 4/8	24 3/8　23 0/8	21 4/8	5　8	Ada County	ID	Vance Gardner	1971	225
179 4/8	22 2/8　24 3/8	19 6/8	5　5	Garfield County	CO	Ed Downard	1984	225
179 4/8	27 2/8　27 5/8	23 4/8	6　5	Crook County	OR	Mark Quant	1995	225
179 4/8	23 6/8　25 2/8	23 5/8	6　7	Luna County	NM	Dale Shiflett	2000	225
179 3/8	26 2/8　24 2/8	20 0/8	5　4	San Miguel County	NM	Robert Montoya	1993	229
179 3/8	23 2/8　25 2/8	20 7/8	5　5	Lane County	KS	Elwin L. Schwartz	1994	229
179 2/8	24 2/8　24 1/8	24 6/8	5　4	Illinois Creek Drainage	unk	Gordon E. Scott	1964	231
*179 2/8	24 3/8　26 3/8	24 1/8	5　4	Chelan County	WA	Michael Darlington	2009	231
179 1/8	24 7/8　24 6/8	27 2/8	6　5	Sierra County	CA	Dan Seaters	1999	233
179 1/8	24 2/8　25 2/8	21 1/8	5　5	Spirit River	ALB	Charles W. Rehor	2006	233
*179 1/8	23 7/8　25 2/8	22 1/8	6　7	Seven Persons	ALB	Earl Chauvin	2010	233
179 0/8	19 1/8　19 4/8	21 4/8	5　6	Sandoval County	NM	D. J. Heckler, Jr.	1969	236
179 0/8	23 6/8　23 4/8	24 1/8	5　5	Lake County	CO	Sam E. Adkins	1978	236
179 0/8	23 5/8　24 4/8	22 4/8	5　5	Elko County	NV	Jerry Vega	1986	236
179 0/8	23 0/8　23 0/8	21 4/8	6　5	Harney County	OR	Cameron Hanes	1991	236
179 0/8	22 6/8　23 0/8	20 4/8	5　5	Lincoln County	WY	Mike Barrett	1991	236
179 0/8	24 0/8　23 7/8	19 1/8	7　5	Baker County	OR	Patrick Strawn	1998	236
179 0/8	23 7/8　23 6/8	23 2/8	5　5	Spring Creek	ALB	Les Baird	1999	236
179 0/8	27 4/8　27 5/8	25 2/8	5　5	Grant County	OR	Larry R. McWilliams	2005	236
179 0/8	22 1/8　21 5/8	19 2/8	5　5	Gila County	AZ	Tony Cuchiara	2006	236
*179 0/8	22 6/8　23 4/8	20 2/8	5　5	Elbert County	CO	Scott Prucha	2006	236
178 7/8	24 5/8　24 5/8	23 5/8	7　5	Utah County	UT	Robert G. Nelson	2004	246
178 6/8	20 5/8　21 1/8	20 0/8	5　5	Billings County	ND	Mark L. Meyer	2004	247
*178 6/8	22 6/8　21 4/8	21 2/8	6　5	Ravalli County	MT	Allen Kitts	2007	247
178 6/8	23 1/8　23 2/8	23 5/8	5　5	Slope County	ND	Joey Wadeson	2008	247
178 5/8	24 2/8　23 3/8	24 7/8	6　6	Rio Blanco County	CO	Rex Schmude	1968	250
178 4/8	24 6/8　25 0/8	23 1/8	5　5	Carter County	MT	R. C. Tucker	1958	251
178 4/8	24 0/8　23 6/8	18 2/8	5　5	Sandoval County	NM	Doug Aikin	1990	251
178 4/8	25 5/8　26 2/8	21 6/8	6　7	Boise County	ID	Thomas M. Szurgot	1990	251
178 4/8	24 7/8　26 1/8	21 5/8	5　6	Klamath County	OR	Jim Harmon	1997	251
*178 4/8	23 1/8　19 4/8	18 2/8	4　4	Garfield County	UT	Steven E. Sheehy	2008	251
178 3/8	28 3/8　27 3/8	28 3/8	5　5	Finney County	KS	Larry Ochs	1968	256
178 3/8	21 3/8　22 2/8	19 5/8	5　5	San Juan County	UT	Shane Barr	1992	256
178 3/8	27 4/8　27 3/8	26 5/8	5　5	Okanogan County	WA	Douglas Duane Kikendall	1992	256
178 3/8	26 2/8　25 7/8	22 5/8	6　5	Taber	ALB	Darcy Miller	1994	256
178 2/8	24 0/8　24 2/8	20 4/8	5　5	Delta County	CO	Larry Bishop	1992	260
178 2/8	23 1/8　25 4/8	24 1/8	5　6	Grand County	UT	Shaun Hirst	2007	260
*178 2/8	22 2/8　23 2/8	23 2/8	5　5	Rio Arriba County	NM	Robinson Dean	2010	260
178 1/8	26 7/8　25 3/8	23 5/8	5　7	Albany County	WY	Shane Woods	2006	263
178 0/8	23 4/8　23 7/8	23 4/8	5　6	Lake County	OR	Ronald C. Halpin	1966	264
178 0/8	24 4/8　23 6/8	24 6/8	5　5	Garfield County	CO	Larry Santek	1985	264
178 0/8	25 0/8　24 4/8	24 6/8	7　6	Lincoln County	MT	Jerry Brown	1986	264
178 0/8	25 1/8　23 5/8	21 4/8	5　5	Ada County	ID	Thomas M. Szurgot	1992	264
178 0/8	21 1/8　22 0/8	18 2/8	5　4	Natrona County	WY	Brian L. Wagner	1993	264
*178 0/8	26 1/8　25 7/8	24 4/8	5　4	Cowley	ALB	Jamie Smith	2006	264
177 7/8	23 2/8　23 7/8	23 2/8	4　4	Routt County	CO	Richard M. Hansen	1964	270
177 7/8	26 1/8　26 2/8	23 1/8	4　4	Gunnison County	CO	Glen Farnum	1978	270
177 7/8	23 6/8　23 0/8	19 3/8	6　6	Mesa County	CO	John D Wood	1984	270
177 7/8	24 3/8　26 4/8	23 1/8	6　5	Coconino County	AZ	James Miner	1987	270
177 7/8	26 1/8　25 3/8	26 7/8	5　5	Elbert County	CO	Robert Nelson	1990	270
*177 7/8	24 1/8　20 7/8	19 7/8	5　5	Pueblo County	CO	Frank Musso	2009	270
177 6/8	27 2/8　26 0/8	32 2/8	6　7	McKinley County	NM	Eloy Salaz	1987	276
177 6/8	22 2/8　22 4/8	24 6/8	5　6	Sublette County	WY	Dana Patrick Furgason	1992	276
177 6/8	25 3/8　24 7/8	20 7/8	6　6	Drumheller	ALB	Tyler Colberg	1994	276
177 6/8	24 5/8　25 0/8	20 6/8	5　5	Grant County	OR	David D. Chapman	1995	276
177 6/8	24 7/8　24 2/8	17 1/8	4　5	Linn County	OR	Jeff Baker	1997	276
177 6/8	26 0/8　22 7/8	27 6/8	5　5	Pueblo County	CO	Peter A. F. Dozois	2001	276
177 5/8	27 7/8　26 4/8	18 0/8	6　6	Buffalo Pound Lake	SAS	Greg Leniuk	2001	282
177 4/8	25 6/8　26 0/8	22 4/8	5　4	Fremont County	WY	Walter Millhollin	1960	283
177 4/8	23 0/8　22 5/8	22 2/8	5　5	Oneida County	ID	J. L. Shelton	1980	283
177 4/8	24 4/8　22 1/8	23 2/8	5　5	Oldman River	ALB	Kevin Wiebe	1991	283

310

MULE DEER (TYPICAL ANTLERS)

Minimum Score 145   Continued

SCORE	LENGTH OF MAIN BEAM R	L	INSIDE SPREAD	NUMBER OF POINTS R	L	AREA	STATE/PROVINCE	HUNTER'S NAME	DATE	RANK
177 4/8	23 2/8	22 6/8	21 4/8	6	7	Sherman County	KS	Brian K. Somers	1994	283
177 4/8	24 4/8	23 0/8	23 0/8	5	4	Ada County	ID	Neil J. Russell	1994	283
177 4/8	24 4/8	25 6/8	22 2/8	4	5	Natrona County	WY	Brian D. Balfour	1996	283
177 3/8	25 5/8	26 4/8	20 7/8	6	6	Caribou County	ID	Jack Daniels	1990	289
177 2/8	22 6/8	23 6/8	28 6/8	6	6	Pima County	AZ	Sherwin Lipsitz	1977	290
177 2/8	21 5/8	23 2/8	20 6/8	6	5	Malheur County	OR	Bennie B. Simpson	1986	290
177 1/8	23 3/8	23 3/8	26 2/8	5	6	Logan County	KS	Thomas Standard	1967	292
177 1/8	23 7/8	24 4/8	22 0/8	4	4	Meagher County	MT	Mike Weitz	1981	292
177 1/8	23 4/8	23 7/8	22 1/8	6	5	La Plata County	CO	James N. Hinson	1987	292
177 1/8	23 5/8	24 4/8	21 3/8	5	5	Albany County	WY	Jerry Bowen	1988	292
177 1/8	23 1/8	23 1/8	22 7/8	5	5	Harney County	OR	Robert Reed	1991	292
177 1/8	25 2/8	26 1/8	25 1/8	5	5	Boulder County	CO	Greg Allen Nichols	1992	292
177 1/8	21 3/8	21 1/8	23 0/8	6	6	Franklin County	ID	Kerry L. Payne	1993	292
177 1/8	24 2/8	24 1/8	21 5/8	5	7	Malheur County	OR	Brian Blackmore	2005	292
177 1/8	24 0/8	24 2/8	20 7/8	5	5	Bannock County	ID	Robert D. Cutler	2008	292
177 1/8	22 4/8	23 3/8	20 3/8	6	5	Tooele County	UT	Randy J. Walk	2009	292
177 0/8	22 0/8	23 6/8	24 4/8	6	5	White Pine County	NV	Dr. Donald Wicher	1961	302
177 0/8	24 4/8	25 5/8	21 4/8	7	6	Garfield County	CO	Steve U'Selis	1967	302
177 0/8	25 1/8	24 5/8	26 2/8	5	6	Delta County	CO	J. T. Kreager	2008	302
*177 0/8	21 7/8	20 6/8	20 0/8	5	5	Ravalli County	MT	Daniel Schurg	2010	302
176 7/8	20 7/8	21 5/8	20 7/8	5	5	Ada County	ID	Neil Russell	1996	306
176 7/8	22 5/8	23 5/8	20 3/8	5	5	Eagle Hill	ALB	Dallas Kaiser	1997	306
176 7/8	23 7/8	25 2/8	20 6/8	6	5	Mankota	SAS	Barry Hanson	1998	306
176 7/8	23 3/8	22 6/8	18 2/8	7	7	Chelan County	WA	Brent Anderson	1998	306
176 6/8	26 3/8	25 1/8	26 0/8	4	5	Yuma County	CO	Mark Sievers	1985	310
176 6/8	27 4/8	26 6/8	22 4/8	5	5	Wasatch County	UT	Doug Strecker	1987	310
176 6/8	25 7/8	24 7/8	25 2/8	5	5	Humboldt County	NV	Robert G. Hopper	1990	310
176 6/8	24 6/8	24 2/8	24 0/8	4	4	Carbon County	WY	Donald A. Carpenter	1990	310
176 6/8	21 7/8	23 4/8	22 2/8	5	5	Morgan County	UT	H. Thomas Stevenson	2004	310
176 5/8	22 5/8	22 2/8	20 6/8	5	6	Lincoln County	WY	Bart DeCora	1989	315
176 5/8	28 0/8	27 6/8	29 7/8	6	6	Weld County	CO	Tim Bradley	1989	315
176 5/8	26 0/8	25 0/8	26 2/8	6	5	Lyman County	SD	Kent Lewis	2004	315
176 4/8	23 4/8	23 5/8	20 0/8	5	5	Ada County	ID	Edward Keeton	1983	318
176 4/8	21 5/8	21 7/8	19 0/8	6	7	Conejos County	CO	Rick Gabbard	1987	318
176 4/8	22 2/8	22 7/8	21 4/8	5	5	Union County	OR	Kevin S. Robins	1994	318
176 4/8	22 1/8	24 7/8	21 7/8	6	7	Rio Arriba County	NM	Richard W. Eustace, Jr.	2006	318
176 3/8	21 0/8	21 1/8	26 3/8	5	5	Torrance County	NM	Frank Johnson	1989	322
176 3/8	21 3/8	21 5/8	22 3/8	5	5	Yuma County	CO	Chad Rockwell	1997	322
176 3/8	21 5/8	24 3/8	21 3/8	5	5	Sonora	MEX	Robert Norotsky	2007	322
176 2/8	22 1/8	24 0/8	20 4/8	5	6	Lincoln County	NE	M. R. Buchtel	1959	325
176 2/8	24 1/8	24 3/8	23 2/8	5	5	Russell County	KS	Duane Mai	1982	325
176 2/8	21 4/8	23 1/8	21 5/8	5	6	Meade County	KS	Roger Davis	1986	325
176 2/8	24 0/8	23 2/8	25 1/8	5	6	Hanna	ALB	David M. Bufkin	1998	325
*176 2/8	24 3/8	23 5/8	21 7/8	6	4	Otero County	NM	Levi Moore	2006	325
176 1/8	24 3/8	24 3/8	23 1/8	7	6	Duchesne County	UT	M.H. 'Bill' Wilkinson, Jr.	1964	330
176 1/8	24 2/8	24 2/8	23 1/8	5	5	Treasure County	MT	Christopher Downs	1993	330
176 1/8	25 1/8	25 1/8	23 6/8	5	6	Rio Arriba County	NM	Aaron Amator	1997	330
176 1/8	28 0/8	25 4/8	26 4/8	7	5	Trego County	KS	Steven W. Hausler	2000	330
176 1/8	24 2/8	25 5/8	27 4/8	5	5	Ravalli County	MT	Colby J. Robinson	2002	330
176 0/8	23 6/8	23 7/8	21 2/8	6	5	San Juan County	UT	Charles Farmer	1964	335
176 0/8	22 3/8	21 5/8	18 6/8	5	5	Coconino County	AZ	Tom Dennis	1972	335
176 0/8	24 7/8	24 7/8	23 6/8	5	6	Cassia County	ID	Earl Peterson	1981	335
176 0/8	22 1/8	23 4/8	21 0/8	6	6	Bingham County	ID	Doug Burkman	1994	335
*176 0/8	21 6/8	22 4/8	21 4/8	5	5	Sully County	SD	Glenn Delabarre	2007	335
*176 0/8	24 4/8	25 6/8	24 3/8	8	5	Elbert County	CO	Eric Nerwin	2009	335
175 7/8	24 5/8	24 1/8	18 0/8	6	9	Presidio County	TX	Neal Bouldin	1987	341
175 7/8	27 7/8	26 6/8	27 0/8	4	7	Cypress Hills	ALB	Russell Gregory Meidinger	1990	341
175 7/8	24 6/8	24 1/8	19 6/8	6	5	Salt Lake County	UT	Scott Fritsch	1997	341
175 7/8	23 0/8	24 2/8	21 6/8	5	6	Scott County	KS	Stacy Hoeme	1998	341
175 7/8	24 6/8	25 4/8	19 1/8	5	4	Elko County	NV	Jim H. Moore	2009	341
175 6/8	22 6/8	22 5/8	22 6/8	5	5	Uintah County	UT	Merlin L. Killpack	1957	346
175 6/8	24 4/8	24 4/8	25 4/8	6	6	Mesa County	CO	Joe Egner	1965	346
175 6/8	24 3/8	25 0/8	22 1/8	4	6	Larimer County	CO	Kevin Vinzant	1986	346
175 6/8	22 4/8	23 1/8	26 7/8	6	5	Flathead County	MT	Kory McGaghy	1992	346
175 6/8	24 2/8	22 5/8	24 5/8	5	5	Ravalli County	MT	Bob L. Walker	2002	346
*175 6/8	24 3/8	24 1/8	23 2/8	5	5	Pershing County	NV	Darrell Gogert	2007	346
175 5/8	23 6/8	25 0/8	21 1/8	4	4	Grant County	OR	Larry Saunders	1985	352
175 5/8	23 4/8	25 3/8	24 7/8	5	5	San Miguel County	NM	Dick McClain	1989	352
175 5/8	25 5/8	24 1/8	24 0/8	6	7	Weld County	CO	Jerry Joseph	1993	352
175 5/8	22 3/8	22 2/8	24 4/8	5	5	Scott County	KS	John C. Walker	1995	352
175 5/8	24 1/8	23 3/8	24 5/8	5	6	Santa Cruz County	AZ	Milton Sommerfeld, Jr.	1997	352
175 5/8	25 4/8	24 7/8	23 1/8	5	5	Deschutes County	OR	Lonnie Walling	2001	352
175 4/8	24 6/8	24 7/8	21 7/8	6	9	Colfax County	NM	Max Crocker	1981	358
175 4/8	21 2/8	20 3/8	21 0/8	5	6	San Juan County	CO	Stan Overstreet	1989	358
175 4/8	25 5/8	23 0/8	21 0/8	6	5	Cheyenne County	CO	Ronald R. Smith	1991	358
175 4/8	23 4/8	24 3/8	24 6/8	6	6	Coconino County	AZ	Mike Meyer	1999	358
175 4/8	23 7/8	21 2/8	18 2/8	6	7	Jefferson County	CO	Mitch Arnold	2002	358
175 3/8	21 5/8	23 1/8	19 5/8	6	7	Park County	CO	Marvin Clyncke	1981	363
175 3/8	24 4/8	24 0/8	23 1/8	5	5	Billings County	ND	Joe Kytoichuk	1983	363
175 3/8	21 2/8	22 2/8	18 1/8	5	5	Frenchman River	SAS	Dennis J. Francais	2000	363
175 3/8	24 1/8	22 7/8	22 3/8	5	5	Salt Lake County	UT	William Jensen	2001	363
175 3/8	26 5/8	26 6/8	26 3/8	4	4	Mesa County	CO	Lester R. Dayton	2003	363
175 3/8	24 3/8	23 3/8	23 5/8	5	5	Boise County	ID	Jacob Buskirk	2006	363
175 2/8	24 1/8	24 4/8	24 4/8	7	6	Emery County	UT	Ron Myers	1958	369
175 2/8	24 6/8	25 3/8	23 6/8	6	7	Garfield County	CO	Robert Pitt	1978	369
175 2/8	23 3/8	23 1/8	21 0/8	5	5	Slope County	ND	Pete Finck	2010	369
175 1/8	24 6/8	27 1/8	27 5/8	5	5	Sawlog Creek	KS	Merle Schulte	1974	372
175 1/8	21 7/8	22 2/8	19 7/8	4	4	Lincoln County	NV	Fred B. Allen III	1975	372
175 1/8	24 1/8	25 4/8	21 5/8	7	8	Delta County	CO	Michael Sturm	1977	372
175 1/8	21 4/8	22 7/8	21 6/8	6	6	Millard County	UT	Jason Woodland	1985	372
175 1/8	23 1/8	23 3/8	25 3/8	5	5	Jefferson County	ID	Brian Rhead	1997	372
175 1/8	23 2/8	25 2/8	19 2/8	5	7	Colfax County	NM	Mark Sullivan	1997	372
175 1/8	22 7/8	23 4/8	22 2/8	6	5	Milk River	ALB	John D. "Jack" Frost	1999	372
175 1/8	24 0/8	25 4/8	20 0/8	5	5	Tehama County	CA	Randy Hamblin	2002	372
175 1/8	22 4/8	22 3/8	21 7/8	4	5	Carseland	ALB	Eric Dirks	2006	372

311

MULE DEER (TYPICAL ANTLERS)

Minimum Score 145   Continued

SCORE	LENGTH OF R MAIN BEAM L	INSIDE SPREAD	NUMBER OF R POINTS L		AREA	STATE/ PROVINCE	HUNTER'S NAME	DATE	RANK
175 0/8	22 6/8	23 4/8	19 5/8	5	6	Manyberries	ALB	Carl A. Miller	1996	381
*175 0/8	23 5/8	23 5/8	19 7/8	5	6	Salt Lake County	UT	Scott Weatherspoon	2004	381
*175 0/8	25 5/8	24 3/8	24 0/8	5	5	Carbon County	WY	Matt Carpenter	2007	381
174 7/8	23 7/8	23 7/8	18 3/8	5	6	Delta County	CO	Paul Dickson	1969	384
174 7/8	22 5/8	21 7/8	23 0/8	5	5	Gallatin County	MT	Bob Savage	1970	384
174 7/8	21 5/8	22 1/8	23 7/8	5	5	Garfield County	CO	Norman L. Richerson	1978	384
174 7/8	25 5/8	23 0/8	28 2/8	5	5	Elbert County	CO	Robert D. Olivier	1981	384
174 7/8	22 5/8	21 2/8	20 3/8	5	5	Rio Arriba County	NM	Nelson Martinez, Jr.	1995	384
174 7/8	23 3/8	24 3/8	22 5/8	5	5	Lassen County	CA	Isaac W. Thornton	2005	384
174 7/8	23 6/8	24 0/8	21 4/8	5	7	Ford County	KS	Gary Shouse	2007	384
174 7/8	24 0/8	23 4/8	23 5/8	5	6	Yuma County	CO	Mike Barrett	2008	384
174 6/8	26 2/8	26 0/8	26 2/8	5	5	Lake County	OR	Gene Lyons	1969	392
174 6/8	24 0/8	23 4/8	21 2/8	5	6	Garfield County	CO	Jewell Petz	1970	392
174 6/8	26 4/8	25 5/8	24 6/8	5	5	Lea County	NM	Eddie Carpenter	1993	392
174 6/8	22 4/8	23 6/8	23 2/8	5	4	Endiang	ALB	Ron McLellan	1997	392
174 6/8	24 7/8	24 6/8	20 0/8	6	5	Elbert County	CO	Tom G. Kelley	2004	392
174 5/8	25 0/8	25 0/8	23 1/8	4	4	Moffat County	CO	Roland C. Gravenkemper	1961	397
174 5/8	23 6/8	22 5/8	19 4/8	6	6	Sevier County	UT	Kenneth L. Shirley	1968	397
174 5/8	22 7/8	23 1/8	20 5/8	7	5	Wichita County	KS	Stacy Hoeme	1990	397
174 5/8	22 6/8	22 5/8	21 1/8	5	5	Pennington County	SD	Ed Heeb	1993	397
174 5/8	24 7/8	24 1/8	20 1/8	8	7	Grant County	OR	William G. Henson	1997	397
174 5/8	23 7/8	24 7/8	21 6/8	5	7	Flagstaff County	ALB	Pride Benson	1997	397
*174 5/8	24 0/8	24 7/8	26 3/8	6	8	Pincher Creek	ALB	Kevin Evans	2006	397
174 4/8	26 0/8	23 5/8	26 4/8	6	5	Mesa County	CO	Douglas D. Watts	1976	404
174 4/8	24 3/8	24 1/8	22 6/8	4	5	Mesa County	CO	Jay Verzuh	1983	404
174 4/8	20 1/8	19 7/8	17 6/8	5	5	Coconino County	AZ	Paul T. Carter	1995	404
174 4/8	25 0/8	24 5/8	19 6/8	5	5	Consort	ALB	Trevor J. Wignall	1997	404
174 4/8	24 0/8	22 3/8	22 2/8	5	5	Milk River	ALB	Tom Hoffman	1999	404
174 4/8	25 1/8	24 6/8	26 5/8	6	5	Meade County	SD	Chris Cammack	2003	404
174 4/8	22 5/8	22 4/8	21 0/8	5	5	Millard County	UT	Cori Kirkpatrick	2008	404
174 4/8	25 3/8	25 5/8	23 2/8	5	5	Haakon County	SD	Jerry L. Ellens	2009	404
174 3/8	21 0/8	23 7/8	23 1/8	6	5	Pima County	AZ	Robert A. Edgar	1982	412
174 3/8	22 5/8	22 6/8	21 5/8	5	5	Lassen County	CA	Rick Pollard	1994	412
174 3/8	24 3/8	24 6/8	23 4/8	6	6	Coconino County	AZ	Eric Vielhauer	1996	412
174 3/8	23 5/8	20 2/8	18 3/8	5	5	Gunnison County	CO	Benjamin Vitkoski	2007	412
174 3/8	23 0/8	20 4/8	21 3/8	5	5	Ravalli County	MT	David A. Kostecki	2007	412
174 2/8	22 7/8	22 6/8	21 2/8	5	5	Natrona County	WY	Pat McAteer	1982	417
174 2/8	23 0/8	22 5/8	23 1/8	5	5	Billings County	ND	Mark Lothspeich	1984	417
174 2/8	25 3/8	23 7/8	25 0/8	6	6	Douglas County	CO	Daniel G. Weippert	1986	417
174 2/8	24 7/8	24 6/8	21 0/8	5	6	Umatilla County	OR	Clifford W. Widel	1991	417
174 2/8	24 1/8	24 6/8	25 6/8	5	5	Catron County	NM	Eddie Claypool	1996	417
174 1/8	21 5/8	23 0/8	22 0/8	6	5	Gray County	KS	Jim Sobba	1994	422
174 1/8	23 6/8	25 1/8	21 3/8	5	4	Powder River County	MT	Thomas Anzalone	2000	422
174 1/8	22 5/8	22 1/8	18 2/8	6	6	Cripple Creek	ALB	Ross McIlwraith	2003	422
174 1/8	20 7/8	20 4/8	18 6/8	6	6	Carbon County	WY	Lee Ford	2005	422
*174 1/8	23 7/8	24 2/8	21 5/8	5	5	Stanley County	SD	Derek Schiefelbein	2008	422
174 0/8	25 0/8	25 1/8	20 6/8	5	5	Ravalli County	MT	John Schulz	1976	427
174 0/8	24 2/8	24 5/8	23 4/8	5	5	Pangman	SAS	Scott Howse	1998	427
*174 0/8	24 6/8	25 4/8	21 4/8	4	5	Fall River County	SD	Lance Verhulst	2005	427
173 7/8	25 3/8	25 2/8	26 0/8	4	4	Uintah County	UT	Hal Wallentine	1962	430
173 7/8	25 4/8	25 4/8	21 0/8	5	5	Garfield County	CO	Danny C. Lloyd	1969	430
173 7/8	24 2/8	24 1/8	22 6/8	7	6	Eagle County	CO	Edward L. Berlier	1970	430
173 7/8	25 0/8	24 5/8	23 5/8	7	7	Okotoks	ALB	Dave Demeter	1981	430
173 7/8	22 5/8	22 4/8	20 3/8	6	5	Fraser River	BC	Don Sankey	1995	430
173 6/8	25 3/8	24 4/8	23 5/8	7	5	Sevier County	UT	Morris Stuart	1972	435
173 6/8	23 6/8	24 0/8	20 4/8	6	5	Boulder County	CO	Floyd Sullivan	1982	435
173 6/8	21 4/8	22 0/8	22 4/8	6	5	Humboldt County	NV	Joel C. Lenz	1984	435
173 6/8	25 4/8	20 3/8	27 4/8	5	6	Meadow Lake	BC	Chip Young	1987	435
173 6/8	24 6/8	22 5/8	18 6/8	5	5	Boise County	ID	Thomas M. Szurgot	1991	435
173 6/8	25 1/8	24 5/8	19 7/8	5	6	Calgary	ALB	Dave Browne	2000	435
173 6/8	23 2/8	23 2/8	19 2/8	5	5	Lake County	OR	Denny Carter	2003	435
173 6/8	23 0/8	23 2/8	21 4/8	5	5	La Plata County	CO	Duane Bolick	2006	435
173 5/8	24 6/8	24 7/8	23 7/8	5	5	Morton County	ND	Pat Sullivan	1957	443
173 5/8	25 1/8	25 5/8	25 2/8	7	5	Pima County	AZ	Joe Nochta	1959	443
173 5/8	21 4/8	21 1/8	21 0/8	6	7	Chaffee County	CO	Lee Rowe	1966	443
173 5/8	23 3/8	23 7/8	24 5/8	5	5	San Juan County	UT	Robert G. Hester	1972	443
173 5/8	23 5/8	22 7/8	22 7/8	5	6	Natrona County	WY	M. Robert DeLaney	1995	443
173 5/8	23 0/8	23 1/8	21 3/8	5	5	Box Elder County	UT	Alan Pringle	2004	443
173 4/8	24 3/8	24 2/8	27 2/8	5	6	Garfield County	CO	Don Mayen	1966	449
173 4/8	22 1/8	22 1/8	20 4/8	6	7	Ada County	ID	David D. Howard	1971	449
173 4/8	23 5/8	24 4/8	21 0/8	4	6	Mesa County	CO	G. Fred Asbell	1974	449
173 4/8	21 5/8	20 4/8	21 2/8	5	5	Montrose County	CO	Chip Greene	1978	449
173 4/8	23 6/8	23 3/8	20 4/8	5	5	Eagle County	CO	Donald R. Hoard	1992	449
173 4/8	24 0/8	22 4/8	20 4/8	5	6	Larimer County	CO	Eric Vance	1995	449
173 4/8	23 3/8	24 1/8	21 5/8	8	7	Montezuma County	CO	Marvin Reichenau	2000	449
*173 4/8	25 0/8	24 6/8	26 5/8	5	5	Bow Island	ALB	Earl Chauvin	2008	449
173 3/8	22 4/8	24 1/8	24 7/8	5	5	Coconino County	AZ	Jack Richards	1958	457
173 3/8	23 0/8	23 5/8	23 5/8	5	5	Sevier County	UT	Robert J. Shumway	1969	457
173 3/8	21 5/8	22 6/8	22 0/8	6	6	Caribou County	ID	Jim Walton	1983	457
173 3/8	22 0/8	22 3/8	22 2/8	5	6	Chelan County	WA	David J. Yonaka	2003	457
173 2/8	22 6/8	23 1/8	22 6/8	6	6	Millard County	UT	George Kendall	1959	461
173 2/8	25 5/8	25 1/8	22 4/8	5	5	Dolores County	CO	Jack Acree	1969	461
173 2/8	24 0/8	24 0/8	21 4/8	5	7	Bernalillo County	NM	Rolland Hanna	1972	461
173 2/8	25 1/8	24 3/8	24 3/8	6	5	Carbon County	UT	Demar Guymon	1982	461
173 2/8	27 6/8	27 2/8	25 6/8	7	7	Norton County	KS	Mark S. Myers	1991	461
173 2/8	25 6/8	24 4/8	26 4/8	5	5	Socorro County	NM	Anthony J. Turrietta	1995	461
173 2/8	23 0/8	21 7/8	18 2/8	6	5	Logan County	KS	Walter E. Lovins	1997	461
173 2/8	21 7/8	23 2/8	23 0/8	4	6	San Juan County	NM	Jason Hoyungowa	2000	461
173 2/8	23 4/8	22 5/8	18 3/8	5	6	Uinta County	WY	Rob Harris	2006	461
*173 2/8	21 0/8	23 3/8	20 4/8	5	5	Campbell County	SD	Troy Hanson	2007	461
173 2/8	24 2/8	26 4/8	24 2/8	4	4	Adams County	CO	Dan Goodnight	2007	461
173 2/8	24 2/8	25 6/8	24 2/8	6	6	Garfield County	CO	Lisa M. Ameen	2008	461
173 1/8	26 3/8	25 0/8	21 3/8	5	5	Coconino County	AZ	H. H. Harter	1961	473
173 1/8	23 3/8	24 1/8	20 5/8	5	5	Teton County	ID	Paul Beesley	1976	473
173 1/8	22 1/8	22 5/8	21 6/8	5	6	Bear Lake County	ID	Steven A. Dewey	1985	473

312

MULE DEER (TYPICAL ANTLERS)

Minimum Score 145   Continued

SCORE	LENGTH OF R MAIN BEAM L	INSIDE SPREAD	NUMBER OF R POINTS L	AREA	STATE/ PROVINCE	HUNTER'S NAME	DATE	RANK
173 1/8	23 3/8 22 2/8	23 0/8	5 7	Deschutes County	OR	Jonathan Roy Manbeck	1987	473
173 1/8	25 3/8 25 2/8	26 1/8	4 5	Millarville	ALB	David S. Elcombe	1998	473
173 1/8	22 1/8 21 0/8	17 7/8	6 5	Big Horn County	WY	Dan Selvig	1999	473
173 1/8	24 4/8 24 2/8	20 7/8	6 5	Brooks	ALB	Neil Summers	1999	473
173 1/8	25 2/8 24 0/8	24 2/8	7 6	Rockyview	ALB	Cameron Foss	2005	473
173 0/8	23 4/8 24 0/8	24 1/8	5 5	Gray County	KS	Bob Barnes	1966	481
173 0/8	21 5/8 22 2/8	24 5/8	4 5	Mesa County	CO	Floyd Kendall	1966	481
173 0/8	26 6/8 26 5/8	23 5/8	6 6	Edmonton	ALB	Brian Berrecloth	1981	481
173 0/8	25 4/8 25 4/8	26 7/8	6 5	Carbon County	UT	Tom Riebe	1983	481
173 0/8	22 2/8 22 2/8	18 2/8	5 5	Caribou County	ID	Larry Jaeger	1985	481
173 0/8	24 3/8 22 4/8	22 2/8	5 5	Boise County	ID	Kenneth A. Hyde	1988	481
172 7/8	22 6/8 22 2/8	20 2/8	6 5	Boise County	ID	Marlin Tullis	1982	487
172 7/8	22 2/8 22 5/8	22 7/8	5 5	Cabri	SAS	Clarence R. Hughes	1989	487
172 7/8	22 5/8 23 3/8	18 7/8	6 5	Colfax County	NM	Joe Amador	1991	487
172 7/8	22 5/8 22 5/8	21 1/8	4 5	Cache County	UT	David Teuscher	1992	487
172 7/8	26 0/8 25 0/8	21 1/8	5 6	Scott County	KS	Brett Eisenhour	1995	487
172 7/8	22 7/8 22 6/8	23 4/8	4 4	Natrona County	WY	Steve Lamb	2004	487
172 7/8	24 3/8 23 7/8	22 2/8	5 6	Rich County	UT	Peggie Feller	2007	487
172 6/8	21 5/8 21 6/8	16 7/8	6 5	Bowman County	ND	Leroy Brandenburger	1967	494
172 6/8	28 7/8 26 3/8	28 7/8	6 6	Rio Arriba County	NM	Kerino H. Revel	1968	494
172 6/8	21 7/8 22 4/8	19 4/8	5 4	Ada County	ID	Ronald B. Jones	1971	494
172 6/8	23 4/8 24 0/8	20 7/8	7 5	San Juan County	UT	Harold Boyack	1975	494
172 6/8	22 3/8 23 0/8	20 6/8	4 5	Mabel Lake	BC	Mark Siegmueller	1984	494
172 6/8	23 1/8 22 5/8	22 0/8	4 4	Rio Blanco County	CO	Brad Murray	1985	494
172 6/8	23 3/8 23 1/8	20 4/8	5 5	Franklin County	ID	Lance Henderson	1992	494
172 6/8	23 2/8 22 2/8	23 6/8	6 6	Coconino County	AZ	David Baldwin	1996	494
172 6/8	25 6/8 24 0/8	24 0/8	5 6	Las Animas County	CO	Todd Wickens	1999	494
172 6/8	24 2/8 25 0/8	21 4/8	5 5	Moffat County	CO	Frank S. Noska IV	2000	494
172 6/8	22 2/8 23 2/8	22 2/8	5 5	Albany County	WY	Derek Long II	2001	494
172 6/8	25 6/8 25 5/8	27 7/8	5 5	Morrow County	OR	Robert Seubert	2007	494
172 6/8	24 0/8 23 2/8	22 4/8	5 5	Sublette County	WY	Shannon Brewer	2008	494
172 5/8	23 6/8 24 2/8	22 3/8	5 5	Bernalillo County	NM	Noble Sinclair	1982	507
172 5/8	22 4/8 20 7/8	20 4/8	5 6	Lincoln County	WY	Mike Barrett	1990	507
172 5/8	24 0/8 23 3/8	19 5/8	5 5	Lincoln County	CO	Joseph A. Vigueria	2000	507
172 5/8	24 3/8 24 2/8	23 1/8	5 6	Big Horn County	WY	Jerome S. Giudice	2009	507
172 4/8	24 3/8 22 7/8	24 3/8	6 5	Malheur County	OR	Carl R. Stone	1957	511
172 4/8	25 3/8 25 4/8	24 2/8	5 5	Owyhee County	ID	Don Rosenvall	1961	511
172 4/8	25 6/8 23 6/8	20 3/8	5 5	Chelan County	WA	Timothy E Pflugh	1984	511
172 4/8	25 4/8 25 7/8	22 2/8	6 6	Mesa County	CO	DeWayne Young	1986	511
172 4/8	21 3/8 22 2/8	22 4/8	5 7	Union County	OR	Carl M. Nelson	1992	511
172 4/8	25 7/8 24 4/8	16 1/8	6 7	Teton County	WY	Dallas Smith	1995	511
172 4/8	24 7/8 25 2/8	28 1/8	5 5	Montezuma County	CO	Bryon D. Long	1996	511
*172 4/8	25 5/8 23 5/8	20 1/8	6 6	Oyen	ALB	Bryce Dillabough	2007	511
*172 4/8	29 2/8 27 6/8	25 2/8	3 4	Davis County	UT	Danl Anselmo	2008	511
172 4/8	24 4/8 25 3/8	21 6/8	8 6	Jefferson County	CO	Robert G. Lane	2009	511
172 3/8	23 3/8 22 6/8	21 6/8	5 7	Garfield County	CO	Kenneth Rapp	1974	521
172 3/8	22 0/8 22 0/8	20 3/8	5 5	Ouray County	CO	Don Castrup	1975	521
172 3/8	25 3/8 25 4/8	23 0/8	6 6	Shasta County	CA	Russell Browning	1983	521
172 3/8	24 5/8 24 1/8	23 0/8	5 6	Norton County	KS	Greg J. McCall	1985	521
172 3/8	23 7/8 22 5/8	24 4/8	5 5	Montrose County	CO	Greg Blackburn	1986	521
172 3/8	25 4/8 25 5/8	21 7/8	5 5	Calgary	ALB	Dave Browne	1999	521
172 3/8	23 1/8 23 0/8	21 7/8	5 5	Caribou County	ID	John B. Heintzelman	2003	521
*172 3/8	24 4/8 24 2/8	19 7/8	5 5	Eagle County	CO	Kurt W. Keskimaki	2007	521
172 3/8	26 0/8 25 4/8	23 1/8	5 5	Lincoln County	NM	Lerry D. Bond	2008	521
172 2/8	24 4/8 25 3/8	21 0/8	6 7	Rock Creek	CO	Louis Prestridge	1961	530
172 2/8	26 0/8 26 0/8	25 6/8	5 5	Wasatch County	UT	Bill Dean	1965	530
172 2/8	21 4/8 22 3/8	19 2/8	5 5	Caribou County	ID	Bret Davis	1991	530
172 2/8	24 1/8 25 0/8	23 2/8	5 5	Sheridan County	WY	Charles F. Neisess	1995	530
172 2/8	23 6/8 23 5/8	25 5/8	6 5	Coconino County	AZ	Mike George	2003	530
172 1/8	24 1/8 24 6/8	24 5/8	5 5	Rio Grande County	CO	Marvin Tompkins	1960	535
172 1/8	22 3/8 22 3/8	18 1/8	4 4	Lake County	OR	Ralph Hoover	1964	535
172 1/8	24 0/8 24 4/8	23 7/8	5 6	Sevier County	UT	Bob Covington	1965	535
172 1/8	21 1/8 22 2/8	20 7/8	5 5	Saguache County	CO	Rick Duggan	1984	535
172 1/8	20 3/8 20 6/8	20 6/8	5 6	Perkins County	SD	Travis Bies	1988	535
172 1/8	22 4/8 23 3/8	21 0/8	6 5	Bowman County	ND	Scott P. Bradac	1992	535
172 1/8	23 7/8 24 6/8	23 5/8	6 5	Salt Lake County	UT	Mike Raetz	1997	535
172 1/8	24 3/8 23 6/8	24 3/8	5 5	Stanley County	SD	Derek Schiefelbein	2006	535
172 0/8	26 1/8 26 3/8	26 1/8	4 5	Baker County	OR	James D. Hanley	1960	543
172 0/8	25 6/8 26 0/8	21 4/8	4 5	Beechy	SAS	Terry Carruthers	1987	543
172 0/8	22 3/8 22 4/8	22 2/8	5 5	Gunnison County	CO	Darrell Jones	1995	543
172 0/8	25 1/8 25 6/8	22 4/8	6 5	Deschutes County	OR	Bruce Williamson	2002	543
172 0/8	24 3/8 24 5/8	20 5/8	6 5	Apache County	AZ	Kurt Wood	2004	543
172 0/8	24 2/8 23 6/8	21 2/8	5 5	Eagle County	CO	William Kyle Ansel	2008	543
172 0/8	24 0/8 25 0/8	24 0/8	5 5	Charles Mix County	SD	Travis T. Theilen	2009	543
171 7/8	23 4/8 23 5/8	27 2/8	5 5	Uintah County	UT	Alvin Sisam	1966	550
171 7/8	26 4/8 24 5/8	24 5/8	4 5	Lancer	SAS	Del Erickson	1976	550
171 7/8	20 3/8 20 5/8	17 7/8	5 5	Larimer County	CO	Mike Kolano	1985	550
171 7/8	23 1/8 24 1/8	25 5/8	9 5	Scott County	KS	Mike Stoppel	1986	550
171 6/8	23 0/8 22 7/8	22 2/8	5 5	Carbon County	WY	Steve Parker	1974	554
171 6/8	22 7/8 21 6/8	23 3/8	8 8	Teton County	MT	James Dean	1977	554
171 6/8	24 7/8 25 4/8	21 6/8	5 6	Delta County	CO	Louis A. Brunett	1983	554
171 6/8	24 2/8 24 3/8	24 4/8	5 5	Teton County	WY	Guy Williamson	1992	554
171 6/8	25 6/8 24 6/8	25 1/8	6 5	Maricopa County	AZ	Larry Drake	1995	554
171 6/8	25 7/8 25 5/8	27 0/8	6 7	San Juan County	NM	Mark Teahan	1998	554
171 6/8	24 7/8 25 5/8	23 0/8	5 5	Malheur County	OR	Clint L. Fillmore	1998	554
171 6/8	23 2/8 23 3/8	22 5/8	5 6	Lincoln County	MT	Ron Halvorson	2000	554
171 6/8	22 0/8 21 7/8	19 0/8	6 5	Brooks	ALB	Joe Given	2001	554
171 6/8	21 4/8 23 2/8	18 0/8	5 5	Buffalo	ALB	Ron Dixon	2008	554
171 6/8	23 6/8 23 6/8	19 0/8	5 5	Jackson County	SD	Sean C. Fulton	2008	554
171 5/8	24 3/8 24 3/8	23 2/8	6 5	Harney County	OR	Chuck Warner	1977	565
171 5/8	23 5/8 24 0/8	19 1/8	4 5	Sweetwater County	WY	Keith Dana	1983	565
171 5/8	24 0/8 24 0/8	25 3/8	5 7	Las Animas County	CO	Gary Lehnherr	1995	565
171 5/8	24 5/8 25 1/8	25 4/8	4 5	Red Deer River	ALB	Bob J. Schriever	2005	565
171 5/8	21 2/8 21 0/8	17 7/8	6 5	Elbert County	CO	Al Baldwin	2008	565
171 4/8	21 6/8 23 3/8	25 2/8	5 6	Uncompahgre N.F.	CO	Vito Benedetto	1976	570

313

MULE DEER (TYPICAL ANTLERS)

Minimum Score 145   Continued

SCORE	LENGTH OF R MAIN BEAM L		INSIDE SPREAD	NUMBER OF R POINTS L		AREA	STATE/ PROVINCE	HUNTER'S NAME	DATE	RANK
171 4/8	24 4/8	24 3/8	21 2/8	5	5	Billings County	ND	Harold Hugelen	1977	570
171 4/8	23 0/8	22 6/8	22 3/8	6	5	Clark County	KS	Dan Fenton	1980	570
171 4/8	24 7/8	25 6/8	23 6/8	4	4	Baker County	OR	Mike Raney	1987	570
171 4/8	24 3/8	24 6/8	21 4/8	5	5	Salt Lake County	UT	Don Adams	2001	570
171 4/8	23 6/8	23 3/8	29 3/8	5	5	Morgan County	CO	Filiberto Lopez	2010	570
171 3/8	23 4/8	23 5/8	22 5/8	6	6	Ravalli County	MT	Joe Wandstrath	1980	576
171 3/8	24 5/8	25 5/8	26 5/8	5	5	Chaffee County	CO	Bruce Fish	1981	576
171 3/8	26 6/8	24 2/8	20 3/8	4	4	Lake County	OR	Michael Wright	1991	576
171 3/8	24 1/8	22 3/8	23 1/8	6	7	Scott County	KS	Dean Hamilton	1993	576
*171 3/8	23 4/8	24 0/8	24 2/8	6	6	Kitscoty	ALB	Dave MacKenzie	1996	576
171 3/8	26 1/8	25 1/8	24 1/8	5	6	Fall River County	SD	Jon Hardesty	2005	576
171 3/8	23 7/8	25 0/8	16 4/8	6	7	Taos County	NM	Darrin Kasper	2006	576
171 2/8	23 2/8	23 6/8	20 2/8	4	5	Summit County	UT	Kent Garfield	1959	583
171 2/8	24 0/8	23 7/8	19 2/8	5	5	Richland County	MT	Dennis Engle	1966	583
171 2/8	21 5/8	22 0/8	16 2/8	5	6	Routt County	CO	Joe Mucka	1975	583
171 2/8	22 6/8	24 2/8	24 7/8	5	5	McKenzie County	ND	Andrew Johnson	1992	583
171 2/8	23 3/8	21 4/8	18 3/8	5	6	Teton County	WY	Deon F. Heiner	1993	583
171 2/8	23 2/8	23 7/8	20 2/8	5	5	Gunnison County	CO	Butch A. Todd	1996	583
171 2/8	24 6/8	24 2/8	20 4/8	6	5	Newell	ALB	Ray Francingues III	2002	583
171 2/8	23 4/8	23 4/8	22 2/8	5	5	Mesa County	CO	David M. Gant	2004	583
171 2/8	23 6/8	23 1/8	28 2/8	5	6	Garfield County	CO	Steve Hammond	2005	583
171 2/8	23 3/8	24 6/8	22 3/8	7	7	Fremont County	ID	Carl A. Passino	2005	583
171 2/8	22 3/8	23 4/8	21 0/8	5	5	Fremont County	WY	Gary Martin	2008	583
171 1/8	28 0/8	26 4/8	22 4/8	8	7	Wasatch County	UT	Frank Snyder	1959	594
171 1/8	25 4/8	25 3/8	24 7/8	7	6	Millard County	UT	Shirley B. Pace	1962	594
171 1/8	23 3/8	23 2/8	22 7/8	5	5	Juab County	UT	Farren Anderson	1964	594
171 1/8	20 7/8	22 7/8	22 2/8	6	7	Mesa County	CO	Curtis Bateman	1983	594
171 1/8	22 7/8	23 2/8	21 5/8	5	5	Garden County	NE	Monte Shaul	1985	594
171 1/8	21 5/8	22 3/8	21 3/8	5	5	Coconino County	AZ	Paul T. Carter	2002	594
*171 1/8	24 5/8	23 5/8	18 4/8	6	5	Lyman County	SD	Gary Ambur	2009	594
171 0/8	21 7/8	23 0/8	21 6/8	5	5	Meade County	KS	Keith Whitney	1986	601
171 0/8	25 1/8	23 0/8	25 4/8	5	8	Adams County	ID	Alan Dehlin	1992	601
171 0/8	23 3/8	23 0/8	21 4/8	4	4	Weld County	CO	Chet Trivette	1997	601
171 0/8	27 6/8	26 2/8	22 3/8	6	6	Chelan County	WA	Daniel Gilyard	2000	601
171 0/8	24 5/8	24 3/8	20 5/8	6	5	Ravalli County	MT	Bob L. Walker	2004	601
170 7/8	21 1/8	22 7/8	19 3/8	4	4	Beaver County	UT	Richard L. Anderson	1960	606
170 7/8	22 7/8	21 5/8	24 4/8	5	5	Bernalillo County	NM	Dr. E. J. Bowser	1971	606
170 7/8	23 4/8	22 1/8	19 6/8	6	5	Uncompahgre N.F.	CO	Allen G. Hughes	1974	606
170 7/8	23 3/8	22 6/8	17 6/8	5	7	Red Willow County	NE	William E. Peck, Jr.	1992	606
170 7/8	22 5/8	23 1/8	20 7/8	4	5	Boise County	ID	Doug Hawker	1992	606
170 7/8	23 2/8	24 4/8	22 7/8	6	5	Garfield County	CO	William S. Drake	1995	606
170 6/8	22 7/8	22 4/8	22 6/8	5	6	Chelan County	WA	Gerald Weiss	1967	612
170 6/8	25 2/8	24 5/8	25 0/8	5	5	Uintah County	UT	Eugene Damron	1974	612
170 6/8	25 4/8	25 7/8	25 4/8	6	6	Kit Carson County	CO	Larry Schaal	1988	612
170 6/8	24 4/8	24 5/8	21 7/8	5	7	Baker County	OR	Luke Maher	1994	612
170 6/8	23 2/8	23 1/8	21 4/8	5	6	Elmore County	ID	Rod Bradley	1996	612
170 6/8	24 1/8	24 3/8	20 6/8	5	4	Salt Lake County	UT	Darin N. Miller	1996	612
170 6/8	25 5/8	24 1/8	21 6/8	5	5	Manyberries	ALB	Carl A. Miller	1997	612
170 6/8	23 7/8	24 0/8	21 2/8	4	5	Ravalli County	MT	Bob L. Walker	2003	612
*170 6/8	23 0/8	22 4/8	18 1/8	5	5	Grant County	ND	Clay Daniels	2009	612
*170 6/8	25 2/8	25 5/8	24 4/8	8	9	Custer County	SD	William S. Seaborne	2009	612
170 5/8	24 7/8	25 6/8	19 7/8	5	6	Garfield County	CO	Robert H. Pitt	1971	622
170 5/8	24 5/8	23 6/8	23 7/8	5	4	Okanogan County	WA	Rick Wichers	2007	622
170 5/8	23 0/8	22 6/8	18 3/8	5	5	Uintah County	UT	Lynn Pomeroy	2010	622
170 4/8	23 2/8	23 0/8	22 0/8	5	5	Carbon County	WY	James E. Lawrence	1971	625
170 4/8	21 1/8	21 5/8	20 1/8	6	5	Humboldt County	NV	Vic Christison	1982	625
170 4/8	26 0/8	24 4/8	25 0/8	5	4	Torrance County	NM	Henry Montoya	1988	625
170 4/8	24 3/8	23 3/8	18 1/8	6	5	Camas County	ID	Bruce McStay	1988	625
170 4/8	23 0/8	23 1/8	19 6/8	5	5	Brunson Lake	BC	Daryl Buchholtz	1991	625
170 4/8	24 4/8	21 1/8	20 0/8	5	6	Mellette County	SD	Robert J. Genske	2004	625
170 4/8	23 1/8	25 1/8	23 6/8	5	6	Bow River	ALB	Dennis Zahn	2009	625
170 3/8	20 7/8	19 4/8	21 4/8	5	5	Ada County	ID	Jim Spearman	1970	632
170 3/8	23 6/8	24 5/8	19 7/8	5	5	Chelan County	WA	Dave Johnson	1977	632
170 3/8	21 0/8	21 0/8	20 0/8	5	6	Harney County	OR	Chuck Warner	1979	632
170 3/8	23 4/8	23 3/8	19 6/8	6	6	Caribou County	ID	Gregg Welch	1988	632
170 3/8	23 2/8	23 2/8	21 6/8	5	6	Chelan County	WA	Wayne Pippin	1991	632
170 3/8	23 4/8	24 2/8	20 3/8	5	5	Meagher County	MT	Michael L. McHugh	1993	632
170 3/8	23 4/8	24 0/8	23 3/8	5	5	Kimball County	NE	Kurt S. Brower	1999	632
170 3/8	23 0/8	22 4/8	21 1/8	5	5	Lincoln County	MT	John Lindstedt	2003	632
170 2/8	24 7/8	23 7/8	24 2/8	6	6	Slope County	ND	Jim Peters	1954	640
170 2/8	23 1/8	23 1/8	20 1/8	5	7	Fishlake National Forest	UT	Stan Rock	1961	640
170 2/8	23 0/8	23 3/8	20 1/8	7	5	Rio Arriba County	NM	Robert H. Keadle	1966	640
170 2/8	21 3/8	20 4/8	20 4/8	7	7	McKenzie County	ND	Don Davidson	1982	640
170 2/8	23 7/8	25 0/8	24 4/8	4	5	Colfax County	NM	Michael A. Sisneros	1991	640
170 2/8	22 5/8	22 4/8	19 2/8	5	5	Bernalillo County	NM	Barron Freeman	1992	640
170 2/8	24 4/8	24 6/8	26 5/8	5	5	Teton County	WY	Donald R. Williamson	1995	640
170 2/8	24 2/8	24 0/8	24 6/8	4	5	Pima County	AZ	James H. Caves III	1997	640
170 2/8	20 4/8	22 7/8	22 0/8	5	5	Baca County	CO	James O. Pittman, Jr.	1999	640
*170 2/8	24 2/8	24 4/8	25 6/8	5	5	Milk River	ALB	M. Blake Patton	2008	640
170 1/8	23 3/8	24 0/8	19 7/8	5	5	Gray County	KS	Dick Masters	1968	650
170 1/8	22 7/8	22 7/8	20 3/8	5	5	Thomas County	KS	Gerald Paxton	1987	650
170 1/8	24 6/8	24 0/8	22 1/8	6	5	Grand County	CO	Paul T. Jones	1999	650
170 1/8	23 6/8	22 5/8	23 3/8	5	5	S. Saskatchewan River	SAS	Glen A. Miller	2001	650
170 1/8	24 1/8	24 6/8	21 1/8	6	6	Malheur County	OR	Michael Adkins	2002	650
170 1/8	24 5/8	25 7/8	20 3/8	4	4	Okanogan County	WA	Lewis Monteith	2005	650
170 0/8	22 4/8	23 0/8	20 6/8	4	5	Routt County	CO	Robert Syvertson, Jr.	1975	656
170 0/8	22 3/8	22 2/8	23 6/8	7	7	Pima County	AZ	James M. Fry	1975	656
170 0/8	23 5/8	22 7/8	19 7/8	5	6	Grant County	OR	Timothy D. Palmore	1976	656
170 0/8	23 3/8	23 7/8	24 2/8	5	6	Uncompahgre N.F.	CO	Robert Meyler IV	1976	656
170 0/8	24 2/8	24 0/8	26 3/8	5	5	Saguache County	CO	Pat Schambow	1985	656
170 0/8	21 4/8	22 2/8	19 0/8	5	5	Norton County	KS	David Bainter	1988	656
170 0/8	26 0/8	24 6/8	25 2/8	6	4	Klamath County	OR	Jeffrey A. Eder	1992	656
170 0/8	25 0/8	25 3/8	23 2/8	5	5	Lake County	OR	Jim DeCaire	1994	656
170 0/8	24 0/8	22 4/8	22 7/8	5	6	Johnson County	WY	John C. Yoder	1997	656
170 0/8	24 4/8	25 0/8	22 0/8	5	5	Garfield County	CO	Robin Justin Baptist	1998	656

314

MULE DEER (TYPICAL ANTLERS)

Minimum Score 145   Continued

SCORE	LENGTH OF R MAIN BEAM L	INSIDE SPREAD	NUMBER OF R POINTS L	AREA	STATE/ PROVINCE	HUNTER'S NAME	DATE	RANK
170 0/8	25 0/8 25 2/8	24 4/8	5 6	Mesa County	CO	Bill L. Conn	1998	656
170 0/8	22 3/8 22 7/8	19 2/8	5 5	Chelan County	WA	John Kernaghan	2001	656
170 0/8	22 0/8 22 3/8	20 2/8	4 5	Gunnison County	CO	Scott Hargrove	2002	656
170 0/8	24 7/8 24 4/8	24 0/8	6 5	Laramie County	WY	Rick Parish	2007	656
*170 0/8	25 4/8 25 1/8	26 1/8	5 5	Nevada County	CA	Les Troncao	2009	656
170 0/8	22 0/8 21 4/8	18 2/8	5 5	Lincoln County	WY	Jeff Whitney	2010	656
169 7/8	23 3/8 22 7/8	24 3/8	4 5	Caribou County	ID	Chet Hopkins	1968	672
169 7/8	24 1/8 24 1/8	21 1/8	5 5	Larimer County	CO	Ron Morgan	1993	672
169 7/8	23 4/8 22 2/8	22 7/8	4 4	Lane County	KS	Dean Hamilton	1996	672
169 6/8	23 0/8 23 3/8	23 0/8	5 5	Garfield County	CO	C. W. Gilbreath	1967	675
169 6/8	25 0/8 23 0/8	22 2/8	4 4	Platte County	WY	Jerry Bowen	1976	675
169 6/8	22 0/8 23 0/8	22 2/8	5 5	Elbert County	CO	Mike Amendt	1981	675
169 6/8	21 7/8 22 2/8	20 0/8	5 5	Garfield County	CO	Eddy Oliger	1986	675
169 6/8	22 3/8 22 3/8	20 4/8	5 6	Camas County	ID	Jim Walters	1988	675
169 6/8	20 6/8 19 7/8	17 2/8	5 5	Valley County	ID	Neil Thagard	1992	675
169 6/8	22 0/8 20 7/8	20 2/8	5 6	Elkwater	ALB	Bruce R. Schoeneweis	1995	675
169 6/8	23 3/8 22 7/8	23 1/8	6 6	Edmonton	ALB	Marven Fehlauer	1996	675
169 6/8	24 1/8 26 5/8	26 3/8	6 5	Yuma County	CO	Mike Barrett	2005	675
*169 6/8	18 2/8 19 4/8	19 2/8	5 5	Dunn County	ND	Christopher Reed	2006	675
*169 6/8	22 5/8 24 3/8	22 0/8	4 4	Klamath County	OR	Randy Ruttledge	2008	675
169 5/8	24 3/8 24 3/8	22 0/8	5 7	Lincoln County	MT	Harold Leslie	1980	686
169 5/8	26 0/8 25 5/8	19 5/8	9 8	Garfield County	CO	Jay A. Keeler	1984	686
169 5/8	22 6/8 22 2/8	20 5/8	5 4	Eagle County	CO	Michael Dziekan	1988	686
169 5/8	24 4/8 24 6/8	21 1/8	4 4	Adams County	ID	Keenar C. Roberts	1998	686
169 5/8	24 3/8 23 0/8	22 5/8	5 5	Lane County	KS	Dean Hamilton	1999	686
169 5/8	24 0/8 23 6/8	20 4/8	5 6	Albany County	WY	Willard Woods	2000	686
169 5/8	22 0/8 23 4/8	19 1/8	4 4	Carbon County	WY	Randy Evans	2007	686
169 4/8	23 0/8 23 3/8	26 7/8	5 5	Owyhee County	ID	Dwane Marler	1955	693
169 4/8	21 3/8 22 1/8	19 6/8	5 5	Bowman County	ND	Scott Bradac	1994	693
169 3/8	22 5/8 22 2/8	26 2/8	5 5	Norton County	KS	Joseph E. Schroeder	1979	695
169 3/8	21 4/8 22 3/8	19 5/8	5 5	McKinley County	NM	Hayden Lambson	1979	695
169 3/8	20 4/8 22 3/8	22 3/8	5 5	Elmore County	ID	Steve Bresnahan	1980	695
169 3/8	22 3/8 22 0/8	19 3/8	5 5	Box Elder County	UT	Bob Doutre	1981	695
169 3/8	20 1/8 20 5/8	19 5/8	5 5	Park County	WY	William D. Rhodes	1992	695
169 3/8	24 1/8 24 2/8	20 5/8	5 7	Grant County	OR	Brian Allen Sorensen	1998	695
169 2/8	22 3/8 21 6/8	23 4/8	6 5	Chelan County	WA	Larry Lockhart	1966	701
169 2/8	26 0/8 26 0/8	20 6/8	5 5	Umatilla County	OR	Dennis Hernley	1987	701
169 2/8	24 6/8 23 6/8	21 1/8	6 5	Pinal County	AZ	Robert Wakefield	1991	701
169 2/8	25 3/8 26 4/8	26 0/8	6 6	Comanche County	KS	Greg Hill	1996	701
169 2/8	25 0/8 24 6/8	24 5/8	5 5	McKenzie County	ND	Corey Hugelen	2000	701
*169 2/8	24 3/8 22 7/8	21 2/8	4 5	Yuma County	CO	Rodney A. Lindsten	2007	701
169 2/8	22 4/8 21 3/8	23 4/8	6 5	Santa Cruz County	AZ	Miguel F. Morales	2009	701
169 2/8	23 6/8 23 7/8	22 7/8	6 7	Quappelle Valley	SAS	Matthew Hauser	2010	701
169 1/8	24 2/8 23 4/8	21 1/8	7 6	San Juan County	UT	Dean Wolf	1970	709
169 1/8	23 2/8 24 7/8	21 4/8	6 7	Elmore County	ID	Champ Church	1986	709
169 1/8	25 1/8 24 0/8	23 2/8	5 5	Dolores County	CO	Eugene Davenport	1990	709
169 1/8	23 7/8 24 1/8	20 3/8	4 5	Hand County	SD	Fred Kober	1991	709
169 2/8	22 5/8 23 0/8	22 1/8	5 5	Klamath County	OR	Theodore A. Davis	1992	709
169 1/8	23 4/8 22 3/8	21 1/8	5 6	Bingham County	ID	Todd F. Lewis	1992	709
169 1/8	22 6/8 23 5/8	17 3/8	5 5	Elko County	NV	John V. Bottari	1995	709
169 1/8	19 6/8 20 5/8	22 0/8	5 6	Barrhead	ALB	Phil Wierenga	1995	709
169 1/8	22 1/8 22 2/8	20 3/8	5 5	Natrona County	WY	Mark Miller	1997	709
169 1/8	23 3/8 23 3/8	21 6/8	6 6	Mesa County	CO	Rick L. Cooper	2000	709
169 0/8	22 0/8 21 5/8	20 0/8	5 4	Colfax County	NM	Gary Ginther	1973	719
169 0/8	23 5/8 24 6/8	22 6/8	5 5	Fremont County	CO	Bill W. Canterbury	1975	719
169 0/8	23 2/8 24 6/8	24 3/8	6 5	San Juan County	UT	Harold Boyack	1978	719
169 0/8	25 1/8 24 7/8	21 2/8	7 7	Bernalillo County	NM	John L. Padilla	1989	719
169 0/8	24 1/8 20 3/8	22 4/8	5 5	Elmore County	ID	David E. Sass	1991	719
169 0/8	22 5/8 23 2/8	24 4/8	5 5	Hanna	ALB	Glen Hutton	1994	719
169 0/8	21 6/8 21 4/8	19 7/8	7 5	Caribou County	ID	Randy K. Guinn	1994	719
169 0/8	22 4/8 20 5/8	22 2/8	4 4	Mesa County	CO	Michael Conn	1997	719
169 0/8	25 0/8 23 7/8	21 4/8	5 7	Jerome County	ID	John Wells, Jr.	1997	719
169 0/8	26 4/8 24 3/8	19 4/8	5 5	La Plata County	CO	Travis Bryant	2004	719
*169 0/8	24 6/8 24 0/8	22 6/8	5 5	Fort Macleod	ALB	Jonathan Brink	2010	719
168 7/8	21 1/8 21 1/8	24 2/8	5 5	Cache County	UT	Carl Rousn	1979	730
168 7/8	21 6/8 24 3/8	22 7/8	5 6	Park County	CO	Jim Johnson	1980	730
168 7/8	21 3/8 22 3/8	21 5/8	5 5	Union County	OR	Jerry W. Simmons	1982	730
168 7/8	24 6/8 25 3/8	22 6/8	6 5	Boise County	ID	Champ Church	1992	730
168 7/8	23 4/8 23 6/8	21 5/8	5 5	Fergus County	MT	Mark L. Gilkey	1999	730
168 7/8	23 1/8 22 4/8	20 7/8	5 5	Kane County	UT	Wally Schwartz	2001	730
168 7/8	25 2/8 25 7/8	25 3/8	6 5	Elbert County	CO	Turk Wendell	2001	730
168 7/8	23 4/8 21 4/8	15 6/8	7 5	Logan County	CO	Ron Kelly Crawford	2007	730
168 6/8	23 1/8 24 2/8	20 6/8	5 4	Baker County	OR	Joe Williamsen	1959	738
168 6/8	24 7/8 24 3/8	23 4/8	5 5	Little Belt Mtns.	MT	James Ployhar	1969	738
168 6/8	21 5/8 21 5/8	17 6/8	6 5	Ravalli County	MT	Bob Brill	1977	738
168 6/8	20 5/8 19 0/8	19 2/8	5 6	Umatilla County	OR	Donald E. Durland	1983	738
168 6/8	22 4/8 23 0/8	17 4/8	5 5	Mesa County	CO	J.D. 'Butch' Shivers	1985	738
168 6/8	23 7/8 24 5/8	21 4/8	6 6	San Miguel County	CO	Jay Scott	1986	738
168 6/8	24 2/8 24 4/8	25 3/8	5 5	Boulder County	CO	Craig Archer	1996	738
*168 6/8	22 7/8 24 4/8	23 0/8	5 5	Cochrane	ALB	Ron Serwa	2008	738
168 6/8	23 1/8 24 1/8	20 4/8	5 5	Rio Arriba County	NM	Clint Engebretsen	2009	738
168 5/8	20 6/8 21 5/8	18 3/8	5 5	Gunnison County	CO	Edward Maxfield Vanderslice	1991	747
168 5/8	20 5/8 22 7/8	22 3/8	5 4	Stillwater County	MT	Dr. Dale Schlehuber	1992	747
168 5/8	23 7/8 25 5/8	25 6/8	4 5	Columbia County	WA	David Kent	1993	747
168 5/8	23 7/8 24 0/8	21 3/8	5 5	Brooks	ALB	Brandon Ray	2000	747
168 5/8	24 0/8 23 5/8	20 3/8	5 7	Rosalind	ALB	Tyrel Herder	2000	747
168 5/8	21 6/8 21 0/8	19 1/8	5 5	Gray County	KS	Andrew O. McIntire	2003	747
168 4/8	24 6/8 24 7/8	21 6/8	5 5	Utah County	UT	Garland Bray	1970	753
168 4/8	23 4/8 22 4/8	23 7/8	5 5	Uncompahgre N.F.	CO	Paul R. Holmes	1974	753
168 4/8	22 2/8 21 6/8	22 5/8	4 4	Carbon County	WY	David Paskett	1990	753
168 4/8	21 3/8 22 2/8	20 4/8	5 5	Pennington County	SD	Douglas E. McDonald	1994	753
168 4/8	24 2/8 24 5/8	22 4/8	7 5	Yuma County	CO	Jerry Bowen	1998	753
168 4/8	22 7/8 22 2/8	19 6/8	5 5	Jefferson County	CO	Larry J. Jones	2001	753
168 4/8	23 2/8 22 3/8	23 0/8	5 5	Cibola County	NM	Derek Gentile	2002	753
168 4/8	26 3/8 25 3/8	22 6/8	5 5	Yavapai County	AZ	James Benigar	2004	753

315

MULE DEER (TYPICAL ANTLERS)

Minimum Score 145   Continued

SCORE	LENGTH OF R MAIN BEAM L	INSIDE SPREAD	NUMBER OF R POINTS L	AREA	STATE/PROVINCE	HUNTER'S NAME	DATE	RANK
168 4/8	24 3/8 25 0/8	23 0/8	5 5	Tooele County	UT	Randy J. Walk	2005	753
168 3/8	23 5/8 23 3/8	17 5/8	5 5	Chelan County	WA	George Wells	1960	762
168 3/8	22 7/8 22 0/8	19 6/8	5 6	Mineral County	CO	Richard Kolish	1961	762
168 3/8	21 7/8 22 5/8	22 7/8	5 5	Weber County	UT	Dennis L. Shirley	1972	762
168 3/8	24 1/8 23 2/8	22 1/8	5 6	Eureka County	NV	Joel C. Lenz	1986	762
168 3/8	26 5/8 25 6/8	28 0/8	5 6	Cochrane	ALB	Eric R. Smith	2001	762
168 3/8	22 3/8 23 1/8	23 5/8	5 5	Reeves County	TX	Gary J. Oden	2007	762
168 2/8	28 6/8 26 5/8	26 0/8	4 5	Uintah County	UT	S. K. Daniels	1908	768
168 2/8	25 0/8 24 0/8	21 7/8	5 5	Mesa County	CO	Jack Kenyon	1965	768
168 2/8	22 6/8 24 0/8	22 6/8	5 5	La Plata County	CO	Don Putterbaugh	1966	768
168 2/8	22 0/8 22 6/8	21 4/8	5 5	Mesa County	CO	Joseph Sverak	1968	768
168 2/8	24 1/8 22 1/8	21 4/8	4 4	Chaffee County	CO	Frank A. Morminello	1977	768
168 2/8	25 0/8 24 3/8	20 6/8	5 5	Humboldt County	NV	James A. Dallimore	1983	768
168 2/8	22 0/8 21 4/8	18 6/8	6 5	Caribou County	ID	Gene Keller	1985	768
168 2/8	25 3/8 24 2/8	25 0/8	6 5	Lincoln County	MT	Alan L. Davis	1992	768
168 2/8	22 0/8 22 4/8	17 6/8	4 5	Gilpin County	CO	Bart Thompson	1996	768
168 2/8	20 4/8 20 4/8	18 4/8	5 5	Kiowa County	CO	Paul Weyand	2002	768
168 2/8	23 0/8 23 3/8	22 4/8	5 5	McKenzie County	ND	Michael Tofte	2003	768
*168 2/8	22 5/8 22 5/8	23 2/8	6 5	Jefferson County	CO	Chris J. Hood	2009	768
168 1/8	21 4/8 21 5/8	19 7/8	5 5	Grand County	CO	Lenard Boughton	1968	780
168 1/8	21 3/8 22 2/8	19 7/8	6 6	McKenzie County	ND	Craig A. Ross	1983	780
168 1/8	24 3/8 25 5/8	25 4/8	6 4	Cochrane	ALB	Larry Collins	1990	780
168 1/8	22 6/8 23 0/8	19 5/8	5 5	Okotoks	ALB	Wayne Porterfield	1996	780
168 1/8	23 0/8 22 3/8	18 5/8	5 5	Cochise County	AZ	Henry Karl, Jr.	2001	780
168 1/8	25 0/8 24 6/8	21 4/8	7 5	Laramie County	WY	Dennis Magnusson	2003	780
168 1/8	19 4/8 20 1/8	23 6/8	6 4	Delta County	CO	Custer McLeod	2004	780
168 0/8	25 3/8 24 3/8	23 0/8	4 6	Uncompahgre N.F.	CO	Dick Gulman	1976	787
168 0/8	23 0/8 22 7/8	24 2/8	5 4	Elko County	NV	James A. Algerio	1980	787
168 0/8	24 0/8 22 7/8	23 2/8	5 5	Jefferson County	CO	Robert Anderson	1980	787
168 0/8	23 4/8 24 1/8	20 4/8	5 5	Ada County	ID	Ed Davidson	1994	787
168 0/8	23 4/8 22 5/8	20 0/8	5 5	Calgary	ALB	Archie J. Nesbitt	2000	787
168 0/8	22 1/8 23 2/8	24 2/8	7 5	Cardston	ALB	Camp Newton	2001	787
168 0/8	21 0/8 20 5/8	19 4/8	5 5	Cache County	UT	Chris Brunker	2001	787
168 0/8	23 6/8 23 3/8	23 0/8	5 6	Sheridan County	WY	Michael Wolff	2006	787
168 0/8	22 2/8 23 3/8	22 3/8	5 6	Natrona County	WY	Mark White	2009	787
167 7/8	24 3/8 24 0/8	27 2/8	6 6	Grand County	UT	Bob Paulson	1967	796
167 7/8	23 1/8 22 1/8	22 6/8	6 6	Routt County	CO	Edwin W. Foerster	1987	796
167 7/8	25 1/8 25 1/8	29 0/8	5 5	Pima County	AZ	Carnie R. Marks	1993	796
167 7/8	22 2/8 22 5/8	18 7/8	5 5	Ada County	ID	Trevor Bonfiglio	1995	796
167 7/8	23 4/8 23 3/8	20 1/8	5 5	Salt Lake County	UT	Tom Dangerfield	2003	796
*167 7/8	22 0/8 22 6/8	19 4/8	6 6	Mesa County	CO	Russell Goldfain	2004	796
167 7/8	24 6/8 25 4/8	19 7/8	5 5	Mesa County	CO	Mark Kadnuck	2006	796
167 6/8	21 4/8 20 6/8	18 5/8	5 5	Wallowa County	OR	Leonard Brooks	1967	803
167 6/8	22 7/8 23 5/8	23 0/8	5 5	Boise County	ID	Ed Moser	1982	803
167 6/8	23 5/8 24 5/8	20 2/8	5 6	Okotoks	ALB	Grant Hill	1989	803
167 6/8	23 0/8 23 0/8	21 0/8	5 5	Jerome County	ID	Guy G. Fitzgerald	1992	803
167 6/8	23 6/8 24 7/8	20 4/8	5 5	Dawson County	NE	Monte Koch	1993	803
167 6/8	24 1/8 23 4/8	22 0/8	6 5	Kathyrn	ALB	Dominic Barbario	1996	803
167 6/8	24 4/8 24 5/8	22 0/8	5 5	Graham County	KS	Randy Wilson	1997	803
167 6/8	24 3/8 23 5/8	23 0/8	6 5	Big Horn County	WY	Ron Niziolek	2007	803
167 5/8	21 2/8 22 1/8	26 0/8	5 5	Grand County	CO	Michael A. Contreras	1978	811
167 5/8	24 0/8 23 2/8	21 4/8	5 6	Greenlee County	AZ	Eddie Claypool	1995	811
167 5/8	24 4/8 25 7/8	26 6/8	5 5	Jones County	SD	Mark C. Schwei	2000	811
167 5/8	22 3/8 24 0/8	16 4/8	5 5	Ravalli County	MT	Steve D. Adams	2005	811
*167 5/8	25 2/8 26 2/8	20 5/8	6 6	Fergus County	MT	Stuart Russell	2010	811
167 4/8	20 2/8 20 5/8	19 0/8	5 5	Cascade County	MT	Ron Johnson	1987	816
167 4/8	22 7/8 20 4/8	21 2/8	5 5	Sweet Grass County	MT	Dr. Dale Schlehuber	1990	816
167 4/8	23 4/8 22 6/8	24 0/8	5 5	Wichita County	KS	Jack D. Kuhlmann	1990	816
167 4/8	22 4/8 23 3/8	19 1/8	6 6	Pinal County	AZ	Sonny Nieto	1991	816
167 4/8	22 2/8 22 1/8	17 2/8	4 5	Abbey	SAS	Floyd Forster	1992	816
167 4/8	24 6/8 25 2/8	19 2/8	5 5	Klickitat County	WA	Leon Wells	1992	816
167 4/8	23 7/8 24 1/8	20 4/8	5 5	Adams County	CO	Dan Goodnight	2005	816
*167 4/8	24 4/8 23 3/8	21 2/8	6 5	Pennington County	SD	Mark Hilderbrant	2006	816
167 3/8	21 4/8 21 3/8	19 3/8	5 5	Owyhee County	ID	Eugene R. Mallard	1963	824
167 3/8	25 0/8 25 0/8	19 3/8	7 5	Klamath County	OR	V. Kenneth Murdock	1978	824
167 3/8	21 6/8 22 7/8	19 0/8	5 7	Mesa County	CO	Paul H. Dickson	1984	824
167 3/8	18 7/8 23 0/8	22 1/8	5 5	Baker County	OR	Kevin Kennedy	1987	824
167 3/8	22 5/8 23 7/8	25 3/8	5 5	Washoe County	NV	Ralph L. Albright	1988	824
167 3/8	23 7/8 24 1/8	20 7/8	5 5	Baker County	OR	Jeff McCrary	1991	824
167 3/8	24 0/8 24 2/8	20 5/8	5 5	West Lake	BC	Bob Dunlop	1991	824
167 3/8	24 7/8 24 6/8	22 5/8	7 8	Gunnison County	CO	Duane Lyerly	1992	824
167 3/8	20 3/8 20 1/8	18 3/8	4 4	Rosebud County	MT	Chuck Adams	2001	824
167 3/8	25 1/8 25 0/8	26 2/8	5 7	Jackson County	SD	Dustin D. Lurz	2009	824
167 3/8	20 7/8 21 5/8	20 3/8	5 4	Lincoln County	WY	Ronell Skinner	1980	834
167 2/8	23 0/8 23 0/8	20 6/8	6 5	Mesa County	CO	Jim Bennett	1981	834
167 2/8	25 0/8 24 7/8	23 2/8	5 7	La Plata County	CO	Michael B. Mitchell	1994	834
167 2/8	22 5/8 22 1/8	21 4/8	5 6	Norton County	KS	George J. Campbell	1996	834
167 2/8	24 3/8 23 6/8	23 2/8	5 5	Harney County	OR	Kenneth B. Jenkins	1998	834
167 2/8	21 4/8 22 0/8	20 2/8	5 5	Dundy County	NE	Matt Gideon	1998	834
167 2/8	23 5/8 23 6/8	20 0/8	4 4	Sheridan County	WY	Andy Carpenter	2010	834
167 1/8	26 3/8 24 4/8	21 2/8	5 4	Humboldt County	NV	Jerry Stout	1965	841
167 1/8	21 1/8 19 3/8	18 2/8	6 6	Anahim Lake	BC	Guy Antilla	1965	841
167 1/8	24 1/8 24 2/8	23 7/8	6 7	Gunnison County	CO	Richard L. Geissler	1983	841
167 1/8	22 0/8 21 3/8	19 3/8	5 5	Converse County	WY	Barry J. Smith	1991	841
167 1/8	24 4/8 25 0/8	23 3/8	5 5	Lake County	OR	Mike Slinkard	1996	841
167 1/8	22 1/8 21 6/8	19 1/8	5 6	Gilliam County	OR	Gary Winslow	1999	841
167 1/8	23 4/8 24 1/8	20 5/8	5 5	Catron County	NM	Paul Thorsen	2003	841
*167 1/8	22 5/8 25 2/8	21 3/8	4 5	Sulpher Springs	BC	Kent Fraser	2005	841
167 1/8	23 4/8 23 5/8	19 7/8	5 5	Milk River	ALB	Chris Westergreen	2008	841
*167 1/8	25 1/8 24 4/8	24 0/8	6 6	Ziebach County	SD	Ramon Birkeland	2009	841
167 0/8	23 3/8 24 2/8	22 2/8	4 4	Eagle County	CO	Arvine Routh	1965	851
167 0/8	23 2/8 23 1/8	22 1/8	7 8	Grand County	CO	Michael K. Ward	1973	851
167 0/8	23 3/8 24 4/8	22 0/8	5 5	Mesa County	CO	Mike Gilbert	1973	851
167 0/8	21 2/8 19 7/8	18 4/8	5 5	Mesa County	CO	Glen Hitt	1975	851
167 0/8	23 5/8 22 5/8	20 4/8	5 6	Garfield County	CO	Randy Edwards	1987	851

316

MULE DEER (TYPICAL ANTLERS)

Minimum Score 145   Continued

SCORE	LENGTH OF MAIN BEAM R	L	INSIDE SPREAD	NUMBER OF POINTS R	L	AREA	STATE/ PROVINCE	HUNTER'S NAME	DATE	RANK
167 0/8	22 0/8	22 4/8	22 0/8	7	7	Warner	ALB	Gary Erickson	1991	851
167 0/8	22 7/8	24 1/8	20 0/8	5	5	Calgary	ALB	Dave Browne	1994	851
167 0/8	22 7/8	23 4/8	19 2/8	5	5	Rawlins County	KS	Mike Wilson	2006	851
167 0/8	23 3/8	23 7/8	19 4/8	5	5	Navajo County	AZ	Jim Willems	2007	851
166 7/8	21 2/8	22 0/8	20 5/8	5	5	Uintah County	UT	Orson Stilson	1964	860
166 7/8	21 6/8	22 5/8	19 5/8	5	5	Phillips County	MT	Mark Kostecki	1994	860
166 7/8	22 2/8	23 5/8	23 1/8	5	5	Pima County	AZ	James Dale Casady	1996	860
166 7/8	23 7/8	25 2/8	20 7/8	5	5	Cassia County	ID	Bart Graves	2004	860
166 7/8	23 4/8	22 1/8	20 0/8	6	8	S. Saskatchewan River	SAS	Glen A. Miller	2005	860
166 7/8	24 0/8	24 5/8	21 5/8	6	5	Hinsdale County	CO	Mark E. Johnson	2009	860
166 6/8	25 1/8	25 3/8	24 4/8	5	6	Uintah County	UT	Doug Walker	1967	866
166 6/8	23 4/8	23 0/8	20 2/8	5	5	Adams County	CO	John C. Schmidt	1974	866
166 6/8	24 3/8	23 4/8	23 4/8	5	4	Mesa County	CO	David E. Samuel	1974	866
166 6/8	24 0/8	23 1/8	21 2/8	5	5	Grant County	OR	Paul J. Zink	1998	866
166 6/8	23 1/8	22 2/8	19 6/8	5	5	Apache County	AZ	Mike Spring	2000	866
166 6/8	24 6/8	24 1/8	25 2/8	5	5	Sturgeon	ALB	Doug Long	2003	866
166 5/8	22 6/8	23 0/8	20 1/8	5	5	Baker County	OR	Lloyd V. Christensen	1959	872
166 5/8	23 4/8	23 6/8	23 5/8	5	5	Montezuma County	CO	Marvin Reichenau	1983	872
166 5/8	22 0/8	22 1/8	19 7/8	5	5	Grant County	OR	Ray Kelton	1985	872
166 5/8	24 5/8	24 5/8	22 0/8	5	6	Milk River Ridge	ALB	Brian Carriere	1990	872
166 5/8	23 6/8	22 4/8	22 3/8	5	5	Bernalillo County	NM	Ruben E. Chavez	1992	872
166 5/8	22 6/8	22 4/8	22 1/8	5	4	Calgary	ALB	Gary Gillett	1996	872
166 5/8	22 0/8	21 5/8	18 5/8	5	5	Yakima County	WA	Douglas D. Kikendall	2002	872
166 4/8	23 2/8	24 0/8	22 2/8	7	7	Owyhee County	ID	Bill Payne	1958	879
166 4/8	23 5/8	22 6/8	21 6/8	5	5	Owyhee County	ID	Blake Murphy	1961	879
166 4/8	20 3/8	20 5/8	16 6/8	5	5	Adams County	ID	Jack St. Germain	1986	879
166 4/8	23 6/8	23 3/8	20 0/8	5	4	Morrow County	OR	Phil Jackson	1992	879
166 4/8	23 4/8	22 3/8	21 6/8	5	5	Deschutes County	OR	Edward H. Glaab	1998	879
166 4/8	21 5/8	22 3/8	20 0/8	5	5	Sierra County	CA	Thomas Hansen	1999	879
166 4/8	23 2/8	24 2/8	19 4/8	5	6	Jerome County	ID	Craig Phillips	2001	879
166 4/8	23 5/8	24 5/8	18 7/8	6	5	Albany County	WY	Mark L. Nelson	2006	879
166 4/8	23 3/8	24 5/8	21 2/8	5	5	Coronation	ALB	Russell Hillis	2007	879
166 4/8	22 2/8	22 0/8	18 6/8	5	5	Big Horn County	MT	Christopher Crane	2008	879
166 3/8	21 7/8	22 5/8	21 0/8	6	7	Butte County	SD	L. G. Braun	1957	889
166 3/8	24 6/8	24 3/8	20 1/8	5	6	Lane County	KS	Dean Hamilton	1988	889
166 3/8	21 4/8	22 1/8	20 1/8	5	5	Ada County	ID	Brian Krebs	1992	889
166 3/8	20 5/8	22 3/8	20 1/8	5	5	Jefferson County	CO	Larry J. Jones	1998	889
166 3/8	25 0/8	25 0/8	21 0/8	6	5	Crook County	OR	Charles A. Stivers	1999	889
166 3/8	22 7/8	24 4/8	19 1/8	5	6	Union County	OR	Ray Borges	2001	889
166 2/8	25 2/8	23 1/8	18 0/8	5	5	Mesa County	CO	Lloyd Kell	1967	895
166 2/8	21 3/8	22 2/8	23 6/8	5	5	Garfield County	CO	Jim Walters	1975	895
166 2/8	22 3/8	22 4/8	23 2/8	5	5	Scott County	KS	Mel Jamison	1986	895
166 2/8	24 2/8	25 2/8	20 4/8	5	5	Platte County	WY	Terry Brown	1992	895
166 2/8	22 3/8	21 3/8	17 6/8	5	5	Exshaw	ALB	David Stecker	1992	895
166 2/8	22 3/8	24 7/8	21 0/8	6	5	Billings County	ND	Larry Ellis	1994	895
166 2/8	19 0/8	19 4/8	16 7/8	7	5	Caribou County	ID	Randy K. Guinn	1997	895
166 2/8	24 2/8	25 5/8	19 6/8	5	5	Medicine Hat	ALB	Jerry Bowen	2004	895
166 1/8	21 4/8	22 1/8	18 1/8	5	5	Carbon County	WY	Duncan G. Weibel	1955	903
166 1/8	20 6/8	21 4/8	19 5/8	5	5	Ada County	ID	M. F. Smith	1968	903
166 1/8	20 4/8	22 4/8	21 3/8	5	5	Calgary	ALB	Dean Reed	1981	903
166 1/8	20 7/8	22 3/8	16 1/8	5	5	Davis County	UT	John Glezos	1993	903
*166 1/8	23 3/8	24 1/8	21 5/8	5	5	Sheridan County	WY	Todd Richins	2005	903
166 1/8	23 5/8	23 5/8	22 7/8	5	5	Pennington County	SD	Jason Abelseth	2005	903
166 1/8	20 3/8	21 0/8	20 7/8	5	5	Big Horn County	WY	Jason Stafford	2010	903
166 0/8	20 0/8	20 7/8	19 5/8	6	5	Lincoln County	NE	M. R. Buchtel	1958	910
166 0/8	24 4/8	23 0/8	21 6/8	4	4	Garfield County	CO	Robert G. Kuper	1966	910
166 0/8	19 7/8	21 1/8	17 6/8	5	5	Mohave County	AZ	Norman J. Brown	1966	910
166 0/8	24 6/8	24 4/8	26 0/8	5	5	Cassia County	ID	Jack B. Watts	1968	910
166 0/8	23 4/8	24 0/8	24 2/8	5	4	Lewis & Clark County	MT	Donald Davidson, Jr.	1980	910
166 0/8	22 2/8	23 1/8	17 6/8	6	6	Elbert County	CO	Billy Tillotson	1986	910
166 0/8	22 0/8	23 0/8	22 4/8	5	5	Maricopa County	AZ	Daniel Whitaker	1988	910
166 0/8	21 7/8	22 2/8	22 4/8	6	5	El Paso County	CO	Freeman Howard	1989	910
166 0/8	22 0/8	21 3/8	17 0/8	5	5	Coconino County	AZ	John Coats	1998	910
166 0/8	25 0/8	23 7/8	21 6/8	6	7	Gunnison County	CO	Tony Zawada	2001	910
166 0/8	24 0/8	23 5/8	20 0/8	6	5	Musselshell County	MT	Michael L. Ritter	2001	910
166 0/8	24 5/8	24 6/8	21 4/8	4	4	Rio Arriba County	NM	Dennis G. Doherty	2004	910
166 0/8	24 1/8	24 5/8	24 4/8	6	7	Sully County	SD	John J. Bush	2007	910
165 7/8	23 4/8	25 0/8	25 0/8	9	6	Owyhee County	ID	Thomas Eld	1964	923
165 7/8	23 6/8	25 6/8	20 3/8	5	5	Moffat County	CO	Albert A. Adams	1982	923
165 7/8	22 6/8	22 4/8	25 6/8	6	7	Gray County	KS	Allen D. Bailey	1985	923
165 7/8	25 3/8	25 1/8	20 5/8	5	6	Mesa County	CO	James C. Snortum	1991	923
165 7/8	23 6/8	23 4/8	21 5/8	6	5	Hilda	ALB	Larry Hoffman	1993	923
165 7/8	22 5/8	24 4/8	22 0/8	6	6	Coconino County	AZ	Jack Hightower	1993	923
165 7/8	21 0/8	23 0/8	19 3/8	6	6	Prowers County	CO	Bo Clark	2002	923
165 7/8	21 7/8	21 0/8	26 6/8	6	6	Marsden	SAS	Merle Janish	2005	923
*165 7/8	23 6/8	24 6/8	24 5/8	5	5	Rio Arriba County	NM	Aaron Barnett	2009	923
*165 7/8	22 1/8	22 6/8	22 3/8	5	5	McKenzie County	ND	John Schneider	2009	923
165 7/8	23 2/8	22 5/8	18 1/8	6	8	Meade County	SD	Randy Simkins	2009	923
165 6/8	24 0/8	23 2/8	19 2/8	6	5	Garfield County	CO	John Richard	1972	934
165 6/8	23 6/8	23 4/8	17 2/8	5	5	Grand County	CO	Burt Thompson	1983	934
165 6/8	23 0/8	21 5/8	16 6/8	4	5	Graham County	KS	Randy Wilson	1989	934
165 6/8	22 1/8	22 4/8	20 0/8	6	5	Garfield County	CO	Thomas Smathers	2000	934
165 6/8	23 3/8	23 2/8	20 0/8	5	5	Morton County	ND	Todd Heid	2003	934
165 6/8	25 3/8	24 2/8	22 0/8	5	4	Chelan County	WA	Jeremy Tomilinson	2005	934
165 5/8	21 1/8	21 0/8	20 5/8	5	5	Utah County	UT	Frank Eicholt	1964	940
165 5/8	21 0/8	21 2/8	18 5/8	5	5	Zone 5	SAS	Ward Minifie	1985	940
165 5/8	21 7/8	21 0/8	23 3/8	5	5	McKinley County	NM	Richard W. Eustace, Jr.	1988	940
165 5/8	22 4/8	24 0/8	17 7/8	5	5	Rich County	UT	Colby Steffen Hagen	1992	940
165 5/8	21 5/8	22 5/8	20 7/8	5	5	San Juan County	NM	Steven J. Vittetow	1997	940
165 5/8	23 6/8	23 4/8	19 2/8	8	7	Elbert County	CO	Frank J. Messina	1998	940
165 5/8	23 4/8	23 3/8	18 5/8	5	5	S. Saskatchewan River	SAS	Braden Cherney	2003	940
*165 5/8	23 1/8	25 4/8	23 7/8	4	6	San Juan County	NM	Cody Balok	2005	940
165 5/8	23 4/8	23 4/8	18 0/8	5	5	Garfield County	CO	Greg Easton	2005	940
165 5/8	23 6/8	24 1/8	22 2/8	5	4	Sheridan County	WY	Scott L. Koelzer	2009	940
165 4/8	23 1/8	23 6/8	24 1/8	6	5	Mesa County	CO	Bob Woodhouse	1978	950

MULE DEER (TYPICAL ANTLERS)

Minimum Score 145   Continued

SCORE	LENGTH OF R MAIN BEAM L	INSIDE SPREAD	NUMBER OF R POINTS L	AREA	STATE/ PROVINCE	HUNTER'S NAME	DATE	RANK
165 4/8	22 4/8 23 4/8	19 0/8	5 5	San Miguel County	NM	Louis Baca	1985	950
165 4/8	21 6/8 22 6/8	25 7/8	5 5	Hodgeman County	KS	Charles Fuller	1985	950
165 4/8	24 1/8 24 7/8	19 3/8	7 6	Kane County	UT	Richard Jolley	1986	950
165 4/8	21 0/8 21 5/8	18 3/8	6 5	Billings County	ND	Harold Hugelen	1990	950
165 4/8	25 2/8 25 6/8	28 2/8	4 4	Las Animas County	CO	J. Keith Chastain	1995	950
165 4/8	24 3/8 24 3/8	21 4/8	5 5	Kane County	UT	Peter F. Woeck II	1996	950
165 4/8	23 0/8 23 5/8	18 0/8	5 6	Gilpin County	CO	Mark Kaufman	1996	950
165 4/8	24 6/8 23 3/8	22 1/8	6 6	Lincoln County	MT	Sandy Colville	1996	950
165 4/8	24 2/8 22 5/8	21 0/8	5 5	Rosebud County	MT	Ed Bukoskey	2002	950
165 4/8	24 6/8 23 6/8	25 0/8	5 5	Billings County	ND	Ryan Hugelen	2005	950
*165 4/8	23 4/8 23 4/8	20 0/8	5 4	Meade County	SD	Randy Simkins	2006	950
165 4/8	25 2/8 24 5/8	21 4/8	4 4	Albany County	WY	Dennis Magnusson	2008	950
165 3/8	27 0/8 26 0/8	19 1/8	7 5	Mesa County	CO	Kent Stumpf	1973	963
165 3/8	24 4/8 25 0/8	18 3/8	7 7	Duchesne County	UT	Everett Burson	1984	963
165 3/8	23 2/8 21 2/8	20 0/8	5 6	Boise County	ID	Peter Cintorino	1985	963
165 3/8	22 2/8 22 0/8	17 0/8	6 5	Bonner County	ID	Bob Driggars	1991	963
165 3/8	19 3/8 20 4/8	17 5/8	4 4	Rio Blanco County	CO	Tom L. Buchholz	1993	963
165 3/8	21 5/8 21 4/8	21 6/8	5 5	Jefferson County	CO	Steve Smith	1998	963
165 3/8	22 6/8 23 0/8	21 3/8	4 5	Billings County	ND	Jay Haverluk	2004	963
165 3/8	22 6/8 22 3/8	21 5/8	5 5	Sevier County	UT	Trent Cracraft	2005	963
165 3/8	20 6/8 20 4/8	21 6/8	5 7	Garfield County	CO	Aaron Amator	2007	963
165 3/8	25 0/8 24 0/8	21 6/8	7 5	Sonora	MEX	Frank S. Noska IV	2009	963
165 2/8	26 5/8 27 0/8	25 2/8	5 5	Mesa County	CO	Ray Carpenter	1960	973
165 2/8	20 6/8 20 1/8	18 4/8	5 5	Clear Creek County	CO	John Marolt III	1967	973
165 2/8	20 3/8 21 1/8	20 3/8	6 5	Mora County	NM	Joel P. McHorse	1975	973
165 2/8	22 0/8 21 5/8	19 4/8	5 5	Cassia County	ID	John Wells	1989	973
165 2/8	22 2/8 22 2/8	24 2/8	5 5	Montrose County	CO	Thomas C. Curtis	1998	973
165 2/8	23 1/8 22 6/8	18 6/8	6 5	Billings County	ND	Robert E. Ebert	2001	973
165 2/8	23 5/8 24 3/8	23 6/8	5 5	Moffat County	CO	Doug Beck	2005	973
165 1/8	20 5/8 22 3/8	20 2/8	5 6	Sevier County	UT	Severin Jensen	1959	980
165 1/8	23 2/8 24 0/8	27 3/8	6 6	Douglas County	CO	Dale Slade	1967	980
165 1/8	23 4/8 25 4/8	26 0/8	5 7	Mesa County	CO	George J. Hronkin III	1982	980
165 1/8	21 3/8 22 2/8	20 1/8	5 5	Valley County	ID	Charles "Chuck" Boatman	1985	980
165 1/8	25 6/8 24 2/8	24 3/8	6 6	Fremont County	WY	Jerry A. Bodar	1988	980
165 1/8	24 6/8 24 0/8	20 3/8	5 5	Umatilla County	OR	Richard Schmidt	1997	980
165 1/8	22 6/8 22 5/8	18 5/8	5 7	Iron County	UT	Michael C. Hirschi	1998	980
165 1/8	23 6/8 24 2/8	20 5/8	5 5	Park County	WY	Benjamin Atnip	2003	980
165 1/8	23 6/8 23 1/8	19 6/8	5 6	Albany County	WY	Harold F. Stinchcomb	2005	980
*165 1/8	22 2/8 23 3/8	18 7/8	5 5	Cochise County	AZ	Marlon A. Holden	2008	980
165 0/8	24 3/8 25 0/8	19 7/8	5 6	Rio Arriba County	NM	David L. Chandler	1967	990
165 0/8	23 4/8 22 6/8	23 5/8	5 6	Cochise County	AZ	Richard Dawe, Jr.	1976	990
165 0/8	22 2/8 22 1/8	22 0/8	5 5	Saguache County	CO	Michael Snodgrass	1977	990
165 0/8	26 4/8 25 2/8	25 0/8	4 5	Lake County	OR	Wayne Lamson, Jr.	1981	990
165 0/8	24 6/8 25 6/8	21 4/8	5 5	Los Alamos County	NM	Doug Aikin	1985	990
165 0/8	22 1/8 21 7/8	21 2/8	5 5	Sanders County	MT	Craig Phillips	1990	990
165 0/8	23 3/8 24 4/8	17 2/8	4 4	Larimer County	CO	Mitch Brown	1992	990
165 0/8	24 2/8 24 2/8	18 1/8	5 5	Franklin County	WA	Bill Barnett	1994	990
165 0/8	22 4/8 22 5/8	21 6/8	5 5	Scott County	KS	D. Larry Potts	1994	990
165 0/8	24 0/8 23 3/8	23 6/8	5 6	Pima County	AZ	Carnie R. Marks	1995	990
165 0/8	21 0/8 21 1/8	17 6/8	5 5	Red Deer River	ALB	Richard Milder	1998	990
165 0/8	23 2/8 24 5/8	20 0/8	5 5	Baker County	OR	Eric Buckenberger	1999	990
165 0/8	25 0/8 24 0/8	23 5/8	5 7	Jones County	SD	Clayton Miller	2004	990
165 0/8	26 3/8 25 0/8	25 7/8	7 6	Teller County	CO	Alfred E. Baldwin	2007	990
*165 0/8	22 0/8 21 3/8	20 6/8	5 5	Cheyenne County	CO	Brett L. Foster	2009	990
164 7/8	24 0/8 22 7/8	23 5/8	4 4	Mesa County	CO	Richard Rounds	1973	1005
164 7/8	22 3/8 21 7/8	19 5/8	5 5	Routt County	CO	Paul Blotz	1974	1005
164 7/8	24 3/8 23 0/8	25 5/8	5 5	Piute County	UT	Art Whitby	1992	1005
164 7/8	23 3/8 21 6/8	21 4/8	7 5	Luna County	NM	Gary Shiflett	1993	1005
164 7/8	21 5/8 23 3/8	19 1/8	4 5	Elbert County	CO	Matt Burrows	1994	1005
164 7/8	23 2/8 22 1/8	19 7/8	5 5	Cremona	ALB	Dave Browne	2002	1005
164 7/8	21 4/8 21 0/8	18 1/8	5 6	Harding County	SD	Neal Snyder	2006	1005
164 6/8	22 4/8 21 3/8	18 2/8	5 5	Skyline Drive	UT	George Heath	1964	1012
164 6/8	20 3/8 22 0/8	22 1/8	4 4	White Pine County	NV	Larry T. Gilbertson	1984	1012
164 6/8	24 5/8 24 3/8	20 0/8	4 5	Montrose County	CO	Scott Smith	1997	1012
164 6/8	22 4/8 22 7/8	18 0/8	5 5	Sioux County	NE	Jeff Micek	2000	1012
164 6/8	21 7/8 22 6/8	20 6/8	5 5	Swift Current	SAS	Stacy Bolton	2004	1012
164 6/8	23 4/8 23 7/8	19 4/8	5 5	Cowley	ALB	Andy MacIntyre	2007	1012
164 5/8	25 6/8 26 1/8	24 4/8	5 5	Fox Valley	SAS	Doug Findlay	1977	1018
164 5/8	20 4/8 21 3/8	20 3/8	4 5	Grand County	UT	Don Dvoroznak	1979	1018
164 5/8	22 2/8 23 2/8	19 4/8	5 6	Cassia County	ID	Richard Ponciano	1985	1018
164 5/8	19 5/8 20 7/8	16 6/8	6 5	Mesa County	CO	Don Walsh	1986	1018
164 5/8	23 6/8 24 2/8	21 0/8	6 5	Scott County	KS	Lynn Freese	1987	1018
164 5/8	24 1/8 23 2/8	19 3/8	6 10	Natrona County	WY	Tom Nelson	1999	1018
164 5/8	28 0/8 27 2/8	24 4/8	4 4	Dundy County	NE	Matt Gideon	1999	1018
*164 5/8	23 5/8 22 3/8	19 6/8	5 6	Ravalli County	MT	Michael Terzo	2007	1018
164 4/8	23 2/8 23 6/8	25 4/8	5 5	Calgary	ALB	David Lovo	1979	1026
164 4/8	21 4/8 21 7/8	20 4/8	5 5	Fergus County	MT	Michael B. Bryson	1986	1026
164 4/8	21 4/8 21 6/8	19 2/8	6 6	Lincoln County	WY	Mike Barrett	1989	1026
164 4/8	21 5/8 22 2/8	22 3/8	6 6	Red Deer Lake	ALB	Larry Mandseth	1989	1026
164 4/8	21 4/8 21 4/8	19 0/8	5 5	Wallowa County	OR	Michael J. Bishop	1994	1026
164 4/8	23 0/8 22 3/8	19 4/8	5 5	Powder River County	MT	Don G. Scofield	1994	1026
164 4/8	25 4/8 24 2/8	21 6/8	5 4	Elbert County	CO	Brian Stoner	2000	1026
164 4/8	21 7/8 22 1/8	20 2/8	5 5	Elbert County	CO	Michael Napp	2008	1026
164 3/8	21 7/8 23 0/8	19 7/8	5 5	Siskiyou County	CA	Dale Gatlin	1959	1034
164 3/8	24 6/8 23 4/8	24 6/8	8 8	Elko County	NV	Dick Woltering	1960	1034
164 3/8	22 3/8 22 3/8	23 2/8	5 5	Sheridan County	KS	Kevin J. Ryan	1974	1034
164 3/8	20 1/8 21 4/8	19 0/8	7 7	Conejos County	CO	Frank Holloway	1983	1034
164 3/8	22 5/8 22 2/8	20 1/8	6 5	Routt County	CO	Richard L. Charles, Sr.	1990	1034
164 3/8	23 6/8 22 4/8	19 5/8	5 5	Carbon County	WY	Dean P. Reed	1991	1034
164 3/8	20 4/8 20 7/8	18 3/8	5 5	Lincoln County	WY	Mike Barrett	1992	1034
164 3/8	23 6/8 24 6/8	21 6/8	5 6	Montrose County	CO	T. S. Stern, Jr.	2003	1034
164 3/8	21 7/8 21 6/8	18 6/8	5 5	McKenzie County	ND	Ryan Hugelen	2004	1034
164 3/8	23 6/8 23 6/8	22 1/8	5 8	Lemhi County	ID	Keith Fullenkamp	2005	1034
164 3/8	25 0/8 25 6/8	19 7/8	7 7	Souris River	SAS	Joshua Michel	2008	1034
164 2/8	23 2/8 24 0/8	19 4/8	7 9	Garfield County	CO	D. H. Nolting	1956	1045

318

MULE DEER (TYPICAL ANTLERS)

Minimum Score 145   Continued

Score	Length of Main Beam R	L	Inside Spread	Number of Points R	L	Area	State/Province	Hunter's Name	Date	Rank
164 2/8	22 6/8	21 6/8	22 0/8	6	5	Routt County	CO	John Hale	1975	1045
164 2/8	20 6/8	23 1/8	18 4/8	7	6	Dolores County	CO	Tommy C. Jeffcoat	1977	1045
164 2/8	21 7/8	22 0/8	21 6/8	5	5	Greenlee County	AZ	Steve E. Allen	1980	1045
164 2/8	24 4/8	24 3/8	23 7/8	6	6	Stafford County	KS	Rob Ginest	1982	1045
164 2/8	22 0/8	20 4/8	18 4/8	4	4	Cassia County	ID	Bryan Sprauge	1984	1045
164 2/8	26 6/8	24 1/8	25 7/8	5	4	San Juan County	NM	Ronnie H. Begay	1988	1045
164 2/8	22 7/8	24 1/8	19 2/8	6	5	Kyle	SAS	Terry Chornomud	1995	1045
164 2/8	22 3/8	23 2/8	24 0/8	5	5	Vermilion	ALB	Glenn Moir	1997	1045
164 2/8	24 4/8	24 4/8	22 0/8	5	5	Humboldt County	NV	Sean Shea	1998	1045
164 2/8	20 0/8	21 0/8	18 5/8	6	5	Yuma County	CO	Randy Wilkins	2000	1045
164 2/8	22 6/8	22 2/8	16 6/8	5	5	Petroleum County	MT	Levi Johnson	2002	1045
164 2/8	24 1/8	24 2/8	25 4/8	4	4	Lassen County	CA	Brian B. Anderson	2004	1045
164 2/8	21 5/8	19 0/8	18 0/8	5	5	Brooks	ALB	Mark Nelson	2006	1045
164 2/8	21 7/8	22 3/8	22 7/8	5	5	Rosebud County	MT	Jerry McPherson	2006	1045
164 2/8	23 6/8	23 2/8	20 6/8	5	5	Garfield County	CO	Robert M. Massett	2007	1045
*164 2/8	19 3/8	20 3/8	21 6/8	6	5	McKenzie County	ND	Chris Reed	2007	1045
164 1/8	25 3/8	25 6/8	23 6/8	8	7	Owyhee County	ID	Merlie Hampton	1962	1062
164 1/8	24 0/8	24 6/8	24 6/8	6	5	Summit County	CO	Russell F. Rider	1964	1062
164 1/8	24 4/8	23 1/8	22 7/8	4	4	Garfield County	CO	Roy Hoff	1968	1062
164 1/8	22 3/8	22 1/8	19 3/8	5	5	Columbia County	WA	Wayne Dickhaut	1983	1062
164 1/8	23 4/8	23 1/8	20 7/8	5	5	Kananaskis	ALB	Don Warner	1992	1062
164 1/8	20 5/8	20 6/8	19 0/8	6	5	Albany County	WY	Jerry Bowen	1992	1062
164 1/8	17 3/8	16 7/8	22 2/8	5	5	Boise County	ID	Ken Gettman	1994	1062
164 1/8	22 5/8	23 2/8	20 1/8	5	5	Bear Lake County	ID	Matthew Denning	1996	1062
164 1/8	23 1/8	22 4/8	20 3/8	5	5	Weld County	CO	Casey J. Hatch	1998	1062
164 1/8	23 3/8	22 5/8	19 1/8	5	5	Moffat County	CO	Rob Syvertson	2002	1062
164 1/8	23 6/8	24 2/8	18 1/8	6	5	Grant County	OR	Jonathan Shetler	2003	1062
164 1/8	22 3/8	20 2/8	19 3/8	5	5	Yuma County	CO	Mike Barrett	2003	1062
164 1/8	23 5/8	23 3/8	18 1/8	5	5	Sanders County	MT	Tom M. Benson	2004	1062
*164 1/8	21 1/8	20 4/8	20 1/8	5	5	Eagle County	CO	Robert J. Feeney	2008	1062
164 0/8	19 4/8	20 1/8	19 6/8	5	5	Garfield County	CO	Dr. Lowell L. Eddy	1968	1076
164 0/8	20 7/8	22 0/8	23 3/8	4	4	West Desert	UT	Myron Adams	1969	1076
164 0/8	21 3/8	21 3/8	18 0/8	4	4	Ada County	ID	Richard C. Nichols	1971	1076
164 0/8	24 6/8	25 3/8	23 7/8	7	6	White Pine County	NV	Robert Davie	1983	1076
164 0/8	25 1/8	24 3/8	22 4/8	4	4	Yakima County	WA	Earl Prentice	1990	1076
164 0/8	23 4/8	24 4/8	24 2/8	5	5	Elbert County	CO	Kim Cooper	1992	1076
164 0/8	23 1/8	23 6/8	21 4/8	5	7	Salt Lake County	UT	Bill Plowman	2001	1076
164 0/8	22 2/8	22 1/8	17 2/8	5	7	Brooks	ALB	Randy Weidner	2001	1076
164 0/8	22 4/8	21 7/8	20 0/8	5	5	Las Animas County	CO	Darrell Bozarth	2001	1076
164 0/8	22 5/8	22 5/8	21 0/8	5	5	Lassen County	CA	Kenneth "Max" Tinnin	2008	1076
163 7/8	20 1/8	21 3/8	17 6/8	5	6	Frontier County	NE	Keene Hueftle	1961	1086
163 7/8	19 0/8	20 6/8	18 1/8	5	5	Phillips County	KS	Phillip Pfortmiller	1986	1086
163 7/8	24 3/8	25 7/8	27 3/8	5	5	McKinley County	NM	Dois Chesshir	1989	1086
163 7/8	20 4/8	22 1/8	19 6/8	6	5	Maricopa County	AZ	Richard S. Jones	1990	1086
163 7/8	23 0/8	20 3/8	17 7/8	5	5	Fergus County	MT	Paul L. Reese	1991	1086
163 7/8	24 2/8	23 7/8	23 5/8	6	5	El Paso County	CO	Clyde A. Bayne	1997	1086
163 7/8	22 1/8	22 3/8	21 7/8	5	5	Anchorton	ALB	Brent Kuntz	1998	1086
163 7/8	24 7/8	24 0/8	20 1/8	5	5	Magrath	ALB	Cameron Cook	2004	1086
163 7/8	22 4/8	23 7/8	21 3/8	6	4	Douglas County	CO	Matt Fischer	2007	1086
163 6/8	22 2/8	21 2/8	21 4/8	5	5	Pima County	AZ	Tom Bylina	1988	1095
163 6/8	26 2/8	26 6/8	27 4/8	3	5	Bella Coola	BC	Lawrence Michalchuk	1995	1095
163 6/8	24 6/8	22 5/8	17 0/8	5	5	Boise County	ID	Larry Bryan Skaar	2005	1095
*163 6/8	23 0/8	22 1/8	20 4/8	5	5	Haakon County	SD	Kevin Bertsch	2006	1095
163 5/8	23 3/8	23 2/8	22 3/8	5	5	White Pine County	NV	Joe Marich	1978	1099
163 5/8	19 0/8	19 0/8	17 7/8	5	5	Gallatin County	MT	Jim Diercks	1981	1099
163 5/8	21 2/8	21 0/8	18 1/8	5	5	Mesa County	CO	Edwin L. Porter	1983	1099
163 5/8	20 6/8	20 6/8	22 6/8	6	5	Bear Lake County	ID	Terry Davis	1984	1099
163 5/8	21 6/8	24 3/8	18 7/8	5	5	Eagle Hill	ALB	Ian Kaiser	1994	1099
163 5/8	23 3/8	19 5/8	18 0/8	6	5	Spring Coulee	ALB	Gary Erickson	1996	1099
163 5/8	18 7/8	19 7/8	18 7/8	5	5	Leduc	ALB	Dean Busat	1997	1099
163 5/8	22 3/8	23 3/8	21 1/8	5	5	Brooks	ALB	Mark Nelson	1999	1099
163 5/8	26 0/8	26 2/8	25 6/8	4	5	Okanogan County	WA	Jeff Thorne	2005	1099
*163 5/8	23 1/8	22 7/8	20 4/8	6	5	Lassen County	CA	Darrin Clegg	2005	1099
163 4/8	23 1/8	23 2/8	20 4/8	5	5		UT	Darwin Crawford	1964	1109
163 4/8	24 1/8	24 1/8	25 0/8	5	5	Lake County	OR	William P. Petredis	1972	1109
163 4/8	24 4/8	24 0/8	22 2/8	9	5	Osborne County	KS	Gary Krier	1984	1109
163 4/8	22 4/8	22 7/8	21 4/8	5	5	Albany County	WY	Mark L. Nelson	2003	1109
163 3/8	22 5/8	25 4/8	17 6/8	8	7	Coconino County	AZ	Jake Price	1963	1113
163 3/8	21 6/8	22 1/8	17 5/8	5	5	Gunnison County	CO	Clark Gallup	1970	1113
163 3/8	23 7/8	23 7/8	21 7/8	5	5	Val Marie	SAS	John Vinge	1992	1113
163 3/8	23 4/8	24 2/8	20 5/8	6	5	Lashburn	SAS	Terence Pinder	2001	1113
163 3/8	23 1/8	23 0/8	18 1/8	5	5	Hand County	SD	Chad Parmely	2007	1113
*163 3/8	21 6/8	22 1/8	23 1/8	5	5	East Mountain Lake	SAS	Craig Vanthuyne	2008	1113
163 3/8	24 0/8	22 0/8	20 1/8	5	5	Millard County	UT	J. D. Logston	2008	1113
*163 3/8	21 0/8	20 0/8	17 5/8	5	5	Corson County	SD	John E. Powell, Jr.	2008	1113
163 3/8	22 1/8	23 0/8	19 1/8	5	5	Harney County	OR	Gary Kephart	2009	1113
*163 3/8	24 6/8	23 4/8	24 1/8	5	6	Harding County	SD	Brent Larsen	2009	1113
163 2/8	22 6/8	22 6/8	23 4/8	5	5	Mesa County	CO	Larry D. Tillett	1972	1123
163 2/8	21 5/8	20 1/8	19 7/8	6	6	Chaffee County	CO	J. Melvin Rose	1973	1123
163 2/8	23 7/8	24 3/8	21 2/8	5	4	Coconino County	AZ	Edward R. Allen, Sr.	1974	1123
163 2/8	20 6/8	21 2/8	22 0/8	5	5	Calgary	ALB	Richard P. King	1987	1123
163 2/8	22 0/8	22 7/8	17 2/8	5	5	Kyle	SAS	Brian W. Johns	1991	1123
163 2/8	22 3/8	23 6/8	21 2/8	5	5	Baker County	OR	T. Blaine McKnight	1992	1123
163 2/8	23 4/8	22 1/8	22 2/8	5	4	Yuma County	CO	Mike Barrett	2000	1123
163 2/8	23 4/8	24 0/8	22 2/8	5	5	White Pine County	NV	Michael P. Hendrix	2002	1123
163 2/8	24 6/8	24 4/8	20 5/8	7	5	Jefferson County	OR	Misty M. Macy	2010	1123
163 1/8	20 6/8	22 6/8	19 5/8	4	4	Routt County	CO	Robert H. Blue	1983	1132
163 1/8	21 6/8	21 6/8	20 7/8	4	4	McKenzie County	ND	Mike 'Myron' Rosemore	1986	1132
163 1/8	23 1/8	22 4/8	24 0/8	5	5	Seward County	KS	Travis Leonard	1993	1132
163 1/8	22 3/8	22 0/8	21 5/8	5	5	Milk River	ALB	Craig Chandler	1997	1132
163 1/8	21 7/8	21 4/8	21 5/8	5	5	Adams County	CO	Scott Nelson	2000	1132
163 1/8	21 7/8	21 2/8	20 7/8	5	5	Chelan County	WA	David J. Yonaka	2002	1132
163 1/8	23 3/8	23 5/8	20 7/8	5	5	Moffat County	CO	Greg Sinn	2003	1132
*163 1/8	21 5/8	22 0/8	17 7/8	5	5	Harding County	SD	Daryl Grams	2006	1132
163 1/8	23 4/8	23 2/8	19 5/8	8	7	Meagher County	MT	Jim Kennedy	2009	1132

319

MULE DEER (TYPICAL ANTLERS)

Minimum Score 145 Continued

SCORE	LENGTH OF R MAIN BEAM L	INSIDE SPREAD	NUMBER OF R POINTS L	AREA	STATE/ PROVINCE	HUNTER'S NAME	DATE	RANK
163 0/8	24 2/8 23 4/8	24 2/8	5 7	La Plata County	CO	Bryan B. Owen	1964	1141
163 0/8	23 3/8 25 3/8	20 6/8	5 5	Coconino County	AZ	Larry Hayden	1983	1141
163 0/8	21 3/8 22 5/8	18 2/8	5 5	Teton County	WY	Al Nelson	1985	1141
163 0/8	25 4/8 24 7/8	23 0/8	4 5	Twin Falls County	ID	William Lent	1985	1141
163 0/8	23 1/8 22 4/8	19 6/8	5 5	Rawlins County	KS	Richard Jones	1986	1141
163 0/8	20 7/8 20 0/8	17 6/8	5 5	Mesa County	CO	Jim Hall	1987	1141
163 0/8	22 3/8 23 0/8	21 6/8	5 5	Culberson County	TX	Kyle Johnson	1992	1141
163 0/8	22 3/8 22 3/8	19 0/8	4 4	Yuma County	CO	Garry Neuschwanger	1992	1141
163 0/8	20 6/8 21 2/8	20 6/8	5 5	Hall County	NE	Jason A. Hettler	1994	1141
163 0/8	22 2/8 23 1/8	18 6/8	5 5	Calgary	ALB	Fred V. Kugler	1997	1141
163 0/8	20 4/8 20 4/8	19 6/8	5 5	Pima County	AZ	Darrel Sudduth	1999	1141
163 0/8	25 3/8 24 0/8	18 7/8	6 6	Wasco County	OR	Dan L. Brown	2000	1141
163 0/8	22 4/8 21 6/8	23 6/8	5 5	Lake County	OR	Bill Caldwell	2001	1141
163 0/8	22 4/8 22 6/8	20 7/8	6 5	Boulder County	CO	Peter Christensen	2005	1141
* 163 0/8	24 1/8 21 2/8	21 3/8	6 5	Kit Carson County	CO	Matthew Palmquist	2008	1141
* 163 0/8	23 2/8 22 7/8	17 4/8	4 5	Rosebud County	MT	Ambrose Updegraff	2009	1141
162 7/8	23 6/8 23 7/8	24 1/8	5 4	Elko County	NV	Orrin M. Owens	1966	1157
162 7/8	23 1/8 22 7/8	20 1/8	5 5	Billings County	ND	Allan R. Bottolfson	1981	1157
162 7/8	23 5/8 21 6/8	20 5/8	5 5	Fremont County	CO	Jerry Tiemeyer	1981	1157
162 7/8	20 4/8 20 7/8	19 5/8	5 5	Delta County	CO	Steve Cook	1984	1157
162 7/8	24 0/8 23 6/8	23 5/8	5 5	Umatilla County	OR	Rick L. Evans	1985	1157
162 7/8	20 5/8 21 6/8	18 3/8	6 5	Mesa County	CO	John E. Gross	1993	1157
162 7/8	23 1/8 21 6/8	23 1/8	5 4	San Juan County	NM	Rick Mace	1995	1157
162 7/8	20 7/8 22 3/8	19 5/8	6 5	Cochrane	ALB	Tom Foss	1996	1157
162 7/8	20 4/8 21 4/8	15 5/8	5 5	Coconino County	AZ	Lynn D. Nelson	1996	1157
162 7/8	22 0/8 22 3/8	20 5/8	5 5	Boulder County	CO	Kevin R. Jones	1999	1157
162 7/8	23 3/8 24 1/8	22 5/8	5 5	Shasta County	CA	Randy Spade	2000	1157
162 7/8	21 3/8 22 2/8	19 3/8	6 6	Okanogan County	WA	Pat Ryan	2003	1157
* 162 7/8	26 1/8 25 7/8	27 0/8	5 4	Fall River County	SD	Ronald L. Kimmy, Jr.	2006	1157
* 162 7/8	22 2/8 20 4/8	17 3/8	6 6	Kiowa County	CO	Brandon Reystead	2006	1157
162 7/8	24 0/8 25 0/8	19 1/8	6 7	Calgary	ALB	Giovanni Mazzeo	2007	1157
162 6/8	21 1/8 23 4/8	23 2/8	5 5	Chelan County	WA	Les Eide	1954	1172
162 6/8	23 5/8 24 2/8	18 5/8	5 6	Chelan County	WA	Brian Kayler	1984	1172
162 6/8	22 4/8 24 0/8	19 6/8	5 5	Larimer County	CO	Ron Morgan	1986	1172
162 6/8	22 1/8 23 1/8	22 2/8	5 5	Chelan County	WA	Rod Courter	1986	1172
162 6/8	22 2/8 22 6/8	23 5/8	5 5	Weld County	CO	Dan Wacker	1988	1172
162 6/8	21 7/8 22 6/8	18 2/8	5 5	Uinta County	WY	Frank W. Sheets	1992	1172
162 6/8	22 6/8 22 5/8	21 6/8	5 5	Cheyenne County	KS	David Hamilton	1992	1172
162 6/8	22 7/8 23 6/8	22 3/8	6 5	Coconino County	AZ	David J. Dettorre	1997	1172
162 6/8	24 1/8 25 2/8	21 6/8	6 5	Cache County	UT	Joseph S. Mayers	2009	1172
162 5/8	19 6/8 20 1/8	22 0/8	5 5	Pima County	AZ	Jerry Clarno	1978	1181
162 5/8	22 4/8 21 0/8	21 2/8	7 6	Washoe County	NV	Ed Fuller	1984	1181
162 5/8	21 4/8 21 1/8	20 7/8	5 5	Las Animas County	CO	Chris J. Furia	1986	1181
162 5/8	20 2/8 21 6/8	19 2/8	7 5	Ada County	ID	Ronald L. Cash	1990	1181
162 5/8	22 4/8 23 3/8	19 1/8	6 5	Montrose County	CO	Thomas D. Thompson	1991	1181
162 5/8	24 3/8 24 7/8	21 3/8	5 5	Sheridan County	WY	Butch West	1992	1181
162 5/8	21 7/8 23 4/8	18 1/8	5 5	Highwood River	ALB	Troy W. Clark	1995	1181
162 5/8	18 2/8 21 7/8	22 4/8	4 5	Yuma County	CO	Tobias Dellamano	1996	1181
162 5/8	20 2/8 19 3/8	19 1/8	5 5	Yuma County	CO	Tom Pindell	1997	1181
162 5/8	23 6/8 23 4/8	23 2/8	5 6	Rio Blanco County	CO	Justin Downing	2002	1181
162 5/8	23 1/8 24 1/8	16 5/8	5 5	Crook County	OR	Bryan Piper	2006	1181
* 162 5/8	25 0/8 25 1/8	22 7/8	4 5	Eagle County	CO	Harry S. Mayer	2006	1181
162 5/8	23 0/8 23 2/8	19 5/8	5 5	Boise County	ID	T. J. Gholson	2007	1181
* 162 5/8	25 6/8 24 1/8	27 7/8	6 6	Colfax County	NM	Hedge Fernandez	2008	1181
162 4/8	21 3/8 21 0/8	19 2/8	5 5	Emery County	UT	Kerry Ware	1964	1195
162 4/8	24 5/8 25 7/8	27 6/8	5 8	Leader	SAS	Don Tourand	1982	1195
162 4/8	20 5/8 21 7/8	17 2/8	5 5	Slope County	ND	Todd Seymonski	1983	1195
162 4/8	21 2/8 20 7/8	23 0/8	5 5	Hooker County	NE	Will Boyer	1991	1195
162 4/8	23 0/8 25 0/8	25 6/8	4 5	Yuma County	CO	Jerry Bowen	1997	1195
162 4/8	22 6/8 22 2/8	20 6/8	5 5	Harney County	OR	Joel Haslett	2003	1195
162 4/8	22 6/8 23 0/8	15 6/8	5 5	Elkwater	ALB	Larry Haley	2003	1195
162 4/8	21 4/8 22 5/8	17 7/8	4 5	Millarville	ALB	Darrell Wright	2003	1195
162 4/8	23 1/8 23 3/8	19 6/8	5 5	Elko County	NV	Thomas D. Bors	2005	1195
162 4/8	23 6/8 23 2/8	19 7/8	6 5	Carbon County	WY	Clay J. Evans	2007	1195
* 162 4/8	25 7/8 24 7/8	25 6/8	3 5	Milk River	ALB	M. Blake Patton	2010	1195
162 3/8	25 2/8 25 0/8	22 6/8	7 7	Bear Lake County	ID	Marriner Jensen	1957	1206
162 3/8	25 6/8 26 3/8	27 5/8	4 5	Pima County	AZ	Steve Mikitish	1983	1206
162 3/8	23 0/8 22 7/8	24 3/8	5 6	Mesa County	CO	Billy T. Edwards	1988	1206
162 3/8	23 5/8 24 0/8	18 7/8	5 5	Standard	ALB	Kevin J. Muller	2000	1206
162 2/8	23 3/8 26 2/8	25 0/8	4 5	Owyhee County	ID	Ralph Collins	1960	1210
162 2/8	20 7/8 20 2/8	22 3/8	6 5	Park County	WY	Jim Patterson	1968	1210
162 2/8	22 5/8 23 0/8	17 0/8	5 5	Eureka County	NV	Gordon Diehl	1980	1210
162 2/8	23 5/8 23 2/8	19 6/8	5 5	Lassen County	CA	Chuck Mazza	1984	1210
162 2/8	23 4/8 23 5/8	21 4/8	5 5	Park County	CO	Randy W. Gorby, Jr.	1988	1210
162 2/8	22 3/8 26 4/8	20 0/8	6 5	Bernalillo County	NM	William A. Brandon	1988	1210
162 2/8	22 7/8 22 3/8	19 4/8	5 7	Camas County	ID	James C. O'Connor	1991	1210
162 2/8	21 1/8 21 5/8	19 5/8	4 5	Natrona County	WY	Robert Engleman	1999	1210
162 2/8	22 7/8 22 6/8	22 1/8	6 6	Dunn County	ND	Steven Gimpl	1999	1210
162 2/8	24 3/8 25 2/8	20 7/8	6 7	Cochise County	AZ	Brek L. Haymore	2007	1210
162 2/8	24 5/8 24 3/8	20 4/8	6 5	Pennington County	SD	Dusty J. Johnson	2009	1210
162 1/8	23 7/8 23 6/8	18 1/8	5 5	Fishlake National Forest	UT	R. E. Kerr	1957	1221
162 1/8	23 2/8 22 5/8	22 1/8	5 5	Range Creek	UT	Frank Turner	1965	1221
162 1/8	22 4/8 22 5/8	17 2/8	5 6	Mesa County	CO	Joel Prickett	1973	1221
162 1/8	20 3/8 22 0/8	23 0/8	7 5	Mora County	NM	Michael J. Maes	1977	1221
162 1/8	21 7/8 21 7/8	23 1/8	6 6	Dundy County	NE	Jim Lutz	1980	1221
162 1/8	24 2/8 21 2/8	21 5/8	6 5	Logan County	KS	Mel Jamison	1985	1221
162 1/8	21 2/8 23 0/8	21 7/8	4 5	Ada County	ID	Charlie Perry	2000	1221
162 1/8	24 1/8 24 1/8	18 7/8	5 5	El Dorado County	CA	Scott Lusk	2000	1221
162 1/8	21 7/8 22 2/8	21 1/8	5 5	Weld County	CO	Lane G. Eskew	2002	1221
162 0/8	22 3/8 23 3/8	21 2/8	5 5	Elko County	NV	Larry D Jones	1985	1230
162 0/8	21 5/8 20 7/8	21 0/8	6 6	Rawlins County	KS	Ken Krien	1988	1230
162 0/8	22 3/8 22 4/8	16 4/8	4 5	Lumby	BC	Owen Schoenberger	1990	1230
162 0/8	22 4/8 22 0/8	19 0/8	5 5	Greenlee County	AZ	Richard V. Gray	2000	1230
162 0/8	23 7/8 24 2/8	24 0/8	6 5	Custer County	ID	Nicholas Natoli	2004	1230
162 0/8	23 0/8 24 0/8	28 3/8	5 5	Bingham County	ID	Alan Copeland	2006	1230

MULE DEER (TYPICAL ANTLERS)

Minimum Score 145   Continued

SCORE	LENGTH OF R MAIN BEAM L	INSIDE SPREAD	NUMBER OF R POINTS L		AREA	STATE/ PROVINCE	HUNTER'S NAME	DATE	RANK
162 0/8	24 5/8 23 4/8	19 4/8	5	5	Deschutes County	OR	Lloyd Suydam	2006	1230
162 0/8	24 0/8 23 7/8	21 4/8	5	6	McKenzie County	ND	Timothy A. Collien	2007	1230
161 7/8	21 2/8 21 6/8	20 3/8	4	5	Rio Blanco County	CO	Douglas Kenyon	1964	1238
161 7/8	22 6/8 21 6/8	21 5/8	5	5	Sevier County	UT	Clark Richards	1967	1238
161 7/8	23 0/8 22 1/8	20 0/8	5	5	Rio Blanco County	CO	Leonard Conley	1973	1238
161 7/8	20 4/8 22 5/8	20 7/8	6	6	Beaver County	UT	Joe Cordonier	1975	1238
161 7/8	21 1/8 20 3/8	18 5/8	5	5	Plumas County	CA	John Grochowski, Jr.	1976	1238
161 7/8	24 3/8 24 1/8	20 7/8	5	4	Maricopa County	AZ	Paul N. Rambeau	1981	1238
161 7/8	25 4/8 23 6/8	22 5/8	8	5	Catron County	NM	Richard D. Trapp	1986	1238
161 7/8	24 6/8 25 1/8	22 3/8	4	3	Grant County	WA	Daniel A. Whitmus	1994	1238
161 7/8	21 4/8 21 4/8	22 6/8	5	6	Ada County	ID	Rory Clinton	1994	1238
161 7/8	23 7/8 22 5/8	19 5/8	6	6	Weyburn	SAS	Paul Chinski	1996	1238
161 7/8	22 4/8 22 5/8	28 0/8	5	7	Harding County	SD	Scott Koan	1998	1238
161 7/8	21 7/8 22 1/8	19 1/8	5	5	Baker County	OR	Tyrone E. Nelson	2001	1238
161 7/8	22 7/8 23 3/8	25 6/8	5	6	Sonora	MEX	Archie J. Nesbitt	2003	1238
161 7/8	23 3/8 22 7/8	19 5/8	5	5	Beaverlodge	ALB	Terry Hagman	2007	1238
161 6/8	21 3/8 21 3/8	21 6/8	5	5	Garfield County	CO	Warren Buss	1978	1252
161 6/8	20 5/8 21 5/8	21 2/8	5	5	Elko County	NV	Gregory Higgins	1988	1252
161 6/8	21 2/8 22 2/8	21 2/8	5	5	Campbell County	WY	Loy Peters	1990	1252
161 6/8	22 2/8 22 6/8	21 2/8	6	7	Lincoln County	CO	James Hipps	1992	1252
161 6/8	24 6/8 23 7/8	20 7/8	5	6	Hamilton County	KS	Bobby Myers	1993	1252
161 6/8	21 7/8 21 7/8	18 0/8	5	5	Johnson County	WY	Andy Stanco	1998	1252
161 6/8	20 4/8 23 4/8	21 4/8	5	5	Harney County	OR	Timothy Roth	2000	1252
161 6/8	22 2/8 21 7/8	20 2/8	5	5	Natrona County	WY	Richard Manchur	2000	1252
161 6/8	22 6/8 22 6/8	21 2/8	4	5	Yuma County	CO	Tom Pindell	2000	1252
161 6/8	24 2/8 23 6/8	20 4/8	5	5	Baker County	OR	David H. Moore	2003	1252
161 6/8	24 6/8 24 2/8	27 0/8	4	4	Chelan County	WA	Charles E. Stanton	2003	1252
161 6/8	20 6/8 21 6/8	20 0/8	5	5	Sioux County	NE	Brad Perkins	2004	1252
161 6/8	23 1/8 23 2/8	20 6/8	5	5	Graham County	AZ	Rudy Montano	2006	1252
161 6/8	21 6/8 21 1/8	19 6/8	4	4	San Juan County	NM	Steven J. Vittetow	2009	1252
*161 6/8	24 6/8 26 6/8	21 6/8	6	7	Pincher Creek	ALB	Charles Schoening	2009	1252
161 6/8	21 2/8 21 0/8	20 4/8	4	5	Cherry County	NE	Kent Hochstein	2010	1252
161 6/8	23 2/8 22 0/8	18 0/8	4	4	Cherry County	NE	Reggie Hochstein	2010	1252
161 5/8	20 0/8 22 4/8	19 3/8	5	5	Lander County	NV	Paul Q. Lenz	1984	1269
161 5/8	22 5/8 22 5/8	21 7/8	5	5	Rio Arriba County	NM	Craig A. Pilley	1987	1269
161 5/8	23 5/8 22 3/8	21 6/8	5	6	Ford County	KS	Jeff Cuer	1988	1269
161 5/8	23 5/8 22 5/8	22 6/8	6	5	Converse County	WY	Jeff Reynolds	1990	1269
161 5/8	23 3/8 23 5/8	21 3/8	4	4	Boise County	ID	David Gallegos	1991	1269
161 5/8	23 0/8 22 5/8	23 7/8	6	4	Elbert County	CO	Wayne Roach	2000	1269
161 5/8	20 5/8 20 5/8	20 5/8	5	5	Delta County	CO	Rick Curtis	2004	1269
161 5/8	23 0/8 21 6/8	22 2/8	6	5	Harney County	OR	Richard Retterath	2008	1269
*161 5/8	22 3/8 21 7/8	19 1/8	5	5	Inyo County	CA	Katie Clifton	2009	1269
161 4/8	24 5/8 24 6/8	24 2/8	7	7	Salt Lake County	UT	Frank M. Davis	1957	1278
161 4/8	24 4/8 24 2/8	23 6/8	4	3	Owyhee County	ID	William R. Vanderhoef	1958	1278
161 4/8	22 5/8 23 5/8	19 2/8	5	5	Sheridan County	WY	Mike Barrett	1985	1278
161 4/8	25 6/8 24 1/8	24 6/8	5	7	Apache County	AZ	Robert A. Wood	1987	1278
161 4/8	21 6/8 20 2/8	18 4/8	5	6	Grant County	OR	Jeff McCrary	1990	1278
161 4/8	21 4/8 22 0/8	21 2/8	5	5	Elbert County	CO	Patrick V. Mulhern, Jr.	1990	1278
161 4/8	21 6/8 21 6/8	16 6/8	5	5	Lincoln County	WY	Delmar Bright	1992	1278
161 4/8	21 4/8 21 3/8	19 5/8	6	5	Campbell County	WY	Art Cain	1994	1278
161 4/8	21 5/8 21 6/8	18 4/8	5	5	Natrona County	WY	Kevin D. Hoff	1998	1278
161 4/8	25 5/8 25 0/8	24 4/8	5	4	Garfield County	UT	Mathew K. Peterson	2001	1278
161 3/8	22 5/8 21 7/8	19 1/8	5	5	Elko County	NV	Bert W. Fox	1961	1288
161 3/8	23 2/8 21 6/8	22 3/8	4	4	Box Butte County	NE	Fred H. D. Krueger	1970	1288
161 3/8	18 5/8 21 1/8	22 1/8	6	5	Cochrane	ALB	Colby Robison	1982	1288
161 3/8	22 5/8 22 7/8	22 1/8	5	5	Rush County	KS	Clarence Tuzicka	1990	1288
161 3/8	22 3/8 22 4/8	18 2/8	5	6	Stanislaus County	CA	Ron Crouch	1992	1288
161 3/8	24 2/8 21 5/8	22 5/8	5	5	Okanogan County	WA	Jerry Bruers	2005	1288
*161 3/8	22 6/8 23 1/8	19 5/8	5	5	Cascade County	MT	Troy Schott	2008	1288
161 3/8	24 0/8 23 2/8	21 2/8	6	7	Salt Lake County	UT	Nathan Fox	2009	1288
161 2/8	21 0/8 20 6/8	16 7/8	5	6	Ada County	ID	Ed Moser	1971	1296
161 2/8	24 6/8 23 5/8	20 4/8	3	3	Mesa County	CO	Billy Ellis	1976	1296
161 2/8	23 6/8 25 2/8	25 4/8	5	4	San Juan County	UT	Todd Hurst	1984	1296
161 2/8	23 4/8 22 3/8	17 6/8	5	5	Big Horn County	MT	Mike Barrett	1984	1296
161 2/8	23 7/8 23 0/8	22 4/8	5	5	Billings County	ND	Cally G Marsh	1989	1296
161 2/8	23 0/8 23 1/8	22 4/8	5	5	Apache County	AZ	Johnny C. Parsons	1992	1296
161 2/8	24 4/8 23 4/8	20 6/8	5	5	Apache County	AZ	Bruce Kallenberger	1993	1296
161 2/8	24 0/8 22 0/8	22 2/8	5	5	Colfax County	NM	Stacy Hoeme	1994	1296
161 2/8	22 1/8 21 4/8	19 6/8	6	5	La Plata County	CO	Pat Palmer	1996	1296
161 2/8	21 3/8 20 6/8	19 0/8	6	5	Adams County	CO	Guy Pierce	2001	1296
161 2/8	22 5/8 23 7/8	20 6/8	4	5	Valley County	ID	Curt L. Giese	2002	1296
161 2/8	23 0/8 22 2/8	19 7/8	5	5	Esther	ALB	Todd Thompson	2003	1296
161 2/8	23 6/8 24 0/8	26 2/8	5	5	Sanders County	MT	Tom M. Benson	2003	1296
*161 2/8	22 6/8 23 4/8	24 1/8	5	5	Meade County	SD	Randy Simkins	2007	1296
161 2/8	22 3/8 22 3/8	19 6/8	5	5	Lincoln County	WA	David C. Hubbard	2009	1296
161 1/8	25 0/8 24 0/8	25 0/8	5	5	Los Alamos County	NM	J. R. McDaniels	1960	1311
161 1/8	20 5/8 20 4/8	15 5/8	5	5	Garfield County	CO	John Murray	1963	1311
161 1/8	23 1/8 21 7/8	18 1/8	5	5	San Juan County	CO	Eddie Claypool	1984	1311
161 1/8	24 6/8 25 5/8	20 3/8	5	4	Kittitas County	WA	Sam Grant	1988	1311
161 1/8	19 4/8 20 5/8	16 7/8	5	5	Coconino County	AZ	Richard S. Brown	1998	1311
161 1/8	24 0/8 24 1/8	18 7/8	5	5	Douglas County	CO	Bruce E. Ritts	1999	1311
161 1/8	23 4/8 24 3/8	21 1/8	5	5	Weld County	CO	David D. Brundeen	2000	1311
*161 1/8	23 3/8 22 6/8	23 6/8	5	5	Okanogan County	WA	Mark Pritchard	2008	1311
161 1/8	21 7/8 23 0/8	19 7/8	5	5	Souris River	SAS	Joshua Michel	2009	1311
161 0/8	23 0/8 23 4/8	19 2/8	4	5	Milk River	ALB	Archie Nesbitt	1992	1320
161 0/8	22 4/8 23 3/8	25 2/8	5	6	Colfax County	NM	Mark Sullivan	1995	1320
161 0/8	22 5/8 22 3/8	18 2/8	6	5	Coconino County	AZ	William C. Rhodes	1996	1320
161 0/8	22 1/8 23 0/8	16 0/8	6	5	Niobrara County	WY	Gary Morse	1998	1320
161 0/8	20 4/8 20 6/8	21 7/8	5	5	Elbert County	CO	Richard Skiles	2000	1320
161 0/8	22 3/8 24 3/8	20 0/8	5	4	Cascade County	MT	Gary Lampkins	2006	1320
*161 0/8	20 0/8 20 3/8	19 1/8	5	7	Davis County	UT	Craig Germond	2008	1320
160 7/8	24 0/8 23 5/8	22 3/8	4	5	Teton County	ID	Gary S. Paynter	1987	1327
160 7/8	21 4/8 21 2/8	18 7/8	5	5	Haakon County	SD	Melvin Buchheim	1993	1327
160 7/8	21 3/8 21 3/8	21 6/8	5	6	Teton County	WY	Arron J. Wagner	1993	1327
160 7/8	20 5/8 21 3/8	16 1/8	5	5	Colfax County	NM	Bruce Imig	1995	1327

321

MULE DEER (TYPICAL ANTLERS)

Minimum Score 145 — Continued

SCORE	LENGTH OF R MAIN BEAM L	INSIDE SPREAD	NUMBER OF R POINTS L		AREA	STATE/ PROVINCE	HUNTER'S NAME	DATE	RANK
160 7/8	25 3/8	24 2/8	22 1/8	5	5	Rio Arriba County	NM	Wally Schwartz	1996	1327
160 7/8	22 4/8	22 6/8	20 1/8	5	5	Rio Blanco County	CO	Jennifer D. Filener	1998	1327
160 7/8	24 1/8	22 2/8	20 1/8	5	5	Frenchman River	SAS	Garrett Francais	2001	1327
160 7/8	26 3/8	24 6/8	23 1/8	5	6	Prowers County	CO	Bo Clark	2005	1327
160 7/8	23 2/8	22 0/8	20 3/8	4	4	Billings County	ND	Mark L. Meyer	2007	1327
160 6/8	20 6/8	21 4/8	21 5/8	5	5	Colfax County	NM	Carl Osborne	1965	1336
160 6/8	22 6/8	22 4/8	21 1/8	7	6	Chelan County	WA	Paul Cohoon	1967	1336
160 6/8	21 3/8	22 2/8	26 7/8	6	6	San Juan County	UT	Dale Warren	1972	1336
160 6/8	22 4/8	22 6/8	15 4/8	5	4	Washoe County	NV	Lawrence Heward	1974	1336
160 6/8	20 5/8	20 3/8	19 4/8	5	5	Boise County	ID	Mike McCollum	1975	1336
160 6/8	21 0/8	22 4/8	21 4/8	5	5	Grand County	CO	Terry J. Kramer	1978	1336
160 6/8	21 7/8	23 2/8	19 2/8	6	5	Thomas County	KS	Darren Andrews	1986	1336
160 6/8	22 2/8	21 1/8	19 6/8	6	7	Archuleta County	CO	James Daugherty	1987	1336
160 6/8	24 6/8	25 0/8	28 2/8	5	7	Washoe County	NV	Tom Hauptman	1988	1336
160 6/8	23 4/8	21 6/8	24 3/8	7	9	Cheyenne County	CO	Monte Baker	1990	1336
160 6/8	23 0/8	23 3/8	18 0/8	6	5	Baker County	OR	Mike Raney	1992	1336
160 6/8	22 0/8	22 0/8	20 3/8	5	7	Finney County	KS	Eddie Rojas, Jr.	1996	1336
160 6/8	21 6/8	22 5/8	18 6/8	5	5	Otero County	NM	Jerry Bales	1997	1336
160 6/8	22 6/8	21 6/8	20 6/8	5	5	Rio Arriba County	NM	Patrick Lovato	1997	1336
160 6/8	20 7/8	22 0/8	21 2/8	5	5	Ada County	ID	Greg McTee	1998	1336
160 6/8	24 4/8	24 1/8	26 1/8	5	4	Coconino County	AZ	Paul T. Carter	2003	1336
160 6/8	23 4/8	25 2/8	20 1/8	6	6	Hanna	ALB	Walter Palmer	2006	1336
160 5/8	20 5/8	20 5/8	19 7/8	4	4	Humboldt County	NV	Mike Toone	1961	1353
160 5/8	22 3/8	22 1/8	24 7/8	5	5	San Juan County	UT	Russell Smith	1971	1353
160 5/8	21 1/8	21 2/8	20 7/8	5	5	Routt County	CO	Mark Chapman	1975	1353
160 5/8	21 1/8	21 6/8	17 7/8	4	4	Moffat County	CO	Glenn Pritchard	1985	1353
160 5/8	23 5/8	23 3/8	21 5/8	5	5	Nevada County	CA	Richard L. Westervelt	1992	1353
160 5/8	24 0/8	25 2/8	27 0/8	5	6	Teton County	WY	Ronell Skinner	1992	1353
160 5/8	22 6/8	22 6/8	25 4/8	5	6	Park County	MT	Nathan Broell	1993	1353
160 5/8	22 0/8	22 6/8	19 3/8	5	5	Garfield County	CO	Rodney K. Snider	1999	1353
160 5/8	22 2/8	23 0/8	20 5/8	5	5	Pima County	AZ	Rick Forrest	2000	1353
160 5/8	23 2/8	23 1/8	19 7/8	5	5	Jumping Pound Creek	ALB	Lindsey Paterson	2004	1353
* 160 5/8	22 1/8	22 7/8	21 5/8	5	5	Pennington County	SD	Matt Burrows	2007	1353
160 4/8	23 6/8	23 1/8	20 0/8	7	8	Elko County	NV	Robert Narrimore	1963	1364
160 4/8	23 5/8	23 5/8	18 0/8	5	5	Lemhi County	ID	Robert J. Eckardt	1978	1364
160 4/8	23 0/8	22 2/8	23 6/8	5	5	Washoe County	NV	Robert L. Brooks, Jr.	1983	1364
160 4/8	23 3/8	24 1/8	16 6/8	6	6	Platte County	WY	Dennis Crew	1995	1364
160 4/8	24 1/8	23 7/8	24 0/8	6	5	Boulder County	CO	James A. MacPherson	2002	1364
160 4/8	21 1/8	22 4/8	18 4/8	5	5	Charles Mix County	SD	Ron Ream	2003	1364
160 4/8	21 4/8	21 2/8	21 5/8	4	5	Rosebud County	MT	Chuck Adams	2003	1364
* 160 4/8	20 3/8	21 3/8	18 2/8	6	4	Douglas County	CO	Jake Cloyed	2004	1364
* 160 4/8	22 2/8	22 1/8	22 4/8	5	6	Grant County	ND	Jason J. Zins	2008	1364
160 4/8	22 7/8	22 6/8	20 6/8	5	5	Prowers County	CO	Bo Clark	2008	1364
160 3/8	22 7/8	22 3/8	18 0/8	5	6	Iron County	UT	Clair Adams	1958	1374
160 3/8	22 4/8	22 4/8	18 2/8	6	6	Mesa County	CO	Ed Adkins	1974	1374
160 3/8	20 6/8	22 1/8	20 1/8	4	4	Mesa County	CO	Ralph Ertz	1980	1374
160 3/8	22 0/8	23 4/8	19 1/8	6	6	Jefferson County	CO	Steve Rehm	1984	1374
160 3/8	24 4/8	22 2/8	22 0/8	6	6	Pima County	AZ	Ronald J. Hover	1987	1374
160 3/8	23 3/8	23 5/8	20 3/8	5	5	Lake County	OR	Carl E. Garner	1991	1374
160 3/8	22 1/8	21 5/8	23 7/8	5	5	Cochrane	ALB	Tom Foss	1994	1374
160 3/8	20 0/8	22 3/8	17 5/8	5	5	Pennington County	SD	Brian Heidbrink	1999	1374
160 3/8	24 5/8	23 4/8	22 7/8	5	5	Klamath County	OR	Philip Q. Kiely	2002	1374
160 3/8	22 2/8	21 5/8	17 6/8	8	7	Chelan County	WA	Matthew Gunter	2002	1374
160 3/8	19 6/8	20 2/8	19 7/8	5	5	Chelan County	WA	Chad Dohlgren	2003	1374
160 3/8	20 6/8	21 0/8	20 1/8	5	5	Phillips County	MT	David L. Skiff	2004	1374
160 3/8	22 7/8	22 0/8	20 5/8	5	5	McKenzie County	ND	Corey Hugelen	2004	1374
160 3/8	24 1/8	25 4/8	20 7/8	5	5	Okanogan County	WA	Robert D. Howe	2005	1374
* 160 3/8	22 1/8	22 5/8	18 7/8	5	5	Oliver County	ND	Gary A. Gierke	2006	1374
160 3/8	21 0/8	22 1/8	20 4/8	6	5	Rosebud County	MT	Doug Stevens	2009	1374
160 2/8	19 2/8	21 2/8	19 0/8	5	5	Millard County	UT	Scott Chesley	1962	1390
160 2/8	19 6/8	21 2/8	20 6/8	5	5	Lemhi County	ID	Kemper McMaster	1978	1390
160 2/8	20 5/8	21 1/8	17 0/8	5	5	Mesa County	CO	Bill Dunbar	1984	1390
160 2/8	25 6/8	24 6/8	23 3/8	6	6	Scott County	KS	Michael E. Woodard	1984	1390
160 2/8	21 4/8	20 5/8	20 6/8	5	5	Gooding County	ID	Robert Dowen	1986	1390
160 2/8	21 6/8	22 6/8	18 0/8	4	4	Sioux County	NE	Wayne Depperschmidt	1989	1390
160 2/8	23 7/8	22 2/8	18 2/8	6	6	Montrose County	CO	Jackie Wright	1995	1390
160 2/8	23 3/8	23 1/8	19 0/8	6	6	Lake Diefenbaker	SAS	Darren Breckner	1995	1390
160 2/8	22 0/8	22 6/8	18 2/8	4	4	Boise County	ID	Dwayne Sturbaum	1995	1390
160 2/8	22 2/8	22 1/8	25 0/8	5	5	Jefferson County	OR	Travis Williams	1997	1390
160 2/8	21 0/8	18 2/8	19 0/8	5	5	Chain Lakes	ALB	Norman Hopkins	2000	1390
160 2/8	23 0/8	22 7/8	22 2/8	5	5	Haakon County	SD	Ron Flottmeyer	2003	1390
160 2/8	22 6/8	24 2/8	18 4/8	5	4	Grant County	OR	Larry G. Burton	2009	1390
160 2/8	26 5/8	26 2/8	16 2/8	6	5	Drumheller	ALB	Douglas North	2009	1390
160 1/8	20 2/8	20 7/8	19 7/8	5	5	Meagher County	MT	Mickey Anderson, Jr.	1966	1404
160 1/8	23 6/8	22 2/8	24 0/8	5	5	Moffat County	CO	Ron Hopkins	1970	1404
160 1/8	22 7/8	22 7/8	23 3/8	5	5	Mesa County	CO	Gary J. Oden	1988	1404
160 1/8	22 1/8	22 6/8	20 1/8	5	5	Deschutes County	OR	R. Sean Glaab	1992	1404
160 1/8	19 0/8	18 6/8	15 5/8	5	5	Ravalli County	MT	Michael A. Dunwell	1994	1404
160 1/8	24 0/8	23 6/8	27 0/8	5	5	Malheur County	OR	Steven Nichols	1996	1404
160 1/8	22 3/8	21 3/8	18 1/8	5	6	Weld County	CO	Reggie Spiegelberg	1996	1404
160 1/8	23 1/8	23 3/8	22 0/8	6	5	Chase County	NE	William Baker	1999	1404
160 1/8	25 2/8	24 5/8	25 1/8	4	4	Stanley County	SD	Derek Schlefelbein	2005	1404
160 0/8	22 4/8	21 7/8	20 2/8	5	5	Chaffee County	CO	Paul J. Zeisler	1964	1413
160 0/8	23 0/8	22 7/8	20 3/8	6	5	Gunnison County	CO	Wayne Depperschmidt	1973	1413
160 0/8	24 4/8	23 2/8	25 0/8	4	4	Coconino County	AZ	Bruce McIntyre	1979	1413
160 0/8	21 4/8	21 7/8	19 2/8	5	5	Linn County	OR	Mary Cook	1980	1413
160 0/8	23 3/8	24 2/8	20 2/8	5	5	Saguache County	CO	Russell Hull	1980	1413
160 0/8	26 2/8	25 1/8	25 0/8	5	5	La Plata County	CO	Michael R. Hinson	1986	1413
160 0/8	21 7/8	22 5/8	17 6/8	5	5	Cherry County	NE	Lloyd C. Smith	1990	1413
160 0/8	21 1/8	22 1/8	19 2/8	5	5	Garfield County	UT	Steve Fitch	1998	1413
160 0/8	21 6/8	22 6/8	19 0/8	5	5	Okotoks	ALB	Mark Gaudry	1998	1413
160 0/8	19 3/8	20 2/8	18 7/8	4	4	Fort Assinibione	ALB	Cedric "Buddy" Malone	2006	1413
* 160 0/8	20 6/8	21 4/8	17 4/8	5	5	Scotts Bluff County	NE	Kerry Keane	2009	1413
159 7/8	24 2/8	25 0/8	19 4/8	5	6	Colfax County	NM	James Kelly	1957	1424
159 7/8	20 7/8	21 6/8	21 6/8	5	5	Liberty County	MT	Kenneth Aaberge	1960	1424

MULE DEER (TYPICAL ANTLERS)

Minimum Score 145   Continued

SCORE	LENGTH OF MAIN BEAM R	L	INSIDE SPREAD	NUMBER OF POINTS R	L	AREA	STATE/PROVINCE	HUNTER'S NAME	DATE	RANK
159 7/8	22 5/8	23 0/8	18 7/8	5	5	Sanders County	MT	Walt Borgmann	1968	1424
159 7/8	23 1/8	21 3/8	17 3/8	5	5	Bernalillo County	NM	Lee Burnett	1972	1424
159 7/8	25 4/8	22 4/8	21 0/8	6	6	Mesa County	CO	Ronald E. Stull	1974	1424
159 7/8	21 5/8	22 3/8	20 1/8	5	5	Okotoks	ALB	Cam Cook	1990	1424
159 7/8	19 7/8	20 6/8	19 2/8	6	6	Ellsworth County	KS	Rod Buchholz	1997	1424
159 7/8	22 3/8	23 4/8	19 2/8	6	6	Jefferson County	CO	Larry J. Jones	2002	1424
159 6/8	23 4/8	22 7/8	22 3/8	7	7	Owyhee County	ID	Gilbert Martin	1960	1432
159 6/8	22 2/8	21 4/8	19 4/8	5	5	Beaver County	UT	Joe Cordonier	1974	1432
159 6/8	22 0/8	22 0/8	20 6/8	4	4	Kamloops	BC	Barry Anderson	1982	1432
159 6/8	21 2/8	21 3/8	18 6/8	5	5	Albany County	WY	Jerry Bowen	1984	1432
159 6/8	22 6/8	23 2/8	20 6/8	5	5	Labette County	KS	Steve Cooper	1986	1432
159 6/8	21 3/8	22 0/8	22 0/8	5	4	Caribou County	ID	Paul Persano	1986	1432
159 6/8	23 7/8	24 2/8	20 6/8	8	6	Norton County	KS	Eldon L. Myers	1991	1432
159 6/8	25 7/8	26 6/8	20 4/8	5	5	Kane County	UT	William D. Hofeling	1993	1432
159 6/8	21 1/8	22 5/8	22 2/8	5	5	Sheridan County	WY	Bruce Kramer	1993	1432
159 6/8	21 4/8	20 4/8	16 2/8	6	5	Gove County	KS	Carl L. Ghan, Jr.	1993	1432
159 6/8	22 2/8	21 6/8	18 6/8	5	5	Garfield County	MT	Corey Hugelen	1994	1432
159 6/8	23 0/8	22 0/8	19 2/8	5	5	Carbon County	WY	Glen H. Burns	1995	1432
159 6/8	23 4/8	20 4/8	21 0/8	5	5	Jerome County	ID	John Wells, Jr.	1996	1432
159 6/8	20 1/8	22 1/8	19 4/8	5	5	Converse County	WY	Gene Mathias	2001	1432
159 6/8	20 2/8	20 7/8	20 0/8	5	5	White Pine County	NV	Dolph Bowman, Jr.	2002	1432
159 6/8	23 1/8	21 5/8	19 2/8	5	5	Sheridan County	WY	Nathan Stiens	2003	1432
159 6/8	21 5/8	23 0/8	22 1/8	6	5	Ground Birch	BC	Darren Dunbar	2006	1432
*159 6/8	21 6/8	21 4/8	16 6/8	5	5	Carbon County	WY	Patrick Malone	2007	1432
159 5/8	22 7/8	22 5/8	25 3/8	5	5	Gove County	KS	Alan Kaiser	1986	1450
159 5/8	24 5/8	23 6/8	20 1/8	7	6	Crook County	OR	Kent Gutches	1991	1450
159 5/8	21 5/8	23 3/8	22 7/8	5	5	Milk River	ALB	Charles W. Rehor	2004	1450
159 5/8	24 0/8	24 0/8	20 5/8	7	5	Johnson County	WY	Craig Grant	2005	1450
*159 5/8	21 5/8	20 6/8	19 5/8	5	5	El Paso County	CO	Brandon Schawe	2008	1450
159 4/8	20 5/8	21 0/8	17 6/8	5	5	Franklin County	ID	Curtis Henderson	1992	1455
159 4/8	21 7/8	21 1/8	22 0/8	5	6	Grant County	OR	Bill Hueckman	1993	1455
159 4/8	23 1/8	23 6/8	21 6/8	5	5	Elbert County	CO	Jason Dirscherl	1995	1455
159 4/8	23 0/8	23 6/8	22 2/8	5	5	McKenzie County	ND	Michael Wavra	1999	1455
159 4/8	22 2/8	23 4/8	26 1/8	5	5	Rio Arriba County	NM	Daniel G. Willems	2000	1455
159 4/8	21 2/8	21 4/8	22 2/8	5	5	Blairmore	ALB	Kevin Williams	2000	1455
159 4/8	22 6/8	22 3/8	20 3/8	6	5	Campbell County	WY	Mark Johnson	2003	1455
159 4/8	16 7/8	19 7/8	19 4/8	5	5	Campbell County	WY	Gary Roney	2004	1455
159 4/8	20 4/8	21 4/8	23 6/8	6	5	Carbon County	WY	Zach Herold	2006	1455
159 4/8	22 5/8	23 7/8	23 0/8	5	5	Uintah County	UT	Jim Winjum	2008	1455
159 4/8	20 6/8	22 4/8	15 4/8	5	5	Big Horn County	WY	Chuck Sullivan	2009	1455
159 4/8	22 7/8	24 5/8	18 4/8	5	5	Sheridan County	WY	Mike Barrett	2009	1455
159 3/8	21 1/8	20 4/8	16 5/8	4	4	Millard County	UT	Dean Todd	1956	1467
159 3/8	22 4/8	22 7/8	18 4/8	5	5	Wasco County	OR	Bill Neary	1966	1467
159 3/8	22 1/8	21 4/8	19 1/8	4	4	Adams County	NE	Virgil Vaughn	1995	1467
159 3/8	22 2/8	22 1/8	20 3/8	5	4	Kiowa County	CO	Mike Edwards	1996	1467
159 3/8	22 3/8	22 5/8	20 7/8	5	5	Johnson County	WY	Richard A. Tesch	1997	1467
159 3/8	21 3/8	20 5/8	22 0/8	5	5	Goshen County	WY	Matt Burrows	1999	1467
159 3/8	22 7/8	24 3/8	23 3/8	5	5	Salt Lake County	UT	Joe Bruscato	2001	1467
159 3/8	22 1/8	22 0/8	23 7/8	4	5	Elmore County	ID	David R. Kooch	2002	1467
159 3/8	22 5/8	21 4/8	19 7/8	5	5	Gilpin County	CO	Scott Powers	2003	1467
159 3/8	23 4/8	23 6/8	23 0/8	6	5	Medicine Hat	ALB	Mike Barrett	2004	1467
*159 3/8	22 3/8	18 4/8	20 0/8	6	5	Oyen	ALB	Rod Shepley	2005	1467
159 2/8	21 1/8	20 4/8	17 2/8	5	5	Garfield County	CO	Robert Pitt	1978	1478
159 2/8	19 6/8	20 0/8	17 6/8	4	4	Crook County	WY	Mark L. Shumate	1986	1478
159 2/8	22 2/8	22 7/8	18 0/8	6	6	Converse County	WY	Rick L. Morley	1996	1478
*159 2/8	24 2/8	23 3/8	26 3/8	5	5	Pima County	AZ	Michael A. Elmer	2004	1478
159 2/8	23 6/8	23 0/8	24 2/8	6	6	Haakon County	SD	Matt Donnelly	2004	1478
159 2/8	22 2/8	22 5/8	22 2/8	5	4	Phillips County	KS	Christopher Whitney	2004	1478
159 1/8	22 6/8	21 6/8	20 5/8	5	7	Garfield County	CO	Jack Peters	1963	1484
159 1/8	23 0/8	23 2/8	18 7/8	4	5	Garfield County	CO	Donald J. Walsh	1977	1484
159 1/8	21 1/8	22 0/8	20 7/8	5	5	White Pine County	NV	Steve Wood	1978	1484
159 1/8	25 6/8	26 2/8	27 5/8	5	7	Maricopa County	AZ	George Toot	1980	1484
159 1/8	24 0/8	22 7/8	20 5/8	5	5	Clear Creek County	CO	Dave Skiff	1982	1484
159 1/8	17 5/8	19 3/8	19 4/8	4	4	Jefferson County	CO	Calvin Farner	1986	1484
*159 1/8	22 7/8	23 5/8	21 5/8	5	5	Deschutes County	OR	John Stone	2007	1484
159 1/8	22 6/8	20 7/8	18 3/8	5	5	Willow Creek	ALB	James Nichols Gray, Jr.	2008	1484
*159 1/8	22 1/8	20 5/8	20 2/8	5	6	Weld County	CO	Derek Foster	2009	1484
159 0/8	24 4/8	24 3/8	22 6/8	4	4	Elko County	NV	Bill L. Conn	1971	1493
159 0/8	22 3/8	21 2/8	25 2/8	5	5	Ada County	ID	Deloy Desaro	1973	1493
159 0/8	20 6/8	21 1/8	17 1/8	5	6	Montrose County	CO	David M. Gant	1977	1493
159 0/8	21 3/8	22 7/8	22 2/8	6	5	San Juan County	CO	Dennis Atwater	1978	1493
159 0/8	22 4/8	22 6/8	19 6/8	5	5	Lincoln County	MT	Christopher C. Crooks	1991	1493
159 0/8	22 7/8	23 3/8	19 2/8	5	5	Rio Arriba County	NM	Matthew Quintana	1994	1493
159 0/8	22 3/8	21 4/8	17 2/8	5	5	Rio Arriba County	NM	Eudane Vicenti	2002	1493
*159 0/8	22 7/8	22 7/8	23 3/8	6	6	Hanna	ALB	David M. Bufkin	2006	1493
159 0/8	24 4/8	22 6/8	24 4/8	4	4	Sonora	MEX	Carol Kindred	2007	1493
158 7/8	20 1/8	19 7/8	22 1/8	5	5	Sevier County	UT	Mike Otten	1973	1502
158 7/8	21 2/8	22 6/8	21 7/8	5	5	Elmore County	ID	Peter J Cintorino	1981	1502
158 7/8	20 4/8	19 4/8	21 4/8	5	6	Carbon County	WY	Daniel S. Christie	1982	1502
158 7/8	22 7/8	22 2/8	17 0/8	5	5	Klamath County	OR	Harold McCraven	1986	1502
158 7/8	21 7/8	22 0/8	17 5/8	5	5	Chase County	NE	John F. Burke	1987	1502
158 7/8	24 6/8	26 3/8	24 0/8	5	5	Yavapai County	AZ	Wally Schwartz	1989	1502
158 7/8	22 2/8	21 4/8	21 5/8	6	5	La Plata County	CO	Michael R. Hinson	1989	1502
158 7/8	20 0/8	21 4/8	18 1/8	5	6	Logan County	KS	James Beougher	1989	1502
158 7/8	23 2/8	23 5/8	22 3/8	6	6	Crystal Springs	ALB	James R. Godlonton	1993	1502
158 7/8	24 4/8	25 1/8	19 3/8	5	4	Baker County	OR	Bill Swoyer	2006	1502
158 6/8	21 3/8	22 3/8	22 0/8	5	5	Lake County	OR	Lyle Reeder	1954	1512
158 6/8	21 6/8	20 7/8	17 0/8	6	4	Stacy	MT	Dewey Olsen	1960	1512
158 6/8	21 1/8	20 7/8	22 0/8	4	5	Platte County	WY	Jerry Bowen	1987	1512
158 6/8	22 3/8	23 3/8	20 4/8	4	4	Lassen County	CA	David Gallegos	1988	1512
158 6/8	19 5/8	19 1/8	19 0/8	5	5	Campbell County	WY	Richard Hettinga	1990	1512
158 6/8	21 5/8	20 7/8	21 2/8	5	5	Malheur County	OR	Steve C. Scott	1992	1512
158 6/8	20 5/8	20 2/8	17 0/8	5	5	Cypress	ALB	Dan David	1993	1512
158 6/8	22 1/8	23 0/8	19 6/8	4	5	Albany County	WY	Jerry Bowen	1994	1512
158 6/8	21 1/8	22 1/8	20 3/8	6	5	Prowers County	CO	Randy Wright	1994	1512

323

MULE DEER (TYPICAL ANTLERS)

Minimum Score 145 — Continued

SCORE	LENGTH OF R MAIN BEAM L	INSIDE SPREAD	NUMBER OF R POINTS L	AREA	STATE/ PROVINCE	HUNTER'S NAME	DATE	RANK
158 6/8	20 2/8 20 2/8	19 0/8	5 5	McKenzie County	ND	Andy Leer	2006	1512
158 6/8	22 0/8 23 2/8	19 4/8	5 5	Coutts	ALB	Cody Spencer	2009	1512
*158 6/8	21 1/8 21 7/8	21 7/8	4 5	Grand County	UT	Joseph Kinney	2010	1512
158 5/8	22 2/8 22 5/8	18 1/8	6 6	Weber County	UT	Bruce N. Moss	1974	1524
158 5/8	22 1/8 22 3/8	18 5/8	6 5	Hodgeman County	KS	Ron Adams	1985	1524
158 5/8	21 7/8 20 7/8	17 6/8	6 5	Morton County	KS	Kevin E. White	1987	1524
158 5/8	21 3/8 22 5/8	21 5/8	5 5	Rio Arriba County	NM	Eudane Vicenti	1995	1524
158 5/8	27 2/8 25 5/8	21 3/8	6 5	Mesa County	CO	Mark Boarman	1996	1524
158 5/8	20 7/8 20 2/8	18 7/8	5 6	Airdrie	ALB	Garth D. Bruneau	2000	1524
158 5/8	21 3/8 21 5/8	17 7/8	5 5	Albany County	WY	Mark L. Nelson	2002	1524
158 5/8	23 1/8 23 7/8	22 5/8	5 6	Yuma County	CO	Mike Barrett	2002	1524
158 5/8	20 3/8 23 1/8	19 5/8	5 5	Wallowa County	OR	Roderick Mosman	2003	1524
158 5/8	23 4/8 23 3/8	25 0/8	7 6	Kiowa County	CO	Bo Clark	2004	1524
158 5/8	22 5/8 19 7/8	17 3/8	5 5	Bow River	ALB	Blake Howland	2005	1524
*158 5/8	22 6/8 23 4/8	21 7/8	5 5	Rosebud County	MT	Danny Felts	2010	1524
158 4/8	23 3/8 23 6/8	22 6/8	4 4	Albany County	WY	Nelson W. Brower	1979	1536
158 4/8	21 0/8 19 6/8	18 2/8	5 5	Greeley County	KS	Keith Foster	1981	1536
158 4/8	20 0/8 20 3/8	15 4/8	5 5	Lane County	KS	Hurley T. Smith	1982	1536
158 4/8	24 2/8 23 2/8	18 4/8	5 4	Garfield County	CO	Orvie E. Linsin	1989	1536
158 4/8	19 5/8 18 5/8	18 4/8	6 6	Maricopa County	AZ	Lawrence Drake	1992	1536
158 4/8	22 1/8 20 2/8	19 2/8	5 5	Douglas County	CO	Kenneth H. Karbon	1992	1536
158 4/8	24 0/8 22 7/8	30 2/8	5 5	Ada County	ID	Robert D. Dower	1992	1536
158 4/8	20 7/8 23 0/8	16 4/8	5 4	Lincoln County	WA	Chris Lesher	1995	1536
*158 4/8	20 6/8 20 1/8	20 4/8	4 4	Billings County	ND	Kenneth A. Osmer	2003	1536
158 4/8	22 2/8 23 0/8	19 6/8	5 4	Billings County	ND	Wayne Yocum, Jr.	2004	1536
158 4/8	20 4/8 21 4/8	20 0/8	5 5	Laramie County	WY	Rick Parish	2008	1536
158 3/8	25 1/8 21 1/8	20 1/8	6 5	Sheridan County	NE	Gerald J. McKinney	1974	1547
158 3/8	24 5/8 24 2/8	21 3/8	4 6	Ada County	ID	Robert E. Stauts	1979	1547
158 3/8	22 5/8 23 3/8	20 1/8	4 5	Mesa County	CO	James C. Kennedy	1995	1547
158 3/8	26 5/8 24 7/8	26 5/8	4 5	La Plata County	CO	Terry Grimes	2004	1547
158 3/8	22 0/8 22 6/8	18 3/8	4 5	Dunn County	ND	Scott L. Sprenger	2007	1547
*158 3/8	23 0/8 23 5/8	22 4/8	6 5	Sioux County	NE	James L. Skinner, Jr.	2008	1547
158 2/8	23 4/8 19 3/8	21 4/8	6 4	Caribou County	ID	Gary L. Vaughn	1969	1553
158 2/8	23 4/8 22 1/8	20 0/8	6 7	Gosper County	NE	Johnny Hemelstrand	1972	1553
158 2/8	19 7/8 20 1/8	19 2/8	5 5	Las Animas County	CO	Byron E. Brown	1984	1553
158 2/8	21 2/8 21 2/8	20 0/8	6 5	Butte County	ID	Gene Fitzgerald	1985	1553
158 2/8	22 6/8 22 6/8	19 5/8	6 5	Pinal County	AZ	Mark Ovitt	1990	1553
158 2/8	23 0/8 22 4/8	23 0/8	5 5	Billings County	ND	Mark Buehrer	1990	1553
158 2/8	20 4/8 22 3/8	19 4/8	5 4	McKenzie County	ND	Terry Sivertson	1991	1553
158 2/8	23 0/8 23 0/8	15 7/8	6 5	Washington County	CO	Larry Wagner	1993	1553
158 2/8	24 2/8 23 1/8	23 7/8	6 8	Caribou County	ID	Ronald Dye	1994	1553
158 2/8	20 7/8 22 5/8	22 0/8	4 5	Ada County	ID	Charlie B. Perry	2000	1553
158 2/8	25 0/8 23 3/8	22 6/8	4 5	Sublette County	WY	Brett I. Ritter	2001	1553
*158 2/8	21 2/8 19 5/8	19 2/8	5 5	Coconino County	AZ	Robert V. Mitchell	2007	1553
158 1/8	20 7/8 20 0/8	18 3/8	5 5		UT	Gordon Young	1963	1565
158 1/8	21 0/8 22 3/8	24 0/8	6 6	Rio Blanco County	CO	Jerry R. Bowen	1970	1565
158 1/8	21 2/8 20 6/8	18 3/8	5 5	Mesa County	CO	David H. Boland	1978	1565
158 1/8	20 6/8 20 3/8	17 7/8	5 4	Texas County	OK	J. Alva Hammond	1981	1565
158 1/8	21 4/8 21 6/8	18 5/8	5 5	Boulder County	CO	Mike Miller	1987	1565
158 1/8	21 5/8 21 7/8	21 3/8	5 5	Osborne County	KS	Blaine Parrott	1989	1565
158 1/8	21 5/8 21 1/8	18 2/8	5 6	Converse County	WY	James Saunoris	1991	1565
158 1/8	23 5/8 23 0/8	18 5/8	5 5	Moffat County	CO	Kieth Hardy	1991	1565
158 1/8	22 6/8 24 4/8	28 0/8	8 5	Lane County	KS	Dean Hamilton	1991	1565
158 1/8	21 0/8 22 0/8	21 5/8	5 5	Jefferson County	CO	Jerry L. Grueneberg	1992	1565
158 1/8	21 7/8 21 0/8	19 1/8	5 6	Culberson County	TX	Gary J. Oden	1992	1565
*158 1/8	23 0/8 21 4/8	20 7/8	5 5	Calgary	ALB	Ron R. Maguire	2003	1565
158 1/8	22 2/8 22 2/8	19 5/8	5 5	Brooks	ALB	Bret Scott	2004	1565
158 1/8	18 2/8 20 7/8	20 3/8	4 4	Spruce Grove	ALB	Randy Kottke	2005	1565
158 1/8	23 1/8 20 7/8	18 1/8	5 5	Lacombe	ALB	Steve McKenzie	2005	1565
158 0/8	21 4/8 21 0/8	21 4/8	7 7	Golden Valley County	ND	Bob Ross	1959	1580
158 0/8	22 2/8 23 3/8	21 2/8	5 5	Owyhee County	ID	R. W. McIntire	1961	1580
158 0/8	25 4/8 24 4/8	24 4/8	3 3	Garfield County	CO	Jimmy R. Speer	1970	1580
158 0/8	21 7/8 22 6/8	19 2/8	5 5	Mesa County	CO	Matt Spohnhauer	1975	1580
158 0/8	24 7/8 24 1/8	21 0/8	6 7	Elbert County	CO	Quince Hale	1989	1580
158 0/8	23 5/8 23 0/8	22 6/8	5 5	Rosebud County	MT	Irvin May	1990	1580
158 0/8	21 3/8 21 1/8	17 0/8	6 5	Rosebud County	MT	Chuck Adams	1996	1580
158 0/8	20 6/8 22 1/8	18 5/8	6 5	Sheridan County	WY	Chris Apel	1997	1580
158 0/8	22 5/8 23 6/8	21 6/8	4 4	Harney County	OR	Paul G. Okita	1998	1580
158 0/8	20 2/8 20 3/8	20 2/8	4 4	Boise County	ID	Gary Gapp	1998	1580
158 0/8	22 4/8 22 3/8	17 0/8	5 5	Valley County	ID	Jim Akenson	2001	1580
158 0/8	23 2/8 23 2/8	23 2/8	6 7	Hanna	ALB	Dewayne Mullins	2002	1580
158 0/8	23 7/8 18 6/8	22 2/8	5 5	El Paso County	CO	Peter Dozois	2003	1580
158 0/8	21 5/8 22 6/8	19 6/8	5 5	Rosebud County	MT	James F. Hirrlinger	2007	1580
157 7/8	23 6/8 24 0/8	21 3/8	4 5	Rio Arriba County	NM	Larry Wright	1972	1594
157 7/8	20 2/8 22 2/8	22 5/8	5 6	Owyhee County	ID	Duane Zemliska	1985	1594
157 7/8	21 6/8 22 0/8	21 4/8	5 6	Mesa County	CO	Jerol W. Vaughn	1985	1594
157 7/8	20 7/8 21 2/8	19 2/8	6 7	Jackson County	CO	Vance E Phelps II	1989	1594
157 7/8	22 6/8 22 6/8	21 3/8	5 5	Culberson County	TX	Gary J. Oden	1989	1594
157 7/8	19 7/8 19 6/8	18 3/8	5 5	Billings County	ND	Terry Buechler	1991	1594
157 7/8	21 0/8 22 5/8	16 5/8	7 6	Harris	SAS	Joe Schmidt	1994	1594
157 7/8	21 6/8 21 6/8	24 1/8	5 6	Coaldale	ALB	Doug Doram	1994	1594
157 7/8	21 5/8 22 3/8	21 0/8	6 5	Trego County	KS	Kent Hensley	1994	1594
157 7/8	22 4/8 23 0/8	23 7/8	7 7	La Plata County	CO	Larry D. Mead	1998	1594
157 7/8	21 1/8 21 5/8	21 5/8	5 5	Converse County	WY	Jim Van Norman	2002	1594
157 7/8	23 0/8 23 1/8	20 1/8	4 5	Edgerton	ALB	Shane Mascarin	2005	1594
157 7/8	22 6/8 21 1/8	20 4/8	6 5	Baker County	OR	Dale Mack	2008	1594
157 6/8	23 7/8 23 4/8	23 7/8	6 6	Owyhee County	ID	Roland Duram	1964	1607
157 6/8	22 5/8 23 3/8	21 0/8	5 5	Mesa County	CO	Terry J. Gerber	1976	1607
157 6/8	21 6/8 21 4/8	22 6/8	5 5	Elmore County	ID	Harold Lefler	1981	1607
157 6/8	20 4/8 23 2/8	19 0/8	4 4	Archuleta County	CO	Bryan Rumbo	1989	1607
157 6/8	19 0/8 19 3/8	19 3/8	6 5	Converse County	WY	Jerry Miller	1992	1607
157 6/8	22 0/8 20 0/8	18 4/8	5 6	Grant County	OR	Phil Grunert	1995	1607
157 6/8	22 2/8 22 3/8	21 0/8	5 6	Manyberries	ALB	Michael R. Deschamps	1995	1607
157 6/8	19 0/8 19 5/8	16 4/8	5 5	Natrona County	WY	Casey Middleton	1998	1607
*157 6/8	20 1/8 20 0/8	21 4/8	7 5	Cochrane	ALB	Eric R. Smith	2004	1607

324

MULE DEER (TYPICAL ANTLERS)

Minimum Score 145 — Continued

SCORE	LENGTH OF R MAIN BEAM L	INSIDE SPREAD	NUMBER OF R POINTS L	AREA	STATE/ PROVINCE	HUNTER'S NAME	DATE	RANK
157 6/8	20 5/8	19 7/8	18 0/8	5	5	Salt Lake County	UT	Rich Brunt	2005	1607
157 6/8	24 6/8	24 4/8	21 0/8	5	5	Hooker County	NE	Andrew L. Glidden	2007	1607
157 6/8	22 4/8	23 5/8	22 6/8	6	5	El Rancho Carriva	MEX	Walter J. Palmer	2009	1607
157 6/8	19 6/8	21 5/8	24 4/8	5	5	Owyhee County	ID	Fred Audette	1960	1619
157 5/8	19 6/8	20 0/8	18 3/8	5	5	Montezuma County	CO	Marvin Reichenau	1973	1619
157 5/8	20 3/8	21 2/8	18 0/8	6	5	Rawlins County	KS	Richard Jones	1979	1619
157 5/8	24 1/8	23 4/8	21 7/8	5	5	Washoe County	NV	Donald J. Taysom	1984	1619
157 5/8	23 6/8	24 1/8	20 3/8	9	5	Cheyenne County	KS	Chet Gardner	1984	1619
157 5/8	23 0/8	22 3/8	20 5/8	4	4	McKinley County	NM	Frank Hausner	1991	1619
157 5/8	23 6/8	24 5/8	26 5/8	5	5	Maricopa County	AZ	William L. Tuvell	1992	1619
157 5/8	21 0/8	21 6/8	19 4/8	6	5	Elko County	NV	Bob Sneed	1997	1619
157 5/8	25 2/8	16 0/8	23 3/8	5	5	Las Animas County	CO	Lon E. Lauber	1999	1619
157 5/8	21 1/8	21 5/8	19 3/8	6	5	Natrona County	WY	Steve Schulz	2001	1619
157 5/8	22 1/8	22 3/8	19 3/8	5	5	Sonora	MEX	Dwight S. Wolf	2002	1619
157 5/8	22 7/8	23 5/8	23 0/8	6	8	Harney County	OR	Jason Radinovich	2006	1619
157 5/8	21 3/8	21 2/8	16 3/8	5	5	Cheyenne County	KS	John Hastert	2006	1619
157 5/8	23 6/8	25 0/8	23 7/8	4	5	San Juan County	NM	Charlie Schlosser	2009	1619
157 4/8	23 1/8	23 3/8	23 2/8	5	6	Grand County	UT	Dean Caldwell	1960	1633
157 4/8	22 2/8	22 4/8	19 4/8	5	5	Garfield County	CO	Bob Gulman	1966	1633
157 4/8	18 5/8	19 2/8	16 0/8	4	4	Bernalillo County	NM	William R. Johnson	1969	1633
157 4/8	22 1/8	20 2/8	21 0/8	5	6	Carter County	MT	Edward Susa	1983	1633
157 4/8	22 3/8	23 5/8	20 6/8	5	5	Mesa County	CO	Paul H. Dickson	1986	1633
157 4/8	21 4/8	21 0/8	19 2/8	5	5	Powder River County	MT	Mark L. Frank	1989	1633
157 4/8	22 0/8	23 7/8	21 7/8	5	6	Yavapai County	AZ	Greg Allen Huyett	1993	1633
157 4/8	22 4/8	21 1/8	21 0/8	5	5	Pennington County	SD	Gary Buckley	1993	1633
157 4/8	21 4/8	22 0/8	18 4/8	5	5	Powell County	MT	Marlon Clapham	1995	1633
157 4/8	24 7/8	25 3/8	20 4/8	4	5	Morgan County	UT	Poncho McCoy	2001	1633
157 4/8	22 6/8	21 6/8	19 5/8	5	6	Sonora	MEX	Dwight S. Wolf	2004	1633
*157 4/8	23 6/8	23 7/8	19 0/8	4	5	Jefferson County	CO	Michael Desmarteau	2004	1633
157 4/8	21 4/8	20 5/8	17 6/8	5	5	Sheridan County	NE	Arthur Cain	2008	1633
157 4/8	21 5/8	23 2/8	17 5/8	5	6	Jackson County	SD	Sean C. Fulton	2008	1633
157 3/8	26 2/8	26 0/8	21 2/8	7	6	Sevier County	UT	Dale Gardner	1958	1647
157 3/8	21 6/8	20 0/8	20 0/8	6	6	Routt County	CO	Bing Kemp	1966	1647
157 3/8	24 1/8	24 1/8	23 3/8	6	7	Montrose County	CO	James A. Davison	1984	1647
157 3/8	17 4/8	19 0/8	16 3/8	5	5	Albany County	WY	Paul Ayotte	1985	1647
157 3/8	21 0/8	21 0/8	20 5/8	5	5	Caribou County	ID	Gary Hunt	1986	1647
157 3/8	22 1/8	22 7/8	17 7/8	6	5	Cypress	ALB	Mike Maloney	1991	1647
157 3/8	23 5/8	23 2/8	25 6/8	4	5	Rawlins County	KS	Craig Doll	1994	1647
157 3/8	22 6/8	23 0/8	19 5/8	5	5	Catron County	NM	Richard V. Gray	1999	1647
157 3/8	18 6/8	21 5/8	19 5/8	5	5	Meade County	SD	Edwin L. DeYoung	2004	1647
157 3/8	22 4/8	22 5/8	20 3/8	5	5	Weld County	CO	Reggie Spiegelberg	2005	1647
157 2/8	22 5/8	21 4/8	20 6/8	6	6	McKenzie County	ND	Roy Mitten	1956	1657
157 2/8	21 5/8	21 4/8	16 4/8	5	5	Bernalillo County	NM	Robert F. Knight	1970	1657
157 2/8	24 4/8	24 2/8	20 1/8	6	5	Wheeler County	OR	Darrell J. Scheffer	1990	1657
157 2/8	20 2/8	22 3/8	22 6/8	4	5	Bear Lake County	ID	Daved E. English	1991	1657
157 2/8	22 5/8	22 7/8	18 0/8	7	5	Sioux County	NE	Jerry Overstreet	1993	1657
157 2/8	21 3/8	21 3/8	21 2/8	5	5	Catron County	NM	Tony Burrola, Jr.	1999	1657
157 2/8	21 4/8	22 3/8	18 6/8	5	5	Larimer County	CO	Charlie Hicks	2004	1657
157 2/8	20 4/8	21 4/8	16 0/8	5	6	Baker County	OR	DeLoy Desaro	2008	1657
*157 2/8	25 3/8	25 6/8	26 0/8	6	7	Rosebud County	MT	Jeffrey Lee	2008	1657
157 2/8	22 7/8	23 1/8	19 4/8	5	5	Meade County	SD	Gary English	2009	1657
157 2/8	23 6/8	23 5/8	25 2/8	4	4	La Paz County	AZ	Jack Smith	2010	1657
157 1/8	22 0/8	23 4/8	23 3/8	6	4	Harney County	OR	Gary Soeth	1980	1668
157 1/8	23 6/8	23 3/8	20 7/8	6	7	Boise County	ID	Gary Kinney	1981	1668
157 1/8	21 4/8	21 6/8	20 5/8	5	5	Clear Creek County	CO	Janet Schreur	1987	1668
157 1/8	21 5/8	21 1/8	19 0/8	5	7	Calgary	ALB	Stuart Sinclair-Smith	1987	1668
157 1/8	23 0/8	20 7/8	21 6/8	5	6	Meade County	KS	Randy Blehm	1989	1668
157 1/8	21 1/8	20 4/8	16 3/8	5	5	Boyd County	NE	Glenn T. Zink	1990	1668
157 1/8	22 2/8	21 7/8	19 5/8	5	5	Campbell County	WY	David Westmoreland	1994	1668
157 1/8	23 4/8	23 5/8	20 2/8	5	6	Gove County	KS	Joshua Hoeme	1997	1668
157 1/8	21 4/8	22 7/8	22 7/8	5	5	Magrath	ALB	Cameron Cook	1997	1668
157 1/8	20 7/8	20 2/8	19 1/8	5	5	Coconino County	AZ	Roy E. Grace	2003	1668
157 1/8	18 5/8	20 4/8	18 5/8	5	5	Cascade County	MT	Timothy Carter	2007	1668
157 0/8	21 4/8	21 5/8	18 0/8	5	5	Mesa County	CO	Robert O. Bash	1976	1679
157 0/8	22 6/8	21 4/8	16 0/8	5	5	Lassen County	CA	Tom McMurphy	1977	1679
157 0/8	21 6/8	20 3/8	18 6/8	5	5	Lane County	KS	Dean Hamilton	1978	1679
157 0/8	21 4/8	20 7/8	16 5/8	6	6	Deer Lodge County	MT	Mike Softich	1981	1679
157 0/8	23 7/8	23 7/8	18 6/8	4	4	Clackamas County	OR	Thomas L. Carter	1984	1679
157 0/8	21 4/8	21 1/8	23 3/8	5	6	Baker County	OR	Chuck Warner	1988	1679
157 0/8	22 4/8	23 1/8	20 0/8	5	6	Pennington County	SD	Tim J. Hoeck	1990	1679
157 0/8	20 5/8	22 3/8	21 6/8	5	5	Ada County	ID	Robert Dowen	1994	1679
157 0/8	23 3/8	22 7/8	23 0/8	5	5	Rosebud County	MT	Chuck Adams	1998	1679
157 0/8	22 1/8	23 0/8	25 2/8	5	4	Lake County	OR	Mike Slinkard	1999	1679
157 0/8	20 5/8	20 5/8	19 6/8	5	5	Campbell County	WY	Gary Roney	2001	1679
157 0/8	22 4/8	22 1/8	23 1/8	4	4	Cochrane	ALB	Eric R. Smith	2002	1679
157 0/8	22 4/8	22 6/8	18 4/8	5	5	Jones County	SD	Auston J. Butt	2009	1679
156 7/8	24 3/8	24 0/8	23 2/8	4	4	Garfield County	CO	John Lamicq, Jr.	1966	1692
156 7/8	20 2/8	20 2/8	19 2/8	4	4	Rio Blanco County	CO	George David Epperson	1983	1692
156 7/8	23 5/8	21 6/8	21 7/8	5	5	McKenzie County	ND	Steve Rehak	1985	1692
156 7/8	21 4/8	20 2/8	15 7/8	5	5	Teller County	CO	Butch Smerkonich	1985	1692
156 7/8	23 2/8	22 3/8	21 2/8	6	5	Chelan County	WA	Brian Kayler	1985	1692
156 7/8	25 3/8	22 7/8	22 3/8	5	5	Laramie County	WY	Duane Christensen	1991	1692
156 7/8	22 1/8	21 4/8	20 7/8	4	5	Fort St. John	BC	Steven W. Hiebert	1992	1692
156 7/8	25 2/8	23 4/8	19 3/8	6	5	Harney County	OR	Terry D. Brumley	1994	1692
156 7/8	24 3/8	25 1/8	26 2/8	4	4	Brooks	ALB	Bruce T. Saunders	1995	1692
156 7/8	21 3/8	22 0/8	16 7/8	5	5	Slope County	ND	Jon Brewer	1996	1692
156 7/8	21 7/8	22 1/8	19 5/8	6	6	Converse County	WY	Jack Dilts	1996	1692
156 7/8	19 7/8	19 4/8	19 7/8	6	6	Eagle Hill	ALB	Dallas Kaiser	1999	1692
156 7/8	21 4/8	20 6/8	18 5/8	5	5	Lyman County	SD	Jody J. Marcks	2004	1692
156 7/8	21 2/8	22 2/8	22 1/8	5	5	Meade County	SD	Jim Van Stensel	2007	1692
156 6/8	23 2/8	24 2/8	20 0/8	6	6	Uintah County	UT	Terry Peck	1964	1706
156 6/8	22 5/8	22 6/8	19 4/8	5	5	Mesa County	CO	Ed Meyer	1967	1706
156 6/8	21 6/8	22 6/8	23 4/8	5	6	Wallowa County	OR	Randy Hopp	1979	1706
156 6/8	22 0/8	22 0/8	22 1/8	5	6	Routt County	CO	Moulton Larmay	1981	1706
156 6/8	24 0/8	22 7/8	25 0/8	6	6	Lane County	KS	Dean Hamilton	1982	1706

325

MULE DEER (TYPICAL ANTLERS)

Minimum Score 145   Continued

SCORE	LENGTH OF R MAIN BEAM L		INSIDE SPREAD	NUMBER OF R POINTS L		AREA	STATE/ PROVINCE	HUNTER'S NAME	DATE	RANK
156 6/8	23 2/8	22 2/8	18 4/8	4	5	Kittitas County	WA	Rich Carnahan	1982	1706
156 6/8	22 5/8	24 1/8	19 6/8	5	5	Garfield County	CO	Perry Trujillo	1983	1706
156 6/8	23 7/8	22 6/8	22 0/8	4	4	Lemhi County	ID	Glen Palmer	1988	1706
156 6/8	20 5/8	20 6/8	19 2/8	5	5	Weld County	CO	Dale Elliott	1991	1706
156 6/8	23 1/8	25 0/8	20 6/8	4	5	Nevada County	CA	Stan Boyer	1995	1706
156 6/8	19 7/8	20 2/8	21 5/8	5	5	Greenlee County	AZ	Eddie Claypool	1996	1706
156 6/8	20 6/8	20 6/8	23 2/8	5	5	Siskiyou County	CA	Brian E. Neuschafer	1997	1706
*156 6/8	23 6/8	21 3/8	21 4/8	5	5	Bow River	ALB	Blake Howland	2007	1706
156 5/8	21 2/8	21 3/8	20 3/8	5	5	Slope County	ND	Vern R. Keim	1959	1719
156 5/8	20 1/8	21 1/8	22 3/8	5	5	Rio Blanco County	CO	Jim Pickering	1966	1719
156 5/8	20 0/8	21 6/8	18 6/8	6	6	Larimer County	CO	Leslie McKenzie	1970	1719
156 5/8	21 7/8	21 0/8	19 3/8	7	6	Lower Arrow Lake	BC	Gerald Bond	1983	1719
156 5/8	20 7/8	18 5/8	18 6/8	6	5	Caribou County	ID	Michael Aldrich	1984	1719
156 5/8	23 4/8	23 5/8	20 4/8	5	6	Writing On Stone Park	ALB	Ryan Krampl/John Krampl	1994	1719
156 5/8	21 1/8	21 2/8	17 1/8	4	5	Lemhi County	ID	John Bennett	1995	1719
156 5/8	19 1/8	21 1/8	19 7/8	4	5	Twin Falls County	ID	Darrell Nunez	2002	1719
156 5/8	21 5/8	20 1/8	17 5/8	5	5	Tooele County	UT	Randy J. Walk	2004	1719
156 4/8	21 7/8	22 1/8	22 0/8	5	4	Weston County	WY	Thomas L. A. Pucci	1956	1728
156 4/8	20 0/8	20 0/8	19 2/8	5	5	Owyhee County	ID	Bill Leisi	1961	1728
156 4/8	22 2/8	24 2/8	20 3/8	4	5	Summit County	UT	Richard Douglass	1964	1728
156 4/8	23 1/8	21 4/8	20 4/8	4	4	Elko County	NV	Paul Dinan	1968	1728
156 4/8	23 1/8	20 7/8	19 2/8	4	4	Chouteau County	MT	Michael R. Buesse er	1971	1728
156 4/8	20 7/8	21 3/8	22 5/8	5	6	Gunnison County	CO	Jim Jarvis	1974	1728
156 4/8	22 5/8	23 6/8	21 4/8	5	5	Campbell County	WY	James P. Smith	1983	1728
156 4/8	22 0/8	20 6/8	18 4/8	5	5	Grant County	OR	Jeffrey A. Young	1986	1728
156 4/8	22 2/8	22 7/8	17 6/8	4	5	Humboldt County	NV	Monte D. Fuller	1988	1728
156 4/8	25 1/8	23 3/8	19 6/8	5	5	Boise County	ID	Kevin J.P. Stephenson	1988	1728
156 4/8	22 0/8	21 1/8	22 5/8	5	6	Coconino County	AZ	Michael Chase	1994	1728
156 4/8	25 2/8	25 0/8	21 4/8	4	4	Powder River County	MT	Paul T. Shore	1996	1728
156 4/8	21 0/8	21 6/8	20 2/8	4	4	Manyberries	ALB	Carl A. Miller	1999	1728
156 4/8	23 2/8	22 3/8	24 2/8	6	7	Malheur County	OR	Marshall Witty	2000	1728
156 4/8	19 4/8	20 0/8	18 0/8	5	5	Campbell County	WY	Calvin Taylor	2003	1728
156 4/8	21 0/8	20 5/8	18 6/8	5	5	Sweetwater County	WY	Michael G. Moeller	2003	1728
*156 4/8	20 1/8	19 6/8	14 0/8	5	5	Judith Basin County	MT	Mark D. Hartwig	2004	1728
156 4/8	24 2/8	20 7/8	22 4/8	5	5	Teller County	CO	Macky Myers	2006	1728
*156 4/8	22 7/8	23 0/8	23 5/8	5	5	Converse County	WY	Michael L. Ritter, Jr.	2007	1728
*156 4/8	18 7/8	20 4/8	16 6/8	5	5	Powder River County	MT	Shawn Wahl	2009	1728
156 4/8	22 4/8	23 2/8	17 6/8	5	7	Lomand	ALB	Ian Gazeley	2009	1728
*156 4/8	25 2/8	25 4/8	26 2/8	5	4	Jackson County	SD	Mark T. DeVries	2009	1728
*156 4/8	24 5/8	23 4/8	24 4/8	5	5	Coconino County	AZ	Lonnie Kesterson	2010	1728
156 3/8	21 6/8	22 6/8	25 0/8	5	6	Owyhee County	ID	Bill Kerr	1962	1751
156 3/8	25 5/8	24 6/8	23 5/8	3	3	Mohave County	AZ	Bill Cross	1963	1751
156 3/8	21 2/8	24 5/8	25 3/8	7	6	Lake County	OR	Orvil Winters	1965	1751
156 3/8	24 5/8	24 2/8	23 4/8	5	7	Cottle County	TX	Mike Ramage	1991	1751
156 3/8	21 2/8	21 5/8	20 5/8	5	5	Converse County	WY	Steve Williams	1993	1751
156 3/8	23 5/8	24 1/8	21 7/8	5	5	Colfax County	NM	Jerry Gallegos	1996	1751
156 3/8	22 2/8	23 0/8	21 5/8	5	5	Logan County	CO	Reggie Spiegelberg	2001	1751
156 3/8	22 3/8	25 0/8	20 3/8	4	5	Butte County	ID	Roudy K. Keller	2002	1751
156 3/8	22 6/8	22 2/8	20 7/8	5	5	Lincoln County	WA	David C. Hubbard	2003	1751
156 3/8	22 2/8	22 5/8	23 0/8	5	5	Campbell County	WY	Debbra S. Roney	2003	1751
156 3/8	21 0/8	20 6/8	20 5/8	5	5	Garfield County	CO	Dave Davis	2005	1751
156 3/8	24 6/8	24 7/8	24 3/8	4	4	Colfax County	NM	Joseph Landon Bell	2008	1751
*156 3/8	24 5/8	24 1/8	19 5/8	5	4	Albany County	WY	Jason McMahon	2010	1751
156 2/8	21 5/8	20 6/8	20 0/8	5	5	Mesa County	CO	Donald Aaron	1971	1764
156 2/8	20 5/8	20 2/8	19 2/8	5	5	Clark County	KS	Rod Lies	1976	1764
156 2/8	22 6/8	21 2/8	21 2/8	5	5	Eureka County	NV	David Sharpe	1990	1764
156 2/8	22 0/8	21 3/8	19 2/8	5	5	Minidoka County	ID	Steven Lee Morrison	1994	1764
156 2/8	23 1/8	23 0/8	19 4/8	4	5	Salt Lake County	UT	Jerry Dee Slaugh	1997	1764
156 2/8	25 2/8	26 0/8	21 1/8	7	6	Coconino County	AZ	Jim Machac	1997	1764
156 2/8	20 6/8	21 1/8	20 4/8	5	5	Dolores County	CO	Rick Mohr	1998	1764
156 2/8	24 1/8	21 6/8	21 7/8	6	7	Kane County	UT	Jay Foxworthy	2007	1764
156 2/8	20 6/8	20 4/8	16 7/8	6	7	Lincoln County	WY	Gavin Steve Lovell	2009	1764
156 1/8	20 6/8	20 7/8	20 2/8	5	6	Millard County	UT	Jerry White	1962	1773
156 1/8	25 1/8	25 6/8	18 5/8	5	5	Rio Arriba County	NM	Gary Isom	1985	1773
156 1/8	24 0/8	23 6/8	21 1/8	5	5	Billings County	ND	Jeff Strunk	1998	1773
156 1/8	22 4/8	22 3/8	18 7/8	4	5	Billings County	ND	Tom Fitch	1998	1773
156 1/8	20 5/8	21 1/8	16 7/8	5	5	Gallatin County	MT	Lance DeHaan	1999	1773
156 1/8	22 5/8	22 2/8	20 7/8	5	6	Harney County	OR	Kenneth B. Jenkins	2001	1773
*156 1/8	22 5/8	21 2/8	22 3/8	5	7	Yuma County	CO	Rodney A. Lindsten	2006	1773
156 1/8	22 3/8	22 3/8	20 3/8	5	5	Sheridan County	WY	Chris Boll	2009	1773
156 0/8	21 4/8	21 0/8	18 2/8	5	5	Iron County	UT	Ken McKnight	1966	1781
156 0/8	20 0/8	20 1/8	18 2/8	5	6	Chelan County	WA	Steve Gorr	1975	1781
156 0/8	22 1/8	20 7/8	18 6/8	5	5	Powder River County	MT	Dan Brockman	1986	1781
156 0/8	22 6/8	22 3/8	16 3/8	5	6	Drumheller	ALB	Stephen K. Wilton	1991	1781
156 0/8	21 4/8	21 6/8	19 2/8	4	4	Powder River County	MT	Eugene Arndt	1996	1781
156 0/8	21 3/8	20 7/8	18 0/8	5	5	Coconino County	AZ	Terry Hart	1998	1781
156 0/8	20 2/8	21 1/8	18 6/8	5	5	Milk River	ALB	Jason Spenst	1999	1781
156 0/8	21 5/8	24 5/8	19 0/8	5	5	Chelan County	WA	Dan L. Kohlman	1999	1781
156 0/8	21 3/8	21 4/8	17 2/8	7	6	Klickitat County	WA	Robert Richart	2000	1781
156 0/8	20 1/8	19 2/8	20 3/8	5	6	Salt Lake County	UT	Kirk L. Holt	2001	1781
156 0/8	22 6/8	22 7/8	22 4/8	4	6	Washakie County	WY	Michael A. Lee	2004	1781
156 0/8	24 7/8	24 2/8	19 4/8	5	5	Otero County	NM	C. Nathan Daugherty	2006	1781
156 0/8	22 6/8	23 2/8	19 2/8	4	4	Sheridan County	WY	Casey L. Dinkel	2008	1781
156 0/8	22 4/8	21 0/8	21 4/8	5	5	Vermilion	ALB	Brad Rieland	2008	1781
155 7/8	21 4/8	21 6/8	20 0/8	5	6	McKenzie County	ND	Mark E. Ferry	1981	1795
155 7/8	22 5/8	23 1/8	22 3/8	5	5	Caribou County	ID	Randy J. Stephens	1988	1795
155 7/8	24 1/8	21 0/8	27 4/8	5	5	San Juan County	NM	Curtis K. Owen	1994	1795
155 7/8	23 3/8	23 1/8	23 3/8	5	4	Powder River County	MT	Don G. Scofield	1996	1795
155 7/8	21 0/8	21 6/8	19 3/8	4	4	Big Horn County	WY	Russell Hookstead	2000	1795
155 7/8	24 5/8	24 5/8	25 4/8	4	4	Apache County	AZ	Bill VanBuskirk	2001	1795
155 7/8	22 4/8	20 6/8	16 6/8	5	7	Manyberries	ALB	Christopher J. Forbes	2002	1795
155 7/8	20 6/8	21 2/8	19 1/8	6	5	Ravalli County	MT	Bobby Rummel	2004	1795
*155 7/8	23 4/8	20 7/8	18 7/8	5	5	Walworth County	SD	Kurt VanRyswyk	2006	1795
155 7/8	20 0/8	20 6/8	16 5/8	4	4	Quappelle Valley	SAS	Matthew Hauser	2008	1795
155 6/8	24 1/8	24 1/8	22 0/8	3	4	Owyhee County	ID	Lynn Thomas	1960	1805

MULE DEER (TYPICAL ANTLERS)

Minimum Score 145 — Continued

SCORE	LENGTH OF R MAIN BEAM L	INSIDE SPREAD	NUMBER OF R POINTS L	AREA	STATE/ PROVINCE	HUNTER'S NAME	DATE	RANK
155 6/8	22 2/8 21 3/8	18 4/8	4 5	Garfield County	CO	Henery Jaman	1966	1805
155 6/8	21 4/8 21 4/8	20 0/8	5 6	White Pine County	NV	Roger A. Picchi	1986	1805
155 6/8	22 0/8 21 1/8	19 0/8	6 5	Sheridan County	WY	Stan Chiras	1988	1805
155 6/8	22 5/8 21 5/8	17 6/8	5 7	Hitchcock	SAS	Gerald Steinke	1993	1805
155 6/8	22 2/8 22 6/8	21 2/8	5 5	Springbank	ALB	David R. Coupland	1994	1805
155 6/8	22 7/8 21 3/8	20 4/8	5 5	Duchesne County	UT	Rusty Farnsworth	2004	1805
155 6/8	18 5/8 18 0/8	16 4/8	5 5	Custer County	ID	Boone B. Peterson	2004	1805
155 6/8	20 1/8 20 2/8	19 3/8	6 6	Yellowstone County	MT	Anthony George	2005	1805
155 6/8	21 0/8 20 6/8	21 0/8	4 4	McKenzie County	ND	David Weltikol	2008	1805
155 6/8	22 2/8 22 6/8	21 2/8	4 5	Saskatoon Mtn.	ALB	Terry Hagman	2008	1805
155 5/8	23 2/8 23 3/8	22 3/8	5 6	Chelan County	WA	R. F. Kelly	1960	1816
155 5/8	20 7/8 20 4/8	21 6/8	5 5	Elko County	NV	Frank M. Davis	1967	1816
155 5/8	23 3/8 23 1/8	17 5/8	6 6	Albany County	WY	Jerry Bowen	1974	1816
155 5/8	22 4/8 22 3/8	19 5/8	5 5	Dolores County	CO	Jay Jaburg	1975	1816
155 5/8	24 0/8 25 6/8	22 0/8	7 5	Coconino County	AZ	Robert G. Arcieri	1977	1816
155 5/8	21 0/8 20 5/8	18 1/8	4 4	Carbon County	WY	Robert K. Paulson	1979	1816
155 5/8	21 0/8 20 4/8	18 7/8	5 5	Garfield County	CO	Joe Wiater	1982	1816
155 5/8	21 4/8 20 4/8	17 7/8	5 5	Platte County	WY	James D. Wagner	1982	1816
155 5/8	20 5/8 20 5/8	19 1/8	5 5	Carbon County	WY	Andy Lindahl	1984	1816
155 5/8	19 5/8 19 7/8	20 4/8	5 4	Dunn County	ND	Todd Boechler	1989	1816
155 5/8	20 2/8 20 0/8	19 5/8	4 4	Powder River County	MT	Dewey R. Woodall	1993	1816
155 5/8	22 3/8 21 7/8	17 1/8	5 5	Colfax County	NM	Robert H. Torstenson	1994	1816
155 5/8	20 5/8 21 1/8	17 5/8	5 5	Arapahoe County	CO	Ivan Littlejohn	1995	1816
155 5/8	24 3/8 21 4/8	22 3/8	4 4	Converse County	WY	Kim Pruitt	1998	1816
155 5/8	19 0/8 19 3/8	17 0/8	5 6	Coconino County	AZ	Wally Schwartz	2001	1816
155 5/8	22 7/8 24 0/8	21 5/8	4 5	Sheridan County	WY	Mike Barrett	2001	1816
155 5/8	22 4/8 24 0/8	19 1/8	5 5	Washington County	CO	Martin R. Kilen	2003	1816
155 5/8	19 6/8 19 6/8	18 7/8	5 5	Park County	CO	Kevin Derks	2004	1816
*155 5/8	20 4/8 19 6/8	17 1/8	5 5	Teller County	CO	Macky Myers	2007	1816
*155 5/8	22 0/8 23 2/8	21 4/8	6 5	Custer County	SD	Keith Pullins	2009	1816
155 4/8	22 2/8 23 6/8	23 2/8	5 4	Millard County	UT	Shirl Pace	1966	1836
155 4/8	19 4/8 21 0/8	19 6/8	5 5	Wayne County	UT	Harold Boyack	1968	1836
155 4/8	21 0/8 21 6/8	22 4/8	5 5	Lake County	OR	Wayne Lamson, Jr.	1980	1836
155 4/8	21 7/8 22 0/8	19 0/8	5 5	Albany County	WY	Jerry Bowen	1985	1836
155 4/8	21 6/8 20 4/8	21 0/8	5 5	Los Alamos County	NM	Doug Aikin	1987	1836
155 4/8	22 7/8 21 4/8	17 4/8	5 6	Chelan County	WA	Danny Kohlman	1991	1836
155 4/8	25 2/8 25 0/8	26 4/8	4 4	Walla Walla County	WA	Lance R. Rea	1992	1836
155 4/8	22 1/8 21 0/8	18 2/8	5 5	Crook County	WY	Dean Ransbottom	1994	1836
155 4/8	22 2/8 20 0/8	22 2/8	5 5	Campbell County	WY	Kevin D. O'Brien	1997	1836
155 4/8	25 6/8 24 7/8	19 0/8	3 4	Jefferson County	CO	Dennis Modlin	1997	1836
155 4/8	20 4/8 24 0/8	20 1/8	5 4	El Paso County	CO	Brook D. Neva	2000	1836
155 4/8	24 4/8 24 4/8	24 2/8	4 4	Cassia County	ID	K. C. Ramsey	2002	1836
155 4/8	22 2/8 23 2/8	20 0/8	5 5	Peace River	ALB	Mike Longtin	2004	1836
155 3/8	22 4/8 22 2/8	25 2/8	5 6	Bow River	ALB	Michael D. Coupland	1986	1849
155 3/8	21 1/8 20 5/8	19 7/8	5 5	Teller County	CO	James L. Anderson	1987	1849
155 3/8	21 0/8 20 7/8	16 4/8	6 6	Routt County	CO	Gary Halbritter	1995	1849
155 3/8	21 5/8 20 5/8	17 7/8	5 5	Lassen County	CA	Wayne Wood	2001	1849
155 3/8	21 2/8 21 3/8	21 3/8	5 5	Ada County	ID	Robert Dowen	2001	1849
155 3/8	23 5/8 23 1/8	22 7/8	4 4	Custer County	MT	Johnnie R. Walters	2002	1849
155 3/8	20 6/8 20 6/8	19 3/8	5 5	Natrona County	WY	Shawn Wagner	2003	1849
155 3/8	24 5/8 23 7/8	29 5/8	5 4	Gove County	KS	Jared Ness	2005	1849
155 3/8	25 0/8 23 1/8	22 7/8	5 6	Mesa County	CO	Scott Andersen	2007	1849
155 2/8	20 2/8 19 4/8	19 2/8	5 5	Owyhee County	ID	Ralph O. Collins	1957	1858
155 2/8	23 6/8 24 2/8	22 4/8	6 5	Ada County	ID	Ronald K. White	1971	1858
155 2/8	20 7/8 21 3/8	22 7/8	6 5	Uncompahgre N.F.	CO	Donald Click	1979	1858
155 2/8	21 3/8 22 0/8	24 1/8	6 4	Box Elder County	UT	Richard Hess	1981	1858
155 2/8	22 0/8 22 6/8	19 4/8	5 5	Lake County	OR	Chuck Warner	1981	1858
155 2/8	21 7/8 22 1/8	17 6/8	5 5	Mesa County	CO	Rudy Wilkison	1984	1858
155 2/8	19 1/8 20 6/8	18 5/8	6 5	Colfax County	NM	Dean K. Oatman	1985	1858
155 2/8	21 0/8 22 4/8	19 6/8	5 5	Eagle County	CO	Tom Tietz	1985	1858
155 2/8	23 5/8 24 0/8	24 7/8	5 4	Elbert County	CO	Billy Tillotson	1985	1858
155 2/8	24 1/8 22 5/8	20 0/8	6 7	Hitchcock County	NE	Roger Lewis	1986	1858
155 2/8	20 4/8 21 4/8	16 0/8	6 5	Payette County	ID	Jon Skinner	1994	1858
155 2/8	24 1/8 23 2/8	19 6/8	5 5	Lethbridge	ALB	Doug Doram	1996	1858
155 2/8	22 5/8 21 4/8	16 2/8	5 5	Wasco County	OR	Michael K. Miller	1997	1858
155 2/8	20 5/8 21 4/8	17 6/8	5 5	Blackfalds	ALB	Colin Campbell	1997	1858
155 2/8	23 0/8 21 7/8	20 2/8	5 5	Modoc County	CA	William German	1997	1858
155 2/8	23 4/8 24 0/8	29 2/8	5 5	Yuma County	CO	Dennis Naylor	1998	1858
155 2/8	20 2/8 21 0/8	16 4/8	5 5	Douglas County	CO	Randall Chastain	2000	1858
155 2/8	21 7/8 21 3/8	20 3/8	5 4	Salt Lake County	UT	Robert C. Coulter	2001	1858
155 2/8	22 1/8 20 7/8	19 2/8	5 5	Petroleum County	MT	Dale Haines	2003	1858
155 2/8	23 2/8 22 4/8	21 2/8	5 5	Converse County	WY	Mark McDonald	2004	1858
155 2/8	21 7/8 22 4/8	23 3/8	5 5	Campbell County	WY	Debhra S. Roney	2004	1858
155 2/8	19 4/8 20 1/8	17 0/8	5 5	Sheridan County	KS	Paul Babcock	2004	1858
155 2/8	23 5/8 22 4/8	21 6/8	5 5	Klamath County	OR	Duane Rogers	2005	1858
*155 2/8	22 1/8 21 1/8	21 2/8	5 5	Corson County	SD	John E. Powell, Jr.	2007	1858
*155 2/8	21 3/8 21 4/8	15 7/8	6 6	Elbow	SAS	Chad Gessner	2008	1858
155 2/8	22 6/8 22 1/8	17 5/8	6 6	Delta County	CO	Rick Bohl	2010	1858
155 1/8	21 2/8 21 3/8	17 7/8	6 5	Sevier County	UT	Ray Shepard	1965	1884
155 1/8	22 0/8 22 6/8	22 5/8	5 7	Lane County	KS	Dean Hamilton	1983	1884
155 1/8	21 5/8 20 0/8	21 1/8	5 6	Custer County	NE	John Slack	1988	1884
155 1/8	19 0/8 20 4/8	18 3/8	5 5	Powder River County	MT	Gene Smith	1991	1884
155 1/8	21 6/8 22 2/8	21 3/8	5 5	Osborne County	KS	Dennis Fisk	1992	1884
155 1/8	22 3/8 22 2/8	16 5/8	5 5	Harney County	OR	Edward Reed	1994	1884
155 1/8	21 6/8 21 5/8	16 3/8	5 5	Manyberries	ALB	Robert G. Barden	1997	1884
155 1/8	21 2/8 21 1/8	17 1/8	6 5	Jefferson County	ID	Adam Torgerson	1999	1884
155 1/8	23 6/8 23 3/8	21 1/8	5 4	Cardston	ALB	Joe Keathley	2005	1884
155 1/8	20 0/8 19 6/8	18 4/8	6 6	Klamath County	OR	Curt Crook	2006	1884
155 0/8	23 2/8 21 4/8	22 0/8	5 4	Lake County	OR	Bill Chahon	1967	1894
155 0/8	23 4/8 23 0/8	23 0/8	6 5	Broadwater County	MT	Larry P. Stevens	1968	1894
155 0/8	19 7/8 22 4/8	17 6/8	4 4	Summit County	CO	Harley Smith	1976	1894
155 0/8	22 6/8 23 0/8	21 2/8	6 6	Rio Blanco County	CO	Larry Streiff	1978	1894
155 0/8	24 2/8 24 4/8	26 0/8	4 3	Mesa County	CO	Duane Beenblossom	1979	1894
155 0/8	21 7/8 22 0/8	20 1/8	5 5	Mesa County	CO	Clarence Bowers, Jr.	1979	1894
155 0/8	21 2/8 22 6/8	21 6/8	4 4	Slope County	ND	Bill Schwendinger	1982	1894

327

MULE DEER (TYPICAL ANTLERS)

Minimum Score 145   Continued

SCORE	LENGTH OF R MAIN BEAM L		INSIDE SPREAD	NUMBER OF R POINTS L		AREA	STATE/ PROVINCE	HUNTER'S NAME	DATE	RANK
155 0/8	20 5/8	19 3/8	18 4/8	5	5	Bernalillo County	NM	Doug Aikin	1983	1894
155 0/8	21 2/8	21 6/8	21 4/8	5	5	Boise County	ID	Larry S. Zurgot	1985	1894
155 0/8	22 6/8	23 2/8	18 6/8	5	5	Bernalillo County	NM	Joseph L. Moyer	1988	1894
155 0/8	21 4/8	21 4/8	20 2/8	5	5	Sundre	ALB	Larry K. Nielsen	1989	1894
155 0/8	18 3/8	19 0/8	20 6/8	4	5	Wallace County	KS	Dave Hale	1992	1894
155 0/8	22 3/8	21 3/8	23 2/8	5	6	Weld County	CO	John P. Johnson	1994	1894
155 0/8	24 0/8	22 4/8	23 2/8	5	5	Calgary	ALB	Bill A. Riel	1995	1894
155 0/8	22 3/8	22 6/8	21 6/8	5	5	Elmore County	ID	Gary Gapp	1997	1894
155 0/8	22 5/8	22 2/8	22 0/8	5	5	Sheridan County	WY	Jerry Shatek	1998	1894
155 0/8	19 7/8	19 2/8	17 4/8	7	5	Charles Mix County	SD	Alan Summerville	1998	1894
155 0/8	21 7/8	22 6/8	19 2/8	5	5	Moffat County	CO	Steven Soehren	1999	1894
155 0/8	22 6/8	23 0/8	25 6/8	4	4	Campbell County	WY	Robert N. Rust	2003	1894
155 0/8	23 0/8	22 4/8	18 0/8	5	5	Cowley	ALB	Scott Holberton	2007	1894
*155 0/8	21 7/8	21 4/8	22 3/8	6	6	Natrona County	WY	Brent Willadsen	2008	1894
155 0/8	21 4/8	21 7/8	19 0/8	5	5	Irricana	ALB	Dusty Maxwell	2009	1894
154 7/8	22 3/8	23 4/8	23 3/8	5	5	Dolores County	CO	Oscar A. Harden	1957	1916
154 7/8	19 4/8	21 2/8	19 2/8	5	6	Millard County	UT	Dale Moore	1961	1916
154 7/8	21 6/8	21 7/8	16 7/8	4	4	Elko County	NV	Jim Cox	1974	1916
154 7/8	21 5/8	22 3/8	18 3/8	5	6	Elko County	NV	John S. Chace, Jr.	1982	1916
154 7/8	24 1/8	24 7/8	18 5/8	4	5	Catron County	NM	Richard V. Gray	1994	1916
154 7/8	20 4/8	21 0/8	18 7/8	5	5	Pinal County	AZ	Gary D. Rancher	1994	1916
154 7/8	21 1/8	21 1/8	18 1/8	5	5	Larimer County	CO	Patrick Wensman	1994	1916
154 7/8	21 1/8	19 6/8	20 7/8	5	5	Jefferson County	CO	Larry J. Jones	1996	1916
154 7/8	20 7/8	22 4/8	18 3/8	6	5	Powder River County	MT	James Gorder	1998	1916
154 7/8	20 2/8	20 6/8	16 7/8	5	5	Lander County	NV	Larry Wellert	2001	1916
154 7/8	21 7/8	21 6/8	18 1/8	5	5	Elbert County	CO	Clay Hall	2007	1916
154 7/8	23 5/8	24 1/8	26 3/8	5	6	Donalda	ALB	John Paul Schaffer	2010	1916
154 6/8	23 1/8	22 7/8	20 2/8	4	5	Montrose County	CO	Dave Reitz	1983	1928
154 6/8	17 5/8	20 1/8	13 4/8	5	5	EL Paso County	CO	Michael Thompson	1984	1928
154 6/8	20 3/8	20 4/8	22 4/8	5	5	Mesa County	CO	R. L. Harrison III	1985	1928
154 6/8	22 5/8	22 7/8	17 7/8	5	5	Elbert County	CO	Randy Kendrick	1998	1928
154 6/8	24 5/8	25 0/8	21 2/8	5	4	Hooker County	NE	Andrew L. Glidden	1999	1928
154 6/8	21 1/8	21 1/8	18 0/8	5	5	Union County	OR	Joe Corrado	2002	1928
*154 6/8	21 2/8	21 7/8	17 6/8	5	5	Bernalillo County	NM	Gabriel Lovato	2005	1928
154 6/8	22 2/8	21 6/8	20 0/8	6	5	McKenzie County	ND	Corey Hugelen	2007	1928
154 5/8	20 3/8	21 7/8	21 7/8	5	5	Lincoln County	NV	Larry Gehre	1963	1936
154 5/8	21 3/8	19 3/8	16 7/8	4	5	Garfield County	CO	Tommy Biffle	1975	1936
154 5/8	23 6/8	23 2/8	20 0/8	5	8	San Juan County	UT	Bruce Gordon	1980	1936
154 5/8	20 1/8	19 5/8	19 5/8	5	5	Lake County	OR	Dale A. Bolin	1983	1936
154 5/8	19 6/8	21 1/8	18 7/8	5	5	Pennington County	SD	Scott Lindgren	1986	1936
154 5/8	20 1/8	19 4/8	21 3/8	5	5	Crook County	WY	Calvin Farner	1986	1936
154 5/8	22 3/8	21 3/8	19 3/8	5	6	Montrose County	CO	Eugene Roesler	1989	1936
154 5/8	21 5/8	22 6/8	21 1/8	5	5	Garfield County	WA	Lee Campbell	1990	1936
154 5/8	19 1/8	20 0/8	17 1/8	5	5	Pima County	AZ	Jeff Ferri	1990	1936
154 5/8	22 4/8	21 2/8	17 1/8	5	5	Wallowa County	OR	Dwayne Heikes	1991	1936
154 5/8	21 6/8	21 3/8	17 7/8	6	6	Millarville	ALB	Joel Bickler	1991	1936
154 5/8	24 4/8	24 0/8	19 7/8	5	6	Washington County	UT	Neil Stratton	1992	1936
154 5/8	20 2/8	20 3/8	25 1/8	7	5	Converse County	WY	Ron Miller	1994	1936
154 5/8	21 6/8	21 0/8	20 1/8	5	5	Gray County	KS	Matthew Stark	1997	1936
154 5/8	18 3/8	18 2/8	19 6/8	5	5	Montezuma County	CO	Bryon D. Long	1998	1936
154 5/8	25 7/8	23 5/8	26 3/8	4	5	Empress	ALB	Tim Sailer	2003	1936
154 5/8	20 7/8	20 6/8	17 7/8	5	5	Moffat County	CO	Joseph Fedorko	2004	1936
154 4/8	22 3/8	22 0/8	22 2/8	5	5	Washoe County	NV	Gary Van Ness	1959	1953
154 4/8	22 3/8	22 5/8	21 0/8	6	6	Routt County	CO	Douglas J. Peterson	1965	1953
154 4/8	22 5/8	24 0/8	18 1/8	6	6	Frontier County	NE	Mark Stencel	1986	1953
154 4/8	20 2/8	20 0/8	22 3/8	6	7	Pima County	AZ	Rick Forrest	1992	1953
154 4/8	19 6/8	19 6/8	21 7/8	5	5	Weld County	CO	Gerald Rasmussen, Jr.	1995	1953
154 4/8	19 1/8	19 6/8	18 0/8	5	5	Weston County	WY	Bill Snodgrass	1997	1953
154 4/8	20 4/8	22 3/8	21 6/8	4	4	Salt Lake County	UT	Jeremy T. Eldredge	2003	1953
*154 4/8	21 3/8	19 1/8	18 2/8	5	5	Chouteau County	MT	Pat J. O'Boyle	2004	1953
*154 4/8	24 3/8	24 2/8	23 0/8	4	3	Las Animas County	CO	Fred Eichler	2004	1953
154 4/8	24 4/8	24 0/8	19 6/8	5	4	Porcupine Hills	ALB	Mark Chindavat	2007	1953
154 3/8	21 7/8	23 1/8	20 5/8	4	5	Pawnee County	KS	Robert E. Lagree	1970	1963
154 3/8	18 0/8	18 1/8	17 5/8	5	5	Yavapai County	AZ	James R. Reckas	1989	1963
154 3/8	25 6/8	26 1/8	27 0/8	3	4	Elbert County	CO	Douglas Cringan	1991	1963
154 3/8	21 5/8	22 3/8	17 3/8	4	4	Powder River County	MT	Joseph A. Borgna	1995	1963
154 3/8	23 7/8	23 4/8	21 3/8	6	5	San Juan County	NM	Randy Sweetland	1997	1963
154 3/8	23 2/8	20 1/8	19 2/8	4	5	Sherman County	OR	Everett A. Proctor	1999	1963
154 3/8	22 6/8	22 7/8	19 1/8	5	5	Converse County	WY	Gary Kautz	2001	1963
154 3/8	22 0/8	20 1/8	19 3/8	5	4	Jefferson County	CO	Gilbert Zarate	2002	1963
154 3/8	23 2/8	24 6/8	17 6/8	5	6	Ravalli County	MT	Miranda M. Martin	2005	1963
154 2/8	21 7/8	21 5/8	17 4/8	8	8	Grant County	OR	Lloyd V. Christensen	1960	1972
154 2/8	22 5/8	22 3/8	19 5/8	4	4	Mesa County	CO	Jimmy E. Ash	1966	1972
154 2/8	22 2/8	21 2/8	21 0/8	7	8	Kirby	WY	Steve Gorr	1970	1972
154 2/8	20 5/8	20 0/8	19 2/8	5	5	Moffat County	CO	Mary E. Nussberger	1978	1972
154 2/8	21 2/8	23 7/8	22 4/8	5	5	Blaine County	ID	Dean Muchow	1979	1972
154 2/8	21 2/8	21 5/8	18 6/8	5	5	Mesa County	CO	Carl Phillips	1980	1972
154 2/8	23 4/8	23 0/8	19 1/8	5	6	Chelan County	WA	Daniel S Nelson	1984	1972
154 2/8	24 4/8	23 2/8	24 4/8	5	4	Lassen County	CA	Steve Thurmon	1999	1972
154 2/8	22 2/8	20 6/8	18 0/8	5	5	Manyberries	ALB	Daniel J. Kelly	1999	1972
154 2/8	20 3/8	20 4/8	17 2/8	5	5	Garfield County	CO	Erik Watts	2000	1972
154 2/8	19 2/8	22 2/8	20 5/8	7	6	Las Animas County	CO	Pat Powell	2000	1972
154 2/8	23 0/8	23 2/8	21 0/8	5	5	Dunn County	ND	Charles Dougherty	2001	1972
154 2/8	22 6/8	22 2/8	19 6/8	6	6	McKenzie County	ND	Corey Hugelen	2002	1972
154 2/8	22 0/8	21 4/8	19 0/8	5	5	Climax	SAS	Reg Smith	2003	1972
154 2/8	20 0/8	21 0/8	17 4/8	5	5	Saguache County	CO	Jarrod Bowers	2005	1972
*154 2/8	22 4/8	21 6/8	17 1/8	4	5	Fort Macleod	ALB	Lucas Osellame	2007	1972
*154 2/8	22 6/8	22 2/8	19 1/8	6	5	Maricopa County	AZ	Lonny Penner	2008	1972
154 2/8	20 6/8	21 3/8	19 6/8	5	5	Albany County	WY	Dubie Bonner	2008	1972
154 2/8	20 5/8	20 3/8	19 0/8	5	5	Washoe County	NV	Matt P. Miller	2008	1972
*154 2/8	24 0/8	22 2/8	17 0/8	5	7	Pennington County	SD	Gordon A. Howie	2009	1972
154 1/8	18 3/8	16 6/8	16 1/8	5	7	Carbon County	UT	Lieb D. Miller	1959	1992
154 1/8	19 6/8	20 5/8	18 1/8	5	6	Jefferson County	OR	Doris T. Barden	1960	1992
154 1/8	21 4/8	21 4/8	20 4/8	4	4	Rio Grande County	CO	Kenneth G. McCombs	1969	1992
154 1/8	20 3/8	21 0/8	16 0/8	5	6	Montrose County	CO	Arthur L. Pace	1974	1992

MULE DEER (TYPICAL ANTLERS)

Minimum Score 145　　Continued

SCORE	LENGTH OF MAIN BEAM R	L	INSIDE SPREAD	NUMBER OF POINTS R	L	AREA	STATE/PROVINCE	HUNTER'S NAME	DATE	RANK
154 1/8	23 5/8	21 6/8	23 6/8	4	4	Montrose County	CO	Don Allen, Jr.	1979	1992
154 1/8	22 6/8	22 5/8	22 5/8	5	4	Malheur County	OR	Jim Nielsen	1988	1992
154 1/8	22 1/8	21 0/8	19 3/8	5	4	Albany County	WY	Jerry Bowen	1990	1992
154 1/8	21 0/8	21 3/8	20 5/8	5	4	Converse County	WY	Herb Mielke	1992	1992
154 1/8	19 1/8	18 1/8	18 0/8	6	5	Teller County	CO	Rodney W. Purvis	1995	1992
154 1/8	22 0/8	22 7/8	18 2/8	6	5	Wasco County	OR	Dana L. Doney	1996	1992
154 1/8	21 7/8	21 1/8	22 4/8	5	5	Apache County	AZ	Frank Hausner	2001	1992
154 1/8	22 5/8	20 5/8	23 4/8	6	6	Malheur County	OR	Ryan Remmer	2001	1992
154 1/8	22 1/8	22 0/8	19 5/8	5	5	San Juan County	UT	Jack Satterfield, Jr.	2002	1992
154 1/8	24 7/8	21 7/8	21 7/8	5	5	Lemhi County	ID	Gary Gapp	2005	1992
*154 1/8	20 2/8	20 2/8	19 7/8	5	5	Potter County	SD	Jason Overby	2008	1992
154 1/8	20 6/8	21 0/8	19 5/8	4	4	Golden Valley County	ND	Curt Bradbury	2010	1992
154 0/8	22 7/8	22 6/8	20 6/8	7	6	Coconino County	AZ	Stuart Diehl	1962	2008
154 0/8	22 0/8	22 2/8	19 4/8	5	5	Mesa County	CO	Al Dawson	1964	2008
154 0/8	24 6/8	24 4/8	29 0/8	5	4	Grant County	OR	Chuck Lynde	1972	2008
154 0/8	25 2/8	24 4/8	21 2/8	5	4	Mesa County	CO	Dale Anderson	1973	2008
154 0/8	20 4/8	21 4/8	19 3/8	6	5	Calgary	ALB	Manfred Grewe	1981	2008
154 0/8	22 7/8	23 6/8	22 5/8	9	7	Lake County	OR	Charles F. Brown	1985	2008
154 0/8	20 3/8	20 2/8	17 2/8	5	4	Converse County	WY	Lee Jernigan	1987	2008
154 0/8	22 1/8	22 1/8	18 0/8	5	4	Elmore County	ID	Timothy J. Conrads	1988	2008
154 0/8	18 5/8	18 5/8	16 4/8	5	4	Baker County	OR	John A. Eyers	1990	2008
154 0/8	22 0/8	22 5/8	20 0/8	6	5	Sublette County	WY	Nelson J. Capestany	1991	2008
154 0/8	21 3/8	22 3/8	19 0/8	5	5	Weld County	CO	Gary L. Clancy	1991	2008
154 0/8	22 2/8	23 2/8	22 3/8	6	5	San Juan County	CO	Jeff Kelly	1994	2008
154 0/8	24 2/8	25 2/8	21 6/8	5	4	Converse County	WY	G. Lowe Morrison	1995	2008
154 0/8	20 3/8	20 5/8	19 2/8	5	5	Mesa County	CO	Roger D. Bailey	2004	2008
153 7/8	19 5/8	19 2/8	19 1/8	6	5	Meagher County	MT	Leroy Dukes	1972	2022
153 7/8	22 6/8	21 7/8	16 6/8	6	6	Rio Blanco County	CO	Kevin Jackson	1973	2022
153 7/8	22 4/8	19 6/8	17 7/8	5	5	Uintah County	UT	Matt Brooks	1974	2022
153 7/8	23 3/8	22 4/8	23 1/8	6	6	Baker County	OR	Randy Jennings	1981	2022
153 7/8	22 5/8	23 3/8	19 2/8	6	6	Pinal County	AZ	Jesse Pena	1988	2022
153 7/8	20 5/8	20 0/8	19 3/8	5	5	Oneida County	ID	Dave Scott	1990	2022
153 7/8	23 1/8	23 1/8	21 7/8	6	6	Billings County	ND	Steve Schaper	1990	2022
153 7/8	21 7/8	20 0/8	16 3/8	5	5	San Juan County	UT	Randy J. Walk	1991	2022
153 7/8	24 2/8	23 4/8	22 6/8	6	5	Lincoln County	CO	Michael B. Lamade	1992	2022
153 7/8	20 7/8	21 2/8	19 7/8	5	5	Garfield County	CO	Kelly P. Bowe	1993	2022
153 7/8	19 6/8	19 7/8	16 1/8	5	5	Powder River County	MT	Rich Driscoll	1994	2022
153 7/8	20 5/8	21 2/8	20 5/8	5	5	Bannock County	ID	Bracken Henderson	1994	2022
153 7/8	25 1/8	22 2/8	19 7/8	6	7	Deschutes County	OR	Randy Stockwell	1997	2022
153 7/8	20 3/8	21 4/8	15 3/8	5	5	Sheridan County	WY	Gary Challoner	1997	2022
153 7/8	20 0/8	20 1/8	20 2/8	5	5	Natrona County	WY	Jim Van Norman	1998	2022
153 7/8	24 0/8	24 3/8	21 1/8	5	5	Fraser River	BC	Guy Sawatsky	1998	2022
153 7/8	22 5/8	20 1/8	21 0/8	4	5	McKenzie County	ND	Corey Hugelen	1998	2022
153 7/8	20 6/8	21 3/8	15 5/8	5	5	Knife Creek	BC	Rick Paquette	1999	2022
153 7/8	26 1/8	25 7/8	28 5/8	5	5	Lake Diefenbaker	SAS	John Enns	2003	2022
153 7/8	21 2/8	19 6/8	22 2/8	6	5	McKenzie County	ND	Corey Hugelen	2006	2022
153 7/8	24 5/8	24 3/8	19 7/8	8	5	Deschutes County	OR	Hank S. Baxter	2007	2022
153 7/8	20 4/8	20 4/8	15 3/8	5	4	Morrow County	OR	Gerald Lee Ford	2008	2022
*153 7/8	19 3/8	21 5/8	19 1/8	5	5	Ravalli County	MT	Craig Cellini	2010	2022
153 6/8	23 0/8	23 6/8	24 4/8	5	5	Siskiyou County	CA	Kenneth B. Jenkins	1958	2045
153 6/8	23 0/8	21 7/8	18 0/8	5	5	Dawes County	NE	William W. Plooster	1958	2045
153 6/8	22 5/8	22 7/8	24 5/8	6	6	Cherry County	NE	Albert Selk	1995	2045
153 6/8	20 0/8	20 6/8	18 0/8	5	5	Bonneville County	ID	Thomas Thiel	1997	2045
153 6/8	20 6/8	21 1/8	16 6/8	5	5	Kittitas County	WA	Randy S. Forman	2000	2045
153 6/8	20 6/8	19 3/8	22 6/8	5	5	Flagstaff	ALB	Brent Kuntz	2002	2045
153 6/8	21 7/8	21 1/8	21 1/8	7	5	Lane County	KS	Tod Anthony	2002	2045
153 6/8	23 2/8	23 0/8	22 4/8	5	5	Rockyview	ALB	Cam T. Foss	2002	2045
153 6/8	23 2/8	23 0/8	22 4/8	5	5	Cochrane	ALB	Cam Foss	2002	2045
153 6/8	22 6/8	24 3/8	18 0/8	5	7	Eagle Hill	ALB	Dallas Kaiser	2003	2045
153 6/8	20 5/8	22 4/8	17 4/8	5	5	Twin Falls County	ID	Darrell Nunez	2003	2045
153 6/8	23 4/8	23 4/8	20 6/8	5	5	Sheridan County	WY	Justin Ammons	2004	2045
153 6/8	21 0/8	21 7/8	18 6/8	5	5	Red Deer River	ALB	Grant Petersen	2005	RANK
153 6/8	21 2/8	20 6/8	19 2/8	5	5	Wembley	ALB	Duane Hagman	2006	2045
153 6/8	21 0/8	22 3/8	14 0/8	6	5	Crossfield	ALB	Dan Lemieux	2007	2045
153 6/8	20 4/8	20 2/8	23 3/8	6	5	Socorro County	NM	Alfred Gallegos	2009	2045
153 5/8	22 0/8	22 4/8	20 7/8	4	4	Billings County	ND	Ed Bry, Jr.	1957	2061
153 5/8	21 0/8	20 7/8	17 7/8	6	7	Moffat County	CO	Zenus E. Cozart	1962	2061
153 5/8	21 4/8	21 4/8	18 7/8	5	6	Moffat County	CO	Hugh Cox	1971	2061
153 5/8	22 3/8	22 7/8	23 3/8	5	5	Pinal County	AZ	James M. Fry	1974	2061
153 5/8	22 6/8	23 1/8	24 0/8	5	5	Routt County	CO	Lee R. Hoxit	1978	2061
153 5/8	21 4/8	21 1/8	19 7/8	4	4	Milk River Ridge	ALB	Don Gibb	1992	2061
153 5/8	21 5/8	23 1/8	20 1/8	5	5	Grant County	WA	J. G. "Rusty" Watson	1997	2061
*153 5/8	21 0/8	20 5/8	19 3/8	5	4	Mellette County	SD	Mark Kayser	2009	2061
153 4/8	22 5/8	21 7/8	22 4/8	5	5	San Juan County	UT	Roy D. Chesley	1963	2069
153 4/8	23 0/8	23 0/8	17 4/8	6	5	Brown County	NE	Seth Fritzler	1965	2069
153 4/8	20 1/8	22 1/8	20 2/8	6	5	Wasatch County	UT	Don Callister	1967	2069
153 4/8	21 2/8	22 0/8	22 4/8	4	4	Slope County	ND	Todd Seymanski	1991	2069
153 4/8	21 7/8	22 1/8	17 4/8	5	5	Mesa County	CO	Joseph M. Schmidt	1992	2069
153 4/8	23 3/8	22 2/8	20 2/8	5	5	Yavapai County	AZ	Patrick M. Kirby	1993	2069
153 4/8	21 5/8	20 4/8	18 4/8	5	4	Graham County	AZ	John A. Bierhaus	1999	2069
153 4/8	21 2/8	20 2/8	19 2/8	5	4	Lincoln County	CO	Thomas A. Hornby	2000	2069
153 4/8	22 2/8	23 1/8	19 0/8	6	4	Union County	OR	Shane Merrill	2003	2069
153 4/8	23 0/8	22 6/8	25 3/8	6	5	Baca County	CO	Ryan Albert	2003	2069
153 4/8	23 1/8	24 4/8	25 5/8	5	5	Boise County	ID	Ray Simpson	2005	2069
153 4/8	21 2/8	21 2/8	16 6/8	5	5	Delta County	CO	Steve Edwards	2006	2069
153 4/8	21 3/8	20 5/8	18 7/8	5	6	Carbon County	WY	Zach Herold	2006	2069
*153 4/8	20 6/8	18 6/8	22 5/8	5	4	Cheyenne County	CO	Chad Ford	2006	2069
153 4/8	22 3/8	23 0/8	20 2/8	5	5	Garfield County	CO	Wade Steffenhagen	2008	2069
*153 4/8	20 0/8	21 0/8	16 6/8	6	5	Pecos County	TX	Milton Harrell	2009	2069
*153 4/8	25 0/8	23 1/8	26 3/8	4	5	Deschutes County	OR	James Wade	2010	2069
153 3/8	22 1/8	21 1/8	21 1/8	4	4	Garfield County	CO	John Nottingham	1974	2086
153 3/8	19 6/8	21 1/8	22 5/8	5	5	Meagher County	MT	Chuck Adams	1979	2086
153 3/8	22 0/8	23 1/8	21 2/8	5	6	Weld County	CO	Gary Thurow	1988	2086
153 3/8	20 1/8	19 3/8	18 1/8	5	5	Carbon County	WY	Peter Schinke	1989	2086
153 3/8	21 3/8	21 6/8	21 1/8	4	3	Rio Arriba County	NM	James Michael Bridges	1989	2086

329

MULE DEER (TYPICAL ANTLERS)

Minimum Score 145   Continued

SCORE	LENGTH OF R MAIN BEAM L	INSIDE SPREAD	NUMBER OF R POINTS L	AREA	STATE/ PROVINCE	HUNTER'S NAME	DATE	RANK
153 3/8	24 5/8 24 5/8	21 4/8	4 5	Sheridan County	WY	Ron Niziolek	1993	2086
153 3/8	19 3/8 19 0/8	26 6/8	5 5	Campbell County	WY	Tim Lammle	1995	2086
153 3/8	18 7/8 19 2/8	17 7/8	4 5	Nevada County	CA	Kevil Pelton	1997	2086
153 3/8	20 4/8 20 5/8	20 1/8	5 5	Milk River	ALB	Joe Coleman	2000	2086
153 3/8	20 2/8 19 4/8	17 7/8	5 6	Claresholm	ALB	Quely Cotter	2003	2086
153 3/8	22 7/8 22 2/8	28 2/8	5 5	Custer County	NE	Kent J. Leibhart	2003	2086
153 3/8	20 1/8 20 7/8	17 5/8	5 4	Billings County	ND	Lou Edelis	2003	2086
153 3/8	22 5/8 22 7/8	18 5/8	5 5	Garfield County	CO	Kurt Allen Grimm	2006	2086
153 2/8	21 0/8 21 0/8	20 0/8	5 5	Custer County	MT	Gene T. Buck	1961	2099
153 2/8	21 4/8 21 3/8	17 6/8	5 5	Garfield County	CO	Randy Gilmore	1982	2099
153 2/8	21 2/8 20 3/8	20 0/8	6 6	Coconino County	AZ	Richard S Jones	1985	2099
153 2/8	19 4/8 20 0/8	15 6/8	5 5	Gregory County	SD	Terry Marcukaitis	1985	2099
153 2/8	20 1/8 20 6/8	14 6/8	6 5	Washoe County	NV	Ronald W. Lindquist	1986	2099
153 2/8	20 3/8 22 3/8	20 0/8	5 5	Billings County	ND	Gary J. Peters	1987	2099
153 2/8	21 6/8 22 0/8	23 0/8	5 5	Campbell County	WY	David A. O'Brien	1993	2099
153 2/8	22 5/8 22 2/8	20 5/8	7 6	Turin	ALB	Raymond Bahr	1994	2099
153 2/8	21 2/8 22 1/8	16 4/8	5 5	Converse County	WY	Bill Randles	1995	2099
153 2/8	23 1/8 22 5/8	25 0/8	6 5	Montrose County	CO	Jim Holdenried	1995	2099
153 2/8	23 6/8 24 5/8	26 0/8	5 5	Cochise County	AZ	Louie Herrera	1995	2099
153 2/8	22 3/8 23 3/8	18 6/8	5 5	Chelan County	WA	Leroy E. House	1996	2099
153 2/8	22 0/8 22 4/8	22 5/8	5 6	Brooks	ALB	Mark Nelson	2000	2099
153 2/8	20 6/8 19 5/8	20 2/8	5 5	Elbert County	CO	Tom Kelley	2002	2099
153 2/8	21 7/8 21 4/8	20 3/8	6 7	Chaffee County	CO	Phillip Gaines	2004	2099
*153 2/8	20 2/8 20 6/8	25 2/8	5 5	Montrose County	CO	William C. Creel	2007	2099
153 2/8	22 7/8 23 0/8	19 6/8	5 5	Lincoln County	NM	Jerry Simmons	2009	2099
153 1/8	22 0/8 22 3/8	24 0/8	5 4	Millard County	UT	Milton F. McQueary	1961	2116
153 1/8	23 5/8 25 2/8	20 2/8	5 4	Rio Blanco County	CO	Thomas Nicholls	1967	2116
153 1/8	22 0/8 21 5/8	21 5/8	5 4	Garfield County	CO	Lester Meredith	1974	2116
153 1/8	21 5/8 22 3/8	22 3/8	5 5	Park County	WY	Jim Dinkins	1978	2116
153 1/8	21 0/8 22 7/8	18 7/8	7 5	Converse County	WY	Ted Jaycox	1982	2116
153 1/8	21 6/8 21 4/8	19 7/8	4 5	Chelan County	WA	Don McNees, Jr.	1983	2116
153 1/8	19 5/8 19 7/8	19 1/8	5 5	Dolores County	CO	Mark Beeler	1992	2116
153 1/8	21 7/8 21 3/8	19 7/8	5 5	Klamath County	OR	Jake S. Schorr	1994	2116
153 1/8	23 5/8 21 4/8	21 1/8	6 5	Delia	ALB	Brian Kakuk	1996	2116
153 1/8	22 1/8 23 0/8	18 7/8	5 6	Hays	ALB	David R. Coupland	1996	2116
153 1/8	21 4/8 19 7/8	16 6/8	5 6	Weld County	CO	Reggie Spiegelberg	1997	2116
153 1/8	20 7/8 21 2/8	17 5/8	5 5	Slope County	ND	Pete Finck	1999	2116
153 1/8	24 1/8 23 3/8	20 7/8	4 4	Brule County	SD	Tony Nogy	2002	2116
153 1/8	21 4/8 22 7/8	21 1/8	5 7	Arapahoe County	CO	Craig J. Appel	2002	2116
153 1/8	18 4/8 18 5/8	14 7/8	4 5	Meagher County	MT	Jim Kennedy	2003	2116
153 1/8	21 1/8 21 1/8	21 4/8	5 5	Douglas County	CO	W. Henry Ferguson	2004	2116
*153 1/8	20 7/8 21 2/8	17 3/8	5 5	Larimer County	CO	Ed Fanchin	2007	2116
153 1/8	20 2/8 20 5/8	20 3/8	5 5	Adams County	CO	Joe Goodnight	2007	2116
153 0/8	21 1/8 22 1/8	23 2/8	5 6	Golden Valley County	MT	Tim Ford	1979	2134
153 0/8	21 7/8 22 6/8	20 2/8	6 5	Valley County	ID	James J. Akenson	1988	2134
153 0/8	22 0/8 21 6/8	19 0/8	5 6	Vertigris Lake	ALB	Keith Heppler	1989	2134
153 0/8	21 5/8 24 0/8	21 6/8	5 5	Lake County	OR	Mike Benton	1990	2134
153 0/8	22 2/8 21 6/8	21 2/8	5 5	Elmore County	ID	Gary Gapp	1990	2134
153 0/8	17 6/8 20 0/8	20 2/8	6 5	Colfax County	NM	Justin L. Sanchez	1990	2134
153 0/8	26 5/8 26 1/8	25 6/8	3 3	Hartley County	TX	Todd Hodnett	1992	2134
153 0/8	24 0/8 24 0/8	21 6/8	4 4	Billings County	ND	John Holdorf	1995	2134
153 0/8	21 5/8 22 4/8	13 6/8	6 6	Catron County	NM	Richard V. Gray	1997	2134
153 0/8	22 1/8 22 4/8	21 6/8	5 5	Luna County	NM	Kevin Schmid/Diane Schmid	1998	2134
153 0/8	23 1/8 18 7/8	19 6/8	6 6	Milk River	ALB	Tom Taylor	2002	2134
153 0/8	22 3/8 22 0/8	25 5/8	6 5	Plumas County	CA	Jerry Dollard	2003	2134
153 0/8	22 5/8 25 6/8	22 0/8	4 4	Sonora	MEX	Carol Kindred	2006	2134
*153 0/8	19 5/8 19 5/8	17 6/8	5 4	Fergus County	MT	Doug Yoder	2007	2134
*153 0/8	18 5/8 18 6/8	20 5/8	6 5	Jefferson County	CO	Robert Brandstetter	2007	2134
153 0/8	22 6/8 22 7/8	14 6/8	7 6	Platte County	WY	Jerry Bowen	2009	2134
152 7/8	20 7/8 21 7/8	20 1/8	6 6	Gove County	KS	Alan D. Beougher	1970	2150
152 7/8	20 4/8 21 7/8	15 3/8	4 4	White River N.F.	CO	Leonard Steiner	1978	2150
152 7/8	22 1/8 23 0/8	21 3/8	5 6	Gila County	AZ	Steven Weekley	1985	2150
152 7/8	21 2/8 20 2/8	18 7/8	5 5	Lincoln County	CO	Cotty Hayes	1992	2150
152 7/8	22 0/8 22 7/8	21 7/8	5 4	Custer County	ID	Kevin Pearce	1994	2150
152 7/8	22 6/8 22 4/8	18 7/8	6 5	Kittitas County	WA	Jeff Thorpe	1994	2150
152 7/8	23 1/8 20 7/8	21 3/8	6 7	Trego County	KS	Ryan Hagans	1995	2150
152 7/8	22 6/8 22 3/8	21 1/8	5 5	Las Animas County	CO	James Brooks	1999	2150
152 7/8	21 7/8 21 4/8	23 0/8	5 5	Elko County	NV	Kevin Myers	2001	2150
152 7/8	22 0/8 22 3/8	18 7/8	6 5	Las Animas County	CO	Bud Smedley	2001	2150
152 7/8	19 0/8 19 3/8	22 0/8	5 5	Buffalo	ALB	Darryl Kublik	2003	2150
152 7/8	22 2/8 21 3/8	17 7/8	5 5	Grassy Lake	ALB	Paul Deme	2004	2150
152 6/8	21 6/8 21 0/8	21 6/8	6 5	Graham County	AZ	Herbert Tom	1981	2162
152 6/8	22 0/8 21 4/8	22 0/8	5 4	Delta County	CO	Timothy L. McKay	1990	2162
152 6/8	24 0/8 22 6/8	21 2/8	5 5	Converse County	WY	M. R. James	1991	2162
152 6/8	19 5/8 19 1/8	18 0/8	4 4	Billings County	ND	William E. Lee, Jr.	1991	2162
152 6/8	19 7/8 21 1/8	17 0/8	5 6	Albany County	WY	Tom Pindell	1994	2162
152 6/8	19 6/8 21 1/8	18 1/8	5 5	Laramie County	WY	Brian Rhead	1995	2162
152 6/8	21 6/8 21 2/8	20 0/8	4 4	Dolores County	CO	Richard C. Johnston	1996	2162
152 6/8	19 2/8 19 2/8	17 0/8	5 5	Elk River	ALB	Dave Bathke	1996	2162
152 6/8	20 2/8 21 6/8	19 6/8	5 5	Cochise County	AZ	Rick Forrest	1998	2162
152 6/8	19 6/8 19 3/8	20 0/8	5 5	Maricopa County	AZ	Matthew Liljenquist	1998	2162
152 6/8	20 4/8 19 2/8	19 2/8	4 6	Prowers County	CO	Skip Valentine	1999	2162
152 6/8	20 5/8 23 0/8	23 5/8	4 4	Las Animas County	CO	Fred Eichler	2001	2162
152 6/8	19 0/8 18 3/8	18 2/8	5 5	Lincoln County	WY	Terry Ripple	2005	2162
152 6/8	23 2/8 22 5/8	23 7/8	6 5	Brooks	ALB	Chris Barker	2008	2162
152 5/8	21 3/8 21 5/8	20 3/8	4 4	Elko County	NV	Bill Freeman	1961	2176
152 5/8	22 0/8 22 3/8	22 3/8	5 5	Fremont County	WY	Gene Farley	1964	2176
152 5/8	23 3/8 23 4/8	19 4/8	7 5	Valley County	ID	James J. Akenson	1984	2176
152 5/8	22 4/8 22 1/8	21 6/8	6 6	Mesa County	CO	Don Rogers	1986	2176
152 5/8	19 5/8 16 4/8	22 6/8	5 4	Wichita County	KS	Jack D. Kuhlmann	1986	2176
152 5/8	20 2/8 19 7/8	19 1/8	5 5	Graham County	KS	Danny G. Coday	1989	2176
152 5/8	20 7/8 22 1/8	20 3/8	4 4	Humboldt County	NV	Rob Fletcher	1991	2176
152 5/8	22 3/8 23 0/8	20 7/8	5 5	San Juan County	CO	Joseph Testerman	1993	2176
152 5/8	22 7/8 22 7/8	23 6/8	5 5	Taber	ALB	Scott Godown	2000	2176
152 5/8	24 1/8 24 5/8	27 4/8	4 6	Treasure County	MT	Chuck Adams	2000	2176

330

MULE DEER (TYPICAL ANTLERS)

Minimum Score 145   Continued

SCORE	LENGTH OF R MAIN BEAM L	INSIDE SPREAD	NUMBER OF R POINTS L	AREA	STATE/ PROVINCE	HUNTER'S NAME	DATE	RANK
152 5/8	22 7/8 23 6/8	21 5/8	5 5	Lincoln County	CO	Derek R. Egbert	2001	2176
*152 5/8	21 5/8 22 1/8	18 1/8	5 5	Bow River	ALB	Blake Howland	2006	2176
*152 5/8	24 4/8 23 7/8	20 7/8	6 5	Pennington County	SD	Kris C. Weinberger	2007	2176
*152 5/8	23 3/8 22 5/8	24 0/8	5 5	Pennington County	SD	Matt Burrows	2008	2176
152 4/8	28 7/8 27 7/8	24 4/8	4 3	Montrose County	CO	John A. Wilk	1978	2190
152 4/8	21 1/8 20 7/8	17 5/8	5 6	Madison County	MT	Tony Rebich	1982	2190
152 4/8	21 6/8 21 7/8	16 6/8	5 5	Harney County	OR	Jim Hodson	1988	2190
152 4/8	21 6/8 21 2/8	20 4/8	5 5	Harney County	OR	Michael J. Bradeen	1989	2190
152 4/8	22 4/8 22 1/8	23 3/8	5 5	Calgary	ALB	Dave Browne	1991	2190
152 4/8	21 7/8 24 1/8	22 0/8	5 5	Greenlee County	AZ	Dan Martin	1994	2190
152 4/8	23 0/8 22 3/8	18 6/8	4 4	Converse County	WY	Lee Jernigan	1997	2190
152 4/8	20 4/8 19 6/8	23 1/8	5 5	Delta County	CO	Rick Curtis	1997	2190
152 4/8	24 0/8 23 0/8	22 2/8	4 5	Jefferson County	OR	Jay Roth	1998	2190
152 4/8	20 1/8 21 1/8	21 1/8	5 7	Powder River County	MT	Dion Brown	2001	2190
152 4/8	22 4/8 22 4/8	20 2/8	5 5	Butte County	ID	Roudy K. Keller	2001	2190
152 4/8	20 4/8 19 6/8	18 4/8	4 5	Lincoln County	WA	Charles Berg	2005	2190
152 4/8	21 2/8 20 3/8	18 4/8	5 5	Crockett County	TX	Robert Earl Kincaid, Jr.	2006	2190
152 4/8	21 1/8 21 2/8	18 4/8	5 6	Billings County	ND	Les Krogstad	2006	2190
*152 4/8	23 3/8 21 1/8	19 2/8	6 5	Cheyenne County	CO	Jim Kerth	2008	2190
152 3/8	20 6/8 20 7/8	20 2/8	5 6	Carbon County	UT	John C. Loutzenhiser	1969	2205
152 3/8	23 0/8 21 7/8	22 4/8	4 4	Montrose County	CO	Viron Barbay	1985	2205
152 3/8	20 7/8 21 3/8	19 3/8	5 5	Cochise County	AZ	Stan Wacker	1989	2205
152 3/8	22 7/8 23 0/8	19 5/8	6 6	Mesa County	CO	Jeffrey M. Davis	1994	2205
152 3/8	24 1/8 22 0/8	20 7/8	5 5	Larimer County	CO	Gene DeVore, Jr.	1997	2205
152 3/8	21 6/8 22 0/8	24 0/8	5 4	Rockyview	ALB	Charles Martin	1998	2205
152 3/8	25 0/8 25 2/8	20 3/8	4 4	Elbert County	CO	Turk Wendell	1999	2205
152 3/8	20 1/8 20 5/8	20 3/8	5 5	Delta County	CO	Judi A. DeRusha	2002	2205
152 3/8	21 3/8 20 4/8	17 3/8	5 4	Carter County	MT	DuWayne M. Larson	2002	2205
152 3/8	23 6/8 23 0/8	21 5/8	6 7	Millarville	ALB	Jeff Ensor	2002	2205
152 3/8	26 3/8 25 7/8	20 7/8	5 5	Pitkin County	CO	Mike Minnick	2003	2205
152 3/8	21 0/8 20 1/8	17 1/8	5 6	Porcupine Hills	ALB	Glen Guenter	2003	2205
152 3/8	21 2/8 20 2/8	21 0/8	8 7	Garfield County	MT	Mark Meyer	2006	2205
*152 3/8	21 1/8 21 1/8	19 3/8	5 5	Stanley County	SD	Mark J. Clausen	2007	2205
152 3/8	20 5/8 21 1/8	19 3/8	5 5	Park County	WY	Clayton Tucker	2007	2205
152 3/8	21 0/8 20 5/8	18 7/8	5 5	Dunn County	ND	James W. Casto III	2007	2205
152 3/8	23 1/8 24 0/8	22 2/8	6 5	Cheyenne County	CO	Steve Keithley	2007	2205
152 3/8	22 0/8 20 4/8	20 3/8	4 5	Pennington County	SD	James Augustine	2008	2205
152 2/8	21 0/8 21 0/8	19 0/8	5 6	Grand County	UT	Roger Smith	1962	2223
152 2/8	19 3/8 20 4/8	20 4/8	5 5	Elko County	NV	Jack Konvalin	1963	2223
152 2/8	26 0/8 26 0/8	22 0/8	4 4	Garfield County	CO	Jim Dougherty	1968	2223
152 2/8	21 5/8 21 7/8	21 5/8	5 5	Millard County	UT	David G. Snyder	1968	2223
152 2/8	21 0/8 21 0/8	24 6/8	6 6	Madison County	MT	Dave Bonczyk	1972	2223
152 2/8	20 1/8 20 2/8	18 0/8	4 4	Billings County	ND	Harold Hugelen	1995	2223
152 2/8	23 5/8 22 6/8	22 2/8	5 5	Yuma County	CO	Jerry Bowen	1996	2223
152 2/8	22 3/8 23 4/8	24 1/8	5 5	Eagle County	CO	Greg Close	1997	2223
152 2/8	21 7/8 22 6/8	23 1/8	5 6	Ellis County	KS	Rick Cunningham	1997	2223
152 1/8	20 1/8 20 1/8	18 1/8	5 5	Cochise County	AZ	John Behrends	1969	2232
152 1/8	23 4/8 22 5/8	23 6/8	6 6	Ross Lake	ALB	Darcy Barrett	1988	2232
152 1/8	21 2/8 21 1/8	16 1/8	5 5	White Pine County	NV	Larry D. Draper	1994	2232
152 1/8	20 7/8 21 2/8	18 4/8	6 5	Twin Falls County	ID	Darrell Nunez	1994	2232
152 1/8	21 6/8 22 1/8	18 5/8	5 5	Garfield County	UT	L. Grant Foster	1996	2232
152 1/8	22 0/8 24 2/8	19 1/8	6 5	Kiowa County	CO	Mike Mrdjenovich	1999	2232
152 1/8	25 4/8 25 1/8	24 6/8	5 4	Johnson County	WY	Jason Stephenson	2004	2232
152 1/8	21 2/8 22 1/8	23 0/8	5 5	Washoe County	NV	Darrin Rice	2005	2232
152 1/8	20 2/8 22 7/8	17 6/8	6 5	Bennett County	SD	Michael J. Keegan	2008	2232
*152 1/8	22 3/8 22 5/8	22 7/8	4 4	Mojave County	AZ	Michael D. Wall	2009	2232
*152 1/8	23 0/8 24 1/8	28 7/8	5 6	Mesa County	CO	Christopher T. Beyer	2009	2232
152 0/8	20 0/8 20 6/8	17 3/8	8 7	Garfield County	UT	Bob Mackinnon	1970	2243
152 0/8	19 3/8 19 5/8	18 0/8	5 5	Bowman County	ND	Mark Loutzenhiser	1985	2243
152 0/8	20 2/8 22 7/8	18 6/8	6 6	Elko County	NV	LeRoy McQueen	1986	2243
152 0/8	21 2/8 21 2/8	22 1/8	5 5	Harney County	OR	Billy Jack Elbert	1989	2243
152 0/8	19 6/8 20 6/8	21 4/8	5 4	Yavapai County	AZ	Nick Arnett	1994	2243
152 0/8	23 4/8 24 5/8	23 0/8	5 5	Mesa County	CO	Bill L. Conn	2000	2243
152 0/8	23 6/8 23 3/8	21 5/8	6 6	Garfield County	CO	Steve Hammond	2000	2243
152 0/8	22 0/8 21 6/8	20 0/8	5 5	Johnson County	WY	Zack Burkett III	2002	2243
152 0/8	21 0/8 21 3/8	20 1/8	5 6	Garfield County	MT	Mark L. Meyer	2003	2243
152 0/8	20 5/8 19 7/8	17 6/8	5 5	Garfield County	CO	Larrie Hazen	2005	2243
152 0/8	23 5/8 23 0/8	21 1/8	5 6	Grant County	NE	Kent Hochstein	2008	2243
151 7/8	22 0/8 22 2/8	20 0/8	6 8	Duchesne County	UT	Rowland S. Enomoto	1965	2254
151 7/8	22 0/8 21 2/8	21 7/8	5 4	Chelan County	WA	L. James Bailey	1977	2254
151 7/8	22 1/8 22 7/8	21 5/8	7 5	Pima County	AZ	Douglas L. Sweepe	1988	2254
151 7/8	21 2/8 21 2/8	18 3/8	5 5	Bergen	ALB	Sandy Watt	1990	2254
151 7/8	25 1/8 25 4/8	23 1/8	4 4	Powder River County	MT	Keith Furgerson	1992	2254
151 7/8	21 6/8 22 4/8	18 1/8	5 5	Powder River County	MT	Richard Driscoll	1995	2254
151 7/8	23 3/8 23 2/8	19 2/8	5 7	Elbert County	CO	Bobby D. Benison	1996	2254
151 7/8	23 2/8 23 1/8	19 7/8	5 4	Stanley County	SD	Ryan Taylor	2005	2254
151 7/8	20 5/8 22 1/8	22 1/8	5 5	Jumping Pound Creek	ALB	Dave Browne	2006	2254
151 6/8	20 3/8 20 2/8	21 4/8	4 5	Garfield County	MT	Herman Hass	1961	2263
151 6/8	18 7/8 21 7/8	21 7/8	6 6	Rio Blanco County	CO	Doug Kenyon	1967	2263
151 6/8	17 5/8 15 4/8	14 4/8	5 5	Garfield County	CO	Roger Smith	1973	2263
151 6/8	22 5/8 21 0/8	20 0/8	5 5	Mesa County	CO	Steve Fossen	1974	2263
151 6/8	19 3/8 21 6/8	16 5/8	5 5	Grand County	CO	Mark Chapman	1978	2263
151 6/8	20 3/8 20 4/8	15 7/8	7 7	Mesa County	CO	Jack O. Rothwell	1979	2263
151 6/8	20 0/8 20 4/8	19 0/8	5 5	Lane County	KS	Dean Hamilton	1985	2263
151 6/8	21 0/8 20 2/8	18 2/8	5 6	Carbon County	WY	Rene Suda	1990	2263
151 6/8	19 7/8 20 2/8	19 7/8	6 5	Platte County	WY	Jason W. Dirscherl	1994	2263
151 6/8	23 0/8 21 6/8	21 5/8	4 5	Osborne County	KS	Robert Grabast	1994	2263
151 6/8	19 6/8 20 2/8	20 5/8	5 5	San Juan County	NM	Bert Poulton	1996	2263
151 6/8	20 3/8 20 6/8	20 0/8	5 5	Culberson County	TX	Robert L. Childress	1998	2263
151 6/8	20 2/8 23 1/8	22 0/8	5 5	Converse County	WY	Peter F. Woeck II	2003	2263
*151 6/8	21 1/8 21 2/8	15 6/8	5 5	Deschutes County	OR	Neal Korpela	2007	2263
151 6/8	21 3/8 21 6/8	15 2/8	5 5	Jackson County	SD	Sean C. Fulton	2007	2263
151 5/8	21 5/8 20 5/8	20 0/8	5 5	Garfield County	UT	Dick Gulman	1968	2278
151 5/8	20 2/8 18 7/8	18 1/8	6 6	Chaffee County	CO	Eugene K. Post	1971	2278
151 5/8	20 5/8 20 5/8	18 1/8	5 5	Mesa County	CO	Richard E. Davis, Jr.	1977	2278

331

MULE DEER (TYPICAL ANTLERS)

Minimum Score 145   Continued

SCORE	LENGTH OF R MAIN BEAM L		INSIDE SPREAD	NUMBER OF R POINTS L		AREA	STATE/ PROVINCE	HUNTER'S NAME	DATE	RANK
151 5/8	19 4/8	20 3/8	16 3/8	6	5	Phillips County	KS	Michael L. Hoft	1985	2278
151 5/8	20 0/8	20 1/8	20 2/8	5	5	Billings County	ND	Greg Obrigewitch	1987	2278
151 5/8	22 4/8	22 2/8	21 1/8	5	5	Caribou County	ID	Roger Wright	1990	2278
151 5/8	21 4/8	21 4/8	18 3/8	5	5	Medicine Hat	ALB	John Carber, Jr.	1997	2278
151 5/8	21 4/8	21 0/8	17 1/8	5	6	Campbell County	WY	Leon R. Nyreen	1997	2278
151 5/8	20 3/8	21 6/8	17 7/8	7	5	Cochrane	ALB	Tom Foss	1997	2278
151 5/8	20 1/8	20 0/8	20 4/8	6	6	Logan County	CO	Scott Withrow	2000	2278
151 5/8	20 1/8	21 0/8	20 1/8	4	5	Elbert County	CO	Bill McGowan	2002	2278
151 5/8	20 6/8	21 4/8	19 4/8	6	5	Fall River County	SD	John McKeever	2003	2278
151 5/8	23 0/8	23 3/8	19 7/8	5	5	Custer County	MT	J. Dale Hale	2005	2278
151 5/8	23 0/8	22 5/8	21 4/8	6	6	Campbell County	SD	Preston W. Huber	2007	2278
151 5/8	22 4/8	22 2/8	21 6/8	7	5	Mesa County	CO	Jynecca Cronk	2008	2278
*151 5/8	19 6/8	20 5/8	16 5/8	4	5	Gove County	KS	Scott Stedman	2008	2278
*151 5/8	19 4/8	19 5/8	17 7/8	5	5	Milk River	ALB	M. Blake Patton	2009	2278
151 4/8	24 5/8	24 5/8	26 2/8	4	6	Bingham County	ID	Craig A. Young	1982	2295
151 4/8	21 7/8	22 0/8	18 6/8	5	5	Grant County	OR	Karl Geaney	1994	2295
151 4/8	23 0/8	21 3/8	18 3/8	5	4	Carter County	MT	Larry L. Lawman	1995	2295
151 4/8	24 2/8	24 5/8	22 6/8	4	5	Jefferson County	OR	Steve Davis	1995	2295
151 4/8	22 4/8	22 7/8	21 2/8	4	5	Modoc County	CA	Wayne Wood	1997	2295
151 4/8	21 1/8	18 7/8	19 2/8	5	6	Hawks Creek	BC	Allan Tew	1997	2295
151 4/8	20 0/8	18 3/8	21 4/8	5	5	Weld County	CO	Nathan L. Andersohn	1998	2295
151 4/8	23 5/8	22 4/8	22 6/8	5	5	Montrose County	CO	Richard "Dick" Wood	1999	2295
151 4/8	21 2/8	21 4/8	20 4/8	5	6	Seven Persons	ALB	Jesse Schowengerdt	2002	2295
151 4/8	21 1/8	21 2/8	22 1/8	5	5	Jefferson County	CO	Larry J. Jones	2003	2295
151 4/8	22 0/8	22 1/8	21 6/8	5	5	Phillips County	MT	Dave Kothbauer	2003	2295
151 4/8	24 4/8	23 3/8	20 4/8	4	4	Cherry County	NE	Kyle Hochstein	2003	2295
151 4/8	22 2/8	19 2/8	18 4/8	4	4	Rich County	UT	Aaron Yarnell	2005	2295
151 3/8	22 4/8	19 2/8	19 1/8	5	5	Dolores County	CO	Dennis Atwater	1979	2308
151 3/8	22 0/8	21 5/8	21 7/8	5	5	Washoe County	NV	David J. Fujii	1981	2308
151 3/8	19 0/8	20 5/8	21 4/8	5	5	Lane County	KS	Dean Hamilton	1986	2308
151 3/8	22 7/8	22 1/8	17 1/8	4	4	Mesa County	CO	Dennis Kelly	1991	2308
151 3/8	21 0/8	22 0/8	18 3/8	4	6	Caribou County	ID	Randon Wright	1991	2308
151 3/8	22 2/8	21 6/8	20 6/8	6	5	Sheridan County	WY	David L. Willis	1992	2308
151 3/8	24 6/8	19 4/8	19 6/8	6	5	Lake County	OR	Jevon A. Struve	2001	2308
*151 3/8	22 2/8	21 4/8	18 5/8	6	5	Mohave County	AZ	William Redding	2009	2308
151 3/8	20 7/8	20 7/8	17 6/8	5	6	Dunn County	ND	Tim Belland	2010	2308
151 2/8	22 7/8	19 2/8	16 4/8	5	5	Chelan County	WA	G. H. Malinoski	1959	2317
151 2/8	24 5/8	23 1/8	24 5/8	7	6	Bear Lake County	ID	Keith V. Hymos	1961	2317
151 2/8	23 2/8	22 7/8	22 4/8	5	4	Chelan County	WA	Ron Carpenter	1973	2317
151 2/8	20 6/8	22 6/8	22 0/8	7	5	Uncompahgre N.F.	CO	Clifford Patterson	1976	2317
151 2/8	21 4/8	21 3/8	20 0/8	5	5	Phillips County	MT	Brian Roness	1984	2317
151 2/8	21 0/8	20 6/8	17 0/8	7	5	Stanley County	SD	Dale DeBoer	1985	2317
151 2/8	24 5/8	25 7/8	19 1/8	7	5	Dundy County	NE	Michael C. Dysh	1988	2317
151 2/8	22 5/8	21 3/8	19 2/8	4	4	Black Diamond	ALB	Marc Nyrose	1989	2317
151 2/8	22 4/8	21 0/8	22 6/8	5	5	County of 40 Mile	ALB	Tammy Glass	1992	2317
151 2/8	21 7/8	21 5/8	19 6/8	6	5	Otero County	NM	Frank Rodriguez	1993	2317
151 2/8	21 2/8	22 6/8	20 2/8	5	4	Milk River	ALB	Will Pick	1999	2317
151 2/8	20 3/8	20 1/8	20 2/8	5	4	Brooks	ALB	Steven E. Sheehy	2000	2317
151 2/8	22 2/8	23 4/8	21 4/8	5	6	Wallowa County	OR	Harry Paul Waterman	2001	2317
151 2/8	20 4/8	20 6/8	21 0/8	5	5	Deschutes County	OR	Charlotte R. Brittner	2001	2317
151 2/8	24 2/8	24 4/8	19 2/8	4	5	Newell	ALB	Ray Francingues III	2003	2317
151 2/8	20 3/8	20 6/8	17 6/8	5	5	Missoula County	MT	Dan Ermatinger	2003	2317
151 2/8	21 6/8	22 4/8	21 2/8	5	5	Big Cooley	ALB	Bob Ameen	2006	2317
*151 2/8	21 1/8	21 2/8	19 6/8	5	5	Johnson County	WY	David Bilotti	2006	2317
151 2/8	21 7/8	23 3/8	22 2/8	5	5	Maricopa County	AZ	Dave Goitia	2007	2317
151 2/8	20 6/8	20 3/8	21 3/8	5	5	Powder River County	MT	Mike Barrett	2009	2317
*151 2/8	23 0/8	21 5/8	24 0/8	4	5	Pueblo County	CO	John E. Brandstatter	2009	2317
151 1/8	21 4/8	22 2/8	20 2/8	6	7	Butte County	SD	John Kirk	1958	2338
151 1/8	23 7/8	22 7/8	20 1/8	4	5	Mesa County	CO	Bill Martens	1984	2338
151 1/8	20 3/8	20 6/8	16 7/8	5	5	McKenzie County	ND	Kurt T. Hovet	1988	2338
151 1/8	19 0/8	19 2/8	13 7/8	5	5	Boise County	ID	Ken Dory	1989	2338
151 1/8	20 6/8	21 1/8	19 3/8	7	6	Valmarie	SAS	Steve Von Hagen	1992	2338
151 1/8	20 7/8	21 0/8	20 5/8	5	5	Stillwater County	MT	Gary F. Bogner	1994	2338
151 1/8	20 3/8	21 2/8	22 1/8	5	5	El Paso County	CO	Ed Ruroede	1996	2338
151 1/8	20 7/8	20 2/8	20 5/8	5	5	Okotoks	ALB	Maurice Pike	2000	2338
*151 1/8	23 6/8	24 2/8	22 2/8	6	6	Jackson County	CO	Sturg Cumberford	2002	2338
*151 1/8	20 1/8	22 1/8	18 4/8	5	6	Brooks	ALB	Gary Joseph	2005	2338
*151 1/8	21 0/8	23 0/8	19 7/8	5	5	Campbell County	SD	Doug Gorhring	2005	2338
151 1/8	21 2/8	22 1/8	20 5/8	5	5	Pennington County	SD	Harry J. Powell	2005	2338
151 1/8	19 6/8	20 1/8	19 2/8	4	6	Pershing County	NV	Bill Pemberton	2008	2338
151 1/8	24 6/8	19 0/8	21 4/8	5	5	Buckley River	BC	Marco Mellace	2008	2338
*151 1/8	22 7/8	23 4/8	23 1/8	5	5	Lomand	ALB	Bev Emigh	2009	2338
150 0/8	22 1/8	22 0/8	20 6/8	5	7	Chelan County	WA	Deryl E. Bland	1964	2353
150 0/8	18 4/8	21 2/8	17 4/8	5	5	Moffat County	CO	Wayne Liskey	1966	2353
150 0/8	22 0/8	19 1/8	23 2/8	5	4	Uncompahgre N.F.	CO	Roy Miller	1972	2353
150 0/8	20 1/8	21 0/8	22 2/8	6	5	Rio Arriba County	NM	Howard Payne	1984	2353
150 0/8	20 3/8	21 4/8	19 0/8	5	5	Platte County	WY	Jody Nordin	1984	2353
150 0/8	19 0/8	18 4/8	19 4/8	5	5	Maricopa County	AZ	Dave Barnhart	1986	2353
150 0/8	22 4/8	20 6/8	20 2/8	5	5	Coconino County	AZ	Randy Barnes	1986	2353
150 0/8	25 1/8	24 7/8	23 1/8	4	6	Cochrane	ALB	Denny Williamson	1989	2353
150 0/8	19 4/8	19 2/8	20 1/8	5	5	Abbey	SAS	Clarence Hughes	1990	2353
150 0/8	21 3/8	21 4/8	22 1/8	5	5	Eagle County	CO	John J. Collins	1991	2353
150 0/8	20 6/8	20 4/8	21 6/8	6	5	Humboldt County	NV	Fred C. Church	1992	2353
150 0/8	18 0/8	18 4/8	22 2/8	5	5	Elbert County	CO	Kim Cooper	1993	2353
150 0/8	20 6/8	21 2/8	19 6/8	5	5	Pennington County	SD	Scott R. Marsich	1994	2353
150 0/8	22 2/8	22 6/8	23 3/8	5	5	Harris	SAS	Joe Schmidt	1995	2353
150 0/8	23 3/8	24 1/8	19 4/8	4	4	Empress	ALB	Dave Holt	1995	2353
150 0/8	20 5/8	21 2/8	20 5/8	4	5	Natrona County	WY	Shawn Wagner	2000	2353
150 0/8	22 4/8	22 1/8	20 4/8	5	5	Harney County	OR	Scott Widner	2001	2353
150 0/8	23 4/8	22 1/8	25 2/8	6	6	Pima County	AZ	Barry R. Sopher	2007	2353
150 7/8	22 4/8	23 3/8	20 0/8	6	6	Hockberry Creek	KS	Dale Redmond	1967	2371
150 7/8	22 5/8	19 3/8	25 3/8	5	4	San Juan County	UT	Ken Ciarelli	1968	2371
150 7/8	22 6/8	22 6/8	20 1/8	6	6	Fremont County	CO	Dave Elliotti	1976	2371
150 7/8	20 4/8	20 2/8	19 1/8	5	5	Idaho County	ID	Gary Belvoir	1981	2371
150 7/8	20 1/8	21 1/8	16 1/8	5	5	Coconino County	AZ	Les Shelton	1984	2371

332

MULE DEER (TYPICAL ANTLERS)

Minimum Score 145 — Continued

SCORE	R MAIN BEAM L	INSIDE SPREAD	R POINTS L	AREA	STATE/PROVINCE	HUNTER'S NAME	DATE	RANK
150 7/8	20 3/8 20 7/8	17 5/8	4 4	Washington County	UT	E. Kip Fowler	1993	2371
150 7/8	20 6/8 20 6/8	18 7/8	5 5	Las Animas County	CO	Jeffrey A. Falkner	1995	2371
150 7/8	22 6/8 23 6/8	23 4/8	5 6	Umatilla County	OR	Richard Schmidt	1996	2371
150 7/8	21 1/8 23 0/8	20 3/8	5 5	Billings County	ND	Mark L. Meyer	1998	2371
150 7/8	23 6/8 22 4/8	20 6/8	4 6	Eagle County	CO	Laurence W. Trotter II	2000	2371
150 7/8	21 1/8 20 7/8	19 1/8	5 5	Duchesne County	UT	Sean P. Davis	2000	2371
150 7/8	25 2/8 23 3/8	23 3/8	5 5	Converse County	WY	Steve Schulz	2006	2371
150 7/8	22 5/8 20 5/8	24 5/8	4 4	Elko County	NV	Amy Boykin	2006	2371
150 7/8	22 4/8 22 2/8	18 4/8	6 6	Valley County	ID	James Akenson	2007	2371
150 6/8	20 5/8 20 3/8	20 5/8	5 6	Washington County	UT	Jack Richards	1960	2385
150 6/8	20 2/8 20 0/8	18 2/8	5 5	Bernalillo County	NM	Lee Braudt	1968	2385
150 6/8	21 6/8 22 1/8	22 4/8	4 5	Hamilton County	KS	Mike Gilbert	1976	2385
150 6/8	22 5/8 21 2/8	23 2/8	5 6	Box Elder County	UT	Steven B. Perry	1980	2385
150 6/8	21 2/8 20 6/8	18 4/8	5 5	Grant County	OR	Rodney Keenon	1982	2385
150 6/8	22 4/8 22 6/8	19 0/8	5 4	County of Warner	ALB	Giuliano Coslovi	1987	2385
150 6/8	25 7/8 23 2/8	25 0/8	4 5	Lassen County	CA	Rick Pollard	1992	2385
150 6/8	20 1/8 20 6/8	16 6/8	5 5	Boise County	ID	Jeff L. Varner	1994	2385
150 6/8	24 6/8 24 2/8	24 2/8	4 5	Elko County	NV	Tim Bottari	2000	2385
150 6/8	19 4/8 19 3/8	18 4/8	5 5	Brooks	ALB	David L. Butler	2004	2385
150 6/8	21 2/8 21 5/8	21 0/8	5 5	Lyman County	SD	Kyle Reedy	2005	2385
150 6/8	20 4/8 20 5/8	19 4/8	5 5	Cochise County	AZ	Roy E. Grace	2007	2385
150 6/8	21 7/8 22 1/8	20 6/8	5 5	Dunn County	ND	Mark Sailer	2008	2385
150 6/8	23 2/8 24 6/8	22 7/8	4 5	Swift Current	SAS	Stacy Bolton	2009	2385
150 5/8	24 2/8 24 7/8	19 6/8	6 5	Bernalillo County	NM	Alan Spitznagle	1982	2399
150 5/8	22 3/8 22 4/8	16 1/8	5 5	Grant County	NM	Mark Garrison	1989	2399
150 5/8	20 1/8 19 5/8	21 0/8	5 5	Boise County	ID	David R. Heck	1991	2399
150 5/8	19 3/8 19 4/8	18 1/8	5 5	McKenzie County	ND	Matt Leer	2001	2399
150 5/8	23 4/8 23 5/8	20 0/8	6 5	Airdrie	ALB	Todd Kersten	2001	2399
150 5/8	22 1/8 21 7/8	18 6/8	6 5	Gallatin County	MT	Michael J. Ott	2004	2399
150 5/8	23 1/8 24 5/8	20 3/8	5 6	Armstrong County	TX	Clint Hukill	2007	2399
150 4/8	21 6/8 22 0/8	21 5/8	5 6	Pima County	AZ	Tony Don	1980	2406
150 4/8	21 4/8 21 4/8	19 4/8	5 4	Garfield County	CO	Keith Backhaus	1981	2406
150 4/8	22 0/8 21 6/8	22 5/8	5 5	Carbon County	UT	C. J. Coleman	1987	2406
150 4/8	21 3/8 20 6/8	18 0/8	6 5	Wallowa County	OR	Billy L. Moores	1996	2406
150 4/8	23 3/8 22 5/8	21 2/8	5 5	Caribou County	ID	Dan A. Whitmus	2000	2406
150 4/8	21 4/8 21 2/8	22 2/8	5 5	Golden Valley County	ND	Chris Haug	2001	2406
150 4/8	23 5/8 23 4/8	21 0/8	6 6	Logan County	CO	Justin Duncan	2003	2406
150 4/8	27 0/8 25 5/8	20 4/8	4 5	Platte County	WY	Bill Hinz	2004	2406
150 4/8	20 6/8 21 0/8	18 0/8	4 4	Douglas County	CO	Staci Ferguson	2004	2406
150 4/8	21 5/8 22 4/8	25 0/8	5 4	Cascade County	MT	Gary Lampkins	2005	2406
150 4/8	23 0/8 22 5/8	21 2/8	4 5	Pennington County	SD	Gary D. English	2010	2406
150 3/8	22 6/8 22 7/8	15 5/8	4 5	Summit County	UT	Clifton Rees	1962	2417
150 3/8	19 6/8 20 3/8	19 7/8	4 5	Grand County	UT	Lowell W. Dobson	1968	2417
150 3/8	21 0/8 21 0/8	15 7/8	5 5	Bernalillo County	NM	Michael M. Emery	1973	2417
150 3/8	21 6/8 21 1/8	19 7/8	5 5	Washoe County	NV	Fred C. Church	1983	2417
150 3/8	20 0/8 20 0/8	21 1/8	5 5	Lane County	KS	Dean Hamilton	1984	2417
150 3/8	20 5/8 20 1/8	22 7/8	5 4	Cascade County	MT	Bennie J. Rossetto	1990	2417
150 3/8	22 1/8 20 6/8	20 1/8	5 5	Boise County	ID	Russ Meyer	1991	2417
150 3/8	19 7/8 19 4/8	23 7/8	4 4	Chouteau County	MT	Dwight P. Martin	1992	2417
150 3/8	19 2/8 18 6/8	16 1/8	5 5	McKenzie County	ND	Brent Smith	1993	2417
150 3/8	20 7/8 21 2/8	19 6/8	5 6	Ford County	KS	J. C. Falco	1993	2417
150 3/8	21 1/8 21 2/8	19 7/8	5 5	Harney County	OR	Tyler Saunders	1996	2417
150 3/8	15 4/8 19 1/8	18 7/8	5 5	Dawes County	NE	Roger Westemeier	1998	2417
150 3/8	21 3/8 22 2/8	20 7/8	5 5	McKenzie County	ND	Don Davidson	1999	2417
150 3/8	21 6/8 21 4/8	19 7/8	5 5	Hanna	ALB	Christopher L. Johnson	2001	2417
150 3/8	23 1/8 21 7/8	18 5/8	6 5	Burleigh County	ND	Tyler Auck	2007	2417
150 3/8	19 4/8 19 6/8	15 5/8	5 5	Custer County	CO	Logan Canterbury	2008	2417
150 2/8	13 0/8 19 7/8	15 3/8	3 6	Boise County	ID	Ralph Hoobing	1964	2433
150 2/8	21 3/8 22 1/8	23 7/8	4 4	Valley County	MT	Andy Hicks	1981	2433
150 2/8	22 1/8 22 1/8	20 4/8	6 5	Maricopa County	AZ	Mike Ottenbacher	1987	2433
150 2/8	22 1/8 22 0/8	15 6/8	5 5	Wasatch County	UT	Ronald Whaley	1987	2433
150 2/8	22 2/8 22 4/8	22 0/8	4 5	Union County	OR	Brian J. Scott	1990	2433
150 2/8	21 4/8 24 3/8	24 0/8	4 3	Bow River	ALB	Bob Gruszecki	1991	2433
150 2/8	22 1/8 19 2/8	20 7/8	5 6	Bernalillo County	NM	Anthony Ortega	1992	2433
150 2/8	20 3/8 21 7/8	19 6/8	5 5	Rio Blanco County	CO	Chris Hofer	1994	2433
150 2/8	19 3/8 21 0/8	20 0/8	5 5	Crook County	OR	David Sonnenburg	1995	2433
150 2/8	20 5/8 21 2/8	18 6/8	5 5	Huerfano County	CO	Alan Blair	1996	2433
150 2/8	20 3/8 21 7/8	19 4/8	5 5	Campbell County	SD	Douglas A. Goehring	1996	2433
150 2/8	19 6/8 21 4/8	21 2/8	4 5	Salt Lake County	UT	Norman Kevin Davis	1996	2433
150 2/8	25 4/8 26 0/8	20 6/8	6 5	Salt Lake County	UT	Bill Plowman	1999	2433
150 2/8	21 6/8 21 0/8	20 1/8	6 7	Conrich	ALB	John Evans	2000	2433
150 2/8	24 2/8 24 0/8	28 5/8	4 5	Fergus County	MT	Rob Miller	2003	2433
150 2/8	20 6/8 19 6/8	18 4/8	5 4	Caribou County	ID	Mike Barrett	2003	2433
150 2/8	21 6/8 20 3/8	17 6/8	5 5	Armstrong County	TX	Brandon Ray	2009	2433
150 1/8	18 3/8 18 5/8	17 3/8	6 7	Garfield County	CO	J. B. Hogan	1961	2450
150 1/8	24 7/8 26 2/8	24 0/8	5 5	Deschutes County	OR	Walter M. Graham	1963	2450
150 1/8	22 3/8 22 2/8	18 3/8	5 5	Jackson County	CO	William B. Tutt	1964	2450
150 1/8	22 6/8 22 7/8	22 3/8	4 4	Gove County	KS	Merton Ikenberry	1966	2450
150 1/8	21 3/8 21 4/8	20 1/8	5 5	Washoe County	NV	Felton Hickman	1970	2450
150 1/8	21 4/8 22 5/8	24 1/8	4 4	Cochrane	ALB	Jim Hillstead	1989	2450
150 1/8	23 2/8 24 2/8	20 5/8	5 5	Campbell County	WY	John Keenan	1993	2450
150 1/8	24 7/8 23 0/8	17 1/8	5 4	Oldman River	ALB	Doug Doram	1993	2450
150 1/8	25 7/8 25 0/8	20 7/8	5 4	Empress	ALB	Michael E. Kessler	1993	2450
150 1/8	20 1/8 20 5/8	19 4/8	5 6	Lincoln County	NE	Tyron Lenz	1994	2450
150 1/8	21 6/8 22 7/8	15 1/8	5 5	Rosebud County	MT	Chuck Adams	1997	2450
150 1/8	21 2/8 22 5/8	19 4/8	5 6	Rio Arriba County	NM	Richard W. Eustace, Jr.	1998	2450
150 1/8	22 0/8 23 3/8	19 7/8	4 6	Converse County	WY	Anthony "Del" DelMastro	1999	2450
*150 1/8	22 5/8 22 6/8	18 3/8	5 5	100 Mile House	BC	Dan Real	2005	2450
150 1/8	22 3/8 22 5/8	25 2/8	5 5	Teller County	CO	Rod J. Hoekert	2007	2450
150 1/8	21 3/8 21 7/8	20 7/8	4 4	Rich County	UT	Glen O. Hallows	2007	2450
*150 1/8	22 7/8 22 0/8	20 1/8	4 4	Porcupine Hills	ALB	Nick Trehearne	2007	2450
150 1/8	24 4/8 24 1/8	19 1/8	5 5	Keya Paha County	NE	R. Kirk Sharp	2008	2450
150 0/8	21 2/8 22 4/8	24 4/8	4 4	Eureka County	NV	B. Verlyn Ownes	1963	2468
150 0/8	18 7/8 18 6/8	16 3/8	5 6	Garfield County	UT	Dick Gulman	1966	2468
150 0/8	19 3/8 21 4/8	20 7/8	5 5	Elko County	NV	Dick Woltering	1968	2468

333

MULE DEER (TYPICAL ANTLERS)

Minimum Score 145   Continued

SCORE	LENGTH OF R MAIN BEAM L	INSIDE SPREAD	NUMBER OF R POINTS L	AREA	STATE/ PROVINCE	HUNTER'S NAME	DATE	RANK
150 0/8	20 0/8 20 1/8	18 1/8	6 6	Larimer County	CO	Tom Tietz	1979	2468
150 0/8	22 4/8 21 7/8	18 4/8	5 4	White Pine County	NV	Scott Faiman	1987	2468
150 0/8	24 2/8 23 2/8	20 4/8	6 4	Pima County	AZ	Rick Betten	1991	2468
150 0/8	19 3/8 17 2/8	16 0/8	4 4	Weber County	UT	Robert G. Petersen	1992	2468
150 0/8	20 2/8 21 0/8	18 2/8	5 5	Jefferson County	CO	David Scott Brown	2000	2468
150 0/8	21 1/8 22 0/8	16 1/8	5 6	Airdrie	ALB	Steven Tebay	2000	2468
150 0/8	24 2/8 25 6/8	23 7/8	4 5	Stewart Valley	SAS	Ron R. Vandermeulen	2002	2468
150 0/8	21 5/8 22 6/8	20 0/8	4 5	Pima County	AZ	Michael James Holberg	2004	2468
150 0/8	23 0/8 22 1/8	23 0/8	5 5	Ada County	ID	Rick D. Ambroz	2005	2468
150 0/8	20 5/8 19 1/8	18 0/8	6 4	Dunn County	ND	Thomas Spence	2006	2468
150 0/8	20 4/8 20 4/8	17 2/8	5 5	Ziebach County	SD	Wesley Koehler	2008	2468
*150 0/8	23 1/8 23 1/8	19 5/8	6 5	Foard County	TX	Thomas Franklin	2009	2468
149 7/8	21 2/8 23 0/8	20 5/8	4 4	Sevier County	UT	Milt McQueary	1964	2483
149 7/8	20 1/8 20 1/8	17 3/8	5 5	Trego County	KS	Larry Pearson	1974	2483
149 7/8	23 5/8 22 6/8	26 2/8	4 4	Pima County	AZ	Michael B. Cachero	1985	2483
149 7/8	20 0/8 22 2/8	19 2/8	6 4	Platte County	WY	G. Fred Asbell	1988	2483
149 7/8	21 0/8 20 7/8	19 7/8	4 5	Billings County	ND	Kevin Clyde	1989	2483
149 7/8	21 4/8 21 5/8	19 5/8	5 4	McKenzie County	ND	Wade Leer	1990	2483
149 7/8	20 4/8 22 0/8	18 3/8	5 5	Furnas County	NE	Walter S. Wright	1991	2483
149 7/8	22 7/8 22 7/8	21 5/8	4 3	Campbell County	WY	Steve Boster	1991	2483
149 7/8	22 1/8 20 5/8	17 7/8	5 5	Boise County	ID	Jerry E. Burt	1992	2483
149 7/8	22 2/8 22 2/8	20 1/8	5 5	Milk River	ALB	Bud Smedley	2001	2483
149 7/8	22 3/8 19 2/8	21 5/8	4 5	Fall River County	SD	Michael J. Jarding	2004	2483
149 7/8	19 7/8 18 5/8	12 7/8	5 5	Platte County	WY	Jerry Bowen	2005	2483
149 7/8	22 0/8 22 1/8	17 7/8	5 5	Adams County	CO	Gene Moore	2005	2483
149 7/8	22 3/8 22 4/8	20 2/8	6 4	Morrill County	NE	Mark Didier	2007	2483
149 7/8	21 3/8 20 4/8	20 3/8	5 5	Billings County	ND	John Stuchlik, Jr.	2008	2483
149 6/8	21 3/8 21 1/8	19 6/8	4 4	Garfield County	CO	Skip Candahl	1966	2498
149 6/8	26 5/8 27 5/8	25 0/8	7 4	Uncompahgre Plateau	CO	Jim Moan	1976	2498
149 6/8	20 6/8 21 1/8	22 1/8	6 6	Mesa County	CO	Parker Leon	1984	2498
149 6/8	22 1/8 21 6/8	19 5/8	5 5	Baker County	OR	Chuck Warner	1986	2498
149 6/8	23 6/8 23 6/8	24 2/8	5 4	Armstrong	BC	Tim Meissner	1992	2498
149 6/8	26 2/8 26 3/8	26 6/8	5 5	Fall River County	SD	Bruce Briesemeister	1993	2498
149 6/8	18 2/8 19 4/8	19 6/8	5 5	Elko County	NV	Jay A. Doke	1995	2498
149 6/8	22 4/8 23 4/8	21 6/8	6 6	McKenzie County	ND	Ike Crimmins	1999	2498
149 6/8	21 3/8 21 0/8	18 4/8	5 5	Baker County	OR	Glen Berry	2000	2498
149 6/8	22 0/8 21 5/8	26 4/8	5 6	San Juan County	NM	Steven J. Vittetow	2001	2498
*149 6/8	21 0/8 21 7/8	20 2/8	5 5	Gunnison County	CO	Les White	2004	2498
*149 6/8	21 2/8 21 4/8	15 2/8	5 5	Garfield County	MT	Joshua Kochin	2005	2498
149 6/8	25 0/8 22 4/8	22 2/8	4 4	Wimborne	ALB	Jason Pierson	2009	2498
149 6/8	21 0/8 21 2/8	19 6/8	5 6	Yuma County	CO	Jerry Bowen	2009	2498
149 5/8	18 1/8 20 7/8	17 7/8	5 5	Rio Blanco County	CO	Joseph H. French	1972	2512
149 5/8	21 2/8 20 2/8	19 1/8	6 8	Canmore	ALB	Karl Pachonik	1982	2512
149 5/8	21 6/8 22 0/8	18 3/8	6 4	Boise County	ID	Tom Weston	1984	2512
149 5/8	20 6/8 22 1/8	18 7/8	5 5	Nye County	NV	Ed Fuller	1986	2512
149 5/8	22 3/8 21 4/8	22 5/8	5 5	Johnson County	WY	Edward H. Carmichael	1989	2512
149 5/8	22 3/8 22 7/8	22 7/8	5 5	Garfield County	CO	John W. Borlang	1990	2512
149 5/8	24 5/8 20 5/8	23 0/8	4 6	Gallatin County	MT	Doug Stackhouse	1992	2512
149 5/8	22 7/8 24 2/8	25 6/8	4 5	Rosebud County	MT	Jack Ferguson	1998	2512
149 5/8	20 3/8 20 7/8	19 1/8	6 5	Platte County	WY	Jerry Bowen	1998	2512
149 5/8	24 3/8 22 6/8	20 5/8	5 4	Nevada County	CA	Darrel Sudduth	2001	2512
149 5/8	17 2/8 19 4/8	17 0/8	6 5	Newell	ALB	Ray Francingues III	2001	2512
149 5/8	21 4/8 20 1/8	20 1/8	5 5	Yuma County	CO	John Sarvis	2001	2512
149 5/8	21 2/8 21 1/8	15 5/8	6 5	Powder River County	MT	Michael A. Betts	2002	2512
149 5/8	19 7/8 20 2/8	18 1/8	5 5	Campbell County	WY	Gary Roney	2003	2512
149 5/8	22 5/8 23 2/8	19 3/8	6 5	Morrill County	NE	Andrew Leisy	2009	2512
149 4/8	22 2/8 22 4/8	19 2/8	4 4	Colfax County	NM	Ed Foster	1966	2527
149 4/8	22 2/8 22 4/8	24 4/8	5 5	Montrose County	CO	John A. Wilk	1977	2527
149 4/8	21 1/8 20 5/8	20 0/8	6 5	Valencia County	NM	Frank Johnson	1985	2527
149 4/8	21 4/8 20 7/8	23 0/8	5 5	Delta County	CO	Larry Tiner	1986	2527
149 4/8	21 0/8 21 3/8	18 4/8	5 5	Valencia County	NM	Frank Johnson	1987	2527
149 4/8	19 0/8 20 4/8	21 2/8	5 5	Meade County	KS	Randy Blehm	1988	2527
149 4/8	21 3/8 23 4/8	22 0/8	5 6	Pinal County	AZ	John R. Villegas	1993	2527
149 4/8	21 3/8 21 6/8	19 2/8	5 8	Grant County	OR	Monte Wade Hack	1999	2527
*149 4/8	20 6/8 21 6/8	15 2/8	5 5	Harding County	SD	Shawn A. Willey	2008	2527
149 3/8	22 4/8 21 6/8	17 1/8	4 4	Okanogan County	WA	Irl Stamps	1939	2536
149 3/8	22 4/8 20 4/8	19 1/8	5 7	Baker County	OR	Chuck Brackin	1964	2536
149 3/8	21 5/8 22 5/8	20 7/8	5 4	Mesa County	CO	John Smith	1964	2536
149 3/8	23 0/8 24 0/8	22 4/8	4 4	White Pine County	NV	Milo W. Burt	1971	2536
149 3/8	22 6/8 22 1/8	19 2/8	6 4	San Juan County	UT	Randy Radant	1984	2536
149 3/8	20 7/8 21 6/8	20 6/8	6 5	Jackson County	OR	Greg Chakarun	1985	2536
149 3/8	22 4/8 21 2/8	20 7/8	5 6	Coconino County	AZ	Duane R. Richardson	1987	2536
149 3/8	21 2/8 21 7/8	17 7/8	5 5	Jackson County	OR	Jason Tarrant	1988	2536
149 3/8	20 2/8 20 0/8	17 1/8	5 5	Slope County	ND	Todd Seymanski	1990	2536
149 3/8	22 3/8 22 5/8	20 1/8	6 5	Morrill County	NE	R. Matthew Bilby	1990	2536
149 3/8	21 2/8 22 3/8	21 5/8	4 5	Pima County	AZ	Samuel Fatovich	1995	2536
149 3/8	21 4/8 21 1/8	18 3/8	5 5	Randall County	TX	Brandon Ray	2000	2536
149 3/8	21 1/8 20 7/8	19 5/8	5 6	Albany County	WY	Brent Swanson	2001	2536
149 3/8	20 3/8 19 3/8	21 5/8	5 5	Valhalla Centre	ALB	Terry Hagman	2002	2536
149 3/8	20 4/8 21 1/8	20 5/8	5 4	Eagle Hill	ALB	Dallas Kaiser	2005	2536
149 2/8	22 6/8 22 5/8	21 4/8	4 4	Lake County	CO	Thomas V. Sieverd ng	1972	2551
149 2/8	25 5/8 25 2/8	25 0/8	6 4	Lincoln County	WY	Mike Barrett	1984	2551
149 2/8	22 3/8 22 5/8	21 4/8	5 5	Garfield County	CO	James P. Speck	1984	2551
149 2/8	19 4/8 20 4/8	19 0/8	5 5	Grant County	OR	Gary Kiepert	1990	2551
149 2/8	21 0/8 21 2/8	21 4/8	4 5	Billings County	ND	Dale R. Zietz	1993	2551
149 2/8	22 1/8 22 1/8	22 0/8	4 4	Jefferson County	CO	Larry J. Jones	1995	2551
149 2/8	21 3/8 22 0/8	19 0/8	7 9	Val Marie	SAS	Brad Dixon	2001	2551
149 1/8	24 4/8 24 0/8	18 1/8	6 5	Washoe County	NV	Cecil D. Martin	1987	2558
149 1/8	24 6/8 24 6/8	23 0/8	4 6	Kiowa County	CO	Danny Ellis	1998	2558
149 1/8	21 2/8 20 2/8	18 3/8	6 5	Lane County	KS	Dean Hamilton	2000	2558
*149 1/8	21 2/8 20 1/8	19 7/8	5 5	Powder River County	MT	Cameron Hanes	2001	2558
149 1/8	22 2/8 21 6/8	18 3/8	5 4	White Pine County	NV	Max W. Ahlvers	2004	2558
149 1/8	23 2/8 23 1/8	17 7/8	4 4	Mesa County	CO	Joshua Snortum	2004	2558
149 1/8	21 6/8 21 2/8	18 5/8	4 4	Powder River County	MT	Don Scofield	2005	2558
149 1/8	21 0/8 21 1/8	17 5/8	5 6	Golden Valley County	ND	Mark Anderson	2007	2558

MULE DEER (TYPICAL ANTLERS)

Minimum Score 145   Continued

SCORE	LENGTH OF R MAIN BEAM L	INSIDE SPREAD	NUMBER OF R POINTS L	AREA	STATE/ PROVINCE	HUNTER'S NAME	DATE	RANK
*149 1/8	22 6/8 21 4/8	17 6/8	5 6	Springbank	ALB	David R. Coupland	2007	2558
*149 1/8	24 5/8 23 6/8	18 7/8	6 7	Delta County	CO	Steve Meng	2009	2558
149 0/8	24 0/8 22 5/8	22 4/8	4 4	Mesa County	CO	Tom Hentrick	1974	2568
149 0/8	20 4/8 19 6/8	23 4/8	5 5	Lincoln County	WY	Vaughn Cross	1978	2568
149 0/8	25 3/8 24 3/8	22 4/8	5 5	Beaver County	UT	William H. Chilvers	1987	2568
149 0/8	24 2/8 22 7/8	22 7/8	5 7	Elmore County	ID	Brian J. Brewster	1998	2568
149 0/8	20 1/8 20 4/8	19 4/8	4 4	Ellis County	KS	Rick Cunningham	1999	2568
149 0/8	23 0/8 22 0/8	20 4/8	5 5	Walla Walla County	WA	Todd Randall	2003	2568
149 0/8	20 7/8 20 4/8	20 2/8	5 5	Elbert County	CO	Jeff Lampe	2003	2568
149 0/8	21 6/8 20 4/8	16 0/8	5 6	Albany County	WY	Marlin Stapleton	2007	2568
149 0/8	22 6/8 22 0/8	18 1/8	6 5	Medicine Hat	ALB	Bailey Simpson	2007	2568
149 0/8	21 4/8 21 3/8	20 0/8	5 4	Carbon County	WY	Solomon Griffith	2008	2568
*149 0/8	22 2/8 22 7/8	15 7/8	7 8	Chelan County	WA	Travis Maitland	2009	2568
148 7/8	19 4/8 19 6/8	20 2/8	5 6	Garfield County	CO	Charles E. Whaley	1974	2579
148 7/8	22 3/8 23 5/8	20 3/8	6 4	Hodgeman County	KS	James Wiggins	1978	2579
148 7/8	22 3/8 23 3/8	21 3/8	4 4	Crook County	OR	Vernon Simpson	1982	2579
148 7/8	24 1/8 24 3/8	20 7/8	5 5	Gunnison County	CO	Mike Reedy	1992	2579
148 7/8	21 7/8 22 1/8	21 6/8	6 4	Boise County	ID	Edward Keeton	1994	2579
148 7/8	26 1/8 27 1/8	25 4/8	5 5	Las Animas County	CO	Thomas E. Rothrock	1999	2579
148 7/8	24 0/8 22 0/8	21 3/8	4 5	Natrona County	WY	Steven J. Torok	2000	2579
148 7/8	21 1/8 21 4/8	19 7/8	5 5	Golden Valley County	ND	Brent Swanson	2004	2579
148 7/8	20 6/8 19 2/8	17 7/8	5 5	Douglas County	CO	Mike Leczel	2004	2579
148 7/8	22 7/8 22 5/8	19 7/8	5 5	Okotoks	ALB	Jordan Cook	2004	2579
148 7/8	20 6/8 22 4/8	19 0/8	6 6	Valley County	ID	James Akenson	2006	2579
148 7/8	19 2/8 21 1/8	21 4/8	5 5	Claresholm	ALB	Irwin Horsey	2008	2579
148 7/8	23 6/8 23 1/8	21 2/8	5 6	Beinfait	SAS	Lynn Hrywkiw	2008	2579
148 6/8	20 7/8 20 6/8	13 2/8	5 4	Okanogan County	WA	Dennis N. Johnson	1971	2592
148 6/8	21 3/8 20 5/8	15 7/8	5 7	Lane County	KS	Vernon L. McBee	1971	2592
148 6/8	21 0/8 22 3/8	21 3/8	5 6	Umatilla County	OR	Loren R. Olsen	1981	2592
148 6/8	19 4/8 20 7/8	19 4/8	5 5	Converse County	WY	Greg Popie	1982	2592
148 6/8	22 6/8 23 4/8	19 6/8	5 4	Siskiyou County	CA	Jim Langley	1984	2592
148 6/8	21 2/8 20 0/8	17 6/8	5 5	Sioux County	NE	Jeffrey Sales	1985	2592
148 6/8	25 0/8 23 7/8	20 2/8	4 4	Garfield County	CO	Tom Urbenek	1988	2592
148 6/8	21 2/8 21 1/8	20 6/8	5 4	Gove County	KS	Joel Beougher	1989	2592
148 6/8	21 1/8 19 1/8	18 4/8	5 5	Campbell County	WY	Paul E. Korn	1997	2592
148 6/8	20 7/8 20 5/8	19 2/8	6 6	Calgary	ALB	Dave Browne	1998	2592
148 6/8	21 1/8 20 7/8	19 5/8	5 5	Pinal County	AZ	Wayne Husted	1999	2592
148 6/8	21 6/8 24 1/8	19 6/8	7 6	Converse County	WY	Gary Kautz	2000	2592
148 6/8	21 5/8 22 6/8	21 2/8	5 5	Teton County	MT	Mark Adler	2000	2592
148 6/8	19 2/8 19 5/8	14 4/8	5 5	Spring Lake	ALB	Terry Hagman	2001	2592
148 6/8	22 6/8 22 0/8	20 1/8	7 6	Custer County	MT	Mitchell Butler	2004	2592
148 6/8	24 0/8 21 7/8	21 7/8	7 6	Campbell County	WY	Lorie Gleason	2007	2592
148 5/8	21 3/8 18 7/8	23 6/8	5 5	Park County	CO	Ed Zehner	1972	2608
148 5/8	24 4/8 23 7/8	23 2/8	6 6	Chelan County	WA	Ted A. Kinsey	1983	2608
148 5/8	22 0/8 22 0/8	21 1/8	5 5	Albany County	WY	Kevin Anderson	1988	2608
148 5/8	21 7/8 21 3/8	23 1/8	5 7	Harney County	OR	Patrick E. Wheeler	1990	2608
148 5/8	22 5/8 22 5/8	18 7/8	4 5	Moffat County	CO	Larry Dean Bicknase	1992	2608
148 5/8	20 5/8 21 0/8	15 5/8	5 5	Crook County	OR	Frank Sanders	1992	2608
148 5/8	22 4/8 22 4/8	20 7/8	4 4	Campbell County	WY	Jon Lammle	1995	2608
148 5/8	25 7/8 25 1/8	23 3/8	4 5	Bernalillo County	NM	Alex Jaramillo, Jr.	1996	2608
148 5/8	21 3/8 21 5/8	19 2/8	5 6	Millard County	UT	Alan K. Manley	2002	2608
148 5/8	19 3/8 19 2/8	18 5/8	5 5	Mineral County	CO	Ron Fief	2005	2608
148 4/8	19 4/8 19 0/8	17 0/8	5 5	Boise County	ID	Floyd Audette	1964	2618
148 4/8	21 7/8 19 7/8	19 2/8	7 6	Perkins County	SD	Dr. David W. Schrody	1979	2618
148 4/8	21 7/8 22 4/8	20 4/8	5 5	Campbell County	WY	Carrol D. Wert	1979	2618
148 4/8	22 2/8 22 6/8	20 4/8	5 5	Converse County	WY	James D. Miller	1980	2618
148 4/8	22 0/8 21 7/8	19 6/8	5 4	San Juan County	UT	Bill Clink	1985	2618
148 4/8	20 7/8 22 2/8	20 2/8	5 5	Harney County	OR	Douglas Modey	1993	2618
148 4/8	19 5/8 21 0/8	19 4/8	5 5	Springbank	ALB	Bry Loyd	1994	2618
148 4/8	20 6/8 21 2/8	17 2/8	4 4	Lake County	OR	Tim Larocco	1996	2618
148 4/8	22 0/8 21 4/8	15 4/8	7 7	Dunn County	ND	Wade Murray	1999	2618
148 4/8	22 4/8 22 1/8	23 2/8	5 4	Black Diamond	ALB	Allen J. O'Brien	2000	2618
148 4/8	22 2/8 23 1/8	19 4/8	5 5	Prowers County	CO	Chester Allen	2001	2618
148 4/8	22 4/8 21 5/8	20 2/8	5 5	Jackson County	CO	Scott R. Essen	2005	2618
148 4/8	23 4/8 23 7/8	22 6/8	6 4	Sheridan County	WY	Will LaDuke	2007	2618
*148 4/8	20 6/8 20 4/8	19 6/8	5 5	Vulcan	ALB	Robert Larsen	2010	2618
148 3/8	22 5/8 23 5/8	18 5/8	5 4	Huerfano County	CO	Loren Johnson	1966	2632
148 3/8	21 1/8 20 4/8	21 5/8	5 5	Carbon County	WY	Rod Schmidt	1984	2632
148 3/8	23 2/8 24 2/8	28 5/8	6 4	Pueblo County	CO	Dean Aggson	1992	2632
148 3/8	20 5/8 19 6/8	17 3/8	5 5	Colfax County	NM	Robert J. Sedlacko	1996	2632
148 3/8	21 0/8 19 1/8	17 3/8	5 6	Teton County	WY	Justin Bliss	1996	2632
148 3/8	20 3/8 19 5/8	17 5/8	5 5	Grant County	OR	Paul J. Zink	1997	2632
148 3/8	20 5/8 21 2/8	16 7/8	4 4	Chelan County	WA	Randall Moore	1998	2632
148 3/8	18 4/8 18 6/8	17 5/8	5 5	Cochrane	ALB	Eric R. Smith	1999	2632
148 3/8	22 4/8 21 7/8	22 1/8	4 4	Foremost	ALB	Buck Horn	2001	2632
148 3/8	22 4/8 23 7/8	21 4/8	5 5	Conrich	ALB	Jeremy Evans	2002	2632
148 3/8	24 1/8 23 3/8	20 7/8	6 5	Johnson County	WY	Clay Harrison	2003	2632
*148 3/8	22 4/8 22 3/8	17 6/8	5 5	McKenzie County	ND	Ryan Bowne	2007	2632
148 3/8	19 6/8 20 6/8	18 3/8	5 5	Lyman County	SD	Robert E. Reedy, Jr.	2007	2632
148 3/8	22 6/8 21 7/8	20 4/8	6 4	Brooks	ALB	Ricardo Longoria	2009	2632
148 3/8	20 7/8 20 3/8	18 5/8	4 5	Salt Lake County	UT	William H. Bryant	2009	2632
148 2/8	20 3/8 21 0/8	17 6/8	5 5	Fergus County	MT	Bob Wanner	1977	2647
148 2/8	20 1/8 20 6/8	20 4/8	5 5	Billings County	ND	Thomas Treto	1982	2647
148 2/8	22 0/8 23 1/8	21 1/8	4 5	Cochrane	ALB	David Richardson	1983	2647
148 2/8	21 5/8 21 2/8	20 4/8	4 5	Chelan County	WA	Joe Lilley	1988	2647
148 2/8	19 2/8 21 0/8	20 4/8	5 5	Cassia County	ID	Monte B. Carlson	1989	2647
148 2/8	22 5/8 21 1/8	21 0/8	6 5	Pima County	AZ	Daniel C. Hicks	1991	2647
148 2/8	23 5/8 23 3/8	20 4/8	5 4	Baker County	OR	Mike Raney	1994	2647
148 2/8	20 0/8 19 2/8	16 6/8	5 5	Beaverhead County	MT	Robert C. Howard	1995	2647
148 2/8	18 7/8 19 1/8	17 6/8	5 5	Elko County	NV	Felton Hickman	1996	2647
148 2/8	18 7/8 20 0/8	13 6/8	5 5	Pima County	AZ	Terence Richard Ziehmer	1998	2647
148 2/8	20 0/8 22 1/8	18 4/8	5 5	Albany County	WY	Rick L. Parish	2000	2647
148 2/8	19 1/8 20 0/8	18 0/8	5 5	Milk River	ALB	Wayne A. Nicholson	2000	2647
148 2/8	19 6/8 19 6/8	18 6/8	5 5	Harney County	OR	Jesse Shetler	2003	2647
148 2/8	21 6/8 21 6/8	20 2/8	5 5	Larimer County	CO	Bradley J. Baldwin	2004	2647

335

MULE DEER (TYPICAL ANTLERS)

Minimum Score 145   Continued

SCORE	LENGTH OF R MAIN BEAM L	INSIDE SPREAD	NUMBER OF R POINTS L	AREA	STATE/ PROVINCE	HUNTER'S NAME	DATE	RANK
148 2/8	20 0/8	18 0/8	17 6/8	5	5	Montrose County	CO	Pat Reilly	2009	2647
148 1/8	20 4/8	21 7/8	22 7/8	9	4	Emery County	UT	Bob Jacobsen	1961	2662
148 1/8	23 0/8	22 3/8	19 5/8	4	4	Pitkin County	CO	William F. Havel	1962	2662
148 1/8	21 7/8	21 7/8	21 5/8	4	5	Lake County	OR	Richard G. Speer	1964	2662
148 1/8	20 0/8	21 0/8	21 0/8	4	5	Ford County	KS	Aubrey Ballard	1966	2662
148 1/8	20 7/8	20 1/8	18 5/8	5	4	Grand County	CO	Judd Cooney	1969	2662
148 1/8	19 0/8	19 3/8	18 5/8	5	5	Carbon County	UT	Leonard Thompson	1973	2662
148 1/8	20 3/8	21 5/8	21 2/8	6	5	Sheridan County	KS	Tom Reedy	1980	2662
148 1/8	22 3/8	21 7/8	23 3/8	4	4	Lake County	OR	Jerry Mosteller	1981	2662
148 1/8	21 4/8	19 6/8	18 5/8	4	5	Mesa County	CO	Jay Verzuh	1982	2662
148 1/8	21 4/8	22 1/8	19 3/8	5	4	Sheridan County	WY	Mike Barrett	1983	2662
148 1/8	21 5/8	21 0/8	21 0/8	6	6	Michichi	ALB	Rodney Dyck	1991	2662
148 1/8	20 4/8	20 1/8	21 2/8	7	7	Hettinger County	ND	Scott Wiseman	1991	2662
148 1/8	23 6/8	23 0/8	18 0/8	6	6	Fraser River	BC	Rick Paquette	1991	2662
148 1/8	20 5/8	21 0/8	17 5/8	7	7	Red Deer Lake	ALB	J. Linley Biblow	1991	2662
148 1/8	23 0/8	23 1/8	23 7/8	5	5	Dundy County	NE	Clay Burrell	1993	2662
148 1/8	19 6/8	19 5/8	17 3/8	5	5	Golden Valley County	MT	Ronald G. Junkert	1994	2662
148 1/8	26 0/8	25 6/8	24 1/8	4	4	Nevada County	CA	Harry Pelton	1995	2662
148 1/8	24 6/8	24 4/8	21 7/8	6	5	Jefferson County	OR	Guy P. Hurlbert	1996	2662
148 1/8	22 6/8	23 3/8	18 2/8	5	5	Brooks	ALB	Chuck Adams	1999	2662
148 1/8	20 0/8	20 0/8	17 7/8	5	5	Ada County	ID	Steve Groening	2001	2662
148 1/8	20 6/8	21 7/8	21 6/8	6	7	Converse County	WY	Lee Jernigan	2005	2662
148 1/8	23 5/8	23 7/8	19 3/8	5	4	Weld County	CO	Michael A. Lee	2005	2662
148 1/8	21 4/8	21 1/8	15 3/8	5	5	Cochrane	ALB	Michael Serwa	2007	2662
148 1/8	22 7/8	23 6/8	20 5/8	4	3	Stanley County	SD	Lance Peery	2008	2662
148 0/8	21 7/8	21 4/8	21 1/8	6	6	White River N.F.	CO	Paul M. Ramsey	1959	2686
148 0/8	20 5/8	20 7/8	16 6/8	6	6	Jones County	SD	Gene M. Hove	1990	2686
148 0/8	19 6/8	19 5/8	20 0/8	5	5	Slope County	ND	Todd Seymanski	1994	2686
148 0/8	23 6/8	23 0/8	26 6/8	5	4	Colfax County	NM	Ray Valerio	1994	2686
148 0/8	20 5/8	19 0/8	17 4/8	4	4	Sheridan County	WY	Larry Burtis	1995	2686
148 0/8	23 6/8	23 0/8	21 2/8	3	3	Billings County	ND	Gary Fleishauer	1996	2686
148 0/8	23 0/8	24 2/8	22 0/8	5	5	Placer County	CA	Scott Lusk	1997	2686
148 0/8	20 7/8	21 5/8	18 6/8	5	5	Calgary	ALB	Jim Wondzell	2001	2686
148 0/8	20 6/8	20 4/8	18 0/8	4	4	McKenzie County	ND	Corey Hugelen	2003	2686
* 148 0/8	23 4/8	21 4/8	19 2/8	5	5	Sevier County	UT	McKay Sorenson	2007	2686
147 7/8	22 3/8	24 0/8	23 3/8	3	4	Millard County	UT	Milton F. McQueary	1958	2696
147 7/8	21 2/8	21 0/8	18 0/8	5	6	Deschutes County	OR	Joe Reynolds	1967	2696
147 7/8	21 5/8	22 0/8	21 5/8	5	5	Johnson County	WY	Scott L. Koelzer	1978	2696
147 7/8	23 3/8	23 7/8	24 0/8	5	4	Mesa County	CO	Garvin H. Gibbins	1984	2696
147 7/8	23 7/8	22 7/8	20 7/8	5	4	Mesa County	CO	Richard Kunevicius	1985	2696
147 7/8	22 2/8	21 0/8	21 5/8	5	4	Washoe County	NV	Cecil D. Martin	1986	2696
147 7/8	22 1/8	21 4/8	19 7/8	5	5	Bernalillo County	NM	Chett Britton	1992	2696
147 7/8	21 7/8	21 7/8	21 7/8	4	5	McGrath	ALB	Cameron Cook	1993	2696
147 7/8	20 5/8	21 0/8	19 3/8	5	4	Billings County	ND	Ryan Hugelen	1999	2696
147 7/8	21 1/8	21 3/8	18 3/8	5	5	Uintah County	UT	Brian Wagar	2000	2696
147 7/8	23 5/8	23 2/8	22 2/8	5	3	Powder River County	MT	Gene Smith	2001	2696
147 7/8	21 6/8	21 4/8	17 5/8	6	5	Albany County	WY	Rick Parish	2002	2696
147 7/8	20 3/8	21 6/8	18 1/8	7	6	Ravalli County	MT	Craig Hobbs	2003	2696
147 7/8	21 7/8	23 5/8	20 1/8	5	3	Elkwater	ALB	Robert J. Haley	2004	2696
147 7/8	19 2/8	19 6/8	19 5/8	5	4	Bashaw	ALB	Alan Brimacombe	2006	2696
* 147 7/8	18 5/8	18 5/8	16 1/8	5	5	Las Animas County	CO	Dave Holt	2006	2696
147 6/8	20 0/8	20 2/8	20 2/8	5	4	Garfield County	CO	Steve Love	1972	2712
147 6/8	19 4/8	21 0/8	21 0/8	5	5	Routt County	CO	John P. Hale	1974	2712
147 6/8	20 5/8	21 6/8	15 6/8	7	5	Garfield County	CO	Edwin Hurt	1980	2712
147 6/8	22 5/8	22 2/8	20 5/8	5	5	Boise County	ID	Matt March, Jr.	1983	2712
147 6/8	17 6/8	22 0/8	20 0/8	4	4	Malheur County	OR	Steve Savage	1985	2712
147 6/8	24 1/8	22 3/8	22 6/8	5	4	McKenzie County	ND	Bryan R. Stein	1988	2712
147 6/8	21 1/8	22 0/8	20 0/8	5	5	Innisfail	ALB	Derrill Herman	1997	2712
147 6/8	19 4/8	17 6/8	18 4/8	5	5	Logan County	CO	Mike Stanley	1998	2712
147 6/8	22 2/8	23 4/8	22 2/8	5	5	Empress	ALB	Michael Ripp	2005	2712
147 6/8	21 7/8	22 0/8	20 0/8	4	4	Dunn County	ND	Scott Wahl	2005	2712
147 6/8	20 4/8	19 4/8	18 4/8	5	6	Bannock County	ID	Thomas F. Call	2006	2712
147 6/8	19 4/8	18 7/8	17 4/8	5	5	Powder River County	MT	Mike Barrett	2006	2712
* 147 6/8	22 0/8	24 3/8	18 4/8	5	5	Magrath	ALB	Keith Bach	2007	2712
147 6/8	20 0/8	20 0/8	19 2/8	5	5	Millard County	UT	Cori Kirkpatrick	2009	2712
147 5/8	21 6/8	21 4/8	20 1/8	5	5	Sevier County	UT	Rowland Enomoto	1963	2726
147 5/8	23 0/8	23 0/8	24 2/8	5	6	San Juan County	UT	Jack Howard	1966	2726
147 5/8	19 1/8	17 0/8	21 0/8	6	5	Grant County	OR	Arthur Redinger	1972	2726
147 5/8	21 1/8	18 7/8	17 5/8	5	4	Sevier County	UT	Robert W. Shilling	1974	2726
147 5/8	25 2/8	24 2/8	22 1/8	7	5	Garfield County	CO	Terry Bridgman	1978	2726
147 5/8	18 6/8	18 7/8	21 0/8	5	4	Elbert County	CO	Calvin Farner	1984	2726
147 5/8	21 7/8	22 7/8	25 2/8	3	3	Butte County	SD	Glenn D Priebe	1984	2726
147 5/8	22 7/8	23 2/8	18 5/8	6	4	Rio Arriba County	NM	Craig Sanchez	1996	2726
147 5/8	21 4/8	22 2/8	20 4/8	6	5	Cassia County	ID	Greg Betts, Jr.	1996	2726
147 5/8	21 1/8	21 5/8	20 4/8	9	7	Deschutes County	OR	Keenan Howard	1999	2726
147 5/8	20 7/8	23 0/8	21 1/8	4	5	Hooker County	NE	Dave Bichlmeier	2000	2726
147 5/8	19 5/8	19 5/8	20 1/8	5	5	Campbell County	WY	John Baadsgaard	2003	2726
147 5/8	20 7/8	20 6/8	25 4/8	4	5	Bear Lake County	ID	Scott O. Roberts	2004	2726
147 5/8	23 0/8	23 0/8	19 1/8	4	4	Chelan County	WA	James Barker	2005	2726
147 5/8	22 6/8	22 2/8	22 1/8	4	4	La Paz County	AZ	Jack Smith	2005	2726
147 5/8	20 6/8	20 7/8	22 5/8	5	5	Washoe County	NV	Kevin J. Retterath	2008	2726
* 147 5/8	22 2/8	21 7/8	19 0/8	8	7	Bowman County	ND	Brian Moser	2009	2726
147 4/8	22 1/8	22 2/8	19 4/8	5	5	Bernalillo County	NM	Larry W. Johnson	1969	2743
147 4/8	21 2/8	22 1/8	19 0/8	5	5	Boulder County	CO	Jack Frank	1970	2743
147 4/8	21 0/8	21 0/8	18 5/8	5	5	Garfield County	CO	Paul R. Shannon	1975	2743
147 4/8	22 3/8	21 5/8	17 4/8	5	5	Maricopa County	AZ	Stephen C. Christensen	1976	2743
147 4/8	20 1/8	20 5/8	19 6/8	5	5	Routt County	CO	Tom N. Garvin	1983	2743
147 4/8	23 0/8	24 0/8	24 0/8	6	6	Sweetwater County	WY	Vic Dana	1983	2743
147 4/8	24 2/8	22 2/8	20 2/8	4	5	Harney County	OR	Gary D. Nyden	1985	2743
147 4/8	19 5/8	19 5/8	16 6/8	5	5	Coconino County	AZ	Steven H. Cook	1989	2743
147 4/8	22 4/8	23 0/8	21 2/8	5	5	Converse County	WY	George A. Zanoni	1991	2743
147 4/8	19 4/8	20 6/8	17 2/8	5	6	Converse County	WY	Harry Cerutti	1991	2743
147 4/8	20 5/8	21 3/8	14 6/8	7	5	Lumby	BC	Owen Schoenberger	1991	2743
147 4/8	22 2/8	24 1/8	24 0/8	5	4	Modoc County	CA	Wayne Wood	1993	2743
147 4/8	20 7/8	20 4/8	19 2/8	5	5	Cardston	ALB	Chuck Adams	2002	2743

MULE DEER (TYPICAL ANTLERS)

Minimum Score 145   Continued

SCORE	LENGTH OF R MAIN BEAM L	INSIDE SPREAD	NUMBER OF R POINTS L	AREA	STATE/ PROVINCE	HUNTER'S NAME	DATE	RANK
147 4/8	20 5/8 21 0/8	20 0/8	4 5	Lincoln County	WY	Derek Germann	2003	2743
147 4/8	20 3/8 19 2/8	15 0/8	5 4	Jenner	ALB	Barry M. Ver Meer	2005	2743
147 4/8	20 4/8 22 5/8	17 4/8	4 4	Huerfano County	CO	Kevin D. Day	2008	2743
147 3/8	23 4/8 23 2/8	20 3/8	5 6	Cherry County	NE	Jack E. Joseph	1961	2759
147 3/8	19 4/8 20 4/8	16 5/8	4 5	Latah County	ID	Chas. A. McDonald	1965	2759
147 3/8	19 0/8 21 0/8	18 1/8	5 5	Johnson County	WY	Mike E. Neilson	1994	2759
147 3/8	22 0/8 22 0/8	20 5/8	5 5	Campbell County	WY	Leon R. Nyreen	1996	2759
147 3/8	19 5/8 19 4/8	21 2/8	5 6	Powder River County	MT	Jim Wilkins	1996	2759
147 3/8	19 5/8 19 6/8	17 7/8	5 5	Big Horn County	WY	Donald J. Kane	1997	2759
147 3/8	21 5/8 22 5/8	23 2/8	5 4	Converse County	WY	Brandon Ray	2001	2759
147 3/8	20 2/8 20 0/8	21 2/8	5 6	Drumheller	ALB	Dean Kirkeby	2001	2759
147 3/8	19 4/8 19 7/8	15 7/8	5 5	Union County	OR	Jeff Cusumano	2003	2759
*147 3/8	19 4/8 21 7/8	20 2/8	5 6	Sioux County	NE	Marcus Paczosa	2003	2759
147 3/8	21 5/8 21 4/8	19 2/8	6 6	Red River	ALB	Matthew Liljenquist	2003	2759
*147 3/8	23 1/8 22 2/8	17 3/8	7 6	Golden Valley County	ND	Pete Finck	2005	2759
147 3/8	21 6/8 22 0/8	21 6/8	6 7	Hutchinson County	SD	Craig Roth	2005	2759
*147 3/8	20 4/8 20 2/8	19 1/8	5 5	McKenzie County	ND	Thomas E. Rothrock	2007	2759
147 3/8	20 4/8 20 5/8	18 4/8	6 5	Malheur County	OR	David Boyd	2009	2759
147 2/8	22 7/8 23 2/8	17 0/8	6 6	Cherry County	NE	Ken Hollpeter	1979	2774
147 2/8	21 4/8 21 3/8	19 4/8	4 5	El Paso County	CO	Rick C. Wilson	1996	2774
147 2/8	22 7/8 22 4/8	16 4/8	5 5	Powder River County	MT	Thomas W. Detrick	2000	2774
147 2/8	21 1/8 21 3/8	16 2/8	5 5	Montrose County	CO	Mark Klusty	2003	2774
147 2/8	22 0/8 22 0/8	22 6/8	4 4	McKenzie County	ND	Joce Hugelen	2003	2774
147 2/8	19 6/8 20 6/8	17 0/8	5 4	Pennington County	SD	Neil Hamerlinck	2003	2774
147 2/8	22 4/8 22 4/8	22 2/8	4 5	Grant County	OR	Robert Wenzel	2004	2774
147 2/8	19 1/8 21 2/8	17 3/8	4 6	Salt Lake County	UT	Darin C. Galley	2004	2774
147 2/8	21 6/8 21 6/8	21 4/8	6 5	Converse County	WY	Peter F. Woeck II	2005	2774
*147 2/8	20 7/8 21 0/8	20 1/8	6 6	Big Horn County	WY	Kevin Merrill	2008	2774
147 2/8	23 4/8 22 1/8	19 4/8	6 6	Routt County	CO	Steven Brown, MD	2008	2774
147 2/8	23 4/8 22 1/8	22 0/8	7 5	Sweet Grass County	MT	Thomas Orrison	2009	2774
147 2/8	20 4/8 21 4/8	15 4/8	5 5	Wild Horse	ALB	Jordan Williams	2009	2774
147 2/8	21 5/8 22 4/8	20 6/8	6 5	Black Diamond	ALB	Mike Bryski	2009	2774
147 1/8	20 5/8 20 1/8	16 7/8	5 5	Uintah County	UT	Rolland Esterline	1967	2788
147 1/8	19 6/8 23 6/8	17 0/8	6 5	Baker County	OR	Larry Garoutte	1970	2788
147 1/8	22 6/8 21 2/8	19 5/8	5 5	Moffat County	CO	Larry Bicknase	1991	2788
147 1/8	20 1/8 19 6/8	19 7/8	5 5	Esther	ALB	Steven J. Parkin	1996	2788
147 1/8	22 3/8 23 0/8	17 3/8	6 5	Weld County	CO	Nathan Andersohn	2000	2788
147 1/8	18 6/8 20 4/8	18 3/8	4 4	Butte County	SD	Gary English	2001	2788
*147 1/8	21 0/8 21 2/8	18 3/8	5 5	Gallatin County	MT	Kirk Stovall	2006	2788
147 1/8	24 5/8 24 4/8	20 5/8	4 5	Benton County	WA	Troy E. Gose	2006	2788
147 0/8	20 3/8 20 7/8	20 2/8	5 5	Uintah County	UT	Merlin L. Killpack	1958	2796
147 0/8	25 4/8 25 0/8	23 5/8	7 5	Grand County	UT	William W. Selby	1974	2796
147 0/8	21 6/8 21 7/8	20 6/8	5 5	Dawson County	MT	Smucky Mann	1975	2796
147 0/8	19 1/8 20 1/8	19 2/8	5 5	Platte County	WY	Robert V. Kiser	1978	2796
147 0/8	20 5/8 21 6/8	19 2/8	5 5	Laramie County	WY	Ronald J. Wedge	1978	2796
147 0/8	20 4/8 20 4/8	17 2/8	5 5	Stanley County	SD	George Hipple	1982	2796
147 0/8	24 0/8 25 0/8	19 6/8	5 9	Lincoln County	MT	R. C. Peters	1983	2796
147 0/8	21 6/8 21 3/8	18 2/8	5 5	Powder River County	MT	Max Miller	1990	2796
147 0/8	22 6/8 22 3/8	20 2/8	6 6	Franklin County	ID	Dale Holpainen	1991	2796
147 0/8	23 0/8 23 0/8	24 5/8	5 4	Sioux County	ND	James Red Tomahawk	1995	2796
147 0/8	21 3/8 20 6/8	18 1/8	6 5	Weld County	CO	Timothy Bradley	1995	2796
147 0/8	21 1/8 20 6/8	19 2/8	6 5	Rimbey	ALB	Gary Bruns	1996	2796
147 0/8	20 5/8 19 7/8	18 0/8	6 5	Fergus County	MT	Judy Adams	1997	2796
147 0/8	22 1/8 22 6/8	23 3/8	5 5	Rawlins County	KS	Todd Fugate	1997	2796
147 0/8	25 3/8 24 1/8	24 6/8	5 4	Yuma County	CO	Tom Pindell	1998	2796
147 0/8	21 7/8 17 7/8	22 1/8	4 6	Rosebud County	MT	George Harms	2000	2796
147 0/8	20 0/8 19 7/8	16 6/8	5 6	Uinta County	WY	Michael Boddicker	2004	2796
*147 0/8	22 2/8 21 0/8	20 4/8	6 5	Montrose County	CO	Donald H. Grimoldi	2004	2796
147 0/8	19 7/8 19 3/8	19 0/8	4 5	Platte County	WY	William Hinz	2007	2796
147 0/8	17 4/8 17 7/8	16 2/8	5 5	Kittitas County	WA	Harris Emmons IV	2009	2796
147 0/8	22 1/8 20 5/8	17 3/8	6 7	Rockyview	ALB	Michael L. Solomon	2009	2796
146 7/8	19 5/8 20 1/8	20 1/8	5 5	Grand County	UT	Norm Goodwin	1960	2817
146 7/8	23 4/8 23 1/8	23 4/8	5 4	Emery County	UT	Bruce Ware	1961	2817
146 7/8	19 2/8 20 0/8	18 5/8	5 4	Baker County	OR	James E. Hodson	1966	2817
146 7/8	21 3/8 20 7/8	21 2/8	4 4	Carbon County	WY	John Swanson	1966	2817
146 7/8	20 7/8 21 2/8	21 3/8	5 5	Meade County	SD	Kenneth McNenny	1967	2817
146 7/8	21 2/8 21 4/8	18 7/8	5 5	Saguache County	CO	Skip Mulso	1974	2817
146 7/8	21 0/8 20 2/8	18 3/8	4 4	Routt County	CO	Bob Stevens	1975	2817
146 7/8	21 4/8 21 6/8	19 3/8	3 3	Clark County	ID	Robert Daniels	1978	2817
146 7/8	20 3/8 21 5/8	20 3/8	6 5	Sheridan County	WY	David Shoop	1980	2817
146 7/8	23 6/8 21 6/8	24 1/8	5 9	Pima County	AZ	Stacy Tompkinson	1984	2817
146 7/8	19 7/8 20 4/8	17 3/8	5 5	Mesa County	CO	Gary L. Hoekman	1986	2817
146 7/8	20 3/8 20 2/8	17 7/8	5 5	Orion	ALB	Kent Hillard	1990	2817
146 7/8	22 0/8 23 1/8	26 7/8	6 5	Calgary	ALB	Archie Nesbitt	1991	2817
146 7/8	24 7/8 22 6/8	18 5/8	5 8	Routt County	CO	Richard Gjerde	1993	2817
146 7/8	21 7/8 21 7/8	17 7/8	5 5	Placer County	CA	Doug Burgard	1993	2817
146 7/8	19 7/8 21 6/8	15 5/8	5 5	Raymond	ALB	Dr. Chuck Leidheiser	1996	2817
146 7/8	19 5/8 19 4/8	19 7/8	5 5	Natrona County	WY	Brian Wagner	2002	2817
146 7/8	22 7/8 22 0/8	20 5/8	5 4	Ground Birch	BC	Tom Taylor	2005	2817
146 7/8	21 0/8 19 5/8	15 1/8	5 5	Cochrane	ALB	Thanos Natras	2007	2817
*146 7/8	22 5/8 22 5/8	19 0/8	6 4	Milo	ALB	Grant W. Markoski	2009	2817
146 7/8	20 5/8 21 3/8	22 4/8	4 4	Cherry County	NE	Reggie Hochstein	2009	2817
146 6/8	19 6/8 20 3/8	15 7/8	4 4	Owyhee County	ID	Seneth Ward	1960	2838
146 6/8	21 1/8 20 2/8	20 3/8	6 5	Mesa County	CO	Dennis Kelly	1981	2838
146 6/8	20 4/8 19 7/8	19 0/8	6 7	Elbert County	CO	Donald Ace Morgan	1983	2838
146 6/8	23 3/8 24 2/8	22 2/8	4 4	Pitkin County	CO	Bill Krenz	1983	2838
146 6/8	18 7/8 20 1/8	19 6/8	5 5	Carbon County	WY	Rod Schmidt	1988	2838
146 6/8	21 5/8 22 4/8	16 2/8	6 5	Meade County	KS	Mike Heinson	1989	2838
146 6/8	21 6/8 21 0/8	22 5/8	6 5	Culberson County	TX	Curtis W. Mathis	1992	2838
146 6/8	22 6/8 22 6/8	24 1/8	4 5	Pima County	AZ	Fred Slone	1992	2838
146 6/8	19 1/8 18 2/8	16 4/8	5 5	Stillwater County	MT	Gary F. Bogner	1993	2838
146 6/8	21 0/8 20 7/8	18 6/8	5 5	Sioux County	NE	Richard A. Skiles	1993	2838
146 6/8	20 3/8 21 0/8	17 4/8	4 5	Archuleta County	CO	Donald B. Myers	1996	2838
146 6/8	19 6/8 21 3/8	19 1/8	5 6	Rosalind	ALB	Sylvester "Sly" Baier	1997	2838
146 6/8	23 3/8 24 4/8	19 2/8	5 5	Tehama County	CA	Richard Hall	1998	2838

337

MULE DEER (TYPICAL ANTLERS)

Minimum Score 145 — Continued

SCORE	R MAIN BEAM L	INSIDE SPREAD	R POINTS L	AREA	STATE/PROVINCE	HUNTER'S NAME	DATE	RANK
146 6/8	19 6/8 22 2/8	17 0/8	5 5	Cochise County	AZ	Christopher B. Heilman	2000	2838
146 6/8	24 3/8 21 0/8	25 2/8	7 7	Weld County	CO	Monty Ace Morgan	2001	2838
146 6/8	23 5/8 23 3/8	19 2/8	5 4	Big Horn County	WY	Chris Jerup	2002	2838
146 6/8	20 6/8 19 7/8	18 1/8	6 5	Albany County	WY	Marlin Stapleton	2006	2838
146 6/8	20 2/8 20 6/8	16 0/8	5 5	Johnson County	WY	Bret Scott	2007	2838
*146 6/8	20 0/8 22 0/8	17 0/8	4 4	Elkwater	ALB	Jesse J. Arndt	2008	2838
146 5/8	22 0/8 22 6/8	18 7/8	5 5	Chelan County	WA	Gerald King	1963	2857
146 5/8	20 5/8 20 3/8	20 6/8	5 5	Johnson County	WY	Gary Olsen	1979	2857
146 5/8	20 6/8 21 0/8	20 7/8	5 5	Uintah County	UT	Dave Lund	1987	2857
146 5/8	21 2/8 22 2/8	15 7/8	4 5	Lemhi County	ID	Mike Muguira	1988	2857
146 5/8	20 1/8 21 1/8	20 3/8	5 5	Sheridan County	WY	Mark Frank	1990	2857
146 5/8	19 2/8 19 0/8	18 1/8	6 8	Wheatland County	MT	Jim Winjum	1992	2857
146 5/8	20 4/8 19 2/8	17 5/8	4 4	Gunnison County	CO	Robert H. Johnson	1997	2857
146 5/8	20 4/8 21 4/8	18 5/8	5 5	Powder River County	MT	Donald Gresh	1998	2857
146 5/8	23 2/8 23 0/8	22 3/8	4 5	Converse County	WY	Mark Kronyak	2001	2857
146 5/8	18 5/8 19 1/8	17 3/8	4 4	Custer County	MT	Johnnie R. Walters	2003	2857
146 4/8	23 3/8 23 0/8	21 0/8	4 5	Wayne County	UT	Harold Boyack	1968	2867
146 4/8	22 7/8 24 4/8	19 4/8	5 5	Mariposa County	CA	Robert D. Downs	1977	2867
146 4/8	20 0/8 20 7/8	19 4/8	5 4	Mesa County	CO	Kaye B. McCrory	1978	2867
146 4/8	24 0/8 26 5/8	23 0/8	7 6	Eagle County	CO	Dave Mendoza	1983	2867
146 4/8	22 4/8 22 3/8	20 4/8	5 5	Piute County	UT	Tim Sayer	1984	2867
146 4/8	22 3/8 22 1/8	19 6/8	5 4	Rio Grande County	CO	Jerry Woodland	1984	2867
146 4/8	21 0/8 23 2/8	22 4/8	5 5	Bowman County	ND	Dwight Eckart	1984	2867
146 4/8	21 7/8 22 4/8	16 7/8	5 8	Cache County	UT	Robert Bronson	1985	2867
146 4/8	21 4/8 21 2/8	18 0/8	5 5	Mesa County	CO	John Papenfuss	1988	2867
146 4/8	18 6/8 19 2/8	19 3/8	5 5	Warner	ALB	Keith Heppler	1991	2867
146 4/8	21 5/8 20 1/8	19 6/8	5 4	Frenchman River	SAS	Dennis J. Francais	2001	2867
146 4/8	21 1/8 22 4/8	18 0/8	6 6	Millard County	UT	Josey J. Parsons	2004	2867
146 4/8	22 1/8 25 4/8	25 6/8	5 4	Elbow	SAS	Chad Gessner	2005	2867
146 4/8	20 3/8 20 7/8	19 5/8	7 5	Gove County	KS	Tod Anthony	2006	2867
146 4/8	19 2/8 20 0/8	18 6/8	5 5	Scurry County	TX	T. Gene Flowers	2007	2867
146 4/8	21 2/8 21 4/8	18 0/8	4 4	Drumheller	ALB	Gunther Tondeleir	2007	2867
*146 4/8	20 5/8 19 3/8	15 6/8	5 5	Yellowstone County	MT	Robert Rodriguez	2008	2867
146 3/8	19 0/8 19 0/8	17 3/8	5 5	Mohave County	AZ	George Kili	1964	2884
146 3/8	20 2/8 21 1/8	19 1/8	5 5	Grand County	UT	Bob Paulson	1967	2884
146 3/8	21 0/8 21 2/8	19 5/8	5 5	Mesa County	CO	Curtis W. Dorroh	1979	2884
146 3/8	22 1/8 22 2/8	22 5/8	7 6	Lane County	KS	Dean Hamilton	1980	2884
146 3/8	19 2/8 21 2/8	19 3/8	4 4	Boulder County	CO	Al Miller	1983	2884
146 3/8	20 4/8 21 3/8	19 5/8	4 6	San Miguel County	NM	Ricardo Roybal	1984	2884
146 3/8	21 1/8 19 4/8	21 4/8	5 5	Billings County	ND	Roy Boots	1985	2884
146 3/8	24 7/8 24 6/8	24 3/8	4 4	Fall River County	SD	Michael A. Judas	1990	2884
146 3/8	19 5/8 21 1/8	26 0/8	4 5	Salt Lake County	UT	Lance Brown	1996	2884
146 3/8	18 4/8 22 7/8	15 7/8	3 4	Sonora	MEX	Ben B. Wallace	2004	2884
146 3/8	21 2/8 21 1/8	19 1/8	5 5	Converse County	WY	Peter F. Woeck II	2004	2884
146 3/8	21 6/8 21 3/8	20 5/8	4 4	Eagle County	CO	William Kyle Ansel	2006	2884
146 3/8	21 1/8 21 6/8	20 1/8	5 5	Dunn County	ND	Stephen A. Dougherty	2008	2884
146 2/8	25 4/8 23 6/8	23 4/8	5 5	Las Animas County	CO	Tom Valamdro	1967	2897
146 2/8	21 0/8 20 2/8	19 1/8	7 6	Gallatin County	MT	Scott Koelzer	1969	2897
146 2/8	21 4/8 21 4/8	20 0/8	5 5	Powder River County	MT	Charles R. Maloney	1973	2897
146 2/8	22 4/8 22 0/8	19 0/8	4 5	Powder River County	MT	Mike Barrett	1985	2897
146 2/8	18 6/8 18 4/8	18 2/8	5 5	Cache County	UT	John A. Bogucki	1988	2897
146 2/8	22 6/8 21 7/8	25 5/8	5 5	Hidalgo County	NM	Steven Tisdale	1992	2897
146 2/8	19 1/8 20 2/8	19 0/8	5 5	Dog Pond Creek	ALB	Dale G. Robison	1998	2897
146 2/8	19 0/8 19 1/8	18 6/8	5 5	Converse County	WY	Dave Canfield	2002	2897
146 2/8	18 2/8 19 2/8	17 4/8	5 5	Washington County	CO	Gregory White	2003	2897
146 2/8	21 5/8 21 1/8	20 6/8	4 4	N. Saskatchewan River	ALB	Ken Byram	2004	2897
146 2/8	18 1/8 18 7/8	16 4/8	5 5	Grant County	NM	Joel Edwards	2007	2897
146 1/8	20 6/8 19 0/8	15 7/8	5 5	Ada County	ID	Jim Wenzel	1971	2908
146 1/8	21 0/8 20 3/8	16 5/8	5 5	Clark County	ID	Max Heberling	1989	2908
146 1/8	20 6/8 22 2/8	22 1/8	5 5	Graham County	KS	Jim Kerbaugh	1989	2908
146 1/8	19 6/8 20 6/8	18 5/8	6 5	Morgan County	CO	Laszlo Nobi	1991	2908
146 1/8	20 5/8 22 2/8	17 7/8	5 5	Otero County	NM	Roger Schoolcraft	1992	2908
146 1/8	23 0/8 21 7/8	19 1/8	5 4	Bernalillo County	NM	Kenneth Jaramillo, Sr.	1995	2908
146 1/8	23 3/8 24 0/8	20 3/8	4 4	Morrow County	OR	Jeffrey H. Edwards	1996	2908
146 1/8	18 1/8 18 3/8	18 7/8	5 5	Powder River County	MT	Gene Smith	1998	2908
146 1/8	21 3/8 22 7/8	19 1/8	5 5	Malheur County	OR	Mike L. Moore	1999	2908
146 1/8	21 4/8 21 4/8	19 1/8	5 5	Chelan County	WA	Eric Strumpfer	2003	2908
146 1/8	20 4/8 21 3/8	21 7/8	4 4	Dunn County	ND	Stephen A. Dougherty	2008	2908
146 0/8	20 4/8 20 2/8	18 2/8	5 5	Elko County	NV	Howard Hill	1944	2919
146 0/8	21 2/8 21 3/8	20 2/8	5 5	Mesa County	CO	William F. DeEsch	1966	2919
146 0/8	18 6/8 19 7/8	17 0/8	5 5	Decatur County	KS	A. E. 'Butch' Whelchel	1977	2919
146 0/8	19 6/8 19 2/8	20 6/8	5 5	Converse County	WY	David A. Widby	1990	2919
146 0/8	22 0/8 19 2/8	23 3/8	5 5	Niobrara County	WY	John H. Williams	1991	2919
146 0/8	19 0/8 20 0/8	16 6/8	4 4	Fergus County	MT	Josef Rud	1998	2919
146 0/8	18 4/8 18 4/8	18 7/8	4 4	Placer County	CA	Adam Schultz	2001	2919
146 0/8	18 5/8 19 3/8	18 6/8	5 4	Catron County	NM	Mike Weaver	2002	2919
146 0/8	20 0/8 19 3/8	20 4/8	5 5	Billings County	ND	Gary Fleishauer	2002	2919
*146 0/8	20 6/8 20 1/8	20 7/8	5 5	Stark County	ND	Duff Donelson	2006	2919
146 0/8	20 2/8 20 0/8	19 2/8	5 5	McKenzie County	ND	Matt Leer	2006	2919
146 0/8	20 7/8 20 3/8	19 2/8	5 5	Williams Lake	BC	Paul Koester	2006	2919
146 0/8	21 4/8 20 5/8	21 7/8	5 5	Powder River County	MT	Tony Dawson	2008	2919
146 0/8	21 5/8 21 0/8	16 5/8	5 7	Cottle County	TX	Clark Peterson	2008	2919
145 7/8	21 1/8 20 4/8	20 5/8	5 6	Madera County	CA	Rodney York	1978	2933
145 7/8	20 1/8 20 3/8	19 5/8	4 4	Chelan County	WA	Rick Morgan	1984	2933
145 7/8	20 0/8 20 0/8	17 7/8	5 5	Valley County	ID	Robert Bruno	1988	2933
145 7/8	21 5/8 22 0/8	19 1/8	5 4	Billings County	ND	Tom Schills	1988	2933
145 7/8	20 1/8 19 1/8	15 1/8	5 5	Carbon County	WY	Joseph Parziale	1992	2933
145 7/8	22 2/8 23 1/8	17 7/8	5 5	Lake County	OR	Claude Babb	1993	2933
145 7/8	21 4/8 20 0/8	17 0/8	6 5	Ravalli County	MT	W. "Red" Chavez	1993	2933
145 7/8	20 2/8 20 2/8	18 1/8	5 4	Meade County	SD	Mike Weyer	1993	2933
145 7/8	22 1/8 23 5/8	20 1/8	5 5	Dorothy	ALB	Stephen K. Witon	1999	2933
145 7/8	22 5/8 21 0/8	19 3/8	4 4	Grant County	OR	Teddy E. Nickerson III	2000	2933
145 7/8	20 4/8 20 4/8	18 7/8	5 5	Dunn County	ND	Stephen A. Dougherty	2001	2933
145 7/8	20 0/8 22 2/8	18 2/8	6 6	Dawson County	MT	Tanner Kreiman	2008	2933
145 6/8	17 0/8 18 3/8	16 0/8	5 5	Lake County	OR	George Rajnus	1961	2945

338

MULE DEER (TYPICAL ANTLERS)

Minimum Score 145 — Continued

SCORE	LENGTH OF R MAIN BEAM L	INSIDE SPREAD	NUMBER OF R POINTS L	AREA	STATE/ PROVINCE	HUNTER'S NAME	DATE	RANK
145 6/8	22 2/8 24 3/8	21 4/8	5 3	Sevier County	UT	James R. Bell	1964	2945
145 6/8	24 1/8 21 3/8	24 2/8	6 6	Chaffee County	CO	Gary Ginther	1973	2945
145 6/8	22 3/8 22 0/8	20 2/8	5 5	Pecos County	TX	Butch Floyd	1975	2945
145 6/8	21 3/8 19 4/8	17 0/8	5 4	Albany County	WY	Jerry Bowen	1980	2945
145 6/8	20 6/8 22 0/8	21 0/8	6 5	Cheyenne County	KS	Kendall Helton	1988	2945
145 6/8	22 5/8 24 2/8	17 3/8	6 5	Bernalillo County	NM	Alvin Chewiwi	1990	2945
145 6/8	22 0/8 20 3/8	22 6/8	5 5	Wasco County	OR	Sean Corbin	1991	2945
145 6/8	19 4/8 23 4/8	21 7/8	5 6	Estevan	SAS	Myron Duff	1992	2945
145 6/8	19 4/8 19 2/8	17 2/8	5 5	Otero County	NM	Greg Perkins	1995	2945
145 6/8	19 4/8 18 4/8	18 2/8	5 5	Sheridan County	WY	Gary L. Challoner	1995	2945
145 6/8	21 4/8 21 2/8	16 6/8	5 5	Devon	ALB	Steve MacKenzie	1997	2945
145 6/8	23 4/8 21 2/8	18 1/8	6 6	Medicine Hat	ALB	Joe T. Soto, Jr.	1999	2945
145 6/8	19 4/8 21 0/8	21 5/8	5 5	McKenzie County	ND	Jason Babinchak	2000	2945
145 6/8	20 6/8 20 7/8	16 4/8	5 5	Eagle Hill	ALB	Dallas Kaiser	2001	2945
145 6/8	21 5/8 20 4/8	18 6/8	5 5	Cessford	ALB	Ronald Murphy	2004	2945
145 6/8	22 0/8 22 3/8	15 0/8	6 6	Fergus County	MT	John "Rosey" Roseland	2006	2945
145 6/8	21 7/8 21 0/8	18 2/8	5 5	Ziebach County	SD	Ramon Birkeland	2007	2945
145 6/8	18 4/8 19 2/8	19 4/8	5 5	Grant County	NM	Jason Edwards	2008	2945
145 5/8	21 0/8 20 4/8	17 5/8	4 4	Grant County	OR	Charlie Endicott	1979	2964
145 5/8	22 5/8 21 2/8	21 7/8	4 5	Ellis County	KS	Mark A. Murphey	1983	2964
145 5/8	22 0/8 22 5/8	20 3/8	7 6	Rich County	UT	Wade Steffenhagen	1992	2964
145 5/8	21 1/8 21 5/8	19 5/8	5 5	Larimer County	CO	Steve Banowetz	1998	2964
145 5/8	18 6/8 20 5/8	16 5/8	5 5	Cochrane	ALB	Patrick D. Quinn	1998	2964
145 5/8	18 4/8 18 4/8	17 1/8	5 5	Campbell County	WY	Michael R. O'Connell	1999	2964
145 5/8	22 4/8 22 5/8	20 5/8	5 4	San Juan County	NM	Dale Drilling	2000	2964
145 5/8	19 5/8 19 2/8	19 5/8	5 5	Haakon County	SD	Chad Ramsey	2003	2964
145 5/8	21 7/8 22 0/8	19 3/8	4 5	Lassen County	CA	Garrett Gantenbein	2005	2964
*145 5/8	23 0/8 19 7/8	22 5/8	5 4	Corson County	SD	John E. Powell, Jr.	2007	2964
145 5/8	24 0/8 25 7/8	27 1/8	5 4	Pima County	AZ	Danny Gifford	2008	2964
145 5/8	21 7/8 23 5/8	18 7/8	5 5	Deschutes County	OR	Randy Flanary	2009	2964
*145 5/8	21 4/8 20 4/8	17 3/8	5 5	Routt County	CO	Darryl Papineau	2009	2964
145 4/8	20 5/8 18 4/8	19 4/8	6 6	Boulder County	CO	Bob Byerly	1967	2977
145 4/8	19 6/8 14 2/8	18 4/8	7 7	Pima County	AZ	Peter C. Knagge	1976	2977
145 4/8	21 5/8 21 6/8	19 6/8	5 5	Sioux County	NE	Steve Woitaszewski	1983	2977
145 4/8	21 7/8 22 4/8	20 4/8	5 4	Converse County	WY	Frank N. Moore	1984	2977
145 4/8	18 4/8 19 4/8	16 6/8	4 4	Platte County	WY	Dave Hiiva	1985	2977
145 4/8	23 3/8 23 5/8	22 4/8	5 5	Lassen County	CA	Wayne Wood	1985	2977
145 4/8	21 2/8 20 5/8	21 5/8	4 4	Jackson County	OR	Ron Schmelzer	1991	2977
145 4/8	17 1/8 20 1/8	14 4/8	6 6	Sioux County	NE	Mike A. Ellingson	1992	2977
145 4/8	22 2/8 21 7/8	20 6/8	4 4	McKenzie County	ND	Ryan Ferrell	1996	2977
145 4/8	20 3/8 19 1/8	19 6/8	4 4	Billings County	ND	Mark L. Meyer	1999	2977
145 4/8	20 6/8 20 4/8	18 4/8	6 6	Carbon County	WY	Barak Capron	2001	2977
145 4/8	21 2/8 22 7/8	20 2/8	5 5	El Paso County	CO	Lee J. Dexter	2001	2977
145 4/8	21 0/8 21 4/8	20 5/8	8 5	Natrona County	WY	Mark Kronyak	2002	2977
145 4/8	20 4/8 20 2/8	19 0/8	5 5	Converse County	WY	Roger Grider	2005	2977
145 4/8	22 1/8 21 7/8	22 1/8	6 4	Boise County	ID	Marty Goffin	2006	2977
145 4/8	22 2/8 23 2/8	22 2/8	6 5	Davis County	UT	Chance Bailey	2007	2977
145 4/8	21 0/8 20 7/8	21 1/8	6 5	Harding County	SD	Doug Braun	2009	2977
145 3/8	27 2/8 26 5/8	26 2/8	5 4	Moffat County	CO	Scott Showalter	1971	2994
145 3/8	21 1/8 20 4/8	19 7/8	4 4	Sioux County	NE	William A. Voor Vart	1978	2994
145 3/8	21 6/8 22 0/8	21 7/8	4 4	Summit County	UT	Larry Dickerson	1985	2994
145 3/8	19 7/8 19 4/8	20 6/8	5 5	Larimer County	CO	Dane Dutrisac	1992	2994
145 3/8	19 7/8 19 6/8	20 1/8	4 4	Caribou County	ID	Michael Sparks	1992	2994
145 3/8	22 0/8 22 1/8	22 1/8	5 4	Pennington County	SD	Gary English	1992	2994
145 3/8	21 5/8 22 1/8	19 1/8	5 5	Dundy County	NE	Matt Gideon	1993	2994
145 3/8	23 1/8 22 1/8	20 5/8	5 4	Weld County	CO	Nathan L. Andersohn	1996	2994
145 3/8	22 7/8 23 3/8	18 7/8	5 5	Lincoln County	NM	Mark Russell	2000	2994
145 3/8	17 0/8 18 6/8	20 6/8	7 6	Coconino County	AZ	Paul T. Carter	2001	2994
145 3/8	22 0/8 20 7/8	15 1/8	5 5	Millarville	ALB	Kyle Sinclair-Smith	2002	2994
145 3/8	19 4/8 20 2/8	23 4/8	5 6	Mellette County	SD	Mark Satre	2004	2994
145 3/8	21 2/8 20 6/8	18 1/8	5 5	Gunnison County	CO	Sheryle Deuter	2007	2994
145 2/8	24 0/8 24 4/8	19 6/8	4 4	Bernalillo County	NM	Robert Bulcock, Jr.	1969	3007
145 2/8	20 1/8 20 2/8	16 2/8	5 5	Uncompahgre N.F.	CO	Larry Holak	1979	3007
145 2/8	22 4/8 23 1/8	17 4/8	5 5	Mesa County	CO	Paul T Brown	1985	3007
145 2/8	22 2/8 22 7/8	19 7/8	6 7	Norton County	KS	Gary Long	1987	3007
145 2/8	21 4/8 21 4/8	18 2/8	5 5	Natrona County	WY	Larry Nelson	1989	3007
145 2/8	20 4/8 20 2/8	20 5/8	5 5	Sandy Point	ALB	Tim Sailer	1990	3007
145 2/8	17 4/8 21 1/8	18 3/8	6 5	Bernalillo County	NM	Mark Sullivan	1994	3007
145 2/8	23 5/8 21 7/8	21 6/8	5 5	Columbia County	WA	Robert C. Allan	1995	3007
145 2/8	21 5/8 22 0/8	22 1/8	5 4	Brooks	ALB	Tim Walsh	1999	3007
145 2/8	20 6/8 20 2/8	18 6/8	6 6	Brooks	ALB	Brandon Ray	1999	3007
145 2/8	21 2/8 19 2/8	28 2/8	5 5	Slope County	ND	Jeff Clark	2000	3007
145 2/8	21 6/8 23 1/8	22 6/8	5 5	Dunn County	ND	Brad Perkins	2000	3007
145 2/8	22 0/8 21 0/8	18 6/8	7 7	Carter County	MT	Jeff Pals	2006	3007
145 2/8	19 4/8 20 6/8	17 4/8	5 5	Converse County	WY	Thomas Hansen II	2008	3007
*145 2/8	20 6/8 18 6/8	17 0/8	6 5	Converse County	WY	Sam Boyles	2008	3007
145 2/8	19 4/8 20 6/8	21 4/8	4 5	Maricopa County	AZ	Matthew Liljenquist	2008	3007
*145 2/8	21 2/8 21 5/8	18 4/8	5 5	Claresholm	ALB	Ryan M. Fleig	2009	3007
145 1/8	23 0/8 23 3/8	22 7/8	5 4	Natrona County	WY	Bill Wade	1970	3024
145 1/8	21 6/8 19 3/8	19 1/8	4 5	Eagle County	CO	Rick Duggan	1981	3024
145 1/8	19 4/8 20 3/8	17 5/8	5 4	Coconino County	AZ	Dick Tone	1981	3024
145 1/8	23 4/8 21 3/8	20 7/8	4 4	Summit County	CO	Mark Anderson	1982	3024
145 1/8	18 5/8 19 4/8	17 5/8	4 4	Routt County	CO	Ronald P. Kelley, Sr.	1985	3024
145 1/8	22 5/8 21 7/8	21 5/8	3 4	Baker County	OR	Arthur Marc Whisler	1986	3024
145 1/8	22 2/8 22 3/8	17 7/8	4 4	Yakima County	WA	Robt. "Andy" Anderson	1986	3024
145 1/8	21 3/8 20 6/8	19 1/8	4 5	Calgary	ALB	Jim Chapman	1991	3024
145 1/8	20 5/8 22 5/8	21 1/8	6 6	Grant County	OR	Ken Arveson, Jr.	1992	3024
145 1/8	19 4/8 20 7/8	16 1/8	5 5	Fergus County	MT	John P. Hartman	2003	3024
145 1/8	21 7/8 23 1/8	22 5/8	5 6	Routt County	CO	Karyn Ries	2004	3024
*145 1/8	20 6/8 20 7/8	24 6/8	5 5	Natrona County	WY	Craig Talbot	2005	3024
145 1/8	20 1/8 20 1/8	21 5/8	5 5	Carter County	MT	Jeff Pals	2005	3024
145 1/8	20 7/8 20 0/8	23 6/8	4 4	Vermilion	ALB	Glenn Moir	2009	3024
145 0/8	22 1/8 21 6/8	17 6/8	5 5	El Paso County	CO	Thomas M. Farmer	1961	3038
145 0/8	22 4/8 22 2/8	21 0/8	5 6	Trego County	KS	Don Howard	1966	3038
145 0/8	22 1/8 22 4/8	21 2/8	5 5	Plumas County	CA	Wayne Ghidossi	1977	3038

339

MULE DEER (TYPICAL ANTLERS)

Minimum Score 145   Continued

SCORE	LENGTH OF R MAIN BEAM L		INSIDE SPREAD	NUMBER OF R POINTS L		AREA	STATE/ PROVINCE	HUNTER'S NAME	DATE	RANK
145 0/8	22 7/8	24 2/8	27 1/8	5	5	Cochise County	AZ	Joe F. Acosta	1986	3038
145 0/8	20 5/8	20 4/8	19 4/8	4	5	Salt Lake County	UT	Lance Dalton	1989	3038
145 0/8	19 7/8	19 7/8	17 4/8	5	5	Fremont County	WY	Gary Nyman	1990	3038
145 0/8	22 2/8	20 7/8	19 2/8	6	5	Saguache County	CO	Mike Chatin	1991	3038
145 0/8	17 4/8	19 0/8	19 6/8	5	5	Union County	OR	Russ Hultberg	1991	3038
145 0/8	24 4/8	23 4/8	22 0/8	4	4	Vermilion	ALB	Graydon Bishop	1992	3038
145 0/8	20 0/8	20 6/8	17 2/8	5	5	Gallatin County	MT	Craig L. Newman	1995	3038
145 0/8	20 5/8	21 5/8	22 2/8	6	5	Jefferson County	OR	Jim Merrill	1997	3038
145 0/8	19 3/8	19 2/8	16 6/8	5	6	Milk River	ALB	Mark Zastrow	2000	3038
145 0/8	22 5/8	22 0/8	23 7/8	6	6	Jefferson County	OR	John Dick	2002	3038
145 0/8	20 0/8	20 0/8	19 6/8	5	5	Albany County	WY	Brent Swanson	2004	3038
*145 0/8	19 6/8	20 3/8	19 3/8	8	6	Jones County	SD	Austin J. Butt	2008	3038
*145 0/8	19 6/8	21 3/8	19 0/8	6	6	Rosebud County	MT	Steve Updegraff	2009	3038

MULE DEER (TYPICAL VELVET ANTLERS)

Minimum Score 145

SCORE	LENGTH OF R MAIN BEAM L		INSIDE SPREAD	NUMBER OF R POINTS L		AREA	STATE/ PROVINCE	HUNTER'S NAME	DATE	RANK
209 1/8	26 5/8	26 1/8	25 3/8	6	6	Mohave County	AZ	Bradley M. Hunter	2010	*
*205 1/8	25 0/8	25 0/8	27 0/8	6	5	Mesa County	CO	Tim W. Roberts	2006	*
*204 6/8	27 7/8	28 1/8	24 4/8	6	5	Weber County	UT	Patrick H. Grieco	2007	*
202 4/8	25 7/8	26 2/8	21 6/8	5	5	Kane County	UT	Charlie Crosby	2008	*
*200 3/8	25 5/8	26 5/8	25 5/8	5	6	Wayne County	UT	Paul Dallin	2008	*
196 4/8	26 6/8	27 1/8	22 4/8	6	4	Mesa County	CO	Jeff Draper	2008	*
*196 1/8	29 0/8	24 6/8	25 1/8	5	5	Eagle County	CO	William Kyle Ansel	2007	*
195 0/8	24 5/8	24 2/8	16 2/8	7	5	Silver Valley	ALB	Jason Frank	2009	*
*194 7/8	27 0/8	27 1/8	17 5/8	5	5	Garfield County	CO	Felton C. Leverette	2005	*
194 7/8	26 7/8	27 7/8	25 4/8	7	6	Deschutes County	OR	Nick Mickelson	2007	*
194 5/8	25 0/8	24 6/8	22 5/8	5	5	Montezuma County	CO	Vern A. Stiegelmeyer	2009	*
194 3/8	27 7/8	27 1/8	26 5/8	5	5	Wayne County	UT	Craig Brown	2007	*
193 7/8	26 3/8	25 5/8	22 7/8	5	5	Garfield County	UT	Lucas M. Ramsay	2009	*
193 6/8	23 5/8	24 1/8	23 6/8	5	5	Garfield County	UT	Howard C. Kirkpatrick	2008	*
192 4/8	23 4/8	25 1/8	22 4/8	5	6	Morrow County	OR	Robert McKibbin	2007	*
191 3/8	27 6/8	26 4/8	25 0/8	8	6	Wayne County	UT	Brady R. Larsen	2007	*
190 7/8	25 0/8	25 1/8	22 7/8	5	5	Apache County	AZ	Jason Yepa	2006	*
190 7/8	24 5/8	24 0/8	20 5/8	5	5	Nye County	NV	Clifford D. Raymond	2009	*
190 4/8	27 0/8	26 1/8	25 4/8	6	7	Montrose County	CO	Derik Yarnell	2008	*
190 2/8	25 2/8	25 3/8	21 6/8	6	7	Delta County	CO	Steve Edwards	2007	*
*189 4/8	25 3/8	23 1/8	22 0/8	5	5	Gunnison County	CO	Brandon J. Hockenberry	2010	*
188 5/8	24 1/8	23 1/8	24 1/8	5	5	Delta County	CO	Ty N. Terry	2005	*
*187 4/8	25 6/8	24 5/8	21 0/8	5	6	Carbon County	UT	Nevin Jensen	2009	*
187 3/8	21 4/8	22 5/8	19 1/8	5	5	Juab County	UT	Roger H. Bliss	2006	*
*186 1/8	25 5/8	24 6/8	20 5/8	5	5	Gunnison County	CO	Jeremy Houghtaling	2004	*
186 0/8	23 4/8	23 6/8	26 3/8	4	6	Washington County	UT	Michael C. Hirschi	2007	*
186 0/8	24 6/8	25 0/8	21 0/8	5	7	Iron County	UT	Thad Fife	2008	*
185 6/8	23 5/8	24 5/8	23 2/8	5	5	Washington County	UT	Russel G. Todd	2008	*
185 5/8	23 2/8	24 0/8	23 3/8	5	5	Morgan County	UT	Lane J. Wayment	2006	*
*185 1/8	25 2/8	23 3/8	21 3/8	5	5	Rich County	UT	Travis Hobbs	2009	*
*184 7/8	25 6/8	25 0/8	20 7/8	5	5	Gunnison County	CO	Walter Hamner	2008	*
184 6/8	25 0/8	24 5/8	20 0/8	4	4	Millard County	UT	Joseph W. Olsen	2007	*
183 7/8	25 3/8	24 6/8	21 5/8	5	5	Bingham County	ID	L. Garland Nelson, Jr.	2005	*
*183 6/8	24 6/8	23 7/8	21 0/8	5	5	Gunnison County	CO	Jay T. Ortega	2004	*
183 3/8	23 3/8	23 2/8	23 3/8	5	5	Salt Lake County	UT	Sam Fitzgerald	2008	*
183 3/8	23 6/8	23 7/8	23 1/8	7	6	Teller County	CO	Neal Alberts	2009	*
182 6/8	23 5/8	24 7/8	21 2/8	7	6	Iron County	UT	Darin Marx	2010	*
*182 5/8	23 1/8	23 3/8	20 1/8	5	5	Jefferson County	OR	Allan Sanford	2007	*
182 3/8	24 5/8	27 3/8	24 2/8	6	6	Peace River	ALB	Douglas Erickson	2005	*
182 3/8	24 1/8	23 2/8	24 1/8	5	5	Garfield County	UT	Michael Brown	2009	*
182 2/8	25 2/8	25 2/8	20 3/8	5	6	Wasatch County	UT	Jace Sager	2005	*
182 2/8	24 0/8	24 2/8	26 4/8	6	6	Garfield County	UT	Jeff Frier	2008	*
182 1/8	25 7/8	25 7/8	19 5/8	5	5	Mesa County	CO	Richard E. Davis	2009	*
*181 6/8	22 5/8	21 7/8	18 3/8	6	5	Grand County	UT	Clark A. Moss	2010	*
181 5/8	23 6/8	23 6/8	21 1/8	5	5	Vermilion	ALB	Glenn Moir	2008	*
181 5/8	21 6/8	24 3/8	25 6/8	6	7	Vermilion	ALB	Brad Rieland	2010	*
*181 2/8	24 2/8	24 6/8	22 6/8	6	6	Eagle County	CO	Greg Spurgeon	2005	*
*181 1/8	23 4/8	23 4/8	23 1/8	5	5	Mesa County	CO	Ben Johnson	2006	*
180 7/8	22 4/8	23 1/8	18 5/8	5	5	Grand County	CO	Andrew Murphy	2004	*
180 6/8	26 3/8	24 5/8	21 0/8	7	6	Grant County	OR	Richard Waters	2001	*
180 6/8	25 2/8	27 1/8	24 1/8	7	4	Peace River	ALB	Nate Jacobson	2006	*
180 5/8	24 5/8	24 6/8	20 4/8	6	5	San Juan County	CO	Kelly Baird	2007	*
180 4/8	23 4/8	24 6/8	25 0/8	6	5	Chaffee County	CO	John Walke	2007	*
180 1/8	21 1/8	23 0/8	21 5/8	5	6	La Plata County	CO	Michael Fischer	2005	*
180 0/8	24 0/8	23 5/8	18 7/8	5	6	Dolores County	CO	Dennis Doherty	2009	*
*179 4/8	25 1/8	24 6/8	22 2/8	5	5	Fremont County	CO	Lance Mulso	2000	*
179 4/8	23 3/8	22 1/8	19 4/8	5	6	La Plata County	CO	Mindy Paulek	2007	*
179 2/8	24 1/8	25 5/8	21 2/8	5	6	Weber County	UT	John Pilarczyk	2007	*
179 1/8	27 0/8	27 6/8	23 5/8	6	6	Wasatch County	UT	Gerald F. Fillmore	1999	*
178 7/8	22 1/8	23 1/8	26 2/8	5	5	Riverhurst	SAS	Russell Long	2005	*
*178 5/8	23 4/8	24 1/8	24 1/8	6	5	Park County	CO	Chris Zimmerman	2010	*
*178 3/8	25 3/8	25 0/8	21 7/8	4	4	Humboldt County	NV	Jesse Haw	2009	*
177 7/8	24 7/8	24 1/8	26 4/8	5	5	Elko County	NV	Dewey Ray Smith	2005	*
*177 7/8	22 7/8	24 4/8	21 5/8	5	5	Chaffee County	CO	Caleb Barclay	2009	*
177 7/8	24 4/8	25 2/8	22 4/8	6	6	La Plata County	CO	Lew Webb	2009	*
*177 5/8	24 2/8	25 1/8	26 2/8	5	5	Elko County	NV	Jonas Vass	2008	*
177 5/8	24 4/8	25 0/8	22 3/8	5	6	Sheridan County	WY	Luke Roush	2010	*
*177 0/8	20 3/8	21 5/8	20 6/8	5	5	Elko County	NV	Robert E. Ziegenbein	2010	*
176 5/8	22 2/8	23 0/8	20 7/8	5	5	San Juan County	UT	Trent Daves	2002	*
*176 5/8	23 4/8	24 1/8	21 5/8	5	6	Lone Rock	SAS	Joshua Corpe	2008	*
*176 2/8	24 4/8	23 7/8	23 4/8	5	5	Grand County	UT	Roy K. Keefer	2007	*
*176 1/8	26 0/8	25 6/8	24 1/8	5	5	Gunnison County	CO	Richard L. Krug	2006	*
176 1/8	23 3/8	24 2/8	14 7/8	6	6	Mora County	NM	Luke C. Kellogg	2007	*
176 0/8	24 3/8	24 5/8	23 6/8	5	5	Larimer County	CO	Jeremiah Bowe	2005	*
175 7/8	24 4/8	23 6/8	24 3/8	7	6	Blueberry Mtn.	ALB	Gary Gillett	2005	*
175 7/8	23 0/8	23 3/8	23 5/8	5	5	Deschutes County	OR	Ross Weaver	2009	*
*175 5/8	24 5/8	24 1/8	24 4/8	5	6	Garfield County	UT	Lance Harris	2010	*
175 3/8	22 0/8	22 4/8	18 0/8	6	5	East River	ALB	Rick Curley	2005	*
175 2/8	26 0/8	23 3/8	23 6/8	5	5	Caribou County	ID	Bill Friedel	1983	*
*175 1/8	24 6/8	23 7/8	20 1/8	5	5	Morgan County	UT	Brandon T. Wicks	2005	*
174 2/8	25 2/8	24 6/8	27 0/8	4	5	Lac Pelletier	SAS	Timothy E. Loran	2004	*
174 1/8	22 2/8	21 6/8	20 6/8	6	6	Mesa County	CO	Mark Rezin	2004	*
174 0/8	23 3/8	23 1/8	19 2/8	5	5	Crook County	WY	Tim Ozmun	1994	*
*173 7/8	24 6/8	23 2/8	23 3/8	6	5	Natrona County	WY	Shawn Wagner	2010	*
173 4/8	25 5/8	25 5/8	21 3/8	5	6	Cassia County	ID	Lee Blankenship	2006	*
*173 3/8	25 3/8	26 0/8	21 4/8	5	7	Deschutes County	OR	Javan H. Shull	2008	*
173 2/8	20 0/8	19 7/8	20 4/8	5	6	Dolores County	CO	Norman L. Stuckman	2007	*
173 1/8	22 7/8	22 2/8	18 1/8	5	5	Jefferson County	CO	Glen Summers	2004	*
173 1/8	24 3/8	24 4/8	22 2/8	5	5	Last Mountain Lake	SAS	Clay Sazynski	2010	*
*173 0/8	20 5/8	22 5/8	22 0/8	5	5	Sanpete County	UT	Russell Larsen	2004	*
172 7/8	22 5/8	23 2/8	21 5/8	5	5	La Plata County	CO	Kevin Neil	2006	*
172 7/8	27 6/8	25 7/8	24 3/8	5	5	Coconino County	AZ	Tony Seddon	2008	*
*172 6/8	22 3/8	23 1/8	19 2/8	5	5	Kane County	UT	Jeremy Littleford	2008	*
172 3/8	23 7/8	22 6/8	18 4/8	6	5	Grand County	CO	Marvin R. Sanchez	2006	*
*172 3/8	23 0/8	23 3/8	25 0/8	5	5	Bow River	ALB	Blake Howland	2008	*

341

MULE DEER (TYPICAL VELVET ANTLERS)

Minimum Score 145   Continued

SCORE	LENGTH OF MAIN BEAM R	L	INSIDE SPREAD	NUMBER OF POINTS R	L	AREA	STATE/ PROVINCE	HUNTER'S NAME	DATE	RANK
172 1/8	23 6/8	24 2/8	22 4/8	4	5	Peace River	ALB	George Pieros, Jr.	2006	*
172 0/8	24 3/8	25 0/8	22 0/8	5	5	Garfield County	UT	Lucas M. Ramsay	2008	*
171 7/8	22 1/8	22 5/8	23 4/8	5	5	Salt Lake County	UT	Dustin Pennington	2005	*
*171 7/8	23 6/8	23 3/8	19 5/8	5	5	Fairview	ALB	Dwayne Huggins	2005	*
171 3/8	25 1/8	25 2/8	24 7/8	3	4	Dolores County	CO	Cory Tunnell	2005	*
171 2/8	23 4/8	23 4/8	21 0/8	4	4	Sublette County	WY	Brian Costello	2004	*
171 2/8	21 2/8	21 4/8	21 0/8	5	5	Morgan County	UT	Randy Springborn	2006	*
170 7/8	23 5/8	22 7/8	21 2/8	6	6	Valhalla	ALB	Jeff Guy	2006	*
170 7/8	24 2/8	24 6/8	26 5/8	6	6	Toole County	MT	Scott Thielmann	2008	*
170 6/8	23 1/8	23 0/8	20 0/8	5	5	Carbon County	UT	Brandon Elegante	2008	*
170 5/8	19 5/8	18 7/8	18 3/8	5	5	Rio Blanco County	CO	Paul Allan Carr	2004	*
*170 5/8	24 5/8	23 7/8	20 1/8	5	5	Las Animas County	CO	Stanley Dwight Taylor	2006	*
170 4/8	22 6/8	24 3/8	18 4/8	5	5	Union County	OR	Robert H. Moxley	2005	*
170 3/8	22 0/8	21 4/8	19 1/8	5	5	Iron County	UT	Colby B. Batty	2003	*
170 3/8	25 3/8	25 0/8	22 3/8	5	5	Grand County	UT	Zachary S. Henseler	2007	*
*170 3/8	25 1/8	25 3/8	19 5/8	5	5	Mesa County	CO	Cody Welch	2007	*
170 2/8	21 0/8	21 5/8	18 4/8	5	5	Custer County	CO	Pamela Mize Hunsaker	2007	*
170 1/8	24 0/8	23 6/8	20 5/8	5	5	Kane County	UT	Guy Smith	2007	*
170 1/8	23 2/8	22 0/8	18 3/8	5	5	Gunnison County	CO	Kathleen L. Gillenwater	2009	*
169 7/8	22 2/8	23 4/8	21 5/8	5	5	Klamath County	OR	Theodore A. Davis	2007	*
169 6/8	24 2/8	22 7/8	19 4/8	5	5	Archuleta County	CO	Phillip Baca	2006	*
169 5/8	19 7/8	19 6/8	16 5/8	5	5	La Plata County	CO	Joseph LaBonte	2004	*
169 3/8	24 6/8	23 6/8	19 5/8	5	5	Garfield County	CO	Benjamin C. Hoesl	2004	*
169 3/8	24 0/8	22 3/8	19 7/8	5	5	Sanpete County	UT	Scott Barclay	2009	*
169 3/8	21 2/8	21 7/8	21 3/8	5	5	Mesa County	CO	Todd Brackett	2009	*
*169 1/8	23 0/8	22 3/8	22 7/8	4	5	Fairview	ALB	Gary Gillett	2008	*
*169 0/8	23 5/8	23 6/8	22 1/8	4	5	San Juan County	NM	Kelly Baird	2009	*
168 7/8	21 7/8	22 7/8	19 5/8	5	5	Carbon County	UT	Duane J. Wood	2008	*
168 6/8	24 2/8	22 1/8	21 2/8	4	4	Maple Creek	SAS	Austin Mawson	2008	*
168 4/8	20 3/8	20 2/8	19 2/8	5	5	Millard County	UT	Andrew A. Ward	2003	*
168 4/8	24 7/8	25 3/8	18 6/8	4	4	Washoe County	NV	Terry Whitney, Jr.	2007	*
168 4/8	22 4/8	22 2/8	20 0/8	5	5	Salt Lake County	UT	Scott Weatherspoon	2008	*
168 4/8	23 1/8	23 4/8	24 3/8	5	5	Gunnison County	CO	Scott Hargrove	2008	*
168 4/8	23 4/8	24 0/8	20 4/8	6	5	Maple Creek	SAS	Dwayne Onofriechuck	2008	*
168 4/8	24 0/8	23 6/8	21 0/8	5	5	Grand County	UT	Tom Langston	2009	*
168 0/8	24 2/8	24 6/8	22 4/8	5	5	Owyhee County	ID	Tim Craft	2006	*
*167 6/8	24 4/8	25 3/8	20 7/8	6	6	Elko County	NV	Wesley A. Wise	2008	*
*167 5/8	27 0/8	25 2/8	19 2/8	7	5	Morrow County	OR	Jack Fowler	2008	*
167 3/8	23 1/8	22 7/8	22 6/8	6	5	Battle River	ALB	J. P. McDonald	2007	*
*167 2/8	21 4/8	22 4/8	20 0/8	5	5	La Plata County	CO	Matthew Dufva	2010	*
167 1/8	23 1/8	22 6/8	21 7/8	5	6	Custer County	CO	Randall Gasch	2006	*
*167 1/8	23 0/8	23 3/8	22 1/8	6	6	Vauxhall	ALB	Branden Martin	2008	*
*167 0/8	24 2/8	23 5/8	20 2/8	5	5	San Juan County	UT	Mark William Christiansen	2007	*
166 6/8	23 0/8	23 0/8	20 0/8	5	5	100 Mile House	BC	Ron Klassen	2004	*
166 6/8	22 2/8	21 2/8	18 0/8	4	5	Morgan County	UT	Dennis "Poncho" McCoy	2005	*
*166 6/8	22 6/8	22 2/8	15 1/8	6	5	Fremont County	CO	William Colon	2007	*
166 6/8	21 7/8	21 3/8	16 2/8	5	5	Clear Creek County	CO	Kyle M. Ouzts	2009	*
*166 5/8	22 7/8	25 2/8	21 2/8	5	6	Medicine Hat	ALB	Perry Robitaille	2007	*
166 4/8	23 6/8	24 2/8	22 3/8	5	6	Conejos County	CO	Lewis Machen	2005	*
*166 4/8	22 2/8	22 0/8	17 5/8	7	6	Ouray County	CO	John R. Keener	2007	*
166 4/8	24 0/8	23 4/8	21 2/8	5	5	Elko County	NV	Alan Wakefield	2008	*
166 4/8	24 7/8	24 4/8	19 4/8	4	4	Wasatch County	UT	Dustin Makin	2008	*
166 4/8	21 7/8	23 1/8	19 0/8	7	6	Lincoln County	NV	Joe Lund	2008	*
166 2/8	20 3/8	20 2/8	16 6/8	8	5	Albany County	WY	Brent Swanson	2005	*
*166 1/8	22 0/8	21 7/8	18 4/8	7	6	Uintah County	UT	Britt Hazelbush	2006	*
165 6/8	20 5/8	22 0/8	18 0/8	5	5	Jackson County	CO	John O. Rosenboom	2006	*
165 6/8	23 4/8	23 4/8	21 4/8	7	7	San Juan County	UT	David Wayne Morgan	2008	*
165 6/8	22 0/8	21 3/8	20 0/8	5	5	Montrose County	CO	Tim L. Donnelly	2009	*
165 5/8	24 4/8	20 6/8	24 3/8	5	6	Navajo County	AZ	Brad Sunkenberg	1998	*
165 5/8	21 3/8	22 3/8	20 3/8	5	5	Elko County	NV	Todd Bresemann	2006	*
165 3/8	23 2/8	22 5/8	21 7/8	5	5	Sierra County	CA	Thomas Hansen	2009	*
165 2/8	23 1/8	25 6/8	22 4/8	5	5	Montrose County	CO	Bruce Barrie	2004	*
*165 2/8	22 1/8	22 6/8	19 0/8	5	5	Hardisty	ALB	Ian Strachan	2008	*
165 1/8	24 0/8	22 2/8	20 7/8	5	5	Boulder County	CO	Joseph Yang	2009	*
165 0/8	19 5/8	19 6/8	16 4/8	5	5	Jackson County	CO	Seth McEvoy	2007	*
164 7/8	18 5/8	18 0/8	19 3/8	5	5	Gunnison County	CO	Fred V. Smith	2006	*
164 7/8	21 5/8	22 5/8	16 1/8	5	5	Tooele County	UT	Gary Durfee	2010	*
164 6/8	21 3/8	22 0/8	21 0/8	5	5	Saddle Hills	ALB	Duane Hagman	2004	*
164 6/8	25 5/8	24 0/8	23 0/8	6	6	Malheur County	OR	Tim P. Brown	2005	*
164 5/8	21 3/8	22 4/8	19 7/8	5	5	Eagle County	CO	Rick Adams	2010	*
164 3/8	21 1/8	22 3/8	20 6/8	6	6	Cache County	UT	Joe Mayers	2007	*
*164 3/8	25 6/8	26 3/8	25 3/8	4	4	San Juan County	UT	Bruce Marshall	2009	*
*164 0/8	22 6/8	23 1/8	19 0/8	4	5	Teller County	CO	Brian A. Depue	2007	*
164 0/8	25 0/8	25 5/8	21 2/8	4	5	Dolores County	CO	Clayton C. Wolter	2009	*
*163 7/8	22 3/8	22 6/8	18 5/8	5	5	Larimer County	CO	Cathy Bucknum	2007	*
163 6/8	22 1/8	20 0/8	19 0/8	5	5	Garfield County	UT	Alan Thompson	2005	*
163 6/8	22 7/8	23 3/8	22 1/8	5	8	Hinsdale County	CO	John Johnson	2009	*
*163 5/8	22 7/8	24 4/8	23 1/8	4	5	Spirit River	ALB	Troy Dzioba	2006	*
*163 5/8	22 1/8	21 0/8	17 3/8	6	6	Garfield County	UT	Lance W. Zobell	2006	*
*163 5/8	19 5/8	22 5/8	17 3/8	5	5	Elko County	NV	Rhonda Kay Meyer	2009	*
*163 4/8	22 6/8	21 1/8	20 4/8	4	5	Grand County	CO	Win Betteridge	2005	*
163 4/8	23 4/8	22 6/8	19 7/8	6	7	Valley County	ID	Kyle W. Odom	2008	*
*163 4/8	25 0/8	24 4/8	22 3/8	6	6	Coconino County	AZ	Dustin Overturf	2008	*
*163 1/8	21 7/8	21 5/8	18 1/8	4	4	Lincoln County	NM	Shane Hohman	2004	*
163 1/8	28 2/8	28 1/8	29 5/8	4	6	Grant County	OR	Brian Spivey	2005	*
163 1/8	22 4/8	22 0/8	19 1/8	4	4	Dunn County	ND	Bill Haase	2006	*
163 0/8	23 6/8	23 7/8	21 4/8	4	4	Sanpete County	UT	Jesse Betteridge	2006	*
*163 0/8	23 4/8	23 5/8	20 2/8	5	5	San Juan County	UT	Bruce Marshall	2007	*
162 7/8	22 2/8	22 6/8	20 6/8	7	6	Peace River	ALB	Chester Dodgson	2009	*
162 4/8	21 1/8	21 6/8	28 0/8	5	5	Coconino County	AZ	Danny Alen Robison	2005	*
162 4/8	21 0/8	21 6/8	22 6/8	5	5	Rich County	UT	Blake Poppleton	2006	*
162 3/8	22 4/8	21 2/8	18 7/8	5	4	Bear Lake County	ID	Travis Bailey	2010	*
162 2/8	21 6/8	22 0/8	19 6/8	5	5	Spirit River	ALB	Stephen Kotz	2005	*
162 2/8	22 4/8	21 5/8	20 4/8	5	5	Humboldt County	NV	James F. Crowley	2007	*
*162 2/8	24 0/8	23 7/8	21 4/8	5	5	Trochu	ALB	Brett Samson	2008	*

MULE DEER (TYPICAL VELVET ANTLERS)

Minimum Score 145 Continued

SCORE	LENGTH OF R MAIN BEAM L	INSIDE SPREAD	NUMBER OF R POINTS L	AREA	STATE/ PROVINCE	HUNTER'S NAME	DATE	RANK
162 1/8	23 2/8 24 7/8	19 5/8	5 5	San Juan County	UT	Randy J. Walk	1995	*
162 1/8	24 1/8 24 1/8	21 0/8	5 6	Bad Heart River	ALB	Rick Martin	2003	*
162 1/8	20 6/8 21 5/8	18 1/8	5 5	Iron County	UT	Mitchell Day	2006	*
162 0/8	23 0/8 18 5/8	23 4/8	4 6	Washington County	UT	Ben Batty	2004	*
*162 0/8	21 6/8 20 2/8	22 4/8	5 5	Greenlee County	AZ	Eric Jeffrey Burgan	2006	*
*161 7/8	22 5/8 23 4/8	21 3/8	4 4	Carter County	MT	Colin Pearson	2007	*
*161 6/8	23 0/8 23 7/8	21 0/8	5 5	Park County	CO	Laura L. Sawyer	2007	*
*161 4/8	22 6/8 23 3/8	22 4/8	5 6	Fremont County	CO	Lance Mulso	2006	*
161 4/8	21 6/8 23 2/8	23 6/8	5 4	Gunnison County	CO	Christopher Carlson	2006	*
*161 4/8	21 2/8 25 0/8	21 0/8	4 4	Jefferson County	CO	Josh Hillegass	2009	*
161 3/8	25 2/8 22 6/8	23 3/8	4 3	Garfield County	UT	Scott Wilson	1999	*
161 2/8	22 7/8 21 6/8	17 6/8	5 5	Greenlee County	AZ	Johnny Blizzard	2000	*
*161 2/8	22 6/8 22 2/8	18 4/8	5 5	Iron County	UT	Tony Lyle	2006	*
161 2/8	21 6/8 22 0/8	19 1/8	5 6	Boulder County	CO	Dustin Christensen	2006	*
161 2/8	24 6/8 23 6/8	20 6/8	4 5	Lincoln County	NV	Herbert Holtam	2007	*
161 2/8	21 4/8 20 5/8	15 6/8	5 5	Custer County	MT	Bradford E. Sink	2007	*
*161 1/8	25 2/8 23 1/8	19 1/8	4 4	Salt Lake County	UT	Kenneth J. Oetker	2005	*
*161 1/8	22 3/8 21 3/8	19 3/8	6 6	La Plata County	CO	Michael D. Robeson	2005	*
161 1/8	21 2/8 21 0/8	20 1/8	4 5	Lander County	NV	Joseph G. DeAngelis	2009	*
*161 1/8	22 3/8 23 3/8	25 6/8	4 4	Millard County	UT	Mike Blair	2009	*
161 0/8	22 0/8 22 2/8	20 2/8	5 5	Gunnison County	CO	Phillip White	2005	*
161 0/8	23 0/8 24 4/8	17 4/8	5 7	Valhalla Centre	ALB	Robert D. Hancock, Jr.	2005	*
161 0/8	21 3/8 21 7/8	16 0/8	7 5	Peace River	ALB	Rodney J. Kelly	2009	*
160 7/8	25 7/8 25 7/8	21 1/8	7 5	McKinley County	NM	Syverson Homer	1988	*
*160 6/8	20 4/8 20 5/8	18 6/8	5 5	Gunnison County	CO	Brandon J. Hockenberry	2008	*
160 5/8	26 1/8 26 5/8	25 3/8	5 4	Mesa County	CO	Erik L. Kantner	2005	*
*160 3/8	23 4/8 23 0/8	20 5/8	5 7	Gunnison County	CO	Travis Schwartz	2007	*
*160 3/8	22 7/8 23 2/8	16 7/8	5 4	Grand County	CO	Pete Timpano	2008	*
160 1/8	20 2/8 20 4/8	14 3/8	5 5	Huerfano County	CO	Lynette Trujillo	2009	*
160 0/8	21 2/8 19 4/8	17 4/8	5 5	Routt County	CO	Nick Ross	2004	*
160 0/8	25 0/8 23 0/8	20 6/8	4 4	Eureka County	NV	Eddie Alves	2008	*
160 0/8	22 6/8 23 3/8	21 4/8	5 5	Converse County	WY	Bill Stewart	2008	*
*159 7/8	20 4/8 20 4/8	18 3/8	4 5	San Juan County	UT	Kyle M. West	2009	*
159 5/8	22 0/8 24 0/8	18 4/8	5 5	Peace River	ALB	Craig Crawford	2004	*
*159 2/8	23 4/8 23 5/8	20 4/8	5 4	Montrose County	CO	James Hennen	2010	*
*159 1/8	22 5/8 22 3/8	19 1/8	5 5	Duchesne County	UT	Dollie D. Denton	2005	*
159 1/8	19 2/8 20 3/8	20 3/8	5 5	Gunnison County	CO	Roy E. Grace	2007	*
*159 1/8	26 5/8 26 2/8	20 4/8	6 3	Elko County	NV	John Bottari	2010	*
158 7/8	23 1/8 25 5/8	24 3/8	5 5	Jefferson County	CO	Barry Himmelman	2006	*
*158 7/8	23 4/8 23 7/8	19 7/8	4 4	Albany County	WY	Ron Mason	2008	*
158 6/8	21 1/8 21 5/8	20 0/8	5 5	Garfield County	CO	Robert Barrie	2004	*
*158 2/8	21 1/8 21 4/8	21 4/8	4 4	Nye County	NV	Lee Rankin	2010	*
158 0/8	23 0/8 22 6/8	24 4/8	5 5	Lincoln County	NV	Stewart D. Fifield	2007	*
*157 7/8	21 1/8 21 5/8	21 3/8	5 5	Moffat County	CO	Jason Bienek	2006	*
*157 7/8	21 2/8 21 6/8	20 1/8	5 5	Douglas County	CO	Timothy A. Laing	2010	*
157 6/8	22 7/8 21 5/8	16 2/8	6 7	Mesa County	CO	Eric J. Curtis	2004	*
157 5/8	19 3/8 20 7/8	17 7/8	5 5	Douglas County	CO	William Ferguson	2007	*
*157 5/8	21 4/8 21 7/8	15 3/8	5 7	Juab County	UT	Blake Peterson	2008	*
157 3/8	21 1/8 21 3/8	19 5/8	5 5	Moffat County	CO	Michael R. O'Connell	2003	*
157 3/8	23 2/8 23 3/8	21 7/8	5 5	El Paso County	CO	Daniel D. Hughes	2007	*
*157 3/8	22 4/8 22 7/8	17 3/8	4 4	Salt Lake County	UT	Kenneth Oetker	2010	*
157 2/8	21 7/8 24 0/8	26 1/8	5 5	San Juan County	UT	Donald Newman	2007	*
157 2/8	20 5/8 22 6/8	20 4/8	5 5	Sheridan County	WY	William R. Crocker	2008	*
157 0/8	23 2/8 23 1/8	21 4/8	5 5	Montrose County	CO	Roger G. Niewiadomski	2004	*
156 7/8	21 7/8 22 0/8	18 0/8	7 5	Delta County	CO	Steve Edwards	2008	*
156 7/8	22 3/8 22 6/8	21 5/8	5 5	Elko County	NV	Joan D. Holland	2010	*
156 6/8	21 3/8 19 7/8	20 0/8	4 5	Custer County	MT	Steve Krutzfeldt	2005	*
*156 6/8	20 1/8 19 2/8	16 2/8	5 5	Cassia County	ID	L. Garland Nelson, Jr.	2010	*
156 5/8	22 3/8 21 3/8	18 0/8	5 5	Eagle County	CO	William Kyle Ansel	2010	*
156 4/8	22 0/8 23 0/8	23 1/8	5 5	Fresno County	CA	Owen Kimberling	2005	*
156 4/8	19 3/8 20 5/8	20 4/8	4 5	Montezuma County	CO	Bryon D. Long	2005	*
156 4/8	23 6/8 23 3/8	19 4/8	5 5	Uintah County	UT	David Thornberry	2008	*
156 3/8	22 7/8 20 7/8	19 5/8	4 4	Nye County	NV	Remi Joseph Warren	2005	*
156 3/8	23 1/8 23 5/8	23 5/8	5 5	Summit County	UT	John Pearce	2007	*
*156 3/8	22 5/8 21 6/8	16 5/8	5 5	Uintah County	UT	Bodee Sessions	2009	*
*156 2/8	23 4/8 24 0/8	24 5/8	4 4	San Miguel County	CO	Darin Gardner	2007	*
*156 2/8	23 3/8 23 4/8	17 6/8	4 4	Grand County	UT	Jeff DeWaal	2009	*
156 2/8	24 7/8 24 3/8	16 4/8	4 4	Jefferson County	CO	Josh Hillegass	2010	*
*156 1/8	21 4/8 20 4/8	20 5/8	5 5	Grand County	CO	Tom Mullinex	2008	*
156 0/8	20 3/8 20 7/8	16 3/8	7 7	Teller County	CO	Larry Clark	2009	*
155 5/8	23 3/8 22 4/8	26 2/8	4 4	Mono County	CA	Charles Millhollin	2004	*
155 5/8	22 2/8 22 5/8	18 1/8	5 5	Pitkin County	CO	Randy Harms	2004	*
155 4/8	17 4/8 23 2/8	21 3/8	7 5	Red Creek	BC	Andrew Snucins	2005	*
*155 3/8	21 2/8 22 5/8	21 0/8	5 6	Elko County	NV	Myles Nance	2010	*
*155 1/8	26 5/8 25 5/8	24 3/8	3 4	Elko County	NV	John Bottari	2008	*
*155 0/8	25 0/8 24 4/8	22 1/8	6 5	Utah County	UT	Zack Mitani	2010	*
154 7/8	21 7/8 21 3/8	17 0/8	6 5	Morgan County	UT	Hal Stauff	2005	*
154 7/8	21 6/8 21 4/8	19 1/8	5 5	McKenzie County	ND	Scott L. Sprenger	2005	*
*154 5/8	24 1/8 22 7/8	21 5/8	4 5	San Juan County	UT	Tom Logan IV	2007	*
154 4/8	22 6/8 23 0/8	16 3/8	5 6	Leader	SAS	Jerry Frankfurt	1982	*
154 4/8	23 1/8 22 3/8	22 0/8	5 5	Elko County	NV	Christopher Faiman	2005	*
154 3/8	23 6/8 25 2/8	19 7/8	5 5	Elko County	NV	Jody Cyr	2005	*
154 3/8	21 0/8 20 2/8	17 7/8	5 5	Utah County	UT	Joe Bruscato	2009	*
154 2/8	22 4/8 21 6/8	19 2/8	5 6	Peace River	ALB	Rick Curley	2006	*
*154 2/8	19 4/8 19 3/8	19 5/8	5 5	Sevier County	UT	Ryan Rickenbach	2007	*
154 2/8	21 2/8 21 1/8	17 6/8	6 5	Garfield County	UT	Bill Van Buskirk	2008	*
154 1/8	23 0/8 23 0/8	22 3/8	5 5	Santa Barbara County	CA	Noel Carter	2005	*
153 7/8	23 1/8 23 7/8	20 3/8	6 5	Sanpete County	UT	Chance Platt	2006	*
153 7/8	23 3/8 23 5/8	23 1/8	5 5	Lassen County	CA	Heath L. Jones	2007	*
153 7/8	23 5/8 22 2/8	22 2/8	5 6	Grand County	CO	Roy E. Grace	2009	*
153 6/8	21 6/8 21 1/8	21 0/8	4 4	Elko County	NV	Lon E. Lauber	2006	*
153 6/8	23 0/8 23 1/8	25 1/8	6 5	Mesa County	CO	Larry M. Peterson	2007	*
153 4/8	21 1/8 23 0/8	26 1/8	5 5	Lincoln County	NV	Randy J. Walk	2009	*
153 2/8	24 7/8 24 5/8	21 1/8	5 6	San Miguel County	CO	Darin Gardner	2006	*
153 1/8	19 5/8 19 6/8	16 6/8	6 5	Summit County	CO	Marvin Clyncke	2010	*

343

MULE DEER (TYPICAL VELVET ANTLERS)

Minimum Score 145 Continued

SCORE	LENGTH OF R MAIN BEAM L	INSIDE SPREAD	NUMBER OF R POINTS L	AREA	STATE/ PROVINCE	HUNTER'S NAME	DATE	RANK
153 0/8	19 1/8 20 3/8	16 2/8	5 5	Iron County	UT	Arnold DeCastro	2010	*
*152 7/8	23 1/8 21 5/8	23 3/8	5 5	Taos County	NM	David L. Sanchez	2009	*
*152 7/8	22 1/8 22 4/8	21 1/8	5 5	Gunnison County	CO	Brandon J. Hockenberry	2009	*
152 6/8	21 1/8 21 5/8	16 4/8	5 5	Weber County	UT	Dennis Turner	2006	*
152 6/8	19 3/8 21 3/8	18 2/8	5 4	Shaunavon	SAS	Garry Leslie	2006	*
*152 5/8	22 6/8 22 4/8	22 0/8	6 5	Sheridan County	WY	Roy L. Walk	2008	*
*152 5/8	19 7/8 21 2/8	18 5/8	5 5	Apache County	AZ	Frank Hausner	2008	*
*152 4/8	20 3/8 20 6/8	18 0/8	5 5	Humboldt County	NV	Cameron R. Hanes	2005	*
152 1/8	20 1/8 19 4/8	16 3/8	5 6	White Pine County	NV	Roy K. Keefer	2004	*
152 1/8	19 7/8 22 0/8	21 1/8	4 4	Greenlee County	AZ	Roy Jimenez	2006	*
*152 0/8	24 0/8 22 0/8	23 0/8	5 4	Grand County	UT	Todd Grossenbach	2009	*
*152 0/8	22 0/8 22 1/8	20 2/8	5 5	Sheridan County	WY	Jamie Graetz	2009	*
*152 0/8	25 3/8 24 3/8	23 1/8	5 6	Washington County	UT	Beau Gledhill	2010	*
*151 7/8	18 0/8 17 5/8	16 5/8	5 5	Spirit River	ALB	James C. Kelly	2004	*
151 6/8	21 6/8 21 4/8	20 0/8	6 6	Coconino County	AZ	Mike Acheson	2009	*
*151 5/8	21 3/8 20 3/8	19 2/8	5 6	Carbon County	UT	Bryan Pierce	2005	*
*151 4/8	21 5/8 23 2/8	20 2/8	5 5	San Juan County	UT	Ron Seifert	2009	*
151 4/8	21 5/8 20 2/8	17 4/8	5 5	Uintah County	UT	Jason Nickell	2009	*
151 3/8	21 4/8 22 1/8	22 1/8	4 5	White Pine County	NV	Donald C. Martin	2008	*
151 2/8	19 6/8 20 7/8	19 6/8	5 5	Routt County	CO	Michael M. McCombs	2004	*
*151 2/8	22 2/8 21 4/8	21 6/8	5 5	Golden Valley County	ND	Pete Finck	2007	*
150 7/8	21 2/8 19 5/8	18 1/8	4 4	Malheur County	OR	Gordon Childers	2010	*
*150 5/8	24 3/8 23 4/8	20 3/8	5 5	Sheridan County	WY	Rick Davidson	2006	*
150 4/8	19 0/8 20 2/8	15 2/8	5 5	Powder River County	MT	Kurt V. Howell	2007	*
150 4/8	22 4/8 22 0/8	18 0/8	5 5	Peace River	ALB	Kaitlyn Popson	2010	*
150 1/8	21 5/8 21 3/8	20 5/8	5 4	Wayne County	UT	Ben E. Pace	2009	*
150 0/8	21 2/8 21 5/8	19 2/8	6 7	Harney County	OR	Jonell Haslett	2005	*
149 5/8	22 0/8 22 0/8	17 5/8	5 4	La Plata County	CO	Donna Crask	2004	*
149 5/8	18 6/8 17 6/8	20 0/8	6 6	Coconino County	AZ	Brian Fuller	2006	*
*149 5/8	21 4/8 20 7/8	17 3/8	5 5	Park County	CO	Spencer Esch	2008	*
149 4/8	21 6/8 21 5/8	19 4/8	4 4	Linn County	OR	Geraldine Emerson	1996	*
149 4/8	19 7/8 19 5/8	19 2/8	5 4	Garfield County	UT	Gary McCain	2008	*
149 4/8	23 0/8 21 6/8	18 6/8	6 6	Jefferson County	CO	Randy Verfaillie	2010	*
*149 3/8	21 4/8 20 7/8	14 7/8	6 6	Summit County	UT	Robert A. Patey	2008	*
149 2/8	23 2/8 21 1/8	20 0/8	5 5	Kiskatinaw River	BC	Terry Barber	2004	*
*149 2/8	22 3/8 21 3/8	17 6/8	4 5	Custer County	CO	James "Kip" Carson	2008	*
*149 1/8	21 4/8 21 4/8	20 1/8	4 4	Alpine County	CA	Randy Redfern	2004	*
*149 1/8	20 4/8 20 0/8	20 2/8	7 6	Smoky River	ALB	Greg Sutley	2006	*
149 0/8	19 0/8 22 3/8	21 5/8	6 5	Wayne County	UT	David Hansen	2005	*
*149 0/8	20 6/8 20 6/8	20 0/8	5 5	Rosebud County	MT	Courtney Tyree	2008	*
148 7/8	21 0/8 23 6/8	17 7/8	5 4	Dunn County	ND	Vance Meadows	2006	*
*148 7/8	21 5/8 22 0/8	19 5/8	4 5	Shaunavon	SAS	Garry Leslie	2007	*
148 6/8	21 0/8 21 6/8	20 6/8	5 5	Chaffee County	CO	Bryan Nelson	2008	*
148 5/8	20 7/8 21 0/8	16 7/8	4 4	Bonneville County	ID	Cass Dopp	2005	*
148 5/8	22 0/8 21 4/8	18 5/8	4 4	Mesa County	CO	Steven K. Easterling	2009	*
148 4/8	19 6/8 19 3/8	15 4/8	5 5	Mesa County	CO	Travis Crowley	2007	*
148 3/8	19 1/8 20 0/8	16 7/8	5 4	Gem County	ID	Sam Rohrbacher	2008	*
148 2/8	22 7/8 23 2/8	23 7/8	4 4	Grand County	UT	Brad Crocco	2005	*
148 1/8	24 4/8 23 1/8	18 3/8	4 5	Fairview	ALB	Eric Rauhanen	2007	*
148 1/8	21 0/8 21 0/8	19 7/8	5 5	Chetwynd	BC	Roy Goodwin	2009	*
148 0/8	23 2/8 22 2/8	20 3/8	4 5	Morgan County	UT	Rick Wilson	2005	*
148 0/8	22 1/8 21 4/8	19 4/8	4 4	Coconino County	AZ	Gary McCain	2007	*
147 6/8	21 0/8 19 4/8	18 4/8	5 5	Gunnison County	CO	Patrick Lorenz	2006	*
147 1/8	23 1/8 22 1/8	18 5/8	5 5	Carbon County	WY	Neil Thagard	2007	*
*147 1/8	20 5/8 20 4/8	18 1/8	5 5	Carbon County	WY	Ryan Malone	2007	*
146 7/8	25 4/8 24 7/8	19 5/8	4 6	Deschutes County	OR	Allan Sanford	1993	*
146 7/8	22 3/8 19 5/8	16 1/8	5 4	Delta County	CO	Steve Parry	1997	*
146 7/8	19 5/8 19 5/8	17 7/8	5 5	Tooele County	UT	Randy J. Walk	2003	*
146 6/8	20 6/8 21 4/8	17 2/8	5 5	Madison County	ID	Sarah Perry	2005	*
146 6/8	20 5/8 21 1/8	16 2/8	4 4	Elbow	SAS	Chad Gessner	2006	*
*146 4/8	19 5/8 21 2/8	19 1/8	6 5	Douglas County	CO	Henry Ferguson	2010	*
146 3/8	23 1/8 22 1/8	23 0/8	5 5	Uintah County	UT	Jason Nickell	2002	*
146 3/8	24 7/8 23 4/8	25 5/8	5 6	Mohave County	AZ	Michael Drake	2010	*
146 2/8	19 3/8 19 2/8	18 6/8	5 5	Montrose County	CO	Travis Schwartz	2005	*
*146 2/8	19 5/8 20 0/8	17 0/8	4 4	Nye County	NV	David Millsaps	2009	*
146 0/8	24 0/8 24 6/8	20 1/8	6 5	McKenzie County	ND	James D. Herring	2005	*
*145 7/8	23 6/8 24 1/8	24 3/8	5 4	Garfield County	CO	Dylon Stafford	2007	*
145 5/8	21 0/8 20 5/8	15 7/8	4 4	Lake Diefenbaker	SAS	Garry Leslie	2005	*
145 4/8	20 2/8 20 6/8	20 4/8	4 4	Salt Lake County	UT	Glenn Jackson	2005	*
*145 4/8	23 2/8 22 1/8	23 2/8	4 5	Salt Lake County	UT	Scott Weatherspoon	2007	*
*145 4/8	20 4/8 20 5/8	19 4/8	5 5	Uintah County	UT	Jonathan Hansen	2008	*
145 4/8	24 3/8 23 2/8	20 4/8	4 5	Carbon County	WY	Timothy W. Stancsheck	2008	*
145 3/8	20 0/8 21 2/8	19 5/8	5 4	Tehama County	CA	Craig Joseph Bucini	2005	*
145 3/8	16 1/8 17 7/8	17 7/8	5 5	Elko County	NV	William Newman	2010	*
145 0/8	19 1/8 19 7/8	17 0/8	5 5	El Paso County	CO	Daniel D. Hughes	2009	*

344

WORLD RECORD MULE DEER
Non-Typical Antlers
Score: 274 7/8
Location: Morgan County, Colorado
Date: 1987
Hunter: Kenneth W. Plank

Non-Typical Mule Deer

by Kenneth W. Plank

We crawled and duck-walked and crept up to within 100 yards of the herd. As we crawled along a fence, a fork horn buck came up over the hill and stood at the top of a small rise about 30 yards from me and about 40 yards from my friend. Seeing another deer behind him, I waited until the second deer came out of the grass. At about 20 yards I saw the nose and eyes and the huge antlers that literally looked like tree branches. This buck was behind a large tree and all I could see was the head. I was on my knees and I drew back and stayed at full draw as long as I could, waiting for him to come out from behind the tree. Apparently the buck had seen my partner, because he wheeled around and disappeared. I was not able to get a shot at all, but I did get a good look at him. There was no way I could count how many points it had, even from 20 yards.

Several days later, I snuck into the grass before dawn and sat down to wait. The first deer I saw was this huge buck. He was over to the left of me in a field. There was no cover for him at all and he seemed to know that something was wrong. He ducked his head down and walked fast, as low to the ground as he could, across the field. He came straight toward me.

As soon as he was at the edge of the weed patch, I was on my knees still hidden by the weeds. Just before he got to the patch, I drew back and waited a second to get a good hold and make sure I had my anchor point. I let go of the arrow and it hit him behind the shoulder.

After about five minutes I peeked out and there were 25 deer on the other side of the weed patch, going on their way. Thoughts of me missing him somehow…that he was going to get away…were running through my mind. It was really hard to sit any longer. But, I waited another ten minutes before I got up. I went to where I had hit him and saw several tracks in the snow… but no other sign. I followed the tracks about 50 yards into the weeds and saw what looked like a tree branch sticking up. There he was!

MULE DEER (NON-TYPICAL ANTLERS)

Minimum Score 170   *Odocoileus hemionus* and certain related subspecies

SCORE	LENGTH OF R MAIN BEAM L	INSIDE SPREAD	NUMBER OF R POINTS L		AREA	STATE/ PROVINCE	HUNTER'S NAME	DATE	RANK
274 7/8	23 7/8 26 2/8	27 0/8	23	12	Morgan County	CO	Kenneth W. Plank	1987	1
274 4/8	28 6/8 29 0/8	21 1/8	12	12	Lincoln County	MT	Andrew Keim	1978	2
274 2/8	25 7/8 25 6/8	25 3/8	15	12	Shackleton	SAS	Glen A. Miller	2003	3
269 0/8	24 7/8 24 0/8	23 6/8	10	14	Lane County	KS	Dean Hamilton	1989	4
258 2/8	26 6/8 26 7/8	24 0/8	13	11	Mesa County	CO	David Glick	1976	5
257 7/8	25 6/8 25 0/8	19 1/8	18	14	Klamath County	OR	Brad Smith	1992	6
257 0/8	23 1/8 23 2/8	23 2/8	15	13	Lincoln County	ID	Zach Shetler	2001	7
*251 2/8	27 1/8 27 4/8	23 6/8	7	10	Last Mountain Lake	SAS	Dave Fuller	2010	8
250 2/8	24 4/8 25 2/8	23 7/8	9	10	Jefferson County	CO	Larry J. Jones	1994	9
246 6/8	25 1/8 27 4/8	24 6/8	12	11	Mesa County	CO	Dean Derby II	1976	10
245 7/8	20 0/8 20 0/8	21 6/8	13	14	Decatur County	KS	David Bainter	1993	11
245 4/8	26 6/8 26 0/8	29 0/8	14	8	Chase County	NE	Gavin McClintock	1999	12
*237 7/8	24 2/8 22 7/8	25 5/8	12	12	Gove County	KS	Matthew Palmquist	2006	13
236 6/8	25 2/8 25 7/8	24 2/8	14	12	Bear Hills	SAS	Tom Jiricka	2003	14
236 5/8	25 6/8 26 5/8	22 2/8	12	11	Lincoln County	NV	Ronald N. Anderson	2001	15
236 2/8	24 1/8 25 6/8	21 1/8	10	8	Souris River	SAS	Darryl Mutrie	2010	16
236 1/8	25 5/8 25 2/8	18 3/8	10	11	Coconino County	AZ	Stanley L. McIntyre	1965	17
235 1/8	24 1/8 23 6/8	20 6/8	13	13	Garfield County	CO	Mark Martin	1997	18
234 4/8	26 4/8 27 2/8	23 7/8	10	8	Juab County	UT	Dennis M. Hickman	1972	19
233 3/8	25 0/8 26 1/8	21 7/8	11	9	S. Saskatchewan River	SAS	Jim Clary	2003	20
232 5/8	26 3/8 24 7/8	20 3/8	11	10	Rio Blanco County	CO	Harold Boyack	1979	21
232 3/8	23 2/8 21 2/8	23 0/8	12	14	Arapahoe County	CO	James P. Verney	1974	22
*231 3/8	22 5/8 22 0/8	24 2/8	13	13	Gove County	KS	Matthew Palmquist	2009	23
229 7/8	27 5/8 28 0/8	25 7/8	6	7	Lambs Canyon	UT	Lee Lindley	1942	24
229 6/8	23 6/8 22 5/8	19 6/8	8	9	Uintah County	UT	Derek Sutton	2009	25
228 7/8	25 3/8 23 4/8	22 4/8	13	6	Warner	ALB	Matthew Beckman	2003	26
228 0/8	25 0/8 25 1/8	25 2/8	10	8	Garfield County	CO	Leo W. Bange	1994	27
227 4/8	24 1/8 27 1/8	26 4/8	9	12	Norton County	KS	David Bainter	1997	28
226 5/8	24 0/8 23 6/8	22 4/8	12	8	Crook County	WY	Charles Lee Smith	1987	29
226 4/8	23 5/8 27 6/8	19 2/8	9	11	Iron County	UT	Neil "Bud" Rhodes	1959	30
226 4/8	24 2/8 23 7/8	20 4/8	8	11	Carbon County	WY	John R. Hansen	2000	30
226 2/8	19 1/8 22 1/8	19 5/8	12	11	Wichita County	KS	Stacy Hoeme	1992	32
225 4/8	23 4/8 23 2/8	22 0/8	10	13	Herd Unit 54	UT	John C. Balch	1965	33
225 2/8	24 2/8 24 2/8	23 1/8	12	7	Garfield County	CO	Dennis Quinn	1972	34
224 6/8	25 5/8 25 5/8	22 4/8	9	9	Ferry County	WA	Romie Hilderbrant	1963	35
224 1/8	25 7/8 24 6/8	24 2/8	10	9	Washakie County	WY	William T. Ivey	1987	36
224 0/8	25 6/8 23 5/8	25 6/8	8	12	Lake County	OR	Jeff Eggleston	1986	37
224 0/8	24 2/8 23 1/8	25 4/8	10	10	Rio Arriba County	NM	Donald Cost	1993	37
224 0/8	25 5/8 26 0/8	26 5/8	10	11	Malheur County	OR	John E. Milleson	2001	37
223 7/8	27 5/8 26 4/8	24 4/8	12	9	Uncompahgre Mtns.	CO	Steve Haynes	1972	40
223 0/8	27 2/8 24 2/8	25 3/8	8	10	Hardisty	ALB	Robert Klinger	2007	41
222 6/8	21 0/8 22 4/8	21 2/8	13	8	Lane County	KS	Dean Hamilton	1990	42
*222 6/8	22 1/8 23 4/8	20 1/8	8	7	Hartley County	TX	Jim Finch	2007	42
222 4/8	24 6/8 23 7/8	25 3/8	9	8	Barber County	KS	Perry Smith	1990	44
222 3/8	27 1/8 27 4/8	22 5/8	11	11	DeWinton	ALB	Blaine Southgate	1991	45
222 3/8	26 5/8 25 5/8	24 4/8	7	15	Harris	SAS	Anne Schmidt	1994	45
222 1/8	23 2/8 23 7/8	19 4/8	8	7	San Juan County	UT	Louie Arko	1972	47
222 1/8	25 5/8 24 5/8	20 4/8	8	10	Montrose County	CO	LaVern Rucker	1975	47
221 4/8	24 3/8 24 0/8	20 3/8	7	8	Salt Lake County	UT	Travis Gates	2008	49
221 3/8	22 7/8 26 4/8	18 5/8	10	10	Sheridan County	WY	Mike Barrett	2003	50
221 1/8	26 4/8 26 1/8	22 6/8	11	11	Bernalillo County	NM	Timothy Dwyer	1985	51
221 1/8	24 2/8 26 0/8	24 5/8	11	13	Jefferson County	OR	Michael Barden	1993	51
220 6/8	20 4/8 18 4/8	19 0/8	15	12	Coconino County	AZ	Placido Alderette	1978	53
220 4/8	25 3/8 25 1/8	24 4/8	9	7	Wainwright	ALB	Shawn Monsen	2007	54
220 3/8	27 3/8 27 1/8	23 1/8	11	7	Sanpete County	UT	I. B. 'Blackie' Owen	1964	55
220 3/8	22 1/8 23 7/8	21 0/8	6	11	Weber County	UT	Timothy E. Brown	1998	55
220 2/8	26 6/8 26 0/8	24 7/8	8	9	Uncompahgre Plateau	CO	Michael T. Schwitters	1971	57
220 2/8	27 0/8 26 4/8	22 0/8	8	10	S. Saskatchewan River	SAS	Jim Clary	2001	57
220 0/8	27 6/8 26 5/8	26 2/8	5	6	Elbert County	CO	Jim Early	1992	59
220 0/8	24 0/8 22 7/8	20 3/8	14	9	Union County	OR	Jon D. Silver	1995	59
219 7/8	25 0/8 25 4/8	20 4/8	9	13	Larimer County	CO	John Winzenried	1979	61
219 6/8	24 2/8 25 2/8	20 5/8	9	9	Trego County	KS	Robert Walt	1993	62
219 5/8	21 2/8 23 1/8	26 0/8	9	8	Mesa County	CO	Roger Lewis	1980	63
219 5/8	25 6/8 26 3/8	24 0/8	7	9	Yuma County	CO	Garry Neuschwanger	1993	63
219 2/8	24 2/8 22 6/8	22 4/8	8	8	Kiowa County	CO	Paul Weyand	2003	65
218 5/8	25 4/8 24 0/8	19 1/8	9	8	Rio Arriba County	NM	Kyle G. Woffinden	1993	66
218 5/8	25 3/8 26 0/8	23 1/8	7	8	Lake Diefenbaker	SAS	Murray Murdoch	1999	66
218 1/8	22 0/8 24 1/8	16 5/8	9	8	Lincoln County	WY	Mike Barrett	1987	68
218 0/8	27 0/8 27 5/8	27 0/8	7	9	San Juan County	UT	Harold Boyack	1974	69
218 0/8	26 1/8 25 0/8	25 0/8	8	9	Garfield County	CO	Bob Hill	1979	69
218 0/8	25 6/8 26 2/8	21 0/8	8	8	Park County	MT	Frank Hallett	1986	69
217 6/8	25 6/8 26 4/8	23 6/8	8	10	Caribou County	ID	James C. Ashley	1977	72
217 6/8	25 5/8 24 5/8	22 5/8	12	13	White Pine County	NV	Russell Suminski	1981	72
217 4/8	27 2/8 25 5/8	23 2/8	10	9	Jefferson County	OR	Bryan Clifton Piper	1995	74
217 2/8	23 5/8 23 7/8	21 0/8	14	7	Beaverhead County	MT	Bob L. Walker	1992	75
*216 7/8	26 4/8 25 5/8	26 6/8	11	7	Sibbald	ALB	Daine Studer	2007	76
216 6/8	23 4/8 24 4/8	22 0/8	9	12	Garfield County	CO	Richard Lepak	1975	77
216 6/8	21 6/8 21 0/8	24 5/8	10	13	Cheyenne County	CO	Marion Keith Almand	2007	78
216 2/8	21 7/8 22 5/8	19 4/8	8	9	Mohave County	AZ	William Cross	1965	79
216 2/8	22 2/8 23 4/8	18 6/8	12	7	Harney County	OR	Glen Shelley	1994	79
215 7/8	23 5/8 24 5/8	20 7/8	9	8	Clark County	KS	Dan Fenton	1988	81
215 7/8	23 5/8 24 2/8	21 6/8	10	14	Weld County	CO	Jon Brodie	1993	81
215 5/8	21 3/8 23 0/8	16 6/8	7	10	Uintah County	UT	Jon E Bingham	1969	83
215 2/8	23 0/8 24 3/8	21 3/8	14	7	Summerland	BC	Dave Johnston	2006	84
*215 0/8	25 5/8 28 0/8	24 5/8	10	12	Bow River	ALB	Terry L. Raymond	2007	85
214 6/8	25 7/8 27 3/8	31 3/8	9	7	McKinley County	NM	R. Grant Clawson	1987	86
214 6/8	24 2/8 25 1/8	20 7/8	7	6	Salt Lake County	UT	Heath Cullimore	2001	86
214 3/8	24 7/8 24 1/8	27 0/8	11	8	Decatur County	KS	Matthew Weibert	1998	88
214 2/8	22 2/8 23 1/8	18 3/8	8	7	Sheridan County	KS	David Rall	1999	89
214 2/8	26 2/8 26 1/8	22 2/8	9	10	Fremont County	CO	Jake Blair	2008	89
214 0/8	25 3/8 25 4/8	22 3/8	8	9	McCone County	MT	James F. Kosi	1974	91
213 7/8	24 4/8 26 2/8	24 3/8	9	11	Barrhead	ALB	Ryan Fisher	2004	92
213 5/8	26 0/8 26 0/8	24 2/8	7	9	Scott County	KS	Edward Stewart	1993	93
213 3/8	27 2/8 28 7/8	20 4/8	8	9	Deschutes County	OR	Craig Williams	1994	94
213 0/8	22 2/8 23 3/8	18 7/8	10	9	Caribou County	ID	Bob McAteer	1966	95

348

MULE DEER (NON-TYPICAL ANTLERS)

Minimum Score 170 — Continued

SCORE	LENGTH OF R MAIN BEAM L	INSIDE SPREAD	NUMBER OF R POINTS L	AREA	STATE/ PROVINCE	HUNTER'S NAME	DATE	RANK
212 7/8	25 2/8 25 0/8	21 2/8	9 8	Halkirk	ALB	Dan Measures	2004	96
212 6/8	23 4/8 23 3/8	24 4/8	8 8	Ness County	KS	Ralph Stum	1966	97
212 6/8	25 4/8 22 6/8	20 5/8	8 11	Logan County	CO	Dan Fox	1997	97
212 5/8	23 7/8 23 6/8	22 3/8	10 9	Red Deer Lake	ALB	Kyle Sinclair-Smith	2003	99
212 2/8	25 1/8 24 0/8	24 4/8	8 9	Sherman County	KS	Wayne Luckert	1987	100
212 2/8	24 3/8 25 1/8	24 7/8	8 7	Dundy County	NE	Matt Gideon	1996	100
*212 1/8	22 6/8 23 4/8	17 1/8	12 9	Rosebud County	MT	Michael Dennehy	2008	102
212 0/8	21 0/8 20 5/8	19 5/8	10 9	Calgary	ALB	Bert Frelink	1985	103
*211 7/8	26 7/8 26 7/8	20 0/8	13 8	Barrhead	ALB	Craig Schmidt	2007	104
211 4/8	23 5/8 26 0/8	23 2/8	11 12	Cochise County	AZ	Dagen Haymore	2008	105
211 1/8	23 5/8 24 4/8	20 6/8	7 7	Uintah County	UT	Vern Hatch	1962	106
211 0/8	27 2/8 26 6/8	22 3/8	7 7	Grant County	OR	Ed Woods	1957	107
211 0/8	25 4/8 24 6/8	19 6/8	11 6	Douglas County	CO	Joshua J. Kelley	2001	107
210 7/8	23 3/8 24 6/8	21 1/8	7 8	Lake Diefenbaker	SAS	Jim Clary	2002	109
210 6/8	21 5/8 20 1/8	22 7/8	8 10	Elbert County	CO	Louis Phillippe	2002	110
210 4/8	24 3/8 25 0/8	27 5/8	7 8	Montrose County	CO	Thomas Gloden	1963	111
210 4/8	24 2/8 22 3/8	22 1/8	7 7	San Juan County	NM	Steven J. Vittetow	2000	111
210 2/8	22 2/8 27 6/8	27 2/8	4 7	Mesa County	CO	Art Cook	1972	113
210 1/8	24 0/8 24 7/8	22 5/8	9 9	Catron County	NM	Duane Luper	2009	114
209 7/8	25 4/8 22 6/8	23 0/8	10 9	Caribou County	ID	Ray Kagel	1992	115
209 6/8	26 5/8 26 2/8	26 1/8	10 8	Minidoka County	ID	Joe Dolan	1952	116
209 5/8	26 0/8 24 0/8	26 2/8	10 7	Caribou County	ID	Mike Barrett	1994	117
*209 5/8	24 1/8 25 7/8	22 2/8	7 8	Ribstone Creek	ALB	Craig Temple	2009	117
209 3/8	25 1/8 24 0/8	24 0/8	6 7	Coconino County	AZ	Lee A. Payne	2004	119
209 1/8	26 1/8 26 1/8	28 1/8	8 8	Garfield County	CO	Mark Martin	1995	120
209 0/8	23 2/8 23 5/8	21 1/8	9 7	Garfield County	CO	Kyle Okeson	2008	121
208 7/8	26 6/8 27 1/8	22 7/8	10 8	Duchesne County	UT	Smiley Arrowchis	1989	122
208 7/8	25 3/8 26 5/8	24 3/8	6 8	Dundurn	SAS	Christopher A. Thurlow	1997	122
*208 4/8	25 0/8 25 1/8	22 5/8	12 8	Huerfano County	CO	Stephen M. Teegardin	2008	124
208 3/8	23 6/8 26 7/8	23 6/8	10 8	Adams County	ID	Donnie Lee Voss	1986	125
208 2/8	25 6/8 25 1/8	25 5/8	9 7	Gove County	KS	Dean Hamilton	1992	126
208 1/8	26 5/8 25 5/8	21 7/8	8 8	Grand County	UT	Charles Denver	1986	127
207 7/8	25 4/8 25 4/8	22 4/8	7 7	Osborne County	KS	Bill Wilson	1997	128
207 5/8	25 0/8 25 0/8	23 1/8	7 9	Decatur County	KS	Joan M. Metz	2002	129
207 4/8	24 3/8 25 1/8	22 7/8	8 7	Montrose County	CO	Barry Kerley	1980	130
207 2/8	28 0/8 26 1/8	25 1/8	7 10	Elbert County	CO	Richard Boss	1999	131
207 0/8	24 2/8 23 0/8	20 6/8	7 5	Elmore County	ID	Deloy Desaro	1972	132
206 7/8	22 2/8 24 1/8	22 1/8	7 9	Lemhi County	ID	A. LaVerne Hokanson	1967	133
206 5/8	24 1/8 25 6/8	17 2/8	10 8	Baker County	OR	Bill Lancaster	2002	134
206 4/8	24 4/8 21 4/8	18 0/8	7 8	Eagle County	CO	Robert Turner	1985	135
206 1/8	23 3/8 23 5/8	16 0/8	9 8	Ravalli County	MT	Steve Lizotte	2005	136
205 7/8	25 5/8 25 6/8	24 5/8	6 7	Montezuma County	CO	Jason B. Carruth	2004	137
205 3/8	24 2/8 24 0/8	22 0/8	8 8	Grand County	UT	C. B. 'John' Olsen	1958	138
205 2/8	26 4/8 26 0/8	20 3/8	5 8	Elbert County	CO	Matt Burrows	1996	139
205 2/8	23 4/8 24 2/8	23 2/8	7 6	Yavapai County	AZ	Tracy Jordan	2007	139
205 1/8	22 7/8 20 7/8	20 6/8	7 8	Cabri	SAS	Gene Andreas	1987	141
204 7/8	24 4/8 24 5/8	25 4/8	8 10	Washoe County	NV	Sean Shea	1997	142
204 7/8	24 6/8 21 7/8	22 4/8	8 7	Yuma County	CO	Wade Smith	2004	142
204 5/8	25 7/8 24 7/8	25 0/8	6 6	Elbow	SAS	Chad Gessner	1997	144
204 4/8	26 2/8 22 6/8	17 5/8	7 9	Fishlake National Forest	UT	Dick Kerr	1955	145
204 3/8	23 6/8 25 3/8	18 1/8	8 8	Mesa County	CO	Don Zanow	1976	146
204 2/8	25 1/8 25 6/8	23 1/8	6 8	Fergus County	MT	Paul Cosman	1991	147
204 2/8	26 2/8 25 6/8	19 7/8	6 7	Malheur County	OR	Clint Fillmore	2000	147
204 1/8	25 3/8 26 2/8	17 2/8	11 10	Umatilla County	OR	Dan Follett	1982	149
204 1/8	26 0/8 26 1/8	25 2/8	8 8	Routt County	CO	Dennis Rowley	1987	149
203 2/8	25 0/8 22 1/8	25 1/8	9 7	Elbert County	CO	Kirk Mulkin	2002	151
203 1/8	22 3/8 23 7/8	19 3/8	8 9	Missoula County	MT	Randal Siemens	2007	152
203 0/8	25 1/8 23 6/8	25 2/8	9 7	Brooks	ALB	Chuck Adams	1998	153
203 0/8	21 2/8 23 0/8	21 6/8	7 8	Main Center	SAS	Tracey Munroe	2002	153
202 5/8	26 0/8 25 3/8	23 3/8	6 7	Garfield County	CO	A. H. Sandidge	1972	155
202 4/8	22 0/8 21 5/8	16 4/8	9 8	Sioux County	NE	Douglas Buckley	1982	156
202 4/8	26 5/8 27 3/8	24 2/8	7 7	Ness County	KS	Chris E. Rupp	2008	156
202 3/8	21 7/8 21 5/8	20 3/8	7 9	Summit County	UT	Lynn C. Maxfield	1986	158
202 1/8	23 7/8 23 6/8	18 1/8	9 8	Lane County	KS	Dean Hamilton	1994	159
202 1/8	22 1/8 20 3/8	13 6/8	8 7	Natrona County	WY	Jim Van Norman	1999	159
202 1/8	27 3/8 26 1/8	26 1/8	8 9	Saskatchewan River	SAS	Robert Clarey	2010	159
201 6/8	21 4/8 22 5/8	22 0/8	9 8	Caribou County	ID	Dennis Dockstader	1969	162
201 6/8	24 4/8 25 4/8	22 7/8	7 10	Nanton	ALB	Art Bowman	2006	162
201 5/8	21 5/8 23 4/8	21 4/8	10 9	Gunnison County	CO	Mark Martin	1994	164
*201 4/8	26 0/8 25 7/8	25 6/8	8 7	Coconino County	AZ	James T. Swann	1999	165
201 3/8	24 0/8 23 1/8	25 1/8	6 8	Wasatch County	UT	Cory Carlson	2005	166
201 2/8	23 3/8 25 7/8	23 4/8	10 7	Kittitas County	WA	Jon R. Alma	2005	167
200 7/8	25 3/8 24 1/8	22 4/8	7 6	Caribou County	ID	Shawn Stockton	1992	168
200 6/8	25 1/8 25 6/8	25 6/8	7 8	Lane County	KS	Matthew Shull	2003	168
200 5/8	25 2/8 23 6/8	24 6/8	6 8	Morgan County	CO	Tim Kroskob	2002	170
200 4/8	22 6/8 23 4/8	20 5/8	8 10	Cochrane	ALB	Dave Carles	1991	171
200 3/8	24 4/8 24 3/8	19 4/8	8 9	Farm Creek	UT	Tex Ross	1966	172
200 2/8	27 5/8 26 2/8	19 1/8	9 8	Montezuma County	CO	Bryon C. Neeley	1971	173
200 1/8	23 7/8 22 1/8	20 2/8	7 8	Pima County	AZ	Jim Johnson	1981	174
*200 0/8	25 5/8 26 0/8	24 7/8	8 6	Chelan County	WA	Eric Stewart	2008	175
199 6/8	25 4/8 24 7/8	24 4/8	9 7	Twin Falls County	ID	Marvin Hedberg	1995	176
199 1/8	22 6/8 23 4/8	19 1/8	9 10	Mesa County	CO	James R. Boyles	1971	177
199 1/8	26 0/8 24 5/8	26 1/8	8 6	Teller County	CO	Ricky D. Conner II	2009	177
199 0/8	22 5/8 22 2/8	22 5/8	8 7	Pima County	AZ	Barry R. Sopher	2008	179
198 7/8	27 2/8 25 4/8	21 5/8	9 8	Medicine Hat	ALB	Roger Hillestad	2008	180
198 5/8	21 6/8 22 6/8	23 4/8	9 8	Franklin County	KS	John R. Coblentz	1966	181
198 5/8	24 1/8 23 3/8	19 2/8	5 11	Teller County	CO	Robert Runkles	1986	181
198 3/8	23 7/8 27 1/8	24 6/8	7 9	Pueblo County	CO	Daniel Wyberg	1993	183
198 3/8	23 0/8 21 1/8	22 6/8	8 8	Pima County	AZ	Tracy G. Hardy	1994	183
198 2/8	22 0/8 22 2/8	17 4/8	7 7	Laramie County	WY	Dennis Magnusson	2004	185
198 2/8	25 5/8 24 4/8	22 5/8	6 6	Cheyenne County	CO	Marion Keith Almand	2008	185
198 1/8	25 3/8 25 1/8	26 7/8	9 6	Eagle County	CO	Mark Martin	1996	187
198 1/8	24 1/8 23 0/8	18 6/8	8 6	Cardston	ALB	Chuck Adams	2003	187
198 0/8	21 5/8 22 0/8	19 0/8	8 9	Routt County	CO	Bruce F. Davison	1968	189
198 0/8	27 2/8 25 7/8	28 4/8	6 6	Ravalli County	MT	Rick Hicks	2004	189

349

MULE DEER (NON-TYPICAL ANTLERS)

Minimum Score 170   Continued

SCORE	LENGTH OF R MAIN BEAM L	INSIDE SPREAD	NUMBER OF R POINTS L		AREA	STATE/PROVINCE	HUNTER'S NAME	DATE	RANK
197 7/8	26 5/8 26 3/8	25 0/8	9	7	Lincoln County	MT	Gary Weber	1978	191
197 7/8	23 0/8 24 0/8	21 2/8	7	8	Blaine County	ID	R. Todd Sanders	2002	191
197 7/8	23 0/8 24 2/8	20 7/8	6	7	Carbon County	WY	Steve Schulz	2002	191
197 7/8	23 1/8 23 7/8	23 7/8	5	5	Cypress Hills	SAS	Perry Holmgren	2007	191
197 5/8	22 0/8 21 1/8	20 5/8	10	8	Elmore County	ID	Jerry G. Fetters	1970	195
197 5/8	23 0/8 23 1/8	20 0/8	8	7	Eagle County	CO	Donald R. Hoard	1989	195
197 4/8	24 6/8 24 4/8	25 5/8	9	7	Morton County	KS	Kevin White	1982	197
*197 4/8	25 7/8 24 6/8	26 0/8	7	5	Fall River County	SD	Lance Verhulst	2003	197
*197 4/8	25 3/8 25 2/8	20 6/8	8	8	Wasatch County	UT	Mark Broderick	2006	197
*197 3/8	18 6/8 23 5/8	27 0/8	8	10	Yavapai County	AZ	Ernie Batcheller	2005	200
197 2/8	23 6/8 23 0/8	29 4/8	7	6	Pima County	AZ	Adam Pence	1998	201
197 1/8	22 4/8 22 4/8	15 3/8	7	8	Bingham County	ID	John Gregan	1998	202
197 1/8	21 0/8 21 6/8	24 5/8	11	7	Warman	SAS	Laverne Hamm	2002	202
*197 1/8	24 0/8 24 4/8	23 0/8	7	9	Flathead County	MT	Cameron Hockett	2007	202
197 1/8	22 6/8 22 6/8	21 0/8	6	4	Arapahoe County	CO	Ryan Hein	2008	202
197 0/8	23 4/8 23 4/8	16 6/8	9	10	Coconino County	AZ	Roy E. Grace	2000	206
196 6/8	23 4/8 25 2/8	24 3/8	9	6	Bear Canyon	ALB	Bill Himmelsbach	2005	207
196 5/8	23 0/8 22 7/8	19 7/8	9	8	Eureka County	NV	Randy Buffington	1993	208
196 5/8	26 2/8 22 6/8	23 3/8	9	7	Hughes County	SD	Gary R. Spencer	2010	208
196 4/8	24 0/8 24 7/8	17 4/8	8	7	Rio Blanco County	CO	Justin Downing	2004	210
*196 4/8	23 5/8 23 4/8	20 0/8	8	7	Delta County	CO	Custer McLeod	2005	210
196 3/8	28 6/8 27 2/8	25 5/8	6	7	Campbell County	SD	Troy Hanson	1996	212
196 3/8	22 3/8 22 3/8	18 4/8	8	7	Moffat County	CO	Clay J. Evans	2007	212
196 2/8	22 4/8 22 2/8	20 7/8	8	6	La Plata County	CO	Leroy A. Martinez	1999	214
195 7/8	25 0/8 24 6/8	22 6/8	6	7	Lemhi County	ID	James Stuart	1982	215
195 6/8	21 2/8 22 6/8	19 3/8	9	9	Weld County	CO	Densel Bolin	1974	216
195 6/8	23 7/8 26 7/8	18 1/8	8	7	Sanders County	MT	Jerry V. Finley	1989	216
195 4/8	25 2/8 23 2/8	22 3/8	9	14	Garfield County	CO	Douglas Kenyon	1964	218
195 1/8	24 5/8 24 0/8	24 2/8	8	8	Eagle County	CO	Mark Martin	1998	219
195 1/8	24 1/8 23 6/8	22 5/8	8	7	Sheridan County	WY	Bruce Kramer	1999	219
195 0/8	23 4/8 22 3/8	18 7/8	7	10	County of Taber	ALB	Quincy Jensen	1990	221
195 0/8	22 2/8 22 4/8	21 0/8	5	8	Carbon County	WY	Tracy Villwok	2007	221
194 7/8	23 0/8 22 7/8	19 7/8	6	7	Finney County	KS	Jay Sloan	1967	223
194 7/8	26 5/8 25 3/8	22 3/8	6	7	Duchesne County	UT	Frank Warburton	1969	223
194 7/8	23 5/8 24 0/8	21 6/8	7	7	La Plata County	CO	Jason Lenberg	2007	223
194 6/8	25 1/8 25 5/8	20 0/8	9	7	Deschutes County	OR	Don M. Green	2008	226
194 6/8	21 4/8 22 6/8	23 7/8	7	8	Cache County	UT	Nathan Allred	2010	226
194 5/8	27 0/8 25 2/8	25 0/8	7	7	Bonneville County	ID	Robert A. Balser	1998	228
194 5/8	24 3/8 24 5/8	24 4/8	8	9	Lac Pelletier	SAS	Todd Binner	2000	228
194 4/8	21 6/8 23 3/8	23 4/8	6	7	Finnegan Ferry	ALB	Stephen K. Wilton	1998	230
194 1/8	25 6/8 24 4/8	22 4/8	7	6	Dolores County	CO	Richard Hasler	1996	231
194 0/8	19 2/8 20 1/8	20 1/8	6	6	Jefferson County	CO	Rob Sparks	2002	232
193 7/8	23 4/8 24 0/8	22 1/8	9	7	Baker County	OR	B. G. Shurtleff	1980	233
193 7/8	22 4/8 23 5/8	23 2/8	8	5	Kearny County	KS	Robert J. Price	1985	233
193 7/8	27 3/8 26 3/8	27 2/8	12	10	Yakima County	WA	James R. Lucas	1990	233
193 6/8	22 5/8 22 6/8	20 0/8	9	9	Utah County	UT	Ivan B. Henderson Jr.	1959	236
193 4/8	20 5/8 22 0/8	22 4/8	6	5	Riverhurst	SAS	Jeff Ewen	2007	237
193 3/8	22 3/8 22 1/8	19 1/8	7	7	Adams County	CO	Dale Harrington	1992	238
193 2/8	22 3/8 22 3/8	19 4/8	12	14	Franklin County	ID	Jason Vogel	1996	239
193 2/8	24 4/8 24 0/8	23 3/8	9	7	Montezuma County	CO	James Stetson Conrad	2007	239
*193 1/8	25 7/8 25 7/8	26 0/8	5	6	Sanpete County	UT	Brennon J. Butler	2010	241
192 7/8	19 7/8 20 4/8	16 5/8	12	11	Scott County	KS	Stacy Hoeme	1994	242
192 5/8	25 0/8 26 6/8	19 0/8	7	10	Modoc County	CA	Scott Young	1996	243
192 4/8	24 4/8 25 0/8	21 3/8	6	7	Caribou County	ID	Mack Tigert	1985	244
192 4/8	24 2/8 22 3/8	17 7/8	6	6	Delta County	CO	Larick F. Spencer	1996	244
192 3/8	26 3/8 25 5/8	24 4/8	9	7	Albany County	WY	Dennis Magnussor	2009	246
192 0/8	24 1/8 22 7/8	25 0/8	6	6	Goshen County	WY	Justin Lovercheck	2001	247
191 7/8	22 2/8 19 1/8	17 6/8	7	12	Bell Marsh Canyon	ID	Loren H. Dunn	1965	248
191 7/8	24 7/8 25 6/8	27 7/8	7	8	Weld County	CO	Kevin Yerian	1999	248
191 7/8	21 4/8 21 4/8	17 7/8	7	8	Chouteau County	MT	Tom Willson	2010	248
191 6/8	22 0/8 22 7/8	18 7/8	11	9	Jackson County	OR	David W. Rose	1982	251
191 6/8	25 6/8 23 5/8	19 5/8	8	9	Ardill	SAS	Todd Binner	1998	251
191 4/8	23 2/8 24 3/8	17 1/8	5	10	Garfield County	CO	J. D. Jones	1971	253
191 4/8	23 6/8 23 6/8	20 6/8	7	8	Grant County	OR	Joe Mengore	1981	253
191 4/8	23 4/8 23 6/8	19 4/8	8	9	Grant County	NM	John H. Trewern	1997	253
191 3/8	25 1/8 25 0/8	21 5/8	8	6	Klamath County	OR	Bruce G. Wales	1993	256
191 3/8	26 2/8 26 6/8	21 0/8	8	7	Malheur County	OR	Dave M. Seida	2008	256
191 1/8	23 1/8 24 3/8	22 0/8	7	9	Smith County	KS	Linton Haresnape	1981	258
191 0/8	23 6/8 21 2/8	16 2/8	8	9	Imperial County	CA	Michael S. Flynn	1986	259
191 0/8	23 2/8 23 7/8	20 3/8	5	8	Starland	ALB	Jason Watts	2004	259
191 0/8	22 4/8 21 7/8	17 2/8	7	7	Sioux County	NE	Ross E. Connell	2009	259
190 7/8	24 4/8 24 3/8	22 5/8	8	8	Ouray County	CO	Daniel J. Niebrugge	2002	262
190 6/8	23 5/8 22 4/8	21 3/8	6	7	Huerfano County	CO	Ron Johnson	1970	263
190 5/8	19 4/8 21 1/8	18 0/8	7	8	Claresholm	ALB	Gary Gapp	2007	264
190 5/8	21 7/8 23 4/8	22 2/8	7	10	Monarch	ALB	Dylan Forsyth	2007	264
190 4/8	19 4/8 20 4/8	21 4/8	6	8	La Plata County	CO	Lew Webb	2007	266
190 1/8	23 3/8 25 0/8	24 2/8	8	6	Kit Carson County	CO	L. Grant Foster	2006	267
189 7/8	23 3/8 23 3/8	22 5/8	9	7	Custer County	MT	Keith M. Polesky	2001	268
*189 7/8	22 3/8 22 4/8	18 0/8	6	6	Blaine County	NE	Nathan Rooney	2007	268
189 6/8	23 3/8 23 0/8	27 7/8	6	10	Caribou County	ID	Joe Given	2000	270
189 5/8	21 0/8 21 5/8	20 7/8	11	9	Lane County	KS	Dean Hamilton	1998	271
189 5/8	23 1/8 23 6/8	23 1/8	7	7	Sheridan County	KS	Paul Babcock	2005	271
*189 5/8	23 5/8 22 6/8	18 3/8	7	9	70 Mile House	BC	Dan Real	2006	271
189 4/8	23 4/8 23 4/8	17 2/8	7	8	Johnson County	WY	Charles Jahnke	1979	274
189 3/8	26 2/8 25 4/8	16 7/8	11	16	Lincoln County	MT	Darryl L. Lyght	1992	275
189 2/8	25 5/8 25 6/8	22 1/8	5	6	Gaspard Creek	BC	Daryl Buchholtz	1998	276
189 2/8	23 6/8 23 4/8	19 5/8	7	7	Scott County	KS	Stacy Hoeme	1999	276
189 2/8	23 1/8 25 0/8	25 5/8	8	7	Salt Lake County	UT	Larry Rasband	2000	276
*189 2/8	22 2/8 20 0/8	22 2/8	6	8	Saskatoon Lake	ALB	Derek Bruce	2010	276
189 1/8	20 1/8 22 2/8	19 3/8	6	8	Garfield County	CO	Robert C. McCardell	1974	280
*189 1/8	21 1/8 26 7/8	19 6/8	8	9	Fall River County	SD	Bryce W. Packard	2006	280
189 0/8	25 1/8 24 6/8	25 2/8	12	11	Dawson County	MT	Monte Dassinger	1973	282
189 0/8	20 0/8 22 3/8	16 7/8	8	6	Garfield County	CO	Stephen Kennedy	1975	282
188 7/8	25 1/8 26 6/8	19 5/8	10	8	Harney County	OR	Frank Abernathy	1999	284
188 6/8	20 5/8 20 2/8	17 1/8	6	7	Brooks	ALB	Mark Nelson	2007	285

350

MULE DEER (NON-TYPICAL ANTLERS)

Minimum Score 170   Continued

SCORE	LENGTH OF MAIN BEAM R L	INSIDE SPREAD	NUMBER OF POINTS R L	AREA	STATE/ PROVINCE	HUNTER'S NAME	DATE	RANK
188 5/8	22 5/8 22 4/8	20 3/8	7 6	Avonlea	SAS	Bryan Bogdan	2003	286
188 3/8	27 2/8 27 6/8	27 7/8	6 7	Logan County	KS	Stacy Hoeme	2000	287
*188 0/8	23 2/8 23 5/8	20 4/8	9 7	Sulpher Springs	BC	Sebastien Therrien	2006	288
187 7/8	17 1/8 22 1/8	16 3/8	12 8	Grand County	UT	Lee Allred	1958	289
*187 7/8	23 7/8 23 1/8	24 1/8	7 8	Malheur County	OR	Morgan E. Webber	2009	289
187 6/8	23 3/8 23 1/8	20 3/8	9 6	Routt County	CO	Thane Anderson	1993	291
187 5/8	22 3/8 24 7/8	23 0/8	7 6	Leduc	ALB	Mike Pewarchuk	1996	292
187 5/8	25 1/8 25 0/8	21 2/8	7 7	Taber	ALB	Darren Gillies	2006	292
*187 4/8	20 5/8 21 0/8	19 6/8	8 9	Sheridan County	KS	J. Scott Stedman	2005	294
187 3/8	25 0/8 25 1/8	21 4/8	8 7	Albany County	WY	Larry Hudson	1996	295
187 3/8	24 0/8 24 4/8	19 0/8	7 6	Millard County	UT	David Edwards	2002	295
187 3/8	25 0/8 25 6/8	23 2/8	9 8	Grant County	OR	Andy Day	2006	295
187 2/8	22 0/8 22 0/8	21 2/8	6 6	Eagle County	CO	Gary O. Glenn	1978	298
187 2/8	24 1/8 23 3/8	22 0/8	7 10	Dundy County	NE	Matt Gideon	1995	298
187 2/8	26 4/8 27 1/8	21 2/8	6 6	Rio Arriba County	NM	Robert J. Seeds	1998	298
187 1/8	23 1/8 22 1/8	20 4/8	8 6	Calgary	ALB	Dave Browne	1995	301
187 1/8	23 3/8 22 7/8	19 6/8	7 6	Willow Creek	ALB	Eric Kuhlman	2006	301
186 7/8	23 1/8 22 4/8	23 4/8	6 8	Jefferson County	CO	Trent D. Robinson	2002	303
186 6/8	25 6/8 22 1/8	24 6/8	8 6	Dolores County	CO	Michael W. Forth	1978	304
186 6/8	24 3/8 22 0/8	23 7/8	7 7	Platte County	WY	Jerry Bowen	1996	304
186 5/8	23 0/8 23 6/8	22 6/8	8 9	Pin Horn Range	ALB	Giuliano Coslovi	1988	306
186 5/8	20 6/8 21 6/8	21 6/8	10 6	Ponteix	SAS	Kevin Pastachak	2002	306
186 4/8	25 5/8 24 2/8	27 0/8	6 5	Pueblo County	CO	Dale Norman Bigger	1994	308
186 4/8	21 1/8 23 7/8	23 3/8	6 6	Kiowa County	CO	Steven F. Wolk	1998	308
186 3/8	20 0/8 20 7/8	15 2/8	9 8	Fergus County	MT	John Fleharty	2004	310
186 3/8	23 4/8 23 0/8	20 3/8	9 7	Park County	CO	Glenn Goldsmith	2005	310
186 3/8	21 4/8 20 4/8	15 5/8	7 10	Sheridan County	WY	Mike Barrett	2008	310
186 2/8	23 3/8 23 3/8	20 5/8	7 7	Boise County	ID	Ray Simpson	2003	313
186 2/8	23 7/8 22 3/8	22 2/8	7 7	Yuma County	CO	Jerry Bowen	2007	313
186 1/8	22 0/8 22 3/8	20 7/8	9 8	Wheeler County	OR	Jeremy Nauta	2000	315
*186 1/8	21 0/8 25 3/8	21 1/8	8 8	Albany County	WY	Joel Bickler	2007	315
186 0/8	23 3/8 24 2/8	21 4/8	8 8	Chaffee County	CO	John D. Hambleton	1975	317
186 0/8	23 1/8 21 5/8	21 0/8	8 7	Ravalli County	MT	Ed Barrett	1983	317
186 0/8	23 0/8 23 1/8	21 0/8	5 6	Powder River County	MT	Joseph A. Borgna	1999	317
186 0/8	22 7/8 22 0/8	18 7/8	6 7	Rio Arriba County	NM	Eudane Vicenti	2007	317
185 7/8	22 7/8 22 3/8	18 0/8	11 8	Klamath County	OR	Charles A. Warner	1975	321
185 7/8	23 6/8 23 0/8	22 2/8	7 6	Carbon County	WY	Clay J. Evans	2005	321
185 6/8	23 7/8 25 5/8	21 7/8	9 7	Medicine Hat	ALB	Perry Robitaille	2003	323
185 4/8	21 0/8 21 4/8	18 5/8	9 9	Hanna	ALB	Dale Drummond	1992	324
185 2/8	22 5/8 20 5/8	23 6/8	8 7	Scott County	KS	Richard B. Spencer	1986	325
*184 7/8	24 1/8 22 2/8	22 6/8	6 6	Dinsmore	SAS	Jason Federspiel	2006	326
184 3/8	22 2/8 23 0/8	20 6/8	8 7	Culberson County	TX	Joe Montoya	1996	327
184 2/8	20 5/8 21 5/8	19 3/8	8 6	Duchesne County	UT	Dean Reynolds	1961	328
184 0/8	23 0/8 22 3/8	17 2/8	7 11	Rosebud County	MT	Rick Miller	1997	329
183 5/8	20 3/8 20 0/8	15 3/8	7 9	Didsbury	ALB	Paul Boody	1993	330
183 5/8	25 5/8 24 4/8	22 3/8	6 7	Okotoks	ALB	Martin Gottinger	2003	330
183 3/8	25 5/8 25 1/8	25 0/8	6 7	Franklin County	ID	Doug Ransom	1985	332
183 3/8	20 2/8 19 6/8	17 7/8	6 6	Laramie County	WY	Brian Rhead	1998	332
183 3/8	24 1/8 24 0/8	20 4/8	7 8	Calgary	ALB	Thomas Jay Little	2008	332
183 3/8	21 2/8 21 5/8	18 4/8	7 13	Inyo County	CA	Jerry Maytum	2009	332
183 2/8	22 7/8 23 4/8	20 2/8	7 6	Scott County	KS	Stacy Hoeme	1995	336
183 2/8	22 3/8 22 1/8	21 0/8	7 6	Carbon County	UT	Casey Mills	2003	336
183 2/8	21 1/8 20 2/8	21 0/8	6 8	La Plata County	CO	Michael J. DeWitt	2004	336
183 2/8	21 5/8 23 5/8	22 3/8	9 9	Lincoln County	NM	Dwight S. Wolf	2005	336
182 7/8	25 3/8 24 3/8	25 0/8	7 7	Garfield County	UT	Kim S. Ades	2004	340
182 7/8	26 3/8 26 4/8	22 5/8	8 6	Wallowa County	OR	Ric Nichols	2005	340
182 5/8	19 5/8 19 5/8	16 3/8	7 7	Valley County	ID	Charles "Chuck" Boatman	1986	342
182 5/8	23 2/8 21 5/8	23 4/8	7 7	Sheridan County	WY	Mike Barrett	2004	342
182 4/8	21 3/8 22 1/8	18 4/8	8 5	Hughes County	SD	Roy Warner	2005	344
182 3/8	24 3/8 23 2/8	24 3/8	6 6	Sheridan County	WY	Tim Goss	2003	345
182 3/8	22 0/8 21 0/8	19 5/8	6 6	Maricopa County	AZ	Matthew Liljenquist	2006	345
182 2/8	22 0/8 22 6/8	20 3/8	6 8	Weld County	CO	Frank Piacentino	2007	347
182 1/8	22 3/8 20 6/8	17 7/8	6 6	Colfax County	NM	M. Blake Patton	2005	348
182 0/8	25 0/8 24 4/8	23 7/8	7 8	Kootenai County	ID	Rodney W. Willis	1977	349
181 7/8	22 7/8 23 5/8	19 5/8	7 6	Russell County	KS	Drew McCartney	1993	350
181 7/8	25 0/8 23 1/8	25 2/8	6 7	Scott County	KS	John C. Walker	1996	350
181 7/8	23 3/8 23 5/8	22 6/8	6 6	Caribou County	ID	Matt Seever	1998	350
181 6/8	25 3/8 24 5/8	20 7/8	7 10	Red Deer Lake	ALB	Jeff Thomson	1996	353
181 5/8	27 0/8 24 3/8	23 4/8	7 9	Chelan County	WA	David M. Bartholemew	1967	354
181 4/8	27 5/8 26 3/8	27 4/8	5 7	Park County	CO	John Cliff	1967	355
181 3/8	23 1/8 22 6/8	23 0/8	9 8	Wichita County	KS	Stacy C. Hoeme	1986	356
181 2/8	25 6/8 26 2/8	25 2/8	6 7	Lane County	KS	Dean Hamilton	1995	357
181 0/8	22 1/8 20 7/8	19 3/8	8 9	McKenzie County	ND	Harvey K. Schlosser	1996	358
181 0/8	21 6/8 23 2/8	19 3/8	7 8	Blairmore	ALB	Mike Park	2009	358
180 7/8	22 5/8 23 3/8	21 0/8	6 6	Gray County	KS	James R. Sobba	1991	360
180 7/8	22 1/8 24 3/8	19 5/8	6 5	Twin Falls County	ID	Ernie Owen	1995	360
180 7/8	23 2/8 24 1/8	22 0/8	5 9	Dona Ana County	NM	Kyle Traylor	1998	360
180 6/8	24 6/8 25 3/8	24 1/8	5 5	Pima County	AZ	Robert Forrest	1998	363
180 6/8	20 4/8 21 3/8	20 7/8	4 5	Natrona County	WY	Shawn M. Porter	2004	363
180 4/8	21 1/8 22 5/8	21 3/8	7 5	Utah County	UT	Frank Warburton	1972	365
180 4/8	26 2/8 26 7/8	27 2/8	6 6	Salt Lake County	UT	Levi Sexton	2001	365
180 2/8	23 4/8 24 4/8	27 5/8	9 7	Ness County	KS	Jed Bain	1992	367
180 1/8	22 4/8 24 4/8	19 4/8	9 7	Caribou County	ID	Ronald L. Owens	1998	368
180 1/8	20 5/8 22 5/8	18 1/8	6 8	Shaunavon	SAS	Darryl Vause	2001	368
180 1/8	20 4/8 19 4/8	20 3/8	5 9	Washoe County	NV	John Sarvis	2007	368
180 0/8	23 5/8 25 1/8	23 1/8	7 8	Lassen County	CA	Jeff Gravano	1994	371
180 0/8	21 7/8 21 6/8	24 5/8	9 8	Baker County	OR	Richard Condos	1998	371
179 6/8	26 1/8 25 2/8	24 4/8	6 6	Converse County	WY	Lee Jernigan	1998	373
179 5/8	24 7/8 23 7/8	21 2/8	7 7	Coconino County	AZ	Randy Ballinger	1998	374
179 5/8	23 1/8 22 4/8	23 2/8	9 12	Converse County	WY	Dale Good	2000	374
179 3/8	23 7/8 24 0/8	22 7/8	6 7	Morrow County	OR	Russ Brannon	1997	376
179 2/8	23 6/8 25 3/8	27 2/8	5 6	Rio Arriba County	NM	Shanahan Largo	2007	377
179 1/8	28 3/8 29 3/8	28 0/8	4 4	Las Animas County	CO	Brian Brochu	1998	378
179 0/8	23 4/8 23 4/8	19 5/8	7 6	Jefferson County	OR	Brett Henderson	1995	379
179 0/8	20 0/8 20 0/8	18 2/8	6 7	Coconino County	AZ	James E. Riner	1998	379

MULE DEER (NON-TYPICAL ANTLERS)

Minimum Score 170   Continued

SCORE	LENGTH OF R MAIN BEAM L	INSIDE SPREAD	NUMBER OF R POINTS L	AREA	STATE/ PROVINCE	HUNTER'S NAME	DATE	RANK
*179 0/8	21 6/8 22 0/8	18 2/8	6 6	Fergus County	MT	Mark Gilkey	2004	379
178 7/8	23 3/8 24 2/8	23 5/8	7 4	Lane County	KS	Dean Hamilton	1998	382
178 5/8	25 3/8 24 6/8	31 0/8	6 7	San Juan County	UT	Guy Gates	1970	383
178 4/8	26 2/8 25 0/8	20 2/8	7 7	Fremont County	WY	Rene Suda	2001	384
*178 4/8	21 4/8 22 6/8	16 3/8	7 6	Lincoln County	CO	David N. Wildenstein	2006	384
178 3/8	22 4/8 20 6/8	18 5/8	5 7	Boulder County	CO	Heath Dillon	1997	386
178 2/8	22 3/8 23 7/8	24 6/8	8 4	Calgary	ALB	Lindsey Paterson	1990	387
178 0/8	20 2/8 20 7/8	18 3/8	8 8	Las Animas County	CO	Michael A. Mattoreno	1989	388
177 7/8	21 2/8 18 6/8	20 2/8	6 7	Garfield County	CO	Steve Byerly	1980	389
177 4/8	24 4/8 22 2/8	26 1/8	9 7	Rio Arriba County	NM	Michael D. Bruce	1986	390
177 4/8	22 2/8 20 2/8	19 0/8	6 7	Billings County	ND	Douglas Kerska	1993	390
177 4/8	22 2/8 21 2/8	20 2/8	9 6	Elko County	NV	Tim Pruitt	1996	390
177 3/8	21 1/8 22 4/8	23 3/8	9 8	Dawson County	MT	Gerald Polesky	1970	393
177 3/8	21 0/8 21 5/8	18 4/8	5 7	Lane County	KS	Tod Anthony	2001	393
177 0/8	23 4/8 23 0/8	19 3/8	6 5	Calgary	ALB	Dave Browne	1997	395
176 7/8	20 5/8 22 5/8	21 2/8	7 7	Rock Creek	CO	Adolph Kuhns	1961	396
176 6/8	25 1/8 22 4/8	27 0/8	6 5	Grant County	OR	Chuck Warner	1983	397
176 5/8	21 4/8 19 6/8	15 0/8	8 7	Decatur County	KS	Darroll Banzet	2009	398
176 4/8	23 6/8 24 3/8	18 2/8	6 9	Grant County	OR	Cory Smith	2000	399
176 2/8	22 2/8 22 1/8	22 4/8	6 7	Converse County	WY	Rick H. Arnold	2005	400
176 0/8	23 3/8 23 5/8	20 4/8	6 6	Scott County	KS	Vince Strickler	1975	401
176 0/8	22 1/8 23 0/8	17 4/8	7 7	Gove County	KS	Rick Kreuter	1991	401
176 0/8	22 3/8 22 2/8	20 5/8	6 6	Park County	WY	Tracy A. LaFollette	1994	401
175 7/8	19 4/8 20 7/8	18 6/8	6 6	Routt County	CO	Chuck Nemec	1974	404
175 7/8	25 0/8 24 6/8	25 1/8	6 7	Jackson County	CO	Timothy Lee Nichols	1994	404
175 7/8	23 4/8 22 6/8	21 2/8	4 7	Laramie County	WY	Dennis Magnussan	2005	404
175 6/8	24 4/8 24 7/8	20 2/8	6 7	Cardston	ALB	Chuck Adams	2001	407
175 3/8	20 6/8 24 2/8	29 0/8	9 9	Ness County	KS	Pete McBee	1969	408
175 3/8	24 2/8 23 3/8	17 3/8	7 8	Culberson County	TX	Gary Oden	1985	408
175 0/8	20 2/8 22 0/8	22 1/8	8 8	Coconino County	AZ	Dave Saquella	1999	410
174 7/8	21 6/8 22 6/8	19 5/8	5 6	Herbert	SAS	Garry Leslie	2001	411
174 6/8	22 5/8 21 2/8	24 0/8	6 9	Custer County	CO	Kurt Keskimaki	1981	412
174 6/8	22 1/8 21 7/8	19 2/8	6 6	Natrona County	WY	Casey Middleton	2000	412
174 5/8	22 4/8 23 3/8	19 6/8	6 6	Milk River	ALB	Stan Godfrey	1997	414
174 3/8	23 4/8 24 3/8	23 5/8	7 8	Dawson County	MT	Richard Harms	1972	415
174 3/8	21 1/8 21 2/8	22 1/8	6 7	Platte County	WY	Jerry Bowen	1995	415
174 2/8	23 6/8 23 1/8	22 0/8	9 10	Mesa County	CO	Art Cook	1958	417
*174 2/8	19 4/8 21 4/8	18 5/8	6 7	100 Mile House	BC	Dan Real	2005	417
174 1/8	25 7/8 24 5/8	18 7/8	7 5	Carbon County	UT	B. E. Epperson	1971	419
174 1/8	20 0/8 21 4/8	20 2/8	6 7	Custer County	MT	Wayne Peeples	2000	419
174 1/8	21 6/8 21 5/8	20 5/8	7 7	Garfield County	CO	David L. Duncan	2005	419
173 7/8	20 7/8 21 0/8	20 3/8	7 5	Lane County	KS	Dean Hamilton	1997	422
173 7/8	23 3/8 23 2/8	18 7/8	7 7	Slope County	ND	Ken Radach	2008	422
*173 5/8	22 3/8 21 3/8	17 0/8	7 6	Granite County	MT	Justin David Benson	2005	424
173 5/8	23 0/8 22 4/8	20 4/8	7 6	Morgan County	CO	John Pursley, Sr.	2006	424
173 4/8	24 3/8 25 2/8	27 2/8	7 6	Union County	OR	Larry G. R. Crompton	2004	426
173 4/8	17 2/8 15 5/8	19 1/8	17 14	Jefferson County	CO	Mitchel C. Arnold	2005	426
173 3/8	20 4/8 26 6/8	20 3/8	6 5	Morrow County	OR	Ray Kelton	1976	428
173 2/8	21 2/8 21 3/8	21 4/8	8 8	Elmore County	ID	Peter J. Cintorino	1980	429
173 2/8	21 2/8 23 0/8	19 4/8	6 6	Grant County	OR	Jason A. West	2000	429
173 2/8	24 4/8 26 0/8	20 3/8	7 8	Bingham County	ID	Steven Nelson	2001	429
173 1/8	19 7/8 22 1/8	17 1/8	8 7	Dawes County	NE	LaVerne J. Weber	1975	432
173 0/8	22 1/8 21 3/8	16 1/8	7 6	Culberson County	TX	Gary J. Oden	1988	433
173 0/8	23 2/8 23 3/8	20 3/8	8 6	Campbell County	SD	Douglas Goehring	1995	433
173 0/8	21 4/8 21 7/8	21 4/8	8 7	Rawlins County	KS	Danny Carmen	2003	433
172 7/8	25 6/8 26 4/8	29 0/8	6 6	Grant County	OR	Ray Kelton	1980	436
172 7/8	23 4/8 24 3/8	22 2/8	8 5	Slope County	ND	Todd Seymanski	1982	436
172 7/8	24 0/8 24 6/8	20 6/8	9 7	Chouteau County	MT	Mike Chouinard	1995	436
172 7/8	22 5/8 22 7/8	25 4/8	6 8	Grant County	NM	Justin Britton	2001	436
172 6/8	20 0/8 18 5/8	19 2/8	11 7	Rawlins County	KS	Richard Jones	1987	440
172 6/8	20 2/8 20 1/8	21 0/8	7 8	Traverse Dam	ALB	Harrison Emigh	2001	440
*172 6/8	22 6/8 22 2/8	19 6/8	6 7	Sonora	MEX	Jake Baker	2010	440
172 5/8	23 4/8 23 5/8	22 3/8	9 6	Kane County	UT	Peter F. Woeck II	1999	443
172 4/8	20 5/8 22 4/8	20 7/8	7 10	Taber	ALB	Gary Peters	1997	444
171 7/8	24 0/8 23 4/8	20 3/8	5 7	Campbell County	WY	Paul Vomela	1992	445
171 7/8	19 0/8 19 5/8	15 7/8	7 10	Coconino County	AZ	Dustin Movius	2000	445
171 7/8	23 4/8 23 5/8	18 7/8	5 7	Frontier County	NE	Chris Demuth	2000	445
171 6/8	20 0/8 20 1/8	18 6/8	6 6	Buffalo Creek	ALB	Dwayne Van Schaick	2000	448
171 5/8	22 0/8 20 6/8	20 1/8	6 6	Douglas County	CO	Bruce Hoover	1994	449
171 5/8	21 4/8 22 5/8	21 5/8	7 5	Coconino County	AZ	Brad Sutton	1998	449
171 4/8	22 2/8 20 1/8	16 3/8	5 12	Mesa County	CO	Paul H. Dickson	1985	451
171 4/8	25 1/8 23 1/8	19 1/8	6 6	Salt Lake County	UT	Jason Yates	2006	451
171 3/8	21 1/8 22 1/8	21 1/8	8 6	Meade County	KS	Richard A. Nordyke	1971	453
171 3/8	18 7/8 21 3/8	18 3/8	8 6	Magrath	ALB	Cameron Cook	1994	453
171 3/8	22 6/8 21 1/8	19 5/8	6 6	El Paso County	CO	Kenneth E. Lacy	2000	453
171 2/8	24 2/8 23 6/8	23 1/8	6 6	Albany County	WY	Leonard Verrelli	2005	456
171 2/8	19 1/8 21 0/8	19 0/8	7 8	Milk River	ALB	Gene Welle	2005	456
171 1/8	23 0/8 23 7/8	20 2/8	7 5	Niobrara County	WY	Rickey E. Morse	1998	458
171 0/8	23 5/8 24 0/8	21 5/8	5 8	Billings County	ND	Michael H. Cummings	1996	459
170 7/8	18 4/8 20 0/8	17 1/8	6 6	Wallowa County	OR	Wayne van Zwoll	1977	460
170 6/8	23 6/8 24 1/8	21 2/8	7 7	Valley County	ID	John Pyle	1978	461
170 5/8	22 0/8 22 1/8	16 3/8	6 5	Lake County	OR	Bill Hendrick	1964	462
170 5/8	20 3/8 19 5/8	20 4/8	5 7	McCone County	MT	David Tofte	1985	462
*170 5/8	21 7/8 23 0/8	16 3/8	6 7	Pecos County	TX	Brandon Harrell	2009	462
170 3/8	19 0/8 22 2/8	19 3/8	8 6	Cardston	ALB	Bob W. Ehle	1996	465
170 3/8	22 0/8 20 3/8	19 2/8	10 6	Hand County	SD	Dylan Deuter	2010	465
170 0/8	19 5/8 17 5/8	19 5/8	7 5	Finney County	KS	Rod Lies	1968	467
170 0/8	25 6/8 15 5/8	21 0/8	6 6	Bingham County	ID	Tim Moon	1996	467

MULE DEER (NON-TYPICAL VELVET ANTLERS)

Minimum Score 170

SCORE	LENGTH OF R MAIN BEAM L	INSIDE SPREAD	NUMBER OF R POINTS L	AREA	STATE/ PROVINCE	HUNTER'S NAME	DATE	RANK
271 4/8	24 3/8 23 6/8	20 3/8	16 17	Bad Hills	SAS	Ron Cordes /Richard Burton	2005	*
260 2/8	24 6/8 27 1/8	20 5/8	10 12	Gunnison County	CO	Jed Lowe	2005	*
*258 2/8	26 6/8 26 5/8	22 6/8	10 12	Utah County	UT	Robert D. Clark	2005	*
255 1/8	24 2/8 24 7/8	16 1/8	9 15	Ada County	ID	Wendell P. Thompson	2007	*
243 1/8	23 5/8 25 4/8	20 4/8	11 11	Jefferson County	CO	David M. Bodine	2006	*
240 5/8	24 7/8 23 5/8	21 6/8	10 10	Boulder County	CO	William A. Janowsky	2006	*
239 6/8	26 2/8 25 0/8	21 5/8	8 12	Maple Creek	SAS	Landon Middleton	2006	*
*230 5/8	25 5/8 24 6/8	22 2/8	9 9	Washington County	UT	Michael C. Hirschi	2009	*
227 4/8	24 2/8 24 1/8	22 0/8	7 8	Teller County	CO	Ron W. Largent	2006	*
227 0/8	26 0/8 25 4/8	20 0/8	11 10	Claydon	SAS	Lornie Casat	2006	*
226 5/8	22 6/8 22 5/8	18 7/8	8 9	Lassen County	CA	Brandon Phillips	2005	*
225 3/8	22 7/8 24 4/8	19 5/8	13 11	Jefferson County	OR	Christopher B. Dunlap	2007	*
*224 4/8	28 1/8 28 7/8	22 6/8	10 7	Kane County	UT	Travis Holmes	2008	*
*223 7/8	25 2/8 25 3/8	19 4/8	8 7	Morgan County	UT	Justin Smith	2008	*
*222 5/8	24 3/8 23 5/8	18 1/8	7 6	Mohave County	AZ	Chance Gledhill	2008	*
*220 7/8	24 4/8 25 3/8	20 5/8	12 7	Jefferson County	CO	Rob Sparks	2009	*
*220 0/8	28 3/8 26 7/8	32 0/8	8 6	Peace River	ALB	Garret Doll	2006	*
*220 0/8	26 2/8 26 0/8	26 2/8	7 8	Salt Lake County	UT	Edwin Kip Fowler	2007	*
216 5/8	25 2/8 25 0/8	24 6/8	9 7	Dolores County	CO	Foy Chandler	2007	*
216 3/8	22 6/8 22 6/8	21 7/8	7 7	Jefferson County	CO	Robert Ramsey	2009	*
*215 5/8	25 7/8 24 7/8	21 6/8	8 10	Summit County	UT	Kevin P. Adamson	2009	*
215 2/8	25 4/8 26 4/8	21 3/8	9 8	Eagle County	CO	Raymond Tenbrook	2010	*
213 0/8	25 6/8 25 0/8	23 2/8	8 6	Lincoln County	NV	Billy Batty	2006	*
*210 3/8	21 2/8 20 6/8	16 7/8	8 7	Salt Lake County	UT	William Jensen	2009	*
209 7/8	24 4/8 24 0/8	20 6/8	7 7	Sevier County	UT	Thomas Russell Nielson	2005	*
*208 2/8	26 0/8 24 3/8	21 2/8	8 6	St. Isidore	ALB	Peter P. Settineri	2007	*
*208 2/8	24 6/8 24 0/8	21 1/8	8 9	San Juan County	UT	Adam Taylor	2010	*
208 1/8	26 2/8 25 0/8	16 2/8	12 10	Plumas County	CA	Travis Kingdon	2005	*
207 3/8	26 0/8 25 4/8	24 2/8	6 7	Garfield County	UT	Kyle Brown	2009	*
206 6/8	26 5/8 25 6/8	23 6/8	8 11	San Juan County	UT	Brian Johnson	1996	*
206 6/8	17 5/8 16 6/8	20 7/8	11 6	El Dorado County	CA	David Wilson	2006	*
206 0/8	25 2/8 25 1/8	23 2/8	7 8	Sevier County	UT	Riley Tidlund	2006	*
205 0/8	26 4/8 26 6/8	25 6/8	5 7	Garfield County	UT	Dace L. Chynoweth	2009	*
*204 6/8	25 6/8 24 5/8	22 7/8	5 7	Grant County	OR	James M. DiMugno	2007	*
*204 0/8	21 6/8 21 2/8	18 6/8	7 8	Garfield County	UT	Scott Wilson	1998	*
*203 7/8	24 0/8 22 3/8	19 7/8	7 8	Salt Lake County	UT	Devin Leonard	2008	*
203 0/8	24 7/8 24 5/8	24 3/8	7 6	Rio Arriba County	NM	Lionel Velarde	2004	*
201 7/8	23 1/8 25 0/8	20 0/8	9 9	Jefferson County	CO	Robert Marshall	2005	*
199 7/8	22 5/8 22 5/8	20 7/8	6 9	Teller County	CO	Nickelous V. Wagner	2007	*
199 7/8	26 1/8 26 2/8	18 1/8	8 8	Malheur County	OR	Justin Simpson	2007	*
*199 1/8	24 3/8 25 7/8	22 1/8	8 7	Lincoln County	NV	Jesse W. Tatman	2009	*
*197 5/8	23 5/8 24 0/8	18 6/8	9 8	La Plata County	CO	Mindy Pawlek	2010	*
*195 6/8	24 4/8 24 3/8	21 2/8	7 6	Garfield County	CO	Robert Peterson	2008	*
195 2/8	22 6/8 22 6/8	21 3/8	7 6	Mineral County	CO	Bob Bartoshesky	2007	*
*195 0/8	20 1/8 19 6/8	18 3/8	8 9	Dunn County	ND	Scott Sprenger	2009	*
194 5/8	23 7/8 24 6/8	20 4/8	7 6	La Plata County	CO	Steven J. Vittetow	2005	*
194 1/8	25 3/8 25 4/8	21 6/8	8 9	Davis County	UT	Jeff Jensen	2010	*
193 7/8	24 2/8 23 6/8	21 1/8	6 6	Spirit River	ALB	Stephen Kotz	2006	*
191 4/8	22 1/8 23 7/8	22 5/8	8 6	Kane County	UT	Travis Holmes	2004	*
*191 4/8	24 6/8 25 1/8	22 1/8	7 7	Rio Arriba County	NM	Trish Cassados	2009	*
191 2/8	23 2/8 25 7/8	17 0/8	6 7	La Plata County	CO	John L. Gardner	2006	*
191 0/8	24 0/8 24 4/8	24 5/8	5 7	Nevada County	CA	Robert Borden	2007	*
190 3/8	20 5/8 21 0/8	16 5/8	7 7	Iron County	UT	Billy Batty	2006	*
190 2/8	22 0/8 22 4/8	21 0/8	7 7	Delta County	CO	Cody A. Rapke	2009	*
*189 3/8	24 1/8 24 7/8	24 2/8	6 9	Mohave County	AZ	Steven E. Sheehy	2008	*
189 0/8	26 5/8 26 2/8	20 6/8	7 5	Mesa County	CO	Larry M. Peterson	2006	*
188 2/8	24 4/8 25 2/8	25 5/8	7 7	Elko County	NV	Kenneth J. Wilkinson	2005	*
188 2/8	22 6/8 23 0/8	21 0/8	8 6	Jefferson County	CO	Rick Duggan	2006	*
*186 4/8	21 2/8 20 4/8	20 3/8	6 7	Slope County	ND	Travis Kirkeide	2008	*
186 0/8	23 3/8 22 3/8	22 5/8	6 8	El Paso County	CO	Daren Abbiehl	2005	*
*184 6/8	23 5/8 22 4/8	22 6/8	9 8	Coconino County	AZ	Rich Janssen	2008	*
184 4/8	21 4/8 21 0/8	21 1/8	7 6	Eatonia	SAS	Tyson Craney	2008	*
183 2/8	20 7/8 21 6/8	17 5/8	8 6	Dunn County	ND	Scott L. Sprenger	2008	*
*181 3/8	23 1/8 22 7/8	18 2/8	8 5	Elko County	NV	David E. Evanow	2008	*
180 6/8	27 4/8 25 3/8	21 6/8	6 8	Park County	CO	Dave Gusky	1975	*
179 3/8	20 7/8 21 4/8	23 4/8	8 8	Carbon County	UT	Boyd Marsing	2009	*
*178 5/8	26 7/8 26 0/8	20 2/8	6 8	Fresno County	CA	Ron Redding, Jr.	2006	*
*178 0/8	22 4/8 23 6/8	17 6/8	8 11	Spirit River	ALB	Joseph F. Rada	2004	*
177 7/8	17 2/8 24 7/8	21 2/8	6 8	Garfield County	CO	Leo Bange	2009	*
*177 2/8	25 4/8 23 7/8	20 4/8	9 8	Gunnison County	CO	Blayne St. James	2005	*
*176 5/8	22 7/8 22 6/8	18 4/8	9 7	McLaren Lake	SAS	Brad Miller	2007	*
174 7/8	23 6/8 23 0/8	20 3/8	8 8	Lake County	OR	Stuart Schuttpelz	2006	*
174 6/8	22 7/8 22 6/8	22 0/8	7 7	Plumas County	CA	Robert Reimers	2005	*
171 1/8	21 5/8 21 3/8	19 2/8	6 6	Carbon County	WY	Kirby Berger	2006	*

WORLD RECORD WHITETAIL DEER
Typical Antlers
Score: 204 4/8
Location: Peoria County, Illinois
Date: 1965
Hunter: Mel Johnson

Typical Whitetail Deer

by Mel Johnson

The year was 1965. I was hunting the edge of a soybean field near Peoria, Illinois. Deer, including a big buck, fed here nightly.

I had no blind in this area so I quickly cleared the oak leaves from a brushy spot, nocked an arrow and settled back. My camouflage clothing blended nicely with the background and the wind was in my face. Everything seemed right for the evening wait.

I had just started relaxing when a deer appeared at the far corner of the field, walking in my direction. My breath caught in my throat at the sight of the large rack that swung gently with every step. I realized if he kept coming he would pass directly in front of my stand. My hand grasped the bow.

The buck cautiously made his way along the field's edge, stopping to check for danger from time to time. The wind was still in my favor as he moved nearer. After what seemed to be an entire deer season, the big whitetail was directly in front of me and my heart almost stopped as he turned and stared right through me. But a moment later he casually turned his massive head and walked on.

One step. Two steps. In one continuous motion I raised slightly, came to full draw and released my arrow. It sliced through his middle and he jumped forward, running toward the center of the field. There was a slight rise in the beanfield and I lost sight of him as he bounded over it. I automatically nocked another arrow and when I looked up he was standing near the rise, looking back in my direction. Then he turned and disappeared again.

I got to my feet and started after him. Soon I saw my arrow on the ground and I placed it back in my quiver. A few more steps and I could see him lying just beyond the rise.

WHITETAIL DEER (TYPICAL ANTLERS)

Minimum Score 125 *Odocoileus virginianus* and certain related subspecies

SCORE	LENGTH OF R MAIN BEAM L	INSIDE SPREAD	NUMBER OF R POINTS L	AREA	STATE/ PROVINCE	HUNTER'S NAME	DATE	RANK
204 4/8	27 5/8 26 6/8	23 5/8	7 6	Peoria County	IL	M. J. Johnson	1965	1
203 3/8	25 7/8 27 2/8	19 3/8	6 6	Sturgeon River	SAS	Hubert "Tiggy" Collins	2003	2
198 3/8	26 7/8 26 0/8	19 4/8	7 7	Muskingum County	OH	Tim Reed	2004	3
197 6/8	25 6/8 26 4/8	18 6/8	7 7	Monroe County	IA	Lloyd Goad	1962	4
197 6/8	29 1/8 30 2/8	20 4/8	6 5	Wright County	MN	Curt Van Lith	1986	4
197 1/8	30 0/8 27 7/8	29 0/8	6 7	Edmonton	ALB	Don McGarvey	1991	6
*196 6/8	29 6/8 27 6/8	19 5/8	5 7	Adams County	OH	Justin Lee Metzner	2006	7
195 7/8	26 1/8 27 7/8	20 5/8	6 6	Anoka County	MN	Barry Peterson	1995	8
195 2/8	29 3/8 27 4/8	19 1/8	9 8	Rock Island County	IL	Kent Anderson	1999	9
194 2/8	26 5/8 25 0/8	21 0/8	6 6	Jones County	IA	Robert L. Miller	1977	10
194 0/8	25 6/8 25 3/8	23 6/8	6 7	Logan County	CO	Stuart Clodfelder	1981	11
194 0/8	27 4/8 27 1/8	19 0/8	5 5	Johnson County	IA	Steven E. Tyer	1994	11
193 7/8	26 4/8 25 2/8	17 1/8	8 7	Wabaunsee County	KS	Brad Henry	2001	13
193 6/8	29 0/8 28 4/8	20 6/8	6 8	Kane County	IL	Ray Schremp	2000	14
193 5/8	29 4/8 29 0/8	19 6/8	7 7	Monroe County	IA	Roy Allison	1995	15
193 3/8	28 4/8 27 3/8	21 0/8	8 6	Henry County	IA	Sam Collora	1996	16
193 2/8	28 3/8 27 7/8	22 2/8	8 6	Jackson County	MI	Craig Calderone	1986	17
193 2/8	27 1/8 27 3/8	15 2/8	7 7	Harper County	KS	Keith Manca	2007	17
192 6/8	27 0/8 26 4/8	19 0/8	5 6	Morris	MAN	Gordon J. Coates	2006	19
191 0/8	28 1/8 27 1/8	20 2/8	5 6	Scott County	IA	Jeffery L. Whisker	1993	20
*190 6/8	22 6/8 27 3/8	22 6/8	6 5	Randolph County	IL	Joel D. Eggers	2007	21
190 5/8	27 0/8 27 1/8	18 0/8	5 7	Warren County	IA	Richard Swim	1981	22
190 4/8	28 6/8 28 3/8	20 0/8	5 5	Parke County	IN	B. Dodd Porter	1985	23
190 2/8	28 6/8 30 3/8	24 4/8	5 5	Delaware County	OH	J. T. Kreager	2010	24
189 4/8	25 4/8 24 7/8	20 0/8	6 7	Monmouth County	NJ	Scott William Borcen	1995	25
189 1/8	27 3/8 28 3/8	20 1/8	8 7	Kearney County	NE	Robert Vrbsky	1978	26
189 1/8	27 6/8 28 3/8	20 1/8	6 6	Allamakee County	IA	Randy Petersburg	1996	26
188 7/8	28 2/8 27 3/8	19 2/8	6 7	Shelby County	IL	James M. Holley	1995	28
188 6/8	27 4/8 27 4/8	25 0/8	5 6	Stafford County	KS	Robin L. Austin	2002	29
188 5/8	27 7/8 26 6/8	24 1/8	6 6	Pottawatomie County	KS	Jerry H. DeFoor	1998	30
188 4/8	30 3/8 30 6/8	21 3/8	8 7	Macon County	MO	Eugene Bausch	2001	31
188 4/8	27 7/8 27 7/8	17 2/8	6 6	Logan County	OH	Anthony Partington	2009	31
188 3/8	28 3/8 29 1/8	22 4/8	10 10	Montgomery County	IL	Travis Hartman	1999	33
188 2/8	25 3/8 26 2/8	17 7/8	8 10	Marion County	KY	Tim Raikes	1996	34
188 1/8	28 6/8 27 3/8	22 2/8	8 8	Des Moines County	IA	Kevin Peterson	1989	35
188 0/8	25 7/8 26 2/8	17 4/8	5 5	St. Louis County	MO	Aaron K. McCauley	1999	36
187 7/8	26 6/8 27 4/8	18 0/8	7 7	Neosho County	KS	Gary C. Freeman	1995	37
*187 5/8	29 1/8 29 0/8	21 3/8	5 5	Harvey County	KS	Paula Wiggers	2005	38
187 4/8	27 3/8 26 6/8	23 5/8	7 7	Taylor County	IA	Adam L. Weldon	2005	39
187 2/8	28 6/8 29 4/8	20 4/8	5 7	Nemaha County	KS	Doug Selbe	1995	40
*187 2/8	27 4/8 28 0/8	18 1/8	9 7	Dunn County	WI	Barry A. Rose	2006	40
187 0/8	29 5/8 29 0/8	18 0/8	7 6	Warren County	IL	John K. Poole	1994	42
186 7/8	24 5/8 24 6/8	16 4/8	7 8	Lee County	IA	Dan Enger	2003	43
186 5/8	24 4/8 24 7/8	16 7/8	7 10	Langlade County	WI	Fred J. Hofmann	1994	44
186 5/8	27 1/8 26 4/8	21 4/8	7 8	Buffalo County	WI	Ken Shane	2000	44
186 3/8	28 7/8 27 7/8	20 3/8	7 7	Franklin County	KS	Steve Edwards	2001	46
186 2/8	27 6/8 29 0/8	20 0/8	5 5	Ogle County	IL	Geoff Lester	2000	47
186 2/8	25 6/8 26 6/8	18 0/8	7 7	Adams County	OH	Larry David Napier	2001	47
186 1/8	25 3/8 24 0/8	16 7/8	6 8	Sumner County	KS	Greg Hill	1988	49
186 1/8	31 2/8 30 5/8	24 0/8	5 8	Morris County	KS	Craig Johnson	1991	49
186 1/8	27 6/8 27 3/8	20 1/8	5 5	Buchanan County	IA	Garry W. Rasmussen	1994	49
185 7/8	28 6/8 27 3/8	20 5/8	7 7	Franklin County	OH	Mark A. Scheel	2003	52
185 6/8	26 3/8 26 2/8	20 7/8	8 8	Bryan County	OK	Larry Luman	1997	53
185 1/8	25 7/8 26 3/8	20 3/8	9 7	Jackson County	IL	Mark Guetersloh	1990	54
185 1/8	27 7/8 26 3/8	17 0/8	8 6	Williams County	OH	Brad McNalley	2000	54
*185 1/8	27 2/8 27 7/8	18 7/8	5 5	Macoupin County	IL	Jess Gilpin	2003	54
*185 1/8	29 6/8 27 6/8	19 6/8	5 8	Outagamie County	WI	James W. Ernst	2005	54
184 5/8	29 0/8 27 3/8	21 6/8	7 9	Edgar County	IL	Rev Jack D. Hoffman	2000	59
184 5/8	24 0/8 26 1/8	19 1/8	6 8	Edgar County	IL	Christopher Newhart	2001	59
184 5/8	26 5/8 26 7/8	18 7/8	5 5	Lorain County	OH	Gregory Hildebrand	2009	59
*184 4/8	27 0/8 25 4/8	19 0/8	6 7	Kleberg County	TX	Terry Hall	2008	62
184 3/8	26 5/8 26 0/8	19 0/8	6 6	Keokuk County	IA	Randy Schmidt	1995	63
184 1/8	31 2/8 32 0/8	20 0/8	6 7	Marshall County	KS	Roger D. Seematter	1994	64
184 1/8	26 5/8 27 1/8	19 2/8	6 7	Christian County	IL	Timothy Purcell	2003	64
184 1/8	28 2/8 28 3/8	17 7/8	5 5	Buffalo County	WI	Bill Remington	2005	64
184 1/8	25 1/8 26 1/8	17 3/8	6 6	Waukesha County	WI	Andrae D'Acquisto	2005	64
*184 0/8	25 7/8 26 5/8	18 4/8	9 8	Clay County	KS	Jeffrey W. Severson	2004	68
183 7/8	26 5/8 26 5/8	18 5/8	6 6	Adams County	IA	Greg Andrews	2000	69
183 7/8	28 6/8 29 0/8	24 2/8	6 6	Buffalo County	WI	Dan Bernarde	2009	69
183 6/8	28 1/8 27 4/8	26 4/8	5 5	Jackson County	IA	George W. Horst	2001	71
*183 6/8	27 6/8 28 0/8	22 4/8	5 5	Woodbury County	IA	Gary T. Roan	2006	71
183 5/8	28 4/8 28 2/8	18 1/8	5 5	Clay County	IL	Scott Fritschle	2002	73
183 4/8	26 4/8 27 2/8	16 2/8	5 5	Monona County	IA	Dave Zima	1996	74
183 4/8	28 1/8 27 2/8	19 5/8	8 7	Sangamon County	IL	Wesley A. Rogers	2006	74
183 3/8	27 5/8 27 1/8	20 1/8	5 5	Talbot County	MD	Petey Councell	1994	76
183 3/8	27 2/8 27 1/8	17 5/8	7 6	Ripley County	IN	Mark A. Bonnewell	2004	76
183 2/8	29 2/8 28 3/8	20 4/8	5 6	Shawnee County	KS	Mark W. Young	1990	78
183 2/8	28 5/8 27 5/8	24 2/8	7 7	Kankakee County	IL	Zachary Thomas	2003	78
183 1/8	26 5/8 25 6/8	18 0/8	7 6	Buffalo County	WI	Wally Sitka	2007	80
*183 1/8	27 1/8 28 1/8	17 7/8	5 5	Buffalo County	WI	Mark Weber	2009	80
182 7/8	26 3/8 25 7/8	21 1/8	5 5	Lincoln County	SD	Curtis Courtney	2004	82
182 6/8	26 7/8 26 1/8	19 0/8	5 5	Roanoke County	VA	Dwayne Webster	1999	83
182 6/8	28 3/8 27 5/8	21 6/8	5 5	Cherokee County	IA	Aaron Smith	2000	83
*182 6/8	27 1/8 28 2/8	20 4/8	6 6	Marathon County	WI	Mark Woller	2010	83
182 5/8	28 5/8 28 5/8	19 2/8	7 5	Republic County	KS	Jody Hadachek	1995	86
182 5/8	25 2/8 24 6/8	23 1/8	5 5	Kendall County	IL	Reese Bernier	2004	86
*182 5/8	27 1/8 26 4/8	22 1/8	6 7	Hartley County	TX	Bucky Powell	2009	86
*182 5/8	27 5/8 28 1/8	21 1/8	5 6	Marion County	IA	Terry Carr	2009	86
182 4/8	26 3/8 26 4/8	15 4/8	6 7	Jackson County	IN	Rocky Deakin	1985	90
182 4/8	29 0/8 29 0/8	19 0/8	6 6	Bremer County	IA	Dave Elmore	1992	90
182 4/8	27 0/8 28 4/8	19 2/8	6 6	Franklin County	IL	Tim Broy	1997	90
182 4/8	27 4/8 27 3/8	17 6/8	5 5	Poweshiek County	IA	Hoyt Elliott, Jr.	2001	90
182 4/8	29 1/8 29 2/8	21 5/8	6 5	Preble County	OH	Mike McCabe	2003	90
182 4/8	28 5/8 29 0/8	25 0/8	6 6	Holmes County	OH	Dale Mohler	2003	90
182 3/8	29 6/8 28 2/8	20 0/8	6 5	Hamilton County	IL	Kevin Steele	2007	96

356

WHITETAIL DEER (TYPICAL ANTLERS)

Minimum Score 125   Continued

SCORE	LENGTH OF R MAIN BEAM L	INSIDE SPREAD	NUMBER OF R POINTS L	AREA	STATE/ PROVINCE	HUNTER'S NAME	DATE	RANK
182 2/8	27 2/8 / 28 3/8	21 1/8	8 / 6	Jefferson County	KS	John Welborn	1982	97
182 2/8	30 1/8 / 30 0/8	19 2/8	5 / 5	Hancock County	IL	Jeff L. Akers	2000	97
182 2/8	27 4/8 / 27 4/8	19 2/8	6 / 6	Sullivan County	IN	John Griswold	2005	97
*182 1/8	27 2/8 / 27 5/8	21 5/8	5 / 5	Clay County	IL	Tim Williams	2004	100
182 0/8	26 5/8 / 28 6/8	22 1/8	6 / 7	Jefferson County	KS	Michael J. Rose	1982	101
182 0/8	25 0/8 / 24 1/8	22 6/8	5 / 6	Henderson County	IL	Nicky J. Clark, Jr.	1999	101
181 7/8	28 6/8 / 27 0/8	21 6/8	5 / 7	Greenwood County	KS	Boyd Schneider	1984	103
181 7/8	26 6/8 / 26 5/8	21 7/8	7 / 6	Dakota County	MN	Eugene Lengsfeld	1985	103
181 7/8	25 3/8 / 27 3/8	21 3/8	5 / 5	Logan County	IL	Terry Lee Rich	1986	103
181 7/8	27 2/8 / 26 5/8	19 6/8	6 / 7	Jefferson County	OH	Brad L. Eibel	1988	103
181 7/8	27 7/8 / 26 3/8	20 3/8	7 / 8	Phillips County	KS	Glen Eller	1993	103
181 7/8	27 4/8 / 26 5/8	20 5/8	6 / 6	Van Buren County	IA	Michael C. Mott	1995	103
181 7/8	26 5/8 / 26 5/8	20 4/8	7 / 7	Washington County	MN	Daniel F. Gallagher	2001	103
181 6/8	26 1/8 / 26 4/8	17 6/8	5 / 5	Wabasha County	MN	Lee G. Partington	1971	110
181 6/8	27 5/8 / 27 7/8	21 4/8	5 / 5	Sussex County	DE	Donald Betts	1989	110
181 6/8	27 5/8 / 28 3/8	21 2/8	6 / 6	Bourbon County	KS	Larry Daly	1990	110
181 5/8	30 5/8 / 30 0/8	19 4/8	7 / 5	Grundy County	IL	Wesley Holm	1968	113
181 5/8	24 7/8 / 25 6/8	24 1/8	6 / 5	Racine County	WI	Andrae D'Acquisto	1996	113
181 5/8	24 5/8 / 24 0/8	14 4/8	7 / 6	Allen County	KS	Frank Sanders	2005	113
*181 5/8	25 0/8 / 26 1/8	20 3/8	5 / 5	Warren County	OH	Greg Grupenhof	2009	113
181 4/8	29 6/8 / 29 5/8	24 2/8	6 / 5	Keya Paha County	NE	Steve R. Pecsenye	1966	117
181 4/8	26 0/8 / 28 5/8	18 6/8	9 / 7	Fulton County	IL	Arnold Hegele	1968	117
181 4/8	26 5/8 / 26 7/8	24 4/8	5 / 6	North Norfolk	MAN	Lloyd Lintott	1986	117
181 4/8	25 7/8 / 26 7/8	19 0/8	8 / 5	Reno County	KS	Charles McHaley, Jr.	1994	117
181 4/8	26 3/8 / 25 3/8	17 3/8	7 / 6	La Salle County	TX	Glenn Thurman	2004	117
181 3/8	27 0/8 / 27 4/8	17 6/8	5 / 7	Lawrence County	IL	Charles Morehead	2002	122
*181 3/8	28 1/8 / 25 4/8	22 1/8	6 / 5	Fulton County	IL	Edward G. Kruzan	2004	122
181 3/8	27 4/8 / 28 5/8	23 6/8	6 / 9	Warren County	MO	Steve M. Micke	2008	122
181 2/8	26 2/8 / 25 2/8	22 2/8	5 / 6	Will County	IL	Joseph Skubisz	1996	125
181 2/8	29 5/8 / 28 7/8	22 7/8	6 / 6	McHenry County	IL	Gary E. Konopasek	1997	125
181 2/8	25 5/8 / 25 1/8	21 2/8	5 / 7	Wilkin County	MN	James Komestakes	2008	125
181 1/8	30 1/8 / 29 1/8	22 3/8	6 / 8	Waushara County	WI	Kenneth G. Wilson	2001	128
181 1/8	24 0/8 / 23 6/8	15 7/8	7 / 7	Webster County	IA	Dave C. Hainzinger	2003	128
181 1/8	28 6/8 / 27 7/8	20 1/8	6 / 6	Price County	WI	Michael Kosmer	2005	128
181 0/8	25 4/8 / 25 0/8	23 4/8	8 / 6	Anderson County	KS	Michael A. Irvin	2003	131
180 6/8	25 5/8 / 25 4/8	17 0/8	6 / 6	Tazewell County	IL	Daniel Raube	2009	132
*180 6/8	26 2/8 / 27 1/8	21 6/8	6 / 5	Houston County	MN	Donny H. Chase	2010	132
180 5/8	26 6/8 / 26 4/8	20 5/8	5 / 5	Jefferson County	KS	Ron Artzer	1987	134
180 4/8	24 7/8 / 26 4/8	21 0/8	5 / 5	Henry County	IA	Jeff L. Weigert	1991	135
180 4/8	29 4/8 / 27 7/8	21 4/8	8 / 5	Ross County	OH	Gerald F. Hamm	1991	135
180 4/8	26 1/8 / 25 6/8	18 5/8	6 / 6	Perry County	IL	Mike Schneider	1991	135
180 4/8	26 4/8 / 27 0/8	19 2/8	5 / 5	Washburn County	WI	Tim Clare	1998	135
180 4/8	27 1/8 / 26 6/8	20 1/8	6 / 5	Rock Island County	IL	Douglas J. Hood	2002	135
180 4/8	25 5/8 / 24 5/8	21 3/8	9 / 7	Van Buren County	IA	Gary Faley	2003	135
180 4/8	28 3/8 / 28 4/8	18 1/8	5 / 6	Trempealeau County	WI	Matt Seifert	2010	135
180 3/8	26 5/8 / 27 5/8	19 5/8	7 / 8	Dakota County	MN	Bill Urbaniak	1996	142
180 3/8	30 7/8 / 28 5/8	21 4/8	6 / 8	Westchester County	NY	Richard Johnson	1998	142
180 3/8	27 0/8 / 25 7/8	19 5/8	8 / 7	Butler County	OH	Ken Russell	1999	142
180 3/8	27 6/8 / 28 1/8	19 7/8	7 / 6	Allamakee County	IA	Joe Lieb	2002	142
180 2/8	25 3/8 / 25 6/8	20 1/8	8 / 6	Jefferson County	WI	Randy Latsch	1995	146
180 2/8	27 0/8 / 26 6/8	20 2/8	5 / 5	Clinton County	MI	John L. Benedict	2002	146
180 2/8	24 0/8 / 23 4/8	17 3/8	9 / 6	Cass County	IL	Robert L. Kizer	2007	146
180 1/8	25 4/8 / 24 2/8	17 5/8	6 / 6	Winona County	MN	Kenneth W. Schreiber	1980	149
180 1/8	30 6/8 / 30 6/8	21 2/8	7 / 5	Mahoning County	OH	Robert A. Haney	1987	149
180 1/8	30 2/8 / 29 1/8	23 5/8	8 / 9	Waukesha County	WI	Kevin A. McNeven	2000	149
180 0/8	24 2/8 / 22 6/8	18 0/8	6 / 6	Maverick County	TX	Ryan Friedkin	2006	152
*180 0/8	29 7/8 / 29 2/8	19 1/8	9 / 9	Linn County	IA	Kevin L. McDonald	2007	152
179 7/8	27 5/8 / 27 4/8	18 5/8	5 / 5	Warren County	IA	Jason Henle	2003	154
*179 6/8	25 7/8 / 27 2/8	19 2/8	6 / 5	Hamilton County	IL	Kevin Tinsley	2006	155
179 6/8	25 2/8 / 25 4/8	18 2/8	5 / 6	Iron County	WI	Ron Macak	2008	155
179 5/8	26 6/8 / 25 7/8	20 7/8	7 / 8	Lac qui Parle County	MN	Mary A. Barvels	1978	157
179 5/8	25 4/8 / 25 3/8	21 6/8	5 / 6	Van Buren County	IA	Blane A. Frey	1993	157
179 5/8	27 1/8 / 27 2/8	19 1/8	5 / 5	Riley County	KS	Brent Harper	1999	157
179 5/8	26 3/8 / 25 6/8	19 3/8	6 / 6	Pike County	IL	Dale B. Karns	2002	157
179 5/8	26 6/8 / 25 4/8	20 3/8	5 / 5	Ford County	KS	Tony Stegman	2008	157
179 4/8	28 1/8 / 28 3/8	19 6/8	6 / 6	Clarke County	IA	Rodney D. Hommer	1990	162
179 4/8	25 2/8 / 25 2/8	19 4/8	5 / 5	Macoupin County	IL	Kurt A. Bohl	1997	162
179 4/8	28 4/8 / 28 5/8	16 4/8	5 / 5	Ellsworth County	KS	Jim Willems	2007	162
179 3/8	26 2/8 / 26 5/8	17 3/8	5 / 5	Marshall County	SD	Phyllis Roehr	1976	165
179 3/8	26 1/8 / 26 6/8	22 0/8	8 / 6	Anoka County	MN	Tom Evertz	1996	165
179 3/8	27 0/8 / 26 5/8	20 2/8	7 / 5	Lafayette County	WI	David A. Carey	2004	165
179 1/8	28 1/8 / 27 7/8	24 6/8	5 / 6	Osage County	KS	Ralph Batchelor, Jr.	1985	168
179 1/8	25 6/8 / 25 6/8	16 3/8	6 / 5	Macoupin County	IL	William T. Wiser, Sr.	1994	168
179 1/8	28 3/8 / 28 1/8	20 7/8	5 / 5	Porter County	IN	Herbert Roy Smith	2001	168
179 1/8	25 7/8 / 25 6/8	17 4/8	9 / 6	N. Saskatchewan River	SAS	Miles Johnson	2003	168
179 1/8	28 3/8 / 28 1/8	21 2/8	7 / 6	Schuyler County	IL	Jim Crane	2004	168
179 1/8	26 3/8 / 25 4/8	21 1/8	5 / 5	Winona County	MN	Tom Holzer	2004	168
179 1/8	26 2/8 / 27 3/8	18 3/8	5 / 5	Morgan County	IL	Terry J. Day	2006	168
179 0/8	25 7/8 / 25 7/8	22 1/8	6 / 6	Scotland County	MO	David Smith	1985	175
179 0/8	27 2/8 / 26 1/8	19 2/8	5 / 5	Wapello County	IA	Robert L. McDowell	1985	175
179 0/8	26 6/8 / 26 6/8	17 6/8	6 / 5	Edgar County	IL	Edward A. Inman	1985	175
179 0/8	27 3/8 / 27 7/8	19 3/8	7 / 7	Des Moines County	IA	Glen M. Thompson	1987	175
179 0/8	27 7/8 / 29 1/8	21 4/8	6 / 6	Union County	IA	Richard Reed	1996	175
178 7/8	26 3/8 / 28 0/8	21 0/8	7 / 8	Washington County	IA	Ronald A. Murphy	1990	180
178 7/8	30 0/8 / 29 4/8	18 1/8	5 / 5	Whiteside County	IL	Bernard Higley, Jr.	1990	180
178 7/8	29 4/8 / 28 4/8	21 2/8	6 / 7	Butler County	KS	Don Williamson	1993	180
*178 7/8	28 1/8 / 28 3/8	17 7/8	5 / 5	Greenup County	KY	Jessy Kegley	2009	180
178 6/8	26 3/8 / 27 0/8	20 1/8	7 / 6	Macon County	MO	Luke Shoemaker	2006	184
178 5/8	26 4/8 / 26 1/8	20 7/8	7 / 7	La Salle County	IL	Larry G. Simmons	1995	185
178 5/8	25 0/8 / 24 7/8	17 1/8	6 / 6	Noble County	IN	William M. Hart, Jr.	2001	185
178 4/8	26 2/8 / 25 0/8	21 2/8	5 / 6	Meade County	KS	Tim Ross	1985	187
178 4/8	25 1/8 / 25 0/8	18 4/8	5 / 5	Fulton County	IL	Locie L. Murphy	1985	187
178 4/8	25 1/8 / 25 4/8	19 4/8	5 / 5	Firdale	MAN	Randy Bean	1988	187
178 4/8	25 2/8 / 25 2/8	19 1/8	6 / 8	Buffalo County	WI	Ed Brannen	2001	187
178 4/8	28 6/8 / 28 4/8	19 0/8	6 / 7	Jackson County	MI	Paul L. Calvert	2003	187

357

WHITETAIL DEER (TYPICAL ANTLERS)

Minimum Score 125   Continued

SCORE	LENGTH OF MAIN BEAM R	L	INSIDE SPREAD	NUMBER OF POINTS R	L	AREA	STATE/PROVINCE	HUNTER'S NAME	DATE	RANK
178 4/8	26 4/8	26 5/8	24 4/8	6	5	Livingston County	IL	Scott Fowler	2004	187
178 3/8	25 2/8	26 4/8	21 2/8	7	8	McPherson County	KS	Larry Daniels	1967	193
178 3/8	25 5/8	26 2/8	19 5/8	7	8	Rockyview	ALB	Charles Martin	2005	193
178 3/8	23 5/8	24 0/8	16 7/8	6	6	Buffalo County	WI	Andy Arbs	2006	193
178 3/8	27 0/8	27 2/8	18 3/8	7	7	Fayette County	IA	Kevin Korman	2008	193
178 2/8	25 0/8	24 6/8	21 6/8	5	6	Marion County	IA	Lowdell Taylor	1999	197
*178 2/8	27 1/8	26 4/8	18 4/8	6	6	Allegheny County	PA	Michael J. Nicola, Sr.	2004	197
*178 2/8	22 2/8	22 5/8	22 4/8	5	5	McCurtain County	OK	Johnny Watkins	2006	197
178 2/8	28 2/8	30 0/8	21 0/8	5	5	Vermilion County	IL	Jeff Kepling	2006	197
178 1/8	26 5/8	27 0/8	22 0/8	6	5	Lucas County	OH	Jim Carpenter	1997	201
*178 1/8	29 1/8	28 2/8	19 3/8	6	5	Crittenden County	KY	Floyd Carpenter	2004	201
*178 1/8	25 7/8	26 3/8	18 2/8	6	6	Harford County	MD	Mark Rogowski	2007	201
178 0/8	27 5/8	27 3/8	21 4/8	5	5	Carroll County	IL	Art Heinze	1988	204
178 0/8	25 6/8	25 2/8	22 4/8	6	7	Ford County	KS	Scott Evans	1997	204
178 0/8	29 1/8	29 1/8	23 6/8	6	6	Sedgwick County	KS	Russell Jerome Barbeau	2000	204
178 0/8	27 4/8	27 5/8	21 0/8	6	5	Arapahoe County	CO	Michael D. Palmer	2004	204
177 7/8	24 3/8	24 0/8	18 5/8	5	6	Harper County	OK	Scott Davis	1993	208
177 6/8	25 6/8	25 6/8	18 6/8	5	5	Jefferson County	WI	Ryan Ritacca	2004	209
177 5/8	25 7/8	25 3/8	18 6/8	6	7	Fulton County	IL	Justin Hillman	2002	210
*177 5/8	26 0/8	25 1/8	19 5/8	6	8	Morrison County	MN	Cory D. Williams	2009	210
177 4/8	26 3/8	26 2/8	20 4/8	6	5	Swan River	MAN	Myles Keller	1994	212
177 4/8	27 6/8	26 6/8	20 5/8	6	6	Pike County	IL	Chad Lankford	2001	212
177 4/8	26 2/8	25 2/8	17 4/8	6	7	Dickinson County	KS	Brad Anderson	2003	212
177 4/8	26 6/8	27 4/8	25 0/8	6	5	Cass County	IN	Kenny W. Sallee	2009	212
177 4/8	27 4/8	27 5/8	21 6/8	7	5	Fulton County	IL	Chuck E. Thome	2009	212
177 3/8	27 1/8	26 3/8	20 3/8	6	5	Greene County	IA	Roger V. Carson	1973	217
177 3/8	28 3/8	28 1/8	18 6/8	6	6	Wayne County	OH	Gary E. Landry	1975	217
177 3/8	27 3/8	26 5/8	20 7/8	5	7	Jones County	IA	Ken Dausener	1984	217
177 3/8	25 2/8	25 1/8	16 4/8	8	6	Miami County	KS	Keith L. Groshong	1991	217
177 3/8	26 5/8	27 2/8	20 3/8	6	6	Isanti County	MN	Jay Patchen	1994	217
177 3/8	28 7/8	27 7/8	19 0/8	6	6	Warren County	IA	Charles Guhl	2003	217
177 3/8	25 0/8	26 2/8	17 7/8	6	6	Greenwood County	KS	William N. Donges	2007	217
177 3/8	27 0/8	26 2/8	22 3/8	5	5	Trempealeau County	WI	Stephen P. Satterlund	2009	217
177 2/8	27 5/8	26 3/8	17 3/8	8	7	Montgomery County	KY	Bobby M. Dale	1986	225
177 2/8	29 7/8	29 0/8	22 4/8	9	6	Miami County	KS	Carl C. Hughes	1995	225
177 2/8	25 4/8	24 6/8	21 6/8	5	5	Grundy County	IL	Brandon Smith	2001	225
177 2/8	25 0/8	25 1/8	20 4/8	5	5	Allamakee County	IA	Mark E. Walleser	2002	225
177 1/8	28 4/8	26 6/8	20 2/8	6	7	Washington County	IA	Ernie Aronson	1985	229
177 1/8	27 1/8	28 6/8	21 2/8	7	5	St. Croix County	WI	Phillip R. Hovde	1990	229
*177 1/8	26 1/8	24 7/8	18 5/8	5	5	Otter Tail County	MN	William J. Wagner	2006	229
177 0/8	28 2/8	28 1/8	18 3/8	8	6	Baltimore County	MD	Richard B. Traband	1990	232
177 0/8	25 7/8	27 3/8	19 0/8	6	6	Muscatine County	IA	Gary Stauffer	1995	232
*177 0/8	26 5/8	26 0/8	17 2/8	5	6	Schuyler County	IL	Glenn Bensinger	2004	232
*177 0/8	28 4/8	27 3/8	24 6/8	5	7	N. Saskatchewan River	ALB	Duane Davies	2010	232
176 7/8	27 5/8	27 0/8	18 4/8	5	5	Will County	IL	David Davis	1990	236
176 7/8	25 7/8	25 3/8	17 4/8	6	5	Sullivan County	IN	Larry A. Nash	1995	236
176 7/8	26 0/8	26 0/8	18 7/8	6	5	Henderson County	IL	Dee C. Steinheiser	2003	236
176 7/8	27 0/8	26 6/8	20 3/8	5	7	Schuyler County	IL	Rob Bartlett	2003	236
*176 7/8	24 3/8	24 7/8	17 3/8	7	8	La Crosse County	WI	Heath Tschumper	2008	236
*176 7/8	24 6/8	24 6/8	17 1/8	7	7	Atchison County	KS	Scott Wyss	2009	236
176 6/8	25 2/8	25 0/8	23 4/8	6	6	Marshall County	KS	Ray A. Mosher	1966	242
176 6/8	26 4/8	25 6/8	20 2/8	6	6	Muscatine County	IA	Don McCullough	1980	242
176 6/8	27 4/8	26 0/8	22 7/8	7	5	McHenry County	IL	Gene Melby	1988	242
176 6/8	25 7/8	25 1/8	21 4/8	6	6	Kane County	IL	Mark DuLong	1991	242
176 6/8	26 4/8	25 2/8	18 6/8	5	5	Clay County	KS	Randy Schumock	1997	242
176 6/8	22 7/8	25 2/8	19 0/8	5	5	Jewell County	KS	David Green	2004	242
176 6/8	25 0/8	26 6/8	21 0/8	7	7	Dane County	WI	Nicholas D. Ring	2006	242
*176 6/8	25 6/8	26 4/8	23 4/8	5	5	Edgar County	IL	Clark Piper	2008	242
176 5/8	26 2/8	26 5/8	21 4/8	5	6	Oconto County	WI	Dean Kegel	1999	250
176 5/8	23 1/8	22 7/8	17 1/8	6	8	Buffalo County	WI	Michael A. Ward	2001	250
176 5/8	25 3/8	24 4/8	20 1/8	5	5	Will County	IL	Jeff S. Miller	2002	250
*176 5/8	24 1/8	25 0/8	18 7/8	6	7	Elk County	KS	Tom McFadden	2007	250
176 4/8	28 3/8	28 1/8	21 6/8	9	6	Morgan County	OH	John Hite	1991	254
176 4/8	25 7/8	25 3/8	21 4/8	10	10	Davis County	IA	Jeffrey A. Getz	1991	254
176 4/8	25 5/8	24 3/8	20 2/8	5	5	Lincoln County	MT	James Hershberger	1994	254
176 4/8	27 2/8	26 6/8	20 3/8	6	5	Linn County	IA	David Heck	1994	254
176 4/8	25 6/8	26 1/8	17 7/8	8	6	Phillips County	KS	James D. Helget	1995	254
176 4/8	28 3/8	28 0/8	18 3/8	7	10	Muscatine County	IA	Tim Kroul	1997	254
176 4/8	24 6/8	24 2/8	24 0/8	5	5	Marion County	IA	Joseph C. Laird	1998	254
*176 4/8	25 4/8	25 5/8	19 2/8	5	6	Casey County	KY	Brad Calvert	2005	254
176 3/8	24 6/8	26 4/8	18 3/8	6	6	Edmonton	ALB	Kevin D. Curry	1995	262
*176 3/8	27 0/8	27 0/8	20 4/8	7	7	Wayne County	KY	Michael Dobbs	2006	262
*176 3/8	26 0/8	24 4/8	18 2/8	7	8	Crawford County	WI	Mark Giese	2007	262
176 2/8	28 2/8	27 5/8	21 0/8	7	5	Houston County	MN	John Zahrte	1981	265
176 2/8	28 0/8	28 6/8	21 2/8	5	6	Kingman County	KS	Gerald Stroot	1981	265
176 2/8	23 6/8	23 3/8	19 4/8	8	7	Walworth County	WI	Tom Senft	1993	265
176 2/8	28 6/8	27 5/8	20 0/8	5	6	Republic County	KS	Larry D. Woodman	2000	265
176 2/8	25 2/8	26 4/8	21 2/8	6	5	Will County	IL	Don Yarnell	2001	265
*176 2/8	27 2/8	26 6/8	19 5/8	7	6	Cecil County	MD	Patrick J. Simpkins	2007	265
*176 2/8	25 6/8	25 7/8	21 2/8	5	5	Wabasha County	MN	Chad E. Schmit	2007	265
*176 2/8	26 3/8	24 7/8	19 4/8	5	5	Pepin County	WI	David S. Prissel	2008	265
176 2/8	26 3/8	26 3/8	19 0/8	5	5	Henderson County	IL	Adam Silvers	2008	265
176 1/8	25 1/8	26 1/8	21 0/8	7	5	Lewis County	KY	Alfred Simms	1985	274
176 1/8	28 3/8	27 4/8	25 1/8	7	7	Clay County	KS	Larry L. Thompson	1988	274
176 1/8	27 1/8	27 4/8	23 5/8	6	5	Johnson County	MO	James Stephens	1990	274
176 1/8	28 0/8	28 2/8	18 7/8	6	9	Rock Island County	IL	Gary D. Hodge	2004	274
*176 1/8	25 6/8	25 5/8	19 3/8	5	5	Riley County	KS	Jim Franson	2007	274
176 0/8	25 5/8	23 6/8	25 5/8	6	5	Clay County	KS	Rayford W. Willingham	1985	279
176 0/8	30 0/8	29 5/8	20 7/8	4	6	Butler County	OH	Chris Allen	1994	279
176 0/8	25 2/8	25 6/8	19 1/8	7	7	Washington County	KS	Ronald Montague	2001	279
176 0/8	27 4/8	27 1/8	18 4/8	5	5	Vinton County	OH	Mike Gilliland	2009	279
175 7/8	27 3/8	26 4/8	24 4/8	7	6	Kandiyohi County	MN	Eldon Hauser	1969	283
175 7/8	27 0/8	28 0/8	20 1/8	5	5	Kosciusko County	IN	Jeremiah A. Lotz	2000	283
175 7/8	27 3/8	26 7/8	21 7/8	6	5	Kosciusko County	IN	Richard C. Gamber	2009	283
175 6/8	26 2/8	27 4/8	17 4/8	7	6	Clay County	IL	Scott Fritschle	1991	286

358

WHITETAIL DEER (TYPICAL ANTLERS)

Minimum Score 125 — Continued

SCORE	LENGTH OF R MAIN BEAM L	INSIDE SPREAD	NUMBER OF R POINTS L	AREA	STATE/ PROVINCE	HUNTER'S NAME	DATE	RANK
175 6/8	29 5/8 28 6/8	21 0/8	5 5	Kent County	MI	Ron Visser	1992	286
*175 6/8	25 6/8 26 4/8	21 6/8	5 6	Washburn County	WI	Allen Spaeth	2004	286
*175 6/8	27 3/8 26 6/8	18 4/8	5 5	Pike County	OH	Jason Nathan	2004	286
175 6/8	27 7/8 27 3/8	21 6/8	5 5	McLean County	IL	Chris Hawkins	2006	286
*175 6/8	26 4/8 26 7/8	20 7/8	6 5	Vernon County	WI	Ryan J. Howell	2009	286
*175 6/8	25 6/8 26 4/8	24 4/8	6 6	Pulaski County	IN	William U. Elza	2010	286
175 5/8	29 0/8 28 6/8	21 3/8	4 4	Burnett County	WI	Myles Keller	1977	293
175 5/8	25 4/8 25 2/8	22 2/8	7 7	Pratt County	KS	Gary Brehm	1984	293
175 5/8	26 0/8 25 6/8	22 2/8	5 6	Dickinson County	KS	Gary Stroda	1985	293
175 5/8	24 1/8 23 4/8	17 3/8	7 7	Woodbury County	IA	Paul Federsen	1988	293
175 5/8	25 5/8 25 6/8	19 3/8	7 7	Lucas County	IA	Dean Chandler	1991	293
175 5/8	30 5/8 28 6/8	23 3/8	5 5	Bucks County	PA	Albert J. Muntz	1995	293
175 5/8	27 6/8 28 3/8	21 7/8	5 5	Knox County	IL	Dick DeMay	1996	293
175 5/8	25 6/8 25 5/8	20 1/8	6 7	Sheboygan County	WI	Bob Siech	2002	293
175 5/8	27 6/8 28 1/8	19 7/8	6 6	Menard County	IL	Andrae D'Acquisto	2006	293
175 5/8	27 3/8 27 0/8	21 2/8	7 9	Vermilion County	IL	Richard Huckstadt	2006	293
*175 5/8	23 6/8 24 2/8	18 1/8	6 6	Woodford County	IL	Kyle L. Marquardt	2007	293
*175 5/8	25 6/8 26 0/8	20 0/8	8 8	Riley County	KS	Jon Massie	2007	293
175 4/8	26 0/8 25 4/8	17 7/8	9 5	Murray County	MN	Steven Wynia	1973	305
175 4/8	27 5/8 27 3/8	22 6/8	5 5	Jo Daviess County	IL	Richard McCartin	1991	305
*175 4/8	27 6/8 27 0/8	18 2/8	5 5	Jefferson County	OH	Jason Woodward	2003	305
175 4/8	26 3/8 26 7/8	17 6/8	6 5	Adams County	IL	Frank Welsch	2003	305
*175 4/8	25 7/8 26 0/8	20 4/8	7 6	Rockingham County	NH	Scot E. Chevalier	2004	305
175 4/8	25 7/8 26 2/8	15 6/8	7 6	Trempealeau County	WI	Mike Krynicki	2005	305
175 4/8	24 6/8 24 1/8	18 0/8	5 5	Scott County	IA	Randy Templeton	2005	305
*175 4/8	26 6/8 27 6/8	21 3/8	5 5	Niagara County	NY	Salvatore Alessandra	2006	305
*175 4/8	25 4/8 27 0/8	20 7/8	6 6	Woodford County	IL	Rodney Fandel	2006	305
175 4/8	27 1/8 27 0/8	17 6/8	5 6	Rice County	KS	Scott White	2008	305
175 4/8	25 1/8 23 3/8	20 2/8	6 6	Appanoose County	IA	C. Allen Currin	2008	305
175 4/8	26 3/8 26 4/8	22 2/8	6 5	Harrison County	IA	Ronald M. Stevens	2009	305
175 3/8	25 7/8 26 5/8	19 7/8	5 5	Ottawa County	KS	Gary Gans	1985	317
175 3/8	28 4/8 29 0/8	19 0/8	5 6	Pottawatomie County	KS	Doug Selbe	1997	317
175 3/8	28 2/8 28 0/8	19 2/8	8 6	Mills County	IA	Robert Brewer	1997	317
175 3/8	26 3/8 26 2/8	21 7/8	4 4	Nobleton	ONT	Jack Leggo	2001	317
175 3/8	25 0/8 24 7/8	20 1/8	5 5	Pueblo County	CO	Ivan Muzljakovich	2005	317
175 2/8	28 5/8 27 2/8	23 5/8	6 6	Sangamon County	IL	Wm. Richard Olsen	1978	322
175 2/8	26 1/8 25 7/8	20 0/8	6 6	St. Mary Parish	LA	Shannon Presley	1981	322
175 2/8	28 3/8 27 4/8	21 2/8	5 5	Henderson County	KY	Donald K. White	1987	322
175 2/8	25 4/8 25 4/8	22 6/8	6 7	Piatt County	IL	Jerry Rudisill	1999	322
175 2/8	26 5/8 25 7/8	20 2/8	5 5	Kane County	IL	Patrick Assell	2000	322
175 2/8	26 0/8 28 3/8	21 3/8	7 5	Logan County	OH	Larry Pooler	2000	322
175 2/8	28 7/8 27 6/8	19 1/8	8 7	Pike County	IL	Lewis W. Henry, Jr.	2000	322
175 2/8	26 7/8 28 4/8	20 6/8	9 8	Lorain County	OH	John Henricks	2003	322
175 2/8	24 7/8 25 0/8	18 6/8	5 5	Shawano County	WI	Tim Wockenfus	2003	322
*175 2/8	24 7/8 25 3/8	19 6/8	7 6	Nodaway County	MO	Brian Raney	2006	322
*175 2/8	28 2/8 28 6/8	23 0/8	5 5	Grayson County	TX	Jim Lillis	2007	322
175 1/8	24 4/8 24 4/8	21 5/8	5 6	Marion County	IA	Gordon Hayes	1973	333
175 1/8	26 3/8 28 0/8	21 3/8	7 9	Dodge County	MN	Bill Chase	1976	333
175 1/8	26 5/8 26 4/8	22 7/8	7 9	Bayfield County	WI	Bob Jaskowiak	1994	333
175 1/8	27 0/8 26 7/8	20 1/8	6 6	Scott County	IA	Jeffrey R. Coonts	1996	333
175 1/8	25 7/8 27 1/8	19 5/8	6 7	Spokane County	WA	Michael G. McBride	1999	333
*175 1/8	26 6/8 27 0/8	17 6/8	6 5	Anderson County	KS	Alan Rihner	2004	333
175 0/8	27 6/8 28 6/8	19 0/8	6 6	Lee County	IA	Stephen Douglas McKeehan, Jr.	1989	339
175 0/8	28 4/8 27 7/8	19 2/8	7 9	Jefferson County	IL	Curtis L. Rapp	1993	339
175 0/8	28 3/8 28 5/8	21 0/8	5 7	Schuyler County	IL	Marc S. Anthony	1995	339
*175 0/8	27 3/8 28 2/8	20 2/8	6 6	Adams County	WI	Kevin Weber	2006	339
*175 0/8	28 6/8 28 5/8	20 1/8	6 6	Jo Daviess County	IL	Dan "Boone" Kirchner	2010	339
174 6/8	24 0/8 25 2/8	20 7/8	7 6	Randolph County	IL	Jack D. Carter	1988	344
174 6/8	27 3/8 28 4/8	18 0/8	8 7	Licking County	OH	Steve Trickle	2001	344
174 6/8	27 0/8 27 0/8	20 3/8	8 7	Grundy County	IL	Mathew Summerlin	2003	344
*174 6/8	27 5/8 27 5/8	19 3/8	6 7	Pike County	MO	Jim DeRousse	2003	344
174 6/8	25 1/8 25 4/8	17 3/8	5 6	Ottawa County	KS	Steve Marcotte	2004	344
*174 6/8	27 0/8 26 7/8	18 2/8	5 5	Miami County	IN	Marcus L. Otto	2006	344
174 5/8	25 1/8 25 7/8	18 7/8	5 5	Pickaway County	OH	Hunter R. Certain	1985	350
174 5/8	25 1/8 25 0/8	16 5/8	5 5	Livingston County	MI	Nicholas Scott Converse	1987	350
174 5/8	27 0/8 28 1/8	22 1/8	5 6	Douglas County	KS	Melvin Dark	2004	350
*174 5/8	25 5/8 26 1/8	21 7/8	6 6	Ramsey County	MN	Jim Tuerk	2004	350
174 5/8	26 4/8 27 0/8	20 7/8	6 6	Tazewell County	IL	Marc Anthony	2007	350
174 4/8	25 4/8 24 7/8	17 2/8	7 5	Toole County	MT	Dale Farnes	1979	355
174 4/8	25 6/8 25 6/8	19 6/8	5 5	Chariton County	MO	Roger D. Guilford	1988	355
174 4/8	30 1/8 28 6/8	22 5/8	7 6	Randolph County	IL	William Simmons	1998	355
174 4/8	28 0/8 27 2/8	20 5/8	6 6	Jackson County	IA	Randy P. Steines	2002	355
*174 4/8	25 7/8 26 0/8	17 4/8	6 7	Callaway County	MO	Dan Thomas	2003	355
174 4/8	25 4/8 25 6/8	18 6/8	6 6	Dimmit County	TX	Dan Friedell, Jr.	2004	355
174 4/8	26 5/8 27 0/8	18 5/8	6 7	Plymouth County	IA	Todd Laughton	2005	355
174 3/8	25 5/8 24 3/8	18 3/8	5 5	Taylor County	KY	Barry Eastridge	1987	362
174 3/8	28 4/8 27 6/8	20 3/8	7 7	Grant County	WI	Charles P. Fralick	1996	362
174 3/8	27 6/8 27 3/8	22 3/8	5 5	Osage County	KS	Evans Woehlecke	1997	362
174 3/8	26 7/8 26 7/8	18 5/8	6 7	Sullivan County	NY	Domenick DeMaria	1998	362
174 3/8	26 0/8 25 1/8	20 2/8	5 7	Fulton County	IL	Robert Stevenson	1999	362
174 3/8	24 4/8 25 6/8	23 1/8	5 5	Polk County	MO	Kevin Fulks	2005	362
174 2/8	27 7/8 27 0/8	21 2/8	5 5	Ashland County	WI	Kelly McClaire	1986	368
174 2/8	24 2/8 24 6/8	18 2/8	5 5	Mower County	MN	Jason Blom	1987	368
174 2/8	25 5/8 25 5/8	18 6/8	6 6	Wabaunsee County	KS	Henry C. Boss II	1991	368
174 2/8	30 0/8 30 5/8	21 5/8	6 6	Miami County	OH	Mike Newman	1996	368
174 2/8	26 5/8 25 1/8	20 6/8	6 6	Polk County	MN	Steven Cornell	2000	368
174 2/8	27 4/8 26 4/8	18 3/8	7 7	Scott County	IN	Bobby Brock	2007	368
*174 2/8	25 2/8 25 2/8	16 7/8	7 6	Berrien County	MI	Matthew L. Wheeler	2007	368
*174 2/8	26 5/8 27 2/8	19 3/8	6 6	Henry County	IL	Joel Hansen	2009	368
174 1/8	23 2/8 23 5/8	18 6/8	9 7	Logan County	IL	Gregory C. Gobleman	1981	376
174 1/8	26 2/8 25 2/8	17 2/8	8 7	Cass County	IL	Chris Gosset	2002	376
174 1/8	26 0/8 26 3/8	18 1/8	6 6	Taylor County	IA	Nathan P. Stiens	2004	376
174 1/8	25 1/8 25 5/8	20 5/8	6 5	Douglas County	WI	Doug Anderson	2004	376
174 1/8	26 6/8 26 5/8	19 3/8	6 6	Appanoose County	IA	Bartt Carney	2008	376
174 0/8	26 3/8 26 2/8	17 6/8	6 6	Harrison County	IA	Ricky G. Seydel	1989	381

359

WHITETAIL DEER (TYPICAL ANTLERS)

Minimum Score 125 — Continued

SCORE	LENGTH OF R MAIN BEAM L	INSIDE SPREAD	NUMBER OF R POINTS L		AREA	STATE/ PROVINCE	HUNTER'S NAME	DATE	RANK
174 0/8	28 0/8	27 4/8	22 4/8	6	5	Cuyahoga County	OH	Charles E. Suk	1994	381
174 0/8	25 7/8	26 3/8	23 0/8	8	5	Vermilion County	IL	Alex L. Ramm	1995	381
174 0/8	29 3/8	29 7/8	19 0/8	4	4	Johnson County	KS	Kevin Hancock	1996	381
174 0/8	26 4/8	26 4/8	18 0/8	5	5	La Salle County	IL	Mike Armstrong	1996	381
*174 0/8	26 2/8	26 0/8	20 0/8	7	6	Marshall County	IL	James R. Kleiber	2004	381
174 0/8	24 4/8	24 7/8	16 7/8	7	6	Calhoun County	IL	Travis Simpson	2005	381
173 7/8	24 0/8	24 2/8	19 1/8	5	5	Noble County	OK	Danny McCants	1968	388
173 7/8	27 4/8	25 5/8	16 3/8	5	6	Pike County	MO	Jim Holdenried	1982	388
173 7/8	26 3/8	27 7/8	21 4/8	6	6	Will County	IL	Harry Hammock	1995	388
173 7/8	24 6/8	25 7/8	16 5/8	6	6	Clay County	MO	David Ruth	1995	388
173 7/8	25 3/8	26 2/8	20 2/8	7	6	Blue Earth County	MN	Jeffery Lee Zimmerman	1995	388
173 7/8	27 6/8	26 6/8	18 4/8	4	6	Wilbarger County	TX	John T. Wright	1998	388
173 7/8	26 6/8	29 0/8	20 5/8	7	7	Buffalo County	WI	Jeff N. Tirri	2002	388
173 7/8	27 1/8	27 1/8	19 5/8	6	6	Delaware County	OH	Jeff Daily	2003	388
*173 7/8	26 4/8	30 2/8	22 2/8	6	5	McLean County	IL	Jeremy Mayfield	2005	388
*173 7/8	25 3/8	25 3/8	18 4/8	7	7	Putnam County	IN	Chris S. Brotherton	2006	388
*173 7/8	28 4/8	27 0/8	20 6/8	7	5	Trempealeau County	WI	Tim Engel	2009	388
173 6/8	26 6/8	27 1/8	19 7/8	7	5	Mercer County	IL	Floyd A. Clark	1961	399
173 6/8	26 1/8	25 0/8	21 5/8	6	5	Winneshiek County	IA	Herbert Amundson	1985	399
173 6/8	25 3/8	26 0/8	18 2/8	5	5	Crawford County	IA	Ed Willroth	1991	399
173 6/8	25 0/8	23 6/8	22 3/8	7	5	Haskell County	KS	Neal Heaton	1993	399
173 6/8	30 0/8	31 2/8	19 6/8	7	7	Union County	KY	Robert C. Caudill	1995	399
173 6/8	27 4/8	26 4/8	21 2/8	6	5	Brown County	IL	Michael Postema	1997	399
173 6/8	26 5/8	26 5/8	20 7/8	7	7	Allamakee County	IA	Joe Lieb	1998	399
173 6/8	30 5/8	29 5/8	20 5/8	6	5	Erie County	OH	James W. Zimmerman	2002	399
173 6/8	25 1/8	24 3/8	19 0/8	5	5	Richland County	WI	Greg Beighley	2003	399
173 6/8	25 1/8	25 0/8	20 2/8	7	8	Jasper County	IL	Tom Shelton	2003	399
173 6/8	26 0/8	25 5/8	18 6/8	7	7	Dunn County	WI	Christopher W. Koele	2009	399
173 6/8	25 0/8	24 4/8	19 0/8	6	6	Sauk County	WI	Tanner S. Mulock	2010	399
173 5/8	26 2/8	26 0/8	22 3/8	6	7	Muskingum County	OH	David R. Hatfield	1980	411
173 5/8	30 1/8	30 0/8	25 3/8	6	5	Jackson County	MO	Mike Sytkowski	1995	411
173 5/8	25 3/8	25 1/8	19 4/8	8	7	Buffalo County	WI	James R. Gabrick	1996	411
173 5/8	24 3/8	23 6/8	20 5/8	5	5	Pottawattamie County	IA	Steve Stuart	1997	411
173 5/8	26 4/8	27 4/8	20 0/8	8	5	Kankakee County	IL	Tim Lynch	1999	411
173 5/8	25 5/8	25 5/8	19 7/8	5	5	Jo Daviess County	IL	William B. Bland	2001	411
*173 5/8	27 6/8	26 6/8	19 1/8	5	5	Pike County	IL	Rickey Cleveland	2003	411
173 5/8	27 6/8	29 3/8	22 1/8	6	6	Winona County	MN	Keith Nelson	2006	411
173 4/8	26 2/8	27 1/8	23 4/8	6	5	Lac qui Parle County	MN	Dale W. Shackelford	1981	419
173 4/8	25 7/8	27 0/8	23 0/8	5	5	McHenry County	IL	Gordon Sunderlage	1987	419
173 4/8	27 0/8	26 4/8	18 6/8	6	5	St. Louis County	MN	James Bong	1988	419
173 4/8	29 6/8	29 2/8	17 6/8	6	5	Pike County	IL	Wayne S. Jones	1996	419
173 4/8	25 3/8	23 6/8	17 6/8	6	5	Louisa County	IA	Todd Goss	1997	419
173 4/8	28 1/8	27 4/8	21 0/8	5	6	Chisago County	MN	Robert C. Palmer	1999	419
173 4/8	27 4/8	29 3/8	22 0/8	5	5	Appanoose County	IA	Randy Andreiri	1999	419
173 4/8	25 4/8	25 4/8	19 4/8	5	7	Trempealeau County	WI	Ross Lambert	2001	419
173 4/8	26 0/8	26 5/8	20 6/8	5	5	Greene County	IL	Ryan Swearingn	2001	419
173 4/8	28 2/8	28 5/8	21 1/8	7	5	Clark County	IL	Barry Howe	2002	419
173 3/8	26 4/8	26 5/8	20 1/8	5	6	Warren County	IL	Larry C. Harding	1974	429
173 3/8	26 3/8	24 6/8	16 5/8	6	5	Bent County	CO	Rick J. Tokarski	1994	429
173 3/8	27 2/8	27 0/8	28 7/8	5	6	Kane County	IL	James Meyer	1995	429
173 3/8	24 5/8	24 5/8	21 3/8	6	5	Sauk County	WI	Eric R. Sorge	1996	429
173 3/8	27 3/8	27 3/8	22 1/8	7	7	McHenry County	ND	Mark A. Palda	2000	429
173 3/8	25 2/8	25 7/8	15 3/8	6	7	Butler County	KS	Chris Elinski	2003	429
173 3/8	28 3/8	27 3/8	22 1/8	4	4	McHenry County	IL	George G. Gilpin, Jr.	2003	429
*173 3/8	26 6/8	26 4/8	19 4/8	7	7	Montgomery County	IA	Shawn Peterson	2004	429
173 3/8	26 0/8	25 7/8	18 0/8	6	5	Jessamine County	KY	Rick McGlothen	2007	429
173 3/8	23 5/8	23 1/8	19 1/8	8	6	Bayfield County	WI	Rodney Hipsher	2008	429
173 2/8	26 0/8	26 3/8	22 5/8	5	6	Miami County	KS	Dan R. Moore	1982	439
173 2/8	27 6/8	28 1/8	18 0/8	7	7	Monroe County	IN	Jake Wineinger	1990	439
173 2/8	24 2/8	25 0/8	19 0/8	5	5	Butler County	MO	Marcus O. Milligan	1997	439
173 2/8	26 5/8	26 5/8	24 6/8	5	5	Pickaway County	OH	Tim Ritchie	1997	439
173 2/8	26 2/8	26 2/8	22 0/8	7	7	Preble County	OH	Gary H. Vest	1999	439
173 2/8	25 4/8	26 5/8	20 5/8	6	6	Iowa County	WI	Michael A. Benish	1999	439
*173 2/8	24 5/8	25 0/8	18 2/8	6	6	Beaver County	PA	Robert E. Davenport	2002	439
173 2/8	27 2/8	27 1/8	18 2/8	7	6	Clark County	IL	Raymond C. Kezler	2006	439
*173 2/8	26 3/8	27 4/8	21 4/8	8	6	Olmsted County	MN	Eric Ronningen	2007	439
173 1/8	28 0/8	28 2/8	21 5/8	7	7	Dunn County	WI	Jack K. Dodge	1987	448
173 1/8	28 6/8	27 6/8	19 3/8	4	4	Morrison County	MN	John McDonald	1993	448
173 1/8	25 5/8	24 2/8	23 3/8	5	5	Nemaha County	KS	Edward E. Daily	1994	448
173 1/8	27 2/8	28 2/8	20 0/8	5	6	Buffalo County	WI	Tom Johnson	1997	448
173 1/8	28 0/8	28 5/8	23 0/8	6	5	Coles County	IL	Ron Osborne	2000	448
173 1/8	27 7/8	26 2/8	17 7/8	5	5	Porter County	IN	Joseph J. Marlow	2001	448
173 1/8	24 7/8	24 1/8	20 0/8	6	7	Pickaway County	OH	Walter Kerschner	2004	448
*173 1/8	24 4/8	23 0/8	15 7/8	6	6	Appanoose County	IA	Tad D. Proudlove	2006	448
173 1/8	23 6/8	25 5/8	22 1/8	6	5	Stafford County	KS	Matthew W. Richardson	2006	448
173 0/8	25 6/8	25 5/8	19 4/8	5	5	St. Louis County	MO	Kenny E. Harwell	2008	448
173 0/8	25 4/8	26 1/8	15 2/8	6	5	White County	IN	Eric L. Mohler	1978	458
173 0/8	25 4/8	27 1/8	19 4/8	9	8	Russell County	KS	Michael J. Pasek	1990	458
173 0/8	27 3/8	27 0/8	19 7/8	7	6	Clay County	MO	Neal B. Breshears	1996	458
173 0/8	24 7/8	24 7/8	20 4/8	5	5	Pratt County	KS	Jerry L. Hawrylak	2006	458
172 7/8	27 6/8	27 1/8	18 5/8	5	6	Isanti County	MN	Ward D. Pierson	2007	458
172 7/8	27 2/8	27 7/8	19 7/8	5	5	Vermilion County	IL	Ed Gudgel	1988	463
172 7/8	25 5/8	26 5/8	21 5/8	6	5	Walworth County	WI	Robert Peterson	1988	463
172 7/8	24 7/8	25 3/8	15 1/8	5	5	Minnehaha County	SD	Dan Anderson	2001	463
*172 7/8	26 6/8	24 4/8	18 7/8	6	7	Clark County	OH	Jason Stull	2004	463
*172 7/8	26 4/8	26 4/8	19 2/8	7	7	Brown County	OH	Steven B. Coney	2005	463
172 7/8	27 0/8	26 5/8	19 1/8	7	8	Spink County	SD	Marv Miller	2006	463
172 7/8	26 1/8	27 7/8	17 6/8	8	9	Kleberg County	TX	Charles A. "Chuck" Meloy	2008	463
172 6/8	26 7/8	27 6/8	25 7/8	6	6	Hancock County	IL	Alan N. Jenkins	2009	463
172 6/8	25 4/8	25 1/8	19 4/8	5	5	Mower County	MN	Art McKenzie	1972	471
172 6/8	26 6/8	25 5/8	16 4/8	5	5	Ripley County	IN	Steve A. Allen	1982	471
172 6/8	25 1/8	24 7/8	18 6/8	6	5	Sullivan County	TN	C. Alan Altizer	1984	471
172 6/8	27 6/8	28 5/8	18 7/8	7	5	Saline County	KS	Bruce Brown	1986	471
172 6/8	27 6/8	28 5/8	18 7/8	7	5	Fairfield County	OH	James Carmichael	1988	471
172 6/8	27 6/8	28 5/8	18 7/8	7	5	Pike County	IL	Jimmy Howard	1989	471

WHITETAIL DEER (TYPICAL ANTLERS)

Minimum Score 125 — Continued

SCORE	LENGTH OF R MAIN BEAM L	INSIDE SPREAD	NUMBER OF R POINTS L		AREA	STATE/ PROVINCE	HUNTER'S NAME	DATE	RANK
172 6/8	28 0/8 28 7/8	19 2/8	6	5	Moultrie County	IL	Joe Nelson	1991	471
172 6/8	25 4/8 25 4/8	17 4/8	6	7	Keokuk County	IA	Michael A. Veres	1995	471
172 6/8	24 5/8 27 5/8	21 1/8	6	6	Union County	SD	Scott Staum	1997	471
172 6/8	27 3/8 27 5/8	18 0/8	6	5	Monroe County	MO	Shelton Wheelan	1999	471
172 6/8	24 4/8 25 2/8	18 4/8	6	5	Tioga County	NY	Daniel E. Walp	2000	471
172 6/8	25 6/8 24 6/8	18 0/8	5	6	Mercer County	PA	Michael D. Heckathorn	2000	471
*172 6/8	28 5/8 27 3/8	18 6/8	9	6	Monroe County	WI	Steve Bjerke	2003	471
172 6/8	26 7/8 25 7/8	18 7/8	6	8	Adams County	WI	John P. Nawrot	2004	471
172 6/8	26 7/8 26 7/8	19 4/8	6	5	Des Moines County	IA	Blake Brindle	2006	471
*172 6/8	27 3/8 27 3/8	18 2/8	8	7	Winona County	MN	Jonny Mullen	2009	471
*172 6/8	26 7/8 25 2/8	18 0/8	7	5	Barron County	WI	Matthew J. Lindstedt	2010	471
172 5/8	26 7/8 27 1/8	18 7/8	5	5	Rosebud County	MT	Michael E Gayheart	1989	488
172 5/8	26 7/8 27 1/8	19 2/8	5	6	Lyon County	KS	Dale Hellman	1990	488
172 5/8	26 0/8 26 1/8	22 3/8	6	6	Smith County	KS	Jon Weavers	1998	488
172 5/8	25 1/8 24 7/8	20 7/8	5	5	Washington County	IA	Bradly Balcar	2003	488
*172 5/8	26 5/8 25 7/8	19 3/8	5	6	Buffalo County	WI	Corinne Brenner	2007	488
172 4/8	26 0/8 26 0/8	18 2/8	7	6	Lucas County	IA	Jim Barlow	1985	493
172 4/8	26 4/8 26 4/8	15 2/8	5	5	Scotland County	MO	Charlie L. Smith	1985	493
172 4/8	27 3/8 27 3/8	18 2/8	5	6	Shelby County	IL	Gene E. Thoele	1991	493
172 4/8	24 5/8 26 2/8	16 6/8	5	5	Bond County	IL	Bill Brown	1995	493
172 4/8	24 7/8 24 6/8	21 0/8	5	5	Knox County	IL	Dan Courtright	1997	493
172 4/8	24 4/8 24 7/8	23 6/8	5	5	Keokuk County	IA	Mike Wells	2000	493
*172 4/8	27 6/8 29 0/8	22 3/8	6	5	Shawano County	WI	Cory Bohlman	2000	493
*172 4/8	25 3/8 25 2/8	18 2/8	5	6	Warren County	OH	John B. Luchini	2004	493
172 4/8	26 1/8 25 7/8	18 4/8	5	5	Montgomery County	KS	Michael L. Peterson	2005	493
172 4/8	27 0/8 27 2/8	18 2/8	7	7	Switzerland County	IN	Chris Gross	2007	493
172 3/8	26 3/8 24 0/8	18 6/8	6	7	Clinton County	IL	James D. Rueter	1984	503
172 3/8	26 6/8 26 4/8	21 3/8	5	5	Marshall County	IA	Dale E. Smith	1988	503
172 3/8	27 0/8 26 7/8	19 1/8	5	5	Johnson County	KS	David Reed	1990	503
172 3/8	29 6/8 30 2/8	21 2/8	4	6	Prince Georges County	MD	Lance D. Canter	1993	503
172 3/8	26 0/8 24 6/8	24 5/8	5	5	Walworth County	WI	Daniel Miller	2000	503
172 3/8	26 4/8 27 1/8	17 4/8	8	6	Douglas County	KS	Brad Robbins	2000	503
172 3/8	26 0/8 26 1/8	18 7/8	5	4	Harrison County	OH	Tom Newman	2006	503
*172 3/8	25 0/8 24 7/8	21 4/8	5	7	Porter County	IN	John R. Brigham	2009	503
*172 3/8	26 7/8 27 0/8	22 1/8	5	5	Hancock County	IL	Josh J. Gronewold	2009	503
172 2/8	26 1/8 25 3/8	19 2/8	5	6	Iowa County	IA	Ardith Lockridge	1965	512
172 2/8	27 3/8 25 1/8	18 4/8	5	5	Clinton County	IA	Robert S. Stankee	1985	512
172 2/8	27 6/8 26 5/8	19 4/8	5	5	Butler County	PA	Ralph W. Stoltenberg, Jr.	1986	512
172 2/8	26 7/8 27 6/8	26 2/8	6	5	Saunders County	NE	John I. Kunert	1986	512
172 2/8	25 1/8 26 4/8	19 6/8	5	5	Clay County	KS	Scott Otto	1989	512
172 2/8	25 0/8 25 2/8	17 4/8	9	6	Delaware County	OK	Bruce Hicks	1990	512
172 2/8	28 1/8 28 4/8	22 0/8	4	5	Champaign County	IL	Justin Park	1992	512
172 2/8	25 0/8 25 7/8	19 0/8	6	6	Des Moines County	IA	James E. Howie	1996	512
172 2/8	27 4/8 27 4/8	19 0/8	6	6	Green County	WI	Tom Cisewski	1998	512
172 2/8	26 1/8 25 0/8	20 0/8	6	6	Knox County	OH	David K. Palmer	1998	512
172 2/8	25 7/8 26 0/8	18 0/8	5	5	Berrien County	MI	Mike C. Payne	2000	512
172 2/8	23 3/8 22 6/8	17 0/8	6	6	Bartholomew County	IN	Dustin G. Prewitt	2001	512
172 2/8	30 0/8 28 6/8	24 3/8	7	6	Champaign County	OH	Shawn Johnson	2003	512
172 2/8	27 7/8 27 5/8	19 4/8	6	7	Taylor County	IA	Casey D. Knight	2008	512
*172 2/8	26 4/8 27 2/8	20 0/8	5	7	Ringgold County	IA	Scott Bradley	2008	512
172 1/8	26 4/8 26 3/8	19 5/8	7	6	Rice County	MN	Mike Sannan	1989	526
172 1/8	27 6/8 26 6/8	17 7/8	7	7	Russell County	KS	James H. Skucius	1990	526
172 1/8	25 1/8 24 6/8	22 5/8	8	8	Lake County	IL	Mark J. Kramer	1990	526
172 1/8	24 2/8 24 7/8	19 5/8	5	6	Wyandotte County	KS	Earl A. Cooksey	1992	526
172 1/8	29 3/8 30 2/8	21 0/8	7	8	Rock County	WI	Steven Kravick	1996	526
172 1/8	28 6/8 27 4/8	22 4/8	5	6	Greene County	OH	Jay M. Skrabacz	1997	526
172 1/8	25 5/8 24 1/8	22 5/8	6	6	Monroe County	IA	Jeff Butler	1999	526
172 1/8	24 5/8 24 4/8	18 5/8	5	5	Buffalo County	WI	Dave Lyga	2000	526
172 1/8	26 2/8 25 6/8	22 7/8	5	5	Lake County	IL	Derrell Listhartke	2000	526
172 1/8	25 3/8 25 4/8	17 1/8	7	8	Winneshiek County	IA	Peter DeJardin	2004	526
172 1/8	23 3/8 22 6/8	16 3/8	6	6	Washington County	KS	Scott B. Carpenter	2004	526
172 1/8	27 2/8 27 5/8	18 5/8	7	7	Worcester County	MA	Paul A. Buccacio	2006	526
172 1/8	23 5/8 23 5/8	20 5/8	5	6	Hartford County	CT	Christopher J. Belisle	2008	526
*172 1/8	25 2/8 25 0/8	18 7/8	6	6	Dunn County	WI	Bob Joubert	2009	526
172 0/8	27 0/8 26 6/8	21 2/8	5	5	Greene County	IN	Jason Anderson	1991	540
172 0/8	25 6/8 25 2/8	17 7/8	5	6	Nicollet County	MN	Bruce Kramer	1991	540
172 0/8	25 4/8 23 4/8	16 6/8	6	6	McMullen County	TX	Steve Best	1991	540
172 0/8	28 1/8 28 1/8	21 1/8	5	6	Greene County	IL	Kenny Tally, Jr.	1995	540
172 0/8	26 3/8 26 4/8	20 2/8	7	7	Pottawatomie County	KS	Dale R. Larson	1995	540
172 0/8	26 6/8 25 3/8	22 1/8	6	6	Shawnee County	KS	Richard Matyak	1997	540
172 0/8	26 2/8 26 2/8	19 2/8	5	5	Delaware County	IA	Chuck Fessler	1997	540
172 0/8	27 0/8 26 6/8	22 2/8	5	5	Tazewell County	IL	Joe L. Beach, Jr.	2002	540
*172 0/8	29 6/8 29 6/8	17 1/8	7	7	Prince Georges County	MD	James Printz	2003	540
*172 0/8	25 2/8 25 7/8	17 0/8	5	5	Sarpy County	NE	Rocky Maas	2007	540
*172 0/8	24 6/8 24 1/8	17 6/8	5	7	Pierce County	WI	Van Howe	2008	540
*172 0/8	28 3/8 28 2/8	23 2/8	5	4	Clay County	NE	James Hamik	2008	540
171 7/8	26 2/8 26 4/8	24 1/8	5	5	Scotland County	MO	David Smith	1984	552
171 7/8	28 5/8 28 0/8	20 7/8	8	7	Linn County	IA	Charles Bemer	1985	552
171 7/8	27 5/8 26 6/8	21 5/8	6	6	Lucas County	IA	Tim M. Whitlatch	1989	552
171 7/8	26 3/8 25 4/8	21 3/8	5	5	Henderson County	KY	Aaron D. Parrish	1995	552
171 7/8	26 7/8 25 5/8	19 5/8	5	6	Moniteau County	MO	Randy Wilson	1999	552
171 7/8	27 4/8 26 2/8	14 5/8	6	6	Fayette County	IL	Levi Tolka	2000	552
171 7/8	27 7/8 27 4/8	21 1/8	5	6	Larue County	KY	Gary Polly	2001	552
171 7/8	26 1/8 28 3/8	21 3/8	8	5	Wayne County	IL	Don Riley	2002	552
*171 7/8	24 1/8 23 3/8	21 7/8	5	5	Monroe County	MI	Michael Paul Kiley	2003	552
171 7/8	26 1/8 25 5/8	17 3/8	6	6	Crawford County	WI	James Balistreri	2003	552
*171 7/8	24 3/8 24 4/8	20 3/8	5	5	Henderson County	KY	Nick Sandefur	2005	552
171 7/8	27 2/8 26 7/8	18 7/8	8	8	Winnebago County	WI	Zach Stromske	2005	552
*171 7/8	26 2/8 26 4/8	19 7/8	8	6	Washington County	KS	Brian S. Spradling	2008	552
171 7/8	26 2/8 26 0/8	18 7/8	7	5	Ottawa County	OH	Frank Despones	2008	552
171 7/8	24 6/8 25 6/8	18 2/8	6	7	Lee County	IA	Eric Bussiere	2008	552
171 7/8	24 4/8 24 3/8	19 3/8	5	5	White County	IN	Aaron Ault	2009	552
171 6/8	26 7/8 26 6/8	25 2/8	7	8	Richland County	ND	Todd Funfar	1982	568
171 6/8	28 1/8 27 1/8	17 6/8	7	6	Carroll County	OH	Randy S Mulheim	1983	568
171 6/8	24 6/8 23 4/8	20 6/8	5	5	Dunn County	WI	James W. Belmore	1991	568

WHITETAIL DEER (TYPICAL ANTLERS)

Minimum Score 125   Continued

Score	R Main Beam	L Main Beam	Inside Spread	R Points	L Points	Area	State/Province	Hunter's Name	Date	Rank
171 6/8	28 0/8	28 0/8	20 6/8	7	8	Edmonton	ALB	Warren Witherspoon	1991	568
171 6/8	25 7/8	26 5/8	18 6/8	6	9	Todd County	MN	Chead D. Wessel	1993	568
171 6/8	26 4/8	26 5/8	19 0/8	5	5	Osage County	OK	Don Gaddis	1995	568
171 6/8	26 6/8	26 5/8	18 6/8	7	6	Anderson County	KS	Gary Shields	1996	568
171 6/8	26 0/8	25 0/8	16 3/8	6	8	Dakota County	MN	Vincent LaCroix	1998	568
171 6/8	25 3/8	25 7/8	18 5/8	5	6	Cookson	SAS	Bry Loyd	1999	568
171 6/8	25 7/8	24 7/8	20 1/8	6	10	Adams County	OH	Larry D. Napier	2000	568
171 6/8	26 5/8	27 0/8	18 3/8	7	6	Mills County	IA	Henry Joslin, Jr.	2000	568
171 6/8	27 1/8	27 0/8	21 4/8	5	5	Waukesha County	WI	Ryan Bischop	2002	568
*171 6/8	26 0/8	26 0/8	15 4/8	5	6	McMullen County	TX	Kirk M. Folsom	2004	568
*171 6/8	26 5/8	27 6/8	18 6/8	6	5	Kendall County	IL	Steve Chivari	2005	568
*171 6/8	26 3/8	27 0/8	19 0/8	5	5	Dubois County	IN	Aaron M. Birk	2009	568
171 5/8	24 6/8	24 0/8	17 3/8	6	6	Calgary	ALB	Scott Simi	1979	583
171 5/8	25 3/8	25 2/8	20 3/8	8	6	Cowley County	KS	Michael L. Snyder	1985	583
171 5/8	26 3/8	25 5/8	19 3/8	5	5	Logan County	KY	Alan Scott	1987	583
171 5/8	25 0/8	25 4/8	21 3/8	5	5	Linn County	KS	Robert R. Goodwin	1994	583
171 5/8	23 6/8	23 4/8	19 7/8	6	6	Fergus County	MT	D. Mitch Kottas	1995	583
171 5/8	26 0/8	26 5/8	19 5/8	5	5	Grundy County	IL	Joseph Gray	1997	583
171 5/8	25 0/8	25 0/8	20 3/8	6	6	Douglas County	NE	Bryan Kindler	1997	583
171 5/8	26 5/8	24 5/8	18 4/8	6	7	Clayton County	IA	Chris Borcherding	1997	583
171 5/8	27 0/8	27 4/8	26 6/8	8	8	Fayette County	IL	Andy A. Wessel	2003	583
171 5/8	24 1/8	24 6/8	15 5/8	5	5	Sangamon County	IL	Matt Strawn	2003	583
171 5/8	24 5/8	24 3/8	19 3/8	6	7	Delaware County	IA	Will Roling	2003	583
171 5/8	27 1/8	27 1/8	18 3/8	7	7	Scioto County	OH	James R. Arnett, Jr.	2004	583
171 5/8	26 4/8	26 7/8	17 0/8	5	5	Lyon County	KS	David Layton	2009	583
171 4/8	24 3/8	23 2/8	16 6/8	6	6	Ellsworth County	KS	Jim Willems	1985	596
171 4/8	24 4/8	25 4/8	19 6/8	6	6	Vermilion County	IL	Ken Becicka	1991	596
171 4/8	26 2/8	26 0/8	21 4/8	6	6	Louisa County	IA	Mike Noble	1992	596
171 4/8	22 5/8	22 2/8	16 1/8	6	7	Kleberg County	TX	Mike Lemker	1997	596
171 4/8	24 6/8	26 4/8	20 0/8	5	5	Suffolk County	NY	Robert Janke	2000	596
171 4/8	26 0/8	25 1/8	18 3/8	6	7	Morgan County	IN	David L. Wolford	2002	596
171 4/8	26 6/8	26 6/8	21 6/8	5	7	Humboldt County	IA	Jerry B. Tokheim	2003	596
171 4/8	24 4/8	23 1/8	18 5/8	6	7	Belair	MAN	Allan H. Niemar	2005	596
171 4/8	24 6/8	25 3/8	21 0/8	5	5	Dane County	WI	Wade M. Mapes	2006	596
*171 4/8	24 0/8	25 0/8	18 4/8	7	6	Polk County	WI	Thomas Coach	2006	596
171 3/8	22 4/8	23 7/8	24 7/8	6	6	Cass County	ND	Warren Buss	1966	606
171 3/8	23 7/8	24 5/8	18 7/8	5	5	Harrison County	IA	R. A. Cronk	1985	606
171 3/8	27 4/8	27 6/8	21 3/8	7	6	Washington County	IL	Robert Schneicer	1985	606
171 3/8	27 3/8	26 5/8	26 0/8	8	8	Jefferson County	WI	Gary Moyer	1987	606
171 3/8	24 1/8	24 7/8	18 5/8	6	6	Sangamon County	IL	Michael R. Vincent	1991	606
171 3/8	23 7/8	24 2/8	15 5/8	6	5	Johnson County	KS	Dave Ward	1993	606
171 3/8	27 2/8	27 0/8	17 7/8	5	5	Charles County	MD	Patrick E. Langley	1997	606
171 3/8	28 2/8	27 5/8	18 5/8	8	5	Logan County	WV	Terry McGrady	1997	606
171 3/8	25 7/8	27 2/8	19 3/8	5	5	Dearborn County	IN	Nick T. Lobenstein	2001	606
171 3/8	24 3/8	25 7/8	19 5/8	5	5	Anderson County	KS	Bob Cutshaw	2001	606
171 3/8	27 2/8	27 1/8	24 1/8	5	5	Randolph County	IL	James E. Mraz	2003	606
*171 3/8	26 3/8	26 6/8	17 6/8	7	6	Hamilton County	OH	Wayne Bolton	2007	606
*171 3/8	26 6/8	27 1/8	19 5/8	7	7	Warren County	IA	Michael Leih	2008	606
171 3/8	26 0/8	26 5/8	16 3/8	5	5	Moniteau County	MO	Donald L. Welch	2008	606
171 3/8	26 0/8	26 0/8	24 1/8	5	5	Clay County	IN	Travis L. Nicosin	2009	606
171 2/8	25 1/8	23 2/8	20 6/8	5	6	Adams County	IA	Gary D. Maatsch	1990	621
171 2/8	25 0/8	25 5/8	20 2/8	5	5	Bartholomew County	IN	Gary Owsley	1995	621
171 2/8	25 5/8	25 7/8	19 2/8	5	5	Sedgwick County	KS	Julio C. Lazcano	1995	621
171 2/8	25 5/8	25 7/8	21 7/8	5	6	Jefferson County	WI	Fred Koehn	1996	621
171 2/8	25 6/8	24 5/8	18 2/8	5	5	Benton County	IA	Tim McLaud	1997	621
171 2/8	27 1/8	28 7/8	22 0/8	7	7	Madison County	OH	Bart Howerton	2000	621
171 2/8	23 2/8	25 2/8	24 4/8	6	7	Scott County	IA	Jeffrey R. Coonts	2002	621
171 2/8	25 4/8	26 2/8	19 4/8	5	5	Buffalo County	WI	Mark Ferman	2003	621
*171 2/8	26 2/8	26 3/8	18 0/8	8	5	Lake County	IN	Todd Jenkins	2009	621
171 2/8	25 0/8	24 4/8	17 2/8	6	6	Winnebago County	WI	Anthony Kapral	2009	621
171 1/8	26 3/8	26 4/8	20 5/8	5	5	Itasca County	MN	John Parmeter	1964	631
171 1/8	23 5/8	24 0/8	16 7/8	6	6	Piatt County	IL	Ronald E. Waugh	1971	631
171 1/8	24 3/8	23 2/8	17 4/8	8	7	Morton County	ND	Tony Schatz	1974	631
171 1/8	25 2/8	24 2/8	21 1/8	6	6	Tazewell County	IL	John P. Condis	1987	631
171 1/8	27 0/8	25 6/8	18 3/8	5	6	Bourbon County	KS	Larry Daly	1988	631
171 1/8	25 3/8	25 2/8	20 1/8	5	5	Clark County	OH	Lafayette Boggs III	1991	631
171 1/8	25 7/8	25 3/8	20 3/8	5	5	McHenry County	IL	Mike Fischer	1993	631
171 1/8	25 2/8	24 6/8	18 4/8	8	7	Sauk County	WI	Dave Zimmerman	1999	631
171 1/8	27 6/8	29 0/8	18 3/8	5	6	Ripley County	IN	Domenick Mitchell	2003	631
*171 1/8	24 4/8	25 2/8	20 7/8	5	5	Menard County	IL	Mike G. Staggs	2004	631
171 1/8	25 0/8	24 6/8	18 3/8	5	5	Outagamie County	WI	Richard J. Verkuilen	2004	631
*171 1/8	28 0/8	29 2/8	22 2/8	6	9	Mille Lacs County	MN	David Piatz	2006	631
171 1/8	25 7/8	26 1/8	18 4/8	6	6	Livingston County	MO	Brett Dawkins	2007	631
171 1/8	26 0/8	25 7/8	22 5/8	5	5	Davis County	IA	David R. Byrd	2007	631
*171 1/8	23 1/8	23 2/8	18 5/8	5	5	Posey County	IN	Ethan Paul	2007	631
*171 1/8	28 3/8	29 5/8	24 2/8	7	7	Dubuque County	IA	Mitch McDermott	2007	631
*171 1/8	24 6/8	25 4/8	16 2/8	9	9	Davis County	IA	Greg Sims	2008	631
171 1/8	29 6/8	29 7/8	23 3/8	5	5	Warren County	IL	Ernest Girdley	2009	631
171 0/8	30 0/8	27 5/8	19 5/8	5	8	Belmont County	OH	Charles J. Wilson	1979	649
171 0/8	27 4/8	27 4/8	22 2/8	5	5	Parke County	IN	Fred Sills	1985	649
171 0/8	24 7/8	24 7/8	21 1/8	7	7	Kleberg County	TX	Darwin D. Baucum	1994	649
171 0/8	26 5/8	26 5/8	18 4/8	5	5	Minnehaha County	SD	Carl L. Murra	1996	649
171 0/8	26 4/8	27 0/8	19 0/8	6	7	Becker County	MN	Jeff Holmer	1998	649
171 0/8	27 4/8	27 7/8	21 3/8	7	7	Shawano County	WI	Joel Gehm	2002	649
171 0/8	25 1/8	26 5/8	19 6/8	5	5	Rock Island County	IL	Scott Kave	2003	649
171 0/8	25 2/8	25 2/8	20 4/8	5	6	Fulton County	IL	Michael C. Vaka	2003	649
171 0/8	27 0/8	27 4/8	20 6/8	8	7	Wabaunsee County	KS	Dylan Smith	2005	649
171 0/8	27 3/8	27 1/8	19 0/8	6	7	Baltimore County	MD	Andrew Hacke	2006	649
*171 0/8	26 1/8	26 3/8	20 7/8	8	7	Decatur County	IA	Mike Buckingham	2006	649
171 0/8	27 7/8	27 4/8	21 3/8	7	10	Warren County	OH	Tim Bishop	2006	649
*171 0/8	26 1/8	26 7/8	17 2/8	6	5	Taylor County	WI	Todd Frombach	2010	649
170 7/8	27 6/8	27 5/8	18 4/8	6	8	Republic County	KS	Carroll Couture	1986	662
170 7/8	27 4/8	28 4/8	21 4/8	7	8	Leavenworth County	KS	Jacob W. Dragieff	1987	662
170 7/8	25 6/8	25 7/8	22 1/8	6	6	Bureau County	IL	Steve W. Hayes	1990	662
170 7/8	27 0/8	27 3/8	19 1/8	6	5	Mercer County	WV	Billy Bishop	1999	662

362

WHITETAIL DEER (TYPICAL ANTLERS)

Minimum Score 125   Continued

SCORE	LENGTH OF R MAIN BEAM L	INSIDE SPREAD	NUMBER OF R POINTS L	AREA	STATE/ PROVINCE	HUNTER'S NAME	DATE	RANK
170 7/8	24 7/8 24 4/8	18 1/8	5 5	Clark County	KS	Lynn Leonard	1999	662
170 7/8	25 6/8 25 4/8	20 6/8	6 7	Pierce County	WI	Donnie G. Frandrup	2002	662
170 7/8	23 7/8 23 7/8	20 1/8	5 5	Clark County	KS	Paul Sims	2003	662
*170 7/8	26 5/8 26 7/8	20 6/8	7 7	Pepin County	WI	John Biederman	2006	662
*170 7/8	25 1/8 24 5/8	16 7/8	5 6	Richland County	IL	Mike Wilson	2007	662
170 7/8	24 5/8 25 5/8	17 6/8	6 6	Lake County	IL	John R. Hoffman	2009	662
170 7/8	24 2/8 23 3/8	17 1/8	7 7	Worth County	MO	Jeffrey C. Lewis	2009	662
*170 7/8	25 1/8 25 3/8	15 5/8	7 6	Tuscarawas County	OH	Keith Yutzy	2009	662
170 6/8	26 1/8 25 3/8	17 4/8	5 5	Mitchell County	IA	Dan Block	1981	674
170 6/8	26 7/8 28 1/8	19 6/8	5 5	Racine County	WI	Anthony J Wozniak	1985	674
170 6/8	24 5/8 23 5/8	14 6/8	6 7	Jackson County	MI	Richard J. Galicki	1991	674
170 6/8	28 4/8 26 7/8	18 7/8	5 6	Tazewell County	IL	Steve R. Larimore	1995	674
170 6/8	24 6/8 25 3/8	15 4/8	6 5	Decatur County	IA	Mark Boswell	1996	674
170 6/8	26 0/8 28 0/8	20 6/8	6 6	Greene County	IN	Jesse D. Yeryar	2001	674
170 6/8	25 7/8 25 1/8	20 0/8	5 6	Morrison County	MN	Robert Durant	2003	674
170 6/8	25 7/8 25 5/8	19 1/8	7 6	Jones County	IA	Mark Stahlberg	2003	674
170 6/8	25 1/8 24 4/8	19 2/8	5 5	Parke County	IN	Mike Vore	2005	674
*170 6/8	23 4/8 25 5/8	17 6/8	9 7	Cedar County	IA	Scott Shulista	2006	674
170 6/8	29 0/8 28 4/8	16 4/8	5 6	Monroe County	IA	Kevin Yonkura	2008	674
170 6/8	24 0/8 24 2/8	17 2/8	6 7	Butler County	KS	David R. Rogers	2008	674
*170 6/8	28 2/8 27 3/8	19 2/8	4 4	Guthrie County	IA	Darren L. Osche	2009	674
170 5/8	26 3/8 25 5/8	18 3/8	5 6	Vermilion County	IL	Mark Pittman	1980	687
170 5/8	23 6/8 23 4/8	16 5/8	6 6	Teton County	MT	James R. Dean	1983	687
170 5/8	26 1/8 26 2/8	18 5/8	7 5	Schuyler County	MO	Mike Meinhardt	1989	687
170 5/8	25 7/8 25 5/8	22 4/8	6 5	Brown County	IL	Timothy I. Burkins	1992	687
170 5/8	24 7/8 25 7/8	17 1/8	5 5	Ogle County	IL	Dick V. Lalowski	1992	687
170 5/8	28 5/8 28 0/8	18 7/8	6 7	Mason County	IL	Doug Jallas	1994	687
170 5/8	26 5/8 28 0/8	17 4/8	7 5	Montgomery County	MD	Scott Wilson	1995	687
170 5/8	26 4/8 25 3/8	18 2/8	6 6	Spruce Lake	SAS	Shaun Bleakney	1996	687
170 5/8	26 6/8 27 5/8	20 1/8	6 6	Williamsburg County	SC	A. Hugh Gaskins	1998	687
170 5/8	27 5/8 29 0/8	18 4/8	6 7	Pickaway County	OH	Douglas L. Falter	2000	687
170 5/8	27 3/8 27 7/8	18 1/8	5 5	Fond du Lac County	WI	Victor Ketchpaw	2000	687
170 5/8	26 1/8 26 4/8	19 5/8	7 6	Mason County	IL	Randall Ballard	2001	687
*170 5/8	25 5/8 26 0/8	17 5/8	6 5	Walworth County	WI	Jeff Hynous	2003	687
170 5/8	29 7/8 30 6/8	23 3/8	5 4	Highland County	OH	Bruce Thompson	2006	687
*170 5/8	26 1/8 24 4/8	18 3/8	5 5	Jessamine County	KY	Danny Preston, Jr.	2007	687
170 5/8	29 1/8 29 5/8	20 0/8	6 4	Morgan County	IN	Michael L. Ikemire	2008	687
170 4/8	25 1/8 25 4/8	20 2/8	5 4	Des Moines County	IA	Bob Fudge	1966	703
170 4/8	25 3/8 24 7/8	20 0/8	6 6	Vilas County	WI	Rick R. Lax	1990	703
170 4/8	26 3/8 26 0/8	19 6/8	5 5	Rock Island County	IL	Joseph V. De Schepper	1991	703
170 4/8	29 0/8 29 3/8	19 1/8	6 5	Cerro Gordo County	IA	Chuck Harris	1991	703
170 4/8	24 6/8 24 5/8	18 0/8	7 7	Pawnee County	NE	Kenneth C. Mort	1991	703
170 4/8	26 1/8 26 5/8	21 5/8	6 8	Livingston County	IL	Alan Gray	1994	703
170 4/8	25 6/8 26 0/8	25 0/8	5 5	Marion County	IA	Henry Moore	1994	703
170 4/8	25 6/8 25 1/8	21 3/8	5 6	Geauga County	OH	Noah R. Troyer	2000	703
170 4/8	27 6/8 28 7/8	19 4/8	7 6	Licking County	OH	Mark E. McCoy	2002	703
170 4/8	26 2/8 26 2/8	18 0/8	6 7	Schuyler County	IL	Rocky Griggs	2003	703
170 4/8	23 5/8 23 4/8	18 5/8	6 6	Otter Tail County	MN	Rick S. Miller	2004	703
170 4/8	26 7/8 25 5/8	19 0/8	5 5	Peoria County	IL	Terry Setterlund	2005	703
*170 4/8	26 5/8 25 6/8	19 0/8	5 5	Morgan County	IL	Bradley Fricke	2006	703
170 4/8	26 2/8 25 6/8	23 6/8	6 7	Hocking County	OH	John Westhoven	2006	703
*170 4/8	23 3/8 23 1/8	24 1/8	6 7	Trempealeau County	WI	Matthew G. Galewski	2007	703
170 4/8	24 3/8 25 4/8	19 4/8	6 6	Neosho County	KS	David L. Bailey	2008	703
170 4/8	26 5/8 28 1/8	20 0/8	5 5	Erie County	NY	Stephen Hess	2008	703
*170 4/8	26 2/8 25 6/8	24 4/8	4 4	Jackson County	IL	Josh Shelton	2009	703
170 3/8	28 5/8 28 2/8	21 6/8	6 4	Hall County	NE	Gust Bergman	1965	721
170 3/8	25 5/8 26 3/8	17 7/8	6 5	Decatur County	IA	Julian Toney	1982	721
170 3/8	27 0/8 26 1/8	20 3/8	5 5	Ogle County	IL	John E. Lawson	1985	721
170 3/8	27 3/8 28 4/8	18 5/8	7 6	Howard County	IA	Clarence Mincks	1991	721
170 3/8	27 4/8 27 6/8	22 2/8	6 7	Crawford County	KS	Dave E. Onelio	1994	721
170 3/8	26 3/8 26 2/8	20 1/8	5 6	Pierce County	WI	Timothy B. Hasty	1994	721
170 3/8	25 4/8 24 7/8	16 7/8	6 7	Pulaski County	IL	Andrew French III	1995	721
170 3/8	23 0/8 23 2/8	17 3/8	6 6	McHenry County	IL	Donald E. Hoey	1996	721
170 3/8	26 6/8 27 2/8	22 4/8	6 6	Jo Daviess County	IL	Cliff Perry	1998	721
170 3/8	26 0/8 25 6/8	18 7/8	6 6	E. Carroll Parish	LA	David Roselle	1998	721
170 3/8	25 4/8 24 7/8	19 6/8	6 6	Washington County	MN	David Flipp	2001	721
170 3/8	26 6/8 25 2/8	19 3/8	5 6	Benton County	MO	Gary Brandes	2003	721
170 3/8	24 4/8 25 4/8	18 2/8	5 6	Fond du Lac County	WI	Andrew Leonard	2005	721
170 3/8	26 0/8 26 2/8	20 4/8	8 8	Barber County	KS	David Downard	2006	721
*170 3/8	25 2/8 25 4/8	19 3/8	7 8	Carlyle	SAS	David Blaise	2008	721
170 3/8	28 3/8 26 7/8	21 7/8	6 6	Tippecanoe County	IN	Steven R. Rider	2009	721
*170 3/8	27 6/8 28 2/8	20 5/8	4 4	Adams County	IL	Luke G. Terstriep	2009	721
170 3/8	23 6/8 23 3/8	16 3/8	5 5	Golden Valley County	ND	Brandon Zinne	2010	721
*170 3/8	25 7/8 26 2/8	21 3/8	6 6	Renville County	ND	Charles C. Duchsherer	2010	721
170 2/8	27 1/8 27 2/8	21 0/8	4 4	Lee County	AL	George P. Mann	1980	740
170 2/8	25 4/8 26 1/8	19 1/8	5 6	Clayton County	IA	Myles Keller	1989	740
170 2/8	26 0/8 25 4/8	19 1/8	8 8	Hocking County	OH	Kim Stevelt	1992	740
170 2/8	24 2/8 24 3/8	19 5/8	6 7	Crowley County	CO	Judy F. Hallman	1993	740
170 2/8	24 0/8 24 6/8	18 6/8	6 6	Davis County	IA	Chuck Riggenbach	1997	740
170 2/8	26 3/8 26 1/8	18 4/8	8 8	Hubbard County	MN	Michael E. Greetan	1998	740
170 2/8	26 0/8 25 5/8	16 4/8	7 5	Christian County	KY	Brian Oatts	1999	740
170 2/8	24 7/8 24 2/8	21 0/8	5 6	Polk County	WI	Les Mortimer	1999	740
170 2/8	23 4/8 23 7/8	17 2/8	6 6	Lake County	IL	Jeff Keller	2002	740
170 2/8	26 2/8 27 0/8	21 0/8	6 6	Maverick County	TX	Rex Dacus	2003	740
170 2/8	23 6/8 24 0/8	16 6/8	6 5	Rockyview	ALB	Gene Parent	2004	740
170 2/8	25 2/8 25 4/8	23 0/8	6 5	Hendricks County	IN	Ray Eldredge	2004	740
170 2/8	25 4/8 23 6/8	18 0/8	5 5	Edgar County	IL	Joseph T. Hankins	2004	740
170 2/8	28 4/8 28 3/8	23 5/8	4 5	Lawrence County	OH	Gregory A. Sullivan	2007	740
170 2/8	22 4/8 22 7/8	16 5/8	6 5	Miller County	MO	Henry T. Rallo, Jr.	2007	740
*170 2/8	26 5/8 26 6/8	19 6/8	5 5	Stafford County	KS	Darrell Wright	2007	740
170 2/8	22 1/8 22 7/8	15 4/8	6 6	La Crosse County	WI	Mark W. Viner	2009	740
170 1/8	26 1/8 27 1/8	22 1/8	5 5	Edwards County	KS	Jay Schaller	1968	757
170 1/8	25 4/8 25 7/8	22 2/8	6 7	Winona County	MN	Roger Traxler	1980	757
170 1/8	25 6/8 25 2/8	21 3/8	5 5	Mower County	MN	Robert D. Plumb	1984	757
170 1/8	26 7/8 26 0/8	20 7/8	5 6	Harford County	MD	Ed Garrison	1987	757

WHITETAIL DEER (TYPICAL ANTLERS)

Minimum Score 125 — Continued

SCORE	LENGTH OF R MAIN BEAM L	INSIDE SPREAD	NUMBER OF R POINTS L		AREA	STATE/ PROVINCE	HUNTER'S NAME	DATE	RANK
170 1/8	25 4/8 26 4/8	17 4/8	10	8	Washington County	IA	Marlin Derby	1987	757
170 1/8	26 0/8 26 4/8	18 1/8	7	6	Miami County	KS	Keith Groshong	1988	757
170 1/8	23 3/8 27 4/8	20 5/8	5	5	Racine County	WI	Michael H. Poeschel	1989	757
170 1/8	25 0/8 27 0/8	19 3/8	5	5	Winnebago County	IA	Matthew Modeland	1990	757
170 1/8	26 6/8 26 4/8	24 2/8	6	6	La Crosse County	WI	Scott R. Wavra	1991	757
170 1/8	28 2/8 27 4/8	22 3/8	6	5	Lake County	IL	John W. Schnider	1992	757
170 1/8	27 1/8 26 0/8	21 7/8	6	6	Henry County	IL	Dave Oleson	1994	757
170 1/8	25 3/8 27 2/8	17 0/8	5	6	Dunn County	WI	Clarence Janota	1995	757
170 1/8	24 6/8 24 2/8	21 3/8	6	7	Otter Tail County	MN	Randy Litke	1995	757
170 1/8	25 4/8 24 3/8	19 5/8	6	6	Ashland County	OH	Steve Orchard	1996	757
170 1/8	24 0/8 24 2/8	19 7/8	7	5	Monona County	IA	John Marinaccio	1997	757
170 1/8	27 2/8 26 5/8	19 2/8	7	7	Kleberg County	TX	Robert Nichols	1997	757
170 1/8	24 6/8 23 6/8	18 1/8	6	6	Kenedy County	TX	Jarred W. Peeples	1998	757
170 1/8	25 0/8 24 7/8	19 1/8	5	5	Prowers County	CO	Jim Matuszewski	1998	757
170 1/8	25 7/8 26 4/8	16 7/8	7	6	Lake of the Woods County	MN	Kevin Olson	2000	757
170 1/8	25 4/8 26 0/8	19 7/8	5	6	Buffalo County	WI	Dan Folkedahl	2000	757
170 1/8	24 1/8 24 2/8	20 6/8	6	6	Lincoln County	SD	Brian Larson	2001	757
170 1/8	25 6/8 22 6/8	20 0/8	6	8	Kane County	IL	Paul Mazur	2003	757
170 1/8	24 3/8 25 0/8	15 6/8	6	6	Hartney	MAN	Brett Hermanson	2006	757
170 1/8	24 6/8 25 3/8	21 5/8	6	7	Eau Claire County	WI	Kevin D. Schippers	2007	757
170 1/8	25 0/8 26 0/8	18 4/8	7	6	Dodge County	WI	Travis Pasbrig	2008	757
170 1/8	24 7/8 24 6/8	20 3/8	5	5	Clinton County	KY	Richard L. Richardson	2009	757
170 0/8	26 1/8 26 6/8	20 0/8	5	5	Scott County	KS	Monte L. Barker	1973	783
170 0/8	29 4/8 29 0/8	20 4/8	6	6	Puslinch Township	ONT	Richard Foss	1980	783
170 0/8	28 0/8 28 6/8	19 5/8	6	5	Jo Daviess County	IL	Bart Blocklinger	1982	783
170 0/8	25 1/8 24 7/8	19 1/8	8	8	Plymouth County	IA	David Erdmann	1987	783
170 0/8	25 1/8 25 5/8	19 6/8	5	5	Battle River	SAS	Gordon Stefanuk	1989	783
170 0/8	26 0/8 27 0/8	19 4/8	6	5	Jackson County	MI	Michael D. Fitzgerald	1990	783
170 0/8	25 4/8 23 4/8	21 0/8	5	5	Harvey County	KS	Dan Stahl	1991	783
170 0/8	28 7/8 27 3/8	23 1/8	5	6	McHenry County	IL	Daniel Doherty	1992	783
170 0/8	25 4/8 26 7/8	25 1/8	5	8	Wabaunsee County	KS	Henry C. Boss II	1995	783
170 0/8	28 4/8 27 2/8	21 6/8	5	5	Cross County	AR	Clay Bassham	1996	783
170 0/8	24 6/8 25 4/8	19 2/8	5	5	Kane County	IL	Brad Lundsteen	1998	783
170 0/8	29 3/8 28 6/8	18 0/8	6	6	Neosho County	KS	Frank Pechacek	1999	783
170 0/8	26 3/8 25 5/8	18 6/8	5	5	Marion County	KS	Travis R. Sargents	2002	783
170 0/8	24 7/8 25 3/8	16 4/8	5	5	Waupaca County	WI	Richard A. Hedtke	2003	783
170 0/8	23 7/8 27 4/8	24 2/8	6	7	Kingman County	KS	Nick C. White	2004	783
*170 0/8	24 2/8 24 4/8	18 0/8	8	6	Jennings County	IN	Chris Fischvogt	2006	783
170 0/8	26 1/8 25 1/8	21 4/8	5	5	Iowa County	WI	Gary L. Johannsen	2007	783
170 0/8	23 7/8 24 6/8	19 6/8	6	6	Washington County	AR	Michael Franks	2007	783
*170 0/8	24 1/8 25 4/8	19 3/8	6	7	Clark County	MO	John Miller	2008	783
169 7/8	25 7/8 25 3/8	17 2/8	6	7	Neosho County	KS	Matt R. Morgan	1992	802
169 7/8	24 4/8 24 4/8	22 3/8	5	5	Walworth County	WI	James W. May	1995	802
169 7/8	25 0/8 24 6/8	19 7/8	5	5	La Salle	MAN	Maurice Trudeau	1998	802
*169 7/8	27 3/8 28 1/8	21 5/8	5	7	Wabash County	IL	Chris Johnson	2004	802
169 7/8	28 0/8 28 2/8	19 7/8	4	4	Sullivan County	NY	Domenick DeMaria	2005	802
169 6/8	26 0/8 27 3/8	20 6/8	4	4	Decatur County	IA	Bruce Jermyn	1979	807
169 6/8	29 6/8 29 2/8	27 0/8	6	6	Coffey County	KS	Jack McCullough	1984	807
169 6/8	26 5/8 26 5/8	16 5/8	5	6	Cass County	IL	Don Coufal	1988	807
169 6/8	26 7/8 26 7/8	24 3/8	7	6	Wyoming County	WV	James Blankenship	1994	807
169 6/8	25 5/8 26 4/8	22 3/8	6	6	Monroe County	WI	Timothy E. Slonka	1994	807
169 6/8	23 5/8 23 2/8	16 4/8	5	6	Warren County	IA	Nicholas Romano	1997	807
169 6/8	26 4/8 26 5/8	17 6/8	6	9	Carberry	MAN	Lance Schultz	2002	807
169 6/8	23 7/8 21 7/8	19 0/8	6	7	Cumberland County	IL	Brad Metcalf	2003	807
169 6/8	24 1/8 24 7/8	20 4/8	7	6	Bearspaw	ALB	Bry Loyd	2006	807
*169 6/8	27 4/8 28 3/8	26 2/8	5	5	Somerset County	PA	Justin S. Keith	2008	807
169 5/8	24 0/8 23 4/8	22 1/8	6	7	Neosho County	KS	Jeff Friederich	1992	817
169 5/8	26 4/8 26 2/8	22 1/8	5	5	Fremont County	IA	Chris Barton	2002	817
169 5/8	22 4/8 22 2/8	14 6/8	6	7	Burleigh County	ND	Tracy Whitney	2005	817
169 5/8	26 3/8 27 3/8	18 3/8	5	5	Cass County	IL	Jake Van Linn	2006	817
169 4/8	23 7/8 25 2/8	17 7/8	6	7	Charles Mix County	SD	Dan Carda	1974	821
169 4/8	24 6/8 24 6/8	18 7/8	7	7	Hennepin County	MN	Mark Kirkwold	1989	821
169 4/8	23 3/8 24 6/8	17 2/8	6	6	Harvey County	KS	Ron Hershberger	1989	821
169 4/8	26 0/8 25 4/8	22 4/8	7	6	Rock Island County	IL	Leo Hoogerwerf	1990	821
169 4/8	24 6/8 24 6/8	19 2/8	5	5	Lafayette County	WI	E. Michael Kitra	1991	821
169 4/8	26 3/8 26 3/8	20 0/8	7	7	Grundy County	IL	Robert Alfonso Jr.	1996	821
169 4/8	28 2/8 28 6/8	14 3/8	6	5	Boone County	KY	Tim Adams	1998	821
169 4/8	27 3/8 25 7/8	19 2/8	7	5	Langlade County	WI	Nicholas Steger	1999	821
169 4/8	27 6/8 27 4/8	22 2/8	5	6	Cook County	IL	Richard Bielik, Sr.	1999	821
169 4/8	25 6/8 26 4/8	23 2/8	5	6	Harper County	KS	Cecil L. Hatcher	2000	821
169 4/8	23 2/8 23 1/8	17 4/8	7	6	Spencer County	KY	Keith King	2001	821
*169 4/8	26 2/8 25 4/8	18 7/8	5	6	Marathon County	WI	Scott Venzke	2005	821
*169 4/8	26 3/8 26 1/8	20 2/8	5	5	Dickinson County	KS	Ron Fitch	2008	821
169 4/8	25 5/8 25 0/8	17 2/8	5	6	Van Buren County	IA	Bryan Scott Perry	2008	821
169 4/8	26 0/8 27 4/8	21 5/8	5	6	Knox County	IL	Don Owen	2009	821
169 3/8	23 5/8 24 5/8	19 2/8	7	7	Perry County	IN	Ronald J. Phillips	1973	836
169 3/8	27 1/8 27 5/8	22 1/8	5	5	Hamilton County	OH	Christopher J. Ludwig	1990	836
169 3/8	27 5/8 27 2/8	20 5/8	6	6	Knox County	IL	Robert J. Hinckley	1991	836
169 3/8	25 2/8 24 7/8	20 5/8	6	6	Niagara Township	ONT	Andre' Secco	1992	836
169 3/8	25 5/8 24 2/8	17 5/8	7	7	Dakota County	MN	Tom Leach	1993	836
169 3/8	27 7/8 28 4/8	19 5/8	5	7	Jefferson County	WI	Mark S. Chesney	1994	836
169 3/8	28 1/8 26 1/8	20 7/8	6	6	Goodhue County	MN	Marv Betcher	1996	836
169 3/8	25 6/8 25 6/8	18 4/8	6	7	Christian County	KY	Kelly Slone	1999	836
169 3/8	25 2/8 24 0/8	20 1/8	6	6	Guthrie County	IA	Michael Henry	2003	836
*169 3/8	25 3/8 25 4/8	19 1/8	6	5	Scott County	IN	Mark Hildebrand	2004	836
*169 3/8	26 4/8 25 6/8	20 6/8	7	8	Knox County	IL	Carl Hunt	2004	836
169 3/8	25 1/8 25 3/8	19 1/8	7	6	Hancock County	IL	Robert Zalkus	2007	836
*169 3/8	24 4/8 25 4/8	17 2/8	6	6	Posey County	IN	Paul Murray	2008	836
169 3/8	25 3/8 25 5/8	19 5/8	5	5	Buffalo County	WI	Steve Ritscher	2008	836
169 2/8	26 1/8 27 2/8	21 6/8	6	5	Ashland County	OH	Darrell Huff	1985	850
169 2/8	25 4/8 25 2/8	19 7/8	6	5	McLean County	IL	Arthur L. Garrson	1992	850
169 2/8	25 1/8 24 6/8	21 4/8	5	5	Lee County	IL	Paul Harmon	1995	850
169 2/8	28 1/8 26 7/8	20 2/8	5	5	Woodson County	KS	Clint Shockley	1997	850
169 2/8	26 7/8 26 2/8	23 2/8	5	6	Oregon County	MO	Woodrow J. Parrott	1999	850
169 2/8	27 1/8 26 6/8	19 0/8	5	5	Hopkins County	KY	William Poe	2002	850

364

WHITETAIL DEER (TYPICAL ANTLERS)

Minimum Score 125   Continued

SCORE	LENGTH OF R MAIN BEAM L		INSIDE SPREAD	NUMBER OF R POINTS L		AREA	STATE/ PROVINCE	HUNTER'S NAME	DATE	RANK
169 2/8	26 4/8	26 7/8	19 6/8	7	6	Harlan County	NE	Darrell Jones	2002	850
169 2/8	26 1/8	26 2/8	21 5/8	5	6	Drumbo	ONT	Daryl Koch	2004	850
*169 2/8	24 0/8	23 1/8	17 6/8	5	5	Clayton County	IA	Steven V. Hansel	2004	850
169 2/8	21 4/8	22 2/8	15 0/8	7	7	Kenedy County	TX	Mickey W. Hellickson	2004	850
*169 2/8	26 5/8	27 2/8	21 0/8	5	5	Warren County	IL	Larry Shepard	2006	850
*169 2/8	25 0/8	24 4/8	19 0/8	6	5	Wyoming County	WV	Michael Workman	2007	850
169 2/8	26 2/8	25 6/8	18 5/8	5	6	Mingo County	WV	Charles Wellman	2008	850
169 2/8	25 2/8	26 2/8	18 7/8	5	6	Juneau County	WI	John P. Mooney	2009	850
169 1/8	28 6/8	28 2/8	19 3/8	6	5	La Salle County	IL	Dave Mrowicki	1985	864
169 1/8	26 7/8	27 2/8	19 2/8	7	7	Parkland	ALB	Allan Gates	1995	864
169 1/8	25 3/8	25 4/8	21 5/8	6	5	Barber County	KS	Tom Langford	1998	864
169 1/8	25 3/8	27 0/8	19 7/8	7	8	Rock County	WI	Curtis Wallisch	2000	864
169 1/8	25 3/8	26 2/8	18 1/8	5	5	Pike County	IL	Steve M. Schuwerk	2003	864
169 1/8	26 0/8	27 4/8	17 2/8	10	6	Holmes County	OH	Aaron Day	2005	864
*169 1/8	26 3/8	26 6/8	17 5/8	5	5	Gallatin County	IL	David Carver	2007	864
169 0/8	25 6/8	26 0/8	18 0/8	7	5	Warren County	IA	Brad Vonk	1980	871
169 0/8	25 5/8	25 2/8	20 5/8	5	6	Marion County	KS	Max Williams	1985	871
169 0/8	27 2/8	26 7/8	22 2/8	5	5	Grant County	WI	Richard Hein	1986	871
169 0/8	24 5/8	25 6/8	20 3/8	6	7	Lyon County	KS	Steve Coe	1996	871
169 0/8	28 3/8	28 2/8	20 1/8	6	7	Metcalfe County	KY	Buddy Gentry	1997	871
169 0/8	25 2/8	24 6/8	20 1/8	5	6	Renville County	MN	Pat Jenniges	1999	871
169 0/8	27 7/8	26 7/8	19 0/8	7	5	Sauk County	WI	Ken Gher	2002	871
*169 0/8	25 1/8	24 7/8	19 2/8	5	8	Washington County	IL	Jason McKinley	2004	871
*169 0/8	23 6/8	23 6/8	17 6/8	5	5	Buffalo County	WI	Ron Jilot	2004	871
*169 0/8	24 0/8	24 3/8	17 2/8	6	6	Scott County	IL	Doug Mosher	2004	871
169 0/8	23 7/8	24 6/8	17 1/8	6	7	Clark County	MO	Steve Gross	2007	871
*169 0/8	25 0/8	25 7/8	18 4/8	5	5	Cooper County	MO	Jerry Lee Masek	2007	871
*169 0/8	27 4/8	29 0/8	17 5/8	7	7	Clermont County	OH	Tom W. Barker	2008	871
*169 0/8	23 0/8	25 1/8	17 4/8	6	5	Manitowoc County	WI	Tom Schneider	2008	871
168 7/8	24 3/8	24 4/8	20 7/8	5	5	Jackson County	IA	Al Weidenbacher	1984	885
168 7/8	27 4/8	27 0/8	19 0/8	5	6	Washington County	MN	Ronald Jacobson	1985	885
168 7/8	22 1/8	22 5/8	22 1/8	6	5	Jefferson County	IL	Rudy Moore	1987	885
168 7/8	23 4/8	23 4/8	18 3/8	6	6	Allamakee County	IA	Patrick Schellsmidt	1993	885
168 7/8	24 6/8	28 6/8	18 7/8	7	7	Geauga County	OH	Dan Shrock	1998	885
168 7/8	31 4/8	30 5/8	19 7/8	5	6	Gallia County	OH	Philip Blaetz	2001	885
168 6/8	27 7/8	27 0/8	16 6/8	7	7	Muskingum County	OH	Gerald Shepler	1988	891
168 6/8	27 1/8	26 6/8	22 1/8	5	6	McLean County	IL	Willie Martin	1993	891
168 6/8	24 5/8	23 6/8	18 6/8	5	5	Fulton County	IL	Alan Miller	1996	891
168 6/8	25 5/8	24 2/8	20 2/8	5	5	Rawlins County	KS	Jim Brennan	1999	891
168 6/8	27 7/8	27 6/8	16 6/8	7	7	Hardin County	KY	Eddie Miller	2003	891
168 6/8	23 3/8	24 5/8	17 2/8	5	5	Lyon County	KS	Kirk Hammond	2005	891
168 6/8	27 0/8	25 3/8	20 3/8	5	9	Wapiti River	ALB	Terry Hagman	2006	891
168 6/8	25 7/8	26 2/8	17 4/8	6	5	Clermont County	OH	Matt Whalen	2007	891
*168 6/8	24 6/8	25 6/8	17 4/8	5	5	Butler County	OH	Timothy J. Smith	2008	891
168 6/8	22 5/8	22 7/8	17 6/8	6	6	Cass County	ND	Justin Newman	2009	891
168 5/8	26 2/8	26 0/8	18 5/8	5	6	Des Moines County	IA	Michael P. Anderson	1977	901
168 5/8	26 3/8	26 1/8	20 6/8	5	6	Mahoning County	OH	Jeff J Hartman	1984	901
168 5/8	25 0/8	24 5/8	17 1/8	7	7	Calhoun County	IL	Dennis A. Kendall	1985	901
168 5/8	25 7/8	25 7/8	22 1/8	5	5	Taylor County	WI	Bradley Cornell	1986	901
168 5/8	26 7/8	27 6/8	20 6/8	6	6	Hancock County	OH	Robert E. Ebert	1988	901
168 5/8	25 6/8	25 6/8	19 5/8	5	5	Winnebago County	IA	Jim Orthel	1990	901
168 5/8	26 0/8	26 1/8	18 3/8	8	7	Harrison County	KY	Sam Blackburn	1991	901
168 5/8	24 7/8	25 4/8	21 6/8	6	7	Delaware County	OH	Steve Downey	1994	901
168 5/8	25 7/8	26 4/8	17 3/8	7	6	Fountain County	IN	Scott James	1999	901
168 5/8	25 0/8	26 3/8	20 7/8	5	6	McDonough County	IL	Rick Balzer	1999	901
168 5/8	20 3/8	19 6/8	19 0/8	6	8	Lyon County	KY	Derek West	2000	901
168 5/8	24 1/8	23 4/8	17 6/8	8	5	Anderson County	KS	Kyle Evans	2002	901
168 5/8	27 2/8	27 0/8	17 4/8	6	5	Calhoun County	IL	Scott T. Krauser	2003	901
168 5/8	26 2/8	25 5/8	19 2/8	6	6	Nuckolls County	NE	Justin T. Lowery	2004	901
168 5/8	26 7/8	25 6/8	20 1/8	6	7	Marquette County	WI	Chad R. Kravick	2005	901
168 5/8	27 1/8	26 4/8	20 1/8	6	7	Bond County	IL	Brian Hulvey	2005	901
168 5/8	28 5/8	28 5/8	22 7/8	4	4	Benton County	IN	Jay E. Spitznagle	2007	901
168 5/8	26 1/8	26 6/8	19 3/8	6	6	Barber County	KS	Dwayne Boney	2007	901
168 5/8	26 3/8	26 0/8	21 4/8	6	9	Muscatine County	IA	Vince Gaeta, Jr.	2007	901
*168 5/8	25 4/8	25 4/8	19 1/8	5	5	Buffalo County	WI	Dan Ory	2008	901
168 4/8	24 0/8	24 7/8	18 6/8	5	5	Lincoln County	KS	Gerald Huehl	1985	921
168 4/8	23 7/8	23 4/8	16 6/8	6	5	Grayson County	KY	John David Johnson	1989	921
168 4/8	23 0/8	22 0/8	21 6/8	5	5	Carroll County	MD	Mark A. Robinson	1993	921
168 4/8	24 7/8	25 1/8	20 2/8	5	5	Buffalo County	WI	Jeffrey Fisher	1997	921
168 4/8	24 6/8	23 5/8	16 0/8	5	6	Johnson County	IA	Darrin Pelland	2004	921
*168 4/8	25 2/8	26 0/8	19 0/8	5	6	Chester County	PA	Jack A. Horosky	2005	921
*168 4/8	26 6/8	26 2/8	21 4/8	7	9	Douglas County	IL	George N. Hatchel	2006	921
*168 4/8	28 3/8	26 0/8	18 4/8	5	7	Macon County	IL	Glenn Williams	2006	921
168 4/8	26 2/8	26 2/8	16 4/8	5	5	Athens County	OH	Andrew D. Proseus	2008	921
168 4/8	26 0/8	25 4/8	18 4/8	6	5	Clay County	KY	Kevin Rice	2008	921
*168 4/8	23 4/8	23 4/8	15 6/8	5	5	Huntington County	IN	Lynn W. Gray	2008	921
*168 4/8	24 7/8	24 7/8	17 0/8	5	5	Madison County	IL	Troy Huffman	2008	921
168 3/8	25 1/8	26 1/8	19 5/8	5	5	Jefferson County	IL	Ben Howard	1988	933
168 3/8	25 0/8	24 6/8	19 3/8	5	5	Kingsbury County	SD	Donald B. Johnson	1989	933
168 3/8	24 6/8	25 2/8	21 3/8	6	7	Oconto County	WI	Peter M. Meeuwsen	1993	933
168 3/8	26 2/8	25 2/8	19 2/8	8	8	Shelby County	IL	Robert W. Bowman, Jr.	1993	933
168 3/8	26 1/8	25 6/8	22 6/8	6	5	Houston County	MN	Bruce C. Norton	1995	933
168 3/8	27 2/8	27 5/8	21 1/8	6	6	Outagamie County	WI	Rodney R. Schutt	1998	933
168 3/8	25 7/8	24 6/8	17 5/8	5	5	Trempealeau County	WI	Ross Lambert	2002	933
*168 3/8	27 5/8	26 5/8	18 5/8	5	6	St. Louis County	MN	Harland Haglin	2005	933
*168 3/8	25 2/8	25 3/8	18 1/8	5	6	Talbot County	MD	J. Richard Jablin	2005	933
*168 3/8	25 6/8	25 6/8	23 6/8	5	7	Henderson County	KY	Robert A. Cates	2009	933
168 3/8	24 2/8	24 2/8	17 5/8	5	5	Buffalo County	WI	Jeremy Brunner	2009	933
168 2/8	27 0/8	26 5/8	19 2/8	5	7	Cowley County	KS	Larry G. Gann	1975	944
168 2/8	25 0/8	24 4/8	21 2/8	5	5	Macon County	IL	Larry D. Smith	1985	944
168 2/8	27 2/8	26 7/8	20 4/8	5	6	Lyon County	KS	John R. Clifton	1985	944
168 2/8	25 4/8	25 1/8	20 3/8	7	5	Mercer County	KY	Steve Baxter	1989	944
168 2/8	24 1/8	25 0/8	17 4/8	5	5	Knox County	IL	Gale Harriman	1991	944
168 2/8	24 4/8	24 6/8	22 0/8	5	5	Piatt County	IL	Michael F. Bily	1996	944
168 2/8	27 2/8	27 4/8	22 0/8	5	6	Macon County	IL	Scott Hartman	2001	944

WHITETAIL DEER (TYPICAL ANTLERS)

Minimum Score 125 — Continued

SCORE	LENGTH OF R MAIN BEAM L	INSIDE SPREAD	NUMBER OF R POINTS L		AREA	STATE/ PROVINCE	HUNTER'S NAME	DATE	RANK
168 2/8	29 0/8	28 2/8	24 0/8	5	5	Mahoning County	OH	James C. Fleet	2007	944
168 2/8	25 5/8	24 7/8	16 6/8	6	6	Trempealeau County	WI	Aaron J. Bagniewski	2007	944
168 2/8	25 2/8	23 7/8	22 4/8	5	5	Champaign County	OH	Michael Maurice	2008	944
168 2/8	25 6/8	25 6/8	19 4/8	5	6	Juneau County	WI	Aaron E. Bigalke	2010	944
168 1/8	24 6/8	24 6/8	20 1/8	6	5	Murray County	MN	Marvin Brouwer	1971	955
168 1/8	27 0/8	27 7/8	20 1/8	6	6	Blue Earth County	MN	Rich Detjen	1984	955
168 1/8	26 6/8	26 0/8	18 0/8	6	6	Clearwater County	ID	Emerald Hutchins	1994	955
168 1/8	25 3/8	25 4/8	18 3/8	5	5	Dakota County	MN	Craig Gill	1996	955
168 1/8	25 3/8	26 0/8	19 0/8	7	7	Houston County	MN	Jay M. Crandall	1998	955
168 1/8	27 6/8	29 3/8	19 7/8	5	5	Marshall County	KS	Lance Stowell	1998	955
168 1/8	27 7/8	27 5/8	20 3/8	5	5	Sullivan County	NY	Domenick DeMaria	1999	955
168 1/8	28 7/8	29 2/8	19 5/8	7	9	Pike County	IL	Gary E. Gerhart	2001	955
168 1/8	26 1/8	25 5/8	19 1/8	6	5	Outagamie County	WI	Thomas Bessette	2002	955
*168 1/8	26 6/8	26 6/8	16 2/8	7	6	Warren County	IA	Bert Lynch	2003	955
*168 1/8	27 0/8	25 6/8	18 7/8	8	5	Vigo County	IN	Jonathan F. Pounds	2003	955
168 1/8	26 4/8	26 2/8	17 3/8	5	5	Dane County	WI	Greg A. Frisch	2006	955
*168 1/8	27 5/8	27 4/8	19 1/8	5	5	Cloud County	KS	John Carolan IV	2009	955
168 0/8	27 2/8	25 7/8	19 0/8	5	5	Vinton County	OH	Ronald E. Morgan	1978	968
168 0/8	26 0/8	25 6/8	19 1/8	10	5	Amherst County	VA	William Dixon Morgan	1980	968
168 0/8	25 4/8	23 7/8	15 6/8	7	7	De Witt County	IL	William R. Henson	1982	968
168 0/8	24 5/8	24 5/8	21 4/8	6	7	Jo Daviess County	IL	Dick Tasch	1989	968
168 0/8	25 1/8	26 1/8	18 2/8	5	5	Lincoln County	SD	Floyd McElroy	1996	968
168 0/8	23 3/8	25 4/8	16 6/8	6	7	Vigo County	IN	Marc E. Weaver	1999	968
168 0/8	26 6/8	26 6/8	22 4/8	6	6	Buffalo County	WI	John G. Erickson	2000	968
168 0/8	24 4/8	25 2/8	19 4/8	6	6	Westchester County	NY	Michael S. Abbruzzi	2004	968
*168 0/8	26 4/8	26 2/8	19 6/8	6	5	Doniphan County	KS	Todd Gray	2004	968
168 0/8	26 5/8	27 1/8	21 4/8	7	6	Greene County	IA	J. R. Miller	2004	968
167 7/8	27 6/8	27 7/8	21 2/8	6	6	Brown County	OH	David Grayson	1976	978
167 7/8	26 0/8	25 5/8	20 3/8	5	6	Clay County	IL	Tom Corry	1985	978
167 7/8	25 3/8	24 3/8	19 1/8	7	7	Bartholomew County	IN	Doug Shepherd	1990	978
167 7/8	27 5/8	27 4/8	24 0/8	8	7	Clark County	IA	Gregory A. Torode	1992	978
167 7/8	26 2/8	26 5/8	27 7/8	5	5	Mercer County	IL	Neil A. Hamerlinck	1993	978
167 7/8	23 7/8	23 3/8	20 5/8	6	6	Washington County	MN	John Bronk	1994	978
167 7/8	25 5/8	26 0/8	21 4/8	5	5	Tompkins County	NY	Paul F. Stone	1996	978
167 7/8	25 2/8	25 3/8	21 1/8	5	5	Bureau County	IL	Edward Joiner	1997	978
167 7/8	24 6/8	25 0/8	19 3/8	6	6	Mason County	IL	David Session	1997	978
167 7/8	29 5/8	28 3/8	18 6/8	5	7	Ross County	OH	David Miller	1999	978
167 7/8	27 4/8	26 0/8	20 6/8	7	7	Monroe County	IA	Terry C. Williams	1999	978
167 7/8	25 7/8	25 2/8	18 3/8	5	4	Laclede County	MO	James Hendrix	1999	978
167 7/8	23 6/8	23 2/8	17 0/8	6	8	Clay County	IN	Eric Ditmars	2001	978
167 7/8	26 3/8	25 6/8	20 7/8	5	5	Randolph County	IL	Larry Deutschmann	2002	978
167 7/8	27 1/8	27 1/8	22 0/8	6	9	Ashland County	WI	Thomas O. Griffith	2003	978
167 7/8	28 2/8	28 6/8	19 5/8	4	4	Winnebago County	WI	Ron Will	2007	978
167 7/8	22 6/8	23 4/8	17 5/8	5	6	Manitowoc County	WI	Walter Hansmann	2010	978
167 6/8	26 4/8	26 2/8	19 6/8	5	5	Monona County	IA	Douglas M. Bonine	1985	995
167 6/8	27 2/8	27 1/8	21 2/8	5	5	Coffey County	KS	Edward L. Bess	1985	995
167 6/8	25 0/8	25 4/8	21 3/8	6	5	Nelson County	KY	Wayne Bodine	1994	995
167 6/8	28 4/8	28 4/8	20 0/8	6	6	Auglaize County	OH	Gary L. Hughes	1994	995
167 6/8	25 5/8	23 7/8	19 0/8	6	6	Christian County	KY	Tommy Clark	1997	995
167 6/8	26 4/8	26 6/8	19 1/8	6	6	La Crosse County	WI	Stephen J. Rusch	1999	995
167 6/8	26 6/8	26 2/8	20 6/8	6	6	Marquette County	WI	Randy J. Gruber	1999	995
167 6/8	25 6/8	25 2/8	18 6/8	7	5	Rogers County	OK	Bert Jones	2002	995
167 6/8	25 0/8	24 2/8	17 1/8	7	5	Pierce County	WI	Doug Hines	2005	995
167 6/8	28 0/8	27 5/8	19 7/8	5	7	Dubuque County	IA	Joe Hill	2007	995
167 6/8	25 5/8	24 5/8	15 6/8	5	5	Trempealeau County	WI	Mark J. Lange	2008	995
167 6/8	26 7/8	25 7/8	21 5/8	6	5	Will County	IL	David Babich	2008	995
167 6/8	25 6/8	24 3/8	20 4/8	6	7	Sangamon County	IL	Andrew Clapper	2009	995
167 5/8	27 7/8	26 6/8	20 7/8	7	7	Chase County	KS	William E. Drummond	1984	1008
167 5/8	23 6/8	23 1/8	15 0/8	7	7	Meigs County	OH	Rick Bolin	1987	1008
167 5/8	24 0/8	24 1/8	17 7/8	5	5	Leavenworth County	KS	John W. Garrison	1990	1008
167 5/8	22 4/8	23 0/8	18 7/8	6	5	Washita County	OK	Alan Cooper	1991	1008
167 5/8	28 1/8	27 7/8	20 6/8	6	4	Macoupin County	IL	Justin Bonnell	1991	1008
167 5/8	29 0/8	29 0/8	19 2/8	7	5	Fulton County	IL	Robert A. Hammerich	1991	1008
167 5/8	25 2/8	24 2/8	17 6/8	5	6	Boone County	MO	Hosie E. Roberts, Jr.	1993	1008
167 5/8	27 6/8	28 2/8	18 6/8	5	6	Amherst Island	ONT	Bill Fenwick	1993	1008
167 5/8	26 6/8	26 7/8	18 1/8	7	7	Pittsburg County	OK	Brett Foster	1994	1008
167 5/8	23 4/8	24 5/8	24 1/8	6	5	Perry County	IL	Wilbur Engelhardt	1994	1008
167 5/8	26 2/8	29 4/8	20 2/8	6	7	Richland County	IL	Dennis Graves	1995	1008
167 5/8	25 3/8	26 0/8	19 5/8	5	5	Gallia County	OH	Dwane Rees	1995	1008
167 5/8	24 2/8	25 0/8	20 5/8	5	5	Geary County	KS	Jamie Farr	2001	1008
167 5/8	23 6/8	24 1/8	18 5/8	5	5	Vinton County	OH	Truman E. Wilson	2002	1008
167 5/8	23 0/8	23 4/8	19 6/8	5	6	Carrot River	SAS	Marvin Pinkowski	2004	1008
*167 5/8	26 6/8	27 1/8	22 7/8	5	5	Sullivan County	IN	Paul Pula, Jr.	2004	1008
167 5/8	25 3/8	26 1/8	19 3/8	6	8	Sangamon County	IL	Bill Bozarth	2004	1008
167 5/8	25 0/8	25 0/8	17 0/8	7	8	Adams County	IL	Matthew W. Hinkamper	2004	1008
167 5/8	25 6/8	25 7/8	19 3/8	6	6	Calhoun County	IL	Franklin Louie Justus	2004	1008
167 5/8	25 3/8	25 5/8	17 4/8	6	8	Douglas County	WI	Allen W. Michael, Jr.	2005	1008
167 4/8	22 4/8	23 1/8	18 4/8	5	5	Jefferson County	NE	Justin Niederklein	2009	1008
167 4/8	23 3/8	24 0/8	21 4/8	6	6	Washington County	KS	Bill R. Mallean	1974	1029
167 4/8	26 4/8	26 0/8	21 0/8	7	7	Coffey County	KS	Glen Stohs	1987	1029
167 4/8	26 6/8	26 0/8	19 4/8	6	5	Sawyer County	WI	Gary R. Christman	1989	1029
167 4/8	26 1/8	26 7/8	21 2/8	5	5	Winneshiek County	IA	Tom Gossman	1990	1029
167 4/8	27 0/8	26 5/8	18 7/8	5	6	Pike County	IL	Timothy Fulmer	1990	1029
167 4/8	23 3/8	23 2/8	17 2/8	5	6	Montgomery County	VA	Edward R. Sowers	1991	1029
167 4/8	26 7/8	26 7/8	17 7/8	7	8	Linn County	KS	Willard W. Wills III	1992	1029
167 4/8	26 0/8	24 3/8	18 6/8	5	5	Morgan County	IN	Steve Long	1995	1029
167 4/8	25 5/8	26 2/8	18 4/8	7	6	St. Clair County	IL	Joe Little	1997	1029
167 4/8	26 6/8	26 6/8	19 2/8	7	6	Dubuque County	IA	Doug Biermann	1997	1029
167 4/8	24 2/8	24 2/8	18 7/8	5	6	Decatur County	IN	Dan Caudill	1999	1029
167 4/8	25 2/8	25 3/8	23 0/8	5	5	Jackson County	WI	Christopher R. Boettcher	1999	1029
167 4/8	27 5/8	26 6/8	21 2/8	5	5	Ellsworth County	KS	Rod Buchholz	1999	1029
167 4/8	26 3/8	26 4/8	20 2/8	5	5	Buffalo County	WI	Jay Snopek	2000	1029
167 4/8	23 5/8	24 2/8	17 6/8	6	7	Trempealeau County	WI	Robert W. Olson	2006	1029
167 4/8	24 4/8	24 1/8	20 6/8	6	6	Ottawa County	KS	Scott M. Bill	2009	1029
167 4/8						Adams County	WI	Russell J. Rupert	2009	1029

366

WHITETAIL DEER (TYPICAL ANTLERS)

Minimum Score 125 — Continued

SCORE	R MAIN BEAM L	INSIDE SPREAD	R POINTS L		AREA	STATE/PROVINCE	HUNTER'S NAME	DATE	RANK
167 4/8	25 6/8 25 3/8	19 6/8	5	5	Lee County	GA	David Campbell	2009	1029
167 3/8	25 1/8 25 0/8	20 5/8	5	7	Sauk County	WI	Daniel Kaczmar	1985	1047
167 3/8	28 5/8 28 4/8	19 2/8	6	6	Sumner County	KS	Don Braddy	1986	1047
167 3/8	28 6/8 26 1/8	20 1/8	5	6	Coshocton County	OH	Harold E. Frank	1989	1047
167 3/8	24 6/8 24 2/8	19 3/8	5	5	Dawson County	MT	Jerry Fevold	1992	1047
167 3/8	25 7/8 26 2/8	23 1/8	5	5	Waukesha County	WI	Kelvin E. Sandel	1992	1047
167 3/8	28 5/8 27 6/8	19 5/8	5	5	Lake County	IL	Roger Redmond	1994	1047
167 3/8	25 7/8 26 6/8	18 3/8	6	5	Dakota County	NE	Kevin Hohenstein	1997	1047
167 3/8	27 1/8 27 2/8	19 5/8	5	6	Bristol County	MA	Paul Reusch, Jr.	2000	1047
167 3/8	25 4/8 25 7/8	18 3/8	5	6	Douglas County	NE	Ernie Buttry	2000	1047
167 3/8	25 7/8 25 2/8	20 2/8	6	5	Portage County	WI	Al Hottenstine	2003	1047
167 3/8	25 0/8 24 6/8	19 7/8	7	5	Queen Annes County	MD	Don Huggins	2004	1047
167 3/8	28 3/8 28 2/8	16 2/8	5	6	Jefferson County	IN	Travis Skinner	2004	1047
167 3/8	25 4/8 26 1/8	17 7/8	5	5	Grundy County	IL	David Both	2006	1047
*167 3/8	25 0/8 25 1/8	18 7/8	5	5	Licking County	OH	Kenneth Brian Blankenship	2008	1047
167 3/8	24 3/8 23 7/8	18 2/8	5	6	Marshall County	IA	John M. Ruopp	2008	1047
*167 3/8	24 7/8 25 4/8	15 4/8	9	5	Kenton County	KY	Dennis S. Flerlage	2010	1047
167 3/8	25 1/8 25 5/8	18 5/8	5	5	Barron County	WI	Eric Schalley	2010	1047
167 2/8	25 2/8 26 2/8	17 2/8	7	6	Todd County	KY	Glendeal Sigers	1987	1064
167 2/8	24 3/8 24 3/8	21 4/8	5	6	Marion County	IA	Brad Van Dusseldorp	1992	1064
167 2/8	25 7/8 26 0/8	21 6/8	6	5	Grundy County	IL	Michael Dunbar	1995	1064
167 2/8	25 3/8 24 6/8	16 6/8	5	5	Douglas County	WI	Mark E. Henck	1998	1064
167 2/8	27 7/8 27 6/8	18 7/8	6	5	Kent County	MD	David Black	1999	1064
167 2/8	24 0/8 22 2/8	19 6/8	5	7	McLean County	KY	Sarah Bullock	2000	1064
167 2/8	27 3/8 26 5/8	22 2/8	4	5	Sauk County	WI	Josh Ringham	2001	1064
167 2/8	29 2/8 28 2/8	22 6/8	6	7	Ashtabula County	OH	Mark R. Johnson	2004	1064
167 2/8	25 1/8 24 4/8	21 5/8	5	6	Gasconade County	MO	Aaron Coen	2005	1064
*167 2/8	26 4/8 26 5/8	16 2/8	5	5	Elk County	KS	Allen Webb	2005	1064
167 2/8	23 3/8 23 4/8	16 2/8	5	5	Buffalo County	WI	Trevor Adams	2007	1064
*167 2/8	27 6/8 28 0/8	21 0/8	5	5	Tallahatchie County	MS	Rob Stockett III	2007	1064
167 2/8	25 1/8 25 2/8	18 5/8	5	4	Buffalo County	WI	Jeremy T. Vogel	2008	1064
*167 2/8	25 6/8 24 4/8	19 4/8	6	7	White County	AR	Raymond King	2008	1064
167 2/8	26 5/8 26 6/8	24 2/8	6	6	Johnson County	NE	Stephen Jarvis	2009	1064
167 1/8	24 5/8 24 7/8	18 6/8	5	5	Chase County	KS	Ronald E. Rhodes	1985	1079
167 1/8	22 5/8 22 6/8	25 2/8	5	7	Dodge County	MN	Myles Keller	1985	1079
167 1/8	25 1/8 25 6/8	20 3/8	6	6	Reno County	KS	R. D. Loudenback	1987	1079
167 1/8	23 4/8 24 0/8	18 5/8	6	5	McHenry County	IL	Charlie Rand	1989	1079
167 1/8	25 2/8 25 4/8	18 7/8	6	5	Fulton County	IL	Michael Taff	1991	1079
167 1/8	27 1/8 27 1/8	21 4/8	7	6	Douglas County	WI	Jeff Brantley	2003	1079
167 1/8	24 3/8 24 7/8	16 1/8	6	6	Kiowa County	KS	Thomas F. Terral	2004	1079
*167 1/8	27 1/8 27 7/8	18 6/8	6	7	Mason County	KY	Ron Welch	2006	1079
167 1/8	24 4/8 24 6/8	18 7/8	5	5	Winona County	MN	Christopher W. Fechner	2007	1079
167 1/8	25 3/8 25 4/8	16 3/8	6	6	Rockcastle County	KY	Larry D. Carter	2007	1079
167 0/8	28 0/8 27 6/8	19 0/8	6	5	Clay County	MN	Ryan Hines	1986	1089
167 0/8	26 0/8 26 1/8	18 2/8	5	5	Montgomery County	IN	Joe W. Woodrow	1988	1089
167 0/8	25 5/8 24 6/8	18 2/8	5	5	Montgomery County	TN	Larry Lee Murphy	1989	1089
167 0/8	26 3/8 25 7/8	18 3/8	6	6	Fountain County	IN	Steve McQueen	1991	1089
167 0/8	27 0/8 26 6/8	22 4/8	6	5	Wilson County	KS	Ed Barton	1994	1089
167 0/8	26 4/8 25 6/8	21 4/8	6	5	Otoe County	NE	Tom Tomes	1995	1089
167 0/8	27 7/8 26 6/8	24 0/8	5	5	Fulton County	IL	Rick Northeimer	1999	1089
167 0/8	26 0/8 27 2/8	21 5/8	7	7	Washington County	IL	Doug Brinkmann	1999	1089
167 0/8	27 0/8 27 1/8	18 5/8	6	6	Bureau County	IL	Dustin Pierceson	2001	1089
167 0/8	27 5/8 25 4/8	20 0/8	4	4	Barber County	KS	Bruce Swartley	2001	1089
167 0/8	27 3/8 26 5/8	17 4/8	5	5	St. Louis County	MN	Marc Miller	2003	1089
167 0/8	26 0/8 25 1/8	18 1/8	7	7	Christian County	IL	Luigi Belcastro	2003	1089
*167 0/8	27 2/8 25 5/8	19 6/8	5	5	Allegan County	MI	Kevin R. Leith	2003	1089
167 0/8	24 4/8 24 7/8	16 4/8	5	5	Jasper County	IL	Jake Geier	2007	1089
167 0/8	23 5/8 23 5/8	22 3/8	5	6	Lenore Lake	SAS	Floyd Forster	2008	1089
166 7/8	26 4/8 26 4/8	20 1/8	7	5	Saline County	NE	Scott Theis	1982	1104
166 7/8	25 2/8 24 5/8	21 1/8	6	6	Geary County	KS	Dennis L. Gillam	1986	1104
166 7/8	26 6/8 26 2/8	19 5/8	6	5	Jackson County	OH	Charles E. Cogdill	1990	1104
166 7/8	23 7/8 24 2/8	19 4/8	8	6	Lake County	MN	Mark Hal Tucker	1991	1104
166 7/8	27 4/8 27 1/8	20 5/8	4	4	Douglas County	WI	James N. Johnson	1992	1104
166 7/8	27 5/8 27 1/8	22 4/8	5	4	St. Marys County	MD	Ricky D. Menard	1993	1104
166 7/8	24 1/8 23 0/8	20 7/8	5	5	Parkland	ALB	Mark Williams	1994	1104
166 7/8	26 5/8 26 1/8	22 5/8	7	6	Maverick County	TX	Gary Miller	1995	1104
166 7/8	26 6/8 26 3/8	16 6/8	7	7	Adams County	IL	Beatrice J. Walmsley	2003	1104
166 7/8	25 2/8 25 0/8	18 4/8	7	8	Mercer County	IL	Joseph DeSchepper	2003	1104
*166 7/8	24 2/8 23 6/8	19 4/8	6	7	Dunn County	WI	David Frank	2005	1104
166 7/8	28 1/8 27 5/8	19 7/8	5	5	Sauk County	WI	Evan Steinhorst	2005	1104
*166 7/8	24 5/8 23 4/8	18 1/8	5	6	Taylor County	IA	Chad Price	2005	1104
166 7/8	25 5/8 24 6/8	18 7/8	5	7	Lucas County	IA	Mike Carter	2007	1104
166 7/8	24 7/8 25 0/8	18 6/8	7	5	Coshocton County	OH	Leon J. Corl, Jr.	2009	1104
166 6/8	24 3/8 24 0/8	21 6/8	6	7	Lanigan	SAS	Bob Tempel	1985	1119
166 6/8	27 3/8 26 6/8	17 6/8	5	5	Allegan County	MI	Larry Deater	1989	1119
166 6/8	26 6/8 25 6/8	16 6/8	6	6	Cerro Gordo County	IA	Bill Alger	1992	1119
166 6/8	28 0/8 28 3/8	18 6/8	6	7	Monroe County	IN	Jeff A. Long	1992	1119
166 6/8	23 0/8 23 4/8	17 2/8	7	7	Dubois County	IN	Edward Helming	1993	1119
166 6/8	24 2/8 23 6/8	16 2/8	5	5	Pike County	IL	Gregory S. Guerrieri	1994	1119
166 6/8	27 3/8 28 2/8	19 7/8	6	6	Kiowa County	KS	Jorge Martinez	1998	1119
166 6/8	26 0/8 24 4/8	20 0/8	6	7	Page County	IA	Ray F. Stark	2000	1119
166 6/8	26 6/8 26 2/8	21 7/8	5	6	Sumner County	KS	Michael Turner	2000	1119
166 6/8	25 1/8 26 1/8	18 7/8	8	6	Forest County	WI	Robert Karl	2001	1119
166 6/8	23 6/8 26 1/8	22 4/8	5	6	Greene County	OH	Rick Spyker	2001	1119
166 6/8	26 0/8 26 7/8	19 2/8	6	6	Pittsburg County	OK	Dale Atwood	2001	1119
166 6/8	24 5/8 26 1/8	23 4/8	5	5	Washington County	WI	David J. Lex	2002	1119
*166 6/8	28 0/8 27 0/8	24 0/8	4	4	Jefferson County	IA	Jess Swanson	2003	1119
166 6/8	26 0/8 26 0/8	19 6/8	5	7	Onondaga County	NY	Mike Weinerth	2003	1119
166 6/8	26 5/8 26 0/8	18 5/8	8	6	Des Moines County	IA	Chad W. Clark	2004	1119
*166 6/8	29 1/8 28 0/8	20 3/8	6	6	Muscatine County	IA	Ray Brisker	2004	1119
166 6/8	25 5/8 26 0/8	21 6/8	5	6	Winona County	MN	Brent Bailey	2004	1119
166 6/8	25 0/8 25 0/8	20 7/8	8	6	Fulton County	IL	Ryan Elenbaas	2005	1119
166 6/8	26 1/8 26 3/8	20 4/8	5	5	Shawano County	WI	Gary Gevaert	2006	1119
166 6/8	24 1/8 23 7/8	19 0/8	7	7	Kenosha County	WI	Bill Cheney	2006	1119
166 6/8	26 0/8 25 7/8	19 5/8	6	5	Newport County	RI	Stephen C. Ponte	2006	1119

WHITETAIL DEER (TYPICAL ANTLERS)

Minimum Score 125 — Continued

SCORE	LENGTH OF R MAIN BEAM L	INSIDE SPREAD	NUMBER OF R POINTS L	AREA	STATE/ PROVINCE	HUNTER'S NAME	DATE	RANK
166 6/8	27 2/8 27 2/8	18 4/8	6 6	Robertson County	KY	Chris Caldwell	2009	1119
*166 6/8	24 2/8 24 1/8	17 5/8	7 7	Lake County	IL	Trent Schneider	2009	1119
*166 6/8	29 0/8 29 0/8	16 7/8	6 5	Guilford County	NC	Andrew E. Kerman	2009	1119
*166 6/8	25 0/8 25 0/8	18 2/8	5 5	Fulton County	KY	Tommy Stewart	2010	1119
166 5/8	26 7/8 27 4/8	19 5/8	5 5	Lyon County	MN	Gene Gustafson	1982	1145
166 5/8	25 2/8 25 0/8	17 5/8	6 7	Meade County	KS	Tim Ross	1987	1145
166 5/8	26 4/8 25 0/8	17 2/8	6 8	Johnson County	IN	Joe F. Heath, Jr.	1989	1145
166 5/8	25 0/8 25 2/8	21 3/8	8 6	Sarpy County	NE	Roy Symanietz	1990	1145
166 5/8	25 5/8 25 5/8	21 5/8	7 8	Mills County	IA	Ted Love	1996	1145
166 5/8	25 4/8 25 6/8	21 2/8	6 6	Chippewa County	WI	Al Larson	1998	1145
166 5/8	26 7/8 27 2/8	21 1/8	4 5	Calhoun County	IL	Ed Fanning	2001	1145
166 5/8	25 6/8 26 2/8	19 7/8	6 5	St. Joseph County	MI	Donald L. Preston	2002	1145
166 5/8	24 2/8 24 6/8	19 6/8	7 5	Allamakee County	IA	Randy Ruth	2002	1145
166 5/8	26 2/8 25 4/8	19 1/8	5 5	Wood County	WI	Jerome Tork	2003	1145
166 5/8	28 7/8 28 4/8	19 5/8	5 5	Clay County	IL	Frank Fulk	2004	1145
*166 5/8	27 2/8 27 5/8	17 6/8	9 6	Houston County	MN	Bill Clink	2005	1145
166 5/8	23 3/8 24 1/8	17 6/8	5 6	Hamlin County	SD	Russell Somsen	2006	1145
*166 5/8	25 3/8 25 4/8	18 0/8	6 6	Monroe County	AR	Todd Norris	2006	1145
166 4/8	27 6/8 28 4/8	21 4/8	5 7	Juniper	NBW	Ron Peterson	1989	1159
166 4/8	26 0/8 26 6/8	19 0/8	5 4	Pierce County	WI	Garrett "Gary" L. Fleishauer	1991	1159
166 4/8	24 6/8 24 4/8	19 0/8	7 7	Buffalo County	WI	Dale Frost	1992	1159
166 4/8	27 2/8 27 0/8	19 6/8	5 5	Gallia County	OH	Mike Wellman	1993	1159
166 4/8	26 7/8 25 4/8	19 4/8	5 5	Hand County	SD	Kevin Bertsch	1993	1159
166 4/8	25 4/8 26 1/8	18 2/8	5 5	Pottawatomie County	KS	Scott Hadsall	1994	1159
166 4/8	26 2/8 26 5/8	17 2/8	6 6	Wayne County	IA	Scott Bunnell	1994	1159
166 4/8	27 4/8 27 1/8	23 0/8	7 6	Marion County	IA	LeRoy Hansaker	1995	1159
166 4/8	26 2/8 25 5/8	22 3/8	4 5	Winneshiek County	IA	Jeff Berns	1996	1159
166 4/8	25 5/8 25 5/8	19 1/8	6 7	Bartholomew County	IN	Shane Sweeney	1998	1159
166 4/8	25 7/8 26 1/8	18 6/8	5 5	Bourbon County	KS	Martin Funk	1998	1159
166 4/8	23 4/8 24 3/8	17 1/8	5 6	Scott County	MN	Michael J. Dickie	1999	1159
166 4/8	27 2/8 26 1/8	20 4/8	5 5	Portage County	OH	Daniel S. Behm	2000	1159
166 4/8	25 7/8 28 1/8	20 4/8	7 5	Marion County	IA	Leonard Grimes	2000	1159
166 4/8	23 6/8 25 4/8	21 2/8	6 5	Franklin County	IN	Darren Westerfeld	2002	1159
166 4/8	26 3/8 25 4/8	21 0/8	6 6	Jo Daviess County	IL	Gary F. Schoenfeld	2003	1159
*166 4/8	24 0/8 23 2/8	17 4/8	5 5	Ogle County	IL	Tod Haefner	2003	1159
166 4/8	24 4/8 24 6/8	17 6/8	5 5	Hamilton County	IL	Todd Oliver	2005	1159
166 4/8	26 4/8 26 3/8	20 6/8	5 5	Waukesha County	WI	Larry Hermann	2006	1159
166 4/8	23 7/8 24 7/8	13 6/8	5 5	Montgomery County	MD	Robert W. Ridenour	2006	1159
*166 4/8	25 0/8 24 7/8	18 3/8	6 6	Mills County	IA	Lloyd E. Barten	2007	1159
166 3/8	26 6/8 26 4/8	17 1/8	6 6	Clarke County	IA	Dwight E. Green	1965	1180
166 3/8	26 3/8 26 0/8	18 2/8	8 5	Yankton County	SD	Roger Irwin	1985	1180
166 3/8	25 2/8 25 1/8	17 6/8	9 7	Lake County	MN	Daniel H. Hall	1991	1180
166 3/8	25 6/8 25 4/8	19 7/8	8 5	Suffolk County	NY	John Bennett	1993	1180
166 3/8	27 4/8 25 4/8	18 1/8	5 5	Waupaca County	WI	Steven D. Breaker	1994	1180
166 3/8	25 6/8 25 6/8	18 7/8	5 5	Rockingham County	VA	Thomas R. Keener	1995	1180
166 3/8	27 1/8 26 5/8	21 1/8	5 7	Linn County	IA	Chad Huschka	1995	1180
166 3/8	27 1/8 27 0/8	18 7/8	5 7	Clayton County	IA	David L. White	1995	1180
166 3/8	25 5/8 25 5/8	18 2/8	7 6	Buffalo County	WI	Bob Lorenz	1999	1180
166 3/8	23 7/8 25 0/8	18 7/8	5 5	Ripley County	IN	Steve A. Allen	2001	1180
166 3/8	26 0/8 25 3/8	20 3/8	6 6	Kleberg County	TX	Michael McFerrin	2002	1180
166 3/8	25 2/8 25 3/8	18 1/8	8 5	Decatur County	IN	George A. Fischer	2002	1180
166 3/8	25 4/8 25 3/8	18 7/8	5 5	Isanti County	MN	Daniel R. Hasser	2003	1180
*166 3/8	28 7/8 29 2/8	24 5/8	6 5	Logan County	OH	Abe Meyers	2004	1180
*166 3/8	25 5/8 25 2/8	17 1/8	5 5	Clark County	KS	Kelly C. Ison	2006	1180
166 3/8	28 1/8 27 5/8	20 7/8	5 5	Van Buren County	IA	Baree Weber	2007	1180
*166 3/8	26 6/8 26 2/8	19 2/8	6 6	Marshall County	IN	Richard A. Fites	2007	1180
166 3/8	25 6/8 27 4/8	20 1/8	5 5	Marion County	IN	Jeff D. Vaughan	2007	1180
166 3/8	24 6/8 24 5/8	17 3/8	5 5	Buffalo County	WI	Brady Blaschko	2010	1180
166 2/8	29 3/8 29 4/8	21 5/8	6 4	Monona County	IA	G. K. Tuttle	1967	1199
166 2/8	27 4/8 27 1/8	20 2/8	9 6	Republic County	KS	Virgil Graham	1986	1199
166 2/8	25 1/8 26 7/8	19 1/8	6 6	Monroe County	IA	Cliff VanZee	1987	1199
166 2/8	26 2/8 27 2/8	19 2/8	7 7	Mower County	MN	Kerry Schroeder	1988	1199
166 2/8	24 5/8 24 7/8	19 2/8	7 7	Kane County	IL	Roy Howard	1991	1199
166 2/8	25 7/8 26 4/8	18 4/8	6 5	Hancock County	IL	Doug Huls	1992	1199
166 2/8	24 0/8 23 7/8	17 2/8	6 6	Piscataquis County	ME	Kelly D. Easler	1996	1199
166 2/8	23 3/8 25 0/8	18 5/8	9 7	Vermilion County	IL	Jerry M. Courson	1997	1199
166 2/8	25 2/8 24 1/8	18 6/8	6 5	Dane County	WI	Mike Elmore	1998	1199
166 2/8	27 3/8 26 7/8	19 1/8	5 5	Phelps County	NE	Gordon Hinrichs	1999	1199
166 2/8	23 0/8 24 2/8	17 2/8	5 5	Louisa County	IA	Robert McCulley	1999	1199
166 2/8	26 5/8 26 3/8	19 3/8	6 8	Washtenaw County	MI	Eric A. Braun	2000	1199
166 2/8	25 6/8 25 0/8	20 0/8	6 7	Morgan County	IL	Jeff Cosner	2001	1199
166 2/8	27 0/8 27 4/8	19 2/8	5 6	Meadow Lake	SAS	Rick Cull	2001	1199
166 2/8	28 1/8 28 0/8	16 3/8	6 7	Adams County	OH	Jim H. Williamson	2003	1199
*166 2/8	25 7/8 25 1/8	19 0/8	5 4	Clark County	IL	Thomas E. Rothrock	2006	1199
*166 2/8	26 1/8 25 2/8	19 0/8	6 5	Warren County	IA	Gary R. Sullivan, Jr.	2007	1199
166 2/8	26 3/8 26 4/8	19 4/8	7 6	Lee County	IL	Lee A. Dixon	2008	1199
*166 2/8	24 1/8 24 0/8	18 2/8	7 8	Wabasha County	MN	Bill Schad	2008	1199
166 2/8	25 7/8 26 2/8	18 1/8	6 5	Chase County	KS	Kent Wartick	2009	1199
166 1/8	23 3/8 23 5/8	19 3/8	5 5	Morrison County	MN	Corey Loney	1963	1219
166 1/8	27 0/8 27 1/8	18 0/8	5 6	Stearns County	MN	Bruce C. Meade	1978	1219
166 1/8	25 6/8 25 2/8	21 2/8	5 4	Texas County	OK	Max Crocker	1986	1219
166 1/8	25 4/8 25 0/8	19 5/8	4 5	Chase County	KS	Lee Ayers	1987	1219
166 1/8	24 5/8 24 5/8	17 1/8	5 6	Bartholomew County	IN	Bryan D. Cook	1989	1219
166 1/8	23 4/8 23 2/8	17 2/8	7 6	White County	IN	Kerry Dean Morton	1989	1219
166 1/8	27 3/8 28 7/8	20 2/8	8 5	Wayne County	IL	Ronald Riley	1990	1219
166 1/8	25 4/8 26 0/8	18 4/8	7 6	Ross County	OH	Keith W. Orr	1991	1219
166 1/8	24 2/8 25 2/8	21 1/8	6 6	Sibley County	MN	Robert M. Boettcher	1993	1219
166 1/8	27 7/8 27 7/8	19 5/8	5 6	Jo Daviess County	IL	Dick V. Lalowski	1995	1219
166 1/8	25 5/8 26 6/8	19 1/8	6 5	Washington County	IA	Al Chapman	1995	1219
166 1/8	28 1/8 26 5/8	21 4/8	7 5	Macomb County	MI	Jeffery P. Merritt	2000	1219
166 1/8	24 0/8 24 0/8	18 3/8	5 5	Chisago County	MN	Jerry Smith	2000	1219
166 1/8	27 4/8 26 7/8	21 4/8	7 7	Jefferson County	IL	Nathan Mays	2000	1219
166 1/8	23 4/8 23 5/8	22 7/8	7 6	La Salle County	IL	Mark K. Atherton	2002	1219
166 1/8	30 1/8 27 4/8	21 0/8	6 5	Rock Island County	IL	Jerry Ballard, Sr.	2004	1219
166 1/8	25 1/8 26 1/8	20 1/8	6 7	Talbot County	MD	James Brandow	2005	1219

368

WHITETAIL DEER (TYPICAL ANTLERS)

Minimum Score 125   Continued

SCORE	LENGTH OF R MAIN BEAM L	INSIDE SPREAD	NUMBER OF R POINTS L	AREA	STATE/ PROVINCE	HUNTER'S NAME	DATE	RANK
*166 1/8	24 7/8 25 4/8	18 7/8	5 5	Walworth County	WI	Raymond A. Kawalec	2006	1219
166 1/8	23 4/8 23 3/8	16 1/8	5 5	Jefferson County	IA	Wayne A. Menard, Jr.	2007	1219
166 1/8	25 1/8 24 1/8	20 1/8	8 5	Wapello County	IA	Connie Pitzen	2007	1219
*166 1/8	25 5/8 27 0/8	17 1/8	7 6	Cass County	IL	Robert W. Muti	2007	1219
166 1/8	23 2/8 23 7/8	19 0/8	6 8	Union County	SD	Chris Hasenbank	2007	1219
166 1/8	25 4/8 25 7/8	20 4/8	6 8	Decatur County	IA	Kevin Hewlett	2007	1219
166 1/8	24 6/8 24 2/8	19 7/8	6 5	Pike County	IL	Brad A. DeJohn	2008	1219
166 0/8	27 5/8 26 7/8	23 4/8	5 5	Clinton County	IA	Loy J. Brooker	1964	1243
166 0/8	23 4/8 23 5/8	18 0/8	5 5	Bon Homme County	SD	Delbert Newman	1964	1243
166 0/8	26 1/8 28 4/8	21 6/8	7 6	Shelby County	IL	Ernest D. Richardson	1977	1243
166 0/8	26 6/8 24 2/8	22 7/8	6 6	Anoka County	MN	John A. Cardinal	1979	1243
166 0/8	24 5/8 25 2/8	20 4/8	6 5	Tazewell County	IL	Jerry W. Kammerer	1981	1243
166 0/8	24 4/8 25 5/8	19 2/8	5 5	Sedgwick County	KS	Louis Turner	1988	1243
166 0/8	26 1/8 26 4/8	19 0/8	5 5	Martin County	IN	Terry L. McCrary	1988	1243
166 0/8	25 2/8 26 1/8	18 6/8	5 5	McHenry County	IL	Brent A. Smith	1994	1243
166 0/8	26 2/8 26 5/8	19 4/8	5 5	Tay Township	ONT	Kevin Dutton	2002	1243
166 0/8	26 5/8 27 6/8	19 5/8	4 6	Anderson County	KS	Gary Shields	2003	1243
166 0/8	27 6/8 28 1/8	17 6/8	5 5	Cedar County	NE	David B. Cull	2003	1243
*166 0/8	25 2/8 25 5/8	19 7/8	6 5	Cedar County	NE	Erik Watts	2007	1243
*166 0/8	24 5/8 25 2/8	20 2/8	5 5	La Crosse County	WI	Mitch Baker	2007	1243
166 0/8	25 1/8 24 1/8	19 2/8	5 5	Red Deer	ALB	Jerry Wall	2009	1243
165 7/8	23 4/8 23 4/8	16 3/8	5 5	Wapello County	IA	Richard L. Larsen	1976	1257
165 7/8	25 4/8 26 1/8	17 5/8	7 6	Licking County	OH	Pat Walker	1978	1257
165 7/8	27 2/8 27 0/8	19 5/8	5 5	Prowers County	CO	Edward Henson	1980	1257
165 7/8	23 0/8 26 0/8	18 1/8	5 5	Vermilion County	IL	Dick Bayer	1987	1257
165 7/8	26 2/8 25 6/8	20 0/8	7 5	Weld County	CO	Mark Houtchens	1991	1257
165 7/8	27 7/8 27 6/8	16 5/8	6 4	Madison County	IL	Tom Wieseman	1993	1257
165 7/8	24 0/8 25 1/8	17 6/8	7 8	Fisher Branch	MAN	Frank Hall	1994	1257
165 7/8	24 5/8 24 4/8	20 1/8	6 5	Madison County	MO	Tony Joe Helm	1994	1257
165 7/8	26 1/8 26 2/8	20 6/8	7 7	Woodford County	IL	Greg Gullett	1999	1257
165 7/8	27 6/8 28 0/8	20 5/8	5 5	Buffalo County	WI	Gary Fleishauer	2000	1257
165 7/8	25 1/8 24 7/8	20 3/8	5 6	Winnebago County	IL	Brad S. Revell	2001	1257
165 7/8	28 3/8 28 3/8	21 5/8	7 6	Lawrence County	IL	John C. Waugh	2003	1257
165 7/8	26 4/8 26 3/8	18 7/8	7 5	Lake County	IN	Joe Banek	2003	1257
*165 7/8	24 7/8 24 6/8	19 1/8	5 5	Wayne County	IL	George A. Weiss	2003	1257
165 7/8	23 1/8 22 0/8	17 7/8	5 5	Motley County	TX	Shane Steen	2003	1257
165 7/8	25 7/8 24 5/8	25 2/8	5 7	Fulton County	IL	William Major	2005	1257
165 7/8	28 3/8 29 0/8	19 4/8	8 8	Livingston County	MI	Jeanetta "Jeanie" Flanery	2006	1257
*165 7/8	24 4/8 25 1/8	18 7/8	5 5	Beltrami County	MN	Lloyd Sobieck	2007	1257
*165 7/8	22 1/8 22 4/8	15 5/8	7 6	Ringgold County	IA	Gordon Clift	2007	1257
165 7/8	25 0/8 25 4/8	20 3/8	6 5	Brown County	WI	Marty Bruecker	2007	1257
165 7/8	27 5/8 26 2/8	19 7/8	5 6	Union County	IN	Brian Cheatham	2007	1257
*165 7/8	27 0/8 26 7/8	21 5/8	5 5	St. Louis County	MN	Camron Vollbrecht	2008	1257
*165 7/8	24 4/8 24 5/8	18 4/8	8 7	Fremont County	IA	Jim Gross	2008	1257
165 6/8	27 0/8 26 1/8	19 0/8	7 6	Pottawattamie County	IA	Dan Bowen	1968	1280
165 6/8	28 1/8 25 7/8	18 4/8	5 6	Darke County	OH	Dean Neff	1988	1280
165 6/8	25 1/8 25 1/8	19 0/8	7 6	Morrison County	MN	Rodney Mysliwiec	1988	1280
165 6/8	25 1/8 26 2/8	18 3/8	5 6	Ottawa County	KS	Patrick E. Helget	1988	1280
165 6/8	25 4/8 25 2/8	21 3/8	5 6	Randolph County	IL	David Uchtmann	1992	1280
165 6/8	25 0/8 24 3/8	19 4/8	5 5	Vigo County	IN	Tim Jones	1994	1280
165 6/8	25 7/8 24 3/8	16 4/8	7 6	Pike County	IL	Huston Martin III	1994	1280
165 6/8	24 1/8 23 6/8	18 0/8	6 6	Shawnee County	KS	Willie Konrade	1995	1280
165 6/8	25 5/8 27 1/8	19 4/8	5 5	Cass County	MN	Brent Beimert	1998	1280
165 6/8	24 4/8 25 4/8	18 4/8	5 6	Allegheny County	PA	Gary Adams	1998	1280
165 6/8	24 6/8 25 4/8	20 4/8	5 5	Appanoose County	IA	Melvin T. Digman	2000	1280
165 6/8	25 0/8 25 2/8	19 5/8	5 8	Lucas County	OH	Larry Benedict	2001	1280
165 6/8	25 3/8 25 4/8	14 7/8	7 8	Pierce County	WI	Kenneth Smith	2002	1280
165 6/8	27 4/8 25 4/8	26 6/8	4 5	St. Marys County	MD	John S. Hurt	2003	1280
*165 6/8	25 0/8 23 3/8	20 0/8	5 5	Schuyler County	IL	Mark A. Edwards	2004	1280
*165 6/8	26 7/8 27 2/8	17 6/8	4 5	Woodbury County	IA	Mike Julius	2007	1280
*165 6/8	26 0/8 26 0/8	20 3/8	6 6	Fairfield County	OH	Michael C. Colby, Jr.	2009	1280
165 5/8	29 0/8 29 2/8	20 2/8	6 8	Preble County	OH	Alan W. Risner	1992	1297
165 5/8	26 6/8 25 6/8	19 4/8	7 7	Adams County	IL	Joseph T. Hankins	2001	1297
165 5/8	24 3/8 24 7/8	16 4/8	6 6	Rogers County	OK	Jesse Newton	2001	1297
165 5/8	25 0/8 23 4/8	17 7/8	5 5	Yuma County	CO	Alan White	2002	1297
165 5/8	24 7/8 24 3/8	23 1/8	5 5	Lyon County	KY	Jace Cagle	2002	1297
165 5/8	24 5/8 23 5/8	20 3/8	6 7	Wayne County	IL	Rick Miller	2003	1297
165 5/8	27 3/8 26 4/8	21 6/8	7 7	Issaquena County	MS	Carl E. Taylor	2004	1297
165 5/8	22 7/8 23 4/8	16 5/8	5 5	Henry County	IN	Frank Chesher	2004	1297
*165 5/8	26 6/8 27 0/8	17 1/8	7 6	Beaver County	PA	Bill Golgosky	2005	1297
165 5/8	27 0/8 26 4/8	23 1/8	6 6	Dauphin County	PA	Scott Cisney	2005	1297
*165 5/8	26 4/8 27 2/8	21 2/8	6 5	Will County	IL	Ron Jones	2006	1297
165 5/8	24 0/8 25 0/8	19 1/8	6 5	Marion County	MO	Geene A. Denish	2006	1297
165 5/8	25 2/8 25 2/8	19 7/8	5 5	Greene County	OH	Aaron Chaney	2008	1297
165 5/8	26 1/8 23 7/8	22 1/8	5 5	Calhoun County	MI	Bradley S. Osborn	2009	1297
165 5/8	27 6/8 27 1/8	21 7/8	6 5	Cook County	IL	Kirby E. Miller	2010	1297
165 4/8	25 6/8 25 1/8	21 0/8	5 5	Kent County	MD	Kent Price	1962	1312
165 4/8	23 2/8 22 5/8	19 4/8	6 6	Peoria County	IL	Larry T Oppe	1984	1312
165 4/8	29 1/8 28 3/8	18 1/8	7 8	Buffalo County	WI	Patrick Ryan	1985	1312
165 4/8	27 6/8 27 5/8	21 0/8	6 5	Will County	IL	Donald R. Spence	1988	1312
165 4/8	25 6/8 27 2/8	22 0/8	5 5	Cherry County	NE	Jack Joseph	1990	1312
165 4/8	26 1/8 25 2/8	20 0/8	5 5	Ohio County	KY	Dwight Keith	1994	1312
165 4/8	27 0/8 25 5/8	16 2/8	7 7	Rockingham County	NC	Jerry Garland Chilton	1995	1312
165 4/8	25 7/8 27 0/8	21 6/8	5 5	Guthrie County	IA	Larry Alexander	1995	1312
165 4/8	23 3/8 23 3/8	17 2/8	6 6	Cochrane	ALB	Rob Valnoski	1996	1312
165 4/8	27 0/8 26 7/8	21 1/8	6 5	Van Buren County	IA	Alan Andrews	1996	1312
165 4/8	25 0/8 24 7/8	19 4/8	6 7	Ogle County	IL	James L. Morgan	1996	1312
165 4/8	23 6/8 25 2/8	20 1/8	6 7	Dallas County	IA	Bret Renshaw	1997	1312
165 4/8	24 4/8 23 7/8	19 3/8	8 5	Lehigh County	PA	Raymond Nechetsky, Sr.	2000	1312
165 4/8	23 7/8 23 4/8	19 0/8	5 5	Richland County	ND	Brian Bernotas	2000	1312
165 4/8	24 7/8 25 6/8	17 2/8	6 6	Guthrie County	IA	Jason Jones	2004	1312
165 4/8	24 4/8 23 0/8	20 4/8	5 5	Allamakee County	IA	Donald R. Larson	2007	1312
165 4/8	26 2/8 26 0/8	19 2/8	6 6	Avoyelles Parish	LA	Jeff Newton	2008	1312
165 4/8	24 2/8 24 7/8	18 3/8	5 6	Macon County	MO	Nathan L. Winkler	2009	1312
165 4/8	24 2/8 23 4/8	16 0/8	5 6	Eau Claire County	WI	Heath Fremstad	2009	1312

WHITETAIL DEER (TYPICAL ANTLERS)

Minimum Score 125 Continued

SCORE	LENGTH OF R MAIN BEAM L	INSIDE SPREAD	NUMBER OF R POINTS L	AREA	STATE/ PROVINCE	HUNTER'S NAME	DATE	RANK
165 3/8	23 7/8 25 6/8	17 1/8	5 7	Owen County	KY	Joseph Caruso	1977	1331
165 3/8	27 0/8 27 2/8	22 5/8	7 7	Grundy County	IL	Gary R. Kuriger	1978	1331
165 3/8	27 5/8 28 1/8	21 3/8	5 5	Marshall County	KS	Theodore J. Martin	1979	1331
165 3/8	26 2/8 26 0/8	20 0/8	5 8	Victoria	MAN	David Wiklund	1984	1331
165 3/8	26 1/8 24 1/8	20 3/8	5 5	Guthrie County	IA	Scott C. Kemble	1989	1331
165 3/8	25 2/8 26 0/8	17 7/8	5 6	Hancock County	IN	Gary Dusang	1991	1331
165 3/8	25 6/8 24 7/8	16 5/8	6 7	Rock Island County	IL	Roman H. Atnip	1991	1331
165 3/8	25 6/8 25 6/8	20 1/8	5 5	Baca County	CO	Eddie Claypool	1991	1331
165 3/8	26 4/8 25 6/8	18 6/8	5 6	Monroe County	MO	Larry Meier	1993	1331
165 3/8	23 2/8 24 0/8	15 7/8	6 6	Coffey County	KS	Max A. Nichols	1993	1331
165 3/8	26 0/8 26 1/8	19 7/8	7 6	Vermilion County	IL	Keith Downing	1993	1331
165 3/8	27 0/8 27 4/8	20 1/8	5 6	Cass County	MI	Jim Hollingsworth	1995	1331
165 3/8	26 5/8 25 6/8	17 7/8	5 6	Oconto County	WI	Ronald Thomson	1998	1331
165 3/8	25 6/8 26 3/8	17 0/8	5 6	Lake County	IL	Jeffery Allard	1998	1331
165 3/8	25 1/8 25 5/8	17 5/8	5 5	Rolette County	ND	Scott Moen	1999	1331
165 3/8	23 4/8 23 4/8	20 1/8	5 5	Uvalde County	TX	Erik Ahart	2002	1331
165 3/8	28 2/8 29 4/8	20 5/8	5 7	Allamakee County	IA	Jon Syverson	2002	1331
165 3/8	25 4/8 26 5/8	15 5/8	5 4	Brown County	IN	George E. Mann	2003	1331
*165 3/8	26 0/8 27 0/8	19 4/8	7 6	Davis County	IA	Arvid Goettsche	2003	1331
165 3/8	26 0/8 25 4/8	18 7/8	5 5	Cherokee County	IA	Cody Brandes	2003	1331
165 3/8	23 1/8 23 6/8	16 4/8	6 6	Spokane County	WA	Ray Bunny	2003	1331
165 3/8	24 1/8 24 1/8	17 7/8	5 5	Will County	IL	Mike LaReau	2003	1331
165 3/8	24 5/8 24 5/8	18 6/8	5 6	Westmoreland County	PA	William E. Cunningham	2004	1331
165 3/8	25 4/8 24 5/8	21 3/8	5 5	Kane County	IL	Dennis H. Kein, Jr.	2004	1331
*165 3/8	26 4/8 25 6/8	22 5/8	5 5	Elgin County	ONT	Shane Good	2006	1331
165 3/8	24 5/8 25 7/8	17 7/8	5 7	Shelby County	IL	William K. Lindsey	2006	1331
*165 3/8	27 3/8 27 1/8	18 7/8	5 6	Waukesha County	WI	Justin Bernklau	2006	1331
*165 3/8	25 4/8 24 0/8	21 5/8	6 7	Columbia County	WI	David A. Schroud, Jr.	2007	1331
165 3/8	26 4/8 26 5/8	18 3/8	6 5	Kingsbury County	SD	Jason Converse	2007	1331
165 2/8	26 5/8 24 6/8	18 1/8	6 6	McPherson County	KS	Daniel Willems	1981	1360
165 2/8	25 6/8 24 2/8	18 2/8	5 5	Clermont County	OH	Nick Lung	1985	1360
165 2/8	25 6/8 25 6/8	21 5/8	5 6	Dubuque County	IA	Paul J. Kluesner	1988	1360
165 2/8	26 0/8 25 1/8	19 3/8	6 6	Wapello County	IA	Robert L. McDowell	1988	1360
165 2/8	25 0/8 24 7/8	18 6/8	7 7	Dunn County	WI	Lamoine Roatch	1989	1360
165 2/8	24 4/8 25 2/8	19 0/8	6 6	Harvey County	KS	Bob Stroble	1989	1360
165 2/8	26 7/8 25 1/8	22 2/8	7 4	Mercer County	NJ	William E. Baker	1993	1360
165 2/8	26 2/8 26 4/8	18 4/8	8 5	Sangamon County	IL	Daran Harn	1996	1360
165 2/8	25 2/8 26 1/8	17 2/8	6 6	Lincoln County	WI	Robin Klade	1998	1360
165 2/8	24 3/8 25 0/8	18 6/8	6 6	Randolph County	IL	David Uchtmann	1999	1360
165 2/8	25 6/8 25 0/8	22 0/8	6 5	Bureau County	IL	Aaron Isaacson	2003	1360
165 2/8	26 0/8 26 7/8	16 5/8	7 7	Cedar County	IA	Thomas Cinadr	2004	1360
*165 2/8	25 1/8 23 3/8	17 6/8	5 5	Licking County	OH	Christopher L. Schnipke	2006	1360
*165 2/8	23 2/8 24 4/8	20 2/8	6 6	Wood County	WI	Ken Kasner	2007	1360
165 2/8	24 4/8 24 7/8	18 4/8	6 8	Peoria County	IL	Michael A. Kelly	2007	1360
165 2/8	27 6/8 28 0/8	19 1/8	7 7	Edgar County	IL	Roy A. Lowe III	2007	1360
165 2/8	26 2/8 25 3/8	18 6/8	5 5	Houston County	MN	Randy Thesing	2008	1360
165 2/8	24 4/8 23 7/8	16 6/8	5 6	Callaway County	MO	David L. Wisdom	2008	1360
*165 2/8	23 5/8 23 5/8	19 2/8	5 5	Vermillion County	IN	Frank L. Turchi	2008	1360
165 2/8	25 6/8 24 2/8	16 4/8	7 8	Taylor County	WI	Ryan Kenner	2009	1360
165 2/8	25 1/8 26 2/8	18 0/8	6 5	Richland County	WI	Daniel Hellenbrand	2009	1360
165 2/8	25 5/8 25 4/8	22 2/8	5 5	Wichita County	KS	Kyle L. Roberts	2009	1360
165 1/8	25 3/8 25 5/8	21 7/8	5 5	Barry County	MI	Jim Birmingham	1977	1382
165 1/8	22 1/8 18 1/8	21 7/8	6 6	Iowa County	IA	David Roberts	1980	1382
165 1/8	24 0/8 24 2/8	20 1/8	6 6	Sawyer County	WI	Robert N. Dale	1980	1382
165 1/8	25 4/8 25 7/8	22 4/8	9 7	Wilson County	KS	Dr. Steven G. Mitchell	1987	1382
165 1/8	25 6/8 25 3/8	17 5/8	5 5	Berrien County	MI	Ronald E. Aalfs	1989	1382
165 1/8	24 4/8 23 2/8	16 7/8	6 6	Franklin County	IL	Terry Killgrove	1993	1382
165 1/8	26 2/8 25 0/8	18 4/8	6 7	Jennings County	IN	Jerry W. St. John	1997	1382
165 1/8	25 5/8 24 5/8	17 7/8	5 5	Bay County	MI	Terry L. Horner	1997	1382
165 1/8	25 5/8 25 7/8	18 1/8	7 6	Brown County	IL	Dennis Cloninger	1997	1382
165 1/8	24 7/8 25 1/8	19 1/8	5 5	Madison County	MT	James C. Kennedy	1999	1382
165 1/8	25 0/8 25 2/8	18 5/8	6 6	Langlade County	WI	Michael T. Spalding	2000	1382
165 1/8	25 3/8 26 5/8	19 3/8	5 5	Marion County	OH	Jeff Mitchell	2001	1382
165 1/8	24 3/8 26 3/8	19 5/8	8 6	Dearborn County	IN	Dan Ginn	2002	1382
165 1/8	25 3/8 25 6/8	20 5/8	5 5	Sumner County	KS	Tim Hearlson	2002	1382
165 1/8	28 4/8 27 0/8	19 3/8	5 5	Stokes County	NC	Greg J. Robertson	2003	1382
165 1/8	27 2/8 26 6/8	17 4/8	6 7	Waushara County	WI	Peter A. Rynders	2004	1382
*165 1/8	25 3/8 24 0/8	18 4/8	6 5	Decatur County	IA	George Richison	2005	1382
*165 1/8	24 2/8 23 3/8	18 7/8	5 5	Marion County	IA	Mark McMurry	2006	1382
*165 1/8	26 6/8 27 0/8	20 3/8	4 4	Barber County	KS	Joe Simpson	2007	1382
165 0/8	26 0/8 24 6/8	18 3/8	6 5	Vilas County	WI	Jonathon Kostreva	1975	1401
165 0/8	26 0/8 25 7/8	20 0/8	5 5	Bond County	IL	Douglas Howard	1978	1401
165 0/8	25 2/8 23 5/8	19 0/8	6 6	Stony Plain	ALB	Wayne C. Prier	1983	1401
165 0/8	24 1/8 24 2/8	17 6/8	5 5	Doniphan County	KS	Richard Williams	1983	1401
165 0/8	25 6/8 25 4/8	20 4/8	5 5	Jefferson County	KS	Emmet Copeland	1989	1401
165 0/8	25 2/8 25 4/8	18 4/8	5 5	Montgomery County	IL	Steven L. Traylor	1989	1401
165 0/8	27 2/8 28 1/8	19 6/8	5 5	Crawford County	IL	Charles E. Guyer	1990	1401
165 0/8	29 0/8 30 1/8	23 5/8	6 6	Randolph County	IL	Bob Theobald	1990	1401
165 0/8	25 1/8 25 3/8	19 4/8	5 5	Geary County	KS	Philip J. Palmer	1991	1401
165 0/8	27 0/8 25 7/8	20 2/8	6 6	Stewart County	TN	Alan Coope	1992	1401
165 0/8	23 7/8 25 0/8	19 0/8	7 6	Cook County	IL	Mark Stanley	1994	1401
165 0/8	26 0/8 25 1/8	15 3/8	5 7	Jefferson County	WI	Robert N. Miller	1996	1401
165 0/8	26 0/8 26 3/8	17 6/8	5 5	Pike County	IL	George R. Metcalf	1998	1401
165 0/8	25 5/8 25 4/8	18 7/8	5 6	Oconto County	WI	Brian Belongea	1999	1401
165 0/8	28 1/8 27 6/8	19 5/8	5 6	Wyoming County	WV	Randall Cook	1999	1401
165 0/8	24 6/8 24 6/8	19 2/8	5 5	Buffalo County	WI	John W. Charles	2000	1401
165 0/8	26 2/8 26 4/8	19 4/8	7 7	Peoria County	IL	Andy Szewczyk	2004	1401
165 0/8	25 6/8 24 2/8	19 3/8	5 5	Morgan County	IN	George F. Alexander	2006	1401
*165 0/8	23 7/8 23 3/8	15 6/8	6 6	Mifflin County	PA	Adam Stout	2007	1401
165 0/8	23 2/8 22 6/8	17 2/8	6 6	Teton County	ID	Gregory R. Pimentel	2007	1401
165 0/8	26 0/8 24 0/8	19 4/8	5 5	Livingston County	MI	Mick A. LaFountain	2007	1401
*165 0/8	24 5/8 24 0/8	17 7/8	7 9	Shawano County	WI	Brett Olson	2008	1401
165 0/8	28 6/8 28 4/8	18 3/8	5 6	Miami County	KS	Richard Meyer	2009	1401
165 0/8	25 2/8 26 2/8	19 1/8	5 7	Logan County	OH	Van Roger Williams	2009	1401
165 0/8	24 2/8 24 7/8	17 1/8	7 5	Fort a La Corne	SAS	Jeff Smith	2010	1401

WHITETAIL DEER (TYPICAL ANTLERS)

Minimum Score 125   Continued

SCORE	LENGTH OF R MAIN BEAM L	INSIDE SPREAD	NUMBER OF R POINTS L	AREA	STATE/ PROVINCE	HUNTER'S NAME	DATE	RANK
164 7/8	28 0/8 25 1/8	20 1/8	4 5	Kane County	IL	James A. Anderson	1980	1426
164 7/8	25 4/8 26 2/8	19 3/8	5 5	Peoria County	IL	Joe R. McCord	1983	1426
164 7/8	24 7/8 25 0/8	17 1/8	5 5	Elkhart County	IN	Joe Leszczynski	1984	1426
164 7/8	25 0/8 25 4/8	19 3/8	6 6	Gray County	KS	Ralph W. Herron	1984	1426
164 7/8	26 1/8 25 6/8	21 7/8	6 6	Madison County	MT	Gordan Sampson	1986	1426
164 7/8	25 4/8 26 0/8	21 3/8	6 7	Coles County	IL	Ralph Garland	1988	1426
164 7/8	26 5/8 27 3/8	18 7/8	5 5	Richland County	OH	Erwin Merkli	1988	1426
164 7/8	27 5/8 27 6/8	23 1/8	7 7	Butler County	OH	Will McQueen	1989	1426
164 7/8	26 4/8 25 4/8	17 7/8	6 5	Osage County	OK	Joe Admire, Sr.	1993	1426
164 7/8	24 7/8 25 7/8	18 5/8	5 5	Christian County	KY	Kelly Jones	1995	1426
164 7/8	26 2/8 27 6/8	20 7/8	6 7	Anne Arundel County	MD	William Gabriel III	1996	1426
164 7/8	24 4/8 24 6/8	19 1/8	5 5	Le Sueur County	MN	Frank Kammerdiener, Jr.	1998	1426
164 7/8	27 2/8 26 7/8	18 6/8	7 6	Wright County	MO	Brian O'Dell	1999	1426
164 7/8	27 7/8 26 4/8	25 1/8	6 5	Issaquena County	MS	James R. House	1999	1426
164 7/8	26 5/8 27 1/8	20 1/8	5 5	Pierce County	WI	Doug Toenjes	2003	1426
164 7/8	24 2/8 24 3/8	20 7/8	5 5	Guthrie County	IA	Marc Nelson	2004	1426
164 7/8	26 2/8 26 5/8	20 1/8	6 6	Hamilton County	OH	Dan McKinney	2004	1426
164 7/8	25 7/8 25 6/8	21 7/8	4 6	Grundy County	IL	Ryan Kohl	2004	1426
164 7/8	23 0/8 23 7/8	16 3/8	5 5	Stark County	ND	Loren Adams	2006	1426
164 7/8	27 0/8 27 1/8	19 6/8	7 7	Clark County	IL	Donald McWilliams, Jr.	2006	1426
164 7/8	25 5/8 24 6/8	18 6/8	6 5	Powell County	MT	Chris Dahl	2007	1426
*164 7/8	26 3/8 25 4/8	18 5/8	5 6	Hart County	KY	Joe Miller	2008	1426
*164 7/8	24 0/8 24 2/8	21 7/8	6 6	Van Buren County	IA	Ernie Merydith	2008	1426
164 6/8	28 1/8 26 5/8	20 7/8	8 5	Shelby County	OH	Jerry Atkinson	1975	1449
164 6/8	26 4/8 28 2/8	22 2/8	5 6	Highland County	OH	Daniel L. Henges	1976	1449
164 6/8	27 5/8 26 0/8	15 6/8	5 5	Sanilac County	MI	Michael J. Wines	1981	1449
164 6/8	26 0/8 26 2/8	20 6/8	5 5	Macoupin County	IL	John E. Eldred	1985	1449
164 6/8	26 5/8 26 5/8	26 4/8	8 5	Sullivan County	IN	John W. Hale	1988	1449
164 6/8	23 6/8 22 3/8	20 2/8	5 5	La Salle County	IL	Randy Hooper	1988	1449
164 6/8	24 5/8 24 5/8	17 0/8	5 5	Macon County	IL	Cal Heseman	1988	1449
164 6/8	24 2/8 24 4/8	15 2/8	5 5	Emmet County	IA	Steven L. Reighard, Sr.	1990	1449
164 6/8	27 7/8 26 6/8	19 5/8	6 7	Lincoln County	NE	Steve Stumbo	1996	1449
164 6/8	26 1/8 25 1/8	17 6/8	5 5	Waukesha County	WI	Christopher E. Toutant	1997	1449
164 6/8	25 1/8 26 0/8	18 4/8	5 5	Clay County	IL	Richard Stock	1997	1449
164 6/8	25 3/8 24 2/8	19 2/8	6 7	Pawnee County	NE	Tom Dupell	2000	1449
164 6/8	26 0/8 27 5/8	22 0/8	8 6	Preble County	OH	Mike McCabe	2000	1449
164 6/8	24 7/8 25 6/8	19 5/8	7 7	Wicomico County	MD	C. L. "Dutch" Workman	2000	1449
164 6/8	23 5/8 22 4/8	20 2/8	5 5	Lake County	IL	Jerry Dobbs	2001	1449
*164 6/8	27 1/8 26 3/8	21 0/8	5 6	Monroe County	WI	James Belcher	2001	1449
164 6/8	24 5/8 24 7/8	22 4/8	5 5	Pawnee County	KS	Diana L. Faris	2002	1449
*164 6/8	24 5/8 24 6/8	18 6/8	5 5	Gallatin County	IL	Cody Smith	2004	1449
*164 6/8	23 1/8 23 2/8	17 6/8	6 6	Decatur County	IA	Zach Thomas	2005	1449
164 6/8	26 6/8 25 7/8	19 4/8	8 6	Fillmore County	MN	Eric Feine	2005	1449
*164 6/8	23 4/8 24 1/8	17 6/8	7 7	Lincoln County	MO	Thomas R. Gibson	2007	1449
164 6/8	23 7/8 23 6/8	22 6/8	5 5	McLean County	ND	Vance Tomlinson	2009	1449
164 5/8	25 2/8 23 5/8	18 5/8	8 6	Sumner County	KS	Archie A. Stralow	1967	1471
164 5/8	26 3/8 24 6/8	20 6/8	5 6	Sedgwick County	CO	Brad Ham	1973	1471
164 5/8	25 7/8 25 7/8	19 3/8	6 6	Fayette County	IA	Jerry Brown	1989	1471
164 5/8	26 5/8 25 4/8	20 4/8	6 6	Saginaw County	MI	William J. Twarog	1990	1471
164 5/8	25 6/8 26 1/8	18 0/8	8 7	McDonough County	IL	Scott Schauble	1994	1471
164 5/8	26 3/8 26 5/8	22 4/8	6 6	Clark County	IL	Jason D. Wallace	1994	1471
164 5/8	22 6/8 22 5/8	17 2/8	6 6	Rock County	WI	David R. Dummer, Jr.	1995	1471
164 5/8	26 0/8 25 5/8	21 1/8	5 6	Portage County	WI	Jonah Reese	1995	1471
164 5/8	25 4/8 24 5/8	20 6/8	6 6	Edgar County	IL	Joe Schmitt	1995	1471
164 5/8	25 5/8 25 3/8	22 4/8	6 7	Ogle County	IL	Matt A. Mlsna	1996	1471
164 5/8	26 5/8 24 6/8	19 1/8	5 5	Pottawattamie County	IA	Rodney P. Stahlnecker	1996	1471
164 5/8	25 0/8 24 3/8	18 1/8	5 5	Parke County	IN	Stephen J. Jones	1998	1471
164 5/8	25 7/8 25 6/8	19 0/8	6 8	Richland County	OH	Tim Stortz	1999	1471
164 5/8	27 6/8 25 7/8	21 3/8	5 5	Rusk County	WI	Doug S. Nitek	2000	1471
164 5/8	24 3/8 24 6/8	22 3/8	5 5	Richland County	WI	Virgil Hill II	2000	1471
164 5/8	23 4/8 24 4/8	20 1/8	5 5	Meigs County	OH	Robert L. Craft	2000	1471
164 5/8	24 7/8 24 7/8	19 1/8	4 5	Rockyview	ALB	Brian A. Meyers	2002	1471
*164 5/8	25 6/8 27 2/8	20 5/8	5 5	Dallas County	IA	Jason Moore	2007	1471
164 5/8	26 0/8 25 5/8	18 3/8	5 5	Hamilton County	IA	Timothy Doering	2007	1471
164 5/8	25 5/8 26 1/8	21 2/8	6 7	Woodbury County	IA	Justin L. Donaghu	2008	1471
164 4/8	23 7/8 24 3/8	18 6/8	5 5	Morton County	ND	Butch Sammons	1985	1491
164 4/8	27 5/8 27 0/8	19 3/8	5 6	Trempealeau County	WI	Keith Lynch	1985	1491
164 4/8	23 5/8 23 5/8	20 7/8	6 6	Bond County	IL	Roger Munie	1987	1491
164 4/8	26 3/8 26 4/8	18 6/8	7 6	Montgomery County	OH	Michael L. Mrusek	1990	1491
164 4/8	26 7/8 26 6/8	17 0/8	5 5	Anoka County	MN	Paul Landberg	1991	1491
164 4/8	26 0/8 27 1/8	18 2/8	6 5	Iroquois County	IL	Troy Gullquist	1992	1491
164 4/8	27 4/8 27 0/8	22 1/8	7 7	Sauk County	WI	Douglas Kerska	1998	1491
164 4/8	24 1/8 24 0/8	19 0/8	6 6	La Crosse County	WI	Don Earley	1999	1491
164 4/8	26 2/8 26 0/8	22 6/8	4 5	Jackson County	IA	Dale H. Anderson	1999	1491
164 4/8	27 4/8 28 0/8	18 4/8	5 6	Boone County	MO	Brandon Beissenherz	2000	1491
164 4/8	23 7/8 24 5/8	18 7/8	6 5	Marion County	IA	Lowdell Taylor	2000	1491
164 4/8	27 2/8 26 4/8	21 2/8	5 9	Comanche County	KS	Jon Yokomizo	2001	1491
164 4/8	27 5/8 27 1/8	20 4/8	6 6	Cass County	IL	Nick Wenskunas	2002	1491
164 4/8	25 5/8 26 5/8	18 2/8	6 8	Franklin County	OH	Mike McConnell	2005	1491
164 4/8	26 4/8 25 4/8	19 7/8	6 6	Tazewell County	IL	Marc Anthony	2006	1491
*164 4/8	24 0/8 24 2/8	17 2/8	6 6	Hutchinson County	TX	Craig Franklin Cowden	2006	1491
164 4/8	27 0/8 27 0/8	19 6/8	5 7	Pepin County	WI	Robert L. Cataract	2007	1491
164 4/8	27 4/8 27 3/8	21 6/8	4 6	Howard County	IN	Clint Van Natter	2008	1491
164 4/8	24 7/8 24 7/8	17 3/8	7 7	Pottawattamie County	IA	Luke Warren	2009	1491
*164 4/8	23 5/8 23 6/8	17 2/8	6 5	Stutsman County	ND	Dustin T. Kleingartner	2010	1491
164 3/8	25 4/8 25 4/8	19 6/8	8 7	Norman County	MN	Gilbert Guttormson	1953	1511
164 3/8	21 4/8 21 6/8	16 5/8	6 6	Wibaux County	MT	Gerald Polesky	1959	1511
164 3/8	28 4/8 28 0/8	20 4/8	7 8	Trigg County	KY	Charles Stahl	1965	1511
164 3/8	25 1/8 25 2/8	18 3/8	5 5	Cottonwood County	MN	Jim Hansen	1972	1511
164 3/8	26 4/8 25 5/8	17 3/8	7 7	Madison County	MT	Jim Schilke	1978	1511
164 3/8	25 6/8 25 4/8	20 1/8	5 7	Saginaw County	MI	Larry Steinley	1979	1511
164 3/8	27 1/8 27 5/8	20 7/8	4 4	Hardin County	OH	Anthony A. Krummrey	1982	1511
164 3/8	28 0/8 27 5/8	21 1/8	6 8	Fayette County	OH	Steven J. Guess	1984	1511
164 3/8	26 7/8 27 0/8	20 7/8	4 4	Louisa County	IA	Roger Gipple	1984	1511
164 3/8	26 6/8 27 7/8	21 3/8	5 6	Perth	ONT	Michael Burwell	1986	1511

WHITETAIL DEER (TYPICAL ANTLERS)

Minimum Score 125 — Continued

SCORE	LENGTH OF MAIN BEAM R	L	INSIDE SPREAD	NUMBER OF POINTS R	L	AREA	STATE/PROVINCE	HUNTER'S NAME	DATE	RANK
164 3/8	26 7/8	25 5/8	18 7/8	5	5	Colfax County	NE	Dennis Indra	1987	1511
164 3/8	25 2/8	24 6/8	20 5/8	5	5	Rock Island County	IL	Mike Mitten	1989	1511
164 3/8	26 2/8	26 2/8	15 7/8	5	5	Scotland County	MO	David Westmoreland	1991	1511
164 3/8	29 5/8	26 5/8	17 7/8	5	4	Van Buren County	MI	Kenneth J. Gillan	1991	1511
164 3/8	24 7/8	25 2/8	16 4/8	6	6	Iron County	WI	Tom Brye	1992	1511
164 3/8	25 6/8	24 6/8	22 0/8	6	5	Sturgeon	ALB	Neal Heaton	1992	1511
164 3/8	25 2/8	26 1/8	17 3/8	5	6	Clark County	IL	Alan Lee	1992	1511
164 3/8	25 6/8	24 7/8	18 0/8	5	8	Breckinridge County	KY	Richard P. Bagley	1994	1511
164 3/8	25 4/8	25 0/8	17 6/8	6	6	Jefferson County	KS	Douglas J. Dee	1994	1511
164 3/8	23 6/8	23 7/8	17 1/8	5	5	White County	IL	Bruce Hillyard	1994	1511
164 3/8	26 5/8	26 3/8	18 7/8	6	5	Henry County	KY	Tom Jenkins	1995	1511
164 3/8	24 4/8	24 2/8	17 1/8	5	5	Doniphan County	KS	Brian Pickman	1998	1511
164 3/8	24 0/8	23 6/8	17 3/8	5	5	Madison County	IA	Gary Knoll	1999	1511
164 3/8	26 2/8	26 1/8	16 3/8	5	6	Niagara County	NY	Mark Irlbacher	2002	1511
164 3/8	25 2/8	25 0/8	18 0/8	6	5	Wabasha County	MN	Jody Wilson	2002	1511
164 3/8	26 7/8	25 4/8	21 1/8	5	5	Suffolk County	NY	James Luppens, Jr.	2002	1511
164 3/8	25 5/8	25 7/8	19 1/8	5	6	Ontario County	NY	Joseph A. Dammen	2006	1511
164 3/8	25 4/8	24 2/8	20 3/8	5	5	Shackelford County	TX	John R. Bass, Jr.	2007	1511
164 3/8	26 4/8	27 4/8	16 6/8	8	6	Sangamon County	IL	Jerry Weisenberger	2007	1511
164 3/8	26 7/8	25 5/8	19 1/8	7	7	Logan County	WV	Carson Birchfield	2007	1511
164 3/8	27 4/8	25 4/8	21 3/8	5	5	Polk County	WI	Matt Andersen	2007	1511
*164 3/8	26 3/8	25 2/8	25 1/8	5	9	Jefferson County	MS	Michael C. Burkley	2008	1511
164 3/8	24 4/8	24 4/8	18 1/8	6	5	Pike County	IL	John P. Lovell	2009	1511
164 3/8	25 2/8	25 4/8	20 3/8	5	5	Clayton County	IA	Mitch Kirby	2009	1511
*164 3/8	25 6/8	25 7/8	19 1/8	5	5	Portage County	WI	Brian Mrozck	2009	1511
164 2/8	27 2/8	26 2/8	21 0/8	11	7	Grundy County	IL	Jerome M. Fris	1972	1546
164 2/8	26 7/8	26 2/8	17 5/8	6	5	Buffalo County	WI	Mark Busch	1986	1546
164 2/8	26 0/8	25 6/8	19 0/8	5	5	Morrison County	MN	Tim Steinhoff	1987	1546
164 2/8	26 6/8	27 1/8	19 6/8	6	5	Pike County	IL	Roger Pepper	1987	1546
164 2/8	25 1/8	24 2/8	17 0/8	5	5	Mason County	IL	Richard J. "Buck" Fuller	1988	1546
164 2/8	23 6/8	22 3/8	22 0/8	8	9	Kendall County	IL	Christopher Kiernan	1989	1546
164 2/8	22 0/8	22 5/8	17 4/8	6	6	Lake County	IL	Steven Tjader	1989	1546
164 2/8	26 7/8	27 5/8	20 6/8	5	7	Clark County	IL	Cole Lee	1990	1546
164 2/8	23 4/8	24 4/8	19 0/8	6	5	Guthrie County	IA	Joe Dowell	1991	1546
164 2/8	25 0/8	27 1/8	22 3/8	6	5	Montgomery County	IA	Dick Paul	1993	1546
164 2/8	24 3/8	25 2/8	21 0/8	5	5	St. Croix County	WI	Tony Rizzo	1994	1546
164 2/8	26 3/8	26 4/8	21 0/8	4	5	Ringgold County	IA	Steve Snow	1996	1546
164 2/8	28 2/8	29 0/8	21 6/8	4	4	Jefferson County	IL	Gail Campbell	1997	1546
164 2/8	26 1/8	25 4/8	18 4/8	8	6	Jefferson County	KS	Lyle Beers	1997	1546
*164 2/8	24 1/8	23 5/8	20 1/8	6	5	Du Page County	IL	Demetrios Malamis	1999	1546
164 2/8	26 3/8	25 6/8	17 6/8	5	6	Shawano County	WI	Keith Wilcox	1999	1546
164 2/8	24 3/8	26 3/8	20 4/8	7	5	Clark County	IL	Jim Collier	1999	1546
164 2/8	27 4/8	27 0/8	23 6/8	5	5	Webster County	IA	Ed Ulicki	2001	1546
164 2/8	27 0/8	25 5/8	18 6/8	5	5	Greene County	IN	Timothy W. Shipp	2002	1546
164 2/8	26 1/8	26 4/8	21 0/8	5	5	Hamilton County	OH	Peter Cielenski	2004	1546
164 2/8	24 2/8	24 2/8	19 0/8	5	5	Lafayette County	WI	Matt Reising	2004	1546
164 2/8	29 3/8	28 0/8	27 2/8	5	5	Caledon	ONT	Piero Silvaroli	2005	1546
164 2/8	26 4/8	26 1/8	17 2/8	5	5	Waushara County	WI	Tom Tuchscherer	2006	1546
*164 2/8	26 4/8	27 7/8	20 1/8	6	8	Warren County	IL	Barry L. Robinson	2006	1546
*164 2/8	24 5/8	24 7/8	20 1/8	5	7	Kanawha County	WV	James Embrey	2006	1546
164 2/8	26 3/8	26 0/8	20 3/8	5	7	Jackson County	MO	Ted Butler	2007	1546
164 2/8	23 4/8	24 0/8	16 4/8	6	6	Livingston County	MO	James McCauley	2010	1546
164 1/8	26 5/8	26 3/8	18 2/8	6	5	Morrison County	MN	Lloyd Neuman	1971	1573
164 1/8	26 2/8	26 4/8	22 5/8	5	5	Washington County	OH	Roger Pape	1980	1573
164 1/8	24 6/8	24 5/8	16 5/8	5	6	Dundy County	NE	John Crump	1983	1573
164 1/8	26 6/8	27 4/8	20 1/8	6	4	Adams County	IL	John Shaffer	1985	1573
164 1/8	26 5/8	26 3/8	18 3/8	6	6	Otoe County	NE	Dale A. Hall	1989	1573
164 1/8	25 4/8	26 1/8	20 5/8	6	5	Lawrence County	IN	Michael R. Davidson	1992	1573
164 1/8	24 6/8	24 5/8	19 5/8	5	5	Spokane County	WA	Mike Ambach	1992	1573
164 1/8	23 2/8	22 6/8	20 7/8	9	6	Nodaway County	MO	Lanny Guthrie	1993	1573
164 1/8	24 2/8	24 2/8	19 3/8	7	8	Logan County	WV	Terry J. Cline	1993	1573
164 1/8	24 6/8	24 5/8	17 6/8	5	5	Adair County	MO	Rodney Baumgartner	1993	1573
164 1/8	24 5/8	25 4/8	17 1/8	5	6	Monroe County	WI	Gary Wright	1994	1573
164 1/8	25 0/8	24 4/8	21 5/8	5	5	Republic County	KS	Gary Dahl	1997	1573
164 1/8	26 0/8	26 2/8	18 6/8	7	5	Pike County	IL	Jerry Anderson	1998	1573
164 1/8	25 0/8	24 5/8	22 7/8	5	5	Moultrie County	IL	Gary F. Saveley	2000	1573
164 1/8	22 7/8	23 6/8	15 3/8	5	5	Outagamie County	WI	Matt R. Heimann	2002	1573
164 1/8	23 1/8	24 5/8	20 3/8	5	5	Macoupin County	IL	Brian Genetti	2002	1573
164 1/8	26 2/8	25 5/8	21 0/8	6	7	Carver County	MN	Robert J. Evans	2002	1573
164 1/8	27 3/8	27 3/8	19 6/8	7	7	La Porte County	IN	Adam Novak	2003	1573
*164 1/8	25 0/8	25 2/8	20 5/8	5	7	Grayson County	KY	Denny Baxter	2004	1573
*164 1/8	23 4/8	23 3/8	17 2/8	7	5	Nemaha County	NE	Ken Hatten	2004	1573
164 1/8	24 2/8	24 6/8	22 1/8	5	5	Tazewell County	IL	Marc Anthony	2004	1573
164 1/8	23 5/8	24 0/8	18 0/8	7	6	Johnson County	NE	Brett Bock	2004	1573
164 1/8	25 2/8	24 5/8	18 7/8	5	5	Columbia County	WI	Randy M. Baerwolf	2004	1573
164 1/8	26 3/8	26 0/8	17 3/8	6	6	St. Croix County	WI	Dennis Saathoff	2004	1573
164 1/8	26 1/8	25 3/8	21 2/8	6	6	Putnam County	IL	Sean Shofner	2006	1573
*164 1/8	23 7/8	23 0/8	17 1/8	7	6	Vigo County	IN	Cindy Rothrock	2007	1573
164 1/8	24 4/8	24 0/8	17 1/8	5	5	Washington County	IA	Don Kieler	2007	1573
164 1/8	26 0/8	25 5/8	21 1/8	5	6	Louisa County	IA	Stuart Robinson	2008	1573
164 1/8	25 6/8	26 3/8	19 1/8	4	5	Union County	IA	Michael Turner	2008	1573
*164 1/8	25 2/8	24 4/8	24 6/8	5	7	Pierce County	WI	Tom J. McNurlin	2010	1573
164 0/8	24 3/8	25 0/8	16 6/8	5	5	Olmsted County	MN	Robert Meyer	1969	1603
164 0/8	25 1/8	25 5/8	23 3/8	5	7	Morrison County	MN	Bruce Edberg	1977	1603
164 0/8	28 0/8	26 4/8	22 6/8	5	5	Buffalo County	WI	Gerald Palmer	1986	1603
164 0/8	25 5/8	26 5/8	19 6/8	6	5	Burnett County	WI	Gary A. Johnson	1989	1603
164 0/8	25 4/8	25 2/8	22 2/8	7	6	Lawrence County	IL	Tom Childress	1992	1603
164 0/8	23 5/8	24 1/8	17 4/8	7	7	Harlan County	KY	Gilbert E. Hensley	1992	1603
164 0/8	24 0/8	24 6/8	19 2/8	6	5	Dallas County	IA	Iner Joelson	1994	1603
164 0/8	26 4/8	26 1/8	19 2/8	4	5	Steuben County	IN	Kevin Smith	1995	1603
164 0/8	26 4/8	26 0/8	19 6/8	5	5	Hennepin County	MN	Douglas Leo Moore	1997	1603
164 0/8	25 2/8	25 3/8	15 4/8	5	5	Morrill County	NE	Tim Ray	1997	1603
164 0/8	25 4/8	25 2/8	21 3/8	6	5	Jefferson County	IA	Robin Giebel	1997	1603
164 0/8	25 0/8	22 7/8	22 4/8	6	5	Kleberg County	TX	Johnnie R. Walters	2000	1603
164 0/8	26 1/8	25 2/8	17 6/8	6	7	Bureau County	IL	George R. Glover	2000	1603

372

WHITETAIL DEER (TYPICAL ANTLERS)

Minimum Score 125 — Continued

SCORE	LENGTH OF R MAIN BEAM L	INSIDE SPREAD	NUMBER OF R POINTS L		AREA	STATE/ PROVINCE	HUNTER'S NAME	DATE	RANK
164 0/8	24 7/8 25 2/8	17 6/8	5	5	Le Sueur County	MN	Brian Wilde	2000	1603
164 0/8	26 4/8 25 3/8	21 4/8	6	5	Mason County	IL	Virgil R. Hester	2001	1603
164 0/8	26 0/8 25 4/8	18 4/8	5	5	McHenry County	IL	Kyle J. Resheske	2003	1603
164 0/8	26 2/8 26 6/8	18 5/8	6	6	Jefferson County	IL	Matt Jack	2004	1603
164 0/8	24 2/8 23 3/8	17 0/8	6	6	Halifax County	VA	Steven W. Blosser	2005	1603
164 0/8	25 7/8 25 5/8	16 4/8	6	8	Arkansas County	AR	Rob Jones	2006	1603
164 0/8	25 4/8 26 0/8	22 0/8	4	5	Stafford County	KS	Steve Keithley	2007	1603
*164 0/8	25 3/8 25 2/8	16 2/8	5	5	Chippewa County	WI	Bob Ewings	2008	1603
164 0/8	25 7/8 25 3/8	17 0/8	6	5	Chautauqua County	KS	Lee Norman	2008	1603
164 0/8	24 5/8 24 5/8	19 4/8	5	6	Ozaukee County	WI	Mark Rohde	2009	1603
163 7/8	26 3/8 26 4/8	19 3/8	9	10	Caldwell County	KY	Daniel R. Keith	1988	1626
163 7/8	27 1/8 27 3/8	22 1/8	6	7	Cass County	IL	Richard Chase/Henry Susong	1993	1626
163 7/8	23 4/8 24 6/8	18 3/8	5	5	Craig County	OK	Kelly Dougherty	1995	1626
163 7/8	25 3/8 25 5/8	18 5/8	5	6	Wayne County	NY	Rick Martin	1997	1626
163 7/8	24 1/8 24 5/8	18 6/8	5	6	Comanche County	KS	Darrell Allen	1997	1626
163 7/8	23 4/8 25 0/8	19 1/8	5	5	Adams County	WI	Eric Johnson	1997	1626
163 7/8	23 4/8 23 6/8	19 2/8	6	7	Fond du Lac County	WI	Shane Bauer	1999	1626
163 7/8	29 5/8 29 2/8	24 0/8	5	4	Macon County	IL	Jerry J. Wilson	1999	1626
163 7/8	24 7/8 25 7/8	19 2/8	6	7	Oakland County	MI	Michael L. Senia	1999	1626
163 7/8	25 0/8 25 1/8	20 7/8	5	5	Maidstone	SAS	Richard Nosek	2000	1626
163 7/8	25 5/8 24 7/8	16 3/8	5	6	Lewis County	KY	Michael Graf	2002	1626
163 7/8	28 6/8 27 3/8	18 0/8	7	7	Jefferson County	IN	Brian Oldfather	2002	1626
163 7/8	22 1/8 20 2/8	17 7/8	6	6	Armstrong County	PA	Richard Hankey	2002	1626
163 7/8	26 4/8 26 7/8	23 5/8	6	5	Jackson County	IA	Larry Curtis	2002	1626
163 7/8	25 6/8 25 0/8	18 3/8	5	5	Ashland County	OH	Matt A. Schumaker	2003	1626
163 7/8	24 5/8 24 2/8	19 6/8	6	6	Butler County	KY	Dennis McElhannon	2003	1626
163 7/8	25 4/8 25 4/8	18 7/8	6	6	Jefferson County	OH	Francis Szymoniak	2004	1626
163 7/8	25 4/8 25 3/8	17 1/8	6	5	Calumet County	WI	Brett Wilkens	2004	1626
163 7/8	28 2/8 29 2/8	17 0/8	5	6	Louisa County	IA	Bradley D. Cole	2005	1626
163 7/8	26 2/8 25 6/8	19 6/8	8	9	Saline County	KS	Jeff Jordan	2006	1626
*163 7/8	25 1/8 25 0/8	19 3/8	5	5	Scott County	MN	James O'Brien	2008	1626
163 7/8	26 2/8 26 0/8	17 1/8	6	6	Muhlenberg County	KY	Dustin Flener	2009	1626
163 7/8	25 0/8 26 1/8	18 3/8	5	6	Waukesha County	WI	Rick A. Bungert	2009	1626
163 7/8	24 1/8 24 4/8	17 5/8	5	6	Barber County	KS	Scott Koelzer	2009	1626
163 6/8	23 6/8 26 5/8	19 2/8	5	5	Fayette County	IA	Bob Nicolay	1981	1650
163 6/8	23 5/8 25 4/8	19 4/8	7	8	Porter County	IN	Raymond T. Satterblom	1983	1650
163 6/8	23 5/8 24 7/8	17 5/8	6	5	Graham County	KS	Russell Hull	1987	1650
163 6/8	27 4/8 27 6/8	20 2/8	5	6	Clark County	IL	Gerald Shaffner	1991	1650
163 6/8	23 0/8 23 7/8	18 3/8	7	5	Cook County	IL	Mike Ryan	1992	1650
163 6/8	24 3/8 24 0/8	17 0/8	5	6	Cowley County	KS	Larry J. McKean	1992	1650
163 6/8	24 4/8 25 1/8	17 6/8	5	5	Lee County	IA	Troy Matter	1994	1650
163 6/8	26 4/8 27 1/8	18 7/8	6	6	Schuyler County	IL	Bruce Clements	1995	1650
163 6/8	24 6/8 26 4/8	19 7/8	6	6	Page County	IA	Justin Blake	1997	1650
163 6/8	25 2/8 26 1/8	20 6/8	5	6	Black Hawk County	IA	Kenneth A. Lewis, Sr.	1999	1650
163 6/8	26 6/8 26 0/8	19 7/8	5	5	Harper County	KS	Brian Hamilton	2000	1650
163 6/8	25 1/8 25 1/8	17 7/8	5	6	Spokane County	WA	Gordon Hoffnagle	2000	1650
163 6/8	25 5/8 26 0/8	19 4/8	5	5	Harrison County	IA	Ron Fleck	2002	1650
163 6/8	27 6/8 26 3/8	21 0/8	5	5	Pierce County	WI	Brian G. Ingli	2003	1650
163 6/8	25 4/8 24 2/8	18 0/8	6	6	Wayne County	IA	Andy C. Decker	2003	1650
163 6/8	24 7/8 23 4/8	18 2/8	5	5	Morrill County	NE	Mark Didier	2004	1650
163 6/8	24 0/8 26 4/8	19 1/8	7	8	Buffalo County	WI	Robert Pacocha	2008	1650
163 5/8	25 6/8 25 4/8	21 6/8	5	5	Phillips County	KS	Bill Duncan	1969	1667
163 5/8	26 5/8 26 1/8	21 3/8	6	7	Lawrence County	IL	Larry K. Karns	1975	1667
163 5/8	25 5/8 25 1/8	19 3/8	5	5	Wright County	MN	Rick Heberling	1978	1667
163 5/8	26 4/8 25 1/8	19 2/8	6	7	Fulton County	IL	Mike Reatherford	1982	1667
163 5/8	25 1/8 25 4/8	19 4/8	6	8	Jackson County	MO	Chris Shotton	1985	1667
163 5/8	25 4/8 26 2/8	19 0/8	6	7	Franklin County	IN	Roger Mullins	1987	1667
163 5/8	23 4/8 23 1/8	19 3/8	5	6	Carver County	MN	Ryan Jopp	1991	1667
163 5/8	21 3/8 21 2/8	15 1/8	6	5	Somerset County	MD	Mike Nichols	1992	1667
163 5/8	26 3/8 29 0/8	21 0/8	8	6	Vermilion County	IL	James D. Rueter	1992	1667
163 5/8	25 0/8 25 4/8	17 1/8	4	6	Billings County	ND	Ohne L. Raasch	1994	1667
163 5/8	26 3/8 27 0/8	19 1/8	5	5	Henry County	MO	Keith Lawson	1996	1667
163 5/8	26 2/8 26 5/8	22 1/8	8	6	Ramsey County	MN	Robert Meyer	1998	1667
163 5/8	27 0/8 26 4/8	20 7/8	6	6	Vigo County	IN	Robert C. Ford	1998	1667
163 5/8	25 2/8 25 2/8	18 3/8	7	7	Noble County	OK	Donald R. Kramer	1998	1667
163 5/8	24 0/8 24 6/8	19 7/8	5	5	Allamakee County	IA	Forrest Goodman	1999	1667
163 5/8	24 5/8 24 3/8	19 5/8	5	7	Coffey County	KS	J. C. Gilliam	2000	1667
163 5/8	23 6/8 23 1/8	16 7/8	6	5	Goodhue County	MN	Scott J. Dunbar	2000	1667
163 5/8	26 5/8 26 1/8	23 7/8	7	6	Grayson County	TX	Mark A. Wade	2000	1667
163 5/8	25 5/8 25 7/8	19 5/8	6	6	Mills County	TX	David L. Petterson, Jr.	2002	1667
163 5/8	27 4/8 28 0/8	19 2/8	6	7	Henderson County	IL	Lee Fields	2003	1667
163 5/8	22 6/8 24 7/8	17 7/8	6	6	Nodaway County	MO	Adam Weldon	2004	1667
163 5/8	23 3/8 24 7/8	19 7/8	6	5	St. Louis County	MN	Richard Van Valkenburg	2005	1667
163 5/8	25 1/8 25 5/8	17 7/8	5	5	Putnam County	MO	Eric J. Madison	2008	1667
163 5/8	24 6/8 23 6/8	18 1/8	5	7	Lincoln County	WI	Tom Schmeltzer	2009	1667
163 4/8	25 4/8 25 5/8	18 0/8	5	7	Renville County	ND	Bobby Triplett	1958	1691
163 4/8	23 4/8 23 0/8	17 6/8	5	5	Wright County	MN	Dale Guetzkow	1978	1691
163 4/8	28 1/8 30 0/8	23 2/8	5	5	Lawrence County	OH	Berkley Pennington, Sr.	1981	1691
163 4/8	24 7/8 23 6/8	21 6/8	8	6	Racine County	WI	Greg A. Hanson	1991	1691
163 4/8	24 1/8 24 2/8	20 7/8	7	7	Will County	IL	Clark Davis	1992	1691
163 4/8	25 1/8 25 0/8	20 4/8	5	5	Macon County	AL	George P. Mann	1994	1691
163 4/8	22 7/8 23 3/8	17 2/8	8	6	Otter Tail County	MN	Kurt Melancon	1994	1691
163 4/8	27 0/8 26 6/8	18 2/8	4	4	Lapeer County	MI	Bruce R. Byrnes	1994	1691
163 4/8	21 7/8 21 2/8	16 5/8	6	7	Waupaca County	WI	Jeffrey F. Hietpas	1994	1691
163 4/8	26 0/8 25 1/8	19 4/8	6	6	Guthrie County	IA	Regi Goodale	1994	1691
163 4/8	26 2/8 25 2/8	19 1/8	6	6	Seward County	KS	Josh Leonard	1994	1691
163 4/8	25 3/8 26 2/8	19 0/8	5	5	Davis County	IA	Neil A. Adams	1995	1691
163 4/8	28 6/8 27 7/8	21 2/8	4	5	Guthrie County	IA	Matthew J. Ewing	1996	1691
163 4/8	26 6/8 26 7/8	21 4/8	6	6	Washtenaw County	MI	Troy J. Satterthwaite	1996	1691
163 4/8	24 1/8 23 0/8	14 0/8	5	5	Pike County	IL	Jim Morgan	1997	1691
163 4/8	23 5/8 24 2/8	18 6/8	6	6	Logan County	IL	Gunnar Darnall	1998	1691
163 4/8	24 1/8 18 2/8	18 2/8	5	5	Marion County	KS	Dennis Ballweg	1999	1691
163 4/8	24 3/8 24 3/8	21 2/8	5	5	Grundy County	IL	Donald Rose	1999	1691
163 4/8	27 4/8 26 3/8	21 6/8	6	5	Morrison County	MN	Corey A. Harmening	1999	1691
163 4/8	22 5/8 23 2/8	19 6/8	5	5	Wayne County	NY	Terry S. Young	2000	1691

373

WHITETAIL DEER (TYPICAL ANTLERS)

Minimum Score 125 Continued

SCORE	LENGTH OF R MAIN BEAM L	INSIDE SPREAD	NUMBER OF R POINTS L	AREA	STATE/PROVINCE	HUNTER'S NAME	DATE	RANK
163 4/8	26 3/8 26 3/8	21 4/8	6 5	Buffalo County	WI	Gerald Todd	2000	1691
163 4/8	27 0/8 26 7/8	21 3/8	4 6	Forest County	PA	Brady Mortimer	2002	1691
163 4/8	24 3/8 24 2/8	17 1/8	7 6	Walworth County	WI	John E. Jutz, Sr.	2003	1691
163 4/8	27 5/8 27 7/8	20 2/8	5 6	Buffalo County	WI	Jackson Serum	2003	1691
163 4/8	25 4/8 26 1/8	16 4/8	6 5	Monroe County	IA	Tim C. Deskin	2003	1691
163 4/8	25 0/8 24 1/8	16 6/8	5 5	Marwayne	ALB	Bob Parker	2004	1691
163 4/8	27 2/8 27 0/8	20 4/8	4 5	Waupaca County	WI	Scott Olsen	2005	1691
163 4/8	24 1/8 23 1/8	18 5/8	6 6	Jersey County	IL	Brandon Fontenot	2006	1691
*163 4/8	23 2/8 24 4/8	15 1/8	5 6	Grant County	WI	Donald Zimmerman	2007	1691
*163 4/8	24 2/8 23 7/8	13 2/8	5 5	Shawano County	WI	Mark A. Weisnicht	2009	1691
*163 4/8	29 1/8 29 0/8	21 6/8	4 5	Montgomery County	OH	Earl England	2009	1691
163 4/8	24 6/8 25 1/8	17 0/8	6 6	Allen County	IN	Thomas E. Burns	2009	1691
163 3/8	24 4/8 22 7/8	22 1/8	5 5	Linn County	IA	Delmar Phillips	1960	1723
163 3/8	24 3/8 23 7/8	17 5/8	8 7	Morrison County	MN	Alvin A. Diemert	1973	1723
163 3/8	26 4/8 26 2/8	20 5/8	5 5	Scott County	KY	Garry Hoffman	1982	1723
163 3/8	26 1/8 26 7/8	15 3/8	6 7	Chase County	KS	John Moore	1983	1723
163 3/8	24 4/8 25 0/8	19 0/8	8 8	Winnebago County	IL	Bradley S. Conrad	1984	1723
163 3/8	27 2/8 26 1/8	19 1/8	5 5	Eaton County	MI	Dennis Orr	1987	1723
163 3/8	24 7/8 24 7/8	19 1/8	6 8	Jefferson County	IL	Ray Leneave	1993	1723
163 3/8	25 5/8 26 5/8	14 5/8	5 5	Barrhead	ALB	Ryan Bielert	1995	1723
163 3/8	25 0/8 25 7/8	18 5/8	5 5	Polk County	MN	Jim Ross	1995	1723
163 3/8	27 6/8 26 1/8	22 2/8	6 7	Baltimore County	MD	Christian M. Phillips	1995	1723
163 3/8	24 2/8 24 0/8	16 7/8	5 5	Republic County	KS	Lonnie Boman	1996	1723
163 3/8	26 0/8 25 3/8	23 4/8	6 5	Page County	IA	Bob Hilton, Jr.	1996	1723
163 3/8	24 5/8 26 3/8	20 4/8	7 6	Jackson County	IL	Mark Bennett	1997	1723
163 3/8	26 4/8 26 7/8	21 4/8	7 6	Jackson County	IA	Doug Lange	1999	1723
163 3/8	25 7/8 26 2/8	20 3/8	5 5	Grant County	IN	William Harris	2000	1723
163 3/8	25 7/8 25 7/8	20 3/8	5 5	Boyd County	KY	Brandon Layman	2001	1723
163 3/8	25 3/8 27 2/8	21 0/8	6 4	Harvey County	KS	Tim S. Ross	2001	1723
163 3/8	22 7/8 22 1/8	17 1/8	7 5	Carroll County	KY	Stephen Harris	2001	1723
163 3/8	26 1/8 25 6/8	19 1/8	7 7	Morrison County	MN	Dean T. Thurston	2003	1723
163 3/8	26 2/8 24 4/8	16 4/8	6 6	Johnson County	MO	Jerry Ayler	2005	1723
163 3/8	23 1/8 23 0/8	18 5/8	5 5	Montgomery County	IA	David Means	2007	1723
*163 3/8	22 3/8 24 1/8	17 7/8	6 7	Saline County	KS	Al Marklevits	2007	1723
*163 3/8	22 1/8 22 7/8	17 4/8	7 8	Jackson County	KS	Thad Wende	2007	1723
163 3/8	20 4/8 27 0/8	18 4/8	7 6	Putnam County	IN	Jonathan D. Chadd	2008	1723
*163 3/8	27 2/8 25 1/8	21 7/8	5 5	Athabasca	ALB	Glen A. Monson	2010	1723
163 2/8	28 2/8 27 3/8	23 7/8	6 6	Brown County	IL	Keith E. Meiser	1981	1748
163 2/8	25 7/8 29 2/8	22 6/8	8 5	Drew County	AR	Larry Standley	1982	1748
163 2/8	25 4/8 25 5/8	19 6/8	5 5	Mason County	KY	R. Kenton Ring	1982	1748
163 2/8	26 1/8 24 6/8	16 3/8	5 7	Licking County	OH	Don Conrad	1985	1748
163 2/8	24 1/8 24 4/8	21 2/8	5 5	Sumner County	KS	Kevin Disney	1985	1748
163 2/8	23 3/8 23 7/8	19 0/8	5 7	Carroll County	MD	Jason Carder	1988	1748
163 2/8	26 4/8 27 2/8	21 5/8	7 5	Kiowa County	KS	Jesse Zook	1989	1748
163 2/8	25 4/8 26 7/8	19 2/8	5 4	Crawford County	KS	Melinda S. Nutt	1991	1748
163 2/8	24 2/8 24 3/8	20 4/8	5 5	Hennepin County	MN	Larry Watson	1991	1748
163 2/8	27 1/8 28 3/8	20 4/8	5 5	Ross County	OH	Sam Detty	1992	1748
163 2/8	23 0/8 22 7/8	17 0/8	7 7	Houston County	MN	Aaron Augedahl	1992	1748
163 2/8	24 2/8 24 2/8	17 4/8	5 5	Rock County	WI	Richard T. Hall	1993	1748
163 2/8	25 1/8 23 3/8	19 4/8	5 6	Linn County	IA	Randy Gardner	1994	1748
163 2/8	28 2/8 27 3/8	22 4/8	4 4	Sangamon County	IL	Robert N. Kirk	1995	1748
163 2/8	25 1/8 24 7/8	17 6/8	5 6	Boone County	WV	Harold McCoy	1996	1748
163 2/8	25 6/8 24 1/8	20 2/8	5 5	Hardin County	OH	Nathan King	1996	1748
163 2/8	24 6/8 26 0/8	18 6/8	5 7	Hamilton County	OH	Jay Knight	1998	1748
163 2/8	26 0/8 25 3/8	20 2/8	5 5	Adams County	IL	Sarah Salukas	1998	1748
163 2/8	25 5/8 26 2/8	18 6/8	5 5	Kenosha County	WI	Larry M. Brevitz, Jr.	1999	1748
163 2/8	24 2/8 24 4/8	20 4/8	6 5	Buffalo County	WI	Jeff Owen	2000	1748
163 2/8	26 3/8 26 0/8	18 4/8	6 5	Buffalo County	WI	Paul Hofer	2004	1748
*163 2/8	26 4/8 25 6/8	19 5/8	6 7	Phelps County	MO	James J. Pelikan	2004	1748
*163 2/8	26 4/8 25 6/8	20 0/8	5 5	Lambton County	ONT	Aldo Pernasilici	2005	1748
163 2/8	22 0/8 21 4/8	17 4/8	6 7	Clay County	IA	Thomas Ray Gross	2006	1748
*163 2/8	26 2/8 26 4/8	17 6/8	5 6	Plymouth County	MA	Fernando A. Cristina	2007	1748
163 2/8	25 6/8 25 5/8	17 6/8	5 7	Jennings County	IN	Jason M. Egly	2007	1748
163 2/8	24 5/8 24 7/8	22 0/8	5 5	Washington County	CO	Brandon Powell	2007	1748
*163 2/8	26 1/8 26 4/8	21 3/8	6 6	Buffalo County	WI	Barry Orne	2008	1748
*163 2/8	26 5/8 28 2/8	19 0/8	6 7	Rock County	WI	Brian Duoss	2008	1748
163 2/8	27 2/8 26 4/8	17 6/8	5 6	Iowa County	WI	Brian Schultz	2008	1748
163 2/8	24 4/8 24 3/8	18 3/8	6 7	Waupaca County	WI	Wesley Smits	2008	1748
163 2/8	25 1/8 25 3/8	17 0/8	6 5	Putnam County	IN	Christopher J. Cooper	2010	1748
163 1/8	24 2/8 26 0/8	16 4/8	7 7	Logan County	WV	Gilbert Sexton	1963	1780
163 1/8	27 6/8 27 5/8	18 6/8	8 5	Knox County	OH	Robert L. Hammond	1983	1780
163 1/8	25 3/8 25 0/8	20 0/8	6 6	Lake County	IL	Andrew Holst	1987	1780
163 1/8	25 1/8 25 6/8	21 3/8	6 5	Logan County	OH	Jerrod Pooler	1988	1780
163 1/8	22 5/8 24 3/8	18 7/8	5 7	Clayton County	IA	Daniel J. Brady	1988	1780
163 1/8	25 6/8 25 2/8	18 5/8	5 5	Wright County	MN	Jerry Goodale	1990	1780
163 1/8	24 6/8 26 4/8	18 0/8	6 6	Bayfield County	WI	Steve Polkoski	1992	1780
163 1/8	26 2/8 26 2/8	20 1/8	6 5	Edwards County	IL	Roger D. Shelby	1992	1780
163 1/8	25 3/8 24 0/8	19 7/8	8 8	La Salle County	TX	Francis D. Elias	1992	1780
163 1/8	27 7/8 26 7/8	23 3/8	5 5	Tensas Parish	LA	Joe Hatton	1995	1780
163 1/8	27 2/8 26 7/8	23 3/8	4 5	Peoria County	IL	Larry Pollack	1995	1780
163 1/8	23 2/8 23 6/8	18 3/8	6 5	Clark County	KS	Dan Pianalto	2000	1780
163 1/8	25 4/8 25 4/8	19 2/8	5 7	Clark County	MO	Kevin Gutknecht	2001	1780
163 1/8	25 7/8 26 6/8	21 6/8	5 6	Tompkins County	NY	Randall McMullen	2002	1780
163 1/8	27 4/8 26 4/8	18 1/8	5 5	Waupaca County	WI	Lee R. Platta	2002	1780
163 1/8	25 4/8 23 3/8	20 5/8	7 6	McDonough County	IL	Chad Sperry	2002	1780
163 1/8	25 6/8 26 1/8	17 6/8	6 5	Knox County	MO	Randy G. Craig	2003	1780
163 1/8	24 6/8 25 4/8	19 5/8	5 5	Adams County	WI	Eric Wichman	2003	1780
*163 1/8	20 6/8 21 7/8	18 7/8	5 5	Adams County	IL	Tim D. Walmsley	2004	1780
*163 1/8	25 3/8 24 4/8	19 5/8	5 5	Meigs County	OH	Gregory S. Ruppenthal	2004	1780
163 1/8	23 2/8 23 4/8	15 7/8	5 6	Cass County	MI	Ronald Kruger	2005	1780
163 1/8	23 4/8 23 7/8	19 2/8	5 5	Brown County	WI	Don Vanden Avond	2005	1780
163 1/8	27 0/8 27 4/8	16 3/8	5 5	Miami County	OH	Ralph J. Bateman	2005	1780
163 1/8	27 0/8 27 4/8	19 1/8	8 5	Portage County	OH	Daniel Troyer	2006	1780
163 1/8	23 0/8 23 1/8	17 6/8	8 7	Dallas County	IA	Joshua Benson	2007	1780
*163 1/8	23 5/8 24 7/8	17 5/8	7 5	Green Lake County	WI	Brian Shulz	2007	1780

374

WHITETAIL DEER (TYPICAL ANTLERS)

Minimum Score 125
Continued

SCORE	LENGTH OF R MAIN BEAM L	INSIDE SPREAD	NUMBER OF R POINTS L	AREA	STATE/ PROVINCE	HUNTER'S NAME	DATE	RANK
163 1/8	24 3/8 24 2/8	21 0/8	5 6	Laclede County	MO	Josh Maddux	2008	1780
163 1/8	27 3/8 27 6/8	19 3/8	5 4	Buffalo County	WI	Kevin Rotering	2008	1780
*163 1/8	24 5/8 23 7/8	18 3/8	6 5	Peoria County	IL	Blake Plattner	2008	1780
*163 1/8	28 0/8 28 1/8	19 5/8	6 6	Shawano County	WI	David D. Hohn	2009	1780
163 1/8	26 2/8 26 3/8	19 1/8	5 6	Schuylkill County	PA	Ronald D. Atkinson	2009	1780
163 1/8	25 5/8 25 1/8	17 0/8	6 5	Shawano County	WI	Dale Diedrick	2009	1780
163 0/8	24 0/8 24 6/8	20 0/8	5 5	Dickinson County	IA	Harold Ehrp	1959	1812
163 0/8	25 2/8 25 0/8	15 1/8	6 6	Texas County	OK	Edward F. Bryan, Jr.	1976	1812
163 0/8	26 3/8 25 3/8	22 0/8	7 8	Switzerland County	IN	Richard W. Keebler	1977	1812
163 0/8	25 1/8 24 3/8	16 4/8	5 5	Ashland County	WI	Sid Kilger	1982	1812
163 0/8	27 5/8 26 6/8	21 0/8	8 8	Gibson County	IN	Phil Scott	1986	1812
163 0/8	25 6/8 24 2/8	20 0/8	5 6	Marshall County	KS	Tim Wanklyn	1986	1812
163 0/8	24 6/8 24 0/8	19 2/8	6 6	Jefferson County	IN	Don Field	1987	1812
163 0/8	27 4/8 27 2/8	19 3/8	6 8	Clarke County	IA	Gary Cobb	1988	1812
163 0/8	24 4/8 24 1/8	20 4/8	5 6	Clermont County	OH	Larry W. Van	1990	1812
163 0/8	20 7/8 19 6/8	15 0/8	6 7	Macoupin County	IL	Rick Tigo	1992	1812
163 0/8	21 6/8 22 2/8	17 4/8	6 6	Will County	IL	Ray T. Guzak	1993	1812
163 0/8	25 1/8 25 5/8	20 4/8	6 6	Will County	IL	Steve Connors	1994	1812
163 0/8	23 4/8 23 7/8	21 4/8	5 5	Lincoln County	CO	Dennis Goody	1994	1812
163 0/8	25 5/8 26 4/8	18 1/8	6 5	Fayette County	IL	Terry L. Jones	1996	1812
163 0/8	25 5/8 26 1/8	19 2/8	5 5	Putnam County	MO	James W. Ross	1996	1812
163 0/8	26 4/8 25 2/8	19 7/8	6 5	Washington County	IA	Joe Goodell	1998	1812
163 0/8	24 7/8 24 4/8	17 6/8	5 5	Langlade County	WI	Wayne R. Wildman, Sr.	1999	1812
163 0/8	24 2/8 24 2/8	16 0/8	5 6	Ashland County	WI	Stanley E. Hopfensperger	1999	1812
163 0/8	24 2/8 22 4/8	15 6/8	5 5	Leavenworth County	KS	William L. Boice	2000	1812
163 0/8	25 6/8 25 5/8	19 0/8	5 5	Dunleath	SAS	Bill Leslie	2001	1812
163 0/8	27 6/8 27 2/8	20 2/8	5 6	Waupaca County	WI	Marshall Henricks	2002	1812
163 0/8	25 0/8 25 3/8	18 4/8	5 5	Chenango County	NY	James A. Robinson	2002	1812
163 0/8	24 5/8 24 4/8	21 1/8	7 6	Pottawattamie County	IA	Rodney P. Stahlnecker	2002	1812
163 0/8	23 1/8 22 5/8	18 0/8	6 5	Morton County	ND	Brian Schmidt	2003	1812
163 0/8	25 1/8 24 4/8	17 1/8	5 6	Lyman County	SD	Mark Rohlfing	2003	1812
*163 0/8	26 5/8 27 2/8	18 4/8	6 6	Barton County	MO	Dustin L. Chasteen	2004	1812
163 0/8	25 7/8 25 5/8	17 2/8	4 4	Jones County	IA	Kevin Muehlenkamp	2004	1812
*163 0/8	27 2/8 27 0/8	19 0/8	5 5	Lucas County	IA	Phillip L. Rich	2004	1812
*163 0/8	26 6/8 26 3/8	16 0/8	6 6	Lake County	SD	Larry R. Masterson	2004	1812
*163 0/8	28 4/8 28 6/8	20 2/8	6 5	Jo Daviess County	IL	David D. Waldschmidt	2006	1812
163 0/8	24 4/8 23 6/8	19 0/8	5 5	Washington County	WI	Stanley Kaminski	2006	1812
163 0/8	28 1/8 28 1/8	23 6/8	5 6	Lyon County	IA	Mark Bauman	2006	1812
163 0/8	26 4/8 24 4/8	21 4/8	5 5	Jackson County	IA	Larry Galliart	2007	1812
163 0/8	23 4/8 24 6/8	22 0/8	5 5	Shelby County	OH	Ben Sherman	2007	1812
163 0/8	26 6/8 25 0/8	19 0/8	5 5	Woodford County	IL	Marc Anthony	2007	1812
162 7/8	29 0/8 30 4/8	19 0/8	6 8	Queen Annes County	MD	L. P. Stephens, Jr.	1962	1847
162 7/8	24 6/8 24 6/8	22 4/8	6 7	Cowley County	KS	Kenneth Highfill	1968	1847
162 7/8	26 6/8 26 7/8	19 5/8	5 5	Lee County	IA	Mike Bentler	1983	1847
162 7/8	24 0/8 23 5/8	22 3/8	5 5	Perry County	IL	Kevin Tate	1989	1847
162 7/8	25 0/8 25 0/8	18 5/8	5 5	Baltimore County	MD	Bruce Hoover	1991	1847
162 7/8	26 7/8 27 3/8	18 6/8	5 5	Edmonton	ALB	Mark Daniel Stanley	1991	1847
162 7/8	23 1/8 24 2/8	16 5/8	5 5	Cuyahoga County	OH	Brett A. Hahner	1994	1847
162 7/8	27 2/8 26 1/8	18 3/8	6 6	Sawyer County	WI	Tim Wozniak	1994	1847
162 7/8	23 7/8 24 4/8	20 5/8	5 5	Chippewa County	WI	Terry Geist	1994	1847
162 7/8	25 7/8 25 6/8	18 5/8	6 6	Outagamie County	WI	Pat Vande Hei	1995	1847
162 7/8	25 4/8 25 0/8	16 3/8	4 4	Mason County	IL	David C. Session	1995	1847
162 7/8	23 4/8 23 3/8	18 0/8	8 6	Scott County	MN	Rob Sieh	1996	1847
162 7/8	27 3/8 27 0/8	21 7/8	4 5	McHenry County	IL	Troy Erckfritz	1996	1847
162 7/8	22 0/8 22 4/8	19 3/8	6 5	Jackson County	IL	John Joiner	1996	1847
162 7/8	22 7/8 24 0/8	17 7/8	6 5	Pike County	IL	Dan Perez	1997	1847
162 7/8	25 4/8 26 3/8	14 7/8	5 6	Waukesha County	WI	Kevin Pavloski	1997	1847
162 7/8	24 5/8 24 7/8	18 7/8	6 6	Jefferson County	MO	David Keith Wiley	1997	1847
162 7/8	26 3/8 26 4/8	18 2/8	5 7	Logan County	OH	Robert Smith	1998	1847
162 7/8	24 0/8 24 6/8	18 1/8	5 5	Gallia County	OH	Nathan Imel	1999	1847
162 7/8	22 4/8 23 2/8	20 1/8	5 5	Jefferson County	KS	Steven E. Harvey	2001	1847
162 7/8	22 5/8 22 5/8	17 7/8	5 5	Trempealeau County	WI	Courtney Kotlarz	2002	1847
162 7/8	26 1/8 26 2/8	18 4/8	5 7	Henry County	MO	David Graham	2002	1847
162 7/8	23 3/8 24 0/8	18 7/8	8 7	Schuyler County	IL	Kent Greening	2002	1847
162 7/8	25 1/8 25 0/8	19 0/8	5 6	Coshocton County	OH	C. Brian Mosholder	2002	1847
*162 7/8	23 7/8 23 6/8	18 5/8	5 5	La Porte County	IN	Tony M. Sikora	2003	1847
162 7/8	25 1/8 25 4/8	15 7/8	5 5	Chippewa County	WI	Delbert H. Helland	2003	1847
162 7/8	24 3/8 23 6/8	19 5/8	6 6	Gallia County	OH	Terry Jones	2003	1847
162 7/8	26 1/8 26 1/8	19 2/8	5 5	Van Wert County	OH	Troy R. Schumm	2005	1847
*162 7/8	25 5/8 26 1/8	16 1/8	7 7	Williams County	OH	Monte J. Perry	2006	1847
162 7/8	25 0/8 25 0/8	16 7/8	6 6	Monongalia County	WV	Mark Gump	2007	1847
162 7/8	27 4/8 28 0/8	21 1/8	5 5	Hampden County	MA	Dean R. Porter	2008	1847
162 7/8	23 0/8 22 1/8	16 6/8	6 7	Walworth County	WI	Nick Nottestad	2010	1847
162 7/8	23 7/8 24 0/8	17 7/8	5 5	Fulton County	KY	Ken Landry	2010	1847
162 6/8	24 2/8 26 2/8	20 6/8	6 7	Rice County	MN	Ken Bakken	1957	1880
162 6/8	24 6/8 25 1/8	19 4/8	5 5	Fayette County	IA	John Nagel	1969	1880
162 6/8	26 2/8 26 2/8	19 4/8	5 6	Clayton County	IA	Dale Kartman	1984	1880
162 6/8	24 1/8 24 7/8	17 4/8	5 5	Ozaukee County	WI	Joe Seaman	1989	1880
162 6/8	24 2/8 25 2/8	18 5/8	5 5	Cedar County	IA	John Shepherd	1994	1880
162 6/8	26 4/8 25 7/8	21 4/8	6 6	Parke County	IN	Tim Wilson	1997	1880
162 6/8	26 2/8 26 7/8	17 6/8	9 6	Dallas County	IA	Robert Sullivan	1997	1880
162 6/8	24 4/8 25 4/8	26 0/8	5 4	Parke County	IN	Charles A. Paxton	1998	1880
162 6/8	24 7/8 23 4/8	20 2/8	6 5	Ferry County	WA	Steve Brown	1999	1880
162 6/8	25 1/8 25 5/8	16 4/8	8 7	Penobscot County	ME	Phil McTigue	1999	1880
162 6/8	26 2/8 27 3/8	20 4/8	5 4	Vernon County	WI	David Whalen	2001	1880
162 6/8	25 0/8 26 5/8	21 0/8	5 5	Geauga County	OH	Alan C. Snyder	2002	1880
162 6/8	25 4/8 26 0/8	21 0/8	5 5	Waupaca County	WI	Edward Mertins	2002	1880
162 6/8	24 6/8 24 0/8	18 2/8	5 5	Muscatine County	IA	Doug Abney	2002	1880
162 6/8	24 6/8 24 4/8	17 6/8	5 5	Grant County	IN	J. Travis Barnett	2003	1880
162 6/8	26 4/8 26 4/8	19 4/8	5 5	Jones County	IA	Tim McDonough	2004	1880
162 6/8	25 7/8 26 3/8	18 2/8	6 6	Kosciusko County	IN	Rodney C. Spurlin	2005	1880
162 6/8	25 4/8 26 0/8	20 2/8	6 5	Breckinridge County	KY	Jack Hayden	2005	1880
*162 6/8	25 0/8 25 1/8	19 6/8	7 5	Stutsman County	ND	Jason Falk	2006	1880
162 6/8	23 6/8 23 4/8	18 4/8	6 5	Kosciusko County	IN	Kevin Brown	2006	1880
*162 6/8	23 4/8 23 6/8	18 0/8	5 5	Forest County	WI	Dan Brezinski	2006	1880

WHITETAIL DEER (TYPICAL ANTLERS)

Minimum Score 125 — Continued

SCORE	LENGTH OF R MAIN BEAM L	INSIDE SPREAD	NUMBER OF R POINTS L	AREA	STATE/PROVINCE	HUNTER'S NAME	DATE	RANK
*162 6/8	25 4/8 25 1/8	20 4/8	7 6	Adams County	IL	Mike Lepkowski, Jr.	2007	1880
162 6/8	24 1/8 23 4/8	16 2/8	6 6	Clay County	MO	Lance Poage	2007	1880
162 6/8	25 7/8 24 7/8	17 4/8	5 5	Linn County	IA	Bert Carmer	2007	1880
162 6/8	27 2/8 27 2/8	20 1/8	8 8	Marquette County	WI	Troy Huffman	2008	1880
162 6/8	22 5/8 23 3/8	16 4/8	6 7	Mills County	IA	John R. Horn	2008	1880
*162 6/8	25 7/8 25 6/8	16 7/8	7 6	Dinorwic	ONT	Jamie Wisnoski	2008	1880
162 6/8	23 6/8 25 3/8	20 0/8	6 5	Jasper County	IL	Chuck Roberts	2009	1880
*162 6/8	26 1/8 25 5/8	16 2/8	8 5	Madison County	IA	Jon Miller	2009	1880
*162 6/8	23 0/8 22 4/8	19 0/8	5 5	Crook County	WY	Mike Schmid	2010	1880
162 5/8	26 2/8 24 0/8	20 7/8	8 7	Marshall County	KS	Gary W. Tobin	1966	1910
162 5/8	26 4/8 27 5/8	20 3/8	4 4	Saunders County	NE	Robert Parkins	1967	1910
162 5/8	26 6/8 26 6/8	21 5/8	5 7	Henry County	IL	Lewis E. Burson	1976	1910
162 5/8	25 2/8 24 7/8	20 1/8	4 5	Lucas County	IA	Bill Brown	1979	1910
162 5/8	25 2/8 25 3/8	15 7/8	5 8	Crawford County	KS	Fred Geier	1981	1910
162 5/8	27 2/8 27 4/8	19 7/8	5 5	St. Charles County	MO	Roland Heiliger	1985	1910
162 5/8	25 3/8 24 3/8	16 4/8	7 5	Buffalo County	WI	Paul Schultz	1986	1910
162 5/8	25 4/8 25 3/8	16 3/8	7 5	Hubbard County	MN	Nick J. Thill, Jr.	1987	1910
162 5/8	24 1/8 23 1/8	19 0/8	6 6	Pike County	IL	Leroy Leonard	1987	1910
162 5/8	25 0/8 25 1/8	20 3/8	6 6	Cerro Gordo County	IA	R. C. Field	1989	1910
162 5/8	26 3/8 26 7/8	17 7/8	5 7	Wyandot County	OH	David Weininger	1991	1910
162 5/8	25 6/8 25 7/8	18 2/8	6 6	Jennings County	IN	Guy F. Euler	1992	1910
162 5/8	24 1/8 23 0/8	18 7/8	5 6	Jefferson County	IL	Edgar Knaus	1993	1910
162 5/8	25 4/8 25 7/8	20 7/8	5 5	Washington County	WI	Edwin M. Ruege	1996	1910
162 5/8	23 6/8 24 7/8	20 0/8	6 5	Suffolk County	NY	Rob Catalano	1997	1910
162 5/8	31 3/8 29 4/8	18 1/8	5 5	Lake County	IL	Scott A. Strickfaden	1997	1910
162 5/8	24 5/8 24 1/8	20 3/8	5 5	Trempealeau County	WI	Kenny Przybilla	1998	1910
162 5/8	23 7/8 24 5/8	22 1/8	7 5	Washington County	MN	Richard J. Hoffman	1999	1910
162 5/8	22 5/8 23 2/8	19 5/8	6 6	Ringgold County	IA	Thomas J. Majors	2000	1910
162 5/8	25 6/8 24 7/8	15 2/8	5 6	Jennings County	IN	Curtis Haines	2000	1910
162 5/8	27 2/8 26 0/8	19 0/8	5 5	Platte County	MO	Sean Witthar	2001	1910
162 5/8	24 4/8 24 0/8	19 3/8	8 5	Macoupin County	IL	Curtis A. Reznicek	2001	1910
162 5/8	24 3/8 24 3/8	17 1/8	8 8	Clay County	IN	Jim Wheeler	2001	1910
162 5/8	26 4/8 27 2/8	18 0/8	6 5	St. Clair County	MO	Delbert L. Bybee	2002	1910
*162 5/8	24 7/8 25 0/8	23 7/8	4 4	Brown County	IL	Thad Townsend	2003	1910
162 5/8	26 5/8 26 0/8	19 7/8	5 6	Madison County	MT	Jeff Allen	2004	1910
162 5/8	24 0/8 25 1/8	16 7/8	5 5	Trempealeau County	WI	Eric A. Theisen	2004	1910
162 5/8	25 3/8 27 0/8	16 3/8	5 5	Ashtabula County	OH	Daniel Feke	2005	1910
162 5/8	28 0/8 27 2/8	18 4/8	5 6	Vigo County	IN	Jack D. Fields II	2006	1910
162 5/8	27 0/8 27 3/8	20 4/8	8 5	Woodbury County	IA	Lee Williams	2007	1910
162 5/8	23 2/8 23 1/8	18 4/8	6 7	Buffalo County	WI	Dustin Rucinski	2008	1910
162 4/8	23 6/8 23 6/8	21 0/8	7 6	Branch County	MI	Randy Massey	1981	1941
162 4/8	25 2/8 25 1/8	19 6/8	6 8	Louisa County	IA	Michael Bell	1983	1941
162 4/8	25 4/8 27 0/8	18 6/8	5 5	Allegheny County	PA	Christopher T. Joyce	1985	1941
162 4/8	26 0/8 26 4/8	22 0/8	5 5	Dundy County	NE	Bradley Wiese	1985	1941
162 4/8	24 3/8 24 4/8	21 1/8	5 6	Stearns County	MN	Pat Gross	1986	1941
162 4/8	23 1/8 24 1/8	18 0/8	6 6	Vermilion County	IL	Sandra Downing	1986	1941
162 4/8	25 5/8 24 6/8	21 0/8	6 7	Will County	IL	Joseph R. Franco	1986	1941
162 4/8	25 5/8 25 5/8	17 1/8	5 6	Anoka County	MN	Kim Van Tassel	1987	1941
162 4/8	24 1/8 24 7/8	19 4/8	5 5	Champaign County	OH	Alan Shafer, Jr.	1993	1941
162 4/8	24 5/8 24 0/8	18 2/8	5 8	Cass County	MI	Bruce Woodill	1995	1941
162 4/8	27 2/8 27 2/8	20 7/8	5 7	Coles County	IL	Chris R. Eaton	2000	1941
162 4/8	26 1/8 25 3/8	19 3/8	5 8	Oakland County	MI	Keith Headley	2000	1941
162 4/8	26 0/8 26 2/8	18 7/8	6 5	Kane County	IL	Ken Hefferle	2001	1941
162 4/8	24 0/8 25 0/8	16 4/8	5 5	La Porte County	IN	Gary Leslie	2001	1941
162 4/8	25 7/8 25 1/8	15 6/8	5 5	Howard County	MO	Tim Cundiff	2002	1941
162 4/8	24 4/8 23 3/8	20 6/8	5 5	Clayton County	IA	Duwayne Fabert	2002	1941
162 4/8	25 1/8 25 4/8	18 2/8	7 5	Polk County	MN	Randal Dufault	2003	1941
162 4/8	26 5/8 22 5/8	24 2/8	6 7	Will County	IL	Jack Haviland	2003	1941
162 4/8	26 1/8 25 4/8	18 0/8	5 5	Major County	OK	Ty Stapleton	2003	1941
162 4/8	25 2/8 24 4/8	17 0/8	5 5	Livingston County	NY	Harley Doneburg	2004	1941
162 4/8	26 0/8 26 0/8	16 3/8	10 6	Bourbon County	KS	Shane Smith	2006	1941
162 4/8	25 2/8 24 3/8	23 2/8	5 5	Marathon County	WI	Heather Woodward	2008	1941
*162 4/8	23 2/8 24 4/8	17 0/8	6 7	Butler County	KS	Gregg Johnson	2008	1941
162 4/8	24 7/8 22 6/8	16 6/8	5 5	Lincoln County	KS	Erik Watts	2009	1941
162 4/8	25 1/8 25 1/8	19 2/8	6 6	Vernon County	WI	Joe Kabat	2009	1941
162 3/8	24 2/8 24 6/8	19 7/8	5 5	Barber County	KS	Glen Snell	1982	1966
162 3/8	27 2/8 27 2/8	19 6/8	5 6	Lake County	IL	Donald M. Hewkin	1986	1966
162 3/8	25 3/8 25 6/8	21 6/8	5 6	Menard County	IL	Mitchell Coffey	1987	1966
162 3/8	23 4/8 23 3/8	20 5/8	5 5	Ogle County	IL	Jeffrey S. Burke	1989	1966
162 3/8	24 7/8 24 4/8	14 7/8	5 5	Morrison County	MN	Edward J. Kastner	1989	1966
162 3/8	27 7/8 28 0/8	19 4/8	8 7	Edmonton	ALB	Dale Spooner	1992	1966
162 3/8	25 5/8 25 5/8	17 2/8	5 7	Whiteside County	IL	Clint Walker	1995	1966
162 3/8	26 6/8 25 3/8	21 5/8	5 5	Washington County	IA	James Cluney	1995	1966
162 3/8	25 5/8 24 3/8	19 3/8	6 6	Dane County	WI	Ronald E. Goodrich	1997	1966
162 3/8	24 0/8 24 7/8	17 2/8	6 6	Oakland County	MI	Matthew A. Jameson	1997	1966
162 3/8	24 5/8 23 7/8	17 5/8	6 8	Bourbon County	KS	Don Slinkard	1997	1966
162 3/8	24 5/8 25 0/8	18 7/8	6 6	Iowa County	WI	Rich Purin	2001	1966
162 3/8	24 5/8 25 3/8	20 7/8	5 5	Wyoming County	WV	Roscoe R. Cook	2001	1966
162 3/8	23 7/8 23 5/8	17 5/8	5 5	Jackson County	IA	David J. Fredericksen	2002	1966
162 3/8	25 3/8 26 0/8	22 3/8	6 5	Johnson County	IN	Ricky Hall, Sr.	2002	1966
162 3/8	25 4/8 25 3/8	21 3/8	5 5	Maverick County	TX	Rex Dacus	2003	1966
*162 3/8	24 1/8 24 0/8	15 6/8	5 8	Jersey County	IL	Kenneth Griffin	2004	1966
162 3/8	26 4/8 24 4/8	19 6/8	6 6	Jewell County	KS	Kevin L. Dahl	2004	1966
*162 3/8	24 4/8 24 5/8	19 4/8	5 6	Wabasha County	MN	Chris Ratz	2006	1966
162 3/8	25 5/8 26 1/8	19 3/8	6 6	Jo Daviess County	IL	Joseph C. Hinderman	2006	1966
162 3/8	28 1/8 29 1/8	19 3/8	6 6	Knox County	OH	Jeff Stutz	2006	1966
162 3/8	24 7/8 25 6/8	16 1/8	4 5	Shelby County	IL	Kevin Roley	2007	1966
*162 3/8	25 7/8 26 1/8	20 7/8	4 5	Warren County	IA	D. Scott Woods	2009	1966
162 3/8	24 2/8 26 1/8	20 7/8	6 8	Logan County	WV	Jason Kerns	2009	1966
*162 3/8	23 0/8 23 3/8	17 5/8	5 5	E. Carroll Parish	LA	Reece Hutson	2010	1966
*162 3/8	28 2/8 27 0/8	18 3/8	6 5	Marion County	IA	Eric Goemaat	2010	1966
162 2/8	22 2/8 24 7/8	17 6/8	6 5	Kingsbury County	SD	Dale Peterson	1972	1992
162 2/8	24 6/8 24 0/8	16 2/8	5 5	Plymouth County	IA	Gary Mitchell	1980	1992
162 2/8	24 1/8 24 2/8	20 4/8	6 5	Le Sueur County	MN	Joe Rybus	1981	1992
162 2/8	24 7/8 24 2/8	19 0/8	5 5	Marion County	KS	Leslie Lalouette	1983	1992

376

WHITETAIL DEER (TYPICAL ANTLERS)

Minimum Score 125   Continued

SCORE	LENGTH OF R MAIN BEAM L	INSIDE SPREAD	NUMBER OF R POINTS L	AREA	STATE/ PROVINCE	HUNTER'S NAME	DATE	RANK
162 2/8	25 3/8 24 7/8	17 6/8	5 5	Trego County	KS	Craig Doll	1985	1992
162 2/8	24 0/8 23 4/8	16 6/8	5 5	Hendricks County	IN	Leon Smith	1986	1992
162 2/8	21 6/8 22 3/8	16 2/8	5 5	Oneida County	WI	Mark Nelis	1987	1992
162 2/8	26 2/8 25 7/8	16 4/8	8 6	Litchfield County	CT	Warren Hensel	1988	1992
162 2/8	21 4/8 23 7/8	21 2/8	6 5	Miller County	MO	Steve Wyrick	1990	1992
162 2/8	25 5/8 26 0/8	16 2/8	6 6	Will County	IL	Mike O'Connor	1991	1992
162 2/8	25 1/8 23 7/8	19 6/8	6 6	Henry County	IA	Myles Keller	1991	1992
162 2/8	27 0/8 27 0/8	21 3/8	6 8	Vermilion County	IL	Alan Colwell	1995	1992
162 2/8	26 0/8 25 2/8	22 0/8	6 5	Douglas County	KS	Keith Jones	1996	1992
162 2/8	23 6/8 24 4/8	16 7/8	6 5	Butler County	KS	Gary L. Church	1999	1992
162 2/8	23 5/8 23 0/8	16 2/8	5 6	Atchison County	MO	Pink Atkins	2001	1992
162 2/8	25 2/8 23 3/8	17 6/8	6 7	Lake County	IL	Dorge O'Some Huang	2001	1992
162 2/8	27 2/8 24 4/8	18 2/8	6 6	Will County	IL	Bruce W. Spittal	2002	1992
*162 2/8	24 5/8 24 7/8	19 6/8	5 5	Buffalo County	WI	Paul D. Mample	2002	1992
162 2/8	26 1/8 26 0/8	21 0/8	5 5	Richland County	OH	Derrick D. Fair	2004	1992
162 2/8	24 4/8 24 7/8	17 4/8	6 5	Woodbury County	IA	Jason W. Hempey	2004	1992
*162 2/8	24 7/8 25 6/8	18 7/8	6 5	Page County	VA	Mike S. Turner	2004	1992
162 2/8	25 4/8 25 1/8	17 2/8	5 5	Schuyler County	IL	Tom J. Ingles	2004	1992
162 2/8	25 1/8 25 4/8	20 6/8	5 5	Muhlenberg County	KY	Jeff L. Vincent	2005	1992
162 2/8	23 1/8 23 3/8	18 0/8	5 5	Ingham County	MI	Mark D. McCrackin	2005	1992
162 2/8	24 5/8 24 3/8	15 6/8	5 6	Washtenaw County	MI	Shawn Spilak	2005	1992
*162 2/8	27 7/8 29 0/8	21 1/8	7 8	Green Lake County	WI	Matthew J. Reilly	2005	1992
*162 2/8	24 7/8 24 7/8	22 4/8	5 5	Marion County	IA	Nathan Ysker	2005	1992
*162 2/8	24 1/8 24 6/8	19 2/8	5 5	Clayton County	IA	Scott Germundson	2005	1992
162 2/8	23 2/8 23 7/8	17 0/8	6 7	Clark County	IL	Pistol Young	2006	1992
162 2/8	25 6/8 27 3/8	21 4/8	6 6	Knox County	IL	Tom Chadwick	2006	1992
*162 2/8	25 3/8 24 6/8	20 1/8	6 5	Greene County	IL	Frank Lyerla	2008	1992
162 2/8	26 3/8 25 4/8	16 0/8	5 5	St. Croix County	WI	Keith Gehrman	2010	1992
162 1/8	23 6/8 24 7/8	17 6/8	6 6	Buffalo County	WI	Bruce Curtis	1983	2024
162 1/8	23 4/8 24 2/8	20 4/8	6 5	Winnebago County	IL	Jeffrey A. Saxby	1984	2024
162 1/8	25 2/8 26 0/8	16 4/8	8 6	Monroe County	IA	Larry Whitson	1985	2024
162 1/8	27 5/8 24 7/8	18 1/8	6 7	Lafayette County	WI	Charles D. Potter	1986	2024
162 1/8	25 6/8 26 4/8	21 4/8	7 7	Clinton County	OH	Mark A. Ross	1988	2024
162 1/8	26 7/8 27 0/8	18 7/8	5 5	Adams County	IL	Randall Lummer	1990	2024
162 1/8	27 0/8 25 0/8	22 4/8	5 5	Newbrook	ALB	Jim Helling	1994	2024
162 1/8	25 1/8 25 7/8	18 1/8	5 5	Buffalo County	WI	Terry Krahn	1994	2024
162 1/8	26 4/8 25 5/8	21 5/8	6 5	Bureau County	IL	Ned L. Thompson	1994	2024
162 1/8	26 2/8 26 1/8	17 6/8	5 6	Fulton County	IL	C. Wayne Miller	1995	2024
162 1/8	24 0/8 24 6/8	17 4/8	7 7	Cole County	MO	Carl Rackers	1996	2024
162 1/8	26 0/8 26 6/8	17 0/8	6 5	Lake County	IL	Terry Nelson	1997	2024
162 1/8	26 6/8 27 0/8	21 6/8	6 6	Rooks County	KS	Marc D. Gray	1997	2024
162 1/8	25 2/8 25 2/8	17 7/8	5 5	Lancaster County	NE	Jon Navratil	1998	2024
162 1/8	26 7/8 26 0/8	26 5/8	7 6	Harvey County	KS	Dan Stahl	1999	2024
*162 1/8	24 6/8 25 6/8	20 3/8	6 7	Du Page County	IL	Rich S. Pawelczyk	2002	2024
162 1/8	25 1/8 27 1/8	24 1/8	5 5	Harvey County	KS	John Wiebe	2003	2024
*162 1/8	24 6/8 25 1/8	23 4/8	8 7	Winnebago County	WI	Jari Boyce	2004	2024
162 1/8	24 1/8 23 6/8	14 5/8	6 5	Calhoun County	IL	Paul Holland	2004	2024
162 1/8	24 1/8 24 5/8	15 2/8	6 5	Putnam County	MO	Tony M. Freeman	2004	2024
162 1/8	25 3/8 25 5/8	20 1/8	6 7	Barber County	KS	Jeff Wilson	2004	2024
162 1/8	24 3/8 23 6/8	18 5/8	6 7	Linn County	KS	Clint Bennett	2005	2024
162 1/8	26 3/8 26 5/8	19 3/8	6 7	Anoka County	MN	Robert Bozovsky	2005	2024
*162 1/8	26 1/8 25 5/8	18 7/8	8 8	Raleigh County	WV	William R. Worley	2006	2024
162 1/8	27 3/8 28 2/8	20 2/8	7 5	Licking County	OH	Jay Larrison	2006	2024
162 1/8	24 7/8 23 6/8	18 3/8	6 6	Steuben County	IN	Bradley Hancock	2006	2024
*162 1/8	25 1/8 25 5/8	17 7/8	5 5	Waushara County	WI	Alvin Elliot	2007	2024
*162 1/8	25 4/8 25 4/8	21 2/8	6 6	Jackson County	IA	Jesse T. Davis	2007	2024
*162 1/8	25 6/8 24 0/8	19 1/8	5 6	Calhoun County	IL	Tim Sickles	2007	2024
*162 1/8	24 2/8 24 7/8	21 2/8	6 6	Freeborn County	MN	Scott Crabtree	2008	2024
162 1/8	26 7/8 26 7/8	17 7/8	6 6	Winnebago County	WI	Gregory L. Niemuth	2008	2024
162 1/8	26 7/8 27 4/8	21 5/8	6 6	Chester County	PA	Craig A. Heffentrager	2009	2024
162 0/8	25 0/8 27 1/8	20 4/8	8 6	Bond County	IL	Larry Nelson	1976	2056
162 0/8	24 2/8 24 2/8	17 2/8	5 5	Wabash County	IL	Ron Hawf	1978	2056
162 0/8	24 3/8 27 2/8	19 2/8	6 6	Edgar County	IL	John J. Dillon	1985	2056
162 0/8	25 7/8 24 7/8	23 7/8	5 7	Marion County	KS	Don Bredemeier	1987	2056
162 0/8	26 0/8 27 7/8	19 2/8	6 5	Mahoning County	OH	Mark A. Brooks	1988	2056
162 0/8	28 0/8 28 6/8	19 0/8	6 5	Anoka County	MN	Dean Smith	1990	2056
162 0/8	25 7/8 26 2/8	20 5/8	6 6	Tolland County	CT	Bruce Moore	1990	2056
162 0/8	23 1/8 24 4/8	17 0/8	6 7	Richland County	ND	Tim Poehls	1992	2056
162 0/8	24 0/8 24 1/8	17 7/8	7 6	Peoria County	IL	Steven R. Williams	1992	2056
162 0/8	25 4/8 25 0/8	17 7/8	6 7	Morrison County	MN	Kevin Windschitl	1993	2056
162 0/8	25 1/8 28 0/8	23 4/8	7 5	Ashland County	OH	Larry G. Hammon	1993	2056
162 0/8	24 5/8 24 2/8	18 2/8	5 6	Dane County	WI	Richard Graf, Jr.	1994	2056
162 0/8	28 6/8 27 1/8	21 4/8	5 5	Hancock County	OH	Bradley D. DePuy	1994	2056
162 0/8	28 1/8 27 6/8	18 0/8	4 5	Hancock County	IL	Frank Hanks	1995	2056
162 0/8	24 7/8 24 7/8	17 0/8	5 5	Marathon County	WI	Gregg Danke	1996	2056
162 0/8	25 0/8 25 0/8	20 4/8	5 5	Prince Georges County	MD	Charles Figgins	1996	2056
162 0/8	26 5/8 25 3/8	19 0/8	6 7	Livingston County	IL	Matthew Leigh	1997	2056
162 0/8	25 6/8 25 4/8	19 4/8	5 7	Bayfield County	WI	Todd Miller	1998	2056
162 0/8	25 4/8 25 1/8	20 0/8	5 5	Benton County	IA	Ron Tuttle	1998	2056
162 0/8	24 2/8 24 4/8	19 2/8	5 5	Johnson County	IL	Doug A. Summers	2001	2056
162 0/8	24 0/8 22 0/8	20 4/8	5 6	McDonough County	IL	Richard Manchur	2001	2056
162 0/8	24 6/8 25 2/8	17 4/8	6 5	Appanoose County	IA	Mark Muir	2002	2056
162 0/8	25 0/8 24 0/8	19 4/8	5 5	Champaign County	OH	Steven Lininger	2003	2056
*162 0/8	23 5/8 23 5/8	16 6/8	5 6	Carroll County	KY	Greg Green	2004	2056
162 0/8	27 1/8 25 0/8	22 0/8	4 5	Ogle County	IL	Dr. Todd Anderson	2004	2056
162 0/8	26 6/8 26 7/8	22 4/8	6 5	Grant County	WI	Jeramie D. Pluemer	2005	2056
162 0/8	25 0/8 24 3/8	20 3/8	5 7	Fayette County	IA	Nathan Steere	2007	2056
161 7/8	23 4/8 25 4/8	18 3/8	5 5	Saunders County	NE	David Strimple	1961	2083
161 7/8	24 2/8 24 1/8	20 4/8	5 5	Douglas County	NE	Noel Miller	1970	2083
161 7/8	23 5/8 24 0/8	17 6/8	7 7	Fulton County	IL	Bob Neal	1981	2083
161 7/8	26 0/8 27 2/8	20 7/8	5 5	Greene County	OH	Charles O. Hill	1982	2083
161 7/8	25 3/8 26 0/8	20 6/8	7 7	Tuscarawas County	OH	Gary Stevens	1982	2083
161 7/8	23 3/8 22 2/8	16 0/8	6 6	Brandon	MAN	Gary Kaluzniak	1985	2083
161 7/8	26 5/8 25 5/8	18 3/8	6 5	Winona County	MN	Tim Rislow	1986	2083
161 7/8	24 2/8 24 7/8	17 6/8	8 5	Jones County	IA	Paul Johnson	1986	2083

377

WHITETAIL DEER (TYPICAL ANTLERS)

Minimum Score 125   Continued

SCORE	LENGTH OF R MAIN BEAM L	INSIDE SPREAD	NUMBER OF R POINTS L		AREA	STATE/ PROVINCE	HUNTER'S NAME	DATE	RANK
161 7/8	23 4/8 24 4/8	16 5/8	5	5	Marion County	MO	James Schaefer	1987	2083
161 7/8	23 1/8 23 2/8	18 3/8	5	5	Jefferson County	WI	Adam Achilli	1988	2083
161 7/8	21 5/8 24 4/8	17 5/8	7	6	Ontario County	NY	Adam T. Kupis	1989	2083
161 7/8	27 0/8 27 7/8	18 0/8	9	6	Mahoning County	OH	Nicholas Young	1990	2083
161 7/8	25 6/8 25 6/8	21 1/8	5	4	Stark County	IL	Adam Shane	1995	2083
161 7/8	28 2/8 27 5/8	19 0/8	9	6	Union County	IL	Gary Towell	1995	2083
161 7/8	28 4/8 28 6/8	18 5/8	5	5	Anne Arundel County	MD	Steve Walker	1996	2083
161 7/8	27 4/8 27 1/8	19 1/8	5	5	Webster County	MO	Jack J. Hubbell	1997	2083
161 7/8	23 2/8 22 2/8	20 1/8	5	6	Salem County	NJ	Don R. D'Antonio	1998	2083
161 7/8	26 1/8 25 3/8	22 1/8	6	8	Wayne County	IL	Danny Jennings	1999	2083
161 7/8	24 1/8 24 7/8	17 4/8	6	5	Jersey County	IL	Timothy S. Douglas	2000	2083
161 7/8	26 7/8 26 4/8	23 5/8	5	5	Washtenaw County	MI	Rocky H. Frazier	2001	2083
161 7/8	23 7/8 25 1/8	17 2/8	7	7	DeKalb County	IL	Jack E. Dolder	2003	2083
161 7/8	26 0/8 25 6/8	16 3/8	4	5	Peoria County	IL	Kevin Wood	2003	2083
161 7/8	23 1/8 24 5/8	18 3/8	5	5	Waukesha County	WI	Jeff Mislang	2004	2083
*161 7/8	28 7/8 29 5/8	20 1/8	7	7	St. Louis County	MN	Larry Kline	2006	2083
161 7/8	24 3/8 25 0/8	18 7/8	5	5	Benton County	IA	Chad W. Clark	2006	2083
161 7/8	25 3/8 26 6/8	20 3/8	7	6	Hennepin County	MN	Larry R. Carlson	2006	2083
161 7/8	23 4/8 23 6/8	15 0/8	7	5	Jersey County	IL	Herman W. Kovar, Sr.	2006	2083
*161 7/8	24 4/8 22 1/8	17 1/8	9	6	Monroe County	MI	Richard L. Martin	2007	2083
*161 7/8	25 3/8 24 7/8	19 3/8	5	5	De Kalb County	MO	Michael D. Jager	2007	2083
*161 7/8	26 5/8 27 3/8	19 1/8	5	5	Madison County	KY	Travis Byrd	2009	2083
*161 7/8	24 2/8 24 2/8	17 5/8	6	6	Otter Tail County	MN	Patrick D. Tobkin	2009	2083
161 7/8	25 6/8 26 0/8	17 4/8	7	7	Marathon County	WI	Brandon Hoppe	2010	2083
161 6/8	27 3/8 26 0/8	27 1/8	4	5	Lake County	IL	David Mitten	1987	2115
161 6/8	22 6/8 23 6/8	17 6/8	5	6	Jo Daviess County	IL	Timothy T. Westemeier	1987	2115
161 6/8	27 7/8 26 7/8	21 2/8	6	6	Pike County	IL	Brad Stamp	1988	2115
161 6/8	26 2/8 24 0/8	19 0/8	6	6	Montgomery County	TN	Zane Mason	1991	2115
161 6/8	25 1/8 25 2/8	20 0/8	6	6	McHenry County	IL	Rick Lagerhausen	1991	2115
161 6/8	23 6/8 23 7/8	21 5/8	7	5	Hancock County	IL	Jerry Pryor	1992	2115
161 6/8	25 0/8 24 7/8	20 0/8	5	5	La Grange County	IN	Mark Robbins	1993	2115
161 6/8	23 4/8 23 1/8	16 2/8	5	5	Clark County	IL	Paul Baird	1994	2115
161 6/8	24 3/8 23 5/8	18 4/8	5	5	Westchester County	NY	Robert Olivier	1994	2115
161 6/8	26 6/8 26 2/8	18 3/8	5	6	Starbuck	MAN	Greg Shirtliff	1996	2115
161 6/8	24 6/8 24 7/8	18 1/8	5	6	Jasper County	IL	Hank Baltzell	1998	2115
161 6/8	25 3/8 26 1/8	22 7/8	6	7	Raleigh County	WV	Theodore R. Stover	2001	2115
161 6/8	26 4/8 27 0/8	19 1/8	7	6	Clark County	MO	Jon Manley	2002	2115
*161 6/8	25 0/8 25 0/8	19 4/8	5	5	Outagamie County	WI	Dan Van Zeeland	2003	2115
*161 6/8	27 5/8 27 6/8	20 2/8	6	5	Coshocton County	OH	Daniel J. Tomon	2003	2115
*161 6/8	25 7/8 24 7/8	18 6/8	4	4	Marion County	IN	Todd D. Day	2003	2115
161 6/8	25 0/8 24 2/8	20 4/8	6	5	Marinette County	WI	Gerald Krause	2004	2115
161 6/8	23 5/8 23 7/8	17 4/8	5	5	Lenawee County	MI	Harold D. Sylvester, Jr.	2004	2115
*161 6/8	25 4/8 23 6/8	16 2/8	6	6	McDowell County	WV	Stephen Beckner	2005	2115
161 6/8	24 1/8 24 1/8	20 0/8	5	5	Bonneville County	ID	Jared Johnson	2007	2115
*161 6/8	24 2/8 24 4/8	18 2/8	5	5	Houston County	MN	Brian Parent	2008	2115
161 6/8	24 3/8 24 7/8	18 2/8	5	5	Crosby County	TX	Ray Grappe	2010	2115
161 5/8	23 3/8 23 1/8	14 5/8	6	6	Dunn County	WI	Leonard Hines	1970	2137
161 5/8	22 6/8 22 5/8	18 6/8	5	6	Juneau County	WI	Harlan Steindl	1971	2137
161 5/8	25 0/8 25 5/8	19 1/8	6	6	Jefferson County	IL	Rick Osborn	1982	2137
161 5/8	22 5/8 24 3/8	17 7/8	5	5	Butler County	KS	Mike Turner	1982	2137
161 5/8	26 3/8 24 4/8	16 4/8	5	6	Butler County	KS	Ronald Tilson	1983	2137
161 5/8	27 2/8 24 4/8	18 1/8	7	8	Franklin County	KS	Dennis Ballweg	1987	2137
161 5/8	25 4/8 24 2/8	19 1/8	5	5	Woodford County	IL	Lynn Roseman	1989	2137
161 5/8	24 4/8 24 1/8	17 1/8	5	6	Forest County	WI	Daniel G. Van Hoosen	1990	2137
161 5/8	26 3/8 26 1/8	20 0/8	6	8	Buffalo County	WI	Gerald Todd, Jr.	1992	2137
161 5/8	24 0/8 24 0/8	16 3/8	5	5	E. Carroll Parish	LA	F. Lane Mitchell	1993	2137
161 5/8	25 3/8 25 4/8	21 5/8	5	5	Comanche County	KS	Jack Brannan	1993	2137
161 5/8	24 0/8 24 3/8	19 1/8	7	7	Hamilton County	OH	Robert E. Plasters	1995	2137
161 5/8	23 3/8 25 0/8	15 7/8	6	6	Logan County	WV	Robert Lee Adams, Jr.	1995	2137
161 5/8	26 2/8 26 1/8	19 1/8	6	5	Franklin County	OH	Craig Bonham	1996	2137
161 5/8	24 6/8 26 5/8	20 1/8	5	5	Guthrie County	IA	Kenneth E. Briggs	1996	2137
161 5/8	23 6/8 23 6/8	18 1/8	5	5	Shawnee County	KS	Dwight Streeter	1997	2137
161 5/8	28 0/8 27 7/8	24 3/8	5	5	McHenry County	IL	Tom M. Toenies	1998	2137
161 5/8	25 3/8 24 4/8	20 3/8	5	6	Dane County	WI	Alden J. Bosben	1998	2137
161 5/8	26 4/8 25 2/8	16 2/8	7	6	Fulton County	IL	Tim Atchley	2001	2137
161 5/8	23 1/8 23 5/8	20 1/8	5	5	Jackson County	OH	David Haynes	2002	2137
161 5/8	23 5/8 24 1/8	22 1/8	5	5	Noble County	IN	Richard A. Green	2002	2137
*161 5/8	23 2/8 24 2/8	15 5/8	7	7	Graves County	KY	John Oldham	2003	2137
161 5/8	27 1/8 27 6/8	20 0/8	5	6	Jefferson County	IL	Carrol Bates	2003	2137
161 5/8	25 0/8 24 4/8	17 3/8	5	5	Madison County	IA	Shane Tuttle	2003	2137
161 5/8	22 7/8 23 7/8	16 2/8	7	6	Clay County	IA	Thomas Ray Gross	2004	2137
161 5/8	26 4/8 23 2/8	16 4/8	6	7	Marshall County	IA	Garry Brandenburg	2005	2137
*161 5/8	22 7/8 23 3/8	18 7/8	5	5	Mason County	MI	Bradley R. McClure	2006	2137
161 5/8	26 7/8 24 4/8	17 6/8	5	7	Tipton County	IN	Skip Servies	2006	2137
161 5/8	27 2/8 26 2/8	20 5/8	6	5	Clarke County	IA	Kyle R. Poindexter	2006	2137
*161 5/8	25 5/8 25 3/8	18 5/8	4	5	Olmsted County	MN	Jeremy Hebl	2007	2137
*161 5/8	22 7/8 24 4/8	17 6/8	6	8	Coles County	IL	Anthony Chrisagis	2007	2137
161 5/8	25 5/8 25 6/8	20 3/8	5	6	Anderson County	KY	Chris Hanks	2008	2137
161 4/8	26 1/8 26 1/8	19 2/8	5	4	Bond County	IL	Sam White	1974	2169
161 4/8	26 0/8 25 6/8	17 4/8	8	6	E. Feliciana Parish	LA	James K. Morgan	1977	2169
161 4/8	25 2/8 27 0/8	20 2/8	5	5	Sumner County	KS	Phill Allton	1983	2169
161 4/8	28 4/8 28 3/8	22 1/8	5	5	Jones County	IA	David A. Leuchs	1984	2169
161 4/8	23 3/8 24 1/8	18 4/8	6	5	Cass County	NE	Ray Brock	1985	2169
161 4/8	27 1/8 26 5/8	18 5/8	4	5	Crawford County	KS	Fred Geier	1988	2169
161 4/8	26 1/8 26 6/8	16 7/8	5	6	Oconto County	WI	Jeffery J. Brabant	1989	2169
161 4/8	25 0/8 25 1/8	18 7/8	6	7	Clinton County	IL	Tracy Hawes	1989	2169
161 4/8	26 1/8 26 4/8	18 6/8	5	5	Dane County	WI	Greg Berndt	1990	2169
161 4/8	24 6/8 25 3/8	19 2/8	5	5	Van Buren County	IA	Jim Francois	1990	2169
161 4/8	25 2/8 25 5/8	18 0/8	6	5	Washburn County	WI	Larry Allen Blaylock	1991	2169
161 4/8	25 1/8 24 0/8	19 0/8	6	5	McLean County	IL	Larry Alvis	1993	2169
161 4/8	25 2/8 26 0/8	19 2/8	6	7	Henderson County	IL	Bob K. Agans	1994	2169
161 4/8	22 7/8 23 1/8	16 6/8	5	5	Ripley County	IN	Steve A. Allen	1995	2169
161 4/8	25 5/8 26 5/8	22 6/8	6	7	Anoka County	MN	Walter Slowikowski	1996	2169
161 4/8	24 4/8 24 4/8	18 2/8	5	5	Hocking County	OH	Dave Hanson	1997	2169
161 4/8	27 0/8 27 5/8	24 2/8	6	7	Clay County	KS	Tom E. Bowman	1997	2169

WHITETAIL DEER (TYPICAL ANTLERS)

Minimum Score 125 Continued

SCORE	LENGTH OF R MAIN BEAM L	INSIDE SPREAD	NUMBER OF R POINTS L	AREA	STATE/ PROVINCE	HUNTER'S NAME	DATE	RANK
161 4/8	26 5/8 27 0/8	17 3/8	10 6	Oconto County	WI	Richard L. Rosio	1998	2169
161 4/8	24 5/8 25 0/8	20 2/8	5 5	Washtenaw County	MI	Gordie Berenson	1999	2169
161 4/8	25 1/8 22 7/8	23 6/8	6 5	Wabaunsee County	KS	David Johnson	1999	2169
161 4/8	28 3/8 28 2/8	17 2/8	6 5	Crawford County	KS	Roger L. Hensley	2000	2169
161 4/8	28 2/8 27 2/8	14 4/8	5 7	Shawnee County	KS	Zachary S. Leonetti	2000	2169
161 4/8	24 2/8 25 2/8	19 4/8	6 6	Jasper County	IA	Don N. Morris	2003	2169
161 4/8	23 5/8 23 5/8	18 2/8	5 5	Saline County	KS	Tom Rathmann	2003	2169
161 4/8	24 7/8 24 1/8	18 0/8	5 5	Dunn County	WI	Andy Benrud	2004	2169
161 4/8	24 5/8 24 4/8	16 2/8	7 7	Black Hawk County	IA	Craig Swenson	2005	2169
161 4/8	24 6/8 26 1/8	22 4/8	5 5	Wyoming County	WV	Ricky Carter	2006	2169
161 4/8	24 6/8 24 3/8	20 7/8	5 7	Hamilton County	IN	Timothy L. Mylin	2007	2169
161 4/8	27 0/8 25 6/8	18 0/8	7 6	Monroe County	NY	William Ladd	2008	2169
*161 4/8	26 4/8 26 5/8	17 6/8	5 5	McDonough County	IL	John P. Condis	2009	2169
161 4/8	23 0/8 22 6/8	17 3/8	8 6	Fayette County	IL	Robert J. Nelling III	2009	2169
161 4/8	26 4/8 26 3/8	18 6/8	5 5	Branch County	MI	Mark R. Bassage	2009	2169
161 4/8	24 2/8 25 3/8	19 0/8	5 5	Franklin County	IL	Cliff Thomas	2010	2169
161 3/8	25 0/8 23 6/8	16 6/8	8 7	Wyandotte County	KS	George F. Bigelow	1967	2202
161 3/8	26 4/8 25 4/8	19 1/8	6 6	Sumner County	KS	Larry Wycoff	1980	2202
161 3/8	29 1/8 27 2/8	23 4/8	7 8	Clark County	OH	Kenneth Preston	1982	2202
161 3/8	27 2/8 25 4/8	22 3/8	4 6	Fayette County	IL	Bill Holman	1983	2202
161 3/8	23 1/8 23 0/8	19 1/8	6 5	Auglaize County	OH	Lee Atha	1983	2202
161 3/8	23 0/8 24 1/8	14 5/8	5 5	Butler County	KS	David R. Rogers	1985	2202
161 3/8	27 7/8 27 1/8	19 3/8	4 4	Grant County	WI	Chris Nelson	1986	2202
161 3/8	25 1/8 27 2/8	15 7/8	7 6	Anderson County	TN	John Johnson	1987	2202
161 3/8	24 6/8 24 6/8	19 6/8	5 7	Lake County	IN	David R. Turbin	1988	2202
161 3/8	26 4/8 25 1/8	19 0/8	6 6	Waukesha County	WI	Dirk Stolz	1989	2202
161 3/8	25 1/8 25 3/8	19 1/8	5 5	McPherson County	KS	Daniel Willems	1990	2202
161 3/8	27 0/8 26 7/8	19 4/8	6 6	Buffalo County	WI	Jason Windsor	1993	2202
161 3/8	26 4/8 26 1/8	16 2/8	5 7	Switzerland County	IN	Rick Bogue	1994	2202
161 3/8	25 2/8 25 5/8	20 7/8	5 5	Refugio County	TX	Terry George Arnim	1995	2202
161 3/8	24 3/8 25 0/8	18 4/8	7 8	Lane County	KS	Dean Hamilton	1997	2202
161 3/8	23 7/8 25 0/8	17 2/8	6 5	Spokane County	WA	Steve Mitchell	1997	2202
161 3/8	25 0/8 25 0/8	16 7/8	6 7	McHenry County	IL	Timothy L. Harkness	1998	2202
161 3/8	23 6/8 24 4/8	21 5/8	6 6	Grande Prairie	ALB	Norris Bates	1998	2202
161 3/8	29 5/8 29 6/8	19 0/8	8 5	Parke County	IN	Michael Vore	1999	2202
161 3/8	25 1/8 25 5/8	17 6/8	6 6	Jefferson County	KS	John Welborn	1999	2202
161 3/8	24 7/8 24 5/8	20 7/8	6 5	Otoe County	NE	Keith Merkel	2000	2202
161 3/8	28 6/8 28 5/8	19 0/8	6 7	Montgomery County	MD	Jeffrey L. Harrison	2002	2202
161 3/8	24 2/8 24 3/8	19 2/8	6 6	Corson County	SD	John E. Powell, Jr.	2002	2202
161 3/8	26 5/8 24 6/8	19 1/8	5 5	Jefferson County	WI	Bill Peterson	2002	2202
161 3/8	25 4/8 25 2/8	20 7/8	5 5	Delaware County	OH	Dave Orndorf	2002	2202
161 3/8	24 0/8 25 0/8	18 7/8	5 5	Chippewa County	WI	Trenton Ty Sweeney	2003	2202
*161 3/8	22 3/8 21 7/8	18 1/8	6 6	Johnson County	IL	Jeffrey D. Carter	2004	2202
*161 3/8	27 7/8 25 7/8	17 7/8	6 5	St. Joseph County	IN	Joseph R. Furore	2004	2202
161 3/8	25 2/8 25 3/8	20 4/8	8 7	Ozaukee County	WI	Jerry Norberg	2004	2202
161 3/8	27 1/8 24 6/8	18 2/8	5 6	Franklin County	OH	Mike Grenier	2005	2202
161 3/8	24 1/8 22 6/8	18 1/8	5 5	Porter County	IN	Tom Lenburg	2005	2202
161 3/8	24 3/8 23 2/8	22 6/8	5 7	Somerset County	NJ	Stephen Kotz	2006	2202
161 3/8	25 1/8 23 7/8	16 1/8	5 5	Floyd County	IA	Spencer Kelly	2006	2202
*161 3/8	26 2/8 23 6/8	19 0/8	6 9	Alexander County	IL	Gary Slusher	2006	2202
161 3/8	27 0/8 28 0/8	20 1/8	6 5	Floyd County	IA	Clay Schneckloth	2007	2202
161 3/8	28 0/8 26 6/8	21 0/8	6 6	Decatur County	KS	Floyd Boan	2008	2202
*161 3/8	25 5/8 23 5/8	21 7/8	4 5	Pepin County	WI	Jason Fitzsimons	2009	2202
161 3/8	24 1/8 24 0/8	16 0/8	6 6	Jefferson County	KS	Tom Schweda	2009	2202
161 2/8	24 2/8 24 0/8	20 0/8	5 5	Muskingum County	OH	Lee E Wilson	1984	2240
161 2/8	23 3/8 24 7/8	18 7/8	6 6	Graham County	KS	Chris Jolly	1984	2240
161 2/8	24 2/8 24 6/8	17 6/8	5 5	Sauk County	WI	Hank Loncki	1989	2240
161 2/8	27 1/8 25 6/8	19 2/8	8 10	Cowley County	KS	Dwayne Graham	1990	2240
161 2/8	24 6/8 24 7/8	16 7/8	6 5	Knox County	IL	Fred E. Miller	1992	2240
161 2/8	24 6/8 24 3/8	19 0/8	6 5	Linn County	KS	Phil Dawson	1994	2240
161 2/8	25 3/8 25 2/8	18 4/8	5 5	Shelby County	IL	Mike Cauble	1994	2240
161 2/8	24 7/8 23 2/8	20 5/8	6 5	Lancaster County	NE	Clint Burge	1996	2240
161 2/8	24 0/8 23 0/8	15 2/8	5 5	St. Walburg	SAS	Murray Davidson	1998	2240
161 2/8	24 0/8 24 1/8	18 0/8	5 6	Polk County	WI	Kevin L. Jones	1998	2240
161 2/8	25 1/8 25 3/8	21 0/8	6 6	Coshocton County	OH	Norman M. Mast	1998	2240
161 2/8	26 0/8 25 7/8	19 6/8	5 5	Logan County	OH	Greg Brooks	1998	2240
161 2/8	22 7/8 23 2/8	16 6/8	5 5	Morrison County	MN	David Schlumpberger	1998	2240
161 2/8	27 0/8 27 0/8	22 3/8	4 6	Warren County	IA	Will F. Pirtle	1999	2240
161 2/8	29 1/8 30 2/8	21 7/8	7 4	Richland County	OH	Ron Swanger	1999	2240
161 2/8	23 6/8 23 2/8	27 7/8	6 5	Marshall County	IN	Cody W. Leed	2003	2240
*161 2/8	26 2/8 25 2/8	19 4/8	5 5	Noble County	IN	Frank A. Kimmell	2003	2240
161 2/8	23 5/8 25 3/8	26 3/8	7 9	Columbia County	WI	Jim Scheberl	2003	2240
161 2/8	22 5/8 23 0/8	15 4/8	5 5	Saunders County	NE	Mark C. Booth	2003	2240
161 2/8	25 1/8 25 0/8	20 2/8	4 5	Kearny County	KS	Loren R. Goss	2004	2240
161 2/8	23 7/8 23 5/8	17 0/8	5 5	Marathon County	WI	Mark Kilty	2005	2240
*161 2/8	24 3/8 25 0/8	17 4/8	5 5	Winona County	MN	Robert A. Hofschulte	2006	2240
161 2/8	25 5/8 25 6/8	19 3/8	9 5	Clay County	KS	Ken Meadors II	2006	2240
*161 2/8	25 6/8 25 0/8	21 6/8	4 4	La Crosse County	WI	Jerry Jorgensen	2007	2240
161 2/8	24 0/8 24 2/8	17 6/8	5 5	Will County	IL	Craig Olthoff	2008	2240
*161 2/8	24 4/8 25 1/8	18 2/8	5 5	Le Sueur County	MN	Chris Smith	2008	2240
*161 2/8	24 2/8 23 4/8	16 6/8	5 5	Bolivar County	MS	Lance Johnson	2008	2240
*161 2/8	25 1/8 24 5/8	19 2/8	5 5	Shawano County	WI	Bradley J. Vander Kelen	2009	2240
*161 2/8	22 7/8 22 6/8	18 5/8	7 7	Lyman County	SD	Michael Ambur	2010	2240
*161 2/8	23 4/8 23 5/8	15 6/8	6 5	Chautauqua County	KS	Timothy Broughton	2010	2240
161 1/8	26 0/8 27 1/8	18 2/8	6 5	Clark County	IN	Frank Mauk, Jr.	1966	2270
161 1/8	24 2/8 25 1/8	16 7/8	5 5	Marinette County	WI	Dale J. Hanson	1985	2270
161 1/8	24 3/8 25 4/8	21 5/8	5 5	Lake County	IL	John Schnider	1987	2270
161 1/8	23 6/8 23 3/8	17 6/8	5 6	Polk County	IA	Jim Garton, Jr.	1989	2270
161 1/8	24 2/8 24 5/8	18 5/8	5 5	Wayne County	IL	Will Sapia	1990	2270
161 1/8	26 0/8 24 0/8	20 3/8	5 5	Butler County	OH	Dale Gross	1990	2270
161 1/8	25 4/8 25 1/8	20 5/8	5 5	Missoula County	MT	Vinnie Pisani	1993	2270
161 1/8	27 6/8 27 6/8	19 7/8	4 6	Paulding County	OH	Tim Lamb	1994	2270
161 1/8	23 3/8 24 1/8	16 1/8	5 9	Eau Claire County	WI	Anthony Johnson	1994	2270
161 1/8	22 5/8 22 2/8	18 4/8	6 5	Rawlins County	KS	James Koggie	1994	2270
161 1/8	25 4/8 26 2/8	16 4/8	5 6	Geary County	KS	Tim Stephens	1995	2270

379

WHITETAIL DEER (TYPICAL ANTLERS)

Minimum Score 125 — Continued

SCORE	LENGTH OF R MAIN BEAM L	INSIDE SPREAD	NUMBER OF R POINTS L	AREA	STATE/ PROVINCE	HUNTER'S NAME	DATE	RANK
161 1/8	26 4/8 26 5/8	20 0/8	9 6	Iron County	WI	Bryan Bellows	1995	2270
161 1/8	26 6/8 27 1/8	20 5/8	6 7	St. Croix County	WI	Burl G. Johnson	1995	2270
161 1/8	24 6/8 25 0/8	18 1/8	5 7	Green Lake	SAS	Pink Atkins	1996	2270
161 1/8	25 0/8 25 4/8	16 7/8	5 6	Goodhue County	MN	Bill Prigge	1997	2270
161 1/8	23 5/8 24 3/8	17 3/8	6 5	Sussex County	DE	Andrew James Phillips	1998	2270
161 1/8	24 6/8 24 6/8	18 3/8	6 5	Monroe County	NY	Dane Edwards	1999	2270
161 1/8	24 7/8 24 1/8	18 4/8	5 6	Buffalo County	WI	Curtis Rotering	2000	2270
161 1/8	24 0/8 24 2/8	17 3/8	5 6	Pottawattamie County	IA	Rodney P. Stahlnecker	2000	2270
161 1/8	25 4/8 25 6/8	19 1/8	5 6	Langlade County	WI	Tom Androschko	2000	2270
161 1/8	24 2/8 23 7/8	19 1/8	5 5	Jefferson County	IA	Josef K. Rud	2000	2270
161 1/8	26 6/8 27 0/8	21 0/8	7 5	Vigo County	IN	Sam J. Lane	2002	2270
*161 1/8	23 7/8 24 7/8	20 3/8	5 5	Dallas County	IA	Ryan McClanahan	2004	2270
161 1/8	26 0/8 25 5/8	21 5/8	5 5	Douglas County	WI	Jason Springer	2006	2270
161 1/8	25 6/8 26 1/8	19 5/8	5 4	Marathon County	WI	Jim Jaworski	2006	2270
*161 1/8	24 3/8 24 2/8	21 1/8	5 6	Brown County	OH	Brian T. Gavin	2006	2270
161 1/8	25 6/8 25 1/8	21 2/8	6 8	Greene County	IL	Mike T. Mecimore	2006	2270
161 1/8	25 3/8 25 5/8	19 4/8	6 5	Noble County	OH	Michael D. Rang	2007	2270
161 1/8	26 4/8 26 6/8	19 5/8	5 5	Traill County	ND	Thomas Pederson	2008	2270
*161 1/8	26 1/8 27 2/8	20 7/8	5 5	Coahuila	MEX	Rick Morgan, Jr.	2008	2270
*161 1/8	22 5/8 22 5/8	19 1/8	5 6	Jackson County	WI	Brian A. Smith	2009	2270
*161 1/8	24 7/8 27 5/8	17 5/8	4 5	Madison Parish	LA	Teri Henley	2010	2270
161 1/8	26 3/8 26 4/8	19 4/8	6 6	Guernsey County	OH	Jeremy T. Joyner	2010	2270
161 0/8	26 2/8 25 1/8	19 4/8	5 5	La Crosse County	WI	Ray Howell	1977	2303
161 0/8	28 0/8 27 3/8	23 4/8	4 4	Jefferson County	IN	Donnie Ball	1984	2303
161 0/8	27 7/8 26 4/8	21 3/8	6 5	Morris County	KS	Craig Johnson	1985	2303
161 0/8	27 2/8 27 1/8	19 2/8	5 5	Orange County	NC	R. J. Hickman	1987	2303
161 0/8	27 1/8 26 0/8	22 2/8	4 4	Lucas County	IA	Gary Goering	1987	2303
161 0/8	24 1/8 23 4/8	18 5/8	7 6	Butler County	OH	Fred S Spurlin	1987	2303
161 0/8	25 0/8 24 4/8	16 4/8	5 6	Fond du Lac County	WI	David E. Stubbe	1988	2303
161 0/8	24 5/8 24 0/8	15 3/8	6 6	Lawrence County	IN	Dale Waldbieser	1988	2303
161 0/8	22 5/8 24 1/8	19 2/8	5 5	Dakota County	MN	Dave Vomela	1988	2303
161 0/8	26 0/8 25 4/8	16 0/8	6 5	Day County	SD	Jim Madsen	1990	2303
161 0/8	26 3/8 27 4/8	21 4/8	4 4	McHenry County	IL	Richard A. Houge	1991	2303
161 0/8	22 0/8 22 0/8	15 4/8	5 5	Marion County	IA	Dwight T. Robuck	1991	2303
161 0/8	23 3/8 23 7/8	20 6/8	5 5	Peoria County	IL	Robert E. Grainger	1991	2303
161 0/8	27 4/8 26 7/8	19 7/8	6 4	Pottawatomie County	KS	Stan Mangas	1992	2303
161 0/8	25 4/8 24 5/8	18 2/8	5 5	Knox County	IL	John S. Barrett	1993	2303
161 0/8	25 1/8 25 1/8	19 4/8	5 5	Geary County	KS	Kevin Foerschler	1995	2303
161 0/8	25 6/8 25 7/8	16 6/8	7 6	Buffalo County	WI	Dennis Palmer	1995	2303
161 0/8	24 0/8 24 4/8	17 2/8	5 5	Butler County	PA	David Craig Snyder	1996	2303
161 0/8	25 1/8 24 4/8	19 0/8	5 5	Jackson County	IL	Carl Vandeloo	1996	2303
161 0/8	25 4/8 26 3/8	21 4/8	4 4	Lawrence County	IL	William Mack McFarland	1998	2303
161 0/8	26 7/8 26 3/8	17 4/8	5 5	St. Croix County	WI	Mark H. Johnson	1998	2303
161 0/8	25 1/8 25 1/8	22 2/8	5 5	Pike County	IL	Randy Williams	2000	2303
161 0/8	24 0/8 22 6/8	18 4/8	5 5	Juneau County	WI	Scott Wafle	2000	2303
161 0/8	25 1/8 24 3/8	20 0/8	5 5	Fayette County	IL	Scott Hunt	2000	2303
161 0/8	29 5/8 29 6/8	23 0/8	6 5	Kane County	IL	Daniel R. Petska	2001	2303
161 0/8	24 3/8 22 7/8	17 7/8	7 6	Pope County	IL	Jerry F. Thomas	2002	2303
161 0/8	25 5/8 25 4/8	23 4/8	4 4	Will County	IL	Ronald Burgess	2003	2303
161 0/8	24 1/8 23 4/8	15 6/8	7 7	Howard County	MO	John Calfee	2003	2303
161 0/8	25 6/8 25 4/8	17 6/8	6 7	Douglas County	WI	Jeffrey D. Waters	2003	2303
161 0/8	24 4/8 23 5/8	20 4/8	7 9	Greene County	IL	Thaddeus J. Lauer	2003	2303
161 0/8	28 5/8 27 5/8	20 6/8	4 4	Pike County	IL	Benjamin D. Huth	2003	2303
*161 0/8	22 2/8 22 2/8	19 0/8	6 5	Anoka County	MN	Neil L. Hubbard	2003	2303
161 0/8	26 0/8 27 1/8	18 7/8	5 7	Fayette County	IN	Boyd Lunsford	2005	2303
161 0/8	23 7/8 23 1/8	18 4/8	6 6	Jones County	IA	Mike Shipley	2005	2303
161 0/8	26 1/8 26 1/8	19 4/8	4 4	Lake County	IL	Corey L. Scott	2006	2303
*161 0/8	22 3/8 23 2/8	19 0/8	6 6	Effingham County	IL	Gary Berlin	2006	2303
*161 0/8	25 0/8 25 1/8	18 2/8	6 5	Fairfax County	VA	Jose Murillo	2006	2303
161 0/8	23 4/8 23 4/8	18 7/8	5 6	Schuyler County	IL	Walter Burbela	2007	2303
161 0/8	25 6/8 24 5/8	16 1/8	6 5	Wright County	MN	Tom Bourgeois	2007	2303
*161 0/8	26 7/8 26 2/8	15 6/8	5 5	Blackford County	IN	Josh R. Light	2008	2303
*161 0/8	27 5/8 27 6/8	20 2/8	5 5	Buffalo County	WI	Dennis Wyttenbach	2008	2303
161 0/8	26 1/8 27 0/8	16 5/8	5 7	Mason County	WV	Danny Chandler	2008	2303
161 0/8	24 0/8 22 7/8	20 4/8	5 6	Woodford County	KY	Brent Littleton	2009	2303
161 0/8	26 3/8 26 6/8	20 4/8	5 5	Saline County	KS	Charles Werner	2009	2303
160 7/8	20 5/8 24 0/8	24 3/8	7 5	Frontier County	NE	Vernon Laverack	1959	2347
160 7/8	25 5/8 27 3/8	21 4/8	5 6	Iowa County	IA	Everett Reid	1962	2347
160 7/8	24 2/8 23 4/8	17 6/8	7 5	Smith County	KS	Ron Sturgeon	1965	2347
160 7/8	24 4/8 24 2/8	17 1/8	5 5	Wayne County	WV	Willard Brown	1967	2347
160 7/8	22 6/8 23 1/8	21 1/8	5 5	Lincoln County	MN	Bernie Ahlberg	1974	2347
160 7/8	25 5/8 25 1/8	16 7/8	5 5	Clark County	IL	Wes Romines	1977	2347
160 7/8	24 2/8 23 5/8	19 3/8	5 5	Saline County	KS	Ray Peterman	1979	2347
160 7/8	25 1/8 26 7/8	18 5/8	4 4	Pike County	IL	Richard Dewey	1981	2347
160 7/8	24 5/8 23 4/8	15 3/8	5 6	Leavenworth County	KS	Albert Lyle Karl	1982	2347
160 7/8	25 2/8 25 6/8	19 5/8	7 7	Rockingham County	VA	Jim Burtner	1989	2347
160 7/8	27 7/8 27 6/8	22 4/8	5 7	Clark County	OH	Ron McGuire	1989	2347
160 7/8	28 1/8 28 6/8	21 5/8	4 4	Bond County	IL	James Coleman	1989	2347
160 7/8	23 4/8 23 7/8	21 7/8	5 5	Sangamon County	IL	David C. Jostes	1990	2347
160 7/8	25 2/8 24 1/8	17 1/8	5 5	Butler County	OH	Norman R. Sampson	1991	2347
160 7/8	25 6/8 25 0/8	17 3/8	6 7	Parkland County	ALB	Sam Halabi	1991	2347
160 7/8	27 2/8 25 4/8	18 0/8	5 6	Monroe County	IA	Robert L. McDowell	1992	2347
160 7/8	23 6/8 23 3/8	21 0/8	6 6	Pueblo County	CO	Kenneth H. Karbon	1993	2347
160 7/8	24 3/8 23 6/8	17 5/8	5 5	Ashland County	WI	Joe Bradle	1994	2347
160 7/8	23 5/8 24 0/8	20 3/8	5 5	Fairfield County	OH	Roy Chestnut	1994	2347
160 7/8	24 1/8 23 5/8	23 3/8	5 5	Polk County	AR	Donald Cost	1995	2347
160 7/8	22 6/8 22 6/8	18 3/8	5 5	Washington County	IA	David Hyman	1995	2347
160 7/8	26 0/8 25 5/8	19 6/8	5 7	Dakota County	MN	Gerald Huntington	1995	2347
160 7/8	23 3/8 24 0/8	18 1/8	5 5	Shelby County	KY	Darrel Cox	1998	2347
160 7/8	23 7/8 24 6/8	18 5/8	6 5	Trempealeau County	WI	Brad J. Gamroth	1999	2347
160 7/8	26 1/8 25 6/8	17 2/8	5 6	Clay County	WV	Vincent Dumrongkietiman	1999	2347
160 7/8	26 3/8 26 0/8	19 3/8	7 5	Macoupin County	IL	Rick D. Tigo	1999	2347
160 7/8	28 0/8 25 6/8	20 3/8	5 5	Knox County	IL	Troy Huffman	2002	2347
160 7/8	24 7/8 24 3/8	18 7/8	5 5	Clarke County	IA	Greg Bakken	2003	2347
160 7/8	25 5/8 26 0/8	14 1/8	5 5	Jasper County	IL	Skip Moore	2003	2347

WHITETAIL DEER (TYPICAL ANTLERS)

Minimum Score 125
Continued

SCORE	LENGTH OF R MAIN BEAM L	INSIDE SPREAD	NUMBER OF R POINTS L	AREA	STATE/PROVINCE	HUNTER'S NAME	DATE	RANK
160 7/8	24 7/8 24 5/8	20 7/8	5 5	Marathon County	WI	Peter Kluz	2003	2347
160 7/8	24 5/8 26 0/8	18 1/8	7 6	Johnson County	IA	Keith Hyatt	2004	2347
160 7/8	24 1/8 23 5/8	17 1/8	5 5	Cass County	IL	Bryan Gawlik	2004	2347
160 7/8	27 0/8 26 3/8	19 5/8	4 5	Jackson County	IA	Dave Finch	2004	2347
160 7/8	24 6/8 26 0/8	19 5/8	5 5	Pierce County	WI	Scott C. Behrens	2004	2347
160 7/8	26 3/8 25 6/8	19 1/8	5 6	Lee County	IA	Glenn E. Wagner	2004	2347
*160 7/8	23 3/8 22 2/8	20 3/8	5 5	Jefferson County	NE	Dave Bedlan	2004	2347
160 7/8	23 7/8 24 5/8	17 3/8	5 5	Marathon County	WI	Dean Graveen	2006	2347
160 7/8	24 5/8 25 2/8	19 1/8	6 6	Hendricks County	IN	Brian Hartsock	2006	2347
*160 7/8	27 7/8 27 0/8	21 3/8	5 6	Adams County	OH	Mark Cole	2007	2347
*160 7/8	25 0/8 24 3/8	17 1/8	6 5	Logan County	WV	Lamanda Norman	2009	2347
160 6/8	25 4/8 25 7/8	17 0/8	6 5	Sarpy County	NE	Lawrence A. Klabunde	1968	2387
160 6/8	26 2/8 25 7/8	19 2/8	6 4	Fillmore County	MN	Doyle Tarrence	1974	2387
160 6/8	26 5/8 26 0/8	19 2/8	4 4	Lake County	IL	Charles R. Zradicka	1986	2387
160 6/8	24 0/8 25 0/8	17 2/8	4 4	Webster County	IA	Dave W. Hainzinger	1987	2387
160 6/8	24 3/8 24 2/8	18 6/8	5 7	Muskegon County	MI	Dave Haack	1988	2387
160 6/8	25 4/8 25 2/8	21 6/8	5 5	Bayfield County	WI	Jim Peters	1989	2387
160 6/8	26 2/8 25 3/8	23 2/8	5 6	Dallas County	IA	Kevin J. Lovell	1992	2387
160 6/8	26 0/8 26 7/8	19 0/8	6 5	Franklin County	OH	Lacie Waller	1993	2387
160 6/8	24 3/8 24 4/8	20 4/8	5 5	Edmonton	ALB	Ian Barclay	1993	2387
160 6/8	25 2/8 25 0/8	18 2/8	7 6	Winneshiek County	IA	James Ryant	1994	2387
160 6/8	24 6/8 26 0/8	16 5/8	6 7	Adams County	WI	Steve Paluszynski	1994	2387
160 6/8	28 3/8 27 3/8	20 6/8	5 5	Queen Annes County	MD	Robert Radford	1994	2387
160 6/8	25 7/8 27 0/8	16 7/8	6 5	Macoupin County	IL	Mike Nichols	1994	2387
160 6/8	24 6/8 23 6/8	23 4/8	6 7	Wood County	WI	Daniel J. Lila	1995	2387
160 6/8	23 7/8 24 0/8	18 5/8	6 6	Monroe County	WI	Charles Frederick	1995	2387
160 6/8	26 3/8 27 5/8	18 4/8	8 6	Belmont County	OH	Mike Huber	1995	2387
160 6/8	27 0/8 27 1/8	20 6/8	4 6	Mason County	IL	George Buck	1996	2387
160 6/8	24 6/8 24 6/8	21 2/8	5 5	Knox County	MO	Jim Baker	1997	2387
160 6/8	25 1/8 25 1/8	21 6/8	4 6	Sussex County	DE	Richard A. Davis	1999	2387
160 6/8	23 4/8 23 7/8	18 2/8	6 7	Olmsted County	MN	Jeff Oliver	1999	2387
160 6/8	25 1/8 25 2/8	16 6/8	6 5	Taylor County	IA	Michael A. Jacklin	1999	2387
160 6/8	23 6/8 25 0/8	17 6/8	5 6	Dunn County	WI	Keith Boernke	1999	2387
160 6/8	26 4/8 26 6/8	18 4/8	5 4	Harvey County	KS	Jimmy Hutto	1999	2387
160 6/8	27 0/8 25 7/8	21 4/8	6 7	La Porte County	IN	Jeff G. Kesling	2000	2387
160 6/8	23 7/8 23 7/8	17 7/8	5 6	Jefferson County	NE	Larry Stafford	2001	2387
160 6/8	26 1/8 24 2/8	18 2/8	6 7	Licking County	OH	David Wamer	2002	2387
160 6/8	27 2/8 26 0/8	24 6/8	5 5	St. Croix County	WI	Bruce Bader	2003	2387
*160 6/8	25 3/8 25 3/8	20 0/8	5 5	Douglas County	WI	James T. Schmid	2004	2387
*160 6/8	25 7/8 26 2/8	21 2/8	6 6	Morrison County	MN	Steve Marod	2004	2387
160 6/8	24 6/8 24 2/8	18 6/8	5 5	Jackson County	IA	Branden A. Post	2004	2387
*160 6/8	25 4/8 24 6/8	21 6/8	6 7	Kenosha County	WI	Anthony Fraley	2006	2387
160 6/8	26 3/8 25 1/8	19 2/8	5 5	Lapeer County	MI	Paul M. Feehan	2007	2387
160 6/8	23 5/8 23 6/8	19 6/8	6 6	Cole County	MO	Bryon Paneitz	2007	2387
160 6/8	28 6/8 27 0/8	19 0/8	5 7	Parke County	IN	Louis Giacone	2007	2387
160 6/8	23 5/8 23 2/8	18 2/8	6 6	Duval County	TX	L. Jack Nelson	2008	2387
*160 6/8	25 3/8 25 0/8	21 6/8	7 5	Trempealeau County	WI	Matthew G. Galewski	2008	2387
160 6/8	27 5/8 27 1/8	21 6/8	4 4	Hancock County	OH	Jason A. Lincoln	2008	2387
160 6/8	27 1/8 26 4/8	24 2/8	4 5	Sheridan County	KS	Paul Babcock	2008	2387
160 6/8	24 6/8 23 3/8	16 6/8	5 5	Vermilion County	IL	Todd Wickens	2009	2387
*160 6/8	24 7/8 25 0/8	20 0/8	6 5	Outagamie County	WI	Robert P. Calmes	2010	2387
160 5/8	22 3/8 23 4/8	16 4/8	7 8	Lawrence County	IL	Bob Brian	1971	2427
160 5/8	24 4/8 25 5/8	23 4/8	5 6	Murray County	MN	Paul Beech	1974	2427
160 5/8	22 2/8 21 4/8	15 5/8	5 5	Montcalm County	MI	Rodney Snyder	1980	2427
160 5/8	25 2/8 25 3/8	14 3/8	6 5	Hubbard County	MN	Myles Keller	1982	2427
160 5/8	23 7/8 23 3/8	16 6/8	6 7	Morrison County	MN	Randy Johnson	1986	2427
160 5/8	21 2/8 21 4/8	14 7/8	6 6	Kenedy County	TX	Cal Adger	1987	2427
160 5/8	25 2/8 25 7/8	19 1/8	7 6	Waukesha County	WI	Dick Harris	1988	2427
160 5/8	26 2/8 26 6/8	18 5/8	5 5	Van Buren County	IA	Noel E. Harlan	1988	2427
160 5/8	27 3/8 24 4/8	18 5/8	5 5	Scott County	MN	Kris Huber	1988	2427
160 5/8	26 2/8 24 6/8	19 5/8	5 6	Christian County	IL	Richard Krider	1988	2427
160 5/8	25 1/8 25 6/8	16 6/8	5 6	Allamakee County	IA	Warren W. Woods	1991	2427
160 5/8	26 1/8 27 5/8	19 5/8	7 7	Jefferson County	IL	Lanny Shaw	1995	2427
160 5/8	22 6/8 22 4/8	15 1/8	6 6	Schuyler County	IL	Edd Clack	1995	2427
160 5/8	23 4/8 25 4/8	18 2/8	7 6	Cook County	IL	Jason Gomez	1995	2427
160 5/8	26 7/8 24 7/8	20 5/8	5 5	Jackson County	MO	Scott Liebenguth	1997	2427
160 5/8	28 6/8 28 1/8	21 7/8	5 5	Knox County	OH	Tom Moxley	1997	2427
160 5/8	24 0/8 24 6/8	18 6/8	7 5	Franklin County	KS	Robert Brewer	1998	2427
160 5/8	25 3/8 25 4/8	16 6/8	5 6	Goodhue County	MN	Steve Raymond	1999	2427
160 5/8	26 5/8 26 5/8	16 5/8	6 4	Clark County	IL	Rick C. Davidson	1999	2427
160 5/8	25 3/8 25 5/8	19 6/8	6 5	Crawford County	WI	Van Jacobson	2000	2427
160 5/8	23 1/8 22 7/8	23 3/8	6 6	Greene County	IL	Jimmie G. Goodnight, Jr.	2001	2427
160 5/8	25 4/8 23 6/8	17 5/8	5 5	Clay County	MO	Norman Boos	2002	2427
160 5/8	25 1/8 25 2/8	20 0/8	5 6	Menard County	IL	George E. Hypke	2002	2427
160 5/8	25 3/8 25 1/8	18 7/8	6 9	Houston County	MN	Philip R. Morris	2003	2427
160 5/8	23 6/8 23 3/8	17 5/8	5 5	Sheridan County	KS	Paul Babcock	2003	2427
160 5/8	24 1/8 23 5/8	16 7/8	5 5	Fulton County	IL	Cory Schoonover	2004	2427
*160 5/8	27 2/8 26 0/8	20 5/8	6 4	Sauk County	WI	Tom G. Eggen	2004	2427
*160 5/8	26 0/8 25 0/8	18 7/8	5 5	Henry County	MO	Jason Garrett	2005	2427
160 5/8	22 4/8 22 4/8	17 1/8	5 5	Burleigh County	ND	Terry Friedt	2005	2427
160 5/8	28 0/8 27 7/8	19 7/8	4 5	Republic County	KS	Jared Melton	2005	2427
160 5/8	21 3/8 22 0/8	17 3/8	5 5	Marathon County	WI	Richard Langenhahn	2006	2427
160 5/8	25 3/8 24 4/8	20 4/8	7 5	Union County	SD	David Trudeau	2007	2427
*160 5/8	25 5/8 26 0/8	21 1/8	6 5	Delaware County	OH	Ryan Parrish	2007	2427
160 5/8	25 5/8 25 4/8	19 1/8	7 5	Decatur County	KS	Tom Reedy	2007	2427
160 5/8	24 4/8 24 2/8	17 5/8	5 5	Taylor County	IA	Scott Bebout	2007	2427
160 5/8	24 6/8 24 4/8	19 1/8	7 7	De Kalb County	MO	Bryan Boyer	2008	2427
160 5/8	23 2/8 23 2/8	14 7/8	5 5	Jackson County	WI	Rod Knudtson	2009	2427
160 5/8	27 5/8 27 0/8	18 1/8	5 5	Allen County	IN	Larry J. Herrmann	2009	2427
160 5/8	24 4/8 24 4/8	18 0/8	5 6	Columbia County	WI	Brandon Steinhorst	2009	2427
*160 5/8	27 2/8 27 6/8	22 4/8	5 4	Vernon County	WI	Tim Maedke	2009	2427
160 4/8	26 6/8 25 4/8	20 7/8	7 7	Williams County	ND	John Bloom	1963	2467
160 4/8	27 2/8 28 0/8	21 4/8	5 7	Lyon County	IA	Marvin H. Peterson	1970	2467
160 4/8	23 1/8 22 4/8	19 0/8	6 7	Keith County	NE	Gil Wilkinson	1970	2467
160 4/8	28 5/8 28 2/8	24 2/8	7 7	Fairfield County	OH	Robert A. Fletcher	1977	2467

WHITETAIL DEER (TYPICAL ANTLERS)

Minimum Score 125 — Continued

SCORE	LENGTH OF R MAIN BEAM L	INSIDE SPREAD	NUMBER OF R POINTS L		AREA	STATE/ PROVINCE	HUNTER'S NAME	DATE	RANK
160 4/8	24 2/8	24 7/8	17 6/8	5	6	Dawson County	MT	Frank Legato	1978	2467
160 4/8	26 0/8	26 2/8	19 2/8	5	5	Trempealeau County	WI	Duane Kupietz	1981	2467
160 4/8	24 2/8	24 7/8	19 2/8	6	5	Waukesha County	WI	Donald T. Lurvey	1982	2467
160 4/8	24 4/8	25 0/8	21 0/8	5	5	Daviess County	MO	Sam Boyd	1987	2467
160 4/8	23 7/8	23 7/8	18 0/8	5	5	Jefferson County	OH	Robert E. Howell	1987	2467
160 4/8	21 7/8	21 4/8	17 0/8	6	6	Fremont County	IA	Larry Zach	1987	2467
160 4/8	24 2/8	25 0/8	19 0/8	5	5	Coles County	IL	Randy Rodebaugh	1988	2467
160 4/8	27 3/8	27 2/8	19 1/8	6	4	Wayne County	MO	Carl Roach	1988	2467
160 4/8	26 2/8	26 7/8	18 6/8	5	5	Schuyler County	IL	Tom Grover	1991	2467
160 4/8	25 6/8	23 7/8	17 1/8	5	7	Pike County	IL	Tim Fulmer	1991	2467
160 4/8	26 4/8	25 3/8	19 4/8	9	7	Putnam County	IL	Tony Day	1992	2467
160 4/8	25 7/8	24 7/8	19 6/8	4	5	Olmsted County	MN	Jim Hanson	1992	2467
160 4/8	25 1/8	24 3/8	18 2/8	5	5	Osage County	MO	Leon Luecke	1992	2467
160 4/8	25 1/8	25 0/8	16 0/8	6	7	Lake County	IL	Kirk Short	1993	2467
160 4/8	24 4/8	24 3/8	17 0/8	5	5	Montgomery County	PA	Donald D. Epprecht	1993	2467
160 4/8	25 3/8	25 3/8	22 2/8	5	5	McHenry County	IL	Kenneth G. Wilson	1994	2467
160 4/8	27 0/8	26 6/8	21 0/8	7	5	Price County	WI	Timothy Engel	1995	2467
160 4/8	22 4/8	22 5/8	17 2/8	6	5	Decatur County	IA	Steve Snow	1995	2467
160 4/8	27 0/8	26 5/8	19 0/8	5	5	Providence County	RI	Stephen Burchett	1996	2467
160 4/8	24 0/8	25 0/8	18 6/8	6	6	Dallas County	IA	Tim Lockner	1997	2467
160 4/8	25 3/8	23 6/8	18 5/8	7	5	Porter County	IN	Donald M. Dolph	1997	2467
160 4/8	26 7/8	27 3/8	21 4/8	5	5	Kankakee County	IL	Keith Dvoroznak	1998	2467
160 4/8	26 4/8	26 3/8	18 3/8	6	5	Vermilion County	IL	Bill Whalen	1999	2467
160 4/8	23 2/8	24 3/8	19 7/8	6	5	Stewart County	TN	John C. Hults	1999	2467
160 4/8	26 4/8	25 1/8	24 0/8	5	5	Jackson County	IA	Larry Galliart	1999	2467
160 4/8	22 1/8	23 0/8	15 0/8	7	7	Boone County	MO	Richard L. Nelson	2000	2467
160 4/8	27 7/8	27 6/8	24 2/8	4	5	Carroll County	IL	Scott A. Parker	2001	2467
160 4/8	23 1/8	24 1/8	18 3/8	6	5	Cayuga County	NY	Michael F. Barski, Jr.	2002	2467
160 4/8	24 5/8	23 6/8	18 3/8	6	6	Cabell County	WV	Gregory Surber	2003	2467
*160 4/8	22 2/8	21 7/8	16 2/8	6	6	Greenwood County	KS	W. Louis Seville III	2003	2467
160 4/8	24 7/8	24 7/8	21 0/8	5	5	Winneshiek County	IA	Steve L. Weber	2004	2467
160 4/8	25 3/8	25 6/8	19 2/8	5	5	Gage County	NE	Brian Toalson	2004	2467
160 4/8	25 2/8	25 4/8	21 0/8	5	7	Waushara County	WI	Dan Bray	2004	2467
*160 4/8	27 6/8	27 4/8	19 0/8	5	5	Allamakee County	IA	Richard Schroeder	2005	2467
*160 4/8	25 1/8	25 3/8	23 1/8	7	5	Anoka County	MN	James Rick	2005	2467
160 4/8	24 3/8	23 7/8	17 2/8	5	6	Jefferson County	IN	Blake Deuser	2007	2467
*160 4/8	23 2/8	22 5/8	18 6/8	5	5	Winona County	MN	Ross Greden	2008	2467
160 4/8	25 2/8	26 5/8	20 2/8	4	4	Dubuque County	IA	Chad P. Brandel	2008	2467
*160 4/8	23 3/8	25 1/8	20 7/8	6	7	Lake County	IN	Aaron Lanting	2008	2467
160 4/8	23 6/8	24 7/8	17 0/8	5	5	Knox County	MO	Keith Pulse	2009	2467
160 4/8	28 2/8	28 3/8	17 4/8	6	7	Buffalo County	WI	Ed Twinn	2010	2467
160 3/8	22 2/8	22 4/8	20 2/8	6	6	Sheridan County	NE	Wayne Krotz	1975	2512
160 3/8	24 3/8	24 2/8	17 1/8	5	5	St. Charles County	MO	Dan Schulte	1976	2512
160 3/8	23 6/8	24 7/8	20 1/8	7	6	Barber County	KS	Herbie M. Landwehr, Jr.	1980	2512
160 3/8	27 5/8	26 0/8	19 7/8	4	4	Clark County	IL	Gerald Shaffner	1983	2512
160 3/8	26 4/8	26 5/8	18 3/8	6	5	Hamilton County	IL	Clifford R. Schoolman	1984	2512
160 3/8	23 4/8	25 2/8	19 1/8	6	6	Jefferson County	IL	Jerry Newell	1986	2512
160 3/8	24 2/8	23 5/8	20 3/8	7	5	Saskatoon	SAS	Maurice Parent	1987	2512
160 3/8	23 4/8	23 2/8	19 1/8	6	6	Murray County	MN	Del Determan	1987	2512
160 3/8	23 2/8	23 3/8	19 5/8	5	5	Rock County	WI	Ronald A. Vike, Jr.	1989	2512
160 3/8	25 5/8	25 7/8	18 5/8	5	7	Clay County	MO	James Wollard	1991	2512
160 3/8	24 6/8	25 6/8	19 6/8	5	6	Washita County	OK	Larry Snider	1991	2512
160 3/8	28 5/8	28 6/8	21 2/8	6	5	Jay County	IN	Avery O. Coleman	1992	2512
160 3/8	26 1/8	26 4/8	18 5/8	5	5	Montgomery County	MD	Joel I. Bullard	1993	2512
160 3/8	23 3/8	23 3/8	18 1/8	5	5	Geary County	KS	William Ahlers	1993	2512
160 3/8	26 2/8	26 1/8	17 3/8	5	6	Alamance County	NC	M. Todd Ramsey	1994	2512
160 3/8	25 4/8	24 4/8	16 7/8	5	5	Delaware County	IA	Jason N. Nolz	1994	2512
160 3/8	23 6/8	23 5/8	17 7/8	5	6	Jay County	IN	Robert Lingo	1994	2512
160 3/8	23 1/8	23 3/8	18 3/8	5	6	Polk County	IA	John Flies	1994	2512
160 3/8	25 0/8	24 4/8	15 0/8	6	5	Lincoln County	MO	Scott Creech	1995	2512
160 3/8	26 4/8	27 1/8	19 7/8	5	4	Shelby County	IL	Steve A. Tripp	1995	2512
160 3/8	26 6/8	27 0/8	21 1/8	5	5	Cherokee County	KS	Doug Walden	1995	2512
160 3/8	23 4/8	23 0/8	15 5/8	5	5	Manitowoc County	WI	Wayne "Gaffer" Blaha	1997	2512
160 3/8	25 2/8	25 2/8	16 5/8	7	5	Ness County	KS	Ron Stoecklein	1997	2512
160 3/8	27 4/8	26 0/8	19 6/8	5	5	Vermilion County	IL	John Hubbard	1997	2512
160 3/8	27 2/8	26 4/8	22 2/8	5	6	Jefferson County	OH	Tom Bateman	1997	2512
160 3/8	22 7/8	24 6/8	17 5/8	5	5	Waukesha County	WI	Richard Carlson	1998	2512
160 3/8	25 0/8	24 7/8	19 7/8	6	6	Columbia County	WI	Keith Salzman	1998	2512
160 3/8	26 1/8	26 5/8	20 3/8	4	5	Oneida County	WI	Brian Baumann	1999	2512
160 3/8	25 7/8	24 5/8	16 1/8	5	5	Wilson County	KS	Ronald K. Cole	1999	2512
160 3/8	26 5/8	25 4/8	21 5/8	5	5	Montcalm County	MI	Mark Allen Pitcher	2000	2512
160 3/8	26 0/8	25 5/8	20 1/8	6	6	Knox County	IL	Troy Huffman	2000	2512
160 3/8	23 4/8	22 7/8	16 7/8	7	6	Kleberg County	TX	Robert Nichols	2001	2512
160 3/8	25 0/8	25 5/8	21 7/8	5	5	Geauga County	OH	Andrew F. Ule	2001	2512
160 3/8	27 0/8	26 0/8	22 5/8	4	6	Guthrie County	IA	Dennis Hoover	2001	2512
160 3/8	24 7/8	26 2/8	21 1/8	6	4	Du Page County	IL	James A. Wetmore	2002	2512
160 3/8	23 7/8	23 5/8	17 6/8	6	7	Ward County	ND	Scott Closs	2003	2512
160 3/8	26 0/8	26 0/8	19 0/8	7	6	Callaway County	MO	Mario Kriete	2003	2512
160 3/8	26 6/8	26 6/8	20 1/8	6	8	Marion County	IA	Gerald T. Dowell	2003	2512
160 3/8	24 0/8	23 7/8	16 1/8	6	5	Seward County	KS	Lynn Leonard	2003	2512
160 3/8	27 3/8	26 6/8	20 4/8	6	5	Jersey County	IL	Chad Goetten	2004	2512
160 3/8	25 5/8	24 1/8	18 7/8	6	5	Okotoks	ALB	Jerry Legere	2005	2512
160 3/8	29 4/8	29 6/8	19 1/8	7	7	Butler County	OH	Michael T. Schul	2006	2512
160 3/8	23 4/8	24 0/8	22 0/8	6	5	Wabaunsee County	KS	Jeff Frank	2006	2512
160 3/8	23 5/8	22 7/8	18 1/8	5	5	McLean County	ND	Zack Roberts	2006	2512
160 3/8	24 5/8	24 0/8	15 7/8	5	6	Butler County	IA	Brian Pruin	2006	2512
160 3/8	26 0/8	26 0/8	19 3/8	6	6	Todd County	MN	Richard M. Cook	2006	2512
*160 3/8	25 2/8	25 0/8	20 5/8	5	5	Buffalo County	WI	Matt Foust	2007	2512
*160 3/8	28 3/8	28 0/8	18 4/8	4	5	Champaign County	OH	Brad Fielder	2008	2512
*160 3/8	22 4/8	23 1/8	18 1/8	6	8	Fayette County	IL	Aaron Miller	2008	2512
160 3/8	24 5/8	25 7/8	18 5/8	6	5	Randolph County	MO	Rob G. Rixon	2008	2512
160 3/8	24 2/8	23 5/8	18 5/8	6	5	Carroll County	IL	Chuck Anderson, Jr.	2008	2512
160 3/8	26 0/8	25 5/8	19 4/8	5	4	Osage County	KS	Richard McCarty	2009	2512
*160 3/8	23 5/8	24 1/8	21 4/8	7	7	Parke County	IN	Jeff Cannaday	2009	2512
160 2/8	25 6/8	26 3/8	19 2/8	5	5	Nance County	NE	Ralph I. Hansen	1963	2565

WHITETAIL DEER (TYPICAL ANTLERS)

Minimum Score 125   Continued

SCORE	LENGTH OF R MAIN BEAM L	INSIDE SPREAD	NUMBER OF R POINTS L	AREA	STATE/ PROVINCE	HUNTER'S NAME	DATE	RANK
160 2/8	25 7/8 26 0/8	21 4/8	4 4	Cherokee County	IA	Jerry L. Smith	1969	2565
160 2/8	22 6/8 23 3/8	19 4/8	5 5	Valley County	MT	John 'Rosey' Roseland	1981	2565
160 2/8	23 1/8 23 1/8	18 0/8	6 6	Mills County	IA	Dale R. Clayton	1983	2565
160 2/8	24 5/8 24 6/8	18 1/8	6 6	Phelps County	NE	Bruce Nielsen	1984	2565
160 2/8	24 4/8 24 5/8	18 0/8	5 5	La Salle County	IL	John Thomas	1987	2565
160 2/8	25 2/8 25 6/8	25 1/8	7 6	Lake County	IL	Woody Scruggs	1987	2565
160 2/8	27 0/8 26 4/8	17 5/8	5 6	Ashland County	WI	Steven Roginske	1988	2565
160 2/8	24 0/8 25 7/8	19 0/8	5 5	Rusk County	WI	Shawn Harris	1991	2565
160 2/8	26 0/8 26 5/8	22 6/8	6 5	Winnebago County	IL	Douglas R. Greensides	1991	2565
160 2/8	25 2/8 25 3/8	18 0/8	5 5	Jessamine County	KY	Roger Drury	1992	2565
160 2/8	26 7/8 26 7/8	20 4/8	5 6	Comanche County	KS	Greg Hill	1992	2565
160 2/8	27 1/8 28 0/8	17 4/8	5 6	Macoupin County	IL	Kenny Tate	1992	2565
160 2/8	23 7/8 23 7/8	19 7/8	6 5	Stevens County	WA	Jay Baker	1992	2565
160 2/8	25 2/8 25 6/8	18 4/8	7 7	Kalamazoo County	MI	Tom G. Ahrens	1993	2565
160 2/8	22 6/8 23 0/8	16 6/8	6 6	St. Croix County	WI	Thomas E. Dulon	1993	2565
160 2/8	24 7/8 22 4/8	19 3/8	5 6	Garden County	NE	Tim Heckenlively	1993	2565
160 2/8	25 3/8 25 6/8	21 0/8	5 5	Wayne County	WV	Alex Spaulding	1994	2565
160 2/8	24 5/8 24 7/8	19 0/8	6 7	St. Marys County	MD	Casey W. Moore	1994	2565
160 2/8	27 4/8 27 5/8	19 0/8	5 5	McHenry County	IL	Kevin Lunde	1995	2565
160 2/8	25 6/8 26 2/8	18 6/8	5 5	Kleberg County	TX	Warren Strickland	1995	2565
160 2/8	24 3/8 27 3/8	21 1/8	6 6	Linn County	KS	Malon I. Randall, Jr.	1997	2565
160 2/8	25 4/8 24 6/8	18 4/8	5 6	Waukesha County	WI	John Morrison	1998	2565
160 2/8	24 1/8 24 1/8	16 5/8	6 6	Dane County	WI	Kevin J. Bronkhorst	1998	2565
160 2/8	24 6/8 26 0/8	17 6/8	5 5	Outagamie County	WI	Matthew R. Heimann	1998	2565
160 2/8	27 0/8 25 7/8	19 4/8	5 5	St. Joseph County	IN	Mervin R. Miller	1998	2565
160 2/8	24 3/8 24 7/8	18 5/8	5 6	Richland County	WI	Mike A. Ferguson	1999	2565
160 2/8	27 1/8 26 5/8	19 0/8	5 5	Hillsdale County	MI	Jeffrey D. Gier	1999	2565
160 2/8	27 0/8 24 4/8	18 4/8	5 5	Polk County	WI	Mutt Wilson	1999	2565
160 2/8	24 3/8 24 4/8	21 6/8	5 5	Summit County	OH	Thomas G. Minute	1999	2565
160 2/8	27 0/8 27 1/8	20 4/8	6 6	Waukesha County	WI	Erik Kroll	2000	2565
160 2/8	24 3/8 23 7/8	19 6/8	5 5	Minnehaha County	SD	Chris Schellinger	2000	2565
160 2/8	24 3/8 24 6/8	18 0/8	5 5	Sauk County	WI	Mark Kramer	2000	2565
160 2/8	25 0/8 24 4/8	16 2/8	5 6	Benton County	IA	Travis Clark	2001	2565
160 2/8	23 4/8 23 4/8	16 0/8	6 6	Piatt County	IL	Mike Bily	2001	2565
160 2/8	25 0/8 24 4/8	19 3/8	6 6	Greene County	MO	Buddy Ghan	2002	2565
160 2/8	23 5/8 24 5/8	15 3/8	5 6	Floyd County	IN	Dennis Mayfield	2003	2565
160 2/8	23 6/8 20 2/8	19 6/8	5 6	Hudson Bay	SAS	Eric Shawn Morin	2003	2565
160 2/8	26 0/8 25 7/8	16 5/8	6 6	Jersey County	IL	Stan Gade	2003	2565
160 2/8	25 0/8 25 3/8	23 2/8	4 5	Lac La Biche	ALB	Greg Talley	2004	2565
160 2/8	22 6/8 23 2/8	20 0/8	6 6	Champaign County	IL	Eric Billman	2004	2565
160 2/8	22 2/8 21 7/8	18 0/8	6 6	Nodaway County	MO	Dave Messner	2004	2565
160 2/8	23 2/8 23 7/8	16 4/8	6 6	Pike County	MO	Jeff Parker	2005	2565
160 2/8	27 0/8 26 3/8	23 6/8	6 8	Montgomery County	OH	Jared Garber	2005	2565
160 2/8	26 6/8 26 6/8	18 7/8	6 6	Winnebago County	IA	Kerry Wentworth	2006	2565
*160 2/8	24 4/8 24 7/8	20 2/8	5 5	Guernsey County	OH	Matthew Pyle	2006	2565
160 2/8	23 4/8 21 7/8	16 2/8	5 5	Iowa County	IA	Andrew Graykowski	2006	2565
*160 2/8	24 5/8 24 2/8	17 4/8	7 6	Boone County	IL	Ivin Hammond	2007	2565
160 2/8	24 1/8 24 0/8	20 1/8	6 5	Van Buren County	MI	Bradlee B. Page	2007	2565
*160 2/8	25 5/8 25 3/8	17 7/8	5 6	Sumner County	KS	Kathy Strecker	2007	2565
*160 2/8	25 0/8 25 1/8	19 0/8	6 6	Cass County	MI	Micheal J. Eash	2008	2565
160 2/8	27 4/8 27 4/8	23 3/8	6 6	Fulton County	IL	Gary L. Olsen	2008	2565
160 2/8	23 6/8 22 7/8	15 4/8	5 5	Putnam County	MO	Bryan A. Kottwitz	2009	2565
160 1/8	25 7/8 26 2/8	18 5/8	5 6	Polk County	MN	Scott Gullickson	1985	2618
160 1/8	25 3/8 25 6/8	17 3/8	5 5	Blue Earth County	MN	Darwin Arndt	1985	2618
160 1/8	27 5/8 26 4/8	19 1/8	4 4	Ross County	OH	Randall W. Haines	1986	2618
160 1/8	27 5/8 27 6/8	21 7/8	5 5	Powell County	KY	Orville Fugate	1987	2618
160 1/8	27 2/8 25 5/8	17 3/8	6 7	Coles County	IL	Jim Eveland	1987	2618
160 1/8	28 6/8 29 7/8	21 3/8	5 4	Lafayette County	WI	Jeff J. Kahle	1988	2618
160 1/8	22 3/8 23 0/8	19 1/8	5 5	Clayton County	IA	Wayne M. Lau	1989	2618
160 1/8	23 7/8 25 0/8	21 1/8	5 5	Washington County	MS	Odis Hill, Jr.	1990	2618
160 1/8	25 3/8 26 6/8	18 4/8	7 10	Huntington County	IN	Troy Harris	1991	2618
160 1/8	26 1/8 25 2/8	17 6/8	8 11	Jefferson County	KS	John Welborn	1991	2618
160 1/8	24 1/8 23 1/8	17 1/8	6 6	Fergus County	MT	John Fleharty	1992	2618
160 1/8	22 4/8 22 6/8	14 7/8	5 5	Hamiota	MAN	Terry Lee	1993	2618
160 1/8	25 1/8 24 3/8	18 7/8	5 5	Keith County	NE	Gale Subbert	1994	2618
160 1/8	21 5/8 25 2/8	15 5/8	6 5	Putnam County	MO	Jerry Williams	1994	2618
160 1/8	26 5/8 25 2/8	19 3/8	5 5	Pierce County	WI	Dan Meixner	1994	2618
160 1/8	27 4/8 27 0/8	19 2/8	7 6	Clark County	IL	Jared Hupp	1995	2618
160 1/8	29 1/8 28 3/8	19 2/8	6 7	Allegheny County	PA	Wallace E. Carr	1996	2618
160 1/8	26 4/8 26 3/8	17 5/8	5 5	Effingham County	IL	Michael E. Lee, Sr.	1997	2618
160 1/8	25 0/8 25 4/8	21 3/8	5 5	Clay County	SD	Jeffrey J. Olson	1997	2618
160 1/8	25 0/8 26 2/8	22 4/8	7 6	Schuyler County	IL	Michael S. Helsley, Jr.	1999	2618
160 1/8	24 7/8 25 6/8	18 5/8	5 5	Clark County	MO	Tom Casey	2001	2618
160 1/8	24 7/8 25 3/8	15 3/8	5 5	Peoria County	IL	Andy C. Decker	2001	2618
160 1/8	28 0/8 27 7/8	20 4/8	8 7	Leavenworth County	KS	Daniel G. Salmon	2001	2618
*160 1/8	25 2/8 24 2/8	17 7/8	5 5	Marion County	KY	Jeremy Roberts	2003	2618
160 1/8	23 2/8 22 4/8	22 3/8	5 5	Kleberg County	TX	Gary E. Rope	2003	2618
160 1/8	24 6/8 23 3/8	19 5/8	5 5	Pierce County	WI	Cory Haglund	2003	2618
160 1/8	21 2/8 23 3/8	16 7/8	5 6	Hamilton County	KS	Scott Burns	2003	2618
160 1/8	26 0/8 25 7/8	19 7/8	5 6	Iron County	WI	Roger Adamavich	2003	2618
*160 1/8	23 6/8 24 0/8	16 0/8	6 6	Pocahontas County	IA	Les Traub	2003	2618
*160 1/8	23 3/8 24 1/8	18 1/8	5 5	Osage County	MO	Shay Abel	2004	2618
160 1/8	25 3/8 25 2/8	20 1/8	5 5	Chickasaw County	IA	Cathy Hall	2005	2618
*160 1/8	24 2/8 24 3/8	18 3/8	6 7	Fulton County	IL	Blair G. Burkhart	2005	2618
160 1/8	24 2/8 24 5/8	17 3/8	6 5	Edgar County	IL	Brad Davis	2005	2618
160 1/8	23 1/8 23 6/8	16 0/8	6 6	DeKalb County	IL	George I. Maness, Jr.	2005	2618
160 1/8	24 0/8 24 5/8	17 1/8	7 7	Appanoose County	IA	Albert P. Sindt	2005	2618
160 1/8	25 6/8 25 4/8	18 1/8	5 5	Jackson County	WI	Nick Mueller	2005	2618
*160 1/8	25 1/8 24 2/8	19 2/8	7 7	Calhoun County	IL	Alex Harbison	2006	2618
160 1/8	26 1/8 25 2/8	18 4/8	6 6	Jefferson County	IN	Michael D. Waltz	2006	2618
160 1/8	26 1/8 25 2/8	19 1/8	6 6	Kleberg County	TX	Daryl Brown	2006	2618
160 1/8	26 6/8 25 2/8	19 7/8	7 6	Polk County	IA	Glen Salow	2007	2618
*160 1/8	25 6/8 26 1/8	19 3/8	5 5	Knox County	OH	Bob Baker	2009	2618
*160 1/8	23 7/8 22 1/8	18 3/8	6 6	Adams County	WI	Brad A. Bauer	2009	2618
160 1/8	27 2/8 26 2/8	17 5/8	5 6	Russell County	KS	Glen Merica	2009	2618

WHITETAIL DEER (TYPICAL ANTLERS)

Minimum Score 125 — Continued

SCORE	LENGTH OF R MAIN BEAM L	INSIDE SPREAD	NUMBER OF R POINTS L	AREA	STATE/ PROVINCE	HUNTER'S NAME	DATE	RANK
160 0/8	24 6/8 24 5/8	21 3/8	6 6	Worth County	IA	Terry Lynch	1972	2661
160 0/8	26 3/8 24 7/8	21 6/8	8 5	Winona County	MN	James Enderson	1973	2661
160 0/8	25 4/8 26 0/8	18 6/8	5 5	Faribault County	MN	Darryl Germann	1974	2661
160 0/8	23 0/8 22 3/8	20 0/8	5 5	Cooper County	MO	Nancy Smith	1984	2661
160 0/8	25 4/8 26 0/8	18 2/8	4 5	Stephenson County	IL	Richard K. Kerr	1985	2661
160 0/8	22 7/8 23 0/8	17 2/8	6 5	Morrill County	NE	Michael A. Brening	1985	2661
160 0/8	25 2/8 25 4/8	25 2/8	5 5	Ellsworth County	KS	Dave Fisher	1986	2661
160 0/8	24 6/8 23 4/8	16 5/8	5 8	Charles County	MD	William J. Kovach	1990	2661
160 0/8	23 5/8 25 1/8	20 4/8	5 5	Sawyer County	WI	Todd Carlson	1990	2661
160 0/8	24 2/8 24 2/8	15 2/8	6 5	Buffalo County	WI	Scott Duellman	1990	2661
160 0/8	27 3/8 26 5/8	20 4/8	5 5	Clermont County	OH	John Fischer	1991	2661
160 0/8	23 6/8 23 5/8	18 7/8	5 6	Becker County	MN	Kurt Holland	1992	2661
160 0/8	24 2/8 23 6/8	17 2/8	5 5	Butler County	KS	George Schuttler	1992	2661
160 0/8	27 4/8 28 1/8	19 6/8	5 5	Clarke County	IA	Alan Shields	1993	2661
160 0/8	26 2/8 25 4/8	22 0/8	9 8	Jefferson County	KY	William S. Finney, Jr.	1993	2661
160 0/8	23 3/8 23 7/8	19 2/8	5 5	Mower County	MN	Randy Hegge	1994	2661
160 0/8	25 0/8 25 1/8	17 2/8	5 5	Weld County	CO	Michael Yeary	1994	2661
160 0/8	23 6/8 23 2/8	17 3/8	7 6	Dane County	WI	Mark McCaulley	1994	2661
160 0/8	21 4/8 22 2/8	17 2/8	5 5	Pontotoc County	OK	Bruce A. Hall	1995	2661
160 0/8	26 0/8 25 7/8	18 4/8	5 5	Jefferson County	OH	Chuck Keenan	1995	2661
160 0/8	27 6/8 27 7/8	23 7/8	6 7	Otero County	CO	Troy Cunningham	1995	2661
160 0/8	24 4/8 25 3/8	18 2/8	5 6	Pulaski County	IL	Paul Landewee	1996	2661
160 0/8	26 0/8 27 4/8	22 4/8	6 6	Shannon County	MO	Edward Thomas	1996	2661
160 0/8	26 3/8 26 3/8	18 2/8	7 7	Noble County	OH	Mark A. Hudak	1997	2661
160 0/8	27 1/8 26 6/8	21 3/8	6 5	Mercer County	IL	Dan Bergen	1997	2661
160 0/8	24 2/8 23 7/8	19 5/8	8 6	Outagamie County	WI	Kevin L. Lohrenz	1998	2661
160 0/8	23 4/8 22 1/8	19 0/8	5 6	Monona County	IA	Dr. David Samuel	1998	2661
160 0/8	24 7/8 23 4/8	20 4/8	5 5	Washington County	MN	Mike Gross	1998	2661
160 0/8	25 4/8 23 5/8	17 4/8	5 5	Montgomery County	IN	Larry A. Culley	1999	2661
160 0/8	23 5/8 23 6/8	27 0/8	7 5	Kankakee County	IL	Don A. Schultz	1999	2661
160 0/8	25 6/8 25 0/8	16 0/8	5 5	Taylor County	WI	Thomas Mildbrand	2000	2661
160 0/8	26 4/8 26 4/8	19 2/8	4 5	Morrison County	MN	Charles Karn	2000	2661
160 0/8	28 4/8 26 0/8	23 0/8	6 5	Harford County	MD	Barry Gladstone	2000	2661
160 0/8	26 6/8 26 5/8	21 4/8	4 4	Butler County	PA	Torre Moore	2001	2661
160 0/8	25 6/8 27 3/8	18 5/8	6 5	Calhoun County	IL	Steven L. Donelson, Jr.	2001	2661
160 0/8	24 7/8 24 6/8	19 2/8	6 5	Washington County	PA	Jeff Lowden	2001	2661
*160 0/8	26 3/8 26 1/8	19 3/8	7 6	Fayette County	IN	Joel Gibson	2003	2661
*160 0/8	22 7/8 23 1/8	16 2/8	7 9	Shawnee County	KS	Gary D. Dawdy	2003	2661
160 0/8	24 4/8 26 3/8	18 2/8	5 5	Guthrie County	IA	Patrick O'Brien	2003	2661
160 0/8	24 4/8 26 1/8	17 4/8	6 5	Gallatin County	IL	Matt Duffy	2003	2661
160 0/8	25 0/8 23 5/8	16 2/8	7 7	Spokane County	WA	Chuck Denner	2003	2661
160 0/8	22 7/8 22 5/8	15 4/8	5 5	Sumner County	KS	Julio Lazcano	2003	2661
160 0/8	26 1/8 26 1/8	18 6/8	4 5	Vernon County	WI	Kevin J. Simonsen	2004	2661
*160 0/8	27 3/8 26 0/8	19 4/8	8 8	Newton County	IN	Richard Booker	2004	2661
160 0/8	27 0/8 27 6/8	19 3/8	6 4	McPherson County	KS	Charles A. Fenstermaker	2004	2661
160 0/8	27 0/8 25 2/8	17 3/8	5 7	Douglas County	KS	Mark Young	2004	2661
160 0/8	25 0/8 24 7/8	16 3/8	5 7	Brown County	IL	Kenneth L. Crooks	2005	2661
160 0/8	25 0/8 25 0/8	19 4/8	5 5	Trempealeau County	WI	Chet Pennington	2006	2661
160 0/8	25 7/8 24 5/8	16 4/8	5 7	Butler County	KS	Darrell Allen	2006	2661
160 0/8	26 3/8 25 5/8	23 0/8	5 6	Ohio County	WV	Jack T. Dick	2007	2661
*160 0/8	24 6/8 24 4/8	18 4/8	5 6	Richland County	MT	Richard Ebersold	2007	2661
*160 0/8	24 0/8 23 3/8	19 0/8	5 6	Vernon County	WI	Dan Tollefson	2007	2661
160 0/8	24 2/8 23 4/8	21 1/8	6 6	Wapello County	IA	Todd McNeill	2008	2661
160 0/8	25 0/8 25 5/8	19 6/8	6 6	Knox County	IL	Dan Hicks	2008	2661
*160 0/8	27 0/8 26 1/8	20 4/8	5 5	Trempealeau County	WI	David Franck	2009	2661
160 0/8	26 6/8 25 4/8	21 0/8	6 5	Logan County	IL	Stewart Riedle	2009	2661
159 7/8	22 5/8 22 5/8	18 2/8	5 6	Clark County	KS	William Rule	1983	2717
159 7/8	24 4/8 25 4/8	20 1/8	6 5	Garden County	NE	Wynn Fontenot	1984	2717
159 7/8	25 7/8 25 2/8	19 5/8	5 5	Brown County	NE	Lorne Allen	1988	2717
159 7/8	22 1/8 22 2/8	18 2/8	6 7	Alberta Beach	ALB	Joe Hanson	1991	2717
159 7/8	24 6/8 25 1/8	19 5/8	6 5	Will County	IL	Gene Hagberg	1991	2717
159 7/8	24 4/8 23 4/8	17 5/8	5 6	Douglas County	KS	Ronald G. Nicholson	1991	2717
159 7/8	27 3/8 28 1/8	18 5/8	5 5	Shawano County	WI	John Anderson, Jr.	1992	2717
159 7/8	27 7/8 27 4/8	25 3/8	4 6	Ross County	OH	Robert Williams	1995	2717
159 7/8	24 2/8 24 1/8	18 5/8	5 5	Linn County	KS	James D. Johnson	1995	2717
159 7/8	24 6/8 24 7/8	18 0/8	6 8	Grayson County	VA	Ralph Haga, Jr.	1997	2717
159 7/8	26 0/8 26 2/8	22 2/8	5 6	Wyoming County	WV	Blake Luce	1997	2717
159 7/8	26 0/8 25 4/8	19 6/8	7 7	Pottawattamie County	IA	Clifford Killpack	1998	2717
159 7/8	24 1/8 24 3/8	18 3/8	6 6	La Salle County	IL	Mike Armstrong	1999	2717
159 7/8	26 4/8 26 5/8	19 1/8	5 5	Genesee County	MI	Ronald J. Phillips	2000	2717
159 7/8	24 6/8 25 0/8	18 7/8	5 5	Marathon County	WI	Al Steiner	2000	2717
159 7/8	27 0/8 27 6/8	22 7/8	4 5	Knox County	OH	Patrick Gentry	2001	2717
159 7/8	26 7/8 26 4/8	20 5/8	4 5	Marinette County	WI	Chad Rickling	2002	2717
159 7/8	24 6/8 25 4/8	17 3/8	5 5	Warren County	IN	Michael A. Burnett	2003	2717
159 7/8	28 1/8 29 3/8	19 1/8	4 4	Ripley County	IN	Mike Brandes	2003	2717
*159 7/8	25 2/8 25 3/8	18 1/8	5 5	Buffalo County	WI	Michael Kreibich	2004	2717
159 7/8	23 2/8 23 4/8	17 3/8	5 5	Morgan County	IL	Nicholas Skinner	2004	2717
159 7/8	25 6/8 25 5/8	19 5/8	6 6	Rooks County	KS	Kenny Newell	2005	2717
159 7/8	25 4/8 24 7/8	17 1/8	5 7	Latimer County	OK	Jeremie W. Moore	2006	2717
159 7/8	25 2/8 26 3/8	21 3/8	7 4	Cook County	IL	Kevin Dahm	2007	2717
159 7/8	24 0/8 23 1/8	19 0/8	6 8	Lamoure County	ND	Adam Peterson	2007	2717
159 7/8	24 6/8 25 2/8	19 1/8	5 5	Pottawatomie County	KS	Kevin Thorburn	2007	2717
*159 7/8	26 2/8 27 1/8	24 3/8	5 5	Cumberland County	IL	Curt Taylor	2007	2717
159 7/8	26 2/8 26 6/8	18 5/8	6 6	Scioto County	OH	Jerry Howard	2008	2717
*159 7/8	24 2/8 23 7/8	19 5/8	6 5	Richland County	IL	Jeremiah Brown	2008	2717
159 7/8	23 2/8 23 4/8	16 7/8	5 5	Kossuth County	IA	Roger Townsend	2009	2717
159 6/8	26 5/8 26 6/8	20 0/8	5 5	Winona County	MN	Arlie Herber	1977	2747
159 6/8	21 2/8 21 2/8	17 0/8	5 5	Vanderburgh County	IN	Floyd Jackson	1977	2747
159 6/8	24 1/8 23 2/8	19 6/8	5 6	Sherburne County	MN	Allen Hugget	1981	2747
159 6/8	26 7/8 25 5/8	17 6/8	6 6	Buffalo County	WI	Bill Peterson	1981	2747
159 6/8	25 0/8 25 0/8	18 2/8	5 5	Miami County	KS	Tom Wiggin	1982	2747
159 6/8	25 6/8 25 1/8	20 6/8	4 4	Washington County	MS	Steve Nichols	1986	2747
159 6/8	24 2/8 24 7/8	19 5/8	5 6	Page County	IA	Dave Bayless	1986	2747
159 6/8	24 5/8 23 6/8	18 4/8	5 5	Rock Island County	IL	Russ Courter	1988	2747
159 6/8	26 7/8 27 2/8	17 2/8	4 5	Greenwood County	KS	John Porubski	1989	2747

384

WHITETAIL DEER (TYPICAL ANTLERS)

Minimum Score 125 — Continued

SCORE	R MAIN BEAM L	INSIDE SPREAD	R POINTS L	AREA	STATE/PROVINCE	HUNTER'S NAME	DATE	RANK
159 6/8	26 7/8 26 0/8	19 7/8	7 7	Crawford County	WI	Mitch Staszak	1993	2747
159 6/8	22 7/8 24 0/8	18 6/8	6 5	Stevens County	MN	Nic Magnuson	1994	2747
159 6/8	26 7/8 25 4/8	18 4/8	5 5	Trumbull County	OH	Gregory D. Spano	1994	2747
159 6/8	23 2/8 23 4/8	18 2/8	5 5	Ferry County	WA	Leroy Day/George Schernitzki	1995	2747
159 6/8	24 4/8 24 7/8	18 4/8	5 6	Pike County	IL	Bill Westlake	1996	2747
159 6/8	24 4/8 23 2/8	19 6/8	5 5	Saline County	IL	Marty Stokich	1996	2747
159 6/8	22 7/8 19 5/8	17 6/8	5 5	Dunn County	WI	Eric Huseboe	1997	2747
159 6/8	25 0/8 25 2/8	21 4/8	5 5	Cherokee County	IA	Lucas Edwards	2000	2747
159 6/8	25 0/8 26 2/8	20 0/8	5 5	Greenwood County	KS	Guy Rupert	2000	2747
159 6/8	23 7/8 24 2/8	18 6/8	7 7	Weld County	CO	Roger D. Bechler	2001	2747
159 6/8	25 6/8 25 6/8	16 6/8	5 5	Shawano County	WI	Bill Seip	2001	2747
159 6/8	24 6/8 25 0/8	16 6/8	5 5	Houston County	MN	Billy Twilley	2002	2747
159 6/8	24 3/8 24 2/8	21 4/8	6 5	Clermont County	OH	Ken McCane	2002	2747
159 6/8	24 6/8 23 7/8	19 4/8	5 5	Dane County	WI	Jeff Lange	2002	2747
159 6/8	23 4/8 23 2/8	20 6/8	7 5	Barton County	MO	Richard Ray	2002	2747
159 6/8	26 2/8 26 3/8	20 0/8	4 5	Washington County	IN	Chris Ault	2003	2747
159 6/8	25 3/8 26 4/8	17 0/8	5 5	Vernon County	MO	Jeff Hubbard	2003	2747
159 6/8	25 1/8 26 1/8	18 7/8	6 6	Harrison County	MO	Leland McCall	2003	2747
159 6/8	27 6/8 26 4/8	24 6/8	4 5	Chautauqua County	NY	Joe Anastasi	2004	2747
*159 6/8	28 3/8 28 6/8	20 4/8	4 4	Greene County	IN	Cory Swartzentruber	2007	2747
159 6/8	24 0/8 24 6/8	17 4/8	5 5	Chippewa County	WI	Daniel Berrum	2007	2747
159 6/8	25 7/8 25 2/8	19 3/8	6 6	Adams County	WI	Dale L. Toltzmann	2007	2747
*159 6/8	25 4/8 23 4/8	17 5/8	6 8	Clark County	IL	Raymond Nuxoll	2007	2747
*159 6/8	24 7/8 23 4/8	21 5/8	7 6	Harper County	KS	Jeffrey Morris	2007	2747
*159 6/8	25 0/8 26 5/8	19 4/8	5 5	Montgomery County	IL	Kirk Kampwerth	2009	2747
159 6/8	26 6/8 26 7/8	18 4/8	5 6	Ripley County	IN	Rob Back	2009	2747
159 6/8	24 3/8 24 4/8	18 2/8	6 5	Appanoose County	IA	Richard P. Hillmer	2009	2747
*159 6/8	23 1/8 25 4/8	17 4/8	5 5	Pittsylvania County	VA	Adam Ellis	2010	2747
159 5/8	26 3/8 25 5/8	21 5/8	5 5	Des Moines County	IA	Richard Howard	1964	2784
159 5/8	22 4/8 22 3/8	18 1/8	5 5	Pittsburg County	OK	John Baumann	1977	2784
159 5/8	23 7/8 23 7/8	15 5/8	6 6	Reno County	KS	Richard A. Swisher	1978	2784
159 5/8	24 6/8 23 1/8	18 1/8	5 5	Madison County	IL	Barry Ash	1980	2784
159 5/8	24 5/8 26 1/8	18 5/8	6 5	Muskingum County	OH	Brent L. Taylor	1981	2784
159 5/8	25 4/8 24 7/8	17 7/8	4 4	Ogle County	IL	Charles L. Martoglio	1982	2784
159 5/8	24 6/8 24 6/8	20 7/8	6 5	Watonwan County	MN	Richard Enger	1983	2784
159 5/8	26 2/8 26 2/8	23 6/8	6 6	Cochrane	ALB	Edward Defrancesco	1984	2784
159 5/8	26 1/8 26 2/8	19 1/8	6 7	Ellis County	KS	Allen Landry	1986	2784
159 5/8	23 2/8 24 4/8	16 1/8	6 5	Hamilton County	IA	Stephen L. Cink	1987	2784
159 5/8	23 3/8 23 6/8	15 7/8	6 7	Hennepin County	MN	John Earl Ford	1988	2784
159 5/8	26 2/8 25 7/8	18 0/8	7 6	Sangamon County	IL	Hobart E. Watson	1992	2784
159 5/8	26 6/8 26 6/8	24 2/8	5 4	La Porte County	IN	Drake Matovich	1993	2784
159 5/8	26 4/8 25 7/8	19 7/8	5 6	Kiowa County	KS	Greg Hill	1993	2784
159 5/8	25 6/8 24 4/8	21 7/8	5 5	Columbia County	WI	Patrick W. Jahn	1995	2784
159 5/8	22 0/8 24 1/8	20 7/8	5 5	Page County	VA	Terry Lee Dorman	1995	2784
159 5/8	25 2/8 24 5/8	19 5/8	5 5	Pendleton County	KY	Philip W. Fox	1996	2784
159 5/8	28 0/8 27 7/8	22 2/8	7 6	Boone County	IA	Chuck Stotts	1996	2784
159 5/8	23 5/8 22 7/8	15 7/8	6 6	Rusk County	WI	Marc A. Olivo	1998	2784
159 5/8	25 7/8 27 4/8	21 3/8	5 5	Labette County	KS	Marty Russell	1998	2784
159 5/8	23 2/8 24 5/8	15 5/8	6 6	La Porte County	IN	Homer T. Griffey	1998	2784
159 5/8	27 4/8 26 6/8	21 7/8	8 8	Warren County	IA	Michael Couch	2001	2784
159 5/8	22 4/8 22 0/8	21 2/8	5 6	Peoria County	IL	Ryan J. Schlueter	2002	2784
159 5/8	25 1/8 25 4/8	19 5/8	8 9	Will County	IL	Kenny Bassett	2003	2784
159 5/8	26 1/8 25 2/8	19 0/8	7 8	Webster County	IA	Tim Finucan	2003	2784
159 5/8	24 3/8 24 5/8	17 1/8	6 5	Buffalo County	WI	Robert Andrew Arbs	2003	2784
*159 5/8	26 3/8 25 4/8	23 0/8	5 6	Warren County	MO	Eric Hambach	2004	2784
159 5/8	24 6/8 24 0/8	16 7/8	5 5	Davis County	IA	Kenneth Musgrove	2004	2784
159 5/8	25 4/8 24 1/8	17 3/8	8 5	Ozaukee County	WI	Stanley D. Richards	2005	2784
*159 5/8	20 4/8 20 3/8	18 5/8	6 6	Miami County	OH	Jeff Wheeler	2005	2784
*159 5/8	23 3/8 23 3/8	15 7/8	5 5	Oldham County	KY	Mike Collier	2005	2784
159 5/8	25 2/8 26 5/8	22 7/8	4 5	Hamilton County	IL	Robert L. Musson	2006	2784
159 5/8	26 1/8 26 1/8	17 5/8	5 5	Jackson County	IL	Chris Holifield	2006	2784
159 5/8	24 5/8 25 2/8	19 5/8	5 5	Jackson County	WI	Robert Parker	2006	2784
159 5/8	25 2/8 23 5/8	15 6/8	6 8	Schuyler County	IL	James Long	2006	2784
*159 5/8	27 7/8 26 7/8	16 6/8	6 6	Mingo County	WV	Matthew Cline	2006	2784
*159 5/8	25 1/8 25 6/8	17 1/8	5 5	Houston County	MN	Russ Breeser	2007	2784
159 5/8	28 4/8 27 1/8	17 1/8	5 8	Butler County	KS	Dan Benton	2007	2784
*159 5/8	25 0/8 25 1/8	18 3/8	5 5	St. Charles County	MO	Chris M. Cella	2008	2784
159 5/8	27 0/8 26 1/8	21 0/8	5 5	Plymouth County	IA	Gary McCrill	2008	2784
*159 5/8	24 1/8 23 5/8	18 1/8	6 6	Switzerland County	IN	Abraham Hall	2009	2784
159 5/8	23 0/8 23 2/8	19 0/8	6 5	Richland County	WI	Patrick J. Finucan	2009	2784
159 4/8	27 6/8 27 6/8	25 4/8	4 4	Blue Earth County	MN	Harold Tow	1963	2826
159 4/8	22 6/8 21 5/8	17 5/8	6 5	Wabash County	IL	Tom J. McRaven	1967	2826
159 4/8	24 5/8 24 6/8	21 2/8	5 5	Hocking County	OH	James Allen Downs	1980	2826
159 4/8	22 5/8 22 6/8	18 0/8	5 4	Morris County	KS	Kenneth R. Bryant	1983	2826
159 4/8	24 4/8 24 6/8	18 0/8	5 6	Dade County	MO	Charles A. Myers	1985	2826
159 4/8	24 7/8 27 3/8	18 0/8	6 6	Scott County	IA	Albert Perreault	1985	2826
159 4/8	26 0/8 25 2/8	19 0/8	5 4	Goodhue County	MN	Brad C. Nesseth	1986	2826
159 4/8	24 4/8 25 1/8	18 4/8	5 5	Will County	IL	Larry Elumbaugh	1987	2826
159 4/8	26 6/8 25 7/8	19 0/8	4 4	Linn County	IA	Jim Arp	1989	2826
159 4/8	24 2/8 24 2/8	16 2/8	5 5	Buffalo County	WI	Ronald Brenner	1990	2826
159 4/8	25 2/8 23 4/8	18 3/8	5 6	Foster County	ND	Bryon Hallwachs	1990	2826
159 4/8	24 5/8 24 2/8	18 0/8	5 5	Pike County	IL	Kevin McCallister	1991	2826
159 4/8	25 4/8 25 4/8	20 2/8	5 5	Randolph County	IN	Roy Patterson	1991	2826
159 4/8	25 7/8 24 4/8	24 4/8	5 5	Morgan County	IL	Jon A. Whalen	1993	2826
159 4/8	24 6/8 23 1/8	23 4/8	5 5	Lyon County	IA	Mike Judas	1993	2826
159 4/8	22 7/8 23 5/8	21 2/8	6 5	Butler County	KS	Robert Faris II	1994	2826
159 4/8	27 3/8 27 1/8	21 4/8	6 6	Wyandot County	OH	Mike Saam	1995	2826
159 4/8	25 0/8 25 3/8	20 2/8	5 5	Macon County	IL	Doug Key	1995	2826
159 4/8	25 2/8 26 0/8	19 0/8	5 6	Des Moines County	IA	James L. Reiser	1996	2826
159 4/8	23 6/8 23 3/8	22 2/8	6 6	Will County	IL	Ken Palmer	1997	2826
159 4/8	28 0/8 26 1/8	18 2/8	5 5	Raleigh County	WV	Jackie Lee Davis	1998	2826
159 4/8	26 3/8 24 5/8	18 4/8	6 5	Linn County	KS	Gary A. Monroe	2002	2826
159 4/8	25 4/8 26 1/8	19 2/8	5 5	Pike County	IL	William N. Shelby	2003	2826
*159 4/8	25 1/8 26 2/8	19 2/8	5 4	Jackson County	WI	Charles Comstock	2003	2826
159 4/8	25 2/8 24 4/8	16 4/8	5 5	Howard County	MO	Roger Gerloff, Jr.	2004	2826

WHITETAIL DEER (TYPICAL ANTLERS)

Minimum Score 125   Continued

SCORE	LENGTH OF R MAIN BEAM L	INSIDE SPREAD	NUMBER OF R POINTS L	AREA	STATE/PROVINCE	HUNTER'S NAME	DATE	RANK
159 4/8	25 4/8 25 2/8	18 2/8	5 5	Waupaca County	WI	Mike Janikowski	2004	2826
*159 4/8	21 4/8 23 1/8	18 0/8	6 6	Washington County	IA	Patrick J. Blindauer	2004	2826
159 4/8	24 6/8 26 6/8	18 6/8	6 5	Johnson County	IL	Dennis Shimp	2004	2826
*159 4/8	24 4/8 25 0/8	19 4/8	5 6	Kingman County	KS	Theodore J. Feight	2004	2826
*159 4/8	24 5/8 24 3/8	18 0/8	5 5	Scott County	IA	Robert A. Lytle	2005	2826
*159 4/8	26 6/8 25 4/8	19 2/8	5 5	Shelby County	OH	Nicholas Gaier	2005	2826
159 4/8	24 7/8 24 7/8	21 6/8	5 5	Marathon County	WI	Glen Loppnow	2005	2826
159 4/8	24 0/8 23 4/8	18 2/8	7 6	Saunders County	NE	Mark Jost	2007	2826
*159 4/8	24 6/8 24 6/8	19 7/8	6 6	Fulton County	IL	Dean Singleton	2007	2826
159 4/8	27 5/8 27 1/8	20 2/8	4 4	Madison County	IA	Eric L. Rooney	2007	2826
159 4/8	25 2/8 25 0/8	19 2/8	5 5	Wayne County	IN	Joe Ladd	2007	2826
159 4/8	25 6/8 26 0/8	22 1/8	6 5	Monroe County	WI	Bryan L. Grandall	2009	2826
159 4/8	24 0/8 23 5/8	19 0/8	5 5	Spokane County	WA	Steve Jeffries	2009	2826
159 3/8	27 6/8 27 1/8	22 3/8	4 4	Pike County	OH	Ray C. Pritchett, Jr.	1977	2864
159 3/8	25 5/8 25 4/8	18 5/8	4 4	Washington County	KS	Tony Mann	1985	2864
159 3/8	24 6/8 23 6/8	18 3/8	6 6	Rock Island County	IL	Mike W. Greeno	1988	2864
159 3/8	25 6/8 25 6/8	17 7/8	5 5	Pike County	IL	Phil McEuen	1988	2864
159 3/8	28 0/8 26 2/8	21 3/8	5 5	Houston County	MN	Steve Bjerke	1989	2864
159 3/8	26 0/8 26 0/8	19 1/8	8 5	Hillsdale County	MI	Dennis L. Burlew	1989	2864
159 3/8	26 7/8 26 3/8	18 3/8	4 4	Washtenaw County	MI	Gregory Kuhn	1990	2864
159 3/8	28 0/8 28 0/8	18 5/8	5 4	Chase County	KS	Dave Ward	1992	2864
159 3/8	25 7/8 24 6/8	19 6/8	5 7	Westchester County	NY	Claude "Kenny" Pylant	1994	2864
159 3/8	25 3/8 25 6/8	20 1/8	5 5	Ozaukee County	WI	Jeff Eder	1994	2864
159 3/8	21 7/8 22 0/8	15 3/8	5 5	Van Buren County	IA	David Thornsberry	1995	2864
159 3/8	25 5/8 25 6/8	17 4/8	6 6	Chippewa County	WI	Brian Starck	1997	2864
159 3/8	23 1/8 24 5/8	18 7/8	5 6	Macoupin County	IL	Jerry A. Dittmer	1998	2864
159 3/8	23 0/8 26 2/8	21 3/8	4 4	Henry County	IA	James E. Howie	1999	2864
159 3/8	25 5/8 24 4/8	15 4/8	6 8	Macon County	MO	Russell Reed	2000	2864
159 3/8	23 6/8 23 0/8	17 2/8	6 5	La Salle County	IL	Allan Simons	2000	2864
159 3/8	26 2/8 27 1/8	19 6/8	6 6	Fillmore County	MN	Alex Haagensen	2001	2864
159 3/8	23 0/8 24 1/8	17 1/8	5 6	Buffalo County	WI	Jed T. Kennedy	2002	2864
159 3/8	23 5/8 23 3/8	19 7/8	5 6	Buffalo County	WI	Joel Tomlinson	2002	2864
159 3/8	24 2/8 23 0/8	19 3/8	6 5	Delaware County	IA	Kevin Davis	2002	2864
159 3/8	24 3/8 24 4/8	16 1/8	5 5	Cass County	IN	Tony Williams	2003	2864
*159 3/8	24 3/8 25 1/8	19 7/8	5 5	Jackson County	WI	Greg D. Brauner	2003	2864
159 3/8	25 7/8 24 1/8	21 1/8	7 7	Lee County	IL	Cory Zimmerly	2003	2864
159 3/8	24 3/8 24 3/8	17 2/8	6 6	Decatur County	IA	Duane Hearing	2004	2864
159 3/8	24 0/8 24 1/8	24 1/8	5 5	Dunn County	WI	Christopher L. Holmes	2005	2864
159 3/8	24 7/8 26 0/8	17 7/8	5 5	Alcurve	SAS	Carl Furman	2005	2864
*159 3/8	23 4/8 23 6/8	19 5/8	5 6	Fillmore County	MN	Mike Kelly	2006	2864
159 3/8	26 7/8 25 7/8	18 5/8	6 7	Decatur County	IN	Rusty Scheibler	2006	2864
159 3/8	23 0/8 23 2/8	17 7/8	6 6	Guthrie County	IA	Rodney Benton	2006	2864
*159 3/8	23 5/8 24 6/8	15 7/8	4 5	Kent County	DE	Joseph T. Shockley	2007	2864
159 3/8	25 1/8 24 4/8	19 2/8	5 6	Jackson County	MO	Chris Nelson	2007	2864
159 3/8	26 2/8 27 0/8	19 0/8	5 4	Brown County	KS	Ryan Menold	2007	2864
*159 3/8	24 6/8 24 6/8	18 4/8	5 7	Logan County	IL	Thomas M. Harris, Jr.	2007	2864
159 3/8	23 6/8 23 6/8	17 7/8	6 6	Davis County	IA	Harlan Peterson	2007	2864
159 3/8	22 4/8 21 6/8	11 7/8	6 5	Washington County	KS	Steven L. Line	2007	2864
159 3/8	25 7/8 26 5/8	20 6/8	6 8	Hancock County	IL	Justin Smith	2009	2864
159 3/8	24 4/8 23 7/8	19 7/8	5 5	DeKalb County	IL	Josef K. Rud	2010	2864
159 2/8	22 4/8 24 0/8	20 2/8	6 7	Hamlin County	SD	John R. Gregory	1975	2901
159 2/8	25 1/8 27 6/8	20 6/8	4 4	Yankton County	SD	Michael L. Tacke	1983	2901
159 2/8	23 2/8 23 0/8	16 2/8	5 5	Anne Arundel County	MD	Jim Roy	1985	2901
159 2/8	23 3/8 24 7/8	18 2/8	8 5	Madison County	IA	Tom Arpy	1987	2901
159 2/8	24 2/8 24 3/8	18 2/8	5 5	Cass County	IA	Dan E. Mikkelsen	1988	2901
159 2/8	24 1/8 24 3/8	18 0/8	5 6	Milwaukee County	WI	Terry R. Brandenburg	1989	2901
159 2/8	31 2/8 31 0/8	21 2/8	4 6	Williamson County	IL	Lowell Mausey	1990	2901
159 2/8	25 7/8 25 4/8	16 0/8	5 5	Buffalo County	WI	Larry Bloom	1994	2901
159 2/8	23 6/8 22 4/8	19 0/8	5 5	Fulton County	IN	Dennis L. Kamp	1994	2901
159 2/8	26 4/8 24 4/8	18 1/8	7 8	Dakota County	MN	Steve Huettl	1994	2901
159 2/8	26 5/8 26 2/8	21 2/8	4 5	McLean County	IL	Gayland McKinnerney	1994	2901
159 2/8	26 1/8 25 0/8	17 3/8	7 5	Osborne County	KS	Gary Ozias	1995	2901
159 2/8	24 6/8 24 1/8	17 0/8	5 5	Dane County	WI	Ty Hauden	1995	2901
159 2/8	24 4/8 24 4/8	17 5/8	6 7	Will County	IL	Frank Grigus	1996	2901
159 2/8	27 6/8 27 3/8	20 4/8	5 5	Calhoun County	IL	Richard Graham	1997	2901
159 2/8	24 3/8 23 2/8	17 4/8	6 6	Clark County	IL	Trey Downing	1997	2901
159 2/8	22 3/8 22 0/8	16 4/8	5 5	Wayne County	IL	Jerry Gifford	1997	2901
159 2/8	26 4/8 27 0/8	20 6/8	6 6	La Salle County	IL	Jeff Barnes	1998	2901
159 2/8	22 5/8 21 7/8	19 2/8	6 6	Stornoway	SAS	Terry Yawney	1999	2901
159 2/8	26 0/8 26 7/8	22 0/8	8 6	Pawnee County	NE	Jeff Handly	1999	2901
159 2/8	24 5/8 26 0/8	17 2/8	6 5	Adams County	OH	Larry David Napier	2000	2901
159 2/8	24 3/8 24 2/8	19 5/8	6 7	Richland County	WI	Andrew Wilson	2000	2901
159 2/8	25 3/8 23 5/8	19 1/8	8 7	Dane County	WI	Robert Smith	2001	2901
159 2/8	22 6/8 23 2/8	19 2/8	5 5	La Salle County	IL	Todd Yeager	2001	2901
159 2/8	22 2/8 23 6/8	16 4/8	5 7	Pike County	IL	Lonnie Manalia	2001	2901
159 2/8	25 5/8 25 2/8	18 5/8	5 6	Crow Wing County	MN	Rick Pickar	2002	2901
159 2/8	26 6/8 26 2/8	21 3/8	5 5	Menard County	IL	Don Bacon	2002	2901
159 2/8	25 4/8 26 2/8	21 6/8	4 5	Fulton County	IL	David Courtright	2002	2901
159 2/8	24 4/8 24 4/8	17 6/8	5 5	Richland County	WI	Michael D. Alexander	2004	2901
159 2/8	22 7/8 22 3/8	22 6/8	5 6	Meade County	KS	Richie Bland	2004	2901
159 2/8	24 7/8 24 4/8	20 0/8	4 4	Marshall County	IL	William Pfaff	2005	2901
159 2/8	22 7/8 22 1/8	16 2/8	5 5	Allamakee County	IA	Earl Goodman	2005	2901
*159 2/8	26 2/8 26 2/8	16 4/8	5 5	Dutchess County	NY	James P. Weaver	2006	2901
159 2/8	26 7/8 26 4/8	18 1/8	5 7	Spencer County	KY	Tim Davis	2006	2901
159 2/8	27 1/8 26 4/8	22 2/8	5 5	Douglas County	WI	Joseph Doskey	2006	2901
*159 2/8	25 2/8 25 5/8	20 6/8	6 5	Trempealeau County	WI	Paul Wenaas	2007	2901
*159 2/8	22 5/8 23 0/8	16 6/8	5 5	Clayton County	IA	Brian Oberfoell	2007	2901
159 2/8	23 4/8 24 4/8	14 4/8	5 5	Butler County	KS	Bentley D. Miller	2007	2901
159 2/8	26 4/8 26 1/8	18 2/8	4 5	Iowa County	WI	Jason Hanson	2008	2901
*159 2/8	21 6/8 21 3/8	20 0/8	5 5	Macomb County	MI	James Lockemy	2009	2901
159 1/8	23 7/8 23 0/8	20 1/8	6 6	Lucas County	OH	Martin Higley	1962	2941
159 1/8	26 2/8 25 2/8	23 5/8	4 5	Grundy County	IL	Ed Vitko, Jr.	1976	2941
159 1/8	22 4/8 24 2/8	16 5/8	7 6	Clayton County	IA	Gary Troester	1978	2941
159 1/8	26 2/8 25 6/8	17 4/8	6 6	Heard County	GA	Howard E. Taylor	1980	2941
159 1/8	24 7/8 25 7/8	21 5/8	8 6	Saline County	KS	Raymond Peterman	1984	2941

386

WHITETAIL DEER (TYPICAL ANTLERS)

Minimum Score 125 — Continued

SCORE	LENGTH OF R MAIN BEAM L	INSIDE SPREAD	NUMBER OF R POINTS L		AREA	STATE/ PROVINCE	HUNTER'S NAME	DATE	RANK
159 1/8	25 0/8	25 1/8	18 1/8	5	5	Winona County	MN	Vernon Zachariason	1986	2941
159 1/8	25 1/8	23 5/8	19 7/8	5	5	Allamakee County	IA	Daniel R. Kennedy	1987	2941
159 1/8	23 1/8	23 6/8	18 5/8	5	5	Livingston County	MI	Keith Joseph Daniels	1988	2941
159 1/8	23 2/8	24 2/8	16 5/8	5	5	Vermilion County	IL	Horace E. Marsh	1990	2941
159 1/8	25 5/8	24 5/8	19 1/8	5	6	Stark County	IL	Kevin Heaton	1990	2941
159 1/8	27 2/8	27 5/8	19 2/8	7	5	Douglas County	KS	Paul Gordon	1991	2941
159 1/8	25 1/8	25 2/8	21 7/8	5	5	Clay County	MN	Randy Nelson	1992	2941
159 1/8	22 0/8	22 0/8	18 5/8	5	5	Butler County	KS	David R. Rogers	1992	2941
159 1/8	25 4/8	24 4/8	21 3/8	7	8	Harrison County	OH	Donald A. Gore	1994	2941
159 1/8	25 4/8	25 0/8	20 1/8	5	5	Walworth County	WI	Bob Gallup	1994	2941
159 1/8	25 5/8	26 6/8	22 1/8	4	4	Milwaukee County	WI	Jason Geschke	1997	2941
159 1/8	24 1/8	23 5/8	17 7/8	5	6	McLean County	ND	Mike Lehmann	1998	2941
159 1/8	25 4/8	25 2/8	18 1/8	5	5	Lake County	IL	Roy McClellan	1998	2941
159 1/8	24 6/8	23 6/8	18 3/8	5	5	Somerset County	MD	Robert Pines, Jr.	1998	2941
159 1/8	22 7/8	23 4/8	18 1/8	6	6	Muscatine County	IA	Todd Stammer	1999	2941
159 1/8	26 3/8	27 2/8	22 1/8	5	5	Ashtabula County	OH	Ray A. Youngs	2000	2941
159 1/8	23 6/8	23 4/8	19 6/8	7	7	Webster County	KY	Steve Wilson	2002	2941
159 1/8	24 7/8	25 3/8	18 7/8	6	5	Greenwood County	KS	Steve Bartel	2002	2941
*159 1/8	27 6/8	27 6/8	18 3/8	4	5	Ashland County	OH	Charles Bunt	2003	2941
159 1/8	25 2/8	26 2/8	17 6/8	5	6	Jersey County	IL	Craig Jones	2003	2941
*159 1/8	23 4/8	23 5/8	19 3/8	5	5	Hutchinson County	SD	Michael Fuerst	2003	2941
159 1/8	23 3/8	23 5/8	19 2/8	5	7	Chickasaw County	IA	Dave Boeding	2004	2941
159 1/8	24 5/8	24 4/8	16 5/8	5	5	Door County	WI	Michael E. Hafenbredl	2005	2941
159 1/8	25 7/8	24 6/8	22 4/8	6	5	Goodhue County	MN	Jack Warfel	2005	2941
*159 1/8	24 4/8	24 6/8	18 6/8	7	6	Leavenworth County	KS	Kyle Billand	2006	2941
159 1/8	26 7/8	26 4/8	18 5/8	8	8	Rush County	IN	Larry E. Lawson	2008	2941
159 0/8	25 7/8	26 1/8	17 6/8	5	5	Shelby County	IL	Gary E. Sievers	1971	2972
159 0/8	22 6/8	22 6/8	18 4/8	5	5	Pulaski County	IN	William F. Bean	1977	2972
159 0/8	23 3/8	23 7/8	18 3/8	7	7	Sarpy County	NE	Todd W. Steward	1985	2972
159 0/8	26 0/8	25 6/8	20 0/8	5	5	Switzerland County	IN	Donald R. Barker	1986	2972
159 0/8	24 0/8	24 2/8	16 6/8	5	5	Lawrence County	OH	Kevin Whitt	1986	2972
159 0/8	25 6/8	25 2/8	14 4/8	5	5	Jackson County	MN	Ken Bute	1987	2972
159 0/8	25 2/8	25 4/8	22 2/8	5	7	Pike County	IL	Steven R. Tice	1989	2972
159 0/8	26 6/8	28 2/8	21 3/8	8	7	Clark County	IL	Ronald E. Pender	1989	2972
159 0/8	23 6/8	23 6/8	18 4/8	5	6	Adair County	OK	Dan Mallory	1990	2972
159 0/8	24 4/8	25 1/8	17 4/8	5	5	Davis County	IA	Gilbert H. Paulsen	1992	2972
159 0/8	23 7/8	23 1/8	19 4/8	6	7	Clark County	IL	Stewart Lee	1992	2972
159 0/8	24 4/8	24 2/8	18 2/8	6	5	Douglas County	WI	Russell E. Harvey	1993	2972
159 0/8	24 0/8	23 6/8	19 3/8	7	7	Peoria County	IL	Jonathan Sarver	1994	2972
159 0/8	26 3/8	26 1/8	19 7/8	7	6	Pike County	IL	Buzz Puterbaugh	1994	2972
159 0/8	27 4/8	27 1/8	18 4/8	5	5	Ray County	MO	Kelly D. Holder	1994	2972
159 0/8	23 5/8	22 6/8	17 6/8	5	7	Ottawa County	MI	Ken Melvin	1995	2972
159 0/8	25 4/8	23 7/8	19 5/8	6	5	Refugio County	TX	Matt W. Mayo	1995	2972
159 0/8	25 0/8	26 3/8	19 6/8	5	5	Anderson County	KS	Clifford Spencer	1995	2972
159 0/8	24 6/8	24 3/8	18 2/8	5	5	Cedar County	IA	Rick Regennitter	1997	2972
159 0/8	24 4/8	22 5/8	17 2/8	5	5	Cedar County	IA	Leland P. Kober	1997	2972
159 0/8	24 4/8	25 3/8	19 2/8	5	6	Steuben County	NY	Bill Makitra	1997	2972
159 0/8	22 3/8	23 5/8	15 0/8	5	5	Gainsborough Creek	MAN	Danny Maffenbeier	1998	2972
159 0/8	24 0/8	23 4/8	17 7/8	6	8	Menard County	IL	David Robbins	1998	2972
159 0/8	27 6/8	26 3/8	19 2/8	6	6	Waupaca County	WI	Reed Buetow	2000	2972
159 0/8	25 3/8	24 5/8	17 5/8	7	5	Washburn County	WI	Matthew Parker	2000	2972
159 0/8	23 3/8	23 7/8	21 4/8	5	5	Harrison County	MO	Richard Pemberton	2000	2972
159 0/8	27 1/8	26 4/8	23 1/8	6	6	Hancock County	OH	Curt Cramer	2000	2972
159 0/8	26 2/8	26 7/8	18 6/8	5	5	Clark County	IL	Jerald Davis	2001	2972
159 0/8	26 3/8	27 2/8	20 0/8	6	5	St. Camille	QUE	Marie Sophie Royer	2002	2972
159 0/8	25 2/8	24 1/8	18 2/8	7	5	Polk County	WI	Timothy F. Hutton	2002	2972
159 0/8	26 3/8	27 0/8	21 2/8	4	5	Sauk County	WI	Michael J. Fichter	2003	2972
159 0/8	26 0/8	26 2/8	16 2/8	5	5	Bracken County	KY	Gene Schadle	2003	2972
159 0/8	25 4/8	25 2/8	18 0/8	6	6	Prowers County	CO	Mike Sanders	2003	2972
*159 0/8	25 4/8	25 0/8	16 6/8	6	6	Ottawa County	OH	Michael G. Tye	2004	2972
159 0/8	26 0/8	26 0/8	17 6/8	6	6	Cherokee County	IA	Dan Soellner	2004	2972
159 0/8	24 4/8	23 7/8	18 2/8	5	5	Marion County	IA	Harry DeBold	2004	2972
159 0/8	24 1/8	24 5/8	17 4/8	6	5	McDonough County	IL	Scott A. Knupp	2005	2972
159 0/8	23 5/8	23 2/8	19 2/8	5	5	McHenry County	IL	Gary L. Capps	2006	2972
159 0/8	22 3/8	22 6/8	20 2/8	5	5	Fulton County	IL	Jeff H. Montgomery	2007	2972
*159 0/8	25 4/8	26 1/8	17 5/8	6	6	Tippecanoe County	IN	Steven A. Rider	2007	2972
159 0/8	23 0/8	22 7/8	19 5/8	6	6	Logan County	OH	Kim A. Best	2007	2972
159 0/8	25 0/8	24 3/8	20 5/8	5	6	Knox County	IL	D. Scott Wolfe	2008	2972
*159 0/8	24 4/8	25 2/8	18 4/8	5	5	Trempealeau County	WI	Brady Rumpel	2009	2972
158 7/8	24 7/8	22 4/8	20 3/8	5	6	Pope County	IL	Gary Thomas	1964	3015
158 7/8	27 4/8	25 7/8	18 3/8	8	8	Blue Earth County	MN	Gordon F. Kopischke	1968	3015
158 7/8	24 7/8	24 2/8	18 1/8	6	5	Owen County	IN	Steven Collins	1973	3015
158 7/8	23 1/8	22 4/8	19 7/8	5	5	Sedgwick County	KS	Marion A. Crumm	1974	3015
158 7/8	24 1/8	24 1/8	20 6/8	5	6	Putnam County	IL	David A. Heath	1975	3015
158 7/8	27 2/8	26 7/8	19 4/8	7	8	Crawford County	OH	Charles Ellis	1977	3015
158 7/8	24 4/8	24 1/8	17 7/8	5	5	Charles County	MD	Jim Wright	1986	3015
158 7/8	25 2/8	25 2/8	20 3/8	6	7	Paulding County	OH	Karl A. Langham	1988	3015
158 7/8	26 7/8	26 1/8	22 1/8	6	5	Henry County	MO	LaVern Rucker	1988	3015
158 7/8	23 1/8	23 2/8	17 5/8	5	5	Pottawattamie County	IA	Mike L. Smith	1989	3015
158 7/8	25 1/8	24 3/8	20 1/8	7	7	Marshall County	IA	Mark A. Hedum	1990	3015
158 7/8	27 4/8	27 1/8	17 3/8	6	5	Chippewa County	WI	Dennis Johnson	1990	3015
158 7/8	26 5/8	26 7/8	19 7/8	4	5	Westchester County	NY	Gregg Della Rocca	1991	3015
158 7/8	26 4/8	26 6/8	18 7/8	4	4	Williamson County	IL	Mark Donahue	1993	3015
158 7/8	27 3/8	26 0/8	16 7/8	7	5	Greene County	OH	Mike Kennedy	1993	3015
158 7/8	28 0/8	27 6/8	20 5/8	4	4	Knox County	IL	Todd A. Clayton	1995	3015
158 7/8	26 0/8	25 6/8	17 5/8	6	6	Ross County	OH	John Virgin, Jr.	1995	3015
158 7/8	24 2/8	24 4/8	18 1/8	4	4	Doniphan County	KS	Dennis R. Wisler	1995	3015
158 7/8	24 7/8	24 4/8	20 5/8	5	5	Gibson County	IN	Mark Ice	1996	3015
158 7/8	22 7/8	23 7/8	16 1/8	5	5	E. Carroll Parish	LA	Brian Arceneaux	1998	3015
158 7/8	24 2/8	24 0/8	19 3/8	5	4	Montgomery County	KS	Loren Dickens, Jr.	1998	3015
158 7/8	25 4/8	25 4/8	21 1/8	5	4	Adams County	CO	Lance MacLennan	2001	3015
158 7/8	24 1/8	24 2/8	19 1/8	5	5	Anne Arundel County	MD	Donald L. Fulkoski	2002	3015
158 7/8	26 1/8	25 7/8	14 1/8	6	6	Cedar County	MO	Michael Coleman	2002	3015
158 7/8	24 2/8	25 1/8	17 0/8	6	5	Jefferson County	KY	Tony Korfhage	2002	3015
158 7/8	24 6/8	24 4/8	21 0/8	5	6	Buffalo County	WI	Randy Ralph Wilcox	2003	3015

387

WHITETAIL DEER (TYPICAL ANTLERS)

Minimum Score 125   Continued

SCORE	LENGTH OF R MAIN BEAM L	INSIDE SPREAD	NUMBER OF R POINTS L		AREA	STATE/ PROVINCE	HUNTER'S NAME	DATE	RANK
158 7/8	25 0/8 24 5/8	19 1/8	5	6	Bremer County	IA	Mark L. Haskin	2003	3015
158 7/8	23 4/8 22 7/8	19 3/8	5	5	Adams County	IL	Shawn Williams	2004	3015
158 7/8	24 6/8 24 6/8	23 1/8	5	5	Fulton County	IL	Carl G. Corbin II	2005	3015
158 7/8	23 1/8 23 2/8	15 6/8	7	7	Green County	WI	Terry Plath	2005	3015
*158 7/8	26 2/8 24 7/8	25 3/8	8	7	Fayette County	OH	Brian Wallner	2006	3015
158 7/8	22 1/8 22 2/8	17 7/8	5	5	Lancaster County	NE	Jacob C. Findley	2006	3015
*158 7/8	23 5/8 22 6/8	19 1/8	6	5	Jackson County	MI	Andrew C. May	2006	3015
*158 7/8	25 0/8 24 5/8	19 1/8	5	5	Macon County	IL	Corey Gist	2008	3015
*158 7/8	25 7/8 25 0/8	16 5/8	5	5	Logan County	WV	Bobby Kelly	2008	3015
*158 7/8	24 6/8 24 5/8	18 0/8	9	6	Waukesha County	WI	Tim Bourdo	2009	3015
158 7/8	26 4/8 26 1/8	19 2/8	7	10	Douglas County	KS	Mark Carlson	2009	3015
158 7/8	23 4/8 24 1/8	21 3/8	5	5	Macoupin County	IL	Brad Weidner	2009	3015
158 6/8	22 5/8 22 7/8	15 6/8	7	7	Irion County	TX	John K. Watson	1977	3053
158 6/8	26 5/8 26 5/8	18 6/8	6	6	Dodge County	MN	Mark A. Lenz	1986	3053
158 6/8	25 0/8 25 4/8	19 2/8	5	5	Vernon County	WI	Dan Morrison	1988	3053
158 6/8	25 1/8 24 0/8	20 2/8	5	5	Brooks County	TX	Billy Ellis III	1989	3053
158 6/8	25 6/8 26 2/8	18 6/8	6	7	Howard County	IA	Mike Grube	1992	3053
158 6/8	24 1/8 24 0/8	18 4/8	7	5	Geary County	KS	Mike Fraser	1992	3053
158 6/8	25 1/8 25 3/8	18 6/8	6	6	Nemaha County	KS	Carol Hartter	1992	3053
158 6/8	23 7/8 24 0/8	18 0/8	5	5	Jo Daviess County	IL	Jeff Dais	1994	3053
158 6/8	26 0/8 26 1/8	16 7/8	7	5	Wright County	MN	Travis Drahota	1994	3053
158 6/8	24 4/8 23 3/8	18 7/8	5	6	Fayette County	IL	Kent Goodin	1996	3053
158 6/8	21 3/8 21 3/8	19 4/8	5	5	Louisa County	IA	Kevin Meyer	1996	3053
158 6/8	25 6/8 25 6/8	26 7/8	5	5	Suffolk County	NY	Robert DeMarco	1997	3053
158 6/8	24 4/8 25 2/8	20 3/8	5	4	Polk County	IA	Joe Crippen	1997	3053
158 6/8	23 2/8 24 2/8	18 0/8	6	6	Richland County	MT	Todd Dehner	1998	3053
158 6/8	24 6/8 24 1/8	17 4/8	6	6	Vermillion County	IN	Chad A. Hennis	1998	3053
158 6/8	21 7/8 22 1/8	16 2/8	5	5	Minnehaha County	SD	Darrell Van Ravenswaay	1998	3053
158 6/8	22 7/8 23 2/8	20 4/8	5	5	Redwood County	MN	Todd Gilb	1998	3053
158 6/8	25 0/8 25 3/8	19 0/8	5	4	Knox County	OH	Mike Lowe	1998	3053
158 6/8	22 7/8 23 2/8	17 3/8	7	9	Greene County	IA	Roger V. Carlson	1999	3053
158 6/8	25 1/8 23 4/8	18 0/8	5	5	Livingston County	IL	Jim P. Pflager	1999	3053
158 6/8	27 4/8 27 1/8	16 0/8	6	6	Morrison County	MN	Jason Milless	2000	3053
158 6/8	23 0/8 23 4/8	17 4/8	6	7	Van Buren County	IA	Hugh Shaw	2001	3053
158 6/8	27 1/8 27 7/8	18 6/8	4	5	Penobscot County	ME	Leslie W. Washburn	2002	3053
158 6/8	25 2/8 24 7/8	21 3/8	5	6	Vernon County	WI	Tom Urbanek	2004	3053
158 6/8	23 6/8 23 7/8	19 6/8	6	5	Otoe County	NE	Nate R. Keller	2004	3053
158 6/8	26 4/8 29 0/8	17 6/8	4	5	Morgan County	IL	Justin C. Howell	2004	3053
158 6/8	23 0/8 25 1/8	18 0/8	5	5	McDonough County	IL	Richard S. Burd, Jr.	2005	3053
158 6/8	23 1/8 22 4/8	18 2/8	5	5	Charles Mix County	SD	Bryan L. Barness	2005	3053
158 6/8	24 2/8 25 2/8	19 2/8	5	5	Tuscarawas County	OH	John Saxon	2006	3053
158 6/8	26 1/8 25 4/8	20 4/8	6	6	Martin County	IN	Brian Huber	2006	3053
*158 6/8	27 1/8 26 1/8	18 2/8	5	5	Waterhen River	SAS	Tom Smith	2006	3053
*158 6/8	26 1/8 25 3/8	17 6/8	6	5	Sangamon County	IL	Rick L. Richno	2006	3053
158 6/8	22 6/8 23 4/8	19 2/8	5	5	Pierce County	WI	Mitchell M. Huppert	2007	3053
158 6/8	25 6/8 25 6/8	19 0/8	5	4	Harper County	KS	Gil Winters	2007	3053
*158 6/8	26 7/8 27 6/8	22 0/8	4	4	Divide County	ND	Guy Haugland	2008	3053
158 6/8	23 5/8 22 1/8	23 0/8	5	6	Isanti County	MN	Jay Steele	2008	3053
158 6/8	24 0/8 24 0/8	18 5/8	5	7	Washington County	PA	Ernest C. Banks, Jr.	2008	3053
158 6/8	22 1/8 21 7/8	20 2/8	6	6	Jefferson County	WI	Greg Blumenberg	2008	3053
158 6/8	23 7/8 23 7/8	17 7/8	5	6	Jo Daviess County	IL	Mark Demont	2008	3053
158 6/8	27 7/8 26 7/8	19 1/8	4	5	Outagamie County	WI	David L. Sipple	2008	3053
*158 6/8	22 2/8 23 1/8	16 6/8	5	5	Allamakee County	IA	Jason Ramaker	2009	3053
*158 6/8	26 4/8 25 4/8	18 2/8	5	5	Vernon County	WI	Ryan J. Howell	2009	3053
158 5/8	24 3/8 25 3/8	15 6/8	5	9	Marinette County	WI	Valerie P. Williams	1966	3095
158 5/8	24 4/8 23 6/8	18 5/8	5	5	Shelby County	IL	Jim Helm	1977	3095
158 5/8	25 5/8 26 1/8	18 1/8	4	4	Chariton County	MO	Brian Argetsinger	1986	3095
158 5/8	22 7/8 23 3/8	17 1/8	5	5	Lee County	IA	Jeff Horsey	1989	3095
158 5/8	23 4/8 23 1/8	20 1/8	7	7	Burlington County	NJ	Thomas A. Stevenson, Sr.	1989	3095
158 5/8	26 5/8 27 6/8	19 1/8	5	5	Dane County	WI	Keith Matush	1990	3095
158 5/8	25 2/8 26 0/8	21 4/8	6	5	La Salle County	IL	John Baunach	1992	3095
158 5/8	24 4/8 23 4/8	19 7/8	5	5	Manitowoc County	WI	Jeff Wittmus	1993	3095
158 5/8	26 2/8 26 0/8	19 3/8	4	4	Gallatin County	IL	Kenneth W. Sharp	1995	3095
158 5/8	24 7/8 25 2/8	16 1/8	6	6	Webster County	NE	Bruce Vahlkamp	1995	3095
158 5/8	24 5/8 24 5/8	17 7/8	6	6	Vernon County	WI	Daniel Hyatt	1995	3095
158 5/8	21 4/8 21 1/8	15 1/8	6	6	Brown County	IL	Robert Anderson	1997	3095
158 5/8	26 4/8 26 3/8	18 1/8	5	5	Fairfield County	CT	Frank Giuliani	1998	3095
158 5/8	26 2/8 25 7/8	25 3/8	5	4	Mercer County	NJ	James R. Godown	1998	3095
158 5/8	25 0/8 24 7/8	20 5/8	5	5	Kleberg County	TX	Johnnie R. Walters	1999	3095
158 5/8	27 3/8 27 6/8	21 7/8	5	5	Carroll County	IL	James C. Carlson	1999	3095
158 5/8	22 5/8 23 7/8	17 1/8	6	6	Woodbury County	IA	Brant Kurtz	2000	3095
158 5/8	21 5/8 22 3/8	17 3/8	5	6	Wicomico County	MD	Michael A. Pilchard	2001	3095
158 5/8	27 0/8 26 2/8	18 7/8	4	4	Baltimore County	MD	Bobby Ambrose	2001	3095
158 5/8	25 0/8 25 3/8	17 1/8	6	6	Jackson County	IN	Dustin Fee	2002	3095
158 5/8	26 6/8 27 4/8	21 3/8	5	4	Carroll County	IL	Jeremy Buckner	2002	3095
158 5/8	27 1/8 26 5/8	18 7/8	5	5	Vigo County	IN	Steve Reedy	2004	3095
158 5/8	25 2/8 24 3/8	20 7/8	6	5	Jefferson County	IN	Boyd L. Emerson	2004	3095
158 5/8	22 3/8 22 4/8	18 5/8	8	8	Gove County	KS	Tanner Tuttle	2004	3095
158 5/8	24 2/8 23 5/8	18 5/8	5	5	Outagamie County	WI	Gerry G. Hockers	2005	3095
158 5/8	26 5/8 27 5/8	20 7/8	5	5	Wright County	MN	Art Otten	2005	3095
158 5/8	25 6/8 25 3/8	15 3/8	5	6	Monroe County	AR	Vance Fisher	2005	3095
158 5/8	25 2/8 24 0/8	18 7/8	5	5	Wicomico County	MD	Everett Lee Howard, Jr.	2005	3095
*158 5/8	23 5/8 24 4/8	19 5/8	5	5	Will County	IL	Rick Cerrato	2006	3095
158 5/8	26 5/8 26 4/8	14 5/8	5	6	Jackson County	MN	Randy Olson	2007	3095
158 5/8	27 2/8 27 1/8	18 6/8	6	4	Trempealeau County	WI	Rick Sesvold	2007	3095
158 5/8	26 5/8 26 6/8	20 2/8	8	5	Sauk County	WI	Jeremy McAlister	2008	3095
158 5/8	24 0/8 23 7/8	17 1/8	5	5	Tuscarawas County	OH	John S. Eaton	2008	3095
*158 5/8	27 2/8 27 3/8	18 5/8	7	6	Fulton County	IL	Matthew Beisswanger	2008	3095
158 5/8	24 0/8 24 2/8	19 5/8	5	5	Will County	IL	Charles Gaidamavice	2009	3095
158 5/8	24 0/8 22 5/8	19 5/8	5	5	La Crosse County	WI	Vance Henry	2009	3095
158 4/8	23 5/8 22 3/8	20 0/8	5	6	Chautauqua County	KS	Gordon Reneberg	1965	3131
158 4/8	26 4/8 25 2/8	22 6/8	5	5	Des Moines County	IA	Michael P. Anderson	1978	3131
158 4/8	23 7/8 24 1/8	16 7/8	6	6	Boone County	IA	Chris W. Doran	1984	3131
158 4/8	25 3/8 25 0/8	17 0/8	9	6	Adair County	MO	Terry Clay	1987	3131
158 4/8	27 4/8 26 4/8	19 2/8	5	5	Adams County	MS	John Harvey	1989	3131

WHITETAIL DEER (TYPICAL ANTLERS)

Minimum Score 125   Continued

SCORE	LENGTH OF MAIN BEAM R	LENGTH OF MAIN BEAM L	INSIDE SPREAD	NUMBER OF POINTS R	NUMBER OF POINTS L	AREA	STATE/PROVINCE	HUNTER'S NAME	DATE	RANK
158 4/8	25 3/8	25 0/8	20 6/8	6	6	Douglas County	WI	John Lawler	1991	3131
158 4/8	26 3/8	26 7/8	18 6/8	5	5	Adams County	OH	Larry D. Napier	1991	3131
158 4/8	25 2/8	23 7/8	19 2/8	6	5	Parke County	IN	Greg Spears	1992	3131
158 4/8	22 6/8	23 2/8	19 2/8	5	5	Washington County	MN	Wayne A. Nicholson	1994	3131
158 4/8	24 6/8	25 3/8	22 0/8	5	5	Shawano County	WI	Richard F. Onesti	1994	3131
158 4/8	23 7/8	24 3/8	19 0/8	6	7	Lawrence County	OH	Greg Riggs	1995	3131
158 4/8	24 1/8	24 1/8	19 4/8	5	5	Manitowoc County	WI	Timothy W. Garceau	1995	3131
158 4/8	24 5/8	24 2/8	17 0/8	6	6	Jackson County	IL	Mark Frankford	1996	3131
158 4/8	25 4/8	24 7/8	21 2/8	6	7	Fayette County	IA	Tim Nuss	1997	3131
158 4/8	24 7/8	25 4/8	20 4/8	5	5	Rock Island County	IL	Don Thomsen	1997	3131
158 4/8	24 3/8	24 6/8	18 2/8	5	5	Preble County	OH	Jim Lipps	1997	3131
158 4/8	23 7/8	25 1/8	19 2/8	5	5	Cole County	MO	Carlos Carrender	1998	3131
158 4/8	25 1/8	25 0/8	23 2/8	5	5	Ardrossan	ALB	Mark Walters	1998	3131
158 4/8	24 1/8	25 5/8	17 6/8	5	5	Adams County	IL	Chad A. Cannady	2000	3131
158 4/8	22 4/8	23 4/8	19 0/8	6	5	Berks County	PA	Chris Engle	2001	3131
158 4/8	24 2/8	25 3/8	14 3/8	5	6	Saginaw County	MI	Harold Boehler, Jr.	2002	3131
158 4/8	24 3/8	24 1/8	19 3/8	6	8	Henry County	KY	Scott Tincher	2002	3131
158 4/8	25 4/8	26 1/8	19 6/8	5	5	Harrison County	IN	Darrell Whitehouse	2003	3131
*158 4/8	25 3/8	26 1/8	20 0/8	5	5	Macon County	IL	Robert Funk	2004	3131
158 4/8	27 4/8	26 6/8	18 7/8	8	8	Lake County	IL	Roy Olson	2004	3131
158 4/8	24 7/8	24 1/8	22 3/8	5	6	Calhoun County	IL	Jeffery S. Duncan	2005	3131
*158 4/8	25 0/8	25 2/8	18 3/8	6	5	Iowa County	IA	Michael Walker	2005	3131
158 4/8	26 7/8	28 2/8	22 1/8	5	6	Rice County	MN	Nick Wells	2005	3131
158 4/8	27 0/8	26 1/8	20 2/8	5	6	Loon Lake	SAS	Cliff Lovelace	2006	3131
158 4/8	25 3/8	24 4/8	17 4/8	5	5	Vigo County	IN	Brent McCammon	2007	3131
*158 4/8	25 6/8	25 3/8	19 4/8	4	4	Lawrence County	OH	Mike Hogsten	2007	3131
158 4/8	23 6/8	22 7/8	15 6/8	5	5	Macomb County	MI	Daniel Amore	2008	3131
158 4/8	24 7/8	24 5/8	18 4/8	7	6	Steuben County	IN	Charles W. Humphries	2008	3131
*158 4/8	21 7/8	23 1/8	18 2/8	5	5	Madison Parish	LA	Kevin Johnston	2009	3131
*158 4/8	24 2/8	24 5/8	17 0/8	6	5	Morrison County	MN	Nick Motzko	2010	3131
158 3/8	22 5/8	23 1/8	15 3/8	6	6	Texas County	OK	Edward F. Bryan, Jr.	1980	3166
158 3/8	23 2/8	23 3/8	19 5/8	5	5	Jackson County	MI	Donald L. O'Dell	1984	3166
158 3/8	27 5/8	28 6/8	23 4/8	8	4	Douglas County	WI	Gerald Berg	1988	3166
158 3/8	24 4/8	24 4/8	19 3/8	5	7	Hennepin County	MN	Robert J. Evans, Jr.	1988	3166
158 3/8	24 2/8	24 6/8	20 1/8	5	5	La Porte County	IN	Scott Saliwanchik	1988	3166
158 3/8	25 4/8	24 6/8	19 3/8	5	7	Logan County	IL	Douglas A. Hullinger	1989	3166
158 3/8	26 5/8	26 6/8	20 3/8	7	7	Jo Daviess County	IL	Michael P. Pickel	1990	3166
158 3/8	27 3/8	26 5/8	22 6/8	5	6	Euphrasia	ONT	Tom Perks	1990	3166
158 3/8	24 7/8	26 5/8	18 1/8	5	5	Delaware County	OH	Steve Boham	1991	3166
158 3/8	25 3/8	26 0/8	16 4/8	7	7	Lake County	IL	James C. Carlson	1991	3166
158 3/8	24 5/8	24 5/8	18 5/8	5	5	Ferry County	WA	Shaun L. Henderson	1992	3166
158 3/8	23 1/8	22 0/8	19 1/8	5	5	Treasure County	MT	John Moorhouse	1993	3166
158 3/8	25 0/8	26 0/8	19 6/8	6	5	Newton County	IN	George G. Bogie	1995	3166
158 3/8	27 1/8	27 7/8	18 6/8	5	6	Allamakee County	IA	Gary L. Mezera	1995	3166
158 3/8	26 4/8	26 5/8	18 0/8	7	6	Marinette County	WI	Steve Jones	1997	3166
158 3/8	23 6/8	23 1/8	18 7/8	5	5	Jennings County	IN	Matthew L. Springmeyer	1998	3166
158 3/8	25 3/8	23 4/8	15 7/8	5	6	Warren County	IA	Jeremy Thayer	2000	3166
158 3/8	26 7/8	26 1/8	19 2/8	5	7	Washington County	MN	Wayne Nicholson	2001	3166
158 3/8	25 5/8	24 6/8	17 1/8	5	6	Baltimore County	MD	James P. Gunther	2002	3166
158 3/8	26 1/8	25 2/8	22 1/8	5	5	Webster County	IA	Timothy J. Finucan	2002	3166
158 3/8	26 0/8	26 1/8	20 5/8	5	5	Price County	WI	Richard Kirchmeyer	2003	3166
158 3/8	24 6/8	24 3/8	16 2/8	8	5	Perry County	IN	Kevin Meunier	2003	3166
158 3/8	23 6/8	24 2/8	18 3/8	6	6	Jackson County	MO	Doug Pruitt	2003	3166
158 3/8	23 2/8	24 2/8	18 2/8	6	5	Buffalo County	WI	Craig Kjendle	2003	3166
158 3/8	26 2/8	26 0/8	20 3/8	4	4	Clark County	IL	G. Douglas McPherson	2004	3166
158 3/8	25 0/8	24 6/8	17 3/8	5	7	Vernon County	WI	Patrick J. Imhoff	2005	3166
158 3/8	24 2/8	24 2/8	20 5/8	6	5	Buffalo County	WI	Ross P. Hauswirth	2005	3166
158 3/8	23 5/8	24 2/8	17 7/8	5	5	Jackson County	IA	Brad Ernst	2006	3166
*158 3/8	22 4/8	22 1/8	16 0/8	5	8	Keya Paha County	NE	Kirk Sharp	2006	3166
*158 3/8	24 0/8	23 5/8	18 0/8	5	6	Tippecanoe County	IN	David Jason Little	2008	3166
*158 3/8	26 2/8	26 2/8	18 7/8	5	7	Dunn County	WI	Eric P. Torgerson	2009	3166
*158 3/8	25 6/8	25 7/8	18 4/8	9	5	Price County	WI	Todd Cummings	2010	3166
158 2/8	26 4/8	24 6/8	22 7/8	5	7	Lee County	IA	Gary Frost	1965	3198
158 2/8	25 0/8	26 4/8	21 2/8	5	6	Barron County	WI	Gary Kohlmeyer	1989	3198
158 2/8	27 6/8	26 5/8	21 0/8	4	5	Pottawattamie County	IA	Tim Waldron	1990	3198
158 2/8	26 0/8	25 5/8	24 4/8	5	5	Calhoun County	MI	Hershel Brown	1992	3198
158 2/8	26 7/8	27 2/8	24 4/8	6	5	Carroll County	IL	David Kerr, Jr.	1992	3198
158 2/8	23 4/8	22 4/8	17 0/8	7	6	La Salle County	IL	Lorin D. Gabehart	1993	3198
158 2/8	23 7/8	24 2/8	17 4/8	5	5	Jackson County	IA	David Charles Horst	1994	3198
158 2/8	25 1/8	26 0/8	20 2/8	5	4	Trumbull County	OH	Chuck Taninecz, Jr.	1994	3198
158 2/8	25 2/8	25 6/8	17 4/8	5	5	Warren County	OH	Jeff Smith	1995	3198
158 2/8	23 4/8	24 0/8	18 2/8	5	5	Peoria County	IL	Joel Pollack	1997	3198
158 2/8	24 0/8	24 4/8	18 6/8	5	5	Marquette County	WI	Philip A. Manthey	1998	3198
158 2/8	25 7/8	25 1/8	18 0/8	5	6	St. Marys County	MD	Pete Ropshaw	1999	3198
158 2/8	23 1/8	24 0/8	17 5/8	5	10	Jackson County	IL	Allen Casten	2000	3198
158 2/8	25 0/8	24 1/8	20 0/8	4	4	Worth County	MO	Rusty Ruble	2000	3198
158 2/8	26 0/8	24 6/8	21 2/8	6	5	Champaign County	OH	Steven Lininger	2001	3198
158 2/8	25 2/8	24 1/8	20 2/8	6	5	Livingston County	IL	Alan M. Schrock	2002	3198
158 2/8	26 1/8	27 4/8	17 4/8	5	6	Lewis County	KY	Randy Lewis	2002	3198
158 2/8	24 7/8	25 0/8	23 0/8	5	5	Carroll County	OH	Dean F. Stebner	2004	3198
158 2/8	26 0/8	24 5/8	18 6/8	5	7	Scott County	MN	Joe Wermerskirchen	2004	3198
158 2/8	25 0/8	26 2/8	21 0/8	7	6	Cass County	IL	Brent D. Russcher	2004	3198
158 2/8	23 7/8	24 5/8	21 4/8	5	5	Tazewell County	IL	Richard Frederick	2004	3198
158 2/8	21 7/8	21 0/8	20 7/8	6	6	Fremont County	IA	Bill D. Tysor	2004	3198
*158 2/8	23 2/8	23 7/8	20 4/8	6	6	Monroe County	WI	Dennis Larsen	2004	3198
158 2/8	27 6/8	26 7/8	19 1/8	5	6	Linn County	IA	Steven Rinderknecht	2004	3198
158 2/8	26 3/8	25 4/8	21 6/8	5	5	Burnett County	WI	Micheal L. Bentley	2007	3198
158 2/8	24 3/8	25 5/8	22 2/8	5	5	Dearborn County	IN	David Lykins	2007	3198
*158 2/8	26 0/8	25 5/8	20 0/8	6	5	Greenwood County	KS	Joshua Woodsmall	2008	3198
158 2/8	25 3/8	23 5/8	19 6/8	5	5	Warren County	IA	Randy Brandt	2008	3198
158 2/8	22 5/8	23 0/8	17 2/8	5	5	Boone County	IA	Ken Lonneman	2009	3198
*158 2/8	25 2/8	25 4/8	14 1/8	7	8	Bourbon County	KS	Douglas A. Lang	2009	3198
*158 2/8	25 2/8	24 1/8	19 2/8	5	4	Fayette County	IL	Dennis Slater	2009	3198
158 1/8	25 2/8	25 4/8	16 5/8	5	4	Randolph County	IN	Ron J. Carlin	1973	3229
158 1/8	22 4/8	22 5/8	17 6/8	6	5	Kossuth County	IA	Steve Rochleau	1981	3229

WHITETAIL DEER (TYPICAL ANTLERS)

Minimum Score 125 — Continued

SCORE	LENGTH OF R MAIN BEAM L	INSIDE SPREAD	NUMBER OF R POINTS L	AREA	STATE/ PROVINCE	HUNTER'S NAME	DATE	RANK
158 1/8	25 1/8 24 2/8	21 5/8	5 4	King George County	VA	L. M. 'Ted' Williams	1981	3229
158 1/8	21 6/8 22 7/8	18 7/8	7 5	Monona County	IA	Gary Mitchell	1983	3229
158 1/8	25 2/8 25 4/8	17 7/8	6 6	Jackson County	IA	Jeff W. Ernst	1984	3229
158 1/8	25 5/8 24 7/8	18 2/8	6 6	Brown County	OH	Michael W. Babcock	1985	3229
158 1/8	26 4/8 26 4/8	18 1/8	6 6	Wyandot County	OH	Michael D Saam	1985	3229
158 1/8	25 1/8 25 6/8	15 7/8	5 5	Columbiana County	OH	David S. Landsberger	1986	3229
158 1/8	25 4/8 25 6/8	18 6/8	7 6	Rock Island County	IL	Donald G. Jones	1986	3229
158 1/8	24 1/8 23 3/8	18 5/8	8 9	Racine County	WI	Joe Spang	1987	3229
158 1/8	25 5/8 25 0/8	20 6/8	6 7	Allamakee County	IA	Joe Lieb	1988	3229
158 1/8	26 1/8 27 0/8	20 5/8	4 4	Adams County	IL	Jim Vahle	1988	3229
158 1/8	22 2/8 21 5/8	17 2/8	6 5	Berkeley County	WV	Robert W. Deeds	1990	3229
158 1/8	23 4/8 26 4/8	20 1/8	5 5	Bullitt County	KY	Tim Williams	1991	3229
158 1/8	27 2/8 26 2/8	19 5/8	4 5	Pike County	OH	Robert Irwin Bazell	1993	3229
158 1/8	25 3/8 24 1/8	17 5/8	6 6	Allen County	KS	Mark Spencer	1994	3229
158 1/8	25 1/8 24 4/8	20 1/8	6 5	McDonough County	IL	Brian Sears	1995	3229
158 1/8	25 2/8 25 1/8	20 6/8	8 5	Stark County	OH	Thomas M. Nelson	1996	3229
158 1/8	26 4/8 26 0/8	18 5/8	9 6	Grundy County	IL	Mark Ermer	1996	3229
158 1/8	23 2/8 23 7/8	19 7/8	8 6	Dodge County	WI	Ben Beine	1997	3229
158 1/8	24 0/8 21 6/8	18 7/8	5 5	Lafayette County	WI	Daniel Popp	1997	3229
158 1/8	26 3/8 26 1/8	18 5/8	5 5	Walworth County	WI	Michael Stelske	1997	3229
158 1/8	24 1/8 24 4/8	17 5/8	5 5	Oldham County	KY	Jerry L. Wade	1997	3229
158 1/8	26 3/8 25 4/8	16 5/8	5 5	McDowell County	WV	James Ricky Kemp	1998	3229
158 1/8	25 0/8 25 4/8	20 7/8	4 4	Buffalo County	WI	Steven L. Olson	1999	3229
158 1/8	25 2/8 26 2/8	20 3/8	4 5	Cortland County	NY	Roger W. Coon	1999	3229
158 1/8	29 2/8 28 7/8	17 5/8	4 4	Hamilton County	OH	Don Ehling	2000	3229
158 1/8	24 6/8 24 2/8	19 1/8	5 5	Waupaca County	WI	Dan Herson	2001	3229
158 1/8	25 1/8 25 1/8	18 2/8	6 6	Larue County	KY	Louie Payne	2002	3229
158 1/8	26 4/8 26 4/8	18 6/8	5 5	Preble County	OH	Ed Vanzant	2003	3229
*158 1/8	24 3/8 23 5/8	18 5/8	5 5	Montcalm County	MI	Justin M. Colby	2003	3229
158 1/8	26 0/8 27 0/8	26 6/8	5 5	Dearborn County	IN	Chris Engel	2003	3229
158 1/8	29 4/8 29 7/8	17 7/8	5 5	Clinton County	IA	Craig Black	2003	3229
158 1/8	24 0/8 22 1/8	23 1/8	6 6	McDonough County	IL	Svend Dieffenbach	2004	3229
158 1/8	24 4/8 25 2/8	17 4/8	5 6	Cloud County	KS	Darrell D. Lynn	2004	3229
158 1/8	25 1/8 25 1/8	17 3/8	5 8	Price County	WI	Richard Kirchmeyer	2005	3229
158 1/8	24 3/8 25 0/8	16 1/8	5 5	Trempealeau County	WI	Bill Lanzel	2005	3229
*158 1/8	28 7/8 28 4/8	17 5/8	6 5	Eau Claire County	WI	Daniel J. Gilles	2006	3229
*158 1/8	21 4/8 21 5/8	16 7/8	6 6	Walsh County	ND	Rodney Troftgruben	2007	3229
158 1/8	21 5/8 24 1/8	16 3/8	5 5	Buffalo County	WI	Dean E. Mense	2007	3229
158 1/8	25 5/8 24 4/8	18 1/8	7 5	Hancock County	OH	Robert E. Ebert	2007	3229
158 1/8	22 0/8 22 2/8	18 1/8	5 7	Butler County	KS	Andrew Benton	2007	3229
158 1/8	28 0/8 26 6/8	22 4/8	7 5	Harvey County	KS	Dan Stahl	2008	3229
*158 1/8	29 0/8 27 0/8	20 7/8	5 6	Copiah County	MS	Randy Hooks	2008	3229
*158 1/8	24 0/8 23 6/8	18 4/8	6 5	Waupaca County	WI	William Kroseberg	2009	3229
158 1/8	24 4/8 24 6/8	18 6/8	5 5	Waupaca County	WI	Christopher N. Sands	2009	3229
158 0/8	24 0/8 23 5/8	18 6/8	6 6	Wayne County	IL	Bill Naney	1981	3275
158 0/8	24 0/8 24 0/8	19 1/8	6 6	Lancaster County	NE	Martin Erickson	1983	3275
158 0/8	26 1/8 26 1/8	19 6/8	4 5	Jackson County	OH	Jim Ridge	1986	3275
158 0/8	24 2/8 23 6/8	19 2/8	5 5	Jackson County	IA	Terry Amling	1988	3275
158 0/8	24 5/8 23 0/8	20 0/8	6 6	Houston County	MN	Michael Val Stevens	1989	3275
158 0/8	24 6/8 24 5/8	20 6/8	5 6	Webster County	IA	Mike Jones	1989	3275
158 0/8	24 1/8 24 7/8	17 6/8	5 7	Ogle County	IL	Art Heinze	1990	3275
158 0/8	27 4/8 26 3/8	17 4/8	5 5	Van Buren County	IA	Gerald Palmer	1990	3275
158 0/8	25 6/8 25 7/8	16 0/8	5 5	Bremer County	IA	Virgil Marlette	1991	3275
158 0/8	22 2/8 22 1/8	18 4/8	6 5	Lincoln County	MO	Mark Gnade	1993	3275
158 0/8	25 6/8 24 0/8	20 6/8	8 8	Jackson County	OH	Jordan R. Spyker	1993	3275
158 0/8	25 4/8 24 7/8	16 0/8	6 5	Price County	WI	David L. Sanborn	1993	3275
158 0/8	23 6/8 21 4/8	17 6/8	7 6	Stony Plain	ALB	David Swanson	1993	3275
158 0/8	25 4/8 24 5/8	19 7/8	6 7	Mercer County	PA	Louis A. Nogay	1994	3275
158 0/8	23 4/8 22 7/8	18 0/8	5 5	Keokuk County	IA	Barry Ledger	1994	3275
158 0/8	24 0/8 23 7/8	20 0/8	5 5	Waukesha County	WI	Chris Gorecki	1994	3275
158 0/8	24 4/8 23 6/8	16 0/8	7 6	Franklin County	PA	John E. Heckman	1995	3275
158 0/8	23 4/8 24 2/8	22 0/8	5 5	Butler County	KS	Larry D. Walker, Jr.	1996	3275
158 0/8	23 1/8 23 0/8	18 0/8	6 6	Douglas County	NE	Rodney Sigel	1997	3275
158 0/8	25 0/8 26 1/8	16 2/8	6 6	Adams County	OH	Craig Collins, Jr.	1998	3275
158 0/8	22 4/8 22 6/8	20 0/8	5 6	Peoria County	IL	Jared Schlipf	1999	3275
158 0/8	22 2/8 23 0/8	22 0/8	5 5	Parke County	IN	Michael Vore	2000	3275
158 0/8	22 7/8 24 1/8	21 2/8	5 5	Yuma County	CO	Brandon Ray	2000	3275
158 0/8	23 7/8 23 7/8	16 2/8	5 6	McHenry County	IL	Doug Krahl	2000	3275
158 0/8	24 0/8 23 5/8	14 2/8	6 6	Stokes County	NC	Todd Alley	2001	3275
158 0/8	23 5/8 24 4/8	18 0/8	5 5	Cook County	IL	Timothy L. Harkness	2001	3275
158 0/8	25 6/8 25 5/8	20 0/8	5 5	Roberts County	TX	Jim Hilliard	2001	3275
158 0/8	22 7/8 24 0/8	17 1/8	5 6	Cowley County	KS	Jeff Earnhardt	2001	3275
158 0/8	24 7/8 25 4/8	18 0/8	7 7	Franklin County	IN	Robert Wood	2001	3275
158 0/8	25 5/8 26 0/8	17 7/8	7 7	Shawano County	WI	Steve Hettmann	2001	3275
158 0/8	22 0/8 21 7/8	16 4/8	5 5	Starke County	IN	Joe Voltolina	2002	3275
*158 0/8	27 0/8 26 2/8	18 2/8	5 7	Graves County	KY	Kirk Murphy	2003	3275
158 0/8	26 0/8 25 6/8	20 6/8	4 6	Butler County	KS	Greg Paris	2003	3275
158 0/8	23 2/8 23 1/8	17 6/8	7 5	Crawford County	WI	Matt Albright	2004	3275
158 0/8	26 3/8 26 2/8	17 7/8	6 8	Manitowoc County	WI	Jeffrey L. Binversie	2004	3275
158 0/8	27 2/8 25 0/8	18 2/8	5 5	La Salle County	IL	Norman J. Rogers	2004	3275
*158 0/8	22 5/8 23 2/8	18 4/8	5 5	Trempealeau County	WI	Wayne G. Lee	2005	3275
158 0/8	24 0/8 24 2/8	16 6/8	5 5	Lewis County	MO	Donald E. Bizzle	2005	3275
*158 0/8	23 1/8 23 3/8	19 6/8	5 5	Fulton County	IL	Ken Morris	2005	3275
*158 0/8	24 6/8 24 1/8	21 7/8	7 8	Red Deer	ALB	Scott Leslie Markham	2006	3275
158 0/8	23 4/8 24 0/8	16 3/8	8 6	Shelby County	KY	Mike Perry	2006	3275
158 0/8	25 2/8 24 6/8	15 3/8	6 7	Benton County	IA	Dale Strong	2006	3275
158 0/8	24 1/8 24 3/8	17 6/8	5 6	Shawano County	WI	Jesse Ward	2006	3275
158 0/8	24 3/8 25 4/8	18 6/8	6 6	Barron County	WI	Mark J. Malinowski	2006	3275
158 0/8	25 5/8 25 6/8	18 0/8	6 8	Clarion County	PA	Korban S. Mohney	2006	3275
158 0/8	25 4/8 24 6/8	18 4/8	5 5	Jefferson County	WI	Larry Braatz	2007	3275
158 0/8	26 1/8 26 2/8	21 0/8	5 6	Hancock County	IL	Roy Campbell	2007	3275
*158 0/8	24 7/8 24 4/8	20 2/8	5 5	Dunn County	WI	Mark Baier	2008	3275
*158 0/8	25 5/8 26 1/8	19 2/8	5 5	Fulton County	IL	Kevin Mercer	2008	3275
158 0/8	23 7/8 23 6/8	18 3/8	4 6	Will County	IL	Chris Fals	2009	3275
158 0/8	25 2/8 26 3/8	19 4/8	5 5	Will County	IL	Mark A. Shandro	2009	3275

WHITETAIL DEER (TYPICAL ANTLERS)

Minimum Score 125   Continued

SCORE	LENGTH OF R MAIN BEAM L	INSIDE SPREAD	NUMBER OF R POINTS L	AREA	STATE/ PROVINCE	HUNTER'S NAME	DATE	RANK
*158 0/8	22 6/8 22 3/8	16 0/8	5 5	Carroll County	MS	Michael S. McCrory	2009	3275
158 0/8	23 3/8 23 3/8	17 2/8	5 5	Henry County	KY	K. C. Adams	2010	3275
157 7/8	23 0/8 25 0/8	19 5/8	5 5	Meeker County	MN	Russell T. Nelson	1974	3328
157 7/8	28 5/8 28 6/8	25 7/8	4 4	Goodhue County	MN	John "Jack" Cordes	1975	3328
157 7/8	23 7/8 24 1/8	16 4/8	5 7	Harvey County	KS	P. Bruce Mosiman	1984	3328
157 7/8	26 5/8 27 2/8	19 1/8	5 6	Boone County	MO	Robert Hagans	1986	3328
157 7/8	27 2/8 25 6/8	17 2/8	6 7	Calhoun County	MI	Jeff Edward Titus	1986	3328
157 7/8	26 6/8 26 7/8	21 1/8	5 5	Vermilion County	IL	James D. Rueter	1987	3328
157 7/8	21 2/8 22 6/8	16 5/8	5 7	Butler County	KS	Jim P. Smith	1987	3328
157 7/8	24 2/8 24 2/8	19 7/8	5 5	Sedgwick County	KS	Jim Molitor	1988	3328
157 7/8	23 3/8 22 6/8	18 2/8	6 5	Boone County	IA	Jim Humberg	1988	3328
157 7/8	24 0/8 23 7/8	14 6/8	5 7	Simpson County	KY	Mike Stovall	1990	3328
157 7/8	22 4/8 25 2/8	17 5/8	5 5	Sherburne County	MN	Ron Makarrall	1993	3328
157 7/8	24 6/8 24 7/8	17 5/8	5 5	Smoky Lake	ALB	Brendle S. Daugherty	1994	3328
157 7/8	26 4/8 26 5/8	21 1/8	4 4	Jackson County	MI	Gerald A. Slusarczyk	1994	3328
157 7/8	25 6/8 25 7/8	20 3/8	7 5	Vigo County	IN	Ryan Howard	1994	3328
157 7/8	26 0/8 26 2/8	21 3/8	7 5	Richardson County	NE	Donald J. Wickham, Jr.	1995	3328
157 7/8	24 5/8 24 5/8	20 0/8	6 5	Fayette County	IL	Paul McConkey	1995	3328
157 7/8	23 7/8 24 1/8	20 7/8	6 7	Benton County	IA	Mike Miner	1996	3328
157 7/8	23 0/8 23 3/8	18 3/8	5 5	Somerset County	PA	Lynn A. Henry	1996	3328
157 7/8	25 1/8 25 6/8	20 5/8	5 6	Miami County	OH	Terry L. Brower	1996	3328
157 7/8	25 7/8 26 7/8	20 3/8	5 4	Waukesha County	WI	Paul A. Samuelson	1997	3328
157 7/8	24 3/8 23 1/8	19 3/8	5 5	Buffalo County	WI	Marty Mattes	1997	3328
157 7/8	25 0/8 25 1/8	16 7/8	6 5	Shawano County	WI	Ken Westphal	1998	3328
157 7/8	24 1/8 24 7/8	18 5/8	5 5	Carroll County	MD	Matthew J. Leonard	1999	3328
157 7/8	29 2/8 27 2/8	20 4/8	5 5	Ringgold County	IA	Myles Keller	1999	3328
157 7/8	24 0/8 24 0/8	20 0/8	5 6	Highland County	OH	Richard D. Farkas	1999	3328
157 7/8	23 6/8 22 4/8	18 3/8	5 5	Pike County	IL	Michael R. Vitale	1999	3328
157 7/8	25 1/8 25 0/8	19 5/8	5 7	Bremer County	IA	Gerald Springer	2000	3328
157 7/8	24 6/8 23 5/8	17 3/8	5 5	Marshall County	KY	Chad Darnall	2001	3328
157 7/8	23 5/8 23 2/8	21 1/8	5 5	Dubuque County	IA	Mike Kane	2001	3328
157 7/8	24 0/8 24 6/8	16 5/8	5 5	Comanche County	KS	Tom Langford	2001	3328
157 7/8	23 7/8 23 6/8	18 2/8	5 8	Appanoose County	IA	Mark Muir	2003	3328
157 7/8	25 0/8 26 3/8	20 5/8	4 5	Buffalo County	WI	Steve Schroeder	2004	3328
157 7/8	23 1/8 23 1/8	15 1/8	6 6	Monroe County	WI	Al Owen	2004	3328
157 7/8	26 0/8 26 0/8	17 7/8	5 5	Athens County	OH	Mike A. Thomas	2004	3328
157 7/8	27 2/8 26 7/8	19 5/8	6 4	Barber County	KS	Jemmie Plasse	2004	3328
157 7/8	21 7/8 22 0/8	18 7/8	6 6	Spokane County	WA	Brandon Enevold	2004	3328
157 7/8	24 4/8 24 3/8	18 1/8	5 6	Sauk County	WI	Michael E. Cole	2005	3328
157 7/8	25 0/8 24 4/8	16 1/8	6 5	Boone County	MO	Mike Burks	2005	3328
*157 7/8	25 4/8 26 0/8	22 1/8	6 5	Peoria County	IL	Kevin Ensor II	2005	3328
157 7/8	22 5/8 23 3/8	17 0/8	6 5	Meade County	KS	Douglas A. Twitty	2005	3328
157 7/8	24 2/8 24 1/8	18 7/8	5 5	Waupaca County	WI	Jacob F. Geurts	2006	3328
*157 7/8	25 3/8 24 4/8	15 7/8	5 7	Adams County	IL	Justin E. Collins	2006	3328
157 7/8	26 3/8 24 4/8	18 4/8	6 7	Lawrence County	IN	Gabriel A. Blanton	2006	3328
*157 7/8	23 4/8 23 2/8	18 3/8	7 10	Jersey County	IL	Kenny Griffin	2006	3328
*157 7/8	21 5/8 22 3/8	15 3/8	7 6	Jefferson County	NE	Nathan M. Francis	2007	3328
157 7/8	24 1/8 24 2/8	17 1/8	5 5	Dorintosh	SAS	Walter Wood	2007	3328
157 7/8	24 6/8 24 3/8	19 1/8	5 5	Jo Daviess County	IL	William L. Holden	2007	3328
*157 7/8	25 6/8 25 3/8	17 3/8	5 5	Shawano County	WI	Michael A. Kroll	2008	3328
157 7/8	26 5/8 26 3/8	19 7/8	6 5	Hancock County	OH	William C. Van Atta, Jr.	2009	3328
*157 7/8	26 4/8 27 4/8	19 2/8	6 7	Saline County	KS	Eddie Benoit	2009	3328
*157 7/8	22 5/8 22 3/8	15 7/8	6 5	Lyman County	SD	Charley E. Larson	2010	3328
157 6/8	23 7/8 24 2/8	15 4/8	5 5	Lyon County	MN	M. Dean Holm	1976	3379
157 6/8	23 4/8 23 3/8	18 4/8	5 5	Phillips County	KS	Lavern A. Wheaton	1978	3379
157 6/8	25 3/8 26 1/8	19 5/8	6 6	Des Moines County	IA	David Bollei	1979	3379
157 6/8	24 7/8 25 2/8	21 4/8	4 6	Geauga County	OH	John A. Suszynski	1981	3379
157 6/8	24 4/8 24 4/8	16 4/8	4 5	Oconto County	WI	Richard E. Liss	1983	3379
157 6/8	23 3/8 23 6/8	17 1/8	6 6	Leavenworth County	KS	John Garrison	1983	3379
157 6/8	23 6/8 23 6/8	17 5/8	8 5	Des Moines County	IA	Ken Thorndyke	1984	3379
157 6/8	26 6/8 25 3/8	19 4/8	5 5	Genesee County	MI	Alfred L. Allen	1987	3379
157 6/8	25 1/8 25 4/8	18 4/8	4 5	Martin County	IN	Terry Kirkman	1987	3379
157 6/8	27 6/8 28 6/8	19 2/8	5 5	Shawnee County	KS	Steven E. Deever	1988	3379
157 6/8	23 4/8 22 7/8	18 2/8	7 5	Yankton County	SD	Alan Peterson	1988	3379
157 6/8	25 4/8 25 4/8	21 4/8	4 4	McLean County	IL	Jim Dicken	1991	3379
157 6/8	23 0/8 25 4/8	21 2/8	4 4	Vermilion	ALB	Glenn Moir	1992	3379
157 6/8	25 5/8 25 1/8	18 5/8	6 5	Oakland County	MI	Bryan K. Malone	1992	3379
157 6/8	25 2/8 25 1/8	16 1/8	7 5	Winneshiek County	IA	Gerald M. Hunter	1992	3379
157 6/8	23 5/8 23 2/8	16 0/8	7 8	Benton County	MO	Rodney Owen	1992	3379
157 6/8	26 0/8 26 0/8	18 6/8	5 5	Kalamazoo County	MI	Jeffrey A. Wisser	1993	3379
157 6/8	24 1/8 25 2/8	15 2/8	4 4	Green County	WI	Timothy J. Scott	1993	3379
157 6/8	26 5/8 25 2/8	19 2/8	6 5	Jefferson County	IN	Andrew W. Pickett	1994	3379
157 6/8	25 1/8 24 6/8	17 7/8	5 5	Dodge County	MN	Dan Rendler	1994	3379
157 6/8	24 3/8 25 1/8	18 2/8	4 4	Crawford County	IL	Jerry Waggoner	1994	3379
157 6/8	23 0/8 23 7/8	21 5/8	7 7	Grant County	KS	Brandon D. Henson	1995	3379
157 6/8	24 0/8 22 7/8	17 2/8	6 6	Pike County	IL	Buzz Puterbaugh	1995	3379
157 6/8	26 3/8 26 5/8	18 2/8	5 4	Genesee County	NY	Richard C. Cooper	1996	3379
157 6/8	24 0/8 23 2/8	18 4/8	5 5	Allamakee County	IA	Duane C. Baumler	1996	3379
157 6/8	24 4/8 24 4/8	19 0/8	7 7	Warren County	IA	Bruce Hupke	1997	3379
157 6/8	25 6/8 24 5/8	18 6/8	5 6	Lawrence County	OH	Denny Tieman	1998	3379
157 6/8	23 5/8 23 1/8	15 4/8	5 5	Jackson County	WI	Russell Stricker	1998	3379
157 6/8	22 4/8 22 1/8	19 0/8	5 5	Otter Tail County	MN	Philip Doll	1999	3379
157 6/8	24 6/8 24 3/8	19 6/8	6 6	Dane County	WI	Joseph Pertzborn	1999	3379
157 6/8	26 7/8 26 1/8	21 0/8	6 7	Crawford County	IL	Paul Hardiek	1999	3379
157 6/8	25 0/8 25 1/8	17 6/8	4 5	Randolph County	IL	Ed Young	1999	3379
157 6/8	21 5/8 22 4/8	18 4/8	5 5	Lafayette County	WI	Robert E. Schober	1999	3379
157 6/8	25 7/8 27 1/8	16 6/8	6 6	Tuscola County	MI	Kurt R. Weiss	1999	3379
157 6/8	30 3/8 31 0/8	16 0/8	4 4	Pulaski County	KY	Dale Prather	2000	3379
157 6/8	24 5/8 24 1/8	18 4/8	5 5	Crawford County	WI	David J. Zirbel	2000	3379
157 6/8	24 5/8 26 4/8	22 6/8	5 4	Cambria County	PA	Daniel Misner	2000	3379
157 6/8	26 5/8 26 3/8	19 0/8	5 4	Washington County	IN	Chris Peacock	2000	3379
157 6/8	25 1/8 25 4/8	19 1/8	6 5	Seneca County	NY	Philip R. Jensen	2001	3379
157 6/8	26 3/8 25 5/8	18 2/8	5 5	Richland County	WI	Chad Raschein	2002	3379
157 6/8	25 0/8 25 1/8	20 0/8	5 6	Jefferson County	IN	Steve Meadows	2003	3379
157 6/8	23 3/8 22 5/8	17 6/8	5 5	Fulton County	OH	Doug Boger	2003	3379

WHITETAIL DEER (TYPICAL ANTLERS)

Minimum Score 125 Continued

SCORE	LENGTH OF R MAIN BEAM L	INSIDE SPREAD	NUMBER OF R POINTS L		AREA	STATE/ PROVINCE	HUNTER'S NAME	DATE	RANK
157 6/8	25 2/8	24 6/8	18 4/8	5	5	Fulton County	IL	Peter Tuttle	2003	3379
157 6/8	24 3/8	25 4/8	20 2/8	6	5	Jones County	IA	Rod Wilson	2003	3379
157 6/8	24 2/8	25 4/8	20 4/8	5	5	Polk County	IA	James D. Vandenburg	2003	3379
157 6/8	27 2/8	27 6/8	20 3/8	8	7	Douglas County	WI	Paul Renman	2005	3379
157 6/8	27 4/8	27 3/8	21 4/8	4	6	Wabash County	IN	Todd Stoffel	2005	3379
*157 6/8	25 2/8	27 0/8	24 0/8	5	5	Richland County	WI	Dan Cupp	2005	3379
157 6/8	24 4/8	22 7/8	14 2/8	5	5	Anderson County	KS	Rod Zupon	2005	3379
*157 6/8	23 0/8	23 5/8	15 7/8	6	5	Waupaca County	WI	Kent Patrick	2006	3379
*157 6/8	25 6/8	24 7/8	20 0/8	5	6	Putnam County	IN	Robert D. Young	2006	3379
157 6/8	24 0/8	23 6/8	18 4/8	6	6	Dundy County	NE	Bryan Holley	2006	3379
157 6/8	22 7/8	23 2/8	16 0/8	5	6	Crawford County	WI	Bob Pettit	2006	3379
157 6/8	26 4/8	26 0/8	19 0/8	6	6	Bayfield County	WI	Joseph N. Liska	2006	3379
157 6/8	24 1/8	24 2/8	17 2/8	5	5	Columbia County	WI	Ronald D. Bittner	2007	3379
157 6/8	26 1/8	26 5/8	18 1/8	7	7	Cayuga County	NY	Cody Buehler	2007	3379
157 6/8	25 5/8	25 4/8	19 0/8	5	5	Carroll County	IL	D. Scott Wolfe	2007	3379
157 6/8	23 4/8	23 3/8	18 2/8	5	6	Wayne County	IA	William R. Spencer	2008	3379
*157 6/8	24 4/8	23 7/8	18 0/8	5	6	Buffalo County	WI	Daniel Chrislaw	2009	3379
*157 6/8	22 6/8	22 3/8	16 2/8	6	6	Dane County	WI	Doug Bair	2009	3379
*157 6/8	26 3/8	25 2/8	20 4/8	5	6	Mifflin County	PA	Ryan S. Coleman	2009	3379
157 6/8	25 4/8	24 7/8	18 1/8	7	7	St. Louis County	MN	Max Childs	2009	3379
157 5/8	22 4/8	23 2/8	16 5/8	6	7	Marion County	KS	Ron Hershberger	1982	3441
157 5/8	22 7/8	24 2/8	18 7/8	5	6	Fulton County	AR	Lynn Luther	1983	3441
157 5/8	27 4/8	27 2/8	21 1/8	5	6	Saline County	KS	Richard Cockroft	1985	3441
157 5/8	24 3/8	23 7/8	19 5/8	5	5	Bartholomew County	IN	Jean E. Sneed	1986	3441
157 5/8	24 1/8	24 0/8	15 7/8	6	6	Atoka County	OK	Patrick C. Patton	1988	3441
157 5/8	25 5/8	26 0/8	21 1/8	5	5	Morgan County	IL	Roger Smith	1989	3441
157 5/8	26 0/8	26 1/8	21 3/8	5	6	Wayne County	MO	Rod Bowling	1989	3441
157 5/8	24 4/8	25 3/8	22 2/8	4	7	McHenry County	IL	Dennis Huhn	1990	3441
157 5/8	27 2/8	25 7/8	19 7/8	4	4	Howard County	MD	William H. Ingram	1991	3441
157 5/8	25 0/8	24 7/8	19 1/8	6	6	Wood County	WI	Michael L. Hewitt	1991	3441
157 5/8	24 3/8	25 3/8	20 6/8	5	6	Du Page County	IL	Ron Knebel	1991	3441
157 5/8	24 3/8	24 5/8	18 0/8	6	7	Washington County	IA	Chris Davies	1991	3441
157 5/8	23 3/8	23 5/8	20 5/8	5	5	Ozaukee County	WI	Richard Kropp	1992	3441
157 5/8	23 4/8	23 4/8	17 1/8	6	6	Brooks County	TX	Tom Buckner	1993	3441
157 5/8	24 2/8	23 1/8	16 5/8	6	6	Noble County	IN	Glen Steele	1993	3441
157 5/8	26 7/8	27 0/8	22 1/8	4	4	Montgomery County	MD	Donald R. Nycum	1994	3441
157 5/8	24 2/8	24 4/8	16 7/8	7	9	Woodford County	IL	Bobby J. Evans	1994	3441
157 5/8	22 1/8	25 4/8	16 6/8	5	7	Louisa County	IA	Dan Brauns	1994	3441
157 5/8	23 7/8	23 7/8	19 3/8	5	5	Burnett County	WI	William L. LaPage	1994	3441
157 5/8	28 3/8	26 0/8	18 3/8	5	5	Waukesha County	WI	Joe Loterbauer	1995	3441
157 5/8	24 6/8	24 0/8	16 4/8	5	5	Lee County	IA	Brian J. Mehaffy	1996	3441
157 5/8	21 7/8	22 0/8	15 7/8	5	5	Saline County	NE	Neil Formanek	1996	3441
157 5/8	25 1/8	26 0/8	18 2/8	6	6	Harrison County	IA	Ben McDonald	1996	3441
157 5/8	25 6/8	24 4/8	17 1/8	5	7	Monona County	IA	Randal Dufault	1997	3441
157 5/8	23 7/8	24 2/8	21 3/8	5	5	Kankakee County	IL	Joseph R. Pergram	1997	3441
157 5/8	27 2/8	27 5/8	25 0/8	6	6	Dodge County	WI	Jeff Meyer	1998	3441
157 5/8	26 0/8	26 1/8	17 6/8	7	7	Athens County	OH	Rod Nutter	1998	3441
157 5/8	26 6/8	26 3/8	19 3/8	5	4	Hampshire County	MA	Todd Frenier	1998	3441
157 5/8	24 7/8	23 0/8	22 5/8	5	5	Kleberg County	TX	W. Scott Brandon	1998	3441
157 5/8	25 4/8	26 0/8	18 0/8	5	6	Buffalo County	WI	Jeff Rumpel	1999	3441
157 5/8	25 1/8	25 2/8	21 5/8	5	5	Kendall County	IL	Richard Bolden	1999	3441
157 5/8	25 5/8	25 0/8	20 4/8	7	6	Winneshiek County	IA	Duane C. Baumler	2001	3441
157 5/8	22 2/8	22 4/8	18 2/8	6	5	Millarville	ALB	Joel Bickler	2001	3441
157 5/8	24 5/8	25 5/8	20 1/8	5	5	Butler County	OH	Mark A. Globig	2001	3441
157 5/8	24 1/8	24 6/8	20 5/8	6	5	Pike County	IL	Rick N. Elliott	2001	3441
157 5/8	22 6/8	22 4/8	17 1/8	6	5	Major County	OK	Blake Pearson	2001	3441
157 5/8	24 4/8	23 6/8	19 2/8	7	6	St. Charles County	MO	Terry Walton	2002	3441
157 5/8	28 4/8	28 1/8	16 7/8	5	5	Franklin County	OH	Shawn Lewis	2002	3441
*157 5/8	26 6/8	26 2/8	21 1/8	4	4	Buffalo County	WI	Michael Minch	2003	3441
157 5/8	24 3/8	24 1/8	17 1/8	5	5	Buffalo County	WI	Tony Heil	2004	3441
157 5/8	23 0/8	23 4/8	18 1/8	6	6	Clark County	KS	Gary Head	2004	3441
*157 5/8	25 3/8	26 2/8	18 2/8	5	6	Pottawattamie County	IA	Jerry Peterson, Jr.	2005	3441
157 5/8	23 6/8	24 2/8	18 3/8	5	5	Price County	WI	Daniel E. Berg	2006	3441
157 5/8	24 5/8	24 4/8	15 4/8	7	5	Coles County	IL	Rick Boyer	2006	3441
157 5/8	24 3/8	24 4/8	18 1/8	6	6	Columbia County	WI	Randel B. Weihert	2006	3441
157 5/8	23 5/8	24 4/8	17 3/8	5	5	Buffalo County	WI	Mark R. Batterson	2006	3441
157 5/8	25 3/8	25 6/8	19 5/8	5	5	Ottawa County	OK	Micah Littlejohn	2007	3441
157 5/8	27 7/8	27 5/8	17 6/8	5	5	Lake County	IL	Greg A. Hanson	2007	3441
157 5/8	24 6/8	24 6/8	17 3/8	6	6	Stevens County	WA	Brian Johnson	2007	3441
*157 5/8	23 0/8	23 4/8	18 6/8	6	7	DeWinton	ALB	Andy A. Giacomin	2008	3441
157 5/8	26 3/8	26 4/8	19 6/8	6	6	Monroe County	IA	Chad Allen	2008	3441
157 5/8	25 6/8	26 5/8	18 2/8	5	6	Bedford County	PA	Craig A. Reasy	2008	3441
*157 5/8	22 4/8	22 2/8	18 1/8	5	6	Jay County	IN	T. J. Westgerdes	2008	3441
157 5/8	24 6/8	26 0/8	16 5/8	10	7	Starke County	IN	Danny Fischer	2009	3441
*157 5/8	26 2/8	25 7/8	18 1/8	5	5	Franklin County	IN	Edward A. Dierckmar	2009	3441
*157 5/8	23 4/8	23 6/8	21 4/8	5	7	Vinton County	OH	Michael David Itnyre	2009	3441
157 5/8	27 4/8	28 0/8	18 7/8	6	5	Columbiana County	OH	Tom Leskosky	2009	3441
157 4/8	25 7/8	25 7/8	17 2/8	4	4	Marion County	IA	Charles H. Walter	1967	3498
157 4/8	22 7/8	23 5/8	18 0/8	5	5	Kalamazoo County	MI	Guy Stutzman	1979	3498
157 4/8	24 2/8	24 4/8	13 6/8	5	5	Webster County	IA	Larry K. Fossen	1980	3498
157 4/8	23 1/8	22 4/8	20 4/8	4	6	Henry County	VA	Mike Weaver	1986	3498
157 4/8	23 5/8	22 6/8	21 1/8	5	6	Jackson County	OH	Steven L. Roe	1987	3498
157 4/8	23 5/8	23 4/8	19 2/8	5	5	Hardin County	IL	Larry Hall	1988	3498
157 4/8	22 6/8	21 7/8	16 2/8	6	6	Grundy County	IL	Brian Bergmann	1988	3498
157 4/8	24 7/8	24 3/8	18 4/8	4	5	Hennepin County	MN	Mike Hintzen	1990	3498
157 4/8	21 3/8	27 3/8	21 4/8	5	5	Crawford County	IL	Steve Parker	1990	3498
157 4/8	24 1/8	24 3/8	19 2/8	6	6	Sawyer County	WI	Gary Haus	1991	3498
157 4/8	25 4/8	25 7/8	20 0/8	4	4	Lake County	IL	Russ Tallman	1992	3498
157 4/8	23 4/8	23 6/8	17 6/8	6	6	Boone County	IA	Bart Bollie	1992	3498
157 4/8	24 4/8	23 1/8	15 0/8	5	5	Chase County	KS	Gregory G. Windler	1992	3498
157 4/8	27 1/8	27 3/8	20 2/8	4	5	Champaign County	IL	Joe Stark	1995	3498
157 4/8	26 5/8	26 4/8	18 6/8	5	6	Wyandotte County	KS	William Danyale McDonald	1996	3498
157 4/8	25 7/8	24 7/8	23 7/8	7	7	Jackson County	IL	Tim Cobin	1996	3498
157 4/8	23 7/8	23 1/8	16 6/8	5	5	Steuben County	NY	Michael Dutcher	1997	3498
157 4/8	26 4/8	26 2/8	19 7/8	5	4	Lake County	OH	Al DiLiberto	1997	3498

WHITETAIL DEER (TYPICAL ANTLERS)

Minimum Score 125
Continued

SCORE	LENGTH OF R MAIN BEAM L	INSIDE SPREAD	NUMBER OF R POINTS L		AREA	STATE/ PROVINCE	HUNTER'S NAME	DATE	RANK
157 4/8	24 6/8 25 6/8	20 6/8	4	4	Cedar County	IA	Keith Roszell	1997	3498
157 4/8	25 1/8 24 1/8	17 4/8	6	5	McKean County	PA	Dale G. Robison	1998	3498
157 4/8	26 4/8 26 6/8	20 2/8	6	5	Warren County	IA	John T. Theiler	1998	3498
157 4/8	25 7/8 25 2/8	19 0/8	5	6	Reno County	KS	John R. Richardson	2000	3498
157 4/8	27 2/8 26 6/8	21 4/8	5	5	Morris County	NJ	Mark Spoto	2002	3498
157 4/8	24 6/8 24 4/8	19 0/8	7	6	Dane County	WI	Jon Kelter	2002	3498
157 4/8	23 7/8 23 7/8	16 4/8	5	6	St. Louis County	MN	Miika Otava	2002	3498
157 4/8	26 0/8 26 2/8	20 1/8	6	6	Washington County	WI	Jordan Rathke	2002	3498
157 4/8	27 0/8 27 0/8	22 0/8	6	6	Cass County	IL	C. William Groesch	2002	3498
157 4/8	25 6/8 26 5/8	14 2/8	6	5	Buffalo County	WI	Jamie Davis	2003	3498
157 4/8	22 2/8 24 0/8	17 0/8	5	5	Barron County	WI	Ryan Ebner	2003	3498
*157 4/8	23 7/8 23 4/8	20 6/8	6	8	Independence County	AR	Charles Barnett	2004	3498
157 4/8	23 5/8 24 1/8	18 5/8	6	5	Carroll County	MO	Dave Swearingin	2004	3498
157 4/8	25 3/8 24 1/8	20 4/8	4	4	Hampshire County	MA	Christopher R. Talbot	2004	3498
*157 4/8	25 2/8 25 2/8	21 0/8	7	5	Buffalo County	WI	John Sligh	2005	3498
157 4/8	24 7/8 24 3/8	17 6/8	4	5	Kingman County	KS	John Sheppard	2005	3498
157 4/8	23 6/8 25 2/8	20 6/8	5	5	Hendricks County	IN	Trevor Perrault	2006	3498
157 4/8	25 4/8 25 1/8	18 0/8	5	5	Geary County	KS	David Rubin	2006	3498
157 4/8	25 6/8 25 2/8	18 6/8	7	5	Butler County	KS	Matthew Bump	2006	3498
157 4/8	25 5/8 25 5/8	20 4/8	7	6	Manitowoc County	WI	Gregory A. Valenta	2006	3498
157 4/8	26 6/8 26 3/8	20 2/8	6	7	Hennepin County	MN	John P. Nagengast	2007	3498
*157 4/8	26 1/8 25 0/8	21 0/8	7	5	Lorain County	OH	Richard F. Gedeon	2007	3498
*157 4/8	25 3/8 25 4/8	19 2/8	5	5	Washington County	MN	Jeff Kasprzak	2007	3498
*157 4/8	23 5/8 22 3/8	18 1/8	6	6	Schuyler County	IL	Clyde McMullen	2007	3498
157 4/8	23 0/8 23 5/8	15 6/8	5	5	Brown County	WI	Jamie Sprutles	2009	3498
157 4/8	24 7/8 23 7/8	20 0/8	5	5	Jefferson County	IL	Kenny Buchanan	2009	3498
157 4/8	23 4/8 22 6/8	20 4/8	5	5	Warren County	IA	Bruce Hupke	2009	3498
*157 4/8	25 5/8 24 5/8	21 4/8	5	5	Fayette County	IL	Keith Daugherty	2009	3498
157 4/8	25 6/8 25 3/8	21 0/8	5	5	Floyd County	IA	Jason Gallup	2009	3498
157 3/8	23 0/8 23 2/8	22 7/8	5	5	Adams County	IL	John Musolino	1966	3545
157 3/8	23 5/8 23 2/8	16 3/8	5	5	Harrison County	KY	Kevin Poe	1984	3545
157 3/8	24 4/8 23 1/8	16 1/8	6	5	Yuma County	CO	Chuck Anderson, Sr.	1985	3545
157 3/8	24 4/8 24 4/8	19 1/8	4	4	Vermilion County	IL	Russell J. Sill	1989	3545
157 3/8	24 6/8 24 2/8	17 7/8	6	6	Price County	WI	Mike Case	1990	3545
157 3/8	24 7/8 25 2/8	15 3/8	6	5	Pickaway County	OH	Willard Dean Clemmons	1992	3545
157 3/8	24 7/8 25 5/8	19 7/8	5	5	Worcester County	MA	Roberta Davis	1992	3545
157 3/8	24 6/8 23 6/8	18 1/8	5	5	Jefferson County	WI	Dale Schilt	1993	3545
157 3/8	26 4/8 26 4/8	19 2/8	6	5	Cloud County	KS	Robert H. Gilbert	1994	3545
157 3/8	24 5/8 24 1/8	18 7/8	6	5	Seneca County	OH	Shawn P. Bradner	1995	3545
157 3/8	23 3/8 22 7/8	15 0/8	5	6	Reno County	KS	Michael L. Murphy	1995	3545
157 3/8	27 5/8 26 7/8	20 2/8	7	5	Columbia County	WI	Kent Kirn	1995	3545
157 3/8	25 4/8 25 1/8	18 1/8	5	5	Clermont County	OH	Todd M. Whitmer	1997	3545
157 3/8	23 1/8 22 5/8	16 7/8	5	5	Sauk County	WI	Dave Malecki	1997	3545
157 3/8	24 3/8 24 2/8	20 3/8	5	5	Stoddard County	MO	Weldon E. Stroup	1998	3545
157 3/8	25 4/8 26 2/8	18 3/8	5	5	Clayton County	IA	Justin Hoeppner	1998	3545
157 3/8	25 7/8 25 3/8	17 5/8	5	5	Vernon County	WI	Roger Conaway	1999	3545
157 3/8	23 5/8 23 7/8	17 1/8	6	7	Douglas County	WI	Scott D. Jones	2000	3545
157 3/8	26 6/8 27 3/8	17 7/8	6	7	Jackson County	OH	Gary D. Rowan	2000	3545
157 3/8	23 6/8 25 3/8	17 7/8	6	8	Hall County	NE	Chris Casteel	2000	3545
157 3/8	26 2/8 26 2/8	18 5/8	4	4	Grafton County	NH	Jeffrey D. Stout	2000	3545
157 3/8	23 2/8 24 0/8	20 1/8	5	5	Morrow County	OH	Lonny Carroll	2001	3545
157 3/8	22 2/8 22 7/8	18 5/8	5	5	Door County	WI	Grant W. Swagel	2003	3545
157 3/8	25 0/8 24 7/8	19 2/8	6	7	Champaign County	OH	Joe Edwards	2004	3545
157 3/8	25 1/8 26 1/8	20 1/8	4	5	Van Buren County	IA	Mark Elsinger	2004	3545
157 3/8	24 3/8 25 3/8	20 3/8	4	4	Douglas County	IL	Seth McGaughey	2004	3545
157 3/8	26 5/8 25 4/8	19 7/8	5	5	St. Francis County	AR	Preston Parkman	2004	3545
*157 3/8	25 2/8 25 2/8	19 3/8	5	5	Morrow County	OH	Michael Sanders	2005	3545
157 3/8	25 3/8 26 2/8	16 2/8	7	7	Audubon County	IA	Rick Scott	2006	3545
157 3/8	23 0/8 23 5/8	17 0/8	6	6	Jefferson County	IN	Darren W. Webb	2006	3545
157 3/8	23 2/8 23 5/8	17 1/8	5	5	Cook County	IL	Douglas Vines	2006	3545
157 3/8	27 2/8 27 4/8	19 0/8	5	5	Woodson County	KS	Jim Bob Brundidge	2007	3545
*157 3/8	24 1/8 25 5/8	18 5/8	6	6	Parke County	IN	Alan Moore	2007	3545
157 3/8	21 3/8 22 2/8	13 4/8	6	7	Carroll County	IA	Dale Wittrock	2007	3545
*157 3/8	26 1/8 26 0/8	19 6/8	5	7	Monroe County	WI	Todd Erickson	2008	3545
157 3/8	23 4/8 24 5/8	20 5/8	6	6	Oakland County	MI	Chris LaFountain	2008	3545
157 3/8	24 0/8 25 4/8	18 1/8	4	4	Richland County	WI	Logan Alexander	2009	3545
157 3/8	23 3/8 24 2/8	16 1/8	5	5	McHenry County	IL	James Didier	2009	3545
157 2/8	22 3/8 23 2/8	16 4/8	5	5	Mountrail County	ND	Dean A. Rehak	1963	3583
157 2/8	23 1/8 22 6/8	16 2/8	6	6	Johnson County	IL	Jim Casey	1963	3583
157 2/8	22 3/8 22 2/8	21 1/8	8	5	Cottonwood County	MN	Brian Grothe	1978	3583
157 2/8	27 6/8 27 6/8	22 3/8	5	6	Jessamine County	KY	David Cartwright	1979	3583
157 2/8	21 1/8 22 4/8	19 7/8	6	5	Lenawee County	MI	Rodney Lee Wilt	1980	3583
157 2/8	25 4/8 25 0/8	17 6/8	5	6	Argyle	MAN	Russ Snell	1982	3583
157 2/8	26 2/8 28 0/8	20 4/8	8	5	Westchester County	NY	Ralph Finacchiaro	1983	3583
157 2/8	25 5/8 26 2/8	17 0/8	5	5	Chickasaw County	IA	Theodore J. Steege IV	1987	3583
157 2/8	25 2/8 25 0/8	20 4/8	5	5	Ashland County	OH	Bert P. Reynolds	1989	3583
157 2/8	23 5/8 23 6/8	19 7/8	7	6	Elbert County	CO	Tom Kelley	1990	3583
157 2/8	24 5/8 23 4/8	22 0/8	6	7	Allegheny County	PA	James K. Stewart	1990	3583
157 2/8	23 6/8 23 3/8	18 0/8	5	5	Houston County	MN	Rob Larson	1991	3583
157 2/8	25 0/8 24 5/8	17 4/8	6	6	Chisago County	MN	Chris Peterson	1991	3583
157 2/8	26 0/8 26 5/8	23 2/8	5	5	Priddis	ALB	Rennie F. Sherman	1992	3583
157 2/8	25 7/8 24 4/8	18 2/8	5	5	Brown County	KS	Tony French	1992	3583
157 2/8	25 1/8 24 4/8	17 4/8	5	5	Winnebago County	IL	Pat Van Barriger	1993	3583
157 2/8	23 1/8 24 2/8	17 0/8	5	5	Washington County	KS	Doug Kruse	1994	3583
157 2/8	23 5/8 23 1/8	17 2/8	7	6	Van Buren County	IA	Jeff Propst	1995	3583
157 2/8	25 2/8 24 7/8	20 6/8	6	5	Cass County	IL	James Deppe	1996	3583
157 2/8	28 3/8 27 4/8	18 2/8	5	5	Patrick County	VA	Jimmy Hall	1996	3583
157 2/8	24 1/8 26 2/8	21 5/8	5	6	Jones County	IA	Chad R. Machart	1997	3583
157 2/8	25 5/8 25 2/8	17 4/8	4	5	Marion County	IA	Roger DeMoss	1998	3583
157 2/8	27 0/8 26 7/8	19 4/8	4	4	Strafford County	NH	Norman E. Brooks, Jr.	1999	3583
157 2/8	25 3/8 25 5/8	18 3/8	5	6	Barron County	WI	Karl Klatt	1999	3583
157 2/8	27 3/8 25 1/8	20 5/8	5	5	Otter Tail County	MN	Douglas H. Kramer	1999	3583
157 2/8	25 4/8 26 0/8	20 4/8	6	8	La Salle County	IL	Terry Lynn Mullins	1999	3583
157 2/8	27 4/8 27 4/8	21 4/8	4	4	De Witt County	IL	Bob Black	1999	3583
157 2/8	25 7/8 26 7/8	17 5/8	5	6	Warren County	KY	Billy Carder	2001	3583

WHITETAIL DEER (TYPICAL ANTLERS)

Minimum Score 125   Continued

SCORE	LENGTH OF MAIN BEAM R / L	INSIDE SPREAD	NUMBER OF POINTS R / L	AREA	STATE/ PROVINCE	HUNTER'S NAME	DATE	RANK
157 2/8	26 1/8 25 5/8	19 4/8	5 5	Massac County	IL	Jack Lambert	2001	3583
157 2/8	27 1/8 27 2/8	23 6/8	7 5	Reno County	KS	Ron Ediger	2001	3583
157 2/8	24 6/8 22 5/8	16 0/8	5 5	Marshall County	IL	Denis Coventry	2002	3583
157 2/8	23 6/8 24 3/8	18 2/8	5 5	Jewell County	KS	Gary Dahl	2003	3583
*157 2/8	25 2/8 23 1/8	16 4/8	5 6	Ionia County	MI	Rick Anderson	2003	3583
157 2/8	24 0/8 24 2/8	18 4/8	6 6	Winnebago County	IL	Bud Meadows	2003	3583
157 2/8	28 0/8 27 0/8	18 7/8	5 6	Darke County	OH	Mark Hatfield	2004	3583
157 2/8	24 2/8 24 4/8	20 4/8	5 5	La Salle County	IL	James Snaidauf	2005	3583
*157 2/8	23 7/8 23 3/8	17 4/8	5 5	Clark County	WI	Preston Wolf	2005	3583
*157 2/8	25 7/8 26 3/8	19 1/8	6 6	Seward County	KS	Lynn Leonard	2005	3583
157 2/8	24 7/8 23 5/8	19 0/8	6 6	Monroe County	WI	Jeffrey W. Vieth	2006	3583
*157 2/8	23 6/8 24 0/8	19 2/8	5 5	Chariton County	MO	Doug Cruse	2006	3583
157 2/8	25 1/8 25 6/8	20 4/8	5 5	Dakota County	MN	Brian LeMay	2006	3583
*157 2/8	23 1/8 23 6/8	18 4/8	5 5	Hand County	SD	Kevin Bertsch	2006	3583
157 2/8	24 6/8 25 2/8	18 4/8	5 5	Sauk County	WI	Jerehmy D. Griffiths	2006	3583
*157 2/8	24 4/8 24 4/8	18 1/8	5 5	Cass County	MN	Mike Schneider	2007	3583
157 2/8	27 0/8 25 6/8	19 6/8	6 7	Buffalo County	WI	Kent Worzalla	2007	3583
*157 2/8	25 2/8 25 0/8	16 1/8	6 6	Washington County	IA	Ken Beachy	2007	3583
157 2/8	26 4/8 26 6/8	21 1/8	5 5	Dane County	WI	Nick Olday	2008	3583
157 2/8	22 2/8 23 4/8	16 0/8	5 6	Adams County	IL	Jimmy Wheat	2008	3583
157 2/8	24 6/8 25 4/8	19 4/8	7 5	Jefferson County	KS	Darin Holman	2008	3583
*157 2/8	25 7/8 25 1/8	16 6/8	5 5	Hamilton County	OH	Tom Koch	2009	3583
157 2/8	23 5/8 25 0/8	18 5/8	8 7	Noble County	OH	Brian Lewandowski	2009	3583
*157 2/8	22 2/8 25 2/8	22 0/8	5 5	Columbia County	WI	Dutch H. Ladwig	2009	3583
157 2/8	26 6/8 28 0/8	20 4/8	6 6	Shawano County	WI	John P. Uttecht	2009	3583
157 1/8	25 3/8 26 1/8	18 5/8	6 6	Puslinch Township	ONT	Jeff Sinclair	1977	3636
157 1/8	25 4/8 24 4/8	23 3/8	6 5	Fairfax County	VA	Chris Jackson	1986	3636
157 1/8	25 7/8 22 4/8	16 4/8	7 5	Eaton County	MI	Bryan Coburn	1990	3636
157 1/8	23 5/8 22 4/8	18 5/8	5 5	McHenry County	IL	Rich Matras	1991	3636
157 1/8	25 6/8 25 7/8	18 7/8	6 4	Dakota County	MN	Vince LaCroix	1992	3636
157 1/8	24 5/8 23 0/8	18 7/8	5 5	Buffalo County	WI	Doug Kensmoe	1992	3636
157 1/8	26 4/8 25 5/8	19 7/8	4 4	Hennepin County	MN	Tony Welch	1993	3636
157 1/8	26 3/8 24 4/8	18 0/8	6 6	Forest County	WI	Anthony J. Swiontek	1993	3636
157 1/8	25 2/8 26 0/8	20 3/8	7 7	Adams County	WI	Michael S. Stammen	1994	3636
157 1/8	26 0/8 26 1/8	19 2/8	6 6	Clayton County	IA	Randy R. Mack	1994	3636
157 1/8	27 3/8 26 5/8	19 4/8	6 5	Beadle County	SD	Brian W. Diede	1994	3636
157 1/8	22 4/8 21 7/8	17 5/8	5 5	Chariton County	MO	Tim Groves	1994	3636
157 1/8	21 4/8 22 6/8	18 3/8	6 5	Jackson County	MN	John Jacobson	1995	3636
157 1/8	25 7/8 25 5/8	19 7/8	6 6	Parke County	IN	Jeff Foster	1996	3636
157 1/8	27 1/8 26 7/8	18 7/8	6 6	Ozaukee County	WI	Mark J. Oleszak	1998	3636
157 1/8	24 3/8 24 3/8	20 7/8	6 6	Buffalo County	WI	Glen Axness	1999	3636
157 1/8	24 6/8 25 3/8	24 1/8	5 5	Buffalo County	WI	Marty Weiss	2000	3636
157 1/8	24 4/8 24 6/8	19 7/8	5 5	Ford County	IL	Michael P. McCartney	2000	3636
157 1/8	26 0/8 24 6/8	17 7/8	5 5	Racine County	WI	Steve Stys	2000	3636
157 1/8	23 7/8 24 2/8	17 5/8	6 6	Fayette County	IA	Jeremy Whittle	2001	3636
157 1/8	25 7/8 25 5/8	19 3/8	6 7	Carroll County	IL	Steven M. Cooper	2002	3636
157 1/8	25 2/8 25 3/8	19 2/8	6 5	Suffolk County	NY	Seth Needelman	2002	3636
157 1/8	23 5/8 23 6/8	14 5/8	6 5	Peoria County	IL	Thomas Peterson	2002	3636
157 1/8	25 3/8 25 7/8	17 1/8	4 6	Waukesha County	WI	Jim Frutchey III	2003	3636
*157 1/8	28 0/8 28 0/8	17 5/8	5 4	Anoka County	MN	Brent Parent	2005	3636
157 1/8	25 3/8 26 3/8	17 3/8	5 7	Union County	IN	T. Jay Maddox	2005	3636
157 1/8	25 1/8 24 3/8	19 3/8	5 5	Knox County	OH	Tim Wolford	2006	3636
157 1/8	22 7/8 22 5/8	14 7/8	5 5	Union County	SD	Troy Van Roekel	2006	3636
157 1/8	23 5/8 23 0/8	15 7/8	5 5	Crawford County	KS	Tim A. Jones	2006	3636
157 1/8	23 4/8 23 7/8	16 5/8	6 6	Jersey County	IL	Bill Rodgers	2006	3636
157 1/8	24 2/8 22 4/8	18 2/8	6 7	Oconto County	WI	Anthony "Tony" Janecek	2006	3636
157 1/8	26 3/8 26 6/8	18 4/8	10 6	Newton County	MO	David Heath Crowder	2007	3636
*157 1/8	25 1/8 24 6/8	18 4/8	6 6	Chickasaw County	IA	Patrick D. Kleppert	2007	3636
157 1/8	25 4/8 26 4/8	16 7/8	6 6	Jo Daviess County	IL	Steven J. Knasko	2007	3636
157 1/8	26 1/8 26 4/8	18 1/8	6 5	St. Paul	ALB	John Drew Moriarity	2008	3636
157 1/8	24 1/8 23 4/8	20 3/8	6 6	Johnson County	KS	J. Zachary Anthony	2008	3636
157 1/8	24 6/8 25 2/8	18 1/8	5 5	Linn County	MO	Michael D. Lampkins	2008	3636
157 1/8	23 4/8 24 0/8	18 7/8	5 5	Buffalo County	WI	Matt Prieur	2008	3636
157 1/8	22 4/8 22 7/8	17 3/8	6 6	Rolette County	ND	Nathan Casavant	2009	3636
157 1/8	23 4/8 23 3/8	20 7/8	6 5	McCurtain County	OK	Brian Keith Snider	2009	3636
*157 1/8	23 7/8 21 0/8	18 3/8	5 5	Trempealeau County	WI	Allen Mock	2009	3636
157 0/8	25 7/8 26 0/8	16 5/8	6 7	Watonwan County	MN	Dave Ellertson	1973	3677
157 0/8	25 3/8 26 0/8	15 6/8	7 8	McKenzie County	ND	Donald Olson	1974	3677
157 0/8	24 3/8 26 0/8	18 6/8	8 6	Ashland County	OH	William Kucic	1985	3677
157 0/8	23 6/8 23 7/8	20 7/8	7 6	McLean County	IL	Daryle W. Tipsord	1985	3677
157 0/8	24 5/8 23 4/8	17 5/8	5 6	Kiowa County	KS	Royce E. Frazier	1986	3677
157 0/8	25 3/8 25 7/8	21 4/8	5 4	Blue Earth County	MN	Tom Lacina	1987	3677
157 0/8	24 7/8 26 7/8	18 0/8	5 5	Roane County	TN	Larry T. Cook	1988	3677
157 0/8	24 6/8 23 0/8	20 3/8	8 9	Lake County	IL	Mike Mitten	1988	3677
157 0/8	23 6/8 23 4/8	18 2/8	6 7	Parke County	IN	Jeff Myers	1989	3677
157 0/8	27 0/8 27 0/8	19 7/8	6 5	Clayton County	IA	Curt Ferguson	1989	3677
157 0/8	22 4/8 22 2/8	18 0/8	6 7	Fayette County	WV	Jeff Stephenson	1993	3677
157 0/8	27 3/8 27 5/8	18 6/8	7 8	Richland County	OH	Russ Winkler	1994	3677
157 0/8	23 1/8 22 4/8	19 4/8	5 6	Nemaha County	KS	Darryl Becker	1994	3677
157 0/8	24 6/8 24 2/8	18 0/8	5 5	Adams County	IL	Michael Bowles	1995	3677
157 0/8	27 1/8 25 4/8	19 4/8	7 8	Morgan County	KY	Glenn Hance	1996	3677
157 0/8	25 5/8 26 4/8	17 4/8	5 5	Edmonton	ALB	Clay Wilson	1996	3677
157 0/8	22 6/8 22 7/8	15 3/8	6 6	Clark County	IL	James P. Weisheit	1996	3677
157 0/8	23 2/8 22 7/8	21 0/8	5 5	Carrot Creek	ALB	Curtis Dennis, Jr.	1997	3677
157 0/8	24 2/8 22 4/8	17 6/8	6 6	Fayette County	IL	Drew Miller	1998	3677
157 0/8	23 4/8 22 6/8	17 6/8	5 5	Manitowoc County	WI	Gregg A. Hetue	1998	3677
157 0/8	23 7/8 23 2/8	19 4/8	5 5	Tunica County	MS	James D. Morris	1998	3677
157 0/8	24 5/8 23 1/8	18 6/8	5 5	Kenedy County	TX	Mark McQueen	1999	3677
*157 0/8	25 5/8 24 7/8	19 3/8	6 7	Miami County	OH	Richard Hunt	1999	3677
157 0/8	23 7/8 23 0/8	19 5/8	6 5	Pike County	IL	Mike Colombo	1999	3677
157 0/8	24 0/8 24 0/8	16 5/8	5 7	Fulton County	IL	Richard Luton	2000	3677
157 0/8	24 1/8 24 3/8	19 2/8	5 5	Rock County	WI	Kurt Kersten	2001	3677
157 0/8	23 6/8 22 5/8	15 4/8	6 6	Grant County	WI	Sandy Schuppner	2001	3677
*157 0/8	24 2/8 25 3/8	19 4/8	7 5	Cass County	IL	Charles Swilley	2003	3677
157 0/8	25 1/8 25 2/8	19 2/8	5 5	Marion County	IA	Bill Sytsma	2004	3677

WHITETAIL DEER (TYPICAL ANTLERS)

Minimum Score 125   Continued

SCORE	LENGTH OF R MAIN BEAM L	INSIDE SPREAD	NUMBER OF R POINTS L		AREA	STATE/PROVINCE	HUNTER'S NAME	DATE	RANK
*157 0/8	26 1/8 25 2/8	18 6/8	4	4	Athens County	OH	Bob Weffler	2004	3677
*157 0/8	24 5/8 25 5/8	19 2/8	6	5	Dubuque County	IA	Dan Habel	2004	3677
157 0/8	28 0/8 27 4/8	22 0/8	4	4	Massac County	IL	Gary Roepke	2005	3677
157 0/8	24 1/8 24 4/8	19 0/8	5	5	Webster County	IA	Jon M. Myers	2005	3677
*157 0/8	23 7/8 23 6/8	16 6/8	5	5	Morrison County	MN	Shawn Janson	2006	3677
*157 0/8	23 4/8 25 1/8	20 0/8	6	5	St. Louis County	MN	Todd Steven Haedrich	2006	3677
157 0/8	26 1/8 26 5/8	18 6/8	5	7	Henderson County	KY	Edward B. Sauerheber	2006	3677
157 0/8	26 5/8 25 1/8	17 2/8	7	6	Buffalo County	WI	Sam Sobotta	2007	3677
157 0/8	27 5/8 26 1/8	20 0/8	4	4	St. Croix County	WI	Wayne Rydberg	2007	3677
*157 0/8	22 3/8 22 2/8	22 3/8	5	6	Richland County	IL	Dewitt Ashley	2008	3677
157 0/8	23 7/8 23 4/8	18 0/8	5	8	Madison County	IL	John Leskera	2009	3677
156 7/8	28 7/8 26 6/8	19 7/8	5	5	Chippewa County	MN	Paul D. Lundgren	1969	3717
156 7/8	25 6/8 25 4/8	19 7/8	6	5	Lake County	IL	Dennis P. Schor	1979	3717
156 7/8	25 2/8 24 5/8	19 7/8	6	5	Johnson County	KS	Jim Laybourne	1979	3717
156 7/8	27 1/8 25 0/8	21 3/8	5	6	Clearwater County	MN	Dennis Engerbretson	1980	3717
156 7/8	23 7/8 23 7/8	19 5/8	5	5	Cherokee County	IA	Dan Roberts	1982	3717
156 7/8	24 0/8 23 7/8	18 0/8	6	6	Butler County	KS	William D. George	1986	3717
156 7/8	23 6/8 24 4/8	19 6/8	5	6	Atoka County	OK	Kevin W. Guinn	1987	3717
156 7/8	26 6/8 26 4/8	20 1/8	5	5	Eugenia	ONT	Ron Lusher	1987	3717
156 7/8	25 1/8 24 1/8	20 2/8	6	5	Franklin County	IA	Ron Hansen	1990	3717
156 7/8	28 4/8 28 2/8	18 5/8	8	8	Talbot County	MD	Ray Kinsey	1992	3717
156 7/8	24 5/8 23 4/8	19 1/8	6	5	Morrison County	MN	Stephan Felix	1992	3717
156 7/8	26 0/8 26 0/8	21 3/8	4	4	Harrison County	IA	Albert Selk	1994	3717
156 7/8	25 0/8 24 6/8	19 5/8	5	5	Suffolk County	NY	Tim Connor	1994	3717
156 7/8	24 5/8 24 1/8	19 3/8	5	6	Dodge County	WI	Don Gourlie	1996	3717
156 7/8	25 0/8 24 4/8	18 1/8	5	6	Dodge County	MN	Myles Keller	1996	3717
156 7/8	25 4/8 25 4/8	20 7/8	5	6	Lawrence County	OH	Burnard Gibson	1997	3717
156 7/8	23 3/8 23 7/8	19 7/8	5	5	McHenry County	IL	Scott Wulf	1997	3717
156 7/8	26 0/8 25 7/8	17 3/8	5	5	Gallia County	OH	Gary C. Casto	1997	3717
156 7/8	25 5/8 25 1/8	21 6/8	6	6	Carroll County	OH	Scott J. Williams	1998	3717
156 7/8	26 3/8 26 1/8	20 7/8	4	4	Jo Daviess County	IL	Joseph C. Hinderman	1998	3717
156 7/8	25 4/8 25 6/8	18 0/8	5	5	La Salle County	IL	Lonnie Reppine	1998	3717
156 7/8	23 0/8 24 2/8	15 7/8	5	5	Armstrong County	PA	Roger Clawson	1999	3717
156 7/8	23 6/8 22 6/8	19 7/8	6	7	Nemaha County	NE	Roger L. Kuhn	2000	3717
156 7/8	21 4/8 21 7/8	14 5/8	5	6	Dane County	WI	Robert Keel	2000	3717
156 7/8	27 7/8 27 2/8	23 5/8	6	5	Will County	IL	John E. Quinlan	2000	3717
156 7/8	23 6/8 23 7/8	18 1/8	5	5	Elliot County	KY	Timmy Thornsberry	2000	3717
156 7/8	23 6/8 23 4/8	16 2/8	6	6	Harrison County	KY	Charles G. Turner	2001	3717
156 7/8	25 6/8 26 0/8	19 7/8	6	4	Butler County	KS	Darin Bennett	2001	3717
*156 7/8	25 7/8 26 3/8	19 2/8	5	4	Schuyler County	IL	Ryan E. Settles	2002	3717
156 7/8	24 6/8 25 1/8	18 7/8	5	5	Kiowa County	KS	Rodney M. Alexander	2002	3717
156 7/8	25 4/8 24 6/8	19 5/8	6	6	Knox County	OH	Jay Robertson	2003	3717
156 7/8	25 6/8 25 1/8	19 2/8	7	5	Dubuque County	IA	Bruce G. Scheffert	2003	3717
156 7/8	27 0/8 28 0/8	17 2/8	5	6	Vernon County	WI	Mike Masterson	2003	3717
156 7/8	25 0/8 25 4/8	18 3/8	5	6	Richardson County	NE	Aaron Stalder	2003	3717
156 7/8	24 1/8 23 3/8	19 0/8	7	6	Monroe County	IA	Michael J. Prucha	2003	3717
156 7/8	25 3/8 25 4/8	19 3/8	5	5	Clinton County	IL	Ron Sample	2003	3717
156 7/8	24 1/8 22 6/8	18 7/8	5	5	Kootenai County	ID	Don Houk	2003	3717
156 7/8	23 2/8 23 0/8	15 3/8	5	5	Wabash County	IL	Jerry M. Summers	2005	3717
156 7/8	23 5/8 23 1/8	19 1/8	5	5	Winnebago County	IL	James P. Arco	2005	3717
156 7/8	22 3/8 22 2/8	16 0/8	6	5	Hancock County	IL	Dee C. Steinheiser	2005	3717
156 7/8	25 1/8 25 4/8	17 1/8	4	4	Cass County	IL	Jake Van Linn	2005	3717
*156 7/8	25 3/8 25 1/8	18 7/8	5	5	Renville County	ND	Jason Overby	2006	3717
156 7/8	24 7/8 25 3/8	19 0/8	6	5	Tuscarawas County	OH	Owen Yoder	2006	3717
156 7/8	26 2/8 25 5/8	21 1/8	5	5	Adams County	WI	Tony Scaffido	2006	3717
156 7/8	26 1/8 25 6/8	16 0/8	5	5	Clark County	WI	Mitch Schindler	2006	3717
156 7/8	28 2/8 27 0/8	21 7/8	4	4	Childress County	TX	Clinton P. Gowin	2007	3717
156 7/8	29 3/8 27 2/8	18 7/8	5	5	Boone County	MO	Brett P. Steinbrecher	2008	3717
*156 7/8	24 2/8 25 3/8	18 7/8	5	5	Douglas County	KS	Ronald F. Lax	2008	3717
*156 7/8	26 5/8 26 6/8	18 7/8	5	5	Morrison County	MN	Scott Rothenberger	2009	3717
*156 7/8	24 6/8 25 5/8	17 2/8	5	5	Niagara County	NY	Justin Van Hoff	2009	3717
*156 7/8	24 1/8 23 7/8	17 0/8	7	7	Wilkinson County	MS	Rick Thomsen	2010	3717
156 6/8	27 1/8 26 5/8	20 5/8	5	5	Lincoln County	WV	Gary Smith	1970	3768
156 6/8	24 1/8 24 0/8	16 6/8	5	5	Meigs County	OH	Brian Kelley	1982	3768
156 6/8	26 7/8 26 4/8	20 0/8	6	5	Des Moines County	IA	Don Smith	1986	3768
156 6/8	24 4/8 24 2/8	16 2/8	6	7	Clark County	IL	Gary Taylor	1986	3768
156 6/8	24 4/8 24 4/8	20 2/8	5	4	Howard County	IA	Terry Larson	1987	3768
156 6/8	25 4/8 24 6/8	19 2/8	5	5	Washington County	IL	Bruce Diedrich	1987	3768
156 6/8	23 0/8 24 0/8	16 7/8	7	5	Walworth County	WI	Brian Strickler	1988	3768
156 6/8	22 6/8 23 5/8	18 2/8	5	5	Miami County	OH	Gary L. Tipps	1988	3768
156 6/8	26 4/8 26 5/8	18 4/8	6	5	Lapeer County	MI	Wayne Coulman	1990	3768
156 6/8	23 7/8 24 2/8	15 6/8	5	5	County of Parkland	ALB	Rob Kubicek	1992	3768
156 6/8	26 1/8 25 5/8	23 2/8	6	6	Suffolk County	NY	Herbert F. DeArmitt III	1992	3768
156 6/8	25 4/8 25 1/8	18 0/8	5	5	Isabella County	MI	Robert J. Warner	1993	3768
156 6/8	25 4/8 25 4/8	19 2/8	5	5	Sawyer County	WI	Alan A. Meyers	1993	3768
156 6/8	23 6/8 25 6/8	20 6/8	5	5	Brown County	OH	James K. Kuntz	1993	3768
156 6/8	25 3/8 24 7/8	19 5/8	5	6	Ozaukee County	WI	Greg Highstrom	1994	3768
156 6/8	25 4/8 24 5/8	19 2/8	6	6	Price County	WI	Frank Plyer	1994	3768
156 6/8	24 0/8 24 6/8	17 2/8	5	5	Hennepin County	MN	Rodney Jansen	1994	3768
156 6/8	22 6/8 23 5/8	20 3/8	7	7	Pope County	IL	Richard Riddle	1995	3768
156 6/8	24 5/8 25 0/8	21 4/8	5	5	Allegany County	NY	Stephen J. Lewandowsk	1995	3768
156 6/8	22 4/8 23 1/8	18 0/8	5	5	Jasper County	IN	Peter J. Kohne	1996	3768
156 6/8	21 5/8 22 0/8	17 0/8	5	5	Washington County	WI	Warren Leemon	1998	3768
156 6/8	23 7/8 23 6/8	16 2/8	5	5	Goodhue County	MN	John "Jack" Cordes	1999	3768
156 6/8	28 6/8 29 6/8	23 2/8	4	3	Wapello County	IA	Keith McIntosh	1999	3768
156 6/8	24 6/8 25 1/8	19 6/8	6	5	Waukesha County	WI	Kevin M. Servi	1999	3768
156 6/8	25 2/8 26 4/8	18 2/8	6	5	Redwood County	MN	Todd Gilb	1999	3768
156 6/8	25 4/8 26 4/8	18 4/8	4	4	Chautauqua County	NY	Wade C. Dellow	2000	3768
156 6/8	25 4/8 25 0/8	17 4/8	5	5	Warren County	IA	Reginald Goodale	2000	3768
156 6/8	27 3/8 27 1/8	17 6/8	5	5	Knox County	IN	Brook Fuller	2001	3768
156 6/8	26 4/8 26 3/8	20 2/8	5	5	Winnebago County	IL	Bud Meadows	2001	3768
156 6/8	26 7/8 26 6/8	19 2/8	4	4	Sauk County	WI	Carl D. Haase	2001	3768
156 6/8	24 1/8 25 2/8	18 2/8	7	8	Lyon County	IA	Duane L. Middle	2001	3768
156 6/8	25 3/8 26 0/8	18 3/8	6	5	Larue County	KY	Paul B. Dunbar	2003	3768
156 6/8	25 2/8 26 6/8	16 6/8	5	5	Wilson County	KS	Sean Wallace	2003	3768

395

WHITETAIL DEER (TYPICAL ANTLERS)

Minimum Score 125   Continued

	LENGTH OF	INSIDE	NUMBER OF		STATE/	HUNTER'S		
SCORE	R MAIN BEAM L	SPREAD	R POINTS L	AREA	PROVINCE	NAME	DATE	RANK
*156 6/8	27 2/8 26 3/8	20 1/8	5 4	Knox County	OH	Jimmy Naber	2003	3768
156 6/8	25 4/8 25 2/8	13 6/8	5 4	Marathon County	WI	Ronald Lavicka	2004	3768
156 6/8	26 5/8 26 5/8	20 2/8	7 6	Shawano County	WI	Carl Prien	2004	3768
*156 6/8	24 1/8 23 1/8	17 0/8	5 5	Marshall County	IN	David S. Fehrer	2004	3768
156 6/8	24 0/8 24 1/8	17 4/8	5 5	Saunders County	NE	Rich Eckstein	2004	3768
156 6/8	24 3/8 23 7/8	18 2/8	5 5	Darke County	OH	Dean Powell	2004	3768
*156 6/8	23 1/8 24 4/8	17 1/8	5 6	Mercer County	IL	David Knupp	2004	3768
156 6/8	23 2/8 24 2/8	17 4/8	5 6	Bent County	CO	Carl Brickell	2004	3768
*156 6/8	25 1/8 25 2/8	16 4/8	6 5	Sullivan County	IN	Steve L. Hobbs	2004	3768
*156 6/8	26 0/8 25 6/8	18 0/8	4 5	La Salle County	IL	Melvin D. Johnson	2004	3768
156 6/8	23 2/8 22 0/8	18 3/8	6 6	Hardin County	IA	Bruce C. Skartvedt	2005	3768
156 6/8	22 4/8 21 5/8	15 1/8	6 5	Adams County	IL	Jason L. Campbell	2005	3768
*156 6/8	26 1/8 26 7/8	22 4/8	4 5	Allamakee County	IA	Randy Petersburg	2005	3768
*156 6/8	25 0/8 24 2/8	19 6/8	5 4	La Salle County	IL	Jason Goodwin	2006	3768
156 6/8	24 2/8 25 2/8	19 5/8	7 8	Stark County	OH	Andy Tormasi	2006	3768
156 6/8	26 7/8 26 3/8	20 0/8	5 5	Knox County	IL	Gregg Schilling	2007	3768
156 6/8	22 2/8 22 3/8	16 5/8	6 6	Callahan County	TX	Porcious Potter	2007	3768
*156 6/8	25 5/8 25 5/8	14 6/8	5 5	Greenwood County	KS	John MacPeak	2007	3768
156 6/8	23 5/8 22 6/8	20 4/8	6 5	Perry County	PA	James A. Flickinger	2009	3768
*156 6/8	26 6/8 26 4/8	19 4/8	5 5	Finney County	KS	Brandon T. Hendrix	2009	3768
156 5/8	26 1/8 25 2/8	20 2/8	6 6	Grant County	WI	Walter Edge	1957	3821
156 5/8	24 6/8 26 3/8	19 5/8	5 4	Traverse County	MN	Roland L. Hausmann	1960	3821
156 5/8	22 7/8 25 0/8	19 6/8	7 7	Des Moines County	IA	E. E. Smith	1965	3821
156 5/8	23 7/8 24 1/8	18 7/8	7 7	Nicollet County	MN	Thomas J. Merkley	1967	3821
156 5/8	27 3/8 26 2/8	21 5/8	5 5	Queen Annes County	MD	Charles Milford Squires	1969	3821
156 5/8	24 7/8 24 3/8	21 1/8	6 5	Wabaunsee County	KS	Tom Willard	1983	3821
156 5/8	22 0/8 22 2/8	16 1/8	6 8	Kossuth County	IA	Ron Burton	1985	3821
156 5/8	24 3/8 24 3/8	19 3/8	5 5	Johnson County	IA	Larry Hermanstorfer	1987	3821
156 5/8	22 6/8 23 3/8	20 7/8	5 5	Price County	WI	Larry Halvorson	1990	3821
156 5/8	24 5/8 24 4/8	18 7/8	5 5	Eaton County	MI	Dudley Miller, Jr.	1990	3821
156 5/8	25 3/8 25 6/8	16 3/8	6 6	Chariton County	MO	Nathan Leonard	1991	3821
156 5/8	23 0/8 23 0/8	16 7/8	11 5	Leavenworth County	KS	Michael Paul	1994	3821
156 5/8	25 6/8 25 7/8	22 3/8	8 7	DeKalb County	IL	Josef K. Rud	1994	3821
156 5/8	23 6/8 21 7/8	14 6/8	6 5	Lee County	IL	Cory J. Zimmerly	1994	3821
156 5/8	25 0/8 24 2/8	17 6/8	6 5	Monroe County	WI	Tim J. Cabasos	1995	3821
156 5/8	25 5/8 25 6/8	18 5/8	5 5	Polk County	WI	David R. Daniels	1996	3821
156 5/8	22 4/8 22 2/8	20 5/8	5 5	Marathon County	WI	Ryan Voigt	1998	3821
156 5/8	24 3/8 25 0/8	19 3/8	5 5	Racine County	WI	Kevin McNeven	1999	3821
156 5/8	25 0/8 25 1/8	18 3/8	5 5	Marshall County	IL	Kevin Carrithers	1999	3821
156 5/8	24 3/8 24 4/8	19 1/8	5 6	Des Moines County	IA	Randy Templeton	1999	3821
156 5/8	23 0/8 23 2/8	15 4/8	6 6	Henry County	IA	Troy Alan Fenton	2000	3821
156 5/8	22 1/8 22 6/8	21 1/8	5 6	Allegheny County	PA	Jeffrey Rebich	2000	3821
156 5/8	26 5/8 26 7/8	19 2/8	5 5	Montgomery County	MD	Bret A. Giuliani	2000	3821
156 5/8	22 4/8 23 4/8	17 1/8	5 5	Dubois County	IN	Faron Schuetter	2001	3821
156 5/8	24 0/8 24 3/8	19 5/8	5 5	Jones County	IA	Robert A. Lange	2001	3821
156 5/8	25 2/8 25 1/8	17 3/8	5 5	Maries County	MO	Kent A. Walters	2002	3821
156 5/8	26 5/8 26 5/8	17 4/8	5 5	Saline County	MO	Mike Beach	2002	3821
156 5/8	22 0/8 22 3/8	13 7/8	7 6	Guthrie County	IA	Joel Johnson	2002	3821
156 5/8	24 7/8 25 0/8	21 4/8	5 6	Columbiana County	OH	Alex Shaffo	2002	3821
156 5/8	24 2/8 23 5/8	20 7/8	5 5	McHenry County	IL	Daniel W. Kozanecki	2003	3821
156 5/8	24 6/8 23 7/8	18 3/8	5 5	Macoupin County	IL	Eric D. Neathery	2003	3821
156 5/8	23 4/8 23 6/8	18 0/8	6 5	Dane County	WI	Mark D. Pauli	2004	3821
156 5/8	29 1/8 27 6/8	23 7/8	5 4	Sauk County	WI	John F. Albert III	2004	3821
156 5/8	25 2/8 25 2/8	24 1/8	5 6	Fulton County	IL	Michael Vaka	2004	3821
156 5/8	23 1/8 23 6/8	18 7/8	5 5	Effingham County	IL	Dan Woltman	2004	3821
156 5/8	23 5/8 22 5/8	19 1/8	5 5	Washington County	IL	Jim Lohman	2005	3821
*156 5/8	23 2/8 22 1/8	20 0/8	6 5	Marion County	IL	Todd M. Hogan	2005	3821
*156 5/8	22 6/8 23 1/8	16 1/8	5 5	Appanoose County	IA	Justin White	2005	3821
*156 5/8	24 6/8 24 0/8	17 6/8	6 5	Gregory County	SD	Dean Hovey	2005	3821
156 5/8	24 6/8 24 2/8	17 2/8	6 5	Dane County	WI	Stephen Field	2006	3821
156 5/8	23 0/8 22 4/8	19 5/8	6 5	Leavenworth County	KS	Scott Craig	2006	3821
156 5/8	23 1/8 22 2/8	19 1/8	5 5	Hamilton County	IN	Michael Musselman	2006	3821
156 5/8	20 6/8 23 1/8	20 4/8	6 7	Stark County	OH	Mitchell S. Thorpe	2007	3821
156 5/8	25 3/8 25 2/8	19 1/8	6 6	Linn County	MO	Daryl E. Miller	2007	3821
156 5/8	21 6/8 22 5/8	17 1/8	5 5	Union County	KY	Jason Jordy	2007	3821
156 5/8	25 0/8 22 6/8	17 1/8	5 5	Decatur County	GA	Derek Maxwell	2008	3821
156 5/8	25 2/8 24 0/8	19 7/8	6 6	Washington County	WI	Dan Bernarde	2008	3821
156 5/8	23 7/8 23 7/8	18 2/8	5 6	Casey County	KY	Larry Underwood	2008	3821
156 5/8	23 7/8 24 0/8	19 2/8	6 6	La Salle County	IL	Jason A. Goodwin	2009	3821
156 5/8	22 2/8 22 2/8	21 7/8	5 5	Lawrence County	IL	John Adams	2009	3821
*156 5/8	24 3/8 24 4/8	17 3/8	7 9	Texas County	MO	Ray Allen	2010	3821
156 4/8	26 4/8 25 7/8	22 5/8	4 5	Williamson County	IL	Roy Williams	1960	3872
156 4/8	26 3/8 24 4/8	17 4/8	5 6	Forest County	WI	Daniel Radder	1968	3872
156 4/8	24 1/8 23 3/8	15 0/8	6 5	Jones County	IA	Gary McCormick	1977	3872
156 4/8	23 7/8 24 1/8	18 3/8	6 6	Graham County	KS	Russell Hull	1979	3872
156 4/8	24 4/8 23 6/8	21 4/8	5 5	Waukesha County	WI	Steve Hoelz	1987	3872
156 4/8	27 0/8 27 5/8	19 1/8	6 6	McLeod County	MN	Craig Hrkal	1988	3872
156 4/8	24 3/8 21 0/8	19 4/8	5 5	Jackson County	OH	Michael L. Cornett	1988	3872
156 4/8	25 4/8 25 5/8	17 6/8	7 7	Osage County	KS	Gerald Britschge	1988	3872
156 4/8	22 0/8 24 0/8	19 3/8	6 8	Macoupin County	IL	Rick D. Tigo	1990	3872
156 4/8	23 6/8 24 1/8	18 0/8	5 5	Clarke County	IA	Mark G. Backstrom	1992	3872
156 4/8	25 3/8 24 6/8	18 2/8	5 5	Nemaha County	KS	Steven L. Hanzlik	1992	3872
156 4/8	24 2/8 23 4/8	18 7/8	6 8	Clark County	IL	Paul Baird	1993	3872
156 4/8	26 7/8 28 0/8	23 4/8	4 4	Macon County	AL	Craig G. Shook	1995	3872
156 4/8	22 2/8 23 5/8	18 6/8	5 6	Stafford County	KS	Bill Duncan	1995	3872
156 4/8	27 5/8 27 5/8	19 4/8	4 4	Coshocton County	OH	John Zaayer	1996	3872
156 4/8	24 6/8 26 0/8	18 4/8	6 5	Lawrence County	IL	David Fleming	1996	3872
156 4/8	25 1/8 23 3/8	18 4/8	6 5	Clay County	IL	Rusty Windle	1997	3872
156 4/8	24 7/8 24 1/8	15 6/8	5 5	Waupaca County	WI	Jason J. Firkus	1997	3872
156 4/8	26 2/8 25 0/8	20 6/8	5 5	Osborne County	KS	Blake Grabast	1997	3872
156 4/8	25 4/8 24 7/8	20 7/8	6 6	Jefferson County	WI	Charles E. Kiupelis	1997	3872
156 4/8	25 4/8 25 1/8	19 3/8	5 6	Barton County	KS	Don Herter	1997	3872
156 4/8	24 7/8 25 4/8	18 2/8	4 5	Marquette County	WI	Thomas J. Roll	1998	3872
156 4/8	21 2/8 22 6/8	19 0/8	7 6	Mercer County	IL	Terry Barrett	1998	3872
156 4/8	25 5/8 25 5/8	18 7/8	6 6	Van Buren County	IA	Michael D. Roberts	1998	3872

396

WHITETAIL DEER (TYPICAL ANTLERS)

Minimum Score 125 — Continued

SCORE	LENGTH OF R MAIN BEAM L	INSIDE SPREAD	NUMBER OF R POINTS L	AREA	STATE/ PROVINCE	HUNTER'S NAME	DATE	RANK
156 4/8	27 3/8 26 4/8	20 1/8	7 8	Crow Wing County	MN	Jason Anderson	2000	3872
156 4/8	23 3/8 24 0/8	17 6/8	5 5	Madison County	KY	Doug Ridner	2003	3872
156 4/8	25 4/8 25 4/8	19 2/8	5 5	Steuben County	IN	Mark Houlton	2003	3872
156 4/8	22 4/8 23 0/8	16 4/8	5 5	Vermillion County	IN	Ben Hanson	2003	3872
156 4/8	24 6/8 23 7/8	15 3/8	6 7	Venango County	PA	Darren D. Wenner	2003	3872
156 4/8	27 3/8 27 6/8	19 0/8	6 6	Schuyler County	IL	Jason O. Lane	2003	3872
156 4/8	26 4/8 26 3/8	20 3/8	4 7	Washington County	IN	Alvin Scott Jones, Jr.	2003	3872
156 4/8	22 6/8 21 7/8	16 0/8	5 5	Ward County	ND	Ed Fogarty	2004	3872
156 4/8	26 6/8 23 6/8	17 1/8	6 6	Edmonson County	KY	Darrell Hennion	2004	3872
156 4/8	23 6/8 24 0/8	16 1/8	5 6	Richland County	ND	Lyle Fritz	2004	3872
156 4/8	24 0/8 24 5/8	18 2/8	5 5	Jefferson County	WI	Butch Carley	2004	3872
156 4/8	23 7/8 23 6/8	17 0/8	6 6	Douglas County	WI	Michael J. Schaaf	2004	3872
156 4/8	25 0/8 25 0/8	16 0/8	7 5	Adams County	IL	Martin Danny Lamb	2004	3872
156 4/8	23 4/8 23 0/8	20 6/8	5 5	McLean County	IL	Scott Darnall	2005	3872
*156 4/8	22 0/8 22 5/8	18 0/8	5 5	Dallas County	IA	James Kelter	2005	3872
156 4/8	24 7/8 24 2/8	19 4/8	4 4	Vermillion County	IN	Frank Mediate	2005	3872
*156 4/8	23 3/8 22 4/8	18 6/8	5 5	Beaver County	PA	Larry O'Neill	2005	3872
156 4/8	24 6/8 23 7/8	15 5/8	5 8	Fulton County	IL	Jeff Pals	2005	3872
*156 4/8	24 6/8 25 1/8	18 5/8	6 6	McHenry County	ND	Wayne Larcombe	2006	3872
156 4/8	24 5/8 25 4/8	21 1/8	7 7	Columbia County	WI	Mark A. Wheeler	2006	3872
156 4/8	26 0/8 26 4/8	21 6/8	6 5	Lake County	IN	Wayne A. Kiser, Jr.	2006	3872
156 4/8	26 5/8 26 6/8	18 5/8	8 6	Moultrie County	IL	Arthur Hughes	2006	3872
*156 4/8	25 1/8 25 2/8	17 2/8	5 5	Olmsted County	MN	Bill Clink	2007	3872
156 4/8	25 3/8 25 7/8	19 6/8	4 4	Monroe County	WI	Josh Wiegand	2007	3872
156 4/8	22 5/8 22 4/8	16 2/8	5 5	Clark County	WI	Mike Baehr	2007	3872
156 4/8	26 6/8 26 7/8	19 0/8	4 5	Jackson County	AR	Kurt Garland	2007	3872
*156 4/8	25 7/8 27 2/8	19 0/8	6 7	Guthrie County	IA	Thomas Buckroyd III	2007	3872
156 4/8	23 2/8 24 3/8	19 0/8	7 6	Jo Daviess County	IL	Mark Jacobson	2007	3872
*156 4/8	27 7/8 26 0/8	16 7/8	6 6	Hamilton County	OH	Gary Blair, Jr.	2008	3872
156 4/8	25 3/8 25 5/8	18 7/8	7 5	Madison County	IA	Todd Murry	2008	3872
*156 4/8	25 5/8 26 4/8	22 0/8	4 4	Randolph County	IN	Cody L. Hunter	2008	3872
156 4/8	24 1/8 23 7/8	17 2/8	5 6	Osage County	KS	Jonathan Melton	2009	3872
156 3/8	27 0/8 25 5/8	20 0/8	8 6	Hamilton County	KS	Mike Gilbert	1977	3928
156 3/8	25 0/8 25 2/8	18 4/8	6 8	Russell County	KS	John W. Frost	1983	3928
156 3/8	24 4/8 24 3/8	21 5/8	6 6	Mills County	IA	Douglas R. Roll	1986	3928
156 3/8	25 4/8 25 2/8	16 7/8	6 5	Vernon County	WI	David Penchi	1987	3928
156 3/8	22 1/8 23 4/8	17 1/8	6 7	Trempealeau County	WI	Ginger Molitor	1988	3928
156 3/8	22 4/8 23 4/8	14 7/8	6 7	Polk County	WI	Jon Mattson	1989	3928
156 3/8	25 0/8 24 5/8	20 5/8	5 4	Effingham County	IL	Tim Dillow	1989	3928
156 3/8	24 4/8 24 2/8	19 7/8	5 7	Sioux County	IA	Owen Sandbulte	1991	3928
156 3/8	27 4/8 26 4/8	21 4/8	6 6	Lawrence County	OH	Richard L. Carte	1991	3928
156 3/8	22 6/8 21 6/8	17 6/8	5 5	Parke County	IN	Louis Murphy	1992	3928
156 3/8	24 5/8 24 1/8	18 3/8	6 7	Strathcona	ALB	Mark Johnson	1992	3928
156 3/8	26 2/8 27 2/8	19 1/8	5 5	Brown County	IL	Thomas J. Lavery	1993	3928
156 3/8	23 3/8 22 5/8	18 3/8	5 6	Menard County	TX	Steve Cocanower	1995	3928
156 3/8	22 2/8 22 2/8	17 1/8	6 6	Buchanan County	MO	Randy Clinton	1996	3928
156 3/8	24 1/8 24 1/8	18 5/8	5 5	Clark County	WI	Tom Brown	1997	3928
156 3/8	26 7/8 25 7/8	21 7/8	4 4	Monona County	IA	Eddie J. Miller	1998	3928
156 3/8	25 0/8 24 7/8	20 0/8	8 7	Jefferson County	IL	Gene R. Gardner	1999	3928
156 3/8	26 7/8 26 3/8	18 2/8	6 7	McLean County	IL	Scott Darnall	1999	3928
156 3/8	25 5/8 25 1/8	19 2/8	6 5	Lucas County	IA	Bill Brown	2000	3928
156 3/8	26 0/8 26 4/8	18 7/8	5 5	Waukesha County	WI	William Christenson	2002	3928
156 3/8	26 0/8 26 5/8	19 3/8	4 4	Rice County	KS	M. Robert DeLaney	2002	3928
156 3/8	24 6/8 25 2/8	21 7/8	6 7	Clark County	KS	Dean N. Anderson	2002	3928
156 3/8	25 1/8 25 2/8	20 6/8	5 6	White County	IL	John W. Scheitinger	2003	3928
156 3/8	23 3/8 23 5/8	19 7/8	7 5	Dane County	WI	Mark R. Pfaff	2003	3928
156 3/8	25 0/8 24 7/8	18 7/8	4 4	Pepin County	WI	Hank Koss III	2003	3928
156 3/8	21 7/8 22 4/8	19 5/8	5 6	Allamakee County	IA	Michael J. Manning	2003	3928
156 3/8	26 6/8 26 3/8	19 5/8	6 5	Ontario County	NY	Ronald G. Perryman	2004	3928
*156 3/8	23 5/8 22 3/8	17 1/8	6 6	Waushara County	WI	Brandon Meyer	2005	3928
156 3/8	24 1/8 24 0/8	20 5/8	5 5	Morrison County	MN	Andrew Trelstad	2005	3928
156 3/8	25 4/8 25 0/8	19 5/8	5 7	McMullen County	TX	James F. Siddons	2005	3928
*156 3/8	25 3/8 23 0/8	19 5/8	5 8	Brown County	WI	Patty R. Kraynik	2006	3928
156 3/8	25 0/8 25 3/8	17 4/8	7 5	Franklin County	MO	Wayne Blankenship	2007	3928
156 3/8	28 4/8 25 2/8	19 0/8	4 5	Coles County	IL	Rick Boyer	2007	3928
156 3/8	26 2/8 27 6/8	19 7/8	6 7	Schuyler County	IL	Tom A. Grover	2007	3928
*156 3/8	24 5/8 24 3/8	19 5/8	5 5	Pottawattamie County	IA	Ricky Griffis	2007	3928
*156 3/8	24 4/8 24 6/8	18 7/8	6 6	Butler County	IA	David Magnuson	2007	3928
156 3/8	28 0/8 27 3/8	19 1/8	7 6	Barber County	KS	Stephen Teague	2008	3928
156 3/8	23 5/8 22 2/8	17 1/8	6 6	Newton County	GA	Kyle Ellis	2009	3928
*156 3/8	23 5/8 24 1/8	19 2/8	6 7	Dodge County	WI	Jim Franke	2009	3928
*156 3/8	25 2/8 25 4/8	17 7/8	5 5	Wyandotte County	KS	Henry Norris, Jr.	2009	3928
156 2/8	26 1/8 26 4/8	21 0/8	6 6	Butler County	KS	Ralph R. Belt	1967	3968
156 2/8	25 0/8 23 2/8	18 0/8	9 6	Palo Alto County	IA	Earl J. Gustafson	1972	3968
156 2/8	23 3/8 23 6/8	16 6/8	5 5	Fulton County	IL	Sam Smith	1973	3968
156 2/8	25 3/8 25 3/8	23 6/8	5 6	Winona County	MN	Daniel McIntire	1979	3968
156 2/8	22 2/8 22 7/8	16 6/8	5 5	Garfield County	MT	Larry H. Hoyt	1982	3968
156 2/8	25 2/8 26 2/8	18 6/8	6 5	Stevens County	WA	Tom Duffey	1983	3968
156 2/8	25 5/8 26 1/8	19 0/8	4 5	Ogle County	IL	Gary D. Shaw	1984	3968
156 2/8	25 1/8 26 0/8	19 4/8	5 5	Oakland County	MI	David B. Tater	1984	3968
156 2/8	24 2/8 24 6/8	21 0/8	5 4	Cass County	IL	Dale Milstead	1985	3968
156 2/8	26 6/8 27 4/8	19 7/8	5 6	Washington County	IL	Tracy D. Hawes	1986	3968
156 2/8	26 2/8 27 0/8	20 0/8	5 5	Washington County	IA	Carl Stogdill	1986	3968
156 2/8	24 5/8 24 3/8	20 6/8	8 5	Kankakee County	IL	Al Weissbohn	1988	3968
156 2/8	26 4/8 26 1/8	16 0/8	4 4	Washburn County	WI	Cullan Hanacek	1989	3968
156 2/8	27 0/8 26 6/8	22 2/8	5 7	Lafayette County	WI	Mike Sigafus	1989	3968
156 2/8	25 1/8 25 0/8	20 6/8	5 5	La Salle County	TX	Dr. F. D. Elias	1990	3968
156 2/8	25 5/8 24 5/8	18 6/8	6 5	Mitchell County	IA	Don Weber	1990	3968
156 2/8	25 6/8 25 3/8	18 4/8	5 5	Wilbarger County	TX	Kenneth W. Baker	1992	3968
156 2/8	23 6/8 23 6/8	17 6/8	5 7	Johnston County	OK	Barbara L. Bray	1993	3968
156 2/8	23 0/8 23 4/8	18 4/8	5 5	Allamakee County	IA	Jerry Custer	1994	3968
156 2/8	24 5/8 23 4/8	17 6/8	5 5	E. Carroll Parish	LA	Bill Bailey	1994	3968
156 2/8	23 5/8 23 1/8	19 0/8	5 5	Jefferson County	IN	Robert E. Bode	1995	3968
156 2/8	25 3/8 24 2/8	16 1/8	5 6	Spencer County	IN	Jim Durlauf	1995	3968
156 2/8	23 5/8 22 6/8	17 0/8	5 5	Pottawattamie County	IA	Robert Copenhaver	1996	3968

397

WHITETAIL DEER (TYPICAL ANTLERS)

Minimum Score 125 — Continued

SCORE	R MAIN BEAM	L MAIN BEAM	INSIDE SPREAD	R POINTS	L POINTS	AREA	STATE/PROVINCE	HUNTER'S NAME	DATE	RANK
156 2/8	27 6/8	28 4/8	22 1/8	6	7	Brown County	OH	Ronald J. Ballein	1996	3968
156 2/8	26 1/8	25 6/8	20 6/8	5	5	De Soto County	MS	Chris Cordell	1997	3968
156 2/8	23 4/8	23 5/8	20 2/8	6	5	Rice County	MN	Jerome D. Larson	1997	3968
156 2/8	25 2/8	25 6/8	20 2/8	5	5	Madison County	KY	Gary W. Langford	1997	3968
156 2/8	24 2/8	23 2/8	20 6/8	5	5	Floyd County	IA	Darwin Goddard	1998	3968
156 2/8	25 1/8	25 0/8	17 7/8	6	5	Wood County	WI	Gary A. Carlson	1998	3968
156 2/8	20 5/8	22 1/8	14 3/8	7	7	Brown County	OH	Randy King	1998	3968
156 2/8	24 2/8	26 0/8	20 0/8	6	6	Cross County	AR	Mack McCuan	1998	3968
156 2/8	27 7/8	26 5/8	23 4/8	6	6	Franklin County	NE	Nathan Andersohn	1999	3968
156 2/8	25 2/8	24 6/8	18 7/8	6	6	Midland County	MI	Eugene Gilbert Parsons	2000	3968
156 2/8	24 1/8	23 7/8	18 6/8	5	6	Clearfield County	PA	L. Thomas Hobson, Jr.	2000	3968
156 2/8	25 3/8	25 7/8	19 2/8	4	4	Monroe County	OH	Tim Kaiser	2000	3968
156 2/8	23 4/8	22 4/8	18 5/8	5	8	E. Carroll Parish	LA	Robert Jarvis	2000	3968
156 2/8	24 1/8	23 4/8	20 0/8	5	5	Cumberland County	ME	Andrew MacDonald	2001	3968
156 2/8	24 3/8	23 2/8	16 6/8	5	5	Armstrong County	PA	Matthew D. Silicki	2002	3968
156 2/8	23 4/8	23 5/8	18 6/8	5	5	Pike County	IL	Rodney King	2002	3968
156 2/8	25 6/8	25 0/8	20 7/8	6	5	Jackson County	WI	Seth Parker	2003	3968
156 2/8	24 5/8	24 3/8	16 7/8	5	7	Union County	SD	Craig A. Zoss	2003	3968
156 2/8	23 2/8	23 2/8	18 2/8	5	5	Sauk County	WI	Jerehmy D. Griffiths	2003	3968
156 2/8	24 3/8	24 5/8	22 3/8	5	6	Carroll County	IL	Del Roberts	2004	3968
*156 2/8	25 6/8	28 2/8	19 6/8	5	5	Floyd County	IN	Kevin Condra	2004	3968
156 2/8	27 7/8	28 4/8	21 6/8	9	7	Logan County	OH	Jim Steve	2004	3968
156 2/8	26 6/8	27 0/8	21 4/8	5	4	Elbow	SAS	Chad Gessner	2005	3968
156 2/8	24 1/8	24 2/8	19 6/8	6	6	Bon Homme County	SD	Chad Bietz	2005	3968
*156 2/8	23 1/8	24 0/8	25 2/8	5	6	Ingham County	MI	Ernie Pribik	2005	3968
*156 2/8	25 0/8	25 1/8	21 6/8	6	6	Columbia County	WI	Mike Lehrmann	2006	3968
*156 2/8	24 2/8	24 4/8	17 7/8	6	5	Trempealeau County	WI	Gary Clark	2006	3968
*156 2/8	27 2/8	25 3/8	19 6/8	7	7	Fulton County	IL	Roy A. Haydt	2006	3968
156 2/8	28 3/8	28 2/8	22 3/8	5	5	Marion County	IA	Leonard Grimes	2006	3968
156 2/8	26 0/8	26 0/8	20 5/8	8	6	McDonough County	IL	Les Twidell	2007	3968
156 2/8	25 4/8	25 6/8	18 2/8	4	4	Mecklenburg County	NC	Dennis Cook	2009	3968
*156 2/8	23 4/8	24 3/8	18 4/8	7	7	Holt County	MO	Zachary Kerns	2009	3968
156 2/8	22 4/8	22 2/8	15 4/8	5	7	Pierce County	WI	Van Howe	2009	3968
156 2/8	24 3/8	24 1/8	24 1/8	7	7	Cass County	MI	Hubert D. Whitehead	2009	3968
156 2/8	24 2/8	24 1/8	20 7/8	7	5	Kewaunee County	WI	Cal Wickman	2010	3968
156 2/8	25 6/8	25 6/8	20 2/8	5	5	Waushara County	WI	Rich Crim	2010	3968
156 1/8	25 4/8	25 2/8	19 1/8	5	5	Crawford County	IL	Mickie L. Purcell	1972	4027
156 1/8	24 3/8	23 7/8	19 7/8	5	5	Ravalli County	MT	Vernon L. Cooper	1977	4027
156 1/8	25 4/8	25 6/8	19 1/8	5	5	Tompkins County	NY	Alan C. Boda	1981	4027
156 1/8	22 6/8	23 2/8	17 7/8	5	5	Monroe County	OH	Wendell Newhouse	1982	4027
156 1/8	24 3/8	25 0/8	19 7/8	7	8	Douglas County	NE	Oran L. Foxworthy	1984	4027
156 1/8	25 5/8	24 6/8	22 1/8	4	4	Sumner County	KS	Ralph Shaver	1984	4027
156 1/8	22 1/8	25 7/8	17 1/8	7	5	Cloud County	KS	Richard Bieker	1985	4027
156 1/8	24 5/8	24 4/8	18 1/8	5	5	Prowers County	CO	Lynn Leonard	1988	4027
156 1/8	24 5/8	26 0/8	17 5/8	7	5	Osage County	KS	Daniel Beavers	1989	4027
156 1/8	25 3/8	26 3/8	21 4/8	6	6	Sarpy County	NE	Gregg E. Lind	1990	4027
156 1/8	25 4/8	27 0/8	19 4/8	6	6	Jackson County	IA	David Shepherd	1990	4027
156 1/8	25 6/8	25 0/8	23 3/8	6	6	Hamilton County	OH	Dave Brackett	1990	4027
156 1/8	27 6/8	28 1/8	20 1/8	7	5	Wayne County	IL	James Isles	1990	4027
156 1/8	24 7/8	25 0/8	18 1/8	5	5	Jo Daviess County	IL	Brian Smith	1991	4027
156 1/8	21 5/8	20 7/8	17 1/8	6	6	Morrison County	MN	Craig Haupt	1993	4027
156 1/8	24 1/8	24 2/8	17 7/8	5	5	Fillmore County	MN	Justin R. Brown	1993	4027
156 1/8	22 1/8	21 0/8	17 7/8	5	5	Lee County	IL	Dennis Staats	1993	4027
156 1/8	24 7/8	25 2/8	20 7/8	5	6	Lake County	IL	Wayne K. Johnson	1994	4027
156 1/8	22 6/8	22 2/8	16 3/8	5	5	Bottineau County	ND	Larry Tooke	1994	4027
156 1/8	25 1/8	25 3/8	19 0/8	4	6	Sawyer County	WI	James R. Pollak	1995	4027
156 1/8	23 4/8	24 0/8	15 7/8	5	5	Nemaha County	KS	Monty G. Noland	1995	4027
156 1/8	23 6/8	24 2/8	21 1/8	5	5	Anoka County	MN	Robert Feigum	1995	4027
156 1/8	24 5/8	24 3/8	18 7/8	4	4	Scott County	IA	Rodney Stalder	1995	4027
156 1/8	23 3/8	24 0/8	19 5/8	8	6	Comanche County	KS	Greg Hill	1995	4027
156 1/8	24 5/8	24 6/8	17 3/8	5	5	Kewaunee County	WI	Ronald F. McClure	1999	4027
*156 1/8	24 5/8	25 6/8	18 4/8	5	6	Steuben County	IN	Steve Nichols	1999	4027
156 1/8	24 7/8	25 0/8	19 5/8	6	6	Wyoming County	WV	Dwight Canada	1999	4027
156 1/8	26 2/8	26 6/8	21 3/8	6	6	Linn County	IA	Steve Madura	2000	4027
156 1/8	26 7/8	26 0/8	16 7/8	6	5	Pike County	IL	Dan Perez	2000	4027
156 1/8	24 2/8	23 7/8	15 7/8	7	5	Platte County	MO	Jeff Graham	2000	4027
156 1/8	23 6/8	22 4/8	15 7/8	5	5	Comanche County	KS	Jay Yokomizo	2001	4027
156 1/8	25 5/8	25 3/8	19 3/8	5	5	Morgan County	IL	Kris Walden	2001	4027
156 1/8	26 5/8	26 1/8	19 0/8	6	4	Kane County	IL	Dean V. Ashton	2002	4027
156 1/8	24 5/8	24 5/8	19 5/8	5	5	St. Clair County	MO	Mark Gumm	2002	4027
156 1/8	27 3/8	25 7/8	19 4/8	6	5	Lehigh County	PA	Michael C. Vaka	2002	4027
156 1/8	25 7/8	25 6/8	19 3/8	5	5	Defiance County	OH	George L. Decker	2002	4027
156 1/8	24 5/8	24 4/8	17 5/8	5	5	Eau Claire County	WI	Patrick McGuire	2003	4027
156 1/8	24 1/8	24 7/8	21 2/8	7	5	Morgan County	IN	Elliott J. Fiscus	2003	4027
156 1/8	26 7/8	27 1/8	18 7/8	5	4	Lake County	IL	John T. Anderson	2003	4027
156 1/8	24 6/8	24 4/8	17 1/8	4	4	Hampden County	MA	Elwood Burtt	2004	4027
156 1/8	21 6/8	22 1/8	16 1/8	5	5	Hillsdale County	MI	Ryan Manore	2004	4027
156 1/8	23 7/8	25 3/8	22 0/8	5	5	Dodge County	WI	Steven E. Twardokus	2004	4027
156 1/8	27 3/8	28 3/8	19 6/8	4	5	Riley County	KS	Chad L. Blockcolsky	2004	4027
156 1/8	25 3/8	24 0/8	17 3/8	5	5	Gallatin County	IL	Dennis George	2005	4027
*156 1/8	23 3/8	24 6/8	16 4/8	9	8	Montgomery County	IL	Robert Meyer	2005	4027
156 1/8	26 5/8	25 6/8	16 7/8	5	5	Fairfax County	VA	James Watkins	2006	4027
156 1/8	24 7/8	23 7/8	17 0/8	6	5	Jennings County	IN	Anthony W. Carter	2007	4027
*156 1/8	24 2/8	24 4/8	17 4/8	6	8	Cowley County	KS	Erin E. Frederick	2007	4027
156 1/8	23 2/8	22 5/8	16 7/8	10	7	Osage County	KS	Barry Clark	2007	4027
*156 1/8	23 5/8	24 0/8	19 6/8	5	8	Steuben County	NY	Steven E. Calderwood	2008	4027
156 1/8	25 6/8	26 2/8	20 5/8	5	5	Christian County	KY	Michael Robertson	2008	4027
*156 1/8	26 7/8	25 0/8	17 2/8	7	6	Kenton County	KY	Paul E. Cooper III	2008	4027
156 1/8	23 4/8	22 7/8	18 7/8	6	6	Saline County	MO	Randy Reese	2008	4027
156 1/8	23 4/8	22 7/8	18 7/8	5	5	Shawano County	WI	Daniel J. Uttecht	2008	4027
156 1/8	21 1/8	21 1/8	17 7/8	5	5	Trego County	KS	David Gillan	2008	4027
156 0/8	26 0/8	27 1/8	16 4/8	4	4	Bertie County	NC	Gordon Gardner	1975	4082
156 0/8	23 4/8	23 7/8	19 6/8	5	5	Stark County	OH	Don Cerosky	1979	4082
156 0/8	25 1/8	24 4/8	20 3/8	6	8	Brown County	IL	Lowell Leslie, Jr.	1980	4082
156 0/8	25 5/8	25 6/8	19 6/8	4	4	Louisa County	IA	Roger Gipple	1982	4082

WHITETAIL DEER (TYPICAL ANTLERS)

Minimum Score 125 — Continued

SCORE	LENGTH OF R MAIN BEAM L	INSIDE SPREAD	NUMBER OF R POINTS L	AREA	STATE/ PROVINCE	HUNTER'S NAME	DATE	RANK
156 0/8	22 2/8 22 5/8	19 6/8	7 7	Perry County	IL	Terry Queen	1983	4082
156 0/8	24 2/8 24 2/8	17 6/8	5 7	Owen County	IN	Michael A. Miller	1986	4082
156 0/8	26 5/8 25 2/8	18 4/8	7 6	Licking County	OH	Robert R. Hutchison	1989	4082
156 0/8	24 1/8 23 3/8	18 0/8	5 5	Alpena County	MI	Samuel Lee Freese	1989	4082
156 0/8	23 1/8 22 7/8	18 2/8	5 5	Trempealeau County	WI	Dane Zielke	1989	4082
156 0/8	22 7/8 24 5/8	16 7/8	6 7	Butler County	KS	Dave Cornish	1989	4082
156 0/8	25 2/8 25 0/8	20 2/8	5 6	Carver County	MN	Brian Klingelhutz	1990	4082
156 0/8	24 6/8 24 4/8	18 0/8	8 8	Oklahoma County	OK	Greg Boydston	1990	4082
156 0/8	24 0/8 25 5/8	18 5/8	5 7	Warren County	IL	Brian P. Monroe	1990	4082
156 0/8	25 3/8 25 2/8	19 0/8	4 5	Clearwater County	ID	Robert Willkas	1990	4082
156 0/8	26 1/8 24 6/8	22 0/8	7 6	Jasper County	IL	Dan Songer	1991	4082
156 0/8	24 7/8 23 7/8	20 4/8	5 5	Macon County	IL	Charlie DeBose, Jr.	1991	4082
156 0/8	23 3/8 24 4/8	18 2/8	5 5	Will County	IL	Larry G. Koerner	1991	4082
156 0/8	27 3/8 26 1/8	18 1/8	6 5	Wright County	MN	Dave Herzan	1992	4082
156 0/8	23 2/8 23 3/8	17 4/8	7 6	Grayson County	TX	Johnny Haddad	1992	4082
156 0/8	26 7/8 26 7/8	19 0/8	5 5	Allamakee County	IA	Gene A. Hall	1993	4082
156 0/8	25 3/8 25 7/8	21 0/8	6 5	Hamilton County	IL	Mark Snow	1993	4082
156 0/8	27 4/8 27 0/8	21 0/8	6 6	Dane County	WI	Andy Maier	1993	4082
156 0/8	25 6/8 25 6/8	20 4/8	6 4	Montgomery County	IL	Larry D. Whitley	1993	4082
156 0/8	25 3/8 24 0/8	15 6/8	5 6	Edwards County	IL	Walter W. Troyer	1993	4082
156 0/8	24 7/8 25 2/8	17 6/8	4 4	Saline County	IL	Rick Carr	1993	4082
156 0/8	25 2/8 25 5/8	17 0/8	5 5	Woodbury County	IA	Douglas Sweeney	1994	4082
156 0/8	24 1/8 23 4/8	21 3/8	7 6	Lenawee County	MI	Ronald E. Cross	1995	4082
156 0/8	22 6/8 23 4/8	18 4/8	5 5	Hillsdale County	MI	Cora J. Fink	1995	4082
156 0/8	23 4/8 23 6/8	17 6/8	7 5	Beltrami County	MN	Scott La Coursiere	1995	4082
156 0/8	24 4/8 23 1/8	18 6/8	5 5	Phillips County	KS	Gary Niblock	1995	4082
156 0/8	24 2/8 24 4/8	19 2/8	5 5	Vermilion County	IL	Mark Lourance	1996	4082
156 0/8	23 6/8 24 7/8	20 0/8	7 7	Buffalo County	WI	Joseph Potter	1996	4082
156 0/8	22 6/8 23 4/8	18 2/8	5 5	Dane County	WI	Rory Rossman	1996	4082
156 0/8	27 3/8 26 6/8	21 1/8	4 5	Henderson County	KY	Edward Croft	1997	4082
156 0/8	25 5/8 26 3/8	19 0/8	4 5	Greene County	PA	R. Adrian Whipkey	1998	4082
156 0/8	24 5/8 25 4/8	18 0/8	5 5	Livingston County	NY	Bradley Weese	1998	4082
156 0/8	25 2/8 25 0/8	21 6/8	5 5	Livingston County	NY	Earl Beardsley	2000	4082
156 0/8	25 5/8 25 2/8	16 3/8	6 7	Linn County	KS	Gary Robertson	2000	4082
156 0/8	24 1/8 24 1/8	17 4/8	5 6	Cloud County	KS	Jordon Koster	2000	4082
156 0/8	23 6/8 23 6/8	19 5/8	5 8	Green County	WI	Nick Sheesley	2001	4082
156 0/8	25 0/8 25 4/8	20 0/8	7 5	Decatur County	IA	Jared Goering	2001	4082
156 0/8	25 5/8 24 6/8	17 4/8	5 7	Adair County	MO	Richard Beckemeyer	2001	4082
156 0/8	22 7/8 23 1/8	17 0/8	6 6	Allamakee County	IA	Randy Jones	2001	4082
156 0/8	24 5/8 23 2/8	17 6/8	6 6	Bond County	IL	Daren Elam	2002	4082
156 0/8	27 0/8 25 1/8	17 7/8	6 6	Merrimack County	NH	Michael D. Rossen	2002	4082
156 0/8	24 4/8 23 6/8	18 6/8	5 5	Pike County	OH	Lenny Downs	2002	4082
156 0/8	23 1/8 23 2/8	18 4/8	5 5	Will County	IL	Craig Olthoff	2003	4082
156 0/8	24 2/8 24 2/8	17 5/8	6 5	Douglas County	MN	Darrick Menk	2003	4082
156 0/8	23 0/8 24 0/8	18 4/8	6 6	Pike County	IL	Steve Fielder	2003	4082
156 0/8	23 1/8 23 3/8	20 3/8	6 7	Hamilton County	OH	Tim Stegmuller	2003	4082
156 0/8	24 4/8 26 6/8	15 6/8	5 5	Livingston County	MI	Bradley Paddock	2003	4082
156 0/8	24 7/8 24 1/8	17 3/8	8 7	Schuyler County	IL	Gregory B. Creasey	2003	4082
156 0/8	25 2/8 26 0/8	18 2/8	6 6	Clay County	IA	Thomas Ray Gross	2003	4082
156 0/8	24 6/8 25 0/8	19 6/8	4 5	Brown County	OH	Jesse B. Fisher	2003	4082
156 0/8	24 6/8 25 2/8	16 1/8	6 6	Elbert County	CO	Cameron R. Hanes	2004	4082
156 0/8	23 3/8 23 4/8	19 2/8	6 6	Monroe County	IA	Robert Smith	2004	4082
156 0/8	23 1/8 23 1/8	17 6/8	5 5	Polk County	WI	Ronald A. Peterson	2004	4082
156 0/8	23 6/8 23 2/8	17 6/8	5 5	Bartholomew County	IN	Scott Rosenberger	2004	4082
*156 0/8	23 6/8 23 7/8	18 3/8	6 6	Taylor County	IA	Daniel B. Miers	2005	4082
156 0/8	24 1/8 26 4/8	20 4/8	5 5	Grundy County	IL	Charles Feuillan, Jr.	2005	4082
156 0/8	23 3/8 22 4/8	19 3/8	7 5	Chase County	KS	Jim Purcaro	2005	4082
156 0/8	26 7/8 26 2/8	19 0/8	5 5	Marquette County	WI	Tim Koenen	2005	4082
*156 0/8	24 6/8 25 1/8	20 6/8	4 5	Cumberland County	IL	Michael D. Kauffman	2005	4082
*156 0/8	23 0/8 22 0/8	17 6/8	7 9	Dane County	WI	John E. Schuchart	2006	4082
*156 0/8	22 1/8 22 0/8	16 0/8	5 5	Decatur County	IA	Greg Glesinger	2007	4082
*156 0/8	27 5/8 26 2/8	23 0/8	7 7	Huntington County	IN	Adam L. Douglas	2007	4082
*156 0/8	22 7/8 22 7/8	18 2/8	5 6	Wabasha County	MN	Nathan Pfeilsticker	2007	4082
156 0/8	26 6/8 26 2/8	16 0/8	6 5	Iowa County	WI	Tom McKinlay	2007	4082
156 0/8	24 4/8 23 5/8	16 6/8	6 5	Baylor County	TX	O. P. "Trey" Carpenter III	2008	4082
*156 0/8	24 4/8 24 2/8	20 2/8	6 6	White County	IN	Jon J. Baker	2009	4082
*156 0/8	22 4/8 24 1/8	17 6/8	5 5	Newton County	IN	Daniel E. Walstra	2009	4082
156 0/8	23 7/8 22 4/8	15 1/8	7 7	Brown County	WI	Justin Hewitt	2009	4082
*156 0/8	24 2/8 24 6/8	18 0/8	5 5	St. Louis County	MN	Joe Doskey	2009	4082
156 0/8	24 6/8 24 6/8	16 4/8	5 5	Oakland County	MI	Linc LaFountain	2009	4082
155 7/8	24 7/8 24 4/8	19 7/8	5 5	Frontier County	NE	Charles Druse	1963	4156
155 7/8	24 3/8 24 5/8	15 5/8	5 5	Harrison County	IA	Clarence N. Jackson, Jr.	1963	4156
155 7/8	26 0/8 24 5/8	17 3/8	6 8	Neosho County	KS	Jeff Friederich	1983	4156
155 7/8	25 4/8 25 1/8	16 7/8	5 5	Macon County	IL	Mike Nickell	1985	4156
155 7/8	24 7/8 24 5/8	20 4/8	6 7	Becker County	MN	Paul Adams	1988	4156
155 7/8	22 5/8 22 7/8	18 1/8	5 5	Bremer County	IA	John W. Breitbach	1989	4156
155 7/8	26 7/8 26 5/8	23 1/8	5 5	Charles County	MD	Scott Bressler	1990	4156
155 7/8	26 6/8 25 6/8	16 2/8	7 6	Anderson County	KS	Kurt A. Sayers	1990	4156
155 7/8	22 1/8 23 5/8	21 5/8	6 5	Hardin County	IA	Tom Catlin	1990	4156
155 7/8	22 1/8 20 6/8	21 5/8	5 5	Jackson County	WI	Calvin J. Haag	1991	4156
155 7/8	26 0/8 25 3/8	18 7/8	5 5	Carroll County	IA	Cory Hulsing	1991	4156
155 7/8	23 3/8 22 7/8	20 3/8	5 5	Tippecanoe County	IN	Steve Rider	1992	4156
155 7/8	25 4/8 25 0/8	19 0/8	6 7	Trempealeau County	WI	Duane Dubiel	1992	4156
155 7/8	25 1/8 24 1/8	18 1/8	5 5	Kankakee County	IL	Charles Gaidamavice	1992	4156
155 7/8	24 1/8 23 5/8	16 5/8	5 5	Saunders County	NE	Joe Crnkovich	1993	4156
155 7/8	24 7/8 24 6/8	22 5/8	5 5	Coahoma County	MS	Charles B. Neely	1994	4156
155 7/8	25 7/8 27 0/8	20 7/8	5 6	Warren County	IA	Scott Messamaker	1994	4156
155 7/8	24 5/8 24 2/8	17 5/8	6 6	Cass County	IL	Ron McCarthy	1994	4156
155 7/8	22 7/8 23 6/8	22 3/8	5 5	Fulton County	IL	Bret L. Epkins	1995	4156
155 7/8	24 2/8 23 6/8	19 7/8	6 5	Seward County	KS	Lynn Leonard	1995	4156
155 7/8	25 7/8 25 4/8	21 5/8	6 5	Hopkins County	KY	Ben Hudson	1996	4156
155 7/8	25 2/8 26 0/8	18 1/8	4 5	Treasure County	MT	Rob Seelye	1996	4156
155 7/8	22 3/8 21 7/8	18 4/8	6 5	Kleberg County	TX	W. Scott Brandon	1996	4156
155 7/8	26 5/8 26 4/8	21 2/8	6 6	Du Page County	IL	James A. Wetmore	1997	4156
155 7/8	25 0/8 24 7/8	19 3/8	5 5	Jefferson County	MS	John A. Windham	1997	4156

WHITETAIL DEER (TYPICAL ANTLERS)

Minimum Score 125 — Continued

SCORE	LENGTH OF R MAIN BEAM L	INSIDE SPREAD	NUMBER OF R POINTS L		AREA	STATE/ PROVINCE	HUNTER'S NAME	DATE	RANK
155 7/8	24 4/8 23 1/8	15 5/8	6	5	Muskingum County	OH	Dan Jennings	1997	4156
155 7/8	22 5/8 25 5/8	21 7/8	6	6	Dane County	WI	Jesse Duhr	1998	4156
155 7/8	24 5/8 25 2/8	18 7/8	5	5	Jackson County	WI	Robert Chamberlain	1999	4156
155 7/8	23 2/8 23 5/8	24 6/8	6	6	Refugio County	TX	Brent A. Tucker	1999	4156
155 7/8	25 3/8 25 6/8	19 2/8	6	5	Clark County	IL	Dan Willett	1999	4156
155 7/8	27 2/8 27 7/8	19 3/8	6	6	St. Louis County	MO	John Mueller	2000	4156
155 7/8	24 0/8 25 6/8	20 5/8	5	6	Johnson County	KS	Keith Canant	2000	4156
155 7/8	23 0/8 22 5/8	17 3/8	6	5	Collingsworth County	TX	Coty Ivey	2001	4156
*155 7/8	25 6/8 26 1/8	17 3/8	6	5	Stark County	IL	Ryan Labedis	2001	4156
155 7/8	25 1/8 24 1/8	17 5/8	6	6	Allegany County	NY	Norbert Schnorr	2001	4156
*155 7/8	25 4/8 25 5/8	20 5/8	5	5	Uvalde County	TX	David Sadler	2002	4156
155 7/8	24 4/8 24 2/8	15 3/8	5	5	Saline County	KS	Daryl DePeel	2002	4156
155 7/8	23 6/8 24 0/8	17 5/8	5	5	Clark County	WI	Donald Damask	2002	4156
155 7/8	22 7/8 23 0/8	19 1/8	5	5	Niagara County	NY	Troy S. Wilson	2002	4156
*155 7/8	25 5/8 25 4/8	18 5/8	4	4	Champaign County	OH	Scott Pflaumer	2002	4156
155 7/8	24 1/8 23 1/8	16 7/8	5	6	Des Moines County	IA	Randy Templeton	2002	4156
155 7/8	25 2/8 24 4/8	18 0/8	6	6	Warren County	IA	Dan Young	2003	4156
155 7/8	23 2/8 22 6/8	18 3/8	5	5	Livingston County	IL	Alan Gray	2003	4156
155 7/8	25 6/8 26 2/8	17 1/8	5	4	Shawano County	WI	Sally A. Reedy	2004	4156
155 7/8	25 3/8 25 0/8	18 7/8	5	5	Buffalo County	WI	Dave Fredrickson	2004	4156
155 7/8	24 1/8 23 1/8	17 3/8	6	5	St. Louis County	MN	Ryland Nelson	2004	4156
155 7/8	19 3/8 21 4/8	16 3/8	5	5	Gove County	KS	Skip Moore	2005	4156
155 7/8	23 6/8 22 2/8	18 5/8	5	5	Cook County	IL	Douglas Vines	2005	4156
155 7/8	25 2/8 24 0/8	21 1/8	6	5	Buffalo County	WI	Troy R. Rauwerdink	2005	4156
*155 7/8	24 2/8 23 5/8	18 3/8	6	5	Linn County	KS	Mark Mortimer	2005	4156
155 7/8	27 6/8 26 4/8	19 1/8	6	5	McLean County	ND	Danny D. Boger	2005	4156
155 7/8	22 0/8 22 4/8	17 6/8	5	7	Rock County	MN	Dominic J. Maras	2006	4156
155 7/8	24 4/8 23 6/8	19 3/8	6	7	Ogle County	IL	Thomas J. Beissel	2006	4156
155 7/8	26 0/8 25 6/8	19 3/8	4	4	Audubon County	IA	Craig Sander	2006	4156
155 7/8	25 0/8 24 7/8	17 6/8	7	5	Oconto County	WI	Steve Linzmeyer	2006	4156
155 7/8	24 3/8 23 5/8	17 1/8	5	5	Sauk County	WI	Bill Boyd	2007	4156
155 7/8	23 4/8 24 3/8	19 1/8	5	5	Furnas County	NE	Anthony Scarlin	2007	4156
155 7/8	25 4/8 25 4/8	19 6/8	5	7	Dane County	WI	Ron A. Zeman	2007	4156
*155 7/8	25 2/8 25 1/8	20 3/8	6	5	La Crosse County	WI	Todd Delaney	2007	4156
155 7/8	24 7/8 25 1/8	17 1/8	5	5	Walworth County	WI	Jeffery L. Nelson	2007	4156
*155 7/8	25 4/8 26 0/8	18 1/8	5	7	Worcester County	MD	Jim T. Hughes	2007	4156
155 7/8	23 7/8 23 5/8	18 6/8	5	5	Piatt County	IL	Hansel Lee Moore, Jr.	2007	4156
*155 7/8	23 7/8 25 0/8	16 6/8	5	6	Woodson County	KS	Clinton Shockley	2007	4156
155 7/8	26 3/8 25 2/8	16 7/8	5	7	Waukesha County	WI	Matthew W. Walker	2008	4156
155 7/8	23 1/8 22 6/8	17 1/8	6	5	Knox County	OH	Alvie Pay	2008	4156
*155 7/8	21 6/8 22 0/8	18 1/8	5	5	Bartholomew County	IN	Dan Barlow	2008	4156
155 7/8	24 6/8 23 7/8	20 1/8	5	5	Becker County	MN	Richard Olie Barten	2009	4156
155 7/8	24 3/8 24 5/8	18 4/8	6	6	Yuma County	CO	Jeff Davis	2009	4156
155 7/8	25 1/8 25 2/8	17 3/8	5	5	Taylor County	WI	Derek Laher	2010	4156
155 6/8	25 1/8 24 4/8	18 4/8	4	5	Madison County	NE	Dick Gambill	1967	4225
155 6/8	24 4/8 24 5/8	21 6/8	5	5	Shawano County	WI	Steve Hauk	1978	4225
155 6/8	23 0/8 23 6/8	19 2/8	5	6	Monroe County	IA	John Vollmer	1982	4225
155 6/8	24 0/8 23 6/8	16 7/8	5	6	Area 28	MAN	Gary Kaluzniak	1983	4225
155 6/8	21 6/8 20 5/8	16 4/8	6	6	McHenry County	IL	Michael D. Patrick	1984	4225
155 6/8	25 2/8 24 1/8	20 2/8	5	5	Lawrence County	MO	David T. Kail	1984	4225
155 6/8	23 7/8 23 5/8	18 2/8	5	5	Morrison County	MN	Thomas Barron, Jr.	1987	4225
155 6/8	24 5/8 24 6/8	16 2/8	5	6	Des Moines County	IA	Pat Stallman	1988	4225
155 6/8	26 0/8 26 2/8	16 6/8	5	5	Allamakee County	IA	Dan Brimeyer	1988	4225
155 6/8	23 4/8 23 1/8	18 4/8	5	5	Marion County	IA	Thomas L. Tucker	1988	4225
155 6/8	22 2/8 22 2/8	16 0/8	5	6	Troup County	GA	James E. Hogan	1989	4225
155 6/8	24 0/8 24 0/8	14 4/8	5	6	Shelby County	IL	Brian Herzog	1991	4225
155 6/8	22 7/8 24 0/8	17 1/8	6	5	Allamakee County	IA	Ernie Burroughs	1992	4225
155 6/8	24 6/8 25 5/8	17 5/8	6	5	Laclede County	MO	Roy McCann	1992	4225
155 6/8	24 6/8 24 1/8	18 6/8	5	5	Washington County	WI	Terry Farnham	1993	4225
155 6/8	24 1/8 23 5/8	20 4/8	5	6	Gogebic County	MI	R. J. Spang	1993	4225
155 6/8	26 1/8 26 6/8	20 6/8	5	5	Jefferson County	WI	Eddie Spiegelhoff	1994	4225
155 6/8	27 1/8 26 5/8	19 2/8	6	5	Calvert County	MD	Bruce Williams	1995	4225
155 6/8	26 2/8 26 0/8	21 4/8	4	4	Edgar County	IL	Joe Schmitt	1995	4225
155 6/8	22 7/8 23 0/8	20 0/8	5	6	Rockingham County	NC	Martin E. Mabe	1996	4225
155 6/8	23 2/8 24 5/8	18 5/8	7	7	Richland County	IL	Tony Prosser	1996	4225
155 6/8	26 6/8 25 7/8	20 0/8	4	4	White County	IL	Bob Curtis	1996	4225
155 6/8	26 6/8 26 6/8	20 6/8	4	4	Edgar County	IL	Greg Stuck	1997	4225
155 6/8	21 4/8 21 2/8	18 0/8	5	5	Douglas County	WI	Tony Ernst	1998	4225
155 6/8	25 3/8 25 3/8	17 0/8	7	5	Dane County	WI	Randy K. Hatch	1998	4225
155 6/8	24 6/8 24 5/8	17 4/8	6	5	Walworth County	WI	Brian Annen	1998	4225
155 6/8	24 4/8 24 5/8	19 2/8	4	5	Christian County	KY	Brent Ezell	1999	4225
155 6/8	18 4/8 23 1/8	18 3/8	8	7	Douglas County	KS	Jim Bieker	1999	4225
155 6/8	22 3/8 23 2/8	21 0/8	5	5	Hand County	SD	Kevin Bertsch	1999	4225
155 6/8	26 0/8 25 4/8	20 7/8	5	6	Shelby County	IL	Rick G. Cobb	2000	4225
155 6/8	27 4/8 25 7/8	19 7/8	5	7	Jones County	IA	David Kramer	2000	4225
155 6/8	23 4/8 22 3/8	19 0/8	5	5	Edwards County	IL	George Maxwell	2001	4225
155 6/8	25 4/8 25 3/8	18 4/8	6	7	Peach County	GA	Travis Harvill	2002	4225
155 6/8	25 7/8 25 6/8	17 5/8	5	4	Fayette County	IA	Ryan Ladeburg	2002	4225
*155 6/8	26 0/8 25 0/8	20 6/8	5	5	Eau Claire County	WI	Brian Markowski	2002	4225
155 6/8	24 2/8 24 3/8	16 4/8	4	5	St. Louis County	MN	Richard W. VanValkenburg	2003	4225
155 6/8	22 4/8 22 3/8	17 0/8	5	5	Buffalo County	WI	Corey W. Fuhrmann	2003	4225
155 6/8	24 2/8 23 7/8	17 6/8	5	5	Vigo County	IN	Greg Spurgeon	2004	4225
155 6/8	25 4/8 27 1/8	17 2/8	5	5	Anoka County	MN	Andy Nelson	2004	4225
*155 6/8	25 0/8 25 0/8	16 2/8	5	6	Marathon County	WI	Lowell Block	2005	4225
155 6/8	24 3/8 22 5/8	15 6/8	6	5	Buffalo County	WI	Danny Hanson	2005	4225
155 6/8	24 5/8 24 7/8	20 1/8	6	6	Winona County	MN	Lyndon Peterson	2006	4225
155 6/8	23 4/8 25 6/8	18 4/8	6	6	Clayton County	IA	Robert Camp	2007	4225
*155 6/8	27 2/8 28 0/8	21 3/8	5	4	Lyon County	KS	Tyson Wolf	2007	4225
*155 6/8	24 6/8 24 4/8	19 2/8	5	5	Scioto County	OH	Jason A. Rhoton	2008	4225
155 6/8	25 3/8 25 6/8	17 4/8	5	5	Grundy County	IL	David A. Both	2008	4225
155 6/8	24 6/8 25 2/8	20 2/8	5	5	Morris County	KS	Glenn Sereda	2009	4225
*155 6/8	23 3/8 23 3/8	18 0/8	7	6	Porter County	IN	James T. Olaughlin	2009	4225
*155 6/8	23 7/8 23 7/8	20 6/8	5	5	Gallia County	OH	Clint Price	2009	4225
155 6/8	24 2/8 25 0/8	18 4/8	5	5	Charles Mix County	SD	Curtis Soulek	2009	4225
155 5/8	25 5/8 26 0/8	19 1/8	5	6	Rice County	KS	Gordon Leo Rayl	1967	4275

400

WHITETAIL DEER (TYPICAL ANTLERS)

Minimum Score 125 — Continued

SCORE	LENGTH OF MAIN BEAM R	L	INSIDE SPREAD	NUMBER OF POINTS R	L	AREA	STATE/ PROVINCE	HUNTER'S NAME	DATE	RANK
155 5/8	22 5/8	23 0/8	18 5/8	5	5	Anne Arundel County	MD	Gene Hyatt	1976	4275
155 5/8	23 7/8	22 5/8	19 1/8	7	5	Harrison County	IA	Alfred S. Foster	1978	4275
155 5/8	25 2/8	23 7/8	17 1/8	5	5	Trempealeau County	WI	Greg Halpern	1982	4275
155 5/8	25 7/8	25 3/8	20 5/8	4	4	Clayton County	IA	Gerald W. Kluesner	1986	4275
155 5/8	24 5/8	23 3/8	18 7/8	5	5	Chase County	KS	Jerry Keller	1986	4275
155 5/8	25 6/8	27 3/8	20 4/8	9	7	Perry County	IL	Jerry M. Smith	1987	4275
155 5/8	26 6/8	28 0/8	18 5/8	5	5	Logan County	OH	Dan Jergens	1987	4275
155 5/8	23 6/8	25 0/8	17 5/8	5	5	Pierce County	WI	Greg Koehler	1988	4275
155 5/8	23 3/8	23 0/8	18 5/8	6	6	Kane County	IL	James A. Anderson	1989	4275
155 5/8	23 6/8	23 7/8	15 2/8	6	5	Brown County	IN	Frank Cross	1989	4275
155 5/8	25 1/8	24 1/8	18 3/8	4	4	Fairfield County	CT	Stephen M. Ruttkamp	1989	4275
155 5/8	24 3/8	24 5/8	19 3/8	5	5	Morrison County	MN	James Anderson	1990	4275
155 5/8	23 3/8	22 7/8	18 1/8	5	5	Kingman County	KS	Ed Laverentz	1991	4275
155 5/8	25 1/8	24 7/8	15 7/8	5	5	Cook County	MN	Richard D. Nelson	1991	4275
155 5/8	25 6/8	25 7/8	18 5/8	6	7	Union County	KY	Charles E. Hobbs	1992	4275
155 5/8	22 3/8	21 6/8	16 3/8	5	5	Willowbrook	SAS	John W. Makowetski	1993	4275
155 5/8	24 2/8	23 3/8	16 1/8	6	6	Jackson County	WI	Glen R. Loppnow	1993	4275
155 5/8	24 5/8	23 2/8	18 1/8	5	5	Grundy County	MO	Gary Vernon	1993	4275
155 5/8	22 7/8	23 2/8	17 3/8	5	5	Winnebago County	WI	John H. Hay	1994	4275
155 5/8	26 1/8	26 2/8	17 3/8	5	6	Cass County	MI	Fred Kruger	1995	4275
155 5/8	24 6/8	23 6/8	17 3/8	5	5	Mercer County	NJ	Richard E. Cincilla	1996	4275
155 5/8	24 3/8	25 2/8	18 2/8	8	7	Waukesha County	WI	Sid Hennekens	1997	4275
155 5/8	24 2/8	24 6/8	18 3/8	5	5	Powell County	MT	Seth Rogers	1998	4275
155 5/8	22 4/8	22 5/8	15 7/8	6	5	Buffalo County	WI	Randy C. Reidt	1998	4275
155 5/8	25 7/8	26 0/8	18 1/8	4	4	Clark County	IL	Dane Thompson	1999	4275
155 5/8	24 2/8	23 4/8	16 1/8	6	5	Richland County	WI	Jack Hendricks	1999	4275
155 5/8	26 0/8	26 6/8	18 1/8	5	5	Madison County	OH	Mike Dillion	1999	4275
155 5/8	24 5/8	24 3/8	20 0/8	5	4	Walworth County	WI	Robert Chelminiak	1999	4275
155 5/8	25 1/8	24 4/8	16 1/8	5	5	Madison County	IA	Doug Burgett	2000	4275
155 5/8	26 3/8	27 7/8	22 2/8	6	4	Caroline County	MD	Vincent Manship	2000	4275
155 5/8	23 0/8	23 0/8	19 0/8	6	5	Boyd County	KY	Don Nickles	2001	4275
155 5/8	23 0/8	23 7/8	18 5/8	7	6	Lake County	IN	William M. Peddycord	2001	4275
155 5/8	22 5/8	24 2/8	17 3/8	6	5	Waupaca County	WI	Kevin R. Sorge	2002	4275
155 5/8	24 3/8	24 5/8	18 1/8	5	5	Mercer County	IL	James C. Jackson	2002	4275
155 5/8	25 5/8	27 2/8	19 1/8	5	5	Knox County	IL	Chris Schmitt	2002	4275
155 5/8	23 7/8	24 6/8	15 7/8	5	6	Salem County	NJ	Larry Hunt	2003	4275
155 5/8	23 4/8	23 4/8	22 5/8	5	5	Priddis	ALB	Lorne D. Rinkel	2003	4275
155 5/8	27 0/8	26 2/8	19 0/8	8	7	McLean County	IL	Scott Darnall	2003	4275
155 5/8	27 0/8	27 0/8	21 7/8	6	6	Gallia County	OH	Mike Connett	2003	4275
*155 5/8	26 2/8	25 5/8	18 1/8	4	4	Montcalm County	MI	Austin R. Shotwell	2004	4275
155 5/8	26 1/8	25 2/8	21 3/8	5	6	Ogle County	IL	Jeff A. Gugle	2005	4275
*155 5/8	24 0/8	24 6/8	17 3/8	5	5	Peoria County	IL	Jason Casteel	2006	4275
*155 5/8	26 1/8	25 5/8	20 5/8	6	5	Rock Island County	IL	Dave Miller	2007	4275
*155 5/8	25 1/8	25 4/8	18 1/8	5	5	Schuyler County	IL	Gerry W. McCoige	2007	4275
*155 5/8	26 4/8	26 2/8	18 7/8	4	4	Highland County	OH	Matt Beachy	2007	4275
155 5/8	25 4/8	23 6/8	16 7/8	5	5	Sherburne County	MN	Ronald Wright	2007	4275
*155 5/8	22 4/8	23 4/8	19 7/8	5	5	Marion County	IA	Jacob Sytsma	2007	4275
155 5/8	26 5/8	26 2/8	20 6/8	6	5	La Salle County	IL	John H. Newcome	2008	4275
*155 5/8	24 7/8	25 6/8	17 5/8	5	5	Elkhart County	IN	Brian J. Brown	2008	4275
155 5/8	22 2/8	21 6/8	17 1/8	5	5	Reno County	KS	W. A. Ladd	2010	4275
155 4/8	23 2/8	25 5/8	18 6/8	7	7	Westchester County	NY	Bernard J. Crescione	1960	4326
155 4/8	25 5/8	25 5/8	16 4/8	5	5	Marion County	IA	Thomas L. Tucker	1967	4326
155 4/8	26 2/8	25 4/8	22 3/8	5	6	Dubuque County	IA	Kurt Cable	1973	4326
155 4/8	23 6/8	25 2/8	19 5/8	7	7	Flathead County	MT	Ralph Ertz	1977	4326
155 4/8	22 3/8	22 3/8	18 1/8	5	6	Lucas County	IA	Lance Brauer	1980	4326
155 4/8	23 2/8	23 6/8	16 6/8	5	5	Lyon County	KS	Ronald E. Rhodes	1981	4326
155 4/8	27 0/8	26 2/8	20 0/8	4	4	Houston County	MN	Gary L. Maier	1985	4326
155 4/8	24 1/8	24 0/8	19 4/8	5	5	Marinette County	WI	John Floriano	1985	4326
155 4/8	23 4/8	24 0/8	20 0/8	5	5	Posey County	IN	Duane Daws	1985	4326
155 4/8	25 1/8	24 6/8	18 0/8	5	6	Washburn County	WI	Wayne Dahlstrom	1986	4326
155 4/8	25 7/8	26 3/8	22 0/8	7	6	Winnebago County	IL	Vaughn Zimmerman	1986	4326
155 4/8	23 7/8	25 6/8	16 4/8	5	5	Forest County	WI	Robert R. Rost	1987	4326
155 4/8	25 1/8	24 4/8	16 4/8	6	5	Jackson County	MO	Charles C. Shotton	1987	4326
155 4/8	23 3/8	24 1/8	16 2/8	5	6	Hennepin County	MN	Delmer Bentz	1988	4326
155 4/8	25 1/8	24 2/8	19 7/8	8	7	Meeker County	MN	Pete Roeser	1990	4326
155 4/8	24 7/8	25 6/8	22 4/8	4	4	Morgan County	IL	Gerald L. Stone	1990	4326
155 4/8	27 4/8	24 4/8	22 2/8	6	6	Rush County	IN	Daniel D. Drysdale	1991	4326
155 4/8	24 3/8	24 1/8	18 3/8	7	8	Jefferson County	OH	Michael W. Brown	1991	4326
155 4/8	26 3/8	26 2/8	22 0/8	4	4	Montgomery County	OH	Kim Hammontree	1991	4326
155 4/8	23 5/8	24 6/8	16 6/8	6	6	Waupaca County	WI	James H. Dimpfl	1992	4326
155 4/8	23 2/8	24 2/8	17 6/8	7	6	Bon Homme County	SD	Mike Peterson	1993	4326
155 4/8	24 2/8	25 6/8	16 1/8	6	6	Pike County	IL	Paul Barry Salmon	1995	4326
155 4/8	25 0/8	25 6/8	20 4/8	6	6	Van Buren County	IA	Jim Chambers	1996	4326
155 4/8	23 3/8	23 3/8	18 6/8	6	5	Spokane County	WA	Skip March	1996	4326
155 4/8	25 1/8	24 4/8	16 4/8	5	5	Blackford County	IN	Dennis K. Decker	1997	4326
155 4/8	25 1/8	25 3/8	17 4/8	4	7	Union County	IL	Ronald Ury	1997	4326
155 4/8	27 0/8	27 1/8	20 4/8	4	4	Crawford County	IL	Chad House	1998	4326
155 4/8	25 6/8	24 6/8	16 2/8	5	5	Dakota County	MN	Michael R. Zaudke	1998	4326
155 4/8	22 4/8	23 5/8	18 0/8	5	5	Valley County	NE	Willard F. Dancer, Jr.	1998	4326
155 4/8	27 2/8	27 2/8	22 0/8	5	4	Madison County	OH	Loren Hershberger	1999	4326
155 4/8	25 0/8	25 3/8	18 2/8	6	6	Kane County	IL	Roy H. Desmond	2000	4326
155 4/8	23 0/8	25 0/8	17 0/8	6	6	Massac County	IL	Rex Fuller	2000	4326
155 4/8	23 3/8	23 3/8	19 1/8	6	5	Richardson County	NE	Aaron Stalder	2001	4326
155 4/8	25 7/8	25 3/8	18 4/8	4	5	Lake County	IL	Robert J. Guarnaccio	2001	4326
155 4/8	25 4/8	25 4/8	20 0/8	5	6	Hocking County	OH	Dan Turvey	2002	4326
155 4/8	24 5/8	23 5/8	18 2/8	5	5	Hancock County	OH	Scott E. Cramer	2002	4326
155 4/8	23 2/8	23 0/8	17 2/8	5	6	Monroe County	IA	Jeffrey D. Lindsey	2004	4326
155 4/8	23 6/8	24 0/8	17 0/8	5	5	Saunders County	NE	Brad Novak	2004	4326
155 4/8	23 7/8	23 4/8	19 0/8	6	5	Douglas County	WI	Bud Halverson	2004	4326
155 4/8	26 0/8	25 5/8	19 6/8	5	6	Washington County	WI	John Wilson	2004	4326
155 4/8	25 2/8	24 1/8	18 2/8	5	5	Winneshiek County	IA	Joel Goodman	2004	4326
155 4/8	24 2/8	23 4/8	18 2/8	5	5	Olmsted County	MN	Jerry V. Finley	2005	4326
155 4/8	24 7/8	24 6/8	20 4/8	5	5	Pierce County	WI	Luke Fleming	2005	4326
155 4/8	28 0/8	27 3/8	18 5/8	6	7	Sarpy County	NE	Timothy E. Bandy	2005	4326
*155 4/8	23 5/8	24 3/8	19 6/8	5	5	Arkansas County	AR	Bruce Burnett	2005	4326

401

WHITETAIL DEER (TYPICAL ANTLERS)

Minimum Score 125 — Continued

SCORE	R MAIN BEAM L	INSIDE SPREAD	R POINTS L	AREA	STATE/PROVINCE	HUNTER'S NAME	DATE	RANK
*155 4/8	25 5/8 24 3/8	17 4/8	5 5	Edmonson County	KY	Gregory Meredith	2006	4326
*155 4/8	24 7/8 24 3/8	14 2/8	7 4	Nicholas County	KY	John Stevens	2006	4326
155 4/8	29 0/8 28 4/8	21 6/8	3 3	Waukesha County	WI	Burt Eichstaedt	2006	4326
*155 4/8	23 7/8 22 6/8	17 0/8	5 6	Harrison County	KY	David Garrison	2006	4326
155 4/8	23 1/8 23 2/8	16 6/8	6 6	Yates County	NY	Patrick J. Mulvaney	2006	4326
*155 4/8	23 4/8 22 2/8	16 6/8	8 7	Lucas County	IA	Brian Pollard	2007	4326
155 4/8	26 5/8 26 2/8	19 4/8	4 4	Butler County	OH	Jim Walker	2007	4326
155 4/8	22 1/8 22 3/8	16 6/8	6 6	Clark County	KS	Michael Peter Yacopino	2007	4326
155 4/8	24 4/8 24 4/8	20 0/8	6 6	Warren County	OH	Drew Heffernan	2008	4326
155 4/8	26 7/8 27 3/8	18 0/8	5 5	Warren County	IA	Ken Lonneman	2008	4326
155 4/8	23 7/8 24 6/8	20 3/8	7 8	Newton County	IN	Brad E. Hyde	2008	4326
155 4/8	24 1/8 25 0/8	17 6/8	6 6	Pulaski County	IN	Greg M. Kiser	2009	4326
*155 4/8	22 6/8 23 6/8	20 2/8	5 5	Allegheny County	PA	Jerry Pepe	2009	4326
155 4/8	26 3/8 27 7/8	24 2/8	5 5	Lafayette County	WI	Steve W. Cole	2009	4326
155 3/8	23 5/8 24 0/8	18 4/8	6 7	Finney County	KS	Wray Decker	1966	4385
155 3/8	26 0/8 26 3/8	21 1/8	6 6	Chickasaw County	IA	William A. Harris	1978	4385
155 3/8	23 3/8 24 2/8	16 0/8	6 5	Union County	OH	Jerry Faine	1982	4385
155 3/8	26 2/8 25 5/8	19 6/8	6 4	Dodge County	MN	Jimmie Donald Hanna	1983	4385
155 3/8	29 2/8 28 2/8	19 7/8	6 8	McDonough County	IL	Locie L. Murphy	1983	4385
155 3/8	24 6/8 24 3/8	20 3/8	5 6	Codington County	SD	Mark Beutow	1983	4385
155 3/8	24 4/8 24 5/8	21 3/8	5 5	Suffolk County	NY	John C. Wehrs	1984	4385
155 3/8	21 4/8 22 0/8	15 5/8	5 6	McKenzie County	ND	Brent Smith	1985	4385
155 3/8	23 7/8 23 6/8	16 5/8	5 5	Cherry County	NE	Gary Galloway	1985	4385
155 3/8	25 4/8 25 6/8	20 3/8	7 5	Pulaski County	MO	Bruce Agee	1986	4385
155 3/8	25 2/8 26 2/8	23 1/8	5 5	Sabine County	TX	Bobby Brundidge	1986	4385
155 3/8	29 6/8 28 7/8	20 7/8	5 6	Highland County	OH	William E. Lee, Jr.	1987	4385
155 3/8	24 6/8 24 5/8	18 1/8	5 5	Vermilion County	IL	Gary L. Wilford	1988	4385
155 3/8	26 3/8 25 4/8	20 0/8	4 5	Butler County	KS	Mike Demel	1990	4385
155 3/8	22 6/8 23 0/8	15 0/8	5 8	Menard County	IL	Norman Horn	1991	4385
155 3/8	24 0/8 24 1/8	16 5/8	5 5	Fillmore County	MN	Danny L. Cole	1991	4385
155 3/8	25 0/8 24 6/8	19 3/8	5 5	Dakota County	MN	Gene Lorentz	1992	4385
155 3/8	23 5/8 23 4/8	16 7/8	5 7	Breckinridge County	KY	John Goins	1993	4385
155 3/8	28 2/8 26 6/8	19 3/8	4 5	Stark County	OH	Bill Hall	1993	4385
155 3/8	24 4/8 24 0/8	17 1/8	7 6	Bates County	MO	Mike Wheeler	1996	4385
155 3/8	25 7/8 25 0/8	18 0/8	6 6	Ashland County	WI	Curt Walker	1996	4385
155 3/8	25 3/8 26 2/8	18 6/8	6 5	Tuscarawas County	OH	Ronnie L. Duplain, Sr	1996	4385
155 3/8	26 2/8 26 1/8	17 5/8	4 4	Washington County	MN	Tony Joseph	1996	4385
155 3/8	25 4/8 24 0/8	18 4/8	6 5	Coshocton County	OH	Mario Costanzo	1997	4385
155 3/8	25 2/8 25 6/8	21 0/8	5 5	Mercer County	IL	Dan Bergen	1997	4385
155 3/8	25 4/8 24 5/8	16 7/8	5 5	Howell County	MO	Carl Hicks	1997	4385
155 3/8	24 5/8 25 3/8	16 1/8	5 5	Nodaway County	MO	Tony Flora	1997	4385
155 3/8	24 3/8 24 4/8	16 7/8	5 5	Clayton County	IA	Jim Hankes	1997	4385
155 3/8	27 5/8 26 4/8	18 7/8	4 4	Jersey County	IL	Jeff Dugger	1998	4385
155 3/8	24 6/8 24 4/8	18 4/8	6 5	Trempealeau County	WI	Irvin L. Hovell	1998	4385
155 3/8	24 2/8 24 3/8	21 5/8	5 5	Monroe County	IA	Mike Ballew	1998	4385
155 3/8	24 3/8 24 5/8	18 1/8	5 5	Dunn County	WI	Todd Kostman	1999	4385
155 3/8	26 4/8 25 7/8	19 7/8	4 5	Washington County	NE	Saylor Clements	2000	4385
155 3/8	25 0/8 25 3/8	16 6/8	8 7	Lawrence County	OH	Larry Pinkerman	2000	4385
155 3/8	24 2/8 24 7/8	18 7/8	5 5	Wyoming County	WV	Eric R. Jennings	2001	4385
155 3/8	24 3/8 23 4/8	17 4/8	5 7	Washington County	WI	Scott Matula	2001	4385
155 3/8	25 7/8 25 3/8	23 7/8	5 5	Knox County	IL	Randy Stone	2001	4385
155 3/8	27 3/8 28 3/8	21 3/8	4 4	McHenry County	IL	Steven Schmieding	2001	4385
155 3/8	23 5/8 23 7/8	18 1/8	5 5	Will County	IL	Dale Hoekstra	2001	4385
155 3/8	24 4/8 24 5/8	15 6/8	6 8	Schuyler County	NY	Anthony J. Ventra	2001	4385
155 3/8	25 5/8 25 6/8	18 1/8	4 4	Porter County	IN	Donald M. Dolph	2002	4385
155 3/8	23 2/8 24 1/8	19 1/8	5 5	Chippewa County	WI	Bruce D. Olson	2002	4385
155 3/8	23 6/8 24 7/8	19 1/8	6 6	Erie County	NY	Daniel Damato	2002	4385
155 3/8	25 3/8 25 4/8	16 5/8	4 6	Monona County	IA	Larry M. Monell	2002	4385
155 3/8	26 1/8 24 7/8	24 1/8	6 8	Jo Daviess County	IL	Leonard Scarborough	2002	4385
155 3/8	24 4/8 24 6/8	16 5/8	6 6	Dallas County	IA	David R. Martin	2002	4385
155 3/8	22 7/8 23 1/8	20 1/8	7 7	Clayton County	IA	Nathaniel White	2002	4385
155 3/8	25 2/8 24 5/8	23 4/8	6 6	Daviess County	KY	Jeremy Higdon	2002	4385
155 3/8	23 1/8 23 5/8	18 5/8	5 5	Clark County	WI	Harold P. Frazee	2003	4385
155 3/8	23 6/8 24 0/8	17 7/8	6 6	Lawrence County	OH	Chad D. Hale	2003	4385
*155 3/8	23 3/8 23 4/8	17 1/8	6 5	Carlton County	MN	John Jones	2003	4385
155 3/8	24 5/8 24 1/8	16 7/8	5 5	Marion County	IA	Leonard Grimes	2003	4385
155 3/8	24 0/8 22 6/8	17 0/8	7 5	Green County	WI	Terry Plath	2004	4385
*155 3/8	24 0/8 23 5/8	18 1/8	5 5	Richardson County	NE	Jack D. Day, Sr.	2004	4385
155 3/8	23 0/8 23 2/8	18 7/8	6 6	Wright County	IA	Rick Brooks	2004	4385
155 3/8	22 3/8 22 2/8	18 3/8	5 5	Sheboygan County	WI	Todd Thiel	2004	4385
155 3/8	23 3/8 23 6/8	18 1/8	5 5	Woodbury County	IA	Tony C. Flesjer, Jr.	2005	4385
155 3/8	23 4/8 23 4/8	17 1/8	6 5	Appanoose County	IA	George D. Scott	2005	4385
155 3/8	24 4/8 23 2/8	17 7/8	5 5	Jersey County	IL	Ryan Niemeyer	2005	4385
155 3/8	25 4/8 25 4/8	21 5/8	4 7	Marion County	OH	Jeff Mitchell	2005	4385
155 3/8	24 4/8 25 5/8	18 5/8	5 4	Cass County	NE	Roger L. Kuhn	2005	4385
*155 3/8	23 4/8 22 2/8	18 4/8	6 6	Kankakee County	IL	Brian Kats	2006	4385
155 3/8	26 0/8 25 6/8	16 7/8	5 5	Ripley County	IN	Grant E. Brown	2006	4385
*155 3/8	24 7/8 24 2/8	18 7/8	8 10	Cass County	IL	Kenneth J. Klein	2006	4385
155 3/8	24 5/8 25 0/8	20 2/8	6 8	Cumberland County	IL	Jason Titus	2006	4385
155 3/8	24 4/8 24 4/8	19 4/8	5 6	Guilford County	NC	Joshua P. Readling	2007	4385
*155 3/8	24 6/8 23 5/8	16 7/8	7 6	Shelby County	IL	James Anderson	2007	4385
*155 3/8	25 4/8 26 0/8	18 3/8	4 5	Butler County	OH	Greg Grupenhof	2007	4385
155 3/8	25 3/8 25 4/8	17 7/8	5 6	Henderson County	KY	Robert W. Grubb	2007	4385
155 3/8	23 3/8 22 5/8	17 3/8	5 6	Kanawha County	WV	Dwight S. Buckner	2007	4385
155 3/8	29 0/8 30 5/8	19 4/8	5 5	La Salle County	IL	Everett Noble	2008	4385
155 3/8	25 3/8 25 2/8	18 4/8	8 6	Juneau County	WI	Steve Klicko	2008	4385
155 3/8	21 7/8 22 1/8	18 3/8	6 6	McMullen County	TX	Mark Ginn	2008	4385
*155 3/8	23 7/8 23 7/8	16 1/8	5 5	Pierce County	WI	Jim Fuchs	2009	4385
*155 3/8	25 0/8 24 6/8	18 3/8	7 6	Athens County	OH	William Haney	2009	4385
*155 3/8	25 2/8 25 0/8	18 3/8	9 7	Washington County	OH	Brad Biehl	2009	4385
155 3/8	25 0/8 25 4/8	22 7/8	5 5	Madison County	ID	Glen McRae	2009	4385
*155 3/8	24 5/8 25 4/8	17 4/8	5 7	Grant County	SD	Sean Pinkert	2009	4385
155 2/8	22 0/8 21 6/8	17 4/8	6 6	Benton County	IA	Gene Pollock	1958	4463
155 2/8	25 0/8 25 5/8	18 3/8	5 6	Floyd County	IA	Richard G. Long	1967	4463
155 2/8	26 4/8 25 4/8	15 2/8	6 6	Scott County	VA	Hugh McConnell	1978	4463

402

WHITETAIL DEER (TYPICAL ANTLERS)

Minimum Score 125   Continued

SCORE	LENGTH OF MAIN BEAM R	L	INSIDE SPREAD	NUMBER OF POINTS R	L	AREA	STATE/PROVINCE	HUNTER'S NAME	DATE	RANK
155 2/8	21 6/8	21 7/8	20 0/8	5	5	Des Moines County	IA	Brad Entsminger	1980	4463
155 2/8	24 5/8	24 2/8	15 4/8	5	6	Knox County	OH	Robert Hammond	1980	4463
155 2/8	23 7/8	24 3/8	17 1/8	5	6	Richland County	MT	Wynn Privratsky	1980	4463
155 2/8	25 3/8	25 4/8	18 4/8	5	5	Licking County	OH	Richard E Pipes	1984	4463
155 2/8	24 4/8	24 1/8	18 0/8	6	6	Lake County	MI	John Mudrovich	1984	4463
155 2/8	26 6/8	27 4/8	17 0/8	4	6	Allamakee County	IA	Ernie Burroughs	1985	4463
155 2/8	27 0/8	25 4/8	21 6/8	4	5	Ogle County	IL	Vernon Rasmussen	1986	4463
155 2/8	26 4/8	26 7/8	17 2/8	5	5	Holmes County	OH	Wanda L. Horwath	1988	4463
155 2/8	27 0/8	26 0/8	18 6/8	5	5	Buffalo County	WI	Gary R. Stutz	1988	4463
155 2/8	28 2/8	27 5/8	20 4/8	5	4	Parke County	IN	Charles Paxton	1989	4463
155 2/8	23 7/8	25 2/8	18 0/8	6	5	Jefferson County	KS	Leon Lemons	1989	4463
155 2/8	24 5/8	24 4/8	15 4/8	5	5	Burnett County	WI	William F. Hurley	1990	4463
155 2/8	24 7/8	24 6/8	20 2/8	5	6	Appanoose County	IA	Steven P. Salmieri	1990	4463
155 2/8	25 6/8	26 4/8	19 2/8	5	5	Monroe County	KY	Joyneta Wilkerson	1993	4463
155 2/8	23 7/8	23 4/8	16 6/8	5	5	Lawrence County	IL	Vergil Jerrell	1993	4463
155 2/8	26 7/8	26 5/8	17 0/8	6	6	Coles County	IL	Bill Davis	1994	4463
155 2/8	25 2/8	25 2/8	17 6/8	5	5	Waukesha County	WI	Donald Wehr	1994	4463
155 2/8	27 5/8	26 5/8	17 2/8	5	5	Beaver County	PA	Eric Kasunic	1994	4463
155 2/8	23 5/8	26 0/8	21 0/8	6	5	Franklin County	KY	Larry B. Goode	1995	4463
155 2/8	29 0/8	28 0/8	18 6/8	5	6	Warren County	IA	Mike Metz	1995	4463
155 2/8	23 5/8	23 6/8	15 6/8	6	6	Fayette County	IN	Chris L. Mustin	1995	4463
155 2/8	25 4/8	25 3/8	16 0/8	5	5	Northampton County	VA	D. Richard Felker II	1995	4463
155 2/8	23 6/8	24 4/8	19 4/8	5	4	McPherson County	KS	Kendall Shaw	1995	4463
155 2/8	26 4/8	25 4/8	18 6/8	5	5	Scott County	IA	Don Brunning	1996	4463
155 2/8	24 3/8	24 5/8	16 7/8	6	9	Osage County	KS	Mike Vandevord	1997	4463
155 2/8	24 6/8	24 7/8	17 4/8	5	5	Douglas County	WI	Kenneth W. Moen	1998	4463
155 2/8	24 4/8	24 1/8	21 6/8	5	7	Washington County	WI	Doug Hart	1998	4463
155 2/8	25 3/8	26 1/8	19 6/8	6	7	Kenosha County	WI	William J. Umnus	1998	4463
155 2/8	24 5/8	23 2/8	14 0/8	5	5	Cecil County	MD	John D. Matherly III	1999	4463
155 2/8	23 5/8	22 6/8	16 2/8	5	5	Racine County	WI	Mike Nowak	2000	4463
155 2/8	23 3/8	23 1/8	17 6/8	6	6	Fillmore County	MN	Jim Rislove	2000	4463
155 2/8	24 0/8	24 2/8	20 1/8	5	6	Morgan County	IL	John B. Luchini	2000	4463
155 2/8	23 6/8	23 7/8	18 4/8	9	7	Parkland	ALB	Frank J. Caza	2000	4463
155 2/8	25 7/8	25 3/8	20 0/8	5	5	York County	ME	Eric Childs	2002	4463
155 2/8	24 6/8	26 7/8	18 6/8	6	6	Daviess County	IN	Michael B. Toon	2002	4463
155 2/8	23 1/8	22 5/8	20 0/8	5	5	Monroe County	MO	Dallas Miller	2002	4463
155 2/8	27 4/8	28 7/8	20 2/8	5	5	Guilford County	NC	Rusty Moore	2002	4463
155 2/8	23 0/8	21 6/8	17 2/8	5	5	Marathon County	WI	Kurt A. Evje	2002	4463
155 2/8	26 3/8	26 2/8	19 0/8	4	5	McPherson County	KS	Marty Case	2002	4463
155 2/8	24 3/8	25 0/8	17 7/8	6	7	Buffalo County	WI	John M. Sabelko	2002	4463
155 2/8	22 4/8	22 1/8	19 2/8	6	5	Trempealeau County	WI	Dave Franck	2003	4463
155 2/8	23 5/8	24 0/8	20 2/8	5	5	Buffalo County	WI	Dave Beeler	2003	4463
155 2/8	23 4/8	23 6/8	20 6/8	5	5	Montgomery County	NY	John J. Tesi	2003	4463
155 2/8	26 5/8	25 0/8	20 0/8	4	5	La Crosse County	WI	Al Thurston	2003	4463
155 2/8	24 4/8	25 0/8	18 4/8	4	5	Minnehaha County	SD	Wayne Huebert	2004	4463
155 2/8	25 6/8	24 2/8	17 6/8	5	5	Will County	IL	Marco DiAnni	2005	4463
155 2/8	24 2/8	24 1/8	16 4/8	6	5	Sangamon County	IL	Rick Richno	2005	4463
155 2/8	24 4/8	24 6/8	18 0/8	5	5	Outagamie County	WI	Tony Ashauer	2006	4463
155 2/8	22 7/8	21 6/8	17 7/8	5	6	Winnebago County	IA	Michael D. Kirschbaum	2006	4463
*155 2/8	26 5/8	26 4/8	21 2/8	6	8	Waushara County	WI	Steven Robert Laudon	2007	4463
155 2/8	22 0/8	22 1/8	18 2/8	5	5	Ogle County	IL	Douglas P. McNames	2008	4463
*155 2/8	23 5/8	23 7/8	21 3/8	5	7	Leavenworth County	KS	Andrew Morgan	2008	4463
*155 2/8	25 0/8	24 4/8	21 4/8	4	4	Jasper County	IL	Jay King	2008	4463
155 2/8	24 1/8	23 4/8	17 6/8	5	7	Douglas County	WI	Rose Marie Janowicz	2008	4463
155 2/8	26 4/8	26 4/8	22 3/8	5	5	Edmonson County	KY	Darrell R. Basham	2009	4463
*155 2/8	24 0/8	24 0/8	18 5/8	7	7	Fulton County	IL	Tyson Rogers	2009	4463
155 2/8	25 1/8	25 0/8	15 7/8	6	5	Waupaca County	WI	Scott A. Bauman	2009	4463
155 2/8	24 0/8	26 0/8	18 0/8	4	4	McDonough County	IL	Beau Below	2009	4463
*155 2/8	24 2/8	24 4/8	16 2/8	5	5	Wayne County	MI	Bradley Scott Slaven	2009	4463
*155 2/8	26 0/8	24 0/8	17 0/8	5	5	Trempealeau County	WI	Steve Podjaski	2010	4463
155 1/8	24 7/8	24 7/8	17 3/8	5	5	Roberts County	SD	Roland L. Hausmann	1959	4526
155 1/8	25 2/8	24 7/8	19 3/8	6	6	Madison County	KY	Sonny Barker	1965	4526
155 1/8	25 6/8	25 0/8	19 7/8	6	5	Morrison County	MN	Timothy L. Kampa	1984	4526
155 1/8	24 7/8	25 7/8	19 7/8	5	5	Calhoun County	MI	Steve D. Munier	1985	4526
155 1/8	29 0/8	26 6/8	22 0/8	5	4	Vermilion County	IL	Allen Walker	1986	4526
155 1/8	25 7/8	25 4/8	17 3/8	5	5	Pawnee County	KS	Carol Moffatt	1986	4526
155 1/8	24 4/8	24 7/8	16 7/8	5	5	Barron County	WI	Tom Lindquist	1987	4526
155 1/8	25 4/8	26 7/8	19 7/8	6	5	Allegan County	MI	Craig S. Shaw	1989	4526
155 1/8	24 1/8	23 2/8	14 6/8	8	6	Chisago County	MN	James Lehman	1990	4526
155 1/8	24 2/8	23 7/8	22 7/8	5	5	Clermont County	OH	Paul L. Voshell	1992	4526
155 1/8	25 0/8	25 3/8	21 2/8	7	5	Will County	IL	Mike D. Francus	1992	4526
155 1/8	23 5/8	23 2/8	15 3/8	5	5	Allamakee County	IA	Brian Keuning	1992	4526
155 1/8	25 0/8	24 5/8	19 3/8	4	5	Sherburne County	MN	Cary Larson	1994	4526
155 1/8	28 4/8	27 0/8	19 3/8	5	6	Linn County	IA	Dan Andrews	1994	4526
155 1/8	26 1/8	27 3/8	18 3/8	7	5	Columbia County	WI	Douglas A. Jarzynski	1995	4526
155 1/8	24 0/8	23 2/8	17 1/8	6	5	Coles County	IL	Cliff Campbell	1995	4526
155 1/8	25 5/8	26 2/8	20 4/8	6	6	Charles Mix County	SD	Justin Plooster	1995	4526
155 1/8	26 6/8	25 7/8	19 3/8	5	6	Butler County	KS	Jeffrey Howington	1995	4526
155 1/8	24 0/8	24 2/8	18 7/8	5	6	Pipestone County	MN	Jim Lorenzen	1995	4526
155 1/8	24 6/8	24 7/8	21 4/8	6	5	Plymouth County	IA	Guy H. Hempey	1997	4526
155 1/8	23 7/8	23 6/8	20 4/8	6	6	Dane County	WI	Mike Padrutt	1997	4526
155 1/8	21 7/8	21 7/8	19 6/8	6	5	Outagamie County	WI	Neil P. Merkes	1998	4526
155 1/8	24 0/8	22 2/8	17 3/8	5	6	Johnson County	IA	Pat Ogden	1998	4526
155 1/8	24 1/8	26 4/8	26 6/8	4	7	Waukesha County	WI	Rodney J. Luchinske	1998	4526
155 1/8	23 0/8	23 3/8	15 1/8	5	5	Warren County	MS	Jim Agent	1998	4526
155 1/8	25 6/8	25 5/8	19 1/8	5	6	Franklin County	IN	Dustin Fee	1999	4526
155 1/8	25 3/8	25 6/8	19 1/8	5	5	Christian County	IL	Jim Davis	1999	4526
155 1/8	23 6/8	24 4/8	19 1/8	5	5	Comanche County	KS	Michael Stegman	1999	4526
155 1/8	24 7/8	24 5/8	17 7/8	5	5	Washtenaw County	MI	Darrin Gotts	2000	4526
155 1/8	24 6/8	25 5/8	18 3/8	6	5	Fayette County	WV	David Kinningham	2000	4526
155 1/8	24 6/8	24 6/8	23 3/8	5	5	Clermont County	OH	Andy Bankemper	2000	4526
155 1/8	24 3/8	24 3/8	20 1/8	5	5	Seward County	KS	James Matuszewski	2000	4526
155 1/8	24 4/8	21 1/8	17 5/8	5	5	Macon County	IL	Mark Beck	2001	4526
155 1/8	25 6/8	26 0/8	18 2/8	5	6	Buffalo County	WI	Mark Beeler	2002	4526
*155 1/8	23 4/8	22 7/8	16 5/8	5	6	Livingston County	NY	Jason D. Wolfanger	2003	4526

403

WHITETAIL DEER (TYPICAL ANTLERS)

Minimum Score 125 — Continued

SCORE	LENGTH OF MAIN BEAM R	L	INSIDE SPREAD	NUMBER OF POINTS R	L	AREA	STATE/ PROVINCE	HUNTER'S NAME	DATE	RANK
155 1/8	23 5/8	24 3/8	17 1/8	5	5	Meigs County	OH	Eric R. Smith	2003	4526
155 1/8	26 1/8	23 7/8	17 6/8	5	5	McCurtain County	OK	John Winship	2003	4526
155 1/8	22 5/8	23 3/8	19 1/8	5	5	Dickson County	TN	Joe L. Uselton	2004	4526
155 1/8	24 7/8	23 7/8	17 5/8	6	5	Hopkins County	KY	Michael L. Gibson	2004	4526
155 1/8	26 2/8	27 3/8	21 6/8	4	5	Clark County	OH	Noel Coy	2004	4526
*155 1/8	26 2/8	26 4/8	18 5/8	4	5	Washington County	IN	Bobby Parker, Jr.	2004	4526
155 1/8	23 6/8	25 0/8	17 7/8	5	6	Fulton County	IL	Charles L. Tanski	2004	4526
*155 1/8	23 4/8	24 0/8	17 5/8	5	5	Washington County	OH	Michael F. Burkhart	2004	4526
155 1/8	27 3/8	26 5/8	17 7/8	7	5	Atchison County	MO	Chris Barton	2004	4526
155 1/8	23 6/8	24 3/8	20 2/8	5	5	Buffalo County	WI	Chad E. Thompson	2004	4526
155 1/8	23 7/8	23 7/8	15 0/8	7	7	Marion County	IA	Kyle Goodwin	2005	4526
155 1/8	23 3/8	23 2/8	13 7/8	6	6	Bottineau County	ND	Brent Moum	2005	4526
*155 1/8	28 3/8	28 1/8	21 0/8	5	4	Belknap County	NH	Mike Amaral	2006	4526
155 1/8	26 5/8	26 2/8	18 4/8	6	7	Washington County	WI	Eric Bell	2007	4526
155 1/8	25 3/8	25 5/8	19 5/8	6	5	Cass County	NE	Allan Dangerfield	2007	4526
*155 1/8	26 2/8	26 0/8	19 5/8	6	5	Harper County	KS	Jonathan Gregory	2007	4526
155 1/8	23 1/8	23 7/8	16 1/8	5	6	Arkansas County	AR	Ed McKinley	2008	4526
*155 1/8	24 0/8	24 6/8	17 3/8	5	5	Clark County	IL	Brian A. McCammon	2008	4526
155 1/8	24 0/8	26 0/8	18 4/8	6	4	Erie County	NY	Raymond Wolford	2008	4526
*155 1/8	26 2/8	27 3/8	22 7/8	4	4	Shawano County	WI	Grant Bystol	2008	4526
155 1/8	24 6/8	24 5/8	16 7/8	6	5	Polk County	IA	Kevin Freymiller	2008	4526
155 1/8	22 3/8	22 2/8	18 3/8	5	5	Vernon County	MO	Kirk Buck	2009	4526
*155 1/8	25 1/8	24 6/8	17 7/8	5	5	Branch County	MI	Bret R. Cary	2009	4526
155 1/8	23 3/8	22 2/8	19 4/8	7	9	Buffalo County	WI	Keith Karlen	2009	4526
155 1/8	23 3/8	23 1/8	20 3/8	6	6	Franklin County	NE	Derek Ingram	2009	4526
155 1/8	22 1/8	23 4/8	17 1/8	5	5	Phillips County	KS	John "Jack" Cordes	2009	4526
155 0/8	23 7/8	24 5/8	18 6/8	7	7	Pope County	MN	John Myhre	1982	4587
155 0/8	24 6/8	24 1/8	22 7/8	6	7	Montgomery County	IL	Keith Pierce	1983	4587
155 0/8	20 5/8	24 0/8	15 7/8	9	7	Lee County	IA	Ralph D. Zaehringer	1985	4587
155 0/8	23 5/8	22 2/8	18 5/8	8	7	Clayton County	IA	Daniel L. Parker	1986	4587
155 0/8	25 2/8	26 6/8	17 1/8	6	5	Barber County	KS	Robert Ricke	1987	4587
155 0/8	24 7/8	24 6/8	16 4/8	6	5	Wayne County	MO	Steve Rueck	1988	4587
155 0/8	25 3/8	25 1/8	18 6/8	7	8	Sawyer County	WI	Greg Peterson	1989	4587
155 0/8	24 0/8	24 5/8	17 7/8	7	5	Jefferson County	WI	Scott Bolson	1989	4587
155 0/8	27 1/8	26 2/8	21 2/8	5	7	St. Clair County	IL	Andy T. Contratto	1989	4587
155 0/8	22 2/8	24 3/8	17 4/8	4	4	Wapello County	IA	Larry Johns	1990	4587
155 0/8	23 6/8	23 1/8	18 4/8	6	6	Coffey County	KS	David W. Bess	1990	4587
155 0/8	25 0/8	25 4/8	16 6/8	5	4	Marion County	KS	Ron Hershberger	1990	4587
155 0/8	25 1/8	25 0/8	18 6/8	6	5	Polk County	MN	Steven Cornell	1990	4587
155 0/8	25 7/8	25 4/8	18 0/8	5	5	Pope County	MN	Bradley D. Rosten	1991	4587
155 0/8	27 4/8	27 3/8	23 6/8	5	6	Bent County	CO	Jay Waring	1991	4587
155 0/8	26 4/8	25 1/8	19 4/8	7	4	Caroline County	MD	Jeff Towers	1991	4587
155 0/8	22 2/8	21 6/8	23 1/8	5	6	Codington County	SD	Marty Lukonen	1993	4587
155 0/8	24 0/8	24 1/8	18 4/8	5	6	Ogle County	IL	Douglas McNames	1994	4587
155 0/8	23 2/8	22 4/8	19 4/8	5	5	Union County	KY	Tony Noe	1994	4587
155 0/8	26 0/8	24 2/8	19 0/8	5	5	Jefferson County	KY	John Gutterman	1995	4587
155 0/8	25 6/8	26 7/8	20 4/8	5	5	Washington County	WI	Jeffrey R. Gall	1996	4587
155 0/8	22 6/8	22 4/8	17 6/8	7	5	Scott County	IA	John S. Carlin	1996	4587
155 0/8	25 0/8	24 3/8	20 0/8	6	5	Montgomery County	IL	Marty Leitschuh	1996	4587
155 0/8	25 1/8	24 0/8	15 2/8	4	4	Garfield County	NE	Jeff Breitkreutz	1997	4587
155 0/8	24 1/8	24 5/8	17 5/8	7	7	Decatur County	IA	Richard Panke	1997	4587
155 0/8	24 3/8	24 2/8	17 2/8	5	6	Washington County	IA	John Sabel	1997	4587
155 0/8	26 1/8	26 3/8	21 5/8	6	8	Logan County	WV	Harold Sayers	1997	4587
155 0/8	24 3/8	24 7/8	18 6/8	7	6	Greene County	IA	Matt Carlson	1997	4587
155 0/8	25 4/8	26 4/8	18 2/8	5	5	Scott County	MN	Derrick Long	1998	4587
155 0/8	26 1/8	26 5/8	18 2/8	5	5	Washington County	WI	Benjamin A. Curtes	1998	4587
155 0/8	24 3/8	25 5/8	21 2/8	5	5	Tioga County	NY	Shane Marshall	1998	4587
155 0/8	23 6/8	24 1/8	18 5/8	6	5	Greene County	IL	Dale Sandage	1998	4587
155 0/8	25 4/8	24 0/8	20 2/8	6	5	Will County	IL	Peter Voss	1998	4587
155 0/8	28 1/8	27 3/8	20 5/8	5	4	Gallatin County	IL	Michael Reehle	1999	4587
155 0/8	26 6/8	25 3/8	20 6/8	5	6	Polk County	IA	Dan Warren	1999	4587
155 0/8	23 6/8	23 4/8	19 2/8	5	6	Russell	MAN	Mike Guenther	2000	4587
155 0/8	25 6/8	26 1/8	18 0/8	6	6	De Kalb County	IN	Dave Hurley	2000	4587
155 0/8	23 2/8	23 2/8	20 0/8	6	9	Bond County	IL	Steve Stinnett	2000	4587
155 0/8	25 1/8	25 4/8	19 0/8	6	5	Marquette County	WI	Gregory R. Clark	2000	4587
155 0/8	26 4/8	26 3/8	15 7/8	4	5	Clayton County	IA	Dan Thole	2000	4587
155 0/8	24 1/8	22 2/8	16 0/8	4	4	Greenwood County	KS	Rodney Alexander	2000	4587
155 0/8	22 7/8	22 6/8	18 6/8	6	5	Prowers County	CO	John Westfall	2000	4587
155 0/8	23 1/8	23 2/8	18 4/8	8	7	Clayton County	IA	Kyle Kuehl	2002	4587
155 0/8	22 4/8	22 4/8	18 1/8	5	7	Peoria County	IL	Ross Edwards	2002	4587
155 0/8	22 7/8	22 2/8	16 6/8	5	5	Mingo County	WV	Isaac Walters	2002	4587
155 0/8	25 0/8	25 2/8	16 6/8	6	5	Grayson County	KY	Charles Van Meter	2003	4587
155 0/8	24 4/8	24 3/8	19 6/8	5	5	Livingston County	IL	Bob Long	2003	4587
*155 0/8	24 7/8	25 4/8	20 4/8	5	5	Racine County	WI	Terry Weis	2003	4587
155 0/8	25 6/8	25 4/8	17 0/8	4	4	Kane County	IL	Ray Schremp	2003	4587
*155 0/8	26 2/8	26 4/8	19 6/8	6	5	Decatur County	IA	William M. Adrianse	2004	4587
*155 0/8	21 3/8	21 6/8	21 5/8	6	5	Shelby County	IL	Jim Schnell	2004	4587
*155 0/8	26 0/8	26 4/8	20 6/8	4	5	Franklin County	IN	Jim Carley	2004	4587
*155 0/8	24 0/8	23 2/8	18 6/8	5	5	Dickinson County	KS	Adam Beason	2004	4587
155 0/8	23 5/8	23 1/8	17 6/8	5	5	Outagamie County	WI	Rob Ruys	2005	4587
*155 0/8	23 6/8	24 0/8	18 2/8	5	6	Fulton County	IL	Frank J. Mancuso	2005	4587
155 0/8	21 1/8	22 4/8	15 2/8	5	5	Buffalo County	WI	Chris Barry	2005	4587
155 0/8	27 0/8	27 0/8	20 4/8	5	5	Winona County	MN	Kurt Knuesel	2005	4587
155 0/8	23 1/8	23 2/8	19 0/8	4	5	Daviess County	IN	Jon Webster	2005	4587
155 0/8	27 2/8	27 5/8	21 2/8	6	7	Worcester County	MD	Jack W. Lynch	2005	4587
155 0/8	24 7/8	25 1/8	16 6/8	6	9	Page County	IA	Chris Barton	2005	4587
*155 0/8	23 3/8	23 0/8	17 5/8	7	6	Jefferson County	IA	James M. Burton	2006	4587
155 0/8	25 6/8	24 4/8	18 2/8	6	5	Noble County	OH	Matthew Sustaric	2006	4587
155 0/8	23 2/8	22 5/8	15 5/8	7	7	Poweshiek County	IA	Robert White	2007	4587
155 0/8	23 6/8	24 1/8	16 7/8	5	6	Buffalo County	WI	Joe Leschke	2007	4587
*155 0/8	26 2/8	25 1/8	21 1/8	8	7	Highland County	OH	Brian Christopher	2007	4587
155 0/8	24 0/8	27 6/8	20 1/8	7	6	Holmes County	OH	Joseph Kauffman	2008	4587
*155 0/8	22 2/8	22 5/8	18 6/8	5	6	Iroquois County	IL	Raymond Holohan	2008	4587
*155 0/8	25 6/8	25 2/8	17 2/8	6	5	Wabash County	IL	Ray Penrod	2008	4587
*155 0/8	25 5/8	23 7/8	21 0/8	7	7	Barnes County	ND	Jon Skalicky	2009	4587

404

WHITETAIL DEER (TYPICAL ANTLERS)

Minimum Score 125   Continued

SCORE	LENGTH OF R MAIN BEAM L	INSIDE SPREAD	NUMBER OF R POINTS L	AREA	STATE/ PROVINCE	HUNTER'S NAME	DATE	RANK
*155 0/8	23 2/8 23 4/8	17 0/8	5 5	Sterling County	TX	Ryan Dupriest	2009	4587
*155 0/8	24 0/8 24 5/8	17 4/8	5 6	Fillmore County	MN	Joel Goodman	2009	4587
155 0/8	25 7/8 25 2/8	19 6/8	5 5	Walworth County	WI	Randy J. Hackbarth	2009	4587
155 0/8	23 4/8 23 1/8	18 4/8	6 6	Worth County	IA	Mark Yates	2009	4587
154 7/8	26 7/8 25 7/8	18 2/8	5 5	Murray County	MN	Craig Cohrs	1968	4660
154 7/8	26 5/8 25 6/8	17 6/8	7 8	Pendleton County	KY	Thomas P. Jones	1969	4660
154 7/8	22 5/8 23 2/8	23 1/8	6 6	Auglaize County	OH	Gary L. Dues	1979	4660
154 7/8	23 4/8 23 5/8	16 4/8	5 4	Kingsbury County	SD	Dan R. Limmer	1981	4660
154 7/8	23 0/8 24 0/8	19 5/8	5 5	Hennepin County	MN	Harold Greseth	1983	4660
154 7/8	23 4/8 23 7/8	16 4/8	10 6	Lincoln County	MN	Paul Erickson	1983	4660
154 7/8	24 2/8 23 6/8	19 1/8	4 5	Blue Earth County	MN	Rory Deutchman	1984	4660
154 7/8	24 1/8 24 5/8	19 5/8	6 5	Dane County	WI	Casey A. Blum	1986	4660
154 7/8	25 3/8 24 5/8	23 5/8	5 5	Nelson County	KY	Tom Blincoe	1987	4660
154 7/8	26 7/8 26 2/8	15 4/8	4 7	Mason County	IL	Mark Meyer	1988	4660
154 7/8	24 4/8 25 7/8	18 4/8	7 6	Washtenaw County	MI	William G. Knight	1988	4660
154 7/8	24 7/8 26 4/8	21 7/8	7 5	Morris County	NJ	Craig Werder	1989	4660
154 7/8	23 3/8 24 4/8	16 1/8	6 5	Traill County	ND	Paul Teegarden	1990	4660
154 7/8	24 4/8 24 2/8	17 1/8	7 7	Brown County	WI	Michael J. Rasmussen	1990	4660
154 7/8	24 4/8 24 6/8	21 5/8	5 4	Champaign County	IL	Robert A. Bryant	1990	4660
154 7/8	25 5/8 25 0/8	19 7/8	5 5	Massac County	IL	Terry B. Lewis	1990	4660
154 7/8	23 5/8 24 2/8	17 6/8	6 5	Dakota County	MN	Thomas Leach, Jr.	1991	4660
154 7/8	23 0/8 23 3/8	20 5/8	6 6	Bureau County	IL	Gregory A. Bowers	1991	4660
154 7/8	25 3/8 24 1/8	15 6/8	5 6	McLean County	IL	Daniel Rogers	1991	4660
154 7/8	25 2/8 25 4/8	18 5/8	7 6	Edmunds County	SD	Russell D. Leair	1992	4660
154 7/8	24 0/8 24 2/8	18 5/8	5 5	Cass County	MI	Scott E. Grice	1993	4660
154 7/8	25 2/8 25 3/8	18 7/8	5 5	Hancock County	IL	Tim Hiland	1994	4660
154 7/8	24 0/8 23 5/8	18 1/8	5 5	Webster County	IA	Dennis Vulgamott	1994	4660
154 7/8	26 0/8 24 6/8	20 7/8	4 5	Lake County	IL	Alvin Roberts	1994	4660
154 7/8	25 2/8 26 1/8	20 5/8	5 4	Johnson County	IA	Darrel Ballantyne	1995	4660
154 7/8	26 0/8 26 0/8	18 3/8	5 5	Page County	IA	Bob Athen	1996	4660
154 7/8	28 4/8 26 4/8	18 7/8	6 5	Madison County	MS	Rusty Crawford	1997	4660
154 7/8	24 2/8 23 6/8	20 3/8	6 5	Union County	OH	Brad LeMaster	1999	4660
154 7/8	26 5/8 27 2/8	20 2/8	8 7	Clermont County	OH	Jim K. Kuntz	1999	4660
154 7/8	22 6/8 23 2/8	20 3/8	5 5	Marquette County	WI	Jeff J. Winn	1999	4660
154 7/8	24 4/8 25 0/8	19 5/8	4 4	Poweshiek County	IA	Jim Hall	2000	4660
154 7/8	23 1/8 23 4/8	19 7/8	5 5	Marion County	MO	Kyn Gordon	2000	4660
154 7/8	25 4/8 25 3/8	18 5/8	5 5	La Crosse County	WI	Terry Larson	2000	4660
154 7/8	26 0/8 26 1/8	20 3/8	5 5	Buffalo County	WI	Rod Springborn	2000	4660
154 7/8	25 6/8 26 0/8	23 5/8	5 4	Waushara County	WI	Robert E. Mitchell	2000	4660
154 7/8	26 1/8 25 2/8	18 4/8	7 6	Coshocton County	OH	Terry Watson	2000	4660
154 7/8	27 0/8 27 6/8	22 5/8	7 6	Pike County	IL	Corey Melton	2001	4660
154 7/8	23 1/8 22 7/8	16 3/8	7 5	Madison County	IA	Eric L. Rooney	2002	4660
154 7/8	23 4/8 23 2/8	16 6/8	6 5	Linn County	IA	Mike Feuerbach	2003	4660
154 7/8	24 5/8 24 6/8	18 2/8	5 6	Monroe County	NY	Dan Dutton	2003	4660
154 7/8	23 3/8 23 5/8	13 1/8	7 6	Clay County	SD	Kevin Johnson	2003	4660
154 7/8	24 6/8 24 2/8	20 2/8	5 6	Dubuque County	IA	F. Michael Gruber	2004	4660
154 7/8	25 0/8 25 5/8	18 7/8	5 5	Monroe County	WI	Jonathan Stakston	2004	4660
154 7/8	24 1/8 24 1/8	21 7/8	5 5	Plymouth County	IA	Chad Ping	2004	4660
154 7/8	22 1/8 22 0/8	17 6/8	5 6	Custer County	MT	Scott L. Koelzer	2005	4660
154 7/8	25 4/8 25 7/8	17 4/8	8 8	Marquette County	WI	Rick Bolton	2006	4660
*154 7/8	24 2/8 23 3/8	18 4/8	6 6	Calumet County	WI	Andrew Schumacher	2006	4660
154 7/8	25 0/8 24 3/8	17 3/8	5 5	Bucks County	PA	Jared R. Kipp	2007	4660
154 7/8	25 4/8 25 2/8	17 5/8	5 5	Pepin County	WI	Craig Brusky	2007	4660
154 7/8	23 6/8 22 4/8	15 0/8	6 6	Cowley County	KS	Stephen C. Van Hoose	2007	4660
*154 7/8	27 3/8 27 5/8	20 1/8	4 4	Vernon County	WI	Lee M. Sheldon	2008	4660
154 7/8	23 5/8 23 6/8	16 1/8	5 5	Sanborn County	SD	Robert Fuerst	2008	4660
154 7/8	23 6/8 23 6/8	21 5/8	5 5	Pierce County	WI	Jonathan Sgarlata	2008	4660
154 7/8	23 2/8 23 4/8	19 1/8	5 5	Madison County	MS	Bob Lloyd	2008	4660
154 7/8	25 6/8 25 5/8	17 4/8	7 8	Tuscarawas County	OH	Steve Archer	2009	4660
*154 7/8	26 4/8 26 4/8	20 6/8	8 7	Sauk County	WI	Scott W. Steinhorst	2009	4660
154 7/8	26 6/8 26 1/8	17 4/8	5 5	Queen Annes County	MD	Kent Uhrich	2009	4660
154 6/8	24 1/8 22 5/8	17 2/8	5 5	Minnehaha County	SD	Clifford Sudenga	1962	4717
154 6/8	25 1/8 25 1/8	21 0/8	5 4	Cottonwood County	MN	Rodney Bailey	1975	4717
154 6/8	24 0/8 23 0/8	18 4/8	5 5	Van Buren County	MI	Rick Reese	1980	4717
154 6/8	24 7/8 25 6/8	20 0/8	5 5	Gray County	KS	Allen D. Bailey	1980	4717
154 6/8	25 1/8 21 7/8	18 4/8	6 4	Mills County	IA	Doug Roll	1985	4717
154 6/8	24 6/8 24 6/8	19 4/8	6 6	Seward County	KS	Lynn Leonard	1987	4717
154 6/8	23 1/8 23 4/8	16 2/8	5 5	Wright County	MN	Rob Johnson	1987	4717
154 6/8	24 5/8 24 4/8	18 3/8	6 5	Lincoln County	NE	Timothy M. Budin	1990	4717
154 6/8	25 6/8 26 5/8	16 2/8	9 7	Pike County	IL	Stan Chamberlain	1990	4717
154 6/8	24 2/8 24 7/8	18 2/8	8 6	Taylor County	WI	Barry Kappel	1991	4717
154 6/8	24 0/8 24 4/8	17 3/8	7 5	Des Moines County	IA	Daniel W. Wegener	1991	4717
154 6/8	25 0/8 25 5/8	20 4/8	5 5	Lewis County	KY	Alfred Lee Simms	1992	4717
154 6/8	26 2/8 25 6/8	19 4/8	5 5	Anoka County	MN	Randy Gajeski	1993	4717
154 6/8	24 4/8 23 6/8	23 0/8	5 5	Macoupin County	IL	Michael Dalton	1994	4717
154 6/8	24 2/8 26 2/8	18 2/8	5 5	Marinette County	WI	Mitch Vincent	1994	4717
154 6/8	24 6/8 24 3/8	18 0/8	6 5	Carroll County	IL	Harry R. Charneski	1994	4717
154 6/8	24 3/8 25 0/8	20 6/8	5 5	Jackson County	IA	David W. Schrody	1994	4717
154 6/8	25 7/8 26 2/8	20 7/8	4 5	Somerset County	NJ	Vincent Mancini	1995	4717
154 6/8	26 3/8 25 7/8	18 7/8	5 6	Ross County	OH	Brian Sowers	1995	4717
154 6/8	26 0/8 25 7/8	20 4/8	4 4	Marshall County	IL	Jeff Neuhalfen	1996	4717
154 6/8	26 6/8 26 3/8	18 4/8	5 5	Cedar County	NE	David B. Cull	1997	4717
154 6/8	24 7/8 24 7/8	21 5/8	6 5	Waukesha County	WI	Mike Scaff	1997	4717
154 6/8	26 1/8 25 0/8	18 2/8	5 5	Union County	IL	Andy Sadler	1997	4717
154 6/8	22 6/8 23 4/8	18 2/8	5 5	Dakota County	MN	Brian T. Lemay	1998	4717
154 6/8	24 3/8 25 0/8	17 0/8	5 5	Waupaca County	WI	Mike Crist	1998	4717
154 6/8	22 6/8 22 2/8	21 5/8	6 5	Fulton County	IL	Nate Walz	1999	4717
154 6/8	25 0/8 25 3/8	18 4/8	5 5	Jackson County	MO	Jonathon McGinness	1999	4717
154 6/8	27 4/8 26 1/8	18 4/8	4 5	Carroll County	IN	Marc Bruce	2000	4717
154 6/8	25 0/8 24 0/8	19 1/8	5 6	Dunn County	WI	Kevin M. Reitz	2000	4717
154 6/8	24 4/8 23 1/8	22 3/8	5 7	Onondaga County	NY	Peter Lucyszyn	2000	4717
154 6/8	23 4/8 22 2/8	18 2/8	5 5	Dodge County	WI	James Schoen	2001	4717
154 6/8	27 3/8 26 5/8	17 4/8	5 6	St. Clair County	IL	Michael A. Gantner	2001	4717
154 6/8	23 5/8 24 4/8	17 7/8	6 5	McDonough County	IL	Jack Laverdiere	2001	4717
154 6/8	25 1/8 25 4/8	17 6/8	6 6	Guernsey County	OH	William Bender, Jr.	2002	4717

WHITETAIL DEER (TYPICAL ANTLERS)

Minimum Score 125 — Continued

SCORE	LENGTH OF MAIN BEAM R	LENGTH OF MAIN BEAM L	INSIDE SPREAD	NUMBER OF POINTS R	NUMBER OF POINTS L	AREA	STATE/PROVINCE	HUNTER'S NAME	DATE	RANK
154 6/8	26 5/8	25 3/8	20 2/8	5	5	Pike County	IL	Jarrett Morgan	2002	4717
154 6/8	22 3/8	23 0/8	20 0/8	5	5	Tippecanoe County	IN	John Bowlin	2003	4717
154 6/8	23 4/8	23 2/8	18 2/8	4	5	Strathcona	ALB	Wayne Sheridan	2003	4717
154 6/8	24 6/8	23 6/8	22 2/8	5	7	Boone County	MO	Hamil B. Goen, Jr.	2004	4717
154 6/8	21 6/8	22 4/8	16 0/8	5	5	Wilson County	KS	Warren C. Townsenc	2004	4717
154 6/8	23 1/8	25 2/8	16 6/8	5	5	Anoka County	MN	Jason Gulbranson	2004	4717
*154 6/8	23 6/8	24 4/8	21 2/8	5	5	Chester County	PA	Ryan R. Shrum	2004	4717
*154 6/8	24 4/8	24 4/8	15 4/8	7	7	McDowell County	WV	Jerry M. Elliott	2004	4717
*154 6/8	26 5/8	26 0/8	15 6/8	6	5	Clay County	IN	Mark Harbin	2005	4717
154 6/8	23 1/8	24 0/8	20 3/8	5	6	Pepin County	WI	Richard Bauer	2006	4717
154 6/8	25 3/8	25 6/8	19 4/8	6	5	Tazewell County	IL	Kerry Lusher	2006	4717
*154 6/8	28 2/8	28 6/8	19 0/8	8	6	Webster County	IA	Robert Ramthun	2006	4717
154 6/8	24 0/8	23 4/8	22 1/8	6	7	Denton County	TX	Micah Daboub	2006	4717
*154 6/8	22 2/8	23 0/8	19 0/8	5	5	Bandera County	TX	Ray Turner	2007	4717
154 6/8	21 4/8	20 5/8	19 0/8	5	5	La Salle County	IL	Everett Brown	2007	4717
154 6/8	26 5/8	25 5/8	19 6/8	5	5	Shelby County	OH	Chris Walker	2007	4717
154 6/8	24 2/8	24 0/8	18 6/8	5	5	Lafayette County	WI	Lance Flannery	2007	4717
154 6/8	25 3/8	25 3/8	21 4/8	4	4	Washington County	MN	Mike Duppong	2007	4717
*154 6/8	25 1/8	24 1/8	18 0/8	6	7	Nicollet County	MN	Dan Doman	2008	4717
154 6/8	25 0/8	24 2/8	18 4/8	4	4	Athens County	OH	Chris Callahan	2008	4717
*154 6/8	24 6/8	25 0/8	18 0/8	5	5	Anne Arundel County	MD	Steven M. Sylvester, Jr.	2008	4717
154 6/8	22 4/8	22 2/8	16 0/8	5	5	Richland County	WI	Jay Petermann	2008	4717
154 6/8	24 3/8	24 1/8	18 6/8	5	5	Barron County	WI	Jon Fenske	2009	4717
154 6/8	25 0/8	25 2/8	20 0/8	6	7	Clinton County	MI	Roland H. Hensley	2009	4717
*154 6/8	24 7/8	25 2/8	18 6/8	6	5	Camden County	MO	Scott Wanko	2009	4717
*154 6/8	25 2/8	25 3/8	18 2/8	5	5	Buffalo County	WI	Tony Heil	2010	4717
154 5/8	25 4/8	26 2/8	18 6/8	5	6	Jackson County	MN	Eugene C. La Maack	1955	4777
154 5/8	23 7/8	24 0/8	20 7/8	4	4	Buchanan County	IA	Frank Sanderson	1983	4777
154 5/8	25 4/8	24 5/8	21 3/8	4	4	Anne Arundel County	MD	Jim Roy	1984	4777
154 5/8	24 3/8	25 4/8	17 2/8	7	8	Miami County	KS	Gary Wurdack	1985	4777
154 5/8	26 1/8	25 4/8	21 3/8	4	4	Dunnville	ONT	Randy Robins	1985	4777
154 5/8	26 2/8	26 3/8	18 3/8	5	5	Kingman County	KS	Dan J. Jacobs	1985	4777
154 5/8	25 3/8	26 0/8	19 2/8	5	5	Scott County	IA	Howard A. Goettsch	1987	4777
154 5/8	25 6/8	25 6/8	19 3/8	5	5	Pierce County	WI	Greg Koehler	1987	4777
154 5/8	22 0/8	25 0/8	19 1/8	5	5	Henderson County	IL	Timothy H. Allaman	1989	4777
154 5/8	25 3/8	23 0/8	22 6/8	8	5	McLean County	IL	Marvin RexRoat	1990	4777
154 5/8	26 3/8	25 5/8	19 3/8	7	6	Gallia County	OH	Darres Craig	1990	4777
154 5/8	23 6/8	24 5/8	16 2/8	7	5	Lincoln County	MO	Scott Hager	1991	4777
154 5/8	24 4/8	24 7/8	17 5/8	5	5	Will County	IL	Rick Johns	1991	4777
154 5/8	22 4/8	22 2/8	19 0/8	7	9	La Salle County	TX	Francis D. Elias	1992	4777
154 5/8	24 0/8	22 1/8	20 5/8	6	7	Wyandotte County	KS	Earl A. Cooksey	1992	4777
154 5/8	27 7/8	27 4/8	21 7/8	5	5	Charles County	MD	Frank J. Furr	1993	4777
154 5/8	24 4/8	23 0/8	16 6/8	6	6	Stewart County	TN	Barry A. Elkins	1994	4777
154 5/8	23 6/8	23 5/8	18 5/8	5	5	Nodaway County	MO	Max Harden	1996	4777
154 5/8	22 4/8	22 0/8	19 0/8	6	6	Union County	KY	Jason Wooldridge	1997	4777
154 5/8	26 2/8	26 4/8	20 5/8	6	5	Effingham County	IL	Philip R. Burke	1997	4777
154 5/8	26 0/8	25 3/8	19 3/8	5	5	Clay County	IL	Don Williams	1998	4777
154 5/8	23 2/8	25 6/8	17 5/8	5	5	Lake County	IL	Steven Hysell	1998	4777
154 5/8	21 4/8	21 6/8	16 4/8	6	5	Dearborn County	IN	Gary Senitza	1999	4777
154 5/8	24 2/8	24 4/8	19 7/8	4	4	Walworth County	WI	Gordon T. Meeker	1999	4777
154 5/8	26 2/8	26 3/8	21 4/8	5	4	Wabash County	IL	J. C. Linson	1999	4777
154 5/8	23 6/8	24 0/8	18 1/8	5	6	Fayette County	IA	Rayford Castille	2000	4777
154 5/8	24 2/8	24 4/8	16 1/8	7	5	De Witt County	IL	Russell Davenport	2000	4777
154 5/8	26 3/8	26 0/8	20 3/8	4	4	St. Joseph County	IN	Jesse L. Thompson	2001	4777
154 5/8	24 6/8	25 4/8	22 1/8	4	4	Allen County	OH	Jerry Rex	2001	4777
154 5/8	24 6/8	24 4/8	22 5/8	5	5	Will County	IL	Rick Johns	2001	4777
154 5/8	27 1/8	27 0/8	19 1/8	7	6	Coles County	IL	John W. Clough	2001	4777
154 5/8	24 7/8	26 0/8	20 3/8	5	5	Harrison County	IA	Ted K. Jaycox	2001	4777
*154 5/8	26 2/8	26 0/8	17 5/8	4	4	Pickaway County	OH	John D. Rogers	2002	4777
154 5/8	23 2/8	22 5/8	14 5/8	5	6	Randolph County	IL	Brad Stanek	2002	4777
154 5/8	24 2/8	24 4/8	18 3/8	6	6	Linn County	IA	James L. Corkery	2002	4777
*154 5/8	25 0/8	26 1/8	17 0/8	6	6	Ashtabula County	OH	Casey R. Gildersleeve	2003	4777
154 5/8	25 5/8	25 2/8	18 3/8	4	5	Mercer County	IL	Chuck Fiser	2003	4777
154 5/8	22 7/8	23 3/8	19 1/8	5	5	Carroll County	MO	Jamie Foley	2003	4777
154 5/8	25 5/8	26 1/8	19 7/8	5	5	Linn County	IA	Kevin Martin	2003	4777
*154 5/8	26 5/8	26 7/8	21 5/8	5	4	Marquette County	WI	Chad Dillinger	2004	4777
*154 5/8	24 4/8	25 5/8	16 7/8	9	5	Buffalo County	WI	Aaron Dobbs	2005	4777
154 5/8	27 0/8	27 2/8	20 2/8	6	6	Middlesex County	MA	Christopher Trainor	2005	4777
154 5/8	24 3/8	23 4/8	18 3/8	7	6	Rock County	WI	James Lamb	2005	4777
154 5/8	26 1/8	26 5/8	17 1/8	5	5	Des Moines County	IA	Chris King	2005	4777
154 5/8	24 4/8	24 5/8	17 2/8	6	8	Irion County	TX	David Rogers	2006	4777
*154 5/8	25 6/8	25 0/8	17 3/8	6	8	Black Hawk County	IA	Chad Hoffman	2006	4777
*154 5/8	26 2/8	25 1/8	19 6/8	8	8	Taylor County	WI	Matt Neumueller	2007	4777
154 5/8	27 1/8	26 2/8	18 5/8	6	6	Waupaca County	WI	Matthew D. Lorge	2007	4777
*154 5/8	25 7/8	24 7/8	18 3/8	5	5	Morrison County	MN	Gregg Kapsner	2008	4777
154 5/8	22 5/8	22 4/8	18 3/8	5	5	St. Louis County	MN	Joshua Carey	2008	4777
154 5/8	25 5/8	25 1/8	22 3/8	5	5	Carroll County	IN	Gregory L. Fouts	2009	4777
154 5/8	25 3/8	23 3/8	18 1/8	8	8	Randolph County	MO	Mike Schanzmeyer	2009	4777
*154 5/8	23 7/8	24 2/8	18 3/8	6	8	Dunn County	WI	Nicholas S. Frase	2009	4777
154 4/8	24 0/8	24 3/8	23 2/8	5	5	Allamakee County	IA	Dayton Jones	1968	4830
154 4/8	23 6/8	24 5/8	18 6/8	5	5	Davis County	IA	Ronald L. Simmons	1970	4830
154 4/8	22 6/8	22 6/8	16 6/8	6	6	Fillmore County	MN	James J. Johnston	1974	4830
154 4/8	25 3/8	24 1/8	18 0/8	5	5	Will County	IL	Fred Lukanc	1978	4830
154 4/8	24 4/8	24 0/8	19 3/8	7	8	Waupaca County	WI	Gary L. Hintz	1978	4830
154 4/8	24 4/8	23 6/8	20 0/8	5	5	Phillips County	KS	Dennis Fredrickson	1983	4830
154 4/8	24 3/8	25 4/8	20 6/8	5	7	Monona County	IA	Bob Reitan	1986	4830
154 4/8	25 1/8	25 6/8	23 0/8	4	4	Washington County	MN	Kenneth Brandl	1987	4830
154 4/8	23 4/8	23 5/8	18 4/8	6	7	Kent County	MD	Donald P. Travis	1987	4830
154 4/8	25 0/8	25 7/8	21 0/8	6	6	Fairfax County	VA	Michael E. Bury	1989	4830
154 4/8	26 1/8	25 0/8	22 6/8	6	6	Litchfield County	CT	Eugene J. Wrabel, Jr.	1990	4830
154 4/8	26 4/8	25 4/8	16 7/8	5	4	Adams County	OH	David W. Gilbert	1990	4830
154 4/8	22 7/8	22 5/8	20 4/8	5	5	Letellier	MAN	Todd Amenrud	1991	4830
154 4/8	24 6/8	25 5/8	18 0/8	5	5	Jefferson County	WI	Mark Stinebrink	1991	4830
154 4/8	22 6/8	22 4/8	17 3/8	6	5	Geary County	KS	Dallas A. Pane	1992	4830
154 4/8	23 4/8	23 1/8	18 2/8	5	6	Iron County	WI	Bruce Dianich	1992	4830

WHITETAIL DEER (TYPICAL ANTLERS)

Minimum Score 125 — Continued

SCORE	LENGTH OF R MAIN BEAM L	INSIDE SPREAD	NUMBER OF R POINTS L	AREA	STATE/ PROVINCE	HUNTER'S NAME	DATE	RANK
154 4/8	24 4/8 24 1/8	19 1/8	6 5	Hennepin County	MN	Robert J. Evans, Jr.	1994	4830
154 4/8	25 1/8 26 1/8	17 4/8	6 5	Cherokee County	KS	Paul Atkins	1995	4830
154 4/8	24 2/8 24 4/8	17 2/8	6 6	Lake County	IL	Joseph G. Wicinski	1995	4830
154 4/8	23 1/8 21 4/8	17 6/8	5 5	Livingston County	IL	Donnie Griswold	1996	4830
154 4/8	23 3/8 23 4/8	19 2/8	7 5	Mercer County	NJ	Marty H. Beekman, Jr.	1996	4830
154 4/8	24 5/8 23 2/8	18 4/8	6 5	Chippewa County	WI	Lee Craker	1998	4830
154 4/8	26 4/8 26 0/8	20 4/8	5 6	Morgan County	IL	Corey Suter	1998	4830
154 4/8	24 7/8 24 0/8	21 2/8	4 4	Grundy County	IL	Mark Anderson	1998	4830
154 4/8	23 1/8 24 0/8	16 3/8	5 6	Kewaunee County	WI	Bill Foucault	1999	4830
154 4/8	25 1/8 25 3/8	18 0/8	6 5	Tompkins County	NY	John E. Huether	2000	4830
154 4/8	24 6/8 25 0/8	18 4/8	5 5	Pittsburg County	OK	Blake Stephens	2000	4830
154 4/8	24 2/8 24 0/8	18 1/8	6 7	Clark County	KS	A. Ronnie Everett	2000	4830
154 4/8	24 2/8 26 5/8	13 2/8	6 5	Harford County	MD	Bill Woolford	2001	4830
154 4/8	28 7/8 27 5/8	21 7/8	6 5	Strafford County	NH	Brian Turgeon	2002	4830
154 4/8	24 7/8 24 7/8	13 6/8	5 5	Reynolds County	MO	Jeffrey S. Barnes	2002	4830
154 4/8	21 6/8 21 3/8	18 0/8	5 5	Crittenden County	KY	Robert Klumm	2003	4830
154 4/8	24 2/8 24 2/8	21 4/8	5 5	Champaign County	OH	Andy Hiltibran	2003	4830
154 4/8	23 2/8 22 7/8	15 6/8	5 6	Clermont County	OH	Faye Kirschbaum	2003	4830
154 4/8	27 1/8 26 6/8	19 3/8	6 5	Dallas County	MO	Jim Salaki	2003	4830
*154 4/8	24 1/8 24 5/8	18 0/8	5 5	Adams County	WI	Daniel Marsicek	2003	4830
154 4/8	24 6/8 25 5/8	16 2/8	5 5	Dallas County	IA	Martin Mock	2003	4830
154 4/8	24 5/8 24 3/8	18 4/8	5 6	Spokane County	WA	Scott Brosvik	2003	4830
154 4/8	22 7/8 24 1/8	17 3/8	5 6	Morrison County	MN	Kevin Will	2004	4830
154 4/8	24 7/8 25 0/8	21 2/8	5 5	Sullivan County	IN	Steve Siscoe	2004	4830
*154 4/8	24 2/8 23 7/8	17 1/8	5 6	Lake County	IN	Scott R. Eggert	2005	4830
154 4/8	22 5/8 23 2/8	17 2/8	6 5	Marathon County	WI	Bruce Stieber	2005	4830
154 4/8	23 2/8 23 2/8	18 2/8	5 6	Roanoke County	VA	William J. Davenport	2005	4830
*154 4/8	22 0/8 22 2/8	19 2/8	5 5	Day County	SD	Dwayne Sass	2005	4830
*154 4/8	25 0/8 24 6/8	16 0/8	5 5	Lake County	IN	Joe Banek	2005	4830
154 4/8	24 1/8 24 7/8	20 1/8	5 5	Cedar County	IA	Brandon L. Hudson	2005	4830
154 4/8	24 2/8 24 3/8	19 1/8	6 5	Menard County	IL	Rodney R. Ruch	2006	4830
154 4/8	25 1/8 25 5/8	18 6/8	6 4	Van Buren County	IA	Dave Nelson	2006	4830
154 4/8	21 4/8 22 5/8	17 4/8	5 5	Lake County	IL	Alan Simonds	2006	4830
154 4/8	28 2/8 26 7/8	21 2/8	5 4	Warren County	OH	Richard L. Newsom	2006	4830
154 4/8	25 5/8 24 1/8	17 6/8	5 5	Sheridan County	ND	Burnell Schuh	2007	4830
*154 4/8	27 2/8 26 1/8	21 2/8	6 6	Houston County	MN	Brent Parent	2007	4830
154 4/8	25 7/8 24 6/8	21 0/8	7 5	Morgan County	OH	Joe Freeman	2007	4830
*154 4/8	25 0/8 25 2/8	18 6/8	4 5	Becker County	MN	Paul Michael Okeson	2008	4830
*154 4/8	24 2/8 24 7/8	19 3/8	5 7	Steuben County	IN	Derek Wyatt	2008	4830
*154 4/8	24 0/8 23 6/8	18 5/8	6 5	Lucas County	OH	Michael Gula	2008	4830
154 4/8	26 0/8 26 2/8	18 4/8	5 5	Bureau County	IL	Greg Bowers	2009	4830
154 4/8	25 6/8 26 0/8	15 4/8	7 6	Gage County	NE	Samuel D. Cowan III	2009	4830
*154 4/8	21 6/8 21 6/8	18 4/8	5 5	Lake County	IN	John T. Lotz	2009	4830
154 4/8	24 3/8 23 4/8	20 6/8	6 5	Jefferson County	WI	John Mitchell	2009	4830
154 4/8	24 4/8 24 4/8	17 2/8	5 6	Warren County	IA	Clifton Rooney	2009	4830
154 4/8	22 1/8 21 7/8	16 2/8	5 5	Clay County	TX	Mike Thompson	2010	4830
154 3/8	23 4/8 24 3/8	18 5/8	7 7	Wythe County	VA	C. D. Tarter	1961	4892
154 3/8	27 2/8 26 0/8	21 5/8	4 4	Martin County	IN	Bill Clark	1967	4892
154 3/8	25 3/8 25 2/8	19 1/8	4 4	Jefferson County	IL	Kirby Laur	1981	4892
154 3/8	23 1/8 24 0/8	21 1/8	5 5	Sherman County	KS	Keith A. Foster	1984	4892
154 3/8	24 2/8 23 5/8	17 1/8	5 5	Polk County	WI	Doug Greene	1986	4892
154 3/8	24 3/8 24 2/8	18 5/8	5 5	Darke County	OH	Roy W. Ditty	1986	4892
154 3/8	23 5/8 22 2/8	17 7/8	5 5	Highland County	OH	Martin Bullock	1986	4892
154 3/8	24 3/8 23 7/8	20 5/8	5 5	Jackson County	WI	Daryl Lanphere	1987	4892
154 3/8	23 3/8 22 7/8	17 5/8	6 5	Lake County	IL	James W. Smith	1988	4892
154 3/8	24 4/8 24 4/8	19 5/8	6 6	St. Clair County	MI	Randy Shaffer	1988	4892
154 3/8	25 3/8 25 3/8	17 5/8	4 4	Clay County	IL	Mike Fry	1988	4892
154 3/8	25 1/8 25 4/8	17 2/8	6 5	Ottawa County	KS	James Helget	1990	4892
154 3/8	23 5/8 25 1/8	18 5/8	4 4	Weld County	CO	Larry Gann	1991	4892
154 3/8	25 0/8 25 0/8	20 6/8	5 6	Logan County	WV	Jimmy Diamond	1991	4892
154 3/8	24 7/8 25 1/8	18 7/8	6 7	Howard County	IA	Roger Meirick	1992	4892
154 3/8	25 0/8 24 1/8	20 3/8	6 4	Chester County	PA	Daniel Haines	1993	4892
154 3/8	26 4/8 23 5/8	18 7/8	5 6	Clark County	OH	Ronnie Todd Cochran	1994	4892
154 3/8	24 7/8 24 7/8	20 6/8	7 6	Ingham County	MI	Craig Prether	1994	4892
154 3/8	26 7/8 25 7/8	18 1/8	5 5	Montgomery County	VA	Curtis L. Coleman	1995	4892
154 3/8	25 5/8 25 4/8	18 5/8	5 6	Macon County	IL	James R. Wilson	1995	4892
154 3/8	23 7/8 24 2/8	16 5/8	5 6	Martin County	IN	Steven W. Sargent	1996	4892
154 3/8	24 2/8 22 5/8	16 2/8	5 6	Spokane County	WA	Joel Enevold	1996	4892
154 3/8	23 0/8 23 3/8	17 5/8	5 5	Battle River	ALB	Harley Rea	1997	4892
154 3/8	24 1/8 23 4/8	19 3/8	6 7	Decatur County	IA	Dave J. Lamberts	1997	4892
154 3/8	24 7/8 24 4/8	18 1/8	5 5	Warren County	IA	Jeff Hoover	1997	4892
154 3/8	23 0/8 26 0/8	20 0/8	5 5	Lake County	IL	Jeremy Bruns	1998	4892
154 3/8	23 5/8 23 1/8	16 3/8	6 6	Greene County	OH	Tim Chenoweth	1998	4892
154 3/8	27 0/8 27 5/8	19 7/8	5 6	Warren County	IA	Todd Reese	1998	4892
154 3/8	25 6/8 25 4/8	17 4/8	6 6	Yorkton	SAS	Ron Vandermeulen	1999	4892
154 3/8	21 6/8 22 7/8	17 1/8	5 5	Lincoln County	SD	Daniel K. Alexander	1999	4892
154 3/8	24 0/8 24 1/8	18 5/8	6 6	Ashland County	WI	Frank Peterson	1999	4892
154 3/8	23 6/8 24 7/8	21 3/8	6 6	Shawnee County	KS	Shane Saia	1999	4892
154 3/8	25 6/8 23 4/8	18 7/8	4 6	Jasper County	IL	Terry Waggoner	1999	4892
154 3/8	27 6/8 26 6/8	19 1/8	5 6	Itasca County	MN	Everett Bonneville	2000	4892
154 3/8	25 1/8 24 5/8	17 1/8	5 5	Trempealeau County	WI	Scott Davis	2000	4892
154 3/8	28 3/8 27 1/8	21 7/8	4 4	Clarke County	IA	James Nelson	2001	4892
154 3/8	24 7/8 24 1/8	19 1/8	5 5	Marshall County	IL	John Phillips	2002	4892
154 3/8	26 1/8 23 7/8	17 7/8	6 5	Wayne County	NY	Elery J. Mayo, Jr.	2003	4892
154 3/8	24 2/8 23 2/8	16 0/8	5 7	Anoka County	MN	Chris Roy	2004	4892
*154 3/8	22 7/8 22 1/8	13 6/8	5 6	Sevier County	AR	Danny Rackley	2004	4892
154 3/8	23 4/8 23 1/8	18 1/8	8 10	Hillsdale County	MI	Ronald W. Riddle, Sr.	2005	4892
154 3/8	23 5/8 25 0/8	17 3/8	6 6	Green Lake County	WI	Kelly S. Roehl	2005	4892
154 3/8	23 1/8 23 2/8	19 3/8	6 6	Mille Lacs County	MN	Pete Schreck	2005	4892
154 3/8	24 6/8 25 5/8	15 7/8	5 5	Nuevo Leon	MEX	John "Jack" C. Culpepper III	2005	4892
154 3/8	25 1/8 24 3/8	19 6/8	5 7	Champaign County	IL	Brian Frichtl	2005	4892
154 3/8	25 0/8 23 7/8	16 4/8	6 6	Trempealeau County	WI	Curt Miller	2006	4892
*154 3/8	23 6/8 23 2/8	21 1/8	5 6	Taylor County	WI	John Kleczewski	2006	4892
*154 3/8	23 7/8 24 1/8	17 7/8	5 5	Oconto County	WI	Steve Koltz	2006	4892
*154 3/8	22 0/8 20 6/8	18 1/8	5 5	Berrien County	MI	Brian D. Burgoyne	2006	4892

WHITETAIL DEER (TYPICAL ANTLERS)

Minimum Score 125 — Continued

SCORE	LENGTH OF R MAIN BEAM L	INSIDE SPREAD	NUMBER OF R POINTS L	AREA	STATE/PROVINCE	HUNTER'S NAME	DATE	RANK
*154 3/8	24 4/8 24 4/8	21 3/8	7 5	Jasper County	IN	Carl K. Northcutt	2007	4892
*154 3/8	20 7/8 20 6/8	18 7/8	5 5	Mason County	IL	Andy Morrill	2007	4892
154 3/8	24 5/8 23 5/8	18 5/8	7 6	Caldwell County	KY	David Storms	2008	4892
154 3/8	24 6/8 25 2/8	18 5/8	5 5	Brule County	SD	Jim Larson	2008	4892
154 3/8	24 7/8 25 0/8	18 5/8	6 5	Page County	IA	Bob Athen	2008	4892
154 3/8	25 0/8 25 0/8	20 7/8	4 5	Iowa County	WI	Tom McKinlay	2008	4892
*154 3/8	23 6/8 23 6/8	16 6/8	5 7	Green County	WI	Scott W. Matteson	2009	4892
154 3/8	22 6/8 23 1/8	21 1/8	5 5	Washburn County	WI	Steve Degner	2009	4892
*154 3/8	23 2/8 22 6/8	17 7/8	5 5	Coal County	OK	Bobby Akins	2009	4892
154 3/8	26 1/8 25 3/8	18 3/8	4 4	Clark County	MO	Chauncey Wilson	2009	4892
154 3/8	20 7/8 20 6/8	14 7/8	6 7	Jackson County	IN	Dirk Botkin	2009	4892
154 3/8	27 0/8 27 0/8	18 3/8	6 7	Massac County	IL	Rodger L. Willett, Jr.	2009	4892
*154 3/8	23 1/8 22 6/8	17 1/8	5 5	Polk County	WI	David J. Moris	2010	4892
*154 3/8	25 4/8 25 3/8	21 1/8	6 6	Buffalo County	WI	Timothy Grzesiak	2010	4892
154 2/8	25 4/8 27 0/8	16 6/8	6 6	Waupaca County	WI	Carl Schoenike	1948	4955
154 2/8	26 2/8 26 0/8	15 4/8	4 5	Aitkin County	MN	Ervin A. Buck	1959	4955
154 2/8	22 3/8 21 7/8	16 6/8	6 6	Clark County	MO	Myles Keller	1981	4955
154 2/8	25 1/8 25 7/8	17 6/8	5 6	Cloud County	KS	Jerrold L. Istas	1981	4955
154 2/8	22 6/8 22 6/8	17 4/8	5 5	Burleigh County	ND	Tony Niemann	1984	4955
154 2/8	23 6/8 23 1/8	17 6/8	6 6	White County	IL	Bruce Masser	1984	4955
154 2/8	24 6/8 23 1/8	18 0/8	8 7	Comanche County	KS	Tommie A. Berger	1985	4955
154 2/8	24 3/8 23 7/8	18 3/8	5 6	Dane County	WI	Eric L. Hamele	1987	4955
154 2/8	26 5/8 26 4/8	18 2/8	8 7	Coles County	IL	Rob King	1987	4955
154 2/8	27 5/8 26 3/8	23 1/8	6 4	Rock Island County	IL	Vernon G. Moon	1988	4955
154 2/8	23 2/8 23 1/8	18 4/8	5 5	Millarville	ALB	Stuart Sinclair-Smith	1989	4955
154 2/8	21 7/8 21 5/8	15 2/8	6 6	Fulton County	IL	Bruce A. Flynn	1989	4955
154 2/8	23 6/8 23 0/8	19 2/8	6 5	Ashland County	WI	Joseph A. Schutte	1990	4955
154 2/8	25 7/8 25 0/8	16 6/8	5 5	Washington County	MN	Lance Edward Vandeberg	1990	4955
154 2/8	24 0/8 24 7/8	20 7/8	5 6	Highland County	OH	David Doyle	1991	4955
154 2/8	25 0/8 25 2/8	15 1/8	7 6	Fayette County	IL	Mike Myers	1991	4955
154 2/8	25 7/8 24 5/8	18 6/8	4 4	Anoka County	MN	Dan Kluth	1992	4955
154 2/8	23 0/8 24 0/8	17 2/8	6 5	Louisa County	IA	Rick Stroud	1992	4955
154 2/8	25 7/8 24 3/8	20 4/8	7 7	Montgomery County	IL	Steve Barricklow	1992	4955
154 2/8	25 7/8 25 2/8	21 0/8	5 6	Ashland County	WI	Dave Matis	1993	4955
154 2/8	25 1/8 26 2/8	19 6/8	5 5	Cecil County	MD	Wallace Pleasanton	1993	4955
154 2/8	22 5/8 21 6/8	19 2/8	5 5	Van Buren County	IA	Deric Saunders	1993	4955
154 2/8	23 1/8 22 4/8	19 6/8	5 5	Strathcona	ALB	Mark Irla	1993	4955
154 2/8	23 2/8 24 1/8	19 2/8	5 5	Marathon County	WI	Mark Jon Miller	1994	4955
154 2/8	27 6/8 26 3/8	21 6/8	6 5	Bucks County	PA	Richard A. McCurdy, Jr.	1994	4955
154 2/8	23 6/8 24 2/8	17 6/8	5 5	Worth County	IA	Larry Porter	1995	4955
154 2/8	27 6/8 27 4/8	18 4/8	4 4	St. Louis County	MO	Jesse Wiggins	1996	4955
154 2/8	26 3/8 25 6/8	18 2/8	5 5	Ripley County	IN	Dan Castner	1996	4955
154 2/8	25 4/8 25 6/8	18 7/8	7 6	Spokane County	WA	Phil Monroe	1997	4955
154 2/8	23 6/8 24 2/8	21 0/8	4 4	Stark County	IL	Ronald Ellington	1997	4955
154 2/8	22 2/8 23 2/8	16 2/8	5 5	McCracken County	KY	Robert Collins	1998	4955
154 2/8	22 6/8 23 2/8	18 0/8	5 5	Trempealeau County	WI	Frank G. Hood II	1999	4955
154 2/8	27 4/8 27 0/8	19 2/8	5 5	Walworth County	WI	Don Teubel	1999	4955
154 2/8	26 2/8 25 1/8	19 6/8	4 4	Monroe County	WI	John A. Korish	1999	4955
154 2/8	25 4/8 25 4/8	17 6/8	6 5	Columbia County	WI	Dennis J. Dreyer	1999	4955
154 2/8	23 1/8 23 2/8	20 6/8	5 6	Hancock County	IL	Lloyd N. Meyers, Jr.	2000	4955
154 2/8	25 4/8 22 6/8	18 6/8	5 5	McLean County	IL	Ron Brandel	2000	4955
154 2/8	21 7/8 22 4/8	17 4/8	5 5	Sherburne County	MN	Greg Maros	2000	4955
154 2/8	24 3/8 24 1/8	15 2/8	5 5	Jefferson County	IN	Brian Scott Smith	2001	4955
154 2/8	25 0/8 23 7/8	19 0/8	7 5	Macoupin County	IL	Christopher Gleason	2001	4955
154 2/8	24 5/8 24 7/8	18 5/8	5 5	Ashtabula County	OH	Steve J. DiGiacomo	2001	4955
154 2/8	26 1/8 25 7/8	16 5/8	7 5	Comanche County	KS	Brad Coleman	2001	4955
154 2/8	24 4/8 24 0/8	17 4/8	5 5	McCreary County	KY	Dana Gibson	2003	4955
154 2/8	22 7/8 22 4/8	14 1/8	6 6	Clinton County	OH	Matt Lamb	2003	4955
154 2/8	24 4/8 24 4/8	20 4/8	5 5	Marathon County	WI	Bill White	2003	4955
*154 2/8	26 3/8 26 0/8	18 4/8	6 5	Clark County	OH	James J. Suzel	2003	4955
154 2/8	25 4/8 25 4/8	18 6/8	4 4	Marathon County	WI	Robert W. Hertz, Jr.	2003	4955
154 2/8	27 3/8 26 4/8	18 1/8	5 7	Elk County	KS	Bill Worrell	2003	4955
154 2/8	25 5/8 25 7/8	19 6/8	7 5	Green County	WI	Mike Kane	2003	4955
154 2/8	24 4/8 25 4/8	15 4/8	5 5	Woodford County	IL	Marc Anthony	2004	4955
*154 2/8	25 1/8 23 6/8	18 2/8	6 5	Allegheny County	PA	Tom Aitken	2004	4955
*154 2/8	23 2/8 23 0/8	15 4/8	5 5	Dickinson County	KS	Mario M. Vasquez	2005	4955
154 2/8	25 2/8 24 6/8	16 2/8	5 5	Crawford County	MO	Louis C. Marnati	2005	4955
*154 2/8	25 3/8 25 5/8	16 0/8	5 5	Pike County	OH	Steve Patrick	2005	4955
*154 2/8	24 1/8 23 1/8	19 6/8	6 6	La Salle County	IL	Norman D. Eggleston	2005	4955
154 2/8	22 5/8 22 1/8	20 4/8	6 5	Laclede County	MO	Jim Atkinson	2006	4955
154 2/8	24 3/8 23 5/8	19 0/8	5 6	Polk County	WI	Kyle W. Backes	2006	4955
*154 2/8	23 5/8 22 5/8	20 2/8	5 5	Riley County	KS	Brad Morris	2006	4955
154 2/8	23 7/8 25 4/8	18 4/8	5 5	Waukesha County	WI	Douglas Trapp	2006	4955
154 2/8	24 7/8 25 0/8	20 0/8	6 6	Wyoming County	NY	Daniel Nugent	2006	4955
*154 2/8	26 0/8 26 0/8	18 6/8	7 8	Dearborn County	IN	John J. Hooten	2007	4955
*154 2/8	23 0/8 22 0/8	18 4/8	5 5	Washington County	IN	David Everage	2007	4955
154 2/8	23 6/8 23 3/8	20 0/8	5 6	Crawford County	WI	Robert E. McCann	2007	4955
154 2/8	22 5/8 22 2/8	16 0/8	6 6	Goodhue County	MN	Jim Duppong	2008	4955
154 2/8	25 3/8 24 2/8	21 6/8	6 6	Wayne County	IN	Phillip S. Ross	2009	4955
154 2/8	25 4/8 24 0/8	19 2/8	6 7	Lincoln County	MO	James Catalano	2009	4955
*154 2/8	25 6/8 24 2/8	19 1/8	6 5	Harrison County	KY	Alex Lyons	2009	4955
154 2/8	24 6/8 24 3/8	19 7/8	5 6	Anoka County	MN	Matthew Contons	2009	4955
*154 2/8	25 2/8 26 6/8	22 5/8	6 5	Calvert County	MD	Bruce A. Hudson	2010	4955
154 1/8	24 6/8 23 7/8	15 5/8	5 5	Brown County	IN	Glen E. Parton	1970	5024
154 1/8	24 6/8 25 5/8	20 4/8	5 7	Noble County	OH	Donald J. Mace	1973	5024
154 1/8	24 6/8 23 4/8	19 6/8	5 7	Shawano County	WI	John Popp	1980	5024
154 1/8	23 5/8 23 7/8	19 5/8	5 5	Stoddard County	MO	Gary Barton	1980	5024
154 1/8	23 0/8 23 1/8	18 7/8	6 7	Faribault County	MN	Carlton Eastvold, Jr.	1982	5024
154 1/8	26 5/8 26 2/8	20 1/8	6 7	Nelson County	KY	Tom Bullock	1983	5024
154 1/8	23 7/8 23 4/8	18 3/8	5 5	Merrick County	NE	Lauren N Erickson	1985	5024
154 1/8	22 6/8 24 7/8	17 5/8	5 5	Miami County	IN	Charles Wecht	1986	5024
154 1/8	28 0/8 27 1/8	25 1/8	4 4	Buffalo County	WI	Frank Frost	1987	5024
154 1/8	22 5/8 21 2/8	19 5/8	5 5	Poinsett County	AR	Barry Deckelman	1988	5024
154 1/8	26 4/8 26 1/8	17 5/8	6 7	Saline County	KS	Shane Roberts	1989	5024
154 1/8	24 4/8 24 1/8	19 5/8	5 4	Phillips County	KS	Gary Fritzler	1990	5024

WHITETAIL DEER (TYPICAL ANTLERS)

Minimum Score 125   Continued

SCORE	LENGTH OF R MAIN BEAM L	INSIDE SPREAD	NUMBER OF R POINTS L	AREA	STATE/ PROVINCE	HUNTER'S NAME	DATE	RANK
154 1/8	24 0/8	24 0/8	16 1/8	5	5	Marion County	IA	Frank M. Hashman	1991	5024
154 1/8	25 2/8	25 6/8	20 5/8	5	7	Harrison County	IA	Gerald D. Dickman	1991	5024
154 1/8	26 1/8	25 7/8	21 4/8	5	5	Calhoun County	MI	Hershel Brown	1992	5024
154 1/8	26 7/8	28 7/8	19 1/8	7	5	Jefferson County	IN	Frank McClain	1992	5024
154 1/8	24 1/8	23 0/8	18 0/8	5	6	Cheyenne County	CO	Travis Leonard	1992	5024
154 1/8	23 0/8	22 2/8	16 5/8	5	5	Osage County	OK	Dan Gaston	1993	5024
154 1/8	24 4/8	25 0/8	22 5/8	5	4	McHenry County	IL	Gary Pfaffinger	1993	5024
154 1/8	24 5/8	25 2/8	17 7/8	5	5	Todd County	MN	Scott Swanson	1994	5024
154 1/8	24 6/8	25 3/8	15 7/8	6	6	Portage County	OH	Timothy Scott Fitzgerald	1995	5024
154 1/8	25 6/8	27 4/8	20 3/8	5	5	Shelby County	OH	Stephen A. Davis	1995	5024
154 1/8	21 6/8	21 5/8	17 1/8	5	4	Frontier County	NE	Donald Bergantz	1995	5024
154 1/8	21 3/8	22 7/8	16 6/8	6	5	Brown County	IN	Alan D. Baxter	1995	5024
154 1/8	23 7/8	23 1/8	20 5/8	5	5	Cass County	IA	Mark Armstrong	1995	5024
154 1/8	28 4/8	27 5/8	19 4/8	7	7	McHenry County	IL	Gary T. Lackhouse	1996	5024
154 1/8	24 3/8	24 0/8	18 7/8	5	4	Kane County	IL	Dean V. Ashton	1997	5024
154 1/8	25 7/8	25 6/8	19 3/8	5	5	Knox County	KY	Rickey C. Bates	1997	5024
154 1/8	22 7/8	23 3/8	19 1/8	5	5	Johnson County	IL	Roger Dubson	1997	5024
154 1/8	21 1/8	20 1/8	14 0/8	7	6	Barron County	WI	Travis Ebner	1999	5024
154 1/8	28 1/8	26 6/8	18 7/8	4	4	Crawford County	KS	Jeff Kavanagh	1999	5024
154 1/8	23 7/8	22 5/8	20 5/8	6	5	Ford County	KS	David M. Crnkovich	1999	5024
154 1/8	25 6/8	27 0/8	20 1/8	4	4	Trempealeau County	WI	Mike Engen	2000	5024
154 1/8	24 5/8	24 5/8	16 5/8	5	5	McHenry County	IL	Jay Larkin	2000	5024
154 1/8	23 7/8	24 1/8	16 0/8	6	6	Taylor County	IA	Steve W. Jennett	2000	5024
154 1/8	23 6/8	23 5/8	16 7/8	4	5	Madison County	IL	Darin Opel	2001	5024
154 1/8	24 0/8	25 0/8	19 6/8	5	5	Suffolk County	NY	John Hansen	2002	5024
154 1/8	24 2/8	24 1/8	17 3/8	5	5	Kane County	IL	Mike Bombardiere	2003	5024
154 1/8	24 4/8	24 7/8	20 1/8	5	5	Greene County	OH	Christopher Smith	2003	5024
154 1/8	20 7/8	21 7/8	19 5/8	6	6	Page County	IA	Bob Athen	2004	5024
154 1/8	23 4/8	25 0/8	20 4/8	6	5	Washtenaw County	MI	Ryan K. Valik	2004	5024
*154 1/8	24 4/8	25 3/8	17 4/8	4	5	Clark County	IL	Dale Brasfield	2005	5024
154 1/8	24 2/8	26 0/8	19 3/8	5	5	Morgan County	OH	Jeffrey D. Eddy	2005	5024
154 1/8	25 3/8	25 4/8	18 0/8	6	5	Marion County	IA	Al Bane	2005	5024
154 1/8	27 3/8	26 7/8	20 3/8	4	4	Vernon County	WI	William Wissestad	2006	5024
154 1/8	24 2/8	25 0/8	19 5/8	4	4	Calhoun County	MI	David Foote	2006	5024
*154 1/8	23 6/8	23 0/8	16 7/8	5	5	Meadow Lake	SAS	Joshua D. Waskowitz	2006	5024
154 1/8	26 4/8	26 2/8	21 4/8	6	6	Guthrie County	IA	Paul Scott	2006	5024
*154 1/8	21 4/8	20 7/8	16 3/8	6	5	Osage County	KS	Kyle Yoder	2006	5024
*154 1/8	23 5/8	25 5/8	17 5/8	6	5	Morrison County	MN	John Edward Kahl	2006	5024
*154 1/8	22 1/8	21 6/8	15 7/8	5	5	Jersey County	IL	Mark H. Hayes	2006	5024
154 1/8	24 5/8	23 6/8	19 1/8	6	5	Yankton County	SD	Jim Jorgensen	2006	5024
154 1/8	24 3/8	23 6/8	16 3/8	5	5	Dubuque County	IA	Robert K. Burris	2006	5024
*154 1/8	23 1/8	22 2/8	19 1/8	5	5	Athens County	OH	Mathew A. Norris	2007	5024
*154 1/8	24 2/8	23 3/8	17 7/8	5	5	Marinette County	WI	Robert Ledvina, Jr.	2008	5024
*154 1/8	24 4/8	23 4/8	20 2/8	7	4	Starke County	IN	Rudy Miller	2008	5024
*154 1/8	25 2/8	25 6/8	20 5/8	4	5	McHenry County	IL	John P. Georgean	2009	5024
154 0/8	26 2/8	26 1/8	17 6/8	5	5	Marshall County	KS	Tim Wanklyn	1976	5081
154 0/8	26 5/8	26 5/8	19 1/8	4	4	Guthrie County	IA	Gordon Headlee	1977	5081
154 0/8	27 2/8	25 7/8	18 4/8	6	4	Knox County	IL	James C. Drake	1979	5081
154 0/8	27 0/8	26 7/8	19 2/8	6	6	Kosciusko County	IN	Charles L. Baker	1979	5081
154 0/8	22 4/8	22 1/8	18 2/8	5	5	Price County	WI	Jim Sorensen	1982	5081
154 0/8	24 4/8	24 5/8	17 4/8	5	5	Monroe County	MO	Dallas L. Miller	1985	5081
154 0/8	24 6/8	24 3/8	15 4/8	5	5	Clay County	IN	Terry L. Dewey	1985	5081
154 0/8	25 1/8	24 1/8	19 2/8	5	5	Kent County	MD	J. Richard Herr	1985	5081
154 0/8	25 1/8	23 1/8	21 1/8	6	6	Tuscarawas County	OH	Stephen Hinkley	1986	5081
154 0/8	27 1/8	27 2/8	17 4/8	5	5	Waukesha County	WI	Duane Turinske	1989	5081
154 0/8	22 3/8	23 4/8	21 0/8	7	8	Jones County	GA	John Bragg	1990	5081
154 0/8	25 0/8	25 7/8	20 4/8	5	4	Henry County	MO	Matt Hull	1991	5081
154 0/8	25 2/8	26 1/8	18 6/8	4	4	Sarpy County	NE	Timothy R. Mathewson	1992	5081
154 0/8	24 3/8	25 4/8	20 1/8	6	7	Oakland County	MI	William Lacy	1993	5081
154 0/8	23 2/8	24 2/8	18 6/8	5	6	Spokane County	WA	Luke Clausen	1993	5081
154 0/8	24 4/8	23 3/8	20 6/8	5	5	Hamilton County	OH	Charlie Bledsoe	1994	5081
154 0/8	22 7/8	23 7/8	15 5/8	6	7	Woodbury County	IA	Dennis Weisz	1995	5081
154 0/8	23 5/8	23 3/8	16 0/8	5	5	Washington County	IA	Rich Albright	1995	5081
154 0/8	23 1/8	23 2/8	23 0/8	5	5	Boundary County	ID	Damon Severson	1996	5081
154 0/8	25 6/8	25 3/8	18 0/8	5	6	Dane County	WI	Scott Moran	1996	5081
154 0/8	22 7/8	22 0/8	18 6/8	5	5	Wabasha County	MN	Gene Hippe	1997	5081
154 0/8	25 2/8	24 7/8	22 0/8	4	5	Kent County	DE	D. Jeremy Henderson	1998	5081
154 0/8	27 2/8	26 5/8	16 4/8	5	5	Jackson County	IL	Derrick P. DeWilde	1998	5081
154 0/8	22 6/8	22 6/8	17 2/8	5	5	Brown County	IL	Ricky Thomas Wensil	1998	5081
154 0/8	23 7/8	23 3/8	18 5/8	6	5	McHenry County	IL	Tim Zimmerman	1999	5081
154 0/8	20 2/8	21 2/8	17 4/8	6	7	Shelby County	KY	Josh Pulliam	1999	5081
154 0/8	24 2/8	24 4/8	23 0/8	5	7	Coshocton County	OH	Robert Yates	1999	5081
154 0/8	25 0/8	26 2/8	17 2/8	6	4	La Salle County	IL	Dewayne Mullins	1999	5081
154 0/8	25 3/8	25 1/8	20 4/8	6	4	Morrison County	MN	Tim Fobbe	2000	5081
154 0/8	23 0/8	22 0/8	17 4/8	5	5	Washington County	WI	Bob Lewis	2000	5081
154 0/8	23 4/8	24 0/8	18 0/8	5	5	Talbot County	MD	Jack Dell	2000	5081
154 0/8	23 4/8	23 0/8	16 2/8	6	6	Morgan County	IN	Steven M. Simpson	2000	5081
154 0/8	24 2/8	24 4/8	18 5/8	6	7	Calhoun County	IL	Derek P. Driesenga	2000	5081
154 0/8	23 0/8	23 1/8	18 4/8	6	4	Dunn County	WI	Eric Torgerson	2001	5081
154 0/8	23 2/8	22 6/8	20 0/8	7	6	Pike County	IL	Edward M. Meyer	2002	5081
154 0/8	24 7/8	24 2/8	17 1/8	7	5	Brown County	WI	David J. Schroeder	2002	5081
154 0/8	25 1/8	25 1/8	22 1/8	4	5	Hand County	SD	Kevin Bertsch	2002	5081
154 0/8	24 3/8	24 1/8	18 6/8	7	5	Scott County	MN	Joshua Gross	2002	5081
154 0/8	23 2/8	24 6/8	17 6/8	4	4	Pike County	IL	William J. Smith	2002	5081
154 0/8	28 2/8	26 3/8	20 6/8	6	5	Barton County	KS	Joel Schneider	2002	5081
154 0/8	24 7/8	25 2/8	21 3/8	5	6	Vernon County	MO	Tom Hood	2003	5081
154 0/8	25 4/8	24 0/8	17 6/8	6	5	Dodge County	MN	Allen Iverson	2003	5081
154 0/8	23 6/8	24 1/8	17 0/8	5	5	Manitowoc County	WI	Ralph E. Schuh	2003	5081
154 0/8	27 4/8	27 0/8	20 4/8	5	4	Calhoun County	IL	Taylor Roberts	2003	5081
154 0/8	22 5/8	23 4/8	18 0/8	6	5	Crook County	WY	Mike Schmid	2004	5081
154 0/8	25 3/8	24 4/8	19 7/8	6	7	Ontario County	NY	Robert A. Newfrock	2004	5081
154 0/8	26 1/8	27 5/8	18 2/8	4	4	Jo Daviess County	IL	Kenneth Pluym	2004	5081
154 0/8	23 5/8	23 5/8	17 4/8	5	5	Pierce County	WI	Jerry M. Zimmer	2004	5081
154 0/8	24 2/8	23 4/8	21 2/8	5	5	La Salle County	IL	Alan Pierson	2004	5081
154 0/8	25 5/8	24 6/8	21 6/8	5	5	Dearborn County	IN	Chris M. Huser	2004	5081

409

WHITETAIL DEER (TYPICAL ANTLERS)

Minimum Score 125 Continued

SCORE	LENGTH OF R MAIN BEAM L	INSIDE SPREAD	NUMBER OF R POINTS L	AREA	STATE/ PROVINCE	HUNTER'S NAME	DATE	RANK
154 0/8	23 0/8 23 4/8	19 2/8	5 5	Gallatin County	KY	Jim Carlson	2004	5081
*154 0/8	23 5/8 22 2/8	16 3/8	5 7	Washington County	NE	Michael Zeringue	2004	5081
154 0/8	22 4/8 23 0/8	19 6/8	5 6	Albany County	WY	Craig Jamison	2005	5081
154 0/8	22 4/8 23 3/8	17 7/8	5 7	Wayne County	MO	Lonnie C. Wood	2005	5081
154 0/8	27 2/8 26 0/8	18 4/8	6 5	Sangamon County	IL	Brian Mullen	2005	5081
154 0/8	25 4/8 27 2/8	19 0/8	5 5	Baker County	GA	Glenn Paschal	2005	5081
154 0/8	26 4/8 25 3/8	21 6/8	6 8	Shawano County	WI	Paul Eberhardt	2005	5081
*154 0/8	24 1/8 24 0/8	21 4/8	6 5	Jefferson County	OH	Mike Scott	2005	5081
154 0/8	26 2/8 25 6/8	23 0/8	5 5	Green County	WI	Greg Rufenacht	2006	5081
154 0/8	27 2/8 26 1/8	18 2/8	5 5	Monroe County	MI	Bob Vining	2006	5081
154 0/8	24 0/8 24 4/8	20 6/8	6 6	Jackson County	MI	David M. Lindeman, Jr.	2007	5081
*154 0/8	22 7/8 22 6/8	20 0/8	5 5	Ballard County	KY	Scott Record	2008	5081
154 0/8	24 0/8 23 4/8	19 6/8	5 5	Allamakee County	IA	Danny Pfiffner	2008	5081
154 0/8	28 5/8 27 7/8	20 0/8	5 5	Huron County	OH	Kevin K. Garner	2008	5081
*154 0/8	23 4/8 23 4/8	18 4/8	4 4	Dunn County	WI	Josh Perrin	2008	5081
*154 0/8	24 2/8 23 4/8	16 2/8	6 5	Greene County	PA	Todd Bland	2009	5081
154 0/8	23 3/8 24 2/8	18 4/8	6 6	Moniteau County	MO	Carlos Hoback	2009	5081
*154 0/8	22 2/8 22 2/8	15 7/8	6 6	Gwinnett County	GA	Stephen Kocis	2009	5081
154 0/8	20 2/8 21 4/8	15 2/8	6 5	Madison County	IN	John D. Adams	2009	5081
153 7/8	25 5/8 24 5/8	23 4/8	5 6	Lee County	IA	Chris Fowler	1980	5150
153 7/8	22 6/8 22 2/8	17 5/8	5 5	McLean County	ND	Terry Cossette	1983	5150
153 7/8	25 6/8 26 0/8	17 1/8	7 7	Black Hawk County	IA	Gary Schoeberl	1985	5150
153 7/8	25 7/8 26 0/8	20 5/8	4 5	Bedford County	VA	Julian A. McFaden III	1986	5150
153 7/8	24 2/8 24 6/8	18 7/8	5 5	Franklin County	IL	Dave Freeman	1987	5150
153 7/8	24 4/8 25 4/8	19 7/8	6 6	Chase County	KS	Jerry Keller	1988	5150
153 7/8	25 3/8 25 1/8	17 1/8	4 4	Stephenson County	IL	Richard Wickersham	1989	5150
153 7/8	22 2/8 22 7/8	20 2/8	5 6	Cass County	ND	Dean Honrud	1991	5150
153 7/8	23 6/8 23 1/8	17 5/8	6 6	Mason County	IL	Christopher Thomas Novak	1993	5150
153 7/8	22 0/8 22 6/8	16 7/8	6 6	Washington County	WI	Gary Bell	1993	5150
153 7/8	27 1/8 26 1/8	20 7/8	5 5	Pike County	IL	Eddie Claypool	1994	5150
153 7/8	23 5/8 24 4/8	17 5/8	5 5	St. Croix County	WI	Don Bock	1994	5150
153 7/8	22 4/8 22 6/8	17 0/8	5 6	Appanoose County	IA	Richard Doll	1994	5150
153 7/8	24 1/8 24 6/8	18 7/8	5 5	Ogle County	IL	Jeff Wiedel	1996	5150
153 7/8	26 2/8 23 3/8	18 2/8	7 6	Rock Island County	IL	Oscar Ellis	1996	5150
153 7/8	23 6/8 23 4/8	16 3/8	6 6	Rock County	WI	Matt Wellenkotter	1996	5150
153 7/8	25 0/8 24 4/8	19 3/8	5 5	Eau Claire County	WI	Joel Stuttgen	1997	5150
153 7/8	22 6/8 23 4/8	18 7/8	5 5	Randolph County	MO	Don Whitefield	1997	5150
153 7/8	25 5/8 26 2/8	17 1/8	7 6	Clark County	IL	Dane Thompson	1997	5150
153 7/8	22 5/8 23 3/8	23 6/8	5 5	Delaware County	IA	Kevin Dempster	1997	5150
153 7/8	23 7/8 23 4/8	19 5/8	6 5	Columbia County	WI	Stephen A. Heiman	1998	5150
153 7/8	25 6/8 25 7/8	20 5/8	5 5	Belknap County	NH	Rodger Matthewman	1998	5150
153 7/8	25 0/8 25 2/8	17 1/8	5 5	Osage County	MO	Paul Stockman, Jr.	1999	5150
153 7/8	22 1/8 25 0/8	18 5/8	5 8	Livingston County	IL	Jeff Bohm	1999	5150
153 7/8	24 3/8 24 2/8	16 7/8	5 5	Prince Georges County	MD	Scott W. Ainsworth	1999	5150
153 7/8	23 4/8 24 3/8	18 7/8	5 5	Clark County	KS	Lynn Leonard	2000	5150
153 7/8	25 0/8 25 7/8	16 3/8	5 6	Saline County	MO	Don Bradshaw	2000	5150
153 7/8	24 2/8 23 5/8	18 2/8	6 7	Mellette County	SD	Douglas E. Hofer	2000	5150
153 7/8	24 2/8 24 5/8	20 3/8	5 5	Muskingum County	OH	Mark Snyder	2000	5150
153 7/8	23 6/8 23 3/8	17 6/8	6 7	Jackson County	IA	David Schrody	2001	5150
153 7/8	23 6/8 24 0/8	17 7/8	5 5	McMullen County	TX	Daniel D. Countiss	2001	5150
153 7/8	25 0/8 25 0/8	19 5/8	5 7	Tazewell County	IL	Mike Reatherford	2002	5150
153 7/8	25 2/8 25 7/8	20 1/8	6 5	Muskingum County	OH	Todd Head	2002	5150
153 7/8	25 5/8 24 6/8	19 1/8	6 6	Dearborn County	IN	Tom Jacobs	2003	5150
153 7/8	23 6/8 24 1/8	16 2/8	6 5	Warren County	OH	Chris Elliott	2003	5150
153 7/8	22 4/8 22 4/8	16 6/8	6 5	Sheboygan County	WI	Glen J. Klug	2003	5150
153 7/8	24 5/8 23 6/8	20 5/8	7 5	Shannon County	MO	Shawn Eggert	2003	5150
153 7/8	23 7/8 24 2/8	19 7/8	7 5	Lee County	IL	Charles W. Rehor	2003	5150
153 7/8	25 1/8 25 3/8	19 3/8	9 10	Schuyler County	IL	Charles Zandstra	2003	5150
153 7/8	24 5/8 24 7/8	19 7/8	5 5	Buffalo County	WI	Thomas J. Kovach	2003	5150
153 7/8	22 4/8 22 3/8	14 7/8	5 5	Saline County	MO	Willie Tichenor	2004	5150
153 7/8	28 4/8 27 4/8	18 3/8	5 5	Howard County	MD	Noah Graham Plauge	2004	5150
*153 7/8	24 2/8 24 2/8	17 3/8	5 6	Marshall County	IN	Bernie L. Reichard	2005	5150
153 7/8	26 7/8 25 6/8	19 1/8	5 4	Breckinridge County	KY	Wendell M. Adams, Jr.	2005	5150
*153 7/8	24 3/8 24 2/8	17 3/8	5 5	Saline County	IL	Mark E. McCowan	2005	5150
*153 7/8	25 4/8 24 7/8	20 5/8	4 5	Sauk County	WI	Brian P. Harms	2006	5150
153 7/8	26 4/8 25 2/8	19 5/8	5 4	Noble County	OH	Justin M. Roberts	2006	5150
153 7/8	29 0/8 29 6/8	20 5/8	4 4	Clinton County	OH	Rich Vinup	2006	5150
153 7/8	24 3/8 24 4/8	19 3/8	5 6	Cottonwood County	MN	Curtis Fast	2006	5150
*153 7/8	23 4/8 23 6/8	17 7/8	5 5	Wilkinson County	MS	Luke Martin, Jr.	2006	5150
153 7/8	26 6/8 27 2/8	21 7/8	6 6	Marathon County	WI	Roger Ewan	2007	5150
153 7/8	23 3/8 23 4/8	17 6/8	6 5	Waushara County	WI	John Michalski	2007	5150
*153 7/8	25 2/8 26 5/8	21 3/8	5 5	Marshall County	IN	Frank Vojtasek	2007	5150
153 7/8	24 3/8 23 6/8	17 3/8	6 6	Zapata County	TX	John D. Hall	2007	5150
153 7/8	22 2/8 22 0/8	18 2/8	7 5	Schuyler County	IL	Edward Poirier	2008	5150
153 7/8	26 2/8 25 3/8	16 5/8	4 4	Fulton County	IN	Henry L. Kidd	2008	5150
153 7/8	24 4/8 24 0/8	18 1/8	5 5	Jackson County	WI	Richard C. Hampe	2009	5150
*153 7/8	25 3/8 25 2/8	18 7/8	5 6	Meigs County	OH	Devon G. Baum	2009	5150
153 6/8	22 1/8 22 7/8	17 0/8	5 5	Kent County	MD	S. Russell Edie	1966	5208
153 6/8	24 5/8 25 1/8	18 2/8	6 5	Lee County	IL	George Nevins	1976	5208
153 6/8	23 3/8 24 3/8	18 0/8	5 5	Lincoln County	SD	Mike Pederson	1979	5208
153 6/8	24 1/8 23 7/8	16 0/8	5 5	Jasper County	MO	Steve Lewis	1983	5208
153 6/8	24 5/8 23 6/8	18 0/8	5 5	Kenosha County	WI	John Schnider, Jr.	1984	5208
153 6/8	25 1/8 24 7/8	18 4/8	5 5	Morrison County	MN	John Erdrich	1984	5208
153 6/8	24 2/8 23 3/8	19 4/8	5 5	Chisago County	MN	Blair Rawlings	1985	5208
153 6/8	22 7/8 23 0/8	17 7/8	5 6	Crook County	WY	Steven Blair	1986	5208
153 6/8	25 5/8 25 0/8	19 5/8	6 6	Adair County	MO	Roger Roberts	1986	5208
153 6/8	23 5/8 23 6/8	20 6/8	6 6	Hennepin County	MN	Steve Clark	1987	5208
153 6/8	24 2/8 23 2/8	22 4/8	5 5	Idaho County	ID	Ron Beitelspacher	1988	5208
153 6/8	24 2/8 24 2/8	17 0/8	7 6	St. Croix County	WI	Steve Huppert	1988	5208
153 6/8	24 0/8 23 2/8	23 2/8	4 4	Fulton County	IL	John Koster	1989	5208
153 6/8	21 6/8 21 5/8	17 1/8	6 5	Lucas County	IA	Orval W. Bedell	1990	5208
153 6/8	22 4/8 23 2/8	16 2/8	5 5	Winnebago County	IL	Mark P. Stock	1991	5208
153 6/8	24 4/8 25 3/8	20 3/8	4 5	Priddis	ALB	Lorne D. Rinkel	1991	5208
153 6/8	25 7/8 26 4/8	22 0/8	5 4	Baraga County	MI	David C. Sikorsky	1991	5208
153 6/8	24 0/8 25 7/8	16 5/8	7 7	Atchison County	MO	Tom Nauman	1991	5208

WHITETAIL DEER (TYPICAL ANTLERS)

Minimum Score 125 — Continued

SCORE	LENGTH OF R MAIN BEAM L	INSIDE SPREAD	NUMBER OF R POINTS L	AREA	STATE/ PROVINCE	HUNTER'S NAME	DATE	RANK
153 6/8	24 4/8 24 0/8	22 4/8	5 7	Suffolk County	NY	Richard Supinsky	1991	5208
153 6/8	23 5/8 23 5/8	21 2/8	6 5	Jackson County	IL	Sharen Oliver	1993	5208
153 6/8	22 1/8 23 1/8	18 6/8	6 6	Adams County	OH	Larry David Napier	1993	5208
153 6/8	23 4/8 24 2/8	21 4/8	7 7	Chippewa County	WI	Steve L. Craker	1994	5208
153 6/8	23 7/8 22 6/8	17 0/8	6 6	Saline County	KS	Stan E. Cox	1994	5208
153 6/8	24 0/8 24 6/8	16 6/8	5 5	Pike County	IL	Gregory S. Guerrieri	1995	5208
153 6/8	29 6/8 27 7/8	20 6/8	5 4	Warren County	OH	Scot Weyrauch	1995	5208
153 6/8	24 2/8 23 7/8	18 2/8	5 6	Brown County	OH	Richard Schmalz	1996	5208
153 6/8	27 5/8 29 2/8	19 1/8	7 5	Fayette County	IL	Rollin C. Wilson	1996	5208
153 6/8	28 6/8 29 1/8	19 2/8	6 5	Miami County	OH	Richard M. Harvey, Sr.	1996	5208
153 6/8	24 6/8 23 4/8	18 2/8	6 5	Buffalo County	NE	Gary Mike Hubbard	1996	5208
153 6/8	24 6/8 23 5/8	21 4/8	5 5	La Crosse County	WI	Michael Herde	1998	5208
153 6/8	22 4/8 22 7/8	14 2/8	5 5	Kearney County	NE	Wayne R. Wall	1998	5208
153 6/8	22 3/8 21 1/8	14 6/8	6 5	Knox County	KY	Roger Dale McDonald, Jr.	1998	5208
153 6/8	24 2/8 25 0/8	20 6/8	5 4	McHenry County	IL	Brad Wiehr	1998	5208
153 6/8	23 7/8 24 2/8	16 6/8	5 6	Crook County	WY	Raymond King	1999	5208
153 6/8	24 1/8 24 4/8	22 4/8	4 5	Harford County	MD	Corey Grace	1999	5208
153 6/8	26 4/8 25 6/8	17 2/8	6 5	Allamakee County	IA	Darrell Moose	1999	5208
153 6/8	24 1/8 24 2/8	17 5/8	7 6	Putnam County	MO	Troy Foote	2000	5208
153 6/8	26 6/8 27 7/8	19 1/8	5 4	Kendall County	IL	Joseph M. Solita	2001	5208
153 6/8	25 0/8 25 2/8	19 4/8	5 5	Ontario County	NY	Sean Barry	2001	5208
153 6/8	21 6/8 23 0/8	16 6/8	5 5	Will County	IL	Thomas S. Spence	2002	5208
153 6/8	21 7/8 23 4/8	15 1/8	6 6	Greene County	IN	John R. Brod	2002	5208
153 6/8	23 1/8 22 4/8	19 6/8	5 6	Peoria County	IL	Mike Fehl	2002	5208
153 6/8	22 3/8 22 4/8	19 4/8	5 5	Pierce County	WI	Mike J. Schommer	2002	5208
153 6/8	23 7/8 23 7/8	16 2/8	6 5	Wyoming County	NY	Victor Albano	2002	5208
153 6/8	26 1/8 26 1/8	18 0/8	4 4	Fremont County	IA	Rick Cain	2002	5208
153 6/8	22 6/8 22 5/8	19 3/8	6 6	Jackson County	IA	Branden A. Post	2002	5208
153 6/8	26 1/8 26 2/8	21 0/8	6 6	Holt County	MO	Greg Clement	2003	5208
153 6/8	24 6/8 24 6/8	16 3/8	6 5	Henry County	IA	Jason Helling	2003	5208
153 6/8	26 2/8 26 2/8	16 4/8	5 5	Washington County	OH	Mark Dye	2003	5208
153 6/8	27 1/8 26 5/8	23 3/8	6 6	Washington County	IL	Dave Burke	2004	5208
*153 6/8	23 7/8 23 5/8	17 6/8	5 5	La Porte County	IN	Christopher C. Fronk	2004	5208
153 6/8	24 6/8 26 3/8	16 6/8	6 5	Allegheny County	PA	Robert R. Robinson	2004	5208
153 6/8	25 0/8 25 0/8	21 4/8	6 5	Buffalo County	WI	Mike Huff	2005	5208
*153 6/8	26 6/8 26 4/8	19 0/8	5 5	Clay County	TX	Mike Thompson	2005	5208
153 6/8	23 3/8 23 2/8	20 6/8	5 5	Brown County	IL	Alan L. Stout	2005	5208
153 6/8	26 3/8 27 0/8	18 6/8	5 4	Appanoose County	IA	Todd Maziarz	2006	5208
*153 6/8	22 3/8 21 5/8	16 6/8	5 5	Elkhart County	IN	Jeff E. Miller	2006	5208
153 6/8	25 2/8 26 2/8	17 6/8	6 5	Morgan County	OH	Jerry Paul Owen	2007	5208
153 6/8	23 7/8 24 2/8	21 4/8	4 6	Boone County	IA	Martin Bruder	2007	5208
*153 6/8	22 6/8 22 0/8	15 6/8	5 5	Fulton County	IL	Steven Brown	2008	5208
*153 6/8	26 3/8 26 3/8	17 2/8	6 6	Clay County	KS	Robby Still	2008	5208
153 6/8	23 6/8 22 7/8	16 7/8	7 7	Marion County	IL	Steve Armstrong	2008	5208
153 6/8	27 6/8 27 4/8	24 4/8	7 5	Jones County	IA	Jim Belcher	2008	5208
153 6/8	22 1/8 22 2/8	16 7/8	5 6	Ford County	KS	Jerry L. Tuttle	2009	5208
153 6/8	24 2/8 24 2/8	15 5/8	5 6	Geary County	KS	Brian Schroyer	2009	5208
153 5/8	23 4/8 23 0/8	22 4/8	5 7	Harris	SAS	Garry Benson	1966	5273
153 5/8	26 5/8 26 6/8	18 5/8	7 5	Hamilton County	IA	Harold Brown	1971	5273
153 5/8	26 0/8 25 2/8	18 1/8	7 5	Halton Hills	ONT	Don Lewis	1978	5273
153 5/8	23 4/8 24 0/8	18 7/8	5 5	Dorchester County	MD	David Logan White	1983	5273
153 5/8	23 7/8 23 3/8	18 3/8	5 5	Cass County	IL	Kevin Duckwiler	1984	5273
153 5/8	26 0/8 25 5/8	21 1/8	6 5	Will County	IL	John Madonis	1984	5273
153 5/8	25 4/8 25 7/8	20 5/8	5 5	Stephenson County	IL	Clarence E. Hille, Jr.	1984	5273
153 5/8	23 0/8 23 0/8	19 5/8	5 5	Sauk County	WI	Michael H. Smith	1986	5273
153 5/8	24 0/8 24 4/8	19 6/8	5 6	Butler County	KS	Robert VanDeventer	1987	5273
153 5/8	25 2/8 24 6/8	18 0/8	6 8	Lorain County	OH	Daniel T. Fortney	1988	5273
153 5/8	25 0/8 25 0/8	17 7/8	5 5	Marathon County	WI	Paul Tuttle	1989	5273
153 5/8	27 4/8 26 7/8	20 6/8	6 4	Allamakee County	IA	Raymond Boland	1989	5273
153 5/8	25 7/8 24 7/8	17 5/8	5 6	Madison County	IA	Fred "Bud" Allen	1991	5273
153 5/8	26 1/8 25 5/8	19 1/8	6 6	Boone County	IA	Dave Rimathe	1992	5273
153 5/8	24 7/8 24 3/8	18 6/8	4 6	Outagamie County	WI	Scott M. Snortum	1992	5273
153 5/8	26 5/8 26 1/8	22 5/8	5 5	Logan County	CO	Robert L. Syvertson, Jr.	1992	5273
153 5/8	24 1/8 23 7/8	21 7/8	5 5	Howe Island	ONT	Nick Milonas	1993	5273
153 5/8	25 0/8 25 3/8	17 3/8	5 5	Monroe County	WI	Aaron Seielstad	1994	5273
153 5/8	23 1/8 23 4/8	17 1/8	5 5	Jackson County	MI	Randall J. Job	1995	5273
153 5/8	23 3/8 24 6/8	18 1/8	4 4	Lake County	IL	William L. Snelgrove	1995	5273
153 5/8	24 3/8 24 0/8	24 6/8	5 5	Renville County	ND	Dan Marler	1995	5273
153 5/8	31 2/8 30 2/8	23 0/8	8 6	McDonough County	IL	Max Wike	1996	5273
153 5/8	24 6/8 24 5/8	20 5/8	5 5	Kane County	IL	Bob Perkins	1996	5273
153 5/8	25 7/8 25 7/8	20 1/8	5 6	Keokuk County	IA	Kenneth P. Martin	1996	5273
153 5/8	22 2/8 21 5/8	17 3/8	5 5	Pike County	IL	Keith K. Klink	1996	5273
153 5/8	24 3/8 24 6/8	17 2/8	5 5	Highland County	OH	Klay Maynard	1996	5273
153 5/8	23 3/8 22 7/8	14 1/8	5 7	Lyon County	IA	Scott Hanson	1997	5273
153 5/8	26 3/8 26 7/8	18 5/8	5 5	Sawyer County	WI	Mike Freismuth	1997	5273
153 5/8	23 6/8 23 1/8	17 7/8	5 6	Columbia County	WI	Jim See	1998	5273
153 5/8	24 7/8 25 3/8	20 3/8	5 5	Washington County	KS	Richard Reith	1998	5273
153 5/8	24 0/8 24 0/8	18 7/8	5 5	Shawano County	WI	Daniel J. Payne	1999	5273
153 5/8	23 0/8 23 5/8	19 7/8	5 5	Buffalo County	WI	Stan Godfrey	2000	5273
153 5/8	25 0/8 24 7/8	19 7/8	6 5	Brown County	IL	Rick Lynch	2000	5273
153 5/8	23 0/8 23 6/8	19 0/8	6 6	Shawano County	WI	Daniel J. Borcherding	2000	5273
153 5/8	26 3/8 25 4/8	22 4/8	6 5	Marquette County	WI	Dan Vogelsang	2000	5273
153 5/8	22 3/8 21 6/8	16 3/8	6 5	Lucas County	IA	Frank Garton	2001	5273
153 5/8	22 3/8 22 7/8	15 7/8	5 6	Cortland County	NY	Bert E. Neff III	2001	5273
153 5/8	23 0/8 22 6/8	19 3/8	5 5	Ottawa County	MI	Scott Knauf	2002	5273
153 5/8	24 0/8 22 4/8	20 1/8	5 5	Marion County	IN	Brian Brady	2002	5273
153 5/8	26 6/8 26 7/8	20 5/8	4 4	Fairfield County	CT	Daniel R. DiSisto III	2002	5273
153 5/8	25 6/8 25 0/8	19 0/8	5 7	Pocahontas County	IA	Matt Pohlman	2002	5273
153 5/8	23 2/8 22 7/8	16 5/8	5 5	Bottineau County	ND	Frank McHard	2003	5273
153 5/8	23 3/8 23 2/8	20 1/8	5 6	Trigg County	KY	Sidney Wade, Jr.	2003	5273
*153 5/8	22 6/8 22 5/8	17 1/8	5 5	Montgomery County	IL	Tom Robbins	2003	5273
153 5/8	23 3/8 23 5/8	16 3/8	5 5	Barnes County	ND	Neil Pederson	2004	5273
*153 5/8	24 4/8 26 0/8	17 5/8	7 7	Johnson County	IL	Joshua Allen	2004	5273
153 5/8	22 3/8 22 2/8	17 1/8	5 5	Cherry County	NE	Joe Smisek	2005	5273
153 5/8	24 4/8 23 7/8	15 0/8	6 5	Buffalo County	WI	Jason Sturz	2006	5273

411

WHITETAIL DEER (TYPICAL ANTLERS)

Minimum Score 125 — Continued

SCORE	LENGTH OF MAIN BEAM R	L	INSIDE SPREAD	NUMBER OF POINTS R	L	AREA	STATE/PROVINCE	HUNTER'S NAME	DATE	RANK
153 5/8	24 1/8	23 5/8	18 3/8	5	6	Schleicher County	TX	Chris Mertz	2007	5273
153 5/8	22 6/8	22 4/8	17 1/8	5	5	Wabasha County	MN	Tom Kothenbeutel	2007	5273
153 5/8	23 7/8	23 0/8	17 7/8	5	5	Dunn County	WI	Scott A. Schmidt	2008	5273
*153 5/8	25 1/8	24 7/8	20 3/8	7	6	Athabasca	ALB	Donald H. Corey	2008	5273
153 5/8	22 7/8	25 2/8	18 6/8	7	5	Cerro Gordo County	IA	Cindy Roberts	2008	5273
153 5/8	21 7/8	22 2/8	18 1/8	5	5	Tulsa County	OK	Carlos Gomez	2008	5273
*153 5/8	23 4/8	23 6/8	16 3/8	5	5	Trempealeau County	WI	Bill Shepherd	2009	5273
153 5/8	21 5/8	22 5/8	15 4/8	5	6	Traill County	ND	Brody Peterson	2009	5273
153 4/8	25 7/8	25 2/8	19 3/8	7	6	Jackson County	MN	Lyle Babcock	1973	5329
153 4/8	25 1/8	23 6/8	22 0/8	6	5	Knox County	OH	John L. Yarman, Jr.	1975	5329
153 4/8	23 5/8	24 1/8	20 6/8	6	5	Billings County	ND	David L. Torkelson	1976	5329
153 4/8	25 5/8	25 7/8	23 4/8	6	5	Logan County	KY	Milton C. Gaddie	1979	5329
153 4/8	26 2/8	26 0/8	23 2/8	6	6	Douglas County	KS	Richard D. Brown	1979	5329
153 4/8	24 4/8	24 2/8	16 2/8	5	6	Columbia County	FL	Robert Ballard	1980	5329
153 4/8	22 5/8	22 4/8	14 6/8	5	5	Callaway County	MO	Marvin Giboney	1980	5329
153 4/8	24 7/8	24 6/8	17 4/8	5	5	Vinton County	OH	Mike Laferty	1982	5329
153 4/8	25 3/8	25 2/8	17 6/8	6	6	Morrison County	MN	Dennis Midas	1983	5329
153 4/8	22 5/8	22 5/8	17 0/8	6	7	Licking County	OH	Jeff Fowls	1986	5329
153 4/8	24 6/8	25 3/8	16 2/8	5	4	Trempealeau County	WI	David A. Stegemeyer	1987	5329
153 4/8	24 6/8	24 1/8	19 0/8	5	5	Dubuque County	IA	Patrick J. McAndrew	1988	5329
153 4/8	24 5/8	24 2/8	17 4/8	5	5	Ashland County	WI	Dennis A. Schmitt	1990	5329
153 4/8	26 0/8	24 4/8	16 6/8	5	5	Barber County	KS	Tom Langford	1990	5329
153 4/8	24 1/8	23 5/8	18 4/8	6	6	Montgomery County	MS	John M. Johnson	1991	5329
153 4/8	23 5/8	24 1/8	17 2/8	5	7	Randolph County	MO	Harold Montgomery	1991	5329
153 4/8	26 2/8	26 6/8	17 7/8	5	6	Knox County	IL	James Schmidt	1991	5329
153 4/8	25 1/8	24 2/8	17 7/8	6	6	Lee County	IA	Dale Clark	1991	5329
153 4/8	23 1/8	22 7/8	16 4/8	7	7	Hitchcock County	NE	Gary Gibson	1991	5329
153 4/8	24 5/8	24 7/8	22 4/8	5	5	Iroquois County	IL	Randy Hiltz	1992	5329
153 4/8	25 4/8	24 6/8	22 4/8	5	4	Peoria County	IL	Lee Lewis	1993	5329
153 4/8	23 0/8	22 4/8	15 0/8	6	6	Mason County	WV	Larry McCarty	1993	5329
153 4/8	22 1/8	22 6/8	17 2/8	5	5	Seward County	KS	Lynn Leonard	1994	5329
153 4/8	25 4/8	25 0/8	18 0/8	4	5	Morris County	KS	Roy De Hoff	1995	5329
153 4/8	25 1/8	25 2/8	16 4/8	5	6	Buffalo County	WI	Burton Goodenough	1995	5329
153 4/8	25 5/8	25 1/8	17 6/8	5	5	Guthrie County	IA	Todd E. Castle	1995	5329
153 4/8	22 6/8	23 1/8	18 4/8	5	7	Lonoke County	AR	Billy L. Gilliam	1995	5329
153 4/8	26 1/8	25 3/8	17 2/8	5	4	Franklin County	IL	Darrell Roberts	1995	5329
153 4/8	26 7/8	26 6/8	20 0/8	4	4	Edgar County	IL	Darrell Bozarth	1996	5329
153 4/8	24 7/8	23 5/8	20 1/8	4	6	Winnebago County	IL	James R. Petersen	1996	5329
153 4/8	25 4/8	24 3/8	19 4/8	5	4	Carroll County	IL	John Tomczak	1996	5329
153 4/8	30 1/8	31 2/8	21 3/8	5	7	Knox County	IL	Larry C. Harding	1996	5329
153 4/8	23 4/8	26 0/8	18 0/8	8	5	Lenawee County	MI	Michael A. Urbanczyk	1997	5329
153 4/8	24 4/8	24 5/8	23 0/8	5	5	Kleberg County	TX	Andy Milam	1997	5329
153 4/8	23 0/8	22 5/8	17 2/8	5	5	Brown County	SD	Bryan B. Aaron	1997	5329
153 4/8	24 5/8	24 7/8	22 0/8	7	6	Adams County	OH	Andy F. Yutzy	1997	5329
153 4/8	23 6/8	23 4/8	17 6/8	6	5	Yuma County	CO	Jeff Lee	1998	5329
153 4/8	25 2/8	25 3/8	21 3/8	6	6	Shawano County	WI	Richard A. Pluger	1998	5329
153 4/8	27 0/8	26 3/8	21 2/8	5	5	Sawyer County	WI	Edward J. Kwiecien	1998	5329
153 4/8	23 0/8	23 5/8	16 7/8	7	6	Iron County	WI	Kurt Meyer	1999	5329
153 4/8	26 2/8	25 6/8	18 0/8	5	5	Crawford County	WI	Robert McCann	1999	5329
153 4/8	27 5/8	27 1/8	20 0/8	5	5	Piatt County	IL	Robert W. James	1999	5329
153 4/8	28 6/8	29 0/8	17 4/8	5	6	Ogle County	IL	Brodie R. Arndt	2000	5329
153 4/8	23 4/8	23 1/8	18 1/8	5	7	Allamakee County	IA	Kevin R. Kelly	2000	5329
153 4/8	22 2/8	21 7/8	16 2/8	5	5	Morris	MAN	Rod McGrath	2001	5329
153 4/8	26 6/8	26 3/8	19 3/8	4	5	Union County	KY	Sam Cotton	2001	5329
153 4/8	20 2/8	22 6/8	17 4/8	7	6	Clark County	IL	James Coyle	2001	5329
153 4/8	26 2/8	25 6/8	17 6/8	5	5	Madison County	NY	Bill Nye	2001	5329
153 4/8	20 7/8	23 4/8	17 6/8	5	5	Clark County	MO	Don Davidson	2002	5329
153 4/8	22 5/8	21 6/8	17 6/8	5	5	Iowa County	WI	Ohne Raasch	2003	5329
153 4/8	24 1/8	24 1/8	19 4/8	4	4	Swan Lake	MAN	Chris Mondor	2003	5329
153 4/8	23 4/8	23 7/8	18 2/8	5	5	Winnebago County	IL	Paul U. Robins	2003	5329
153 4/8	23 3/8	23 2/8	16 0/8	5	5	McLean County	ND	Tim Tomlinson	2004	5329
153 4/8	24 0/8	23 6/8	17 4/8	5	5	Cass County	MO	Ronald Raines	2004	5329
153 4/8	24 2/8	24 2/8	18 4/8	5	6	Fayette County	IA	Jason Hurd	2004	5329
153 4/8	25 0/8	25 0/8	18 4/8	4	4	Ottawa County	KS	John Nelson	2004	5329
*153 4/8	25 6/8	25 2/8	17 3/8	9	6	Jefferson County	IL	Zack Thompson	2005	5329
*153 4/8	24 3/8	25 3/8	19 7/8	5	6	Tioga County	NY	John Olsen	2006	5329
153 4/8	26 4/8	25 0/8	16 1/8	6	5	Clark County	IL	Fred Eichler	2006	5329
153 4/8	24 6/8	25 2/8	21 0/8	5	5	Schuylkill County	PA	Ernie Moyer	2007	5329
153 4/8	25 7/8	25 1/8	20 6/8	5	6	Lincoln County	OK	Ken Petros	2007	5329
153 4/8	26 1/8	26 2/8	19 4/8	4	5	Logan County	WV	Ronald Barnette	2008	5329
153 4/8	24 6/8	24 5/8	18 0/8	5	5	Hunterdon County	NJ	Michael R. Pongratz	2008	5329
153 4/8	23 7/8	23 4/8	17 2/8	5	5	Trempealeau County	WI	Eric Boberg	2008	5329
*153 4/8	25 7/8	24 0/8	18 2/8	5	5	Livingston County	NY	Cecil Edwards	2009	5329
*153 4/8	25 4/8	24 4/8	16 0/8	7	6	Marquette County	WI	Tim McFaul	2009	5329
153 4/8	26 1/8	24 6/8	17 2/8	4	4	Sanborn County	SD	Brandon Goergen	2009	5329
153 3/8	25 5/8	24 7/8	19 4/8	5	6	Grundy County	IL	Ed Vitko, Jr.	1972	5396
153 3/8	21 2/8	22 3/8	19 0/8	7	6	Morrison County	MN	Robert R. Ganzer	1973	5396
153 3/8	25 5/8	27 6/8	21 1/8	4	4	Knox County	IL	Bill Richards	1981	5396
153 3/8	25 1/8	24 3/8	19 3/8	4	4	Webster County	WV	Charles P. Green	1982	5396
153 3/8	22 7/8	22 7/8	20 6/8	7	7	Macoupin County	IL	Charles M. Woolfolk	1983	5396
153 3/8	24 7/8	24 7/8	17 7/8	6	7	Calumet County	WI	Matt Fuchs	1986	5396
153 3/8	24 2/8	26 1/8	18 6/8	6	6	McHenry County	IL	Lenny Vohasek	1987	5396
153 3/8	28 4/8	29 4/8	21 7/8	4	5	Dakota County	NE	Keith R. Claypool	1987	5396
153 3/8	28 4/8	27 6/8	21 3/8	4	4	Howard County	MD	Chris Apostolakos	1987	5396
153 3/8	23 1/8	22 7/8	20 3/8	5	5	Morgan County	CO	Michael Paul Hansen	1988	5396
153 3/8	25 2/8	24 6/8	17 5/8	5	5	Suffolk County	NY	Ronald W. Tybaert	1988	5396
153 3/8	25 5/8	24 2/8	19 1/8	5	5	Greene County	MO	Don M. Andrews	1988	5396
153 3/8	24 4/8	24 4/8	18 2/8	5	6	Webb County	TX	Gilberto Guajardo, Jr.	1989	5396
153 3/8	24 4/8	25 4/8	20 4/8	5	6	Lake County	IL	Mark Nelsen	1990	5396
153 3/8	25 4/8	25 3/8	20 3/8	5	5	Racine County	WI	Dave L. Krupp	1990	5396
153 3/8	25 4/8	25 3/8	16 1/8	5	5	Jefferson County	IA	Robin L. Geibel	1990	5396
153 3/8	23 1/8	22 6/8	19 7/8	5	5	Westchester County	NY	Michael A. Chirico	1990	5396
153 3/8	28 4/8	26 4/8	18 3/8	4	5	Bracken County	KY	George Clark	1990	5396
153 3/8	24 2/8	24 6/8	18 0/8	5	7	Tazewell County	IL	Charles F. Estes	1991	5396
153 3/8	25 1/8	25 2/8	19 1/8	4	4	McHenry County	IL	Roger A. Bacon	1992	5396

WHITETAIL DEER (TYPICAL ANTLERS)

Minimum Score 125 Continued

SCORE	LENGTH OF R MAIN BEAM L	INSIDE SPREAD	NUMBER OF R POINTS L	AREA	STATE/PROVINCE	HUNTER'S NAME	DATE	RANK
153 3/8	23 5/8 22 7/8	20 3/8	6 6	Macon County	IL	Joe Sapp	1993	5396
153 3/8	26 1/8 26 4/8	19 3/8	5 4	Scott County	IL	Gene E. Meier	1993	5396
153 3/8	26 4/8 27 0/8	18 7/8	6 5	Linn County	IA	Hunter B. Techau	1993	5396
153 3/8	24 6/8 25 2/8	15 3/8	5 6	Turner County	SD	Tony Waltner	1994	5396
153 3/8	25 0/8 25 2/8	20 4/8	6 7	Macoupin County	IL	Joe Clements	1995	5396
153 3/8	25 6/8 25 5/8	21 5/8	5 6	Butler County	KS	Kirk Kelly	1995	5396
153 3/8	24 0/8 23 4/8	17 7/8	5 5	Logan County	WV	William L.T. Pack	1996	5396
153 3/8	23 6/8 23 4/8	19 7/8	6 6	Van Buren County	IA	Mark Story	1996	5396
153 3/8	24 3/8 23 6/8	20 1/8	5 5	Winnebago County	IL	Randy K. Thompson	1997	5396
153 3/8	24 5/8 25 0/8	16 3/8	5 7	Cedar County	NE	Scott Aase	1998	5396
153 3/8	27 5/8 27 6/8	16 0/8	10 7	Brown County	IL	David R. Herschelman	1998	5396
153 3/8	22 3/8 22 3/8	17 5/8	5 6	Clayton County	IA	Gary L. Mezera	1998	5396
153 3/8	22 7/8 23 5/8	18 7/8	5 5	Appanoose County	IA	Larry R. Shondel	1998	5396
153 3/8	23 1/8 23 1/8	18 1/8	5 5	Spokane County	WA	Robert Pfeifer	1998	5396
153 3/8	23 0/8 22 5/8	19 5/8	6 6	Clark County	MO	B. Mike Fischer	1999	5396
153 3/8	24 2/8 24 0/8	17 7/8	5 5	Schuyler County	IL	Ken Shaw	2000	5396
153 3/8	24 7/8 25 4/8	17 1/8	5 5	Floyd County	VA	Les Hall	2001	5396
153 3/8	25 0/8 25 5/8	16 3/8	4 5	Brown County	IL	Ricky Thomas Wensil	2001	5396
153 3/8	23 7/8 23 5/8	16 3/8	5 5	Blackford County	IN	Gary L. Winder	2001	5396
153 3/8	23 3/8 23 2/8	16 4/8	6 7	Webster County	IA	Edward E. Ulicki	2002	5396
153 3/8	23 5/8 22 7/8	17 5/8	5 5	Dane County	WI	Mark J. Vils	2003	5396
153 3/8	25 3/8 24 2/8	17 7/8	5 5	Whiteside County	IL	Kevin Pinski	2003	5396
153 3/8	24 1/8 23 3/8	20 6/8	7 5	Guthrie County	IA	Mark Van Houten	2003	5396
153 3/8	23 2/8 23 4/8	20 3/8	6 6	Ellis County	OK	Ronnie Rabe	2003	5396
*153 3/8	23 5/8 24 7/8	19 3/8	6 5	Polk County	IA	Steve Flanagan	2003	5396
*153 3/8	24 6/8 25 7/8	23 4/8	5 6	Bracken County	KY	Adam Engnes	2004	5396
153 3/8	26 1/8 25 4/8	17 3/8	5 5	Hartford County	CT	David Iskra	2004	5396
153 3/8	25 6/8 25 5/8	20 7/8	7 7	Taylor County	WI	Lorin Dassow	2005	5396
153 3/8	25 0/8 24 4/8	21 4/8	6 5	Iroquois County	IL	Steven Clark	2005	5396
153 3/8	24 5/8 24 5/8	19 7/8	5 5	Sawyer County	WI	Tom Christensen	2005	5396
153 3/8	21 0/8 22 0/8	16 2/8	8 6	Yellowstone County	MT	Ron Hein	2006	5396
153 3/8	24 7/8 24 7/8	20 6/8	7 7	Fayette County	KY	Don Jenkins	2006	5396
*153 3/8	27 1/8 27 3/8	18 2/8	6 5	Macoupin County	IL	Kevin Bowman	2006	5396
153 3/8	23 6/8 23 7/8	17 1/8	5 5	Trempealeau County	WI	Richard Bryson	2006	5396
153 3/8	24 0/8 24 6/8	17 0/8	6 6	Marinette County	WI	Ben Bruette	2006	5396
*153 3/8	25 3/8 25 3/8	18 1/8	6 9	Defiance County	OH	Jeremy R. Nadler	2007	5396
153 3/8	25 6/8 27 0/8	18 7/8	6 6	Hennepin County	MN	Dean Basch	2007	5396
*153 3/8	25 3/8 24 5/8	16 5/8	6 5	Hendricks County	IN	James R. McBay	2007	5396
153 3/8	23 0/8 22 6/8	17 3/8	5 6	Guthrie County	IA	Kevin Forke	2007	5396
153 3/8	23 6/8 24 4/8	17 0/8	6 6	Grand Forks County	ND	Jeff Monson	2008	5396
153 3/8	23 4/8 23 3/8	18 1/8	5 5	Wayne County	NY	Chris Loveless	2008	5396
153 3/8	23 5/8 23 4/8	18 7/8	5 5	Tazewell County	IL	Mark E. Jones	2009	5396
153 3/8	24 0/8 23 0/8	22 7/8	6 7	Phillips County	AR	Chad Foster	2009	5396
*153 3/8	24 0/8 23 1/8	16 7/8	6 6	Carroll County	OH	Marvin Morrison, Jr.	2009	5396
*153 3/8	26 1/8 26 1/8	16 5/8	5 5	Jefferson County	NE	Andy Berkenpas	2009	5396
153 3/8	24 1/8 23 4/8	19 3/8	6 6	Fremont County	IA	Seth Carlock	2009	5396
*153 3/8	23 4/8 23 4/8	17 2/8	6 8	Dunn County	WI	Robert A. Seidmore	2009	5396
153 3/8	24 4/8 23 7/8	18 7/8	6 6	McLean County	ND	Vance Tomlinson	2010	5396
153 3/8	26 1/8 25 2/8	18 0/8	7 6	Shawano County	WI	Denis A. Oswald	2010	5396
153 2/8	24 4/8 24 3/8	24 4/8	5 6	Burt County	NE	Harold W. Hawkins	1966	5465
153 2/8	26 0/8 26 7/8	20 6/8	6 6	Winnebago County	IA	Ronald Gordon	1972	5465
153 2/8	22 5/8 22 3/8	20 4/8	5 5	Lincoln County	NE	Greg Wingfield	1978	5465
153 2/8	21 6/8 21 7/8	15 0/8	5 5	Wood County	WI	James Wilke	1984	5465
153 2/8	26 3/8 25 2/8	18 4/8	7 5	Butler County	KS	Larry Womack	1984	5465
153 2/8	24 3/8 23 6/8	20 2/8	5 5	Jackson County	MN	Bill Vangsness	1985	5465
153 2/8	22 1/8 23 3/8	17 1/8	9 5	Seminole County	OK	James V. Flowers III	1986	5465
153 2/8	24 4/8 24 7/8	19 0/8	5 5	Frederick County	MD	Grayson Mercer, Jr.	1986	5465
153 2/8	25 0/8 25 5/8	19 5/8	9 6	Morgan County	IL	Sam Alfand	1986	5465
153 2/8	23 0/8 24 2/8	19 0/8	5 5	Wapello County	IA	Jim Smith	1987	5465
153 2/8	23 4/8 24 7/8	17 0/8	7 5	Pulaski County	IN	Steve Knebel	1988	5465
153 2/8	25 1/8 25 1/8	21 6/8	4 4	Stephenson County	IL	Robert J. Schiffman	1989	5465
153 2/8	24 6/8 24 4/8	20 4/8	7 5	Edmonton	ALB	Dale Spooner	1991	5465
153 2/8	23 7/8 23 4/8	18 2/8	5 5	Coffey County	KS	Douglas Gilkison	1992	5465
153 2/8	25 1/8 24 3/8	21 7/8	5 6	Carroll County	IL	Ed Smetana	1993	5465
153 2/8	26 3/8 26 2/8	19 1/8	5 6	Kent County	MD	Robert G. Griffin	1994	5465
153 2/8	24 3/8 23 6/8	14 4/8	6 8	Boone County	IA	James Perkins	1994	5465
153 2/8	24 1/8 23 2/8	18 2/8	5 5	Piatt County	IL	Robert W. James	1995	5465
153 2/8	24 2/8 23 7/8	24 0/8	6 7	Will County	IL	Timothy A. Butler	1995	5465
153 2/8	24 0/8 23 5/8	20 3/8	6 5	Fayette County	IA	David Kemmerer	1995	5465
153 2/8	23 1/8 23 4/8	17 3/8	8 5	Buffalo County	WI	David J. Brion	1995	5465
153 2/8	23 3/8 23 5/8	19 2/8	5 6	Page County	IA	Chris Barton	1996	5465
153 2/8	24 3/8 23 7/8	19 4/8	5 6	Adams County	WI	Michael J. Yates	1998	5465
153 2/8	23 2/8 24 6/8	19 2/8	4 5	Crawford County	IL	Matthew D. Elliott	1998	5465
153 2/8	23 6/8 23 4/8	16 5/8	6 5	Marquette County	WI	Robert Sarbacker	1999	5465
153 2/8	25 2/8 24 1/8	20 5/8	5 7	Fairfield County	CT	James E. Dubuc	2001	5465
153 2/8	25 1/8 25 0/8	17 4/8	6 5	Hamilton County	OH	Robert A. Henry	2001	5465
153 2/8	24 4/8 24 3/8	16 1/8	6 6	Cole County	MO	Mike Distler	2001	5465
153 2/8	23 4/8 23 4/8	18 1/8	5 6	Wayne County	IA	Brent Clodfelter	2001	5465
153 2/8	24 5/8 25 5/8	18 7/8	6 6	Chester County	PA	Raymond P. Dabitz	2002	5465
153 2/8	24 6/8 23 1/8	18 1/8	6 7	Buffalo County	WI	Stan Godfrey	2002	5465
153 2/8	25 4/8 24 2/8	21 4/8	5 5	Jackson County	WI	John Schulte	2002	5465
153 2/8	25 0/8 24 7/8	17 2/8	6 5	Iowa County	WI	Bradford Pittman	2002	5465
153 2/8	26 1/8 26 6/8	20 0/8	4 4	Buffalo County	WI	Ross Goulette	2003	5465
153 2/8	26 3/8 25 6/8	18 6/8	5 5	Fond du Lac County	WI	Gregory R. Marshall	2004	5465
153 2/8	21 4/8 21 4/8	19 3/8	5 6	Woodbury County	IA	Shane Bainbridge	2004	5465
153 2/8	27 4/8 26 6/8	18 0/8	4 4	Green County	WI	Jerry Benson, Jr.	2004	5465
153 2/8	25 6/8 26 0/8	18 2/8	5 6	Allamakee County	IA	Joe Lieb	2004	5465
153 2/8	23 1/8 23 4/8	17 6/8	5 5	Huntington County	IN	Ronnie Douglas	2005	5465
*153 2/8	28 0/8 26 7/8	22 0/8	5 5	Du Page County	IL	Anton Hruby	2005	5465
153 2/8	24 6/8 24 4/8	21 0/8	5 5	Waukesha County	WI	Cormac Palmer	2005	5465
153 2/8	20 6/8 22 2/8	16 4/8	5 5	De Kalb County	IN	Terry Keenan	2006	5465
153 2/8	25 5/8 25 7/8	18 7/8	6 5	Buffalo County	WI	Dave Hale	2006	5465
153 2/8	22 0/8 22 1/8	20 0/8	5 5	DeKalb County	IL	Milferd R. Schwersenska	2006	5465
153 2/8	25 5/8 25 5/8	17 5/8	6 6	Vernon County	WI	Jesse A. Blum	2007	5465
153 2/8	25 2/8 25 0/8	19 0/8	5 6	Montgomery County	OH	Brad Lupton	2007	5465

413

WHITETAIL DEER (TYPICAL ANTLERS)

Minimum Score 125 — Continued

SCORE	R MAIN BEAM L	INSIDE SPREAD	R POINTS L	AREA	STATE/PROVINCE	HUNTER'S NAME	DATE	RANK
153 2/8	23 4/8 23 0/8	17 6/8	5 6	Pike County	IL	Gary Nunn	2007	5465
153 2/8	25 4/8 25 3/8	20 4/8	5 5	Green County	WI	Jeffrey Zanow	2007	5465
153 2/8	24 3/8 24 4/8	20 4/8	6 5	Hemphill County	TX	Shay Read	2008	5465
153 2/8	21 6/8 23 3/8	18 0/8	5 6	Trempealeau County	WI	Dalton Nephew	2008	5465
153 2/8	25 7/8 27 2/8	18 2/8	5 4	Jefferson County	KY	Ron Sonne	2008	5465
153 2/8	24 1/8 24 0/8	17 5/8	7 6	Marinette County	WI	Chad Rickling	2009	5465
153 2/8	27 0/8 25 5/8	19 5/8	5 6	Washburn County	WI	Brandon Degner	2009	5465
*153 2/8	25 1/8 25 3/8	15 4/8	5 5	Chicot County	AR	John S. Ingram	2009	5465
153 1/8	25 2/8 25 0/8	18 5/8	4 5	Lincoln County	NE	Rich Birch	1965	5519
153 1/8	25 6/8 25 1/8	19 1/8	6 5	Christian County	IL	Michael Miloncus	1983	5519
153 1/8	25 6/8 25 1/8	17 1/8	7 6	Moody County	SD	Paul Schlobohm	1983	5519
153 1/8	27 2/8 27 1/8	27 2/8	6 5	Lee County	IA	Ronald Elbe	1986	5519
153 1/8	22 5/8 21 3/8	18 1/8	5 5	White County	AR	Harold Dwain Marlin	1987	5519
153 1/8	20 4/8 21 6/8	18 5/8	5 5	St. Clair County	IL	Jim Fetters	1987	5519
153 1/8	24 3/8 24 3/8	16 5/8	5 6	Lake County	IL	Steve Andrews	1988	5519
153 1/8	22 6/8 23 1/8	17 3/8	7 8	Walworth County	WI	Charles Palmer	1990	5519
153 1/8	25 4/8 25 2/8	19 3/8	5 5	Monroe County	NY	Dan Scorza	1990	5519
153 1/8	23 7/8 22 7/8	17 6/8	7 5	Washington County	OH	Scott J. Cogar	1992	5519
153 1/8	24 3/8 24 1/8	20 4/8	6 5	Henry County	IA	William J. Wilson	1992	5519
153 1/8	25 7/8 25 2/8	18 3/8	5 4	Wood County	OH	Mark Kubacki	1994	5519
153 1/8	22 5/8 22 7/8	18 1/8	5 5	York County	PA	Joseph Kingston	1994	5519
153 1/8	23 1/8 23 5/8	15 7/8	5 5	Livingston County	MI	Ted Thomas Ford	1994	5519
153 1/8	24 0/8 24 2/8	17 7/8	5 5	Litchfield County	CT	Antonio E. Cacela	1995	5519
153 1/8	25 0/8 24 2/8	20 3/8	5 6	Shelby County	MO	Glen Mertens	1995	5519
153 1/8	24 1/8 23 3/8	15 1/8	6 6	Richland County	WI	Mickel R. Whitfield	1998	5519
153 1/8	23 5/8 24 0/8	19 3/8	6 6	Litchfield County	CT	Kenneth R. Beeler, Jr.	1998	5519
153 1/8	22 4/8 22 5/8	16 5/8	5 5	Washtenaw County	MI	Todd W. Farmer	1998	5519
153 1/8	25 5/8 26 0/8	16 3/8	5 5	Jo Daviess County	IL	Kenneth Pluym	1998	5519
153 1/8	22 7/8 24 3/8	18 3/8	7 5	Fayette County	IA	Wayne Squires	1998	5519
153 1/8	25 6/8 25 3/8	18 5/8	5 4	Muscatine County	IA	Mark Seefeldt, Jr.	1998	5519
153 1/8	20 0/8 20 2/8	16 5/8	6 6	Haskell County	OK	David L. Rose	1998	5519
153 1/8	21 3/8 22 3/8	18 7/8	6 7	Ogle County	IL	Allen Hedges	1999	5519
153 1/8	23 5/8 23 3/8	21 6/8	8 6	Pepin County	WI	Robert Cataract	1999	5519
153 1/8	25 3/8 24 5/8	17 3/8	5 5	Butler County	IA	David W. Diercks	1999	5519
153 1/8	24 0/8 24 0/8	20 3/8	5 5	Buffalo County	WI	Joe Sanks	2000	5519
153 1/8	25 7/8 27 0/8	21 0/8	4 6	Dane County	WI	Patrick J. Sutter	2000	5519
153 1/8	24 2/8 25 4/8	16 7/8	5 5	Lincoln County	WV	John Ramey	2000	5519
153 1/8	26 4/8 25 3/8	18 0/8	7 5	St. Louis County	MO	Larry D. Simmons, Jr.	2001	5519
153 1/8	24 4/8 23 3/8	17 1/8	5 5	McHenry County	IL	Richard Pope	2001	5519
153 1/8	28 2/8 27 6/8	20 1/8	6 7	Montgomery County	IL	Chris Cvengros	2001	5519
153 1/8	24 1/8 23 0/8	18 7/8	5 5	McLean County	IL	Dave Baker	2002	5519
153 1/8	24 7/8 24 5/8	19 1/8	5 5	Washington County	WI	Joel W. Wicklund	2002	5519
153 1/8	25 4/8 25 5/8	21 6/8	7 5	Kane County	IL	Dean V. Ashton	2002	5519
153 1/8	24 1/8 23 1/8	18 5/8	6 6	Iron County	WI	Jack Bradley III	2002	5519
*153 1/8	24 1/8 23 0/8	16 7/8	6 6	Bourbon County	KS	Dale Gauthier	2003	5519
153 1/8	25 0/8 27 0/8	17 5/8	5 5	Ashland County	OH	Nathan Clint Lozier	2003	5519
153 1/8	24 2/8 24 2/8	18 5/8	5 5	Outagamie County	WI	Al Conger	2004	5519
153 1/8	25 3/8 24 3/8	16 3/8	6 7	Sumner County	KS	Jeff Aldrich	2004	5519
153 1/8	28 0/8 28 1/8	22 3/8	5 4	Clinton County	IA	Tim Bartels	2004	5519
*153 1/8	25 1/8 23 2/8	20 1/8	4 5	Lake County	IL	John F. Kahon III	2005	5519
153 1/8	23 3/8 22 7/8	15 1/8	5 5	Van Buren County	IA	James Fitzgerald	2005	5519
153 1/8	22 7/8 23 1/8	16 4/8	8 6	Mason County	IL	Robert Stinauer	2005	5519
153 1/8	25 1/8 25 2/8	18 3/8	5 5	Mitchell County	IA	Kyle Wedeking	2005	5519
153 1/8	23 5/8 23 7/8	18 2/8	6 6	Van Buren County	IA	Kevin McDonald	2006	5519
*153 1/8	25 2/8 25 7/8	19 1/8	4 4	Stokes County	NC	Todd Rothrock	2007	5519
*153 1/8	24 1/8 22 6/8	16 5/8	5 5	Wythe County	VA	Ricky King	2007	5519
153 1/8	22 0/8 25 3/8	14 6/8	7 6	Waupaca County	WI	Craig Konrad	2007	5519
153 1/8	26 2/8 24 2/8	22 4/8	6 7	Fairfield County	OH	Robert Strait	2007	5519
153 1/8	26 5/8 25 3/8	17 5/8	5 5	St. Marys County	MD	Craig Buist	2007	5519
153 1/8	23 1/8 23 1/8	18 1/8	5 4	Tippecanoe County	IN	Eric Braund	2007	5519
153 1/8	25 2/8 24 2/8	14 4/8	5 9	Richland County	OH	Eric Saterfield	2007	5519
*153 1/8	22 3/8 22 5/8	18 5/8	6 5	Washington County	OH	David C. Brewer	2008	5519
153 1/8	25 2/8 25 6/8	18 6/8	6 5	Waukesha County	WI	Michael J. Braund	2008	5519
153 1/8	22 0/8 21 6/8	17 5/8	7 9	Barber County	KS	Mike Gallop	2008	5519
153 1/8	23 1/8 22 1/8	19 0/8	6 4	Rice County	KS	Russell Hammer	2009	5519
153 1/8	28 6/8 29 2/8	18 6/8	5 4	Lawrence County	PA	James R. Mayberry	2009	5519
153 1/8	23 6/8 23 4/8	20 7/8	6 6	Jefferson County	PA	Tony Medvetz	2009	5519
*153 1/8	22 1/8 22 2/8	16 1/8	6 7	Lawrence County	OH	David Massie	2009	5519
*153 1/8	23 0/8 21 0/8	15 3/8	5 6	Chippewa County	WI	Nathan Woolever	2009	5519
153 1/8	23 1/8 23 1/8	17 5/8	6 6	Owen County	IN	James D. Baird	2009	5519
153 1/8	26 0/8 25 2/8	18 6/8	7 6	Dunn County	WI	Robert Shaw	2009	5519
153 1/8	23 5/8 24 5/8	15 4/8	8 7	Harris County	GA	Jay Foxworthy	2009	5519
153 1/8	23 2/8 23 2/8	20 2/8	6 7	Dane County	WI	Daniel W. Zenker	2010	5519
153 0/8	25 0/8 25 2/8	17 4/8	5 5	Cambria County	PA	Andrew J. Getsy	1965	5584
153 0/8	21 3/8 21 1/8	16 4/8	5 5	Burleigh County	ND	Jim Balzer	1977	5584
153 0/8	24 7/8 25 1/8	16 3/8	5 6	Koochiching County	MN	Dr. Thomas Zbaracki	1980	5584
153 0/8	23 2/8 23 6/8	16 0/8	5 5	Lawrence County	PA	Wayne Edwards	1981	5584
153 0/8	23 5/8 23 6/8	15 7/8	6 6	Shelby County	IL	Bill D. Pesch	1983	5584
153 0/8	23 7/8 24 3/8	18 4/8	5 5	Trumbull County	OH	Art Stanton	1985	5584
153 0/8	25 3/8 25 2/8	19 4/8	4 5	Dane County	WI	Joe Eugster	1986	5584
153 0/8	26 1/8 26 5/8	19 3/8	4 5	Mason County	IL	Gregory B. Snider	1986	5584
153 0/8	24 2/8 24 2/8	21 6/8	5 6	Lake County	IL	Roger A. Bacon	1987	5584
153 0/8	24 0/8 25 4/8	23 1/8	5 5	Lake County	IL	Kris Laho	1987	5584
153 0/8	26 1/8 26 3/8	22 2/8	5 4	Craig County	OK	Eddie Claypool	1988	5584
153 0/8	26 0/8 26 3/8	18 4/8	5 4	Sangamon County	IL	Randy Black	1988	5584
153 0/8	26 2/8 25 5/8	15 1/8	5 5	Saline County	NE	Don Kohout	1990	5584
153 0/8	26 1/8 24 4/8	15 5/8	6 5	Kay County	OK	Guy L. LeMonnier, Jr.	1990	5584
153 0/8	22 3/8 22 1/8	15 0/8	5 5	Henry County	IA	Paul Ginkens	1990	5584
153 0/8	22 0/8 21 5/8	17 7/8	8 7	Washburn County	WI	Dennis Regenauer	1990	5584
153 0/8	26 0/8 25 4/8	19 0/8	4 4	Vinton County	OH	Randy Boggs	1991	5584
153 0/8	25 3/8 26 4/8	18 3/8	6 6	Buffalo County	WI	Brad Johnson	1992	5584
153 0/8	24 0/8 25 2/8	17 3/8	5 6	Edwards County	KS	Sheila Wood	1992	5584
153 0/8	23 0/8 22 5/8	16 2/8	6 5	Casey County	KY	Carroll Gibson	1993	5584
153 0/8	23 6/8 23 1/8	16 4/8	5 5	McLean County	IL	Robert F. Keith	1993	5584
153 0/8	23 6/8 23 6/8	16 4/8	5 5	Racine County	WI	Calvin Kamrath	1994	5584

WHITETAIL DEER (TYPICAL ANTLERS)

Minimum Score 125 — Continued

SCORE	LENGTH OF R MAIN BEAM L	INSIDE SPREAD	NUMBER OF R POINTS L	AREA	STATE/ PROVINCE	HUNTER'S NAME	DATE	RANK
153 0/8	27 3/8 26 4/8	21 3/8	6 5	Vernon County	WI	Tim Hoeth	1995	5584
153 0/8	23 6/8 22 5/8	18 4/8	5 5	Fond du Lac County	WI	Tim Frank	1995	5584
153 0/8	22 0/8 21 2/8	17 6/8	5 5	Washington County	WI	Rick Bertoni	1995	5584
153 0/8	23 5/8 24 5/8	15 4/8	6 7	Meigs County	OH	Tim Smith	1995	5584
153 0/8	24 3/8 23 3/8	21 7/8	7 6	Edmonton	ALB	Lynn R. Parrish	1995	5584
153 0/8	27 2/8 28 0/8	21 0/8	4 4	Monroe County	NY	Robert Ferrarone	1995	5584
153 0/8	25 3/8 25 0/8	19 0/8	5 4	Jefferson County	IA	Dennis Douthart	1996	5584
153 0/8	25 5/8 24 1/8	22 4/8	6 5	Lincoln County	NE	Jason K. Swanson	1996	5584
153 0/8	27 0/8 25 7/8	23 2/8	4 4	Somerset County	NJ	Andrew A. Confortini	1997	5584
153 0/8	24 5/8 25 0/8	18 2/8	5 5	Waukesha County	WI	Doug Kennedy	1997	5584
153 0/8	23 0/8 24 6/8	21 0/8	5 6	Knox County	OH	Wayne Zollars	1998	5584
153 0/8	22 7/8 22 5/8	18 0/8	5 5	Williams County	OH	Nicholas Lloyd	1998	5584
153 0/8	23 0/8 24 3/8	17 6/8	6 7	Fayette County	IA	Roger Bagg	1998	5584
153 0/8	25 5/8 26 3/8	19 6/8	5 5	Trempealeau County	WI	Ross Lambert	1999	5584
153 0/8	25 4/8 24 7/8	20 2/8	4 5	Jo Daviess County	IL	Mike Kane	1999	5584
153 0/8	24 3/8 24 7/8	17 1/8	6 6	Boone County	IA	Shawn Hornberg	1999	5584
153 0/8	24 0/8 25 6/8	17 0/8	4 5	Will County	IL	Jerry LeVault	1999	5584
153 0/8	25 5/8 25 1/8	20 1/8	4 6	Douglas County	KS	Wiley Burnett	1999	5584
153 0/8	22 0/8 24 4/8	18 1/8	6 6	Callaway County	MO	Shannon Baumgartner	2000	5584
153 0/8	23 7/8 23 7/8	18 2/8	5 6	Freeborn County	MN	Kevin Nelsen	2000	5584
153 0/8	20 4/8 24 1/8	21 6/8	7 5	Delaware County	OH	Steve Boham	2000	5584
*153 0/8	25 3/8 26 5/8	17 6/8	5 5	Henry County	IN	Gregg Watt	2001	5584
153 0/8	24 3/8 24 1/8	20 5/8	6 7	Steuben County	IN	Joseph S. Hutter	2001	5584
153 0/8	24 0/8 23 3/8	17 4/8	4 4	Lenawee County	MI	Scott W. Cramer	2002	5584
153 0/8	23 1/8 23 4/8	17 1/8	6 6	McDonald County	MO	Brian Sharp	2002	5584
*153 0/8	23 3/8 24 1/8	20 1/8	6 5	Grant County	IN	Matt Swain	2003	5584
153 0/8	22 5/8 24 0/8	15 4/8	5 5	Scotland County	MO	Jerry Dwayne Smith	2003	5584
153 0/8	24 0/8 23 0/8	20 2/8	5 5	Buffalo County	WI	Samuel D. Schleicher	2003	5584
153 0/8	23 5/8 22 7/8	18 4/8	5 5	Keokuk County	IA	David DeFrance	2003	5584
153 0/8	23 6/8 22 5/8	17 6/8	5 5	Trempealeau County	WI	Tom R. Speltz	2003	5584
*153 0/8	22 6/8 23 3/8	19 2/8	6 6	Miller County	MO	Chad Williams	2004	5584
153 0/8	27 2/8 28 2/8	18 1/8	6 6	Queen Annes County	MD	Eric Johnson	2004	5584
*153 0/8	24 7/8 24 3/8	17 0/8	5 5	Oregon County	MO	Jason Record	2005	5584
153 0/8	24 1/8 24 3/8	18 2/8	6 6	Nemaha County	NE	Jason A. Swanson	2005	5584
153 0/8	25 6/8 25 2/8	20 7/8	5 7	St. Louis County	MN	Jamie Majchrzak	2005	5584
153 0/8	24 2/8 24 2/8	21 2/8	4 4	Montcalm County	MI	Terry Lee Goodell	2005	5584
*153 0/8	27 1/8 27 0/8	19 4/8	4 4	Cochrane	ALB	Eric R. Smith	2005	5584
*153 0/8	23 1/8 23 4/8	16 4/8	5 5	Morton County	ND	Jerrid Soupir	2005	5584
153 0/8	22 2/8 20 6/8	16 4/8	6 7	Kane County	IL	Dean V. Ashton	2006	5584
153 0/8	22 4/8 22 1/8	14 4/8	5 5	Warren County	MO	Larry Molitor	2006	5584
*153 0/8	25 1/8 25 0/8	20 6/8	5 5	Adams County	IL	Timothy D. Walmsley	2007	5584
153 0/8	22 5/8 22 3/8	16 2/8	5 5	Appanoose County	IA	Bryan Cassady	2007	5584
153 0/8	24 5/8 25 5/8	19 2/8	5 5	Clark County	WI	Roy A. Gregorich	2008	5584
153 0/8	23 6/8 23 2/8	15 4/8	5 5	Wayne County	NY	Anthony P. Mastrangelo	2008	5584
*153 0/8	22 4/8 22 3/8	17 7/8	6 5	Barber County	KS	Dean Avagnano	2008	5584
153 0/8	22 1/8 23 4/8	16 4/8	6 7	Dunn County	WI	Nikolas Sheppard	2009	5584
*153 0/8	26 4/8 25 2/8	19 0/8	4 4	McKean County	PA	Harry Frazier III	2009	5584
*153 0/8	22 6/8 23 3/8	18 6/8	6 6	Carroll County	IN	Eric Hall	2009	5584
152 7/8	21 4/8 22 0/8	18 7/8	5 5	Polk County	WI	Wendle Johnson	1969	5654
152 7/8	23 2/8 22 2/8	18 4/8	7 5	Morgan County	CO	Dr. Stuart Clodfelder	1974	5654
152 7/8	22 1/8 23 0/8	17 0/8	6 5	Sullivan County	IN	Kenny Pirtle	1975	5654
152 7/8	24 3/8 24 2/8	20 7/8	5 6	Missoula County	MT	Rick L. Stone	1981	5654
152 7/8	23 2/8 23 4/8	19 1/8	6 5	Delaware County	PA	John A. Lashinsky	1984	5654
152 7/8	24 2/8 24 2/8	20 3/8	5 5	Washington County	WI	Lee A. Richard	1984	5654
152 7/8	21 6/8 22 2/8	19 7/8	5 5	Henry County	IL	Willard "Woody" Moore	1986	5654
152 7/8	25 1/8 26 1/8	16 7/8	5 5	Highland County	OH	Jeffrey A. Swerlein	1988	5654
152 7/8	23 2/8 23 0/8	20 1/8	6 6	Wayne County	WV	Larry Sarver	1988	5654
152 7/8	23 3/8 23 6/8	19 2/8	5 8	Guthrie County	IA	Leonard H. Mussell	1989	5654
152 7/8	23 7/8 23 7/8	20 5/8	5 6	Olmsted County	MN	Chris A. Valli	1989	5654
152 7/8	22 6/8 22 2/8	18 1/8	5 5	Sauk County	WI	Hank Lee	1989	5654
152 7/8	22 2/8 22 3/8	16 2/8	5 6	Chisago County	MN	John R. Palmer	1989	5654
152 7/8	24 3/8 24 4/8	17 1/8	4 4	Oconto County	WI	Gary DeBauch	1990	5654
152 7/8	26 0/8 25 7/8	20 2/8	6 5	Strafford County	NH	William S. Carlsen	1990	5654
152 7/8	23 3/8 21 0/8	17 5/8	6 6	McHenry County	IL	William D. Lilly	1990	5654
152 7/8	27 4/8 27 2/8	21 1/8	5 5	Lawrence County	OH	Bobby L. Willis	1991	5654
152 7/8	23 1/8 23 6/8	21 6/8	6 5	Creek County	OK	Carmon G. Romine, Jr.	1991	5654
152 7/8	25 0/8 25 1/8	17 1/8	6 6	Loudoun County	VA	Michael R. Mutkus	1992	5654
152 7/8	24 1/8 23 4/8	16 6/8	5 6	Langlade County	WI	Thomas H. Kubiaczyk	1993	5654
152 7/8	22 4/8 22 5/8	17 0/8	5 7	Bullitt County	KY	Andy Cox	1994	5654
152 7/8	25 1/8 24 6/8	21 7/8	5 5	Allegheny County	PA	Daniel A. Urbas	1995	5654
152 7/8	24 6/8 24 4/8	20 1/8	5 5	Jefferson County	IA	D. Greiffendorf	1995	5654
152 7/8	24 3/8 23 5/8	18 5/8	5 5	Grayson County	TX	Lynn Burkhead	1996	5654
152 7/8	25 1/8 26 6/8	19 7/8	7 7	Marion County	KS	Michael Sowell	1996	5654
152 7/8	26 6/8 26 3/8	21 5/8	4 5	Hamilton County	KS	Bill Kreie	1997	5654
152 7/8	24 4/8 24 7/8	23 5/8	5 5	Montour County	PA	Gilbert H. Riley	1998	5654
152 7/8	23 0/8 21 3/8	18 1/8	5 5	Kossuth County	IA	Charles Greg Arnold	1998	5654
152 7/8	22 0/8 22 3/8	15 3/8	5 5	Waupaca County	WI	Dave Roberts	1998	5654
152 7/8	25 6/8 25 0/8	17 7/8	4 4	Ripley County	IN	Dennis Bergman	1999	5654
152 7/8	24 0/8 22 6/8	16 7/8	6 6	Logan County	CO	Mark Vogt	1999	5654
152 7/8	22 2/8 23 4/8	16 6/8	6 6	Fayette County	IA	Steve Rinderknecht	2000	5654
152 7/8	23 5/8 23 3/8	16 1/8	5 5	Columbia County	WI	Paul E. Johnson	2000	5654
*152 7/8	23 5/8 23 3/8	17 5/8	5 5	Hancock County	IL	Ryan Settles	2001	5654
152 7/8	23 6/8 23 4/8	18 1/8	5 5	Waukesha County	WI	Dave Steger	2001	5654
152 7/8	25 3/8 24 4/8	15 4/8	5 5	Franklin County	KS	Darby Beck	2001	5654
152 7/8	24 7/8 25 1/8	20 3/8	5 5	Sumner County	KS	Ted Benvin	2001	5654
152 7/8	21 3/8 25 3/8	18 2/8	5 6	Wyandotte County	KS	Brian J. Sundnas	2002	5654
152 7/8	24 3/8 24 3/8	16 6/8	6 6	Adams County	OH	Mike Hydler	2002	5654
152 7/8	22 4/8 23 0/8	17 7/8	5 5	Yellowhead	ALB	Dwayne Huggins	2002	5654
152 7/8	25 4/8 26 4/8	18 3/8	6 6	Marion County	IA	Shawn Van Wyk	2003	5654
152 7/8	25 5/8 25 7/8	17 0/8	7 5	Pike County	IL	Dell Kirby	2003	5654
152 7/8	24 7/8 23 1/8	18 3/8	5 5	Berks County	PA	Joseph A. Hoster	2004	5654
152 7/8	24 2/8 24 2/8	21 2/8	6 6	Union County	KY	Steve Helton	2004	5654
152 7/8	23 2/8 23 7/8	21 3/8	6 6	Chautauqua County	KS	Mark Melton	2004	5654
152 7/8	24 1/8 23 6/8	19 2/8	5 6	Vigo County	IN	Wes Isbell	2005	5654
152 7/8	26 0/8 24 5/8	19 3/8	5 6	Logan County	IL	Jim Jones	2005	5654

415

WHITETAIL DEER (TYPICAL ANTLERS)

Minimum Score 125   Continued

SCORE	LENGTH OF R MAIN BEAM L	INSIDE SPREAD	NUMBER OF R POINTS L	AREA	STATE/ PROVINCE	HUNTER'S NAME	DATE	RANK
*152 7/8	26 0/8 24 4/8	24 5/8	6 7	Tazewell County	IL	Joe Getz	2006	5654
*152 7/8	24 2/8 26 1/8	24 3/8	7 6	Iowa County	WI	Tom Mitchell	2006	5654
*152 7/8	22 7/8 23 0/8	16 5/8	6 6	Marks Township	ONT	Jay Hickman	2006	5654
152 7/8	23 4/8 22 0/8	15 7/8	5 6	Brookings County	SD	Tyler Erickson	2007	5654
*152 7/8	22 3/8 22 6/8	17 7/8	5 5	New Castle County	DE	Nicky Ferrara	2007	5654
152 7/8	24 1/8 23 4/8	18 7/8	5 5	Green County	WI	Steve Gobeli	2008	5654
152 7/8	26 3/8 26 0/8	22 5/8	4 5	Buffalo County	WI	Brad Juaire	2008	5654
152 7/8	26 4/8 26 7/8	17 5/8	6 6	Vernon County	WI	Andrew Blum	2008	5654
152 7/8	22 5/8 22 3/8	20 0/8	8 7	Brown County	IL	Mancel W. Sherrer	2008	5654
152 7/8	26 6/8 26 1/8	22 5/8	5 6	Bureau County	IL	Robert D. Everhart	2009	5654
152 7/8	25 4/8 26 0/8	19 3/8	4 4	Stephenson County	IL	Brian Kimpel	2009	5654
152 7/8	26 2/8 25 0/8	19 5/8	6 7	Defiance County	OH	Todd R. Twigg	2009	5654
152 6/8	25 6/8 25 1/8	21 2/8	4 5	Jefferson County	IN	Robert Schmidt	1959	5713
152 6/8	24 6/8 23 2/8	17 7/8	7 7	Winona County	MN	Donald M. Bzoskie	1978	5713
152 6/8	24 7/8 24 1/8	21 0/8	4 4	Randolph County	IL	Steven Wydeck	1979	5713
152 6/8	25 2/8 24 3/8	18 4/8	5 5	Saginaw County	MI	Jack W. Bare	1981	5713
152 6/8	23 3/8 23 0/8	20 0/8	5 5	Morrison County	MN	Floyd Foslien	1981	5713
152 6/8	25 0/8 25 2/8	17 6/8	6 6	Holt County	MO	Frank Berkemeier	1984	5713
152 6/8	22 6/8 22 2/8	14 2/8	6 5	Rogers County	OK	Byron Jasper	1984	5713
152 6/8	27 0/8 27 2/8	16 4/8	4 5	Roane County	TN	Rod Brown	1986	5713
152 6/8	25 4/8 26 2/8	18 2/8	5 5	Texas County	OK	Don Callaway	1986	5713
152 6/8	23 2/8 23 6/8	18 2/8	5 6	Logan County	OH	Richard D. Fullerton	1988	5713
152 6/8	26 3/8 28 3/8	22 3/8	4 5	Vermilion County	IL	John E. Fry	1989	5713
152 6/8	26 1/8 25 5/8	17 0/8	6 5	Lawrence County	IL	Ron Wells	1989	5713
152 6/8	22 3/8 21 4/8	17 4/8	6 5	Winnebago County	IL	Drake R. Branca	1990	5713
152 6/8	23 4/8 23 2/8	17 7/8	6 5	Ohio County	IN	Gary Copeland	1991	5713
152 6/8	25 0/8 24 0/8	18 0/8	5 6	Cass County	MI	Kim C. Deda	1991	5713
152 6/8	24 4/8 24 7/8	20 3/8	6 7	Worcester County	MA	Peter J. Warakomski	1991	5713
152 6/8	24 6/8 24 4/8	20 4/8	5 5	Morrison County	MN	Ward Fiebiger	1992	5713
152 6/8	22 2/8 22 4/8	18 3/8	6 6	Rock County	MN	Jim Lorenzen	1993	5713
152 6/8	25 0/8 25 7/8	19 0/8	5 5	Greene County	OH	Mark A. Marsh	1994	5713
152 6/8	27 2/8 26 4/8	21 2/8	5 4	Allamakee County	IA	Robyn Henderson	1996	5713
152 6/8	22 7/8 23 3/8	15 0/8	5 6	Porter County	IN	Bob Rowles	1997	5713
152 6/8	22 4/8 23 4/8	15 4/8	6 5	Warren County	OH	Jeffery S. Frieszell	1998	5713
152 6/8	25 6/8 25 3/8	20 2/8	4 4	McLean County	IL	Jeff S. Jordan	1998	5713
152 6/8	23 0/8 23 7/8	19 4/8	5 5	Clark County	IL	Kelly Norton	1999	5713
152 6/8	24 5/8 24 0/8	18 4/8	6 6	Sauk County	WI	Randy Smith	1999	5713
152 6/8	24 6/8 25 2/8	19 2/8	5 5	Buffalo County	WI	Dean Dieckman	1999	5713
152 6/8	25 4/8 25 1/8	21 2/8	4 4	Pike County	IL	Kenneth C. Long, Jr.	1999	5713
152 6/8	25 1/8 25 1/8	18 2/8	4 5	Sedgwick County	KS	Dale Segraves	1999	5713
152 6/8	25 0/8 24 3/8	19 3/8	6 5	Yorkton	SAS	Phyllis Vandermeulen	1999	5713
152 6/8	24 1/8 24 5/8	18 5/8	4 7	Appanoose County	IA	Rick Seavey	1999	5713
152 6/8	23 2/8 24 0/8	19 7/8	7 6	St. Joseph County	IN	H. Bruce Weaver	2000	5713
152 6/8	22 3/8 21 7/8	16 6/8	5 6	Monroe County	IA	Michael Seals	2000	5713
152 6/8	24 6/8 24 6/8	18 4/8	5 5	St. Louis County	MO	Bob Hostetler	2000	5713
152 6/8	24 7/8 24 3/8	18 4/8	7 7	Hudson Bay	SAS	Steve Johnson	2000	5713
152 6/8	23 1/8 22 0/8	20 6/8	5 5	Vilas County	WI	Phil Dreger	2001	5713
152 6/8	25 0/8 25 0/8	19 6/8	5 4	Polk County	WI	Kevin Lucas	2001	5713
152 6/8	28 4/8 27 6/8	22 1/8	5 5	Jones County	IA	Doug Kramer	2001	5713
152 6/8	26 1/8 23 7/8	20 6/8	5 4	Butler County	OH	Murphy Napier	2001	5713
152 6/8	27 6/8 27 1/8	24 2/8	4 4	Butler County	KS	David R. Rogers	2001	5713
152 6/8	27 1/8 25 6/8	22 1/8	6 5	Carroll County	NH	James C. Town	2002	5713
*152 6/8	24 0/8 24 3/8	18 2/8	7 6	Plymouth County	IA	David R. Lorenz	2003	5713
152 6/8	26 4/8 26 4/8	22 0/8	5 5	Sumner County	KS	Barry Wiley	2003	5713
152 6/8	26 4/8 25 3/8	20 6/8	5 4	Lawrence County	IL	Donald Kiser	2004	5713
*152 6/8	24 4/8 25 7/8	21 3/8	6 5	Douglas County	WI	Loren H. Johnson	2005	5713
*152 6/8	19 2/8 20 7/8	12 3/8	6 5	Breckinridge County	KY	Silas Dudley	2005	5713
152 6/8	23 2/8 22 7/8	13 6/8	5 5	Tippecanoe County	IN	Joseph Blando	2005	5713
152 6/8	23 6/8 24 2/8	18 2/8	4 4	Hancock County	IL	Michael Martress	2005	5713
*152 6/8	23 5/8 22 7/8	18 4/8	5 5	Queen Annes County	MD	Douglas Brissey	2005	5713
152 6/8	23 4/8 24 6/8	19 6/8	5 5	Marathon County	WI	Clayton Schmitt	2005	5713
*152 6/8	24 3/8 24 5/8	20 2/8	5 4	Oneida County	NY	Brian Doyle	2005	5713
152 6/8	25 7/8 25 2/8	21 4/8	5 5	Lycoming County	PA	Terry J. O'Connor	2006	5713
152 6/8	22 3/8 24 4/8	19 2/8	7 6	Delaware County	OH	Matt Scarbury	2006	5713
*152 6/8	22 1/8 22 3/8	16 0/8	5 5	Newton County	IN	Robert L. Byars	2006	5713
*152 6/8	23 6/8 22 7/8	17 4/8	5 4	Howard County	IA	Martin M. Weeks	2006	5713
*152 6/8	22 6/8 24 1/8	15 2/8	6 7	Knox County	MO	Clinton Hankins III	2006	5713
152 6/8	21 7/8 21 6/8	17 0/8	6 10	Hinds County	MS	Caleb Cope	2006	5713
152 6/8	22 5/8 21 7/8	18 7/8	6 6	St. Croix County	WI	Mike G. Walsh	2007	5713
152 6/8	24 2/8 24 3/8	18 0/8	5 5	Monroe County	GA	Chip Salem	2007	5713
152 6/8	23 4/8 23 4/8	16 0/8	5 5	Polk County	WI	Ron Peterson	2007	5713
152 6/8	23 5/8 24 0/8	15 2/8	5 5	Sarpy County	NE	Ryan C. Cronk	2007	5713
*152 6/8	22 5/8 23 5/8	21 2/8	5 5	Anderson County	KY	Henry Ray Brooks	2007	5713
*152 6/8	26 1/8 26 1/8	18 2/8	7 5	McDowell County	WV	David Rash	2007	5713
152 6/8	22 6/8 22 2/8	18 6/8	5 5	La Crosse County	WI	Rob Nelson	2008	5713
*152 6/8	25 1/8 25 3/8	18 0/8	6 6	Poweshiek County	IA	Dean A. Huls	2008	5713
152 6/8	25 4/8 24 5/8	18 0/8	5 5	Calhoun County	MI	Robert L. Milano	2008	5713
152 6/8	22 7/8 23 1/8	17 7/8	6 5	Richland County	WI	Michael Stewart	2008	5713
152 6/8	24 1/8 24 7/8	18 2/8	5 5	Bear Lake	ALB	Stanley Alexander	2009	5713
152 6/8	27 2/8 27 3/8	19 4/8	5 5	Macon County	GA	David Sams	2009	5713
152 6/8	24 4/8 24 4/8	18 2/8	5 5	Fond du Lac County	WI	Clint S. Beck	2009	5713
152 6/8	24 0/8 23 7/8	19 0/8	5 5	Dunn County	WI	Randy Mittlestadt	2009	5713
*152 6/8	23 3/8 23 3/8	19 0/8	5 5	Stoddard County	MO	Andie McClain	2009	5713
152 6/8	24 0/8 22 6/8	18 4/8	5 5	Wyoming County	WV	Jerry Hutchinson	2009	5713
152 5/8	23 5/8 24 5/8	19 7/8	6 5	Ralls County	MO	Donald Curless	1959	5785
152 5/8	23 2/8 23 0/8	17 2/8	5 6	Monroe County	MO	Carl T. Peak	1968	5785
152 5/8	25 6/8 25 3/8	17 7/8	5 5	McLean County	IL	Mike Turner	1981	5785
152 5/8	23 1/8 24 0/8	16 1/8	6 5	Roseau County	MN	Dave Hovda	1982	5785
152 5/8	24 5/8 24 0/8	19 4/8	7 7	Delaware County	IA	Chet Goldsberry	1982	5785
152 5/8	22 7/8 22 5/8	16 3/8	5 5	Lyon County	MN	Dwight A. Hemme	1984	5785
152 5/8	25 2/8 22 5/8	17 1/8	5 5	Marathon County	WI	Marcell Wieloch	1986	5785
152 5/8	22 6/8 24 2/8	17 7/8	7 6	Carver County	MN	Steve Polston	1986	5785
152 5/8	26 0/8 25 0/8	20 5/8	4 4	Marion County	IA	Steven F. Donnelly, Jr.	1986	5785
152 5/8	26 2/8 25 7/8	17 1/8	4 4	Forest County	WI	Greg Lenz	1988	5785
152 5/8	23 0/8 21 2/8	17 3/8	5 5	Crawford County	IL	Steve Newkirk	1989	5785

416

WHITETAIL DEER (TYPICAL ANTLERS)

Minimum Score 125   Continued

SCORE	LENGTH OF R MAIN BEAM L	INSIDE SPREAD	NUMBER OF R POINTS L	AREA	STATE/PROVINCE	HUNTER'S NAME	DATE	RANK
152 5/8	23 6/8 22 5/8	19 3/8	5 5	Winnebago County	IL	Tom Sanderson	1990	5785
152 5/8	21 4/8 21 1/8	17 1/8	6 6	Hennepin County	MN	Dan Kittok	1990	5785
152 5/8	21 0/8 21 1/8	15 1/8	5 5	Leavenworth County	KS	Thomas H. Rendall	1990	5785
152 5/8	26 4/8 26 1/8	23 1/8	6 7	Pike County	IL	Rick Conrad	1991	5785
152 5/8	25 3/8 26 0/8	18 2/8	6 6	Clinton County	IA	Shawn Petersen	1991	5785
152 5/8	22 0/8 22 0/8	16 3/8	6 6	McPherson County	KS	Daniel G. Willems	1993	5785
152 5/8	23 3/8 24 1/8	19 7/8	5 5	Guthrie County	IA	Gary D. Stewart	1994	5785
152 5/8	23 0/8 23 1/8	18 7/8	7 6	Whiteside County	IL	Abraham Wuebben	1994	5785
152 5/8	22 0/8 23 2/8	15 3/8	6 6	Maverick County	TX	Gary Miller	1995	5785
152 5/8	22 1/8 23 0/8	15 7/8	6 5	Buffalo County	WI	Jesse D. Bloom	1995	5785
152 5/8	24 2/8 24 5/8	16 5/8	5 6	Jackson County	MI	Mark Douglas Kelley	1995	5785
152 5/8	23 2/8 22 4/8	17 7/8	4 4	Wilson County	KS	Roy L. Walk	1995	5785
152 5/8	23 4/8 22 6/8	20 7/8	8 7	Will County	IL	Mark Anderson	1995	5785
*152 5/8	21 5/8 23 4/8	18 1/8	6 6	Meeker County	MN	Robert Mattila	1996	5785
152 5/8	25 5/8 24 4/8	23 5/8	5 5	Kendall County	IL	Jim Childs	1996	5785
152 5/8	23 5/8 24 0/8	20 5/8	5 5	Delaware County	OH	Tim Stamm	1996	5785
152 5/8	23 6/8 24 0/8	18 1/8	5 5	Ozaukee County	WI	Bob Butler	1999	5785
152 5/8	25 2/8 24 6/8	16 7/8	7 4	Pike County	OH	Lynn Henry	1999	5785
152 5/8	25 4/8 26 4/8	19 3/8	5 4	Preble County	OH	Mike McCabe	1999	5785
152 5/8	23 2/8 23 3/8	18 3/8	5 5	Refugio County	TX	Leroy Reinecke	1999	5785
152 5/8	23 4/8 22 2/8	16 0/8	6 6	St. Joseph County	IN	Phillip J. Groves	2000	5785
152 5/8	24 3/8 24 5/8	20 1/8	5 5	Clayton County	IA	Michael Wohlers	2000	5785
152 5/8	23 2/8 23 4/8	20 1/8	5 5	Sheboygan County	WI	Randy P. Van Ess	2000	5785
152 5/8	23 6/8 22 4/8	18 2/8	5 6	Kane County	IL	Carl Kwak	2001	5785
152 5/8	23 4/8 23 2/8	19 7/8	5 5	La Salle County	IL	John Thomas	2001	5785
152 5/8	23 3/8 24 3/8	19 7/8	5 5	Lycoming County	PA	Ken Hakes	2001	5785
152 5/8	23 0/8 23 0/8	16 7/8	5 5	Coffey County	KS	Chad Powell	2001	5785
152 5/8	26 0/8 25 1/8	20 6/8	6 7	Knox County	OH	Carl Stricker	2002	5785
152 5/8	24 1/8 24 7/8	17 5/8	5 5	Montcalm County	MI	Marco Kenneth Bilello	2002	5785
152 5/8	23 4/8 23 5/8	16 3/8	5 5	Allamakee County	IA	P. J. Connelly	2002	5785
*152 5/8	27 1/8 26 4/8	20 7/8	4 4	Grant County	WI	Kevin R. Kelly	2003	5785
152 5/8	23 6/8 25 0/8	16 6/8	5 6	Morgan County	MO	Chantz S. Brown	2003	5785
152 5/8	24 0/8 24 0/8	20 5/8	5 5	Hutchinson County	SD	Douglas Mercier	2003	5785
152 5/8	23 5/8 22 7/8	18 2/8	8 9	Tazewell County	IL	Jon D. Christopher	2003	5785
152 5/8	27 3/8 27 4/8	24 5/8	5 6	Lehigh County	PA	Mike Deskiewicz	2003	5785
152 5/8	24 6/8 24 5/8	18 1/8	5 4	Woodbury County	IA	Wendell Van Beek	2003	5785
152 5/8	25 7/8 24 7/8	18 7/8	5 5	Trempealeau County	WI	Matt R. Andersen	2004	5785
152 5/8	24 0/8 22 6/8	19 1/8	5 5	Berkshire County	MA	Tom Hynes	2004	5785
152 5/8	24 3/8 23 1/8	17 3/8	5 6	Miami County	KS	Randy Francis	2004	5785
152 5/8	24 7/8 24 4/8	18 4/8	6 6	Polk County	WI	Brian Seidel	2004	5785
152 5/8	23 1/8 23 2/8	18 7/8	5 5	Clinton County	IA	Jeremy White	2005	5785
152 5/8	23 4/8 23 6/8	19 1/8	5 5	Madison County	ID	Gregory Ryan Pimentel	2005	5785
152 5/8	21 0/8 21 0/8	17 3/8	6 6	Lancaster County	NE	Mark Benes	2006	5785
152 5/8	24 2/8 24 6/8	18 7/8	5 7	Adair County	MO	Anthony P. Mihalevich	2006	5785
*152 5/8	25 4/8 24 0/8	16 7/8	6 8	Allamakee County	IA	Chris Van Gerpen	2006	5785
152 5/8	24 0/8 24 0/8	18 1/8	5 5	Wythe County	VA	James E. Wright	2006	5785
*152 5/8	23 1/8 24 5/8	16 1/8	6 7	Stewart County	TN	Taylor Teets	2006	5785
*152 5/8	24 3/8 23 4/8	16 1/8	5 5	Clermont County	OH	Tony Jones	2006	5785
152 5/8	23 6/8 23 7/8	17 7/8	5 5	Ward County	ND	John R. Plesuk	2006	5785
152 5/8	24 2/8 24 5/8	17 2/8	7 6	Duval County	TX	Larry Teel	2007	5785
152 5/8	23 7/8 24 6/8	19 3/8	6 6	Kendall County	IL	Joe Onderisin	2007	5785
*152 5/8	24 1/8 24 0/8	17 3/8	5 5	Winona County	MN	Greg Marmsoler	2007	5785
152 5/8	22 5/8 22 7/8	16 5/8	5 5	O'Brien County	IA	Jerry W. Culbertson	2007	5785
152 5/8	22 6/8 23 2/8	15 2/8	6 7	Caldwell County	MO	Christopher L. Lein	2007	5785
152 5/8	29 2/8 28 0/8	19 1/8	5 4	Lenawee County	MI	Billy J. Thompson	2007	5785
152 5/8	21 6/8 22 2/8	17 4/8	5 6	Barron County	WI	David McPhail	2007	5785
152 5/8	24 6/8 24 0/8	17 2/8	6 6	Rockingham County	NC	Michael L. Shelton	2007	5785
*152 5/8	24 1/8 23 3/8	19 3/8	5 5	Monroe County	MI	James Robert Horney, Jr.	2007	5785
152 5/8	27 7/8 27 6/8	22 1/8	4 4	Stephenson County	IL	Joe Daughenbaugh	2007	5785
152 5/8	23 2/8 23 4/8	16 3/8	5 5	Bond County	IL	William T. Rench	2008	5785
*152 5/8	25 2/8 24 0/8	18 7/8	5 5	Clarion County	PA	Todd Bowser	2008	5785
152 5/8	26 4/8 25 4/8	19 1/8	7 5	Knox County	IL	Robert Aldred	2008	5785
152 5/8	23 3/8 22 4/8	18 6/8	6 6	Highland County	OH	Pat Harm	2009	5785
*152 5/8	26 0/8 25 6/8	20 7/8	6 5	York County	PA	Donald C. Laughman	2009	5785
*152 5/8	25 0/8 25 6/8	20 7/8	4 4	Ohio County	KY	Kenny Morphew	2009	5785
*152 5/8	26 3/8 19 4/8	17 3/8	6 5	Richland County	IL	Toby Schrock	2009	5785
*152 5/8	23 0/8 22 6/8	15 1/8	5 5	Divide County	ND	Len Shafer, Jr.	2009	5785
152 4/8	24 6/8 24 0/8	19 2/8	8 6	Hardin County	KY	Jimmy D. Neal	1973	5863
152 4/8	28 7/8 26 2/8	19 2/8	5 5	Somerset County	MD	Burgess Blevins	1974	5863
152 4/8	24 3/8 24 0/8	19 2/8	5 5	Scott County	MN	Dean Jansen	1976	5863
152 4/8	25 6/8 27 4/8	18 3/8	7 5	Westchester County	NY	Jack Dykstra	1986	5863
152 4/8	21 5/8 21 3/8	18 6/8	5 5	Provost	ALB	Harvey McNalley	1987	5863
152 4/8	24 5/8 25 5/8	20 4/8	7 7	Lake County	IL	Ted Bellefeuille	1987	5863
152 4/8	23 6/8 24 6/8	17 6/8	5 5	Harris County	TX	John Hall	1987	5863
152 4/8	23 0/8 22 7/8	19 0/8	6 6	Pike County	OH	Raymond McComas	1988	5863
152 4/8	23 3/8 23 5/8	17 7/8	5 6	Lehigh County	PA	Steve C. Metzger	1989	5863
152 4/8	26 1/8 27 4/8	21 6/8	5 5	Hocking County	OH	Chad Krahel	1990	5863
152 4/8	25 6/8 25 5/8	20 3/8	5 6	St. Francois County	MO	Adam Ashby	1991	5863
152 4/8	25 1/8 25 0/8	19 4/8	4 4	Wilkes County	NC	Joe Butcher	1992	5863
152 4/8	23 1/8 23 2/8	16 5/8	7 6	Starke County	IN	Michael Palm	1992	5863
152 4/8	24 1/8 23 1/8	15 2/8	5 5	Taylor County	WI	Dave Gebert	1992	5863
152 4/8	26 0/8 25 5/8	18 2/8	5 4	Washington County	WI	Tony Snow	1992	5863
152 4/8	23 6/8 24 3/8	19 4/8	4 4	Marion County	IL	Gary Rose	1992	5863
152 4/8	26 3/8 27 0/8	22 5/8	5 5	Licking County	OH	Thomas E. Lott	1992	5863
152 4/8	24 7/8 24 5/8	18 6/8	4 4	Ogle County	IL	Thomas W. Johnson	1992	5863
152 4/8	22 7/8 23 6/8	15 6/8	5 5	Jay County	IN	Danny M. Bost	1993	5863
152 4/8	23 4/8 23 4/8	18 0/8	5 5	Harrison County	OH	Ron Fishel	1994	5863
152 4/8	25 1/8 25 2/8	22 6/8	4 5	Pulaski County	IL	Lawrence Helton	1994	5863
152 4/8	25 4/8 25 4/8	16 0/8	6 6	Butler County	OH	Adam E. Wurzelbacher	1995	5863
152 4/8	22 7/8 21 0/8	16 6/8	5 5	Ford County	IL	Gail Reiners	1995	5863
152 4/8	23 6/8 22 3/8	20 6/8	5 5	Burleigh County	ND	Wes Berg	1995	5863
152 4/8	25 0/8 25 1/8	21 4/8	5 5	E. Carroll Parish	LA	Mike Edwards	1995	5863
152 4/8	27 7/8 26 2/8	22 2/8	4 4	Tensas Parish	LA	Kenney Dunham	1996	5863
152 4/8	23 5/8 23 3/8	21 2/8	5 5	Van Buren County	MI	Eric Vollrath	1996	5863
152 4/8	25 0/8 24 5/8	17 6/8	5 5	Fayette County	OH	Whitlow Wyatt	1996	5863

417

WHITETAIL DEER (TYPICAL ANTLERS)

Minimum Score 125 — Continued

SCORE	R MAIN BEAM L	INSIDE SPREAD	R POINTS L	AREA	STATE/PROVINCE	HUNTER'S NAME	DATE	RANK
152 4/8	22 6/8 23 2/8	19 0/8	5 5	Fremont County	IA	Dave Holt	1997	5863
152 4/8	23 2/8 22 3/8	16 4/8	5 6	Shawnee County	KS	Roy Shafer	1997	5863
152 4/8	25 2/8 24 7/8	19 4/8	4 4	Coweta County	GA	Rick Harris	1997	5863
152 4/8	24 1/8 22 7/8	21 2/8	5 5	McDowell County	WV	Eli Meadows	1998	5863
152 4/8	24 6/8 25 4/8	19 2/8	4 6	Fountain County	IN	Kris Key	1998	5863
152 4/8	23 5/8 24 3/8	18 0/8	6 5	Vilas County	WI	Less Ryan	1998	5863
152 4/8	24 3/8 24 7/8	18 4/8	5 5	Adams County	WI	Jeffery K. Lien	1998	5863
152 4/8	23 4/8 23 2/8	16 1/8	7 6	Brown County	MN	Michael Billmeier	1999	5863
152 4/8	25 4/8 23 5/8	19 0/8	5 5	Jackson County	OH	Ken Conley	1999	5863
152 4/8	23 0/8 22 2/8	15 2/8	6 6	Irion County	TX	Kenny Ellis	2000	5863
152 4/8	24 3/8 23 5/8	18 0/8	5 6	Marathon County	WI	Dan Walsh	2000	5863
152 4/8	23 4/8 23 2/8	17 0/8	6 8	Marion County	IA	Patrick J. Hagens	2001	5863
152 4/8	24 4/8 24 0/8	18 6/8	5 7	Marshall County	IL	Wayne Macha	2001	5863
152 4/8	23 4/8 24 1/8	20 4/8	5 5	Christian County	IL	Jim Davis	2001	5863
152 4/8	29 6/8 29 2/8	16 7/8	7 6	Fulton County	IL	Floyd Cunningham	2001	5863
152 4/8	26 3/8 26 6/8	18 2/8	7 6	Winona County	MN	Lincoln H. Kreofsky	2002	5863
*152 4/8	23 2/8 22 6/8	17 5/8	7 7	De Kalb County	IN	Hans Martin	2002	5863
152 4/8	20 2/8 20 4/8	18 4/8	5 5	Comanche County	KS	Jeff Ehlers	2002	5863
152 4/8	24 6/8 24 6/8	18 6/8	5 5	Ontario County	NY	Raymond "Bo" Snyder	2002	5863
152 4/8	24 1/8 24 3/8	15 0/8	5 6	Bedford County	VA	Troy D. Bennett	2003	5863
152 4/8	24 4/8 25 2/8	20 2/8	4 5	Jackson County	IA	Joe Lieb	2003	5863
152 4/8	25 0/8 24 0/8	19 6/8	5 6	McPherson County	KS	Bill J. Zerger	2003	5863
152 4/8	23 5/8 23 6/8	18 2/8	5 5	Jasper County	IL	Gary Michl	2003	5863
152 4/8	25 5/8 25 3/8	20 4/8	6 5	Houston County	MN	Lee J. Keim	2003	5863
152 4/8	24 5/8 21 2/8	15 6/8	6 5	Buffalo County	WI	Kevin J. Averbeck	2004	5863
152 4/8	25 1/8 25 0/8	22 0/8	5 5	Coles County	IL	Paul D. Briggerman	2004	5863
*152 4/8	23 6/8 20 1/8	19 0/8	6 9	Clayton County	IA	John Bauer	2004	5863
*152 4/8	24 0/8 24 2/8	16 2/8	5 5	Charles County	MD	Ronald F. Hortie	2004	5863
152 4/8	23 0/8 23 6/8	17 2/8	6 5	Shelby County	TN	Michael McDivitt	2004	5863
152 4/8	25 0/8 26 1/8	21 2/8	4 5	Jackson County	IL	Tim Cobin	2004	5863
152 4/8	20 6/8 20 6/8	20 0/8	6 7	Tom Green County	TX	Mark Mullin	2004	5863
152 4/8	23 2/8 23 3/8	15 4/8	5 5	Kingman County	KS	Mark B. Steffen	2005	5863
152 4/8	22 4/8 22 6/8	18 4/8	5 5	Marshall County	IA	Robert F. Boswell	2005	5863
152 4/8	27 6/8 27 4/8	19 3/8	6 7	Fond du Lac County	WI	Barry Kasuboski	2006	5863
152 4/8	26 5/8 26 6/8	30 4/8	7 5	Maverick County	TX	Corbin Friedkin	2006	5863
*152 4/8	22 6/8 24 1/8	17 2/8	5 5	Winneshiek County	IA	Jeff Stenzel	2006	5863
*152 4/8	23 0/8 23 6/8	17 4/8	5 5	Wayne County	IA	Randell Danish	2006	5863
152 4/8	20 3/8 21 2/8	15 2/8	6 7	Gage County	NE	Carl Parker	2006	5863
*152 4/8	21 3/8 22 1/8	15 1/8	6 8	Ramsey County	ND	Lee Myklebust	2007	5863
*152 4/8	22 5/8 23 1/8	18 4/8	5 5	Independence County	AR	Witt Stephens, Jr.	2007	5863
152 4/8	24 2/8 24 2/8	17 0/8	5 5	Van Buren County	IA	Richard M. Penn	2007	5863
152 4/8	23 3/8 23 0/8	17 1/8	5 7	Dane County	WI	Robert Boss	2008	5863
*152 4/8	25 2/8 25 2/8	20 6/8	4 5	Highland County	OH	Todd Daugherty	2008	5863
152 4/8	26 3/8 26 5/8	19 6/8	5 5	Linn County	IA	James L. Corkery	2008	5863
*152 4/8	23 7/8 24 1/8	18 4/8	5 6	Pepin County	WI	Chris Berger	2009	5863
152 4/8	25 0/8 23 2/8	17 4/8	6 6	Columbia County	WI	Anthony J. Kopfhamer	2009	5863
152 4/8	26 0/8 25 7/8	19 5/8	6 5	Trempealeau County	WI	Matthew A. Ninko	2009	5863
*152 4/8	21 7/8 21 5/8	17 0/8	5 5	Marathon County	WI	Otto B. Johnson, Jr.	2009	5863
152 3/8	24 7/8 24 7/8	18 5/8	8 6	Pope County	IL	Dr. H. Neil Becker	1968	5939
152 3/8	25 4/8 25 4/8	17 6/8	8 7	Jasper County	IA	Edward L. Stevens	1976	5939
152 3/8	24 5/8 24 3/8	19 1/8	4 4	Guthrie County	IA	Barry Chalfant	1979	5939
152 3/8	23 2/8 24 7/8	18 3/8	6 5	Schuyler County	IL	Stephen J. McCoy	1979	5939
152 3/8	22 5/8 21 6/8	17 3/8	5 5	Butler County	KS	John Schwartz	1981	5939
152 3/8	24 6/8 24 6/8	16 3/8	5 5	Oceana County	MI	J. C. Ingram	1982	5939
152 3/8	24 7/8 25 3/8	19 7/8	4 4	Yorkton	SAS	Ron Vandermeulen	1983	5939
152 3/8	24 0/8 24 4/8	19 5/8	5 5	Jewell County	KS	Rod Rose	1984	5939
152 3/8	22 3/8 23 2/8	18 5/8	6 5	Kenosha County	WI	Howard Moore	1984	5939
152 3/8	24 3/8 25 0/8	19 7/8	5 5	Logan County	IL	Charles E. Dumire	1984	5939
152 3/8	25 0/8 24 3/8	17 2/8	5 8	Franklin County	KS	Joe Maloney	1985	5939
152 3/8	23 0/8 22 5/8	17 7/8	5 6	Gasconade County	MO	John R Hawkins	1985	5939
152 3/8	25 6/8 24 7/8	17 2/8	8 5	Washington County	KS	Stan Brustowicz	1985	5939
152 3/8	26 6/8 29 1/8	21 1/8	6 5	Bullitt County	KY	Todd A. Edwards	1990	5939
152 3/8	23 7/8 24 7/8	19 3/8	6 6	Pueblo County	CO	Steve Mayo	1990	5939
152 3/8	25 3/8 25 4/8	17 7/8	5 4	Jackson County	IL	Tracy D. Hawes	1991	5939
152 3/8	23 1/8 23 4/8	19 5/8	5 5	Porter County	IN	William Dials	1991	5939
152 3/8	26 1/8 25 2/8	18 5/8	5 7	Belmont County	OH	Chad Krahel	1991	5939
152 3/8	22 4/8 21 5/8	17 7/8	5 5	Codington County	SD	Jerry Redlin	1991	5939
152 3/8	26 0/8 25 2/8	20 7/8	5 7	Macomb County	MI	Paul L. Carabelli	1993	5939
152 3/8	23 7/8 24 3/8	19 7/8	5 5	Poinsett County	AR	William Tyler	1993	5939
152 3/8	25 6/8 25 7/8	19 7/8	5 4	Crawford County	IL	Charlie Guyer	1994	5939
152 3/8	23 6/8 23 2/8	19 0/8	6 5	Adams County	IL	Larry D. Grant	1994	5939
152 3/8	24 5/8 23 4/8	17 3/8	5 5	Chisago County	MN	Mike Shanahan	1994	5939
152 3/8	22 2/8 22 1/8	16 5/8	7 5	Will County	IL	James E. Giese	1995	5939
152 3/8	24 4/8 25 5/8	17 3/8	5 5	McLean County	KY	Joseph A. Rhodes	1996	5939
152 3/8	21 6/8 21 6/8	14 3/8	6 5	Duck Mtns.	MAN	Keith L. Vandever	1996	5939
152 3/8	21 5/8 21 6/8	16 3/8	5 6	Pawnee County	NE	Gary R. Dowse	1996	5939
152 3/8	26 6/8 26 5/8	18 7/8	4 4	Fulton County	IL	Dave Voorhees	1996	5939
152 3/8	24 7/8 24 7/8	17 5/8	6 5	Cowley County	KS	Pat Sackett	1996	5939
152 3/8	24 1/8 25 1/8	16 6/8	5 5	Adams County	WI	Clifford W. Krentz	1997	5939
152 3/8	25 2/8 23 2/8	20 5/8	6 5	Houston County	MN	Daniel W. Strasser	1997	5939
152 3/8	25 6/8 26 1/8	17 1/8	6 7	Knox County	IN	Marcie Arnold	1997	5939
152 3/8	24 7/8 25 2/8	14 7/8	7 6	Morgan County	IL	Shaun Nickel	1997	5939
152 3/8	27 1/8 26 5/8	18 3/8	6 5	Harvey County	KS	John Wiebe	1997	5939
152 3/8	24 1/8 25 3/8	17 7/8	4 4	Mason County	WV	Larry W. McCarty	1997	5939
152 3/8	25 3/8 25 4/8	20 3/8	5 5	Waushara County	WI	Jack Kaercher	1998	5939
152 3/8	26 1/8 28 2/8	19 4/8	5 4	Prowers County	CO	Neal Heaton	1998	5939
152 3/8	23 1/8 23 2/8	18 3/8	6 6	Lucas County	OH	Stephen P. Siegfried	1998	5939
152 3/8	24 6/8 24 3/8	17 7/8	5 5	Barren County	KY	Mike Binder	1998	5939
152 3/8	24 0/8 23 3/8	20 6/8	7 7	Chase County	KS	Troy Chapman	1999	5939
152 3/8	25 2/8 25 0/8	18 3/8	5 5	Dubuque County	IA	Ron Johnson	1999	5939
152 3/8	21 4/8 20 6/8	17 3/8	6 6	Winneshiek County	IA	Jeff Feickert	1999	5939
152 3/8	25 3/8 25 0/8	18 1/8	5 5	Chicot County	AR	Frank Greenlee	1999	5939
152 3/8	23 0/8 23 2/8	20 5/8	4 5	Peoria County	IL	Roger Albertson	2000	5939
152 3/8	25 0/8 23 7/8	16 4/8	6 6	Barton County	MO	Bob Blank	2000	5939
152 3/8	24 7/8 24 6/8	17 3/8	7 6	Otter Tail County	MN	Douglas H. Kramer	2001	5939

WHITETAIL DEER (TYPICAL ANTLERS)

Minimum Score 125 — Continued

SCORE	LENGTH OF R MAIN BEAM L	INSIDE SPREAD	NUMBER OF R POINTS L	AREA	STATE/ PROVINCE	HUNTER'S NAME	DATE	RANK
152 3/8	24 1/8 24 5/8	19 3/8	5 5	Harford County	MD	Dave O'Connell	2002	5939
152 3/8	25 0/8 26 0/8	21 1/8	5 5	Dane County	WI	Cody Helmer	2002	5939
152 3/8	22 2/8 23 6/8	18 7/8	5 5	Polk County	IA	Shane Tuttle	2002	5939
152 3/8	24 4/8 23 4/8	17 0/8	6 5	Logan County	OH	Travis Tracey	2003	5939
152 3/8	25 0/8 25 7/8	21 4/8	5 6	Monroe County	IL	William J. Ziebold	2003	5939
152 3/8	24 5/8 23 2/8	16 2/8	7 6	Pratt County	KS	Scott Rozier	2003	5939
152 3/8	25 6/8 25 4/8	19 3/8	9 6	Winnebago County	WI	Brian Trebiatowski	2004	5939
152 3/8	22 6/8 24 2/8	15 7/8	5 5	Pike County	IL	Jason Boyd	2004	5939
152 3/8	23 0/8 24 3/8	17 1/8	5 7	Story County	IA	Jim Chittenden	2004	5939
152 3/8	24 4/8 24 4/8	20 1/8	5 5	Cloud County	KS	Kenneth R. Lynn	2004	5939
152 3/8	23 3/8 23 4/8	17 2/8	6 5	Pike County	IL	James T. Walters	2004	5939
152 3/8	25 7/8 25 3/8	18 6/8	5 7	Washington County	WI	Leann Karoses	2004	5939
*152 3/8	25 7/8 26 1/8	21 6/8	6 7	Polk County	WI	Mark E. Henck	2004	5939
152 3/8	24 7/8 24 6/8	18 7/8	5 5	Cass County	MN	Gary Trout	2004	5939
*152 3/8	23 4/8 22 7/8	17 5/8	5 5	Jefferson County	KS	Bill Clink	2004	5939
152 3/8	23 3/8 23 3/8	16 4/8	5 6	Hunterdon County	NJ	Daniel LaVerde	2005	5939
152 3/8	25 2/8 24 5/8	18 7/8	5 5	Sauk County	WI	Gerald Holt	2005	5939
152 3/8	24 5/8 24 4/8	18 3/8	5 5	La Salle County	IL	Stanley C. Petty	2005	5939
152 3/8	23 3/8 24 0/8	16 6/8	7 5	Phillips County	KS	Martin Seemann	2005	5939
152 3/8	22 6/8 23 1/8	20 5/8	4 5	Bon Homme County	SD	Jim Kostal	2005	5939
152 3/8	23 0/8 23 1/8	16 0/8	6 6	Mountrail County	ND	Bryan Gray	2006	5939
152 3/8	23 7/8 24 3/8	16 0/8	6 6	Brown County	IL	Roy H. Desmond	2006	5939
152 3/8	24 2/8 24 2/8	17 7/8	5 5	Baltimore County	MD	Ulysses D. Perry	2006	5939
*152 3/8	22 4/8 22 4/8	16 3/8	5 5	Dubuque County	IA	Ron Kueter	2006	5939
152 3/8	23 3/8 22 6/8	18 6/8	5 6	Iowa County	IA	Kurt Chizek	2006	5939
152 3/8	21 5/8 23 1/8	18 0/8	6 5	Jackson County	WI	Cole Beaudin	2006	5939
*152 3/8	24 4/8 22 5/8	19 3/8	5 6	Rooks County	KS	Dave Holt	2006	5939
152 3/8	25 5/8 25 0/8	19 3/8	5 6	Houston County	MN	Matt Enfield	2007	5939
152 3/8	23 2/8 25 1/8	17 3/8	6 6	Jersey County	IL	Charles Hamilton	2007	5939
152 3/8	23 5/8 22 7/8	19 5/8	6 7	Gage County	NE	Ben Vilda	2008	5939
152 3/8	25 6/8 24 2/8	16 7/8	5 7	Marion County	KS	Dennis Ballweg	2008	5939
152 3/8	23 3/8 23 6/8	19 1/8	5 5	Cedar County	MO	Jacob Berning	2008	5939
*152 3/8	22 7/8 23 1/8	17 1/8	6 6	Jackson County	OH	Mark Bradford	2008	5939
*152 3/8	24 3/8 23 0/8	20 7/8	5 5	Gasconade County	MO	Chad J. Hatfield	2008	5939
152 3/8	23 3/8 24 1/8	18 7/8	5 5	Cass County	ND	Dan Davidson	2008	5939
*152 3/8	23 1/8 23 0/8	17 1/8	7 8	Union County	IN	Clint Woeste	2008	5939
152 3/8	22 3/8 22 6/8	22 5/8	5 5	Greene County	MO	Brian Sutherland	2009	5939
*152 3/8	23 3/8 23 5/8	18 6/8	6 5	Buffalo County	WI	Troy Mahutga	2009	5939
*152 3/8	22 5/8 22 3/8	18 1/8	6 5	Dunn County	WI	Jason M. Mountin	2009	5939
152 2/8	27 6/8 27 3/8	15 5/8	6 6	Grundy County	IL	Wesley Holm	1971	6025
152 2/8	24 6/8 24 4/8	18 4/8	5 5	Cowley County	KS	Michael L. Snyder	1978	6025
152 2/8	28 4/8 27 4/8	20 2/8	4 4	Winona County	MN	Leonard Anglewitz	1978	6025
152 2/8	22 6/8 22 7/8	15 7/8	6 10	Clay County	IA	Larry Sippel	1981	6025
152 2/8	24 5/8 24 4/8	20 2/8	6 7	Miami County	KS	Brian J. Hammond	1982	6025
152 2/8	24 2/8 23 5/8	17 4/8	6 4	Marshall County	KS	Dean C. Bookwalter	1982	6025
152 2/8	22 2/8 21 7/8	19 5/8	5 7	Morrison County	MN	Willard L. Voight, Jr.	1984	6025
152 2/8	24 3/8 23 4/8	16 6/8	6 5	Highland County	OH	James Stephens	1984	6025
152 2/8	25 6/8 24 2/8	19 2/8	8 7	La Crosse County	WI	Kenne A. Happel	1985	6025
152 2/8	25 3/8 25 3/8	21 6/8	5 5	Middlesex County	CT	Felix Nosewicz	1985	6025
152 2/8	24 4/8 25 0/8	18 6/8	4 4	Marathon County	WI	Mark Schneider	1985	6025
152 2/8	23 3/8 25 3/8	19 7/8	6 5	Columbia County	WI	Jeff A. Obrion	1986	6025
152 2/8	25 6/8 25 6/8	18 6/8	5 4	Dubuque County	IA	Randy Miller	1989	6025
152 2/8	25 4/8 25 1/8	18 6/8	7 5	Jasper County	IL	Eric Brooks	1989	6025
152 2/8	26 4/8 25 7/8	19 1/8	7 5	Schuyler County	MO	Jim Pierceall	1990	6025
152 2/8	24 4/8 24 1/8	15 2/8	5 6	Putnam County	OH	Pat Will	1990	6025
152 2/8	24 4/8 24 1/8	17 6/8	5 5	Allamakee County	IA	Dennis L. Weber	1990	6025
152 2/8	22 2/8 21 6/8	18 6/8	6 5	Spencer County	IN	Allen Kramer	1991	6025
152 2/8	22 6/8 22 7/8	18 0/8	5 5	Winneshiek County	IA	David G. Baumler	1991	6025
152 2/8	23 5/8 22 7/8	16 3/8	5 6	Rush County	KS	John Denk	1991	6025
152 2/8	26 1/8 26 2/8	18 2/8	4 4	Sumner County	KS	Warren C. Townsend	1991	6025
152 2/8	23 1/8 22 7/8	20 2/8	5 5	Kleberg County	TX	Wayne Peeples	1992	6025
152 2/8	26 0/8 27 0/8	18 1/8	5 7	Tama County	IA	Tim Rowden	1994	6025
152 2/8	22 6/8 22 7/8	17 6/8	5 5	Wayne County	MO	Carl Watkins	1995	6025
152 2/8	24 4/8 24 2/8	17 6/8	6 6	Kane County	IL	Richard Hight	1995	6025
152 2/8	24 3/8 24 2/8	22 6/8	6 5	Vermilion County	IL	Harvey Dove	1996	6025
152 2/8	24 5/8 25 7/8	19 5/8	6 6	Adams County	IL	Tim Walmsley	1996	6025
152 2/8	23 1/8 23 1/8	18 4/8	5 6	Carroll County	IL	Allen G. Comstock	1997	6025
152 2/8	22 1/8 23 3/8	18 0/8	5 5	Clay County	SD	Jeffrey J. Olson	1998	6025
152 2/8	24 0/8 23 6/8	16 6/8	8 6	Johnson County	KS	Jeff G. Woodroof	1998	6025
152 2/8	24 7/8 24 1/8	19 1/8	5 6	Wabasha County	MN	Marc R. Hanson	1999	6025
152 2/8	23 6/8 22 0/8	22 2/8	5 5	Ulster County	NY	Frank Fackovec	1999	6025
152 2/8	23 4/8 23 4/8	16 2/8	5 6	Monroe County	NY	Marc Emiliano	1999	6025
152 2/8	25 2/8 24 4/8	17 0/8	5 5	Adams County	IL	Jason A. Wollbrink	2000	6025
152 2/8	26 7/8 25 7/8	19 5/8	5 4	Polk County	IA	Jason Jones	2000	6025
152 2/8	21 2/8 21 1/8	23 7/8	5 5	Clay County	KS	Chris Redline	2000	6025
152 2/8	22 6/8 22 6/8	20 2/8	5 6	McHenry County	IL	Michael L. Hervey	2001	6025
152 2/8	25 1/8 24 7/8	20 0/8	4 4	Wayne County	IL	Jim Spihlmann	2002	6025
152 2/8	25 0/8 25 0/8	17 2/8	5 5	Carter County	KY	Rodney Carroll	2002	6025
152 2/8	21 4/8 22 4/8	17 0/8	5 5	Douglas County	WI	Robert Chammings	2002	6025
152 2/8	24 6/8 26 0/8	23 0/8	5 6	Warren County	IA	Rodney D. Parker	2002	6025
152 2/8	22 2/8 22 4/8	16 2/8	5 6	White County	IL	Phillip S. Helms	2002	6025
152 2/8	25 2/8 25 4/8	19 2/8	5 6	Wabash County	IN	William C. Hadaway	2002	6025
*152 2/8	24 7/8 24 4/8	17 6/8	5 6	Fayette County	OH	Bill Qvick, Jr.	2003	6025
152 2/8	25 2/8 25 0/8	18 4/8	5 5	Dearborn County	IN	Cody Baker	2003	6025
152 2/8	23 4/8 24 0/8	18 1/8	5 6	Pierce County	WI	Jason Young	2003	6025
152 2/8	24 6/8 25 1/8	18 6/8	5 6	Atchison County	MO	Chris Barton	2003	6025
152 2/8	24 0/8 24 4/8	20 6/8	5 5	Adair County	KY	Robert Hayes	2003	6025
152 2/8	26 0/8 25 5/8	16 6/8	6 5	Allegheny County	PA	Daniel P. Miller	2003	6025
152 2/8	24 5/8 24 6/8	20 0/8	4 5	McHenry County	IL	Michael Cummings	2003	6025
*152 2/8	23 6/8 23 6/8	19 2/8	5 5	Floyd County	IA	Philip Parcher	2003	6025
152 2/8	24 1/8 24 0/8	21 4/8	5 4	Monona County	IA	Rocco Verelli	2004	6025
152 2/8	24 0/8 24 2/8	18 0/8	4 5	Hand County	SD	Travis Sivertsen	2004	6025
152 2/8	24 3/8 24 1/8	21 0/8	5 5	Clay County	KY	Glen Nantz	2004	6025
152 2/8	25 3/8 23 7/8	16 3/8	8 7	Fond du Lac County	WI	David Hahn	2004	6025
152 2/8	25 7/8 24 6/8	17 4/8	5 5	Greenwood County	KS	Michael J. Coyne III	2004	6025

419

WHITETAIL DEER (TYPICAL ANTLERS)

Minimum Score 125 — Continued

SCORE	LENGTH OF MAIN BEAM R	L	INSIDE SPREAD	NUMBER OF POINTS R	L	AREA	STATE/ PROVINCE	HUNTER'S NAME	DATE	RANK
152 2/8	24 3/8	24 4/8	18 1/8	7	8	Webster County	IA	Roger F. Taylor	2004	6025
152 2/8	21 6/8	23 0/8	16 6/8	5	5	Douglas County	WI	Wayne Smith	2005	6025
*152 2/8	25 0/8	24 4/8	18 6/8	5	6	Adams County	OH	Greg Hawk	2005	6025
152 2/8	22 6/8	25 1/8	18 2/8	5	5	Marquette County	WI	Michael Yeska	2006	6025
*152 2/8	26 1/8	25 6/8	19 6/8	6	5	Buffalo County	WI	Dave Fredrickson	2006	6025
152 2/8	23 6/8	25 5/8	20 4/8	5	4	Will County	IL	Dale Hoekstra	2006	6025
*152 2/8	21 7/8	22 0/8	17 0/8	5	5	Riley County	KS	Alan Shadow	2006	6025
152 2/8	23 1/8	22 5/8	15 5/8	8	7	Cascade County	MT	Carl Schroeder	2007	6025
152 2/8	22 7/8	23 4/8	14 4/8	5	5	Warren County	IL	Todd Jones	2007	6025
152 2/8	24 4/8	25 2/8	19 2/8	4	4	Jo Daviess County	IL	Jason E. Dupasquier	2007	6025
152 2/8	26 5/8	25 7/8	20 4/8	6	7	Outagamie County	WI	Duane Froehlich	2007	6025
152 2/8	25 0/8	25 5/8	17 2/8	4	4	Allegan County	MI	Matt Vanden Heuvel	2008	6025
152 2/8	22 7/8	22 2/8	18 2/8	6	5	Fulton County	IN	Jordan A. Howell	2008	6025
152 2/8	24 4/8	24 7/8	18 0/8	6	7	Jefferson County	PA	Kenneth Woodrow	2008	6025
*152 2/8	27 2/8	25 6/8	19 2/8	4	5	Clark County	KY	Roger Smith	2009	6025
152 2/8	24 6/8	24 5/8	21 2/8	5	5	Eaton County	MI	Byran Adcock	2009	6025
*152 2/8	23 6/8	24 0/8	16 4/8	5	5	Faulk County	SD	Eugene Field	2009	6025
152 1/8	21 4/8	24 2/8	21 3/8	5	4	Owen County	IN	Edward L. Armstrong	1967	6098
152 1/8	25 6/8	26 1/8	20 3/8	6	4	Watonwan County	MN	David Raney	1972	6098
152 1/8	22 4/8	22 3/8	18 3/8	5	6	Ogle County	IL	Chuck Bowman	1974	6098
152 1/8	25 1/8	25 3/8	17 1/8	6	6	Louisa County	IA	Duane O'Donnell	1979	6098
152 1/8	25 3/8	25 1/8	17 6/8	5	6	Olmsted County	MN	Tom Kothenbeutel	1980	6098
152 1/8	24 1/8	24 5/8	19 3/8	5	5	Schuyler County	NY	Steve Herforth	1981	6098
152 1/8	24 4/8	24 4/8	20 7/8	4	4	Iowa County	IA	Rick Ransom	1985	6098
152 1/8	23 6/8	24 1/8	16 4/8	7	6	Pawnee County	KS	Karl E. Elmore	1987	6098
152 1/8	24 7/8	22 7/8	18 1/8	5	5	Brooks County	TX	Jim L. McCrory	1988	6098
152 1/8	24 2/8	24 0/8	17 1/8	6	5	Mercer County	ND	William F. Jensen	1989	6098
152 1/8	23 1/8	23 2/8	19 5/8	5	6	Washington County	WI	Glenn E. Becker	1989	6098
152 1/8	21 0/8	21 5/8	17 2/8	6	6	Pike County	IN	Keith M. Witte	1989	6098
152 1/8	24 5/8	25 3/8	22 7/8	4	5	Monona County	IA	Rick Archer	1989	6098
152 1/8	25 1/8	25 3/8	18 7/8	4	4	Scott County	IA	Gary Faley	1989	6098
152 1/8	22 4/8	22 6/8	17 3/8	5	5	Powder River County	MT	Rich Driscoll	1990	6098
152 1/8	24 4/8	24 0/8	17 3/8	4	4	Bond County	IL	James Grider	1990	6098
152 1/8	24 3/8	24 0/8	20 7/8	4	5	Will County	IL	Robert L. Kamenjarin	1990	6098
152 1/8	25 4/8	25 2/8	17 5/8	4	4	Kandiyohi County	MN	Elroy Thorson	1991	6098
152 1/8	23 5/8	23 0/8	16 6/8	8	8	Clark County	MO	Duane Wilson	1991	6098
152 1/8	22 4/8	23 7/8	16 1/8	4	4	Henry County	VA	Mike Weaver	1991	6098
152 1/8	26 2/8	25 7/8	19 2/8	4	6	Franklin County	IL	Tom Haag	1991	6098
152 1/8	25 3/8	25 3/8	19 0/8	5	7	Wabash County	IN	Mike Rees	1992	6098
152 1/8	23 7/8	23 6/8	20 5/8	5	5	Todd County	MN	Bruce Hudalla	1992	6098
152 1/8	25 3/8	25 4/8	20 1/8	5	5	Warren County	IA	Ken Sharp	1992	6098
152 1/8	23 3/8	22 7/8	18 2/8	5	7	Oneida County	WI	David Simon	1993	6098
152 1/8	23 0/8	23 2/8	16 3/8	5	5	Greenwood County	KS	Danny Linnebur	1993	6098
152 1/8	23 3/8	23 2/8	19 7/8	5	5	St. Croix County	WI	Chad Olsen	1994	6098
152 1/8	25 1/8	26 0/8	19 1/8	5	5	Porter County	IN	Robert E. Ford, Jr.	1994	6098
152 1/8	25 1/8	24 4/8	18 5/8	6	5	Harford County	MD	Bruce W. Summers	1994	6098
152 1/8	25 2/8	25 6/8	15 7/8	7	6	Pike County	IL	Dave Webel	1994	6098
152 1/8	22 4/8	22 4/8	22 1/8	7	6	Lincoln County	MO	Steve Dietiker	1995	6098
152 1/8	23 5/8	22 7/8	17 6/8	8	5	Worcester County	MD	Randall M. Hastings	1995	6098
152 1/8	24 1/8	25 2/8	18 2/8	4	5	Scott County	IA	Daniel Hosaflook	1995	6098
152 1/8	21 1/8	20 5/8	18 7/8	6	7	Hennepin County	MN	Timothy K. Hatch	1996	6098
152 1/8	24 7/8	24 7/8	21 5/8	5	5	Pulaski County	VA	Michael P. Miller	1996	6098
152 1/8	25 5/8	26 2/8	16 7/8	5	5	Aiken County	SC	Allan Gilbert	1997	6098
152 1/8	24 4/8	24 3/8	21 5/8	4	4	Appanoose County	IA	Ronnie Everett	1997	6098
152 1/8	23 4/8	24 1/8	17 1/8	5	5	Sawyer County	WI	Gary J. Gedart	1998	6098
152 1/8	24 2/8	24 0/8	16 5/8	5	5	Columbia County	WI	Timothy G. Haas	1998	6098
152 1/8	23 6/8	23 7/8	18 3/8	6	5	Kane County	IL	Mark Anderson	1998	6098
152 1/8	22 5/8	22 4/8	18 1/8	5	5	Gray County	TX	Martin Wallis	1998	6098
152 1/8	26 4/8	26 5/8	18 5/8	4	5	St. Clair County	IL	Jason Doty	1999	6098
152 1/8	25 7/8	26 1/8	20 4/8	4	6	Buffalo County	WI	Gary E. Ott	2001	6098
152 1/8	27 1/8	26 3/8	16 0/8	5	6	Providence County	RI	Louis Bibby	2001	6098
152 1/8	23 4/8	27 1/8	20 3/8	6	5	Brown County	WI	Jim J. Dequaine	2001	6098
152 1/8	24 5/8	24 3/8	16 3/8	7	6	Morgan County	OH	Jeremy Wayne	2001	6098
152 1/8	24 5/8	24 3/8	17 7/8	5	5	Muskegon County	MI	Ron Langlois	2002	6098
152 1/8	26 2/8	25 4/8	18 7/8	6	6	Sawyer County	WI	Bruce Beckwith	2002	6098
152 1/8	26 3/8	26 3/8	18 5/8	6	6	McHenry County	IL	Scott Kunzie	2002	6098
152 1/8	26 2/8	26 0/8	18 2/8	5	5	Lawrence County	IL	Virgil Lane	2002	6098
152 1/8	23 7/8	23 1/8	22 7/8	6	5	Dubuque County	IA	Ryan M. Gruber	2002	6098
152 1/8	25 0/8	24 7/8	16 0/8	5	6	Scioto County	OH	Brian Hopper	2002	6098
*152 1/8	25 3/8	25 0/8	17 2/8	6	6	Mahoning County	OH	Matt Hartman	2003	6098
152 1/8	24 1/8	23 7/8	16 3/8	5	5	Ozaukee County	WI	Patrick C. Swan	2003	6098
152 1/8	24 3/8	24 2/8	16 7/8	5	5	Chester County	PA	Michael L. Brooks	2003	6098
152 1/8	24 1/8	24 4/8	18 2/8	7	5	Effingham County	IL	Mike Barns	2003	6098
*152 1/8	24 2/8	23 5/8	19 3/8	5	7	Hamilton County	OH	Rodney Strayer	2003	6098
*152 1/8	23 2/8	22 6/8	16 3/8	5	6	Jefferson County	WI	Richard J. Randall	2003	6098
*152 1/8	22 0/8	22 0/8	18 3/8	6	7	Cloud County	KS	Rick Jarvis	2003	6098
*152 1/8	24 0/8	23 7/8	16 5/8	6	6	Texas County	MO	Matt Little	2003	6098
*152 1/8	26 1/8	26 4/8	17 7/8	4	5	Polk County	WI	Jim R. Radke	2004	6098
*152 1/8	26 0/8	25 2/8	18 5/8	4	4	Winona County	MN	Adam Delort	2004	6098
*152 1/8	25 4/8	25 2/8	16 3/8	5	5	Fayette County	IA	Ryan Ladeburg	2004	6098
152 1/8	26 1/8	25 1/8	20 2/8	7	5	Dakota County	NE	Treff DeRoin	2004	6098
152 1/8	24 4/8	23 5/8	19 7/8	6	6	Coles County	IL	Bill Hernandez	2004	6098
152 1/8	24 4/8	24 1/8	18 7/8	8	6	Clinton County	OH	Bryan Achtermann	2004	6098
*152 1/8	25 4/8	25 7/8	17 5/8	5	4	Bureau County	IL	Lamont Littlefield	2004	6098
152 1/8	25 4/8	26 0/8	19 1/8	6	7	Mason County	IL	Bob Stinauer	2004	6098
152 1/8	23 7/8	24 5/8	19 1/8	5	6	Winnebago County	WI	Andy Worm	2004	6098
152 1/8	22 4/8	21 5/8	15 7/8	5	5	St. Charles County	MO	Steven Gentz	2004	6098
*152 1/8	24 4/8	23 4/8	14 7/8	6	6	Saline County	NE	Rick L. Cox	2005	6098
152 1/8	24 4/8	22 1/8	17 3/8	5	7	Dearborn County	IN	John Small	2005	6098
152 1/8	23 7/8	23 5/8	18 1/8	5	5	Webster County	IA	Lyle Kauffman	2005	6098
152 1/8	23 4/8	24 0/8	21 2/8	6	6	Reagan County	TX	Dean Titsworth	2005	6098
*152 1/8	25 4/8	25 4/8	16 3/8	5	5	Branch County	MI	Patrick W. Lieby, Jr.	2006	6098
152 1/8	27 0/8	26 2/8	18 1/8	5	8	Trempealeau County	WI	Zach Bisek	2006	6098
152 1/8	25 3/8	25 1/8	19 5/8	4	4	Traill County	ND	Brody Peterson	2006	6098
152 1/8	24 0/8	24 0/8	19 3/8	6	5	Greene County	IL	David J. Mansey	2006	6098

WHITETAIL DEER (TYPICAL ANTLERS)

Minimum Score 125 / Continued

SCORE	LENGTH OF R MAIN BEAM L	INSIDE SPREAD	NUMBER OF R POINTS L		AREA	STATE/ PROVINCE	HUNTER'S NAME	DATE	RANK
*152 1/8	24 6/8 24 1/8	18 5/8	5	5	Lenawee County	MI	Samuel D. Forche	2006	6098
152 1/8	23 1/8 24 2/8	21 6/8	7	8	Carroll County	IL	John B. McNamara	2006	6098
*152 1/8	24 5/8 24 5/8	17 5/8	6	5	Ogle County	IL	Steven MacLaren	2006	6098
152 1/8	26 0/8 25 2/8	21 5/8	4	4	Morgan County	CO	Pete Lauer	2006	6098
*152 1/8	20 7/8 20 7/8	16 3/8	6	6	Allamakee County	IA	Bryan Todd Zeller	2007	6098
152 1/8	22 4/8 23 0/8	17 3/8	7	6	Lincoln County	SD	Scott Schemmel	2008	6098
*152 1/8	23 5/8 22 6/8	17 7/8	6	6	Buffalo County	WI	Devin L. Pronschinske	2008	6098
152 1/8	26 6/8 27 4/8	21 1/8	7	5	Steuben County	IN	Tim R. Troyer	2008	6098
152 1/8	25 7/8 25 5/8	18 1/8	4	4	Licking County	OH	Tony Casagrande	2008	6098
*152 1/8	24 3/8 24 4/8	18 7/8	5	5	Pierce County	WI	Nathan Brenner	2009	6098
152 1/8	26 1/8 24 7/8	20 7/8	5	5	Lawrence County	PA	Joseph W. Kursel	2009	6098
*152 1/8	23 7/8 24 1/8	18 7/8	6	6	Warren County	MS	Andy Taunton	2009	6098
152 0/8	24 0/8 24 6/8	20 2/8	5	5	Finney County	KS	Howard Haug, Jr.	1973	6188
152 0/8	23 0/8 23 0/8	16 0/8	5	5	Allen County	KY	Johnny Upton	1976	6188
152 0/8	22 1/8 22 1/8	16 2/8	5	6	Marshall County	SD	Merle Funston	1982	6188
152 0/8	26 6/8 26 3/8	17 6/8	5	4	Clay County	MN	Anthony Laddusaw	1985	6188
152 0/8	24 6/8 24 6/8	17 6/8	7	6	Dakota County	MN	Tom Esslinger	1985	6188
152 0/8	24 6/8 24 3/8	17 6/8	5	5	Itasca County	MN	Thomas A. Leedham	1985	6188
152 0/8	22 7/8 23 1/8	17 0/8	5	5	Champaign County	IL	John W. Chumbley	1985	6188
152 0/8	24 6/8 24 6/8	20 4/8	4	5	Winnebago County	IL	Ronald R. DeMus	1986	6188
152 0/8	23 1/8 23 6/8	19 0/8	5	6	Houston County	MN	Bob L. Billings	1987	6188
152 0/8	27 0/8 26 3/8	17 4/8	5	5	Lincoln County	MO	Donald E. Thompson, Jr.	1989	6188
152 0/8	22 6/8 22 0/8	18 4/8	6	4	Cass County	NE	Mike Wright	1989	6188
152 0/8	22 6/8 23 0/8	20 4/8	5	5	Iron County	WI	John A. Franke	1990	6188
152 0/8	23 0/8 22 0/8	17 0/8	5	5	Yankton County	SD	Daryl Miller	1990	6188
152 0/8	24 2/8 24 3/8	19 6/8	5	4	Logan County	IL	James Booth	1991	6188
152 0/8	26 3/8 26 3/8	20 2/8	7	6	Jackson County	MI	Robert J. Riddle	1992	6188
152 0/8	22 2/8 22 0/8	17 2/8	6	6	Buffalo County	WI	Barry Ritscher	1992	6188
152 0/8	24 5/8 24 6/8	18 4/8	5	5	Mercer County	IL	Richard D. Dochterman	1992	6188
152 0/8	23 5/8 24 3/8	18 0/8	4	4	McHenry County	IL	Richard G. Hoey	1992	6188
152 0/8	24 0/8 22 4/8	17 6/8	5	5	Columbia County	WI	Robert A. Williams	1992	6188
152 0/8	27 6/8 27 4/8	20 4/8	4	4	Will County	IL	John Kamarauskas	1992	6188
152 0/8	21 2/8 22 6/8	18 2/8	6	5	Ionia County	MI	Steve Jancar	1993	6188
152 0/8	22 7/8 22 6/8	16 0/8	6	6	Kleberg County	TX	W. J. Lucas III	1993	6188
152 0/8	22 5/8 22 2/8	18 3/8	5	6	Douglas County	MN	John P. Herd	1993	6188
152 0/8	24 5/8 24 5/8	19 4/8	5	5	Buffalo County	WI	Edmund Smieja	1993	6188
152 0/8	23 7/8 24 7/8	16 2/8	6	6	Montgomery County	PA	Tom Killoran	1993	6188
152 0/8	25 2/8 24 4/8	19 2/8	5	8	Ellis County	KS	Dan Cross	1993	6188
152 0/8	24 0/8 25 4/8	18 4/8	4	4	Christian County	KY	Barry Gant	1993	6188
152 0/8	24 0/8 26 2/8	16 0/8	5	7	Seneca County	NY	Scott C. Smith	1993	6188
152 0/8	24 0/8 23 1/8	16 6/8	5	5	Crawford County	PA	Angelo S. Iavarone, Jr.	1994	6188
152 0/8	25 1/8 26 1/8	19 2/8	5	5	Athens County	OH	David A. Hawk	1994	6188
152 0/8	21 2/8 22 0/8	16 6/8	5	5	Kerr County	TX	Robert L. Parker, Jr.	1994	6188
152 0/8	26 5/8 26 3/8	20 0/8	4	5	Linn County	IA	Randal J. Willey	1994	6188
152 0/8	24 2/8 26 0/8	19 0/8	4	4	Hennepin County	MN	Joe Bilek	1994	6188
152 0/8	26 6/8 26 0/8	19 5/8	6	7	St. Louis County	MN	Nathan M. Samarzia	1995	6188
152 0/8	23 5/8 24 1/8	21 0/8	6	5	Prince Georges County	MD	Tracy Ford	1995	6188
152 0/8	23 2/8 22 4/8	16 2/8	5	5	Cavalier County	ND	James B. Sondeland	1995	6188
152 0/8	26 6/8 24 3/8	19 6/8	5	5	Will County	IL	Brian Smith	1996	6188
152 0/8	24 1/8 24 1/8	18 0/8	5	7	Scott County	IA	Patrick E. Lucas	1996	6188
152 0/8	24 2/8 23 6/8	15 0/8	5	5	Taylor County	WI	Dave Gebert	1996	6188
152 0/8	28 0/8 28 3/8	19 2/8	4	4	Adams County	OH	Larry D. Napier	1996	6188
152 0/8	24 4/8 23 6/8	17 3/8	6	7	Rocky Rapids	ALB	Harvey Seguin	1997	6188
152 0/8	24 6/8 24 7/8	20 0/8	5	6	Shawnee County	KS	Eldon Johnson	1997	6188
152 0/8	25 0/8 25 4/8	15 6/8	5	6	Atchison County	KS	Richard Morgan	1997	6188
152 0/8	24 5/8 23 0/8	19 0/8	6	5	Jo Daviess County	IL	Jack Rife	1997	6188
152 0/8	24 4/8 23 1/8	18 3/8	5	6	Chippewa County	WI	Scott Steinmetz	1997	6188
152 0/8	23 6/8 24 7/8	18 0/8	4	4	Kane County	IL	Ken Dubois	1997	6188
152 0/8	25 1/8 25 1/8	20 0/8	5	4	Knox County	IL	Roger A. Sheetz	1997	6188
152 0/8	25 3/8 25 2/8	18 6/8	5	5	Chippewa County	WI	Keith Hager	1998	6188
152 0/8	23 3/8 23 4/8	20 4/8	4	4	St. Marys County	MD	Ronald W. McKenzie	1998	6188
152 0/8	25 2/8 25 4/8	20 2/8	5	6	Wabash County	IL	Dan Hinderliter	1998	6188
152 0/8	23 0/8 23 2/8	21 0/8	5	5	Pope County	IL	Carlos "Chip" Powers	1998	6188
152 0/8	24 7/8 25 5/8	21 2/8	6	6	Athens County	OH	Charles Montgomery	1998	6188
152 0/8	22 6/8 22 6/8	17 4/8	5	6	Lancaster County	NE	Clarence Poteet	1999	6188
152 0/8	22 2/8 22 2/8	18 0/8	5	5	Providence County	RI	Daniel T. Strong	2000	6188
152 0/8	25 3/8 24 1/8	18 2/8	6	6	Randolph County	MO	Tim Scott	2000	6188
152 0/8	25 0/8 24 3/8	18 6/8	7	7	Daviess County	MO	Tim Harrell	2001	6188
152 0/8	23 7/8 23 7/8	18 6/8	5	6	Burleigh County	ND	William D. Helphrey	2001	6188
152 0/8	22 1/8 23 4/8	16 1/8	5	5	Sauk County	WI	Joe Rohloff	2002	6188
152 0/8	21 7/8 21 2/8	17 5/8	6	7	Irion County	TX	Kenny Ellis	2002	6188
152 0/8	25 6/8 26 0/8	15 4/8	4	5	Preble County	OH	Buell Harris	2002	6188
152 0/8	21 4/8 22 2/8	16 6/8	5	5	Fulton County	IL	David Courtright	2003	6188
*152 0/8	21 6/8 22 2/8	18 6/8	7	6	Jefferson County	IA	Shawn Smith	2003	6188
152 0/8	21 4/8 20 7/8	16 5/8	6	5	Riley County	KS	Tony W. Cleveland	2003	6188
152 0/8	24 5/8 25 2/8	21 2/8	5	4	Osage County	MO	Kenny Hoeller	2004	6188
152 0/8	21 6/8 21 5/8	15 6/8	6	7	Coles County	IL	Dan Milburn	2004	6188
152 0/8	25 6/8 25 4/8	17 7/8	6	5	Sandusky County	OH	Robert Missler	2004	6188
152 0/8	22 6/8 22 0/8	14 6/8	5	5	Pike County	IL	Ken Ash	2004	6188
152 0/8	24 7/8 21 2/8	16 6/8	5	7	Kankakee County	IL	Steven W. Nelson	2004	6188
152 0/8	26 0/8 25 4/8	16 6/8	6	4	Clinton County	IA	Kyle McGarry	2004	6188
152 0/8	22 2/8 23 2/8	18 0/8	5	5	Columbiana County	OH	Terry Melott, Jr.	2004	6188
152 0/8	25 5/8 24 6/8	16 6/8	6	6	Bates County	MO	Clint Bennett	2005	6188
152 0/8	20 7/8 20 6/8	18 6/8	6	6	Kit Carson County	CO	Scott Haeder	2005	6188
152 0/8	25 0/8 24 5/8	18 6/8	5	5	Forest County	WI	Jeff Ternes	2005	6188
152 0/8	23 5/8 25 6/8	19 2/8	6	9	Noxubee County	MS	Wayne Stewart, Jr.	2005	6188
152 0/8	25 3/8 24 0/8	17 0/8	6	5	Knox County	MO	Art Hendrickson	2006	6188
152 0/8	23 5/8 23 0/8	18 6/8	5	6	Washington County	OH	Roger L. Pape	2006	6188
152 0/8	22 4/8 26 5/8	23 2/8	7	7	Monmouth County	NJ	Humberto Herrera	2006	6188
152 0/8	21 3/8 20 2/8	17 6/8	6	7	Chautauqua County	NY	Tim Morrison	2006	6188
*152 0/8	22 2/8 22 7/8	17 4/8	6	5	Green Lake County	WI	Randy Raith	2006	6188
152 0/8	24 6/8 24 4/8	17 6/8	5	5	Guernsey County	OH	Tim R. King	2006	6188
*152 0/8	22 4/8 22 7/8	17 0/8	9	8	Walworth County	WI	Jason A. Richmond	2006	6188
152 0/8	25 0/8 22 6/8	17 7/8	5	7	Oconto County	WI	Tim Gorman	2007	6188
*152 0/8	22 1/8 21 4/8	20 2/8	5	6	Ramsey County	ND	Jason Ramberg	2007	6188

421

WHITETAIL DEER (TYPICAL ANTLERS)

Minimum Score 125   Continued

SCORE	LENGTH OF R MAIN BEAM L	INSIDE SPREAD	NUMBER OF R POINTS L		AREA	STATE/PROVINCE	HUNTER'S NAME	DATE	RANK
152 0/8	24 1/8	23 0/8	19 2/8	6	6	Pierce County	WI	Kevin Brantner	2008	6188
152 0/8	23 5/8	23 4/8	15 6/8	5	5	De Kalb County	IN	W. H. Cannon	2008	6188
152 0/8	22 2/8	23 3/8	15 6/8	5	5	Taylor County	WI	Ronald B. Young II	2008	6188
*152 0/8	23 5/8	24 2/8	17 6/8	6	6	Vernon County	WI	Todd Suiter	2008	6188
152 0/8	25 7/8	25 6/8	20 4/8	5	5	Knotts County	KY	David Lee Bailey	2008	6188
*152 0/8	24 2/8	24 2/8	21 4/8	5	5	Allamakee County	IA	John Papp	2009	6188
152 0/8	25 2/8	24 1/8	17 4/8	6	6	Edgar County	IL	Roy Lowe III	2009	6188
152 0/8	24 1/8	23 0/8	20 0/8	6	6	Edgar County	IL	Brian Crockett	2009	6188
151 7/8	27 1/8	28 0/8	18 6/8	5	5	Morrison County	MN	Steve Smythe	1968	6279
151 7/8	24 3/8	24 7/8	18 3/8	5	5	Davis County	IA	George C. Francis	1979	6279
151 7/8	23 7/8	23 7/8	17 6/8	6	6	Tama County	IA	Kirk Lundberg	1980	6279
151 7/8	26 1/8	25 6/8	18 0/8	5	7	Brown County	SD	Jan Hinrichs	1981	6279
151 7/8	24 6/8	24 4/8	19 1/8	5	5	Will County	IL	Ike Rhodes	1984	6279
151 7/8	24 6/8	25 4/8	18 1/8	6	6	McCook County	SD	James C. Perkins	1984	6279
151 7/8	24 4/8	23 6/8	15 5/8	5	5	Grant County	WI	William Stetler	1985	6279
151 7/8	25 1/8	24 5/8	16 7/8	7	6	Waukesha County	WI	Perry Scott Brummer	1986	6279
151 7/8	24 1/8	22 3/8	17 2/8	6	5	Lewis County	MO	Sam Smith	1986	6279
151 7/8	26 3/8	26 3/8	24 3/8	4	5	Peoria County	IL	Dick McKown	1986	6279
151 7/8	23 7/8	23 4/8	19 7/8	5	5	Livingston County	MI	Charles D. Lemay	1987	6279
151 7/8	21 6/8	21 5/8	17 3/8	6	6	Laurel County	KY	Jerry Hubbard	1987	6279
151 7/8	25 3/8	24 5/8	17 0/8	5	8	Kingman County	KS	Terry Morisse	1988	6279
151 7/8	25 4/8	25 5/8	22 7/8	6	5	Whitley County	IN	Frank J. Yaquinto	1990	6279
151 7/8	22 1/8	22 2/8	16 1/8	5	6	Edmonton	ALB	Rick Bell	1991	6279
151 7/8	24 0/8	22 4/8	15 3/8	5	5	Rock County	WI	Fred J. Townsend	1992	6279
151 7/8	25 0/8	25 4/8	19 2/8	7	8	Graham County	KS	Russell Hull	1992	6279
151 7/8	22 4/8	23 5/8	18 5/8	5	5	Allamakee County	IA	Mark A. Kamm	1993	6279
151 7/8	23 4/8	23 7/8	19 7/8	5	5	Graves County	KY	Jamie Mason	1993	6279
151 7/8	24 5/8	24 1/8	16 5/8	5	5	Dunn County	WI	Dan Wolf	1993	6279
151 7/8	26 0/8	26 0/8	18 7/8	6	5	Morrison County	MN	Ross Engstran	1993	6279
151 7/8	27 6/8	27 5/8	25 5/8	6	4	Washington County	MS	Frank Greenlee	1994	6279
151 7/8	24 6/8	23 6/8	20 3/8	5	6	Union County	KY	Jimmy Vaught	1994	6279
151 7/8	24 2/8	23 0/8	17 3/8	5	5	Strathcona	ALB	Tom Chadwick	1994	6279
151 7/8	24 7/8	24 6/8	17 0/8	7	6	Douglas County	KS	John Hackathorn	1994	6279
151 7/8	22 2/8	21 4/8	14 0/8	6	5	Kerr County	TX	Bobbie E. Kimbro	1995	6279
151 7/8	25 4/8	25 5/8	17 7/8	7	6	Greene County	IN	Tony Richards	1995	6279
151 7/8	22 1/8	22 1/8	21 0/8	7	6	Sherburne County	MN	Phil Hinkemeyer	1995	6279
151 7/8	24 1/8	24 2/8	19 7/8	4	4	Jefferson County	WI	Dennis Messmann	1996	6279
151 7/8	22 5/8	23 4/8	16 7/8	6	6	Wayne County	NY	Thomas A. Mitchell	1996	6279
151 7/8	25 4/8	24 2/8	20 7/8	4	4	Issaquena County	MS	Chris Malinowski	1997	6279
151 7/8	23 5/8	22 5/8	17 3/8	5	5	Stark County	IL	Jeff D. Schweigert	1997	6279
151 7/8	23 7/8	24 0/8	20 3/8	5	5	Meigs County	OH	Phillip R. King	1997	6279
151 7/8	24 0/8	25 4/8	18 7/8	5	5	Allamakee County	IA	Jeffrey R. Paulus	1997	6279
151 7/8	24 4/8	24 4/8	17 5/8	5	5	Shawnee County	KS	Frank Brennan	1997	6279
151 7/8	22 6/8	23 0/8	18 7/8	6	6	Edmonton	ALB	Robert A. Mochilar	1997	6279
151 7/8	24 1/8	23 0/8	20 4/8	7	6	Dakota County	MN	Todd Grieger	1997	6279
151 7/8	26 2/8	25 3/8	16 5/8	4	4	Montgomery County	OH	Len Willenbrink	1998	6279
151 7/8	22 2/8	23 2/8	15 3/8	5	5	Muskingum County	OH	Todd J. Wagner	1998	6279
151 7/8	24 0/8	24 3/8	20 5/8	5	5	Branch County	MI	Troy A. Lane	1999	6279
151 7/8	22 6/8	23 0/8	19 5/8	5	5	Berrien County	MI	Brian E. Gregg	1999	6279
151 7/8	25 5/8	24 4/8	19 1/8	4	4	Butler County	KS	Claude Allen	1999	6279
151 7/8	23 0/8	23 2/8	19 1/8	5	5	Pottawattamie County	IA	Randy Feller	2000	6279
151 7/8	25 6/8	26 1/8	18 3/8	5	5	Buffalo County	WI	James D. Laehn	2000	6279
151 7/8	23 4/8	23 6/8	16 3/8	5	5	Monroe County	MO	Shelton Wheelan	2000	6279
151 7/8	25 5/8	26 0/8	16 6/8	6	5	Waukesha County	WI	Steven Biksadski	2000	6279
151 7/8	21 1/8	24 7/8	18 2/8	7	7	Pope County	IL	Wade C. Atchley	2000	6279
151 7/8	23 4/8	23 4/8	18 7/8	6	5	Clark County	WI	Bruce R. Stone	2000	6279
151 7/8	24 4/8	23 7/8	16 2/8	5	6	Sioux County	IA	Brian Oordt	2000	6279
151 7/8	26 4/8	26 6/8	19 7/8	4	4	Summit County	OH	James Bill Geralis	2001	6279
151 7/8	24 6/8	23 2/8	15 1/8	6	6	Marquette County	WI	Tim Landolt	2001	6279
151 7/8	22 6/8	28 0/8	17 6/8	5	5	McLean County	IL	James D. Olsen	2001	6279
151 7/8	24 0/8	23 5/8	22 1/8	5	5	Winona County	MN	Robert A. Markwardt	2002	6279
151 7/8	22 6/8	22 3/8	18 7/8	4	4	Buffalo County	WI	Jason Hunger	2002	6279
151 7/8	24 6/8	25 5/8	20 0/8	7	7	Clark County	IL	Troy Biddle	2002	6279
151 7/8	24 4/8	24 2/8	18 3/8	5	5	Winona County	MN	Robert Wick	2002	6279
*151 7/8	24 5/8	23 7/8	17 7/8	6	8	Decatur County	IA	John Thomas	2002	6279
151 7/8	24 4/8	25 4/8	19 1/8	6	7	Warren County	IA	Eric Sowers	2002	6279
151 7/8	27 5/8	29 2/8	20 7/8	4	4	Calvert County	MD	Keith R. Balderson	2002	6279
151 7/8	24 7/8	23 7/8	16 1/8	5	5	Polk County	WI	Corey Mackenzie	2003	6279
151 7/8	25 2/8	22 6/8	27 4/8	7	8	Adams County	WI	Kevin Weber	2003	6279
151 7/8	24 6/8	25 1/8	17 7/8	6	6	Boone County	MO	Gene Simmerman	2003	6279
151 7/8	24 0/8	24 3/8	16 7/8	5	5	Monroe County	NY	Ronald E. Michael, Jr.	2003	6279
151 7/8	26 4/8	25 4/8	20 1/8	7	6	Madison County	ID	Doug Kauer	2004	6279
151 7/8	23 7/8	23 4/8	23 4/8	7	5	Buffalo County	WI	Deric Lindstrom	2004	6279
151 7/8	22 7/8	23 0/8	17 0/8	6	6	Richland County	IL	Carl Waggle	2004	6279
151 7/8	24 2/8	24 4/8	22 6/8	5	6	Madison County	ID	Cornell A. Hansen	2004	6279
151 7/8	28 5/8	29 0/8	18 4/8	5	7	Worth County	GA	Eric Mullis	2005	6279
151 7/8	24 1/8	24 5/8	16 3/8	5	5	Kewaunee County	WI	Randal J. Gilson	2005	6279
*151 7/8	25 0/8	25 2/8	20 7/8	7	5	Dunn County	WI	Matt Benrud	2005	6279
151 7/8	25 0/8	24 5/8	15 7/8	5	5	Branch County	MI	Bradley D. Keith	2005	6279
151 7/8	24 6/8	24 4/8	19 1/8	5	5	Pawnee County	OK	Peter Jackson	2005	6279
151 7/8	24 5/8	22 2/8	21 0/8	6	7	Mahoning County	OH	Ron Osborne	2006	6279
151 7/8	23 3/8	23 5/8	19 1/8	5	5	Ohio County	IN	Brandon Wright	2006	6279
151 7/8	22 2/8	23 4/8	17 6/8	8	6	Peoria County	IL	Mike Reatherford	2006	6279
*151 7/8	24 7/8	24 2/8	20 0/8	8	7	Franklin County	IL	Billy Joe Lovett	2006	6279
151 7/8	24 0/8	23 3/8	18 6/8	6	5	Vernon County	WI	Andrew Blum	2006	6279
151 7/8	25 1/8	24 6/8	19 7/8	5	6	Athens County	OH	Andrew D. Proseus	2007	6279
151 7/8	25 0/8	24 7/8	19 7/8	6	6	Cass County	IL	Larry C. Holcomb	2007	6279
151 7/8	26 2/8	26 1/8	19 7/8	6	6	Grayson County	TX	John Henderson	2007	6279
*151 7/8	21 6/8	21 5/8	17 7/8	5	5	Pike County	IL	Angela K. Walk	2008	6279
151 7/8	22 5/8	22 0/8	17 1/8	5	5	Hughes County	SD	Robert Truax	2008	6279
151 7/8	24 4/8	25 1/8	19 3/8	5	5	Morgan County	MO	Paul Fergerson	2008	6279
151 7/8	24 1/8	23 5/8	22 1/8	5	4	Buffalo County	WI	Greg Reedy	2009	6279
*151 7/8	23 1/8	23 4/8	19 2/8	6	4	Ross County	OH	William R. Lott, Jr.	2009	6279
151 7/8	25 1/8	25 5/8	19 1/8	4	5	Logan County	WV	Brian Adkins	2009	6279
*151 7/8	23 2/8	23 1/8	16 5/8	6	5	Alfalfa County	OK	Darren Titsworth	2009	6279

WHITETAIL DEER (TYPICAL ANTLERS)

Minimum Score 125 — Continued

SCORE	LENGTH OF R MAIN BEAM L	INSIDE SPREAD	NUMBER OF R POINTS L		AREA	STATE/ PROVINCE	HUNTER'S NAME	DATE	RANK
151 6/8	22 1/8	23 2/8	15 4/8	6	5	Flathead County	MT	Jerry D. Almos	1970	6366
151 6/8	25 4/8	24 7/8	21 0/8	8	6	Warren County	OH	Lundy Lewis	1981	6366
151 6/8	25 0/8	24 7/8	17 4/8	5	5	Murray County	MN	Dennis Lunderborg	1982	6366
151 6/8	25 7/8	22 1/8	20 1/8	5	9	Columbiana County	OH	Bill Lawrence	1983	6366
151 6/8	23 7/8	24 0/8	21 4/8	4	4	Beaver County	OK	Max Crocker	1984	6366
151 6/8	27 6/8	26 6/8	19 7/8	5	5	Champaign County	OH	Thomas R. Weaver	1984	6366
151 6/8	24 2/8	24 0/8	21 5/8	5	6	Madison County	IA	Todd L. Fuson	1986	6366
151 6/8	27 2/8	26 0/8	21 4/8	4	5	Greenwood County	KS	Jerry Ramshaw	1986	6366
151 6/8	23 5/8	23 4/8	16 3/8	6	7	Wabasha County	MN	Wayne Techaw, Jr.	1987	6366
151 6/8	25 4/8	26 6/8	18 2/8	6	5	Ogle County	IL	Jim Hill	1987	6366
151 6/8	24 1/8	23 4/8	20 4/8	4	4	Bond County	IL	Allen D. Ellsworth	1987	6366
151 6/8	25 5/8	26 1/8	18 6/8	6	9	Pulaski County	IL	Garrett Wilson	1988	6366
151 6/8	25 5/8	24 6/8	21 4/8	4	5	Christian County	IL	Lee Penn	1988	6366
151 6/8	23 3/8	23 6/8	17 0/8	5	5	Greene County	IA	Glen Garnett	1990	6366
151 6/8	25 4/8	24 3/8	16 1/8	7	5	Ross County	OH	Randy Johnson	1990	6366
151 6/8	24 7/8	25 0/8	19 6/8	4	4	St. Clair County	MI	Lawrence S. Cowhy	1991	6366
151 6/8	24 1/8	23 6/8	17 6/8	6	5	Pottawattamie County	IA	Allan T. Carmichael	1992	6366
151 6/8	25 5/8	23 7/8	19 4/8	5	7	Hocking County	OH	Chris R. Cetone	1992	6366
151 6/8	24 0/8	23 4/8	18 2/8	5	5	Lancaster County	PA	Douglas D. Shiffler	1992	6366
151 6/8	23 1/8	22 5/8	16 4/8	5	5	Cherry Lake	BC	Anthony P. Zielinski	1992	6366
151 6/8	24 1/8	23 7/8	20 4/8	5	5	Shawano County	WI	Todd M. Krause	1992	6366
151 6/8	24 1/8	22 5/8	19 7/8	6	5	McHenry County	IL	Zach Dagel	1992	6366
151 6/8	24 2/8	24 0/8	19 5/8	6	5	Washington County	MN	Dave Vadnais	1993	6366
151 6/8	25 5/8	25 5/8	18 6/8	4	4	Jersey County	IL	David Bailey, Jr.	1994	6366
151 6/8	23 0/8	23 3/8	21 2/8	5	5	Nowata County	OK	Jeff Fitts	1994	6366
151 6/8	24 1/8	23 3/8	20 4/8	5	6	Gratiot County	MI	Jeff Watson	1995	6366
151 6/8	23 7/8	24 1/8	17 4/8	5	6	Keya Paha County	NE	John H. Smith	1995	6366
151 6/8	22 3/8	22 0/8	20 2/8	5	5	Monroe County	IL	Dan Young	1995	6366
151 6/8	27 1/8	27 4/8	22 7/8	6	5	La Crosse County	WI	Terry Wieman	1996	6366
151 6/8	23 1/8	23 2/8	18 3/8	5	6	Fayette County	IA	Steve Stern	1996	6366
151 6/8	26 6/8	25 2/8	22 0/8	6	5	Worth County	IA	John Janssen	1996	6366
151 6/8	27 5/8	26 6/8	22 1/8	8	6	Morgan County	IL	Ray Rabon	1996	6366
151 6/8	23 1/8	25 6/8	16 4/8	6	6	Vigo County	IN	Eric W. Corbin	1997	6366
151 6/8	25 7/8	26 3/8	18 5/8	6	6	Milwaukee County	WI	Jeremy Meyer	1997	6366
151 6/8	25 0/8	24 0/8	19 3/8	5	7	Des Moines County	IA	Robin Schneider	1997	6366
151 6/8	24 6/8	24 5/8	19 6/8	4	4	Stony Plain	ALB	Jim Paplawski	1998	6366
151 6/8	26 4/8	26 6/8	20 2/8	5	4	Delaware County	OH	Larry Eberhard	1998	6366
151 6/8	21 7/8	22 3/8	18 1/8	7	7	Cass County	ND	Roy Aafedt	1999	6366
151 6/8	24 4/8	23 7/8	18 0/8	5	5	Crawford County	IL	Duane J. Newlin	1999	6366
151 6/8	23 7/8	23 5/8	16 0/8	8	6	Marion County	IA	Gerald T. Dowell	1999	6366
151 6/8	24 7/8	25 7/8	18 6/8	5	5	Edmonton	ALB	Steve Grue	1999	6366
151 6/8	26 4/8	25 6/8	19 0/8	5	4	Monroe County	IA	Ken W. Cobb	1999	6366
151 6/8	21 7/8	21 5/8	17 2/8	5	5	Rooks County	KS	Shawn W. Harding	2000	6366
151 6/8	24 0/8	25 4/8	23 4/8	4	4	Mercer County	NJ	Steve Ficarro	2000	6366
151 6/8	22 4/8	21 7/8	14 2/8	6	6	Edmonton	ALB	Ryk Visscher	2000	6366
*151 6/8	24 1/8	23 7/8	17 0/8	5	5	Stokes County	NC	Floyd R. Inman	2001	6366
151 6/8	27 0/8	26 7/8	20 0/8	5	4	Lake County	IL	Rob B. Getz	2001	6366
151 6/8	25 6/8	24 6/8	17 2/8	5	6	Henry County	KY	Winston G. Irvin, Jr.	2001	6366
151 6/8	23 1/8	23 2/8	17 2/8	6	6	Christian County	MO	Russell E. Alexander	2002	6366
151 6/8	24 1/8	23 6/8	18 2/8	5	5	Kane County	IL	Daniel R. Petska	2003	6366
*151 6/8	27 3/8	28 0/8	19 3/8	6	4	Fayette County	IL	Jon Washburn	2003	6366
*151 6/8	26 3/8	26 3/8	18 6/8	5	5	Dubuque County	IA	Mike Schwartz	2003	6366
151 6/8	23 2/8	23 4/8	19 4/8	6	5	Adams County	WI	Frank Knaus I	2004	6366
151 6/8	22 2/8	22 7/8	19 0/8	5	5	Meeker County	MN	David Tipka	2004	6366
*151 6/8	24 4/8	25 0/8	19 0/8	4	4	Dubuque County	IA	Dan Kieffer	2004	6366
151 6/8	23 4/8	23 6/8	16 4/8	5	5	Weld County	CO	Greg Hamilton	2004	6366
151 6/8	26 3/8	26 2/8	17 2/8	5	5	Grant County	IN	Junior Hoheimer	2005	6366
*151 6/8	21 4/8	23 1/8	17 0/8	5	5	Butler County	PA	Michael Miller	2005	6366
151 6/8	24 5/8	23 2/8	22 4/8	5	5	Jefferson County	OH	Joshua O. Switzer	2006	6366
151 6/8	24 3/8	24 7/8	17 7/8	6	5	Marquette County	WI	Randall J. Crook	2006	6366
*151 6/8	21 3/8	21 1/8	14 6/8	5	5	Polk County	WI	Chad M. Cunningham	2006	6366
*151 6/8	25 7/8	25 4/8	18 4/8	5	5	Outagamie County	WI	Jim W. Ernst	2006	6366
151 6/8	23 3/8	23 5/8	20 0/8	5	5	Coles County	IL	Todd Smith	2006	6366
*151 6/8	24 4/8	24 7/8	20 4/8	5	5	Polk County	WI	Vincent E. Graf	2006	6366
151 6/8	23 2/8	23 2/8	19 0/8	5	5	Wainwright	ALB	Shane Mascarin	2007	6366
*151 6/8	23 2/8	23 2/8	17 4/8	5	5	Flagstaff	ALB	Lori Keeler	2007	6366
*151 6/8	25 1/8	24 1/8	17 0/8	5	5	Steuben County	NY	Terry Clark, Jr.	2007	6366
*151 6/8	24 1/8	23 5/8	17 2/8	7	7	Winona County	MN	Shawn W. Dunlap	2007	6366
*151 6/8	25 4/8	26 7/8	17 4/8	4	5	La Salle County	IL	Michael Martin, Jr.	2007	6366
151 6/8	25 7/8	25 4/8	20 2/8	5	5	Dane County	WI	Steve Lane	2007	6366
151 6/8	23 4/8	23 6/8	19 5/8	8	3	Jasper County	IL	Derek Ginder	2007	6366
*151 6/8	24 2/8	24 1/8	17 6/8	5	6	Winnebago County	IA	Donald Elbert	2007	6366
151 6/8	24 6/8	24 5/8	20 0/8	5	5	Nodaway County	MO	John Judah	2007	6366
151 6/8	23 1/8	22 6/8	16 2/8	6	7	Polk County	MN	James A. Gunufson	2008	6366
*151 6/8	25 6/8	25 7/8	19 6/8	6	6	Russell County	KS	Jamie W. Andrew	2008	6366
151 6/8	23 4/8	23 7/8	22 2/8	5	5	Houston County	MN	Lee Michael Books	2008	6366
151 6/8	24 2/8	24 0/8	17 2/8	5	5	De Kalb County	IN	Paul Branch	2008	6366
151 6/8	22 6/8	23 2/8	19 0/8	7	6	Green County	WI	Nicholas Jarvis	2008	6366
*151 6/8	24 5/8	23 4/8	16 0/8	5	5	Clark County	IL	Jeff Bordwell	2008	6366
*151 6/8	25 1/8	25 7/8	18 4/8	4	4	Vernon County	WI	Chris Dahl	2008	6366
*151 6/8	24 6/8	26 7/8	19 6/8	4	4	Washington County	MN	Lee M. Firminger	2008	6366
*151 6/8	23 6/8	23 6/8	19 0/8	5	6	Coahuila	MEX	Rick Morgan	2009	6366
151 6/8	23 1/8	23 5/8	16 2/8	5	6	Jefferson County	MO	Michael Meuser	2009	6366
151 6/8	24 3/8	23 3/8	20 2/8	5	6	Guthrie County	IA	Levi Wittrock	2009	6366
*151 6/8	25 4/8	23 7/8	19 0/8	5	6	Morrow County	OH	Bob Branstetter	2009	6366
151 5/8	26 2/8	24 7/8	20 6/8	6	6	Franklin County	KS	Kenneth Heinitz	1966	6451
151 5/8	24 2/8	24 3/8	18 7/8	4	4	Douglas County	WI	Larry Allen Blaylock	1978	6451
151 5/8	26 0/8	24 3/8	18 3/8	6	6	Reno County	KS	Dan Ropp	1981	6451
151 5/8	26 6/8	26 1/8	17 3/8	4	4	Carter County	KY	Herbie Jackson	1982	6451
151 5/8	25 6/8	25 4/8	21 5/8	6	7	Green County	WI	Alex Elkins	1982	6451
151 5/8	26 6/8	26 5/8	17 5/8	4	4	Jackson County	OH	Jeffrey L. Walters	1984	6451
151 5/8	24 7/8	25 2/8	20 7/8	5	5	Vermilion County	IL	Bill Fitton	1984	6451
151 5/8	22 2/8	23 2/8	16 5/8	6	6	Fremont County	IA	Mike Laughlin	1989	6451
151 5/8	25 7/8	25 3/8	21 7/8	5	4	Ringgold County	IA	Dale L. Clark	1989	6451
151 5/8	25 1/8	25 3/8	20 3/8	5	5	St. Louis County	MO	Michael T. Horn	1989	6451

WHITETAIL DEER (TYPICAL ANTLERS)

Minimum Score 125 — Continued

SCORE	LENGTH OF R MAIN BEAM L	INSIDE SPREAD	NUMBER OF R POINTS L	AREA	STATE/PROVINCE	HUNTER'S NAME	DATE	RANK
151 5/8	23 4/8 22 2/8	20 1/8	5 5	Jefferson County	ID	Brent D. Barber	1990	6451
151 5/8	24 5/8 24 4/8	20 4/8	6 6	Hunterdon County	NJ	Jack Baker	1990	6451
151 5/8	26 0/8 24 2/8	16 0/8	6 6	Lee County	IA	Larry Galliart	1991	6451
151 5/8	22 6/8 24 4/8	17 4/8	8 5	Wyandotte County	KS	Bruce McComb	1991	6451
151 5/8	21 4/8 21 6/8	19 7/8	5 7	Pike County	IL	Robert Sacher	1993	6451
151 5/8	22 3/8 22 4/8	18 1/8	5 5	Millarville	ALB	Leo Comeau	1993	6451
151 5/8	23 6/8 23 4/8	16 7/8	5 5	Highland County	OH	Paul A. Eldridge	1993	6451
151 5/8	23 4/8 23 3/8	20 1/8	7 5	Clay County	AR	Stephen E. White	1993	6451
151 5/8	24 1/8 24 2/8	18 1/8	5 5	Chester County	PA	Robert J. Dupoldt	1994	6451
151 5/8	24 0/8 27 0/8	18 7/8	5 5	Caledon	ONT	Robert Urquhart	1995	6451
151 5/8	23 5/8 23 7/8	17 5/8	5 8	Jones County	IA	Tim McDonough	1995	6451
151 5/8	21 6/8 21 6/8	19 7/8	5 5	La Salle County	IL	Paul Garrison	1996	6451
151 5/8	23 7/8 23 5/8	18 3/8	8 5	Polk County	IA	David Mongar	1996	6451
151 5/8	22 1/8 22 2/8	19 7/8	5 5	Allamakee County	IA	Steven W. Amann	1996	6451
151 5/8	26 2/8 27 2/8	17 5/8	5 4	Clinton County	IL	Mike Timmons	1997	6451
151 5/8	22 0/8 21 3/8	16 6/8	5 5	Morrison County	MN	Ben Brazil	1997	6451
151 5/8	23 1/8 23 4/8	17 7/8	5 4	Brown County	IL	Erich Elendt	1997	6451
151 5/8	24 2/8 23 3/8	17 2/8	5 6	Dubuque County	IA	Jay Konzen	1998	6451
151 5/8	24 4/8 24 0/8	15 7/8	7 6	Monroe County	WV	David Allen	1998	6451
151 5/8	24 0/8 24 2/8	17 1/8	5 5	Dubois County	IN	Eric Smith	1998	6451
151 5/8	24 2/8 24 3/8	21 5/8	5 5	Henderson County	KY	Kelly Woods	1999	6451
151 5/8	25 4/8 25 2/8	17 3/8	5 5	Hillsborough County	NH	Kevin Foster	2000	6451
151 5/8	22 6/8 22 4/8	15 5/8	5 5	Cottonwood County	MN	Chad Magnussen	2000	6451
151 5/8	23 2/8 23 1/8	18 1/8	5 6	Clay County	MN	Craig Enervold	2001	6451
151 5/8	24 7/8 25 2/8	19 3/8	5 7	Buffalo County	WI	Rick A. Olson	2001	6451
151 5/8	23 3/8 23 3/8	20 3/8	6 5	Ogle County	IL	Bill B. Winebaugh	2001	6451
151 5/8	25 1/8 25 1/8	20 0/8	7 5	Wood County	WI	Jon Zinthefer	2002	6451
151 5/8	23 4/8 24 5/8	18 5/8	5 5	Buffalo County	WI	Jim Kamla	2002	6451
151 5/8	25 6/8 25 3/8	18 3/8	5 4	Wyoming County	NY	David Mager	2002	6451
151 5/8	21 6/8 21 2/8	15 7/8	5 5	McLean County	ND	Scott G. Hettinger	2002	6451
151 5/8	22 1/8 22 3/8	18 7/8	5 5	Shawano County	WI	Ross Berkhahn	2003	6451
151 5/8	24 6/8 24 2/8	15 5/8	5 5	Houston County	MN	James J. Willard	2003	6451
151 5/8	23 0/8 21 7/8	15 3/8	5 5	Person County	NC	Kirk Oakley	2003	6451
151 5/8	24 4/8 24 6/8	18 1/8	7 4	Henry County	IA	David Pawloski	2003	6451
151 5/8	26 3/8 25 6/8	20 0/8	6 6	Adams County	IA	David Keith	2003	6451
151 5/8	25 2/8 22 5/8	18 5/8	7 5	Webb County	TX	Norman E. Speer	2003	6451
151 5/8	22 2/8 20 5/8	18 7/8	6 6	La Porte County	IN	Rick A. Salzer	2004	6451
151 5/8	22 5/8 22 7/8	15 6/8	6 6	Concho County	TX	Bill Young	2004	6451
151 5/8	24 0/8 24 2/8	16 2/8	5 5	Davis County	IA	Allen F. Weber	2004	6451
151 5/8	24 1/8 23 4/8	17 6/8	6 5	Ashtabula County	OH	Charles K. Ellsworth	2004	6451
151 5/8	25 5/8 26 0/8	21 6/8	4 6	Jewell County	KS	Nathan Andersohn	2004	6451
151 5/8	26 0/8 23 7/8	19 4/8	6 6	Harper County	KS	John Add Benson	2004	6451
151 5/8	22 5/8 23 0/8	17 5/8	5 5	Polk County	WI	Dale Leisch	2004	6451
151 5/8	24 2/8 24 5/8	17 7/8	6 6	Allegheny County	PA	William Miller	2005	6451
151 5/8	24 4/8 24 4/8	22 4/8	7 5	Steuben County	IN	Cory Armstrong	2005	6451
151 5/8	22 1/8 23 1/8	15 3/8	5 7	Union County	IA	Robert R. Spratt	2005	6451
151 5/8	24 2/8 24 1/8	18 7/8	5 5	Edgar County	IL	Brad Davis	2006	6451
151 5/8	24 5/8 26 0/8	18 7/8	6 5	Scott County	MN	Chad Stocker	2006	6451
151 5/8	22 1/8 22 7/8	17 5/8	7 7	Belmont County	OH	Sam Wells	2006	6451
151 5/8	24 1/8 23 1/8	17 7/8	5 5	Kane County	IL	William W. Wishon, Jr.	2006	6451
151 5/8	25 7/8 26 6/8	22 2/8	5 6	Darke County	OH	Gregory L. Knick	2006	6451
*151 5/8	24 4/8 23 3/8	15 0/8	9 7	Waupaca County	WI	Earl H. Clement	2007	6451
*151 5/8	22 4/8 22 1/8	16 4/8	6 7	Eau Claire County	WI	Eric Sturz	2007	6451
151 5/8	24 4/8 24 4/8	18 3/8	6 6	Winneshiek County	IA	Larry Mestad	2007	6451
151 5/8	23 1/8 23 1/8	17 5/8	6 6	Dodge County	WI	Don Gourlie, Jr.	2007	6451
151 5/8	26 3/8 26 4/8	20 3/8	4 5	Calumet County	WI	Bryce D. Bodway	2007	6451
151 5/8	25 6/8 24 4/8	19 1/8	6 6	Vernon County	WI	Randy C. Hooverson	2007	6451
151 5/8	24 5/8 24 7/8	19 2/8	5 7	Spokane County	WA	Mickey Hough	2007	6451
*151 5/8	27 0/8 26 3/8	21 3/8	5 5	Wyandot County	OH	Cory Rife	2008	6451
*151 5/8	23 5/8 23 1/8	16 6/8	7 8	Ottawa County	KS	Jason Leeper	2008	6451
*151 5/8	23 0/8 22 7/8	15 1/8	5 6	St. Joseph County	IN	Michael J. McNarney	2008	6451
*151 5/8	24 2/8 24 4/8	16 5/8	6 6	Herkimer County	NY	Art Bass	2009	6451
151 5/8	24 3/8 22 2/8	17 1/8	7 8	Marquette County	WI	Kori A. Coddington	2009	6451
151 5/8	22 3/8 23 7/8	21 3/8	6 5	Jackson County	IA	Matthew Franks	2009	6451
*151 5/8	27 5/8 26 5/8	24 7/8	6 6	Winneshiek County	IA	Zachary Holkesvik	2009	6451
*151 5/8	22 4/8 23 2/8	15 5/8	6 6	Wood County	WI	Tim Rhodes	2009	6451
151 5/8	24 0/8 24 0/8	17 3/8	5 5	Chase County	KS	Wesley Blank	2009	6451
151 5/8	25 0/8 23 6/8	17 1/8	5 5	Lapeer County	MI	John Benedict	2009	6451
151 4/8	23 2/8 22 5/8	16 0/8	6 6	Gogebic County	MI	Fred Felbab	1959	6529
151 4/8	23 2/8 22 7/8	16 2/8	5 5	Murray County	MN	Jim F. Wyffels	1968	6529
151 4/8	21 1/8 21 7/8	18 6/8	6 5	Brown County	SD	Duane Trost	1973	6529
151 4/8	24 2/8 24 3/8	19 4/8	5 5	Marshall County	IL	William J. McNutt	1979	6529
151 4/8	23 6/8 22 5/8	17 3/8	6 5	Pittsburg County	OK	Harry Milican	1983	6529
151 4/8	26 4/8 26 0/8	20 2/8	4 4	Mason County	IL	David C. Gillespie	1984	6529
151 4/8	21 3/8 21 5/8	19 0/8	5 5	Lincoln County	MT	Glenn W. Gibson	1985	6529
151 4/8	22 7/8 22 4/8	17 0/8	5 5	Buffalo County	WI	Gerald Palmer	1985	6529
151 4/8	24 4/8 24 7/8	23 0/8	5 5	Riley County	KS	L. F. Howerton	1985	6529
151 4/8	25 1/8 25 1/8	21 2/8	5 4	Pierce County	WI	Dave Clare	1985	6529
151 4/8	26 3/8 25 0/8	18 2/8	5 5	Polk County	WI	Todd C. Swenson	1986	6529
151 4/8	22 4/8 21 4/8	18 0/8	6 5	McLeod County	MN	Ed Homan	1986	6529
151 4/8	21 5/8 23 0/8	17 6/8	8 5	Day County	SD	Sandy Heuer	1987	6529
151 4/8	24 2/8 25 2/8	17 2/8	4 6	Morrison County	MN	Troy Brown	1988	6529
151 4/8	26 7/8 27 2/8	19 0/8	4 4	Pierce County	WI	Victor Howe	1988	6529
151 4/8	24 2/8 23 3/8	17 4/8	5 5	Sumner County	KS	Lynn Reed	1988	6529
151 4/8	25 6/8 23 5/8	18 0/8	5 5	Fayette County	IA	Jim Smith	1989	6529
151 4/8	24 7/8 25 0/8	19 6/8	5 5	Lewis County	MO	Blaine Emrick	1990	6529
151 4/8	23 7/8 23 2/8	16 0/8	5 5	Otero County	CO	Ron Rockwell	1990	6529
151 4/8	26 1/8 25 1/8	16 4/8	5 5	Tuscarawas County	OH	Karl Paulik	1991	6529
151 4/8	22 1/8 21 3/8	17 2/8	5 5	Steuben County	IN	Barry Bowers	1991	6529
151 4/8	25 3/8 25 4/8	15 2/8	5 5	Lake County	IL	Steven Hysell	1992	6529
151 4/8	23 0/8 25 2/8	20 4/8	7 6	Hamilton County	OH	Ronnie L. Smith	1992	6529
151 4/8	26 6/8 25 5/8	22 0/8	4 4	Pike County	OH	Jim Borchelt	1993	6529
151 4/8	24 0/8 24 0/8	17 0/8	6 6	Burnett County	WI	Steven R. Brink	1994	6529
151 4/8	24 3/8 25 3/8	17 6/8	5 5	Kanawha County	WV	David Roberts	1994	6529
151 4/8	26 0/8 26 1/8	19 3/8	7 5	Decatur County	IA	Richard D. Panke	1994	6529

424

WHITETAIL DEER (TYPICAL ANTLERS)

Minimum Score 125 — Continued

SCORE	LENGTH OF R MAIN BEAM L	INSIDE SPREAD	NUMBER OF R POINTS L		AREA	STATE/PROVINCE	HUNTER'S NAME	DATE	RANK
151 4/8	26 1/8	24 6/8	15 4/8	9	6	Douglas County	KS	Steven W. Stumbo	1994	6529
151 4/8	26 5/8	26 1/8	17 0/8	4	5	Benton County	MO	Jim Pennington, Jr.	1995	6529
151 4/8	25 7/8	25 7/8	19 3/8	6	6	Jefferson County	WI	Aaron Persinger	1995	6529
151 4/8	24 1/8	23 7/8	17 4/8	5	5	Chester County	PA	Steve Mihalcik	1995	6529
151 4/8	23 1/8	25 6/8	17 6/8	6	5	Knox County	IL	Gale Harriman	1995	6529
151 4/8	25 0/8	23 4/8	18 4/8	5	5	Christian County	IL	George Eftink	1996	6529
151 4/8	25 3/8	23 7/8	19 0/8	5	5	Dane County	WI	Robert A. Ebert	1997	6529
151 4/8	21 6/8	22 5/8	17 2/8	5	5	Morrison County	MN	Bill Bosaaen	1997	6529
151 4/8	22 1/8	22 2/8	15 6/8	5	5	Jefferson County	WI	Paul Minning	1998	6529
151 4/8	24 0/8	25 1/8	18 4/8	5	4	Lancaster County	NE	Chris Navratil	1998	6529
151 4/8	26 3/8	26 4/8	21 1/8	7	4	Douglas County	KS	Robert Michel	1998	6529
151 4/8	26 0/8	25 6/8	17 7/8	5	6	Allen County	OH	Ted Smith	1998	6529
151 4/8	22 6/8	23 1/8	17 1/8	6	6	Monroe County	IA	Jerry Ohlendorf	1998	6529
151 4/8	24 1/8	25 4/8	16 6/8	5	6	Bolivar County	MS	Duke Morgan, Jr.	2000	6529
151 4/8	22 7/8	22 6/8	16 3/8	5	6	Pottawattamie County	IA	Scott Huenniger	2000	6529
151 4/8	23 7/8	23 1/8	16 6/8	5	5	Bracken County	KY	Gene Schadle	2001	6529
151 4/8	23 6/8	24 1/8	15 0/8	5	5	Daviess County	IN	David E. Aishe	2001	6529
151 4/8	24 1/8	26 0/8	18 0/8	5	5	La Crosse County	WI	Kevin R. Johnson	2001	6529
151 4/8	22 0/8	22 0/8	17 0/8	5	5	Osage County	KS	Gene Helmick	2001	6529
151 4/8	24 4/8	24 6/8	18 0/8	8	5	Delaware County	OH	Bob Weinberg III	2001	6529
151 4/8	22 2/8	22 6/8	17 2/8	5	5	Adams County	IL	Neal C. Meyer	2002	6529
151 4/8	22 6/8	23 0/8	19 3/8	6	6	Coles County	IL	Brad Metcalf	2002	6529
151 4/8	24 0/8	21 5/8	22 4/8	5	5	Somerset County	NJ	Mark Spoto	2003	6529
151 4/8	25 7/8	26 6/8	21 3/8	7	6	Licking County	OH	Gary Roser	2003	6529
151 4/8	22 7/8	22 7/8	19 2/8	5	5	Vigo County	IN	Daniel R. Green	2003	6529
151 4/8	23 1/8	23 4/8	20 2/8	5	5	Decatur County	IA	Gene Banas	2003	6529
151 4/8	26 4/8	26 1/8	17 4/8	7	5	Howard County	MD	Christopher L. Fischer	2003	6529
151 4/8	21 7/8	22 0/8	17 2/8	6	6	Buffalo County	WI	James N. Mayer, Jr.	2004	6529
151 4/8	23 7/8	24 3/8	16 5/8	7	6	Buffalo County	WI	Gary Rucinski	2004	6529
*151 4/8	24 4/8	23 4/8	19 2/8	5	4	Anoka County	MN	Russell Christen	2004	6529
151 4/8	23 0/8	24 2/8	20 0/8	5	5	Portage County	WI	Justin Palbrach	2005	6529
*151 4/8	24 2/8	24 0/8	19 0/8	4	5	Hinds County	MS	Dee Perkins	2005	6529
151 4/8	23 5/8	24 7/8	17 2/8	5	5	Eau Claire County	WI	Christopher L. Nelson	2005	6529
*151 4/8	24 0/8	22 6/8	19 7/8	5	7	Wayne County	MO	Kenny Cochman	2005	6529
151 4/8	24 5/8	23 2/8	16 6/8	7	5	Marathon County	WI	Jeffrey E. Thompson	2005	6529
151 4/8	25 6/8	24 5/8	17 7/8	5	7	Osceola County	IA	Douglas Roth	2005	6529
*151 4/8	24 6/8	24 4/8	20 4/8	5	5	Morgan County	OH	Daniel A. Briggs	2006	6529
*151 4/8	22 5/8	22 6/8	14 6/8	5	5	St. Charles County	MO	Derek Dirnberger	2006	6529
*151 4/8	22 4/8	23 1/8	18 3/8	5	6	Pike County	IL	Gary W. Penn	2006	6529
151 4/8	23 4/8	23 2/8	18 0/8	4	4	Butler County	KS	Kent Wartick	2006	6529
151 4/8	25 1/8	25 5/8	19 6/8	6	6	Comanche County	KS	Frank G. Hood	2006	6529
151 4/8	23 6/8	23 3/8	16 2/8	6	5	Bolivar County	MS	Rob Dawkins	2007	6529
*151 4/8	22 7/8	22 0/8	18 2/8	7	6	Franklin County	IN	Rob K. Rich	2007	6529
*151 4/8	24 6/8	23 2/8	18 6/8	4	5	White County	IN	Kurtis Welk	2007	6529
151 4/8	23 3/8	23 4/8	15 7/8	6	7	Spencer County	IN	John E. Johnson	2007	6529
151 4/8	25 6/8	25 4/8	19 0/8	5	5	Berks County	PA	David M. Maloney	2008	6529
*151 4/8	26 6/8	26 4/8	21 2/8	5	8	Coshocton County	OH	Chad M. Simpson	2009	6529
151 4/8	23 3/8	23 2/8	18 5/8	5	6	Palo Pinto County	TX	Rocky Pitre	2009	6529
151 4/8	23 4/8	23 1/8	19 0/8	6	6	Allegany County	NY	Thomas Haley	2009	6529
151 3/8	26 3/8	25 4/8	15 6/8	6	7	Martin County	IN	Robert E. Sloan	1968	6605
151 3/8	23 2/8	23 7/8	19 1/8	5	5	Amherst County	VA	Jerry Armes	1975	6605
151 3/8	23 4/8	24 0/8	18 3/8	5	6	Morris County	NJ	Phil D'Ottavio	1980	6605
151 3/8	23 4/8	23 1/8	17 7/8	5	5	Langlade County	WI	Larry Petts	1983	6605
151 3/8	26 1/8	26 1/8	18 0/8	5	7	Clay County	MN	Randy Swanson	1984	6605
151 3/8	26 2/8	26 4/8	17 7/8	5	5	Osage County	KS	Gene Beam	1984	6605
151 3/8	22 3/8	22 4/8	18 5/8	5	5	Trempealeau County	WI	Michael Baer	1984	6605
151 3/8	25 2/8	25 4/8	17 3/8	6	5	Sauk County	WI	Casey A. Blum	1985	6605
151 3/8	25 5/8	25 0/8	17 7/8	5	5	Posey County	IN	Donald R. Koester	1986	6605
151 3/8	22 0/8	22 6/8	15 7/8	7	6	Stearns County	MN	Chuck Thies	1987	6605
151 3/8	26 3/8	26 3/8	20 3/8	4	4	Roberts County	SD	Myles Keller	1987	6605
151 3/8	24 1/8	23 5/8	17 3/8	4	4	Eaton County	MI	John A. Lee	1988	6605
151 3/8	21 4/8	22 5/8	18 7/8	6	5	Logan County	IL	Eldon R. Broster	1989	6605
151 3/8	23 5/8	23 5/8	17 5/8	5	5	Prince Georges County	MD	Sam Lyon	1989	6605
151 3/8	25 6/8	24 1/8	17 7/8	5	5	Lake County	IL	Jeffery L. Allard	1989	6605
151 3/8	22 5/8	22 5/8	17 7/8	5	5	Clayton County	IA	Robert C. Ungs	1990	6605
151 3/8	25 7/8	24 7/8	20 7/8	6	5	Knox County	OH	Stan Tyson	1990	6605
151 3/8	23 0/8	23 4/8	19 0/8	7	5	Cook County	IL	Dean Assink	1990	6605
151 3/8	26 3/8	25 0/8	18 5/8	5	5	Dakota County	MN	Jeff Kamrud	1991	6605
151 3/8	25 5/8	24 5/8	20 7/8	4	4	McHenry County	IL	Dave Pederson	1992	6605
151 3/8	24 1/8	23 5/8	17 5/8	5	5	Morrison County	MN	Joe Adrian	1993	6605
151 3/8	24 6/8	25 7/8	19 2/8	5	6	Chautauqua County	KS	Roy Urban	1993	6605
151 3/8	23 7/8	23 2/8	17 6/8	6	7	Rockland County	NY	Ben Risley	1993	6605
151 3/8	26 2/8	26 3/8	18 1/8	4	4	Bayfield County	WI	Larry Fischer	1993	6605
151 3/8	24 7/8	24 7/8	19 0/8	5	4	Johnson County	IL	Randall L. Steinmetz, Jr.	1993	6605
151 3/8	26 5/8	27 0/8	22 6/8	5	7	Seneca County	OH	Dennis J. Heilman	1993	6605
151 3/8	27 0/8	26 6/8	20 1/8	4	4	Southampton County	VA	John B. Mitchell	1994	6605
151 3/8	25 3/8	26 6/8	21 4/8	7	5	Boone County	IL	Dwight Gunderson	1994	6605
151 3/8	25 1/8	24 7/8	19 6/8	6	5	Jersey County	IL	Jeff Phipps	1994	6605
151 3/8	26 1/8	25 3/8	19 7/8	6	7	Pope County	IL	Dale Cain	1994	6605
151 3/8	21 2/8	21 0/8	15 1/8	5	6	Hudson Bay	SAS	Ted K. Jaycox	1994	6605
151 3/8	24 3/8	24 1/8	20 5/8	4	4	Fayette County	IA	Dennis Welsh	1994	6605
151 3/8	20 6/8	21 6/8	19 3/8	6	6	Du Page County	IL	Paul Tikusis	1995	6605
151 3/8	23 1/8	24 2/8	15 1/8	6	5	Warren County	KY	Greg Green	1995	6605
151 3/8	24 0/8	24 0/8	18 0/8	7	7	Lincoln County	KY	Randy Yocum	1995	6605
151 3/8	25 2/8	25 6/8	20 3/8	5	4	Peoria County	IL	Paul Clay	1995	6605
151 3/8	25 3/8	24 0/8	18 3/8	4	5	Winona County	MN	Dustin N. Luedtke	1996	6605
151 3/8	23 6/8	23 4/8	18 0/8	7	6	Davis County	IA	Ben Cox	1996	6605
151 3/8	22 6/8	23 0/8	19 1/8	5	5	Trumbull County	OH	Jerry McConahy	1996	6605
151 3/8	23 0/8	23 1/8	19 7/8	5	5	Somerset County	ME	Mark T. Thomas	1997	6605
151 3/8	25 6/8	26 2/8	18 4/8	6	6	Floyd County	IA	Darwin R. Goddard	1997	6605
151 3/8	25 5/8	26 0/8	17 6/8	6	6	Monroe County	IA	Larry Zach	1997	6605
151 3/8	25 1/8	24 4/8	15 5/8	5	5	Union County	OH	Kevin A. Habyan	1997	6605
151 3/8	26 3/8	25 1/8	20 3/8	4	4	Steuben County	IN	Rick A. Roemke	1998	6605
151 3/8	25 0/8	24 7/8	19 5/8	4	4	Meadow Lake	SAS	Tom Miranda	1998	6605
151 3/8	24 0/8	23 7/8	17 4/8	7	7	Lee County	IA	Joseph T. Digman	1998	6605

WHITETAIL DEER (TYPICAL ANTLERS)

Minimum Score 125 — Continued

SCORE	LENGTH OF MAIN BEAM R	L	INSIDE SPREAD	NUMBER OF POINTS R	L	AREA	STATE/PROVINCE	HUNTER'S NAME	DATE	RANK
151 3/8	25 2/8	25 2/8	20 1/8	5	5	Richland County	WI	Michael S. Gillingham	1999	6605
151 3/8	24 0/8	23 5/8	17 1/8	5	5	Fayette County	WV	Teddy Mills	1999	6605
151 3/8	22 2/8	22 5/8	15 5/8	5	5	Iowa County	IA	Kevin McDonald	1999	6605
151 3/8	24 5/8	25 2/8	17 7/8	4	4	La Crosse County	WI	Nathan L. Tucker	2000	6605
151 3/8	23 1/8	23 6/8	15 5/8	6	5	Pike County	IL	Dennis George	2000	6605
151 3/8	23 6/8	24 1/8	17 3/8	5	5	Orleans County	NY	Duane Seiler II	2000	6605
151 3/8	24 0/8	24 1/8	19 1/8	5	5	Allamakee County	IA	Michael J. Manning	2000	6605
151 3/8	22 2/8	23 2/8	19 3/8	5	5	Will County	IL	Timothy Aftanas	2000	6605
151 3/8	23 4/8	24 1/8	18 6/8	6	5	Allegany County	NY	William Gary Taylor	2002	6605
151 3/8	26 0/8	25 2/8	19 3/8	5	5	Phillips County	KS	Martin Seemann	2002	6605
151 3/8	23 4/8	26 0/8	20 6/8	7	5	Harrison County	OH	Keith D. Spencer	2003	6605
151 3/8	22 5/8	22 4/8	16 7/8	6	6	Coffey County	KS	Randy Stahl	2003	6605
151 3/8	24 1/8	24 1/8	18 4/8	9	9	Cowley County	KS	Derek Frazier	2003	6605
151 3/8	26 6/8	25 3/8	17 6/8	5	6	Warren County	IA	Randy Manuel	2004	6605
151 3/8	27 2/8	26 7/8	15 1/8	5	4	Hancock County	OH	Tim Carles	2004	6605
151 3/8	25 1/8	24 3/8	16 1/8	5	6	Livingston County	MI	Robert Mars	2004	6605
151 3/8	25 3/8	25 3/8	18 7/8	5	5	Fulton County	GA	Chuck Birchfield	2004	6605
151 3/8	23 5/8	22 6/8	19 3/8	5	5	Atoka County	OK	Ralph Dale Mobbs	2005	6605
151 3/8	22 4/8	22 0/8	17 7/8	6	6	Hot Springs County	WY	Jay Steadman	2006	6605
151 3/8	26 2/8	26 6/8	17 1/8	6	5	Dunn County	WI	Brian Bonesteel	2006	6605
*151 3/8	22 6/8	22 1/8	18 5/8	5	5	Mahoning County	OH	Jeff Hartman	2006	6605
151 3/8	23 0/8	22 7/8	18 3/8	6	5	La Salle County	IL	Donald Greathouse	2006	6605
151 3/8	23 0/8	24 4/8	14 7/8	5	5	Riley County	KS	Richard Yarborough	2007	6605
*151 3/8	23 1/8	24 0/8	19 3/8	7	7	McHenry County	ND	Travis Clemens	2007	6605
*151 3/8	23 7/8	24 5/8	20 1/8	5	6	Grand Forks County	ND	Austin W. Moffett	2007	6605
*151 3/8	24 2/8	24 1/8	17 6/8	7	6	Obion County	TN	Robby Mulcahy	2007	6605
*151 3/8	22 1/8	22 4/8	14 7/8	5	6	Dallas County	AL	Johnny Harris	2008	6605
*151 3/8	22 6/8	23 4/8	17 7/8	7	7	Stoddard County	MO	Lawson Metcalf	2008	6605
*151 3/8	27 3/8	26 4/8	19 3/8	4	4	Wabasha County	MN	Bill Schad	2009	6605
151 3/8	25 1/8	26 3/8	21 5/8	5	6	Randolph County	IL	Jay J. Carr	2009	6605
151 2/8	25 5/8	25 6/8	17 2/8	4	4	Fillmore County	MN	David Carson	1967	6681
151 2/8	24 1/8	23 4/8	14 1/8	7	5	Blue Earth County	MN	Rory Duetchman	1974	6681
151 2/8	22 1/8	22 4/8	18 2/8	6	6	Clark County	SD	Dean L. Myers	1975	6681
151 2/8	25 0/8	24 4/8	18 0/8	5	5	La Salle County	IL	John Sullivan	1977	6681
151 2/8	25 3/8	24 6/8	18 6/8	4	5	Litchfield County	CT	Donald R. Groody	1982	6681
151 2/8	23 4/8	24 4/8	17 6/8	7	5	Warrick County	IN	Thomas Scheucher	1982	6681
151 2/8	26 2/8	25 3/8	18 0/8	5	5	Cowley County	KS	Michael L. Snyder	1984	6681
151 2/8	22 4/8	22 3/8	13 7/8	6	5	Livingston County	IL	Tom Roe	1987	6681
151 2/8	24 7/8	21 4/8	16 4/8	5	5	Benton County	IA	Jeff L. Jacobi	1987	6681
151 2/8	24 1/8	23 5/8	17 0/8	5	6	Clarke County	GA	Terry Pahl	1988	6681
151 2/8	23 4/8	22 5/8	20 1/8	7	5	Washburn County	WI	John Galvin	1988	6681
151 2/8	22 6/8	23 7/8	20 2/8	5	5	Iroquois County	IL	Eric Edwards	1988	6681
151 2/8	24 5/8	24 3/8	20 5/8	5	4	Fulton County	GA	John Brooks	1989	6681
151 2/8	24 4/8	25 4/8	19 0/8	5	8	Fulton County	IL	Don DeRenzy	1990	6681
151 2/8	26 1/8	26 0/8	15 0/8	5	5	Franklin County	VA	S. Gregory Venning	1990	6681
151 2/8	24 5/8	25 1/8	17 6/8	5	5	Will County	IL	Ty Orgas	1990	6681
151 2/8	25 0/8	25 2/8	15 6/8	5	5	Burlington County	NJ	Elliston M. Jacobs	1991	6681
151 2/8	24 3/8	24 3/8	19 4/8	4	5	Madison County	IL	Kevin Moore	1991	6681
151 2/8	22 3/8	24 2/8	18 4/8	8	6	Tazewell County	IL	Ronald J. Ghighi	1992	6681
151 2/8	20 0/8	21 1/8	18 6/8	5	5	McHenry County	IL	Michael F. Riske	1992	6681
151 2/8	25 3/8	24 7/8	18 2/8	4	4	Coles County	IL	Alan Batson	1992	6681
151 2/8	24 6/8	23 1/8	21 6/8	5	5	Waukesha County	WI	James Sackett	1993	6681
151 2/8	22 7/8	24 4/8	19 2/8	5	6	Warren County	IA	Philip Martin	1993	6681
151 2/8	21 4/8	20 4/8	15 0/8	6	6	Shoshone County	ID	Dana D. Atwood, Jr.	1993	6681
151 2/8	22 2/8	22 0/8	14 0/8	5	5	Wayne County	MI	John K. Anderson	1994	6681
151 2/8	25 7/8	24 7/8	18 1/8	7	6	Polk County	WI	Larry E. Carlson	1995	6681
151 2/8	23 7/8	24 5/8	21 2/8	4	5	Lee County	IL	John Friel	1995	6681
151 2/8	23 3/8	22 6/8	19 4/8	5	5	McLean County	IL	Kelly Spence	1995	6681
151 2/8	23 3/8	23 2/8	18 7/8	5	6	Washburn County	WI	Tim Clare	1996	6681
151 2/8	27 3/8	27 6/8	17 4/8	5	5	Portage County	WI	Alan R. Ruechel	1997	6681
151 2/8	23 7/8	23 4/8	16 6/8	7	6	Pittsburg County	OK	Joe G. Arms	1997	6681
151 2/8	24 0/8	25 0/8	16 0/8	6	5	Plymouth County	IA	Todd M. Laughton	1997	6681
151 2/8	26 6/8	26 2/8	23 5/8	5	5	Lee County	IL	Gary Wyatt	1998	6681
151 2/8	23 5/8	23 4/8	15 0/8	5	4	Beltrami County	MN	Mike Oelrich	1998	6681
151 2/8	22 1/8	23 2/8	16 4/8	5	5	Crawford County	PA	Blaine Eppeheimer	1999	6681
151 2/8	22 5/8	21 3/8	16 3/8	5	6	Waupaca County	WI	Brian Dey	2000	6681
151 2/8	23 3/8	23 1/8	17 4/8	6	5	Olmsted County	MN	Steven Tebay	2000	6681
151 2/8	22 6/8	22 0/8	19 0/8	6	6	Clinton County	IN	Barry L. Morphew	2000	6681
151 2/8	25 7/8	26 0/8	19 0/8	4	5	Linn County	IA	Curt M. Jorgensen	2000	6681
151 2/8	24 6/8	24 3/8	19 2/8	5	5	Tuscarawas County	OH	Kris W. Albaugh	2001	6681
151 2/8	22 1/8	23 2/8	20 2/8	5	5	Warren County	IA	Daniel Hawthorne	2001	6681
151 2/8	23 1/8	23 4/8	22 1/8	5	7	Harford County	MD	Ernie Welsh	2002	6681
151 2/8	24 1/8	24 4/8	19 7/8	6	6	La Salle County	IL	Anthony Allison	2002	6681
151 2/8	24 7/8	21 5/8	18 4/8	6	5	Yankton County	SD	Dan Benson	2002	6681
151 2/8	24 4/8	23 5/8	17 2/8	5	6	Livingston County	MO	Robert T. Evans	2002	6681
151 2/8	25 6/8	25 4/8	18 2/8	4	4	Coos County	NH	Lawrence F. Blakely, Jr.	2002	6681
151 2/8	25 1/8	24 3/8	14 7/8	5	7	Waupaca County	WI	Adam J. Lorge	2003	6681
151 2/8	23 7/8	23 3/8	17 4/8	5	6	Dodge County	WI	Keith Beilke	2003	6681
151 2/8	24 3/8	25 0/8	18 6/8	4	4	La Porte County	IN	Robert R. Evans	2003	6681
151 2/8	23 7/8	23 5/8	18 2/8	5	5	Hamilton County	OH	Robert Wood	2003	6681
151 2/8	24 3/8	25 1/8	18 6/8	5	5	Greene County	AR	Rodney Lanier	2003	6681
*151 2/8	25 1/8	26 1/8	21 1/8	5	6	Kane County	IL	Paul Mazur	2004	6681
151 2/8	23 2/8	22 7/8	17 0/8	6	7	Oliver County	ND	Douglas Moen	2004	6681
151 2/8	24 6/8	24 7/8	18 6/8	4	4	Clark County	KS	Gary Russell	2004	6681
151 2/8	25 0/8	24 0/8	17 6/8	5	5	Owen County	IN	Richard M. Malad	2004	6681
*151 2/8	21 6/8	21 7/8	19 1/8	5	6	Grant County	WI	Mickel R. Whitfield	2005	6681
151 2/8	24 6/8	24 2/8	16 3/8	6	5	Navarro County	TX	John Harper	2005	6681
*151 2/8	26 0/8	26 6/8	17 6/8	6	5	Allegan County	MI	David Selvig	2005	6681
151 2/8	27 7/8	28 1/8	20 0/8	7	5	Washington County	WI	Michael Berend	2005	6681
151 2/8	24 0/8	24 2/8	18 6/8	5	5	Dodge County	WI	Milan Jelic	2006	6681
151 2/8	24 4/8	23 4/8	19 6/8	5	5	Buffalo County	WI	Aaron Dobbs	2006	6681
151 2/8	25 0/8	25 1/8	18 7/8	5	5	Trempealeau County	WI	Jeremy J. Ouellette	2006	6681
151 2/8	24 3/8	23 2/8	17 3/8	8	6	Paipoonge	ONT	Glenn Rivard	2006	6681
151 2/8	24 5/8	24 5/8	20 6/8	6	5	Douglas County	WI	Jay Paniagua	2006	6681
*151 2/8	24 6/8	24 5/8	18 4/8	5	5	Delaware County	OH	Randy Rice	2006	6681

WHITETAIL DEER (TYPICAL ANTLERS)

Minimum Score 125   Continued

SCORE	LENGTH OF R MAIN BEAM L		INSIDE SPREAD	NUMBER OF R POINTS L		AREA	STATE/ PROVINCE	HUNTER'S NAME	DATE	RANK
*151 2/8	23 1/8	22 4/8	18 6/8	6	6	Linn County	MO	Bill Jared	2007	6681
151 2/8	22 3/8	22 1/8	18 4/8	5	5	La Crosse County	WI	Chris Colburn	2007	6681
151 2/8	24 1/8	24 6/8	19 0/8	5	5	Jefferson County	NE	Scott Heselmeyer	2007	6681
151 2/8	25 5/8	24 4/8	17 2/8	5	5	Bolivar County	MS	Rob Dawkins	2007	6681
151 2/8	22 7/8	22 5/8	14 0/8	5	5	Allamakee County	IA	Jake Needham	2008	6681
151 2/8	21 7/8	22 6/8	15 6/8	6	6	Decatur County	IA	John Theiler	2008	6681
151 2/8	27 2/8	25 6/8	18 2/8	5	5	Washington County	KS	Worley L. Sewell III	2008	6681
151 2/8	25 4/8	26 6/8	18 5/8	6	4	Hardin County	OH	Haulie R. Marshall	2009	6681
151 2/8	23 0/8	23 5/8	20 2/8	5	5	Sarpy County	NE	Brian Frans	2009	6681
*151 2/8	23 6/8	22 5/8	18 6/8	5	5	Clayton County	IA	Tracey Groth	2009	6681
*151 2/8	25 3/8	24 3/8	20 0/8	7	6	Wyoming County	WV	Mark Cook	2009	6681
151 1/8	27 4/8	24 7/8	16 2/8	6	6	Adams County	IL	John C. Robinson	1967	6757
151 1/8	22 3/8	23 4/8	18 4/8	7	7	Adair County	MO	Dr. Eddy Transano	1971	6757
151 1/8	25 6/8	24 4/8	19 3/8	5	5	Lucas County	OH	Gail A. Rice	1978	6757
151 1/8	22 6/8	22 6/8	17 4/8	7	6	Wood County	WI	Scott Arneson	1979	6757
151 1/8	23 4/8	21 4/8	18 3/8	5	5	Minnehaha County	SD	Bradley D. Swier	1982	6757
151 1/8	23 1/8	23 2/8	17 1/8	5	5	Barren County	KY	Steve England	1983	6757
151 1/8	25 2/8	24 0/8	20 7/8	4	5	Franklin County	KS	Don Hrabe	1985	6757
151 1/8	24 2/8	26 5/8	17 3/8	5	5	Bond County	IL	Gary Netzler	1987	6757
151 1/8	24 5/8	23 4/8	17 7/8	5	5	Grant County	WI	Joe Devlin	1987	6757
151 1/8	22 0/8	23 2/8	16 3/8	5	5	Jefferson County	MO	Steve North	1988	6757
151 1/8	23 3/8	23 6/8	19 5/8	5	6	Okotoks	ALB	Dave Richardson	1989	6757
151 1/8	25 1/8	24 7/8	19 1/8	5	5	Hamilton County	OH	Keith Casey	1989	6757
151 1/8	22 2/8	21 0/8	17 1/8	5	5	Saline County	KS	James R. Weldy	1990	6757
151 1/8	23 1/8	23 5/8	17 5/8	7	9	De Kalb County	MO	Jim W. Martin	1990	6757
151 1/8	24 0/8	23 7/8	18 6/8	7	6	Stearns County	MN	Paul M. Froseth	1991	6757
151 1/8	23 3/8	23 1/8	17 7/8	6	7	Duval County	TX	Dean Oatman	1992	6757
151 1/8	25 6/8	26 0/8	18 0/8	6	4	Jackson County	IA	Dick Barker	1992	6757
151 1/8	22 6/8	23 2/8	14 1/8	5	5	Coles County	IL	Mark Cooper	1992	6757
151 1/8	22 5/8	22 5/8	17 7/8	6	5	Allamakee County	IA	Thomas J. Brimeyer	1992	6757
151 1/8	26 4/8	25 4/8	20 0/8	4	4	Mason County	IL	Gregory B. Snider	1992	6757
151 1/8	23 3/8	23 7/8	17 7/8	6	6	Kenedy County	TX	James Hill	1992	6757
151 1/8	27 4/8	27 4/8	18 4/8	5	4	Prairie County	AR	Ed Smith	1992	6757
151 1/8	25 2/8	24 2/8	15 5/8	6	5	Dane County	WI	Trevor J. Neuman	1993	6757
151 1/8	26 4/8	25 4/8	17 5/8	4	4	Iron County	WI	David Flowers	1993	6757
151 1/8	22 7/8	23 3/8	22 5/8	4	5	Johnson County	IA	Thomas Jensen	1994	6757
151 1/8	23 6/8	23 6/8	16 5/8	5	5	Monroe County	IA	Ed McDaniel	1994	6757
151 1/8	25 1/8	25 1/8	16 7/8	7	6	Hamilton County	OH	Randall E. Sanders	1994	6757
151 1/8	23 0/8	23 0/8	16 7/8	5	5	Breckinridge County	KY	James Bowles	1994	6757
151 1/8	22 2/8	22 2/8	17 7/8	5	5	Winnebago County	IL	John Duggan	1995	6757
151 1/8	21 6/8	20 7/8	18 7/8	5	6	Marshall County	KS	Robert Thompson	1996	6757
151 1/8	24 4/8	24 2/8	15 5/8	4	4	Hampden County	MA	Stanley Marko	1996	6757
151 1/8	25 5/8	24 6/8	18 5/8	4	5	Wyoming County	WV	Brian Janutolo	1997	6757
151 1/8	24 0/8	23 1/8	19 0/8	6	6	Moultrie County	IL	Bret Guin	1997	6757
151 1/8	23 4/8	23 7/8	16 7/8	5	5	Buchanan County	IA	Scott Smith	1997	6757
151 1/8	23 2/8	22 7/8	18 1/8	5	5	Webster County	MO	Scott Stevens	1997	6757
151 1/8	23 2/8	23 3/8	17 5/8	6	5	Vilas County	WI	Jay Kidd	1998	6757
151 1/8	26 4/8	27 0/8	18 5/8	4	4	Dodge County	WI	Robert J. Brunker	1998	6757
151 1/8	24 3/8	25 3/8	22 1/8	4	4	Union County	IA	Rob Crabb	1998	6757
151 1/8	24 7/8	24 2/8	17 5/8	6	6	Pottawatomie County	KS	Marlin Harrison	1998	6757
151 1/8	25 1/8	23 5/8	19 2/8	6	7	Champaign County	OH	Kenny Farvour	1998	6757
151 1/8	23 5/8	22 7/8	17 1/8	5	5	Wilson County	KS	Newell Easley	1998	6757
151 1/8	25 0/8	26 2/8	17 5/8	5	7	St. Louis County	MO	J. Andy Patt	1998	6757
151 1/8	24 1/8	23 3/8	19 5/8	5	5	Jackson County	WI	Allan Jahneke	1999	6757
151 1/8	22 3/8	23 6/8	16 1/8	7	6	Chase County	KS	Jerry Keller	1999	6757
151 1/8	24 7/8	24 4/8	17 5/8	5	6	Columbia County	WI	Keith Corbett	2000	6757
151 1/8	22 1/8	23 5/8	16 5/8	5	5	Talbot County	MD	Sean P. Fisher	2000	6757
151 1/8	24 5/8	23 6/8	22 1/8	5	5	Columbia County	WI	Gene A. Waterworth	2000	6757
151 1/8	23 5/8	24 6/8	15 3/8	5	5	St. Charles County	MO	Richard L. Shaiper	2000	6757
151 1/8	23 0/8	24 1/8	18 4/8	6	7	Nicollet County	MN	Jeff W. Flood	2001	6757
151 1/8	23 0/8	22 3/8	18 1/8	5	6	Morrison County	MN	Rand J. Kramer	2001	6757
151 1/8	24 2/8	24 0/8	19 0/8	6	7	Sedgwick County	KS	Dennis Brack	2002	6757
*151 1/8	22 2/8	22 5/8	18 5/8	6	8	Pike County	IL	John Sligh	2003	6757
151 1/8	23 7/8	23 3/8	16 3/8	6	5	Wayne County	IL	Patrick Halbert	2003	6757
151 1/8	25 3/8	25 3/8	19 5/8	5	6	Ross County	OH	Kenny "William" Curry	2003	6757
151 1/8	25 4/8	24 6/8	23 3/8	5	5	Livingston County	NY	Gregory Boquard	2003	6757
*151 1/8	23 1/8	23 1/8	17 6/8	6	5	McLean County	ND	Earl Anderson	2003	6757
151 1/8	26 6/8	25 0/8	17 3/8	5	6	Boone County	IA	Russell Page	2004	6757
151 1/8	25 3/8	24 3/8	18 0/8	5	6	Lafayette County	WI	Jeffery Redfearn	2004	6757
151 1/8	22 4/8	22 4/8	17 1/8	6	5	Clay County	IL	Chad McGee	2004	6757
151 1/8	23 4/8	23 4/8	20 3/8	5	5	Sullivan County	IN	Jerry Ross	2004	6757
151 1/8	22 0/8	23 3/8	15 5/8	6	6	Clark County	WI	Dick Urban	2005	6757
151 1/8	23 4/8	23 4/8	18 0/8	7	6	Spencer County	KY	Jeff Tinsley	2005	6757
151 1/8	23 2/8	24 2/8	19 7/8	5	5	Holt County	NE	Tom Neibauer	2005	6757
*151 1/8	24 2/8	24 1/8	15 3/8	7	7	Morris County	KS	Jon Winkelried	2005	6757
151 1/8	25 1/8	24 7/8	16 4/8	7	5	Tazewell County	IL	Brian Devine	2005	6757
151 1/8	21 7/8	22 5/8	16 1/8	5	5	Ward County	ND	Dennis W. Russin	2006	6757
151 1/8	22 3/8	23 4/8	17 0/8	7	6	Perry County	PA	Gregory W. Reisinger	2006	6757
*151 1/8	26 0/8	26 2/8	18 0/8	5	5	Pike County	IL	Patrick J. Shoppell	2006	6757
151 1/8	22 4/8	23 2/8	16 1/8	5	5	Lamoure County	ND	Eugene Sandness	2007	6757
151 1/8	24 7/8	24 0/8	19 0/8	5	8	Mercer County	IL	Darin Neal	2007	6757
151 1/8	25 7/8	26 7/8	23 1/8	5	5	Preble County	OH	Ronald Downs	2007	6757
151 1/8	25 5/8	26 2/8	19 6/8	5	6	Fairfield County	OH	Bob Markowski	2007	6757
*151 1/8	23 4/8	23 2/8	17 5/8	5	6	Sioux County	ND	Rock J. Powell	2008	6757
151 1/8	25 4/8	25 0/8	17 5/8	7	6	Mecklenburg County	NC	Sterling Austin	2008	6757
151 1/8	26 0/8	23 6/8	16 4/8	5	6	Linn County	KS	Tony J. Mitchem	2008	6757
151 1/8	24 2/8	24 2/8	24 1/8	5	5	Northampton County	PA	Don Brink	2008	6757
151 1/8	25 6/8	25 6/8	19 4/8	6	6	Owen County	IN	Bob Sturgis	2008	6757
151 1/8	23 6/8	23 6/8	16 7/8	5	5	Dunn County	WI	Charles Burns	2008	6757
151 1/8	24 4/8	23 5/8	14 5/8	5	5	Fulton County	IL	Tyler Anderson	2008	6757
*151 1/8	24 3/8	24 3/8	18 4/8	7	7	Schuyler County	MO	John E. Robinson	2009	6757
151 1/8	26 1/8	26 2/8	21 7/8	4	4	Harrison County	OH	Roger J. Cox	2009	6757
151 0/8	25 0/8	26 0/8	16 6/8	5	5	Warrick County	IN	Gerald G. Taylor	1970	6838
151 0/8	23 6/8	24 5/8	19 6/8	5	5	Polk County	WI	Bryan Anderson	1976	6838
151 0/8	30 1/8	29 0/8	20 2/8	7	5	Gray County	KS	Paul Meininger	1980	6838

WHITETAIL DEER (TYPICAL ANTLERS)

Minimum Score 125   Continued

SCORE	LENGTH OF R MAIN BEAM L	INSIDE SPREAD	NUMBER OF R POINTS L		AREA	STATE/ PROVINCE	HUNTER'S NAME	DATE	RANK
151 0/8	23 2/8	23 5/8	21 2/8	5	5	Grant County	WI	Doug J. Leibfried	1981	6838
151 0/8	25 3/8	24 0/8	17 4/8	5	5	Columbia County	WI	Jeffrey M. Ballweg	1984	6838
151 0/8	23 7/8	23 3/8	20 0/8	5	5	White County	IL	Eric D. Devore	1985	6838
151 0/8	26 5/8	27 1/8	20 4/8	4	4	Appanoose County	IA	Steven P. Widmar	1986	6838
151 0/8	26 7/8	24 5/8	18 0/8	5	4	Marshall County	IL	Bryan Blair	1987	6838
151 0/8	24 4/8	24 6/8	18 2/8	5	5	Jefferson County	WI	Gary Goldbeck	1987	6838
151 0/8	27 2/8	25 2/8	18 6/8	5	6	Northampton County	VA	Stanley I. Long	1988	6838
151 0/8	26 0/8	25 4/8	19 0/8	6	6	Woodford County	IL	Stan Bocian	1988	6838
151 0/8	25 6/8	23 6/8	21 2/8	5	5	Davis County	IA	Clayton Eakins	1990	6838
151 0/8	23 3/8	24 4/8	19 6/8	5	5	Kosciusko County	IN	Ronald D. Newcomer	1990	6838
151 0/8	24 5/8	25 0/8	18 4/8	6	6	Fayette County	IL	Kelly Tarter	1990	6838
151 0/8	23 6/8	22 4/8	18 4/8	7	7	Pope County	MN	David Strickler	1991	6838
151 0/8	24 6/8	23 3/8	24 6/8	6	5	Kenedy County	TX	Carl Walker	1991	6838
151 0/8	24 7/8	25 5/8	17 6/8	6	6	Jasper County	IL	David Staley	1991	6838
151 0/8	23 7/8	24 1/8	20 1/8	6	6	Price County	WI	Myron Sales	1993	6838
151 0/8	24 1/8	23 6/8	19 4/8	7	7	Clark County	OH	David L. Stull	1993	6838
151 0/8	24 3/8	24 2/8	17 0/8	4	6	Morgan County	IL	Kevin Mitchell	1993	6838
151 0/8	24 1/8	25 0/8	18 0/8	5	5	Fond du Lac County	WI	Brian Grade	1994	6838
151 0/8	24 1/8	22 7/8	19 4/8	5	5	Milwaukee County	WI	Joseph Banach	1995	6838
151 0/8	24 1/8	24 6/8	17 0/8	5	5	Morgan County	OH	Richard Newsom	1995	6838
151 0/8	21 4/8	22 2/8	18 2/8	6	6	Iowa County	IA	Karey Garringer	1995	6838
151 0/8	26 2/8	26 3/8	19 6/8	5	6	Decatur County	IA	Corey A. Christopherson	1995	6838
151 0/8	24 7/8	23 0/8	16 6/8	5	5	Morgan County	MO	Bob Sutton	1996	6838
151 0/8	25 2/8	26 7/8	20 7/8	6	6	Suffolk County	NY	John Bennett	1996	6838
151 0/8	25 0/8	25 4/8	18 2/8	6	6	Laurel County	KY	Mark Fields	1997	6838
151 0/8	23 7/8	22 1/8	16 4/8	6	5	Dawson County	MT	Ray E. Peters	1997	6838
151 0/8	26 6/8	27 4/8	21 4/8	4	4	McHenry County	IL	Donald R. Hanrahan	1997	6838
151 0/8	21 5/8	22 0/8	16 4/8	5	5	Pike County	IL	Stan Chamberlain	1997	6838
151 0/8	24 3/8	24 2/8	16 6/8	4	4	Edmonton	ALB	John Young	1997	6838
151 0/8	25 4/8	25 6/8	20 0/8	4	5	Morrison County	MN	Daniel Kremers	1998	6838
151 0/8	22 4/8	23 1/8	17 4/8	6	5	Sawyer County	WI	Brian Denzine	1998	6838
151 0/8	22 4/8	25 4/8	19 1/8	7	8	Oak Lake	MAN	David Sawatsky	1998	6838
151 0/8	22 5/8	24 7/8	17 4/8	5	5	Lake County	IL	Steve Hysell	1998	6838
151 0/8	22 6/8	23 2/8	17 0/8	5	5	La Salle County	IL	Mark D. Hunter	1999	6838
151 0/8	19 3/8	22 7/8	19 0/8	7	6	Lake County	IL	Eugene R. Noska	1999	6838
151 0/8	22 3/8	22 6/8	18 0/8	5	6	Winnebago County	WI	D. Jon Behm	1999	6838
151 0/8	23 1/8	24 1/8	21 0/8	6	5	Polk County	IA	John M. Myers	1999	6838
151 0/8	26 4/8	26 5/8	17 2/8	6	6	Logan County	WV	Larry Kade, Jr.	1999	6838
151 0/8	24 2/8	24 0/8	16 2/8	5	5	Pike County	IL	Gary W. Penn	2000	6838
151 0/8	24 4/8	24 2/8	15 6/8	5	5	Winnebago County	IL	Gaylord M. Winterberg	2000	6838
151 0/8	23 6/8	23 0/8	19 2/8	5	5	Chautauqua County	KS	Mike Thornton	2000	6838
151 0/8	25 6/8	25 6/8	18 4/8	4	4	Mills County	IA	Frank Bachman	2000	6838
151 0/8	25 7/8	25 7/8	16 1/8	5	7	Winnebago County	WI	Ron W. Kolosky	2001	6838
151 0/8	25 1/8	24 6/8	19 2/8	4	4	Montgomery County	MD	Charles B. Jones	2001	6838
151 0/8	23 5/8	23 5/8	17 4/8	6	6	Morgan County	IN	Nathan K. Lowder	2002	6838
151 0/8	23 1/8	23 2/8	16 4/8	5	5	Ogle County	IL	Tim Broos	2002	6838
151 0/8	24 1/8	23 6/8	21 0/8	5	5	Edgar County	IL	Jerry R. David	2002	6838
151 0/8	24 4/8	23 1/8	18 2/8	5	5	Parkland	ALB	Troy Dzioba	2002	6838
151 0/8	24 4/8	25 4/8	20 0/8	4	5	Crawford County	OH	Klinton L. Wood	2003	6838
151 0/8	23 5/8	22 1/8	18 0/8	5	5	Buffalo County	WI	Ben Vazquez	2003	6838
151 0/8	25 1/8	24 3/8	15 0/8	5	5	Decatur County	IA	Carl Rowson	2003	6838
151 0/8	23 0/8	22 6/8	18 0/8	5	5	Cross County	AR	Robert Brawner	2003	6838
151 0/8	23 1/8	23 2/8	15 0/8	6	8	Boone County	MO	Randy Garrett	2004	6838
151 0/8	25 3/8	24 1/8	17 0/8	5	5	Marathon County	WI	Matthew Groshek	2004	6838
151 0/8	23 2/8	23 0/8	15 2/8	5	5	Oconto County	WI	John Block	2004	6838
151 0/8	27 4/8	28 0/8	17 3/8	5	4	Richland County	OH	Brian L. McClintock	2004	6838
151 0/8	22 3/8	23 1/8	16 0/8	6	5	Shawano County	WI	Bryan J. Bender	2004	6838
151 0/8	24 7/8	24 3/8	19 0/8	5	5	Thayer County	NE	Ross Graveling	2004	6838
151 0/8	23 0/8	24 0/8	20 2/8	6	5	Phillips County	KS	Gary Niblock	2004	6838
151 0/8	25 3/8	24 2/8	18 0/8	5	4	Linn County	KS	T. J. Herrick	2004	6838
151 0/8	25 2/8	25 7/8	20 5/8	5	6	Richardson County	NE	Michael G. Newlun	2004	6838
151 0/8	24 4/8	24 7/8	18 6/8	4	5	Pierce County	WI	Lars H. Loberg	2005	6838
*151 0/8	24 3/8	24 2/8	19 0/8	5	5	Dunn County	WI	Jon Johansen	2005	6838
*151 0/8	23 4/8	24 0/8	18 2/8	6	9	Plymouth County	IA	Michael L. Wheat	2005	6838
*151 0/8	23 5/8	23 5/8	13 2/8	5	6	Clay County	IL	Anthony Pagel	2005	6838
*151 0/8	25 7/8	18 1/8	17 2/8	8	5	Holt County	MO	Jim Bauer	2005	6838
151 0/8	24 1/8	24 3/8	19 0/8	8	6	Champaign County	IL	Duane Eby	2005	6838
151 0/8	22 5/8	22 1/8	16 4/8	5	6	Jackson County	IA	Daryl Parker	2005	6838
*151 0/8	22 0/8	23 4/8	15 6/8	5	5	Lawrence County	OH	Jared Redmond	2005	6838
*151 0/8	26 1/8	26 0/8	17 4/8	4	5	Ft. Bend County	TX	Chris Helms	2005	6838
151 0/8	27 1/8	26 5/8	18 3/8	7	6	Licking County	OH	Thomas Black	2006	6838
151 0/8	24 0/8	23 5/8	16 4/8	5	5	Buffalo County	WI	Robert E. Toonen	2006	6838
151 0/8	21 7/8	22 7/8	16 6/8	5	6	Lincoln County	WI	Bob Reichelt	2006	6838
151 0/8	23 3/8	22 0/8	16 4/8	5	6	Knox County	NE	Justin Zila	2007	6838
151 0/8	21 5/8	21 7/8	17 4/8	5	6	Hall County	GA	Marty Jarrard	2007	6838
*151 0/8	23 4/8	23 2/8	16 6/8	5	5	Wyandotte County	KS	Henry Norris	2007	6838
151 0/8	24 3/8	24 6/8	20 6/8	5	7	Vinton County	OH	Carl R. Salmons	2007	6838
151 0/8	24 5/8	24 3/8	15 4/8	5	5	Sullivan County	IN	Tim Sherman	2008	6838
151 0/8	26 1/8	27 0/8	19 2/8	5	5	Dearborn County	IN	Dave Goodwin	2008	6838
*151 0/8	24 3/8	25 5/8	15 3/8	7	6	Allamakee County	IA	Jason Davis	2008	6838
*151 0/8	23 6/8	23 5/8	18 6/8	5	6	Defiance County	OH	Mike Dewyse	2009	6838
151 0/8	22 4/8	21 2/8	19 0/8	5	6	Buffalo County	WI	Dennis V. Palmer	2009	6838
151 0/8	23 4/8	24 4/8	17 2/8	6	6	Graham County	KS	Travis Becker	2009	6838
151 0/8	22 7/8	23 3/8	18 6/8	7	6	Buffalo County	WI	Brady Laufenberg	2009	6838
151 0/8	21 2/8	21 0/8	16 6/8	7	7	Guthrie County	IA	Allen L. Henry	2009	6838
*151 0/8	23 1/8	23 4/8	15 6/8	5	5	Butler County	PA	Steve M. Chambers	2009	6838
151 0/8	23 4/8	24 1/8	15 0/8	6	6	Cooper County	MO	Christian Loesing	2009	6838
150 7/8	23 2/8	22 2/8	18 1/8	5	5	Trempealeau County	WI	Phillip Lunde	1969	6928
150 7/8	22 6/8	22 5/8	20 1/8	5	5	Harlan County	NE	Edwin Witte	1973	6928
150 7/8	24 3/8	22 5/8	17 5/8	7	6	Lancaster County	PA	J. John Buhay	1980	6928
150 7/8	26 0/8	26 0/8	21 1/8	5	5	Kent County	MI	Robert Ten Eyck	1980	6928
150 7/8	22 5/8	23 1/8	18 3/8	6	6	Cumberland County	ME	David C. Smart	1984	6928
150 7/8	23 2/8	22 7/8	17 6/8	6	6	Washington County	IA	David Greenlee	1986	6928
150 7/8	23 0/8	22 2/8	20 5/8	6	6	Becker County	MN	Arnold F. Ostgarden	1987	6928
150 7/8	24 0/8	23 6/8	20 3/8	6	7	Butler County	KS	Rodney Koehn	1987	6928

428

WHITETAIL DEER (TYPICAL ANTLERS)

Minimum Score 125 — Continued

SCORE	R MAIN BEAM L	INSIDE SPREAD	R POINTS L	AREA	STATE/PROVINCE	HUNTER'S NAME	DATE	RANK
150 7/8	24 4/8 23 2/8	20 5/8	5 5	Hopkins County	KY	Albert Hargis	1987	6928
150 7/8	27 5/8 27 3/8	18 0/8	6 6	Menard County	IL	Darrell Holliday	1987	6928
150 7/8	23 6/8 24 3/8	17 5/8	7 6	De Kalb County	IN	Eric L. Ditmars	1988	6928
150 7/8	28 6/8 27 4/8	19 4/8	5 6	Lawrence County	IL	Roger D. Wallace	1989	6928
150 7/8	26 1/8 24 7/8	21 3/8	4 4	Black Hawk County	IA	Craig Cornelius	1989	6928
150 7/8	22 0/8 22 0/8	18 3/8	6 5	Brown County	IL	Lowell Leslie, Jr.	1991	6928
150 7/8	24 5/8 24 2/8	17 5/8	5 5	Dickinson County	KS	George M. Havice	1991	6928
150 7/8	24 4/8 23 6/8	17 0/8	5 6	Butler County	OH	Michael L. Gibbs	1992	6928
150 7/8	26 1/8 27 2/8	21 6/8	5 5	Iron County	WI	Roger "Bucky" Adamovich	1992	6928
150 7/8	24 2/8 23 3/8	17 3/8	5 5	Ellis County	KS	Stan Honas	1993	6928
150 7/8	24 7/8 24 7/8	16 0/8	7 6	Clark County	WI	Darin E. Degenhardt	1993	6928
150 7/8	25 1/8 24 6/8	18 6/8	7 5	Branch County	MI	Arthur L. Shirey, Sr.	1994	6928
150 7/8	22 4/8 22 3/8	16 3/8	7 7	Letellier	MAN	Todd Amenrud	1994	6928
150 7/8	23 6/8 24 6/8	18 3/8	5 6	Okanogan County	WA	Kevin P. Skirko	1994	6928
150 7/8	26 4/8 26 5/8	17 7/8	7 7	Iron County	WI	Dave Matis	1995	6928
150 7/8	23 3/8 23 3/8	15 4/8	7 5	Putnam County	MO	P. Mike O'Reilly	1995	6928
150 7/8	22 6/8 23 4/8	19 1/8	5 6	Pike County	IL	Jay Verzuh	1995	6928
150 7/8	25 7/8 26 0/8	19 5/8	6 5	Webster County	IA	Darle Myers	1995	6928
150 7/8	24 6/8 24 7/8	19 7/8	5 5	Mitchell County	IA	Jerry Lee Mead	1996	6928
150 7/8	24 1/8 23 5/8	16 1/8	6 6	Putnam County	IL	Gene Koehler	1996	6928
150 7/8	23 1/8 22 0/8	16 5/8	5 5	Kleberg County	TX	Johnnie R. Walters	1997	6928
150 7/8	21 5/8 21 7/8	16 5/8	5 5	Taylor County	WI	Lyle Peterson	1998	6928
150 7/8	21 3/8 23 0/8	16 6/8	6 5	Winnebago County	IL	Fred Isom	1998	6928
150 7/8	24 7/8 25 7/8	19 6/8	4 5	Adams County	IL	Kevin J. Elbus	1998	6928
150 7/8	25 1/8 24 4/8	18 2/8	6 5	Trempealeau County	WI	Dale Hein	1998	6928
150 7/8	24 4/8 24 1/8	17 5/8	5 5	Columbia County	WI	Frank A. Cagney	1998	6928
150 7/8	26 0/8 26 3/8	18 3/8	6 5	Des Moines County	IA	Jeff Kimmel	1998	6928
150 7/8	26 1/8 26 5/8	19 5/8	4 4	Hampshire County	MA	Nathan Hurd	1998	6928
150 7/8	25 6/8 25 5/8	21 1/8	4 4	Talbot County	MD	Steve Mitchell	1999	6928
150 7/8	22 7/8 22 6/8	14 7/8	6 7	Ingham County	MI	Bruce Caltrider	1999	6928
150 7/8	24 4/8 24 7/8	19 0/8	6 5	Greene County	MO	Wave Nunnally	1999	6928
150 7/8	22 3/8 22 2/8	16 4/8	7 6	Davison County	SD	Brad Feterl	2000	6928
150 7/8	25 0/8 25 4/8	18 1/8	5 6	Putnam County	MO	Trevor Blanchard	2000	6928
150 7/8	25 4/8 25 3/8	22 7/8	5 5	Macon County	IL	Charlie DeBose	2000	6928
150 7/8	23 5/8 23 3/8	17 7/8	6 6	Scott County	KY	Ronnie Jacobs	2001	6928
150 7/8	21 4/8 21 1/8	20 1/8	7 7	Vermilion	ALB	Tim Pardely	2001	6928
150 7/8	25 4/8 26 5/8	20 0/8	5 6	La Grange County	IN	James M. Schiltz	2001	6928
150 7/8	25 6/8 26 6/8	16 7/8	4 4	Randolph County	IL	Michael P. McIntyre	2001	6928
150 7/8	24 6/8 23 7/8	16 1/8	7 5	Montgomery County	KS	Leland D. McCall	2001	6928
150 7/8	24 1/8 26 0/8	18 5/8	5 5	Kent County	MD	George Harms	2001	6928
150 7/8	21 7/8 22 1/8	21 3/8	5 5	Monona County	IA	Brian G. Mann	2003	6928
*150 7/8	26 7/8 26 1/8	18 7/8	5 5	Carroll County	NH	James Stockman	2003	6928
150 7/8	24 5/8 25 3/8	18 1/8	5 5	Jim Hogg County	TX	Norman E. Speer	2003	6928
150 7/8	23 1/8 23 0/8	19 1/8	4 5	Dunn County	ND	Doug Strecker	2004	6928
*150 7/8	26 4/8 27 3/8	20 5/8	5 5	Beltrami County	MN	Craig Dahl	2004	6928
150 7/8	23 1/8 21 7/8	17 1/8	5 5	Clark County	KS	Kelly C. Ison	2004	6928
150 7/8	22 7/8 23 2/8	18 1/8	5 4	Forest County	WI	Don Armatoski	2004	6928
150 7/8	24 1/8 23 3/8	15 2/8	6 6	Dunn County	WI	Dave R. Lieffort	2004	6928
150 7/8	24 3/8 25 2/8	19 1/8	6 6	Montgomery County	IA	Dan Pratt	2004	6928
150 7/8	24 7/8 26 1/8	22 5/8	6 5	Lorain County	OH	Steven D. Reinhold	2004	6928
150 7/8	25 0/8 24 5/8	16 5/8	6 7	Allegany County	NY	Charles Piosenka	2005	6928
150 7/8	21 4/8 21 7/8	18 5/8	6 6	Van Buren County	MI	Douglas Paul Myers	2005	6928
150 7/8	23 6/8 22 1/8	22 3/8	6 7	Greene County	OH	Geoff Maki	2005	6928
150 7/8	23 0/8 23 1/8	17 2/8	8 5	Langlade County	WI	Allen Aird	2005	6928
150 7/8	22 6/8 23 1/8	17 3/8	5 5	Greene County	IL	Gerald Nutt	2006	6928
*150 7/8	23 6/8 23 3/8	19 7/8	5 5	Clark County	WI	Mike Oberle	2006	6928
150 7/8	26 3/8 25 6/8	21 5/8	5 6	Douglas County	IL	Rob Grace	2006	6928
150 7/8	26 6/8 23 5/8	21 7/8	6 4	Allegheny County	PA	Russel Sienko	2006	6928
*150 7/8	21 7/8 21 5/8	16 1/8	5 5	Eau Claire County	WI	Tommy Vehrs	2006	6928
150 7/8	24 0/8 23 2/8	17 5/8	5 5	Coles County	IL	Ron Osborne	2006	6928
150 7/8	23 1/8 22 4/8	19 7/8	5 5	Orleans County	NY	Michael R. Plummer	2007	6928
*150 7/8	21 5/8 21 4/8	18 7/8	5 6	Peoria County	IL	Philip Alvey, Jr.	2007	6928
150 7/8	23 2/8 23 2/8	16 3/8	5 5	Van Buren County	IA	Dustin A. Hoffmann	2007	6928
150 7/8	25 3/8 25 2/8	20 3/8	6 6	Clayton County	IA	Bart Osterhaus	2007	6928
150 7/8	26 5/8 26 2/8	18 2/8	5 6	Logan County	WV	Jason Lowe	2007	6928
150 7/8	23 5/8 24 1/8	19 3/8	5 6	Todd County	MN	Jared McGhee	2008	6928
*150 7/8	21 5/8 22 6/8	15 7/8	6 5	Poweshiek County	IA	Brian Lowry	2008	6928
*150 7/8	25 3/8 24 0/8	19 3/8	5 5	Comanche County	KS	Chris J. Hood	2008	6928
150 7/8	24 5/8 24 2/8	17 4/8	6 5	Walworth County	WI	Michael Senft	2009	6928
150 7/8	22 7/8 22 3/8	17 6/8	7 5	Mercer County	ND	Byron W. Borlaug	2009	6928
*150 7/8	22 3/8 23 5/8	16 1/8	5 5	Jackson County	WI	Matthew Sedelbauer	2009	6928
150 7/8	25 3/8 25 7/8	17 6/8	6 6	Rogers County	OK	John Battle	2009	6928
*150 7/8	24 0/8 24 3/8	15 1/8	4 4	Comanche County	KS	Bruce B. Aughtry	2010	6928
150 6/8	22 3/8 22 0/8	16 4/8	5 5	Redwood County	MN	Irvin Plotz	1975	7009
150 6/8	22 2/8 21 7/8	19 0/8	5 6	Allegan County	MI	Lane Humphreys	1979	7009
150 6/8	24 4/8 23 7/8	18 6/8	6 6	Columbia County	WI	Jerry Ulrich	1980	7009
150 6/8	25 2/8 24 6/8	19 6/8	5 6	Jo Daviess County	IL	Michael Muehleip	1981	7009
150 6/8	25 3/8 25 3/8	20 1/8	4 6	Winnebago County	IL	Fred L. Smith	1985	7009
150 6/8	24 6/8 24 6/8	16 4/8	5 5	Wayne County	IL	Ginger Harvey	1986	7009
150 6/8	22 5/8 23 3/8	19 2/8	6 5	Floyd County	IA	Mark Koenigsfeld	1986	7009
150 6/8	24 6/8 24 5/8	27 1/8	5 5	Greenwood County	KS	Ray Penner	1986	7009
150 6/8	21 2/8 21 4/8	21 6/8	5 5	Clearwater County	ID	Gordon Fout	1987	7009
150 6/8	24 6/8 25 1/8	21 4/8	4 4	Boone County	IA	Dave Rimathe	1988	7009
150 6/8	22 6/8 21 6/8	15 6/8	5 5	Hocking County	OH	James Earl Roberts, Jr.	1988	7009
150 6/8	25 4/8 25 1/8	17 2/8	4 4	Suffolk County	NY	Ed Viola	1988	7009
150 6/8	21 5/8 21 7/8	17 0/8	6 5	Prince William County	VA	Jeff Redding	1990	7009
150 6/8	25 3/8 24 0/8	18 7/8	5 6	Webster County	IA	Darrell Promes	1990	7009
150 6/8	24 1/8 24 0/8	16 6/8	4 4	Linn County	IA	David Hotz	1990	7009
150 6/8	24 3/8 23 0/8	19 2/8	5 6	Wapello County	IA	Joseph Mayhew	1991	7009
150 6/8	24 0/8 24 4/8	20 2/8	5 5	Price County	WI	Michael J. Lobner	1991	7009
150 6/8	24 5/8 24 7/8	18 6/8	6 6	Shawano County	WI	David M. Zachow	1993	7009
150 6/8	23 1/8 23 0/8	21 2/8	5 5	Henry County	VA	Mike Weaver	1993	7009
150 6/8	22 6/8 23 7/8	19 0/8	5 5	Knox County	IL	Robert J. Hinckley	1993	7009
150 6/8	24 4/8 24 0/8	19 2/8	4 6	Sheboygan County	WI	Dennis P. Walter	1994	7009
150 6/8	25 2/8 25 5/8	18 6/8	4 4	Kendall County	IL	David Musser	1994	7009

WHITETAIL DEER (TYPICAL ANTLERS)

Minimum Score 125 — Continued

SCORE	LENGTH OF R MAIN BEAM L	INSIDE SPREAD	NUMBER OF R POINTS L	AREA	STATE/ PROVINCE	HUNTER'S NAME	DATE	RANK
150 6/8	27 2/8 27 5/8	20 2/8	5 7	Will County	IL	Rick Buchmeier	1994	7009
150 6/8	23 4/8 23 6/8	19 2/8	5 5	Sauk County	WI	Chad Price	1996	7009
150 6/8	21 7/8 21 4/8	18 0/8	5 5	Dane County	WI	Dean E. Goecks	1996	7009
150 6/8	24 7/8 23 2/8	19 0/8	5 5	Jackson County	IL	Ron Braun	1996	7009
150 6/8	24 5/8 24 0/8	19 0/8	5 5	Buffalo County	WI	Gerald Palmer	1997	7009
150 6/8	23 7/8 25 3/8	18 0/8	5 5	Union County	IL	Mark Landewee	1997	7009
150 6/8	24 6/8 25 1/8	19 2/8	5 6	Dane County	WI	Daryl Endres	1998	7009
150 6/8	21 5/8 22 4/8	20 0/8	6 5	Livingston County	NY	James R. Cromwell	1998	7009
150 6/8	25 3/8 25 5/8	19 3/8	7 5	Monona County	IA	Warren E. Jensen	1998	7009
150 6/8	23 0/8 23 0/8	17 0/8	5 5	Jackson County	IA	Mike Driscoll	1998	7009
150 6/8	23 7/8 23 7/8	17 2/8	5 5	Wyoming County	WV	Robert McGee	1998	7009
150 6/8	25 2/8 25 6/8	21 4/8	5 5	Kanawha County	WV	Donald R. Atkins	1998	7009
150 6/8	30 3/8 29 7/8	17 6/8	5 5	Carroll County	KY	Raetta Porter	1999	7009
150 6/8	25 6/8 22 7/8	18 6/8	5 6	Licking County	OH	Denny Ridgeway	1999	7009
150 6/8	21 2/8 21 2/8	18 2/8	5 5	Rawlins County	KS	Zack Leonetti	1999	7009
150 6/8	23 4/8 23 6/8	16 4/8	6 6	Oconto County	WI	Anthony P. Mercier	1999	7009
150 6/8	21 4/8 21 3/8	15 7/8	6 5	Traill County	ND	Tim Sorteberg	1999	7009
150 6/8	22 0/8 22 0/8	17 6/8	5 5	Williams County	ND	Jerry Brevik	2000	7009
150 6/8	24 5/8 24 2/8	18 6/8	5 5	Butler County	MO	Steve Rueck	2001	7009
150 6/8	24 1/8 23 6/8	16 2/8	5 5	Warren County	KY	Billy Carder	2002	7009
150 6/8	24 6/8 23 5/8	17 0/8	5 5	Shelby County	IL	Rick G. Cobb	2003	7009
150 6/8	24 1/8 25 3/8	17 6/8	6 5	Lacombe	ALB	Mark Stuart	2003	7009
*150 6/8	23 2/8 22 3/8	16 2/8	5 5	Lincoln County	MS	Nathan Martin	2003	7009
150 6/8	24 5/8 24 1/8	21 6/8	5 5	DeKalb County	IL	Josef K. Rud	2003	7009
150 6/8	25 0/8 24 1/8	19 3/8	4 5	Bucks County	PA	John McArthur	2003	7009
150 6/8	22 4/8 24 4/8	19 1/8	6 6	Brown County	WI	Paul G. Staeven	2003	7009
150 6/8	22 7/8 23 4/8	16 4/8	5 4	Decatur County	IA	Steve Snow	2004	7009
150 6/8	25 2/8 25 2/8	15 0/8	5 5	Guthrie County	IA	Richard L. Grosteffon, Jr.	2004	7009
150 6/8	24 0/8 23 3/8	18 2/8	5 5	Barber County	KS	Joel D. Miller	2004	7009
*150 6/8	24 2/8 24 4/8	15 3/8	5 4	Rutherford County	TN	Dale Ford	2005	7009
*150 6/8	22 6/8 21 3/8	18 0/8	5 6	Fulton County	IN	Steven A. Robinson	2005	7009
*150 6/8	23 3/8 23 0/8	16 3/8	6 7	Allen County	KS	Kortney McGraw	2005	7009
*150 6/8	22 6/8 22 0/8	17 0/8	6 6	Morrison County	MN	Kevin Karger	2005	7009
150 6/8	23 4/8 23 6/8	22 1/8	6 7	Nuevo Leon	MEX	John Hoffmann	2005	7009
150 6/8	24 0/8 24 3/8	18 2/8	5 5	Buffalo County	WI	Mike Danzinger	2005	7009
150 6/8	24 3/8 26 2/8	18 4/8	4 4	Racine County	WI	Scott R. Holler	2006	7009
150 6/8	25 0/8 24 6/8	15 2/8	5 5	Sullivan County	PA	L. W. Miller	2006	7009
*150 6/8	24 2/8 23 3/8	16 4/8	5 4	Howard County	MO	John C. Sizemore	2006	7009
150 6/8	26 3/8 26 3/8	20 2/8	4 5	Rockingham County	NH	John A. Page, Sr.	2006	7009
150 6/8	21 7/8 21 5/8	14 2/8	5 6	Johnson County	IA	Andy Fuhrmeister	2007	7009
*150 6/8	25 3/8 24 2/8	16 6/8	4 5	Jennings County	IN	Eric McIntosh	2007	7009
150 6/8	24 4/8 25 6/8	18 3/8	5 4	St. Joseph County	IN	Brad E. Feece	2007	7009
*150 6/8	24 4/8 24 2/8	17 6/8	5 5	St. Joseph County	MI	Scott Maurer	2007	7009
*150 6/8	20 6/8 20 7/8	15 6/8	5 5	Valley County	MT	Shannon Stanley	2008	7009
150 6/8	22 7/8 22 6/8	17 4/8	5 5	Fond du Lac County	WI	Ben Isaac	2008	7009
*150 6/8	24 0/8 24 7/8	21 0/8	5 5	Washington County	OH	Luke Kuchta	2008	7009
*150 6/8	22 4/8 22 6/8	17 6/8	6 6	Mercer County	OH	Christopher Ruchty	2009	7009
150 6/8	23 4/8 24 0/8	16 6/8	5 5	Buffalo County	WI	Jerry Waara	2009	7009
150 6/8	21 3/8 22 3/8	16 4/8	6 5	Morgan County	OH	Jerry Paul Owen	2009	7009
150 6/8	23 6/8 24 3/8	18 0/8	7 6	Dane County	WI	Jeff Lien	2009	7009
150 6/8	22 4/8 22 5/8	18 2/8	6 5	Pierce County	NE	Joe Beltz	2009	7009
*150 6/8	26 4/8 26 3/8	16 3/8	6 6	Logan County	WV	Dwayne C. Cline	2009	7009
150 6/8	23 5/8 23 3/8	17 2/8	5 5	Tom Green County	TX	Ronnie Parsons	2009	7009
150 5/8	21 0/8 22 7/8	19 3/8	6 5	Madison County	NE	Darwin Heppner	1967	7084
150 5/8	22 7/8 22 6/8	22 1/8	5 6	Eaton County	MI	Greg Hoefler	1982	7084
150 5/8	24 4/8 23 4/8	18 1/8	7 5	Pratt County	KS	Scott Haworth	1984	7084
150 5/8	22 7/8 22 5/8	18 5/8	5 5	Ashland County	OH	Lyle Bennett	1984	7084
150 5/8	22 3/8 22 3/8	17 3/8	5 5	Chippewa County	WI	Tim Walters	1985	7084
150 5/8	25 6/8 24 5/8	21 7/8	5 5	Randolph County	IL	Loren Eggemeyer	1987	7084
150 5/8	27 3/8 27 5/8	21 1/8	5 5	Adams County	IL	James A. Stupavsky	1988	7084
150 5/8	26 2/8 26 1/8	18 5/8	5 5	Randolph County	AR	Joey White	1990	7084
150 5/8	25 0/8 23 4/8	18 1/8	7 6	Randolph County	IL	Gary Vanpelt	1991	7084
150 5/8	24 5/8 23 6/8	18 5/8	5 5	Comanche County	KS	Randy Eddy	1992	7084
150 5/8	23 3/8 22 5/8	18 3/8	5 5	Elnora	ALB	Barry Mitchell	1993	7084
150 5/8	24 6/8 24 0/8	20 5/8	5 6	Manitoulin Island	ONT	Greg Clark	1993	7084
150 5/8	20 0/8 22 3/8	18 3/8	7 6	Montgomery County	IA	Buzz Dicks	1993	7084
150 5/8	24 0/8 24 0/8	18 2/8	6 7	Livingston County	NY	Alan Tubbs	1994	7084
150 5/8	25 6/8 24 5/8	16 5/8	5 5	Middlesex County	MA	Thomas B. Hickey, Jr.	1995	7084
150 5/8	22 7/8 21 6/8	14 6/8	7 6	Anoka County	MN	Larry Cooke	1996	7084
150 5/8	23 7/8 24 4/8	17 3/8	6 6	Kleberg County	TX	Mike Lemker	1996	7084
150 5/8	23 4/8 24 0/8	18 7/8	5 5	Stony Plain	ALB	David Paplawski	1997	7084
150 5/8	25 2/8 23 1/8	18 2/8	7 6	Mahoning County	OH	Terry L. Van Tassel	1997	7084
150 5/8	24 3/8 25 4/8	19 1/8	4 4	Shelby County	KY	James L. Jamison	1998	7084
150 5/8	26 2/8 26 3/8	20 4/8	5 6	Fulton County	IL	Lyndel Lingenfelter	1998	7084
150 5/8	27 1/8 26 2/8	17 5/8	5 5	Gallia County	OH	Scott Phillips	1998	7084
150 5/8	22 0/8 21 2/8	21 1/8	5 6	Dodge County	WI	Peter P. Griese	1998	7084
150 5/8	25 7/8 25 7/8	19 3/8	4 4	Lake County	IL	Steve Andrews	1998	7084
150 5/8	23 6/8 25 0/8	19 7/8	4 4	Stephenson County	IL	Dwight D. Peterson	1998	7084
150 5/8	22 6/8 21 6/8	17 5/8	7 6	Chester County	PA	Kyle D. Tholan	1999	7084
150 5/8	24 4/8 23 6/8	18 4/8	6 7	Anoka County	MN	John Strecker	1999	7084
150 5/8	24 1/8 23 7/8	16 5/8	5 5	Lee County	IA	Troy M. Matter	1999	7084
150 5/8	24 3/8 23 6/8	16 3/8	5 5	Breckinridge County	KY	Steve McMillen	1999	7084
150 5/8	24 2/8 25 3/8	17 7/8	5 5	Decatur County	IA	Robert D. Deskin	1999	7084
150 5/8	23 2/8 23 4/8	19 7/8	5 6	Dodge County	WI	David Schrab	1999	7084
150 5/8	23 2/8 23 2/8	19 1/8	5 5	McHenry County	IL	Robert C. Wagner	2000	7084
150 5/8	25 2/8 24 5/8	19 5/8	5 5	Jefferson County	OH	Harold C. Knight III	2000	7084
150 5/8	26 4/8 25 4/8	17 5/8	5 5	Waupaca County	WI	Gary Roth	2000	7084
150 5/8	23 2/8 23 6/8	15 7/8	5 5	Madison County	NY	Scott Clark	2000	7084
150 5/8	26 2/8 25 7/8	18 1/8	4 6	McHenry County	IL	Ken Stewart	2000	7084
150 5/8	23 3/8 23 2/8	16 5/8	6 6	Hamilton County	IA	Scott R. McCaulley	2000	7084
150 5/8	24 5/8 25 5/8	18 3/8	5 5	Eaton County	MI	Matt M. Merryfield	2001	7084
150 5/8	21 7/8 22 4/8	19 3/8	5 5	Davis County	IA	Jeff J. Dudgeon	2002	7084
150 5/8	24 1/8 23 4/8	20 1/8	4 5	Wood County	WI	Jeff Lynn	2002	7084
150 5/8	23 0/8 23 0/8	17 7/8	5 5	Rock County	WI	Allen Kilcoyne	2003	7084
150 5/8	26 0/8 26 1/8	18 3/8	5 5	Fond du Lac County	WI	William Theyerl	2004	7084

WHITETAIL DEER (TYPICAL ANTLERS)

Minimum Score 125   Continued

SCORE	LENGTH OF R MAIN BEAM L	INSIDE SPREAD	NUMBER OF R POINTS L	AREA	STATE/ PROVINCE	HUNTER'S NAME	DATE	RANK
150 5/8	23 7/8 22 5/8	18 3/8	4 5	Shelby County	IN	William A. Leach, Jr.	2004	7084
*150 5/8	22 4/8 22 1/8	18 6/8	5 6	St. Louis County	MO	Michael Brown	2005	7084
*150 5/8	26 3/8 25 0/8	24 1/8	4 4	Ogle County	IL	Michael R. Williams	2005	7084
150 5/8	24 0/8 23 4/8	17 7/8	5 5	Buffalo County	WI	Matt Buchan	2006	7084
*150 5/8	26 3/8 25 7/8	19 0/8	5 7	Marshall County	IA	Tim Kacmarynski	2006	7084
*150 5/8	25 3/8 24 1/8	19 7/8	7 7	Clayton County	IA	Chad Breuer	2006	7084
*150 5/8	23 2/8 23 1/8	13 4/8	6 5	Medina County	OH	Robert Kane Henderson	2006	7084
*150 5/8	24 7/8 24 7/8	17 1/8	5 5	Greene County	IL	Craig Vanausdoll	2006	7084
150 5/8	21 3/8 21 2/8	15 4/8	7 7	Coshocton County	OH	Mike Bay	2007	7084
150 5/8	24 0/8 24 6/8	19 2/8	5 7	Bayfield County	WI	Brian Humes	2007	7084
150 5/8	24 4/8 23 5/8	16 5/8	5 5	Highland County	OH	Claud "Chris" Dopel, Jr.	2007	7084
*150 5/8	22 7/8 22 6/8	16 4/8	8 7	Wichita County	TX	Shawn Price	2007	7084
*150 5/8	23 5/8 23 5/8	19 0/8	6 7	Dodge County	MN	Mark Lenz	2007	7084
150 5/8	26 2/8 25 7/8	20 1/8	6 7	Clark County	KY	Charles W. Saylor	2008	7084
*150 5/8	22 7/8 22 1/8	16 1/8	6 6	Washington County	NE	James Lode	2008	7084
150 5/8	25 4/8 25 7/8	15 5/8	4 5	Marquette County	WI	Michael P. Glover	2008	7084
150 5/8	23 1/8 21 5/8	18 3/8	5 6	Clark County	WI	Randy Hinker	2008	7084
*150 5/8	24 6/8 24 4/8	19 3/8	5 4	Essex County	MA	Harold Otto	2008	7084
150 5/8	26 1/8 26 0/8	18 7/8	5 7	Hartford County	CT	Brian T. Bennett	2008	7084
*150 5/8	27 2/8 27 0/8	19 6/8	6 5	Kanabec County	MN	Travis Nelson	2009	7084
150 5/8	21 6/8 22 5/8	18 7/8	5 5	Scotland County	MO	Chris Zeringue	2009	7084
150 5/8	24 7/8 24 3/8	18 1/8	6 5	Whitley County	IN	Johnny L. Walthour, Jr.	2009	7084
150 5/8	24 2/8 24 0/8	19 1/8	5 6	Brown County	SD	Ryan Casey	2009	7084
150 5/8	22 3/8 22 7/8	17 7/8	5 5	Cecil County	MD	Shirley Hitchens	2009	7084
*150 5/8	24 1/8 24 4/8	19 3/8	6 6	Tensas Parish	LA	Todd Cerniglia	2009	7084
150 4/8	24 4/8 24 4/8	18 6/8	5 4	Scott County	IA	Howard A. Goettsch	1974	7151
150 4/8	22 5/8 22 3/8	14 7/8	6 7	Wabasha County	MN	Lee Partington	1975	7151
150 4/8	21 4/8 21 6/8	15 6/8	6 6	Dunn County	WI	Mary Nussberger	1976	7151
150 4/8	24 7/8 24 7/8	17 6/8	5 5	Guernsey County	OH	Miltos Stefanitais	1979	7151
150 4/8	22 1/8 22 0/8	20 4/8	5 5	Woodford County	IL	Roger Miller	1980	7151
150 4/8	23 6/8 23 4/8	19 0/8	5 5	Schuyler County	NY	Donald L. Lane	1980	7151
150 4/8	26 3/8 25 0/8	18 4/8	5 4	Miami County	OH	Richard G. Williamson	1981	7151
150 4/8	24 2/8 25 1/8	19 4/8	4 4	Monroe County	WI	Dirk Gillette	1981	7151
150 4/8	24 7/8 27 2/8	28 1/8	5 4	Greenwood County	KS	Ray Penner	1984	7151
150 4/8	23 6/8 22 3/8	16 0/8	4 4	Osage County	KS	Bill Senne	1985	7151
150 4/8	26 2/8 26 2/8	18 2/8	4 4	Pepin County	WI	Myles Keller	1985	7151
150 4/8	23 4/8 23 2/8	17 1/8	5 7	Florence County	WI	Carolyn Lemanski	1986	7151
150 4/8	26 0/8 26 1/8	20 3/8	7 6	Knox County	MO	Roger Gipple	1986	7151
150 4/8	24 4/8 25 6/8	19 2/8	5 5	La Salle County	IL	James Pierson	1989	7151
150 4/8	23 5/8 24 6/8	18 0/8	5 5	Gregory County	SD	Dan Swiler	1990	7151
150 4/8	24 6/8 24 7/8	17 4/8	5 5	Stoddard County	MO	Ken Heuer	1990	7151
150 4/8	23 1/8 22 5/8	17 2/8	5 5	Ravalli County	MT	Mark Moreland	1991	7151
150 4/8	22 7/8 23 1/8	17 0/8	5 5	Jackson County	WI	Scott R. Hanson	1991	7151
150 4/8	25 0/8 24 4/8	19 6/8	5 4	Prowers County	CO	Neal Heaton	1991	7151
150 4/8	23 6/8 22 4/8	18 1/8	6 6	Comanche County	KS	Randall Eddy	1991	7151
150 4/8	21 6/8 22 0/8	17 6/8	5 5	Saginaw County	MI	Jerry D. Pratt	1991	7151
150 4/8	24 1/8 25 2/8	18 6/8	5 4	Claiborne County	MS	Tripp Stennett	1992	7151
150 4/8	27 4/8 18 5/8	18 6/8	7 7	Randolph County	IN	Ted Mooneyhan	1992	7151
150 4/8	21 3/8 21 6/8	16 0/8	5 5	Clarke County	IA	William L. Tuttle	1992	7151
150 4/8	22 7/8 22 6/8	20 4/8	5 5	Anoka County	MN	Paul Landberg	1993	7151
150 4/8	23 0/8 24 2/8	18 0/8	5 5	Montgomery County	MD	DeWayne A. Leslie	1993	7151
150 4/8	23 3/8 23 3/8	18 2/8	7 7	McDonough County	IL	Dane Metcalf	1993	7151
150 4/8	24 5/8 26 2/8	15 5/8	7 6	Todd County	KY	Thomas Allen Haley	1994	7151
150 4/8	22 4/8 22 0/8	20 2/8	5 5	Champaign County	IL	James Smith	1994	7151
150 4/8	23 4/8 22 7/8	19 4/8	6 7	Jasper County	IA	Randy Taylor	1994	7151
150 4/8	23 2/8 23 4/8	17 0/8	5 5	Hunterdon County	NJ	Charles Reinhart	1994	7151
150 4/8	22 6/8 22 4/8	18 6/8	5 5	Lake County	IL	Brent A. Nelson	1995	7151
150 4/8	25 7/8 22 5/8	18 1/8	5 6	Peoria County	IL	Denny Masching	1995	7151
150 4/8	23 2/8 23 4/8	17 4/8	5 5	Bourbon County	KS	Chad Holt	1995	7151
150 4/8	25 2/8 26 5/8	16 4/8	5 4	Washington County	KS	Doug Kruse	1996	7151
150 4/8	24 6/8 25 0/8	17 4/8	7 7	Montgomery County	IL	Kevin Seely	1996	7151
150 4/8	25 0/8 26 2/8	20 7/8	5 6	Webster County	WV	Jeff Bowman	1996	7151
150 4/8	21 7/8 22 0/8	18 0/8	7 5	McDonald County	MO	Brian K. Sharp	1997	7151
150 4/8	24 5/8 25 1/8	18 0/8	5 5	Northampton County	PA	William A. Car, Jr.	1997	7151
150 4/8	23 2/8 23 2/8	15 2/8	5 5	Chautauqua County	KS	Daniel L. Hubert	1997	7151
150 4/8	24 4/8 25 1/8	21 6/8	5 5	Winneshiek County	IA	Shawn Bartz	1997	7151
150 4/8	23 7/8 24 4/8	17 3/8	6 5	Highland County	OH	Jason Sowders	1997	7151
150 4/8	24 1/8 23 5/8	18 7/8	6 6	Ohio County	KY	Robbie Hinton	1998	7151
150 4/8	21 2/8 21 1/8	17 1/8	6 7	Sanborn County	SD	Brian J. Carmody	1999	7151
150 4/8	23 4/8 23 4/8	16 1/8	6 5	Morrison County	MN	Mark Edlund	1999	7151
150 4/8	25 4/8 26 5/8	21 0/8	5 4	Clinton County	IA	Terry Frahm	1999	7151
150 4/8	24 4/8 25 2/8	18 6/8	5 5	Muskingum County	OH	Todd Popek	1999	7151
150 4/8	26 2/8 26 1/8	22 2/8	5 4	Buffalo County	WI	Tim Hagmann	2000	7151
150 4/8	24 7/8 25 2/8	17 4/8	5 5	Clare County	MI	Joe Slocum	2000	7151
150 4/8	25 5/8 25 5/8	18 5/8	5 5	Martin County	IN	Mark Huber	2000	7151
150 4/8	27 4/8 27 2/8	19 6/8	5 4	Baltimore County	MD	Ronald P. Bowers, Jr.	2000	7151
150 4/8	26 4/8 24 4/8	18 6/8	6 5	Jefferson County	WV	Paxton Jones	2000	7151
150 4/8	23 7/8 23 0/8	22 0/8	5 5	Kent County	DE	John W. Forbes	2001	7151
150 4/8	24 1/8 23 4/8	17 6/8	5 5	Bradford County	PA	Thomas McAndrew	2001	7151
150 4/8	26 4/8 25 6/8	21 4/8	5 5	Will County	IL	Alex Billings	2001	7151
150 4/8	24 1/8 23 6/8	18 2/8	4 4	La Salle County	IL	Pat Purdue	2001	7151
150 4/8	22 1/8 22 3/8	16 0/8	5 5	Winneshiek County	IA	Steve Weber	2001	7151
150 4/8	25 2/8 24 5/8	16 3/8	5 6	Woodson County	KS	Michael Linnebur	2001	7151
150 4/8	24 2/8 24 1/8	17 4/8	6 7	Saline County	KS	John R. Moling	2001	7151
150 4/8	25 1/8 24 7/8	18 3/8	6 5	McDonough County	IL	William M. Brown	2002	7151
150 4/8	24 3/8 22 4/8	19 7/8	6 6	Allegheny County	PA	Chris Rusiewicz	2002	7151
150 4/8	23 7/8 24 1/8	19 2/8	5 5	Licking County	OH	Wayne F. Farnsworth, Jr.	2002	7151
150 4/8	24 1/8 24 1/8	17 5/8	5 7	Menifee County	KY	Mike Penna	2003	7151
150 4/8	27 1/8 25 0/8	20 6/8	5 5	Suffolk County	NY	Richard Kiely	2003	7151
*150 4/8	25 6/8 25 6/8	17 3/8	6 5	Green Lake County	WI	Andrew P. Knurowski	2003	7151
*150 4/8	25 0/8 24 0/8	19 6/8	5 5	Jackson County	MI	Adam M. Bemis	2004	7151
150 4/8	25 2/8 24 4/8	18 6/8	6 6	Shelby County	MO	Matt Gill	2004	7151
150 4/8	27 0/8 27 3/8	21 4/8	4 5	Rock Island County	IL	Mikel Angel	2004	7151
150 4/8	25 3/8 25 6/8	18 0/8	6 5	Richardson County	NE	Mason Nall	2004	7151
150 4/8	22 6/8 23 0/8	18 2/8	5 5	Hinds County	MS	James Mordica	2005	7151

WHITETAIL DEER (TYPICAL ANTLERS)

Minimum Score 125 — Continued

SCORE	LENGTH OF R MAIN BEAM L	INSIDE SPREAD	NUMBER OF R POINTS L	AREA	STATE/ PROVINCE	HUNTER'S NAME	DATE	RANK
*150 4/8	24 1/8 24 2/8	18 0/8	6 6	Clearwater County	MN	Nathan Higginbotham	2005	7151
150 4/8	23 0/8 21 5/8	20 5/8	6 6	Christian County	KY	Jerred Matthews	2005	7151
*150 4/8	25 6/8 25 2/8	20 4/8	4 4	Carroll County	OH	Ryan Irwin	2005	7151
150 4/8	23 1/8 23 1/8	17 6/8	5 5	Keokuk County	IA	Eric J. Stein	2005	7151
150 4/8	24 1/8 24 3/8	17 6/8	5 5	Des Moines County	IA	Gary Grassi	2005	7151
*150 4/8	26 5/8 25 6/8	18 1/8	5 4	Columbia County	WI	Todd Campnell	2006	7151
150 4/8	24 1/8 24 0/8	14 6/8	5 5	Mitchell County	IA	Neal Keeling	2006	7151
*150 4/8	22 4/8 22 4/8	17 2/8	5 5	Jefferson County	IL	Zack Thompson	2006	7151
*150 4/8	23 7/8 24 2/8	19 0/8	4 4	Barber County	KS	Charlie Jones	2006	7151
*150 4/8	25 5/8 26 2/8	18 6/8	5 5	Harlan County	KY	Bobby Kelly	2007	7151
150 4/8	25 0/8 24 4/8	18 6/8	5 5	Sarpy County	NE	Craig Stine	2007	7151
150 4/8	22 4/8 22 4/8	17 2/8	5 5	Richmond County	GA	Jack U. Baker, Jr.	2007	7151
150 4/8	23 0/8 24 3/8	16 6/8	5 5	Dane County	WI	Dave Dilley	2007	7151
150 4/8	25 3/8 26 0/8	19 0/8	5 5	Columbia County	WI	Earl Adam Eichline	2007	7151
*150 4/8	26 6/8 26 4/8	18 0/8	5 5	Putnam County	IN	Rodney Graham	2007	7151
150 4/8	24 2/8 25 2/8	18 2/8	4 5	Rock County	WI	Jeff Gray	2007	7151
*150 4/8	23 4/8 21 7/8	16 1/8	5 7	Delaware County	IN	Jamin McQuitty	2008	7151
*150 4/8	24 7/8 25 0/8	19 2/8	5 5	Fond du Lac County	WI	Josh Pipping	2008	7151
150 4/8	24 1/8 24 2/8	19 4/8	5 5	Portage County	WI	Dan Karl	2008	7151
150 4/8	26 4/8 26 4/8	17 0/8	4 4	Morgan County	IL	Terry L. Day	2008	7151
*150 4/8	24 0/8 24 1/8	19 1/8	4 6	Tensas Parish	LA	James Allen Doyle	2009	7151
150 4/8	23 3/8 23 1/8	18 6/8	5 5	Clarion County	PA	Jamie S. Rex	2009	7151
150 4/8	22 4/8 22 5/8	17 3/8	6 6	Parke County	IN	James E. McCalister	2009	7151
150 4/8	23 4/8 21 7/8	21 2/8	6 6	Trempealeau County	WI	Don Baardseth	2009	7151
*150 4/8	22 7/8 21 7/8	17 0/8	5 5	Polk County	WI	Jesse Ashton	2009	7151
150 4/8	25 2/8 24 2/8	20 1/8	6 6	Lake County	OH	Thomas J. Udovic	2009	7151
150 4/8	25 0/8 24 1/8	22 5/8	6 5	Jefferson County	WI	Dawn Traub	2009	7151
*150 4/8	24 2/8 23 4/8	16 1/8	6 8	Rimbey	ALB	Shane Jensen	2010	7151
150 4/8	23 3/8 22 2/8	18 2/8	5 5	St. Joseph County	IN	Douglas K. Dieterly	2010	7151
150 3/8	24 5/8 24 5/8	22 5/8	4 4	Oneida County	WI	Philip Hildebrand	1967	7250
150 3/8	28 0/8 27 4/8	20 5/8	4 5	Jones County	GA	Sid Hester	1969	7250
150 3/8	20 4/8 21 2/8	16 7/8	5 5	Langlade County	WI	Herbert Buettner	1970	7250
150 3/8	24 0/8 23 4/8	15 4/8	5 5	Juneau County	WI	Anthony Wulin	1977	7250
150 3/8	23 3/8 23 5/8	18 3/8	6 7	Graham County	KS	Russell Hull	1977	7250
150 3/8	22 2/8 22 3/8	15 3/8	5 5	Souris River	MAN	Garry William Kaluzniak	1980	7250
150 3/8	26 0/8 24 4/8	16 4/8	9 8	Oakland County	MI	Donald J. Fisher	1981	7250
150 3/8	25 1/8 25 0/8	17 2/8	5 5	Jackson County	MO	Marvin Thomey	1983	7250
150 3/8	23 1/8 22 3/8	16 4/8	5 6	Dakota County	MN	Dave Vomela	1985	7250
150 3/8	23 1/8 23 5/8	19 5/8	7 7	Yuma County	CO	Richard King	1985	7250
150 3/8	24 0/8 24 2/8	16 4/8	6 6	Benton County	IA	Okee Walker	1986	7250
150 3/8	26 1/8 26 1/8	16 6/8	7 5	Jackson County	OH	Robert E. Thomas, Jr.	1987	7250
150 3/8	24 2/8 23 2/8	18 5/8	4 5	Clark County	IL	Max M. LeCrone	1988	7250
150 3/8	24 0/8 25 2/8	15 4/8	5 7	Clark County	OH	Rick Rounds	1988	7250
150 3/8	23 4/8 24 0/8	16 7/8	5 7	Branch County	MI	James E. Marvin	1990	7250
150 3/8	23 0/8 22 5/8	20 1/8	5 5	Mason County	IL	Jeff Heilman	1990	7250
150 3/8	24 0/8 24 4/8	20 7/8	5 5	Suffolk County	NY	Bruce R. Dickerson	1990	7250
150 3/8	25 3/8 25 6/8	19 1/8	5 5	Greene County	OH	Rodney Curtis Bailey	1990	7250
150 3/8	23 6/8 25 3/8	17 5/8	4 4	Vinton County	OH	Burl Keesee	1991	7250
150 3/8	24 3/8 24 3/8	17 5/8	5 5	Throckmorton County	TX	Darrel Bewley	1992	7250
150 3/8	23 2/8 23 4/8	19 7/8	5 5	Stearns County	MN	Brent Helgeson	1992	7250
150 3/8	25 4/8 24 3/8	20 7/8	4 4	Scott County	IA	Randy Templeton	1992	7250
150 3/8	24 7/8 24 6/8	21 1/8	5 4	Roberts County	SD	Myles Keller	1992	7250
150 3/8	27 1/8 26 1/8	17 1/8	5 5	Cheshire County	NH	Bud Croteau	1994	7250
150 3/8	23 0/8 24 0/8	17 3/8	5 5	Washington County	IA	James Cluney	1994	7250
150 3/8	23 4/8 22 4/8	15 7/8	6 6	Callaway County	MO	Gene Cogorno	1994	7250
150 3/8	24 4/8 25 0/8	19 5/8	5 5	La Salle County	IL	Eduardo Rojas	1994	7250
150 3/8	20 4/8 21 3/8	16 3/8	7 6	Douglas County	KS	Mark Young	1996	7250
150 3/8	24 3/8 25 1/8	19 7/8	5 5	Green County	WI	Jamie Grinder	1997	7250
150 3/8	23 0/8 23 0/8	16 5/8	5 5	Kane County	IL	Jeffery A. Girls	1998	7250
150 3/8	23 6/8 24 1/8	20 2/8	5 6	Clermont County	OH	Robert Lemme	1999	7250
150 3/8	20 1/8 20 6/8	14 2/8	6 5	Irion County	TX	Terry M. Tadsen	1999	7250
150 3/8	22 3/8 23 3/8	19 1/8	5 5	Ottawa County	KS	Patrick E. Helget	1999	7250
150 3/8	23 5/8 21 7/8	19 2/8	5 6	Waushara County	WI	Mark J. Kalata	2000	7250
150 3/8	24 5/8 25 3/8	19 2/8	5 7	Shawano County	WI	David E. Hull	2000	7250
150 3/8	26 3/8 26 1/8	18 7/8	4 4	Alexander County	IL	Mark W. Pasmore	2000	7250
150 3/8	25 7/8 25 5/8	21 1/8	4 4	Dodge County	WI	Scott Bautch	2001	7250
150 3/8	26 0/8 26 6/8	24 1/8	6 6	Pottawattamie County	IA	Jack Kalstrup	2001	7250
150 3/8	23 2/8 23 5/8	17 7/8	5 5	Grant County	KY	Thomas Schumer	2002	7250
150 3/8	25 0/8 25 5/8	16 0/8	5 5	Carroll County	MO	William Brown	2002	7250
150 3/8	22 3/8 22 3/8	18 1/8	6 6	Wayne County	IA	Jake Taylor	2002	7250
150 3/8	23 3/8 24 1/8	15 7/8	6 6	Breckinridge County	KY	Steve McMillen	2002	7250
150 3/8	22 6/8 24 0/8	15 7/8	6 5	Dakota County	MN	Todd William Hogan	2002	7250
150 3/8	26 0/8 26 4/8	17 3/8	4 5	Cedar County	NE	David B. Cull	2003	7250
150 3/8	24 0/8 23 5/8	16 5/8	6 6	Union County	OH	Ronnie Allen	2003	7250
150 3/8	28 7/8 28 6/8	18 2/8	5 5	Humphreys County	MS	James C. Kennedy	2003	7250
150 3/8	22 6/8 23 0/8	16 5/8	6 5	Clark County	IL	Jay Tarble	2004	7250
150 3/8	22 1/8 20 1/8	20 5/8	5 5	Columbia County	WI	Steven L. Rohn	2004	7250
150 3/8	26 0/8 25 0/8	17 5/8	5 8	Bremer County	IA	Dave MacDonald	2004	7250
150 3/8	27 1/8 25 6/8	18 5/8	5 4	Thayer County	NE	Earl V. Hillman, Jr.	2004	7250
150 3/8	24 4/8 24 1/8	18 3/8	4 4	Cedar County	NE	Marlyn Wiebelhaus	2004	7250
*150 3/8	22 4/8 22 3/8	17 5/8	5 5	Clarke County	IA	Jed Howe	2005	7250
150 3/8	23 6/8 23 0/8	18 1/8	5 5	Fulton County	IL	Michael Hopping	2005	7250
150 3/8	22 7/8 23 3/8	18 3/8	5 5	Lincoln County	WI	Patrick "Norm" Kahle	2005	7250
150 3/8	22 1/8 22 4/8	20 0/8	5 6	McHenry County	IL	Donald Freeman	2005	7250
*150 3/8	25 0/8 24 3/8	20 0/8	7 7	Casey County	KY	John E. Barrows III	2006	7250
150 3/8	24 7/8 24 6/8	18 0/8	5 5	Montgomery County	OH	Barry L. Howich	2006	7250
*150 3/8	25 3/8 25 3/8	16 4/8	6 6	Gallia County	OH	Jeff Skinner	2006	7250
*150 3/8	24 3/8 25 0/8	18 1/8	4 4	Coles County	IL	Chris R. Eaton	2006	7250
*150 3/8	23 3/8 24 6/8	23 0/8	6 7	Buffalo County	WI	Chad G. Halama	2007	7250
150 3/8	25 0/8 23 6/8	21 5/8	5 4	Van Buren County	IA	Richard Lesan	2007	7250
150 3/8	22 2/8 20 5/8	16 1/8	5 5	Van Buren County	IA	Mark Elsinger	2007	7250
150 3/8	22 0/8 21 5/8	18 6/8	6 7	Bond County	IL	Scott Abbott	2007	7250
150 3/8	20 3/8 20 0/8	16 0/8	6 6	Morris County	KS	Daniel C. Rude	2007	7250
*150 3/8	24 6/8 25 1/8	18 5/8	4 4	Carroll County	OH	Glen L. Stark	2008	7250
150 3/8	25 2/8 24 3/8	18 7/8	6 6	Hillsdale County	MI	Michael J. Zachary	2008	7250

WHITETAIL DEER (TYPICAL ANTLERS)

Minimum Score 125   Continued

SCORE	LENGTH OF R MAIN BEAM L	INSIDE SPREAD	NUMBER OF R POINTS L	AREA	STATE/ PROVINCE	HUNTER'S NAME	DATE	RANK
150 3/8	23 6/8 23 2/8	18 2/8	6 5	Tazewell County	IL	Michael L. Gore	2008	7250
150 3/8	25 1/8 25 3/8	16 4/8	7 6	Hancock County	IL	Max Bell	2008	7250
150 3/8	22 0/8 22 5/8	20 2/8	6 6	Kingman County	KS	Collen L. Steffen	2008	7250
*150 3/8	22 3/8 21 3/8	15 4/8	6 6	Fountain County	IN	Brian L. Walls	2009	7250
150 3/8	23 0/8 22 2/8	18 3/8	5 5	Columbia County	WI	Jonathon A. Herrmann	2009	7250
150 3/8	24 7/8 25 3/8	17 6/8	4 5	St. Joseph County	IN	Chris T. Mammolenti	2009	7250
*150 3/8	24 3/8 24 4/8	20 1/8	5 5	Renville County	ND	Ryan Ones	2009	7250
150 2/8	23 5/8 23 3/8	17 2/8	6 6	Jackson County	WI	Roger Reinart	1972	7323
150 2/8	26 0/8 24 2/8	19 0/8	4 5	Spink County	SD	Gerald A. Kettering	1978	7323
150 2/8	23 3/8 23 5/8	14 0/8	5 5	Cottonwood County	MN	Leonard P. Thiner	1978	7323
150 2/8	25 2/8 27 1/8	19 4/8	4 4	Fulton County	IL	William L. Beaird	1984	7323
150 2/8	23 3/8 22 7/8	17 2/8	5 5	Marathon County	WI	Kevin Denzine	1985	7323
150 2/8	25 1/8 25 2/8	16 7/8	7 5	Dodge County	WI	Fran Hallmeyer	1986	7323
150 2/8	23 1/8 24 0/8	16 2/8	5 5	Price County	WI	Ben Grapa	1987	7323
150 2/8	24 4/8 24 5/8	18 4/8	5 5	Wyoming	ONT	Pierre Parent	1987	7323
150 2/8	24 4/8 25 3/8	17 1/8	7 5	Lawrence County	IL	James R. Griggs	1987	7323
150 2/8	25 5/8 26 6/8	23 2/8	6 6	Meigs County	OH	Earl M. Johnson	1987	7323
150 2/8	23 1/8 24 4/8	15 2/8	5 6	Crowley County	CO	Chuck Anderson, Sr.	1987	7323
150 2/8	26 3/8 26 6/8	19 4/8	5 5	Howard County	MD	David Wilson	1988	7323
150 2/8	24 0/8 23 7/8	20 3/8	4 7	Webster County	IA	Scott L. Powers	1988	7323
150 2/8	22 4/8 23 1/8	18 1/8	6 7	Butler County	KS	Jack Evans	1988	7323
150 2/8	23 6/8 24 2/8	16 6/8	5 5	Cass County	MI	Donald Zehrung	1988	7323
150 2/8	25 3/8 24 1/8	19 2/8	4 4	Webster County	IA	Curtis Martens	1988	7323
150 2/8	21 7/8 22 0/8	17 4/8	6 6	Buffalo County	WI	Gary Stutz	1989	7323
150 2/8	24 6/8 24 6/8	19 3/8	6 6	Lawrence County	OH	Scott Johnson	1989	7323
150 2/8	24 1/8 24 0/8	17 1/8	6 8	Douglas County	WI	Steve Wittke	1990	7323
150 2/8	21 4/8 21 5/8	15 2/8	5 5	Bremer County	IA	Rod Heidemann	1990	7323
150 2/8	28 4/8 27 4/8	24 2/8	6 4	Napanee	ONT	Tim McCabe	1990	7323
150 2/8	23 2/8 22 2/8	24 0/8	5 7	Kleberg County	TX	Wayne Peeples	1991	7323
150 2/8	23 4/8 23 0/8	15 6/8	5 5	Monroe County	MO	Montie R. Haupt	1991	7323
150 2/8	23 4/8 23 5/8	16 0/8	6 6	Sauk County	WI	Fred Hess	1991	7323
150 2/8	25 0/8 24 7/8	21 2/8	4 4	Lincoln County	WI	Mark Wimmer	1992	7323
150 2/8	26 4/8 26 0/8	17 2/8	5 6	Wyandot County	OH	James D. Herring	1992	7323
150 2/8	23 4/8 22 6/8	17 6/8	5 5	Mahaska County	IA	Greg Springer	1992	7323
150 2/8	24 0/8 24 3/8	18 4/8	5 5	Uvalde County	TX	Michael R. Geller	1993	7323
150 2/8	25 6/8 25 2/8	16 3/8	7 6	Plymouth County	IA	Jon T. Saunders	1994	7323
150 2/8	23 1/8 22 7/8	20 4/8	5 5	Sawyer County	WI	Eugene J. Fleming	1995	7323
150 2/8	26 1/8 26 6/8	21 4/8	5 5	Effingham County	IL	Gary Miller	1995	7323
150 2/8	25 3/8 23 3/8	21 4/8	5 5	Marshall County	IL	Rich Shanklin	1995	7323
150 2/8	24 1/8 22 6/8	16 7/8	5 6	Livingston County	IL	David Hoerner	1996	7323
150 2/8	25 5/8 24 5/8	20 6/8	4 4	Shelby County	IL	Kris E. Knox	1996	7323
150 2/8	23 4/8 22 7/8	19 4/8	5 5	Marquette County	WI	Charles Weyh	1996	7323
150 2/8	23 7/8 24 5/8	16 5/8	7 6	Trempealeau County	WI	Sam D. Severson	1997	7323
150 2/8	23 2/8 23 1/8	18 4/8	5 5	Christian County	KY	Chester Stewart	1997	7323
150 2/8	22 2/8 22 6/8	16 6/8	5 5	Fayette County	IA	Gary Sefert	1997	7323
150 2/8	20 5/8 20 7/8	14 4/8	7 7	Fremont County	WY	Scott Foster	1998	7323
150 2/8	25 2/8 25 2/8	19 5/8	7 7	Price County	WI	Tim Fritz	1998	7323
150 2/8	24 1/8 23 4/8	20 0/8	5 5	Gage County	NE	Ben Navratil	1998	7323
150 2/8	21 6/8 23 0/8	18 2/8	5 5	Marshall County	IN	Larry D. Hochstetler	1998	7323
150 2/8	23 1/8 24 7/8	17 6/8	5 4	Sullivan County	IN	Brian Wright	1998	7323
150 2/8	24 1/8 23 7/8	19 2/8	5 5	Jefferson County	WI	Mark Zimmerman	1998	7323
150 2/8	22 7/8 23 1/8	17 2/8	5 5	Fayette County	PA	Larry Landman	1999	7323
150 2/8	20 7/8 21 0/8	15 2/8	6 5	Callahan County	TX	Elvan L. Goode	1999	7323
150 2/8	25 6/8 25 7/8	22 4/8	5 5	Dodge County	WI	Jerry Leair	1999	7323
150 2/8	25 0/8 26 6/8	21 5/8	5 5	Jo Daviess County	IL	James C. Berning	1999	7323
150 2/8	21 5/8 21 3/8	17 0/8	6 6	Ohio County	KY	Kenny Morphew	1999	7323
150 2/8	25 0/8 24 7/8	20 2/8	4 5	Frederick County	MD	Jeffrey A. Eyler	2000	7323
150 2/8	24 0/8 23 2/8	17 2/8	5 6	Fulton County	GA	Rick Polsean	2001	7323
150 2/8	24 6/8 24 0/8	18 4/8	6 6	Crow Wing County	MN	Douglas Richert	2001	7323
150 2/8	26 2/8 26 6/8	16 6/8	4 5	Worth County	GA	Shane Calhoun	2001	7323
150 2/8	23 3/8 24 5/8	17 6/8	4 5	St. Brieux	SAS	Floyd Forster	2001	7323
150 2/8	22 7/8 23 3/8	19 6/8	5 5	Chester County	PA	William E. Gerhardt	2002	7323
150 2/8	23 6/8 23 4/8	19 2/8	5 6	Kingman	ALB	Sly Baier	2002	7323
150 2/8	23 2/8 22 4/8	17 4/8	5 5	Grant County	WI	Roger Wallace	2002	7323
150 2/8	24 6/8 23 6/8	19 4/8	5 5	Richland County	WI	Michael D. Alexander	2002	7323
150 2/8	22 2/8 21 7/8	15 0/8	5 5	Hodgeman County	KS	Ivan Muzljakovich	2002	7323
150 2/8	25 0/8 23 2/8	19 2/8	5 5	Tuscarawas County	OH	George Croftcheck	2002	7323
150 2/8	26 4/8 26 4/8	21 0/8	5 5	Pike County	IL	Andrew J. Swope	2003	7323
*150 2/8	26 4/8 24 4/8	19 4/8	4 5	Tuscarawas County	OH	Terry Zingery	2003	7323
150 2/8	24 0/8 24 3/8	16 4/8	5 5	Linn County	MO	John Jordan	2003	7323
150 2/8	25 3/8 24 3/8	22 0/8	5 5	St. Croix County	WI	Daniel G. Weishaar	2003	7323
150 2/8	23 7/8 24 2/8	16 0/8	6 5	Plymouth County	IA	Tim Sanow	2004	7323
150 2/8	25 7/8 25 3/8	20 0/8	6 5	Buffalo County	WI	Zachary Dieckman	2004	7323
*150 2/8	25 0/8 23 6/8	17 0/8	5 5	Jackson County	WI	Brooke Anderson	2004	7323
150 2/8	28 4/8 28 4/8	17 2/8	5 8	Floyd County	IA	Justin Crum	2004	7323
150 2/8	21 6/8 21 6/8	15 3/8	6 6	Rooks County	KS	Jim Dougherty	2004	7323
*150 2/8	24 0/8 24 4/8	22 4/8	6 5	Monmouth County	NJ	George Duncan	2005	7323
150 2/8	23 4/8 23 2/8	18 0/8	6 6	Putnam County	WV	Terry Rowh	2005	7323
150 2/8	23 4/8 23 0/8	18 6/8	5 5	Fond du Lac County	WI	Joel B. Landaal	2005	7323
150 2/8	24 2/8 24 2/8	22 4/8	4 4	Surry County	VA	Dwight S. Wolf	2005	7323
150 2/8	27 6/8 27 5/8	18 5/8	5 5	Jefferson County	IN	Henry Reynolds	2005	7323
150 2/8	23 3/8 23 5/8	18 2/8	6 6	Sussex County	DE	Rudy D. Miller	2005	7323
*150 2/8	21 4/8 20 5/8	18 4/8	6 5	Renville County	ND	Cody Hammer	2006	7323
*150 2/8	27 0/8 26 6/8	17 4/8	5 5	Adams County	OH	Stephen C. Budig	2007	7323
*150 2/8	24 5/8 23 6/8	17 0/8	5 5	Dane County	WI	Tim Hellenbrand	2007	7323
150 2/8	22 4/8 23 0/8	15 0/8	5 5	Macoupin County	IL	Matthew M. Davis	2008	7323
*150 2/8	26 2/8 25 1/8	18 4/8	5 5	Washington County	MN	Josh Hall	2008	7323
150 2/8	21 7/8 22 6/8	17 0/8	6 5	Otoe County	NE	Mike Kinney	2008	7323
150 2/8	24 4/8 23 5/8	20 0/8	5 5	Greenwood County	KS	Frank S. Noska IV	2008	7323
150 2/8	24 3/8 24 1/8	18 4/8	5 5	Vernon County	WI	Greg A. Miller	2009	7323
*150 2/8	23 3/8 22 4/8	15 6/8	6 6	Montgomery County	MO	Jaron R. Freie	2009	7323
150 2/8	24 0/8 25 1/8	19 6/8	4 5	Buffalo County	WI	Ryan Roberts	2009	7323
*150 2/8	24 1/8 24 4/8	20 7/8	6 5	Anne Arundel County	MD	Nicholas DiMauro	2009	7323
150 2/8	23 0/8 22 2/8	15 6/8	5 6	Morgan County	IL	Jeremy Braner	2009	7323
150 1/8	24 3/8 23 4/8	21 1/8	6 6	Luzerne County	PA	Edward Prutzman	1953	7410

433

WHITETAIL DEER (TYPICAL ANTLERS)

Minimum Score 125   Continued

SCORE	LENGTH OF R MAIN BEAM L	INSIDE SPREAD	NUMBER OF R POINTS L	AREA	STATE/ PROVINCE	HUNTER'S NAME	DATE	RANK
150 1/8	23 5/8 23 0/8	16 7/8	5 6	Johnson County	IA	Jim Keefer	1969	7410
150 1/8	22 5/8 23 7/8	16 1/8	5 5	Guthrie County	IA	Bill Barringen	1975	7410
150 1/8	24 2/8 24 5/8	16 7/8	5 5	Freeborn County	MN	Robert Haney	1977	7410
150 1/8	20 6/8 20 2/8	18 1/8	6 6	Richland County	ND	Lyle Fritz	1978	7410
150 1/8	26 0/8 26 2/8	19 0/8	4 5	Butler County	OH	Roger S. Trigg	1979	7410
150 1/8	24 7/8 26 2/8	19 7/8	5 6	Anoka County	MN	Patricia Barry	1980	7410
150 1/8	22 1/8 22 4/8	17 7/8	5 5	Dearborn County	IN	Mike Serio	1982	7410
150 1/8	22 7/8 22 5/8	17 1/8	5 4	Oldham County	KY	Phillip Burba	1985	7410
150 1/8	23 4/8 24 2/8	17 3/8	4 5	Jefferson County	WI	Patrick Thiede	1985	7410
150 1/8	24 4/8 24 3/8	20 1/8	7 8	Lake County	IL	James C. Carlson	1985	7410
150 1/8	23 3/8 22 2/8	17 1/8	6 6	Guthrie County	IA	John D. Hambleton	1989	7410
150 1/8	25 6/8 25 2/8	19 3/8	7 4	Leavenworth County	KS	Travis McGraw	1990	7410
150 1/8	25 7/8 25 1/8	22 3/8	5 4	Perry County	IL	Roger D. Pyron	1990	7410
150 1/8	22 6/8 22 4/8	21 1/8	5 6	Louisa County	IA	Larry H. Thumann, Sr.	1990	7410
150 1/8	23 3/8 22 2/8	18 6/8	7 6	Marion County	IL	R. Andrew Read	1991	7410
150 1/8	26 2/8 24 6/8	20 7/8	4 5	Henry County	VA	Mike Weaver	1992	7410
150 1/8	25 6/8 26 2/8	20 1/8	6 6	Iowa County	WI	Bob Washa	1992	7410
150 1/8	25 3/8 25 2/8	23 0/8	5 5	Stephenson County	IL	George N. Miller	1992	7410
150 1/8	26 7/8 27 2/8	23 5/8	6 6	McCreary County	KY	Eddie Howard	1992	7410
150 1/8	23 3/8 24 1/8	17 1/8	5 5	Sedgwick County	KS	Ronnie Helsel	1992	7410
150 1/8	24 1/8 23 1/8	16 5/8	5 5	Ashland County	WI	Jason Lawver	1992	7410
150 1/8	27 1/8 27 2/8	21 1/8	4 4	Trempealeau County	WI	John Geske	1993	7410
150 1/8	25 3/8 26 6/8	17 5/8	5 6	Clark County	OH	Lafayette Boggs III	1993	7410
150 1/8	23 1/8 22 2/8	19 3/8	5 6	Lincoln County	WI	Marty Sosnovske	1993	7410
150 1/8	23 3/8 23 4/8	15 2/8	7 5	De Witt County	IL	Joe Burzinski	1993	7410
150 1/8	23 4/8 20 1/8	19 3/8	7 6	Brooke County	WV	Russell L. James	1993	7410
150 1/8	26 3/8 25 5/8	18 0/8	4 6	Calhoun County	IL	Jeffery B. Foiles	1994	7410
150 1/8	23 1/8 23 0/8	14 7/8	5 5	Forest County	WI	Donald J. Goffard	1994	7410
150 1/8	22 5/8 23 3/8	16 7/8	5 5	Dimmit County	TX	Bob George	1994	7410
150 1/8	25 6/8 25 4/8	21 6/8	5 4	Schuyler County	IL	John Johnston	1994	7410
150 1/8	23 1/8 23 3/8	16 5/8	5 6	Jackson County	MI	Terry J. Filipek	1994	7410
150 1/8	25 4/8 25 6/8	23 7/8	6 5	McIntosh County	OK	Brad Lanham	1995	7410
150 1/8	22 7/8 22 5/8	19 7/8	5 5	Lee County	IL	Andy McCoy	1995	7410
150 1/8	25 0/8 24 2/8	21 3/8	4 4	Montgomery County	IL	Dale H. Lessman	1995	7410
150 1/8	23 7/8 24 6/8	20 1/8	7 6	Grant County	WI	Wayne A. Willkomm	1995	7410
150 1/8	23 0/8 23 1/8	17 7/8	5 6	Eau Claire County	WI	Dick Kraft	1995	7410
150 1/8	24 7/8 25 5/8	19 7/8	5 4	Montgomery County	IN	Chad M. Neukam	1995	7410
150 1/8	25 7/8 25 6/8	23 1/8	4 6	Carroll County	IL	James C. Carlson	1997	7410
150 1/8	24 4/8 25 7/8	19 7/8	5 5	Walworth County	WI	Jeffery Nelson	1997	7410
150 1/8	24 3/8 25 0/8	18 7/8	6 5	Greene County	OH	Bob Galloway	1997	7410
150 1/8	27 0/8 27 4/8	21 1/8	6 6	Carroll County	IL	Dick V. Lalowski	1998	7410
150 1/8	23 4/8 23 1/8	23 1/8	5 5	Becker County	MN	Craig Rossman	1998	7410
150 1/8	26 6/8 24 0/8	20 3/8	4 6	Mercer County	OH	Hud Baker	1999	7410
150 1/8	26 7/8 25 4/8	22 3/8	4 5	McHenry County	IL	Donald Hanrahan	1999	7410
150 1/8	26 3/8 27 0/8	19 6/8	5 5	Scioto County	OH	Kenneth Davis	1999	7410
150 1/8	22 1/8 22 2/8	16 3/8	6 5	Sherburne County	MN	Eric Abbott	1999	7410
150 1/8	23 4/8 23 5/8	16 2/8	5 5	Charles County	MD	Randall Simmons	2000	7410
150 1/8	25 5/8 27 2/8	20 7/8	5 4	Brown County	WI	Avery Smith	2000	7410
150 1/8	23 4/8 23 2/8	15 5/8	6 5	Kenedy County	TX	Mickey W. Hellickson	2000	7410
150 1/8	23 3/8 23 6/8	15 1/8	6 5	Breckinridge County	KY	Steve McMillen	2001	7410
150 1/8	25 1/8 26 0/8	18 3/8	6 5	Sauk County	WI	Scott Zasada	2001	7410
150 1/8	24 6/8 24 6/8	19 4/8	5 6	Crawford County	WI	Jeff Westra	2001	7410
150 1/8	25 5/8 24 6/8	19 7/8	5 5	Adams County	IA	David L. Keith	2001	7410
150 1/8	23 3/8 22 2/8	16 6/8	6 5	Adams County	IL	Johnny Simmons	2001	7410
150 1/8	21 3/8 21 4/8	19 5/8	5 5	Millarville	ALB	Darrell Wright	2002	7410
150 1/8	21 2/8 22 3/8	15 1/8	6 6	Trempealeau County	WI	John B. Rhude	2002	7410
150 1/8	23 0/8 22 5/8	17 7/8	5 5	Grant County	WI	Mike Richards	2003	7410
150 1/8	25 1/8 25 0/8	19 5/8	5 5	Kenton County	KY	Rick Mounce	2003	7410
150 1/8	23 4/8 22 7/8	17 1/8	5 5	Allamakee County	IA	Howard J. Beeson	2003	7410
*150 1/8	26 2/8 25 4/8	19 1/8	5 5	Dunn County	WI	Tom Hendrickson	2003	7410
150 1/8	25 4/8 24 6/8	22 3/8	4 4	Spokane County	WA	James A. Bertolero	2003	7410
150 1/8	24 1/8 23 2/8	18 7/8	6 6	Henry County	IN	Charles Reese	2003	7410
150 1/8	22 2/8 22 1/8	20 3/8	5 6	Graves County	KY	Casey D. Kuppart	2004	7410
*150 1/8	25 0/8 25 5/8	19 5/8	4 4	Ross County	OH	Randy Johnson	2004	7410
*150 1/8	23 2/8 23 0/8	16 7/8	5 5	Lincoln County	KS	Erik Watts	2004	7410
*150 1/8	25 0/8 25 4/8	17 5/8	6 5	Lafayette County	WI	Duane Eilbes	2005	7410
150 1/8	23 0/8 23 4/8	18 7/8	5 5	Pottawatomie County	KS	David Kuttler	2005	7410
150 1/8	24 3/8 25 2/8	20 5/8	4 5	Lee County	IL	Charles W. Rehor	2005	7410
150 1/8	24 0/8 24 2/8	17 1/8	5 5	Ramsey County	ND	Ernie Olson	2006	7410
150 1/8	23 6/8 23 5/8	19 6/8	5 6	Waupaca County	WI	Peter Bodway	2006	7410
150 1/8	23 4/8 23 0/8	18 5/8	5 6	Waukesha County	WI	Christopher DeQuardo	2006	7410
*150 1/8	25 0/8 23 1/8	18 3/8	7 5	Dubuque County	IA	Frank Fincel	2006	7410
150 1/8	23 4/8 22 4/8	18 5/8	5 5	La Crosse County	WI	Brad Lueck	2007	7410
*150 1/8	23 4/8 24 1/8	17 5/8	4 4	Plymouth County	IA	Wayne R. Nesje	2007	7410
150 1/8	26 6/8 26 3/8	18 5/8	4 4	Houston County	MN	Andy Beissel	2007	7410
150 1/8	24 5/8 23 6/8	19 2/8	5 6	Montgomery County	IN	John P. Beaman	2007	7410
150 1/8	24 4/8 23 3/8	18 3/8	6 7	Jackson County	WI	Jeff Zwiefelhofer	2007	7410
*150 1/8	22 2/8 22 7/8	16 1/8	8 9	Webster County	KY	Bradley A. Curry	2007	7410
*150 1/8	22 6/8 23 0/8	21 7/8	5 5	Davis County	IA	Larry D. Sylvester	2007	7410
150 1/8	22 6/8 23 4/8	18 7/8	4 4	Clay County	SD	Jeffrey J. Olson	2007	7410
*150 1/8	23 3/8 23 0/8	17 7/8	6 8	Trempealeau County	WI	Chris J. Hood	2008	7410
150 1/8	23 6/8 23 7/8	19 3/8	5 6	Coleman County	TX	Don Albrecht	2008	7410
150 1/8	21 1/8 22 5/8	14 6/8	5 6	Brown County	IL	Ron Wahl	2008	7410
150 1/8	24 1/8 24 1/8	16 7/8	5 6	Coshocton County	OH	Shane Donley	2008	7410
*150 1/8	25 4/8 22 3/8	15 6/8	6 7	Washington County	PA	Danny R. Kisner	2008	7410
150 1/8	23 4/8 23 3/8	16 5/8	6 5	Republic County	KS	Eddie Gore	2008	7410
*150 1/8	22 2/8 24 1/8	16 6/8	7 5	Jackson County	KY	Tony A. Mahaffey	2008	7410
150 1/8	22 6/8 24 0/8	16 2/8	5 6	Bollinger County	MO	Brandon Lynch	2009	7410
150 1/8	25 7/8 26 3/8	16 5/8	8 6	Geauga County	OH	David Fellenstein	2009	7410
*150 1/8	23 2/8 23 0/8	20 1/8	5 6	Dubuque County	IA	Martin Kearney	2009	7410
150 1/8	22 1/8 22 3/8	18 3/8	5 6	Brown County	SD	Todd Severson	2009	7410
150 1/8	22 1/8 22 3/8	13 5/8	5 6	Southampton County	VA	Joseph Bunn	2009	7410
*150 1/8	22 3/8 21 5/8	17 7/8	5 5	Jo Daviess County	IL	Richard Phillips	2009	7410
150 1/8	20 6/8 22 2/8	15 1/8	6 6	Pope County	IL	Carles Sutton	2009	7410
150 0/8	25 3/8 24 3/8	15 6/8	5 6	Adams County	WI	Daniel Becker	1957	7505

434

WHITETAIL DEER (TYPICAL ANTLERS)

Minimum Score 125 — Continued

SCORE	LENGTH OF R MAIN BEAM L	INSIDE SPREAD	NUMBER OF R POINTS L	AREA	STATE/PROVINCE	HUNTER'S NAME	DATE	RANK
150 0/8	26 6/8 27 1/8	17 6/8	5 4	Benton County	IA	Robert L. Walker	1961	7505
150 0/8	26 4/8 26 4/8	18 4/8	5 5	Shelby County	IA	Einar Leistad	1970	7505
150 0/8	22 0/8 23 2/8	17 2/8	5 6	Ozaukee County	WI	Rand Krueger	1980	7505
150 0/8	24 5/8 23 0/8	17 4/8	5 5	Kosciusko County	IN	Gil Reed	1981	7505
150 0/8	22 1/8 22 0/8	17 2/8	5 5	Lake County	IL	Daniel M. Bott	1983	7505
150 0/8	22 3/8 22 4/8	17 1/8	6 6	Carroll County	AR	Larry Gasaway	1984	7505
150 0/8	24 4/8 24 1/8	18 1/8	4 6	Penobscot County	ME	Kris T. Saunders	1985	7505
150 0/8	21 0/8 21 4/8	15 7/8	4 5	Wabash County	IL	Paul Benham	1985	7505
150 0/8	22 5/8 23 4/8	16 5/8	5 7	Tazewell County	IL	William H. Ray	1985	7505
150 0/8	25 4/8 24 7/8	17 5/8	6 6	Livingston County	IL	James B. Smith	1985	7505
150 0/8	23 7/8 23 3/8	20 0/8	5 5	White County	IL	Eric D. Devare	1985	7505
150 0/8	23 6/8 24 2/8	17 0/8	5 5	Chase County	KS	Dan McClure	1985	7505
150 0/8	22 2/8 21 4/8	16 4/8	5 6	Berkshire County	MA	Alan Ziegler	1986	7505
150 0/8	25 1/8 25 3/8	20 0/8	4 4	Champaign County	OH	Douglas L. Hudson	1987	7505
150 0/8	24 2/8 23 3/8	19 2/8	5 5	Ashtabula County	OH	Mike Morehouse	1988	7505
150 0/8	25 6/8 26 2/8	18 4/8	5 5	Coles County	IL	Ron Osborne	1988	7505
150 0/8	24 0/8 23 6/8	18 1/8	5 7	Lake County	IL	James D. Maricle	1989	7505
150 0/8	22 3/8 22 5/8	15 0/8	6 6	Dane County	WI	Rick Krause	1990	7505
150 0/8	23 5/8 23 0/8	18 2/8	5 5	Cedar County	IA	George R. Briggs	1990	7505
150 0/8	24 4/8 25 2/8	20 2/8	6 6	Inglewood	ONT	Jack Leggo	1990	7505
150 0/8	23 4/8 23 3/8	15 4/8	5 5	Allamakee County	IA	Rodney Smed	1991	7505
150 0/8	24 6/8 24 4/8	19 0/8	4 4	Mercer County	NJ	Scott Lysenko	1991	7505
150 0/8	25 6/8 26 2/8	20 0/8	4 4	Todd County	MN	Brad G. Lorentz	1991	7505
150 0/8	24 6/8 25 7/8	20 6/8	6 6	Buffalo County	WI	John W. Zahrte	1991	7505
150 0/8	26 0/8 26 2/8	17 2/8	4 4	Portage County	WI	Robert J. Karnowski	1992	7505
150 0/8	24 6/8 24 4/8	16 6/8	5 5	Fremont County	IA	Dave Holt	1992	7505
150 0/8	24 4/8 24 3/8	18 6/8	5 5	Brown County	IL	Kevin Weeks	1992	7505
150 0/8	22 1/8 23 5/8	19 4/8	5 5	Tuscarawas County	OH	Josh Deubner	1993	7505
150 0/8	25 7/8 24 4/8	21 2/8	5 4	Jo Daviess County	IL	Jeff Parks	1993	7505
150 0/8	24 4/8 24 0/8	18 4/8	5 6	Shawano County	WI	Brian M. Buckarma	1993	7505
150 0/8	24 5/8 24 7/8	19 1/8	7 5	Crawford County	KS	Ron Mason	1993	7505
150 0/8	22 2/8 21 4/8	17 4/8	5 5	Goodhue County	MN	Steve Puppe	1994	7505
150 0/8	25 3/8 26 2/8	17 0/8	6 6	Dodge County	WI	Larry Spittel	1994	7505
150 0/8	23 4/8 23 0/8	18 6/8	5 5	Wayne County	MI	Gregory Kuhn	1994	7505
150 0/8	23 6/8 24 3/8	15 0/8	5 5	St. Marys County	MD	Shawn Day	1995	7505
150 0/8	22 0/8 21 7/8	17 4/8	7 8	Kent County	MI	Jason Leslie Eaton	1995	7505
150 0/8	24 0/8 22 7/8	15 7/8	5 6	Harrison County	IA	Bob Siech	1995	7505
150 0/8	23 3/8 22 1/8	20 4/8	5 5	Black Hawk County	IA	Bill Glenny	1996	7505
150 0/8	22 6/8 23 1/8	18 6/8	5 5	Des Moines County	IA	Tim Wallin	1996	7505
150 0/8	24 2/8 24 3/8	22 0/8	5 5	Cook County	IL	F. Dan Dinelli	1997	7505
150 0/8	21 4/8 21 3/8	19 6/8	6 6	Saginaw County	MI	William R. Jerome	1997	7505
150 0/8	24 3/8 24 0/8	17 4/8	4 5	Dane County	WI	Mike Grosse	1997	7505
150 0/8	23 6/8 23 7/8	15 0/8	5 6	Holt County	MO	Juston W. Carr	1997	7505
150 0/8	23 7/8 24 6/8	16 4/8	5 5	Morgan County	IN	Mike G. Graber	1997	7505
150 0/8	22 4/8 21 5/8	19 0/8	5 5	Refugio County	TX	William D. Baker	1997	7505
150 0/8	24 1/8 24 4/8	20 6/8	4 4	Buffalo County	WI	Dennis Palmer	1997	7505
150 0/8	24 2/8 24 1/8	19 2/8	5 5	Comanche County	OK	Scott Lovell	1998	7505
150 0/8	26 4/8 26 6/8	19 3/8	5 5	Buffalo County	WI	Ron Brenner	1998	7505
150 0/8	24 6/8 24 3/8	17 6/8	4 5	Scott County	IA	Milo Fred Brown, Jr.	1998	7505
150 0/8	23 2/8 22 6/8	17 6/8	5 5	Webster County	IA	Nicholas Brantner	1998	7505
150 0/8	22 7/8 22 7/8	17 4/8	5 5	Douglas County	WI	Ron Aho	1998	7505
150 0/8	23 6/8 23 7/8	18 6/8	4 4	Rock Island County	IL	Bob Nash	1999	7505
150 0/8	27 1/8 26 7/8	24 6/8	4 4	Caledon East	ONT	Henry Quittard	1999	7505
150 0/8	23 4/8 23 6/8	19 2/8	7 7	Knox County	OH	Mike Patterson	1999	7505
*150 0/8	23 5/8 23 3/8	17 4/8	5 5	Wilcox County	GA	Marvin Smith	1999	7505
150 0/8	23 7/8 24 2/8	16 1/8	6 6	Meadow Lake	SAS	Jonathan Paul	2000	7505
150 0/8	24 2/8 24 6/8	17 7/8	6 6	Iron County	WI	Butch Syring	2000	7505
150 0/8	25 2/8 25 0/8	20 2/8	6 7	Des Moines County	IA	Chad W. Clark	2000	7505
150 0/8	25 1/8 24 7/8	19 3/8	6 6	Pottawatomie County	KS	Tom L. Nihart	2000	7505
150 0/8	23 4/8 21 4/8	19 6/8	5 5	Pike County	IN	Victor A. Jennings	2000	7505
150 0/8	24 6/8 24 3/8	16 4/8	6 6	Jefferson County	OH	William S. LaRue	2000	7505
150 0/8	23 7/8 24 2/8	16 2/8	5 5	Knox County	OH	Chad Ford	2000	7505
150 0/8	21 7/8 23 3/8	14 0/8	5 5	Taylor County	KY	Jeff Valentine	2001	7505
150 0/8	21 5/8 21 7/8	15 4/8	5 5	Meigs County	OH	Bill Wyan	2001	7505
150 0/8	26 2/8 25 4/8	19 2/8	6 5	Green County	WI	Shawn O'Neill	2002	7505
150 0/8	26 2/8 28 1/8	19 3/8	4 6	Miami County	OH	David Tarter	2002	7505
150 0/8	24 0/8 25 1/8	17 4/8	7 6	Peoria County	IL	Terry Setterlund	2002	7505
150 0/8	26 2/8 25 0/8	22 2/8	4 5	Henderson County	IL	Angelo Soyangco	2002	7505
150 0/8	27 0/8 27 3/8	18 5/8	5 5	Grafton County	NH	Hans Ingemundsen	2003	7505
150 0/8	25 0/8 23 7/8	17 2/8	6 5	Shawano County	WI	David J. Haas	2003	7505
150 0/8	23 6/8 23 3/8	18 6/8	5 5	Vernon County	WI	Jeff Prucha	2003	7505
150 0/8	26 1/8 23 4/8	19 0/8	6 8	Geauga County	OH	Jon Newcomb	2003	7505
150 0/8	21 4/8 21 0/8	15 1/8	6 5	Guthrie County	IA	Rob Bish	2003	7505
150 0/8	23 0/8 24 2/8	19 0/8	6 5	Montgomery County	PA	Dave Stercula	2004	7505
150 0/8	24 7/8 24 5/8	18 6/8	5 5	Dane County	WI	Tom Graff	2004	7505
150 0/8	21 4/8 21 6/8	17 4/8	5 6	Calhoun County	IL	Wayne Kiel	2004	7505
*150 0/8	25 0/8 24 4/8	19 6/8	5 5	Waushara County	WI	Tyler Jazdzewski	2005	7505
*150 0/8	24 4/8 24 1/8	16 6/8	6 5	Allamakee County	IA	Terry Johnson	2005	7505
150 0/8	23 1/8 23 5/8	17 4/8	7 5	Montgomery County	IL	Jeff Burdick	2005	7505
150 0/8	25 6/8 25 0/8	19 5/8	5 5	Ogle County	IL	Todd Hasara	2005	7505
150 0/8	25 5/8 24 3/8	20 1/8	5 6	Erie County	NY	Jarred Hudson	2005	7505
*150 0/8	26 5/8 26 6/8	16 5/8	5 5	Howard County	IA	Lynn Scheidel	2005	7505
150 0/8	23 5/8 25 3/8	16 7/8	7 5	Jennings County	IN	Tony L. Beatty	2006	7505
150 0/8	24 3/8 24 2/8	21 2/8	5 5	Green Lake County	WI	Casey Schwandt	2006	7505
*150 0/8	23 4/8 23 4/8	20 4/8	5 5	Phillips County	AR	Joey Hopper	2006	7505
*150 0/8	24 6/8 25 3/8	19 0/8	5 5	Crawford County	OH	Chad A. Liming	2007	7505
150 0/8	23 1/8 23 3/8	16 5/8	8 7	Macoupin County	IL	Jack Behnke	2007	7505
*150 0/8	25 5/8 25 2/8	19 2/8	5 5	Washburn County	WI	Steven Des Jardins	2007	7505
150 0/8	25 6/8 23 0/8	17 6/8	6 6	Atchison County	MO	Robert Michniak	2007	7505
150 0/8	23 6/8 22 6/8	19 3/8	5 6	Doniphan County	KS	Hayes Petteway	2007	7505
*150 0/8	26 0/8 26 1/8	18 4/8	5 5	Knox County	OH	J. Chris Lepley	2007	7505
*150 0/8	22 6/8 23 3/8	17 0/8	6 7	Sheboygan County	WI	Terry Knier	2007	7505
150 0/8	24 6/8 25 2/8	22 0/8	5 5	Woodbury County	IA	Calvin Armstrong	2007	7505
150 0/8	22 4/8 20 6/8	19 0/8	5 5	Russell County	KS	Adam L. Cregger	2007	7505
150 0/8	23 1/8 23 0/8	17 6/8	5 5	Webb County	TX	Norman E. Speer	2007	7505

435

WHITETAIL DEER (TYPICAL ANTLERS)

Minimum Score 125 — Continued

SCORE	LENGTH OF R MAIN BEAM L	INSIDE SPREAD	NUMBER OF R POINTS L		AREA	STATE/PROVINCE	HUNTER'S NAME	DATE	RANK
150 0/8	26 5/8 25 7/8	19 5/8	6	6	Christian County	KY	Jason Ross	2008	7505
150 0/8	24 7/8 25 0/8	22 2/8	4	6	Pierce County	WI	Lance J. Olson	2008	7505
150 0/8	26 6/8 26 4/8	17 5/8	5	6	Henderson County	KY	Chip Crafton	2008	7505
150 0/8	24 6/8 23 7/8	21 0/8	5	5	Carver County	MN	David Brueggemeier	2008	7505
150 0/8	24 2/8 24 5/8	17 5/8	7	7	Jackson County	OH	Kenneth Mike Frash	2009	7505
150 0/8	23 2/8 22 5/8	21 0/8	5	7	Spencer County	IN	William F. Cody II	2009	7505
150 0/8	25 1/8 25 1/8	19 2/8	6	6	Allegany County	NY	William Pearce, Jr.	2009	7505
150 0/8	26 1/8 26 2/8	20 4/8	5	5	Tioga County	PA	Gerald W. Fusner, Jr.	2009	7505
150 0/8	24 4/8 24 6/8	17 0/8	5	7	Rock Island County	IL	Craig Black	2009	7505
150 0/8	25 3/8 25 3/8	18 6/8	4	4	Pope County	IL	Bobby L. Huckaby	2009	7505
149 7/8	26 0/8 25 6/8	20 3/8	4	4	Pulaski County	VA	Ray S. Carter	1962	7611
149 7/8	21 6/8 21 1/8	17 3/8	5	5	Adams County	IL	Lyndall W. Heyen	1967	7611
149 7/8	24 6/8 24 1/8	20 1/8	6	6	Will County	IL	Jerry Yost	1978	7611
149 7/8	23 5/8 23 5/8	17 1/8	5	5	Scott County	KY	Mike Northcut	1980	7611
149 7/8	25 1/8 24 1/8	18 7/8	6	6	Dauphin County	PA	Larry D. Wiestling	1983	7611
149 7/8	25 0/8 25 0/8	17 5/8	5	5	Pittsburg County	OK	Doug Larimer	1985	7611
149 7/8	22 0/8 22 1/8	17 0/8	7	6	Cumberland County	NJ	Bob Eisele	1986	7611
149 7/8	24 6/8 25 4/8	16 4/8	6	6	Madison County	IL	Frank W. Gavillet	1986	7611
149 7/8	24 7/8 24 4/8	17 7/8	6	5	Allegheny County	PA	George M. Conway	1987	7611
149 7/8	25 0/8 24 2/8	19 6/8	6	4	Nicollet County	MN	Neil Treml	1987	7611
149 7/8	25 1/8 24 3/8	20 7/8	5	4	Meade County	KS	Keith Whitney	1987	7611
149 7/8	23 0/8 23 5/8	17 3/8	6	5	Jackson County	MO	Ty Easley	1988	7611
149 7/8	24 4/8 24 1/8	16 4/8	6	6	Arenac County	MI	Jim Gall	1989	7611
149 7/8	23 3/8 23 2/8	18 4/8	5	6	Kenosha County	WI	Thomas C. Zeihen	1989	7611
149 7/8	26 0/8 26 3/8	21 7/8	4	6	Dodge County	WI	Steve Moritz	1991	7611
149 7/8	23 1/8 24 2/8	17 6/8	5	5	Graham County	KS	Jim Kerbaugh	1991	7611
149 7/8	25 4/8 26 1/8	16 5/8	5	5	Edgar County	IL	Dale Good	1992	7611
149 7/8	22 5/8 23 2/8	17 4/8	5	6	De Witt County	IL	Charlie DeBose	1992	7611
149 7/8	26 1/8 27 0/8	19 5/8	6	7	Washington County	KS	Ronald Montague	1993	7611
149 7/8	23 2/8 23 6/8	18 3/8	5	5	Boone County	MO	Bruce Richardson	1994	7611
149 7/8	26 5/8 26 1/8	18 4/8	5	5	Allegany County	NY	Christopher Enders	1994	7611
149 7/8	24 3/8 24 3/8	23 3/8	6	4	Clarke County	IA	David C. Curnes	1994	7611
149 7/8	26 0/8 25 0/8	18 3/8	5	8	Allegan County	MI	David L. Delpiere	1995	7611
149 7/8	27 0/8 26 4/8	23 3/8	5	5	Greene County	OH	Joe Wright	1995	7611
149 7/8	24 2/8 24 7/8	21 1/8	5	5	Anderson County	KS	Dennis L. Dahlke	1995	7611
149 7/8	24 4/8 24 0/8	17 4/8	6	5	Norman County	MN	Les Krogstad	1996	7611
149 7/8	22 0/8 21 4/8	19 6/8	5	6	Sawyer County	WI	Timothy J. Drover	1996	7611
149 7/8	25 2/8 25 4/8	19 1/8	5	5	Ross County	OH	Alan Parsons	1996	7611
149 7/8	25 5/8 25 3/8	20 5/8	5	5	Hillsdale County	MI	Bruce J. Pearson	1997	7611
149 7/8	25 0/8 25 4/8	21 7/8	5	4	Warren County	IA	Jacob Schuler	1997	7611
149 7/8	23 3/8 23 4/8	17 3/8	7	6	Livingston County	NY	Mark T. Rumfola	1998	7611
149 7/8	25 1/8 24 4/8	23 1/8	6	6	Hardin County	IA	Jeff Pabst	1998	7611
149 7/8	24 2/8 24 0/8	19 5/8	4	4	Macoupin County	IL	Bill Langheim	1998	7611
149 7/8	25 6/8 23 3/8	19 1/8	5	6	Randolph County	IL	Leo Dufrenne, Jr.	1998	7611
149 7/8	25 1/8 25 2/8	15 6/8	7	5	Oconto County	WI	Leslie "Butch" Vorpah	1999	7611
149 7/8	24 3/8 24 1/8	19 2/8	8	5	Lenawee County	MI	Rocky H. Frazier	1999	7611
149 7/8	22 5/8 22 3/8	18 3/8	6	6	Door County	WI	Wayne Lautenbach	1999	7611
149 7/8	26 7/8 25 5/8	17 7/8	4	5	St. Croix County	WI	Alex Williams	2000	7611
149 7/8	22 3/8 23 0/8	19 3/8	5	5	Dane County	WI	Dave Dilley	2000	7611
149 7/8	21 5/8 20 6/8	14 3/8	5	5	Buchanan County	VA	Curtis Lester	2000	7611
149 7/8	23 6/8 23 5/8	18 1/8	8	5	Monmouth County	NJ	Joseph J. Meglio	2001	7611
149 7/8	24 3/8 23 4/8	19 7/8	5	7	Coshocton County	OH	Gary Parrigan	2001	7611
149 7/8	25 3/8 25 3/8	17 5/8	5	6	Pike County	IL	Brian D. Russell	2001	7611
149 7/8	24 5/8 24 4/8	17 5/8	7	5	Jersey County	IL	David Schneider	2001	7611
149 7/8	24 5/8 24 2/8	17 5/8	4	4	Tipton County	IN	Don Cole	2001	7611
149 7/8	25 1/8 24 0/8	18 7/8	5	7	Richardson County	NE	Jerry N. Roever	2001	7611
149 7/8	22 2/8 22 2/8	15 3/8	5	5	Victoria County	TX	Ronald Rychetsky	2002	7611
149 7/8	24 5/8 24 3/8	19 2/8	6	8	Dane County	WI	David W. Platt	2002	7611
149 7/8	22 3/8 22 3/8	18 5/8	5	5	Champaign County	OH	Roger R. Donohoe	2002	7611
149 7/8	23 1/8 23 6/8	20 1/8	5	7	Posey County	IN	Brian G. Merkley	2002	7611
149 7/8	23 3/8 21 7/8	19 3/8	5	5	Marquette County	WI	Randy Strupp	2002	7611
149 7/8	23 6/8 24 0/8	17 4/8	6	9	Sangamon County	IL	Bob Lanser	2003	7611
149 7/8	24 2/8 23 6/8	16 7/8	5	5	Des Moines County	IA	Randy Templeton	2003	7611
149 7/8	25 7/8 25 3/8	18 1/8	4	4	Clinton County	OH	Greg Klink, Jr.	2004	7611
149 7/8	24 3/8 23 7/8	16 2/8	5	7	Bremer County	IA	Gregg Lamphier	2004	7611
*149 7/8	22 5/8 21 7/8	16 1/8	5	5	Jackson County	IA	Steve Williams	2004	7611
*149 7/8	27 0/8 26 0/8	16 7/8	7	5	Mahaska County	IA	Mike Shrader	2004	7611
149 7/8	23 2/8 22 5/8	16 3/8	5	5	Ripley County	MO	Eric Ormsby	2004	7611
149 7/8	26 3/8 24 1/8	18 3/8	6	6	Van Buren County	IA	Doug Guise	2004	7611
149 7/8	23 1/8 22 6/8	18 5/8	6	5	Maverick County	TX	H. Mike Palmer	2005	7611
149 7/8	25 4/8 24 3/8	20 7/8	5	5	Belair	MAN	Bruce J. Gray	2005	7611
*149 7/8	23 6/8 23 4/8	15 7/8	5	5	Clay County	MO	Ben Von Bargen	2005	7611
149 7/8	23 6/8 23 4/8	17 1/8	5	5	Webb County	TX	Randi Hardesty	2005	7611
149 7/8	25 1/8 25 1/8	19 4/8	5	6	Graham County	KS	Mick Cheshire	2005	7611
149 7/8	23 5/8 24 4/8	19 3/8	6	5	Allegheny County	PA	Raymond W. Powell	2005	7611
149 7/8	23 5/8 23 3/8	18 3/8	6	5	Will County	IL	Thomas M. Stepanek	2005	7611
149 7/8	25 1/8 24 0/8	19 1/8	6	5	Buffalo County	WI	Jeff Wendorf	2005	7611
149 7/8	22 1/8 22 3/8	20 5/8	6	5	Clark County	IL	Samuel Cade	2005	7611
149 7/8	24 2/8 25 2/8	16 2/8	6	6	Linn County	IA	Larry Wiley	2005	7611
*149 7/8	23 1/8 23 1/8	16 1/8	5	4	Petroleum County	MT	Eric Jolma	2006	7611
149 7/8	24 5/8 24 6/8	21 0/8	5	5	Van Buren County	MI	Jeff R. Cerven	2006	7611
*149 7/8	25 0/8 26 3/8	18 5/8	5	5	Ashland County	OH	Adam W. Hiller	2006	7611
149 7/8	22 0/8 22 0/8	18 5/8	5	5	Towner County	ND	Jordan Klein	2006	7611
*149 7/8	24 7/8 24 1/8	17 7/8	6	11	Jackson County	SD	Kyle P. Battell	2007	7611
149 7/8	23 7/8 24 2/8	17 0/8	6	5	DeKalb County	IL	Josef K. Rud	2007	7611
*149 7/8	26 6/8 26 6/8	17 4/8	5	7	Sharp County	AR	Witt Stephens, Jr.	2007	7611
149 7/8	24 0/8 23 7/8	16 1/8	6	5	Marshall County	IA	Garry Brandenburg	2007	7611
149 7/8	25 4/8 26 4/8	19 7/8	4	4	Warren County	MS	Justin Boler	2008	7611
*149 7/8	25 2/8 24 3/8	17 7/8	5	6	Monroe County	WI	Greg Sondreal	2008	7611
*149 7/8	24 0/8 23 6/8	18 3/8	5	5	Warren County	IA	Mark E. Carpenter	2008	7611
*149 7/8	24 6/8 25 4/8	23 3/8	4	4	Columbiana County	OH	Kenneth Henry	2009	7611
149 7/8	24 0/8 23 0/8	20 1/8	6	5	Wilbarger County	TX	Si Schur	2009	7611
149 7/8	23 7/8 24 1/8	18 2/8	5	6	Fort Macleod	ALB	Dan Neels	2009	7611
149 7/8	23 4/8 22 1/8	18 2/8	6	6	Winnebago County	WI	Ted Luehring	2009	7611
149 7/8	24 2/8 25 1/8	18 4/8	6	5	Kiowa County	CO	Kevin Railsback	2009	7611

436

WHITETAIL DEER (TYPICAL ANTLERS)

Minimum Score 125   Continued

SCORE	LENGTH OF R MAIN BEAM L	INSIDE SPREAD	NUMBER OF R POINTS L	AREA	STATE/ PROVINCE	HUNTER'S NAME	DATE	RANK
149 7/8	22 4/8 22 2/8	17 7/8	4 5	Harper County	KS	Jason M. Bond	2009	7611
149 7/8	22 6/8 23 2/8	19 6/8	5 6	Sanford	MAN	Ed Parker	2009	7611
149 6/8	23 4/8 23 5/8	17 1/8	7 6	Gull Lake	SAS	Keith Roney	1978	7698
149 6/8	23 6/8 24 7/8	21 6/8	4 4	Branch County	MI	Howard W. Loehr	1983	7698
149 6/8	25 1/8 26 0/8	20 6/8	4 5	Piatt County	IL	Marvin R. Salmon	1983	7698
149 6/8	25 0/8 24 5/8	17 4/8	5 5	La Salle County	IL	Gary Tabor	1984	7698
149 6/8	26 1/8 25 7/8	21 5/8	6 6	Anderson County	TN	Daniel W. Chase	1985	7698
149 6/8	25 6/8 23 3/8	18 1/8	6 6	Douglas County	KS	Samuel J. Tunget	1985	7698
149 6/8	23 7/8 23 2/8	19 2/8	5 7	Hocking County	OH	John E Furderer	1987	7698
149 6/8	24 3/8 25 2/8	18 3/8	5 6	Kane County	IL	Steven J. Kamp	1988	7698
149 6/8	25 6/8 24 7/8	19 4/8	6 7	Adams County	OH	Richard O. Ramsey	1990	7698
149 6/8	21 5/8 21 7/8	18 5/8	5 8	Sangamon County	IL	Matthew W. Cloyd	1990	7698
149 6/8	23 4/8 23 7/8	20 4/8	6 5	Waukesha County	WI	Mike Scaff	1991	7698
149 6/8	24 1/8 23 5/8	20 0/8	5 5	Macoupin County	IL	James Olroyd	1992	7698
149 6/8	23 4/8 24 3/8	17 5/8	6 5	Upson County	GA	Tony O. Chapman	1992	7698
149 6/8	24 4/8 24 7/8	16 7/8	5 5	Iron County	MO	Teresa L. Campbell	1992	7698
149 6/8	24 0/8 24 2/8	18 4/8	6 7	Yuma County	CO	Kevin Shively	1993	7698
149 6/8	23 2/8 22 0/8	19 1/8	6 5	Millarville	ALB	Joel Bickler	1993	7698
149 6/8	24 3/8 24 1/8	21 6/8	5 4	Pike County	MO	Cordell Queathem, Jr.	1993	7698
149 6/8	23 1/8 22 3/8	19 1/8	6 6	Crawford County	PA	Richard W. Marks	1994	7698
149 6/8	24 0/8 22 6/8	17 4/8	6 5	Walworth County	WI	Ernie Meinen	1995	7698
149 6/8	22 6/8 22 6/8	16 2/8	8 6	Licking County	OH	Tom Lott	1995	7698
149 6/8	24 2/8 24 7/8	17 0/8	7 5	Sawyer County	WI	Ed Schimke	1995	7698
149 6/8	23 5/8 24 6/8	15 4/8	7 7	Vinton County	OH	Mark Meadows	1995	7698
149 6/8	23 4/8 23 4/8	16 6/8	5 5	La Salle County	IL	Michael Elbrecht	1995	7698
149 6/8	25 2/8 25 3/8	19 0/8	6 5	McHenry County	IL	Joe Florent	1995	7698
149 6/8	25 3/8 25 4/8	19 6/8	4 4	McLean County	IL	Dale McKinnerney	1995	7698
149 6/8	26 5/8 27 0/8	19 0/8	5 4	Boone County	NE	Jeff Beckwith	1997	7698
149 6/8	25 1/8 24 5/8	16 0/8	5 5	Athens County	OH	Michael A. Rex	1997	7698
149 6/8	27 3/8 26 7/8	19 0/8	4 4	Livingston County	IL	Richard D. Green	1997	7698
149 6/8	26 2/8 27 6/8	21 4/8	5 6	Logan County	WV	James D. Collins II	1997	7698
149 6/8	25 4/8 25 2/8	19 6/8	5 8	Ozaukee County	WI	Joseph V. Spata	1997	7698
149 6/8	24 1/8 25 1/8	21 6/8	6 4	Cerro Gordo County	IA	Corey Martin	1997	7698
149 6/8	22 6/8 24 0/8	18 4/8	5 5	Howard County	MD	Robert W. Evans, Jr.	1998	7698
149 6/8	22 7/8 23 1/8	18 5/8	6 6	Stephenson County	IL	Greg Wedig	1998	7698
149 6/8	25 0/8 24 2/8	18 4/8	6 5	Clark County	IL	Jeremy W. Jobst	1998	7698
149 6/8	22 0/8 22 4/8	16 6/8	6 5	Ashland County	WI	Carl Hawkinson	1999	7698
149 6/8	22 0/8 22 5/8	21 2/8	5 5	Sussex County	DE	David A. Ritter	1999	7698
149 6/8	25 6/8 26 2/8	21 2/8	6 6	Lumpkin County	GA	Jack N. Jones	2000	7698
149 6/8	26 3/8 25 1/8	19 0/8	5 5	Essex County	MA	Bruce Palmacci	2000	7698
149 6/8	24 4/8 24 6/8	19 6/8	4 5	Louisa County	IA	Mike Lange	2000	7698
149 6/8	22 7/8 24 2/8	19 0/8	5 5	Reno County	KS	Brian L. Wickey	2000	7698
149 6/8	24 4/8 24 0/8	16 6/8	5 6	Warren County	IA	Rich Onder	2000	7698
149 6/8	28 6/8 28 7/8	21 4/8	4 4	Washington County	OH	Justin Hoon	2000	7698
149 6/8	26 2/8 24 7/8	16 0/8	6 5	Marquette County	WI	Brian L. Elger	2001	7698
149 6/8	24 2/8 23 5/8	19 4/8	5 4	Bremer County	IA	David L. MacDonald	2001	7698
149 6/8	26 6/8 26 7/8	20 2/8	4 4	Jackson County	MO	Scott Liebenguth	2001	7698
149 6/8	24 1/8 24 2/8	17 0/8	5 5	Clinton County	IA	Charles L. Gifford	2001	7698
149 6/8	24 6/8 24 5/8	18 6/8	5 5	Trempealeau County	WI	Bob McDonah	2002	7698
149 6/8	25 0/8 26 0/8	17 0/8	4 4	Calhoun County	IL	Matt Bichsel	2002	7698
149 6/8	25 6/8 25 0/8	17 2/8	4 4	Taylor County	IA	Todd Tobin	2002	7698
149 6/8	23 2/8 23 5/8	18 2/8	6 5	Shelby County	IL	David Walbright	2002	7698
149 6/8	23 4/8 22 4/8	17 4/8	6 6	Dubuque County	IA	Daniel Houselog	2002	7698
149 6/8	24 0/8 22 1/8	19 0/8	5 5	Oneida County	WI	Shawn Swiontek	2003	7698
149 6/8	21 1/8 20 5/8	19 2/8	5 5	Genesee County	MI	Michael P. Treiger	2003	7698
149 6/8	22 6/8 21 6/8	18 3/8	6 6	Linn County	IA	Brad Erger	2003	7698
149 6/8	24 4/8 25 4/8	19 0/8	7 7	Crawford County	IL	Michael W. Elliott	2003	7698
149 6/8	26 5/8 27 0/8	17 3/8	5 5	Anderson County	KS	Steve Zupon	2003	7698
149 6/8	22 5/8 22 5/8	17 7/8	6 5	Clark County	WI	Randy Sebesta	2004	7698
149 6/8	25 4/8 25 3/8	18 4/8	5 6	Clark County	WI	Josh Meissner	2004	7698
*149 6/8	23 7/8 24 4/8	18 4/8	5 7	Clark County	KS	Fred Eichler	2004	7698
149 6/8	26 0/8 25 6/8	17 6/8	5 6	Madison County	IL	Christopher Lind	2004	7698
*149 6/8	23 7/8 23 6/8	16 2/8	4 5	Appanoose County	IA	Bryan Cassady	2004	7698
149 6/8	25 2/8 25 6/8	19 0/8	4 4	Morrow County	OH	Jeff Weisner	2004	7698
149 6/8	23 0/8 22 3/8	18 6/8	5 5	Dimmit County	TX	Rick Knape	2005	7698
149 6/8	24 5/8 24 6/8	15 7/8	5 6	Harrison County	KY	Kevin Poe	2005	7698
*149 6/8	21 7/8 20 1/8	18 7/8	5 5	Noble County	IN	Jeremy Robertson	2005	7698
149 6/8	25 6/8 24 4/8	18 2/8	5 5	Oakland County	MI	Paul Caster	2006	7698
*149 6/8	24 3/8 24 5/8	17 4/8	5 5	Trempealeau County	WI	Eric R. Boberg	2006	7698
*149 6/8	25 1/8 26 1/8	19 6/8	5 5	Coshocton County	OH	Chris Coverdale	2006	7698
149 6/8	23 2/8 21 6/8	16 1/8	7 7	Van Buren County	MI	Todd J. Tapper	2006	7698
149 6/8	24 2/8 23 7/8	22 6/8	6 4	O'Brien County	IA	Daryl Tjaden	2006	7698
149 6/8	24 6/8 25 3/8	21 5/8	5 6	Westchester County	NY	Gus Congemi	2006	7698
149 6/8	24 0/8 24 1/8	19 6/8	5 5	Botetourt County	VA	Thomas Dwayne Martin	2007	7698
*149 6/8	22 4/8 21 7/8	17 6/8	6 5	Stoddard County	MO	Rayvan Patterson	2007	7698
149 6/8	22 4/8 23 2/8	17 6/8	4 4	Fulton County	GA	Jamie Weaver	2007	7698
149 6/8	27 4/8 26 2/8	17 7/8	5 6	Olmsted County	MN	Kerry Olson	2008	7698
149 6/8	25 0/8 24 4/8	18 0/8	5 5	Dane County	WI	Chuck Guastella	2008	7698
*149 6/8	23 4/8 22 4/8	22 0/8	6 5	McPherson County	KS	Nelson S. Burnette	2008	7698
*149 6/8	23 5/8 23 6/8	18 4/8	5 5	Lawrence County	IN	Jeremy W. Smith	2008	7698
149 6/8	22 1/8 22 5/8	18 1/8	6 5	Berks County	PA	Aaron B. Ogden	2009	7698
149 6/8	25 2/8 24 5/8	18 2/8	5 5	Columbia County	WI	Daniel Hellenbrand	2009	7698
*149 6/8	26 3/8 27 1/8	19 4/8	6 6	Taylor County	WI	Michael Arrowood	2009	7698
*149 6/8	25 0/8 23 4/8	18 7/8	5 5	Orleans County	NY	Jeff Haseley	2009	7698
*149 6/8	20 4/8 21 3/8	15 0/8	5 5	Republic County	KS	Robert M. Young	2009	7698
149 5/8	25 6/8 25 3/8	18 5/8	6 6	La Salle County	IL	Timothy L. Kakara	1975	7781
149 5/8	25 4/8 25 2/8	20 1/8	6 5	Chase County	KS	John Moore	1981	7781
149 5/8	24 5/8 25 2/8	20 1/8	5 7	Sheboygan County	WI	Leon Schultz	1983	7781
149 5/8	22 4/8 23 5/8	20 1/8	5 5	Johnson County	NE	Brad Seitz	1984	7781
149 5/8	23 1/8 23 1/8	16 5/8	6 6	York County	NE	Harold Bowman	1985	7781
149 5/8	25 1/8 23 2/8	17 5/8	6 6	Livingston County	NY	John J. Valle	1985	7781
149 5/8	22 7/8 23 3/8	21 1/8	5 5	Osage	SAS	Fred Paslawski	1986	7781
149 5/8	25 1/8 25 0/8	16 7/8	5 4	McPherson County	KS	George E. Hoke	1986	7781
149 5/8	27 3/8 28 6/8	20 3/8	5 6	Delaware County	IA	Robert J. Becker	1987	7781
149 5/8	24 3/8 24 3/8	19 1/8	5 4	Kiowa County	KS	Karl L. Ballard	1987	7781

WHITETAIL DEER (TYPICAL ANTLERS)

Minimum Score 125 — Continued

SCORE	R MAIN BEAM L	INSIDE SPREAD	R POINTS L	AREA	STATE/PROVINCE	HUNTER'S NAME	DATE	RANK
149 5/8	26 4/8 26 1/8	20 7/8	4 4	Montgomery County	IL	Martin L. Leitschuh	1987	7781
149 5/8	26 4/8 26 4/8	21 0/8	7 6	Jefferson County	IL	Terry Storey	1988	7781
149 5/8	23 4/8 24 3/8	18 6/8	6 6	Fayette County	IA	Mike Barker	1989	7781
149 5/8	23 4/8 22 3/8	17 1/8	5 5	Ripley County	IN	Kevin D. Hall	1989	7781
149 5/8	24 3/8 25 3/8	18 2/8	7 6	Carroll County	IL	Art Heinze	1989	7781
149 5/8	23 2/8 22 4/8	18 3/8	5 5	Crow Wing County	MN	Mike Brandes	1989	7781
149 5/8	24 4/8 24 2/8	19 4/8	6 5	Macon County	IL	Gary Wayne Scheland, Sr.	1990	7781
149 5/8	26 2/8 27 3/8	19 4/8	5 4	Jo Daviess County	IL	Ronald J. Blauwkamp	1990	7781
149 5/8	24 5/8 24 5/8	20 2/8	6 5	Barber County	KS	Jim F. Shadid	1991	7781
149 5/8	24 1/8 23 7/8	17 7/8	5 5	Otter Tail County	MN	Craig Smith	1991	7781
149 5/8	24 4/8 24 7/8	15 5/8	6 6	Pottawatomie County	KS	Nathan Figge	1992	7781
149 5/8	24 7/8 25 2/8	15 4/8	7 5	Howell County	MO	Thomas E. French	1992	7781
149 5/8	26 0/8 26 0/8	16 0/8	6 7	Strathcona	ALB	Gord MacDonald	1992	7781
149 5/8	21 3/8 21 4/8	15 5/8	6 6	Boone County	IA	Kevin L. Holm	1992	7781
149 5/8	26 6/8 26 2/8	20 5/8	7 6	Hancock County	IL	Ryan D. Biery	1993	7781
149 5/8	22 4/8 21 7/8	16 4/8	5 6	Winnebago County	WI	John Hay	1993	7781
149 5/8	27 0/8 25 7/8	24 1/8	4 4	Clinton County	IN	Donny L. Pickell	1993	7781
149 5/8	20 4/8 19 1/8	15 5/8	5 6	Iroquois County	IL	Doug Post	1993	7781
149 5/8	24 3/8 24 2/8	18 0/8	7 6	Woodbury County	IA	Todd T. Carr	1993	7781
149 5/8	23 3/8 22 4/8	18 7/8	5 5	Boone County	WV	Mark Summers	1994	7781
149 5/8	26 0/8 24 2/8	21 2/8	5 5	Monroe County	IA	Bob McDowell	1994	7781
149 5/8	24 4/8 24 3/8	16 5/8	5 5	Clinton County	IL	Jim Lohman	1994	7781
149 5/8	24 6/8 24 6/8	20 7/8	7 5	Brooke	ONT	Bill Majovsky	1995	7781
149 5/8	24 0/8 23 6/8	19 3/8	5 5	Kent County	MD	Charles W. Smith, Jr.	1995	7781
149 5/8	25 0/8 25 5/8	21 0/8	7 5	Kankakee County	IL	Calvin R. Cox	1995	7781
149 5/8	26 2/8 27 6/8	21 6/8	8 5	DeKalb County	IL	James G. Tippitt	1995	7781
149 5/8	22 4/8 22 2/8	16 3/8	5 5	Madison Parish	LA	Jason Elrod	1996	7781
149 5/8	26 6/8 26 7/8	18 7/8	5 5	Osborne County	KS	Blake Grabast	1996	7781
149 5/8	22 4/8 23 2/8	17 6/8	5 6	Lyon County	IA	Paul E. Blotz	1996	7781
149 5/8	25 6/8 27 4/8	24 4/8	4 6	Winneshiek County	IA	Gary L. Mezera	1996	7781
149 5/8	25 0/8 25 0/8	17 3/8	5 5	Tensas Parish	LA	Robert T. Buller	1997	7781
149 5/8	25 7/8 25 7/8	18 1/8	5 5	Wyoming County	WV	Robert Adams	1997	7781
149 5/8	25 1/8 25 4/8	19 3/8	6 7	Waukesha County	WI	Dean Wintersberger	1997	7781
149 5/8	24 2/8 22 6/8	20 6/8	4 6	Scott County	IA	Ric Bishop	1997	7781
149 5/8	24 1/8 24 1/8	20 3/8	6 5	Dane County	WI	Mark Gerhardt	1997	7781
149 5/8	26 6/8 24 2/8	17 6/8	8 8	Miami County	KS	Larry Hermann	1997	7781
149 5/8	22 7/8 24 2/8	16 1/8	7 5	Montgomery County	KS	Claude McCullough	1998	7781
149 5/8	24 4/8 24 1/8	15 3/8	5 5	Todd County	MN	Marlen Schmitz	1998	7781
149 5/8	23 3/8 23 4/8	18 3/8	5 5	E. Carroll Parish	LA	Laurent E. Barbe, Jr.	1998	7781
149 5/8	23 0/8 23 3/8	20 5/8	5 5	Fairfield County	CT	John Michelotti	1998	7781
149 5/8	26 2/8 26 4/8	18 5/8	5 4	Eau Claire County	WI	Dan Gilles	1998	7781
149 5/8	23 7/8 24 0/8	19 5/8	5 5	Black Hawk County	IA	Michael Judas	1999	7781
149 5/8	22 4/8 23 4/8	17 3/8	5 5	Hancock County	IA	Ken Lonneman	1999	7781
149 5/8	20 6/8 20 5/8	18 5/8	5 6	Chautauqua County	NY	Christopher R. May	1999	7781
149 5/8	24 2/8 24 0/8	16 5/8	5 5	Sauk County	WI	David E. Zeman	2000	7781
149 5/8	25 0/8 25 0/8	18 7/8	5 4	Livingston County	IL	Lyle Molen	2000	7781
149 5/8	25 0/8 24 7/8	18 3/8	6 6	Oconto County	WI	Mark A. Zuller, Sr.	2001	7781
149 5/8	26 7/8 26 6/8	17 7/8	4 4	Wayne County	MI	Robert A. Stevens	2001	7781
149 5/8	25 2/8 25 1/8	19 5/8	4 4	Pepin County	WI	Jim Kraft	2001	7781
149 5/8	22 3/8 22 0/8	21 3/8	7 5	Calhoun County	IL	Neal Furlow	2001	7781
149 5/8	23 4/8 22 3/8	19 3/8	6 6	Chippewa County	WI	Jim Ramharter	2001	7781
149 5/8	26 0/8 25 5/8	19 3/8	5 8	La Salle County	IL	Mark D. Hunter	2002	7781
149 5/8	24 0/8 26 0/8	18 1/8	4 4	Adams County	IL	Warren Cottingham	2002	7781
149 5/8	26 0/8 25 2/8	17 1/8	5 4	Greene County	IN	Kenneth J. Hert	2002	7781
149 5/8	25 0/8 26 4/8	18 5/8	4 4	Dunn County	WI	James Belmore	2002	7781
149 5/8	21 6/8 22 4/8	20 7/8	6 6	Jefferson County	IA	Wendall R. Matson	2002	7781
149 5/8	24 6/8 23 2/8	21 3/8	5 5	Jefferson County	IN	Thomas E. Heitman	2002	7781
149 5/8	23 4/8 23 2/8	15 7/8	5 7	Hamilton County	KS	Charlie Hanawalt	2002	7781
149 5/8	25 1/8 24 0/8	16 1/8	5 5	Union County	IL	Nick Kramer	2003	7781
149 5/8	22 5/8 24 0/8	18 1/8	5 5	Greene County	IN	Tim Neal	2003	7781
149 5/8	26 2/8 25 3/8	18 4/8	6 4	Montgomery County	PA	Aaron C. Weinsteiger	2003	7781
149 5/8	21 4/8 21 4/8	16 3/8	5 5	Will County	IL	Dale Hoekstra	2003	7781
149 5/8	22 1/8 21 7/8	19 1/8	5 5	Shawano County	WI	Shane Ouellette	2003	7781
*149 5/8	22 2/8 23 1/8	16 1/8	6 5	Sullivan County	MO	Ronald P. Smith	2004	7781
149 5/8	24 3/8 24 2/8	17 3/8	5 5	Waupaca County	WI	Craig J. Zwiers	2004	7781
*149 5/8	24 0/8 23 2/8	17 3/8	6 6	Schuyler County	IL	Keith Conner	2004	7781
149 5/8	25 2/8 25 0/8	19 7/8	6 6	Kewaunee County	WI	Tim Mathu	2005	7781
*149 5/8	22 0/8 22 0/8	20 1/8	8 6	St. Joseph County	IN	Andrew G. Riffel	2005	7781
*149 5/8	26 5/8 26 4/8	19 3/8	4 6	Greene County	IL	John Adcock	2005	7781
149 5/8	25 0/8 25 2/8	17 7/8	4 4	Montgomery County	MO	Marvin Cobb	2005	7781
149 5/8	21 7/8 22 1/8	17 5/8	5 5	Clayton County	IA	Andy Belk	2005	7781
*149 5/8	23 5/8 23 7/8	16 7/8	5 5	Comanche County	KS	Michele Eichler	2005	7781
149 5/8	24 4/8 24 6/8	17 7/8	4 4	Saline County	MO	Kevin Mikels	2006	7781
149 5/8	20 7/8 21 5/8	16 1/8	5 5	Clayton County	IA	Du Wayne Fabert	2006	7781
149 5/8	22 7/8 23 4/8	16 5/8	5 5	La Crosse County	WI	Chris Barry	2006	7781
*149 5/8	24 0/8 22 5/8	16 5/8	6 5	Green County	WI	Dean W. Lederman	2006	7781
149 5/8	22 4/8 21 3/8	15 7/8	6 5	Scott County	IL	Tim Garner	2006	7781
149 5/8	26 2/8 24 6/8	20 4/8	9 5	Carberry	MAN	Gerard Rosset	2007	7781
149 5/8	22 3/8 21 4/8	19 3/8	5 5	Polk County	WI	Greg Marek	2007	7781
*149 5/8	22 6/8 23 6/8	19 5/8	5 5	Adams County	OH	Joe Thomas	2007	7781
149 5/8	25 1/8 25 4/8	17 5/8	4 5	Price County	WI	Roger A. Niewiadomski, Sr.	2007	7781
149 5/8	25 3/8 24 5/8	17 1/8	8 8	Jackson County	MN	Nic Rowe	2007	7781
149 5/8	23 3/8 22 5/8	17 5/8	5 5	Adams County	WI	Ron Gehrig	2007	7781
149 5/8	25 0/8 23 7/8	16 2/8	5 6	Wayne County	IL	Brad Almaroad	2007	7781
*149 5/8	26 4/8 26 7/8	21 1/8	4 5	Trempealeau County	WI	James D. Fox	2008	7781
*149 5/8	22 1/8 22 1/8	16 7/8	5 5	Pike County	IL	Charles DeBenedittis	2008	7781
149 5/8	24 3/8 24 6/8	16 7/8	6 6	Doniphan County	KS	Brian Pollard	2008	7781
*149 5/8	24 4/8 24 4/8	17 5/8	7 5	Reynolds County	MO	Steven Watson	2009	7781
149 5/8	25 5/8 25 6/8	21 1/8	4 5	Putnam County	IN	Robbie Farrow	2009	7781
*149 5/8	23 7/8 22 7/8	18 1/8	4 4	Morris County	KS	David J. Nache, Jr.	2009	7781
*149 5/8	23 7/8 24 4/8	17 4/8	5 7	Rusk County	WI	Ron Zahorski	2009	7781
*149 5/8	26 6/8 28 0/8	17 1/8	6 6	Gallia County	OH	Tom Fulks	2009	7781
149 4/8	23 3/8 26 0/8	20 2/8	5 5	Woodbury County	IA	Don Gothier	1962	7883
149 4/8	25 3/8 25 2/8	18 7/8	8 8	Westchester County	NY	Steve Solomon	1963	7883
149 4/8	23 2/8 23 2/8	17 1/8	6 5	Newton County	IN	Gerald R. Metros	1973	7883

438

WHITETAIL DEER (TYPICAL ANTLERS)

Minimum Score 125   Continued

SCORE	LENGTH OF R MAIN BEAM L	INSIDE SPREAD	NUMBER OF R POINTS L		AREA	STATE/ PROVINCE	HUNTER'S NAME	DATE	RANK
149 4/8	22 5/8 22 3/8	17 4/8	7	5	Ogle County	IL	Jerome Bruns	1983	7883
149 4/8	24 5/8 25 2/8	17 0/8	5	5	Sedgwick County	KS	Bob Shull	1984	7883
149 4/8	25 3/8 25 0/8	21 4/8	4	4	Shawnee County	KS	Jim Dultmeier	1985	7883
149 4/8	23 4/8 23 7/8	16 3/8	7	6	Platte County	WY	Jerry Bowen	1986	7883
149 4/8	25 4/8 25 7/8	17 4/8	6	5	Dane County	WI	John Podebradsky	1986	7883
149 4/8	23 5/8 24 5/8	22 0/8	5	5	Keokuk County	IA	Mike Krier	1986	7883
149 4/8	22 6/8 22 3/8	16 7/8	6	5	Polk County	WI	Blaine Mortimer	1987	7883
149 4/8	26 1/8 25 5/8	22 6/8	5	4	Lee County	IL	Rick Hornung	1988	7883
149 4/8	23 1/8 21 6/8	19 6/8	5	7	Kossuth County	IA	Bruce K. Leeck	1989	7883
149 4/8	28 2/8 25 2/8	19 0/8	5	6	Lancaster County	NE	Bog Spicha	1990	7883
149 4/8	24 2/8 19 0/8	20 7/8	5	7	Buffalo County	WI	Matthew J. Gorniak	1990	7883
149 4/8	25 0/8 24 4/8	18 4/8	6	5	Champaign County	IL	Bud Barnes	1991	7883
149 4/8	24 2/8 23 6/8	18 6/8	5	4	Clayton County	IA	Joseph C. Hinderman	1991	7883
149 4/8	23 1/8 24 0/8	16 7/8	6	5	Ravalli County	MT	Michael R. Lindquist	1993	7883
149 4/8	23 6/8 23 0/8	16 1/8	6	6	Morrison County	MN	Terry F. Much	1993	7883
149 4/8	24 6/8 24 6/8	17 4/8	4	4	Lake County	IL	Dr. John R. Thodos	1993	7883
149 4/8	23 1/8 23 1/8	16 2/8	5	5	Marathon County	WI	Dean J. Novitzke	1993	7883
149 4/8	21 5/8 23 2/8	16 4/8	5	5	McKenzie County	ND	Dennis Carns	1994	7883
149 4/8	25 0/8 25 0/8	20 2/8	6	5	Dakota County	MN	Keith A. Klingborg	1995	7883
149 4/8	24 3/8 23 7/8	16 2/8	5	6	Preble County	OH	Jason Hines	1995	7883
149 4/8	21 1/8 26 2/8	19 1/8	6	5	Pierceland	SAS	Bruce A. Hatch	1995	7883
149 4/8	25 2/8 26 0/8	16 5/8	6	6	Ross County	OH	David L. Buckler	1996	7883
149 4/8	24 4/8 24 6/8	18 4/8	5	4	Logan County	CO	Janet L. George	1996	7883
149 4/8	22 3/8 24 0/8	17 0/8	5	5	Deschaillons	QUE	Bruno Martin L'Herault	1996	7883
149 4/8	22 5/8 24 1/8	16 2/8	5	5	Buffalo County	WI	Christopher S. Dellger	1996	7883
149 4/8	25 3/8 24 5/8	17 6/8	5	5	Mills County	IA	Elaine D. Brown	1996	7883
149 4/8	26 1/8 24 7/8	19 7/8	6	5	Marion County	IA	Lowdell Taylor	1997	7883
149 4/8	22 4/8 21 3/8	17 6/8	5	5	Jackson County	WI	Todd Herrington	1997	7883
149 4/8	23 7/8 24 6/8	19 6/8	5	5	Guthrie County	IA	Rollie Schultz	1998	7883
149 4/8	23 4/8 23 2/8	17 2/8	5	5	Marathon County	WI	Allan Brusky	1998	7883
149 4/8	23 3/8 23 1/8	16 6/8	5	5	Morrison County	MN	Allen J. Germscheid	1998	7883
149 4/8	24 4/8 24 6/8	17 4/8	5	5	Henry County	IL	Gregg Schilling	1999	7883
149 4/8	22 4/8 22 4/8	19 4/8	5	5	Garfield County	MT	Cary Roper	2000	7883
149 4/8	25 2/8 24 6/8	16 4/8	5	5	Brown County	IL	Kevin Wort	2000	7883
149 4/8	24 4/8 24 4/8	20 0/8	5	4	Dickinson County	KS	Rodney Althiser	2000	7883
149 4/8	26 7/8 25 7/8	22 6/8	4	5	Fulton County	IL	James B. Powell	2000	7883
149 4/8	23 7/8 23 2/8	17 4/8	4	5	Oakland County	MI	Don E. Blalock	2001	7883
149 4/8	24 3/8 22 7/8	15 6/8	5	5	Van Buren County	IA	Bob Bellmer	2001	7883
149 4/8	20 0/8 21 2/8	14 2/8	5	5	Madison County	IA	Kevin Hulsing	2001	7883
149 4/8	22 3/8 21 3/8	16 4/8	6	8	Dunn County	WI	Ryan Langman	2003	7883
149 4/8	27 4/8 25 0/8	20 1/8	5	8	Stark County	OH	Larry Scheetz III	2003	7883
149 4/8	23 0/8 26 3/8	18 0/8	5	5	Walworth County	WI	Eli Nieuwenhuis	2003	7883
149 4/8	24 5/8 24 5/8	20 4/8	6	6	Clinton County	OH	Jason E. Davis	2003	7883
*149 4/8	23 0/8 21 6/8	14 2/8	6	5	Keya Paha County	NE	R. Kirk Sharp	2004	7883
149 4/8	24 1/8 24 2/8	20 6/8	5	5	Sawyer County	WI	Matt Farley	2005	7883
*149 4/8	23 0/8 22 5/8	18 0/8	4	4	Jersey County	IL	Bill Wilson	2005	7883
*149 4/8	23 1/8 23 1/8	16 2/8	6	5	Howard County	IA	Rebecca Burke	2005	7883
*149 4/8	23 7/8 22 1/8	18 0/8	6	5	Clark County	IL	Rick Davidson	2006	7883
*149 4/8	21 1/8 21 4/8	15 6/8	5	6	Brown County	OH	Lawton Shafer	2006	7883
*149 4/8	25 3/8 24 6/8	18 6/8	5	8	Oconto County	WI	Craig Gerndt	2006	7883
*149 4/8	24 5/8 24 4/8	15 4/8	5	7	Lancaster County	NE	Brett Hillis	2006	7883
*149 4/8	24 7/8 25 3/8	16 1/8	6	6	Pike County	IL	Michael Daniels	2007	7883
*149 4/8	23 1/8 22 6/8	15 4/8	5	6	Kewaunee County	WI	Steven D. Seiler	2007	7883
149 4/8	23 5/8 23 5/8	16 0/8	5	6	Fayette County	IN	William E. Wayson, Jr.	2007	7883
*149 4/8	24 0/8 23 4/8	17 2/8	5	6	Fillmore County	MN	Tim Johnson	2008	7883
149 4/8	22 4/8 22 7/8	18 2/8	6	5	Buffalo County	WI	Bill Kriesel	2008	7883
149 4/8	24 4/8 25 2/8	19 6/8	5	6	Trempealeau County	WI	Jamie Back	2008	7883
*149 4/8	24 2/8 23 0/8	21 2/8	4	6	Barron County	WI	Brad Dostal	2008	7883
149 4/8	22 7/8 22 1/8	17 4/8	6	6	Edwards County	IL	Josh R. Shelby	2008	7883
149 4/8	26 1/8 25 7/8	18 6/8	6	6	Brown County	SD	Bill Fluke	2009	7883
*149 4/8	25 6/8 26 0/8	19 3/8	5	5	Yell County	AR	John Thomas	2009	7883
149 4/8	24 1/8 24 6/8	15 6/8	5	5	Jennings County	IN	Moses Manuel	2010	7883
*149 4/8	23 7/8 23 3/8	16 0/8	6	6	Buffalo County	WI	Jim Wondzell	2010	7883
149 3/8	26 6/8 25 4/8	22 1/8	4	4	Westchester County	NY	George Ferber	1957	7949
149 3/8	23 4/8 23 3/8	15 7/8	5	5	Madison County	KY	Robert Young	1963	7949
149 3/8	23 1/8 24 4/8	19 3/8	5	5	Newton County	IN	Philip Kozlowski	1968	7949
149 3/8	23 7/8 23 2/8	15 7/8	5	5	Buffalo County	WI	Daniel J. Brunner	1969	7949
149 3/8	24 1/8 24 2/8	19 3/8	5	5	Lawrence County	OH	Ronald E. Burnette	1971	7949
149 3/8	23 7/8 23 4/8	17 5/8	5	5	Waushara County	WI	Ronald Anunson	1974	7949
149 3/8	22 2/8 23 1/8	15 7/8	6	6	Lac qui Parle County	MN	Ron Patzer	1980	7949
149 3/8	24 1/8 25 3/8	19 7/8	5	6	Perry County	IL	Vern Quillman	1981	7949
149 3/8	24 2/8 23 3/8	19 3/8	6	7	Charles County	MD	Frank A. Rankin	1981	7949
149 3/8	24 0/8 25 2/8	17 4/8	5	4	Washington County	OH	Charles E. Vaughan	1983	7949
149 3/8	25 5/8 25 0/8	20 4/8	4	5	Noble County	OK	Bill Hughes	1984	7949
149 3/8	22 5/8 22 6/8	15 5/8	5	5	Morgan County	CO	Stan Kingcade	1985	7949
149 3/8	24 2/8 23 5/8	21 3/8	6	6	Iroquois County	IL	Dale W. Duits	1986	7949
149 3/8	24 7/8 26 5/8	16 5/8	6	6	Athens County	OH	Ron Sallee	1986	7949
149 3/8	26 6/8 24 7/8	17 7/8	5	4	Marshall County	IL	Bryan Blair	1987	7949
149 3/8	21 7/8 23 4/8	18 7/8	6	6	Ozaukee County	WI	Mark Hoelz	1987	7949
149 3/8	23 5/8 24 0/8	17 2/8	4	6	Sandusky County	OH	James Moll	1988	7949
149 3/8	21 5/8 21 1/8	17 3/8	5	5	Morden	MAN	Allen K. Martens	1988	7949
149 3/8	25 3/8 25 1/8	19 5/8	5	5	Muskingum County	OH	John W. Keefe	1988	7949
149 3/8	23 1/8 22 5/8	18 7/8	4	5	Somerset County	NJ	Peter Paradise	1989	7949
149 3/8	24 1/8 24 5/8	18 7/8	5	5	Buffalo County	WI	Randall Martin	1990	7949
149 3/8	24 4/8 24 4/8	19 0/8	7	7	Johnson County	IA	Kevin Deets	1990	7949
149 3/8	26 0/8 25 5/8	19 6/8	5	6	Monona County	IA	Richard Kelly	1990	7949
149 3/8	27 0/8 25 4/8	21 1/8	5	4	Burt County	NE	Michael L. Johnson	1990	7949
149 3/8	24 1/8 23 5/8	19 3/8	5	5	Stearns County	MN	Jeff Skinner	1991	7949
149 3/8	24 6/8 26 2/8	20 7/8	6	6	McHenry County	IL	Brian Witte	1991	7949
149 3/8	25 1/8 25 2/8	15 2/8	6	6	Owen County	KY	Robert C. Long, Jr.	1991	7949
149 3/8	22 1/8 21 5/8	19 7/8	5	5	Grand Forks County	ND	Kendall J. Allgaier	1992	7949
149 3/8	27 2/8 26 4/8	19 1/8	4	6	Johnson County	IL	Mike Stafford	1992	7949
149 3/8	24 4/8 24 7/8	20 4/8	5	5	Crawford County	KS	William F. Nauyok III	1992	7949
149 3/8	23 7/8 24 2/8	17 5/8	5	5	Hitchcock County	NE	Rob Seybold	1993	7949
149 3/8	25 2/8 23 5/8	18 6/8	6	5	Ozaukee County	WI	William J. Ferguson	1993	7949

WHITETAIL DEER (TYPICAL ANTLERS)

Minimum Score 125 — Continued

SCORE	LENGTH OF R MAIN BEAM L	INSIDE SPREAD	NUMBER OF R POINTS L	AREA	STATE/ PROVINCE	HUNTER'S NAME	DATE	RANK
149 3/8	27 4/8 25 4/8	17 5/8	4 5	Queen Annes County	MD	Charles M. Pierson	1994	7949
149 3/8	26 2/8 25 1/8	21 5/8	4 4	Trempealeau County	WI	Jim P. Konkel	1994	7949
149 3/8	23 7/8 23 6/8	19 3/8	5 5	Jefferson County	WI	Karen Raasch	1994	7949
149 3/8	29 0/8 28 6/8	25 1/8	6 6	Wayne County	MI	Mark E. Oprisiu	1994	7949
149 3/8	23 7/8 23 2/8	18 3/8	5 5	Winnebago County	IL	Dave Fisher	1994	7949
149 3/8	24 4/8 25 2/8	18 2/8	5 7	Shelby County	IN	Dan Cord	1995	7949
149 3/8	25 4/8 24 2/8	22 1/8	5 4	Allegan County	MI	William D. Brooks	1995	7949
149 3/8	25 0/8 23 0/8	18 5/8	4 6	Buffalo County	WI	Dan Lee	1995	7949
149 3/8	25 4/8 25 2/8	19 1/8	5 5	Grundy County	MO	Keith Vandevender	1995	7949
149 3/8	24 4/8 24 7/8	18 7/8	4 5	Linn County	IA	Jamie Washburn	1995	7949
149 3/8	24 3/8 24 0/8	19 1/8	5 6	Morrison County	MN	Jim Klassen	1996	7949
149 3/8	26 3/8 24 7/8	18 7/8	5 5	Marquette County	WI	Arthur J. Gruner	1996	7949
149 3/8	23 4/8 23 5/8	17 3/8	6 7	Neosho County	KS	Roger L. Barriger	1996	7949
149 3/8	26 5/8 27 3/8	17 5/8	5 5	Clark County	IL	Todd Murphy	1996	7949
149 3/8	23 1/8 23 5/8	21 7/8	6 5	Kanawha County	WV	Rick Boggess	1997	7949
149 3/8	23 0/8 22 5/8	15 7/8	5 5	Blue Earth County	MN	Dan Friedrichs	1997	7949
149 3/8	24 0/8 24 0/8	19 5/8	4 4	Iowa County	IA	Tim Krauss	1997	7949
149 3/8	24 3/8 24 6/8	18 2/8	7 5	Wayne County	NY	Angus Hopkins	1997	7949
149 3/8	23 0/8 23 0/8	18 5/8	5 5	Irion County	TX	David L. Duncan	1997	7949
149 3/8	24 6/8 23 6/8	19 3/8	5 5	Orange County	IN	Randy Whalin	1998	7949
149 3/8	23 1/8 23 0/8	16 3/8	6 5	Washington County	PA	Dennis Gondella	1998	7949
149 3/8	25 4/8 26 3/8	18 5/8	4 4	Perry County	OH	Tim Strohl	1998	7949
149 3/8	24 6/8 24 2/8	17 2/8	6 5	Switzerland County	IN	James Reed	1998	7949
149 3/8	26 0/8 25 2/8	19 3/8	4 4	Mercer County	IL	A. J. Cummings	1998	7949
149 3/8	26 3/8 25 6/8	16 7/8	5 4	Weats	SAS	Roy Ihlenfeld	1999	7949
149 3/8	23 7/8 23 0/8	17 7/8	6 6	La Salle County	IL	Paul W. Wilken	1999	7949
149 3/8	24 1/8 23 1/8	17 3/8	5 6	Waupaca County	WI	Adam S. Reetz	1999	7949
149 3/8	25 6/8 25 5/8	18 5/8	5 5	Logan County	OH	Jeff Reeves	1999	7949
149 3/8	25 7/8 25 5/8	20 3/8	6 5	Lawrence County	IN	Rick Mowery	1999	7949
149 3/8	23 5/8 24 5/8	18 1/8	4 5	Wyoming County	NY	Gerald Zylinski, Jr.	2000	7949
149 3/8	25 3/8 25 7/8	19 0/8	7 6	Lee County	IL	Duane Rod	2000	7949
149 3/8	23 5/8 23 4/8	18 5/8	5 5	Lyon County	KS	Marvin D. Scalf	2000	7949
149 3/8	24 0/8 24 3/8	20 2/8	6 7	Kittson County	MN	Mark Kukowski	2001	7949
149 3/8	23 0/8 23 4/8	17 7/8	5 5	Bertwell	SAS	Gordon Faust	2001	7949
149 3/8	24 3/8 23 7/8	18 7/8	7 6	Douglas County	WI	Andy C. Schmidt	2001	7949
149 3/8	25 1/8 24 7/8	19 5/8	5 5	Alexander County	IL	Scott R. Frakes	2001	7949
149 3/8	23 0/8 24 0/8	16 3/8	5 6	Johnson County	KS	Curtis Shupe	2002	7949
149 3/8	25 3/8 24 6/8	21 0/8	5 6	Sauk County	WI	Joe Buckles	2002	7949
149 3/8	27 2/8 27 0/8	24 1/8	5 4	Carroll County	IL	Barry Morgan	2002	7949
149 3/8	22 6/8 23 5/8	20 2/8	7 7	Sumner County	KS	Troy Whaley	2002	7949
149 3/8	23 2/8 22 4/8	14 7/8	5 5	La Crosse County	WI	John Freybler	2003	7949
149 3/8	22 4/8 22 4/8	15 3/8	5 5	Cass County	MI	Kim M. Vaughn	2003	7949
149 3/8	22 7/8 22 1/8	17 5/8	5 6	Buffalo County	WI	Dirk Derse	2003	7949
*149 3/8	26 0/8 24 6/8	19 2/8	6 6	Carroll County	IN	Loren Root	2003	7949
149 3/8	23 3/8 27 3/8	18 6/8	6 6	Knox County	IL	Joe Needham	2003	7949
149 3/8	22 6/8 21 2/8	17 3/8	5 5	Eau Claire County	WI	Charles R. Jensen	2004	7949
149 3/8	24 2/8 24 3/8	21 3/8	6 6	Meigs County	OH	Leslie W. Matherly	2004	7949
*149 3/8	25 5/8 25 6/8	21 3/8	5 5	La Crosse County	WI	Tom Weber	2004	7949
149 3/8	22 2/8 22 1/8	16 3/8	5 6	Daviess County	MO	David McGinness	2005	7949
149 3/8	25 0/8 25 2/8	20 7/8	5 5	Vernon County	WI	Steven Nestingen	2005	7949
149 3/8	25 2/8 22 4/8	16 5/8	5 6	Howard County	IN	Jeff Cass	2005	7949
149 3/8	22 3/8 22 1/8	15 7/8	6 6	Winnebago County	IA	Jim Foos	2005	7949
*149 3/8	23 7/8 25 2/8	17 7/8	5 5	Pike County	IL	Randy C. Oitker	2005	7949
*149 3/8	22 1/8 22 2/8	18 1/8	5 6	Polk County	IA	Vincent Stefanski	2005	7949
149 3/8	21 7/8 21 6/8	15 3/8	7 6	Monroe County	IA	Gary Charipar	2005	7949
149 3/8	24 2/8 26 0/8	17 1/8	7 6	Brown County	IL	Jody Yancey	2005	7949
149 3/8	22 4/8 22 2/8	15 2/8	6 5	Osage County	KS	Aaron Cowing	2005	7949
149 3/8	24 0/8 23 5/8	14 6/8	5 6	Crow Wing County	MN	Bela Smude	2006	7949
149 3/8	26 6/8 24 6/8	17 2/8	6 6	Cass County	IA	Jacob Clarken	2006	7949
149 3/8	20 7/8 21 2/8	15 3/8	5 5	Macon County	IL	Owen Sullivan	2006	7949
149 3/8	20 4/8 22 2/8	15 1/8	6 6	McKenzie County	ND	David Weltikol	2007	7949
149 3/8	24 2/8 24 4/8	20 7/8	6 6	Parke County	IN	Andrew Horning	2007	7949
*149 3/8	22 4/8 24 2/8	18 5/8	5 5	Clark County	IL	Rick Davidson	2007	7949
149 3/8	25 1/8 25 6/8	18 6/8	6 6	Clayton County	IA	John Hansen	2007	7949
149 3/8	24 7/8 25 4/8	17 3/8	5 4	Madison County	IA	John Spahn	2007	7949
149 3/8	22 2/8 22 3/8	17 7/8	6 6	Buffalo County	NE	Mike Walker	2007	7949
*149 3/8	24 7/8 24 2/8	18 1/8	5 5	Stutsman County	ND	Brandon Carlson	2007	7949
*149 3/8	24 7/8 25 2/8	18 5/8	4 5	La Crosse County	WI	Roger Fish	2008	7949
*149 3/8	26 7/8 26 4/8	21 1/8	5 4	Macoupin County	IL	Kyle Nolan	2008	7949
149 3/8	22 4/8 20 6/8	15 5/8	7 5	Cumberland County	IL	David Pontious	2009	7949
*149 3/8	25 0/8 25 1/8	16 3/8	6 6	Jackson County	OH	Rick Davis	2009	7949
*149 3/8	25 2/8 25 2/8	18 7/8	6 7	Vigo County	IN	Tim L. Sherman	2009	7949
149 2/8	25 3/8 24 6/8	20 4/8	5 5	Westchester County	NY	Joseph H. Keeler	1957	8053
149 2/8	22 0/8 22 1/8	16 6/8	5 5	Will County	IL	Daniel R. Altiery	1973	8053
149 2/8	22 7/8 22 6/8	20 6/8	4 5	Auglaize County	OH	Fred Rostorfer	1980	8053
149 2/8	23 3/8 23 4/8	15 3/8	5 7	Livingston County	MI	John Richmond	1981	8053
149 2/8	23 4/8 22 6/8	18 6/8	6 6	Columbia County	WI	Gene R. Elsing	1981	8053
149 2/8	20 7/8 21 7/8	14 0/8	5 5	Lincoln County	MT	R. C. Peters	1984	8053
149 2/8	24 0/8 22 1/8	17 4/8	5 5	Washtenaw County	MI	Fred Johnson	1984	8053
149 2/8	27 4/8 26 2/8	20 2/8	7 7	Fulton County	IL	Locie L Murphy	1984	8053
149 2/8	23 6/8 23 4/8	18 0/8	5 5	Jackson County	MO	Marvin Thomey	1984	8053
149 2/8	23 4/8 23 2/8	19 4/8	6 5	Otter Tail County	MN	Kelly Shannon	1987	8053
149 2/8	24 2/8 24 2/8	16 7/8	5 5	Warren County	KY	Jerry Sympson	1987	8053
149 2/8	26 2/8 25 1/8	19 6/8	6 4	Tama County	IA	Travis Hansen	1988	8053
149 2/8	23 1/8 23 7/8	17 0/8	5 4	Vinton County	OH	Brian D. Ehrhart	1989	8053
149 2/8	21 6/8 19 7/8	15 6/8	5 5	Ashe County	NC	Marshall "Footsie" Eller	1991	8053
149 2/8	24 2/8 24 1/8	18 2/8	5 5	Rusk County	WI	Ed Madlon	1992	8053
149 2/8	23 5/8 22 6/8	20 2/8	5 5	E. Carroll Parish	LA	Robert H. Jarvis	1993	8053
149 2/8	23 3/8 23 3/8	15 4/8	5 6	Adams County	OH	Kenneth Ashcraft, Jr.	1993	8053
149 2/8	20 5/8 26 0/8	18 6/8	5 4	Morrison County	MN	Kirt M. Dotzler	1993	8053
149 2/8	24 4/8 24 6/8	15 7/8	6 6	Oconto County	WI	Wade Kempka	1993	8053
149 2/8	24 4/8 24 2/8	18 7/8	6 6	Cass County	ND	Rob Dooley	1993	8053
149 2/8	24 0/8 23 6/8	16 2/8	5 5	Brown County	MN	Paul Berg	1994	8053
149 2/8	22 0/8 23 2/8	19 6/8	5 5	Muscatine County	IA	James E. Quinn	1994	8053
149 2/8	24 1/8 24 2/8	17 6/8	5 5	Allamakee County	IA	Joe Lieb	1994	8053

WHITETAIL DEER (TYPICAL ANTLERS)

Minimum Score 125 — Continued

SCORE	LENGTH OF R MAIN BEAM L	INSIDE SPREAD	NUMBER OF R POINTS L	AREA	STATE/ PROVINCE	HUNTER'S NAME	DATE	RANK
149 2/8	26 2/8 26 0/8	18 0/8	5 6	Pierce County	WI	Jeff Schoeder	1994	8053
149 2/8	23 2/8 24 1/8	18 6/8	7 5	Washington County	IL	Kevin Woker	1995	8053
149 2/8	24 5/8 24 5/8	17 4/8	5 5	Montgomery County	NC	Ricky E. Jennings	1995	8053
149 2/8	23 3/8 24 5/8	22 4/8	5 6	Plymouth County	MA	Daniel E. Chisholm	1995	8053
149 2/8	24 5/8 24 6/8	19 7/8	7 5	Delaware County	IA	Daniel G. Putz	1995	8053
149 2/8	21 7/8 22 0/8	19 2/8	6 5	Peoria County	IL	Joe Cooper	1995	8053
149 2/8	23 3/8 23 5/8	17 4/8	5 5	Waukesha County	WI	Jane Stolz	1995	8053
149 2/8	24 5/8 26 6/8	19 0/8	5 6	Howe Island	ONT	Nick Milonas	1995	8053
149 2/8	26 1/8 25 0/8	20 0/8	5 5	Henry County	IL	Robert Aldred	1996	8053
149 2/8	23 4/8 22 3/8	14 6/8	5 5	Sheboygan County	WI	Jim Gruber, Jr.	1996	8053
149 2/8	24 7/8 25 3/8	17 2/8	4 4	Newton County	TX	Brian Babin	1996	8053
149 2/8	25 6/8 25 7/8	17 2/8	5 4	Allamakee County	IA	Justin Grove	1996	8053
149 2/8	23 4/8 22 7/8	20 0/8	5 5	La Salle County	IL	Dennis Brown	1996	8053
149 2/8	25 7/8 25 0/8	20 1/8	4 6	Buena Vista County	IA	Dan D. Soellner	1996	8053
149 2/8	26 2/8 26 2/8	21 5/8	6 5	Branch County	MI	Gregory J. Raatz	1997	8053
149 2/8	20 3/8 20 4/8	14 6/8	6 6	Jefferson County	IL	Todd Jimmie Reed	1997	8053
149 2/8	23 3/8 25 4/8	20 3/8	5 4	Wicomico County	MD	Michael Pilchard	1997	8053
149 2/8	26 3/8 26 2/8	22 4/8	4 7	McHenry County	IL	Darrell J. Prielipp	1997	8053
149 2/8	29 0/8 28 4/8	22 6/8	4 4	Knox County	OH	Bill Banner	1997	8053
149 2/8	24 2/8 24 1/8	18 6/8	5 5	Graves County	KY	Casey Kuppart	1998	8053
149 2/8	22 0/8 21 4/8	19 1/8	6 6	Ozaukee County	WI	Mark B. Kosobucki	1998	8053
149 2/8	23 6/8 23 2/8	17 2/8	5 5	Clark County	IL	Gerald "Gabe" Shaffner	1998	8053
149 2/8	25 7/8 25 7/8	19 4/8	4 4	Pike County	IL	Lance Johnson	1998	8053
149 2/8	24 1/8 23 4/8	18 3/8	5 6	Cass County	MI	Darren M. Karenke	1998	8053
149 2/8	22 5/8 22 5/8	18 1/8	5 6	Douglas County	NE	Todd Wendt	1998	8053
149 2/8	23 4/8 23 4/8	18 0/8	6 6	Pike County	OH	John R. Ribic	1998	8053
149 2/8	22 4/8 22 2/8	16 6/8	6 5	Bayfield County	WI	Jim Kanicky	1998	8053
149 2/8	20 7/8 22 7/8	15 2/8	6 5	Adair County	MO	Bob Wagner	1999	8053
149 2/8	25 2/8 24 6/8	16 6/8	7 5	Riley County	KS	Scott Breitsprecher	1999	8053
149 2/8	24 0/8 23 6/8	16 6/8	5 5	Somerset County	NJ	Carmen Santucci	1999	8053
149 2/8	24 6/8 25 2/8	19 0/8	5 5	Jackson County	WI	Richard A. Kopacz	2000	8053
149 2/8	23 0/8 23 1/8	19 4/8	5 5	Waushara County	WI	Mark Menting	2000	8053
149 2/8	25 3/8 25 6/8	19 4/8	5 5	Wayne County	OH	Brian M. Bilinovich	2000	8053
149 2/8	25 5/8 24 6/8	18 4/8	5 4	La Crosse County	WI	Curt Horman	2000	8053
149 2/8	26 0/8 25 4/8	28 5/8	5 5	Northampton County	PA	William A. Car	2000	8053
149 2/8	22 5/8 21 7/8	19 0/8	5 5	Wabasha County	MN	Paul C. Irlbeck	2000	8053
149 2/8	23 0/8 22 4/8	19 2/8	7 7	Stearns County	MN	Russ Braegelmann	2000	8053
149 2/8	22 3/8 22 4/8	16 6/8	5 5	Greene County	IN	Peter M. Sartoris	2001	8053
149 2/8	24 4/8 22 6/8	19 5/8	7 7	Gregory County	SD	Mark Kayser	2001	8053
149 2/8	25 0/8 24 0/8	18 4/8	5 4	Marion County	IA	Leonard Grimes	2001	8053
149 2/8	23 0/8 22 5/8	17 4/8	5 5	Rice County	KS	L. W. Miller	2001	8053
149 2/8	23 4/8 23 7/8	18 0/8	5 6	Sibley County	MN	Mark Herd	2001	8053
149 2/8	25 0/8 23 5/8	18 0/8	6 6	McIntosh County	OK	Perry Kendall	2002	8053
149 2/8	25 3/8 26 3/8	17 1/8	6 6	Iowa County	IA	Kurt Chizek	2002	8053
149 2/8	25 6/8 25 5/8	17 3/8	5 4	Nemaha County	KS	John McIntire	2002	8053
149 2/8	23 4/8 24 0/8	17 6/8	5 5	Coos County	NH	Robert LaFrance	2002	8053
149 2/8	24 0/8 24 6/8	21 0/8	6 5	Columbiana County	OH	Terry Melott, Jr.	2003	8053
149 2/8	25 3/8 24 6/8	17 2/8	8 6	Greene County	OH	Tom Grace	2003	8053
149 2/8	25 0/8 24 7/8	18 7/8	5 8	Delaware County	IA	Rick Miersen	2003	8053
149 2/8	22 6/8 23 0/8	17 6/8	5 5	Maverick County	TX	John J. Wyble	2004	8053
149 2/8	21 3/8 22 3/8	16 4/8	5 5	Charles Mix County	SD	Darryl Deurmier	2004	8053
149 2/8	21 4/8 22 0/8	17 6/8	5 5	Taylor County	IA	Russ Scott	2004	8053
149 2/8	23 0/8 25 4/8	19 1/8	5 7	Auglaize County	OH	Anthony Gerdeman	2005	8053
149 2/8	22 5/8 23 6/8	14 6/8	5 6	Goodsoil	SAS	Richard Service	2005	8053
149 2/8	23 7/8 23 2/8	17 4/8	7 7	Houston County	MN	Tony Folcey	2005	8053
149 2/8	22 5/8 23 2/8	18 2/8	5 5	Nemaha County	NE	Roger G. Kuhn	2005	8053
*149 2/8	26 1/8 25 2/8	18 2/8	5 6	Cass County	ND	Paul Rohrer	2006	8053
149 2/8	24 0/8 23 7/8	20 2/8	5 5	Mercer County	IL	Kenneth Yeater	2006	8053
*149 2/8	22 4/8 23 3/8	18 6/8	4 5	Sumner County	KS	Randy Hoffman	2006	8053
149 2/8	24 1/8 23 7/8	21 1/8	6 7	Shawano County	WI	Kevin Prien	2007	8053
149 2/8	24 2/8 22 6/8	16 1/8	5 6	Kiskatinaw River	BC	Wayne Chmelyk	2007	8053
149 2/8	22 3/8 21 7/8	16 5/8	6 5	Goodhue County	MN	Mitchell Gadient	2007	8053
*149 2/8	20 6/8 20 7/8	18 2/8	5 5	Kewaunee County	WI	Jamie Charles	2007	8053
*149 2/8	24 4/8 23 4/8	18 2/8	5 5	Adams County	IL	Johnny Shields	2007	8053
149 2/8	24 1/8 23 4/8	14 6/8	5 5	Hartford County	CT	John Miller	2007	8053
*149 2/8	24 3/8 23 3/8	17 0/8	5 4	Fulton County	GA	Bob Coombs	2007	8053
149 2/8	25 6/8 23 5/8	15 7/8	6 7	Adams County	IA	Travis Paul	2008	8053
149 2/8	22 0/8 22 7/8	16 6/8	5 6	Randolph County	NC	Leon Kyle Lamb	2009	8053
149 2/8	22 7/8 22 4/8	18 1/8	5 6	Grand Forks County	ND	Aaron Christ Johnson	2009	8053
149 2/8	23 4/8 23 6/8	17 4/8	5 5	Taylor County	IA	Steven Corey Melton	2009	8053
149 2/8	21 0/8 20 6/8	14 5/8	5 6	Genesee County	MI	Dustin Terwilliger	2009	8053
*149 2/8	22 1/8 21 5/8	17 0/8	5 6	Woodward County	OK	Chris Edwards	2009	8053
149 2/8	20 6/8 20 4/8	14 3/8	5 6	Butler County	KS	Travis B. Henderson	2009	8053
*149 2/8	23 1/8 23 0/8	16 7/8	6 6	St. Louis County	MN	Kevin Busche	2009	8053
149 1/8	25 4/8 25 0/8	17 0/8	5 7	Bon Homme County	SD	Terry Gretschman	1974	8150
149 1/8	23 3/8 22 0/8	19 6/8	6 5	Coles County	IL	Bill Spaniol	1976	8150
149 1/8	25 7/8 23 2/8	19 7/8	5 5	Clark County	IL	Gerald D. Shaffner	1984	8150
149 1/8	24 0/8 24 6/8	19 4/8	6 6	Phillips County	KS	Bryan Henry	1984	8150
149 1/8	22 3/8 24 2/8	17 2/8	6 5	Traill County	ND	Dale Grindeland	1986	8150
149 1/8	26 1/8 27 3/8	19 5/8	7 7	Morrison County	MN	Jeff Moris	1987	8150
149 1/8	25 6/8 24 7/8	16 3/8	5 4	Union County	KY	Joseph K. "Bo" Girten	1988	8150
149 1/8	25 7/8 26 3/8	20 5/8	4 4	Washington County	MN	Scott Ralidak	1989	8150
149 1/8	25 1/8 24 1/8	16 7/8	6 5	Vilas County	WI	Craig Hanson	1989	8150
149 1/8	22 3/8 22 6/8	15 5/8	5 5	Stearns County	MN	Duane Gertken	1989	8150
149 1/8	21 5/8 23 0/8	20 7/8	5 5	Peoria County	IL	Tom Missen	1989	8150
149 1/8	23 1/8 23 0/8	17 1/8	11 8	Clinton County	IL	Tracy Hawes	1990	8150
149 1/8	23 6/8 24 4/8	18 3/8	5 6	Crow Wing County	MN	Shane Gunderson	1991	8150
149 1/8	24 2/8 25 4/8	16 3/8	7 7	Sarpy County	NE	Bernard J. Kubat, Jr.	1991	8150
149 1/8	23 7/8 24 3/8	20 3/8	5 5	Iron County	WI	Kevin J. Genisot	1991	8150
149 1/8	22 2/8 23 0/8	16 3/8	5 5	Neosho County	KS	Scotty Manbeck	1992	8150
149 1/8	23 3/8 24 1/8	15 3/8	6 5	Hancock County	OH	Bruce O'Rear	1992	8150
149 1/8	26 4/8 25 4/8	19 5/8	5 5	Noxubee County	MS	Chuck Allen	1993	8150
149 1/8	26 1/8 24 2/8	18 7/8	4 5	Guilford County	NC	Wanda L. Peeples	1993	8150
149 1/8	26 1/8 25 3/8	21 7/8	6 4	Peoria County	IL	Tom Missen	1993	8150
149 1/8	22 0/8 23 1/8	17 7/8	5 5	Stevens County	WA	Greg Sorensen	1994	8150

441

WHITETAIL DEER (TYPICAL ANTLERS)

Minimum Score 125   Continued

SCORE	LENGTH OF R MAIN BEAM L		INSIDE SPREAD	NUMBER OF R POINTS L		AREA	STATE/ PROVINCE	HUNTER'S NAME	DATE	RANK
149 1/8	24 0/8	25 0/8	21 1/8	5	5	Kenosha County	WI	Jamie Boyd	1994	8150
149 1/8	25 0/8	25 2/8	18 1/8	5	4	Scott County	MN	Norman J. Williams	1994	8150
149 1/8	25 3/8	24 3/8	17 7/8	5	6	Whiteside County	IL	Clint Walker	1995	8150
149 1/8	22 7/8	23 2/8	20 3/8	5	5	Waukesha County	WI	Tom Gorski	1995	8150
149 1/8	26 0/8	24 7/8	20 4/8	4	5	Sangamon County	IL	Kent J. Sturhahn	1995	8150
149 1/8	26 6/8	27 0/8	21 1/8	5	5	Brown County	IL	Bill Cross	1995	8150
149 1/8	23 3/8	23 2/8	18 1/8	4	7	Linn County	MO	Marc Amer	1995	8150
149 1/8	22 0/8	21 6/8	17 5/8	5	5	Lake County	IL	Gary Hannigan	1996	8150
149 1/8	23 2/8	23 2/8	18 4/8	5	7	Grayson County	TX	Shane Wilson	1996	8150
149 1/8	25 2/8	25 3/8	18 7/8	5	5	Worth County	GA	Ian Wolfgang Hindle	1997	8150
149 1/8	23 6/8	23 2/8	17 5/8	5	5	Montgomery County	MD	Steven Nocket	1998	8150
149 1/8	24 0/8	24 4/8	18 5/8	5	4	Lancaster County	NE	Bryan Bjorkman	1998	8150
149 1/8	24 0/8	24 0/8	17 5/8	5	5	Scott County	IN	Jason Reynolds	1998	8150
149 1/8	23 6/8	24 6/8	19 3/8	5	5	La Crosse County	WI	Dirk W. Hunter	1998	8150
149 1/8	22 2/8	24 4/8	15 7/8	6	6	Rock Island County	IL	Robert P. Moore	1998	8150
149 1/8	22 4/8	22 6/8	17 7/8	5	5	Jo Daviess County	IL	Edward C. Schultz	1998	8150
149 1/8	21 0/8	22 1/8	18 3/8	5	5	Burnett County	WI	Bruce A. Thomas	1998	8150
149 1/8	24 7/8	24 2/8	17 7/8	5	5	Adams County	WI	Jeffrey Bellmer	1999	8150
149 1/8	24 4/8	23 6/8	17 3/8	5	5	Oneida County	WI	Marty Smith	1999	8150
149 1/8	21 3/8	22 3/8	18 7/8	5	5	Adams County	IL	David Wedding	1999	8150
149 1/8	23 7/8	23 7/8	16 4/8	6	5	White County	IN	Rickey Adams	1999	8150
149 1/8	23 7/8	23 4/8	17 3/8	5	5	Washington County	MO	John Kolisch	1999	8150
149 1/8	24 3/8	25 5/8	17 7/8	5	5	Ross County	OH	James Silvers	1999	8150
149 1/8	22 2/8	21 4/8	14 7/8	6	6	Adams County	WI	Keith C. Redding	1999	8150
149 1/8	24 4/8	24 1/8	15 5/8	5	5	Wyoming County	WV	Steve Davis	1999	8150
149 1/8	25 1/8	24 5/8	16 5/8	8	7	Lincoln County	WI	Scott Gipple	2000	8150
149 1/8	24 0/8	23 3/8	20 7/8	4	4	Boone County	IL	Quentin E. Paul	2000	8150
149 1/8	22 6/8	22 4/8	18 5/8	5	4	Tippecanoe County	IN	Tom McIntyre	2000	8150
149 1/8	24 6/8	25 7/8	21 0/8	5	6	Crawford County	IL	Michele Fitts	2001	8150
149 1/8	23 2/8	22 5/8	17 7/8	5	5	Marquette County	WI	David E. Tearney	2001	8150
149 1/8	23 7/8	25 1/8	19 1/8	6	5	Niagara County	NY	Chris Reid	2001	8150
149 1/8	24 3/8	23 1/8	17 3/8	5	5	Greenwood County	KS	Guy Rupert	2001	8150
*149 1/8	23 7/8	24 2/8	18 0/8	6	5	St Pierre de Broughton	QUE	Jimmy Cliché	2002	8150
149 1/8	25 5/8	24 4/8	19 2/8	5	5	Dodge County	WI	Jeffrey Pankow	2002	8150
*149 1/8	25 2/8	25 3/8	19 3/8	5	5	Macon County	IL	Lou Cullum	2003	8150
149 1/8	25 1/8	25 0/8	18 5/8	5	5	Bayfield County	WI	Brian Weber	2003	8150
149 1/8	24 7/8	24 6/8	16 7/8	8	5	Lake County	IN	Wayne Raper	2003	8150
149 1/8	24 1/8	24 3/8	21 6/8	7	6	Calhoun County	IL	Craig Kittstein	2003	8150
149 1/8	23 1/8	22 1/8	16 3/8	7	6	Van Buren County	IA	Blake Swanson	2004	8150
149 1/8	24 7/8	25 4/8	19 3/8	4	5	Sarpy County	NE	James J. Beebe	2005	8150
*149 1/8	23 2/8	22 6/8	16 7/8	6	5	De Kalb County	IN	Phil L. Pulley	2005	8150
*149 1/8	22 4/8	22 2/8	19 5/8	6	6	Blackford County	IN	Mark Lechien	2005	8150
*149 1/8	24 2/8	23 4/8	17 6/8	5	5	Jackson County	OH	Jeremy Kerns	2005	8150
149 1/8	22 5/8	21 2/8	20 5/8	5	6	Allen County	IN	Justin M. Edwards	2005	8150
149 1/8	23 1/8	22 4/8	17 1/8	4	4	Brown County	IL	George D. Reed, Jr.	2005	8150
*149 1/8	21 7/8	23 2/8	19 0/8	5	5	Greene County	IL	Frank Lyerla	2006	8150
149 1/8	22 0/8	23 3/8	19 5/8	6	5	Pepin County	WI	John Meade	2006	8150
149 1/8	22 6/8	23 4/8	19 3/8	6	6	McLean County	ND	Tim Tomlinson	2006	8150
*149 1/8	22 7/8	22 7/8	18 1/8	5	5	Parkland	ALB	Dale Johnson	2006	8150
*149 1/8	24 5/8	24 0/8	16 5/8	5	5	Barber County	KS	Blayne St. James	2006	8150
149 1/8	23 1/8	22 2/8	17 0/8	5	6	Scott County	KY	Thomas H. Marshall	2007	8150
*149 1/8	21 5/8	21 5/8	18 7/8	5	5	Throckmorton County	TX	Ched J. Kinler	2007	8150
*149 1/8	25 7/8	25 7/8	16 5/8	6	6	Fayette County	IN	Merle Seeley	2007	8150
149 1/8	24 4/8	25 2/8	16 0/8	6	6	Racine County	WI	Ian Schrank	2008	8150
*149 1/8	26 6/8	26 2/8	18 1/8	4	4	Armstrong County	PA	Nicholas D. Freemar	2008	8150
149 1/8	24 0/8	24 0/8	20 1/8	5	5	Marquette County	WI	Clay Campbell	2008	8150
149 1/8	26 5/8	26 3/8	18 5/8	5	4	Labette County	KS	Rodney J. Kelly	2008	8150
*149 1/8	27 1/8	28 0/8	18 7/8	5	5	Weld County	CO	Dave Culter	2008	8150
*149 1/8	24 7/8	24 4/8	18 3/8	4	4	Johnson County	IA	Brian Oberfoell	2008	8150
149 1/8	21 7/8	23 2/8	16 3/8	6	8	Dane County	WI	Travis Simplot	2009	8150
*149 1/8	24 5/8	23 3/8	16 6/8	7	7	Meigs County	OH	Joe Pursley	2009	8150
149 1/8	25 1/8	27 0/8	19 5/8	5	4	Madison County	ID	Michael Larson	2009	8150
149 0/8	25 7/8	23 5/8	19 4/8	6	5	Mitchell County	IA	Elmer Krueger	1961	8233
149 0/8	25 0/8	25 0/8	19 4/8	5	4	Black Hawk County	IA	Robert Riggle	1975	8233
149 0/8	23 4/8	22 5/8	15 4/8	5	5	Pickaway County	OH	Weldon R. Snyder	1980	8233
149 0/8	24 4/8	23 4/8	19 6/8	5	5	Marion County	KS	David C. Hett	1980	8233
149 0/8	24 6/8	25 1/8	19 2/8	6	5	Warren County	IA	Grant Poindexter	1981	8233
149 0/8	25 5/8	24 5/8	18 6/8	4	5	Kiowa County	KS	Dan Manwarren	1984	8233
149 0/8	25 1/8	24 6/8	17 7/8	6	5	Calhoun County	MI	Larry C. Holcomb	1984	8233
149 0/8	21 5/8	21 6/8	20 0/8	5	5	Atchison County	KS	Larry Bleier	1985	8233
149 0/8	26 0/8	26 2/8	18 3/8	4	5	Morrison County	MN	Craig Krafthefer	1986	8233
149 0/8	27 1/8	27 6/8	20 6/8	4	4	Dunn County	WI	Mark Sokup	1987	8233
149 0/8	23 3/8	24 6/8	17 6/8	6	5	Marinette County	WI	Philip E. Bretl	1987	8233
149 0/8	23 4/8	22 4/8	15 2/8	7	6	Kenosha County	WI	Alois Jeske, Sr.	1987	8233
149 0/8	23 5/8	23 4/8	21 1/8	6	7	Washtenaw County	MI	Frank Schmidt, Jr.	1987	8233
149 0/8	23 0/8	22 7/8	17 4/8	5	6	Clay County	IL	David Thompson	1987	8233
149 0/8	24 1/8	24 4/8	19 1/8	6	7	Ozaukee County	WI	Jack Klotz	1988	8233
149 0/8	25 7/8	24 4/8	19 6/8	5	5	San Augustine County	TX	Ed Gunter	1988	8233
149 0/8	22 0/8	22 2/8	17 2/8	5	5	Hardin County	IA	William Stonebraker	1988	8233
149 0/8	26 3/8	25 2/8	19 2/8	6	6	Kane County	IL	Bill Yoakum	1988	8233
149 0/8	23 3/8	22 6/8	18 6/8	5	5	Dubuque County	IA	James A. Deckert	1990	8233
149 0/8	23 0/8	22 4/8	17 7/8	6	6	Greene County	AR	Mike Croy	1990	8233
149 0/8	24 0/8	24 0/8	19 2/8	5	4	Brown County	IN	Dale Snyder	1991	8233
149 0/8	24 4/8	26 2/8	15 4/8	5	5	Schuyler County	IL	Bill Daugherty	1991	8233
149 0/8	21 5/8	22 5/8	17 2/8	5	5	Bledsoe County	TN	Marty N. Swafford	1991	8233
149 0/8	25 3/8	25 0/8	19 0/8	5	5	Du Page County	IL	Peter Schumacher	1991	8233
149 0/8	24 3/8	24 1/8	19 2/8	5	5	Racine County	WI	Brek M. Zortman	1991	8233
149 0/8	24 5/8	25 1/8	21 2/8	5	5	Taylor County	WI	Logan W. Winger	1992	8233
149 0/8	24 1/8	24 7/8	20 6/8	5	5	Surry County	VA	Jeff S. Davis	1992	8233
149 0/8	22 5/8	22 1/8	17 6/8	5	5	Lake County	IL	Wayne Johnson	1992	8233
149 0/8	21 7/8	20 7/8	18 4/8	6	6	Menard County	IL	Ronald J. Wadsworth	1992	8233
149 0/8	22 4/8	24 2/8	20 3/8	5	5	Livingston County	IL	Rick DeFauw	1993	8233
149 0/8	24 1/8	23 6/8	18 0/8	5	5	Butler County	OH	James W. Burnes	1994	8233
149 0/8	21 5/8	21 3/8	14 5/8	6	6	Dawes County	NE	Gary L. Mason	1994	8233
149 0/8	21 5/8	21 3/8	14 5/8	6	6	Worcester County	MD	Kip Melson	1994	8233

442

WHITETAIL DEER (TYPICAL ANTLERS)

Minimum Score 125
Continued

SCORE	LENGTH OF R MAIN BEAM L	INSIDE SPREAD	NUMBER OF R POINTS L	AREA	STATE/ PROVINCE	HUNTER'S NAME	DATE	RANK
149 0/8	24 7/8 24 7/8	17 2/8	6 6	Houston County	MN	Bob Borowiak	1995	8233
149 0/8	22 3/8 22 4/8	14 6/8	5 5	Livingston County	MI	Mark L. Klett	1995	8233
149 0/8	24 7/8 25 0/8	17 2/8	5 5	Louisa County	IA	Robert McCulley	1995	8233
149 0/8	24 0/8 22 4/8	16 0/8	8 6	Jackson County	MO	Stephen D. Vincent	1995	8233
149 0/8	21 3/8 21 1/8	17 4/8	5 5	Dodge County	MN	Kerry Webster	1996	8233
149 0/8	26 1/8 26 6/8	19 1/8	6 6	Kenedy County	TX	Richard M. Ley	1996	8233
149 0/8	25 2/8 23 6/8	17 2/8	5 6	Walworth County	WI	James May	1997	8233
149 0/8	20 2/8 20 4/8	14 0/8	7 7	Montgomery County	KS	Dr. Daniel J. Gray	1997	8233
149 0/8	24 1/8 23 0/8	16 2/8	5 5	Athens County	OH	Charles Thompson	1997	8233
149 0/8	23 3/8 22 3/8	16 4/8	5 5	Duval County	TX	F. H. Becker	1997	8233
149 0/8	24 2/8 24 1/8	18 4/8	5 5	Carroll County	TN	Rex Walter Robinson	1998	8233
149 0/8	24 4/8 25 4/8	17 2/8	4 5	Linn County	IA	Christopher J. Swanke	1998	8233
149 0/8	27 7/8 27 6/8	19 7/8	4 5	Waukesha County	WI	Dan Infalt	1998	8233
149 0/8	24 1/8 24 7/8	16 2/8	5 5	Ohio County	IN	Darrin Christerson	1998	8233
149 0/8	25 7/8 25 4/8	20 0/8	5 4	Jones County	IA	Jason Tapken	1998	8233
149 0/8	25 2/8 25 1/8	18 2/8	6 7	Lancaster County	NE	Dave Allder	1998	8233
149 0/8	24 0/8 23 5/8	20 6/8	8 7	Winnebago County	WI	Neal E. Roebke	1999	8233
149 0/8	25 2/8 24 6/8	20 2/8	5 5	Grant County	WI	Randy L. Rech	1999	8233
149 0/8	22 4/8 22 0/8	19 2/8	5 5	Winnebago County	IL	James R. Petersen	1999	8233
149 0/8	21 4/8 20 3/8	17 4/8	6 6	Oconto County	WI	Ralph H. Torbeck	1999	8233
149 0/8	23 6/8 23 7/8	18 2/8	4 4	Morgan County	IL	Chuck Woodward	1999	8233
149 0/8	22 2/8 23 1/8	18 6/8	5 4	Houston County	MN	Raymond L. Howell, Sr.	1999	8233
149 0/8	24 3/8 24 0/8	19 0/8	5 5	Jo Daviess County	IL	Edward C. Schultz	2000	8233
149 0/8	27 6/8 27 7/8	15 6/8	4 5	Trempealeau County	WI	Walter J. Hofer	2000	8233
149 0/8	24 0/8 23 6/8	16 0/8	6 6	Monmouth County	NJ	Tim Shipman	2000	8233
149 0/8	24 0/8 22 5/8	20 4/8	5 5	Jefferson County	WI	Robert Peot, Jr.	2001	8233
149 0/8	22 2/8 24 0/8	19 4/8	5 5	Warren County	IA	Cody Ryan Frye	2001	8233
149 0/8	25 3/8 26 7/8	17 0/8	6 6	Van Buren County	IA	Michael D. Thornton	2001	8233
149 0/8	24 5/8 24 6/8	18 4/8	4 4	Oneida County	WI	George F. Kvatek	2002	8233
149 0/8	25 4/8 25 5/8	20 1/8	5 6	Niagara County	NY	Martin Stephenson	2002	8233
149 0/8	24 5/8 24 2/8	16 6/8	4 5	Rusk County	WI	Mitch Baker	2002	8233
149 0/8	22 4/8 24 4/8	16 6/8	6 5	Marion County	IL	Vernice Young	2002	8233
149 0/8	23 4/8 25 4/8	17 5/8	8 7	Waukesha County	WI	Jeffrey Hecyk	2003	8233
149 0/8	23 7/8 23 2/8	19 4/8	5 5	Martin County	IN	John R. Butcher	2003	8233
149 0/8	24 6/8 24 4/8	22 1/8	4 5	Richland County	IL	Daryl Zuber	2003	8233
149 0/8	24 7/8 26 3/8	16 6/8	5 5	Macon County	IL	Dave Elliott	2003	8233
149 0/8	25 3/8 25 1/8	16 4/8	6 6	Comanche County	KS	Dennis F. Craft	2003	8233
*149 0/8	26 1/8 25 7/8	15 2/8	6 4	Yell County	AR	Trinidad Escovedo, Jr.	2004	8233
149 0/8	24 5/8 23 6/8	22 0/8	6 8	Rockland County	NY	Hugh Artrip	2004	8233
*149 0/8	25 4/8 25 1/8	19 2/8	5 5	Washington County	OH	Tulsa Green	2004	8233
*149 0/8	23 4/8 23 7/8	21 2/8	4 4	Nobles County	MN	Chad Jeffers	2004	8233
149 0/8	23 7/8 22 7/8	14 3/8	7 6	Pawnee County	NE	Bill Phillips	2004	8233
*149 0/8	23 4/8 24 1/8	17 6/8	5 5	Trempealeau County	WI	Alan P. Suchla	2005	8233
149 0/8	22 2/8 22 1/8	18 3/8	6 6	Marshall County	WV	David Yoho	2005	8233
149 0/8	22 3/8 23 7/8	16 3/8	5 7	Priddis	ALB	Lorne D. Rinkel	2005	8233
*149 0/8	23 5/8 24 0/8	15 5/8	6 6	Union County	SD	Tate Glader	2006	8233
149 0/8	23 6/8 23 4/8	17 5/8	5 6	Polk County	WI	John A. Fredrick, Jr.	2006	8233
149 0/8	23 0/8 22 2/8	18 1/8	7 7	St. Croix County	WI	Robert J. Evans	2006	8233
149 0/8	24 4/8 22 6/8	17 2/8	5 5	Monona County	IA	John E. Seward	2006	8233
149 0/8	27 1/8 27 1/8	19 1/8	4 6	Plymouth County	IA	Eric J. Ellensohn	2006	8233
149 0/8	23 2/8 23 6/8	17 4/8	5 5	Livingston County	KY	William E. Joiner	2007	8233
149 0/8	23 2/8 22 6/8	16 1/8	6 9	Doniphan County	KS	David Hurd II	2007	8233
149 0/8	21 6/8 21 5/8	18 0/8	5 5	Trempealeau County	WI	Jeff Helmers	2008	8233
149 0/8	23 0/8 23 5/8	19 0/8	4 5	Buffalo County	WI	Beau Hensen	2008	8233
149 0/8	25 0/8 25 0/8	17 2/8	5 5	Rooks County	KS	Shawn W. Harding	2008	8233
149 0/8	24 2/8 23 5/8	19 7/8	6 6	Marquette County	WI	John Steuck	2008	8233
149 0/8	24 2/8 24 3/8	18 5/8	6 6	Wyandot County	OH	David Ware	2009	8233
149 0/8	25 0/8 25 1/8	21 0/8	4 5	Souris	MAN	Bryan Klein	2009	8233
*149 0/8	21 5/8 21 4/8	15 7/8	5 7	Shawano County	WI	Brian W. Ratayczak	2009	8233
*149 0/8	22 5/8 23 2/8	16 4/8	5 5	Waupaca County	WI	Todd A. Kurszewski	2009	8233
149 0/8	22 5/8 23 2/8	16 4/8	5 5	Buffalo County	WI	Tom Wolfe	2009	8233
148 7/8	15 4/8 26 0/8	19 4/8	5 7	Lincoln County	WI	Ronald Pond	1961	8327
148 7/8	24 6/8 24 0/8	18 7/8	4 5	Grant County	SD	Larry Turbak	1964	8327
148 7/8	23 1/8 23 1/8	18 4/8	6 4	Knox County	OH	John E. Bumpus	1971	8327
148 7/8	23 1/8 23 1/8	19 3/8	5 4	Clayton County	IA	Ralph Edward Livingston	1984	8327
148 7/8	24 2/8 22 7/8	17 2/8	6 5	Clay County	KS	Larry Reed	1985	8327
148 7/8	23 0/8 23 1/8	16 5/8	5 5	Erie County	NY	Martin Dollard	1986	8327
148 7/8	25 2/8 24 4/8	17 7/8	4 4	Pepin County	WI	Denton Hoyt	1987	8327
148 7/8	24 3/8 22 7/8	20 3/8	6 6	Caledon Township	ONT	Jack Leggo	1988	8327
148 7/8	24 4/8 26 2/8	18 5/8	4 4	Iroquois County	IL	Andrew C. McTaggart	1989	8327
148 7/8	22 3/8 20 0/8	16 1/8	6 6	Lee County	IL	Marcus Nettz	1990	8327
148 7/8	23 0/8 23 0/8	17 1/8	5 5	Fillmore County	MN	Brad Sutton	1990	8327
148 7/8	24 6/8 25 0/8	21 1/8	5 5	Anoka County	MN	Bob Ross	1990	8327
148 7/8	26 1/8 27 6/8	18 5/8	5 5	Heard County	GA	Jeffery T. Jackson	1990	8327
148 7/8	22 0/8 22 7/8	18 5/8	5 5	Burleigh County	ND	Don Bieber	1991	8327
148 7/8	24 1/8 24 6/8	19 7/8	6 6	Dane County	WI	Matthew A. Shimniok	1991	8327
148 7/8	20 3/8 19 3/8	13 7/8	6 6	Nodaway County	MO	Ron Browning	1991	8327
148 7/8	24 5/8 24 2/8	19 2/8	6 6	Stafford County	KS	Dan Schaad	1991	8327
148 7/8	26 3/8 26 5/8	19 0/8	7 6	Buffalo County	WI	Ron Books	1992	8327
148 7/8	24 7/8 24 5/8	18 3/8	5 4	Cass County	MI	William L. Bethard, Jr.	1992	8327
148 7/8	24 3/8 23 6/8	20 1/8	4 4	Knox County	IL	Dennis Landon	1992	8327
148 7/8	23 4/8 23 4/8	17 1/8	7 6	Brown County	SD	Brad Dinger	1993	8327
148 7/8	22 7/8 24 1/8	17 3/8	5 5	Washington County	IA	Rich Albright	1993	8327
148 7/8	24 2/8 25 3/8	20 1/8	6 5	Harding Township	ONT	Larry Ferguson	1993	8327
148 7/8	24 6/8 24 5/8	19 3/8	4 5	Hillsdale County	MI	Terry J. Gerber	1994	8327
148 7/8	26 0/8 25 6/8	20 7/8	5 4	Preble County	OH	Dean Ketring	1994	8327
148 7/8	23 0/8 23 4/8	15 3/8	5 5	Shelby County	IL	Jonathan L. Gifford	1994	8327
148 7/8	23 0/8 22 6/8	17 5/8	5 5	Osage County	KS	Tim Sparks	1994	8327
148 7/8	24 5/8 25 4/8	18 5/8	5 5	Adams County	WI	Russell Scoville	1995	8327
148 7/8	23 2/8 23 0/8	15 2/8	6 6	Clark County	IL	Gerald "Gabe" Shaffner	1995	8327
148 7/8	23 3/8 22 4/8	19 4/8	7 5	Parke County	IN	Tom James	1996	8327
148 7/8	22 6/8 22 2/8	17 5/8	5 5	Hendricks County	IN	James W. Thompson	1996	8327
148 7/8	25 2/8 24 6/8	17 5/8	5 5	Lorain County	OH	Steve Reinhold	1996	8327
148 7/8	24 1/8 24 1/8	15 7/8	5 5	Winona County	MN	Steven Krage	1996	8327
148 7/8	24 1/8 23 1/8	19 7/8	5 5	Morris County	NJ	David Barth	1996	8327

443

WHITETAIL DEER (TYPICAL ANTLERS)

Minimum Score 125   Continued

SCORE	LENGTH OF R MAIN BEAM L	INSIDE SPREAD	NUMBER OF R POINTS L	AREA	STATE/ PROVINCE	HUNTER'S NAME	DATE	RANK
148 7/8	21 7/8 22 0/8	17 5/8	5 5	Buffalo County	WI	John Larson	1996	8327
148 7/8	23 6/8 25 2/8	21 3/8	6 5	Polk County	WI	Larry Selzler	1996	8327
148 7/8	25 4/8 25 4/8	17 7/8	12 10	Grant County	IN	Kevin Kidwell	1997	8327
148 7/8	23 6/8 24 2/8	18 3/8	7 6	Des Moines County	IA	Eric S. Rankin	1997	8327
148 7/8	28 1/8 28 0/8	20 7/8	5 4	Preble County	OH	Mike McCabe	1997	8327
148 7/8	25 3/8 25 6/8	17 4/8	5 6	Marion County	IL	Brent Holzhausen	1997	8327
148 7/8	27 7/8 28 0/8	20 5/8	5 6	Richland County	OH	Craig Hallabrin	1997	8327
148 7/8	24 1/8 25 0/8	17 5/8	6 5	Waukesha County	WI	Brad Lenhardt	1997	8327
148 7/8	27 4/8 27 5/8	21 5/8	4 5	Montgomery County	PA	Jeff Steigelmann	1998	8327
148 7/8	23 4/8 24 3/8	18 4/8	6 5	Kewaunee County	WI	Randy L. Flentje	1998	8327
148 7/8	23 6/8 23 3/8	17 3/8	6 6	Waushara County	WI	Ralph Spanbauer	1998	8327
148 7/8	23 4/8 24 1/8	18 1/8	5 5	Somerset County	NJ	Spiro J. Stilianessis	1998	8327
148 7/8	23 3/8 23 7/8	18 2/8	6 7	Sarpy County	NE	Jim Camenzind	1999	8327
148 7/8	25 0/8 24 2/8	20 2/8	5 6	Marathon County	WI	Randall L. Moe	2000	8327
148 7/8	22 3/8 22 4/8	19 1/8	5 5	Holt County	NE	Gerry L. Schaaf	2000	8327
148 7/8	24 3/8 24 6/8	18 5/8	5 5	Sumner County	KS	Wayne K. Lillie	2000	8327
148 7/8	21 6/8 21 3/8	19 6/8	7 7	Warren County	IA	Steve Wells	2000	8327
148 7/8	23 4/8 23 6/8	18 1/8	6 6	Dane County	WI	Brian Campbell	2001	8327
148 7/8	23 0/8 23 5/8	17 1/8	5 5	Greene County	IL	Neil "Pete" Sickinger	2001	8327
148 7/8	23 7/8 24 1/8	18 1/8	5 5	Montgomery County	MD	Robert E. Yokley	2002	8327
148 7/8	25 0/8 23 5/8	18 7/8	5 5	Monroe County	WI	Andy Tetzlaff	2002	8327
148 7/8	23 1/8 24 4/8	18 3/8	5 5	Adams County	WI	Len Hamman	2002	8327
148 7/8	24 3/8 24 4/8	19 3/8	4 5	Houston County	MN	Leon McNutt	2002	8327
148 7/8	26 3/8 26 4/8	17 3/8	5 6	Mercer County	WV	Kevin Standifur	2002	8327
148 7/8	23 0/8 23 1/8	17 5/8	5 5	Carroll County	AR	Wesley Chaney	2002	8327
148 7/8	23 7/8 23 2/8	18 1/8	5 5	Lewis County	MO	Curt Thompson	2002	8327
148 7/8	23 2/8 23 6/8	17 5/8	5 5	Lake County	IL	Ted Hysell	2002	8327
148 7/8	20 6/8 21 7/8	18 6/8	7 5	Ogle County	IL	Marc Brumbly	2002	8327
148 7/8	26 0/8 26 3/8	19 6/8	4 5	Madison County	IL	Jerry Malone	2003	8327
148 7/8	24 6/8 26 0/8	18 1/8	4 4	Osage County	MO	Paul Heckemeyer	2003	8327
148 7/8	23 7/8 23 1/8	17 0/8	5 5	Moultrie County	IL	Bret Guin	2003	8327
148 7/8	23 4/8 22 3/8	17 5/8	5 5	Page County	IA	Dick Paul	2003	8327
148 7/8	23 6/8 23 3/8	16 5/8	5 5	Hardin County	IA	Bruce Off	2003	8327
148 7/8	22 5/8 23 3/8	15 1/8	5 5	Rice County	KS	Jeffrey David Morris	2004	8327
*148 7/8	25 1/8 25 2/8	16 2/8	6 5	Franklin County	NE	Steven D. Osterbuhr	2004	8327
148 7/8	25 3/8 24 6/8	16 6/8	5 6	Jo Daviess County	IL	Jim Horneck	2005	8327
148 7/8	25 2/8 24 5/8	18 3/8	4 4	Fayette County	IL	Jim Myers	2005	8327
*148 7/8	23 0/8 22 1/8	17 7/8	5 5	Jefferson County	WI	Dan Buckingham	2006	8327
148 7/8	25 4/8 24 4/8	17 5/8	5 5	Logan County	IL	Greg Broughton	2006	8327
148 7/8	23 4/8 25 0/8	19 7/8	5 5	Buchanan County	MO	Richard Roe	2006	8327
148 7/8	23 5/8 23 7/8	16 0/8	7 6	Parke County	IN	Mike Vore	2006	8327
*148 7/8	22 4/8 22 3/8	17 2/8	5 6	Richland County	ND	Brian Bernatos	2006	8327
148 7/8	21 5/8 22 5/8	19 5/8	5 5	La Salle County	IL	Al Kwiatkowski	2006	8327
148 7/8	21 1/8 22 6/8	18 1/8	5 5	Putnam County	IN	Tim French	2006	8327
148 7/8	22 4/8 21 4/8	17 3/8	5 5	Fond du Lac County	WI	Kevin J. Lefeber	2006	8327
*148 7/8	23 1/8 23 0/8	15 3/8	6 5	Buffalo County	WI	Josh Chelf	2007	8327
*148 7/8	23 0/8 23 7/8	19 1/8	6 7	Polk County	IA	Sean Roberts	2007	8327
148 7/8	25 0/8 24 6/8	19 5/8	5 5	Marinette County	WI	Robert Johnson	2007	8327
148 7/8	24 1/8 24 7/8	21 5/8	6 6	Benton County	IA	Chad W. Clark	2007	8327
*148 7/8	23 0/8 24 4/8	19 3/8	5 4	Lancaster County	NE	Tim Miller	2007	8327
148 7/8	23 4/8 24 2/8	18 1/8	5 5	Buffalo County	WI	Jeffrey Jones	2007	8327
*148 7/8	26 0/8 26 2/8	20 0/8	9 6	Madison County	IA	Brian Gray	2007	8327
148 7/8	23 7/8 24 1/8	18 4/8	5 6	Stevens County	WA	Chuck Berg	2007	8327
*148 7/8	25 2/8 26 0/8	22 3/8	4 4	New Castle County	DE	Nicky Ferrara	2008	8327
*148 7/8	24 0/8 23 7/8	17 2/8	5 5	Cloud County	KS	Bill Deckman	2008	8327
*148 7/8	22 7/8 23 0/8	17 7/8	5 5	St. Louis County	MN	Brian Johnson	2008	8327
148 7/8	22 7/8 24 0/8	17 0/8	6 5	Rock Island County	IL	David Miller	2009	8327
148 7/8	25 4/8 26 4/8	20 5/8	5 5	Goodhue County	MN	Sue Cushing	2009	8327
148 7/8	24 4/8 24 4/8	22 5/8	5 5	Rush County	KS	Craig Goettl	2009	8327
148 7/8	22 4/8 22 5/8	16 5/8	6 5	Pike County	IL	Rob Jones	2009	8327
148 6/8	25 1/8 25 7/8	18 0/8	4 5	Lincoln County	MO	Robert Remmert, Sr.	1960	8421
148 6/8	25 2/8 25 2/8	19 6/8	5 5	Iowa County	IA	Russ Sill	1967	8421
148 6/8	23 0/8 23 0/8	18 4/8	5 5	Jefferson County	IN	Jim Coldiron	1969	8421
148 6/8	21 3/8 21 1/8	19 1/8	6 5	Brown County	SD	Bill Franklin	1972	8421
148 6/8	22 0/8 21 7/8	16 5/8	7 5	Schuylkill County	PA	Scott Bond	1979	8421
148 6/8	24 2/8 23 4/8	22 6/8	6 7	Brookings County	SD	Larry Bohls	1982	8421
148 6/8	24 1/8 23 6/8	17 2/8	5 5	Boone County	IA	Earl Taylor	1982	8421
148 6/8	22 6/8 22 6/8	16 6/8	5 6	Reno County	KS	Davis J. Ediger	1982	8421
148 6/8	22 6/8 22 3/8	15 2/8	5 4	Pierce County	ND	James Olson	1983	8421
148 6/8	23 2/8 23 3/8	18 0/8	6 5	Kingsbury County	SD	Scott L. Laudenslager	1984	8421
148 6/8	23 2/8 23 0/8	16 5/8	7 6	Jefferson County	WI	Steve Behm	1985	8421
148 6/8	22 0/8 22 0/8	17 0/8	5 5	Monroe County	IN	Dene Snoddy	1986	8421
148 6/8	23 1/8 25 3/8	18 7/8	6 5	Morgan County	IL	Steve North	1986	8421
148 6/8	25 0/8 25 0/8	22 0/8	8 5	Jasper County	IA	William E. Webster	1987	8421
148 6/8	25 0/8 23 4/8	17 5/8	5 6	Clermont County	OH	Timothy M. Singler	1988	8421
148 6/8	22 3/8 22 1/8	17 7/8	7 6	Winona County	MN	Tom Kothenbeutel	1988	8421
148 6/8	24 0/8 23 0/8	17 0/8	5 5	Muscatine County	IA	Lyle Sindt	1988	8421
148 6/8	25 1/8 25 0/8	18 6/8	5 5	Middlesex County	MA	Joe R. Shepard	1988	8421
148 6/8	24 1/8 24 1/8	16 2/8	6 6	Chippewa County	MN	Paul D. Gill	1988	8421
148 6/8	22 2/8 22 2/8	16 5/8	8 6	Edmonton	ALB	Dave Dickson	1990	8421
148 6/8	23 1/8 23 3/8	16 6/8	5 5	Bon Homme County	SD	Leonard J. Magee	1990	8421
148 6/8	24 6/8 25 2/8	24 3/8	5 5	Anne Arundel County	MD	Jim Roy	1990	8421
148 6/8	23 4/8 23 5/8	18 2/8	5 5	Champaign County	IL	Terry Evans	1991	8421
148 6/8	25 1/8 24 4/8	21 1/8	6 5	Bourbon County	KS	Larry Daly	1991	8421
148 6/8	24 7/8 23 6/8	22 0/8	4 4	Zavala County	TX	Barry Powell	1992	8421
148 6/8	23 5/8 22 2/8	17 2/8	5 5	Seward County	KS	Lynn Leonard	1992	8421
148 6/8	26 1/8 25 2/8	18 5/8	7 7	Manitowoc County	WI	Daniel J. Kleiber	1992	8421
148 6/8	24 4/8 24 3/8	22 4/8	4 4	Fairfield County	CT	Stephen Rohaly	1992	8421
148 6/8	22 2/8 21 3/8	16 2/8	6 5	Holt County	MO	Jim Zawodny	1992	8421
148 6/8	23 3/8 26 4/8	18 3/8	8 5	Iroquois County	IL	Dennis Clark	1993	8421
148 6/8	25 1/8 24 5/8	21 0/8	5 5	Kenosha County	WI	Timothy Cox	1994	8421
148 6/8	24 4/8 24 7/8	18 4/8	5 5	Henry County	IA	Mark Weber	1994	8421
148 6/8	24 4/8 24 4/8	17 2/8	5 5	Dunn County	WI	Brian R. Bonesteel	1994	8421
148 6/8	26 4/8 24 6/8	19 4/8	5 6	Montgomery County	IA	Dick Paul	1994	8421
148 6/8	24 2/8 24 0/8	18 6/8	5 5	Jackson County	IL	Terri Lively	1994	8421

444

WHITETAIL DEER (TYPICAL ANTLERS)

Minimum Score 125   Continued

SCORE	LENGTH OF R MAIN BEAM L	INSIDE SPREAD	NUMBER OF R POINTS L	AREA	STATE/PROVINCE	HUNTER'S NAME	DATE	RANK
148 6/8	22 4/8 22 1/8	17 3/8	5 6	Granby River	BC	Randy Workman	1994	8421
148 6/8	24 0/8 24 0/8	17 4/8	5 6	Knox County	IL	Frank T. Cain	1994	8421
148 6/8	23 7/8 23 5/8	18 2/8	5 5	Oneida County	WI	David Klotzbuecher	1995	8421
148 6/8	22 7/8 22 2/8	19 2/8	6 5	Walworth County	WI	Randy Vinge	1995	8421
148 6/8	26 4/8 26 7/8	18 2/8	5 6	Athens County	OH	Charlie Grubbs	1995	8421
148 6/8	22 1/8 23 1/8	19 0/8	5 5	Pottawattamie County	IA	Donald Combs	1996	8421
148 6/8	24 2/8 24 2/8	21 0/8	6 6	Marshall County	IL	Timothy Myers	1997	8421
148 6/8	29 5/8 28 1/8	21 0/8	4 6	Calhoun County	MI	Toby M. Wendt	1997	8421
148 6/8	24 1/8 24 4/8	18 0/8	5 5	Cass County	IL	Kevin Duckwiler	1997	8421
148 6/8	27 0/8 27 4/8	21 2/8	4 4	Lorain County	OH	Steven D. Reinhold	1997	8421
148 6/8	20 6/8 21 3/8	15 6/8	5 5	Kane County	IL	Fred Lehman	1997	8421
148 6/8	20 4/8 22 5/8	18 2/8	5 5	Sandusky County	OH	Michael A. Gonya	1997	8421
148 6/8	22 4/8 22 4/8	16 2/8	6 6	Webster County	MS	Kenny May	1998	8421
148 6/8	22 5/8 22 4/8	20 2/8	6 6	Pierce County	WI	Brent A. Schuler	1998	8421
148 6/8	22 5/8 23 0/8	18 7/8	5 6	Morrison County	MN	Derek Tykwinski	1998	8421
148 6/8	26 0/8 25 0/8	16 2/8	4 4	Richland County	WI	Douglas Elliott	1998	8421
148 6/8	23 1/8 24 3/8	15 4/8	6 6	Harrison County	OH	Jerry Dickerson	1998	8421
148 6/8	26 4/8 25 5/8	19 3/8	5 7	Jasper County	IL	Steve Gray	1998	8421
148 6/8	25 2/8 25 3/8	20 2/8	6 4	Johnston County	NC	Ronnie Lee Shirley, Jr.	1999	8421
148 6/8	26 1/8 27 0/8	20 6/8	5 5	Washington County	MS	Bobby R. Woods	1999	8421
148 6/8	24 2/8 25 1/8	15 2/8	5 5	Montgomery County	TX	Jason R. Pelton	1999	8421
148 6/8	24 5/8 24 4/8	16 6/8	5 5	Shelby County	IL	Jim Harbert	1999	8421
148 6/8	21 1/8 21 4/8	16 5/8	5 6	Pike County	IL	Philip D. Riley	1999	8421
148 6/8	23 4/8 24 0/8	16 3/8	5 7	Houston County	GA	Jim Dawson	1999	8421
148 6/8	23 5/8 23 6/8	17 6/8	4 4	Douglas County	NE	David Welch	1999	8421
148 6/8	22 5/8 22 5/8	15 2/8	5 5	Buffalo County	WI	Chuck Schultz	2000	8421
148 6/8	26 7/8 26 5/8	17 2/8	5 4	Monroe County	MI	Kenneth D. Locke	2000	8421
148 6/8	26 7/8 26 0/8	20 2/8	4 5	Delaware County	OH	Robert Seitz	2000	8421
148 6/8	23 4/8 22 4/8	17 6/8	5 5	Callaway County	MO	Willis Vance	2000	8421
148 6/8	23 4/8 23 3/8	16 6/8	5 5	Dubuque County	IA	Douglas M. Oberfoell	2000	8421
148 6/8	25 0/8 24 4/8	17 1/8	4 5	Edgar County	IL	Trent Herring	2000	8421
148 6/8	22 1/8 22 0/8	19 0/8	6 4	Lincoln County	SD	Chris Engberg	2001	8421
148 6/8	26 5/8 24 6/8	16 2/8	6 7	Effingham County	IL	Roger Loy	2001	8421
148 6/8	21 6/8 22 2/8	18 4/8	5 5	Iowa County	WI	Travis W. Halverson	2002	8421
148 6/8	25 2/8 25 2/8	20 0/8	7 7	Allamakee County	IA	Mike Peterson	2002	8421
148 6/8	23 0/8 24 2/8	14 7/8	8 5	Portage County	WI	Jeremy Wittmann	2002	8421
148 6/8	22 7/8 24 4/8	16 4/8	5 5	Vernon County	WI	Jim Koskovich	2002	8421
148 6/8	25 4/8 25 1/8	19 2/8	6 5	Summit County	OH	Larry Martin	2002	8421
148 6/8	22 7/8 22 0/8	15 7/8	5 6	Brown County	WI	Kurt Jordan	2002	8421
148 6/8	23 2/8 23 2/8	17 0/8	5 5	Scott County	MN	David S. Larson	2003	8421
*148 6/8	24 0/8 24 0/8	17 4/8	5 5	Grundy County	MO	Kenny Brewer	2004	8421
148 6/8	25 1/8 24 5/8	20 0/8	6 6	Todd County	KY	Harry Reagan	2004	8421
148 6/8	22 4/8 23 2/8	16 0/8	5 5	Calhoun County	MI	Mark R. Reynolds	2004	8421
148 6/8	25 0/8 25 5/8	20 6/8	4 6	Lee County	IL	Dale Dye	2004	8421
148 6/8	25 6/8 23 5/8	19 5/8	5 6	Warren County	IL	Daniel J. Semenza	2004	8421
148 6/8	23 7/8 23 7/8	21 3/8	5 5	New Haven County	CT	David Conroy	2004	8421
148 6/8	26 2/8 25 1/8	16 6/8	6 6	Montgomery County	KS	Mike Gevaert	2004	8421
148 6/8	23 7/8 23 0/8	20 5/8	5 5	Buffalo County	WI	Paul Teska	2005	8421
148 6/8	23 5/8 23 0/8	16 2/8	4 5	Logan County	AR	Rodney Canada	2005	8421
*148 6/8	24 2/8 24 2/8	16 3/8	5 6	Van Buren County	MI	Scott E. Austin	2005	8421
148 6/8	23 5/8 22 4/8	19 0/8	5 5	Knox County	OH	McCray Coates	2005	8421
148 6/8	25 2/8 24 7/8	15 0/8	5 5	Desha County	AR	David W. Bush	2005	8421
148 6/8	25 3/8 25 5/8	18 4/8	5 5	Eau Claire County	WI	Jeffrey J. Endvick	2006	8421
148 6/8	23 3/8 22 4/8	15 3/8	7 6	Page County	IA	Jeffery Slaymaker	2006	8421
*148 6/8	24 4/8 24 3/8	19 2/8	6 5	Van Buren County	MI	Matthew A. Scharl	2006	8421
148 6/8	27 1/8 25 7/8	19 5/8	6 6	Bradford County	PA	Tony Johnson	2006	8421
148 6/8	24 0/8 26 1/8	19 4/8	6 6	Anoka County	MN	Alan Muyres	2006	8421
*148 6/8	22 4/8 23 2/8	18 0/8	5 5	Washington County	KS	Brian P. Bishop	2006	8421
148 6/8	23 1/8 23 0/8	19 7/8	7 5	Caldwell County	MO	Tim Edwards	2007	8421
148 6/8	26 0/8 25 1/8	21 0/8	4 5	Lenawee County	MI	Scott D. Norkey	2007	8421
*148 6/8	23 0/8 21 4/8	18 4/8	6 6	Woodford County	IL	Bruno A. Albiero	2007	8421
*148 6/8	26 7/8 25 7/8	20 6/8	4 4	Cass County	IN	Todd R. Cripe	2007	8421
148 6/8	21 6/8 20 6/8	15 0/8	6 7	Wayne County	IN	Mark Seal	2007	8421
148 6/8	22 7/8 23 4/8	17 5/8	5 5	Billings County	ND	John Hild	2007	8421
148 6/8	21 5/8 21 2/8	17 2/8	6 5	Calloway County	KY	Tim J. Hobbs	2008	8421
148 6/8	25 2/8 24 7/8	18 0/8	5 5	Outagamie County	WI	Jaime Rettler	2008	8421
*148 6/8	23 4/8 23 7/8	16 3/8	6 5	Lake County	IN	James R. Burnett	2009	8421
148 6/8	23 5/8 23 0/8	23 0/8	4 4	Dunn County	WI	Robert J. Knops	2009	8421
*148 6/8	22 0/8 22 2/8	18 4/8	7 9	Bon Homme County	SD	Mark W. Sedlacek	2009	8421
*148 6/8	23 0/8 24 3/8	19 0/8	6 5	Linn County	KS	Michael Brian Jameson	2009	8421
148 5/8	25 2/8 25 3/8	17 7/8	5 5	Newton County	IN	Larry Boezeman	1971	8526
148 5/8	21 7/8 22 0/8	14 7/8	5 6	Pulaski County	MO	Ron Poston	1972	8526
148 5/8	26 7/8 26 6/8	23 1/8	6 5	Coshocton County	OH	Charles H. Vlasek, Jr.	1979	8526
148 5/8	23 0/8 22 6/8	22 1/8	5 5	Marion County	IA	Leonard Grimes	1981	8526
148 5/8	23 1/8 24 5/8	18 6/8	5 5	Tuscola County	MI	Patrick C. Lewis	1983	8526
148 5/8	25 6/8 25 6/8	19 6/8	6 5	Niobrara County	WY	Kenneth Fluck	1985	8526
148 5/8	19 3/8 21 7/8	20 5/8	6 6	Dunn County	WI	Richard Urbaniak	1985	8526
148 5/8	25 5/8 25 0/8	19 2/8	5 6	Piatt County	IL	David E. DeMoss	1985	8526
148 5/8	22 1/8 24 1/8	20 5/8	5 5	Hancock County	WV	William Gary Rusinovich	1986	8526
148 5/8	23 3/8 23 5/8	17 7/8	5 5	Price County	WI	Dave A. Radosta	1987	8526
148 5/8	26 4/8 25 7/8	18 5/8	4 5	Wabasha County	MN	Keith A. Ramthun	1988	8526
148 5/8	20 3/8 21 3/8	16 7/8	5 5	Somerset County	PA	Brian Jones	1988	8526
148 5/8	24 1/8 24 4/8	19 5/8	5 5	Sedgwick County	KS	Kent Lawson	1988	8526
148 5/8	24 4/8 24 4/8	17 5/8	7 7	Chippewa County	MN	Gary Laughlin	1988	8526
148 5/8	25 2/8 24 7/8	16 7/8	5 5	Crawford County	KS	Jim W. Heardt	1988	8526
148 5/8	26 6/8 25 3/8	19 5/8	4 6	Hardin County	IL	Charles E. Spear	1989	8526
148 5/8	23 1/8 24 2/8	19 5/8	4 5	Bureau County	IL	Gregory A. Bowers	1989	8526
148 5/8	22 7/8 23 3/8	16 3/8	5 5	Rock County	WI	R. Wayne Douglas	1989	8526
148 5/8	22 3/8 22 0/8	15 4/8	6 7	Licking County	OH	Randy Marcum	1990	8526
148 5/8	23 2/8 23 1/8	18 5/8	5 5	Oneida County	WI	John L. Mueller	1990	8526
148 5/8	23 4/8 22 6/8	18 5/8	5 7	Jackson County	MO	Donald Dutton	1991	8526
148 5/8	22 1/8 22 6/8	18 3/8	5 8	Selkirk	MAN	Kerry Minsky	1991	8526
148 5/8	24 1/8 24 1/8	18 5/8	5 5	Ogle County	IL	Thomas W. Sharkey	1991	8526
148 5/8	20 7/8 21 3/8	19 1/8	6 8	Clinton County	OH	Vaughn Wright	1991	8526
148 5/8	23 3/8 23 7/8	19 0/8	5 6	Warren County	IA	Mark Motsinger	1991	8526

445

WHITETAIL DEER (TYPICAL ANTLERS)

Minimum Score 125 — Continued

SCORE	LENGTH OF R MAIN BEAM L	INSIDE SPREAD	NUMBER OF R POINTS L	AREA	STATE/ PROVINCE	HUNTER'S NAME	DATE	RANK
148 5/8	24 6/8 25 0/8	17 0/8	6 5	Price County	WI	Charles Pasewald	1992	8526
148 5/8	24 3/8 23 2/8	19 1/8	5 5	Hamilton County	IA	Steve Doering	1992	8526
148 5/8	23 5/8 23 0/8	19 3/8	4 4	Dallas County	IA	John Flies	1992	8526
148 5/8	24 7/8 25 0/8	20 3/8	6 5	La Salle County	IL	Phill Pulfer	1993	8526
148 5/8	24 2/8 24 4/8	18 6/8	5 6	Sauk County	WI	Rick Krumenauer	1993	8526
148 5/8	23 3/8 23 6/8	16 3/8	6 6	Iroquois County	IL	Howard Brady	1994	8526
148 5/8	26 2/8 23 3/8	15 4/8	5 6	Wapello County	IA	David Meyer	1994	8526
148 5/8	24 4/8 25 4/8	19 4/8	5 7	Jackson County	WI	Michael Coleman	1995	8526
148 5/8	25 3/8 24 0/8	19 5/8	5 5	Pepin County	WI	Kirk Peterson	1995	8526
148 5/8	25 3/8 24 7/8	18 3/8	4 4	Knox County	IL	Gerald Duane Smith	1995	8526
148 5/8	24 5/8 23 5/8	16 5/8	5 5	Louisa County	IA	Rick Stroud	1995	8526
148 5/8	25 5/8 23 6/8	18 5/8	5 5	Starke County	IN	F. James Harris	1995	8526
148 5/8	23 3/8 23 5/8	19 1/8	5 6	Kenosha County	WI	Thomas T. King	1995	8526
148 5/8	25 0/8 24 5/8	21 1/8	5 5	Champaign County	OH	Roland A. Chamberlin	1995	8526
148 5/8	25 4/8 24 7/8	20 3/8	6 5	Orange County	NC	Bob Arnao	1996	8526
148 5/8	23 1/8 23 7/8	17 2/8	6 5	Benton County	IA	Chris Swanke	1996	8526
148 5/8	23 6/8 23 6/8	17 1/8	6 6	Clay County	KS	Larry Bloomfield	1997	8526
148 5/8	28 5/8 27 5/8	21 7/8	5 5	Douglas County	WI	Roland R. Peterson	1997	8526
148 5/8	22 6/8 22 7/8	17 5/8	7 7	Cotton County	OK	Scott Crew	1997	8526
148 5/8	22 0/8 23 0/8	21 1/8	5 5	Switzerland County	IN	Jeff Middendorf	1998	8526
148 5/8	23 6/8 23 2/8	14 2/8	5 6	Washburn County	WI	Tim Schmidt	1998	8526
148 5/8	23 4/8 24 0/8	19 2/8	6 6	Vinton County	OH	James A. Koch, Jr.	1998	8526
148 5/8	23 6/8 24 6/8	19 1/8	4 5	Sauk County	WI	Patrick M. Bloom	1998	8526
148 5/8	23 7/8 23 0/8	19 3/8	6 6	La Grange County	IN	Ron J. Gingerich	1999	8526
148 5/8	25 4/8 24 4/8	18 1/8	5 6	Floyd County	IA	Jerry Newton	1999	8526
148 5/8	24 3/8 24 7/8	15 7/8	5 5	Richland County	ND	Tom Hatlestad	2000	8526
148 5/8	24 4/8 25 7/8	20 0/8	6 5	Wyoming County	NY	Anthony Franklin	2000	8526
148 5/8	21 3/8 22 0/8	16 3/8	5 5	Ogle County	IL	Charles P. Lanzendorf	2000	8526
148 5/8	21 3/8 20 4/8	16 3/8	5 5	Putnam County	MO	Dennis Burk	2000	8526
148 5/8	23 7/8 23 3/8	17 3/8	5 5	Carroll County	MO	Mark L. Samuels	2000	8526
148 5/8	24 3/8 24 4/8	17 2/8	5 6	Preble County	OH	Stanley Jennings	2000	8526
148 5/8	25 5/8 25 1/8	20 7/8	6 5	Jackson County	MN	Steven Soehren	2001	8526
148 5/8	26 2/8 26 6/8	21 5/8	4 4	Edgar County	IL	Jack D. Hoffman	2001	8526
148 5/8	23 3/8 22 7/8	20 5/8	7 6	Sheboygan County	WI	Travis S. Luedtke	2001	8526
148 5/8	24 4/8 24 2/8	20 1/8	8 5	Ogle County	IL	Michael K. Jones	2001	8526
148 5/8	24 3/8 24 3/8	19 7/8	4 5	Clay County	KS	Bill Plowman	2001	8526
148 5/8	24 0/8 23 1/8	18 3/8	5 5	Greenwood County	KS	Frank S. Noska IV	2002	8526
148 5/8	21 5/8 22 0/8	17 6/8	6 5	Hamilton County	IA	Scott R. McCaulley	2002	8526
148 5/8	26 1/8 26 7/8	19 7/8	4 3	Westchester County	NY	Stephen Cook	2002	8526
148 5/8	25 3/8 26 6/8	18 2/8	5 5	Bartholomew County	IN	Dan Mace	2003	8526
148 5/8	23 5/8 22 3/8	17 1/8	5 6	Ottawa County	KS	Patrick E. Helget	2003	8526
*148 5/8	22 7/8 23 4/8	16 7/8	5 5	Perry County	OH	Steve Abram	2003	8526
148 5/8	24 6/8 21 6/8	21 0/8	6 6	Schuyler County	IL	Tom A. Grover	2003	8526
148 5/8	24 6/8 24 0/8	19 5/8	4 7	Douglas County	NE	Rodney Sigel	2004	8526
148 5/8	22 4/8 22 4/8	17 5/8	5 5	Grant County	IN	Donald Lee Monroe, Jr.	2004	8526
148 5/8	27 4/8 26 2/8	18 5/8	7 4	Phillips County	KS	Dennis J. Erkinger	2004	8526
148 5/8	23 6/8 23 3/8	18 1/8	5 4	Will County	IL	Thomas S. Spence	2004	8526
*148 5/8	23 0/8 22 7/8	15 1/8	7 5	Columbia County	WI	Timothy R. Brown	2005	8526
148 5/8	24 0/8 24 7/8	19 0/8	5 5	Muscatine County	IA	John Ager	2005	8526
148 5/8	26 4/8 25 6/8	17 1/8	4 4	Clinton County	IA	Ronald Feuss	2005	8526
148 5/8	24 2/8 23 6/8	17 2/8	5 5	Hartford County	CT	John Miller	2005	8526
*148 5/8	23 3/8 22 6/8	17 1/8	5 5	Trempealeau County	WI	Allan D. Stuhr	2005	8526
148 5/8	24 6/8 25 1/8	18 3/8	4 4	Mifflin County	PA	Michael Mathews	2006	8526
*148 5/8	23 5/8 23 4/8	18 2/8	6 5	Mitchell County	IA	Phil Brumm	2006	8526
148 5/8	24 5/8 25 1/8	17 4/8	7 5	Adams County	OH	Jeff Yost	2006	8526
148 5/8	24 4/8 24 2/8	16 0/8	6 7	Morrison County	MN	James Halupczok	2007	8526
148 5/8	23 6/8 24 7/8	18 3/8	5 5	Pottawattamie County	IA	Craig Benson	2007	8526
148 5/8	23 2/8 23 5/8	17 5/8	5 5	Republic County	KS	Bradley Deneault	2007	8526
148 5/8	23 3/8 21 2/8	16 2/8	5 6	Carroll County	IL	Jim Carlson	2007	8526
148 5/8	26 4/8 27 3/8	21 0/8	6 6	Randolph County	IL	Jerry Brown, Jr.	2007	8526
148 5/8	23 4/8 23 4/8	20 0/8	5 8	Marshall County	KS	Richard Dovey	2007	8526
148 5/8	22 2/8 24 2/8	17 4/8	7 6	Ferry County	WA	Shaun Honeycutt	2007	8526
*148 5/8	23 6/8 23 7/8	17 2/8	6 5	Johnson County	IA	Brad Myszka	2008	8526
*148 5/8	24 7/8 24 3/8	19 3/8	6 6	Hancock County	IL	James R. Presnell	2008	8526
148 5/8	22 1/8 22 0/8	18 3/8	6 6	Marion County	IL	Kevin Chambers	2008	8526
*148 5/8	22 4/8 21 4/8	17 1/8	5 5	Jackson County	OK	Jason S. Jones	2008	8526
*148 5/8	24 4/8 24 4/8	18 5/8	6 5	Jefferson County	WI	Moses Stiemke	2008	8526
*148 5/8	24 6/8 25 4/8	18 1/8	5 5	Mahoning County	OH	Steve Scott	2008	8526
*148 5/8	24 1/8 24 3/8	19 6/8	5 6	Northampton County	PA	Cory Nansteel	2009	8526
148 5/8	24 5/8 23 7/8	18 1/8	7 5	Van Buren County	IA	Charles W. Rehor	2009	8526
148 5/8	27 5/8 25 5/8	20 6/8	4 5	Washington County	IN	Shayne Spurgeor	2009	8526
148 5/8	23 3/8 21 7/8	16 1/8	5 5	Logan County	CO	Michael Dziekan	2009	8526
148 5/8	25 0/8 24 2/8	19 1/8	5 5	Atchison County	KS	Kyle Schrick	2009	8526
148 5/8	22 4/8 22 2/8	18 5/8	5 4	Lincoln County	AR	Wade Hill	2010	8526
148 4/8	23 0/8 22 4/8	20 1/8	4 5	Murray County	MN	Mike Molitor	1968	8625
148 4/8	20 7/8 21 4/8	16 6/8	5 5	Rock County	WI	Bruce Douglas	1978	8625
148 4/8	26 0/8 22 5/8	18 0/8	5 5	Woodford County	IL	James M. Bill, Jr.	1982	8625
148 4/8	24 2/8 24 5/8	21 5/8	5 5	Martin County	MN	Dean Roben	1982	8625
148 4/8	25 1/8 24 4/8	16 6/8	5 5	Grant County	WI	William P Rodenkirch	1983	8625
148 4/8	23 0/8 23 6/8	17 7/8	5 6	Pepin County	WI	Roger Anderson	1984	8625
148 4/8	23 7/8 25 2/8	19 4/8	5 4	Jefferson County	OH	Larry C. Riggle	1984	8625
148 4/8	25 5/8 24 2/8	18 4/8	5 5	Randolph County	IL	Conel H. Rogers, Jr.	1985	8625
148 4/8	24 3/8 24 5/8	20 6/8	7 6	Meade County	KS	Randall J. VanDegrift	1985	8625
148 4/8	22 2/8 22 2/8	19 6/8	5 5	Seward County	KS	Stuart G. Hazard III	1985	8625
148 4/8	25 6/8 22 0/8	19 1/8	8 7	Kings County	NBW	Ken Kirkpatrick	1986	8625
148 4/8	23 6/8 25 0/8	19 0/8	5 5	Edmonson County	KY	Marvin T. Pate	1987	8625
148 4/8	26 2/8 26 1/8	18 6/8	6 6	Waukesha County	WI	Ron V. Schneider	1987	8625
148 4/8	26 0/8 27 5/8	19 0/8	4 4	Orange County	NC	Todd McDonald	1988	8625
148 4/8	27 3/8 27 1/8	20 2/8	4 4	Lawrence County	IL	Russell Morris	1988	8625
148 4/8	21 6/8 21 4/8	17 6/8	5 5	Scott County	MN	Donald T. Turner	1989	8625
148 4/8	22 1/8 23 1/8	15 2/8	5 6	Burleigh County	ND	Robert Matzke	1989	8625
148 4/8	23 1/8 23 4/8	18 4/8	5 5	Woodford County	IL	Larry Messer	1989	8625
148 4/8	24 3/8 24 2/8	16 4/8	6 5	Polk County	WI	Daniel Carlson	1989	8625
148 4/8	22 5/8 22 7/8	17 2/8	5 5	Caldwell County	KY	Boyd Smith	1990	8625
148 4/8	26 0/8 25 5/8	21 4/8	7 6	Cedar County	IA	Brian Barclay	1990	8625

WHITETAIL DEER (TYPICAL ANTLERS)

Minimum Score 125 Continued

SCORE	LENGTH OF R MAIN BEAM L	INSIDE SPREAD	NUMBER OF R POINTS L	AREA	STATE/ PROVINCE	HUNTER'S NAME	DATE	RANK
148 4/8	22 6/8 22 3/8	18 6/8	5 5	Oneida County	WI	Jeff Aulik	1990	8625
148 4/8	25 2/8 26 0/8	16 7/8	5 5	Cumberland County	ME	Chester L. Brooks	1991	8625
148 4/8	21 5/8 23 5/8	17 4/8	5 5	Warren County	IA	Dan Mork	1991	8625
148 4/8	22 4/8 22 4/8	19 2/8	5 5	Baltimore County	MD	Bruce Hoover	1992	8625
148 4/8	20 4/8 21 1/8	16 6/8	6 5	Hardin County	OH	Kevin Stahler	1992	8625
148 4/8	23 6/8 23 3/8	17 6/8	5 5	Eau Claire County	WI	Jack T. Lawler	1992	8625
148 4/8	23 5/8 22 2/8	18 4/8	5 5	Wayne County	MI	Ronald A. Stolberg	1992	8625
148 4/8	26 3/8 25 7/8	19 4/8	5 7	Oneida County	WI	Jeffrey Roell	1993	8625
148 4/8	22 7/8 23 3/8	18 4/8	5 5	Iowa County	WI	Dennis Cliff	1993	8625
148 4/8	27 0/8 26 3/8	15 4/8	4 4	Iron County	WI	Gerold Schaff	1994	8625
148 4/8	24 7/8 24 5/8	18 2/8	4 4	Outagamie County	WI	Gerald A. Snortum	1994	8625
148 4/8	23 4/8 24 4/8	16 0/8	5 5	Lawrence County	OH	Robert Sturgill	1994	8625
148 4/8	24 4/8 24 3/8	18 0/8	6 5	Pike County	IL	Mark Beeler	1994	8625
148 4/8	25 1/8 25 1/8	16 2/8	5 5	Lake County	IL	Jim Tahaney	1996	8625
148 4/8	25 5/8 25 4/8	19 5/8	4 6	Allamakee County	IA	Jeff Wirth	1996	8625
148 4/8	22 2/8 22 3/8	16 0/8	5 5	Dubuque County	IA	Doug Westhoff	1996	8625
148 4/8	24 2/8 21 6/8	18 1/8	7 6	Ramsey County	MN	Robert Meyer, Jr.	1997	8625
148 4/8	24 6/8 26 2/8	19 0/8	5 5	Martin County	IN	Kevin Olinger	1997	8625
148 4/8	23 6/8 24 2/8	18 6/8	5 5	Allen County	IN	Randy Zion	1997	8625
148 4/8	24 3/8 24 3/8	19 0/8	5 5	Kewaunee County	WI	Joe J. Dax	1997	8625
148 4/8	23 2/8 24 2/8	22 2/8	4 4	Somerset County	NJ	James C. Kelly	1998	8625
148 4/8	24 7/8 23 5/8	15 4/8	7 5	Washburn County	WI	Nick Haus	1998	8625
148 4/8	22 2/8 21 5/8	17 2/8	7 6	Oneida County	WI	Steven J. Rainville	1998	8625
148 4/8	24 3/8 23 6/8	19 0/8	5 5	Shawano County	WI	David J. Yonker	1998	8625
148 4/8	24 0/8 23 1/8	19 3/8	5 6	Wood County	WI	Scott Leibl	1998	8625
148 4/8	22 4/8 22 0/8	17 4/8	5 6	Cumberland County	IL	Raymond Watkins	1998	8625
148 4/8	23 6/8 22 5/8	17 2/8	6 7	Winnebago County	IL	Robert H. Torstenson	1998	8625
148 4/8	23 2/8 24 3/8	19 3/8	6 6	Manitowoc County	WI	Gregory A. Valenta	1999	8625
148 4/8	24 2/8 23 1/8	17 1/8	5 6	Langlade County	WI	Greg Below	1999	8625
148 4/8	21 6/8 23 3/8	19 4/8	7 7	Stephenson County	IL	Dan Bumphrey	1999	8625
148 4/8	23 0/8 22 1/8	15 6/8	5 5	Hancock County	KY	Brian A. Nichols	1999	8625
148 4/8	26 6/8 26 0/8	18 4/8	5 5	Monroe County	NY	John Phillips	1999	8625
148 4/8	23 5/8 23 3/8	18 4/8	5 5	Davis County	IA	Bob Farthing	1999	8625
148 4/8	23 7/8 24 1/8	19 2/8	4 5	Chester County	PA	Walt Kowalczyk	1999	8625
148 4/8	22 6/8 21 2/8	17 0/8	5 5	Clayton County	GA	Wayne Boyd	1999	8625
148 4/8	22 5/8 22 4/8	20 0/8	5 5	Webb County	TX	H. I. "Hank" Bussa, Jr.	1999	8625
148 4/8	24 2/8 23 5/8	18 4/8	5 4	Fairfield County	CT	Joseph A. De Bone, Jr.	2000	8625
148 4/8	22 3/8 21 7/8	17 2/8	5 5	Ottawa County	KS	Shannon Reeves	2000	8625
148 4/8	22 0/8 23 0/8	17 4/8	5 5	Oconto County	WI	Brian Van Horn	2000	8625
148 4/8	27 4/8 26 6/8	22 5/8	5 5	Seneca County	NY	Timothy N. Thomas	2001	8625
148 4/8	23 7/8 23 3/8	20 1/8	5 4	Darke County	OH	Matthew Watercutter	2002	8625
148 4/8	23 6/8 22 4/8	16 2/8	5 5	Montgomery County	KS	Robert L. Mills	2002	8625
148 4/8	23 2/8 23 1/8	17 3/8	6 7	Freeborn County	MN	Beau Jensen	2002	8625
148 4/8	23 1/8 22 3/8	16 6/8	5 5	Adams County	WI	Dan Seward	2003	8625
*148 4/8	23 0/8 22 5/8	17 2/8	6 7	E. Feliciana Parish	LA	Bill Fromenthal	2003	8625
148 4/8	22 4/8 22 6/8	16 4/8	5 6	Rock Island County	IL	Mike Milam	2003	8625
148 4/8	24 6/8 25 1/8	18 0/8	4 5	Richland County	IL	Tony Prosser	2003	8625
148 4/8	25 0/8 24 4/8	19 0/8	4 4	Benton County	MO	Kenneth Tanner	2004	8625
148 4/8	25 6/8 26 0/8	20 2/8	4 4	Carroll County	OH	Steve Waers	2004	8625
148 4/8	23 7/8 23 7/8	19 2/8	4 5	Freeborn County	MN	Chris Brennecke	2004	8625
*148 4/8	23 6/8 23 3/8	19 2/8	5 9	Union County	SD	Matt Marx	2004	8625
148 4/8	23 5/8 23 0/8	16 2/8	5 6	Buffalo County	WI	Michael A. Miller	2004	8625
*148 4/8	24 5/8 23 4/8	17 4/8	5 6	Langlade County	WI	Jeff Van Rossum	2004	8625
148 4/8	25 2/8 24 0/8	17 6/8	6 5	Jo Daviess County	IL	Dennis Heineman	2004	8625
*148 4/8	24 3/8 24 0/8	19 2/8	4 4	Pierce County	WI	Mark Hotter	2004	8625
*148 4/8	26 7/8 26 4/8	21 2/8	5 6	Wyoming County	WV	J. Matthew Brown	2004	8625
148 4/8	24 1/8 25 5/8	19 2/8	4 4	Butler County	KS	David Kuttler	2004	8625
*148 4/8	22 4/8 22 3/8	17 2/8	6 7	Union County	SD	Charles Burrell	2005	8625
148 4/8	23 6/8 22 7/8	17 4/8	5 5	Cattaraugus County	NY	Paul Kowalski	2005	8625
148 4/8	25 7/8 25 2/8	18 0/8	5 5	Grand Traverse County	MI	Greg Hamilton	2005	8625
148 4/8	22 5/8 23 4/8	18 4/8	5 5	Clinton County	MI	Kelly E. Russell	2005	8625
148 4/8	22 2/8 22 2/8	17 6/8	5 5	Chase County	KS	Charles Swift	2005	8625
*148 4/8	24 6/8 23 7/8	16 4/8	5 4	Pulaski County	IL	Michael Bates	2005	8625
148 4/8	25 2/8 26 1/8	17 4/8	6 4	Clay County	SD	Jeffrey J. Olson	2005	8625
148 4/8	22 7/8 23 4/8	15 4/8	5 5	Woodbury County	IA	Shane Bainbridge	2005	8625
148 4/8	25 5/8 26 3/8	19 3/8	5 5	Waupaca County	WI	Brett H. Vanden Hoogen	2006	8625
148 4/8	20 6/8 22 0/8	15 3/8	5 6	Van Buren County	IA	Joel M. Riotto	2006	8625
*148 4/8	24 0/8 24 7/8	17 2/8	4 5	De Kalb County	MO	Wes R. Martin	2006	8625
148 4/8	23 3/8 23 3/8	17 0/8	5 5	Winnebago County	WI	Tim Meilahn	2006	8625
148 4/8	24 1/8 23 0/8	17 2/8	5 5	White County	IL	Samuel P. Vonella	2006	8625
148 4/8	26 3/8 25 3/8	18 6/8	4 5	Buffalo County	WI	Ryan M. Kane	2006	8625
148 4/8	23 4/8 23 6/8	17 0/8	5 5	Trempealeau County	WI	John S. McKeeth	2006	8625
148 4/8	23 0/8 23 0/8	17 2/8	8 5	Marshall County	WV	David B. Yoho	2006	8625
148 4/8	27 6/8 26 3/8	19 2/8	4 4	Anne Arundel County	MD	Mark D. Sanders	2006	8625
*148 4/8	28 1/8 28 2/8	21 0/8	4 4	Madison County	MS	D. R. Bozeman	2007	8625
148 4/8	23 1/8 24 0/8	21 1/8	5 7	Venango County	PA	Jeff Stephenson	2007	8625
148 4/8	24 5/8 23 5/8	17 4/8	5 5	Moniteau County	MO	Chris Allee	2007	8625
*148 4/8	25 1/8 26 4/8	19 4/8	4 4	Calvert County	MD	David Robert Alianti	2007	8625
148 4/8	25 3/8 24 7/8	20 4/8	5 6	Jasper County	IA	Roger Amundson	2007	8625
*148 4/8	24 6/8 25 0/8	22 0/8	5 4	Hunterdon County	NJ	Timothy M. Dockery	2008	8625
148 4/8	25 2/8 25 4/8	20 5/8	7 5	Osborne County	KS	John B. Triplett, Jr.	2008	8625
148 4/8	24 2/8 25 6/8	16 6/8	5 5	McHenry County	IL	Kevin Muench	2008	8625
*148 4/8	24 2/8 24 0/8	16 6/8	5 5	Greene County	PA	Patrick V. Ford	2009	8625
148 4/8	25 2/8 25 7/8	15 6/8	5 5	Coffey County	KS	Scott Jankowski	2009	8625
148 3/8	25 6/8 26 7/8	22 2/8	9 5	Scott County	MN	Bob Gregory	1967	8730
148 3/8	23 5/8 23 7/8	17 5/8	5 5	Monroe County	NY	Robert J. Ranalletta	1976	8730
148 3/8	23 0/8 23 4/8	18 0/8	6 7	Ballard County	KY	Gregory Joles	1978	8730
148 3/8	22 5/8 22 1/8	17 5/8	6 6	Watonwan County	MN	Joe Graif	1981	8730
148 3/8	23 5/8 23 7/8	24 1/8	6 6	Fairfield County	OH	Jim Jordan	1982	8730
148 3/8	22 1/8 22 6/8	18 1/8	5 5	Morrison County	MN	Robert Redmann	1984	8730
148 3/8	23 7/8 22 7/8	17 0/8	7 5	Fayette County	IN	Chris L. Mustin	1984	8730
148 3/8	24 6/8 25 5/8	19 1/8	5 5	Baltimore County	MD	Donald Layne	1985	8730
148 3/8	24 3/8 24 2/8	18 1/8	6 6	Phillips County	KS	Julius E. Schoenberger	1985	8730
148 3/8	22 2/8 23 6/8	16 7/8	5 5	Ottawa County	KS	Wayne E. Smith	1985	8730
148 3/8	22 0/8 21 7/8	17 5/8	7 7	Carter County	OK	Charles W. Chatham	1986	8730

447

WHITETAIL DEER (TYPICAL ANTLERS)

Minimum Score 125   Continued

SCORE	LENGTH OF R MAIN BEAM L	INSIDE SPREAD	NUMBER OF R POINTS L	AREA	STATE/PROVINCE	HUNTER'S NAME	DATE	RANK
148 3/8	23 0/8 22 4/8	19 3/8	5 5	Macoupin County	IL	Don Snyder	1986	8730
148 3/8	25 3/8 25 0/8	16 7/8	6 5	Noble County	IN	Daniel J. Bidwell	1987	8730
148 3/8	24 5/8 24 2/8	22 0/8	5 4	Wright County	IA	Mark D. Slining	1987	8730
148 3/8	23 2/8 23 0/8	20 1/8	5 6	Grant County	KY	Richard L. Koors	1988	8730
148 3/8	23 4/8 23 4/8	19 3/8	5 6	Ionia County	MI	James E. Allen	1988	8730
148 3/8	22 5/8 22 5/8	17 3/8	4 5	Morgan County	OH	Stacey Triplet	1989	8730
148 3/8	22 5/8 24 4/8	18 3/8	5 5	Lewis & Clark County	MT	Sonny Templeton	1989	8730
148 3/8	25 5/8 24 5/8	18 7/8	4 5	Stoddard County	MO	Clint Barnfield	1990	8730
148 3/8	24 4/8 24 2/8	20 5/8	5 5	Boone County	IL	Wilmer V. Garlick	1990	8730
148 3/8	27 0/8 23 6/8	18 3/8	4 4	Middlesex County	CT	Fredrick J. Massini	1990	8730
148 3/8	26 1/8 25 6/8	19 1/8	4 6	Tama County	IA	Harold Cox	1990	8730
148 3/8	27 3/8 27 5/8	18 5/8	5 4	Barton County	MO	Gregory W. Benander	1990	8730
148 3/8	22 6/8 22 1/8	20 1/8	5 5	Kandiyohi County	MN	Bob Sampson	1991	8730
148 3/8	27 0/8 26 0/8	18 1/8	9 6	Webster County	IA	Terry Rial	1992	8730
148 3/8	26 4/8 25 6/8	21 2/8	6 4	Washington County	MN	Keith Johnson	1992	8730
148 3/8	24 3/8 23 0/8	16 3/8	7 7	La Salle County	IL	Pete Stoneberg	1993	8730
148 3/8	21 1/8 20 4/8	15 7/8	5 5	Roseau County	MN	Dillon Janousek	1993	8730
148 3/8	22 1/8 23 2/8	17 6/8	6 6	Washington County	KS	Bob Funke	1993	8730
148 3/8	24 2/8 24 2/8	16 2/8	7 5	Buffalo County	WI	John Charles	1994	8730
148 3/8	23 0/8 22 7/8	17 1/8	5 5	Columbia County	WI	Ryan Traut	1994	8730
148 3/8	26 2/8 27 7/8	20 5/8	4 4	Westchester County	NY	William J. Evans	1994	8730
148 3/8	24 1/8 24 5/8	22 4/8	6 4	Chautauqua County	KS	Eddie Claypool	1994	8730
148 3/8	24 2/8 24 1/8	18 1/8	5 5	Scotland County	MO	Steve Stoltz	1994	8730
148 3/8	24 7/8 23 1/8	17 4/8	6 5	Winona County	MN	Roger Merchlewitz	1994	8730
148 3/8	23 7/8 24 2/8	19 2/8	5 6	Sullivan County	NH	Don Goodwin	1995	8730
148 3/8	24 6/8 24 4/8	16 7/8	4 5	Madison County	IL	Leo N. Brinson, Jr.	1995	8730
148 3/8	23 4/8 24 4/8	19 7/8	5 5	Marshall County	KS	Terry Gunn	1995	8730
148 3/8	26 1/8 26 0/8	19 3/8	4 4	Nemaha County	KS	Darryl Becker	1995	8730
148 3/8	23 4/8 23 3/8	18 7/8	5 6	Lincoln County	WI	Trevor Sorce	1995	8730
148 3/8	20 6/8 20 7/8	15 5/8	5 5	Okanogan County	WA	Kirk Sapp	1996	8730
148 3/8	23 7/8 23 4/8	17 3/8	4 6	Fulton County	IL	Lyndel Lingenfelter	1996	8730
148 3/8	26 5/8 24 0/8	15 7/8	8 6	Butler County	IA	Curt J. Chase	1996	8730
148 3/8	24 5/8 23 1/8	19 4/8	5 5	Clinton County	IL	Trey Johnson	1996	8730
148 3/8	23 4/8 23 3/8	17 5/8	5 5	Kalamazoo County	MI	Mark S. Vlietstra	1997	8730
148 3/8	22 5/8 20 3/8	20 1/8	6 5	Dallas County	IA	Les Nelson	1998	8730
148 3/8	23 5/8 25 1/8	16 6/8	4 6	Madison County	IL	John Phillips, Jr.	1998	8730
148 3/8	24 6/8 25 4/8	17 0/8	6 5	Jackson County	MI	Emilio Troiani	1999	8730
148 3/8	23 4/8 23 0/8	17 7/8	5 5	Boone County	MO	Kris Steinbeck	1999	8730
148 3/8	23 2/8 24 1/8	20 5/8	4 5	Pike County	IL	Charles R. Hudson	1999	8730
148 3/8	25 0/8 23 5/8	17 0/8	6 6	Walworth County	WI	Alan Chalmers	1999	8730
148 3/8	23 4/8 23 0/8	18 0/8	5 6	Chippewa County	WI	Jason Roper	1999	8730
148 3/8	23 2/8 23 4/8	17 7/8	5 5	Hennepin County	MN	Dean Basch	2000	8730
148 3/8	23 5/8 23 0/8	16 4/8	5 5	Linn County	MO	Jim Kiel	2000	8730
*148 3/8	23 1/8 22 6/8	17 3/8	6 9	Brown County	SD	Rick Lipp	2000	8730
148 3/8	24 0/8 24 4/8	21 1/8	5 4	Buffalo County	WI	Jeff Ewens	2000	8730
148 3/8	23 6/8 24 0/8	18 7/8	4 5	McKenzie County	ND	Lance Keator	2000	8730
148 3/8	21 6/8 22 2/8	15 6/8	7 6	Crawford County	KS	Jeff Kavanagh	2000	8730
148 3/8	25 0/8 24 3/8	17 4/8	5 6	Coffey County	KS	Steve Edwards	2000	8730
148 3/8	22 1/8 21 4/8	17 2/8	5 6	Olmsted County	MN	Jeffrey W. Brobst	2001	8730
148 3/8	27 2/8 26 6/8	20 3/8	5 5	Carroll County	IL	Thomas E. Gumpert	2001	8730
148 3/8	21 6/8 21 7/8	21 1/8	5 5	Kenton County	KY	Wayne Smith	2001	8730
148 3/8	20 4/8 21 3/8	14 2/8	6 7	Shawnee County	KS	Arthur E. Fletcher, Jr.	2001	8730
148 3/8	23 1/8 22 3/8	18 1/8	6 5	Carter County	MT	Ronald W. Dendy	2001	8730
148 3/8	27 4/8 26 0/8	19 3/8	4 4	La Crosse County	WI	David E. Lesky	2001	8730
148 3/8	22 3/8 19 5/8	23 0/8	5 5	Van Buren County	IA	Allen Huff	2001	8730
148 3/8	22 7/8 22 7/8	15 7/8	6 6	Lac La Biche	ALB	Mike Butler	2002	8730
148 3/8	24 3/8 23 5/8	17 0/8	6 6	Buffalo County	WI	Scott R. Glenz	2002	8730
148 3/8	22 1/8 22 0/8	16 5/8	5 5	Buffalo County	WI	Matt Foust	2002	8730
148 3/8	25 5/8 25 4/8	16 7/8	4 4	Richland County	IL	Pete Seals	2002	8730
148 3/8	23 0/8 25 0/8	19 5/8	7 5	Beaver County	PA	Larry O'Neill	2003	8730
148 3/8	24 7/8 23 7/8	17 6/8	5 7	Knox County	IL	Roy Gamber	2003	8730
*148 3/8	23 6/8 23 3/8	16 5/8	5 5	McKenzie County	ND	Robert E. Cochrane	2003	8730
148 3/8	22 7/8 23 6/8	21 1/8	5 4	Lee County	IL	Matthew C. Rehor	2003	8730
148 3/8	22 3/8 22 5/8	16 4/8	6 5	Franklin County	IL	Cedric "Buddy" Malone, Jr.	2003	8730
148 3/8	23 5/8 22 7/8	18 4/8	7 6	Tuscarawas County	OH	Robert Rozich	2003	8730
148 3/8	22 2/8 22 2/8	17 1/8	5 6	Knox County	IL	Randy A. Bozarth	2003	8730
*148 3/8	22 1/8 22 2/8	15 7/8	5 5	Jefferson County	IN	Jordan Key	2003	8730
148 3/8	21 4/8 20 7/8	15 7/8	5 6	Comanche County	OK	John P. Sklaney, Jr.	2004	8730
148 3/8	23 6/8 23 4/8	14 1/8	5 5	Johnson County	IN	Scott Farley	2004	8730
148 3/8	21 5/8 21 2/8	15 6/8	6 5	Montcalm County	MI	Andy Berkenpas	2005	8730
148 3/8	23 7/8 24 6/8	16 4/8	8 6	Preble County	OH	Paul D. Price	2005	8730
148 3/8	25 4/8 25 3/8	17 3/8	5 5	Knox County	IN	Warren Riker, Jr.	2005	8730
148 3/8	23 0/8 23 4/8	17 1/8	5 5	Richland County	ND	Dell K. Sprecher	2006	8730
*148 3/8	24 1/8 23 1/8	16 3/8	5 5	Washington County	MN	Joe Ricker	2006	8730
148 3/8	23 7/8 23 4/8	15 1/8	6 7	Buffalo County	WI	Mark Forster	2006	8730
148 3/8	22 4/8 21 5/8	15 0/8	6 6	Washington County	WI	Jason Stange	2006	8730
*148 3/8	24 7/8 25 0/8	18 7/8	5 5	Buffalo County	WI	Scott D. Emond	2006	8730
148 3/8	23 4/8 24 0/8	16 0/8	8 9	Big Stone County	MN	Terry Schneider	2007	8730
*148 3/8	23 2/8 22 6/8	21 1/8	5 7	Pulaski County	IN	Joe Martino	2007	8730
*148 3/8	26 2/8 24 6/8	18 5/8	5 5	Buffalo County	WI	Timothy Piparo	2007	8730
148 3/8	24 6/8 25 2/8	15 4/8	7 6	Erie County	OH	Glenn Shupe	2007	8730
*148 3/8	24 4/8 24 6/8	24 3/8	5 5	Reno County	KS	Caley J. Ediger	2007	8730
*148 3/8	24 2/8 23 4/8	20 3/8	5 5	Hampden County	MA	Steven Coulter	2007	8730
148 3/8	22 5/8 23 3/8	16 1/8	5 5	Phillips County	MT	Wyatt Smith	2008	8730
*148 3/8	26 5/8 27 1/8	24 3/8	4 4	Adams County	PA	Tim Deal	2008	8730
*148 3/8	25 0/8 25 0/8	18 1/8	5 5	Northumberland County	PA	Joseph Knapick	2008	8730
*148 3/8	23 0/8 24 0/8	18 1/8	5 5	Cedar County	MO	Mark A. Long	2009	8730
148 3/8	23 3/8 23 0/8	18 1/8	5 5	Trempealeau County	WI	Jon Wozney	2009	8730
*148 3/8	23 4/8 23 1/8	17 3/8	6 5	Yankton County	SD	Trenton Haffley	2009	8730
148 2/8	22 3/8 21 6/8	16 2/8	5 5	Walworth County	SD	Irvin Guthmiller	1956	8830
148 2/8	22 7/8 21 5/8	18 2/8	5 5	Harrison County	IA	James W. Glasscock	1968	8830
148 2/8	25 1/8 24 1/8	15 4/8	5 5	Woodbury County	IA	Guy Hempey	1969	8830
148 2/8	24 5/8 24 7/8	24 0/8	5 5	Jackson County	IL	Darrell Fritsche	1973	8830
148 2/8	20 7/8 22 2/8	16 4/8	5 5	Pittsburg County	OK	Bill Hisle	1975	8830
148 2/8	24 2/8 23 4/8	18 0/8	5 7	Latah County	ID	Don A. West	1976	8830

WHITETAIL DEER (TYPICAL ANTLERS)

Minimum Score 125   Continued

SCORE	LENGTH OF R MAIN BEAM L	INSIDE SPREAD	NUMBER OF R POINTS L		AREA	STATE/ PROVINCE	HUNTER'S NAME	DATE	RANK
148 2/8	26 5/8	24 3/8	19 7/8	6	8	Coshocton County	OH	Charles N. McDonald	1977	8830
148 2/8	23 0/8	22 2/8	20 7/8	4	5	Sanford	MAN	Wayne Rodgers	1979	8830
148 2/8	24 7/8	25 1/8	18 0/8	5	5	Winnebago County	IL	Fred Kelley	1981	8830
148 2/8	24 6/8	23 3/8	16 5/8	4	6	Clark County	KS	Casey V. Rudd	1981	8830
148 2/8	23 4/8	23 1/8	22 6/8	6	10	Marion County	IL	Paul Duncan	1982	8830
148 2/8	27 3/8	27 0/8	20 7/8	5	6	Washington County	WI	Steve Karoses	1983	8830
148 2/8	26 0/8	26 2/8	17 5/8	8	6	Adair County	MO	Tim Richardson	1983	8830
148 2/8	23 0/8	23 6/8	17 0/8	5	5	Pierce County	WI	Mitchell C. Nelson	1984	8830
148 2/8	21 2/8	21 6/8	18 4/8	5	5	Kenosha County	WI	Marty Daniels	1985	8830
148 2/8	25 7/8	26 0/8	20 0/8	4	4	Polk County	MN	Warren Nelson	1986	8830
148 2/8	20 7/8	21 5/8	18 6/8	5	6	Butler County	KS	David R. Rogers	1986	8830
148 2/8	24 2/8	23 6/8	16 3/8	6	5	Polk County	IA	Robert E. Morterud	1987	8830
148 2/8	23 0/8	24 1/8	21 4/8	6	5	Clay County	MN	James F. Thompson	1987	8830
148 2/8	25 7/8	26 4/8	18 2/8	5	5	Cross County	AR	Rickey W. Proctor	1987	8830
148 2/8	22 7/8	24 1/8	19 5/8	6	6	Allen County	KS	Curt Stahl	1988	8830
148 2/8	24 7/8	25 7/8	19 6/8	4	4	Belmont County	OH	Chad Krahel	1989	8830
148 2/8	26 0/8	26 4/8	19 4/8	6	6	Will County	IL	Dennis J. Lake	1990	8830
148 2/8	23 5/8	23 0/8	20 4/8	5	7	Jersey County	IL	Judy Kovar	1990	8830
148 2/8	23 2/8	23 3/8	17 0/8	7	5	Marshall County	OK	James B. Evans, Jr.	1990	8830
148 2/8	26 0/8	26 3/8	18 3/8	4	5	Lake County	IL	Donald R. Powers	1990	8830
148 2/8	25 3/8	23 3/8	19 6/8	6	8	Phillips County	KS	Charles Bockhorn	1991	8830
148 2/8	23 4/8	23 7/8	19 0/8	5	5	Steuben County	NY	Mark S. O'Donal	1991	8830
148 2/8	22 5/8	22 0/8	17 4/8	5	5	Vermilion County	IL	Jeffery Parkerson	1991	8830
148 2/8	27 6/8	27 2/8	17 6/8	5	6	Howard County	MO	Bodie Beach	1991	8830
148 2/8	25 1/8	24 4/8	17 5/8	7	6	Fayette County	IL	Mike Ziemba	1991	8830
148 2/8	25 0/8	24 4/8	18 0/8	5	5	Pike County	IL	Jerry Pennock	1991	8830
148 2/8	24 3/8	25 0/8	16 7/8	9	8	Hennepin County	MN	Todd J. Zwak	1991	8830
148 2/8	24 5/8	24 5/8	18 0/8	6	7	Dane County	WI	Alan Corlett	1991	8830
148 2/8	24 0/8	24 7/8	19 4/8	4	5	Houston County	MN	Travis Peterson	1992	8830
148 2/8	23 7/8	23 5/8	17 4/8	4	4	Knox County	IL	Gregg E. Moore	1993	8830
148 2/8	24 7/8	25 3/8	17 4/8	5	8	Pembina County	ND	Myles Keller	1993	8830
148 2/8	25 5/8	24 7/8	16 4/8	7	5	Butler County	KS	Frank Boyer	1994	8830
148 2/8	21 2/8	22 0/8	16 4/8	5	6	Noble County	OH	Charles D. Bennethum, Jr.	1995	8830
148 2/8	24 4/8	23 5/8	16 5/8	6	5	Coles County	IL	Jim Eveland	1995	8830
148 2/8	24 4/8	23 2/8	19 6/8	5	5	Ogle County	IL	Jeff Blascoe	1995	8830
148 2/8	23 7/8	23 5/8	16 2/8	5	5	Clermont County	OH	Zachary J. Watkins	1995	8830
148 2/8	22 0/8	22 1/8	19 0/8	6	5	Jackson County	IA	David H. Lincoln	1995	8830
148 2/8	23 4/8	24 4/8	19 4/8	5	5	Bon Homme County	SD	Todd Hornstra	1995	8830
148 2/8	24 6/8	24 6/8	19 4/8	5	5	Marion County	IA	Kyle Goodwin	1995	8830
148 2/8	25 0/8	25 0/8	17 2/8	5	5	Pike County	IL	Don Dye, Jr.	1995	8830
148 2/8	24 5/8	24 0/8	17 4/8	5	5	Casey County	KY	Carroll Gibson	1996	8830
148 2/8	25 1/8	24 5/8	17 4/8	5	5	Woods County	OK	Lloyd Mark Evans	1996	8830
148 2/8	25 4/8	25 5/8	20 4/8	5	5	Jefferson County	WI	Randolph M. Moots	1996	8830
148 2/8	22 1/8	22 2/8	19 2/8	6	5	Dane County	WI	Joe Hoff	1997	8830
148 2/8	23 4/8	24 0/8	16 4/8	6	5	Sauk County	WI	Scott E. Kotlowski	1997	8830
148 2/8	20 7/8	20 5/8	19 4/8	6	6	Huron County	MI	David Charles Wille	1997	8830
148 2/8	21 0/8	20 6/8	16 4/8	5	5	Treasure County	MT	Steve Trimble	1998	8830
148 2/8	26 2/8	25 5/8	21 0/8	6	5	Sawyer County	WI	Eric D. Riegler	1998	8830
148 2/8	22 0/8	22 1/8	20 6/8	5	5	Dane County	WI	Benjamin X. Smith	1998	8830
148 2/8	25 0/8	24 7/8	18 2/8	6	6	Marathon County	WI	Wally Raczkowski	1998	8830
148 2/8	22 6/8	25 1/8	23 1/8	7	6	Linn County	KS	Bobby G. Medlin	1998	8830
148 2/8	23 7/8	25 0/8	18 3/8	7	5	Ontario County	NY	Albert S. Martin	1998	8830
148 2/8	23 0/8	26 4/8	21 1/8	8	6	Lancaster County	NE	Brad Konen	1998	8830
148 2/8	22 6/8	23 6/8	18 2/8	5	5	Ogle County	IL	Tim Hasara	1998	8830
148 2/8	23 7/8	24 1/8	19 2/8	5	5	Claiborne County	MS	P. C. Aughtry III	1998	8830
148 2/8	22 7/8	23 7/8	18 4/8	4	4	Dore Lake	SAS	Ricky Bishop	1998	8830
148 2/8	24 3/8	23 7/8	17 2/8	5	5	New Haven County	CT	Steven Marino	1999	8830
148 2/8	23 0/8	23 4/8	18 2/8	5	5	Houston County	GA	David Testerman	1999	8830
148 2/8	23 7/8	24 3/8	17 6/8	5	5	Pepin County	WI	Jim Wold	1999	8830
148 2/8	22 6/8	23 4/8	20 2/8	5	5	Richland County	WI	Gregg P. Ely	1999	8830
148 2/8	23 3/8	26 2/8	19 4/8	7	5	Tuscarawas County	OH	Kris Albaugh	1999	8830
148 2/8	27 1/8	26 4/8	19 1/8	6	8	Chautauqua County	KS	Robert Daniels	1999	8830
148 2/8	21 6/8	21 5/8	18 0/8	5	5	Hardin County	OH	Bethel Nickles	1999	8830
148 2/8	23 2/8	23 1/8	19 2/8	6	6	Dunn County	WI	Todd R. Kurtzhals	1999	8830
148 2/8	25 6/8	25 6/8	18 4/8	6	6	Lake County	IL	Mark Nelsen	1999	8830
148 2/8	24 3/8	19 5/8	15 3/8	5	6	Monroe County	NY	Ralph G. Faull	1999	8830
148 2/8	22 5/8	22 4/8	15 2/8	5	5	Bucks County	PA	Scott S. Benek	2001	8830
148 2/8	25 7/8	25 0/8	18 5/8	6	6	Adams County	IL	Cory Naderhoff	2001	8830
148 2/8	26 4/8	25 3/8	20 0/8	4	5	Brown County	IL	Robert Brent Price	2001	8830
148 2/8	25 3/8	25 4/8	18 7/8	6	5	Noble County	OK	Dan Gaston	2001	8830
148 2/8	25 1/8	26 2/8	17 6/8	5	5	Warren County	IA	Todd Reese	2002	8830
148 2/8	22 0/8	22 0/8	17 4/8	5	5	Buffalo County	WI	Eric J. Tepley	2002	8830
148 2/8	22 4/8	21 7/8	16 4/8	5	5	Massac County	IL	Joseph M. Scarpy	2002	8830
*148 2/8	24 2/8	24 2/8	18 4/8	5	5	Brown County	WI	Nick Van Lanen	2002	8830
148 2/8	22 5/8	22 4/8	18 3/8	6	7	Tama County	IA	Brent Allee	2003	8830
148 2/8	24 4/8	24 1/8	16 6/8	5	5	Adams County	WI	Mark Mertens	2003	8830
148 2/8	24 6/8	25 1/8	20 3/8	5	5	Winnebago County	IL	John Prenot	2003	8830
148 2/8	21 3/8	20 7/8	16 2/8	5	6	Polk County	IA	Vincent Stefanski	2003	8830
148 2/8	25 1/8	24 6/8	18 2/8	4	4	Larue County	KY	Davy Coffey	2003	8830
*148 2/8	23 3/8	22 6/8	18 6/8	5	6	Schuyler County	IL	Joe Martin	2003	8830
148 2/8	25 2/8	22 7/8	19 4/8	5	4	Sherburne County	MN	John "Jack" Purkis	2003	8830
148 2/8	23 4/8	23 2/8	16 6/8	4	5	Lenore Lake	SAS	Floyd Forster	2003	8830
148 2/8	21 1/8	20 7/8	22 2/8	6	6	Lewis County	MO	Brian Kuepfert	2004	8830
148 2/8	22 6/8	22 6/8	14 4/8	6	7	Burnett County	WI	Terry L. Olson	2004	8830
148 2/8	27 0/8	24 3/8	20 0/8	4	5	Comanche County	KS	Mark Voth	2004	8830
*148 2/8	23 6/8	24 2/8	16 2/8	5	4	Jefferson County	AR	Felix G. Smart VI	2004	8830
*148 2/8	20 3/8	21 7/8	16 2/8	5	6	Washington County	IL	Barry Craig	2005	8830
148 2/8	25 5/8	24 0/8	20 6/8	4	5	Stephenson County	IL	Scott Raisbeck	2005	8830
*148 2/8	22 6/8	22 6/8	16 6/8	5	5	Cheyenne County	CO	Chad Ford	2005	8830
148 2/8	24 7/8	26 0/8	22 1/8	5	5	Kane County	IL	Dean V. Ashton	2005	8830
148 2/8	24 3/8	25 1/8	20 0/8	5	5	Peoria County	IL	Anthony R. Miche Morefield	2006	8830
148 2/8	23 2/8	23 1/8	17 4/8	4	5	Putnam County	IL	Kenneth J. Sona	2006	8830
*148 2/8	25 2/8	24 3/8	17 2/8	5	5	Washington County	WI	Tim Cull	2007	8830
148 2/8	25 7/8	26 3/8	17 0/8	4	4	Northampton County	VA	Gary M. West	2007	8830
148 2/8	24 2/8	24 6/8	20 2/8	4	6	Beaverlodge	ALB	Duane Hagman	2007	8830

449

WHITETAIL DEER (TYPICAL ANTLERS)

Minimum Score 125 — Continued

SCORE	LENGTH OF R MAIN BEAM L	INSIDE SPREAD	NUMBER OF R POINTS L	AREA	STATE/ PROVINCE	HUNTER'S NAME	DATE	RANK
*148 2/8	22 3/8 22 5/8	17 2/8	6 5	Door County	WI	Alex Brauer	2007	8830
*148 2/8	24 0/8 24 0/8	15 4/8	5 5	Monona County	IA	David Klocke	2007	8830
148 2/8	20 4/8 21 7/8	17 0/8	5 5	Ketchamoot Creek	ALB	Neil Kercher	2007	8830
148 2/8	26 3/8 26 0/8	20 0/8	5 6	Vernon County	WI	Adam Casper	2008	8830
*148 2/8	24 6/8 24 6/8	18 2/8	4 5	Buffalo County	WI	Patrick Barwick	2008	8830
148 2/8	28 3/8 26 6/8	18 0/8	7 5	Lafayette County	WI	Nick Neff	2008	8830
*148 2/8	21 0/8 24 6/8	19 1/8	6 6	Green Lake County	WI	Daniel R. Seymer	2008	8830
*148 2/8	22 5/8 21 3/8	16 5/8	8 6	Noble County	IN	Tim Nussbaum	2008	8830
148 2/8	23 6/8 24 2/8	19 7/8	5 6	Auglaize County	OH	Rick Hirschfeld	2009	8830
148 2/8	25 4/8 25 1/8	18 4/8	4 4	Rockingham County	NC	Brad Kendrick	2009	8830
148 2/8	21 3/8 23 0/8	15 0/8	5 5	Lewis County	KY	Dale May	2009	8830
*148 2/8	23 7/8 24 4/8	19 3/8	5 5	Olmsted County	MN	Jason Skrukrud	2009	8830
*148 2/8	22 2/8 22 6/8	19 4/8	5 5	Morrow County	OH	Brody Young	2009	8830
148 2/8	23 3/8 23 2/8	18 4/8	6 5	Schuyler County	IL	Reece Whitley	2009	8830
148 2/8	26 2/8 26 6/8	21 2/8	5 5	Steuben County	IN	Lonnie P. Ingledue	2009	8830
*148 2/8	22 5/8 23 0/8	17 4/8	5 5	Ravalli County	MT	Logan Miller	2010	8830
148 1/8	24 2/8 24 2/8	20 5/8	4 4	Erie County	NY	William R. Helmich	1975	8947
148 1/8	23 0/8 22 5/8	17 2/8	5 5	Wellington County	ONT	Barry Marshall	1975	8947
148 1/8	27 3/8 27 5/8	21 6/8	6 6	Tazewell County	IL	David Huser	1980	8947
148 1/8	24 2/8 22 5/8	19 3/8	5 5	Uvalde County	TX	Jim Jordan	1986	8947
148 1/8	23 3/8 22 7/8	18 5/8	5 5	Calumet County	WI	Joseph R. Mader	1986	8947
148 1/8	23 6/8 24 5/8	17 6/8	5 8	Cass County	ND	Rodney P. Mathison	1986	8947
148 1/8	23 2/8 24 0/8	19 5/8	6 5	Brown County	WI	Andy Dobesh	1987	8947
148 1/8	22 6/8 22 3/8	18 2/8	5 5	Hickory County	MO	David Langton	1987	8947
148 1/8	23 7/8 23 6/8	20 3/8	5 5	Crow Wing County	MN	Bob Brown	1988	8947
148 1/8	24 4/8 25 0/8	19 5/8	5 5	Pike County	IL	Ray Hatfield	1988	8947
148 1/8	22 4/8 22 7/8	20 1/8	5 6	Sawyer County	WI	Brad B. Christensen	1989	8947
148 1/8	25 2/8 25 5/8	18 2/8	5 6	Iron County	WI	D. J. Sullivan	1990	8947
148 1/8	23 0/8 22 4/8	21 1/8	5 5	Burnett County	WI	Sheldon Wendorf	1990	8947
148 1/8	25 0/8 24 5/8	20 5/8	4 5	McHenry County	IL	Dennis E. Straumann	1990	8947
148 1/8	24 2/8 23 5/8	14 1/8	6 6	Whiteside County	IL	Abraham Wuebben	1991	8947
148 1/8	25 3/8 25 0/8	17 7/8	8 5	Stoddard County	MO	Ken Heuer	1991	8947
148 1/8	24 0/8 24 6/8	20 5/8	4 5	Somerset County	MD	Mark Labo	1992	8947
148 1/8	23 2/8 23 7/8	17 7/8	5 5	Laclede County	MO	Richard Blackman	1992	8947
148 1/8	24 1/8 24 0/8	18 2/8	4 5	De Witt County	IL	James L. Nicholson	1992	8947
148 1/8	22 7/8 22 4/8	22 1/8	5 5	Lake County	IL	Jeff Miller	1993	8947
148 1/8	21 2/8 23 0/8	13 6/8	6 5	Platte County	MO	Clint Woods	1994	8947
148 1/8	24 7/8 24 5/8	17 5/8	5 4	Macon County	IL	Mark Cecil Sutton	1994	8947
148 1/8	23 3/8 23 7/8	19 3/8	6 5	Waukesha County	WI	Dana Hoppe	1994	8947
148 1/8	25 1/8 24 6/8	17 7/8	4 4	Huron County	OH	Rodney L. Gribble	1994	8947
148 1/8	25 7/8 26 3/8	20 2/8	5 4	McDowell County	WV	Roger Wolfe, Jr.	1994	8947
148 1/8	24 6/8 24 7/8	19 3/8	5 4	Montgomery County	MO	Arthur Bader	1994	8947
148 1/8	24 7/8 25 4/8	20 5/8	5 5	Kleberg County	TX	Robert Nichols	1995	8947
148 1/8	23 0/8 23 2/8	18 3/8	5 5	Wright County	MN	Michael Halberg	1995	8947
148 1/8	23 5/8 24 3/8	18 6/8	4 5	Porter County	IN	James S. Friday	1996	8947
148 1/8	25 4/8 23 4/8	17 6/8	5 8	Buffalo County	WI	Mark Klatt	1996	8947
148 1/8	27 6/8 26 3/8	17 5/8	7 5	Seneca County	OH	Ronald Bivens	1996	8947
148 1/8	22 0/8 22 2/8	16 1/8	5 5	Taylor County	WI	W. David Windle	1996	8947
148 1/8	21 6/8 21 4/8	15 7/8	5 6	Holmes County	MS	Billy Ellis III	1997	8947
148 1/8	24 3/8 24 0/8	20 5/8	6 7	Harford County	MD	Bret Mower	1997	8947
148 1/8	24 4/8 24 3/8	18 7/8	5 5	Washington Parish	LA	Hunter Lewis	1997	8947
148 1/8	22 4/8 22 0/8	17 3/8	5 5	Douglas County	WI	Charles R. Pattee	1997	8947
148 1/8	22 4/8 23 6/8	16 7/8	5 5	Wayne County	IL	Andy Schlichting	1997	8947
148 1/8	24 6/8 24 4/8	21 1/8	5 5	Vilas County	WI	Gary Thomson	1997	8947
148 1/8	20 2/8 22 2/8	20 3/8	6 5	Thunder Bay	ONT	David Nuttall	1998	8947
148 1/8	24 5/8 23 5/8	18 1/8	5 5	Buffalo County	WI	Roger Comero	1998	8947
148 1/8	23 5/8 24 1/8	20 7/8	6 4	Iron County	WI	Matthew K. Schneider	1998	8947
148 1/8	20 4/8 21 3/8	17 1/8	5 5	Van Buren County	IA	David M. Ackland, Jr.	1999	8947
148 1/8	24 3/8 23 6/8	19 1/8	4 4	Audrain County	MO	Eric Dellenbaugh	1999	8947
148 1/8	24 6/8 24 1/8	17 1/8	5 5	Monroe County	NY	Angelo Licciardello	1999	8947
148 1/8	23 1/8 22 4/8	19 1/8	5 6	Jefferson County	IA	Steve Stoltz	1999	8947
148 1/8	25 5/8 25 7/8	19 3/8	6 5	Stephenson County	IL	Donald Packard	1999	8947
148 1/8	24 0/8 22 3/8	18 0/8	5 7	Macon County	AL	Norman Parks	2000	8947
148 1/8	22 0/8 20 5/8	17 1/8	5 5	Warren County	MS	Bobby McMillian	2000	8947
148 1/8	21 6/8 21 1/8	17 4/8	6 6	Williams County	OH	Dave Keesbery	2000	8947
148 1/8	25 1/8 24 6/8	21 5/8	4 6	Plymouth County	MA	Michael Prisco	2000	8947
148 1/8	23 2/8 23 3/8	17 5/8	5 5	Pike County	IL	Virgil R. Klepper, Jr.	2000	8947
148 1/8	23 2/8 23 0/8	16 5/8	5 5	Mountrail County	ND	James Domaskin	2000	8947
148 1/8	21 3/8 20 4/8	16 4/8	5 6	Spencer County	IN	Roger Wilkinson	2001	8947
148 1/8	26 1/8 26 1/8	20 1/8	4 5	Allegheny County	PA	Harold W. Soose	2001	8947
148 1/8	24 4/8 24 1/8	19 4/8	5 7	Wells County	IN	Bryan L. Schwartz	2001	8947
148 1/8	24 1/8 24 1/8	16 2/8	6 5	Carroll County	IN	Robert Bishop	2001	8947
148 1/8	23 7/8 25 1/8	18 7/8	4 4	Pike County	IL	Corey Melton	2002	8947
148 1/8	23 2/8 22 4/8	20 5/8	5 5	Carroll County	IL	James Carlson	2002	8947
148 1/8	23 3/8 22 3/8	17 1/8	6 8	Franklin County	IN	Trevor Abernathy	2003	8947
148 1/8	24 6/8 24 4/8	19 3/8	4 5	Fulton County	IL	John Groen	2003	8947
148 1/8	26 4/8 27 4/8	21 3/8	4 5	Washington County	RI	Thomas Simpson	2003	8947
*148 1/8	22 6/8 23 5/8	22 1/8	5 5	Waukesha County	WI	Jason Cawley	2004	8947
*148 1/8	23 0/8 24 1/8	18 2/8	8 11	Sawyer County	WI	Bill Roehl	2004	8947
148 1/8	22 4/8 22 4/8	17 1/8	5 5	Trempealeau County	WI	Mike Hestekin	2005	8947
*148 1/8	23 3/8 25 4/8	15 7/8	5 5	Cowley County	KS	George B. Smith	2005	8947
148 1/8	23 2/8 23 2/8	17 4/8	6 5	Fulton County	IL	James Schapen	2005	8947
148 1/8	24 4/8 24 1/8	22 5/8	5 5	Calhoun County	IL	Daniel H. Zecker	2005	8947
148 1/8	24 1/8 23 5/8	18 4/8	4 6	Minnehaha County	SD	Brad Struck	2005	8947
*148 1/8	23 7/8 24 2/8	18 1/8	7 5	Williamson County	TN	James H. Byram	2006	8947
148 1/8	21 2/8 21 0/8	16 2/8	5 6	Fillmore County	MN	Joseph Osland	2006	8947
148 1/8	22 7/8 22 7/8	17 3/8	5 5	Sawyer County	WI	Craig Melger	2006	8947
148 1/8	21 4/8 21 6/8	14 7/8	5 5	Pennington County	SD	Gary A. Marowelli	2006	8947
*148 1/8	25 5/8 25 1/8	21 3/8	4 5	Indiana County	PA	Carmen J. Gett	2007	8947
*148 1/8	22 7/8 22 5/8	16 4/8	6 5	Sangamon County	IL	Dennis Whitley	2007	8947
148 1/8	23 2/8 24 6/8	17 5/8	5 5	Pike County	IL	Scott Rupert	2007	8947
*148 1/8	23 0/8 22 2/8	19 5/8	4 4	Jackson County	WI	Charles Comstock	2007	8947
148 1/8	22 5/8 23 4/8	18 5/8	5 5	Calhoun County	MI	Garry F. Mainstone	2007	8947
148 1/8	22 5/8 23 0/8	17 3/8	6 5	Dakota County	NE	Glen A. Paulsen	2007	8947
148 1/8	23 5/8 23 3/8	18 1/8	5 6	Defiance County	OH	Mike Dewyse	2007	8947

450

WHITETAIL DEER (TYPICAL ANTLERS)

Minimum Score 125 · Continued

SCORE	LENGTH OF R MAIN BEAM L	INSIDE SPREAD	NUMBER OF R POINTS L	AREA	STATE/ PROVINCE	HUNTER'S NAME	DATE	RANK
*148 1/8	26 2/8 26 0/8	15 6/8	5 6	Bullitt County	KY	Shannon Ray Hall	2008	8947
148 1/8	25 0/8 26 4/8	17 7/8	6 5	Russell County	KS	Don Herter	2008	8947
148 1/8	25 4/8 25 0/8	17 7/8	6 7	Jefferson County	KS	Logan J. Bouwman	2009	8947
148 1/8	25 1/8 23 5/8	18 3/8	5 5	Douglas County	IL	Seth McGaughey	2009	8947
*148 1/8	23 5/8 24 4/8	18 2/8	6 5	Trego County	KS	Terry Chambers	2009	8947
148 0/8	22 1/8 22 2/8	14 6/8	5 5	Stanley County	SD	Brad Taylor	1979	9031
148 0/8	23 5/8 23 1/8	18 6/8	5 6	Uvalde County	TX	M.H. 'Bill' Wilkinson, Jr.	1980	9031
148 0/8	22 6/8 23 1/8	17 6/8	5 5	Green County	WI	E. Dussault	1983	9031
148 0/8	25 2/8 25 2/8	18 3/8	5 5	Buffalo County	WI	Daniel Folkedahl	1984	9031
148 0/8	24 6/8 25 5/8	23 6/8	4 5	Clay County	MN	Keith J Fischer	1984	9031
148 0/8	24 3/8 25 0/8	18 3/8	6 8	McIntosh County	ND	Garnes Ruff	1985	9031
148 0/8	22 4/8 22 0/8	15 3/8	5 6	Norman County	MN	Les Krogstad	1985	9031
148 0/8	25 7/8 27 7/8	16 7/8	7 6	Madison County	NY	Lloyd Weigel	1985	9031
148 0/8	20 0/8 23 1/8	22 4/8	6 5	Dorchester County	MD	Bob Reinert	1985	9031
148 0/8	24 2/8 24 3/8	19 5/8	6 5	Kittson County	MN	Steve Lindberg	1986	9031
148 0/8	24 1/8 24 4/8	15 6/8	5 6	Vernon County	WI	Harry J. Curtis	1986	9031
148 0/8	27 3/8 28 1/8	19 0/8	5 5	Putnam County	IN	Kevin W. Jones	1986	9031
148 0/8	22 1/8 22 6/8	21 0/8	5 5	Suffolk County	NY	Steven Schoen	1987	9031
148 0/8	23 6/8 23 6/8	18 4/8	6 6	Bremer County	IA	LeRoy Matthias	1988	9031
148 0/8	23 6/8 25 4/8	21 0/8	4 4	Marathon County	WI	Steven Marvin	1989	9031
148 0/8	25 3/8 24 2/8	20 2/8	5 5	Shelby County	IL	David E. Varvil	1989	9031
148 0/8	26 2/8 26 1/8	23 1/8	6 6	De Witt County	IL	Chris Dilks	1989	9031
148 0/8	24 0/8 24 0/8	18 5/8	7 6	Williamson County	IL	Charles Tessone	1989	9031
148 0/8	24 2/8 23 0/8	19 2/8	7 6	Allamakee County	IA	Tim Waid	1990	9031
148 0/8	23 1/8 22 7/8	17 4/8	4 4	Boundary County	ID	Mike Hittle	1991	9031
148 0/8	22 0/8 22 4/8	16 4/8	6 5	Deuel County	NE	Dirk Gosnell	1991	9031
148 0/8	25 4/8 26 5/8	18 6/8	4 4	Vermilion County	IL	Darin Duitsman	1991	9031
148 0/8	22 7/8 23 1/8	15 2/8	5 5	Chisago County	MN	Bill Barzydlo	1991	9031
148 0/8	24 5/8 24 5/8	15 3/8	6 5	Clayton County	IA	Thomas Schremser	1991	9031
148 0/8	24 1/8 23 5/8	16 6/8	7 6	Gallia County	OH	Gary Griffith	1991	9031
148 0/8	25 1/8 23 2/8	16 4/8	5 5	Van Buren County	IA	Dan Brockman	1991	9031
148 0/8	22 5/8 22 3/8	19 0/8	5 5	Jackson County	WI	Glen R. Loppnow	1992	9031
148 0/8	23 4/8 24 5/8	18 4/8	5 5	Powell County	MT	George Croft	1992	9031
148 0/8	25 2/8 25 5/8	17 1/8	7 7	Spokane County	WA	Dan E. Kersey	1992	9031
148 0/8	24 4/8 25 4/8	20 6/8	5 5	Cuyahoga County	OH	Mark R. Johnson	1993	9031
148 0/8	24 2/8 24 1/8	19 6/8	5 4	Steuben County	IN	Michael L. Osborne	1994	9031
148 0/8	24 0/8 24 2/8	18 1/8	7 6	Jefferson County	WI	Craig Wetterling	1994	9031
148 0/8	24 5/8 24 5/8	20 2/8	5 5	Jackson County	IN	Ray A. Strong	1994	9031
148 0/8	26 3/8 26 1/8	21 4/8	4 6	Clayton County	IA	Daniel J. Brimeyer	1995	9031
148 0/8	23 6/8 23 5/8	19 4/8	4 5	Pulaski County	IN	Daniel A. Beal	1995	9031
148 0/8	24 0/8 24 3/8	21 6/8	4 4	Woodford County	KY	Daniel E. Jackson II	1995	9031
148 0/8	23 0/8 24 1/8	17 4/8	6 5	Sussex County	DE	Don Fiedler	1997	9031
148 0/8	22 2/8 23 1/8	21 2/8	5 6	Randolph County	IL	Mark Bradley	1997	9031
148 0/8	24 2/8 24 2/8	17 0/8	5 5	Sussex County	DE	David A. Ritter	1998	9031
148 0/8	22 4/8 22 3/8	18 0/8	5 6	Jackson County	MI	Steve L. Bell	1998	9031
148 0/8	24 0/8 26 1/8	19 2/8	4 4	Calhoun County	IL	Robert G. Fulton	1998	9031
148 0/8	23 4/8 23 5/8	17 2/8	5 6	Jefferson County	WI	Ben Sikhart	1998	9031
148 0/8	24 4/8 26 0/8	20 0/8	5 6	Polk County	NE	Chris Yates	1998	9031
148 0/8	24 5/8 25 2/8	16 2/8	5 5	McDowell County	WV	Dennis Mahaffey, Sr.	1998	9031
148 0/8	22 1/8 21 3/8	19 3/8	7 5	Des Moines County	IA	Mark Thomson	1998	9031
148 0/8	23 4/8 23 7/8	18 2/8	5 6	Iron County	WI	Kenneth Funk	1998	9031
148 0/8	21 6/8 21 1/8	16 6/8	6 5	Montgomery County	NC	W. Lee Stafford, Jr.	1999	9031
148 0/8	21 3/8 21 2/8	15 6/8	5 5	Oconto County	WI	Dale Missall	1999	9031
148 0/8	24 7/8 24 0/8	19 1/8	6 6	Waukesha County	WI	Scott Kulick	1999	9031
148 0/8	25 5/8 24 7/8	21 0/8	4 6	Kalamazoo County	MI	Joseph King	1999	9031
148 0/8	22 7/8 23 4/8	19 2/8	7 7	Ohio County	KY	Steven Fulton	2000	9031
148 0/8	22 6/8 22 2/8	16 1/8	7 5	Outagamie County	WI	Randy Muthig	2000	9031
148 0/8	24 2/8 25 2/8	19 6/8	4 4	Chippewa County	WI	Michael R. Sedlacek	2000	9031
148 0/8	21 4/8 21 4/8	16 0/8	5 5	Will County	IL	Dale Hoekstra	2001	9031
148 0/8	23 5/8 24 3/8	18 4/8	5 6	Sangamon County	IL	Robert Sankey	2001	9031
148 0/8	18 5/8 23 3/8	18 2/8	6 5	Flathead County	MT	Shawn Price	2001	9031
148 0/8	24 4/8 24 6/8	19 4/8	5 5	Allamakee County	IA	Mark Tlusty	2001	9031
148 0/8	26 1/8 26 2/8	19 0/8	4 4	Talbot County	MD	Michael Haddock	2001	9031
148 0/8	22 6/8 22 1/8	16 4/8	5 5	Buffalo County	WI	Paul Krueger	2002	9031
148 0/8	22 1/8 22 1/8	16 2/8	5 5	Morrison County	MN	Vince Meyer	2002	9031
148 0/8	22 0/8 23 2/8	19 0/8	5 5	Clay County	NE	Lyle Skalka	2002	9031
148 0/8	24 7/8 25 2/8	13 7/8	5 6	Macon County	GA	David Austin	2002	9031
148 0/8	21 0/8 21 7/8	14 5/8	6 7	Pike County	IL	Brad Stamp	2002	9031
148 0/8	24 6/8 25 7/8	16 6/8	5 6	Linn County	IA	Rick Peterson	2003	9031
148 0/8	26 3/8 27 2/8	18 0/8	5 5	Stearns County	MN	Duane Scepaniak	2003	9031
*148 0/8	23 5/8 23 1/8	16 0/8	5 5	Clayton County	IA	Dennis Ulbrich	2003	9031
148 0/8	22 0/8 21 5/8	17 2/8	5 7	Crawford County	IL	Bob Dowdy	2003	9031
148 0/8	22 6/8 24 7/8	19 0/8	5 6	Brown County	IL	Sean Christopher Broyles	2003	9031
148 0/8	24 4/8 24 6/8	20 0/8	5 5	Gallatin County	IL	Doug Londal	2003	9031
148 0/8	23 0/8 21 6/8	17 6/8	5 5	Doniphan County	KS	John J. Rosson	2003	9031
148 0/8	23 7/8 25 3/8	18 4/8	4 4	Guthrie County	IA	Richard Grunsted	2003	9031
148 0/8	25 5/8 26 4/8	21 0/8	5 5	Clayton County	IA	Forrest Ladwig	2003	9031
148 0/8	23 5/8 23 3/8	19 0/8	5 5	Clay County	SD	Douglas Hayes	2003	9031
148 0/8	24 7/8 24 1/8	18 5/8	7 6	Cook County	IL	Don Sons	2003	9031
148 0/8	23 0/8 22 2/8	22 0/8	5 6	Cedar County	NE	Brandon Fischer	2003	9031
148 0/8	23 0/8 23 3/8	18 1/8	7 5	Kent County	DE	Dwayne Boney	2004	9031
148 0/8	23 3/8 23 3/8	17 0/8	5 5	Trempealeau County	WI	Steven G. Follansbee	2004	9031
148 0/8	25 7/8 27 3/8	22 2/8	5 6	Hillsdale County	MI	Kevin Jump	2004	9031
148 0/8	23 5/8 23 5/8	17 1/8	7 6	Woodbury County	IA	Blake Miller	2004	9031
148 0/8	21 5/8 23 4/8	19 0/8	5 5	Crawford County	WI	Dave Shaffer	2004	9031
148 0/8	22 2/8 22 6/8	16 4/8	6 5	Shawano County	WI	Lee C. Papendorf	2004	9031
*148 0/8	24 7/8 23 7/8	21 0/8	5 4	Clay County	AR	Chris Tarno	2004	9031
148 0/8	24 1/8 23 4/8	16 0/8	5 5	Douglas County	WI	Kenneth Fedyn	2004	9031
*148 0/8	25 6/8 25 2/8	23 2/8	6 6	Cass County	IL	Lance Hemken	2004	9031
148 0/8	26 6/8 24 6/8	24 4/8	5 5	Pike County	IL	Stephen W. Manker	2004	9031
148 0/8	25 0/8 25 2/8	19 2/8	4 4	Price County	WI	Donald L. Wanie	2004	9031
*148 0/8	24 5/8 23 6/8	18 4/8	5 4	Jackson County	WI	Brooke Anderson	2005	9031
148 0/8	23 7/8 24 0/8	18 4/8	4 5	Dodge County	WI	Bob Schultz	2005	9031
148 0/8	24 7/8 24 7/8	18 2/8	5 5	Clark County	WI	Shannon Nelson	2005	9031
148 0/8	23 4/8 23 7/8	17 0/8	5 5	Taylor County	WI	Joseph J. Frombach	2005	9031

451

WHITETAIL DEER (TYPICAL ANTLERS)

Minimum Score 125 Continued

SCORE	LENGTH OF R MAIN BEAM L	INSIDE SPREAD	NUMBER OF R POINTS L	AREA	STATE/ PROVINCE	HUNTER'S NAME	DATE	RANK
148 0/8	22 4/8 22 7/8	17 6/8	5 5	Gage County	NE	Larry G. Lottman	2005	9031
148 0/8	28 2/8 26 6/8	18 4/8	6 5	DeKalb County	IL	William McCoy	2005	9031
148 0/8	26 5/8 25 3/8	17 1/8	5 5	Polk County	WI	Todd Montgomery	2005	9031
148 0/8	25 4/8 25 4/8	18 4/8	5 7	Randolph County	IN	Jeff Geesaman	2005	9031
*148 0/8	26 1/8 26 3/8	19 4/8	5 5	Greene County	OH	Nick Ison	2005	9031
*148 0/8	23 3/8 22 7/8	18 6/8	5 5	Adams County	IL	Gerard J. West	2005	9031
148 0/8	24 6/8 25 1/8	18 2/8	5 7	Anoka County	MN	Dan Kasper	2005	9031
*148 0/8	21 2/8 21 1/8	16 2/8	5 5	Columbia County	WI	Jason Stenberg	2006	9031
148 0/8	24 4/8 23 2/8	17 0/8	4 5	Fulton County	IL	William D. Hardesty III	2006	9031
148 0/8	24 1/8 23 1/8	18 6/8	4 6	Cecil County	MD	David Joseph Wunder	2006	9031
*148 0/8	22 5/8 23 3/8	15 3/8	7 5	Greene County	IN	Bill Mullis	2006	9031
148 0/8	25 0/8 23 2/8	21 2/8	5 5	Richland County	WI	Dale R. Ripp	2006	9031
148 0/8	25 0/8 24 7/8	18 0/8	6 5	Dane County	WI	Scott Zoromski	2006	9031
148 0/8	25 7/8 25 4/8	24 2/8	6 5	Richland County	WI	Joseph A. Pizer	2006	9031
*148 0/8	22 7/8 22 4/8	17 2/8	6 6	Vinton County	OH	Jason Harris	2006	9031
148 0/8	24 3/8 23 5/8	18 2/8	4 5	Bayfield County	WI	Tom Walters	2006	9031
148 0/8	24 6/8 25 2/8	19 4/8	4 4	Clark County	MO	George Vinal	2006	9031
148 0/8	22 5/8 23 2/8	17 0/8	5 5	Jackson County	WI	Joshua T. Wyss	2007	9031
148 0/8	23 6/8 23 4/8	22 4/8	6 5	Cass County	IN	Dempsey Gross	2007	9031
*148 0/8	23 2/8 23 1/8	17 6/8	5 5	Portage County	WI	Nathan Kedrowicz	2008	9031
*148 0/8	28 1/8 25 7/8	19 6/8	5 5	Ste. Genevieve County	MO	David C. Jacobs	2008	9031
148 0/8	22 2/8 22 3/8	16 1/8	6 6	McDonough County	IL	Richard S. Bard	2008	9031
*148 0/8	24 7/8 23 3/8	18 2/8	5 5	Waukesha County	WI	Mark Adams	2008	9031
148 0/8	24 7/8 25 3/8	19 0/8	5 5	Richland County	WI	Daniel Snider	2008	9031
*148 0/8	23 4/8 25 6/8	19 1/8	6 8	Johnson County	IA	Kevin L. McDonald	2008	9031
148 0/8	23 5/8 24 0/8	17 2/8	7 6	Pepin County	WI	Jesse Seifert	2009	9031
148 0/8	24 0/8 24 2/8	21 6/8	5 7	Williams County	OH	David Gustafson	2009	9031
148 0/8	21 7/8 21 6/8	17 6/8	6 6	Marquette County	WI	David A. Janssen	2009	9031
148 0/8	22 5/8 23 7/8	15 6/8	4 4	Republic County	KS	Greg Larsen	2009	9031
*148 0/8	23 3/8 23 7/8	16 6/8	5 5	Pembina County	ND	Christa Brodina	2010	9031
148 0/8	24 6/8 24 6/8	18 4/8	4 5	Lincoln County	WI	Robert LePage	2010	9031
147 7/8	21 7/8 22 2/8	18 5/8	5 5	Green Lake County	WI	Al Hubbell	1974	9152
147 7/8	25 6/8 24 7/8	21 7/8	4 4	Anne Arundel County	MD	James E. Roy	1977	9152
147 7/8	22 2/8 22 3/8	18 5/8	5 5	Iron County	MI	David C. Tarsi	1978	9152
147 7/8	26 3/8 25 5/8	17 5/8	4 4	Lafayette County	WI	Kim D. Gruenberg	1979	9152
147 7/8	20 6/8 21 6/8	18 4/8	6 6	Cass County	NE	David R. Kempnich	1981	9152
147 7/8	27 0/8 26 0/8	23 2/8	4 6	Cowley County	KS	Virgil Dwayne Graham	1982	9152
147 7/8	25 1/8 26 1/8	21 6/8	5 6	McHenry County	IL	Greg Herdrich	1983	9152
147 7/8	24 5/8 24 0/8	19 5/8	5 5	Guthrie County	IA	Vernie W. Grasty	1983	9152
147 7/8	23 4/8 24 2/8	15 2/8	5 6	Harris County	TX	John Hall	1985	9152
147 7/8	21 7/8 22 2/8	17 7/8	5 5	Butler County	OH	James Lynch	1985	9152
147 7/8	21 2/8 21 1/8	19 6/8	6 6	Rice County	KS	David L. Boedeker	1986	9152
147 7/8	23 4/8 23 0/8	14 5/8	5 5	Langlade County	WI	Mark Helgeson	1986	9152
147 7/8	23 6/8 23 3/8	18 2/8	6 6	Wabaunsee County	KS	Jim Hagan	1986	9152
147 7/8	23 4/8 23 4/8	20 3/8	5 5	Lake County	IL	David Mitten	1987	9152
147 7/8	23 3/8 24 3/8	18 5/8	5 5	Dakota County	MN	Fred Kober	1988	9152
147 7/8	22 1/8 22 3/8	15 5/8	6 6	Scott County	IA	Gary W. Gilkison	1988	9152
147 7/8	25 0/8 24 3/8	15 7/8	6 6	Chippewa County	WI	Joseph L. Couey	1989	9152
147 7/8	22 1/8 22 6/8	17 1/8	5 5	Macon County	IL	Earl Nelson	1989	9152
147 7/8	24 5/8 25 1/8	19 5/8	4 4	Eau Claire County	WI	Robert W. Hall	1990	9152
147 7/8	26 0/8 25 5/8	23 3/8	4 4	Allamakee County	IA	Kevin Sweeney	1990	9152
147 7/8	25 7/8 26 3/8	19 5/8	4 4	Lake County	IL	Allen G. Comstock	1990	9152
147 7/8	23 3/8 23 1/8	16 7/8	5 6	Waukesha County	WI	Andrae D'Acquisto	1991	9152
147 7/8	24 1/8 22 4/8	16 4/8	6 6	Redwood County	MN	Gary Schunk	1992	9152
147 7/8	23 2/8 23 0/8	17 0/8	7 7	La Salle County	TX	Jeremy Elias	1992	9152
147 7/8	26 6/8 26 5/8	18 1/8	4 4	Calvert County	MD	Charles J. Wade	1993	9152
147 7/8	25 0/8 25 0/8	18 0/8	5 8	Schuyler County	IL	Gregory Runkle	1993	9152
147 7/8	22 6/8 23 2/8	17 5/8	5 6	Jackson County	OH	Edsel D. Duty	1993	9152
147 7/8	24 7/8 25 2/8	18 7/8	4 5	Sauk County	WI	Michael J. McGann	1994	9152
147 7/8	26 2/8 26 4/8	19 5/8	4 5	Knox County	IL	Kevin Engels	1994	9152
147 7/8	24 4/8 24 2/8	17 1/8	6 5	Wapello County	IA	Ralph McConaughey	1995	9152
147 7/8	26 5/8 26 1/8	14 6/8	7 6	Buffalo County	WI	Daniel H. Folkedahl	1995	9152
147 7/8	26 2/8 25 7/8	19 2/8	4 6	Shelby County	IL	Joseph Hoene	1996	9152
147 7/8	24 2/8 24 5/8	17 5/8	6 5	Jackson County	MI	Clare C. Butler	1996	9152
147 7/8	24 1/8 24 7/8	18 6/8	7 6	Pike County	IL	Pat Davis	1996	9152
147 7/8	24 7/8 24 7/8	16 4/8	5 5	Clay County	IL	Richard Stock	1996	9152
147 7/8	22 5/8 22 4/8	21 5/8	5 5	Minnehaha County	SD	Tim Zoellner	1996	9152
147 7/8	21 3/8 21 7/8	14 5/8	5 5	St. Clair County	MI	Jeffrey Curtis Vargo	1997	9152
147 7/8	22 7/8 22 5/8	19 3/8	5 5	Missoula County	MT	Karl E. Evans	1997	9152
147 7/8	21 5/8 20 7/8	15 3/8	5 6	Waupaca County	WI	Ronald L. Lutzewitz	1997	9152
147 7/8	22 7/8 23 3/8	20 1/8	6 5	Bayfield County	WI	Jeff Ottman	1997	9152
147 7/8	22 4/8 21 6/8	17 7/8	5 5	St. Charles County	MO	Daniel Gentz	1997	9152
147 7/8	21 7/8 23 2/8	16 5/8	6 6	Bremer County	IA	Dean Reiter	1998	9152
147 7/8	22 3/8 22 7/8	20 1/8	5 5	Kalamazoo County	MI	Thomas N. Reichert	1998	9152
147 7/8	23 4/8 24 4/8	18 5/8	5 5	Schoharie County	NY	Richard A. Lally, Jr.	1998	9152
147 7/8	22 1/8 21 3/8	18 3/8	5 5	Fairfield County	CT	Douglas E. LoBasso	1998	9152
147 7/8	23 3/8 22 6/8	18 5/8	5 6	Winnebago County	IL	Fred W. Cook	1999	9152
147 7/8	22 7/8 22 2/8	20 7/8	5 5	Woodford County	IL	Darin M. Steffen	1999	9152
147 7/8	24 3/8 24 7/8	17 5/8	4 5	Saline County	NE	Smoke Filip	1999	9152
147 7/8	24 6/8 25 1/8	18 6/8	9 6	Oneida County	WI	Mike Berger	1999	9152
147 7/8	24 1/8 23 0/8	19 2/8	6 6	Rock Island County	IL	Shawn Van Alsburg	2000	9152
147 7/8	23 6/8 23 4/8	17 5/8	5 5	Plymouth County	IA	Jerry Goodmanson	2000	9152
147 7/8	23 1/8 22 6/8	16 3/8	5 5	Waushara County	WI	Harvey Kalbus	2000	9152
147 7/8	24 1/8 22 2/8	18 7/8	5 6	Monroe County	WI	Dave Keene	2001	9152
147 7/8	23 0/8 22 7/8	19 7/8	5 5	Henrico County	VA	James R. Bowles III	2001	9152
147 7/8	23 5/8 24 4/8	20 7/8	5 5	Dubuque County	IA	Scott Klein	2001	9152
147 7/8	21 6/8 21 7/8	18 5/8	5 5	Scott County	IA	Henry Peters, Jr.	2001	9152
147 7/8	22 2/8 22 5/8	17 1/8	5 5	Daviess County	IN	David R. Knepp	2001	9152
147 7/8	26 7/8 25 7/8	17 2/8	7 5	Clermont County	OH	Bob Lemme	2002	9152
*147 7/8	24 2/8 25 6/8	19 1/8	5 5	Buffalo County	WI	David Kiesow	2002	9152
147 7/8	22 3/8 22 6/8	22 4/8	6 7	Ogle County	IL	Gary Martin	2002	9152
147 7/8	21 7/8 22 5/8	16 7/8	5 5	Pike County	IL	Joe Netzler	2002	9152
147 7/8	22 7/8 22 7/8	18 3/8	5 5	Cass County	IL	Daniel W. Kirkes	2002	9152
*147 7/8	26 1/8 26 2/8	17 1/8	5 5	McPherson County	KS	Bryan D. Zerger	2002	9152
147 7/8	25 2/8 25 0/8	19 4/8	6 5	Kiowa County	KS	Chuck Adams	2002	9152

452

WHITETAIL DEER (TYPICAL ANTLERS)

Minimum Score 125 Continued

SCORE	LENGTH OF R MAIN BEAM L	INSIDE SPREAD	NUMBER OF R POINTS L		AREA	STATE/ PROVINCE	HUNTER'S NAME	DATE	RANK
*147 7/8	24 3/8 22 2/8	18 4/8	6	6	Ashland County	WI	Deane Halverson	2003	9152
*147 7/8	23 3/8 22 6/8	18 3/8	9	7	Decatur County	IA	Ken Roddey	2003	9152
147 7/8	23 6/8 23 5/8	21 5/8	5	5	Nemaha County	NE	Danny E. Williams	2003	9152
147 7/8	25 6/8 24 2/8	19 1/8	5	5	Cerro Gordo County	IA	Chad Novak	2003	9152
147 7/8	24 4/8 24 7/8	18 7/8	5	6	Hancock County	OH	Scott E. Cramer	2004	9152
147 7/8	25 5/8 25 4/8	19 1/8	4	6	La Salle County	IL	Ben Beddingfield	2004	9152
147 7/8	23 4/8 23 6/8	17 3/8	5	6	Schuyler County	IL	Dennis D. Taylor	2004	9152
147 7/8	21 5/8 22 4/8	12 7/8	5	5	Jasper County	IL	Todd Probst	2004	9152
147 7/8	24 2/8 24 4/8	19 1/8	5	5	Kane County	IL	Dean Ashton	2004	9152
147 7/8	23 5/8 23 6/8	16 7/8	5	5	Clayton County	IA	Aaron Green	2005	9152
*147 7/8	21 4/8 21 6/8	15 3/8	5	5	Hancock County	IL	Clifford Goodreau	2005	9152
147 7/8	23 7/8 24 6/8	19 1/8	5	5	Harrison County	IN	Kenny R. Missi	2005	9152
*147 7/8	22 5/8 22 3/8	16 7/8	5	5	Logan County	CO	Brad Baldwin	2005	9152
*147 7/8	22 7/8 24 0/8	16 5/8	5	5	Wyoming County	WV	Steven Rowan	2005	9152
147 7/8	25 6/8 25 5/8	17 1/8	4	5	Rogers County	OK	David T. Garnecky	2006	9152
147 7/8	25 6/8 26 0/8	22 1/8	4	4	Sauk County	WI	Jon M. Craker	2006	9152
147 7/8	21 7/8 21 2/8	14 7/8	6	6	Ray County	MO	Cody S. Niemchick	2006	9152
147 7/8	24 1/8 23 4/8	16 5/8	8	7	Montgomery County	IN	Tim Congleton	2006	9152
*147 7/8	23 6/8 24 0/8	22 5/8	4	5	Posey County	IN	Josh Milliner	2006	9152
147 7/8	22 6/8 22 2/8	16 7/8	5	5	Van Buren County	IA	Blake Swanson	2006	9152
*147 7/8	26 0/8 27 6/8	19 1/8	5	5	Franklin County	IN	Brandon Watkins	2006	9152
147 7/8	25 4/8 24 4/8	17 1/8	4	6	Sedgwick County	KS	Clinton Davis	2006	9152
147 7/8	23 0/8 22 7/8	18 0/8	6	5	Stearns County	MN	Randy Laage	2007	9152
147 7/8	23 0/8 23 3/8	16 3/8	6	6	Rockingham County	NC	Barry Joyce	2007	9152
147 7/8	24 6/8 24 6/8	16 3/8	7	5	Garfield County	OK	Joe Peeper	2007	9152
147 7/8	26 2/8 26 1/8	22 4/8	5	8	Taylor County	IA	Travis Crowley	2007	9152
*147 7/8	25 5/8 25 6/8	19 1/8	6	5	Macon County	IL	Doug Perry	2007	9152
147 7/8	23 0/8 23 1/8	20 6/8	7	5	Wadena County	MN	Ben Walsvik	2008	9152
147 7/8	24 0/8 23 1/8	16 6/8	6	6	Carter County	KY	Rodney Carroll	2008	9152
147 7/8	24 2/8 25 0/8	18 3/8	5	5	Warren County	KY	Jeff Goodwin	2008	9152
147 7/8	25 0/8 24 7/8	20 6/8	6	5	Garvin County	OK	Chris Raper	2008	9152
*147 7/8	25 2/8 25 5/8	18 3/8	5	5	Hart County	KY	David Paige	2008	9152
147 7/8	21 5/8 23 6/8	18 1/8	5	5	Wyandot County	OH	Sean Welty	2008	9152
147 7/8	21 3/8 21 1/8	17 1/8	5	5	Allegan County	MI	Matthew P. Krcatovich	2008	9152
147 7/8	25 0/8 23 5/8	17 2/8	5	6	Kingman County	KS	Chad Pipkin	2008	9152
147 7/8	20 1/8 19 5/8	13 5/8	7	6	Calhoun County	IL	Blaine W. Pazero	2008	9152
147 7/8	24 3/8 24 6/8	16 5/8	6	6	Morgan County	CO	John Cannon	2009	9152
*147 7/8	23 0/8 22 7/8	19 1/8	5	5	Jackson County	IN	Jerry G. Ames, Jr.	2009	9152
147 7/8	23 6/8 23 3/8	13 5/8	7	6	Sumner County	KS	Donald R. McGuire	2009	9152
147 7/8	20 3/8 22 0/8	16 7/8	5	5	McHenry County	ND	Scott Hettinger	2009	9152
147 7/8	23 7/8 23 7/8	19 3/8	7	5	Kingman County	KS	Collen L. Steffen	2009	9152
*147 7/8	23 6/8 24 3/8	17 1/8	5	5	Effingham County	IL	Tyler Rickelman	2009	9152
*147 7/8	25 1/8 23 1/8	20 3/8	6	6	Jackson County	MI	Adam R. Armstrong	2010	9152
147 6/8	23 4/8 23 2/8	16 0/8	5	5	Morrison County	MN	John Zwickey	1955	9259
147 6/8	23 5/8 24 3/8	16 6/8	6	7	Morrison County	MN	Allen E. Farmes	1957	9259
147 6/8	25 3/8 24 5/8	19 7/8	6	5	Jo Daviess County	IL	Jerry Fritz	1971	9259
147 6/8	24 1/8 25 6/8	19 0/8	5	5	Dickinson County	MI	Myles Keller	1976	9259
147 6/8	24 6/8 23 0/8	17 6/8	6	6	Butler County	KY	O. D. Phelps	1977	9259
147 6/8	24 0/8 24 2/8	17 2/8	6	5	Harlan County	NE	Ron Breitsprecher	1978	9259
147 6/8	22 3/8 22 1/8	17 4/8	4	4	Mercer County	ND	Steven J. Prock	1980	9259
147 6/8	22 1/8 22 2/8	19 6/8	5	5	Union County	IL	Karen Mason	1980	9259
147 6/8	25 6/8 24 6/8	18 0/8	5	5	Jackson County	IA	Carl Severson	1982	9259
147 6/8	23 2/8 23 1/8	18 0/8	5	5	Sumner County	KS	Danny S. Holden	1982	9259
147 6/8	22 3/8 22 4/8	21 2/8	4	4	Kingsbury County	SD	Mack Butler	1984	9259
147 6/8	22 5/8 23 2/8	19 2/8	5	6	Stafford County	KS	Larry E Bowser	1985	9259
147 6/8	21 2/8 21 7/8	16 0/8	8	8	Macoupin County	IL	Leonard Koniak	1987	9259
147 6/8	23 7/8 23 6/8	17 2/8	6	6	Crawford County	IL	Gary Bickers	1987	9259
147 6/8	24 0/8 24 0/8	20 0/8	5	5	Iroquois County	IL	Gregory A. Hiser	1989	9259
147 6/8	23 7/8 24 2/8	18 3/8	6	7	Monroe County	NY	Tim Bumbarger	1990	9259
147 6/8	25 2/8 25 6/8	22 2/8	4	4	Delaware County	OH	Doug Fuller	1991	9259
147 6/8	26 4/8 26 2/8	19 5/8	6	7	Clinton County	OH	Kevin L. Wilson	1991	9259
147 6/8	22 1/8 21 6/8	18 4/8	8	7	Cedar County	IA	Paul Dykstra	1991	9259
147 6/8	22 7/8 23 7/8	17 3/8	8	9	Marshall County	MN	Jeremy Beck	1992	9259
147 6/8	24 3/8 23 2/8	21 5/8	6	6	Knox County	IL	Lee Murray	1992	9259
147 6/8	24 0/8 24 4/8	16 6/8	5	5	Pittsburg County	OK	Roy Ward	1992	9259
147 6/8	24 3/8 24 4/8	18 2/8	5	5	Calhoun County	IL	Randy Watters	1992	9259
147 6/8	24 0/8 23 1/8	17 6/8	5	6	Wabaunsee County	KS	Ron Arand	1992	9259
147 6/8	24 4/8 21 4/8	16 7/8	7	5	Harrison County	IA	Jamen Cates	1993	9259
147 6/8	22 2/8 22 5/8	16 6/8	5	5	Morrison County	MN	Richard Asp	1994	9259
147 6/8	25 4/8 25 5/8	19 6/8	6	4	Dane County	WI	Jeffrey Lee Zanow	1994	9259
147 6/8	23 7/8 23 4/8	19 4/8	5	5	Ogle County	IL	Roy Nichols	1994	9259
147 6/8	24 1/8 24 1/8	20 2/8	5	4	Barber County	KS	Tom Langford	1994	9259
147 6/8	23 3/8 23 4/8	20 6/8	5	5	Washtenaw County	MI	Richard N. Lane	1995	9259
147 6/8	24 7/8 24 3/8	19 1/8	7	7	Allegheny County	PA	Richard J. Blauser	1995	9259
147 6/8	22 2/8 23 2/8	16 2/8	5	5	Kenosha County	WI	Joseph C. Albright	1995	9259
147 6/8	23 5/8 24 4/8	18 1/8	6	5	Delaware County	IN	Steve Minard	1995	9259
147 6/8	25 2/8 24 2/8	17 2/8	5	5	Appanoose County	IA	Dennis Palmer	1996	9259
147 6/8	21 4/8 21 4/8	16 0/8	5	5	Jackson County	MO	Dennis W. Patrick	1996	9259
147 6/8	23 1/8 23 2/8	19 0/8	6	7	Licking County	OH	Kerry Proctor	1996	9259
147 6/8	24 0/8 24 6/8	20 2/8	7	5	Butler County	KY	David Whitehouse	1996	9259
147 6/8	23 4/8 24 3/8	18 7/8	6	6	Ferry County	WA	Doug Kikendall	1997	9259
147 6/8	25 5/8 25 6/8	21 6/8	5	5	Ozark County	MO	Donny James	1997	9259
147 6/8	28 0/8 21 0/8	21 6/8	7	6	Buffalo County	WI	Bill Barzydlo	1997	9259
147 6/8	25 3/8 24 4/8	19 0/8	4	4	Cook County	IL	Timothy L. Harkness	1997	9259
147 6/8	25 6/8 25 5/8	17 6/8	4	4	Cherokee County	KS	Paul Atkins	1997	9259
147 6/8	25 0/8 25 6/8	18 0/8	4	4	Harford County	MD	Andrew Hacke	1997	9259
147 6/8	21 6/8 21 5/8	19 2/8	5	5	Clay County	IA	Thomas Ray Gross	1997	9259
147 6/8	25 2/8 25 2/8	18 2/8	5	5	Putnam County	NY	Jesse Jaycox	1998	9259
147 6/8	23 7/8 25 5/8	19 5/8	5	4	Lake County	IN	Michael G. Turner	1998	9259
147 6/8	24 4/8 25 2/8	20 2/8	5	4	Adams County	WI	Jerry J. Hoffman	1998	9259
147 6/8	23 2/8 22 3/8	17 0/8	5	5	Winona County	MN	Todd Miller	1999	9259
147 6/8	23 2/8 23 5/8	19 0/8	5	6	Belmont County	OH	Brent Burkhart	1999	9259
147 6/8	26 6/8 25 7/8	17 2/8	5	5	Buffalo County	WI	Gary R. Stutz	1999	9259
147 6/8	23 6/8 23 5/8	18 1/8	7	5	Osage County	OK	Ty Stapleton	1999	9259
147 6/8	24 5/8 24 0/8	20 4/8	5	5	Jones County	IA	Vic Boeding	1999	9259

453

WHITETAIL DEER (TYPICAL ANTLERS)

Minimum Score 125 — Continued

SCORE	LENGTH OF R MAIN BEAM L	INSIDE SPREAD	NUMBER OF R POINTS L		AREA	STATE/PROVINCE	HUNTER'S NAME	DATE	RANK
147 6/8	23 0/8 23 4/8	17 4/8	6	6	Pulaski County	AR	Francis M. Elton	1999	9259
147 6/8	26 3/8 25 2/8	21 0/8	5	6	Dane County	WI	Dave Weber	2000	9259
147 6/8	23 7/8 25 7/8	22 4/8	4	5	Schuyler County	NY	Leonard D. Knapp	2000	9259
147 6/8	24 6/8 25 0/8	20 3/8	5	6	Sherburne County	MN	Richard A. Iano	2000	9259
147 6/8	24 4/8 24 4/8	19 2/8	5	5	Chippewa County	WI	Andrew Seidlitz	2000	9259
147 6/8	23 5/8 22 5/8	17 7/8	6	5	Otter Tail County	MN	Robert Westby	2001	9259
147 6/8	26 1/8 27 2/8	17 0/8	4	5	Macon County	MO	Roger Johnston	2001	9259
147 6/8	23 5/8 22 5/8	18 4/8	5	7	Vigo County	IN	Devin Smith	2001	9259
147 6/8	23 2/8 22 5/8	16 4/8	5	6	Marquette County	WI	Edward M. Rundgren, Jr.	2002	9259
147 6/8	22 2/8 22 4/8	18 0/8	6	6	Linn County	MO	Robert V. Mitchell	2002	9259
147 6/8	22 5/8 24 2/8	19 6/8	5	4	Sullivan County	PA	Frank Skoranski, Jr.	2002	9259
147 6/8	24 2/8 25 0/8	20 6/8	4	4	Dodge County	MN	Dan Nelson	2002	9259
147 6/8	25 0/8 24 4/8	20 0/8	4	6	Highland County	OH	Brad Russ	2003	9259
147 6/8	23 2/8 23 2/8	17 0/8	5	5	Allen County	KS	Todd D. Robbins	2003	9259
147 6/8	22 5/8 22 4/8	15 6/8	5	5	Jennings County	IN	Ricky Hoyle	2003	9259
147 6/8	25 3/8 26 2/8	20 6/8	4	4	Alexander County	IL	Mark W. Pasmore	2003	9259
147 6/8	22 3/8 23 5/8	18 3/8	5	6	Pike County	IL	Lee Durden	2003	9259
147 6/8	23 4/8 23 7/8	16 2/8	6	5	St. Louis County	MN	John Abdo	2003	9259
147 6/8	23 0/8 23 3/8	17 0/8	5	5	Wyandot County	OH	James D. Herring	2004	9259
147 6/8	22 6/8 22 2/8	16 4/8	6	5	Burnett County	WI	Randy Krone	2004	9259
147 6/8	25 2/8 25 0/8	14 4/8	4	5	Pulaski County	IL	Bill Spaulding	2004	9259
147 6/8	23 0/8 23 4/8	18 2/8	8	8	Pierce County	WI	Kevin Winger	2005	9259
147 6/8	25 0/8 25 2/8	20 6/8	6	5	Buffalo County	WI	Cardell Potter	2005	9259
147 6/8	25 6/8 25 6/8	20 7/8	4	5	Rock County	WI	Joshua E. Wells	2005	9259
*147 6/8	22 6/8 23 0/8	19 4/8	5	5	Warren County	NJ	Ryan L. Eastridge	2005	9259
*147 6/8	24 1/8 24 1/8	18 4/8	5	5	Harrison County	KY	Todd Morris	2005	9259
147 6/8	21 5/8 21 7/8	18 4/8	5	5	Pike County	IL	Jeff Dale	2005	9259
147 6/8	25 4/8 24 0/8	20 6/8	4	5	Mercer County	PA	Joe Stephenson	2005	9259
147 6/8	21 4/8 21 2/8	17 6/8	6	5	Lincoln County	MO	Josh Lenk	2005	9259
*147 6/8	23 6/8 23 6/8	18 6/8	4	5	Mitchell County	IA	Eric Johnston	2005	9259
147 6/8	23 5/8 24 2/8	15 2/8	4	4	Ralls County	MO	Todd Scheibe	2005	9259
147 6/8	23 2/8 23 5/8	18 2/8	5	5	St. Croix County	WI	Tony Rizzo	2005	9259
147 6/8	25 2/8 24 6/8	16 1/8	7	6	Lyon County	KS	Johnny W. Drake	2005	9259
147 6/8	22 6/8 23 4/8	23 2/8	6	6	Taylor County	IA	Jeremy Tobin	2005	9259
*147 6/8	22 7/8 22 6/8	18 6/8	5	5	Buffalo County	WI	Ronald Walski	2006	9259
147 6/8	22 5/8 21 7/8	16 7/8	5	7	Buffalo County	WI	Jeff Doucette	2006	9259
*147 6/8	22 1/8 20 0/8	17 4/8	7	6	Phillips County	KS	Darren Diederich	2006	9259
147 6/8	24 1/8 24 0/8	16 4/8	5	5	Blue Earth County	MN	Grant Halverson	2006	9259
*147 6/8	24 5/8 24 6/8	18 6/8	7	4	La Crosse County	WI	Mike Kammel	2006	9259
147 6/8	24 4/8 24 3/8	17 7/8	6	7	Waukesha County	WI	Richard Thayer	2006	9259
147 6/8	23 0/8 22 6/8	18 4/8	5	5	Dodge County	WI	Ken Strahota	2006	9259
147 6/8	24 1/8 24 0/8	18 2/8	7	6	Grant County	WI	Brandon Becker	2006	9259
147 6/8	23 2/8 24 6/8	19 0/8	6	6	Scott County	TN	Richard Slaven	2006	9259
147 6/8	22 2/8 22 4/8	17 6/8	6	5	Buffalo County	WI	Wayne Olson	2007	9259
147 6/8	24 0/8 24 4/8	20 4/8	4	4	Warren County	IN	Roger L. Neal	2007	9259
*147 6/8	25 0/8 25 4/8	17 6/8	5	5	Van Buren County	IA	Kyle Murphy	2007	9259
147 6/8	24 2/8 23 1/8	16 2/8	6	8	Outagamie County	WI	Greg Reed	2007	9259
147 6/8	22 0/8 23 0/8	15 2/8	5	5	Van Buren County	IA	Richard Penn	2008	9259
147 6/8	22 5/8 23 3/8	18 6/8	5	5	Dodge County	NE	Dave Wimmer	2008	9259
147 6/8	23 1/8 22 6/8	17 0/8	4	4	Vernon County	WI	Casey A. Blum	2008	9259
147 6/8	26 1/8 25 3/8	20 3/8	7	5	Tallahatchie County	MS	Jim Kennedy	2009	9259
147 6/8	27 6/8 26 5/8	18 6/8	4	5	Warren County	KY	Dallas Clark	2009	9259
147 6/8	22 1/8 23 1/8	22 2/8	5	5	Hamilton County	TX	Doug Kelly	2009	9259
*147 6/8	22 3/8 22 3/8	18 2/8	5	5	Cass County	NE	David Hopp	2009	9259
147 6/8	25 4/8 26 4/8	18 4/8	4	5	Columbia County	WI	Glenn McKay	2009	9259
147 6/8	23 0/8 22 5/8	17 0/8	5	5	Portage County	WI	Mark Ostricki	2009	9259
147 5/8	23 7/8 23 5/8	19 1/8	5	5	Fillmore County	MN	Dale Honsey	1951	9367
147 5/8	24 2/8 26 0/8	20 2/8	6	6	Nicollet County	MN	Thomas J. Merkley	1970	9367
147 5/8	22 7/8 23 2/8	18 1/8	4	4	Wilkin County	MN	Darrel G. Montieth	1978	9367
147 5/8	23 5/8 23 4/8	18 3/8	4	5	Morrison County	MN	Leon Fuchs	1981	9367
147 5/8	22 2/8 22 7/8	16 6/8	6	6	Merrimack County	NH	Jerry Smith	1982	9367
147 5/8	24 7/8 25 3/8	19 5/8	5	6	Peoria County	IL	Joe Shryock, Jr.	1983	9367
147 5/8	24 6/8 25 2/8	17 2/8	5	6	Koochiching County	MN	Terrance L. Jaeger	1983	9367
147 5/8	23 5/8 22 7/8	18 3/8	5	5	De Witt County	IL	John H. Piatt	1983	9367
147 5/8	25 3/8 24 7/8	17 7/8	5	5	Butler County	PA	David L. Travaglio	1986	9367
147 5/8	26 0/8 25 3/8	18 3/8	5	6	Morgan County	OH	Ron Newsom	1986	9367
147 5/8	25 0/8 24 3/8	21 4/8	5	5	Winona County	MN	Rodney Blake	1986	9367
147 5/8	23 1/8 25 6/8	18 7/8	5	5	Rock County	WI	John G. Donstad	1986	9367
147 5/8	24 3/8 24 3/8	18 3/8	6	5	Washington County	MN	Scott Moncur	1987	9367
147 5/8	24 7/8 24 5/8	17 5/8	5	5	Shelby County	IL	Dennis J. Lynch	1987	9367
147 5/8	23 2/8 25 2/8	16 1/8	5	6	Perry County	IL	Scott Rice	1987	9367
147 5/8	27 0/8 26 6/8	21 3/8	4	5	Baltimore County	MD	Kevin Vogt	1990	9367
147 5/8	24 2/8 24 5/8	15 3/8	5	5	Walton County	GA	Kenny Starnes	1991	9367
147 5/8	23 6/8 22 2/8	15 3/8	5	5	Lipscomb County	TX	Rick C. McDowell	1991	9367
147 5/8	25 2/8 25 0/8	17 3/8	7	5	Union County	IL	Donald S. Blakley	1991	9367
147 5/8	23 2/8 23 5/8	20 6/8	4	5	Marion County	KS	Dennis N. Ballweg	1991	9367
147 5/8	23 7/8 22 1/8	18 2/8	5	6	Des Moines County	IA	Harold Lingenfelter	1992	9367
147 5/8	24 7/8 24 6/8	19 5/8	8	8	Guernsey County	OH	Reuben W. Miller	1993	9367
147 5/8	25 5/8 24 7/8	16 6/8	5	5	Washington County	KS	Scott A. Wilkens	1993	9367
147 5/8	24 3/8 25 3/8	18 7/8	5	5	Rusk County	WI	Irving Schneiderwent	1993	9367
147 5/8	22 7/8 23 4/8	15 7/8	5	5	Knox County	OH	Gary Sparks	1994	9367
147 5/8	23 4/8 24 3/8	18 4/8	4	5	Winneshiek County	IA	John Havel	1994	9367
147 5/8	22 3/8 22 3/8	17 3/8	6	5	Dunn County	WI	John S. Fassbinder	1994	9367
147 5/8	23 3/8 24 6/8	18 1/8	5	5	Belmont County	OH	Lewis R. Holcomb	1994	9367
147 5/8	22 5/8 24 1/8	16 5/8	6	6	Marion County	IL	James W. Norman	1994	9367
147 5/8	26 4/8 27 2/8	21 0/8	6	6	Pottawattamie County	IA	Forrest Brown	1994	9367
147 5/8	25 7/8 26 4/8	21 7/8	5	4	Richland County	MT	Brad Hayward	1995	9367
147 5/8	23 6/8 24 2/8	16 5/8	6	5	Dimmit County	TX	Marty Woods	1995	9367
147 5/8	22 7/8 23 3/8	17 2/8	6	5	Van Buren County	IA	Elmer Luce, Jr.	1995	9367
147 5/8	24 5/8 22 6/8	21 7/8	5	5	Woodford County	IL	Shawn Meyer	1995	9367
147 5/8	22 6/8 24 6/8	18 7/8	5	6	Grafton County	NH	Jeff Stout	1995	9367
147 5/8	23 7/8 24 1/8	18 3/8	6	6	Decatur County	IA	Larry Richard	1996	9367
147 5/8	24 0/8 23 6/8	17 7/8	4	4	Butler County	KS	Shiloh Thomas	1996	9367
147 5/8	25 2/8 25 6/8	20 0/8	6	5	Weld County	CO	Kevin Yerian	1996	9367
147 5/8	24 3/8 22 4/8	20 0/8	6	7	Dakota County	MN	Bobby Johnson	1996	9367

454

WHITETAIL DEER (TYPICAL ANTLERS)

Minimum Score 125 Continued

SCORE	LENGTH OF R MAIN BEAM L		INSIDE SPREAD	NUMBER OF R POINTS L		AREA	STATE/ PROVINCE	HUNTER'S NAME	DATE	RANK
147 5/8	23 5/8	23 5/8	17 6/8	6	6	Iowa County	WI	Leslie Ladd	1997	9367
147 5/8	24 0/8	23 7/8	16 4/8	7	6	Poinsett County	AR	Kevin Owens	1997	9367
147 5/8	26 7/8	25 0/8	17 5/8	5	4	Monroe County	NY	Christopher Consler	1997	9367
147 5/8	26 3/8	24 4/8	21 5/8	5	5	Fairfax County	VA	Mike Nyalko	1997	9367
147 5/8	24 3/8	24 6/8	16 7/8	5	5	Fairfield County	OH	David E. Jenkins	1997	9367
147 5/8	25 4/8	23 5/8	17 1/8	4	5	Eau Claire County	WI	Dave Strassman	1998	9367
147 5/8	23 0/8	21 6/8	18 1/8	5	6	Geauga County	OH	Michael Brent	1998	9367
147 5/8	23 7/8	23 6/8	17 0/8	6	5	Marathon County	WI	Dave Richter	1998	9367
147 5/8	24 4/8	25 0/8	18 3/8	5	6	Noble County	OH	Charles Grant	1998	9367
147 5/8	27 0/8	26 3/8	17 6/8	5	6	Forsyth County	NC	Gregory Baugus	1999	9367
147 5/8	25 1/8	24 3/8	14 3/8	5	5	Ohio County	IN	Randy Hastings	1999	9367
147 5/8	24 2/8	25 0/8	19 2/8	4	5	Kankakee County	IL	Dale Van Deursen	1999	9367
147 5/8	25 2/8	21 5/8	22 1/8	4	4	Buffalo County	WI	Frank H. Brenner	2000	9367
147 5/8	24 3/8	26 1/8	21 5/8	5	5	Cass County	MI	Ronald E. Hartline	2000	9367
147 5/8	26 0/8	25 0/8	17 5/8	4	4	New Kent County	VA	Kenny Parker	2000	9367
147 5/8	24 1/8	24 2/8	17 7/8	5	5	Wood County	OH	Edward S. Mahler	2000	9367
147 5/8	24 0/8	24 5/8	18 1/8	6	6	Morgan County	IN	Kevin K. Steinway	2000	9367
147 5/8	24 0/8	24 1/8	14 5/8	6	6	Pottawatomie County	KS	Bryant Shermoe	2000	9367
147 5/8	22 1/8	21 4/8	16 7/8	6	5	Brown County	IL	David Herschelman	2000	9367
147 5/8	23 5/8	23 4/8	14 7/8	6	5	Allen County	KS	Jack Simpson	2000	9367
147 5/8	22 0/8	20 5/8	16 3/8	5	6	Clark County	IL	Jack Fields II	2001	9367
147 5/8	23 0/8	22 6/8	17 3/8	6	5	Jackson County	WI	Jay J. Settersten	2001	9367
147 5/8	24 3/8	23 2/8	18 5/8	5	5	Dakota County	MN	Brian Lemay	2001	9367
147 5/8	25 5/8	25 0/8	18 3/8	5	5	Scott County	IA	David D. Finch	2001	9367
147 5/8	24 3/8	23 2/8	18 7/8	6	7	Clermont County	OH	Randy W. Nueby	2001	9367
*147 5/8	22 6/8	22 4/8	19 5/8	6	5	Hughes County	SD	Chad Mosteller	2002	9367
147 5/8	26 4/8	25 3/8	17 7/8	6	7	McLean County	IL	Bill Frank	2002	9367
147 5/8	24 7/8	24 3/8	16 5/8	4	4	Black Hawk County	IA	Walt Grandon	2002	9367
147 5/8	24 0/8	24 3/8	17 2/8	5	4	Calhoun County	IL	Duane Johnson	2002	9367
147 5/8	23 3/8	23 1/8	17 4/8	6	6	Pine County	MN	John E. Hauwiller	2002	9367
147 5/8	23 1/8	23 7/8	18 5/8	4	5	Jackson County	MO	Ryan Rieder	2002	9367
147 5/8	24 3/8	24 6/8	19 7/8	4	4	Madison County	IL	Scott Lawson	2002	9367
147 5/8	22 0/8	22 6/8	17 4/8	5	6	Lake County	IN	Al Kirkland	2002	9367
147 5/8	28 1/8	28 1/8	20 4/8	4	4	Champlain	ONT	Bob Pytel	2003	9367
147 5/8	24 7/8	23 4/8	17 5/8	5	5	Grayson County	TX	Tim Bedell	2003	9367
147 5/8	25 7/8	25 5/8	22 1/8	4	7	Warren County	IL	Gary Sampson	2003	9367
147 5/8	22 2/8	22 4/8	17 2/8	5	6	Linn County	KS	David Thornberry	2003	9367
147 5/8	22 6/8	23 0/8	15 5/8	5	5	Crow Wing County	MN	Patrick Erdrich	2003	9367
147 5/8	21 4/8	21 7/8	17 0/8	6	6	Taylor County	WI	Derek Nichols	2004	9367
147 5/8	25 0/8	24 0/8	18 7/8	5	6	Furnas County	NE	Blake R. Rotherham	2004	9367
147 5/8	23 2/8	22 5/8	19 5/8	5	4	Dodge County	MN	Myles Keller	2004	9367
147 5/8	24 4/8	24 4/8	18 4/8	6	7	Orange County	NY	Richard Hobart	2004	9367
*147 5/8	22 3/8	22 5/8	16 2/8	5	5	Winnebago County	IL	Fred W. Cook	2004	9367
147 5/8	23 1/8	23 2/8	18 3/8	6	6	Pike County	IL	Jeff Fusco	2004	9367
147 5/8	24 5/8	26 0/8	22 1/8	5	4	Comanche County	KS	Pat Lefemine	2004	9367
147 5/8	25 5/8	25 5/8	18 4/8	5	4	Franklin County	OH	Dennis F. Ruppel	2005	9367
147 5/8	25 7/8	26 7/8	19 7/8	5	7	Todd County	MN	Marshall Zutter	2005	9367
147 5/8	23 5/8	23 5/8	19 3/8	5	5	Monona County	IA	Mathew L. Ritz	2005	9367
*147 5/8	26 1/8	26 4/8	20 2/8	5	4	Lucas County	OH	Steve J. Lucarelli	2005	9367
*147 5/8	23 5/8	22 3/8	18 5/8	5	6	Buffalo County	WI	Joel Helein	2005	9367
147 5/8	25 5/8	26 4/8	18 1/8	5	4	Livingston County	IL	Everett Roe	2005	9367
147 5/8	23 7/8	23 4/8	19 1/8	5	7	Harrison County	IA	Scott Sailors	2005	9367
147 5/8	24 1/8	25 2/8	20 3/8	6	6	Polk County	WI	John Larson	2005	9367
*147 5/8	25 3/8	24 2/8	23 0/8	5	5	Polk County	IA	Glen Salow	2005	9367
147 5/8	21 5/8	22 4/8	14 1/8	6	5	Griggs County	ND	Chris Reinhart	2006	9367
*147 5/8	25 0/8	25 4/8	15 6/8	5	4	Putnam County	IN	Cyree Adair	2006	9367
147 5/8	23 0/8	21 7/8	18 3/8	5	5	Lycoming County	PA	Charles Gingrich	2006	9367
*147 5/8	21 6/8	21 4/8	17 4/8	6	6	Allamakee County	IA	Mark A. Stone	2006	9367
147 5/8	23 0/8	23 2/8	18 6/8	5	5	Hays County	TX	Duane Steffek	2007	9367
147 5/8	25 0/8	24 6/8	17 0/8	5	4	Richland County	OH	Matt Messer	2007	9367
*147 5/8	22 6/8	23 6/8	15 7/8	7	5	Belmont County	OH	Thaddeus Jay White, Jr.	2007	9367
147 5/8	23 6/8	23 5/8	17 0/8	6	5	Coles County	IL	Rick Boyer	2007	9367
*147 5/8	23 0/8	23 2/8	17 5/8	5	5	Madison County	ID	Justin Kostial	2007	9367
*147 5/8	21 7/8	21 7/8	14 7/8	5	7	Columbia County	WI	Jason Stenberg	2008	9367
147 5/8	20 5/8	19 1/8	19 3/8	6	6	Hunterdon County	NJ	Paul J. Long	2008	9367
147 5/8	22 6/8	23 3/8	15 7/8	5	5	Harrison County	OH	Greg Partaka	2008	9367
*147 5/8	23 6/8	25 0/8	19 3/8	6	5	Walworth County	WI	Jason Richmond	2008	9367
147 5/8	24 3/8	24 6/8	17 1/8	5	5	Harrison County	IN	Mike Schmitz	2008	9367
*147 5/8	22 6/8	22 4/8	16 7/8	5	5	Linn County	IA	Michael Wall	2009	9367
147 5/8	22 1/8	21 5/8	19 3/8	5	6	Polk County	MN	James Gunufson	2009	9367
147 5/8	22 5/8	21 5/8	17 7/8	6	5	Gage County	NE	Jason Merchant	2009	9367
*147 5/8	22 4/8	22 7/8	20 6/8	5	5	Priddis	ALB	Kelly Maxwell	2009	9367
*147 5/8	24 6/8	26 7/8	18 0/8	7	7	Warren County	IA	David A. Spacek	2009	9367
147 4/8	22 2/8	22 6/8	18 4/8	4	4	Shawano County	WI	John Schoenike	1960	9479
147 4/8	25 5/8	24 0/8	21 0/8	4	6	Montgomery County	AL	Rett Kelly	1974	9479
147 4/8	23 7/8	23 2/8	16 4/8	7	5	Darke County	OH	Jim Duvall	1977	9479
147 4/8	24 0/8	23 3/8	20 6/8	6	6	Fulton County	OH	Gary R. Bailey	1980	9479
147 4/8	22 6/8	22 2/8	16 6/8	5	5	Burleigh County	ND	James A. Sauvageau	1980	9479
147 4/8	25 3/8	25 6/8	19 0/8	4	5	Blue Earth County	MN	Aaron L. Urke	1981	9479
147 4/8	23 7/8	23 7/8	16 5/8	7	5	Trempealeau County	WI	Donald Skaar	1982	9479
147 4/8	21 0/8	20 5/8	17 6/8	5	5	Cloud County	KS	Jeff Gerard	1982	9479
147 4/8	23 0/8	23 1/8	18 4/8	5	5	St. Charles County	MO	Harry L. Smith	1983	9479
147 4/8	24 1/8	26 0/8	18 6/8	4	4	Prairie County	AR	Joe Moody	1984	9479
147 4/8	25 0/8	25 1/8	19 4/8	5	5	Dane County	WI	John M. Welke, Jr.	1985	9479
147 4/8	23 6/8	23 0/8	14 6/8	5	5	Leader	SAS	Clifton Schneider	1986	9479
147 4/8	26 1/8	26 2/8	19 6/8	6	4	Lincoln County	MO	Terry F. Fry	1986	9479
147 4/8	22 5/8	22 3/8	16 2/8	5	5	Henry County	MO	Cary Dennis	1987	9479
147 4/8	25 6/8	25 0/8	20 7/8	5	7	Jackson County	MI	Scot E. Gazlay	1987	9479
147 4/8	24 3/8	24 3/8	16 4/8	4	5	Woodbury County	IA	Ron Frahm	1987	9479
147 4/8	24 2/8	24 2/8	19 0/8	6	5	Hardin County	IA	William Stonebraker	1987	9479
147 4/8	23 1/8	23 3/8	20 4/8	5	5	Pepin County	WI	Duane Peterson	1988	9479
147 4/8	23 4/8	23 2/8	17 4/8	5	5	Sawyer County	WI	Mike Haegele	1988	9479
147 4/8	24 2/8	24 1/8	17 4/8	5	5	Mahaska County	IA	Larry Smith	1989	9479
147 4/8	26 5/8	22 6/8	19 2/8	5	5	Jersey County	IL	Judy Kovar	1989	9479
147 4/8	23 2/8	23 2/8	20 0/8	5	5	Dickens County	TX	Jim Eppler	1990	9479

WHITETAIL DEER (TYPICAL ANTLERS)

Minimum Score 125 — Continued

SCORE	LENGTH OF R MAIN BEAM L	INSIDE SPREAD	NUMBER OF R POINTS L	AREA	STATE/PROVINCE	HUNTER'S NAME	DATE	RANK
147 4/8	25 4/8 25 1/8	18 0/8	5 5	Pulaski County	GA	Chris Cornelius	1990	9479
147 4/8	25 4/8 25 4/8	23 6/8	4 4	Wayne County	IA	Connie Pherigo	1990	9479
147 4/8	24 0/8 22 7/8	18 3/8	4 6	Clinton County	OH	Robert L. Sargent	1990	9479
147 4/8	23 6/8 24 4/8	17 4/8	5 5	Henry County	IA	Bruce Barrie	1990	9479
147 4/8	25 2/8 24 7/8	17 2/8	5 5	Lawrence County	IN	Gary L. Brown	1991	9479
147 4/8	25 3/8 25 5/8	17 2/8	5 5	Eau Claire County	WI	Wayne R. Brixen	1991	9479
147 4/8	28 0/8 26 3/8	22 3/8	5 5	Bayfield County	WI	Clifton D. Louis	1991	9479
147 4/8	24 0/8 24 7/8	16 0/8	8 7	Muscatine County	IA	Craig A. Owens	1991	9479
147 4/8	22 7/8 23 1/8	14 6/8	5 6	Dubuque County	IA	Curtis G. Steffen	1991	9479
147 4/8	23 5/8 23 0/8	19 5/8	4 5	Henry County	IA	Troy Ailey	1991	9479
147 4/8	21 2/8 20 3/8	16 0/8	5 5	Cochrane	ALB	Tom Foss	1992	9479
147 4/8	22 7/8 23 4/8	16 0/8	5 5	Rockingham County	NC	Richard B. Dyer	1992	9479
147 4/8	22 2/8 22 2/8	15 4/8	5 7	Chautauqua County	KS	William Wilmeth	1992	9479
147 4/8	21 6/8 21 5/8	20 4/8	6 6	Greene County	IN	Zaldy Advincula	1993	9479
147 4/8	25 6/8 24 3/8	18 5/8	5 6	Woodford County	IL	Joseph C. Jerse	1993	9479
147 4/8	22 7/8 22 5/8	15 6/8	4 4	Wayne County	NY	Scott M. Aman	1993	9479
147 4/8	23 4/8 24 2/8	18 2/8	5 5	Fayette County	IA	Marvin Buckmaster	1993	9479
147 4/8	23 4/8 23 1/8	16 2/8	5 6	Cole County	MO	Anthony Norbert Boessen	1994	9479
147 4/8	23 3/8 25 7/8	17 6/8	5 5	Macoupin County	IL	Brad Bellm	1995	9479
147 4/8	23 5/8 24 2/8	18 4/8	5 5	Kane County	IL	George Moeller, Jr.	1995	9479
147 4/8	23 3/8 22 6/8	23 7/8	5 7	Spink County	SD	Mike Hoesing	1995	9479
147 4/8	23 6/8 23 4/8	16 6/8	5 4	Waukesha County	WI	Peter J. Purdy	1995	9479
147 4/8	24 5/8 24 5/8	19 2/8	4 5	Delaware County	IA	William J. Gadient	1996	9479
147 4/8	24 2/8 22 2/8	17 4/8	5 5	Hopkins County	KY	Darrin Eaton	1997	9479
147 4/8	21 4/8 21 4/8	17 6/8	5 5	St. Croix County	WI	Steve Huppert	1997	9479
147 4/8	23 7/8 22 6/8	18 4/8	5 5	Pike County	IL	Jeffrey R. Van Varick	1997	9479
147 4/8	26 0/8 24 6/8	18 1/8	4 5	Jennings County	IN	Kevin D. Hall	1997	9479
147 4/8	23 0/8 22 1/8	16 4/8	5 5	Humboldt County	IA	Dennis Evans	1997	9479
147 4/8	23 0/8 23 7/8	17 2/8	5 4	Clark County	IL	James S. Coyle	1997	9479
147 4/8	26 5/8 27 2/8	18 3/8	5 5	McLean County	IL	David Grizzle	1997	9479
147 4/8	26 2/8 25 5/8	20 0/8	5 5	La Salle County	TX	George W. Semple	1997	9479
147 4/8	21 4/8 19 7/8	16 0/8	5 5	Marinette County	WI	Randy J. Diederich	1998	9479
147 4/8	25 0/8 24 3/8	19 0/8	5 5	La Salle County	IL	Todd J. Yeager	1998	9479
147 4/8	23 5/8 25 1/8	19 6/8	4 4	Benton County	IA	Rodney Dudley	1998	9479
147 4/8	22 6/8 22 2/8	17 7/8	5 6	Oconto County	WI	Ben Baye	1999	9479
147 4/8	25 3/8 24 2/8	17 4/8	5 5	Prairie River	SAS	Jack Chernysh	1999	9479
147 4/8	22 6/8 22 6/8	17 1/8	6 6	Arenac County	MI	Jason Stange	2000	9479
147 4/8	23 5/8 23 0/8	21 0/8	7 6	Fremont County	IA	Mark Armstrong	2000	9479
147 4/8	24 0/8 23 1/8	21 5/8	6 7	Ramsey County	MN	Nick Maras	2000	9479
147 4/8	24 2/8 24 4/8	17 2/8	5 6	Christian County	KY	Richard W. Scott	2001	9479
147 4/8	25 4/8 25 7/8	20 4/8	5 5	Union County	SD	Derrall Minor	2001	9479
147 4/8	24 2/8 24 3/8	18 2/8	5 5	Decatur County	IA	Steve Snow	2001	9479
147 4/8	24 2/8 24 5/8	17 4/8	6 6	Outagamie County	WI	Gregory A. Beyer	2001	9479
147 4/8	22 3/8 22 5/8	17 4/8	5 6	Lincoln County	WI	Mark Schneider	2001	9479
147 4/8	21 0/8 20 7/8	17 2/8	5 5	Hughes County	SD	Jason Smith	2002	9479
147 4/8	23 0/8 22 3/8	17 4/8	5 5	Barry County	MI	Ben F. Henney	2002	9479
*147 4/8	22 5/8 24 2/8	16 6/8	6 5	Harrison County	IA	Bob Sauvain	2002	9479
147 4/8	28 5/8 27 2/8	15 6/8	5 7	Washington County	MN	Matt Cote	2003	9479
147 4/8	25 4/8 24 6/8	22 0/8	4 5	Northampton County	PA	Scott Lechner	2003	9479
*147 4/8	24 0/8 23 2/8	17 6/8	5 5	Miami County	KS	David Haake	2003	9479
147 4/8	24 2/8 23 1/8	14 2/8	6 5	Forest County	WI	David M. Schwartz	2003	9479
147 4/8	24 3/8 23 2/8	19 0/8	6 5	Crawford County	WI	Lance J. Patrouille	2003	9479
147 4/8	26 4/8 25 5/8	22 4/8	6 7	Barber County	KS	Bruce Swartley	2003	9479
147 4/8	22 6/8 23 4/8	19 5/8	6 5	Peoria County	IL	John Landsverk	2003	9479
147 4/8	22 3/8 21 4/8	18 1/8	6 5	Dunn County	ND	Corey Mueller	2003	9479
147 4/8	24 2/8 23 7/8	18 4/8	5 5	Fond du Lac County	WI	Steve Weber	2004	9479
147 4/8	24 0/8 24 0/8	16 0/8	5 5	Fayette County	OH	Mark Sharp	2004	9479
*147 4/8	22 4/8 22 1/8	15 0/8	5 6	Sanilac County	MI	Don King	2004	9479
*147 4/8	23 3/8 24 0/8	17 7/8	6 6	Wayne County	OH	Bob Arnold	2004	9479
*147 4/8	25 3/8 25 2/8	22 2/8	6 5	Steuben County	NY	Ray Cavallaro	2004	9479
*147 4/8	22 4/8 22 6/8	16 2/8	5 5	Frio County	TX	Craig Dishon	2004	9479
147 4/8	23 3/8 23 1/8	18 4/8	5 5	St. Louis County	MO	Phil Ruffino	2005	9479
*147 4/8	23 5/8 22 7/8	15 6/8	5 5	Vernon County	WI	Jose L. Garcia	2005	9479
147 4/8	22 3/8 23 4/8	16 4/8	6 6	Cabell County	WV	James Dillon	2005	9479
147 4/8	22 3/8 22 2/8	16 6/8	5 5	DeKalb County	IL	Mark Swanson	2005	9479
*147 4/8	25 1/8 25 5/8	18 0/8	6 5	Tuscaloosa County	AL	Jeff Gregory	2005	9479
*147 4/8	25 0/8 25 1/8	17 4/8	4 4	Wayne County	IL	Harlan D. Pierce	2006	9479
147 4/8	24 4/8 25 5/8	17 0/8	5 4	Oconto County	WI	Dale Fabry	2006	9479
147 4/8	24 0/8 23 4/8	18 6/8	6 5	Fayette County	IA	Ryan Vsetecka	2006	9479
147 4/8	25 7/8 25 3/8	20 0/8	4 5	McDonough County	IL	Chad Helman	2006	9479
147 4/8	21 5/8 22 4/8	16 4/8	5 6	Trempealeau County	WI	Matt Andersen	2007	9479
147 4/8	23 3/8 23 5/8	15 6/8	5 5	Linn County	KS	Jason Yosick	2007	9479
147 4/8	23 4/8 23 4/8	18 6/8	5 5	Pulaski County	IN	Roger Dean Toczek	2007	9479
147 4/8	24 3/8 22 6/8	15 6/8	8 6	Johnson County	KS	Chris Jennerwein	2007	9479
147 4/8	20 5/8 21 0/8	16 0/8	5 5	Madison County	AR	Preston Harriman	2008	9479
147 4/8	22 1/8 22 2/8	18 3/8	5 6	Trempealeau County	WI	Matt M. Ihrig	2008	9479
147 4/8	22 5/8 23 2/8	15 5/8	5 7	Jefferson County	IA	John L. Wozniak	2008	9479
*147 4/8	24 0/8 23 3/8	20 0/8	5 5	Buffalo County	WI	Pat Resch	2008	9479
*147 4/8	29 2/8 30 0/8	19 5/8	10 7	Morgan County	IL	Charles W. Griffin	2008	9479
147 4/8	22 0/8 22 0/8	18 4/8	6 5	Sauk County	WI	Kraig Heinzman	2009	9479
147 3/8	22 4/8 22 4/8	17 7/8	5 6	Waushara County	WI	Mike Barth	1977	9581
147 3/8	21 5/8 21 5/8	16 3/8	6 5	Lee County	IA	Mark Clemens	1978	9581
147 3/8	25 7/8 26 0/8	18 1/8	5 4	Franklin County	VA	Mike Weaver	1978	9581
147 3/8	28 1/8 28 1/8	19 7/8	5 4	Huntingdon County	PA	John A. Williams	1979	9581
147 3/8	22 5/8 23 7/8	18 3/8	5 5	Guthrie County	IA	Steve Hunerdosse	1982	9581
147 3/8	22 0/8 22 3/8	12 7/8	7 5	Jackson County	MO	Marvin Thomey	1984	9581
147 3/8	21 1/8 20 7/8	15 7/8	6 6	Troup County	GA	Eddie D. Martin	1984	9581
147 3/8	22 4/8 24 2/8	16 5/8	6 5	Union County	IL	Ronald L. Kosydor	1985	9581
147 3/8	22 6/8 23 0/8	18 3/8	5 5	Lee County	IA	Glenn E. Wagner	1985	9581
147 3/8	23 3/8 23 2/8	15 7/8	6 5	Buffalo County	WI	Bill R. Berg	1986	9581
147 3/8	25 6/8 25 1/8	19 5/8	5 4	McHenry County	IL	William R. Bishop, Jr.	1988	9581
147 3/8	23 1/8 22 3/8	19 5/8	5 5	Vermilion County	IL	Dr H. Neil Becker	1988	9581
147 3/8	23 5/8 25 3/8	19 1/8	4 4	Ellsworth County	KS	Rick Kirkpatrick	1989	9581
147 3/8	27 0/8 25 7/8	19 1/8	4 4	Shelby County	IL	Terry Jo Anderson	1989	9581
147 3/8	23 3/8 24 0/8	17 7/8	6 5	Warren County	IL	Bryan E. DeJaynes	1989	9581

456

WHITETAIL DEER (TYPICAL ANTLERS)

Minimum Score 125   Continued

SCORE	LENGTH OF R MAIN BEAM L	INSIDE SPREAD	NUMBER OF R POINTS L	AREA	STATE/ PROVINCE	HUNTER'S NAME	DATE	RANK
147 3/8	23 7/8 22 6/8	18 0/8	5 6	Sussex County	VA	Frank Patterson	1989	9581
147 3/8	22 7/8 21 4/8	16 3/8	5 5	Marathon County	WI	Mark J. Duerr	1989	9581
147 3/8	23 0/8 22 4/8	18 2/8	7 5	Davis County	IA	Robert L. McDowell	1990	9581
147 3/8	22 4/8 22 3/8	19 1/8	4 4	Webb County	TX	Alvin Levy	1991	9581
147 3/8	24 0/8 24 5/8	19 3/8	5 5	Westmoreland County	PA	David Bish	1992	9581
147 3/8	22 6/8 22 3/8	20 0/8	5 6	Price County	WI	Stanley P. Mindock	1992	9581
147 3/8	21 0/8 21 2/8	17 3/8	6 5	Vermilion County	IL	Robert Dave Mitchell	1992	9581
147 3/8	23 7/8 23 5/8	18 3/8	5 5	Reno County	KS	Doug Chapman	1992	9581
147 3/8	22 1/8 23 0/8	18 1/8	5 5	Sullivan County	IN	Joe Rehmel	1993	9581
147 3/8	24 5/8 25 0/8	19 5/8	5 4	Lee County	IL	Craig B. Walter	1993	9581
147 3/8	21 3/8 21 4/8	17 1/8	6 5	Kerr County	TX	Chuck Adams	1993	9581
147 3/8	25 4/8 26 4/8	18 2/8	5 5	Hillsdale County	MI	Matthew C. Sommers	1994	9581
147 3/8	25 6/8 26 1/8	20 1/8	5 5	Cuyahoga County	OH	Mark Johnson	1994	9581
147 3/8	22 6/8 22 4/8	17 5/8	6 6	Walworth County	WI	Bradley Wilson	1994	9581
147 3/8	22 1/8 22 5/8	15 1/8	5 6	Woodbury County	IA	Mark R. Huntley	1994	9581
147 3/8	21 2/8 21 4/8	17 5/8	6 5	Pottawatomie County	KS	James E. Kelty	1995	9581
147 3/8	23 2/8 23 1/8	17 3/8	5 5	Brown County	OH	Troy Conley	1995	9581
147 3/8	24 1/8 24 4/8	17 3/8	6 7	Rock County	WI	Dennis Krueger	1995	9581
147 3/8	26 1/8 27 7/8	14 5/8	4 4	Douglas County	KS	Denzil L. Hackathorn	1996	9581
147 3/8	24 0/8 21 2/8	19 7/8	5 5	Blackford County	IN	Mark Garrison	1996	9581
147 3/8	22 7/8 22 3/8	14 7/8	5 5	Dane County	WI	Tom Pasold	1996	9581
147 3/8	24 4/8 24 6/8	17 2/8	8 6	Grundy County	IL	Brian L. Crawford	1996	9581
147 3/8	25 7/8 25 7/8	20 7/8	4 4	McHenry County	IL	Jody Kellnhofer	1996	9581
147 3/8	23 1/8 23 2/8	19 1/8	5 5	Taylor County	WI	Brian Knusta	1998	9581
147 3/8	25 0/8 25 1/8	17 0/8	5 7	Hillsdale County	MI	Mike Sarns	1998	9581
147 3/8	24 5/8 23 1/8	19 1/8	4 4	Calhoun County	IL	Steve McCluskey	1998	9581
147 3/8	24 0/8 24 1/8	20 2/8	6 6	Washington County	WI	Timothy L. Bauer	1998	9581
147 3/8	22 4/8 21 4/8	18 2/8	5 5	Woodbury County	IA	Stuart J. Nitzschke	1998	9581
147 3/8	23 7/8 23 6/8	19 5/8	4 5	Columbia County	WI	Matt Winn	1998	9581
147 3/8	25 1/8 23 7/8	15 2/8	6 6	Shawano County	WI	Mark Yuenger	1999	9581
147 3/8	24 1/8 23 4/8	18 1/8	5 6	Olmsted County	MN	Robert Smigelski	1999	9581
147 3/8	22 4/8 23 0/8	16 7/8	5 5	Jo Daviess County	IL	John Westaby	1999	9581
147 3/8	23 7/8 23 3/8	17 1/8	5 6	La Crosse County	WI	Brad Bond	1999	9581
147 3/8	21 4/8 21 2/8	18 0/8	6 5	Peoria County	IL	Roger A. Albertson	1999	9581
147 3/8	23 2/8 23 4/8	14 3/8	5 5	Johnson County	IA	Scott Fuhrmeister	1999	9581
147 3/8	25 0/8 26 2/8	18 5/8	5 6	Johnson County	KS	Tom Acree	2000	9581
147 3/8	25 2/8 25 4/8	17 3/8	5 5	Meigs County	OH	Tim L. Smith	2000	9581
147 3/8	25 0/8 24 2/8	16 7/8	5 5	Wayne County	IN	Stephen Smitley	2000	9581
147 3/8	24 4/8 25 6/8	18 7/8	6 5	Pike County	IL	Matthew Laney	2001	9581
147 3/8	23 4/8 23 1/8	20 3/8	4 4	Jay County	IN	Tom Michael, Jr.	2001	9581
147 3/8	23 3/8 23 3/8	16 6/8	6 6	Sauk County	WI	Dave Zimmerman	2001	9581
147 3/8	21 2/8 22 1/8	16 3/8	5 5	Hamilton County	IA	Keith Brock	2001	9581
147 3/8	23 7/8 23 0/8	21 7/8	5 6	Kleberg County	TX	Eddie Hammond	2002	9581
147 3/8	23 6/8 22 5/8	18 5/8	5 5	Marquette County	WI	J. Scott McIlvoy	2002	9581
147 3/8	24 5/8 25 2/8	17 7/8	5 6	Waukesha County	WI	Jim Stewart	2002	9581
147 3/8	25 7/8 25 6/8	18 1/8	4 4	Riley County	KS	John Duggan	2002	9581
147 3/8	22 6/8 23 3/8	17 4/8	4 5	Winneshiek County	IA	Tim J. Quandahl	2002	9581
147 3/8	23 4/8 23 0/8	15 6/8	7 5	Decatur County	IA	Glenn M. Brauer	2002	9581
147 3/8	24 2/8 23 5/8	18 0/8	6 5	Licking County	OH	Paul White	2002	9581
147 3/8	23 6/8 24 0/8	17 1/8	5 4	E. Carroll Parish	LA	Rodney Crimm	2002	9581
147 3/8	23 0/8 23 2/8	20 4/8	6 5	Door County	WI	Eric Carper	2003	9581
147 3/8	27 3/8 26 1/8	18 6/8	5 7	Cedar County	MO	Brian L. Sumner	2003	9581
*147 3/8	25 6/8 25 5/8	18 2/8	4 5	Erie County	NY	Jack Reekie	2004	9581
147 3/8	23 0/8 22 4/8	15 3/8	5 5	Brown County	IL	Eric D. Ehinger	2004	9581
147 3/8	24 0/8 24 1/8	17 1/8	5 5	Polk County	WI	Jesse M. Ashton	2004	9581
147 3/8	25 1/8 27 0/8	18 1/8	5 6	Houston County	MN	Isaac Alexander	2004	9581
147 3/8	23 4/8 23 4/8	20 3/8	4 4	Stephenson County	IL	Dana Wybourn	2004	9581
147 3/8	23 4/8 24 4/8	17 3/8	4 5	Somerset County	NJ	Harry Nevin Kline	2005	9581
147 3/8	25 0/8 24 6/8	21 7/8	4 5	Will County	IL	Tom Mooi	2005	9581
147 3/8	22 5/8 22 1/8	21 4/8	5 8	Buffalo County	WI	Dean Anderson	2005	9581
147 3/8	24 4/8 24 3/8	22 7/8	5 5	Tompkins County	NY	Jesse W. Miller	2005	9581
147 3/8	22 2/8 22 5/8	16 1/8	5 6	Woodbury County	IA	James K. Webster	2005	9581
147 3/8	24 1/8 23 0/8	17 5/8	6 6	Adams County	WI	Tom Merriam	2005	9581
147 3/8	24 5/8 24 1/8	19 2/8	6 5	Butler County	KS	Anthony Pata	2005	9581
*147 3/8	25 0/8 22 5/8	19 3/8	7 5	Edgar County	IL	Joe Douglas	2005	9581
147 3/8	24 5/8 24 1/8	19 4/8	5 6	Buffalo County	WI	Glen Axness	2006	9581
*147 3/8	24 3/8 23 5/8	17 5/8	4 5	Fond du Lac County	WI	Dan Beattie	2006	9581
147 3/8	25 3/8 25 1/8	19 5/8	4 4	Putnam County	IN	Jeff Elkins	2006	9581
147 3/8	24 3/8 23 2/8	19 7/8	4 4	Douglas County	KS	Ron Shanks	2006	9581
147 3/8	22 0/8 22 1/8	14 3/8	5 5	Pottawattamie County	IA	Loren Short	2006	9581
*147 3/8	23 2/8 22 0/8	16 3/8	6 6	Carroll County	MS	Michael S. McCrory	2006	9581
*147 3/8	24 5/8 24 3/8	19 1/8	4 5	Iowa County	WI	Jason Carden	2007	9581
*147 3/8	24 7/8 24 6/8	18 1/8	6 5	Bayfield County	WI	Shawn Johnson	2007	9581
147 3/8	23 3/8 24 1/8	22 1/8	4 4	Vermilion County	IL	Jeff Toms	2007	9581
147 3/8	21 5/8 21 2/8	16 5/8	5 6	Door County	WI	Eric Carper	2007	9581
147 3/8	24 4/8 24 1/8	16 4/8	5 5	Seward County	NE	Jim Krieser	2008	9581
147 3/8	23 0/8 24 1/8	16 1/8	5 4	Chautauqua County	NY	Rodney Smink	2008	9581
147 3/8	26 3/8 24 4/8	17 7/8	4 4	Brookings County	SD	Christopher L. Engbrecht	2008	9581
147 3/8	21 6/8 20 5/8	18 0/8	6 6	Jackson County	WI	Jeffrey J. Wittkopp	2008	9581
*147 3/8	25 3/8 25 1/8	20 3/8	4 4	Walworth County	WI	Christopher Klein	2009	9581
147 3/8	24 4/8 24 4/8	20 4/8	5 6	Butler County	OH	John P. Carroll	2009	9581
147 3/8	26 4/8 28 0/8	22 6/8	5 6	Phillips County	CO	Shawn Greathouse	2009	9581
147 2/8	23 2/8 25 1/8	20 4/8	9 8	Clay County	IA	Uriah M. Hostetler	1964	9678
147 2/8	23 2/8 22 4/8	19 2/8	5 5	Madison County	IN	Pat Moreland	1969	9678
147 2/8	23 1/8 23 1/8	15 6/8	5 5	Green Lake County	WI	Don Chier	1973	9678
147 2/8	25 2/8 25 2/8	20 6/8	5 5	Fayette County	IA	Terry Cannady	1976	9678
147 2/8	21 3/8 20 6/8	17 4/8	5 5	Iroquois County	IL	Scott L. Mohler	1979	9678
147 2/8	25 7/8 24 3/8	25 4/8	4 4	Parke County	IN	Alan W. Brannan	1980	9678
147 2/8	24 6/8 22 7/8	18 4/8	5 6	Waushara County	WI	Tim J. Terrell	1980	9678
147 2/8	23 2/8 22 6/8	19 2/8	5 7	Pembina County	ND	Roger Furstenau	1983	9678
147 2/8	24 7/8 25 0/8	18 7/8	7 8	Clay County	MN	John Randash	1984	9678
147 2/8	21 5/8 21 6/8	18 2/8	6 5	Grant County	MN	Harold Forcier	1984	9678
147 2/8	24 5/8 24 3/8	18 2/8	6 5	Jackson County	OH	Keith Kuhn	1984	9678
147 2/8	25 1/8 25 6/8	23 2/8	4 4	Gage County	NE	Jerry Miller	1987	9678
147 2/8	20 2/8 21 5/8	20 6/8	5 5	Somerset County	NJ	Harold J. Tallett	1987	9678

457

WHITETAIL DEER (TYPICAL ANTLERS)

Minimum Score 125 Continued

SCORE	LENGTH OF R MAIN BEAM L	INSIDE SPREAD	NUMBER OF R POINTS L	AREA	STATE/ PROVINCE	HUNTER'S NAME	DATE	RANK
147 2/8	25 0/8 23 0/8	14 4/8	7 6	Blue Earth County	MN	Bruce Kramer	1987	9678
147 2/8	21 6/8 20 0/8	17 4/8	6 6	Pottawattamie County	IA	Randall L. Foote	1987	9678
147 2/8	24 0/8 22 6/8	20 6/8	5 5	Monroe County	GA	Patrick Carter	1988	9678
147 2/8	23 1/8 24 6/8	19 7/8	7 7	Vermilion County	IL	Robert G. Downing	1988	9678
147 2/8	24 4/8 22 1/8	21 2/8	6 7	Meigs County	OH	Patrick D. Kearns	1988	9678
147 2/8	25 0/8 25 5/8	23 6/8	4 5	Cook County	IL	Charles Gaidamavice	1989	9678
147 2/8	23 0/8 22 6/8	16 0/8	6 5	Morgan County	CO	Dean Procunier	1990	9678
147 2/8	22 5/8 23 4/8	17 7/8	5 6	Allamakee County	IA	Mark D. Christopherson	1991	9678
147 2/8	29 1/8 28 5/8	22 0/8	4 4	Lawrence County	OH	Randy Boggs	1991	9678
147 2/8	25 1/8 24 1/8	18 6/8	4 5	Flathead County	MT	John C. Bartlett	1992	9678
147 2/8	22 2/8 22 0/8	17 4/8	5 5	Lincoln County	MO	Larry Crouch	1992	9678
147 2/8	23 3/8 21 1/8	21 0/8	5 5	Rock County	WI	Monica A. Freeman	1992	9678
147 2/8	22 7/8 22 7/8	16 6/8	5 5	Cold Lake	ALB	Martin Belisle	1992	9678
147 2/8	24 0/8 23 7/8	17 6/8	4 5	Eau Claire County	WI	Mike Payne	1992	9678
147 2/8	21 5/8 21 5/8	18 6/8	5 5	Fergus County	MT	Mike Sweeney	1992	9678
147 2/8	25 3/8 26 1/8	19 4/8	5 4	Daviess County	IN	Mark Moeller	1993	9678
147 2/8	22 4/8 21 1/8	16 6/8	5 5	Washington County	OH	Ryan Fullenkamp	1994	9678
147 2/8	25 4/8 24 5/8	16 6/8	5 5	Lake County	IL	David Shumway	1994	9678
147 2/8	25 1/8 25 2/8	19 0/8	5 4	Lyon County	KS	Aaron Lazzers	1994	9678
147 2/8	22 6/8 23 6/8	20 6/8	4 6	Lincoln County	SD	Collin C. Benson	1994	9678
147 2/8	25 1/8 24 6/8	17 6/8	5 4	Lawrence County	MO	Jason Graff	1994	9678
147 2/8	24 6/8 24 7/8	21 4/8	5 4	Davis County	IA	Gary Biles	1995	9678
147 2/8	22 0/8 22 3/8	17 4/8	5 5	Dane County	WI	Darren Culles	1995	9678
147 2/8	24 7/8 24 4/8	18 7/8	6 6	Brown County	IL	David Crooks	1995	9678
147 2/8	23 5/8 24 0/8	18 0/8	5 5	Clay County	KS	Dan Ayers	1995	9678
147 2/8	23 6/8 22 6/8	18 3/8	11 8	Dakota County	MN	John J. Boland	1995	9678
147 2/8	21 3/8 20 7/8	16 4/8	5 5	Trempealeau County	WI	John P. Simerson	1996	9678
147 2/8	22 6/8 22 4/8	16 3/8	6 5	Kingsbury County	SD	Jerry Ellingson	1996	9678
147 2/8	22 4/8 22 2/8	16 2/8	6 5	Richardson County	NE	Ted Younker	1996	9678
147 2/8	23 1/8 23 3/8	16 6/8	6 6	Todd County	KY	David D. Haley	1997	9678
147 2/8	22 1/8 22 2/8	19 2/8	6 4	Hardin County	KY	Ricky J. Rankin	1997	9678
147 2/8	20 5/8 21 7/8	18 0/8	6 6	Livingston County	MI	Joseph Metivier	1997	9678
147 2/8	24 5/8 24 6/8	18 6/8	5 6	Grant County	WI	Greg Matthews	1997	9678
147 2/8	26 2/8 24 2/8	16 4/8	5 5	Waukesha County	WI	Louis Kimball	1997	9678
147 2/8	23 2/8 22 2/8	18 6/8	5 5	Henry County	VA	Mike Weaver	1997	9678
147 2/8	23 4/8 23 4/8	17 0/8	6 5	Lincoln County	WI	Joel Wendt	1998	9678
147 2/8	23 0/8 22 7/8	16 0/8	5 5	Clermont County	OH	Robert Lemme	1998	9678
147 2/8	22 7/8 23 2/8	18 2/8	6 5	Carroll County	MO	Mike Stice	1998	9678
147 2/8	21 7/8 23 4/8	16 0/8	5 5	Green Lake County	WI	Burton R. Werch, Jr.	1998	9678
147 2/8	23 2/8 23 5/8	18 4/8	6 5	Marshall County	OK	Jay Don Reed	1998	9678
147 2/8	21 6/8 23 3/8	17 2/8	6 5	Livingston County	MI	Robert B. Vines	1998	9678
147 2/8	27 2/8 26 6/8	17 6/8	8 6	Marion County	KS	Bradley S. Tobias	1998	9678
147 2/8	24 3/8 24 0/8	18 0/8	4 5	Washington County	MN	Tom Makelke	1999	9678
147 2/8	25 1/8 23 6/8	20 2/8	5 5	Hamilton County	IN	Douglas D. Bowen	1999	9678
147 2/8	23 2/8 23 2/8	19 6/8	6 6	Sullivan County	IN	Tim L. Sherman	1999	9678
147 2/8	23 6/8 23 4/8	17 4/8	5 6	Chickasaw County	IA	Chad Seidel	1999	9678
147 2/8	23 4/8 23 4/8	18 7/8	5 4	Fairfax County	VA	Chris Rowlands	1999	9678
147 2/8	21 5/8 21 2/8	18 2/8	6 6	Refugio County	TX	Robert R. White	1999	9678
147 2/8	24 2/8 24 1/8	17 1/8	6 5	Gasconade County	MO	Donnie Jacquin	2000	9678
147 2/8	23 3/8 25 1/8	18 0/8	6 6	Brown County	IL	Nick Stranierо	2000	9678
147 2/8	22 3/8 22 5/8	16 2/8	5 5	Brown County	WI	Dale Metoxen	2001	9678
147 2/8	25 5/8 24 6/8	17 2/8	7 5	Washington County	OH	Steve Walker	2001	9678
147 2/8	24 7/8 24 6/8	17 0/8	5 4	Brown County	IL	Lee Hein	2001	9678
147 2/8	24 4/8 24 5/8	16 4/8	5 5	Henry County	IL	James T. Galloway	2002	9678
147 2/8	22 3/8 22 5/8	18 4/8	6 5	Clark County	WI	James R. Gilbertson	2002	9678
147 2/8	22 4/8 20 4/8	20 4/8	5 7	Porter County	IN	Mike Basich	2003	9678
147 2/8	23 0/8 23 5/8	15 0/8	5 6	Clay County	KY	Charles "Cheese" Burns	2003	9678
147 2/8	22 4/8 23 4/8	16 4/8	6 6	Pierce County	WI	Ben Huppert	2003	9678
147 2/8	24 6/8 23 3/8	17 3/8	5 6	Logan County	IL	Clarence R. Bree	2003	9678
147 2/8	24 1/8 23 1/8	17 0/8	5 4	Will County	IL	John Kamarauskas	2003	9678
147 2/8	23 5/8 23 0/8	18 6/8	5 5	Jackson County	KS	Don Schuyler	2003	9678
147 2/8	21 4/8 22 6/8	19 6/8	6 5	Macon County	IL	David Elliott	2004	9678
147 2/8	21 0/8 22 2/8	15 6/8	5 5	Clay County	SD	Leo Powell	2004	9678
147 2/8	20 6/8 21 0/8	15 6/8	5 5	Jackson County	WI	Ty Bowman	2004	9678
147 2/8	24 5/8 25 1/8	20 0/8	4 4	Buffalo County	NE	Rich Walters	2004	9678
147 2/8	27 0/8 26 4/8	19 7/8	6 5	McLean County	IL	James Bartels	2004	9678
*147 2/8	22 0/8 21 6/8	17 6/8	5 5	Dodge County	WI	Todd Schellpfeffer	2004	9678
147 2/8	23 7/8 24 1/8	19 7/8	6 5	Guernsey County	OH	Alan P. Mann	2004	9678
147 2/8	22 4/8 22 4/8	19 0/8	5 5	Cass County	MN	Gary Ysteboe	2004	9678
147 2/8	21 5/8 22 4/8	17 4/8	5 5	Floyd County	IA	Ryan Kayle	2005	9678
*147 2/8	25 5/8 25 5/8	15 6/8	5 5	De Kalb County	GA	Johnny Johnson	2005	9678
147 2/8	26 0/8 21 4/8	18 6/8	5 5	Onondaga County	NY	Tom Costello	2005	9678
*147 2/8	22 3/8 21 7/8	15 2/8	6 7	Pike County	IL	Ken Cascarella	2005	9678
147 2/8	23 3/8 23 4/8	16 4/8	4 4	Clark County	IL	Lonnie S. Yobst	2005	9678
*147 2/8	23 7/8 22 4/8	15 6/8	5 5	Montgomery County	OH	Brian LaPointe	2005	9678
147 2/8	22 4/8 23 2/8	23 2/8	5 5	St. Joseph County	IN	Jeff E. Besinger	2006	9678
147 2/8	23 0/8 22 6/8	17 6/8	5 5	Buffalo County	WI	Tyler Heil	2006	9678
*147 2/8	25 7/8 25 0/8	19 6/8	6 6	Washington County	NY	Andrew L. Marchaland	2006	9678
147 2/8	24 5/8 25 5/8	18 2/8	5 5	Bradford County	PA	Frank Chrzan	2006	9678
147 2/8	24 6/8 24 2/8	20 4/8	5 4	Dane County	WI	Jeffrey Zanow	2006	9678
147 2/8	21 4/8 21 1/8	16 6/8	6 6	McLean County	ND	Preston Bauer	2007	9678
*147 2/8	22 7/8 23 0/8	16 4/8	5 5	Steele County	ND	Nick Fugleberg	2007	9678
147 2/8	24 0/8 25 2/8	22 2/8	4 4	Jackson County	WI	Dillon Gearing	2007	9678
147 2/8	22 4/8 23 0/8	18 6/8	5 5	Green Lake County	WI	Charles Coon	2007	9678
*147 2/8	26 2/8 27 3/8	20 0/8	5 5	Scott County	IA	Robert Lytle	2007	9678
147 2/8	23 4/8 23 2/8	18 2/8	4 4	Dane County	WI	Jesse A. Blum	2007	9678
147 2/8	23 0/8 21 1/8	19 0/8	4 5	Prowers County	CO	Newell Easley	2007	9678
147 2/8	21 0/8 21 6/8	15 0/8	5 5	Hamilton County	KS	Dennis Carnine	2008	9678
147 2/8	21 5/8 21 7/8	16 1/8	6 7	St. Marys County	MD	Pete Ropshaw	2008	9678
*147 2/8	22 6/8 22 0/8	17 0/8	5 5	Athens County	OH	Michael Hunt	2008	9678
147 2/8	22 0/8 22 0/8	16 6/8	5 5	Shawano County	WI	John A. Lohrentz	2009	9678
147 2/8	22 4/8 23 0/8	19 6/8	5 5	Buffalo County	WI	Steven Blackton	2009	9678
*147 2/8	24 6/8 26 7/8	20 4/8	4 5	Middlesex County	MA	Brian Fillebrown	2009	9678
147 2/8	25 5/8 25 0/8	17 4/8	5 4	Clark County	OH	Scott Clark	2009	9678
*147 2/8	24 0/8 24 2/8	16 2/8	5 6	Wilson County	KS	Mac McPherson	2009	9678

458

WHITETAIL DEER (TYPICAL ANTLERS)

Minimum Score 125   Continued

SCORE	LENGTH OF R MAIN BEAM L	INSIDE SPREAD	NUMBER OF R POINTS L	AREA	STATE/ PROVINCE	HUNTER'S NAME	DATE	RANK
147 2/8	22 6/8	23 6/8	17 3/8	6	5	Peoria County	IL	Chris Noonen	2009	9678
*147 2/8	23 0/8	23 1/8	18 6/8	5	5	Decatur County	IA	Gene Olsen	2009	9678
*147 2/8	25 3/8	25 7/8	20 0/8	5	5	Green Lake County	WI	Luke Ladwig	2010	9678
147 2/8	26 6/8	26 0/8	19 0/8	5	6	Lincoln County	WI	Jack Greil	2010	9678
*147 2/8	25 0/8	25 2/8	21 0/8	9	6	Trempealeau County	WI	Travis Eckman	2010	9678
147 1/8	25 1/8	25 3/8	16 7/8	5	5	Delaware County	IA	Blair Berens	1963	9791
147 1/8	22 6/8	23 1/8	17 5/8	5	6	Iron County	WI	Dr. C. J. Rainaldo	1967	9791
147 1/8	24 7/8	24 4/8	18 4/8	7	7	Red Willow County	NE	Gary Ginther	1967	9791
147 1/8	21 0/8	21 5/8	16 3/8	6	6	Vilas County	WI	Anthony J. Sahulcik, Jr.	1969	9791
147 1/8	25 0/8	24 0/8	18 3/8	4	4	Dodge County	MN	Clark Gallup	1974	9791
147 1/8	24 3/8	25 7/8	18 5/8	4	4	Coffey County	KS	Joyce Wilhite	1974	9791
147 1/8	20 5/8	20 0/8	19 5/8	5	5	Redwood County	MN	Dennis Groebner	1975	9791
147 1/8	25 2/8	24 3/8	18 1/8	5	5	Hancock County	OH	Robert E. Ebert	1981	9791
147 1/8	22 1/8	22 1/8	19 3/8	5	5	Kiowa County	KS	Ralph A. Brown	1981	9791
147 1/8	23 2/8	23 6/8	18 1/8	5	5	Teton County	MT	James R. Toms	1984	9791
147 1/8	27 5/8	27 5/8	21 1/8	4	5	Highland County	OH	Larry K. Snoddy	1984	9791
147 1/8	24 2/8	25 4/8	15 7/8	4	5	Wallace County	KS	Gerry Nix	1985	9791
147 1/8	24 5/8	24 5/8	18 2/8	7	5	Burleigh County	ND	Chuck Welch	1986	9791
147 1/8	24 1/8	24 5/8	15 3/8	6	5	Highland County	OH	Roger Dale Burton	1987	9791
147 1/8	22 4/8	22 7/8	17 3/8	5	5	Vigo County	IN	Bob Miller	1987	9791
147 1/8	23 6/8	23 5/8	19 6/8	6	8	Carroll County	IL	Edward Pannell	1987	9791
147 1/8	24 2/8	23 1/8	17 0/8	5	4	Butler County	KS	Mike Schwelgert	1987	9791
147 1/8	23 1/8	22 4/8	18 6/8	5	6	Phillips County	KS	Phillip Cromwell	1987	9791
147 1/8	22 6/8	23 1/8	19 1/8	4	4	Hardin County	KY	Steve Crabtree	1987	9791
147 1/8	23 3/8	24 0/8	19 5/8	5	4	Lake County	IL	Robert A. Turner	1989	9791
147 1/8	21 1/8	22 0/8	17 5/8	5	5	Codington County	SD	Bryan Monteith	1989	9791
147 1/8	25 4/8	23 6/8	17 4/8	6	5	Worcester County	MA	Terry D. Atwater	1990	9791
147 1/8	25 1/8	23 3/8	18 4/8	7	5	Goodhue County	MN	Scott Johnson	1990	9791
147 1/8	24 4/8	24 0/8	18 1/8	5	5	Marinette County	WI	Robert J. Randerson	1990	9791
147 1/8	22 2/8	22 0/8	17 1/8	5	5	Union County	PA	Matthew McGinnis	1991	9791
147 1/8	24 1/8	25 3/8	23 3/8	5	5	Missoula County	MT	Matthew J. Stout	1992	9791
147 1/8	23 4/8	23 5/8	18 3/8	4	4	Tompkins County	NY	Don Zifchock	1992	9791
147 1/8	26 7/8	26 1/8	18 3/8	5	4	Rush County	IN	Brock Cross	1993	9791
147 1/8	22 3/8	21 4/8	16 1/8	6	6	Daviess County	KY	George Stuart	1993	9791
147 1/8	22 6/8	24 0/8	16 5/8	5	5	Vernon County	MO	Larry D. Bogart	1993	9791
147 1/8	23 5/8	23 1/8	21 1/8	4	5	Sheboygan County	WI	Jim Ziegler, Jr.	1993	9791
147 1/8	23 7/8	23 3/8	19 1/8	5	5	Trempealeau County	WI	Jim Jessessky	1994	9791
147 1/8	22 7/8	22 2/8	17 1/8	5	5	Washtenaw County	MI	Gary Young	1994	9791
147 1/8	25 3/8	23 7/8	18 3/8	4	5	Iowa County	IA	Kevin Kuester	1994	9791
147 1/8	24 0/8	23 3/8	20 1/8	4	6	Rolette County	ND	Doug Stewart	1994	9791
147 1/8	25 2/8	25 6/8	22 1/8	4	5	St. Charles County	MO	Mark J. Shea	1995	9791
147 1/8	26 4/8	26 4/8	18 7/8	7	4	Brown County	IL	Ronald Hanna	1995	9791
147 1/8	23 0/8	21 7/8	17 3/8	6	5	Du Page County	IL	Larry L. Border	1995	9791
147 1/8	22 2/8	22 2/8	18 5/8	4	4	Marion County	IL	Russell Leboff	1995	9791
147 1/8	23 3/8	22 5/8	16 0/8	5	5	Page County	VA	Mark W. Richards, Sr.	1996	9791
147 1/8	26 1/8	25 6/8	20 6/8	6	6	Dane County	WI	Phillip E. Oinonen	1996	9791
147 1/8	22 7/8	23 0/8	16 7/8	4	4	Edgar County	IL	Frank C. Vail III	1996	9791
147 1/8	22 2/8	22 2/8	18 7/8	5	5	Des Moines County	IA	Michael Graham	1996	9791
147 1/8	21 2/8	21 6/8	16 6/8	5	6	Jackson County	AL	Eddie Bolt	1997	9791
147 1/8	26 5/8	27 7/8	18 7/8	4	5	Menard County	IL	Brent Davis	1997	9791
147 1/8	23 1/8	22 6/8	16 7/8	7	7	Eau Claire County	WI	Jim Simon	1997	9791
147 1/8	25 3/8	25 3/8	17 7/8	4	4	Columbia County	WI	Richard A. Schreiber	1997	9791
147 1/8	24 0/8	23 7/8	18 2/8	6	5	Dallas County	IA	Chris Brown	1997	9791
147 1/8	24 3/8	24 6/8	19 5/8	5	6	Jefferson County	KY	Chad Berger	1997	9791
147 1/8	21 5/8	22 1/8	18 6/8	7	8	Wilson County	KS	Warren C. Townsend	1997	9791
147 1/8	23 4/8	23 6/8	15 7/8	7	7	Sawyer County	WI	Fran E. Eilbes	1998	9791
147 1/8	25 5/8	24 4/8	18 3/8	5	7	Grundy County	IL	David Both	1998	9791
147 1/8	25 4/8	23 5/8	16 5/8	5	5	Vernon County	MO	Lawrence Mark Guthrie	1998	9791
147 1/8	25 4/8	25 2/8	18 1/8	4	4	Cedar County	IA	Jerry Simon	1998	9791
147 1/8	20 3/8	20 6/8	13 7/8	5	5	Harford County	MD	David Scott Slaton	1998	9791
147 1/8	24 4/8	24 3/8	21 3/8	6	5	St. Joseph County	IN	Gregory S. Saenz	1998	9791
147 1/8	24 2/8	24 2/8	16 7/8	5	5	Dakota County	MN	Marlene Odahlen-Hinz	1998	9791
147 1/8	23 4/8	23 7/8	16 5/8	6	5	Edgar County	IL	Brad Davis	1999	9791
147 1/8	24 1/8	23 0/8	18 1/8	5	5	Waupaca County	WI	Jeffery J. Stepanski	1999	9791
147 1/8	23 4/8	24 5/8	15 3/8	5	4	Nance County	NE	Scott Frenzen	1999	9791
147 1/8	24 1/8	23 6/8	19 1/8	6	5	Sheboygan County	WI	Todd Schaetz	1999	9791
147 1/8	22 6/8	22 6/8	17 4/8	5	5	Saline County	KS	Philip D. Baltazor	1999	9791
147 1/8	26 2/8	25 5/8	20 2/8	4	5	Green Lake County	WI	Rodney Sommer	2000	9791
147 1/8	24 2/8	24 7/8	19 7/8	5	5	Pike County	IL	Tim Spencer	2000	9791
147 1/8	22 5/8	22 0/8	17 1/8	5	5	Sawyer County	WI	Ed Schimke	2000	9791
147 1/8	21 1/8	21 2/8	16 5/8	5	6	Marquette County	WI	Tim Landolt	2000	9791
147 1/8	24 6/8	24 7/8	21 3/8	4	4	Guernsey County	OH	Billy A. Archer	2000	9791
147 1/8	24 4/8	22 6/8	17 3/8	5	5	Jackson County	IA	Jim Beck	2001	9791
147 1/8	23 2/8	24 6/8	18 3/8	4	5	Winona County	MN	Scott Roberts	2001	9791
147 1/8	23 6/8	23 0/8	15 7/8	5	5	St. Charles County	MO	Chris Holtey	2002	9791
147 1/8	23 6/8	24 1/8	18 5/8	5	5	Johnson County	MO	Mark Thomason	2002	9791
147 1/8	23 6/8	23 6/8	20 6/8	6	5	Harrison County	IA	Jeffrey Goss	2002	9791
147 1/8	25 6/8	25 6/8	18 4/8	6	5	Winona County	MN	Leonard Anglewitz	2002	9791
147 1/8	23 6/8	23 3/8	17 5/8	5	6	Clay County	IA	Rick Petersen	2002	9791
147 1/8	24 7/8	25 6/8	20 1/8	5	5	Ripley County	MO	Thomas Edwin Taylor	2002	9791
147 1/8	24 6/8	25 1/8	18 5/8	4	6	Bingham County	ID	Ray Kagel	2003	9791
147 1/8	24 5/8	24 4/8	17 7/8	4	5	Manitowoc County	WI	Dean R. Schad	2003	9791
147 1/8	21 0/8	21 5/8	20 1/8	5	5	Juneau County	WI	Michael J. Siegler	2003	9791
147 1/8	21 5/8	22 1/8	17 7/8	5	6	Beadle County	SD	Gregory L. Weeldreyer	2003	9791
147 1/8	25 4/8	24 3/8	19 0/8	5	7	Knox County	OH	Randy Frazee	2003	9791
147 1/8	23 6/8	23 7/8	17 3/8	6	6	Burnett County	WI	Byron Hopke	2003	9791
147 1/8	24 1/8	23 2/8	19 7/8	6	5	Grant County	WI	Mark Mezera	2003	9791
147 1/8	23 4/8	23 1/8	19 2/8	6	6	Rolette County	ND	Craig L. Larson	2003	9791
147 1/8	24 5/8	24 4/8	17 0/8	5	5	Muskingum County	OH	Douglas J. Eshenour	2003	9791
147 1/8	22 2/8	22 3/8	18 3/8	4	4	Randall County	TX	Brandon Ray	2003	9791
147 1/8	22 5/8	22 2/8	17 3/8	5	6	Montgomery County	IA	Tom Wright	2004	9791
147 1/8	21 2/8	21 0/8	15 3/8	5	5	Jersey County	IL	Derrick DeWilde	2004	9791
147 1/8	23 0/8	22 7/8	18 1/8	5	5	St. Louis County	MN	Ross Nelson	2004	9791
*147 1/8	23 3/8	23 4/8	17 7/8	4	5	Branch County	MI	Aaron M. Knauss	2005	9791
147 1/8	24 0/8	24 6/8	17 3/8	6	5	La Salle County	IL	Gus D. Leigh	2005	9791

459

WHITETAIL DEER (TYPICAL ANTLERS)

Minimum Score 125 — Continued

SCORE	LENGTH OF R MAIN BEAM L		INSIDE SPREAD	NUMBER OF R POINTS L		AREA	STATE/ PROVINCE	HUNTER'S NAME	DATE	RANK
147 1/8	22 5/8	23 5/8	18 5/8	6	6	Putnam County	IL	Jay L. O'Hara	2005	9791
147 1/8	24 6/8	23 3/8	17 7/8	5	6	Kane County	IL	Steve A. Nistler	2005	9791
147 1/8	25 0/8	23 7/8	19 0/8	6	4	Montcalm County	MI	Jason A. Wiley	2006	9791
147 1/8	20 6/8	21 4/8	17 1/8	5	6	Gallatin County	IL	Michael A. Melton	2006	9791
147 1/8	24 0/8	25 1/8	17 5/8	5	5	Outagamie County	WI	Bill Brennan	2006	9791
147 1/8	22 6/8	23 0/8	21 5/8	5	5	Osage County	OK	Rollin Johnson	2006	9791
147 1/8	23 2/8	21 7/8	19 0/8	7	6	Jewell County	KS	Bob Staples	2006	9791
*147 1/8	20 6/8	21 4/8	17 1/8	5	5	Will County	IL	James Kopca, Sr.	2006	9791
147 1/8	23 3/8	23 6/8	20 1/8	5	6	Guthrie County	IA	Glenn E. Thompson	2006	9791
147 1/8	24 2/8	24 1/8	21 1/8	5	5	Kane County	IL	Jeffrey F. Pyra	2007	9791
147 1/8	24 5/8	25 2/8	17 0/8	6	9	Mercer County	NJ	Kevin Kyle	2007	9791
147 1/8	20 7/8	21 7/8	15 7/8	6	4	Dubuque County	IA	Joseph Hinderman	2007	9791
147 1/8	21 6/8	22 4/8	17 2/8	7	7	Juneau County	WI	Robert R. Fink	2007	9791
*147 1/8	23 4/8	23 0/8	20 5/8	5	5	Columbiana County	OH	Kevin P. Joy	2007	9791
147 1/8	22 6/8	21 6/8	17 3/8	5	6	Atchison County	KS	Jeffrey D. Bell	2007	9791
*147 1/8	25 4/8	25 2/8	21 1/8	4	4	Barber County	KS	Doug Meeks	2007	9791
147 1/8	26 4/8	25 6/8	17 7/8	4	4	Warren County	IA	Doug Dearden	2007	9791
*147 1/8	26 2/8	26 3/8	19 7/8	4	5	Thayer County	NE	Brian Rut	2007	9791
147 1/8	25 6/8	24 5/8	19 5/8	4	4	Rock County	WI	Rick Utzig	2007	9791
147 1/8	23 5/8	23 2/8	19 0/8	7	5	Jackson County	OH	John Yeatts	2007	9791
*147 1/8	24 2/8	24 4/8	18 7/8	5	5	Eddy County	ND	Amanda Andrus	2008	9791
147 1/8	23 2/8	22 7/8	15 5/8	5	5	Wandering River	ALB	James Pike	2008	9791
147 1/8	22 3/8	23 0/8	19 3/8	5	4	Rock Island County	IL	Mikel Angel	2008	9791
147 1/8	23 4/8	23 4/8	14 0/8	4	5	Woodson County	KS	Danny Ferguson	2008	9791
147 1/8	23 5/8	24 1/8	17 1/8	5	4	Fillmore County	MN	David E. Kingsley	2008	9791
*147 1/8	24 3/8	24 2/8	17 1/8	6	6	Winston County	MS	Devon Vowell	2009	9791
147 1/8	23 1/8	24 1/8	15 7/8	5	5	Wayne County	MO	Jeffrey Hale	2009	9791
*147 1/8	24 7/8	24 2/8	20 5/8	4	4	Licking County	OH	Karl Steiner	2010	9791
147 0/8	24 6/8	25 5/8	17 4/8	5	7	Dodge County	WI	Alex B. Feucht	1963	9909
147 0/8	24 3/8	24 7/8	19 2/8	7	7	Dodge County	NE	Donald W. Robinson	1974	9909
147 0/8	23 6/8	24 0/8	20 3/8	6	5	Hancock County	IL	Ron Paul	1974	9909
147 0/8	28 5/8	26 2/8	19 0/8	5	4	Fulton County	IL	Bernard Smith	1974	9909
147 0/8	25 4/8	24 1/8	21 2/8	6	7	Morrison County	MN	Gordon Bayerkohler	1979	9909
147 0/8	23 5/8	23 5/8	20 0/8	5	5	Allamakee County	IA	Don Kieler	1979	9909
147 0/8	25 2/8	25 1/8	19 4/8	4	4	Iroquois County	IL	Bruce Courville	1980	9909
147 0/8	26 4/8	26 2/8	16 0/8	5	7	Gage County	NE	Eldon C. Wellman	1981	9909
147 0/8	25 1/8	25 2/8	19 6/8	7	6	Charles County	MD	David G. Wilson	1981	9909
147 0/8	24 4/8	23 7/8	18 6/8	4	5	Osborne County	KS	Mike Kidwell	1981	9909
147 0/8	22 3/8	22 2/8	18 4/8	5	5	Outagamie County	WI	Jim Vorland	1983	9909
147 0/8	26 1/8	24 2/8	22 0/8	4	5	Dorchester County	MD	Michael F. Blair	1983	9909
147 0/8	23 6/8	24 4/8	17 2/8	5	6	Lee County	IL	Donald E. Moore	1983	9909
147 0/8	23 7/8	23 6/8	20 0/8	5	5	Jefferson County	KS	John Welborn	1984	9909
147 0/8	26 2/8	25 4/8	17 6/8	5	5	Vernon County	MO	Roger L. Hensley	1985	9909
147 0/8	22 5/8	24 0/8	19 2/8	6	8	Cedar County	MO	David Barnard	1986	9909
147 0/8	23 3/8	22 7/8	15 2/8	6	6	Bradley County	AR	Granville Pankey	1987	9909
147 0/8	24 6/8	24 0/8	18 6/8	4	4	Wright County	MN	Dale Florek	1987	9909
147 0/8	23 2/8	24 4/8	15 2/8	5	5	Washington County	MN	Richard Eisinger	1988	9909
147 0/8	23 6/8	24 2/8	17 0/8	5	4	Livingston County	MI	Elmer DePlanche	1988	9909
147 0/8	22 1/8	22 0/8	17 2/8	5	5	Winnebago County	IL	Timothy J. Stuebs	1988	9909
147 0/8	24 6/8	24 6/8	18 0/8	8	7	Richland County	IL	Bill Taylor	1989	9909
147 0/8	23 7/8	23 2/8	16 1/8	6	8	Jefferson County	OH	James Zink	1989	9909
147 0/8	25 4/8	23 7/8	22 5/8	6	5	Woodford County	IL	Stan Bocian	1989	9909
147 0/8	23 3/8	21 6/8	18 2/8	5	5	Warren County	IA	Larry Caldwell	1989	9909
147 0/8	23 1/8	23 2/8	19 4/8	5	4	Boone County	IL	Michael A. Beasley	1989	9909
147 0/8	22 7/8	24 3/8	16 2/8	5	5	Walsh County	ND	Dayton Larson	1990	9909
147 0/8	25 2/8	25 6/8	17 6/8	5	5	Vermilion County	IL	Alexander Ramm	1990	9909
147 0/8	22 3/8	23 1/8	18 6/8	6	5	Waupaca County	WI	Brian Shambeau	1991	9909
147 0/8	24 7/8	24 5/8	18 1/8	6	6	Harrison County	OH	Robert M. Mensinger	1991	9909
147 0/8	24 4/8	25 1/8	23 0/8	4	5	Ernestown	ONT	Detlef Udo Fischer	1991	9909
147 0/8	27 4/8	27 1/8	23 0/8	4	4	Cape May County	NJ	Joseph C. Byrd	1992	9909
147 0/8	25 7/8	27 2/8	19 4/8	5	5	Allen County	IN	Chad E. Nicodemus	1992	9909
147 0/8	24 6/8	25 0/8	17 3/8	6	6	Wright County	MN	Greg Lavallee	1992	9909
147 0/8	25 3/8	25 6/8	20 0/8	4	4	Edgar County	IL	Frank Vail, III	1992	9909
147 0/8	23 2/8	24 1/8	16 6/8	5	7	Iroquois County	IL	Terry Doehring	1993	9909
147 0/8	23 6/8	23 7/8	17 0/8	5	5	Vinton County	OH	Tom Dishong, Jr.	1993	9909
147 0/8	22 6/8	22 3/8	17 4/8	5	5	Worth County	IA	Larry B. Porter	1993	9909
147 0/8	23 0/8	22 6/8	18 2/8	5	6	Buffalo County	WI	Ronald Brenner	1993	9909
147 0/8	26 6/8	25 3/8	20 2/8	6	6	Green Lake County	WI	Dale Dallman	1994	9909
147 0/8	23 1/8	23 1/8	15 7/8	5	6	Richland County	MT	Scott Sundheim	1994	9909
147 0/8	25 3/8	24 6/8	16 6/8	5	5	Waldo County	ME	Carol D. Macaulay	1994	9909
147 0/8	25 5/8	26 0/8	18 4/8	5	6	Jo Daviess County	IL	Daniel Keppen	1994	9909
147 0/8	23 4/8	24 5/8	18 6/8	5	5	Pike County	OH	Perry A. Cantrell	1994	9909
147 0/8	23 2/8	23 2/8	18 0/8	5	5	Muskingum County	OH	James Barbour	1994	9909
147 0/8	24 2/8	24 3/8	20 3/8	4	5	Baraga County	MI	Frank J. Kassuba	1995	9909
147 0/8	24 0/8	23 2/8	15 4/8	5	5	Lake County	IL	Robert H. Fugett	1995	9909
147 0/8	22 5/8	21 3/8	16 4/8	5	5	Ogle County	IL	Roy Nichols	1996	9909
147 0/8	21 6/8	22 5/8	15 4/8	5	5	Osage County	KS	Gerald Britschge	1996	9909
147 0/8	23 1/8	23 4/8	15 2/8	6	6	Des Moines County	IA	Robert J. Lewis	1996	9909
147 0/8	23 1/8	23 0/8	17 6/8	5	5	Cecil County	MD	Robert Allen Shelley	1996	9909
147 0/8	25 2/8	25 0/8	20 0/8	5	5	Buffalo County	WI	Wayne L. Olson	1997	9909
147 0/8	23 5/8	24 0/8	18 6/8	6	6	Kalamazoo County	MI	Cameron Russell Cudney	1997	9909
147 0/8	23 4/8	23 6/8	21 0/8	4	4	Jackson County	IA	Kevin A. Schmidt	1997	9909
147 0/8	21 4/8	21 5/8	15 3/8	6	7	Doniphan County	KS	Stephen D. Wolfram	1997	9909
147 0/8	22 7/8	22 5/8	14 7/8	6	5	Polk County	IA	Robert Howard	1997	9909
147 0/8	21 6/8	21 2/8	19 5/8	5	7	Henry County	IL	Steven R. Capps	1997	9909
147 0/8	23 7/8	23 5/8	19 4/8	5	5	Prowers County	CO	Neal Heaton	1997	9909
147 0/8	24 4/8	23 3/8	19 4/8	5	5	Allegheny County	PA	Wayne Paul Neyman	1998	9909
147 0/8	24 7/8	24 1/8	21 2/8	5	5	Dane County	WI	Bruce Lowrey	1998	9909
147 0/8	22 0/8	21 7/8	15 6/8	5	5	Pike County	IL	Brian McGill	1998	9909
147 0/8	21 5/8	22 4/8	15 2/8	5	6	Butler County	KS	Tim Hommertzheim	1998	9909
147 0/8	24 4/8	25 2/8	19 2/8	4	4	Fulton County	IL	Gus Congemi	1998	9909
147 0/8	27 0/8	26 5/8	20 0/8	4	4	Linn County	IA	Gary L. Havlik	1998	9909
147 0/8	21 0/8	21 2/8	23 0/8	5	5	Dodge County	WI	Richard Kling	1999	9909
147 0/8	23 1/8	24 3/8	16 4/8	5	5	Pike County	MO	Thomas L. Mazurek	1999	9909
147 0/8	22 3/8	20 7/8	16 2/8	5	6	Griggs County	ND	Bryan Hedstrom	1999	9909

460

WHITETAIL DEER (TYPICAL ANTLERS)

Minimum Score 125   Continued

SCORE	LENGTH OF R MAIN BEAM L	INSIDE SPREAD	NUMBER OF R POINTS L	AREA	STATE/ PROVINCE	HUNTER'S NAME	DATE	RANK
147 0/8	24 2/8	22 5/8	16 2/8	5 5	Lowndes County	AL	Joe Middleton	1999	9909
147 0/8	22 2/8	21 5/8	14 6/8	5 5	Scott County	IA	Sohn Smith	1999	9909
147 0/8	24 4/8	23 0/8	17 4/8	6 5	Brown County	IL	G. Merrill Jones	1999	9909
147 0/8	24 5/8	24 4/8	16 2/8	5 5	Ross County	OH	John M. Hinkle, Jr.	1999	9909
147 0/8	23 1/8	23 5/8	18 0/8	6 6	Oconto County	WI	Mathew J. Davis	1999	9909
147 0/8	25 6/8	26 3/8	21 4/8	4 4	Buffalo County	WI	Michael V. Parker	2000	9909
147 0/8	23 1/8	23 4/8	15 0/8	5 5	Loudoun County	VA	Tim Pickering	2000	9909
147 0/8	22 3/8	22 3/8	16 6/8	5 5	Washington County	IA	Mike Hershberger	2000	9909
147 0/8	27 0/8	26 2/8	18 4/8	5 5	Harford County	MD	Dennis Blaine Little	2000	9909
147 0/8	24 0/8	25 4/8	19 4/8	4 4	Missoula County	MT	Robert D. Mattie	2000	9909
147 0/8	22 0/8	23 4/8	16 6/8	5 5	Smith County	KS	Brent Sturges	2001	9909
147 0/8	23 2/8	22 6/8	17 6/8	5 5	McHenry County	IL	Kory Lang	2001	9909
147 0/8	23 7/8	22 5/8	16 4/8	7 6	Oconto County	WI	Chad Hanmann	2002	9909
147 0/8	23 2/8	21 2/8	16 7/8	6 5	Burke County	ND	Jay Hass	2002	9909
147 0/8	23 3/8	22 1/8	18 0/8	5 5	Clay County	SD	Kevin S. Hanson	2002	9909
147 0/8	23 4/8	22 2/8	20 0/8	5 5	Burnett County	WI	John Shepard	2002	9909
147 0/8	26 5/8	25 3/8	17 4/8	4 4	Allen County	IN	Craig Wiseman	2002	9909
147 0/8	25 1/8	26 4/8	19 7/8	5 5	Taylor County	IA	Mark Norcross	2002	9909
147 0/8	23 3/8	23 4/8	15 4/8	4 4	Macoupin County	IL	Mike Lavoie	2002	9909
147 0/8	20 7/8	21 6/8	15 0/8	5 5	Walsh County	ND	Arvid Swendseid	2003	9909
147 0/8	24 5/8	24 0/8	17 0/8	4 4	Refugio County	TX	Brent A. Tucker	2003	9909
147 0/8	25 2/8	26 0/8	17 2/8	6 5	Polk County	MN	Jeff Gullickson	2003	9909
147 0/8	21 5/8	23 5/8	19 0/8	5 6	Valley County	NE	Chuck Green	2003	9909
147 0/8	24 5/8	25 2/8	19 2/8	4 4	McLean County	IL	Scott Darnall	2004	9909
147 0/8	24 0/8	23 5/8	18 6/8	5 5	St. Croix County	WI	Gary D. Benck	2004	9909
147 0/8	22 6/8	22 1/8	21 0/8	6 6	Crawford County	OH	Roger A. France	2004	9909
147 0/8	22 2/8	22 5/8	18 4/8	5 5	Will County	IL	Joel D. Carpenter	2004	9909
147 0/8	22 5/8	23 3/8	15 0/8	5 5	Vernon County	WI	Steve Marsolek	2004	9909
147 0/8	23 4/8	24 0/8	20 0/8	4 5	Chippewa County	WI	Doug Lodahl	2004	9909
147 0/8	21 2/8	21 2/8	17 2/8	7 7	Oswego County	NY	James Sherman	2004	9909
147 0/8	23 4/8	23 5/8	17 2/8	4 5	Rice County	KS	Tom Klimek	2004	9909
147 0/8	26 6/8	26 1/8	22 2/8	4 5	Randolph County	IL	Ed Martin	2004	9909
147 0/8	22 1/8	22 1/8	16 0/8	5 5	Mountrail County	ND	Craig Richardson	2004	9909
147 0/8	25 3/8	22 5/8	17 2/8	5 5	Minnehaha County	SD	Shawn D. Pliska	2004	9909
147 0/8	26 1/8	26 2/8	19 3/8	5 5	Coshocton County	OH	Curtis Murphy	2005	9909
147 0/8	23 0/8	21 3/8	15 6/8	5 5	Ripley County	IN	Michael T. Neuner	2005	9909
*147 0/8	22 6/8	23 2/8	18 0/8	5 6	Cavalier County	ND	Dustin Brodina	2005	9909
147 0/8	23 6/8	23 1/8	19 0/8	5 5	Montgomery County	IA	Dick Paul	2005	9909
*147 0/8	22 7/8	23 5/8	18 0/8	6 5	Monroe County	IA	Tom O'Brien	2005	9909
*147 0/8	25 2/8	26 7/8	18 0/8	4 5	Kent County	MD	Richard Germain	2005	9909
*147 0/8	23 0/8	22 5/8	17 4/8	5 5	Griggs County	ND	Chad A. Haaland	2006	9909
*147 0/8	25 7/8	26 0/8	17 7/8	5 6	Clark County	IN	Rick L. Pelphrey, DVM	2006	9909
147 0/8	22 1/8	22 4/8	18 2/8	5 5	Outagamie County	WI	David D. Kuettel	2006	9909
147 0/8	26 2/8	26 2/8	20 0/8	4 4	Fayette County	OH	Aaron Simonson	2006	9909
147 0/8	22 2/8	23 1/8	19 3/8	5 6	Cole County	MO	Mark Rackers	2007	9909
147 0/8	24 1/8	24 6/8	17 4/8	4 4	Clark County	WI	Jack A. Friemoth	2007	9909
*147 0/8	22 1/8	22 0/8	18 0/8	6 5	Sauk County	WI	Marc J. Terry	2007	9909
147 0/8	21 6/8	22 7/8	19 2/8	6 6	Linn County	IA	James L. Corkery	2007	9909
147 0/8	23 0/8	23 4/8	16 0/8	5 5	Greene County	IN	Jarrod Holtsclaw	2007	9909
*147 0/8	24 2/8	23 1/8	20 0/8	6 7	Osborne County	KS	David Chritz	2007	9909
147 0/8	22 7/8	24 0/8	18 7/8	5 6	Hocking County	OH	Nick Ellis	2008	9909
147 0/8	23 4/8	23 6/8	15 2/8	5 5	Oswego County	NY	Rob Godfrey	2008	9909
147 0/8	24 1/8	23 2/8	19 0/8	5 6	Crawford County	IL	Tom Weinerth	2008	9909
*147 0/8	22 3/8	22 2/8	16 0/8	5 5	Polk County	WI	John Larson	2008	9909
147 0/8	23 0/8	23 6/8	16 0/8	6 5	Richland County	WI	Ben Hooks	2009	9909
*147 0/8	23 3/8	23 2/8	20 4/8	6 6	Kent County	RI	Louis Cote	2009	9909
*147 0/8	23 5/8	23 7/8	16 0/8	5 5	Lake County	IN	Larry Huizenga	2009	9909
146 7/8	24 0/8	24 3/8	22 1/8	5 7	Cass County	ND	Duane H. Olsen	1959	10033
146 7/8	21 5/8	21 0/8	16 3/8	5 5	Buffalo County	NE	Dwight Bond	1970	10033
146 7/8	23 5/8	22 6/8	16 6/8	6 6	Osceola County	IA	Roger Rehborg	1973	10033
146 7/8	22 2/8	21 2/8	19 7/8	5 5	Waushara County	WI	Norman A. Moss	1976	10033
146 7/8	24 2/8	24 2/8	15 5/8	4 4	Martin County	IN	Clarence McIntosh	1976	10033
146 7/8	21 1/8	20 7/8	22 4/8	5 5	Ogle County	IL	Art Heinze	1981	10033
146 7/8	23 1/8	21 6/8	16 1/8	5 5	Day County	SD	Cary Gill	1982	10033
146 7/8	22 6/8	21 6/8	16 1/8	5 5	Jasper County	IA	Mike Needham	1982	10033
146 7/8	25 3/8	25 0/8	18 7/8	5 4	Powhatan County	VA	W. Scott Thorpe	1985	10033
146 7/8	24 7/8	23 5/8	18 3/8	6 6	Jackson County	MI	Randy R. Peck	1986	10033
146 7/8	22 6/8	22 3/8	18 5/8	4 5	Jackson County	IL	Wayne Watt	1986	10033
146 7/8	24 4/8	23 5/8	18 6/8	6 6	Florence County	WI	Mark S. Becker	1987	10033
146 7/8	22 1/8	23 1/8	18 5/8	6 5	Le Flore County	OK	Bill Brannon	1988	10033
146 7/8	23 2/8	25 2/8	17 1/8	6 7	Houston County	MN	James Roth	1988	10033
146 7/8	24 2/8	24 0/8	19 3/8	4 4	Calvert County	MD	David Herbert	1989	10033
146 7/8	23 2/8	22 7/8	15 1/8	5 6	Mercer County	MO	David Gentry	1989	10033
146 7/8	24 5/8	24 2/8	17 4/8	5 7	Jackson County	IL	Steven W. Mifflin	1989	10033
146 7/8	25 3/8	25 6/8	20 5/8	5 4	Queen Annes County	MD	Raymie J. Williams III	1990	10033
146 7/8	23 5/8	20 0/8	18 3/8	6 5	Washington County	IL	Morris Lingle	1990	10033
146 7/8	25 1/8	25 2/8	18 3/8	5 5	Berkshire County	MA	William Drumm	1990	10033
146 7/8	21 6/8	21 6/8	16 5/8	5 5	Coke County	TX	Jack Mark Stone	1990	10033
146 7/8	22 5/8	22 0/8	17 1/8	6 5	Madison County	IL	Ronald Newby	1991	10033
146 7/8	25 6/8	25 7/8	18 5/8	7 5	Keokuk County	IA	Roger Dekok	1991	10033
146 7/8	22 6/8	22 4/8	20 3/8	4 6	Fairfield County	OH	Kevin Blackstone	1991	10033
146 7/8	23 4/8	24 4/8	17 1/8	5 6	Augusta Township	ONT	Henry P. Bouchard	1991	10033
146 7/8	23 4/8	25 5/8	22 6/8	5 5	Guilford County	NC	David L. Hendrix	1992	10033
146 7/8	24 7/8	24 7/8	21 3/8	4 4	Pepin County	WI	David L. Fayerweather	1993	10033
146 7/8	24 2/8	24 2/8	15 4/8	7 5	Cumberland County	IL	Larry Thompson	1993	10033
146 7/8	21 2/8	23 6/8	15 7/8	5 5	Douglas County	WI	J. Mark Wagenschutz	1993	10033
146 7/8	20 2/8	20 3/8	16 4/8	8 9	Genesee County	MI	Linda F. Luna	1993	10033
146 7/8	21 4/8	22 2/8	17 0/8	6 5	Seward County	KS	Lynn Leonard	1993	10033
146 7/8	23 6/8	24 6/8	18 6/8	5 5	Coshocton County	OH	Gary Lynn Fischer	1994	10033
146 7/8	23 2/8	23 1/8	17 6/8	6 7	Park County	WY	Larry Hicks	1994	10033
146 7/8	25 1/8	24 2/8	18 5/8	5 5	Pierce County	WI	Ron Sarnstrom	1994	10033
146 7/8	24 1/8	24 4/8	16 7/8	5 5	Hardin County	IA	William Stonebraker	1994	10033
146 7/8	23 0/8	23 0/8	19 3/8	4 4	Fulton County	IL	Butch Sulteen	1994	10033
146 7/8	27 5/8	28 5/8	17 7/8	4 4	Clermont County	OH	Lee Bumgardner	1994	10033
146 7/8	27 1/8	28 1/8	19 3/8	5 5	McHenry County	IL	Mark Wagner	1994	10033

461

WHITETAIL DEER (TYPICAL ANTLERS)

Minimum Score 125 — Continued

SCORE	LENGTH OF R MAIN BEAM L	INSIDE SPREAD	NUMBER OF R POINTS L		AREA	STATE/PROVINCE	HUNTER'S NAME	DATE	RANK
146 7/8	22 7/8 21 4/8	19 7/8	5	5	Kleberg County	TX	Johnnie R. Walters	1994	10033
146 7/8	19 4/8 20 2/8	16 6/8	5	6	Jackson County	KS	Rick Hummel	1995	10033
146 7/8	26 1/8 27 5/8	21 5/8	5	4	New Haven County	CT	Jeffrey R. Corbett	1995	10033
146 7/8	23 3/8 23 7/8	17 3/8	6	5	Menard County	IL	Mark Singleton	1995	10033
146 7/8	23 0/8 23 7/8	15 5/8	5	6	Davis County	IA	Dennis Dolash	1995	10033
146 7/8	24 3/8 24 1/8	20 2/8	6	6	McHenry County	IL	Rich Swanson	1995	10033
146 7/8	24 7/8 24 7/8	17 5/8	5	5	Morgan County	OH	Ron Newsom	1996	10033
146 7/8	25 0/8 22 7/8	19 7/8	5	5	Walworth County	WI	Jeffrey Nettesheim	1996	10033
146 7/8	26 0/8 26 0/8	18 5/8	5	5	New Haven County	CT	Real J. Masse	1996	10033
146 7/8	25 4/8 25 6/8	20 5/8	4	5	Portage County	OH	Dale A. Holmberg	1996	10033
146 7/8	22 1/8 21 4/8	17 3/8	5	5	Elbert County	CO	Daniel F. Dirscherl	1996	10033
146 7/8	22 2/8 22 6/8	15 3/8	6	5	Kankakee County	IL	Christopher Druckrey	1997	10033
146 7/8	22 0/8 23 4/8	17 5/8	7	5	Brown County	WI	Gregory P. Clabots	1997	10033
146 7/8	24 6/8 23 5/8	17 3/8	5	5	Dunn County	WI	Brian P. Knutson	1997	10033
146 7/8	25 6/8 26 1/8	20 5/8	5	8	Lake County	IL	Art Olson	1997	10033
146 7/8	26 3/8 26 3/8	22 1/8	6	6	Jo Daviess County	IL	Michael J. Pitzen	1998	10033
146 7/8	23 4/8 23 6/8	16 7/8	4	5	Van Buren County	IA	Shannon Shepard	1998	10033
146 7/8	27 4/8 25 5/8	20 5/8	6	7	Crawford County	WI	Louis J. New III	1998	10033
146 7/8	24 0/8 23 5/8	17 5/8	6	5	Dunn County	WI	Scott Kostman	1998	10033
146 7/8	22 5/8 23 7/8	16 2/8	7	5	Monroe County	IA	Bob Veverka	1998	10033
146 7/8	23 0/8 21 5/8	15 5/8	5	7	Buffalo County	WI	John W. Charles	1999	10033
146 7/8	24 3/8 23 6/8	14 7/8	5	6	Peoria County	IL	Philippe W. Boland	1999	10033
146 7/8	23 4/8 22 3/8	19 3/8	6	5	Columbia County	WI	Richard Sutter	2000	10033
146 7/8	25 3/8 25 3/8	16 2/8	5	5	Winona County	MN	Jeffrey R. Fechner	2000	10033
146 7/8	21 1/8 21 3/8	15 5/8	6	5	Macoupin County	IL	Tim Norris	2000	10033
146 7/8	23 6/8 22 2/8	15 4/8	6	5	Portage County	WI	Eric L. Jastromski	2000	10033
146 7/8	26 1/8 24 6/8	20 1/8	7	5	St. Clair County	IL	Dave Pregon	2000	10033
146 7/8	22 2/8 22 0/8	17 7/8	4	4	Preble County	OH	Todd M. Snyder	2000	10033
146 7/8	24 1/8 23 7/8	27 6/8	6	5	Sauk County	WI	Jeremiah D. Jesse	2001	10033
146 7/8	25 3/8 24 0/8	19 1/8	5	5	Adams County	OH	Brandon Prifogle	2001	10033
146 7/8	24 5/8 25 1/8	20 5/8	5	4	Coahoma County	MS	Wayne Strider, Jr.	2001	10033
146 7/8	23 1/8 23 2/8	17 6/8	5	6	Henry County	IA	Eric E. Teall	2001	10033
146 7/8	23 3/8 23 5/8	16 7/8	5	4	Cayuga County	NY	Andrew Ridley	2001	10033
146 7/8	26 2/8 26 5/8	20 7/8	4	5	Dubuque County	IA	F. Michael Gruber	2001	10033
146 7/8	25 5/8 24 4/8	24 0/8	5	6	Frio County	TX	Joe M. Keathley	2002	10033
146 7/8	24 3/8 24 1/8	16 7/8	5	5	Rockingham County	NC	Richard D. Auten	2002	10033
146 7/8	22 3/8 22 7/8	19 7/8	6	5	McLennan County	TX	Mike T. Thrasher	2002	10033
146 7/8	25 0/8 25 2/8	17 7/8	4	6	Roberts County	SD	Wesley Koehler	2002	10033
146 7/8	22 2/8 22 2/8	17 3/8	5	6	Clay County	IA	Thomas Ray Gross	2002	10033
146 7/8	22 1/8 21 7/8	16 3/8	6	5	Chariton County	MO	Billy Joe Kennedy, Jr.	2002	10033
146 7/8	25 0/8 19 1/8	20 3/8	5	5	Worcester County	MA	Andrew Davison	2002	10033
146 7/8	23 4/8 23 6/8	14 6/8	6	8	Du Page County	IL	Jonathan J. Buckman	2002	10033
*146 7/8	24 0/8 24 4/8	18 7/8	4	4	Wagoner County	OK	Rick Wrona	2002	10033
146 7/8	25 1/8 26 0/8	19 6/8	6	5	Northampton County	VA	Skip Valentine	2003	10033
146 7/8	24 0/8 23 4/8	19 3/8	5	5	Fulton County	IN	Matt Campbell	2003	10033
146 7/8	24 0/8 22 4/8	19 1/8	6	6	Hinds County	MS	Will Lyons	2003	10033
146 7/8	23 5/8 23 7/8	20 7/8	5	4	Henry County	IL	James T. Galloway	2003	10033
146 7/8	24 6/8 25 1/8	18 1/8	6	5	Cass County	NE	Marcus Dryak	2003	10033
146 7/8	24 5/8 25 5/8	19 4/8	6	4	Logan County	OH	Harold Clem	2003	10033
146 7/8	24 5/8 23 3/8	16 7/8	5	5	Lane County	KS	Dean Hamilton	2003	10033
146 7/8	22 7/8 22 2/8	18 2/8	5	6	Barron County	WI	Gordy Severude	2003	10033
146 7/8	22 3/8 22 5/8	16 3/8	6	5	Cook County	IL	Timothy L. Harkness	2004	10033
*146 7/8	22 7/8 25 0/8	12 7/8	5	6	Jefferson County	IL	Steve Wiseley	2004	10033
146 7/8	22 7/8 23 3/8	18 2/8	6	5	Mercer County	PA	Paul Hause	2004	10033
146 7/8	24 1/8 25 0/8	18 4/8	6	5	Carver County	MN	Jerry Chalupsky	2004	10033
146 7/8	21 7/8 22 2/8	15 3/8	6	5	Will County	IL	Dale Hoekstra	2004	10033
*146 7/8	23 3/8 23 0/8	15 3/8	7	7	Perry County	OH	Troy Cameron	2004	10033
146 7/8	23 0/8 21 7/8	17 3/8	6	5	Vernon County	WI	Stacy G. Myers	2004	10033
146 7/8	21 2/8 23 2/8	19 1/8	5	5	Grundy County	IL	Rod Phelan	2005	10033
146 7/8	22 2/8 22 6/8	20 3/8	5	5	Grant County	WI	Peter O'Brien	2005	10033
146 7/8	22 2/8 21 4/8	20 1/8	5	5	Buffalo County	WI	Robert A. Weihert	2005	10033
*146 7/8	23 6/8 23 6/8	18 1/8	5	5	Goodsoil	SAS	Richard Service	2006	10033
146 7/8	23 7/8 24 1/8	18 0/8	7	5	Butler County	KS	Raymond Blevins	2006	10033
*146 7/8	24 3/8 23 0/8	20 1/8	6	7	Columbiana County	OH	Michael Piccirilli	2006	10033
146 7/8	22 0/8 23 3/8	19 1/8	6	5	Orleans County	NY	Jeffrey Adams	2006	10033
146 7/8	22 6/8 23 0/8	17 7/8	6	6	Grundy County	IL	Bryan Chapman	2006	10033
146 7/8	24 7/8 23 7/8	20 0/8	6	6	Lincoln County	WI	Clay A. Gavigan	2006	10033
146 7/8	22 2/8 22 1/8	18 3/8	5	5	Richland County	WI	Scott A. Wagner	2006	10033
146 7/8	26 3/8 24 7/8	19 6/8	4	5	Chippewa County	WI	Cary Roper	2006	10033
*146 7/8	25 0/8 24 2/8	19 3/8	4	4	Oconto County	WI	George A. Morales	2006	10033
146 7/8	22 3/8 24 0/8	19 5/8	5	5	Columbia County	WI	Stuart C. Rostad	2007	10033
*146 7/8	23 6/8 23 3/8	18 3/8	5	5	Waupaca County	WI	Thomas Freiesleben	2007	10033
*146 7/8	22 4/8 21 0/8	17 3/8	5	5	Kane County	IL	Fred Lehman	2007	10033
146 7/8	22 2/8 23 0/8	16 0/8	6	5	Lyon County	KY	Duane Clark	2007	10033
146 7/8	21 0/8 21 0/8	15 3/8	6	6	Platte County	MO	Jack Moore	2007	10033
146 7/8	23 3/8 23 5/8	16 5/8	6	5	Battle River	ALB	J. P. McDonald	2008	10033
*146 7/8	24 7/8 25 6/8	16 5/8	5	6	Brown County	OH	Trevor D. Hanna	2008	10033
146 7/8	22 7/8 21 7/8	13 6/8	7	5	Fulton County	GA	Kendall Golightly	2009	10033
*146 7/8	24 1/8 24 2/8	15 3/8	5	6	Guthrie County	IA	Jerome Jensen	2009	10033
*146 7/8	23 0/8 22 4/8	15 7/8	5	5	Yell County	AR	Ronnie Lee Woodard	2009	10033
*146 7/8	24 6/8 26 1/8	18 2/8	7	5	Washington County	WI	Gary A. Scheer	2009	10033
146 6/8	23 6/8 24 1/8	17 0/8	5	4	Allegany County	MD	James Wilhelm	1961	10152
146 6/8	23 3/8 23 1/8	17 6/8	7	8	Roberts County	SD	Robert Hendren	1967	10152
146 6/8	24 6/8 27 0/8	20 2/8	5	4	Neosho County	KS	Carl Walker	1968	10152
146 6/8	26 1/8 25 3/8	18 1/8	4	5	Lee County	IA	Jim Bohnenkamp	1970	10152
146 6/8	25 5/8 25 5/8	18 0/8	5	5	Shelby County	IL	Gary E. Sievers	1972	10152
146 6/8	21 5/8 21 5/8	18 3/8	6	7	Will County	IL	Richard Manegold	1976	10152
146 6/8	23 0/8 25 5/8	16 3/8	6	5	Lafayette County	WI	Greg Penniston	1977	10152
146 6/8	25 4/8 25 6/8	17 3/8	5	5	Tuscarawas County	OH	Tracy Sheaffer	1980	10152
146 6/8	26 1/8 25 3/8	16 0/8	5	4	Waushara County	WI	James L. Reiff, Jr.	1981	10152
146 6/8	24 7/8 25 0/8	18 6/8	5	6	Cedar County	IA	Mike Rummells	1982	10152
146 6/8	25 2/8 24 3/8	18 0/8	5	5	Logan County	OH	David Katterheinrich	1984	10152
146 6/8	21 5/8 22 5/8	22 4/8	5	5	Lincoln County	MO	Jerry Davis, Jr.	1987	10152
146 6/8	26 6/8 25 5/8	24 4/8	5	5	Suffolk County	NY	Joe Barbato	1988	10152
146 6/8	27 0/8 27 3/8	19 0/8	4	5	North Dumphries Township	ONT	Jeff Bendig	1988	10152

WHITETAIL DEER (TYPICAL ANTLERS)

Minimum Score 125 Continued

SCORE	LENGTH OF R MAIN BEAM L	INSIDE SPREAD	NUMBER OF R POINTS L		AREA	STATE/ PROVINCE	HUNTER'S NAME	DATE	RANK
146 6/8	24 0/8	23 1/8	17 2/8	5	4	Howard County	IA	Terry Lee Larson	1988	10152
146 6/8	21 4/8	22 1/8	16 3/8	6	6	Richland County	ND	Allen Perlenfein	1989	10152
146 6/8	22 7/8	22 4/8	18 6/8	5	5	Powell County	MT	Dan D. Boy	1989	10152
146 6/8	24 7/8	25 3/8	18 2/8	4	4	Montgomery County	TN	Julia C. Davidson	1989	10152
146 6/8	23 2/8	23 1/8	19 4/8	5	5	Fergus County	MT	Stan Chiras	1989	10152
146 6/8	20 2/8	20 4/8	15 1/8	6	5	Pulaski County	GA	Dan B. Clifton	1989	10152
146 6/8	26 3/8	26 0/8	19 4/8	5	4	Rusk County	WI	Gordon Bohochik	1990	10152
146 6/8	26 1/8	23 2/8	19 6/8	6	6	Vermilion County	IL	Jack Toms, Jr.	1990	10152
146 6/8	26 0/8	20 2/8	23 1/8	6	6	Osborne County	KS	Cary L. Sommerla	1990	10152
146 6/8	24 2/8	23 2/8	18 0/8	5	5	Morgan County	OH	Mark Donnally	1991	10152
146 6/8	23 6/8	23 0/8	16 6/8	6	6	De Kalb County	MO	Dennis Collins	1991	10152
146 6/8	21 6/8	21 5/8	16 4/8	6	6	Waupaca County	WI	Thomas Conradt	1992	10152
146 6/8	23 7/8	22 7/8	19 0/8	6	5	Cumberland County	IL	Pete Sweitzer	1992	10152
146 6/8	22 1/8	22 0/8	16 0/8	5	5	Waukesha County	WI	Jane Nelson	1992	10152
146 6/8	21 7/8	22 2/8	17 0/8	5	5	Sterling County	TX	Mike Belanger	1992	10152
146 6/8	23 5/8	23 2/8	18 4/8	5	4	Breckinridge County	KY	R. Ray Wix	1993	10152
146 6/8	26 0/8	25 6/8	17 6/8	8	5	Jackson County	IL	Gregg Tucker	1993	10152
146 6/8	25 0/8	25 6/8	21 1/8	7	6	St. Francis County	AR	Tom Thompson	1993	10152
146 6/8	25 5/8	24 6/8	19 0/8	5	5	Adams County	IA	Kenny Vaill	1993	10152
146 6/8	27 0/8	25 2/8	19 0/8	6	8	Bourbon County	KS	Kevin G. Asbury	1993	10152
146 6/8	20 5/8	21 2/8	17 0/8	5	5	Sheridan County	WY	George K. Warner	1994	10152
146 6/8	24 2/8	24 4/8	23 7/8	5	4	Belknap County	NH	Tom Sleeper	1994	10152
146 6/8	26 5/8	25 7/8	20 0/8	4	5	McHenry County	IL	Roger W. Gates	1994	10152
146 6/8	23 6/8	24 0/8	19 0/8	5	7	Clay County	IA	Thomas Ray Gross	1994	10152
146 6/8	25 0/8	24 6/8	18 6/8	5	6	Rice County	MN	Mike Johnson	1995	10152
146 6/8	24 3/8	23 3/8	18 0/8	5	5	Pike County	IL	Troy Richart	1995	10152
146 6/8	25 3/8	22 7/8	19 0/8	6	5	Anne Arundel County	MD	Hillory Dean	1995	10152
146 6/8	23 3/8	23 5/8	19 0/8	4	4	Kankakee County	IL	Bryan Hays	1995	10152
146 6/8	21 4/8	22 3/8	15 4/8	4	4	Van Buren County	IA	James Bohnenkamp	1995	10152
146 6/8	25 6/8	25 4/8	20 2/8	6	4	Mills County	IA	David D. Greenwood	1995	10152
146 6/8	25 6/8	24 7/8	18 0/8	5	5	Hillsdale County	MI	Gale E. Pauken	1996	10152
146 6/8	24 1/8	24 1/8	14 5/8	5	6	Pike County	IL	Nelson Sherman, Jr.	1996	10152
146 6/8	25 7/8	26 7/8	19 4/8	5	4	Pike County	IL	Mike Dixon	1996	10152
146 6/8	23 3/8	22 6/8	20 2/8	5	5	Stoddard County	MO	Don Reynolds	1996	10152
146 6/8	23 1/8	23 6/8	15 6/8	6	7	Kenedy County	TX	Thomas J. Hoffman	1997	10152
146 6/8	24 4/8	24 7/8	21 4/8	4	4	Douglas County	WI	Donald Lietha, Jr.	1997	10152
146 6/8	26 3/8	27 5/8	16 6/8	4	4	Du Page County	IL	Bruno Parzyck	1997	10152
146 6/8	23 6/8	23 7/8	18 2/8	5	6	Iowa County	WI	Robert A. Ramsden	1997	10152
146 6/8	25 5/8	25 4/8	19 4/8	4	4	Somerset County	NJ	Joseph Stavola	1997	10152
146 6/8	23 0/8	22 1/8	20 6/8	5	6	Marathon County	WI	Bill Heil	1998	10152
146 6/8	25 4/8	24 6/8	20 6/8	4	4	Thayer County	NE	Robert J. Baxa	1998	10152
146 6/8	24 2/8	24 1/8	17 3/8	7	7	Lincoln County	NE	Robert Schwanz	1998	10152
146 6/8	23 5/8	23 1/8	16 4/8	5	5	Buffalo County	WI	Bob Pieterick	1999	10152
146 6/8	23 7/8	23 1/8	20 6/8	5	5	Columbia County	WI	William B. Farmer	1999	10152
146 6/8	23 1/8	23 3/8	17 0/8	4	4	Washington County	MN	Todd A. Bentler	2000	10152
146 6/8	23 4/8	23 1/8	16 5/8	7	7	Niobrara County	WY	Darryl Nicks	2000	10152
146 6/8	24 1/8	24 1/8	19 6/8	4	4	Sawyer County	WI	Gary Gedart	2000	10152
146 6/8	24 7/8	25 0/8	20 1/8	5	6	McKenzie County	ND	Corey Hugelen	2000	10152
146 6/8	22 4/8	22 3/8	18 4/8	5	5	Calumet County	WI	Jeff Buechel	2000	10152
146 6/8	22 7/8	22 0/8	17 4/8	5	5	Butler County	KS	Ted Nelson	2000	10152
146 6/8	20 7/8	23 7/8	19 0/8	5	5	Sherburne County	MN	John Nagorski	2000	10152
146 6/8	25 2/8	25 6/8	19 6/8	5	5	Forest County	WI	Michael Doemel	2001	10152
146 6/8	27 2/8	26 4/8	21 6/8	4	4	Jefferson County	OH	Brian Eagleton	2001	10152
146 6/8	22 1/8	22 5/8	20 6/8	5	5	Clinton County	IL	Randall Kampwerth	2001	10152
146 6/8	21 6/8	21 7/8	15 6/8	5	5	Marshall County	KS	John Gomel	2001	10152
146 6/8	23 2/8	22 7/8	17 0/8	5	5	Outagamie County	WI	Mary Jo Grawitch	2002	10152
146 6/8	26 1/8	26 2/8	21 6/8	6	5	Wadena County	MN	Joe Gieske	2002	10152
146 6/8	20 6/8	19 6/8	14 0/8	6	5	Kenedy County	TX	Ken Witt	2002	10152
146 6/8	21 6/8	21 4/8	16 2/8	7	8	Marshall County	IN	Melvin C. Walter	2002	10152
146 6/8	23 7/8	23 3/8	17 4/8	6	6	Black Hawk County	IA	Ray W. Berry	2002	10152
146 6/8	22 7/8	23 5/8	19 2/8	5	6	Genesee County	MI	Timothy M. Dodak	2002	10152
146 6/8	23 4/8	23 4/8	17 2/8	5	4	Livingston County	IL	Gerald T. Shepherd	2002	10152
146 6/8	23 6/8	23 4/8	15 0/8	5	5	Ripley County	IN	Steve Scudder	2003	10152
146 6/8	24 0/8	22 1/8	19 3/8	6	5	Ontonagon County	MI	J. J. Flynn	2003	10152
146 6/8	26 5/8	26 5/8	19 5/8	6	6	Clermont County	OH	David Porter	2003	10152
146 6/8	22 2/8	22 0/8	18 4/8	5	6	Comanche County	KS	Ted K. Jaycox	2003	10152
*146 6/8	23 4/8	23 4/8	19 2/8	6	4	Sauk County	WI	Russell J. Hanson	2004	10152
146 6/8	23 7/8	24 5/8	19 5/8	5	6	Woodford County	IL	Michael R. Davis	2004	10152
146 6/8	23 5/8	23 2/8	19 6/8	4	4	Columbia County	WI	Maurice De Vries	2004	10152
146 6/8	22 6/8	22 5/8	17 7/8	6	8	Calhoun County	IL	Larry J. Clark	2004	10152
*146 6/8	23 6/8	22 7/8	15 2/8	7	5	Sheboygan County	WI	Michael R. Hassinger	2004	10152
146 6/8	21 6/8	22 0/8	15 2/8	5	5	Pulaski County	IN	Chris R. Cirrincione	2004	10152
146 6/8	24 2/8	24 2/8	21 0/8	5	4	Marion County	OH	Mark A. Jamison	2004	10152
146 6/8	24 4/8	25 0/8	18 2/8	5	5	Rockland County	NY	Ben Risley	2004	10152
146 6/8	24 1/8	24 5/8	18 2/8	5	6	Barron County	WI	Karl Klatt	2005	10152
146 6/8	23 0/8	23 3/8	16 4/8	6	7	Douglas County	WI	David D. Paulus	2005	10152
146 6/8	24 4/8	24 1/8	21 4/8	4	4	Washington County	IA	L. W. Miller	2005	10152
146 6/8	22 0/8	22 4/8	15 2/8	5	5	Lawrence County	OH	Michael D. McComas II	2005	10152
146 6/8	24 0/8	21 0/8	20 2/8	5	5	Douglas County	KS	Jeff Gregory	2005	10152
*146 6/8	23 5/8	23 2/8	18 6/8	5	5	Monona County	IA	Daniel H. Larsen	2005	10152
*146 6/8	22 6/8	23 0/8	19 4/8	5	5	Washington County	MN	Mark W. Kujala	2005	10152
146 6/8	25 2/8	23 7/8	16 5/8	5	5	Goodhue County	MN	Christopher J. Cordes	2005	10152
*146 6/8	22 5/8	22 1/8	19 0/8	4	4	St. Louis County	MN	Harald O. Heymann	2005	10152
*146 6/8	25 2/8	25 1/8	18 0/8	4	5	Jefferson County	OH	William H. Ferguson III	2005	10152
*146 6/8	24 0/8	24 1/8	16 6/8	5	7	Cumberland County	IL	Travis Green	2006	10152
146 6/8	21 6/8	23 5/8	17 2/8	6	6	Johnson County	IA	Darren Pingel	2006	10152
146 6/8	21 0/8	25 0/8	21 6/8	5	6	Page County	IA	Bob Athen	2006	10152
146 6/8	24 1/8	23 0/8	16 2/8	6	5	Jersey County	IL	Judy Kovar	2006	10152
146 6/8	25 2/8	25 0/8	18 6/8	4	5	Audrain County	MO	Richard Bagley	2006	10152
146 6/8	24 7/8	24 1/8	17 3/8	4	5	Jackson County	TN	Jerry M. Osborne	2007	10152
146 6/8	23 3/8	23 3/8	18 4/8	6	5	Wizard Lake	ALB	Kevin J. Hetrick	2007	10152
146 6/8	25 6/8	25 2/8	21 2/8	4	4	Dubuque County	IA	Eric Dupont	2007	10152
146 6/8	22 5/8	23 0/8	17 2/8	6	6	Eau Claire County	WI	Tim Sell	2007	10152
146 6/8	26 0/8	25 6/8	19 6/8	7	5	Brown County	IL	Adam Shaughnessy	2007	10152
*146 6/8	23 3/8	23 7/8	17 2/8	5	5	Wayne County	IN	Charles "Chuck" Blevins	2007	10152

463

WHITETAIL DEER (TYPICAL ANTLERS)

Minimum Score 125   Continued

SCORE	LENGTH OF R MAIN BEAM L	INSIDE SPREAD	NUMBER OF R POINTS L	AREA	STATE/ PROVINCE	HUNTER'S NAME	DATE	RANK
146 6/8	23 0/8 22 1/8	18 2/8	5 5	Putnam County	IN	Wesley Ward	2007	10152
*146 6/8	24 4/8 25 0/8	18 4/8	5 5	Houston County	MN	Richard Tenute	2007	10152
146 6/8	24 7/8 22 7/8	18 7/8	6 5	Jersey County	IL	Judy Kovar	2008	10152
*146 6/8	23 1/8 23 4/8	17 4/8	5 5	Beltrami County	MN	Jeffrey Everhart	2008	10152
*146 6/8	24 7/8 24 6/8	22 0/8	4 4	Morrison County	MN	Chad Neuman	2008	10152
146 6/8	23 7/8 23 6/8	16 6/8	4 4	Pike County	OH	Jordan Collins	2008	10152
146 6/8	24 7/8 24 5/8	16 7/8	5 6	Pierce County	WI	Nate Gruber	2008	10152
146 6/8	22 4/8 22 7/8	19 4/8	5 5	Cass County	NE	Kip Fuxa	2008	10152
*146 6/8	24 4/8 24 4/8	17 2/8	5 5	Jefferson County	IN	Eric W. Dickerson	2008	10152
146 6/8	21 5/8 21 2/8	14 4/8	6 6	Bingham County	ID	Rance Dye	2008	10152
146 6/8	22 0/8 21 6/8	17 4/8	6 5	Chetwynd	BC	Roy Goodwin	2009	10152
*146 6/8	22 5/8 22 5/8	16 4/8	5 5	Knox County	OH	Robert Dickinson	2009	10152
*146 6/8	23 4/8 22 5/8	16 4/8	5 5	Noble County	IN	Ford A. Frick, Jr.	2009	10152
146 6/8	23 7/8 24 0/8	18 2/8	6 6	Sedgwick County	KS	George M. Moore	2009	10152
146 6/8	22 3/8 22 4/8	15 2/8	5 6	Trempealeau County	WI	David N. Andersen	2010	10152
146 5/8	22 5/8 22 5/8	18 7/8	4 3	Brown County	SD	Donald Grote	1963	10276
146 5/8	23 2/8 24 1/8	17 3/8	5 6	Buckingham County	VA	Larry D. Baker	1974	10276
146 5/8	25 2/8 25 6/8	18 7/8	4 5	Carroll County	IL	Art Heinze	1978	10276
146 5/8	20 6/8 22 1/8	19 4/8	7 7	Clinton County	IN	Sheldon H. Stoops	1979	10276
146 5/8	24 2/8 24 1/8	18 7/8	6 7	Des Moines County	IA	Larry R. Booth	1979	10276
146 5/8	23 4/8 24 0/8	19 1/8	5 5	Morrison County	MN	Bart Brodt	1984	10276
146 5/8	24 3/8 24 4/8	16 5/8	6 5	Cole County	MO	Norman P. Stucky	1984	10276
146 5/8	24 3/8 24 3/8	16 2/8	8 8	Clark County	MO	Allen L. Courtney	1986	10276
146 5/8	23 6/8 23 4/8	20 3/8	4 5	Kent County	MI	Benjamin V. Lapus, Jr.	1986	10276
146 5/8	24 7/8 24 1/8	17 7/8	5 4	Hartford County	CT	Peter J.M. Kiendzoir	1986	10276
146 5/8	22 4/8 22 0/8	16 1/8	5 6	Wabash County	IL	Robert E. Campbell	1987	10276
146 5/8	24 7/8 25 5/8	20 4/8	5 7	Washington County	WI	Tony Snow	1988	10276
146 5/8	21 7/8 21 2/8	15 5/8	5 5	Nueces County	TX	Wayne Peeples	1989	10276
146 5/8	24 5/8 24 7/8	18 6/8	5 6	Crawford County	KS	Cary R. Rybnick	1989	10276
146 5/8	24 7/8 24 4/8	19 6/8	6 7	Forest County	WI	Jim Sot	1990	10276
146 5/8	22 7/8 23 1/8	17 7/8	5 5	Cecil County	MD	Steven D. Flanagan	1990	10276
146 5/8	24 0/8 24 7/8	16 1/8	5 6	Macomb County	MI	Frank M. Malik, Jr.	1990	10276
146 5/8	25 6/8 25 6/8	19 3/8	5 5	Polk County	IA	Steve Dilling	1990	10276
146 5/8	21 3/8 21 4/8	16 3/8	4 4	Dodge County	MN	Myles Keller	1990	10276
146 5/8	24 0/8 23 1/8	16 3/8	6 6	Giles County	TN	Jerry Case	1991	10276
146 5/8	24 4/8 23 6/8	20 0/8	5 4	Monroe County	IN	Brian K. Lady	1991	10276
146 5/8	21 0/8 21 1/8	16 5/8	5 5	Shawnee County	KS	Dan McConnell	1991	10276
146 5/8	25 5/8 23 6/8	18 1/8	6 5	Ontario County	NY	Robert D. Koutras	1992	10276
146 5/8	23 4/8 22 6/8	16 5/8	5 5	Roane County	WV	Edward Osborne	1992	10276
146 5/8	26 0/8 26 4/8	21 1/8	7 5	Ferndale	MAN	Ed Parker	1992	10276
146 5/8	22 6/8 22 4/8	16 1/8	6 5	Cocke County	TN	Terry Finchum	1993	10276
146 5/8	22 6/8 22 4/8	20 7/8	6 9	Lac qui Parle County	MN	Wade Schmidt	1993	10276
146 5/8	24 1/8 24 6/8	20 6/8	4 5	Morris County	NJ	Russell Davidson	1993	10276
146 5/8	23 1/8 23 1/8	16 5/8	5 5	Dane County	WI	Jeffrey R. DeLaura	1994	10276
146 5/8	24 1/8 23 1/8	18 5/8	5 6	Adams County	IL	Larry D. Grant	1994	10276
146 5/8	24 3/8 23 5/8	16 7/8	6 5	Greene County	IL	Robert Neff	1994	10276
146 5/8	25 2/8 26 2/8	22 5/8	5 4	Warren County	IL	Bryan E. DeJaynes	1994	10276
146 5/8	22 6/8 23 0/8	18 3/8	5 5	Trempealeau County	WI	David Mikrut	1994	10276
146 5/8	23 0/8 23 0/8	18 3/8	5 6	Sawyer County	WI	Greg Biskup	1994	10276
146 5/8	24 0/8 23 5/8	16 1/8	5 5	Miami County	KS	Chuck Buckley	1994	10276
146 5/8	22 3/8 21 7/8	17 5/8	5 5	Sedgwick County	CO	Everett Tarrell	1994	10276
146 5/8	23 2/8 23 0/8	18 7/8	5 5	Berrien County	MI	Craig Miller	1995	10276
146 5/8	25 5/8 24 5/8	22 1/8	4 4	Ogle County	IL	Scott Relien	1995	10276
146 5/8	23 4/8 23 3/8	17 5/8	5 5	Hamilton County	IA	Chad M. Foster	1996	10276
146 5/8	24 0/8 24 4/8	17 2/8	6 5	Grant County	WI	Glen Stangl	1996	10276
146 5/8	22 5/8 21 3/8	16 2/8	6 7	Van Buren County	IA	Russ Miller	1996	10276
146 5/8	24 6/8 23 7/8	20 3/8	5 4	Vilas County	WI	Roger A. Turner	1997	10276
146 5/8	22 7/8 24 1/8	17 1/8	5 5	Crawford County	WI	Chuck Bender	1997	10276
146 5/8	25 4/8 26 3/8	22 2/8	5 6	Montgomery County	OH	Dale Shepard	1997	10276
146 5/8	24 2/8 23 5/8	22 1/8	5 5	Floyd County	IA	Dennis Noling	1997	10276
146 5/8	24 5/8 24 1/8	18 3/8	4 4	Fayette County	WV	David Kinningham	1998	10276
146 5/8	20 4/8 21 0/8	16 7/8	6 5	Pierson	MAN	Mike Minshull	1999	10276
146 5/8	21 3/8 21 6/8	18 5/8	5 5	Phillips County	KS	Terry Moran	1999	10276
146 5/8	25 0/8 24 1/8	18 5/8	5 5	Benton County	IA	Joe Smith	1999	10276
146 5/8	23 1/8 23 1/8	16 7/8	5 5	Kenedy County	TX	Johnnie R. Walters	2000	10276
146 5/8	22 5/8 21 7/8	18 1/8	5 5	Green Lake County	WI	Kenneth D. Zik	2000	10276
146 5/8	24 7/8 24 3/8	18 7/8	4 5	Adams County	WI	Jerome S. Koziczkowski	2000	10276
146 5/8	25 6/8 25 1/8	17 7/8	4 4	Madison County	IL	Don Lockhart	2000	10276
146 5/8	25 4/8 26 1/8	18 5/8	6 5	Shelby County	IL	David "Kent" Sims	2000	10276
146 5/8	26 1/8 25 0/8	17 5/8	4 5	Union County	KY	Tony M. Noe	2000	10276
146 5/8	22 6/8 22 3/8	14 5/8	5 5	Fillmore County	MN	Curt Paulson	2001	10276
146 5/8	23 0/8 22 3/8	18 2/8	6 6	Winona County	MN	Curt Heyer	2001	10276
146 5/8	27 0/8 26 3/8	17 7/8	4 5	Macoupin County	IL	Chris Bettis	2001	10276
146 5/8	23 5/8 23 5/8	17 1/8	4 5	Fulton County	IL	Tim Sweet	2001	10276
146 5/8	23 2/8 22 5/8	18 5/8	5 5	Delaware County	IA	Kris Lenz	2001	10276
146 5/8	24 0/8 24 2/8	17 1/8	6 6	Berkshire County	MA	Bill Crine	2001	10276
146 5/8	23 5/8 23 4/8	20 3/8	4 5	Goodsoil	SAS	Lawrence W. Sylvester	2002	10276
146 5/8	23 6/8 22 4/8	20 7/8	5 6	Stone County	AR	Johnathan Thorn	2002	10276
146 5/8	23 1/8 22 2/8	19 0/8	6 6	Chippewa County	WI	Tom Jakubowicz	2002	10276
146 5/8	20 7/8 22 1/8	17 1/8	5 5	Pike County	IL	Scott Ford	2002	10276
146 5/8	22 5/8 22 1/8	16 5/8	6 5	Vilas County	WI	Eric "Shoob" Schumacher	2002	10276
146 5/8	23 0/8 22 6/8	17 6/8	6 6	Dodge County	WI	Jeffrey L. Miller	2002	10276
146 5/8	23 4/8 25 3/8	16 3/8	6 5	Suffolk County	NY	Alexander Rabuyanov	2002	10276
146 5/8	21 4/8 21 5/8	18 3/8	5 5	Tom Green County	TX	Michael Haack	2003	10276
146 5/8	26 1/8 24 2/8	18 4/8	5 5	Suffolk County	NY	Anthony Minichini	2003	10276
146 5/8	23 5/8 23 2/8	13 5/8	5 6	Lafayette County	MO	Christopher Arnold	2003	10276
146 5/8	21 3/8 21 0/8	13 7/8	5 5	Dodge County	WI	Dean Fredrick	2003	10276
146 5/8	22 5/8 21 4/8	18 3/8	5 5	Peoria County	IL	Lee Lewis	2003	10276
146 5/8	25 0/8 24 2/8	18 5/8	5 5	Knox County	IL	Steve L. Larson	2003	10276
146 5/8	23 7/8 23 5/8	14 5/8	6 6	Holmes County	OH	Scott Miller	2003	10276
146 5/8	22 4/8 21 6/8	19 1/8	6 5	Johnson County	KS	James H. Schneider	2004	10276
146 5/8	25 0/8 24 2/8	16 7/8	5 4	Lee County	IL	Rick Farringer	2004	10276
*146 5/8	27 2/8 24 4/8	20 3/8	6 8	Brown County	OH	Adam Engnes	2004	10276
*146 5/8	25 0/8 23 3/8	15 5/8	5 5	Pike County	IL	Harlan Paul	2004	10276
146 5/8	24 7/8 24 7/8	17 3/8	5 4	Clayton County	IA	Mike Then	2004	10276

464

WHITETAIL DEER (TYPICAL ANTLERS)

Minimum Score 125 — Continued

SCORE	R MAIN BEAM L	INSIDE SPREAD	R POINTS L		AREA	STATE/ PROVINCE	HUNTER'S NAME	DATE	RANK
146 5/8	22 7/8 20 2/8	18 5/8	5	5	Mercer County	PA	Daniel T. Schuller, Jr.	2004	10276
146 5/8	24 3/8 24 1/8	19 7/8	6	6	Mineral County	MT	Bill Schusted	2005	10276
146 5/8	26 0/8 26 1/8	18 1/8	4	5	Buffalo County	WI	Jeff Leirmo	2005	10276
146 5/8	21 2/8 21 7/8	16 3/8	5	5	Monroe County	OH	Bob Cover	2005	10276
146 5/8	23 6/8 23 6/8	16 5/8	5	5	Sauk County	WI	Ron E. Beloungy	2005	10276
146 5/8	23 7/8 22 4/8	17 5/8	6	5	Marion County	IA	Gerald T. Dowell	2005	10276
146 5/8	23 5/8 23 4/8	16 1/8	5	5	Montour County	PA	Denis Beachel	2005	10276
*146 5/8	22 5/8 22 5/8	15 7/8	5	5	Clark County	WI	Chad Naedler	2005	10276
146 5/8	24 5/8 23 6/8	18 3/8	4	5	Outagamie County	WI	Mike Ernst	2005	10276
146 5/8	22 6/8 22 2/8	20 5/8	5	6	Cochrane	ALB	Eric R. Smith	2006	10276
146 5/8	24 1/8 23 6/8	17 1/8	5	5	Jefferson County	WI	Danny Gottschalk	2006	10276
146 5/8	24 2/8 24 1/8	17 1/8	5	4	Gage County	NE	Larry Leitow	2006	10276
*146 5/8	23 2/8 23 1/8	17 5/8	5	5	Westchester County	NY	Joseph Randazzo	2006	10276
*146 5/8	23 3/8 21 5/8	18 3/8	4	5	Kosciusko County	IN	John D. Breading	2006	10276
*146 5/8	23 7/8 23 6/8	20 5/8	5	5	Howard County	MO	Kile Kluck	2006	10276
146 5/8	25 0/8 25 0/8	17 5/8	5	5	Rainy River	ONT	Curtis Lanxton	2007	10276
146 5/8	25 0/8 25 4/8	19 7/8	4	4	St. Croix County	WI	Dave Nelson	2007	10276
146 5/8	21 7/8 22 4/8	16 3/8	5	5	Dickey County	ND	Adam Gramlow	2007	10276
*146 5/8	25 2/8 24 5/8	19 7/8	5	5	Houston County	MN	Greg L. Billings	2008	10276
*146 5/8	26 2/8 26 5/8	20 7/8	4	4	St. Joseph County	MI	Jerry G. Miller	2008	10276
146 5/8	23 1/8 22 5/8	18 1/8	5	5	Columbia County	WI	Patrick C. Stollfus	2008	10276
146 5/8	23 2/8 23 1/8	17 7/8	10	7	Waupaca County	WI	Corey W. Janke	2008	10276
146 5/8	21 4/8 21 1/8	16 1/8	5	5	Mills County	IA	William J. Kroll	2008	10276
146 5/8	23 6/8 21 4/8	17 3/8	5	5	Allen County	KS	Scott Jankowski	2008	10276
146 5/8	24 3/8 24 1/8	18 3/8	4	4	Monroe County	OH	Darby Bender, Jr.	2008	10276
146 5/8	22 3/8 23 0/8	20 5/8	5	5	Franklin County	IL	Joe Richardson	2008	10276
*146 5/8	24 7/8 24 7/8	17 3/8	5	5	St. Louis County	MN	Matthew Carpenter	2008	10276
146 5/8	26 0/8 25 4/8	17 5/8	4	4	Wyandot County	OH	John R. Thomas	2009	10276
146 5/8	23 5/8 22 6/8	16 2/8	5	6	Monroe County	IN	Travis Cheeseman	2009	10276
*146 5/8	22 2/8 22 0/8	16 3/8	4	6	Madison County	MS	Robert G. Dye, Sr.	2009	10276
146 5/8	23 5/8 23 3/8	14 4/8	6	6	Waukesha County	WI	Robert J. Duwe	2009	10276
*146 5/8	23 5/8 23 6/8	18 5/8	5	4	Champaign County	OH	John May	2009	10276
*146 5/8	25 0/8 24 6/8	17 1/8	6	5	Fulton County	IL	Brian Smith	2009	10276
146 5/8	25 2/8 25 0/8	18 6/8	5	5	Shawano County	WI	James Lemke	2009	10276
146 4/8	22 0/8 22 1/8	17 4/8	5	5	Wood County	WI	George Davis	1967	10390
146 4/8	24 4/8 24 0/8	15 0/8	5	5	Amherst County	VA	Garry B. Pruitt	1972	10390
146 4/8	22 0/8 23 3/8	18 0/8	5	5	Vigo County	IN	Richard E. Smith	1973	10390
146 4/8	25 0/8 24 7/8	18 6/8	5	5	Cayuga County	NY	John Andrews, Sr.	1974	10390
146 4/8	24 2/8 25 2/8	17 6/8	6	5	Christian County	IL	Camron Fitzsimmons	1980	10390
146 4/8	23 0/8 24 6/8	19 1/8	6	6	Ashland County	WI	Chris Westlund	1982	10390
146 4/8	26 4/8 25 2/8	17 4/8	4	5	Polk County	MO	James Scott Hogan	1982	10390
146 4/8	24 3/8 24 5/8	18 6/8	4	4	Greene County	IL	Daniel E. Kallal	1983	10390
146 4/8	21 5/8 21 2/8	15 0/8	5	5	Forest County	WI	Eugene A. Pribek	1985	10390
146 4/8	22 3/8 22 7/8	16 0/8	5	5	Ritchie County	WV	Tim Jividen	1985	10390
146 4/8	24 0/8 23 6/8	16 2/8	4	4	Randolph County	IL	Edward J. Lannon	1985	10390
146 4/8	23 0/8 22 5/8	13 4/8	6	6	Trempealeau County	WI	Greg J. Halama	1986	10390
146 4/8	23 4/8 25 3/8	17 0/8	7	7	Washington County	WI	Eric Handeland	1986	10390
146 4/8	26 2/8 26 4/8	18 2/8	5	5	Jackson County	AR	Doug C. Cockrill	1986	10390
146 4/8	22 3/8 22 3/8	17 0/8	4	4	Dunn County	ND	Todd W. Boechler	1986	10390
146 4/8	24 4/8 24 4/8	19 4/8	4	5	Pulaski County	KY	Bobbie Ryan	1986	10390
146 4/8	23 3/8 24 1/8	17 4/8	5	5	Le Sueur County	MN	Joe Rybus	1987	10390
146 4/8	24 6/8 23 4/8	19 4/8	5	5	Rock County	WI	Gary Hookstead	1987	10390
146 4/8	23 3/8 23 2/8	17 7/8	6	5	Cottonwood County	MN	Steven L. Erickson	1987	10390
146 4/8	25 0/8 24 1/8	19 2/8	5	5	Mercer County	NJ	Robert Pazdan	1988	10390
146 4/8	23 1/8 23 4/8	16 4/8	5	5	Langlade County	WI	Dale G. Kemp	1988	10390
146 4/8	22 0/8 21 5/8	17 3/8	6	5	Randolph County	IL	Dale Scherle	1988	10390
146 4/8	24 2/8 23 1/8	19 0/8	5	5	Benton County	IA	Norm Madison	1988	10390
146 4/8	25 0/8 25 7/8	19 0/8	5	7	Greene County	IL	Clayton Whitlock	1989	10390
146 4/8	23 0/8 23 4/8	19 0/8	5	4	Waukesha County	WI	Steven Hamann	1989	10390
146 4/8	25 0/8 25 6/8	16 4/8	5	5	Nelson County	VA	Larry W. Toms	1989	10390
146 4/8	23 0/8 23 4/8	16 0/8	5	5	Boone County	AR	Phillip Vanderpool	1990	10390
146 4/8	25 0/8 24 1/8	21 2/8	5	4	Putnam County	IN	Randy Nippe	1990	10390
146 4/8	27 6/8 25 6/8	18 2/8	5	6	Middlesex County	MA	Jared Apostolakes	1990	10390
146 4/8	23 5/8 23 3/8	18 4/8	5	5	Okotoks	ALB	Randy Brown	1991	10390
146 4/8	23 4/8 24 0/8	24 1/8	5	5	Randolph County	AR	Darrell Hagood	1992	10390
146 4/8	23 5/8 23 6/8	19 7/8	5	5	Union County	KY	Richard Mehlbauer	1992	10390
146 4/8	24 4/8 23 5/8	18 6/8	5	5	Henry County	OH	Doug Michaelis	1992	10390
146 4/8	24 6/8 25 2/8	22 0/8	5	5	Cass County	IL	Carl H. Musch	1992	10390
146 4/8	23 0/8 22 6/8	18 4/8	5	5	Henry County	IA	Jack Bates	1992	10390
146 4/8	23 3/8 22 4/8	19 6/8	5	5	Decatur County	KS	Dave Wilson	1992	10390
146 4/8	26 4/8 24 5/8	18 7/8	8	6	Cass County	MO	John Gardner	1994	10390
146 4/8	23 6/8 23 5/8	19 2/8	4	5	Vilas County	WI	Eugene A. Pribek	1994	10390
146 4/8	23 1/8 23 0/8	18 4/8	5	5	Brown County	OH	Bernard J. Waters	1994	10390
146 4/8	23 4/8 24 0/8	19 6/8	6	5	Cook County	IL	Daniel H. Albaugh	1994	10390
146 4/8	23 0/8 21 2/8	16 0/8	6	5	Macon County	MO	Dean Mayfield	1994	10390
146 4/8	24 5/8 23 6/8	18 4/8	4	4	Coles County	IL	Mike Finney	1995	10390
146 4/8	24 1/8 24 7/8	15 6/8	4	4	Thurston County	NE	Mike Lutt	1995	10390
146 4/8	24 1/8 23 0/8	21 7/8	6	5	Van Buren County	IA	Jim Chambers	1995	10390
146 4/8	21 6/8 22 7/8	15 5/8	6	5	Chippewa County	WI	Dale Helland	1995	10390
146 4/8	20 0/8 20 2/8	16 4/8	5	6	Brown County	SD	Brad Dinger	1995	10390
146 4/8	23 7/8 23 4/8	20 6/8	4	4	Jefferson County	PA	James Kotch	1997	10390
146 4/8	21 7/8 22 5/8	14 5/8	5	6	Edgar County	IL	Jeff Stuthers	1997	10390
146 4/8	23 3/8 22 3/8	18 4/8	5	5	Eau Claire County	WI	Riley Fletschock	1997	10390
146 4/8	24 2/8 21 7/8	17 2/8	5	6	Menard County	IL	Ron Wadsworth	1997	10390
146 4/8	25 2/8 23 7/8	19 2/8	5	5	Hennepin County	MN	David A. Mundahl	1997	10390
146 4/8	25 4/8 23 4/8	16 5/8	7	6	Oakland County	MI	Tim Bostwick	1997	10390
146 4/8	24 4/8 22 3/8	20 0/8	5	5	Allamakee County	IA	Rich Buchli	1997	10390
146 4/8	24 2/8 24 7/8	18 4/8	4	4	Adams County	OH	George P. Hehr	1997	10390
146 4/8	23 4/8 23 6/8	17 5/8	6	8	Muskingum County	OH	Bryan Cooper	1997	10390
146 4/8	23 4/8 23 1/8	17 5/8	6	6	Montgomery County	TN	Walter Wright	1998	10390
146 4/8	22 3/8 23 2/8	22 4/8	5	5	Richland County	WI	Kerry Knutson	1998	10390
146 4/8	24 1/8 23 4/8	18 4/8	5	5	Iowa County	WI	David Tuskowski	1998	10390
146 4/8	24 0/8 23 0/8	17 6/8	5	5	Hocking County	OH	Ray Vining	1998	10390
146 4/8	23 6/8 24 0/8	19 2/8	4	5	Osage County	KS	Mike Vandevord	1998	10390
146 4/8	23 0/8 22 1/8	15 6/8	5	5	Hardin County	OH	Jeff Hites	1998	10390

465

WHITETAIL DEER (TYPICAL ANTLERS)

Minimum Score 125   Continued

SCORE	LENGTH OF R MAIN BEAM L	INSIDE SPREAD	NUMBER OF R POINTS L	AREA	STATE/ PROVINCE	HUNTER'S NAME	DATE	RANK
146 4/8	23 4/8 23 4/8	20 2/8	5 4	Shawano County	WI	Mark Pukall	1999	10390
146 4/8	19 6/8 23 5/8	21 6/8	5 5	St. Louis County	MO	David Hasekamp	1999	10390
146 4/8	20 4/8 21 6/8	18 2/8	5 5	Grundy County	IL	Danny Salyers	1999	10390
146 4/8	26 0/8 25 6/8	18 2/8	4 4	Dubuque County	IA	Jon M. Roraff	1999	10390
146 4/8	24 6/8 24 2/8	17 4/8	5 5	Monroe County	IA	William Weatherman	1999	10390
146 4/8	23 7/8 23 0/8	17 0/8	5 5	Speers	SAS	Kenneth S. Rebeyka	2000	10390
146 4/8	23 7/8 22 5/8	20 6/8	5 5	Buffalo County	WI	Robert A. Arbs	2000	10390
146 4/8	23 1/8 22 5/8	16 6/8	5 5	Lancaster County	NE	Darrell Schroeppel	2000	10390
146 4/8	25 0/8 26 1/8	19 4/8	4 4	Frederick County	MD	Edward Reilly	2000	10390
146 4/8	23 4/8 23 0/8	18 4/8	5 5	Buffalo County	WI	Joe Simerson	2000	10390
146 4/8	26 6/8 27 0/8	20 2/8	4 5	Livingston County	NY	Paul Kennedy	2000	10390
146 4/8	25 2/8 24 5/8	18 4/8	6 4	Jones County	IA	Tracy L. Chappell	2001	10390
146 4/8	27 3/8 25 1/8	16 2/8	5 4	Buffalo County	WI	Greg Reedy	2001	10390
146 4/8	24 3/8 24 1/8	20 2/8	5 5	Caledon East	ONT	Carl Whittier	2001	10390
146 4/8	21 3/8 21 3/8	16 6/8	6 6	Zavala County	TX	Robert Barrie	2001	10390
146 4/8	23 1/8 23 5/8	20 6/8	6 5	Dodge County	WI	Nathan Huebner	2002	10390
146 4/8	23 5/8 25 2/8	17 2/8	5 5	Monona County	IA	Mike Conlon	2002	10390
146 4/8	22 2/8 21 4/8	14 0/8	9 8	Harford County	MD	Forest Wiest	2002	10390
146 4/8	19 2/8 20 1/8	17 7/8	7 6	Traill County	ND	Pam Baird	2003	10390
146 4/8	22 2/8 22 5/8	17 0/8	5 6	Spokane County	WA	Charles Stivers	2003	10390
146 4/8	21 6/8 22 1/8	20 6/8	6 6	Waupaca County	WI	Gary Beyersdorf	2003	10390
146 4/8	24 5/8 23 2/8	19 6/8	4 4	Vinton County	OH	James Anthony	2003	10390
*146 4/8	22 3/8 23 6/8	16 2/8	5 5	Texas County	MO	Wade White	2003	10390
146 4/8	25 5/8 25 1/8	20 4/8	6 5	Dodge County	NE	Jeff Weidert	2003	10390
*146 4/8	24 7/8 25 2/8	23 2/8	5 4	Green Lake County	WI	Mark R. Bornick	2003	10390
*146 4/8	25 5/8 25 6/8	15 2/8	5 5	Chautauqua County	NY	William R. Haskins	2003	10390
146 4/8	24 4/8 24 4/8	21 0/8	4 5	Richland County	OH	Keith D. Levendorf	2003	10390
146 4/8	18 6/8 21 0/8	17 0/8	7 6	Pike County	IL	Frank S. Monberger	2003	10390
146 4/8	23 7/8 25 0/8	18 3/8	6 6	Lyon County	KS	Johnny Drake	2003	10390
146 4/8	22 0/8 22 7/8	15 0/8	5 9	Putnam County	MO	Anthony L. Kottwitz	2003	10390
146 4/8	25 5/8 25 6/8	18 4/8	6 7	Gray County	KS	Andrew McIntire	2004	10390
146 4/8	22 3/8 21 3/8	15 2/8	5 5	Pike County	IN	Kevin L. Woods	2004	10390
146 4/8	22 7/8 23 0/8	19 1/8	5 6	Waushara County	WI	Scott D. Palmer	2004	10390
146 4/8	24 7/8 25 1/8	19 2/8	5 5	Olmsted County	MN	William W. Van Vugt	2004	10390
*146 4/8	21 6/8 23 4/8	18 0/8	4 5	Will County	IL	Andrew W. Manukas	2004	10390
146 4/8	27 1/8 27 3/8	21 3/8	6 6	Elkhart County	IN	Mark A. McDowell	2004	10390
146 4/8	22 3/8 22 7/8	17 6/8	5 5	Rock Island County	IL	Mikel Angel	2005	10390
*146 4/8	22 6/8 21 6/8	18 2/8	6 5	Calumet County	WI	Brett Wilkens	2006	10390
146 4/8	24 3/8 23 6/8	19 6/8	5 5	Fergus County	MT	Derek Mellum	2006	10390
*146 4/8	25 4/8 25 4/8	20 6/8	4 5	Douglas County	MO	Daniel L. Sisco	2006	10390
146 4/8	23 2/8 24 2/8	20 2/8	6 5	Kane County	IL	Michael Ahlman	2006	10390
146 4/8	26 4/8 25 4/8	17 1/8	5 7	Marquette County	WI	Steve Abitz	2006	10390
*146 4/8	23 1/8 23 7/8	18 2/8	6 5	Waushara County	WI	Scott Wilson	2006	10390
146 4/8	21 5/8 21 6/8	17 6/8	5 5	Latah County	ID	Josh Chandler	2007	10390
*146 4/8	26 6/8 25 3/8	16 4/8	4 4	Franklin County	IN	Chris Monroe	2007	10390
146 4/8	22 4/8 23 6/8	16 2/8	4 4	White County	IL	Anthony Firrello, Jr.	2007	10390
146 4/8	23 1/8 22 7/8	16 4/8	5 5	Dubuque County	IA	Martin Kearney	2007	10390
146 4/8	22 2/8 22 3/8	16 2/8	6 6	Clay County	IN	David M. Cruser	2007	10390
146 4/8	25 4/8 25 5/8	21 0/8	4 4	Niagara County	NY	Chris Gatehouse	2007	10390
*146 4/8	24 5/8 24 6/8	21 0/8	6 8	Reynolds County	MO	Steven Watson	2007	10390
*146 4/8	23 0/8 23 2/8	16 6/8	5 6	Juneau County	WI	Richard R. Hale	2007	10390
146 4/8	24 4/8 22 6/8	18 4/8	6 6	Buffalo County	WI	Ken P. Schlager	2007	10390
146 4/8	24 2/8 25 1/8	18 6/8	5 5	Iowa County	WI	Thomas Ridgeman	2007	10390
146 4/8	21 2/8 21 4/8	18 3/8	6 6	Carroll County	IL	Rick Candos	2007	10390
146 4/8	23 5/8 24 3/8	16 6/8	5 5	McHenry County	IL	John Behm	2008	10390
*146 4/8	23 6/8 23 7/8	16 2/8	5 5	Roane County	TN	George Headden, Jr.	2008	10390
146 4/8	26 2/8 24 4/8	18 1/8	5 7	Olmsted County	MN	Rick Mattson	2008	10390
*146 4/8	24 5/8 25 0/8	19 6/8	7 7	Adams County	IA	Brad Herring	2008	10390
146 4/8	25 0/8 25 5/8	19 4/8	4 4	Greene County	IN	Jeremy Graber	2008	10390
146 4/8	24 2/8 24 1/8	17 2/8	4 4	Allamakee County	IA	Dr. Kevin Harmon	2008	10390
146 4/8	27 0/8 26 7/8	18 1/8	5 6	Worth County	GA	Brian McClure	2009	10390
146 4/8	22 2/8 22 4/8	15 4/8	4 6	St. Louis County	MO	Thomas J. Bock	2009	10390
*146 4/8	22 7/8 23 2/8	19 0/8	4 4	Jackson County	WI	Kirk Goetzka	2009	10390
146 4/8	22 6/8 22 2/8	20 3/8	6 5	Marquette County	WI	Arlyn Johnson	2009	10390
146 4/8	21 2/8 21 5/8	16 5/8	8 7	Will County	IL	Jim Saunoris, Jr.	2009	10390
*146 4/8	25 4/8 25 5/8	17 4/8	5 6	Dimmit County	TX	Peter Meaden	2009	10390
146 3/8	23 5/8 23 1/8	27 1/8	5 5	De Kalb County	IN	Stanley Bremer	1969	10517
146 3/8	24 6/8 24 5/8	15 3/8	5 5	Palo Alto County	IA	Kim E. Gustafson	1972	10517
146 3/8	22 7/8 22 4/8	17 1/8	5 5	Shiawassee County	MI	David Asberry	1978	10517
146 3/8	23 1/8 23 6/8	19 2/8	6 6	Chase County	KS	Jim Wilson	1980	10517
146 3/8	23 5/8 23 5/8	20 1/8	5 5	Hamilton County	OH	Jerome R. Buschle, Jr.	1981	10517
146 3/8	23 1/8 23 1/8	17 5/8	4 5	Cecil County	MD	John M. Martino	1981	10517
146 3/8	23 5/8 23 1/8	16 1/8	5 5	Jo Daviess County	IL	David R. Kammerude	1983	10517
146 3/8	22 5/8 22 1/8	16 7/8	6 6	Floyd County	IA	Mike Bull	1983	10517
146 3/8	24 0/8 22 2/8	19 1/8	5 5	Perry County	IL	Richard Kuhnert	1984	10517
146 3/8	24 6/8 25 7/8	20 7/8	5 5	Hamilton County	OH	Bob Miller	1985	10517
146 3/8	24 7/8 23 1/8	19 1/8	5 5	Whitley County	IN	Bradley S. Kissinger	1986	10517
146 3/8	21 0/8 22 0/8	16 1/8	5 5	Wilson County	KS	Kevin D. O'Neill	1986	10517
146 3/8	22 1/8 22 1/8	16 5/8	5 5	Blue Earth County	MN	Paul Busse	1987	10517
146 3/8	23 2/8 24 3/8	17 7/8	4 4	Montgomery County	IL	John Snoddy	1987	10517
146 3/8	23 5/8 23 5/8	19 4/8	5 5	Van Buren County	IA	Clint O'Day	1988	10517
146 3/8	22 6/8 22 2/8	16 3/8	5 5	St. Francis County	AR	Johnny Smith	1989	10517
146 3/8	24 0/8 24 0/8	20 3/8	4 4	Isanti County	MN	Kevin Caldwell	1990	10517
146 3/8	24 0/8 23 2/8	17 3/8	6 5	Brown County	WI	Robert M. McLellan	1990	10517
146 3/8	22 6/8 22 7/8	14 7/8	6 6	Polk County	WI	Barry Peterson	1991	10517
146 3/8	25 4/8 25 0/8	15 4/8	7 6	Shelby County	MO	William P. McQuillen	1991	10517
146 3/8	22 5/8 21 5/8	15 5/8	5 5	Hennepin County	MN	Greg Wermerskirchen	1991	10517
146 3/8	22 4/8 23 4/8	17 5/8	5 5	McHenry County	IL	Donald E. Hoey	1991	10517
146 3/8	24 0/8 24 2/8	19 1/8	4 4	Kane County	IL	Richard Hight	1993	10517
146 3/8	22 6/8 22 4/8	16 4/8	5 5	Sauk County	WI	Bill H. Overson	1993	10517
146 3/8	21 1/8 21 6/8	17 5/8	6 6	Adams County	IA	Bryant Shermoe	1993	10517
146 3/8	20 0/8 21 4/8	15 5/8	5 7	Kenedy County	TX	John W. Wallace	1993	10517
146 3/8	23 4/8 23 7/8	20 0/8	6 6	Cass County	ND	Mark R. Thompson	1993	10517
146 3/8	22 2/8 23 0/8	18 7/8	7 6	Morrison County	MN	John Teschendorf	1994	10517
146 3/8	23 7/8 23 5/8	19 5/8	5 5	Logan County	IL	William Bruner	1994	10517

WHITETAIL DEER (TYPICAL ANTLERS)

Minimum Score 125
Continued

SCORE	LENGTH OF R MAIN BEAM L	INSIDE SPREAD	NUMBER OF R POINTS L	AREA	STATE/ PROVINCE	HUNTER'S NAME	DATE	RANK
146 3/8	24 4/8 24 4/8	16 2/8	9 7	Stewart County	TN	John C. Hults	1995	10517
146 3/8	24 3/8 24 6/8	19 1/8	5 6	Clay County	SD	Richard Brown	1995	10517
146 3/8	25 7/8 26 4/8	19 0/8	6 6	Columbia County	WI	Larry Owens	1995	10517
146 3/8	24 4/8 24 0/8	19 3/8	5 5	Waupaca County	WI	Phil T. Knutzen	1996	10517
146 3/8	24 4/8 25 0/8	18 7/8	4 4	Auglaize County	OH	Ron Wireman	1996	10517
146 3/8	23 2/8 23 1/8	19 1/8	5 6	Sanilac County	MI	William B. Thrash III	1997	10517
146 3/8	21 4/8 22 2/8	15 4/8	6 5	Oakland County	MI	Dwight D. Paslean	1997	10517
146 3/8	26 5/8 26 2/8	20 3/8	5 5	Peoria County	IL	Steven W. Nelson	1997	10517
146 3/8	23 5/8 23 3/8	17 1/8	5 5	New Sarepta	ALB	Dale Fennema	1997	10517
146 3/8	26 7/8 26 0/8	16 1/8	4 4	Knox County	IN	Virgil Lane	1997	10517
146 3/8	22 0/8 22 3/8	16 1/8	5 5	Jefferson County	KS	John Welborn	1997	10517
146 3/8	23 3/8 23 0/8	16 3/8	5 6	Iowa County	WI	Larry G. Fesenfeld	1998	10517
146 3/8	24 5/8 24 4/8	17 1/8	5 5	Wayne County	NY	Mark C. Meyer	1998	10517
146 3/8	26 6/8 26 5/8	22 3/8	4 4	Jo Daviess County	IL	James G. Harkness	1998	10517
146 3/8	26 0/8 25 6/8	19 1/8	5 5	Hardin County	OH	Ray Davis, Jr.	1998	10517
146 3/8	20 3/8 21 0/8	15 1/8	5 5	Van Buren County	IA	Todd Fellows	1998	10517
146 3/8	22 7/8 22 6/8	17 1/8	6 5	Columbia County	WI	Clarence Yaeger	1999	10517
146 3/8	23 4/8 24 0/8	17 1/8	6 8	Tuscarawas County	OH	Dave Blake	1999	10517
146 3/8	24 0/8 24 1/8	13 3/8	5 5	Oktibbeha County	MS	Rodney Kendrick	2000	10517
146 3/8	27 1/8 27 3/8	18 5/8	5 7	Oldham County	KY	W. Austin Musselman, Jr.	2000	10517
146 3/8	25 2/8 25 0/8	17 7/8	7 6	Baca County	CO	Roger A. Smithson	2000	10517
146 3/8	24 4/8 23 2/8	14 7/8	7 6	Richardson County	NE	Daniel J. Jones	2000	10517
146 3/8	22 6/8 23 1/8	18 3/8	6 6	Washington County	NE	Steven T. Pierce	2000	10517
146 3/8	23 0/8 22 4/8	16 7/8	5 5	Martin County	IN	Steven W. Sargent	2000	10517
146 3/8	25 4/8 25 4/8	16 1/8	5 5	Belmont County	OH	Shane Skinner	2000	10517
146 3/8	23 3/8 24 0/8	22 1/8	5 5	Hamilton County	IA	Heath Brock	2000	10517
146 3/8	24 4/8 24 4/8	18 3/8	6 5	Anoka County	MN	Bill Slowikowski	2000	10517
146 3/8	25 2/8 26 1/8	16 3/8	5 5	Hartford County	CT	Ronald Bodach	2001	10517
146 3/8	23 1/8 23 7/8	19 1/8	5 7	La Porte County	IN	Roger J. Roy, Jr.	2001	10517
146 3/8	23 0/8 23 2/8	19 7/8	5 5	Assiniboine River	MAN	Adam Bartsch	2001	10517
146 3/8	22 4/8 23 1/8	15 7/8	5 4	Kingsbury County	SD	Frank Virchow	2001	10517
146 3/8	23 4/8 23 3/8	19 7/8	7 6	Adams County	IL	Raymond L. Voss	2002	10517
*146 3/8	22 7/8 21 4/8	19 7/8	5 5	Fayette County	IL	Rodney Hunt	2002	10517
146 3/8	25 4/8 26 0/8	17 3/8	6 6	Olmsted County	MN	Richard A. Cordie	2002	10517
146 3/8	22 7/8 22 4/8	16 3/8	6 5	Marquette County	WI	David J. Kannel	2002	10517
146 3/8	22 5/8 21 6/8	16 7/8	5 5	Montgomery County	IN	Larry A. Culley	2002	10517
146 3/8	23 4/8 24 4/8	21 1/8	5 5	Howard County	TX	David L. Duncan	2003	10517
146 3/8	23 2/8 23 0/8	15 0/8	6 8	Jackson County	MO	Richard Pemberton	2003	10517
146 3/8	20 4/8 20 7/8	18 5/8	5 5	Ashland County	WI	Douglas B. Thorp	2003	10517
146 3/8	24 5/8 24 0/8	16 5/8	5 5	Knox County	MO	Jeff Gentry	2003	10517
146 3/8	25 4/8 25 3/8	15 3/8	4 6	St. Louis County	MO	Jay T. Powell	2003	10517
146 3/8	24 2/8 24 1/8	16 1/8	5 5	Portage County	WI	Bryan C. Herro	2003	10517
146 3/8	22 0/8 22 5/8	20 7/8	5 5	Green County	WI	Randy L. Goebel	2003	10517
146 3/8	24 2/8 24 3/8	17 1/8	5 4	Lawrence County	SD	Matthew Neisen	2003	10517
146 3/8	21 4/8 21 5/8	19 2/8	5 6	Montgomery County	MD	Glenn E. Hawkins	2004	10517
146 3/8	23 2/8 23 5/8	17 5/8	5 5	New Haven County	CT	Chris Herold	2004	10517
*146 3/8	23 6/8 24 3/8	14 1/8	5 5	Callaway County	MO	Richard Snow	2004	10517
*146 3/8	22 6/8 21 3/8	19 1/8	6 5	Saline County	IL	Nick Dennison	2004	10517
146 3/8	25 3/8 25 2/8	16 7/8	4 5	Holt County	MO	Dave Heath	2004	10517
*146 3/8	24 1/8 23 2/8	18 7/8	5 8	Dunn County	WI	Chad Gaedtke	2004	10517
146 3/8	24 4/8 23 6/8	18 2/8	5 6	Chesterfield County	VA	Mark E. Rapalee	2004	10517
146 3/8	21 0/8 21 1/8	19 6/8	6 5	St. Croix County	WI	Kelsey Iverson	2004	10517
146 3/8	24 0/8 24 2/8	17 3/8	6 5	Winona County	MN	Bob Micheel	2005	10517
*146 3/8	23 0/8 23 3/8	18 5/8	6 6	Saunders County	NE	Brett Scheuler	2005	10517
146 3/8	23 6/8 23 5/8	17 3/8	6 7	Clarke County	VA	Larry R. Tumblin, Sr.	2005	10517
146 3/8	25 6/8 26 3/8	21 6/8	4 5	Pike County	IL	Michael C. Melton	2005	10517
146 3/8	23 1/8 23 0/8	16 3/8	6 5	Brown County	IN	Gordon Braun	2006	10517
146 3/8	26 0/8 25 3/8	21 1/8	7 7	Erie County	PA	Joseph Evanoff	2006	10517
146 3/8	27 1/8 26 1/8	22 5/8	4 5	Lancaster County	VA	Stephen H. James	2006	10517
146 3/8	26 6/8 27 6/8	16 4/8	4 7	Brown County	OH	Chuck Conti	2006	10517
146 3/8	22 4/8 22 3/8	17 3/8	5 5	Jackson County	IL	Tim Cobin	2006	10517
146 3/8	20 4/8 20 1/8	14 7/8	5 5	Randolph County	MO	Web D. Winfrey	2007	10517
146 3/8	24 6/8 24 2/8	18 2/8	5 5	Comanche County	KS	Gary Head	2007	10517
146 3/8	23 5/8 22 6/8	18 7/8	6 6	Susquehanna County	PA	Aaron Harvatine	2007	10517
146 3/8	23 2/8 21 4/8	17 7/8	6 6	Iowa County	WI	Mark Argue	2007	10517
*146 3/8	21 6/8 21 7/8	18 1/8	7 6	Butler County	KY	Doug Grindstaff	2007	10517
146 3/8	22 7/8 23 4/8	18 6/8	6 4	Boone County	KY	James J. Alsip	2007	10517
146 3/8	25 4/8 25 1/8	20 7/8	5 6	Warren County	NJ	Eric Burgess	2007	10517
146 3/8	24 5/8 24 5/8	19 3/8	5 5	Refugio County	TX	Robert R. White	2007	10517
146 3/8	23 2/8 24 0/8	19 5/8	6 6	Logan County	KY	Stanley Meacham	2008	10517
146 3/8	24 4/8 24 3/8	18 7/8	7 6	Gwinnett County	GA	Jerry H. Mann	2008	10517
146 3/8	23 0/8 23 1/8	19 0/8	5 4	Trempealeau County	WI	Ray N. Andersen	2008	10517
*146 3/8	23 2/8 23 2/8	15 7/8	5 5	Houston County	MN	Lon E. Bleess	2008	10517
*146 3/8	23 3/8 22 5/8	15 5/8	6 5	Starke County	IN	Jacob Zachary	2008	10517
146 3/8	25 0/8 25 7/8	18 6/8	6 6	Vermilion County	IL	James Brown	2008	10517
146 3/8	25 7/8 25 5/8	19 3/8	5 6	Franklin County	MA	Brian L. Young	2008	10517
146 3/8	24 4/8 25 4/8	22 2/8	7 5	Macoupin County	IL	John Pocklington, Jr.	2008	10517
146 3/8	24 7/8 24 7/8	20 5/8	6 5	Edmonton	ALB	Gunther Tondeleir	2008	10517
146 3/8	20 4/8 21 5/8	16 7/8	5 5	Edmonton	ALB	Gunther Tondeleir	2008	10517
*146 3/8	25 0/8 25 0/8	19 5/8	5 8	Carroll County	OH	Cody D. Stark	2009	10517
*146 3/8	25 2/8 24 6/8	15 1/8	5 6	Athens County	OH	Matthew Watson	2009	10517
146 3/8	22 2/8 24 4/8	16 0/8	6 7	Duval County	TX	E. J. Hale	2009	10517
*146 3/8	23 1/8 24 5/8	18 3/8	4 4	Ripley County	IN	Joe Cole	2009	10517
146 3/8	23 2/8 24 6/8	17 6/8	5 4	Platte County	MO	Tom Cannon	2009	10517
146 2/8	24 3/8 24 1/8	18 2/8	5 5	Stearns County	MN	Mike Beuning	1945	10630
146 2/8	26 5/8 25 6/8	20 6/8	5 5	Plymouth County	IA	Cash N. Howe	1974	10630
146 2/8	24 6/8 24 1/8	18 2/8	5 5	Butler County	KS	David R. Rogers	1976	10630
146 2/8	21 2/8 21 7/8	21 2/8	5 5	Clark County	KS	Danny R. Fenton	1977	10630
146 2/8	22 7/8 23 5/8	16 5/8	6 6	Lafayette County	WI	Wayne Gassman	1977	10630
146 2/8	24 4/8 24 6/8	15 6/8	4 4	Clark County	IL	Gerald Shaffner	1978	10630
146 2/8	25 1/8 24 2/8	20 2/8	6 4	Union County	OH	Charles Yoakum	1980	10630
146 2/8	24 6/8 24 0/8	19 1/8	5 7	Berkeley County	SC	Hugh Gaskins	1980	10630
146 2/8	25 2/8 25 0/8	17 2/8	5 6	Graham County	KS	Russell Hull	1982	10630
146 2/8	23 6/8 22 5/8	18 0/8	5 5	Brown County	OH	Ronald Akins	1982	10630
146 2/8	24 4/8 24 3/8	19 4/8	5 4	Washington County	WI	J.J. Ziegler	1983	10630

467

WHITETAIL DEER (TYPICAL ANTLERS)

Minimum Score 125 — Continued

SCORE	LENGTH OF R MAIN BEAM L	INSIDE SPREAD	NUMBER OF R POINTS L		AREA	STATE/ PROVINCE	HUNTER'S NAME	DATE	RANK
146 2/8	24 6/8 24 5/8	19 4/8	5	5	Lafayette County	WI	Roger Wand	1983	10630
146 2/8	24 0/8 24 5/8	18 2/8	6	6	Dane County	WI	Roland G. Lettman	1983	10630
146 2/8	26 7/8 26 3/8	16 5/8	7	6	Granville County	NC	Bradley Brann	1984	10630
146 2/8	22 2/8 21 6/8	16 5/8	5	6	Parkland County	ALB	Michel Carigan	1984	10630
146 2/8	26 1/8 25 0/8	18 6/8	5	5	St. Lawrence County	NY	Joseph W. Pudney	1985	10630
146 2/8	25 0/8 22 7/8	14 4/8	4	4	Van Buren County	IA	Tom Weigand	1985	10630
146 2/8	22 6/8 22 0/8	17 5/8	5	6	Dodge County	MN	David Lyke	1985	10630
146 2/8	22 5/8 23 6/8	17 6/8	6	6	Ontonagon County	MI	Paul M. Kilpela	1986	10630
146 2/8	24 3/8 24 5/8	19 1/8	5	6	Redwood County	MN	R. Tetrick/M. Tetrick	1986	10630
146 2/8	24 1/8 25 6/8	20 6/8	6	5	Lake County	IL	Kenneth D. Staples	1986	10630
146 2/8	25 5/8 25 0/8	17 6/8	6	4	Pike County	OH	John Ribic	1987	10630
146 2/8	20 5/8 21 6/8	15 2/8	5	5	Jackson County	MI	Dale M. Leach	1987	10630
146 2/8	24 0/8 22 7/8	19 6/8	4	4	Greenwood County	KS	Brian Deer	1987	10630
146 2/8	21 4/8 22 2/8	18 2/8	6	6	Livingston County	IL	Tom Roe	1989	10630
146 2/8	22 3/8 22 3/8	19 1/8	6	6	Fayette County	IA	Thomas D. Joyner, Jr.	1990	10630
146 2/8	26 6/8 26 6/8	19 4/8	6	5	Pike County	IL	Robert L. Cox	1991	10630
146 2/8	22 4/8 22 2/8	15 1/8	5	5	Sedgwick County	KS	Larry Buchholz	1991	10630
146 2/8	25 0/8 24 3/8	18 4/8	9	7	Cowley County	KS	Larry J. McKean	1991	10630
146 2/8	22 7/8 22 1/8	16 1/8	6	6	Morrison County	MN	Randy Loken	1991	10630
146 2/8	21 2/8 21 4/8	15 3/8	7	6	Eau Claire County	WI	Terry Mueller	1993	10630
146 2/8	22 6/8 23 1/8	20 4/8	5	5	Belmont County	OH	William P. Koval	1993	10630
146 2/8	24 4/8 24 4/8	20 6/8	5	6	Webb County	TX	Norman Speer	1993	10630
146 2/8	23 0/8 23 2/8	18 0/8	5	5	Uvalde County	TX	Michael R. Geller	1993	10630
146 2/8	21 3/8 21 3/8	17 7/8	7	8	Cascade County	MT	Bruce Davidson	1994	10630
146 2/8	22 0/8 21 3/8	16 5/8	6	7	Jefferson County	WI	Jeff McKenzie	1994	10630
146 2/8	22 3/8 22 2/8	19 2/8	6	6	St. Joseph County	IN	Michael R. Ebersole	1994	10630
146 2/8	25 1/8 24 2/8	19 6/8	6	6	Kankakee County	IL	Jim Brandt	1994	10630
146 2/8	23 6/8 23 0/8	19 0/8	5	5	Douglas County	WI	Travis D. Hicks	1994	10630
146 2/8	26 5/8 24 4/8	20 0/8	6	7	Stearns County	MN	Steven H. Moon	1994	10630
146 2/8	22 3/8 21 5/8	17 2/8	5	7	Louisa County	IA	Robert Walker	1994	10630
146 2/8	23 0/8 24 6/8	20 1/8	6	5	Cross County	AR	Aaron W. Curtis III	1995	10630
146 2/8	25 4/8 25 0/8	19 0/8	5	4	Grant County	WI	Charles P. Fralick	1995	10630
146 2/8	22 7/8 23 3/8	19 7/8	5	6	Massac County	IL	Thomas L. Adkins	1995	10630
146 2/8	23 1/8 23 7/8	15 4/8	5	6	Oneida County	WI	Don Psenicka	1995	10630
146 2/8	24 4/8 24 3/8	16 6/8	5	5	Kent County	MI	Frederick H. Syswerda	1995	10630
146 2/8	21 7/8 22 0/8	15 2/8	5	5	Rock County	WI	Robert W. Doerr	1995	10630
146 2/8	21 1/8 22 3/8	20 0/8	6	5	Logan County	WV	Danny Lee Bourne	1995	10630
146 2/8	26 0/8 25 4/8	19 1/8	6	6	Chester County	PA	Joe Joyce	1996	10630
146 2/8	22 4/8 22 4/8	17 2/8	7	6	Buffalo County	WI	Brian Potter	1996	10630
146 2/8	20 6/8 19 5/8	20 3/8	6	5	Fulton County	IL	Greg Pauli	1996	10630
146 2/8	21 4/8 21 3/8	16 6/8	6	6	Bayfield County	WI	Eric Carlson	1996	10630
146 2/8	22 4/8 23 1/8	18 2/8	4	5	Queen Annes County	MD	Marc D. Weiss	1998	10630
146 2/8	24 2/8 24 4/8	19 1/8	6	6	Pike County	IL	Michael Aebel	1998	10630
146 2/8	23 0/8 23 4/8	15 2/8	6	7	Ferry County	WA	Antonio P. Bamba	1998	10630
146 2/8	23 1/8 23 6/8	18 6/8	7	7	Crawford County	PA	Dale A. Prusia	1999	10630
146 2/8	25 6/8 25 3/8	17 0/8	4	4	Forest County	WI	Dale Babcock	1999	10630
146 2/8	26 1/8 26 1/8	19 0/8	5	6	Columbia County	WI	Scot Ulrich	1999	10630
146 2/8	23 4/8 23 7/8	18 4/8	4	4	Trumbull County	OH	Michael Mace	1999	10630
146 2/8	24 2/8 23 6/8	18 0/8	6	5	Lincoln County	OK	Tom E. Quinton	1999	10630
146 2/8	22 0/8 23 0/8	16 6/8	4	4	Henry County	VA	Mike Weaver	1999	10630
146 2/8	21 3/8 22 0/8	23 7/8	5	6	St. Croix County	WI	Stephen R. Olson	2000	10630
146 2/8	24 1/8 23 6/8	17 7/8	5	5	Washington County	WI	Tom Isaac	2000	10630
146 2/8	22 1/8 22 3/8	19 2/8	5	5	Erie County	NY	Scott Felschow	2000	10630
146 2/8	25 0/8 24 6/8	21 6/8	6	6	Pierce County	WI	Ronald Nierenhausen	2000	10630
146 2/8	26 6/8 25 4/8	21 7/8	6	5	Fulton County	IL	Jeff Pals	2000	10630
146 2/8	22 4/8 23 4/8	19 0/8	5	6	Henry County	IA	Chad Manning	2000	10630
146 2/8	24 5/8 24 1/8	16 5/8	6	6	Randolph County	AR	Ron Baxley	2000	10630
146 2/8	22 1/8 21 4/8	17 4/8	5	5	Whitman County	WA	Cameron Heusser	2001	10630
146 2/8	24 7/8 23 1/8	18 0/8	5	5	Wabasha County	MN	Ken Ramthun	2001	10630
146 2/8	24 4/8 24 6/8	16 5/8	4	6	Delaware County	IA	Dean Dempster	2001	10630
146 2/8	23 5/8 34 2/8	18 4/8	5	5	Buffalo County	WI	Fred E. Neitzel	2001	10630
146 2/8	22 6/8 22 5/8	16 4/8	5	5	Adams County	IL	Ken Krause	2001	10630
146 2/8	23 1/8 22 5/8	18 6/8	5	5	Buchanan County	VA	Thomas Dotson	2001	10630
146 2/8	20 3/8 22 4/8	18 2/8	5	5	Shawano County	WI	Jason P. Young	2002	10630
146 2/8	25 3/8 26 0/8	18 6/8	5	5	Hampshire County	MA	Jemmie A. Plasse	2002	10630
146 2/8	22 7/8 23 1/8	16 1/8	7	6	Wabash County	IL	Jeff Duncan	2002	10630
146 2/8	25 4/8 24 7/8	21 6/8	5	5	Davis County	IA	Doug Miller	2002	10630
146 2/8	23 6/8 23 4/8	19 7/8	5	4	Linn County	IA	Steve Rinderknecht	2003	10630
146 2/8	21 3/8 22 0/8	16 6/8	5	5	Shawano County	WI	Jim Diederich	2003	10630
*146 2/8	23 3/8 22 5/8	18 6/8	5	5	Mingo County	WV	Darrin Williams	2003	10630
146 2/8	24 0/8 22 7/8	20 3/8	6	6	Dutton	ONT	Ken Sloetjes	2003	10630
146 2/8	22 2/8 22 4/8	16 4/8	5	5	Morris	MAN	Robert Berard	2003	10630
146 2/8	24 3/8 24 5/8	17 2/8	5	5	Anderson County	TN	Roger A. Presley	2003	10630
146 2/8	22 1/8 21 2/8	17 6/8	5	5	Big Stone County	MN	Joseph M. Lahr	2003	10630
*146 2/8	23 2/8 23 1/8	16 4/8	5	6	McHenry County	ND	Kory Loewen	2004	10630
146 2/8	22 7/8 22 6/8	18 4/8	5	5	Pike County	PA	Charles R. Fletcher, Jr.	2004	10630
146 2/8	22 1/8 22 3/8	16 3/8	6	5	Hand County	SD	Chad Resel	2004	10630
*146 2/8	23 4/8 24 1/8	17 6/8	4	4	Cabarrus County	NC	Darrin Easley	2004	10630
146 2/8	25 2/8 25 1/8	17 2/8	4	4	Pike County	IL	Steve Mason	2004	10630
146 2/8	23 7/8 22 5/8	20 0/8	5	5	White County	IL	Greg Clark	2004	10630
146 2/8	25 4/8 25 7/8	18 2/8	4	5	Highland County	OH	Doug Brandt	2004	10630
146 2/8	25 5/8 25 3/8	17 4/8	5	5	Van Buren County	MI	Randy G. Cramer	2004	10630
146 2/8	26 0/8 25 3/8	21 4/8	4	4	Trempealeau County	WI	Barry Schmitt	2004	10630
146 2/8	23 0/8 24 0/8	22 2/8	5	5	Cowley County	KS	Mike Weaver	2004	10630
146 2/8	24 5/8 24 2/8	15 6/8	5	6	Fairfax County	VA	Mike C. Day	2004	10630
146 2/8	22 6/8 23 7/8	16 5/8	5	6	Gillespie County	TX	Troy Fowler	2005	10630
*146 2/8	22 1/8 22 1/8	22 3/8	6	5	Tippecanoe County	IN	Robert E. Northrup, Jr.	2005	10630
146 2/8	21 0/8 21 0/8	16 0/8	7	5	Steele County	ND	Nick Fugleberg	2006	10630
*146 2/8	24 3/8 24 6/8	15 6/8	5	6	Ripley County	IN	Steve Scudder	2006	10630
146 2/8	23 2/8 22 5/8	17 0/8	5	5	Hubbard County	MN	Bob Ness	2006	10630
146 2/8	25 0/8 25 0/8	18 0/8	6	9	Greene County	IN	Chris Edwards	2006	10630
146 2/8	23 7/8 24 1/8	17 6/8	4	4	Washington County	WI	Joel W. Wicklund	2006	10630
146 2/8	23 3/8 23 4/8	17 0/8	5	5	Davis County	IA	Kelly O'Keefe	2006	10630
146 2/8	24 3/8 22 0/8	21 2/8	6	7	Talbot County	MD	Jody Lee LeCompte	2006	10630
146 2/8	29 3/8 28 0/8	17 5/8	5	7	Webster County	IA	Darle Myers	2006	10630

WHITETAIL DEER (TYPICAL ANTLERS)

Minimum Score 125   Continued

	LENGTH OF	INSIDE	NUMBER OF			STATE/	HUNTER'S		
SCORE	R MAIN BEAM L	SPREAD	R POINTS L		AREA	PROVINCE	NAME	DATE	RANK
*146 2/8	23 4/8 23 5/8	18 6/8	4	4	Monmouth County	NJ	Kenneth J. Dillon	2007	10630
146 2/8	24 1/8 23 7/8	20 6/8	5	5	Oconto County	WI	Wayne De Villers	2007	10630
146 2/8	26 3/8 24 6/8	18 4/8	4	4	Rice County	KS	Tom Klimek	2007	10630
*146 2/8	24 5/8 23 6/8	16 2/8	5	5	Daviess County	KY	Joel Williams	2008	10630
146 2/8	23 7/8 24 0/8	20 2/8	7	7	Ripley County	IN	Gerald Eads	2008	10630
146 2/8	22 3/8 21 5/8	17 6/8	5	6	Hamilton County	OH	Jon Goldsberry	2008	10630
*146 2/8	23 4/8 23 0/8	18 6/8	5	5	Goodhue County	MN	Todd Dalager	2008	10630
146 2/8	23 7/8 23 0/8	18 6/8	4	5	Osage County	KS	Don McKechnie	2008	10630
*146 2/8	22 5/8 22 6/8	17 0/8	5	5	De Kalb County	IN	Warren J. Carnahan	2008	10630
*146 2/8	21 4/8 21 2/8	16 1/8	6	5	Daviess County	MO	Jonathan McGinness	2008	10630
146 2/8	23 6/8 24 3/8	17 6/8	5	5	Jackson County	WI	Richard Swanson	2009	10630
*146 2/8	21 6/8 21 3/8	15 6/8	5	5	Waupaca County	WI	Ryan Braunel	2009	10630
*146 2/8	22 0/8 21 6/8	18 2/8	5	5	Washington County	WI	Luke Vogds	2009	10630
*146 2/8	23 1/8 23 2/8	17 0/8	5	5	Eau Claire County	WI	Gregory W. Bradford	2009	10630
*146 2/8	22 0/8 22 3/8	18 0/8	5	5	Bon Homme County	SD	Mark W. Sedlacek	2009	10630
146 2/8	22 4/8 22 2/8	18 0/8	5	4	Iowa County	WI	Andrew A. Wagner	2010	10630
146 2/8	26 4/8 26 6/8	17 0/8	5	5	Jefferson County	AR	Gary Bell	2010	10630
*146 2/8	21 0/8 21 0/8	17 2/8	5	6	Franklin County	MO	Roger G. Kleekamp	2010	10630
*146 2/8	22 4/8 23 3/8	19 6/8	5	5	Buffalo County	WI	Don Kane	2010	10630
146 1/8	23 5/8 24 5/8	17 7/8	6	8	Delaware County	IA	Douglas G. Dabroski	1975	10755
146 1/8	25 2/8 25 6/8	21 2/8	5	8	Jefferson County	WI	Neil L. Lindemann	1977	10755
146 1/8	24 1/8 25 0/8	18 3/8	5	5	Lamar County	GA	Joe A. Medcalf	1977	10755
146 1/8	25 2/8 23 3/8	18 2/8	6	5	Dickinson County	MI	Edward J. Henkel	1980	10755
146 1/8	25 3/8 25 2/8	19 1/8	5	5	Darke County	OH	Larry Moore	1980	10755
146 1/8	24 2/8 24 2/8	19 3/8	4	4	Chisago County	MN	Richard Brown	1980	10755
146 1/8	25 2/8 25 5/8	17 6/8	5	6	Morrison County	MN	John Strait	1981	10755
146 1/8	24 3/8 23 4/8	14 7/8	6	5	Chisago County	MN	Clancy Lindvall	1982	10755
146 1/8	24 3/8 23 2/8	17 2/8	5	7	Waseca County	MN	Mark Williams	1982	10755
146 1/8	24 6/8 24 2/8	19 7/8	4	5	Douglas County	NE	Ralph Joos, Jr.	1984	10755
146 1/8	23 4/8 21 5/8	16 1/8	5	5	Montcalm County	MI	David Tompsett	1985	10755
146 1/8	25 5/8 25 7/8	20 0/8	5	4	Albert County	NBW	Mike Pugh	1986	10755
146 1/8	23 4/8 23 4/8	15 1/8	6	6	Carlton County	MN	Rick Nelson	1986	10755
146 1/8	23 1/8 23 0/8	14 5/8	5	5	Lucas County	IA	Bill Brown	1986	10755
146 1/8	26 0/8 25 6/8	15 5/8	4	4	Buffalo County	WI	Dale E. Tenner	1987	10755
146 1/8	23 4/8 22 3/8	21 1/8	5	5	Huntington County	IN	R.D. Tessmer /R.S. Tessmer	1988	10755
146 1/8	24 4/8 24 2/8	18 5/8	5	4	Guernsey County	OH	Kerry Mora	1988	10755
146 1/8	25 0/8 23 5/8	16 6/8	7	5	Coshocton County	OH	David M. Croft	1989	10755
146 1/8	23 2/8 23 2/8	19 4/8	6	4	Gibson County	IN	Robert Bump	1990	10755
146 1/8	25 0/8 24 0/8	22 3/8	5	6	Queen Annes County	MD	Ross F. Mills	1990	10755
146 1/8	25 7/8 25 1/8	19 5/8	4	4	Medina County	OH	Chris Postle	1991	10755
146 1/8	22 5/8 20 3/8	17 6/8	6	6	Oceana County	MI	Mark Rollenhagen	1991	10755
146 1/8	21 7/8 21 5/8	15 5/8	5	5	Jo Daviess County	IL	Stan Godfrey	1992	10755
146 1/8	23 1/8 25 1/8	17 7/8	4	4	Poinsett County	AR	Steve Anderson	1992	10755
146 1/8	24 0/8 24 0/8	16 3/8	4	5	Chester County	PA	Bruce Skipper	1993	10755
146 1/8	25 3/8 24 5/8	20 6/8	6	5	Adams County	WI	Douglas R. Shomperlen	1993	10755
146 1/8	22 0/8 21 3/8	17 3/8	5	5	Cumberland County	IL	Gary Jones	1993	10755
146 1/8	26 3/8 24 7/8	17 7/8	5	4	Jefferson County	IN	Terry R. Nelson	1993	10755
146 1/8	24 0/8 23 0/8	19 5/8	4	6	Edmonton	ALB	Gunther Tondeleir	1993	10755
146 1/8	23 0/8 24 1/8	16 7/8	6	5	La Crosse County	WI	Dean Tschumper	1993	10755
146 1/8	23 3/8 23 2/8	20 1/8	7	6	Hardin County	IA	Ronald A. Sunken	1993	10755
146 1/8	23 1/8 23 2/8	17 3/8	5	5	Ransom County	ND	Clyde Williamson	1993	10755
146 1/8	24 6/8 25 0/8	17 3/8	5	5	Buffalo County	WI	Michael J. Barstad	1994	10755
146 1/8	24 2/8 23 1/8	17 3/8	5	5	Scott County	IL	Donald W. Slater	1994	10755
146 1/8	23 7/8 24 6/8	17 3/8	5	5	Washington County	WI	Brian Strachota	1994	10755
146 1/8	22 6/8 22 1/8	16 7/8	5	5	Washtenaw County	MI	Tom Homer	1994	10755
146 1/8	28 1/8 26 2/8	20 4/8	5	7	Monona County	IA	Douglas V. Johnston	1994	10755
146 1/8	25 2/8 24 3/8	18 2/8	5	5	Fayette County	IA	David Bond	1994	10755
146 1/8	26 7/8 27 7/8	21 0/8	6	4	Dubuque County	IA	Ron Johnson	1994	10755
146 1/8	23 1/8 23 5/8	14 7/8	5	5	Ferry County	WA	Shawn Henderson	1995	10755
146 1/8	24 6/8 24 5/8	15 7/8	5	7	Monroe County	IN	Clarence S. Dawson	1995	10755
146 1/8	26 0/8 25 6/8	21 3/8	4	4	Kenosha County	WI	Daniel K. Halladay	1995	10755
146 1/8	22 3/8 23 2/8	15 3/8	5	5	Noble County	IN	Tim Nussbaum	1995	10755
146 1/8	22 0/8 22 7/8	18 7/8	6	5	Grundy County	IL	Wesley Holm	1995	10755
146 1/8	24 4/8 24 4/8	17 6/8	4	6	McMullen County	TX	Rick Daab	1996	10755
146 1/8	24 0/8 24 5/8	16 7/8	5	7	Effingham County	IL	Keith Kirby	1996	10755
146 1/8	23 0/8 23 6/8	17 5/8	6	6	Kent County	MD	John A. Price, Jr.	1996	10755
146 1/8	24 5/8 25 5/8	18 4/8	6	7	Otero County	CO	George Bock	1996	10755
146 1/8	22 0/8 21 7/8	16 3/8	5	5	Manitowoc County	WI	Scott Endries	1996	10755
146 1/8	25 3/8 24 1/8	19 7/8	4	4	Rapides Parish	LA	Roy M. Snow	1996	10755
146 1/8	21 5/8 21 2/8	16 7/8	6	6	Todd County	MN	Paul Drake	1997	10755
146 1/8	23 4/8 23 3/8	18 1/8	6	6	Souris	MAN	Bryan Klein	1997	10755
146 1/8	25 7/8 26 6/8	20 4/8	4	4	Linn County	IA	Duane D. Long	1997	10755
146 1/8	23 4/8 23 5/8	19 0/8	5	5	McKenzie County	ND	Corey Hugelen	1997	10755
146 1/8	25 4/8 23 6/8	21 5/8	5	5	Cochrane	ALB	Tom Foss	1997	10755
146 1/8	23 3/8 23 4/8	20 3/8	5	5	Wyoming County	WV	Perry Tilley	1997	10755
146 1/8	22 1/8 22 0/8	14 4/8	6	6	Stoddard County	MO	Derek Stone	1998	10755
146 1/8	21 3/8 22 3/8	18 7/8	5	5	Dimmit County	TX	Sonny Evans	1999	10755
146 1/8	23 5/8 24 0/8	17 5/8	5	5	Dane County	WI	Todd R. Zeuske	1999	10755
146 1/8	22 2/8 21 7/8	17 4/8	5	6	Berrien County	MI	Ryan P. Flowers	1999	10755
146 1/8	27 0/8 25 5/8	19 0/8	4	5	Jersey County	IL	James A. Thiel	1999	10755
146 1/8	22 1/8 22 7/8	16 5/8	5	4	Iowa County	WI	Mike Jansen	1999	10755
146 1/8	22 7/8 23 6/8	18 1/8	5	4	Greene County	IL	Ron Woodward	1999	10755
146 1/8	23 6/8 23 5/8	16 5/8	5	5	Harrison County	IA	Lane Ostendorf	1999	10755
146 1/8	23 7/8 22 7/8	15 1/8	7	7	Adams County	WI	William Hooyman	1999	10755
146 1/8	24 1/8 24 1/8	17 5/8	4	4	Riley County	KS	Jeff D. Wilson	2000	10755
146 1/8	23 6/8 23 4/8	17 1/8	5	5	Marquette County	WI	James E. Polk	2000	10755
146 1/8	22 6/8 23 6/8	19 4/8	6	6	Wood County	WI	Scott Leibl	2000	10755
146 1/8	25 1/8 24 7/8	19 5/8	5	5	Houston County	MN	Bill Clink	2000	10755
146 1/8	24 5/8 23 7/8	18 1/8	5	5	Marquette County	WI	Kenneth A. Landolt	2000	10755
146 1/8	24 6/8 23 2/8	18 5/8	4	4	Clark County	IL	Randy Rodebaugh	2000	10755
146 1/8	23 5/8 22 7/8	19 6/8	5	6	Hamilton County	IL	Frank Williams	2000	10755
146 1/8	25 0/8 26 0/8	20 3/8	5	5	Lake County	IL	Ken Wodek, Jr.	2000	10755
146 1/8	21 3/8 23 3/8	15 1/8	6	5	Waupaca County	WI	Keith Clegg	2001	10755
146 1/8	25 1/8 25 2/8	21 3/8	5	5	Peoria County	IL	Larry Oppe	2001	10755
146 1/8	23 2/8 24 7/8	13 4/8	6	7	Cooper County	MO	Matt Kollmeyer	2001	10755

469

WHITETAIL DEER (TYPICAL ANTLERS)

Minimum Score 125 — Continued

SCORE	R MAIN BEAM	L MAIN BEAM	INSIDE SPREAD	R POINTS	L POINTS	AREA	STATE/PROVINCE	HUNTER'S NAME	DATE	RANK
146 1/8	26 1/8	26 6/8	17 1/8	5	4	Tuscarawas County	OH	Monroe J. Turner III	2001	10755
146 1/8	25 3/8	24 5/8	17 5/8	5	5	Benton County	IA	Douglas R. Brecht	2001	10755
146 1/8	23 4/8	23 7/8	19 5/8	4	4	Howard County	IA	Mark Thomas	2001	10755
146 1/8	22 1/8	22 0/8	16 7/8	5	5	Barber County	KS	Todd Christiansen	2002	10755
146 1/8	26 4/8	25 6/8	18 2/8	6	5	Lake County	IL	Carl H. Spaeth	2002	10755
146 1/8	24 5/8	23 5/8	19 1/8	6	5	Allegheny County	PA	Kevin P. Hallam	2002	10755
146 1/8	22 7/8	22 6/8	16 3/8	7	5	McLean County	IL	Brett A. Taylor	2003	10755
* 146 1/8	22 5/8	23 0/8	18 7/8	5	5	Fayette County	IN	James B. Marshall	2003	10755
146 1/8	23 0/8	23 7/8	19 5/8	5	5	Blaine County	OK	Ron Westfahl	2003	10755
146 1/8	24 2/8	24 6/8	19 1/8	5	6	Montgomery County	KS	John Layton	2003	10755
146 1/8	23 3/8	22 7/8	17 7/8	6	6	Sumner County	KS	Darin Wiley	2003	10755
146 1/8	22 0/8	21 5/8	17 3/8	6	7	Webb County	TX	Bryan Hurt	2003	10755
* 146 1/8	22 2/8	23 0/8	19 3/8	5	5	Monroe County	NY	Tony Casciani	2004	10755
* 146 1/8	23 4/8	22 6/8	16 1/8	5	5	Washington County	OH	Jeffrey Dewald	2004	10755
146 1/8	24 0/8	24 0/8	18 0/8	7	7	Logan County	OH	Clark Fledderjohann	2005	10755
146 1/8	24 4/8	26 2/8	20 1/8	5	6	Jackson County	WI	Dennis Arkowski	2005	10755
146 1/8	23 1/8	22 7/8	14 1/8	6	5	Lewis County	KY	Randy Lewis	2005	10755
* 146 1/8	23 6/8	22 5/8	17 5/8	5	5	Livingston County	IL	Dave Irvin, Jr.	2005	10755
* 146 1/8	24 4/8	24 1/8	20 3/8	5	5	Itasca County	MN	Brian Berard	2005	10755
* 146 1/8	23 7/8	24 5/8	17 7/8	5	5	Foster County	ND	Derek Briss	2006	10755
146 1/8	20 7/8	20 2/8	17 7/8	6	6	Sauk County	WI	Matt Baughman	2006	10755
146 1/8	22 0/8	22 5/8	15 7/8	5	6	Waupaca County	WI	Christine Diestler	2006	10755
146 1/8	22 7/8	22 6/8	16 3/8	5	5	Taylor County	WI	Randy L. Juedes	2006	10755
146 1/8	24 0/8	23 5/8	16 7/8	6	5	Polk County	WI	Raymond Little	2006	10755
146 1/8	21 4/8	21 4/8	17 1/8	5	5	Shelby County	KY	David Nowlin	2007	10755
146 1/8	27 1/8	27 1/8	21 0/8	6	6	Clark County	OH	Denny Parrett	2007	10755
* 146 1/8	22 4/8	21 4/8	17 3/8	6	5	Fond du Lac County	WI	Tim Lamonska	2007	10755
* 146 1/8	24 5/8	24 2/8	16 0/8	5	6	Allen County	OH	Bill Bellman	2007	10755
146 1/8	26 0/8	25 1/8	17 4/8	6	4	Lafayette County	WI	Bruce Jackson	2007	10755
146 1/8	21 2/8	21 3/8	16 1/8	6	5	Jackson County	MI	Elmer G. Garrett	2007	10755
146 1/8	23 7/8	24 5/8	18 3/8	4	4	Henry County	IA	Mark R. Murphy	2007	10755
146 1/8	25 3/8	25 2/8	17 6/8	7	6	Potter County	PA	Paul Sabo	2007	10755
* 146 1/8	21 2/8	22 0/8	18 0/8	6	5	Clay County	IL	Michael F. Boldt	2007	10755
146 1/8	22 4/8	23 5/8	17 3/8	4	4	Butler County	KS	Paul Wilkins	2007	10755
* 146 1/8	24 6/8	25 4/8	18 6/8	5	4	Grant County	WI	Brian Flynn	2007	10755
146 1/8	25 4/8	25 1/8	15 6/8	5	5	Hubbard County	MN	Mike Schlee	2007	10755
146 1/8	22 6/8	22 4/8	18 2/8	7	8	Lancaster County	NE	Mark Benes	2007	10755
* 146 1/8	22 3/8	22 7/8	17 0/8	5	5	Cerro Gordo County	IA	Landon Schultz	2008	10755
146 1/8	24 3/8	24 2/8	17 2/8	6	4	Buffalo County	WI	Jeremy Case	2008	10755
* 146 1/8	23 5/8	22 5/8	18 1/8	6	5	Washington County	NE	Tim L. Welsh	2008	10755
146 1/8	22 0/8	23 0/8	18 6/8	7	5	Black Hawk County	IA	Bill Kneeskern	2008	10755
* 146 1/8	22 6/8	22 5/8	17 3/8	5	6	Will County	IL	Charles Gaidamavice	2009	10755
* 146 1/8	21 6/8	22 6/8	16 3/8	5	6	Bourbon County	KS	Tracy Finn	2009	10755
146 1/8	24 1/8	25 0/8	17 7/8	5	5	Bourbon County	KS	Gary Lynn Deweese	2009	10755
146 1/8	25 3/8	24 5/8	17 1/8	7	5	Ellsworth County	KS	Coleman Allen III	2009	10755
* 146 1/8	25 0/8	25 3/8	18 5/8	6	5	Jasper County	IL	Brad Beisner	2009	10755
146 1/8	23 6/8	24 2/8	17 3/8	5	5	Adams County	OH	Steve Kinker	2009	10755
* 146 1/8	22 4/8	23 6/8	18 3/8	5	5	Schuyler County	IL	Edd Clack	2009	10755
146 1/8	24 5/8	23 5/8	21 1/8	5	4	Pepin County	WI	Willie Manor	2009	10755
146 0/8	22 1/8	22 2/8	19 2/8	6	6	Richland County	MT	James L. Kelly	1958	10880
146 0/8	21 1/8	20 6/8	17 5/8	5	6	Cass County	IN	William D. Finks	1967	10880
146 0/8	24 0/8	25 0/8	18 4/8	5	5	Will County	IL	Terry Marcukaitis	1971	10880
146 0/8	25 0/8	24 0/8	22 0/8	5	5	Winona County	MN	Henry Scharmack, Jr.	1973	10880
146 0/8	20 5/8	20 5/8	14 3/8	7	8	Murray County	MN	John Stenke	1973	10880
146 0/8	24 1/8	24 4/8	16 0/8	6	6	Keith County	NE	Gerald Spurgin	1975	10880
146 0/8	23 0/8	22 4/8	18 1/8	6	5	Calgary	ALB	Fred Walker	1981	10880
146 0/8	21 6/8	21 5/8	16 2/8	5	5	Saline County	NE	Donald D. Matejka	1982	10880
146 0/8	22 0/8	23 0/8	18 2/8	6	6	Kewaunee County	WI	Harold Blahnik	1982	10880
146 0/8	21 5/8	22 1/8	18 2/8	5	5	Roberts County	SD	John Fridgen	1984	10880
146 0/8	27 0/8	27 2/8	21 6/8	4	4	Morrison County	MN	John Sobaski	1985	10880
146 0/8	24 2/8	23 2/8	15 6/8	5	6	Fulton County	IL	John I. Briggs	1986	10880
146 0/8	23 4/8	22 6/8	19 4/8	5	5	Clayton County	IA	Joe Lieb	1986	10880
146 0/8	24 4/8	24 4/8	19 7/8	6	6	Jo Daviess County	IL	William Stephanopoulos	1986	10880
146 0/8	25 2/8	24 0/8	18 2/8	4	4	Saunders County	NE	Gary Frerichs	1988	10880
146 0/8	25 0/8	23 2/8	21 2/8	5	6	Clay County	MN	Patrick Cox	1989	10880
146 0/8	22 1/8	23 2/8	17 0/8	5	5	Allamakee County	IA	Casey A. Blum	1989	10880
146 0/8	22 0/8	22 3/8	16 4/8	5	5	Robertson County	KY	Jim Whisman	1989	10880
146 0/8	22 0/8	21 0/8	17 0/8	5	5	Heard County	GA	Ray Hand	1990	10880
146 0/8	23 7/8	23 3/8	18 1/8	6	5	Fillmore County	MN	Dean C. Irish	1990	10880
146 0/8	23 3/8	22 6/8	16 0/8	4	5	Westchester County	NY	Ronald Moore	1991	10880
146 0/8	26 3/8	26 4/8	16 2/8	7	5	St. Charles County	MO	Benjamin F. Hamrick	1992	10880
146 0/8	24 1/8	23 0/8	19 2/8	5	5	Winnebago County	IL	David L. Miller	1992	10880
146 0/8	26 1/8	26 1/8	18 4/8	7	5	Newton County	IN	Ralph G. Bogie	1992	10880
146 0/8	26 5/8	27 0/8	17 0/8	4	6	Worcester County	MA	Michael P. Duffy	1992	10880
146 0/8	24 0/8	23 6/8	17 6/8	6	5	Eau Claire County	WI	Tony Aaron	1992	10880
146 0/8	25 2/8	25 2/8	21 6/8	4	4	Baltimore County	MD	Timothy Whitehead	1993	10880
146 0/8	23 1/8	23 5/8	19 4/8	5	6	Allen County	IN	Phillip H. Wiegmann	1993	10880
146 0/8	24 0/8	23 7/8	17 4/8	5	5	Door County	WI	Mark K. Bauldry	1993	10880
146 0/8	20 2/8	23 1/8	18 0/8	5	5	Grundy County	IL	Leonard Erschen	1993	10880
146 0/8	21 6/8	21 4/8	17 6/8	5	5	Henry County	VA	Mike Weaver	1993	10880
146 0/8	21 4/8	22 2/8	18 0/8	6	5	Ottawa County	KS	Robert A. Stegmaier	1993	10880
146 0/8	21 3/8	23 7/8	17 2/8	6	5	Harper County	KS	Scott Lagers	1994	10880
146 0/8	21 3/8	21 3/8	20 4/8	5	5	Kane County	IL	Art P. Toney	1994	10880
146 0/8	24 0/8	24 2/8	19 0/8	5	4	La Salle County	IL	Dewayne Mullins	1995	10880
146 0/8	22 5/8	23 5/8	19 2/8	5	4	Osage County	KS	Gerald Britschge	1995	10880
146 0/8	25 7/8	25 7/8	17 6/8	5	5	Fayette County	IL	James Maske	1995	10880
146 0/8	23 2/8	23 0/8	17 0/8	4	5	Richland County	MT	Kurt A. Bensinger	1996	10880
146 0/8	23 5/8	23 7/8	21 5/8	6	5	Clark County	WI	Michael A. Ruzic	1996	10880
146 0/8	25 2/8	23 7/8	20 0/8	5	6	Marion County	IL	Chris Phillips	1996	10880
146 0/8	22 1/8	22 0/8	18 0/8	5	5	Redwood County	MN	Todd Gilb	1996	10880
146 0/8	22 5/8	21 5/8	17 6/8	5	5	Winona County	MN	Steve R. Strike	1997	10880
146 0/8	24 0/8	23 7/8	18 4/8	5	5	Knox County	IL	Jeff Nelson	1997	10880
146 0/8	24 2/8	24 0/8	18 0/8	5	5	Suffolk County	NY	Neal Heaton	1997	10880
146 0/8	25 1/8	25 2/8	19 6/8	6	5	Tuscarawas County	OH	William C. Gintz	1997	10880
146 0/8	25 0/8	24 2/8	16 4/8	6	5	Manitowoc County	WI	Charles "Chuck" Wilhelm	1997	10880

WHITETAIL DEER (TYPICAL ANTLERS)

Minimum Score 125 — Continued

SCORE	LENGTH OF R MAIN BEAM L	INSIDE SPREAD	NUMBER OF R POINTS L	AREA	STATE/ PROVINCE	HUNTER'S NAME	DATE	RANK
146 0/8	23 0/8 23 3/8	16 0/8	6 5	Miami County	KS	Tom Burgmeier	1998	10880
146 0/8	23 5/8 25 0/8	17 4/8	5 5	Buffalo County	WI	John W. Zahrte	1998	10880
146 0/8	23 5/8 23 0/8	18 2/8	5 5	Montgomery County	PA	David P. Decembrino	1998	10880
146 0/8	24 7/8 24 2/8	16 7/8	7 4	Ashland County	WI	Jeffrey H. Bellmer	1998	10880
146 0/8	25 4/8 26 2/8	17 0/8	4 4	Pike County	IL	Mike Huggins	1998	10880
146 0/8	23 4/8 23 4/8	16 5/8	8 6	Roseau County	MN	Ray Robinson	1998	10880
146 0/8	23 2/8 22 2/8	17 0/8	5 6	Outagamie County	WI	Chris Dombrowski	1999	10880
146 0/8	27 0/8 24 2/8	17 2/8	5 5	Harrison County	OH	Alex Abel	1999	10880
146 0/8	22 0/8 23 4/8	18 0/8	5 5	McKenzie County	ND	Corey Hugelen	1999	10880
146 0/8	21 4/8 22 2/8	17 1/8	6 5	McLean County	IL	Dustin Hinds	2000	10880
146 0/8	26 0/8 26 3/8	20 6/8	4 4	Rock Island County	IL	Douglas Hood	2000	10880
146 0/8	27 5/8 28 1/8	20 2/8	6 6	Lorain County	OH	Mark Lepine	2000	10880
146 0/8	24 0/8 24 4/8	17 0/8	5 5	Chester County	PA	Frank T. Giunta, Jr.	2000	10880
146 0/8	23 7/8 24 6/8	18 6/8	6 6	Roberts County	SD	Dana Holmgren	2001	10880
146 0/8	23 0/8 24 0/8	17 4/8	5 5	Trempealeau County	WI	Chad G. Halama	2001	10880
146 0/8	23 7/8 24 4/8	16 7/8	6 5	Jersey County	IL	Stan Gade	2001	10880
146 0/8	23 4/8 22 7/8	17 2/8	5 7	Washburn County	WI	Nicole Minnick	2001	10880
146 0/8	23 5/8 23 7/8	16 0/8	4 4	Warren County	IA	Mike McKinney	2001	10880
146 0/8	24 1/8 24 1/8	17 2/8	6 5	Pike County	IL	Scott Anthony	2001	10880
146 0/8	21 7/8 23 1/8	16 4/8	5 6	Plymouth County	IA	Robert J. Pierson	2001	10880
146 0/8	22 4/8 22 6/8	17 4/8	5 6	Ford County	KS	David M. Crnkovich	2001	10880
146 0/8	25 4/8 26 2/8	18 2/8	4 4	McHenry County	IL	Brent Smith	2002	10880
146 0/8	23 6/8 23 5/8	17 3/8	6 7	Fairfield County	OH	James E. Marsee	2002	10880
146 0/8	24 3/8 24 2/8	20 0/8	4 4	Lee County	IA	Russ Landes	2002	10880
146 0/8	21 3/8 20 7/8	16 2/8	5 5	Clark County	MO	Frank E. Knox	2002	10880
146 0/8	26 0/8 25 3/8	18 4/8	6 5	Jersey County	IL	Judy Kovar	2002	10880
146 0/8	26 1/8 26 2/8	19 6/8	5 5	Otter Tail County	MN	Lyle Tabbut	2002	10880
146 0/8	23 2/8 23 2/8	17 0/8	6 5	Allegheny County	PA	Leonard Schiavon	2002	10880
146 0/8	25 3/8 25 7/8	22 4/8	5 5	Anne Arundel County	MD	Steve E. Willsey	2002	10880
146 0/8	21 6/8 21 2/8	15 6/8	5 5	New Kent County	VA	John W. Franklin	2003	10880
146 0/8	25 6/8 25 5/8	19 2/8	5 5	Buffalo County	WI	Chris Hill	2003	10880
146 0/8	23 1/8 22 6/8	16 3/8	5 6	Allamakee County	IA	Travis Ebner	2003	10880
146 0/8	23 2/8 22 1/8	19 1/8	7 5	Parke County	IN	Les L. Mink	2003	10880
146 0/8	22 2/8 23 2/8	18 2/8	5 5	Price County	WI	Teresa Heisler	2003	10880
*146 0/8	23 6/8 23 6/8	17 1/8	6 7	Waukesha County	WI	Mark A. Greeneway	2004	10880
146 0/8	23 4/8 22 2/8	17 0/8	8 5	Clinton County	IA	Craig Black	2004	10880
*146 0/8	23 4/8 25 1/8	19 0/8	4 4	Henry County	IL	Edward Finn	2004	10880
146 0/8	24 7/8 24 6/8	17 6/8	5 5	Licking County	OH	Mark Pisto	2004	10880
146 0/8	21 6/8 22 2/8	21 0/8	5 6	Muhlenberg County	KY	Steven Conrad	2004	10880
*146 0/8	23 2/8 24 1/8	18 6/8	4 5	Worth County	MO	David M. Krampitz	2004	10880
146 0/8	21 4/8 20 0/8	16 1/8	6 6	Hennepin County	MN	David Halsey	2004	10880
146 0/8	23 7/8 23 0/8	16 6/8	5 6	Lafayette County	WI	Shawn Buck	2004	10880
*146 0/8	22 6/8 22 5/8	18 7/8	6 5	Fayette County	IL	Devon Graumenz	2004	10880
146 0/8	24 7/8 24 2/8	18 4/8	4 5	Coronation	ALB	Russel Hillis	2005	10880
146 0/8	23 2/8 23 4/8	18 0/8	6 5	Lafayette County	WI	Gary Bald	2005	10880
*146 0/8	21 4/8 21 3/8	16 2/8	5 5	Van Buren County	MI	Bob J. Smola	2005	10880
146 0/8	18 5/8 19 5/8	17 0/8	5 5	Calhoun County	IL	Ben Robertson	2005	10880
146 0/8	24 2/8 23 2/8	17 4/8	4 5	Putnam County	IL	Randy Willoughby	2005	10880
146 0/8	20 0/8 23 4/8	19 0/8	4 4	Fulton County	IL	John M. Yaswinski	2005	10880
146 0/8	25 3/8 25 1/8	17 0/8	4 5	Iowa County	WI	Joe Grimm	2005	10880
146 0/8	21 6/8 22 6/8	19 2/8	5 4	Allamakee County	IA	Jeri Schwartzhoff	2005	10880
146 0/8	22 0/8 22 5/8	14 2/8	4 4	Oakland County	MI	John D. Burkett	2005	10880
146 0/8	23 0/8 23 0/8	17 0/8	6 6	Dunn County	WI	Jeffrey J. Grunderian	2006	10880
*146 0/8	24 7/8 25 3/8	17 7/8	6 7	Dakota County	NE	Randall R. Peters	2006	10880
146 0/8	24 2/8 24 2/8	17 5/8	6 7	Waukesha County	WI	David E. Helm	2006	10880
*146 0/8	24 6/8 24 6/8	18 3/8	6 6	Jefferson County	MO	Ty Thaler	2007	10880
146 0/8	23 7/8 23 3/8	20 4/8	4 4	Steuben County	IN	Scott Kressley	2007	10880
*146 0/8	24 4/8 24 0/8	18 6/8	5 6	Cass County	ND	Dean Warkenthein	2007	10880
146 0/8	24 0/8 24 1/8	18 2/8	6 6	Fond du Lac County	WI	Joseph Schmuhl	2007	10880
*146 0/8	25 4/8 22 3/8	17 2/8	5 5	Knox County	OH	John Dawson	2007	10880
146 0/8	24 6/8 24 0/8	17 6/8	5 5	Buffalo County	WI	Lois J. O'Brien	2007	10880
146 0/8	25 4/8 24 3/8	19 2/8	5 5	Pike County	IL	Fernando Semiao	2007	10880
146 0/8	23 7/8 24 1/8	16 4/8	5 6	Adams County	OH	Paul Gray	2007	10880
*146 0/8	20 2/8 20 1/8	17 6/8	5 6	Henry County	KY	Ray Bruce Combs	2008	10880
*146 0/8	22 4/8 22 7/8	16 7/8	5 7	Portage County	WI	Derek Check	2008	10880
146 0/8	22 7/8 23 1/8	21 3/8	5 6	Boone County	MO	Eric Chism	2008	10880
146 0/8	22 1/8 21 6/8	19 0/8	5 5	Plymouth County	MA	Kevin Provost	2008	10880
146 0/8	20 0/8 19 2/8	14 1/8	6 5	Mitchell County	IA	Thomas Erickson	2008	10880
146 0/8	22 2/8 22 6/8	16 6/8	5 5	Laclede County	MO	Lucas Mackey	2009	10880
146 0/8	23 0/8 21 4/8	17 0/8	5 5	Sauk County	WI	Steven L. Pyfferoen	2009	10880
*146 0/8	24 6/8 24 5/8	16 3/8	5 6	Ripley County	IN	Chris Salyer	2009	10880
146 0/8	23 1/8 22 5/8	17 4/8	5 5	Shawano County	WI	Mark Kropp	2009	10880
*146 0/8	23 2/8 24 1/8	17 4/8	4 5	Richland County	IL	Dewitt Ashley	2009	10880
*146 0/8	20 4/8 23 4/8	18 4/8	6 5	Polk County	WI	Mario J. Battisti	2009	10880
145 7/8	25 1/8 25 0/8	16 3/8	4 5	Wood County	WI	Laddimere Beranek	1959	11000
145 7/8	25 4/8 24 4/8	19 1/8	4 4	Greeley County	NE	Bill W. Bauer	1962	11000
145 7/8	22 4/8 22 7/8	20 7/8	4 8	Lafayette County	WI	James Goetzke	1972	11000
145 7/8	23 3/8 23 1/8	16 1/8	7 8	Polk County	MN	Willie Johnson/Tim Amuinson	1981	11000
145 7/8	21 4/8 22 0/8	15 2/8	5 6	Chase County	KS	John L. Moore	1982	11000
145 7/8	22 6/8 24 4/8	18 7/8	6 5	Lewis & Clark County	MT	Royce Dake	1982	11000
145 7/8	23 5/8 24 0/8	16 5/8	8 5	Manitowoc County	WI	Thomas L. Alfson	1983	11000
145 7/8	22 4/8 22 3/8	20 1/8	5 5	Harvey County	KS	Gregory K. Dirksen	1983	11000
145 7/8	25 1/8 25 2/8	19 1/8	5 5	Monroe County	NY	Pat M. Moore	1987	11000
145 7/8	24 1/8 23 0/8	18 5/8	5 5	Kent County	MD	Steve J. Grabowski, Jr.	1987	11000
145 7/8	25 2/8 27 2/8	17 4/8	5 6	Brown County	IL	Ron Hanna	1988	11000
145 7/8	26 4/8 24 4/8	17 0/8	5 7	Republic County	KS	Gary Dahl	1988	11000
145 7/8	22 7/8 23 1/8	15 0/8	8 5	Shawnee County	KS	Bradley D Porubsky	1989	11000
145 7/8	23 5/8 23 7/8	18 7/8	6 6	Lake County	IL	Mike Serwa	1990	11000
145 7/8	23 7/8 23 5/8	17 1/8	6 5	Barry County	MO	Donald L. Randolph	1990	11000
145 7/8	23 4/8 22 4/8	17 5/8	5 6	Republic County	KS	Jerry A. Thomas	1990	11000
145 7/8	23 0/8 22 2/8	16 5/8	5 5	Arenac County	MI	Daryl Russell	1991	11000
145 7/8	24 6/8 25 5/8	18 1/8	5 5	Aitkin County	MN	Daniel Picht	1991	11000
145 7/8	25 2/8 25 1/8	19 1/8	5 4	Madison County	IA	Gary Knoll	1991	11000
145 7/8	22 2/8 22 4/8	16 3/8	4 5	Washington County	IL	Stanley F. Musial	1991	11000
145 7/8	22 2/8 22 3/8	18 4/8	7 7	Carroll County	IL	Paul Shipman	1991	11000

471

WHITETAIL DEER (TYPICAL ANTLERS)

Minimum Score 125 — Continued

SCORE	LENGTH OF MAIN BEAM R	L	INSIDE SPREAD	NUMBER OF POINTS R	L	AREA	STATE/PROVINCE	HUNTER'S NAME	DATE	RANK
145 7/8	24 0/8	24 0/8	19 3/8	5	6	Johnson County	IA	Bruce Charipar	1992	11000
145 7/8	25 1/8	26 3/8	22 1/8	3	3	Steuben County	IN	Jim Loughran	1992	11000
145 7/8	21 1/8	22 6/8	16 7/8	5	5	Henry County	VA	Mike Weaver	1992	11000
145 7/8	25 0/8	24 4/8	18 0/8	6	7	Dane County	WI	Bennie P. Larson	1993	11000
145 7/8	22 5/8	23 2/8	17 5/8	5	5	Dane County	WI	Stuart Smith	1994	11000
145 7/8	23 6/8	23 4/8	18 0/8	6	5	Buffalo County	WI	David Pfeiffer	1994	11000
145 7/8	22 0/8	22 6/8	17 5/8	5	5	Noble County	OH	John W. Denny	1994	11000
145 7/8	22 4/8	23 0/8	16 3/8	5	5	McHenry County	IL	Troy D. Erckfritz	1995	11000
145 7/8	23 1/8	24 5/8	16 3/8	5	5	Columbia County	WI	Perry L. Dahl	1996	11000
145 7/8	24 5/8	24 3/8	22 4/8	5	5	Waupaca County	WI	Adam J. Lorge	1996	11000
145 7/8	27 0/8	26 5/8	17 5/8	5	5	Dane County	WI	Lawrence O. Bushey	1996	11000
145 7/8	24 4/8	24 6/8	19 1/8	5	5	Buffalo County	WI	Jack R. Dieckman	1996	11000
145 7/8	22 1/8	23 5/8	16 2/8	7	6	Slope County	ND	Dennis Palmer	1996	11000
145 7/8	26 5/8	27 0/8	20 3/8	5	4	La Salle County	IL	Wayne Riebe	1997	11000
145 7/8	25 4/8	26 0/8	20 1/8	5	4	Montgomery County	OH	Christopher L. Lutz	1997	11000
145 7/8	21 5/8	21 7/8	14 7/8	5	5	Martin County	IN	Jay Davis	1997	11000
145 7/8	19 4/8	21 3/8	15 5/8	5	5	Oldham County	KY	Daniel Klingenfus	1997	11000
145 7/8	23 2/8	24 1/8	14 3/8	5	4	Erie County	OH	Kent Hamilton	1997	11000
145 7/8	24 3/8	24 5/8	20 1/8	4	5	Steele County	ND	Andrew Plaine	1998	11000
145 7/8	24 2/8	23 4/8	16 7/8	5	5	Morrison County	MN	Charles Wysocky	1998	11000
145 7/8	23 7/8	24 2/8	19 1/8	5	5	Eau Claire County	WI	Wayne J. Cook	1998	11000
145 7/8	22 2/8	22 3/8	23 5/8	4	4	Montgomery County	MD	Michael L. McCarty	1998	11000
145 7/8	21 1/8	21 2/8	16 2/8	5	5	Ontario County	NY	Donald T. Runyon	1999	11000
145 7/8	24 6/8	24 6/8	21 5/8	4	4	Ashland County	OH	Clay Braden	1999	11000
145 7/8	21 5/8	22 0/8	18 3/8	5	5	Pepin County	WI	Patrick H. Falkner	1999	11000
145 7/8	25 2/8	25 4/8	21 7/8	5	5	Madison County	VA	Steve A. Lillard	1999	11000
145 7/8	22 4/8	22 5/8	16 3/8	5	5	Houston County	MN	Bob Borowiak	1999	11000
145 7/8	23 4/8	22 2/8	17 5/8	5	5	Shawano County	WI	Harvey R. Roth	2000	11000
145 7/8	26 3/8	26 7/8	19 7/8	4	5	Morgan County	OH	Adam Troiano	2000	11000
145 7/8	23 5/8	24 3/8	18 7/8	5	5	White County	AR	Jason Smith	2000	11000
145 7/8	24 5/8	22 6/8	18 1/8	5	5	Lincoln County	WI	Roy R. Albright	2000	11000
145 7/8	22 2/8	22 5/8	17 7/8	6	5	Adams County	IL	Lynn Seckman	2001	11000
145 7/8	22 7/8	22 7/8	17 7/8	6	5	Lancaster County	NE	Scott Oswald	2001	11000
145 7/8	23 3/8	23 6/8	19 1/8	5	5	Marshall County	IA	Jerry W. Hopkins	2001	11000
145 7/8	22 4/8	22 3/8	17 5/8	5	5	Kleberg County	TX	Mickey W. Hellickson	2001	11000
145 7/8	21 4/8	21 0/8	18 3/8	5	7	Audrain County	MO	Mark Johnson	2002	11000
145 7/8	23 5/8	24 0/8	17 7/8	4	5	Vermillion County	IN	Jeff Michalic	2002	11000
145 7/8	23 3/8	23 5/8	17 0/8	6	6	Pike County	IL	John Buffolino	2002	11000
145 7/8	22 7/8	22 6/8	16 1/8	5	5	Black Hawk County	IA	Scott Heit	2002	11000
145 7/8	24 0/8	24 2/8	17 1/8	4	4	Lee County	IL	Doug R. Foster	2002	11000
145 7/8	25 0/8	25 1/8	16 7/8	4	4	Clarke County	IA	Alan Cole	2002	11000
145 7/8	24 6/8	25 3/8	18 1/8	4	4	Chautauqua County	NY	Richard K. Johnson, Jr.	2003	11000
145 7/8	21 5/8	22 5/8	16 6/8	6	5	Atoka County	OK	Brian Mixon	2003	11000
145 7/8	22 6/8	24 2/8	22 5/8	5	5	Allamakee County	IA	Bill Clink	2003	11000
145 7/8	26 2/8	26 2/8	17 5/8	5	6	Geauga County	OH	Edmond J. Geber	2003	11000
*145 7/8	24 7/8	24 0/8	19 3/8	5	6	Morgan County	CO	Jerod Neb	2003	11000
145 7/8	23 0/8	23 0/8	16 4/8	6	5	Washington County	MS	William L. Coppage	2003	11000
145 7/8	25 2/8	24 6/8	18 3/8	5	5	Chariton County	MO	Brandon Maddox	2003	11000
145 7/8	24 0/8	22 6/8	18 2/8	5	7	Fillmore County	MN	Paul Lambrecht	2004	11000
*145 7/8	23 0/8	23 4/8	16 5/8	5	5	Greenwood County	KS	Dr. William L. Connelly	2004	11000
145 7/8	23 7/8	23 3/8	17 1/8	5	5	Wayne County	IN	Ryan Canterbury	2004	11000
145 7/8	25 3/8	26 4/8	21 3/8	4	4	Richland County	WI	T. J. Schultz	2004	11000
145 7/8	23 7/8	24 0/8	19 3/8	5	5	Jennings County	IN	Bradly Summers	2004	11000
145 7/8	23 2/8	23 1/8	16 1/8	6	5	Fillmore County	MN	Nancy Atwood	2004	11000
145 7/8	23 2/8	23 4/8	18 4/8	5	6	Davis County	IA	Scott Kirsch	2004	11000
*145 7/8	24 2/8	25 4/8	14 5/8	5	5	Hancock County	KY	Sean Greenwood	2004	11000
145 7/8	23 3/8	21 1/8	18 3/8	5	6	Saginaw County	MI	Joseph Wachowicz	2004	11000
*145 7/8	22 4/8	24 1/8	18 6/8	5	6	Schuyler County	MO	Brad Fallert	2004	11000
145 7/8	23 5/8	22 1/8	18 2/8	5	6	Kingman County	KS	Eric Eckenrode	2004	11000
145 7/8	22 0/8	22 2/8	15 7/8	6	6	Morgan County	IL	Donald L. Chamberlain	2004	11000
*145 7/8	24 3/8	23 6/8	15 5/8	5	6	Waushara County	WI	Scott Oberst	2005	11000
145 7/8	22 4/8	23 0/8	16 3/8	5	6	Barnes County	ND	Curt Johnson	2005	11000
145 7/8	26 2/8	25 3/8	20 5/8	6	4	Tippecanoe County	IN	Jim K. Esposito	2005	11000
*145 7/8	21 2/8	21 4/8	16 5/8	5	5	Will County	IL	Leroy C. Peart	2005	11000
145 7/8	23 3/8	23 2/8	16 5/8	5	6	Ottawa County	KS	John B. Bowman	2005	11000
*145 7/8	25 4/8	26 5/8	22 1/8	5	5	Cumberland County	ME	Augustus E. Doughty	2005	11000
145 7/8	24 3/8	24 4/8	17 0/8	7	7	Greene County	IN	Kevin James Hobson	2006	11000
145 7/8	25 1/8	24 0/8	19 1/8	5	5	Christian County	IL	Sylvan Purcell, Jr.	2006	11000
145 7/8	23 6/8	23 7/8	16 7/8	5	5	Winnebago County	WI	Jim Stromske	2006	11000
145 7/8	22 1/8	22 6/8	17 2/8	6	6	Jasper County	IL	Tom Shelton	2007	11000
*145 7/8	21 5/8	20 4/8	15 1/8	6	6	Adams County	IL	Steven Parker	2007	11000
145 7/8	25 3/8	25 3/8	18 1/8	4	4	Kane County	IL	Gary Astin	2007	11000
*145 7/8	22 5/8	22 1/8	19 0/8	7	5	Clark County	IL	Greg Finney	2007	11000
145 7/8	25 1/8	24 0/8	16 7/8	6	5	Harrison County	KY	Daniel Terry	2007	11000
*145 7/8	23 2/8	24 2/8	17 5/8	6	5	Jones County	IA	Christopher Delay	2007	11000
145 7/8	23 2/8	23 1/8	19 5/8	7	5	Benson County	ND	Randall J. Simon	2008	11000
145 7/8	22 4/8	23 6/8	15 1/8	6	6	Portage County	WI	Peter J. Waldmann	2008	11000
145 7/8	24 2/8	24 2/8	18 6/8	6	8	Phillips County	KS	Sherwin Van Kooten	2008	11000
145 7/8	25 0/8	24 6/8	18 0/8	10	7	Wayne County	IA	Jared M. Cramer	2008	11000
*145 7/8	24 6/8	23 6/8	17 2/8	7	7	Appanoose County	IA	David Mitchell	2008	11000
145 7/8	23 6/8	21 3/8	19 5/8	5	5	Clark County	KS	David Lock	2008	11000
145 7/8	24 2/8	24 3/8	16 7/8	5	5	Greene County	GA	Michael Mullins	2009	11000
*145 7/8	23 6/8	23 4/8	21 1/8	5	5	Auglaize County	OH	Joseph Wireman	2009	11000
*145 7/8	21 7/8	20 7/8	15 1/8	5	5	Campbell County	SD	Gabe Ellerton	2010	11000
145 6/8	20 0/8	20 5/8	17 0/8	5	6	Okmulgee County	OK	Pat Giulioli	1973	11105
145 6/8	21 5/8	22 4/8	17 0/8	5	5	Monroe County	WI	Bob Besch	1980	11105
145 6/8	22 3/8	23 2/8	16 6/8	4	5	Jefferson County	KS	John Welborn	1981	11105
145 6/8	22 0/8	22 0/8	17 2/8	5	5	Millarville	ALB	Richard Freudenberg	1982	11105
145 6/8	23 2/8	23 4/8	15 5/8	6	5	Ravalli County	MT	Arden R. Cowan	1983	11105
145 6/8	23 0/8	23 1/8	20 0/8	4	5	Aransas County	TX	Dr. Tip Coleman	1985	11105
145 6/8	21 3/8	21 3/8	17 0/8	6	5	Clay County	MN	Darwin Cihak	1986	11105
145 6/8	22 5/8	22 2/8	17 2/8	5	7	Jefferson County	WI	Randy Latsch	1986	11105
145 6/8	23 1/8	22 2/8	15 2/8	6	6	Kenedy County	TX	George Cooper	1987	11105
145 6/8	23 3/8	24 0/8	18 0/8	7	6	Van Buren County	IA	Don Kieler	1987	11105
145 6/8	23 7/8	23 6/8	17 0/8	4	4	Polk County	WI	Andy Bollant	1988	11105

WHITETAIL DEER (TYPICAL ANTLERS)

Minimum Score 125   Continued

SCORE	LENGTH OF R MAIN BEAM L	INSIDE SPREAD	NUMBER OF R POINTS L	AREA	STATE/ PROVINCE	HUNTER'S NAME	DATE	RANK
145 6/8	21 4/8 21 7/8	15 2/8	5 5	Jefferson County	WI	Brad Hering	1989	11105
145 6/8	23 3/8 24 1/8	17 6/8	5 7	St. Croix County	WI	David Saltness	1989	11105
145 6/8	24 3/8 23 7/8	16 3/8	6 6	Linn County	IA	Darryl W. Martin	1989	11105
145 6/8	24 3/8 24 7/8	21 0/8	4 4	Cecil County	MD	Earl McSorley	1989	11105
145 6/8	22 3/8 22 3/8	14 0/8	5 5	Iron County	WI	Scott Hultman	1989	11105
145 6/8	22 3/8 23 5/8	18 4/8	5 5	Meade County	KY	Kevin Anderson	1989	11105
145 6/8	23 3/8 23 7/8	18 1/8	7 7	Wabash County	IL	Gerald E. Wirth	1990	11105
145 6/8	23 4/8 23 4/8	18 2/8	5 6	Worcester County	MA	Mark Doucimo	1990	11105
145 6/8	25 3/8 25 6/8	19 4/8	7 9	Florence County	WI	Steven C. Gevaert	1991	11105
145 6/8	21 5/8 22 2/8	18 4/8	5 4	Mercer County	IL	Dennis Nelson	1991	11105
145 6/8	23 4/8 24 0/8	17 0/8	6 5	Jasper County	IL	Elmer R. Luce, Jr.	1991	11105
145 6/8	21 4/8 21 4/8	17 2/8	5 5	Plymouth County	IA	Cash N. Howe	1991	11105
145 6/8	26 7/8 27 4/8	19 6/8	4 4	Middlesex County	MA	Joe R. Shepard	1991	11105
145 6/8	22 6/8 21 7/8	17 2/8	5 5	Pickett County	TN	Robert E. Lee	1993	11105
145 6/8	24 2/8 25 4/8	20 6/8	6 6	Douglas County	WI	Jens Gregerson III	1993	11105
145 6/8	21 6/8 23 1/8	17 0/8	6 8	Kewaunee County	WI	Phil J. Romdenne	1993	11105
145 6/8	25 6/8 27 5/8	19 6/8	5 4	Knox County	OH	David B. Fowls	1993	11105
145 6/8	25 2/8 25 0/8	20 6/8	4 5	Clinton County	IL	Tracy D. Hawes	1993	11105
145 6/8	24 6/8 24 4/8	18 6/8	5 5	Bayfield County	WI	Joseph Beedlow	1994	11105
145 6/8	23 5/8 22 7/8	21 0/8	4 4	Coles County	IL	Matt Smith	1994	11105
145 6/8	24 7/8 23 3/8	19 7/8	6 6	Rice County	MN	Howard L. Wolf	1994	11105
145 6/8	21 1/8 21 4/8	15 4/8	5 5	Henry County	VA	Mike Weaver	1995	11105
145 6/8	24 7/8 24 2/8	18 2/8	4 4	Franklin County	OH	Gregory J. Rustemeyer	1995	11105
145 6/8	23 0/8 22 2/8	17 6/8	5 5	Jackson County	IN	Max E. Gambrel	1995	11105
145 6/8	23 6/8 25 7/8	21 0/8	6 6	Walworth County	WI	Chuck Palmer	1995	11105
145 6/8	26 2/8 26 7/8	18 4/8	5 5	Whitley County	IN	Scott C. Geist	1995	11105
145 6/8	22 3/8 23 0/8	17 0/8	6 5	Putnam County	IN	Chris Nichols	1996	11105
145 6/8	26 7/8 26 5/8	19 3/8	7 4	Jasper County	IL	Brian Collins	1996	11105
145 6/8	24 7/8 25 6/8	15 4/8	5 5	Adams County	OH	Lonnie Shattuck, Jr.	1997	11105
145 6/8	21 6/8 22 3/8	15 6/8	5 5	Harrison County	IA	Tracy Liddell	1997	11105
145 6/8	25 0/8 25 2/8	19 6/8	6 7	Grant County	WI	Randy Hochhausen	1997	11105
145 6/8	23 0/8 24 5/8	16 6/8	7 5	Cherokee County	IA	Curtis Otto	1997	11105
145 6/8	24 4/8 24 1/8	17 4/8	5 4	Nuevo Laredo	MEX	William Young, Jr.	1997	11105
145 6/8	21 2/8 21 1/8	14 6/8	5 5	Cooper County	MO	David Westmoreland	1998	11105
145 6/8	23 1/8 21 2/8	18 0/8	5 6	Buffalo County	WI	Edward Brannen	1998	11105
145 6/8	24 0/8 25 3/8	20 0/8	6 5	Manitowoc County	WI	Jason J. Orth	1998	11105
145 6/8	23 1/8 24 2/8	15 2/8	5 5	Westmoreland County	PA	William H. Powers, Jr.	1999	11105
145 6/8	22 2/8 22 7/8	20 2/8	7 5	Outagamie County	WI	Russ Diem	1999	11105
145 6/8	25 4/8 24 0/8	20 0/8	5 7	McLean County	IL	Steve Ringger	1999	11105
145 6/8	22 7/8 23 7/8	17 7/8	6 8	Mercer County	IL	Rye Boruff	1999	11105
145 6/8	24 7/8 25 1/8	20 0/8	4 4	Kane County	IL	Scott Sommers	1999	11105
145 6/8	26 6/8 25 5/8	20 4/8	4 4	Ashtabula County	OH	David Allen	1999	11105
145 6/8	26 7/8 26 7/8	18 3/8	6 5	Madison County	IL	Bob Sibley	1999	11105
145 6/8	21 0/8 22 3/8	15 2/8	5 5	Waupaca County	WI	William Peotter	1999	11105
145 6/8	22 6/8 25 6/8	20 1/8	5 6	Dubuque County	IA	Chuck Seipp	2000	11105
145 6/8	22 4/8 22 3/8	17 2/8	8 6	Waupaca County	WI	Travis M. Dittman	2000	11105
145 6/8	23 0/8 22 6/8	15 6/8	5 5	Pike County	IL	Michael Brendle	2000	11105
145 6/8	23 4/8 22 7/8	21 3/8	5 6	Green Lake County	WI	Jamie L. Rataczak	2000	11105
145 6/8	24 4/8 24 4/8	21 4/8	5 5	Langlade County	WI	Daniel S. Konz	2000	11105
145 6/8	24 4/8 25 2/8	20 0/8	4 4	Licking County	OH	Bret Crane	2000	11105
145 6/8	23 1/8 22 7/8	16 7/8	5 9	Pike County	IL	James E. Hummel	2000	11105
145 6/8	23 6/8 22 7/8	16 0/8	7 5	Schuyler County	IL	Chad Ingles	2000	11105
145 6/8	21 7/8 22 5/8	18 6/8	5 5	St. Louis County	MO	Jim Holdenried	2001	11105
145 6/8	23 5/8 23 4/8	17 6/8	4 4	Iowa County	IA	Shawn Smith	2001	11105
145 6/8	22 4/8 22 4/8	17 4/8	5 4	McHenry County	IL	Dieter Gutt	2001	11105
145 6/8	23 7/8 23 0/8	20 4/8	5 5	La Grange County	IN	Troy Sams	2002	11105
145 6/8	25 2/8 25 4/8	17 7/8	5 5	Adams County	IA	Randy Loghry	2002	11105
145 6/8	23 3/8 22 5/8	22 5/8	5 7	Jersey County	IL	Brandon Fontenot	2002	11105
145 6/8	25 1/8 25 1/8	19 6/8	4 4	Frio County	TX	Joe Keathley	2003	11105
145 6/8	25 1/8 26 0/8	17 2/8	4 5	Washington County	OH	Elwood Young, Jr.	2003	11105
145 6/8	25 2/8 25 3/8	19 2/8	4 4	Jones County	IA	Gary Holland	2003	11105
*145 6/8	23 3/8 23 6/8	18 4/8	4 4	Polk County	IA	Dan Womble	2003	11105
145 6/8	22 4/8 23 7/8	18 2/8	5 5	Taylor County	IA	Adam Weldon	2003	11105
145 6/8	25 0/8 25 2/8	20 4/8	5 5	Christian County	KY	Phillip Morgan	2003	11105
145 6/8	24 6/8 24 0/8	18 7/8	5 8	Huron County	OH	Steve Hacker	2003	11105
145 6/8	23 5/8 24 3/8	17 6/8	5 5	McHenry County	IL	Bill Kubik	2003	11105
145 6/8	24 0/8 23 6/8	17 1/8	5 7	Lucas County	IA	Michael Starner	2003	11105
145 6/8	22 5/8 22 4/8	16 6/8	5 4	Jackson County	KS	Curtis Shupe	2003	11105
145 6/8	23 6/8 22 7/8	19 0/8	5 4	Will County	IL	Dale Hoekstra	2003	11105
145 6/8	22 6/8 23 4/8	14 4/8	6 7	Henry County	MO	John Stephen Smith	2003	11105
145 6/8	22 4/8 23 1/8	14 0/8	6 6	Miller County	MO	John Ripperger	2004	11105
*145 6/8	23 2/8 23 4/8	17 4/8	6 5	St. Joseph County	MI	Ron Wickenheiser	2004	11105
145 6/8	24 6/8 23 6/8	17 2/8	7 7	Marion County	IA	Kyle Goodwin	2004	11105
145 6/8	23 2/8 23 4/8	18 6/8	6 5	Jefferson County	WI	Dan Gottschalk	2004	11105
145 6/8	23 4/8 22 5/8	20 1/8	5 6	Ashtabula County	OH	Larry M. Knapp	2004	11105
145 6/8	22 6/8 22 5/8	14 2/8	6 5	Adams County	WI	James Mike Flairty	2004	11105
145 6/8	23 2/8 23 3/8	18 6/8	5 5	Pike County	IL	James D. Rueter	2004	11105
145 6/8	22 6/8 22 2/8	22 2/8	5 5	Duval County	TX	Billy E. Corley	2004	11105
145 6/8	22 7/8 22 2/8	15 6/8	5 5	Mower County	MN	Cameron Landherr	2005	11105
*145 6/8	23 7/8 22 5/8	18 2/8	4 4	Pierce County	WI	Barry J. Hager	2005	11105
145 6/8	23 0/8 23 0/8	15 2/8	6 5	Cumberland County	PA	Alvin Halteman	2005	11105
145 6/8	22 3/8 22 3/8	16 1/8	5 6	Woodford County	IL	Stan Bocian	2005	11105
145 6/8	23 1/8 23 4/8	19 3/8	5 4	Macoupin County	IL	Jim Barry	2005	11105
145 6/8	23 0/8 22 1/8	20 0/8	5 5	Butler County	KS	Kent Wartick	2005	11105
145 6/8	22 5/8 22 6/8	19 2/8	5 5	Ripley County	IN	Johnny Howard	2005	11105
145 6/8	25 1/8 24 5/8	16 4/8	5 5	Holmes County	OH	Jim Reynolds	2006	11105
*145 6/8	22 5/8 23 4/8	18 0/8	5 5	Pike County	MO	Brian G. Dempsey	2006	11105
145 6/8	24 2/8 23 0/8	16 0/8	5 5	Waushara County	WI	Kenneth W. Burch	2006	11105
145 6/8	22 6/8 22 5/8	22 2/8	5 5	Livingston County	NY	Gary E. Grattan, Sr.	2006	11105
145 6/8	25 3/8 24 5/8	19 2/8	5 4	Kankakee County	IL	Stanley L. Gawlinski	2006	11105
*145 6/8	23 4/8 24 3/8	17 6/8	5 6	Warren County	IA	David McDowell	2006	11105
145 6/8	23 4/8 23 0/8	23 0/8	5 5	Marion County	IL	Brent Beighley	2006	11105
*145 6/8	24 4/8 25 1/8	19 6/8	5 5	Itasca County	MN	Shane Hastings	2006	11105
145 6/8	25 0/8 25 0/8	20 0/8	5 5	Bucks County	PA	Bill Belz	2007	11105
145 6/8	23 5/8 23 6/8	14 4/8	5 5	Vernon County	WI	Travis Lee Williams	2007	11105

473

WHITETAIL DEER (TYPICAL ANTLERS)

Minimum Score 125 — Continued

SCORE	LENGTH OF R MAIN BEAM L	INSIDE SPREAD	NUMBER OF R POINTS L		AREA	STATE/ PROVINCE	HUNTER'S NAME	DATE	RANK
*145 6/8	22 0/8 22 0/8	16 7/8	5	6	Daviess County	MO	Jonathan McGinness	2007	11105
*145 6/8	25 3/8 25 4/8	19 6/8	4	5	Republic County	KS	Billy Davis	2007	11105
145 6/8	23 0/8 21 4/8	17 4/8	5	5	Edgar County	IL	Tim B. Taylor	2007	11105
145 6/8	25 4/8 24 0/8	15 3/8	7	8	Geauga County	OH	Rick Marinelli	2008	11105
145 6/8	25 5/8 26 1/8	21 0/8	6	4	Henry County	KY	Barry Buffat	2008	11105
*145 6/8	25 1/8 25 5/8	18 0/8	5	5	Woodson County	KS	Tom Sutherland, Jr.	2008	11105
*145 6/8	22 6/8 23 0/8	15 0/8	6	5	Pulaski County	IN	Marc Kesler	2008	11105
*145 6/8	21 4/8 21 3/8	17 0/8	5	5	Pettis County	MO	Mark W. Goodrich	2008	11105
*145 6/8	24 0/8 23 6/8	18 4/8	8	5	Osage County	KS	John Akin	2008	11105
145 6/8	26 3/8 25 4/8	19 7/8	5	4	Dane County	WI	Rick Sies	2008	11105
145 6/8	25 0/8 24 2/8	19 6/8	5	5	Oneida County	WI	Tim Clawson	2008	11105
145 6/8	23 4/8 25 4/8	20 1/8	5	6	Allamakee County	IA	Michael Adkins, Sr.	2008	11105
*145 6/8	21 6/8 21 0/8	22 5/8	5	5	Bee County	TX	Robert R. White	2008	11105
145 6/8	25 4/8 25 6/8	16 2/8	8	5	Vinton County	OH	Matt Bethel	2009	11105
145 6/8	22 3/8 22 2/8	16 5/8	5	6	Knox County	IL	Don Owen	2009	11105
145 6/8	23 0/8 23 5/8	18 4/8	5	7	Clinton County	MI	Mike Hetherington	2009	11105
*145 6/8	22 3/8 22 6/8	19 6/8	5	5	Morrison County	MN	Rand Joe Kramer	2009	11105
*145 6/8	22 5/8 22 0/8	17 0/8	5	5	Marathon County	WI	Kris M. Kosobucki	2009	11105
145 6/8	22 7/8 23 3/8	17 2/8	5	6	Franklin County	OH	Chuck Gregory	2009	11105
145 6/8	23 2/8 22 7/8	14 2/8	5	5	Johnson County	KS	Rickey Akers	2009	11105
145 6/8	21 2/8 20 5/8	18 4/8	6	5	Buffalo County	WI	Marc N. Shaft	2010	11105
145 5/8	25 1/8 24 4/8	19 7/8	6	5	Waseca County	MN	Robert Barrie	1971	11232
145 5/8	22 5/8 21 5/8	17 4/8	6	6	Moody County	SD	Harvey R. Benton	1976	11232
145 5/8	23 5/8 23 0/8	18 4/8	5	7	Stearns County	MN	Larry Schwarze	1979	11232
145 5/8	23 0/8 23 6/8	17 3/8	5	5	Rich Valley	ALB	Eric Teege	1980	11232
145 5/8	23 2/8 23 4/8	18 1/8	5	5	St. Croix County	WI	Keith Andrea	1981	11232
145 5/8	23 5/8 23 1/8	18 1/8	4	4	Wayne County	IA	Andy C. Decker	1982	11232
145 5/8	24 0/8 24 4/8	18 5/8	6	5	Athens County	OH	Steve Wilkes	1983	11232
145 5/8	26 1/8 25 7/8	18 2/8	5	5	Houston County	GA	Issac W. Horne	1985	11232
145 5/8	22 2/8 22 7/8	15 5/8	6	6	Isanti County	MN	Tim Dugas	1985	11232
145 5/8	24 1/8 23 4/8	19 2/8	5	6	Black Hawk County	IA	John L. Derifield	1985	11232
145 5/8	26 2/8 25 1/8	20 6/8	5	7	Christian County	IL	Carl Tucker	1985	11232
145 5/8	23 2/8 24 3/8	20 4/8	6	5	Coffey County	KS	James Bowman	1985	11232
145 5/8	25 5/8 24 5/8	16 7/8	5	4	Hancock County	OH	Dennis J. Morris	1986	11232
145 5/8	23 3/8 24 2/8	17 5/8	5	5	Isanti County	MN	Jon Anderson	1986	11232
145 5/8	26 5/8 24 3/8	19 7/8	4	5	Johnson County	IL	Jack D. Lambert	1986	11232
145 5/8	24 7/8 25 7/8	23 7/8	6	4	Lake County	IL	Robert Henry Torstenson	1986	11232
145 5/8	27 3/8 27 4/8	20 5/8	4	4	Marion County	IA	Leonard Grimes	1986	11232
145 5/8	24 1/8 22 5/8	18 7/8	4	4	Sawyer County	WI	Dan Sours	1989	11232
145 5/8	22 1/8 22 2/8	19 1/8	6	6	Calgary	ALB	Brent Brown	1989	11232
145 5/8	23 5/8 24 1/8	18 1/8	5	4	Platte County	WY	Jerry Bowen	1991	11232
145 5/8	22 6/8 21 6/8	19 7/8	6	6	Lake County	IL	William A. Murphy	1991	11232
145 5/8	23 0/8 22 6/8	18 1/8	5	5	Lake County	IL	Matt Porter	1991	11232
145 5/8	24 2/8 25 3/8	19 7/8	4	4	McHenry County	IL	Joe Roos	1991	11232
145 5/8	26 5/8 26 0/8	19 4/8	5	6	Kendall County	IL	Douglas W. Musser	1992	11232
145 5/8	24 6/8 26 4/8	17 4/8	4	5	Carbon County	MT	Mike Booke	1992	11232
145 5/8	24 3/8 24 2/8	21 3/8	5	6	Highland County	OH	Rickey M. Davis	1994	11232
145 5/8	25 5/8 25 6/8	16 1/8	5	5	Anoka County	MN	Robert Christensen	1994	11232
145 5/8	21 7/8 21 5/8	15 6/8	5	6	Riley County	KS	Ron Phillips	1994	11232
145 5/8	23 4/8 23 3/8	19 3/8	5	5	Ogle County	IL	Mickey D. Badertscher, Jr.	1994	11232
145 5/8	23 6/8 23 2/8	14 1/8	5	5	Ashland County	WI	James Wilbur	1994	11232
145 5/8	23 6/8 23 5/8	19 7/8	5	5	Chester County	PA	Randy D. Coyle	1994	11232
145 5/8	25 0/8 25 4/8	18 2/8	5	5	Fulton County	IL	Patrick Cebuhar	1994	11232
145 5/8	28 7/8 26 1/8	22 3/8	4	5	Miami County	OH	Richard Hunt	1994	11232
145 5/8	25 0/8 24 5/8	17 1/8	7	5	Barry County	MO	R. Steven Crain	1995	11232
145 5/8	22 6/8 23 2/8	18 5/8	5	6	Olmsted County	MN	John G. Wooldridge	1995	11232
145 5/8	23 4/8 23 1/8	17 3/8	5	5	Berks County	PA	Robert J. Entler, Jr.	1995	11232
145 5/8	23 6/8 22 6/8	18 1/8	5	5	Richland County	WI	Joe Bavlnka	1995	11232
145 5/8	22 4/8 22 2/8	18 1/8	5	5	Buffalo County	WI	Carl Wermeling	1995	11232
145 5/8	24 1/8 24 2/8	15 7/8	5	5	Codington County	SD	Troy A. Richardson	1995	11232
145 5/8	26 3/8 25 3/8	17 7/8	4	4	Vermilion County	IL	Kenneth Roy	1995	11232
145 5/8	24 2/8 23 0/8	20 7/8	5	5	Cape Girardeau County	MO	Darrell Hobbs	1995	11232
145 5/8	24 0/8 24 6/8	19 1/8	4	4	Haskell County	OK	Johnny Traylor	1995	11232
145 5/8	20 6/8 18 7/8	16 1/8	6	6	Monroe County	IN	David Smith	1996	11232
145 5/8	22 4/8 22 6/8	17 1/8	5	5	Winona County	MN	Terrence Wobig	1997	11232
145 5/8	24 2/8 24 2/8	17 6/8	5	6	Williamson County	TN	John Rutledge	1997	11232
145 5/8	21 3/8 21 7/8	17 4/8	5	7	Marquette County	WI	Michael V. Marshall	1997	11232
145 5/8	23 3/8 22 7/8	17 0/8	8	6	Mahaska County	IA	Robert Spoelstra	1997	11232
145 5/8	21 4/8 23 2/8	21 1/8	5	5	Monona County	IA	Mark Jost	1997	11232
145 5/8	20 2/8 20 1/8	19 3/8	5	5	Albany County	WY	Joel R. Bailey	1998	11232
145 5/8	24 4/8 23 2/8	15 1/8	5	5	Kent County	MD	Joseph Flanagan	1998	11232
145 5/8	21 3/8 21 5/8	19 2/8	6	5	Vernon County	WI	Matthew Dahlen	1998	11232
145 5/8	24 5/8 23 4/8	16 4/8	5	6	Muskingum County	OH	Scott R. Popeko	1998	11232
145 5/8	23 6/8 23 1/8	18 5/8	5	5	Webster County	IA	Terry Schulz	1998	11232
145 5/8	23 0/8 23 2/8	18 6/8	5	5	E. Carroll Parish	LA	Alan Schweer	1999	11232
145 5/8	23 7/8 23 7/8	19 2/8	10	7	Stark County	IL	Kenneth Hess	1999	11232
145 5/8	26 3/8 24 7/8	18 4/8	6	5	Republic County	KS	Jerry Thomas	1999	11232
145 5/8	23 4/8 24 4/8	17 6/8	6	6	Union County	SD	Nick Welch	1999	11232
145 5/8	22 7/8 22 4/8	15 5/8	6	5	Columbia County	WI	Robbie Buchanan	1999	11232
145 5/8	24 2/8 23 3/8	17 5/8	5	6	Van Buren County	IA	Pat Welch	1999	11232
145 5/8	23 7/8 23 6/8	15 3/8	7	8	Dane County	WI	John M. Anders	2000	11232
145 5/8	23 7/8 24 2/8	16 7/8	4	4	Cass County	MI	Eric E. Emenaker	2000	11232
145 5/8	26 3/8 26 3/8	18 3/8	4	5	Lafayette County	MS	Eric Roush	2000	11232
145 5/8	23 0/8 22 2/8	14 5/8	5	5	Ashland County	WI	Brad J. Rudie	2001	11232
145 5/8	25 2/8 25 0/8	20 1/8	4	4	Adams County	IL	Ronald Allen Jackson	2001	11232
145 5/8	23 7/8 23 7/8	17 3/8	6	5	La Salle County	IL	Terry Mullins	2001	11232
145 5/8	21 7/8 22 3/8	17 0/8	5	6	Marathon County	WI	Jon Beran	2002	11232
145 5/8	24 3/8 22 4/8	17 3/8	5	5	St. Clair County	MO	Richard Pemberton	2002	11232
145 5/8	25 5/8 25 5/8	18 6/8	4	5	Lake County	IL	Chris Marzahl	2002	11232
145 5/8	24 0/8 22 6/8	21 3/8	6	5	Butler County	KS	Hal Waller	2002	11232
145 5/8	22 1/8 22 0/8	16 7/8	5	5	Wabasha County	MN	Deick Bridley	2003	11232
145 5/8	24 0/8 25 4/8	15 7/8	4	5	Darke County	OH	Jason Gentry	2003	11232
145 5/8	21 4/8 22 6/8	19 0/8	7	5	Kenosha County	WI	Loren W. Esch	2003	11232
*145 5/8	23 6/8 24 3/8	16 1/8	5	5	Oakland County	MI	Albert T. Perry	2003	11232
145 5/8	23 6/8 23 6/8	16 1/8	5	4	Hutchinson County	SD	Kyle J. Bak	2004	11232

474

WHITETAIL DEER (TYPICAL ANTLERS)

Minimum Score 125 — Continued

SCORE	LENGTH OF R MAIN BEAM L	INSIDE SPREAD	NUMBER OF R POINTS L	AREA	STATE/PROVINCE	HUNTER'S NAME	DATE	RANK
145 5/8	22 3/8 24 1/8	19 0/8	7 5	Pike County	MO	David W. Bentele	2004	11232
*145 5/8	22 0/8 22 0/8	17 1/8	4 5	Miner County	SD	Kelly Goldammer	2004	11232
*145 5/8	24 6/8 24 7/8	18 3/8	5 6	Sevier County	AR	Brian Gennings	2004	11232
145 5/8	24 4/8 23 5/8	18 3/8	5 5	Van Buren County	IA	Christopher W. Fechner	2004	11232
145 5/8	21 7/8 22 4/8	17 1/8	5 5	Will County	IL	Paul J. Haugen	2005	11232
*145 5/8	22 5/8 22 4/8	19 5/8	4 5	Morgan County	CO	Jeff Jordan	2005	11232
145 5/8	22 7/8 23 2/8	16 7/8	5 5	Lincoln County	SD	Mike Stevens	2005	11232
145 5/8	22 1/8 22 0/8	15 1/8	5 5	Shelby County	MO	Gerald Trunko	2006	11232
*145 5/8	26 4/8 27 1/8	19 6/8	5 8	Tazewell County	IL	Russell Fuller	2006	11232
145 5/8	21 4/8 22 6/8	22 6/8	6 5	Chippewa County	WI	Josh Eder	2006	11232
145 5/8	23 3/8 23 4/8	17 3/8	5 7	Erie County	NY	Robert Kibler	2006	11232
145 5/8	25 1/8 26 1/8	16 0/8	4 5	Noble County	IN	David Kessel	2006	11232
145 5/8	23 0/8 24 1/8	20 3/8	7 7	Waukesha County	WI	Andrew Kolbeck	2006	11232
145 5/8	26 7/8 26 4/8	22 7/8	6 4	Dodge County	WI	Mark A. Ackerman	2006	11232
*145 5/8	22 1/8 21 3/8	15 1/8	5 5	Iowa County	IA	Mike Rife	2007	11232
*145 5/8	25 4/8 24 6/8	18 1/8	6 6	Franklin County	IL	Gabriel L. Knight	2007	11232
145 5/8	23 0/8 23 0/8	17 1/8	6 6	Dunn County	WI	Jason Herman	2008	11232
145 5/8	23 0/8 23 5/8	18 5/8	5 5	Fairfield County	CT	Vince Beauleau	2008	11232
145 5/8	23 6/8 24 7/8	17 3/8	5 5	Cayuga County	NY	Jay Knapp	2008	11232
145 5/8	24 3/8 24 7/8	15 7/8	5 5	Columbia County	WI	Richard A. Schreiber	2008	11232
*145 5/8	24 0/8 24 0/8	15 1/8	6 9	Franklin County	IN	Nick Obermeyer	2008	11232
*145 5/8	25 7/8 24 0/8	19 6/8	6 6	Wayne County	IN	James Hamilton	2008	11232
145 5/8	21 6/8 22 3/8	20 7/8	5 5	Monona County	IA	Dale DuVal	2008	11232
*145 5/8	25 5/8 25 1/8	19 4/8	8 6	Shawnee County	KS	Mike Kruger	2008	11232
*145 5/8	22 1/8 22 2/8	16 3/8	5 5	Divide County	ND	Guy Haugland	2009	11232
145 5/8	23 4/8 23 2/8	19 5/8	5 7	Nemaha County	NE	Rod Teten	2009	11232
*145 5/8	21 6/8 21 0/8	14 7/8	8 5	Richland County	ND	John Langenwalter	2009	11232
*145 5/8	23 0/8 22 1/8	20 7/8	5 8	La Grange County	IN	Kyler West	2009	11232
145 5/8	23 2/8 22 6/8	17 1/8	5 5	Brown County	IL	David R. Herschelman	2009	11232
145 4/8	23 3/8 24 0/8	17 2/8	6 7	Morton County	ND	Eddy Wallery	1959	11335
145 4/8	25 2/8 24 1/8	18 6/8	5 5	Waupaca County	WI	Craig Shambeau	1968	11335
145 4/8	25 5/8 24 4/8	19 0/8	4 5	Monroe County	WI	Larry Arentz	1977	11335
145 4/8	23 2/8 22 0/8	18 2/8	7 6	Mower County	MN	Walter E. Bauer	1977	11335
145 4/8	24 3/8 23 0/8	20 4/8	5 4	Marion County	IA	Donald Bennett	1977	11335
145 4/8	22 1/8 21 6/8	17 2/8	5 5	Van Buren County	MI	Bob Zedeck	1979	11335
145 4/8	24 3/8 22 7/8	18 1/8	5 6	Lawrence County	AL	Richard McClanahan	1980	11335
145 4/8	23 7/8 24 3/8	20 2/8	4 4	Kent County	MI	Peter Champnoise	1981	11335
145 4/8	24 1/8 24 3/8	21 4/8	7 6	Hamilton County	OH	Jack Ranz	1982	11335
145 4/8	24 0/8 24 1/8	18 7/8	5 4	Scott County	KY	Park Tackett	1984	11335
145 4/8	23 0/8 24 0/8	19 4/8	4 5	Cass County	MI	Lee Davis	1985	11335
145 4/8	24 0/8 22 2/8	18 0/8	6 6	Delaware County	OH	Ronald E. Murphy	1986	11335
145 4/8	23 0/8 24 3/8	18 2/8	6 6	Trego County	KS	Morris Crisler	1986	11335
145 4/8	24 0/8 25 1/8	21 3/8	6 6	Houston County	MN	Bruce Norton	1987	11335
145 4/8	24 6/8 22 2/8	17 0/8	5 5	Jefferson County	MO	Steve North	1987	11335
145 4/8	23 2/8 24 4/8	18 2/8	4 4	Adams County	IL	Gary Nebe	1987	11335
145 4/8	23 6/8 23 7/8	18 4/8	4 4	Chester County	PA	Randy R. Caspersen	1988	11335
145 4/8	24 4/8 24 6/8	17 2/8	4 4	Ravalli County	MT	Chris Landstrom	1988	11335
145 4/8	23 5/8 23 3/8	17 0/8	7 6	Kankakee County	IL	Stanley Gawlinski	1990	11335
145 4/8	25 5/8 25 5/8	18 1/8	5 5	Coles County	IL	Gary Jones	1990	11335
145 4/8	22 3/8 22 4/8	17 4/8	5 5	Price County	WI	Phil Socwell	1990	11335
145 4/8	23 4/8 23 4/8	19 0/8	5 6	Buffalo County	WI	Edward Brannen	1991	11335
145 4/8	22 5/8 23 4/8	16 3/8	5 6	Appanoose County	IA	Steven P. Salmieri	1991	11335
145 4/8	24 3/8 23 2/8	19 4/8	5 6	Baca County	CO	Kurt W. Keskimaki	1991	11335
145 4/8	21 0/8 20 4/8	16 5/8	6 7	Osborne County	KS	Dennis Fisk	1991	11335
145 4/8	25 6/8 25 5/8	16 2/8	5 5	Meade County	KY	Aaron H. Pierce	1992	11335
145 4/8	21 3/8 21 6/8	17 2/8	5 6	Brooks County	TX	Jimmy W. McBee	1992	11335
145 4/8	23 0/8 22 2/8	18 6/8	5 5	Will County	IL	Bob Ourth	1992	11335
145 4/8	24 6/8 24 4/8	17 0/8	5 5	Braxton County	WV	Jeffrey Styers	1992	11335
145 4/8	25 1/8 23 5/8	18 5/8	6 5	Edgar County	IL	Darrell Higgins	1993	11335
145 4/8	26 1/8 25 5/8	18 4/8	5 5	Webb County	TX	David M. Richards	1993	11335
145 4/8	26 0/8 25 5/8	19 0/8	5 4	Williamson County	IL	Tim Flowers	1994	11335
145 4/8	22 1/8 22 5/8	18 2/8	7 7	Outagamie County	WI	Donald J. Calmes	1994	11335
145 4/8	27 6/8 27 0/8	19 4/8	5 4	Brown County	IL	Tom Lavery	1994	11335
145 4/8	23 0/8 23 5/8	17 6/8	5 5	Clay County	WV	Rodney Neal	1994	11335
145 4/8	22 1/8 23 1/8	14 6/8	6 7	Aurora County	SD	Troy Kirsch	1994	11335
145 4/8	24 0/8 22 2/8	18 4/8	4 4	Tazewell County	IL	Steven D. Kroll	1994	11335
145 4/8	23 1/8 22 7/8	20 2/8	6 5	Livingston County	IL	Kurt Hobart	1995	11335
145 4/8	23 4/8 23 3/8	20 2/8	4 4	Barron County	WI	Todd W. Bailey	1995	11335
145 4/8	23 6/8 25 6/8	19 4/8	4 4	Greenwood County	KS	Jon Burgdorf	1995	11335
145 4/8	24 2/8 25 5/8	16 0/8	5 5	Olmsted County	MN	Dave Frost	1995	11335
145 4/8	23 3/8 23 7/8	17 2/8	5 5	Dorchester County	MD	Norman L. Eckels, Jr.	1995	11335
145 4/8	24 4/8 24 2/8	17 2/8	6 9	Carroll County	MO	Larry Cochenour	1995	11335
145 4/8	21 3/8 21 1/8	18 4/8	5 7	Todd County	KY	William E. Page	1996	11335
145 4/8	25 0/8 24 6/8	20 6/8	4 4	Fairfield County	CT	Chris Look III	1997	11335
145 4/8	22 6/8 22 4/8	16 2/8	5 5	Howard County	IA	Scott E. Runde	1997	11335
145 4/8	24 4/8 25 7/8	17 7/8	5 5	Iroquois County	IL	Cary Pence	1997	11335
145 4/8	23 4/8 23 4/8	16 0/8	5 6	Chase County	KS	Tony Cassity	1997	11335
145 4/8	23 3/8 22 6/8	16 6/8	7 6	Boone County	MO	Tate Robb	1998	11335
145 4/8	24 0/8 24 4/8	16 5/8	7 7	Steuben County	IN	Troy R. Portner	1998	11335
145 4/8	25 2/8 24 2/8	20 6/8	5 4	Scott County	IL	Larry Harbison	1998	11335
145 4/8	25 5/8 26 4/8	20 4/8	4 4	Barber County	KS	Ronald Bacon	1998	11335
145 4/8	23 7/8 24 0/8	17 7/8	5 5	Allegheny County	PA	Michael B. Wheale	1998	11335
145 4/8	24 1/8 23 6/8	18 7/8	7 6	Clayton County	IA	Mike Then	1998	11335
145 4/8	23 6/8 23 2/8	18 2/8	5 5	Henry County	IL	Tennie J. Weaver	1998	11335
145 4/8	20 1/8 21 0/8	17 0/8	5 6	Saline County	NE	Douglas Shandera	1998	11335
145 4/8	23 0/8 23 6/8	14 7/8	5 6	Fairfax County	VA	Ricky D. Cook	1999	11335
145 4/8	24 6/8 24 7/8	17 4/8	4 5	Buffalo County	WI	Steven Rucinski	1999	11335
145 4/8	26 7/8 26 4/8	17 0/8	5 6	Logan County	OH	Paul Defibaugh	1999	11335
145 4/8	23 1/8 24 6/8	22 0/8	6 5	Lancaster County	NE	Shaun McDonald	2000	11335
145 4/8	25 4/8 25 2/8	21 2/8	4 4	Waushara County	WI	Mitchell Krueger	2000	11335
145 4/8	25 1/8 26 3/8	18 4/8	4 4	Ripley County	IN	David Ely	2000	11335
145 4/8	22 0/8 22 3/8	18 6/8	6 6	Edmonton	ALB	Branko Androic	2001	11335
145 4/8	23 0/8 23 4/8	12 6/8	5 5	Boone County	MO	Corey Gibson	2001	11335
145 4/8	22 7/8 22 2/8	15 2/8	6 5	McDonough County	IL	Joe Laverdiere	2001	11335
145 4/8	22 6/8 23 0/8	17 4/8	5 5	Gogebic County	MI	William Christopherson	2001	11335

WHITETAIL DEER (TYPICAL ANTLERS)

Minimum Score 125   Continued

SCORE	LENGTH OF R MAIN BEAM L	INSIDE SPREAD	NUMBER OF R POINTS L		AREA	STATE/ PROVINCE	HUNTER'S NAME	DATE	RANK
145 4/8	24 7/8 24 6/8	17 4/8	4	4	Cecil County	MD	Alfred Brooks	2001	11335
145 4/8	20 6/8 21 0/8	15 7/8	6	7	Redwood County	MN	Todd Gilb	2001	11335
*145 4/8	23 2/8 23 3/8	18 0/8	5	4	Columbiana County	OH	Carl R. Lindner	2002	11335
145 4/8	24 0/8 24 4/8	16 4/8	5	5	Russell County	KS	Alan Bullard	2002	11335
145 4/8	24 0/8 23 4/8	18 2/8	5	5	Atchison County	MO	Chris Barton	2002	11335
145 4/8	24 0/8 24 2/8	19 0/8	5	5	Schuyler County	NY	Tim Skinner	2002	11335
145 4/8	24 6/8 24 1/8	19 2/8	6	5	Kleberg County	TX	Hunter Meldman	2002	11335
145 4/8	23 3/8 23 4/8	16 7/8	5	4	Marion County	IA	Eric McCombs	2003	11335
145 4/8	22 4/8 22 6/8	19 6/8	5	5	Kingman County	KS	Mark B. Steffen	2004	11335
145 4/8	24 1/8 26 1/8	20 0/8	5	5	Waukesha County	WI	Todd Krempasky	2004	11335
145 4/8	24 6/8 24 5/8	21 2/8	4	4	La Salle County	IL	Allan Simons	2004	11335
*145 4/8	25 5/8 26 0/8	18 2/8	5	5	Lenawee County	MI	Timothy L. Nieto	2004	11335
145 4/8	22 5/8 22 0/8	16 6/8	5	5	Sauk County	WI	Brandon S. Greenheck	2004	11335
145 4/8	22 3/8 22 2/8	16 5/8	6	7	Sauk County	WI	Jason J. Buchholz	2005	11335
*145 4/8	23 4/8 23 2/8	21 0/8	4	4	Erie County	NY	C. Jack Brzezinski	2005	11335
145 4/8	25 7/8 27 0/8	21 6/8	5	4	Buffalo County	WI	John Ford	2005	11335
145 4/8	23 0/8 25 4/8	22 3/8	6	6	Chester County	PA	Samuel S. Beiler	2005	11335
145 4/8	23 3/8 22 6/8	17 2/8	5	6	Langlade County	WI	Zachary Heenan	2005	11335
*145 4/8	24 3/8 24 4/8	19 2/8	5	5	Jo Daviess County	IL	John H. Rineer, Jr.	2005	11335
*145 4/8	26 1/8 24 3/8	19 0/8	4	4	Ashland County	OH	William DeLosh	2005	11335
145 4/8	20 6/8 21 4/8	19 4/8	5	6	Brookings County	SD	Rick Schultz	2005	11335
145 4/8	24 7/8 24 6/8	20 0/8	4	4	Johnson County	IN	Harley S. Clifton	2005	11335
145 4/8	25 4/8 25 0/8	14 6/8	6	6	Weld County	CO	Nathan Andersohn	2005	11335
145 4/8	25 0/8 24 3/8	18 2/8	5	5	Decatur County	IA	Royce DeCook	2005	11335
145 4/8	23 1/8 24 0/8	16 4/8	4	4	Fayette County	TX	John P. Thompson	2005	11335
*145 4/8	24 7/8 25 5/8	18 0/8	5	5	Lawrence County	AR	Steve Light	2005	11335
145 4/8	24 5/8 24 1/8	15 3/8	5	7	Green Lake County	WI	Ethan E. Schulz	2006	11335
145 4/8	23 2/8 24 0/8	18 2/8	6	6	Blue Earth County	MN	Daniel Doman	2006	11335
*145 4/8	26 5/8 25 0/8	18 6/8	5	5	Lawrence County	OH	Brian Howell	2006	11335
145 4/8	21 4/8 21 5/8	16 0/8	7	5	Macon County	MO	Cullen Oldham	2006	11335
145 4/8	24 1/8 23 7/8	17 7/8	5	5	Pepin County	WI	Patrick Falkner	2006	11335
145 4/8	23 6/8 23 7/8	14 4/8	5	5	Trempealeau County	WI	Chad Losinski	2006	11335
*145 4/8	25 0/8 25 6/8	17 2/8	5	5	Pike County	IL	Kyle Ulander	2007	11335
*145 4/8	24 1/8 23 4/8	17 0/8	4	4	Woodford County	IL	John Heineke	2007	11335
145 4/8	24 2/8 23 2/8	17 6/8	5	5	Lyon County	KS	Shawn Hugg	2007	11335
145 4/8	20 2/8 20 0/8	17 4/8	7	6	Pike County	IL	Steve Veres	2007	11335
145 4/8	21 4/8 20 2/8	14 2/8	5	7	Adams County	IL	Jerry Malone	2007	11335
145 4/8	25 5/8 25 0/8	17 5/8	6	5	Montgomery County	PA	Andy Clemmer	2008	11335
*145 4/8	22 7/8 22 2/8	17 6/8	5	6	Brown County	IL	Jim Cowling	2008	11335
*145 4/8	21 4/8 20 7/8	13 4/8	6	5	La Porte County	IN	Mike E. Falck	2008	11335
145 4/8	21 3/8 21 5/8	15 6/8	7	5	Kingman County	KS	Robert Sloey	2008	11335
*145 4/8	21 3/8 21 6/8	18 2/8	5	5	Clay County	AR	Zack Yancey	2008	11335
145 4/8	25 5/8 25 0/8	16 7/8	6	6	Goodhue County	MN	John "Jack" Cordes	2009	11335
*145 4/8	21 6/8 22 4/8	18 6/8	6	5	Polk County	WI	John Larson	2009	11335
145 4/8	22 5/8 22 3/8	17 4/8	5	5	St. Croix County	WI	Ben Talalla	2009	11335
*145 4/8	25 0/8 23 3/8	17 3/8	7	5	Licking County	OH	Ron Spence	2009	11335
145 4/8	24 0/8 23 6/8	20 6/8	5	6	Casey County	KY	Robert I. Popplewell	2009	11335
145 4/8	21 7/8 23 0/8	17 3/8	6	5	Dickinson County	KS	Andrew Nolet	2009	11335
145 4/8	22 5/8 23 6/8	16 6/8	5	5	Pulaski County	MO	Aaron M. C. Cisco	2010	11335
145 3/8	24 3/8 25 1/8	20 5/8	5	5	Lyon County	KS	Edward Bess	1967	11450
145 3/8	22 4/8 22 5/8	18 1/8	5	5	Morrison County	MN	Gerald A. Young	1971	11450
145 3/8	23 4/8 23 4/8	18 6/8	5	5	Kanawha County	WV	Luther McClure	1973	11450
145 3/8	24 5/8 25 5/8	22 1/8	4	5	Will County	IL	Philip J. Gariboldi	1977	11450
145 3/8	26 7/8 26 3/8	20 2/8	4	4	Jackson County	MI	Scot Gazlay	1977	11450
145 3/8	22 7/8 23 0/8	19 1/8	5	5	Des Moines County	IA	John Jindrich	1979	11450
145 3/8	22 6/8 21 3/8	17 4/8	6	6	Marshall County	SD	Tim Johnson	1980	11450
145 3/8	23 7/8 23 7/8	17 5/8	4	4	Pike County	OH	William H. Koehler	1981	11450
145 3/8	23 3/8 23 6/8	17 2/8	5	4	Jackson County	OH	Joe W. Wright	1982	11450
145 3/8	23 4/8 22 2/8	18 1/8	5	5	Osage County	KS	Gary Hunsicker	1985	11450
145 3/8	22 0/8 21 6/8	17 5/8	5	5	Otter Tail County	MN	Walter Rieckman	1986	11450
145 3/8	23 0/8 23 4/8	17 1/8	6	5	Delaware County	OH	Mark Yarnell	1986	11450
145 3/8	20 4/8 21 0/8	15 1/8	6	6	Bayfield County	WI	James Rohr	1986	11450
145 3/8	24 3/8 24 4/8	18 7/8	4	4	Vilas County	WI	Bruce Jacobson	1987	11450
145 3/8	24 6/8 24 6/8	17 4/8	5	6	Le Sueur County	MN	Donald Attenberger	1988	11450
145 3/8	22 4/8 22 0/8	16 3/8	5	6	McHenry County	IL	Bill Gilstead	1988	11450
145 3/8	25 4/8 24 0/8	19 2/8	5	4	Peoria County	IL	Donald R. Ragain	1988	11450
145 3/8	21 5/8 22 5/8	18 1/8	5	5	Osborne County	KS	Craig E. Pottberg	1988	11450
145 3/8	22 7/8 22 3/8	18 1/8	6	5	Tuscarawas County	OH	Emery Schlabach	1988	11450
145 3/8	23 4/8 24 5/8	16 3/8	7	5	Montgomery County	MD	James C. Dalrymple, Jr.	1988	11450
145 3/8	25 7/8 25 7/8	19 3/8	4	4	Langlade County	WI	David Nelson	1989	11450
145 3/8	24 1/8 23 5/8	18 4/8	5	5	Scott County	KY	Darrell Sharp	1990	11450
145 3/8	23 7/8 23 5/8	16 5/8	5	5	Jennings County	IN	Gregory Dean Tucker	1990	11450
145 3/8	24 2/8 24 2/8	17 7/8	6	7	Cherokee County	IA	Dennis Vaudt	1992	11450
145 3/8	23 5/8 26 0/8	16 4/8	5	9	Crawford County	KS	Kim A. Ryan	1992	11450
145 3/8	23 4/8 22 6/8	17 0/8	7	5	Daviess County	IN	Bob C. Graber	1992	11450
145 3/8	22 6/8 22 2/8	18 3/8	5	7	Scott County	MN	Jason Sorenson	1992	11450
145 3/8	22 2/8 22 3/8	20 1/8	5	5	Cook County	IL	David Daly	1992	11450
145 3/8	22 0/8 22 6/8	19 7/8	4	4	Douglas County	MN	Ryan Augeson	1993	11450
145 3/8	22 5/8 22 0/8	18 4/8	7	7	Du Page County	IL	Gerald Allison	1993	11450
145 3/8	26 0/8 27 6/8	18 5/8	5	5	Milwaukee County	WI	Dennis Napreilla	1993	11450
145 3/8	24 4/8 25 5/8	16 6/8	5	5	Saline County	MO	Brandon E. Isbell	1994	11450
145 3/8	28 0/8 26 4/8	19 4/8	6	7	Morrison County	MN	Roger Whiteoak	1994	11450
145 3/8	24 6/8 24 7/8	17 1/8	5	5	Wabasha County	MN	Tim L. Hansen	1994	11450
145 3/8	21 7/8 23 1/8	19 3/8	4	5	Dane County	WI	Brad Madigan	1994	11450
145 3/8	24 5/8 24 6/8	14 4/8	5	5	Clark County	SD	Don Aarstad	1994	11450
145 3/8	24 6/8 26 3/8	20 3/8	5	5	Suffolk County	NY	Vincent Passero	1995	11450
145 3/8	21 1/8 22 4/8	16 7/8	5	5	Appanoose County	IA	Lynn Moeller	1995	11450
145 3/8	26 0/8 25 6/8	19 5/8	4	4	Plymouth County	IA	Jon T. Saunders	1996	11450
145 3/8	25 0/8 23 7/8	16 7/8	5	5	Kenosha County	WI	Brian Koldeway	1996	11450
145 3/8	23 4/8 22 7/8	20 1/8	5	5	St. Louis County	MO	Dave McConnell	1996	11450
145 3/8	23 1/8 23 4/8	18 6/8	6	6	Sutton County	TX	Sherri K. Dean	1997	11450
145 3/8	23 2/8 23 2/8	17 5/8	5	5	Vilas County	WI	Phillip N. Dreger	1997	11450
145 3/8	22 5/8 23 5/8	16 5/8	5	5	Brown County	IL	Bill Klansek	1997	11450
145 3/8	24 7/8 25 5/8	22 3/8	4	5	Edgar County	IL	Dana R. Cawthon	1997	11450
145 3/8	24 0/8 25 0/8	22 4/8	4	5	Cloud County	KS	Gerald Dockins	1997	11450

WHITETAIL DEER (TYPICAL ANTLERS)

Minimum Score 125   Continued

SCORE	LENGTH OF R MAIN BEAM L	INSIDE SPREAD	NUMBER OF R POINTS L		AREA	STATE/ PROVINCE	HUNTER'S NAME	DATE	RANK
145 3/8	22 1/8	23 2/8	14 7/8	5	5	Madison County	IL	Steve Longhi	1997	11450
145 3/8	25 1/8	25 2/8	19 3/8	7	5	Yorkton	SAS	Al Mehling	1998	11450
145 3/8	26 0/8	24 2/8	21 2/8	5	4	Fairfax County	VA	Samuel Kirby Kerns	1998	11450
145 3/8	21 3/8	22 7/8	17 1/8	5	5	Franklin County	MO	Doug Feth	1998	11450
145 3/8	22 2/8	22 5/8	17 5/8	6	5	Moniteau County	MO	Jimmy Arrowood	1998	11450
145 3/8	24 4/8	22 6/8	16 5/8	5	4	Jackson County	WI	Jeff Olson	1998	11450
145 3/8	23 4/8	23 7/8	17 3/8	5	5	Miami County	OH	Vernon C. Smedley	1998	11450
145 3/8	24 4/8	21 2/8	17 1/8	4	4	Warren County	IA	Richard E. Stanton	1998	11450
145 3/8	23 6/8	24 1/8	17 1/8	6	6	Jones County	IA	Stacy Lee Brown	1999	11450
145 3/8	23 0/8	22 7/8	16 5/8	5	5	Columbia County	WI	Randel B. Weihert	1999	11450
145 3/8	23 6/8	23 5/8	19 0/8	6	6	Adair County	IA	Stan Brown	1999	11450
145 3/8	20 6/8	22 1/8	17 2/8	6	5	Grundy County	MO	Steven Meek	1999	11450
145 3/8	26 4/8	26 1/8	17 2/8	5	4	Jersey County	IL	Robert A. Schnettgoecke	2000	11450
145 3/8	23 0/8	23 2/8	19 1/8	4	5	Waushara County	WI	David G. Meier	2000	11450
145 3/8	21 7/8	22 2/8	16 5/8	5	5	Waukesha County	WI	Michael Veres	2000	11450
145 3/8	25 2/8	23 6/8	15 5/8	4	4	Parke County	IN	Tom E. James	2000	11450
145 3/8	25 4/8	25 3/8	15 5/8	4	4	Franklin County	MO	David Gould	2000	11450
145 3/8	24 5/8	24 0/8	19 3/8	4	4	Johnson County	IA	Gene Witt	2000	11450
145 3/8	24 2/8	22 5/8	20 1/8	5	6	Mercer County	IL	Todd L. Jones	2000	11450
145 3/8	24 5/8	24 1/8	18 1/8	6	7	Clark County	IL	Kelly Norton	2001	11450
145 3/8	23 7/8	22 7/8	17 7/8	5	5	Independence County	AR	Witt Stephens, Jr.	2002	11450
145 3/8	24 3/8	24 6/8	18 7/8	6	5	Franklin County	PA	David Larry Stump	2002	11450
145 3/8	23 4/8	24 2/8	18 1/8	5	6	Buffalo County	WI	Ben Curtis	2002	11450
145 3/8	24 5/8	24 3/8	19 3/8	4	4	Sawyer County	WI	Cody Conner	2002	11450
145 3/8	24 1/8	23 5/8	16 5/8	4	5	Jackson County	MO	Rick Morrison	2002	11450
145 3/8	24 6/8	23 4/8	21 0/8	5	5	Adams County	IL	Steve P. Barry	2002	11450
145 3/8	25 4/8	25 3/8	19 1/8	4	4	Van Buren County	MI	Kirk E. Dale	2003	11450
145 3/8	21 4/8	20 7/8	19 5/8	5	6	Fulton County	IN	Timothy B. Corn	2003	11450
145 3/8	25 0/8	23 2/8	19 3/8	5	5	Mitchell County	GA	Jeff Moss	2003	11450
145 3/8	22 0/8	21 7/8	15 3/8	5	5	Burnett County	WI	Rick L. Derrick	2004	11450
145 3/8	23 5/8	24 3/8	18 1/8	5	5	Dodge County	WI	Jeff K. Rosenthal	2004	11450
145 3/8	26 3/8	26 3/8	19 5/8	5	5	Washington County	OH	Ralph L. Long	2004	11450
145 3/8	24 1/8	24 5/8	17 1/8	5	5	Greene County	IL	Randy Templeton	2004	11450
145 3/8	24 6/8	24 0/8	17 5/8	6	5	St. Charles County	MO	Ken Wortmann	2004	11450
*145 3/8	24 2/8	23 7/8	21 1/8	4	5	McHenry County	IL	David A. Comer	2004	11450
145 3/8	24 6/8	23 7/8	17 3/8	5	5	Buffalo County	WI	Eric Farr	2004	11450
145 3/8	24 1/8	24 0/8	18 1/8	5	5	Pratt County	KS	Kory Lang	2004	11450
145 3/8	25 0/8	25 2/8	19 1/8	5	5	Langlade County	WI	Shannon R. Reinke	2005	11450
145 3/8	22 7/8	22 2/8	20 1/8	6	6	Winnebago County	WI	Mike Boyce	2005	11450
145 3/8	24 0/8	21 7/8	19 4/8	5	4	Cecil County	MD	Michael Till	2005	11450
145 3/8	24 5/8	24 4/8	18 1/8	5	5	Henry County	IA	Judd Shumaker	2005	11450
145 3/8	24 1/8	26 2/8	17 7/8	5	5	Buffalo County	WI	Tod Torgerson	2005	11450
*145 3/8	21 5/8	21 0/8	14 7/8	7	5	Parke County	IN	Dean A. Millikan	2005	11450
*145 3/8	26 3/8	26 0/8	20 3/8	4	4	Tippecanoe County	IN	Chris Quinlisk	2005	11450
*145 3/8	22 2/8	22 2/8	18 3/8	6	5	Montgomery County	MD	Peter N. Angle	2005	11450
145 3/8	22 1/8	21 1/8	16 7/8	5	6	Crook County	WY	Mike Schmid	2006	11450
145 3/8	22 0/8	21 5/8	19 3/8	6	5	Fillmore County	MN	Kevin Wikre	2006	11450
145 3/8	23 1/8	23 3/8	16 3/8	5	5	McKenzie County	ND	Lance Keator	2006	11450
145 3/8	24 4/8	24 2/8	17 6/8	7	7	La Crosse County	WI	Greg Mueller	2006	11450
145 3/8	23 4/8	24 5/8	18 7/8	5	5	Linn County	IA	Kevin McDonald	2006	11450
145 3/8	23 2/8	24 2/8	15 1/8	5	5	Marion County	KY	Philip Sharp	2006	11450
145 3/8	24 5/8	23 4/8	19 0/8	6	6	Houston County	MN	Tony Folcey	2006	11450
*145 3/8	24 0/8	24 5/8	16 3/8	5	5	Washington County	PA	Wilbur R. Wood	2006	11450
145 3/8	21 2/8	23 6/8	18 3/8	5	6	Shawano County	WI	Sally A. Reedy	2006	11450
*145 3/8	24 1/8	24 4/8	18 1/8	5	7	Dubuque County	IA	Terry J. Meyer	2007	11450
*145 3/8	23 2/8	23 0/8	15 4/8	7	7	Audrain County	MO	Ronald "Bill" Casto	2007	11450
*145 3/8	25 0/8	23 6/8	20 7/8	5	4	Marquette County	WI	Michael Cuttill	2007	11450
*145 3/8	24 3/8	24 4/8	20 6/8	8	6	Macon County	IL	David P. Backus	2007	11450
145 3/8	22 4/8	22 3/8	18 2/8	6	6	Waukesha County	WI	David A. Steger	2007	11450
145 3/8	25 7/8	24 6/8	19 0/8	6	6	Gallatin County	IL	Wesley T. Blank	2007	11450
145 3/8	22 7/8	23 7/8	17 3/8	5	6	Orange County	IN	Doug Partenheimer	2007	11450
145 3/8	24 4/8	22 4/8	16 5/8	5	5	Bay County	MI	David Haven	2007	11450
*145 3/8	23 3/8	23 7/8	18 7/8	4	5	Perry County	AR	Brad Windle	2008	11450
*145 3/8	23 2/8	23 7/8	19 1/8	4	6	Prince George County	VA	Charles Wilson	2008	11450
*145 3/8	25 5/8	23 2/8	19 4/8	5	4	Kingman County	KS	Paul Owens	2008	11450
145 3/8	23 3/8	24 3/8	18 5/8	5	4	Monmouth County	NJ	Brett Search	2008	11450
145 3/8	25 3/8	24 6/8	20 1/8	4	4	Wyoming County	PA	Gary Custer	2008	11450
145 3/8	25 3/8	24 4/8	18 1/8	6	6	Sherburne County	MN	Michael Jorgensen	2008	11450
145 3/8	25 2/8	25 5/8	18 3/8	5	4	Scotland County	MO	Joseph J. Faron III	2008	11450
*145 3/8	24 0/8	24 2/8	15 7/8	6	6	Dane County	WI	Mike Grady	2008	11450
*145 3/8	23 2/8	22 7/8	16 4/8	7	5	Milk River	ALB	Terry Vickers	2009	11450
145 3/8	26 1/8	26 6/8	19 1/8	4	4	Jo Daviess County	IL	Chad Gerber	2009	11450
*145 3/8	24 1/8	24 4/8	17 4/8	5	5	Burnett County	WI	Scott McFaggen	2009	11450
145 3/8	24 5/8	23 4/8	16 5/8	4	5	Trempealeau County	WI	James Sylla	2009	11450
*145 3/8	23 0/8	22 5/8	17 4/8	7	7	Dane County	WI	Leon Wipperfurth	2009	11450
145 3/8	23 4/8	23 4/8	20 5/8	7	7	Jackson County	WI	Peter Chandler	2009	11450
145 2/8	21 6/8	21 3/8	18 2/8	5	5	Des Moines County	IA	Gary Biles	1973	11572
145 2/8	22 5/8	22 7/8	17 2/8	5	5	Yankton County	SD	Gordon Orton	1976	11572
145 2/8	23 5/8	23 0/8	16 2/8	5	5	Polk County	IA	Jim Young	1978	11572
145 2/8	23 0/8	22 4/8	15 4/8	7	6	Douglas County	KS	Richard D. Brown	1978	11572
145 2/8	23 7/8	24 4/8	17 5/8	5	5	Livingston County	MI	Alan K. Newberry	1979	11572
145 2/8	21 5/8	21 1/8	19 4/8	5	5	Clark County	AR	Thomas E. Taylor	1982	11572
145 2/8	22 7/8	23 6/8	18 6/8	5	5	Madison County	IA	Stephen W. Kent	1982	11572
145 2/8	26 2/8	25 7/8	22 1/8	6	6	Grant County	WI	Gary Wiest	1982	11572
145 2/8	24 1/8	24 2/8	18 6/8	4	4	Vernon County	WI	David Penchi	1982	11572
145 2/8	24 2/8	22 0/8	22 0/8	5	6	Stephenson County	IL	Dwight Pickard	1983	11572
145 2/8	26 6/8	25 6/8	21 2/8	4	4	Mercer County	NJ	James E. McCloskey, Jr.	1984	11572
145 2/8	22 6/8	21 0/8	16 4/8	5	5	Hennepin County	MN	Robert L. Halverson	1985	11572
145 2/8	23 0/8	23 0/8	15 6/8	5	5	Holt County	NE	Thomas D. Lanz	1986	11572
145 2/8	22 5/8	22 1/8	17 0/8	5	5	Cloud County	KS	Mark Copple	1986	11572
145 2/8	23 5/8	24 7/8	18 4/8	6	5	Lincoln County	MT	Michael F. Shepard	1987	11572
145 2/8	24 6/8	23 4/8	18 6/8	4	4	Issaquena County	MS	Charles A. Peeples	1988	11572
145 2/8	23 2/8	23 0/8	17 2/8	5	5	Peoria County	IL	Lenny Asbell	1988	11572
145 2/8	25 6/8	25 3/8	19 2/8	5	6	Du Page County	IL	Gregg Weck	1988	11572
145 2/8	23 1/8	23 6/8	16 3/8	6	4	Lawrence County	IL	Lary Caddell	1988	11572

477

WHITETAIL DEER (TYPICAL ANTLERS)

Minimum Score 125 — Continued

SCORE	LENGTH OF R MAIN BEAM L	INSIDE SPREAD	NUMBER OF R POINTS L	AREA	STATE/PROVINCE	HUNTER'S NAME	DATE	RANK
145 2/8	25 7/8 25 4/8	21 0/8	4 4	Daviess County	IN	John H. Kenworthy	1989	11572
145 2/8	23 0/8 22 5/8	16 6/8	6 4	Delaware County	IA	Dean Dempster	1989	11572
145 2/8	24 5/8 24 0/8	18 4/8	4 6	Clearwater County	ID	Michael L. McCabe	1990	11572
145 2/8	24 0/8 24 2/8	17 4/8	4 4	Columbia County	PA	Robert Markle	1990	11572
145 2/8	23 1/8 22 0/8	17 2/8	5 5	Seward County	KS	Lynn Leonard	1990	11572
145 2/8	24 4/8 24 6/8	18 0/8	4 4	Rock Island County	IL	Tim Pressly	1990	11572
145 2/8	23 4/8 23 4/8	20 5/8	5 5	Belmont County	OH	Aaron Wiley	1990	11572
145 2/8	22 2/8 22 0/8	17 4/8	5 5	Davis County	IA	Roy Glosser	1990	11572
145 2/8	21 1/8 21 7/8	18 0/8	5 5	Chester County	PA	Stephen Daniels Raeburn	1991	11572
145 2/8	24 0/8 23 5/8	18 0/8	9 6	Wyandotte County	KS	Earl A. Cooksey	1991	11572
145 2/8	23 0/8 23 4/8	19 0/8	7 6	Webster County	IA	Steven W. Hiveley	1992	11572
145 2/8	22 7/8 22 3/8	16 2/8	5 5	Pottawattamie County	IA	Jeffery L. Hodges	1992	11572
145 2/8	22 2/8 22 0/8	16 2/8	5 6	Logan County	WV	Kevin A. Stone	1992	11572
145 2/8	23 4/8 23 2/8	18 0/8	7 7	Cook County	IL	Daniel H. Albaugh	1993	11572
145 2/8	22 1/8 23 2/8	19 6/8	5 5	Somerset County	MD	Michael Alan Pilchard	1993	11572
145 2/8	22 1/8 22 1/8	21 0/8	5 5	Carroll County	IL	Mike Gibson	1993	11572
145 2/8	20 4/8 21 2/8	14 4/8	5 5	Emmet County	IA	Timothy S. McCarthy	1993	11572
145 2/8	24 0/8 23 4/8	17 6/8	5 5	Chippewa County	WI	Loren J. Roth	1994	11572
145 2/8	21 0/8 22 4/8	17 1/8	7 5	Calhoun County	IL	David Triplo	1994	11572
145 2/8	23 0/8 23 4/8	17 2/8	6 5	Lee County	IL	Gary Miller	1994	11572
145 2/8	23 6/8 22 7/8	16 2/8	4 4	Brooks County	TX	Craig Weiland	1994	11572
145 2/8	25 1/8 23 5/8	19 0/8	5 5	Issaquena County	MS	Robert H. Jarvis	1994	11572
145 2/8	23 4/8 23 6/8	19 2/8	6 6	Dunn County	WI	Dave Lieffort	1994	11572
145 2/8	23 0/8 22 2/8	15 6/8	6 5	Lancaster County	NE	Jim Ryan	1994	11572
145 2/8	24 2/8 24 6/8	16 3/8	5 5	Calloway County	KY	Roger Moredock	1995	11572
145 2/8	25 5/8 22 7/8	16 4/8	4 4	Allamakee County	IA	Marlon Jones	1996	11572
145 2/8	24 1/8 22 6/8	17 6/8	5 5	Lawrence County	IN	Kevin Luallen	1996	11572
145 2/8	23 0/8 22 1/8	15 3/8	6 5	La Salle County	IL	John P. Hartman	1997	11572
145 2/8	21 2/8 21 1/8	16 0/8	5 5	Marinette County	WI	Brian Wieting	1997	11572
145 2/8	23 3/8 23 1/8	20 0/8	5 5	Calhoun County	MI	John P. Walters II	1997	11572
145 2/8	26 1/8 24 2/8	17 4/8	7 5	Pike County	IL	Eddie Claypool	1997	11572
145 2/8	26 0/8 24 6/8	20 0/8	6 5	Monona County	IA	Kyle Corey	1997	11572
145 2/8	24 7/8 25 4/8	17 6/8	5 5	Raleigh County	WV	Robert Jarrell	1997	11572
145 2/8	25 6/8 24 4/8	16 6/8	4 5	Warren County	IL	Will Higgins	1998	11572
145 2/8	25 6/8 24 2/8	17 0/8	4 4	Dunn County	WI	Jeffery J. Hoff	1998	11572
145 2/8	24 3/8 25 1/8	18 5/8	6 5	Rock County	WI	Kenneth McKennon	1998	11572
145 2/8	25 2/8 25 7/8	19 5/8	6 5	Tioga County	NY	Robert Nurritto	1998	11572
145 2/8	25 4/8 24 1/8	15 6/8	6 5	Dubuque County	IA	Jim F. Roth	1999	11572
145 2/8	25 4/8 25 0/8	19 1/8	7 4	Leavenworth County	KS	Richard S. Inlow	1999	11572
145 2/8	23 6/8 22 2/8	16 6/8	5 5	Boone County	IL	Jim Kaszynski	1999	11572
145 2/8	24 3/8 25 4/8	21 4/8	6 5	Ozaukee County	WI	Joe Spata	1999	11572
145 2/8	22 3/8 22 4/8	15 6/8	5 5	St. Joseph County	MI	Josh Pant	2000	11572
145 2/8	28 2/8 29 2/8	20 2/8	3 3	Waupaca County	WI	Daniel Herson	2000	11572
145 2/8	25 1/8 25 1/8	19 4/8	6 5	Rice County	KS	Russell L. Hammer	2000	11572
145 2/8	21 6/8 22 2/8	17 0/8	5 8	Grundy County	MO	Dave Wright	2000	11572
145 2/8	24 5/8 25 2/8	21 3/8	5 4	Clayton County	IA	Steve Gobeli	2000	11572
145 2/8	22 2/8 21 5/8	16 4/8	6 5	Decatur County	IA	Steve Snow	2000	11572
145 2/8	24 7/8 24 0/8	19 0/8	4 6	Stephenson County	IL	Jamie A. Hafferty	2000	11572
145 2/8	21 6/8 22 1/8	19 0/8	5 5	Calumet County	WI	Michael G. Schwarz	2000	11572
145 2/8	22 4/8 21 6/8	16 4/8	6 6	Sterling County	TX	Deron C. Gross	2001	11572
145 2/8	23 4/8 23 7/8	18 3/8	6 7	Summit County	OH	William N. Novicky	2001	11572
145 2/8	23 7/8 22 6/8	18 6/8	7 6	Madison County	MS	Kendrick Gross	2001	11572
145 2/8	22 6/8 23 0/8	15 4/8	5 5	Marion County	MO	Chris Harlow	2001	11572
145 2/8	25 0/8 23 4/8	17 1/8	6 6	Coal County	OK	Mike Megee	2001	11572
145 2/8	24 1/8 25 0/8	18 2/8	5 5	Webb County	TX	Hank Bussa	2001	11572
145 2/8	22 4/8 24 0/8	13 4/8	6 5	Lincoln County	AR	Lee Walt	2002	11572
145 2/8	25 0/8 25 6/8	18 4/8	4 4	McHenry County	IL	Scott Attergott	2002	11572
145 2/8	24 7/8 24 4/8	18 6/8	5 5	Roseau County	MN	Luis Jain	2002	11572
145 2/8	21 4/8 22 6/8	19 0/8	5 5	Lake County	IL	Steve Hysell	2002	11572
145 2/8	23 5/8 23 0/8	19 6/8	5 5	Webb County	TX	Dennis Cooke	2002	11572
145 2/8	22 0/8 23 1/8	18 0/8	5 5	Nodaway County	MO	Doug A. Gallagher	2003	11572
145 2/8	23 2/8 22 6/8	17 2/8	5 5	Elkhart County	IN	Donald J. Lambert	2003	11572
145 2/8	24 2/8 25 3/8	18 6/8	7 6	Wood County	WI	Cary Schneider	2003	11572
145 2/8	24 0/8 23 7/8	17 2/8	7 4	Richardson County	NE	Jerry D. Oliver	2003	11572
145 2/8	22 0/8 21 7/8	17 4/8	5 5	Ward County	ND	Harold L. Marten	2003	11572
145 2/8	21 7/8 21 3/8	16 2/8	5 5	Woodbury County	IA	Jon T. Saunders	2003	11572
145 2/8	25 2/8 23 6/8	18 4/8	4 6	Rock County	WI	Carey Passer	2003	11572
145 2/8	22 3/8 23 0/8	19 7/8	6 5	Seward County	NE	Travis Keslar	2003	11572
*145 2/8	24 0/8 24 5/8	19 0/8	5 6	Floyd County	IA	Randy Bouska	2004	11572
145 2/8	23 6/8 25 4/8	20 2/8	4 4	Vernon County	WI	Andrew J. Blum	2004	11572
145 2/8	24 5/8 23 5/8	18 5/8	6 4	Jefferson County	NE	Nicholas R. Koch	2004	11572
145 2/8	21 2/8 23 4/8	19 1/8	5 6	Buffalo County	WI	John G. Erickson	2004	11572
145 2/8	26 1/8 26 0/8	18 5/8	5 5	Edgar County	IL	Dan Cable	2004	11572
145 2/8	21 7/8 21 6/8	15 6/8	5 5	Pope County	IL	Jeff Tupper	2004	11572
*145 2/8	21 3/8 21 3/8	16 3/8	5 5	Jasper County	IL	Steve Miller	2004	11572
*145 2/8	25 1/8 25 1/8	20 4/8	5 5	Shawnee County	KS	Art Fletcher	2004	11572
145 2/8	22 6/8 23 1/8	16 0/8	5 5	Sauk County	WI	Rich G. Thruman	2005	11572
*145 2/8	22 6/8 22 7/8	17 4/8	5 5	Muskingum County	OH	Lenny Palmisano	2005	11572
145 2/8	26 1/8 25 2/8	19 4/8	4 4	Randolph County	IN	Trevor A. Hoover	2005	11572
*145 2/8	23 1/8 23 0/8	18 0/8	6 5	Waukesha County	WI	Whitie Mehlberg	2005	11572
145 2/8	25 1/8 25 6/8	18 6/8	4 4	Lorain County	OH	Giles Russell	2005	11572
145 2/8	24 5/8 24 7/8	20 2/8	4 5	Fairfield County	OH	Andrew L. Cherryhomes	2005	11572
145 2/8	22 0/8 20 0/8	16 0/8	5 5	Montgomery County	MO	Michael R. Vagedes	2005	11572
145 2/8	25 2/8 24 5/8	19 4/8	4 4	Louisa County	IA	Dean Welchman	2005	11572
145 2/8	26 3/8 26 2/8	21 5/8	8 7	Sandusky County	OH	Thomas Olszewski	2005	11572
145 2/8	23 0/8 24 5/8	16 6/8	5 5	Richland County	WI	Paul Henthorn	2006	11572
145 2/8	25 2/8 25 1/8	17 2/8	4 4	Litchfield County	CT	John Coniglio	2006	11572
*145 2/8	24 0/8 25 2/8	19 4/8	4 4	Monroe County	NY	Tony Tumminelli	2006	11572
145 2/8	22 6/8 22 6/8	18 7/8	6 5	Tazewell County	IL	Richard Frederick	2006	11572
145 2/8	25 1/8 23 1/8	19 3/8	7 8	Clarke County	IA	Brian Pollard	2006	11572
145 2/8	22 1/8 23 2/8	16 4/8	5 5	Minnehaha County	SD	Howard W. Burns	2007	11572
145 2/8	22 5/8 23 0/8	15 7/8	6 5	Morgan County	OH	Gregg Woodyard	2007	11572
*145 2/8	24 1/8 24 2/8	16 0/8	5 5	Garson	MAN	John Walczak	2007	11572
145 2/8	25 3/8 24 5/8	21 5/8	5 4	Johnson County	IA	Bo Jackson	2007	11572
*145 2/8	25 1/8 24 3/8	17 4/8	5 5	Wayne County	IN	Claude Reynolds	2007	11572

WHITETAIL DEER (TYPICAL ANTLERS)

Minimum Score 125 Continued

SCORE	LENGTH OF MAIN BEAM R / L	INSIDE SPREAD	NUMBER OF POINTS R / L	AREA	STATE/ PROVINCE	HUNTER'S NAME	DATE	RANK
145 2/8	22 7/8 / 22 2/8	14 6/8	5 / 6	Fulton County	IL	Jeff Pals	2007	11572
145 2/8	22 2/8 / 22 7/8	16 3/8	6 / 5	Anderson County	KS	Gary Hall	2007	11572
*145 2/8	23 3/8 / 22 5/8	16 4/8	7 / 7	Clay County	NE	James Hamik	2007	11572
145 2/8	24 0/8 / 25 2/8	17 4/8	5 / 6	Defiance County	OH	Darren E. Yackee	2007	11572
145 2/8	24 3/8 / 24 3/8	19 0/8	4 / 4	Kane County	IL	Roy H. Desmond	2008	11572
*145 2/8	26 2/8 / 25 6/8	19 5/8	6 / 6	Olmsted County	MN	Michele Leqve	2008	11572
145 2/8	24 7/8 / 24 1/8	19 6/8	4 / 5	Trempealeau County	WI	Matt R. Andersen	2008	11572
145 2/8	24 0/8 / 23 2/8	19 4/8	5 / 6	Wright County	MN	Eric Williamson	2008	11572
*145 2/8	24 3/8 / 24 4/8	19 4/8	5 / 4	Randolph County	IL	Luke Simpson	2008	11572
*145 2/8	23 3/8 / 23 0/8	18 6/8	5 / 6	La Crosse County	WI	Charles Mahlum	2009	11572
*145 2/8	21 4/8 / 21 7/8	18 7/8	6 / 5	Manitowoc County	WI	Terry A. Wiensch	2009	11572
145 2/8	25 0/8 / 24 7/8	21 0/8	4 / 5	Carroll County	OH	Larry James	2009	11572
*145 2/8	22 7/8 / 23 4/8	18 2/8	5 / 5	Shawano County	WI	Thomas G. Kestly	2010	11572
145 1/8	24 7/8 / 25 2/8	22 0/8	5 / 6	Grundy County	IL	Tony Muhich	1975	11699
145 1/8	23 1/8 / 22 7/8	17 1/8	7 / 7	Dearborn County	IN	David Goodwin	1978	11699
145 1/8	22 3/8 / 22 5/8	15 5/8	5 / 5	Kent County	MI	Virgil G. Baker, Jr.	1979	11699
145 1/8	23 6/8 / 23 2/8	18 5/8	5 / 6	Green County	WI	Dan Behring	1979	11699
145 1/8	24 6/8 / 24 0/8	18 5/8	6 / 5	Leavenworth County	KS	Chris Calovich	1982	11699
145 1/8	23 0/8 / 23 0/8	17 3/8	5 / 5	Berkshire County	MA	Richard Scorzafava	1984	11699
145 1/8	21 7/8 / 21 6/8	17 1/8	5 / 5	Calgary	ALB	Dwayne Andrus	1986	11699
145 1/8	22 6/8 / 23 0/8	20 5/8	6 / 6	Floyd County	VA	Jeffery Weddle	1987	11699
145 1/8	23 6/8 / 23 6/8	21 1/8	4 / 4	Montgomery County	OH	Sam Dycus	1987	11699
145 1/8	23 6/8 / 23 4/8	18 6/8	5 / 7	Livingston County	NY	Gary Hartford	1988	11699
145 1/8	23 2/8 / 24 3/8	20 3/8	4 / 5	Stanton County	NE	Gary Frowick	1989	11699
145 1/8	25 4/8 / 25 6/8	18 7/8	4 / 4	Monroe County	IA	Tom Starns	1989	11699
145 1/8	25 3/8 / 24 0/8	19 7/8	4 / 5	Buffalo County	WI	Mark E. Fetting	1990	11699
145 1/8	22 6/8 / 22 2/8	18 1/8	5 / 5	Jones County	IA	Ronald W. Post	1990	11699
145 1/8	24 2/8 / 22 7/8	20 1/8	5 / 5	Carroll County	MD	Bill Roach	1990	11699
145 1/8	22 3/8 / 23 3/8	14 3/8	5 / 5	Cadogan	ALB	Judd Cooney	1991	11699
145 1/8	23 5/8 / 23 5/8	20 7/8	4 / 5	Platte County	MO	Francisco Escobar	1991	11699
145 1/8	22 2/8 / 21 7/8	16 5/8	5 / 5	Crawford County	IL	Charlie Guyer	1991	11699
145 1/8	22 6/8 / 22 3/8	19 3/8	5 / 6	Weslock	ALB	Trevor Edwards	1992	11699
145 1/8	22 2/8 / 22 4/8	18 7/8	4 / 4	Middlesex County	NJ	George A. Costantini	1993	11699
145 1/8	21 1/8 / 21 0/8	13 7/8	5 / 6	Lincoln County	MO	Christopher Scoggins	1993	11699
145 1/8	23 0/8 / 23 4/8	18 1/8	5 / 5	Perry County	IL	Charlie Korte	1993	11699
145 1/8	24 7/8 / 23 7/8	18 3/8	5 / 5	Monroe County	IA	Fred "Bud" Allen	1993	11699
145 1/8	24 7/8 / 25 4/8	20 5/8	4 / 4	Lawrence County	IL	Dan Deisher	1993	11699
145 1/8	21 4/8 / 21 4/8	19 7/8	5 / 5	Valley County	MT	Gene Henck	1993	11699
145 1/8	23 0/8 / 21 5/8	16 5/8	5 / 5	Edgar County	IL	Kenneth Wiehe	1993	11699
145 1/8	24 0/8 / 23 4/8	18 7/8	6 / 5	Pike County	IL	William R. Graham	1993	11699
145 1/8	24 0/8 / 23 2/8	16 1/8	5 / 6	Licking County	OH	Ron Engstrom	1994	11699
145 1/8	25 1/8 / 24 7/8	17 5/8	5 / 5	Sullivan County	IN	Mike Crist	1994	11699
145 1/8	21 4/8 / 24 1/8	17 1/8	6 / 6	Shiawassee County	MI	Chris A. Adolf	1994	11699
145 1/8	21 6/8 / 21 7/8	15 5/8	5 / 5	Parke County	IN	Rick Marshall	1995	11699
145 1/8	21 1/8 / 20 6/8	17 1/8	5 / 5	Edmonton	ALB	Steve MacKenzie	1996	11699
145 1/8	24 1/8 / 23 5/8	18 0/8	4 / 5	Arkansas County	AR	Joe D. Milloway	1996	11699
145 1/8	24 0/8 / 24 1/8	16 6/8	8 / 5	Livingston County	MI	Dave Kasbohm	1996	11699
145 1/8	25 7/8 / 24 0/8	18 3/8	4 / 4	Spencer County	KY	Nathan D. Tucker	1996	11699
145 1/8	24 3/8 / 23 1/8	19 5/8	5 / 5	Waukesha County	WI	Kris Droegkamp	1996	11699
145 1/8	22 5/8 / 22 7/8	18 3/8	5 / 5	Delaware County	IA	Kelly Salow	1996	11699
145 1/8	25 1/8 / 25 3/8	19 3/8	5 / 6	Vermilion County	IL	Jack A. Miller	1996	11699
145 1/8	24 0/8 / 23 5/8	18 5/8	4 / 4	Hampden County	MA	Art Leigner	1996	11699
145 1/8	25 0/8 / 26 2/8	20 7/8	5 / 4	Sussex County	DE	Wade B. Whaley	1997	11699
145 1/8	26 2/8 / 27 1/8	20 4/8	4 / 5	Des Moines County	IA	Jeff Wilson	1997	11699
145 1/8	23 1/8 / 23 3/8	19 2/8	6 / 6	Price County	WI	David Pepper	1997	11699
145 1/8	23 1/8 / 24 1/8	16 5/8	5 / 5	Pike County	IL	Gregory S. Guerrieri	1997	11699
145 1/8	23 5/8 / 23 4/8	17 7/8	5 / 5	Clermont County	OH	Mark D. Wolfson	1997	11699
145 1/8	23 2/8 / 24 1/8	17 7/8	7 / 5	Jersey County	IL	Jeff Fencel	1997	11699
145 1/8	25 0/8 / 24 3/8	17 7/8	4 / 5	Coles County	IL	John H. Hoxmeier	1997	11699
145 1/8	21 2/8 / 21 4/8	19 0/8	6 / 6	Macon County	IL	Dave Elliott	1998	11699
145 1/8	23 5/8 / 23 2/8	20 1/8	4 / 4	Butler County	IA	Ken Van Lengen	1998	11699
145 1/8	24 4/8 / 23 5/8	17 5/8	4 / 4	Walworth County	WI	Eli Nieuwenhuis	1998	11699
145 1/8	25 4/8 / 26 3/8	19 3/8	4 / 4	Buffalo County	WI	Steven L. Olson	1998	11699
145 1/8	26 6/8 / 25 7/8	18 7/8	5 / 5	Columbiana County	OH	Doug Winland	1998	11699
145 1/8	21 6/8 / 22 4/8	19 5/8	5 / 5	Duval County	TX	Gip Friesen	1998	11699
145 1/8	22 5/8 / 21 3/8	15 7/8	5 / 5	Sioux County	NE	Rich Kimball	1999	11699
145 1/8	25 2/8 / 25 3/8	18 5/8	6 / 7	York County	NBW	Terry Dillon	1999	11699
145 1/8	21 4/8 / 22 5/8	17 5/8	5 / 5	Waukesha County	WI	Todd Krempasky	1999	11699
145 1/8	23 4/8 / 23 4/8	21 5/8	5 / 5	Eau Claire County	WI	William A. Ciezki	1999	11699
145 1/8	23 0/8 / 22 4/8	18 3/8	5 / 5	Monona County	IA	Rod Sigel	1999	11699
145 1/8	22 3/8 / 21 0/8	16 3/8	5 / 5	Greene County	IN	Galen L. Miller	1999	11699
145 1/8	24 4/8 / 23 6/8	16 1/8	5 / 7	Monroe County	NY	Thomas G. Hartman	1999	11699
145 1/8	24 1/8 / 25 0/8	23 0/8	4 / 6	La Salle	MAN	Curt Bossuyt	1999	11699
145 1/8	26 5/8 / 26 1/8	19 5/8	4 / 4	Middlesex County	CT	Donald R. Venuti, Jr.	2000	11699
145 1/8	22 5/8 / 21 6/8	16 5/8	5 / 5	Waushara County	WI	Patrick A. Colburn	2000	11699
145 1/8	24 2/8 / 24 0/8	17 5/8	4 / 4	Adams County	WI	Micheal Witkowski	2000	11699
145 1/8	23 7/8 / 22 2/8	19 5/8	5 / 5	Marshall County	IL	William E. Reuscher	2000	11699
145 1/8	22 2/8 / 22 7/8	18 3/8	7 / 6	Poplarfield	MAN	David A. Shupp	2000	11699
145 1/8	23 3/8 / 24 3/8	20 7/8	4 / 4	Nelson County	ND	Jay Estvold	2000	11699
145 1/8	24 2/8 / 24 2/8	19 1/8	5 / 5	Livingston County	IL	Jeffery E. Wilson	2001	11699
145 1/8	21 4/8 / 21 2/8	17 3/8	6 / 5	Green County	WI	Al Martin	2001	11699
*145 1/8	23 5/8 / 23 2/8	17 3/8	5 / 5	Cass County	MI	Todd Schacknies	2001	11699
145 1/8	20 6/8 / 21 7/8	20 3/8	6 / 6	Dane County	WI	Kurt Schaller	2001	11699
145 1/8	22 6/8 / 23 2/8	16 1/8	6 / 6	Clayton County	IA	Joe Lieb	2001	11699
145 1/8	24 4/8 / 24 4/8	16 4/8	5 / 5	Brown County	KS	Jim Holdenried	2001	11699
145 1/8	25 4/8 / 24 7/8	20 5/8	4 / 4	Montgomery County	IL	Richard Doolin	2001	11699
145 1/8	22 0/8 / 23 1/8	17 1/8	6 / 5	McLean County	ND	Larry Rice	2002	11699
145 1/8	22 5/8 / 23 1/8	17 5/8	5 / 5	Polk County	WI	Todd Cunningham	2002	11699
145 1/8	25 0/8 / 25 0/8	16 7/8	6 / 6	La Salle County	IL	John R. Blunk	2002	11699
145 1/8	22 2/8 / 23 6/8	17 3/8	5 / 5	Door County	WI	Chad Jeanquart	2003	11699
145 1/8	24 0/8 / 23 0/8	16 3/8	6 / 7	Pike County	IL	Mark L. Dorty	2003	11699
145 1/8	27 0/8 / 26 1/8	19 7/8	5 / 5	Madison County	IA	Frank Stutsman	2003	11699
145 1/8	24 1/8 / 24 0/8	21 5/8	4 / 4	Kenosha County	WI	Robert D. Bozarth	2003	11699
145 1/8	25 2/8 / 24 4/8	15 7/8	5 / 5	Ashland County	OH	Joseph M. Sammon	2003	11699
145 1/8	22 3/8 / 22 5/8	18 5/8	5 / 5	Dubuque County	IA	Corey P. Klein	2004	11699

479

WHITETAIL DEER (TYPICAL ANTLERS)

Minimum Score 125 — Continued

SCORE	LENGTH OF MAIN BEAM R	L	INSIDE SPREAD	NUMBER OF POINTS R	L	AREA	STATE/PROVINCE	HUNTER'S NAME	DATE	RANK
*145 1/8	24 4/8	25 3/8	18 7/8	4	4	Gwinnett County	GA	Joe Street	2004	11699
145 1/8	23 3/8	22 6/8	17 5/8	5	5	Waupaca County	WI	Dan Loken	2004	11699
145 1/8	24 1/8	24 3/8	19 1/8	4	4	Jersey County	IL	Judy Kovar	2004	11699
145 1/8	26 7/8	26 7/8	17 5/8	4	6	Shelby County	IL	Greg Scribner	2004	11699
145 1/8	23 4/8	23 5/8	17 3/8	4	4	Buffalo County	WI	Al Schroeder	2004	11699
145 1/8	21 6/8	21 7/8	15 1/8	5	6	Plymouth County	IA	Brian J. Emmick	2004	11699
145 1/8	24 4/8	24 0/8	21 7/8	5	5	Dimmit County	TX	Wendell Wallace	2004	11699
145 1/8	25 2/8	25 0/8	19 4/8	6	5	Jo Daviess County	IL	Jim Horneck	2004	11699
145 1/8	22 7/8	23 5/8	20 3/8	5	5	Price County	WI	Jerry Piechowski	2004	11699
145 1/8	21 3/8	21 5/8	15 1/8	5	5	Madison County	IA	Ken Flaherty	2004	11699
145 1/8	23 2/8	23 6/8	18 7/8	5	4	McLean County	IL	John Heinlen	2005	11699
*145 1/8	23 4/8	22 3/8	18 2/8	6	5	Outagamie County	WI	Bryan Lausman	2005	11699
145 1/8	22 6/8	21 7/8	16 1/8	5	6	Jackson County	IA	John Gau	2005	11699
*145 1/8	24 0/8	24 2/8	19 2/8	4	4	Jackson County	IL	Terry Page	2005	11699
145 1/8	21 5/8	21 1/8	16 1/8	5	5	Pike County	IL	Greg Spangler, Sr.	2005	11699
145 1/8	21 7/8	24 4/8	17 5/8	5	5	Audrain County	MO	Lindell Spiers	2005	11699
*145 1/8	25 1/8	24 4/8	17 5/8	5	5	Marshall County	IA	Brad M. Larson	2005	11699
145 1/8	24 4/8	25 0/8	20 5/8	6	6	Marion County	IA	Tyler Naeve	2005	11699
145 1/8	23 2/8	23 0/8	15 0/8	4	6	Comanche County	KS	Fred Eichler	2005	11699
145 1/8	24 5/8	24 5/8	20 5/8	4	4	Sedgwick County	KS	Willie Metzen	2006	11699
145 1/8	22 6/8	25 2/8	17 6/8	6	5	Pike County	IL	Scott Benassi	2006	11699
*145 1/8	24 2/8	23 4/8	18 3/8	4	4	Schuyler County	IL	Steve Pollard	2006	11699
145 1/8	21 7/8	22 3/8	16 4/8	7	6	Walsh County	ND	Gary Monsebroten	2006	11699
145 1/8	25 7/8	24 0/8	16 4/8	7	5	Livingston County	MO	Tom Monehan	2006	11699
145 1/8	21 6/8	21 6/8	16 5/8	5	5	Bonner County	ID	John Schneider	2007	11699
145 1/8	25 3/8	25 7/8	23 3/8	5	4	Genesee County	NY	Steven Marsceill	2007	11699
145 1/8	26 6/8	27 6/8	18 6/8	6	8	Anne Arundel County	MD	Will Rosenberg	2007	11699
145 1/8	23 3/8	23 4/8	15 5/8	5	5	Columbia County	WI	Ryan Vick	2007	11699
145 1/8	23 7/8	23 5/8	17 3/8	7	5	Green County	WI	Paul Ovadal	2008	11699
*145 1/8	24 0/8	26 7/8	19 1/8	4	4	Franklin County	IN	Joel Biltz	2008	11699
145 1/8	22 3/8	20 7/8	17 1/8	6	5	Worth County	IA	Lucas Flugum	2008	11699
145 1/8	24 4/8	25 0/8	17 6/8	5	4	Riley County	KS	Eddie Ripp	2008	11699
145 1/8	23 3/8	22 1/8	16 5/8	6	8	Ramsey County	ND	Josh Worley	2009	11699
*145 1/8	22 1/8	23 1/8	14 7/8	6	5	Shelby County	KY	Scott Barrass	2009	11699
145 1/8	26 5/8	27 5/8	19 5/8	5	5	Phillips County	KS	Jason Van Kooten	2009	11699
145 1/8	23 2/8	22 1/8	19 7/8	5	5	Traill County	ND	Jim Kirkeby	2009	11699
145 1/8	23 6/8	24 4/8	16 5/8	5	7	Greene County	OH	Ed Heigel	2009	11699
*145 1/8	25 4/8	26 7/8	23 6/8	5	5	Carroll County	IN	Kameron Banes	2009	11699
*145 1/8	24 1/8	27 2/8	20 7/8	5	6	Harper County	KS	John Add Benson	2009	11699
145 0/8	22 5/8	21 2/8	14 2/8	6	6	Washington County	IA	Doron Whitlock	1966	11820
145 0/8	24 0/8	24 5/8	20 0/8	4	4	Grant County	SD	Kevin Bronson	1973	11820
145 0/8	24 0/8	22 2/8	15 2/8	6	6	Trigg County	KY	Donald Powell	1974	11820
145 0/8	23 1/8	22 6/8	15 2/8	5	5	Mahaska County	IA	Randy Randall	1978	11820
145 0/8	21 5/8	22 4/8	15 4/8	5	5	Jones County	IA	Jim H. Dougherty	1979	11820
145 0/8	24 2/8	22 1/8	14 1/8	8	6	Ste. Genevieve County	MO	Dr. Dennis Diaz	1980	11820
145 0/8	23 6/8	24 2/8	19 6/8	5	5	Huntingdon County	PA	John A. Williams	1983	11820
145 0/8	20 4/8	21 4/8	16 4/8	5	5	Polk County	MN	Grant Schultz	1984	11820
145 0/8	23 0/8	23 4/8	19 1/8	9	5	St. Joseph County	IN	Monty Layne	1984	11820
145 0/8	24 3/8	24 5/8	16 2/8	5	5	Peoria County	IL	Earl Evans	1985	11820
145 0/8	23 3/8	24 4/8	18 2/8	4	4	Sumter County	AL	Denis Waldrop	1986	11820
145 0/8	22 0/8	23 4/8	19 4/8	5	5	Champaign County	IL	David TenEyck	1986	11820
145 0/8	22 4/8	22 3/8	17 6/8	6	6	Craighead County	AR	Rob Veach	1986	11820
145 0/8	23 7/8	24 4/8	18 0/8	4	4	Bee County	TX	Gary Kraatz	1987	11820
145 0/8	21 4/8	21 4/8	15 6/8	5	5	Traill County	ND	Chuck E. Spicer	1987	11820
145 0/8	24 2/8	26 3/8	16 6/8	5	4	Meigs County	OH	Gale E. Osborne	1988	11820
145 0/8	21 3/8	22 5/8	20 4/8	5	6	Bexar County	TX	Ben Wallace	1990	11820
145 0/8	26 0/8	26 4/8	18 2/8	4	4	Milwaukee County	WI	Tony Snow	1990	11820
145 0/8	24 5/8	23 2/8	16 6/8	5	5	Dougherty County	GA	Michael L. Layfield	1990	11820
145 0/8	24 1/8	23 5/8	19 0/8	5	4	Allamakee County	IA	Timothy E. Lodermeier	1990	11820
145 0/8	21 6/8	21 6/8	17 0/8	5	5	Sumner County	KS	Greg Hill	1990	11820
145 0/8	21 6/8	21 4/8	16 2/8	5	5	Washburn County	WI	Leonard L. Schneider	1991	11820
145 0/8	22 0/8	21 6/8	14 2/8	5	5	Ohio County	IN	Richard English	1991	11820
145 0/8	22 4/8	23 1/8	18 0/8	5	6	Polk County	WI	Vernon H. Simon	1992	11820
145 0/8	24 2/8	24 5/8	17 4/8	4	5	Darke County	OH	Bernard Grillot	1992	11820
145 0/8	21 6/8	23 0/8	16 6/8	5	6	Waushara County	WI	Dean Frater	1992	11820
145 0/8	22 1/8	21 6/8	19 3/8	6	6	Goodhue County	MN	John "Jack" Cordes	1993	11820
145 0/8	23 2/8	23 0/8	19 6/8	5	5	Kankakee County	IL	Kirk Redenius	1993	11820
145 0/8	21 1/8	22 4/8	17 7/8	6	6	Talbot County	MD	Jack Dell	1993	11820
145 0/8	22 3/8	22 2/8	19 0/8	5	5	Williamson County	IL	Mark Frey	1994	11820
145 0/8	23 2/8	24 4/8	19 0/8	5	5	Whiteside County	IL	William S. Milby	1994	11820
145 0/8	21 4/8	16 3/8	17 7/8	6	5	Coles County	IL	Mike Cline	1994	11820
145 0/8	25 2/8	24 6/8	17 0/8	5	5	Appanoose County	IA	Dennis Palmer	1994	11820
145 0/8	23 2/8	24 2/8	20 3/8	5	5	Hardin County	KY	Lewis Graham	1994	11820
145 0/8	23 7/8	23 7/8	16 0/8	5	5	Marathon County	WI	Scott Czerwonka	1995	11820
145 0/8	24 1/8	25 2/8	19 6/8	5	4	Linn County	IA	Steven S. Millius	1995	11820
145 0/8	25 3/8	25 7/8	19 4/8	4	5	Union County	IN	Mike McCabe	1995	11820
145 0/8	24 2/8	24 0/8	15 4/8	5	6	Scott County	IL	Gene Meier	1995	11820
145 0/8	22 4/8	22 6/8	16 4/8	4	4	Jackson County	WV	Robert Buckalew II	1995	11820
145 0/8	25 7/8	26 4/8	21 4/8	6	5	Garden County	NE	Dan Schmid	1995	11820
145 0/8	23 5/8	22 6/8	16 5/8	7	5	Grant County	WI	Josh Kreul	1996	11820
145 0/8	24 0/8	23 2/8	16 2/8	5	5	Hart County	KY	Albert Grimes	1996	11820
145 0/8	21 5/8	21 4/8	17 1/8	6	5	Olmsted County	MN	Bruce R. Long	1996	11820
145 0/8	26 7/8	26 4/8	17 5/8	5	6	Phelps County	MO	Dwayne La Barge	1996	11820
145 0/8	22 1/8	22 3/8	17 4/8	5	5	La Porte County	IN	Christopher M. Beck	1996	11820
145 0/8	23 5/8	23 7/8	18 4/8	5	5	Cook County	IL	Dan Boss	1996	11820
145 0/8	21 7/8	22 0/8	14 4/8	5	6	Wayne County	WV	Emery Dotson	1997	11820
145 0/8	24 5/8	23 6/8	17 0/8	4	4	Union County	SD	Bradley R. Bertrand	1997	11820
145 0/8	23 4/8	23 4/8	17 5/8	5	5	Clarke County	IA	Jeff Jorgensen	1997	11820
145 0/8	24 2/8	25 0/8	18 6/8	5	4	Scott County	IA	Jeffrey R. Coonts	1997	11820
145 0/8	25 3/8	25 2/8	19 0/8	5	5	Putnam County	IL	Michael D. Holmes	1997	11820
145 0/8	22 4/8	22 0/8	17 6/8	5	5	Pike County	IL	Arnie Boccafogli	1997	11820
145 0/8	22 4/8	24 6/8	16 6/8	5	5	Macoupin County	IL	Brad Bellm	1998	11820
145 0/8	23 7/8	23 3/8	14 6/8	5	4	Richland County	MT	Kurt Bensinger	1998	11820
145 0/8	24 6/8	24 1/8	17 1/8	6	5	Hennepin County	MN	Shawn Lynch	1998	11820
145 0/8	25 2/8	25 4/8	15 0/8	4	4	Washington County	KY	Brian A. Mattingly	1999	11820

480

WHITETAIL DEER (TYPICAL ANTLERS)

Minimum Score 125

SCORE	LENGTH OF R MAIN BEAM L		INSIDE SPREAD	NUMBER OF R POINTS L		AREA	STATE/ PROVINCE	HUNTER'S NAME	DATE	RANK
145 0/8	24 6/8	24 5/8	21 0/8	4	4	Suffolk County	NY	Scott Sahlstrom	1999	11820
145 0/8	23 6/8	23 4/8	19 3/8	5	6	Langlade County	WI	Michael W. Fredin	1999	11820
145 0/8	24 0/8	25 1/8	18 6/8	4	4	Green County	WI	Bill Maves	2000	11820
145 0/8	22 0/8	22 1/8	18 0/8	6	5	Berks County	PA	Larry L. Wolfe	2000	11820
145 0/8	23 6/8	24 0/8	13 2/8	6	5	Middlesex County	MA	Stephen T. Slaman	2000	11820
145 0/8	21 1/8	21 4/8	18 2/8	5	5	Fairfax County	VA	Thomas M. Kody	2000	11820
145 0/8	22 5/8	23 3/8	21 4/8	6	5	Brown County	IL	Ralph Sorrentino	2000	11820
145 0/8	23 0/8	23 6/8	17 4/8	5	6	Logan County	KY	Doug Yoder	2001	11820
145 0/8	22 4/8	21 3/8	15 4/8	6	5	Erath County	TX	Lindy McCarty	2001	11820
145 0/8	23 4/8	24 2/8	17 2/8	5	5	Waupaca County	WI	Timm W. Raddatz	2002	11820
145 0/8	23 2/8	23 2/8	18 2/8	4	5	Champaign County	OH	Todd M. Lanich	2002	11820
145 0/8	24 6/8	25 1/8	21 0/8	5	6	Walworth County	WI	Douglas M. Scherer	2002	11820
145 0/8	22 6/8	23 0/8	18 4/8	5	5	Rusk County	WI	Ty Dennis	2003	11820
145 0/8	22 2/8	22 6/8	17 0/8	6	6	Coke County	TX	Bart Wilson	2003	11820
145 0/8	21 7/8	23 1/8	16 4/8	5	5	Logan County	KY	Stan Yoder	2003	11820
*145 0/8	26 4/8	26 0/8	17 5/8	6	4	Wayne County	KY	Jesse Vaughn	2003	11820
*145 0/8	24 2/8	23 0/8	17 0/8	4	4	McHenry County	IL	George Patrick	2003	11820
145 0/8	25 2/8	26 0/8	20 4/8	4	4	Scott County	IA	Bill Starr	2003	11820
145 0/8	25 3/8	26 3/8	18 0/8	4	4	McDonough County	IL	Jack Laverdiere	2003	11820
145 0/8	27 6/8	26 4/8	19 4/8	6	6	Cerro Gordo County	IA	Dan Mujica	2003	11820
*145 0/8	24 4/8	24 1/8	18 1/8	5	5	Calhoun County	MI	Alfred A. Brenner	2004	11820
145 0/8	21 1/8	22 4/8	17 1/8	5	6	Hunterdon County	NJ	Anthony Diecidue	2004	11820
145 0/8	24 1/8	24 0/8	15 0/8	5	5	Cumberland County	PA	Herb Lebo	2004	11820
145 0/8	23 5/8	24 1/8	17 2/8	5	5	Marshall County	IN	Gregg M. Holzwart	2004	11820
*145 0/8	23 1/8	23 5/8	20 1/8	5	5	Chemung County	NY	Lew Parker	2004	11820
145 0/8	24 5/8	25 7/8	18 2/8	5	4	Polk County	AR	Scott Frachiseur	2004	11820
145 0/8	23 6/8	23 2/8	18 0/8	4	5	Kane County	IL	Timothy L. Harkness	2004	11820
145 0/8	20 6/8	20 3/8	17 2/8	6	6	Kane County	IL	Andy Rakowski	2005	11820
145 0/8	23 1/8	23 5/8	20 6/8	5	5	Waukesha County	WI	Carey Stapleton	2005	11820
*145 0/8	23 4/8	24 1/8	17 2/8	4	5	Franklin County	KS	Gary Shields	2005	11820
*145 0/8	25 1/8	25 0/8	15 6/8	7	5	Pike County	IL	Ken Mullen	2005	11820
145 0/8	24 3/8	24 2/8	19 2/8	4	4	Cheyenne County	CO	Mark Mariani	2005	11820
145 0/8	26 0/8	27 5/8	19 3/8	7	7	Iroquois County	IL	James Booi	2005	11820
*145 0/8	23 5/8	24 0/8	18 0/8	6	5	Sullivan County	IN	Mike J. Eslinger	2005	11820
*145 0/8	23 2/8	24 1/8	17 0/8	5	6	Dane County	WI	Stuart Smith	2005	11820
145 0/8	25 7/8	26 1/8	18 5/8	6	4	Columbia County	WI	Corey J. Neuman	2005	11820
145 0/8	27 1/8	26 3/8	17 4/8	6	3	Page County	IA	Chris Barton	2005	11820
145 0/8	23 4/8	23 7/8	17 3/8	5	5	Schuyler County	IL	Donald B. Coufal	2005	11820
*145 0/8	25 1/8	25 2/8	18 4/8	6	7	Douglas County	WI	Kevin Kivisto	2005	11820
*145 0/8	22 3/8	21 6/8	16 4/8	5	5	McMullen County	TX	Chris Cloninger	2005	11820
145 0/8	26 1/8	26 7/8	21 4/8	4	4	Concordia Parish	LA	Brad Mitchell	2006	11820
145 0/8	22 5/8	22 5/8	18 2/8	5	5	Polk County	WI	Justin J. Bergmann	2006	11820
145 0/8	24 0/8	23 0/8	18 1/8	5	7	Waupaca County	WI	Jeffrey T. Parker	2006	11820
145 0/8	24 5/8	24 2/8	24 0/8	5	5	McHenry County	IL	James R. Schultz	2006	11820
145 0/8	21 4/8	21 2/8	15 4/8	5	5	Monroe County	MO	Greta Chase	2006	11820
145 0/8	23 6/8	23 5/8	19 4/8	4	4	Edgar County	IL	Brad Davis	2006	11820
145 0/8	23 2/8	23 4/8	21 0/8	5	4	Livingston County	NY	Shane Moran	2006	11820
145 0/8	23 4/8	26 0/8	19 2/8	5	4	Gibson County	IN	Bruce Matsel	2006	11820
*145 0/8	23 1/8	22 1/8	18 0/8	5	5	Grayson County	TX	Mike Hargrove	2006	11820
*145 0/8	20 6/8	21 2/8	17 2/8	5	5	Fort a La Corne	SAS	Jordan Geall	2007	11820
*145 0/8	23 0/8	22 4/8	16 6/8	6	7	Ashland County	WI	Rory Michalski	2007	11820
145 0/8	24 1/8	25 0/8	20 3/8	5	5	Bourbon County	KS	Jeff Hubbard	2007	11820
*145 0/8	21 7/8	22 7/8	14 3/8	8	5	Calumet County	WI	Michael Schwarz	2007	11820
145 0/8	23 0/8	22 6/8	18 5/8	5	4	Gove County	KS	Albert Leon Ryel	2007	11820
145 0/8	22 5/8	22 0/8	17 1/8	6	6	Eckville	ALB	Ian Tilley	2008	11820
*145 0/8	24 2/8	24 4/8	22 2/8	4	5	Taney County	MO	Robbie Duggan	2008	11820
145 0/8	23 4/8	23 2/8	20 2/8	5	5	Graham County	KS	Ross Reddy	2008	11820
145 0/8	22 6/8	22 3/8	17 6/8	5	6	Rock County	WI	Thomas Waldman	2008	11820
145 0/8	23 2/8	22 3/8	18 7/8	5	6	McHenry County	IL	Brad Wiehr	2008	11820
145 0/8	23 0/8	23 0/8	20 2/8	5	5	Winnebago County	WI	Tim Frank	2008	11820
145 0/8	23 1/8	23 5/8	16 2/8	6	7	White County	IN	Ronnie E. Graham	2008	11820
145 0/8	23 7/8	23 3/8	16 6/8	5	5	Columbia County	WI	Amos D. Schrock	2009	11820
145 0/8	21 6/8	22 4/8	17 0/8	5	5	Porter County	IN	Charles D. Brumley	2009	11820
145 0/8	25 0/8	24 4/8	17 6/8	4	4	Dane County	WI	Chad M. Kruger	2009	11820
*145 0/8	22 2/8	21 6/8	16 2/8	5	5	Barron County	WI	Jeremy Boe	2009	11820
*145 0/8	25 7/8	25 4/8	19 4/8	4	4	Fulton County	GA	Kevin M. Hudec	2010	11820
*145 0/8	21 4/8	22 3/8	17 2/8	5	5	Woodlands County	ALB	Ron Brown	2010	11820
144 7/8	23 0/8	23 4/8	19 7/8	6	6	Wyandotte County	KS	George F. Bigelow	1966	11943
144 7/8	21 7/8	22 3/8	17 1/8	5	6	Sussex County	VA	Alvin D. Skinner	1972	11943
144 7/8	25 1/8	25 0/8	18 3/8	5	6	Louisa County	IA	Harold E. Boysen	1978	11943
144 7/8	25 7/8	25 4/8	21 7/8	4	4	Dallas County	IA	John M. Bascom	1979	11943
144 7/8	20 2/8	20 1/8	15 2/8	6	5	Richland County	MT	Garth N. Kallevig	1980	11943
144 7/8	25 7/8	25 4/8	19 3/8	4	4	Sumner County	KS	Dave Baldwin	1982	11943
144 7/8	23 4/8	22 0/8	18 3/8	4	4	Cerro Gordo County	IA	Earl L. Goodman	1983	11943
144 7/8	22 4/8	22 2/8	20 7/8	4	5	Perry County	IL	Greg Thompson	1985	11943
144 7/8	22 3/8	22 1/8	17 5/8	5	5	Onondaga County	NY	Kim A. Schneider	1985	11943
144 7/8	25 4/8	25 2/8	16 3/8	5	6	Mayes County	OK	John W. Madlock	1985	11943
144 7/8	21 7/8	21 2/8	18 7/8	6	5	Texas County	OK	Max Crocker	1985	11943
144 7/8	21 2/8	21 1/8	18 7/8	5	5	Osborne County	KS	Gary L. Ozias	1985	11943
144 7/8	25 7/8	25 6/8	18 7/8	7	7	Washburn County	WI	William "Mike" Johnson	1987	11943
144 7/8	22 4/8	21 4/8	16 6/8	6	5	Lake County	IL	Carl H. Spaeth	1987	11943
144 7/8	24 6/8	24 4/8	16 2/8	5	5	Dearborn County	IN	Jerry O. Kent	1988	11943
144 7/8	22 4/8	23 4/8	19 5/8	5	4	Buffalo County	WI	Gary Dorn	1988	11943
144 7/8	26 4/8	26 0/8	15 7/8	6	5	Chambers County	AL	Craig Reynolds	1988	11943
144 7/8	22 6/8	22 7/8	17 5/8	5	5	Kossuth County	IA	Robert Barslou	1989	11943
144 7/8	23 3/8	24 1/8	16 5/8	4	5	Mower County	MN	Robert Frost	1989	11943
144 7/8	21 5/8	21 0/8	15 7/8	5	6	Kleberg County	TX	Wayne Peeples	1990	11943
144 7/8	26 4/8	25 1/8	20 7/8	5	5	Berrien County	MI	Larry McLaughlin	1990	11943
144 7/8	23 4/8	23 6/8	18 1/8	4	5	Worcester County	MD	David Johnson	1990	11943
144 7/8	22 7/8	22 5/8	16 6/8	5	6	Pike County	IL	James Kerr	1990	11943
144 7/8	22 7/8	23 7/8	16 1/8	4	4	Union County	IL	Doug Edwards	1990	11943
144 7/8	24 4/8	23 0/8	21 1/8	4	5	Mills County	IA	John Bantz	1990	11943
144 7/8	19 3/8	20 1/8	17 7/8	6	6	Anson County	NC	Tommy Michael Gilmore	1991	11943
144 7/8	23 6/8	25 2/8	17 3/8	4	5	Allamakee County	IA	Bill Saddler	1991	11943
144 7/8	25 3/8	25 6/8	18 1/8	5	4	Ardrossan	ALB	Terry Alan Myroniuk	1991	11943

WHITETAIL DEER (TYPICAL ANTLERS)

Minimum Score 125 — Continued

SCORE	LENGTH OF R MAIN BEAM L	INSIDE SPREAD	NUMBER OF R POINTS L	AREA	STATE/PROVINCE	HUNTER'S NAME	DATE	RANK
144 7/8	23 2/8 23 6/8	19 1/8	5 5	Berks County	PA	Frank P. Dattala	1992	11943
144 7/8	24 4/8 23 3/8	17 2/8	5 6	Iroquois County	IL	Dennis Clark	1992	11943
144 7/8	23 4/8 23 5/8	17 6/8	6 5	Jefferson County	WI	Ernie Turpin	1993	11943
144 7/8	22 2/8 24 0/8	15 3/8	6 7	Lake County	IL	Alvin Roberts	1993	11943
144 7/8	22 6/8 22 4/8	14 7/8	5 5	Waupaca County	WI	Scott Wolfe	1994	11943
144 7/8	24 0/8 23 2/8	17 7/8	5 5	Washington County	OH	Lowell Roberts	1994	11943
144 7/8	23 4/8 25 3/8	20 5/8	5 6	Douglas County	WI	Steven J. Cadotte	1995	11943
144 7/8	23 0/8 20 5/8	17 6/8	7 8	Marion County	IL	Shawn Lowery	1995	11943
144 7/8	24 2/8 24 2/8	19 7/8	5 4	Lac St. Anne	ALB	Dwayne Miller	1996	11943
144 7/8	24 2/8 24 3/8	15 7/8	6 5	Jackson County	MO	Jim Moss	1996	11943
144 7/8	23 7/8 24 7/8	16 7/8	5 5	Trempealeau County	WI	Dan Smith	1996	11943
144 7/8	23 1/8 22 6/8	16 3/8	5 5	Kanawha County	WV	Gregory S. King	1996	11943
144 7/8	21 6/8 21 3/8	19 3/8	7 6	Cook County	IL	Len Kamp	1996	11943
144 7/8	24 3/8 24 3/8	18 7/8	4 4	Pepin County	WI	Larry Gruber	1997	11943
144 7/8	23 5/8 24 4/8	20 6/8	5 6	Christian County	IL	Dwight Rorie	1997	11943
144 7/8	24 3/8 24 1/8	17 5/8	5 6	Putnam County	IL	Dennis M. Mallie	1997	11943
144 7/8	21 3/8 21 6/8	18 3/8	5 5	Kenosha County	WI	Craig Bobula	1997	11943
144 7/8	23 0/8 23 6/8	17 5/8	4 4	Boone County	IA	Gary Steel	1997	11943
144 7/8	25 3/8 26 1/8	17 3/8	6 5	Washington County	OH	Eric Scott Estes	1997	11943
144 7/8	24 7/8 25 4/8	16 6/8	5 4	Montgomery County	IA	Dick Paul	1997	11943
144 7/8	21 5/8 20 6/8	18 3/8	5 5	Rusk County	WI	George Olivo	1997	11943
144 7/8	26 1/8 26 3/8	18 0/8	6 6	Marathon County	WI	Kyle R. Heckendorf	1998	11943
144 7/8	25 5/8 25 6/8	17 1/8	4 5	Buffalo County	WI	Curt Youngbauer	1998	11943
144 7/8	26 2/8 25 2/8	19 1/8	4 4	Jasper County	IA	Henry Moore	1998	11943
144 7/8	22 4/8 23 1/8	19 2/8	6 5	Jackson County	IA	Terry W. Amling	1998	11943
144 7/8	23 4/8 23 7/8	16 0/8	5 6	Washburn County	WI	Dan Duchesneau	1999	11943
144 7/8	22 3/8 22 1/8	15 1/8	5 5	Polk County	MN	Ronald T. Hamerski	1999	11943
144 7/8	23 3/8 23 5/8	17 3/8	5 5	St. Croix County	WI	Bryan J. Brite	1999	11943
144 7/8	25 6/8 25 3/8	20 5/8	6 4	Taylor County	IA	Todd Tobin	1999	11943
144 7/8	23 7/8 25 4/8	19 7/8	4 4	Delaware County	OH	Steven Krakowka	1999	11943
144 7/8	24 1/8 23 0/8	21 2/8	7 6	Waukesha County	WI	Blaine E. Jester	2000	11943
144 7/8	23 7/8 24 1/8	17 5/8	6 4	Luzerne County	PA	Tony Kalinosky	2000	11943
144 7/8	22 2/8 20 3/8	17 5/8	5 7	Orleans County	NY	Dale Hargrave	2000	11943
144 7/8	22 7/8 23 7/8	18 0/8	7 6	Morrison County	MN	Larry Trushenski	2000	11943
144 7/8	23 4/8 23 4/8	18 7/8	5 5	Kalamazoo County	MI	Ted P. Stender	2000	11943
144 7/8	24 5/8 26 5/8	19 1/8	4 7	Jo Daviess County	IL	Ken Plowman	2000	11943
144 7/8	21 0/8 21 4/8	16 6/8	6 5	Sauk County	WI	Bruce J. Mehrens	2000	11943
144 7/8	22 4/8 22 5/8	16 6/8	5 6	Marquette County	WI	James E. Polk	2001	11943
144 7/8	22 2/8 22 2/8	15 1/8	5 6	Warren County	IN	Nathan Grogan	2001	11943
144 7/8	24 2/8 24 6/8	20 1/8	5 7	Sangamon County	IL	Jonathan P. Smith	2001	11943
144 7/8	24 0/8 24 3/8	17 1/8	5 5	Pike County	IL	Frank Barker, Jr.	2001	11943
144 7/8	22 6/8 21 5/8	16 5/8	5 5	Buffalo County	WI	Larry Hestekin	2002	11943
144 7/8	22 2/8 22 4/8	20 7/8	6 5	Marion County	IA	Leonard Grimes	2002	11943
144 7/8	25 2/8 25 5/8	23 5/8	4 6	Woodson County	KS	Frank L. Pechacek	2002	11943
144 7/8	22 1/8 21 5/8	16 7/8	7 5	Summit County	OH	Dave Juchnowski	2002	11943
144 7/8	22 3/8 21 7/8	15 7/8	6 5	Kleberg County	TX	Scott Brown	2003	11943
144 7/8	20 5/8 21 4/8	15 5/8	5 5	Stony Plain	ALB	Cyril Sparrowe	2003	11943
144 7/8	22 6/8 20 7/8	17 5/8	5 5	McDonough County	IL	Brian Eason	2003	11943
144 7/8	23 3/8 23 6/8	17 7/8	5 5	Buffalo County	WI	Jacob J. Curtis	2003	11943
144 7/8	24 2/8 23 5/8	17 0/8	6 5	Madison County	IA	Bruce Tyree	2003	11943
144 7/8	22 1/8 22 4/8	17 7/8	5 5	Cedar County	IA	Collin D. Johnson	2003	11943
144 7/8	23 3/8 25 0/8	17 4/8	6 6	Daviess County	MO	Brett R. DeGraaf	2003	11943
144 7/8	24 0/8 24 2/8	19 0/8	5 4	Chippewa County	WI	Al Larson	2003	11943
144 7/8	22 4/8 21 3/8	16 1/8	6 6	Clark County	KS	Levi Craft	2003	11943
144 7/8	23 5/8 23 7/8	21 4/8	6 5	Cumberland County	IL	Dan Flach	2003	11943
*144 7/8	24 4/8 25 0/8	16 7/8	6 5	Alamance County	NC	John Robert Miller	2003	11943
144 7/8	25 2/8 25 6/8	16 4/8	6 5	Sauk County	WI	Matt Peetz	2004	11943
*144 7/8	26 1/8 24 6/8	21 4/8	5 7	Fulton County	OH	Robert R. Cass	2004	11943
144 7/8	23 4/8 23 2/8	15 1/8	6 6	Tama County	IA	Tim Kacmarynski	2004	11943
144 7/8	25 3/8 24 3/8	16 1/8	6 5	Waukesha County	WI	Mathew Rynearson	2004	11943
144 7/8	24 0/8 23 6/8	22 5/8	4 4	Marshall County	IN	Verle S. Miller	2004	11943
144 7/8	23 0/8 22 7/8	16 3/8	5 5	Sauk County	WI	Dave Zimmerman	2004	11943
144 7/8	24 4/8 24 4/8	15 5/8	4 4	Marathon County	WI	Steven Roeder	2005	11943
144 7/8	24 6/8 25 0/8	17 5/8	5 5	Forest County	WI	Tracy D. Nery	2005	11943
*144 7/8	23 6/8 23 5/8	18 5/8	4 5	Comanche County	KS	Gregg Krikke	2005	11943
144 7/8	23 1/8 23 0/8	19 0/8	6 5	Parke County	IN	Charles A. Paxton	2005	11943
144 7/8	24 3/8 23 6/8	18 1/8	6 6	Franklin County	NE	Rodney Jacobitz	2006	11943
144 7/8	25 3/8 26 1/8	19 6/8	5 6	Clark County	OH	Scott Clark	2006	11943
144 7/8	25 0/8 20 3/8	21 0/8	6 6	Oakland County	MI	Mark Morris	2006	11943
144 7/8	23 1/8 23 2/8	16 3/8	6 4	Page County	IA	Bob Athen	2006	11943
144 7/8	26 0/8 26 0/8	18 7/8	5 4	Jo Daviess County	IL	Jim Carlson	2006	11943
*144 7/8	23 3/8 22 2/8	15 5/8	6 5	Pulaski County	IN	Andrew L. Malott	2006	11943
144 7/8	25 3/8 23 4/8	16 5/8	5 5	Polk County	WI	Corey Chappelear	2006	11943
144 7/8	22 6/8 23 3/8	18 1/8	4 4	Spink County	SD	Doug Braun	2006	11943
*144 7/8	25 6/8 26 1/8	14 7/8	5 5	Bucks County	PA	Jerry B. Koder	2006	11943
144 7/8	23 1/8 23 2/8	16 1/8	5 5	Walworth County	WI	Eric Sterbenz	2006	11943
144 7/8	25 5/8 26 6/8	17 0/8	4 5	Surry County	VA	Dwight S. Wolf	2006	11943
144 7/8	23 4/8 24 1/8	15 5/8	7 5	Muskingum County	OH	Bradley A. Schaeffer	2006	11943
144 7/8	24 0/8 24 0/8	21 3/8	5 5	Wayne County	IN	Chuck A. Turner	2006	11943
144 7/8	23 7/8 23 4/8	19 1/8	5 5	Whitley County	IN	Sean Scott	2006	11943
144 7/8	24 3/8 24 0/8	18 7/8	4 4	Highwood River	ALB	Tara Normand	2007	11943
*144 7/8	21 2/8 21 3/8	17 5/8	6 5	Williams County	ND	Dwayne Hellman	2007	11943
144 7/8	24 2/8 23 6/8	16 2/8	5 6	Tom Green County	TX	Ronnie Parsons	2007	11943
144 7/8	23 5/8 24 6/8	19 3/8	5 5	Buffalo County	WI	Robert Burdick	2007	11943
144 7/8	21 3/8 21 5/8	15 0/8	7 6	Green County	WI	Terry Plath	2007	11943
144 7/8	22 0/8 23 7/8	18 5/8	5 5	Lawrence County	OH	Brian E. Galligan	2007	11943
144 7/8	22 2/8 23 2/8	16 6/8	6 5	Vigo County	IN	Joseph L. Swan	2008	11943
144 7/8	23 1/8 23 1/8	18 4/8	6 5	Waupaca County	WI	Tony E. Fischer	2008	11943
144 7/8	22 5/8 23 3/8	17 1/8	5 5	Scotland County	MO	Brad Martin	2008	11943
*144 7/8	26 1/8 26 0/8	17 6/8	6 5	Vernon County	WI	Paul Colburn	2008	11943
144 7/8	20 3/8 20 6/8	15 5/8	5 6	Clay County	SD	Steve Hansen	2008	11943
*144 7/8	22 3/8 21 5/8	15 7/8	6 5	Indiana County	PA	Don Hess, Jr.	2008	11943
144 7/8	24 1/8 24 2/8	20 7/8	5 5	Marathon County	WI	Kevin Furmanek	2008	11943
144 7/8	22 3/8 22 2/8	18 7/8	6 5	Washington County	IA	Leonard Marine	2008	11943
144 7/8	23 3/8 23 7/8	17 6/8	5 7	Ottawa County	OH	Robert Fleming	2008	11943

WHITETAIL DEER (TYPICAL ANTLERS)

Minimum Score 125 — Continued

SCORE	LENGTH OF MAIN BEAM R	L	INSIDE SPREAD	NUMBER OF POINTS R	L	AREA	STATE/ PROVINCE	HUNTER'S NAME	DATE	RANK
*144 7/8	23 4/8	23 0/8	17 1/8	4	4	Cayuga County	NY	Mike Frank	2009	11943
*144 7/8	24 6/8	25 1/8	21 2/8	6	6	Lebanon County	PA	Eugene Schamber, Jr.	2009	11943
*144 7/8	24 5/8	22 6/8	17 6/8	6	5	Meriwether County	GA	Bradley Haralson	2009	11943
*144 7/8	23 3/8	24 4/8	20 3/8	6	5	La Porte County	IN	Chad A. Schau	2009	11943
144 7/8	23 7/8	23 6/8	15 7/8	6	5	Montgomery County	KS	John M. Dunlap	2009	11943
*144 7/8	23 2/8	24 3/8	17 1/8	5	6	Miami County	IN	Kevin Cox	2009	11943
144 7/8	21 1/8	21 0/8	15 2/8	8	8	Waushara County	WI	Robert E. Mitchell	2009	11943
*144 7/8	26 0/8	26 0/8	21 4/8	8	5	Will County	IL	Andrew Boseo	2009	11943
*144 7/8	23 6/8	23 5/8	18 4/8	4	5	Preble County	OH	Clay Brewer	2009	11943
144 7/8	22 7/8	23 7/8	21 6/8	5	6	Jackson County	IA	Richard Marr	2009	11943
*144 7/8	22 3/8	22 5/8	17 3/8	6	5	Shelby County	TN	Keith Delon	2009	11943
144 7/8	21 3/8	21 1/8	15 7/8	5	5	Custer County	SD	Chad P. Lehman	2010	11943
144 6/8	19 6/8	20 0/8	15 2/8	6	7	Powell County	MT	Danny Moore	1974	12078
144 6/8	21 7/8	22 1/8	17 4/8	6	7	Christian County	IL	Scott M. Cassidy	1983	12078
144 6/8	25 2/8	24 6/8	19 2/8	4	5	Delaware County	PA	James Taylor	1984	12078
144 6/8	21 0/8	21 4/8	17 0/8	5	5	Sumner County	KS	Jeffrey L. Nash	1984	12078
144 6/8	23 4/8	23 0/8	16 2/8	5	4	Powell County	MT	Sonny Templeton	1986	12078
144 6/8	25 7/8	25 4/8	19 0/8	4	4	Lake County	IL	Carl H. Spaeth	1986	12078
144 6/8	24 1/8	25 4/8	18 0/8	4	5	Hancock County	MS	Alan J. Guess	1987	12078
144 6/8	26 4/8	25 2/8	21 4/8	5	4	Lincoln County	ME	Darryl Flagg	1988	12078
144 6/8	24 5/8	23 3/8	18 0/8	5	5	Bent County	CO	Kurt W. Keskimaki	1988	12078
144 6/8	24 7/8	24 6/8	20 4/8	6	4	Clayton County	IA	Jim Kerns	1989	12078
144 6/8	23 0/8	22 2/8	18 6/8	5	5	Fairfield County	OH	John W. Todhunter, Jr.	1989	12078
144 6/8	26 0/8	25 7/8	14 3/8	6	5	Tazewell County	IL	Kevin Eggen	1989	12078
144 6/8	23 7/8	23 7/8	15 6/8	4	5	Lee County	IA	Mark Webb	1989	12078
144 6/8	22 3/8	21 0/8	16 4/8	5	5	Irion County	TX	William Jay Wilson	1989	12078
144 6/8	24 3/8	23 6/8	16 6/8	6	5	Portage County	WI	Mike Kurzinski	1990	12078
144 6/8	21 0/8	21 4/8	17 4/8	5	5	Middlesex	ONT	Kim Slobojin	1990	12078
144 6/8	24 6/8	24 3/8	20 6/8	4	4	La Salle County	IL	Bart Pals	1991	12078
144 6/8	25 7/8	26 2/8	18 2/8	5	5	Door County	WI	Larry Page	1991	12078
144 6/8	22 3/8	22 1/8	18 6/8	5	4	County of St. Hyacinthe	QUE	Guy Turcotte	1991	12078
144 6/8	24 1/8	23 5/8	19 2/8	5	5	Livingston County	IL	Tom Roe	1991	12078
144 6/8	25 0/8	24 1/8	18 2/8	6	5	Waukesha County	WI	Ed Rahberger, Jr.	1992	12078
144 6/8	23 1/8	23 4/8	18 2/8	9	6	Jefferson County	WI	Cory Haseleu	1992	12078
144 6/8	23 4/8	23 1/8	16 6/8	5	5	Parke County	IN	Kyle Laney	1992	12078
144 6/8	22 6/8	23 2/8	17 0/8	6	5	Eau Claire County	WI	Bob J. Grunewald	1993	12078
144 6/8	21 3/8	22 2/8	18 4/8	6	5	Logan County	KY	Timmy Shackelford	1993	12078
144 6/8	23 3/8	23 4/8	16 2/8	5	5	Tompkins County	NY	Allen E. Cobane	1993	12078
144 6/8	25 3/8	25 3/8	19 4/8	6	5	Henry County	IA	Ben Moore	1993	12078
144 6/8	23 7/8	24 3/8	17 3/8	6	6	Tillman County	OK	Edward Wayne Roach	1993	12078
144 6/8	21 5/8	20 7/8	16 4/8	5	5	Flathead County	MT	Dennis Brieske	1994	12078
144 6/8	24 0/8	24 3/8	18 4/8	7	5	Rock County	WI	Keith Hackett II	1994	12078
144 6/8	24 6/8	23 5/8	18 0/8	4	7	Dubuque County	IA	Daniel C. Mehrl	1994	12078
144 6/8	25 5/8	26 0/8	16 2/8	5	5	Limestone County	AL	Neal Baker	1994	12078
144 6/8	24 0/8	24 3/8	17 3/8	6	6	Sawyer County	WI	Bernard Gavre	1994	12078
144 6/8	24 5/8	24 0/8	18 0/8	5	6	Kankakee County	IL	Tim Haut	1994	12078
144 6/8	24 1/8	22 5/8	19 6/8	6	5	Macon County	IL	Norman L. Mathias	1994	12078
144 6/8	23 2/8	22 1/8	19 4/8	5	5	Webb County	TX	Matthew W. Howard	1995	12078
144 6/8	26 1/8	25 5/8	16 5/8	5	6	Marathon County	WI	Dean Hanke	1995	12078
144 6/8	22 7/8	22 4/8	18 4/8	5	5	Mecosta County	MI	Jake Neal	1995	12078
144 6/8	23 5/8	24 4/8	18 4/8	4	4	Washtenaw County	MI	Phil Maly	1995	12078
144 6/8	25 4/8	25 2/8	18 0/8	4	6	Allen County	OH	Mark Spallinger	1995	12078
144 6/8	26 1/8	25 4/8	19 0/8	4	4	Cass County	NE	Roger Maxon	1995	12078
144 6/8	23 3/8	23 7/8	18 0/8	6	5	Carroll County	MS	Tucker Miller III	1995	12078
144 6/8	25 3/8	24 4/8	16 6/8	7	5	Washtenaw County	MI	Michael S. Rose	1996	12078
144 6/8	24 0/8	24 2/8	17 6/8	4	4	Dunn County	WI	Mike Lenz	1996	12078
144 6/8	21 2/8	21 6/8	15 4/8	5	5	Jefferson County	IN	Doug Schwartz	1997	12078
144 6/8	23 1/8	23 5/8	18 0/8	6	5	Allamakee County	IA	Robert Thornley	1997	12078
144 6/8	22 7/8	23 4/8	16 4/8	5	5	Allegheny County	PA	Joseph M. Iusi	1998	12078
144 6/8	24 1/8	23 7/8	18 6/8	4	4	Waushara County	WI	Brad Leary	1998	12078
144 6/8	22 2/8	21 5/8	14 2/8	5	5	Adams County	IL	Ken Doellman	1998	12078
144 6/8	23 6/8	21 7/8	14 6/8	5	6	Fayette County	IA	Gerald E. Hunter	1998	12078
144 6/8	24 5/8	24 2/8	18 1/8	8	6	Crawford County	IL	Justin Childress	1998	12078
144 6/8	23 5/8	23 7/8	21 3/8	7	6	Boone County	IL	Todd Berkenpas	1998	12078
144 6/8	25 4/8	24 4/8	20 2/8	5	5	Bayfield County	WI	Ludwig B. Millhausen	1998	12078
144 6/8	24 1/8	23 4/8	18 4/8	4	4	Cass County	NE	Alfred Cosson	1999	12078
144 6/8	22 6/8	22 1/8	17 2/8	5	5	Seminole County	OK	Mike Wyatt	1999	12078
144 6/8	25 5/8	26 2/8	19 0/8	4	4	Middlesex County	MA	Gregory Holt	1999	12078
144 6/8	23 7/8	22 4/8	16 5/8	6	5	Fulton County	OH	W. Tennyson Krugh	1999	12078
144 6/8	23 2/8	23 1/8	15 7/8	7	6	Winnebago County	WI	Randy B. Gehrt	1999	12078
144 6/8	22 5/8	22 6/8	15 4/8	5	5	Jo Daviess County	IL	Brandon W. Lieber	1999	12078
144 6/8	21 2/8	22 2/8	17 6/8	6	6	Trempealeau County	WI	Zackery Olson	1999	12078
144 6/8	22 0/8	22 0/8	13 6/8	6	7	Calhoun County	IL	Otis S. Darnell	1999	12078
144 6/8	24 0/8	24 2/8	16 4/8	6	6	Suffolk County	NY	Robert Janke	1999	12078
144 6/8	22 0/8	23 0/8	19 4/8	5	5	Crawford County	PA	Robert Royal	2000	12078
144 6/8	23 1/8	23 1/8	16 0/8	5	5	Crawford County	WI	Thomas Brown	2000	12078
144 6/8	23 2/8	23 1/8	20 4/8	6	5	DeKalb County	IL	Mark Swanson	2000	12078
144 6/8	23 7/8	23 7/8	19 2/8	5	5	Ralls County	MO	Mike Fulton	2000	12078
144 6/8	21 7/8	22 3/8	20 6/8	5	6	Kanawha County	WV	Mickey Farmer	2000	12078
144 6/8	21 5/8	22 0/8	15 6/8	5	5	Cedar County	NE	David B. Cull	2000	12078
144 6/8	26 5/8	26 4/8	18 2/8	4	4	Douglas County	WI	Drew Vig	2000	12078
144 6/8	23 4/8	24 1/8	19 4/8	4	5	Washington County	MS	Chris Holifield	2001	12078
144 6/8	23 0/8	23 2/8	18 0/8	5	5	Madison County	MT	Keith Dvoroznak	2001	12078
144 6/8	21 5/8	20 5/8	18 4/8	6	5	Allen County	KY	Jason Holloway	2001	12078
144 6/8	24 1/8	24 0/8	16 4/8	4	4	Susquehanna County	PA	Gus Congemi	2001	12078
144 6/8	23 6/8	22 7/8	17 3/8	5	6	Wyoming County	NY	Erik S. Shaffer	2001	12078
144 6/8	22 5/8	24 0/8	20 2/8	4	4	Taylor County	IA	Nathan Stiens	2001	12078
144 6/8	22 4/8	23 5/8	20 4/8	5	4	Berkeley County	WV	Mike Price	2001	12078
144 6/8	21 3/8	21 6/8	18 2/8	5	5	Franklin County	IA	Lynn Hughes	2001	12078
144 6/8	22 3/8	22 1/8	16 0/8	5	5	Dodge County	WI	James Hanna	2002	12078
144 6/8	21 6/8	20 2/8	15 4/8	6	5	Noble County	IN	Brad L. Smith	2002	12078
144 6/8	22 5/8	23 3/8	18 0/8	6	5	Doniphan County	KS	David Krampitz	2002	12078
144 6/8	23 0/8	22 7/8	16 6/8	4	4	Buffalo County	WI	Donnie Hansen	2002	12078
144 6/8	22 7/8	22 7/8	18 7/8	6	7	Sevier County	AR	Dale Pierce	2002	12078
144 6/8	22 2/8	22 7/8	15 2/8	5	4	Ford County	KS	Shawn W. Harding	2002	12078

483

WHITETAIL DEER (TYPICAL ANTLERS)

Minimum Score 125 — Continued

SCORE	LENGTH OF R MAIN BEAM L	INSIDE SPREAD	NUMBER OF R POINTS L	AREA	STATE/PROVINCE	HUNTER'S NAME	DATE	RANK
144 6/8	25 4/8 25 6/8	22 2/8	5 4	Whiteside County	IL	Gary Friend	2002	12078
144 6/8	21 3/8 21 3/8	15 2/8	5 6	Brown County	SD	Mark White	2002	12078
144 6/8	22 4/8 22 6/8	15 0/8	5 5	Montgomery County	IA	Mark Benda	2002	12078
144 6/8	25 6/8 25 1/8	17 2/8	5 6	Delaware County	OH	Steve Boham	2002	12078
144 6/8	24 3/8 25 0/8	16 2/8	5 5	Harper County	KS	Randy Shipman	2002	12078
144 6/8	24 7/8 24 5/8	18 5/8	6 8	Oconto County	WI	Jim Sachs	2002	12078
*144 6/8	22 2/8 22 4/8	15 4/8	5 5	Franklin County	MO	Carl Lohrer	2002	12078
144 6/8	25 2/8 25 6/8	18 0/8	5 5	Union County	KY	Hugh C. Dickens	2002	12078
144 6/8	24 7/8 24 7/8	19 2/8	5 4	Dallas County	IA	Jeramy Marean	2002	12078
144 6/8	20 4/8 20 4/8	15 2/8	5 5	Sheridan County	WY	Susan K. Barrett	2003	12078
*144 6/8	21 0/8 22 6/8	19 7/8	5 6	Montague County	TX	Brett Cason	2003	12078
144 6/8	22 0/8 21 0/8	18 2/8	5 5	Trempealeau County	WI	Jon Borreson	2003	12078
*144 6/8	24 0/8 22 3/8	19 2/8	4 5	Dunn County	WI	Benjamin R. Heinrich	2003	12078
144 6/8	25 1/8 25 0/8	20 4/8	4 5	Westchester County	NY	Stephen Cook	2003	12078
144 6/8	24 3/8 24 0/8	14 7/8	5 4	Caddo County	OK	Randy McLemore	2003	12078
144 6/8	22 6/8 23 0/8	17 4/8	5 5	Montgomery County	MD	Robert A. Shelley	2003	12078
144 6/8	23 2/8 22 7/8	20 1/8	6 6	Waushara County	WI	Sam Smith	2003	12078
*144 6/8	23 4/8 23 2/8	13 6/8	6 5	Trempealeau County	WI	Mike Hestekin	2003	12078
144 6/8	21 6/8 21 3/8	16 0/8	5 6	Marquette County	WI	Chad Yocum	2003	12078
144 6/8	25 4/8 25 4/8	18 2/8	5 4	Sharp County	AR	Witt Stephens, Jr.	2003	12078
144 6/8	24 4/8 24 4/8	16 0/8	5 5	Northampton County	PA	Mark D. Winter	2004	12078
144 6/8	20 4/8 20 6/8	15 2/8	6 7	Kidder County	ND	Trevor Wick	2004	12078
144 6/8	21 3/8 22 2/8	15 5/8	5 6	Jo Daviess County	IL	Thomas A. Shimak, Jr.	2004	12078
144 6/8	22 4/8 22 5/8	19 0/8	5 5	Buffalo County	WI	Jeffrey J. Ewens	2004	12078
144 6/8	24 0/8 23 6/8	21 2/8	4 5	Erie County	NY	Dan McAuley	2004	12078
144 6/8	25 5/8 24 6/8	17 2/8	4 4	Pepin County	WI	Jess Loewenhagen	2004	12078
144 6/8	24 5/8 25 2/8	17 4/8	5 5	Pike County	IL	Mark Tartaglia	2004	12078
144 6/8	23 4/8 22 7/8	17 4/8	4 4	Isle of Wight County	VA	Dwight S. Wolf	2004	12078
144 6/8	24 4/8 22 4/8	17 6/8	5 6	Livingston County	MI	Butch Hauser	2004	12078
144 6/8	23 5/8 23 6/8	16 2/8	5 5	Delaware County	OH	Steve Boham	2004	12078
144 6/8	21 2/8 21 0/8	17 6/8	5 5	Walsh County	ND	Shawn Cudmore	2004	12078
144 6/8	23 1/8 22 5/8	17 0/8	5 5	Holt County	NE	Eric Carper	2005	12078
144 6/8	22 3/8 21 4/8	18 2/8	5 5	Kankakee County	IL	Timothy Haut	2005	12078
*144 6/8	19 5/8 19 6/8	20 2/8	5 6	Ramsey County	ND	Kelly Durbin	2006	12078
144 6/8	23 6/8 23 5/8	18 2/8	6 5	Delaware County	IA	Kevin D. Dempster	2006	12078
144 6/8	22 6/8 23 5/8	18 0/8	5 5	Owen County	IN	Paxton Davis	2006	12078
144 6/8	23 4/8 23 3/8	16 6/8	5 5	Surry County	VA	John R. Guzik	2006	12078
144 6/8	24 7/8 22 5/8	19 1/8	6 6	Grant County	WI	Bob Deckert	2006	12078
144 6/8	28 2/8 27 0/8	19 2/8	4 4	Dunn County	WI	Randy Samens	2006	12078
144 6/8	20 5/8 22 5/8	21 4/8	5 6	La Crosse County	WI	John M. Brunner	2006	12078
144 6/8	22 7/8 23 6/8	15 0/8	6 6	Bedford County	VA	Thomas G. Lester	2006	12078
*144 6/8	22 5/8 22 3/8	18 6/8	5 5	Washington County	MS	Dr. Larry Ennis	2006	12078
144 6/8	26 0/8 25 6/8	21 1/8	4 5	Dubuque County	IA	Dennis Pregler	2006	12078
144 6/8	22 2/8 24 5/8	18 6/8	5 5	Marion County	IA	Gerald T. Dowell	2006	12078
144 6/8	20 5/8 21 1/8	16 2/8	5 5	Williamson County	TN	Will Jones	2007	12078
144 6/8	22 7/8 23 6/8	17 6/8	4 5	Clay County	SD	Scott E. Hansen	2007	12078
*144 6/8	24 1/8 24 2/8	19 2/8	5 5	Trempealeau County	WI	Rudy Suchla	2008	12078
*144 6/8	21 6/8 22 2/8	16 3/8	5 8	Yell County	AR	David Webb	2008	12078
144 6/8	24 5/8 23 4/8	18 4/8	4 4	Montgomery County	OH	Todd McKinney	2008	12078
144 6/8	25 4/8 25 4/8	22 4/8	5 4	Plymouth County	MA	Dean Harrold	2008	12078
144 6/8	23 4/8 23 5/8	17 2/8	7 7	Pike County	IL	Pittman Edwards, Jr.	2008	12078
*144 6/8	26 4/8 25 7/8	18 4/8	4 6	Rawlins County	KS	Doug Ketchum	2008	12078
144 6/8	22 4/8 22 5/8	16 6/8	5 5	Buffalo County	WI	Jeff Klieforth	2008	12078
144 6/8	20 0/8 20 7/8	18 3/8	5 6	Sheboygan County	WI	Michael R. Payne	2008	12078
144 6/8	25 5/8 25 5/8	17 2/8	5 7	Dane County	WI	Michael P. Stacey	2008	12078
144 6/8	22 6/8 22 2/8	14 2/8	5 4	Marathon County	WI	Sara Leonard	2008	12078
*144 6/8	24 0/8 24 2/8	17 1/8	6 7	La Salle County	TX	Ronnie Satterfield	2008	12078
144 6/8	25 1/8 25 1/8	18 5/8	5 6	Pepin County	WI	Brad J. Glaus	2009	12078
144 6/8	24 4/8 26 1/8	23 2/8	7 6	Trempealeau County	WI	David N. Andersen	2009	12078
144 6/8	23 3/8 23 6/8	15 0/8	5 5	Rockdale County	GA	Tim Hill	2009	12078
*144 6/8	22 0/8 22 2/8	25 0/8	6 6	Lucas County	IA	Roy F. Palmer	2009	12078
144 6/8	23 4/8 23 6/8	13 4/8	5 5	Sumner County	KS	Trey Jones	2009	12078
*144 6/8	23 5/8 24 2/8	19 4/8	5 4	Adair County	MO	David Spangler	2009	12078
144 6/8	21 5/8 21 0/8	20 2/8	5 5	Allegheny County	PA	Rudy Fleck	2009	12078
144 6/8	22 7/8 21 6/8	17 4/8	5 5	Portage County	WI	Erin Kalata	2009	12078
*144 6/8	23 2/8 23 5/8	17 0/8	6 5	Buffalo County	WI	Mitch Palmer	2009	12078
144 5/8	24 0/8 24 4/8	21 3/8	4 4	Spink County	SD	Jerald Shantz	1959	12227
144 5/8	22 1/8 22 1/8	15 7/8	5 5	Rock County	WI	T. Lawrence Hesgard	1966	12227
144 5/8	23 6/8 23 6/8	19 7/8	4 4	Geauga County	OH	Rudy Grecar	1970	12227
144 5/8	24 7/8 26 3/8	21 7/8	5 6	Valley County	MT	Leith Wimmer	1971	12227
144 5/8	22 7/8 22 7/8	17 7/8	5 5	Vermillion County	IN	Robert McClara	1972	12227
144 5/8	23 6/8 24 2/8	16 5/8	5 5	Will County	IL	Joseph Wyer	1978	12227
144 5/8	23 2/8 23 6/8	18 3/8	5 5	Huntingdon County	PA	John A. Williams	1980	12227
144 5/8	24 4/8 22 7/8	16 3/8	5 5	Douglas County	WI	Oren Hanson	1982	12227
144 5/8	22 2/8 21 2/8	18 1/8	4 5	Oconto County	WI	David Nelsen	1982	12227
144 5/8	24 2/8 23 4/8	15 1/8	5 6	Traill County	ND	Arlin Ingebretson	1983	12227
144 5/8	23 0/8 22 1/8	14 5/8	5 5	Price County	WI	Peter Koenig	1983	12227
144 5/8	22 5/8 21 5/8	16 3/8	6 6	Stanley County	SD	Randy Kleinschmidt	1985	12227
144 5/8	24 5/8 25 0/8	19 3/8	4 4	Calvert County	MD	Tom Hosselrode	1986	12227
144 5/8	24 2/8 25 1/8	16 5/8	4 4	Washburn County	WI	Tom Elliot	1987	12227
144 5/8	28 1/8 25 6/8	20 1/8	5 5	Howard County	MD	David Wilson	1988	12227
144 5/8	22 2/8 22 3/8	15 1/8	6 6	Cherokee County	KS	David B. Price	1988	12227
144 5/8	22 7/8 22 4/8	15 5/8	6 5	Pike County	IL	Jim Murphy	1988	12227
144 5/8	23 0/8 23 6/8	17 5/8	5 5	Ramsey County	MN	Rick Westberg	1989	12227
144 5/8	25 3/8 24 0/8	20 7/8	5 5	Lenawee County	MI	Melvin D. Hoffman	1989	12227
144 5/8	22 7/8 23 1/8	19 3/8	6 7	Hopkins County	KY	Tracy Daves	1989	12227
144 5/8	24 6/8 23 5/8	16 7/8	5 5	Prowers County	CO	Daniel Kavalunas	1989	12227
144 5/8	22 7/8 25 0/8	20 5/8	5 6	Jasper County	IA	Brian Vander Velden	1989	12227
144 5/8	25 3/8 26 0/8	22 1/8	5 5	Jo Daviess County	IL	Scott R. Jackson	1989	12227
144 5/8	25 7/8 24 5/8	21 5/8	4 5	Chase County	KS	Rod Koehn	1989	12227
144 5/8	26 0/8 26 3/8	20 1/8	4 4	Fayette County	IL	Dean Harrison	1990	12227
144 5/8	25 3/8 23 5/8	21 6/8	5 5	Montgomery County	MD	Bret Giuliani	1991	12227
144 5/8	23 0/8 23 3/8	20 5/8	4 4	Kankakee County	IL	Jim Wetmore	1991	12227
144 5/8	27 6/8 27 1/8	22 3/8	5 4	Sauk County	WI	Mark A. Parrott	1991	12227
144 5/8	22 0/8 22 2/8	15 1/8	5 5	Carroll County	MS	Jim L. McCrory	1991	12227

484

WHITETAIL DEER (TYPICAL ANTLERS)

Minimum Score 125 — Continued

SCORE	LENGTH OF MAIN BEAM R	L	INSIDE SPREAD	NUMBER OF POINTS R	L	AREA	STATE/ PROVINCE	HUNTER'S NAME	DATE	RANK
144 5/8	22 1/8	21 7/8	19 1/8	4	5	Polk County	WI	Jerry Larsen	1992	12227
144 5/8	24 0/8	24 2/8	16 5/8	6	5	Jay County	IN	Chuck Caster	1993	12227
144 5/8	23 2/8	22 7/8	15 5/8	5	5	Prince William County	VA	Ted Falce	1993	12227
144 5/8	22 5/8	23 5/8	17 1/8	5	4	Lake County	OH	David N. Russell, Jr.	1993	12227
144 5/8	23 0/8	22 3/8	18 1/8	5	5	Chippewa County	WI	Casey Copas	1993	12227
144 5/8	25 0/8	24 6/8	19 1/8	5	5	Buffalo County	WI	John J. Mack	1993	12227
144 5/8	19 6/8	19 6/8	15 3/8	5	5	Livingston County	MI	Richard Powell	1993	12227
144 5/8	20 6/8	23 2/8	16 6/8	6	5	Adair County	MO	Eddie Schmitz	1994	12227
144 5/8	24 7/8	24 7/8	18 4/8	6	5	Chase County	KS	Clayton Shively	1994	12227
144 5/8	26 2/8	25 1/8	16 7/8	4	5	Williamson County	IL	Gerald K. Brueggemann	1995	12227
144 5/8	25 1/8	26 2/8	19 2/8	4	7	Delaware County	OH	Mitch Cole	1995	12227
144 5/8	21 7/8	23 0/8	19 0/8	6	5	La Salle	MAN	Curt Bossuyt	1995	12227
144 5/8	24 5/8	25 0/8	20 1/8	5	5	De Kalb County	GA	Craig Sears	1996	12227
144 5/8	21 2/8	21 3/8	16 3/8	5	4	Lee County	IL	Mark G. Kaleel	1996	12227
144 5/8	27 5/8	27 0/8	19 7/8	5	5	Grant County	WI	Wayne A. Willkomm	1996	12227
144 5/8	22 3/8	24 5/8	15 6/8	5	6	Portage County	WI	Bob F. Jastromski	1996	12227
144 5/8	24 0/8	26 1/8	18 2/8	5	7	Portage County	WI	Ralph L. Gagas	1997	12227
144 5/8	23 7/8	24 3/8	17 1/8	5	5	Edmonson County	KY	Robert Cena	1997	12227
144 5/8	21 6/8	22 0/8	18 7/8	5	6	Iowa County	WI	Ken Yerges	1997	12227
144 5/8	22 3/8	22 2/8	14 5/8	7	5	Hardin County	KY	Roland C. Menton	1997	12227
144 5/8	19 6/8	20 6/8	18 6/8	5	6	Namao	ALB	Randy Tellier	1997	12227
144 5/8	23 2/8	23 2/8	19 3/8	6	6	Calhoun County	IL	Paul Holland	1997	12227
144 5/8	22 4/8	23 1/8	16 1/8	5	5	Lake County	IL	William L. Snelgrove	1997	12227
144 5/8	25 5/8	25 1/8	20 5/8	4	4	Westchester County	NY	Robert Evans	1997	12227
144 5/8	24 1/8	24 6/8	16 5/8	5	5	Douglas County	NE	Scott K. Reed	1997	12227
144 5/8	22 7/8	22 3/8	18 3/8	5	5	Cooper County	MO	Chris Dowling	1998	12227
144 5/8	23 6/8	24 4/8	21 3/8	5	5	Cass County	IL	Glenn Hubbard	1998	12227
144 5/8	20 7/8	21 6/8	17 7/8	6	5	Taylor County	IA	Dave Messner	1998	12227
144 5/8	26 0/8	26 0/8	19 6/8	6	6	Pepin County	WI	Mitchell Gibson	1998	12227
144 5/8	24 0/8	24 5/8	17 5/8	4	4	Geauga County	OH	Dominic Graziano	1998	12227
144 5/8	24 4/8	21 6/8	19 1/8	6	5	Custer County	NE	Stephen C. Christensen	1998	12227
144 5/8	21 7/8	20 7/8	14 6/8	8	7	Boone County	MO	Mike DeShazo	1998	12227
144 5/8	22 0/8	22 5/8	16 1/8	5	5	Price County	WI	Timothy A. Gehrke	1998	12227
144 5/8	23 6/8	24 5/8	16 1/8	4	4	Johnson County	IL	Michael L. Ruebensam	1999	12227
144 5/8	23 2/8	23 0/8	16 7/8	4	4	Bureau County	IL	Todd Batten	1999	12227
144 5/8	23 6/8	24 0/8	18 1/8	5	5	Lewis & Clark County	MT	Sonny Templeton	1999	12227
144 5/8	23 4/8	24 0/8	19 3/8	4	4	Buffalo County	WI	Barry Orne	1999	12227
144 5/8	24 0/8	24 4/8	19 2/8	5	6	Wicomico County	MD	Robert Clyde, Sr.	1999	12227
144 5/8	23 2/8	24 2/8	18 7/8	6	5	Kleberg County	TX	Scott Brandon	1999	12227
144 5/8	20 6/8	21 4/8	17 6/8	7	7	Phillips County	MT	Randy Louck	2000	12227
144 5/8	22 2/8	21 4/8	19 7/8	6	5	Douglas County	WI	Zachary Lieble	2000	12227
144 5/8	24 4/8	25 2/8	21 2/8	6	6	Price County	WI	Ray Jung	2000	12227
144 5/8	24 0/8	24 1/8	16 3/8	4	4	Wyoming County	WV	Damon Vest, Jr.	2000	12227
144 5/8	21 6/8	22 0/8	16 1/8	5	5	Allegheny County	PA	Denny Swarmer III	2001	12227
144 5/8	22 5/8	22 5/8	16 1/8	6	7	St. Croix County	WI	Luke Edin	2001	12227
144 5/8	23 2/8	23 2/8	15 5/8	5	5	Newton County	GA	Vernon S. Prince III	2001	12227
144 5/8	23 7/8	23 6/8	18 7/8	4	4	Edmonson County	KY	Jamie Ashley	2002	12227
144 5/8	23 0/8	22 2/8	16 7/8	5	5	Holt County	NE	Dennis Dale	2002	12227
144 5/8	26 2/8	25 5/8	20 3/8	4	5	Jo Daviess County	IL	Larry Cox	2002	12227
*144 5/8	24 0/8	24 1/8	19 5/8	4	4	Suffolk County	NY	Danny Dost	2002	12227
144 5/8	22 7/8	22 5/8	15 6/8	5	6	Buffalo County	WI	Glen R. Axeness	2002	12227
144 5/8	23 2/8	24 2/8	18 1/8	5	4	Vernon County	WI	Greg A. Miller	2002	12227
*144 5/8	27 5/8	28 4/8	19 7/8	4	4	Knox County	OH	Jason Bywaters	2003	12227
144 5/8	18 2/8	23 4/8	17 3/8	4	5	Sauk County	WI	Wilhelm Hoffmann	2003	12227
144 5/8	23 1/8	23 0/8	18 3/8	5	6	Barber County	KS	Bill Klansek	2003	12227
*144 5/8	23 4/8	23 3/8	17 3/8	5	7	Carter County	MO	LeRoy F. Knupp	2003	12227
144 5/8	23 3/8	23 0/8	16 1/8	5	5	Knox County	MO	Gerald Bruegenhemke	2003	12227
*144 5/8	23 1/8	24 0/8	16 4/8	5	7	Fayette County	IL	Chad Zumwalt	2003	12227
*144 5/8	22 1/8	21 5/8	15 7/8	5	5	Tioga County	NY	Kirk Nielsen	2003	12227
144 5/8	22 0/8	23 2/8	19 1/8	5	5	Lake County	IL	Carl Spaeth	2004	12227
144 5/8	23 4/8	23 4/8	18 0/8	5	6	Marion County	IA	Joe Laird	2004	12227
144 5/8	22 7/8	24 0/8	19 4/8	4	5	McKenzie County	ND	Michael Tofte	2004	12227
144 5/8	22 4/8	22 2/8	15 0/8	5	6	Shawano County	WI	Chad J. Curran	2004	12227
144 5/8	24 1/8	24 0/8	17 3/8	4	4	Irion County	TX	Anthony "Del" DelMastro	2005	12227
144 5/8	24 2/8	23 6/8	18 1/8	4	4	Chippewa County	WI	Tom Jakubowicz	2005	12227
144 5/8	24 4/8	24 1/8	17 3/8	5	5	Erie County	NY	Randy Verel	2005	12227
144 5/8	26 4/8	27 5/8	20 5/8	4	4	Lancaster County	PA	Steve Mellinger	2005	12227
144 5/8	23 7/8	24 1/8	17 3/8	5	5	Waupaca County	WI	Eric M. Mazemke	2005	12227
144 5/8	24 5/8	23 1/8	17 7/8	5	4	Johnson County	IA	Joe Wagner	2005	12227
144 5/8	21 0/8	22 7/8	17 3/8	6	5	Peoria County	IL	Chris Noonen	2006	12227
144 5/8	24 4/8	26 2/8	18 2/8	6	5	La Crosse County	WI	Rod Springborn	2006	12227
144 5/8	23 4/8	23 0/8	16 0/8	6	6	Fayette County	IA	Mike Judas	2006	12227
*144 5/8	23 6/8	23 5/8	16 2/8	7	5	Price County	WI	Randy Simpson	2006	12227
*144 5/8	24 3/8	25 0/8	21 3/8	5	4	Hinds County	MS	Jody V. Sistrunk	2006	12227
*144 5/8	22 2/8	22 2/8	16 1/8	6	5	Bayfield County	WI	Mark "Gutz" Gutsmiedl	2006	12227
144 5/8	22 2/8	21 7/8	19 7/8	5	5	Winnebago County	IA	Keith Frerichs	2006	12227
144 5/8	21 6/8	22 3/8	18 5/8	5	5	Stephenson County	IL	Wesley A. Busse	2007	12227
144 5/8	26 7/8	25 7/8	16 5/8	5	5	Graham County	KS	Mick Cheshire	2007	12227
144 5/8	24 7/8	25 3/8	20 1/8	4	4	Hillsdale County	MI	Scott Bryant	2007	12227
*144 5/8	21 5/8	21 0/8	18 1/8	5	5	Iowa County	IA	Matt Matthes	2008	12227
144 5/8	23 0/8	22 6/8	17 3/8	4	5	Marshall County	IN	Tim E. Figg	2008	12227
*144 5/8	23 4/8	24 5/8	20 4/8	6	6	De Kalb County	MO	Paul Coblentz	2008	12227
*144 5/8	22 3/8	22 5/8	17 6/8	5	4	Kendall County	IL	Todd Borgman	2008	12227
144 5/8	24 0/8	24 3/8	18 3/8	5	5	Clayton County	IA	Aaron L. Green	2008	12227
144 5/8	22 0/8	25 6/8	17 4/8	6	5	Richland County	WI	Jeffery Firari	2008	12227
*144 5/8	22 6/8	22 6/8	18 6/8	6	6	Doniphan County	KS	Jason Wilson	2008	12227
144 5/8	24 1/8	24 3/8	21 5/8	4	4	Clay County	MN	Harold Palmer	2008	12227
*144 5/8	23 7/8	24 0/8	16 1/8	5	5	Stephens County	TX	Wei Wen Wong	2008	12227
*144 5/8	23 2/8	23 7/8	18 5/8	5	5	Buffalo County	WI	Jim Wondzell	2009	12227
144 5/8	27 1/8	27 1/8	21 2/8	5	5	Montgomery County	IN	Scott Starnes	2009	12227
144 5/8	22 4/8	22 6/8	18 2/8	6	5	Fountain County	IN	Greg Evans	2009	12227
*144 5/8	22 1/8	22 2/8	19 1/8	5	5	Cass County	IL	Joseph Furden	2009	12227
*144 5/8	24 6/8	24 4/8	22 0/8	5	7	Webb County	TX	Mark E. Williams	2009	12227
*144 5/8	21 4/8	21 4/8	17 7/8	5	5	Buffalo County	WI	Randy J. Schoeneck	2010	12227
144 4/8	22 6/8	22 6/8	16 3/8	5	7	Hall County	NE	Verne Skow	1958	12350

485

WHITETAIL DEER (TYPICAL ANTLERS)

Minimum Score 125 — Continued

SCORE	LENGTH OF MAIN BEAM R	L	INSIDE SPREAD	NUMBER OF POINTS R	L	AREA	STATE/ PROVINCE	HUNTER'S NAME	DATE	RANK
144 4/8	23 2/8	23 6/8	16 3/8	5	6	Day County	SD	John E. Sigdestad	1963	12350
144 4/8	25 3/8	26 1/8	16 4/8	5	4	Montgomery County	MD	Victor Ezerski	1975	12350
144 4/8	23 1/8	22 2/8	17 2/8	5	5	Winnebago County	IA	Ronald Gorden	1977	12350
144 4/8	23 0/8	24 5/8	14 5/8	6	8	Scott County	MN	Charlie Abeln	1977	12350
144 4/8	23 2/8	22 5/8	18 4/8	5	6	Greene County	OH	Don F. Necina	1981	12350
144 4/8	26 2/8	26 1/8	18 3/8	5	6	Jo Daviess County	IL	Kenneth Pluym	1985	12350
144 4/8	25 6/8	26 4/8	19 7/8	7	7	Madison County	NY	John Loveday	1985	12350
144 4/8	21 7/8	22 0/8	17 0/8	5	5	Morrison County	MN	Will Carlson	1986	12350
144 4/8	25 1/8	24 5/8	19 2/8	4	4	Montgomery County	OH	Anthony W. Miller	1986	12350
144 4/8	21 6/8	22 2/8	15 5/8	7	7	Peoria County	IL	Kevin Walsh	1986	12350
144 4/8	22 3/8	23 3/8	16 4/8	5	5	Lincoln County	MO	Denton C. Raymond	1988	12350
144 4/8	22 4/8	22 2/8	15 1/8	6	5	Howard County	IA	John R. Koschmeder	1988	12350
144 4/8	24 7/8	24 5/8	22 6/8	5	4	Ravalli County	MT	Tom Storm	1988	12350
144 4/8	25 1/8	24 0/8	21 0/8	5	6	Westchester County	NY	Frank Reindl	1988	12350
144 4/8	22 2/8	23 0/8	18 6/8	5	5	Allegheny County	PA	John H. Matthews	1989	12350
144 4/8	24 3/8	23 2/8	21 3/8	5	7	Jefferson County	WI	Mark A. Meyer	1989	12350
144 4/8	23 7/8	24 3/8	21 2/8	6	6	Vermilion County	IL	Robert G. Downing	1989	12350
144 4/8	24 2/8	25 0/8	17 0/8	5	4	Geauga County	OH	Joe Galfidi, Jr.	1990	12350
144 4/8	24 4/8	24 5/8	22 6/8	4	4	Appanoose County	IA	Frank Delouis	1990	12350
144 4/8	23 0/8	23 1/8	18 6/8	4	4	Lewis & Clark County	MT	Sonny Templeton	1990	12350
144 4/8	25 4/8	25 1/8	20 1/8	6	6	Clark County	OH	Randy McConnaughey	1990	12350
144 4/8	26 4/8	26 2/8	20 2/8	5	4	Colchester Township	ONT	Leo Potvin	1990	12350
144 4/8	25 2/8	25 0/8	19 4/8	7	5	Pottawattamie County	IA	Mark E. Raney	1991	12350
144 4/8	24 3/8	23 5/8	19 6/8	5	5	Iowa County	WI	Troy K. Koelzer	1991	12350
144 4/8	22 6/8	23 0/8	18 7/8	5	4	Edgar County	IL	Jerry Lee Watters	1992	12350
144 4/8	22 6/8	23 4/8	15 6/8	5	5	Juneau County	WI	Mark Marcinkowski	1993	12350
144 4/8	25 7/8	24 3/8	20 5/8	5	5	Winneshiek County	IA	Wayne Lamoreux	1993	12350
144 4/8	24 2/8	24 0/8	18 6/8	4	4	Cass County	NE	Bill Cox	1993	12350
144 4/8	24 6/8	23 5/8	14 0/8	6	5	Wilkinson County	MS	Ronnie G. Richardson	1994	12350
144 4/8	23 6/8	23 5/8	20 1/8	5	5	Kankakee County	IL	Rick Renzi	1994	12350
144 4/8	23 6/8	24 1/8	17 0/8	5	5	Jay County	IN	Steve Hammond	1995	12350
144 4/8	23 4/8	24 3/8	16 5/8	6	7	Lawrence County	OH	Richard P. Lynch	1995	12350
144 4/8	24 4/8	23 6/8	17 4/8	5	5	Olmsted County	MN	Charlie L. Flicek	1995	12350
144 4/8	22 6/8	22 5/8	14 6/8	5	5	Bright Sand Lake	SAS	Darren Feist	1996	12350
144 4/8	22 7/8	22 6/8	16 6/8	6	5	Anoka County	MN	Tom Brunner	1996	12350
144 4/8	24 1/8	24 0/8	21 6/8	4	4	Dane County	WI	Dan DiMaggio	1996	12350
144 4/8	24 4/8	23 4/8	18 6/8	6	6	Morgan County	CO	Tony Burmester	1996	12350
144 4/8	23 6/8	22 1/8	20 4/8	5	4	E. Carroll Parish	LA	John Poindexter	1997	12350
144 4/8	25 0/8	24 5/8	14 6/8	4	7	Knox County	OH	Robert Fowler	1997	12350
144 4/8	21 0/8	19 5/8	15 6/8	6	6	Prince Georges County	MD	James D. Gales	1997	12350
144 4/8	24 2/8	24 6/8	17 4/8	6	6	Clay County	IA	Jim R. Montgomery	1997	12350
144 4/8	25 6/8	25 2/8	18 2/8	5	4	Lee County	IL	Gordon C. Gabelmann	1997	12350
144 4/8	25 4/8	22 6/8	17 0/8	6	7	Lake County	IL	Richard W. Good, Jr	1997	12350
144 4/8	24 4/8	26 2/8	16 0/8	5	5	Chester County	PA	Steve Schmeusser	1998	12350
144 4/8	25 2/8	25 1/8	19 2/8	5	5	Richland County	IL	Bill Pearcy	1998	12350
144 4/8	23 4/8	24 2/8	17 2/8	5	4	Clinton County	IN	Mike Ticen	1998	12350
144 4/8	22 3/8	22 6/8	22 5/8	5	7	Pike County	IL	Nelson Sherman, Jr.	1998	12350
144 4/8	24 1/8	24 0/8	17 2/8	6	7	Reno County	KS	David Abernathy	1998	12350
144 4/8	23 7/8	25 7/8	21 7/8	6	5	Lake County	IL	Patrick McClellan	1999	12350
144 4/8	23 2/8	23 6/8	17 0/8	5	5	Eau Claire County	WI	Milt Schmidt	1999	12350
144 4/8	20 5/8	21 2/8	16 4/8	5	6	Columbia County	WI	Mark L. Hamele	1999	12350
144 4/8	20 3/8	21 7/8	13 4/8	5	5	Rutherford County	TN	Ray A. Lane, Sr.	1999	12350
144 4/8	25 6/8	25 5/8	18 4/8	4	4	Pulaski County	VA	Mike McDaniel	1999	12350
144 4/8	22 6/8	23 1/8	18 2/8	5	5	La Crosse County	WI	Mark Sesvold	1999	12350
144 4/8	24 2/8	26 1/8	20 1/8	4	4	Muscatine County	IA	Wade Eagle	1999	12350
144 4/8	23 6/8	25 4/8	17 2/8	5	6	Clay County	IA	Marvin Wooldridge	1999	12350
144 4/8	24 3/8	23 3/8	15 2/8	5	5	McHenry County	IL	Jeffrey J. McCarthy	1999	12350
144 4/8	22 3/8	22 1/8	18 0/8	5	5	Cumberland County	ME	Edwin R. Sprague	1999	12350
144 4/8	22 7/8	24 7/8	22 2/8	4	4	Grant County	WI	Glenn Droessler	2000	12350
144 4/8	23 1/8	23 3/8	16 2/8	5	5	Lapeer County	MI	Ryan A. Fuerst	2000	12350
144 4/8	22 0/8	22 3/8	20 7/8	7	7	Pratt County	KS	Morgan Turner	2000	12350
144 4/8	28 1/8	28 4/8	19 2/8	5	5	Winnebago County	IL	Paul U. Robins	2000	12350
144 4/8	23 4/8	25 0/8	15 4/8	7	8	Green Lake County	WI	Timothy S. Judas	2000	12350
144 4/8	22 6/8	22 4/8	16 4/8	6	6	Peoria County	IL	Lincoln Huber	2000	12350
144 4/8	25 2/8	25 0/8	17 6/8	6	4	Waupaca County	WI	Bill S. Mueller	2001	12350
144 4/8	21 2/8	21 5/8	16 4/8	6	6	Trimble County	KY	Bobby Hall	2001	12350
144 4/8	23 3/8	22 6/8	16 6/8	7	6	Jefferson County	MO	Terry L. Miller	2001	12350
144 4/8	24 4/8	24 7/8	19 3/8	5	4	Columbia County	WI	Michael K. Paulcheck	2001	12350
144 4/8	23 1/8	22 7/8	17 0/8	5	5	Wood County	WV	Dwight Cochran	2001	12350
144 4/8	25 0/8	25 4/8	21 0/8	6	6	McHenry County	IL	Mike Cummings	2001	12350
144 4/8	21 4/8	23 0/8	16 0/8	7	5	Wayne County	IA	Connie Pherigo	2001	12350
144 4/8	21 6/8	21 3/8	14 6/8	5	5	Pottawattamie County	IA	Gary Jungferman	2001	12350
144 4/8	21 6/8	22 0/8	20 3/8	7	6	Morris County	NJ	Peter Paradise	2002	12350
144 4/8	22 7/8	23 3/8	17 4/8	5	5	Wayne County	NY	Richard D. Vanderlirde	2002	12350
144 4/8	23 3/8	23 6/8	18 1/8	6	6	Iowa County	WI	Jake Venden	2002	12350
144 4/8	25 1/8	24 4/8	20 7/8	6	7	Williamson County	TN	Ronnie McCandless	2002	12350
*144 4/8	21 7/8	21 2/8	16 4/8	5	5	Monroe County	WI	Todd Pierce	2003	12350
144 4/8	24 7/8	24 1/8	16 0/8	5	5	Oconto County	WI	Dean Baeten	2003	12350
144 4/8	21 4/8	23 0/8	19 6/8	5	5	Shawano County	WI	Jason Schmidt	2003	12350
144 4/8	24 0/8	26 0/8	19 4/8	4	6	Van Buren County	IA	Ivan Muzljakovich	2003	12350
144 4/8	23 6/8	22 5/8	14 4/8	5	6	Chippewa County	WI	Craig J. Hetchler	2003	12350
144 4/8	25 4/8	25 0/8	18 4/8	4	4	Pinawa	MAN	Mark S. Ilijanic	2003	12350
144 4/8	24 2/8	23 1/8	20 6/8	8	5	Pike County	IL	David R. Burnett	2003	12350
144 4/8	23 3/8	22 6/8	16 6/8	7	5	Clay County	IL	Mike Butts	2003	12350
*144 4/8	25 4/8	23 2/8	20 4/8	5	7	Coshocton County	OH	Frank Antoniacci	2003	12350
144 4/8	22 4/8	22 2/8	14 0/8	5	5	Nelson County	KY	Tana Allgeier	2004	12350
144 4/8	23 5/8	23 5/8	20 6/8	6	5	Mecklenburg County	NC	Jeff Esely, Jr.	2004	12350
144 4/8	22 6/8	22 0/8	15 3/8	6	5	Washburn County	WI	David Schmidt	2004	12350
144 4/8	25 4/8	25 5/8	20 2/8	4	4	Buffalo County	WI	Dave Stuhr	2004	12350
*144 4/8	24 2/8	24 3/8	18 2/8	5	5	Jefferson County	WI	Casey L. Williamson	2004	12350
*144 4/8	23 5/8	23 3/8	13 5/8	5	6	Woodford County	KY	Brett Hornback	2004	12350
144 4/8	22 2/8	21 6/8	16 6/8	5	5	Outagamie County	WI	Chantz Nimmer	2004	12350
144 4/8	22 1/8	23 2/8	18 4/8	5	5	Cayuga County	NY	William F. Walker	2004	12350
144 4/8	25 3/8	25 0/8	19 2/8	4	4	Erie County	NY	James R. Sickau	2004	12350
*144 4/8	25 5/8	24 4/8	18 0/8	5	5	McKenzie County	ND	Wes Slade	2005	12350

WHITETAIL DEER (TYPICAL ANTLERS)

Minimum Score 125 — Continued

SCORE	LENGTH OF R MAIN BEAM L	INSIDE SPREAD	NUMBER OF R POINTS L	AREA	STATE/PROVINCE	HUNTER'S NAME	DATE	RANK
144 4/8	24 5/8 25 7/8	15 5/8	5 7	Van Buren County	IA	Baree Weber	2005	12350
144 4/8	22 2/8 22 0/8	17 2/8	5 5	Hamilton County	OH	Michael W. Powell, Jr.	2005	12350
144 4/8	25 1/8 25 6/8	20 0/8	5 6	Middlesex County	CT	Michael Tavarozzi	2005	12350
144 4/8	24 2/8 24 7/8	20 6/8	5 5	Pike County	IL	Derrick Ellis	2005	12350
144 4/8	22 4/8 23 5/8	17 7/8	6 7	Coles County	IL	Dan Milburn	2005	12350
144 4/8	22 7/8 22 2/8	16 0/8	4 5	Lafayette County	WI	Steve Simmons	2005	12350
*144 4/8	25 5/8 25 0/8	16 0/8	5 5	Monroe County	IA	Chris L. Rivers	2005	12350
144 4/8	23 7/8 23 2/8	19 6/8	5 5	Clark County	IL	Kevin J. Boyer	2005	12350
*144 4/8	23 3/8 23 0/8	18 2/8	4 5	Griggs County	ND	Nicholas L. Dahl	2006	12350
144 4/8	22 5/8 21 6/8	16 2/8	5 5	Cumberland County	NJ	Larry Hunt	2006	12350
144 4/8	23 4/8 22 4/8	18 2/8	6 5	Souris	MAN	Brian Knochenmus	2006	12350
144 4/8	23 0/8 23 1/8	18 4/8	4 4	St. Joseph County	IN	H. Bruce Weaver	2006	12350
144 4/8	23 5/8 23 7/8	15 6/8	4 4	Shawano County	WI	Lee C. Papendorf	2006	12350
144 4/8	24 0/8 24 2/8	19 4/8	4 5	Waushara County	WI	William E. Sennott	2006	12350
144 4/8	24 2/8 24 6/8	16 3/8	6 6	Franklin County	KS	Ronnie Rumford	2006	12350
144 4/8	21 5/8 21 5/8	17 0/8	5 5	Green Lake County	WI	Chris Van Derslice	2007	12350
144 4/8	17 4/8 21 0/8	16 2/8	6 6	Outagamie County	WI	David Gast	2007	12350
144 4/8	23 2/8 23 1/8	21 6/8	4 4	Rogers County	OK	Ty Stapleton	2007	12350
144 4/8	22 5/8 22 0/8	15 4/8	4 4	Outagamie County	WI	Charlie Peterson	2007	12350
144 4/8	24 0/8 23 4/8	18 6/8	6 5	McDowell County	WV	Robert Meadows	2008	12350
144 4/8	23 6/8 23 5/8	19 2/8	6 9	Pepin County	WI	James K. Kraft	2008	12350
144 4/8	22 6/8 23 6/8	18 6/8	5 4	Montgomery County	TN	John Wilson	2008	12350
144 4/8	24 1/8 24 5/8	22 0/8	5 5	Livingston County	NY	David Cambron	2008	12350
*144 4/8	23 3/8 24 7/8	18 2/8	8 4	Waupaca County	WI	Robert Stammer	2008	12350
*144 4/8	23 6/8 24 2/8	15 4/8	7 6	Spencer County	KY	Andrew S. Ware	2009	12350
144 4/8	21 7/8 20 5/8	15 2/8	7 6	Owen County	IN	R. Brad Dragoo	2009	12350
*144 4/8	23 2/8 24 2/8	15 3/8	5 6	Chippewa County	WI	Barry Walters	2009	12350
144 4/8	24 3/8 25 3/8	21 2/8	4 6	Jackson County	WI	Casey Steen	2009	12350
144 4/8	24 1/8 24 3/8	18 3/8	6 7	Sauk County	WI	Casey J. Holloway	2009	12350
144 4/8	26 0/8 25 4/8	18 4/8	6 8	Jefferson County	KS	Darin E. Holman	2009	12350
144 4/8	24 5/8 24 3/8	19 2/8	4 5	Republic County	KS	Donald Stowell	2009	12350
144 4/8	25 0/8 24 3/8	19 3/8	4 6	Marion County	IA	Eric Mohler	2009	12350
*144 4/8	25 0/8 25 0/8	17 6/8	4 4	Jasper County	IA	Don Morris	2009	12350
144 4/8	22 6/8 22 5/8	16 4/8	5 6	Drew County	AR	Tommy Bratton	2009	12350
144 4/8	24 7/8 25 2/8	17 1/8	7 4	Athens County	OH	Dale Ward	2009	12350
144 4/8	22 2/8 21 6/8	15 6/8	6 5	Warren County	MO	Jason Schoppenhorst	2010	12350
144 3/8	23 7/8 23 5/8	17 2/8	6 7	Rock County	NE	Dick Mauch	1963	12482
144 3/8	23 7/8 24 5/8	19 5/8	6 4	Delaware County	OH	Jack R. Hecker	1975	12482
144 3/8	23 6/8 23 6/8	16 4/8	4 5	Columbia County	WI	Ronald Bordson	1976	12482
144 3/8	22 5/8 23 7/8	16 5/8	5 6	Sawyer County	WI	Dave Phillips	1981	12482
144 3/8	22 4/8 23 5/8	16 6/8	5 5	Murray County	MN	John Laundre	1981	12482
144 3/8	23 1/8 22 7/8	17 7/8	6 6	Kingman County	KS	Scott Helmke	1982	12482
144 3/8	23 0/8 23 6/8	19 7/8	5 5	Clayton County	IA	Kenneth Clayton	1982	12482
144 3/8	22 6/8 22 4/8	18 7/8	6 5	Columbia County	WI	Jerry Ulrich	1984	12482
144 3/8	24 1/8 24 4/8	19 5/8	5 6	Morrison County	MN	Rick Hayner	1984	12482
144 3/8	21 6/8 22 1/8	18 3/8	5 5	Ripley County	IN	Dick Gambrel	1984	12482
144 3/8	23 7/8 24 1/8	17 1/8	4 5	Anderson County	TN	Johnny Wayne Jobe	1985	12482
144 3/8	21 1/8 21 5/8	19 7/8	6 5	Sussex County	NJ	Frank Tropona	1987	12482
144 3/8	26 4/8 25 6/8	19 4/8	6 6	Decatur County	IA	Julian Toney	1987	12482
144 3/8	23 5/8 23 1/8	15 3/8	5 6	Blue Earth County	MN	John Chatleain	1987	12482
144 3/8	25 7/8 24 6/8	17 7/8	4 4	Lambton County	ONT	Robert B. Kennedy	1988	12482
144 3/8	24 7/8 25 5/8	19 1/8	4 4	Polk County	IA	Todd Collins	1988	12482
144 3/8	22 3/8 22 0/8	20 7/8	6 5	Anoka County	MN	Greg Seymour	1990	12482
144 3/8	23 1/8 22 2/8	15 6/8	7 6	Beausejour	MAN	Dave DeLeeuw	1991	12482
144 3/8	22 5/8 22 2/8	16 2/8	5 8	Norman County	MN	Joel Gwin	1991	12482
144 3/8	23 1/8 24 0/8	19 1/8	5 6	Goodhue County	MN	John "Jack" Cordes	1991	12482
144 3/8	22 2/8 22 7/8	15 7/8	5 6	Rockdale County	GA	Jim Conway	1991	12482
144 3/8	25 4/8 25 0/8	19 5/8	5 6	Madison County	AR	Gary R. Catron	1991	12482
144 3/8	21 5/8 21 6/8	16 7/8	5 6	Sauk County	WI	Timothy J. Terbilcox	1992	12482
144 3/8	26 1/8 25 3/8	19 3/8	4 4	Lawrence County	IN	William Deaton	1992	12482
144 3/8	23 7/8 24 0/8	19 2/8	8 8	Logan County	KY	Marty Wilkins	1992	12482
144 3/8	22 4/8 23 2/8	17 2/8	7 6	Dane County	WI	Mark Orvick	1992	12482
144 3/8	21 6/8 22 2/8	16 3/8	5 6	Waushara County	WI	Duane Apps	1992	12482
144 3/8	22 4/8 21 4/8	18 5/8	5 5	Crawford County	IL	Kyle Mann	1992	12482
144 3/8	22 3/8 22 6/8	18 5/8	5 5	Sauk County	WI	Rollin W. Sorge	1992	12482
144 3/8	20 5/8 21 7/8	17 7/8	5 5	Leduc	ALB	Gerald P. Wrubleski	1993	12482
144 3/8	24 2/8 24 4/8	18 5/8	4 4	Dakota County	MN	Tim Gaughan	1993	12482
144 3/8	20 7/8 25 1/8	18 4/8	5 5	Harvey County	KS	Ron Hershberger	1993	12482
144 3/8	21 5/8 21 7/8	15 7/8	5 5	Ashland County	WI	Augie Boehm	1993	12482
144 3/8	25 3/8 23 6/8	15 5/8	5 6	Harrison County	MO	Sam Blackburn	1994	12482
144 3/8	24 6/8 24 4/8	20 1/8	4 4	Lake County	IL	John F. Isaacson	1994	12482
144 3/8	22 5/8 23 1/8	18 5/8	4 5	Darke County	OH	Ron Fansler	1994	12482
144 3/8	23 5/8 23 3/8	17 1/8	5 5	Juneau County	WI	Mark E. Miller	1994	12482
144 3/8	22 2/8 23 3/8	20 1/8	5 5	Muskingum County	OH	Greg Morehead	1994	12482
144 3/8	20 4/8 21 3/8	17 3/8	6 5	Oconto County	WI	Jeff Nowak	1994	12482
144 3/8	24 0/8 23 3/8	19 7/8	5 5	Logan County	KY	David L. Yoder	1995	12482
144 3/8	24 4/8 24 5/8	18 3/8	5 5	Caldwell County	MO	Jason Jedlicka	1995	12482
144 3/8	22 2/8 25 0/8	17 1/8	4 5	Ross County	OH	Keith Orr	1995	12482
144 3/8	22 7/8 22 5/8	17 1/8	6 5	Harrison County	OH	Walter Luikart	1995	12482
144 3/8	24 1/8 23 1/8	17 5/8	5 6	Alcona County	MI	Albert Inman	1996	12482
144 3/8	21 5/8 21 1/8	20 1/8	5 5	Nemaha County	KS	Darryl Becker	1996	12482
144 3/8	24 2/8 25 3/8	16 6/8	5 4	Hale County	AL	Patrick Suchey	1996	12482
144 3/8	24 5/8 24 0/8	20 0/8	6 5	La Salle County	IL	Albert W. Marshall	1996	12482
144 3/8	25 5/8 25 4/8	20 3/8	5 5	Sauk County	WI	Adam Lawinger	1996	12482
144 3/8	22 5/8 22 3/8	16 5/8	5 5	Meigs County	OH	William T. Peneston	1996	12482
144 3/8	20 1/8 20 5/8	16 3/8	5 5	Ferry County	WA	Jerry Solie	1996	12482
144 3/8	22 5/8 23 1/8	20 7/8	5 4	Missoula County	MT	Rory J. Zarling	1996	12482
144 3/8	22 3/8 22 3/8	18 6/8	7 6	Pulaski County	KY	Wayne Padgett	1997	12482
144 3/8	25 2/8 25 4/8	17 5/8	4 5	Clark County	IL	Kevin Boyer	1997	12482
144 3/8	24 4/8 24 1/8	18 3/8	6 8	Major County	OK	Elbert Woodrow Jobe	1997	12482
144 3/8	24 0/8 23 6/8	19 5/8	5 4	Hocking County	OH	Harold L. Briedenbaugh	1997	12482
144 3/8	24 2/8 23 0/8	17 5/8	5 5	Washington County	WI	Robert Naylor	1997	12482
144 3/8	25 0/8 25 1/8	18 7/8	4 4	Knox County	IL	David Emken	1997	12482
144 3/8	24 5/8 25 1/8	20 5/8	4 5	Logan County	IL	Danny P. Boward	1997	12482
144 3/8	23 4/8 24 0/8	19 1/8	5 5	Lake County	IL	Myron Hayes	1997	12482

WHITETAIL DEER (TYPICAL ANTLERS)

Minimum Score 125 — Continued

SCORE	R MAIN BEAM L	INSIDE SPREAD	R POINTS L		AREA	STATE/PROVINCE	HUNTER'S NAME	DATE	RANK
144 3/8	24 4/8	24 0/8	16 3/8	4	4	Shawano County	WI	Robert E. Reedy, Jr.	1998	12482
144 3/8	21 0/8	21 2/8	13 7/8	5	5	Pike County	IL	Joe Pitetti, Sr.	1998	12482
144 3/8	24 0/8	23 4/8	16 7/8	7	6	Coles County	IL	John Winnett	1998	12482
144 3/8	23 3/8	23 4/8	19 2/8	5	7	Hutchinson County	SD	Corey Gall	1998	12482
144 3/8	24 1/8	24 7/8	17 1/8	4	4	Jackson County	IN	Brad Lockman	1999	12482
144 3/8	24 2/8	24 2/8	18 0/8	5	5	Callaway County	MO	Stephen Hudson	1999	12482
144 3/8	25 4/8	24 6/8	20 7/8	5	4	Lake County	IL	Van Garner	1999	12482
144 3/8	22 5/8	22 1/8	18 3/8	4	4	Crawford County	IN	Joe M. Thompson	1999	12482
144 3/8	22 3/8	22 2/8	14 1/8	5	5	Hamilton County	OH	Kim Brockhoff	1999	12482
144 3/8	22 4/8	23 0/8	17 3/8	5	5	McMullen County	TX	Bob Gilbert	1999	12482
144 3/8	22 3/8	22 6/8	19 2/8	7	7	Washington County	MS	Kevin W. Busbee	2000	12482
144 3/8	23 3/8	22 1/8	23 4/8	6	4	Queen Annes County	MD	George Dana III	2000	12482
144 3/8	23 3/8	22 7/8	16 4/8	7	5	Texas County	MO	Steve Adey	2000	12482
144 3/8	23 0/8	22 5/8	15 5/8	7	5	Mingo County	WV	Charles Boyce	2000	12482
144 3/8	22 4/8	20 6/8	17 3/8	5	5	Renville County	ND	Jay Hass	2000	12482
144 3/8	23 4/8	23 6/8	20 3/8	5	5	Buffalo County	WI	Mark Johnson	2000	12482
144 3/8	23 0/8	22 6/8	16 7/8	5	5	Douglas County	MO	Don R. Wilson	2000	12482
144 3/8	22 7/8	23 1/8	18 4/8	6	6	Pike County	IL	Pat Corrado, Jr.	2000	12482
144 3/8	24 5/8	23 7/8	21 5/8	7	8	Lake County	IL	Randy C. Reid	2000	12482
144 3/8	26 5/8	26 4/8	25 3/8	4	4	Issaquena County	MS	Rusty Stubbs	2000	12482
144 3/8	23 7/8	24 0/8	16 5/8	5	5	Allamakee County	IA	Duane C. Baumler	2000	12482
144 3/8	23 4/8	23 1/8	21 1/8	5	6	Union County	SD	Nate Schmitz	2001	12482
144 3/8	23 0/8	23 1/8	17 3/8	5	5	Ottawa County	MI	Ed Mascarenas	2002	12482
144 3/8	22 0/8	21 4/8	15 3/8	5	5	Franklin County	IN	Daniel Allen	2002	12482
144 3/8	24 3/8	24 4/8	16 3/8	5	5	Delaware County	IA	Kevin D. Dempster	2002	12482
144 3/8	22 7/8	21 7/8	18 5/8	5	5	Barton County	KS	Chris Pasek	2002	12482
144 3/8	22 6/8	22 3/8	20 3/8	6	6	Ramsey County	MN	Travis P. Muyres	2002	12482
*144 3/8	24 5/8	24 1/8	19 1/8	5	5	Cook County	IL	George S. Del Rio	2002	12482
144 3/8	25 4/8	24 5/8	20 1/8	6	4	Sawyer County	WI	Thomas E. Stieber	2002	12482
144 3/8	20 6/8	21 1/8	19 1/8	5	6	Grundy County	IL	Vince Stills	2002	12482
144 3/8	23 7/8	23 6/8	15 5/8	5	5	Winneshiek County	IA	Randy Kerian	2002	12482
144 3/8	23 5/8	24 3/8	17 5/8	4	4	Fulton County	IL	Mark R. Bertram	2003	12482
144 3/8	24 4/8	25 3/8	19 1/8	5	5	Ogle County	IL	John Bushnell	2003	12482
144 3/8	22 6/8	23 4/8	21 2/8	7	5	Posey County	IN	Brian L. Alderson	2003	12482
144 3/8	24 6/8	26 6/8	19 6/8	6	7	Thayer County	NE	Tim Callahan	2003	12482
144 3/8	21 3/8	22 2/8	17 3/8	5	5	Highland County	OH	Thomas J. Dean II	2003	12482
144 3/8	21 6/8	22 2/8	15 7/8	5	5	Trempealeau County	WI	David N. Andersen	2004	12482
*144 3/8	22 1/8	21 7/8	17 1/8	6	5	Souris	MAN	Jason Lamovec	2004	12482
144 3/8	26 1/8	26 0/8	19 7/8	6	4	Portage County	OH	David E. Stonestreet	2004	12482
144 3/8	25 4/8	23 1/8	16 5/8	5	5	St. Clair County	IL	David Feltman	2004	12482
144 3/8	22 7/8	24 0/8	16 3/8	5	5	Dauphin County	PA	Kent A. Zimmerman	2004	12482
144 3/8	24 6/8	25 4/8	21 3/8	5	5	Collingwood	ONT	James McLenaghen	2004	12482
*144 3/8	22 2/8	22 3/8	16 3/8	5	5	Scott County	IL	Timothy Bolduc	2004	12482
*144 3/8	20 2/8	21 5/8	16 7/8	5	5	McMullen County	TX	Mark Wilson	2004	12482
144 3/8	27 1/8	26 7/8	17 7/8	5	5	Chatham County	NC	Benjamin M. Mann	2005	12482
144 3/8	23 2/8	23 0/8	17 1/8	5	5	Lucas County	IA	Bill Brown	2005	12482
*144 3/8	23 3/8	23 1/8	16 7/8	6	5	Lancaster County	NE	Mike Samson	2005	12482
144 3/8	23 6/8	23 4/8	16 1/8	5	5	Kleberg County	TX	Peeler Lacey	2005	12482
144 3/8	25 4/8	27 1/8	17 4/8	5	6	Jefferson County	IL	James D. Rueter	2005	12482
144 3/8	23 3/8	23 0/8	17 3/8	5	5	Stark County	OH	Dack Warner	2005	12482
*144 3/8	20 2/8	20 2/8	15 0/8	6	7	Pocahontas County	IA	Les Traub	2005	12482
144 3/8	24 0/8	23 3/8	17 5/8	6	5	Knox County	IL	Floyd Steinmetz, Jr.	2005	12482
144 3/8	24 1/8	24 3/8	20 5/8	5	6	Allamakee County	IA	Thor Johnson	2005	12482
*144 3/8	21 7/8	22 5/8	16 7/8	5	5	Marion County	KS	Derrick Dollar	2005	12482
144 3/8	23 2/8	23 4/8	17 5/8	5	5	Brown County	IL	Robert A. Crowe	2005	12482
144 3/8	26 0/8	25 2/8	21 5/8	5	5	Delaware County	OH	Keith Kintner II	2005	12482
*144 3/8	21 3/8	21 4/8	15 5/8	7	5	Portage County	WI	Dan Karl	2006	12482
*144 3/8	25 4/8	24 5/8	18 3/8	5	5	Middlesex County	CT	Anthony Gioco	2006	12482
144 3/8	22 1/8	24 1/8	16 3/8	7	5	McDonough County	IL	Dan Colaianni	2006	12482
144 3/8	25 1/8	23 6/8	17 7/8	5	5	Bradford County	PA	Rick W. Jows	2006	12482
*144 3/8	21 4/8	21 2/8	16 7/8	5	6	Fulton County	IL	Jerome King	2006	12482
144 3/8	24 6/8	22 6/8	22 1/8	6	6	Coryell County	TX	Joshua LeGrande Sears	2006	12482
144 3/8	24 1/8	24 6/8	19 5/8	4	4	N. Saskatchewan River	ALB	Ryan Basaraba	2007	12482
144 3/8	25 6/8	24 2/8	19 1/8	6	6	Fountain County	IN	Andrew Weisgerber	2007	12482
*144 3/8	23 0/8	23 6/8	17 3/8	5	5	Linn County	IA	Mary Benion	2007	12482
*144 3/8	23 3/8	23 2/8	15 1/8	5	5	Gibson County	IN	James S. Wright	2008	12482
*144 3/8	22 6/8	22 4/8	18 5/8	4	4	Parkland	ALB	Jeremy Barrett	2008	12482
144 3/8	20 2/8	20 5/8	16 7/8	5	5	Stutsman County	ND	Cory Smith	2008	12482
144 3/8	26 3/8	26 4/8	18 3/8	4	5	Buffalo County	WI	John W. Charles	2008	12482
144 3/8	24 1/8	24 5/8	20 3/8	4	4	Beaver County	PA	Steve Wory	2008	12482
*144 3/8	21 4/8	20 6/8	18 7/8	6	6	Steele County	ND	Matthew Kern	2009	12482
*144 3/8	20 3/8	20 4/8	16 0/8	6	6	Walsh County	ND	Bryan Olson	2009	12482
*144 3/8	22 6/8	22 6/8	17 3/8	5	5	Jackson County	WI	Richard D. Elmer	2009	12482
*144 3/8	22 1/8	21 4/8	15 6/8	5	6	Waushara County	WI	Brian Haase	2009	12482
144 3/8	23 1/8	24 5/8	19 3/8	5	5	Marquette County	WI	Jason Sengbusch	2009	12482
144 3/8	24 3/8	24 6/8	17 0/8	5	6	Benton County	AR	Cliff Eggert	2009	12482
*144 3/8	23 6/8	23 4/8	17 5/8	6	6	Wapello County	IA	Todd Popek	2009	12482
144 2/8	25 7/8	26 2/8	23 0/8	4	4	Bucks County	PA	Robert Weaver	1923	12618
144 2/8	21 5/8	21 4/8	17 2/8	5	5	Miner County	SD	William Hueners	1965	12618
144 2/8	21 7/8	21 7/8	14 2/8	5	5	Brown County	SD	Harold Larson	1966	12618
144 2/8	20 6/8	20 7/8	15 4/8	5	5	Juneau County	WI	Gordon Stittleburg	1966	12618
144 2/8	22 6/8	23 4/8	17 6/8	5	5	Steele County	MN	Maynard Bauer	1977	12618
144 2/8	24 2/8	22 6/8	19 6/8	5	5	Miami County	OH	Dale Stull	1980	12618
144 2/8	23 2/8	23 4/8	18 4/8	5	5	St. Joseph County	IN	Joe J. Leszczynski	1981	12618
144 2/8	22 7/8	23 2/8	17 0/8	5	5	Coffey County	KS	Marc Chester	1983	12618
144 2/8	20 3/8	20 1/8	15 4/8	5	6	Brown County	KS	Ken Spencer	1983	12618
144 2/8	25 1/8	24 2/8	20 6/8	5	4	Hamilton County	IL	Paul Sebby	1984	12618
144 2/8	24 0/8	24 3/8	19 3/8	7	6	Fairfield County	OH	Merle D. Strope	1986	12618
144 2/8	21 5/8	20 6/8	20 4/8	5	6	Lake County	IL	Mike Mitten	1986	12618
144 2/8	23 5/8	23 0/8	16 2/8	6	6	Cass County	IL	Donald Coufal	1987	12618
144 2/8	24 5/8	23 6/8	16 5/8	5	6	Clay County	IL	William Brummer	1988	12618
144 2/8	23 6/8	23 0/8	16 4/8	6	6	Christian County	IL	David Loyd	1988	12618
144 2/8	29 0/8	28 2/8	19 1/8	5	5	Charles County	MD	Mel Wolfe	1989	12618
144 2/8	22 4/8	22 6/8	14 0/8	5	5	Kenosha County	WI	John R. Griffin	1991	12618
144 2/8	24 6/8	24 7/8	21 2/8	6	5	Beltrami County	MN	Scott LaCoursiere	1992	12618

WHITETAIL DEER (TYPICAL ANTLERS)

Minimum Score 125   Continued

SCORE	LENGTH OF R MAIN BEAM L	INSIDE SPREAD	NUMBER OF R POINTS L	AREA	STATE/ PROVINCE	HUNTER'S NAME	DATE	RANK
144 2/8	24 2/8 24 1/8	20 0/8	4 5	Crawford County	IL	John Hale	1992	12618
144 2/8	24 0/8 24 3/8	16 7/8	6 4	Washington County	PA	Terry L. Kubacka	1993	12618
144 2/8	24 5/8 23 5/8	20 4/8	6 5	Madison County	IA	Roy Mikesell	1993	12618
144 2/8	23 5/8 21 0/8	18 2/8	5 6	Ashland County	WI	Mark Francis Ellias	1994	12618
144 2/8	24 1/8 25 1/8	20 6/8	5 5	Douglas County	NE	Ron Nordell	1994	12618
144 2/8	23 3/8 23 1/8	20 0/8	5 5	Lake County	IL	Mark Nelsen	1994	12618
144 2/8	23 3/8 23 4/8	18 4/8	6 5	Slope County	ND	Jeremy Brockman	1994	12618
144 2/8	21 6/8 22 6/8	16 0/8	6 5	Crawford County	KS	Dave E. Onelio	1995	12618
144 2/8	23 3/8 24 0/8	16 4/8	6 6	Steuben County	IN	Michael R. Chambers	1995	12618
144 2/8	24 3/8 24 4/8	20 2/8	4 5	Ingham County	MI	Paul Wygant	1995	12618
144 2/8	23 1/8 23 2/8	16 0/8	4 4	Henderson County	IL	Steven Hartney	1995	12618
144 2/8	26 2/8 24 6/8	19 6/8	5 5	Bayfield County	WI	Robert DeMars	1995	12618
144 2/8	22 7/8 22 3/8	19 0/8	6 5	Raleigh County	WV	Mark Aliff	1995	12618
144 2/8	23 0/8 23 5/8	16 6/8	6 5	Chitek Lake	SAS	Ken Brock	1995	12618
144 2/8	25 7/8 26 1/8	17 6/8	6 5	Des Moines County	IA	Tyler Messer	1995	12618
144 2/8	25 1/8 25 4/8	20 0/8	4 4	Chautauqua County	NY	Clarence Corbett	1995	12618
144 2/8	23 5/8 22 5/8	19 1/8	6 6	Madison County	ID	Todd Kauer	1996	12618
144 2/8	20 5/8 21 2/8	17 2/8	6 5	Kleberg County	TX	Roderick E. Nutter	1996	12618
144 2/8	24 3/8 23 5/8	17 4/8	6 7	Lee County	IA	Dan E. Glasgow, Sr.	1996	12618
144 2/8	24 6/8 24 6/8	17 5/8	6 5	Furnas County	NE	Gordon R. Smith	1996	12618
144 2/8	22 4/8 21 2/8	14 4/8	7 6	Chariton County	MO	Scott Brooks	1996	12618
144 2/8	22 5/8 22 1/8	15 2/8	5 5	Clarke County	IA	Thomas Stone	1996	12618
144 2/8	22 1/8 23 5/8	18 2/8	4 5	Suffolk County	NY	Steve Kelly	1996	12618
144 2/8	24 0/8 19 0/8	21 6/8	6 5	Suffolk County	NY	Lou Cannizzo	1996	12618
144 2/8	21 7/8 24 1/8	21 5/8	5 4	Vermilion County	IL	Harvey Dove	1996	12618
144 2/8	21 4/8 22 1/8	18 6/8	5 5	Scotland County	MO	James M. Slowinski	1997	12618
144 2/8	24 7/8 25 1/8	20 6/8	4 4	Bucks County	PA	Tom Hooven	1997	12618
144 2/8	22 6/8 21 7/8	15 4/8	8 5	Weld County	CO	Kevin Yerian	1997	12618
144 2/8	22 5/8 21 7/8	17 2/8	5 5	Rock County	WI	Frank A. Cagney	1997	12618
144 2/8	23 6/8 23 7/8	18 2/8	5 5	Boone County	IA	Kevin M. Christensen	1997	12618
144 2/8	23 6/8 23 6/8	17 0/8	5 5	Webb County	TX	Norman E. Speer	1997	12618
144 2/8	22 2/8 23 6/8	18 0/8	5 5	Union County	IA	Roy Mikesell	1997	12618
144 2/8	25 0/8 24 4/8	19 0/8	4 4	Wayne County	NY	Terry Bourgeois	1998	12618
144 2/8	25 3/8 24 4/8	19 3/8	5 6	Putnam County	IL	Alex F. Rolando, Jr.	1998	12618
144 2/8	23 4/8 23 1/8	16 2/8	4 4	Sheboygan County	WI	Douglas Knecht	1998	12618
144 2/8	24 0/8 23 1/8	17 4/8	4 5	Dubuque County	IA	Chad Patrick Brandel	1998	12618
144 2/8	23 6/8 23 0/8	17 0/8	7 5	St. Clair County	MO	Scott Stevens	1998	12618
144 2/8	21 4/8 23 0/8	13 6/8	5 5	St. Louis County	MO	Terry Comely	1998	12618
144 2/8	21 7/8 22 2/8	17 2/8	5 5	Vilas County	WI	Patrick T. Brien	1999	12618
144 2/8	22 6/8 22 5/8	18 4/8	6 5	Hays County	TX	Dalton Elliott, Jr.	1999	12618
144 2/8	22 6/8 23 5/8	16 4/8	4 4	Washburn County	WI	Jay Cornell	1999	12618
144 2/8	21 7/8 22 5/8	18 6/8	5 5	Oneida County	WI	Eric Kloes	1999	12618
144 2/8	24 5/8 25 4/8	18 4/8	4 5	McDowell County	WV	Kevin Kelley	1999	12618
144 2/8	21 2/8 23 1/8	16 4/8	6 7	Lawrence County	OH	Randy Helton	1999	12618
144 2/8	22 5/8 22 4/8	16 3/8	6 5	Dimmit County	TX	Kevin Hilbig	1999	12618
144 2/8	25 4/8 25 7/8	19 4/8	5 5	Mercer County	NJ	Chris Di Meglio	2000	12618
144 2/8	22 7/8 22 4/8	18 7/8	5 6	Benton County	MO	Gerald Schroeder	2000	12618
144 2/8	22 4/8 25 4/8	18 6/8	6 5	Henry County	IA	Chad M. Stearns	2000	12618
*144 2/8	22 1/8 22 7/8	17 6/8	5 4	Doniphan County	KS	Todd Gray	2000	12618
144 2/8	26 2/8 26 3/8	22 6/8	4 4	New Haven County	CT	Paul J. Mead, Jr.	2000	12618
144 2/8	22 4/8 22 1/8	15 6/8	5 5	Madison County	MT	Scott Tollison	2001	12618
144 2/8	21 6/8 21 3/8	15 6/8	5 5	Sullivan County	MO	Mike Otto	2001	12618
144 2/8	23 4/8 23 1/8	16 6/8	5 5	Genesee County	NY	Rocky Velletta	2001	12618
144 2/8	23 4/8 23 2/8	18 4/8	5 5	Plymouth County	MA	Glen D. Costa	2001	12618
144 2/8	24 4/8 23 4/8	20 0/8	5 4	Trempealeau County	WI	Grant Mathson	2001	12618
144 2/8	23 0/8 22 6/8	16 1/8	5 7	Jefferson County	KY	Patrick Hardesty	2001	12618
144 2/8	23 2/8 23 2/8	21 0/8	5 4	Stephenson County	IL	Terry Tregloan	2002	12618
144 2/8	21 1/8 21 1/8	17 4/8	5 5	Union County	SD	Bradley R. Bertrand	2002	12618
144 2/8	23 5/8 23 1/8	15 2/8	5 5	Trempealeau County	WI	Jeff Helmers	2002	12618
144 2/8	24 3/8 25 2/8	19 0/8	6 5	Noble County	IN	Lloyd D. Millhouse	2002	12618
144 2/8	22 6/8 21 7/8	14 6/8	6 5	Jackson County	IA	Roger L. Kafer	2002	12618
144 2/8	23 4/8 23 6/8	15 4/8	4 4	Bureau County	IL	Bob LaPorte III	2002	12618
144 2/8	22 5/8 22 4/8	18 6/8	5 5	Trempealeau County	WI	Ryan Metzler	2002	12618
144 2/8	24 4/8 24 7/8	16 2/8	4 4	Robertson County	TN	David Clardy	2002	12618
144 2/8	21 6/8 22 4/8	16 2/8	5 5	Armstrong County	PA	Herbert L. Stitt	2003	12618
*144 2/8	25 1/8 25 0/8	17 6/8	5 5	Guernsey County	OH	Michael Lipowski	2003	12618
144 2/8	23 1/8 23 0/8	18 2/8	7 5	Trempealeau County	WI	John S. McKeeth	2003	12618
144 2/8	23 5/8 24 1/8	17 6/8	6 5	Johnson County	IA	Gary Miller	2003	12618
144 2/8	21 5/8 23 0/8	17 2/8	5 6	Buffalo County	WI	Loren Bown	2003	12618
144 2/8	25 1/8 23 7/8	21 2/8	5 5	Lake County	IL	Brad Baley	2003	12618
144 2/8	25 7/8 25 5/8	19 0/8	4 5	Hunterdon County	NJ	Daniel S. Deveney	2004	12618
144 2/8	22 6/8 22 2/8	19 2/8	4 4	Warren County	IA	Alan Cole	2004	12618
144 2/8	21 5/8 20 5/8	15 7/8	5 6	Jasper County	IA	Tom McFadden	2004	12618
144 2/8	24 0/8 24 6/8	17 4/8	5 5	Calhoun County	IL	Frank Greenlee	2004	12618
144 2/8	21 7/8 22 4/8	20 4/8	5 6	Webster County	IA	Bret Ming	2004	12618
*144 2/8	21 2/8 21 7/8	15 2/8	5 5	Elk County	KS	Jeri Boley	2004	12618
144 2/8	22 0/8 25 0/8	20 4/8	5 5	Monroe County	IA	David L. Klobnak	2004	12618
*144 2/8	23 6/8 23 4/8	18 2/8	5 5	Nuevo Leon	MEX	David Lynn Shumate	2004	12618
144 2/8	22 3/8 23 0/8	19 1/8	6 5	Barron County	WI	Travis Ebner	2005	12618
144 2/8	22 2/8 22 5/8	16 4/8	6 5	Jasper County	IL	Skip Moore	2005	12618
144 2/8	21 6/8 22 1/8	16 2/8	6 5	Buffalo County	WI	Jim Rzentkowski	2005	12618
144 2/8	24 0/8 23 7/8	17 2/8	5 4	Waukesha County	WI	Steven J. Biksadski	2005	12618
*144 2/8	25 4/8 24 5/8	18 4/8	6 5	Isanti County	MN	Corey Hopkins	2006	12618
*144 2/8	23 4/8 25 1/8	17 5/8	6 5	Tioga County	NY	Robert Crawford, Jr.	2006	12618
144 2/8	23 5/8 22 3/8	16 4/8	5 4	Knox County	IL	Floyd M. Steinmetz, Sr.	2006	12618
144 2/8	23 2/8 23 6/8	19 6/8	6 6	Peoria County	IL	Larry Oppe	2006	12618
144 2/8	22 7/8 23 0/8	16 0/8	5 5	Beadle County	SD	LaRon Klock	2006	12618
144 2/8	27 1/8 26 4/8	20 6/8	4 4	Buffalo County	WI	Brian L. J. Mathiowetz	2006	12618
*144 2/8	25 7/8 24 4/8	16 6/8	6 5	Linn County	MO	Craig Chapman	2006	12618
144 2/8	26 5/8 24 2/8	18 3/8	7 5	Lewis County	MO	Mark Hooks	2006	12618
144 2/8	23 4/8 22 5/8	17 6/8	8 7	Clay County	KS	Keith Merrill	2006	12618
144 2/8	21 4/8 22 7/8	17 0/8	5 5	Branch County	MI	Travis Arver	2006	12618
*144 2/8	25 3/8 25 6/8	17 6/8	4 4	Morgan County	IN	Jared K. Litton	2007	12618
144 2/8	25 5/8 26 5/8	18 4/8	5 5	Middlesex County	CT	Ted Berry	2007	12618
144 2/8	22 1/8 22 0/8	17 0/8	5 5	Barron County	WI	Gary Krecker	2007	12618

489

WHITETAIL DEER (TYPICAL ANTLERS)

Minimum Score 125 Continued

SCORE	LENGTH OF R MAIN BEAM L	INSIDE SPREAD	NUMBER OF R POINTS L		AREA	STATE/ PROVINCE	HUNTER'S NAME	DATE	RANK
144 2/8	23 4/8 23 4/8	18 3/8	6	5	Sangamon County	IL	Steve W. Brown	2007	12618
144 2/8	22 5/8 22 3/8	19 3/8	5	6	Decatur County	IA	Ronnie McCorkell	2007	12618
144 2/8	23 0/8 23 7/8	19 0/8	4	4	Fillmore County	MN	Jeremy Rabe	2008	12618
144 2/8	23 1/8 22 2/8	21 4/8	5	6	Putnam County	IN	Joshua A. Stoner	2008	12618
144 2/8	21 7/8 21 7/8	15 4/8	5	6	Pepin County	WI	David Fayerweather	2008	12618
*144 2/8	23 0/8 24 1/8	18 3/8	7	6	Barber County	KS	Ron Lengen	2008	12618
*144 2/8	26 0/8 25 0/8	19 6/8	7	5	Pulaski County	KY	Marty Flynn	2008	12618
144 2/8	23 0/8 22 7/8	17 4/8	5	5	Champaign County	OH	Ed Zirkle	2008	12618
*144 2/8	25 0/8 25 2/8	20 2/8	7	6	Houston County	MN	Chris Barry	2009	12618
*144 2/8	22 0/8 21 6/8	16 4/8	5	5	Walsh County	ND	Dustin Brodina	2009	12618
*144 2/8	22 4/8 22 5/8	16 7/8	5	6	Buffalo County	WI	Dennis Potter	2009	12618
144 2/8	23 0/8 22 7/8	16 2/8	5	5	La Grange County	IN	Norman R. Carpenter	2009	12618
*144 2/8	23 3/8 22 5/8	19 0/8	5	5	Iowa County	IA	Kevin Clauson	2009	12618
144 2/8	23 5/8 24 4/8	17 6/8	6	6	Cedar County	NE	David B. Cull	2009	12618
144 1/8	21 3/8 21 2/8	17 2/8	5	7	Marshall County	KS	Jack Thornton	1965	12745
144 1/8	25 0/8 24 0/8	17 7/8	5	4	Union County	IL	Pat Mitchell	1974	12745
144 1/8	21 6/8 22 1/8	17 5/8	5	5	Jackson County	IL	Dave Yearian	1979	12745
144 1/8	23 7/8 23 1/8	19 1/8	4	4	Defiance County	OH	Alan Stark	1981	12745
144 1/8	25 0/8 25 7/8	16 0/8	4	5	Vinton County	OH	Randy Fee	1981	12745
144 1/8	21 1/8 21 0/8	17 1/8	5	5	Maverick County	TX	Dean Oatman	1982	12745
144 1/8	22 3/8 21 6/8	14 7/8	7	7	Calumet County	WI	Myron E. Jochmann	1982	12745
144 1/8	26 3/8 26 0/8	20 3/8	3	4	Charles County	MD	Fred Dolinger	1982	12745
144 1/8	21 1/8 21 6/8	17 0/8	7	7	Pittsburg County	OK	Brett Jones	1984	12745
144 1/8	23 1/8 22 7/8	19 4/8	5	4	Des Moines County	IA	Ray Waschkat	1985	12745
144 1/8	22 6/8 22 4/8	17 1/8	5	5	Woodbury County	IA	Ritch A. Stolpe	1985	12745
144 1/8	24 7/8 24 3/8	20 3/8	4	4	Berkeley County	SC	Hugh Gaskins	1986	12745
144 1/8	23 5/8 24 2/8	18 3/8	5	5	Sullivan County	IN	Morris L. Parr	1986	12745
144 1/8	25 3/8 25 1/8	19 5/8	5	4	Shawnee County	KS	Steve Deever	1986	12745
144 1/8	20 7/8 20 2/8	16 2/8	6	5	Hampshire County	MA	Larry Davis	1986	12745
144 1/8	22 2/8 23 2/8	17 2/8	6	7	Hughes County	OK	Randy Fletcher	1987	12745
144 1/8	21 6/8 22 1/8	17 0/8	5	6	Pepin County	WI	Joe Weiss	1987	12745
144 1/8	24 4/8 22 0/8	17 3/8	6	6	Benton County	MO	Curtis A. Powell	1988	12745
144 1/8	23 1/8 23 7/8	19 3/8	5	5	Montgomery County	IL	Mark Everett	1988	12745
144 1/8	21 7/8 22 2/8	17 5/8	5	6	Kenedy County	TX	Pink Atkins	1988	12745
144 1/8	26 2/8 26 0/8	16 6/8	4	5	Surry County	VA	William Allen Rickmond	1989	12745
144 1/8	22 1/8 23 4/8	19 7/8	5	5	Marinette County	WI	Chuck Gerbenskey	1989	12745
144 1/8	25 3/8 24 4/8	19 3/8	5	4	Hennepin County	MN	Ken Fluck	1989	12745
144 1/8	23 4/8 23 7/8	16 1/8	7	7	Blue Earth County	MN	Terry R. Wehr	1989	12745
144 1/8	22 4/8 23 5/8	18 3/8	5	5	Allamakee County	IA	Timothy Macal	1990	12745
144 1/8	23 1/8 22 7/8	13 3/8	5	5	Hood County	TX	Mike Searles	1990	12745
144 1/8	25 0/8 24 1/8	20 7/8	4	4	Ferry County	WA	Don Ohman, Jr.	1990	12745
144 1/8	24 1/8 23 7/8	17 1/8	6	5	Benton County	MO	Kelly Collins	1990	12745
144 1/8	22 7/8 23 1/8	15 1/8	6	6	Cedar County	IA	Ron Petersen	1991	12745
144 1/8	24 0/8 24 2/8	16 6/8	6	6	Hopkins County	KY	Randy Slinger	1991	12745
144 1/8	25 1/8 25 5/8	16 5/8	4	4	Iron County	WI	Daniel J. Van Oss	1991	12745
144 1/8	21 6/8 22 2/8	14 5/8	5	5	Hendricks County	IN	Chester D. Aiduks	1991	12745
144 1/8	25 4/8 26 3/8	17 4/8	6	5	Scotland County	MO	Jim Johnson	1991	12745
144 1/8	25 6/8 25 6/8	19 7/8	6	5	Leduc	ALB	Floyd Brunes	1992	12745
144 1/8	22 7/8 19 2/8	21 5/8	5	5	Marquette County	WI	Dennis P. Gohlke	1992	12745
144 1/8	25 2/8 25 1/8	18 1/8	4	4	Racine County	WI	Tim Steinke	1992	12745
144 1/8	21 1/8 20 4/8	15 7/8	5	5	Livingston County	NY	Jeffrey C. Meredith	1993	12745
144 1/8	23 4/8 23 1/8	18 0/8	5	7	Chester County	PA	Edwin Forteza	1993	12745
144 1/8	24 0/8 23 7/8	18 0/8	6	6	Knox County	OH	Tim Meier	1994	12745
144 1/8	22 3/8 22 3/8	19 7/8	6	5	Ozaukee County	WI	Rick Kropp, Jr.	1994	12745
144 1/8	23 0/8 24 0/8	19 3/8	5	7	Hancock County	IL	Robert Bara	1994	12745
144 1/8	23 4/8 24 2/8	17 4/8	6	6	Pocahontas County	WV	Everette McKinney	1994	12745
144 1/8	20 7/8 20 7/8	16 4/8	7	6	Pottawatomie County	KS	Greg DeVader	1994	12745
144 1/8	27 0/8 25 6/8	23 1/8	5	4	Brown County	IL	Sylvan Purcell, Jr.	1994	12745
144 1/8	23 0/8 23 2/8	20 3/8	4	4	Tazewell County	IL	Jim Querciagrossa	1995	12745
144 1/8	23 2/8 23 7/8	15 7/8	4	5	Calgary	ALB	Bill Riel	1996	12745
144 1/8	23 6/8 23 6/8	18 7/8	5	5	Rock County	WI	Bob Miller	1996	12745
144 1/8	23 1/8 23 5/8	16 4/8	6	5	Dubuque County	IA	Jim Boxleiter	1996	12745
144 1/8	23 5/8 24 4/8	19 3/8	5	5	Washington County	OH	Michael R. Moore	1996	12745
144 1/8	23 4/8 23 7/8	18 4/8	5	4	Cerro Gordo County	IA	Tom S. Hyde	1996	12745
144 1/8	21 6/8 22 2/8	18 3/8	6	6	Braxton County	WV	Edward Clifton	1997	12745
144 1/8	24 6/8 25 3/8	18 0/8	5	6	Pike County	IL	Mike Hogan	1997	12745
144 1/8	20 7/8 20 5/8	17 4/8	6	5	Montcalm County	MI	John Sobie	1997	12745
144 1/8	22 6/8 22 5/8	19 7/8	5	5	Chautauqua County	NY	John Goldberg	1997	12745
144 1/8	25 4/8 24 6/8	18 1/8	5	5	Stark County	IL	Gerald Schaff	1997	12745
144 1/8	22 1/8 22 6/8	18 5/8	5	5	Morgan County	IL	Terry Day	1997	12745
144 1/8	21 2/8 22 3/8	18 5/8	5	5	Penobscot County	ME	Scott H. Hartsgrove	1998	12745
144 1/8	23 6/8 26 5/8	17 5/8	5	6	Vinton County	OH	Thad R. Bright	1998	12745
144 1/8	23 4/8 23 5/8	17 7/8	5	5	Clinton County	IA	Shawn Petersen	1998	12745
144 1/8	24 1/8 24 3/8	15 4/8	6	6	Meigs County	OH	Shawn Rayburn	1998	12745
144 1/8	24 4/8 24 4/8	17 6/8	5	4	Allamakee County	IA	Jim Kieler	1998	12745
144 1/8	22 6/8 21 5/8	16 5/8	6	5	Johnson County	IA	Scott Shrader	1999	12745
144 1/8	25 1/8 23 7/8	18 7/8	4	4	Belmont County	OH	Stormi S. Day	1999	12745
144 1/8	23 0/8 23 0/8	18 3/8	4	4	Allegan County	MI	Jeff R. Weber	1999	12745
144 1/8	25 3/8 25 1/8	18 5/8	4	5	Prince Georges County	MD	Frank J. Furr	1999	12745
144 1/8	21 6/8 21 1/8	16 1/8	4	5	Ogle County	IL	Ronald L. Nelson	1999	12745
144 1/8	23 0/8 21 6/8	17 1/8	5	5	Sauk County	WI	Ken Frank	1999	12745
144 1/8	24 2/8 24 1/8	18 3/8	4	5	Clay County	KS	Chris Redline	1999	12745
144 1/8	23 4/8 22 6/8	16 6/8	6	5	Taylor County	WI	Ray Kliscz	2000	12745
144 1/8	24 6/8 23 1/8	17 3/8	4	4	Becker County	MN	Ross Wothe	2000	12745
144 1/8	22 6/8 22 5/8	20 2/8	5	4	Monroe County	WI	Raymond E. Felos	2000	12745
144 1/8	25 2/8 23 0/8	17 5/8	5	6	Montgomery County	IA	Brian Paul	2000	12745
144 1/8.	24 7/8 25 2/8	20 3/8	6	5	Washtenaw County	MI	Marc E. Keezer	2000	12745
144 1/8	22 2/8 24 4/8	17 1/8	6	6	Grundy County	IL	David Both	2000	12745
144 1/8	21 0/8 20 5/8	16 3/8	5	5	Adams County	WI	Dale M. Bowser	2001	12745
144 1/8	24 2/8 24 7/8	17 5/8	5	5	Washington County	WI	Duane Dvorak	2001	12745
144 1/8	24 4/8 23 2/8	19 6/8	5	5	Halifax	NS	Craig Pembroke	2001	12745
144 1/8	25 1/8 24 5/8	19 4/8	5	4	Iowa County	IA	Kevin McDonald	2001	12745
144 1/8	24 2/8 22 2/8	17 3/8	5	5	Waukesha County	WI	John M. Plese	2001	12745
144 1/8	23 0/8 23 1/8	15 0/8	5	6	Wapello County	IA	Dennis Bradley	2002	12745
144 1/8	24 2/8 20 6/8	16 0/8	6	5	Nemaha County	NE	Randy Striggow	2002	12745

WHITETAIL DEER (TYPICAL ANTLERS)

Minimum Score 125   Continued

SCORE	LENGTH OF MAIN BEAM R	LENGTH OF MAIN BEAM L	INSIDE SPREAD	NUMBER OF POINTS R	NUMBER OF POINTS L	AREA	STATE/ PROVINCE	HUNTER'S NAME	DATE	RANK
144 1/8	24 3/8	24 1/8	19 0/8	5	6	Oneida County	NY	Douglas Mosher	2002	12745
*144 1/8	23 2/8	21 2/8	16 3/8	7	5	Pettis County	MO	Michael Fagg	2003	12745
144 1/8	23 6/8	24 1/8	16 3/8	5	6	Waupaca County	WI	John W. Miller	2003	12745
144 1/8	20 7/8	21 1/8	15 7/8	5	5	Story County	IA	Tom Bell, Jr.	2003	12745
144 1/8	21 5/8	21 3/8	16 7/8	5	6	Jefferson County	NE	J. L. Robinson	2003	12745
144 1/8	25 4/8	24 7/8	19 7/8	5	4	Clay County	IL	Kenneth Haven	2003	12745
144 1/8	24 0/8	23 5/8	15 3/8	8	7	Knox County	IL	Keith Hudson	2003	12745
*144 1/8	22 4/8	22 2/8	17 6/8	5	6	Clermont County	OH	Charles Lee McHenry	2003	12745
144 1/8	25 2/8	24 2/8	19 5/8	4	4	St. Louis County	MN	Duncan Puffer	2003	12745
*144 1/8	23 6/8	21 6/8	14 7/8	4	4	Duval County	TX	P. C. Aughtry III	2004	12745
144 1/8	23 4/8	23 6/8	20 5/8	5	4	Price County	WI	Tim Risch	2004	12745
144 1/8	24 4/8	26 2/8	17 4/8	7	7	Wabasha County	MN	Michael Walker	2004	12745
144 1/8	21 1/8	20 2/8	17 3/8	5	5	Harrison County	MO	Michael Garrett	2004	12745
144 1/8	22 0/8	22 1/8	19 1/8	6	5	Orleans County	NY	Stefan J. Kessel, Jr.	2004	12745
144 1/8	22 2/8	22 3/8	17 7/8	4	4	Logan County	IL	Greg Potter	2004	12745
*144 1/8	24 1/8	24 2/8	16 0/8	4	5	Scotland County	MO	Joe Orsega	2004	12745
144 1/8	23 3/8	24 2/8	17 1/8	5	4	Winnebago County	IL	Michael S. Kloster	2004	12745
144 1/8	23 6/8	22 4/8	16 7/8	5	4	Kewaunee County	WI	Chris Tassoul	2004	12745
144 1/8	23 1/8	22 1/8	18 5/8	5	5	Grant County	WI	Mark D. Toepfer	2004	12745
*144 1/8	25 2/8	25 0/8	15 2/8	6	6	Defiance County	OH	John Ryan Adams	2005	12745
144 1/8	21 4/8	21 6/8	13 5/8	7	6	St. Croix County	WI	Todd Brinker	2005	12745
*144 1/8	23 6/8	23 7/8	19 4/8	5	6	Noble County	IN	Clinton R. Johnston	2005	12745
*144 1/8	26 7/8	24 2/8	17 7/8	5	5	Winona County	MN	Dennis Hengel	2005	12745
*144 1/8	24 7/8	25 4/8	19 3/8	4	4	Linn County	IA	Jerry Merritt	2005	12745
144 1/8	21 0/8	21 4/8	17 7/8	6	6	Sebastian County	AR	Will Beason	2005	12745
*144 1/8	23 2/8	24 2/8	16 7/8	6	7	Waukesha County	WI	Dayton Weed II	2006	12745
144 1/8	21 1/8	21 2/8	16 1/8	5	5	Stearns County	MN	Randy Laage	2006	12745
*144 1/8	21 7/8	21 6/8	16 7/8	5	5	Carberry	MAN	Jesse Larson	2006	12745
144 1/8	24 0/8	24 0/8	19 1/8	5	5	Mille Lacs County	MN	David R. Palmquist	2006	12745
144 1/8	23 6/8	24 3/8	16 4/8	5	5	Parke County	IN	Jeff Eslinger	2006	12745
144 1/8	24 0/8	24 0/8	17 7/8	4	4	McHenry County	IL	Jack Curry	2006	12745
144 1/8	22 6/8	22 3/8	14 4/8	5	7	Davis County	IA	Alan Francis	2006	12745
144 1/8	26 3/8	25 1/8	21 4/8	6	6	Floyd County	IA	Greg Kellogg	2006	12745
144 1/8	24 0/8	22 2/8	16 1/8	6	5	Coshocton County	OH	Gary L. Fischer	2006	12745
*144 1/8	23 7/8	24 2/8	19 2/8	5	4	Warren County	KY	Michael Whittle	2007	12745
144 1/8	23 4/8	25 0/8	15 6/8	5	5	Johnson County	IA	Darren Pingel	2007	12745
144 1/8	21 2/8	20 2/8	18 5/8	5	5	Ward County	ND	Gary Rude	2007	12745
*144 1/8	23 3/8	23 7/8	16 5/8	5	6	Sheboygan County	WI	Robert Babino	2007	12745
*144 1/8	23 7/8	24 7/8	20 6/8	5	6	St. Louis County	MN	Kyle Johnson	2007	12745
144 1/8	26 2/8	26 3/8	19 7/8	5	5	Fillmore County	MN	Timothy J. Daul	2007	12745
144 1/8	24 7/8	25 0/8	21 6/8	7	6	Buffalo County	WI	Adam D. Severson	2007	12745
144 1/8	24 5/8	23 5/8	14 5/8	5	6	Archer County	TX	Jerry Bales	2007	12745
*144 1/8	24 5/8	25 1/8	17 2/8	4	7	Linn County	KS	Doug Simmons	2007	12745
144 1/8	22 4/8	22 5/8	16 3/8	5	5	Logan County	WV	Gary K. Workman	2007	12745
*144 1/8	20 3/8	20 6/8	14 7/8	5	5	Valley County	MT	Todd Wendel	2008	12745
144 1/8	24 0/8	25 2/8	16 7/8	5	5	Dane County	WI	Steven J. Spaeni	2008	12745
*144 1/8	22 5/8	22 0/8	17 4/8	6	6	Ramsey County	ND	Jeff Brodina	2008	12745
144 1/8	24 2/8	25 4/8	19 1/8	5	4	Lehigh County	PA	Kyle Wildoner	2008	12745
144 1/8	24 0/8	24 6/8	19 0/8	8	6	Buffalo County	WI	Curt Rotering	2008	12745
*144 1/8	24 0/8	22 6/8	16 3/8	5	5	Wayne County	IA	Emmett Smith	2008	12745
144 1/8	27 2/8	26 5/8	20 3/8	5	4	Dodge County	WI	Charles Watry	2008	12745
144 1/8	29 5/8	27 3/8	20 1/8	6	5	McDowell County	WV	Bernie Shorter	2008	12745
*144 1/8	28 0/8	26 2/8	19 7/8	4	4	Holmes County	MS	Buddy Clairain	2009	12745
*144 1/8	24 2/8	25 6/8	20 2/8	8	7	Jackson County	IA	Thomas L. Decker	2009	12745
144 1/8	22 2/8	22 4/8	16 5/8	4	4	Marion County	IA	Randy Des Camps	2009	12745
144 1/8	24 3/8	24 1/8	15 0/8	5	5	Pawnee County	NE	Philip G. Koetje	2009	12745
144 1/8	24 0/8	25 3/8	16 3/8	4	7	Warren County	OH	Warren Dorsa	2009	12745
*144 1/8	23 0/8	22 0/8	16 1/8	6	6	Nemaha County	NE	Brian Bradshaw	2009	12745
*144 1/8	25 3/8	27 0/8	18 3/8	5	5	Hancock County	IA	John M. Seglem	2009	12745
144 0/8	21 4/8	22 0/8	16 6/8	5	5	Adams County	IL	Gerald Morton	1963	12885
144 0/8	22 4/8	23 0/8	18 6/8	5	5	Fayette County	IA	Kenneth Durnin	1971	12885
144 0/8	24 4/8	23 5/8	17 6/8	5	4	Wayne County	WV	Eddie Mullins	1976	12885
144 0/8	23 2/8	23 3/8	18 4/8	5	5	Lee County	AL	George P. Mann	1979	12885
144 0/8	24 2/8	24 4/8	18 4/8	5	4	Murray County	MN	Alan Metz	1979	12885
144 0/8	23 4/8	24 0/8	17 2/8	5	5	Hocking County	OH	Greg Bonecutter, Sr.	1979	12885
144 0/8	23 5/8	24 4/8	18 6/8	4	4	Juneau County	WI	Kelly Urban	1980	12885
144 0/8	22 4/8	22 3/8	18 2/8	5	5	Logan County	OH	Mark A. Payne	1981	12885
144 0/8	25 6/8	25 6/8	17 5/8	4	5	Jackson County	OH	Thomas Hart	1981	12885
144 0/8	19 5/8	20 6/8	17 6/8	5	5	Fremont County	IA	Larry Zach	1984	12885
144 0/8	22 0/8	22 1/8	21 7/8	7	8	Hennepin County	MN	Clarence D. Huls	1984	12885
144 0/8	23 5/8	23 6/8	19 2/8	6	4	Franklin County	KS	J. R. Oshel	1985	12885
144 0/8	23 6/8	24 2/8	18 4/8	5	6	Monmouth County	NJ	Cliff Underwood	1985	12885
144 0/8	23 7/8	23 2/8	19 0/8	5	5	Lewis & Clark County	MT	Sonny Templeton	1985	12885
144 0/8	23 7/8	23 0/8	18 0/8	5	5	Hubbard County	MN	Tim Leeseberg	1985	12885
144 0/8	24 1/8	23 5/8	16 5/8	7	8	Henderson County	KY	Michael Embry	1986	12885
144 0/8	25 7/8	24 7/8	17 6/8	4	4	Union County	SD	Derrall Minor	1987	12885
144 0/8	22 4/8	22 0/8	17 3/8	5	7	Mercer County	ND	Chris S. Hadland	1988	12885
144 0/8	24 0/8	23 6/8	18 4/8	4	5	Lycoming County	PA	Peter Salamone	1988	12885
144 0/8	22 4/8	24 7/8	17 2/8	5	5	Kane County	IL	Kurt J. Bird	1988	12885
144 0/8	22 4/8	23 6/8	16 6/8	4	4	Starke County	IN	Daniel H. Chaney	1989	12885
144 0/8	23 4/8	23 6/8	17 4/8	5	5	Du Page County	IL	Richard Maish	1989	12885
144 0/8	25 6/8	26 2/8	16 0/8	6	6	Kankakee County	IL	Al Weissbohn	1989	12885
144 0/8	24 7/8	24 6/8	17 2/8	4	5	Yellow Medicine County	MN	Brent Hassel	1990	12885
144 0/8	22 5/8	22 5/8	16 7/8	7	6	Stark County	ND	Howard Sharpe	1990	12885
144 0/8	24 1/8	25 0/8	18 6/8	5	4	Fulton County	OH	Mike Krasny	1990	12885
144 0/8	24 5/8	24 0/8	19 0/8	4	5	Wapello County	IA	Dave D. Young	1990	12885
144 0/8	26 4/8	25 2/8	17 1/8	6	5	Stokes County	NC	Phillip D. Ring	1991	12885
144 0/8	24 5/8	24 6/8	18 0/8	5	5	McHenry County	IL	Ray Kraeplin	1991	12885
144 0/8	22 4/8	22 4/8	15 0/8	5	5	Patrick County	VA	Ricky D. Boyd	1991	12885
144 0/8	20 3/8	21 5/8	20 4/8	6	6	Cochrane	ALB	Tom Foss	1991	12885
144 0/8	24 3/8	25 3/8	20 1/8	5	5	Lake County	IL	Richard Battaglia	1992	12885
144 0/8	24 0/8	24 2/8	19 6/8	4	4	Black Hawk County	IA	Gregory E. Lough	1992	12885
144 0/8	24 1/8	23 5/8	23 1/8	4	5	Cecil County	MD	Jerry T. Hewitt	1993	12885
144 0/8	23 6/8	24 7/8	17 2/8	6	8	Portage County	WI	Jerry W. Irwin	1993	12885
144 0/8	22 6/8	24 2/8	18 0/8	5	5	Hancock County	IN	Jim Moore	1993	12885

491

WHITETAIL DEER (TYPICAL ANTLERS)

Minimum Score 125 — Continued

SCORE	LENGTH OF R MAIN BEAM L	INSIDE SPREAD	NUMBER OF R POINTS L		AREA	STATE/PROVINCE	HUNTER'S NAME	DATE	RANK
144 0/8	22 1/8	22 7/8	19 2/8	6	6	Tippecanoe County	IN	Mitchell Tuinstra	1993	12885
144 0/8	25 0/8	25 2/8	19 4/8	4	4	Winneshiek County	IA	Gary Pavlovec	1993	12885
144 0/8	23 6/8	23 6/8	20 0/8	5	6	McHenry County	IL	David J. Binz	1994	12885
144 0/8	22 1/8	21 3/8	18 3/8	6	5	Manitowoc County	WI	Dennis Waniger	1994	12885
144 0/8	24 6/8	23 5/8	15 2/8	6	5	Wayne County	KY	Jeff Keith	1994	12885
144 0/8	24 1/8	24 1/8	19 4/8	4	4	Peoria County	IL	Michael H. Reatherford	1994	12885
144 0/8	22 7/8	23 5/8	16 2/8	5	4	Wood County	WI	Eugene "Toby" Keen	1995	12885
144 0/8	22 6/8	22 6/8	17 0/8	6	6	Livingston County	MI	Kenneth Roy	1995	12885
144 0/8	23 2/8	22 5/8	17 0/8	4	4	Irion County	TX	Ronnie L. Whitt	1995	12885
144 0/8	23 2/8	23 3/8	17 2/8	4	4	Grundy County	IL	Russell Robak	1995	12885
144 0/8	23 2/8	23 2/8	17 3/8	6	7	Anoka County	MN	Dennis Hoveland	1995	12885
144 0/8	22 5/8	22 2/8	16 4/8	5	6	Lafayette County	MO	Troy McNeel	1995	12885
144 0/8	24 2/8	24 7/8	17 0/8	5	5	Calhoun County	MI	Danny W. Murphy	1996	12885
144 0/8	21 3/8	22 0/8	18 6/8	5	5	Atlantic County	NJ	Edgar Reinhardt	1996	12885
144 0/8	23 6/8	24 0/8	17 6/8	5	5	Jackson County	MO	David A. Vestal	1996	12885
144 0/8	23 2/8	23 0/8	18 0/8	5	5	Guernsey County	OH	James E. McMasters	1996	12885
144 0/8	21 7/8	23 4/8	18 2/8	5	5	Tensas Parish	LA	Lynn Honeycutt	1997	12885
144 0/8	23 0/8	22 1/8	16 0/8	5	5	Marathon County	WI	Constance M. Welch	1997	12885
144 0/8	24 2/8	23 1/8	17 0/8	5	5	Buffalo County	WI	Chad M. Much	1997	12885
144 0/8	22 2/8	22 0/8	17 1/8	6	7	Grant County	WI	Jeff A. Landon	1997	12885
144 0/8	23 2/8	24 5/8	19 2/8	4	4	La Salle County	IL	Kevin K. Couch	1997	12885
144 0/8	23 7/8	23 2/8	15 0/8	5	5	Winneshiek County	IA	Scott V. Stewart	1997	12885
144 0/8	22 2/8	22 3/8	16 7/8	5	6	Prowers County	CO	Jim Matuszewski	1997	12885
144 0/8	23 0/8	22 1/8	18 4/8	5	5	Kandiyohi County	MN	Jesse Vlaminck	1997	12885
144 0/8	23 4/8	24 4/8	17 2/8	4	4	Winona County	MN	Terry C. Miller	1998	12885
144 0/8	27 4/8	25 3/8	21 7/8	4	5	Huron County	OH	Rob G. Crouse	1998	12885
144 0/8	22 3/8	22 1/8	15 6/8	6	6	Eau Claire County	WI	Mike Erickson	1998	12885
144 0/8	21 7/8	21 5/8	17 6/8	5	5	York County	NE	Ben Collingham	1998	12885
144 0/8	21 6/8	22 1/8	17 5/8	6	6	Grant County	WI	Bill Ackerman	1998	12885
144 0/8	22 6/8	21 3/8	18 0/8	5	5	Shawano County	WI	Kenton Olson	1998	12885
144 0/8	22 0/8	22 6/8	15 2/8	5	5	Shawano County	WI	Charles D. Peterson	1998	12885
144 0/8	24 4/8	23 0/8	17 4/8	5	5	Warren County	IA	Jack Rush	1998	12885
144 0/8	24 3/8	25 0/8	18 4/8	4	4	Jefferson County	WI	Mike Brown	1999	12885
144 0/8	24 7/8	24 0/8	19 3/8	5	7	Dodge County	WI	Michael Lentz	1999	12885
144 0/8	23 4/8	23 5/8	17 4/8	6	5	Pike County	IL	Ronnie Davis	1999	12885
144 0/8	22 5/8	22 4/8	18 0/8	5	5	Dodge County	MN	Darrin Giesler	1999	12885
144 0/8	24 7/8	25 4/8	19 4/8	5	5	Delson	QUE	Bruno Proulx	1999	12885
144 0/8	24 0/8	24 5/8	17 4/8	5	5	McHenry County	IL	Chadd Hartwig	1999	12885
144 0/8	24 2/8	23 6/8	18 6/8	4	4	Clayton County	IA	Jim Hankes	1999	12885
144 0/8	23 2/8	23 1/8	17 4/8	6	5	Dodge County	WI	Mark Salzman	1999	12885
144 0/8	23 5/8	22 4/8	18 3/8	6	6	Fayette County	IA	Gary H. Helgerson	1999	12885
144 0/8	21 6/8	21 4/8	15 2/8	5	5	Souris	MAN	Bryan Klein	2000	12885
144 0/8	21 4/8	21 1/8	18 4/8	5	7	Christian County	KY	Scott Goodwin	2000	12885
144 0/8	21 0/8	21 0/8	15 6/8	5	5	Carroll County	IL	Jerome Ulaszek	2000	12885
144 0/8	22 5/8	22 1/8	18 0/8	6	6	Ogle County	IL	Christopher Morath	2000	12885
144 0/8	22 4/8	22 2/8	17 4/8	5	5	Marion County	KS	Paul Czekuc	2000	12885
144 0/8	19 7/8	22 3/8	17 6/8	5	5	Spokane County	WA	Todd Greiner	2000	12885
144 0/8	22 3/8	22 4/8	15 6/8	5	6	Fillmore County	MN	Duane C. Baumler	2000	12885
144 0/8	25 2/8	25 1/8	19 6/8	4	4	Winn Parish	LA	James E. Baxley	2001	12885
144 0/8	21 0/8	20 5/8	18 4/8	5	5	Lincoln County	MN	Mike Carmody	2001	12885
144 0/8	19 5/8	23 5/8	18 0/8	5	5	Fillmore County	MN	Bill F. Pich	2002	12885
144 0/8	24 6/8	23 5/8	18 2/8	4	4	Schuyler County	IL	Fred G. Lening	2002	12885
144 0/8	23 1/8	23 2/8	15 4/8	5	5	Shawano County	WI	Dennis Gitter	2002	12885
144 0/8	21 4/8	21 7/8	16 0/8	5	5	Eau Claire County	WI	Tony Hagedorn	2002	12885
144 0/8	22 6/8	21 7/8	15 2/8	5	5	Adams County	WI	Bruce Scheehle	2002	12885
*144 0/8	23 6/8	22 5/8	16 0/8	5	5	Coweta County	GA	Randy Metzger	2003	12885
144 0/8	22 1/8	22 3/8	15 0/8	6	5	McHenry County	ND	Carter Medalen	2003	12885
144 0/8	21 2/8	21 4/8	15 6/8	5	5	Gage County	NE	Larry Lottman	2003	12885
144 0/8	24 2/8	24 2/8	20 0/8	5	6	Vigo County	IN	Michael S. Jones	2003	12885
144 0/8	24 0/8	24 4/8	20 2/8	5	4	Edgar County	IL	Kirk E. Allen	2003	12885
*144 0/8	23 6/8	23 4/8	18 2/8	5	4	Jennings County	IN	Eric McIntosh	2003	12885
144 0/8	23 7/8	21 6/8	18 6/8	7	5	Clay County	MO	Christopher Lein	2003	12885
144 0/8	21 4/8	20 7/8	17 2/8	7	7	Sweet Grass County	MT	Jeff Gavne	2004	12885
*144 0/8	24 5/8	25 6/8	19 0/8	7	4	Fayette County	IN	Steve Mitchell	2004	12885
144 0/8	24 2/8	24 0/8	17 2/8	5	4	Calgary	ALB	Greg Moore	2004	12885
144 0/8	22 1/8	20 6/8	17 4/8	6	6	Grant County	WI	Bryce Stetler	2004	12885
*144 0/8	21 3/8	23 2/8	19 2/8	4	4	Will County	IL	Paul L. Leonhardt	2004	12885
144 0/8	23 0/8	23 4/8	18 0/8	5	5	Piatt County	IL	Woodrow David	2004	12885
144 0/8	25 5/8	25 5/8	18 0/8	5	4	Plymouth County	IA	Eric Ellensohn	2004	12885
144 0/8	22 1/8	23 7/8	16 4/8	6	5	Page County	IA	Dave Messner	2004	12885
144 0/8	24 3/8	24 7/8	17 4/8	5	4	Kiowa County	KS	Shane Collier	2004	12885
144 0/8	23 0/8	24 0/8	18 0/8	4	5	Estevan	SAS	Garry Leslie	2004	12885
144 0/8	24 2/8	23 6/8	19 6/8	6	6	Macon County	IL	David Elliott	2004	12885
144 0/8	25 5/8	22 6/8	19 1/8	5	4	Hutchinson County	TX	Marvin Kramer	2004	12885
*144 0/8	25 0/8	24 2/8	20 0/8	4	4	Estill County	KY	Jeff Centers	2004	12885
144 0/8	23 2/8	22 4/8	18 6/8	5	5	Polk County	WI	Greg Orton	2005	12885
*144 0/8	23 2/8	22 3/8	17 2/8	6	5	Clay County	MN	Gregory L. Landa	2005	12885
*144 0/8	22 7/8	22 2/8	19 6/8	5	6	Indiana County	PA	Charles Edward Woodman	2005	12885
144 0/8	24 1/8	24 6/8	16 7/8	6	6	Licking County	OH	Rick Sutton	2005	12885
144 0/8	22 4/8	21 3/8	17 4/8	5	5	Buffalo County	WI	Jake Van Linn	2005	12885
144 0/8	21 5/8	23 0/8	15 6/8	5	5	Johnson County	IL	John A. Whidbee	2005	12885
144 0/8	24 3/8	23 7/8	19 2/8	4	4	Howard County	MD	Christopher Hall	2005	12885
144 0/8	21 6/8	22 3/8	18 3/8	5	6	Ozark County	MO	Carlos A. Gomez	2005	12885
144 0/8	24 5/8	22 5/8	18 4/8	4	4	Bourbon County	KS	Brian Luce	2005	12885
144 0/8	25 2/8	25 3/8	19 1/8	6	4	Boone County	IA	Dustin Gorman	2005	12885
*144 0/8	23 5/8	23 1/8	18 1/8	6	6	Story County	IA	Mike Augustin	2006	12885
144 0/8	26 3/8	25 6/8	20 0/8	5	5	Kosciusko County	IN	Kyle Myers	2006	12885
144 0/8	22 5/8	22 4/8	19 0/8	5	5	Montgomery County	MD	Donald J. Christenson	2006	12885
144 0/8	24 1/8	23 7/8	17 6/8	4	5	Chippewa County	WI	Tim Walters	2006	12885
*144 0/8	26 0/8	26 2/8	17 2/8	5	5	Dubois County	IN	Glen Haase	2006	12885
144 0/8	22 7/8	22 4/8	17 4/8	5	5	White County	IL	Ben LeCroy	2006	12885
*144 0/8	21 6/8	22 3/8	19 2/8	5	5	Phillips County	KS	Gary Niblock	2006	12885
*144 0/8	23 6/8	23 4/8	18 4/8	5	5	Forest County	WI	Thomas S. Karl	2007	12885
144 0/8	21 2/8	21 0/8	18 2/8	5	5	Warren County	IA	Casey Wilson	2007	12885
144 0/8	22 1/8	22 6/8	16 6/8	6	6	Clay County	IN	Michael R. Lowry	2007	12885

WHITETAIL DEER (TYPICAL ANTLERS)

Minimum Score 125   Continued

SCORE	LENGTH OF R MAIN BEAM L	INSIDE SPREAD	NUMBER OF R POINTS L	AREA	STATE/ PROVINCE	HUNTER'S NAME	DATE	RANK
144 0/8	21 3/8 21 3/8	16 4/8	6 6	Pontotoc County	OK	Sherwin R. Farmer	2007	12885
144 0/8	24 5/8 24 0/8	19 2/8	8 5	Schuyler County	IL	Vince Farrow	2007	12885
144 0/8	22 5/8 23 0/8	19 0/8	5 5	Medina County	OH	Dale Collins	2007	12885
*144 0/8	22 3/8 22 2/8	19 2/8	5 6	Waupaca County	WI	Randy Groskreutz	2008	12885
144 0/8	24 0/8 21 4/8	17 4/8	5 5	Berkshire County	MA	Gregg Massini	2008	12885
144 0/8	22 5/8 21 6/8	17 0/8	5 6	Greene County	IL	Travis W. Fowble	2008	12885
144 0/8	22 7/8 22 1/8	17 4/8	6 4	Christian County	IL	Dave Boehler	2008	12885
144 0/8	21 7/8 21 2/8	15 2/8	5 5	Osage County	KS	Bill Cline	2008	12885
144 0/8	23 7/8 23 6/8	14 6/8	5 5	Riley County	KS	Mike Weaver	2008	12885
144 0/8	24 1/8 24 2/8	16 7/8	8 9	Neosho County	KS	Chad Leonard	2009	12885
144 0/8	23 5/8 24 5/8	21 0/8	5 4	Jackson County	WI	Mark Seeley	2009	12885
144 0/8	23 7/8 23 0/8	16 4/8	5 5	Monroe County	NY	Jared Reger	2009	12885
144 0/8	22 6/8 22 7/8	18 7/8	5 6	Keya Paha County	NE	R. Kirk Sharp	2009	12885
*144 0/8	23 7/8 24 3/8	18 4/8	4 4	Brown County	WI	Dave Wiegert, Jr.	2009	12885
144 0/8	23 5/8 23 5/8	15 4/8	4 4	Barber County	KS	Todd L. Mercure	2009	12885
*144 0/8	22 0/8 21 6/8	15 2/8	4 4	Jefferson County	KS	Scott Campbell	2009	12885
144 0/8	23 4/8 23 4/8	19 6/8	5 4	Winnebago County	IA	Mike Vinci	2009	12885
143 7/8	21 5/8 22 2/8	15 7/8	5 5	Oktibbeha County	MS	Frank Cascio, Jr.	1978	13033
143 7/8	23 1/8 23 0/8	19 1/8	4 5	White County	IN	Richard Zaring	1980	13033
143 7/8	22 5/8 21 6/8	14 7/8	6 5	Traverse County	MN	Gary Anderson	1980	13033
143 7/8	27 3/8 26 2/8	19 0/8	5 6	Erie County	NY	Mark A. Bennett	1981	13033
143 7/8	22 1/8 23 1/8	17 3/8	5 5	Taylor County	WI	Tony Kliscz	1981	13033
143 7/8	28 6/8 26 3/8	21 1/8	4 5	Ross County	OH	Jack F. Hatton	1982	13033
143 7/8	24 1/8 23 0/8	17 7/8	6 5	Morrill County	NE	Gerry Hrasky	1983	13033
143 7/8	20 4/8 20 3/8	15 3/8	5 5	Macon County	AL	George P. Mann	1984	13033
143 7/8	24 3/8 23 2/8	19 1/8	7 7	Allegheny County	PA	Richard J. Kudranski	1985	13033
143 7/8	23 4/8 23 5/8	17 5/8	5 5	Ashland County	WI	Neal Turney	1987	13033
143 7/8	26 0/8 26 3/8	21 4/8	7 7	Clinton County	MI	Louie Mrazek	1987	13033
143 7/8	25 5/8 24 2/8	15 7/8	4 4	St. Croix County	WI	Robert K. Weaver	1987	13033
143 7/8	23 6/8 23 5/8	21 5/8	5 5	La Salle County	IL	Gary Tabor	1987	13033
143 7/8	21 2/8 21 6/8	15 5/8	5 5	Allamakee County	IA	Gary P. Cole	1987	13033
143 7/8	21 4/8 22 4/8	18 3/8	5 5	Iroquois County	IL	Jerry Putnam	1987	13033
143 7/8	23 4/8 24 5/8	17 4/8	5 8	Camden County	MO	John Cartwright	1989	13033
143 7/8	22 7/8 22 5/8	18 3/8	6 6	Monroe County	WI	Chuck Underberg	1989	13033
143 7/8	22 6/8 22 2/8	16 3/8	5 5	Hamilton County	IN	Scott Griffin	1990	13033
143 7/8	23 5/8 22 0/8	17 7/8	5 5	Olmsted County	MN	Steven Laudon	1990	13033
143 7/8	27 4/8 26 6/8	21 1/8	5 4	Bartholomew County	IN	James W. Smith	1990	13033
143 7/8	26 2/8 24 6/8	17 5/8	6 4	Winnebago County	IL	Mark P. Stock	1990	13033
143 7/8	25 6/8 25 4/8	22 5/8	4 4	Calhoun County	MI	Greg H. St. John	1991	13033
143 7/8	24 3/8 24 5/8	16 3/8	5 5	Custer County	NE	Dan Dowse	1991	13033
143 7/8	24 0/8 24 2/8	17 7/8	4 4	Porter County	IN	James Frahm	1991	13033
143 7/8	23 7/8 23 0/8	14 5/8	5 5	McKenzie County	ND	Steve Rehak	1991	13033
143 7/8	23 7/8 25 3/8	17 7/8	4 5	Marinette County	WI	Mark W. Johnson	1992	13033
143 7/8	24 5/8 23 4/8	17 2/8	6 7	DeKalb County	IL	Jim Zielinski	1992	13033
143 7/8	25 7/8 26 3/8	17 7/8	4 4	Adams County	IL	Edward Leach	1992	13033
143 7/8	23 7/8 24 4/8	16 7/8	6 5	Shelby County	IL	Jim Harbert	1992	13033
143 7/8	22 3/8 22 6/8	16 5/8	5 5	Kankakee County	IL	Tom Campbell	1992	13033
143 7/8	23 5/8 23 4/8	17 2/8	6 4	Muskingum County	OH	Randy Pennell	1993	13033
143 7/8	19 4/8 20 4/8	15 7/8	5 6	Daviess County	MO	Daniel Terry	1993	13033
143 7/8	23 1/8 23 2/8	15 7/8	5 5	Cape Girardeau County	MO	Martin Blumenthal	1993	13033
143 7/8	21 7/8 22 7/8	15 1/8	5 5	Tazewell County	IL	Thomas Watson	1993	13033
143 7/8	23 4/8 23 7/8	20 3/8	4 4	Hennepin County	MN	Daniel Kittok	1993	13033
143 7/8	22 6/8 22 7/8	18 1/8	4 5	La Salle County	IL	Ray F. Daniels	1993	13033
143 7/8	22 2/8 23 3/8	18 5/8	5 5	Washington County	MN	Tim Dornseif	1994	13033
143 7/8	21 7/8 21 2/8	18 3/8	4 4	Ingham County	MI	Daniel J. Briggs	1994	13033
143 7/8	22 7/8 23 2/8	20 3/8	5 5	St. Croix County	WI	Steve J. Ball	1995	13033
143 7/8	23 3/8 23 2/8	18 3/8	5 5	Mercer County	WV	Dwayne E. Repass	1995	13033
143 7/8	25 0/8 23 6/8	18 4/8	4 6	Greene County	OH	George R. Fischer	1995	13033
143 7/8	25 1/8 24 7/8	19 6/8	5 4	Jefferson County	WI	Matt Grischow	1996	13033
143 7/8	23 4/8 24 0/8	18 1/8	5 5	Juneau County	WI	David W. Reynolds	1996	13033
143 7/8	21 4/8 21 2/8	18 7/8	5 5	Logan County	KY	Russell D. Johnson	1996	13033
143 7/8	24 3/8 24 4/8	20 1/8	4 4	Grant County	SD	Steve Snow	1996	13033
143 7/8	26 3/8 24 6/8	18 7/8	7 6	Chisago County	MN	Buckley Smith	1996	13033
143 7/8	24 1/8 24 0/8	19 1/8	6 5	Dubuque County	IA	Timothy J. Harle	1996	13033
143 7/8	24 3/8 23 5/8	19 4/8	6 5	Calvert County	MD	James "Skip" Edwards	1997	13033
143 7/8	23 5/8 23 0/8	24 4/8	5 5	Fairfax County	VA	James Robert Jones	1997	13033
143 7/8	25 1/8 25 7/8	17 7/8	4 5	Perry County	IL	Ron Pyron	1997	13033
143 7/8	24 6/8 23 6/8	17 7/8	5 5	Muscatine County	IA	Michael A. Owens	1997	13033
143 7/8	21 7/8 21 3/8	16 3/8	6 7	Iowa County	WI	Jeffrey D. Johnston	1998	13033
143 7/8	22 6/8 24 0/8	17 1/8	4 5	Thurston County	NE	Terry D. Kramper	1998	13033
143 7/8	23 7/8 23 3/8	16 1/8	6 9	Atchison County	MO	Pink Atkins	1998	13033
143 7/8	22 6/8 23 6/8	20 1/8	5 5	Bucks County	PA	Frederic G. Lening	1998	13033
143 7/8	23 2/8 22 5/8	18 1/8	5 5	Van Buren County	IA	Gary Bolden	1998	13033
143 7/8	21 0/8 21 6/8	15 3/8	5 5	Clay County	KS	Corey Trumpp	1998	13033
143 7/8	23 5/8 23 5/8	17 1/8	6 6	Waupaca County	WI	Mitzi K. Omit	1998	13033
143 7/8	22 1/8 24 1/8	15 0/8	6 6	Wright County	MO	Darrel Hickman	1999	13033
143 7/8	25 2/8 24 7/8	17 5/8	4 6	Boone County	IL	Larry R. Anderson	1999	13033
143 7/8	22 6/8 23 1/8	19 1/8	6 7	Doniphan County	KS	Robert E. Wilson	1999	13033
143 7/8	20 4/8 21 4/8	17 3/8	5 5	Kosciusko County	IN	Dan J. Krupp	2000	13033
143 7/8	22 2/8 22 6/8	18 1/8	5 7	Rock County	WI	Pat Weberpal	2000	13033
143 7/8	24 4/8 25 2/8	19 3/8	4 4	Cayuga County	NY	Gary J. Cunningham, Jr.	2000	13033
143 7/8	23 2/8 23 1/8	15 5/8	6 5	McHenry County	IL	Sal Agro	2000	13033
143 7/8	22 6/8 23 3/8	15 7/8	6 5	Madison County	IA	Roger Broadbent	2000	13033
143 7/8	22 2/8 21 4/8	18 1/8	5 5	Johnson County	IA	Kevin G. Rocca	2000	13033
143 7/8	23 2/8 24 3/8	20 5/8	4 5	Jefferson County	ID	Robert Davies	2000	13033
143 7/8	21 1/8 21 4/8	17 1/8	5 6	Lucas County	IA	Darren Johnston	2001	13033
*143 7/8	23 6/8 22 2/8	19 1/8	5 4	Beaver County	PA	Robert E. Davenport	2001	13033
143 7/8	22 7/8 22 6/8	16 0/8	6 6	Outagamie County	WI	Joe Van Offeren	2002	13033
143 7/8	24 1/8 24 0/8	17 3/8	4 5	Washington County	PA	Dennis Novak	2002	13033
143 7/8	25 4/8 27 4/8	21 2/8	6 5	Christian County	IL	Roland J. Thoma	2002	13033
143 7/8	24 1/8 22 4/8	18 5/8	5 4	Cumberland County	IL	Larry Hall	2002	13033
143 7/8	23 0/8 23 0/8	18 5/8	5 5	Louisa County	IA	Christopher E. Bennett	2002	13033
143 7/8	24 4/8 24 0/8	16 7/8	5 6	Athens County	OH	Donald E. Lee	2002	13033
143 7/8	25 7/8 25 0/8	20 5/8	5 5	Adams County	IL	Rusty J. Voss	2002	13033
143 7/8	25 4/8 24 0/8	20 1/8	4 7	Logan County	CO	Joe Baird	2002	13033

WHITETAIL DEER (TYPICAL ANTLERS)

Minimum Score 125   Continued

SCORE	LENGTH OF R MAIN BEAM L	INSIDE SPREAD	NUMBER OF R POINTS L	AREA	STATE/ PROVINCE	HUNTER'S NAME	DATE	RANK
143 7/8	22 6/8 23 1/8	21 1/8	5 5	E. Carroll Parish	LA	Randy Steverson	2002	13033
143 7/8	23 2/8 23 3/8	15 5/8	6 5	Milwaukee County	WI	Bruce Gniot	2003	13033
143 7/8	27 0/8 24 5/8	19 3/8	5 5	Trempealeau County	WI	Scott Halama	2003	13033
143 7/8	22 7/8 22 2/8	18 2/8	6 5	Hillsdale County	MI	Andrew C. May	2003	13033
143 7/8	24 7/8 24 6/8	15 4/8	7 5	Steuben County	IN	Shaun Hamilton	2003	13033
143 7/8	26 6/8 27 4/8	22 4/8	5 6	Nodaway County	MO	Ron Browning	2003	13033
143 7/8	24 0/8 24 0/8	19 3/8	5 5	Sawyer County	WI	Curtis R. Stepanek	2003	13033
143 7/8	21 4/8 20 4/8	15 7/8	5 5	Ogle County	IL	John Vos	2003	13033
143 7/8	21 4/8 20 6/8	15 3/8	5 5	Daviess County	MO	Eric Williams	2003	13033
143 7/8	23 6/8 23 2/8	19 0/8	4 6	Dauphin County	PA	Jesse E. Shertzer	2004	13033
143 7/8	21 4/8 23 0/8	16 6/8	7 6	Woodford County	KY	Monti Donovan	2004	13033
143 7/8	25 3/8 25 6/8	22 2/8	5 5	Carroll County	IL	James Carlson	2004	13033
143 7/8	21 1/8 22 5/8	19 1/8	5 6	Montgomery County	IA	Mark Benda	2004	13033
143 7/8	22 3/8 21 7/8	17 3/8	5 5	Shelby County	IA	Neil Werner Gross	2004	13033
143 7/8	23 5/8 23 5/8	18 7/8	4 4	Monona County	IA	Roger B. Reiling	2004	13033
143 7/8	23 1/8 23 2/8	15 5/8	5 5	Bolivar County	MS	Duke Morgan, Jr.	2004	13033
143 7/8	24 5/8 23 5/8	17 3/8	5 5	Outagamie County	WI	Chris G. Kringel	2005	13033
143 7/8	21 0/8 20 6/8	18 4/8	5 6	Cardston	ALB	Gus Congemi	2005	13033
143 7/8	18 5/8 21 2/8	16 5/8	6 5	Winona County	MN	Mark Sherack	2005	13033
143 7/8	23 2/8 23 4/8	17 2/8	6 5	Christian County	KY	Harry W. Kelly, Jr.	2005	13033
143 7/8	23 7/8 23 4/8	15 7/8	5 5	Crow Wing County	MN	David Newenhouse	2005	13033
* 143 7/8	25 6/8 26 1/8	16 6/8	6 7	McHenry County	IL	Scott Truckenbrod	2005	13033
143 7/8	26 1/8 24 7/8	18 7/8	4 5	Vinton County	OH	Darren Coloutti	2005	13033
143 7/8	22 6/8 23 0/8	18 3/8	6 6	Christian County	IL	Brian Elam	2005	13033
143 7/8	24 6/8 25 7/8	18 4/8	5 5	Vigo County	IN	Dale Bozarth	2005	13033
143 7/8	23 4/8 23 3/8	17 1/8	5 5	Yankton County	SD	David W. Mingo	2005	13033
143 7/8	24 2/8 23 2/8	16 4/8	6 4	Dunn County	WI	Brent Forsman	2005	13033
143 7/8	23 2/8 24 3/8	16 7/8	4 4	Washington County	MN	John Donner	2005	13033
143 7/8	24 3/8 25 0/8	16 6/8	5 4	Stearns County	MN	Tim H. Gertken	2005	13033
* 143 7/8	21 7/8 21 5/8	20 1/8	5 5	Anne Arundel County	MD	Terrence M. Beaulac	2006	13033
143 7/8	23 5/8 23 3/8	16 4/8	5 6	Trempealeau County	WI	Scott Guthrie	2006	13033
143 7/8	25 1/8 24 7/8	18 5/8	5 6	Kosciusko County	IN	Troy Gay	2006	13033
* 143 7/8	24 2/8 24 0/8	15 5/8	4 4	Clarion County	PA	Brian Dale Shetler	2006	13033
* 143 7/8	22 0/8 21 5/8	17 5/8	5 5	Livingston County	MO	Scott Hatcher	2006	13033
143 7/8	22 2/8 22 4/8	15 1/8	6 5	Montgomery County	KS	J. Eddy Laton	2006	13033
143 7/8	23 5/8 24 0/8	16 1/8	6 6	Harrison County	IA	Lane L. Ostendorf	2006	13033
143 7/8	21 0/8 20 3/8	16 3/8	5 6	Stark County	ND	Jesse Jalbert	2007	13033
143 7/8	24 0/8 24 4/8	19 5/8	4 4	Morris County	NJ	A. J. Bachman	2007	13033
* 143 7/8	24 2/8 22 5/8	16 5/8	5 6	Floyd County	IN	Eric Sprigler	2007	13033
143 7/8	20 5/8 21 3/8	21 3/8	5 5	Lafayette County	WI	Russell Sharp	2007	13033
143 7/8	23 3/8 23 3/8	18 7/8	5 5	Brookings County	SD	Drew William Olson	2007	13033
* 143 7/8	21 2/8 21 7/8	18 1/8	5 4	Fountain County	IN	Dustin Ward	2007	13033
* 143 7/8	22 3/8 22 2/8	14 5/8	6 5	Johnson County	IL	Roger Cantrell	2007	13033
143 7/8	21 4/8 21 5/8	17 1/8	5 5	Otter Tail County	MN	Alex Kloustad	2007	13033
143 7/8	22 4/8 22 6/8	16 3/8	4 4	Whiteside County	IL	Terry McKenna	2007	13033
143 7/8	25 7/8 24 3/8	18 7/8	4 4	Madison County	MS	John S. Stratton	2008	13033
* 143 7/8	22 6/8 22 4/8	16 6/8	7 5	Waupaca County	WI	Mike Henschel	2008	13033
143 7/8	25 6/8 24 6/8	18 1/8	4 5	Bond County	IL	Daren Elam	2008	13033
143 7/8	23 3/8 23 4/8	16 7/8	5 6	Fulton County	IL	Robert Bahr	2009	13033
* 143 7/8	21 6/8 23 1/8	18 7/8	4 5	Eau Claire County	WI	Joe Polkowske	2009	13033
143 7/8	25 1/8 25 2/8	18 7/8	4 4	Reno County	KS	Eric T. Moomau	2009	13033
* 143 7/8	22 7/8 22 1/8	19 5/8	5 5	Eastland County	TX	Bud Wood	2010	13033
143 6/8	22 3/8 21 0/8	18 6/8	6 10	Ionia County	MI	Bob Jones	1966	13163
143 6/8	23 7/8 23 4/8	19 0/8	4 5	Iron County	WI	Lee C. Dix	1968	13163
143 6/8	22 6/8 23 2/8	19 6/8	6 5	Waseca County	MN	Larry W. Born	1975	13163
143 6/8	21 1/8 21 1/8	17 2/8	7 6	McHenry County	ND	William J. Berg	1978	13163
143 6/8	20 7/8 21 2/8	15 2/8	6 5	Sabine County	TX	Max L. Turner	1982	13163
143 6/8	23 0/8 21 3/8	17 4/8	5 5	Oneida County	WI	Pat Abraham	1983	13163
143 6/8	24 6/8 26 1/8	24 1/8	4 6	Isanti County	MN	Donald Vandermey	1985	13163
143 6/8	24 4/8 25 2/8	21 2/8	6 4	Shawnee County	KS	Kevin Hogan	1985	13163
143 6/8	23 3/8 23 2/8	18 6/8	5 5	Ottawa County	OK	Ed Hammons	1986	13163
143 6/8	24 7/8 25 4/8	19 2/8	5 5	Belmont County	OH	Tony Abranovic, Jr.	1986	13163
143 6/8	23 1/8 23 1/8	17 0/8	5 5	Jackson County	OH	Randy Moore	1986	13163
143 6/8	22 2/8 23 2/8	15 4/8	5 6	Platte County	NE	Brad Marler	1987	13163
143 6/8	25 0/8 24 5/8	18 6/8	5 8	Washington County	MN	Scott Gerry	1987	13163
143 6/8	25 0/8 24 4/8	18 2/8	7 7	Butler County	KS	Claude Allen	1987	13163
143 6/8	24 5/8 23 6/8	18 0/8	6 6	Chester County	PA	Steve Thais	1987	13163
143 6/8	24 1/8 24 2/8	19 4/8	5 5	Cowley County	KS	Warren C. Townsend	1988	13163
143 6/8	22 7/8 24 7/8	18 2/8	4 5	Cloud County	KS	Gerald Dockins	1991	13163
143 6/8	23 7/8 23 2/8	21 5/8	5 5	Clay County	MN	Bill Lunden	1992	13163
143 6/8	24 4/8 23 7/8	18 1/8	6 5	Kleberg County	TX	Tom Winn	1992	13163
143 6/8	25 0/8 26 1/8	16 4/8	6 4	Morgan County	IL	Ed Ward	1992	13163
143 6/8	25 0/8 24 7/8	17 0/8	4 4	Chambers County	AL	Emory E. Lynn	1993	13163
143 6/8	23 1/8 23 0/8	17 0/8	5 5	Iron County	WI	Chris F. Tuszke	1993	13163
143 6/8	23 5/8 23 5/8	18 4/8	4 4	Knox County	IL	Kevin J. Engels	1993	13163
143 6/8	23 0/8 23 0/8	16 0/8	5 5	Brooks County	TX	Ronnie Howard	1993	13163
143 6/8	25 3/8 25 2/8	21 5/8	6 5	Pike County	IL	Jimmy Howard	1993	13163
143 6/8	26 7/8 27 5/8	17 6/8	6 5	Anoka County	MN	Charlie Grove	1993	13163
143 6/8	20 1/8 21 4/8	16 7/8	6 5	Manitowoc County	WI	Roger "Bucky" Wagner	1994	13163
143 6/8	24 3/8 23 7/8	21 0/8	5 5	Sauk County	WI	Jeffrey D. Jensen	1994	13163
143 6/8	24 5/8 25 1/8	17 4/8	4 4	Wayne County	IA	Dennis M. Jones	1994	13163
143 6/8	25 1/8 23 5/8	20 3/8	8 7	Champaign County	IL	Michael R. Melvin	1994	13163
143 6/8	23 2/8 23 1/8	17 0/8	5 5	Polk County	WI	Ron Kantola	1994	13163
143 6/8	24 3/8 24 3/8	19 2/8	6 5	Lake County	OH	Bradley E. Nicholson	1994	13163
143 6/8	23 1/8 22 4/8	16 4/8	5 5	Monroe County	WI	Spyder Akright	1995	13163
143 6/8	23 2/8 23 0/8	16 6/8	5 6	Tazewell County	IL	Dan Gustafson	1995	13163
143 6/8	22 4/8 22 6/8	16 6/8	5 5	Johnson County	IA	Brian J. Bourgeois	1995	13163
143 6/8	24 1/8 24 5/8	16 5/8	4 5	Suffolk County	NY	Neal Heaton	1995	13163
143 6/8	26 0/8 26 0/8	19 0/8	4 4	Douglas County	WI	Glen D. Hope	1995	13163
143 6/8	23 2/8 23 4/8	15 4/8	4 4	Coles County	IL	Rick Campbell	1996	13163
143 6/8	23 0/8 23 0/8	18 2/8	5 4	Marion County	IA	David L. Klobnak	1996	13163
143 6/8	23 4/8 23 0/8	21 4/8	5 5	Oregon County	MO	Johnny Ray Bennett	1996	13163
143 6/8	22 7/8 23 4/8	14 2/8	5 5	Osage County	OK	Bryan Jackson	1996	13163
143 6/8	22 6/8 21 3/8	15 6/8	5 6	La Crosse County	WI	Bob Dearman	1996	13163
143 6/8	22 0/8 22 0/8	16 2/8	5 5	Wood County	OH	Kenneth E. Greulich	1997	13163

494

WHITETAIL DEER (TYPICAL ANTLERS)

Minimum Score 125   Continued

SCORE	LENGTH OF R MAIN BEAM L	INSIDE SPREAD	NUMBER OF R POINTS L	AREA	STATE/PROVINCE	HUNTER'S NAME	DATE	RANK
143 6/8	21 0/8 21 1/8	15 5/8	5 7	St. Croix County	WI	Justin Stahl	1997	13163
143 6/8	22 5/8 22 7/8	18 2/8	5 5	Oakland County	MI	Michael Feeny	1997	13163
143 6/8	21 5/8 21 1/8	17 0/8	5 5	Taylor County	WI	Roger Gebauer	1997	13163
143 6/8	23 3/8 23 3/8	18 7/8	5 4	Mason County	IL	William B. Russell	1997	13163
143 6/8	23 1/8 23 2/8	19 2/8	5 7	Story County	IA	Aaron Scharf	1997	13163
143 6/8	20 1/8 20 4/8	16 6/8	5 5	Grant County	WI	Calvin Rauch	1998	13163
143 6/8	22 6/8 22 7/8	18 2/8	4 5	Macon County	IL	Dial Rasar	1998	13163
143 6/8	22 6/8 23 3/8	18 4/8	5 5	Adams County	IL	Gerald L. Anderson	1998	13163
143 6/8	23 1/8 22 6/8	17 3/8	5 6	Buffalo County	WI	Steven Schroeder	1999	13163
143 6/8	23 0/8 23 1/8	18 0/8	5 5	Stanley County	SD	Barry McLaury	1999	13163
143 6/8	23 0/8 21 7/8	15 6/8	5 5	Floyd County	VA	William M. Davis	1999	13163
143 6/8	24 0/8 24 0/8	17 4/8	4 4	Suffolk County	NY	Hugh P. Miles	1999	13163
143 6/8	26 0/8 24 5/8	20 0/8	5 6	Dubuque County	IA	Jeffrey Steckel	1999	13163
143 6/8	20 1/8 21 5/8	18 0/8	6 6	White County	AR	Jason Smith	2000	13163
*143 6/8	22 4/8 22 7/8	19 0/8	4 4	Saline County	KS	James Craven	2000	13163
143 6/8	25 6/8 26 4/8	21 0/8	4 4	Penobscot County	ME	Garry Allen	2000	13163
143 6/8	21 1/8 22 7/8	17 4/8	6 5	Litchfield County	CT	Albert Leavitt, Jr.	2000	13163
143 6/8	24 7/8 25 5/8	21 2/8	4 4	Clark County	IL	Chris Reedy	2000	13163
143 6/8	24 0/8 24 1/8	18 6/8	5 5	La Grange County	IN	Richard A. Smith	2000	13163
143 6/8	23 0/8 25 7/8	16 4/8	5 5	Webb County	TX	Lloyd B. Swiedom	2001	13163
143 6/8	24 0/8 24 3/8	18 6/8	5 5	Caroline County	MD	Sean T. Stafford	2001	13163
143 6/8	25 0/8 26 7/8	20 1/8	5 5	Lake County	OH	Charles Cerankosky	2001	13163
143 6/8	21 5/8 22 1/8	16 2/8	5 5	Crawford County	KS	Ron Mason	2001	13163
143 6/8	24 2/8 25 1/8	18 4/8	5 5	Logan County	AR	Will Beason	2001	13163
143 6/8	21 3/8 20 6/8	17 6/8	5 5	Buffalo County	WI	Randy Springborn	2001	13163
143 6/8	24 2/8 24 4/8	16 4/8	5 5	Shawano County	WI	Jody Marcks	2002	13163
143 6/8	23 5/8 21 6/8	16 2/8	8 7	Morgan County	KY	Larry York	2002	13163
143 6/8	24 3/8 24 1/8	20 1/8	6 6	Cross County	AR	Jeff D. Smothers	2002	13163
143 6/8	23 2/8 23 1/8	20 5/8	6 6	Parke County	IN	Gary Shay II	2002	13163
143 6/8	24 5/8 24 7/8	22 4/8	4 4	Warren County	PA	Jeffrey A. Hickin	2002	13163
143 6/8	25 6/8 26 3/8	17 6/8	4 4	Lucas County	IA	Bill Brown	2002	13163
143 6/8	23 4/8 23 3/8	19 2/8	5 4	Yates County	NY	John A. Schembra	2002	13163
143 6/8	23 7/8 23 6/8	16 4/8	5 5	Holt County	NE	Scott Keyes	2002	13163
143 6/8	22 0/8 21 6/8	15 5/8	7 6	Pike County	IL	Jason Bumgardner	2003	13163
143 6/8	22 6/8 23 1/8	15 4/8	5 4	Waupaca County	WI	Robert L. Pagel, Sr.	2003	13163
143 6/8	24 5/8 24 4/8	18 4/8	4 4	McHenry County	IL	William D. Weiss	2003	13163
143 6/8	21 0/8 24 4/8	19 4/8	7 5	Noble County	IN	Kyle Jay Gilbert	2003	13163
143 6/8	26 7/8 26 5/8	20 6/8	4 4	Jersey County	IL	Dennis K. Johnson	2003	13163
*143 6/8	24 5/8 24 5/8	18 1/8	5 6	E. Carroll Parish	LA	Michael W. Fisher	2003	13163
143 6/8	24 6/8 25 0/8	13 5/8	7 6	Coweta County	GA	Jack Martin	2004	13163
143 6/8	23 7/8 23 6/8	19 2/8	4 4	Livingston County	MO	Myron R. Ebersold	2004	13163
143 6/8	21 6/8 23 2/8	17 4/8	6 5	Hillsdale County	MI	Thomas Andrew Leach	2004	13163
143 6/8	24 5/8 24 1/8	18 0/8	5 6	Warren County	IA	Eric Sowers	2004	13163
*143 6/8	22 4/8 21 7/8	15 6/8	6 5	Cambria County	PA	James J. Thiec	2004	13163
143 6/8	24 2/8 24 2/8	18 2/8	5 5	Butler County	IA	Dennis Hoeppner	2004	13163
143 6/8	20 5/8 23 2/8	16 2/8	5 5	Comanche County	KS	Louis Lambiotte	2004	13163
143 6/8	23 0/8 23 3/8	16 2/8	5 5	Taylor County	IA	Todd N. Tobin	2005	13163
143 6/8	24 3/8 23 3/8	19 0/8	5 6	Delaware County	IA	Kevin Dempster	2005	13163
143 6/8	23 3/8 23 4/8	17 4/8	5 5	Manitowoc County	WI	Tom Scheuer	2005	13163
143 6/8	22 7/8 23 3/8	17 4/8	5 5	Eaton County	MI	Nate Dickinson	2005	13163
143 6/8	24 4/8 23 4/8	19 0/8	4 6	Will County	IL	Bruce Smith	2005	13163
143 6/8	22 6/8 22 5/8	14 7/8	6 5	Bremer County	IA	Waylen Riley Stauffer	2005	13163
143 6/8	23 6/8 24 7/8	17 0/8	5 7	Oklahoma County	OK	William G. Gustafson II	2005	13163
143 6/8	25 2/8 25 6/8	18 0/8	5 4	Will County	IL	Dale Hoekstra	2006	13163
*143 6/8	23 5/8 23 2/8	17 5/8	7 6	Oneida County	WI	Jeff Johnson	2006	13163
143 6/8	23 5/8 22 7/8	20 6/8	4 4	Worth County	MO	Shane Dulak	2006	13163
143 6/8	25 4/8 25 5/8	21 4/8	4 4	Van Buren County	MI	Russell W. Borden	2006	13163
*143 6/8	24 1/8 24 1/8	20 0/8	4 4	Niagara County	NY	Anthony LaRock	2006	13163
*143 6/8	23 0/8 22 5/8	17 2/8	4 5	Monroe County	WI	Bryan Grandall	2006	13163
143 6/8	24 4/8 23 4/8	20 4/8	5 6	Chippewa County	WI	Eric Wedemeyer	2006	13163
143 6/8	23 5/8 23 6/8	20 3/8	6 5	Polk County	WI	Bill Johnson	2006	13163
*143 6/8	24 5/8 24 5/8	16 2/8	6 5	Sedgwick County	KS	Adam Phillips	2006	13163
*143 6/8	22 2/8 22 0/8	17 7/8	5 6	Tugaske	SAS	Reg Aupperle	2006	13163
*143 6/8	23 4/8 25 0/8	17 4/8	5 5	Sumner County	KS	Jeff Kistler	2006	13163
*143 6/8	23 7/8 23 7/8	17 3/8	5 5	Hamilton County	IL	Kyle Lotz	2007	13163
143 6/8	21 6/8 22 6/8	13 4/8	5 5	Cooper County	MO	Matt Kollmeyer	2007	13163
143 6/8	22 7/8 22 7/8	18 0/8	5 6	Dunn County	WI	Erik Glaus	2007	13163
143 6/8	25 4/8 24 6/8	17 6/8	6 6	Wayne County	IA	Tom Hejduk	2007	13163
143 6/8	22 7/8 22 2/8	18 0/8	4 5	Lenore Lake	SAS	Floyd Forster	2007	13163
143 6/8	23 4/8 23 7/8	18 4/8	7 5	Coshocton County	OH	Gary Fischer	2008	13163
*143 6/8	21 6/8 22 0/8	18 2/8	5 5	Shiawassee County	MI	John K. Dotson	2008	13163
*143 6/8	24 3/8 24 0/8	16 5/8	7 7	Hancock County	OH	Rick Bates	2008	13163
143 6/8	25 0/8 25 4/8	21 0/8	4 4	St. Croix County	WI	Rodney Cain	2008	13163
143 6/8	24 1/8 25 7/8	17 6/8	5 4	Boone County	MO	Jim Cook	2008	13163
143 6/8	22 1/8 21 2/8	16 0/8	5 5	Marinette County	WI	Leroy Hansen	2008	13163
143 6/8	22 0/8 21 2/8	16 2/8	6 6	Switzerland County	IN	Daniel Ashman	2009	13163
143 6/8	21 5/8 22 1/8	16 5/8	6 5	Dunn County	ND	Vance Meadows	2009	13163
143 6/8	24 0/8 24 4/8	18 4/8	6 8	Cass County	NE	Roger Buck	2009	13163
143 6/8	22 1/8 22 2/8	18 2/8	5 5	Allegheny County	PA	David M. Borelle	2009	13163
143 6/8	22 3/8 22 6/8	16 2/8	6 6	Warren County	IA	Bruce Hupke	2009	13163
143 6/8	24 2/8 24 6/8	20 2/8	4 4	Chisago County	MN	Todd Kapsner	2009	13163
143 6/8	22 3/8 22 6/8	19 4/8	5 6	Chautauqua County	NY	Scott Ferry	2009	13163
*143 6/8	24 2/8 23 4/8	17 4/8	5 5	Pierce County	WI	Josh Raab	2009	13163
*143 6/8	23 0/8 22 6/8	18 6/8	5 5	Ringgold County	IA	Bryan W. Bishop	2009	13163
*143 6/8	20 4/8 20 7/8	15 4/8	5 5	Portage County	WI	Adam Drefcinski	2009	13163
143 6/8	21 1/8 22 1/8	17 4/8	7 7	Union County	SD	Bradley D. Mollet	2009	13163
*143 6/8	21 4/8 22 5/8	15 2/8	5 6	Arkansas County	AR	Mickey Joe Smith	2010	13163
143 5/8	22 5/8 23 4/8	17 4/8	6 4	Washington County	MN	Keith Christensen	1975	13293
143 5/8	23 5/8 23 5/8	17 3/8	5 5	Neosho County	KS	Hugh B. Woolard	1976	13293
143 5/8	23 2/8 23 5/8	15 7/8	5 6	Polk County	WI	Ron Simmons	1977	13293
143 5/8	23 3/8 22 4/8	18 6/8	6 8	Houston County	MN	Arden M. Schock	1980	13293
143 5/8	25 0/8 24 7/8	17 5/8	5 4	Miami County	OH	Philip C. Gudorf	1982	13293
143 5/8	24 5/8 24 5/8	19 5/8	4 4	Vinton County	OH	Robert Irwin Bazell	1982	13293
143 5/8	23 7/8 22 7/8	19 7/8	5 5	Randolph County	WV	Charles Byrd	1982	13293
143 5/8	23 6/8 23 4/8	15 3/8	5 5	Union County	OR	Kim Tameris	1983	13293

495

WHITETAIL DEER (TYPICAL ANTLERS)

Minimum Score 125   Continued

Score	Length of Main Beam R	L	Inside Spread	Number of Points R	L	Area	State/Province	Hunter's Name	Date	Rank
143 5/8	23 7/8	23 5/8	18 3/8	6	5	Blue Earth County	MN	LeRoy Urban	1983	13293
143 5/8	23 2/8	24 0/8	19 0/8	5	8	Morrison County	MN	Doug Heath	1984	13293
143 5/8	26 0/8	24 2/8	18 3/8	6	5	Leavenworth County	KS	Terry F. Verkler, Jr.	1984	13293
143 5/8	22 1/8	22 7/8	20 1/8	5	5	Carroll County	IL	Art Heinze	1984	13293
143 5/8	20 1/8	20 6/8	16 4/8	6	6	Pine County	MN	Mike Stauty	1984	13293
143 5/8	25 1/8	23 6/8	16 3/8	7	8	Fayette County	IA	Roger DeKok	1985	13293
143 5/8	23 4/8	24 4/8	20 1/8	4	4	Pike County	IL	Rick L. Rodhouse	1986	13293
143 5/8	23 4/8	23 7/8	18 3/8	6	5	Bremer County	IA	Tom Markussen	1986	13293
143 5/8	23 4/8	22 2/8	17 1/8	5	6	Itasca County	MN	Tom Meyer	1987	13293
143 5/8	22 4/8	23 6/8	17 1/8	5	5	Dane County	WI	Tom Isaac	1987	13293
143 5/8	23 1/8	23 1/8	19 5/8	5	5	Crow Wing County	MN	Tom Aspros	1987	13293
143 5/8	22 3/8	22 5/8	15 7/8	5	7	Roseau County	MN	Stuart Wojciechowsk	1988	13293
143 5/8	24 5/8	25 1/8	17 2/8	6	6	Van Buren County	IA	Jim Francois	1988	13293
143 5/8	23 0/8	23 0/8	19 7/8	4	5	Mahaska County	IA	David Walker, Sr.	1988	13293
143 5/8	22 3/8	22 0/8	18 5/8	6	5	Mingo County	WV	Jerry W. Sammons	1988	13293
143 5/8	23 4/8	23 5/8	17 3/8	5	5	Tompkins	SAS	Clarence R Hughes	1989	13293
143 5/8	21 6/8	21 4/8	17 1/8	4	4	Reno County	KS	Robert Williams	1989	13293
143 5/8	22 5/8	22 3/8	15 3/8	5	5	Isanti County	MN	Greg Seymour	1989	13293
143 5/8	24 4/8	24 1/8	20 1/8	4	4	Henry County	IL	Neal Nelson	1990	13293
143 5/8	24 2/8	24 2/8	17 2/8	5	6	Grand Traverse County	MI	Bill Alpers	1990	13293
143 5/8	23 5/8	24 2/8	19 7/8	5	5	Wright County	MN	Nick Daleiden	1991	13293
143 5/8	22 3/8	22 3/8	20 3/8	4	4	Harrison County	OH	Brent Heavilin	1991	13293
143 5/8	21 0/8	21 1/8	19 6/8	6	6	Monroe County	OH	Darby A. Bender, Jr.	1991	13293
143 5/8	19 4/8	19 6/8	17 3/8	5	5	Tazewell County	IL	Jim Plemmons	1991	13293
143 5/8	21 5/8	21 5/8	16 5/8	7	7	Lewis & Clark County	MT	Scott Shanklin	1992	13293
143 5/8	25 7/8	25 6/8	20 4/8	5	5	Bucks County	PA	Stephen Kollar	1992	13293
143 5/8	25 0/8	24 4/8	17 5/8	6	5	St. Croix County	WI	Tom Jensen	1992	13293
143 5/8	24 0/8	23 3/8	17 5/8	5	5	Price County	WI	Gene Puckhaber	1992	13293
143 5/8	22 3/8	22 5/8	17 0/8	7	5	Jackson County	IA	Elmer E. Kemp	1992	13293
143 5/8	21 1/8	21 4/8	16 7/8	5	6	Dickey County	ND	Mark Wonders	1993	13293
143 5/8	21 5/8	20 4/8	17 7/8	5	5	Marathon County	WI	Daniel W. Pelot	1993	13293
143 5/8	21 2/8	22 0/8	16 3/8	5	5	Latimer County	OK	Bob Ketcher	1993	13293
143 5/8	23 6/8	24 0/8	19 3/8	5	5	Price County	WI	Dan Gotz	1993	13293
143 5/8	23 5/8	22 5/8	18 3/8	5	5	Washington County	NE	Douglas Fiala	1993	13293
143 5/8	22 7/8	23 1/8	16 7/8	5	5	Eaton County	MI	Patrick J. Rankin	1994	13293
143 5/8	25 7/8	25 4/8	17 2/8	5	6	Douglas County	WI	Bradley Olson	1994	13293
143 5/8	23 7/8	25 1/8	21 5/8	7	5	Putnam County	IL	Eric Jeppson	1994	13293
143 5/8	24 1/8	25 4/8	17 7/8	4	4	Reno County	KS	John R. Richardson	1994	13293
143 5/8	24 3/8	24 4/8	18 6/8	5	5	Macoupin County	IL	Frank T. Link	1994	13293
143 5/8	20 6/8	22 7/8	25 2/8	5	6	Fairfield County	CT	Keith Dibble	1994	13293
143 5/8	24 4/8	23 7/8	18 3/8	5	5	Walworth County	WI	Mark Aleckson	1995	13293
143 5/8	22 6/8	22 6/8	17 1/8	6	6	Marquette County	WI	Gregory M. Wolsdorf	1995	13293
143 5/8	24 2/8	24 2/8	16 7/8	4	4	Henry County	IL	Joe DeSchepper	1995	13293
143 5/8	24 0/8	23 4/8	18 7/8	7	6	Lake County	IL	Kevin Dahm	1995	13293
143 5/8	22 6/8	22 2/8	18 1/8	5	5	Delta County	MI	Gerald F. MacKenzie	1995	13293
143 5/8	24 6/8	24 2/8	17 7/8	5	5	Oswego County	NY	Corey Moore	1995	13293
143 5/8	25 6/8	27 2/8	19 4/8	7	7	Hamilton County	OH	David J. Olding	1995	13293
143 5/8	23 7/8	23 4/8	19 0/8	6	5	Lake County	IL	Gregory Homola	1995	13293
143 5/8	22 4/8	22 7/8	16 7/8	5	5	Butler County	IA	Howard Thompson	1996	13293
143 5/8	23 1/8	23 6/8	18 7/8	4	4	Fentress County	TN	Edgar F. Parker III	1996	13293
143 5/8	21 6/8	22 3/8	17 0/8	7	8	Blue Earth County	MN	Dick Sobtzak	1996	13293
143 5/8	24 0/8	22 4/8	16 5/8	5	5	Chester County	PA	Herbert M. Evans	1996	13293
143 5/8	24 4/8	24 4/8	19 4/8	7	5	Franklin County	OH	Mark M. Browning	1997	13293
143 5/8	26 1/8	25 7/8	20 1/8	5	4	Hancock County	WV	Shane B. Murphy	1997	13293
143 5/8	23 3/8	23 6/8	17 1/8	6	5	Tippecanoe County	IN	Frank J. Wolf II	1997	13293
143 5/8	21 5/8	20 3/8	19 1/8	6	5	Vinton County	OH	Carlos J. Blackburn	1997	13293
143 5/8	26 1/8	27 1/8	21 7/8	4	4	Sauk County	WI	Dennis D. Connors	1997	13293
143 5/8	25 6/8	23 4/8	18 7/8	7	7	Appanoose County	IA	Greg Below	1997	13293
143 5/8	22 3/8	22 5/8	20 1/8	6	6	Dodge County	WI	Jeffrey M. Bahls	1997	13293
143 5/8	22 4/8	22 4/8	16 3/8	4	4	Peoria County	IL	Bill Draper	1997	13293
143 5/8	23 1/8	23 0/8	21 1/8	5	5	Arkansas County	AR	Danny Clark	1997	13293
143 5/8	21 3/8	22 1/8	21 3/8	5	5	Kenedy County	TX	M. R. James	1997	13293
143 5/8	24 1/8	23 1/8	19 3/8	5	5	Price County	WI	David Poetzl	1998	13293
143 5/8	23 6/8	24 2/8	16 1/8	5	6	Pierce County	WI	Jeremy Jennings	1998	13293
143 5/8	23 7/8	24 0/8	18 5/8	5	5	Van Buren County	MI	Jonathon Healy	1998	13293
143 5/8	26 7/8	24 6/8	18 3/8	4	5	Greene County	OH	Bob Galloway	1998	13293
143 5/8	26 1/8	25 7/8	21 7/8	4	4	Greene County	IL	Patricia Whitlock	1999	13293
143 5/8	24 4/8	24 5/8	15 5/8	4	5	Kewaunee County	WI	Jesse Dequaine	1999	13293
143 5/8	20 4/8	20 3/8	15 7/8	5	5	Weld County	CO	Roger D. Bechler	1999	13293
143 5/8	21 4/8	22 1/8	18 3/8	5	6	St. Francis County	AR	Tracy Rogers	1999	13293
143 5/8	22 2/8	22 6/8	19 7/8	5	5	McCook County	SD	Dustin Edwards	1999	13293
143 5/8	22 7/8	23 0/8	19 7/8	5	5	Cavalier County	ND	James Sondeland	2000	13293
143 5/8	26 4/8	24 6/8	21 4/8	4	6	Washington County	WI	Guy R. Ringle	2000	13293
143 5/8	27 4/8	28 0/8	16 4/8	4	5	Jedburg	SAS	Danny Mikkonen	2000	13293
143 5/8	25 7/8	26 1/8	17 0/8	4	7	Carberry	MAN	Terry Elliott	2000	13293
143 5/8	22 5/8	22 6/8	17 3/8	5	5	Chautauqua County	NY	David M. Gatto	2000	13293
143 5/8	22 7/8	23 7/8	17 7/8	6	5	Polk County	WI	John B. Larson	2000	13293
143 5/8	23 2/8	23 6/8	19 1/8	5	5	Greenwood County	KS	George Kaplan	2000	13293
143 5/8	24 0/8	23 1/8	18 2/8	6	5	Monroe County	IL	Gary C. Gilbert	2000	13293
143 5/8	22 2/8	23 3/8	17 3/8	5	5	Smith County	KS	Mike Weaver	2000	13293
143 5/8	22 6/8	23 0/8	17 7/8	5	5	Acme	ALB	Greg Letkemann	2001	13293
143 5/8	22 6/8	22 4/8	21 1/8	6	5	Will County	IL	Bill Beaumont	2001	13293
143 5/8	24 0/8	23 5/8	17 5/8	5	5	Becker County	MN	Trevor Bjerke	2001	13293
143 5/8	23 4/8	23 4/8	18 3/8	6	5	Chickasaw County	IA	Peter Schrandt	2001	13293
143 5/8	22 0/8	22 5/8	18 5/8	5	5	Marshall County	KS	David Johnson	2001	13293
143 5/8	23 1/8	22 1/8	15 4/8	6	7	Troup County	GA	Allan Mitchell	2001	13293
143 5/8	24 3/8	24 4/8	17 5/8	5	5	Spokane County	WA	Gordon G. Hoffnagle	2001	13293
143 5/8	22 5/8	22 1/8	17 7/8	5	5	Buffalo County	WI	Jeff Klieforth	2002	13293
143 5/8	24 0/8	25 7/8	18 2/8	5	5	Floyd County	IA	Drew Kelly	2002	13293
143 5/8	23 0/8	22 0/8	16 7/8	5	5	Dubuque County	IA	Wally Rogan	2002	13293
143 5/8	22 7/8	24 2/8	23 1/8	4	4	Sussex County	NJ	Scott Anderson	2002	13293
143 5/8	20 7/8	20 6/8	17 1/8	7	7	Pittsburg County	OK	Tony Robison	2002	13293
143 5/8	24 4/8	24 4/8	17 7/8	5	5	Atascosa County	TX	Fred A. Williams, Jr.	2002	13293
143 5/8	21 6/8	23 0/8	15 7/8	6	6	Cape May County	NJ	Mike DiPalantino	2002	13293
143 5/8	24 4/8	25 1/8	17 3/8	5	6	Dougherty County	GA	Jacob Paschal	2003	13293

WHITETAIL DEER (TYPICAL ANTLERS)

Minimum Score 125   Continued

SCORE	LENGTH OF R MAIN BEAM L	INSIDE SPREAD	NUMBER OF R POINTS L	AREA	STATE/PROVINCE	HUNTER'S NAME	DATE	RANK
143 5/8	21 6/8 22 0/8	16 1/8	6 6	Shawano County	WI	Thomas R. Aleksy	2003	13293
143 5/8	23 4/8 24 4/8	19 3/8	5 6	Dimmit County	TX	Mark Anders	2003	13293
143 5/8	22 0/8 23 2/8	16 3/8	5 5	York County	PA	Noelle L. Feltenberger	2003	13293
143 5/8	19 0/8 18 2/8	16 3/8	5 5	Licking County	OH	Eric Adams	2003	13293
143 5/8	22 1/8 22 2/8	16 6/8	6 5	Barry County	MO	Jerry L. Henderson	2003	13293
143 5/8	22 0/8 22 4/8	19 1/8	9 6	Trempealeau County	WI	Ray N. Andersen	2004	13293
143 5/8	23 1/8 23 3/8	17 3/8	5 5	McDonough County	IL	Curt Myers	2004	13293
*143 5/8	24 3/8 23 0/8	19 5/8	5 6	Lucas County	IA	Roy Palmer	2004	13293
143 5/8	20 2/8 22 3/8	17 5/8	5 5	Sauk County	WI	Brian P. Harms	2004	13293
143 5/8	23 4/8 24 6/8	17 7/8	4 4	Jefferson County	WI	Jeff Leverenz	2004	13293
143 5/8	21 2/8 21 0/8	15 6/8	6 5	Sauk County	WI	Michael J. McGann	2004	13293
143 5/8	22 6/8 23 0/8	16 5/8	5 5	Tate County	MS	Jeff Burkley	2005	13293
143 5/8	22 4/8 21 7/8	17 4/8	6 6	Ransom County	ND	Mike Johnson	2005	13293
143 5/8	19 5/8 20 4/8	15 3/8	5 5	Switzerland County	IN	Joe Bacon	2005	13293
*143 5/8	25 0/8 24 0/8	18 7/8	5 4	Washington County	AR	Dennis Daniels	2005	13293
143 5/8	28 0/8 25 7/8	20 1/8	5 4	Shelby County	IL	Daren R. Drees	2005	13293
143 5/8	24 6/8 24 4/8	18 7/8	5 5	Monmouth County	NJ	Dave Basselini	2006	13293
143 5/8	21 6/8 22 5/8	16 0/8	5 8	Decatur County	IN	Nathan Osting	2006	13293
143 5/8	23 6/8 24 2/8	17 0/8	4 5	Des Moines County	IA	Mark Thomson	2006	13293
143 5/8	25 1/8 25 3/8	19 7/8	4 5	Waukesha County	WI	David Timm	2006	13293
*143 5/8	22 5/8 22 5/8	15 2/8	5 5	Scott County	IA	Milo F. Brown, Jr.	2006	13293
143 5/8	23 6/8 23 3/8	18 5/8	4 4	Randolph County	IL	Clay Curten	2006	13293
*143 5/8	24 5/8 26 0/8	17 3/8	4 4	Caswell County	NC	Matthew R. Powers	2007	13293
*143 5/8	23 6/8 23 6/8	20 5/8	5 5	Howard County	MO	Robert Humphrey	2007	13293
*143 5/8	24 0/8 23 0/8	19 5/8	5 5	Steele County	MN	Nicholas Arndt	2007	13293
*143 5/8	25 3/8 23 4/8	19 1/8	5 5	Richland County	WI	Brian Swanson	2007	13293
143 5/8	22 2/8 22 4/8	16 3/8	5 5	Allegheny County	PA	Michael A. Kienzle	2007	13293
143 5/8	25 4/8 25 4/8	18 1/8	4 4	Logan County	IL	Wayne Clark	2007	13293
143 5/8	22 6/8 23 0/8	17 6/8	7 6	Suffolk County	NY	Andrew Conway	2007	13293
143 5/8	24 1/8 24 0/8	17 7/8	5 5	Meade County	SD	Tony L. Mendoza	2008	13293
*143 5/8	22 2/8 22 0/8	15 3/8	5 5	Live Oak County	TX	Lawrence Alan Bishop	2008	13293
143 5/8	25 4/8 24 7/8	18 5/8	5 5	Shawano County	WI	Kenneth W. Alft	2009	13293
143 5/8	22 2/8 22 5/8	18 1/8	5 6	Dawes County	NE	Gary Hudson	2009	13293
143 5/8	20 5/8 21 2/8	16 1/8	6 6	Grant County	ND	Loren P. Gerhardt	2009	13293
*143 5/8	22 6/8 23 4/8	19 4/8	5 5	Jefferson County	NY	Raul Medina	2009	13293
*143 5/8	24 0/8 24 5/8	20 1/8	5 4	Belmont County	OH	Jody Bonfini	2009	13293
143 5/8	22 0/8 22 1/8	16 5/8	4 5	Massac County	IL	Ronald L. Wells	2009	13293
143 5/8	23 7/8 24 0/8	15 5/8	4 4	Anoka County	MN	Lee A. Hennen	2009	13293
143 4/8	23 7/8 23 0/8	20 0/8	5 7	Traverse County	MN	Roland L. Hausmann	1958	13434
143 4/8	22 5/8 22 7/8	21 4/8	6 6	Ellis County	KS	Lee Couture	1969	13434
143 4/8	24 3/8 25 0/8	17 2/8	5 5	Miami County	KS	Fred Supulver	1969	13434
143 4/8	23 0/8 22 4/8	16 6/8	5 6	Sheboygan County	WI	Gary Mueller	1971	13434
143 4/8	23 4/8 22 1/8	18 4/8	5 5	Saginaw County	MI	Dorm Haskins	1978	13434
143 4/8	23 5/8 22 7/8	19 2/8	4 5	Belmont County	OH	Fred Holub	1980	13434
143 4/8	23 4/8 24 0/8	17 2/8	6 5	Cherokee County	KS	Brett Thomas	1981	13434
143 4/8	24 2/8 24 4/8	17 6/8	5 6	Pike County	OH	Billy Ray Jenkins	1981	13434
143 4/8	24 0/8 23 5/8	17 6/8	4 4	Finney County	KS	Wilferd Nichols	1981	13434
143 4/8	24 5/8 23 3/8	17 0/8	5 5	St. Clair County	MI	Art Brown	1981	13434
143 4/8	23 6/8 23 1/8	18 2/8	7 5	Winona County	MN	Jim Keim	1982	13434
143 4/8	23 6/8 23 1/8	18 6/8	4 4	Stafford County	KS	Larry Hoffman	1982	13434
143 4/8	22 4/8 22 5/8	18 4/8	6 5	Huntingdon County	PA	John A. Williams	1984	13434
143 4/8	24 4/8 23 7/8	17 6/8	5 5	Otter Tail County	MN	Ross R Grothe	1984	13434
143 4/8	25 5/8 25 6/8	17 2/8	7 6	Sheboygan County	WI	Randy Mavis	1985	13434
143 4/8	24 6/8 24 7/8	21 0/8	4 5	Logan County	IL	Mark E. Humbert	1985	13434
143 4/8	23 3/8 25 4/8	19 0/8	6 4	Clayton County	IA	Paul 'Buck' Farni, Jr.	1986	13434
143 4/8	24 6/8 24 4/8	18 2/8	5 5	Henderson County	IL	Steve Fausel	1986	13434
143 4/8	23 1/8 23 5/8	18 0/8	5 5	Lafayette County	WI	James D. Beau	1987	13434
143 4/8	21 1/8 22 6/8	18 6/8	5 5	Blue Earth County	MN	Larry Tapper	1987	13434
143 4/8	26 2/8 27 2/8	18 4/8	4 4	Anoka County	MN	Dean Leshovsky	1988	13434
143 4/8	23 3/8 23 2/8	17 4/8	5 4	La Salle County	IL	Gene Brandolino	1988	13434
143 4/8	22 4/8 22 7/8	16 3/8	7 7	Clay County	IA	Charles Norgaard	1988	13434
143 4/8	22 6/8 22 6/8	16 0/8	5 5	Lewis County	WV	Clyde Moses	1988	13434
143 4/8	24 4/8 24 3/8	19 2/8	5 5	Westchester County	NY	George R. Newman	1988	13434
143 4/8	24 2/8 22 5/8	18 2/8	5 5	Greene County	IL	Leonard S. Walters	1988	13434
143 4/8	22 6/8 22 3/8	19 0/8	6 6	Elk County	KS	Lance McIntosh	1988	13434
143 4/8	24 2/8 23 3/8	17 5/8	6 5	Pottawatomie County	OK	Jerry Braziel	1988	13434
143 4/8	21 6/8 22 6/8	20 4/8	4 5	Baltimore County	MD	William F. Smeltzer	1989	13434
143 4/8	24 5/8 26 0/8	19 6/8	5 5	Winnebago County	IL	Andy L. Ballinger	1989	13434
143 4/8	23 5/8 24 0/8	20 2/8	6 5	Andrew County	MO	Bill Wolf, Jr.	1990	13434
143 4/8	21 3/8 22 3/8	16 2/8	5 6	Will County	IL	James Kamenjarin	1991	13434
143 4/8	23 6/8 23 3/8	17 2/8	4 4	Pike County	MO	Henry F. Benson, Jr.	1991	13434
143 4/8	25 1/8 23 6/8	19 0/8	6 6	Rusk County	WI	Ron Welch	1991	13434
143 4/8	25 0/8 25 6/8	17 6/8	4 4	Macoupin County	IL	Ernie Gagnor	1991	13434
143 4/8	22 4/8 22 4/8	15 0/8	6 6	Madison County	IA	Scott Creger	1991	13434
143 4/8	21 6/8 21 5/8	19 2/8	5 6	Houghton County	MI	Randy Hinton	1992	13434
143 4/8	25 6/8 25 0/8	20 0/8	6 5	Crawford County	WI	Tom Gainor	1992	13434
143 4/8	22 6/8 21 5/8	20 3/8	6 7	Holmes County	OH	Derrick Columbo	1992	13434
143 4/8	25 1/8 25 0/8	19 4/8	8 9	Winona County	MN	Douglas Kerska	1992	13434
143 4/8	22 1/8 23 4/8	24 3/8	5 5	Jefferson County	OH	Bob Uyselt	1992	13434
143 4/8	24 2/8 25 2/8	16 0/8	6 6	Ward County	ND	Lyle Helmers	1993	13434
143 4/8	24 5/8 24 5/8	18 6/8	4 5	Missoula County	MT	James R. Clapham	1993	13434
143 4/8	23 1/8 24 0/8	17 5/8	5 6	Dane County	WI	Rob Anderson	1993	13434
143 4/8	21 5/8 22 1/8	16 4/8	5 5	Vilas County	WI	Dick Schmidt	1993	13434
143 4/8	26 0/8 25 2/8	18 4/8	6 7	Martin County	IN	Charles A. Hamstra	1993	13434
143 4/8	22 5/8 22 4/8	17 7/8	5 5	Sauk County	WI	Dale R. Dahlke	1993	13434
143 4/8	22 7/8 22 1/8	17 3/8	6 5	Owen County	KY	Gary A. Bruewer	1993	13434
143 4/8	23 6/8 24 3/8	17 5/8	6 6	Grundy County	IL	Steven Blanton	1993	13434
143 4/8	20 6/8 21 1/8	14 6/8	5 5	Libau	MAN	Kerry Minsky	1994	13434
143 4/8	21 7/8 22 1/8	18 0/8	6 5	Owen County	IN	Billy J. Beaman	1994	13434
143 4/8	22 2/8 22 5/8	16 4/8	5 5	Scott County	IA	Randy Templeton	1994	13434
143 4/8	26 4/8 26 0/8	20 2/8	4 4	Oneida County	WI	David Groose	1994	13434
143 4/8	23 5/8 23 1/8	20 0/8	5 5	Jackson County	IA	Ronald G. Hellweg	1994	13434
143 4/8	21 6/8 22 2/8	19 2/8	5 5	Peoria County	IL	David A. Goodwin	1994	13434
143 4/8	22 1/8 23 2/8	15 4/8	4 4	Iowa County	WI	Dick A. Scoville	1994	13434
143 4/8	24 2/8 24 6/8	18 0/8	5 5	Peoria County	IL	Brad Christopherson	1994	13434

497

WHITETAIL DEER (TYPICAL ANTLERS)

Minimum Score 125 — Continued

SCORE	LENGTH OF R MAIN BEAM L	INSIDE SPREAD	NUMBER OF R POINTS L		AREA	STATE/PROVINCE	HUNTER'S NAME	DATE	RANK
143 4/8	24 2/8 24 0/8	18 4/8	5	5	Winneshiek County	IA	Randy E. Doyle	1994	13434
143 4/8	25 0/8 25 0/8	17 5/8	6	6	Bowden	ALB	Ken Davidson	1995	13434
143 4/8	25 0/8 26 4/8	17 2/8	6	5	Highland County	OH	Roger Dale Burton	1996	13434
143 4/8	25 0/8 25 3/8	16 6/8	7	4	Martin County	IN	Glen Scott Akles	1996	13434
143 4/8	23 6/8 24 0/8	18 4/8	5	5	Ohio County	KY	Scott Young	1997	13434
143 4/8	23 7/8 23 2/8	16 2/8	4	5	Ottawa County	KS	John G. Nelson	1997	13434
143 4/8	26 1/8 25 7/8	17 0/8	5	4	Pope County	IL	Fred A. Andalora	1997	13434
143 4/8	23 1/8 22 1/8	16 6/8	5	5	Jackson County	IL	Jeff Beckmann	1998	13434
143 4/8	21 6/8 23 1/8	17 4/8	4	6	Juneau County	WI	Phillip Chilson	1998	13434
143 4/8	22 7/8 23 5/8	17 6/8	5	6	Adams County	IL	Loren Schiera	1998	13434
143 4/8	21 3/8 21 3/8	18 2/8	5	5	Pepin County	WI	Jim Drier	1998	13434
143 4/8	24 3/8 24 4/8	18 2/8	6	5	Fayette County	IN	William Wayson, Jr.	1998	13434
143 4/8	21 5/8 21 4/8	20 0/8	5	5	Chippewa County	WI	Mike Folczyk	1999	13434
143 4/8	24 5/8 25 0/8	20 5/8	5	5	Vinton County	OH	David L. Hendrix	1999	13434
143 4/8	21 6/8 21 4/8	17 2/8	5	5	Calgary	ALB	David R. Coupland	1999	13434
143 4/8	24 5/8 24 4/8	15 0/8	5	5	Wilcox County	AL	Donnie Bedsole	2000	13434
143 4/8	20 4/8 21 4/8	16 2/8	5	5	Callahan County	TX	Keith A. Shahan	2000	13434
143 4/8	25 3/8 25 6/8	16 2/8	4	4	Daviess County	IN	Mark Miller	2000	13434
143 4/8	24 0/8 24 2/8	14 6/8	4	5	Story County	IA	Jerry Deters	2000	13434
143 4/8	20 6/8 22 0/8	15 6/8	5	7	Lake County	IN	James Joseph Adams	2000	13434
143 4/8	22 0/8 20 6/8	17 6/8	5	5	Tioga County	NY	Jeffrey Smith	2000	13434
143 4/8	24 6/8 23 5/8	17 2/8	5	5	Hinds County	MS	William J. Van Devender	2000	13434
143 4/8	19 6/8 20 2/8	19 6/8	6	5	Hunterdon County	NJ	James Hrubesh	2000	13434
143 4/8	24 3/8 24 6/8	16 2/8	6	4	La Crosse County	WI	Jason H. Devine	2001	13434
143 4/8	24 1/8 21 7/8	18 2/8	6	5	New Haven County	CT	Edward A. Masse	2001	13434
143 4/8	24 0/8 22 4/8	21 2/8	4	4	Ashtabula County	OH	Mark Johnson	2001	13434
143 4/8	24 1/8 23 5/8	17 0/8	5	5	Jackson County	MO	John Parker	2001	13434
143 4/8	22 0/8 21 7/8	13 6/8	5	5	Bon Homme County	SD	Todd S. Hornstra	2001	13434
143 4/8	23 6/8 24 4/8	18 6/8	5	5	Cass County	IL	Bill Groesch	2001	13434
143 4/8	23 2/8 22 6/8	19 6/8	5	5	Fond du Lac County	WI	Brandon W. Straub	2001	13434
143 4/8	23 0/8 22 7/8	16 6/8	4	5	Macoupin County	IL	Vern Rose	2002	13434
143 4/8	23 3/8 22 0/8	16 2/8	5	5	Davis County	IA	Kenneth Musgrove	2002	13434
143 4/8	23 1/8 21 5/8	16 4/8	5	5	Delaware County	IA	Duane Vaske	2002	13434
*143 4/8	23 7/8 23 0/8	18 2/8	5	4	Crawford County	WI	Randall O. Nash	2002	13434
143 4/8	24 5/8 24 7/8	20 4/8	4	4	Pope County	MN	Roger Mann	2002	13434
143 4/8	22 5/8 22 3/8	17 0/8	5	5	Delaware County	IA	Dean Dempster	2002	13434
143 4/8	23 3/8 22 7/8	16 0/8	4	4	Jackson County	WI	Todd Moseley	2002	13434
143 4/8	25 2/8 20 7/8	17 2/8	5	4	Jackson County	MO	Gregory Robinson	2003	13434
143 4/8	21 6/8 21 7/8	14 7/8	5	6	Marion County	KS	Dennis Ballweg	2003	13434
143 4/8	22 2/8 22 2/8	16 2/8	4	4	Burnett County	WI	Karen Krouch	2003	13434
143 4/8	28 2/8 26 5/8	19 1/8	5	6	Lenawee County	MI	Andrew J. Allshouse	2003	13434
143 4/8	23 7/8 24 2/8	22 2/8	6	5	Jefferson County	WI	Chuck Schroeder	2003	13434
143 4/8	24 0/8 23 7/8	22 3/8	4	6	Salem County	NJ	Ed Carpenter	2003	13434
*143 4/8	21 6/8 22 0/8	15 6/8	7	7	Shelby County	MO	Bud Price	2003	13434
143 4/8	20 6/8 20 2/8	15 6/8	5	5	Day County	SD	Stewart Franzen	2003	13434
143 4/8	23 1/8 22 6/8	16 2/8	5	5	McMullen County	TX	Lannie B. Philley	2004	13434
143 4/8	24 3/8 23 4/8	20 2/8	4	5	Zavala County	TX	Ronald Wardell	2004	13434
143 4/8	24 0/8 24 1/8	19 5/8	6	5	Fayette County	IA	John Christensen	2004	13434
*143 4/8	23 1/8 23 1/8	16 7/8	6	7	Bayfield County	WI	Garrett Monson	2004	13434
143 4/8	23 5/8 23 1/8	19 0/8	5	5	Cayuga County	NY	Rich Raymond	2004	13434
143 4/8	25 3/8 25 4/8	17 4/8	5	4	Trempealeau County	WI	Brian Baumgartner	2004	13434
*143 4/8	24 5/8 24 5/8	15 2/8	4	4	Madison County	IA	Gary Wagner	2005	13434
143 4/8	22 0/8 21 5/8	15 0/8	5	6	Walsh County	ND	David Moe	2005	13434
*143 4/8	21 5/8 22 1/8	17 3/8	7	6	Burke County	GA	Kelvin Rhodes	2005	13434
*143 4/8	21 1/8 21 5/8	15 6/8	5	5	Wayne County	MO	Ken Wienhoff	2005	13434
143 4/8	23 0/8 22 4/8	17 6/8	4	4	Fountain County	IN	Rodney Jay Heston	2005	13434
143 4/8	22 7/8 22 1/8	15 2/8	6	6	Shelby County	IL	Jason Dunaway	2005	13434
143 4/8	23 4/8 23 2/8	16 2/8	5	5	Sawyer County	WI	Barry L. Peterson	2006	13434
*143 4/8	21 7/8 21 4/8	17 3/8	6	6	Grandora	SAS	Don Otsig	2006	13434
143 4/8	24 1/8 23 4/8	19 2/8	5	5	Kent County	MI	Joshua P. Hopkins	2006	13434
143 4/8	21 5/8 21 4/8	17 0/8	5	5	Dane County	WI	Robin "Bud" Rogers	2006	13434
143 4/8	25 0/8 24 6/8	22 5/8	6	4	Fulton County	IL	Gregory S. Guerrier	2006	13434
*143 4/8	24 4/8 24 7/8	18 6/8	4	4	Buchanan County	MO	Chad Angst	2006	13434
*143 4/8	23 7/8 23 7/8	22 3/8	7	5	Starke County	IN	F. James Harris	2006	13434
*143 4/8	23 4/8 21 5/8	20 0/8	6	6	Bayfield County	WI	John K. Klatt	2006	13434
*143 4/8	22 0/8 22 4/8	17 2/8	6	5	Moody County	SD	Wayne R. Nesje	2006	13434
143 4/8	23 2/8 23 5/8	16 0/8	5	5	Washtenaw County	MI	Mark Oldeck	2006	13434
143 4/8	23 0/8 23 5/8	19 3/8	5	6	Richland County	WI	Dan Blando	2006	13434
*143 4/8	23 1/8 22 5/8	18 0/8	5	6	Richland County	WI	Michael Kieler	2006	13434
143 4/8	26 0/8 25 4/8	19 7/8	6	5	Morris County	NJ	Kenneth Baker	2007	13434
143 4/8	22 0/8 22 2/8	22 3/8	4	4	Knox County	NE	Joe Haupt	2007	13434
143 4/8	23 0/8 23 0/8	14 5/8	6	6	Scotland County	MO	Greg Kohne	2007	13434
*143 4/8	21 5/8 21 2/8	19 2/8	5	5	Peoria County	IL	Denny Masching	2007	13434
*143 4/8	24 0/8 24 2/8	20 2/8	5	5	Vernon County	WI	Harold M. Frank	2007	13434
143 4/8	25 5/8 25 6/8	17 5/8	5	5	Cass County	MI	Thomas H. Colley IV	2007	13434
143 4/8	26 0/8 25 3/8	17 5/8	5	4	Gage County	NE	Richard E. Monfelt	2008	13434
*143 4/8	21 2/8 21 5/8	15 6/8	5	5	Pratt County	KS	David Wayne Koonze	2008	13434
*143 4/8	24 0/8 24 1/8	16 0/8	5	6	Hamilton County	IA	Fred Ulven	2008	13434
*143 4/8	22 6/8 23 3/8	17 2/8	6	7	Barber County	KS	Doug Meeks	2008	13434
143 4/8	23 4/8 24 5/8	17 6/8	5	4	Lawrence County	IN	William T. Johnson	2008	13434
*143 4/8	22 4/8 22 4/8	17 6/8	5	5	Marks	ONT	Jay Hickman	2008	13434
143 4/8	23 0/8 23 1/8	15 0/8	5	5	Fulton County	IL	Steve Miller	2009	13434
143 4/8	23 7/8 22 5/8	18 2/8	5	4	Ray County	MO	Robert G. May II	2009	13434
*143 4/8	22 4/8 23 4/8	15 0/8	6	6	Marshall County	IN	John D. Dietl	2009	13434
143 4/8	24 0/8 24 3/8	18 3/8	5	4	Crawford County	IL	Dave Foreman	2009	13434
*143 4/8	23 0/8 23 0/8	20 0/8	4	5	Richland County	WI	Jim Havlik	2009	13434
*143 4/8	22 3/8 23 5/8	19 0/8	5	5	Elk County	KS	Ben Gillon	2009	13434
143 4/8	24 0/8 24 3/8	16 5/8	6	6	Jefferson County	WI	Mike Brown	2009	13434
143 4/8	23 6/8 23 6/8	18 2/8	5	5	Marion County	IA	Leonard G. Grimes	2009	13434
143 4/8	22 6/8 23 4/8	18 2/8	4	4	Burleigh County	ND	Scott Lang	2010	13434
143 3/8	25 0/8 23 6/8	16 3/8	6	5	Otter Tail County	MN	J. P. Maurins	1956	13581
143 3/8	23 0/8 23 1/8	15 7/8	5	5	Comanche County	OK	Kenneth D. Cook	1971	13581
143 3/8	22 2/8 22 0/8	17 2/8	7	7	Morrison County	MN	Glen Marklowitz	1972	13581
143 3/8	22 4/8 22 4/8	20 1/8	4	6	Allamakee County	IA	Jim Schmidt	1974	13581
143 3/8	24 1/8 25 2/8	17 1/8	5	5	Cass County	MN	Richard J. Schabert	1977	13581

WHITETAIL DEER (TYPICAL ANTLERS)

Minimum Score 125 — Continued

SCORE	LENGTH OF R MAIN BEAM L	INSIDE SPREAD	NUMBER OF R POINTS L		AREA	STATE/ PROVINCE	HUNTER'S NAME	DATE	RANK
143 3/8	27 0/8	26 0/8	20 1/8	4	4	Charles County	MD	John Allen Williams	1980	13581
143 3/8	24 1/8	24 0/8	15 5/8	4	5	Saginaw County	MI	Paul Mickey	1981	13581
143 3/8	22 0/8	23 4/8	19 0/8	8	8	Pike County	IL	Steve Carlen	1982	13581
143 3/8	24 1/8	23 7/8	17 5/8	5	5	Green County	WI	B. Duane Byrne	1984	13581
143 3/8	23 6/8	24 3/8	18 1/8	4	4	Ogle County	IL	Dr. Juanito E. Delfinado	1984	13581
143 3/8	25 3/8	24 7/8	19 1/8	4	4	Norman County	MN	Bryan Mickelson	1985	13581
143 3/8	22 7/8	24 2/8	17 7/8	4	4	Walworth County	WI	Gary Jordan	1985	13581
143 3/8	18 6/8	21 0/8	16 3/8	5	5	Slope County	ND	Jack Lefor	1985	13581
143 3/8	24 0/8	23 6/8	22 2/8	5	6	Pennington County	MN	John A. Monroe	1986	13581
143 3/8	22 6/8	22 2/8	20 6/8	6	4	Clayton County	IA	Francis Winter	1986	13581
143 3/8	23 0/8	23 6/8	20 1/8	5	5	Green County	WI	Ernie V. Hutchinson	1986	13581
143 3/8	22 1/8	22 2/8	15 7/8	5	6	Adams County	WI	Danny C. Winchester	1988	13581
143 3/8	23 2/8	22 3/8	19 1/8	5	6	Du Page County	IL	Joseph Keim	1988	13581
143 3/8	24 6/8	25 0/8	17 3/8	7	5	Pierce County	WI	Daniel D. Kern	1988	13581
143 3/8	22 0/8	22 5/8	18 3/8	5	5	Greene County	IL	Mark Petersen	1988	13581
143 3/8	21 3/8	22 3/8	17 1/8	5	7	Dodge County	WI	Jim Bauer	1989	13581
143 3/8	22 5/8	22 1/8	18 1/8	5	5	Burlington County	NJ	Raymond Woodruff	1989	13581
143 3/8	24 4/8	25 0/8	19 3/8	4	4	Mills County	IA	John Bantz	1989	13581
143 3/8	23 6/8	23 5/8	20 1/8	5	5	Lake County	IL	John Roscop	1989	13581
143 3/8	25 4/8	27 4/8	19 5/8	4	4	Montgomery County	PA	Charlie Haydt	1990	13581
143 3/8	23 4/8	24 4/8	17 4/8	4	5	Gibson County	IN	Steve Feller	1990	13581
143 3/8	24 6/8	25 2/8	20 2/8	6	5	Jackson County	OH	Gordon Gibbs	1990	13581
143 3/8	25 2/8	25 1/8	20 5/8	4	6	Caledon Township	ONT	Carl Whittier	1990	13581
143 3/8	24 5/8	24 3/8	16 7/8	4	4	Morris County	NJ	Geoffrey Stewart	1991	13581
143 3/8	22 7/8	23 4/8	19 5/8	4	5	Adams County	WI	Michael E. Rykiel	1991	13581
143 3/8	21 7/8	20 6/8	15 7/8	5	5	Burleigh County	ND	Ron Geffre	1991	13581
143 3/8	23 6/8	23 4/8	17 1/8	5	5	Buckingham County	VA	Barry D. Warner	1992	13581
143 3/8	21 5/8	22 2/8	16 3/8	5	5	Dakota County	NE	Nick Larsen	1992	13581
143 3/8	24 0/8	23 4/8	21 1/8	5	5	Hardin County	IA	Jason P. Jedele	1992	13581
143 3/8	24 1/8	24 0/8	18 2/8	7	6	Dane County	WI	Rick J. Miyagawa	1992	13581
143 3/8	24 6/8	23 6/8	18 1/8	6	5	Green County	WI	Ross D. Daniels	1992	13581
143 3/8	21 7/8	22 5/8	14 1/8	5	5	Will County	IL	Don Oswald	1993	13581
143 3/8	23 2/8	24 0/8	17 1/8	5	5	La Salle County	TX	Gary Pitts	1993	13581
143 3/8	24 2/8	24 2/8	19 3/8	6	5	Rock County	WI	James W. Keller	1993	13581
143 3/8	22 7/8	22 7/8	20 2/8	4	6	Richland County	WI	Bob Wagner	1993	13581
143 3/8	23 0/8	23 3/8	17 1/8	5	5	Nuevo Leon	MEX	Michael T. Thrasher	1993	13581
143 3/8	22 2/8	20 0/8	15 6/8	5	6	Burleigh County	ND	Matthew J. Meidinger	1994	13581
143 3/8	22 7/8	23 3/8	17 4/8	5	6	Shelby County	KY	Larry Duncan	1994	13581
143 3/8	23 5/8	23 1/8	17 5/8	5	5	McHenry County	IL	Ed Fitzgerald	1994	13581
143 3/8	25 3/8	25 2/8	16 7/8	4	5	Fillmore County	MN	Kyle Rosedahl	1994	13581
143 3/8	22 6/8	22 2/8	16 0/8	6	5	Waushara County	WI	Bob Collins	1994	13581
143 3/8	22 5/8	22 4/8	18 3/8	5	6	Marquette County	WI	Michael Vilkoski	1994	13581
143 3/8	24 3/8	24 7/8	20 5/8	5	4	Franklin County	IL	Cathy DeNeal	1994	13581
143 3/8	27 0/8	26 6/8	17 3/8	4	4	Baltimore County	MD	David A. Buchta	1995	13581
143 3/8	22 5/8	23 0/8	15 6/8	6	5	Pike County	IL	Eddie Claypool	1995	13581
143 3/8	25 3/8	25 4/8	19 1/8	4	4	Darke County	OH	Wally Harder	1995	13581
143 3/8	22 4/8	23 4/8	20 1/8	6	6	Goodhue County	MN	Rex Novek	1996	13581
143 3/8	21 3/8	20 6/8	19 3/8	5	5	Branch County	MI	Bret R. Cary	1996	13581
143 3/8	24 1/8	22 3/8	17 7/8	4	4	Kent County	MD	Delmas Foster	1996	13581
143 3/8	24 3/8	26 1/8	20 5/8	4	4	Washington County	MN	Steve Rosa	1996	13581
143 3/8	24 7/8	24 4/8	19 6/8	6	6	Green Lake County	WI	Clarence E. Miller	1996	13581
143 3/8	21 4/8	21 2/8	13 3/8	6	5	Wright County	IA	Steve Claude	1997	13581
143 3/8	22 7/8	23 7/8	18 1/8	5	5	Pike County	MO	Gary Johnston	1997	13581
143 3/8	24 0/8	23 1/8	19 3/8	5	6	Waukesha County	WI	Philip "Nicky" Holland	1997	13581
143 3/8	20 6/8	20 4/8	18 3/8	7	6	Perry County	IL	Jeff Buchler	1997	13581
143 3/8	24 4/8	24 2/8	16 6/8	6	6	Manitowoc County	WI	Robert A. DeGreef	1998	13581
143 3/8	25 4/8	25 2/8	17 2/8	5	6	Adams County	OH	Ken White	1998	13581
143 3/8	20 4/8	22 0/8	14 3/8	5	5	Wyoming County	WV	Trent Rose	1998	13581
143 3/8	26 1/8	25 4/8	18 1/8	5	7	Calhoun County	MI	Daniel B. Libbrecht	1999	13581
143 3/8	21 1/8	20 3/8	13 7/8	5	5	Jo Daviess County	IL	Dan Strohecker	1999	13581
143 3/8	23 1/8	22 7/8	18 5/8	6	6	Buffalo County	WI	Timothy L. Huebner	1999	13581
143 3/8	22 2/8	22 3/8	20 3/8	5	5	Jones County	IA	Tracy L. Meyers	1999	13581
143 3/8	21 4/8	22 0/8	19 3/8	5	5	Eau Claire County	WI	Scott Guthrie	1999	13581
143 3/8	21 3/8	21 6/8	18 1/8	4	4	Black Hawk County	IA	Michael Judas	2000	13581
143 3/8	23 6/8	23 1/8	17 7/8	6	4	Luzerne County	PA	Roy W. Bartlett, Jr.	2000	13581
143 3/8	24 0/8	25 1/8	24 5/8	4	5	Cherry County	NE	Adam Naslund	2000	13581
143 3/8	25 5/8	24 5/8	19 7/8	4	4	Montgomery County	MD	Robert A. Sorrell	2001	13581
143 3/8	24 2/8	24 6/8	18 4/8	5	4	Trumbull County	OH	Mike Palumbo	2001	13581
143 3/8	23 0/8	24 7/8	19 7/8	4	4	Clay County	MN	Walter J. Palmer	2001	13581
143 3/8	23 6/8	23 6/8	20 3/8	5	5	Jones County	IA	Curtis Sabers	2002	13581
143 3/8	21 0/8	20 2/8	13 1/8	5	5	Bourbon County	KS	James Livak	2002	13581
143 3/8	22 0/8	22 2/8	16 3/8	5	5	Menard County	IL	Kevin D. Neese	2002	13581
143 3/8	23 1/8	22 0/8	17 5/8	5	5	Holmes County	OH	Mike Beachy	2002	13581
143 3/8	24 6/8	24 6/8	18 4/8	6	6	Lawrence County	OH	Robin Creswell	2003	13581
143 3/8	21 1/8	21 3/8	17 0/8	6	7	Boone County	IL	Michael J. Bland	2003	13581
143 3/8	21 7/8	20 2/8	18 3/8	5	6	Barron County	WI	David Riebe	2003	13581
143 3/8	22 3/8	22 3/8	15 3/8	6	7	Ralls County	MO	Jeff T. Tammen	2003	13581
* 143 3/8	21 1/8	21 2/8	16 3/8	6	5	Darke County	OH	Kevin Pierce	2003	13581
143 3/8	23 6/8	24 0/8	17 5/8	4	4	Coleman County	TX	Elvan Goode	2003	13581
143 3/8	22 7/8	23 6/8	17 5/8	4	4	Keya Paha County	NE	R. Kirk Sharp	2003	13581
143 3/8	22 1/8	22 2/8	16 5/8	5	5	Lyon County	KY	Matt Colson	2004	13581
143 3/8	23 6/8	24 1/8	15 5/8	5	5	Columbia County	WI	Tomas Winter	2004	13581
143 3/8	23 4/8	23 7/8	15 0/8	5	6	Indiana County	PA	Joseph Slovinsky, Jr.	2004	13581
143 3/8	24 1/8	23 6/8	18 3/8	4	4	Todd County	KY	Eric S. Sears	2004	13581
143 3/8	23 6/8	23 3/8	19 7/8	5	5	Rusk County	WI	Steven Sedani	2004	13581
143 3/8	21 5/8	21 2/8	15 7/8	7	7	Pike County	IL	Donnie Sultan	2004	13581
143 3/8	25 1/8	25 0/8	17 3/8	4	4	Hubbard County	MN	Dale DeVriendt	2004	13581
* 143 3/8	22 3/8	22 3/8	15 3/8	5	5	Pike County	IL	Shannon Quinn	2004	13581
143 3/8	25 2/8	25 3/8	17 5/8	4	4	Pepin County	WI	Dusty Seifert	2004	13581
* 143 3/8	23 6/8	24 0/8	17 3/8	6	5	Union County	SD	Tim M. Dailey	2004	13581
143 3/8	25 4/8	24 2/8	18 4/8	5	6	Shelby County	TN	Timothy V. Murray	2004	13581
143 3/8	23 3/8	23 0/8	15 7/8	5	5	Gallatin County	KY	Monty Jennings	2005	13581
143 3/8	23 4/8	23 3/8	16 7/8	4	4	Harrison County	MO	Dan Bucher	2005	13581
143 3/8	22 3/8	22 3/8	14 3/8	4	4	Traill County	ND	Tim Pederson	2005	13581
143 3/8	21 5/8	21 6/8	16 5/8	6	5	Wabasha County	MN	Jeff Benjamin	2005	13581

WHITETAIL DEER (TYPICAL ANTLERS)

Minimum Score 125   Continued

SCORE	LENGTH OF R MAIN BEAM L	INSIDE SPREAD	NUMBER OF R POINTS L		AREA	STATE/ PROVINCE	HUNTER'S NAME	DATE	RANK
143 3/8	24 4/8 24 7/8	19 5/8	5	4	Jasper County	IN	Charles E. Hershman	2005	13581
143 3/8	24 7/8 25 4/8	15 7/8	4	4	Breckinridge County	KY	Steve Cundiff	2005	13581
*143 3/8	23 6/8 22 4/8	17 7/8	6	6	Buffalo County	WI	Benjamin A. Bodoh	2005	13581
143 3/8	24 0/8 24 3/8	19 6/8	8	8	Fulton County	IL	Mary-Lou Bonneau	2005	13581
143 3/8	22 6/8 23 2/8	17 5/8	5	5	Allamakee County	IA	James Rea	2005	13581
143 3/8	22 6/8 23 0/8	17 7/8	5	5	Chickasaw County	IA	Gene Hall	2005	13581
143 3/8	24 4/8 23 2/8	17 5/8	5	5	Pickaway County	OH	David R. Hurley	2005	13581
143 3/8	22 5/8 21 4/8	15 3/8	5	6	Licking County	OH	David Chrisman	2006	13581
143 3/8	22 5/8 21 7/8	20 1/8	5	5	Columbia County	WI	Mark L. Hamele	2006	13581
*143 3/8	22 2/8 22 2/8	17 4/8	5	6	Cass County	IL	Ron Lewandowski	2006	13581
143 3/8	21 3/8 20 7/8	18 2/8	5	6	Spink County	SD	Shauna Woodward	2006	13581
143 3/8	22 2/8 22 3/8	15 3/8	5	5	Hennepin County	MN	Ross Gramstad	2006	13581
143 3/8	20 3/8 20 4/8	15 2/8	6	5	Wilkes County	NC	Todd Lowe	2007	13581
143 3/8	22 4/8 22 0/8	16 4/8	5	6	Lacombe	ALB	Wade Soderberg	2007	13581
143 3/8	24 1/8 24 1/8	18 1/8	5	6	Washington County	NE	Douglas Lew Detherow	2007	13581
143 3/8	24 4/8 25 2/8	20 5/8	6	6	Manitowoc County	WI	Oscar Dick	2007	13581
143 3/8	22 6/8 21 5/8	17 2/8	6	7	Crow Wing County	MN	Wade Arnold	2007	13581
*143 3/8	22 5/8 23 5/8	19 1/8	7	5	Decatur County	IA	Brad Olsen	2008	13581
*143 3/8	24 7/8 24 3/8	13 7/8	5	5	Walworth County	WI	Tim Cates	2008	13581
143 3/8	22 6/8 21 6/8	16 3/8	5	5	Webb County	TX	Brian Witherspoon	2008	13581
143 3/8	23 4/8 23 1/8	18 7/8	6	5	Ontario County	NY	Aaron Duncan	2008	13581
143 3/8	22 0/8 22 0/8	15 2/8	6	5	Franklin County	KS	Warren Kennedy	2008	13581
143 3/8	22 4/8 22 3/8	14 3/8	5	5	Callaway County	MO	David W. Myers	2008	13581
143 3/8	22 1/8 21 0/8	13 5/8	5	5	Crawford County	IL	Bob Snell	2008	13581
143 3/8	25 6/8 25 0/8	16 2/8	4	5	Kinney County	TX	Federic S. Barton	2008	13581
143 3/8	22 2/8 23 3/8	20 0/8	5	6	Richland County	ND	Nick England	2008	13581
143 3/8	24 1/8 24 5/8	16 5/8	5	5	Taylor County	WI	Todd Frombach	2009	13581
*143 3/8	22 1/8 22 5/8	20 5/8	4	5	Waukesha County	WI	Dave Casper	2009	13581
143 3/8	22 7/8 23 2/8	18 7/8	5	5	Warren County	IA	Donald R. Brandt	2009	13581
*143 3/8	26 2/8 25 6/8	21 4/8	7	6	Mahoning County	OH	Zachary R. Randolph	2009	13581
*143 3/8	23 3/8 24 0/8	15 7/8	5	5	Knox County	ME	Bruce Hendrickson	2009	13581
*143 3/8	24 0/8 24 2/8	21 3/8	5	4	Sauk County	WI	Scott P. Wood	2009	13581
143 3/8	24 5/8 24 2/8	17 7/8	4	5	Outagamie County	WI	Bob Jentz	2010	13581
143 2/8	25 0/8 24 0/8	16 6/8	5	6	Phillips County	AR	Stanley Zellner	1964	13714
143 2/8	25 0/8 23 7/8	19 4/8	5	5	Geauga County	OH	Rudy Grecar	1971	13714
143 2/8	26 0/8 25 0/8	17 4/8	8	7	Comanche County	OK	Lloyd Payne III	1976	13714
143 2/8	25 2/8 26 1/8	18 4/8	4	4	Monroe County	IN	Mike Webb	1977	13714
143 2/8	22 0/8 23 1/8	16 0/8	5	5	Fond du Lac County	WI	Jim Rickmeyer	1979	13714
143 2/8	25 4/8 25 0/8	19 2/8	5	5	Price County	WI	Todd R. Sorensen	1981	13714
143 2/8	24 6/8 25 0/8	18 4/8	5	5	Marion County	TN	Larry Gravitt	1981	13714
143 2/8	21 7/8 21 6/8	18 4/8	5	5	Jefferson County	MT	Bob Peterson	1983	13714
143 2/8	24 2/8 24 6/8	16 2/8	5	6	Green County	WI	Wellington W. Wert	1983	13714
143 2/8	24 3/8 24 3/8	20 0/8	4	4	Edgar County	IL	Benton B. Caldwell	1983	13714
143 2/8	23 2/8 23 3/8	13 4/8	5	5	Hardin County	IA	Rick McDowell	1983	13714
143 2/8	24 5/8 23 4/8	19 0/8	5	4	Fairfield County	OH	Gary Lockwood	1984	13714
143 2/8	23 2/8 22 4/8	18 7/8	5	6	Winona County	MN	Bill Clink	1984	13714
143 2/8	24 3/8 24 6/8	15 6/8	6	6	Cooper County	MO	Vaughn Sell	1985	13714
143 2/8	26 0/8 25 6/8	21 4/8	5	4	Montgomery County	MD	Bobby Ray Waters	1985	13714
143 2/8	23 4/8 23 3/8	16 6/8	5	5	Warren County	IA	Lanny Caligiuri	1985	13714
143 2/8	22 3/8 22 4/8	19 0/8	5	5	Washington County	MN	Ronald H. Krienke	1986	13714
143 2/8	24 3/8 24 2/8	20 6/8	4	4	Greene County	AR	Danny J. Walker	1986	13714
143 2/8	23 5/8 25 1/8	16 4/8	4	4	Sumner County	KS	Robert E. Daley	1986	13714
143 2/8	23 1/8 23 5/8	18 6/8	6	5	Union County	SD	Larry Minter	1987	13714
143 2/8	26 6/8 25 0/8	18 6/8	5	6	Spokane County	WA	Paul Fisher	1988	13714
143 2/8	23 3/8 23 2/8	15 4/8	6	6	Butler County	OH	Robert G. Banks, Jr.	1988	13714
143 2/8	23 1/8 22 5/8	16 6/8	5	5	Jackson County	MI	John R. Ahrens	1988	13714
143 2/8	23 0/8 23 2/8	17 0/8	5	5	Lawrence County	KY	Michael Hatfield	1988	13714
143 2/8	24 0/8 24 1/8	21 0/8	5	4	Hamilton County	OH	George Robert Freudiger	1988	13714
143 2/8	21 7/8 22 2/8	17 2/8	5	5	Hancock County	IL	David Lee Sanderson	1988	13714
143 2/8	24 2/8 25 2/8	21 4/8	5	4	Hamilton County	OH	John L. Cox	1989	13714
143 2/8	24 4/8 23 4/8	22 2/8	4	4	Montcalm County	MI	Rickey P. Allen	1989	13714
143 2/8	21 4/8 21 4/8	16 5/8	6	6	Defiance County	OH	Stanley Knittle	1989	13714
143 2/8	22 5/8 22 4/8	18 0/8	5	5	Goodhue County	MN	Michael Schmidt	1990	13714
143 2/8	22 4/8 21 2/8	17 0/8	6	5	Norton County	KS	Larry H. Hillman	1990	13714
143 2/8	23 0/8 23 1/8	17 6/8	5	5	Greene County	OH	Richard McClelland	1990	13714
143 2/8	26 5/8 26 6/8	19 6/8	6	6	Will County	IL	Chad Elumbaugh	1990	13714
143 2/8	23 6/8 22 6/8	14 0/8	6	5	Licking County	OH	Thomas E. Lott	1991	13714
143 2/8	21 1/8 22 0/8	16 4/8	5	5	Kleberg County	TX	Johnnie R. Walters	1991	13714
143 2/8	22 5/8 23 4/8	17 3/8	8	7	Richland County	WI	Ronald S. Pulcine	1991	13714
143 2/8	22 1/8 24 3/8	17 7/8	6	5	Iowa County	IA	Thomas Dvorak	1991	13714
143 2/8	24 5/8 25 4/8	18 4/8	5	4	Dakota County	MN	Tim L. Gaughan	1991	13714
143 2/8	22 0/8 22 7/8	15 6/8	5	5	Barnes County	ND	Dean Klein	1992	13714
143 2/8	24 1/8 23 7/8	17 6/8	4	4	Trimble County	KY	Todd Calvert	1992	13714
143 2/8	24 6/8 24 5/8	17 6/8	4	5	Adams County	IL	David St. John	1992	13714
143 2/8	22 6/8 22 4/8	17 0/8	5	6	Langlade County	WI	Lonnie Gene Eick	1992	13714
143 2/8	23 5/8 24 2/8	21 2/8	4	5	Preble County	OH	Robert A. Worley	1992	13714
143 2/8	23 6/8 23 7/8	17 4/8	4	6	Lake County	IL	Carl H. Spaeth	1992	13714
143 2/8	24 4/8 23 7/8	19 2/8	4	6	Northumberland County	PA	Chuck Beaver	1993	13714
143 2/8	23 5/8 24 6/8	15 4/8	4	4	Ohio County	IN	Troy Courtney	1993	13714
143 2/8	23 6/8 23 2/8	20 0/8	5	4	Yankton County	SD	David B. Cull	1993	13714
143 2/8	24 4/8 24 0/8	20 6/8	5	6	Walworth County	WI	Charles Palmer	1993	13714
143 2/8	24 2/8 23 1/8	17 2/8	5	5	Burlington County	NJ	Louis J. Palfy, Jr.	1994	13714
143 2/8	21 6/8 21 6/8	20 4/8	5	5	Marinette County	WI	Michael C. Kramer	1994	13714
143 2/8	24 3/8 24 5/8	16 4/8	5	4	Jackson County	MI	Andrew D. Cook	1994	13714
143 2/8	22 7/8 24 0/8	17 2/8	5	5	Green Lake County	WI	Craig A. Rohde	1994	13714
143 2/8	24 4/8 25 6/8	20 6/8	4	4	Walworth County	WI	Steve Jacobson	1994	13714
143 2/8	23 1/8 23 3/8	18 2/8	4	5	La Crosse County	WI	Ron Lichtie	1994	13714
143 2/8	24 2/8 25 3/8	16 6/8	4	5	Harford County	MD	Matthew J. Reheard	1995	13714
143 2/8	22 2/8 22 4/8	20 6/8	5	6	Lee County	IL	Steven Jacobs	1995	13714
143 2/8	25 0/8 24 5/8	21 2/8	8	6	Dallas County	IA	Mike Prince	1995	13714
143 2/8	23 3/8 23 7/8	21 4/8	5	6	Vernon County	MO	Paul Reedy	1995	13714
143 2/8	25 0/8 26 5/8	18 3/8	4	7	Perry County	OH	Butch Samson	1995	13714
143 2/8	24 5/8 24 4/8	18 0/8	6	5	Nicolet	QUE	Onil Provencher	1996	13714
143 2/8	24 6/8 24 0/8	19 2/8	4	4	Yazoo County	MS	Glenn Rose	1996	13714
143 2/8	18 5/8 23 2/8	16 6/8	8	6	Douglas County	KS	Jim Bieker	1996	13714

500

WHITETAIL DEER (TYPICAL ANTLERS)

Minimum Score 125   Continued

Score	Length of R Main Beam L	Inside Spread	Number of R Points L	Area	State/Province	Hunter's Name	Date	Rank
143 2/8	22 4/8 22 4/8	16 4/8	4 5	Jefferson County	WI	Paul Alane	1996	13714
143 2/8	21 5/8 21 4/8	21 2/8	5 5	Chester County	PA	Skip Boyd	1996	13714
143 2/8	19 6/8 21 1/8	18 6/8	5 5	McLean County	IL	Tim Leake	1996	13714
143 2/8	25 0/8 24 4/8	18 0/8	4 4	Lake County	IL	Steven Hysell	1996	13714
143 2/8	19 7/8 22 5/8	18 2/8	6 5	Jefferson County	WV	James L. Jenkins	1997	13714
143 2/8	22 6/8 22 6/8	19 2/8	3 3	Piatt County	IL	Rusty Hunt	1997	13714
143 2/8	23 4/8 24 5/8	19 4/8	4 5	Perry County	PA	Mark Mayberry	1997	13714
143 2/8	23 0/8 23 4/8	15 6/8	5 4	Blackford County	IN	Mike Hatfield	1997	13714
143 2/8	24 2/8 25 2/8	18 2/8	4 4	Forest County	WI	David Schmelebeck	1998	13714
143 2/8	23 7/8 22 4/8	17 0/8	5 5	Worth County	IA	Larry B. Porter	1998	13714
143 2/8	23 4/8 23 3/8	20 0/8	5 5	Woodford County	IL	Timothy P. Devine	1998	13714
143 2/8	23 4/8 22 3/8	17 2/8	5 5	Callaway County	MO	Larry R. Brown, Jr.	1999	13714
143 2/8	22 2/8 23 3/8	16 6/8	5 5	Delaware County	OH	John Stark	1999	13714
143 2/8	22 4/8 23 0/8	17 0/8	6 5	Dane County	WI	John Dimpfl	1999	13714
143 2/8	27 6/8 28 1/8	22 3/8	6 5	Moultrie County	IL	Leroy Petersheim	1999	13714
143 2/8	22 2/8 22 6/8	18 2/8	5 4	Appanoose County	IA	Rick Petersen	1999	13714
143 2/8	23 4/8 23 7/8	16 0/8	4 4	Pawnee County	NE	Roger Wenzl	1999	13714
143 2/8	22 1/8 22 5/8	18 0/8	6 6	Kane County	IL	Dean V. Ashton	1999	13714
143 2/8	24 4/8 24 2/8	18 4/8	5 5	Cayuga County	NY	Kirk W. Lawler	1999	13714
143 2/8	23 6/8 22 6/8	19 0/8	5 6	Marathon County	WI	Willie Reed	1999	13714
143 2/8	21 4/8 23 4/8	15 6/8	6 5	Menard County	IL	Ed Weiskopf III	1999	13714
143 2/8	22 7/8 22 3/8	13 2/8	6 5	Pope County	IL	Robert Johnson	1999	13714
143 2/8	23 7/8 23 5/8	18 1/8	6 6	Valley County	MT	Richard M. Penn	2000	13714
143 2/8	21 7/8 21 7/8	16 6/8	5 6	Fort Steele	BC	George Terpsma	2000	13714
143 2/8	27 7/8 25 7/8	18 3/8	5 5	Starke County	IN	Kenneth L. Kemble	2001	13714
143 2/8	23 0/8 23 7/8	18 2/8	5 5	Rusk County	WI	Timothy S. Bonn	2001	13714
143 2/8	23 0/8 24 5/8	16 5/8	5 4	Pike County	IL	James Williams	2001	13714
143 2/8	24 3/8 23 7/8	19 7/8	5 6	Warren County	IA	Todd Reese	2001	13714
143 2/8	21 3/8 24 2/8	17 6/8	4 4	Polk County	IA	Vincent Stefanski	2001	13714
143 2/8	21 4/8 20 4/8	16 6/8	6 6	Rice County	MN	Bob Moen	2001	13714
143 2/8	22 1/8 22 0/8	14 0/8	5 5	Dearborn County	IN	Gregory M. Gavin	2002	13714
143 2/8	25 0/8 24 2/8	21 7/8	7 7	Chickasaw County	IA	Troy White	2002	13714
143 2/8	21 7/8 22 6/8	17 0/8	5 5	Anoka County	MN	Chad E. Setterholm	2002	13714
143 2/8	22 7/8 23 4/8	18 0/8	4 4	Brown County	WI	Donald A. Poppy	2002	13714
143 2/8	22 0/8 23 2/8	16 0/8	5 5	Vernon County	WI	James Ekern	2002	13714
143 2/8	24 4/8 24 1/8	19 4/8	4 4	Macoupin County	IL	Kenneth Tate	2002	13714
143 2/8	23 4/8 24 3/8	18 4/8	4 4	Rock County	WI	Brian Huber	2002	13714
143 2/8	22 6/8 23 6/8	18 6/8	5 5	McDowell County	WV	Robert Wimmer	2002	13714
143 2/8	22 7/8 23 3/8	15 0/8	5 5	Clay County	MO	Taylor Lein	2003	13714
143 2/8	23 1/8 23 3/8	14 4/8	8 7	Renville County	MN	Stephen Menning	2003	13714
143 2/8	21 6/8 22 2/8	18 2/8	5 5	Dunn County	WI	Jason S. Boda	2003	13714
143 2/8	22 6/8 22 6/8	16 4/8	5 5	Cole County	MO	Dennis Kauffman	2003	13714
143 2/8	21 5/8 22 2/8	17 2/8	5 5	Buffalo County	WI	Dan Evenson	2003	13714
143 2/8	23 4/8 23 3/8	16 6/8	5 5	Portage County	WI	Thomas A. Orlikowski	2003	13714
143 2/8	27 0/8 25 2/8	18 0/8	4 5	Charlotte County	VA	Gordon Shepheard	2003	13714
143 2/8	24 3/8 25 4/8	17 6/8	5 5	Wake County	NC	Scott Kazmierczak	2003	13714
143 2/8	26 6/8 23 0/8	17 6/8	4 4	Kenosha County	WI	Carl H. Spaeth	2003	13714
143 2/8	24 1/8 24 7/8	17 0/8	5 6	Warren County	VA	Steven P. Morgan	2003	13714
143 2/8	26 1/8 25 1/8	13 4/8	5 4	Calhoun County	IL	Donald Wigley	2003	13714
143 2/8	20 3/8 21 1/8	16 6/8	5 5	Buffalo County	WI	Dennis J. Buchholz	2004	13714
143 2/8	23 5/8 23 5/8	18 2/8	5 5	Grand Forks County	ND	Ryan Svoboda	2004	13714
143 2/8	23 0/8 22 6/8	19 1/8	4 6	Edwards County	IL	Scott M. Fassinger	2004	13714
143 2/8	22 6/8 22 2/8	15 6/8	5 6	Jefferson County	WI	Bradley R. Waters	2004	13714
143 2/8	22 5/8 22 6/8	18 5/8	5 5	Hand County	SD	Joseph Sievers	2004	13714
*143 2/8	23 1/8 22 4/8	20 0/8	7 5	Ramsey County	MN	Paul Eckman	2004	13714
143 2/8	25 1/8 25 1/8	15 0/8	5 5	Freeborn County	MN	Jim Palmer	2004	13714
143 2/8	24 6/8 25 5/8	20 0/8	6 4	Anne Arundel County	MD	Samuel G. Willsey	2005	13714
143 2/8	24 2/8 24 2/8	17 3/8	6 5	Douglas County	WI	Aaron Larson	2005	13714
143 2/8	22 4/8 23 7/8	15 5/8	5 5	Harrison County	MO	Brent Forsman	2005	13714
143 2/8	23 6/8 24 2/8	19 2/8	5 6	Bennington County	VT	Ben Morse	2005	13714
143 2/8	25 3/8 24 2/8	18 3/8	5 5	Saline County	KS	Michael Boahn	2005	13714
143 2/8	21 2/8 21 2/8	15 4/8	6 5	Genesee County	MI	Robert D. DuBois	2005	13714
143 2/8	25 4/8 25 6/8	13 6/8	4 4	Trempealeau County	WI	John R. Suchla	2005	13714
*143 2/8	20 6/8 21 0/8	15 0/8	7 6	Simpson County	MS	Joe Rankin	2005	13714
143 2/8	25 0/8 24 0/8	17 6/8	4 5	Edgar County	IL	Brian Crockett	2005	13714
*143 2/8	25 2/8 24 4/8	19 4/8	5 5	Van Buren County	IA	Scott Knauf	2005	13714
143 2/8	25 4/8 25 4/8	16 6/8	4 5	Coffey County	KS	Joseph D. Helget	2005	13714
143 2/8	24 1/8 23 5/8	20 7/8	7 6	Carver County	MN	Brian Weege	2005	13714
143 2/8	21 4/8 23 0/8	14 4/8	5 5	Martin County	IN	Paul Rhodes	2006	13714
143 2/8	22 7/8 23 1/8	17 6/8	5 7	Trempealeau County	WI	Shawn Prudlick	2006	13714
143 2/8	22 6/8 22 4/8	17 2/8	5 5	Waupaca County	WI	Dan Loken	2006	13714
*143 2/8	23 3/8 23 4/8	16 6/8	5 6	Macon County	MO	Dae M. Lederle	2006	13714
*143 2/8	24 1/8 23 6/8	18 4/8	5 6	Dodge County	WI	Michael J. Petruske	2006	13714
143 2/8	22 7/8 23 2/8	18 6/8	4 5	Chickasaw County	IA	Randy Platz	2006	13714
143 2/8	25 0/8 25 4/8	22 5/8	5 4	Ripley County	IN	Sam Durham	2006	13714
143 2/8	22 1/8 21 6/8	17 4/8	5 5	Price County	WI	Eric Peterson	2006	13714
143 2/8	23 6/8 22 6/8	18 4/8	5 5	McHenry County	ND	Don Scofield	2006	13714
143 2/8	21 6/8 21 0/8	18 6/8	4 6	Shelby County	KY	Bert Eisenback	2006	13714
143 2/8	23 5/8 24 0/8	19 4/8	4 4	Vermillion County	IN	Kevin Anderson	2007	13714
143 2/8	28 0/8 26 7/8	19 0/8	4 3	Delaware County	IA	Ahrend Gibson	2007	13714
*143 2/8	24 1/8 23 0/8	17 2/8	6 5	Logan County	WV	Richard Belchor	2007	13714
143 2/8	24 2/8 22 4/8	18 2/8	6 5	Clark County	IL	Kevin Boyer	2007	13714
143 2/8	23 3/8 22 5/8	18 2/8	6 6	Summers County	WV	Rick Lilly	2007	13714
143 2/8	21 0/8 21 6/8	16 0/8	5 5	Duval County	TX	Dayner Roberts	2008	13714
143 2/8	22 6/8 23 0/8	19 0/8	6 5	Huntingdon County	PA	Marty W. Snyder	2008	13714
143 2/8	20 6/8 21 5/8	17 4/8	6 5	Gwinnett County	GA	Joseph A. DeFriece	2008	13714
143 2/8	22 1/8 23 2/8	16 7/8	7 6	Cass County	IN	Cory M. McGuire	2008	13714
143 2/8	21 2/8 20 4/8	18 5/8	6 5	Beadle County	SD	Josh Stanfield	2008	13714
143 2/8	22 2/8 22 1/8	17 4/8	6 6	Benton County	AR	Charlie Woodrum	2008	13714
*143 2/8	23 1/8 22 5/8	17 0/8	5 5	Pike County	IL	Jason M. Hough	2008	13714
143 2/8	18 6/8 19 5/8	15 2/8	5 5	Davis County	IA	Glen Pullin	2008	13714
*143 2/8	23 2/8 23 1/8	20 0/8	5 5	Middlesex County	NJ	Ken Nale	2008	13714
143 2/8	24 2/8 23 4/8	19 4/8	5 5	Otter Tail County	MN	Justin Heide	2009	13714
143 2/8	25 1/8 24 2/8	18 2/8	5 4	Berks County	PA	Jesse R. Border	2009	13714
143 2/8	23 0/8 22 3/8	16 2/8	5 5	Onondaga County	NY	Ricky M. Mills, Jr.	2009	13714

501

WHITETAIL DEER (TYPICAL ANTLERS)

Minimum Score 125 — Continued

SCORE	LENGTH OF R MAIN BEAM L	INSIDE SPREAD	NUMBER OF R POINTS L		AREA	STATE/PROVINCE	HUNTER'S NAME	DATE	RANK
143 2/8	21 7/8	19 6/8	15 4/8	6	5	Barron County	WI	Elmer Meyer	2009	13714
143 2/8	25 4/8	24 4/8	17 5/8	5	7	Ogle County	IL	Rick Leifheit	2009	13714
143 2/8	23 3/8	24 1/8	20 2/8	7	5	Menard County	TX	Stephen Boster	2009	13714
143 2/8	22 2/8	22 0/8	21 2/8	5	5	Kinney County	TX	Richard D. Sommer	2010	13714
143 1/8	23 0/8	23 2/8	17 1/8	5	4	Graham County	KS	Russell Hull	1965	13875
143 1/8	21 7/8	23 2/8	21 5/8	5	5	Linn County	IA	Tom Postel	1979	13875
143 1/8	21 2/8	22 7/8	18 3/8	6	7	Lincoln County	MN	David J. Rouge	1981	13875
143 1/8	22 6/8	22 1/8	18 6/8	6	5	Barry County	MI	Jay W. Gaston	1981	13875
143 1/8	21 6/8	21 2/8	19 5/8	6	6	Holmes County	OH	Dale R. Kaufman	1983	13875
143 1/8	22 5/8	22 4/8	19 5/8	5	5	Missoula County	MT	Greg Munther	1983	13875
143 1/8	20 6/8	20 3/8	18 7/8	6	6	Olmsted County	MN	Brian Veloske	1984	13875
143 1/8	24 6/8	25 4/8	17 7/8	6	7	Riley County	KS	Kenneth W. Lynch	1985	13875
143 1/8	22 2/8	22 1/8	15 7/8	5	5	Washburn County	WI	Michael Elliot	1986	13875
143 1/8	23 0/8	23 2/8	20 0/8	7	5	Iowa County	WI	Brad Burbach	1986	13875
143 1/8	25 0/8	22 2/8	20 1/8	6	5	Crawford County	WI	John Becwar	1987	13875
143 1/8	24 1/8	23 2/8	19 2/8	6	5	Cherry County	NE	Gary Galloway	1987	13875
143 1/8	24 0/8	23 2/8	17 3/8	7	5	Shawnee County	KS	William A. Konrade	1987	13875
143 1/8	24 1/8	22 2/8	22 5/8	4	4	Montcalm County	MI	A. Gene Higginson	1987	13875
143 1/8	24 3/8	24 2/8	20 3/8	5	5	Clayton County	IA	Albert A. Weidenbacher	1987	13875
143 1/8	23 6/8	24 6/8	21 1/8	4	4	Le Sueur County	MN	Randall Mathwig	1988	13875
143 1/8	23 0/8	21 7/8	14 7/8	5	5	Ripley County	IN	Van R. Craft	1988	13875
143 1/8	24 7/8	24 6/8	19 7/8	5	4	Fairfax County	VA	Kevin R. Lake	1989	13875
143 1/8	22 7/8	23 5/8	17 5/8	5	4	Piatt County	IL	David M. James	1991	13875
143 1/8	25 5/8	25 7/8	19 3/8	7	6	Schuyler County	IL	John Johnston	1991	13875
143 1/8	22 0/8	22 4/8	18 5/8	5	5	Crawford County	IL	Charlie Guyer	1991	13875
143 1/8	22 5/8	22 2/8	16 0/8	6	6	Vilas County	WI	Frank E. Caroselli	1991	13875
143 1/8	24 1/8	21 2/8	17 0/8	5	6	Lafayette County	WI	Todd Hanson	1991	13875
143 1/8	22 4/8	23 0/8	19 5/8	5	5	Carter County	MT	Keith L. Folk	1992	13875
143 1/8	21 0/8	22 5/8	16 3/8	5	5	Chester County	PA	Vincent J. Mento	1992	13875
143 1/8	23 7/8	22 7/8	20 1/8	5	5	Delaware County	IA	Eric Klaren	1992	13875
143 1/8	24 0/8	23 2/8	18 7/8	4	4	Iroquois County	IL	Terry Doehring	1992	13875
143 1/8	24 1/8	23 4/8	18 1/8	4	5	Muskingum County	OH	Danny Pyle	1993	13875
143 1/8	22 7/8	21 4/8	19 1/8	5	6	Calhoun County	IL	Randy Cress	1993	13875
143 1/8	25 1/8	24 7/8	18 3/8	4	5	Calhoun County	IL	David E. Willis	1993	13875
143 1/8	22 6/8	22 4/8	17 6/8	5	4	Wilcox County	AL	Scott M. Ware	1994	13875
143 1/8	23 2/8	23 0/8	17 0/8	4	6	Winnebago County	WI	Kenneth C. Walter	1994	13875
143 1/8	25 7/8	24 0/8	18 7/8	4	5	Vermilion County	IL	Terry Everingham	1994	13875
143 1/8	23 6/8	23 1/8	18 6/8	7	5	Langlade County	WI	David A. Nelson	1995	13875
143 1/8	22 3/8	21 2/8	14 2/8	6	6	Muscogee County	GA	Dr. Garland K. "Crow" Gudger	1995	13875
143 1/8	22 3/8	22 7/8	17 5/8	5	5	Polk County	WI	Aaron D. Baillargeon	1995	13875
143 1/8	23 2/8	23 0/8	20 0/8	7	4	Butler County	KS	David R. Rogers	1995	13875
143 1/8	27 4/8	26 6/8	20 5/8	3	6	Bond County	IL	Cory Holcmann	1995	13875
143 1/8	23 7/8	24 3/8	16 1/8	4	4	Hamilton County	IA	Matthew R. Lewis	1996	13875
143 1/8	23 6/8	25 6/8	18 2/8	4	6	Vermilion County	IL	Donald Sollars	1996	13875
143 1/8	23 1/8	23 0/8	17 1/8	5	5	Butler County	KS	Rodney Hommertzheim	1996	13875
143 1/8	23 1/8	24 1/8	17 7/8	5	6	Fond du Lac County	WI	Greg Schleusner	1996	13875
143 1/8	25 6/8	25 5/8	19 2/8	4	6	Allamakee County	IA	Gary Charipar	1996	13875
143 1/8	25 3/8	25 0/8	20 1/8	4	6	Will County	IL	Nick Ginnetti	1997	13875
143 1/8	25 7/8	25 2/8	19 1/8	5	5	Parke County	IN	Chuck Paddock	1997	13875
143 1/8	23 2/8	24 3/8	15 0/8	8	6	Yazoo County	MS	Jimmy Hilderbrand	1997	13875
143 1/8	22 1/8	22 1/8	16 5/8	5	6	Polk County	WI	Rick Heintz	1997	13875
143 1/8	25 1/8	26 1/8	18 3/8	5	6	Meigs County	OH	Patrick D. Kearns	1997	13875
143 1/8	22 1/8	21 6/8	22 2/8	5	5	Trempealeau County	WI	Jeffery Stoll	1997	13875
143 1/8	23 6/8	23 1/8	19 6/8	4	5	Peoria County	IL	Scott Turner	1997	13875
143 1/8	19 7/8	19 7/8	16 1/8	6	6	Lyon County	KS	Michael Esch	1997	13875
143 1/8	20 6/8	20 6/8	17 5/8	5	6	Wright County	IA	Ron Hansen	1997	13875
143 1/8	23 3/8	24 1/8	18 5/8	5	6	Jo Daviess County	IL	Bart Blocklinger	1998	13875
143 1/8	23 2/8	22 7/8	17 5/8	4	5	Robertson County	TN	David Martin	1998	13875
143 1/8	22 1/8	22 1/8	18 1/8	5	5	Sawyer County	WI	Brent Van Vonderen	1999	13875
143 1/8	24 1/8	24 2/8	16 0/8	6	6	Pike County	IL	Jeff Sencenbaugh	1999	13875
143 1/8	24 4/8	24 2/8	19 1/8	6	5	Bureau County	IL	Tim Billhorn	1999	13875
143 1/8	22 2/8	23 1/8	16 3/8	5	5	La Salle County	IL	Bill Weygand	1999	13875
143 1/8	23 6/8	22 5/8	19 0/8	6	7	Sumner County	KS	Barry Wiley	1999	13875
143 1/8	21 2/8	21 6/8	17 0/8	5	5	Massac County	IL	George Brunn	1999	13875
143 1/8	20 4/8	20 4/8	16 7/8	5	5	Warren County	KY	Jack Butler, Jr.	2000	13875
143 1/8	21 5/8	24 2/8	20 1/8	4	4	Dane County	WI	David Trolinger	2000	13875
143 1/8	22 0/8	21 6/8	18 0/8	6	5	Pike County	IL	Steven R. Tice	2000	13875
143 1/8	23 7/8	23 0/8	17 3/8	5	5	Union County	IA	Tim Dunphy	2000	13875
143 1/8	23 1/8	23 2/8	17 7/8	4	4	Peoria County	IL	Barry Bowers	2000	13875
143 1/8	24 0/8	22 5/8	16 3/8	5	5	Oconto County	WI	Eric D. Angus	2001	13875
143 1/8	23 7/8	23 5/8	19 4/8	5	6	Walsh County	ND	Michael Pokrzywinski	2001	13875
143 1/8	24 5/8	24 1/8	18 5/8	4	4	Greene County	OH	Phillip McDougal	2001	13875
143 1/8	21 7/8	21 5/8	14 5/8	6	8	Burnett County	WI	Steve Stoner	2001	13875
143 1/8	25 0/8	25 4/8	19 7/8	5	4	Delaware County	OH	Steve Boham	2001	13875
143 1/8	21 6/8	20 0/8	18 1/8	5	5	Delaware County	IA	Larry F. Heyer	2001	13875
143 1/8	23 5/8	23 4/8	19 3/8	5	5	Buffalo County	WI	James J. Johnson	2001	13875
143 1/8	25 2/8	24 2/8	18 5/8	6	7	Chemung County	NY	Edmond N. Dodge	2001	13875
143 1/8	22 1/8	21 7/8	18 4/8	6	6	Pike County	IL	Otis S. Darnell, Jr.	2001	13875
143 1/8	22 5/8	22 2/8	15 1/8	4	4	Westchester County	NY	Robert Komosinski	2001	13875
143 1/8	25 4/8	25 6/8	20 2/8	5	5	Westchester County	NY	Gus Congemi	2001	13875
143 1/8	22 5/8	22 3/8	15 0/8	5	7	Marathon County	WI	Tomas Winter	2002	13875
143 1/8	23 6/8	23 3/8	14 7/8	5	5	Chippewa County	WI	Derrick McGary	2002	13875
143 1/8	23 4/8	22 6/8	16 3/8	5	5	Olmsted County	MN	Kevin Joyce	2002	13875
143 1/8	27 1/8	26 1/8	23 2/8	5	5	Buffalo County	WI	Daniel Folkedahl	2002	13875
143 1/8	23 2/8	22 7/8	17 5/8	7	6	Montgomery County	IL	Jim Bruns	2002	13875
143 1/8	21 1/8	21 5/8	19 1/8	5	5	Pike County	IL	Gary L. Goldasich	2002	13875
143 1/8	23 6/8	24 2/8	19 1/8	4	4	Caroline County	MD	Jeff Minor	2002	13875
143 1/8	24 0/8	22 2/8	18 4/8	5	7	Robertson County	TN	David Ingram	2002	13875
143 1/8	21 6/8	21 2/8	16 1/8	5	5	Chicot County	AR	Frank Greenlee	2002	13875
143 1/8	23 1/8	23 1/8	17 4/8	6	5	La Salle County	IL	Tom McMurtry	2003	13875
143 1/8	23 4/8	24 2/8	17 5/8	4	4	Dakota County	MN	John Huddock	2003	13875
143 1/8	25 0/8	24 0/8	18 3/8	4	5	Rawlins County	KS	Zack Leonetti	2003	13875
143 1/8	24 3/8	22 6/8	19 7/8	4	4	Clay County	NE	Arnie Svoboda	2003	13875
143 1/8	22 2/8	22 2/8	16 3/8	6	4	Barber County	KS	Stephen Kotz	2003	13875
143 1/8	24 4/8	23 4/8	20 3/8	5	4	Kane County	IL	Todd J. Dorn	2003	13875

WHITETAIL DEER (TYPICAL ANTLERS)

Minimum Score 125 — Continued

SCORE	R MAIN BEAM L	INSIDE SPREAD	R POINTS L	AREA	STATE/PROVINCE	HUNTER'S NAME	DATE	RANK
143 1/8	27 0/8 25 5/8	16 4/8	5 4	Wake County	NC	Jay Adcock	2003	13875
143 1/8	22 5/8 22 4/8	15 5/8	6 6	Marathon County	WI	Max J. Muzynoski	2003	13875
*143 1/8	22 1/8 22 2/8	16 4/8	10 5	Wright County	MO	Ronnie Hightower	2003	13875
143 1/8	24 2/8 22 7/8	19 1/8	4 4	Chicot County	AR	Tucker Miller III	2004	13875
143 1/8	24 2/8 22 6/8	19 1/8	5 5	Benzie County	MI	William Jesse Bailey, Jr.	2004	13875
143 1/8	23 4/8 23 4/8	19 5/8	4 4	Lorain County	OH	Lyle Bennett	2004	13875
*143 1/8	25 4/8 25 1/8	18 7/8	6 5	Trempealeau County	WI	Rick Sterry	2004	13875
143 1/8	24 2/8 25 4/8	16 1/8	6 5	Lawrence County	OH	Robin Creswell	2004	13875
143 1/8	23 7/8 22 6/8	16 3/8	5 5	Pike County	IL	Darin McBeath	2004	13875
143 1/8	22 5/8 22 1/8	16 5/8	5 5	Houston County	MN	Chris Moon	2005	13875
143 1/8	22 2/8 21 6/8	16 5/8	6 5	Allegheny County	PA	Michael Wolff	2005	13875
143 1/8	24 1/8 23 2/8	18 5/8	5 7	Clinton County	OH	Kirk Lee	2005	13875
143 1/8	23 1/8 24 0/8	19 5/8	5 6	Fairfax County	VA	Ricky Cook	2005	13875
*143 1/8	24 6/8 23 5/8	16 3/8	6 6	Jasper County	IL	Garrett Tucker	2005	13875
*143 1/8	21 6/8 21 6/8	14 1/8	5 5	Winona County	MN	John Wise	2005	13875
*143 1/8	26 3/8 22 5/8	18 0/8	6 4	Lewis County	KY	Mike Norris	2005	13875
143 1/8	23 3/8 24 1/8	18 4/8	4 5	Round Lake	SAS	Floyd Forster	2005	13875
*143 1/8	21 1/8 22 7/8	19 1/8	5 6	Somerset County	PA	Bryan Hynicka	2006	13875
143 1/8	24 3/8 23 0/8	18 2/8	8 8	Tompkins County	NY	Joseph G. Ebel	2006	13875
143 1/8	25 1/8 25 2/8	19 0/8	5 7	Cass County	IL	Larry A. Holcomb	2006	13875
*143 1/8	22 7/8 23 2/8	15 5/8	5 5	Vigo County	IN	Thomas E. Rothrock	2006	13875
143 1/8	24 0/8 23 7/8	14 1/8	6 6	Kenedy County	TX	Mickey W. Hellickson	2006	13875
143 1/8	26 4/8 24 0/8	24 0/8	6 8	Macoupin County	IL	Doug Drew-Campbell	2006	13875
143 1/8	24 3/8 24 2/8	19 0/8	5 6	Orleans County	NY	Rick Fullwell	2006	13875
143 1/8	23 0/8 24 2/8	18 5/8	7 5	Juneau County	WI	Mitchell D. Vinz	2007	13875
143 1/8	22 2/8 22 2/8	14 0/8	7 5	Douglas County	WI	Shawn Koosman	2007	13875
*143 1/8	21 4/8 22 5/8	18 0/8	5 7	Monroe County	WI	Daniel Parker	2007	13875
143 1/8	23 4/8 21 7/8	20 5/8	6 5	Lawrence County	PA	Dennis Singer	2007	13875
143 1/8	26 0/8 24 3/8	19 2/8	5 6	Ashland County	WI	Jeffrey L. Steede	2007	13875
143 1/8	22 4/8 23 1/8	17 1/8	5 5	Anne Arundel County	MD	Michael Herpel	2007	13875
*143 1/8	21 7/8 23 2/8	15 3/8	5 5	Worth County	GA	Jordan Kyle Cox	2007	13875
143 1/8	23 0/8 23 6/8	17 3/8	6 5	Fulton County	IL	Craig Talbot	2007	13875
*143 1/8	21 2/8 22 2/8	15 1/8	5 5	Fergus County	MT	Brad Seyfert	2007	13875
143 1/8	22 4/8 22 1/8	18 7/8	5 5	Cochrane	ALB	Byron Albertson	2007	13875
143 1/8	26 0/8 26 3/8	17 4/8	7 6	Decatur County	IN	Eric Mann	2008	13875
*143 1/8	25 2/8 24 5/8	18 1/8	4 5	Page County	IA	Randy Scheel	2008	13875
143 1/8	19 4/8 19 0/8	16 5/8	5 6	Daviess County	MO	Chuck Weldon	2008	13875
*143 1/8	25 4/8 24 5/8	20 1/8	5 4	Christian County	IL	Robert Wemple	2008	13875
*143 1/8	23 7/8 24 0/8	18 1/8	5 5	Callaway County	MO	Marvin Cobb	2009	13875
*143 1/8	23 2/8 23 0/8	16 3/8	4 5	Pike County	OH	Glenn A. Fink	2009	13875
143 1/8	23 2/8 22 3/8	15 7/8	6 6	Bolivar County	MS	Paul Rizzo	2009	13875
*143 1/8	26 5/8 28 0/8	19 7/8	6 8	Fillmore County	MN	Tyler R. Wright	2009	13875
*143 1/8	23 4/8 23 0/8	15 5/8	5 5	Arcola	SAS	Terence Voth	2009	13875
143 0/8	23 5/8 22 0/8	19 4/8	5 5	Wright County	IA	Ronald Gorden	1958	14009
143 0/8	25 1/8 25 6/8	18 4/8	6 7	Aitkin County	MN	Ervin A. Buck	1961	14009
143 0/8	24 0/8 24 5/8	20 5/8	5 5	Pope County	IL	Bob E. Sims	1964	14009
143 0/8	25 4/8 21 0/8	14 6/8	5 6	Ottawa County	KS	Scotty Baugh	1967	14009
143 0/8	22 7/8 21 7/8	16 2/8	5 5	Edwards County	KS	Gerald L. Schaller	1972	14009
143 0/8	20 2/8 19 6/8	15 4/8	5 5	Madison County	IA	Larry L. Cavanaugh	1979	14009
143 0/8	24 3/8 24 4/8	18 1/8	6 5	Black Hawk County	IA	Richard Minahan	1980	14009
143 0/8	24 3/8 25 0/8	18 2/8	4 4	Sawyer County	WI	Steve Olson	1981	14009
143 0/8	22 6/8 22 0/8	19 2/8	5 6	Henry County	VA	Mike Weaver	1981	14009
143 0/8	20 5/8 20 5/8	15 4/8	5 5	Seward County	KS	Lynn Leonard	1983	14009
143 0/8	22 1/8 23 0/8	17 4/8	5 6	Montgomery County	PA	Robert J. Bochnak	1983	14009
143 0/8	24 6/8 23 1/8	22 0/8	6 5	Kankakee County	IL	Rick Renzi	1983	14009
143 0/8	21 0/8 21 4/8	17 6/8	6 7	Des Moines County	IA	Tom Delaney	1985	14009
143 0/8	23 2/8 23 5/8	19 5/8	5 4	La Salle County	IL	LeRoy H. Buckley, Jr.	1986	14009
143 0/8	23 5/8 24 6/8	17 4/8	5 5	Alfalfa County	OK	David W. Dowell	1986	14009
143 0/8	23 1/8 23 4/8	17 0/8	5 6	Sauk County	WI	Richard L. Kirkland	1987	14009
143 0/8	20 3/8 21 1/8	18 2/8	6 5	Columbia County	WI	Howard H. Hill	1987	14009
143 0/8	22 3/8 21 3/8	18 0/8	6 5	Missoula County	MT	Jon Cusker	1987	14009
143 0/8	23 5/8 23 3/8	17 2/8	5 5	Fairfax County	VA	Harry R. Husch, Jr.	1988	14009
143 0/8	22 6/8 24 0/8	18 0/8	5 5	Marathon County	WI	Mark Timken	1988	14009
143 0/8	22 7/8 23 4/8	18 4/8	4 5	Bayfield County	WI	Wayne Zirn	1988	14009
143 0/8	22 5/8 21 4/8	18 2/8	6 6	Licking County	OH	Stoney May	1988	14009
143 0/8	24 4/8 25 0/8	17 2/8	5 5	Beltrami County	MN	Ross Campbell	1988	14009
143 0/8	22 6/8 23 5/8	20 4/8	5 5	Montgomery County	MD	Richard H. Stabler	1989	14009
143 0/8	23 1/8 24 1/8	17 4/8	4 4	Allen County	IN	Randy McIntosh	1989	14009
143 0/8	23 6/8 22 2/8	17 2/8	6 6	Lee County	IA	Russell (Rusty) Robbins	1990	14009
143 0/8	25 2/8 23 4/8	17 6/8	5 5	Christian County	KY	Gary Holbrook	1990	14009
143 0/8	23 5/8 24 0/8	16 0/8	6 9	Wabash County	IL	Troy A. Hinderliter	1990	14009
143 0/8	23 1/8 23 7/8	17 4/8	5 5	Watauga County	NC	Chris Carlton	1991	14009
143 0/8	24 7/8 23 1/8	16 4/8	5 5	Dodge County	MN	Myles Keller	1991	14009
143 0/8	24 6/8 24 3/8	17 0/8	5 5	Lincoln County	MO	Hugh Steavenson	1991	14009
143 0/8	23 1/8 24 5/8	19 4/8	4 5	Jefferson County	OH	Joseph Daniel Nemitt	1991	14009
143 0/8	23 1/8 23 2/8	19 0/8	5 5	Lafayette County	WI	Bradley D. Phillips	1991	14009
143 0/8	22 3/8 22 1/8	17 6/8	5 5	Sebastian County	AR	Jim Garner	1992	14009
143 0/8	24 3/8 24 6/8	17 0/8	4 4	Lake County	IL	Andrew D. Orals	1992	14009
143 0/8	24 3/8 25 1/8	23 6/8	5 4	McHenry County	IL	Kory Lang	1993	14009
143 0/8	23 6/8 23 5/8	18 0/8	4 4	Hendricks County	IN	Aaron Wesley Hamstra	1993	14009
143 0/8	22 1/8 22 4/8	19 2/8	5 5	Berks County	PA	Mark L. Breidegam	1993	14009
143 0/8	26 7/8 27 0/8	18 0/8	5 5	Allegheny County	PA	John M. Stankowski	1993	14009
143 0/8	25 3/8 23 1/8	20 5/8	5 6	Jo Daviess County	IL	Jim Horneck	1993	14009
143 0/8	24 6/8 25 2/8	17 6/8	5 5	Buffalo County	WI	Dave Fredrickson	1993	14009
143 0/8	22 4/8 22 2/8	15 4/8	6 5	Wyoming County	WV	David K. Cox	1993	14009
143 0/8	26 0/8 25 2/8	26 1/8	4 3	Edmonton	ALB	Warren Witherspoon	1993	14009
143 0/8	23 5/8 22 5/8	19 0/8	5 5	Trempealeau County	WI	Rusty Severson	1994	14009
143 0/8	25 6/8 25 6/8	19 6/8	4 5	Scott County	IA	Gary Kiefer	1994	14009
143 0/8	21 2/8 23 2/8	20 0/8	5 5	Fulton County	IL	Barbara Briggs	1994	14009
143 0/8	24 1/8 24 1/8	19 2/8	5 5	Poweshiek County	IA	Keven Gibson	1994	14009
143 0/8	20 0/8 20 2/8	16 4/8	5 5	San Patricio County	TX	William Lee Emmons	1994	14009
143 0/8	22 1/8 21 7/8	19 0/8	5 5	Valley County	MT	Anthony Swiontek	1995	14009
143 0/8	24 1/8 25 0/8	18 2/8	5 5	Screven County	GA	Thomas W. Hughes	1995	14009
143 0/8	23 2/8 22 6/8	20 6/8	4 4	Daviess County	MO	Daniel P. Minor	1995	14009
143 0/8	22 1/8 23 4/8	13 4/8	5 6	Live Oak County	TX	Henry Tucker	1995	14009

WHITETAIL DEER (TYPICAL ANTLERS)

Minimum Score 125 — Continued

SCORE	LENGTH OF R MAIN BEAM L	INSIDE SPREAD	NUMBER OF R POINTS L		AREA	STATE/ PROVINCE	HUNTER'S NAME	DATE	RANK
143 0/8	22 4/8	23 3/8	20 0/8	6	5	Geauga County	OH	John P. Ross	1995	14009
143 0/8	25 0/8	25 3/8	17 2/8	5	4	Dakota County	MN	Derrick L. Bennett	1995	14009
143 0/8	23 6/8	23 2/8	18 6/8	7	6	Davis County	IA	Jeffrey A. Getz	1995	14009
143 0/8	21 6/8	25 3/8	20 2/8	7	4	Buffalo County	WI	Brian Potter	1995	14009
143 0/8	24 0/8	22 4/8	18 0/8	5	5	Boone County	MO	Jim Norden	1995	14009
143 0/8	24 2/8	24 3/8	17 4/8	5	5	Lawrence County	OH	Bob Fruda	1995	14009
143 0/8	25 2/8	25 0/8	18 5/8	5	4	Dakota County	MN	Edwin J. Schneider	1995	14009
143 0/8	26 1/8	26 1/8	16 4/8	5	5	Wayne County	KY	Adrian Bell	1995	14009
143 0/8	25 3/8	25 4/8	20 6/8	5	4	Morris County	NJ	Dr. Dennis M. Noonan	1996	14009
143 0/8	21 7/8	21 7/8	14 7/8	5	7	Kenedy County	TX	Tina M. Peeples	1996	14009
143 0/8	24 6/8	24 7/8	19 5/8	5	5	Trempealeau County	WI	Gary Kupka	1996	14009
143 0/8	24 3/8	24 3/8	20 2/8	5	5	Athens County	OH	Curtis R. Rutter	1996	14009
143 0/8	20 6/8	21 4/8	16 6/8	6	6	Tazewell County	IL	Matthew J. Wells	1996	14009
143 0/8	26 1/8	27 1/8	20 6/8	4	4	Lawrence County	OH	Johnny R. Holbrook	1996	14009
143 0/8	26 0/8	24 5/8	20 0/8	4	4	Dodge County	WI	Earl Zimmerman	1997	14009
143 0/8	24 1/8	23 5/8	19 0/8	4	4	Yankton County	SD	Jerry R. Kolda	1997	14009
143 0/8	24 5/8	25 5/8	20 5/8	4	5	Gasconade County	MO	Arvel L. Schneider	1997	14009
143 0/8	24 3/8	24 2/8	20 6/8	4	4	Tompkins County	NY	Raymond G. Woods	1997	14009
143 0/8	26 6/8	26 4/8	21 4/8	6	6	Gloucester County	NJ	Richard W. Etschman	1997	14009
143 0/8	24 4/8	26 7/8	22 1/8	5	4	McPherson County	KS	Jay Bullinger	1997	14009
143 0/8	22 6/8	22 2/8	18 6/8	5	5	Oconto County	WI	James F. Belongia	1997	14009
143 0/8	23 5/8	21 5/8	15 1/8	6	5	Smoky Lake	ALB	Mike Horton	1998	14009
143 0/8	23 5/8	23 5/8	18 7/8	6	5	Macon County	MO	Russell Riggins	1998	14009
143 0/8	23 2/8	23 5/8	19 0/8	4	4	Champaign County	IL	Dana Reynolds	1998	14009
143 0/8	24 0/8	25 0/8	14 6/8	5	7	Brown County	IL	Thomas Christensen	1998	14009
143 0/8	22 3/8	22 6/8	20 4/8	6	7	Cass County	MI	Andy Brossman	1998	14009
143 0/8	21 4/8	21 3/8	13 4/8	6	5	Putnam County	GA	George Ralph Harper	1999	14009
143 0/8	26 0/8	23 4/8	16 3/8	5	6	Marshall County	IN	J. Michael Umbaugh	1999	14009
143 0/8	22 4/8	24 3/8	15 2/8	7	5	Gallia County	OH	Bill Hood	1999	14009
143 0/8	21 6/8	21 2/8	18 6/8	5	5	Marathon County	WI	Steven Vander Wegen	2000	14009
143 0/8	22 0/8	22 2/8	17 2/8	5	5	Howard County	IA	Christopher Amiot	2000	14009
143 0/8	22 4/8	23 5/8	17 1/8	6	4	Indiana County	PA	Calvin Kostella	2000	14009
143 0/8	23 2/8	22 6/8	17 6/8	6	6	Shawano County	WI	Scott Pluger	2000	14009
143 0/8	22 3/8	23 0/8	15 4/8	6	7	Buffalo County	WI	Jason Meyers	2000	14009
143 0/8	22 6/8	22 3/8	18 4/8	6	7	Todd County	MN	Nathan Reed	2000	14009
143 0/8	21 2/8	21 6/8	16 6/8	7	6	Oconto County	WI	Leslie "Butch" Vorpahl	2000	14009
143 0/8	26 5/8	26 6/8	18 0/8	3	4	Sedgwick County	KS	Gary Voth	2000	14009
143 0/8	23 6/8	23 6/8	15 7/8	6	5	Floyd County	IA	Jason Ritter	2000	14009
143 0/8	22 5/8	21 7/8	18 0/8	6	5	Allegany County	NY	Doug France	2001	14009
143 0/8	25 4/8	25 4/8	20 2/8	4	4	Grant County	WI	Doug Hazen	2001	14009
143 0/8	21 7/8	22 5/8	17 0/8	4	4	Montgomery County	IA	Pink Atkins	2001	14009
143 0/8	26 0/8	25 0/8	20 4/8	5	4	Wayne County	NY	Chris K. Loveless	2002	14009
143 0/8	21 5/8	22 0/8	16 2/8	5	5	Pierce County	WI	Don Linse	2002	14009
143 0/8	22 1/8	21 0/8	17 6/8	6	5	Winnebago County	IL	Thomas T. King	2002	14009
143 0/8	27 0/8	25 4/8	17 1/8	5	7	Pawnee County	NE	Gary Brunberg	2002	14009
143 0/8	23 1/8	23 3/8	17 4/8	6	5	Price County	WI	Eckhard Hoffer	2003	14009
143 0/8	24 3/8	23 3/8	16 5/8	5	6	Roberts County	SD	John A. Meyen	2003	14009
*143 0/8	22 0/8	21 6/8	17 5/8	6	5	Ramsey County	ND	Kelly Durbin	2003	14009
143 0/8	24 0/8	24 5/8	16 0/8	6	5	Macon County	MO	Robert Brundage	2003	14009
143 0/8	28 1/8	28 2/8	23 4/8	5	3	Montgomery County	OH	Trace Morse	2003	14009
143 0/8	22 3/8	22 5/8	17 1/8	6	6	Perry County	MO	Shawn Martin	2003	14009
143 0/8	24 4/8	24 3/8	17 4/8	5	5	New Haven County	CT	William R. Fairchild	2003	14009
143 0/8	23 1/8	22 1/8	16 2/8	5	5	Ohio County	IN	Casey Knigga	2003	14009
*143 0/8	26 7/8	25 0/8	17 0/8	6	6	Calhoun County	MI	David C. Jacob	2003	14009
143 0/8	21 1/8	22 7/8	16 0/8	8	8	Van Buren County	IA	James M. Fitzgerald	2003	14009
143 0/8	21 2/8	23 1/8	19 5/8	6	5	Hamilton County	IL	C. M. "Rusty" Priest	2003	14009
143 0/8	24 0/8	22 6/8	16 2/8	5	5	Macon County	IL	Jerry Wilson	2003	14009
143 0/8	26 2/8	26 6/8	17 0/8	4	4	Fond du Lac County	WI	Terry Wegner	2003	14009
143 0/8	23 1/8	23 2/8	17 0/8	6	5	Jo Daviess County	IL	Nicholas J. Dodds	2003	14009
143 0/8	23 5/8	24 4/8	18 1/8	5	6	Mercer County	PA	Donald F. Cloud	2004	14009
143 0/8	24 2/8	24 3/8	22 4/8	4	4	Ogle County	IL	Tim Hasara	2004	14009
143 0/8	23 5/8	23 5/8	16 2/8	4	5	Stark County	IL	Ron Delbridge	2004	14009
143 0/8	24 2/8	23 6/8	15 0/8	5	5	Davis County	IA	Terry Breeding	2004	14009
143 0/8	23 4/8	23 4/8	19 0/8	4	5	Buffalo County	WI	Nathan Ashwell	2005	14009
*143 0/8	24 6/8	25 6/8	18 4/8	5	5	Jackson County	MO	Clay Cumberford	2005	14009
143 0/8	21 5/8	21 0/8	15 4/8	5	5	Saline County	AR	Mike Mobley	2005	14009
143 0/8	25 6/8	27 6/8	21 0/8	4	4	Meade County	KS	Richie Bland	2005	14009
*143 0/8	22 5/8	22 0/8	18 0/8	5	5	Ringgold County	IA	Dallas Eakes	2005	14009
143 0/8	23 0/8	24 5/8	16 3/8	6	5	Sauk County	WI	George D. Scott	2005	14009
*143 0/8	20 6/8	23 1/8	17 0/8	6	6	McHenry County	ND	Elliot F. Piton	2006	14009
143 0/8	21 7/8	22 1/8	18 1/8	5	6	Washington County	WI	Jeff Mueller	2006	14009
*143 0/8	22 1/8	22 2/8	19 0/8	6	5	Franklin County	PA	Gregory Baer	2006	14009
143 0/8	22 6/8	22 4/8	15 2/8	5	5	McPherson County	KS	Dan Marsh	2006	14009
143 0/8	21 0/8	22 3/8	16 5/8	5	5	Maries County	MO	Joey Braun	2006	14009
143 0/8	23 1/8	22 7/8	19 0/8	5	5	Kewaunee County	WI	Nathan Prevost	2006	14009
143 0/8	21 4/8	23 7/8	18 6/8	5	5	McLean County	KY	William Morgan Jones	2006	14009
*143 0/8	26 1/8	25 2/8	20 2/8	5	5	Bucks County	PA	Douglas Urich	2006	14009
143 0/8	22 7/8	22 3/8	16 4/8	5	5	Estill County	KY	Bill Farmer	2006	14009
*143 0/8	25 3/8	24 1/8	20 2/8	5	5	Schuylkill County	PA	Andrew Drumheller	2006	14009
143 0/8	22 2/8	21 4/8	16 2/8	5	5	Ramsey County	ND	Daniel Erickstad	2006	14009
143 0/8	25 3/8	25 0/8	20 6/8	5	5	Peoria County	IL	Ross Edwards	2006	14009
143 0/8	24 1/8	23 7/8	16 2/8	4	4	Bingham County	ID	Danny R. Henson	2006	14009
*143 0/8	23 6/8	22 6/8	17 2/8	5	5	Peoria County	IL	Randy Beecham	2006	14009
*143 0/8	22 0/8	21 6/8	17 0/8	5	5	Isanti County	MN	Jim Pratt	2007	14009
143 0/8	24 3/8	24 3/8	16 2/8	4	5	Keya Paha County	NE	R. Kirk Sharp	2007	14009
*143 0/8	24 4/8	23 2/8	18 4/8	8	6	White County	IN	Justin E. Rowland	2007	14009
143 0/8	24 5/8	26 4/8	20 4/8	4	4	Wyoming County	WV	Dougie Lester	2007	14009
*143 0/8	24 3/8	24 2/8	15 2/8	4	4	Jasper County	MO	James W. Buchanan	2007	14009
143 0/8	22 7/8	22 5/8	16 0/8	5	5	Sherburne County	MN	Mark P. Bauer	2007	14009
143 0/8	24 1/8	22 7/8	19 6/8	5	5	Mason County	WV	Lewis Holcomb	2007	14009
143 0/8	23 7/8	22 0/8	19 2/8	5	6	Monongalia County	WV	Jason K. Frankhouser	2007	14009
143 0/8	23 2/8	24 7/8	16 4/8	5	5	Lamar County	AL	Jeff Taylor	2007	14009
*143 0/8	21 4/8	22 1/8	16 2/8	5	7	Clark County	WI	Robby G. Roehl	2008	14009
*143 0/8	20 6/8	20 5/8	16 4/8	5	5	Pike County	IL	Pastor Quentin Beard	2008	14009
*143 0/8	21 7/8	22 3/8	18 0/8	5	5	Sauk County	WI	Rick Lehman	2008	14009

WHITETAIL DEER (TYPICAL ANTLERS)

Minimum Score 125 — Continued

SCORE	LENGTH OF R MAIN BEAM L	INSIDE SPREAD	NUMBER OF R POINTS L		AREA	STATE/ PROVINCE	HUNTER'S NAME	DATE	RANK
143 0/8	23 7/8 22 7/8	18 0/8	5	5	Jones County	IA	Milo F. Brown, Jr.	2008	14009
*143 0/8	24 2/8 23 4/8	18 6/8	5	5	Wood County	OH	Jason Albanese	2008	14009
*143 0/8	22 4/8 23 4/8	19 6/8	5	5	Sullivan County	IN	Nathan A. Walton	2008	14009
143 0/8	24 6/8 23 4/8	18 6/8	4	5	Lafayette County	WI	Ken Heinrichs	2008	14009
143 0/8	23 5/8 23 2/8	17 6/8	5	5	Dutchess County	NY	Joe Dziegelewski	2009	14009
143 0/8	22 2/8 22 2/8	16 2/8	5	7	Sullivan County	MO	Roy Haler	2009	14009
143 0/8	24 2/8 23 2/8	17 0/8	5	5	Dane County	WI	Brian M. Shunk	2009	14009
*143 0/8	24 7/8 25 5/8	20 0/8	5	6	Monona County	IA	Rodney Walker	2009	14009
*143 0/8	24 1/8 23 6/8	17 4/8	5	5	Clark County	WI	Jamie Kilty	2009	14009
*143 0/8	22 5/8 24 1/8	18 0/8	6	4	Union County	SD	Troy Van Roekel	2009	14009
143 0/8	25 5/8 25 4/8	18 4/8	4	5	Monona County	IA	Roger VanBeek	2009	14009
142 7/8	20 4/8 20 6/8	16 3/8	5	5	Brown County	SD	Wayne Miller	1971	14167
142 7/8	21 3/8 21 7/8	16 1/8	6	5	Becker County	MN	Kurt Lepping	1972	14167
142 7/8	21 1/8 22 4/8	16 1/8	5	5	Jackson County	WI	Clark Gallup	1972	14167
142 7/8	24 1/8 24 2/8	20 1/8	4	5	Douglas County	NE	Walter Ruff, Jr.	1973	14167
142 7/8	26 2/8 25 6/8	22 2/8	4	4	Carroll County	IL	Donald Lauer	1978	14167
142 7/8	21 0/8 23 5/8	19 6/8	6	5	Teton County	MT	Richard C. Semrad	1979	14167
142 7/8	22 2/8 21 5/8	13 7/8	4	4	St. Louis County	MN	Dan Tanner	1979	14167
142 7/8	22 0/8 23 2/8	18 1/8	4	5	Warren County	IA	Charly Stills	1980	14167
142 7/8	22 7/8 23 0/8	17 1/8	5	6	Redwood County	MN	Kenneth A. Gilb	1980	14167
142 7/8	25 2/8 25 2/8	18 3/8	5	5	Freeborn County	MN	Kermit Askland	1982	14167
142 7/8	21 2/8 21 2/8	16 7/8	5	5	Richland County	MT	Dave McGough	1983	14167
142 7/8	21 0/8 20 4/8	18 0/8	5	6	Jefferson County	NE	Bob Funke	1983	14167
142 7/8	22 3/8 23 1/8	17 7/8	5	4	Shelby County	IL	David Russell	1983	14167
142 7/8	22 3/8 22 0/8	18 7/8	5	5	Winneshiek County	IA	Gary Baumler	1984	14167
142 7/8	23 6/8 23 1/8	16 3/8	5	5	Webster County	IA	Edward E. Ulicki	1984	14167
142 7/8	24 4/8 25 5/8	21 1/8	4	4	Will County	IL	Terry Marcukaitis	1984	14167
142 7/8	24 4/8 24 5/8	20 1/8	5	5	Marshall County	KS	Steve Johnson	1984	14167
142 7/8	24 5/8 24 6/8	20 3/8	6	5	Lafayette County	WI	Larry Rose	1985	14167
142 7/8	25 0/8 26 1/8	15 5/8	4	5	Clark County	IN	Steve Bower	1986	14167
142 7/8	25 5/8 26 6/8	19 2/8	6	5	Florence County	WI	Dale T. Nixon	1988	14167
142 7/8	22 3/8 24 1/8	19 2/8	7	9	Murray County	OK	Charles R. Sanford	1988	14167
142 7/8	24 0/8 24 0/8	17 7/8	6	6	Cass County	MI	Randall Smith	1988	14167
142 7/8	23 4/8 23 2/8	15 1/8	4	4	Atascosa County	TX	Gene Lasseter	1989	14167
142 7/8	23 6/8 23 2/8	20 1/8	4	5	Jo Daviess County	IL	James F. Delaney	1989	14167
142 7/8	23 1/8 24 3/8	17 3/8	5	6	Hardin County	OH	Mark Preston	1989	14167
142 7/8	22 3/8 22 4/8	16 5/8	5	5	Cedar County	NE	Cathy M. Tramp	1990	14167
142 7/8	26 7/8 24 3/8	21 2/8	7	5	White County	IL	Peter P. Fiala	1990	14167
142 7/8	23 6/8 24 5/8	18 1/8	5	4	Crawford County	KS	Shawn Pipkin	1991	14167
142 7/8	25 4/8 24 5/8	20 3/8	5	5	Holmes County	OH	Charles Larue	1991	14167
142 7/8	24 1/8 23 1/8	17 5/8	8	5	Adams County	IL	Steve Cornwell	1991	14167
142 7/8	24 3/8 24 3/8	18 2/8	7	6	Green County	WI	Steve J. Gobeli	1992	14167
142 7/8	21 3/8 22 0/8	16 4/8	6	5	Hennepin County	MN	Michael Mulcare	1992	14167
142 7/8	24 4/8 25 4/8	18 1/8	5	5	Zavala County	TX	Joseph D. Krout, III	1992	14167
142 7/8	25 1/8 26 2/8	19 3/8	4	4	E. Carroll Parish	LA	George R. Bryant	1993	14167
142 7/8	21 1/8 21 5/8	17 0/8	6	6	Bryan County	OK	Randy Cheshier	1993	14167
142 7/8	21 5/8 22 1/8	15 3/8	5	7	Fayette County	WV	Thomas Stevens	1993	14167
142 7/8	21 7/8 22 5/8	15 7/8	5	5	Marquette County	WI	Jay A. Severson	1994	14167
142 7/8	22 6/8 24 7/8	22 2/8	8	8	Stearns County	MN	David Kloeppner	1994	14167
142 7/8	24 0/8 23 3/8	18 3/8	5	5	Jo Daviess County	IL	Bob Bruss	1994	14167
142 7/8	22 4/8 23 3/8	16 5/8	5	5	Crawford County	KS	Ron Mason	1994	14167
142 7/8	24 4/8 24 4/8	21 0/8	5	5	Warren County	IL	Rodney Retherford	1995	14167
142 7/8	22 6/8 22 6/8	19 7/8	5	5	Franklin County	VA	Dolan Baker	1995	14167
142 7/8	23 4/8 23 6/8	17 3/8	5	5	Des Moines County	IA	Craig A. Owens	1995	14167
142 7/8	23 7/8 24 1/8	16 7/8	5	5	Schuyler County	IL	John Johnston	1995	14167
142 7/8	24 6/8 24 3/8	15 7/8	5	4	Caldwell County	KY	Keith Westfall	1995	14167
142 7/8	20 4/8 20 7/8	17 2/8	5	6	Mower County	MN	Ben Williams	1995	14167
142 7/8	23 5/8 23 1/8	17 7/8	5	5	Trempealeau County	WI	Mike Engen	1996	14167
142 7/8	24 6/8 25 5/8	20 7/8	5	4	Elgin	ONT	Mike Renaud	1996	14167
142 7/8	26 2/8 24 7/8	22 3/8	4	4	Nemaha County	KS	Tom Lierz	1996	14167
142 7/8	22 4/8 21 5/8	21 1/8	6	6	Mitchell County	IA	Michael D. Rehnelt	1996	14167
142 7/8	22 7/8 23 1/8	20 7/8	5	5	Worcester County	MA	Ronald Rosenlund	1996	14167
142 7/8	23 1/8 23 0/8	17 1/8	5	4	Pike County	IL	Merlyn Winchell	1996	14167
142 7/8	24 4/8 24 0/8	20 1/8	4	5	Rockingham County	NH	Richard Bourdelais	1996	14167
142 7/8	21 6/8 21 7/8	14 7/8	5	5	Buffalo County	WI	Lynn Moeller	1996	14167
142 7/8	23 4/8 23 5/8	16 5/8	5	5	Richland County	WI	Craig Fairbert	1997	14167
142 7/8	23 1/8 23 4/8	15 5/8	4	4	St. Marys County	MD	Mark B. Goddard	1997	14167
142 7/8	21 2/8 21 3/8	16 6/8	5	5	Hand County	SD	Kevin Bertsch	1997	14167
142 7/8	24 6/8 24 4/8	19 3/8	5	5	Pawnee County	KS	Jason Reece	1997	14167
142 7/8	24 7/8 25 0/8	17 1/8	4	5	Washtenaw County	MI	Walter Pish	1998	14167
142 7/8	24 6/8 25 7/8	22 5/8	5	4	Chester County	PA	Jim Connor	1998	14167
142 7/8	24 3/8 24 0/8	18 1/8	4	4	Chippewa County	WI	Randy Helland	1998	14167
142 7/8	18 5/8 19 2/8	18 1/8	5	5	Gasconade County	MO	Danny L. Marquart	1998	14167
142 7/8	23 5/8 23 1/8	16 1/8	4	4	Jackson County	WI	Kyle Bruley	1998	14167
142 7/8	22 7/8 23 2/8	18 6/8	5	5	Lee County	IL	Bob Lahman	1998	14167
142 7/8	25 5/8 25 2/8	17 5/8	4	5	McDowell County	WV	Robert T. Mullins	1998	14167
142 7/8	23 1/8 23 1/8	20 1/8	4	5	Kosciusko County	IN	Joshua D. Beery	1998	14167
142 7/8	22 7/8 23 6/8	17 3/8	6	7	Calhoun County	IL	George Van Landingham	1998	14167
142 7/8	21 7/8 22 2/8	20 1/8	5	5	Adams County	IL	Tom Moore	1998	14167
142 7/8	21 5/8 21 4/8	17 1/8	5	5	Sheboygan County	WI	Jeff Karoses	1998	14167
142 7/8	23 5/8 23 5/8	20 1/8	5	5	Coleman County	TX	Micah Daboub	1998	14167
142 7/8	22 6/8 22 7/8	18 5/8	5	5	Schuylkill County	PA	Trevor L. Steigerwalt	1999	14167
142 7/8	22 6/8 23 2/8	14 3/8	5	5	Randolph County	MO	John Terry	1999	14167
142 7/8	21 2/8 21 6/8	15 1/8	5	5	Juneau County	WI	Ron Stetzenbach	1999	14167
142 7/8	24 2/8 24 2/8	18 4/8	6	6	Pike County	IL	William J. Smith	1999	14167
142 7/8	21 3/8 20 6/8	16 1/8	5	5	Hardin County	IA	Kevin Heitland	1999	14167
142 7/8	24 6/8 25 0/8	19 0/8	5	4	Waukesha County	WI	Jim Parulski	1999	14167
142 7/8	22 4/8 20 2/8	18 3/8	4	4	Cook County	IL	Timothy L. Harkness	1999	14167
142 7/8	23 6/8 24 6/8	16 2/8	5	5	Neosho County	KS	Bill Ruble	2000	14167
142 7/8	24 6/8 25 1/8	17 7/8	4	5	Clay County	WV	Dale Drennen	2000	14167
142 7/8	23 6/8 24 1/8	18 7/8	5	5	St. Charles County	MO	Lawrence C. Miller	2000	14167
142 7/8	22 2/8 21 5/8	16 1/8	5	5	Outagamie County	WI	Jim Vande Hey	2001	14167
142 7/8	22 3/8 22 0/8	14 1/8	5	6	Portage County	WI	Jeff P. Zelinski	2001	14167
142 7/8	22 3/8 22 3/8	18 1/8	5	5	Pierce County	WI	Don Eldred	2001	14167
142 7/8	23 7/8 23 0/8	18 5/8	4	4	Columbia County	WI	Thomas R. Karel	2001	14167

WHITETAIL DEER (TYPICAL ANTLERS)

Minimum Score 125 — Continued

SCORE	R MAIN BEAM L	INSIDE SPREAD	R POINTS L	AREA	STATE/ PROVINCE	HUNTER'S NAME	DATE	RANK
142 7/8	21 4/8 21 0/8	16 5/8	5 5	Williamson County	IL	Travis Haas	2001	14167
142 7/8	24 3/8 24 2/8	18 5/8	5 4	Hickman County	KY	Jeff Berryhill	2001	14167
142 7/8	23 3/8 21 6/8	15 5/8	5 5	Clinton County	MO	David Bosley	2001	14167
142 7/8	23 2/8 22 7/8	16 1/8	5 5	Herkimer County	NY	Wayne Rockwell	2001	14167
142 7/8	24 3/8 24 6/8	17 5/8	5 5	Taylor County	IA	Brandon Moon	2001	14167
142 7/8	21 3/8 18 1/8	19 3/8	5 6	Wapello County	IA	Jeff Ortner	2001	14167
142 7/8	23 0/8 23 6/8	14 1/8	6 5	Grayson County	TX	Josh Randles	2001	14167
*142 7/8	22 6/8 22 7/8	14 4/8	6 7	Polk County	GA	Dutch Copelan	2002	14167
142 7/8	26 6/8 27 5/8	20 5/8	5 4	Person County	NC	Robert Carter	2002	14167
142 7/8	24 3/8 25 5/8	21 7/8	5 5	Sussex County	NJ	Dennis Hullings	2002	14167
142 7/8	23 0/8 23 1/8	16 6/8	6 6	McHenry County	IL	Rich Swanson	2002	14167
142 7/8	23 3/8 24 5/8	15 7/8	4 4	La Salle County	TX	Wayne Eskew	2002	14167
*142 7/8	25 4/8 25 7/8	17 4/8	6 6	Butler County	OH	Joshua Martin	2002	14167
142 7/8	21 3/8 22 0/8	15 3/8	6 5	Oklahoma County	OK	William S. Duncan	2003	14167
142 7/8	22 7/8 24 0/8	17 7/8	8 7	Montgomery County	IL	Cody Hill	2003	14167
142 7/8	22 4/8 23 5/8	16 7/8	5 5	Ford County	KS	Ford Dye	2003	14167
142 7/8	19 6/8 19 4/8	16 5/8	7 6	Calhoun County	IL	Emmet Watson	2003	14167
142 7/8	23 4/8 23 4/8	18 3/8	5 5	Buffalo County	WI	Alan Gleiter	2003	14167
*142 7/8	25 4/8 23 1/8	19 1/8	4 4	Perry County	OH	Steve Abram	2003	14167
142 7/8	24 3/8 25 3/8	16 6/8	7 6	Fond du Lac County	WI	Cary Literski	2003	14167
142 7/8	27 2/8 25 1/8	20 1/8	5 5	Pike County	IL	Belinda Lankford	2003	14167
142 7/8	21 6/8 22 1/8	17 1/8	5 5	Harrison County	MO	Michael C. Garrett	2003	14167
142 7/8	23 4/8 22 5/8	18 7/8	4 5	McCulloch County	TX	Joshua D. Puryear	2004	14167
142 7/8	22 3/8 21 7/8	16 3/8	5 5	Douglas County	WI	Scott L. Wood	2004	14167
142 7/8	23 2/8 23 1/8	21 1/8	5 5	McKenzie County	ND	Harry Leaver	2004	14167
*142 7/8	24 1/8 22 3/8	21 5/8	4 6	Stephenson County	IL	Rodger Watts	2004	14167
142 7/8	22 4/8 22 1/8	17 4/8	7 6	Lenawee County	MI	Steven C. Robinson	2005	14167
142 7/8	20 5/8 21 7/8	19 5/8	5 5	Jackson County	IA	Chip Brown	2005	14167
142 7/8	25 5/8 26 6/8	17 1/8	5 5	Clark County	WI	Robert Redig	2005	14167
142 7/8	20 3/8 23 6/8	18 2/8	6 5	Warrick County	IN	Eric Stamps	2005	14167
*142 7/8	24 6/8 22 6/8	19 1/8	5 5	Ringgold County	IA	Andrew Bishop	2005	14167
142 7/8	21 4/8 22 3/8	17 3/8	5 5	Howard County	IA	Jacob Cray	2005	14167
142 7/8	24 0/8 24 4/8	17 1/8	4 4	Stanley County	SD	Kent Lewis	2006	14167
142 7/8	25 5/8 21 0/8	20 4/8	5 7	Portage County	OH	Christopher D. Gerbrick	2006	14167
142 7/8	23 2/8 24 2/8	20 5/8	6 7	Lafayette County	WI	Joshua Pink	2006	14167
142 7/8	23 2/8 23 7/8	17 1/8	5 5	Dixon County	NE	Daniel J. Williams	2006	14167
*142 7/8	23 5/8 23 2/8	18 1/8	5 5	Rockcastle County	KY	Tony A. Mahaffey	2007	14167
142 7/8	23 2/8 23 3/8	18 7/8	5 5	Trempealeau County	WI	Ray N. Andersen	2007	14167
142 7/8	23 6/8 23 0/8	18 1/8	5 5	Buffalo County	WI	Gregory A. Hensen	2007	14167
142 7/8	23 2/8 23 4/8	21 0/8	5 5	Boone County	IA	Cameron Jensen	2007	14167
142 7/8	21 4/8 22 3/8	24 3/8	4 6	Fulton County	IL	Jeff Pals	2007	14167
142 7/8	21 5/8 22 3/8	17 0/8	6 5	Washington County	WI	Rick Bertoni	2007	14167
*142 7/8	23 1/8 25 5/8	17 5/8	5 5	Comanche County	KS	Lynn Leonard	2007	14167
142 7/8	27 0/8 26 5/8	24 3/8	5 5	Lucas County	OH	Steve Lucarelli	2008	14167
142 7/8	23 3/8 23 2/8	18 7/8	4 4	Crow Wing County	MN	Nola Remer	2008	14167
*142 7/8	21 3/8 21 0/8	17 7/8	5 5	Parke County	IN	John A. Henderson	2008	14167
*142 7/8	26 1/8 26 0/8	17 2/8	8 8	Lincoln County	KS	Mike Blankenship	2008	14167
142 7/8	22 7/8 22 4/8	18 5/8	5 6	Allegheny County	PA	Mark Busse	2008	14167
*142 7/8	25 3/8 25 2/8	18 7/8	5 5	Monroe County	OH	Luis A. Sanders	2008	14167
142 7/8	24 7/8 24 7/8	21 1/8	4 4	Lee County	IL	Rick Farringer	2008	14167
142 7/8	22 0/8 22 4/8	15 0/8	6 6	Sutton County	TX	Drake Shurley	2009	14167
*142 7/8	20 2/8 20 6/8	14 5/8	5 6	Johnston County	OK	Rollie Lunsford	2009	14167
142 7/8	24 6/8 23 0/8	17 3/8	5 5	Waupaca County	WI	Cole TeBeest	2009	14167
142 7/8	22 2/8 21 4/8	17 4/8	6 6	Trempealeau County	WI	Dan Kampa	2009	14167
142 7/8	25 0/8 24 4/8	17 6/8	5 4	Trempealeau County	WI	Ray Andersen	2010	14167
142 6/8	23 5/8 23 0/8	19 5/8	4 5	Green Lake County	WI	Mark Novitske	1969	14306
142 6/8	22 2/8 21 7/8	18 7/8	6 6	Douglas County	MN	David Koenen	1973	14306
142 6/8	25 3/8 25 4/8	16 6/8	4 4	Darke County	OH	Wayne Goubeaux	1974	14306
142 6/8	25 6/8 25 7/8	16 6/8	4 4	Prairie County	AR	John W. Hogue	1978	14306
142 6/8	21 3/8 21 3/8	18 6/8	5 6	Empress	ALB	Alan R. Francis	1980	14306
142 6/8	22 4/8 21 1/8	19 4/8	4 4	De Kalb County	MO	Mark Garr	1982	14306
142 6/8	23 6/8 24 0/8	19 5/8	6 5	Jefferson County	WI	Jed Kottwitz	1983	14306
142 6/8	24 2/8 23 7/8	19 2/8	5 5	Madison County	AL	Rocky Drake	1983	14306
142 6/8	22 3/8 23 1/8	17 6/8	5 4	Clay County	KS	Larry Reed	1984	14306
142 6/8	21 7/8 22 5/8	15 4/8	5 6	Lycoming County	PA	Kelly J. Cooper	1985	14306
142 6/8	14 4/8 20 0/8	17 4/8	6 6	Waukesha County	WI	John Riehle	1985	14306
142 6/8	22 0/8 22 1/8	17 2/8	5 5	Hamilton County	KS	Scott Showalter	1985	14306
142 6/8	22 1/8 21 6/8	16 0/8	5 6	Cherokee County	TX	John Hall	1986	14306
142 6/8	23 6/8 23 0/8	18 6/8	5 4	Allen County	IN	Denny Emrich	1986	14306
142 6/8	22 3/8 22 4/8	18 2/8	7 7	Lincoln County	MT	David R. Erickson	1987	14306
142 6/8	23 5/8 23 3/8	15 4/8	6 6	Clayton County	IA	Scott W. Miller	1988	14306
142 6/8	24 6/8 26 1/8	24 4/8	5 5	Oneida County	WI	Joseph Kwaterski	1988	14306
142 6/8	20 5/8 21 0/8	16 4/8	6 5	Dodge County	NE	Mike Diers	1988	14306
142 6/8	21 5/8 22 5/8	19 0/8	5 5	Woodford County	IL	Sid Schertz	1988	14306
142 6/8	20 0/8 21 0/8	18 1/8	5 6	New Castle County	DE	Earl McSorley	1988	14306
142 6/8	24 3/8 23 5/8	16 6/8	4 4	Saunders County	NE	Richard Cherovsky	1989	14306
142 6/8	22 3/8 22 5/8	15 0/8	8 7	Cherokee County	OK	Monte Reid	1989	14306
142 6/8	22 1/8 22 7/8	18 4/8	7 7	Price County	WI	Tom G. Verkilen	1989	14306
142 6/8	23 5/8 23 5/8	16 6/8	5 5	Hancock County	IL	William T. Kirby	1989	14306
142 6/8	21 3/8 22 0/8	20 6/8	7 9	Linn County	IA	Craig Cutts	1989	14306
142 6/8	23 0/8 24 1/8	15 0/8	6 5	Tom Green County	TX	Ronnie Parsons	1990	14306
142 6/8	23 2/8 24 3/8	15 4/8	5 5	Allegheny County	PA	David C. Williams	1990	14306
142 6/8	24 1/8 23 3/8	16 2/8	5 5	Eau Claire County	WI	Riley Allen Fletschock	1990	14306
142 6/8	23 4/8 24 5/8	19 2/8	5 5	Effingham County	IL	Roger Loy	1990	14306
142 6/8	23 1/8 23 2/8	18 6/8	6 5	Warren County	OH	Bruce Woods	1991	14306
142 6/8	23 3/8 23 5/8	20 4/8	5 5	Outagamie County	WI	Joe P. DeBruin	1991	14306
142 6/8	23 6/8 23 0/8	18 0/8	4 6	McLean County	IL	Eric B. Hill	1991	14306
142 6/8	22 6/8 22 2/8	17 4/8	5 5	Cavan Township	ONT	Mark J. Dymond	1991	14306
142 6/8	21 4/8 22 1/8	16 7/8	6 8	Ravalli County	MT	Melvin Harold Monson	1992	14306
142 6/8	24 3/8 24 7/8	19 6/8	4 5	Saunders County	NE	William D. Meyers	1992	14306
142 6/8	23 3/8 21 7/8	19 2/8	5 6	McLeod River	ALB	Shayne Wadlow	1992	14306
142 6/8	22 6/8 22 4/8	16 0/8	5 5	McCulloch County	TX	Cecil Carder	1992	14306
142 6/8	22 3/8 23 3/8	18 2/8	5 5	Licking County	OH	Orin Noyes	1992	14306
142 6/8	22 2/8 23 1/8	16 4/8	5 5	La Crosse County	WI	Barry Christenson	1993	14306
142 6/8	23 2/8 23 6/8	19 2/8	5 5	Darke County	OH	Dale L. Detro	1993	14306

506

WHITETAIL DEER (TYPICAL ANTLERS)

Minimum Score 125   Continued

SCORE	LENGTH OF R MAIN BEAM L	INSIDE SPREAD	NUMBER OF R POINTS L	AREA	STATE/ PROVINCE	HUNTER'S NAME	DATE	RANK
142 6/8	23 0/8	23 6/8	18 2/8	4	5	Green County	WI	Doug Cupp	1993	14306
142 6/8	21 1/8	23 5/8	17 2/8	5	5	New Castle County	DE	Bruce Pyle	1993	14306
142 6/8	24 4/8	25 5/8	17 6/8	4	6	St. Louis County	MO	Scott Leuthauser	1994	14306
142 6/8	25 1/8	25 6/8	22 2/8	4	4	Bucks County	PA	William A. Car	1994	14306
142 6/8	21 4/8	21 3/8	17 4/8	5	5	Franklin County	KS	Steven M. Hale	1994	14306
142 6/8	22 5/8	22 5/8	18 6/8	4	4	McHenry County	IL	Kenneth A. Spence	1994	14306
142 6/8	21 0/8	22 2/8	14 2/8	5	6	Portage County	WI	John Lane	1995	14306
142 6/8	15 4/8	27 6/8	20 2/8	7	7	Marion County	IA	James D. Pendroy	1995	14306
142 6/8	22 0/8	21 6/8	18 4/8	5	5	Dubuque County	IA	Adam W. Anglin	1995	14306
142 6/8	25 2/8	25 4/8	16 6/8	6	5	Franklin County	PA	Phares B. Witmer III	1995	14306
142 6/8	22 0/8	21 6/8	16 2/8	5	5	Polk County	IA	Nick Hildreth	1995	14306
142 6/8	22 1/8	22 1/8	17 4/8	5	5	Alexander County	IL	Brian Bard	1995	14306
142 6/8	22 5/8	22 5/8	17 7/8	6	6	Waukesha County	WI	Richard M. Wasielewski	1995	14306
142 6/8	24 1/8	23 3/8	20 2/8	5	4	Adair County	MO	Tom Drury	1996	14306
142 6/8	22 1/8	22 6/8	16 7/8	4	6	Stephenson County	IL	Calvin B. Hanson	1996	14306
142 6/8	27 1/8	26 3/8	23 5/8	5	5	Vinton County	OH	John Oberschlake	1996	14306
142 6/8	24 5/8	25 2/8	16 2/8	5	5	Fairfax County	VA	Bobby J. Gray	1996	14306
142 6/8	24 2/8	25 4/8	19 4/8	5	4	Jackson County	WI	Kenneth A. Olson	1996	14306
142 6/8	23 7/8	23 7/8	17 7/8	7	7	Brown County	IL	Ricky Bishop	1996	14306
142 6/8	24 0/8	22 4/8	15 2/8	5	5	Washington County	WI	David E. Witte	1996	14306
142 6/8	23 1/8	22 6/8	15 6/8	6	5	Columbia County	WI	Eric R. De Venecia	1997	14306
142 6/8	23 7/8	24 2/8	17 4/8	5	5	Ashtabula County	OH	Michael A. Candela	1997	14306
142 6/8	23 4/8	22 7/8	16 0/8	4	5	Houston County	MN	Peter Bonfe	1997	14306
142 6/8	25 6/8	24 4/8	18 6/8	6	5	Johnson County	IA	Jeff Jensen	1997	14306
142 6/8	23 3/8	22 5/8	20 1/8	5	5	Appanoose County	IA	Ralph Lane, Jr.	1997	14306
142 6/8	25 4/8	25 2/8	19 0/8	3	4	Howard County	MD	Mike Dunsmore	1998	14306
142 6/8	19 3/8	19 3/8	15 0/8	6	6	Tom Green County	TX	Ronnie Parsons	1998	14306
142 6/8	26 6/8	26 0/8	23 6/8	5	4	Lucas County	OH	Michael S. Pasztor	1998	14306
142 6/8	21 3/8	21 2/8	13 4/8	6	6	Pike County	IL	Brian Brochu	1998	14306
142 6/8	25 2/8	24 3/8	16 2/8	4	4	Todd County	KY	Mark A. Shanklin	1998	14306
142 6/8	22 6/8	23 4/8	19 0/8	6	5	Nemaha County	NE	Robert E. Plympton	1998	14306
142 6/8	22 2/8	21 6/8	19 6/8	7	7	Price County	WI	Bryan Kennedy	1998	14306
142 6/8	21 5/8	23 2/8	18 2/8	5	5	Harrison County	KY	Lyle T. Fryman	1999	14306
142 6/8	25 7/8	26 3/8	20 0/8	4	5	Clark County	KY	Paul W. Shelton	1999	14306
142 6/8	23 6/8	23 2/8	17 6/8	5	5	Dunn County	WI	David M. Jenson	1999	14306
142 6/8	23 6/8	22 5/8	16 2/8	5	5	Adams County	WI	Scott Wiedmeyer	1999	14306
142 6/8	22 0/8	21 5/8	17 6/8	6	5	Randolph County	IN	Jeremy W. Reynolds	1999	14306
142 6/8	22 3/8	22 3/8	17 3/8	6	5	Buena Vista County	IA	Dan D. Soellner	1999	14306
142 6/8	25 6/8	26 5/8	17 4/8	5	4	Howard County	MD	Paul D. Rick	1999	14306
142 6/8	22 5/8	22 4/8	17 4/8	5	5	Kenedy County	TX	Stephen L. Geller	1999	14306
142 6/8	25 1/8	25 2/8	18 0/8	5	5	Sangamon County	IL	Michael Aebel	1999	14306
142 6/8	23 3/8	23 0/8	21 0/8	5	5	McMullen County	TX	Peter Clifton Swenson	1999	14306
142 6/8	24 0/8	24 5/8	16 1/8	5	5	Terrell County	GA	Randy Bailey	2000	14306
142 6/8	26 0/8	24 2/8	17 6/8	5	5	Marquette County	WI	Lisa R. Steuck	2000	14306
142 6/8	24 2/8	22 4/8	18 4/8	4	4	Jefferson County	NE	Larry G. Lottman	2000	14306
142 6/8	25 1/8	23 5/8	21 4/8	4	4	Fayette County	OH	Rodney L. Garringer	2000	14306
142 6/8	24 7/8	26 2/8	18 0/8	5	5	Calhoun County	MI	Bryan L. Pollman	2000	14306
142 6/8	24 2/8	24 3/8	19 6/8	4	4	Macon County	IL	Tim Stemple	2000	14306
142 6/8	21 6/8	22 2/8	15 4/8	5	5	Ozaukee County	WI	Donald P. Mueller	2000	14306
142 6/8	25 6/8	23 6/8	15 4/8	5	6	Wayne County	NY	Doug Bowman	2000	14306
142 6/8	23 0/8	23 0/8	19 2/8	4	5	Clay County	WV	Jeremy Jones	2000	14306
142 6/8	24 1/8	24 4/8	16 4/8	5	6	Livingston County	MI	Gregg Remer	2000	14306
142 6/8	23 6/8	24 4/8	18 6/8	5	5	Rogers County	OK	Billy Coghill	2001	14306
142 6/8	23 6/8	23 2/8	18 6/8	5	7	Marquette County	WI	John Kurz	2001	14306
142 6/8	23 1/8	21 7/8	18 6/8	6	5	Marshall County	IL	Steve Holloway	2001	14306
142 6/8	23 6/8	23 6/8	16 4/8	6	5	Buffalo County	WI	Dean R. Dieckman	2001	14306
142 6/8	24 6/8	23 4/8	18 2/8	5	6	Murray County	GA	Michael Flood	2001	14306
142 6/8	25 0/8	23 6/8	17 4/8	5	4	Marion County	IN	Randy A. Bartels	2002	14306
142 6/8	22 0/8	22 6/8	18 6/8	5	5	Peoria County	IL	Todd DeGroot	2002	14306
142 6/8	22 7/8	21 4/8	18 3/8	6	5	Fulton County	IL	Dave Merry	2002	14306
142 6/8	26 4/8	25 4/8	15 6/8	5	6	Van Buren County	IA	Wally King	2002	14306
142 6/8	24 5/8	25 2/8	17 6/8	6	6	Licking County	OH	Carl A. Williams	2002	14306
142 6/8	22 4/8	22 0/8	17 6/8	5	5	Becker County	MN	Dane Gigstead	2003	14306
142 6/8	24 1/8	23 1/8	20 4/8	5	5	Knox County	OH	Derrick Palmer	2003	14306
*142 6/8	23 5/8	23 3/8	19 4/8	4	4	Douglas County	SD	Larry Wold	2003	14306
142 6/8	22 4/8	23 3/8	17 0/8	5	5	Winneshiek County	IA	Tim Everding	2003	14306
142 6/8	25 3/8	25 4/8	17 3/8	6	5	McPherson County	KS	Matthew Palmquist	2003	14306
142 6/8	21 2/8	21 1/8	15 2/8	5	5	Cass County	IL	Esh Gearhart	2003	14306
142 6/8	21 7/8	20 7/8	14 4/8	5	5	Hardin County	IA	Lincoln Eekhoff	2004	14306
142 6/8	23 3/8	23 7/8	18 6/8	5	5	Menominee County	WI	Raymond E. Creapeau	2004	14306
142 6/8	23 6/8	22 4/8	17 2/8	5	5	Calhoun County	MI	Joe Mocnik	2004	14306
142 6/8	22 4/8	22 7/8	18 2/8	5	5	Hocking County	OH	Michael McGlynn, Jr.	2004	14306
142 6/8	24 0/8	24 6/8	18 2/8	4	5	Jackson County	IA	Larry Galliart	2004	14306
142 6/8	24 4/8	24 7/8	17 3/8	6	7	Clay County	SD	Jeffrey J. Olson	2004	14306
142 6/8	21 7/8	21 6/8	17 4/8	5	5	Ramsey County	ND	Dale Schonauer	2005	14306
*142 6/8	23 1/8	23 2/8	18 2/8	5	5	Miami County	KS	Lonnie P. Gulley	2005	14306
142 6/8	24 2/8	24 5/8	21 2/8	5	5	Trumbull County	OH	Phillip D. Berg, Jr.	2005	14306
142 6/8	22 4/8	23 0/8	19 2/8	5	4	Jefferson County	KS	Michael K. Dunnaway	2005	14306
*142 6/8	22 1/8	24 0/8	18 4/8	5	5	White County	IL	Ben LeCroy	2005	14306
142 6/8	26 1/8	25 3/8	16 4/8	5	5	Union County	IL	La Rue Parr	2005	14306
142 6/8	23 4/8	23 4/8	17 1/8	5	9	Clarke County	IA	James Oswald	2005	14306
*142 6/8	21 7/8	22 6/8	15 0/8	6	6	Phillips County	AR	Joey Hopper	2005	14306
*142 6/8	24 0/8	24 1/8	17 4/8	5	5	Yazoo County	MS	Blair Rankin	2005	14306
142 6/8	25 2/8	25 0/8	18 6/8	5	5	Fulton County	GA	Kirk Crisler	2006	14306
142 6/8	25 3/8	27 0/8	17 3/8	6	4	Schuyler County	IL	Thomas J. Green	2006	14306
142 6/8	25 4/8	25 4/8	17 6/8	5	4	Fairfield County	OH	Ron Haynes	2006	14306
*142 6/8	24 0/8	24 3/8	18 4/8	4	5	Monroe County	WI	Todd Fahning	2006	14306
142 6/8	26 5/8	27 6/8	23 3/8	5	5	Highland County	OH	Jim Addington	2006	14306
142 6/8	22 0/8	25 5/8	19 0/8	6	4	Yuma County	CO	Dennis Miller	2006	14306
142 6/8	25 0/8	24 6/8	16 6/8	5	5	Buffalo County	WI	Gary Stutz	2007	14306
142 6/8	24 2/8	24 4/8	18 7/8	5	4	Swift County	MN	Justin Sanders	2007	14306
142 6/8	22 3/8	18 3/8	16 4/8	6	6	Sterling County	TX	Bill Potts	2007	14306
*142 6/8	24 1/8	24 7/8	14 7/8	6	4	Buffalo County	WI	Frank Jilot	2007	14306
*142 6/8	22 3/8	23 2/8	19 0/8	5	5	Eau Claire County	WI	Luke Wollenziehn	2007	14306
142 6/8	22 3/8	20 7/8	17 2/8	6	7	Van Buren County	IA	Dennis Bradley	2007	14306

WHITETAIL DEER (TYPICAL ANTLERS)

Minimum Score 125 — Continued

SCORE	LENGTH OF R MAIN BEAM L	INSIDE SPREAD	NUMBER OF R POINTS L	AREA	STATE/ PROVINCE	HUNTER'S NAME	DATE	RANK
*142 6/8	21 3/8 22 1/8	18 2/8	5 5	Daviess County	MO	Jonathan McGinness	2008	14306
*142 6/8	22 4/8 21 3/8	16 0/8	5 5	Scott County	IL	David Ward	2008	14306
142 6/8	26 5/8 26 2/8	17 4/8	4 4	Brown County	WI	Thomas D. Huempfner	2008	14306
142 6/8	23 4/8 23 6/8	18 2/8	5 5	Grant County	OK	Brent Hibbets	2008	14306
*142 6/8	24 3/8 24 5/8	17 0/8	5 4	Highland County	OH	Tom Peterson	2008	14306
*142 6/8	23 2/8 23 2/8	17 6/8	5 4	Jo Daviess County	IL	Dave Martinek	2008	14306
142 6/8	24 1/8 23 4/8	16 7/8	8 5	Bourbon County	KS	Mickey Parish	2008	14306
142 6/8	23 4/8 24 0/8	18 7/8	7 6	Otoe County	NE	Jason A. Swanson	2008	14306
142 6/8	21 6/8 21 7/8	18 0/8	6 5	Wilson County	KS	A. J. Lynch	2008	14306
142 6/8	25 1/8 26 0/8	20 1/8	8 6	Crawford County	WI	Gary Bald	2008	14306
*142 6/8	25 1/8 25 3/8	19 6/8	6 5	Concordia Parish	LA	Rodney Wiley	2009	14306
142 6/8	25 6/8 26 0/8	18 2/8	4 4	Erie County	NY	Robert Christopher	2009	14306
*142 6/8	22 6/8 22 6/8	18 6/8	5 6	Otter Tail County	MN	Michael Miller	2009	14306
*142 6/8	22 2/8 21 7/8	16 4/8	5 5	Fulton County	IL	Jeffery J. Hokanson	2009	14306
*142 6/8	23 2/8 22 5/8	21 4/8	4 4	Schuyler County	MO	Andrew C. May	2009	14306
*142 6/8	23 3/8 22 6/8	20 2/8	5 5	Kosciusko County	IN	Scott A. Amsden	2009	14306
*142 6/8	24 5/8 25 3/8	19 4/8	4 4	Hampden County	MA	James Janisieski	2009	14306
142 6/8	23 7/8 25 1/8	18 0/8	4 5	Niagara County	NY	Charles Jaenecke	2009	14306
142 5/8	24 2/8 22 7/8	15 5/8	5 5	Fleming County	KY	Dewey Miller	1976	14459
142 5/8	23 5/8 22 7/8	19 2/8	7 5	Boone County	IA	Harold Luke	1980	14459
142 5/8	22 2/8 22 3/8	18 5/8	5 5	Richland County	OH	Joey A. Garcia	1980	14459
142 5/8	22 0/8 22 2/8	16 7/8	5 5	Chase County	KS	Lanny Deering	1981	14459
142 5/8	25 6/8 25 4/8	16 4/8	4 6	Darke County	OH	Norbert D. Schlecty	1981	14459
142 5/8	22 5/8 22 2/8	18 1/8	6 6	Waukesha County	WI	Mike Edlebeck	1982	14459
142 5/8	24 7/8 24 1/8	18 1/8	5 5	Dane County	WI	Dean Stolen	1982	14459
142 5/8	24 0/8 24 2/8	20 3/8	5 5	Cochrane	ALB	Kenneth Bills	1982	14459
142 5/8	20 1/8 20 6/8	16 4/8	6 5	Simpson County	KY	Murrell Ray Knight	1984	14459
142 5/8	21 4/8 22 3/8	15 7/8	7 5	Pepin County	WI	James D. Williams	1984	14459
142 5/8	22 6/8 22 5/8	20 3/8	5 4	Berkshire County	MA	Richard Scorzafava	1985	14459
142 5/8	23 6/8 23 0/8	16 7/8	6 7	Stafford County	KS	Larry Hamby	1986	14459
142 5/8	24 0/8 24 0/8	20 0/8	6 5	Page County	IA	Chris Barton	1987	14459
142 5/8	22 5/8 23 6/8	16 3/8	6 8	Kossuth County	IA	Roger M. Batt	1987	14459
142 5/8	25 1/8 24 1/8	18 5/8	4 4	Westchester County	NY	Kenneth Martin	1987	14459
142 5/8	21 5/8 22 0/8	15 1/8	5 5	Will County	IL	Thomas J. Suggs	1987	14459
142 5/8	25 4/8 25 3/8	17 7/8	4 4	Jackson County	IL	Dan Young	1988	14459
142 5/8	23 1/8 20 4/8	18 7/8	5 5	Kalamazoo County	MI	Vern Kuipers	1988	14459
142 5/8	22 3/8 23 0/8	17 0/8	7 6	Fairfield County	OH	Dean J. Kiourtsis	1988	14459
142 5/8	25 3/8 24 5/8	19 1/8	5 5	Chickasaw County	IA	T. J. Colburn	1989	14459
142 5/8	26 6/8 26 4/8	20 5/8	4 3	Scotland County	MO	John Emerson	1989	14459
142 5/8	23 1/8 23 4/8	18 5/8	4 4	Parkland County	ALB	Sam Halabi	1990	14459
142 5/8	26 7/8 26 2/8	17 6/8	8 7	Martin County	KY	James W. Howard	1990	14459
142 5/8	23 6/8 23 3/8	19 0/8	5 5	Clark County	IL	Kenneth G. Geibel	1990	14459
142 5/8	22 0/8 23 0/8	16 0/8	6 5	Buffalo County	WI	Eric Matheson	1990	14459
142 5/8	22 6/8 22 4/8	16 7/8	6 7	Will County	IL	Joseph E. Voltolina	1990	14459
142 5/8	24 0/8 22 5/8	18 7/8	5 6	St. Joseph County	IN	Mike Ritter	1991	14459
142 5/8	23 5/8 24 5/8	18 0/8	4 4	Mission Creek	BC	Colin L. Fazan	1991	14459
142 5/8	23 3/8 23 1/8	18 0/8	6 5	Vilas County	WI	Phil Dreger	1991	14459
142 5/8	26 3/8 26 1/8	18 7/8	5 5	Louisa County	IA	Jeff Sindt	1991	14459
142 5/8	24 1/8 27 1/8	19 2/8	6 5	Cumberland County	IL	Lonnie Finks	1992	14459
142 5/8	22 4/8 23 1/8	16 1/8	5 5	Traill County	ND	Don Kluck	1992	14459
142 5/8	25 1/8 25 5/8	20 4/8	5 5	Pike County	OH	Lynn A. Henry	1992	14459
142 5/8	24 5/8 25 4/8	20 7/8	5 4	Brown County	IL	Jason Garthaus	1993	14459
142 5/8	24 1/8 24 7/8	20 1/8	6 6	Allegheny County	PA	Paul W. Zoller	1993	14459
142 5/8	24 6/8 24 5/8	22 7/8	4 4	Sauk County	WI	Timothy J. Terbilcox	1993	14459
142 5/8	22 5/8 22 3/8	16 7/8	5 5	La Crosse County	WI	James Pike	1993	14459
142 5/8	24 5/8 23 5/8	16 7/8	4 4	Goshen County	WY	Eddie Claypool	1993	14459
142 5/8	24 4/8 24 1/8	16 1/8	5 5	New Castle County	DE	Jeff Flanagan	1993	14459
142 5/8	22 4/8 21 6/8	18 6/8	6 5	Ross County	OH	Charles A. Hawkins	1994	14459
142 5/8	20 5/8 21 1/8	17 2/8	6 6	Clay County	IN	Doug Myers	1994	14459
142 5/8	24 0/8 23 3/8	17 6/8	7 6	Spokane County	WA	Mike Ambach	1994	14459
142 5/8	21 4/8 21 6/8	16 5/8	5 5	Pittsburg County	OK	Rick Pingleton	1995	14459
142 5/8	25 3/8 24 5/8	18 6/8	5 5	Bayfield County	WI	Gene Huettl	1995	14459
142 5/8	23 3/8 23 2/8	15 7/8	5 4	Nemaha County	KS	David Shumaker	1995	14459
142 5/8	23 4/8 22 0/8	19 5/8	5 5	Suffolk County	NY	John J. Gattuso	1995	14459
142 5/8	22 4/8 21 1/8	19 1/8	4 4	Worcester County	MA	Brian Archambeault	1995	14459
142 5/8	24 6/8 27 3/8	19 7/8	5 5	Jo Daviess County	IL	Jerry J. Smith	1995	14459
142 5/8	23 6/8 23 6/8	18 3/8	5 5	Shelby County	IL	Stephan Tripp	1996	14459
142 5/8	22 1/8 22 5/8	18 5/8	5 5	Montgomery County	AL	Price Bishop	1996	14459
142 5/8	25 5/8 24 6/8	19 5/8	6 6	Allegheny County	PA	Dale Fleck	1996	14459
142 5/8	24 4/8 24 4/8	17 1/8	5 5	Raleigh County	WV	Jimmy Barker	1997	14459
142 5/8	23 1/8 24 0/8	18 7/8	5 5	Jackson County	MI	Roger A. Dodt	1997	14459
142 5/8	24 4/8 23 4/8	18 3/8	4 5	Pike County	IL	Michael Mitale	1997	14459
142 5/8	25 2/8 24 4/8	16 3/8	4 4	Jackson County	MO	Jonathan McGinness	1997	14459
142 5/8	24 2/8 23 6/8	16 6/8	4 5	Appanoose County	IA	Bill Breeding	1997	14459
142 5/8	23 7/8 23 1/8	20 3/8	7 5	Hughes County	OK	Will F. Tobey	1997	14459
142 5/8	22 5/8 23 5/8	18 1/8	4 4	Winneshiek County	IA	Dean Miller	1997	14459
142 5/8	24 4/8 24 1/8	17 4/8	5 5	Lake County	IL	Tom Bobula	1998	14459
142 5/8	22 5/8 23 3/8	19 0/8	5 5	Van Buren County	IA	Lee Wittman	1998	14459
142 5/8	21 5/8 24 2/8	18 5/8	6 6	Grant County	WI	Herman Pockelwald	1999	14459
142 5/8	23 0/8 23 6/8	18 7/8	4 5	Sawyer County	WI	Lance Ewert	2000	14459
142 5/8	22 7/8 22 3/8	17 5/8	5 5	Hot Spring County	AR	Elgin A. Hamner III	2000	14459
142 5/8	23 2/8 23 3/8	19 6/8	4 4	Bay County	MI	Paul Atton	2000	14459
142 5/8	25 5/8 24 3/8	15 5/8	6 6	Pike County	IL	John Sobie	2000	14459
142 5/8	23 0/8 24 1/8	20 1/8	5 6	Buffalo County	WI	Kristine Brockman	2000	14459
142 5/8	22 7/8 24 1/8	18 1/8	4 4	Kiowa County	KS	Steve Atkinson	2000	14459
142 5/8	25 1/8 24 6/8	17 5/8	4 4	Noble County	IN	Timothy L. Gienger	2000	14459
142 5/8	25 1/8 24 5/8	17 1/8	4 4	Nowata County	OK	Robert Park	2000	14459
142 5/8	23 0/8 23 6/8	16 7/8	5 5	Portage County	OH	K. Michael Page	2000	14459
142 5/8	21 6/8 23 2/8	17 0/8	6 6	Butler County	OH	Mark Weingartner	2000	14459
142 5/8	24 3/8 24 7/8	16 1/8	5 5	Hartford County	CT	Donovan Valley	2001	14459
142 5/8	20 1/8 21 7/8	18 3/8	6 6	Franklin County	MO	David Nadler	2001	14459
142 5/8	24 1/8 24 2/8	16 3/8	5 5	Switzerland County	IN	Michael W. Oatman	2001	14459
142 5/8	23 3/8 23 3/8	18 5/8	5 5	Dearborn County	IN	Earl Baumann	2001	14459
142 5/8	23 1/8 23 0/8	17 5/8	5 5	Montgomery County	OH	Michael E. Alspaugh, Sr.	2001	14459
142 5/8	25 0/8 23 4/8	18 4/8	5 6	Belmont County	OH	Terry Duvall	2002	14459

WHITETAIL DEER (TYPICAL ANTLERS)

Minimum Score 125   Continued

SCORE	LENGTH OF R MAIN BEAM L	INSIDE SPREAD	NUMBER OF R POINTS L		AREA	STATE/ PROVINCE	HUNTER'S NAME	DATE	RANK
142 5/8	23 6/8	23 6/8	16 3/8	5	5	Cass County	MI	Kirt M. Ullig	2002	14459
142 5/8	24 3/8	24 0/8	16 7/8	4	4	Hamilton County	IL	Joseph Poole	2002	14459
142 5/8	23 1/8	23 0/8	17 2/8	6	5	Adair County	IA	Wayne Haas	2002	14459
142 5/8	22 5/8	23 1/8	17 1/8	5	5	Jackson County	MI	Andrew M. Kershaw	2003	14459
142 5/8	22 0/8	22 0/8	16 7/8	7	7	Callaway County	MO	Tim Atterberry	2003	14459
142 5/8	21 2/8	21 7/8	17 7/8	6	6	Calhoun County	IL	Brent R. Biller	2003	14459
142 5/8	25 3/8	26 6/8	19 5/8	4	4	Fulton County	IN	Dave Koch	2003	14459
*142 5/8	23 6/8	23 7/8	19 1/8	5	5	Clayton County	IA	Brian Oberfoell	2003	14459
142 5/8	25 2/8	23 3/8	17 7/8	4	4	Logan County	OH	Chad Best	2003	14459
142 5/8	23 3/8	22 2/8	16 1/8	6	4	Pierce County	WI	Charles R. Holland	2004	14459
*142 5/8	21 1/8	20 5/8	15 5/8	5	5	Lampasas County	TX	James L. Walker	2004	14459
*142 5/8	22 5/8	22 7/8	19 1/8	4	4	Mellette County	SD	Douglas E. Hofer	2004	14459
142 5/8	24 5/8	23 3/8	17 1/8	5	7	Cass County	MI	Chad J. Priebe	2004	14459
142 5/8	23 6/8	22 6/8	16 5/8	4	4	Champaign County	IL	Brian McClure	2004	14459
142 5/8	22 1/8	21 7/8	17 5/8	5	6	Taylor County	IA	Chris A. Burns	2004	14459
142 5/8	23 3/8	23 2/8	23 4/8	5	5	Holmes County	OH	C. Shane Donley	2004	14459
142 5/8	23 4/8	23 2/8	18 5/8	7	6	Goshen County	WY	Don B. Gaskin	2005	14459
*142 5/8	24 5/8	23 6/8	18 1/8	5	5	Hocking County	OH	Chuck Moneypenny	2005	14459
142 5/8	20 2/8	20 7/8	15 3/8	6	5	Washburn County	WI	Douglas G. Williams	2005	14459
142 5/8	24 5/8	23 1/8	19 3/8	5	5	Hancock County	IN	James D. Over	2005	14459
*142 5/8	24 5/8	24 5/8	16 6/8	6	7	Woodbury County	IA	Jon Johnson	2005	14459
*142 5/8	22 0/8	22 6/8	17 7/8	5	5	Franklin County	KY	Daryl W. Couch	2006	14459
*142 5/8	24 0/8	22 3/8	17 7/8	4	4	Dunn County	ND	Dean Hochhalter	2006	14459
142 5/8	22 4/8	22 2/8	15 2/8	5	7	Daviess County	IN	Raymond D. Raber	2006	14459
142 5/8	23 1/8	23 2/8	17 5/8	5	4	Butler County	KS	Brandon Hendrix	2006	14459
*142 5/8	23 4/8	23 1/8	14 4/8	7	6	Chase County	KS	Jim Weberry	2006	14459
*142 5/8	24 6/8	24 5/8	18 7/8	4	5	Wood County	WI	William Reimer	2006	14459
*142 5/8	26 0/8	25 0/8	19 0/8	5	5	Hardin County	IA	Roger Demiter	2006	14459
142 5/8	24 1/8	22 4/8	20 5/8	4	5	Suffolk County	NY	Andrew Conway	2006	14459
142 5/8	23 0/8	23 7/8	19 1/8	5	5	Kalamazoo County	MI	William J. Vlietstra	2007	14459
142 5/8	20 7/8	21 1/8	15 7/8	6	6	Wabasha County	MN	Brian Schroeder	2007	14459
142 5/8	22 1/8	21 7/8	17 3/8	5	5	McKenzie County	ND	Jocelyn Hugelen	2007	14459
*142 5/8	23 4/8	23 5/8	16 6/8	6	7	Cass County	IL	Randall Dyal	2007	14459
142 5/8	22 6/8	20 4/8	17 4/8	5	5	St. Joseph County	IN	Kenneth S. Solnoky, Jr.	2007	14459
142 5/8	23 4/8	21 2/8	16 3/8	5	5	Chippewa County	WI	Joshua Barnier	2007	14459
*142 5/8	23 7/8	23 6/8	13 7/8	7	6	Sullivan County	IN	Brian McCammon	2007	14459
142 5/8	25 0/8	24 3/8	16 1/8	6	5	Taylor County	IA	Todd Tobin	2007	14459
142 5/8	21 4/8	21 7/8	18 7/8	5	8	Wayne County	IA	Dave Shuey	2007	14459
142 5/8	25 0/8	24 4/8	17 7/8	5	6	Clayton County	IA	Craig A. Bries	2007	14459
142 5/8	24 3/8	24 6/8	20 2/8	5	5	Brown County	IN	Jensen E. Scott	2007	14459
142 5/8	24 0/8	23 5/8	18 2/8	6	6	Dodge County	WI	Eric Kuehn	2007	14459
142 5/8	22 5/8	22 2/8	16 5/8	5	5	Johnson County	IA	Reed Bleeker	2007	14459
142 5/8	22 3/8	21 5/8	14 3/8	5	6	Wyoming County	WV	Shad Rice	2007	14459
142 5/8	22 1/8	22 2/8	18 5/8	6	7	Washington County	MN	Patrick Ellias	2007	14459
142 5/8	24 5/8	22 4/8	16 1/8	4	5	Clermont County	OH	Mike Ingold	2008	14459
*142 5/8	21 4/8	21 7/8	16 1/8	5	6	Greene County	PA	Michael Effinger	2008	14459
142 5/8	24 7/8	23 5/8	19 5/8	4	5	Lawrence County	IL	John Barrick	2008	14459
142 5/8	22 5/8	21 5/8	19 2/8	5	6	Rock Island County	IL	Vernon Moon	2008	14459
*142 5/8	22 4/8	22 1/8	18 1/8	5	5	Armstrong County	PA	Doug Kolich	2008	14459
142 5/8	22 7/8	23 3/8	17 7/8	5	5	Athens County	OH	James R. Harper	2008	14459
142 5/8	21 0/8	20 4/8	15 5/8	5	5	Green Lake County	WI	Laurence W. Trotter II	2008	14459
142 5/8	23 2/8	23 0/8	17 7/8	5	5	Preble County	OH	Jeff Cornett	2008	14459
142 5/8	22 7/8	22 6/8	18 5/8	5	5	Portage County	WI	Chuck Jurgella	2008	14459
*142 5/8	22 7/8	23 3/8	14 1/8	5	6	Decatur County	IA	D. Jason Bollman	2008	14459
*142 5/8	25 4/8	25 1/8	21 7/8	4	4	Kendall County	IL	Todd M. Borgman	2009	14459
*142 5/8	22 5/8	23 4/8	17 5/8	7	5	Taylor County	WI	Brady A. Schmidt	2009	14459
142 5/8	22 7/8	23 2/8	17 1/8	6	6	Greenwood County	KS	Ray Penner	2009	14459
142 5/8	23 4/8	23 4/8	19 7/8	5	5	McDonough County	IL	Scott Wolford	2009	14459
142 5/8	22 6/8	22 7/8	14 7/8	5	5	Grenada County	MS	Al Hankins	2010	14459
142 4/8	22 5/8	22 4/8	19 0/8	5	5	Newton County	IN	Jim Manes	1963	14595
142 4/8	23 3/8	23 4/8	18 4/8	4	4	Winnebago County	IA	Duane Peterson	1966	14595
142 4/8	22 0/8	21 1/8	14 6/8	6	6	Dunn County	WI	John J. Logan	1970	14595
142 4/8	24 7/8	24 0/8	19 6/8	4	4	Ballard County	KY	Archie Jacobs	1977	14595
142 4/8	24 7/8	24 3/8	19 3/8	6	5	Jackson County	IL	Mark A. Bollman	1979	14595
142 4/8	23 7/8	22 6/8	17 0/8	5	5	Musselshell County	MT	Larry W. Ostermiller	1979	14595
142 4/8	24 2/8	24 3/8	20 6/8	5	5	Robertson County	KY	Glen Arnold	1981	14595
142 4/8	23 5/8	24 1/8	15 6/8	5	5	Treasure County	MT	Scott Brockway	1981	14595
142 4/8	21 0/8	20 6/8	16 3/8	5	6	Winona County	MN	Ron J. Parks	1981	14595
142 4/8	21 0/8	21 5/8	18 4/8	6	5	Jo Daviess County	IL	Kelly John Arnold	1981	14595
142 4/8	22 5/8	23 2/8	20 1/8	5	6	Murray County	MN	David Swanson	1983	14595
142 4/8	22 0/8	22 2/8	14 6/8	5	5	McKenzie County	ND	David Tofte	1983	14595
142 4/8	23 7/8	23 6/8	18 2/8	4	4	Bon Homme County	SD	Leon Somsen	1984	14595
142 4/8	20 4/8	20 4/8	16 0/8	5	5	McLean County	ND	Curt Radke	1985	14595
142 4/8	22 6/8	24 4/8	19 3/8	4	5	Lyon County	KS	Frank Mowdey	1986	14595
142 4/8	24 7/8	25 0/8	19 3/8	5	5	Vilas County	WI	David Jablonski	1987	14595
142 4/8	24 2/8	23 5/8	19 2/8	4	5	Jo Daviess County	IL	Brian Spillane	1988	14595
142 4/8	20 4/8	20 3/8	16 4/8	5	5	Camrose	ALB	Dave Gerber	1988	14595
142 4/8	25 4/8	25 6/8	17 5/8	5	5	Gallia County	OH	Alan Runyon	1988	14595
142 4/8	23 0/8	24 6/8	18 3/8	6	6	Kingman County	KS	Ed Laverentz	1988	14595
142 4/8	25 0/8	25 2/8	18 5/8	6	7	Bowman County	ND	Stan Chiras	1988	14595
142 4/8	24 0/8	24 2/8	20 4/8	5	7	Shawnee County	KS	Randy Hildreth	1989	14595
142 4/8	22 5/8	23 1/8	17 0/8	4	4	Crawford County	IL	Jim Sexton	1989	14595
142 4/8	22 4/8	21 4/8	17 0/8	4	6	Dakota County	MN	Joseph Butler	1989	14595
142 4/8	21 1/8	20 5/8	14 5/8	5	5	Hardin County	KY	Eugene Cotton	1990	14595
142 4/8	23 7/8	23 0/8	17 4/8	5	5	Vilas County	WI	Dick Mutsch	1990	14595
142 4/8	22 0/8	21 6/8	17 5/8	6	5	Adams County	WI	Mark Hoffman	1990	14595
142 4/8	22 6/8	23 7/8	18 0/8	4	4	De Kalb County	GA	Michael Flowers	1990	14595
142 4/8	24 3/8	24 5/8	18 6/8	5	5	Lincoln County	MO	Greg Grooms	1990	14595
142 4/8	21 2/8	22 6/8	16 6/8	6	5	Wilkin County	MN	Brad Buth	1991	14595
142 4/8	21 5/8	22 5/8	16 0/8	5	5	Mason County	IL	Jeff Heilman	1991	14595
142 4/8	25 0/8	26 0/8	20 0/8	4	5	Charlevoix County	MI	Thomas B. Bacon	1991	14595
142 4/8	23 2/8	21 6/8	16 4/8	5	5	Des Moines County	IA	Tom Lingenfelter	1991	14595
142 4/8	21 0/8	21 4/8	17 5/8	5	5	Shawnee County	KS	Daniel L. Amspacker	1991	14595
142 4/8	21 0/8	21 1/8	16 5/8	5	5	McHenry County	IL	Richard Tudor	1992	14595
142 4/8	25 0/8	24 0/8	19 4/8	4	4	Harrison County	MO	Scott Shoemate	1993	14595

509

WHITETAIL DEER (TYPICAL ANTLERS)

Minimum Score 125 — Continued

SCORE	LENGTH OF R MAIN BEAM L	INSIDE SPREAD	NUMBER OF R POINTS L	AREA	STATE/ PROVINCE	HUNTER'S NAME	DATE	RANK
142 4/8	24 6/8 24 2/8	14 5/8	6 6	Monroe County	MO	Todd Martens	1993	14595
142 4/8	23 3/8 22 0/8	14 4/8	5 5	Logan County	CO	Pete Lauer	1993	14595
142 4/8	22 6/8 22 7/8	15 6/8	5 5	Cottonwood County	MN	Jeff Radtke	1993	14595
142 4/8	21 2/8 22 2/8	16 2/8	5 5	Will County	IL	Jack Haviland	1994	14595
142 4/8	21 5/8 20 7/8	17 0/8	5 5	Polk County	WI	Kevin Jones	1994	14595
142 4/8	21 6/8 21 6/8	16 4/8	5 5	Rockland County	NY	Scott Sahlstrom	1994	14595
142 4/8	22 0/8 22 0/8	19 4/8	5 4	Passaic County	NJ	Erich Reuter	1995	14595
142 4/8	24 3/8 25 3/8	17 0/8	4 4	Rock County	WI	Cory Mielke	1995	14595
142 4/8	25 2/8 23 2/8	18 6/8	4 6	Fremont County	IA	Richard Delanty	1995	14595
142 4/8	21 5/8 21 1/8	16 2/8	5 5	Hand County	SD	Craig E. "Curly" Hargens	1995	14595
142 4/8	21 6/8 22 4/8	17 6/8	5 5	Lee County	IA	Robert Lane	1995	14595
142 4/8	23 4/8 23 5/8	16 6/8	5 5	Montgomery County	MS	Tony Arnold	1995	14595
142 4/8	23 6/8 23 6/8	16 4/8	7 6	Ross County	OH	Paggie Peters	1996	14595
142 4/8	23 6/8 23 7/8	18 2/8	4 4	Coffee County	GA	Scott Miller	1996	14595
142 4/8	22 5/8 22 5/8	16 3/8	7 6	Gallia County	OH	Robert E. Lee	1996	14595
142 4/8	21 2/8 21 2/8	18 0/8	6 6	Winneshiek County	IA	Duane C. Baumler	1996	14595
142 4/8	23 5/8 24 3/8	17 4/8	4 4	Peoria County	IL	Stan Parkerson	1996	14595
142 4/8	25 1/8 25 6/8	21 6/8	5 4	Buffalo County	WI	Tony Heil	1996	14595
142 4/8	24 2/8 23 0/8	19 4/8	4 5	Jo Daviess County	IL	Joseph G. Daube	1996	14595
142 4/8	23 6/8 24 4/8	20 3/8	5 5	Dimmit County	TX	Chuck Adams	1997	14595
142 4/8	22 2/8 22 2/8	17 0/8	6 7	Rusk County	WI	Stacy Volk	1997	14595
142 4/8	24 3/8 24 6/8	17 6/8	5 5	Jackson County	MO	George Dusselier	1997	14595
142 4/8	23 6/8 24 5/8	22 1/8	6 6	Bucks County	PA	Richard Franklin	1997	14595
142 4/8	26 4/8 27 0/8	20 4/8	4 4	Cowley County	KS	Loy D. Peters	1997	14595
142 4/8	21 4/8 21 5/8	18 0/8	5 5	Logan County	NE	James B. Meador	1997	14595
142 4/8	21 7/8 22 1/8	16 4/8	6 6	Wayne County	MI	Dennis A. Schramm	1997	14595
142 4/8	22 2/8 22 1/8	17 0/8	4 4	Prince Georges County	MD	Donald A. Molnar, Jr.	1997	14595
142 4/8	22 4/8 24 4/8	18 3/8	5 5	Scott County	IA	John Sailor	1997	14595
142 4/8	22 0/8 22 5/8	17 0/8	5 5	Washington County	KS	Delmer Wilgers	1997	14595
142 4/8	22 4/8 22 4/8	17 2/8	6 5	Ferry County	WA	Michael Cassaday	1998	14595
142 4/8	23 0/8 22 5/8	16 4/8	5 5	Langlade County	WI	Christopher Pownell	1998	14595
142 4/8	25 5/8 25 3/8	17 4/8	5 5	Coshocton County	OH	Troy Jones	1998	14595
142 4/8	22 6/8 23 2/8	15 6/8	5 5	Ashland County	WI	Jeff Steede	1998	14595
142 4/8	25 3/8 24 2/8	18 4/8	5 5	Chase County	KS	Scottie Dewayne Blair	1998	14595
142 4/8	21 0/8 21 4/8	18 4/8	5 5	Dubuque County	IA	Patrick J. Sweeney	1999	14595
142 4/8	23 6/8 22 1/8	17 6/8	5 5	Boone County	WV	James Prince	1999	14595
142 4/8	22 4/8 23 1/8	15 0/8	5 5	Wayne County	WV	Steven Karr	1999	14595
142 4/8	23 4/8 24 2/8	21 4/8	4 4	Rock County	WI	Mike Nanstad	2000	14595
142 4/8	24 4/8 24 7/8	15 2/8	6 6	Butler County	OH	Eric Davidson	2000	14595
142 4/8	24 4/8 23 5/8	17 2/8	4 5	Peoria County	IL	Tom Chadwick	2000	14595
142 4/8	25 2/8 26 0/8	18 5/8	6 5	Hennepin County	MN	Gary S. Kroells	2000	14595
142 4/8	25 5/8 25 0/8	17 0/8	4 4	Rock County	WI	Larry Keith	2000	14595
142 4/8	26 0/8 26 3/8	20 4/8	3 4	Lake County	IL	Gary Gardner	2000	14595
142 4/8	26 3/8 25 5/8	17 0/8	6 6	Venango County	PA	Terry Joseph Anderson	2000	14595
142 4/8	23 2/8 23 1/8	18 0/8	5 5	Iowa County	IA	Kevin McDonald	2000	14595
142 4/8	23 3/8 22 3/8	13 6/8	5 5	Green Lake County	WI	Edward D. Froelich	2000	14595
142 4/8	23 6/8 23 4/8	19 4/8	6 4	Sawyer County	WI	Greg Biskup	2000	14595
142 4/8	24 1/8 24 3/8	18 6/8	4 4	Clarke County	IA	Don Mealey	2000	14595
142 4/8	21 4/8 23 3/8	17 4/8	5 6	Pawnee County	NE	Michael G. Newlun	2000	14595
142 4/8	22 1/8 21 7/8	17 1/8	6 5	Cass County	NE	Robert Wright	2000	14595
142 4/8	24 2/8 24 5/8	20 2/8	5 5	Clay County	IA	Rick Petersen	2001	14595
142 4/8	21 0/8 20 4/8	15 6/8	5 5	Will County	IL	Robert Gaskin	2001	14595
142 4/8	24 4/8 24 1/8	18 4/8	5 5	Appanoose County	IA	Troy McGinnis	2001	14595
142 4/8	23 0/8 22 2/8	17 0/8	5 6	Ontario County	NY	Steve Payne	2001	14595
142 4/8	21 3/8 21 7/8	16 2/8	5 5	Clarke County	IA	Don Mealey	2001	14595
142 4/8	22 6/8 21 5/8	17 6/8	6 5	Trempealeau County	WI	David N. Andersen	2002	14595
142 4/8	25 1/8 19 0/8	20 2/8	5 5	Buffalo County	WI	Al R. Zerby	2002	14595
142 4/8	21 7/8 22 7/8	16 3/8	4 5	Kenedy County	TX	Marc Bartoskewitz	2002	14595
142 4/8	27 0/8 27 6/8	22 6/8	5 7	Crawford County	WI	Bill Wright	2002	14595
142 4/8	24 2/8 23 7/8	17 0/8	5 5	La Crosse County	WI	Michael Hess	2002	14595
142 4/8	21 5/8 22 5/8	17 2/8	6 5	Fayette County	IL	John Lotz	2002	14595
142 4/8	22 6/8 22 2/8	14 4/8	6 6	Knox County	OH	Les Harmeyer	2002	14595
142 4/8	22 6/8 22 1/8	18 2/8	5 6	Sauk County	WI	Allen M. Winecke	2003	14595
142 4/8	24 6/8 26 0/8	19 0/8	5 4	Talbot County	MD	Tara Quinn	2003	14595
142 4/8	23 2/8 23 1/8	19 2/8	5 5	Will County	IL	Andy L. Suligoy	2003	14595
*142 4/8	22 5/8 23 7/8	15 2/8	5 7	Jackson County	WI	Chuck Hutchens	2003	14595
142 4/8	24 0/8 26 0/8	19 1/8	5 5	Pottawatomie County	KS	Ronald D. Artzer	2003	14595
142 4/8	20 1/8 21 0/8	17 2/8	6 5	Page County	IA	Chris Barton	2003	14595
142 4/8	22 4/8 22 5/8	15 4/8	5 5	Kenedy County	TX	David Wylie	2003	14595
142 4/8	23 7/8 24 2/8	20 2/8	4 4	La Salle County	IL	Ron Wagner	2004	14595
142 4/8	25 0/8 24 2/8	18 2/8	5 5	Butler County	KY	Mike Sale	2004	14595
142 4/8	22 7/8 22 4/8	17 0/8	5 5	Itasca County	MN	Dieter Metzig	2004	14595
142 4/8	22 4/8 22 5/8	18 2/8	5 5	Sturgeon	ALB	Dan Hartley	2004	14595
142 4/8	22 3/8 20 5/8	16 7/8	5 6	Spink County	SD	Ron Miller	2004	14595
142 4/8	24 3/8 24 2/8	20 5/8	5 4	Trempealeau County	WI	Bobby E. Lince	2004	14595
142 4/8	21 0/8 19 6/8	14 6/8	7 6	Morrison County	MN	Kevin Read	2004	14595
*142 4/8	22 1/8 24 2/8	20 2/8	5 6	Grant County	ND	Alan Malm	2004	14595
142 4/8	23 1/8 24 0/8	17 1/8	5 6	Sawyer County	WI	Jeff Williamson	2004	14595
142 4/8	21 2/8 21 5/8	19 0/8	5 6	Columbia County	WI	Robert L. Wenger	2005	14595
142 4/8	23 2/8 23 6/8	16 4/8	5 5	Barron County	WI	Gordon Severude	2005	14595
142 4/8	23 4/8 21 6/8	16 2/8	5 5	Jefferson County	KS	Jeff Flynn	2005	14595
*142 4/8	23 1/8 24 2/8	19 2/8	4 4	Boone County	IL	Ryan B. Culvey	2005	14595
142 4/8	22 4/8 23 1/8	19 2/8	6 4	Kingsbury County	SD	Tyler Henriksen	2005	14595
142 4/8	23 2/8 23 3/8	16 4/8	4 4	Rice County	KS	Sandra L. Willems	2005	14595
142 4/8	21 4/8 20 6/8	15 4/8	5 5	Meeker County	MN	Joe Miller	2006	14595
142 4/8	24 2/8 23 3/8	17 2/8	7 6	Jackson County	MO	Chantz Brown	2006	14595
142 4/8	26 0/8 25 4/8	17 2/8	6 6	Jennings County	IN	Steve Ludlow	2006	14595
*142 4/8	23 1/8 21 7/8	15 4/8	5 5	Jones County	SD	Dusty Carroll	2006	14595
142 4/8	24 1/8 24 0/8	20 2/8	5 5	Bucks County	PA	Steve A. Boccella	2006	14595
142 4/8	24 0/8 23 6/8	17 3/8	6 5	Wyoming County	NY	Daniel O'Connor	2006	14595
142 4/8	24 1/8 22 4/8	18 2/8	6 5	Brown County	WI	Michael R. Zirbel	2006	14595
142 4/8	25 3/8 26 1/8	17 2/8	5 4	Monmouth County	NJ	Conover White	2006	14595
*142 4/8	24 0/8 23 3/8	17 2/8	4 4	Fayette County	TN	Jimmy Cotham	2006	14595
142 4/8	20 2/8 22 0/8	18 2/8	5 5	Henderson County	IL	Ray Watts	2007	14595
142 4/8	22 4/8 23 5/8	16 3/8	7 5	Portage County	WI	Terry Craig	2007	14595

WHITETAIL DEER (TYPICAL ANTLERS)

Minimum Score 125 — Continued

SCORE	LENGTH OF R MAIN BEAM L	INSIDE SPREAD	NUMBER OF R POINTS L	AREA	STATE/ PROVINCE	HUNTER'S NAME	DATE	RANK
*142 4/8	24 6/8 25 5/8	16 6/8	4 5	Randall County	TX	Brandon Ray	2007	14595
142 4/8	20 1/8 21 5/8	16 6/8	7 6	Saskatoon Mtn.	ALB	Brent Watson	2007	14595
*142 4/8	23 6/8 23 3/8	18 2/8	6 7	Lorain County	OH	Steven D. Reinhold	2007	14595
*142 4/8	22 4/8 22 3/8	17 7/8	7 7	Linn County	MO	Darren Shaw	2007	14595
142 4/8	25 1/8 25 3/8	15 2/8	5 5	Grant County	NE	David Peters	2007	14595
142 4/8	23 7/8 23 6/8	18 6/8	5 5	Huron County	MI	Timothy J. Hatch	2007	14595
142 4/8	23 1/8 23 0/8	16 0/8	6 10	Benton County	MO	Brian K. Bell	2008	14595
*142 4/8	24 1/8 23 1/8	17 5/8	4 8	Worcester County	MA	Jeff D'Amico	2008	14595
142 4/8	21 5/8 21 1/8	15 6/8	5 5	Clay County	MO	Christopher L. Lein	2008	14595
142 4/8	21 6/8 21 7/8	18 6/8	5 5	Harrison County	OH	Ben L. Nastal	2008	14595
*142 4/8	24 6/8 25 4/8	21 4/8	5 5	Sullivan County	IN	Brian A. McCammon	2008	14595
142 4/8	24 1/8 24 5/8	16 0/8	4 5	Waupaca County	WI	John W. Miller	2008	14595
142 4/8	23 3/8 23 1/8	18 0/8	5 5	Parke County	IN	Jeffrey E. Wilson	2008	14595
142 4/8	22 1/8 24 0/8	14 2/8	5 5	Steuben County	IN	Robert Harris	2008	14595
142 4/8	24 2/8 24 7/8	16 6/8	4 6	Decatur County	IA	Adam Wamsher	2008	14595
142 4/8	21 3/8 23 0/8	20 4/8	5 7	La Porte County	IN	Darryl Jones	2009	14595
142 4/8	22 7/8 21 7/8	16 2/8	6 7	Powder River County	MT	Jeffrey A. Noble	2009	14595
142 4/8	23 3/8 23 3/8	18 4/8	5 5	Burke County	GA	Brian Josey	2009	14595
142 4/8	25 7/8 25 0/8	17 7/8	5 9	Lake County	MN	Randall J. Bowe	2009	14595
*142 4/8	22 3/8 22 5/8	15 5/8	4 5	Marshall County	KY	Harley Reese Johnson	2009	14595
142 4/8	22 2/8 22 7/8	15 6/8	5 5	Lucas County	IA	Todd Michael Johnston	2009	14595
142 4/8	23 3/8 22 3/8	18 2/8	5 5	Jefferson County	NE	Nick Hahn	2009	14595
*142 4/8	23 1/8 23 4/8	18 3/8	5 6	Dane County	WI	Jeremy Grabandt	2009	14595
142 3/8	25 4/8 24 3/8	20 7/8	4 5	Mercer County	NJ	John K. Deveney	1975	14749
142 3/8	21 5/8 21 5/8	15 1/8	5 5	Wapello County	IA	Larry Terrell	1977	14749
142 3/8	23 4/8 22 4/8	18 1/8	5 5	Jersey County	IL	Jerry Cover	1979	14749
142 3/8	22 0/8 21 6/8	16 7/8	5 4	Henry County	VA	Mike Weaver	1980	14749
142 3/8	21 1/8 24 4/8	20 4/8	6 6	St. Charles County	MO	Edward J. Davidson	1980	14749
142 3/8	22 5/8 22 0/8	18 1/8	5 5	Washtenaw County	MI	Philip John Maly	1983	14749
142 3/8	23 4/8 23 6/8	17 3/8	4 4	Champaign County	IL	Robert E. Mabry	1983	14749
142 3/8	21 4/8 22 5/8	17 5/8	6 7	Barton County	KS	Craig Doll	1984	14749
142 3/8	20 6/8 21 0/8	17 5/8	5 5	Hardin County	TX	Mike Allen	1985	14749
142 3/8	24 2/8 26 5/8	16 1/8	4 4	Wright County	MN	Donald J. Emons	1985	14749
142 3/8	20 0/8 19 5/8	19 3/8	5 5	Shelby County	MO	Willard Otto	1985	14749
142 3/8	24 6/8 23 5/8	19 1/8	4 4	Bremer County	IA	Dave Sullivan	1986	14749
142 3/8	22 2/8 22 4/8	16 1/8	7 5	Wilson County	KS	Keith Jabben	1986	14749
142 3/8	25 5/8 26 4/8	19 7/8	4 4	Benton County	IA	Ted Walton	1986	14749
142 3/8	23 2/8 24 5/8	17 1/8	5 5	Muhlenberg County	KY	Kent Rhoads	1987	14749
142 3/8	24 3/8 24 6/8	17 3/8	4 4	Kent County	MI	Frank J. Tusch	1987	14749
142 3/8	22 6/8 25 2/8	15 6/8	5 6	Cumberland County	KY	Michael Groce	1987	14749
142 3/8	20 4/8 20 3/8	17 0/8	6 6	Kenedy County	TX	Cal Adger	1988	14749
142 3/8	22 4/8 22 4/8	17 3/8	5 5	St. Charles County	MO	Marty Marler	1988	14749
142 3/8	23 0/8 24 2/8	16 5/8	5 6	Iron County	WI	Robert Peltonen	1988	14749
142 3/8	23 2/8 23 2/8	17 2/8	8 6	Peoria County	IL	Larry Oppe	1988	14749
142 3/8	22 6/8 24 6/8	18 2/8	6 6	Fairfield County	CT	Mitchell R. Ziemba	1988	14749
142 3/8	23 3/8 23 2/8	16 1/8	4 4	Meade County	SD	Frank E. Virchow	1989	14749
142 3/8	21 6/8 21 5/8	16 3/8	8 6	Osage County	KS	Mike VandeVord	1989	14749
142 3/8	24 4/8 25 1/8	18 3/8	5 5	Knox County	IL	Brad Wunder	1990	14749
142 3/8	22 5/8 23 2/8	16 3/8	5 5	Henderson County	TN	Pat Davis	1990	14749
142 3/8	21 4/8 22 3/8	19 1/8	4 5	Monona County	IA	Patrick Salmen	1990	14749
142 3/8	23 2/8 23 5/8	13 2/8	7 9	Allegheny County	PA	Paul W. Zoller	1991	14749
142 3/8	24 5/8 24 4/8	16 6/8	7 7	De Witt County	IL	Jack Bray	1991	14749
142 3/8	25 5/8 25 5/8	19 7/8	4 4	Hampshire County	MA	Eric Jalque	1991	14749
142 3/8	22 4/8 22 7/8	16 7/8	4 5	Comal County	TX	Jim Butcher	1991	14749
142 3/8	25 0/8 25 7/8	14 6/8	5 5	Cumberland County	NJ	Bob Eisele	1992	14749
142 3/8	23 6/8 22 5/8	17 5/8	4 4	St. Croix County	WI	Bruce R. Guck	1992	14749
142 3/8	22 2/8 21 4/8	15 5/8	6 6	Kenosha County	WI	John R. Griffin	1992	14749
142 3/8	22 1/8 22 0/8	16 7/8	6 5	Lincoln County	NE	Dave Hinton	1993	14749
142 3/8	24 3/8 25 2/8	21 6/8	6 8	Wilkin County	MN	Dave Balken	1993	14749
142 3/8	23 1/8 23 3/8	17 3/8	3 4	Yuma County	CO	Alan White	1993	14749
142 3/8	23 2/8 23 2/8	18 7/8	5 5	McHenry County	IL	Norton Baum	1993	14749
142 3/8	20 7/8 21 3/8	16 2/8	6 6	Fayette County	WV	Bryan Berry	1993	14749
142 3/8	27 5/8 27 1/8	20 1/8	9 6	Guernsey County	OH	D. Keith Kinney	1994	14749
142 3/8	22 7/8 22 2/8	14 7/8	7 6	Marion County	MO	John Boskovich	1994	14749
142 3/8	21 4/8 21 7/8	17 1/8	5 5	La Salle County	IL	Brian G. Dobberke	1994	14749
142 3/8	21 4/8 22 6/8	18 5/8	5 5	Jackson County	MO	Jeff Estes	1994	14749
142 3/8	24 5/8 24 0/8	22 3/8	4 4	Hillsborough County	NH	Bill Helstein	1994	14749
142 3/8	23 6/8 25 3/8	18 3/8	4 4	Logan County	WV	Tom Green	1994	14749
142 3/8	24 2/8 24 2/8	18 1/8	5 5	Stark County	IL	Gary Krause	1995	14749
142 3/8	21 1/8 22 4/8	20 5/8	6 6	Osage County	OK	Donnie Gabbard	1995	14749
142 3/8	22 4/8 22 6/8	16 3/8	5 5	Cayuga County	NY	Terry Van Wie	1995	14749
142 3/8	23 6/8 24 0/8	18 6/8	4 5	Tazewell County	IL	Andy Payne	1996	14749
142 3/8	23 1/8 24 1/8	18 5/8	5 5	Warren County	IA	Mike Schaefer	1996	14749
142 3/8	22 3/8 23 0/8	20 5/8	5 5	McHenry County	IL	Donald R. Hanrahan	1996	14749
142 3/8	25 3/8 25 1/8	20 3/8	5 4	Clark County	WI	Curt D. Zielke	1996	14749
142 3/8	22 5/8 21 6/8	17 1/8	5 5	Coles County	IL	Morris L. Parr	1996	14749
142 3/8	23 3/8 24 6/8	16 5/8	4 4	Marion County	IN	Dan Esterline	1996	14749
142 3/8	22 0/8 21 6/8	17 3/8	4 4	McHenry County	IL	Brent A. Smith	1996	14749
142 3/8	22 7/8 22 5/8	15 7/8	5 5	Boundary County	ID	Kenton Clairmont	1997	14749
142 3/8	22 4/8 23 0/8	18 7/8	6 5	Buffalo County	WI	Bradley H. Goulet	1997	14749
142 3/8	24 0/8 22 7/8	22 5/8	5 7	Spiritwood	SAS	Lizette Lohan	1997	14749
142 3/8	24 0/8 24 0/8	16 2/8	6 5	Eau Claire County	WI	Scott Kunz	1997	14749
142 3/8	22 7/8 23 2/8	19 2/8	6 5	McHenry County	IL	Steven Beda	1997	14749
142 3/8	22 4/8 22 6/8	16 3/8	5 5	Burnett County	WI	Michael G. Washburn	1997	14749
142 3/8	24 4/8 25 2/8	18 2/8	6 6	Putnam County	MO	John Freihaut	1997	14749
142 3/8	21 3/8 20 5/8	18 4/8	6 6	Allegheny County	PA	Charles LaBernz	1997	14749
142 3/8	21 3/8 22 1/8	14 7/8	6 5	Madison County	MT	Jim Kennedy	1998	14749
142 3/8	23 1/8 23 3/8	15 3/8	5 5	Buchanan County	MO	David Bryan	1998	14749
142 3/8	21 1/8 21 1/8	16 5/8	5 5	Polk County	WI	Ron Ekstrand	1998	14749
142 3/8	23 0/8 22 4/8	18 3/8	5 5	New Haven County	CT	Stephen A. Marino	1998	14749
142 3/8	23 3/8 23 1/8	18 3/8	5 5	St. Croix County	WI	Bryn L. Briesemeister	1998	14749
142 3/8	24 4/8 23 6/8	17 3/8	5 5	Montmorency County	MI	James Kvasnovsky	1998	14749
142 3/8	23 5/8 23 5/8	23 5/8	4 4	Suffolk County	NY	Stephen Haufsk	1998	14749
142 3/8	24 7/8 24 0/8	19 7/8	4 5	Butler County	KY	Lloyd D. Washer	1999	14749
142 3/8	22 6/8 21 4/8	18 4/8	7 5	Price County	WI	Vicki Lemke	1999	14749

WHITETAIL DEER (TYPICAL ANTLERS)

Minimum Score 125 — Continued

SCORE	LENGTH OF R MAIN BEAM L	INSIDE SPREAD	NUMBER OF R POINTS L		AREA	STATE/PROVINCE	HUNTER'S NAME	DATE	RANK
142 3/8	22 6/8 22 5/8	22 1/8	5	5	Jackson County	MI	Marlin J. Winchell	1999	14749
142 3/8	22 4/8 22 5/8	16 7/8	5	5	Buffalo County	WI	Dave Fredrickson	1999	14749
142 3/8	26 5/8 26 1/8	17 7/8	4	4	Meigs County	OH	Jeffrey T. Mardis	1999	14749
142 3/8	26 0/8 26 2/8	18 5/8	4	4	Osage County	OK	Jimmy Russell	1999	14749
142 3/8	21 3/8 22 0/8	17 5/8	5	5	Sioux County	NE	John Wietecha	2000	14749
142 3/8	23 5/8 23 7/8	16 3/8	5	6	Ashland County	WI	Randy Wayerski	2000	14749
142 3/8	22 0/8 22 7/8	18 1/8	5	7	Allegheny County	PA	Gary J. Snyder	2000	14749
142 3/8	25 0/8 23 4/8	19 5/8	5	4	Wabaunsee County	KS	David Bedore	2000	14749
142 3/8	22 5/8 22 5/8	16 3/8	6	7	Sauk County	WI	Kurt R. Muchow	2000	14749
142 3/8	23 6/8 23 6/8	20 1/8	5	6	Warren County	IA	Gene Evans	2000	14749
142 3/8	22 4/8 22 3/8	14 7/8	5	5	Van Buren County	IA	Ernie Merydith	2000	14749
142 3/8	21 7/8 21 2/8	18 0/8	8	5	Washburn County	WI	Jim Gobel	2001	14749
142 3/8	23 2/8 21 6/8	16 7/8	5	5	Dane County	WI	Charles A. Bollig	2001	14749
142 3/8	21 1/8 22 6/8	16 0/8	5	6	Allegheny County	PA	Thomas Hagner	2001	14749
142 3/8	22 6/8 22 3/8	15 5/8	4	4	Kingman County	KS	Jimmy Montgomery	2001	14749
142 3/8	22 4/8 21 5/8	18 1/8	6	5	Lafayette County	WI	Todd Hanson	2001	14749
142 3/8	21 7/8 21 5/8	16 6/8	6	5	Dubuque County	IA	Robert Mace	2001	14749
142 3/8	20 0/8 20 0/8	16 1/8	5	6	McHenry County	IL	Lonny Neil Black	2001	14749
142 3/8	22 1/8 21 3/8	16 7/8	4	5	Owen County	IN	Cody Snodgrass	2001	14749
142 3/8	22 3/8 21 7/8	16 1/8	4	4	Cloud County	KS	Steve Snow	2001	14749
142 3/8	25 2/8 24 7/8	17 4/8	5	6	Issaquena County	MS	Tom I. Alexander	2001	14749
142 3/8	21 3/8 21 0/8	15 7/8	5	5	Meigs County	OH	Justin S. Brewer	2002	14749
142 3/8	23 1/8 23 7/8	15 2/8	5	6	Durham County	NC	Dan Glosson	2002	14749
142 3/8	25 2/8 25 2/8	18 3/8	5	5	Outagamie County	WI	Jason Van Handel	2002	14749
142 3/8	23 3/8 23 5/8	17 1/8	5	5	Schuyler County	IL	Mark A. Sargent	2002	14749
142 3/8	24 6/8 24 3/8	18 1/8	4	4	Montgomery County	IN	Michael L. Hufford	2002	14749
*142 3/8	24 0/8 23 0/8	18 7/8	4	4	Cherokee County	KS	Ted Shinn	2002	14749
142 3/8	24 4/8 23 4/8	20 3/8	5	5	Montgomery County	MD	Lothar Weber	2002	14749
142 3/8	22 2/8 22 3/8	15 6/8	5	7	Hopkins County	KY	Greg Bonecutter, Sr.	2003	14749
142 3/8	23 7/8 24 5/8	19 1/8	6	5	Carroll County	NH	Dave Guyer, Jr.	2003	14749
142 3/8	26 6/8 25 2/8	19 1/8	5	5	Switzerland County	IN	Douglas Acra	2003	14749
142 3/8	21 0/8 21 5/8	17 5/8	4	4	Nemaha County	NE	Larry Goertz	2003	14749
142 3/8	25 0/8 24 6/8	15 7/8	4	4	Burlington County	NJ	Paul Bogdan	2003	14749
142 3/8	22 4/8 22 7/8	18 5/8	4	4	Wyoming County	WV	Phillip Paynter	2003	14749
142 3/8	22 6/8 22 4/8	17 1/8	5	5	Steuben County	NY	Donald W. Heerdt	2003	14749
142 3/8	24 2/8 24 0/8	19 7/8	5	5	Ontario County	NY	Stephen W. Doudt	2003	14749
142 3/8	24 6/8 23 4/8	18 1/8	5	4	Miami County	IN	Kyle A. Tolliver	2003	14749
142 3/8	24 5/8 24 2/8	21 3/8	5	5	Ozaukee County	WI	Eric Lehner	2003	14749
142 3/8	24 2/8 22 4/8	19 3/8	5	5	Fairfield County	CT	Dave Booth	2003	14749
142 3/8	24 7/8 25 3/8	18 7/8	4	4	Washington County	MN	Michael Gross	2003	14749
*142 3/8	23 5/8 23 6/8	19 3/8	7	5	Will County	IL	Ron Zavesky	2004	14749
142 3/8	23 1/8 22 3/8	15 5/8	5	5	Fillmore County	MN	Mike Blees	2004	14749
142 3/8	23 4/8 22 5/8	18 7/8	5	5	Marathon County	WI	Robert Peskie	2004	14749
142 3/8	23 5/8 24 4/8	18 7/8	5	6	Brown County	OH	Greg Gavin	2004	14749
142 3/8	22 3/8 23 6/8	17 7/8	5	5	McLean County	IL	Mark Talaski	2004	14749
142 3/8	24 5/8 25 0/8	16 5/8	4	4	Grayson County	KY	Jeffrey Scott Yount	2004	14749
*142 3/8	24 0/8 24 0/8	18 1/8	7	5	Jackson County	MI	Rock W. Soles	2004	14749
*142 3/8	22 3/8 21 3/8	16 7/8	5	5	Columbia County	WI	Jeff A. Rhodes	2004	14749
142 3/8	23 2/8 24 2/8	19 3/8	5	4	Will County	IL	Greg Humphrey	2004	14749
142 3/8	23 6/8 23 4/8	18 4/8	5	6	Barber County	KS	Bill Klansek	2004	14749
142 3/8	20 1/8 20 2/8	15 5/8	5	5	Pike County	IL	Darrell Nichols	2004	14749
*142 3/8	20 4/8 20 3/8	16 1/8	5	7	Kidder County	ND	Ben Buntrock	2005	14749
*142 3/8	25 5/8 23 6/8	18 1/8	5	5	Forsyth County	NC	George Raymond Drawdy	2005	14749
142 3/8	22 7/8 22 4/8	15 7/8	4	4	Trempealeau County	WI	Adam Pronschinske	2005	14749
142 3/8	24 0/8 25 0/8	17 5/8	5	5	Isanti County	MN	Brandon Bistedeau	2005	14749
*142 3/8	21 7/8 20 6/8	19 3/8	5	5	Kane County	IL	Mike Bombardiere	2005	14749
142 3/8	24 4/8 22 6/8	19 1/8	5	5	Fulton County	IL	Norman B. Gorsuch	2005	14749
*142 3/8	24 3/8 24 3/8	18 5/8	5	6	Linn County	MO	Chris Forster	2005	14749
142 3/8	21 2/8 21 7/8	17 3/8	5	5	Allen County	OH	Dave Newland	2005	14749
142 3/8	21 4/8 20 5/8	18 0/8	6	6	Monmouth County	NJ	Brian Baum	2005	14749
142 3/8	24 0/8 25 2/8	18 1/8	4	5	Polk County	WI	Jason Kerkow	2006	14749
142 3/8	26 0/8 24 7/8	19 1/8	6	7	Worth County	MO	Mark Sander	2006	14749
*142 3/8	22 3/8 22 0/8	16 5/8	5	5	Washington County	MN	Joseph Ferguson	2006	14749
142 3/8	24 4/8 23 1/8	17 5/8	4	4	Pulaski County	IN	Gerald Sheperd	2006	14749
142 3/8	22 2/8 21 4/8	19 1/8	5	5	Clark County	MO	Kyle Zinnert	2006	14749
142 3/8	23 5/8 25 0/8	17 7/8	6	5	Fairfield County	OH	Andrew L. Cherryhomes	2006	14749
*142 3/8	20 1/8 21 0/8	15 5/8	7	7	Carter County	OK	J. Scott Stedman	2006	14749
142 3/8	22 3/8 20 2/8	18 3/8	5	6	Snyder County	PA	Jason W. Weller	2007	14749
*142 3/8	21 6/8 22 1/8	20 5/8	6	5	Dodge County	WI	Chris Friess	2007	14749
142 3/8	24 6/8 22 1/8	19 7/8	7	7	Franklin County	KS	Heath Powers	2007	14749
142 3/8	24 2/8 22 5/8	14 7/8	6	5	Carroll County	MS	Chris Covington	2007	14749
142 3/8	22 7/8 23 2/8	17 7/8	4	4	Jay County	IN	Kip W. VanSkyock	2008	14749
*142 3/8	22 6/8 24 6/8	17 2/8	5	5	Whitley County	IN	Tony A. Hill	2008	14749
*142 3/8	23 2/8 23 3/8	14 7/8	6	6	Stokes County	NC	Timothy Joe Watkins	2008	14749
*142 3/8	24 0/8 23 0/8	19 1/8	4	4	Polk County	WI	Jeff Holdt	2008	14749
142 3/8	27 3/8 26 1/8	16 6/8	5	5	Schuyler County	IL	Steven Rinckey	2008	14749
142 3/8	24 2/8 24 0/8	16 2/8	4	5	Union County	IA	Clayton R. Bodoh, Jr.	2008	14749
142 3/8	21 4/8 21 2/8	15 2/8	6	5	Waupaca County	WI	Adam J. Lorge	2008	14749
142 3/8	25 0/8 24 6/8	18 6/8	5	6	Harper County	KS	Shawn Baker	2008	14749
*142 3/8	23 5/8 23 6/8	16 5/8	5	5	Licking County	OH	Stephen Pomerleau	2008	14749
*142 3/8	24 2/8 24 2/8	19 1/8	5	5	Chautauqua County	KS	Timothy Broughton	2008	14749
142 3/8	23 0/8 22 2/8	19 3/8	6	6	Comanche County	KS	Frank G. Hood	2008	14749
*142 3/8	24 7/8 24 7/8	18 3/8	5	6	Garrard County	KY	Bradley W.	2008	14749
142 3/8	26 1/8 25 3/8	20 3/8	4	4	Ogle County	IL	Douglas P. McNames	2009	14749
142 3/8	23 2/8 23 5/8	15 7/8	4	4	Worth County	GA	Brian McClure	2009	14749
*142 3/8	23 2/8 23 5/8	17 4/8	5	6	Rock Island County	IL	Phillip E. Blunt	2009	14749
142 3/8	26 2/8 25 0/8	22 1/8	4	4	Lafayette County	WI	Russell Sharp	2009	14749
142 3/8	25 5/8 26 2/8	18 4/8	6	8	Jackson County	WI	Thomas J. Zdrojewski	2009	14749
*142 3/8	23 7/8 23 7/8	17 5/8	4	4	Fulton County	IN	Jodi M. Mikesell	2009	14749
142 3/8	21 5/8 22 1/8	13 6/8	6	6	Llano County	TX	Kyle Maruska	2009	14749
*142 3/8	24 0/8 24 4/8	19 3/8	5	5	Hall County	GA	Marty Jarrard	2010	14749
142 3/8	22 5/8 23 4/8	17 5/8	5	7	Ionia County	MI	Andrew C. VanDeusen	2010	14749
142 2/8	23 3/8 24 0/8	20 0/8	4	5	McLean County	ND	Robert Loftin	1959	14913
142 2/8	23 2/8 22 6/8	17 6/8	5	6	Grant County	WI	Bob Woods	1962	14913
142 2/8	21 1/8 22 2/8	18 1/8	6	4	Morrison County	MN	Dale Nieters	1971	14913

WHITETAIL DEER (TYPICAL ANTLERS)

Minimum Score 125 — Continued

SCORE	R MAIN BEAM L	INSIDE SPREAD	R POINTS L		AREA	STATE/PROVINCE	HUNTER'S NAME	DATE	RANK
142 2/8	21 2/8 21 1/8	17 1/8	6	5	Sabine County	TX	Norman D. Davis	1972	14913
142 2/8	24 3/8 23 7/8	19 6/8	4	4	Gallatin County	KY	Thomas W. Roberts	1976	14913
142 2/8	24 1/8 24 1/8	17 0/8	6	5	Le Sueur County	MN	Gene Solyntjes	1976	14913
142 2/8	27 3/8 28 5/8	19 6/8	4	5	Harrison County	OH	Joe Cola	1976	14913
142 2/8	22 4/8 23 6/8	19 0/8	7	5	Jones County	IA	Donald Bohlken	1978	14913
142 2/8	21 7/8 21 0/8	17 0/8	6	6	Dodge County	MN	Myles Keller	1980	14913
142 2/8	21 1/8 20 3/8	18 2/8	5	5	Edgar County	IL	Rory Steidl	1983	14913
142 2/8	24 7/8 24 3/8	21 4/8	5	5	Jackson County	MI	Russell P. Blair	1983	14913
142 2/8	22 7/8 24 5/8	18 0/8	5	5	Buffalo County	WI	Patrick Myers	1985	14913
142 2/8	23 5/8 26 1/8	18 3/8	5	6	Eau Claire County	WI	Kenneth A. Sweeny	1985	14913
142 2/8	21 4/8 22 0/8	18 4/8	5	5	Lake County	IL	Robert K. Lapacek	1986	14913
142 2/8	22 5/8 22 2/8	17 2/8	5	5	Crawford County	IL	Robert L. Harvey	1987	14913
142 2/8	24 0/8 25 0/8	17 2/8	6	4	Licking County	OH	Robert H. Wise	1987	14913
142 2/8	22 6/8 23 3/8	16 1/8	7	6	Roberts County	SD	Myles Keller	1988	14913
142 2/8	22 2/8 22 4/8	16 4/8	5	5	Cherokee County	IA	Brad Husman	1988	14913
142 2/8	22 5/8 23 2/8	18 2/8	6	6	Jackson County	WI	Glen R. Loppnow	1989	14913
142 2/8	20 7/8 20 7/8	15 4/8	5	5	Miller County	MO	John Patterson	1989	14913
142 2/8	25 7/8 24 6/8	19 2/8	4	5	Dunn County	WI	Michael E. Suckow	1989	14913
142 2/8	25 3/8 26 5/8	18 3/8	5	5	Hamilton County	IA	Larry Haren	1989	14913
142 2/8	25 0/8 23 3/8	17 4/8	6	4	Leavenworth County	KS	Jacob W. Dragieff	1989	14913
142 2/8	24 4/8 25 1/8	19 2/8	5	5	Madison County	OH	Timothy A. Chenoweth	1990	14913
142 2/8	22 3/8 23 4/8	16 4/8	5	5	Wetzel County	WV	Paul Pichardo	1990	14913
142 2/8	23 5/8 24 1/8	16 4/8	4	5	Ashland County	WI	Lawrence D. Wollock	1990	14913
142 2/8	25 2/8 25 6/8	22 6/8	5	5	Burlington County	NJ	Frank R. Buckman	1990	14913
142 2/8	25 2/8 25 2/8	19 6/8	4	4	Clayton County	IA	Richard A. Preston	1990	14913
142 2/8	25 5/8 26 3/8	21 2/8	4	4	Livingston County	IL	Tom Roe	1991	14913
142 2/8	21 0/8 22 1/8	16 4/8	5	5	Cross County	AR	Wilburn Holt	1992	14913
142 2/8	24 3/8 23 0/8	15 6/8	4	5	Towner County	ND	Troy Peterson	1992	14913
142 2/8	24 4/8 23 4/8	15 3/8	5	6	Cecil County	MD	Michael L. Boyle	1992	14913
142 2/8	20 4/8 22 2/8	19 0/8	5	4	Knox County	IL	Troy D. Huffman	1992	14913
142 2/8	24 2/8 24 2/8	18 0/8	5	6	Pierce County	WI	Steve Borton	1992	14913
142 2/8	24 2/8 23 5/8	19 5/8	5	6	Cass County	ND	Shane Kautzman	1993	14913
142 2/8	21 0/8 21 3/8	16 2/8	5	5	Wood County	WI	Tom Krutzik	1993	14913
142 2/8	22 7/8 22 5/8	15 4/8	6	6	Marathon County	WI	Shawn G. Stubbe	1993	14913
142 2/8	22 4/8 21 5/8	19 2/8	5	5	Fairfield County	CT	Stephen T. Shay	1993	14913
142 2/8	24 5/8 24 0/8	22 0/8	5	5	Mason County	MI	Brian Petersen	1994	14913
142 2/8	24 7/8 25 4/8	19 6/8	6	5	Warren County	IA	James M. Engle	1994	14913
142 2/8	23 1/8 22 0/8	17 4/8	4	4	Ross County	OH	Ben Fout	1994	14913
142 2/8	23 4/8 23 4/8	18 5/8	5	6	Worcester County	MA	Russell Gray	1994	14913
142 2/8	27 2/8 26 1/8	19 3/8	4	5	Perry County	OH	Thomas E. Kunkler	1994	14913
142 2/8	26 2/8 27 2/8	21 0/8	5	4	Jefferson County	IA	Chris E. Dodds	1994	14913
142 2/8	22 7/8 22 0/8	16 6/8	5	5	Uvalde County	TX	Todd Alexander	1995	14913
142 2/8	24 5/8 26 3/8	17 4/8	6	4	Montgomery County	AL	Zane Caudill	1995	14913
142 2/8	24 1/8 24 0/8	16 2/8	4	4	Barron County	WI	Dwight Stuart	1995	14913
142 2/8	24 2/8 23 7/8	19 4/8	4	4	Baltimore County	MD	Robert Coffman	1995	14913
142 2/8	27 1/8 26 6/8	18 2/8	4	4	Poinsett County	AR	Kevin Owens	1995	14913
142 2/8	23 7/8 24 3/8	20 2/8	5	4	Milwaukee County	WI	Jeff Gricar	1996	14913
142 2/8	21 0/8 20 5/8	15 6/8	5	5	Montgomery County	TN	Brandan Ty Motsinger	1996	14913
142 2/8	23 4/8 21 5/8	18 4/8	5	7	Monmouth County	NJ	Lido D. Panfili	1996	14913
142 2/8	24 4/8 22 3/8	18 6/8	5	4	Perry County	OH	Butch Samson	1996	14913
142 2/8	21 4/8 21 4/8	18 0/8	5	5	Washington County	MN	Scott R. Nelson	1996	14913
142 2/8	22 4/8 23 0/8	16 2/8	5	7	Winneshiek County	IA	Paul Styve	1997	14913
142 2/8	22 6/8 24 0/8	20 4/8	5	4	Jo Daviess County	IL	Scott Byrne	1997	14913
142 2/8	22 0/8 21 7/8	20 2/8	4	4	Butler County	KS	Kent Wartick	1997	14913
142 2/8	23 6/8 22 2/8	14 6/8	6	5	Hand County	SD	Jason D. Resel	1997	14913
142 2/8	25 4/8 25 4/8	21 0/8	5	4	Tazewell County	IL	Richard Frederick	1997	14913
142 2/8	21 5/8 21 7/8	16 0/8	5	5	Osage County	KS	Walter S. Church IV	1997	14913
142 2/8	22 3/8 23 5/8	16 2/8	5	5	Randolph County	IL	Rob Boyd	1997	14913
142 2/8	23 6/8 23 6/8	23 0/8	5	5	Harper County	KS	Frederick Koehn	1997	14913
142 2/8	24 0/8 23 4/8	19 2/8	4	4	Concordia Parish	LA	Bill Dondero	1997	14913
142 2/8	22 1/8 22 5/8	19 2/8	5	4	Maverick County	TX	Dennis J. Marbach	1997	14913
142 2/8	22 4/8 22 2/8	13 6/8	6	5	Upton County	TX	Dean Titsworth	1997	14913
142 2/8	24 2/8 23 7/8	16 4/8	4	4	Door County	WI	Eric Andersen	1998	14913
142 2/8	23 3/8 23 3/8	17 6/8	4	6	Jackson County	WI	Leo J. George	1998	14913
142 2/8	21 6/8 21 3/8	16 0/8	5	5	Juneau County	WI	Scott McKay	1998	14913
142 2/8	23 3/8 24 6/8	18 0/8	6	6	Porter County	IN	Jerry Sherman	1998	14913
142 2/8	22 6/8 21 7/8	14 3/8	5	6	Menominee County	WI	Keith M. Goodwill	1998	14913
142 2/8	25 5/8 26 4/8	21 2/8	4	5	Prince Georges County	MD	Chuck Tedesco	1998	14913
142 2/8	23 2/8 22 6/8	17 6/8	4	4	Crandall	MAN	Gord Lee	1999	14913
142 2/8	24 2/8 23 4/8	16 4/8	4	4	Bristol County	MA	Steve Rogers	1999	14913
142 2/8	23 6/8 24 1/8	17 0/8	5	5	Adams County	WI	Thomas J. Griffin	1999	14913
142 2/8	22 3/8 22 1/8	13 2/8	5	5	Claiborne County	MS	James O. Carpenter	1999	14913
142 2/8	23 6/8 24 1/8	19 1/8	6	5	Stony Plain	ALB	Bart Schutz	1999	14913
142 2/8	23 7/8 23 0/8	19 6/8	6	6	Jackson County	IN	Jeffery Vance	1999	14913
142 2/8	23 6/8 24 1/8	18 0/8	4	5	Livingston County	IL	John D. Landrus	1999	14913
142 2/8	21 7/8 21 0/8	15 4/8	5	5	Waupaca County	WI	Jacob Balthazon	2000	14913
142 2/8	24 4/8 24 7/8	18 4/8	4	4	Greene County	IN	Ray Farmer	2000	14913
142 2/8	22 6/8 22 6/8	15 0/8	6	6	Crawford County	WI	Jim Kozelka	2000	14913
142 2/8	20 7/8 25 4/8	20 1/8	6	6	Greene County	IL	Joseph Eiche	2000	14913
142 2/8	23 3/8 23 0/8	17 2/8	5	5	McDonough County	IL	Dane Metcalf	2000	14913
142 2/8	22 2/8 23 0/8	17 6/8	5	5	Iron County	WI	Howard Becker	2000	14913
142 2/8	20 2/8 20 7/8	15 2/8	5	5	Ogle County	IL	Steven J. Vittetow	2000	14913
142 2/8	22 2/8 21 6/8	16 0/8	5	6	Kalkaska County	MI	Jesse James Patrick	2001	14913
142 2/8	23 5/8 23 0/8	20 4/8	4	4	Lee County	IL	Cory J. Zimmerly	2001	14913
142 2/8	23 1/8 23 5/8	16 4/8	6	5	Wayne County	NY	Jeffrey A. MacNeal	2001	14913
142 2/8	23 2/8 23 3/8	17 6/8	4	4	Stephenson County	IL	Ron Kaderly	2001	14913
142 2/8	25 1/8 24 5/8	19 0/8	5	5	Fairfield County	CT	Keith Strychalsky	2002	14913
142 2/8	23 4/8 21 7/8	17 6/8	5	5	Pettis County	MO	Christopher J. Smith	2002	14913
142 2/8	22 0/8 23 1/8	17 4/8	7	5	Pike County	IL	Doug Wheelehon	2002	14913
142 2/8	22 2/8 24 1/8	19 0/8	5	5	Buffalo County	WI	Gary Fleishauer	2002	14913
142 2/8	22 7/8 22 3/8	16 2/8	4	4	Linn County	KS	Gary Cox	2002	14913
142 2/8	23 6/8 23 5/8	22 0/8	5	5	Lake County	IL	Ken Wodek, Jr.	2003	14913
142 2/8	24 2/8 27 2/8	19 0/8	5	4	St. Joseph County	IN	David Adams	2003	14913
142 2/8	23 4/8 21 7/8	14 4/8	5	5	Mahaska County	IA	Chip J. Terpstra	2003	14913
*142 2/8	21 0/8 21 0/8	14 1/8	6	5	Butler County	KY	Jamie Renfrow	2003	14913

513

WHITETAIL DEER (TYPICAL ANTLERS)

Minimum Score 125
Continued

SCORE	LENGTH OF R MAIN BEAM L	INSIDE SPREAD	NUMBER OF R POINTS L		AREA	STATE/PROVINCE	HUNTER'S NAME	DATE	RANK
142 2/8	22 4/8	22 6/8	16 1/8	6	6	Juneau County	WI	Chase Seebecker	2003	14913
*142 2/8	24 1/8	23 4/8	17 4/8	4	4	Owen County	IN	Clarence S. Dawson	2003	14913
142 2/8	22 7/8	23 1/8	19 0/8	5	4	Knox County	OH	Lewis Holdren	2003	14913
142 2/8	23 4/8	24 6/8	18 0/8	4	5	Comanche County	KS	Harold Leslie	2003	14913
*142 2/8	23 0/8	23 2/8	15 0/8	5	5	Bullitt County	KY	Roger McMillion, Jr.	2004	14913
*142 2/8	22 7/8	22 1/8	14 0/8	5	5	Cobb County	GA	Terry White	2004	14913
142 2/8	24 1/8	23 5/8	17 0/8	6	7	Mahaska County	IA	Michael Olson	2004	14913
142 2/8	19 4/8	22 4/8	18 2/8	7	6	Tazewell County	IL	Brian Devine	2004	14913
*142 2/8	26 4/8	26 3/8	21 0/8	4	4	Dunn County	WI	Charles W. Bowell	2004	14913
142 2/8	24 1/8	22 6/8	15 0/8	5	5	Pike County	IL	Billy Riggs	2004	14913
142 2/8	24 5/8	24 7/8	19 6/8	5	5	Charles County	MD	Lance Schiemer	2004	14913
*142 2/8	22 0/8	22 6/8	17 0/8	5	5	Crawford County	KS	Matthew S. Sanders	2004	14913
142 2/8	23 0/8	22 5/8	16 4/8	5	5	Todd County	MN	Ryan Augeson	2004	14913
142 2/8	21 4/8	23 4/8	19 2/8	5	5	Spokane County	WA	Glen Berry	2004	14913
142 2/8	23 3/8	24 0/8	18 4/8	4	5	Calhoun County	MI	George I. Swan, Jr.	2004	14913
*142 2/8	23 1/8	23 7/8	18 0/8	5	6	Alfalfa County	OK	Greg Justice	2004	14913
142 2/8	22 6/8	22 1/8	18 3/8	5	6	Hamilton County	IA	Scott Wiese	2005	14913
142 2/8	23 4/8	23 2/8	21 2/8	6	5	Price County	WI	Mitchell Burger	2005	14913
142 2/8	21 7/8	21 6/8	21 6/8	5	5	Buffalo County	WI	Dean Mense	2005	14913
142 2/8	25 0/8	25 0/8	16 2/8	4	4	Clarke County	VA	Martin E. Stonesifer	2005	14913
*142 2/8	21 2/8	21 4/8	15 4/8	5	5	Schleicher County	TX	Timmy Browning	2005	14913
*142 2/8	23 4/8	22 5/8	13 6/8	5	5	Mercer County	MO	Bryan Kissinger	2005	14913
142 2/8	23 6/8	22 5/8	21 4/8	4	4	Grant County	WI	Mike Richards	2005	14913
142 2/8	21 2/8	21 5/8	17 4/8	5	5	Winnebago County	WI	Tim Meilahn	2005	14913
142 2/8	22 5/8	22 3/8	18 4/8	5	5	Vernon County	WI	Ryan Howell	2005	14913
142 2/8	24 2/8	24 4/8	20 2/8	5	6	Lake County	IL	Steven Hysell	2005	14913
142 2/8	24 2/8	23 3/8	18 3/8	4	6	Suffolk County	NY	George C. Johnson, Jr	2005	14913
*142 2/8	24 0/8	24 5/8	16 2/8	4	5	Sevier County	AR	Jeff Eaves	2005	14913
*142 2/8	24 5/8	23 4/8	17 0/8	4	4	Jackson County	IN	Robert G. Klakamp	2006	14913
142 2/8	24 5/8	24 5/8	19 4/8	5	5	Cass County	IL	Larry C. Holcomb	2006	14913
*142 2/8	25 5/8	24 7/8	19 6/8	4	4	Muskingum County	OH	Troy William Engleha-t	2006	14913
142 2/8	24 3/8	24 5/8	15 6/8	4	4	Adair County	MO	Robert Stewart	2006	14913
142 2/8	23 7/8	24 4/8	19 6/8	5	5	Anoka County	MN	Pat McKenzie	2006	14913
142 2/8	23 2/8	23 4/8	18 0/8	7	6	Marquette County	WI	Joseph Zauner	2006	14913
142 2/8	23 3/8	23 6/8	17 0/8	5	7	Monroe County	NY	Chris Brower	2006	14913
*142 2/8	22 4/8	22 0/8	18 4/8	6	7	Columbia County	WI	Bruce F. Udell	2006	14913
*142 2/8	22 4/8	21 4/8	16 6/8	8	5	Pike County	IL	Truit Acosta	2006	14913
142 2/8	20 4/8	20 5/8	15 6/8	5	5	Lenore Lake	SAS	Floyd Forster	2006	14913
142 2/8	23 2/8	24 4/8	21 4/8	4	4	Lorain County	OH	Patrick Reddinger	2007	14913
142 2/8	24 7/8	25 2/8	18 4/8	5	4	Henrico County	VA	Bruce Scott	2007	14913
142 2/8	23 1/8	23 4/8	20 2/8	5	5	Chautauqua County	NY	Kim Olson	2007	14913
*142 2/8	23 1/8	23 4/8	17 0/8	5	6	Kosciusko County	IN	Chad A. Zartman	2007	14913
142 2/8	21 1/8	20 4/8	16 0/8	5	5	Johnson County	IA	Leon Schlueter	2007	14913
142 2/8	24 0/8	23 0/8	17 2/8	4	5	Macon County	IL	Todd Williams	2007	14913
142 2/8	23 5/8	23 4/8	19 2/8	8	5	Buffalo County	WI	Glen Axness	2007	14913
142 2/8	21 7/8	22 2/8	17 2/8	4	4	Douglas County	NE	Mark Jost	2007	14913
142 2/8	26 2/8	25 2/8	18 2/8	5	4	Knox County	IL	Don Owen	2007	14913
*142 2/8	22 6/8	24 5/8	19 0/8	5	6	Richland County	OH	Douglas A. Hamman	2007	14913
142 2/8	23 7/8	23 6/8	21 0/8	5	4	Niagara County	NY	Travis Diez	2008	14913
142 2/8	22 4/8	22 1/8	19 2/8	5	5	Trempealeau County	WI	Craig Marsolek	2008	14913
142 2/8	22 5/8	22 6/8	14 4/8	5	5	Fairfield County	CT	Joe Fedorko	2008	14913
142 2/8	22 1/8	21 1/8	15 6/8	5	5	Fayette County	PA	Michael J. Yeager	2008	14913
142 2/8	23 2/8	23 4/8	17 7/8	6	5	Green Lake County	WI	Tim M. Tabbert	2008	14913
142 2/8	24 1/8	23 2/8	19 6/8	5	5	Woods County	OK	Wilbur Ramos	2008	14913
*142 2/8	24 4/8	22 0/8	22 2/8	5	5	Washington County	IL	Ronnie Berry	2008	14913
*142 2/8	25 6/8	23 6/8	17 0/8	5	6	Carroll County	MS	Michael S. McCrory	2008	14913
142 2/8	21 2/8	22 1/8	16 6/8	5	5	Wood County	WI	Dan Luther	2009	14913
142 2/8	22 3/8	22 1/8	17 6/8	8	7	Matagorda County	TX	Wesley R. Smolik	2009	14913
142 2/8	22 3/8	20 5/8	16 5/8	6	4	Marquette County	WI	Gary F. Thalacker	2009	14913
142 2/8	23 1/8	22 5/8	18 0/8	5	5	Comanche County	KS	Daryl P. Guest	2009	14913
*142 2/8	25 4/8	26 1/8	18 2/8	6	5	Wood County	OH	Matt Stone	2009	14913
142 2/8	24 2/8	24 0/8	18 2/8	4	5	Chautauqua County	NY	Eric Green	2009	14913
142 2/8	24 3/8	23 2/8	19 0/8	4	4	Clarke County	IA	Don Mealey	2009	14913
*142 2/8	24 1/8	24 6/8	20 6/8	5	5	Winona County	MN	Chad Anderson	2009	14913
142 2/8	21 6/8	22 0/8	14 0/8	5	5	Lincoln County	OK	John Tse	2010	14913
142 1/8	23 1/8	22 7/8	18 6/8	5	5	Huron County	OH	Thomas Sheldon	1956	15076
142 1/8	23 6/8	23 1/8	15 3/8	6	6	Morgan County	GA	Jerry Wall	1966	15076
142 1/8	25 0/8	25 2/8	20 3/8	6	6	Faribault County	MN	Timothy Anderson	1970	15076
142 1/8	24 2/8	25 7/8	22 1/8	5	4	Pope County	AR	Danny L. Mathis	1971	15076
142 1/8	24 2/8	24 0/8	18 3/8	6	6	Buffalo County	WI	Myles Keller	1973	15076
142 1/8	23 7/8	23 7/8	17 5/8	5	5	Port Perry	ONT	Ken Steele	1979	15076
142 1/8	23 4/8	23 4/8	16 7/8	4	4	Ripley County	IN	Dick Gambrel	1981	15076
142 1/8	22 7/8	22 2/8	16 3/8	5	5	McPherson County	KS	James Willems	1981	15076
142 1/8	22 1/8	21 6/8	14 5/8	5	5	Charles County	MD	John L. Penny	1982	15076
142 1/8	20 1/8	20 5/8	13 7/8	5	5	Juneau County	WI	Dennis Dreischmeier	1982	15076
142 1/8	24 6/8	25 3/8	18 1/8	4	4	Lawrence County	OH	Carl G. Coburn	1982	15076
142 1/8	26 0/8	25 0/8	22 1/8	6	6	Medina County	OH	Bruce Hamilton	1983	15076
142 1/8	21 2/8	21 4/8	16 5/8	6	6	Washington County	MD	David M. Kumsher	1985	15076
142 1/8	25 0/8	24 2/8	18 3/8	6	7	Ohio County	IN	Ernest Frady	1985	15076
142 1/8	20 2/8	20 7/8	17 0/8	6	5	Trego County	KS	William R. Whitworth	1985	15076
142 1/8	25 0/8	24 6/8	17 7/8	4	4	Logan County	CO	Kent Sump	1985	15076
142 1/8	24 4/8	25 2/8	19 1/8	4	5	Waushara County	WI	Lester W. Lant, Jr.	1986	15076
142 1/8	23 3/8	22 3/8	18 5/8	4	5	Somerset County	NJ	John Maddaluna	1986	15076
142 1/8	22 3/8	22 1/8	17 5/8	5	5	Pope County	AR	Todd Fountain	1987	15076
142 1/8	24 0/8	24 3/8	16 2/8	5	6	Winnebago County	IA	Jerry Reynolds	1987	15076
142 1/8	25 0/8	24 5/8	19 1/8	5	5	Rock County	WI	Gary Schiefelbein	1987	15076
142 1/8	24 6/8	25 4/8	19 5/8	5	5	Jackson County	KS	Dayton R. Wright	1987	15076
142 1/8	26 3/8	26 1/8	19 1/8	4	4	Charles County	MD	Douglas M. Garcia	1988	15076
142 1/8	21 6/8	22 2/8	17 5/8	5	5	Noble County	IN	Frank M. McDonald	1989	15076
142 1/8	25 7/8	25 5/8	22 7/8	7	6	Dubuque County	IA	Ken Treanor	1989	15076
142 1/8	22 4/8	23 0/8	17 5/8	7	5	Saline County	MO	Jerry Underwood	1989	15076
142 1/8	23 3/8	24 5/8	16 4/8	5	6	Logan County	IL	Donald D. Stiner	1989	15076
142 1/8	23 2/8	23 6/8	17 7/8	5	5	Langlade County	WI	Robert A. Winkler	1990	15076
142 1/8	25 3/8	24 5/8	20 7/8	4	4	Renville County	MN	Tom Neubauer	1990	15076
142 1/8	23 4/8	24 1/8	17 3/8	5	5	Cass County	MO	Mike R. Wheeler	1990	15076

514

WHITETAIL DEER (TYPICAL ANTLERS)

Minimum Score 125   Continued

SCORE	LENGTH OF R MAIN BEAM L	INSIDE SPREAD	NUMBER OF R POINTS L		AREA	STATE/ PROVINCE	HUNTER'S NAME	DATE	RANK
142 1/8	25 4/8	23 3/8	17 1/8	4	4	Crawford County	IL	Steve L. Hobbs	1990	15076
142 1/8	19 6/8	19 6/8	18 7/8	5	5	Weld County	CO	Dave Culter	1990	15076
142 1/8	22 3/8	21 7/8	18 3/8	5	5	Winneshiek County	IA	Lonnie Tiedt	1990	15076
142 1/8	24 0/8	22 6/8	17 3/8	5	6	Bucks County	PA	Michael J. Mullin	1991	15076
142 1/8	21 1/8	21 5/8	18 7/8	5	5	Kendall County	IL	John D. Rogers II	1991	15076
142 1/8	24 4/8	24 1/8	16 7/8	5	5	Lawrence County	OH	Jerry L. Scythes	1991	15076
142 1/8	23 0/8	22 3/8	16 7/8	5	5	Chariton County	MO	Dennis Meyers	1991	15076
142 1/8	22 0/8	22 0/8	17 3/8	6	5	Crawford County	IL	Jim Liffick	1991	15076
142 1/8	22 2/8	22 4/8	20 3/8	4	5	La Salle County	IL	Robert L. McAtee	1992	15076
142 1/8	24 0/8	23 6/8	18 7/8	5	5	Buffalo County	WI	Michael J. Barstad	1993	15076
142 1/8	23 5/8	22 5/8	14 0/8	6	5	Richland County	IL	Troy A. Hinderliter	1993	15076
142 1/8	22 2/8	21 5/8	17 7/8	5	5	Forest County	WI	Randy R. Lepak	1993	15076
142 1/8	20 2/8	20 2/8	19 7/8	6	7	Montcalm County	MI	Christopher Fedewa	1993	15076
142 1/8	22 4/8	21 5/8	16 5/8	7	7	Okanogan County	WA	Fred Zissel	1994	15076
142 1/8	24 1/8	22 5/8	16 4/8	6	5	Laclede County	MO	Gary Lemery	1994	15076
142 1/8	25 0/8	23 4/8	15 5/8	5	5	Cedar County	MO	Mark A. Frieze	1994	15076
142 1/8	23 5/8	24 0/8	19 5/8	6	5	Weld County	CO	Tim Mangina	1994	15076
142 1/8	22 3/8	24 1/8	18 5/8	5	6	Worth County	IA	Mark Johnson	1994	15076
142 1/8	24 1/8	23 4/8	19 1/8	6	5	Jefferson County	WI	Jack Findlay	1994	15076
142 1/8	20 0/8	21 1/8	15 3/8	5	5	Chautauqua County	KS	John C. Ford	1994	15076
142 1/8	21 5/8	24 4/8	15 5/8	5	5	Cass County	MI	Calvin Percy	1994	15076
142 1/8	24 1/8	23 5/8	15 7/8	5	7	Waupaca County	WI	Merlin Reinke	1995	15076
142 1/8	21 5/8	22 2/8	15 5/8	5	5	Hopkins County	KY	Greg Belk	1995	15076
142 1/8	23 5/8	23 3/8	15 5/8	5	5	Franklin County	MO	Dennis Ross	1995	15076
142 1/8	24 0/8	23 6/8	17 1/8	6	7	St. Louis County	MO	Robert O. Werges	1995	15076
142 1/8	22 7/8	22 0/8	20 3/8	5	6	Washington County	KS	William B. Wilgers	1995	15076
142 1/8	23 3/8	23 3/8	17 3/8	5	5	Delaware County	OH	Jeff Daily	1995	15076
142 1/8	19 7/8	20 0/8	17 5/8	5	5	Pike County	KY	Leroy Hamilton	1995	15076
142 1/8	23 7/8	24 0/8	19 5/8	4	5	Charles Mix County	SD	Larry Hansum	1995	15076
142 1/8	23 7/8	23 0/8	18 5/8	5	5	Webster County	KY	Robert Tatro, Jr.	1996	15076
142 1/8	22 1/8	22 4/8	15 7/8	5	5	Seneca County	OH	Tom Weimerskirch	1996	15076
142 1/8	26 2/8	24 3/8	19 7/8	4	4	Trempealeau County	WI	John Sobczak	1997	15076
142 1/8	23 0/8	24 4/8	17 2/8	5	5	Pierce County	WI	Perry Goetsch	1997	15076
142 1/8	23 0/8	23 3/8	13 7/8	4	5	De Kalb County	IN	Gordon Velpel III	1997	15076
142 1/8	21 5/8	20 5/8	18 3/8	6	5	Henry County	IA	Tracy C. Krebsbach	1997	15076
142 1/8	21 3/8	20 6/8	16 7/8	5	5	Comanche County	OK	William Early Wilkins	1997	15076
142 1/8	22 3/8	22 4/8	16 3/8	5	5	Douglas County	WI	Jeffrey N. Breitzmann	1997	15076
142 1/8	23 1/8	24 7/8	23 3/8	8	5	Ogle County	IL	Danny Nichols	1997	15076
142 1/8	25 0/8	26 0/8	19 7/8	5	5	Rusk County	WI	Anthony M. Olivo	1998	15076
142 1/8	22 7/8	23 2/8	19 6/8	6	6	Putnam County	MO	Randy Cooling	1998	15076
142 1/8	22 4/8	23 1/8	21 3/8	4	4	Rock Island County	IL	Kurt Frakes	1998	15076
142 1/8	23 1/8	23 1/8	15 7/8	5	5	Ripley County	IN	Mark Brooks	1998	15076
142 1/8	24 3/8	24 3/8	21 4/8	6	4	Kingman County	KS	Mark Hancock	1998	15076
142 1/8	25 4/8	25 0/8	18 1/8	6	4	Price County	WI	Michael W. Ullenbrauck	1999	15076
142 1/8	23 1/8	23 1/8	16 4/8	5	6	Sauk County	WI	Mike McGann	1999	15076
142 1/8	23 7/8	23 7/8	17 1/8	6	6	Sabine County	TX	Michael Lee DeFee	1999	15076
142 1/8	22 4/8	22 2/8	16 1/8	5	5	Adams County	IL	Doug A. Tucker	1999	15076
142 1/8	26 1/8	24 5/8	18 5/8	4	4	La Porte County	IN	Brian E. Waldo	1999	15076
142 1/8	21 7/8	20 4/8	16 1/8	5	5	Ashtabula County	OH	Robert R. Payne, Jr.	1999	15076
142 1/8	24 5/8	25 2/8	27 4/8	6	5	Summit County	OH	Kasey Lukacs	1999	15076
142 1/8	22 0/8	22 5/8	17 5/8	5	5	Ontario County	NY	Doug F. Johncox	1999	15076
142 1/8	24 2/8	24 3/8	17 1/8	7	5	Union County	SD	Bradley D. Mollet	1999	15076
142 1/8	21 4/8	21 7/8	17 2/8	6	5	Buena Vista County	IA	Brent Schnetter	1999	15076
142 1/8	25 1/8	24 7/8	18 7/8	6	6	Peoria County	IL	Roger A. Albertson	1999	15076
142 1/8	23 4/8	21 7/8	20 1/8	5	5	Jefferson County	MT	Elmer Schonscheck	2000	15076
142 1/8	20 4/8	20 4/8	17 1/8	5	6	Jackson County	MO	Tony Standiford	2000	15076
142 1/8	23 7/8	23 6/8	18 1/8	5	5	Eau Claire County	WI	Loren Lone	2000	15076
142 1/8	23 2/8	22 3/8	16 7/8	5	5	Buffalo County	WI	Teresa Fredrickson	2000	15076
142 1/8	22 2/8	21 5/8	15 6/8	5	6	Franklin County	KS	Matthew Ferguson	2000	15076
142 1/8	25 4/8	24 3/8	18 5/8	4	4	Sherburne County	MN	Keith Asfeld	2000	15076
142 1/8	24 6/8	25 3/8	19 7/8	5	4	Claiborne County	MS	Lance Stroud	2000	15076
142 1/8	25 1/8	25 2/8	22 7/8	4	5	Goodhue County	MN	Earl Robinson	2001	15076
142 1/8	24 1/8	24 0/8	20 1/8	6	6	Monroe County	IA	Bruce Kirkpatrick	2001	15076
142 1/8	23 7/8	24 4/8	22 1/8	5	4	Holt County	NE	Theron Dewine	2002	15076
142 1/8	24 2/8	23 5/8	20 1/8	4	4	Jay County	IN	Jeremy L. Davis	2002	15076
142 1/8	24 0/8	24 0/8	19 3/8	4	5	Lenawee County	MI	Josh Weage	2002	15076
142 1/8	24 0/8	24 7/8	17 5/8	5	5	Champaign County	IL	Aric Carney	2002	15076
142 1/8	22 6/8	22 6/8	17 5/8	5	6	Lawrence County	MO	Grant Gaddy	2002	15076
142 1/8	22 1/8	22 7/8	20 2/8	5	8	Sarpy County	NE	Ryan Cronk	2002	15076
142 1/8	21 5/8	21 7/8	18 3/8	5	5	Sherburne County	MN	Ronald S. Wright	2002	15076
142 1/8	24 4/8	24 0/8	20 3/8	5	5	Calumet County	WI	Jesse Schneider	2002	15076
142 1/8	24 7/8	24 4/8	16 1/8	6	6	Lincoln County	MO	Jason Schieffer	2002	15076
142 1/8	23 7/8	24 7/8	18 4/8	4	5	Page County	IA	Kevin Oleson	2002	15076
142 1/8	22 1/8	21 1/8	14 5/8	5	5	Holt County	NE	Larry A. Hermsmeyer	2002	15076
142 1/8	23 0/8	23 5/8	17 5/8	7	6	Fayette County	IL	Mark Luster	2002	15076
142 1/8	23 7/8	24 1/8	16 1/8	5	5	Iron County	MI	Tom Mancl	2003	15076
142 1/8	21 0/8	21 1/8	17 1/8	5	5	Licking County	OH	Eric McKenzie	2003	15076
142 1/8	26 1/8	26 2/8	22 5/8	6	4	Kosciusko County	IN	Jon D. Cook	2003	15076
142 1/8	20 1/8	20 2/8	19 5/8	5	5	Boone County	MO	Mike Schanzmeyer	2003	15076
142 1/8	21 5/8	22 7/8	16 5/8	5	5	La Porte County	IN	Brian A. Thompson	2003	15076
142 1/8	26 6/8	27 1/8	18 4/8	5	6	Ripley County	IN	Blake Comer	2003	15076
142 1/8	22 7/8	23 2/8	15 4/8	6	6	Sangamon County	IL	Brian Bergmann	2004	15076
142 1/8	22 6/8	23 6/8	15 6/8	7	5	Crook County	WY	Perry G. Groshek	2004	15076
142 1/8	21 6/8	22 3/8	15 5/8	5	5	Burleson County	TX	Bradley Muske	2004	15076
142 1/8	23 2/8	23 2/8	14 5/8	5	5	Cass County	MI	Brian P. Watson	2004	15076
142 1/8	24 4/8	24 0/8	16 6/8	6	4	Johnson County	IA	Mike McGowan	2004	15076
142 1/8	24 4/8	21 3/8	15 3/8	6	5	Osage County	OK	Tommy Wagner	2004	15076
142 1/8	23 1/8	22 3/8	16 6/8	6	7	Trempealeau County	WI	David A. Lyngen	2004	15076
142 1/8	22 6/8	22 7/8	16 1/8	5	6	Pike County	MO	Adam Orf	2004	15076
142 1/8	22 1/8	21 3/8	15 5/8	5	5	Brown County	IL	Marty Chester	2004	15076
*142 1/8	24 0/8	23 4/8	18 5/8	4	4	Adams County	WI	Bill Schrank	2004	15076
142 1/8	23 3/8	23 3/8	16 5/8	5	5	Mills County	IA	Jerry Peterson	2004	15076
*142 1/8	22 6/8	22 5/8	17 1/8	5	5	Green Lake County	WI	Scott J. Sullivan	2005	15076
142 1/8	23 4/8	24 1/8	18 0/8	5	6	Pierce County	WI	Tom Kirchner	2005	15076
142 1/8	22 6/8	24 3/8	17 0/8	6	6	Burnett County	WI	Paul V. Holmquist	2005	15076

WHITETAIL DEER (TYPICAL ANTLERS)

Minimum Score 125 — Continued

SCORE	LENGTH OF R MAIN BEAM L	INSIDE SPREAD	NUMBER OF R POINTS L	AREA	STATE/PROVINCE	HUNTER'S NAME	DATE	RANK
142 1/8	25 0/8 25 0/8	17 7/8	5 5	Sauk County	WI	Sherman Raschein	2005	15076
142 1/8	24 0/8 24 0/8	19 2/8	5 6	Cedar County	IA	Shobin Finley	2005	15076
142 1/8	23 6/8 23 6/8	18 2/8	7 8	Lawrence County	OH	Mike Triplett	2006	15076
142 1/8	20 7/8 21 4/8	17 2/8	6 6	Buffalo County	WI	Joel E. Mann	2006	15076
142 1/8	25 3/8 23 2/8	15 3/8	4 4	Vernon County	WI	Casey Blum	2006	15076
142 1/8	23 7/8 24 0/8	17 3/8	6 6	Howard County	IA	Dennis Douglas	2006	15076
*142 1/8	24 0/8 22 3/8	18 6/8	4 5	Eaton County	MI	Jeffery K. Duits	2006	15076
142 1/8	26 3/8 26 4/8	21 1/8	4 4	Lucas County	OH	Gary A. Romstadt, Jr.	2006	15076
*142 1/8	22 1/8 23 3/8	18 5/8	6 6	Taylor County	GA	Lisa K. Smith	2006	15076
*142 1/8	21 0/8 21 5/8	15 3/8	5 5	Sherburne County	MN	Ronald S. Wright	2006	15076
142 1/8	23 5/8 23 6/8	17 1/8	5 6	Williams County	OH	Doug Zastrow	2006	15076
142 1/8	22 3/8 24 3/8	18 7/8	5 6	Wood County	OH	Tyler Brown	2007	15076
142 1/8	20 6/8 20 3/8	17 3/8	5 5	Tom Green County	TX	Ronnie Parsons	2007	15076
142 1/8	22 2/8 20 5/8	18 5/8	5 5	St. Clair County	MI	Mark Zelazny	2007	15076
142 1/8	23 6/8 22 6/8	19 4/8	5 6	Houston County	MN	Stephen A. Dougherty	2007	15076
*142 1/8	24 0/8 23 4/8	18 1/8	5 5	Barron County	WI	Larry C. Nelson	2007	15076
142 1/8	24 2/8 24 2/8	19 7/8	4 4	Delaware County	OH	Doug Fadely	2007	15076
142 1/8	23 4/8 22 5/8	15 7/8	6 7	Harrison County	KY	Rodney Milner	2007	15076
142 1/8	22 2/8 23 6/8	16 7/8	6 6	Beaverlodge	ALB	Terry Hagman	2007	15076
142 1/8	22 5/8 21 7/8	20 0/8	5 6	Manitowoc County	WI	Jason Orth	2008	15076
142 1/8	22 5/8 23 4/8	16 4/8	6 6	Cass County	NE	Neil Chandler	2008	15076
*142 1/8	21 2/8 21 7/8	18 1/8	5 5	Benton County	IA	Harvey Dirks	2008	15076
142 1/8	22 7/8 24 1/8	17 3/8	4 4	Monona County	IA	Rene Curran	2008	15076
*142 1/8	23 4/8 23 4/8	17 3/8	5 5	Scott County	IA	Tim Carlson	2008	15076
142 1/8	21 6/8 22 6/8	16 6/8	6 5	Shawano County	WI	Adam J. De Bauch	2008	15076
142 1/8	21 6/8 21 6/8	18 2/8	5 4	Monroe County	IA	Kurt Schroeder	2008	15076
142 1/8	24 3/8 24 0/8	18 5/8	6 5	Dunn County	WI	Steven C. Crites	2008	15076
142 1/8	22 6/8 22 4/8	18 3/8	5 5	Calumet County	WI	Jim Allwardt	2009	15076
*142 1/8	22 7/8 21 7/8	16 5/8	5 5	McHenry County	ND	David Miller	2009	15076
*142 1/8	23 2/8 24 6/8	18 7/8	4 4	Cherokee County	OK	Bob Sherbourne	2009	15076
142 1/8	21 6/8 21 5/8	16 5/8	6 6	Eau Claire County	WI	Michael Falkner	2009	15076
142 1/8	24 5/8 25 1/8	15 7/8	7 6	Winneshiek County	IA	Ryan Ebner	2009	15076
142 1/8	23 3/8 22 4/8	20 3/8	4 4	Carroll County	IL	Alan D. Herum	2009	15076
*142 1/8	21 5/8 21 3/8	17 3/8	5 5	Columbiana County	OH	John P. Bellanca	2009	15076
142 1/8	22 7/8 22 0/8	19 3/8	5 5	East Ferris Township	ONT	Ken Leppert	2009	15076
142 1/8	26 7/8 25 4/8	18 0/8	5 5	Ottawa County	OK	Ron McCorkell	2009	15076
142 0/8	22 4/8 23 0/8	17 2/8	6 5	Logan County	IL	Irwin L. Miller	1976	15237
142 0/8	24 1/8 24 1/8	17 6/8	5 6	Winona County	MN	Clayton Bentson	1977	15237
142 0/8	24 0/8 23 7/8	15 5/8	5 6	Bayfield County	WI	James J. Messerschmidt	1979	15237
142 0/8	24 5/8 24 4/8	18 6/8	4 4	Woodford County	IL	Byron L. Davenport	1980	15237
142 0/8	20 7/8 19 5/8	18 2/8	5 5	Shelby County	IL	Richard W. Neumann	1982	15237
142 0/8	23 4/8 21 6/8	19 6/8	5 7	Union County	IL	Randy Cronk	1983	15237
142 0/8	27 0/8 27 0/8	20 0/8	4 4	Ravalli County	MT	Harry Potton	1983	15237
142 0/8	22 2/8 22 5/8	18 5/8	5 7	Will County	IL	Joseph R. Pergram	1983	15237
142 0/8	21 5/8 20 5/8	17 6/8	5 5	Dubuque County	IA	Joe Lieb	1984	15237
142 0/8	23 1/8 23 3/8	16 6/8	5 5	Dane County	WI	Joseph A. Radecki	1984	15237
142 0/8	20 6/8 20 6/8	17 0/8	5 5	Shawnee County	KS	Eldon Johnson	1985	15237
142 0/8	24 5/8 24 4/8	15 2/8	5 5	Morrison County	MN	Stan Spychalla	1986	15237
142 0/8	22 6/8 23 2/8	16 0/8	5 5	Fergus County	MT	Mike Sweeney	1986	15237
142 0/8	21 3/8 21 0/8	15 6/8	5 5	Burnett County	WI	Doug Anderson	1987	15237
142 0/8	21 6/8 23 3/8	16 4/8	5 5	La Salle County	IL	William Weygand	1988	15237
142 0/8	22 0/8 22 5/8	16 4/8	5 5	Buffalo County	WI	Jeff Wendorf	1988	15237
142 0/8	23 0/8 22 7/8	16 6/8	5 5	Creek County	OK	Larry V Fears	1988	15237
142 0/8	21 6/8 22 3/8	17 4/8	6 5	Pierce County	WI	Robert Barrie	1989	15237
142 0/8	25 0/8 24 2/8	16 4/8	4 5	St. Croix County	WI	Keith Andrea	1990	15237
142 0/8	23 0/8 23 6/8	19 0/8	4 4	Putnam County	WV	Forrest R. Woodard	1990	15237
142 0/8	24 4/8 24 6/8	18 1/8	5 5	Suffolk County	NY	John Jeff Pfeifer	1990	15237
142 0/8	21 0/8 20 6/8	18 0/8	5 5	Cooper County	MO	Fred Storozyszyn	1990	15237
142 0/8	22 4/8 22 5/8	17 2/8	5 7	Winona County	MN	Dennis Marg	1991	15237
142 0/8	23 3/8 24 0/8	18 6/8	5 5	Madison County	KY	Gary W. Langford	1991	15237
142 0/8	24 5/8 23 4/8	20 0/8	6 5	Henderson County	KY	Lawrence F. Smithhart	1991	15237
142 0/8	22 1/8 21 7/8	17 2/8	6 5	Poweshiek County	IA	Kevin Kudart	1991	15237
142 0/8	24 2/8 24 3/8	17 0/8	7 6	Cook County	MN	Bruce Zimpel	1991	15237
142 0/8	22 6/8 21 3/8	19 2/8	5 5	Sharkey County	MS	Kirby Deer, Jr.	1992	15237
142 0/8	23 5/8 23 6/8	21 0/8	4 4	Chester County	PA	William J. Combs, Jr.	1992	15237
142 0/8	24 7/8 24 6/8	19 0/8	8 6	Jefferson County	WI	Mike Leslie	1992	15237
142 0/8	22 6/8 23 3/8	19 6/8	5 5	Adams County	IL	Timothy D. Walmsley	1992	15237
142 0/8	24 3/8 21 5/8	22 1/8	5 5	Summit County	OH	Tim E. Gall	1992	15237
142 0/8	20 2/8 20 6/8	14 2/8	5 5	McKenzie County	ND	Shawn A. Koosman	1993	15237
142 0/8	23 7/8 23 5/8	19 4/8	4 5	Jo Daviess County	IL	Ronald R. Gawlik	1993	15237
142 0/8	24 2/8 22 6/8	18 4/8	5 5	Hennepin County	MN	Greg A. Maciej	1993	15237
142 0/8	22 3/8 21 6/8	18 6/8	5 5	Ottawa County	MI	Kurtis C. Boeve	1994	15237
142 0/8	25 6/8 26 3/8	18 0/8	5 5	Orange County	NC	Derek J. Green	1994	15237
142 0/8	22 7/8 23 0/8	17 0/8	5 5	Buffalo County	WI	Robert J. Seckora	1994	15237
142 0/8	24 4/8 24 2/8	17 6/8	4 4	Polk County	WI	Dave Neville	1994	15237
142 0/8	24 5/8 23 2/8	19 0/8	5 5	Shawnee County	KS	James Creviston II	1994	15237
142 0/8	24 4/8 23 5/8	17 1/8	5 6	Anoka County	MN	Stanley Grygelko	1994	15237
142 0/8	25 5/8 25 2/8	17 4/8	4 4	Cuyahoga County	OH	Kenneth D. Walter	1994	15237
142 0/8	21 4/8 21 1/8	15 4/8	5 5	Spink County	SD	Randy Schultz	1994	15237
142 0/8	25 1/8 24 6/8	17 4/8	4 4	St. Clair County	MI	James Glombowski	1995	15237
142 0/8	22 6/8 22 4/8	17 0/8	5 5	Lapeer County	MI	Russell Martin	1995	15237
142 0/8	23 6/8 25 3/8	19 7/8	5 6	Will County	IL	Nathan A. Teske	1995	15237
142 0/8	23 4/8 22 6/8	17 2/8	5 5	Jackson County	MI	Richard Quentin Walker	1995	15237
142 0/8	23 4/8 22 4/8	17 4/8	5 5	Buffalo County	WI	Bob Kostecki	1995	15237
142 0/8	22 4/8 19 6/8	19 6/8	5 5	New Haven County	CT	Jason Cuda	1995	15237
142 0/8	24 0/8 24 2/8	18 4/8	4 4	Baltimore County	MD	Jack Schatz	1995	15237
142 0/8	24 3/8 23 4/8	17 6/8	5 5	Marion County	KS	Dennis N. Ballweg	1995	15237
142 0/8	22 4/8 23 0/8	18 0/8	5 5	Marshall County	IN	Jeff A. Ellinger	1995	15237
142 0/8	23 6/8 23 3/8	16 5/8	7 9	Douglas County	KS	Mark Young	1995	15237
142 0/8	23 3/8 22 0/8	16 4/8	5 5	Oakland County	MI	Gary Allen	1996	15237
142 0/8	24 6/8 24 6/8	15 0/8	5 5	Coles County	IL	Bob Weber	1996	15237
142 0/8	25 0/8 24 5/8	17 6/8	4 4	Marion County	IA	Merle Schulz	1996	15237
142 0/8	23 4/8 23 1/8	17 2/8	5 4	Clarke County	IA	Don Mealey	1996	15237
142 0/8	21 5/8 21 3/8	15 4/8	5 5	E. Carroll Parish	LA	Robert Songin	1996	15237
142 0/8	25 0/8 25 0/8	20 3/8	6 6	Walworth County	WI	Mike Brady	1997	15237

WHITETAIL DEER (TYPICAL ANTLERS)

Minimum Score 125   Continued

SCORE	LENGTH OF R MAIN BEAM L	INSIDE SPREAD	NUMBER OF R POINTS L	AREA	STATE/ PROVINCE	HUNTER'S NAME	DATE	RANK
142 0/8	22 2/8	22 6/8	17 4/8	5 5	Gwinnett County	GA	Jeff Crowell	1997	15237
142 0/8	24 5/8	23 2/8	18 6/8	5 5	Hardin County	OH	Lori Podhorsky	1997	15237
142 0/8	22 7/8	22 3/8	16 7/8	6 5	Belmont County	OH	Rick Dufford	1997	15237
142 0/8	24 4/8	24 7/8	18 2/8	6 6	Macoupin County	IL	Kevin Fones	1997	15237
142 0/8	23 1/8	22 6/8	18 4/8	5 5	Benton County	IA	Kevin Nolan	1997	15237
142 0/8	24 3/8	24 5/8	17 4/8	5 5	Westchester County	NY	Carl Colasacco	1997	15237
142 0/8	21 1/8	21 1/8	14 7/8	6 5	Columbia County	WI	Steven L. Rohn	1998	15237
142 0/8	24 4/8	24 7/8	20 0/8	5 5	Lawrence County	OH	Richard Lyall	1998	15237
142 0/8	22 1/8	22 4/8	17 5/8	5 6	Sanilac County	MI	Joel Edward Haynes	1998	15237
142 0/8	23 2/8	23 5/8	17 2/8	5 5	Calumet County	WI	Jeffrey J. Zwiers	1998	15237
142 0/8	22 7/8	22 4/8	16 1/8	5 5	Suffolk County	NY	James Matuszewski	1998	15237
142 0/8	22 2/8	21 4/8	17 2/8	6 5	Meade County	KY	Chris Beck	1999	15237
142 0/8	21 3/8	21 2/8	16 4/8	5 5	Washington County	KS	Doug Kruse	1999	15237
142 0/8	24 4/8	24 5/8	18 0/8	4 5	Martin County	IN	Richard L. Miller	1999	15237
142 0/8	22 3/8	23 0/8	17 2/8	5 4	Adams County	IA	Todd Crill	1999	15237
142 0/8	23 4/8	23 0/8	21 6/8	5 5	Marquette County	WI	Chanc L. Vogel	1999	15237
142 0/8	23 3/8	24 2/8	17 0/8	5 5	Menominee County	WI	Keith Goodwill	1999	15237
142 0/8	21 5/8	22 2/8	17 0/8	5 5	Crawford County	IL	Clint House	2000	15237
142 0/8	22 7/8	22 2/8	15 4/8	5 5	Columbia County	WI	Lance Braaksma	2000	15237
142 0/8	22 7/8	23 0/8	19 7/8	7 7	Buffalo County	WI	Gregory Cugliari	2000	15237
142 0/8	23 1/8	22 6/8	15 3/8	5 6	Highland County	OH	Willie Davis	2000	15237
142 0/8	22 2/8	23 1/8	19 6/8	5 5	Sarpy County	NE	Trevor Hefley	2001	15237
142 0/8	23 4/8	22 1/8	17 4/8	5 6	Jackson County	WI	Eugene Krohn	2001	15237
142 0/8	25 2/8	25 7/8	19 0/8	7 5	Franklin County	PA	John Marcoux	2001	15237
142 0/8	24 2/8	23 7/8	18 6/8	5 5	Outagamie County	WI	Alois "Tom" Leisgang	2001	15237
142 0/8	22 4/8	22 6/8	16 6/8	6 7	Van Buren County	IA	Todd Rumsey	2001	15237
142 0/8	24 6/8	23 4/8	15 0/8	5 7	Muskingum County	OH	Scott Bare, Jr.	2001	15237
142 0/8	21 4/8	23 0/8	15 4/8	4 4	Mountrail County	ND	Bryan Gray	2002	15237
142 0/8	22 0/8	21 5/8	16 1/8	6 5	Morrison County	MN	Vaughn Cornelius	2002	15237
142 0/8	23 6/8	24 5/8	19 5/8	7 5	Allen County	IN	Chuck Moughler	2002	15237
142 0/8	26 7/8	26 6/8	20 7/8	5 5	Middlesex County	MA	Delfo Ferranti	2002	15237
142 0/8	20 1/8	20 1/8	15 0/8	5 5	Lyman County	SD	Bob Karlen	2002	15237
142 0/8	25 5/8	25 1/8	19 6/8	4 4	Suffolk County	NY	Sean Abrams	2002	15237
142 0/8	23 6/8	22 3/8	18 6/8	6 6	Fayette County	IL	Lance Chapman	2002	15237
142 0/8	25 3/8	24 2/8	17 1/8	6 4	Barber County	KS	Stephen Brecq	2003	15237
142 0/8	20 4/8	20 7/8	17 4/8	6 5	Cherokee County	KS	Casey Roberts	2003	15237
*142 0/8	23 5/8	23 5/8	18 0/8	5 5	Fond du Lac County	WI	Benjamin Giese	2003	15237
142 0/8	24 5/8	23 6/8	20 6/8	4 4	Harrison County	OH	William R. Patterson	2003	15237
142 0/8	25 0/8	24 0/8	18 2/8	5 6	Dane County	WI	James A. Zbigniewicz	2003	15237
*142 0/8	23 4/8	23 3/8	16 5/8	6 4	Rock Island County	IL	John Klossing	2003	15237
*142 0/8	22 4/8	23 4/8	21 0/8	6 6	Washington County	IN	Neil Coyle	2004	15237
142 0/8	24 6/8	26 1/8	19 2/8	5 5	Nodaway County	MO	Lee Swearingen	2004	15237
142 0/8	25 0/8	25 1/8	19 2/8	4 4	Clark County	WI	John N. Schneider	2004	15237
142 0/8	23 6/8	22 5/8	19 4/8	5 5	Eau Claire County	WI	John Susa	2004	15237
142 0/8	23 3/8	22 7/8	17 1/8	5 6	Marathon County	WI	Floyd D. Matteson	2004	15237
142 0/8	22 5/8	24 3/8	19 6/8	6 5	Knox County	NE	Ron Ekstrand	2004	15237
*142 0/8	23 1/8	23 0/8	16 6/8	5 4	Traverse County	MN	Gordon Krumwiede	2004	15237
142 0/8	24 3/8	24 2/8	17 2/8	5 5	Buffalo County	WI	Jeff Klieforth	2004	15237
142 0/8	24 1/8	23 0/8	16 0/8	5 5	Macon County	IL	Donald Smith	2004	15237
142 0/8	26 2/8	26 4/8	20 6/8	5 5	Geauga County	OH	Jeff Randles	2004	15237
142 0/8	22 3/8	20 1/8	15 6/8	5 5	White County	IL	Travis Conrad	2004	15237
*142 0/8	23 4/8	23 6/8	17 4/8	5 5	W. Feliciana Parish	LA	Matthew Aldridge	2005	15237
*142 0/8	24 6/8	24 0/8	17 6/8	5 4	Marion County	IL	Dannie White	2005	15237
142 0/8	25 0/8	24 2/8	18 4/8	6 5	Knox County	IL	Zach Sharp	2005	15237
142 0/8	23 4/8	23 3/8	19 0/8	5 5	Trempealeau County	WI	Chad Gill	2005	15237
142 0/8	19 4/8	20 5/8	15 2/8	5 5	Clinton County	MI	William J. Irrer	2005	15237
*142 0/8	24 3/8	23 7/8	17 6/8	5 5	St. Croix County	WI	Paul E. Korn	2005	15237
142 0/8	23 4/8	23 2/8	16 6/8	6 5	Monona County	IA	Gary J. Smith	2005	15237
142 0/8	25 0/8	25 5/8	17 2/8	6 5	Reno County	KS	Greg Sims	2005	15237
142 0/8	25 0/8	25 5/8	20 4/8	4 5	Shawano County	WI	Shawn M. Fletcher	2005	15237
142 0/8	23 2/8	23 5/8	18 6/8	5 6	Clarke County	IA	Brad Northway	2005	15237
142 0/8	22 3/8	22 6/8	18 1/8	5 6	Round Lake	SAS	Floyd Forster	2006	15237
142 0/8	24 4/8	23 6/8	16 2/8	8 8	Camden County	MO	Ryan Gibson	2006	15237
*142 0/8	23 1/8	23 1/8	15 6/8	5 5	Wake County	NC	Miles A. Dean, Jr.	2006	15237
142 0/8	23 3/8	25 3/8	19 5/8	6 5	Bartholomew County	IN	Gary S. Walters	2006	15237
*142 0/8	22 2/8	22 6/8	15 7/8	5 6	Clearwater County	MN	Steve Wraa	2006	15237
142 0/8	24 6/8	25 4/8	14 7/8	7 6	Pike County	IL	Bruce Schulz	2006	15237
*142 0/8	22 1/8	21 6/8	17 6/8	4 5	Marathon County	WI	Jay Heeg	2006	15237
142 0/8	22 5/8	22 2/8	18 6/8	6 6	Saline County	IL	Clint Price	2006	15237
142 0/8	23 1/8	23 1/8	19 0/8	5 5	Vernon County	WI	Bill Collins	2007	15237
142 0/8	23 4/8	23 0/8	14 6/8	5 6	Jasper County	IA	Don Morris	2007	15237
142 0/8	21 7/8	21 4/8	14 6/8	5 6	Pushmataha County	OK	Dirk Megee, Sr.	2007	15237
142 0/8	22 0/8	22 5/8	17 4/8	6 6	Auglaize County	OH	Shane McCollum	2007	15237
142 0/8	24 5/8	23 2/8	19 6/8	4 4	Story County	IA	Dan Baxter	2007	15237
*142 0/8	25 0/8	25 1/8	22 6/8	4 4	Barber County	KS	John Files	2007	15237
*142 0/8	22 0/8	22 0/8	18 2/8	5 6	Mitchell County	IA	Royce R. Schultz	2007	15237
*142 0/8	22 2/8	23 4/8	14 6/8	5 5	Scott County	IL	Roger D. Scott	2007	15237
*142 0/8	25 2/8	25 7/8	17 0/8	4 6	Greenup County	KY	Chris Bentley	2008	15237
142 0/8	23 1/8	23 2/8	19 6/8	5 6	Green Lake County	WI	Michael J. Sina	2008	15237
142 0/8	24 2/8	24 3/8	20 6/8	5 5	Calumet County	WI	Alan R. Miller	2008	15237
*142 0/8	23 6/8	24 1/8	22 2/8	5 4	Butler County	OH	Jim Harvey	2008	15237
142 0/8	21 5/8	22 5/8	18 0/8	5 6	Coshocton County	OH	Donald Hale	2009	15237
*142 0/8	22 7/8	22 3/8	17 6/8	5 4	Venango County	PA	Jason Kontaxes	2009	15237
*142 0/8	24 3/8	24 5/8	15 6/8	4 4	Estill County	KY	Jason Freeman	2009	15237
*142 0/8	21 5/8	20 4/8	16 2/8	5 5	Woodford County	KY	Brett Hornback	2009	15237
*142 0/8	23 6/8	23 3/8	18 5/8	6 6	Richland County	WI	Andy Keller	2009	15237
*142 0/8	22 6/8	21 5/8	12 4/8	6 6	Barnes County	ND	Dean Breske	2009	15237
*142 0/8	24 6/8	23 4/8	17 0/8	5 5	Allegan County	MI	Kenneth Gibbie	2009	15237
141 7/8	24 2/8	24 5/8	23 3/8	4 6	Jackson County	IA	Thomas L. Berkley	1959	15384
141 7/8	23 0/8	22 0/8	20 1/8	5 4	Pottawattamie County	IA	Gary A. Green	1968	15384
141 7/8	21 0/8	19 6/8	15 2/8	5 5	Lincoln County	SD	Kai R. Anderson	1972	15384
141 7/8	23 6/8	22 1/8	17 1/8	5 5	Stony Plain	ALB	Barry A. Olsen	1979	15384
141 7/8	26 0/8	26 2/8	20 5/8	4 4	Hocking County	OH	Paul T. Sater	1979	15384
141 7/8	23 7/8	23 3/8	17 3/8	4 5	Pine County	MN	Jack Pichotta	1980	15384
141 7/8	25 5/8	26 2/8	18 3/8	4 4	Shelby County	OH	Kenneth E. Huffman	1982	15384

WHITETAIL DEER (TYPICAL ANTLERS)

Minimum Score 125   Continued

SCORE	LENGTH OF R MAIN BEAM L	INSIDE SPREAD	NUMBER OF R POINTS L		AREA	STATE/ PROVINCE	HUNTER'S NAME	DATE	RANK
141 7/8	26 2/8	26 3/8	21 0/8	5	6	Coshocton County	OH	Mike Stumph	1983	15384
141 7/8	21 2/8	20 6/8	18 3/8	5	5	Dunn County	WI	Bruce Olson	1983	15384
141 7/8	25 1/8	24 7/8	20 5/8	5	5	Kent County	ONT	John McGuigan	1984	15384
141 7/8	25 7/8	24 4/8	19 5/8	4	4	Muskingum County	OH	Rick A. Goodin	1984	15384
141 7/8	23 6/8	23 6/8	17 3/8	4	5	Camden County	MO	Steve West	1985	15384
141 7/8	24 7/8	24 4/8	16 1/8	5	5	Anderson County	SC	J. Alan Wilson, Jr.	1985	15384
141 7/8	25 3/8	24 6/8	20 0/8	5	5	Seneca County	NY	Dominic D'Amico	1985	15384
141 7/8	22 6/8	21 1/8	18 3/8	5	5	Richland County	WI	Jerry L. Gander	1986	15384
141 7/8	24 1/8	23 3/8	14 3/8	5	4	Waushara County	WI	Douglas F. Kornel	1987	15384
141 7/8	24 6/8	25 2/8	21 3/8	5	8	Carroll County	IL	Art Heinze	1987	15384
141 7/8	23 5/8	22 2/8	19 6/8	5	4	Kane County	IL	Carl S. Diesel	1987	15384
141 7/8	20 6/8	21 7/8	17 5/8	6	6	Hunterdon County	NJ	Bob Petner	1987	15384
141 7/8	23 6/8	25 0/8	22 5/8	4	5	Suffolk County	NY	Dennis Marinuzzi	1987	15384
141 7/8	23 7/8	23 5/8	15 7/8	5	5	Kane County	IL	Bruce R. Cummins	1988	15384
141 7/8	19 7/8	19 2/8	15 6/8	5	6	Burleigh County	ND	Gordon Smith	1988	15384
141 7/8	21 4/8	21 4/8	18 7/8	5	5	Kittson County	MN	James B Frederick	1989	15384
141 7/8	23 0/8	23 7/8	17 2/8	5	6	Calhoun County	MI	Edward A. Conkell	1989	15384
141 7/8	24 2/8	24 6/8	22 3/8	4	4	Somerset County	NJ	Bob Santiago	1990	15384
141 7/8	21 7/8	22 1/8	17 3/8	5	5	Schuyler County	IL	John Johnston	1990	15384
141 7/8	23 3/8	24 1/8	22 3/8	4	5	Crawford County	WI	Ivan Heisz	1991	15384
141 7/8	24 4/8	25 1/8	19 3/8	5	6	Allegheny County	PA	Michael Barberich	1991	15384
141 7/8	24 2/8	23 6/8	18 7/8	4	5	Massac County	IL	David T. Harris	1991	15384
141 7/8	24 0/8	24 0/8	18 5/8	4	4	Webster County	IA	Edward E. Ulicki	1991	15384
141 7/8	26 1/8	26 1/8	18 1/8	4	4	Marion County	OH	Sam M. Derugen	1991	15384
141 7/8	26 5/8	26 5/8	17 5/8	4	4	Hamilton County	TX	David Parrish	1992	15384
141 7/8	23 2/8	23 3/8	19 0/8	7	6	Douglas County	WI	Charles A. Wright	1992	15384
141 7/8	22 4/8	23 6/8	16 1/8	4	4	Burleigh County	ND	Mike Sahli	1992	15384
141 7/8	21 2/8	21 3/8	18 1/8	5	4	St. Charles County	MO	Mark Gutermuth	1992	15384
141 7/8	23 0/8	23 1/8	19 1/8	4	4	Dawson County	NE	Jim McConathy, Jr.	1993	15384
141 7/8	25 1/8	25 5/8	16 0/8	5	5	Scott County	MN	Mike Genty	1993	15384
141 7/8	25 5/8	25 1/8	18 1/8	5	4	Montgomery County	MD	Mark A. Coletta	1993	15384
141 7/8	23 3/8	23 6/8	19 1/8	6	6	Dunn County	WI	James W. Suckow	1994	15384
141 7/8	23 6/8	23 4/8	17 4/8	4	5	Madison County	MO	Junior Shy	1994	15384
141 7/8	21 5/8	21 5/8	23 0/8	4	4	Fremont County	IA	Curtis L. Athen	1995	15384
141 7/8	28 6/8	28 0/8	20 1/8	5	4	La Salle County	IL	David Both	1995	15384
141 7/8	23 3/8	22 3/8	19 3/8	7	5	Allegheny County	PA	Scott E. Walters	1995	15384
141 7/8	24 7/8	24 7/8	15 7/8	5	5	Vinton County	OH	Robert J. Smith	1995	15384
141 7/8	26 4/8	23 2/8	19 3/8	5	7	La Salle County	IL	Donald Greathouse	1995	15384
141 7/8	24 2/8	24 2/8	17 4/8	5	6	Logan County	WV	Roger D. Maynard	1995	15384
141 7/8	21 1/8	21 0/8	20 4/8	5	6	Talbot County	MD	J. Matthew Getsinger	1995	15384
141 7/8	21 5/8	20 6/8	17 5/8	5	6	Carroll County	KY	Tim Dermon	1996	15384
141 7/8	23 2/8	23 0/8	16 3/8	5	5	Becker County	MN	Joe Skarie	1996	15384
141 7/8	26 3/8	27 4/8	23 3/8	4	4	Fairfax County	VA	Jack B. Yeager	1996	15384
141 7/8	20 5/8	20 5/8	17 5/8	5	6	Des Moines County	IA	Gary Grassi	1996	15384
141 7/8	22 4/8	23 2/8	18 5/8	5	5	Clayton County	IA	Wayne Salow	1996	15384
141 7/8	23 1/8	25 4/8	13 3/8	7	7	Shawnee County	KS	Shawn Beuchat	1996	15384
141 7/8	22 4/8	21 7/8	17 3/8	4	4	Lake County	IL	William L. Snelgrove	1997	15384
141 7/8	23 3/8	24 1/8	17 5/8	5	5	St. Clair County	IL	Jeffery Gross	1997	15384
141 7/8	24 1/8	24 0/8	18 5/8	4	4	Ralls County	MO	Chad Nepple	1997	15384
141 7/8	21 7/8	23 0/8	16 7/8	5	4	Shackelford County	TX	Randy Rifenburgh	1997	15384
141 7/8	22 5/8	22 5/8	17 7/8	5	5	Cass County	MI	Fred Kruger	1997	15384
141 7/8	25 4/8	25 5/8	15 5/8	4	4	Monroe County	WI	Mark Jacobson	1997	15384
141 7/8	24 6/8	25 2/8	22 4/8	6	5	E. Carroll Parish	LA	Randy Duncan	1997	15384
141 7/8	23 4/8	23 4/8	17 5/8	5	5	Dimmit County	TX	Rodney E. Bellett	1997	15384
141 7/8	23 2/8	23 4/8	18 3/8	5	5	Juneau County	WI	Gilbert Lee	1998	15384
141 7/8	19 4/8	20 3/8	18 5/8	5	5	Monona County	IA	Kevin Rittenhouse	1998	15384
141 7/8	26 2/8	26 0/8	23 1/8	3	3	Grayson County	KY	Kelvin Stanton	1998	15384
141 7/8	21 0/8	20 7/8	16 5/8	5	5	Coryell County	TX	Joshua L. Sears	1998	15384
141 7/8	23 3/8	24 2/8	18 6/8	6	5	Todd County	KY	George Addison, Jr.	1998	15384
141 7/8	24 1/8	22 6/8	18 4/8	7	5	Mercer County	PA	Josh Burk	1999	15384
141 7/8	25 0/8	25 7/8	21 4/8	5	6	Prowers County	CO	Dennis L. Howell	1999	15384
141 7/8	23 7/8	23 4/8	20 3/8	6	6	Brown County	MN	Dave Larson	1999	15384
141 7/8	20 0/8	22 3/8	14 1/8	6	7	Pittsburg County	OK	J. Michael Goodnight	1999	15384
141 7/8	22 5/8	22 0/8	14 7/8	5	5	Monroe County	WI	Michael Downing	1999	15384
141 7/8	20 7/8	20 2/8	16 3/8	5	5	Iroquois County	IL	Stanley R. Heimerl	1999	15384
141 7/8	19 5/8	20 4/8	13 3/8	6	5	Southampton County	VA	W. T. Drake, Jr.	1999	15384
141 7/8	23 5/8	21 5/8	23 6/8	6	5	Waukesha County	WI	Neal P. Luterbach	1999	15384
141 7/8	23 3/8	23 2/8	18 1/8	5	5	Richland County	IL	Edward F. Wilson	1999	15384
141 7/8	23 6/8	24 4/8	18 3/8	5	4	Winona County	MN	Scott Roberts	1999	15384
141 7/8	23 0/8	22 6/8	18 5/8	4	6	Delaware County	IA	Gary Havlik	1999	15384
141 7/8	21 4/8	22 0/8	20 5/8	6	5	Shelby County	IL	Tyler Sims	2000	15384
141 7/8	21 1/8	21 5/8	15 3/8	5	5	Adams County	WI	Daniel L. Finup	2000	15384
141 7/8	25 0/8	25 6/8	21 1/8	4	5	Buffalo County	WI	Mark A Witcepalek Brouchoud	2000	15384
141 7/8	20 7/8	22 3/8	16 5/8	6	6	Rockingham County	VA	Keith Dean	2000	15384
141 7/8	20 1/8	20 2/8	14 5/8	5	5	Williamson County	TN	Fred Harvey	2000	15384
141 7/8	22 7/8	21 6/8	15 5/8	7	5	Pepin County	WI	Kenneth E. Nimmo	2000	15384
141 7/8	25 1/8	25 6/8	18 5/8	6	6	Steuben County	NY	Timothy Olszowy	2000	15384
141 7/8	24 5/8	26 2/8	19 5/8	5	5	Winnebago County	IL	Carl Stricker	2000	15384
141 7/8	26 2/8	24 4/8	18 4/8	5	6	Jersey County	IL	Mark Stephens	2000	15384
141 7/8	23 1/8	22 7/8	16 5/8	5	5	Richland County	WI	Gregory L. Beighley	2000	15384
141 7/8	22 3/8	23 0/8	19 1/8	5	5	Eau Claire County	WI	Tom Harris, Jr.	2000	15384
141 7/8	25 6/8	24 6/8	20 7/8	5	6	Warren County	VA	Timothy W. Harmon	2000	15384
141 7/8	23 0/8	22 1/8	16 3/8	5	5	Harper County	KS	John Files	2000	15384
141 7/8	22 2/8	18 1/8	17 5/8	5	7	Jasper County	IA	Albert Augustin	2000	15384
141 7/8	22 6/8	23 5/8	18 1/8	4	5	Henry County	IN	Daniel E. Waples	2001	15384
141 7/8	25 7/8	27 1/8	19 2/8	6	7	Greene County	IN	Ray Farmer	2001	15384
141 7/8	23 4/8	25 0/8	17 4/8	5	4	Will County	IL	Karl F. Lange	2001	15384
141 7/8	25 4/8	25 4/8	20 7/8	4	4	Delaware County	IA	Richard P. Smith	2001	15384
141 7/8	22 2/8	22 4/8	21 3/8	4	4	La Crosse County	WI	Jerry Jorgensen	2001	15384
141 7/8	24 1/8	23 7/8	18 6/8	6	6	Shelby County	OH	Jarrod D. Whitehead	2001	15384
141 7/8	21 2/8	21 1/8	14 5/8	5	6	Hancock County	OH	Jason L. Collert	2001	15384
141 7/8	23 0/8	24 4/8	21 0/8	7	6	Mason County	IL	Robert Stinauer	2002	15384
141 7/8	22 4/8	22 3/8	15 1/8	5	5	Vernon County	WI	Wade Carney	2002	15384
141 7/8	21 0/8	20 0/8	17 7/8	5	6	Traill County	ND	Pam Baird	2002	15384
141 7/8	22 0/8	22 0/8	14 1/8	5	5	Boone County	IA	Tejay Meredith	2002	15384

518

WHITETAIL DEER (TYPICAL ANTLERS)

Minimum Score 125 — Continued

SCORE	LENGTH OF R MAIN BEAM L	INSIDE SPREAD	NUMBER OF R POINTS L	AREA	STATE/PROVINCE	HUNTER'S NAME	DATE	RANK
*141 7/8	25 1/8 25 3/8	19 2/8	5 5	Washtenaw County	MI	Brian F. Miller	2002	15384
141 7/8	22 6/8 21 6/8	17 0/8	6 6	Marion County	IN	Larry Jones	2002	15384
141 7/8	24 4/8 23 6/8	22 3/8	6 5	Ogle County	IL	Dr. Todd M. Anderson	2002	15384
141 7/8	26 2/8 26 0/8	21 1/8	4 4	Chicot County	AR	Scott Plunkett	2002	15384
141 7/8	22 5/8 23 3/8	16 3/8	5 6	Conecuh County	AL	H. Eldon Scott III	2003	15384
*141 7/8	23 2/8 22 4/8	14 2/8	6 7	Elk County	KS	Robert Boley	2003	15384
141 7/8	24 6/8 24 2/8	18 5/8	5 4	Niagara County	NY	Michael Lobczowski	2003	15384
*141 7/8	22 0/8 21 7/8	17 1/8	4 4	Adams County	IL	Barry Estes	2003	15384
141 7/8	22 7/8 24 2/8	16 3/8	5 5	Mercer County	MO	Buck Keltner	2004	15384
141 7/8	25 4/8 25 3/8	17 5/8	5 4	Christian County	KY	John Blakeley	2004	15384
141 7/8	27 2/8 25 4/8	21 1/8	5 4	Sangamon County	IL	Brian Bergmann	2004	15384
141 7/8	24 0/8 23 4/8	18 4/8	5 5	Montgomery County	AR	Kevin Partain	2004	15384
141 7/8	21 5/8 22 1/8	16 7/8	5 5	Hubbard County	MN	Michael E. Greetan	2004	15384
141 7/8	21 1/8 20 0/8	15 7/8	5 5	Brown County	OH	David E. Vitori	2004	15384
141 7/8	23 1/8 23 7/8	17 1/8	5 5	Arkansas County	AR	Chris Youngblood	2004	15384
141 7/8	24 7/8 25 7/8	20 1/8	4 5	Montgomery County	KS	John Layton	2004	15384
141 7/8	23 1/8 23 2/8	18 1/8	5 5	Taylor County	WI	Gary French	2004	15384
141 7/8	23 5/8 23 6/8	15 7/8	5 5	Onondaga County	NY	Don Myers	2005	15384
141 7/8	24 0/8 24 4/8	18 3/8	4 4	Somerset County	MD	Michael J. Hinman	2005	15384
141 7/8	22 1/8 22 3/8	17 7/8	5 5	Daviess County	IN	Abraham L. Knepp	2005	15384
141 7/8	23 1/8 22 6/8	17 5/8	8 7	Kosciusko County	IN	Brett Anthony	2005	15384
141 7/8	23 0/8 22 7/8	15 7/8	6 6	Traill County	ND	Steven W. Larson	2005	15384
141 7/8	21 5/8 21 4/8	13 1/8	5 5	Daviess County	KY	Rodney Adkins	2005	15384
141 7/8	20 2/8 20 7/8	15 7/8	5 5	Buffalo County	WI	Dave Justmann	2005	15384
*141 7/8	23 5/8 22 5/8	20 5/8	4 5	Anne Arundel County	MD	Bob Carlson	2005	15384
141 7/8	23 6/8 25 1/8	17 5/8	4 6	Issaquena County	MS	Andy White	2006	15384
141 7/8	21 4/8 22 2/8	14 0/8	5 5	Boone County	MO	Steve Washam	2006	15384
*141 7/8	24 7/8 24 5/8	18 5/8	4 4	Pepin County	WI	Greg Bethel	2006	15384
*141 7/8	25 3/8 25 1/8	16 6/8	6 6	Monroe County	IA	Scott Prucha	2006	15384
141 7/8	24 5/8 24 6/8	18 7/8	7 6	Kearny County	KS	Gary Shumate	2006	15384
141 7/8	22 2/8 22 1/8	17 5/8	5 5	Cottle County	TX	Terry Rice	2006	15384
141 7/8	23 2/8 22 6/8	17 3/8	5 5	Burnett County	WI	Steven F. Blanchette	2006	15384
141 7/8	22 2/8 22 4/8	17 7/8	5 5	Buffalo County	WI	Gary Fleishauer	2006	15384
141 7/8	22 7/8 23 1/8	19 5/8	5 5	Sawyer County	WI	Steve Loker	2007	15384
*141 7/8	24 0/8 23 0/8	19 3/8	5 5	Monroe County	WI	Larry L. Gilles	2007	15384
*141 7/8	20 2/8 21 5/8	18 1/8	5 5	Houston County	TX	Clint Sorensen	2007	15384
*141 7/8	22 3/8 22 0/8	16 7/8	5 5	McCulloch County	TX	Grover C. Tuggle, Jr.	2007	15384
*141 7/8	23 1/8 22 6/8	18 3/8	5 5	Eau Claire County	WI	Shanon Moon	2007	15384
*141 7/8	22 5/8 22 4/8	14 6/8	5 6	Logan County	WV	Marcus Lambert	2007	15384
141 7/8	25 6/8 25 6/8	16 3/8	6 6	Rogers County	OK	Corbin Rowe	2007	15384
141 7/8	22 7/8 22 4/8	18 7/8	5 5	Polk County	MN	Joe Ramerth	2007	15384
141 7/8	24 4/8 24 4/8	17 6/8	6 7	Meigs County	OH	Brian Stupp	2007	15384
141 7/8	25 1/8 24 4/8	17 3/8	4 5	Wells County	IN	Kelvin Michael	2007	15384
141 7/8	24 4/8 25 5/8	19 7/8	5 5	Mercer County	NJ	Ricky Fallon	2007	15384
*141 7/8	24 5/8 24 5/8	17 3/8	5 4	Monroe County	PA	Herb Courtright	2008	15384
141 7/8	23 3/8 23 4/8	14 3/8	5 5	Wyandot County	OH	Monte D. Saam	2008	15384
*141 7/8	22 5/8 22 6/8	15 5/8	5 5	Martin County	IN	Bryan C. Fox	2008	15384
141 7/8	20 1/8 19 7/8	15 3/8	6 7	El Paso County	CO	Thomas J. Baca	2008	15384
141 7/8	21 1/8 20 7/8	13 7/8	6 6	Portage County	WI	James A. Koziczkowski	2008	15384
141 7/8	23 0/8 22 2/8	18 5/8	5 5	Avery County	NC	Douglas Tennant	2009	15384
*141 7/8	24 2/8 22 7/8	19 0/8	6 6	Whiteside County	IL	Clint Walker	2009	15384
141 7/8	23 4/8 24 3/8	15 7/8	5 5	Jefferson County	WI	Ernie Turpin	2009	15384
*141 7/8	23 6/8 23 1/8	17 6/8	5 6	McDonough County	IL	David G. Misner	2009	15384
*141 7/8	23 0/8 23 0/8	20 4/8	5 4	Adams County	IA	Dennis Coenen, Jr.	2009	15384
141 7/8	23 1/8 23 0/8	17 3/8	5 5	McDowell County	WV	Bernard Shorter	2009	15384
*141 7/8	22 5/8 21 4/8	17 1/8	5 7	Washington County	MS	Dr. Larry Ennis	2009	15384
*141 7/8	23 3/8 21 5/8	20 3/8	5 5	Bolivar County	MS	Duke Morgan, Jr.	2009	15384
141 6/8	24 3/8 24 2/8	20 0/8	4 4	Morrison County	MN	Rodney W. Olson	1958	15543
141 6/8	21 6/8 22 3/8	15 2/8	5 5	Eau Claire County	WI	Gordy Robinson	1962	15543
141 6/8	23 6/8 23 7/8	17 4/8	5 4	Dodge County	MN	Cy Champa	1969	15543
141 6/8	23 6/8 24 4/8	24 0/8	4 4	Newton County	IN	Denny Raper	1980	15543
141 6/8	20 5/8 22 6/8	17 2/8	5 5	Alpena County	MI	Michael E. Kaiser	1981	15543
141 6/8	24 7/8 24 2/8	20 2/8	4 4	Todd County	MN	Ted Pilgrim	1981	15543
141 6/8	26 2/8 25 2/8	22 6/8	4 4	Johnson County	NE	Ronald G. Filip	1981	15543
141 6/8	24 4/8 23 2/8	17 2/8	5 6	Pittsburg County	OK	Richard H. Gill	1984	15543
141 6/8	21 4/8 21 4/8	17 2/8	5 7	Hughes County	SD	Kent D. Keenlyne	1984	15543
141 6/8	21 4/8 21 2/8	16 1/8	5 6	Lyon County	MN	Randy S Van Overbeke	1985	15543
141 6/8	24 1/8 24 3/8	19 2/8	5 5	Strathcona	ALB	Jack Kempf	1985	15543
141 6/8	20 6/8 21 2/8	16 4/8	5 5	Jefferson County	WI	Mike Leslie	1986	15543
141 6/8	21 7/8 22 1/8	16 2/8	6 5	Audrain County	MO	Darrell Miller	1986	15543
141 6/8	25 5/8 25 7/8	18 5/8	7 5	Meigs County	OH	James J. Vitale, Jr.	1987	15543
141 6/8	23 1/8 23 7/8	17 1/8	6 6	Mower County	MN	Jeffrey L. Boucher	1987	15543
141 6/8	25 2/8 25 1/8	18 2/8	4 4	Chisago County	MN	Patrick Smith	1988	15543
141 6/8	23 1/8 23 5/8	19 4/8	5 6	Lee County	IL	Tim Robinson	1988	15543
141 6/8	25 0/8 25 0/8	16 5/8	4 5	York	ONT	Dave Barnacal	1989	15543
141 6/8	22 3/8 22 3/8	15 4/8	5 5	Caldwell County	MO	Michael C. Burr	1989	15543
141 6/8	23 3/8 23 1/8	19 2/8	6 5	Will County	IL	Ronald R. Henson	1990	15543
141 6/8	23 1/8 23 1/8	17 2/8	4 4	Brazos County	TX	John Dury	1990	15543
141 6/8	27 4/8 26 3/8	18 3/8	5 8	Ross County	OH	Don Rawn	1990	15543
141 6/8	22 2/8 22 6/8	16 0/8	5 5	Clay County	MO	John Godfrey	1991	15543
141 6/8	22 6/8 23 0/8	19 2/8	5 5	Columbia County	WI	Richard A. Prescott	1991	15543
141 6/8	23 6/8 23 4/8	19 4/8	5 5	Tipton County	IN	Don Cole	1991	15543
141 6/8	21 7/8 21 5/8	17 0/8	5 5	New Castle County	DE	Earl McSorley	1991	15543
141 6/8	22 0/8 22 1/8	15 1/8	7 6	Oneida County	WI	David J. Hoppe	1991	15543
141 6/8	23 5/8 22 3/8	17 0/8	4 4	Mercer County	IL	Charles L. Winston	1991	15543
141 6/8	21 2/8 22 0/8	16 0/8	6 6	Buffalo County	WI	James K. Kraft	1992	15543
141 6/8	25 5/8 25 4/8	17 3/8	5 6	Lawrence County	OH	Brian Massie	1992	15543
141 6/8	24 1/8 25 1/8	20 1/8	6 8	Berrien County	MI	David Kennedy	1992	15543
141 6/8	23 4/8 24 1/8	14 4/8	8 5	Oneida County	WI	Jeff A. Fehrenbach	1992	15543
141 6/8	23 1/8 22 3/8	19 0/8	4 5	La Salle County	IL	James D. Lockhart	1992	15543
141 6/8	24 7/8 24 7/8	19 6/8	4 4	Chase County	KS	Ron Smith	1992	15543
141 6/8	21 5/8 21 5/8	16 3/8	6 5	Hennepin County	MN	Richard Williams	1993	15543
141 6/8	21 3/8 21 4/8	16 6/8	5 5	Edmonson County	KY	Vernon Decker	1993	15543
141 6/8	20 5/8 20 0/8	15 4/8	7 6	Hubbard County	MN	Bob Ness	1993	15543
141 6/8	21 7/8 23 2/8	16 6/8	4 4	Butler County	KY	Ricky L. Harper	1993	15543

WHITETAIL DEER (TYPICAL ANTLERS)

Minimum Score 125   Continued

SCORE	LENGTH OF R MAIN BEAM L	INSIDE SPREAD	NUMBER OF R POINTS L		AREA	STATE/ PROVINCE	HUNTER'S NAME	DATE	RANK
141 6/8	24 1/8 23 6/8	16 3/8	5	6	Appanoose County	IA	Jeff Van Tress	1993	15543
141 6/8	24 5/8 23 4/8	17 5/8	6	5	Hopkins County	KY	W. G. Hayden, Jr.	1993	15543
141 6/8	27 4/8 28 2/8	22 2/8	6	4	Todd County	KY	Jerald Tabb	1993	15543
141 6/8	25 0/8 24 4/8	22 0/8	4	5	Menard County	IL	Russ Dixon	1993	15543
141 6/8	23 4/8 24 3/8	18 2/8	5	6	Tallapoosa County	AL	Wesley Ashcraft	1994	15543
141 6/8	25 1/8 24 6/8	19 1/8	7	5	Crawford County	WI	Russ Gillitzer	1994	15543
141 6/8	25 0/8 25 3/8	15 2/8	4	5	Monroe County	WI	Robert C. Stout	1994	15543
141 6/8	23 4/8 23 4/8	19 6/8	4	5	Union County	KY	Huey K. Long	1994	15543
141 6/8	23 0/8 23 1/8	19 4/8	4	4	Haskell County	KS	Neal Heaton	1994	15543
141 6/8	20 2/8 21 2/8	17 4/8	5	5	Will County	IL	James A. Wetmore	1994	15543
141 6/8	21 7/8 21 6/8	17 4/8	5	5	Jackson County	WI	Dan R. Merritt	1995	15543
141 6/8	21 6/8 21 4/8	16 6/8	5	5	Crook County	WY	Scott Fullerton	1995	15543
141 6/8	20 7/8 20 6/8	16 3/8	6	5	Washington County	NE	Don Sundell	1995	15543
141 6/8	23 3/8 23 2/8	19 6/8	6	5	Brown County	SD	Jon Russell	1995	15543
141 6/8	24 0/8 25 3/8	20 2/8	5	5	Westchester County	NY	Carl G. Schuster	1995	15543
141 6/8	21 0/8 22 1/8	17 4/8	5	5	Manitowoc County	WI	Randy Flentje	1995	15543
141 6/8	25 3/8 24 2/8	19 0/8	4	4	De Witt County	IL	Terry Poppe	1995	15543
141 6/8	26 6/8 26 0/8	19 3/8	5	6	Knox County	OH	Jason Elliott	1995	15543
141 6/8	22 7/8 21 7/8	18 2/8	4	4	Rock County	WI	Christopher A. Leach	1996	15543
141 6/8	23 6/8 24 4/8	19 3/8	5	5	Wayne County	NY	Jim Mourey	1996	15543
141 6/8	24 0/8 22 3/8	18 6/8	5	4	Morris County	NJ	John G. Belanger	1996	15543
141 6/8	23 6/8 22 7/8	20 6/8	6	6	St. Charles County	MO	Jeff Narzinski	1996	15543
141 6/8	21 4/8 21 5/8	18 2/8	4	4	Marshall County	KS	Roger Seematter	1996	15543
141 6/8	22 7/8 23 3/8	19 6/8	5	5	Millarville	ALB	Joel Bickler	1996	15543
141 6/8	24 6/8 24 6/8	20 2/8	5	4	Vermillion County	IN	John Moore	1996	15543
141 6/8	20 2/8 20 6/8	17 0/8	5	6	Fond du Lac County	WI	Kenneth E. Fischer	1996	15543
141 6/8	24 5/8 24 6/8	18 2/8	4	5	Steuben County	NY	Raymond Nisbet	1997	15543
141 6/8	22 6/8 22 7/8	18 2/8	5	5	Genesee County	NY	Bill Nicoll	1997	15543
141 6/8	23 7/8 23 5/8	18 4/8	5	5	Olmsted County	MN	Chad Powell	1997	15543
141 6/8	24 1/8 23 0/8	19 4/8	5	5	Burnett County	WI	Kent Bassett	1998	15543
141 6/8	24 7/8 25 3/8	18 4/8	4	4	Dane County	WI	Troy Williams	1998	15543
141 6/8	24 5/8 23 2/8	20 2/8	4	5	Sawyer County	WI	Jeff Williamson	1998	15543
141 6/8	25 3/8 26 5/8	20 4/8	6	4	Newton County	IN	Todd James	1998	15543
141 6/8	26 0/8 26 1/8	15 0/8	5	6	Madison County	IL	Patrick Kelly	1998	15543
141 6/8	24 1/8 23 1/8	18 0/8	4	4	Hancock County	IL	Mike Lamade	1998	15543
141 6/8	24 7/8 24 5/8	17 4/8	4	4	Panola County	MS	Fred Hentz	1999	15543
141 6/8	25 7/8 24 4/8	15 4/8	5	5	Calvert County	MD	Curtis W. Benko	1999	15543
141 6/8	23 5/8 24 4/8	19 4/8	4	4	Waukesha County	WI	Mike Malinowski	1999	15543
141 6/8	26 0/8 25 4/8	17 4/8	7	5	Phelps County	MO	Eugene Skyles	1999	15543
141 6/8	24 7/8 22 7/8	19 7/8	5	4	Muskingum County	OH	Daren Gillespie	1999	15543
141 6/8	25 3/8 24 2/8	16 1/8	4	5	Lenawee County	MI	Terry A. Brooks	1999	15543
141 6/8	21 6/8 22 2/8	21 4/8	5	5	Burke County	ND	Jay Hass	1999	15543
141 6/8	22 0/8 22 1/8	17 4/8	5	5	Douglas County	WI	Dwayne Perry	1999	15543
141 6/8	21 3/8 22 2/8	18 2/8	5	5	Spokane County	WA	Brian V. Taylor	2000	15543
141 6/8	23 3/8 21 2/8	16 6/8	4	4	Somerset County	NJ	Joseph Raio	2000	15543
141 6/8	24 3/8 24 2/8	17 2/8	5	5	Clayton County	IA	Duane Fox	2000	15543
141 6/8	24 4/8 23 4/8	19 6/8	5	4	Chester County	PA	Brian Buzzard	2000	15543
141 6/8	26 0/8 26 6/8	16 4/8	5	4	Lawrence County	OH	Jim Downs	2000	15543
141 6/8	22 4/8 23 2/8	15 4/8	4	4	Ogle County	IL	Jeremy Bruns	2000	15543
141 6/8	23 1/8 22 3/8	16 6/8	5	5	Walworth County	WI	Dennis Mohr	2000	15543
141 6/8	22 2/8 23 1/8	19 2/8	4	4	Lake County	IL	Carl Spaeth	2000	15543
141 6/8	22 3/8 21 2/8	15 6/8	5	5	Nuckolls County	NE	Arnie Svoboda	2001	15543
141 6/8	24 6/8 23 1/8	19 6/8	4	5	Lorain County	OH	Lyle Bennett	2001	15543
141 6/8	23 2/8 22 6/8	19 6/8	5	5	Lincoln County	CO	Steven J. Hipps	2001	15543
141 6/8	23 0/8 23 2/8	21 0/8	5	7	Warren County	IA	Bruce Hupke	2001	15543
141 6/8	24 6/8 22 3/8	21 0/8	7	6	Saskatoon Mtn.	ALB	Ken Kitzmann	2001	15543
141 6/8	25 4/8 24 1/8	15 3/8	5	6	Somerset County	MD	David Vaxmonsky	2002	15543
141 6/8	22 0/8 22 0/8	20 2/8	5	5	Trempealeau County	WI	Craig Markham	2002	15543
141 6/8	23 3/8 21 7/8	17 2/8	5	6	Richardson County	NE	Todd A. Baker	2002	15543
141 6/8	20 3/8 20 3/8	16 7/8	6	5	Morgan County	IL	Michael Grove	2002	15543
141 6/8	23 1/8 24 2/8	15 2/8	5	5	Bourbon County	KS	Michael W. Andrews	2002	15543
141 6/8	22 4/8 22 4/8	18 0/8	5	5	Sauk County	WI	Brian Taggart	2002	15543
141 6/8	22 7/8 22 0/8	17 0/8	5	4	Ogle County	IL	Terry Parkhouse	2002	15543
141 6/8	22 3/8 21 7/8	16 4/8	5	5	Winona County	MN	Ross Greden	2002	15543
141 6/8	23 6/8 24 4/8	15 0/8	5	5	Iowa County	WI	Steve Zaemisch	2003	15543
141 6/8	22 1/8 22 4/8	16 4/8	7	6	Edwards County	TX	Wendell P. Barnes	2003	15543
141 6/8	25 2/8 25 7/8	18 6/8	7	7	Harrison County	KY	Kevin Poe	2003	15543
*141 6/8	22 3/8 22 4/8	16 0/8	6	7	Pike County	IN	Nathan R. Levitte	2003	15543
141 6/8	24 0/8 23 3/8	16 6/8	4	4	Washington County	IN	Brian K. Taylor	2003	15543
141 6/8	24 1/8 23 2/8	18 6/8	5	5	Marshall County	IL	Mike Rinehart	2003	15543
141 6/8	24 0/8 24 6/8	18 2/8	4	5	Warrick County	IN	Bradley S. Meneely	2003	15543
141 6/8	22 3/8 21 6/8	17 6/8	5	5	Bartholomew County	IN	Boyd L. Emerson	2003	15543
141 6/8	22 7/8 22 5/8	14 6/8	5	5	Madison County	IL	Dale McCain	2003	15543
141 6/8	24 0/8 23 3/8	19 6/8	5	5	Walworth County	WI	Steven Toth	2003	15543
141 6/8	23 0/8 24 7/8	16 4/8	4	4	Macoupin County	IL	Dale Edwards	2003	15543
141 6/8	21 4/8 21 7/8	15 2/8	5	5	Clark County	KS	Ernie Merydith	2003	15543
141 6/8	19 7/8 21 5/8	17 0/8	5	5	Wyoming County	WV	Andy Stewart	2003	15543
141 6/8	24 2/8 22 7/8	18 5/8	6	5	McMullen County	TX	Peter Swenson	2004	15543
141 6/8	22 2/8 22 6/8	17 6/8	5	5	Madison County	MT	Jim Kennedy	2004	15543
141 6/8	22 0/8 21 1/8	16 5/8	5	6	Adams County	WI	Gregory R. Batchelor	2004	15543
141 6/8	21 5/8 23 0/8	18 2/8	5	5	Parke County	IN	Timothy L. Mylin	2004	15543
141 6/8	23 3/8 25 1/8	17 7/8	7	4	Mahoning County	OH	David Rickert	2004	15543
*141 6/8	21 7/8 21 4/8	15 4/8	5	5	McHenry County	ND	Jeremy Dosch	2004	15543
*141 6/8	26 3/8 25 4/8	21 5/8	4	5	Winnebago County	WI	Todd C. Neubauer	2004	15543
141 6/8	22 0/8 22 1/8	17 0/8	4	4	Woodward County	OK	Mike Mohr	2004	15543
141 6/8	23 2/8 22 2/8	19 0/8	4	4	Marion County	IA	Randy Des Camps	2005	15543
141 6/8	23 3/8 23 3/8	19 4/8	6	5	Linn County	MO	Marvin Jackson	2005	15543
141 6/8	23 0/8 24 0/8	19 6/8	4	4	Summit County	OH	Richard Sestito	2005	15543
141 6/8	25 0/8 24 7/8	17 2/8	5	5	St. Clair County	MI	Mark Zelazny	2005	15543
*141 6/8	22 6/8 22 1/8	16 4/8	5	4	Morgan County	MO	David Haake	2006	15543
*141 6/8	23 5/8 21 4/8	18 0/8	4	4	Hamilton County	IL	Michael Southern	2006	15543
*141 6/8	22 1/8 22 2/8	17 0/8	5	5	Clark County	IL	Warren Carr	2006	15543
141 6/8	23 6/8 22 5/8	20 6/8	4	5	Tazewell County	IL	Marc Anthony	2006	15543
141 6/8	22 3/8 24 0/8	19 2/8	5	5	Cattaraugus County	NY	Ron Bull	2006	15543
141 6/8	21 6/8 21 0/8	17 2/8	5	5	Mills County	IA	Devron Moore	2006	15543

WHITETAIL DEER (TYPICAL ANTLERS)

Minimum Score 125   Continued

SCORE	LENGTH OF R MAIN BEAM L	INSIDE SPREAD	NUMBER OF R POINTS L		AREA	STATE/ PROVINCE	HUNTER'S NAME	DATE	RANK
*141 6/8	20 1/8 21 1/8	16 0/8	6	5	Ft. Bend County	TX	Chris Helms	2006	15543
141 6/8	23 1/8 22 7/8	17 3/8	7	5	Spokane County	WA	John Schneider	2006	15543
*141 6/8	23 1/8 21 7/8	19 2/8	5	5	Callahan County	TX	Matthew D. Stark	2007	15543
*141 6/8	22 6/8 22 0/8	14 2/8	5	5	Holt County	MO	Mitch Baker	2007	15543
141 6/8	23 3/8 23 6/8	19 2/8	4	4	Butler County	IA	Mike Klahsen	2007	15543
*141 6/8	24 2/8 24 3/8	17 0/8	5	5	Elk County	PA	Nathan Weinzierl	2007	15543
*141 6/8	22 6/8 23 1/8	16 6/8	4	4	Clinton County	MI	Pete G. Smith	2007	15543
*141 6/8	23 6/8 24 3/8	14 4/8	4	5	La Crosse County	WI	James A. Larson	2007	15543
141 6/8	25 4/8 24 3/8	16 4/8	5	5	St. Clair County	IL	Mark Laquet	2007	15543
141 6/8	22 5/8 20 1/8	16 5/8	5	7	Waukesha County	WI	Jerry Briski	2007	15543
141 6/8	22 2/8 23 2/8	16 6/8	5	4	Macoupin County	IL	Chris Bettis	2007	15543
141 6/8	24 6/8 25 4/8	17 0/8	6	5	Johnson County	KS	Eric M. Johnson	2007	15543
141 6/8	22 5/8 22 4/8	16 4/8	5	5	Northampton County	NC	William W. Whitley, Jr.	2008	15543
141 6/8	23 3/8 24 1/8	17 4/8	5	5	Henry County	VA	Darrell Joyce	2008	15543
*141 6/8	22 6/8 23 2/8	13 4/8	6	6	Pawnee County	NE	Michael G. Newlun	2008	15543
141 6/8	23 7/8 25 0/8	18 4/8	7	6	Shelby County	OH	Darrell R. Sanders	2008	15543
*141 6/8	20 4/8 22 2/8	18 0/8	5	5	Jefferson County	WI	Clint Dehnert	2008	15543
*141 6/8	20 5/8 20 5/8	13 6/8	5	5	Prowers County	CO	Daniel Orcutt	2008	15543
141 6/8	21 6/8 22 0/8	15 0/8	5	5	Buffalo County	WI	Sue Falkner	2009	15543
141 6/8	22 1/8 22 3/8	14 4/8	7	7	St. Louis County	MO	Greg J. Bock	2009	15543
*141 6/8	19 6/8 20 3/8	16 0/8	6	6	Manitowoc County	WI	Martin Wilfert	2009	15543
141 6/8	24 1/8 22 3/8	17 4/8	5	5	Wadena County	MN	Matthew Rousslang	2009	15543
*141 6/8	24 4/8 24 1/8	14 5/8	6	5	Wythe County	VA	Charles William Shoemaker III	2009	15543
141 6/8	23 7/8 23 4/8	19 7/8	7	6	Winnebago County	WI	Chris Karoses	2009	15543
*141 6/8	22 6/8 22 6/8	16 7/8	5	5	Riley County	KS	Brian Brochu	2009	15543
141 6/8	24 1/8 25 3/8	20 6/8	4	4	Clinton County	MI	Troy B. Braman	2009	15543
*141 6/8	22 2/8 21 6/8	17 2/8	4	4	Hillsdale County	MI	Ken L. Plum	2009	15543
141 6/8	22 4/8 22 5/8	16 6/8	5	7	Randolph County	MO	Web Winfrey	2009	15543
141 6/8	23 0/8 22 1/8	17 0/8	5	5	Marion County	KS	Dennis Ballweg	2009	15543
141 6/8	22 6/8 22 1/8	17 0/8	5	5	Jo Daviess County	IL	Tim Streight	2009	15543
*141 6/8	23 1/8 23 2/8	18 0/8	5	5	Coffey County	KS	Don Erbert	2009	15543
141 5/8	24 0/8 24 3/8	21 6/8	6	3	Allegan County	MI	Stan Skorch	1967	15707
141 5/8	23 3/8 23 5/8	19 5/8	4	5	Crawford County	IL	Jim Earleywine	1978	15707
141 5/8	21 7/8 23 0/8	19 7/8	4	5	Shelby County	IL	Ed Ikemire	1979	15707
141 5/8	24 5/8 24 6/8	17 2/8	5	6	Gallia County	OH	Buck Blankenship	1981	15707
141 5/8	24 7/8 23 7/8	20 1/8	5	4	Roane County	TN	Thomas K. Grause	1981	15707
141 5/8	25 2/8 26 0/8	18 1/8	4	4	Highland County	OH	Douglas Ambroza	1982	15707
141 5/8	23 3/8 22 3/8	19 2/8	5	6	Missoula County	MT	Bob Jacobsen	1982	15707
141 5/8	25 5/8 26 0/8	18 3/8	5	4	Dane County	WI	Don Magnuson	1983	15707
141 5/8	22 2/8 23 2/8	18 1/8	5	5	Grant County	WI	Randy Dressler	1984	15707
141 5/8	22 0/8 22 1/8	17 1/8	5	5	Yellow Medicine County	MN	Harold Greseth	1985	15707
141 5/8	21 7/8 22 4/8	15 5/8	4	4	Sedgwick County	KS	Vince Albert	1986	15707
141 5/8	22 4/8 22 4/8	17 1/8	6	7	Slope County	ND	Dick Cheatley	1987	15707
141 5/8	22 3/8 22 4/8	16 3/8	5	5	Fillmore County	MN	Jim Vagts	1987	15707
141 5/8	23 2/8 22 3/8	17 1/8	5	5	Ozaukee County	WI	Michael Karrels	1988	15707
141 5/8	23 5/8 26 2/8	19 0/8	7	7	Rock County	WI	Dale Snyder	1988	15707
141 5/8	22 3/8 23 2/8	18 1/8	5	5	Wagoner County	OK	Terry Moody	1988	15707
141 5/8	22 7/8 22 6/8	17 1/8	4	4	Strathcona	ALB	Ryk Visscher	1989	15707
141 5/8	24 4/8 23 2/8	17 3/8	7	7	Butler County	KS	Mike Demel	1989	15707
141 5/8	23 4/8 23 7/8	15 4/8	7	8	Sawyer County	WI	Dan Pleoger	1990	15707
141 5/8	22 7/8 22 6/8	18 5/8	6	4	Washington County	MN	Rodney P. Bailey	1990	15707
141 5/8	25 7/8 25 5/8	18 4/8	7	5	Tama County	IA	Dan Yuska	1990	15707
141 5/8	23 4/8 23 6/8	16 6/8	6	5	Wyandot County	OH	Richard V. Ebert	1990	15707
141 5/8	22 6/8 22 0/8	21 1/8	5	5	Boone County	IL	Anthony T. Smith	1990	15707
141 5/8	22 3/8 23 0/8	19 6/8	5	6	Athens County	OH	Michael A. Rex	1991	15707
141 5/8	25 1/8 26 1/8	18 0/8	5	6	Vermilion County	IL	Lonnie D. Massengale	1991	15707
141 5/8	24 1/8 22 0/8	17 7/8	5	4	Martin County	IN	Casey S. Jones	1992	15707
141 5/8	21 5/8 22 0/8	18 5/8	5	5	Pearl River County	MS	Tommy L. Rose	1993	15707
141 5/8	22 3/8 23 4/8	15 6/8	7	6	Poplarfield	MAN	Richard Schweitzer	1993	15707
141 5/8	23 0/8 22 6/8	17 1/8	5	6	Buffalo County	WI	Glenn Vinton	1993	15707
141 5/8	22 4/8 23 1/8	16 7/8	5	5	Crowley County	CO	Frank G. Hallman	1993	15707
141 5/8	23 6/8 23 0/8	15 1/8	5	6	La Salle County	TX	Kirk M. Folsom	1994	15707
141 5/8	26 0/8 25 6/8	21 6/8	4	6	McHenry County	IL	Ernie Meinen	1994	15707
141 5/8	24 6/8 25 2/8	16 5/8	4	5	Harrison County	MO	Mark Gann	1994	15707
141 5/8	23 5/8 23 0/8	14 3/8	5	6	Logan County	AR	William Campbell	1994	15707
141 5/8	24 1/8 23 1/8	20 3/8	4	5	Parke County	IN	Chuck Paddock	1994	15707
141 5/8	25 4/8 25 6/8	18 3/8	4	4	Darke County	OH	Thomas E. Warner	1994	15707
141 5/8	24 1/8 22 5/8	16 7/8	5	6	Crawford County	WI	Emerald A. Faulkner, Jr.	1994	15707
141 5/8	21 2/8 21 1/8	16 4/8	5	5	Travis County	TX	Jerrell Greenwalt	1994	15707
141 5/8	24 6/8 26 0/8	16 7/8	4	5	Kent County	MD	Bruce Fair	1994	15707
141 5/8	24 4/8 24 1/8	18 5/8	5	5	Pope County	MN	LeRoy Olson	1994	15707
141 5/8	20 1/8 21 5/8	15 5/8	5	5	Buffalo County	WI	Joe J. Meinerz	1995	15707
141 5/8	25 1/8 22 6/8	17 1/8	5	5	Bracken County	KY	Tony Schumann	1995	15707
141 5/8	23 4/8 24 0/8	18 4/8	6	4	Marion County	IA	Gerald T. Dowell	1995	15707
141 5/8	22 7/8 23 1/8	20 4/8	6	5	Winnebago County	IL	Dave Judy	1995	15707
141 5/8	22 5/8 22 6/8	15 1/8	5	5	Waupaca County	WI	James J. Hlaban	1996	15707
141 5/8	22 2/8 22 2/8	15 0/8	7	5	Lee County	IA	J. D. White	1996	15707
141 5/8	25 0/8 25 4/8	19 7/8	6	6	Bayfield County	WI	Roger Lemler	1996	15707
141 5/8	26 1/8 26 0/8	20 1/8	5	4	Creek County	OK	Dan R. Massey	1996	15707
141 5/8	23 0/8 23 3/8	19 5/8	4	4	Kosciusko County	IN	Jerry R. Hyde, Jr.	1996	15707
141 5/8	24 2/8 24 1/8	17 7/8	6	5	Crawford County	WI	Mark N. Livingston	1997	15707
141 5/8	23 0/8 23 6/8	18 5/8	5	5	Sauk County	WI	John F. Klus	1997	15707
141 5/8	22 4/8 23 3/8	16 1/8	5	5	Hamilton County	OH	Josh Hamilton	1997	15707
141 5/8	22 4/8 22 3/8	15 6/8	5	4	Washington County	MN	Jason Bellomy	1997	15707
141 5/8	21 5/8 20 0/8	16 3/8	5	5	Manitowoc County	WI	Fran Nellis	1997	15707
141 5/8	22 2/8 23 4/8	18 5/8	4	4	Wapello County	IA	Arnold E. Vest	1997	15707
141 5/8	21 1/8 21 5/8	15 3/8	5	5	Powder River County	MT	Tom Detrick	1998	15707
141 5/8	22 6/8 22 6/8	19 5/8	4	5	Fond du Lac County	WI	Wayne Schumacher	1998	15707
141 5/8	21 1/8 20 2/8	16 1/8	6	5	Waupaca County	WI	Rollie J. Hermes	1998	15707
141 5/8	24 0/8 24 0/8	19 5/8	4	5	Dane County	WI	Mark Maier	1998	15707
141 5/8	21 4/8 21 7/8	15 1/8	6	5	Marathon County	WI	Ken Schreiner	1998	15707
141 5/8	20 7/8 21 7/8	19 1/8	5	5	Ontario County	NY	Richard Young	1998	15707
141 5/8	22 7/8 23 2/8	17 3/8	5	6	Belmont County	OH	Robert L. Lewis	1998	15707
141 5/8	21 7/8 22 1/8	16 7/8	5	6	Lake County	IL	Nick Heelein	1998	15707
141 5/8	23 2/8 23 3/8	18 7/8	4	4	Iowa County	WI	Darles D. Hoffman	1998	15707

521

WHITETAIL DEER (TYPICAL ANTLERS)

Minimum Score 125 — Continued

SCORE	LENGTH OF R MAIN BEAM L	INSIDE SPREAD	NUMBER OF R POINTS L	AREA	STATE/PROVINCE	HUNTER'S NAME	DATE	RANK
141 5/8	23 3/8	24 1/8	18 7/8	6 5	Waukesha County	WI	Nathan Bourdo	1998	15707
141 5/8	23 4/8	24 4/8	18 2/8	5 4	Kootenai County	ID	Jim Nursall	1999	15707
141 5/8	21 0/8	21 7/8	14 0/8	6 8	Crook County	WY	Thomas Hancharuk	1999	15707
141 5/8	22 7/8	22 3/8	17 1/8	5 5	Butler County	KS	Michael Boahn	1999	15707
141 5/8	26 4/8	27 5/8	17 5/8	5 6	Essex County	MA	Jim Owen	1999	15707
141 5/8	22 5/8	21 7/8	18 3/8	5 5	Burnett County	WI	Randy Thomas	1999	15707
141 5/8	25 5/8	26 4/8	21 0/8	8 6	Columbia County	WI	Scott J. Clemmons	1999	15707
141 5/8	24 2/8	23 7/8	19 5/8	4 4	Clark County	IL	Gerald "Gabe" Shaffner	1999	15707
141 5/8	21 0/8	21 5/8	16 3/8	5 5	York County	PA	Donald Sedam	1999	15707
141 5/8	22 1/8	22 0/8	23 4/8	5 5	Carroll County	IL	Lawrence R. Fetzer	1999	15707
141 5/8	24 0/8	24 0/8	16 5/8	5 6	Sharp County	AR	Witt Stephens	2000	15707
141 5/8	21 6/8	23 2/8	16 5/8	5 6	Williams County	OH	James Pearson	2000	15707
141 5/8	22 4/8	23 0/8	17 5/8	4 5	Richland County	MT	Charles S. Caley	2000	15707
141 5/8	24 0/8	24 5/8	22 0/8	5 7	Lee County	IL	Mark Swanson	2000	15707
141 5/8	24 7/8	23 6/8	18 3/8	5 4	Dakota County	MN	Eric Drenckhahn	2000	15707
141 5/8	20 6/8	20 6/8	16 1/8	6 6	Wood County	WI	Bruce B. Leberg, Jr.	2001	15707
141 5/8	24 4/8	24 3/8	16 1/8	4 4	Pike County	IL	Steve R. Swain	2001	15707
141 5/8	23 0/8	22 4/8	17 3/8	5 6	Dodge County	MN	Carl Mergen	2001	15707
141 5/8	20 6/8	21 4/8	15 7/8	5 5	Pike County	OH	August McGinnis	2001	15707
141 5/8	21 2/8	22 0/8	16 2/8	5 6	Dane County	WI	Daniel A. Haun	2001	15707
141 5/8	20 0/8	20 5/8	20 5/8	5 5	Cattaraugus County	NY	Daniel Carroll	2001	15707
141 5/8	22 1/8	22 5/8	20 4/8	7 5	Ottawa County	KS	John B. Bowman	2001	15707
141 5/8	21 2/8	21 6/8	18 5/8	5 5	Switzerland County	IN	Brian Gavin	2002	15707
141 5/8	20 2/8	20 1/8	15 3/8	5 6	Brookings County	SD	Ryan Gruber	2002	15707
141 5/8	24 5/8	24 2/8	17 5/8	4 5	Butler County	PA	Mike Gillespie	2002	15707
141 5/8	22 7/8	23 2/8	18 1/8	5 5	Sheboygan County	WI	Jayson Brendel	2002	15707
141 5/8	23 6/8	23 3/8	17 5/8	4 4	Pickaway County	OH	Thomas J. Preston	2002	15707
141 5/8	23 6/8	24 2/8	17 4/8	6 6	Dauphin County	PA	Kenneth Miller	2002	15707
141 5/8	22 4/8	22 5/8	18 4/8	6 6	Trempealeau County	WI	Ray N. Andersen	2002	15707
141 5/8	25 4/8	25 0/8	16 7/8	4 4	Monroe County	IA	David A. Markham	2002	15707
141 5/8	22 5/8	23 5/8	17 0/8	5 4	Crawford County	PA	Carl Oxley	2002	15707
141 5/8	28 4/8	29 3/8	19 7/8	4 5	Coshocton County	OH	Thomas A. Patsy	2002	15707
141 5/8	22 5/8	23 2/8	19 1/8	5 6	Fayette County	IL	Larry Cripe	2002	15707
141 5/8	22 2/8	21 3/8	15 4/8	7 5	Adams County	IL	Ken Doellman	2002	15707
141 5/8	20 7/8	20 4/8	15 2/8	5 6	Fairfield County	OH	Garry Miller	2002	15707
141 5/8	23 1/8	23 2/8	20 3/8	5 5	Frio County	TX	Joe Keathley	2002	15707
141 5/8	23 0/8	24 0/8	17 0/8	10 5	Pike County	MO	Steve Barnard	2003	15707
141 5/8	22 3/8	21 6/8	18 2/8	6 5	Randolph County	AR	Blake Ashton McCord	2003	15707
141 5/8	24 4/8	25 5/8	19 5/8	4 5	Buffalo County	WI	Ryan Zenk	2003	15707
141 5/8	24 3/8	23 6/8	19 0/8	5 6	Jackson County	IA	Stacy Brown	2003	15707
*141 5/8	25 5/8	26 4/8	19 6/8	6 5	Juneau County	WI	Mike Barreau	2004	15707
141 5/8	20 5/8	19 6/8	17 5/8	5 5	Traill County	ND	Larry Berg	2004	15707
141 5/8	22 0/8	22 1/8	14 3/8	7 6	Chickasaw County	IA	Brad Stendel	2004	15707
141 5/8	25 3/8	24 7/8	19 3/8	5 4	Bucks County	PA	Donald Tarasiewicz Jr.	2004	15707
*141 5/8	23 1/8	23 0/8	17 3/8	5 5	Wayne County	IA	Emmett Smith	2004	15707
141 5/8	22 3/8	22 2/8	17 1/8	5 4	Jackson County	WI	George Laufenberg	2004	15707
141 5/8	23 4/8	23 5/8	22 3/8	4 4	Van Buren County	MI	James R. Casey	2004	15707
141 5/8	24 4/8	25 2/8	20 5/8	4 5	Lucas County	OH	Gerald E. Koralewski	2004	15707
141 5/8	22 1/8	21 5/8	19 7/8	4 4	Erie County	PA	Michael L. Stives	2004	15707
141 5/8	23 0/8	22 1/8	14 7/8	5 5	Wyoming County	WV	Brian E. Glass	2004	15707
141 5/8	24 4/8	21 3/8	14 5/8	5 5	Pike County	IL	Allen Buffington	2004	15707
*141 5/8	22 5/8	22 0/8	16 1/8	5 5	Tom Green County	TX	Rusty Touchstone	2005	15707
141 5/8	24 5/8	24 1/8	19 3/8	5 5	Dane County	WI	Bob Keel	2005	15707
141 5/8	24 2/8	24 3/8	16 3/8	5 5	Pulaski County	IN	David R. Cannon	2005	15707
*141 5/8	22 5/8	23 7/8	17 1/8	5 5	Buffalo County	WI	Matt Foust	2005	15707
141 5/8	23 0/8	24 7/8	19 1/8	5 6	Columbia County	WI	Daniel L. Katsma	2005	15707
*141 5/8	26 6/8	25 7/8	20 1/8	4 4	Shawano County	WI	Walter J. Moesch	2006	15707
*141 5/8	24 5/8	24 0/8	19 4/8	6 7	Wood County	OH	Nickalas Sangregory	2006	15707
141 5/8	21 3/8	21 7/8	16 5/8	5 5	Fond du Lac County	WI	Robert J. Schumacher	2006	15707
141 5/8	26 0/8	25 3/8	20 5/8	4 4	Kane County	IL	Michael A. Steib	2006	15707
*141 5/8	23 6/8	23 5/8	18 5/8	7 8	Buffalo County	WI	Mark Beeler	2006	15707
141 5/8	23 7/8	22 3/8	19 0/8	7 9	Miami County	OH	Tyrone McGhee	2006	15707
141 5/8	23 0/8	21 5/8	23 3/8	4 6	Walworth County	WI	Al Ortmann	2006	15707
*141 5/8	21 6/8	21 3/8	17 6/8	7 6	Allen County	OH	Tim Wurst	2006	15707
*141 5/8	22 4/8	22 5/8	16 3/8	5 5	Hardin County	IA	Jason Jedele	2006	15707
*141 5/8	24 2/8	25 0/8	16 6/8	6 5	Kingman County	KS	Robert Sloey	2006	15707
141 5/8	23 4/8	25 3/8	18 0/8	7 4	Greenwood County	KS	Jeremy Sickles	2006	15707
141 5/8	24 0/8	23 4/8	19 1/8	4 4	Grant County	KY	Elmer Klaber	2007	15707
141 5/8	26 1/8	24 6/8	17 5/8	5 4	Boone County	MO	Eddie Schultz	2007	15707
*141 5/8	23 4/8	22 4/8	18 5/8	5 6	Livingston County	MI	Samuel L. Hoyt	2007	15707
141 5/8	21 2/8	21 4/8	16 2/8	6 6	Burt County	NE	Donald Combs	2007	15707
*141 5/8	23 1/8	22 1/8	17 3/8	5 4	Ross County	OH	Dustin A. Bethel	2007	15707
141 5/8	22 7/8	23 6/8	15 6/8	6 6	La Crosse County	WI	Michael Wadel	2007	15707
*141 5/8	22 2/8	22 3/8	16 3/8	4 4	Iowa County	WI	Randy Statz	2007	15707
141 5/8	23 6/8	24 6/8	18 3/8	4 5	Carlton County	MN	Mike Benson	2007	15707
141 5/8	21 0/8	23 2/8	17 7/8	5 5	Jackson County	MI	Robert Wade Miller	2007	15707
141 5/8	25 1/8	25 4/8	21 5/8	4 5	Kane County	IL	Ray Schremp	2007	15707
*141 5/8	24 1/8	24 6/8	18 1/8	5 5	Jackson County	OH	Michael Schnatterly	2007	15707
141 5/8	22 3/8	23 5/8	16 1/8	5 5	Sumner County	KS	Barry Wiley	2007	15707
141 5/8	24 4/8	24 0/8	16 7/8	5 5	Barry County	MO	Jesse R. Paulsen	2008	15707
141 5/8	25 3/8	23 7/8	17 5/8	7 7	Barron County	WI	Travis Ebner	2008	15707
141 5/8	21 3/8	20 3/8	18 7/8	4 5	Johnson County	KS	Gregory L. Freese	2008	15707
141 5/8	22 0/8	23 0/8	20 1/8	6 6	Columbia County	WI	Ryan Vick	2008	15707
141 5/8	25 0/8	24 3/8	16 7/8	5 4	Trempealeau County	WI	Dan Kampa	2008	15707
*141 5/8	22 2/8	23 0/8	14 7/8	5 6	Juneau County	WI	Jennifer Lambert	2008	15707
141 5/8	23 6/8	23 3/8	18 1/8	4 5	Hamilton County	IA	Aaron Scharf	2008	15707
*141 5/8	22 4/8	21 1/8	19 3/8	6 7	Indiana County	PA	Eric S. Hilliard	2008	15707
*141 5/8	24 2/8	24 4/8	17 7/8	5 5	Burnett County	WI	Bob Svoboda	2008	15707
*141 5/8	21 2/8	21 6/8	16 7/8	6 7	Allen County	KS	Don Erbert	2008	15707
*141 5/8	22 0/8	22 6/8	18 5/8	5 5	Trempealeau County	WI	Duane Dubiel	2008	15707
141 5/8	23 6/8	23 6/8	19 1/8	5 6	Buffalo County	WI	John W. Smart	2009	15707
*141 5/8	21 3/8	21 7/8	18 4/8	6 8	Dunn County	WI	Aaron Knutson	2009	15707
*141 5/8	24 6/8	24 6/8	15 5/8	4 4	Randolph County	MO	Thomas R. Logan, Jr.	2009	15707
141 5/8	25 6/8	25 3/8	23 7/8	6 8	Mills County	IA	Lynn Schrum	2009	15707
*141 5/8	25 1/8	25 3/8	18 1/8	9 6	Waupaca County	WI	Hunter Muthig	2009	15707

522

WHITETAIL DEER (TYPICAL ANTLERS)

Minimum Score 125 — Continued

SCORE	LENGTH OF R MAIN BEAM L	INSIDE SPREAD	NUMBER OF R POINTS L		AREA	STATE/ PROVINCE	HUNTER'S NAME	DATE	RANK
*141 5/8	25 3/8 26 4/8	21 5/8	5	4	Dubuque County	IA	Bill Rauen	2010	15707
141 4/8	21 1/8 21 4/8	19 6/8	5	5	Hyde County	SD	Gordon Sampson	1974	15867
141 4/8	22 3/8 22 3/8	17 4/8	5	5	Richland County	OH	Walter A. Bartashus	1976	15867
141 4/8	23 3/8 22 7/8	17 3/8	5	7	Trigg County	KY	Wayne R. Brooks	1978	15867
141 4/8	23 6/8 24 4/8	19 0/8	5	5	Jackson County	IA	Thomas E. Maas	1979	15867
141 4/8	22 2/8 22 1/8	16 0/8	5	4	Stephenson County	IL	John Miller	1983	15867
141 4/8	20 6/8 20 7/8	17 0/8	5	5	Cowley County	KS	George B. Smith	1983	15867
141 4/8	22 2/8 22 2/8	20 0/8	6	5	Pepin County	WI	Brian Berger	1984	15867
141 4/8	24 0/8 24 4/8	15 2/8	5	5	Jackson County	IA	Todd Simmons	1984	15867
141 4/8	25 4/8 21 0/8	21 0/8	10	9	Wyandotte County	KS	Robert A. Bentz	1984	15867
141 4/8	27 4/8 25 3/8	20 4/8	6	5	McNairy County	TN	Arlus Ray Burney	1985	15867
141 4/8	22 2/8 22 7/8	17 3/8	7	6	Osborne County	KS	Craig Pottberg	1986	15867
141 4/8	25 5/8 25 6/8	16 4/8	7	6	Knox County	IN	Keith Richard Bosecker	1988	15867
141 4/8	21 7/8 20 6/8	13 2/8	5	6	Langlade County	WI	Mike Sheldon	1988	15867
141 4/8	22 4/8 22 7/8	17 4/8	5	6	Texas County	OK	Max Crocker	1988	15867
141 4/8	21 5/8 22 1/8	17 2/8	5	5	Westchester County	NY	Rayot A. DiFate	1988	15867
141 4/8	24 7/8 24 0/8	20 2/8	5	5	Shawano County	WI	Jeffrey J. Gipp	1988	15867
141 4/8	21 3/8 21 0/8	15 0/8	5	6	McHenry County	IL	James Coley	1989	15867
141 4/8	26 5/8 26 6/8	21 0/8	5	4	Warren County	OH	Russell L. Wiessinger	1989	15867
141 4/8	23 0/8 22 6/8	17 6/8	4	4	Sullivan County	IN	David Ridge	1989	15867
141 4/8	21 6/8 21 4/8	18 4/8	5	5	Monona County	IA	Pat Boyle	1989	15867
141 4/8	23 6/8 23 0/8	18 0/8	4	4	Knox County	OH	Gregg A. Melfe	1989	15867
141 4/8	24 0/8 23 7/8	17 7/8	6	5	Prairie County	AR	Doug Casey	1990	15867
141 4/8	21 5/8 21 7/8	13 6/8	5	7	Powell County	MT	Julian Proctor	1990	15867
141 4/8	22 2/8 21 4/8	16 6/8	6	5	La Porte County	IN	Wayne Wood	1990	15867
141 4/8	22 1/8 22 3/8	18 6/8	5	4	Jo Daviess County	IL	David W. Seas	1990	15867
141 4/8	23 4/8 23 4/8	19 6/8	4	6	McHenry County	IL	Russ Tallman	1990	15867
141 4/8	25 6/8 24 7/8	18 4/8	4	4	Oconto County	WI	John Pashek	1990	15867
141 4/8	22 7/8 22 5/8	15 2/8	5	5	Waupaca County	WI	Jeff Behrens	1991	15867
141 4/8	20 7/8 22 3/8	14 6/8	5	5	Loudoun County	VA	Roger Lane Pearce	1991	15867
141 4/8	22 2/8 22 6/8	22 0/8	5	5	Hocking County	OH	Ernie Glason, Jr.	1991	15867
141 4/8	23 3/8 22 7/8	15 4/8	6	6	Loudoun County	VA	Stephen L. George	1991	15867
141 4/8	22 1/8 20 4/8	18 2/8	5	5	Anderson County	KS	Robert G. Coplen	1991	15867
141 4/8	26 3/8 25 1/8	17 3/8	6	5	Jefferson County	IL	Ron Leek	1991	15867
141 4/8	20 7/8 21 0/8	16 2/8	5	5	Kenedy County	TX	Peeler G. Lacey, MD	1992	15867
141 4/8	22 5/8 22 7/8	15 4/8	5	5	Muskingum County	OH	Mike Wilson	1992	15867
141 4/8	24 2/8 23 4/8	17 2/8	4	4	Richland County	ND	Robert Kapaun, Jr.	1992	15867
141 4/8	24 1/8 24 0/8	18 0/8	4	4	Brown County	OH	Robert T. Walker	1992	15867
141 4/8	22 2/8 22 7/8	17 3/8	5	6	Calhoun County	IL	Dewaine Slinkard	1992	15867
141 4/8	22 0/8 22 0/8	19 0/8	5	5	Kiowa County	KS	Karl Ballard	1992	15867
141 4/8	22 1/8 22 5/8	16 4/8	4	4	Jackson County	WI	Dave Eckel	1992	15867
141 4/8	23 5/8 23 3/8	17 2/8	4	4	Stevens County	WA	Dennis Olson	1992	15867
141 4/8	22 6/8 23 4/8	19 4/8	5	5	Kankakee County	IL	Jeffery J. Schneider	1993	15867
141 4/8	22 1/8 23 5/8	20 3/8	7	8	Hawkins County	TN	Mark S. Rogers	1993	15867
141 4/8	23 4/8 23 6/8	16 5/8	6	5	Schoharie County	NY	Bill Clapper, Jr.	1993	15867
141 4/8	24 7/8 25 0/8	20 6/8	5	4	Bureau County	IL	Ronald L. Smith	1993	15867
141 4/8	24 2/8 25 0/8	16 6/8	4	5	Pembina County	ND	Roger Furstenau	1993	15867
141 4/8	21 0/8 21 2/8	17 2/8	5	6	Chautauqua County	NY	John J. Burkholder	1994	15867
141 4/8	22 6/8 23 4/8	17 2/8	5	5	Dallas County	IA	Patrick J. Riley	1994	15867
141 4/8	23 3/8 22 3/8	17 0/8	5	4	Worth County	IA	Larry Porter	1994	15867
141 4/8	23 0/8 23 1/8	17 0/8	5	5	Macoupin County	IL	Lonnie Manalia	1994	15867
141 4/8	25 6/8 27 5/8	20 4/8	8	6	Jasper County	IL	Kenneth Huss	1995	15867
141 4/8	21 6/8 21 7/8	17 2/8	5	5	Adams County	IL	Ken J. Doellman	1995	15867
141 4/8	19 4/8 19 2/8	14 2/8	6	5	Cherry County	NE	Paul Brakhage	1995	15867
141 4/8	24 6/8 23 0/8	18 4/8	4	4	Tolland County	CT	Raymond Bienia	1995	15867
141 4/8	21 3/8 21 1/8	17 0/8	5	6	Wapello County	IA	Dennis Bradley	1995	15867
141 4/8	22 3/8 21 6/8	15 6/8	6	6	Pike County	IL	Dan Perez	1995	15867
141 4/8	25 2/8 25 1/8	17 0/8	4	4	Lawrence County	IN	Arter V. Thompson	1995	15867
141 4/8	25 4/8 23 7/8	21 7/8	5	5	Baltimore County	MD	Robert E. Roberts	1995	15867
141 4/8	21 5/8 22 1/8	15 2/8	6	5	Madison County	MT	J. Dudley Ottley, Sr.	1995	15867
141 4/8	21 6/8 21 7/8	19 2/8	6	5	Washington County	KS	Colby Manley	1995	15867
141 4/8	23 4/8 22 7/8	17 4/8	5	5	Otter Tail County	MN	Scott Rude	1996	15867
141 4/8	22 2/8 22 3/8	17 0/8	5	5	Columbia County	WI	Michael K. Paulcheck	1996	15867
141 4/8	20 7/8 20 6/8	15 6/8	6	6	Pike County	IL	Robert Sacher	1996	15867
141 4/8	22 3/8 22 6/8	19 6/8	6	5	Fayette County	IN	Gregg Mustin	1996	15867
141 4/8	22 3/8 22 2/8	18 4/8	4	4	Fond du Lac County	WI	Devin Hill	1996	15867
141 4/8	23 0/8 23 6/8	15 4/8	5	5	Washington County	MN	Patrick J. Ellias	1997	15867
141 4/8	27 3/8 25 1/8	20 2/8	4	4	Prince Georges County	MD	William "Gordon" Bowers, Jr.	1997	15867
141 4/8	20 0/8 21 6/8	17 2/8	5	5	Appanoose County	IA	Paul Cockriel	1997	15867
141 4/8	22 6/8 23 0/8	16 2/8	4	4	Broome County	NY	Dan Blanchard	1997	15867
141 4/8	22 6/8 22 0/8	18 6/8	6	5	Logan County	OH	Mike Anderson	1997	15867
141 4/8	25 2/8 25 0/8	19 6/8	5	4	Schuylkill County	PA	Terry Schwalm	1997	15867
141 4/8	21 3/8 21 0/8	18 4/8	6	6	Bureau County	IL	Gregory A. Bowers	1997	15867
141 4/8	24 5/8 24 0/8	17 0/8	5	4	Licking County	OH	Thomas L. Derugen	1997	15867
141 4/8	22 3/8 23 4/8	22 4/8	4	4	Hanover County	VA	David Wayne Hardiman	1997	15867
141 4/8	23 4/8 24 1/8	16 0/8	6	5	Racine County	WI	Deane Friend	1998	15867
141 4/8	27 6/8 27 7/8	20 4/8	4	4	Portage County	OH	Robert L. Fogel	1998	15867
141 4/8	24 3/8 24 5/8	16 4/8	5	5	Vernon County	WI	Bill Kyser	1998	15867
141 4/8	24 6/8 22 6/8	20 0/8	7	5	Allegheny County	PA	Brian Senovich	1998	15867
141 4/8	21 4/8 22 1/8	17 2/8	7	7	Love County	OK	Ronny Langston	1998	15867
141 4/8	24 7/8 24 6/8	18 6/8	4	4	Jackson County	IA	Ronald G. Uthe, Sr.	1999	15867
141 4/8	22 1/8 21 7/8	14 2/8	5	5	Montgomery County	IL	Tracy Schau	1999	15867
141 4/8	22 2/8 22 4/8	17 2/8	5	5	Suffolk County	NY	Michael Fenezia	1999	15867
141 4/8	23 3/8 24 4/8	17 2/8	6	5	Ste. Genevieve County	MO	Steven E. Rosso	1999	15867
141 4/8	21 4/8 21 0/8	15 2/8	4	5	Nuevo Leon	MEX	Skip Valentine	1999	15867
141 4/8	25 1/8 25 0/8	17 2/8	4	6	Washington County	KS	Stanley Brustowicz	1999	15867
141 4/8	24 2/8 23 1/8	18 6/8	5	5	Schuyler County	NY	Michael J. Naylor	2000	15867
141 4/8	24 0/8 23 2/8	19 7/8	6	6	Poweshiek County	IA	Jeff Schneekloth	2000	15867
141 4/8	24 4/8 24 0/8	20 0/8	4	4	Crawford County	WI	Robert A. Pettit	2000	15867
141 4/8	24 0/8 24 0/8	19 2/8	5	5	Westmoreland County	PA	Frank Carns	2000	15867
141 4/8	21 5/8 22 2/8	17 2/8	5	5	Hudson Bay	SAS	Max E. Hatfield	2000	15867
141 4/8	21 0/8 23 5/8	15 6/8	5	5	Dubuque County	IA	Scott Klein	2000	15867
141 4/8	23 2/8 23 0/8	19 6/8	4	4	Bolivar County	MS	Duke Morgan, Jr.	2000	15867
141 4/8	23 2/8 22 6/8	15 0/8	6	5	Madison County	IN	Randall A. Hobbs	2001	15867
141 4/8	22 5/8 21 6/8	16 2/8	5	6	Brown County	WI	Larry N. Lemmen	2001	15867

523

WHITETAIL DEER (TYPICAL ANTLERS)

Minimum Score 125 — Continued

SCORE	LENGTH OF R MAIN BEAM L	INSIDE SPREAD	NUMBER OF R POINTS L		AREA	STATE/ PROVINCE	HUNTER'S NAME	DATE	RANK
141 4/8	22 2/8	22 0/8	19 2/8	5	5	Marathon County	WI	Robert L. Peskie	2001	15867
141 4/8	23 5/8	22 6/8	19 6/8	5	5	Harding County	SD	Bob D. Oliver	2001	15867
141 4/8	21 2/8	21 4/8	15 5/8	5	6	Ogle County	IL	Dr. Todd M. Anderson	2001	15867
141 4/8	21 0/8	20 6/8	14 4/8	6	6	Monongalia County	WV	Nick Yokopovich	2001	15867
141 4/8	22 5/8	22 4/8	17 6/8	5	5	Jefferson County	IN	Alan Baxter	2001	15867
141 4/8	23 4/8	24 4/8	19 6/8	5	4	Comanche County	KS	Frank G. Hood	2002	15867
141 4/8	20 2/8	19 6/8	15 0/8	5	5	Venango County	PA	Gerald L. Miller II	2002	15867
141 4/8	23 3/8	24 4/8	20 2/8	6	5	Morris County	NJ	Kenneth Baker	2002	15867
141 4/8	21 6/8	24 6/8	17 2/8	6	6	Elkhart County	IN	Donald J. Lambert	2002	15867
141 4/8	22 7/8	23 3/8	21 2/8	5	5	Suffolk County	NY	Tom Hauser	2002	15867
141 4/8	22 3/8	23 1/8	16 0/8	5	5	Monroe County	IA	Bill Bridges	2002	15867
141 4/8	21 3/8	21 5/8	16 0/8	5	5	Johnson County	IA	Josh Amelon	2002	15867
141 4/8	22 5/8	24 2/8	19 4/8	6	7	Peoria County	IL	Dennis D. Litterst	2002	15867
141 4/8	23 6/8	23 4/8	21 4/8	5	5	Westlock	ALB	Joe Videtich	2003	15867
141 4/8	21 0/8	21 0/8	17 6/8	5	5	Red Deer	ALB	Pat Bayley	2003	15867
141 4/8	23 0/8	22 4/8	17 5/8	5	4	Garland County	AR	Wayne Brown	2003	15867
141 4/8	26 0/8	25 0/8	18 7/8	5	5	Randolph County	AR	Kent Bridges	2003	15867
141 4/8	20 5/8	20 0/8	17 4/8	5	5	Anoka County	MN	Mike Fitzpatrick	2003	15867
141 4/8	22 1/8	22 2/8	16 4/8	5	5	Washington County	OH	Elwood Young, Jr.	2004	15867
141 4/8	22 7/8	23 0/8	16 5/8	4	5	Franklin County	IL	Shannon L. Arrowood	2004	15867
141 4/8	23 4/8	23 3/8	17 1/8	6	5	Meskanaw	SAS	Floyd Forster	2004	15867
141 4/8	21 5/8	21 7/8	14 4/8	5	5	Wells County	ND	Joel Willey	2005	15867
141 4/8	20 3/8	21 4/8	15 0/8	6	6	Meade County	SD	Paul D. Bovard	2005	15867
*141 4/8	23 4/8	22 3/8	19 0/8	6	6	Auglaize County	OH	Doug Crowe	2005	15867
141 4/8	23 4/8	21 3/8	16 4/8	5	5	Montgomery County	IL	Brett Goldsmith	2005	15867
141 4/8	25 0/8	22 6/8	21 0/8	4	5	Defiance County	OH	Josh Burkholder	2005	15867
141 4/8	24 5/8	23 6/8	18 4/8	5	5	Armstrong County	PA	David Cushey	2005	15867
*141 4/8	23 4/8	23 0/8	18 2/8	5	5	Wood County	WI	Todd Tuskowski	2005	15867
*141 4/8	23 3/8	22 5/8	16 2/8	5	5	Montgomery County	OH	Adam Harris	2005	15867
141 4/8	23 4/8	23 4/8	18 4/8	5	4	Hampshire County	MA	James McKemmie	2006	15867
141 4/8	22 5/8	23 1/8	19 3/8	5	4	Lane County	KS	Dean Hamilton	2006	15867
*141 4/8	20 0/8	20 4/8	15 6/8	5	5	Jefferson County	IN	Eric Dickerson	2006	15867
141 4/8	22 2/8	21 4/8	17 0/8	5	6	Fond du Lac County	WI	Steve Giese	2006	15867
*141 4/8	22 0/8	21 1/8	17 6/8	5	5	Cass County	MI	Jeffrey A. Went	2006	15867
141 4/8	26 1/8	25 1/8	18 0/8	5	5	Jo Daviess County	IL	Donald W. Hansen, Jr.	2006	15867
141 4/8	22 2/8	23 0/8	15 2/8	4	5	Dodge County	WI	Keith Kanzenbach	2006	15867
141 4/8	26 4/8	25 1/8	20 1/8	5	6	Brown County	OH	Robert Hauke	2006	15867
*141 4/8	22 2/8	22 0/8	16 2/8	6	5	Carter County	MT	John Crook	2007	15867
141 4/8	24 2/8	24 0/8	19 1/8	5	4	Grant County	WI	Troy J. Collins	2007	15867
141 4/8	23 4/8	22 7/8	17 0/8	5	5	Switzerland County	IN	Kaleb Scott	2007	15867
*141 4/8	21 2/8	22 2/8	18 2/8	5	5	Buffalo County	WI	Mike LaBelle	2007	15867
*141 4/8	21 0/8	20 7/8	16 4/8	5	5	Miami County	IN	Clinton B. Lawson	2007	15867
*141 4/8	23 0/8	23 0/8	17 4/8	5	5	Val Verde County	TX	Michael L. Stilley	2007	15867
141 4/8	23 4/8	24 2/8	15 4/8	4	4	Buffalo County	WI	Mike Johnson	2007	15867
*141 4/8	23 2/8	24 3/8	15 0/8	6	6	Schuyler County	NY	Walter D. Johns	2007	15867
141 4/8	22 4/8	22 2/8	21 2/8	5	4	Monroe County	IN	Brian K. Lady	2007	15867
*141 4/8	21 2/8	22 4/8	18 2/8	5	5	Lucas County	IA	Shirley Allen	2007	15867
141 4/8	23 7/8	23 6/8	19 4/8	5	5	Delaware County	IA	Dean Dempster	2007	15867
141 4/8	24 7/8	25 2/8	15 2/8	4	7	Rogers County	OK	Allen Prior	2007	15867
141 4/8	21 0/8	20 7/8	16 4/8	5	5	Allegheny County	PA	Steve Martinelli	2008	15867
*141 4/8	22 3/8	22 3/8	15 2/8	6	6	Scott County	KY	David Beach	2008	15867
141 4/8	22 3/8	21 2/8	18 6/8	5	5	Mineral County	MT	Bob Sandberg	2008	15867
141 4/8	23 1/8	22 0/8	17 1/8	6	4	Clay County	IA	Mitchell Gross	2008	15867
141 4/8	22 4/8	23 4/8	16 0/8	5	6	Dimmit County	TX	John D. Hall	2008	15867
141 4/8	23 5/8	23 5/8	19 6/8	4	5	Richland County	IL	Ray Smith	2008	15867
*141 4/8	22 6/8	22 5/8	15 6/8	6	5	Vernon County	MO	Tanner W. Stever	2008	15867
*141 4/8	23 0/8	21 2/8	17 0/8	5	5	Will County	IL	Matt Copot	2008	15867
*141 4/8	25 4/8	26 4/8	22 1/8	5	5	Wood County	WI	Dan Dahlstrom	2008	15867
*141 4/8	23 6/8	23 5/8	20 3/8	5	4	Fulton County	IL	Larry Burgard	2008	15867
*141 4/8	27 0/8	26 7/8	18 7/8	4	7	Trimble County	KY	Andrew W. Pickett	2008	15867
*141 4/8	24 0/8	23 7/8	20 2/8	5	6	Jackson County	TN	Wesley G. Faust	2008	15867
*141 4/8	23 3/8	23 3/8	18 4/8	4	4	Ramsey County	MN	Joseph Mailer	2009	15867
141 4/8	23 4/8	24 3/8	18 2/8	4	5	Johnson County	IN	Larry D. Hazelwood	2009	15867
*141 4/8	21 4/8	22 1/8	18 2/8	5	5	Washington County	PA	Thomas R. Harris	2009	15867
*141 4/8	22 0/8	24 3/8	19 5/8	5	7	Dunn County	WI	Brandon Marion	2009	15867
*141 4/8	23 1/8	25 1/8	16 7/8	6	6	Buffalo County	WI	Chad Collins	2009	15867
141 4/8	23 2/8	23 0/8	18 2/8	6	5	Clark County	SD	Kevin Robling	2009	15867
*141 4/8	20 4/8	20 2/8	15 2/8	5	5	Porter County	IN	Tim Yankauskas	2009	15867
141 4/8	23 7/8	23 5/8	15 6/8	5	5	Pawnee County	OK	Chad Warren	2009	15867
*141 4/8	23 6/8	23 7/8	15 2/8	4	5	Sioux County	IA	Owen Sandbulte	2009	15867
*141 4/8	26 7/8	25 1/8	17 3/8	5	6	Adams County	OH	Chadin D. Miller	2009	15867
*141 4/8	23 3/8	22 7/8	17 0/8	5	5	Jackson County	OH	Randy Westmoreland	2009	15867
*141 4/8	20 7/8	20 0/8	15 4/8	6	5	Waupaca County	WI	Todd P. Kelsey	2010	15867
*141 4/8	22 0/8	22 0/8	16 3/8	7	7	Keya Paha County	NE	R. Kirk Sharp	2010	15867
141 3/8	23 3/8	22 4/8	17 1/8	7	6	Hughes County	SD	Ross Krull	1969	16035
141 3/8	24 5/8	26 3/8	16 3/8	5	6	Vilas County	WI	Dennis W. Essers	1976	16035
141 3/8	22 0/8	21 2/8	21 7/8	6	6	Elk County	KS	Marvin Whitehead	1978	16035
141 3/8	24 6/8	24 5/8	18 2/8	6	10	Seneca County	OH	Bruce R. Stover	1980	16035
141 3/8	24 0/8	23 1/8	19 7/8	5	5	Mitchell County	KS	Charlie Stevens	1981	16035
141 3/8	23 5/8	23 3/8	17 4/8	7	5	Warren County	VA	Ronnie Wines	1981	16035
141 3/8	22 3/8	21 5/8	15 1/8	5	5	Eau Claire County	WI	Terry R. Zich	1982	16035
141 3/8	24 7/8	24 0/8	16 7/8	5	4	Burleigh County	ND	Andrew M. Schneider	1982	16035
141 3/8	24 6/8	24 6/8	19 2/8	5	7	Putnam County	WV	James H. Myers	1983	16035
141 3/8	25 1/8	25 0/8	19 7/8	5	4	Fayette County	IL	Mike Kistler	1983	16035
141 3/8	22 2/8	22 1/8	18 5/8	4	5	Clermont County	OH	Harold A. Thompson, Jr.	1983	16035
141 3/8	27 7/8	26 2/8	18 5/8	7	5	Boone County	IA	Dan A. Dillavou	1984	16035
141 3/8	23 5/8	23 4/8	18 5/8	5	5	Dakota County	MN	Brad Bieber	1984	16035
141 3/8	21 2/8	23 0/8	19 5/8	6	9	Louisa County	IA	Jay Schmelzer	1985	16035
141 3/8	23 5/8	23 2/8	15 2/8	6	5	Kay County	OK	Guy LeMonnier	1985	16035
141 3/8	25 5/8	25 3/8	19 5/8	4	5	Jackson County	MN	Merlin Jurgens	1985	16035
141 3/8	18 6/8	23 1/8	15 5/8	5	5	Lake County	IL	Robert H. Fugett	1985	16035
141 3/8	21 7/8	23 0/8	16 2/8	5	7	Jackson County	IA	David Schrody	1985	16035
141 3/8	24 5/8	22 7/8	17 5/8	5	5	Howard Township	ONT	Wm. K. Jamieson	1985	16035
141 3/8	22 6/8	23 1/8	19 3/8	5	5	Greene County	OH	Daniel J. Gereg	1987	16035
141 3/8	23 5/8	23 1/8	16 1/8	5	5	Langlade County	WI	Bernhardt Behlke	1987	16035

524

WHITETAIL DEER (TYPICAL ANTLERS)

Minimum Score 125   Continued

SCORE	LENGTH OF R MAIN BEAM L	INSIDE SPREAD	NUMBER OF R POINTS L	AREA	STATE/ PROVINCE	HUNTER'S NAME	DATE	RANK
141 3/8	26 1/8 26 1/8	18 5/8	5 5	Fairfield County	OH	Thomas Moore	1988	16035
141 3/8	23 6/8 22 3/8	18 2/8	5 6	Douglas County	WI	Perry Cunningham	1988	16035
141 3/8	23 1/8 22 3/8	16 3/8	5 4	Licking County	OH	Ron Lohrman, Sr.	1988	16035
141 3/8	19 7/8 21 4/8	15 3/8	4 5	Wapello County	IA	Stephen A. Cullinan	1989	16035
141 3/8	25 3/8 25 6/8	18 3/8	5 5	Racine County	WI	Mark Wilcox	1989	16035
141 3/8	25 4/8 26 4/8	18 7/8	5 4	Grant County	WI	Clifford T. Bailey	1990	16035
141 3/8	23 1/8 23 0/8	17 0/8	7 6	Douglas County	WI	William James Back	1991	16035
141 3/8	22 6/8 22 6/8	18 5/8	5 6	Douglas County	WI	Jeff Paulus	1991	16035
141 3/8	21 3/8 21 2/8	15 5/8	5 5	Jackson County	MO	Wendell Hood	1991	16035
141 3/8	23 2/8 23 2/8	18 3/8	5 5	Bayfield County	WI	Arthur E. Hyde	1992	16035
141 3/8	20 3/8 20 3/8	15 7/8	5 5	St. Joseph County	IN	Michael L. Ritter	1992	16035
141 3/8	23 5/8 23 4/8	20 3/8	5 5	Olmsted County	MN	Kyle T. Hutchinson	1992	16035
141 3/8	22 4/8 22 5/8	20 1/8	6 6	Letellier	MAN	John Haspel	1992	16035
141 3/8	20 6/8 20 5/8	16 2/8	6 6	Jasper County	IA	Gary W. Vasseau	1992	16035
141 3/8	23 0/8 22 0/8	17 3/8	5 5	Duval County	TX	Ray Hinojosa	1992	16035
141 3/8	22 3/8 23 4/8	14 1/8	7 6	Pettis County	MO	Travis G. Lorenz	1992	16035
141 3/8	22 1/8 21 6/8	16 7/8	6 6	Iroquois County	IL	Daniel Marzano	1993	16035
141 3/8	24 1/8 23 3/8	19 3/8	5 5	La Salle County	IL	Gary L. Tabor, Sr.	1993	16035
141 3/8	21 4/8 21 4/8	16 1/8	5 5	Langlade County	WI	Jeffrey C. Mishler	1993	16035
141 3/8	23 1/8 23 0/8	18 1/8	5 5	Mercer County	IL	Lonnie Dickey	1993	16035
141 3/8	23 1/8 22 0/8	17 3/8	6 6	Real County	TX	Ben B. Wallace	1994	16035
141 3/8	23 5/8 23 2/8	17 3/8	6 5	Vinton County	OH	Les Loranzan, Jr.	1994	16035
141 3/8	23 6/8 22 3/8	19 0/8	6 6	La Grange County	IN	David V. Chupp	1994	16035
141 3/8	26 0/8 25 4/8	19 1/8	4 5	Edgar County	IL	Dale Bozarth	1994	16035
141 3/8	21 7/8 19 3/8	17 5/8	5 5	Pottawattamie County	IA	Doug Clayton	1994	16035
141 3/8	23 1/8 23 5/8	18 7/8	5 5	Lehigh County	PA	Dale F. Arner	1995	16035
141 3/8	24 0/8 22 7/8	16 7/8	5 5	Ionia County	MI	Jeff L. Fidler	1995	16035
141 3/8	21 1/8 22 4/8	20 0/8	6 5	Bayfield County	WI	Stephen M. Sorenson	1995	16035
141 3/8	23 7/8 23 0/8	15 2/8	5 7	Lapeer County	MI	Jeff Douglas	1995	16035
141 3/8	24 0/8 24 3/8	17 3/8	5 5	Kingman County	KS	Terry Morisse	1995	16035
141 3/8	24 0/8 24 3/8	19 1/8	4 4	Charles County	MD	Billy Moore	1995	16035
141 3/8	22 7/8 23 5/8	17 1/8	4 5	Washington County	MO	Jimmy J. O'Neal, Jr.	1995	16035
141 3/8	20 4/8 21 0/8	13 5/8	5 5	Montgomery County	MD	Richard L. Latimer, Jr.	1995	16035
141 3/8	22 5/8 23 3/8	22 2/8	4 6	Major County	OK	Mike Hein	1996	16035
141 3/8	25 1/8 24 7/8	20 2/8	4 6	Iowa County	WI	Sheldon Ward	1996	16035
141 3/8	23 1/8 23 3/8	17 3/8	4 4	Jefferson County	KS	Jeff Dunn	1996	16035
141 3/8	23 6/8 25 1/8	18 1/8	4 4	Sumner County	KS	Roger L. Emley	1996	16035
141 3/8	21 3/8 21 3/8	17 1/8	5 5	Lee County	IL	Mike Burrs	1996	16035
141 3/8	21 7/8 22 1/8	17 3/8	5 5	Racine County	WI	Thomas C. Berczyk	1997	16035
141 3/8	23 0/8 22 6/8	18 3/8	5 5	Pike County	MO	Dale Whittington	1997	16035
141 3/8	21 6/8 22 5/8	16 7/8	6 5	Pike County	IL	David W. Reese	1997	16035
141 3/8	23 3/8 24 5/8	20 4/8	6 5	Alexander County	IL	Donnie Blaney	1997	16035
141 3/8	22 1/8 22 3/8	18 6/8	6 5	Des Moines County	IA	Craig A. Owens	1997	16035
141 3/8	23 2/8 23 4/8	17 1/8	6 6	Sawyer County	WI	Jeffrey P. Tomesh	1997	16035
141 3/8	23 5/8 22 7/8	19 1/8	5 5	Monroe County	IA	Larry Zach	1997	16035
141 3/8	22 2/8 22 5/8	17 3/8	6 6	Breckinridge County	KY	Kevin Vessels	1997	16035
141 3/8	24 3/8 24 6/8	18 7/8	5 5	Isanti County	MN	Robert Michaletz	1997	16035
141 3/8	25 1/8 24 6/8	19 0/8	7 5	La Crosse County	WI	Greg Mueller	1997	16035
141 3/8	24 0/8 23 4/8	17 7/8	4 4	St. Clair County	MI	Todd D. Louks	1998	16035
141 3/8	22 2/8 22 4/8	15 7/8	5 5	Montgomery County	MD	Rod J. McKim	1998	16035
141 3/8	24 0/8 23 3/8	17 5/8	7 6	Dane County	WI	Scott Marty	1998	16035
141 3/8	24 4/8 24 6/8	19 4/8	5 5	Somerset County	PA	Randy McCall	1998	16035
141 3/8	25 1/8 24 5/8	22 3/8	4 4	Perry County	OH	Rod Eppley	1998	16035
141 3/8	23 1/8 22 0/8	18 3/8	5 5	Buffalo County	WI	Denny Richardson	1999	16035
141 3/8	23 2/8 24 4/8	16 7/8	6 5	Lewis County	KY	Wes Fisher	1999	16035
141 3/8	22 1/8 22 2/8	19 2/8	5 6	Forest County	WI	Jeremiah Voigt	1999	16035
141 3/8	22 0/8 21 1/8	14 7/8	5 5	Buffalo County	WI	Ed Brannen	1999	16035
141 3/8	23 5/8 24 4/8	19 1/8	4 7	Shawnee County	KS	B. J. Young	1999	16035
141 3/8	23 3/8 23 5/8	18 5/8	5 5	Vernon County	WI	Jeffery R. Meinertz	1999	16035
141 3/8	23 0/8 22 5/8	16 5/8	4 5	Brown County	IL	Michael Postema	1999	16035
141 3/8	22 5/8 24 0/8	21 1/8	5 5	Waushara County	WI	Dave Chase	1999	16035
141 3/8	22 2/8 22 2/8	20 2/8	6 5	Chippewa County	WI	Don Lunemann	1999	16035
141 3/8	22 3/8 21 7/8	15 5/8	5 5	Crawford County	WI	Mark Gerhard	1999	16035
141 3/8	21 7/8 21 0/8	18 1/8	5 5	Meigs County	OH	Mike Whitlatch	1999	16035
141 3/8	23 0/8 24 0/8	19 2/8	6 4	Suffolk County	NY	Mike Mattera	1999	16035
141 3/8	24 7/8 24 4/8	21 1/8	5 5	Fairfax County	VA	Michael Mecimore	1999	16035
141 3/8	23 5/8 22 6/8	19 1/8	5 5	Fayette County	PA	Terry R. Brady	2000	16035
141 3/8	21 7/8 21 6/8	14 3/8	5 5	Crook County	WY	Clay Harrison	2000	16035
141 3/8	23 2/8 23 7/8	18 3/8	5 5	Clark County	KS	E. L. McDaniel	2000	16035
141 3/8	23 0/8 22 2/8	20 3/8	5 5	Clayton County	IA	Travis Slama	2000	16035
141 3/8	23 6/8 23 4/8	18 1/8	6 6	Marquette County	WI	Thomas G. Bloomingdale	2000	16035
141 3/8	21 3/8 22 2/8	17 0/8	6 5	Jefferson County	KS	Kevin G. Newman	2000	16035
141 3/8	23 5/8 22 4/8	16 2/8	6 6	Buffalo County	WI	Rusty Severson	2001	16035
141 3/8	21 4/8 21 2/8	17 5/8	5 5	Callaway County	MO	Lonnie Giboney	2001	16035
141 3/8	24 6/8 24 6/8	17 3/8	5 4	Fulton County	IL	Seth A. Hintz	2001	16035
141 3/8	22 6/8 22 7/8	18 3/8	5 5	Fairfax County	VA	Thomas M. Kody	2001	16035
141 3/8	24 6/8 25 4/8	22 5/8	5 7	Jefferson County	KY	Allen Emmett	2001	16035
141 3/8	24 6/8 23 0/8	18 3/8	5 4	Mercer County	IL	Randal J. Dixon	2002	16035
141 3/8	21 0/8 21 1/8	17 0/8	5 6	La Crosse County	WI	David Nyhus	2002	16035
141 3/8	26 3/8 25 5/8	18 1/8	6 3	Brown County	IL	Mark Edwards	2002	16035
141 3/8	24 5/8 24 5/8	20 5/8	4 4	Holmes County	OH	Craig Stitzlein	2002	16035
141 3/8	23 7/8 23 5/8	16 4/8	5 5	Jo Daviess County	IL	Todd M. Wasmund	2003	16035
141 3/8	21 1/8 21 4/8	20 1/8	6 5	Fond du Lac County	WI	Daniel Williston	2003	16035
141 3/8	24 4/8 24 0/8	19 7/8	4 4	York County	ME	Al Raychard	2003	16035
141 3/8	22 6/8 23 5/8	20 3/8	6 6	Trumbull County	OH	Jeffrey W. Orth	2003	16035
141 3/8	23 4/8 22 3/8	18 1/8	4 4	Montgomery County	PA	Ralph K. Kappenstein, Jr.	2003	16035
141 3/8	21 6/8 21 1/8	17 5/8	5 5	Polk County	IA	Christopher J. Green	2003	16035
141 3/8	21 3/8 20 1/8	14 7/8	6 5	McCurtain County	OK	J. Heath Martin	2003	16035
141 3/8	23 0/8 22 2/8	20 1/8	6 6	E. Carroll Parish	LA	Clifford Edward Dunigan, Jr.	2004	16035
141 3/8	22 6/8 23 1/8	19 3/8	5 5	Allegheny County	PA	A. J. Votedian	2004	16035
141 3/8	24 3/8 24 6/8	16 7/8	5 5	Vigo County	IN	Daniel R. Green	2004	16035
141 3/8	24 5/8 24 0/8	18 1/8	4 4	Geauga County	OH	Jeffrey J. Blechschmid	2004	16035
*141 3/8	23 5/8 22 4/8	14 5/8	4 5	Adair County	MO	Gerald Linneweh	2004	16035
141 3/8	25 6/8 26 3/8	20 1/8	5 4	Linn County	IA	Nathan Goodlove	2004	16035
141 3/8	23 4/8 23 0/8	18 2/8	5 5	La Salle County	TX	John W. Ellas	2004	16035

525

WHITETAIL DEER (TYPICAL ANTLERS)

Minimum Score 125 Continued

SCORE	LENGTH OF R MAIN BEAM L	INSIDE SPREAD	NUMBER OF R POINTS L	AREA	STATE/ PROVINCE	HUNTER'S NAME	DATE	RANK
141 3/8	21 6/8 22 1/8	16 3/8	5 5	Round Lake	SAS	Floyd Forster	2005	16035
*141 3/8	22 4/8 22 3/8	18 1/8	5 5	Outagamie County	WI	Douglas Bricco	2005	16035
141 3/8	25 6/8 26 0/8	20 7/8	4 5	Tippecanoe County	IN	Kenneth L. Stigers	2005	16035
141 3/8	20 0/8 20 5/8	16 6/8	6 6	Harrison County	IA	Tom Pluhar	2005	16035
141 3/8	21 5/8 21 2/8	19 1/8	5 5	Pierce County	WI	Cory Haglund	2005	16035
141 3/8	23 3/8 24 0/8	17 5/8	4 5	Trempealeau County	WI	Jon Borreson	2005	16035
141 3/8	22 1/8 22 1/8	18 0/8	6 5	Clay County	MN	Walter J. Palmer	2005	16035
141 3/8	24 4/8 24 4/8	22 1/8	4 4	Jones County	IA	Jerry Casey	2005	16035
141 3/8	25 2/8 22 7/8	15 5/8	5 5	Cowley County	KS	Arlene Giulioli	2005	16035
141 3/8	20 4/8 20 1/8	18 0/8	5 7	Jefferson County	MO	Rodger W. Ernst	2005	16035
*141 3/8	19 7/8 20 1/8	17 1/8	7 6	Madison County	MT	Eric J. Henrich	2006	16035
141 3/8	21 2/8 21 6/8	15 1/8	6 6	Walsh County	ND	John Tweten	2006	16035
141 3/8	23 0/8 23 1/8	18 1/8	5 7	Oneida County	WI	Randall Sankey	2006	16035
141 3/8	24 1/8 21 4/8	22 3/8	4 4	Steuben County	IN	Robert Harris	2006	16035
*141 3/8	24 4/8 24 4/8	15 6/8	6 5	Polk County	WI	Eric Larson	2006	16035
*141 3/8	23 4/8 23 1/8	20 1/8	5 5	Buffalo County	WI	Mike Loesel	2006	16035
141 3/8	22 6/8 24 3/8	19 2/8	6 5	Clark County	IL	Jason H. Bowering	2006	16035
141 3/8	24 4/8 24 2/8	18 5/8	4 4	Richland County	WI	Rick Monson	2006	16035
*141 3/8	22 2/8 22 1/8	15 4/8	6 7	Appanoose County	IA	Russell A. Nichols	2006	16035
141 3/8	25 2/8 25 5/8	21 0/8	6 5	Wayne County	IN	Chris E. Edwards	2006	16035
141 3/8	25 5/8 25 6/8	17 3/8	5 4	Adams County	IA	Dean Lammers	2006	16035
141 3/8	22 7/8 23 7/8	20 7/8	4 4	Steuben County	IN	Mike Trick	2007	16035
*141 3/8	20 7/8 22 2/8	19 7/8	5 5	Morrison County	MN	Jared Schiller	2007	16035
*141 3/8	21 4/8 21 4/8	17 4/8	5 6	Marshall County	IN	Jeffrey L. Miller	2007	16035
*141 3/8	23 1/8 22 4/8	17 3/8	5 4	Jo Daviess County	IL	Wil R. Rossman	2007	16035
*141 3/8	22 6/8 22 0/8	16 1/8	5 5	Ward County	ND	Wayne Larcombe	2007	16035
*141 3/8	24 2/8 24 1/8	17 0/8	5 5	Trumbull County	OH	Scott Chapman	2007	16035
*141 3/8	23 0/8 23 5/8	18 3/8	5 5	Fulton County	IL	Steven Brown	2007	16035
141 3/8	21 3/8 22 0/8	14 5/8	5 5	McHenry County	ND	Jeff Jacob	2007	16035
*141 3/8	23 4/8 22 3/8	14 0/8	5 6	Webster County	MO	Matt Dill	2007	16035
*141 3/8	19 3/8 20 0/8	14 7/8	5 6	Lyon County	KY	Todd Duncan	2008	16035
141 3/8	24 4/8 24 4/8	19 6/8	6 6	Carroll County	OH	Terry Rosenberg	2008	16035
141 3/8	24 3/8 24 1/8	18 3/8	4 4	Wyoming County	NY	Jim Heckathorn	2008	16035
141 3/8	24 5/8 24 3/8	17 7/8	4 4	Cattaraugus County	NY	Marvin Shantler	2008	16035
141 3/8	24 1/8 24 0/8	17 0/8	4 6	Columbia County	WI	Dallas J. Lasche	2008	16035
*141 3/8	23 2/8 23 3/8	20 5/8	5 5	Waushara County	WI	Arthur Benotti	2008	16035
141 3/8	20 6/8 21 7/8	17 3/8	5 5	Randolph County	IL	Clay Curten	2008	16035
*141 3/8	22 6/8 21 5/8	14 7/8	6 5	Highland County	OH	Daniel Myers	2008	16035
*141 3/8	24 2/8 25 0/8	16 4/8	5 5	Barber County	KS	Dan Argenti	2008	16035
*141 3/8	23 0/8 24 7/8	16 0/8	6 5	Mercer County	IL	Robert Rice	2008	16035
*141 3/8	24 3/8 23 7/8	17 4/8	7 5	Richland County	IL	Trent Yonaka	2008	16035
141 3/8	21 3/8 21 0/8	16 6/8	6 5	Cascade County	MT	Gary Owen	2008	16035
141 3/8	23 7/8 23 7/8	18 7/8	4 4	Waukesha County	WI	Douglas Doughty	2008	16035
141 3/8	25 0/8 23 5/8	17 1/8	5 5	Wabasha County	MN	Jody Wilson	2009	16035
141 3/8	22 0/8 22 0/8	15 5/8	5 5	Woodson County	KS	Andrew Bell III	2009	16035
141 3/8	24 6/8 24 6/8	20 1/8	4 4	Clay County	KS	Matthew J. Hoobler	2009	16035
141 3/8	23 5/8 22 4/8	19 1/8	5 7	Howard County	IA	Phil Henry	2009	16035
141 3/8	22 7/8 22 7/8	17 1/8	5 5	Sauk County	WI	James L. Litscher	2010	16035
141 2/8	24 4/8 23 1/8	16 6/8	5 5	Lee County	IA	Terry E. Woodworth	1973	16199
141 2/8	22 5/8 23 1/8	22 2/8	4 5	Bon Homme County	SD	Jeff Miedema	1978	16199
141 2/8	23 3/8 23 2/8	17 2/8	5 5	Cottonwood County	MN	Robert K. Vincent	1978	16199
141 2/8	25 7/8 25 7/8	20 4/8	5 4	Douglas County	KS	Russell Stevens	1978	16199
141 2/8	24 2/8 23 4/8	20 2/8	4 5	DeKalb County	IL	Bob Broos	1980	16199
141 2/8	21 6/8 20 2/8	16 0/8	7 6	Grant County	WI	Thomas A. Franseen	1982	16199
141 2/8	22 4/8 22 4/8	20 3/8	5 6	Allamakee County	IA	Glen A. Jones	1983	16199
141 2/8	24 4/8 25 7/8	20 6/8	6 5	Powell County	MT	Steve Pocha	1984	16199
141 2/8	21 6/8 20 5/8	19 2/8	6 5	Green County	WI	Randall A. Schupbach	1984	16199
141 2/8	24 4/8 23 2/8	21 0/8	4 6	Fayette County	IL	Charlie Gelsinger, Jr.	1985	16199
141 2/8	26 1/8 26 1/8	18 4/8	5 4	Lawrence County	OH	Don Nickles	1985	16199
141 2/8	24 5/8 24 3/8	20 2/8	5 6	Pike County	OH	Harry R. Fite	1985	16199
141 2/8	23 3/8 23 3/8	16 2/8	4 4	Kandiyohi County	MN	Jeffrey L. Danielson	1986	16199
141 2/8	23 7/8 23 1/8	15 6/8	4 4	Green County	WI	Michael J. Beckwith	1986	16199
141 2/8	21 4/8 20 7/8	19 6/8	5 5	Mercer County	OH	Rick Kaud, Sr.	1986	16199
141 2/8	23 0/8 23 0/8	19 5/8	5 6	Portage County	WI	Philip P. Kalata	1987	16199
141 2/8	21 1/8 21 5/8	19 6/8	5 6	Weld County	CO	Dale A. Elliott	1988	16199
141 2/8	22 3/8 22 1/8	18 0/8	6 6	Price County	WI	Gerald Kozey	1988	16199
141 2/8	22 7/8 23 3/8	18 4/8	5 5	La Salle County	TX	Dr. F. D. Elias	1989	16199
141 2/8	23 0/8 23 1/8	16 2/8	5 5	Brown County	WI	David J. Schauer	1989	16199
141 2/8	24 2/8 23 7/8	17 5/8	6 6	Berrien County	MI	Michael Holy	1989	16199
141 2/8	20 0/8 21 4/8	16 4/8	5 5	Osborne County	KS	Craig E. Pottberg	1989	16199
141 2/8	24 3/8 25 4/8	17 4/8	6 7	Hennepin County	MN	Rob't Nash	1990	16199
141 2/8	23 5/8 24 3/8	15 2/8	5 5	Screven County	GA	Don L. Allex	1990	16199
141 2/8	23 4/8 23 6/8	20 3/8	6 6	Calgary	ALB	David R. Coupland	1990	16199
141 2/8	24 2/8 25 4/8	21 7/8	5 5	Monroe County	NY	Dane R. Edwards	1990	16199
141 2/8	22 5/8 22 3/8	18 0/8	5 5	Walworth County	WI	Ernie Meinen	1990	16199
141 2/8	22 1/8 22 1/8	17 0/8	10 9	Delaware County	IA	Jeffrey J. Tobin	1991	16199
141 2/8	23 5/8 22 3/8	18 0/8	5 5	Walworth County	WI	Robert R. Friend	1991	16199
141 2/8	24 2/8 22 7/8	18 2/8	8 6	Holt County	MO	Collis Bosworth	1991	16199
141 2/8	21 0/8 21 7/8	16 1/8	7 5	McHenry County	IL	Scott Kunzie	1992	16199
141 2/8	24 4/8 21 5/8	20 0/8	6 6	Wapello County	IA	Ronald L. Simmons	1992	16199
141 2/8	20 5/8 22 0/8	17 0/8	5 5	Douglas County	WI	Steve Wittke	1992	16199
141 2/8	22 2/8 22 0/8	15 2/8	5 5	Carter County	MO	Bob Benedick	1992	16199
141 2/8	24 0/8 23 4/8	19 2/8	5 4	Whiteside County	IL	Bernard J. Higley, Sr.	1992	16199
141 2/8	22 2/8 23 1/8	18 4/8	4 4	Coles County	IL	James G. Aldrich	1992	16199
141 2/8	24 4/8 23 4/8	20 0/8	4 4	Buffalo County	WI	Daniel Brockman	1993	16199
141 2/8	21 0/8 20 6/8	18 3/8	7 6	Oldham County	KY	Irv Turpen	1993	16199
141 2/8	23 2/8 24 4/8	18 2/8	4 5	Cass County	IL	Neal Kellam	1993	16199
141 2/8	25 1/8 24 3/8	19 0/8	4 4	Allegheny County	PA	Thomas W. Eiler	1994	16199
141 2/8	24 6/8 25 1/8	19 4/8	4 4	Logan County	IL	Michael C. Geskey	1994	16199
141 2/8	21 2/8 21 2/8	23 5/8	5 5	Ontario County	NY	Timothy E. Serviss	1995	16199
141 2/8	21 7/8 22 4/8	15 2/8	5 5	Douglas County	KS	Danzil L. Hackathorn	1995	16199
141 2/8	23 0/8 21 5/8	17 6/8	5 6	Allamakee County	IA	Jim J. Oberfoell	1995	16199
141 2/8	24 0/8 24 4/8	18 2/8	4 5	Waupaca County	WI	Marlin Stapleton, Jr.	1995	16199
141 2/8	24 2/8 24 0/8	20 4/8	4 4	Eau Claire County	WI	Arnie Roytek	1995	16199
141 2/8	23 7/8 23 7/8	16 5/8	6 6	Jefferson County	KY	Kent Stroud	1995	16199

WHITETAIL DEER (TYPICAL ANTLERS)

Minimum Score 125 — Continued

SCORE	LENGTH OF R MAIN BEAM L		INSIDE SPREAD	NUMBER OF R POINTS L		AREA	STATE/ PROVINCE	HUNTER'S NAME	DATE	RANK
141 2/8	22 6/8	22 4/8	19 5/8	5	6	San Patricio County	TX	Lane Feazell	1995	16199
141 2/8	25 0/8	24 7/8	17 0/8	4	5	Berks County	PA	Frank M. Maddona	1996	16199
141 2/8	22 5/8	23 5/8	20 4/8	6	5	Oktibbeha County	MS	Kim Vickers	1996	16199
141 2/8	22 4/8	21 1/8	15 1/8	8	6	Grundy County	MO	Ethan Griffin	1996	16199
141 2/8	26 2/8	25 5/8	20 0/8	4	5	Berks County	PA	John A. Weir	1996	16199
141 2/8	22 2/8	21 1/8	16 6/8	5	5	Meigs County	OH	Matt Wilson	1996	16199
141 2/8	25 1/8	25 3/8	21 0/8	8	5	Jersey County	IL	John Mueller	1996	16199
141 2/8	24 0/8	23 2/8	19 5/8	5	7	Jackson County	IA	Russell G. Goldsmith	1996	16199
141 2/8	24 2/8	24 4/8	16 6/8	5	5	Marathon County	WI	Kurt Schreiner	1996	16199
141 2/8	22 7/8	22 2/8	15 6/8	6	6	Ogle County	IL	Robert D. Bradley	1996	16199
141 2/8	25 4/8	25 6/8	17 3/8	5	5	Queen Annes County	MD	Eric Miller	1997	16199
141 2/8	24 1/8	23 6/8	22 0/8	4	5	Clark County	OH	Brian Loveless	1997	16199
141 2/8	23 2/8	23 4/8	17 2/8	4	5	Brown County	IL	David R. Herschelman	1997	16199
141 2/8	25 6/8	25 1/8	20 1/8	5	5	Dubuque County	IA	Joey Sarazin	1997	16199
141 2/8	24 7/8	24 7/8	18 0/8	5	6	Anderson County	KS	Windell R. Johnson	1997	16199
141 2/8	21 7/8	21 5/8	18 0/8	5	5	Houghton County	MI	Michael Monette	1998	16199
141 2/8	23 1/8	22 0/8	20 4/8	4	4	Walworth County	WI	John Osborne	1998	16199
141 2/8	22 5/8	22 1/8	16 6/8	5	5	Olmsted County	MN	Mark W. Karppi	1998	16199
141 2/8	24 1/8	24 0/8	18 6/8	4	4	Claiborne County	MS	James Cassell, Jr.	1998	16199
141 2/8	24 6/8	26 2/8	14 6/8	4	5	Gage County	NE	Gene Tupa	1998	16199
141 2/8	24 5/8	25 0/8	20 4/8	6	7	Boone County	IA	Robert R. Sherrard	1998	16199
141 2/8	22 4/8	21 3/8	18 7/8	5	6	Buffalo County	WI	Eric F. Farr	1998	16199
141 2/8	23 3/8	23 7/8	16 0/8	4	7	Rock County	WI	Robert S. Larson	1998	16199
141 2/8	21 2/8	22 6/8	15 4/8	6	6	Fond du Lac County	WI	Kenneth E. Fischer	1998	16199
141 2/8	23 2/8	22 6/8	16 6/8	5	5	Appanoose County	IA	Todd L. Fuller	1998	16199
141 2/8	20 5/8	21 2/8	18 0/8	6	7	Lincoln County	WI	Dan Detert	1998	16199
141 2/8	21 6/8	20 5/8	15 6/8	5	5	Harrison County	KY	Terry Turner	1999	16199
141 2/8	24 0/8	23 1/8	15 4/8	4	4	Scioto County	OH	Brent Hobbs	1999	16199
141 2/8	22 4/8	23 2/8	19 2/8	6	6	Morrison County	MN	Vincent A. LaCroix	1999	16199
141 2/8	22 1/8	21 7/8	18 0/8	6	5	Pike County	IL	Rusty Smith	1999	16199
141 2/8	24 4/8	24 2/8	20 6/8	4	4	Marshall County	IN	Rob G. Konopinski	1999	16199
141 2/8	24 5/8	23 3/8	18 2/8	5	5	Iroquois County	IL	Doug Hettinger	1999	16199
141 2/8	22 7/8	22 1/8	14 4/8	5	5	Hamilton County	IA	Keith Brock	1999	16199
141 2/8	21 5/8	21 2/8	16 2/8	5	5	O'Brien County	IA	Kent Miller	1999	16199
141 2/8	23 5/8	22 3/8	17 0/8	5	5	Reno County	KS	Richard W. Hedger	2000	16199
141 2/8	23 6/8	23 7/8	20 0/8	4	4	Fayette County	IN	Roy L. Grizzell	2000	16199
141 2/8	22 5/8	22 6/8	18 4/8	5	5	Harper County	KS	Paul Chackan	2000	16199
141 2/8	25 2/8	26 1/8	20 4/8	4	4	Miami County	OH	Craig Peters	2000	16199
141 2/8	26 2/8	26 2/8	17 2/8	4	4	Jackson County	IL	Char Speth	2000	16199
141 2/8	23 4/8	22 7/8	18 4/8	4	4	Marshall County	KS	Timothy A. Baker	2000	16199
141 2/8	20 4/8	20 3/8	17 4/8	5	5	Matagorda County	TX	Wesley Smolik	2001	16199
141 2/8	24 1/8	23 3/8	15 6/8	7	6	Lapeer County	MI	Rusty Clark	2001	16199
141 2/8	24 2/8	23 3/8	17 6/8	5	5	Greene County	MO	Junior C. Combs	2001	16199
141 2/8	23 1/8	23 0/8	15 0/8	6	5	Maries County	MO	Dwain Melton	2001	16199
141 2/8	22 5/8	22 6/8	19 0/8	5	5	Woodbury County	IA	Dan Flammang	2001	16199
141 2/8	23 6/8	22 4/8	17 4/8	5	4	Chickasaw County	IA	Randy Ruiter	2001	16199
141 2/8	22 1/8	21 3/8	18 6/8	5	5	Walworth County	WI	Jeff Ellis	2002	16199
141 2/8	21 6/8	22 7/8	18 0/8	5	5	Massac County	IL	Dustan Koger	2002	16199
141 2/8	23 2/8	23 4/8	14 6/8	7	7	Medina County	OH	Dave Goode	2003	16199
141 2/8	23 4/8	20 3/8	18 4/8	5	5	Chautauqua County	NY	Mark Hycner	2003	16199
141 2/8	21 1/8	21 0/8	15 6/8	5	5	Lucas County	IA	Bill Brown	2003	16199
141 2/8	20 5/8	22 6/8	15 0/8	5	5	Buffalo County	WI	Brian R. Bonesteel	2003	16199
141 2/8	22 5/8	21 6/8	17 4/8	5	6	Iowa County	IA	Kevin McDonald	2003	16199
141 2/8	25 2/8	24 7/8	18 5/8	6	5	Luzerne County	PA	Chris Denmon	2003	16199
*141 2/8	24 7/8	24 3/8	19 0/8	4	5	Wayne County	IN	Tyson Booher	2004	16199
141 2/8	24 4/8	24 7/8	17 2/8	5	4	Lyman County	SD	Brad Golay	2004	16199
141 2/8	22 5/8	23 2/8	18 0/8	5	5	Vernon County	WI	Jeffrey R. Fechner	2004	16199
*141 2/8	22 6/8	24 0/8	16 2/8	5	6	Madison County	IL	Mike Harris	2004	16199
141 2/8	23 3/8	23 5/8	16 2/8	6	6	Jasper County	SC	Travis Malphrus	2004	16199
141 2/8	23 7/8	24 5/8	17 2/8	5	5	Livingston County	NY	Jeremy W. Ruscitto	2004	16199
141 2/8	23 1/8	23 5/8	18 5/8	5	7	Grant County	WI	Tod R. Fleming	2004	16199
141 2/8	23 0/8	22 6/8	16 7/8	5	6	Indiana County	PA	Mike Zaffuto	2004	16199
141 2/8	21 2/8	20 7/8	16 6/8	5	6	Walsh County	ND	Brian Janikowski	2005	16199
141 2/8	24 3/8	23 5/8	20 6/8	4	4	Columbia County	WI	Jeff G. Plenty	2005	16199
141 2/8	21 1/8	22 0/8	17 0/8	5	5	Benson County	ND	Brett Kenner	2005	16199
*141 2/8	22 7/8	23 0/8	19 0/8	6	5	Missoula County	MT	Jake Sol	2005	16199
141 2/8	23 0/8	23 2/8	20 5/8	6	6	Mercer County	PA	Mark J. King	2005	16199
*141 2/8	24 1/8	22 5/8	17 2/8	4	4	Richland County	WI	Randall Hilgers	2005	16199
141 2/8	23 0/8	23 6/8	22 4/8	4	5	Keokuk County	IA	Larry Garber	2005	16199
141 2/8	22 3/8	22 3/8	18 2/8	5	5	Dodge County	WI	Tony Lefeber	2005	16199
141 2/8	23 1/8	25 1/8	18 4/8	4	4	Piatt County	IL	Doug Benjamin Williams	2005	16199
*141 2/8	24 7/8	23 2/8	18 6/8	5	5	Bayfield County	WI	Jim Messerschmidt	2005	16199
141 2/8	22 3/8	22 2/8	15 4/8	5	5	Oconto County	WI	Einard E. Staidl	2005	16199
141 2/8	21 4/8	21 0/8	20 3/8	6	6	Choctaw County	OK	Kenneth Pate	2005	16199
*141 2/8	21 6/8	21 3/8	15 7/8	6	5	Vermillion County	IN	Mitchell L. Fisher	2006	16199
141 2/8	26 2/8	27 1/8	23 6/8	3	3	La Salle County	IL	John G. Sykes	2006	16199
141 2/8	26 3/8	26 1/8	21 0/8	4	4	Buffalo County	WI	Bo Klevgard	2006	16199
141 2/8	23 3/8	23 0/8	15 1/8	5	5	Oakland County	MI	Daniel Ward Parker	2006	16199
*141 2/8	22 1/8	21 6/8	15 0/8	6	9	Noble County	IN	Frank A. Kimmell	2006	16199
141 2/8	22 6/8	23 1/8	17 1/8	5	6	Cherokee County	IA	Russell Schmidt	2007	16199
*141 2/8	22 1/8	22 0/8	14 4/8	4	4	Cass County	ND	LeRoy Cossette	2007	16199
141 2/8	22 3/8	22 3/8	15 2/8	5	5	Trempealeau County	WI	Andy George	2007	16199
*141 2/8	26 4/8	25 5/8	17 6/8	4	5	Muskingum County	OH	Brad Little	2007	16199
141 2/8	21 0/8	20 3/8	17 4/8	6	6	Stanley County	SD	Cullan Deis	2007	16199
141 2/8	22 2/8	22 0/8	16 4/8	5	5	Marion County	KS	Dennis Ballweg	2007	16199
141 2/8	22 6/8	21 1/8	16 5/8	5	6	Yankton County	SD	Rick Bak	2007	16199
*141 2/8	21 7/8	21 4/8	15 4/8	5	5	Jersey County	IL	Lucas Fontenot	2008	16199
141 2/8	20 3/8	22 7/8	16 3/8	6	7	Prince William County	VA	Ricky Cook	2008	16199
141 2/8	25 1/8	23 0/8	19 2/8	5	4	Sauk County	WI	Russell J. Balfanz, Jr.	2008	16199
*141 2/8	23 2/8	24 2/8	17 2/8	5	5	Fond du Lac County	WI	Nick Leonard	2008	16199
*141 2/8	22 2/8	23 0/8	15 3/8	5	6	Clayton County	IA	Brian G. Kluesner	2008	16199
141 2/8	21 7/8	23 4/8	18 6/8	5	5	Jefferson County	OH	William G. Rusinovich	2008	16199
*141 2/8	22 3/8	22 1/8	18 0/8	5	5	Jefferson County	WI	Jeremy T. Clark	2008	16199
*141 2/8	26 0/8	25 3/8	22 3/8	4	5	Will County	IL	Charles Gaidamavice	2008	16199
141 2/8	23 5/8	23 0/8	18 0/8	5	6	Polk County	WI	Kevin D. O'Brien	2008	16199

WHITETAIL DEER (TYPICAL ANTLERS)

Minimum Score 125 Continued

SCORE	LENGTH OF R MAIN BEAM L		INSIDE SPREAD	NUMBER OF R POINTS L		AREA	STATE/ PROVINCE	HUNTER'S NAME	DATE	RANK
141 2/8	24 7/8	25 2/8	18 6/8	6	6	Whiteside County	IL	Cole Young	2009	16199
141 2/8	22 2/8	21 1/8	15 6/8	5	5	Cascade County	MT	Carl Schroeder	2009	16199
141 2/8	22 6/8	22 0/8	16 2/8	5	4	Fillmore County	MN	Bob Gossman	2009	16199
*141 2/8	22 6/8	23 0/8	19 4/8	6	5	Randolph County	IL	Jacob Kiefer	2009	16199
141 2/8	22 5/8	23 2/8	17 2/8	4	4	Jackson County	WI	Allan W. Storandt	2009	16199
141 2/8	23 5/8	21 6/8	14 4/8	5	5	Marion County	IN	Jesse Denson	2009	16199
141 2/8	22 1/8	22 0/8	16 5/8	6	5	McDowell County	WV	Adam Meadows	2009	16199
141 2/8	22 4/8	22 1/8	17 0/8	5	6	Perry County	OH	Kyle P. Lane	2009	16199
*141 2/8	21 3/8	21 3/8	19 4/8	5	5	Marshall County	SD	Terry Fredrickson	2009	16199
141 2/8	21 5/8	24 0/8	18 1/8	4	5	Davis County	IA	Neric D. Smith	2009	16199
*141 2/8	22 6/8	21 5/8	16 4/8	5	5	Kalamazoo County	MI	Michael L. Geesaman	2009	16199
141 1/8	26 2/8	27 6/8	19 0/8	4	5	Dodge County	NE	Gary Trost	1961	16352
141 1/8	21 5/8	22 2/8	17 5/8	5	6	Talbot County	MD	Gary W. Sommers	1979	16352
141 1/8	22 0/8	24 2/8	18 1/8	4	6	Shelby County	IL	Ron Ragan	1979	16352
141 1/8	24 2/8	24 6/8	17 1/8	5	4	Tuscaloosa County	AL	Bobby Hemphill	1981	16352
141 1/8	24 0/8	23 1/8	23 3/8	5	5	Pittsburg County	OK	Dave Jilge	1981	16352
141 1/8	25 0/8	25 0/8	17 2/8	6	6	Jefferson County	OH	William J. Fedor	1981	16352
141 1/8	22 1/8	22 7/8	19 0/8	6	5	Des Moines County	IA	David R. Bessine	1982	16352
141 1/8	23 7/8	22 1/8	17 7/8	5	5	Stanley County	SD	Jim P. Hallock	1983	16352
141 1/8	22 5/8	21 7/8	15 4/8	8	7	Boone County	MO	Craig S Gemming	1984	16352
141 1/8	27 1/8	26 6/8	18 0/8	4	5	Boone County	MO	Dale Robb	1984	16352
141 1/8	22 4/8	22 2/8	21 0/8	6	6	Wabaunsee County	KS	Charles Bisnette	1985	16352
141 1/8	24 3/8	24 2/8	19 1/8	4	4	Kit Carson County	CO	Kenneth Assmus	1986	16352
141 1/8	22 4/8	23 2/8	15 6/8	7	6	Texas County	OK	Max Crocker	1986	16352
141 1/8	23 3/8	21 1/8	18 4/8	5	5	Jefferson County	IN	Dan Oliver	1986	16352
141 1/8	24 1/8	23 3/8	17 5/8	5	5	Oneida County	WI	Rollie H. Bessett	1986	16352
141 1/8	22 3/8	22 4/8	16 7/8	5	6	Harvey County	KS	Mark M. Jones	1987	16352
141 1/8	22 5/8	21 7/8	17 5/8	4	4	Jasper County	MO	Roger Lindsey	1988	16352
141 1/8	21 6/8	22 6/8	17 1/8	5	5	Buffalo County	WI	Bruce B. Pronschinske	1988	16352
141 1/8	25 0/8	25 4/8	22 7/8	6	5	Randolph County	IL	Ron Dunker	1988	16352
141 1/8	22 2/8	23 1/8	18 5/8	5	5	Madison County	IL	Roger Downer	1988	16352
141 1/8	23 3/8	23 4/8	18 1/8	4	5	Plymouth County	IA	Timm M. Banks	1989	16352
141 1/8	20 7/8	21 3/8	19 1/8	5	5	Indiana County	PA	David W. Magiera	1990	16352
141 1/8	25 1/8	24 2/8	17 1/8	6	5	Anoka County	MN	Tim Dugas	1990	16352
141 1/8	22 2/8	22 6/8	16 5/8	5	5	St. Charles County	MO	Carlis Stephens	1991	16352
141 1/8	22 4/8	22 4/8	15 5/8	5	5	Kandiyohi County	MN	David Rannestad	1991	16352
141 1/8	24 0/8	23 7/8	21 0/8	5	5	Allamakee County	IA	Cody Hawkins	1991	16352
141 1/8	23 5/8	23 0/8	20 1/8	5	5	Anne Arundel County	MD	J. J. Fegan	1991	16352
141 1/8	24 7/8	24 2/8	17 3/8	4	5	McHenry County	IL	Ernie Meinen	1991	16352
141 1/8	26 1/8	25 2/8	20 6/8	4	5	Letcher County	KY	Terry Mullins	1992	16352
141 1/8	21 5/8	21 3/8	18 5/8	5	5	Burleigh County	ND	Terry Lee Johnson	1992	16352
141 1/8	23 2/8	24 1/8	18 3/8	5	6	Waushara County	WI	Ben Sullivan	1992	16352
141 1/8	23 0/8	22 0/8	16 5/8	5	4	Flathead County	MT	Dan Perez	1993	16352
141 1/8	21 6/8	21 7/8	17 2/8	6	5	Beltrami County	MN	Jon H. Becker	1993	16352
141 1/8	22 6/8	22 7/8	17 3/8	4	4	Monroe County	IN	Russell L. Edwards	1993	16352
141 1/8	21 4/8	21 6/8	16 3/8	6	5	Goodhue County	MN	Richard W. Rolls	1993	16352
141 1/8	22 1/8	22 0/8	19 7/8	5	5	Green County	WI	John W. Elsner	1993	16352
141 1/8	23 1/8	23 6/8	16 3/8	4	5	Chester County	PA	Edward F. McConnel	1993	16352
141 1/8	23 5/8	22 6/8	17 3/8	5	5	La Porte County	IN	Dwayne E. Wireman	1994	16352
141 1/8	25 5/8	26 2/8	17 1/8	6	7	Ripley County	IN	Eric Sampson	1994	16352
141 1/8	19 7/8	20 4/8	14 3/8	5	5	Morrison County	MN	Duane E. Eilbes	1994	16352
141 1/8	23 2/8	22 2/8	15 7/8	6	5	Dane County	WI	Steve Mulcahy	1994	16352
141 1/8	26 2/8	25 4/8	21 7/8	4	5	Anne Arundel County	MD	Joseph W. Keller, Jr.	1994	16352
141 1/8	22 6/8	24 1/8	16 7/8	5	5	Ashland County	WI	Leland Wertepny	1994	16352
141 1/8	22 4/8	22 0/8	17 5/8	4	4	Scotland County	MO	Jay Smith	1994	16352
141 1/8	22 5/8	22 4/8	16 1/8	5	6	Ashland County	WI	Patrick Mohr	1995	16352
141 1/8	21 7/8	22 6/8	16 1/8	4	5	Crawford County	IA	Dick Frazier	1995	16352
141 1/8	23 3/8	22 7/8	18 1/8	5	5	Forest County	WI	Daniel Brezinski	1995	16352
141 1/8	24 1/8	23 4/8	16 5/8	5	5	Jackson County	WI	Michael R. Abel	1995	16352
141 1/8	25 4/8	25 2/8	20 3/8	5	5	Perry County	OH	Todd J. Krieg	1996	16352
141 1/8	24 0/8	22 0/8	15 3/8	9	6	Hale County	AL	Tim Kohlenberg	1996	16352
141 1/8	22 0/8	22 3/8	15 7/8	5	6	Goshen County	WY	Reggie Theus	1996	16352
141 1/8	23 3/8	23 1/8	18 1/8	4	4	Harper County	KS	Bryan Naccarato	1996	16352
141 1/8	23 5/8	24 1/8	18 5/8	5	5	Macon County	IL	Dave M. Elliott	1996	16352
141 1/8	24 7/8	22 1/8	16 5/8	4	4	Kent County	MI	Bernie Arthur Brunges III	1996	16352
141 1/8	24 0/8	23 5/8	20 2/8	6	5	Woodruff County	AR	Tom Clark	1997	16352
141 1/8	24 1/8	23 5/8	17 7/8	4	4	Henry County	GA	Rocky Thompson	1997	16352
141 1/8	24 5/8	25 1/8	19 5/8	5	5	Sullivan County	NH	Rick Eaton	1997	16352
141 1/8	22 4/8	24 0/8	20 6/8	5	6	Waukesha County	WI	Douglas S. Giesen	1997	16352
141 1/8	26 7/8	24 5/8	19 0/8	6	6	Chatham County	NC	William Phillips	1997	16352
141 1/8	24 1/8	24 7/8	19 3/8	5	5	Fayette County	IL	Brady Philpot	1997	16352
141 1/8	21 3/8	21 7/8	16 3/8	5	5	Kleberg County	TX	Robert Nichols	1997	16352
141 1/8	23 0/8	22 4/8	17 6/8	4	5	Wayne County	OH	Kim D. Gochnauer	1998	16352
141 1/8	22 2/8	22 4/8	15 1/8	5	5	Wood County	WI	John P. Tauschek	1998	16352
141 1/8	23 4/8	23 2/8	18 3/8	6	5	Morris County	NJ	Peter Settineri	1998	16352
141 1/8	25 7/8	25 2/8	17 7/8	5	4	Iroquois County	IL	Michael Cordes	1998	16352
141 1/8	23 4/8	23 5/8	18 7/8	5	5	Dakota County	MN	Curt LeMay	1998	16352
141 1/8	23 4/8	23 5/8	16 5/8	6	7	Pierce County	WI	John Kuesel, Jr.	1999	16352
141 1/8	21 4/8	21 7/8	18 7/8	5	5	Haakon County	SD	Scott Hettinger	1999	16352
141 1/8	22 0/8	21 7/8	14 5/8	5	5	Jackson County	WI	Matt Staff	1999	16352
141 1/8	23 7/8	24 4/8	21 1/8	4	4	Washington County	MS	Odis Hill, Jr.	1999	16352
141 1/8	26 0/8	26 3/8	21 1/8	4	4	Clayton County	IA	Larry Bird	1999	16352
141 1/8	20 0/8	21 4/8	18 7/8	6	5	Scott County	MN	Rob Sieh	1999	16352
141 1/8	19 7/8	20 3/8	19 0/8	7	7	Cecil County	MD	Matt Doughten	2000	16352
141 1/8	23 5/8	23 4/8	17 3/8	4	4	Fremont County	IA	Patrick Athen	2000	16352
141 1/8	21 5/8	22 3/8	18 5/8	5	5	Schuyler County	IL	Tom Spence	2000	16352
141 1/8	22 6/8	22 5/8	19 3/8	5	5	Parke County	IN	Darren L. Waymire	2000	16352
141 1/8	20 3/8	22 6/8	15 1/8	5	5	Missoula County	MT	Tom M. Benson	2000	16352
141 1/8	23 3/8	21 7/8	17 5/8	5	5	Houston County	MN	Delane A. Frauenkron	2000	16352
141 1/8	26 2/8	26 6/8	16 7/8	5	4	Muskingum County	OH	Drew D. Handwork	2001	16352
141 1/8	21 6/8	22 2/8	15 1/8	5	5	Jasper County	IN	George Shaw	2001	16352
141 1/8	23 2/8	24 5/8	17 3/8	5	5	Vilas County	WI	Doug Gast	2001	16352
141 1/8	22 4/8	22 1/8	16 7/8	5	5	Douglas County	NE	Kevin M. Currin	2001	16352
141 1/8	22 6/8	23 2/8	15 3/8	5	5	Pittsburg County	OK	Marlon Moore	2001	16352
141 1/8	24 6/8	24 6/8	17 0/8	6	5	Litchfield County	CT	Robert Wozniak	2002	16352

WHITETAIL DEER (TYPICAL ANTLERS)

Minimum Score 125 — Continued

SCORE	LENGTH OF R MAIN BEAM L	INSIDE SPREAD	NUMBER OF R POINTS L	AREA	STATE/PROVINCE	HUNTER'S NAME	DATE	RANK
141 1/8	21 4/8 23 2/8	18 7/8	5 4	Vigo County	IN	Charles Tharp	2002	16352
141 1/8	24 5/8 23 5/8	19 1/8	5 5	Iowa County	IA	Kevin McDonald	2002	16352
141 1/8	24 0/8 23 1/8	15 7/8	5 5	Butler County	OH	Steve Tanner II	2002	16352
141 1/8	26 0/8 25 6/8	20 1/8	5 5	Coahuila	MEX	Mike Pillow	2002	16352
*141 1/8	21 6/8 22 0/8	19 0/8	7 5	Warren County	IL	David L. Freeman	2003	16352
141 1/8	22 5/8 17 6/8	21 7/8	5 5	Washington County	MN	Nick Howe	2003	16352
141 1/8	21 4/8 22 0/8	20 1/8	4 4	Polk County	IA	Jason Rosonke	2003	16352
141 1/8	25 0/8 26 1/8	18 3/8	5 6	Crawford County	KS	John Adam Gariglietti	2003	16352
141 1/8	24 6/8 26 4/8	17 5/8	4 4	Medina County	OH	Jason Martin	2003	16352
141 1/8	21 3/8 22 3/8	16 2/8	6 5	Caldwell County	MO	Harold D. Baker, Jr.	2003	16352
141 1/8	23 6/8 22 0/8	18 0/8	5 6	Marquette County	WI	Tim O'Donnell	2004	16352
141 1/8	22 0/8 22 1/8	14 6/8	7 5	Todd County	KY	Jonathan Wells	2004	16352
*141 1/8	22 2/8 22 4/8	16 3/8	6 5	Prowers County	CO	Jeff Travis	2004	16352
141 1/8	24 4/8 23 6/8	18 5/8	5 4	Grant County	WI	Thomas J. Schmidt	2004	16352
141 1/8	24 2/8 24 5/8	18 0/8	6 5	Floyd County	IA	Jeff H. Nordman	2004	16352
141 1/8	20 6/8 21 1/8	15 7/8	6 5	Scott County	IL	Steve Tice	2004	16352
141 1/8	22 6/8 22 4/8	18 1/8	5 6	Barron County	WI	Justin Lewis	2004	16352
*141 1/8	23 1/8 23 6/8	19 3/8	7 6	Washington County	WI	Randy Puestow	2004	16352
141 1/8	23 6/8 22 3/8	16 2/8	5 6	Marathon County	WI	Robert L. Oksiuta	2004	16352
141 1/8	22 5/8 21 4/8	16 1/8	4 5	Vigo County	IN	Daniel R. Green	2005	16352
141 1/8	23 0/8 23 3/8	16 5/8	5 4	Marshall County	IN	Galen L. Miller	2005	16352
141 1/8	24 0/8 22 0/8	17 1/8	5 5	Carroll County	MO	Glen Whipkins	2005	16352
141 1/8	20 6/8 21 0/8	16 5/8	5 5	Butler County	PA	Sean Swidzinski	2005	16352
141 1/8	24 7/8 24 4/8	19 1/8	5 6	Dorchester County	MD	Brad Hughes	2005	16352
141 1/8	25 2/8 24 4/8	19 3/8	5 5	Crawford County	WI	John Papenfuss	2005	16352
141 1/8	22 7/8 22 6/8	19 1/8	4 5	Polk County	WI	Jon A. Leisch	2005	16352
141 1/8	19 4/8 19 1/8	15 7/8	5 5	Idaho County	ID	DeLoy Desaro	2005	16352
*141 1/8	23 0/8 23 3/8	16 3/8	5 5	Pike County	IL	Mike J. Wood	2005	16352
141 1/8	22 1/8 23 1/8	18 5/8	4 4	Waukesha County	WI	Jeff Mislang	2006	16352
141 1/8	23 0/8 22 7/8	17 0/8	5 7	Somerset County	NJ	Robert Staudt, Jr.	2006	16352
*141 1/8	23 7/8 22 5/8	16 1/8	6 5	Licking County	OH	Mark W. Zabel	2006	16352
141 1/8	23 2/8 22 3/8	19 2/8	4 5	Olmsted County	MN	Steve Wendt	2006	16352
*141 1/8	23 3/8 23 2/8	15 2/8	5 6	Lincoln County	KS	Erik Watts	2006	16352
141 1/8	22 6/8 22 6/8	15 5/8	6 5	Harper County	KS	Charles L. Palmer	2006	16352
141 1/8	24 6/8 24 4/8	15 7/8	4 5	Bradford County	PA	Nathan Gallow	2007	16352
141 1/8	23 4/8 25 0/8	19 0/8	5 5	Outagamie County	WI	Nicholas K. Kamba	2007	16352
*141 1/8	23 0/8 22 6/8	16 7/8	5 6	Clayton County	IA	Daniel R. Kennedy	2007	16352
141 1/8	19 6/8 19 6/8	15 2/8	6 5	Humboldt County	IA	Patrick Ulrich	2007	16352
141 1/8	24 4/8 23 4/8	16 3/8	4 4	Clinton County	OH	Ron Wilt	2007	16352
141 1/8	25 4/8 24 4/8	15 1/8	5 5	Scoble Township	ONT	Douglas Rivard	2007	16352
*141 1/8	24 5/8 24 1/8	16 7/8	5 5	Buffalo County	WI	Bill Clink	2008	16352
141 1/8	18 5/8 18 5/8	12 6/8	6 5	McLean County	ND	Scott Lang	2008	16352
141 1/8	22 7/8 23 1/8	17 5/8	5 4	Lawrence County	IN	Greg Day	2008	16352
141 1/8	23 6/8 23 0/8	19 1/8	4 4	Grant County	WI	Phillip Breuer	2008	16352
*141 1/8	24 0/8 24 1/8	17 5/8	4 4	Franklin County	MS	Wade Hester	2008	16352
141 1/8	26 3/8 24 5/8	20 2/8	6 6	Ottawa County	KS	Richard Womble	2008	16352
*141 1/8	19 3/8 19 3/8	19 5/8	6 6	Bighorn	ALB	David Dickson	2008	16352
141 1/8	21 4/8 21 6/8	17 2/8	6 5	Gallatin County	IL	Paul Morgan	2009	16352
*141 1/8	22 6/8 24 6/8	17 7/8	4 5	Clark County	SD	Wade Stobbs	2009	16352
141 1/8	23 1/8 22 0/8	21 3/8	4 3	Iowa County	WI	Thomas F. Ridgeman	2009	16352
*141 1/8	26 3/8 24 6/8	20 3/8	5 5	Columbia County	WI	Bruce F. Udell	2009	16352
141 1/8	22 2/8 22 2/8	18 3/8	4 4	McCook County	SD	Jacob Boom	2009	16352
141 1/8	23 0/8 23 0/8	16 0/8	6 5	Jackson County	IA	Jeffrey A. Berg	2009	16352
141 0/8	22 2/8 21 7/8	16 0/8	4 5	Hand County	SD	Robert Werdel	1963	16489
141 0/8	24 2/8 24 4/8	18 0/8	5 4	Vermilion County	IL	Larry Mollet	1974	16489
141 0/8	21 5/8 22 0/8	16 0/8	4 5	Nobles County	MN	Rod McNab	1974	16489
141 0/8	24 2/8 24 1/8	18 3/8	4 4	Ohio County	IN	Mike Meyer	1979	16489
141 0/8	22 4/8 22 4/8	16 2/8	5 5	Marion County	IA	Steven F. Donnelly, Jr.	1982	16489
141 0/8	22 5/8 23 1/8	15 4/8	6 5	Marion County	WV	Samuel F. Clingan	1983	16489
141 0/8	21 2/8 22 0/8	17 1/8	6 5	Floyd County	IA	Dennis Grauerholz	1983	16489
141 0/8	24 3/8 23 5/8	18 1/8	5 4	Pine County	MN	Dave Hartl	1984	16489
141 0/8	23 4/8 23 3/8	21 2/8	5 5	Flathead County	MT	Wes Plummer	1984	16489
141 0/8	23 4/8 23 4/8	19 4/8	5 6	Douglas County	KS	Russell Stevens	1984	16489
141 0/8	24 3/8 24 1/8	17 2/8	4 4	Pottawatomie County	KS	Loyd C. Flowers, Sr.	1984	16489
141 0/8	24 5/8 23 7/8	17 4/8	5 4	Chatham County	NC	James T. Noonan III	1984	16489
141 0/8	22 3/8 21 5/8	18 6/8	4 4	Cass County	NE	Roger E. Buck	1985	16489
141 0/8	25 1/8 25 1/8	20 6/8	4 4	Prince Georges County	MD	Robert O. Turner II	1985	16489
141 0/8	21 4/8 17 2/8	17 0/8	5 6	Guernsey County	OH	Todd E. Feichter	1986	16489
141 0/8	25 0/8 24 5/8	17 6/8	5 5	Waterloo	ONT	John Wyszynski	1986	16489
141 0/8	25 0/8 24 2/8	19 2/8	4 4	Williams County	OH	Timothy L. Garber	1987	16489
141 0/8	23 1/8 23 6/8	18 4/8	5 4	Forest County	WI	Robert DuFek	1987	16489
141 0/8	24 1/8 25 4/8	19 1/8	6 6	Westchester County	NY	Wayne Alan Simko	1987	16489
141 0/8	23 0/8 23 0/8	15 2/8	4 4	Grundy County	IL	Jim W. Zientek	1987	16489
141 0/8	24 5/8 23 3/8	22 0/8	5 5	Warren County	IL	Jim M. Bratkovic	1988	16489
141 0/8	24 0/8 23 1/8	18 0/8	5 5	Chemung County	NY	Kim E. Womer	1988	16489
141 0/8	23 6/8 24 3/8	18 5/8	5 5	Wayne County	IL	Paul Fearn	1988	16489
141 0/8	21 3/8 21 4/8	15 4/8	6 5	Livingston County	IL	Michael G. Keesee	1989	16489
141 0/8	24 7/8 24 7/8	18 0/8	5 4	Riley County	KS	Robert L. Gardner	1989	16489
141 0/8	21 4/8 22 2/8	15 0/8	6 6	Thorsby	ALB	John Trout, Jr.	1989	16489
141 0/8	23 0/8 23 0/8	17 2/8	4 4	Burleigh County	ND	Jim Domaskin	1989	16489
141 0/8	25 4/8 25 2/8	16 0/8	4 4	Anderdon Township	ONT	Leo Potvin	1989	16489
141 0/8	26 0/8 26 2/8	19 0/8	5 5	La Salle County	TX	Dr. F. D. Elias	1990	16489
141 0/8	23 6/8 23 3/8	20 5/8	5 5	Mercer County	NJ	Frank Prato	1990	16489
141 0/8	23 2/8 22 7/8	17 0/8	5 5	Guthrie County	IA	John D. Hambleton	1990	16489
141 0/8	22 2/8 22 4/8	15 2/8	5 5	Franklin County	IA	Arlynn Ahrens	1990	16489
141 0/8	23 0/8 24 1/8	17 0/8	5 6	Weld County	CO	Chuck Brewer	1990	16489
141 0/8	23 4/8 22 5/8	17 0/8	5 6	Gallia County	OH	Bobby Clenney	1991	16489
141 0/8	22 7/8 23 3/8	17 3/8	5 5	Woodson County	KS	Joe Chippeaux	1991	16489
141 0/8	23 4/8 21 6/8	17 2/8	4 4	Ontario County	NY	Neil R. Ross	1991	16489
141 0/8	29 4/8 29 0/8	19 0/8	4 4	Richardson County	NE	Perry Oates	1991	16489
141 0/8	21 6/8 20 2/8	15 0/8	5 5	McHenry County	IL	William D. Weiss	1991	16489
141 0/8	25 3/8 25 1/8	18 4/8	5 5	Warren County	OH	W. H. "Billy" Brock III	1991	16489
141 0/8	22 4/8 22 6/8	17 0/8	5 5	Lake County	MN	Larry Antonich	1991	16489
141 0/8	22 1/8 21 0/8	15 2/8	6 6	Wood Mtn.	SAS	A. Jeff Best	1992	16489
141 0/8	27 0/8 27 5/8	18 4/8	5 4	Geauga County	OH	Richard W. Rudnay	1992	16489

WHITETAIL DEER (TYPICAL ANTLERS)

Minimum Score 125 — Continued

SCORE	LENGTH OF R MAIN BEAM L	INSIDE SPREAD	NUMBER OF R POINTS L		AREA	STATE/ PROVINCE	HUNTER'S NAME	DATE	RANK
141 0/8	24 1/8	22 3/8	15 7/8	4 5	Brown County	IL	Charles R. Figge	1992	16489
141 0/8	23 0/8	22 4/8	17 5/8	6 6	Christian County	IL	Philip Estell	1992	16489
141 0/8	25 7/8	25 1/8	17 6/8	4 4	Camden County	GA	John Bragg	1992	16489
141 0/8	23 0/8	23 6/8	15 4/8	6 6	Boone County	IL	Thomas C. Baker	1992	16489
141 0/8	22 6/8	23 6/8	18 1/8	6 4	Linn County	IA	David Elsbury	1993	16489
141 0/8	23 0/8	22 0/8	13 4/8	5 6	St. Louis County	MN	Jeff Montgomery	1993	16489
141 0/8	22 4/8	23 3/8	13 4/8	6 5	Buffalo County	WI	Ron Schultz	1993	16489
141 0/8	25 3/8	23 1/8	19 2/8	4 4	Suffolk County	NY	Neal Heaton	1993	16489
141 0/8	22 5/8	22 3/8	17 6/8	5 5	Henry County	VA	Mike Weaver	1993	16489
141 0/8	23 4/8	23 4/8	16 6/8	5 5	Dubuque County	IA	Mark W. Breitsprecker	1993	16489
141 0/8	24 5/8	25 0/8	18 2/8	4 5	Dallas County	IA	Joe Uedelhofen	1993	16489
141 0/8	22 7/8	23 7/8	20 2/8	4 4	Vermilion County	IL	David A. Downing	1993	16489
141 0/8	27 4/8	26 6/8	22 6/8	4 3	Saline County	IL	Mark L. Maynard	1993	16489
141 0/8	24 2/8	24 2/8	16 4/8	6 5	Macoupin County	IL	John Wesbrook	1993	16489
141 0/8	24 1/8	23 1/8	19 0/8	5 6	Sauk County	WI	Jerry Groth	1994	16489
141 0/8	23 3/8	23 0/8	15 4/8	5 6	Kent County	MD	Tom Scilipoti	1994	16489
141 0/8	21 0/8	20 6/8	15 2/8	6 5	Dodge County	MN	Terry Krahn	1994	16489
141 0/8	23 6/8	22 3/8	17 2/8	6 5	Cecil County	MD	Raymond M. Cook	1994	16489
141 0/8	23 5/8	22 6/8	16 2/8	5 4	Washington County	KS	Toby M. Bruna	1994	16489
141 0/8	23 2/8	23 4/8	16 0/8	5 5	Jasper County	IL	Marty Draves	1994	16489
141 0/8	24 4/8	23 1/8	19 6/8	4 4	Cumberland County	IL	Tom Koester	1995	16489
141 0/8	25 5/8	23 4/8	19 3/8	6 6	Kennebec County	ME	Sue D. LaRue	1995	16489
141 0/8	25 4/8	25 1/8	19 2/8	4 4	Tazewell County	IL	Tom McClary, Jr.	1995	16489
141 0/8	23 1/8	21 7/8	19 6/8	5 5	Edgar County	IL	Dale Good	1995	16489
141 0/8	23 7/8	24 0/8	19 0/8	5 6	Sawyer County	WI	Steven J. Olson	1995	16489
141 0/8	24 4/8	24 2/8	18 0/8	4 4	Cumberland County	IL	Randy Rodebaugh	1995	16489
141 0/8	23 1/8	23 2/8	17 2/8	5 5	Van Buren County	TN	Dwight Bottoms	1995	16489
141 0/8	24 4/8	24 6/8	17 4/8	4 5	Mingo County	WV	Clifford Hall	1995	16489
141 0/8	22 4/8	23 1/8	19 5/8	6 5	Du Page County	IL	James A. Wetmore	1995	16489
141 0/8	22 2/8	22 2/8	16 2/8	5 5	Goodhue County	MN	Peter Collins	1996	16489
141 0/8	27 2/8	26 0/8	20 6/8	4 5	McHenry County	IL	Gary T. Lackhouse	1996	16489
141 0/8	22 7/8	24 0/8	17 6/8	5 4	St. Louis County	MN	Brad Ronning	1996	16489
141 0/8	22 4/8	23 5/8	18 4/8	5 5	Polk County	IA	John W. Flies	1996	16489
141 0/8	23 6/8	23 4/8	20 0/8	4 5	Schuyler County	IL	Marc Anthony	1996	16489
141 0/8	22 6/8	23 0/8	20 5/8	6 8	Butler County	OH	Michael Rumpler	1996	16489
141 0/8	23 1/8	22 2/8	18 0/8	5 5	Montcalm County	MI	Duane Keeler	1997	16489
141 0/8	23 0/8	23 0/8	17 0/8	5 5	Trempealeau County	WI	Adam James Jarozewski	1997	16489
141 0/8	22 2/8	22 0/8	18 0/8	5 5	Waushara County	WI	Brett C. Larsen	1997	16489
141 0/8	21 4/8	21 6/8	16 4/8	4 5	Winona County	MN	Shawn E. Eyre	1997	16489
141 0/8	22 4/8	22 3/8	15 4/8	7 5	Chautauqua County	KS	Foster V. Yancey, Jr.	1997	16489
141 0/8	21 7/8	21 7/8	16 6/8	5 6	Walsh County	ND	Darrell W. Deutz	1998	16489
141 0/8	23 7/8	24 2/8	16 4/8	4 4	Price County	WI	Roger A. Niewiadomski	1998	16489
141 0/8	23 4/8	23 7/8	18 2/8	5 4	Wyoming County	WV	Robert Holden	1998	16489
141 0/8	23 4/8	23 7/8	18 0/8	4 4	Trempealeau County	WI	Scott Gunderson	1998	16489
141 0/8	22 4/8	22 3/8	17 4/8	5 5	Chester County	PA	Bob Horkey	1998	16489
141 0/8	22 5/8	24 0/8	16 7/8	6 5	Warren County	IA	Brent Hines	1998	16489
141 0/8	22 7/8	22 4/8	19 4/8	6 6	Brookings County	SD	Fred T. Meyer	1998	16489
141 0/8	21 6/8	21 6/8	15 0/8	5 6	Bayfield County	WI	Aaron Bloomquist	1998	16489
141 0/8	23 3/8	23 3/8	17 4/8	5 4	Mercer County	PA	Sam Conover	1999	16489
141 0/8	24 6/8	23 6/8	18 0/8	7 6	Marshall County	IN	Craig Highland	1999	16489
141 0/8	22 0/8	22 0/8	15 2/8	5 5	Winnebago County	IL	Richard C. McCormick	1999	16489
141 0/8	22 5/8	22 7/8	16 4/8	7 5	Madison County	NY	William F. O'Brien IV	1999	16489
141 0/8	22 2/8	22 4/8	16 3/8	7 6	Polk County	IA	Joe Case	1999	16489
141 0/8	22 7/8	22 4/8	17 4/8	7 5	Lawrence County	IN	Michael Bartley	1999	16489
141 0/8	21 5/8	22 1/8	14 6/8	5 5	Meigs County	OH	Norman Gray	1999	16489
141 0/8	22 6/8	23 6/8	18 7/8	7 7	Macon County	MO	Steve Hurst	1999	16489
141 0/8	24 0/8	23 0/8	19 2/8	5 8	Bureau County	IL	Scott Orlandi	1999	16489
141 0/8	23 4/8	22 3/8	18 0/8	9 7	Pike County	IL	Al Schult	1999	16489
141 0/8	24 6/8	25 1/8	19 7/8	7 6	Gage County	NE	Tom Hottovy	1999	16489
141 0/8	24 4/8	23 1/8	18 2/8	5 6	Pike County	IL	Jim Coleman	1999	16489
141 0/8	22 3/8	22 7/8	16 0/8	5 5	Pike County	IL	Lee Denney	1999	16489
141 0/8	26 2/8	25 2/8	19 6/8	6 5	Scott County	IA	Jeffrey R. Coonts	1999	16489
141 0/8	23 4/8	23 7/8	21 0/8	4 5	Queen Annes County	MD	Chris E. Fifer	1999	16489
141 0/8	20 6/8	22 2/8	15 0/8	5 5	Cumberland County	NJ	Bob Eisele	1999	16489
141 0/8	22 1/8	21 6/8	13 4/8	5 5	Marquette County	WI	Mike Guenther	2000	16489
141 0/8	24 7/8	23 5/8	19 2/8	5 5	Carter County	MO	Richard Orchard	2000	16489
141 0/8	26 3/8	26 5/8	22 1/8	5 4	Frederick County	MD	Holmes Stoner III	2000	16489
141 0/8	26 5/8	24 0/8	19 0/8	6 6	Linn County	IA	Greg Hofmuster	2000	16489
141 0/8	24 6/8	23 4/8	14 4/8	5 5	Oconto County	WI	Jeff Belongea	2000	16489
141 0/8	21 1/8	21 1/8	17 4/8	6 5	Madison County	IL	Kelly Harper	2000	16489
141 0/8	23 6/8	20 6/8	17 0/8	5 5	Tioga County	NY	John M. Briggs	2000	16489
141 0/8	21 7/8	22 3/8	20 0/8	4 4	Lyon County	IA	Michael Judas	2000	16489
141 0/8	23 6/8	23 6/8	16 4/8	5 5	Mingo County	WV	Bobby Starr	2000	16489
141 0/8	21 0/8	21 0/8	17 6/8	5 5	Park County	MT	Scott Norquist	2001	16489
141 0/8	24 7/8	22 6/8	15 2/8	5 5	Houston County	GA	Paul Brown	2001	16489
141 0/8	22 3/8	22 2/8	19 4/8	4 4	Winona County	MN	Steve Speltz	2001	16489
141 0/8	24 1/8	24 6/8	17 7/8	4 5	Vermilion County	IL	Jeff Parkerson	2001	16489
141 0/8	23 0/8	23 2/8	15 4/8	6 6	Venango County	PA	James E. Casteel	2001	16489
141 0/8	23 0/8	23 1/8	16 0/8	7 5	Iron County	WI	Brian A. Bartkowiak	2001	16489
141 0/8	24 4/8	24 4/8	15 0/8	4 5	Waushara County	WI	Brian F. Wenzel	2001	16489
141 0/8	22 0/8	23 1/8	18 4/8	4 5	Delaware County	IA	Daniel G. Putz	2001	16489
141 0/8	22 1/8	21 4/8	16 2/8	5 5	Otter Tail County	MN	Trent Ament	2001	16489
141 0/8	20 2/8	21 1/8	16 7/8	5 6	Porter County	IN	Ellis E. Ponton	2002	16489
141 0/8	22 1/8	22 0/8	19 7/8	5 5	Posey County	IN	Frank Davis	2002	16489
141 0/8	21 3/8	20 7/8	16 0/8	7 8	Warren County	IN	Nathan Grogan	2002	16489
141 0/8	21 6/8	21 2/8	16 4/8	6 5	Morris County	NJ	Dennis George	2002	16489
141 0/8	25 0/8	26 6/8	23 2/8	4 5	Livingston County	NY	Chad Draper	2002	16489
141 0/8	24 4/8	24 1/8	16 4/8	5 5	Charles County	MD	Patrick E. Langley	2002	16489
141 0/8	20 6/8	21 2/8	14 6/8	4 4	Geauga County	OH	Gregory A. Anderson	2002	16489
141 0/8	22 6/8	23 3/8	15 6/8	5 5	Osage County	MO	Forrest Fortune	2002	16489
141 0/8	28 2/8	27 5/8	16 5/8	7 7	Edmonson County	KY	Don Decker	2002	16489
*141 0/8	22 5/8	21 7/8	18 2/8	7 8	Dodge County	MN	Kevin Cain	2003	16489
141 0/8	22 7/8	22 7/8	16 4/8	5 5	Marquette County	WI	Riley McLaughlin	2003	16489
141 0/8	23 0/8	23 4/8	17 4/8	6 6	Wood County	WI	James D. Curtin	2003	16489
141 0/8	23 4/8	22 7/8	15 5/8	6 5	Hudson Bay	SAS	Jeff Brigham	2003	16489

WHITETAIL DEER (TYPICAL ANTLERS)

Minimum Score 125   Continued

SCORE	LENGTH OF R MAIN BEAM L	INSIDE SPREAD	NUMBER OF R POINTS L	AREA	STATE/ PROVINCE	HUNTER'S NAME	DATE	RANK
141 0/8	23 5/8 23 4/8	18 0/8	4 5	Washington County	IL	Adam Kempfer	2003	16489
141 0/8	24 6/8 25 2/8	17 4/8	5 5	Buffalo County	WI	David W. Pfeiffer	2003	16489
141 0/8	19 7/8 20 4/8	16 2/8	5 5	Pierce County	WI	Bruce Barrie	2003	16489
141 0/8	23 5/8 22 4/8	18 0/8	5 5	Wood County	WI	Mike Bohn	2003	16489
141 0/8	24 4/8 26 3/8	17 7/8	9 8	Republic County	KS	Jason A. Miller	2003	16489
141 0/8	22 3/8 21 6/8	15 7/8	4 5	Jackson County	KY	Darren Day	2003	16489
*141 0/8	23 3/8 23 1/8	20 3/8	6 6	Boone County	MO	Daniel Finke	2004	16489
*141 0/8	24 6/8 25 2/8	19 0/8	5 5	Roberts County	SD	Wesley Koehler	2004	16489
141 0/8	20 3/8 20 2/8	18 6/8	5 9	Marshall County	IL	William T. Trainor, Jr.	2004	16489
*141 0/8	24 0/8 25 3/8	17 3/8	7 7	Worcester County	MA	Joseph Leofanti	2004	16489
141 0/8	23 2/8 23 0/8	19 4/8	5 5	Buffalo County	WI	Glen Axness	2004	16489
141 0/8	25 3/8 24 6/8	17 0/8	4 4	Cass County	IL	Chet Hollar	2004	16489
141 0/8	25 7/8 25 1/8	20 2/8	6 4	Tensas Parish	LA	Kris Fulmer	2004	16489
*141 0/8	24 7/8 24 0/8	15 6/8	5 5	Hopkins County	KY	William Cartwright, Jr.	2005	16489
*141 0/8	23 4/8 22 6/8	17 4/8	4 5	Champaign County	IL	Doug McClure	2005	16489
141 0/8	23 0/8 22 5/8	18 6/8	4 5	Will County	IL	Darren Van Essen	2005	16489
141 0/8	25 4/8 25 5/8	16 7/8	6 7	Christian County	IL	Jim Davis	2005	16489
141 0/8	23 1/8 21 7/8	20 0/8	5 5	Dawson County	NE	Shawn Church	2005	16489
141 0/8	24 5/8 24 6/8	17 2/8	10 5	Scott County	IN	Bob Craig	2005	16489
141 0/8	23 1/8 22 7/8	14 6/8	4 5	Calhoun County	IL	Ronald Thieme	2005	16489
141 0/8	25 4/8 24 3/8	20 2/8	6 5	Tuscarawas County	OH	Zach Kaiser	2005	16489
*141 0/8	22 3/8 22 0/8	18 4/8	4 5	Will County	IL	Adam Marcukaitis	2005	16489
*141 0/8	23 2/8 22 1/8	17 5/8	6 5	Prowers County	CO	Phillip Gaines	2005	16489
141 0/8	22 0/8 21 7/8	16 0/8	5 5	Cass County	IL	Chet Hollar	2005	16489
141 0/8	20 2/8 20 2/8	14 6/8	5 5	Polk County	WI	Kyle A. Ward	2005	16489
*141 0/8	24 4/8 25 5/8	17 1/8	8 5	Jefferson County	NY	Jack Newman	2005	16489
*141 0/8	24 4/8 24 0/8	18 0/8	5 5	Avoyelles Parish	LA	Tammy Lemoine	2006	16489
141 0/8	25 3/8 24 2/8	17 2/8	5 6	Stokes County	NC	Jerrold Wade	2006	16489
141 0/8	22 2/8 21 6/8	18 3/8	6 7	Kleberg County	TX	Matt Plitt	2006	16489
141 0/8	23 2/8 23 7/8	21 0/8	4 4	Union County	SD	Todd A. Halverson	2006	16489
141 0/8	25 6/8 25 3/8	18 4/8	5 4	Steuben County	IN	Gregory J. Raatz	2006	16489
141 0/8	22 5/8 22 6/8	18 0/8	4 5	Houston County	MN	Jay Ougel	2006	16489
141 0/8	22 7/8 21 5/8	15 2/8	5 5	Lincoln County	MO	Ernest Durlas	2007	16489
141 0/8	23 1/8 23 6/8	16 7/8	5 4	Taylor County	WV	Charles W. Boyce	2007	16489
141 0/8	23 7/8 25 2/8	17 6/8	4 4	Hancock County	IN	Brian Davidson	2007	16489
141 0/8	23 3/8 22 4/8	20 4/8	5 5	Lancaster County	PA	Frank D. Rice	2007	16489
141 0/8	23 4/8 23 1/8	16 4/8	5 5	Wayne County	IA	John Anderson	2007	16489
141 0/8	22 0/8 22 5/8	15 0/8	6 6	Ellsworth County	KS	Henry E. Crosby, Jr.	2007	16489
*141 0/8	22 3/8 22 3/8	15 2/8	5 5	Marion County	IL	Jack Thomas	2007	16489
*141 0/8	25 7/8 25 2/8	19 0/8	5 4	Sawyer County	WI	Bruce Beckwith	2008	16489
*141 0/8	21 2/8 21 1/8	18 2/8	8 6	McKenzie County	ND	Tom Zebro	2008	16489
*141 0/8	22 3/8 22 5/8	15 0/8	5 5	Madison Parish	LA	Clay Abraham	2008	16489
*141 0/8	22 0/8 22 6/8	24 4/8	5 5	Jackson County	OH	Jody Rus	2008	16489
141 0/8	25 2/8 25 6/8	15 6/8	4 4	Hampden County	MA	Roger Pyzocha	2008	16489
*141 0/8	23 0/8 23 2/8	19 6/8	5 5	Green Lake County	WI	Luke Ladwig	2008	16489
141 0/8	24 5/8 23 5/8	17 2/8	4 4	Menard County	IL	George G. Bogie	2008	16489
141 0/8	23 6/8 23 5/8	18 6/8	5 7	Loon Lake	SAS	Lanny Nault	2009	16489
*141 0/8	21 1/8 20 4/8	19 4/8	5 5	Polk County	WI	David J. Moris	2009	16489
*141 0/8	24 4/8 24 7/8	18 6/8	5 5	Jay County	IN	David Garke	2009	16489
141 0/8	24 6/8 22 4/8	17 4/8	6 5	Saline County	MO	Brian Inlow	2009	16489
141 0/8	23 5/8 23 5/8	19 2/8	4 6	Grundy County	IL	Michael J. Fraley	2009	16489
141 0/8	22 4/8 23 4/8	21 4/8	5 6	Jefferson County	WI	Eric Ericson	2009	16489
*141 0/8	23 0/8 22 6/8	22 0/8	5 5	Winnebago County	IL	Steven B. McGaw, Jr.	2009	16489
141 0/8	21 6/8 21 2/8	16 4/8	5 6	Sullivan County	MO	J. Todd Fry	2009	16489
141 0/8	23 6/8 25 2/8	18 0/8	4 4	Warren County	NJ	Jared M. Cramer	2009	16489
*141 0/8	19 5/8 20 2/8	15 1/8	5 6	Scotland County	MO	Jason Pedersen	2009	16489
*141 0/8	26 3/8 26 1/8	19 1/8	7 5	Clayton County	IA	James Scherf	2009	16489

Deer entries below 141 0/8, that appeared in the 6th Edition, are not included here, but are included on the accompanying CD (see page 119), and also in the Club's Records Archives.

140 7/8	24 4/8 24 1/8	16 5/8	4 4	Harper County	KS	Terrence Horan	2002	16683
140 7/8	24 6/8 24 4/8	19 3/8	7 4	Issaquena County	MS	Luke Parker	2003	16683
140 7/8	25 5/8 26 0/8	20 0/8	4 5	Madison County	IA	Keith R. Mickley	2003	16683
140 7/8	22 6/8 22 7/8	19 3/8	6 5	Bureau County	IL	Greg Bowers	2003	16683
*140 7/8	21 3/8 20 6/8	17 1/8	5 5	Mercer County	ND	Jesse Carter	2004	16683
140 7/8	19 5/8 20 1/8	16 1/8	5 5	Fond du Lac County	WI	Michael J. Gantner	2004	16683
140 7/8	23 4/8 23 4/8	17 5/8	6 5	St. Louis County	MN	Mitchell Vidor	2004	16683
*140 7/8	23 1/8 23 0/8	18 6/8	5 4	Henderson County	IL	Bruce Smith	2004	16683
140 7/8	21 0/8 21 0/8	15 3/8	5 5	Boone County	IA	Jason D. Loecker	2004	16683
*140 7/8	27 3/8 26 5/8	17 6/8	6 8	Berrien County	MI	Randy Luthringer	2004	16683
140 7/8	20 0/8 21 2/8	19 3/8	5 5	Vinton County	OH	Mark Gifford	2004	16683
*140 7/8	25 7/8 24 7/8	17 6/8	5 8	Jefferson County	KS	Tom Brandt	2004	16683
140 7/8	19 6/8 20 3/8	14 0/8	6 6	Livingston County	MO	Tony E. Lister	2004	16683
140 7/8	22 7/8 23 4/8	17 7/8	4 4	Portage County	OH	Randal A. Battista	2004	16683
*140 7/8	24 5/8 24 1/8	17 4/8	5 4	Kent County	DE	Robert Z. Barrett	2005	16683
140 7/8	22 0/8 20 6/8	14 7/8	6 5	Sioux County	IA	Jeffrey S. Nibbelink	2005	16683
140 7/8	21 0/8 20 4/8	17 3/8	5 5	Worth County	MO	Peter Dale	2005	16683
140 7/8	23 1/8 24 4/8	17 1/8	4 4	Knox County	IN	Brian Fellows	2005	16683
140 7/8	23 0/8 22 5/8	15 3/8	5 5	Miner County	SD	Nathan Kizer	2005	16683
*140 7/8	21 3/8 21 4/8	17 5/8	5 5	Washington County	WI	Dennis M. Kratz, Jr.	2005	16683
140 7/8	23 0/8 21 7/8	20 7/8	5 4	Henry County	VA	Mike Weaver	2005	16683
*140 7/8	22 4/8 22 3/8	17 1/8	5 5	Val Verde County	TX	Eleazar Pena	2005	16683
140 7/8	24 6/8 23 7/8	16 5/8	4 5	Buffalo County	WI	Andrew Sturz	2006	16683
140 7/8	22 5/8 23 2/8	15 7/8	5 5	Jefferson County	OH	Brady J. Baker, Jr.	2006	16683
*140 7/8	24 2/8 23 7/8	19 1/8	4 4	Montgomery County	OH	Dean A. Stover	2006	16683
140 7/8	24 0/8 22 6/8	21 1/8	5 5	Shawano County	WI	Jason H. J. Stammer	2006	16683
140 7/8	24 0/8 23 5/8	21 3/8	4 4	Pierce County	WI	David Hovel	2006	16683
140 7/8	23 6/8 23 1/8	17 3/8	5 6	Jackson County	OH	Randell Cockerham	2006	16683
140 7/8	22 3/8 22 2/8	17 7/8	5 5	Marathon County	WI	Chad J. Curtis	2007	16683
140 7/8	22 2/8 22 3/8	19 7/8	5 5	Screven County	GA	Ryan Beasley	2007	16683
140 7/8	24 3/8 24 0/8	17 5/8	4 4	Dane County	WI	Kevin Bronkhorst	2007	16683
140 7/8	21 6/8 21 1/8	15 6/8	7 7	Allen County	IN	R. James Zehr	2007	16683
140 7/8	25 0/8 21 6/8	17 3/8	5 4	Buffalo County	WI	Travis Althoff	2007	16683

Deer entries below 141 0/8, that appeared in the 6th Edition, are not included here, but are included on the accompanying CD (see page 119), and also in the Club's Records Archives.

WHITETAIL DEER (TYPICAL ANTLERS)

Minimum Score 125 Continued

SCORE	LENGTH OF R MAIN BEAM L	INSIDE SPREAD	NUMBER OF R POINTS L	AREA	STATE/ PROVINCE	HUNTER'S NAME	DATE	RANK
140 7/8	21 4/8 22 0/8	16 7/8	5 5	La Crosse County	WI	Daniel A. Knutson	2007	16683
140 7/8	24 2/8 25 5/8	16 0/8	6 6	Dunn County	WI	David Z. Zoellick	2007	16683
140 7/8	22 4/8 22 2/8	17 3/8	6 6	Vernon County	WI	Keith Peetz	2007	16683
*140 7/8	23 4/8 23 0/8	15 1/8	4 5	Fayette County	IA	Todd A. Grimes	2007	16683
*140 7/8	19 7/8 20 3/8	16 1/8	5 5	Mercer County	ND	Steve Borlaug	2008	16683
*140 7/8	24 2/8 24 2/8	17 3/8	4 4	Allen County	KY	Clay Kirby	2008	16683
140 7/8	23 6/8 24 3/8	19 3/8	5 4	Chester County	PA	Dave Kochel	2008	16683
*140 7/8	23 4/8 23 4/8	18 1/8	4 4	Pierce County	WI	David M. Krampitz	2008	16683
140 7/8	21 4/8 22 2/8	18 1/8	5 5	Buffalo County	WI	Bill Katula	2008	16683
140 7/8	21 0/8 19 7/8	19 7/8	5 7	Pulaski County	IN	Mark Narantic	2008	16683
140 7/8	23 6/8 22 7/8	17 1/8	5 5	Columbia County	WI	Mark Livingston	2008	16683
140 7/8	22 4/8 23 4/8	19 3/8	4 5	Day County	SD	David Larson	2008	16683
140 7/8	23 6/8 23 1/8	18 3/8	6 6	Olmsted County	MN	Steve Strickland	2008	16683
140 7/8	23 0/8 22 7/8	19 3/8	5 5	Bosque County	TX	Keith Finstad	2008	16683
140 7/8	23 7/8 23 6/8	16 7/8	4 4	Red Deer	ALB	Wayne Soderberg	2009	16683
140 7/8	24 0/8 23 1/8	17 6/8	6 5	Orleans County	NY	Craig Heidemann	2009	16683
*140 7/8	22 3/8 22 5/8	19 5/8	5 6	Iowa County	WI	Jesse M. Parpart	2009	16683
*140 7/8	23 7/8 22 3/8	18 2/8	5 6	Whitley County	IN	Andy M. Straub	2009	16683
140 7/8	23 6/8 22 2/8	18 0/8	7 7	Outagamie County	WI	Mike Ernst	2009	16683
140 7/8	21 0/8 20 4/8	15 6/8	6 6	Ross County	OH	Tari Myers	2009	16683
140 7/8	24 0/8 24 7/8	19 4/8	6 4	Henry County	IA	Joe McSorley	2009	16683
140 7/8	25 3/8 24 2/8	20 5/8	5 5	Medina County	OH	Bill Hanzel	2009	16683
140 6/8	21 2/8 21 6/8	18 0/8	6 5	Sussex County	DE	Charlie Sewell	2000	16838
140 6/8	22 6/8 23 3/8	19 6/8	5 5	Ripley County	IN	Michael Thomas Neuner	2000	16838
140 6/8	23 5/8 24 0/8	18 2/8	5 5	Jasper County	IL	Carl Waggle	2003	16838
140 6/8	23 1/8 22 7/8	17 6/8	4 4	Buffalo County	WI	Fred Baures	2003	16838
140 6/8	23 2/8 23 1/8	18 5/8	5 5	Jo Daviess County	IL	Mike Feldermann	2004	16838
140 6/8	22 6/8 22 4/8	16 6/8	6 5	Schuyler County	IL	Rick E. Park	2004	16838
140 6/8	25 5/8 25 6/8	19 1/8	4 5	Grant County	WI	Jason Dalsing	2004	16838
140 6/8	25 2/8 25 1/8	17 4/8	5 5	Jackson County	IN	Douglas S. Stickles	2004	16838
140 6/8	23 0/8 22 3/8	17 1/8	7 7	Adams County	IL	Randy Kurz	2004	16838
140 6/8	22 6/8 24 0/8	15 6/8	4 5	Waupaca County	WI	Robert L. Pagel, Sr.	2004	16838
140 6/8	22 2/8 24 1/8	18 2/8	4 5	Harper County	KS	Warren Hatcher	2004	16838
140 6/8	25 4/8 25 1/8	19 2/8	5 4	Coles County	IL	Rick Boyer	2004	16838
140 6/8	22 1/8 22 4/8	21 0/8	4 4	Rusk County	WI	Ronald Frohn	2004	16838
140 6/8	24 7/8 26 7/8	25 2/8	7 6	Warren County	MS	Al Guido	2004	16838
140 6/8	23 6/8 23 7/8	16 4/8	4 5	Greene County	IL	Gerald Nutt	2005	16838
140 6/8	24 4/8 24 0/8	21 6/8	4 4	Fairfield County	CT	Donald H. Kuhn II	2005	16838
*140 6/8	21 4/8 20 7/8	17 7/8	5 6	Griggs County	ND	Chad Haaland	2005	16838
*140 6/8	20 2/8 20 1/8	17 0/8	5 4	Griggs County	ND	Peter Schwieters	2005	16838
140 6/8	21 5/8 21 2/8	15 6/8	5 5	Traill County	ND	Mike Strand	2005	16838
*140 6/8	22 4/8 23 1/8	18 2/8	5 4	De Kalb County	IN	Ronald L. Kline	2005	16838
140 6/8	23 6/8 25 2/8	20 0/8	5 6	Howard County	IA	Thomas R. Cray	2005	16838
140 6/8	25 1/8 24 4/8	17 3/8	7 9	Chautauqua County	NY	Jeff Sample	2005	16838
140 6/8	23 4/8 24 6/8	18 0/8	4 5	Ontario County	NY	Matt Fritz	2005	16838
*140 6/8	23 7/8 25 1/8	17 2/8	4 4	Dubuque County	IA	Joseph Raio	2005	16838
140 6/8	24 1/8 23 3/8	16 6/8	7 6	Piatt County	IL	Johnnie Richardson	2005	16838
140 6/8	23 6/8 23 6/8	20 4/8	4 5	Hartford County	CT	Frank Aleria	2005	16838
140 6/8	22 5/8 21 6/8	18 0/8	5 5	Maverick County	TX	Ralph Peterson	2006	16838
140 6/8	23 4/8 22 7/8	19 2/8	5 5	Elk County	KS	Jeffrey Fitts	2006	16838
140 6/8	24 4/8 23 4/8	17 2/8	4 4	Will County	IL	Tom Mooi	2006	16838
*140 6/8	23 3/8 23 3/8	17 4/8	5 5	Putnam County	OH	Tom Stant	2006	16838
140 6/8	21 6/8 22 1/8	15 6/8	6 6	Greene County	PA	Zachary Policz	2006	16838
140 6/8	21 1/8 21 0/8	14 3/8	5 6	Gasconade County	MO	Michael C. Spurgeon	2006	16838
140 6/8	21 7/8 22 4/8	18 2/8	6 5	Brown County	IL	Ross Surratt	2006	16838
140 6/8	22 6/8 22 4/8	17 2/8	6 7	Boone County	MO	Robert Morton	2006	16838
140 6/8	27 2/8 25 4/8	22 0/8	5 5	Peoria County	IL	Tim Heinz	2006	16838
140 6/8	22 6/8 22 3/8	17 2/8	5 5	Mingo County	WV	Clint Doyle	2006	16838
140 6/8	22 4/8 22 6/8	17 4/8	5 5	Sedgwick County	KS	Todd Wilson	2006	16838
140 6/8	20 0/8 20 6/8	14 2/8	5 5	Tippecanoe County	IN	Michael J. Smith	2007	16838
*140 6/8	25 2/8 26 3/8	20 1/8	7 8	St. Croix County	WI	Mel Jirasek	2007	16838
140 6/8	24 5/8 23 7/8	17 1/8	6 7	Rice County	MN	Bob Favro	2007	16838
140 6/8	24 6/8 25 4/8	17 2/8	4 4	Keya Paha County	NE	R. Kirk Sharp	2007	16838
*140 6/8	21 3/8 21 1/8	16 0/8	5 5	McDonough County	IL	Randy Huizenga	2007	16838
*140 6/8	23 7/8 25 0/8	17 7/8	5 4	Polk County	IA	James D. Steele	2007	16838
140 6/8	23 4/8 24 6/8	16 3/8	7 5	Harper County	KS	Charles L. Palmer	2007	16838
140 6/8	21 7/8 21 5/8	17 6/8	6 5	Eaton County	MI	William Emenhiser	2007	16838
*140 6/8	24 3/8 24 3/8	18 0/8	4 4	Lincoln County	KS	Erik Watts	2007	16838
140 6/8	22 0/8 21 5/8	17 3/8	6 7	Hodgeman County	KS	Dan Bernarde	2007	16838
*140 6/8	22 7/8 23 2/8	15 6/8	5 5	Jasper County	IN	Clay B. Whaley	2007	16838
140 6/8	20 7/8 20 7/8	15 2/8	5 5	Vernon County	WI	Ryan Holte	2008	16838
140 6/8	21 4/8 23 0/8	17 4/8	5 5	Carroll County	MS	Ryan Taylor	2008	16838
*140 6/8	23 0/8 22 3/8	17 0/8	5 5	Meade County	KY	Shannon Ray Hall	2008	16838
140 6/8	23 3/8 22 6/8	16 2/8	5 7	Chitek Lake	SAS	Kevin Mulkeran	2008	16838
*140 6/8	24 0/8 24 2/8	15 4/8	5 5	Houston County	MN	Andrew Sackrison	2008	16838
*140 6/8	22 4/8 22 5/8	19 0/8	5 5	Rock County	WI	Ryan Hogenmiller	2008	16838
140 6/8	23 2/8 22 2/8	17 2/8	5 6	Monroe County	IN	Louie Kitcoff	2008	16838
140 6/8	23 0/8 22 3/8	18 2/8	5 5	Fairfax County	VA	Thomas M. Kody	2008	16838
140 6/8	22 1/8 22 7/8	20 4/8	4 5	Jackson County	WI	Darrell L. Armbruster	2008	16838
*140 6/8	24 3/8 23 6/8	18 6/8	4 5	Las Animas County	CO	Dustin Mincic	2008	16838
140 6/8	25 1/8 24 7/8	16 6/8	4 4	Jackson County	MI	Vince Smith	2009	16838
140 6/8	23 0/8 22 3/8	18 4/8	6 5	Fillmore County	MN	Kevin Wikre	2009	16838
140 6/8	22 3/8 22 3/8	16 4/8	5 5	Custer County	NE	Zac Bartak	2009	16838
140 6/8	24 3/8 23 6/8	19 6/8	4 4	Door County	WI	Bart A. Falish	2009	16838
140 6/8	24 4/8 25 1/8	20 4/8	5 5	Buffalo County	WI	Douglas R. Trapp	2009	16838
140 6/8	25 3/8 23 6/8	17 6/8	5 6	Vernon County	WI	Erik Jensen	2009	16838
140 6/8	25 3/8 25 2/8	17 6/8	4 4	Gage County	NE	Gene Tupa	2009	16838
*140 6/8	22 4/8 23 3/8	15 6/8	5 5	Chautauqua County	KS	Jason Birmingham	2009	16838
*140 6/8	25 3/8 23 6/8	13 5/8	7 7	St. Croix County	WI	Chris Meyers	2010	16838
140 5/8	24 2/8 24 6/8	16 4/8	5 6	Wabasha County	MN	Robert A. Hofschulte	1999	17018
140 5/8	24 0/8 24 6/8	22 1/8	5 6	Monona County	IA	Dave Newman	1999	17018
140 5/8	24 0/8 23 4/8	16 4/8	5 5	Atchison County	MO	Raymond Gebhards, Jr.	2000	17018
140 5/8	21 3/8 22 1/8	15 4/8	7 7	Howard County	IA	Lynn Scheidel	2000	17018
*140 5/8	24 2/8 22 6/8	16 5/8	4 4	Adams County	OH	Joe Wiesman	2002	17018
*140 5/8	24 5/8 22 5/8	18 3/8	5 5	Daviess County	IN	Rodney Swartzentruber	2003	17018

532

WHITETAIL DEER (TYPICAL ANTLERS)

Minimum Score 125 — Continued

SCORE	LENGTH OF R MAIN BEAM L	INSIDE SPREAD	NUMBER OF R POINTS L	AREA	STATE/ PROVINCE	HUNTER'S NAME	DATE	RANK
140 5/8	21 6/8 22 4/8	16 1/8	5 5	Randolph County	MO	Matt Fleming	2003	17018
140 5/8	23 3/8 24 7/8	16 6/8	5 6	Jackson County	OK	Lawrence K. Wilks	2003	17018
140 5/8	22 6/8 22 6/8	17 4/8	7 5	Tuscarawas County	OH	Gary J. Czatt	2004	17018
140 5/8	23 4/8 22 7/8	18 1/8	5 5	Jackson County	WI	Nancie S. Cooper	2004	17018
140 5/8	21 0/8 22 0/8	15 5/8	5 5	Clark County	MO	Kristopher Brewer	2004	17018
140 5/8	22 1/8 21 2/8	16 7/8	7 5	Sharp County	AR	Witt Stephens, Jr.	2004	17018
140 5/8	23 3/8 23 1/8	16 1/8	5 6	Logan County	KY	Doug Yoder	2004	17018
140 5/8	22 5/8 23 3/8	17 2/8	6 5	Kane County	IL	Marcus Withey	2004	17018
140 5/8	22 0/8 20 6/8	17 1/8	6 6	Scott County	IL	Chris McCormack	2004	17018
140 5/8	21 7/8 22 2/8	15 3/8	5 6	Upson County	GA	Britt Owens	2004	17018
140 5/8	22 4/8 22 6/8	16 1/8	6 5	Fulton County	IL	Gregory S. Guerrieri	2004	17018
* 140 5/8	22 0/8 21 7/8	15 1/8	5 5	Butler County	PA	Donald R. Garvin	2004	17018
140 5/8	27 3/8 27 1/8	16 5/8	4 5	Kent County	MD	Timothy S. Bressler	2004	17018
* 140 5/8	21 4/8 21 7/8	15 3/8	5 5	Richland County	MT	Paul Bryant	2005	17018
140 5/8	20 6/8 20 5/8	16 1/8	6 5	Webster County	NE	Jerrod Meyer	2005	17018
140 5/8	22 7/8 23 0/8	18 7/8	4 4	Dane County	WI	Casey Preimesberger	2005	17018
140 5/8	22 5/8 22 0/8	17 5/8	5 6	Dubuque County	IA	Jerry Comer	2005	17018
140 5/8	23 3/8 23 0/8	17 1/8	4 4	Chippewa County	WI	Rick Wulterkens	2005	17018
140 5/8	23 3/8 23 7/8	18 1/8	5 5	Muskingum County	OH	Cory Jones	2005	17018
140 5/8	23 1/8 23 1/8	18 3/8	6 6	Clay County	IA	Thomas Gross	2005	17018
140 5/8	24 2/8 24 2/8	17 3/8	4 4	Licking County	OH	Mike Dillman	2005	17018
140 5/8	23 4/8 24 0/8	21 1/8	5 5	Howard County	MD	Kevin Patrick Crowell	2005	17018
140 5/8	23 6/8 23 7/8	18 3/8	4 4	Douglas County	WI	Douglas S. Nelson	2006	17018
140 5/8	22 1/8 21 7/8	20 3/8	5 5	Houston County	MN	Jeffrey D. McKenzie	2006	17018
* 140 5/8	20 6/8 20 7/8	14 5/8	7 5	Valley County	MT	Evan Guenther	2006	17018
140 5/8	21 1/8 21 2/8	14 5/8	6 5	Waupaca County	WI	Greg Guderjohn	2006	17018
140 5/8	22 2/8 22 6/8	15 1/8	6 5	McPherson County	KS	Allan W. Mitchell	2006	17018
140 5/8	24 4/8 23 0/8	16 5/8	5 4	Hamilton County	OH	Mike Bier	2006	17018
140 5/8	21 4/8 21 5/8	16 1/8	5 5	Cerro Gordo County	IA	Tom O'Neill	2006	17018
140 5/8	22 7/8 21 6/8	15 1/8	5 5	Pepin County	WI	Brent Risler	2006	17018
140 5/8	24 4/8 24 3/8	17 3/8	5 4	Coshocton County	OH	Joel Coffman	2006	17018
140 5/8	24 3/8 23 6/8	18 1/8	5 7	Carroll County	IL	Robert G. Gaul	2007	17018
140 5/8	23 2/8 23 3/8	17 1/8	5 7	Kosciusko County	IN	Jason Hall	2007	17018
140 5/8	21 4/8 20 4/8	17 1/8	5 5	Sutton County	TX	Daniel Welker	2007	17018
* 140 5/8	24 1/8 25 0/8	19 7/8	4 4	Clinton County	IA	Jason Loose	2007	17018
140 5/8	23 0/8 24 2/8	17 5/8	5 6	Clayton County	IA	Aaron Green	2007	17018
140 5/8	26 2/8 27 2/8	19 4/8	5 6	Delaware County	IA	Edward Gibbs	2007	17018
* 140 5/8	24 4/8 23 6/8	21 7/8	6 7	Grayson County	TX	Justin Jackson	2007	17018
140 5/8	23 2/8 22 0/8	21 1/8	6 5	Carroll County	IL	James Connor	2008	17018
* 140 5/8	23 0/8 22 3/8	16 2/8	6 7	Parke County	IN	Wesley A. Mendez	2008	17018
140 5/8	20 7/8 21 3/8	18 3/8	5 5	Cedar County	MO	Mark A. Long	2008	17018
140 5/8	23 3/8 24 6/8	19 1/8	5 5	Fond du Lac County	WI	Kurt Freund	2008	17018
140 5/8	22 5/8 23 0/8	16 6/8	5 6	Marquette County	WI	Patrick Primising	2008	17018
140 5/8	20 4/8 21 2/8	16 1/8	5 6	Mercer County	MO	Larry L. Darnell	2008	17018
* 140 5/8	25 0/8 24 3/8	18 1/8	4 4	Calhoun County	MI	Gerry S. Demars	2008	17018
140 5/8	22 4/8 21 6/8	17 0/8	8 7	Marshall County	IN	Steven E. Yoder	2008	17018
140 5/8	25 2/8 24 0/8	18 4/8	7 7	Rawlins County	KS	Eileen Porubsky	2008	17018
* 140 5/8	25 7/8 23 1/8	20 0/8	6 6	Henderson County	IL	Fortunato Cuevas	2008	17018
140 5/8	22 6/8 22 6/8	16 7/8	5 4	Fulton County	IL	Gregory S. Guerrieri	2008	17018
140 5/8	20 4/8 20 4/8	17 1/8	5 5	Carver County	MN	Jerry D. Chalupsky	2009	17018
140 5/8	22 4/8 21 2/8	19 0/8	5 6	Perry County	PA	Scott Matthews	2009	17018
* 140 5/8	22 0/8 21 5/8	17 5/8	5 5	Kanabec County	MN	Michael Erickson	2009	17018
* 140 5/8	22 3/8 21 4/8	16 3/8	5 5	Greene County	IN	Josh Wilkie	2009	17018
140 5/8	21 4/8 20 2/8	16 7/8	5 5	Scott County	MN	Allan Kasper	2009	17018
* 140 5/8	20 7/8 19 7/8	15 1/8	5 5	Adams County	WI	Mica Weber	2009	17018
* 140 5/8	22 2/8 20 6/8	15 3/8	6 5	Sedgwick County	KS	Eric N. Wilson	2009	17018
140 5/8	24 6/8 25 2/8	19 5/8	5 5	Knox County	OH	Donald J. Billa, Sr.	2009	17018
* 140 5/8	23 6/8 24 1/8	22 2/8	6 5	Bradford County	PA	Steve Canfield	2009	17018
* 140 5/8	22 5/8 21 0/8	15 7/8	4 5	Atchison County	MO	Danny Crow	2009	17018
* 140 5/8	24 0/8 24 1/8	19 4/8	5 6	Warren County	OH	Jim Confer	2009	17018
* 140 5/8	23 2/8 22 6/8	17 6/8	5 4	Marquette County	WI	Eric Flood	2009	17018
140 5/8	22 7/8 22 4/8	15 5/8	5 6	Irion County	TX	Ronnie Parsons	2009	17018
* 140 5/8	21 4/8 22 0/8	19 7/8	5 5	Custer County	OK	Matthew Baker	2009	17018
140 5/8	22 1/8 21 7/8	16 0/8	5 5	Wabasha County	MN	Jody Wilson	2010	17018
140 4/8	22 2/8 24 0/8	15 7/8	6 7	La Porte County	IN	Robert R. Rossi, Sr.	2001	17194
140 4/8	24 0/8 25 0/8	19 6/8	5 5	Washington County	IA	Bob Bellmer	2003	17194
140 4/8	24 6/8 25 5/8	17 6/8	4 5	Jackson County	WI	Ryan Foust	2004	17194
140 4/8	26 3/8 24 3/8	20 4/8	4 4	Hartford County	CT	Richard Mitchell	2004	17194
140 4/8	21 6/8 22 7/8	17 3/8	5 6	Lincoln County	SD	Raymond C. Baysore	2004	17194
140 4/8	21 6/8 23 2/8	16 3/8	5 6	Appanoose County	IA	Curt J. Holder	2004	17194
140 4/8	24 3/8 23 3/8	18 6/8	5 6	Dodge County	WI	Tony Sabo	2004	17194
140 4/8	24 0/8 24 0/8	14 4/8	4 4	Vernon County	WI	Scott J. Jonas	2004	17194
140 4/8	22 3/8 21 7/8	15 6/8	8 7	Hillsdale County	MI	Jason Osting	2004	17194
140 4/8	23 0/8 22 4/8	16 2/8	5 7	Marathon County	WI	Larry Jansen	2004	17194
140 4/8	24 0/8 24 0/8	16 2/8	5 5	Knox County	IL	Floyd M. Steinmetz, Sr.	2004	17194
140 4/8	22 1/8 22 3/8	17 3/8	6 6	Barber County	KS	Robert R. Spratt	2004	17194
140 4/8	22 7/8 22 5/8	14 2/8	5 5	Linn County	IA	Clinton Harris	2004	17194
140 4/8	26 6/8 24 3/8	17 1/8	6 4	Fulton County	IL	Dan Perich	2004	17194
* 140 4/8	22 0/8 21 3/8	17 2/8	5 5	Livingston County	MI	Robert J. Redmond	2005	17194
* 140 4/8	23 1/8 22 3/8	15 3/8	6 5	Cass County	IN	Walter K. Kosiak	2005	17194
140 4/8	22 2/8 22 6/8	19 0/8	5 4	Oconto County	WI	Chad A. Hanmann	2005	17194
140 4/8	21 4/8 20 6/8	15 4/8	6 5	Buffalo County	WI	James K. Kraft	2005	17194
* 140 4/8	24 7/8 25 1/8	18 0/8	5 5	Middlesex County	MA	Larry Gagnon	2005	17194
140 4/8	22 5/8 23 1/8	17 6/8	5 5	Vinton County	OH	Jeff Cornett	2005	17194
* 140 4/8	25 7/8 26 1/8	18 0/8	4 4	Harrison County	IA	Bob Sauvain	2005	17194
* 140 4/8	23 4/8 23 5/8	18 4/8	6 5	Greene County	IN	Frank Caddell	2005	17194
140 4/8	25 1/8 25 0/8	20 4/8	4 5	Allegheny County	PA	Timothy D. Scherer	2005	17194
140 4/8	22 5/8 22 4/8	17 2/8	4 5	Wayne County	IL	Tim Gillespie	2005	17194
* 140 4/8	23 3/8 22 6/8	16 2/8	4 4	Washington County	TN	Gary R. Mitchell	2005	17194
140 4/8	25 4/8 22 7/8	20 4/8	4 5	Parke County	IN	William J. Haase, Jr.	2006	17194
* 140 4/8	22 2/8 22 4/8	20 4/8	8 7	Tulsa County	OK	Glen McGuire	2006	17194
140 4/8	24 5/8 24 0/8	18 3/8	5 7	Macoupin County	IL	Kalen S. Hutchings	2006	17194
140 4/8	20 5/8 21 5/8	17 6/8	5 6	Waukesha County	WI	Chris Smith	2006	17194
* 140 4/8	22 2/8 22 6/8	15 7/8	6 6	Hamilton County	IA	Paul Whitmore	2006	17194
* 140 4/8	22 4/8 21 2/8	19 2/8	5 5	Wyandot County	OH	James A. Thiel	2006	17194

Deer entries below 141 0/8, that appeared in the 6th Edition, are not included here, but are included on the accompanying CD (see page 119), and also in the Club's Records Archives.

WHITETAIL DEER (TYPICAL ANTLERS)

Minimum Score 125 — Continued

SCORE	R MAIN BEAM	L	INSIDE SPREAD	R POINTS	L	AREA	STATE/PROVINCE	HUNTER'S NAME	DATE	RANK
140 4/8	19 5/8	20 0/8	16 0/8	5	5	St. Louis County	MN	Ken Davis, Jr.	2007	17194
*140 4/8	24 5/8	23 6/8	18 0/8	5	5	Trempealeau County	WI	Frank G. Hood	2007	17194
140 4/8	23 0/8	23 2/8	18 4/8	4	4	Putnam County	IN	David Parent	2007	17194
140 4/8	22 2/8	22 1/8	17 6/8	4	4	Dauphin County	PA	Joe Petroski	2007	17194
140 4/8	25 0/8	24 1/8	19 2/8	4	5	Collingsworth County	TX	Sloan Brown	2007	17194
140 4/8	23 4/8	23 1/8	15 2/8	5	5	Isabella County	MI	Bryan Lee McBride	2007	17194
140 4/8	23 2/8	22 6/8	15 5/8	5	7	McPherson County	KS	Larry E. Garner, Jr.	2007	17194
*140 4/8	21 5/8	24 1/8	18 2/8	4	5	Newton County	IN	Jason M. Helfrich	2007	17194
140 4/8	24 4/8	24 1/8	18 4/8	4	4	Fording Mtn.	BC	Randy Reid	2007	17194
*140 4/8	22 6/8	22 6/8	16 0/8	5	5	Otter Tail County	MN	Dan Daleiden	2008	17194
*140 4/8	24 0/8	23 5/8	15 4/8	5	5	Dubois County	IN	Doug Lampert	2008	17194
140 4/8	22 4/8	22 3/8	18 2/8	6	7	Osage County	OK	John K. DeLong	2008	17194
140 4/8	22 1/8	22 1/8	16 0/8	5	5	Polk County	WI	Duane Bethke	2008	17194
140 4/8	22 6/8	21 5/8	16 6/8	6	6	Desha County	AR	Tucker Miller III	2008	17194
140 4/8	26 2/8	24 5/8	16 2/8	5	4	Cass County	MI	Mike Rewa	2009	17194
*140 4/8	21 7/8	22 0/8	15 6/8	6	5	Dunn County	ND	Greg Pruitt	2009	17194
140 4/8	21 1/8	20 5/8	17 7/8	5	7	Cheatham County	TN	Tommy Nicholson	2009	17194
140 4/8	20 3/8	20 3/8	15 2/8	6	5	Wyoming County	NY	Gregory Hoffmeister	2009	17194
140 4/8	23 3/8	23 6/8	14 4/8	4	4	Snyder County	PA	Steve Knepp	2009	17194
140 4/8	19 7/8	19 6/8	16 1/8	6	6	Spink County	SD	Douglas L. Stahl	2009	17194
*140 4/8	21 3/8	20 5/8	14 6/8	5	5	McMullen County	TX	Benjamin A. Siddons	2009	17194
140 4/8	22 2/8	21 7/8	15 6/8	6	6	Flathead County	MT	Harvey C. Swanson	2010	17194
140 4/8	23 6/8	24 2/8	13 6/8	8	7	Barron County	WI	Timothy Widiker	2010	17194
140 3/8	24 1/8	24 5/8	18 6/8	4	7	Alexander County	IL	Ron Miller	2003	17375
*140 3/8	23 6/8	22 3/8	17 5/8	5	5	Wabasha County	MN	Todd B. Greseth	2004	17375
*140 3/8	24 0/8	25 0/8	19 1/8	4	5	Richland County	WI	Randall R. Hilgers	2004	17375
140 3/8	26 1/8	25 3/8	17 7/8	4	4	Jefferson County	WI	James C. Hettich	2004	17375
*140 3/8	22 2/8	22 4/8	15 7/8	5	4	Putnam County	IN	Todd Farris	2004	17375
*140 3/8	26 0/8	24 6/8	18 6/8	8	5	Geauga County	OH	Don Becker	2005	17375
140 3/8	24 6/8	25 5/8	19 4/8	4	6	Mercer County	PA	Todd R. Bromley	2005	17375
140 3/8	22 2/8	21 2/8	17 3/8	5	6	Winnebago County	IL	Michael S. Kloster	2005	17375
140 3/8	22 3/8	22 3/8	16 1/8	7	7	Greene County	IL	Gary M. Brown	2005	17375
140 3/8	24 1/8	24 1/8	18 1/8	5	5	Ashland County	WI	Jerry Schaff	2005	17375
140 3/8	23 4/8	23 4/8	16 3/8	5	5	Linn County	KS	Trent Little	2005	17375
*140 3/8	23 1/8	23 5/8	16 3/8	6	5	Macon County	MO	Tony Winkler	2005	17375
140 3/8	22 0/8	21 2/8	17 7/8	5	5	Bracken County	KY	Ian Kelsch	2006	17375
140 3/8	23 6/8	23 3/8	17 3/8	5	5	Price County	WI	Ted Ironside	2006	17375
140 3/8	22 6/8	25 2/8	20 4/8	6	5	Van Buren County	IA	Marty V. Cairns	2006	17375
140 3/8	23 2/8	22 3/8	15 6/8	5	6	Richland County	WI	Michael D. Alexander	2006	17375
140 3/8	23 3/8	23 0/8	17 1/8	4	5	Calhoun County	IL	Frank Greenlee	2006	17375
140 3/8	27 0/8	26 0/8	19 5/8	5	4	Hocking County	OH	Jeffery Bever	2006	17375
140 3/8	20 0/8	19 5/8	18 5/8	5	5	Emmet County	IA	Douglas M. Fitzgerald	2006	17375
140 3/8	22 6/8	22 2/8	16 1/8	5	5	Dane County	WI	Josh Maier	2006	17375
*140 3/8	25 0/8	24 4/8	16 1/8	5	5	Mason County	WV	Scott Roush, Jr.	2006	17375
140 3/8	24 0/8	23 3/8	17 0/8	6	4	Steuben County	IN	Phil Worden	2007	17375
140 3/8	20 6/8	21 2/8	16 7/8	5	5	Outagamie County	WI	Michael Ernst	2007	17375
*140 3/8	24 6/8	24 1/8	18 5/8	4	5	Warren County	VA	Jason A. Foster	2007	17375
140 3/8	24 2/8	23 6/8	18 3/8	4	4	Hunterdon County	NJ	Donald Hoffman	2007	17375
140 3/8	22 4/8	22 7/8	16 7/8	5	5	Johnson County	NE	Dale Doeden	2007	17375
140 3/8	23 7/8	24 0/8	21 3/8	8	7	Sawyer County	WI	Herb Kirchner	2007	17375
140 3/8	24 5/8	23 7/8	17 5/8	4	5	Monmouth County	NJ	Nick Francisco	2008	17375
*140 3/8	22 0/8	22 5/8	15 5/8	5	5	Jackson County	IA	Cody Decker	2008	17375
140 3/8	20 5/8	20 4/8	17 1/8	5	5	Irion County	TX	Craig Horn	2008	17375
*140 3/8	24 4/8	24 3/8	17 0/8	6	7	Fayette County	IL	John Wilson	2008	17375
*140 3/8	22 1/8	22 1/8	21 3/8	5	5	Clay County	TX	Terry Meek	2008	17375
*140 3/8	23 4/8	21 5/8	19 7/8	5	5	Chester County	PA	John D. Miller	2008	17375
*140 3/8	21 4/8	20 6/8	16 1/8	5	5	Montgomery County	MO	Michael V. Loebach	2008	17375
140 3/8	20 5/8	20 6/8	15 3/8	5	5	Spink County	SD	Richard Binger	2008	17375
*140 3/8	23 0/8	23 3/8	17 1/8	5	5	Shawano County	WI	Ronald Serwa	2008	17375
140 3/8	25 2/8	26 7/8	19 4/8	6	5	Gallia County	OH	Roy Lane	2008	17375
140 3/8	23 1/8	23 0/8	19 0/8	6	5	Southampton County	VA	James Janisieski	2008	17375
*140 3/8	21 5/8	22 2/8	15 4/8	9	7	Alfalfa County	OK	Matt Rigdon	2008	17375
140 3/8	23 4/8	23 6/8	17 4/8	6	6	Clinton County	MO	Tom Allen	2008	17375
*140 3/8	22 6/8	23 2/8	15 7/8	5	5	Macon County	GA	Chad E. Morrison	2008	17375
*140 3/8	22 3/8	21 2/8	16 6/8	6	5	Mercer County	OH	Mike Hamberg	2009	17375
*140 3/8	21 5/8	22 5/8	15 3/8	7	7	Ross County	OH	Chris Chapin	2009	17375
140 3/8	23 1/8	23 5/8	16 4/8	4	5	Barron County	WI	Brad Knutson	2009	17375
*140 3/8	22 6/8	24 0/8	19 3/8	5	5	Jackson County	OH	Gerald L. Miller II	2009	17375
140 3/8	22 4/8	21 5/8	17 7/8	5	7	Jo Daviess County	IL	Todd Graf	2010	17375
140 2/8	23 1/8	21 4/8	18 3/8	5	6	Perry County	IL	Donald G. Robinson	1990	17546
140 2/8	22 6/8	22 6/8	18 2/8	5	4	Lincoln County	WI	Derik Erickson	1999	17546
140 2/8	25 2/8	24 5/8	16 0/8	4	4	Alexander County	IL	Terry Kepley	1999	17546
140 2/8	22 1/8	22 0/8	15 2/8	6	5	Cass County	MO	Jim Clarke	2002	17546
*140 2/8	23 2/8	23 3/8	17 0/8	5	5	Bartholomew County	IN	Randy Birchfield	2002	17546
140 2/8	24 4/8	23 4/8	17 1/8	6	8	Waushara County	WI	Sam Druecke	2003	17546
*140 2/8	22 6/8	23 0/8	17 2/8	5	5	Reynolds County	MO	Allen Murray	2003	17546
140 2/8	22 6/8	22 6/8	16 7/8	8	7	La Crosse County	WI	Mark D. Clements	2003	17546
*140 2/8	21 5/8	22 5/8	15 2/8	5	6	Ransom County	ND	Travis Dick	2004	17546
140 2/8	23 3/8	23 0/8	16 7/8	6	6	Victoria County	TX	Cliff Eckberg	2004	17546
140 2/8	20 0/8	22 3/8	16 6/8	4	5	Manitowoc County	WI	Roger Lauersdorf	2004	17546
140 2/8	24 0/8	24 6/8	16 2/8	4	5	Chippewa County	WI	Chad R. Halvorson	2004	17546
*140 2/8	23 4/8	23 4/8	17 2/8	4	4	Essex County	MA	Brian Healy	2004	17546
140 2/8	24 4/8	24 1/8	21 0/8	5	7	Marquette County	WI	Frank Roidt	2004	17546
140 2/8	22 2/8	22 6/8	18 4/8	5	5	Marshall County	IL	Rich Lingemann	2004	17546
140 2/8	21 1/8	20 1/8	18 5/8	6	4	Moody County	SD	Toby Johnson	2004	17546
*140 2/8	22 4/8	22 3/8	18 3/8	6	5	Webb County	TX	Patric Coldewey	2004	17546
140 2/8	23 2/8	23 4/8	16 0/8	4	4	Rosebud County	MT	Joel D. Harris	2005	17546
*140 2/8	21 0/8	21 5/8	13 4/8	5	5	Floyd County	IA	Philip Parcher	2005	17546
140 2/8	22 4/8	20 7/8	19 0/8	5	5	Southampton County	VA	John Stout	2005	17546
*140 2/8	24 1/8	23 7/8	21 5/8	4	6	Hamilton County	OH	Don Clements	2005	17546
140 2/8	22 6/8	22 4/8	15 4/8	5	5	Pennington County	SD	Jeff Lick	2005	17546
140 2/8	23 6/8	23 6/8	16 4/8	5	5	Leavenworth County	KS	Rob Gardner	2005	17546
140 2/8	22 0/8	21 5/8	17 6/8	5	5	Walla Walla County	WA	Todd Randall	2006	17546
*140 2/8	22 3/8	22 3/8	16 6/8	5	5	Kosciusko County	IN	Brian G. Likens	2006	17546
140 2/8	22 0/8	21 7/8	18 4/8	5	5	Buffalo County	WI	Rod Springborn	2007	17546

534

WHITETAIL DEER (TYPICAL ANTLERS)

Minimum Score 125   Continued

SCORE	LENGTH OF MAIN BEAM R L	INSIDE SPREAD	NUMBER OF POINTS R L	AREA	STATE/ PROVINCE	HUNTER'S NAME	DATE	RANK
140 2/8	21 5/8 21 2/8	17 6/8	6 7	Dane County	WI	Jody A. Bartnick	2007	17546
*140 2/8	23 6/8 23 4/8	22 4/8	4 6	Brown County	SD	Bill Fluke	2007	17546
140 2/8	20 7/8 20 0/8	16 6/8	5 6	Fillmore County	MN	Kyle Hutchinson	2008	17546
140 2/8	25 0/8 23 7/8	18 2/8	4 4	Houston County	MN	Robert Boland	2008	17546
140 2/8	20 0/8 20 3/8	18 6/8	5 5	Hancock County	OH	Craig E. Spieker	2008	17546
*140 2/8	23 2/8 23 2/8	18 6/8	5 5	Jackson County	MI	Larry S. Brown	2008	17546
140 2/8	23 7/8 23 1/8	16 0/8	5 5	Texas County	MO	Carl Hicks	2008	17546
140 2/8	23 5/8 24 4/8	17 3/8	5 6	Delaware County	IN	Randy Duerr	2008	17546
140 2/8	24 3/8 25 0/8	16 6/8	8 7	Richland County	OH	Rick Whiteside	2008	17546
140 2/8	24 0/8 23 7/8	17 0/8	6 4	Fremont County	IA	Curtis Athen	2008	17546
140 2/8	22 7/8 22 4/8	20 4/8	4 4	Waushara County	WI	Eric J. Haag	2008	17546
140 2/8	20 4/8 21 0/8	16 6/8	5 5	Mercer County	IL	Kelli Weeks	2008	17546
140 2/8	20 4/8 20 3/8	15 4/8	5 5	Comanche County	KS	Ronald Rockwell	2008	17546
*140 2/8	23 5/8 23 6/8	19 0/8	6 8	Port Perry	ONT	Jason Scott	2008	17546
140 2/8	23 3/8 23 2/8	16 4/8	5 5	Barton County	MO	Jerrit Gardner	2009	17546
140 2/8	25 6/8 24 1/8	17 6/8	5 4	Dane County	WI	James P. Jorstad	2009	17546
*140 2/8	22 4/8 22 1/8	15 2/8	5 5	Jefferson County	OK	Brandan M. Walterscheid	2009	17546
*140 2/8	24 0/8 24 1/8	17 5/8	5 6	Ferry County	WA	Tim G. Wallis	2009	17546
140 1/8	23 4/8 21 3/8	18 7/8	4 5	Callaway County	MO	Christopher Gray	2003	17713
140 1/8	22 3/8 22 6/8	16 4/8	6 5	Jackson County	IA	Dana Lawrence	2004	17713
140 1/8	22 5/8 22 5/8	19 3/8	5 5	Payne County	OK	Shane Collier	2004	17713
140 1/8	19 7/8 20 7/8	18 7/8	6 7	Jim Hogg County	TX	Parten Wakefield	2005	17713
*140 1/8	19 1/8 23 0/8	21 7/8	4 4	Trempealeau County	WI	Dylan Hess	2005	17713
140 1/8	22 1/8 21 4/8	16 4/8	7 5	Bartholomew County	IN	Thomas J. Johnson	2005	17713
140 1/8	22 5/8 23 3/8	19 3/8	4 4	Dakota County	MN	Timothy J. Pladson	2005	17713
140 1/8	21 4/8 21 7/8	17 5/8	5 5	Brown County	WI	Tim Daul	2005	17713
140 1/8	19 4/8 21 1/8	15 7/8	5 5	Jones County	IA	Scott Kirsch	2005	17713
140 1/8	22 2/8 23 2/8	15 1/8	6 5	Rusk County	WI	James R. Lange	2005	17713
140 1/8	22 6/8 22 0/8	15 1/8	6 7	Clark County	MO	Joe Wuelling	2005	17713
140 1/8	21 5/8 21 4/8	17 5/8	4 5	Scott County	IN	Jim Brown	2005	17713
*140 1/8	24 5/8 23 6/8	15 7/8	5 6	Auglaize County	OH	Mark Agler	2005	17713
*140 1/8	22 1/8 23 0/8	18 6/8	5 6	Eau Claire County	WI	Greg Steinacker	2005	17713
140 1/8	23 4/8 23 3/8	18 5/8	4 5	Elk River	BC	Randy Reid	2005	17713
140 1/8	22 7/8 23 0/8	17 1/8	5 5	Sutton County	TX	Alan Young	2005	17713
140 1/8	22 5/8 21 7/8	17 7/8	5 5	Douglas County	WI	Walter J. Palmer	2005	17713
140 1/8	25 4/8 24 7/8	19 1/8	5 6	Lorain County	OH	Steven Reinhold	2005	17713
140 1/8	22 7/8 23 1/8	16 1/8	4 4	Pike County	IL	Eric Mohrman	2005	17713
*140 1/8	23 5/8 23 3/8	19 2/8	8 6	Ralls County	MO	Scott A. Doering	2006	17713
140 1/8	20 2/8 21 7/8	16 5/8	5 5	Kingsbury County	SD	Jason L. Converse	2006	17713
*140 1/8	21 6/8 21 4/8	15 1/8	5 5	Griggs County	ND	Taylor Musland	2006	17713
140 1/8	22 4/8 23 2/8	17 4/8	5 4	Hocking County	OH	Charles B. Rosier	2006	17713
140 1/8	24 6/8 24 2/8	21 1/8	5 6	Marion County	IN	Dustin VanTreese	2006	17713
140 1/8	23 0/8 22 6/8	19 1/8	5 5	Neeb	SAS	Matthew Kozloski	2006	17713
140 1/8	21 6/8 21 5/8	16 0/8	6 7	Schuyler County	IL	Joseph A. Blankenship	2006	17713
*140 1/8	22 5/8 22 2/8	16 3/8	5 5	Cedar County	IA	Bill Hillyer	2006	17713
140 1/8	21 4/8 22 2/8	18 7/8	5 5	Wells County	ND	Ted Lowery	2006	17713
140 1/8	23 7/8 23 5/8	17 1/8	4 4	Buffalo County	WI	David Walchle	2006	17713
140 1/8	21 4/8 22 2/8	17 1/8	8 5	La Porte County	IN	Jay Cress	2006	17713
140 1/8	22 3/8 23 1/8	17 3/8	5 5	Waukesha County	WI	Nicholas R. Vander Molen	2006	17713
140 1/8	22 2/8 21 2/8	15 3/8	5 5	Sauk County	WI	Michael J. Fichter	2006	17713
140 1/8	25 5/8 24 6/8	17 4/8	5 5	Hocking County	OH	Mark Brown	2006	17713
140 1/8	21 3/8 21 1/8	21 4/8	4 5	Powell County	MT	Anthony J. Scharf	2006	17713
*140 1/8	23 5/8 22 5/8	17 5/8	4 5	Lancaster County	NE	Brett Pesek	2007	17713
140 1/8	22 5/8 23 2/8	17 3/8	4 4	Meeker County	MN	Steve Schultz	2007	17713
*140 1/8	23 0/8 23 2/8	23 6/8	4 5	Stephenson County	IL	Gerald Erbsen	2007	17713
140 1/8	23 2/8 23 6/8	18 3/8	4 6	Allegheny County	PA	Frederick Salay, Jr.	2007	17713
*140 1/8	22 3/8 22 2/8	17 7/8	7 5	Starke County	IN	Kevin C. Gal	2007	17713
140 1/8	26 4/8 26 2/8	19 5/8	5 5	Morrow County	OH	James E. Murray	2007	17713
140 1/8	24 0/8 22 0/8	20 5/8	4 5	Knox County	OH	Ben Woolison	2007	17713
140 1/8	22 2/8 23 1/8	15 4/8	6 6	Webb County	TX	Norman E. Speer	2007	17713
*140 1/8	24 4/8 24 5/8	18 5/8	4 4	Franklin County	IA	Benjamin Gaffney	2008	17713
140 1/8	23 4/8 23 2/8	19 1/8	5 4	Oswego County	NY	Frank Paino	2008	17713
*140 1/8	22 0/8 22 2/8	15 5/8	5 5	Somerset County	PA	Steven Fogle	2008	17713
140 1/8	24 2/8 24 4/8	16 1/8	5 4	Kingman County	KS	James Collins	2008	17713
*140 1/8	21 4/8 22 5/8	18 5/8	5 6	Will County	IL	Kurt Pavey	2008	17713
140 1/8	24 4/8 25 4/8	19 1/8	5 6	Norfolk County	MA	Bill Feeney	2008	17713
*140 1/8	23 3/8 23 3/8	18 2/8	5 5	Elmore County	AL	Tyler Hill	2009	17713
140 1/8	22 0/8 21 7/8	17 4/8	6 6	Clark County	KY	Robert "Ben" Redmon	2009	17713
140 1/8	23 4/8 23 4/8	17 7/8	5 5	Outagamie County	WI	Chris Kern	2009	17713
*140 1/8	21 0/8 22 0/8	16 1/8	5 6	Clayton County	IA	William Tighe	2009	17713
140 1/8	21 2/8 20 5/8	20 0/8	6 6	Jefferson County	IA	Rod J. Hoekert	2009	17713
140 1/8	21 0/8 21 2/8	15 5/8	5 5	Wells County	IN	Brandon A. Leas	2009	17713
140 1/8	19 7/8 20 3/8	18 1/8	5 5	Andrew County	MO	Brent Hesterly	2009	17713
140 1/8	22 6/8 23 0/8	16 7/8	5 5	Vilas County	WI	Alan Sauer	2009	17713
140 1/8	25 6/8 26 0/8	20 7/8	4 4	Buffalo County	WI	Jeffrey A. Johnson	2009	17713
*140 0/8	22 5/8 23 5/8	17 0/8	4 4	Linn County	IA	Clinton Harris	1996	17900
140 0/8	24 3/8 23 3/8	19 6/8	6 5	Fond du Lac County	WI	Andrew Leonard	1998	17900
*140 0/8	22 5/8 24 2/8	17 3/8	6 7	Pennington County	SD	Chris D. Hamm	2003	17900
*140 0/8	25 0/8 24 1/8	16 0/8	4 5	Ross County	OH	Randy Johnson	2003	17900
140 0/8	24 6/8 25 4/8	17 2/8	5 5	Woodford County	IL	Rocky Pulliam	2003	17900
*140 0/8	23 6/8 23 6/8	17 6/8	7 4	Jefferson County	IN	Kenneth Routh	2004	17900
140 0/8	25 0/8 25 0/8	20 6/8	4 4	Geauga County	OH	Leonard Blackie	2004	17900
140 0/8	21 5/8 21 5/8	15 3/8	4 5	Pierce County	WI	Myles Keller	2004	17900
140 0/8	23 2/8 23 1/8	17 0/8	5 4	Nemaha County	KS	Daryl Darling	2004	17900
140 0/8	25 3/8 24 5/8	19 0/8	6 4	Chickasaw County	IA	Randy Sinwell	2004	17900
140 0/8	21 6/8 21 7/8	15 2/8	5 5	Olmsted County	MN	Bruce Smith	2004	17900
140 0/8	23 3/8 22 6/8	16 0/8	6 5	Marquette County	WI	Robert L. Kampen	2004	17900
*140 0/8	22 1/8 22 2/8	15 4/8	5 5	Shawano County	WI	Randy Lemke	2004	17900
*140 0/8	22 0/8 21 1/8	14 2/8	6 6	Nodaway County	MO	Todd Gray	2004	17900
140 0/8	22 4/8 23 2/8	17 6/8	5 5	Lorain County	OH	Jason M. Smith	2004	17900
140 0/8	23 2/8 24 0/8	16 0/8	5 5	Monroe County	IA	Duane Harthoorn	2004	17900
140 0/8	24 2/8 23 3/8	19 0/8	4 4	Linn County	IA	James L. Corkery	2005	17900
*140 0/8	23 6/8 23 7/8	15 7/8	6 5	Waushara County	WI	Jason Chase	2005	17900
*140 0/8	23 2/8 23 2/8	21 1/8	4 4	Clark County	IN	Danny L. McCurry	2005	17900
140 0/8	23 5/8 23 5/8	16 6/8	4 4	Barron County	WI	Donald K. Isaacson	2005	17900

Deer entries below 141 0/8, that appeared in the 6th Edition, are not included here, but are included on the accompanying CD (see page 119), and also in the Club's Records Archives.

535

WHITETAIL DEER (TYPICAL ANTLERS)

Minimum Score 125 — Continued

SCORE	LENGTH OF R MAIN BEAM L		INSIDE SPREAD	NUMBER OF R POINTS L		AREA	STATE/ PROVINCE	HUNTER'S NAME	DATE	RANK
*140 0/8	21 1/8	21 3/8	17 0/8	6	6	Delaware County	IA	Rick Smith	2005	17900
140 0/8	23 4/8	22 7/8	18 4/8	7	6	Pike County	IL	Frank E. Stossel	2005	17900
*140 0/8	26 4/8	25 6/8	18 1/8	5	7	Huntington County	IN	Nick Gray	2005	17900
140 0/8	23 3/8	20 3/8	18 1/8	5	6	Fulton County	IL	Carl "Chopper" Muth, Jr.	2005	17900
140 0/8	23 0/8	22 6/8	14 4/8	5	5	Kosciusko County	IN	Kevin R. Burkholder	2005	17900
140 0/8	23 2/8	23 4/8	17 4/8	5	5	Montgomery County	IA	Steven Paul	2005	17900
*140 0/8	23 7/8	23 5/8	16 6/8	5	5	Van Buren County	MI	Travis Taylor	2005	17900
140 0/8	21 5/8	22 1/8	16 6/8	5	5	Berks County	PA	Thad A. Lantz	2005	17900
140 0/8	20 2/8	21 0/8	17 6/8	5	5	Calhoun County	IL	Taylor Roberts	2005	17900
140 0/8	20 5/8	20 2/8	19 2/8	5	5	Missoula County	MT	Nicholas Best	2005	17900
140 0/8	22 6/8	22 4/8	16 1/8	6	4	Fillmore County	MN	Glenn E. Hisey	2006	17900
140 0/8	22 7/8	23 4/8	18 3/8	5	6	St. Croix County	WI	Brian Sturgul	2006	17900
*140 0/8	24 4/8	23 6/8	17 6/8	4	4	Wilkes County	NC	Marty A. Parsons	2006	17900
140 0/8	23 1/8	23 2/8	17 4/8	5	5	Lake County	MI	Joe Vanderlinde	2006	17900
*140 0/8	23 6/8	25 0/8	17 2/8	6	5	Wayne County	NY	Charlie Phalen	2006	17900
*140 0/8	21 5/8	21 6/8	21 2/8	6	7	Clayton County	IA	Brian Oberfoell	2006	17900
140 0/8	25 6/8	26 6/8	19 2/8	5	5	Linn County	MO	John Brink	2006	17900
140 0/8	22 7/8	22 7/8	18 6/8	4	5	Sauk County	WI	Gary A. Steinhorst	2006	17900
*140 0/8	24 1/8	23 6/8	18 0/8	4	5	Adams County	IL	Jeffrey W. Lineberry	2006	17900
140 0/8	24 1/8	24 3/8	19 4/8	7	5	Monmouth County	NJ	Thomas McComb	2006	17900
140 0/8	26 2/8	22 6/8	17 3/8	6	4	Granville County	NC	Larry B. Fischer III	2007	17900
140 0/8	22 3/8	22 4/8	15 4/8	9	7	Warren County	KY	Charlie Durbin	2007	17900
140 0/8	21 4/8	20 7/8	18 2/8	5	6	Douglas County	WI	Miika Otava	2007	17900
140 0/8	27 0/8	25 5/8	25 5/8	7	7	Dodge County	WI	Jeffrey C. Higgins	2007	17900
140 0/8	23 5/8	22 7/8	19 2/8	4	4	Ward County	ND	Levi Tomlinson	2008	17900
140 0/8	23 1/8	21 6/8	15 4/8	5	5	McHenry County	IL	Donald Ellis	2008	17900
140 0/8	23 0/8	23 7/8	19 6/8	5	4	Dinwiddie County	VA	Gary Wayne Adams	2008	17900
140 0/8	23 0/8	23 0/8	17 0/8	5	5	Winneshiek County	IA	Randy E. Doyle	2008	17900
*140 0/8	24 5/8	24 6/8	17 7/8	5	6	Marquette County	WI	Robert Sarbacker	2008	17900
*140 0/8	25 6/8	25 1/8	16 1/8	5	4	Lancaster County	PA	Leon M. Wenger	2008	17900
*140 0/8	22 6/8	22 6/8	14 2/8	5	5	Monona County	IA	Brian D. Clausen	2008	17900
140 0/8	23 0/8	23 1/8	19 4/8	4	4	Woodbury County	IA	Gary T. Roan	2008	17900
*140 0/8	25 2/8	25 0/8	16 6/8	4	5	McDonald County	MO	Jeff Cook	2008	17900
140 0/8	21 1/8	21 2/8	18 2/8	5	6	Fond du Lac County	WI	Andy "Bubba" Kastein	2008	17900
*140 0/8	23 4/8	22 0/8	19 0/8	8	5	Columbia County	WI	Rich Semrad	2009	17900
*140 0/8	24 4/8	25 2/8	21 0/8	6	5	Delaware County	OH	Randy Rice	2009	17900
*140 0/8	24 0/8	24 5/8	15 2/8	4	4	Hancock County	IA	Dale James	2009	17900
*140 0/8	23 7/8	25 1/8	20 1/8	4	5	Burnett County	WI	Tim Burnham	2009	17900
140 0/8	24 1/8	24 2/8	20 2/8	4	4	Licking County	OH	Zack Brooks	2009	17900
140 0/8	24 7/8	24 7/8	18 0/8	5	4	Columbia County	PA	Stephen Toczylousky	2009	17900
*140 0/8	21 3/8	22 1/8	18 4/8	5	5	Brown County	KS	Leslie Brittian	2009	17900
140 0/8	21 7/8	22 2/8	18 6/8	4	4	St. Louis County	MO	Jason D. Mathes	2009	17900
*140 0/8	24 1/8	24 0/8	14 2/8	5	6	Polk County	MO	Tyler Lee Gerling	2010	17900
139 7/8	23 4/8	25 4/8	16 5/8	4	4	Henry County	VA	Richard B. Dyer	1988	18111
139 7/8	25 6/8	25 4/8	15 0/8	5	4	Fulton County	IL	Parrish Brown	1993	18111
139 7/8	21 2/8	21 6/8	17 1/8	5	7	Beaver County	PA	Doug Margetic	2004	18111
139 7/8	24 2/8	24 6/8	15 5/8	5	5	Guilford County	NC	David L. Adams	2004	18111
139 7/8	21 3/8	21 4/8	17 2/8	6	5	Clark County	IL	Brad Conine	2004	18111
*139 7/8	22 3/8	20 4/8	16 1/8	5	6	Macoupin County	IL	Christopher L. Gleason	2004	18111
139 7/8	23 0/8	23 0/8	17 3/8	5	5	Hampden County	MA	Bruce Zebrowski	2004	18111
139 7/8	23 7/8	24 3/8	18 5/8	4	4	Scott County	IA	Alan Humphrey	2005	18111
*139 7/8	20 7/8	20 2/8	18 1/8	5	5	Door County	WI	Christiaan Jeanquart	2005	18111
139 7/8	23 5/8	23 5/8	18 1/8	5	5	Washington County	WI	Daniel Joel	2005	18111
*139 7/8	22 3/8	23 3/8	13 7/8	5	5	Branch County	MI	John L. Ganton	2005	18111
*139 7/8	21 6/8	21 7/8	16 7/8	5	5	Fillmore County	MN	Michael Billmeier	2005	18111
139 7/8	22 2/8	22 1/8	16 7/8	7	8	Hillsdale County	MI	Jeff Miazgowicz	2005	18111
139 7/8	23 7/8	23 6/8	18 5/8	4	5	Jefferson County	WI	Larry L. Braatz	2005	18111
*139 7/8	21 4/8	22 2/8	14 7/8	5	5	Todd County	KY	Jamie S. Reagan	2005	18111
139 7/8	23 7/8	24 0/8	17 3/8	5	5	Ross County	OH	Kenneth Frank	2005	18111
139 7/8	24 0/8	25 0/8	18 1/8	6	4	Green County	WI	Robert Krueger	2005	18111
139 7/8	21 5/8	20 2/8	17 4/8	6	5	Washington County	WI	Christopher DeQuardo	2005	18111
139 7/8	21 2/8	21 6/8	16 3/8	5	5	Otter Tail County	MN	Christopher Jay Roley	2005	18111
139 7/8	22 7/8	22 6/8	17 3/8	4	4	Buffalo County	WI	Dave Fredrickson	2005	18111
139 7/8	22 4/8	23 1/8	15 5/8	4	5	Clay County	IN	Steve Myers	2005	18111
139 7/8	23 4/8	23 3/8	16 7/8	5	5	Griggs County	ND	A. D. Alstad	2006	18111
139 7/8	21 0/8	20 5/8	18 1/8	4	5	Barnes County	ND	Travis Kunze	2006	18111
*139 7/8	21 6/8	22 0/8	16 3/8	6	5	San Saba County	TX	Jason Rudel	2006	18111
*139 7/8	24 1/8	25 6/8	17 2/8	5	4	Wayne County	IN	Matt Brennan	2006	18111
139 7/8	25 7/8	24 0/8	14 6/8	5	7	Anoka County	MN	Douglas R. Smith	2006	18111
139 7/8	21 6/8	22 3/8	16 1/8	5	5	Haskell County	OK	James Sterling Clayton	2007	18111
*139 7/8	22 4/8	23 0/8	18 5/8	5	5	Clark County	IL	Rick Davidson	2007	18111
*139 7/8	22 3/8	22 3/8	14 7/8	5	5	Monroe County	NY	Michael Brien	2007	18111
139 7/8	21 7/8	22 0/8	15 7/8	5	5	Sanilac County	MI	Troy R. Tank	2007	18111
139 7/8	22 5/8	23 6/8	15 1/8	6	6	Douglas County	IL	Luke Cain	2007	18111
*139 7/8	25 1/8	23 6/8	20 1/8	5	6	Taylor County	IA	Matt Morris	2007	18111
139 7/8	21 1/8	19 6/8	15 3/8	5	5	Harper County	KS	Jim Downing	2007	18111
139 7/8	27 2/8	27 1/8	24 4/8	5	3	Norton County	KS	Brian Boyd	2007	18111
139 7/8	24 0/8	24 4/8	18 1/8	5	4	Juneau County	WI	Dave Puhl	2007	18111
139 7/8	23 5/8	23 0/8	17 1/8	5	5	Jefferson County	WI	Robert C. Haseleu	2008	18111
139 7/8	23 7/8	22 3/8	19 3/8	5	5	Noble County	IN	Todd J. McCulloch	2008	18111
139 7/8	23 0/8	22 4/8	16 5/8	5	5	Dunn County	WI	Troy Waller	2008	18111
139 7/8	23 6/8	24 4/8	19 5/8	4	4	Pierce County	WI	Michael A. Trudeau	2008	18111
*139 7/8	23 5/8	23 2/8	17 0/8	7	5	Jasper County	IL	Paul Hardiek	2008	18111
139 7/8	23 1/8	23 1/8	18 5/8	5	5	Dubuque County	IA	Seth Ferrie	2008	18111
*139 7/8	21 6/8	21 4/8	19 5/8	5	5	Berks County	PA	Bruce Gauker	2009	18111
139 7/8	23 7/8	23 0/8	15 4/8	5	7	Barron County	WI	Ryan Ebner	2009	18111
*139 7/8	23 7/8	23 5/8	19 4/8	6	7	Barber County	KS	Robert Spratt	2009	18111
139 7/8	23 5/8	23 6/8	17 7/8	4	4	Kane County	IL	Casey K. Bowgren	2009	18111
139 7/8	21 3/8	21 2/8	15 2/8	5	5	Bottineau County	ND	Christina Clark	2009	18111
139 7/8	26 1/8	23 2/8	19 1/8	5	4	Suffolk County	NY	Eugene Tripodo	2009	18111
*139 7/8	23 4/8	23 4/8	18 7/8	5	6	Martin County	IN	Roy Montgomery	2010	18111
139 6/8	23 4/8	23 1/8	17 2/8	5	5	McKenzie County	ND	Jeff Jacob	1997	18257
139 6/8	22 1/8	21 7/8	18 0/8	5	5	Allegheny County	PA	Kirk Benson	2002	18257
139 6/8	22 3/8	21 3/8	12 4/8	5	5	Butler County	KS	Michael Wilson	2003	18257
139 6/8	23 3/8	22 7/8	17 6/8	4	4	Marion County	IN	Rick Dietz	2003	18257

536

WHITETAIL DEER (TYPICAL ANTLERS)

Minimum Score 125   Continued

SCORE	LENGTH OF R MAIN BEAM L	INSIDE SPREAD	NUMBER OF R POINTS L	AREA	STATE/ PROVINCE	HUNTER'S NAME	DATE	RANK
139 6/8	21 3/8 21 1/8	15 0/8	5 5	Macomb County	MI	Carl Kline	2003	18257
139 6/8	22 6/8 22 3/8	17 5/8	6 5	Pend Oreille County	WA	W. Dale Crum	2004	18257
*139 6/8	24 3/8 24 3/8	14 6/8	5 4	Grayson County	KY	Ronnie Whobrey	2004	18257
139 6/8	20 2/8 19 5/8	12 3/8	5 6	Scotland County	MO	Ryan Clark	2004	18257
139 6/8	23 0/8 22 4/8	20 6/8	6 5	Sharp County	AR	Witt Stephens, Jr.	2004	18257
*139 6/8	24 3/8 23 5/8	17 0/8	5 5	La Grange County	IN	Daven King	2004	18257
139 6/8	23 2/8 23 6/8	17 2/8	7 5	Calhoun County	MI	Thomas K. Piepkow, Jr.	2004	18257
139 6/8	25 3/8 25 6/8	18 4/8	6 5	Gage County	NE	Eric P. Garton	2004	18257
139 6/8	23 0/8 22 5/8	19 4/8	5 4	Trempealeau County	WI	Michael Krajewski	2004	18257
139 6/8	23 5/8 22 0/8	18 4/8	6 6	Buffalo County	WI	Ty Johnson	2004	18257
139 6/8	24 4/8 24 3/8	17 2/8	5 4	Meade County	KS	Rollie Lunsford	2004	18257
*139 6/8	24 5/8 24 2/8	17 0/8	5 5	New Castle County	DE	John J. Lloyd	2004	18257
139 6/8	22 0/8 21 1/8	17 4/8	5 5	Beltrami County	MN	Randy Gregg	2005	18257
*139 6/8	24 1/8 24 6/8	20 2/8	5 5	Richland County	WI	Rick Fruit	2005	18257
*139 6/8	23 1/8 23 6/8	18 3/8	6 5	Greene County	IL	John J. Rosser	2005	18257
139 6/8	20 7/8 20 6/8	16 4/8	5 5	Buffalo County	WI	Timothy Grzesiak	2005	18257
139 6/8	24 1/8 23 2/8	19 6/8	4 4	Hardin County	TN	Roger Hylton	2006	18257
139 6/8	23 3/8 23 3/8	17 0/8	5 5	Marinette County	WI	Scott Dyer	2006	18257
*139 6/8	25 7/8 26 0/8	16 0/8	5 4	Butler County	PA	Martin J. Kuss	2006	18257
139 6/8	26 1/8 26 2/8	19 5/8	7 5	Kent County	MD	Kevin Harms	2006	18257
139 6/8	23 5/8 24 3/8	22 2/8	4 5	Buffalo County	WI	Rich Nielson	2006	18257
139 6/8	22 6/8 22 6/8	20 4/8	4 4	Rock County	WI	Kevin McLaughlin	2006	18257
139 6/8	23 0/8 23 7/8	17 2/8	4 4	White County	IL	Brian Turgeon	2006	18257
139 6/8	23 0/8 23 0/8	13 6/8	4 5	Richland County	WI	Jacob M. Elder	2006	18257
*139 6/8	26 6/8 27 0/8	17 0/8	4 4	Worth County	GA	Terry Dewayne Weaver	2006	18257
139 6/8	23 3/8 23 3/8	17 6/8	5 5	Elk County	KS	Mike Weaver	2006	18257
139 6/8	23 5/8 23 5/8	16 6/8	5 5	Preston County	WV	Lawrence P. Neidert	2007	18257
139 6/8	23 3/8 22 6/8	17 0/8	5 5	N. Saskatchewan River	SAS	Curtis Lee	2007	18257
139 6/8	22 6/8 23 2/8	16 0/8	4 4	Wabasha County	MN	John D. Bazey	2007	18257
139 6/8	22 2/8 21 5/8	14 7/8	5 6	Brown County	SD	Chad Jurgens	2007	18257
*139 6/8	23 4/8 23 5/8	22 0/8	5 5	De Kalb County	MO	Dennis Cannell	2007	18257
139 6/8	25 0/8 25 7/8	22 7/8	6 6	Dubuque County	IA	Terry Freiburger	2007	18257
*139 6/8	21 4/8 21 4/8	16 6/8	4 5	Pike County	IL	Barry Potteiger	2007	18257
139 6/8	23 6/8 23 3/8	19 0/8	5 5	Jackson County	WI	David Stahl	2007	18257
*139 6/8	21 7/8 22 0/8	16 0/8	5 6	Pope County	IL	Thomas Levalley	2007	18257
*139 6/8	23 6/8 23 7/8	16 2/8	5 5	Schuyler County	IL	David Karr	2007	18257
139 6/8	22 6/8 24 4/8	20 0/8	8 9	Appanoose County	IA	Chris Dickens	2007	18257
*139 6/8	21 3/8 21 4/8	18 2/8	4 4	Polk County	WI	Jeff Niemann	2008	18257
139 6/8	22 5/8 22 2/8	19 4/8	6 5	Venango County	PA	Joshua J. VanSise	2008	18257
*139 6/8	21 7/8 21 2/8	16 0/8	6 5	Dane County	WI	James Zbigniewicz	2008	18257
*139 6/8	22 1/8 22 4/8	15 7/8	7 6	Adams County	IL	Ronnie Myer	2008	18257
139 6/8	24 4/8 23 7/8	21 6/8	6 4	Chippewa County	WI	Bronson Stelzer	2008	18257
*139 6/8	22 1/8 22 6/8	18 6/8	4 5	Essex County	MA	Sam Kalil	2008	18257
139 6/8	21 6/8 21 6/8	19 2/8	4 4	Washburn County	WI	Jeffrey D. Larson	2009	18257
*139 6/8	23 4/8 23 6/8	19 6/8	5 5	Houston County	MN	Andrew J. Sackrison	2009	18257
*139 6/8	24 0/8 23 0/8	15 6/8	5 6	Buffalo County	WI	Jeff Bennett	2009	18257
*139 6/8	25 4/8 24 3/8	17 4/8	4 4	Kiowa County	KS	Clipper Strickland	2009	18257
*139 6/8	23 0/8 23 6/8	19 0/8	4 4	Williamson County	IL	Nicholas Wilson	2009	18257
*139 6/8	25 6/8 24 5/8	16 4/8	5 5	Wabash County	IN	Kevin M. Eltzroth	2009	18257
*139 6/8	22 7/8 22 1/8	16 2/8	5 6	Oconto County	WI	Travis Schindel	2009	18257
*139 6/8	24 0/8 22 3/8	16 3/8	6 7	Marquette County	WI	Roman R. Konczal	2010	18257
*139 6/8	23 4/8 23 7/8	19 0/8	4 4	Clearwater County	MN	Kaylin Erickson	2010	18257
139 5/8	24 3/8 24 7/8	18 1/8	4 4	Lyon County	MN	Bruce Grow	1971	18426
139 5/8	24 6/8 24 5/8	18 1/8	4 5	Madison County	IA	Marc A. Headington	1998	18426
*139 5/8	22 0/8 24 0/8	16 2/8	6 6	Williams County	OH	Jimmy Allen Ernest	2002	18426
139 5/8	22 0/8 23 2/8	16 6/8	7 4	Muhlenberg County	KY	Robert L. Stark II	2003	18426
139 5/8	21 4/8 21 7/8	15 7/8	5 5	Hardin County	IA	Matt Kuester	2003	18426
139 5/8	23 0/8 22 4/8	16 1/8	6 5	Bon Homme County	SD	Mark W. Sedlacek	2004	18426
139 5/8	24 5/8 24 3/8	16 1/8	5 5	Ionia County	MI	Cory McDiarmid	2004	18426
*139 5/8	21 6/8 21 7/8	19 4/8	6 5	Cass County	IL	David Soden	2004	18426
139 5/8	21 6/8 21 6/8	17 3/8	5 5	Waupaca County	WI	Robert Bazile	2004	18426
*139 5/8	24 2/8 26 0/8	14 6/8	7 6	Ransom County	ND	Terry Anderson	2005	18426
139 5/8	22 0/8 20 6/8	15 3/8	6 7	Atascosa County	TX	Alan Peters	2005	18426
*139 5/8	23 7/8 23 2/8	14 1/8	6 5	Ashland County	WI	Lief Blom	2005	18426
139 5/8	22 2/8 23 0/8	16 1/8	5 5	Worth County	MO	David C. Schoenberger	2005	18426
139 5/8	24 0/8 23 0/8	18 2/8	4 6	Outagamie County	WI	Benjamin S. VanGeffen	2006	18426
139 5/8	26 4/8 26 2/8	19 7/8	4 4	Bradford County	PA	Ike Deemer	2006	18426
*139 5/8	21 5/8 21 6/8	19 5/8	5 7	Walworth County	WI	Patrick Scheurell	2006	18426
139 5/8	21 4/8 21 6/8	16 5/8	5 4	Goodsoil	SAS	Robert Vogel	2006	18426
*139 5/8	22 1/8 22 0/8	15 7/8	5 5	Mercer County	NJ	Ron Ricciardi	2006	18426
*139 5/8	22 1/8 22 3/8	18 4/8	5 5	Walsh County	ND	Patrick Novak	2006	18426
139 5/8	22 4/8 20 3/8	15 5/8	5 5	Pierce County	WI	Eric Duchnowski	2006	18426
139 5/8	22 3/8 23 2/8	16 7/8	5 4	Anderson County	KS	Chase Doherty	2006	18426
139 5/8	24 2/8 24 2/8	18 7/8	7 5	Benton County	IA	Brett Albertsen	2006	18426
139 5/8	24 1/8 24 2/8	18 5/8	4 4	Henry County	IN	Todd A. Wallace	2006	18426
139 5/8	23 6/8 24 3/8	16 7/8	5 4	La Crosse County	WI	Anthony J. Bottcher	2006	18426
139 5/8	23 6/8 23 2/8	19 1/8	5 4	Chemung County	NY	Stephen D. Horton	2006	18426
139 5/8	22 1/8 21 5/8	19 7/8	5 5	Plymouth County	MA	Doug Wight	2006	18426
139 5/8	24 3/8 24 0/8	16 7/8	5 5	Van Buren County	IA	Levi Weaver, Jr.	2006	18426
*139 5/8	21 7/8 21 2/8	18 4/8	4 5	Clay County	IA	Terry Betz	2006	18426
139 5/8	22 2/8 22 3/8	16 1/8	5 5	Pike County	MO	Mark A. Kohl	2007	18426
139 5/8	22 0/8 22 0/8	17 3/8	5 5	Shawano County	WI	Tim Van Camp	2007	18426
139 5/8	25 4/8 25 2/8	19 2/8	6 6	Bureau County	IL	Darin Bittner	2007	18426
*139 5/8	24 2/8 23 2/8	20 4/8	4 5	Douglas County	KS	Ronald F. Lax	2007	18426
139 5/8	25 5/8 26 1/8	18 5/8	4 4	Anne Arundel County	MD	Nicholas DiMauro	2007	18426
139 5/8	21 1/8 21 6/8	19 7/8	7 5	Randolph County	IL	Clay Curten	2007	18426
*139 5/8	20 5/8 20 3/8	16 7/8	4 4	Dunn County	ND	Lynn Brew	2008	18426
139 5/8	23 0/8 21 4/8	15 6/8	5 6	Reno County	KS	Gary L. Yoder	2008	18426
139 5/8	21 7/8 21 7/8	20 1/8	4 5	Allen County	OH	Rodney Diemer	2008	18426
*139 5/8	21 7/8 21 2/8	17 3/8	5 5	Grand Traverse County	MI	Sean Whalen	2008	18426
*139 5/8	23 0/8 23 0/8	18 1/8	4 5	Pottawatomie County	KS	David Johnson	2008	18426
139 5/8	24 1/8 23 3/8	18 2/8	6 6	Washburn County	WI	Todd M. Johnson	2009	18426
139 5/8	22 0/8 22 4/8	14 5/8	6 7	Logan County	OH	Robert Lee	2009	18426
139 5/8	22 1/8 22 1/8	15 0/8	6 6	Christian County	KY	Andy Naghtin	2009	18426
*139 5/8	26 4/8 26 0/8	19 3/8	4 4	Whitley County	IN	Tony Nix	2009	18426

Deer entries below 141 0/8, that appeared in the 6th Edition, are not included here, but are included on the accompanying CD (see page 119), and also in the Club's Records Archives.

WHITETAIL DEER (TYPICAL ANTLERS)

Minimum Score 125   Continued

SCORE	LENGTH OF R MAIN BEAM L	INSIDE SPREAD	NUMBER OF R POINTS L	AREA	STATE/ PROVINCE	HUNTER'S NAME	DATE	RANK
*139 5/8	22 3/8 23 5/8	17 4/8	6 6	Columbia County	WI	Wayne A. Buckley	2009	18426
139 5/8	23 2/8 23 3/8	16 3/8	4 5	Ward County	ND	Jeff Jacob	2010	18426
139 5/8	21 1/8 21 4/8	19 3/8	4 4	Will County	IL	Jim Saunoris, Jr.	2010	18426
139 5/8	22 3/8 22 3/8	18 1/8	6 5	Grant County	WI	Brad Hellenbrand	2010	18426
139 4/8	22 7/8 23 2/8	16 4/8	4 5	Harding County	SD	Scott Garner	2000	18574
139 4/8	24 2/8 24 1/8	17 1/8	6 5	Will County	IL	James E. Giese	2001	18574
139 4/8	23 5/8 23 6/8	15 0/8	5 6	Belmont County	OH	David Boltz	2001	18574
139 4/8	23 3/8 23 2/8	17 2/8	5 4	Ashland County	WI	Robert Wiezorek	2004	18574
139 4/8	22 0/8 21 5/8	16 2/8	5 5	Buffalo County	WI	Randy Springborn	2004	18574
139 4/8	21 1/8 21 3/8	15 2/8	7 6	Yankton County	SD	Scott Cutler	2004	18574
139 4/8	24 1/8 23 7/8	16 4/8	5 4	Buffalo County	WI	Tod J. Torgerson	2004	18574
139 4/8	24 4/8 24 2/8	13 6/8	5 5	Hart County	KY	Michael Sloan	2004	18574
139 4/8	24 1/8 24 4/8	18 6/8	6 5	Dawes County	NE	Scott G. Johnson	2004	18574
139 4/8	22 4/8 22 1/8	16 4/8	4 4	Dunn County	WI	Jason Lewis	2004	18574
139 4/8	23 1/8 23 4/8	18 2/8	5 5	La Salle County	IL	Nathan Clift	2004	18574
139 4/8	23 3/8 23 0/8	16 2/8	4 4	Burnett County	WI	Martin C. Shutt	2004	18574
139 4/8	22 0/8 23 1/8	17 2/8	5 5	Jo Daviess County	IL	Charles C. Lawrence	2004	18574
139 4/8	22 5/8 24 1/8	15 6/8	5 5	Somerset County	PA	Randy R. Ferry	2004	18574
139 4/8	23 6/8 23 6/8	16 2/8	5 5	Stark County	OH	Dack Warner	2004	18574
139 4/8	22 0/8 22 3/8	17 4/8	4 4	Williamson County	TN	Robert V. Russell	2004	18574
*139 4/8	22 2/8 23 3/8	18 4/8	5 4	Wyoming County	WV	Lyndell Perry	2004	18574
139 4/8	23 4/8 23 6/8	18 4/8	4 5	Webster County	IA	David Grunwald	2005	18574
139 4/8	22 0/8 23 0/8	16 6/8	5 5	Trempealeau County	WI	Ryan Metzler	2005	18574
*139 4/8	24 5/8 23 3/8	19 6/8	5 4	Morrison County	MN	David Sapletal	2005	18574
139 4/8	22 4/8 23 5/8	17 0/8	5 5	Laclede County	MO	Timothy Sherrer	2005	18574
139 4/8	23 0/8 21 6/8	17 1/8	6 5	Woodford County	IL	Marc Anthony	2005	18574
139 4/8	22 3/8 22 3/8	19 2/8	5 5	Bond County	IL	J. T. Scott	2005	18574
139 4/8	24 0/8 23 5/8	16 4/8	5 4	Buffalo County	WI	Dan Evenson	2005	18574
*139 4/8	21 7/8 22 0/8	14 6/8	5 5	Kanawha County	WV	Robert Young	2005	18574
139 4/8	22 7/8 20 5/8	18 0/8	5 5	Madison County	MS	Ken Pugh	2006	18574
139 4/8	21 3/8 21 5/8	17 4/8	5 5	Mountrail County	ND	Sjon Zunich	2006	18574
*139 4/8	23 2/8 23 5/8	19 4/8	5 6	Jackson County	IA	John Gau	2006	18574
139 4/8	23 3/8 22 7/8	18 4/8	4 4	Valley County	MT	Richard Penn	2006	18574
*139 4/8	23 2/8 21 2/8	17 2/8	5 6	Walworth County	WI	J. R. Deschner	2006	18574
139 4/8	23 6/8 23 6/8	19 6/8	5 5	Newton County	AR	Barry Greenhaw	2006	18574
139 4/8	21 7/8 21 2/8	17 4/8	5 4	Waupaca County	WI	Richard A. Hedtke	2006	18574
139 4/8	21 7/8 21 5/8	17 1/8	5 7	Catahoula Parish	LA	Dolan Pendarvis	2006	18574
139 4/8	23 1/8 23 6/8	19 4/8	4 4	Suffolk County	NY	Donald J. Tasch	2006	18574
*139 4/8	22 7/8 23 6/8	16 6/8	5 4	Oconto County	WI	Brian B. Gross	2007	18574
139 4/8	17 2/8 20 1/8	17 0/8	5 5	Garden County	NE	Rob Schneider	2007	18574
*139 4/8	24 1/8 24 3/8	17 6/8	4 4	Muskegon County	MI	Andrew Kent	2007	18574
139 4/8	23 2/8 22 7/8	15 0/8	7 6	Whiteside County	IL	Cole Young	2007	18574
*139 4/8	24 0/8 23 7/8	18 7/8	6 6	Lancaster County	PA	Chris Linderman	2007	18574
139 4/8	24 1/8 24 6/8	18 0/8	4 5	Harper County	KS	John Add Benson	2007	18574
139 4/8	25 1/8 24 6/8	17 4/8	7 6	Fremont County	IA	Patrick Athen	2007	18574
*139 4/8	21 5/8 21 4/8	17 6/8	5 6	Brown County	SD	Shaun Opsahl	2007	18574
139 4/8	22 3/8 24 7/8	17 3/8	5 4	Linn County	IA	Tyler Carmer	2007	18574
139 4/8	22 1/8 22 0/8	16 1/8	5 4	Howard County	MO	Kevin Pape	2008	18574
139 4/8	21 5/8 21 5/8	16 0/8	5 6	Jackson County	MO	Chris Nelson	2008	18574
*139 4/8	22 6/8 22 4/8	18 4/8	5 5	Steuben County	IN	Dan Weigel	2008	18574
139 4/8	23 4/8 22 7/8	16 7/8	5 6	Grundy County	IL	David A. Both	2008	18574
139 4/8	22 0/8 22 5/8	16 4/8	5 5	Madison County	AL	Andy Cobb	2008	18574
*139 4/8	23 1/8 23 3/8	17 4/8	4 4	New Haven County	CT	John M. Jillson	2008	18574
*139 4/8	21 7/8 22 1/8	16 0/8	5 5	Buffalo County	WI	Michael R. Senft	2008	18574
139 4/8	22 0/8 20 6/8	14 2/8	5 5	Atchison County	MO	Chuck Linthicum	2008	18574
139 4/8	22 2/8 21 3/8	14 1/8	5 6	Allegan County	MI	Craig W. Hansen	2008	18574
139 4/8	23 7/8 24 0/8	18 2/8	5 5	Fairfax County	VA	Robert F. Lafferty IV	2008	18574
139 4/8	25 5/8 26 4/8	18 2/8	5 6	Warren County	IA	Todd Gentry	2008	18574
*139 4/8	21 6/8 22 2/8	15 6/8	5 5	Queen Annes County	MD	Richard Edward Drechsler	2008	18574
*139 4/8	20 7/8 20 6/8	15 2/8	6 5	Lamoure County	ND	Bradley Jans	2009	18574
139 4/8	24 1/8 23 5/8	15 7/8	5 5	Waupaca County	WI	Adam J. Lorge	2009	18574
*139 4/8	25 3/8 24 4/8	17 4/8	5 5	Cherry County	NE	David Nicolai	2009	18574
139 4/8	22 5/8 21 2/8	15 4/8	5 7	Lyon County	KS	Richard E. Rattay	2009	18574
139 4/8	21 7/8 22 3/8	14 6/8	5 5	Yankton County	SD	David B. Cull	2009	18574
*139 4/8	22 6/8 22 7/8	19 6/8	5 6	Fulton County	GA	Derrick Burden	2010	18574
139 3/8	24 5/8 25 2/8	18 6/8	5 4	St. Clair County	MO	Joe Florido	2001	18746
139 3/8	24 1/8 23 7/8	18 2/8	5 7	Jackson County	IN	James Slaughter	2002	18746
139 3/8	23 4/8 23 4/8	14 2/8	5 5	Marshall County	TN	Scott Jackson	2004	18746
139 3/8	21 3/8 22 7/8	19 3/8	5 5	Marquette County	WI	Kyle McReath	2004	18746
139 3/8	23 7/8 23 5/8	17 1/8	4 4	Phelps County	NE	Donald Ace Morgan	2004	18746
*139 3/8	24 0/8 24 7/8	18 1/8	5 4	White County	IL	Eric Gholson	2004	18746
*139 3/8	22 0/8 21 5/8	14 3/8	6 6	Coffey County	KS	Don Erbert	2004	18746
139 3/8	20 3/8 20 7/8	17 4/8	6 5	Sauk County	WI	Rick Newman	2005	18746
139 3/8	21 7/8 22 0/8	17 1/8	5 5	Chariton County	MO	Josh Boeger	2005	18746
*139 3/8	24 7/8 25 2/8	20 0/8	7 6	Calhoun County	IL	Chris Ford	2005	18746
139 3/8	21 4/8 22 2/8	17 0/8	6 5	Reno County	KS	Dave Benson	2005	18746
139 3/8	22 2/8 22 1/8	19 0/8	5 7	Jerauld County	SD	George Bright	2005	18746
139 3/8	23 3/8 23 6/8	13 7/8	7 8	Concordia Parish	LA	Joel Prejean	2005	18746
139 3/8	23 5/8 23 0/8	17 7/8	5 5	Rock County	WI	Michael Muenchow	2006	18746
139 3/8	24 1/8 24 4/8	17 3/8	5 4	St. Croix County	WI	Greg Schmitz	2006	18746
139 3/8	22 5/8 23 0/8	18 1/8	4 4	Washburn County	WI	Timothy A. Nashton	2006	18746
139 3/8	22 1/8 23 6/8	17 3/8	5 5	Buffalo County	WI	Kevin D. McClure	2006	18746
*139 3/8	22 7/8 22 2/8	16 3/8	6 6	Seward County	NE	Monte Mares	2007	18746
139 3/8	25 1/8 23 0/8	18 7/8	5 5	Houston County	MN	Ray N. Andersen	2007	18746
*139 3/8	25 0/8 22 0/8	22 6/8	7 6	Crawford County	WI	Mitch Holliday	2007	18746
139 3/8	22 5/8 22 1/8	20 3/8	4 4	Macon County	IL	Owen P. Sullivan	2007	18746
139 3/8	24 5/8 23 6/8	20 3/8	5 4	Jackson County	IL	Anthony J. Caminiti	2007	18746
139 3/8	24 5/8 24 2/8	16 4/8	5 5	Wheeler County	TX	Steve Snelgrooes	2007	18746
139 3/8	23 6/8 23 1/8	17 5/8	4 4	Rockingham County	NH	Tod Rinfret	2007	18746
*139 3/8	22 4/8 22 0/8	18 1/8	5 5	Atascosa County	TX	William D. Huspek	2007	18746
*139 3/8	22 1/8 22 3/8	17 1/8	5 5	Sussex County	DE	Matthew Megee	2008	18746
*139 3/8	20 3/8 20 3/8	17 1/8	5 6	Pierce County	NE	Cody Schnebel	2008	18746
*139 3/8	21 1/8 20 7/8	15 0/8	5 6	Hendricks County	IN	Dustin Nichols	2008	18746
139 3/8	23 7/8 23 6/8	18 7/8	5 4	Jackson County	IA	David Schrody	2008	18746
139 3/8	22 2/8 22 0/8	18 6/8	6 6	Richland County	IL	Bill Pearcy	2008	18746

WHITETAIL DEER (TYPICAL ANTLERS)

Minimum Score 125 — Continued

SCORE	LENGTH OF R MAIN BEAM L	INSIDE SPREAD	NUMBER OF R POINTS L	AREA	STATE/ PROVINCE	HUNTER'S NAME	DATE	RANK
*139 3/8	24 4/8 24 3/8	19 3/8	5 5	St. Croix County	WI	Koby Zahl	2009	18746
*139 3/8	23 2/8 23 0/8	16 5/8	4 5	Schuyler County	IL	Robert Van Munster	2009	18746
*139 3/8	23 1/8 23 1/8	17 4/8	5 5	Allamakee County	IA	Steve Blow	2009	18746
139 3/8	22 2/8 22 7/8	21 1/8	5 6	Trempealeau County	WI	Ella Dorn	2009	18746
*139 3/8	27 0/8 26 0/8	18 3/8	5 5	Vernon County	WI	Jesse Barstad	2009	18746
139 3/8	23 3/8 23 6/8	17 7/8	7 6	Jefferson County	OH	Joseph Blazer	2009	18746
139 3/8	23 3/8 23 0/8	17 4/8	6 6	Clay County	IA	Marc Gustafson	2009	18746
*139 3/8	20 3/8 20 7/8	13 7/8	5 5	Worcester County	MD	Michael E. Seal	2009	18746
*139 3/8	23 3/8 23 2/8	13 5/8	5 5	Ingham County	MI	James L. Taylor	2010	18746
*139 3/8	23 1/8 24 4/8	17 7/8	4 5	Houston County	MN	Doug Sanders	2010	18746
*139 2/8	21 4/8 22 0/8	15 2/8	5 5	Washington County	PA	Shawn McClay	2003	18897
139 2/8	26 7/8 27 3/8	21 4/8	4 4	Essex County	MA	Stephen Chevalier	2003	18897
139 2/8	20 4/8 22 0/8	16 1/8	6 5	Calhoun County	IL	Steve McCluskey	2004	18897
139 2/8	24 4/8 24 2/8	19 0/8	5 5	Madison County	IL	Ron Allen	2004	18897
139 2/8	24 4/8 24 5/8	19 2/8	4 4	Greene County	IL	Mike Weaver	2004	18897
139 2/8	21 1/8 20 7/8	16 7/8	5 6	Buffalo County	WI	Dan Scharmer	2004	18897
139 2/8	23 5/8 22 4/8	16 6/8	5 5	Buffalo County	WI	David W. Pfeiffer	2004	18897
*139 2/8	21 3/8 21 3/8	15 4/8	5 5	Pike County	IL	Keith Edwards	2004	18897
139 2/8	23 6/8 24 4/8	18 0/8	4 4	Adams County	WI	Kevin Peters	2004	18897
139 2/8	23 0/8 21 5/8	16 5/8	5 6	Allamakee County	IA	Dennis Michael Stubbs	2004	18897
139 2/8	23 3/8 24 1/8	15 6/8	4 5	Warren County	OH	Chuck Coffey	2004	18897
139 2/8	25 3/8 24 4/8	15 2/8	5 5	Arkansas County	AR	Justin Marrs	2004	18897
139 2/8	21 7/8 22 2/8	19 2/8	5 5	Vulcan	ALB	Roger Montgomery	2005	18897
*139 2/8	20 6/8 21 5/8	15 6/8	5 5	Ramsey County	ND	Dwight Logie	2005	18897
139 2/8	23 0/8 22 1/8	18 4/8	5 4	Dorintosh	SAS	James Blamy	2005	18897
139 2/8	24 1/8 25 5/8	18 2/8	7 6	Bristol County	MA	Steven Rogers	2005	18897
139 2/8	20 7/8 21 0/8	15 4/8	5 5	Dubuque County	IA	Ron Kueter	2005	18897
139 2/8	21 4/8 21 1/8	16 0/8	5 6	Clark County	WI	Lucas Papierniak	2005	18897
139 2/8	22 3/8 22 1/8	16 4/8	5 5	Turner County	SD	Keith Engbrecht	2005	18897
139 2/8	25 1/8 23 7/8	18 0/8	6 6	Clay County	IA	Thomas Gross	2005	18897
139 2/8	25 0/8 23 5/8	18 7/8	6 5	Buffalo County	WI	Raymond Nachtwey	2006	18897
139 2/8	23 3/8 22 4/8	17 5/8	7 8	Green Lake County	WI	Dustin R. Schmitt	2006	18897
139 2/8	23 1/8 21 6/8	15 4/8	5 5	Worth County	GA	Bryan K. Gregory	2006	18897
139 2/8	24 2/8 25 1/8	15 4/8	5 4	Cortland County	NY	Tim Kellogg	2006	18897
*139 2/8	26 4/8 24 3/8	22 4/8	5 4	Dodge County	WI	Rick Eichorst	2006	18897
139 2/8	24 5/8 25 3/8	19 1/8	6 6	Montgomery County	OH	Jeremy Martin	2006	18897
*139 2/8	24 6/8 25 1/8	18 4/8	4 6	Vernon County	WI	Eric Schickowski	2006	18897
*139 2/8	24 7/8 24 0/8	18 1/8	5 6	Decatur County	IA	John Rippey	2006	18897
139 2/8	21 2/8 19 6/8	16 6/8	5 5	Schuyler County	IL	Matthew Zeigler	2006	18897
139 2/8	24 7/8 24 0/8	18 0/8	4 4	Greene County	IA	Kris Ostrander	2006	18897
*139 2/8	21 4/8 21 7/8	15 4/8	9 9	Montgomery County	MO	Robert K. Jones	2006	18897
139 2/8	23 4/8 24 0/8	17 4/8	5 5	Stevens County	WA	James R. Kerr	2006	18897
*139 2/8	22 0/8 22 1/8	15 5/8	7 8	Harford County	MD	Jason Thomas Boothe	2007	18897
139 2/8	22 7/8 23 2/8	19 6/8	8 9	Lawrence County	SD	Scott Paramo	2007	18897
139 2/8	25 4/8 23 4/8	16 4/8	4 4	De Kalb County	IN	David Sauders	2007	18897
139 2/8	25 6/8 25 4/8	22 6/8	4 4	Buffalo County	WI	Gregory A. Hanneman	2007	18897
*139 2/8	21 3/8 20 5/8	16 4/8	6 6	Cass County	IN	Randall E. Roark	2007	18897
139 2/8	20 2/8 23 0/8	18 0/8	4 4	Buffalo County	WI	Jeffrey G. Crary	2007	18897
139 2/8	23 6/8 21 5/8	19 1/8	8 6	Worth County	IA	Dave Reyerson	2007	18897
*139 2/8	24 4/8 23 5/8	17 6/8	5 6	Dubuque County	IA	Timothy J. Harle	2007	18897
*139 2/8	21 1/8 22 0/8	18 0/8	5 5	Parke County	IN	Roger Cooper	2007	18897
139 2/8	22 6/8 22 6/8	20 1/8	6 6	St. Louis County	MN	Marc Miller	2007	18897
*139 2/8	24 5/8 24 2/8	18 3/8	4 6	Jo Daviess County	IL	Glenn Evans	2007	18897
139 2/8	21 3/8 22 3/8	18 6/8	6 4	McDonough County	IL	Jason B. Amato	2007	18897
139 2/8	23 2/8 23 3/8	15 7/8	6 7	Jackson County	IN	Chris Connell	2007	18897
139 2/8	22 7/8 23 1/8	18 2/8	4 4	Lake County	IN	Chester W. Patterson	2007	18897
*139 2/8	23 0/8 24 0/8	18 4/8	4 4	Queen Annes County	MD	William J. Jimeno	2007	18897
139 2/8	22 5/8 22 0/8	17 6/8	6 7	Phelps County	MO	Brandon Skyles	2007	18897
*139 2/8	23 5/8 25 1/8	17 0/8	5 5	Buffalo County	WI	Tim Huebner	2008	18897
139 2/8	21 5/8 21 2/8	17 2/8	5 5	Adams County	WI	Brandon Popp	2008	18897
*139 2/8	21 6/8 22 3/8	15 5/8	6 5	Blue Earth County	MN	Blaine R. Eichstadt	2008	18897
139 2/8	25 5/8 26 1/8	19 0/8	5 6	Linn County	IA	James L. Newman	2008	18897
139 2/8	20 6/8 20 5/8	18 2/8	5 5	Butler County	NE	James Kucera	2008	18897
139 2/8	26 5/8 26 0/8	21 0/8	5 4	Bucks County	PA	Robert Davis	2008	18897
139 2/8	26 0/8 25 2/8	19 7/8	5 4	Queen Annes County	MD	Bruce Wine	2008	18897
139 2/8	24 6/8 24 5/8	17 4/8	5 6	Carrot River	SAS	Steff Stefanovich	2008	18897
139 2/8	22 6/8 22 7/8	18 2/8	4 4	Nodaway County	MO	Todd Tobin	2008	18897
*139 2/8	22 0/8 22 5/8	16 6/8	5 5	Lyon County	MN	Corey Clark	2009	18897
139 2/8	25 2/8 24 6/8	17 0/8	5 5	Richland County	WI	Terry L. Laufenberg	2009	18897
*139 2/8	22 2/8 22 2/8	19 4/8	5 5	Kosciusko County	IN	Mark S. Cass	2009	18897
*139 2/8	22 4/8 22 2/8	14 6/8	4 6	Jackson County	MO	Scott Gray Williams	2009	18897
*139 2/8	22 4/8 23 3/8	17 4/8	4 5	Sauk County	WI	Tim Seils	2009	18897
139 2/8	23 2/8 23 7/8	19 1/8	6 5	Nemaha County	KS	Dennis Harper	2009	18897
139 2/8	21 6/8 22 1/8	16 0/8	5 5	Comanche County	KS	Ronald J. Murphy	2009	18897
139 2/8	25 2/8 23 7/8	20 1/8	7 7	Plymouth County	MA	Jason Zimmer	2009	18897
*139 2/8	20 0/8 21 0/8	16 4/8	5 5	Franklin County	IL	Darin DeNeal	2010	18897
139 1/8	23 0/8 22 7/8	16 7/8	5 5	Richland County	OH	Todd C. Fenner	1997	19078
139 1/8	23 5/8 23 6/8	19 3/8	7 6	Starke County	IN	Sam Vanni	2002	19078
*139 1/8	25 4/8 25 3/8	22 1/8	5 6	Shawano County	WI	Walter J. Moesch	2003	19078
139 1/8	23 2/8 22 2/8	16 0/8	6 6	Cedar County	IA	Devin Petersen	2003	19078
139 1/8	21 3/8 20 4/8	13 1/8	5 6	Cavalier County	ND	James Sonderland	2003	19078
139 1/8	20 7/8 21 0/8	19 1/8	5 5	Marinette County	WI	Joe Fiedorowicz	2004	19078
139 1/8	22 1/8 24 2/8	23 7/8	5 4	Westmoreland County	PA	Heather Waywood	2004	19078
*139 1/8	21 7/8 22 4/8	18 3/8	6 7	Peoria County	IL	Greg Petrakis	2004	19078
139 1/8	24 4/8 24 1/8	18 1/8	4 4	Winnebago County	IL	Michael S. Kloster	2004	19078
*139 1/8	23 0/8 22 5/8	17 7/8	4 4	Kent County	MI	David Stocking	2004	19078
*139 1/8	24 4/8 24 5/8	15 3/8	4 5	Ford County	IL	Brad Weidner	2004	19078
139 1/8	25 5/8 24 0/8	18 7/8	5 5	Bolivar County	MS	Lance Johnson	2004	19078
139 1/8	21 1/8 21 1/8	15 1/8	4 5	Gallatin County	MT	Bob Morton	2005	19078
139 1/8	26 3/8 24 5/8	18 3/8	8 6	Eau Claire County	WI	Scott Williamson	2005	19078
139 1/8	23 6/8 23 3/8	20 6/8	4 4	Hardeman County	TN	Denton Shearin	2005	19078
139 1/8	22 7/8 22 0/8	18 2/8	6 6	Otoe County	NE	Douglas Srb	2005	19078
139 1/8	21 0/8 20 4/8	15 0/8	5 6	Toombs County	GA	Michael Manning	2005	19078
139 1/8	25 5/8 25 5/8	16 7/8	4 4	Windham County	CT	Dieter Bromkamp	2005	19078
139 1/8	20 7/8 22 1/8	17 7/8	4 5	Yankton County	SD	Chris A. Fitch	2005	19078

Deer entries below 141 0/8, that appeared in the 6th Edition, are not included here, but are included on the accompanying CD (see page 119), and also in the Club's Records Archives.

539

WHITETAIL DEER (TYPICAL ANTLERS)

Minimum Score 125 — Continued

SCORE	LENGTH OF R MAIN BEAM L	INSIDE SPREAD	NUMBER OF R POINTS L	AREA	STATE/PROVINCE	HUNTER'S NAME	DATE	RANK
*139 1/8	22 1/8 21 5/8	19 5/8	4 5	Lucas County	IA	Roy Palmer	2005	19078
*139 1/8	23 1/8 23 0/8	15 7/8	5 5	Van Buren County	MI	Jerry R. Johnson	2006	19078
*139 1/8	23 0/8 24 1/8	15 5/8	4 4	Donley County	TX	Ryan Stevens	2006	19078
139 1/8	22 3/8 22 3/8	15 3/8	5 5	Hughes County	OK	Tom Cartwright	2006	19078
139 1/8	24 3/8 25 5/8	17 5/8	4 4	La Crosse County	WI	Cory Stoner	2006	19078
139 1/8	23 6/8 24 0/8	19 0/8	5 4	Genesee County	NY	Scott Blond	2006	19078
139 1/8	24 4/8 23 5/8	18 7/8	4 4	Saline County	AR	Landon Dickerson	2006	19078
*139 1/8	22 7/8 22 1/8	17 5/8	4 4	Allamakee County	IA	Arnie Crum	2006	19078
139 1/8	24 0/8 25 0/8	16 1/8	5 6	Pittsburg County	OK	Bill Williams	2006	19078
139 1/8	23 6/8 23 0/8	17 7/8	7 6	Missoula County	MT	Randolph Chitwood	2006	19078
139 1/8	22 4/8 22 5/8	13 7/8	6 6	Adams County	IL	Ray Burke	2006	19078
139 1/8	24 5/8 24 0/8	15 5/8	5 5	La Salle County	IL	Alan R. Simons	2006	19078
139 1/8	22 1/8 24 1/8	15 5/8	4 5	Warren County	IA	Sue Motzko	2006	19078
139 1/8	23 2/8 23 5/8	19 1/8	4 4	Crawford County	IL	Brad Weger	2006	19078
*139 1/8	25 1/8 25 1/8	17 1/8	4 4	Worcester County	MA	Paul Rich	2006	19078
139 1/8	20 7/8 21 6/8	17 5/8	5 5	Ward County	ND	Tim Tomlinson	2007	19078
*139 1/8	24 2/8 23 4/8	17 5/8	5 5	Washington County	KY	Kevin Devine	2007	19078
139 1/8	21 1/8 21 3/8	16 1/8	5 5	Cadogan	ALB	Walter Krom	2007	19078
139 1/8	20 3/8 20 1/8	17 3/8	7 7	Maverick County	TX	H. Mike Palmer	2007	19078
*139 1/8	20 5/8 20 2/8	17 7/8	5 5	Dawes County	NE	Dwayne E. Ensign	2007	19078
*139 1/8	21 6/8 20 5/8	16 3/8	5 5	Kosciusko County	IN	Greg Brazo	2007	19078
139 1/8	24 1/8 23 7/8	15 0/8	7 6	Gallatin County	IL	Darrin Garner	2007	19078
*139 1/8	24 4/8 24 1/8	16 1/8	4 4	Chickasaw County	IA	Tom Brown	2007	19078
*139 1/8	24 0/8 22 7/8	14 7/8	5 5	Washington County	AR	Kenny Enderland	2007	19078
139 1/8	24 0/8 23 6/8	18 2/8	4 5	Vermillion County	IN	Todd Wickens	2007	19078
*139 1/8	25 3/8 25 5/8	21 2/8	5 6	Isabella County	MI	Anthony Urban	2008	19078
*139 1/8	23 6/8 24 4/8	18 1/8	5 5	Berrien County	MI	Andrew Bierwagen	2008	19078
*139 1/8	24 5/8 24 1/8	17 3/8	5 6	Dearborn County	IN	Dan Pegram	2008	19078
*139 1/8	24 7/8 25 2/8	17 3/8	4 5	Noble County	IN	Kraig L. Keirn	2008	19078
139 1/8	23 0/8 22 0/8	16 6/8	5 5	Kankakee County	IL	Doug A. Duncan	2008	19078
*139 1/8	24 2/8 23 5/8	17 3/8	5 5	Venango County	PA	Matthew James Hite	2008	19078
139 1/8	22 0/8 22 0/8	18 7/8	5 4	Johnson County	IL	Keith Cerny	2008	19078
139 1/8	22 4/8 24 0/8	19 3/8	5 5	Decatur County	IA	Ivan Muzljakovich	2008	19078
*139 1/8	22 4/8 22 3/8	16 7/8	5 4	Owen County	KY	Byron Robertson	2009	19078
139 1/8	21 4/8 21 5/8	15 5/8	5 8	Vilas County	WI	Jon Strick	2009	19078
139 1/8	25 3/8 24 6/8	20 7/8	5 5	Orleans County	NY	John W. Brabon, Jr.	2009	19078
139 1/8	22 2/8 21 3/8	19 0/8	6 5	Clermont County	OH	Jeffrey A. Matthews	2009	19078
*139 1/8	21 7/8 21 3/8	16 1/8	5 4	Jefferson County	PA	Patrick Brennen	2009	19078
139 1/8	20 5/8 20 1/8	16 3/8	5 6	Ramsey County	ND	Dan Erickstad	2009	19078
139 1/8	19 6/8 20 5/8	16 3/8	7 7	Franklin County	IA	Randy Filbrandt	2009	19078
139 1/8	23 3/8 23 0/8	17 1/8	6 5	Grenada County	MS	Al Hankins	2010	19078
*139 1/8	27 1/8 26 0/8	18 1/8	6 5	Livingston County	NY	Karen M. Bernecker	2010	19078
139 0/8	25 3/8 26 0/8	18 3/8	4 5	Suffolk County	NY	Richard Wright	2001	19261
139 0/8	19 6/8 22 1/8	17 4/8	6 6	La Porte County	IN	William J. Patton	2002	19261
139 0/8	21 4/8 22 7/8	17 0/8	4 4	Rockyview	ALB	Cam T. Foss	2002	19261
139 0/8	22 4/8 22 5/8	19 6/8	4 4	Jefferson County	WI	Jay Bowe	2003	19261
139 0/8	21 7/8 20 2/8	15 5/8	6 5	Mitchell County	IA	Phil Brumm	2003	19261
139 0/8	21 7/8 20 2/8	15 6/8	5 5	Macomb County	MI	Michael D. Durst	2004	19261
139 0/8	23 2/8 22 1/8	16 4/8	4 5	Clay County	IA	Thomas Ray Gross	2004	19261
139 0/8	23 1/8 23 2/8	15 3/8	7 5	James City County	VA	Steve Van Kirk	2004	19261
139 0/8	25 2/8 22 5/8	19 0/8	4 5	Jones County	IA	Brian Brunscheen	2004	19261
139 0/8	22 6/8 22 7/8	15 2/8	6 5	Juneau County	WI	Terry Wright	2004	19261
*139 0/8	25 0/8 24 5/8	16 6/8	4 4	Auglaize County	OH	Tom Rindler	2004	19261
*139 0/8	20 6/8 21 5/8	16 6/8	5 5	Clinton County	MI	Tory J. Schneider	2004	19261
139 0/8	21 6/8 21 4/8	16 5/8	5 5	Boyd County	NE	Steve V. Reiser	2004	19261
139 0/8	24 5/8 25 4/8	15 3/8	6 5	Calhoun County	IL	Ben Robertson	2004	19261
*139 0/8	25 6/8 25 6/8	18 1/8	6 6	Coshocton County	OH	Carl Phipps	2005	19261
139 0/8	23 0/8 22 3/8	15 4/8	5 5	Coshocton County	OH	Jesse Fischer	2005	19261
139 0/8	21 2/8 20 7/8	15 6/8	5 5	Toombs County	GA	Mike Morris	2005	19261
139 0/8	22 6/8 23 4/8	18 4/8	5 5	Knox County	MO	Leo Meyer	2005	19261
139 0/8	22 3/8 23 0/8	16 2/8	5 5	Westmoreland County	PA	Scott M. Fassinger	2005	19261
139 0/8	22 2/8 22 4/8	14 4/8	5 6	Audrain County	MO	Trent Silver	2005	19261
*139 0/8	21 5/8 20 6/8	16 6/8	5 5	Bremer County	IA	Howard Schmitz	2005	19261
*139 0/8	23 5/8 23 5/8	15 2/8	4 4	Osage County	KS	Chris Ward	2005	19261
139 0/8	21 0/8 20 2/8	17 7/8	6 6	Jones County	IA	Jason Tjaden	2006	19261
139 0/8	20 5/8 20 6/8	16 6/8	5 5	Dodge County	WI	Jason D. Schlesner	2006	19261
139 0/8	22 0/8 22 3/8	17 2/8	5 5	Franklin County	IN	Jarod K. Wuestefeld	2006	19261
*139 0/8	24 5/8 23 4/8	20 2/8	4 5	Sauk County	WI	Dale T. Curtin	2006	19261
139 0/8	21 6/8 21 7/8	15 6/8	5 5	Jackson County	OH	Kurtis Strickland	2006	19261
139 0/8	22 7/8 22 3/8	19 6/8	6 6	Douglas County	SD	Dwight Mills	2006	19261
139 0/8	24 2/8 24 4/8	17 5/8	5 7	Ottawa County	KS	Patrick E. Helget	2006	19261
*139 0/8	24 2/8 24 0/8	18 0/8	7 5	De Kalb County	IN	Ronald L. Kline	2006	19261
139 0/8	21 5/8 22 4/8	16 2/8	5 5	Dubois County	IN	Bart Schmitt	2007	19261
139 0/8	25 3/8 24 4/8	23 3/8	5 9	Livingston County	MI	Mick A. LaFountain	2007	19261
*139 0/8	22 6/8 22 5/8	16 0/8	6 5	Pepin County	WI	Shaughn Laehn	2007	19261
139 0/8	24 3/8 25 6/8	18 0/8	5 4	Iron County	WI	Chris Fink	2007	19261
139 0/8	23 3/8 23 7/8	16 0/8	5 4	Perry County	PA	Dave Adams	2007	19261
139 0/8	22 3/8 22 5/8	17 4/8	6 5	Buffalo County	WI	Mark T. Eswein	2007	19261
139 0/8	23 4/8 24 0/8	19 4/8	4 4	Brown County	IL	Kenneth Garls	2007	19261
*139 0/8	21 3/8 21 2/8	13 6/8	6 7	Licking County	OH	Ryan Gargasz	2007	19261
139 0/8	21 3/8 22 2/8	15 4/8	5 6	McHenry County	IL	Christopher Hutson	2008	19261
139 0/8	24 4/8 24 4/8	17 6/8	5 5	Will County	IL	Carl Mentzer	2008	19261
*139 0/8	24 2/8 25 4/8	14 2/8	6 5	Woodlands County	ALB	Leonard Verbaas	2008	19261
139 0/8	21 5/8 21 5/8	16 2/8	5 6	Loon Lake	SAS	Lanny Nault	2008	19261
*139 0/8	24 0/8 24 1/8	18 5/8	5 6	Houston County	MN	Brian Jones	2009	19261
139 0/8	21 6/8 22 2/8	22 2/8	7 6	Chisago County	MN	Mike Peterson	2009	19261
139 0/8	21 6/8 22 0/8	17 4/8	6 5	Polk County	WI	Shawn Koosman	2009	19261
*139 0/8	20 1/8 20 2/8	16 2/8	6 5	Wood County	WI	Mike Zdun	2009	19261
*139 0/8	21 3/8 21 7/8	17 4/8	5 5	Polk County	WI	Steven L. Karo	2009	19261
*139 0/8	22 6/8 22 4/8	20 2/8	4 6	Kalamazoo County	MI	Jon Dracht	2009	19261
*139 0/8	23 3/8 24 6/8	17 0/8	6 6	Johnson County	NE	James Terrell Smith	2009	19261
139 0/8	24 3/8 25 4/8	19 4/8	4 4	Lawrence County	PA	Robert H. Davis	2009	19261
138 7/8	23 4/8 24 0/8	18 1/8	4 4	Lorain County	OH	Steven D. Reinhold	1994	19434
138 7/8	25 0/8 24 6/8	18 7/8	5 5	Queen Annes County	MD	Michael A. Schafer, Jr.	2002	19434
*138 7/8	22 3/8 22 6/8	20 1/8	4 5	Boone County	IA	Jared Lenz	2003	19434

WHITETAIL DEER (TYPICAL ANTLERS)

Minimum Score 125   Continued

SCORE	LENGTH OF R MAIN BEAM L	INSIDE SPREAD	NUMBER OF R POINTS L	AREA	STATE/ PROVINCE	HUNTER'S NAME	DATE	RANK
*138 7/8	25 4/8 25 1/8	19 1/8	4 4	Montgomery County	TN	Jeff Winningham	2004	19434
*138 7/8	23 1/8 23 5/8	14 1/8	5 5	Christian County	KY	Nick Sandefur	2004	19434
138 7/8	22 2/8 21 4/8	15 1/8	5 5	Mercer County	PA	Dick Bortz	2004	19434
138 7/8	22 6/8 23 5/8	14 7/8	5 5	Crittenden County	KY	John R. Noland	2004	19434
*138 7/8	24 4/8 24 2/8	16 4/8	4 5	Maverick County	TX	Mike Stegall	2005	19434
138 7/8	25 0/8 26 0/8	19 1/8	5 5	Allegheny County	PA	Raymond R. Drabicki	2005	19434
138 7/8	23 7/8 24 3/8	18 3/8	4 4	Sauk County	WI	Allen J. Ray	2005	19434
138 7/8	23 2/8 24 0/8	16 1/8	5 4	Jasper County	IL	Paul Hardiek	2005	19434
*138 7/8	21 0/8 20 5/8	15 2/8	5 6	Jasper County	IA	Michael A. Riley	2005	19434
*138 7/8	21 5/8 21 5/8	15 7/8	6 5	Smith County	KS	Ronald Reneberg	2005	19434
138 7/8	25 1/8 24 4/8	20 1/8	4 4	Christian County	IL	Sylvan Purcell	2005	19434
138 7/8	24 0/8 23 3/8	19 0/8	6 6	Buffalo County	WI	Scott Swan	2005	19434
138 7/8	24 1/8 22 3/8	15 5/8	5 5	Marshall County	IN	James M. Miller	2005	19434
138 7/8	22 1/8 22 5/8	17 1/8	5 5	Polk County	WI	Jason A. Barr	2005	19434
138 7/8	24 4/8 23 4/8	18 5/8	5 7	Guernsey County	OH	Don Masters	2006	19434
*138 7/8	20 3/8 22 7/8	20 0/8	6 5	Kent County	DE	Robert Piascinski	2006	19434
138 7/8	26 0/8 27 2/8	19 1/8	4 4	Bedford County	VA	W. H. Burks	2006	19434
138 7/8	22 6/8 22 3/8	18 5/8	5 5	Will County	IL	Jeff Pals	2006	19434
138 7/8	22 5/8 22 3/8	16 1/8	7 5	Delaware County	IN	Scott A. Conley	2006	19434
*138 7/8	24 2/8 22 5/8	17 3/8	4 4	Perry County	IL	Pete Drummond	2006	19434
138 7/8	18 7/8 20 1/8	14 5/8	5 5	Jewell County	KS	Donald Klenklen	2006	19434
138 7/8	19 1/8 20 1/8	14 3/8	5 5	Hillsdale County	MI	Paul T. Bortolussi	2006	19434
*138 7/8	24 3/8 24 0/8	18 5/8	5 5	McHenry County	IL	Bobby Barrett	2006	19434
138 7/8	20 0/8 19 6/8	15 7/8	5 5	Des Moines County	IA	Gary Grassi	2006	19434
*138 7/8	25 3/8 24 2/8	18 3/8	6 4	Knox County	IL	Jeff Wood	2007	19434
138 7/8	24 5/8 22 6/8	18 7/8	5 5	Waushara County	WI	Eric J. Haag	2007	19434
138 7/8	24 3/8 23 4/8	19 1/8	4 4	Stanley County	SD	Kyle Carter	2007	19434
*138 7/8	23 4/8 23 0/8	20 7/8	4 4	Allen County	IN	Michael Heastan	2007	19434
*138 7/8	23 0/8 22 7/8	14 3/8	5 5	Waushara County	WI	Patrick J. Rait	2008	19434
138 7/8	24 5/8 25 0/8	18 4/8	7 5	Trempealeau County	WI	Joe P. Neinas	2008	19434
138 7/8	26 1/8 23 7/8	17 1/8	6 5	Noble County	IN	Scott W. Lindsey	2008	19434
138 7/8	24 2/8 24 1/8	17 2/8	5 5	Jackson County	MI	James O. Ward	2008	19434
138 7/8	23 0/8 23 2/8	16 7/8	5 5	Putnam County	TN	Jeff Betcher, Jr.	2008	19434
138 7/8	24 7/8 23 5/8	19 5/8	6 5	Sauk County	WI	Joseph Finnegan	2008	19434
*138 7/8	25 4/8 25 5/8	16 6/8	7 5	Washington County	MN	Derrick Adam Orr	2008	19434
138 7/8	24 2/8 24 6/8	15 2/8	6 9	Grenada County	MS	Andrew Nobile	2009	19434
*138 7/8	21 7/8 22 0/8	15 7/8	5 5	Marshall County	WV	Robert E. Guynn	2009	19434
138 7/8	23 1/8 22 7/8	17 7/8	7 7	Reno County	KS	Roy Hukill	2009	19434
*138 7/8	23 5/8 22 3/8	15 2/8	8 5	Marshall County	IN	Nathaniel R. Yoder	2009	19434
138 7/8	25 0/8 22 0/8	17 5/8	6 5	Allegheny County	PA	Jon M. Taucher	2009	19434
138 7/8	22 4/8 22 3/8	18 3/8	5 6	Comanche County	KS	Thomas J. Pluhar	2009	19434
138 7/8	23 6/8 23 7/8	20 6/8	5 7	Kingman County	KS	Mark B. Steffen	2009	19434
138 7/8	24 6/8 25 3/8	17 0/8	8 6	Jo Daviess County	IL	Jim Collachia	2009	19434
138 7/8	23 0/8 22 0/8	16 5/8	5 5	Dutton Township	ONT	Matt Hill	2009	19434
*138 7/8	24 7/8 24 2/8	17 5/8	5 6	Taylor County	IA	Alan Benton	2009	19434
*138 7/8	22 3/8 22 2/8	20 1/8	4 4	Spink County	SD	Tim Hofer	2009	19434
*138 7/8	20 0/8 20 3/8	15 6/8	5 6	Cooking Lake	ALB	Craig Temple	2009	19434
138 7/8	23 4/8 23 0/8	18 6/8	4 7	Mille Lacs County	MN	Cory Ploeger	2009	19434
*138 7/8	22 6/8 21 6/8	18 5/8	5 5	Webb County	TX	Curtis Abbott	2009	19434
138 7/8	21 7/8 22 0/8	15 1/8	6 6	Winnebago County	WI	Daniel M. Marohn	2009	19434
*138 7/8	23 3/8 23 7/8	17 3/8	5 5	Washington County	PA	Michael W. Falosk	2010	19434
138 6/8	23 2/8 24 5/8	14 0/8	5 5	Genesee County	MI	Thomas Tremblay	1982	19597
138 6/8	21 7/8 21 6/8	15 6/8	5 5	Marquette County	WI	Timothy J. McReath	2003	19597
138 6/8	21 5/8 23 1/8	18 2/8	5 5	Bullitt County	KY	Michael Dennis Minton	2004	19597
138 6/8	23 4/8 24 1/8	15 0/8	4 4	Champaign County	OH	Thomas Flohre	2004	19597
138 6/8	21 7/8 22 7/8	14 2/8	4 5	Sumner County	KS	Ted Benvin	2004	19597
138 6/8	21 7/8 23 1/8	14 6/8	5 7	Ringgold County	IA	Richard Combs	2004	19597
138 6/8	22 6/8 22 2/8	18 2/8	5 6	Van Buren County	MI	James Flory, Jr.	2004	19597
138 6/8	24 1/8 24 1/8	17 6/8	6 6	Lamar County	AL	Ken Swanson	2004	19597
138 6/8	23 0/8 23 0/8	17 6/8	5 5	St. Louis County	MN	Richard Maciejeski	2004	19597
*138 6/8	22 7/8 22 2/8	15 3/8	8 5	Clark County	MO	Alex Del Vecchio	2004	19597
138 6/8	23 7/8 23 1/8	17 2/8	5 6	Washburn County	WI	Mark Vrieze	2004	19597
138 6/8	21 2/8 22 2/8	18 2/8	5 5	La Crosse County	WI	Mark L. Anderson	2004	19597
138 6/8	23 5/8 23 6/8	18 4/8	5 7	Will County	IL	Ron Offerman	2004	19597
138 6/8	22 4/8 23 2/8	15 6/8	5 5	Plymouth County	IA	Gregory T. Bolf	2004	19597
*138 6/8	23 6/8 22 7/8	18 1/8	5 5	Miami County	IN	Wendell Beachy	2005	19597
138 6/8	21 7/8 22 1/8	17 3/8	6 5	Shackelford County	TX	Clint Siddons	2005	19597
138 6/8	21 7/8 22 5/8	17 6/8	5 5	Rice County	MN	Tim Ozmun	2005	19597
138 6/8	24 3/8 24 2/8	17 5/8	4 5	Hillsdale County	MI	Tom St. Bernard	2005	19597
*138 6/8	23 0/8 23 0/8	17 2/8	5 5	Parke County	IN	Mike Fowler	2005	19597
138 6/8	25 1/8 26 0/8	17 5/8	4 6	Warren County	IA	Kent Risbeck	2005	19597
138 6/8	22 2/8 22 5/8	17 1/8	6 5	Plymouth County	IA	Mark Hartman	2005	19597
138 6/8	23 1/8 22 3/8	17 0/8	5 5	Woodbury County	IA	Russ R. Wauhob	2005	19597
138 6/8	23 7/8 24 1/8	18 0/8	4 4	Dakota County	MN	Brian LeMay	2005	19597
*138 6/8	23 0/8 23 0/8	18 0/8	5 4	Union County	SD	Matt Marx	2006	19597
138 6/8	23 6/8 23 5/8	16 2/8	4 4	Monongalia County	WV	Dave Nicola	2006	19597
*138 6/8	23 0/8 23 1/8	17 7/8	7 7	Waukesha County	WI	Keirston E. Peckham	2006	19597
138 6/8	22 0/8 22 7/8	16 0/8	6 4	Green Lake	SAS	Michael Wolff	2006	19597
*138 6/8	20 3/8 20 4/8	16 4/8	5 5	Webster County	MO	Jeff Prewitt	2006	19597
*138 6/8	24 5/8 23 5/8	15 7/8	4 7	Riley County	KS	Ralph Lowell Thomas	2006	19597
138 6/8	24 6/8 24 4/8	19 0/8	4 4	Wayne County	NY	Jeffrey Maynard	2006	19597
138 6/8	21 1/8 19 0/8	14 2/8	5 5	Champaign County	OH	Bob Lacy	2006	19597
*138 6/8	23 2/8 23 0/8	18 4/8	5 5	Eau Claire County	WI	Eric Bunce	2006	19597
138 6/8	23 4/8 23 4/8	16 0/8	5 5	Fairfield County	CT	Larry A. Savo	2006	19597
*138 6/8	23 6/8 23 3/8	17 6/8	5 5	Pike County	IL	Corbet W. Vaughn	2006	19597
*138 6/8	23 3/8 24 1/8	19 4/8	4 4	Brown County	OH	Larry Ferguson	2006	19597
138 6/8	23 6/8 23 2/8	19 0/8	6 4	Phillips County	KS	Dan Pruett	2006	19597
138 6/8	23 5/8 23 3/8	20 2/8	5 4	Stevens County	WA	Mark E. Edin	2006	19597
138 6/8	26 2/8 26 0/8	19 7/8	7 7	Mahoning County	OH	Gary Eugene Fansler	2007	19597
138 6/8	23 5/8 23 1/8	26 2/8	6 6	Murray County	OK	Billy Miller	2007	19597
138 6/8	20 7/8 20 5/8	16 4/8	5 5	Gasconade County	MO	Ed Lansford	2007	19597
138 6/8	24 3/8 24 1/8	14 5/8	6 5	Dubuque County	IA	Brandon Gruber	2007	19597
*138 6/8	22 1/8 22 2/8	16 4/8	5 5	White County	IL	Kenny Thompson	2007	19597
138 6/8	23 1/8 23 0/8	16 2/8	4 4	Vermilion	ALB	Tim Pardely	2007	19597
*138 6/8	22 4/8 21 7/8	16 4/8	5 6	Mitchell County	KS	Toby Barnett	2007	19597

Deer entries below 141 0/8, that appeared in the 6th Edition, are not included here, but are included on the accompanying CD (see page 119), and also in the Club's Records Archives.

WHITETAIL DEER (TYPICAL ANTLERS)

Minimum Score 125   Continued

SCORE	LENGTH OF R MAIN BEAM L		INSIDE SPREAD	NUMBER OF R POINTS L		AREA	STATE/ PROVINCE	HUNTER'S NAME	DATE	RANK
*138 6/8	23 3/8	24 1/8	17 6/8	4	5	Eau Claire County	WI	Jake Davis	2007	19597
*138 6/8	22 5/8	22 3/8	14 4/8	6	5	Jones County	IA	Jeff Abel	2007	19597
138 6/8	27 6/8	28 4/8	20 0/8	4	4	Clinton County	OH	Todd Viars	2007	19597
138 6/8	23 4/8	23 5/8	19 6/8	5	5	Belmont County	OH	Ron Pockl	2007	19597
138 6/8	21 1/8	21 2/8	15 0/8	6	6	Jewell County	KS	Robert Goodloe	2007	19597
138 6/8	24 3/8	25 6/8	23 4/8	6	5	Sullivan County	IN	Scott Boone	2007	19597
138 6/8	21 0/8	20 3/8	14 6/8	5	5	Peoria County	IL	Ralph Spenny	2007	19597
*138 6/8	22 2/8	22 0/8	16 0/8	4	5	Ramsey County	ND	Daniel Erickstad	2007	19597
*138 6/8	22 1/8	22 5/8	20 6/8	5	5	Menard County	TX	J. R. Morgan	2007	19597
138 6/8	24 2/8	23 3/8	16 4/8	5	5	Trempealeau County	WI	David N. Andersen	2008	19597
138 6/8	22 4/8	22 2/8	17 5/8	5	4	Chariton County	MO	James Rodgers	2008	19597
138 6/8	24 6/8	24 4/8	18 5/8	6	5	Keya Paha County	NE	R. Kirk Sharp	2008	19597
*138 6/8	23 6/8	24 7/8	18 6/8	5	5	Columbia County	WI	Shane T. Larson	2008	19597
*138 6/8	23 0/8	23 4/8	18 1/8	6	5	E. Carroll Parish	LA	Scott Owens	2008	19597
138 6/8	26 3/8	21 2/8	20 4/8	5	5	Muskingum County	OH	Dennis Sherman	2008	19597
138 6/8	23 2/8	22 7/8	18 2/8	5	5	Sumner County	KS	Barry Wiley	2009	19597
*138 6/8	21 3/8	21 5/8	14 7/8	6	5	Callaway County	MO	Kevin P. Kennedy	2009	19597
138 6/8	24 2/8	23 7/8	17 1/8	4	6	Jewell County	KS	Steven Pohl	2009	19597
138 6/8	21 6/8	21 6/8	13 2/8	5	5	Kingman County	KS	Charles L. Palmer	2009	19597
*138 6/8	22 2/8	22 3/8	15 4/8	4	4	Erie County	PA	Josh Myers	2009	19597
138 5/8	23 6/8	22 3/8	17 5/8	5	5	Lorain County	OH	Steve Reinhold	1999	19774
138 5/8	27 0/8	25 2/8	19 1/8	4	4	Edwards County	IL	Jordan L. Mason	2001	19774
*138 5/8	20 7/8	20 3/8	17 2/8	6	5	Polk County	WI	Jason Johnson	2003	19774
138 5/8	23 0/8	22 6/8	19 1/8	4	5	Cedar County	MO	Rodney Schroer	2003	19774
138 5/8	19 6/8	20 6/8	18 3/8	5	5	Campbell County	SD	Doug Goehring	2003	19774
138 5/8	22 2/8	21 1/8	17 7/8	4	4	Brown County	SD	Mike DeKam	2003	19774
138 5/8	21 5/8	21 3/8	14 1/8	5	5	Carroll County	IL	Jim A. Morgan	2003	19774
138 5/8	22 7/8	22 4/8	16 1/8	4	4	Crook County	WY	Don Scofield	2004	19774
138 5/8	16 3/8	21 2/8	17 5/8	5	5	Pike County	IL	Timothy R. Wheeley	2004	19774
138 5/8	24 0/8	25 0/8	15 4/8	5	6	Boone County	IL	Tyler S. Streit	2004	19774
138 5/8	17 2/8	18 7/8	17 7/8	6	6	Trigg County	KY	Andy Shepherd	2004	19774
138 5/8	23 2/8	22 6/8	17 1/8	5	4	Warren County	NJ	William Guiles	2004	19774
*138 5/8	24 3/8	24 2/8	19 7/8	5	5	Pepin County	WI	David Holden	2004	19774
138 5/8	23 6/8	23 0/8	20 3/8	5	6	Waupaca County	WI	Joel D. Warner	2004	19774
138 5/8	23 4/8	24 4/8	16 7/8	4	4	Hillsdale County	MI	William C. Marquardt	2004	19774
138 5/8	23 6/8	23 5/8	16 5/8	4	4	Waushara County	WI	Jason A. Hupf	2004	19774
138 5/8	24 1/8	24 3/8	19 1/8	5	5	Hancock County	OH	Todd Noirot	2004	19774
138 5/8	20 7/8	21 3/8	15 2/8	6	6	McCulloch County	TX	Eddy Wathen	2005	19774
*138 5/8	21 0/8	22 4/8	18 5/8	5	5	Randall County	TX	Brandon Ray	2005	19774
138 5/8	24 2/8	24 1/8	18 0/8	7	5	Branch County	MI	Keith Dirschell	2005	19774
138 5/8	23 0/8	22 7/8	15 6/8	6	5	Stutsman County	ND	Jon Sjostrom	2005	19774
*138 5/8	21 5/8	20 6/8	15 2/8	5	6	Hubbard County	MN	Bradley F. Nei	2005	19774
138 5/8	21 1/8	20 6/8	16 4/8	7	5	Shawano County	WI	Erik Wolff	2005	19774
*138 5/8	24 7/8	25 1/8	19 0/8	7	5	Buffalo County	WI	Sarah Schubert	2005	19774
*138 5/8	22 3/8	22 3/8	17 5/8	5	6	Wyandot County	OH	Scott Mouser	2005	19774
138 5/8	22 6/8	22 4/8	16 1/8	5	6	Texas County	MO	Jeff Hansford	2006	19774
*138 5/8	22 2/8	21 0/8	12 7/8	5	5	Stanton County	NE	Jeff Allen	2006	19774
*138 5/8	23 3/8	23 7/8	15 5/8	5	5	Tuscarawas County	OH	Timothy W. Sherman	2006	19774
138 5/8	23 0/8	24 1/8	17 7/8	5	5	Madison County	MS	Parker Stubbs	2006	19774
138 5/8	21 0/8	20 2/8	15 7/8	6	5	Montgomery County	IA	Michael Fuller	2006	19774
138 5/8	22 1/8	22 2/8	18 5/8	5	5	St. Clair County	MI	Gary J. Staniec	2006	19774
*138 5/8	23 2/8	23 0/8	19 1/8	5	4	Kane County	IL	William Kinsinger	2007	19774
*138 5/8	24 3/8	23 4/8	19 4/8	6	7	Dane County	WI	John Miller	2007	19774
138 5/8	23 0/8	21 4/8	16 0/8	5	7	Dodge County	WI	Taylor M. Young	2008	19774
138 5/8	23 4/8	23 4/8	17 7/8	4	4	Wilson County	KS	Gary Greve	2008	19774
*138 5/8	22 6/8	23 3/8	18 3/8	6	6	Iowa County	WI	Ryan F. Lipska	2008	19774
138 5/8	21 2/8	21 6/8	17 5/8	5	5	St. Clair County	MO	Jerry L. Tichenor	2008	19774
*138 5/8	23 0/8	23 6/8	18 2/8	5	4	Allamakee County	IA	Bryon Anderson	2008	19774
138 5/8	24 2/8	23 5/8	20 1/8	4	4	Jasper County	IL	Kent Schafer	2008	19774
138 5/8	20 2/8	19 6/8	15 5/8	7	7	Desha County	AR	Chris Weast	2008	19774
*138 5/8	25 3/8	25 1/8	18 7/8	6	5	Ozaukee County	WI	Jeremy Dandy	2009	19774
*138 5/8	25 4/8	25 5/8	18 2/8	6	6	Oconee County	GA	Matthew D. Ulmer	2009	19774
*138 5/8	25 2/8	24 7/8	18 7/8	4	4	Phelps County	MO	Clarence J. Taylor	2009	19774
138 5/8	21 7/8	22 0/8	17 3/8	4	4	Polk County	WI	Jason Mork	2009	19774
*138 5/8	23 6/8	22 1/8	19 3/8	4	6	Madison County	IA	Travis Nace	2009	19774
138 5/8	24 4/8	24 1/8	19 1/8	7	5	Pepin County	WI	Jerre Lerum	2009	19774
138 5/8	24 0/8	23 4/8	17 5/8	4	4	Wood County	WI	Roger Hansen	2009	19774
138 5/8	22 0/8	22 5/8	18 3/8	4	4	Adams County	IL	Jim Moran	2009	19774
*138 5/8	20 0/8	19 5/8	13 7/8	5	5	Shawano County	WI	Alex Brauer	2010	19774
*138 5/8	21 6/8	20 4/8	22 2/8	5	7	Becker County	MN	Paul Okeson	2010	19774
*138 5/8	22 4/8	22 3/8	17 5/8	4	4	Elkhart County	IN	Loren J. Chupp	2010	19774
138 4/8	25 1/8	25 0/8	20 0/8	5	5	Hand County	SD	Kevin Bertsch	2001	19941
138 4/8	21 5/8	22 4/8	17 6/8	5	5	Cattaraugus County	NY	David W. Bobseine	2003	19941
138 4/8	23 3/8	23 3/8	17 6/8	4	4	Stark County	ND	Terry Buechler	2004	19941
138 4/8	24 0/8	23 0/8	14 4/8	5	6	Pulaski County	KY	Douglas Bray	2004	19941
*138 4/8	20 7/8	20 2/8	15 0/8	4	4	Saunders County	NE	Chris Divis	2004	19941
*138 4/8	23 5/8	22 5/8	18 6/8	4	4	Claiborne County	MS	Mike Eubanks	2004	19941
138 4/8	23 5/8	23 5/8	15 2/8	4	4	Eau Claire County	WI	Jeff Henning	2004	19941
138 4/8	22 1/8	22 7/8	16 5/8	6	6	Knox County	MO	Mike Zimmerman	2004	19941
138 4/8	24 6/8	23 4/8	15 1/8	6	5	Marathon County	WI	Roger Wendorf	2004	19941
138 4/8	25 0/8	23 4/8	17 0/8	5	5	Washington County	WI	Donald M. Olson	2004	19941
138 4/8	24 0/8	24 0/8	19 4/8	4	4	Bucks County	PA	Guy Kunsman	2004	19941
138 4/8	22 4/8	22 7/8	19 2/8	5	5	Macon County	GA	David Campbell	2004	19941
*138 4/8	22 7/8	22 2/8	16 5/8	5	5	Wright County	IA	Jason Campbell	2004	19941
138 4/8	23 0/8	23 4/8	21 0/8	5	6	Bergen County	NJ	Mark Spoto	2004	19941
138 4/8	23 0/8	23 1/8	16 0/8	7	6	Waupaca County	WI	Scott J. Moeller	2004	19941
138 4/8	24 2/8	24 1/8	18 6/8	5	5	Winnebago County	IL	Daniel De Mus	2005	19941
138 4/8	21 1/8	22 2/8	19 4/8	6	6	Buffalo County	WI	Brandon Stenseth	2005	19941
138 4/8	23 2/8	23 3/8	15 0/8	4	6	Cowley County	KS	Gary L. Gray	2005	19941
138 4/8	23 5/8	22 1/8	16 6/8	5	5	Green Lake County	WI	Luke Ladwig	2006	19941
138 4/8	23 1/8	23 0/8	23 0/8	6	6	Itasca County	MN	Scott J. Elich	2006	19941
138 4/8	22 5/8	22 0/8	17 6/8	4	5	Hopkins County	KY	Daniel Meador	2006	19941
138 4/8	24 6/8	23 5/8	19 3/8	6	6	Bucks County	PA	Bill Worrell	2006	19941
138 4/8	25 1/8	24 1/8	17 7/8	5	7	Dane County	WI	Kevin Stoll	2006	19941
*138 4/8	23 2/8	22 1/8	15 5/8	6	6	Genesee County	NY	Thomas Chapell	2006	19941

542

WHITETAIL DEER (TYPICAL ANTLERS)

Minimum Score 125   Continued

SCORE	LENGTH OF R MAIN BEAM L	INSIDE SPREAD	NUMBER OF R POINTS L	AREA	STATE/ PROVINCE	HUNTER'S NAME	DATE	RANK
138 4/8	23 2/8 24 6/8	18 4/8	5 5	Middlesex	ONT	Matthieu Hill	2006	19941
*138 4/8	24 6/8 24 5/8	20 2/8	4 4	Butler County	PA	Matt Drake	2006	19941
138 4/8	23 5/8 24 0/8	20 7/8	4 5	Mercer County	PA	Benjamin Patterson	2006	19941
*138 4/8	24 2/8 24 4/8	20 6/8	4 5	Outagamie County	WI	Charles R. Meltz	2007	19941
138 4/8	24 4/8 25 0/8	20 2/8	5 5	Mercer County	PA	Nick Sernik	2007	19941
138 4/8	23 1/8 23 4/8	16 0/8	5 5	Appanoose County	IA	Brad Sabin	2007	19941
*138 4/8	22 4/8 22 3/8	19 2/8	5 5	Buffalo County	WI	Walt Legge	2007	19941
138 4/8	21 0/8 21 4/8	16 2/8	6 6	Trempealeau County	WI	Tom Kloss	2007	19941
*138 4/8	24 6/8 25 0/8	17 6/8	3 4	Guernsey County	OH	Kenneth Larew	2007	19941
*138 4/8	25 0/8 25 7/8	18 6/8	6 6	Hancock County	IL	Scott R. Eggert	2007	19941
138 4/8	21 7/8 22 7/8	20 4/8	5 4	De Kalb County	IN	Benjamin S. Collier	2007	19941
*138 4/8	22 6/8 23 6/8	20 0/8	4 5	Pepin County	WI	Danny W. Burich	2008	19941
*138 4/8	24 2/8 24 1/8	17 6/8	4 5	Washtenaw County	MI	Michael Troiani	2008	19941
138 4/8	23 1/8 22 5/8	17 5/8	7 5	York County	PA	Steward J. Heikes, Jr.	2008	19941
*138 4/8	24 2/8 24 3/8	15 2/8	5 5	Polk County	IA	Brett L. Hendrickson	2009	19941
*138 4/8	20 7/8 22 3/8	20 2/8	5 5	Preble County	OH	Jennifer A. Olsen	2009	19941
138 4/8	23 3/8 24 1/8	20 4/8	4 5	Lancaster County	NE	Ray Heusinkvelt	2009	19941
138 4/8	20 4/8 21 3/8	14 0/8	6 8	Yankton County	SD	Kyle Hochstein	2009	19941
138 4/8	23 2/8 23 1/8	18 4/8	5 5	Pratt County	KS	Ron McCorkell	2009	19941
138 4/8	22 0/8 21 7/8	19 0/8	5 4	Laclede County	MO	Justin Wasmer	2009	19941
138 4/8	23 4/8 23 5/8	17 4/8	4 4	Edwards County	IL	Samuel Andrew Thompson	2009	19941
*138 4/8	22 2/8 21 5/8	16 4/8	5 5	Chautauqua County	KS	Tony Shrum	2009	19941
138 3/8	24 5/8 24 5/8	16 1/8	4 4	Winona County	MN	Don Gregerson	1998	20093
*138 3/8	22 4/8 21 0/8	17 0/8	7 8	Mason County	IL	Tad Yetter	1998	20093
*138 3/8	23 6/8 22 1/8	18 3/8	7 6	Clark County	IL	Mark Kezler	2002	20093
138 3/8	21 7/8 22 6/8	15 0/8	6 6	Marquette County	WI	Dennis Kaebisch	2003	20093
*138 3/8	23 0/8 25 6/8	18 5/8	4 4	New Castle County	DE	Nicky Ferrara	2003	20093
138 3/8	23 6/8 24 0/8	16 4/8	10 8	Allamakee County	IA	James Chizek	2003	20093
138 3/8	23 0/8 23 0/8	20 1/8	5 4	Marion County	IA	Randy Des Camps	2003	20093
138 3/8	24 0/8 23 7/8	16 5/8	6 6	Moultrie County	IL	Bret Guin	2004	20093
138 3/8	22 0/8 21 6/8	20 1/8	4 4	Fillmore County	MN	Jim Dequaine	2004	20093
138 3/8	23 0/8 23 0/8	15 4/8	6 5	Pulaski County	KY	Gary Epperson	2004	20093
138 3/8	24 5/8 24 7/8	17 1/8	5 4	Kalamazoo County	MI	Corey Viegelahn	2004	20093
138 3/8	23 7/8 24 0/8	17 5/8	5 5	Racine County	WI	Jason Kuschewski	2005	20093
138 3/8	23 3/8 25 3/8	16 3/8	5 4	Dooly County	GA	Wayne Howell	2005	20093
138 3/8	22 7/8 23 3/8	17 3/8	7 6	Allen County	IN	Pete M. Felkner	2005	20093
138 3/8	22 5/8 22 7/8	16 3/8	5 5	Pike County	IL	Brad Stamp	2005	20093
138 3/8	23 3/8 24 0/8	19 3/8	6 5	Buffalo County	WI	Benjaman M. Parker	2005	20093
*138 3/8	23 5/8 24 0/8	15 5/8	5 5	Marion County	KY	Jude Buckman	2005	20093
*138 3/8	22 5/8 24 3/8	18 7/8	4 6	Greene County	IN	Gary Graves	2005	20093
138 3/8	26 3/8 23 5/8	18 4/8	5 5	Washtenaw County	MI	Chris D. Denning	2005	20093
138 3/8	22 5/8 21 6/8	17 7/8	6 5	Washington County	IL	Carl H. Komora	2005	20093
*138 3/8	23 6/8 21 7/8	16 1/8	6 5	Hennepin County	MN	Jason Tietz	2006	20093
138 3/8	23 2/8 24 3/8	19 5/8	4 4	Hopkins County	KY	Kelly N. Smith	2006	20093
138 3/8	21 7/8 22 0/8	14 7/8	5 5	Barry County	MI	Robert C. McKay	2006	20093
138 3/8	24 5/8 24 3/8	16 7/8	6 5	Allegheny County	PA	John R. DeRoss	2006	20093
138 3/8	21 2/8 21 5/8	13 7/8	5 5	Trinity County	TX	Richard Warner	2006	20093
138 3/8	25 0/8 24 5/8	19 7/8	4 4	Oneida County	WI	John W. Huebner	2006	20093
*138 3/8	21 0/8 20 7/8	17 3/8	6 5	Rusk County	WI	Justin Marks	2006	20093
*138 3/8	21 5/8 22 1/8	15 6/8	5 4	Pike County	MO	David H. Dillon, Jr.	2006	20093
*138 3/8	20 6/8 21 4/8	17 7/8	5 7	Tioga County	PA	Gary D. Krieger	2006	20093
138 3/8	21 3/8 22 2/8	16 3/8	4 5	Linn County	MO	Marc Fagen	2006	20093
138 3/8	22 0/8 21 1/8	14 3/8	5 5	Logan County	KS	James Austin	2006	20093
138 3/8	22 2/8 23 4/8	20 1/8	6 5	Monona County	IA	David Albers	2006	20093
138 3/8	23 0/8 25 1/8	17 5/8	5 5	Peoria County	IL	Larry T. Schmitt	2006	20093
138 3/8	25 0/8 24 6/8	21 2/8	5 6	Prince Georges County	MD	Bruce Chase	2007	20093
*138 3/8	25 0/8 25 2/8	18 7/8	4 4	Dickinson County	KS	Nicholas Simon	2007	20093
*138 3/8	21 6/8 22 3/8	15 5/8	5 5	Limestone County	AL	Richard Brock	2007	20093
138 3/8	21 5/8 22 3/8	17 3/8	5 5	Mercer County	PA	Raymond P. Mozes	2007	20093
138 3/8	22 0/8 21 5/8	18 3/8	4 4	Beaver County	PA	Anthony Presutti	2007	20093
138 3/8	22 6/8 23 0/8	18 5/8	4 4	Jackson County	MI	Lawrence B. Avison III	2007	20093
138 3/8	21 0/8 20 7/8	16 4/8	6 5	Yankton County	SD	Joe Steiner	2007	20093
138 3/8	22 0/8 23 3/8	18 3/8	4 4	Genesee County	MI	Kevin M. Brown	2007	20093
*138 3/8	22 6/8 22 0/8	17 2/8	6 8	Washington County	NE	Scott Opfer	2007	20093
*138 3/8	22 5/8 22 1/8	17 1/8	5 5	Walworth County	WI	Brian Kilpin	2007	20093
138 3/8	22 6/8 23 6/8	14 5/8	5 5	Fillmore County	MN	David E. Kingsley	2007	20093
138 3/8	21 6/8 21 6/8	18 2/8	6 6	Wood County	WI	Harry Jonas	2007	20093
*138 3/8	21 1/8 21 3/8	14 1/8	6 5	Lawrence County	SD	Daniel P. Axlund	2008	20093
*138 3/8	23 3/8 23 3/8	19 7/8	4 5	Worcester County	MA	Jamie Chumsae	2008	20093
138 3/8	22 5/8 22 6/8	17 7/8	5 5	Burke County	ND	Kyle Hass	2008	20093
*138 3/8	24 3/8 25 4/8	19 1/8	4 4	Champaign County	OH	Ryan Maurice	2008	20093
*138 3/8	22 3/8 22 3/8	16 3/8	4 5	Meeker County	MN	Jason Schwartz	2008	20093
138 3/8	23 5/8 24 5/8	18 1/8	4 5	Adams County	WI	Tom Baggs	2008	20093
138 3/8	23 0/8 23 4/8	21 5/8	7 5	Jefferson County	MO	Larry A. Stolle	2008	20093
*138 3/8	20 1/8 19 6/8	16 3/8	5 5	Meade County	SD	Chad Stolicker	2008	20093
138 3/8	24 0/8 24 2/8	19 2/8	5 5	Stoddard County	MO	Dolan Pendarvis	2008	20093
*138 3/8	20 2/8 20 4/8	16 3/8	5 5	Ellis County	KS	Drew McCartney	2009	20093
*138 3/8	23 0/8 22 6/8	21 5/8	5 4	Lincoln County	KS	Ron Kosmala	2009	20093
138 3/8	22 4/8 22 3/8	16 7/8	7 5	Elkhart County	IN	David K. Allison	2009	20093
*138 3/8	23 1/8 22 0/8	18 7/8	5 6	Dane County	WI	Leonard Jung	2009	20093
138 3/8	21 1/8 20 6/8	17 0/8	6 6	Lancaster County	NE	Clarence Poteet	2009	20093
138 3/8	25 2/8 22 6/8	17 3/8	4 4	Leavenworth County	KS	Charles K. Clayborn	2009	20093
*138 3/8	22 4/8 22 1/8	17 4/8	6 7	Parke County	IN	Brannon Fowler	2009	20093
138 3/8	22 3/8 22 4/8	15 5/8	5 5	Juneau County	WI	Phillip R. Pahlke	2009	20093
*138 3/8	21 5/8 20 0/8	16 3/8	5 5	Clayton County	IA	Brian Kluesner	2009	20093
*138 3/8	23 0/8 22 1/8	17 2/8	5 6	Allegan County	MI	John M. Luscomb	2009	20093
138 3/8	25 0/8 23 6/8	19 3/8	5 4	Worcester County	MD	Christopher J. Jordan	2009	20093
138 3/8	19 5/8 20 2/8	17 7/8	5 5	Greene County	PA	Ronald R. Whipkey	2010	20093
138 2/8	23 0/8 21 2/8	15 2/8	5 5	Jasper County	IL	Travis Gephart	2001	20287
138 2/8	22 6/8 23 7/8	19 0/8	5 5	Teton County	MT	Shanun Rammell	2002	20287
*138 2/8	24 1/8 22 2/8	15 4/8	5 5	Edmonson County	KY	Jim Whobrey	2002	20287
138 2/8	22 7/8 23 7/8	19 2/8	5 4	Kalamazoo County	MI	Paul Thrasher	2003	20287
138 2/8	21 5/8 22 6/8	20 0/8	6 6	Pike County	IL	Frank Vannell	2003	20287
138 2/8	24 0/8 24 6/8	17 2/8	4 4	Kleberg County	TX	Christopher M. Crain	2003	20287
*138 2/8	22 2/8 22 1/8	17 6/8	6 7	Winnebago County	IA	John R. Carlson	2004	20287

Deer entries below 141 0/8, that appeared in the 6th Edition, are not included here, but are included on the accompanying CD (see page 119), and also in the Club's Records Archives.

543

WHITETAIL DEER (TYPICAL ANTLERS)

Minimum Score 125 — Continued

SCORE	LENGTH OF R MAIN BEAM L	INSIDE SPREAD	NUMBER OF R POINTS L	AREA	STATE/ PROVINCE	HUNTER'S NAME	DATE	RANK
138 2/8	24 0/8 23 6/8	17 4/8	4 5	Sauk County	WI	David R. Melvin	2004	20287
*138 2/8	23 5/8 24 0/8	15 6/8	4 4	Lawrence County	IL	Michael Ray Roper	2004	20287
138 2/8	25 0/8 24 3/8	16 6/8	5 5	Waukesha County	WI	Jay Trudell	2005	20287
138 2/8	23 0/8 22 7/8	16 3/8	6 5	Portage County	WI	Adam Schroer	2005	20287
138 2/8	21 1/8 22 2/8	18 4/8	5 6	Floyd County	IA	Robert Webb	2005	20287
138 2/8	21 6/8 21 5/8	16 0/8	5 5	Vernon County	WI	Andrew J. Blum	2005	20287
*138 2/8	20 5/8 20 6/8	16 1/8	6 6	Dane County	WI	Joshua Mersberger	2005	20287
138 2/8	22 1/8 22 2/8	16 6/8	5 5	Madison County	MO	Doug Rehkop	2005	20287
*138 2/8	20 0/8 21 2/8	18 0/8	5 5	Christian County	KY	Robert E. Morse III	2005	20287
138 2/8	24 5/8 25 3/8	19 4/8	6 6	Floyd County	IA	Frank Kelly	2005	20287
*138 2/8	22 3/8 22 4/8	16 0/8	5 6	Outagamie County	WI	Albert J. Ruys	2006	20287
138 2/8	22 1/8 22 4/8	18 0/8	5 6	Henderson County	KY	Clint Girten	2006	20287
138 2/8	25 6/8 24 5/8	17 4/8	4 4	Logan County	OH	Edward Zirkle, Jr.	2006	20287
138 2/8	22 5/8 22 2/8	20 4/8	6 5	Plymouth County	IA	Scott H. Boylan	2006	20287
138 2/8	24 6/8 25 0/8	17 4/8	4 4	Marquette County	WI	Troy Huffman	2006	20287
138 2/8	23 4/8 23 3/8	19 4/8	5 4	Taylor County	IA	Todd Tobin	2006	20287
138 2/8	20 2/8 20 3/8	16 0/8	5 5	Bayfield County	WI	Dale Nixon	2006	20287
138 2/8	23 4/8 24 0/8	18 6/8	4 4	Wood County	TX	Cody Hunt	2006	20287
138 2/8	22 4/8 21 6/8	17 4/8	8 8	Dodge County	WI	Steve Beske	2007	20287
138 2/8	21 5/8 21 6/8	16 0/8	6 5	Newton County	IN	David Ramirez	2007	20287
138 2/8	20 7/8 20 5/8	15 2/8	5 5	Dodge County	WI	Gerald W. Backhaus	2007	20287
138 2/8	23 2/8 23 1/8	18 6/8	4 4	Fillmore County	MN	Jason Churchill	2007	20287
138 2/8	22 1/8 22 6/8	18 2/8	5 5	Ashland County	OH	Jimmy Hemp	2007	20287
138 2/8	22 1/8 22 0/8	17 6/8	5 5	Armstrong County	PA	Pressley R. Shearer	2007	20287
138 2/8	23 4/8 22 7/8	16 4/8	5 5	Peoria County	IL	Chris Noonen	2007	20287
*138 2/8	23 4/8 21 6/8	17 2/8	4 4	Adams County	WI	Bruce Scheehle	2007	20287
138 2/8	25 0/8 25 0/8	20 4/8	4 5	Dearborn County	IN	Casey Roberts	2008	20287
138 2/8	23 6/8 23 0/8	17 4/8	4 4	Boyd County	KY	Greg Wallace	2008	20287
*138 2/8	22 5/8 23 4/8	19 2/8	5 5	Morrison County	MN	Eric Craine	2008	20287
138 2/8	22 3/8 22 2/8	16 2/8	4 4	Lake County	IL	Bill J. Meyer III	2008	20287
*138 2/8	21 5/8 22 3/8	18 0/8	5 5	Shelby County	IL	Luke Wasson	2008	20287
138 2/8	19 5/8 22 0/8	20 2/8	5 5	Seneca County	NY	Roger J. Smith, Sr.	2008	20287
*138 2/8	23 7/8 24 2/8	19 5/8	7 5	Grant County	WI	Josh Miller	2008	20287
*138 2/8	22 3/8 23 2/8	17 6/8	4 4	Shelby County	IN	Anthony M. Bordenkecher	2008	20287
138 2/8	21 2/8 21 2/8	20 0/8	5 5	Hunterdon County	NJ	Gary W. Kenthack	2008	20287
138 2/8	22 6/8 22 5/8	17 4/8	5 5	Wayne County	IA	Dave Shuey	2008	20287
*138 2/8	25 5/8 23 7/8	18 2/8	5 4	Walworth County	WI	Tim Cates	2009	20287
138 2/8	23 3/8 24 5/8	19 5/8	5 7	Clayton County	IA	Gerald E. Hunter	2009	20287
*138 2/8	20 1/8 20 3/8	16 0/8	5 5	Jefferson County	IN	Scott Rauch	2009	20287
138 2/8	24 4/8 22 3/8	20 2/8	5 6	Fulton County	PA	William C. Dovey, Jr.	2009	20287
138 2/8	23 1/8 22 5/8	18 0/8	5 5	Crawford County	PA	Dwayne Trimble	2009	20287
*138 2/8	21 6/8 22 0/8	19 0/8	6 6	Monona County	IA	Evan Bruhn	2009	20287
138 2/8	22 7/8 22 4/8	17 3/8	5 6	Polk County	WI	Ron Peterson	2010	20287
*138 1/8	22 3/8 23 4/8	20 7/8	5 5	Yorkton	SAS	Shawn Frankfurt	2000	20463
138 1/8	25 2/8 24 6/8	22 3/8	5 6	Buffalo County	WI	Bryan Tamke	2003	20463
138 1/8	23 6/8 24 0/8	19 0/8	5 5	Cumberland County	PA	Robert L. Bailey, Jr.	2003	20463
138 1/8	26 3/8 25 4/8	18 7/8	5 5	Buffalo County	WI	Dave Fredrickson	2003	20463
138 1/8	23 7/8 23 3/8	17 2/8	8 6	Marshall County	IN	Richard D. Murray, Jr.	2004	20463
138 1/8	22 2/8 22 6/8	19 4/8	5 5	Bristol County	MA	Steven Rogers	2004	20463
138 1/8	24 5/8 25 0/8	17 4/8	4 5	Columbia County	WI	Wayne A. Buckley	2004	20463
*138 1/8	21 3/8 22 1/8	18 7/8	5 5	Clark County	IL	Steve L. Hobbs	2004	20463
138 1/8	25 4/8 25 3/8	16 7/8	5 5	Pike County	IL	Barron Naar	2004	20463
138 1/8	23 1/8 22 7/8	16 3/8	5 4	La Crosse County	WI	Eric Jandro	2004	20463
138 1/8	22 7/8 22 5/8	17 3/8	6 6	Jefferson County	WI	Chad Montalbano	2004	20463
138 1/8	24 6/8 25 4/8	18 2/8	3 5	Van Buren County	IA	Joel Hoenk	2004	20463
*138 1/8	23 0/8 23 4/8	14 5/8	5 5	Chautauqua County	NY	Mark Irlbacher	2004	20463
*138 1/8	24 1/8 24 5/8	14 3/8	4 4	Hampshire County	MA	Charles Boissonneault	2004	20463
138 1/8	22 1/8 22 0/8	14 1/8	5 4	Elk County	KS	Mike Worrell	2004	20463
138 1/8	23 7/8 23 4/8	19 0/8	4 5	Knox County	IL	Gary Baranowski	2004	20463
138 1/8	23 3/8 23 0/8	19 3/8	4 4	Ocean County	NJ	Brian A. Bock	2005	20463
138 1/8	22 4/8 23 0/8	18 1/8	5 5	Muskingum County	OH	Ryan Berry	2005	20463
138 1/8	24 1/8 24 1/8	16 3/8	5 4	Marathon County	WI	Jon Shuda	2005	20463
138 1/8	24 2/8 24 3/8	16 0/8	6 6	Schuyler County	MO	Ronnie Fallert	2005	20463
138 1/8	21 1/8 20 7/8	17 3/8	5 5	Huntington County	IN	Tyler Sprinkle	2005	20463
*138 1/8	23 5/8 23 2/8	20 0/8	5 5	Adams County	IL	Tim Walmsley	2005	20463
138 1/8	22 6/8 23 2/8	16 4/8	6 5	Vermilion County	IL	Andy Pierce	2005	20463
138 1/8	21 2/8 21 3/8	18 5/8	4 5	Monona County	IA	J. Mark Lary	2005	20463
138 1/8	23 7/8 23 5/8	15 7/8	6 6	Calhoun County	IL	Aaron Miller	2005	20463
*138 1/8	21 4/8 20 7/8	17 4/8	6 6	Palo Alto County	IA	Leo James Moser	2005	20463
138 1/8	23 2/8 22 3/8	17 3/8	4 4	Republic County	KS	Jeremy Heitman	2005	20463
*138 1/8	25 2/8 23 4/8	23 1/8	4 4	Lake County	IL	John F. Kahon III	2006	20463
138 1/8	21 6/8 21 5/8	18 7/8	5 4	Auglaize County	OH	Scott Grant	2006	20463
138 1/8	22 0/8 21 2/8	16 1/8	5 5	Clark County	IL	G. Douglas McPherson	2006	20463
*138 1/8	20 1/8 20 2/8	18 3/8	5 5	Hancock County	IL	Michael C. Galla	2006	20463
*138 1/8	21 3/8 22 5/8	21 6/8	6 6	Will County	IL	Blair E. Konczal	2006	20463
138 1/8	21 7/8 21 6/8	16 5/8	5 5	Dodge County	MN	Bill Archer	2006	20463
138 1/8	24 6/8 25 7/8	16 7/8	5 5	Fulton County	IL	Jeff Pals	2006	20463
138 1/8	22 1/8 23 0/8	19 5/8	5 5	Fond du Lac County	WI	Jim Wesenberg	2006	20463
138 1/8	21 6/8 22 0/8	18 3/8	5 6	Harford County	MD	Ed Koehnlein III	2006	20463
138 1/8	20 2/8 20 2/8	16 1/8	5 5	Callaway County	MO	Joseph R. Lang	2006	20463
138 1/8	21 0/8 23 3/8	16 6/8	7 5	Calhoun County	MI	Phillip T. Bennett	2006	20463
*138 1/8	20 1/8 19 6/8	17 3/8	5 5	Nodaway County	MO	Dave Messner	2006	20463
138 1/8	23 0/8 23 1/8	16 6/8	6 5	Taylor County	WI	Dale G. Lee	2007	20463
*138 1/8	23 4/8 25 0/8	19 0/8	6 7	Schuylkill County	PA	William J. Shiner	2007	20463
138 1/8	20 6/8 20 6/8	17 4/8	5 7	Iowa County	WI	Benjamin D. Henner	2007	20463
*138 1/8	23 5/8 23 6/8	18 2/8	5 5	Kenosha County	WI	Joseph McHugh	2007	20463
138 1/8	22 5/8 22 2/8	16 4/8	4 5	Green County	WI	Cody D. Williams	2007	20463
*138 1/8	23 3/8 23 4/8	17 5/8	5 5	Hopkins County	KY	Daniel Meador	2007	20463
*138 1/8	22 1/8 22 5/8	16 1/8	4 4	Brown County	IL	Ryan Hogenmiller	2007	20463
138 1/8	22 6/8 22 0/8	17 5/8	6 5	Grand Forks County	ND	John Brewinski	2008	20463
138 1/8	24 2/8 23 4/8	17 4/8	6 6	Sullivan County	MO	Justin A. Johnson	2008	20463
*138 1/8	21 0/8 21 2/8	15 7/8	5 6	Gage County	NE	Chad L. Morgan	2008	20463
*138 1/8	20 7/8 19 2/8	13 3/8	6 6	Marion County	MO	Louis R. Garrett	2008	20463
*138 1/8	24 1/8 24 2/8	19 1/8	5 4	Stark County	OH	David B. Hodgekin	2008	20463
*138 1/8	22 3/8 22 6/8	20 1/8	7 6	Carroll County	OH	Michael L. Parrish	2008	20463

WHITETAIL DEER (TYPICAL ANTLERS)

Minimum Score 125   Continued

SCORE	LENGTH OF MAIN BEAM R	LENGTH OF MAIN BEAM L	INSIDE SPREAD	NUMBER OF POINTS R	NUMBER OF POINTS L	AREA	STATE/ PROVINCE	HUNTER'S NAME	DATE	RANK
138 1/8	20 6/8	20 6/8	20 0/8	7	5	Columbia County	WI	Norbert Wipperfurth	2009	20463
138 1/8	23 4/8	22 2/8	16 1/8	5	5	Pulaski County	MO	Ken Morgan	2009	20463
*138 1/8	21 6/8	21 6/8	15 1/8	5	5	Manitowoc County	WI	Max LeClair	2009	20463
138 1/8	22 2/8	22 1/8	18 7/8	5	4	Cass County	ND	Darrell Poll	2009	20463
138 1/8	22 4/8	21 6/8	18 1/8	5	5	Peoria County	IL	Ross Edwards	2009	20463
*138 1/8	22 5/8	22 3/8	17 3/8	6	5	Pulaski County	MO	Benjamin N. Allen	2009	20463
138 1/8	23 1/8	22 4/8	16 1/8	4	5	Harvey County	KS	John O. Wiebe	2009	20463
138 1/8	20 3/8	21 2/8	15 7/8	5	5	Brown County	WI	Dennis Flavion	2009	20463
*138 1/8	19 3/8	20 2/8	14 4/8	6	6	Pennington County	SD	Paul E. Nelson	2010	20463
138 0/8	23 6/8	19 3/8	19 2/8	5	5	Monroe County	NY	Brad Nanna	2001	20645
138 0/8	23 2/8	23 7/8	18 4/8	6	7	Cedar County	IA	Dewey Behrle	2003	20645
138 0/8	23 3/8	23 2/8	17 4/8	5	5	Burnett County	WI	Daniel Ellie	2003	20645
*138 0/8	23 0/8	22 4/8	21 0/8	4	4	Peoria County	IL	Jeremy Etnyre	2004	20645
138 0/8	21 6/8	21 7/8	17 1/8	6	5	Fillmore County	MN	John Marzolf	2004	20645
138 0/8	24 1/8	23 3/8	16 0/8	4	4	La Salle County	IL	Todd J. Yeager	2004	20645
138 0/8	20 5/8	21 3/8	14 2/8	5	5	Pike County	IL	Scott DePompe	2004	20645
138 0/8	25 0/8	25 1/8	18 2/8	4	4	Allegan County	MI	Brian Veen	2004	20645
138 0/8	22 0/8	22 4/8	15 4/8	5	5	Jackson County	MO	Ryan Rieder	2004	20645
138 0/8	22 5/8	22 5/8	20 0/8	4	4	McHenry County	IL	Brad Wiehr	2004	20645
138 0/8	23 0/8	22 3/8	24 0/8	4	4	Bow River	ALB	Cam T. Foss	2004	20645
138 0/8	24 0/8	23 5/8	17 2/8	5	4	Lake County	IL	Steven Hysell	2004	20645
*138 0/8	23 1/8	23 2/8	16 5/8	6	4	Pike County	IL	Kevin Tinsley	2005	20645
138 0/8	21 3/8	21 2/8	15 6/8	5	6	Buffalo County	WI	Larry Carlson	2005	20645
138 0/8	22 0/8	21 1/8	16 6/8	5	5	Pottawatomie County	KS	Matthew E. Fiala	2005	20645
*138 0/8	22 7/8	22 4/8	15 0/8	5	5	Scioto County	OH	David B. Phillips	2005	20645
*138 0/8	20 6/8	20 6/8	15 4/8	5	5	St. Louis County	MN	Bradley L. Salo	2005	20645
138 0/8	21 7/8	23 0/8	16 2/8	5	5	St. Joseph County	IN	Rodney A. Lowry	2005	20645
138 0/8	22 6/8	22 4/8	17 4/8	5	4	Buffalo County	WI	Greg Heiman	2005	20645
138 0/8	22 4/8	21 7/8	15 6/8	5	5	Lucas County	IA	Kevin Foltz	2005	20645
138 0/8	23 2/8	22 4/8	19 6/8	4	4	Richland County	WI	Adam Kirschbaum	2005	20645
138 0/8	23 1/8	22 5/8	15 6/8	6	4	Washington County	WI	James Van Roo	2005	20645
138 0/8	18 7/8	19 4/8	14 4/8	5	5	Vinton County	OH	James D. Davis	2005	20645
*138 0/8	21 1/8	20 6/8	17 2/8	4	5	Polk County	WI	Jack G. Fleming	2005	20645
138 0/8	25 0/8	24 5/8	19 6/8	4	4	Somerset County	NJ	William J. Hutnik	2005	20645
138 0/8	24 1/8	23 5/8	14 6/8	6	5	Outagamie County	WI	Jacob A. Smith	2005	20645
138 0/8	22 1/8	22 1/8	16 2/8	5	5	Buffalo County	WI	Jeff Moris	2005	20645
138 0/8	22 0/8	22 4/8	15 6/8	5	5	Lamoure County	ND	Adam Peterson	2005	20645
*138 0/8	23 1/8	23 5/8	17 4/8	5	6	Burleigh County	ND	Ben Buntrock	2006	20645
138 0/8	20 5/8	20 0/8	16 7/8	5	6	Coleman County	TX	Danny Mitcham	2006	20645
138 0/8	22 4/8	22 7/8	18 4/8	4	4	Adams County	IL	Beatrice J. Walmsley	2006	20645
*138 0/8	21 3/8	21 0/8	15 4/8	5	6	Pike County	MO	Scott Corley	2006	20645
*138 0/8	22 0/8	21 4/8	17 2/8	6	7	Hanson County	SD	Brian Hellman	2006	20645
138 0/8	23 4/8	23 6/8	19 0/8	4	5	Oconto County	WI	Gustav A. Otto	2006	20645
138 0/8	21 2/8	21 6/8	17 0/8	5	5	Allamakee County	IA	Brian Wisinski	2006	20645
138 0/8	20 4/8	20 7/8	17 6/8	5	4	Pope County	IL	Earl Allbright	2006	20645
138 0/8	25 6/8	23 4/8	16 4/8	5	5	Dunn County	WI	Jerold R. Olson	2006	20645
138 0/8	24 5/8	24 6/8	19 1/8	5	6	Rice County	KS	Shane Collier	2006	20645
138 0/8	23 0/8	22 4/8	16 2/8	5	5	Kent County	RI	Joyce Morris	2007	20645
138 0/8	21 0/8	21 2/8	15 4/8	6	5	Jo Daviess County	IL	Mike Feldermann	2007	20645
138 0/8	23 4/8	23 4/8	18 0/8	4	5	Green County	WI	Jeff E. McArdle	2007	20645
138 0/8	23 2/8	23 0/8	19 2/8	4	4	Genesee County	NY	John Schembra	2007	20645
*138 0/8	22 1/8	22 2/8	15 0/8	5	5	Jefferson County	IN	Chris E. Barron	2007	20645
*138 0/8	24 3/8	24 3/8	20 4/8	5	6	Carroll County	IN	Brian R. Whitus	2007	20645
*138 0/8	21 7/8	22 2/8	16 0/8	5	5	Harrison County	IN	Isaac Knable	2007	20645
138 0/8	25 6/8	24 0/8	17 2/8	4	4	Jefferson County	IL	Ed Knaus	2007	20645
138 0/8	23 0/8	21 2/8	16 4/8	6	5	Franklin County	IL	Dale McCain, Sr.	2007	20645
138 0/8	23 2/8	23 7/8	18 1/8	6	5	Owen County	IN	Brandon Mescall	2007	20645
138 0/8	25 0/8	22 4/8	16 6/8	5	5	Putnam County	MO	Chandlar Graham	2007	20645
*138 0/8	20 2/8	20 2/8	16 2/8	5	5	Lyon County	KS	Deidra Rattay	2007	20645
*138 0/8	24 4/8	23 4/8	19 3/8	7	6	Sarpy County	NE	Ray Turkle	2007	20645
138 0/8	22 6/8	22 7/8	17 2/8	5	5	Lycoming County	PA	James J. Jenzano	2008	20645
138 0/8	22 5/8	22 4/8	19 4/8	4	4	Jackson County	WI	Aaron D. Eberhardt	2008	20645
138 0/8	22 7/8	22 0/8	17 4/8	5	5	Gove County	KS	Brian May	2008	20645
138 0/8	20 7/8	21 3/8	17 0/8	5	5	White County	IN	Evan Martin	2008	20645
138 0/8	21 1/8	23 3/8	17 0/8	5	5	Delaware County	IN	Samuel J. Bales	2008	20645
138 0/8	21 7/8	22 1/8	19 0/8	4	4	Venango County	PA	Frank Carolas	2008	20645
138 0/8	21 4/8	21 6/8	15 0/8	5	5	Sauk County	WI	Darin Kuhnke	2008	20645
*138 0/8	20 2/8	21 5/8	17 4/8	5	6	Hamilton County	IL	John Harold Silvester	2008	20645
138 0/8	22 5/8	22 4/8	17 0/8	6	7	Clay County	AR	Brett McMillon	2008	20645
138 0/8	25 7/8	25 6/8	18 2/8	3	5	Calvert County	MD	Christopher Bartlett	2009	20645
138 0/8	22 4/8	22 1/8	16 7/8	6	4	Stearns County	MN	Steve Schaefer	2009	20645
*138 0/8	21 6/8	21 1/8	15 4/8	5	5	Rockdale County	GA	Nelson Garmon	2009	20645
138 0/8	21 5/8	22 2/8	16 6/8	6	6	Fulton County	IL	Jason A. Denton	2009	20645
138 0/8	23 4/8	22 6/8	16 2/8	7	6	Brooke County	WV	Travis Young	2009	20645
138 0/8	21 3/8	20 4/8	17 2/8	6	5	Archer County	TX	Jerry Bales	2009	20645
138 0/8	21 1/8	21 7/8	16 6/8	5	6	Peach County	GA	David Sams	2009	20645
*138 0/8	22 0/8	22 1/8	17 6/8	5	5	Berks County	PA	Brendan M. Fink	2009	20645
*138 0/8	23 4/8	24 3/8	18 4/8	6	5	Anne Arundel County	MD	Ken Huntzberry	2009	20645
138 0/8	22 6/8	21 2/8	18 2/8	4	4	Iowa County	WI	Nic Segebrecht	2010	20645
138 0/8	23 7/8	23 1/8	15 6/8	6	7	Washington County	PA	Dennis Gondella	2010	20645
*138 0/8	21 0/8	21 4/8	16 4/8	5	5	Indiana County	PA	Aaron J. Limrick	2010	20645
137 7/8	21 4/8	23 0/8	18 7/8	5	5	Grand Forks County	ND	Michael Whiteside	2000	20859
137 7/8	23 1/8	23 7/8	18 5/8	5	5	Saunders County	NE	David F. Jirovsky	2000	20859
137 7/8	22 6/8	22 3/8	13 4/8	6	5	Seminole County	OK	Tony Bevelhymer	2003	20859
137 7/8	23 0/8	21 7/8	22 3/8	6	6	Goodsoil	SAS	Richard Service	2003	20859
137 7/8	22 5/8	22 4/8	17 0/8	6	6	Martin County	IN	Brian Huber	2003	20859
137 7/8	23 6/8	22 4/8	18 1/8	4	4	Logan County	IL	Wesley Liesman	2003	20859
137 7/8	25 3/8	23 6/8	19 4/8	5	7	Boone County	IN	Terry J. Bohl	2004	20859
137 7/8	22 0/8	22 4/8	17 3/8	5	5	Cass County	IL	Brian Hafkey	2004	20859
*137 7/8	22 5/8	22 3/8	16 5/8	5	7	Wells County	ND	Darwin Manz	2005	20859
137 7/8	21 1/8	20 3/8	16 3/8	6	5	Beaverhead County	MT	Neal Davis	2005	20859
137 7/8	22 7/8	22 3/8	15 5/8	6	5	Oconto County	WI	Edward M. Russell	2005	20859
137 7/8	21 6/8	22 6/8	16 1/8	5	5	Price County	WI	Jeff J. Ernest	2005	20859
137 7/8	21 7/8	23 0/8	15 3/8	5	5	Waupaca County	WI	Pace Faskell	2005	20859
137 7/8	23 2/8	22 6/8	16 7/8	5	6	Athens County	OH	Richard Hocutt	2005	20859

Deer entries below 141 0/8, that appeared in the 6th Edition, are not included here, but are included on the accompanying CD (see page 119), and also in the Club's Records Archives.

WHITETAIL DEER (TYPICAL ANTLERS)

Minimum Score 125 — Continued

SCORE	R MAIN BEAM L	INSIDE SPREAD	R POINTS L		AREA	STATE/ PROVINCE	HUNTER'S NAME	DATE	RANK
*137 7/8	25 6/8 24 4/8	18 5/8	4	5	Licking County	OH	Rich Ruddle	2005	20859
*137 7/8	26 5/8 25 0/8	19 0/8	4	7	Bracken County	KY	Ryan Dale Fryman	2006	20859
137 7/8	22 6/8 22 7/8	14 4/8	5	4	Shackelford County	TX	Brandon Ray	2006	20859
137 7/8	23 3/8 23 5/8	18 3/8	6	5	Gage County	NE	Garry L. Mueller	2006	20859
137 7/8	22 5/8 21 6/8	20 1/8	6	6	Trempealeau County	WI	Bill J. Baardseth	2006	20859
137 7/8	24 4/8 24 0/8	16 6/8	5	5	Pike County	IL	Larry Peterson, Jr.	2006	20859
*137 7/8	22 3/8 23 5/8	17 3/8	5	5	Vigo County	IN	Greg Spurgeon	2006	20859
137 7/8	24 4/8 24 4/8	15 7/8	4	5	Muhlenburg County	KY	Brandon Wright	2006	20859
137 7/8	21 4/8 20 7/8	20 3/8	5	5	Dunn County	WI	Ryan Benitz	2006	20859
*137 7/8	22 6/8 20 6/8	18 5/8	6	4	Franklin County	NE	Brad Hawpe	2006	20859
137 7/8	24 5/8 24 6/8	18 5/8	5	4	La Grange County	IN	Chad A. Helsel	2006	20859
137 7/8	23 7/8 23 7/8	23 7/8	4	4	Bradford County	PA	Carrie Brown	2006	20859
137 7/8	21 5/8 21 5/8	17 5/8	5	6	Jo Daviess County	IL	Mike Felderman	2006	20859
*137 7/8	22 7/8 23 4/8	18 6/8	5	7	Butler County	KS	Jeff Myers	2006	20859
137 7/8	21 7/8 22 3/8	16 3/8	5	5	East Kootenay	BC	Paul Langenbach	2006	20859
137 7/8	22 0/8 21 7/8	13 5/8	5	5	Putnam County	TN	Troy M. Davenport	2007	20859
137 7/8	24 6/8 23 3/8	16 1/8	7	6	Cass County	MI	John Wayne Isabel	2007	20859
*137 7/8	23 7/8 24 3/8	18 4/8	5	5	Stark County	IL	Lance Terry	2007	20859
*137 7/8	21 5/8 20 5/8	15 7/8	5	5	Woodson County	KS	Frank L. Pechacek	2007	20859
137 7/8	22 6/8 23 5/8	15 5/8	5	5	Iowa County	WI	William J. Garcia	2007	20859
137 7/8	25 0/8 24 4/8	20 5/8	4	4	Buffalo County	WI	Dan Johnson	2007	20859
*137 7/8	23 1/8 23 0/8	19 7/8	5	5	Dubuque County	IA	Ryan Gruber	2007	20859
137 7/8	21 3/8 21 3/8	16 3/8	6	5	Sauk County	WI	Kevin Yineman	2007	20859
137 7/8	21 5/8 21 2/8	14 5/8	5	4	Otoe County	NE	Dale D. Kopf	2007	20859
137 7/8	23 0/8 23 3/8	17 7/8	7	6	Crawford County	PA	Ron W. Deems III	2007	20859
*137 7/8	24 6/8 26 0/8	18 3/8	4	4	Champaign County	IL	Brandon Roberts	2007	20859
137 7/8	20 1/8 20 6/8	16 5/8	5	5	Lake County	MN	Tom Walker	2007	20859
137 7/8	22 3/8 22 3/8	17 7/8	6	6	Belmont County	OH	Michael A. Frey	2008	20859
137 7/8	21 7/8 21 3/8	15 4/8	5	6	Westmoreland County	PA	Brian P. Harr	2008	20859
*137 7/8	20 1/8 21 0/8	13 0/8	7	6	Crook County	WY	Mike Schmid	2008	20859
137 7/8	21 5/8 20 5/8	16 1/8	5	5	Washington County	WI	Brian Hart	2008	20859
137 7/8	22 4/8 22 7/8	15 3/8	5	5	Atchison County	MO	Chris Barton	2008	20859
137 7/8	22 6/8 24 3/8	19 1/8	4	5	Marshall County	IN	Jim D. Hart III	2008	20859
*137 7/8	23 0/8 22 4/8	16 5/8	6	6	Clinton County	IA	Michael Harlson	2008	20859
137 7/8	25 4/8 25 1/8	17 3/8	4	5	Noble County	OH	Jimmie D. Bates	2008	20859
137 7/8	23 4/8 24 2/8	17 3/8	5	5	Kewaunee County	WI	Jon Mueller	2008	20859
137 7/8	21 0/8 21 6/8	14 3/8	5	6	Mercer County	ND	Tom Nelson	2009	20859
*137 7/8	22 0/8 21 6/8	17 7/8	5	5	Greene County	GA	Haywood Crumbley	2009	20859
*137 7/8	24 5/8 23 1/8	19 7/8	4	4	Tazewell County	IL	Dillon Weishaupt	2009	20859
137 7/8	22 6/8 20 7/8	18 2/8	7	8	Brookings County	SD	Mark D. Larson	2009	20859
137 7/8	22 4/8 23 1/8	15 1/8	4	4	Ozaukee County	WI	Glenn Dehne	2009	20859
137 7/8	22 1/8 22 4/8	15 3/8	5	5	Dunn County	ND	Stephen A. Dougherty	2009	20859
*137 7/8	24 1/8 23 6/8	21 1/8	6	5	Waupaca County	WI	David A. Voigt	2010	20859
*137 7/8	24 2/8 24 0/8	19 3/8	4	5	Sauk County	WI	Josh Selck	2010	20859
*137 7/8	25 2/8 23 1/8	18 6/8	7	5	Barron County	WI	Sonja Diedrich	2010	20859
*137 7/8	21 7/8 22 0/8	16 5/8	5	5	Shawano County	WI	Kevin J. Herrmann	2010	20859
137 6/8	21 4/8 21 0/8	14 6/8	4	4	Lorain County	OH	Steven Reinhold	1992	21043
137 6/8	23 4/8 23 0/8	17 2/8	4	4	Orange County	IN	Jerry L. Crone	2002	21043
137 6/8	21 4/8 21 2/8	15 4/8	4	4	Woodbury County	IA	Russ R. Wauhob	2002	21043
137 6/8	23 1/8 23 0/8	18 2/8	4	5	Fairfield County	OH	David J. Gonzalez	2003	21043
137 6/8	20 2/8 20 2/8	16 4/8	5	6	Adams County	OH	Jerry Wilcher	2004	21043
137 6/8	21 6/8 22 1/8	17 4/8	5	6	Goodhue County	MN	Cyle Warwick	2004	21043
137 6/8	20 3/8 22 0/8	17 2/8	6	5	Portage County	WI	Dan Haedt	2004	21043
137 6/8	21 4/8 21 3/8	18 6/8	4	4	Brown County	IN	Jim R. Byers	2004	21043
137 6/8	21 5/8 21 7/8	18 4/8	5	6	Hancock County	IL	Georgia Oliver	2004	21043
137 6/8	21 1/8 20 5/8	15 6/8	5	5	Waupaca County	WI	Christofer D. Schultz	2004	21043
137 6/8	23 3/8 23 4/8	16 6/8	4	4	Jersey County	IL	Ken Feazel	2004	21043
*137 6/8	23 6/8 23 3/8	16 0/8	6	5	Trumbull County	OH	Joe Evans	2004	21043
137 6/8	22 5/8 22 5/8	19 5/8	6	5	Manitowoc County	WI	Kurk T. Bessler	2004	21043
137 6/8	22 1/8 22 6/8	15 4/8	5	5	Columbia County	WI	Richard A. Schreiber	2004	21043
137 6/8	25 2/8 24 4/8	20 0/8	5	5	Trumbull County	OH	Cory Bradley	2004	21043
137 6/8	24 7/8 23 4/8	18 2/8	5	4	Pepin County	WI	Josh Brantner	2004	21043
137 6/8	22 6/8 22 0/8	16 4/8	4	5	Foster County	ND	Tyler Ingebretson	2005	21043
137 6/8	23 3/8 22 3/8	21 0/8	4	4	Dunn County	WI	Jeffrey Steven Dooley	2005	21043
137 6/8	20 2/8 20 4/8	15 2/8	5	5	Jackson County	WI	Bart D. Friday	2005	21043
137 6/8	22 7/8 23 0/8	18 2/8	5	5	Brown County	IL	Michael Blasé	2005	21043
137 6/8	21 0/8 20 1/8	16 4/8	5	5	Vernon County	WI	Kevin J. Simonsen	2005	21043
137 6/8	23 6/8 22 2/8	15 0/8	6	5	White County	IN	Milton Lee Kinder	2005	21043
137 6/8	22 4/8 22 4/8	15 0/8	5	5	Coshocton County	OH	George Robey	2005	21043
*137 6/8	24 2/8 23 1/8	17 7/8	5	6	Will County	IL	Dave Connors	2005	21043
137 6/8	20 4/8 22 1/8	18 0/8	5	5	Holt County	NE	Jesse Grenier	2005	21043
137 6/8	22 4/8 23 2/8	19 4/8	4	5	Steuben County	IN	Bill Spurgeon	2005	21043
137 6/8	21 4/8 21 7/8	15 5/8	6	7	Outagamie County	WI	Robert McCarthy	2005	21043
137 6/8	23 5/8 23 0/8	18 6/8	5	5	Price County	WI	Kyle Tokarski	2005	21043
137 6/8	23 7/8 22 5/8	16 6/8	5	4	Parke County	IN	Tom E. James	2005	21043
*137 6/8	21 6/8 20 5/8	17 6/8	7	7	Polk County	IA	Steve Davis	2005	21043
137 6/8	21 4/8 21 5/8	17 2/8	4	5	Buffalo County	WI	Jim Wondzell	2005	21043
137 6/8	22 6/8 22 2/8	18 4/8	6	5	Wapello County	IA	Gary Bix, Jr.	2005	21043
*137 6/8	21 2/8 21 4/8	19 2/8	5	5	Hardin County	IA	Roger Demiter	2005	21043
137 6/8	23 3/8 23 6/8	18 0/8	6	5	Waushara County	WI	Adam J. Blader	2005	21043
137 6/8	22 4/8 21 5/8	14 0/8	5	5	Shackelford County	TX	Scott A. Carlisle	2005	21043
137 6/8	24 1/8 26 2/8	17 2/8	4	4	Oconto County	WI	Bret H. Jossie	2006	21043
137 6/8	22 2/8 23 0/8	16 6/8	4	5	La Crosse County	WI	Todd C. Cudo	2006	21043
137 6/8	23 3/8 22 4/8	15 0/8	5	6	Tom Green County	TX	Ronnie Parsons	2006	21043
137 6/8	23 0/8 23 1/8	20 6/8	4	5	Washington County	MS	Odis Hill, Jr.	2006	21043
*137 6/8	22 7/8 22 5/8	18 3/8	5	6	Ripley County	IN	Jack Day, Jr.	2006	21043
137 6/8	22 1/8 22 7/8	19 2/8	5	5	Sauk County	WI	Chris Dischler	2006	21043
137 6/8	23 1/8 24 1/8	18 0/8	6	4	Ford County	KS	Andy White	2006	21043
137 6/8	19 5/8 19 5/8	14 4/8	5	5	Logan County	KY	Stan Yoder	2006	21043
137 6/8	21 3/8 20 5/8	16 6/8	6	5	Marquette County	WI	Jay Severson	2006	21043
137 6/8	26 3/8 25 5/8	18 4/8	6	5	Northampton County	PA	Jerome Kroboth	2006	21043
137 6/8	26 1/8 25 4/8	19 0/8	4	4	Bolivar County	MS	Brandon Harrington	2006	21043
*137 6/8	21 6/8 23 4/8	14 6/8	5	5	Scott County	IA	Rodney C. Stock	2006	21043
*137 6/8	21 3/8 21 4/8	16 0/8	4	5	Howard County	MD	Chris Leonard Fischer	2006	21043
137 6/8	21 7/8 22 2/8	13 4/8	5	5	Oldham County	KY	Woodford Long	2006	21043

546

WHITETAIL DEER (TYPICAL ANTLERS)

Minimum Score 125
Continued

SCORE	LENGTH OF R MAIN BEAM L	INSIDE SPREAD	NUMBER OF R POINTS L	AREA	STATE/PROVINCE	HUNTER'S NAME	DATE	RANK
137 6/8	21 7/8 22 4/8	22 2/8	8 7	Grayson County	TX	Randy Henderson	2006	21043
137 6/8	22 5/8 23 1/8	17 6/8	5 4	Woodbury County	IA	Jon G. Danke	2006	21043
137 6/8	23 4/8 22 7/8	17 4/8	4 4	Osborne County	KS	Gary Ozias	2006	21043
*137 6/8	23 1/8 22 7/8	16 4/8	4 4	Adams County	WI	Jacob C. Prasalowicz	2007	21043
137 6/8	21 6/8 21 4/8	15 2/8	6 5	Shelby County	MO	Danny Copenhaver	2007	21043
*137 6/8	20 6/8 20 6/8	15 4/8	6 7	Will County	IL	Darvin Loyd	2007	21043
*137 6/8	23 7/8 24 1/8	16 7/8	5 5	Vermilion County	IL	Monty E. Ollis	2007	21043
*137 6/8	23 7/8 21 6/8	16 6/8	5 5	Pike County	IL	Scott Harper	2007	21043
*137 6/8	19 5/8 20 3/8	14 7/8	8 6	Stafford County	KS	Grant White	2007	21043
137 6/8	22 4/8 22 6/8	18 0/8	4 4	Crawford County	WI	Chad Smethurst	2007	21043
*137 6/8	21 0/8 21 7/8	18 4/8	5 5	Concho County	TX	Jack Jetton	2008	21043
137 6/8	22 7/8 23 2/8	18 2/8	5 4	McLean County	ND	Ben Stremick	2008	21043
137 6/8	21 2/8 22 1/8	14 0/8	5 6	Cass County	MI	Jeremiah J. Rezente	2008	21043
*137 6/8	21 7/8 21 4/8	16 0/8	5 5	Price County	WI	Glenn Seitz	2008	21043
137 6/8	23 0/8 22 5/8	16 4/8	5 5	Steuben County	IN	Henry Smith	2008	21043
137 6/8	23 6/8 23 1/8	17 5/8	5 5	Adams County	WI	Kevin Scott Kowalski	2008	21043
137 6/8	23 4/8 21 6/8	17 0/8	5 4	Dane County	WI	Chris Nuenthel	2008	21043
*137 6/8	23 7/8 21 1/8	17 6/8	4 4	Cloud County	KS	Wade Deckman	2008	21043
*137 6/8	23 6/8 24 6/8	14 6/8	5 5	Portage County	WI	Tim Raflik	2008	21043
137 6/8	23 0/8 22 5/8	13 4/8	5 5	Stephens County	TX	Clif Allen	2008	21043
137 6/8	20 5/8 20 1/8	23 1/8	6 5	Cumberland County	PA	Darby Bender, Jr.	2009	21043
*137 6/8	23 6/8 23 5/8	17 7/8	6 7	Buffalo County	WI	Jesse J. Kuri	2009	21043
*137 6/8	21 7/8 20 6/8	18 0/8	4 5	Waupaca County	WI	Jason R. Sweere	2009	21043
137 6/8	21 3/8 23 6/8	18 6/8	6 5	Pike County	OH	Mark Leer	2009	21043
*137 6/8	23 6/8 24 3/8	19 1/8	6 4	Dunn County	WI	Josh Clayton	2009	21043
137 6/8	22 1/8 22 1/8	18 0/8	5 5	Spink County	SD	Mark Grote	2009	21043
*137 6/8	20 6/8 21 0/8	18 4/8	5 5	Juneau County	WI	Guy Metzger	2009	21043
137 6/8	21 7/8 22 4/8	18 2/8	5 5	Fremont County	IA	Mark Armstrong	2009	21043
137 6/8	22 4/8 22 5/8	15 4/8	5 5	Cook County	GA	Maxwell V. Gresham	2009	21043
*137 6/8	23 3/8 23 0/8	17 5/8	6 6	Barron County	WI	Adam Sadowski	2010	21043
*137 5/8	21 7/8 23 0/8	17 3/8	5 5	Jefferson County	WI	John Fonslow	1999	21267
137 5/8	22 0/8 22 4/8	14 7/8	5 5	Becker County	MN	Richard Olie Barton	2000	21267
137 5/8	23 5/8 23 5/8	16 3/8	4 5	Wayne County	IA	Randy Cooling	2000	21267
*137 5/8	21 6/8 23 0/8	15 4/8	5 6	Marshall County	WV	John T. Erazmus III	2003	21267
137 5/8	22 3/8 21 2/8	16 1/8	5 5	Orange County	NC	Todd McDonald	2004	21267
137 5/8	21 6/8 21 3/8	18 1/8	5 5	Redwood County	MN	Todd Gilb	2004	21267
137 5/8	22 3/8 19 6/8	15 1/8	6 6	Roberts County	SD	Jason Fonder	2004	21267
137 5/8	21 0/8 21 0/8	17 7/8	5 5	Sumter County	AL	Gary M. Kellum	2004	21267
137 5/8	22 3/8 22 3/8	17 5/8	4 4	Schuyler County	IL	Homer E. McSwain, Jr.	2004	21267
137 5/8	20 3/8 22 0/8	15 7/8	4 5	Codington County	SD	Michael Robbins	2004	21267
137 5/8	24 0/8 22 5/8	17 6/8	5 5	Bayfield County	WI	Myron Gilomen	2004	21267
*137 5/8	22 7/8 22 7/8	19 2/8	6 7	Cowley County	KS	George B. Smith	2004	21267
137 5/8	21 4/8 20 7/8	17 3/8	5 4	Monroe County	WI	Allen Hart	2004	21267
137 5/8	25 4/8 24 7/8	16 3/8	6 5	Plymouth County	IA	William P. Conlon	2004	21267
*137 5/8	24 3/8 23 2/8	17 2/8	7 6	McDowell County	WV	Michael East, Jr.	2004	21267
137 5/8	22 4/8 23 0/8	17 6/8	7 8	Walsh County	ND	Chris Hoenke	2005	21267
137 5/8	22 2/8 21 6/8	15 1/8	5 5	Walsh County	ND	Darrell W. Deutz	2005	21267
137 5/8	21 6/8 21 2/8	16 7/8	4 5	Monroe County	WI	Tom Thurston	2005	21267
*137 5/8	22 5/8 23 0/8	16 7/8	5 5	Hancock County	IL	Kenneth G. Reed	2005	21267
137 5/8	20 5/8 20 0/8	14 3/8	5 6	Barnes County	ND	Gary L. Koch	2005	21267
*137 5/8	20 3/8 20 4/8	15 5/8	5 5	Livingston County	MI	Timothy A. Eilola	2005	21267
*137 5/8	26 0/8 26 0/8	19 1/8	3 3	Clark County	IL	Phil Buchanan	2005	21267
137 5/8	24 3/8 24 3/8	19 1/8	5 4	Will County	IL	Jack R. Haviland	2005	21267
137 5/8	21 5/8 22 1/8	18 7/8	5 5	Clayton County	IA	Joe Lieb	2005	21267
*137 5/8	22 2/8 22 2/8	16 3/8	6 7	St. Francois County	MO	Kyle Miller	2006	21267
*137 5/8	20 0/8 20 2/8	18 1/8	5 5	Indiana County	PA	Paul Fairman	2006	21267
137 5/8	24 0/8 24 2/8	16 1/8	5 5	Westchester County	NY	Joe DeVito	2006	21267
137 5/8	23 1/8 24 0/8	18 1/8	4 5	Buffalo County	WI	Robert J. Pacocha	2006	21267
137 5/8	22 1/8 23 1/8	15 3/8	5 5	Clayton County	IA	Landon Uhlenhopp	2006	21267
137 5/8	21 7/8 22 4/8	14 6/8	6 5	Calhoun County	MI	Martin S. Campbell	2006	21267
*137 5/8	24 4/8 25 0/8	20 7/8	5 4	Keya Paha County	NE	David E. Kuhn	2006	21267
137 5/8	23 0/8 23 3/8	17 7/8	5 5	Waupaca County	WI	Joe Breznik	2006	21267
*137 5/8	22 4/8 23 2/8	19 0/8	7 5	Buffalo County	WI	Jason W. Hess	2006	21267
137 5/8	24 3/8 22 6/8	14 1/8	4 4	Shelby County	IL	Luke Wasson	2006	21267
137 5/8	22 4/8 23 2/8	17 5/8	4 5	Cook County	GA	Mark W. Futch	2006	21267
137 5/8	22 3/8 19 2/8	17 5/8	5 5	Dunn County	WI	Luke Edin	2007	21267
137 5/8	20 0/8 19 6/8	15 2/8	5 6	Shawano County	WI	John A. Lohrentz	2007	21267
*137 5/8	22 7/8 22 3/8	20 3/8	4 5	Perry County	PA	Benjamin Mann Jones	2007	21267
*137 5/8	23 2/8 23 2/8	16 5/8	7 6	Adams County	IL	Bruce Eller	2007	21267
*137 5/8	21 0/8 21 2/8	16 1/8	5 5	Concho County	TX	Randy Martin	2007	21267
137 5/8	21 6/8 21 4/8	16 6/8	6 5	Vermilion County	IL	Shawn Schermann	2007	21267
*137 5/8	23 3/8 22 6/8	19 1/8	4 4	Berks County	PA	Vincent Skimski	2007	21267
137 5/8	22 6/8 23 0/8	18 3/8	6 4	Parke County	IN	David P. Phelan	2007	21267
137 5/8	23 1/8 23 4/8	19 3/8	5 5	Warren County	IA	Al Thayer	2007	21267
*137 5/8	23 0/8 22 6/8	18 7/8	5 5	Allegheny County	PA	John Mator II	2007	21267
*137 5/8	20 7/8 20 5/8	17 4/8	7 7	Woodford County	KY	Joe Lacefield	2007	21267
137 5/8	24 0/8 24 1/8	15 4/8	5 5	Chemung County	NY	William P. Thomas	2007	21267
137 5/8	23 7/8 24 3/8	17 3/8	5 6	Russell County	KS	Craig Paul Rennhack	2007	21267
137 5/8	23 5/8 23 0/8	17 7/8	5 6	Jewell County	KS	David L. Duncan	2007	21267
137 5/8	20 2/8 20 4/8	15 5/8	5 5	Buffalo County	WI	Ron Janicek, Jr.	2008	21267
*137 5/8	23 4/8 23 0/8	17 3/8	4 4	Portage County	WI	Chris Pliska	2008	21267
*137 5/8	22 2/8 23 0/8	18 7/8	5 4	Creek County	OK	Brad D. Matherly	2008	21267
137 5/8	20 2/8 20 6/8	15 7/8	5 5	Baylor County	TX	Stephen Marshall	2008	21267
*137 5/8	22 2/8 22 1/8	16 1/8	5 5	Harrison County	WV	Suzanne Bishop	2008	21267
137 5/8	24 6/8 22 7/8	17 0/8	6 7	Clermont County	OH	Gene Schadle	2008	21267
*137 5/8	22 1/8 22 7/8	15 3/8	5 5	Barnes County	ND	Larry M. Wagner	2008	21267
*137 5/8	22 5/8 21 1/8	17 7/8	5 5	Barron County	WI	Todd Larson	2008	21267
137 5/8	23 1/8 23 0/8	16 3/8	4 5	Montgomery County	TN	Wilson L. Christy	2008	21267
137 5/8	23 2/8 24 0/8	15 7/8	5 5	Winneshiek County	IA	Michael Ehrig	2008	21267
137 5/8	22 6/8 22 6/8	16 3/8	4 4	Kit Carson County	CO	L. Grant Foster	2008	21267
*137 5/8	19 1/8 19 5/8	17 3/8	6 5	Yankton County	SD	Gabriel Laber	2009	21267
137 5/8	24 1/8 24 2/8	16 2/8	8 7	Sauk County	WI	Scott M. Vater	2009	21267
*137 5/8	21 2/8 22 1/8	17 5/8	5 5	Allamakee County	IA	Randy Kaster	2009	21267
137 5/8	23 1/8 22 3/8	19 1/8	5 5	Creek County	OK	Steve A. Nall	2010	21267
137 5/8	23 4/8 23 1/8	17 5/8	5 5	Indiana County	PA	Brad T. Lowmaster	2010	21267

Deer entries below 141 0/8, that appeared in the 6th Edition, are not included here, but are included on the accompanying CD (see page 119), and also in the Club's Records Archives.

WHITETAIL DEER (TYPICAL ANTLERS)

Minimum Score 125 — Continued

SCORE	LENGTH OF R MAIN BEAM L	INSIDE SPREAD	NUMBER OF R POINTS L		AREA	STATE/ PROVINCE	HUNTER'S NAME	DATE	RANK
137 4/8	21 4/8 21 7/8	15 2/8	4	5	Green County	WI	Ritch Miller	1997	21469
137 4/8	20 0/8 21 2/8	15 6/8	6	6	Maverick County	TX	T. J. Neal	2000	21469
137 4/8	22 5/8 21 0/8	18 4/8	4	5	Clark County	IL	Joseph T. Hankins	2003	21469
*137 4/8	22 5/8 22 3/8	15 6/8	5	5	Clark County	IL	Todd Hunter	2003	21469
137 4/8	24 2/8 24 3/8	16 0/8	4	5	Waupaca County	WI	Jon Voight	2004	21469
137 4/8	21 6/8 20 6/8	15 0/8	5	6	Greene County	IL	Larry R. Morris	2004	21469
137 4/8	19 6/8 20 0/8	13 6/8	6	8	Kenedy County	TX	Kip M. Melancon	2004	21469
137 4/8	22 3/8 22 6/8	17 4/8	5	5	Walsh County	ND	David Moe	2004	21469
137 4/8	22 7/8 23 2/8	15 6/8	5	5	Wyandot County	OH	John Thomas	2004	21469
137 4/8	23 6/8 23 6/8	18 4/8	5	4	Carroll County	OH	Michael P. Cirignano	2004	21469
137 4/8	21 7/8 22 0/8	17 6/8	5	6	Will County	IL	Andy Suligoy	2004	21469
137 4/8	22 6/8 23 1/8	18 4/8	5	4	Ashtabula County	OH	Jeffrey W. Reed	2004	21469
137 4/8	22 4/8 23 5/8	19 2/8	5	5	Adams County	IL	Douglas "Chico" Partlowe	2004	21469
137 4/8	20 5/8 21 1/8	16 0/8	5	5	Ransom County	ND	Mark Lemieux	2004	21469
*137 4/8	22 3/8 20 7/8	14 2/8	5	5	Atoka County	OK	Dwight S. Mullins	2004	21469
*137 4/8	22 4/8 22 4/8	14 7/8	6	5	Southampton County	VA	Kenneth J. Vick	2004	21469
*137 4/8	23 2/8 24 1/8	20 6/8	5	7	Piatt County	IL	Ben Williams	2004	21469
137 4/8	25 6/8 24 4/8	19 0/8	4	4	Schuyler County	IL	Matthew Nezich	2004	21469
137 4/8	23 1/8 23 1/8	17 2/8	4	4	Pike County	IL	Don J. Papczynski	2004	21469
137 4/8	24 5/8 24 2/8	15 2/8	4	4	Madison County	OH	John Piccione	2004	21469
*137 4/8	22 7/8 22 6/8	20 4/8	5	4	St. Louis County	MN	Brian R. Landrigan	2004	21469
137 4/8	20 1/8 20 6/8	13 4/8	5	5	Owen County	IN	Richard Malad II	2005	21469
137 4/8	22 1/8 23 2/8	18 4/8	5	4	Lancaster County	PA	Phares Beiler	2005	21469
137 4/8	20 4/8 21 6/8	18 6/8	4	5	Winona County	MN	Jason Struckmann	2005	21469
137 4/8	22 0/8 22 6/8	15 0/8	5	5	Collingsworth County	TX	Ken R. Witt	2005	21469
*137 4/8	24 1/8 23 2/8	18 0/8	4	4	Steuben County	IN	Scott Feller	2005	21469
137 4/8	24 0/8 21 5/8	18 2/8	4	4	Sherburne County	MN	Curtis G. Nelson	2005	21469
137 4/8	23 4/8 23 4/8	18 4/8	4	5	Fulton County	IL	Mark R. Bertram	2005	21469
137 4/8	20 2/8 21 3/8	18 4/8	5	5	Hand County	SD	Jim L. Aalbers	2005	21469
137 4/8	21 5/8 21 3/8	16 3/8	5	4	De Witt County	IL	Francis E. Holman	2005	21469
137 4/8	24 6/8 23 5/8	19 0/8	4	4	Allamakee County	IA	Ken G. Raflik	2005	21469
*137 4/8	22 7/8 22 0/8	16 6/8	4	5	Portage County	WI	Bill P. Stoltenberg	2005	21469
*137 4/8	22 3/8 22 6/8	17 4/8	5	5	Monroe County	IA	Macky Myers	2005	21469
137 4/8	21 3/8 21 4/8	17 4/8	6	5	Sheboygan County	WI	Lucas Roe	2006	21469
137 4/8	25 5/8 25 3/8	18 4/8	5	4	Carbon County	PA	Craig A. Zeigenfuss	2006	21469
*137 4/8	24 2/8 23 4/8	16 6/8	5	5	Strafford County	NH	Arthur Cardinal, Jr.	2006	21469
137 4/8	21 2/8 21 4/8	16 4/8	5	5	Jackson County	WI	Derrick S. Craft	2006	21469
137 4/8	22 1/8 22 2/8	18 0/8	4	4	Pierce County	WI	Adam F. Frandrup	2006	21469
137 4/8	21 5/8 22 6/8	15 0/8	5	5	Brown County	SD	Lynn Jensen	2006	21469
137 4/8	21 2/8 21 2/8	15 2/8	5	5	Rusk County	WI	Shane Traczyk	2006	21469
137 4/8	22 7/8 23 0/8	20 2/8	5	5	Buffalo County	WI	Ron Welch	2006	21469
*137 4/8	22 3/8 23 0/8	12 7/8	5	7	Steuben County	IN	Jake Sanders	2006	21469
137 4/8	24 1/8 23 7/8	13 0/8	5	5	Hartford County	CT	Richard J. Langer	2006	21469
137 4/8	22 7/8 23 6/8	17 5/8	7	4	Montgomery County	PA	David M. Stinley	2006	21469
137 4/8	20 4/8 24 5/8	17 6/8	6	6	Shawnee County	KS	Stuart Hazard	2006	21469
137 4/8	23 4/8 23 4/8	16 6/8	4	4	Dallas County	IA	Bryce N. Sitter	2006	21469
137 4/8	23 2/8 24 7/8	15 0/8	4	4	Washington County	KS	Richard Reith	2006	21469
*137 4/8	23 5/8 23 7/8	17 4/8	4	4	Adams County	MS	Patrick Kelleher	2006	21469
137 4/8	21 4/8 20 4/8	15 4/8	5	5	Waupaca County	WI	Gary Roth	2007	21469
137 4/8	21 0/8 21 1/8	15 2/8	5	5	Dodge County	NE	Thomas Henry	2007	21469
137 4/8	20 0/8 21 2/8	17 2/8	5	6	Will County	IL	Glenn Mathias	2007	21469
*137 4/8	19 7/8 20 0/8	15 0/8	6	5	Defiance County	OH	William Riley	2007	21469
137 4/8	23 2/8 25 0/8	16 0/8	4	5	Green Lake County	WI	David Kummerow	2007	21469
137 4/8	22 6/8 21 2/8	18 0/8	4	4	Brown County	SD	Ryan Weigel	2007	21469
137 4/8	22 2/8 22 3/8	18 2/8	5	5	Livingston County	NY	Andrew C. Wright	2007	21469
137 4/8	25 4/8 25 5/8	18 6/8	4	4	Clark County	KS	Don Myers	2007	21469
*137 4/8	23 6/8 22 4/8	16 4/8	6	5	Scott County	IA	Milo F. Brown, Jr.	2007	21469
*137 4/8	22 2/8 20 7/8	17 4/8	6	5	Marathon County	WI	Scot Thompson	2008	21469
137 4/8	21 4/8 21 3/8	15 4/8	6	6	Jefferson County	WI	Larry R. Roth	2008	21469
137 4/8	20 6/8 20 7/8	16 2/8	5	5	Warren County	MO	Marc Owen	2008	21469
137 4/8	22 1/8 22 6/8	18 2/8	5	6	Barber County	KS	R. Gary Goldman	2008	21469
137 4/8	22 3/8 23 0/8	15 0/8	5	4	Iowa County	WI	Justin Lipska	2008	21469
137 4/8	21 2/8 21 7/8	19 2/8	5	5	Ramsey County	ND	Cassie Logie	2009	21469
*137 4/8	24 5/8 23 0/8	18 4/8	4	6	Waukesha County	WI	Casey Grimm	2009	21469
*137 4/8	23 7/8 23 1/8	18 7/8	6	5	Gregory County	SD	Mark W. Sedlacek	2009	21469
137 4/8	22 2/8 25 6/8	22 4/8	4	5	Lorain County	OH	Tom Hall	2009	21469
137 4/8	20 6/8 22 0/8	17 2/8	4	4	Steuben County	IN	Robert Harris	2009	21469
137 4/8	25 4/8 25 2/8	17 6/8	4	4	Dimmit County	TX	John Henry Holloway III	2009	21469
137 4/8	23 0/8 22 1/8	18 5/8	6	5	Dane County	WI	Scott C. Broughton	2009	21469
*137 4/8	19 6/8 18 5/8	18 2/8	5	5	Dauphin County	PA	Robert M. Kreamer	2009	21469
137 4/8	23 4/8 23 3/8	17 4/8	5	5	Oneida County	WI	Tim Clawson	2009	21469
137 4/8	23 7/8 24 2/8	17 4/8	5	4	Mercer County	MO	Larry Brown	2009	21469
*137 4/8	23 2/8 23 0/8	17 6/8	5	5	Cass County	IL	Steve Deming	2009	21469
*137 4/8	22 5/8 22 7/8	17 3/8	5	4	Sauk County	WI	Edward Hasse	2009	21469
*137 4/8	22 0/8 21 0/8	18 4/8	5	4	Greene County	IL	Matthew Cheek	2009	21469
137 4/8	24 3/8 22 6/8	16 6/8	5	5	Clark County	KS	Scott Hettinger	2009	21469
137 4/8	23 1/8 22 5/8	15 1/8	4	5	Upton County	TX	Dean Titsworth	2010	21469
137 3/8	22 4/8 23 5/8	16 4/8	4	5	Mahoning County	OH	Michael Engstrom	2001	21657
137 3/8	22 2/8 22 2/8	17 1/8	4	4	Pike County	IL	Kent Stewart	2002	21657
137 3/8	24 1/8 22 3/8	16 0/8	6	4	Dundurn	SAS	Jean L. Camirand, Jr.	2003	21657
*137 3/8	23 4/8 22 1/8	18 5/8	5	6	Marathon County	WI	John Sattler	2003	21657
*137 3/8	23 4/8 24 3/8	18 7/8	6	6	La Porte County	IN	Mark Beyler	2004	21657
137 3/8	21 0/8 20 2/8	16 2/8	7	5	Warren County	KY	Russell Brown	2004	21657
137 3/8	23 6/8 24 0/8	18 5/8	5	5	Frederick County	VA	Rick Brannon	2004	21657
137 3/8	23 2/8 22 1/8	17 7/8	6	5	Jackson County	WI	Joey Arneson	2004	21657
137 3/8	23 3/8 16 5/8	18 3/8	5	5	Ottawa County	MI	Douglas J. Grotenrath	2004	21657
*137 3/8	20 5/8 20 5/8	17 6/8	5	6	Shiawassee County	MI	Larry W. Delaney	2004	21657
137 3/8	23 0/8 22 7/8	17 5/8	5	5	Clayton County	IA	Glen E. Pauly	2004	21657
137 3/8	24 3/8 24 6/8	19 1/8	4	5	Saskatoon Mtn.	ALB	Wilf Lehners	2004	21657
137 3/8	22 1/8 20 7/8	16 3/8	5	6	Edgar County	IL	Brad Davis	2004	21657
137 3/8	23 1/8 22 3/8	18 2/8	7	6	Ravalli County	MT	Rusty G. Wandler	2005	21657
137 3/8	20 4/8 21 1/8	14 7/8	5	5	Green County	WI	Charles S. Buttke	2005	21657
137 3/8	22 7/8 23 7/8	17 0/8	4	5	Howell County	MO	Stace Kerley	2005	21657
137 3/8	21 5/8 23 0/8	18 0/8	5	6	Jo Daviess County	IL	Bill Salzmann	2005	21657
*137 3/8	23 6/8 24 0/8	16 2/8	5	5	Jennings County	IN	Curtis Haines	2005	21657

548

WHITETAIL DEER (TYPICAL ANTLERS)

Minimum Score 125 — Continued

SCORE	R MAIN BEAM L	INSIDE SPREAD	R POINTS L		AREA	STATE/PROVINCE	HUNTER'S NAME	DATE	RANK
137 3/8	22 5/8 22 0/8	18 1/8	5	5	Waupaca County	WI	Brian J. Emerson	2005	21657
137 3/8	21 3/8 20 7/8	17 4/8	6	6	Pawnee County	NE	Bill Phillips	2005	21657
137 3/8	23 0/8 23 7/8	17 3/8	4	6	Adams County	MS	Boo Brumfield	2005	21657
*137 3/8	21 7/8 21 3/8	18 2/8	6	6	Coles County	IL	Darren Stafford	2005	21657
137 3/8	24 2/8 23 5/8	18 1/8	5	5	Anderson County	SC	Jimmy C. Fricks	2005	21657
137 3/8	23 6/8 23 3/8	17 5/8	6	5	Washington County	WI	Jim Kirsch, Jr.	2006	21657
137 3/8	23 1/8 23 1/8	16 6/8	6	5	Rankin County	MS	Tee Murtagh	2006	21657
137 3/8	22 5/8 22 2/8	16 3/8	6	7	Trempealeau County	WI	Jeffrey Steinke	2006	21657
*137 3/8	23 5/8 24 1/8	18 5/8	4	4	Chester County	PA	Brian Meilinger	2006	21657
137 3/8	19 4/8 19 6/8	13 1/8	5	5	Camden County	MO	Tommy J. Jones	2006	21657
137 3/8	21 4/8 21 4/8	17 0/8	5	8	Waupaca County	WI	Dean Pitt	2006	21657
*137 3/8	21 7/8 21 5/8	13 5/8	5	5	Ohio County	KY	Keith Cook	2006	21657
*137 3/8	23 3/8 23 2/8	18 5/8	4	4	Jasper County	IN	Jeffrey T. Scheurich	2006	21657
137 3/8	24 7/8 25 3/8	18 4/8	6	6	Adams County	WI	Russell J. Rupert	2006	21657
*137 3/8	23 5/8 23 0/8	16 1/8	5	5	Taylor County	WI	Gene Rizzi	2007	21657
137 3/8	19 2/8 19 6/8	17 3/8	5	5	Walsh County	ND	Randal J. Schuster	2007	21657
137 3/8	22 4/8 22 6/8	17 5/8	5	5	Rockingham County	NC	Kevin Gilley	2007	21657
*137 3/8	23 7/8 22 5/8	17 1/8	5	5	Ross County	OH	Tim Nussbaum	2007	21657
*137 3/8	22 6/8 24 1/8	17 5/8	5	4	Adams County	OH	Christopher M. Swain	2007	21657
137 3/8	21 7/8 21 5/8	16 4/8	7	5	Lancaster County	NE	William Stolzer	2007	21657
*137 3/8	23 6/8 23 6/8	14 3/8	4	5	Brown County	SD	Robert Baker	2007	21657
137 3/8	22 0/8 21 7/8	19 5/8	5	5	Douglas County	WI	Eric L. Gucinski	2007	21657
137 3/8	22 0/8 23 2/8	18 5/8	4	4	Hunterdon County	NJ	Peter Tilstra	2007	21657
*137 3/8	23 2/8 22 2/8	17 7/8	4	5	Pierce County	WI	Van Howe	2007	21657
*137 3/8	21 6/8 22 6/8	16 5/8	4	4	Allen County	IN	Adam Sims	2007	21657
137 3/8	21 6/8 21 7/8	16 5/8	5	5	Kendall County	IL	Matt Wohead	2007	21657
137 3/8	22 2/8 21 1/8	16 3/8	5	6	Columbia County	WI	Curt Stam	2007	21657
*137 3/8	23 4/8 24 6/8	19 3/8	4	4	Wyoming County	WV	Danny P. Toler	2007	21657
137 3/8	22 4/8 22 7/8	16 2/8	5	6	Rockyview	ALB	Tara Normand	2008	21657
*137 3/8	22 1/8 22 4/8	16 0/8	5	6	Taylor County	GA	Chase Brinson	2008	21657
137 3/8	23 5/8 26 1/8	19 3/8	6	7	Black Hawk County	IA	Chad Schmidt	2008	21657
137 3/8	21 1/8 21 0/8	15 3/8	6	6	Sterling County	TX	Jonathan Ewing	2008	21657
*137 3/8	21 4/8 21 2/8	17 1/8	5	5	Claiborne County	MS	Ricky Grafton	2008	21657
137 3/8	22 1/8 22 3/8	18 1/8	5	4	Olmsted County	MN	Daniel "Boone" Bell	2008	21657
137 3/8	21 0/8 21 3/8	17 7/8	5	5	Mercer County	IL	Todd Jones	2008	21657
137 3/8	22 1/8 22 4/8	18 3/8	5	5	La Crosse County	WI	Vance Henry	2008	21657
*137 3/8	19 7/8 20 1/8	15 5/8	5	5	Jefferson County	NE	Adam Kriz	2008	21657
137 3/8	22 5/8 22 0/8	18 7/8	5	5	Grant County	WI	Brian Koeller	2008	21657
137 3/8	22 3/8 22 2/8	16 7/8	5	6	Montgomery County	IL	Randy J. Farrar	2008	21657
*137 3/8	23 3/8 22 4/8	16 6/8	5	5	Webster County	IA	Jared Lenz	2008	21657
137 3/8	24 7/8 22 7/8	18 2/8	6	7	Decatur County	GA	Bert Parker	2009	21657
*137 3/8	25 6/8 24 3/8	17 4/8	4	5	Vermilion County	IL	Randall Keith Johnson, Jr.	2009	21657
137 3/8	23 5/8 22 3/8	15 5/8	5	5	Hamilton County	IL	J. T. Kreager	2009	21657
*137 3/8	22 7/8 22 1/8	15 1/8	4	4	Adams County	IN	Adam Kaehr	2009	21657
137 3/8	22 0/8 21 7/8	19 3/8	5	5	Coffey County	KS	Andy Lee	2009	21657
*137 3/8	22 1/8 23 2/8	15 4/8	5	6	Dane County	WI	Cody P. Statz	2009	21657
*137 3/8	20 7/8 20 3/8	16 5/8	5	5	Adams County	IL	Steve Preziosi	2009	21657
137 3/8	23 2/8 22 2/8	18 1/8	5	5	Shelby County	OH	Travis Lawson	2009	21657
137 3/8	23 0/8 22 4/8	21 0/8	6	7	Cook County	IL	Ron Smith	2009	21657
*137 3/8	23 4/8 23 4/8	16 5/8	8	6	Muhlenberg County	KY	Steve Conrad	2010	21657
137 2/8	23 2/8 23 3/8	16 6/8	5	5	Fairfield County	OH	Hobert Payne	1998	21850
137 2/8	19 2/8 19 3/8	13 4/8	5	5	Kenedy County	TX	Bruce R. Schoeneweis	1998	21850
137 2/8	21 1/8 21 2/8	16 4/8	5	5	Madison County	MT	Robert Reed	2001	21850
137 2/8	26 7/8 25 7/8	20 5/8	4	6	Steuben County	IN	Matthew D. Farnham	2001	21850
137 2/8	20 2/8 20 4/8	13 6/8	6	6	Green Lake County	WI	John R. Buttke	2002	21850
*137 2/8	21 5/8 21 4/8	16 2/8	4	4	Calhoun County	MI	Rick Alan Combs	2002	21850
137 2/8	23 7/8 24 2/8	19 0/8	5	5	Henderson County	IL	Tom Hagner	2003	21850
*137 2/8	25 1/8 25 2/8	19 2/8	4	4	Lincoln County	WI	Chris Freymuth	2003	21850
137 2/8	21 3/8 19 7/8	16 0/8	5	5	Fulton County	IN	Dennis Kamp	2004	21850
137 2/8	21 2/8 21 5/8	16 6/8	4	4	Winnebago County	IL	Philip J. Guarino, Jr.	2004	21850
137 2/8	22 3/8 22 5/8	17 6/8	4	4	Chickasaw County	IA	Marshall Phillips	2004	21850
137 2/8	22 6/8 22 5/8	17 7/8	6	6	Woodbury County	IA	Steve Schrank	2004	21850
137 2/8	21 4/8 21 5/8	18 2/8	5	5	Issaquena County	MS	Ben Robertson	2004	21850
137 2/8	21 5/8 22 2/8	15 4/8	5	5	Blue Earth County	MN	David Schroepfer	2004	21850
137 2/8	22 7/8 23 0/8	19 4/8	5	4	Clark County	KS	Ernie Merydith	2005	21850
137 2/8	24 0/8 24 2/8	18 6/8	4	4	Pike County	MO	Sam Pickard	2005	21850
*137 2/8	22 4/8 21 4/8	17 0/8	5	5	Yell County	AR	Sidney W. Autrey	2005	21850
137 2/8	21 7/8 23 1/8	14 0/8	5	5	Lincoln County	WI	George Harer	2005	21850
137 2/8	22 0/8 22 7/8	16 5/8	6	5	Greene County	MO	Travis Crowley	2005	21850
137 2/8	21 7/8 22 2/8	18 0/8	5	6	Manitowoc County	WI	Jeff J. MacDonald	2005	21850
137 2/8	22 3/8 22 4/8	20 2/8	5	5	Greenwood County	KS	John MacPeak	2005	21850
137 2/8	23 4/8 23 3/8	18 2/8	5	4	Vermilion County	IL	Jason Shirkey	2005	21850
137 2/8	23 1/8 21 3/8	17 2/8	5	5	Richland County	IL	Austin Ridgely	2005	21850
137 2/8	23 2/8 23 6/8	18 6/8	5	6	Hancock County	IL	Bradley J. Swanson	2005	21850
137 2/8	21 6/8 21 4/8	16 0/8	5	5	Grand Forks County	ND	Brian Nord	2006	21850
137 2/8	22 1/8 22 1/8	18 2/8	5	6	Henry County	IN	Jeremy Adkins	2006	21850
137 2/8	24 3/8 24 6/8	19 2/8	4	4	Licking County	OH	N. Dale Radcliff	2006	21850
*137 2/8	21 5/8 21 2/8	18 2/8	5	5	Wabash County	IN	T. J. Eads	2006	21850
137 2/8	23 2/8 21 7/8	18 6/8	6	5	Floyd County	IA	Danny Bean	2006	21850
137 2/8	20 5/8 22 3/8	15 2/8	5	5	Columbia County	WI	Peter J. McCormick	2006	21850
137 2/8	21 7/8 21 2/8	16 1/8	6	5	Dodge County	WI	Troy Kirchoff	2006	21850
137 2/8	23 7/8 21 7/8	17 4/8	5	5	Clark County	IL	Ernest D. Parker	2006	21850
137 2/8	19 2/8 19 1/8	16 2/8	5	5	Pepin County	WI	Eric Carlson	2006	21850
137 2/8	23 2/8 22 6/8	16 2/8	5	7	Outagamie County	WI	Matt Lorge	2006	21850
137 2/8	22 2/8 23 4/8	15 0/8	5	5	Bedford County	VA	Charles Allen Poole	2006	21850
137 2/8	24 2/8 24 3/8	19 2/8	4	4	Bucks County	PA	Dan Day	2006	21850
137 2/8	23 7/8 23 5/8	19 6/8	4	4	Lee County	IL	Thomas Sawyer	2006	21850
137 2/8	22 4/8 22 5/8	16 6/8	5	5	Bayfield County	WI	Mike McCormick	2006	21850
137 2/8	20 3/8 20 6/8	15 2/8	8	5	Chippewa County	MN	Zach Bothun	2006	21850
137 2/8	23 0/8 22 4/8	15 2/8	5	5	Larimer County	CO	David L. Duncan	2006	21850
137 2/8	21 7/8 21 2/8	15 6/8	5	5	Ferry County	WA	Chad Berry	2006	21850
137 2/8	21 5/8 22 3/8	16 0/8	5	5	Waupaca County	WI	William R. Ganiere	2007	21850
*137 2/8	23 0/8 21 6/8	21 4/8	4	6	Monroe County	WI	Robert D. Berg	2007	21850
*137 2/8	22 6/8 22 2/8	17 7/8	6	5	Dutchess County	NY	Mark Phillips	2007	21850
137 2/8	24 1/8 25 5/8	18 1/8	5	5	Buffalo County	WI	Raymond Nachtwey	2007	21850

Deer entries below 141 0/8, that appeared in the 6th Edition, are not included here, but are included on the accompanying CD (see page 119), and also in the Club's Records Archives.

WHITETAIL DEER (TYPICAL ANTLERS)

Minimum Score 125 — Continued

SCORE	R MAIN BEAM	L MAIN BEAM	INSIDE SPREAD	R POINTS	L POINTS	AREA	STATE/PROVINCE	HUNTER'S NAME	DATE	RANK
*137 2/8	23 7/8	23 1/8	19 0/8	4	6	Cambria County	PA	Dean L. Albright	2007	21850
*137 2/8	24 3/8	24 2/8	16 5/8	6	5	Peoria County	IL	Brian Vande Mark	2007	21850
137 2/8	20 5/8	20 4/8	14 1/8	7	7	Barber County	KS	Keith A. Dana	2007	21850
*137 2/8	22 4/8	21 5/8	16 4/8	5	5	Suffolk County	NY	Thomas J. Focazio	2007	21850
*137 2/8	23 5/8	22 6/8	19 3/8	6	5	Green County	WI	Greg Wedig	2008	21850
137 2/8	20 4/8	21 3/8	17 2/8	5	6	Victoria County	TX	E. W. "Scooter" Douglass	2008	21850
*137 2/8	22 3/8	22 1/8	16 6/8	5	5	Dane County	WI	Christian Ruck	2008	21850
137 2/8	24 3/8	22 1/8	17 0/8	4	4	Middlesex County	NJ	Craig Fallon	2008	21850
137 2/8	23 3/8	23 2/8	19 3/8	4	5	Sedgwick County	KS	Bob Campbell	2008	21850
137 2/8	21 6/8	21 5/8	18 0/8	5	5	Pike County	IL	Kim Bettinger	2008	21850
137 2/8	23 7/8	24 1/8	19 2/8	4	5	Otero County	CO	Todd Bandemer	2008	21850
137 2/8	22 4/8	23 1/8	18 7/8	5	6	Fulton County	IL	Greg Lingenfelter	2008	21850
*137 2/8	21 2/8	21 3/8	15 6/8	5	5	Isabella County	MI	Jerry R. Griffin	2008	21850
137 2/8	20 0/8	20 5/8	16 3/8	6	5	Wayne County	NE	Mike Beiermann	2009	21850
137 2/8	22 7/8	22 4/8	20 4/8	4	4	Dimmit County	TX	John Henry Holloway III	2009	21850
*137 2/8	23 2/8	23 0/8	18 2/8	6	4	Shawano County	WI	David L. Schmidt	2009	21850
*137 2/8	27 3/8	25 0/8	18 6/8	4	4	Buffalo County	WI	Bob Decker	2009	21850
137 2/8	22 7/8	22 4/8	13 5/8	4	6	Gage County	NE	Gary Stohs	2009	21850
137 2/8	23 0/8	23 7/8	18 4/8	5	5	Niagara County	NY	Marc S. Britt	2009	21850
137 2/8	22 7/8	21 4/8	17 1/8	9	5	Kiowa County	KS	Rick Duggan	2009	21850
*137 2/8	22 6/8	23 3/8	18 0/8	5	4	Floyd County	IA	Philip Parcher	2009	21850
137 2/8	21 1/8	22 2/8	15 5/8	6	5	Franklin County	IL	Dave Pankow	2009	21850
*137 1/8	22 0/8	21 2/8	18 1/8	5	5	Mercer County	KY	Stevie Elliott	2003	22055
*137 1/8	23 5/8	24 4/8	18 5/8	6	5	Vinton County	OH	Jason M. Good	2004	22055
137 1/8	24 5/8	22 7/8	18 1/8	5	7	Rockland County	NY	David J. Hoehmann	2004	22055
137 1/8	20 6/8	21 5/8	15 5/8	5	6	Clark County	SD	Bob Syring	2004	22055
*137 1/8	22 5/8	23 4/8	16 1/8	5	4	Vernon County	MO	Brian W. Hollands	2004	22055
137 1/8	24 2/8	25 4/8	16 1/8	4	4	Kankakee County	IL	Allen R. Messier	2004	22055
*137 1/8	20 4/8	20 4/8	16 5/8	5	5	Somerset County	PA	Jason Siwula	2004	22055
137 1/8	23 2/8	22 7/8	18 3/8	4	4	Cass County	IL	Jason Griffin	2004	22055
137 1/8	23 5/8	22 6/8	18 3/8	5	5	Tarrant County	TX	Angel Flores	2004	22055
137 1/8	20 0/8	21 0/8	17 5/8	5	4	Rosebud County	MT	William Elfland	2004	22055
137 1/8	20 4/8	21 4/8	15 3/8	5	6	Wilkinson County	GA	Tim Burke	2005	22055
137 1/8	22 5/8	23 2/8	17 3/8	5	5	Otsego County	NY	Greg Packard	2005	22055
137 1/8	24 7/8	25 3/8	16 5/8	4	4	Buffalo County	WI	Mick Kulig	2005	22055
137 1/8	23 2/8	23 5/8	13 5/8	6	6	Linn County	KS	F. David Thornberry	2005	22055
137 1/8	22 6/8	23 2/8	17 3/8	6	5	Jackson County	IA	Stacy Brown	2005	22055
137 1/8	23 1/8	22 6/8	15 7/8	5	5	Dubuque County	IA	Chad P. Brandel	2006	22055
137 1/8	21 7/8	21 1/8	16 0/8	6	5	Burnett County	WI	Thomas E. Swenson	2006	22055
137 1/8	22 2/8	22 0/8	15 5/8	5	5	Ashland County	WI	Mike Petroski, Jr.	2006	22055
137 1/8	21 1/8	20 4/8	15 7/8	6	5	Douglas County	WI	Marty Kasinskas	2006	22055
*137 1/8	21 7/8	21 5/8	16 7/8	4	4	Jackson County	OH	William Parise	2006	22055
137 1/8	24 1/8	24 5/8	21 1/8	4	4	Sauk County	WI	Zach Klemp	2006	22055
137 1/8	21 4/8	21 2/8	17 5/8	5	5	Buffalo County	WI	John W. Charles	2006	22055
*137 1/8	23 6/8	24 5/8	17 3/8	8	6	Portage County	WI	Travis McIntee	2006	22055
137 1/8	25 2/8	24 3/8	17 1/8	4	4	Van Buren County	IA	Mark Elsinger	2006	22055
137 1/8	20 5/8	20 4/8	13 7/8	5	5	Monroe County	IA	Phil Blaetz	2006	22055
137 1/8	20 4/8	21 2/8	15 3/8	5	5	Wayne County	IA	Dennis N. Doggett	2006	22055
*137 1/8	20 5/8	20 1/8	14 4/8	6	5	Comanche County	KS	John Thomas	2006	22055
137 1/8	25 0/8	24 5/8	20 3/8	5	4	Rock County	WI	Gilbert Sparhawk	2006	22055
137 1/8	21 6/8	21 3/8	16 7/8	6	6	Polk County	WI	Ethan Cook	2007	22055
*137 1/8	22 3/8	21 6/8	17 6/8	5	6	Erie County	PA	Todd S. Meeker	2007	22055
137 1/8	23 4/8	21 0/8	17 1/8	6	5	Baker County	GA	Jacob Paschal	2007	22055
137 1/8	22 2/8	22 1/8	18 1/8	7	6	Woodbury County	IA	Tim Susie	2007	22055
137 1/8	22 4/8	22 3/8	17 1/8	6	5	Crawford County	IL	Brock Hardiek	2007	22055
137 1/8	22 7/8	22 0/8	18 1/8	5	5	Chariton County	MO	Roger Fraley	2007	22055
*137 1/8	23 5/8	23 3/8	16 0/8	5	6	Harford County	MD	Robert P. Brown, Jr.	2007	22055
137 1/8	23 1/8	23 0/8	18 3/8	5	5	Buffalo County	WI	Tony Heil	2007	22055
137 1/8	21 6/8	20 5/8	17 0/8	7	6	Clermont County	OH	Gene Schadle	2007	22055
137 1/8	22 2/8	20 5/8	16 2/8	6	5	Linn County	IA	Scott D. Moon	2007	22055
137 1/8	22 6/8	21 4/8	17 1/8	4	5	Jackson County	IA	Tom Avery	2007	22055
137 1/8	24 6/8	23 2/8	17 3/8	5	4	Berks County	PA	Scott A. Rohrbach	2007	22055
*137 1/8	22 0/8	21 5/8	18 7/8	5	5	Henderson County	KY	Jason Singletary	2007	22055
*137 1/8	23 5/8	22 2/8	15 6/8	5	4	Ashland County	OH	Joseph Hochstetler	2007	22055
*137 1/8	24 0/8	23 6/8	20 7/8	5	4	Sumner County	KS	Stephen W. Muse	2007	22055
137 1/8	19 4/8	19 4/8	15 5/8	5	5	Russell County	KS	Jamie W. Andrew	2007	22055
*137 1/8	21 5/8	21 4/8	16 3/8	5	5	Scioto County	OH	Brent A. Penn	2008	22055
137 1/8	22 1/8	22 0/8	17 3/8	4	5	Big Horn County	WY	Dave Moss	2008	22055
137 1/8	19 7/8	20 0/8	13 7/8	5	5	Adair County	MO	Walter Schaefer	2008	22055
*137 1/8	22 0/8	21 6/8	19 3/8	5	4	Brown County	IL	James W. Hawthorne, Jr.	2008	22055
137 1/8	24 5/8	24 4/8	15 3/8	4	4	Conecuh County	AL	Albert Ward II	2008	22055
137 1/8	20 5/8	20 3/8	16 1/8	5	5	Schuyler County	IL	Mike Weaver	2008	22055
137 1/8	21 4/8	21 5/8	18 1/8	6	5	McHenry County	ND	Scott Hettinger	2008	22055
*137 1/8	20 7/8	21 1/8	17 0/8	7	5	Park County	WY	Jerry Dollard	2009	22055
137 1/8	21 5/8	22 1/8	13 1/8	5	5	Waupaca County	WI	Ron James	2009	22055
137 1/8	24 3/8	24 4/8	16 3/8	4	4	Keya Paha County	NE	Terry Marcukaitis	2009	22055
*137 1/8	22 1/8	23 3/8	19 1/8	5	5	Knox County	NE	Frank Conte	2009	22055
137 1/8	22 5/8	22 1/8	14 5/8	4	4	Brule County	SD	Jeff W. Flood	2009	22055
137 1/8	21 0/8	20 5/8	18 5/8	5	5	Kidder County	ND	Jeffrey D. Hanson	2009	22055
137 1/8	25 4/8	24 6/8	18 3/8	4	5	Marquette County	WI	Brian M. Tyczinski	2009	22055
137 1/8	22 2/8	23 0/8	18 5/8	5	5	Lauderdale County	TN	Jack Swift	2009	22055
137 0/8	20 6/8	21 1/8	14 6/8	5	5	Sauk County	WI	John Michael Ramsey	1995	22242
137 0/8	22 7/8	22 7/8	18 4/8	4	4	Washington County	KS	Richard A. Reith	2003	22242
137 0/8	25 0/8	25 3/8	15 6/8	4	4	Kane County	IL	Casey Bowgren	2003	22242
137 0/8	23 0/8	23 1/8	17 6/8	5	5	Ellsworth County	KS	Jeff Clark	2003	22242
*137 0/8	22 0/8	22 4/8	20 6/8	5	4	Douglas County	WI	Kenneth J. Waldvogel	2004	22242
137 0/8	22 6/8	22 0/8	17 0/8	4	4	Marathon County	WI	Brian E. Matteson	2004	22242
137 0/8	23 3/8	23 1/8	19 2/8	5	5	Morgan County	IL	Harry Savage	2004	22242
*137 0/8	20 6/8	20 4/8	20 0/8	6	4	Wabash County	IL	Nicholaus Johnson	2004	22242
137 0/8	20 6/8	21 0/8	15 6/8	5	5	Union County	SD	Dan Rosenbaum	2004	22242
137 0/8	20 3/8	20 6/8	18 2/8	4	4	Polk County	WI	Rick Hanson	2004	22242
137 0/8	22 4/8	23 3/8	18 0/8	6	5	Vernon County	WI	Dustin J. Nevsimal	2004	22242
*137 0/8	24 0/8	24 7/8	18 6/8	4	5	Middlesex County	MA	Larry Gagnon	2004	22242
137 0/8	20 4/8	20 6/8	15 4/8	5	5	Williams County	ND	Jim Hval	2004	22242
137 0/8	24 2/8	24 6/8	15 4/8	4	4	Fulton County	GA	Lyndon Terrell	2004	22242

550

WHITETAIL DEER (TYPICAL ANTLERS)

Minimum Score 125 — Continued

SCORE	LENGTH OF R MAIN BEAM L	INSIDE SPREAD	NUMBER OF R POINTS L	AREA	STATE/PROVINCE	HUNTER'S NAME	DATE	RANK
137 0/8	25 4/8 24 4/8	15 4/8	4 4	Johnson County	KY	Kevin Osborne	2004	22242
137 0/8	24 5/8 25 2/8	17 6/8	4 4	Essex County	MA	Keith A. Hopkins	2004	22242
137 0/8	22 6/8 23 4/8	15 4/8	5 6	Waupaca County	WI	Ronnie Nollenberg	2005	22242
137 0/8	21 4/8 21 2/8	17 3/8	6 6	Sutton County	TX	Ki Marley	2005	22242
137 0/8	21 2/8 21 7/8	17 6/8	5 5	Green County	WI	Daniel D. Walker	2005	22242
137 0/8	24 6/8 25 0/8	17 2/8	4 4	Johnson County	IA	Duane Long	2005	22242
*137 0/8	21 1/8 21 4/8	15 2/8	5 5	Ottawa County	KS	Terry Mullins	2005	22242
137 0/8	21 2/8 23 2/8	17 4/8	5 5	Olmsted County	MN	Michele Leqve	2005	22242
*137 0/8	21 5/8 21 7/8	18 4/8	5 5	Waupaca County	WI	Bruce Learman	2005	22242
137 0/8	22 5/8 23 6/8	16 0/8	4 4	Barber County	KS	Casmir Domurat	2005	22242
*137 0/8	17 7/8 21 7/8	17 0/8	6 6	Buffalo County	NE	Jess Kucera	2005	22242
*137 0/8	19 6/8 20 0/8	14 6/8	7 5	Sterling County	TX	Ryan Dupriest	2005	22242
137 0/8	20 7/8 21 1/8	13 4/8	5 5	Cavalier County	ND	Jeff Girodat	2005	22242
137 0/8	23 1/8 22 3/8	17 7/8	6 5	Benson County	ND	Lance G. Loken	2006	22242
*137 0/8	19 6/8 19 5/8	16 6/8	6 5	Hennepin County	MN	Todd Stephens	2006	22242
137 0/8	23 4/8 23 0/8	17 2/8	4 4	Todd County	KY	Jeff Larsen	2006	22242
*137 0/8	25 1/8 25 2/8	17 0/8	4 4	Oconto County	WI	James Kryzanek	2006	22242
137 0/8	20 5/8 22 0/8	19 4/8	5 5	Delaware County	IN	Richard A. Kauffman	2006	22242
*137 0/8	22 1/8 22 1/8	14 6/8	5 5	Appanoose County	IA	Joshua R. Stuedemann	2006	22242
137 0/8	22 1/8 21 2/8	17 6/8	5 5	Adams County	MS	Bob Chain, Jr.	2006	22242
137 0/8	21 1/8 21 1/8	14 4/8	5 5	Pike County	IL	Bill Hadlock	2006	22242
137 0/8	23 4/8 24 0/8	17 2/8	4 5	Franklin County	MA	Jacob Allen Salls	2006	22242
137 0/8	22 5/8 22 0/8	18 1/8	5 6	Miami County	IN	Kevin Harshman	2007	22242
137 0/8	25 3/8 23 4/8	21 4/8	5 8	Moultrie County	IL	Greg Scribner	2007	22242
137 0/8	23 4/8 22 7/8	18 2/8	5 4	Clarion County	PA	James A. Mays III	2007	22242
*137 0/8	20 6/8 20 7/8	18 4/8	4 4	Saline County	AR	Kyle Wyatt Ferguson	2007	22242
137 0/8	21 1/8 20 7/8	16 2/8	5 5	Llano County	TX	Ellen Labay	2007	22242
137 0/8	20 6/8 19 6/8	17 6/8	5 5	Edmonton	ALB	Gunther Tondeleir	2007	22242
137 0/8	17 7/8 19 5/8	17 0/8	5 5	Saunders County	NE	Josh Depatie	2007	22242
*137 0/8	21 2/8 21 1/8	17 0/8	5 5	Boone County	IA	Kevin M. Christensen	2007	22242
137 0/8	20 3/8 21 4/8	16 0/8	6 5	Jasper County	IL	Skip Moore	2007	22242
137 0/8	22 4/8 21 2/8	14 4/8	5 5	Knox County	NE	Scott Feldhacker	2007	22242
137 0/8	24 3/8 22 4/8	16 5/8	5 5	Green County	WI	Jacob D. Laube	2007	22242
137 0/8	21 2/8 21 1/8	16 0/8	5 5	McKenzie County	ND	Dan Brockman	2007	22242
137 0/8	19 0/8 19 7/8	17 0/8	5 5	Iowa County	WI	Nic J. Segebrecht	2008	22242
*137 0/8	22 5/8 22 6/8	16 7/8	6 5	Morrison County	MN	Rand Joe Kramer	2008	22242
*137 0/8	20 6/8 21 2/8	15 4/8	5 6	Ramsey County	ND	Dustin Brodina	2008	22242
137 0/8	21 7/8 22 0/8	18 6/8	5 5	Wheeler County	TX	Bence Close	2008	22242
137 0/8	23 1/8 22 2/8	18 4/8	4 4	Hardin County	OH	Haulie Marshall	2008	22242
137 0/8	22 0/8 20 7/8	15 6/8	5 5	Polk County	WI	Nick Lauterbach	2008	22242
137 0/8	22 6/8 23 2/8	17 2/8	5 6	Richland County	WI	Michael D. Alexander	2008	22242
137 0/8	21 7/8 22 1/8	18 2/8	5 5	Lawrence County	PA	Frank Fornataro, Jr.	2009	22242
137 0/8	21 1/8 20 6/8	15 6/8	5 5	Iowa County	WI	David Kammerer	2009	22242
*137 0/8	24 4/8 24 2/8	16 0/8	5 4	Kenton County	KY	Brian Delaney	2009	22242
*137 0/8	23 4/8 24 1/8	19 2/8	5 4	Sangamon County	IL	Eli Cook	2009	22242
137 0/8	20 4/8 20 4/8	17 6/8	5 5	Jefferson County	WI	Gary D. Clark	2009	22242
*137 0/8	25 1/8 25 0/8	15 6/8	5 6	Vigo County	IN	Greg W. Spurgeon	2009	22242
137 0/8	23 3/8 23 4/8	15 4/8	6 6	Linn County	IA	James Newman	2009	22242
137 0/8	24 5/8 24 1/8	19 0/8	4 4	Dubuque County	IA	Ron Johnson	2009	22242
137 0/8	24 1/8 24 2/8	19 2/8	4 5	Shelby County	MO	Raymond G. Jost	2009	22242
*137 0/8	23 6/8 23 0/8	17 4/8	4 4	Will County	IL	Tom Mooi	2009	22242
137 0/8	21 6/8 20 5/8	14 2/8	5 5	Monroe County	IA	Matthew Liljenquist	2009	22242
137 0/8	23 5/8 23 4/8	19 2/8	6 5	Riley County	KS	Michael Schurle	2009	22242
*137 0/8	22 0/8 22 0/8	18 2/8	5 5	Haakon County	SD	Kevin Bertsch	2010	22242
136 7/8	22 6/8 22 3/8	20 4/8	6 4	Clark County	IL	Daniel R. Green	2002	22455
136 7/8	22 7/8 21 6/8	18 1/8	5 5	Guernsey County	OH	Kenneth A. Sumner, Jr.	2002	22455
*136 7/8	21 6/8 21 7/8	17 3/8	5 5	Larue County	KY	Ernie Judd	2003	22455
136 7/8	21 7/8 22 2/8	17 7/8	4 5	Chippewa County	WI	Rob Kendall	2004	22455
136 7/8	23 0/8 23 0/8	16 7/8	5 5	Washburn County	WI	Jeffrey T. Lyons	2004	22455
*136 7/8	22 0/8 21 5/8	15 3/8	5 5	Woodbury County	IA	Brant Kurtz	2004	22455
*136 7/8	23 6/8 23 4/8	28 0/8	4 5	La Crosse County	WI	Jeff Towner	2004	22455
136 7/8	24 1/8 24 1/8	17 7/8	4 4	Hanover County	VA	M. Douglas Armstrong	2004	22455
136 7/8	21 1/8 21 0/8	15 5/8	6 6	Waukesha County	WI	Lee Thurow	2004	22455
136 7/8	22 4/8 22 0/8	15 7/8	5 5	Polk County	WI	David E. Johnson	2004	22455
136 7/8	22 2/8 21 7/8	16 1/8	4 4	Will County	IL	Robert Fisher	2004	22455
136 7/8	22 1/8 21 4/8	16 7/8	5 5	Rockland County	NY	Ben Risley	2004	22455
*136 7/8	22 3/8 22 4/8	17 7/8	7 5	Clark County	MO	Frank Knox	2004	22455
136 7/8	23 7/8 24 0/8	21 1/8	5 5	Nowata County	OK	Cliff Shrum	2004	22455
136 7/8	23 7/8 23 4/8	17 1/8	5 7	Greene County	IL	David Mansey	2004	22455
136 7/8	22 4/8 22 4/8	15 5/8	5 5	E. Carroll Parish	LA	Rodney Crimm	2005	22455
136 7/8	21 2/8 22 4/8	16 3/8	5 5	Outagamie County	WI	Todd Hopkins	2005	22455
136 7/8	23 6/8 24 3/8	18 1/8	6 7	Delaware County	IN	Jason Burcham	2005	22455
136 7/8	21 6/8 23 4/8	17 5/8	5 5	Douglas County	NE	Jessica Sigel	2005	22455
136 7/8	23 3/8 23 6/8	16 1/8	4 5	Washington County	MN	Richard Stromberg	2005	22455
136 7/8	21 6/8 24 4/8	20 5/8	5 4	St. Louis County	MN	John Abdo	2005	22455
*136 7/8	22 4/8 22 4/8	19 7/8	4 5	Cedar County	IA	Eric Brissee	2005	22455
136 7/8	22 0/8 22 0/8	17 1/8	4 4	Harris County	GA	Larry Garner, Jr.	2005	22455
136 7/8	23 3/8 23 3/8	16 1/8	6 5	Henry County	IN	Jessie L. Posey	2005	22455
*136 7/8	24 7/8 24 1/8	17 5/8	6 5	Scott County	IN	Brian J. Smith	2005	22455
136 7/8	22 0/8 22 2/8	15 5/8	5 5	Pike County	IL	Charles L. Palmer	2005	22455
136 7/8	20 3/8 21 5/8	18 1/8	4 4	Pike County	IL	Brian D. Scarnegie	2005	22455
*136 7/8	23 7/8 23 6/8	13 7/8	8 7	Warren County	KY	Patrick Wilson	2006	22455
*136 7/8	21 1/8 20 4/8	17 5/8	5 5	Bucks County	PA	Chuck Vollmer, Jr.	2006	22455
136 7/8	23 0/8 24 5/8	17 5/8	5 6	Lenawee County	MI	Forrest Grosteffon	2006	22455
136 7/8	21 7/8 22 0/8	17 7/8	4 4	Marquette County	WI	Andrew J. Cole	2006	22455
136 7/8	24 6/8 25 2/8	18 4/8	5 5	Jasper County	IL	Kenneth Ferguson	2006	22455
*136 7/8	21 5/8 21 5/8	17 5/8	5 4	Ward County	ND	Gary Rude	2006	22455
136 7/8	21 2/8 22 4/8	20 0/8	6 6	Dodge County	WI	Jim Vergenz	2006	22455
136 7/8	21 3/8 20 4/8	19 1/8	5 5	Hardin County	IA	Duane M. Jackson	2006	22455
136 7/8	24 0/8 23 5/8	18 3/8	4 4	New London County	CT	David Luke, Sr.	2006	22455
136 7/8	23 6/8 24 1/8	19 1/8	5 5	Cherry County	NE	David J. Nicolai	2006	22455
136 7/8	21 5/8 22 2/8	13 0/8	6 6	Macon County	MO	Joe Rowland	2007	22455
*136 7/8	24 2/8 24 2/8	18 7/8	6 6	Lake County	IN	John M. Singel	2007	22455
*136 7/8	23 1/8 21 4/8	17 7/8	4 4	Lawrence County	SD	Cory S. Hemeyer	2007	22455
*136 7/8	21 5/8 20 3/8	13 3/8	5 5	Houston County	TX	Coy Wade	2007	22455

Deer entries below 141 0/8, that appeared in the 6th Edition, are not included here, but are included on the accompanying CD (see page 119), and also in the Club's Records Archives.

WHITETAIL DEER (TYPICAL ANTLERS)

Minimum Score 125 — Continued

SCORE	LENGTH OF R MAIN BEAM L	INSIDE SPREAD	NUMBER OF R POINTS L		AREA	STATE/PROVINCE	HUNTER'S NAME	DATE	RANK
136 7/8	23 6/8 23 4/8	18 1/8	5	4	Auglaize County	OH	Nick Rostorfer	2007	22455
*136 7/8	20 0/8 22 2/8	16 3/8	8	6	Butler County	PA	Donald Garvin	2007	22455
*136 7/8	22 0/8 23 2/8	17 1/8	5	5	Hancock County	IL	Cody Lyons	2007	22455
136 7/8	22 2/8 23 0/8	18 1/8	6	5	Allen County	IN	Randy G. Easterday	2007	22455
136 7/8	22 6/8 23 6/8	18 5/8	4	5	Schuyler County	IL	Richard L. Bothell	2007	22455
*136 7/8	21 7/8 21 7/8	16 1/8	6	6	Parke County	IN	R. Shane Asher	2007	22455
136 7/8	19 5/8 20 5/8	14 5/8	5	5	Warren County	IA	Scott P. Wilson	2007	22455
136 7/8	23 4/8 22 0/8	17 7/8	5	4	Peoria County	IL	Larry Oppe	2007	22455
136 7/8	21 7/8 21 0/8	18 1/8	5	4	Shawano County	WI	Victor L. Kratzke	2007	22455
136 7/8	22 0/8 21 3/8	14 5/8	5	5	Vernon County	MO	Jeff Hubbard	2008	22455
136 7/8	21 6/8 21 3/8	16 1/8	6	6	Cumberland County	PA	Robert Weller	2008	22455
136 7/8	21 7/8 21 5/8	19 4/8	6	4	Cook County	IL	Mark Buehrer	2008	22455
*136 7/8	25 6/8 25 0/8	16 5/8	8	8	McPherson County	KS	Matthew Palmquist	2008	22455
*136 7/8	21 2/8 19 7/8	18 1/8	5	5	Buffalo County	WI	Randy J. Schoeneck	2009	22455
136 7/8	21 7/8 22 7/8	18 3/8	5	7	Buffalo County	WI	Ryan M. Kane	2009	22455
*136 7/8	22 6/8 22 5/8	16 3/8	5	5	Pepin County	WI	Bill Phillips	2009	22455
*136 7/8	23 5/8 23 1/8	15 4/8	4	6	Ward County	ND	Charles Weiser	2009	22455
136 7/8	21 2/8 21 6/8	15 1/8	6	8	Fulton County	IL	Jeff Pals	2009	22455
*136 7/8	20 7/8 21 3/8	16 5/8	5	5	Hempstead County	AR	Jeffrey Eaves	2009	22455
*136 7/8	24 4/8 23 7/8	15 1/8	5	6	Washington County	PA	George A. Kurtich	2010	22455
136 6/8	23 5/8 22 4/8	18 6/8	4	4	Henry County	IA	Ben Moore	2001	22647
136 6/8	23 0/8 22 4/8	18 4/8	5	5	Alcurve	SAS	Carl Furman	2003	22647
*136 6/8	23 7/8 22 4/8	19 4/8	7	5	Sarpy County	NE	Thomas Kelly	2003	22647
136 6/8	22 4/8 23 6/8	18 0/8	5	5	Ross County	OH	John Lawhorn, Jr.	2003	22647
136 6/8	21 7/8 22 6/8	16 4/8	5	5	Bayfield County	WI	Rodney Hipsher	2003	22647
136 6/8	21 0/8 21 5/8	16 0/8	5	6	De Kalb County	MO	Tony McCallan	2004	22647
136 6/8	22 4/8 21 3/8	17 2/8	5	5	Hocking County	OH	Mike Tigner	2004	22647
136 6/8	24 3/8 24 1/8	20 1/8	6	5	Gloucester County	NJ	Ronald Bilotta	2004	22647
136 6/8	22 2/8 21 7/8	17 6/8	5	5	Adams County	MS	Ellis Palasini, Jr.	2004	22647
136 6/8	21 1/8 21 2/8	15 4/8	5	6	Dimmit County	TX	Rick Knape	2004	22647
136 6/8	21 0/8 21 6/8	15 4/8	5	5	Price County	WI	Mason Burger	2004	22647
*136 6/8	23 2/8 22 7/8	19 4/8	4	5	Howard County	MO	Ryan Lueckenhoff	2005	22647
136 6/8	21 2/8 21 1/8	15 6/8	5	5	Burnett County	WI	Kent Bassett	2005	22647
136 6/8	21 4/8 21 6/8	18 2/8	5	5	Brown County	OH	Joe Eskew	2005	22647
136 6/8	21 1/8 21 5/8	16 6/8	5	5	Lake County	MN	Randy Bowe	2005	22647
136 6/8	21 4/8 21 4/8	19 6/8	4	5	Monroe County	OH	Bryan Kahrig	2005	22647
*136 6/8	23 1/8 23 6/8	15 4/8	5	5	Daviess County	IN	Allen Graber	2005	22647
136 6/8	21 5/8 21 5/8	14 2/8	5	5	Jackson County	WI	Brian Rilling	2005	22647
136 6/8	21 0/8 21 7/8	19 4/8	4	5	Winona County	MN	Jim Starks	2005	22647
136 6/8	21 0/8 20 5/8	12 2/8	5	5	Goodsoil	SAS	Robert Vogel	2005	22647
*136 6/8	22 5/8 23 0/8	16 6/8	5	5	Morrison County	MN	Dale Devriendt	2005	22647
136 6/8	23 0/8 22 5/8	19 2/8	5	4	Wabasha County	MN	Ryan Sawinski	2005	22647
*136 6/8	24 2/8 23 6/8	16 0/8	4	5	Madison County	IN	Kennie Roberts	2005	22647
136 6/8	22 2/8 21 6/8	18 4/8	5	5	Gallatin County	IL	Michael Andrew Melton	2005	22647
136 6/8	24 0/8 23 1/8	18 2/8	5	4	Ashland County	OH	Jim Reynolds	2005	22647
*136 6/8	21 6/8 21 2/8	19 2/8	4	4	Oconto County	WI	Jordan C. Schroeder	2005	22647
136 6/8	22 4/8 22 0/8	22 6/8	6	6	Jones County	IA	Matt Kouba	2005	22647
136 6/8	22 2/8 21 7/8	16 7/8	5	6	Columbia County	WI	Larry Lee Prochnow	2005	22647
*136 6/8	23 1/8 23 1/8	15 0/8	5	6	Calhoun County	IL	Jeff Johnson	2005	22647
136 6/8	22 3/8 22 7/8	18 2/8	4	5	Sioux County	IA	Owen Sandbulte	2005	22647
136 6/8	21 4/8 20 4/8	15 0/8	5	5	Ramsey County	ND	Kelly Durbin	2005	22647
136 6/8	24 0/8 22 7/8	19 6/8	5	4	Ashtabula County	OH	Ronnie Queen	2006	22647
*136 6/8	22 6/8 23 1/8	14 4/8	4	6	Vernon County	WI	Kevin Magalsky	2006	22647
136 6/8	21 4/8 20 7/8	17 6/8	5	5	Chester County	PA	Mark J. Zawada	2006	22647
136 6/8	22 1/8 22 2/8	15 2/8	5	6	Pike County	IL	Todd Chapman	2006	22647
136 6/8	20 3/8 19 3/8	15 6/8	5	5	Cass County	IA	Mark Armstrong	2006	22647
*136 6/8	21 4/8 22 2/8	16 4/8	5	5	Marquette County	WI	Gregory S. Weston	2006	22647
*136 6/8	23 2/8 21 2/8	20 4/8	5	5	Madison County	IL	John C. Richardson III	2006	22647
136 6/8	21 7/8 22 2/8	17 2/8	4	5	Buffalo County	WI	Dan Dregney	2006	22647
*136 6/8	24 2/8 23 5/8	19 5/8	4	7	St. Croix County	WI	Barry Peterson	2006	22647
*136 6/8	22 6/8 22 2/8	18 6/8	4	4	Charles County	MD	Donald Leonard Burch	2006	22647
136 6/8	23 7/8 23 7/8	19 4/8	5	5	Fairfield County	CT	Bill Terry, Sr.	2006	22647
136 6/8	23 2/8 23 3/8	17 2/8	4	5	Hand County	SD	Travis Sivertsen	2007	22647
136 6/8	24 0/8 23 2/8	19 6/8	4	4	Lake County	IL	John Shadian	2007	22647
136 6/8	21 0/8 21 4/8	15 0/8	5	5	Lafayette County	WI	Todd Schwenkner	2007	22647
136 6/8	22 4/8 21 4/8	16 2/8	6	5	Jasper County	IA	Dean G. Elbe	2007	22647
*136 6/8	21 7/8 21 6/8	15 0/8	8	7	Comanche County	KS	Pat Lefemine	2007	22647
136 6/8	22 7/8 23 1/8	19 0/8	4	4	St. Croix County	WI	Keith M. Gehrman	2007	22647
*136 6/8	23 6/8 24 3/8	19 3/8	5	5	Adams County	OH	David G. Swain	2008	22647
136 6/8	22 6/8 22 1/8	18 6/8	5	5	Washington County	PA	Richard M. Kolesar	2008	22647
*136 6/8	24 0/8 23 5/8	18 0/8	6	6	Marion County	IL	Timothy Lacey	2008	22647
*136 6/8	21 3/8 21 5/8	17 6/8	5	5	Griggs County	ND	Al Messner	2008	22647
136 6/8	21 3/8 21 7/8	14 4/8	5	5	Wilbarger County	TX	Rodney Alexander	2008	22647
136 6/8	22 4/8 22 5/8	19 4/8	4	5	Pierce County	WI	Scott Brenner	2008	22647
136 6/8	23 0/8 21 6/8	17 0/8	5	5	Dodge County	WI	Duane Winter	2008	22647
*136 6/8	23 4/8 22 3/8	17 4/8	5	5	Cass County	NE	Douglas D. Schmidt	2008	22647
136 6/8	21 6/8 23 1/8	16 5/8	6	5	Monroe County	IN	Jason Howard	2008	22647
136 6/8	23 0/8 22 3/8	16 2/8	5	5	Sheboygan County	WI	Todd Schaetz	2008	22647
*136 6/8	20 4/8 20 2/8	16 4/8	5	5	Marion County	IA	Paul Reese	2008	22647
*136 6/8	22 5/8 22 6/8	17 5/8	7	6	Outagamie County	WI	Nick Schroeder	2008	22647
136 6/8	21 5/8 21 4/8	17 2/8	4	4	Tazewell County	IL	Dillon Weishaupt	2008	22647
*136 6/8	25 0/8 24 4/8	17 4/8	4	4	Shawano County	WI	Joel Minniecheske	2008	22647
*136 6/8	22 0/8 21 7/8	17 1/8	8	8	Polk County	WI	Ken Carrier	2008	22647
*136 6/8	22 7/8 22 5/8	16 6/8	5	5	Clay County	GA	Jeffrey L. Powell	2008	22647
136 6/8	21 0/8 21 3/8	16 4/8	5	5	Rusk County	WI	Cory O'Bryan	2009	22647
136 6/8	20 3/8 20 7/8	17 2/8	5	5	Polk County	WI	Bill Nelson	2009	22647
*136 6/8	21 0/8 20 7/8	20 0/8	5	5	Montague County	TX	Weldon Duff	2009	22647
*136 6/8	24 5/8 23 2/8	14 0/8	6	6	Adams County	OH	Brent Hodges	2009	22647
136 6/8	21 7/8 21 5/8	14 3/8	6	6	Van Buren County	IA	Baree Weber	2009	22647
*136 6/8	23 4/8 22 2/8	15 4/8	5	6	Jones County	IA	Gary Grassi	2009	22647
*136 6/8	21 4/8 21 2/8	17 0/8	5	6	St. Louis County	MN	Garrett Eikanger	2009	22647
136 6/8	21 6/8 21 4/8	18 2/8	5	5	Calhoun County	IL	Larry Stockton	2009	22647
136 6/8	21 0/8 21 0/8	17 2/8	5	5	Allen County	KS	Gordon Lew	2009	22647
*136 6/8	23 4/8 24 2/8	15 4/8	4	4	Sussex County	DE	Mark A. Johnson	2010	22647
136 5/8	21 4/8 21 2/8	16 7/8	5	5	Fulton County	IN	Dennis Kamp	2000	22864

WHITETAIL DEER (TYPICAL ANTLERS)

Minimum Score 125   Continued

SCORE	LENGTH OF R MAIN BEAM L	INSIDE SPREAD	NUMBER OF R POINTS L		AREA	STATE/ PROVINCE	HUNTER'S NAME	DATE	RANK
136 5/8	21 4/8 23 4/8	18 3/8	5	4	Fond du Lac County	WI	Nick Leonard	2002	22864
136 5/8	22 1/8 23 5/8	17 2/8	4	5	St. Clair County	MI	Charles B. Leemhuis	2004	22864
136 5/8	22 4/8 21 7/8	18 5/8	7	5	Williams County	OH	Mike S. Pasztor	2004	22864
*136 5/8	23 3/8 21 3/8	18 1/8	4	5	Red Willow County	NE	Larry J. Pohl	2004	22864
136 5/8	22 1/8 23 5/8	16 5/8	5	4	De Kalb County	IN	John W. Pranger, Jr.	2004	22864
136 5/8	22 4/8 23 4/8	17 7/8	5	5	Monroe County	PA	Jeffrey C. Mikol	2004	22864
136 5/8	20 7/8 22 1/8	16 5/8	5	5	Madison County	IA	Steve A. Marsh	2004	22864
136 5/8	22 3/8 22 2/8	18 5/8	5	4	Lee County	IL	Matthew C. Rehor	2004	22864
136 5/8	24 5/8 24 6/8	17 1/8	4	6	Linn County	KS	Douglas L. Below	2004	22864
*136 5/8	23 1/8 21 7/8	17 3/8	5	6	Jackson County	IA	Scott Hollinhead	2004	22864
136 5/8	24 0/8 24 3/8	16 1/8	4	4	Knox County	OH	Jim Reynolds	2004	22864
136 5/8	22 6/8 22 2/8	21 1/8	7	6	Marquette County	WI	Matt L. Bolstad	2004	22864
136 5/8	22 6/8 21 5/8	14 3/8	7	5	Randolph County	WV	Eric Vanscoy	2004	22864
136 5/8	20 5/8 21 2/8	16 7/8	6	7	Jones County	IA	Gerry W. Carstens	2004	22864
136 5/8	21 5/8 22 3/8	16 4/8	6	6	Norman County	MN	Dennis Warner	2005	22864
136 5/8	23 1/8 24 2/8	17 4/8	5	7	Delaware County	IA	Dean Dempster III	2005	22864
136 5/8	25 4/8 24 0/8	18 7/8	5	5	Dunn County	WI	Bob Knops	2005	22864
*136 5/8	23 1/8 23 2/8	17 7/8	5	4	Clermont County	OH	Matt Abercrombie	2005	22864
*136 5/8	22 0/8 22 6/8	14 6/8	6	6	Lincoln County	WI	Dave Burk	2005	22864
136 5/8	22 2/8 22 0/8	15 0/8	6	6	Cowley County	KS	Randy Patterson	2005	22864
136 5/8	21 6/8 22 2/8	15 7/8	5	5	Rock Island County	IL	Pat Hurley	2005	22864
136 5/8	23 3/8 23 2/8	17 3/8	5	5	Noble County	IN	Harold L. Patrick	2005	22864
*136 5/8	24 3/8 23 4/8	16 1/8	5	5	Concordia Parish	LA	Gary Nance	2005	22864
*136 5/8	23 3/8 23 5/8	17 3/8	5	5	Ashtabula County	OH	Scott Patterson	2005	22864
*136 5/8	22 0/8 24 1/8	19 1/8	5	5	Jackson County	IA	Dana Lawrence	2005	22864
136 5/8	21 6/8 21 1/8	16 5/8	8	5	Wright County	MN	John B. Kasper	2005	22864
136 5/8	26 2/8 22 5/8	16 6/8	6	6	St. Brieux	SAS	Chad Rohel	2006	22864
136 5/8	22 4/8 22 6/8	19 2/8	4	4	Lafayette County	WI	Roger Davis	2006	22864
*136 5/8	23 3/8 23 7/8	20 5/8	4	5	Hillsborough County	NH	Greg Carchidi	2006	22864
136 5/8	23 1/8 23 0/8	15 1/8	4	4	Buffalo County	WI	Kevin J. Averbeck	2006	22864
136 5/8	23 0/8 23 2/8	18 2/8	5	7	Jo Daviess County	IL	Jim Collachia	2006	22864
136 5/8	24 0/8 25 0/8	20 1/8	5	5	Rock County	WI	Barry Bergendale	2006	22864
*136 5/8	22 3/8 22 0/8	16 5/8	6	5	Rock Island County	IL	Steve Mogridge	2006	22864
136 5/8	23 7/8 23 7/8	18 7/8	5	5	Decatur County	IA	Richard Powles	2006	22864
136 5/8	24 2/8 24 4/8	20 4/8	6	4	Knox County	IL	Terry L. Ryder	2006	22864
136 5/8	22 4/8 21 6/8	15 4/8	7	5	Marion County	IA	Kyle Goodwin	2006	22864
136 5/8	23 5/8 23 4/8	17 5/8	6	5	Peoria County	IL	Mark Mellott	2006	22864
*136 5/8	21 1/8 21 4/8	16 1/8	6	5	Shoal Lake	MAN	Terrence H. Gause	2007	22864
*136 5/8	21 2/8 21 6/8	20 7/8	4	4	Crawford County	AR	Paul Thrift	2007	22864
*136 5/8	21 2/8 21 5/8	15 1/8	5	5	La Salle County	IL	Stanley Petty	2007	22864
*136 5/8	22 6/8 23 1/8	17 4/8	5	7	Sauk County	WI	Charles Arndt	2007	22864
136 5/8	21 0/8 21 7/8	16 6/8	5	7	Fairfield County	OH	Adam Perry	2007	22864
136 5/8	23 5/8 23 6/8	16 5/8	4	6	Dubuque County	IA	Mike Lyons	2007	22864
136 5/8	23 2/8 22 7/8	18 6/8	6	5	Bureau County	IL	Loran W. Yoakum	2007	22864
*136 5/8	24 0/8 23 5/8	16 7/8	5	5	Wyoming County	WV	Lonnie Blankenship	2007	22864
136 5/8	22 0/8 22 5/8	19 3/8	4	5	Waukesha County	WI	Chris Smith	2007	22864
136 5/8	20 5/8 20 4/8	16 7/8	5	6	Saline County	AR	Bryan Garner	2008	22864
*136 5/8	22 5/8 22 6/8	17 3/8	5	5	Warren County	VA	Nathan L. Patterson	2008	22864
136 5/8	22 7/8 25 1/8	19 5/8	4	5	Ozaukee County	WI	Carter Prinsen	2008	22864
136 5/8	22 6/8 22 2/8	19 3/8	4	4	Worth County	GA	Grayson G. Roberts	2008	22864
136 5/8	22 0/8 20 7/8	17 7/8	5	5	Columbia County	WI	Steve Rohn	2008	22864
*136 5/8	20 7/8 20 6/8	18 4/8	5	5	Larue County	KY	Chris Choate	2008	22864
136 5/8	22 6/8 22 4/8	15 5/8	5	5	Clayton County	IA	John Christensen	2008	22864
*136 5/8	26 7/8 28 6/8	19 3/8	4	3	Comanche County	KS	Bruce B. Aughtry	2008	22864
136 5/8	26 0/8 25 7/8	16 6/8	5	5	Putnam County	IL	Jason D. Art	2008	22864
*136 5/8	21 7/8 22 4/8	17 0/8	7	6	Shawano County	WI	Nathan Kedrowicz	2009	22864
136 5/8	21 1/8 21 5/8	16 1/8	5	5	Lincoln County	KY	Stephen Burton	2009	22864
*136 5/8	23 0/8 23 1/8	14 3/8	5	5	Steuben County	IN	Jesse R. Ferree	2009	22864
*136 5/8	23 7/8 23 0/8	18 3/8	4	6	Sioux County	IA	Jeffrey S. Nibbelink	2009	22864
*136 5/8	20 4/8 21 5/8	18 3/8	5	5	Marshall County	IN	Michael J. Weber	2009	22864
*136 5/8	22 3/8 21 6/8	17 3/8	4	5	Blue Earth County	MN	Adam Hunt	2009	22864
136 5/8	23 2/8 24 5/8	19 3/8	4	4	Bucks County	PA	Clifford Saxby	2009	22864
*136 4/8	23 5/8 23 4/8	17 7/8	5	6	Switzerland County	IN	Gregg Watt	2000	23055
136 4/8	22 3/8 21 7/8	17 6/8	4	4	Champaign County	OH	John May	2001	23055
136 4/8	23 2/8 23 2/8	16 6/8	4	4	Burleigh County	ND	Ben Buntrock	2002	23055
*136 4/8	22 0/8 21 6/8	16 7/8	5	4	Harrison County	IA	Steven C. Moody, Sr.	2003	23055
136 4/8	23 3/8 23 1/8	17 6/8	5	4	Carroll County	OH	Robert S. Wilson	2004	23055
136 4/8	23 2/8 22 4/8	15 4/8	4	4	Riley County	KS	Ryan D. Hubbard	2004	23055
136 4/8	19 0/8 20 3/8	14 2/8	5	5	Pike County	IL	Larry A. Bassett	2004	23055
*136 4/8	22 3/8 22 2/8	17 5/8	6	5	Stephenson County	IL	Ron E. Kaderly	2004	23055
*136 4/8	23 5/8 24 1/8	18 2/8	5	4	Fayette County	IA	Jeremy Massman	2004	23055
*136 4/8	23 6/8 23 0/8	17 0/8	4	4	Ripley County	IN	Blake Comer	2005	23055
136 4/8	20 0/8 20 5/8	17 4/8	5	6	Price County	WI	Brad Willemssen	2005	23055
*136 4/8	24 1/8 25 4/8	16 0/8	4	4	Logan County	IL	Toby L. Montgomery	2005	23055
136 4/8	24 3/8 23 3/8	17 2/8	5	5	Columbia County	WI	William D. Buckley	2005	23055
136 4/8	21 1/8 20 5/8	17 4/8	5	5	Holt County	NE	Danny Havranek	2005	23055
*136 4/8	22 5/8 22 2/8	18 5/8	6	6	Athens County	OH	Bill Moir	2005	23055
136 4/8	20 6/8 21 1/8	14 0/8	5	5	Meriwether County	GA	Perry Murphy	2005	23055
136 4/8	20 7/8 20 0/8	15 2/8	5	5	Denton County	TX	Ronny Allen	2005	23055
136 4/8	24 6/8 24 1/8	15 2/8	4	4	Morris County	NJ	Kenneth Baker	2006	23055
136 4/8	21 5/8 21 7/8	15 6/8	4	4	Whitley County	IN	Johnny Walthour, Jr.	2006	23055
136 4/8	21 1/8 20 7/8	20 6/8	4	4	Dorintosh	SAS	Walter Wood	2006	23055
*136 4/8	23 7/8 24 6/8	16 4/8	4	5	Columbia County	WI	Bruce F. Udell	2006	23055
136 4/8	22 5/8 22 1/8	17 7/8	6	6	Hancock County	IL	Mike Hardy	2006	23055
*136 4/8	23 6/8 22 4/8	16 2/8	5	5	Fayette County	WV	Warrick Smith, Jr.	2006	23055
136 4/8	21 5/8 22 5/8	17 0/8	4	4	Allamakee County	IA	Tyler A. Blohm	2006	23055
136 4/8	24 5/8 24 0/8	16 7/8	5	7	Fond du Lac County	WI	Robin Stibb	2006	23055
136 4/8	22 3/8 22 3/8	18 0/8	5	4	Woodbury County	IA	Douglas Christiansen	2006	23055
136 4/8	19 6/8 18 1/8	13 6/8	4	4	Green County	WI	Paul Ovadal	2007	23055
136 4/8	23 6/8 24 1/8	16 0/8	6	5	Eau Claire County	WI	Jason Zunker	2007	23055
136 4/8	21 0/8 20 6/8	14 4/8	6	7	Lawrence County	SD	Martin W. Pahkamaa	2007	23055
136 4/8	24 5/8 23 2/8	19 4/8	4	4	Richland County	WI	Jeff Beighley	2007	23055
136 4/8	22 0/8 21 4/8	20 5/8	5	6	Carroll County	IN	Robert Whitus	2007	23055
*136 4/8	22 4/8 22 0/8	17 6/8	5	6	Adair County	MO	Chuck Minick	2007	23055
136 4/8	22 3/8 22 3/8	20 4/8	4	5	Monroe County	WI	Jason M. Kamrath	2007	23055

Deer entries below 141 0/8, that appeared in the 6th Edition, are not included here, but are included on the accompanying CD (see page 119), and also in the Club's Records Archives.

553

WHITETAIL DEER (TYPICAL ANTLERS)

Minimum Score 125 — Continued

SCORE	R MAIN BEAM L	INSIDE SPREAD	R POINTS L	AREA	STATE/PROVINCE	HUNTER'S NAME	DATE	RANK
*136 4/8	25 4/8 25 1/8	17 0/8	4 4	Pike County	OH	Joseph A. Price, Jr.	2007	23055
136 4/8	21 1/8 21 3/8	19 6/8	5 6	Anoka County	MN	Mike Fitzpatrick	2007	23055
136 4/8	20 6/8 21 0/8	16 0/8	6 5	Big River	SAS	David Simmons	2007	23055
*136 4/8	22 5/8 22 4/8	20 2/8	5 4	New Castle County	DE	Michael Zabinko	2007	23055
136 4/8	21 2/8 22 0/8	18 3/8	5 6	Powell County	KY	Jim Jordan	2008	23055
*136 4/8	22 4/8 22 2/8	16 2/8	6 5	Richland County	OH	Daniel L. Crist	2008	23055
136 4/8	20 4/8 21 1/8	18 0/8	5 5	Barron County	WI	Brian Thill	2008	23055
136 4/8	21 2/8 22 6/8	16 3/8	6 5	Morgan County	IL	Gerald E. Hunter	2008	23055
136 4/8	23 0/8 24 1/8	18 4/8	6 5	Buffalo County	WI	Lucas Jones	2008	23055
136 4/8	24 2/8 24 2/8	19 4/8	5 5	Delaware County	PA	Roger Summers	2008	23055
*136 4/8	21 6/8 21 2/8	17 0/8	5 5	Porter County	IN	Chris M. Ryba	2008	23055
136 4/8	21 1/8 21 0/8	17 0/8	5 6	Nemaha County	KS	Kristopher Nolte	2008	23055
136 4/8	23 6/8 24 0/8	19 7/8	5 6	Jefferson County	WI	Larry Braatz	2008	23055
136 4/8	20 3/8 21 0/8	16 0/8	7 5	Winston County	AL	Derek Burleson	2009	23055
136 4/8	20 6/8 20 6/8	16 7/8	8 7	Buffalo County	WI	Mark Miller	2009	23055
136 4/8	22 0/8 20 1/8	16 4/8	5 5	Lincoln County	AR	Matt Miles	2009	23055
136 4/8	23 2/8 22 5/8	17 6/8	4 4	Howard County	IA	Bob Rasmussen	2009	23055
136 3/8	22 0/8 22 4/8	19 3/8	6 5	St. Croix County	WI	Daniel D. Clayton	2003	23241
136 3/8	20 1/8 21 1/8	15 3/8	4 4	Ashland County	WI	Jeremy Anderson	2003	23241
136 3/8	21 7/8 21 2/8	14 1/8	5 5	Orleans County	VT	Albert Lambert	2003	23241
*136 3/8	23 0/8 21 4/8	17 1/8	4 4	Pierce County	ND	Jeff Zavada	2004	23241
*136 3/8	22 2/8 21 7/8	15 7/8	6 7	Polk County	WI	Jon W. Haley	2004	23241
136 3/8	21 1/8 21 3/8	18 1/8	5 5	Jo Daviess County	IL	Dale Goytowski	2004	23241
136 3/8	22 1/8 22 5/8	15 4/8	5 5	Waupaca County	WI	Ryan Braunel	2004	23241
*136 3/8	22 2/8 22 1/8	17 3/8	4 4	Shawano County	WI	Chris Sperberg	2004	23241
136 3/8	23 7/8 22 7/8	18 3/8	4 4	Taylor County	WI	Gregg Peters	2004	23241
136 3/8	19 3/8 19 6/8	14 5/8	5 5	Chautauqua County	KS	Marcel Bergeron	2004	23241
136 3/8	22 2/8 21 0/8	21 5/8	4 5	Comanche County	KS	Mark Gerrald	2004	23241
136 3/8	21 7/8 21 6/8	15 2/8	6 5	Jackson County	WV	Lew King	2004	23241
136 3/8	24 2/8 25 1/8	17 2/8	5 5	Peoria County	IL	Jon Calzavara, Jr.	2004	23241
136 3/8	22 2/8 22 1/8	14 7/8	4 4	Pike County	IL	Steve W. Sowers	2004	23241
136 3/8	23 4/8 23 6/8	17 2/8	4 5	Buffalo County	WI	Leonard Moeller	2004	23241
136 3/8	21 7/8 21 6/8	16 5/8	5 6	Dimmit County	TX	Rick Knape	2005	23241
136 3/8	22 7/8 23 7/8	16 5/8	6 5	Warren County	IA	Mark Jenkins	2005	23241
136 3/8	22 1/8 22 5/8	16 4/8	5 6	Columbia County	WI	Jeff Brock	2005	23241
136 3/8	22 1/8 22 7/8	16 3/8	5 5	Wood County	WI	Kevin Bonkoski	2005	23241
136 3/8	25 7/8 25 0/8	23 0/8	7 6	Green Lake County	WI	Douglas B. Werch	2005	23241
136 3/8	24 4/8 23 4/8	18 3/8	5 4	Atascosa County	TX	Darrell Kainer	2005	23241
136 3/8	22 1/8 21 6/8	15 3/8	4 4	Allegheny County	PA	Russell Hottenfeller	2005	23241
*136 3/8	21 0/8 23 0/8	17 6/8	6 6	Oklahoma County	OK	Jack L. Hodgkinson, Jr.	2005	23241
136 3/8	19 6/8 19 5/8	12 4/8	7 7	Switzerland County	IN	Ashley Jellison	2005	23241
136 3/8	22 7/8 22 5/8	17 3/8	5 5	Randolph County	IL	Joseph E. Defibaugh	2005	23241
136 3/8	23 6/8 23 2/8	16 3/8	4 4	Logan County	KS	Clinton Davis	2005	23241
136 3/8	19 7/8 20 6/8	15 5/8	6 5	Cascade County	MT	Stephen Tylinski	2005	23241
*136 3/8	25 2/8 24 7/8	17 5/8	4 4	Coos County	NH	Jason Foster	2005	23241
136 3/8	21 6/8 21 5/8	15 5/8	6 6	Scott County	MN	Robin Sieh	2006	23241
*136 3/8	23 5/8 24 4/8	16 3/8	4 4	Newton County	MS	Luther Boone	2006	23241
*136 3/8	21 2/8 22 0/8	16 1/8	6 6	Jersey County	IL	Greg Haney	2006	23241
136 3/8	22 7/8 22 4/8	17 3/8	5 5	Green Lake County	WI	Jake Ladwig	2006	23241
136 3/8	20 6/8 21 1/8	16 5/8	5 5	Jerauld County	SD	Greg Ham	2006	23241
136 3/8	21 6/8 22 2/8	16 6/8	5 6	Montgomery County	IL	Brett Goldsmith	2006	23241
136 3/8	23 4/8 23 2/8	16 1/8	4 4	Hardin County	IL	Joseph P. Petrus	2006	23241
136 3/8	21 1/8 21 1/8	16 7/8	5 5	Scott County	KY	Jeremy Hanna	2007	23241
136 3/8	23 0/8 24 0/8	16 0/8	5 5	Winnebago County	IL	David Clark	2007	23241
136 3/8	23 4/8 24 3/8	16 5/8	4 4	Dunn County	WI	Michael Shields	2007	23241
136 3/8	22 7/8 22 4/8	16 7/8	6 5	Ashland County	WI	Steven Warden	2007	23241
136 3/8	20 6/8 20 6/8	16 2/8	6 5	Sauk County	WI	Tod R. Fleming	2007	23241
136 3/8	24 4/8 23 2/8	17 7/8	4 4	Bayfield County	WI	John Herrmann	2007	23241
*136 3/8	22 4/8 22 4/8	14 7/8	5 5	Schleicher County	TX	Mark Hunt	2008	23241
*136 3/8	22 6/8 22 1/8	19 5/8	5 5	Pepin County	WI	James L. Elberg	2008	23241
136 3/8	19 7/8 20 5/8	14 1/8	5 5	Allegheny County	PA	Jeffrey M. Theobald	2008	23241
136 3/8	20 1/8 19 7/8	16 7/8	5 5	Carrot River	SAS	Tom Nelson	2008	23241
*136 3/8	22 2/8 22 3/8	14 5/8	4 5	Steuben County	IN	Derek Lipely	2008	23241
136 3/8	24 5/8 24 7/8	23 1/8	4 4	Lancaster County	PA	Kevin R. Zynn	2008	23241
*136 3/8	23 0/8 17 0/8	18 4/8	6 5	Fountain County	IN	Jeff W. Frazier	2008	23241
*136 3/8	26 6/8 26 1/8	21 3/8	4 5	Forsyth County	NC	Dan Allen Boyer	2008	23241
*136 3/8	23 0/8 22 7/8	16 6/8	7 4	Natchitoches Parish	LA	Ronald Courville	2008	23241
*136 3/8	23 5/8 23 3/8	19 3/8	4 4	Kearny County	KS	Thomas G. Barton	2008	23241
136 3/8	21 2/8 21 1/8	16 1/8	5 5	St. Tammany Parish	LA	Michael Jourdan	2008	23241
136 3/8	21 6/8 20 4/8	16 3/8	5 6	Somerset County	PA	Jake Tuck	2009	23241
136 3/8	22 2/8 21 5/8	16 7/8	5 5	Jones County	GA	Grady Brantley	2009	23241
*136 3/8	23 1/8 22 7/8	18 1/8	5 4	Elkhart County	IN	Arnold E. Miller	2009	23241
*136 3/8	23 7/8 23 3/8	19 3/8	4 4	Posey County	IN	Joe Darr	2009	23241
*136 3/8	20 7/8 21 1/8	15 5/8	6 5	Hubbard County	MN	Warren Wilcox	2009	23241
136 3/8	22 4/8 20 6/8	18 7/8	5 5	Hillsdale County	MI	Andrew J. Paulsen	2009	23241
*136 3/8	21 2/8 21 6/8	18 1/8	5 7	Richland County	WI	Derek Goplin	2009	23241
136 3/8	19 7/8 19 0/8	13 6/8	5 6	Kewaunee County	WI	Davey Delcore	2009	23241
136 2/8	24 6/8 25 0/8	18 2/8	5 6	Ohio County	IN	Pat Sweeney	1996	23424
136 2/8	21 0/8 20 7/8	18 5/8	5 6	Miami County	IN	Mark Ross	1998	23424
*136 2/8	22 5/8 22 4/8	18 3/8	4 5	Blackmud Lake	ALB	Dean Bromberger	2000	23424
136 2/8	23 3/8 23 5/8	18 6/8	4 4	Wyandot County	OH	Nathan Elliott	2002	23424
*136 2/8	21 7/8 21 6/8	16 2/8	5 5	Muhlenberg County	KY	Robert Cena	2003	23424
136 2/8	23 2/8 23 6/8	18 6/8	4 4	Marathon County	WI	Collin Running	2003	23424
136 2/8	23 4/8 25 4/8	20 7/8	6 4	Worth County	MO	Bruce Barrie	2003	23424
136 2/8	23 2/8 25 2/8	21 2/8	6 5	Live Oak County	TX	John D. Hall	2004	23424
136 2/8	22 4/8 22 1/8	16 6/8	5 6	St. Louis County	MO	Ronald Leuthauser	2004	23424
136 2/8	22 6/8 21 7/8	19 4/8	4 4	Wyandot County	OH	David Ware	2004	23424
136 2/8	22 6/8 22 6/8	16 4/8	4 4	Pettis County	MO	Shawn Ellis	2004	23424
*136 2/8	21 4/8 21 5/8	15 6/8	5 5	Callaway County	MO	Brad Suthoff	2004	23424
136 2/8	21 0/8 20 7/8	13 6/8	5 5	Calhoun County	IL	Paul Hall	2004	23424
136 2/8	18 7/8 20 5/8	17 5/8	5 6	Polk County	WI	Dennis G. Psick	2004	23424
*136 2/8	23 0/8 23 4/8	17 2/8	6 7	Van Buren County	IA	Eric Sandiford	2004	23424
136 2/8	21 6/8 22 2/8	17 4/8	4 4	Green Lake County	WI	Luke A. Ladwig	2004	23424
*136 2/8	23 2/8 22 5/8	15 6/8	4 4	Vernon County	WI	Daniel Downing	2005	23424
136 2/8	23 4/8 23 3/8	18 6/8	4 4	Baltimore County	MD	Erik W. Nutter	2005	23424

554

WHITETAIL DEER (TYPICAL ANTLERS)

Minimum Score 125 — Continued

SCORE	R MAIN BEAM L	INSIDE SPREAD	R POINTS L		AREA	STATE/PROVINCE	HUNTER'S NAME	DATE	RANK
*136 2/8	25 2/8 24 1/8	19 7/8	6	4	Montgomery County	PA	Josh Bell	2005	23424
*136 2/8	22 7/8 24 2/8	16 5/8	7	5	Pike County	IL	Angela K. Walk	2005	23424
136 2/8	23 4/8 24 2/8	18 2/8	6	6	Iron County	WI	John Boss	2005	23424
*136 2/8	24 6/8 24 2/8	16 4/8	4	5	Sussex County	DE	Brian W. Sherwood	2005	23424
136 2/8	22 2/8 21 7/8	17 0/8	4	5	Platte County	MO	Jack Moore	2005	23424
136 2/8	21 1/8 20 6/8	14 6/8	5	6	Osage County	MO	Janice Riley	2005	23424
136 2/8	20 1/8 22 0/8	16 4/8	5	5	Mitchell County	IA	Phil Brumm	2005	23424
*136 2/8	21 2/8 21 4/8	16 2/8	5	5	Irion County	TX	Dusty McDaniel	2005	23424
136 2/8	20 3/8 20 3/8	14 4/8	5	5	Pike County	IL	John Randal Adamson IV	2005	23424
*136 2/8	23 2/8 25 3/8	25 0/8	7	4	Bucks County	PA	Robert W. Mott	2005	23424
136 2/8	25 6/8 25 4/8	20 0/8	4	4	Kent County	MI	Scott Bolser	2005	23424
136 2/8	22 1/8 22 3/8	17 2/8	4	4	Jefferson County	WI	Jeff J. Winn	2005	23424
136 2/8	21 7/8 21 6/8	14 5/8	6	7	Powder River County	MT	Richard Driscoll	2006	23424
136 2/8	21 3/8 21 5/8	16 6/8	4	5	Sully County	SD	Jerry J. Bush	2006	23424
*136 2/8	19 1/8 18 7/8	16 6/8	5	5	Newton County	GA	Dexter Leach	2006	23424
136 2/8	22 0/8 21 4/8	16 2/8	5	5	Guernsey County	OH	Jimmie Bates	2006	23424
136 2/8	24 4/8 23 5/8	17 0/8	6	5	Clark County	WI	Floyd J. Vancil	2006	23424
136 2/8	21 4/8 24 5/8	19 2/8	4	5	Henderson County	IL	Fortunato J. Cuevas	2006	23424
136 2/8	24 2/8 25 3/8	15 7/8	7	5	Athens County	OH	Ty Holdcroft	2006	23424
136 2/8	20 1/8 19 3/8	15 4/8	5	5	Grant County	WI	Jeff Steinback	2006	23424
136 2/8	21 0/8 21 1/8	14 2/8	5	5	Clark County	IL	Derek Loser	2006	23424
136 2/8	22 6/8 23 6/8	17 1/8	5	5	Warren County	NJ	Joseph Prinzo	2006	23424
*136 2/8	21 3/8 21 6/8	17 2/8	5	5	Woodson County	KS	Thomas M. Sutherland, Jr.	2006	23424
136 2/8	20 7/8 20 5/8	17 2/8	5	5	Lincoln County	NE	Henry R. Obermeier	2006	23424
136 2/8	23 6/8 23 6/8	16 7/8	5	6	Harrison County	OH	Donna Harper	2006	23424
*136 2/8	23 2/8 23 6/8	18 3/8	5	5	Van Buren County	MI	Bryan A. Hemenway	2006	23424
*136 2/8	23 5/8 22 4/8	19 2/8	4	5	Dubuque County	IA	Stefan Mumm	2006	23424
136 2/8	20 2/8 20 1/8	14 0/8	5	5	Woodlands	ALB	Leonard Verbaas	2007	23424
136 2/8	24 1/8 24 0/8	16 0/8	4	4	Franklin County	PA	Mark Baker	2007	23424
*136 2/8	22 6/8 22 6/8	15 4/8	4	6	Clark County	WI	Jim Ley	2007	23424
136 2/8	23 1/8 23 3/8	18 6/8	4	4	Tom Green County	TX	Dayne Rice	2007	23424
136 2/8	22 1/8 22 7/8	19 0/8	4	4	Monroe County	IA	Jerry Ohlendorf	2007	23424
136 2/8	21 5/8 21 1/8	15 4/8	5	5	Pike County	IL	Jacob Paschal	2007	23424
136 2/8	23 3/8 24 2/8	19 2/8	5	5	Meriwether County	GA	Kyle W. Crawford	2007	23424
136 2/8	24 0/8 24 1/8	21 4/8	4	4	Warren County	IN	Matthew Booth	2007	23424
*136 2/8	23 5/8 22 1/8	17 3/8	5	4	Madison County	IA	Marc Headington	2007	23424
136 2/8	25 0/8 23 3/8	17 4/8	5	4	Vance County	NC	Charles Grantham, Jr.	2008	23424
136 2/8	23 0/8 22 5/8	15 0/8	5	5	Washburn County	WI	Todd Muska	2008	23424
*136 2/8	20 3/8 19 2/8	13 4/8	5	5	Nelson County	KY	Eric Culver	2008	23424
136 2/8	23 0/8 20 7/8	22 0/8	5	5	Baylor County	TX	Richard L. Thurman	2008	23424
*136 2/8	22 1/8 21 4/8	18 4/8	4	4	Osage County	KS	Stephen Van Nieuwenhuyse	2008	23424
*136 2/8	23 2/8 23 0/8	17 6/8	4	4	Osage County	MO	Shawn Newcomb	2008	23424
136 2/8	20 5/8 20 7/8	15 7/8	6	7	Douglas County	NE	Rod Sigel	2009	23424
136 2/8	21 6/8 21 0/8	14 6/8	5	5	Buffalo County	WI	Marc N. Shaft	2009	23424
136 2/8	21 3/8 20 7/8	16 2/8	4	4	Waupaca County	WI	Daniel J. Mueller	2009	23424
*136 2/8	21 6/8 22 1/8	17 2/8	5	5	Knox County	IL	Gregg Simpson	2009	23424
*136 2/8	23 6/8 21 4/8	18 0/8	5	5	Kosciusko County	IN	Jeff Metcalf	2009	23424
*136 2/8	24 5/8 24 5/8	17 5/8	5	7	Jackson County	WI	Ramon Knudtson	2009	23424
136 2/8	25 0/8 24 2/8	17 0/8	5	5	St. Croix County	WI	Travis Schaffan	2009	23424
136 2/8	24 0/8 23 3/8	17 2/8	5	5	Clark County	MO	Toby J. Wood	2009	23424
136 2/8	23 2/8 22 5/8	14 2/8	5	4	Fayette County	TX	Rick Knape	2009	23424
136 2/8	23 1/8 22 7/8	19 0/8	6	5	Mitchell County	KS	William M. Johnson	2009	23424
136 2/8	18 7/8 19 3/8	15 4/8	6	6	Chautauqua County	KS	Dr. Kevin Harmon	2009	23424
*136 2/8	22 6/8 22 7/8	20 0/8	5	6	Tunica County	MS	Charles B. Johnson, Jr.	2009	23424
*136 2/8	25 2/8 24 7/8	15 7/8	4	8	Shackelford County	TX	Mike Pedigo	2009	23424
136 1/8	25 3/8 24 5/8	21 5/8	4	3	Vernon County	WI	Donald E. Oliver	1999	23653
136 1/8	22 0/8 21 2/8	16 0/8	7	5	McDonough County	IL	Frederick G. McFarland, Jr.	1999	23653
136 1/8	24 1/8 23 7/8	17 7/8	6	4	Gibson County	IN	David Weyer	2001	23653
136 1/8	23 4/8 22 7/8	16 5/8	4	5	Huntington County	IN	Mark Whitacre	2002	23653
136 1/8	22 3/8 22 5/8	19 0/8	4	5	Stephenson County	IL	Don J. Packard	2004	23653
136 1/8	20 7/8 22 1/8	17 3/8	5	5	Adams County	WI	Byron Cook	2004	23653
136 1/8	24 0/8 24 2/8	15 3/8	5	4	Grundy County	MO	Keith Vandevender	2004	23653
*136 1/8	23 7/8 23 2/8	19 3/8	5	4	Moody County	SD	Jason Zemlicka	2004	23653
136 1/8	20 3/8 21 0/8	14 1/8	5	5	Dallas County	MO	Norm Fogt	2004	23653
136 1/8	22 3/8 22 2/8	20 3/8	4	4	Hancock County	IA	Ken Lonneman	2004	23653
136 1/8	24 1/8 23 5/8	19 7/8	5	4	Cass County	IL	C. William Groesch	2004	23653
136 1/8	22 1/8 21 3/8	16 7/8	5	5	Randolph County	MO	Web Winfrey	2004	23653
136 1/8	24 3/8 23 6/8	17 1/8	5	5	Muskingum County	OH	Oscar Coleman	2004	23653
136 1/8	21 5/8 22 2/8	15 5/8	5	6	Marinette County	WI	Kenneth Ganter	2004	23653
136 1/8	24 1/8 21 0/8	18 0/8	6	6	Vernon County	WI	Richard L. Williams	2004	23653
136 1/8	23 2/8 23 0/8	19 1/8	4	4	Vernon County	WI	Dave R. Jackson	2004	23653
136 1/8	25 4/8 25 0/8	19 1/8	4	4	Barber County	KS	Lew Webb	2004	23653
136 1/8	21 1/8 22 1/8	17 3/8	5	5	Bell County	TX	Tomme R. Actkinson	2004	23653
136 1/8	22 3/8 25 2/8	18 3/8	5	4	Macon County	IL	Woodrow David	2004	23653
136 1/8	22 7/8 22 0/8	16 3/8	4	5	Madison County	IL	Mike Bertelsmann	2004	23653
136 1/8	23 2/8 23 7/8	17 3/8	4	4	Middlesex County	CT	Richard Wade	2005	23653
136 1/8	21 1/8 21 4/8	14 3/8	4	4	Carroll County	MO	Scott Englert	2005	23653
*136 1/8	22 1/8 21 4/8	17 5/8	5	5	Tom Green County	TX	Robert Kincaid, Jr.	2005	23653
136 1/8	23 0/8 23 4/8	19 3/8	4	4	Bucks County	PA	Shane Meenan	2005	23653
*136 1/8	22 1/8 22 3/8	14 3/8	5	5	Dubuque County	IA	Jeff Bettcher	2005	23653
*136 1/8	20 5/8 21 4/8	16 3/8	5	5	Callaway County	MO	Tim Underwood	2005	23653
*136 1/8	19 5/8 20 1/8	14 1/8	6	7	Pike County	IL	David Pritchard	2005	23653
136 1/8	22 3/8 24 3/8	17 5/8	8	5	Vernon County	MO	Brian Callaghan	2005	23653
*136 1/8	19 5/8 19 7/8	17 5/8	5	5	Rusk County	WI	Michael J. Kelenic	2005	23653
136 1/8	22 4/8 21 6/8	16 7/8	5	5	Sauk County	WI	James P. Merfeld	2005	23653
136 1/8	24 1/8 23 4/8	16 4/8	6	6	Athens County	OH	Chris Baynham	2005	23653
136 1/8	25 6/8 25 5/8	19 7/8	7	7	Lee County	IL	Gordon C. Gabelmann	2005	23653
136 1/8	22 0/8 23 0/8	17 7/8	5	5	Grayson County	TX	Chet Hough	2005	23653
*136 1/8	25 5/8 26 1/8	19 4/8	4	5	Stokes County	NC	Todd Rothrock	2006	23653
136 1/8	22 6/8 22 5/8	17 3/8	4	4	Clarendon County	SC	David B. Baker	2006	23653
136 1/8	25 1/8 24 2/8	19 3/8	5	5	Dodge County	WI	Bob Haseleu	2006	23653
*136 1/8	23 5/8 23 5/8	16 4/8	4	6	Woodford County	KY	James Humphrey	2006	23653
136 1/8	21 3/8 22 5/8	17 7/8	5	5	Buffalo County	WI	Glenn Klomaten	2006	23653
136 1/8	22 6/8 22 7/8	19 1/8	5	4	Wright County	MN	Andrew Tilbury	2006	23653
136 1/8	22 7/8 23 1/8	16 1/8	6	8	Sheboygan County	WI	Brian Reeder	2006	23653

Deer entries below 141 0/8, that appeared in the 6th Edition, are not included here, but are included on the accompanying CD (see page 119), and also in the Club's Records Archives.

555

WHITETAIL DEER (TYPICAL ANTLERS)

Minimum Score 125 — Continued

SCORE	R MAIN BEAM L	INSIDE SPREAD	R POINTS L		AREA	STATE/PROVINCE	HUNTER'S NAME	DATE	RANK
*136 1/8	21 4/8 21 0/8	16 5/8	5	5	Chautauqua County	NY	Gregory A. Lucas	2006	23653
136 1/8	23 6/8 23 6/8	17 0/8	5	5	Wayne County	NY	Gerald Smith	2006	23653
*136 1/8	23 3/8 23 2/8	17 4/8	7	5	Switzerland County	IN	Tim Caldwell	2006	23653
136 1/8	23 2/8 23 2/8	18 3/8	4	4	Comanche County	KS	Gary Head	2006	23653
136 1/8	21 5/8 21 7/8	15 3/8	5	5	Pottawatomie County	KS	Andrew Engholm	2006	23653
*136 1/8	20 4/8 20 2/8	18 1/8	7	5	Pike County	IL	Billy Riggs	2006	23653
*136 1/8	23 2/8 23 3/8	17 7/8	5	5	Whitley County	IN	Jason W. Branning	2006	23653
*136 1/8	20 5/8 24 1/8	13 6/8	6	5	Harrison County	OH	Jake Gorrell	2006	23653
136 1/8	24 2/8 22 3/8	17 7/8	4	5	Rock Island County	IL	Paul R. Schultz	2006	23653
136 1/8	26 0/8 25 2/8	19 1/8	4	4	Cumberland County	ME	Matthew W. Slocomb	2006	23653
136 1/8	20 4/8 20 7/8	16 3/8	5	6	Spokane County	WA	Brandon Enevold	2007	23653
136 1/8	21 0/8 21 3/8	16 1/8	5	5	Williams County	ND	Richard Gustafson	2007	23653
136 1/8	20 5/8 20 4/8	15 1/8	5	6	Brown County	IL	Neil W. Grover	2007	23653
*136 1/8	23 2/8 22 3/8	17 5/8	4	4	Wake County	NC	Kenneth Block	2007	23653
136 1/8	23 6/8 23 1/8	18 4/8	6	7	Christian County	IL	Rich Crowley	2007	23653
136 1/8	20 1/8 20 6/8	14 7/8	5	5	Daviess County	MO	M. Garry Pierson	2007	23653
136 1/8	25 2/8 25 4/8	19 5/8	8	6	Muskingum County	OH	Tim Smith	2007	23653
*136 1/8	23 5/8 23 3/8	17 7/8	5	4	Steuben County	IN	Dwayne Ort	2007	23653
136 1/8	22 2/8 22 3/8	15 5/8	5	5	Stafford County	KS	Donald C. Martin	2007	23653
136 1/8	23 4/8 23 1/8	16 0/8	7	5	Jasper County	IN	Frank B. Curles, Jr.	2007	23653
136 1/8	23 4/8 23 6/8	17 6/8	5	5	Greenwood County	KS	Bradley C. Magoon	2007	23653
136 1/8	22 6/8 22 2/8	17 7/8	5	5	Dukes County	MA	Brian T. Welch	2007	23653
136 1/8	25 2/8 25 6/8	16 6/8	5	7	Hocking County	OH	Mark Brown	2007	23653
136 1/8	24 4/8 24 5/8	18 1/8	5	4	Dubuque County	IA	Joe Rokusek	2007	23653
136 1/8	23 1/8 23 4/8	17 6/8	5	5	McMullen County	TX	Benjamin A. Siddons	2007	23653
*136 1/8	24 7/8 24 7/8	19 4/8	5	5	Robertson County	KY	Randy Myers	2008	23653
136 1/8	23 4/8 23 7/8	18 4/8	6	5	Green County	WI	William Copus	2008	23653
136 1/8	23 1/8 22 4/8	20 3/8	5	5	Westchester County	NY	Anthony Drpich	2008	23653
*136 1/8	25 0/8 24 4/8	15 7/8	4	4	Hartford County	CT	Thad M. Stewart	2009	23653
*136 1/8	23 1/8 22 3/8	16 7/8	8	5	Floyd County	IA	Andy Aird	2009	23653
136 1/8	23 5/8 24 0/8	15 5/8	8	6	Pike County	IL	Edward Roskopf	2009	23653
*136 1/8	21 2/8 21 2/8	20 1/8	5	5	Du Page County	IL	John P. Georgean	2010	23653
136 0/8	20 0/8 20 6/8	20 6/8	5	5	Converse County	WY	Frank Rus	1998	23836
136 0/8	21 2/8 21 5/8	13 6/8	5	5	Otter Tail County	MN	Daniel Iacarella	2000	23836
136 0/8	22 5/8 23 5/8	19 2/8	6	5	Westmoreland County	PA	Merle Bohince	2001	23836
136 0/8	22 4/8 23 1/8	17 2/8	4	4	Pike County	IL	Glen Lewis	2002	23836
*136 0/8	23 3/8 22 5/8	15 4/8	4	4	Southampton County	VA	Gerald Corallo	2003	23836
136 0/8	22 4/8 22 1/8	20 0/8	5	5	Monroe County	WI	Kyle D. Carr	2003	23836
136 0/8	22 1/8 22 0/8	16 4/8	4	4	Bracken County	KY	Matt Ernst	2004	23836
*136 0/8	21 6/8 21 2/8	19 2/8	5	5	Becker County	MN	Karl J. Carlson	2004	23836
136 0/8	22 7/8 22 3/8	19 2/8	4	4	Oneida County	WI	Greg D. Haese	2004	23836
136 0/8	21 7/8 20 0/8	14 6/8	5	5	Brown County	IL	Ross Surratt	2004	23836
136 0/8	22 4/8 22 0/8	18 0/8	4	4	Noble County	IN	Shea Greve	2004	23836
136 0/8	24 5/8 24 7/8	19 6/8	4	4	Jackson County	MI	Bryon K. Coppernoll	2004	23836
136 0/8	22 6/8 22 6/8	18 2/8	5	5	Trempealeau County	WI	Troy A. Mahutga	2004	23836
*136 0/8	22 6/8 22 7/8	16 4/8	5	4	Crawford County	WI	Leon Orzechowski	2004	23836
136 0/8	21 4/8 21 4/8	16 7/8	6	6	Clay County	MO	John Stephen Smith	2004	23836
136 0/8	22 5/8 23 3/8	20 5/8	5	7	Washington County	IL	Robert Jack	2004	23836
136 0/8	22 3/8 21 7/8	20 4/8	4	4	Boone County	MO	Bryan Crump	2004	23836
*136 0/8	20 1/8 21 6/8	18 2/8	6	6	Allamakee County	IA	Jay Schroeder	2004	23836
136 0/8	21 2/8 21 2/8	16 2/8	5	5	Lincoln County	CO	Craig Germond	2004	23836
136 0/8	22 5/8 22 0/8	16 0/8	5	4	Kay County	OK	James C. Burnett	2004	23836
136 0/8	22 6/8 22 5/8	15 4/8	6	5	Webb County	TX	James Bailey	2004	23836
136 0/8	22 4/8 22 3/8	18 0/8	5	5	Anoka County	MN	Carl Ganter	2005	23836
136 0/8	22 5/8 23 5/8	17 0/8	4	4	Lawrence County	IN	Charles George	2005	23836
136 0/8	21 0/8 20 3/8	16 4/8	5	5	Jersey County	IL	Judy Kovar	2005	23836
136 0/8	20 4/8 20 1/8	18 6/8	5	5	Atchison County	MO	Pat Athen	2005	23836
136 0/8	22 7/8 23 3/8	17 2/8	5	5	Grant County	WI	Gary Maciolek	2005	23836
*136 0/8	20 2/8 19 0/8	17 2/8	5	5	Montgomery County	IN	Craig Pirtle	2005	23836
136 0/8	21 7/8 22 3/8	16 2/8	4	4	Allamakee County	IA	T. J. Durnin	2005	23836
*136 0/8	20 5/8 20 2/8	16 4/8	4	4	Randolph County	IL	Craig Collins	2005	23836
136 0/8	24 1/8 24 4/8	21 2/8	5	5	Ottawa County	KS	Patrick E. Helget	2005	23836
136 0/8	21 5/8 22 6/8	18 0/8	5	5	Chippewa County	WI	Tim Danielson	2005	23836
*136 0/8	22 4/8 22 6/8	18 3/8	5	4	Hamilton County	IA	Darrel Hogan	2005	23836
136 0/8	25 0/8 24 0/8	17 2/8	4	4	Southampton County	VA	Hunter Patterson	2005	23836
*136 0/8	22 1/8 22 5/8	16 6/8	4	5	Steuben County	NY	Michael Dutcher	2005	23836
136 0/8	22 7/8 23 0/8	17 0/8	5	5	Delaware County	IA	Drew Kuckler	2005	23836
136 0/8	20 2/8 20 2/8	14 0/8	5	5	Carroll County	IL	Steve Gobeli	2005	23836
*136 0/8	23 1/8 22 6/8	18 3/8	7	4	Scott County	KY	Andrew Tackett	2006	23836
136 0/8	22 7/8 22 3/8	19 0/8	5	5	Webster County	NE	Jared Groce	2006	23836
136 0/8	24 3/8 22 7/8	17 4/8	5	6	Labette County	KS	Rodney Kelly	2006	23836
136 0/8	21 7/8 21 7/8	16 2/8	5	5	Jefferson County	WI	Thomas Ehrke	2006	23836
136 0/8	23 1/8 23 3/8	16 0/8	5	6	Madison County	MS	Jamey Evans	2006	23836
136 0/8	22 2/8 22 4/8	16 4/8	5	5	Davis County	IA	Gary Biles	2006	23836
*136 0/8	23 7/8 22 1/8	17 3/8	4	5	Dunn County	WI	Kevin Lechner	2006	23836
136 0/8	24 7/8 24 7/8	16 4/8	5	5	Benton County	AR	Jaysen Evans	2006	23836
*136 0/8	23 0/8 22 6/8	16 7/8	5	6	Worth County	IA	Brian Johnson	2006	23836
136 0/8	23 7/8 23 4/8	17 6/8	4	4	Warren County	OH	Tim Wadsworth	2006	23836
*136 0/8	23 4/8 23 0/8	18 2/8	4	5	Rock County	WI	Ken Rothergass	2006	23836
136 0/8	23 3/8 24 6/8	18 4/8	5	4	Henry County	IN	Todd W. Dawson	2006	23836
136 0/8	21 4/8 22 5/8	15 2/8	6	5	Adams County	WI	Dave Schmitt	2006	23836
136 0/8	22 1/8 21 7/8	16 4/8	4	5	Knox County	MO	Chris Skaggs	2006	23836
*136 0/8	22 6/8 23 7/8	21 0/8	4	4	Washington County	WI	Rodney Erickson	2007	23836
*136 0/8	20 1/8 20 3/8	16 0/8	5	5	Issaquena County	MS	Macky Myers	2007	23836
136 0/8	22 7/8 22 6/8	18 3/8	5	5	Scott County	KY	Jeremy Nettles	2007	23836
136 0/8	23 6/8 23 0/8	16 0/8	4	4	Howard County	TX	David L. Duncan	2007	23836
136 0/8	21 5/8 23 0/8	18 6/8	5	5	Champaign County	IL	Todd Jimmie Reed	2007	23836
*136 0/8	20 7/8 19 5/8	16 0/8	4	4	Lincoln County	MO	Nick Dorsen	2007	23836
136 0/8	23 7/8 23 5/8	15 7/8	6	5	Washington County	KS	Michael P. Comalli	2007	23836
136 0/8	21 5/8 22 0/8	16 1/8	4	4	Rock County	WI	Dan Arnold	2007	23836
*136 0/8	21 6/8 22 4/8	20 7/8	6	5	Buffalo County	WI	Mark Beeler	2007	23836
136 0/8	22 1/8 21 6/8	14 2/8	5	5	Knox County	MO	Martin Dixson	2007	23836
136 0/8	23 4/8 23 0/8	18 3/8	6	4	Cass County	NE	Jeff Bina	2007	23836
136 0/8	22 2/8 21 6/8	16 6/8	5	5	Crockett County	TX	Robert E. Kincaid, Jr.	2007	23836
136 0/8	22 7/8 23 2/8	19 4/8	4	5	Duval County	TX	Mikki Lackey	2007	23836

556

WHITETAIL DEER (TYPICAL ANTLERS)

Minimum Score 125   Continued

SCORE	LENGTH OF R MAIN BEAM L	INSIDE SPREAD	NUMBER OF R POINTS L		AREA	STATE/ PROVINCE	HUNTER'S NAME	DATE	RANK
*136 0/8	21 4/8 21 6/8	17 0/8	4	4	Montgomery County	MO	Robert K. Jones	2008	23836
136 0/8	21 7/8 23 3/8	22 7/8	6	5	Mink Lake	ALB	Andreas Pagenkopf	2008	23836
136 0/8	25 0/8 24 1/8	18 4/8	5	5	Hartford County	CT	Richard J. Langer	2008	23836
136 0/8	22 7/8 23 0/8	16 6/8	6	4	Anderson County	KS	Taylor Edwards	2008	23836
136 0/8	23 1/8 21 7/8	17 1/8	5	4	Hampshire County	MA	Mitchell Mazur	2008	23836
136 0/8	26 1/8 25 3/8	17 0/8	4	4	Jasper County	IL	Keaton Dobbs	2008	23836
*136 0/8	22 5/8 24 0/8	16 4/8	4	5	Kearny County	KS	Gary Shumate	2008	23836
136 0/8	20 6/8 20 4/8	16 6/8	5	4	Burlington County	NJ	Tyler G. Gladd	2008	23836
136 0/8	22 0/8 22 2/8	17 4/8	5	5	Langlade County	WI	Kory Kais	2008	23836
136 0/8	21 2/8 22 1/8	16 7/8	6	6	Pike County	IL	Dan Laurent	2008	23836
*136 0/8	22 3/8 22 5/8	16 0/8	4	5	Traill County	ND	Kurt Borg	2008	23836
*136 0/8	22 1/8 21 3/8	16 4/8	5	7	Knox County	NE	Dan Doman	2009	23836
136 0/8	21 6/8 21 6/8	18 2/8	7	7	Green Lake County	WI	Scott O. Naparalla	2009	23836
*136 0/8	22 7/8 23 1/8	18 6/8	5	5	Hampden County	MA	Bill Ayers, Jr.	2009	23836
136 0/8	21 2/8 21 4/8	19 0/8	5	5	Jackson County	WI	Mike L. DeBranbander	2009	23836
*136 0/8	23 7/8 24 1/8	13 5/8	6	5	Lewis County	MO	Doug Rader	2009	23836
136 0/8	22 6/8 22 6/8	17 0/8	6	7	Ramsey County	MN	Brian Lemay	2009	23836
136 0/8	23 0/8 20 6/8	18 5/8	6	6	Warren County	IN	Michael D. Masterson	2009	23836
136 0/8	23 3/8 23 7/8	16 0/8	6	4	Erie County	PA	John P. Stahon	2009	23836
136 0/8	26 3/8 25 1/8	20 3/8	5	5	Athens County	OH	Chuck Mann	2009	23836
136 0/8	22 6/8 23 2/8	15 6/8	5	5	Washington County	KY	Mike Blevins	2009	23836
*136 0/8	20 6/8 20 5/8	15 4/8	5	5	Hardin County	IL	Linda J. Brandon	2009	23836
*136 0/8	22 3/8 21 3/8	15 5/8	6	6	Brown County	OH	Kent Ballard	2009	23836
135 7/8	22 6/8 22 4/8	17 3/8	4	5	Broadwater County	MT	Bill Hangas	2001	24078
135 7/8	23 5/8 23 6/8	16 5/8	5	5	Warren County	IN	Jason Faulstich	2003	24078
135 7/8	22 1/8 22 1/8	17 2/8	6	5	Scott County	IL	Alan Mitchell	2003	24078
*135 7/8	21 1/8 21 2/8	16 1/8	5	5	Spink County	SD	Norman Humphrey	2003	24078
135 7/8	20 4/8 20 1/8	14 7/8	6	7	Webster County	IA	Jesse M. Ulicki	2004	24078
135 7/8	20 3/8 20 3/8	16 7/8	4	4	Beaver County	OK	Richie Bland	2004	24078
135 7/8	22 2/8 22 3/8	16 5/8	4	4	Dodge County	WI	Duane Nettesheim	2004	24078
135 7/8	27 1/8 27 3/8	16 3/8	5	6	Barron County	WI	Ryan Ebner	2005	24078
135 7/8	23 2/8 22 3/8	17 3/8	5	7	Logan County	KY	Stan Yoder	2005	24078
*135 7/8	23 1/8 23 0/8	18 1/8	5	5	Ward County	ND	Wayne Larcombe	2005	24078
135 7/8	22 4/8 22 7/8	19 1/8	4	5	Fillmore County	MN	John DeGeorge	2005	24078
*135 7/8	21 6/8 22 4/8	18 7/8	4	4	Ramsey County	ND	Ryan Olson	2005	24078
135 7/8	24 2/8 25 2/8	18 0/8	4	6	Mercer County	PA	Theodore N. Knechtel	2005	24078
135 7/8	20 0/8 20 7/8	15 3/8	5	5	Lawrence County	SD	Joseph Hallenbeck, Jr.	2005	24078
*135 7/8	23 5/8 23 4/8	18 7/8	4	3	Macoupin County	IL	Seth Hackler	2005	24078
135 7/8	24 2/8 24 4/8	16 5/8	5	4	Highland County	OH	Willie Davis	2005	24078
135 7/8	22 2/8 24 2/8	19 3/8	4	5	Calhoun County	MI	George I. Swan, Jr.	2006	24078
135 7/8	20 7/8 20 7/8	19 3/8	6	5	Orange County	IN	Mark Verble	2006	24078
*135 7/8	21 7/8 23 1/8	15 6/8	6	5	Ripley County	IN	Mark Wagner	2006	24078
135 7/8	24 2/8 25 5/8	19 1/8	5	5	Waukesha County	WI	Chris Leppin	2006	24078
135 7/8	21 3/8 22 5/8	17 1/8	4	5	Oxford	ONT	Wieslaw Klecki	2006	24078
135 7/8	24 6/8 22 4/8	18 3/8	4	4	Caroline County	MD	Scott B. Schorr	2006	24078
*135 7/8	22 3/8 23 3/8	15 3/8	7	5	Preble County	OH	Kevin Pierce	2006	24078
*135 7/8	22 2/8 22 1/8	14 7/8	5	5	Brown County	WI	Jack Vanden Heuvel	2006	24078
135 7/8	25 6/8 25 5/8	18 6/8	5	7	Portage County	OH	George Strunk	2006	24078
135 7/8	21 1/8 21 2/8	14 4/8	5	6	Oconto County	WI	Bob Milkie, Jr.	2006	24078
*135 7/8	19 7/8 20 2/8	13 7/8	5	5	Tom Green County	TX	Mark Harrington	2007	24078
135 7/8	22 5/8 21 2/8	18 5/8	6	7	Love County	OK	Bill Costin	2007	24078
135 7/8	23 3/8 23 7/8	19 1/8	4	4	Burt County	NE	Heath E. Penny	2007	24078
135 7/8	23 4/8 23 6/8	17 7/8	6	5	Monroe County	NY	Joel D. Henshaw	2007	24078
135 7/8	22 4/8 21 6/8	16 1/8	5	6	Davis County	IA	Russ Kay	2007	24078
135 7/8	19 6/8 20 5/8	13 7/8	5	5	Fond du Lac County	WI	Scott Paulin	2007	24078
135 7/8	23 6/8 23 2/8	19 7/8	4	4	Irion County	TX	Roger Reynolds	2007	24078
*135 7/8	19 2/8 19 0/8	16 5/8	5	5	Bartow County	GA	DeWayne Fuqua	2008	24078
*135 7/8	24 1/8 23 6/8	15 3/8	4	4	Scott County	MN	Joe Caminati	2008	24078
*135 7/8	23 2/8 24 4/8	21 6/8	6	6	Ward County	ND	Dylan Heinze	2008	24078
135 7/8	23 5/8 22 6/8	17 2/8	4	5	Linn County	MO	John Shermaly	2008	24078
135 7/8	22 7/8 23 6/8	15 3/8	4	4	Bradford County	PA	Bob Fuhrman	2008	24078
*135 7/8	25 0/8 24 2/8	21 3/8	4	4	Berks County	PA	John E. Houck, Jr.	2008	24078
135 7/8	22 2/8 21 7/8	18 7/8	5	5	Sac County	IA	Kolin Mueggenberg	2008	24078
*135 7/8	20 7/8 20 4/8	14 1/8	5	5	Montgomery County	AL	Peyton Ashmore	2008	24078
135 7/8	20 5/8 20 5/8	16 5/8	5	5	Buffalo County	WI	Cory Baker	2008	24078
135 7/8	23 7/8 23 6/8	17 7/8	4	4	Garrard County	KY	Bobby G. Reed	2008	24078
*135 7/8	21 1/8 21 0/8	14 5/8	5	5	Bourbon County	KS	Richard Crawford	2008	24078
135 7/8	22 0/8 22 1/8	15 7/8	5	5	Kosciusko County	IN	Scott L. Werstler	2008	24078
135 7/8	21 4/8 22 3/8	17 7/8	4	4	McHenry County	ND	Keith Jones	2008	24078
135 7/8	22 2/8 22 6/8	18 5/8	4	4	Marinette County	WI	Joe Fiedorowicz	2008	24078
*135 7/8	22 4/8 22 0/8	18 7/8	4	4	Dauphin County	PA	Tim Kauffman	2009	24078
135 7/8	20 5/8 22 3/8	14 4/8	6	5	Coweta County	GA	Ken Yearta	2009	24078
135 7/8	22 6/8 23 1/8	17 5/8	5	5	Louisa County	IA	Dan McSorley	2009	24078
135 7/8	22 6/8 23 1/8	23 2/8	4	4	Gregory County	SD	Terry Marcukaitis	2009	24078
135 7/8	23 2/8 22 7/8	15 4/8	6	5	Davis County	IA	George Francis	2009	24078
*135 7/8	21 0/8 19 7/8	15 5/8	5	5	Foster County	ND	Cory Smith	2010	24078
135 6/8	21 7/8 21 2/8	16 4/8	5	6	Oakland County	MI	Robert A. Stevens	1985	24280
135 6/8	24 1/8 22 5/8	18 0/8	4	4	Crittenden County	KY	Denver Townsend	2000	24280
135 6/8	23 2/8 23 6/8	18 5/8	4	5	Chester County	PA	Michael W. Taylor	2002	24280
135 6/8	20 7/8 22 0/8	16 0/8	5	5	Jackson County	WI	Jason Wollberg	2003	24280
135 6/8	21 1/8 20 4/8	16 4/8	5	5	Vilas County	WI	David Fudala	2003	24280
135 6/8	22 3/8 22 1/8	17 7/8	5	5	Osage County	KS	Richard McCarty	2003	24280
135 6/8	21 2/8 21 7/8	19 2/8	4	5	Saline County	IL	George Michael Cannon	2003	24280
135 6/8	22 2/8 22 3/8	15 4/8	5	4	Merrick County	NE	Stacy Morton	2003	24280
135 6/8	23 0/8 23 1/8	17 6/8	5	4	Becker County	MN	Timothy Nicolas Erickson	2004	24280
*135 6/8	23 6/8 23 5/8	18 6/8	4	4	Scott County	MN	Mike Buetow	2004	24280
135 6/8	22 1/8 22 4/8	17 6/8	5	5	Clearwater County	MN	Joe Mantia	2004	24280
135 6/8	22 4/8 21 4/8	16 0/8	5	5	Trempealeau County	WI	Lou Kindred	2004	24280
*135 6/8	21 6/8 22 0/8	18 2/8	5	5	Hillsdale County	MI	Darren R. Councell	2004	24280
135 6/8	23 6/8 23 4/8	16 0/8	4	4	Anne Arundel County	MD	James J. Fegan	2004	24280
135 6/8	24 2/8 23 5/8	17 5/8	4	7	La Salle County	IL	John P. Hartman	2004	24280
135 6/8	22 5/8 23 0/8	18 6/8	5	5	Warren County	IL	Duane D. Freeman	2004	24280
*135 6/8	22 4/8 21 6/8	16 4/8	5	5	Dodge County	WI	Chris Friess	2004	24280
135 6/8	23 7/8 24 5/8	17 6/8	5	5	Pike County	IL	Brett Haas	2004	24280
135 6/8	24 5/8 23 3/8	17 4/8	6	6	Spencer County	IN	Michael Kamuf	2004	24280

Deer entries below 141 0/8, that appeared in the 6th Edition, are not included here, but are included on the accompanying CD (see page 119), and also in the Club's Records Archives.

557

WHITETAIL DEER (TYPICAL ANTLERS)

Minimum Score 125   Continued

SCORE	LENGTH OF R MAIN BEAM L	INSIDE SPREAD	NUMBER OF R POINTS L	AREA	STATE/PROVINCE	HUNTER'S NAME	DATE	RANK
135 6/8	23 3/8 24 3/8	18 6/8	7 5	Trempealeau County	WI	Chad Losinski	2004	24280
135 6/8	21 4/8 20 7/8	17 1/8	7 6	Fairfield County	OH	Nick Hoover	2004	24280
*135 6/8	22 6/8 21 6/8	17 0/8	7 6	Logan County	KY	Robin Rutherford	2005	24280
135 6/8	22 1/8 22 2/8	16 0/8	5 5	Cass County	MO	Chris Findley	2005	24280
*135 6/8	21 4/8 21 0/8	14 4/8	5 5	Crook County	WY	Michele Leqve	2005	24280
*135 6/8	20 2/8 19 5/8	17 0/8	5 5	Harrison County	KY	Lyle T. Fryman	2005	24280
135 6/8	25 5/8 24 4/8	17 0/8	5 5	Crawford County	IN	Tim Durbin	2005	24280
135 6/8	23 2/8 25 0/8	19 0/8	4 4	Erie County	NY	Dan McAuley	2005	24280
*135 6/8	22 2/8 22 4/8	16 1/8	6 5	Mills County	IA	Robert J. Eckes, Jr.	2005	24280
*135 6/8	22 1/8 21 6/8	15 6/8	5 5	Woods County	OK	Mike Dobson	2006	24280
135 6/8	21 0/8 20 2/8	13 4/8	5 5	Dubuque County	IA	Matt Webb	2006	24280
135 6/8	20 2/8 20 4/8	15 5/8	8 6	Harrison County	IN	Kenny R. Missi	2006	24280
135 6/8	21 7/8 21 3/8	18 6/8	5 6	Pottawatomie County	KS	C. Bruce Carroll	2006	24280
135 6/8	21 3/8 20 5/8	15 0/8	5 5	Worth County	MO	Alan Benton	2006	24280
135 6/8	25 0/8 25 5/8	22 0/8	5 4	Whitley County	IN	Daniel W. Barnhart	2006	24280
*135 6/8	21 6/8 22 2/8	16 4/8	5 6	Vigo County	IN	Luke Whitkanack	2006	24280
135 6/8	23 2/8 24 2/8	18 2/8	6 7	Waupaca County	WI	Gary L. Ebert	2006	24280
135 6/8	21 7/8 22 0/8	16 4/8	5 6	Sebastian County	AR	George Talkington	2007	24280
*135 6/8	21 7/8 21 6/8	18 1/8	6 8	Clark County	OH	James J. Suzel	2007	24280
135 6/8	22 4/8 22 1/8	17 0/8	4 4	Shawano County	WI	Harvey R. Roth	2007	24280
135 6/8	22 7/8 21 0/8	18 0/8	5 5	Franklin County	PA	Mark A. Wise	2007	24280
135 6/8	20 7/8 20 3/8	15 0/8	5 6	Adams County	WI	Dennis Konrath	2007	24280
135 6/8	21 1/8 22 2/8	17 0/8	4 4	Switzerland County	IN	J. Chris Robbins	2007	24280
135 6/8	24 2/8 24 1/8	17 6/8	5 4	Marshall County	SD	Shane Rien	2007	24280
*135 6/8	24 5/8 25 6/8	16 0/8	5 7	Monroe County	MI	David A. Kwiatkowski	2007	24280
*135 6/8	24 0/8 23 0/8	17 1/8	5 6	Jasper County	IN	Sam Vanni	2007	24280
135 6/8	23 0/8 22 0/8	15 6/8	6 5	Buffalo County	WI	Kelly Thompson	2007	24280
135 6/8	23 5/8 23 0/8	17 6/8	4 4	Houston County	MN	Steve Skau	2007	24280
135 6/8	22 1/8 21 2/8	18 2/8	6 7	Hardin County	IA	Bruce Off	2007	24280
135 6/8	20 2/8 20 3/8	17 2/8	4 5	Greenwood County	KS	Frank S. Noska IV	2007	24280
*135 6/8	22 7/8 23 7/8	19 4/8	4 4	Issaquena County	MS	Macky Myers	2007	24280
*135 6/8	22 6/8 21 5/8	18 2/8	5 5	Sequoyah County	OK	Jamey Burkhart	2008	24280
135 6/8	21 3/8 21 1/8	16 0/8	5 5	Columbia County	WI	Heath Hagner	2008	24280
*135 6/8	20 0/8 19 4/8	21 4/8	5 5	Albemarle County	VA	Keith Grubbs	2008	24280
*135 6/8	22 3/8 21 7/8	17 2/8	4 4	Ransom County	ND	Ben Hendricks	2008	24280
*135 6/8	22 7/8 23 0/8	18 6/8	4 4	Henry County	IA	Judd Shumaker	2008	24280
*135 6/8	21 2/8 22 1/8	16 0/8	4 4	Jefferson County	WI	Doug Scherer	2008	24280
135 6/8	20 5/8 21 1/8	16 6/8	5 5	Hamilton County	IA	Dave M. Root	2008	24280
*135 6/8	24 0/8 22 7/8	16 6/8	5 4	Saratoga County	NY	Gary Nicol	2008	24280
*135 6/8	23 3/8 24 5/8	19 3/8	6 6	Sumner County	KS	Matthew J. Allmond	2008	24280
*135 6/8	22 4/8 21 0/8	20 6/8	4 5	Comanche County	KS	Ambrose Updegraff	2008	24280
135 6/8	21 5/8 22 6/8	17 0/8	5 4	Nemaha County	NE	Randall Rehmeier	2008	24280
*135 6/8	21 3/8 21 3/8	15 4/8	5 5	Wetzel County	WV	James Banker	2008	24280
135 6/8	22 5/8 23 1/8	16 4/8	7 8	Steuben County	IN	Chris Spaw	2009	24280
*135 6/8	22 3/8 22 4/8	17 0/8	5 7	Wood County	OH	James A. Peterson	2009	24280
*135 6/8	24 6/8 24 7/8	17 6/8	4 5	Winnebago County	WI	Tony Schreiber	2009	24280
*135 6/8	24 1/8 23 7/8	20 3/8	5 5	Vernon County	WI	Richard Anderson	2009	24280
*135 6/8	22 6/8 22 6/8	18 2/8	4 4	Charles County	MD	Lance Schiemer	2009	24280
*135 6/8	22 3/8 23 5/8	16 4/8	7 6	Hocking County	OH	Daniel Zaglewski	2009	24280
*135 6/8	26 5/8 27 5/8	20 3/8	4 6	Greene County	IL	Wayne Stocker	2009	24280
135 6/8	24 2/8 23 6/8	15 5/8	4 5	Livingston County	NY	Philip Powell	2009	24280
135 6/8	23 6/8 23 2/8	15 2/8	4 4	Winona County	MN	Johnny F. Micheel	2009	24280
135 6/8	23 0/8 24 0/8	17 7/8	7 7	Morgan County	MO	John Haake	2009	24280
135 6/8	22 1/8 21 4/8	19 0/8	5 4	Shawano County	WI	Kyle R. Ewald	2009	24280
*135 6/8	23 3/8 23 1/8	18 2/8	5 5	Sandusky County	OH	Brian Streacker	2009	24280
135 6/8	23 7/8 22 3/8	19 1/8	6 5	Crook County	WY	Adam A. Clark	2010	24280
135 5/8	24 6/8 25 7/8	18 0/8	4 6	Cattaraugus County	NY	Ronald Dale Kooser	1978	24517
*135 5/8	21 6/8 21 5/8	17 4/8	5 6	Monroe County	MI	Patrick H. Gabriel	1999	24517
135 5/8	23 7/8 24 4/8	17 7/8	4 4	Marquette County	WI	William Brummond	2000	24517
135 5/8	23 6/8 25 0/8	15 6/8	6 6	Oldham County	KY	Tom Woosley	2002	24517
*135 5/8	23 2/8 23 4/8	17 5/8	6 4	Allegheny County	PA	Robert E. Guynn	2003	24517
135 5/8	24 1/8 23 7/8	17 7/8	5 5	Winnebago County	IL	Peter R. Basile	2003	24517
135 5/8	21 5/8 21 5/8	15 7/8	5 5	Columbia County	WI	Mike Lehrmann	2003	24517
135 5/8	24 1/8 24 0/8	18 7/8	4 5	Comanche County	KS	Ben F. Craft	2003	24517
135 5/8	23 6/8 24 0/8	16 3/8	5 4	Knox County	OH	Aaron Tedrow	2004	24517
135 5/8	20 3/8 20 2/8	17 1/8	5 6	Anne Arundel County	MD	Samuel G. Willsey	2004	24517
*135 5/8	27 2/8 24 6/8	18 2/8	6 6	Trumbull County	OH	Justin Scott Abbott	2004	24517
135 5/8	22 0/8 23 3/8	18 1/8	4 5	Clermont County	OH	Gene Schadle	2004	24517
135 5/8	22 1/8 23 3/8	16 3/8	5 5	York County	PA	Marvin Diller	2004	24517
135 5/8	22 1/8 21 3/8	17 3/8	4 4	Lake County	IN	Vic Peoples	2004	24517
*135 5/8	22 1/8 21 4/8	16 7/8	5 5	Isabella County	MI	Michael William Mackley	2004	24517
135 5/8	24 3/8 25 2/8	16 1/8	5 5	Bond County	IL	Mark Thornton	2004	24517
135 5/8	22 5/8 22 7/8	18 2/8	4 5	Polk County	WI	Frank Taylor	2004	24517
135 5/8	20 5/8 20 2/8	12 3/8	6 7	Van Buren County	IA	Ivan Muzljakovich	2004	24517
135 5/8	24 1/8 24 5/8	17 7/8	5 4	Fayette County	IL	Mike Durbin	2004	24517
*135 5/8	20 7/8 20 4/8	15 5/8	5 5	Lawrence County	SD	Gary Larive	2004	24517
135 5/8	20 4/8 21 0/8	16 5/8	5 5	Buffalo County	WI	Claude B. Klein	2004	24517
135 5/8	21 0/8 21 2/8	19 6/8	6 7	Bond County	IL	Mark Wilkerson	2005	24517
135 5/8	21 3/8 21 1/8	15 3/8	5 5	Washburn County	WI	Johnny Paine	2005	24517
135 5/8	22 5/8 22 1/8	15 5/8	7 5	Logan County	IL	Eldon Broster	2005	24517
135 5/8	22 5/8 21 1/8	13 2/8	6 6	Ripley County	IN	Sam Durham	2005	24517
135 5/8	21 7/8 20 7/8	16 3/8	5 6	Miami County	IN	Bill Burdine	2005	24517
135 5/8	22 2/8 22 5/8	11 7/8	5 5	Pike County	IL	Steve M. Schuwerk	2005	24517
*135 5/8	24 1/8 24 5/8	20 0/8	5 6	McDowell County	WV	Mark Delida	2005	24517
135 5/8	24 6/8 24 4/8	17 7/8	5 5	Oswego County	NY	Kevin Carter	2005	24517
135 5/8	23 5/8 23 3/8	14 7/8	5 5	Nemaha County	KS	Brian Ross	2005	24517
135 5/8	24 1/8 24 2/8	18 1/8	4 4	Sterling County	TX	P. R. Potts	2005	24517
*135 5/8	24 0/8 24 3/8	18 0/8	5 5	Bourbon County	KS	Doyle Slinkard	2005	24517
135 5/8	23 2/8 22 6/8	17 1/8	5 5	Winneshiek County	IA	Curt Jones	2005	24517
135 5/8	21 1/8 20 7/8	15 5/8	5 5	Pend Oreille County	WA	Anthony Rueppel	2006	24517
*135 5/8	24 4/8 22 6/8	17 3/8	4 4	Winnebago County	IL	Andrea Oakes	2006	24517
135 5/8	21 6/8 22 5/8	16 5/8	5 5	Clark County	WI	Jason Lamovec	2006	24517
135 5/8	21 6/8 22 7/8	15 3/8	4 4	Harrison County	MO	Steve Tylinski	2006	24517
135 5/8	23 5/8 23 3/8	17 1/8	5 5	Monroe County	IA	Rick L. Slinger	2006	24517
*135 5/8	22 7/8 23 0/8	18 5/8	5 5	Wabasha County	MN	David Radtke	2006	24517

558

WHITETAIL DEER (TYPICAL ANTLERS)

Minimum Score 125   Continued

SCORE	LENGTH OF R MAIN BEAM L	INSIDE SPREAD	NUMBER OF R POINTS L	AREA	STATE/ PROVINCE	HUNTER'S NAME	DATE	RANK
135 5/8	23 3/8 23 4/8	18 1/8	4 5	Jackson County	IL	Timothy Cobin, Jr.	2006	24517
*135 5/8	19 5/8 19 2/8	15 1/8	5 5	Ransom County	ND	Travis Dick	2007	24517
135 5/8	23 3/8 24 3/8	21 1/8	8 9	Beaverhead County	MT	Donald S. Dvoroznak	2007	24517
135 5/8	26 3/8 26 3/8	18 5/8	5 6	Eaton County	MI	Patrick Jon Rankin	2007	24517
135 5/8	21 0/8 22 0/8	17 1/8	6 5	Green Lake County	WI	Kirk D. Dornfeld	2007	24517
*135 5/8	20 2/8 19 4/8	16 7/8	5 5	Waushara County	WI	Dan Grambsch	2007	24517
135 5/8	23 5/8 23 2/8	18 1/8	4 5	Greene County	IN	Michael D. Beedie	2007	24517
135 5/8	20 6/8 22 2/8	18 7/8	6 5	Fond du Lac County	WI	Dan Leonard	2007	24517
*135 5/8	20 6/8 20 6/8	16 5/8	5 5	Vernon County	WI	Larry Orvold	2007	24517
135 5/8	21 6/8 22 4/8	16 3/8	5 5	Putnam County	IN	Robert S. Ragan	2007	24517
135 5/8	22 4/8 22 5/8	17 3/8	5 6	Onondaga County	NY	Bruce E. Foote	2007	24517
135 5/8	21 0/8 20 6/8	17 5/8	5 5	Peoria County	IL	Mike Reatherford	2007	24517
135 5/8	21 6/8 22 0/8	16 5/8	5 5	Comanche County	KS	William E. Gaunt, Jr.	2007	24517
135 5/8	25 7/8 25 4/8	15 4/8	6 5	Greenwood County	KS	Michael A. Wilson	2007	24517
135 5/8	20 5/8 20 2/8	15 4/8	6 6	Trempealeau County	WI	Garrett Halama	2008	24517
135 5/8	21 6/8 22 1/8	13 6/8	6 5	Chariton County	MO	Mark Schmitt	2008	24517
*135 5/8	23 4/8 23 0/8	19 3/8	4 5	Tippecanoe County	IN	Brian P. Baker	2008	24517
*135 5/8	23 1/8 23 0/8	16 5/8	4 4	Pike County	IL	Todd Hoftiezer	2008	24517
135 5/8	20 4/8 21 2/8	16 0/8	6 9	Baxter County	AR	Dana Friedland, Jr.	2008	24517
135 5/8	22 2/8 21 7/8	14 7/8	6 6	Dane County	WI	Jon McGettigan	2008	24517
135 5/8	22 4/8 21 5/8	18 7/8	5 6	Schuyler County	IL	Tommy Coy Jones	2008	24517
*135 5/8	22 0/8 22 6/8	20 0/8	6 6	Clay County	AR	Bill McCartney	2008	24517
*135 5/8	22 5/8 22 0/8	19 7/8	5 5	McLean County	ND	Sam C. Sager	2008	24517
135 5/8	22 6/8 22 5/8	15 7/8	6 6	Marion County	IA	Gerald T. Dowell	2008	24517
135 5/8	25 7/8 25 1/8	17 6/8	5 6	Pepin County	WI	Dustin Auth	2009	24517
135 5/8	24 1/8 23 6/8	18 4/8	5 7	Shawano County	WI	Scott D. Moon	2009	24517
135 5/8	21 4/8 21 6/8	16 3/8	5 5	Kosciusko County	IN	Tim A. Tubbs	2009	24517
135 5/8	20 4/8 18 2/8	15 3/8	6 5	Tom Green County	TX	Ronnie Parsons	2009	24517
*135 5/8	21 2/8 21 4/8	14 7/8	5 4	Ottawa County	KS	Rod Haley	2009	24517
135 5/8	21 5/8 21 5/8	15 5/8	5 5	Beadle County	SD	Harvey Tschetter	2009	24517
135 5/8	22 5/8 24 7/8	19 1/8	6 5	Moore County	NC	Jonathan Gregson	2009	24517
*135 5/8	22 4/8 22 0/8	15 3/8	5 5	Marks Township	ONT	Jay Hickman	2009	24517
*135 5/8	21 0/8 21 5/8	15 5/8	5 5	Davis County	IA	Kirk Clark	2009	24517
*135 5/8	21 4/8 21 4/8	19 1/8	4 4	Warren County	IA	Dan Semenza	2009	24517
135 5/8	23 7/8 23 6/8	18 3/8	6 5	Monroe County	NY	James Steven Burkhart	2009	24517
135 4/8	20 1/8 19 6/8	15 6/8	5 5	Branch County	MI	Arza J. Harris	1999	24728
135 4/8	20 5/8 21 0/8	15 6/8	5 5	Pike County	MO	Daniel Tow	2000	24728
135 4/8	22 7/8 22 6/8	19 0/8	4 4	Butte County	SD	Reginald E. Faber, Jr.	2001	24728
135 4/8	22 0/8 22 2/8	16 3/8	6 6	Valley County	NE	Gary Dyer	2002	24728
135 4/8	20 5/8 21 2/8	17 2/8	5 5	Shawano County	WI	Lance Olson	2002	24728
*135 4/8	22 1/8 22 4/8	18 0/8	4 5	Stephenson County	IL	Gerald Erbsen	2003	24728
135 4/8	22 3/8 23 4/8	17 2/8	4 4	Eau Claire County	WI	Shawn Vanlandingham	2004	24728
135 4/8	23 0/8 21 6/8	20 4/8	5 5	Sauk County	WI	Joe Litscher	2004	24728
135 4/8	20 4/8 20 6/8	15 0/8	5 5	Victoria County	TX	Ted W. Douglass, Jr.	2004	24728
135 4/8	23 7/8 25 3/8	13 6/8	4 4	Bourbon County	KS	Kevin Asbury	2004	24728
135 4/8	24 6/8 24 4/8	20 2/8	3 3	Brown County	NE	Joel A. Klammer	2004	24728
*135 4/8	21 4/8 21 6/8	15 6/8	5 4	Hickman County	TN	Richard H. Boehms	2004	24728
*135 4/8	22 4/8 21 7/8	15 4/8	6 7	Washita County	OK	Steven Brown	2004	24728
135 4/8	21 0/8 20 6/8	16 6/8	5 5	Rosebud County	MT	Nina Krueger	2005	24728
135 4/8	19 6/8 19 6/8	17 0/8	5 5	Washington County	WI	Thomas Neuburg	2005	24728
135 4/8	22 3/8 23 2/8	19 2/8	4 4	Carroll County	IN	Casey Watson	2005	24728
135 4/8	24 5/8 23 5/8	19 6/8	4 4	Venango County	PA	Denton J. Wenner	2005	24728
135 4/8	20 1/8 20 4/8	16 2/8	5 5	Holt County	MO	Chad Grisim	2005	24728
*135 4/8	21 3/8 21 2/8	15 2/8	5 5	Schuyler County	IL	Daniel L. Cole	2005	24728
135 4/8	23 6/8 23 2/8	17 0/8	4 5	Yates County	NY	Kent Duane	2005	24728
135 4/8	23 5/8 24 5/8	20 2/8	5 6	Ashland County	OH	Gary S. Bellis	2005	24728
*135 4/8	24 5/8 24 3/8	16 4/8	4 4	Linn County	IA	Keith Peterson	2005	24728
*135 4/8	23 5/8 24 2/8	21 4/8	4 4	Essex County	MA	Jay Tripp	2005	24728
135 4/8	22 6/8 21 7/8	18 6/8	5 5	Lancaster County	NE	Jamey Montey	2006	24728
135 4/8	21 4/8 22 6/8	15 0/8	5 4	Marshall County	IN	Kathryn R. Holmes	2006	24728
135 4/8	22 1/8 21 0/8	18 6/8	4 4	Genesee County	NY	Neal Short	2006	24728
135 4/8	24 1/8 24 5/8	15 2/8	4 4	Hillsborough County	NH	Richard Gallant	2006	24728
135 4/8	22 4/8 22 1/8	17 2/8	5 5	Buffalo County	WI	Brian Cepress	2006	24728
135 4/8	23 0/8 22 3/8	17 6/8	5 6	Edmonson County	KY	Craig Browning	2006	24728
135 4/8	23 4/8 23 4/8	18 6/8	6 5	Queen Annes County	MD	Kent Uhrich	2006	24728
135 4/8	23 7/8 21 2/8	20 7/8	6 5	Pierce County	WI	Michael Brickner	2006	24728
135 4/8	23 1/8 22 0/8	18 0/8	5 5	Pottawattamie County	IA	Chad Grisim	2006	24728
135 4/8	21 7/8 22 0/8	20 4/8	5 5	Chicot County	AR	Frank Greenlee	2006	24728
*135 4/8	23 0/8 22 5/8	16 7/8	5 5	Buffalo County	WI	Dave Pfieffer	2006	24728
135 4/8	23 7/8 23 7/8	14 6/8	5 5	Marion County	KY	Ronald Dylan Bright	2007	24728
135 4/8	20 5/8 20 5/8	17 2/8	5 5	Steuben County	IN	Steven Harter	2007	24728
135 4/8	21 0/8 22 0/8	16 6/8	5 5	Cayuga County	NY	Dan Walsh	2007	24728
135 4/8	19 6/8 19 7/8	18 2/8	5 6	Linn County	KS	Larry W. Peterson	2007	24728
135 4/8	23 0/8 22 4/8	13 6/8	4 4	St. Joseph County	IN	Garrett McBride	2007	24728
*135 4/8	22 4/8 24 1/8	20 6/8	5 5	Newton County	IN	Jim Pistello	2007	24728
*135 4/8	23 4/8 23 3/8	16 6/8	4 5	Kenedy County	TX	Daniel J. Moultrie	2007	24728
*135 4/8	21 3/8 22 4/8	15 2/8	6 6	Adair County	MO	Robert C. Stewart	2008	24728
*135 4/8	23 1/8 22 7/8	17 0/8	5 5	Baltimore County	MD	Michael Scott Richardson	2008	24728
135 4/8	21 7/8 22 5/8	15 0/8	5 5	Cass County	MI	Roger S. Thompson	2008	24728
135 4/8	21 4/8 21 4/8	15 2/8	5 5	Cass County	IL	Mark Koonter	2008	24728
135 4/8	23 3/8 23 4/8	16 6/8	5 5	Pike County	IL	Michael Veres	2008	24728
*135 4/8	22 1/8 22 6/8	17 0/8	5 5	Bon Homme County	SD	Mark W. Sedlacek	2008	24728
135 4/8	22 6/8 22 1/8	23 2/8	4 4	Monmouth County	NJ	Tony Monte	2008	24728
*135 4/8	23 5/8 24 4/8	20 1/8	6 6	Screven County	GA	Alan McAllister	2009	24728
135 4/8	23 0/8 21 7/8	18 3/8	6 6	Redwood County	MN	Jamie R. Jenniges	2009	24728
*135 4/8	22 3/8 22 0/8	17 0/8	4 4	Buffalo County	WI	Cody W. Doucette	2009	24728
135 4/8	22 2/8 22 1/8	18 5/8	6 5	Cass County	IL	Henry A. Passerini, Jr.	2009	24728
135 4/8	22 6/8 23 1/8	19 5/8	4 6	Washburn County	WI	Dan Hanson	2009	24728
*135 4/8	21 0/8 22 4/8	17 7/8	5 5	Macomb County	MI	Michael C. Mohan	2009	24728
135 4/8	23 5/8 23 3/8	16 6/8	4 6	Chippewa County	WI	Scott Beaudette	2009	24728
*135 4/8	22 7/8 22 4/8	19 2/8	5 5	McDonald County	MO	Rusty Johnson	2009	24728
*135 4/8	22 6/8 23 1/8	20 1/8	4 4	Clark County	IL	Kevin A. Camp	2009	24728
135 4/8	21 7/8 23 7/8	22 0/8	5 5	Buffalo County	WI	Budd Kadinger	2009	24728
135 4/8	22 6/8 22 5/8	18 2/8	5 5	Armstrong County	PA	William M. Cloak	2009	24728
*135 4/8	22 1/8 21 1/8	15 4/8	5 5	Lawrence County	OH	Shannon Quinn	2009	24728

Deer entries below 141 0/8, that appeared in the 6th Edition, are not included here, but are included on the accompanying CD (see page 119), and also in the Club's Records Archives.

WHITETAIL DEER (TYPICAL ANTLERS)

Minimum Score 125   Continued

SCORE	LENGTH OF R MAIN BEAM L	INSIDE SPREAD	NUMBER OF R POINTS L		AREA	STATE/ PROVINCE	HUNTER'S NAME	DATE	RANK
*135 4/8	19 4/8 20 6/8	16 4/8	6	5	Ramsey County	ND	Amber Logie	2009	24728
135 3/8	21 3/8 21 0/8	16 5/8	5	6	Clarke County	IA	Greg Bakken	2001	24944
135 3/8	24 6/8 25 1/8	19 3/8	5	4	Worcester County	MA	William Haney	2003	24944
135 3/8	20 6/8 20 1/8	16 5/8	5	5	Slope County	ND	John Carpenter	2004	24944
135 3/8	20 3/8 19 6/8	14 4/8	6	5	Lee County	IL	Lee Dixon	2004	24944
135 3/8	22 0/8 23 6/8	17 3/8	6	5	Chester County	PA	Carl F. Nagle	2004	24944
135 3/8	22 7/8 24 1/8	15 7/8	4	4	Fulton County	IN	Jason T. Shoemaker	2004	24944
135 3/8	24 7/8 25 2/8	18 5/8	4	4	Brown County	NE	Keith Karr	2004	24944
135 3/8	23 3/8 22 6/8	14 7/8	6	5	Columbia County	WI	Wayne E. Peters	2004	24944
*135 3/8	23 6/8 24 0/8	20 6/8	7	4	Kent County	MI	Nolan Davis	2004	24944
135 3/8	21 2/8 22 2/8	17 1/8	6	5	Marion County	IA	Randy Des Camps	2004	24944
135 3/8	22 4/8 20 6/8	16 5/8	4	4	Pottawattamie County	IA	Randy Sage	2004	24944
*135 3/8	19 7/8 20 2/8	15 3/8	5	5	St. Clair County	MI	Shawn Eagle	2004	24944
135 3/8	22 5/8 22 5/8	15 3/8	5	5	Clark County	IN	Doc Nash	2004	24944
135 3/8	22 1/8 22 4/8	13 3/8	4	4	Dubuque County	IA	Tom Casey	2004	24944
135 3/8	22 4/8 22 6/8	20 1/8	5	4	Washington County	NE	Clint Barnes	2004	24944
135 3/8	23 3/8 22 0/8	16 5/8	4	4	Fort Assiniboine	ALB	Donald James Cohick	2005	24944
135 3/8	23 3/8 23 6/8	17 3/8	4	4	Kent County	MD	R. Bradford Perry	2005	24944
135 3/8	22 1/8 22 3/8	15 1/8	4	4	Lyon County	IA	Mike Judas	2005	24944
135 3/8	21 5/8 20 2/8	14 3/8	4	4	Branch County	MI	Glenn M. Padmos	2005	24944
135 3/8	24 5/8 24 7/8	20 7/8	5	4	Dougherty County	GA	Michael Layfield	2005	24944
*135 3/8	23 7/8 23 1/8	14 6/8	8	6	Cerro Gordo County	IA	Dick Searle	2005	24944
135 3/8	18 7/8 21 3/8	17 4/8	6	5	Cass County	MI	Andy W. Silverthorn	2005	24944
135 3/8	24 2/8 22 2/8	19 3/8	5	6	Buffalo County	WI	Tony Heil	2005	24944
135 3/8	23 3/8 23 4/8	19 3/8	4	5	Beaver County	PA	Kenneth W. Day	2005	24944
135 3/8	20 6/8 21 2/8	20 1/8	5	4	Des Moines County	IA	Tad Boeding	2005	24944
135 3/8	22 2/8 22 0/8	17 5/8	5	4	Buffalo County	WI	Michael Schleicher	2005	24944
135 3/8	20 3/8 19 6/8	18 1/8	5	5	Carver County	MN	Adam Rametta	2005	24944
135 3/8	24 1/8 24 4/8	17 3/8	4	4	Clayton County	IA	James E. Irwin	2005	24944
*135 3/8	22 6/8 23 4/8	17 4/8	6	6	Lake County	IN	Aaron D. Lanting	2005	24944
*135 3/8	23 7/8 24 5/8	17 1/8	4	4	Hartford County	CT	David Kilgore	2005	24944
135 3/8	22 0/8 21 7/8	16 4/8	6	4	Sumner County	KS	Craig Jones	2005	24944
*135 3/8	23 0/8 24 1/8	16 3/8	5	4	Crittenden County	KY	Robert Gregor	2005	24944
*135 3/8	25 3/8 22 7/8	17 5/8	4	7	Union County	KY	Dustin McCord	2006	24944
135 3/8	21 2/8 22 4/8	17 3/8	5	4	Jo Daviess County	IL	Jack Rife	2006	24944
135 3/8	22 6/8 24 3/8	15 1/8	5	6	Dunn County	WI	Michael J. Lauer	2006	24944
135 3/8	24 5/8 23 4/8	19 7/8	4	5	Jasper County	IA	Douglas J. Van Wyk	2006	24944
*135 3/8	23 3/8 24 3/8	21 1/8	6	6	Lake County	IN	Mike Gudenschwager	2006	24944
135 3/8	23 1/8 22 7/8	17 4/8	5	6	Allegan County	MI	Larry Wennersten	2006	24944
135 3/8	23 5/8 23 6/8	18 1/8	4	4	Barron County	WI	Brett Moravitz	2006	24944
135 3/8	25 0/8 24 6/8	16 5/8	6	6	Montgomery County	MD	Frank H. Wilmot	2006	24944
*135 3/8	23 3/8 22 7/8	17 5/8	5	5	Trempealeau County	WI	Larry A. Bley	2007	24944
*135 3/8	22 2/8 22 6/8	17 7/8	7	5	Outagamie County	WI	Mark B. Menting	2007	24944
*135 3/8	23 6/8 23 2/8	17 3/8	5	5	Callaway County	MO	Les Renn	2007	24944
135 3/8	24 3/8 23 7/8	16 5/8	4	4	Muskingum County	OH	John Hogan	2007	24944
*135 3/8	21 4/8 22 2/8	17 3/8	5	5	Monroe County	MI	Bradley W. Jacobs	2007	24944
135 3/8	24 2/8 23 4/8	14 5/8	5	5	Barton County	MO	D. J. Delgado	2007	24944
*135 3/8	17 6/8 20 3/8	16 1/8	5	5	Beadle County	SD	Scott Hintz	2007	24944
*135 3/8	25 4/8 25 6/8	16 6/8	5	5	Ottawa County	MI	Scott Knauf	2007	24944
135 3/8	25 0/8 23 1/8	17 7/8	4	4	Sullivan County	IN	Randy Shiflett	2007	24944
135 3/8	24 2/8 23 7/8	21 1/8	5	5	Bledsoe County	TN	Michael Bobel	2007	24944
135 3/8	22 2/8 21 2/8	15 6/8	7	6	Randolph County	AR	Derek Kildow	2007	24944
135 3/8	20 7/8 20 7/8	14 1/8	5	5	Pine County	MN	Randy E. Broz	2007	24944
*135 3/8	22 7/8 23 0/8	16 5/8	4	6	Ray County	MO	Jeff Ball	2008	24944
135 3/8	21 5/8 20 6/8	14 3/8	4	5	Scotland County	MO	Monty Allen "Jake" Boytek	2008	24944
135 3/8	22 7/8 23 1/8	17 3/8	4	5	Venango County	PA	Andrew Crocker	2008	24944
*135 3/8	22 7/8 23 4/8	17 6/8	5	7	Crittenden County	KY	Ryan T. Bulle	2008	24944
135 3/8	21 3/8 21 0/8	17 7/8	5	5	Adams County	IL	Phil D. Kelso	2008	24944
135 3/8	25 0/8 23 2/8	20 1/8	4	4	Dane County	WI	Stuart Smith	2008	24944
*135 3/8	21 6/8 22 4/8	18 5/8	5	5	Buffalo County	WI	Mark Beeler	2008	24944
135 3/8	23 2/8 23 5/8	17 2/8	5	6	Dubois County	IN	Seth Wagner	2008	24944
*135 3/8	20 6/8 20 6/8	19 6/8	5	5	Morgan County	OH	Mike Strong	2008	24944
135 3/8	21 1/8 21 6/8	18 3/8	5	5	DeKalb County	IL	Stephen Tarnoki	2008	24944
135 3/8	20 7/8 20 6/8	18 2/8	6	5	Park County	WY	Eric Boley	2009	24944
*135 3/8	22 0/8 21 6/8	16 1/8	5	5	Fayette County	IL	Todd Moreland	2009	24944
*135 3/8	22 6/8 22 3/8	17 1/8	5	6	Jefferson County	NE	Jarred Horsky	2009	24944
135 3/8	24 0/8 24 2/8	17 7/8	4	4	Morris County	NJ	Mark Spoto	2009	24944
135 3/8	23 1/8 23 6/8	15 3/8	5	5	Otter Tail County	MN	Derek Revering	2009	24944
*135 3/8	21 4/8 21 6/8	15 3/8	6	5	Mellette County	SD	Eddie R. Brockhoft	2009	24944
135 3/8	22 7/8 21 3/8	14 7/8	5	5	Somerset County	MD	William "Bill" Collins	2009	24944
135 3/8	23 4/8 22 3/8	22 5/8	4	4	Kent County	MD	James Thompson	2009	24944
135 3/8	23 5/8 23 6/8	14 7/8	4	4	Schuyler County	NY	Michael James Benjamin	2009	24944
135 3/8	22 3/8 22 4/8	17 3/8	4	5	Essex County	NJ	Carmen Cucuzza	2009	24944
135 3/8	22 1/8 21 4/8	16 3/8	4	4	Norton County	KS	Nathan Andersohn	2009	24944
135 2/8	22 4/8 22 4/8	17 4/8	5	5	Coahuila	MEX	Ernest "Kit" Alsop, MD	1998	25162
135 2/8	20 7/8 21 6/8	17 2/8	5	5	Saginaw County	MI	Kent Ballard	2001	25162
*135 2/8	22 1/8 22 1/8	17 2/8	5	5	Ward County	ND	Roger Hodnefield	2002	25162
*135 2/8	21 2/8 21 1/8	14 2/8	5	5	Jefferson County	IN	Richard L. Jones	2003	25162
135 2/8	22 7/8 23 4/8	18 0/8	5	4	Jasper County	IL	Carl Waggle	2003	25162
135 2/8	23 2/8 23 2/8	17 6/8	4	4	Hocking County	OH	Kelly Vaughn	2004	25162
135 2/8	23 2/8 23 2/8	18 3/8	6	6	Berks County	PA	Jason S. Angstadt	2004	25162
135 2/8	23 0/8 24 3/8	17 2/8	4	5	Live Oak County	TX	John D. Hall	2004	25162
135 2/8	22 0/8 21 6/8	19 0/8	5	5	White County	IL	Walt Guthrie	2004	25162
135 2/8	22 2/8 22 6/8	13 4/8	5	5	Buffalo County	WI	Nathan Ashwell	2004	25162
135 2/8	22 1/8 22 1/8	16 2/8	5	4	Waupaca County	WI	Jim Kern	2004	25162
*135 2/8	22 1/8 22 1/8	16 6/8	5	5	Sauk County	WI	Justin M. Acheson	2004	25162
135 2/8	23 4/8 23 3/8	19 2/8	4	4	Huron County	OH	Joseph M. Houghtland	2004	25162
135 2/8	21 5/8 20 0/8	15 6/8	4	5	Eau Claire County	WI	John D. Bergeson	2004	25162
135 2/8	22 3/8 21 6/8	17 4/8	5	5	Dunn County	WI	Kevin Klatt	2004	25162
135 2/8	21 1/8 22 4/8	14 2/8	6	6	Dallas County	IA	J. Alex Wick	2004	25162
135 2/8	21 3/8 20 2/8	15 5/8	5	8	Pike County	IL	Scott Brewer	2004	25162
135 2/8	22 3/8 22 5/8	16 6/8	5	4	Okanogan County	WA	L. Allen Beard	2005	25162
135 2/8	23 1/8 23 0/8	19 2/8	4	4	Somerset County	NJ	Scott Parneg	2005	25162
135 2/8	19 3/8 18 4/8	16 6/8	5	5	Throckmorton County	TX	James Lawler	2005	25162
135 2/8	23 0/8 22 3/8	17 3/8	6	6	McCulloch County	TX	Michael D. Williams	2005	25162

WHITETAIL DEER (TYPICAL ANTLERS)

Minimum Score 125 Continued

SCORE	LENGTH OF R MAIN BEAM L		INSIDE SPREAD	NUMBER OF R POINTS L		AREA	STATE/ PROVINCE	HUNTER'S NAME	DATE	RANK
135 2/8	21 2/8	21 3/8	19 0/8	5	5	Eddy County	ND	Jason Stafford	2005	25162
*135 2/8	23 3/8	23 1/8	18 2/8	4	4	Iowa County	WI	Matthew T. Gleichauf	2005	25162
135 2/8	23 3/8	24 1/8	17 3/8	6	5	Sevier County	AR	Ken Friday	2005	25162
*135 2/8	21 2/8	21 2/8	17 4/8	6	5	Fountain County	IN	Art Brannon	2005	25162
135 2/8	23 0/8	22 4/8	17 6/8	4	4	Vernon County	WI	Danny McGinnis	2005	25162
135 2/8	21 6/8	21 2/8	16 6/8	5	5	Monroe County	NY	David Offen	2005	25162
135 2/8	21 7/8	20 6/8	16 4/8	5	5	Ransom County	ND	Walter J. Palmer	2005	25162
*135 2/8	22 0/8	22 5/8	19 2/8	4	5	Clay County	MN	Craig D. Enervold	2005	25162
135 2/8	22 1/8	22 5/8	17 0/8	5	5	Washington County	PA	James Bateson	2006	25162
135 2/8	22 5/8	24 0/8	16 5/8	5	6	St. Louis County	MO	Vincent A. Brandt, Sr.	2006	25162
135 2/8	21 4/8	21 2/8	16 6/8	7	7	Gallatin County	MT	Bob Morton	2006	25162
*135 2/8	22 4/8	23 0/8	16 4/8	5	5	Kennebec County	ME	Leroy Robinson, Jr.	2006	25162
135 2/8	20 2/8	19 1/8	16 2/8	6	6	Portage County	WI	Dale D. Iwanski	2006	25162
135 2/8	22 4/8	23 5/8	18 2/8	5	5	Carroll County	IN	Dane Hunter Fife	2006	25162
135 2/8	21 4/8	20 4/8	16 4/8	5	5	Van Buren County	IA	Brian Klein, Jr.	2006	25162
135 2/8	23 3/8	24 1/8	17 2/8	4	4	Champaign County	OH	Robert Criss	2006	25162
135 2/8	23 4/8	22 4/8	18 6/8	4	4	Barry County	MI	Jesse J. Noteboom	2006	25162
135 2/8	20 6/8	21 4/8	15 4/8	4	4	Sangamon County	IL	Allen Magie	2006	25162
*135 2/8	23 4/8	23 4/8	17 6/8	4	5	Buffalo County	WI	Greg Pettis	2006	25162
*135 2/8	23 7/8	25 3/8	15 2/8	4	5	Sangamon County	IL	Gary Gould	2006	25162
*135 2/8	22 6/8	22 2/8	16 2/8	4	4	Hancock County	IL	Scott Eggert	2006	25162
135 2/8	26 3/8	27 1/8	21 0/8	4	4	Newport County	RI	Augie Viveiros, Jr.	2006	25162
135 2/8	21 5/8	22 1/8	15 2/8	5	8	Lawrence County	TN	Jeff Hill	2007	25162
135 2/8	20 0/8	21 2/8	12 6/8	7	6	Sutton County	TX	Allen Junek	2007	25162
135 2/8	21 5/8	22 2/8	13 2/8	5	5	Van Buren County	MI	Craig W. Hansen	2007	25162
135 2/8	23 3/8	22 1/8	21 6/8	5	5	Union County	NC	Matt Stegall	2007	25162
*135 2/8	20 5/8	20 1/8	16 4/8	5	5	Goodsoil	SAS	Richard Service	2007	25162
*135 2/8	22 4/8	22 6/8	17 0/8	4	6	Casey County	KY	Ray Weddle	2007	25162
135 2/8	22 3/8	22 1/8	16 6/8	5	5	Athens County	OH	James Harper	2007	25162
*135 2/8	22 5/8	23 5/8	17 4/8	4	4	Lenawee County	MI	Gary F. Davis	2007	25162
135 2/8	21 2/8	22 0/8	16 6/8	4	6	Cass County	NE	Neil Chandler	2007	25162
135 2/8	25 0/8	25 7/8	22 4/8	3	4	Burnett County	WI	Jennifer Humphrey	2007	25162
*135 2/8	22 0/8	21 4/8	17 4/8	4	4	Peoria County	IL	Dalton Bontz	2007	25162
135 2/8	24 2/8	23 6/8	20 0/8	5	6	Iroquois County	IL	Ron Jackson	2007	25162
135 2/8	22 4/8	22 1/8	16 2/8	5	5	Buffalo County	SD	Steve Huppert	2007	25162
135 2/8	21 3/8	20 6/8	16 5/8	7	6	Delaware County	OK	Brandon Houston	2007	25162
135 2/8	16 4/8	23 0/8	19 5/8	6	5	Black Hawk County	IA	Steve J. Miller	2007	25162
*135 2/8	22 0/8	23 2/8	17 1/8	4	6	Brown County	OH	Chuck Conti	2008	25162
*135 2/8	20 7/8	20 6/8	16 4/8	4	5	Lapeer County	MI	Kevin J. VanderPloeg	2008	25162
135 2/8	23 0/8	22 3/8	17 0/8	5	5	Cloud County	KS	Patrick E. Helget	2008	25162
*135 2/8	24 5/8	23 1/8	21 7/8	6	4	Rimbey	ALB	Eric A. Keuling	2008	25162
*135 2/8	23 2/8	24 1/8	17 6/8	4	4	Surry County	VA	Pete Forehand	2008	25162
135 2/8	23 6/8	24 2/8	18 6/8	4	5	Plymouth County	IA	Mike Shea	2008	25162
135 2/8	23 7/8	24 5/8	17 4/8	4	5	Sanborn County	SD	Bob Hetland	2008	25162
135 2/8	25 7/8	25 4/8	19 3/8	4	6	Westchester County	NY	Gus Congemi	2008	25162
135 2/8	24 1/8	24 0/8	17 7/8	5	4	Jo Daviess County	IL	Mark Jacobson	2008	25162
*135 2/8	22 4/8	23 3/8	15 4/8	5	5	Rice County	MN	Scott Koehler	2008	25162
*135 2/8	21 3/8	22 0/8	15 4/8	5	5	Green Lake County	WI	Art Eichmann	2008	25162
135 2/8	23 5/8	24 0/8	19 5/8	4	5	Carroll County	IL	Jim Carlson	2008	25162
135 2/8	23 0/8	22 3/8	18 0/8	5	5	Muskingum County	OH	Tim J. Forsyth	2008	25162
*135 2/8	22 6/8	22 2/8	14 2/8	4	4	Clinton County	IL	Craig Markus	2008	25162
135 2/8	24 6/8	24 2/8	17 7/8	5	8	Licking County	OH	Sam Lantz	2009	25162
135 2/8	23 0/8	22 5/8	17 5/8	5	4	Richland County	WI	Bruce E. Winterberg	2009	25162
135 2/8	23 1/8	22 5/8	21 5/8	6	5	Calhoun County	MI	Franco J. Domingo	2009	25162
135 2/8	19 7/8	21 5/8	17 6/8	5	5	Dunn County	WI	Randall Shay	2009	25162
135 2/8	22 1/8	21 2/8	17 0/8	4	4	St. Joseph County	MI	Andrew D. Gest	2009	25162
135 2/8	21 6/8	22 1/8	15 6/8	5	5	Berrien County	MI	Howard Johnson Kingsley	2009	25162
135 2/8	22 4/8	23 0/8	16 2/8	5	6	Schuyler County	IL	Ashley D. Forbis	2009	25162
135 2/8	22 4/8	22 4/8	18 0/8	5	5	Major County	OK	John Henry Holloway III	2009	25162
135 2/8	23 1/8	22 1/8	16 6/8	6	4	Brown County	IL	Martin Stonesifer	2009	25162
135 2/8	22 7/8	23 3/8	17 7/8	7	6	Erie County	NY	Dennis J. Waiss	2009	25162
135 2/8	23 7/8	23 2/8	19 6/8	4	4	Chicot County	AR	Steven Corey Melton	2009	25162
*135 2/8	21 5/8	21 6/8	24 1/8	5	5	Spirit River	ALB	Jordan Ray Hach	2010	25162
135 2/8	20 4/8	20 3/8	16 4/8	5	5	McKenzie County	ND	John Richardson	2010	25162
135 2/8	22 2/8	22 5/8	16 5/8	7	6	Marathon County	WI	Michael Ullenbrauck	2010	25162
135 2/8	22 3/8	21 7/8	17 6/8	4	5	Rice County	MN	John "Jack" Cordes	2010	25162
135 1/8	19 4/8	20 5/8	15 0/8	6	6	Rusk County	WI	Fred Hennekens	2001	25405
135 1/8	23 2/8	22 7/8	17 6/8	5	4	Trempealeau County	WI	Greg Smith	2002	25405
135 1/8	24 0/8	23 7/8	16 6/8	6	6	Todd County	KY	Troy M. Rains	2003	25405
135 1/8	21 3/8	20 0/8	19 2/8	5	6	Webb County	TX	Matthew Howard	2003	25405
135 1/8	21 1/8	21 5/8	15 1/8	6	6	Madison County	MT	Robert Hind	2004	25405
135 1/8	20 3/8	20 7/8	15 7/8	5	5	Monroe County	IN	Earl L. Stewart	2004	25405
135 1/8	23 2/8	20 5/8	17 2/8	5	6	Buffalo County	WI	Daniel H. Folkedahl	2004	25405
135 1/8	25 6/8	24 0/8	17 5/8	4	5	Greenwood County	KS	Marcus Nall	2004	25405
135 1/8	21 2/8	23 2/8	16 0/8	5	6	Polk County	WI	Brent Traynor	2004	25405
135 1/8	23 2/8	23 2/8	17 7/8	5	5	Richland County	WI	Paul Henthorn	2004	25405
135 1/8	21 6/8	21 7/8	19 7/8	5	4	Buffalo County	WI	Jerry Rucinski	2005	25405
*135 1/8	21 6/8	21 3/8	16 5/8	5	5	Montgomery County	TN	Jason Brown	2005	25405
*135 1/8	24 4/8	23 0/8	18 7/8	4	4	Clark County	KS	Ron Barnett	2005	25405
135 1/8	25 7/8	25 2/8	17 7/8	4	4	Dubuque County	IA	Alan L. Burr	2005	25405
135 1/8	24 4/8	24 0/8	16 7/8	4	4	Filmore County	NE	Jerry Franck	2005	25405
135 1/8	22 6/8	23 0/8	17 5/8	4	5	Cecil County	MD	Tom Ellwood	2005	25405
135 1/8	23 6/8	23 6/8	19 1/8	5	4	Clarion County	PA	Dana J. McCauley	2005	25405
135 1/8	22 6/8	23 4/8	16 7/8	5	5	Ontario County	NY	Tracey Read	2005	25405
*135 1/8	24 6/8	24 6/8	18 3/8	4	4	Forsyth County	NC	Louis F. Harp, Jr.	2005	25405
135 1/8	21 6/8	21 5/8	15 5/8	5	5	Crawford County	KS	Earl Chauvin	2005	25405
135 1/8	20 4/8	20 5/8	17 1/8	5	6	Natrona County	WY	Ryan Kuharski	2006	25405
135 1/8	23 3/8	21 4/8	16 7/8	5	4	Renville County	ND	Tom Alexander	2006	25405
135 1/8	21 4/8	21 7/8	19 7/8	6	6	Refugio County	TX	Robert R. White	2006	25405
135 1/8	22 0/8	22 4/8	17 1/8	5	5	Buffalo County	WI	Dean Dieckman	2006	25405
135 1/8	22 2/8	21 5/8	16 7/8	5	5	Monroe County	WV	Gregory Johnston	2006	25405
135 1/8	21 5/8	21 1/8	17 1/8	5	5	Winneshiek County	IA	Dan Eickelberg	2006	25405
*135 1/8	19 7/8	20 1/8	16 0/8	5	6	Clark County	IL	Kurt "Dusty" Rentrop	2006	25405
135 1/8	21 1/8	21 2/8	15 5/8	4	4	Scott County	IA	Doug Buchanan	2006	25405
*135 1/8	22 5/8	22 6/8	16 5/8	4	5	Sullivan County	MO	Steve Jacobs	2006	25405

Deer entries below 141 0/8, that appeared in the 6th Edition, are not included here, but are included on the accompanying CD (see page 119), and also in the Club's Records Archives.

WHITETAIL DEER (TYPICAL ANTLERS)

Minimum Score 125 Continued

SCORE	LENGTH OF R MAIN BEAM L	INSIDE SPREAD	NUMBER OF R POINTS L		AREA	STATE/ PROVINCE	HUNTER'S NAME	DATE	RANK
135 1/8	22 6/8 23 3/8	17 5/8	4	4	Morrison County	MN	Jay Feigum	2006	25405
135 1/8	22 2/8 22 3/8	17 1/8	5	5	Hidalgo County	TX	Bob Simpson	2007	25405
*135 1/8	22 2/8 22 3/8	15 7/8	4	4	Juneau County	WI	Ethan Engevold	2007	25405
135 1/8	21 1/8 21 2/8	15 7/8	4	4	Jefferson County	WI	Josh Knickmeier	2007	25405
135 1/8	23 0/8 22 6/8	18 1/8	5	4	Buffalo County	WI	Shane Stuhr	2007	25405
135 1/8	23 0/8 23 3/8	19 4/8	4	5	Richland County	WI	Chanc L. Vogel	2007	25405
*135 1/8	21 7/8 22 2/8	17 7/8	4	4	Billings County	ND	Robert H. Peot, Jr.	2007	25405
*135 1/8	19 5/8 20 0/8	17 3/8	5	5	Sargent County	ND	Josh Herzog	2007	25405
*135 1/8	24 4/8 24 5/8	16 5/8	6	6	Jefferson County	WI	Clint Dehnert	2008	25405
135 1/8	21 3/8 21 5/8	16 5/8	5	5	King County	TX	George Wroten	2008	25405
*135 1/8	23 6/8 23 4/8	19 4/8	5	5	Allamakee County	IA	Tim Oberfoell	2008	25405
*135 1/8	21 4/8 21 5/8	16 7/8	5	5	Appanoose County	IA	Larry Howell	2008	25405
135 1/8	24 2/8 24 7/8	19 1/8	4	4	Clay County	IL	Kurt R. Rohl	2008	25405
135 1/8	22 7/8 23 4/8	16 1/8	4	4	Pope County	AR	Beau Dollar	2008	25405
*135 1/8	22 7/8 22 5/8	15 7/8	5	5	Winston County	AL	Shane Blanton	2008	25405
135 1/8	22 1/8 22 0/8	18 7/8	5	4	Logan County	IL	Wayne L. Clark	2008	25405
135 1/8	21 4/8 22 4/8	17 1/8	4	4	Haakon County	SD	Roy E. Warner	2008	25405
135 1/8	24 1/8 23 0/8	23 2/8	7	7	Christian County	KY	Ben H. Gore	2009	25405
135 1/8	23 3/8 23 1/8	15 5/8	4	4	Van Buren County	MI	Daniel A. Noe	2009	25405
*135 1/8	23 0/8 21 3/8	14 1/8	5	6	Scotland County	MO	Russell A. Nichols	2009	25405
*135 1/8	23 2/8 23 3/8	16 5/8	4	5	Kingman County	KS	Mason W. Mock	2009	25405
*135 1/8	21 6/8 23 7/8	16 7/8	4	5	Dodge County	NE	Ethan Muller	2009	25405
*135 1/8	20 3/8 20 4/8	15 2/8	6	5	Rock County	WI	Nicholas G. Punzel	2009	25405
*135 1/8	24 2/8 23 3/8	18 3/8	5	6	Johnson County	IN	Thomas R. Northrip	2009	25405
*135 1/8	25 0/8 24 7/8	16 6/8	9	6	Marquette County	WI	Ethan A. Burns	2009	25405
135 1/8	20 7/8 21 5/8	15 6/8	6	7	Ferry County	WA	Jon Timmer	2009	25405
*135 1/8	22 1/8 21 7/8	18 1/8	4	4	Hall County	GA	Marty Jarrard	2009	25405
*135 1/8	21 6/8 20 7/8	15 2/8	6	6	Okmulgee County	OK	John Mark Veenker	2010	25405
*135 0/8	20 0/8 20 0/8	13 6/8	5	7	Dunn County	WI	Tony Owens	2000	25596
135 0/8	23 0/8 22 5/8	16 6/8	6	4	Kankakee County	IL	Brent Wilson	2000	25596
*135 0/8	25 6/8 25 1/8	21 0/8	5	4	Washington County	WI	Robert M. Shilts	2002	25596
135 0/8	20 7/8 21 4/8	16 0/8	4	5	Perry County	OH	Jay Cheney	2002	25596
135 0/8	21 2/8 21 3/8	16 0/8	5	5	Forest County	WI	Brandon W. Brigham	2003	25596
*135 0/8	23 2/8 22 3/8	16 4/8	4	4	Cross County	AR	Shane South	2003	25596
135 0/8	20 5/8 21 6/8	16 4/8	5	4	Marathon County	WI	Brad Conklin	2004	25596
135 0/8	25 2/8 24 7/8	19 0/8	5	4	Franklin County	IN	Brad Nobbe	2004	25596
*135 0/8	23 2/8 22 6/8	16 6/8	4	4	Pike County	IL	David Tarver	2004	25596
135 0/8	21 0/8 21 0/8	15 0/8	5	5	Grundy County	IL	David Both	2004	25596
135 0/8	20 2/8 21 0/8	17 2/8	5	5	Clay County	IA	William Selzer	2004	25596
135 0/8	22 0/8 21 4/8	16 0/8	5	6	Webb County	TX	Randi Hardesty	2004	25596
*135 0/8	25 2/8 25 2/8	22 2/8	4	4	Fairfield County	CT	J. Christopher Sova	2004	25596
135 0/8	19 4/8 19 4/8	13 2/8	5	5	Tom Green County	TX	Ray Hennig	2004	25596
135 0/8	20 7/8 21 4/8	17 2/8	5	5	Refugio County	TX	Rodney Smith	2004	25596
135 0/8	19 7/8 20 4/8	15 0/8	5	5	Dawson County	MT	Vern Lindquist	2005	25596
*135 0/8	23 0/8 22 6/8	20 0/8	6	5	Jasper County	MO	Travis H. Sageser	2005	25596
135 0/8	24 2/8 24 6/8	21 3/8	6	5	Middlesex County	CT	Scott Hughes	2005	25596
135 0/8	19 7/8 20 0/8	12 6/8	5	5	Ionia County	MI	Dan W. Blunt, Jr.	2005	25596
135 0/8	22 4/8 23 0/8	17 6/8	4	5	Henderson County	KY	George L. Nelson II	2005	25596
135 0/8	20 6/8 21 7/8	17 6/8	5	5	Marshall County	IN	Stephen E. Guzak	2005	25596
135 0/8	23 0/8 22 4/8	14 6/8	5	5	Trempealeau County	WI	Gary R. Benrud	2005	25596
135 0/8	23 3/8 23 4/8	17 2/8	5	6	Adams County	WI	Edward R. Czerkas, Jr.	2005	25596
135 0/8	21 3/8 22 0/8	17 4/8	5	6	Shawano County	WI	J. A. Olszewski	2005	25596
135 0/8	21 7/8 21 5/8	16 0/8	4	4	Barron County	WI	Timothy Widiker	2005	25596
135 0/8	24 4/8 24 4/8	16 4/8	4	4	Bolivar County	MS	Lance Johnson	2005	25596
135 0/8	24 5/8 23 2/8	17 6/8	5	4	Daviess County	IN	Zach Kirchner	2005	25596
*135 0/8	21 4/8 21 1/8	19 6/8	5	4	Lycoming County	PA	Robin Fisher	2006	25596
135 0/8	22 6/8 22 0/8	15 2/8	4	5	Nodaway County	MO	Doug Gallagher	2006	25596
*135 0/8	25 0/8 23 7/8	18 3/8	5	5	Livingston County	MI	Denise M. New	2006	25596
*135 0/8	21 4/8 23 0/8	18 1/8	6	8	Barron County	WI	Douglas R. Kahl	2006	25596
135 0/8	23 0/8 24 0/8	16 5/8	6	4	Marathon County	WI	John Prichard	2006	25596
*135 0/8	23 3/8 23 4/8	16 2/8	4	4	Harrison County	MO	Mike Heckman	2006	25596
*135 0/8	21 2/8 22 6/8	16 0/8	4	5	Otter Tail County	MN	Shannon Starry	2006	25596
135 0/8	20 5/8 20 1/8	16 2/8	6	5	Dunn County	WI	Matthew B. O'Meara	2006	25596
*135 0/8	21 1/8 21 1/8	16 4/8	6	5	Linn County	KS	Nick Yosick	2006	25596
135 0/8	21 0/8 21 4/8	16 5/8	5	6	Buffalo County	WI	Willie Kulig	2006	25596
135 0/8	23 6/8 22 5/8	19 2/8	4	4	Hendricks County	IN	Dustin Nichols	2006	25596
*135 0/8	24 2/8 23 0/8	19 1/8	8	6	Buffalo County	WI	Don Loch	2006	25596
135 0/8	22 6/8 23 1/8	17 4/8	5	5	Benton County	IA	Fred Thiele	2006	25596
135 0/8	21 7/8 22 0/8	16 4/8	5	5	Mason County	IL	Toby L. Shutt	2006	25596
135 0/8	25 2/8 25 2/8	22 2/8	4	7	McPherson County	KS	Larry E. Garner, Jr.	2006	25596
135 0/8	20 4/8 20 4/8	15 4/8	5	5	Ward County	ND	DuWayne Larson	2006	25596
135 0/8	22 1/8 21 7/8	16 0/8	5	5	Hutchinson County	TX	Stewart Garrison	2006	25596
135 0/8	21 7/8 21 2/8	13 6/8	5	5	Sheridan County	ND	Scott Hettinger	2007	25596
135 0/8	20 0/8 21 3/8	20 0/8	5	6	Otero County	NM	David J. Cramer	2007	25596
135 0/8	21 6/8 21 6/8	16 4/8	4	4	Trempealeau County	WI	David Andersen	2007	25596
*135 0/8	20 7/8 21 5/8	14 5/8	5	7	Butler County	MO	Meegan W. Turnbeaugh	2007	25596
135 0/8	23 0/8 23 0/8	16 4/8	5	4	McDonough County	IL	Bruce R. Frazier	2007	25596
135 0/8	22 0/8 22 0/8	15 6/8	4	4	Oconto County	WI	David Elsen	2007	25596
*135 0/8	24 1/8 21 5/8	19 0/8	7	8	Buffalo County	WI	Gunnar J. Hagen	2007	25596
135 0/8	25 3/8 25 7/8	17 4/8	6	5	Vernon County	MO	Thad Smith	2007	25596
*135 0/8	21 0/8 21 4/8	16 4/8	5	6	Waupaca County	WI	Mark Redman	2007	25596
135 0/8	21 4/8 20 5/8	18 4/8	4	4	Elk County	KS	Chad Watson	2007	25596
135 0/8	23 0/8 24 2/8	19 3/8	5	4	Plymouth County	MA	George Main	2007	25596
135 0/8	22 2/8 21 2/8	16 0/8	8	6	Marathon County	WI	Gerard Morris	2007	25596
*135 0/8	21 4/8 23 2/8	15 4/8	6	5	Coffey County	KS	Don Erbert	2007	25596
135 0/8	23 0/8 23 6/8	19 4/8	4	4	Elk County	KS	Mike Weaver	2007	25596
*135 0/8	25 5/8 24 6/8	20 0/8	5	5	Pulaski County	AR	Mark S. Williamson	2007	25596
135 0/8	23 3/8 22 7/8	16 4/8	4	4	Montgomery County	OH	Mike Skilwies	2007	25596
135 0/8	21 0/8 20 2/8	14 7/8	6	6	Williams Lake	BC	Al Campsall	2008	25596
*135 0/8	20 3/8 20 1/8	14 0/8	5	6	Marquette County	WI	Brodie Berriochoa	2008	25596
135 0/8	22 1/8 22 4/8	16 2/8	5	5	Niagara County	NY	Bryan Meigs	2008	25596
135 0/8	22 0/8 22 3/8	19 5/8	6	5	Buffalo County	WI	Jim Wondzell	2008	25596
135 0/8	22 4/8 22 7/8	15 4/8	5	5	Erie County	PA	Lee M. Steadman	2008	25596
135 0/8	21 5/8 21 4/8	17 6/8	5	5	Muscatine County	IA	Brian Sindt	2008	25596
*135 0/8	24 1/8 23 7/8	20 2/8	5	5	Berks County	PA	Scott Ressler	2008	25596

WHITETAIL DEER (TYPICAL ANTLERS)

Minimum Score 125   Continued

SCORE	LENGTH OF R MAIN BEAM L	INSIDE SPREAD	NUMBER OF R POINTS L	AREA	STATE/PROVINCE	HUNTER'S NAME	DATE	RANK
135 0/8	23 5/8 23 1/8	18 4/8	6 3	Vernon County	WI	Adrian J. Amelse	2008	25596
*135 0/8	25 2/8 24 5/8	20 0/8	4 5	Clarion County	PA	Ted A. Memo	2008	25596
*135 0/8	23 0/8 22 6/8	19 5/8	4 6	Wright County	MN	Ambrose Opatz	2008	25596
135 0/8	21 3/8 23 0/8	16 6/8	5 5	McPherson County	KS	Tim Rockefeller	2008	25596
135 0/8	21 3/8 21 4/8	19 0/8	6 6	McHenry County	ND	Don G. Scofield	2008	25596
135 0/8	21 2/8 21 7/8	16 0/8	5 5	Barron County	WI	Bill Peterson	2009	25596
*135 0/8	24 0/8 23 4/8	18 4/8	5 5	Edmonson County	KY	James Cummings	2009	25596
135 0/8	22 2/8 22 3/8	16 6/8	5 5	Redwood County	MN	Jim Buckley	2009	25596
135 0/8	21 5/8 20 4/8	15 0/8	5 5	Green Lake County	WI	Mason Schmidt	2009	25596
135 0/8	24 0/8 23 5/8	17 0/8	4 4	Guthrie County	IA	Kirk James Bond	2009	25596
135 0/8	21 3/8 21 7/8	20 6/8	6 4	Tippecanoe County	IN	Kellen O. Vaught	2009	25596
*135 0/8	22 0/8 21 4/8	15 6/8	5 5	Wayne County	IA	Marc Goldberg	2009	25596
135 0/8	23 7/8 24 5/8	16 4/8	4 4	Fulton County	GA	Lee Edward Johnson	2009	25596
*135 0/8	25 1/8 25 0/8	20 4/8	4 4	Jackson County	IA	Mark Henfrey	2010	25596
135 0/8	22 3/8 21 6/8	17 0/8	4 4	Warren County	NJ	James C. Agens	2010	25596
134 7/8	24 2/8 23 2/8	19 3/8	4 4	Dorchester County	MD	Lothar Weber	1995	25830
134 7/8	22 2/8 21 3/8	17 7/8	4 4	Clark County	KS	Jerry Taylor	2000	25830
*134 7/8	21 4/8 21 6/8	16 7/8	5 6	Henderson County	IL	Bruce Smith	2002	25830
134 7/8	20 5/8 21 3/8	14 2/8	5 6	Dallas County	IA	Jeff Brennan	2003	25830
134 7/8	22 2/8 23 2/8	17 1/8	4 4	Queen Annes County	MD	Virgil R. Klepper, Jr.	2003	25830
134 7/8	21 5/8 21 6/8	16 7/8	5 4	Outagamie County	WI	Dan Stern	2003	25830
134 7/8	23 2/8 23 3/8	19 1/8	4 4	Douglas County	KS	Mike Dunnaway	2003	25830
134 7/8	27 3/8 27 1/8	16 1/8	5 7	Jefferson County	KY	W. Austin Musselman, Jr.	2004	25830
134 7/8	22 4/8 21 0/8	19 4/8	6 5	Suffolk County	NY	Nathan Dahlstrom	2004	25830
134 7/8	22 3/8 22 4/8	17 1/8	5 4	Cass County	MN	Jason Forbord	2004	25830
134 7/8	19 7/8 19 7/8	16 2/8	6 5	Washington County	PA	Bryan Dolanch	2004	25830
*134 7/8	21 3/8 21 1/8	16 5/8	5 5	Sutton County	TX	James Sowell, Jr.	2004	25830
134 7/8	19 6/8 20 0/8	16 1/8	5 5	Jackson County	MI	Kenny W. Gibson	2004	25830
*134 7/8	23 3/8 23 0/8	20 1/8	4 4	Mecosta County	MI	Dennis Floyd LaLonde	2004	25830
134 7/8	20 2/8 21 7/8	18 5/8	5 5	Hancock County	IL	Bradley J. Swanson	2004	25830
134 7/8	21 3/8 21 6/8	16 5/8	5 6	Grant County	SD	David Larson	2004	25830
134 7/8	22 5/8 22 7/8	20 5/8	5 5	Montgomery County	IN	Trent D. Bohn	2004	25830
*134 7/8	21 3/8 21 3/8	16 1/8	5 5	Pike County	IL	Chad Zumwalt	2004	25830
134 7/8	22 6/8 21 4/8	20 1/8	5 5	Jasper County	IA	Don Morris	2004	25830
*134 7/8	21 2/8 21 1/8	16 3/8	4 5	Jefferson County	OH	Dan Fortney	2004	25830
*134 7/8	19 5/8 19 5/8	13 7/8	5 5	Fairfield County	OH	Michael R. Dobbs	2004	25830
134 7/8	24 2/8 23 3/8	18 3/8	6 6	Cass County	IL	Daniel W. Kirkes	2004	25830
*134 7/8	21 4/8 20 2/8	15 1/8	5 6	Howard County	MO	Don Thurman	2004	25830
134 7/8	21 2/8 22 0/8	17 3/8	6 5	Anoka County	MN	Dan Pohl	2004	25830
134 7/8	23 0/8 22 6/8	17 7/8	4 4	Callahan County	TX	Jeff Shaffer	2005	25830
*134 7/8	21 5/8 21 3/8	16 2/8	6 6	Cass County	ND	John M. Gefroh	2005	25830
134 7/8	22 2/8 22 3/8	15 6/8	6 6	Bayfield County	WI	William M. Naleid	2005	25830
134 7/8	21 0/8 20 7/8	16 5/8	5 5	Jo Daviess County	IL	Ken Pluym	2005	25830
134 7/8	23 3/8 22 5/8	14 1/8	4 5	Wayne County	NY	Gary M. Wright	2005	25830
*134 7/8	22 2/8 22 5/8	13 7/8	5 5	Atlantic County	NJ	James Walker	2005	25830
134 7/8	19 1/8 20 0/8	18 7/8	6 6	Randolph County	AR	Blake A. McCord	2005	25830
134 7/8	22 2/8 23 2/8	17 5/8	4 6	Woods County	OK	James B. Carson	2005	25830
*134 7/8	23 1/8 22 7/8	18 1/8	4 4	Houston County	MN	Jason Sichler	2005	25830
134 7/8	22 1/8 21 3/8	17 5/8	5 5	Granby River	BC	Dave Peat	2005	25830
*134 7/8	20 6/8 21 1/8	16 3/8	5 5	Kidder County	ND	Lance Larson	2005	25830
*134 7/8	23 4/8 23 0/8	17 3/8	6 6	Wilson County	TX	Ralph McGrew	2006	25830
134 7/8	23 0/8 23 4/8	16 3/8	4 4	Hamilton County	OH	Kenneth A. Pfierman	2006	25830
134 7/8	22 3/8 22 2/8	14 6/8	5 7	Nemaha County	NE	Tony Pickens	2006	25830
*134 7/8	23 5/8 25 0/8	16 0/8	4 6	Ontario County	NY	Gary B. Van Stean	2006	25830
134 7/8	23 1/8 25 2/8	17 5/8	5 5	Buffalo County	WI	Jake Van Linn	2006	25830
134 7/8	23 5/8 23 2/8	17 1/8	5 5	Buffalo County	WI	Todd Klundt	2006	25830
134 7/8	26 2/8 26 2/8	18 7/8	5 4	Bond County	IL	Gary Netzler	2006	25830
134 7/8	24 0/8 26 1/8	20 5/8	5 5	Trempealeau County	WI	Jerry Krajewski	2006	25830
134 7/8	23 7/8 23 7/8	20 1/8	5 6	Ashland County	WI	Douglas B. Thorp	2006	25830
*134 7/8	23 0/8 24 4/8	15 5/8	5 4	Pope County	IL	Richard H. Britt	2006	25830
*134 7/8	24 1/8 22 4/8	18 3/8	5 4	Guthrie County	IA	Thomas Buckroyd III	2006	25830
*134 7/8	22 5/8 22 4/8	18 1/8	5 5	Washington County	RI	Marc Desjardins	2006	25830
134 7/8	20 4/8 20 3/8	15 3/8	6 5	Marion County	IL	Sid Tingen	2006	25830
134 7/8	24 2/8 24 6/8	17 0/8	6 5	Fairfield County	OH	Matt DeFazio	2006	25830
134 7/8	22 1/8 22 3/8	18 2/8	5 6	Burnett County	WI	Jennifer Bybee	2007	25830
*134 7/8	20 5/8 21 6/8	19 5/8	5 5	Crawford County	PA	Robert L. Foster	2007	25830
134 7/8	20 5/8 21 3/8	15 2/8	8 7	Walsh County	ND	Josh Worley	2007	25830
*134 7/8	22 2/8 23 3/8	14 7/8	5 5	Cooper County	MO	Travis Layne	2007	25830
134 7/8	22 2/8 22 1/8	13 3/8	5 4	Sutton County	TX	George L. Steele	2007	25830
*134 7/8	22 3/8 22 2/8	15 5/8	5 6	Missoula County	MT	Jake A. Sol	2007	25830
134 7/8	20 5/8 20 3/8	16 3/8	5 5	Granby River	BC	Kelly Hoglund	2007	25830
*134 7/8	23 5/8 20 4/8	12 5/8	7 6	Hillsdale County	MI	Scott E. Manore	2007	25830
134 7/8	22 6/8 23 4/8	17 1/8	4 6	Monroe County	WI	Jacob J. Brey	2008	25830
134 7/8	21 3/8 20 5/8	16 5/8	5 5	Jackson County	WI	Marie Harkner	2008	25830
134 7/8	21 3/8 21 3/8	18 0/8	5 4	Seneca County	NY	Jesse Miller	2008	25830
134 7/8	21 2/8 21 2/8	14 5/8	5 5	Van Buren County	IA	Baree Weber	2008	25830
*134 7/8	21 2/8 21 3/8	18 3/8	5 5	Sauk County	WI	Marc J. Terry	2008	25830
*134 7/8	22 6/8 23 1/8	16 3/8	4 5	Miami County	IN	Robert Graber	2008	25830
134 7/8	24 2/8 23 4/8	18 4/8	7 7	Fulton County	IL	Scott Kiefner	2008	25830
*134 7/8	23 2/8 23 3/8	19 1/8	4 4	Walsh County	ND	Max Hoefs	2009	25830
*134 7/8	20 6/8 20 1/8	18 1/8	5 8	Wandering River	ALB	Robert Cooper	2009	25830
*134 7/8	24 2/8 24 5/8	16 6/8	7 6	Cayuga County	NY	Darren L. Moore	2009	25830
134 7/8	24 2/8 25 0/8	20 7/8	4 4	Dauphin County	PA	Andrew Spittle	2009	25830
*134 7/8	24 5/8 24 2/8	16 7/8	5 6	Phillips County	KS	Brian E. Berlier	2009	25830
*134 7/8	23 2/8 23 1/8	17 5/8	7 5	Washington County	PA	Jerry LaSalvia	2009	25830
*134 7/8	23 1/8 21 7/8	18 6/8	6 5	Randolph County	GA	Graham Lovett	2009	25830
134 6/8	21 4/8 21 1/8	17 0/8	5 5	Christian County	KY	Brian Bliese	2002	26033
134 6/8	23 2/8 23 0/8	16 1/8	6 6	Adams County	IL	Brian Gregg	2002	26033
134 6/8	21 2/8 22 1/8	17 0/8	5 5	Parkland	ALB	Paul Parker	2004	26033
134 6/8	22 6/8 24 1/8	15 4/8	6 6	Barber County	KS	Rob Grannis	2004	26033
134 6/8	22 7/8 22 4/8	17 0/8	5 5	Winnebago County	IA	Robert Filbrandt	2004	26033
134 6/8	22 3/8 21 6/8	17 2/8	5 4	Madison County	OH	Phil Acles	2004	26033
134 6/8	21 0/8 21 6/8	13 4/8	7 5	Westchester County	NY	Gus A. Congemi	2004	26033
*134 6/8	23 7/8 22 7/8	14 4/8	5 5	Kemper County	MS	John Alan Anthony	2005	26033
*134 6/8	22 3/8 22 1/8	15 0/8	6 6	Polk County	WI	Lane M. Henck	2005	26033

Deer entries below 141 0/8, that appeared in the 6th Edition, are not included here, but are included on the accompanying CD (see page 119), and also in the Club's Records Archives.

WHITETAIL DEER (TYPICAL ANTLERS)

Minimum Score 125 — Continued

SCORE	LENGTH OF R MAIN BEAM L	INSIDE SPREAD	NUMBER OF R POINTS L		AREA	STATE/ PROVINCE	HUNTER'S NAME	DATE	RANK
*134 6/8	20 7/8	21 0/8	15 4/8	5	5	Rockcastle County	KY	Tony A. Mahaffey	2005	26033
134 6/8	23 4/8	23 4/8	17 4/8	4	4	Linn County	IA	Stuart Slaymaker	2005	26033
134 6/8	20 3/8	20 1/8	13 0/8	5	5	Jackson County	OH	Rich Harless	2005	26033
*134 6/8	24 6/8	25 2/8	16 1/8	7	6	Riley County	KS	Mike Gauntt	2005	26033
134 6/8	23 2/8	25 1/8	20 2/8	4	4	McHenry County	IL	William Snelgrove	2005	26033
*134 6/8	20 7/8	21 2/8	16 4/8	4	5	McHenry County	ND	Scott Piton	2006	26033
134 6/8	22 7/8	21 7/8	20 4/8	4	5	Daviess County	MO	Roy W. Akerson	2006	26033
134 6/8	21 2/8	21 7/8	17 7/8	4	4	Baldwin County	GA	Jon Funderburke	2006	26033
134 6/8	19 7/8	20 5/8	17 1/8	5	4	Nodaway County	MO	Michael Soulen	2006	26033
*134 6/8	21 5/8	21 3/8	17 1/8	6	6	Rusk County	WI	Al Borchardt	2006	26033
134 6/8	21 5/8	23 4/8	20 4/8	5	5	Langlade County	WI	Kyle Kaltz	2006	26033
134 6/8	21 3/8	22 2/8	18 2/8	6	6	Hughes County	SD	Lance Peery	2006	26033
134 6/8	21 4/8	22 0/8	18 4/8	5	6	McMullen County	TX	Chris Varni	2006	26033
134 6/8	21 1/8	22 3/8	15 4/8	5	5	Uvalde County	TX	Greg Ogle	2007	26033
*134 6/8	22 4/8	22 3/8	16 0/8	4	7	Dunn County	ND	Cynthia Zachmeier	2007	26033
134 6/8	21 0/8	21 4/8	15 0/8	8	7	Clare County	MI	William Ray Ezell	2007	26033
134 6/8	25 0/8	23 2/8	17 6/8	4	5	Coshocton County	OH	Jesse Fischer	2007	26033
134 6/8	21 5/8	21 1/8	16 4/8	5	5	Rusk County	WI	Eric Wedemeyer	2007	26033
134 6/8	21 4/8	21 6/8	18 7/8	5	6	Nicollet County	MN	Steve Morasch	2007	26033
134 6/8	22 4/8	21 5/8	14 6/8	5	4	Clark County	IL	Mike Miller	2007	26033
*134 6/8	22 6/8	22 6/8	19 6/8	4	4	Waupaca County	WI	Trevor J. Saeger	2007	26033
134 6/8	24 1/8	23 1/8	15 2/8	4	5	Clinton County	IN	James Hardesty	2007	26033
134 6/8	21 5/8	22 1/8	19 3/8	5	5	Jewell County	KS	John "Jack" Cordes	2007	26033
134 6/8	26 4/8	25 7/8	16 0/8	4	5	Winneshiek County	IA	Shawn Busch	2007	26033
134 6/8	20 5/8	21 0/8	15 2/8	5	5	Allen County	IN	Todd Scheumann	2007	26033
*134 6/8	22 6/8	22 5/8	17 4/8	4	4	Clark County	IL	Clinton D. Marchant	2007	26033
134 6/8	22 2/8	23 0/8	17 6/8	5	5	Anderson County	KY	Kenneth Brooks	2007	26033
134 6/8	22 6/8	23 6/8	18 1/8	7	8	Clayton County	IA	Josh Regal	2007	26033
134 6/8	21 6/8	21 2/8	17 6/8	5	5	Jefferson County	NE	Barry Finkhouse	2008	26033
134 6/8	21 3/8	21 5/8	15 5/8	6	6	Lavaca County	TX	Doug Grahmann	2008	26033
*134 6/8	19 0/8	21 0/8	15 0/8	5	5	Cass County	ND	Mike Svaleson	2008	26033
134 6/8	21 4/8	21 6/8	17 0/8	5	5	Buffalo County	WI	Tod Torgerson	2008	26033
134 6/8	22 1/8	21 3/8	17 7/8	6	5	Lake County	IL	Brian J. Flament	2008	26033
*134 6/8	21 4/8	22 2/8	18 6/8	5	5	Adams County	MS	Patrick Kelleher	2008	26033
134 6/8	22 7/8	23 2/8	18 2/8	8	8	Brown County	SD	Jennifer Thares	2009	26033
134 6/8	23 2/8	24 7/8	23 0/8	5	4	Schuylkill County	PA	Kevin Duke	2009	26033
*134 6/8	20 1/8	19 4/8	15 0/8	5	5	Green Lake	SAS	Anthony Glasso	2009	26033
134 6/8	23 1/8	22 7/8	19 5/8	5	4	Green County	WI	Terry Wolf	2009	26033
*134 6/8	24 7/8	24 5/8	18 5/8	6	5	Tippecanoe County	IN	Brian Rockhill	2009	26033
134 6/8	21 5/8	20 4/8	16 1/8	6	6	Clark County	IL	Brock Griffiths Marietta	2009	26033
134 6/8	24 7/8	24 3/8	19 0/8	5	5	Merrimack County	NH	Christopher Gagne	2009	26033
*134 6/8	20 5/8	20 2/8	18 6/8	5	5	Victoria County	TX	Matt Wheat	2010	26033
*134 6/8	22 4/8	22 1/8	18 7/8	4	5	Manitowoc County	WI	Michael R. Hassinger	2010	26033
134 5/8	23 5/8	24 3/8	16 4/8	7	5	Leflore County	MS	Glenn Carpenter	1999	26231
134 5/8	23 1/8	21 4/8	16 5/8	4	4	Pope County	IL	Scott Matteson	2000	26231
134 5/8	22 3/8	22 2/8	18 3/8	4	4	Cheyenne County	KS	Greg Sinn	2001	26231
134 5/8	22 0/8	22 3/8	17 3/8	6	7	Ottawa County	KS	John B. Bowman	2003	26231
134 5/8	22 6/8	23 2/8	18 7/8	4	5	Jefferson County	ID	Ryan Pimentel	2004	26231
134 5/8	24 7/8	25 3/8	17 2/8	5	7	Lawrence County	PA	G. Steve Zeppelin	2004	26231
134 5/8	22 7/8	22 1/8	18 5/8	5	5	Dunn County	WI	Mark E. Fictum	2004	26231
134 5/8	22 7/8	22 0/8	15 3/8	4	4	Knox County	IL	Zach Sharp	2004	26231
*134 5/8	20 3/8	20 5/8	16 1/8	6	5	Wabasha County	MN	Steve Strickland	2004	26231
134 5/8	23 2/8	24 1/8	17 7/8	5	5	Shelby County	IN	Joe Havlin	2004	26231
134 5/8	22 3/8	22 4/8	18 1/8	4	4	Douglas County	WI	Jim Vanlandschoot	2004	26231
*134 5/8	23 7/8	23 3/8	16 1/8	5	4	Douglas County	WI	Wayne C. Smith	2004	26231
134 5/8	20 6/8	20 3/8	15 5/8	5	5	Tompkins County	NY	Steve Frost	2004	26231
134 5/8	26 6/8	24 4/8	21 0/8	5	6	Miami County	OH	Greg Thacker	2004	26231
134 5/8	23 0/8	23 6/8	15 7/8	4	4	Charles County	MD	William A. Eaton	2005	26231
134 5/8	23 1/8	24 0/8	15 3/8	4	4	Marshall County	MN	Austin Moffett	2005	26231
134 5/8	20 7/8	21 0/8	14 7/8	5	5	Montgomery County	MD	Richard L. Latimer, Jr.	2005	26231
134 5/8	20 0/8	20 0/8	14 3/8	4	4	Will County	IL	Jeff Pals	2005	26231
*134 5/8	24 7/8	24 6/8	17 4/8	4	5	Marshall County	IN	Eric E. Amor	2005	26231
134 5/8	20 4/8	21 7/8	14 0/8	6	5	Buffalo County	WI	Curt Mart	2005	26231
134 5/8	23 0/8	22 1/8	19 1/8	6	6	Dunn County	WI	Jason Lewis	2005	26231
134 5/8	22 0/8	22 1/8	20 0/8	6	6	Macoupin County	IL	Bob Frizzo	2005	26231
134 5/8	21 3/8	21 6/8	16 5/8	6	6	Baker County	GA	J. C. Griffin	2005	26231
*134 5/8	22 2/8	22 7/8	16 3/8	5	6	Douglas County	NE	Brad Lewis	2005	26231
134 5/8	22 6/8	22 6/8	16 1/8	4	4	Martin County	IN	Kent Gingerich	2005	26231
*134 5/8	22 4/8	23 1/8	17 1/8	4	5	Union County	KY	Gabe S. Krantz	2005	26231
*134 5/8	25 6/8	25 3/8	16 4/8	5	6	Bay County	MI	Thomas F. Stein	2005	26231
134 5/8	21 6/8	24 0/8	15 6/8	7	5	Butler County	OH	Tyler C. Hornung	2005	26231
134 5/8	23 0/8	22 5/8	15 7/8	4	5	Paipoonge	ONT	Glenn Rivard	2005	26231
134 5/8	22 7/8	24 2/8	17 5/8	4	4	Bedford County	PA	Robert P. Perrin	2006	26231
134 5/8	21 1/8	20 5/8	14 3/8	5	5	Tom Green County	TX	Calvin Stewart	2006	26231
*134 5/8	25 4/8	25 0/8	17 6/8	5	5	Meigs County	OH	Dana Decker	2006	26231
*134 5/8	23 1/8	23 1/8	16 7/8	4	5	Monroe County	WI	Reuben Lemke	2006	26231
134 5/8	22 5/8	24 2/8	21 3/8	4	5	Wright County	MN	Eric Williamson	2006	26231
134 5/8	24 1/8	24 0/8	16 3/8	5	5	Calhoun County	IL	Brian Van Landingham	2006	26231
*134 5/8	19 4/8	20 0/8	16 5/8	5	5	Putnam County	MO	Josh McConnell	2006	26231
134 5/8	22 2/8	22 0/8	14 5/8	4	4	Atchison County	MO	Pink Atkins	2006	26231
134 5/8	21 1/8	21 4/8	13 7/8	7	6	Steuben County	IN	Dustin Nilson	2006	26231
134 5/8	23 5/8	23 3/8	16 7/8	5	5	Delaware County	OH	David Orndorf	2006	26231
134 5/8	24 1/8	24 0/8	14 5/8	5	5	Platte County	MO	Brett Brown	2007	26231
*134 5/8	23 0/8	24 0/8	23 3/8	4	4	Cabarrus County	NC	Bart Tolson	2007	26231
134 5/8	21 2/8	20 6/8	14 5/8	5	7	Potter County	SD	Randy Mink	2007	26231
134 5/8	22 2/8	22 4/8	17 1/8	5	5	Rusk County	WI	Rich Varsho	2007	26231
*134 5/8	22 6/8	22 2/8	18 3/8	4	4	Dunn County	WI	Richard Hovland	2007	26231
134 5/8	21 7/8	21 1/8	18 1/8	4	5	Winnebago County	IL	Bob L. Haedt	2007	26231
134 5/8	22 3/8	23 3/8	19 5/8	4	4	Parke County	IN	Jeremiah R. Lemmons	2007	26231
*134 5/8	20 4/8	20 5/8	14 1/8	5	6	Seward County	NE	Justin Hetz	2007	26231
134 5/8	22 3/8	22 4/8	16 7/8	4	5	Scioto County	OH	Kenneth Phipps	2007	26231
134 5/8	23 3/8	23 2/8	16 0/8	6	7	Saline County	MO	Dan Hollingsworth	2007	26231
134 5/8	23 7/8	23 5/8	16 1/8	5	5	Pepin County	WI	Brad J. Seifert	2007	26231
*134 5/8	22 2/8	22 7/8	19 5/8	4	5	Calhoun County	IL	David M. DelPrete	2007	26231
134 5/8	22 5/8	22 3/8	18 1/8	5	5	Cass County	NE	Steve Leichleiter	2007	26231

WHITETAIL DEER (TYPICAL ANTLERS)

Minimum Score 125   Continued

SCORE	LENGTH OF R MAIN BEAM L	INSIDE SPREAD	NUMBER OF R POINTS L	AREA	STATE/ PROVINCE	HUNTER'S NAME	DATE	RANK
134 5/8	22 7/8 23 3/8	19 7/8	4 4	Peoria County	IL	Chris Karl	2007	26231
*134 5/8	21 4/8 21 3/8	15 7/8	5 5	Knox County	IL	Gary Owen	2007	26231
134 5/8	20 1/8 20 7/8	16 3/8	5 5	Cook County	GA	Mark W. Futch	2007	26231
134 5/8	21 0/8 21 6/8	16 3/8	5 5	Bolivar County	MS	Brian Van Landingham	2007	26231
134 5/8	25 1/8 24 4/8	17 3/8	4 4	Harris County	GA	Jay Foxworthy	2007	26231
134 5/8	23 1/8 22 1/8	16 5/8	4 5	Hennepin County	MN	Andrew Carlyle	2008	26231
*134 5/8	21 0/8 21 6/8	14 5/8	5 5	Montgomery County	MD	Dwayne A. Remillard	2008	26231
134 5/8	23 4/8 23 3/8	18 3/8	6 6	Brown County	WI	Dale VandenLangenberg	2008	26231
*134 5/8	23 2/8 24 5/8	19 0/8	4 6	Tippecanoe County	IN	Don Pickell	2008	26231
*134 5/8	20 6/8 20 7/8	17 3/8	5 5	Richland County	WI	Randy Hilgers	2008	26231
134 5/8	25 6/8 26 0/8	16 7/8	6 7	Huron County	OH	Dustin Malott	2008	26231
134 5/8	19 6/8 19 5/8	12 2/8	6 6	Tom Green County	TX	Ronnie Parsons	2008	26231
*134 5/8	25 2/8 24 0/8	18 3/8	4 4	Wayne County	IA	Bob Hile	2008	26231
134 5/8	23 0/8 22 2/8	16 7/8	5 4	Rosebud County	MT	Justin Robbe	2009	26231
*134 5/8	22 4/8 22 3/8	16 5/8	7 5	Ralls County	MO	Benjamin J. Sansone	2009	26231
134 5/8	24 5/8 26 0/8	20 3/8	4 4	Southampton County	VA	Derek B. Foster	2009	26231
134 5/8	20 4/8 20 0/8	16 3/8	6 7	Howard County	IA	Joel Cox	2009	26231
*134 5/8	21 7/8 23 0/8	17 1/8	4 4	Sauk County	WI	Hunter Yineman	2009	26231
*134 5/8	23 5/8 25 4/8	22 2/8	7 4	Logan County	CO	Patrick Wensman	2009	26231
*134 5/8	23 7/8 24 1/8	17 3/8	7 4	Putnam County	MO	Brian Loveland	2009	26231
134 5/8	26 4/8 25 2/8	20 7/8	5 5	Kane County	IL	Rick Galvin	2009	26231
134 5/8	22 4/8 22 5/8	19 1/8	4 4	Cedar County	NE	David B. Cull	2009	26231
134 5/8	23 4/8 23 5/8	19 3/8	7 5	Jefferson County	OH	Ronald J. Ault	2010	26231
134 4/8	22 3/8 22 6/8	17 6/8	5 5	Allegheny County	PA	James D. Edwards	1993	26446
134 4/8	22 2/8 22 0/8	16 4/8	5 5	Marshall County	IL	John Phillips	1997	26446
134 4/8	21 1/8 22 3/8	16 1/8	6 6	Van Buren County	MI	Craig W. Hansen	1999	26446
134 4/8	23 7/8 23 1/8	17 4/8	5 5	Newport News County	VA	Dwight S. Wolf	2003	26446
134 4/8	20 4/8 19 3/8	15 2/8	5 5	Cedar County	MO	Kenneth Ferguson	2003	26446
134 4/8	21 7/8 22 2/8	17 2/8	4 4	Fulton County	IN	Jeffrey A. Martin	2003	26446
*134 4/8	22 1/8 21 4/8	16 6/8	4 4	Calvert County	MD	Jonathan Aultman	2004	26446
134 4/8	23 1/8 22 5/8	18 4/8	4 5	Mecosta County	MI	Dave Gentile	2004	26446
134 4/8	22 0/8 22 0/8	14 4/8	5 5	Winona County	MN	Brent Berning	2004	26446
*134 4/8	18 6/8 18 0/8	16 4/8	5 5	Allamakee County	IA	Adam Delphey	2004	26446
*134 4/8	23 6/8 23 6/8	16 6/8	4 4	Harrison County	OH	Duane G. Mayle, Jr.	2004	26446
*134 4/8	23 4/8 23 0/8	16 6/8	6 5	Henry County	KY	Ed Tomlin, Jr.	2004	26446
134 4/8	21 2/8 21 7/8	16 2/8	6 7	McDonough County	IL	Nick Digrino	2004	26446
134 4/8	24 5/8 25 5/8	18 2/8	4 4	Jersey County	IL	Robert Schroeder	2004	26446
134 4/8	17 0/8 22 6/8	16 0/8	6 6	Dallas County	IA	Jeff Brennan	2004	26446
134 4/8	24 2/8 23 2/8	14 2/8	5 5	Ward County	ND	Jack Sorum	2004	26446
134 4/8	24 1/8 23 5/8	18 4/8	4 4	Saskatchewan River	SAS	Gary Fidyk	2004	26446
134 4/8	24 6/8 22 0/8	15 6/8	10 7	St. Louis County	MO	Johnny Durbin, Jr.	2004	26446
134 4/8	23 0/8 23 2/8	15 6/8	4 4	Dane County	WI	Danny M. Francois	2005	26446
134 4/8	21 2/8 21 4/8	17 4/8	4 4	Trempealeau County	WI	Mitchell A. Markham	2005	26446
134 4/8	22 0/8 22 0/8	16 2/8	5 5	Fond du Lac County	WI	Anthony Hidde	2005	26446
134 4/8	23 6/8 23 7/8	15 0/8	4 5	Wilbarger County	TX	Rodney Alexander	2005	26446
*134 4/8	20 3/8 20 4/8	14 6/8	5 6	Macon County	MO	John W. Cozart	2005	26446
134 4/8	20 5/8 21 1/8	16 7/8	5 5	Madison County	GA	Nathan Gammons	2005	26446
134 4/8	20 5/8 19 6/8	15 4/8	5 5	Schuyler County	IL	Doug Stuart	2005	26446
134 4/8	22 5/8 23 1/8	19 0/8	5 5	Prairie River	SAS	Ken H. Taylor	2005	26446
134 4/8	23 6/8 23 6/8	17 1/8	6 6	Plymouth County	MA	Andrew Tenneson	2005	26446
134 4/8	23 2/8 24 3/8	16 2/8	4 6	Steuben County	IN	Thomas A. Gardner	2005	26446
134 4/8	24 6/8 23 6/8	18 2/8	5 6	Buffalo County	WI	Glen Axness	2005	26446
134 4/8	19 5/8 19 1/8	15 4/8	6 5	Van Buren County	IA	Richard M. Penn	2005	26446
134 4/8	25 5/8 23 5/8	19 4/8	4 4	Clark County	WI	Allen Pease	2005	26446
*134 4/8	21 1/8 21 2/8	16 4/8	5 4	Dewey County	OK	Marvin Holt	2005	26446
*134 4/8	22 6/8 22 1/8	18 0/8	5 5	Lincoln County	WI	Clover Spacek	2006	26446
134 4/8	21 4/8 20 1/8	14 7/8	7 7	Clark County	WI	Brian Dix	2006	26446
134 4/8	21 3/8 21 7/8	16 4/8	5 5	Kalamazoo County	MI	John C. Hart, Jr., MD	2006	26446
*134 4/8	20 4/8 21 0/8	15 6/8	5 5	Lincoln County	WI	Joseph Heier, Sr.	2006	26446
134 4/8	22 3/8 22 2/8	17 2/8	5 5	Houston County	MN	Dean R. Krueger	2006	26446
134 4/8	21 2/8 20 4/8	18 0/8	6 5	Anoka County	MN	Brian Chou	2006	26446
134 4/8	22 4/8 22 6/8	16 0/8	4 4	Walworth County	WI	Greg Senft	2006	26446
134 4/8	19 6/8 20 3/8	15 4/8	5 5	Montgomery County	IL	Brett Goldsmith	2006	26446
*134 4/8	23 2/8 24 1/8	18 0/8	4 4	Allamakee County	IA	Rod Vanderwerf	2006	26446
*134 4/8	21 3/8 21 3/8	15 6/8	4 4	Davison County	SD	Eric Hammer	2006	26446
134 4/8	23 4/8 23 2/8	19 0/8	4 4	Cuyahoga County	OH	Jeremy J. Scholzen	2006	26446
134 4/8	20 1/8 20 5/8	14 2/8	6 8	Nodaway County	MO	Paul A. Machovina	2006	26446
134 4/8	23 3/8 23 4/8	14 4/8	4 5	Ottawa County	KS	John B. Bowman	2006	26446
134 4/8	22 2/8 23 0/8	17 4/8	5 5	Jewell County	KS	David L. Duncan	2006	26446
*134 4/8	24 1/8 24 7/8	18 4/8	4 4	Carroll County	OH	Donald Stem	2006	26446
134 4/8	22 7/8 21 2/8	17 6/8	5 8	Jefferson County	MS	Joshua K. Beard	2007	26446
*134 4/8	23 6/8 23 3/8	16 2/8	4 4	Clark County	IL	Todd M. Jobst	2007	26446
134 4/8	22 7/8 23 6/8	18 6/8	7 5	Monroe County	WI	Austin Reinhart	2007	26446
134 4/8	22 0/8 22 4/8	16 0/8	5 4	Waushara County	WI	Wendy Christensen-Senk	2007	26446
134 4/8	22 0/8 20 5/8	16 0/8	5 5	St. Louis County	MN	Scott Schafer	2007	26446
134 4/8	23 6/8 24 2/8	17 0/8	4 4	Tyler County	WV	Allen Belcher	2007	26446
*134 4/8	22 1/8 22 1/8	17 6/8	5 5	Parke County	IN	Dan Ellis	2007	26446
*134 4/8	21 5/8 21 7/8	16 6/8	4 5	Sullivan County	IN	Isaac D. Walton	2007	26446
134 4/8	20 2/8 21 2/8	15 7/8	6 5	Bond County	IL	Dennis Pruitt	2007	26446
134 4/8	21 1/8 21 7/8	17 4/8	4 4	Brown County	TX	Tim Skaggs	2007	26446
*134 4/8	22 5/8 22 5/8	17 6/8	5 5	Hughes County	SD	Rich Paynter	2008	26446
134 4/8	22 0/8 21 2/8	15 2/8	6 6	Montcalm County	MI	Tom Parauka	2008	26446
*134 4/8	22 0/8 21 6/8	19 3/8	6 8	Hancock County	IL	Jason F. Grimsley	2008	26446
134 4/8	21 7/8 22 5/8	16 6/8	5 4	Dane County	WI	Randall Hagen	2008	26446
134 4/8	22 7/8 23 3/8	17 3/8	5 5	Somerset County	PA	Scott E. Clough	2008	26446
134 4/8	23 4/8 25 4/8	19 0/8	5 3	Iowa County	WI	Nick Meyer	2008	26446
134 4/8	22 6/8 23 7/8	16 0/8	6 5	De Kalb County	GA	David Sherrill	2008	26446
*134 4/8	21 3/8 21 4/8	21 4/8	5 5	Raymond	ALB	Larry Stelfox	2009	26446
*134 4/8	21 2/8 21 5/8	16 0/8	6 5	Ripley County	IN	Darren Speer	2009	26446
134 4/8	21 6/8 21 6/8	16 6/8	5 5	Pierce County	WI	Bruce Murray	2009	26446
134 4/8	22 4/8 22 6/8	17 2/8	5 5	Aurora County	SD	Julio F. Medeiros	2009	26446
*134 4/8	21 4/8 21 3/8	16 6/8	5 5	Hocking County	OH	Aaron W. Sager	2009	26446
134 4/8	24 1/8 24 5/8	19 1/8	6 5	Llano County	TX	Eddy L. Maxey	2009	26446
*134 3/8	23 7/8 23 7/8	15 3/8	4 4	Vernon County	MO	Jeff Chambers	2000	26665
134 3/8	21 7/8 21 2/8	14 1/8	6 6	Lincoln County	WI	Dan Detert	2001	26665

Deer entries below 141 0/8, that appeared in the 6th Edition, are not included here, but are included on the accompanying CD (see page 119), and also in the Club's Records Archives.

WHITETAIL DEER (TYPICAL ANTLERS)

Minimum Score 125 — Continued

SCORE	R MAIN BEAM L	INSIDE SPREAD	R POINTS L	AREA	STATE/PROVINCE	HUNTER'S NAME	DATE	RANK
134 3/8	20 0/8 19 7/8	14 7/8	5 5	Grayson County	KY	Billy Davis	2003	26665
134 3/8	24 0/8 23 4/8	16 5/8	5 4	La Salle County	IL	Kevin W. Couch	2003	26665
134 3/8	22 7/8 22 4/8	16 7/8	4 4	Decatur County	IA	Larry L. Darnell	2003	26665
134 3/8	22 3/8 23 3/8	19 7/8	5 5	Greenwood County	KS	Nick Penner	2003	26665
134 3/8	22 3/8 22 0/8	18 3/8	4 4	Kenedy County	TX	Bear Brewer	2004	26665
134 3/8	23 4/8 23 0/8	17 7/8	5 5	Maverick County	TX	Bryant Stein	2004	26665
134 3/8	21 5/8 21 3/8	17 5/8	5 6	Green Lake County	WI	Alex A. Preuss	2004	26665
134 3/8	22 5/8 23 0/8	18 1/8	5 4	Kenosha County	WI	Larry M. Brevitz, Jr.	2004	26665
134 3/8	23 2/8 23 1/8	20 3/8	4 4	New Haven County	CT	Kevin Thorburn	2004	26665
134 3/8	24 4/8 24 3/8	19 6/8	6 4	Lawrence County	IL	Tony East	2004	26665
134 3/8	23 4/8 23 3/8	18 6/8	8 6	Kane County	IL	Rick Jensen	2004	26665
134 3/8	22 2/8 21 0/8	19 1/8	5 4	Bureau County	IL	Greg Bowers	2004	26665
134 3/8	22 2/8 21 5/8	21 6/8	6 7	Scott County	MN	Joe Stensrud	2004	26665
*134 3/8	23 7/8 22 7/8	17 1/8	4 4	Morton County	ND	Dustin M. Grove	2004	26665
134 3/8	22 4/8 21 6/8	17 1/8	5 5	Clearfield County	PA	Ed Veres	2005	26665
134 3/8	20 3/8 20 2/8	17 2/8	6 6	Henry County	IL	Mikel Angel	2005	26665
134 3/8	21 7/8 22 1/8	18 1/8	4 4	Portage County	WI	Mike Bohn	2005	26665
134 3/8	21 2/8 21 2/8	15 1/8	5 5	Oconto County	WI	Gregory Hansen	2005	26665
134 3/8	21 6/8 21 2/8	14 5/8	5 5	Green Lake County	WI	Brian A. Meiller	2005	26665
134 3/8	22 3/8 23 3/8	14 6/8	7 6	Martin County	IN	Cole Heichelbech	2005	26665
134 3/8	21 2/8 20 6/8	15 7/8	5 5	Saginaw County	MI	Scott A. Kemerer	2005	26665
134 3/8	22 5/8 22 4/8	17 5/8	4 4	Delaware County	OH	Clint Warner	2005	26665
134 3/8	24 1/8 25 3/8	19 4/8	6 5	Queen Annes County	MD	Chad Kauffman	2005	26665
*134 3/8	23 5/8 22 3/8	16 7/8	4 5	Knox County	IL	Jeremy Stevens	2005	26665
*134 3/8	20 6/8 21 6/8	14 7/8	5 5	Jefferson County	MS	Macky Myers	2005	26665
*134 3/8	22 1/8 21 4/8	16 6/8	5 6	Dane County	WI	Tony Tantillo	2006	26665
*134 3/8	21 3/8 22 0/8	14 3/8	5 5	Douglas County	WI	Randy Cornell	2006	26665
134 3/8	20 2/8 20 0/8	17 5/8	5 6	Sargent County	ND	Bryan S. Gabel	2006	26665
134 3/8	22 1/8 23 2/8	18 4/8	5 4	Harrison County	IN	Ted Mills, Jr.	2006	26665
*134 3/8	20 7/8 20 5/8	18 1/8	5 5	Cherokee County	KS	Joshua Alan Zahn	2006	26665
134 3/8	21 0/8 21 3/8	16 5/8	4 5	Schuyler County	MO	Richard H. Sapp	2006	26665
*134 3/8	21 7/8 21 2/8	17 1/8	4 4	Lee County	IL	Richard Schroeder	2006	26665
*134 3/8	19 5/8 20 0/8	17 3/8	5 5	Adams County	IL	Rickey Cleveland	2006	26665
*134 3/8	25 5/8 24 7/8	17 0/8	5 6	Carroll County	IN	Victor B. Herr	2006	26665
134 3/8	22 3/8 22 1/8	18 1/8	4 4	Ward County	ND	Harold Marten	2006	26665
134 3/8	21 7/8 23 2/8	15 1/8	5 4	Miami County	IN	Harry Van Dalsen, Jr.	2006	26665
*134 3/8	25 4/8 25 2/8	20 0/8	5 4	Ferry County	WA	Larry Ramsey	2006	26665
*134 3/8	20 7/8 18 1/8	14 3/8	5 6	Buffalo County	WI	Scott Smith	2007	26665
134 3/8	24 4/8 24 4/8	16 3/8	4 5	Lawrence County	SD	John E. Batt	2007	26665
*134 3/8	21 7/8 21 5/8	14 0/8	7 6	Morrison County	MN	Timothy H. Gertken	2007	26665
134 3/8	22 1/8 22 3/8	14 7/8	6 5	Poweshiek County	IA	Ryan Van Tomme	2007	26665
134 3/8	24 6/8 24 0/8	17 3/8	4 4	Richland County	WI	Ryan R. Keegan	2007	26665
134 3/8	24 1/8 24 4/8	17 7/8	5 3	Iowa County	WI	Chris Lindner	2007	26665
134 3/8	20 3/8 21 7/8	17 3/8	5 5	Scott County	MN	Tim Millard	2007	26665
134 3/8	19 5/8 21 5/8	18 3/8	5 5	Wells County	ND	DuWayne Larson	2008	26665
*134 3/8	23 2/8 23 3/8	17 6/8	8 6	Shelby County	KY	Tyler Chase Wininger	2008	26665
*134 3/8	22 7/8 22 4/8	20 3/8	4 4	Shannon County	MO	David Ferguson	2008	26665
*134 3/8	23 1/8 23 1/8	19 0/8	6 5	Juniata County	PA	Charles E. Burkhart	2008	26665
134 3/8	22 4/8 23 0/8	16 6/8	7 7	Vermilion County	IL	Russell Guthrie	2008	26665
134 3/8	23 6/8 23 2/8	18 7/8	5 4	Houston County	MN	Kraig Garmaker	2008	26665
*134 3/8	22 2/8 22 3/8	19 7/8	4 4	Republic County	KS	R. Jeremiah Young	2008	26665
134 3/8	22 3/8 22 6/8	19 6/8	6 5	Trempealeau County	WI	Mike Reed	2008	26665
134 3/8	22 2/8 22 4/8	19 1/8	5 5	Dunn County	WI	Matthew Bartz	2008	26665
134 3/8	21 2/8 20 2/8	15 7/8	5 5	Allen County	OH	Jon Mull	2008	26665
*134 3/8	23 2/8 22 6/8	16 0/8	4 7	Oakland County	MI	Albert T. Perry	2008	26665
134 3/8	21 1/8 22 1/8	14 4/8	4 6	Lee County	IL	Charles W. Rehor	2008	26665
*134 3/8	20 7/8 21 7/8	19 3/8	5 5	Pike County	IL	Jeremy Vandeven	2009	26665
*134 3/8	20 4/8 20 2/8	15 3/8	4 5	De Kalb County	IN	David W. Peters	2009	26665
134 3/8	23 0/8 21 7/8	18 1/8	4 4	Clayton County	IA	Bobby Bailey	2009	26665
*134 3/8	22 1/8 22 2/8	20 1/8	4 4	Vanderburgh County	IN	Nathan Koester	2009	26665
*134 3/8	24 0/8 24 2/8	20 6/8	6 6	McLean County	IL	Brandon Weidman	2009	26665
134 3/8	22 2/8 23 5/8	16 3/8	5 7	Chautauqua County	KS	Dwight S. Wolf	2009	26665
134 3/8	21 1/8 21 2/8	16 7/8	4 4	Jo Daviess County	IL	Chris Toft	2009	26665
*134 3/8	20 0/8 22 0/8	21 5/8	4 5	Barber County	KS	Randy Steverson	2009	26665
134 3/8	22 1/8 23 0/8	19 4/8	5 6	Riley County	KS	Neil Raedel	2009	26665
*134 3/8	22 0/8 21 1/8	17 3/8	6 7	Shelby County	MO	Keith Arnold	2009	26665
134 3/8	20 1/8 21 3/8	16 1/8	6 8	Thurston County	NE	Brandon Combs	2009	26665
134 3/8	23 2/8 23 2/8	16 0/8	6 5	Marion County	OH	Todd R. Flohr	2009	26665
134 3/8	21 4/8 24 2/8	18 7/8	4 4	Woodbury County	IA	Russell J. Johnson	2009	26665
*134 3/8	25 5/8 24 7/8	18 1/8	5 4	Gillespie County	TX	Gerald A. Lusk	2010	26665
134 2/8	22 5/8 21 7/8	16 4/8	4 5	Shelby County	IN	Troy E. Brant	1995	26883
134 2/8	20 5/8 22 3/8	17 4/8	5 5	Pike County	IL	Ronald Harness	1997	26883
134 2/8	23 4/8 24 3/8	17 0/8	6 5	Branch County	MI	Bret R. Cary	2000	26883
134 2/8	22 3/8 21 3/8	19 2/8	5 5	Oneida County	WI	Kenneth A. Wollermann	2001	26883
134 2/8	20 3/8 20 4/8	17 0/8	5 5	Medina County	TX	Roger Wintle	2001	26883
134 2/8	22 2/8 22 7/8	16 6/8	4 4	Crawford County	WI	Robert McCann	2003	26883
134 2/8	23 3/8 23 6/8	17 0/8	4 5	Schuyler County	IL	Robert Paveletz	2003	26883
134 2/8	21 1/8 21 3/8	14 0/8	5 5	Dimmit County	TX	Wendell Wallace	2003	26883
134 2/8	21 0/8 20 3/8	16 2/8	6 5	Dimmit County	TX	Carl Hardin	2004	26883
*134 2/8	20 7/8 22 6/8	16 4/8	5 7	Carroll County	MO	Terry Aversman	2004	26883
134 2/8	23 2/8 23 5/8	18 4/8	4 4	Lake County	OH	Gary F. Nagy	2004	26883
134 2/8	25 3/8 24 6/8	19 6/8	5 6	Monona County	IA	Steve Petersen	2004	26883
134 2/8	21 4/8 23 3/8	14 5/8	6 6	Maverick County	TX	Myron L. Menking	2004	26883
134 2/8	21 3/8 21 6/8	17 7/8	6 4	Buffalo County	WI	Brian Traun	2005	26883
*134 2/8	22 1/8 21 3/8	16 0/8	5 5	Ward County	ND	DuWayne Larson	2005	26883
*134 2/8	19 6/8 21 0/8	19 2/8	5 5	Butler County	PA	Bill Danner	2005	26883
*134 2/8	25 4/8 24 3/8	18 2/8	5 5	Buffalo County	WI	John Sabelko	2005	26883
134 2/8	21 6/8 22 2/8	18 6/8	6 5	Allegheny County	PA	James Filipiak	2005	26883
134 2/8	20 6/8 21 5/8	16 1/8	6 7	Scott County	IA	Steve Buffenbarger	2005	26883
134 2/8	23 0/8 23 0/8	17 2/8	4 5	Dunn County	WI	Mitch Bergeson	2005	26883
134 2/8	21 2/8 20 7/8	15 4/8	4 4	Edgar County	IL	Dale Good	2005	26883
134 2/8	21 0/8 22 0/8	18 0/8	5 5	La Crosse County	WI	Timothy Kendall	2005	26883
134 2/8	21 4/8 22 4/8	15 4/8	5 5	McMullen County	TX	Jason Goertz	2005	26883
134 2/8	24 1/8 24 5/8	18 2/8	4 5	Fairfax County	VA	Curtis Shaw	2006	26883
*134 2/8	23 1/8 24 6/8	18 5/8	6 5	Butler County	PA	Ronald S. Smelscer	2006	26883

566

WHITETAIL DEER (TYPICAL ANTLERS)

Minimum Score 125 — Continued

SCORE	LENGTH OF R MAIN BEAM L	INSIDE SPREAD	NUMBER OF R POINTS L	AREA	STATE/ PROVINCE	HUNTER'S NAME	DATE	RANK
134 2/8	21 2/8 21 3/8	19 2/8	4 5	Burnett County	WI	Rick Derrick	2006	26883
134 2/8	25 0/8 25 0/8	19 0/8	4 5	Cattaraugus County	NY	Richard Thornton	2006	26883
134 2/8	22 4/8 22 6/8	16 2/8	5 6	Waupaca County	WI	Kirt Hoffmann	2006	26883
*134 2/8	22 1/8 20 7/8	17 2/8	4 4	Madison County	IL	Christopher S. Ostresh	2006	26883
134 2/8	23 7/8 22 4/8	18 2/8	4 4	Schuylkill County	PA	Matthew L. Withelder	2006	26883
134 2/8	21 0/8 21 0/8	18 6/8	4 5	Dane County	WI	Jim Purdin	2006	26883
134 2/8	23 5/8 20 6/8	18 7/8	5 5	Republic County	KS	Gary Dahl	2006	26883
*134 2/8	22 0/8 21 7/8	15 5/8	6 6	Wabaunsee County	KS	George Wong	2006	26883
134 2/8	21 6/8 22 4/8	16 6/8	4 4	Stewart County	GA	P. Butler Ball	2006	26883
*134 2/8	22 2/8 22 1/8	18 4/8	6 7	Green Lake County	WI	Tim Trotter	2006	26883
*134 2/8	22 2/8 22 0/8	18 6/8	4 5	Warren County	PA	Ralph F. Ward	2007	26883
134 2/8	22 3/8 20 7/8	16 4/8	5 5	Sherburne County	MN	Daniel Hegge	2007	26883
*134 2/8	21 0/8 22 3/8	16 0/8	6 7	Windham County	CT	Ken Johnson	2007	26883
134 2/8	24 4/8 24 7/8	17 2/8	4 4	Todd County	KY	Kevin Sears	2007	26883
134 2/8	21 6/8 21 2/8	17 2/8	4 5	McIntosh County	OK	Alva Gordon	2007	26883
134 2/8	21 0/8 21 6/8	17 6/8	6 6	Kosciusko County	IN	Ed Kipker	2007	26883
134 2/8	23 3/8 23 5/8	19 0/8	5 5	Lucas County	IA	Charles Arnold	2007	26883
*134 2/8	23 0/8 22 2/8	19 2/8	5 5	Iowa County	IA	Andrew Graykowski	2007	26883
134 2/8	21 4/8 21 2/8	18 0/8	5 5	Frio County	TX	Tom Langston	2007	26883
*134 2/8	20 7/8 21 5/8	16 0/8	5 5	Pine County	MN	Steve Schroeder	2008	26883
134 2/8	21 3/8 23 2/8	15 0/8	5 6	San Saba County	TX	Kelby McCall	2008	26883
*134 2/8	24 6/8 24 3/8	18 0/8	4 4	La Crosse County	WI	Shawn Zellmer	2008	26883
134 2/8	21 6/8 21 3/8	19 6/8	4 4	Goodhue County	MN	Brad Cushing	2008	26883
*134 2/8	22 1/8 21 6/8	14 4/8	4 4	Clay County	IN	Robert W. Mitchell	2008	26883
*134 2/8	22 0/8 20 4/8	16 2/8	5 5	Scott County	AR	David Brewer	2008	26883
134 2/8	21 3/8 22 1/8	14 4/8	4 4	Washington County	OH	Ralph Pinkerton	2008	26883
*134 2/8	20 6/8 21 2/8	14 6/8	5 6	Ben Hill County	GA	Marc Sheffield	2008	26883
134 2/8	21 1/8 22 0/8	17 2/8	6 6	Stearns County	MN	Charlie Huot	2008	26883
134 2/8	23 2/8 24 7/8	16 0/8	8 7	Marshall County	IN	Donny E. Betzner	2009	26883
134 2/8	21 4/8 21 3/8	15 2/8	5 5	Yell County	AR	Clarence Rodrigues	2009	26883
134 2/8	24 4/8 24 0/8	14 3/8	5 5	Monroe County	MI	Jerome Gotha	2009	26883
*134 2/8	22 7/8 22 6/8	16 2/8	4 4	Allamakee County	IA	Dean E. Mense	2009	26883
134 2/8	19 6/8 21 0/8	17 7/8	4 5	Brown County	WI	Brad Linzmeier	2009	26883
134 2/8	21 6/8 21 7/8	17 4/8	6 5	Queen Annes County	MD	Virgil R. Klepper, Jr.	2009	26883
*134 2/8	22 2/8 22 2/8	17 2/8	4 5	Jefferson County	WI	Sherry Lee Vingum	2009	26883
*134 2/8	25 1/8 23 2/8	17 6/8	4 4	Jo Daviess County	IL	Mark DeWitt	2009	26883
134 2/8	21 3/8 20 3/8	17 0/8	5 5	Sauk County	WI	Austin J. Brown	2009	26883
134 2/8	21 1/8 20 6/8	14 4/8	5 5	Pottawatomie County	KS	Brandon Cerkas	2009	26883
134 2/8	20 2/8 20 6/8	21 5/8	5 5	Clark County	KS	David A. Lock	2009	26883
*134 2/8	21 3/8 21 3/8	18 0/8	5 5	Portage County	WI	Jerry Check	2009	26883
*134 2/8	22 0/8 22 0/8	18 2/8	5 5	Barron County	WI	Greg Nelson	2009	26883
134 2/8	24 5/8 23 7/8	18 0/8	5 4	Franklin County	NC	Scott Russell	2009	26883
134 1/8	23 4/8 23 0/8	17 3/8	4 6	Whitley County	IN	Joe Williamson	1991	27089
134 1/8	20 4/8 20 4/8	15 4/8	5 6	Champaign County	IL	Robert E. Mabry	1992	27089
134 1/8	21 7/8 22 2/8	15 1/8	5 5	Notre-Dame-De-Lourde	QUE	Roland Hanser	1999	27089
134 1/8	23 3/8 22 4/8	18 1/8	4 4	Laramie County	WY	Bob V. Danenhower, Sr.	2000	27089
134 1/8	21 5/8 22 4/8	19 5/8	4 4	Kingsbury County	SD	Reginald E. Faber, Jr.	2000	27089
134 1/8	24 4/8 24 5/8	14 3/8	4 4	Newaygo County	MI	Ed Mascarenas	2001	27089
*134 1/8	25 4/8 24 6/8	17 5/8	4 5	Kalamazoo County	MI	Thomas A. Hildebrand	2003	27089
134 1/8	24 0/8 22 2/8	17 5/8	6 4	Ashland County	WI	Jerry Schaff	2003	27089
134 1/8	21 5/8 22 7/8	16 5/8	4 4	Will County	IL	Adam Marcukaitis	2004	27089
134 1/8	21 5/8 22 0/8	19 1/8	4 4	Juneau County	WI	Craig C. Tormoen	2004	27089
134 1/8	22 0/8 21 3/8	17 4/8	4 6	Juneau County	WI	Randall J. Senzig	2004	27089
134 1/8	26 6/8 25 6/8	18 3/8	5 8	Coles County	IL	Joseph D. Price	2004	27089
134 1/8	23 0/8 22 4/8	16 7/8	4 4	Warren County	OH	Steven Alexander	2005	27089
*134 1/8	22 1/8 22 5/8	13 5/8	4 4	Sheboygan County	WI	Robert Babino	2005	27089
134 1/8	22 5/8 22 5/8	19 5/8	4 4	Montgomery County	IN	John P. Beaman	2005	27089
*134 1/8	21 4/8 21 4/8	17 2/8	5 5	Clarke County	MS	Carey Osbon	2005	27089
134 1/8	21 4/8 21 6/8	15 7/8	5 5	Butler County	IA	Landon Uhlenhopp	2005	27089
134 1/8	21 1/8 21 0/8	14 3/8	6 7	Harrison County	MO	Brian Wines	2005	27089
134 1/8	22 0/8 22 4/8	15 6/8	7 5	Jasper County	IL	John Barrick	2005	27089
134 1/8	23 0/8 23 1/8	15 7/8	4 5	Ashland County	WI	John W. Juley	2005	27089
134 1/8	23 0/8 22 4/8	16 3/8	6 6	Gage County	NE	Nate Keller	2005	27089
134 1/8	23 5/8 23 5/8	17 1/8	4 4	Randolph County	NC	Derek S. Cranford	2006	27089
134 1/8	23 6/8 23 7/8	18 3/8	5 4	Jackson County	MI	Jason A. Fryt	2006	27089
*134 1/8	21 2/8 22 6/8	18 6/8	4 6	Monmouth County	NJ	R. J. Krajcsovics	2006	27089
134 1/8	22 0/8 21 6/8	15 5/8	6 6	Moultrie County	IL	Gregory Scribner	2006	27089
134 1/8	21 4/8 21 5/8	15 3/8	5 6	Bucks County	PA	Rudy Blair	2006	27089
*134 1/8	22 4/8 23 0/8	15 3/8	5 5	Wabasha County	MN	Sean M. Corfits	2006	27089
134 1/8	24 3/8 24 3/8	19 7/8	4 3	Pike County	IL	Christopher K. Krista	2006	27089
134 1/8	22 6/8 22 2/8	17 3/8	5 6	Douglas County	WI	Daniel Esselstrom, Jr.	2006	27089
134 1/8	23 7/8 22 7/8	19 5/8	5 4	Knox County	IN	Malcolm E. Dubbs III	2006	27089
134 1/8	22 3/8 21 7/8	14 7/8	5 6	Webster County	IA	Dave Propst	2006	27089
*134 1/8	24 0/8 22 7/8	17 3/8	5 4	Randolph County	AR	Jade Price	2006	27089
134 1/8	24 6/8 24 7/8	20 7/8	4 4	Archer County	TX	Breyden Bales	2006	27089
*134 1/8	22 6/8 21 6/8	14 1/8	5 5	Miami County	KS	David Haake	2006	27089
*134 1/8	23 1/8 22 6/8	17 3/8	5 4	Bedford County	TN	Clint Holden	2007	27089
134 1/8	21 6/8 22 2/8	17 7/8	5 4	Jackson County	WV	James W. Casto III	2007	27089
*134 1/8	24 7/8 24 3/8	18 4/8	6 5	Washington County	RI	Michael Henry, Jr.	2007	27089
134 1/8	21 3/8 22 4/8	18 5/8	4 4	Sheboygan County	WI	Gerald Eigenberger	2007	27089
*134 1/8	22 5/8 22 0/8	15 7/8	6 5	Benton County	AR	Rusty Johnson	2007	27089
134 1/8	21 4/8 22 7/8	18 1/8	5 5	Schuyler County	IL	Matthew Zeigler	2007	27089
134 1/8	22 4/8 22 6/8	15 3/8	5 4	Chautauqua County	NY	Mark Chilberg	2007	27089
134 1/8	22 3/8 22 5/8	15 6/8	4 5	Ward County	ND	Don Scofield	2007	27089
134 1/8	21 5/8 20 7/8	17 5/8	5 5	Shawano County	WI	Wayne Bamke	2007	27089
*134 1/8	23 2/8 23 2/8	17 1/8	5 4	Scott County	KY	Chris Howard	2008	27089
134 1/8	24 5/8 24 2/8	16 0/8	5 6	Rowan County	NC	Ronnie Barrier	2008	27089
134 1/8	25 3/8 25 0/8	13 7/8	5 6	Crow Wing County	MN	Randy Litke	2008	27089
134 1/8	20 6/8 20 6/8	17 0/8	5 7	Fountain County	IN	William Hanna	2008	27089
134 1/8	24 5/8 24 3/8	20 5/8	6 6	Buffalo County	WI	Randy Springborn	2008	27089
*134 1/8	22 5/8 21 4/8	16 3/8	4 6	Fayette County	IA	Matthew Petersen	2008	27089
134 1/8	22 2/8 23 1/8	16 7/8	4 5	Washington County	PA	Richard D. Popeck	2008	27089
134 1/8	22 2/8 25 4/8	15 7/8	6 6	Hardin County	KY	Gary T. Anderson	2008	27089
*134 1/8	21 1/8 21 3/8	12 3/8	5 6	Adams County	IL	Bruce Eller	2008	27089
134 1/8	23 0/8 21 4/8	19 4/8	5 6	Iowa County	WI	Dave Henner	2008	27089

Deer entries below 141 0/8, that appeared in the 6th Edition, are not included here, but are included on the accompanying CD (see page 119), and also in the Club's Records Archives.

WHITETAIL DEER (TYPICAL ANTLERS)

Minimum Score 125 — Continued

SCORE	LENGTH OF MAIN BEAM R	L	INSIDE SPREAD	NUMBER OF POINTS R	L	AREA	STATE/ PROVINCE	HUNTER'S NAME	DATE	RANK
134 1/8	22 1/8	23 1/8	16 6/8	5	6	Coal County	OK	Mark Parkhill	2008	27089
*134 1/8	22 3/8	22 4/8	18 3/8	4	4	Knox County	IL	Brad Palmer	2008	27089
*134 1/8	22 3/8	21 7/8	18 1/8	6	7	McMullen County	TX	John Kovarcik	2009	27089
134 1/8	19 4/8	19 1/8	17 6/8	5	6	Madison County	MT	Chris Dahl	2009	27089
134 1/8	20 5/8	20 4/8	14 5/8	5	5	Hemphill County	TX	Robert Marusak	2009	27089
134 1/8	24 6/8	23 0/8	19 5/8	4	4	Delaware County	OH	Steve Garrett	2009	27089
134 1/8	23 0/8	22 6/8	16 5/8	4	4	Louisa County	IA	Mitch Finke	2009	27089
134 1/8	21 0/8	20 5/8	17 4/8	6	4	Keya Paha County	NE	Terry Marcukaitis	2009	27089
*134 1/8	21 3/8	22 3/8	17 0/8	5	5	Butler County	KS	William Swigart	2009	27089
*134 1/8	22 6/8	23 4/8	19 1/8	5	6	Barber County	KS	Brian E. Barlass	2009	27089
134 1/8	21 5/8	21 7/8	16 3/8	5	5	Fayette County	WV	Adam Bowman	2009	27089
*134 1/8	21 1/8	20 3/8	19 7/8	7	6	Edmunds County	SD	Travis Wagner	2009	27089
*134 1/8	23 3/8	22 0/8	19 0/8	4	5	Coles County	IL	Chris R. Eaton	2009	27089
134 1/8	20 6/8	20 2/8	17 3/8	5	5	McHenry County	ND	John Michael Grunseth	2009	27089
134 0/8	22 6/8	23 0/8	17 4/8	4	4	Oneida County	WI	Randy Sankey	1996	27293
134 0/8	21 7/8	21 4/8	16 4/8	4	5	Madison County	IL	Darrell Smith	2000	27293
134 0/8	21 7/8	20 5/8	18 4/8	4	5	Lincoln County	WI	Tom Schmeltzer	2000	27293
134 0/8	20 4/8	20 5/8	15 6/8	5	5	Rockland County	NY	Benjamin Risley	2003	27293
134 0/8	22 3/8	22 7/8	15 2/8	4	5	Polk County	MN	Doug Holtman	2003	27293
*134 0/8	23 4/8	23 4/8	15 3/8	4	5	Calvert County	MD	Earl E. Burke	2004	27293
134 0/8	22 0/8	21 6/8	19 4/8	4	5	Dawson County	NE	Shawn Church	2004	27293
134 0/8	20 6/8	20 4/8	16 6/8	7	6	Missoula County	MT	Jeffrey G. Taylor	2004	27293
134 0/8	20 2/8	20 2/8	15 0/8	5	5	Waupaca County	WI	Brian Dey	2004	27293
134 0/8	23 4/8	23 1/8	16 2/8	5	5	Hardin County	OH	Jim Spallinger	2004	27293
134 0/8	22 1/8	22 7/8	15 2/8	6	6	Kosciusko County	IN	Henry L. Kidd	2004	27293
134 0/8	22 1/8	22 3/8	18 6/8	8	5	Jackson County	MI	John A. Hay	2004	27293
134 0/8	21 3/8	20 5/8	14 2/8	6	7	Marion County	KY	Terry Edward Colvin	2004	27293
134 0/8	23 1/8	23 7/8	16 0/8	5	5	La Porte County	IN	Roger R. Miller	2004	27293
134 0/8	23 0/8	22 5/8	18 6/8	4	4	Sauk County	WI	Andy Bartnick	2004	27293
134 0/8	21 2/8	21 5/8	17 6/8	4	4	Harper County	KS	John Files	2004	27293
134 0/8	24 2/8	25 7/8	17 0/8	4	4	Orange County	NC	Ken A. Leimone	2004	27293
134 0/8	23 2/8	23 6/8	20 0/8	4	4	Monmouth County	NJ	Mark Kronyak	2004	27293
134 0/8	22 1/8	21 7/8	14 6/8	5	5	Irion County	TX	Andrew Stanco	2005	27293
134 0/8	21 0/8	21 2/8	18 1/8	6	5	Sullivan County	IN	Mike Miller	2005	27293
134 0/8	21 1/8	20 7/8	18 0/8	5	5	Bexar County	TX	John Bass	2005	27293
134 0/8	23 0/8	22 1/8	16 6/8	4	4	Pepin County	WI	Patrick Falkner	2005	27293
134 0/8	24 5/8	25 0/8	17 4/8	4	4	Reno County	KS	Greg Johnson	2005	27293
134 0/8	21 5/8	22 0/8	14 0/8	6	5	Vermilion County	IL	Shawn Schermann	2005	27293
134 0/8	22 0/8	22 7/8	14 0/8	6	5	Yuma County	CO	Scott W. Meszaros	2005	27293
134 0/8	23 5/8	23 0/8	16 2/8	4	4	Holmes County	OH	Larry Elliott	2005	27293
134 0/8	22 6/8	22 3/8	16 4/8	4	4	Fayette County	OH	Whitlow Wyatt	2005	27293
*134 0/8	20 7/8	20 5/8	16 4/8	5	7	Eddy County	ND	Greg Kolstad	2006	27293
*134 0/8	19 2/8	18 7/8	14 2/8	5	6	Crook County	WY	Michele Leqve	2006	27293
134 0/8	24 6/8	24 7/8	16 0/8	3	3	New Haven County	CT	Adam Mastracchio	2006	27293
134 0/8	23 7/8	23 6/8	15 4/8	5	6	Lake of the Woods County	MN	Ed Albrecht	2006	27293
134 0/8	22 0/8	22 0/8	16 2/8	4	4	Anne Arundel County	MD	Rachelle Gertz	2006	27293
*134 0/8	21 4/8	21 5/8	17 7/8	8	5	Lawrence County	PA	Eric Bishop	2006	27293
134 0/8	22 4/8	21 4/8	17 6/8	7	5	Washington County	PA	Jason M. Phillips	2006	27293
134 0/8	23 7/8	24 0/8	18 0/8	4	4	Vernon County	WI	Kevin J. Simonsen	2006	27293
134 0/8	20 3/8	19 6/8	14 4/8	5	6	Richland County	WI	Randy Wielgus	2006	27293
*134 0/8	25 3/8	24 2/8	16 6/8	4	4	Warren County	IA	Alan Cole	2006	27293
134 0/8	23 0/8	24 1/8	21 4/8	4	4	Lenawee County	MI	Nic Austin	2006	27293
134 0/8	22 1/8	25 1/8	18 6/8	4	4	Dearborn County	IN	Ricky Henderson	2006	27293
134 0/8	25 1/8	25 5/8	18 2/8	3	4	Houston County	MN	Jeff Keogh	2006	27293
134 0/8	23 5/8	23 1/8	20 0/8	5	5	Franklin County	MA	Andrew Howard	2006	27293
134 0/8	22 3/8	23 7/8	16 2/8	4	4	Jackson County	IL	Tim Cobin	2006	27293
134 0/8	26 4/8	26 0/8	21 0/8	8	5	Morgan County	OH	Bernie McNamee	2007	27293
134 0/8	24 1/8	22 5/8	15 0/8	8	7	Mason County	IL	Bill Blevins	2007	27293
*134 0/8	21 7/8	22 0/8	15 4/8	5	7	Hocking County	OH	Ed Zagurski	2007	27293
134 0/8	20 2/8	20 3/8	16 2/8	5	5	Washington County	WI	Gregory G. Kuhn	2007	27293
*134 0/8	23 6/8	24 2/8	18 4/8	4	4	Fayette County	IA	Christopher Bierman	2007	27293
134 0/8	21 0/8	22 1/8	18 0/8	4	4	Monroe County	MI	Everett L. Willis	2007	27293
*134 0/8	19 2/8	20 6/8	14 7/8	6	5	Chitek Lake	SAS	Lawrence Newbern	2007	27293
134 0/8	21 7/8	22 2/8	18 4/8	5	5	Kiowa County	KS	Shane Collier	2007	27293
134 0/8	20 4/8	20 4/8	16 6/8	4	5	Clearwater	ALB	Warren Welch	2008	27293
134 0/8	23 1/8	22 5/8	20 0/8	4	4	Clay County	MN	Walter J. Palmer	2008	27293
134 0/8	21 4/8	23 1/8	17 0/8	5	5	Clinton County	MI	Drew S. Cronk	2008	27293
134 0/8	20 3/8	20 3/8	17 4/8	5	6	Northampton County	PA	Keith R. Horn	2008	27293
*134 0/8	23 4/8	23 5/8	18 6/8	6	4	Houston County	MN	Richard Tenute	2008	27293
*134 0/8	25 1/8	25 0/8	17 6/8	5	5	Dubois County	IN	Kirk M. Wyman	2008	27293
134 0/8	23 4/8	21 6/8	17 2/8	4	5	Cumberland County	IL	Raymond Watkins	2008	27293
*134 0/8	23 7/8	24 1/8	20 0/8	3	4	Furnas County	NE	Brad Bounds	2008	27293
134 0/8	24 0/8	23 4/8	19 1/8	5	4	Barber County	KS	Robert Spratt	2008	27293
*134 0/8	22 3/8	22 3/8	17 4/8	5	5	Webb County	TX	Brandon Pickens	2008	27293
*134 0/8	20 5/8	20 7/8	17 0/8	5	5	Live Oak County	TX	James "Ron" Whitmore, Sr.	2008	27293
*134 0/8	23 3/8	23 5/8	17 4/8	4	5	Polk County	IA	Eddie VanDorn	2008	27293
*134 0/8	26 5/8	25 6/8	19 2/8	5	5	Fillmore County	MN	Anthony Watson	2009	27293
134 0/8	22 3/8	22 4/8	15 2/8	6	5	Hampshire County	MA	David J. Benham	2009	27293
*134 0/8	24 0/8	25 0/8	17 4/8	4	5	Black Hawk County	IA	Chad Tobin	2009	27293
134 0/8	22 3/8	23 1/8	14 4/8	4	5	Van Buren County	IA	Jim Reints	2009	27293
134 0/8	21 0/8	21 6/8	19 0/8	8	6	Van Buren County	MI	Kevin M. Hall	2009	27293
*134 0/8	21 7/8	21 4/8	16 6/8	5	5	Vernon County	WI	Gerald J. Schumacher	2009	27293
134 0/8	23 0/8	21 6/8	18 6/8	4	5	Fisher County	TX	Michael Kloth	2010	27293
134 0/8	21 7/8	21 7/8	16 6/8	5	5	Washburn County	WI	Tim Johnson	2010	27293
133 7/8	22 2/8	21 4/8	18 1/8	4	4	Allen County	IN	Matthew R. Myers	1988	27505
133 7/8	22 4/8	22 5/8	18 6/8	4	6	Jackson County	MO	John Stephen Smith	1995	27505
133 7/8	22 1/8	23 1/8	17 1/8	4	5	Sauk County	WI	Scott W. Hill	2003	27505
133 7/8	22 2/8	21 2/8	17 3/8	5	4	Cuming County	NE	Heath Cornett	2003	27505
133 7/8	22 5/8	22 5/8	15 7/8	5	4	Burnett County	WI	Joseph A. Renfrow, Jr.	2003	27505
133 7/8	23 2/8	23 3/8	19 2/8	4	5	Stearns County	MN	Marcus Nettz	2003	27505
133 7/8	19 1/8	18 7/8	13 2/8	6	6	Cherokee County	KS	David Benitz	2003	27505
133 7/8	22 7/8	22 3/8	15 5/8	7	5	Shelby County	KY	Justin Thompson	2004	27505
133 7/8	22 1/8	21 5/8	14 7/8	6	8	Zavala County	TX	Ronald Wardell	2004	27505
*133 7/8	23 7/8	23 3/8	17 5/8	4	6	Douglas County	WI	Robert Thompson	2004	27505
133 7/8	24 4/8	24 4/8	18 4/8	4	7	Fremont County	IA	Mark Armstrong	2004	27505

WHITETAIL DEER (TYPICAL ANTLERS)

Minimum Score 125 — Continued

SCORE	LENGTH OF R MAIN BEAM L	INSIDE SPREAD	NUMBER OF R POINTS L	AREA	STATE/ PROVINCE	HUNTER'S NAME	DATE	RANK
*133 7/8	23 6/8 23 7/8	20 6/8	7 5	Bourbon County	KS	Doyle Slinkard	2004	27505
133 7/8	21 5/8 20 6/8	17 7/8	4 4	Jasper County	IA	Wilbur "Buck" Ringler	2004	27505
133 7/8	20 7/8 20 7/8	16 7/8	5 5	Pratt County	KS	Reggie Hochstein	2004	27505
133 7/8	22 2/8 21 6/8	17 3/8	5 5	Richland County	WI	Jesse Lenz	2004	27505
133 7/8	21 2/8 20 3/8	15 5/8	5 6	Tuscarawas County	OH	Steve Archer	2004	27505
133 7/8	22 6/8 23 3/8	19 3/8	4 4	Ashtabula County	OH	Kevin Dunham	2004	27505
133 7/8	23 1/8 23 1/8	17 3/8	4 5	Riley County	KS	Scott King	2004	27505
133 7/8	22 0/8 21 4/8	16 1/8	5 5	Washington County	OH	Phillip Jarvis	2004	27505
133 7/8	22 4/8 22 7/8	19 5/8	6 6	Plymouth County	MA	Kevin Provost	2004	27505
133 7/8	23 2/8 21 7/8	17 3/8	5 5	Waushara County	WI	Brian Barnes	2005	27505
133 7/8	23 3/8 23 0/8	19 6/8	6 5	Clark County	OH	Eric Keplinger	2005	27505
133 7/8	24 4/8 23 2/8	21 1/8	4 4	La Salle County	IL	Allan Simons	2005	27505
133 7/8	21 7/8 23 3/8	20 1/8	4 4	Tuscarawas County	OH	Roger M. Tyler	2005	27505
*133 7/8	21 7/8 22 1/8	18 5/8	4 4	Jo Daviess County	IL	James G. Harkness	2005	27505
133 7/8	21 5/8 22 3/8	18 5/8	4 4	Dunn County	WI	Dave Lieffort	2005	27505
133 7/8	23 6/8 23 5/8	18 5/8	4 5	Delaware County	IA	Dean Dempster II	2005	27505
133 7/8	23 4/8 23 6/8	18 7/8	5 5	Whiteside County	IL	Clint Walker	2005	27505
*133 7/8	24 2/8 23 2/8	17 1/8	5 4	St. Clair County	MI	Walter McGranahan	2005	27505
133 7/8	22 3/8 21 6/8	17 1/8	5 5	Kent County	MI	Dan Roodvoets	2005	27505
133 7/8	18 4/8 18 6/8	12 7/8	6 6	Cass County	IL	Daniel W. Kirkes	2005	27505
*133 7/8	20 0/8 21 0/8	17 3/8	5 5	Winnebago County	WI	Kevin Malnory	2005	27505
133 7/8	24 5/8 24 3/8	16 6/8	6 6	Franklin County	IL	Darin DeNeal	2005	27505
*133 7/8	21 3/8 20 6/8	18 7/8	4 4	Adams County	IA	John Zilinski	2005	27505
133 7/8	19 6/8 20 4/8	16 5/8	5 5	Berrien County	MI	Dean Heath	2005	27505
*133 7/8	23 2/8 22 6/8	19 5/8	5 5	Chester County	PA	Ryan E. Forrester	2005	27505
133 7/8	21 0/8 20 3/8	18 3/8	6 5	Sarpy County	NE	Philip Zimmerman	2005	27505
133 7/8	24 5/8 25 2/8	17 0/8	5 4	Madison County	IL	Greg Maul	2005	27505
*133 7/8	21 7/8 22 0/8	17 2/8	4 5	Barnes County	ND	Dennis Roberg	2006	27505
133 7/8	23 0/8 23 3/8	15 6/8	7 4	Outagamie County	WI	David Winkel	2006	27505
133 7/8	22 4/8 22 0/8	17 7/8	4 4	Sheridan County	WY	Susan K. Barrett	2006	27505
133 7/8	22 2/8 22 4/8	17 2/8	6 6	Clearwater County	MN	Bryan Dyrdahl	2006	27505
133 7/8	20 7/8 20 4/8	14 1/8	5 6	Moody County	SD	Jason Zemlicka	2006	27505
133 7/8	25 2/8 23 1/8	17 5/8	5 4	Vanderburgh County	IN	Clifford K. Crowe	2006	27505
*133 7/8	20 5/8 20 3/8	17 4/8	5 7	Meade County	KY	Josh Pierce	2006	27505
*133 7/8	22 7/8 23 3/8	19 1/8	6 4	Clark County	IL	Rick Davidson	2006	27505
133 7/8	22 2/8 22 7/8	19 2/8	7 7	St. Joseph County	IN	Charles E. Harbin	2006	27505
133 7/8	21 5/8 22 4/8	16 2/8	5 6	Clark County	IA	Don Mealey	2006	27505
*133 7/8	23 4/8 22 0/8	16 5/8	5 4	Douglas County	WI	Kevin Kivisto	2007	27505
133 7/8	20 6/8 20 6/8	15 5/8	6 7	Vilas County	WI	Timothy Ryan	2007	27505
*133 7/8	22 4/8 21 6/8	16 3/8	5 5	Broadwater County	MT	John Hoyle	2007	27505
133 7/8	22 2/8 21 4/8	14 6/8	6 6	Marquette County	WI	James L. Ziemer	2007	27505
133 7/8	24 0/8 22 5/8	18 6/8	5 6	Iowa County	WI	Rich Foss	2007	27505
133 7/8	21 1/8 20 6/8	16 7/8	5 5	Ashland County	WI	Thomas J. Suttner	2007	27505
133 7/8	21 1/8 21 3/8	13 3/8	5 4	Buffalo County	WI	Michael Schleicher	2007	27505
133 7/8	19 5/8 20 4/8	17 1/8	5 5	Kosciusko County	IN	Zach Stookey	2007	27505
133 7/8	23 2/8 23 4/8	21 2/8	5 7	Dane County	WI	Dennis Kutsche	2007	27505
133 7/8	23 1/8 22 2/8	16 7/8	4 4	Westchester County	NY	John Lombardo, Jr.	2007	27505
133 7/8	22 0/8 21 7/8	17 3/8	5 5	St. Clair County	IL	Wayne M. Kniepkamp	2007	27505
133 7/8	22 3/8 22 5/8	17 5/8	4 4	Cass County	MI	Michael L. Ritter	2007	27505
133 7/8	20 6/8 21 6/8	16 5/8	4 4	Kerr County	TX	Oma Claunch	2007	27505
133 7/8	21 7/8 22 0/8	19 4/8	5 6	Butler County	PA	Brad Fleming	2008	27505
133 7/8	25 0/8 24 7/8	21 1/8	4 4	Scott County	IA	Pamela Templeton	2008	27505
*133 7/8	24 2/8 24 3/8	15 6/8	6 5	Seneca County	OH	Nathan Elliott	2008	27505
*133 7/8	25 7/8 24 3/8	16 1/8	5 4	Berrien County	MI	Andrew J. Bierwagen	2008	27505
133 7/8	22 5/8 23 2/8	17 3/8	6 6	Stafford County	KS	Bob O'Brien	2008	27505
133 7/8	23 3/8 23 3/8	18 5/8	6 6	Douglas County	WI	Kasey Jensen	2008	27505
*133 7/8	24 5/8 24 3/8	15 3/8	6 5	Branch County	MI	Bret Cary	2008	27505
133 7/8	22 5/8 22 6/8	18 6/8	5 5	Burnett County	WI	Gregory Widiker	2008	27505
133 7/8	20 6/8 21 4/8	19 1/8	6 5	Polk County	WI	Ron Ekstrand	2008	27505
133 7/8	25 4/8 24 5/8	19 5/8	5 5	Clinton County	OH	Bill Hall	2008	27505
*133 7/8	25 6/8 24 0/8	18 6/8	4 6	Pike County	OH	Jarrod Bowers	2009	27505
133 7/8	20 2/8 21 0/8	17 5/8	5 5	Putnam County	MO	Gerald W. Webber	2009	27505
133 7/8	21 7/8 22 0/8	19 5/8	5 5	McHenry County	IL	Kevin Muench	2009	27505
133 7/8	22 6/8 23 0/8	19 7/8	5 4	Wood County	WI	Greg Kremer	2009	27505
133 7/8	18 4/8 18 7/8	14 5/8	5 5	Gallatin County	MT	Bob Morton	2009	27505
*133 7/8	19 6/8 21 2/8	19 3/8	4 4	Madison County	IA	Jason Hansen	2009	27505
133 7/8	21 6/8 22 0/8	15 1/8	4 4	Kosciusko County	IN	Jason Hall	2010	27505
133 6/8	24 2/8 24 0/8	17 1/8	6 6	Miami County	IN	Donald P. Dabelow	1998	27728
133 6/8	20 7/8 20 0/8	14 2/8	4 4	Harris County	GA	Kenneth O. Athon, Jr.	2002	27728
133 6/8	24 6/8 24 3/8	17 6/8	4 4	Fayette County	IA	Jerry L. Gallmeyer	2003	27728
133 6/8	22 4/8 23 2/8	15 4/8	5 5	Edmonson County	KY	Mark Klusty	2004	27728
*133 6/8	23 4/8 23 5/8	14 6/8	4 5	Polk County	WI	Dan Cain	2004	27728
*133 6/8	22 0/8 23 6/8	17 1/8	5 8	Franklin County	VA	Travis McPherson	2004	27728
133 6/8	23 0/8 23 2/8	18 0/8	5 5	Calhoun County	IL	John R. King	2004	27728
133 6/8	22 3/8 22 5/8	15 4/8	4 5	Buffalo County	SD	Rob Knippling	2004	27728
133 6/8	21 0/8 20 5/8	17 4/8	5 5	Woodbury County	IA	Jason Ross	2004	27728
*133 6/8	22 6/8 22 1/8	16 2/8	4 4	La Crosse County	WI	Spencer Mashak	2004	27728
133 6/8	23 3/8 24 3/8	15 0/8	4 5	Waushara County	WI	Jonathan J. Lehman	2004	27728
133 6/8	24 4/8 23 2/8	17 0/8	4 4	Hendricks County	IN	Robert Lynch II	2004	27728
133 6/8	20 5/8 20 3/8	16 4/8	5 5	Oconto County	WI	Cody Hendricks	2004	27728
*133 6/8	22 3/8 21 3/8	15 7/8	6 5	Massac County	IL	Kevin Randall	2004	27728
133 6/8	20 0/8 19 5/8	17 4/8	5 5	Cheyenne County	CO	Ken Stieh	2004	27728
*133 6/8	20 1/8 19 7/8	13 0/8	5 5	Pulaski County	AR	Don E. Blakley	2005	27728
133 6/8	24 3/8 24 2/8	17 0/8	4 4	Itasca County	MN	Curt Youngkin	2005	27728
133 6/8	20 6/8 21 0/8	15 2/8	8 5	Kenedy County	TX	Bob Gilbert	2005	27728
*133 6/8	19 0/8 19 0/8	17 4/8	6 6	Mower County	MN	Joseph Landherr	2005	27728
133 6/8	22 4/8 22 4/8	16 2/8	6 5	Fulton County	IL	Michael J. Fazende	2005	27728
133 6/8	23 3/8 23 3/8	18 0/8	4 4	Taylor County	WI	Tom Hefner	2005	27728
133 6/8	22 2/8 22 5/8	15 6/8	4 5	Ashe County	NC	Billy Joe Blevins, Jr.	2005	27728
133 6/8	22 1/8 21 6/8	17 6/8	5 5	Oconto County	WI	Scott C. Mercure	2005	27728
133 6/8	24 0/8 23 4/8	17 2/8	5 6	Pike County	IL	Jeffrey L. Lescalleet	2005	27728
133 6/8	23 1/8 22 3/8	19 3/8	7 5	Somerset County	NJ	Manuel A. Santos	2005	27728
133 6/8	21 1/8 20 4/8	14 4/8	5 5	Webster County	NE	William Grube	2006	27728
133 6/8	21 2/8 20 0/8	16 4/8	5 5	St. Croix County	WI	Dave DeJong	2006	27728
133 6/8	22 0/8 21 3/8	15 2/8	5 5	Callaway County	MO	Jeff Bergsieker	2006	27728

Deer entries below 141 0/8, that appeared in the 6th Edition, are not included here, but are included on the accompanying CD (see page 119), and also in the Club's Records Archives.

WHITETAIL DEER (TYPICAL ANTLERS)

Minimum Score 125 — Continued

SCORE	LENGTH OF R MAIN BEAM L	INSIDE SPREAD	NUMBER OF R POINTS L		AREA	STATE/ PROVINCE	HUNTER'S NAME	DATE	RANK
133 6/8	21 7/8 23 3/8	17 1/8	6	6	Lee County	IA	Mike Gorham	2006	27728
133 6/8	22 3/8 22 1/8	16 6/8	5	5	Franklin County	IA	Larry Fanny	2006	27728
*133 6/8	22 7/8 22 1/8	14 0/8	5	5	Belmont County	OH	Brian Herrin	2006	27728
133 6/8	26 0/8 25 1/8	17 0/8	4	4	Adams County	OH	Jim Williamson	2006	27728
133 6/8	22 0/8 21 6/8	17 0/8	5	5	Niagara County	NY	Mike Jeffords	2006	27728
133 6/8	24 4/8 22 5/8	17 7/8	4	6	Waushara County	WI	Bruce Shine	2006	27728
*133 6/8	24 5/8 24 6/8	25 6/8	4	4	Strafford County	NH	Michael Young	2006	27728
133 6/8	19 5/8 20 5/8	17 1/8	6	5	Monona County	IA	Michael W. McKenna	2006	27728
*133 6/8	22 7/8 24 2/8	18 5/8	6	5	Shelby County	IL	Lee Roadarmel	2007	27728
133 6/8	21 5/8 20 7/8	14 6/8	5	5	Dubuque County	IA	Nathan Feldmann	2007	27728
*133 6/8	19 0/8 21 4/8	14 0/8	6	5	Spencer County	IN	Billy R. Embry	2007	27728
133 6/8	21 5/8 22 5/8	19 6/8	4	4	Ashland County	WI	Elliot Heath	2007	27728
133 6/8	23 6/8 23 0/8	18 4/8	5	6	Marion County	IA	Leonard Grimes	2007	27728
*133 6/8	24 1/8 23 4/8	16 4/8	5	5	Whitley County	IN	Randy Wilkinson	2008	27728
133 6/8	25 3/8 24 5/8	17 2/8	4	4	Dodge County	WI	Brad Brockhaus	2008	27728
133 6/8	22 2/8 23 4/8	16 6/8	5	4	Morris County	NJ	Mark Spoto	2008	27728
*133 6/8	21 1/8 21 1/8	15 0/8	5	5	Ionia County	MI	Joel B. Mitchell	2008	27728
*133 6/8	23 7/8 22 2/8	19 2/8	4	4	Onondaga County	NY	Roy C. Lytle, Jr.	2008	27728
*133 6/8	25 4/8 26 1/8	18 4/8	6	6	Polk County	WI	Brian Stensven	2008	27728
*133 6/8	21 3/8 22 1/8	16 4/8	5	4	Hand County	SD	Travis Sivertsen	2008	27728
133 6/8	23 4/8 22 6/8	21 6/8	4	4	Morris County	KS	Forest Keith	2008	27728
133 6/8	19 6/8 23 7/8	14 4/8	4	4	Jackson County	IA	Mathias Dague	2008	27728
*133 6/8	20 5/8 19 7/8	9 5/8	7	5	Cass County	ND	Craig A. Wendt	2008	27728
*133 6/8	23 6/8 23 2/8	20 0/8	5	5	Webb County	TX	Clyde Miller	2009	27728
133 6/8	21 5/8 21 2/8	16 0/8	4	4	Cass County	ND	Troy Hocking	2009	27728
*133 6/8	20 5/8 20 1/8	13 0/8	6	6	Pike County	IL	Philip Snider	2009	27728
133 6/8	21 5/8 21 6/8	15 5/8	6	6	Mitchell County	IA	Brady Hunter	2009	27728
133 6/8	20 1/8 19 5/8	19 0/8	6	6	Wharton County	TX	Robert Alford	2009	27728
*133 6/8	22 5/8 21 4/8	15 6/8	5	5	Columbia County	WI	Steven J. Schwenke	2009	27728
*133 6/8	21 5/8 21 3/8	16 6/8	5	5	Waukesha County	WI	Gregory S. Weston	2009	27728
*133 6/8	23 4/8 22 2/8	19 0/8	4	4	De Kalb County	IN	Ben Krafft	2009	27728
*133 6/8	22 1/8 22 2/8	15 6/8	5	5	Wayne County	PA	Jeffrey Rutkowski	2009	27728
*133 6/8	21 3/8 20 6/8	16 4/8	5	5	Fillmore County	MN	Brad Horn	2009	27728
133 6/8	24 2/8 23 1/8	18 2/8	5	5	St. Croix County	WI	Dean Gehrman	2009	27728
133 6/8	23 4/8 23 1/8	19 2/8	4	4	Cumberland County	PA	Randy D. Martin	2009	27728
*133 6/8	21 6/8 20 4/8	18 0/8	5	5	Fairfax County	VA	Thomas R. Christie	2009	27728
*133 6/8	23 4/8 24 2/8	18 2/8	5	4	McMullen County	TX	Brad Schmidt	2010	27728
*133 6/8	23 5/8 22 2/8	17 6/8	5	6	Marshall County	KY	Blake Jackson	2010	27728
133 5/8	22 5/8 22 2/8	16 1/8	4	4	Allegany County	NY	David B. McDonald	1981	27961
133 5/8	22 3/8 23 4/8	18 7/8	5	5	Allamakee County	IA	Joe Lieb	1997	27961
133 5/8	21 1/8 22 0/8	17 3/8	4	4	Clarke County	IA	Greg Bakken	1999	27961
133 5/8	24 6/8 24 6/8	17 3/8	4	4	Hampden County	MA	Robbie Ober	1999	27961
133 5/8	25 0/8 23 6/8	17 0/8	5	4	Delaware County	PA	Carl Hill, Jr.	2000	27961
133 5/8	22 0/8 22 4/8	17 3/8	5	5	Buffalo County	WI	David C. Schoenberger	2001	27961
133 5/8	20 7/8 19 7/8	15 3/8	5	4	Wadena County	MN	Joe Gieske	2003	27961
133 5/8	22 0/8 21 7/8	17 4/8	6	6	Howard County	MO	Les Edwards	2003	27961
133 5/8	20 6/8 20 0/8	16 5/8	5	5	Wilbarger County	TX	Rodney Alexander	2003	27961
*133 5/8	20 7/8 20 7/8	16 1/8	5	5	Eaton County	MI	Martin D. Binkowski	2004	27961
133 5/8	22 6/8 21 5/8	16 5/8	4	4	Huntington County	IN	Gary Trimble	2004	27961
133 5/8	22 6/8 23 3/8	17 1/8	7	5	Hand County	SD	Scotty Parmely	2004	27961
*133 5/8	21 3/8 21 4/8	17 3/8	4	4	Clark County	IN	Raymond J. Popp III	2004	27961
133 5/8	24 7/8 22 3/8	18 1/8	5	5	Vermillion County	IN	Bill Payton	2004	27961
133 5/8	24 0/8 24 5/8	18 1/8	4	4	Monroe County	WI	David G. Carr	2004	27961
133 5/8	22 7/8 24 1/8	20 0/8	5	5	York County	PA	Jan R. Dell	2004	27961
133 5/8	19 0/8 20 7/8	15 5/8	5	6	Waukesha County	WI	Casey Grimm	2004	27961
133 5/8	24 4/8 24 4/8	18 5/8	5	4	Adams County	OH	Brian Baker	2004	27961
133 5/8	20 6/8 20 6/8	16 6/8	5	7	Ashland County	OH	William Fry	2004	27961
133 5/8	23 1/8 22 2/8	15 5/8	5	5	Meeker County	MN	Chris Schultz	2004	27961
133 5/8	23 0/8 22 5/8	16 3/8	5	4	Henderson County	NC	James A. Suttles	2004	27961
133 5/8	22 6/8 22 4/8	17 3/8	4	5	Hand County	SD	Kevin Bertsch	2004	27961
133 5/8	21 6/8 23 5/8	17 7/8	4	4	Bayfield County	WI	Rodney Hipsher	2004	27961
*133 5/8	19 7/8 20 5/8	15 5/8	6	6	Lac La Biche	ALB	Rod Shepley	2005	27961
133 5/8	20 3/8 20 6/8	17 1/8	4	4	Woodford County	KY	Chris Stone	2005	27961
133 5/8	24 3/8 24 2/8	17 2/8	7	7	Huron County	OH	Kelly Godfrey	2005	27961
133 5/8	21 4/8 23 3/8	20 3/8	5	4	De Kalb County	IN	Jerry Webber	2005	27961
133 5/8	22 1/8 22 3/8	16 5/8	4	4	Richland County	WI	John J. Dresen, Jr.	2005	27961
*133 5/8	24 5/8 24 6/8	16 7/8	4	5	Trempealeau County	WI	Jim Rand	2005	27961
133 5/8	22 4/8 22 4/8	16 5/8	4	4	Sauk County	WI	Garrick Anderson	2005	27961
133 5/8	21 0/8 20 3/8	16 7/8	6	6	Lincoln County	WI	Brad Kanitz	2005	27961
133 5/8	22 6/8 22 0/8	20 7/8	6	6	Polk County	WI	David T. Borek	2005	27961
133 5/8	24 7/8 24 3/8	18 3/8	4	4	Muskingum County	OH	Robert S. Hageter	2005	27961
*133 5/8	24 0/8 23 6/8	17 5/8	4	4	Jones County	IA	Dean Jacobson	2005	27961
133 5/8	22 4/8 21 6/8	16 7/8	5	5	Jefferson County	WI	Larry L. Braatz	2005	27961
*133 5/8	20 0/8 19 6/8	16 5/8	5	5	Spink County	SD	Norman Humphrey	2005	27961
133 5/8	25 4/8 23 7/8	16 0/8	4	6	Osage County	OK	Bryan White	2005	27961
*133 5/8	21 3/8 21 3/8	17 5/8	6	4	Scott County	IL	David K. Ward	2005	27961
133 5/8	21 3/8 19 5/8	14 7/8	4	4	Gonzales County	TX	Randy Peck	2005	27961
133 5/8	23 7/8 26 0/8	23 7/8	6	5	Mercer County	NJ	Steven Foster	2006	27961
133 5/8	25 1/8 25 2/8	19 1/8	4	5	Grant County	KY	Jeff Dixon	2006	27961
133 5/8	20 7/8 21 3/8	16 1/8	5	5	Lincoln County	MS	Karl Adams	2006	27961
*133 5/8	20 6/8 19 4/8	17 0/8	6	8	Sharp County	AR	Witt Stephens	2006	27961
*133 5/8	20 2/8 22 5/8	16 5/8	5	5	Chemung County	NY	Robert Diehr, Jr.	2006	27961
133 5/8	24 1/8 24 1/8	20 1/8	5	6	Ohio County	IN	David K. Miller	2006	27961
133 5/8	21 1/8 22 1/8	16 5/8	5	5	Linn County	MO	Gary Lampkins	2006	27961
133 5/8	22 5/8 22 2/8	17 3/8	5	5	Saunders County	NE	Jacob Komenda	2006	27961
133 5/8	22 6/8 22 4/8	15 1/8	5	4	Pike County	IL	Kim Bettinger	2006	27961
*133 5/8	21 6/8 20 2/8	17 1/8	6	6	Monroe County	NY	Stephen R. Miller	2006	27961
*133 5/8	19 0/8 21 0/8	16 3/8	5	5	Clay County	KS	Kevin Turgeon	2006	27961
133 5/8	22 2/8 22 6/8	18 3/8	5	5	Coles County	IL	Robert F. Hartbank	2006	27961
133 5/8	23 2/8 23 3/8	19 3/8	5	4	Mountrail County	ND	Craig Richardson	2007	27961
133 5/8	21 5/8 22 0/8	17 7/8	5	5	Duval County	TX	Dayner Roberts	2007	27961
133 5/8	23 5/8 21 5/8	17 3/8	4	5	Coahoma County	MS	Richard Fyfe	2007	27961
*133 5/8	22 0/8 22 1/8	16 3/8	5	5	Newaygo County	MI	Brian Rottier	2007	27961
133 5/8	23 4/8 22 1/8	19 5/8	4	4	Winona County	MN	Paul Georgeson	2007	27961
133 5/8	23 5/8 22 1/8	21 1/8	5	6	Wandering River	ALB	Pierre Giguere	2007	27961

WHITETAIL DEER (TYPICAL ANTLERS)

Minimum Score 125   Continued

SCORE	LENGTH OF R MAIN BEAM L	INSIDE SPREAD	NUMBER OF R POINTS L	AREA	STATE/ PROVINCE	HUNTER'S NAME	DATE	RANK
*133 5/8	21 3/8 21 0/8	17 0/8	5 6	Barron County	WI	Brad Knutson	2007	27961
133 5/8	21 7/8 21 7/8	16 6/8	5 5	Leflore County	MS	Barry A. McDonald	2007	27961
133 5/8	25 1/8 23 5/8	17 3/8	4 5	Cass County	MI	Tristan J. Weaver	2007	27961
133 5/8	26 4/8 25 3/8	17 7/8	5 4	McDowell County	WV	Robert Wimmer	2007	27961
133 5/8	21 4/8 21 2/8	17 7/8	4 5	Madison County	ID	Doug Kauer	2007	27961
133 5/8	22 0/8 22 4/8	17 4/8	5 7	Republic County	KS	Steven J. Dutton	2008	27961
133 5/8	24 2/8 23 0/8	17 7/8	5 5	Buffalo County	WI	Kory Rud	2008	27961
*133 5/8	20 4/8 20 3/8	19 1/8	5 5	Logan County	CO	Brad Baldwin	2008	27961
*133 5/8	22 3/8 20 6/8	15 3/8	5 5	Polk County	WI	Jordan Niemann	2008	27961
*133 5/8	22 0/8 22 1/8	21 1/8	5 4	Washington County	MD	Randy A. Working	2008	27961
133 5/8	20 7/8 21 2/8	16 1/8	4 4	Ionia County	MI	Michael J. Trombly	2008	27961
133 5/8	21 2/8 22 1/8	16 5/8	5 4	Crawford County	WI	Cody McCann	2008	27961
133 5/8	23 3/8 23 0/8	16 5/8	4 4	Fremont County	IA	Scott Wayne Overly	2008	27961
133 5/8	24 2/8 24 6/8	19 5/8	5 4	Jefferson County	OH	Steve Peperis	2009	27961
*133 5/8	22 7/8 23 0/8	15 3/8	5 5	Morrison County	MN	Art Betker	2009	27961
*133 5/8	23 6/8 23 7/8	18 3/8	5 5	Allen County	OH	Jeff Koslakiewicz	2009	27961
*133 5/8	23 5/8 21 0/8	18 1/8	4 4	Knox County	OH	Steve Doyle	2009	27961
*133 5/8	23 1/8 23 6/8	18 1/8	6 6	McHenry County	ND	Jeff Hintze	2009	27961
*133 5/8	24 0/8 23 7/8	16 6/8	5 5	Buffalo County	WI	Chris D. McCuin	2009	27961
*133 5/8	23 4/8 23 0/8	16 3/8	5 5	Winneshiek County	IA	Patrick Falkner	2009	27961
*133 5/8	23 1/8 23 2/8	17 0/8	6 5	Douglas County	WI	Ryan Hoerchner	2009	27961
*133 5/8	23 6/8 23 2/8	17 2/8	5 5	Phillips County	KS	Bill Hahn	2009	27961
133 5/8	21 0/8 21 0/8	14 7/8	5 5	Decatur County	KS	Johnny Watson	2009	27961
*133 5/8	24 1/8 25 1/8	16 6/8	5 5	Berrien County	MI	Chad A. Schau	2009	27961
*133 5/8	22 2/8 21 6/8	18 0/8	6 5	Ford County	KS	Ford Dye	2009	27961
133 4/8	22 4/8 23 4/8	14 0/8	6 5	Vernon County	WI	Steve Munson	1992	28192
133 4/8	22 2/8 21 5/8	17 2/8	4 5	Orange County	NY	James L. Conklin, Jr.	2003	28192
133 4/8	21 6/8 21 4/8	15 4/8	5 4	Morgan County	IL	Brandon Downs	2003	28192
133 4/8	23 1/8 24 2/8	17 6/8	4 4	Madison County	MS	Ken Pugh	2003	28192
133 4/8	20 4/8 21 2/8	18 1/8	7 6	Sherburne County	MN	Ronald S. Wright	2004	28192
*133 4/8	22 3/8 21 6/8	14 4/8	5 5	Minnehaha County	SD	Chuck Powers	2004	28192
133 4/8	18 6/8 19 4/8	13 4/8	5 5	Knox County	NE	Ryan Hochstein	2004	28192
133 4/8	21 5/8 21 5/8	16 0/8	5 5	Boone County	IL	Brad A. Betke	2004	28192
133 4/8	24 1/8 23 4/8	19 4/8	4 4	Lake County	IL	Ted Hysell	2004	28192
133 4/8	20 5/8 21 2/8	16 2/8	5 5	Buffalo County	WI	Gregory A. Brueshaber	2004	28192
133 4/8	22 4/8 21 4/8	14 2/8	5 6	Jackson County	WI	Richard C. Hampe	2004	28192
133 4/8	22 3/8 21 6/8	16 2/8	6 5	Waupaca County	WI	Roger Boushley	2004	28192
133 4/8	21 7/8 21 1/8	15 4/8	5 5	Franklin County	IL	James O. Chase, Jr.	2004	28192
133 4/8	23 3/8 17 3/8	16 6/8	5 5	Greene County	IL	Ron McCarthy	2004	28192
133 4/8	22 1/8 21 2/8	18 6/8	5 5	Dodge County	WI	David R. Spellman	2005	28192
*133 4/8	21 6/8 20 6/8	16 1/8	6 6	Winona County	MN	Gene Gerry	2005	28192
133 4/8	24 4/8 24 2/8	18 4/8	5 5	Kosciusko County	IN	Cass Kruckeberg	2005	28192
133 4/8	20 4/8 18 3/8	16 4/8	4 4	Starke County	IN	Jerry W. Bennett	2005	28192
133 4/8	21 2/8 21 6/8	18 2/8	4 4	Monmouth County	NJ	Lou Cornine	2005	28192
133 4/8	20 7/8 21 0/8	16 4/8	5 5	Kane County	IL	Jim Gellner	2005	28192
133 4/8	21 4/8 20 5/8	14 2/8	5 5	Portage County	WI	William E. Stormoen	2005	28192
*133 4/8	22 7/8 23 4/8	16 6/8	7 6	Dutchess County	NY	Peter Cilione	2005	28192
133 4/8	22 7/8 22 4/8	14 6/8	5 5	Susquehanna County	PA	William Feduchak	2005	28192
133 4/8	22 2/8 21 2/8	15 4/8	5 4	Highland County	OH	Craig Craddock	2005	28192
*133 4/8	21 0/8 21 0/8	18 0/8	5 5	Lycoming County	PA	Tom Stopper	2005	28192
133 4/8	23 6/8 23 6/8	20 5/8	5 4	McLean County	KY	Ronnie Dickens	2005	28192
*133 4/8	22 4/8 21 6/8	16 2/8	4 4	Vernon County	WI	Richard Schroeder	2005	28192
133 4/8	24 3/8 23 3/8	17 6/8	4 5	Jackson County	WV	James W. Casto III	2005	28192
133 4/8	22 0/8 21 0/8	16 6/8	5 5	Dimmit County	TX	Rick Knape	2005	28192
*133 4/8	20 0/8 20 3/8	16 0/8	6 7	Wabasha County	MN	John Wooldridge	2005	28192
*133 4/8	23 5/8 24 0/8	17 6/8	4 4	Duval County	TX	Michael Corley	2005	28192
133 4/8	23 0/8 23 4/8	17 4/8	4 4	Westchester County	NY	Adam Greto	2005	28192
133 4/8	20 1/8 21 3/8	18 6/8	5 5	Anderson County	KY	Timothy Paul Drury	2006	28192
133 4/8	22 0/8 22 4/8	18 2/8	5 5	Waupaca County	WI	Dean Thiel	2006	28192
133 4/8	22 2/8 22 4/8	18 4/8	6 5	Vernon County	WI	James Ekern	2006	28192
*133 4/8	23 4/8 22 6/8	17 5/8	7 5	Bon Homme County	SD	Mark W. Sedlacek	2006	28192
133 4/8	22 4/8 23 4/8	14 1/8	6 5	Warren County	IA	Edward Hyde	2006	28192
133 4/8	20 4/8 19 3/8	15 7/8	5 7	Trempealeau County	WI	Ryan Bautch	2006	28192
*133 4/8	20 5/8 21 1/8	19 0/8	5 5	White County	IL	Michael L. Ritter, Jr.	2006	28192
133 4/8	21 2/8 21 3/8	16 6/8	4 4	Jasper County	IL	Gordon Kreke	2006	28192
133 4/8	23 4/8 24 4/8	19 2/8	5 5	Arkansas County	AR	Evan Benthal	2006	28192
133 4/8	20 6/8 20 4/8	12 7/8	6 6	McCulloch County	TX	Harry W. Kelly	2007	28192
133 4/8	21 7/8 22 5/8	14 6/8	5 5	Atchison County	MO	Chris Barton	2007	28192
133 4/8	21 5/8 22 3/8	17 6/8	5 4	Chenango County	NY	Randy Wilcox, Jr.	2007	28192
133 4/8	22 0/8 22 1/8	16 5/8	6 6	Monona County	IA	Dan Schemmel	2007	28192
133 4/8	22 7/8 23 3/8	18 2/8	7 7	Trempealeau County	WI	Rick Bryson	2007	28192
133 4/8	21 6/8 22 0/8	12 6/8	5 5	Muskegon County	MI	Rob J. Stein	2007	28192
133 4/8	22 7/8 22 1/8	16 0/8	6 5	Pike County	IL	Tim Webb	2007	28192
*133 4/8	23 2/8 23 6/8	17 0/8	5 5	Marshall County	WV	John T. Erazmus III	2007	28192
133 4/8	21 7/8 21 7/8	17 4/8	5 5	St. Croix County	WI	John Stoffel	2007	28192
*133 4/8	22 4/8 22 6/8	18 4/8	4 4	Buffalo County	WI	Josh J. Miller	2007	28192
133 4/8	21 0/8 21 2/8	16 4/8	5 5	Van Buren County	IA	George C. Francis	2007	28192
133 4/8	21 7/8 23 2/8	16 2/8	7 6	Sheridan County	WY	Johnny Watson	2008	28192
133 4/8	18 7/8 19 6/8	16 4/8	7 6	Charlie Lake	BC	Keith Rande	2008	28192
133 4/8	24 0/8 23 7/8	16 6/8	7 8	Fond du Lac County	WI	Bob Sondalle	2008	28192
133 4/8	22 0/8 22 6/8	16 5/8	6 7	Columbia County	WI	Kenneth W. Schrader	2008	28192
*133 4/8	20 3/8 19 4/8	16 6/8	5 5	Moniteau County	MO	Chuck Hammers	2008	28192
133 4/8	22 0/8 21 4/8	16 0/8	5 5	Houston County	AL	Gary "Todd" Anderson	2008	28192
133 4/8	24 4/8 24 3/8	20 3/8	6 5	Columbia County	WI	Alex A. Preuss	2008	28192
133 4/8	19 6/8 20 0/8	16 5/8	6 4	Calhoun County	MI	George Swan, Jr.	2008	28192
133 4/8	21 4/8 21 6/8	16 2/8	5 5	Howard County	IA	Lynn Scheidel	2008	28192
*133 4/8	21 1/8 21 4/8	15 6/8	5 4	Houston County	MN	Chris Carriere	2008	28192
133 4/8	22 4/8 22 6/8	18 2/8	4 7	Wayne County	NY	Brian Neal	2008	28192
133 4/8	23 0/8 22 7/8	16 4/8	4 5	Iowa County	WI	Gerald A. Endres	2008	28192
*133 4/8	26 6/8 26 7/8	17 6/8	4 3	White County	IL	Jason Garman	2008	28192
133 4/8	21 2/8 20 3/8	14 6/8	5 5	Price County	WI	Brian Roush	2008	28192
133 4/8	23 4/8 24 1/8	18 0/8	4 5	Hillsborough County	NH	Brian LeFrancois	2009	28192
133 4/8	20 0/8 19 0/8	15 4/8	5 5	Childress County	TX	David Moore	2009	28192
133 4/8	20 1/8 21 1/8	15 0/8	4 6	Leflore County	MS	Marc Archer	2009	28192
*133 4/8	23 3/8 23 2/8	17 6/8	4 4	Wood County	WV	Elmer H. Parker, Sr.	2009	28192

Deer entries below 141 0/8, that appeared in the 6th Edition, are not included here, but are included on the accompanying CD (see page 119), and also in the Club's Records Archives.

WHITETAIL DEER (TYPICAL ANTLERS)

Minimum Score 125 — Continued

SCORE	LENGTH OF R MAIN BEAM L	INSIDE SPREAD	NUMBER OF R POINTS L	AREA	STATE/ PROVINCE	HUNTER'S NAME	DATE	RANK
133 4/8	24 5/8 24 0/8	15 7/8	5 6	Tuscarawas County	OH	Lance A. Tyler	2009	28192
133 4/8	21 3/8 20 0/8	18 2/8	5 5	Buffalo County	WI	Duane Powell	2009	28192
*133 4/8	21 1/8 22 3/8	18 5/8	7 5	Pike County	IL	Paul Lewis	2009	28192
133 4/8	21 4/8 21 2/8	16 4/8	4 4	Comanche County	KS	Gary Head	2009	28192
*133 4/8	25 2/8 26 2/8	15 7/8	4 6	Perry County	AR	Dale Roper	2009	28192
133 4/8	20 7/8 22 5/8	15 4/8	5 5	Logan County	NE	Mark Warner	2009	28192
*133 4/8	22 0/8 22 7/8	18 4/8	4 5	Clarke County	GA	Kyle E. Coleman	2009	28192
133 4/8	22 2/8 23 2/8	19 6/8	5 5	Erie County	NY	Lee J. Weisbeck	2009	28192
*133 4/8	21 7/8 21 7/8	16 4/8	4 5	La Salle County	IL	Fred Centko	2009	28192
*133 4/8	21 1/8 20 1/8	15 2/8	4 5	Sumner County	KS	David L. Butler	2009	28192
133 4/8	22 4/8 22 4/8	14 4/8	6 6	Hancock County	OH	Robert E. Ebert	2010	28192
133 3/8	20 4/8 20 4/8	14 3/8	5 5	Linn County	MO	Allan Boesch	2002	28426
133 3/8	21 0/8 20 6/8	16 7/8	5 6	Coryell County	TX	Joshua Sears	2003	28426
133 3/8	20 4/8 20 6/8	16 7/8	4 5	Hardin County	IL	James Weldon, Jr.	2003	28426
133 3/8	22 2/8 22 4/8	15 7/8	4 5	Coweta County	GA	Jack Martin	2004	28426
133 3/8	23 6/8 24 0/8	17 7/8	5 5	Dane County	WI	Joshua J. Mersberger	2004	28426
133 3/8	21 2/8 21 1/8	14 5/8	5 5	Fulton County	IL	Roger L. Hensley	2004	28426
133 3/8	20 5/8 20 2/8	16 5/8	5 5	Dodge County	WI	Nic Zoellick	2004	28426
*133 3/8	22 0/8 21 4/8	12 1/8	5 5	Buffalo County	WI	Denver Reese	2004	28426
133 3/8	20 7/8 21 6/8	14 1/8	5 5	Pike County	OH	Justin Hamilton	2004	28426
*133 3/8	24 6/8 24 1/8	17 3/8	4 5	Jersey County	IL	Walter McPherson	2004	28426
133 3/8	21 0/8 20 4/8	15 5/8	5 5	Wood County	WI	Ryan R. Wilhorn	2004	28426
133 3/8	23 2/8 22 6/8	17 2/8	5 4	Hamilton County	IN	James P. Tomasik	2004	28426
133 3/8	22 1/8 21 6/8	15 7/8	4 4	Columbia County	WI	Jeremy Williams	2005	28426
*133 3/8	23 5/8 23 4/8	18 5/8	5 4	Parke County	IN	S. Bradley Link	2005	28426
*133 3/8	21 5/8 21 3/8	17 1/8	4 4	Custer County	OK	Mike Dobson	2005	28426
133 3/8	20 3/8 21 2/8	16 2/8	6 6	York County	PA	Tom G. Mable	2005	28426
133 3/8	23 5/8 22 2/8	16 1/8	5 5	Trempealeau County	WI	John Suchla	2005	28426
*133 3/8	22 3/8 21 7/8	17 1/8	4 5	Cass County	IL	Steven Parker	2005	28426
133 3/8	22 2/8 22 7/8	17 7/8	4 4	Dallas County	IA	Jeff Brennan	2005	28426
133 3/8	22 2/8 21 1/8	15 3/8	5 5	Morrison County	MN	Mark Grams	2005	28426
*133 3/8	21 0/8 22 0/8	16 2/8	6 6	Burleigh County	ND	Kari Ann Buntrock	2006	28426
*133 3/8	21 0/8 21 6/8	16 5/8	4 4	Dunn County	WI	Seth T. Hulback	2006	28426
*133 3/8	20 7/8 21 0/8	14 5/8	5 5	Blanco County	TX	Earl Chauvin	2006	28426
133 3/8	21 5/8 22 3/8	16 1/8	5 5	Indiana County	PA	George Douglas, Jr.	2006	28426
*133 3/8	23 4/8 23 5/8	18 1/8	4 5	Webster County	NE	Keelan Brumbelow	2006	28426
133 3/8	21 4/8 20 7/8	20 4/8	6 6	Jackson County	OH	Steve Sherman	2006	28426
133 3/8	21 3/8 22 6/8	18 0/8	6 7	Licking County	OH	Brandon Salyer	2007	28426
133 3/8	20 2/8 21 2/8	17 4/8	7 5	Brown County	SD	Todd Severson	2007	28426
133 3/8	23 0/8 22 5/8	15 2/8	7 4	Fillmore County	MN	Greg Bergan	2007	28426
*133 3/8	21 4/8 24 1/8	16 1/8	5 5	Stanley County	SD	Kent Lewis	2007	28426
*133 3/8	22 2/8 21 4/8	17 2/8	6 6	Winnebago County	IA	Bradley W. Huntington	2007	28426
133 3/8	19 2/8 21 0/8	14 3/8	5 5	Crawford County	WI	Nick Krueger	2007	28426
133 3/8	24 0/8 23 2/8	18 1/8	4 4	Dane County	WI	Josh Holzapfel	2007	28426
133 3/8	20 4/8 19 0/8	14 7/8	6 5	St. Croix County	WI	Mike Johnson	2007	28426
*133 3/8	24 4/8 24 0/8	18 2/8	5 6	Jo Daviess County	IL	Ryan O'Connell	2007	28426
133 3/8	24 3/8 21 4/8	21 1/8	4 4	Dane County	WI	Steven Grinder	2007	28426
133 3/8	22 0/8 23 5/8	15 1/8	6 6	Brown County	OH	Daniel W. Sheppard	2007	28426
133 3/8	24 3/8 24 7/8	19 7/8	4 5	Dougherty County	GA	Grayson G. Roberts	2007	28426
133 3/8	24 3/8 22 4/8	20 7/8	4 4	Iowa County	WI	Roger Venden	2008	28426
*133 3/8	22 4/8 22 2/8	17 5/8	5 5	Ashe County	NC	David Bowers	2008	28426
133 3/8	23 3/8 23 6/8	20 0/8	5 5	Dunn County	WI	Erik Glaus	2008	28426
133 3/8	21 4/8 20 7/8	19 0/8	5 4	Howard County	IA	Jason Niedert	2008	28426
*133 3/8	23 7/8 20 5/8	17 7/8	5 4	Hopkins County	KY	Justin Creekmur	2008	28426
133 3/8	20 7/8 19 7/8	19 1/8	6 5	Buffalo County	WI	Scott Smith	2008	28426
*133 3/8	23 4/8 23 0/8	19 7/8	5 5	Ontario County	NY	David C. Olsen	2008	28426
133 3/8	20 5/8 21 0/8	15 6/8	5 6	Cooper County	MO	Matt Kollmeyer	2008	28426
133 3/8	20 7/8 22 0/8	18 5/8	5 5	Vernon County	WI	Arnold Hatfield	2008	28426
*133 3/8	20 3/8 19 4/8	15 7/8	5 5	Lancaster County	PA	William E. Mehaffey	2008	28426
*133 3/8	22 4/8 22 1/8	16 5/8	4 5	Putnam County	MO	Dusty Loveland	2008	28426
133 3/8	24 2/8 23 2/8	20 1/8	5 5	Ross County	OH	T. M. Gilmore	2008	28426
133 3/8	24 5/8 24 2/8	15 4/8	5 5	Coffey County	KS	Ricky Orr	2008	28426
*133 3/8	25 7/8 24 7/8	17 4/8	6 7	Fond du Lac County	WI	Jason J. Karst	2009	28426
133 3/8	23 2/8 23 0/8	17 7/8	4 4	Waupaca County	WI	Richard A. Hedtke	2009	28426
*133 3/8	21 5/8 22 2/8	19 5/8	4 4	Buffalo County	WI	Dean Spychalski	2009	28426
133 3/8	23 1/8 23 0/8	17 3/8	4 4	Montgomery County	MO	Brian S. Wagner	2009	28426
*133 3/8	22 2/8 22 7/8	18 5/8	5 5	Marion County	IN	Brett Hankins	2009	28426
133 3/8	22 6/8 22 7/8	17 3/8	4 6	Shawano County	WI	Rickey Ashman	2009	28426
*133 3/8	22 6/8 23 1/8	15 6/8	6 5	Adams County	OH	Scott L. Heatley	2009	28426
133 3/8	21 6/8 22 5/8	18 1/8	4 4	Henry County	IA	Gerald Allen	2009	28426
133 3/8	22 2/8 22 3/8	16 3/8	4 5	Greene County	MO	Norm Nothnagel	2009	28426
*133 3/8	23 5/8 23 1/8	18 3/8	4 4	Pierce County	WI	Brian Nielson	2009	28426
133 3/8	21 6/8 21 5/8	17 7/8	4 5	Nodaway County	MO	Doug A. Gallagher	2009	28426
133 3/8	24 4/8 24 1/8	18 1/8	4 5	Outagamie County	WI	Steve Lamers	2009	28426
*133 3/8	21 6/8 21 4/8	17 5/8	5 4	Henry County	IL	Brett Reeder	2009	28426
*133 3/8	20 7/8 21 6/8	16 5/8	5 5	Clayton County	IA	Zach Etringer	2009	28426
*133 3/8	21 3/8 22 0/8	17 2/8	5 5	Montgomery County	TN	Ben Stanley Haywood	2009	28426
133 3/8	23 2/8 23 2/8	21 4/8	4 6	St. Louis County	MN	Joseph W. Thomson	2009	28426
133 3/8	21 3/8 21 3/8	16 3/8	5 4	Wayne County	NE	Robert W. Hawkins	2010	28426
*133 3/8	20 4/8 19 3/8	14 7/8	5 6	Jackson County	WI	Matthew Sedelbauer	2010	28426
133 2/8	21 7/8 22 2/8	16 1/8	6 7	Douglas County	WI	Michael J. Jarvis	1999	28628
133 2/8	20 7/8 21 4/8	16 4/8	5 5	Kerr County	TX	Tres Childs	2000	28628
133 2/8	22 0/8 22 0/8	14 0/8	4 5	Polk County	WI	Joe Jensen	2002	28628
133 2/8	23 0/8 23 7/8	17 6/8	5 5	Buffalo County	WI	Daniel H. Folkedahl	2003	28628
133 2/8	21 5/8 21 1/8	15 0/8	6 5	Racine County	WI	Daniel Seitz	2003	28628
133 2/8	21 4/8 23 0/8	18 0/8	5 5	Dodge County	NE	Nathan Bates	2004	28628
133 2/8	25 3/8 27 0/8	20 1/8	4 6	Clark County	IN	Don R. Taylor	2004	28628
133 2/8	21 7/8 21 2/8	16 0/8	5 5	Greene County	OH	Jeremy L. Short	2004	28628
133 2/8	22 6/8 22 0/8	15 6/8	4 5	Jefferson County	AR	Richie Bridges	2004	28628
133 2/8	23 6/8 24 0/8	15 4/8	4 4	Kosciusko County	IN	Todd J. McCulloch	2004	28628
133 2/8	19 4/8 19 4/8	18 1/8	5 6	Burnett County	WI	Lee Thomas	2004	28628
133 2/8	23 2/8 21 3/8	16 2/8	5 5	Calumet County	WI	Pete Halbach	2004	28628
*133 2/8	24 0/8 24 0/8	19 1/8	4 5	Eau Claire County	WI	Dan Brown	2004	28628
133 2/8	22 5/8 22 6/8	18 2/8	5 5	Richland County	WI	Brian Wisinski	2004	28628
*133 2/8	20 6/8 20 7/8	16 6/8	5 5	Waukesha County	WI	Jason Popp	2004	28628

572

WHITETAIL DEER (TYPICAL ANTLERS)

Minimum Score 125 — Continued

SCORE	LENGTH OF R MAIN BEAM L	INSIDE SPREAD	NUMBER OF R POINTS L	AREA	STATE/ PROVINCE	HUNTER'S NAME	DATE	RANK
133 2/8	24 5/8 24 1/8	17 7/8	5 6	Platte County	MO	Mike Cherner	2004	28628
133 2/8	20 5/8 21 0/8	15 6/8	5 5	Allegany County	NY	Glenn Smith	2004	28628
133 2/8	23 4/8 22 6/8	16 6/8	5 5	Lewis & Clark County	MT	Steve Kamps	2004	28628
*133 2/8	22 0/8 22 1/8	16 4/8	5 4	Ford County	KS	Ford Dye	2005	28628
133 2/8	20 7/8 22 6/8	14 0/8	5 5	Crawford County	IN	William E. Beals	2005	28628
133 2/8	22 1/8 22 4/8	15 4/8	5 4	Clark County	IL	Rich Foote	2005	28628
*133 2/8	22 0/8 23 1/8	18 6/8	5 5	Olmsted County	MN	David A. Radtke	2005	28628
133 2/8	23 2/8 23 0/8	20 4/8	4 5	Sarpy County	NE	Tom Kelly	2005	28628
133 2/8	20 1/8 20 1/8	12 4/8	5 5	Hardin County	KY	Randy Sherrard	2005	28628
133 2/8	23 4/8 23 1/8	16 0/8	4 4	Berks County	PA	Frank Kast	2005	28628
133 2/8	24 2/8 24 2/8	18 4/8	4 4	Norfolk County	MA	Joe Brown	2005	28628
133 2/8	24 3/8 24 4/8	18 2/8	4 4	St. Louis County	MO	Jay T. Powell	2005	28628
*133 2/8	20 4/8 21 6/8	17 0/8	7 6	Scott County	MN	Andy Lynch	2006	28628
133 2/8	21 7/8 21 3/8	17 0/8	5 5	Jo Daviess County	IL	John G. Baunach	2006	28628
*133 2/8	24 0/8 22 7/8	15 4/8	4 4	Bottineau County	ND	Jeff Gregory	2006	28628
133 2/8	23 2/8 22 7/8	15 6/8	5 5	Chisago County	MN	Ron Ekstrand	2006	28628
133 2/8	21 2/8 21 0/8	17 0/8	5 5	Buffalo County	SD	Rob Knippling	2006	28628
133 2/8	21 6/8 22 0/8	18 0/8	4 4	Adams County	IL	Richard Fleischman	2006	28628
133 2/8	23 6/8 22 7/8	17 5/8	6 5	Orange County	IN	Nick Horton	2006	28628
133 2/8	21 4/8 21 7/8	16 0/8	5 5	Kent County	MI	Vinson C. Videan	2007	28628
133 2/8	23 5/8 23 7/8	17 4/8	5 5	Harrison County	OH	Randall Eaglen	2007	28628
133 2/8	21 0/8 20 2/8	17 6/8	5 5	Berrien County	MI	Clay Ackerman	2007	28628
133 2/8	23 0/8 23 7/8	14 4/8	4 4	La Crosse County	WI	Matt W. Pagliaro	2007	28628
133 2/8	21 0/8 22 1/8	18 0/8	5 5	Concho County	TX	Bill Young	2007	28628
133 2/8	21 0/8 21 6/8	15 2/8	4 4	Adams County	WI	Daniel J. Schwartz	2007	28628
133 2/8	22 3/8 22 4/8	18 2/8	5 5	Venango County	PA	Guy F. Wingard	2007	28628
133 2/8	18 6/8 20 1/8	18 4/8	5 5	Traill County	ND	John Baird	2007	28628
133 2/8	26 0/8 23 3/8	15 2/8	5 4	Allen County	KS	Gary Greve	2007	28628
133 2/8	23 1/8 22 7/8	15 6/8	9 8	Kent County	MI	Matthew McCauley	2007	28628
133 2/8	25 5/8 24 6/8	18 6/8	5 4	Carroll County	IN	Brian J. Curwick	2007	28628
133 2/8	24 5/8 23 6/8	17 4/8	4 4	Marquette County	MI	Matthew Scheuren	2007	28628
*133 2/8	22 5/8 22 0/8	18 6/8	4 4	Traill County	ND	Troy A. Johnson	2008	28628
133 2/8	22 6/8 23 2/8	17 0/8	5 6	Marquette County	WI	Daniel Schmitt	2008	28628
133 2/8	24 2/8 24 1/8	14 3/8	5 5	Licking County	OH	Jacob Denuit	2008	28628
133 2/8	21 7/8 20 5/8	19 2/8	5 5	Fulton County	IL	Russel Rudy	2008	28628
*133 2/8	23 6/8 22 6/8	18 4/8	7 7	Fulton County	IL	Larry M. Young, Jr.	2008	28628
133 2/8	24 1/8 25 0/8	18 3/8	6 3	La Crosse County	WI	Gary Priem	2008	28628
*133 2/8	21 3/8 22 0/8	16 0/8	5 5	Bolivar County	MS	Lance Johnson	2008	28628
133 2/8	22 2/8 21 7/8	16 5/8	8 6	Sauk County	WI	Keith Peetz	2008	28628
133 2/8	23 2/8 23 1/8	17 4/8	4 4	Cross County	AR	Kurt Brawner	2008	28628
*133 2/8	23 0/8 22 3/8	18 4/8	4 4	Camden County	MO	Leo Marler	2009	28628
133 2/8	23 3/8 23 6/8	14 0/8	4 5	Dunn County	WI	John Forster	2009	28628
133 2/8	23 3/8 21 7/8	18 0/8	4 4	Whitley County	IN	Scott D. Miller	2009	28628
*133 2/8	23 2/8 22 0/8	17 6/8	5 5	Monroe County	WI	Eric Senkowski	2009	28628
*133 2/8	20 3/8 21 5/8	17 3/8	5 6	Vernon County	WI	Thomas E. Erie	2009	28628
*133 2/8	26 1/8 27 7/8	17 6/8	3 4	Vernon County	WI	Steve Munson	2009	28628
*133 2/8	23 0/8 23 3/8	18 6/8	5 5	Meigs County	OH	Wallace Mullis	2009	28628
133 2/8	21 4/8 21 0/8	16 1/8	4 5	Craig County	OK	John Dunlap	2009	28628
*133 2/8	22 1/8 22 4/8	18 4/8	4 4	Crittenden County	KY	Lee Colquitt	2010	28628
*133 2/8	20 4/8 21 3/8	14 2/8	5 5	Estevan	SAS	Garry Leslie	2010	28628
133 2/8	20 7/8 21 6/8	15 4/8	5 5	Granville County	NC	Chad Browning	2010	28628
*133 2/8	20 2/8 19 1/8	15 7/8	8 6	Fillmore County	MN	Mike Kelly	2010	28628
133 1/8	22 2/8 21 5/8	16 3/8	5 5	Lee County	IA	Glenn E. Wagner	1992	28882
133 1/8	23 1/8 23 0/8	19 3/8	5 5	Yankton County	SD	Jeff Simonsen	1996	28882
133 1/8	21 4/8 21 2/8	18 1/8	4 5	Lafayette County	WI	Brian Zimmerman	1997	28882
133 1/8	21 5/8 20 6/8	15 2/8	6 6	Steuben County	IN	Lynn A. Barrows	1998	28882
133 1/8	23 0/8 23 2/8	18 0/8	4 6	Will County	IL	James E. Giese	1999	28882
133 1/8	23 5/8 23 7/8	17 5/8	5 4	Cook County	GA	Mark W. Futch	2003	28882
133 1/8	23 2/8 23 1/8	15 6/8	4 6	York County	VA	Rodger L. Willett, Jr.	2004	28882
133 1/8	23 1/8 22 6/8	15 0/8	4 8	Hancock County	IL	Jay Smith	2004	28882
*133 1/8	21 6/8 21 3/8	17 3/8	5 5	Menifee County	KY	Joshua M. Brown	2004	28882
133 1/8	25 0/8 24 4/8	17 7/8	5 4	Knox County	MO	Keith Pulse	2004	28882
133 1/8	24 7/8 24 4/8	17 7/8	4 5	Delaware County	IN	Jeff S. Bell	2004	28882
133 1/8	21 3/8 23 5/8	18 5/8	5 5	Queen Annes County	MD	Thomas W. Fisher	2004	28882
133 1/8	21 2/8 21 6/8	14 3/8	5 5	Pike County	IL	Gary L. McGhee	2004	28882
*133 1/8	23 1/8 24 6/8	20 6/8	4 5	Cortland County	NY	Barry Baldwin	2004	28882
133 1/8	24 6/8 24 6/8	17 5/8	4 4	Morgan County	IN	Timothy L. Gentry	2004	28882
133 1/8	20 0/8 22 0/8	16 1/8	6 6	Meigs County	OH	Eric Harris	2004	28882
133 1/8	21 6/8 21 4/8	19 7/8	6 6	Berks County	PA	Jason R. Wentzel	2004	28882
133 1/8	23 0/8 22 6/8	17 1/8	4 4	Washington County	PA	Raymond Mosco	2004	28882
133 1/8	24 7/8 23 6/8	17 5/8	5 6	Adams County	IL	Kerry Anderson	2004	28882
133 1/8	23 1/8 25 7/8	19 4/8	5 4	Newport County	RI	Mark Robertson	2004	28882
133 1/8	23 5/8 23 1/8	23 0/8	6 4	Elk County	KS	Jim Frey	2004	28882
133 1/8	20 7/8 20 2/8	15 1/8	5 5	Waupaca County	WI	Aren R. Nugent	2005	28882
133 1/8	21 2/8 21 7/8	16 1/8	5 5	Pennington County	SD	Raymond Hughes	2005	28882
133 1/8	25 0/8 24 5/8	19 2/8	7 7	De Witt County	IL	Ben Estes	2005	28882
*133 1/8	24 6/8 23 5/8	18 3/8	5 4	Chester County	PA	Rico DiFilippo	2005	28882
133 1/8	22 1/8 22 0/8	18 3/8	6 5	Clark County	SD	Mark Turner	2005	28882
133 1/8	22 0/8 22 0/8	18 5/8	4 4	Coleman County	TX	William D. Burns	2005	28882
*133 1/8	22 3/8 22 2/8	17 2/8	5 5	Clay County	AR	Jade Price	2005	28882
133 1/8	23 5/8 22 4/8	15 1/8	6 5	Jennings County	IN	Calvin Dean Elmore	2006	28882
133 1/8	23 4/8 23 0/8	16 3/8	5 5	Woodford County	KY	Chris Stone	2006	28882
133 1/8	21 6/8 22 4/8	12 5/8	4 5	Jackson County	MO	Jim Hinson	2006	28882
133 1/8	22 6/8 25 0/8	16 5/8	4 5	Franklin County	PA	Eric J. Lehman	2006	28882
133 1/8	22 3/8 20 3/8	17 7/8	5 7	Polk County	WI	Tom Weaver	2006	28882
*133 1/8	21 3/8 21 2/8	17 3/8	5 5	Mitchell County	IA	Royce R. Schultz	2006	28882
*133 1/8	21 5/8 22 3/8	17 5/8	5 5	Posey County	IN	Alan Erwin	2006	28882
133 1/8	23 7/8 25 2/8	19 1/8	4 4	Waushara County	WI	David L. Seidl	2006	28882
133 1/8	23 5/8 24 5/8	18 3/8	6 5	Pierce County	WI	Ryan Magee	2006	28882
133 1/8	21 7/8 21 4/8	16 5/8	5 4	Waukesha County	WI	Bob Rajnicek	2006	28882
*133 1/8	22 7/8 24 0/8	19 3/8	4 5	Marinette County	WI	Robert Seefeldt	2006	28882
133 1/8	22 4/8 21 7/8	18 7/8	4 4	Hendricks County	IN	Brian Lamb	2006	28882
133 1/8	22 7/8 22 0/8	14 4/8	6 7	Pembina County	ND	Rick Pfau	2006	28882
133 1/8	22 0/8 22 0/8	19 3/8	4 4	Duval County	TX	Dayner Roberts	2007	28882
*133 1/8	22 5/8 21 7/8	17 0/8	5 6	Shackelford County	TX	Jim Rummage	2007	28882

Deer entries below 141 0/8, that appeared in the 6th Edition, are not included here, but are included on the accompanying CD (see page 119), and also in the Club's Records Archives.

WHITETAIL DEER (TYPICAL ANTLERS)

Minimum Score 125 Continued

SCORE	LENGTH OF R MAIN BEAM L	INSIDE SPREAD	NUMBER OF R POINTS L		AREA	STATE/ PROVINCE	HUNTER'S NAME	DATE	RANK
133 1/8	24 2/8 24 2/8	17 7/8	4	4	Champaign County	IL	John Wyman Hovey	2007	28882
133 1/8	20 6/8 20 0/8	15 4/8	6	5	Perry County	PA	Anthony E. Kyler	2007	28882
*133 1/8	21 0/8 21 3/8	17 3/8	5	5	Monroe County	WI	Paul M. Mueller	2007	28882
133 1/8	22 5/8 22 7/8	16 7/8	5	5	Sioux Narrows	ONT	Chris Jensen	2007	28882
133 1/8	21 2/8 21 5/8	16 7/8	4	4	Talbot County	MD	David Lighty	2007	28882
*133 1/8	18 2/8 19 3/8	19 7/8	5	5	Somerset County	PA	Art Berkebile	2007	28882
133 1/8	20 4/8 20 3/8	16 1/8	5	5	La Salle County	IL	Shawn T. Kelley	2007	28882
*133 1/8	24 5/8 25 4/8	21 0/8	5	4	Steuben County	IN	Darwin "Bear" Griva	2007	28882
133 1/8	20 2/8 20 4/8	18 7/8	4	4	Berrien County	MI	Michael Holy	2007	28882
133 1/8	21 2/8 20 4/8	15 3/8	5	5	Lapeer County	MI	Travis Swoish	2007	28882
*133 1/8	22 2/8 21 7/8	20 3/8	4	5	Tensas Parish	LA	Kris Fulmer	2007	28882
*133 1/8	22 5/8 22 5/8	20 7/8	5	5	Madison County	MS	D. R. Bozeman	2007	28882
133 1/8	18 2/8 20 1/8	16 4/8	6	5	Park County	MT	George Kamps	2008	28882
*133 1/8	21 7/8 21 6/8	16 6/8	8	6	Juneau County	WI	Sam Coppernoll	2008	28882
133 1/8	23 3/8 23 5/8	17 1/8	4	4	Hancock County	OH	Bruce S. O'Rear	2008	28882
133 1/8	20 7/8 21 1/8	17 1/8	5	5	Waupaca County	WI	Susan J. Sawitski	2008	28882
133 1/8	27 3/8 27 2/8	18 3/8	7	5	Winnebago County	IL	Jeffery J. Reuter	2008	28882
*133 1/8	22 3/8 23 3/8	17 7/8	5	6	Trempealeau County	WI	Allan Stuhr	2008	28882
133 1/8	22 2/8 20 0/8	16 0/8	5	6	Grant County	WI	Tony Reynolds	2008	28882
133 1/8	26 0/8 27 2/8	18 4/8	6	6	Buffalo County	NE	Brian Pollema	2008	28882
133 1/8	21 3/8 21 7/8	16 1/8	5	5	McHenry County	IL	John B. McNamara	2008	28882
*133 1/8	20 7/8 21 2/8	16 3/8	5	5	Black Hawk County	IA	Steve Finegan	2008	28882
133 1/8	20 1/8 20 4/8	14 3/8	5	5	Fond du Lac County	WI	Jerome D. Isaac	2008	28882
133 1/8	21 4/8 21 4/8	14 5/8	5	4	Sweet Grass County	MT	Colton J. Gavne	2009	28882
133 1/8	21 0/8 22 0/8	16 7/8	4	4	Marathon County	WI	Dean Haen	2009	28882
133 1/8	22 1/8 22 6/8	17 7/8	4	4	Niagara County	NY	Christopher Pusateri	2009	28882
133 1/8	27 0/8 27 0/8	20 0/8	4	5	Vernon County	WI	Reid Ekern	2009	28882
*133 1/8	24 0/8 23 3/8	17 5/8	5	5	Parke County	IN	Tim Wadkins	2009	28882
133 1/8	23 3/8 23 5/8	16 7/8	4	4	Marathon County	WI	Russell Wendorf	2009	28882
133 1/8	19 6/8 19 1/8	15 1/8	5	6	Sully County	SD	Randi Erickson	2009	28882
*133 1/8	21 4/8 21 7/8	17 1/8	4	4	Wyoming County	NY	Keith Dixon	2009	28882
133 1/8	23 4/8 25 0/8	19 5/8	5	5	Will County	IL	Jake Saunoris	2010	28882
133 0/8	23 5/8 22 4/8	17 4/8	4	5	Logan County	KY	Randy Cash	1996	29113
133 0/8	23 1/8 22 5/8	19 0/8	4	5	Norman County	MN	Bruce Doerfler	2001	29113
133 0/8	25 2/8 25 3/8	17 2/8	4	4	Surry County	VA	Dwight S. Wolf	2002	29113
133 0/8	22 5/8 22 2/8	14 6/8	5	5	Buffalo County	WI	Robert J. Decker	2002	29113
133 0/8	23 7/8 23 4/8	16 3/8	5	6	Pottawattamie County	IA	Gary Jungferman	2002	29113
133 0/8	22 0/8 22 0/8	18 0/8	4	7	Lincoln County	MO	John Ilgenfritz	2002	29113
133 0/8	22 7/8 22 6/8	16 2/8	5	4	Rogers County	OK	Ty Stapleton	2002	29113
133 0/8	22 6/8 22 3/8	16 0/8	5	5	Clermont County	OH	Rod Bullock	2003	29113
133 0/8	20 5/8 20 5/8	15 4/8	5	5	Clark County	WI	Steven R. Finder	2003	29113
133 0/8	21 5/8 21 6/8	18 0/8	4	5	Trempealeau County	WI	Jon Brady	2004	29113
133 0/8	20 6/8 21 3/8	17 4/8	5	5	Iowa County	WI	Clint Rickey	2004	29113
133 0/8	22 4/8 22 7/8	18 6/8	5	5	Marquette County	WI	Mark Guderski	2004	29113
133 0/8	22 4/8 23 2/8	16 2/8	4	5	Fulton County	IL	Thomas Hartman	2004	29113
133 0/8	24 2/8 23 3/8	18 0/8	5	5	St. Louis County	MN	Matt Russell	2004	29113
133 0/8	21 7/8 21 4/8	16 2/8	4	5	Winona County	MN	John W. Zahrte	2004	29113
133 0/8	20 5/8 22 0/8	17 4/8	5	5	Fulton County	IL	Gary L. Morse	2004	29113
133 0/8	21 0/8 21 0/8	15 4/8	6	5	Clay County	MN	Walt Palmer	2004	29113
133 0/8	22 0/8 21 4/8	15 6/8	5	5	Orange County	IN	Brandon Parks	2004	29113
133 0/8	20 6/8 21 0/8	16 0/8	5	5	Eau Claire County	WI	Michael K. Benrud	2004	29113
*133 0/8	21 5/8 21 7/8	15 6/8	7	6	Palo Alto County	IA	Les Traub	2004	29113
133 0/8	20 5/8 20 2/8	17 0/8	5	5	Missoula County	MT	Eric Kress	2004	29113
*133 0/8	24 0/8 22 4/8	16 3/8	5	4	Kiowa County	KS	Shane Patterson	2004	29113
133 0/8	22 6/8 22 6/8	18 6/8	5	4	Henry County	VA	Mike Weaver	2004	29113
133 0/8	20 6/8 20 7/8	16 6/8	5	6	Jackson County	WI	Keith Skadahl	2005	29113
133 0/8	22 0/8 23 0/8	15 2/8	5	5	Zavala County	TX	Joe Braun	2005	29113
133 0/8	24 6/8 23 6/8	16 4/8	4	4	Goodhue County	MN	John "Jack" Cordes	2005	29113
133 0/8	19 6/8 19 2/8	17 0/8	5	5	Sauk County	WI	Joshua E. Wendorf	2005	29113
*133 0/8	22 0/8 21 7/8	20 0/8	4	5	Holmes County	MS	Lonnie Jones	2005	29113
*133 0/8	21 5/8 23 2/8	17 6/8	5	5	Lincoln County	WV	Matt Thompson	2005	29113
*133 0/8	21 5/8 21 5/8	17 4/8	5	4	Allegany County	NY	William G. Costello II	2005	29113
133 0/8	22 6/8 23 5/8	17 5/8	5	6	Pope County	IL	Mike Remsburger	2005	29113
133 0/8	20 3/8 20 6/8	15 6/8	5	5	Pike County	IL	Scott Craft	2005	29113
*133 0/8	22 0/8 21 6/8	15 4/8	6	5	Anoka County	MN	Brian Parent	2005	29113
133 0/8	20 0/8 20 5/8	14 4/8	5	5	Crawford County	IL	Russell T. Wachtel	2005	29113
133 0/8	20 0/8 20 2/8	17 0/8	5	5	Lewis & Clark County	MT	Steven B. Kamps	2005	29113
133 0/8	26 1/8 24 1/8	21 6/8	4	4	Darke County	OH	Gene Maher III	2005	29113
133 0/8	24 2/8 23 7/8	16 2/8	4	4	Essex County	NJ	Carmen Cucuzza	2005	29113
133 0/8	20 2/8 20 3/8	17 4/8	5	5	Shelby County	TN	Todd Gray	2005	29113
133 0/8	25 4/8 25 4/8	19 0/8	4	4	Webb County	TX	Bob Gilbert	2005	29113
*133 0/8	21 4/8 21 5/8	16 0/8	4	4	Sauk County	WI	Matthew C. Stanley	2006	29113
133 0/8	22 6/8 23 3/8	18 5/8	6	8	Camden County	MO	Shawn Mankey	2006	29113
133 0/8	20 3/8 21 7/8	18 4/8	5	5	Dane County	WI	Matthew A. Brown	2006	29113
133 0/8	22 0/8 22 4/8	16 0/8	4	4	Alexander County	IL	Christopher A. Jenkins	2006	29113
133 0/8	22 6/8 21 7/8	17 0/8	4	4	Polk County	WI	Steven Peterson	2006	29113
133 0/8	23 2/8 22 3/8	17 2/8	5	4	Allamakee County	IA	Arlyn Meinders	2006	29113
133 0/8	20 3/8 20 3/8	16 6/8	5	5	Wells County	IN	Jim Harden	2006	29113
133 0/8	22 6/8 23 6/8	20 2/8	4	5	Butler County	OH	Randy Young	2006	29113
133 0/8	22 4/8 22 5/8	16 0/8	4	4	Woodbury County	IA	David A. Hesse	2006	29113
*133 0/8	21 1/8 21 4/8	15 0/8	5	5	Randolph County	AL	Matthew Jennings	2006	29113
*133 0/8	23 4/8 23 3/8	19 2/8	4	5	Dunn County	ND	Timothy Zachmeier	2007	29113
133 0/8	24 2/8 23 2/8	16 4/8	5	6	Cambria County	PA	Joseph S. Milchak	2007	29113
133 0/8	22 0/8 21 6/8	16 0/8	5	5	Trempealeau County	WI	Richard Sterry	2007	29113
*133 0/8	22 4/8 23 0/8	16 6/8	5	5	Houston County	MN	Douglas Sanders	2007	29113
*133 0/8	22 1/8 22 6/8	22 0/8	4	4	Monroe County	WI	Larry E. Rezin	2007	29113
133 0/8	25 1/8 24 4/8	19 5/8	6	4	Boone County	KY	Travis A. Dunhoft	2007	29113
*133 0/8	21 2/8 22 1/8	16 4/8	5	5	Kemper County	MS	Dwayne E. Ensign	2007	29113
133 0/8	22 6/8 21 6/8	16 2/8	6	6	Allen County	IN	Mike Densel	2007	29113
133 0/8	21 6/8 22 5/8	15 6/8	4	5	Ripley County	IN	Jeff Cumberworth	2007	29113
133 0/8	21 6/8 22 2/8	15 6/8	5	6	Montgomery County	PA	Ken Barnett	2007	29113
133 0/8	19 7/8 20 5/8	12 2/8	5	5	Dickson County	TN	Gary P. Jenkins	2007	29113
133 0/8	23 3/8 21 5/8	16 0/8	5	5	Douglas County	NE	Craig Overman	2007	29113
*133 0/8	22 4/8 24 5/8	20 0/8	5	4	Randolph County	NC	Scott Key	2008	29113
*133 0/8	21 4/8 22 3/8	17 7/8	5	7	Coshocton County	OH	Jesse Fischer	2008	29113

WHITETAIL DEER (TYPICAL ANTLERS)

Minimum Score 125 — Continued

SCORE	LENGTH OF R MAIN BEAM L	INSIDE SPREAD	NUMBER OF R POINTS L	AREA	STATE/ PROVINCE	HUNTER'S NAME	DATE	RANK
*133 0/8	20 2/8 20 6/8	14 0/8	5 5	Victoria County	TX	Brian Rohde	2008	29113
*133 0/8	23 0/8 22 6/8	17 0/8	4 4	Waukesha County	WI	Robert Rajnicek	2008	29113
*133 0/8	20 6/8 20 2/8	14 6/8	5 5	Fulton County	IL	Anthony Galletti	2008	29113
*133 0/8	21 4/8 22 7/8	18 0/8	5 4	Columbia County	WI	Bruce F. Udell	2008	29113
133 0/8	21 6/8 25 3/8	15 0/8	6 6	Carver County	MN	Jason Martinetto	2008	29113
*133 0/8	23 4/8 23 7/8	16 6/8	5 5	Benton County	AR	Anthony Hughes	2008	29113
133 0/8	24 1/8 24 3/8	17 4/8	5 4	Kent County	MI	Ryan W. Leonard	2008	29113
133 0/8	24 0/8 24 0/8	21 4/8	4 4	Washington County	MS	Odis Hill, Jr.	2009	29113
133 0/8	24 2/8 23 4/8	17 0/8	7 7	Carroll County	MS	John Kenneth Brower	2009	29113
133 0/8	21 5/8 22 5/8	17 0/8	6 5	Coles County	IL	Terry Waggoner	2009	29113
*133 0/8	23 3/8 23 1/8	17 4/8	5 4	Houston County	MN	Wayne J. Hood, Jr.	2009	29113
133 0/8	19 6/8 21 0/8	15 2/8	6 5	Delaware County	OH	J. T. Kreager	2009	29113
133 0/8	24 3/8 24 6/8	15 4/8	4 4	Butler County	KS	Paul Wilkens	2009	29113
133 0/8	22 4/8 23 2/8	18 0/8	4 4	Putnam County	IN	John E. Jacobs	2009	29113
133 0/8	18 6/8 19 6/8	18 0/8	6 8	Pike County	IL	Scott Brewer	2009	29113
*133 0/8	22 6/8 22 7/8	16 0/8	5 6	Tulsa County	OK	Daniel Hendricks	2009	29113
*133 0/8	22 5/8 22 6/8	19 4/8	5 5	Burnett County	WI	Kevin Fossum	2009	29113
133 0/8	19 7/8 20 2/8	17 2/8	5 5	Westmoreland County	PA	Daniel K. Kuehn	2010	29113
133 0/8	20 2/8 21 1/8	16 3/8	7 7	Parke County	IN	Kyle M. Stark	2010	29113
132 7/8	20 2/8 20 4/8	15 4/8	6 5	Callaway County	MO	Marc Owen	1998	29369
132 7/8	21 6/8 22 2/8	15 4/8	5 7	Washington County	KS	Lynn Moeller	2000	29369
132 7/8	22 7/8 23 1/8	16 5/8	4 6	Greene County	PA	David M. O'Hara	2003	29369
132 7/8	21 1/8 19 2/8	15 7/8	5 5	Camden County	MO	Alan Blair	2004	29369
*132 7/8	20 4/8 19 1/8	14 2/8	6 8	Marshall County	SD	Michael William Werner	2004	29369
132 7/8	22 7/8 23 0/8	17 3/8	4 4	Lincoln County	WI	Rich Ashbrenner	2004	29369
132 7/8	23 1/8 22 6/8	19 3/8	4 4	St. Croix County	WI	Dick Prescott	2004	29369
132 7/8	20 7/8 20 7/8	15 3/8	5 5	Spink County	SD	Paul R. Tremblay	2004	29369
132 7/8	21 0/8 21 4/8	18 3/8	4 5	Ramsey County	ND	Mark Armentrout	2004	29369
132 7/8	21 3/8 21 5/8	16 7/8	4 5	Fond du Lac County	WI	Bob Sabel	2005	29369
132 7/8	22 2/8 21 1/8	15 3/8	7 6	Portage County	WI	Chris J. Lockery	2005	29369
*132 7/8	21 3/8 22 0/8	14 7/8	5 5	Tazewell County	IL	Chad Mason	2005	29369
132 7/8	21 3/8 21 3/8	18 7/8	5 5	Richland County	WI	Paul R. Turgasen	2005	29369
132 7/8	20 1/8 20 2/8	14 2/8	7 5	San Saba County	TX	Adam Huggins	2005	29369
132 7/8	22 0/8 22 0/8	17 0/8	6 6	Crockett County	TX	Byron Krueger	2005	29369
132 7/8	24 0/8 21 1/8	17 5/8	5 7	Winnebago County	WI	Al Hansen	2005	29369
132 7/8	24 1/8 23 6/8	18 3/8	5 4	Morrison County	MN	Andrew Breth	2005	29369
132 7/8	21 4/8 19 7/8	16 2/8	6 5	Allegheny County	PA	Pat Capatolla	2005	29369
132 7/8	20 6/8 21 2/8	15 3/8	5 5	Queen Annes County	MD	John Patrick	2005	29369
132 7/8	26 6/8 25 3/8	18 6/8	4 4	Montgomery County	OH	Robert C. Warnick, Jr.	2005	29369
132 7/8	20 7/8 21 6/8	17 5/8	4 6	Dubuque County	IA	Paul Hill	2005	29369
132 7/8	24 0/8 23 2/8	18 5/8	5 6	Gallatin County	IL	Marcel Veenstra	2005	29369
*132 7/8	20 3/8 19 2/8	18 3/8	6 6	Madison County	AL	Paul Robinette	2006	29369
132 7/8	20 3/8 20 1/8	14 0/8	5 6	Ozaukee County	WI	Mitchell Hencke	2006	29369
132 7/8	23 1/8 23 2/8	14 3/8	5 5	Pike County	IL	Timothy Schroeder	2006	29369
132 7/8	22 6/8 22 5/8	15 2/8	7 9	Cayuga County	NY	Dustin O'Hara	2006	29369
132 7/8	21 3/8 20 5/8	16 3/8	7 5	Jersey County	IL	Brad Brundies	2006	29369
132 7/8	21 3/8 20 7/8	15 7/8	5 5	Trempealeau County	WI	David A. Lyngen	2006	29369
*132 7/8	24 6/8 25 1/8	15 3/8	4 4	Mecklenburg County	VA	Terry J. Copeland	2006	29369
132 7/8	21 6/8 23 2/8	18 3/8	4 5	Van Buren County	IA	Kent Uhrich	2006	29369
132 7/8	22 5/8 23 1/8	19 1/8	4 5	Montgomery County	MD	Lon D. Santis	2006	29369
*132 7/8	22 3/8 22 5/8	20 3/8	5 4	Cass County	MI	Wendell Pompey	2006	29369
132 7/8	21 6/8 20 6/8	16 7/8	6 5	Bristol County	MA	William Medeiros, Jr.	2006	29369
*132 7/8	21 1/8 20 4/8	15 7/8	5 5	Brown County	WI	Patrick Berg	2006	29369
132 7/8	23 4/8 23 1/8	17 1/8	5 5	Washburn County	WI	Jack Harrington	2006	29369
*132 7/8	21 6/8 22 1/8	16 5/8	4 5	Outagamie County	WI	Rick Steffens	2006	29369
132 7/8	23 1/8 20 3/8	18 3/8	5 6	Logan County	CO	Mark Vogt	2006	29369
132 7/8	27 2/8 26 7/8	18 5/8	8 5	Maries County	MO	Tomas Newman	2006	29369
132 7/8	22 7/8 23 0/8	17 1/8	5 5	Cooke County	TX	Don Frazier	2007	29369
132 7/8	26 2/8 23 7/8	19 6/8	5 5	Iowa County	WI	Steven Massey	2007	29369
*132 7/8	25 5/8 25 1/8	20 0/8	4 4	Erie County	NY	Brian Zawacki	2007	29369
*132 7/8	19 7/8 18 7/8	16 5/8	6 6	Buffalo County	WI	Rod Smith	2007	29369
132 7/8	20 2/8 20 5/8	16 1/8	5 5	Yell County	AR	John Hogue	2007	29369
132 7/8	22 2/8 20 7/8	18 2/8	5 6	Dundy County	NE	Ronald King	2007	29369
132 7/8	23 5/8 22 6/8	17 1/8	5 5	Barron County	WI	Travis Ebner	2007	29369
132 7/8	24 7/8 23 0/8	15 1/8	4 7	Washington County	PA	Herbert M. Pratt	2007	29369
132 7/8	21 0/8 21 4/8	18 1/8	4 4	Muskingum County	OH	Michael Cline	2007	29369
*132 7/8	22 1/8 22 2/8	14 4/8	6 4	Monroe County	GA	Joe Bufford	2007	29369
*132 7/8	20 2/8 21 1/8	17 3/8	5 5	Delaware County	PA	Drew J. Baum	2008	29369
132 7/8	23 2/8 23 3/8	16 4/8	5 4	Morris County	NJ	Mark Spoto	2008	29369
*132 7/8	20 6/8 21 0/8	17 7/8	5 5	Kosciusko County	IN	Donald H. Gest	2008	29369
132 7/8	22 2/8 22 6/8	19 5/8	4 5	Gasconade County	MO	Kurt Kottwitz	2008	29369
132 7/8	19 1/8 22 0/8	15 3/8	5 5	Noble County	IN	Duane Douglas Ewell	2008	29369
*132 7/8	20 7/8 22 1/8	15 3/8	4 4	Buffalo County	WI	Gunnar Hagen	2008	29369
132 7/8	22 6/8 22 0/8	15 3/8	4 4	Washington County	WI	Kevin Ramthun	2008	29369
132 7/8	22 7/8 22 3/8	15 5/8	4 5	Jay County	IN	Rob Kaiser	2008	29369
132 7/8	23 0/8 23 0/8	19 1/8	6 5	Payne County	OK	Riley A. Reigh	2008	29369
132 7/8	20 3/8 20 6/8	17 3/8	5 5	Johnson County	NE	Doug Eltiste	2008	29369
132 7/8	25 2/8 24 4/8	15 6/8	6 5	Wicomico County	MD	Thomas Calloway	2008	29369
*132 7/8	19 2/8 19 0/8	15 3/8	6 6	Stanley County	SD	Kris Herren	2008	29369
132 7/8	18 1/8 19 0/8	12 2/8	6 7	Converse County	WY	Adam Fackelman	2009	29369
132 7/8	22 3/8 22 1/8	16 3/8	4 4	Morgan County	GA	Andrew C. Curtis	2009	29369
*132 7/8	22 3/8 21 1/8	16 5/8	5 5	Marshall County	IN	David V. Haag	2009	29369
132 7/8	23 0/8 23 6/8	14 2/8	4 6	Mercer County	MO	James Rantz	2009	29369
*132 7/8	24 0/8 24 2/8	18 6/8	4 5	Carroll County	MS	Casey Stanford	2009	29369
132 7/8	25 3/8 24 2/8	15 5/8	3 5	Decatur County	IA	Jack Theiler	2009	29369
*132 7/8	19 4/8 20 1/8	16 1/8	4 4	Ramsey County	ND	Dwight Logie	2009	29369
*132 7/8	23 3/8 22 6/8	14 7/8	5 5	Madison County	MS	Howard Parish	2010	29369
*132 7/8	21 6/8 21 4/8	15 1/8	4 4	Willowbrook	SAS	Brian Aamodt	2010	29369
132 6/8	24 4/8 24 2/8	20 4/8	4 4	Washington County	PA	James A. Gibson	1999	29587
132 6/8	22 0/8 22 5/8	18 2/8	4 5	Dodge County	MN	Jesse Stevenson	2003	29587
132 6/8	25 1/8 24 0/8	16 4/8	4 5	Jennings County	IN	Mike Mowery	2003	29587
132 6/8	21 0/8 21 1/8	13 5/8	6 6	Saunders County	NE	Rich Eckstein	2003	29587
132 6/8	19 0/8 19 3/8	15 4/8	5 5	Lincoln County	MO	Bob Brodt	2003	29587
132 6/8	23 1/8 21 0/8	15 4/8	4 4	Knox County	IL	Luke Creswell	2003	29587
132 6/8	21 6/8 21 6/8	15 6/8	4 4	Wilcox County	AL	Timothy D. Bassett	2004	29587

Deer entries below 141 0/8, that appeared in the 6th Edition, are not included here, but are included on the accompanying CD (see page 119), and also in the Club's Records Archives.

575

WHITETAIL DEER (TYPICAL ANTLERS)

Minimum Score 125 — Continued

SCORE	R MAIN BEAM L	INSIDE SPREAD	R POINTS L		AREA	STATE/PROVINCE	HUNTER'S NAME	DATE	RANK
*132 6/8	24 4/8 25 2/8	19 4/8	4	4	Beltrami County	MN	Ben Jordan	2004	29587
132 6/8	21 7/8 21 2/8	18 6/8	5	5	Young County	TX	Bryan Edward Sanders	2004	29587
132 6/8	25 3/8 26 0/8	19 2/8	4	4	Jackson County	IA	Chip Pregler	2004	29587
*132 6/8	21 4/8 23 0/8	17 6/8	4	5	Dubuque County	IA	Todd Templen	2004	29587
132 6/8	21 5/8 21 2/8	17 2/8	4	4	Lucan	ONT	Don Cunningham	2004	29587
132 6/8	22 7/8 21 6/8	15 4/8	5	5	Converse County	WY	Peter R. Schoonmaker	2004	29587
132 6/8	20 2/8 20 4/8	16 0/8	5	5	Berks County	PA	Bruce R. Kent	2004	29587
132 6/8	23 2/8 23 2/8	17 1/8	5	4	Hancock County	IL	Greg Bonecutter, Sr.	2004	29587
*132 6/8	23 5/8 25 2/8	16 1/8	5	5	Buffalo County	WI	Gregory J. Pettis	2004	29587
*132 6/8	20 6/8 20 7/8	18 4/8	5	5	Comanche County	KS	Chris Howard	2004	29587
132 6/8	19 5/8 19 3/8	15 4/8	6	5	Waupaca County	WI	Kirt A. Kettenhoven	2004	29587
132 6/8	22 0/8 22 6/8	20 2/8	4	4	Webster County	IA	Edward E. Ulicki	2004	29587
132 6/8	22 7/8 22 2/8	15 2/8	5	5	Noble County	OH	Jim Schoolcraft	2004	29587
132 6/8	21 3/8 21 4/8	18 2/8	4	4	Coahoma County	MS	Jarrett Morgan	2004	29587
132 6/8	21 1/8 20 0/8	18 0/8	5	4	Oakland County	MI	William R. Groves	2004	29587
132 6/8	22 4/8 22 0/8	17 2/8	5	5	Trempealeau County	WI	Ralph Lyon	2004	29587
*132 6/8	22 4/8 23 2/8	14 1/8	5	6	Kalamazoo County	MI	Tony G. Hegedus	2004	29587
132 6/8	22 3/8 22 5/8	18 2/8	5	5	Jim Hogg County	TX	Rayburn L. Gerke	2004	29587
132 6/8	22 0/8 22 1/8	17 0/8	6	6	Shawano County	WI	Timothy Klitzke	2005	29587
*132 6/8	22 5/8 22 0/8	18 6/8	5	5	Allegheny County	PA	Dean Dorsch	2005	29587
*132 6/8	23 3/8 21 5/8	19 1/8	6	5	Pike County	IL	David D. Shawley	2005	29587
132 6/8	21 4/8 21 0/8	17 6/8	5	5	Barron County	WI	David W. Leschisin	2005	29587
132 6/8	20 0/8 21 1/8	14 0/8	5	6	Adams County	IA	Travis Paul	2005	29587
132 6/8	23 5/8 23 2/8	17 7/8	4	5	Essex County	VA	Jason Butler	2005	29587
*132 6/8	22 0/8 21 3/8	16 3/8	5	5	Columbia County	WI	John M. Salzman	2005	29587
132 6/8	19 4/8 21 2/8	16 2/8	5	5	Buffalo County	WI	Greg Hensen	2005	29587
*132 6/8	22 1/8 22 2/8	14 4/8	4	5	Van Buren County	IA	Gary Kephart	2005	29587
132 6/8	20 7/8 20 5/8	18 6/8	5	5	Cass County	MI	Randy R. Wilcox	2005	29587
132 6/8	19 5/8 19 4/8	15 6/8	5	5	La Salle County	IL	Jeffrey Oscepinski	2005	29587
132 6/8	23 6/8 23 0/8	17 6/8	5	4	Ramsey County	ND	Bryston Berg	2005	29587
132 6/8	20 0/8 20 3/8	17 0/8	5	7	Creston	BC	Jason Wall	2005	29587
*132 6/8	23 3/8 23 3/8	15 0/8	5	6	Washington County	OH	Luke G. Kuchta	2006	29587
132 6/8	24 5/8 23 4/8	19 4/8	4	5	Tuscarawas County	OH	Ron Hower	2006	29587
*132 6/8	22 4/8 21 6/8	18 2/8	4	4	Garfield County	OK	Tim Bonnewell	2006	29587
132 6/8	21 4/8 21 4/8	16 2/8	4	4	Grand Forks County	ND	David Lueker	2006	29587
*132 6/8	22 6/8 22 4/8	18 0/8	5	5	Jackson County	IA	Ron Goedken	2006	29587
132 6/8	21 3/8 21 1/8	15 3/8	7	7	Audubon County	IA	Mark Baier	2006	29587
*132 6/8	22 4/8 22 0/8	16 4/8	4	4	Taylor County	WI	James Ebert	2006	29587
*132 6/8	21 0/8 22 3/8	19 1/8	4	4	Lorain County	OH	Jason Schwartz	2006	29587
132 6/8	21 2/8 22 3/8	16 6/8	5	6	Tioga County	NY	Michael A. Struble	2006	29587
*132 6/8	22 2/8 22 6/8	19 6/8	4	4	Adams County	WI	Charles A. Schweiger	2006	29587
*132 6/8	21 1/8 21 1/8	13 6/8	4	4	Bollinger County	MO	Tyler G. Wagner	2007	29587
*132 6/8	23 6/8 23 1/8	16 7/8	4	6	Hastings Lake	ALB	Dean Bromberger	2007	29587
*132 6/8	22 5/8 22 0/8	19 4/8	4	4	Mason County	TX	Gary Kneese	2007	29587
*132 6/8	22 5/8 23 2/8	16 4/8	4	5	Halifax County	VA	Tommy Hatcher	2007	29587
132 6/8	21 2/8 22 0/8	15 4/8	5	5	Ross County	OH	Dustin Baker	2007	29587
*132 6/8	21 3/8 21 7/8	14 0/8	5	6	Bartholomew County	IN	Brandon Weidman	2007	29587
132 6/8	20 6/8 20 2/8	15 2/8	6	7	Putnam County	IN	Denny Smith	2007	29587
132 6/8	22 1/8 22 2/8	16 7/8	5	7	Monroe County	NY	John J. Martone	2007	29587
*132 6/8	23 7/8 23 7/8	15 4/8	4	4	Duval County	TX	Hunter Teel	2007	29587
132 6/8	22 7/8 21 4/8	15 2/8	4	4	Ward County	ND	John R. Plesuk	2007	29587
*132 6/8	19 1/8 20 1/8	17 2/8	5	5	Monroe County	KY	Steven Lyon	2008	29587
132 6/8	22 5/8 22 7/8	16 7/8	4	6	Pottawatomie County	KS	Brian Artzer	2008	29587
132 6/8	22 1/8 22 0/8	20 2/8	5	6	Polk County	WI	Jeff D. Everson	2008	29587
*132 6/8	23 4/8 23 3/8	20 4/8	5	4	Sauk County	WI	Charles Arndt	2008	29587
*132 6/8	22 4/8 22 1/8	15 6/8	5	5	Jackson County	MI	Jennifer Ann Crawford	2008	29587
132 6/8	21 4/8 21 6/8	15 4/8	5	5	Polk County	WI	Jesse Weber	2008	29587
132 6/8	20 0/8 21 0/8	15 4/8	6	5	Kingman County	KS	Rich Kimball	2008	29587
132 6/8	21 2/8 22 4/8	17 0/8	5	5	Adams County	IA	Mike Weaver	2008	29587
132 6/8	22 0/8 22 2/8	17 0/8	4	4	Athens County	OH	Richard H. Whitaker III	2008	29587
*132 6/8	20 4/8 20 5/8	17 6/8	5	5	Mahoning County	OH	David Rickert	2008	29587
*132 6/8	23 5/8 23 6/8	18 2/8	4	4	Columbia County	WI	Brian R. Schmidt	2008	29587
*132 6/8	21 1/8 20 7/8	16 0/8	4	4	Burlington County	NJ	Michael Stevenson	2009	29587
*132 6/8	21 3/8 23 1/8	17 2/8	5	5	Rusk County	WI	Todd Sauerwein	2009	29587
132 6/8	23 1/8 23 2/8	15 0/8	5	5	Labette County	KS	Rodney J. Kelly	2009	29587
132 6/8	22 0/8 23 0/8	17 2/8	5	4	Stoddard County	MO	John Dolan Pendarvis	2009	29587
132 6/8	24 5/8 24 4/8	17 2/8	4	4	Berks County	PA	Tony E. Torrence	2009	29587
*132 6/8	21 4/8 22 0/8	17 5/8	5	6	Dunn County	WI	Tim Holmstadt	2009	29587
*132 6/8	21 6/8 22 4/8	16 3/8	6	9	Young County	TX	Zack Burkett III	2009	29587
132 6/8	20 5/8 20 0/8	15 0/8	6	7	Plymouth County	IA	Randy Collins	2010	29587
*132 5/8	22 2/8 23 1/8	13 7/8	5	4	Calhoun County	MI	Robert W. Peet	2000	29815
132 5/8	19 5/8 20 5/8	15 3/8	5	6	Winnebago County	WI	Scott Wuest	2002	29815
132 5/8	23 4/8 23 4/8	18 1/8	4	4	La Salle County	IL	Dale F. Long	2003	29815
132 5/8	23 7/8 23 6/8	20 3/8	7	7	Trempealeau County	WI	Manfred Vonuhl	2003	29815
132 5/8	25 4/8 25 2/8	16 6/8	4	5	Adams County	IL	Melvin Linder II	2003	29815
132 5/8	21 4/8 21 3/8	16 3/8	5	4	Carroll County	MO	Jamie B. Foley	2004	29815
132 5/8	21 6/8 25 0/8	19 1/8	4	5	Allamakee County	IA	Arnie Crum	2004	29815
132 5/8	20 2/8 21 0/8	13 6/8	6	7	Sawyer County	WI	Wayne Krenz	2004	29815
132 5/8	25 5/8 26 4/8	20 4/8	7	6	Buffalo County	WI	David L. Halverson	2004	29815
132 5/8	21 0/8 22 0/8	17 3/8	4	4	Chickasaw County	IA	Steve Murray	2004	29815
132 5/8	22 3/8 23 2/8	18 7/8	5	6	Johnson County	IA	Randy J. Prybil	2004	29815
132 5/8	21 2/8 21 3/8	18 3/8	5	4	Marshall County	SD	Doug Miiller	2004	29815
132 5/8	23 2/8 23 2/8	17 1/8	4	4	Tom Green County	TX	Jerry Dean Hebert	2004	29815
132 5/8	19 7/8 18 1/8	16 3/8	5	6	Zavala County	TX	Hal Hargis	2004	29815
132 5/8	20 1/8 20 7/8	13 5/8	5	5	Marquette County	WI	Jake Ladwig	2005	29815
132 5/8	23 4/8 23 6/8	22 1/8	5	5	Monroe County	WI	Jason M. Kamrath	2005	29815
132 5/8	18 0/8 18 2/8	16 7/8	8	7	Wayne County	OH	Matthew C. Stutzman	2005	29815
*132 5/8	18 3/8 18 4/8	13 3/8	5	5	Butler County	KY	Randy Ward	2005	29815
132 5/8	23 5/8 24 5/8	19 7/8	5	4	Washington County	IA	Bradly Balcar	2005	29815
132 5/8	22 4/8 23 0/8	17 1/8	4	5	Calhoun County	IL	Evan Steinhorst	2005	29815
132 5/8	22 1/8 21 6/8	17 7/8	4	5	Beaver County	PA	Jason A. Hrelec	2005	29815
132 5/8	20 4/8 20 4/8	15 5/8	4	5	Allen County	IN	Jim Harden	2005	29815
132 5/8	21 1/8 23 1/8	18 5/8	4	4	Black Hawk County	IA	Roger Boyd	2005	29815
132 5/8	24 1/8 22 7/8	17 1/8	4	4	Butler County	PA	Thomas Mohanan, Jr.	2005	29815
132 5/8	23 3/8 23 2/8	16 6/8	6	7	Clarion County	PA	Jay B. Heckethorn	2005	29815

WHITETAIL DEER (TYPICAL ANTLERS)

Minimum Score 125　　　　　　　　　　　　　　　　　　　　　　　　　　　　　　　　　　　　　　Continued

SCORE	LENGTH OF R MAIN BEAM L	INSIDE SPREAD	NUMBER OF R POINTS L		AREA	STATE/ PROVINCE	HUNTER'S NAME	DATE	RANK
132 5/8	21 3/8　21 5/8	17 2/8	6	6	Union County	SD	Tim Heaton	2005	29815
*132 5/8	24 6/8　24 3/8	18 1/8	5	4	Brown County	IN	William A. "Tony" Williams	2005	29815
132 5/8	24 4/8　22 6/8	16 1/8	5	7	Vigo County	IN	William Howard	2005	29815
132 5/8	23 3/8　24 3/8	15 2/8	4	5	Sawyer County	WI	Gary Schnitzler	2005	29815
132 5/8	21 2/8　20 1/8	16 3/8	5	5	Meriwether County	GA	Michael Newman	2006	29815
132 5/8	20 6/8　19 7/8	16 7/8	8	5	Hancock County	IN	Roy Hargrove	2006	29815
*132 5/8	22 6/8　22 0/8	18 3/8	6	5	Marquette County	WI	Timothy J. O'Leary	2006	29815
*132 5/8	21 6/8　21 5/8	17 7/8	4	4	Scott County	IL	Tom Goldasich	2006	29815
*132 5/8	23 2/8　22 5/8	14 7/8	5	5	Washington County	OH	Tyler Spence	2006	29815
132 5/8	22 5/8　22 3/8	18 5/8	4	5	Carroll County	MO	Warren L. Standley	2006	29815
132 5/8	22 0/8　23 6/8	17 1/8	4	5	Calhoun County	MI	Dale J. Trescott	2006	29815
*132 5/8	21 3/8　20 6/8	16 2/8	6	7	Richland County	ND	Nick England	2006	29815
132 5/8	22 6/8　22 4/8	19 5/8	4	4	Chautauqua County	NY	Ronald Ferry	2006	29815
*132 5/8	20 4/8　19 4/8	16 1/8	6	6	Marquette County	WI	Lee A. Smet	2006	29815
132 5/8	22 1/8　20 7/8	17 5/8	5	5	La Salle County	TX	John W. Elias	2006	29815
132 5/8	19 5/8　18 4/8	18 3/8	5	5	Putnam County	MO	Mike Schanzmeyer	2007	29815
*132 5/8	21 2/8　20 5/8	15 3/8	5	5	Harrison County	KY	Lyle T. Fryman	2007	29815
*132 5/8	23 4/8　22 4/8	19 3/8	4	4	Franklin County	NC	David E. Robbins, Jr.	2007	29815
*132 5/8	21 7/8　21 7/8	17 1/8	5	4	Outagamie County	WI	Jim Ernst	2007	29815
*132 5/8	25 5/8　22 7/8	18 0/8	5	6	Crawford County	PA	Donald Sutton	2007	29815
132 5/8	21 0/8　21 5/8	16 1/8	5	5	Wabasha County	MN	Keith Ramthun	2007	29815
*132 5/8	25 0/8　25 2/8	20 7/8	4	4	Charlotte County	VA	William Keith Stewart	2007	29815
132 5/8	21 5/8　21 5/8	15 3/8	5	5	Schleicher County	TX	Rusty Bryant	2007	29815
132 5/8	24 0/8　24 6/8	20 4/8	4	4	Vermillion County	IN	Tim Ditto	2007	29815
132 5/8	22 0/8　22 4/8	15 1/8	4	4	Wayne County	IA	Wayne Boyer	2007	29815
132 5/8	23 0/8　23 5/8	17 7/8	8	7	Dorion Township	ONT	Chris Height	2007	29815
*132 5/8	22 6/8　23 3/8	14 7/8	4	4	Sangamon County	IL	Doc Kauffman	2007	29815
132 5/8	22 5/8　24 2/8	20 1/8	4	4	Hardin County	KY	Derrick Peters	2007	29815
132 5/8	22 1/8　22 1/8	19 6/8	5	6	Oklahoma County	OK	Ken Jose	2007	29815
132 5/8	20 7/8　21 6/8	15 5/8	5	5	Spokane County	WA	Josh Rieger	2007	29815
132 5/8	22 6/8　21 7/8	15 7/8	5	5	Bonneville County	ID	Gregory R. Pimentel	2007	29815
132 5/8	18 6/8　18 5/8	13 5/8	5	5	Harris County	TX	Billybob Hornback	2007	29815
*132 5/8	21 1/8　21 1/8	16 7/8	5	5	Bayfield County	WI	Dale Goytowski	2007	29815
132 5/8	22 4/8　22 5/8	18 7/8	4	5	Polk County	WI	Sarah Droher	2008	29815
*132 5/8	20 4/8　20 1/8	18 3/8	5	5	Lewis & Clark County	MT	Mike McVicker	2008	29815
132 5/8	22 7/8　22 4/8	17 3/8	4	4	Van Buren County	MI	Ryan K. Oliver	2008	29815
*132 5/8	24 0/8　24 2/8	15 2/8	6	4	Defiance County	OH	William Riley	2008	29815
132 5/8	19 5/8　21 1/8	18 5/8	5	5	Ontario County	NY	Craig Van Schaick	2008	29815
*132 5/8	20 3/8　20 3/8	16 3/8	5	5	Lake County	IN	John T. Nelson	2008	29815
132 5/8	24 2/8　23 3/8	20 3/8	4	5	Butler County	PA	Dale Brown	2008	29815
132 5/8	24 4/8　24 2/8	18 7/8	4	5	Fairfield County	CT	Anthony Cardinale	2008	29815
132 5/8	20 7/8　20 7/8	16 1/8	5	5	Queen Annes County	MD	Eric D. Ford	2008	29815
*132 5/8	24 3/8　22 3/8	17 5/8	6	5	Salem County	NJ	Daniel P. Smick	2008	29815
132 5/8	24 0/8　23 4/8	16 7/8	4	4	Athens County	OH	Jeffrey D. Eddy	2008	29815
*132 5/8	21 4/8　21 0/8	15 7/8	6	5	Sullivan County	IN	Conrad J. Kittle	2008	29815
*132 5/8	24 1/8　22 1/8	16 5/8	4	4	Belknap County	NH	Ron Taylor, Jr.	2008	29815
132 5/8	22 4/8　22 5/8	16 7/8	4	6	Boone County	IA	Thomas Baum	2008	29815
*132 5/8	19 1/8　21 3/8	14 3/8	6	5	St. Clair County	MO	Blane Baker	2008	29815
132 5/8	20 1/8　20 4/8	19 3/8	5	7	Hillsdale County	MI	Daniel K. Timmons	2008	29815
132 5/8	21 7/8　23 0/8	17 3/8	4	4	Mountrail County	ND	John Richardson	2009	29815
132 5/8	22 1/8　22 0/8	17 5/8	4	4	Cass County	MI	Ronald E. Hartline, Jr.	2009	29815
132 5/8	23 2/8　22 0/8	20 3/8	4	5	Monmouth County	NJ	Mark Kronyak	2009	29815
*132 5/8	22 0/8　22 7/8	16 7/8	6	6	Fond du Lac County	WI	Benjamin S. Giese	2009	29815
132 5/8	24 0/8　23 3/8	18 1/8	4	4	Whitley County	IN	Bart A. Bailey	2009	29815
132 5/8	21 7/8　20 0/8	14 5/8	5	5	Lincoln County	MO	Ernest Durlas	2009	29815
132 5/8	25 1/8　23 7/8	20 2/8	6	5	Juneau County	WI	Richard A. Laabs	2009	29815
132 5/8	23 4/8　23 4/8	21 7/8	4	5	Licking County	OH	David Chrisman	2009	29815
132 4/8	19 7/8　21 5/8	16 0/8	5	5	Lawrence County	SD	Micheal D. Hudson	1983	30053
132 4/8	23 6/8　23 1/8	15 6/8	4	5	Ripley County	IN	Jack D. Day, Sr.	1986	30053
132 4/8	23 6/8　22 7/8	17 0/8	4	4	Clayton County	IA	Gabe Oldfather	2001	30053
*132 4/8	22 4/8　24 0/8	19 7/8	6	4	Washington County	OH	Tulsa Green	2001	30053
132 4/8	19 5/8　20 4/8	16 4/8	5	6	Black Hawk County	IA	Mike Judas	2003	30053
132 4/8	19 2/8　19 6/8	16 0/8	6	5	Sussex County	VA	William Edwards	2004	30053
132 4/8	22 7/8　21 7/8	19 0/8	5	4	Crawford County	WI	Doug Krachey	2004	30053
132 4/8	20 7/8　20 3/8	14 6/8	6	5	Buffalo County	WI	Michael R. Senft	2004	30053
132 4/8	22 7/8　22 2/8	13 6/8	6	6	Pike County	IL	Gerald Polachak	2004	30053
132 4/8	20 3/8　19 5/8	15 1/8	6	6	Waukesha County	WI	Patrick T. McNamee	2004	30053
132 4/8	21 5/8　21 5/8	18 2/8	4	4	Dane County	WI	David Cummings	2004	30053
132 4/8	22 2/8　21 1/8	17 6/8	4	4	Vigo County	IN	Jim Conley, Jr.	2004	30053
*132 4/8	23 7/8　22 7/8	20 0/8	4	4	Allen County	IN	Lyle Felger	2004	30053
*132 4/8	20 7/8　20 2/8	15 2/8	5	5	Door County	WI	Billy Charles	2004	30053
132 4/8	22 7/8　23 4/8	19 6/8	4	4	Adams County	WI	Edward S. Biebesheimer	2004	30053
132 4/8	23 5/8　22 6/8	18 6/8	5	4	Lake County	IN	Marc Maloian	2004	30053
132 4/8	21 7/8　21 0/8	15 0/8	7	6	Johnson County	NE	Brian Brinkman	2004	30053
132 4/8	20 5/8　20 2/8	14 6/8	5	5	Harper County	KS	Paul Wilkens	2004	30053
132 4/8	19 5/8　21 2/8	15 6/8	6	6	Washington County	PA	Barrett Brown	2004	30053
*132 4/8	22 1/8　23 2/8	19 6/8	4	4	Fairfield County	CT	John Matluck	2004	30053
*132 4/8	22 1/8　22 5/8	18 0/8	4	4	Clay County	IN	Shane White	2005	30053
132 4/8	22 0/8　22 1/8	16 0/8	5	5	Stratten	ONT	Bernie Goebel	2005	30053
*132 4/8	24 1/8　22 3/8	17 0/8	4	5	Jackson County	WI	Steve Snyder	2005	30053
132 4/8	23 4/8　23 1/8	18 6/8	5	3	Vernon County	WI	Mark R. See	2005	30053
132 4/8	24 3/8　25 5/8	20 4/8	5	4	Dearborn County	IN	Corey Bruns	2005	30053
*132 4/8	22 4/8　21 6/8	15 6/8	5	5	Buffalo County	WI	Scott D. Emond	2005	30053
132 4/8	21 0/8　22 0/8	16 2/8	5	5	La Crosse County	WI	Steven A. Parker	2005	30053
132 4/8	21 1/8　20 3/8	16 4/8	5	6	Greene County	IL	Patrick Bartlett	2005	30053
132 4/8	23 6/8　21 4/8	20 4/8	4	4	Clermont County	OH	Jody Beck	2005	30053
*132 4/8	21 1/8　20 7/8	14 4/8	5	4	La Salle County	TX	Mike Rust	2005	30053
132 4/8	20 0/8　19 0/8	14 2/8	5	5	Peoria County	IL	Larry Oppe	2005	30053
132 4/8	23 1/8　23 3/8	18 6/8	4	5	Green Lake County	WI	Tim Syvrud	2005	30053
132 4/8	23 7/8　23 4/8	18 7/8	8	7	Marshall County	KS	James L. Ungerer	2005	30053
*132 4/8	23 0/8　23 5/8	18 4/8	4	5	Claiborne County	MS	Fred P. Shaw	2006	30053
132 4/8	23 1/8　21 7/8	16 2/8	4	4	Christian County	KY	Art Powers	2006	30053
132 4/8	23 1/8　23 7/8	16 4/8	4	6	Tippecanoe County	IN	Bill Shallenberger	2006	30053
132 4/8	20 4/8　20 3/8	14 4/8	6	6	Green County	WI	Scott Blumer	2006	30053
*132 4/8	22 4/8　22 6/8	16 4/8	5	4	Franklin County	MO	Greg Van Leer	2006	30053

Deer entries below 141 0/8, that appeared in the 6th Edition, are not included here, but are included on the accompanying CD (see page 119), and also in the Club's Records Archives.

WHITETAIL DEER (TYPICAL ANTLERS)

Minimum Score 125   Continued

SCORE	LENGTH OF R MAIN BEAM L	INSIDE SPREAD	NUMBER OF R POINTS L	AREA	STATE/PROVINCE	HUNTER'S NAME	DATE	RANK
*132 4/8	19 3/8 20 4/8	16 2/8	5 5	Brown County	IL	Derrick Ellis	2006	30053
*132 4/8	21 6/8 22 4/8	15 5/8	6 5	Hand County	SD	Damon Brueggeman	2006	30053
132 4/8	22 0/8 20 6/8	18 0/8	4 4	Monona County	IA	Dean Dittenber	2006	30053
132 4/8	20 4/8 20 2/8	15 2/8	7 7	Maury County	TN	Noah Joe Carr	2007	30053
132 4/8	22 5/8 23 0/8	16 7/8	6 6	Taylor County	WI	Raymond A. Kliscz	2007	30053
132 4/8	21 2/8 21 3/8	17 2/8	5 5	Polk County	NE	Ron Kutschkau	2007	30053
132 4/8	22 7/8 22 5/8	18 1/8	5 5	Desha County	AR	Tucker Miller III	2007	30053
132 4/8	20 7/8 21 4/8	17 7/8	7 6	Winnebago County	WI	Ron W. Kolosky	2007	30053
132 4/8	22 2/8 21 3/8	14 4/8	5 6	Sanilac County	MI	Eric L. Rooney	2007	30053
*132 4/8	22 3/8 23 2/8	14 4/8	6 7	Mills County	IA	Henry Joslin III	2007	30053
132 4/8	22 2/8 22 5/8	16 4/8	5 5	Houston County	MN	Chris Moon	2007	30053
132 4/8	20 5/8 21 3/8	16 4/8	5 5	Summers County	WV	Jeff Cooper	2007	30053
132 4/8	19 6/8 19 5/8	14 6/8	5 5	Polk County	WI	Steven L. Karo	2007	30053
*132 4/8	23 1/8 23 0/8	18 2/8	4 4	Livingston County	MI	Donald Mitchell	2007	30053
132 4/8	22 4/8 21 3/8	16 2/8	4 4	Mobile County	AL	Pat Lods	2008	30053
132 4/8	21 5/8 23 1/8	19 5/8	6 6	Freestone County	TX	Dennis Grimsley	2008	30053
132 4/8	23 0/8 23 1/8	16 7/8	5 5	Irion County	TX	Ronnie Parsons	2008	30053
132 4/8	20 3/8 24 0/8	17 0/8	6 5	Barron County	WI	Les Karpiel	2008	30053
*132 4/8	20 2/8 19 6/8	14 7/8	7 6	Pepin County	WI	Patrick Falkner	2008	30053
132 4/8	22 5/8 22 6/8	16 0/8	4 5	Monroe County	WI	Ethan L. Sullivan	2008	30053
132 4/8	21 3/8 23 3/8	18 7/8	5 5	Pike County	OH	Glenn A. Fink	2008	30053
132 4/8	20 5/8 21 0/8	16 5/8	6 5	Rusk County	WI	Robert R. Pelland	2009	30053
*132 4/8	21 7/8 19 2/8	14 6/8	5 5	Valley County	MT	David Bowers	2009	30053
132 4/8	21 4/8 23 0/8	16 2/8	4 5	Douglas County	MN	Richard Johnson	2009	30053
*132 4/8	21 5/8 21 3/8	15 4/8	5 4	Lawrence County	MO	Craig Freitag	2009	30053
*132 4/8	20 6/8 20 3/8	13 5/8	7 5	Harrison County	OH	Josh Henderson	2009	30053
132 4/8	20 7/8 20 7/8	14 3/8	8 6	Wood County	WI	Ron Rosplock	2009	30053
*132 4/8	21 1/8 21 2/8	14 5/8	5 4	Putnam County	IN	Mark D. Weileman	2009	30053
*132 4/8	19 7/8 20 4/8	15 4/8	5 7	W. Feliciana Parish	LA	Cathy Munson	2009	30053
*132 4/8	19 7/8 20 1/8	16 7/8	6 6	St. Croix County	WI	Dan Nottestad	2009	30053
132 4/8	22 0/8 22 4/8	15 6/8	5 5	Monona County	IA	Dan Schemmel	2009	30053
132 4/8	21 1/8 20 6/8	16 4/8	5 5	Le Flore County	OK	Shane Womack	2009	30053
*132 4/8	24 0/8 22 5/8	19 0/8	4 4	Crawford County	WI	Matt Fernette	2009	30053
*132 4/8	22 5/8 23 3/8	17 0/8	4 5	Noble County	IN	Chad A. Eryman	2009	30053
*132 4/8	24 6/8 25 0/8	18 0/8	5 4	Barber County	KS	Dean Avagnano	2009	30053
132 4/8	20 3/8 20 7/8	14 2/8	5 5	Kleberg County	TX	Daniel Brown	2009	30053
132 4/8	21 2/8 20 7/8	15 4/8	6 7	Delaware County	OH	Jeremiah Waugh	2010	30053
132 3/8	18 6/8 21 7/8	15 7/8	4 5	Shawano County	WI	Duane Hafner	2003	30321
*132 3/8	20 1/8 20 1/8	15 5/8	5 5	Carroll County	KY	Greg Green	2003	30321
132 3/8	21 0/8 21 7/8	16 3/8	4 4	Bureau County	IL	Scott Grimmer	2003	30321
132 3/8	22 5/8 22 4/8	14 5/8	4 5	Polk County	WI	Steven J. Snell	2004	30321
132 3/8	22 0/8 22 3/8	19 1/8	5 4	Burleigh County	ND	Alan W. Smith	2004	30321
132 3/8	18 3/8 19 0/8	16 3/8	6 6	Harrison County	MO	Ken Collins	2004	30321
132 3/8	23 4/8 22 5/8	18 7/8	5 4	Waukesha County	WI	Ron Strauss	2005	30321
132 3/8	21 6/8 22 5/8	18 3/8	5 5	Monroe County	IL	George Dee Bankhead	2005	30321
132 3/8	23 4/8 23 3/8	17 3/8	3 4	Johnson County	IN	Joe A. Brewer	2005	30321
*132 3/8	21 2/8 22 0/8	17 5/8	5 6	Pike County	IN	Larry Daub	2005	30321
132 3/8	23 5/8 23 1/8	15 5/8	5 4	Clarke County	IA	Dan Young	2005	30321
132 3/8	20 0/8 19 2/8	14 3/8	5 5	Calhoun County	MI	Joseph W. Michilizzi	2005	30321
*132 3/8	22 0/8 22 4/8	16 1/8	4 5	Outagamie County	WI	Bill Schuh	2005	30321
132 3/8	21 1/8 22 3/8	17 4/8	7 6	Licking County	OH	Scott Burkhart	2005	30321
*132 3/8	20 6/8 21 1/8	18 1/8	6 5	Hand County	SD	Charles Fawcett	2005	30321
132 3/8	21 0/8 20 7/8	16 4/8	7 6	Pike County	IL	Zach Rogers	2005	30321
132 3/8	22 7/8 19 3/8	15 3/8	6 6	Shelby County	IL	Robert Baldwin	2005	30321
132 3/8	22 3/8 20 0/8	17 3/8	6 5	Jefferson County	IL	Harry Bellock	2005	30321
132 3/8	21 4/8 21 5/8	18 1/8	5 5	Fauquier County	VA	C. Jeffrey Lawson	2005	30321
132 3/8	22 7/8 21 7/8	18 5/8	5 4	Dodge County	WI	Matthew Aumann	2006	30321
132 3/8	23 2/8 22 1/8	20 5/8	6 7	Stutsman County	ND	Adam Hofmann	2006	30321
132 3/8	23 2/8 22 2/8	19 1/8	4 4	Holmes County	MS	Scott Mardis	2006	30321
132 3/8	21 3/8 22 0/8	15 3/8	5 5	Hardeman County	TX	Matt Shelton	2006	30321
*132 3/8	21 4/8 21 3/8	15 7/8	5 5	Towner County	ND	Ron James	2006	30321
132 3/8	21 3/8 20 4/8	15 1/8	5 5	Marquette County	WI	Robert L. Kampen	2006	30321
132 3/8	20 5/8 22 6/8	19 4/8	6 5	Boone County	IA	Jason Loecker	2006	30321
132 3/8	20 7/8 20 4/8	14 6/8	4 7	Adams County	IL	John M. Troutman	2006	30321
*132 3/8	21 3/8 20 7/8	17 6/8	4 7	Nodaway County	MO	Christopher B. Franklin	2006	30321
132 3/8	22 1/8 24 4/8	20 5/8	4 4	Marquette County	WI	Michael E. Kohnke	2006	30321
132 3/8	20 4/8 20 3/8	14 1/8	5 4	Montgomery County	IA	Mark Moser	2006	30321
*132 3/8	22 6/8 23 1/8	18 1/8	5 5	Logan County	WV	Perry Bailey, Jr.	2006	30321
*132 3/8	22 1/8 21 6/8	21 2/8	5 5	Monroe County	NY	Thomas R. Buss	2006	30321
*132 3/8	20 5/8 21 3/8	17 3/8	6 5	Mille Lacs County	MN	Jake Vlieger	2007	30321
132 3/8	19 4/8 20 5/8	16 5/8	5 5	McMullen County	TX	Jerome Bischoffberger	2007	30321
*132 3/8	21 1/8 20 5/8	17 7/8	4 5	Kalamazoo County	MI	Nicholas Waldron	2007	30321
132 3/8	21 2/8 21 5/8	17 3/8	5 8	Buffalo County	WI	John G. Erickson	2007	30321
132 3/8	22 2/8 23 4/8	20 1/8	4 4	Dubois County	IN	Isaac Heeke	2007	30321
132 3/8	22 5/8 22 6/8	17 7/8	6 7	Kewaunee County	WI	Mark Nelis	2007	30321
*132 3/8	21 4/8 20 3/8	15 5/8	5 5	Shawnee County	KS	Michael J. Kruger	2007	30321
132 3/8	21 3/8 21 7/8	17 7/8	6 6	Vernon County	WI	Dennis Von Ruden	2007	30321
132 3/8	21 4/8 22 5/8	16 3/8	4 4	Parke County	IN	Ron Martin	2007	30321
132 3/8	22 3/8 21 2/8	16 4/8	5 5	Gallatin County	IL	Mark K. Jackson	2007	30321
*132 3/8	21 6/8 21 5/8	15 6/8	5 5	Pike County	IL	Timothy J. Comes	2007	30321
132 3/8	23 7/8 24 3/8	18 3/8	4 4	Cayuga County	NY	Keith R. Mantey	2007	30321
*132 3/8	21 0/8 21 1/8	17 0/8	5 6	Early County	GA	Franklin Ford	2007	30321
132 3/8	21 4/8 21 4/8	16 4/8	6 7	Marquette County	WI	Shane Steffen	2008	30321
*132 3/8	23 6/8 23 5/8	18 1/8	4 4	Ocean County	NJ	Kyle O'Donnell	2008	30321
132 3/8	23 2/8 23 4/8	15 7/8	5 6	Sangamon County	IL	Michael G. Bushue	2008	30321
132 3/8	22 4/8 22 1/8	18 6/8	6 7	Hodgeman County	KS	Chad Jones	2008	30321
*132 3/8	22 5/8 23 7/8	19 7/8	4 4	Polk County	WI	Marc A. Montpetit	2008	30321
132 3/8	23 5/8 23 1/8	15 5/8	5 6	Kent County	MD	Joseph Batel	2008	30321
132 3/8	21 2/8 21 4/8	18 5/8	4 5	Carroll County	IL	Paul P. Brescia	2008	30321
132 3/8	25 0/8 25 1/8	18 5/8	6 4	Grant County	WI	Steve Dobson	2008	30321
132 3/8	22 0/8 23 0/8	18 1/8	5 5	Livingston County	NY	Gary Lee Hartford	2008	30321
132 3/8	22 1/8 19 3/8	18 1/8	5 5	Indiana County	PA	William Platt	2008	30321
*132 3/8	25 2/8 21 7/8	18 1/8	4 6	Hardin County	IA	Bruce Off	2008	30321
132 3/8	20 6/8 21 1/8	17 7/8	5 5	Carroll County	MS	Trent Trussell	2008	30321
*132 3/8	21 0/8 20 1/8	16 3/8	5 6	Grenada County	MS	Chuck Rose	2008	30321

WHITETAIL DEER (TYPICAL ANTLERS)

Minimum Score 125   Continued

SCORE	LENGTH OF R MAIN BEAM L		INSIDE SPREAD	NUMBER OF R POINTS L		AREA	STATE/ PROVINCE	HUNTER'S NAME	DATE	RANK
*132 3/8	21 3/8	21 5/8	23 0/8	4	4	Tippecanoe County	IN	Daniel R. Phillips	2009	30321
132 3/8	20 0/8	20 6/8	15 1/8	5	5	Pike County	IL	David J. Luedde	2009	30321
132 3/8	25 4/8	24 6/8	21 5/8	4	5	Marshall County	IL	Dennis Chalkey	2009	30321
*132 3/8	19 4/8	23 2/8	21 0/8	8	4	Berks County	PA	Henry Wooleyhand, Jr.	2009	30321
132 3/8	21 5/8	21 0/8	16 7/8	6	5	Clay County	MO	Christopher Lein	2009	30321
132 3/8	20 5/8	21 5/8	16 1/8	4	5	Manitowoc County	WI	Jason Thiel	2009	30321
132 3/8	23 6/8	23 6/8	18 3/8	5	7	Pike County	IN	Jason R. Scheller	2009	30321
*132 3/8	19 6/8	19 6/8	13 7/8	5	5	Osborne County	KS	Kirk Rexroat	2009	30321
*132 3/8	23 6/8	23 5/8	18 3/8	4	5	Monroe County	NY	Matthew Beres	2009	30321
132 3/8	21 4/8	22 4/8	17 5/8	4	5	Barry County	MI	Jeff Neeley	2010	30321
132 3/8	24 5/8	23 5/8	17 0/8	4	5	Greene County	IL	Gary Brown	2010	30321
132 2/8	24 4/8	24 0/8	17 2/8	6	4	Jasper County	IL	Mike Tonn	2001	30557
132 2/8	20 1/8	20 2/8	15 2/8	5	5	Ward County	ND	Stephen Erickson	2004	30557
132 2/8	21 7/8	22 0/8	16 2/8	4	5	Juneau County	WI	Rick Dogs	2004	30557
132 2/8	22 4/8	20 5/8	18 2/8	5	5	Chautauqua County	NY	Richard K. Johnson, Jr.	2004	30557
132 2/8	22 4/8	22 1/8	16 2/8	4	4	Clarke County	IA	Nate Ogbourne	2004	30557
*132 2/8	22 0/8	21 7/8	19 6/8	4	4	Vernon County	MO	Steve Schroeder	2004	30557
132 2/8	22 3/8	21 1/8	17 2/8	4	4	St. Joseph County	IN	Michael L. Ritter	2004	30557
*132 2/8	21 5/8	21 7/8	18 7/8	6	5	Logan County	CO	Sonya Garcia	2004	30557
132 2/8	22 3/8	23 4/8	19 0/8	5	4	St. Charles County	MO	Lon Ostman	2004	30557
132 2/8	21 3/8	20 5/8	16 4/8	5	9	Franklin County	NE	Michael Henry	2004	30557
*132 2/8	20 5/8	20 4/8	14 2/8	5	5	Buffalo County	NE	Greg Kush	2004	30557
132 2/8	23 1/8	22 4/8	17 6/8	5	6	Dunn County	WI	Steve Schaefer	2004	30557
132 2/8	23 4/8	22 4/8	15 6/8	4	4	Kingman County	KS	Rich Kimball	2004	30557
*132 2/8	23 1/8	24 1/8	16 5/8	5	5	Atchison County	MO	Mark Cascio	2004	30557
132 2/8	22 4/8	22 2/8	16 0/8	4	4	Stillwater County	MT	Norman Colbert, Jr.	2004	30557
132 2/8	19 6/8	19 5/8	15 0/8	5	5	Sawyer County	WI	Bruce Beckwith	2004	30557
*132 2/8	20 4/8	20 4/8	15 6/8	5	5	Erskine	ALB	Brian Champnella	2005	30557
132 2/8	18 4/8	19 0/8	14 2/8	7	6	Simpson County	KY	Shawn Gregory	2005	30557
132 2/8	22 7/8	17 4/8	17 6/8	5	5	Wright County	MN	Allan E. Kasper	2005	30557
132 2/8	22 1/8	21 5/8	15 6/8	5	5	Adams County	IL	Earl S. Grant	2005	30557
132 2/8	22 7/8	22 6/8	18 6/8	5	6	New Haven County	CT	Bob Hammond	2005	30557
132 2/8	21 7/8	21 7/8	17 6/8	4	5	Mercer County	PA	Gary Kasbee	2005	30557
132 2/8	23 2/8	23 3/8	16 0/8	5	4	Buffalo County	WI	Rich Thole	2005	30557
*132 2/8	21 4/8	21 0/8	14 3/8	5	6	Brown County	IL	Donald A. Beveridge	2005	30557
132 2/8	22 1/8	22 6/8	19 4/8	4	4	DeKalb County	IL	Ronald G. Allen	2005	30557
132 2/8	23 0/8	23 6/8	16 5/8	7	7	Belmont County	OH	Robert Scott	2005	30557
*132 2/8	23 4/8	22 1/8	15 4/8	6	5	Mason County	WV	Randy Searls	2005	30557
132 2/8	22 4/8	22 1/8	15 0/8	4	5	Clinton County	IA	Charles L. Gifford	2005	30557
132 2/8	23 4/8	23 4/8	17 4/8	4	6	Green County	WI	Steve Gobeli	2005	30557
132 2/8	22 1/8	23 3/8	21 4/8	4	7	Gage County	NE	Brian Toalson	2005	30557
*132 2/8	20 1/8	20 4/8	13 2/8	5	5	Crawford County	KS	Matthew Sanders	2005	30557
132 2/8	22 0/8	20 3/8	17 6/8	4	5	Eau Claire County	WI	Daniel Bruder	2006	30557
132 2/8	19 4/8	18 4/8	17 0/8	4	5	Mason County	MI	Derek S. Sanders	2006	30557
132 2/8	21 5/8	21 3/8	15 6/8	5	5	Buffalo County	WI	Jeff Wendorf	2006	30557
132 2/8	19 5/8	20 5/8	16 0/8	5	5	Hardin County	IL	Michael Mroz	2006	30557
132 2/8	23 6/8	23 4/8	20 6/8	4	5	Charles County	MD	Patrick E. Langley	2006	30557
132 2/8	20 4/8	20 3/8	13 3/8	8	5	Jefferson County	NY	Enoch S. Studley, Jr.	2006	30557
*132 2/8	22 4/8	22 7/8	16 4/8	4	4	Chautauqua County	NY	Scott Forbes	2006	30557
132 2/8	24 4/8	23 2/8	19 4/8	4	4	Chester County	PA	Jeffrey A. Dunlap	2006	30557
132 2/8	22 0/8	22 2/8	19 0/8	4	4	Ashland County	OH	Chris Smith	2006	30557
132 2/8	25 1/8	23 1/8	15 0/8	5	5	Venango County	PA	Clarence Sam Lee	2006	30557
*132 2/8	24 4/8	23 4/8	17 2/8	6	5	Walworth County	WI	Joe Dorn	2006	30557
132 2/8	20 0/8	20 5/8	14 5/8	6	5	Delaware County	IA	Kelly Salow	2006	30557
*132 2/8	22 1/8	22 2/8	17 0/8	4	5	Cass County	IA	Jerry Groth	2006	30557
*132 2/8	22 4/8	22 2/8	15 2/8	5	5	Richland County	OH	Keith Levendorf	2006	30557
132 2/8	20 4/8	20 5/8	15 1/8	5	5	Monroe County	AR	Tommy Gerlach	2006	30557
132 2/8	20 4/8	20 6/8	18 4/8	5	5	San Saba County	TX	Bruce Kipley	2006	30557
132 2/8	22 4/8	22 0/8	14 6/8	5	5	Page County	IA	Chris Barton	2007	30557
132 2/8	22 2/8	21 7/8	15 6/8	5	5	Morris County	NJ	Jason Anzelmo	2007	30557
*132 2/8	19 1/8	18 4/8	16 6/8	5	5	Brown County	WI	Ken Romuald	2007	30557
*132 2/8	23 6/8	24 6/8	18 4/8	4	5	Simpson County	MS	Scott Maddox	2007	30557
132 2/8	21 7/8	23 0/8	17 2/8	4	5	Harper County	KS	Nelson Goss	2007	30557
132 2/8	20 7/8	22 2/8	17 6/8	4	4	Tippecanoe County	IN	Stacy Rogers	2007	30557
*132 2/8	21 0/8	21 3/8	14 0/8	5	5	Johnson County	IA	David DeHaan	2007	30557
132 2/8	21 0/8	20 4/8	17 0/8	5	5	La Crosse County	WI	Shawn Zellmer	2007	30557
*132 2/8	21 4/8	20 0/8	16 2/8	4	4	Perry County	IN	Austin L. Carpenter	2007	30557
132 2/8	21 3/8	20 7/8	15 4/8	5	5	Randolph County	MO	John A. Antonacci	2007	30557
132 2/8	20 4/8	21 2/8	16 5/8	5	5	St. Croix County	WI	Donovan Johnson	2007	30557
132 2/8	21 0/8	22 5/8	16 2/8	6	6	Union County	IA	Robert Spratt	2007	30557
132 2/8	22 4/8	21 6/8	15 4/8	5	5	Comanche County	KS	Blake Swicord	2007	30557
132 2/8	20 7/8	21 2/8	15 2/8	6	5	Green County	WI	Derek Scheidegger	2007	30557
*132 2/8	21 1/8	20 4/8	15 4/8	6	4	St. Joseph County	IN	Jeffery M. Hoshaw	2007	30557
132 2/8	22 0/8	23 0/8	17 4/8	4	4	Callaway County	MO	Robert W. Fagan	2007	30557
*132 2/8	20 2/8	20 5/8	15 7/8	5	5	Guadalupe County	TX	Keith W. Majors	2008	30557
132 2/8	24 0/8	22 5/8	19 0/8	7	5	Northampton County	PA	John P. Barto III	2008	30557
*132 2/8	25 1/8	24 1/8	21 2/8	4	4	Franklin County	PA	Wayne E. Brensinger	2008	30557
*132 2/8	22 6/8	23 0/8	16 2/8	5	7	Sauk County	WI	Keith Johnson	2008	30557
*132 2/8	20 7/8	21 2/8	18 0/8	4	4	Grant County	SD	Bert Veen	2008	30557
*132 2/8	20 3/8	20 3/8	16 2/8	5	5	Oconto County	WI	Linda M. Gasser	2008	30557
132 2/8	22 0/8	21 5/8	19 0/8	4	5	Monroe County	IA	Scott Hargrove	2008	30557
*132 2/8	21 7/8	22 2/8	17 2/8	4	4	Fayette County	PA	Ron Kozak	2008	30557
132 2/8	22 4/8	23 2/8	14 3/8	5	5	Clay County	KS	Greg Kirby	2008	30557
132 2/8	23 3/8	22 3/8	18 6/8	4	4	Gratiot County	MI	Ralph E. Madden	2008	30557
132 2/8	24 0/8	26 1/8	18 6/8	5	6	Washington County	KS	Steve Line	2008	30557
*132 2/8	22 1/8	22 3/8	14 2/8	5	5	Clay County	TX	Mike Thompson	2008	30557
132 2/8	20 2/8	21 6/8	17 3/8	4	5	Brown County	WI	Anthony Gaura	2009	30557
132 2/8	21 6/8	22 2/8	17 0/8	4	4	Scott County	KY	Gregory T. Callaghan	2009	30557
*132 2/8	22 2/8	23 6/8	16 4/8	5	5	Pepin County	WI	Byron Nichols	2009	30557
132 2/8	22 2/8	22 2/8	15 6/8	5	5	Ohio County	IN	Brad Henry	2009	30557
*132 2/8	20 2/8	21 7/8	18 6/8	6	5	Flathead County	MT	Stephen Milheim	2010	30557
*132 2/8	21 5/8	21 1/8	19 6/8	5	5	Sheridan County	WY	Todd Richins	2010	30557
132 1/8	23 1/8	21 4/8	16 5/8	5	4	St. Croix County	WI	Tim Hyland	1998	30824
132 1/8	24 1/8	23 3/8	17 7/8	6	6	Churchville	NS	Chris Tobin	1999	30824
132 1/8	19 2/8	19 7/8	14 7/8	5	5	Kerr County	TX	Tres Childs	2000	30824

Deer entries below 141 0/8, that appeared in the 6th Edition, are not included here, but are included on the accompanying CD (see page 119), and also in the Club's Records Archives.

WHITETAIL DEER (TYPICAL ANTLERS)

Minimum Score 125 — Continued

SCORE	LENGTH OF R MAIN BEAM L	INSIDE SPREAD	NUMBER OF R POINTS L	AREA	STATE/PROVINCE	HUNTER'S NAME	DATE	RANK
132 1/8	20 1/8 20 6/8	14 3/8	5 5	Dakota County	MN	Joe Stensrud	2002	30824
132 1/8	21 3/8 20 5/8	15 5/8	5 5	Van Buren County	MI	Daniel E. Abbott	2003	30824
132 1/8	20 6/8 20 6/8	14 5/8	4 5	Edmonson County	KY	Jamie Ashley	2004	30824
132 1/8	23 4/8 23 6/8	19 1/8	5 4	Dunn County	WI	Brian Bonesteel	2004	30824
132 1/8	21 3/8 21 5/8	15 5/8	4 4	Delaware County	IA	Mark Nahra	2004	30824
132 1/8	24 1/8 24 7/8	18 1/8	6 5	McLean County	IL	Anthony Stolfa	2004	30824
132 1/8	22 5/8 20 5/8	15 1/8	5 4	McHenry County	IL	Donald E. Hoey	2004	30824
*132 1/8	21 5/8 21 0/8	14 3/8	6 5	Clark County	WI	Chris Vandeberg	2004	30824
*132 1/8	22 3/8 20 0/8	15 6/8	5 5	Knox County	IN	Derek Cardinal	2005	30824
*132 1/8	21 4/8 21 1/8	15 3/8	5 5	McHenry County	ND	Billy Joe Lovett	2005	30824
132 1/8	23 2/8 23 1/8	16 1/8	4 5	Adams County	MS	John Jenkins	2005	30824
132 1/8	21 0/8 21 0/8	14 3/8	6 5	McKenzie County	ND	Tim Novak	2005	30824
132 1/8	23 1/8 23 2/8	17 3/8	4 4	Madison Parish	LA	Steve Parks	2005	30824
132 1/8	21 0/8 21 2/8	17 1/8	5 6	Morris County	NJ	Mark Spoto	2006	30824
*132 1/8	22 4/8 23 3/8	20 3/8	4 4	Union County	PA	Bryon Waltman	2006	30824
*132 1/8	19 4/8 20 1/8	15 1/8	6 5	Stutsman County	ND	Jeff Schuchard	2006	30824
*132 1/8	21 2/8 22 0/8	17 7/8	5 7	Dodge County	MN	Allen Iverson	2006	30824
132 1/8	23 3/8 23 3/8	17 6/8	6 6	Fulton County	IL	Jeffery J. Hokanson	2006	30824
132 1/8	21 5/8 21 6/8	15 1/8	5 5	Dunn County	WI	Mike Klinger	2006	30824
132 1/8	24 5/8 24 0/8	16 7/8	4 5	Mifflin County	PA	Cody C. Specht	2006	30824
*132 1/8	24 2/8 23 3/8	20 3/8	5 5	Rock County	WI	James Uhe	2006	30824
132 1/8	22 7/8 20 6/8	16 1/8	5 5	Adams County	IL	Jim Moran	2006	30824
132 1/8	21 1/8 21 5/8	16 1/8	5 6	Winona County	MN	Andy Krage	2007	30824
132 1/8	25 0/8 24 7/8	18 2/8	7 6	Sheridan County	KS	Jerry Bowen	2007	30824
132 1/8	21 0/8 21 7/8	16 5/8	5 6	Buffalo County	WI	Stan Godfrey	2007	30824
*132 1/8	23 0/8 23 0/8	15 7/8	6 5	Sawyer County	WI	David A. Stevens	2007	30824
132 1/8	22 2/8 22 2/8	17 5/8	4 5	Jefferson County	IA	Josef K. Rud	2007	30824
132 1/8	20 7/8 21 7/8	17 1/8	5 5	Edmonton	ALB	Gunther Tondeleir	2007	30824
132 1/8	21 5/8 21 1/8	20 1/8	4 4	Fergus County	MT	Rick Catron	2008	30824
*132 1/8	23 6/8 22 3/8	14 7/8	5 6	Bath County	VA	Jim McVey	2008	30824
132 1/8	21 4/8 21 2/8	16 2/8	6 6	Scotland County	MO	Russell A. Nichols	2008	30824
*132 1/8	21 3/8 22 1/8	16 1/8	5 5	Schuyler County	IL	Mark Smith	2008	30824
132 1/8	22 6/8 22 6/8	17 5/8	5 5	Reno County	KS	Greig Sims	2008	30824
*132 1/8	20 6/8 20 4/8	14 3/8	5 5	Anderson County	KY	Jeffrey Bennett	2009	30824
*132 1/8	21 7/8 21 2/8	16 6/8	6 5	Taylor County	WI	Rocky Olsen	2009	30824
*132 1/8	22 1/8 22 5/8	18 5/8	5 5	Ottawa County	MI	Douglas J. Grotenrath	2009	30824
132 1/8	18 6/8 19 4/8	13 4/8	5 6	Cumberland County	IL	Terrance Althoff	2009	30824
132 1/8	23 1/8 23 3/8	17 7/8	5 5	Sussex County	NJ	Wayne Johnson, Jr.	2009	30824
*132 1/8	23 1/8 22 6/8	14 3/8	5 5	Pike County	IL	Tom Goldasich	2009	30824
132 1/8	22 2/8 22 5/8	16 1/8	5 5	Randolph County	WV	Todd A. Schoonover	2009	30824
132 1/8	23 1/8 23 1/8	16 5/8	4 4	Buffalo County	WI	David Walchle	2010	30824
*132 1/8	21 1/8 20 5/8	17 5/8	5 4	Brooks County	TX	Moses Vernon	2010	30824
*132 1/8	21 0/8 20 7/8	15 7/8	5 5	Meade County	SD	Gabe Ellerton	2010	30824
*132 1/8	23 0/8 23 5/8	19 1/8	4 5	Rockingham County	NH	Guy Cilluffo	2010	30824
132 0/8	21 4/8 21 0/8	14 5/8	7 6	Clark County	IN	Dexter A. Smith	1985	31029
132 0/8	22 2/8 21 0/8	18 4/8	4 4	Muskingum County	OH	Ben Risley	1993	31029
132 0/8	22 4/8 22 4/8	19 4/8	4 4	Decatur County	GA	Charles S. Caley	1999	31029
132 0/8	21 3/8 21 3/8	18 6/8	6 6	Licking County	OH	William Nixon	2000	31029
132 0/8	24 3/8 23 0/8	21 6/8	5 5	Fairfield County	OH	Hobert Payne	2001	31029
132 0/8	20 7/8 21 4/8	18 6/8	5 5	Pike County	IL	Bill Bailey	2002	31029
*132 0/8	20 6/8 20 7/8	16 2/8	4 4	Washington County	IN	Neil Coyle	2003	31029
132 0/8	21 5/8 21 3/8	14 6/8	5 5	Monroe County	WI	Isaac Wissestad	2003	31029
132 0/8	25 3/8 22 1/8	16 4/8	4 4	Montgomery County	MD	James C. Dalrymple	2003	31029
132 0/8	20 3/8 20 7/8	13 4/8	6 5	Freestone County	TX	Jerry Irons	2004	31029
132 0/8	23 4/8 23 1/8	16 6/8	4 5	Gallatin County	IL	Justin Martin	2004	31029
132 0/8	23 6/8 23 0/8	16 2/8	4 4	Spencer County	IN	Lance Stephens	2004	31029
132 0/8	23 0/8 22 5/8	15 4/8	6 5	Cambria County	PA	Jeff Davis	2004	31029
*132 0/8	21 7/8 22 5/8	17 4/8	5 4	Fountain County	IN	Matthew Hanna	2004	31029
132 0/8	19 4/8 21 2/8	19 4/8	5 5	Branch County	MI	Chad L. Frohriep	2004	31029
132 0/8	20 1/8 20 7/8	15 6/8	5 5	Sauk County	WI	Dennis V. Slaght	2004	31029
132 0/8	24 7/8 24 6/8	16 6/8	4 4	Hampden County	MA	Patrick Kelly	2004	31029
132 0/8	23 1/8 21 7/8	16 0/8	4 4	Marathon County	WI	Keith C. Juedes	2004	31029
132 0/8	21 4/8 21 6/8	17 2/8	5 5	Scott County	IA	James Halsey	2004	31029
132 0/8	22 1/8 22 7/8	18 6/8	4 4	Hunterdon County	NJ	Kevin Klenke	2004	31029
*132 0/8	24 3/8 23 0/8	18 4/8	5 5	Sullivan County	NY	Paul S. Veidenheimer	2004	31029
132 0/8	25 2/8 24 4/8	19 0/8	5 4	Jasper County	IL	Dave Fleming	2004	31029
132 0/8	23 2/8 22 3/8	21 4/8	4 4	Bergen County	NJ	Mark Spoto	2005	31029
*132 0/8	21 3/8 20 7/8	17 2/8	5 5	Sutton County	TX	Rene Mouton	2005	31029
132 0/8	23 4/8 24 4/8	16 2/8	5 6	Morgan County	OH	Gregg Woodyard	2005	31029
132 0/8	19 3/8 19 4/8	15 0/8	5 5	Waupaca County	WI	Matthew S. Moeller	2005	31029
*132 0/8	24 1/8 25 2/8	21 4/8	5 5	Chester County	PA	Bryan Murdaugh	2005	31029
132 0/8	21 4/8 20 1/8	18 0/8	5 5	Price County	WI	Donald Heisler	2005	31029
132 0/8	23 2/8 23 7/8	19 4/8	5 5	Steuben County	IN	Keith Goodrow	2005	31029
132 0/8	23 0/8 22 5/8	18 2/8	5 6	Rush County	IN	George M. Ruth	2005	31029
132 0/8	22 2/8 22 2/8	15 3/8	5 9	Marion County	KY	Billy Thompson	2005	31029
132 0/8	22 4/8 22 5/8	15 0/8	5 4	Livingston County	MO	Russel C. Harris	2005	31029
*132 0/8	17 7/8 19 0/8	13 3/8	7 7	Shawano County	WI	James C. Snortum	2005	31029
*132 0/8	21 7/8 22 1/8	18 0/8	4 5	Anoka County	MN	Tom LaBelle	2005	31029
132 0/8	22 2/8 23 0/8	15 4/8	5 5	Eau Claire County	WI	Derek Jon Pierce	2005	31029
132 0/8	24 4/8 24 4/8	19 6/8	4 4	Jewell County	KS	Nathan Andersohn	2005	31029
132 0/8	23 7/8 23 1/8	19 4/8	5 5	Monroe County	NY	Ken Oliver	2005	31029
*132 0/8	23 0/8 22 4/8	15 4/8	5 5	Marathon County	WI	Bradley A. Myszka	2005	31029
132 0/8	21 2/8 21 2/8	18 0/8	4 4	Tyler County	WV	Matthew Allan Hayes	2005	31029
132 0/8	23 1/8 23 1/8	15 7/8	6 6	Washington County	KS	Rod Kriz	2005	31029
132 0/8	21 0/8 21 3/8	14 6/8	4 4	Goodhue County	MN	Dave Cordes	2005	31029
*132 0/8	24 4/8 24 6/8	16 5/8	6 5	Webster County	NE	Derek Wayne	2006	31029
*132 0/8	21 3/8 22 3/8	18 0/8	6 6	Clayton County	IA	Kenneth Lewis, Jr.	2006	31029
132 0/8	23 4/8 22 7/8	15 0/8	5 5	Polk County	WI	Brian Pedersen	2006	31029
132 0/8	21 4/8 20 6/8	19 2/8	5 5	Adams County	WI	Zachary E. Zachow	2006	31029
132 0/8	21 3/8 20 3/8	16 4/8	5 4	Buffalo County	WI	Jim Rzentkowski	2006	31029
132 0/8	20 1/8 21 1/8	14 2/8	4 5	Spencer County	IN	Todd Hammond	2006	31029
*132 0/8	25 0/8 19 7/8	18 0/8	5 4	Allamakee County	IA	Gordon Severude	2006	31029
132 0/8	23 0/8 23 0/8	15 2/8	4 4	Knox County	IL	Stacy Morton	2006	31029
132 0/8	22 6/8 22 7/8	18 0/8	6 6	DeKalb County	IL	Josef K. Rud	2006	31029
132 0/8	22 3/8 21 6/8	15 7/8	6 5	Turner County	GA	Frank Gettig	2006	31029

WHITETAIL DEER (TYPICAL ANTLERS)

Minimum Score 125 — Continued

SCORE	LENGTH OF R MAIN BEAM L	INSIDE SPREAD	NUMBER OF R POINTS L	AREA	STATE/ PROVINCE	HUNTER'S NAME	DATE	RANK
*132 0/8	20 6/8 20 6/8	16 3/8	6 5	Ramsey County	ND	Richard Burt	2006	31029
*132 0/8	20 1/8 19 5/8	13 4/8	5 5	Trempealeau County	WI	Gordon R. Heule	2007	31029
132 0/8	20 4/8 20 2/8	16 1/8	5 6	Marquette County	WI	Wendell "Butch" Howes, Jr.	2007	31029
*132 0/8	23 2/8 22 3/8	14 3/8	6 5	Union County	KY	Josh Lockard	2007	31029
*132 0/8	22 7/8 24 0/8	16 3/8	5 6	Highland County	OH	William A. Morlik, Jr.	2007	31029
132 0/8	21 5/8 20 7/8	17 2/8	5 5	Sauk County	WI	John T. Been	2007	31029
132 0/8	20 4/8 21 0/8	16 1/8	6 5	Chippewa County	WI	Tim Danielson	2007	31029
*132 0/8	24 4/8 24 4/8	16 0/8	4 4	Jefferson County	KS	Marty Flynn	2007	31029
132 0/8	22 2/8 22 2/8	19 0/8	5 4	Butler County	KY	Jeff Roeder	2008	31029
132 0/8	21 6/8 23 3/8	15 2/8	5 5	Washtenaw County	MI	Channing J. Hutchins	2008	31029
132 0/8	20 5/8 21 2/8	18 2/8	5 4	Appanoose County	IA	Rick Petersen	2008	31029
*132 0/8	26 1/8 25 4/8	22 2/8	7 7	Chautauqua County	NY	Dillon Titus	2008	31029
132 0/8	20 7/8 20 3/8	15 4/8	5 5	Jackson County	WI	Ryan D. Baumann	2008	31029
132 0/8	18 7/8 19 4/8	16 2/8	5 5	Lemhi County	ID	Gary Gapp	2008	31029
*132 0/8	21 7/8 18 3/8	15 6/8	5 6	Sullivan County	IN	Travis C. Kittle	2008	31029
132 0/8	22 0/8 21 5/8	18 0/8	6 5	Union County	SD	Tim Heaton	2009	31029
*132 0/8	23 0/8 22 3/8	20 0/8	6 5	Cattaraugus County	NY	Joseph Ansel	2009	31029
132 0/8	22 6/8 24 0/8	16 6/8	4 4	Monroe County	WI	Todd Weibel	2009	31029
*132 0/8	27 3/8 26 0/8	19 2/8	4 5	Hampden County	MA	Michael Morrissey	2009	31029
132 0/8	23 1/8 23 3/8	18 4/8	5 5	Kent County	MI	Ryan Lind	2009	31029
*132 0/8	18 5/8 19 2/8	16 6/8	5 5	Thurston County	NE	Kevin Howell	2009	31029
*132 0/8	21 6/8 22 2/8	17 2/8	5 5	Williams County	OH	Joseph A. King, Sr.	2009	31029
*132 0/8	21 3/8 20 3/8	17 4/8	4 4	Saginaw County	MI	Travis A. Maike	2009	31029
132 0/8	23 1/8 23 1/8	17 0/8	4 4	Wilbarger County	TX	Rodney Alexander	2009	31029
132 0/8	24 0/8 25 0/8	20 0/8	5 6	Decatur County	IA	Bobby W. Hooven	2010	31029
131 7/8	20 1/8 20 3/8	16 0/8	6 5	Champaign County	IL	Robert E. Mabry	1991	31287
*131 7/8	21 4/8 21 3/8	15 5/8	5 5	Vernon County	WI	Harold M. Frank	2002	31287
131 7/8	22 6/8 22 0/8	16 2/8	5 6	Marshall County	IN	Chad D. Pendill	2003	31287
131 7/8	22 3/8 23 3/8	15 1/8	5 5	Buffalo County	WI	Jason Sturz	2004	31287
131 7/8	22 5/8 22 0/8	18 3/8	5 5	Harris County	TX	Jared Janak	2004	31287
131 7/8	26 5/8 25 6/8	18 2/8	6 4	Washington County	NE	Rick Fitchhorn, Jr.	2004	31287
131 7/8	23 2/8 21 5/8	18 3/8	4 4	Knox County	IN	Brian Evans	2004	31287
*131 7/8	20 3/8 20 4/8	14 7/8	4 4	Richardson County	NE	Randy Heckenlively	2004	31287
131 7/8	20 6/8 20 7/8	17 1/8	5 5	Chautauqua County	KS	Johnnie R. Walters	2004	31287
131 7/8	20 2/8 20 3/8	18 1/8	5 5	Will County	IL	Daniel A. Wait	2005	31287
*131 7/8	22 4/8 22 0/8	20 5/8	5 4	Effingham County	IL	Mark Schabbing	2005	31287
131 7/8	21 2/8 20 1/8	15 6/8	6 5	Waupaca County	WI	Scott J. Moeller	2005	31287
131 7/8	23 6/8 23 6/8	17 2/8	4 7	Kent County	MD	Michael Travis	2005	31287
131 7/8	22 6/8 21 5/8	14 3/8	4 5	Madison County	IL	Kennon Sutter	2005	31287
131 7/8	22 2/8 23 1/8	16 3/8	5 5	Ozaukee County	WI	Tom Bloomingdale	2005	31287
131 7/8	21 1/8 21 6/8	18 3/8	6 6	Douglas County	WI	Scott Soden	2005	31287
131 7/8	23 0/8 21 4/8	16 3/8	5 4	Washington County	WI	William W. Evert	2005	31287
131 7/8	22 0/8 22 0/8	16 7/8	5 5	Hillsdale County	MI	Brian Mulins	2005	31287
131 7/8	23 0/8 22 4/8	17 1/8	3 3	Lincoln County	SD	Jesse Hartman	2005	31287
131 7/8	21 0/8 20 7/8	17 3/8	4 4	Fergus County	MT	Josef K. Rud	2006	31287
131 7/8	24 4/8 22 7/8	15 5/8	5 4	Robertson County	KY	Paul Andrew Shelton	2006	31287
*131 7/8	21 3/8 21 3/8	15 1/8	5 5	Delaware County	IA	Dean Salow	2006	31287
131 7/8	23 3/8 22 0/8	19 1/8	4 4	Trempealeau County	WI	Erich Von Uhl	2006	31287
*131 7/8	20 0/8 20 5/8	16 4/8	6 6	Marion County	IA	Troy M. Hawkshead	2006	31287
131 7/8	21 0/8 22 2/8	19 1/8	4 4	Pierce County	WI	Joseph Leroy Linder	2006	31287
131 7/8	23 3/8 23 7/8	17 7/8	4 4	Johnson County	IL	John Domurot, Jr.	2006	31287
131 7/8	24 6/8 23 5/8	18 4/8	6 4	Coshocton County	OH	Randy R. Mabe	2006	31287
*131 7/8	20 5/8 21 2/8	15 7/8	5 5	Suffolk County	NY	Reno Rosa	2006	31287
*131 7/8	23 6/8 24 0/8	14 7/8	5 5	Orleans County	NY	Michael Roffe	2006	31287
*131 7/8	19 7/8 20 7/8	14 5/8	6 5	Wood County	WI	Joe Murray, Jr.	2006	31287
131 7/8	21 1/8 21 7/8	15 7/8	5 5	McHenry County	IL	Brad Wiehr	2006	31287
131 7/8	21 2/8 18 6/8	15 5/8	5 4	Kinney County	TX	Federic S. Barton	2006	31287
*131 7/8	23 2/8 23 7/8	18 3/8	4 4	Hancock County	WV	James Troy Barron	2006	31287
131 7/8	21 4/8 21 0/8	14 3/8	5 6	Montgomery County	TN	Keith Vaughn	2007	31287
131 7/8	20 7/8 21 6/8	15 1/8	5 6	Kosciusko County	IN	Mark A. Karczewski	2007	31287
131 7/8	24 2/8 23 4/8	17 1/8	4 5	Reynolds County	MO	Terry Turner	2007	31287
131 7/8	21 4/8 23 4/8	16 2/8	7 6	Lancaster County	NE	Gary Kurtzer	2007	31287
*131 7/8	24 3/8 24 3/8	16 3/8	5 5	Allamakee County	IA	Kyle Kothenbeutel	2007	31287
*131 7/8	19 6/8 19 3/8	15 1/8	5 5	Indiana County	PA	Keith A. Rhine	2007	31287
*131 7/8	22 4/8 23 6/8	15 3/8	5 5	Brown County	IN	Tim R. Bailey	2007	31287
*131 7/8	19 7/8 19 7/8	18 2/8	6 6	Shelby County	KY	Eric F. Burge	2008	31287
131 7/8	22 2/8 22 0/8	15 3/8	4 4	Conway County	AR	Roger Young	2008	31287
131 7/8	21 6/8 21 7/8	17 5/8	5 5	Young County	TX	Clif Allen	2008	31287
*131 7/8	22 2/8 22 1/8	18 1/8	4 4	Pepin County	WI	Brian Juliot	2008	31287
131 7/8	22 3/8 21 4/8	16 1/8	4 5	Trempealeau County	WI	Don Kreibich	2008	31287
131 7/8	21 0/8 21 0/8	16 3/8	4 5	Marion County	IA	Gerald T. Dowell	2008	31287
131 7/8	20 6/8 20 2/8	16 4/8	5 6	Polk County	WI	Kurt Marquardt	2008	31287
131 7/8	20 0/8 20 6/8	18 1/8	5 6	Marathon County	WI	Gary Lee Olson	2008	31287
131 7/8	22 3/8 22 7/8	14 0/8	6 7	Burt County	NE	Don Combs	2008	31287
131 7/8	23 6/8 24 5/8	18 5/8	4 4	Owen County	IN	Ty K. Hampe	2008	31287
131 7/8	24 0/8 23 4/8	18 2/8	5 5	Marquette County	WI	Tim Koenen	2008	31287
131 7/8	23 4/8 23 1/8	14 5/8	4 4	Ford County	KS	Bryan Harris	2008	31287
*131 7/8	20 7/8 21 5/8	14 5/8	5 5	Lewis & Clark County	MT	Jeremy M. Foster	2009	31287
131 7/8	22 2/8 22 4/8	14 4/8	4 7	Ashland County	OH	Eli Yoder	2009	31287
*131 7/8	21 0/8 21 7/8	17 0/8	4 5	Perry County	OH	Philip I. Black	2009	31287
131 7/8	22 4/8 22 6/8	16 6/8	6 5	Bureau County	IL	Josef K. Rud	2009	31287
*131 7/8	23 3/8 23 2/8	17 5/8	4 4	Lewis County	KY	Joshua Phillips	2009	31287
131 7/8	21 7/8 22 6/8	14 2/8	4 5	Menominee County	WI	Raymond E. Creapeau, Jr.	2009	31287
*131 7/8	26 7/8 24 4/8	21 3/8	5 5	Buffalo County	WI	Adam L. Pronschinske	2009	31287
*131 7/8	22 5/8 22 6/8	16 2/8	5 4	Wyoming County	WV	Michael Jamison	2009	31287
*131 7/8	23 1/8 22 6/8	21 3/8	4 4	Winnebago County	IL	Darrin P. Oakes	2009	31287
131 7/8	23 6/8 23 3/8	18 1/8	4 4	Bureau County	IL	David M. Dierzen	2009	31287
131 7/8	21 0/8 20 4/8	16 3/8	5 6	Lincoln County	WI	Phil Borchardt	2009	31287
*131 7/8	24 4/8 23 4/8	16 2/8	6 6	Pickaway County	OH	John D. Rogers	2009	31287
*131 7/8	22 6/8 22 4/8	20 7/8	5 5	Westchester County	NY	James P. Cottrell	2009	31287
*131 7/8	20 3/8 20 1/8	16 5/8	5 5	Tompkins County	NY	Eduardo Torres	2010	31287
131 7/8	24 4/8 22 3/8	18 3/8	7 7	Union County	OH	Tyler Thompson	2010	31287
131 7/8	21 3/8 22 1/8	15 5/8	6 5	Becker County	MN	Dusty Jasken	2010	31287
131 6/8	20 6/8 21 7/8	19 4/8	5 5	Champaign County	IL	Robert E. Mabry	1978	31536
131 6/8	22 5/8 22 4/8	17 6/8	5 6	Morris County	NJ	Mark Spoto	1989	31536

Deer entries below 141 0/8, that appeared in the 6th Edition, are not included here, but are included on the accompanying CD (see page 119), and also in the Club's Records Archives.

WHITETAIL DEER (TYPICAL ANTLERS)

Minimum Score 125 — Continued

SCORE	R MAIN BEAM L	INSIDE SPREAD	R POINTS L		AREA	STATE/PROVINCE	HUNTER'S NAME	DATE	RANK
131 6/8	22 1/8 22 4/8	17 2/8	4	5	Waupaca County	WI	Paul M. Schuelke	2001	31536
131 6/8	21 5/8 21 1/8	16 2/8	5	5	Fauquier County	VA	C. Jeffery Lawson	2001	31536
131 6/8	23 0/8 23 2/8	15 6/8	5	4	Angelina County	TX	William DuPree	2004	31536
131 6/8	20 6/8 22 1/8	17 4/8	4	5	McLean County	IL	John Forbes	2004	31536
131 6/8	22 0/8 22 7/8	21 0/8	4	4	Vigo County	IN	Brent L. McCammon	2004	31536
131 6/8	24 3/8 25 0/8	16 5/8	5	5	Boyle County	KY	Keith Smith	2004	31536
131 6/8	20 1/8 21 0/8	16 4/8	5	5	Albany County	WY	Ron Mason	2005	31536
131 6/8	23 3/8 23 2/8	15 2/8	6	5	Sumter County	GA	Tony Morris	2005	31536
*131 6/8	22 7/8 23 2/8	16 0/8	5	5	Washington County	PA	Keith Cartier	2005	31536
131 6/8	20 6/8 20 7/8	16 0/8	5	4	Buffalo County	WI	Marc N. Shaft	2005	31536
131 6/8	22 4/8 21 4/8	17 2/8	5	5	Benton County	MN	Kurt Clitty	2005	31536
131 6/8	24 0/8 23 4/8	18 4/8	5	4	Lawrence County	IL	Jerry Dunn	2005	31536
131 6/8	21 4/8 21 3/8	17 3/8	5	6	Young County	TX	Brad Hawpe	2005	31536
*131 6/8	23 4/8 22 2/8	19 4/8	5	4	Somerset County	NJ	Joseph Raio	2005	31536
*131 6/8	23 4/8 25 7/8	16 4/8	7	5	Harper County	KS	Justin Stutts	2005	31536
131 6/8	20 6/8 20 0/8	15 2/8	5	5	Penobscot County	ME	Charles Laversa	2005	31536
131 6/8	21 4/8 22 0/8	15 4/8	9	6	Adams County	IL	Wayne L. Carter	2005	31536
131 6/8	21 0/8 20 4/8	15 2/8	5	5	McKenzie County	ND	Dean Halseth	2005	31536
*131 6/8	23 5/8 23 6/8	18 6/8	5	4	Johnson County	IA	Scott Fuhrmeister	2005	31536
131 6/8	23 2/8 23 2/8	23 6/8	5	5	Tensas Parish	LA	Connor Wood	2005	31536
131 6/8	21 2/8 20 3/8	14 6/8	5	5	Powell County	MT	Paul R. Tremblay	2006	31536
131 6/8	22 7/8 23 0/8	17 7/8	6	4	Butler County	PA	Timothy Morgus	2006	31536
131 6/8	22 7/8 22 6/8	18 4/8	4	4	Marshall County	WV	Kevin Druschel	2006	31536
*131 6/8	24 0/8 23 2/8	18 0/8	5	5	Vernon County	WI	Michael D. Preuss	2006	31536
131 6/8	22 7/8 24 2/8	14 0/8	6	5	Winneshiek County	IA	Travis Ebner	2006	31536
131 6/8	22 3/8 22 6/8	17 6/8	5	5	Calhoun County	IL	David G. DeHaan	2006	31536
131 6/8	23 4/8 23 0/8	18 0/8	4	4	Monroe County	NY	Christopher Wegman	2006	31536
131 6/8	23 0/8 22 2/8	17 4/8	4	4	Fillmore County	MN	David E. Kingsley	2006	31536
131 6/8	23 2/8 23 0/8	18 7/8	6	4	Houston County	MN	David J. Nicolai	2006	31536
131 6/8	23 6/8 22 3/8	18 0/8	4	3	Edwards County	IL	Daniel Weber	2006	31536
131 6/8	22 2/8 21 7/8	17 2/8	4	5	Ford County	KS	Bryan Harris	2006	31536
*131 6/8	23 0/8 24 1/8	15 4/8	4	3	Rock Island County	IL	Dave Ripple	2006	31536
131 6/8	21 3/8 22 2/8	19 0/8	5	4	Lake County	IL	Steven Hysell	2007	31536
*131 6/8	22 2/8 19 6/8	16 2/8	5	5	Tippecanoe County	IN	G. Shane Crum	2007	31536
131 6/8	23 3/8 24 1/8	18 2/8	5	5	E. Carroll Parish	LA	Phillip Morgan	2007	31536
131 6/8	22 3/8 22 1/8	16 4/8	5	5	Douglas County	IL	Keith Findley	2007	31536
131 6/8	21 2/8 19 6/8	16 2/8	5	5	Will County	IL	Greg Humphrey	2007	31536
131 6/8	21 5/8 22 4/8	15 0/8	4	4	Marchand	MAN	Jody Schmitz	2007	31536
*131 6/8	22 0/8 21 2/8	19 6/8	4	5	Taylor County	WI	Allen Emmerich	2007	31536
131 6/8	22 1/8 20 0/8	15 3/8	6	6	Hillsdale County	MI	Jim Campbell	2007	31536
131 6/8	22 5/8 21 4/8	18 0/8	5	5	Crawford County	KS	Eric Kuhlman	2007	31536
131 6/8	22 2/8 23 5/8	18 0/8	5	5	Jackson County	IA	Sean Hughes	2007	31536
131 6/8	20 4/8 21 5/8	20 0/8	4	4	Faulk County	SD	Michael J. Yost	2007	31536
*131 6/8	21 4/8 21 3/8	16 2/8	5	5	Sheridan County	ND	Terry Weltz	2007	31536
131 6/8	21 2/8 21 4/8	19 2/8	5	5	Fulton County	GA	Steve Pollard	2007	31536
131 6/8	21 1/8 20 7/8	18 6/8	4	4	Independence County	AR	H. Ford Trotter	2008	31536
131 6/8	23 0/8 23 2/8	16 3/8	5	6	Chautauqua County	NY	Stephen Hutten	2008	31536
131 6/8	21 3/8 21 6/8	18 0/8	4	5	Logan County	OH	Clark Fledderjohann	2008	31536
*131 6/8	20 0/8 20 4/8	15 0/8	5	5	Dane County	WI	Jason P. Ramaker	2008	31536
131 6/8	21 2/8 22 4/8	17 0/8	4	4	Madison County	NY	Carl Conklin	2008	31536
*131 6/8	19 6/8 19 3/8	17 2/8	5	5	Butler County	PA	Chuck Kelly	2008	31536
131 6/8	21 0/8 20 0/8	16 2/8	5	5	Carroll County	OH	Chuck Secrist	2008	31536
*131 6/8	23 4/8 23 4/8	18 2/8	4	4	Harper County	KS	Nelson Goss	2008	31536
*131 6/8	22 5/8 23 0/8	19 6/8	4	5	Pike County	IL	Brian Hickman	2008	31536
*131 6/8	19 1/8 18 4/8	15 0/8	5	5	Anoka County	MN	Kenneth Fink	2008	31536
131 6/8	21 1/8 22 4/8	17 3/8	4	4	New Castle County	DE	F. Grier Wakefield, Jr.	2008	31536
*131 6/8	24 3/8 23 5/8	19 3/8	6	4	Suffolk County	NY	Charles Mulham	2009	31536
131 6/8	22 7/8 22 7/8	17 0/8	4	5	Starke County	IN	Dave Kooienga	2009	31536
131 6/8	21 5/8 21 0/8	16 2/8	5	5	Trempealeau County	WI	Jeff Helmers	2009	31536
*131 6/8	21 4/8 21 6/8	16 0/8	5	5	Bradford County	PA	Kyle D. Johnson	2009	31536
*131 6/8	22 4/8 20 0/8	13 0/8	4	4	Jackson County	WI	Travis Janke	2009	31536
131 6/8	23 0/8 21 4/8	18 0/8	6	5	Waupaca County	WI	Dave Justmann	2009	31536
131 6/8	22 6/8 22 5/8	16 0/8	4	4	Pike County	IL	Kenneth Woods	2009	31536
*131 6/8	22 3/8 21 6/8	15 0/8	6	6	Fairfield County	CT	Mark Dorosh	2009	31536
131 6/8	23 0/8 22 5/8	17 6/8	4	4	Saunders County	NE	Frank Albrecht	2009	31536
*131 6/8	23 4/8 22 5/8	18 2/8	4	5	Belmont County	OH	Jason M. Shell	2009	31536
*131 6/8	27 2/8 26 2/8	17 0/8	7	6	Harper County	KS	Jonathan Gregory	2009	31536
*131 6/8	23 1/8 22 2/8	17 2/8	5	5	Rogers County	OK	Rollie Lunsford	2009	31536
131 6/8	22 1/8 22 7/8	18 6/8	5	4	Worcester County	MA	William M. Roach	2009	31536
131 5/8	19 4/8 21 0/8	17 1/8	5	4	Lake County	IN	Ryan A. Huseman	2000	31792
131 5/8	21 1/8 21 5/8	13 6/8	4	6	Dunn County	WI	Jerold R. Olson	2002	31792
131 5/8	22 1/8 23 3/8	18 1/8	5	5	Chippewa County	WI	Derrick McGary	2003	31792
131 5/8	23 4/8 23 4/8	18 3/8	5	6	Walworth County	WI	Mark Soderland	2003	31792
131 5/8	21 5/8 22 0/8	16 5/8	4	4	Houston County	MN	Steve Skau	2003	31792
131 5/8	21 7/8 22 7/8	20 0/8	5	4	La Grange County	IN	Troy Sams	2004	31792
*131 5/8	24 2/8 23 5/8	18 1/8	4	4	Franklin County	IN	Rick Smith	2004	31792
*131 5/8	21 3/8 22 1/8	18 1/8	4	5	Tippecanoe County	IN	Gene Mills	2004	31792
131 5/8	23 3/8 24 6/8	17 3/8	4	4	Fulton County	IL	Steve Miller	2004	31792
*131 5/8	21 0/8 20 7/8	18 5/8	5	5	Knox County	IN	Josh Hammelman	2004	31792
*131 5/8	22 0/8 21 0/8	15 3/8	4	4	Schuyler County	IL	Homer E. McSwain, Sr.	2004	31792
131 5/8	23 0/8 22 3/8	20 1/8	4	5	Dodge County	NE	Norman Poppe	2004	31792
131 5/8	21 1/8 22 2/8	16 5/8	6	4	Chautauqua County	KS	Steve Gevaert	2004	31792
131 5/8	20 5/8 21 3/8	17 1/8	5	5	Rock County	WI	Christopher W. Hendricks	2004	31792
131 5/8	21 6/8 21 7/8	14 5/8	4	4	Lyon County	KS	Johnny W. Drake	2004	31792
131 5/8	21 7/8 22 2/8	17 7/8	4	4	Pend Oreille County	WA	Eric White	2004	31792
*131 5/8	22 5/8 22 7/8	15 7/8	4	5	Wayne County	IN	Eric A. Baumer	2005	31792
131 5/8	22 2/8 22 0/8	16 7/8	5	5	Parker County	TX	Bill A. Potts	2005	31792
131 5/8	20 4/8 20 1/8	13 7/8	6	5	Young County	TX	Zack Burkett III	2005	31792
*131 5/8	25 0/8 24 3/8	21 1/8	4	4	Haywood County	TN	John Swords	2005	31792
131 5/8	23 6/8 23 5/8	17 7/8	5	5	Buffalo County	WI	Wayne Olson	2005	31792
131 5/8	23 6/8 24 3/8	20 5/8	4	5	Burlington County	NJ	John Hoefling, Jr.	2005	31792
131 5/8	22 1/8 23 5/8	19 0/8	6	4	Ashtabula County	OH	Jeffrey W. Reed	2005	31792
131 5/8	22 5/8 23 4/8	18 0/8	4	5	Butler County	PA	Chad Gettemy	2005	31792
131 5/8	23 0/8 22 5/8	17 5/8	5	5	Pepin County	WI	Tony Doehrmann	2005	31792
*131 5/8	23 4/8 22 1/8	19 5/8	4	5	Kent County	DE	C. Melvin Wyatt, Jr.	2005	31792

582

WHITETAIL DEER (TYPICAL ANTLERS)

Minimum Score 125 — Continued

SCORE	R MAIN BEAM L	INSIDE SPREAD	R POINTS L	AREA	STATE/PROVINCE	HUNTER'S NAME	DATE	RANK
*131 5/8	22 0/8 23 4/8	19 1/8	5 6	Duval County	TX	Brandon Ray	2005	31792
131 5/8	22 2/8 22 7/8	16 3/8	8 7	Hocking County	OH	Jerry Haynes	2006	31792
131 5/8	17 0/8 21 6/8	17 7/8	6 6	McHenry County	ND	Ron Olson	2006	31792
131 5/8	20 3/8 20 4/8	16 1/8	5 5	Waupaca County	WI	Andrew Sternagel	2006	31792
131 5/8	21 7/8 22 2/8	16 7/8	5 5	St. Louis County	MN	Marc Miller	2006	31792
131 5/8	20 3/8 20 7/8	15 7/8	4 5	McKenzie County	ND	Jocelyn Hugelen	2006	31792
*131 5/8	20 1/8 22 2/8	14 7/8	5 5	Granville County	NC	Jason E. Clayton	2006	31792
131 5/8	24 1/8 22 7/8	16 3/8	4 4	Shelby County	OH	Buck Siler	2006	31792
131 5/8	19 4/8 21 1/8	15 3/8	5 5	Cleveland County	AR	Chris E. Burford	2006	31792
*131 5/8	20 4/8 20 6/8	17 1/8	5 5	Coshocton County	OH	Harold W. Stried	2006	31792
131 5/8	23 4/8 22 2/8	18 2/8	6 4	Decatur County	IA	John Theiler	2006	31792
*131 5/8	23 2/8 24 0/8	20 2/8	5 4	Clark County	OH	James J. Suzel	2006	31792
131 5/8	20 3/8 21 3/8	16 5/8	5 5	Noble County	OH	David Berdanier	2006	31792
131 5/8	20 7/8 20 6/8	14 3/8	7 5	Decatur County	IA	Larry L. Darnell	2006	31792
131 5/8	23 3/8 22 3/8	17 3/8	5 5	Edgar County	IL	Jack D. Fields II	2006	31792
*131 5/8	21 1/8 21 4/8	13 7/8	5 6	Macon County	MO	Brad Goodapple	2006	31792
131 5/8	18 4/8 20 2/8	13 1/8	5 5	Logan County	OH	Van Roger Williams	2006	31792
131 5/8	24 4/8 24 0/8	18 3/8	6 5	Fillmore County	MN	Kyle T. Hutchinson	2007	31792
*131 5/8	23 4/8 22 3/8	18 5/8	4 4	Manistee County	MI	Alex Ringel	2007	31792
131 5/8	18 1/8 18 0/8	14 7/8	5 5	Tippecanoe County	IN	Jim R. Esposito	2007	31792
*131 5/8	22 2/8 23 3/8	18 7/8	4 4	Adams County	IN	Shannon W. Smitley	2007	31792
131 5/8	21 6/8 22 3/8	13 7/8	5 5	Sarpy County	NE	Ryan C. Cronk	2007	31792
131 5/8	20 2/8 20 0/8	16 5/8	5 5	Monona County	IA	Will Beason	2007	31792
*131 5/8	24 0/8 24 2/8	18 0/8	5 7	Logan County	OH	Jeff Covault	2007	31792
131 5/8	22 2/8 22 2/8	17 5/8	3 4	Columbia County	WI	David A. Krueger	2007	31792
131 5/8	22 3/8 22 1/8	17 3/8	4 5	Benton County	AR	Michael Pointer	2007	31792
131 5/8	20 3/8 20 5/8	14 5/8	6 5	Clay County	KS	Erik Franzen	2007	31792
*131 5/8	22 5/8 22 3/8	16 5/8	4 4	Ashland County	OH	Justin Garver	2007	31792
131 5/8	21 3/8 21 7/8	19 5/8	4 4	Clayton County	IA	Du Wayne Fabert	2007	31792
131 5/8	22 7/8 21 7/8	16 1/8	4 4	Bolivar County	MS	Lance Johnson	2007	31792
*131 5/8	20 5/8 20 2/8	16 1/8	5 5	Ward County	ND	Casey S. Sidener	2008	31792
*131 5/8	25 2/8 24 2/8	18 7/8	5 4	Waushara County	WI	Brian F. Wenzel	2008	31792
*131 5/8	21 4/8 21 1/8	14 3/8	5 5	Jackson County	TX	Kelvin Billington	2008	31792
131 5/8	21 4/8 20 7/8	15 5/8	5 5	Burleson County	TX	Cary Balcar	2008	31792
131 5/8	21 5/8 20 3/8	15 5/8	5 5	Tuscola County	MI	Mark Jae Timko	2008	31792
*131 5/8	22 5/8 21 5/8	15 3/8	5 5	Hall County	TX	Gene Sharp	2008	31792
*131 5/8	21 7/8 22 2/8	16 4/8	6 5	St. Louis County	MN	Bill Hebl	2008	31792
*131 5/8	21 5/8 21 6/8	17 7/8	4 5	Beadle County	SD	Scott Hintz	2008	31792
131 5/8	22 0/8 25 0/8	21 0/8	6 5	Broome County	NY	Ward E. Coe	2008	31792
131 5/8	23 6/8 22 0/8	17 7/8	6 6	Powhatan County	VA	Johnny E. Worsham	2008	31792
*131 5/8	25 6/8 25 4/8	17 3/8	5 6	Coffey County	KS	Rob Kanmore	2008	31792
131 5/8	21 5/8 22 5/8	16 5/8	6 5	Lamoure County	ND	Jordan Thoreson	2009	31792
*131 5/8	21 2/8 21 0/8	16 1/8	5 5	Barron County	WI	Jim Bayerle	2009	31792
131 5/8	20 6/8 20 4/8	16 1/8	4 4	Erie County	PA	Michael L. Stives	2009	31792
*131 5/8	20 6/8 20 4/8	18 3/8	6 5	Dane County	WI	Joshua LaFevre	2009	31792
*131 5/8	23 7/8 23 3/8	15 3/8	4 4	Tuscarawas County	OH	Seth J. Rieger	2009	31792
*131 5/8	20 4/8 21 5/8	15 1/8	5 6	Tompkins County	NY	John E. Huether	2009	31792
131 5/8	21 4/8 24 2/8	17 3/8	4 4	Portage County	WI	Kevin Raflik	2009	31792
131 5/8	23 2/8 23 2/8	17 3/8	7 5	Linn County	KS	Douglas L. Below	2009	31792
*131 5/8	22 3/8 22 4/8	19 7/8	4 4	Carroll County	AR	Terry Lee Mattox	2009	31792
131 5/8	22 1/8 21 4/8	15 4/8	4 7	Putnam County	MO	Tim Staelens	2009	31792
131 4/8	22 4/8 22 0/8	15 4/8	5 5	Ashland County	WI	Thomas J. Dezotell	1994	32015
131 4/8	22 1/8 22 1/8	17 0/8	4 4	Ashland County	OH	Gary L. Fowler	2001	32015
131 4/8	21 4/8 21 1/8	15 5/8	4 6	Stokes County	NC	Eddie Priddy	2003	32015
*131 4/8	24 0/8 23 3/8	14 3/8	6 6	Lewis County	MO	Stephen Coleman	2003	32015
*131 4/8	20 6/8 20 6/8	14 2/8	5 5	Jefferson County	NE	William D. Peperkorn	2004	32015
131 4/8	22 2/8 21 2/8	17 2/8	4 4	Allegheny County	PA	William Miller	2004	32015
*131 4/8	25 1/8 24 5/8	16 4/8	4 4	Tompkins County	NY	Dustin Kryszczuk	2004	32015
131 4/8	21 5/8 21 5/8	17 0/8	4 4	La Salle County	IL	Jonah L. Dunning	2004	32015
131 4/8	22 2/8 23 0/8	17 0/8	4 4	Rock County	WI	Jamie Ashley	2004	32015
131 4/8	22 2/8 22 6/8	15 2/8	5 5	Pike County	IL	Fortunato J. Cuevas	2004	32015
131 4/8	24 1/8 25 3/8	19 2/8	4 5	Guthrie County	IA	Scott A. Ayres	2004	32015
131 4/8	22 6/8 22 5/8	16 6/8	5 5	Dubuque County	IA	David L. Prine	2004	32015
131 4/8	22 5/8 22 4/8	18 0/8	6 5	Dodge County	GA	James W. Rogers, Sr.	2004	32015
131 4/8	20 5/8 23 1/8	15 0/8	4 4	Waushara County	WI	Brian Rieves	2004	32015
131 4/8	20 7/8 23 2/8	16 2/8	5 4	Logan County	KS	Steve Boham	2004	32015
*131 4/8	20 6/8 21 1/8	14 4/8	5 5	Cooke County	TX	Tim Williams	2004	32015
131 4/8	19 1/8 18 5/8	15 0/8	5 5	Carroll County	MS	Casey Stanford	2005	32015
131 4/8	21 7/8 22 1/8	18 6/8	5 5	Dodge County	MN	Terry Benda	2005	32015
*131 4/8	20 7/8 21 2/8	14 4/8	5 5	Faulkner County	AR	Kevin Lee Sanson	2005	32015
131 4/8	22 4/8 22 4/8	16 6/8	4 5	Union County	SD	Douglas Wagner	2005	32015
131 4/8	23 0/8 22 3/8	17 2/8	4 5	Wyoming County	WV	David Detrick	2005	32015
131 4/8	20 3/8 20 3/8	15 0/8	4 5	Tom Green County	TX	Ronnie Parsons	2005	32015
131 4/8	23 5/8 23 7/8	15 2/8	4 4	Worcester County	MA	Mark Stevens	2005	32015
131 4/8	21 2/8 22 2/8	17 0/8	5 5	Clayton County	IA	Craig A. Bries	2005	32015
131 4/8	20 1/8 20 6/8	14 2/8	6 5	Boone County	IA	Jason Loecker	2005	32015
131 4/8	22 6/8 22 2/8	15 2/8	6 5	Bolivar County	MS	Duke Morgan	2005	32015
*131 4/8	22 6/8 21 7/8	19 1/8	5 6	Adams County	IL	Timothy D. Walmsley	2006	32015
*131 4/8	21 0/8 20 2/8	17 6/8	4 4	Monmouth County	NJ	Tom Glowacka, Jr.	2006	32015
*131 4/8	20 3/8 20 6/8	15 2/8	4 4	Steuben County	IN	Rich McCarty	2006	32015
131 4/8	21 6/8 22 4/8	16 0/8	5 5	Waupaca County	WI	Chris Widoff	2006	32015
*131 4/8	23 5/8 23 6/8	17 3/8	4 5	Jefferson County	OH	Steve Peperis	2006	32015
131 4/8	21 0/8 20 4/8	19 2/8	4 5	Putnam County	IN	Monty Keyt	2006	32015
131 4/8	22 0/8 22 0/8	15 0/8	5 6	Pulaski County	KY	Calvin Rollyson	2006	32015
*131 4/8	20 5/8 19 5/8	16 6/8	5 4	Vernon County	WI	John Skau	2006	32015
*131 4/8	21 4/8 22 3/8	14 7/8	6 4	Floyd County	IA	Jason Crum	2006	32015
131 4/8	21 2/8 21 6/8	16 4/8	7 7	Green Lake County	WI	Chad R. Hoinacki	2006	32015
131 4/8	24 5/8 24 5/8	19 0/8	4 4	Woodson County	KS	Evan Hendricks	2006	32015
131 4/8	22 2/8 23 6/8	17 0/8	6 7	Marion County	IN	Brian J. Lamping	2006	32015
131 4/8	23 7/8 23 4/8	17 0/8	4 4	Madison Parish	LA	Joseph Gex	2006	32015
131 4/8	23 3/8 24 1/8	19 0/8	6 5	Livingston County	IL	Everett G. Roe, Jr.	2006	32015
131 4/8	20 6/8 18 2/8	15 0/8	5 5	Rosebud County	MT	Chad P. Lehman	2007	32015
131 4/8	22 7/8 23 7/8	17 4/8	4 5	Morris County	NJ	Lou Cornine	2007	32015
131 4/8	21 1/8 22 2/8	19 1/8	6 7	Thurston County	NE	Eric Ducklow	2007	32015
131 4/8	20 2/8 19 7/8	15 2/8	5 5	Sutton County	TX	Drake Shurley	2007	32015

Deer entries below 141 0/8, that appeared in the 6th Edition, are not included here, but are included on the accompanying CD (see page 119), and also in the Club's Records Archives.

WHITETAIL DEER (TYPICAL ANTLERS)

Minimum Score 125   Continued

SCORE	LENGTH OF R MAIN BEAM L	INSIDE SPREAD	NUMBER OF R POINTS L	AREA	STATE/ PROVINCE	HUNTER'S NAME	DATE	RANK
131 4/8	24 3/8 / 22 5/8	18 2/8	4 / 5	Polk County	WI	Shaun Hughes	2007	32015
131 4/8	21 3/8 / 21 0/8	18 6/8	4 / 5	Henry County	IL	Doug Gibson	2007	32015
131 4/8	23 2/8 / 23 5/8	14 1/8	8 / 6	Marion County	KS	Ron Selby	2007	32015
*131 4/8	23 1/8 / 23 5/8	15 1/8	5 / 4	Cloud County	KS	Jason Rourke	2007	32015
131 4/8	20 5/8 / 20 4/8	19 2/8	5 / 5	Taylor County	IA	Todd Tobin	2007	32015
131 4/8	21 3/8 / 20 7/8	13 6/8	5 / 5	Slope County	ND	Dion Waniorek	2007	32015
131 4/8	22 3/8 / 21 3/8	20 2/8	4 / 4	Hampden County	MA	Donald McLeod	2008	32015
131 4/8	21 1/8 / 20 3/8	16 2/8	6 / 5	Kosciusko County	IN	Brandon D. Salmons	2008	32015
*131 4/8	22 0/8 / 21 3/8	16 0/8	4 / 4	Ransom County	ND	Mike Johnson	2008	32015
131 4/8	20 4/8 / 21 2/8	15 2/8	5 / 5	Pulaski County	IN	Bryce C. Rasmussen	2008	32015
131 4/8	23 2/8 / 21 6/8	20 2/8	4 / 4	Hand County	SD	Dylan Deuter	2008	32015
*131 4/8	22 4/8 / 21 2/8	12 4/8	6 / 7	Westmoreland County	PA	William Flower	2008	32015
131 4/8	24 0/8 / 22 0/8	20 2/8	5 / 4	Charles County	MD	Lance Schiemer	2008	32015
131 4/8	21 2/8 / 19 6/8	19 0/8	5 / 6	Rock County	WI	Steven Woodstock	2009	32015
*131 4/8	22 7/8 / 22 1/8	20 6/8	5 / 5	Adams County	IL	George McCabe	2009	32015
*131 4/8	22 0/8 / 22 3/8	18 0/8	5 / 5	Trempealeau County	WI	Chad Prudlick	2009	32015
131 4/8	22 7/8 / 23 1/8	19 0/8	5 / 4	Fulton County	IL	Mike J. Trone	2009	32015
131 4/8	23 0/8 / 23 7/8	19 2/8	4 / 4	Marshall County	KS	Billy Silvia, Jr.	2009	32015
131 4/8	23 7/8 / 22 4/8	15 6/8	4 / 6	Portage County	WI	Jim Lilyquist	2009	32015
131 4/8	22 5/8 / 22 0/8	18 2/8	4 / 4	Monona County	IA	Thomas J. Pluhar	2009	32015
*131 4/8	22 4/8 / 22 4/8	20 4/8	5 / 4	Iron County	WI	Dan Geiger	2009	32015
131 4/8	23 3/8 / 23 7/8	18 4/8	5 / 4	Baker County	GA	Leon Spurlin	2010	32015
*131 4/8	22 3/8 / 22 1/8	16 2/8	4 / 5	Buffalo County	WI	Ed Romanowski	2010	32015
131 3/8	21 7/8 / 21 1/8	15 5/8	5 / 5	Chickasaw County	IA	James A. Harris	1994	32268
131 3/8	23 4/8 / 23 6/8	19 1/8	5 / 5	Benton County	IA	Thomas Harrelson	1995	32268
131 3/8	22 1/8 / 21 2/8	15 6/8	5 / 4	Lorain County	OH	Steven Reinhold	1998	32268
131 3/8	20 7/8 / 21 5/8	16 7/8	4 / 5	Pierce County	WI	Travis Wolf	1999	32268
131 3/8	20 1/8 / 19 6/8	15 1/8	5 / 5	Johnson County	IL	Alex Hensley	2000	32268
131 3/8	20 6/8 / 21 1/8	15 3/8	4 / 4	Outagamie County	WI	Gary Krull	2003	32268
131 3/8	21 4/8 / 21 2/8	14 7/8	5 / 5	Yankton County	SD	Scott Cutler	2003	32268
131 3/8	22 0/8 / 22 2/8	17 3/8	4 / 5	Franklin County	IN	Travis Isaacs	2003	32268
131 3/8	22 3/8 / 22 2/8	15 7/8	4 / 4	Sussex County	DE	Jeff Minor	2003	32268
*131 3/8	22 3/8 / 22 2/8	15 7/8	5 / 5	Waupaca County	WI	Greg Biggar	2004	32268
131 3/8	22 4/8 / 22 4/8	17 7/8	4 / 4	Branch County	MI	Bret R. Cary	2004	32268
131 3/8	22 7/8 / 23 3/8	20 1/8	6 / 5	Dauphin County	PA	David Swanger	2004	32268
*131 3/8	22 0/8 / 22 4/8	16 7/8	5 / 5	Anoka County	MN	Josh Johnson	2004	32268
131 3/8	24 0/8 / 23 6/8	18 1/8	4 / 6	Iowa County	IA	Dan Blount	2004	32268
131 3/8	24 5/8 / 24 4/8	22 1/8	3 / 3	Wood County	WI	Craig Hahm	2004	32268
131 3/8	23 2/8 / 23 6/8	20 2/8	4 / 5	Dunn County	WI	Paul Lindstrom	2004	32268
131 3/8	21 7/8 / 21 6/8	16 0/8	6 / 4	Montgomery County	IA	Dick Paul	2004	32268
131 3/8	23 6/8 / 25 0/8	18 2/8	5 / 5	Shelby County	IN	Marcus W. Eads	2004	32268
131 3/8	22 3/8 / 24 5/8	16 4/8	4 / 5	Lyon County	KS	Dusty Smart	2004	32268
131 3/8	21 7/8 / 22 1/8	18 5/8	6 / 7	Kewaunee County	WI	Andrew Zommers	2004	32268
131 3/8	21 5/8 / 21 7/8	16 1/8	5 / 5	Missoula County	MT	John T. Mandell	2005	32268
131 3/8	23 7/8 / 24 4/8	17 5/8	4 / 4	Walworth County	WI	Jessy Senft	2005	32268
131 3/8	21 1/8 / 21 1/8	15 1/8	5 / 5	Jefferson County	WI	Jason Turnacliff	2005	32268
*131 3/8	22 3/8 / 23 2/8	16 1/8	6 / 4	Sussex County	NJ	Tom Babcock	2005	32268
131 3/8	21 5/8 / 21 5/8	15 2/8	5 / 4	De Kalb County	IN	DeWayne Fiedler	2005	32268
131 3/8	23 4/8 / 17 1/8	20 5/8	5 / 5	Pike County	IL	Richard J. Van Buskirk	2005	32268
131 3/8	24 2/8 / 24 4/8	18 1/8	5 / 5	Harrison County	MO	C. Jeffery Lawson	2005	32268
*131 3/8	20 5/8 / 21 0/8	14 4/8	6 / 5	Woodson County	KS	Chad Grant	2005	32268
131 3/8	21 3/8 / 21 4/8	16 5/8	4 / 4	Cowley County	KS	Pat Giulioli	2005	32268
131 3/8	23 6/8 / 23 6/8	15 7/8	5 / 5	Anoka County	MN	Larry Hudson	2005	32268
131 3/8	22 0/8 / 21 4/8	16 7/8	4 / 4	Monroe County	NY	Robert Symonds	2005	32268
131 3/8	19 7/8 / 20 7/8	14 7/8	5 / 5	Powder River County	MT	Louis Sarris	2006	32268
131 3/8	20 1/8 / 20 3/8	15 3/8	5 / 5	Irwin County	GA	William M. Rousey, Jr.	2006	32268
*131 3/8	22 6/8 / 22 1/8	15 5/8	5 / 5	Sterling County	TX	Judd Adcock	2006	32268
131 3/8	21 6/8 / 22 2/8	20 1/8	5 / 5	Monroe County	NY	Christopher Whitmore	2006	32268
*131 3/8	22 6/8 / 22 6/8	16 1/8	4 / 4	Jackson County	OH	Casey Adkins	2006	32268
131 3/8	20 6/8 / 21 1/8	16 7/8	5 / 5	Waupaca County	WI	Daniel J. Bodway	2006	32268
131 3/8	23 1/8 / 23 6/8	17 5/8	5 / 5	Hand County	SD	Kevin R. Hvam	2006	32268
131 3/8	21 0/8 / 22 7/8	19 7/8	6 / 6	Potter County	PA	Dick Hillyard	2006	32268
*131 3/8	21 2/8 / 20 7/8	14 7/8	5 / 5	Schuyler County	IL	Robert Van Munster	2006	32268
131 3/8	23 1/8 / 23 1/8	17 3/8	4 / 4	Clark County	WI	Rick Hasler	2006	32268
*131 3/8	20 7/8 / 18 5/8	17 5/8	5 / 5	Dubuque County	IA	Kevin Schmidt	2006	32268
131 3/8	19 6/8 / 21 3/8	15 7/8	5 / 6	Mills County	TX	Luke Drolet	2006	32268
131 3/8	20 1/8 / 20 0/8	15 7/8	5 / 5	Lake County	IL	Bill Barrett	2007	32268
131 3/8	21 7/8 / 21 5/8	17 4/8	5 / 6	Greene County	OH	Charles J. Cooper	2007	32268
131 3/8	18 2/8 / 17 6/8	14 1/8	6 / 5	Montcalm County	MI	Travis M. Opper	2007	32268
131 3/8	23 4/8 / 23 1/8	19 3/8	4 / 4	Livingston County	NY	John Burns	2007	32268
*131 3/8	21 6/8 / 21 3/8	17 7/8	5 / 5	Logan County	WV	Travis Belcher	2007	32268
131 3/8	21 7/8 / 21 3/8	18 1/8	4 / 5	Hendricks County	IN	Joe Johnson	2007	32268
*131 3/8	20 5/8 / 20 5/8	16 5/8	5 / 5	Putnam County	MO	Mark G. DeGenova	2007	32268
*131 3/8	22 4/8 / 22 4/8	17 3/8	5 / 5	Monroe County	NY	Paul R. Swanger	2007	32268
*131 3/8	21 1/8 / 22 0/8	14 5/8	4 / 5	Sauk County	WI	Tim Seils	2007	32268
131 3/8	22 1/8 / 22 3/8	20 3/8	5 / 5	Huntington County	IN	Mark Whitacre	2007	32268
*131 3/8	21 1/8 / 21 0/8	17 0/8	6 / 5	Linn County	KS	Gregory Jones	2007	32268
131 3/8	21 5/8 / 21 1/8	17 1/8	4 / 4	Trempealeau County	WI	Scott Schock	2007	32268
*131 3/8	20 6/8 / 21 4/8	18 1/8	5 / 5	Houston County	MN	Joe Magee	2008	32268
*131 3/8	23 3/8 / 25 1/8	17 7/8	5 / 4	Delaware County	OH	Rob Donahue	2008	32268
131 3/8	21 4/8 / 21 7/8	16 1/8	5 / 5	Marquette County	WI	Robert L. Kampen	2008	32268
131 3/8	22 0/8 / 22 2/8	17 5/8	5 / 5	Halifax County	NC	John Clark Purvis, Sr.	2008	32268
*131 3/8	24 4/8 / 25 0/8	18 5/8	3 / 4	Salem County	NJ	John Catalano	2008	32268
*131 3/8	23 6/8 / 25 6/8	24 1/8	3 / 3	Berks County	PA	JoAnn Eshleman	2008	32268
131 3/8	23 0/8 / 23 7/8	18 4/8	5 / 5	Carroll County	IL	Jeff Carlson	2008	32268
131 3/8	21 5/8 / 23 0/8	15 7/8	5 / 5	Clayton County	IA	Joey Pierce	2008	32268
131 3/8	23 0/8 / 23 4/8	16 6/8	5 / 5	Wyoming County	WV	Jared Lee Garrison	2008	32268
131 3/8	20 5/8 / 20 5/8	16 5/8	5 / 5	Dunn County	WI	Scott Freiermuth	2008	32268
*131 3/8	23 0/8 / 21 7/8	18 7/8	5 / 5	Dickinson County	KS	Adam Beason	2008	32268
131 3/8	22 2/8 / 23 2/8	21 7/8	4 / 4	Monmouth County	NJ	Frank Bennett	2008	32268
*131 3/8	23 2/8 / 23 0/8	15 2/8	5 / 5	Montgomery County	IL	Jeremy Shipman	2008	32268
131 3/8	24 3/8 / 23 0/8	15 7/8	6 / 5	Dougherty County	GA	Glenn Paschal	2009	32268
131 3/8	23 1/8 / 21 2/8	17 0/8	6 / 8	Sullivan County	MO	Casey A. Blum	2009	32268
131 3/8	21 4/8 / 21 4/8	19 1/8	4 / 5	Jackson County	OH	Roger Brewer	2009	32268
*131 3/8	19 6/8 / 20 3/8	16 7/8	5 / 5	Meeker County	MN	Shawn Nelson	2009	32268

WHITETAIL DEER (TYPICAL ANTLERS)

Minimum Score 125   Continued

SCORE	LENGTH OF MAIN BEAM R	LENGTH OF MAIN BEAM L	INSIDE SPREAD	NUMBER OF POINTS R	NUMBER OF POINTS L	AREA	STATE/ PROVINCE	HUNTER'S NAME	DATE	RANK
131 3/8	21 7/8	22 0/8	18 1/8	5	5	Saginaw County	MI	Daniel R. Wendling	2009	32268
131 3/8	21 6/8	21 4/8	15 1/8	5	5	Buffalo County	WI	Dean Dieckman	2009	32268
131 3/8	20 5/8	19 7/8	14 1/8	5	5	Franklin County	IN	Casey Prifogle	2009	32268
131 3/8	23 2/8	22 5/8	14 3/8	5	5	Marquette County	WI	Dennis J. Kohlmeyer	2009	32268
*131 3/8	22 5/8	23 3/8	18 4/8	5	5	Bayfield County	WI	Daryl Jensen	2009	32268
131 3/8	25 5/8	24 6/8	15 2/8	5	7	Monroe County	WI	Michael K. Miller	2009	32268
131 3/8	23 0/8	21 5/8	18 6/8	4	5	Douglas County	NE	Steve Combs	2009	32268
131 3/8	23 5/8	23 1/8	19 3/8	4	5	Burnett County	WI	Kent Bassett	2009	32268
*131 3/8	22 5/8	22 4/8	17 7/8	4	4	Waupaca County	WI	Andrew Millard	2010	32268
131 2/8	20 0/8	21 0/8	16 0/8	5	5	Faribault County	MN	Bryan Schroeder	1988	32496
131 2/8	21 6/8	21 6/8	15 7/8	6	6	Cedar County	NE	Kent Hochstein	2000	32496
131 2/8	20 5/8	20 4/8	15 6/8	5	6	Lyon County	IA	John L. Stillson	2000	32496
131 2/8	20 7/8	21 0/8	16 4/8	5	4	Clearwater	ALB	Terry Brew	2000	32496
131 2/8	21 3/8	22 6/8	19 0/8	4	5	La Crosse County	WI	Gary Thompson	2002	32496
131 2/8	19 6/8	19 0/8	18 0/8	5	5	Bear Creek	ALB	Rick Martin	2002	32496
131 2/8	21 4/8	22 2/8	17 6/8	5	5	Itasca County	MN	Curt Youngkin	2003	32496
131 2/8	20 2/8	21 1/8	16 0/8	6	5	Grant County	WI	Jerod J. Ray	2003	32496
131 2/8	24 3/8	24 4/8	20 1/8	3	5	Sangamon County	IL	Scot Harvey	2003	32496
131 2/8	21 5/8	20 4/8	17 4/8	4	4	Will County	IL	James E. Giese	2003	32496
131 2/8	24 2/8	25 0/8	19 6/8	4	4	Berks County	PA	Glenn A. Sunday	2003	32496
131 2/8	22 2/8	20 7/8	16 6/8	4	5	Iowa County	IA	Mike Rife	2003	32496
131 2/8	23 7/8	22 7/8	17 2/8	4	6	Slope County	ND	Jim Schwendinger	2004	32496
131 2/8	21 6/8	21 4/8	16 2/8	8	6	Nodaway County	MO	Jeremy R. Tobin	2004	32496
131 2/8	22 3/8	21 7/8	17 4/8	5	5	Barron County	WI	Cody Kruger	2004	32496
131 2/8	21 7/8	22 6/8	18 5/8	5	5	La Salle County	IL	Michael J. Fenwick	2004	32496
*131 2/8	24 0/8	24 4/8	18 4/8	5	6	Halifax County	VA	Paul Riggs	2004	32496
*131 2/8	23 5/8	23 6/8	14 2/8	4	5	Buffalo County	WI	Joe Jilot	2004	32496
*131 2/8	20 1/8	20 1/8	16 0/8	5	6	Freeborn County	MN	Scott Crabtree	2004	32496
*131 2/8	23 3/8	24 0/8	17 0/8	6	5	Stark County	IL	Mark Vancil	2004	32496
131 2/8	21 6/8	23 0/8	16 6/8	5	4	Chickasaw County	IA	Carlie Schnoebelen	2004	32496
131 2/8	21 7/8	22 5/8	16 2/8	5	5	Adams County	WI	Richard H. Christensen	2004	32496
*131 2/8	21 4/8	21 1/8	16 4/8	5	5	Ottawa County	MI	Doug Lezman	2004	32496
131 2/8	24 0/8	23 5/8	18 3/8	6	5	Nowata County	OK	Brandon McClain	2004	32496
131 2/8	22 2/8	22 2/8	17 4/8	5	4	Defiance County	OH	William D. Riley	2004	32496
*131 2/8	23 2/8	22 7/8	17 4/8	4	4	Waukesha County	WI	Joel P. Smith	2004	32496
131 2/8	22 6/8	23 0/8	16 4/8	5	5	Cass County	ND	Paul Muscha	2004	32496
131 2/8	21 5/8	20 2/8	16 2/8	4	4	Bottineau County	ND	Jeffery Hoff	2005	32496
*131 2/8	24 1/8	25 5/8	17 7/8	5	5	Green County	WI	John Albrecht	2005	32496
131 2/8	21 3/8	22 2/8	15 4/8	5	5	Dauphin County	PA	Curtis J. Hoy	2005	32496
131 2/8	21 6/8	22 5/8	17 0/8	4	4	Wood County	WV	Jeffrey D. Eddy	2005	32496
131 2/8	23 3/8	22 0/8	17 0/8	4	6	Vernon County	WI	Kevin W. Bauman	2005	32496
131 2/8	21 6/8	21 4/8	16 4/8	5	5	Pratt County	KS	Lonnie Desmarais	2005	32496
131 2/8	22 5/8	22 7/8	22 2/8	4	4	Pepin County	WI	Jerre Lerum	2005	32496
131 2/8	21 5/8	21 4/8	16 0/8	4	5	Marquette County	WI	Craig Coda	2005	32496
131 2/8	22 2/8	22 1/8	17 6/8	4	4	Dougherty County	GA	Thomas Edmonds	2005	32496
131 2/8	22 1/8	22 2/8	15 2/8	5	5	Muskingum County	OH	James Hamilton, Jr.	2005	32496
131 2/8	20 3/8	19 5/8	12 6/8	5	6	Stevens County	WA	Steve Mitchell	2005	32496
131 2/8	23 7/8	24 7/8	19 4/8	4	4	James City County	VA	Jerry F. Thomas	2005	32496
131 2/8	21 0/8	21 0/8	16 5/8	5	5	Beaverhead County	MT	Donald S. Dvoroznak	2006	32496
131 2/8	21 6/8	21 6/8	16 0/8	4	4	Flathead County	MT	Ryan Shima	2006	32496
*131 2/8	22 7/8	22 1/8	19 2/8	4	4	Isabella County	MI	Paul R. Weber	2006	32496
131 2/8	21 6/8	20 6/8	17 6/8	5	4	Linn County	KS	Larry W. Peterson	2006	32496
*131 2/8	20 6/8	22 3/8	19 4/8	6	4	Lake County	IN	Richard T. Booker	2006	32496
131 2/8	22 0/8	21 7/8	17 2/8	5	5	Brown County	KS	Garen McGinnis	2006	32496
131 2/8	20 6/8	20 5/8	17 6/8	5	5	Buffalo County	WI	Michael J. Zuhlsdorf	2006	32496
131 2/8	20 4/8	19 6/8	15 4/8	5	4	Charles Mix County	SD	Bryan L. Barness	2006	32496
*131 2/8	21 5/8	20 2/8	16 5/8	6	5	Refugio County	TX	Gary Hayek	2006	32496
131 2/8	23 1/8	24 1/8	16 6/8	4	4	New Castle County	DE	Seawraj Vidyanand	2006	32496
131 2/8	22 1/8	21 3/8	17 4/8	4	5	Douglas County	WI	Timothy G. Stroik	2006	32496
131 2/8	20 0/8	20 6/8	14 0/8	5	5	Kenedy County	TX	Marc Bartoskewitz	2006	32496
131 2/8	21 5/8	20 7/8	17 2/8	5	5	San Saba County	TX	Adam Huggins	2007	32496
131 2/8	21 4/8	21 4/8	14 4/8	4	4	Gasconade County	MO	Brady Hicks	2007	32496
*131 2/8	23 6/8	19 3/8	22 5/8	6	7	Morgan County	OH	Jeff Bryant	2007	32496
131 2/8	21 7/8	21 6/8	18 4/8	4	5	Ionia County	MI	Robert Bevington	2007	32496
131 2/8	21 6/8	22 5/8	19 4/8	6	5	Cass County	MI	Fred R. Grice	2007	32496
*131 2/8	20 3/8	20 5/8	15 0/8	5	5	Knox County	MO	Bruce Wilken	2007	32496
*131 2/8	22 2/8	22 1/8	15 7/8	7	9	Holmes County	OH	Joseph Camera	2007	32496
131 2/8	22 3/8	22 7/8	16 3/8	6	4	Shawano County	WI	Whitney K. Pluger	2007	32496
131 2/8	23 4/8	23 6/8	19 0/8	5	5	Schuyler County	NY	Sam Wright	2007	32496
131 2/8	20 4/8	19 0/8	18 4/8	5	5	Winnebago County	WI	Dick Palecek	2007	32496
*131 2/8	22 4/8	22 4/8	17 2/8	4	4	Shawano County	WI	Ron Vander Kelen	2007	32496
*131 2/8	22 0/8	22 1/8	17 0/8	5	4	Rice County	KS	Paul W. Townes III	2007	32496
131 2/8	20 4/8	21 0/8	17 0/8	5	5	Washington County	KS	Tony Perri	2007	32496
131 2/8	23 3/8	23 4/8	18 6/8	4	5	Cottle County	TX	Terry Rice	2007	32496
131 2/8	23 2/8	21 6/8	13 4/8	5	6	Coal County	OK	Wayne Pyron	2007	32496
131 2/8	20 7/8	22 0/8	19 2/8	4	4	Edmunds County	SD	John Carney	2008	32496
131 2/8	23 0/8	22 7/8	18 6/8	4	5	Harrison County	WV	Stephen Felosa	2008	32496
131 2/8	21 4/8	23 1/8	15 0/8	5	5	Indiana County	PA	Joseph L. Pacconi	2008	32496
131 2/8	21 0/8	20 6/8	14 2/8	4	4	Macon County	GA	Doug Lloyd	2008	32496
131 2/8	20 4/8	21 0/8	16 2/8	5	6	Brown County	SD	Tyler Efraimson	2008	32496
131 2/8	22 6/8	22 4/8	16 6/8	7	6	Indiana County	PA	James A. Capitosti	2008	32496
131 2/8	22 0/8	21 5/8	16 0/8	4	4	Woodbury County	IA	Michael L. Wheat	2008	32496
*131 2/8	21 1/8	19 3/8	16 6/8	5	5	Anderson County	KS	Royce J. Carter	2008	32496
131 2/8	24 1/8	22 4/8	17 4/8	5	4	Mercer County	PA	Cliff Baker	2008	32496
131 2/8	22 1/8	22 3/8	19 2/8	7	6	Ripley County	IN	Bryan Miller	2008	32496
*131 2/8	21 7/8	22 7/8	14 6/8	4	5	Chester County	PA	Mark Mummert	2008	32496
*131 2/8	22 7/8	23 1/8	17 0/8	4	5	Clayton County	IA	Brian M. Oberfoell	2008	32496
131 2/8	22 4/8	21 6/8	16 6/8	5	5	Clermont County	OH	Kyle Smith	2008	32496
*131 2/8	22 7/8	21 6/8	15 4/8	5	6	Washington County	OH	James A. Sallee	2008	32496
*131 2/8	26 7/8	26 0/8	16 2/8	6	7	Gallia County	OH	Jefferson D. Miller, Jr.	2009	32496
131 2/8	19 2/8	19 5/8	14 3/8	5	6	Becker County	MN	Dominic L. Johnson	2009	32496
131 2/8	20 1/8	19 6/8	16 4/8	5	5	Pierce County	WI	Michael J. Gunderson	2009	32496
*131 2/8	22 1/8	21 6/8	15 3/8	4	5	Keith County	NE	Brad J. Baldwin	2009	32496
131 2/8	23 4/8	23 4/8	18 5/8	5	5	Morris County	KS	Stephen Hathcock	2009	32496
*131 2/8	22 7/8	23 4/8	14 6/8	5	4	St. Croix County	WI	Darin Gilbertson	2009	32496

Deer entries below 141 0/8, that appeared in the 6th Edition, are not included here, but are included on the accompanying CD (see page 119), and also in the Club's Records Archives.

WHITETAIL DEER (TYPICAL ANTLERS)

Minimum Score 125   Continued

SCORE	LENGTH OF MAIN BEAM R	LENGTH OF MAIN BEAM L	INSIDE SPREAD	NUMBER OF POINTS R	NUMBER OF POINTS L	AREA	STATE/ PROVINCE	HUNTER'S NAME	DATE	RANK
*131 2/8	21 4/8	22 1/8	17 0/8	5	4	Ontario County	NY	John M. Gallo	2009	32496
*131 2/8	21 6/8	22 4/8	16 4/8	5	4	Cumberland County	IL	Nicholas Watkins	2009	32496
131 2/8	21 7/8	22 0/8	20 0/8	4	4	Columbia County	WI	Todd D. Lerum	2009	32496
131 2/8	24 4/8	23 0/8	17 4/8	6	5	Delaware County	OH	Michael Finamore	2009	32496
131 2/8	24 6/8	24 0/8	18 3/8	5	5	Fayette County	OH	Casey Long	2009	32496
131 1/8	23 6/8	22 4/8	18 1/8	4	4	Buffalo County	WI	Jerry Rucinski	2002	32758
131 1/8	24 7/8	23 2/8	21 7/8	6	7	Bucks County	PA	R. Brett Hoffman	2002	32758
131 1/8	21 6/8	23 1/8	17 3/8	5	4	Bucks County	PA	Glenn L. Weiss	2002	32758
131 1/8	22 4/8	21 7/8	17 0/8	4	5	Clay County	MO	Paul S. Ehinger	2003	32758
131 1/8	21 4/8	21 3/8	18 3/8	5	5	Jackson County	WI	Christopher Cornelius	2004	32758
131 1/8	21 5/8	21 6/8	19 1/8	5	4	Chicot County	AR	Louis Lambiotte	2004	32758
131 1/8	21 7/8	23 0/8	15 3/8	4	5	Hanover County	VA	Wayne Hardiman	2004	32758
131 1/8	23 2/8	24 0/8	19 1/8	4	4	Jefferson County	WI	Scott Maass	2004	32758
131 1/8	23 1/8	23 1/8	16 4/8	5	5	Schuylkill County	PA	Thomas Bright	2004	32758
*131 1/8	21 5/8	22 0/8	20 0/8	5	5	Middlesex County	MA	Peter Carpinteri	2004	32758
131 1/8	24 2/8	23 7/8	17 5/8	5	4	Ashland County	OH	Tomas G. Constance	2004	32758
*131 1/8	25 1/8	23 4/8	15 1/8	5	6	Pike County	IL	Barry G. Estes	2004	32758
131 1/8	21 7/8	23 1/8	18 1/8	4	5	Morgan County	IL	David Troxell	2004	32758
131 1/8	21 5/8	20 0/8	16 0/8	6	5	Jackson County	IL	Tim Cobin, Jr.	2004	32758
131 1/8	23 3/8	22 4/8	18 1/8	4	4	Lake County	IL	Ken Wodek III	2004	32758
131 1/8	24 2/8	25 4/8	17 1/8	5	4	Harvey County	KS	Richard Krehbiel	2004	32758
131 1/8	20 1/8	20 6/8	15 7/8	5	4	San Saba County	TX	Kenneth M. Thompson	2004	32758
131 1/8	21 4/8	22 6/8	18 1/8	4	4	Nodaway County	MO	Warren Hurley	2004	32758
*131 1/8	23 5/8	23 0/8	19 1/8	4	6	Charles County	MD	Tristan Taylor	2005	32758
131 1/8	22 6/8	22 6/8	16 3/8	5	5	Alachua County	FL	Glenn Harrell	2005	32758
131 1/8	22 0/8	21 7/8	20 2/8	5	4	Grundy County	IL	David Both	2005	32758
131 1/8	20 5/8	21 5/8	14 3/8	5	5	Dunn County	WI	Eric Stuart	2005	32758
131 1/8	21 7/8	22 1/8	16 1/8	6	8	Pike County	MO	Aaron Straube	2005	32758
131 1/8	21 6/8	21 6/8	15 7/8	5	5	Tioga County	NY	Greg J. Nichols	2005	32758
*131 1/8	21 2/8	20 5/8	14 5/8	5	5	Green Lake County	WI	Ron Bachand	2005	32758
131 1/8	22 1/8	22 2/8	15 5/8	4	5	Boone County	MO	Stephen Claypool	2005	32758
131 1/8	19 7/8	20 5/8	16 7/8	5	5	Edgar County	IL	Robert Agnew	2005	32758
*131 1/8	25 0/8	24 4/8	20 6/8	5	5	Caroline County	MD	Tom Scott	2005	32758
*131 1/8	23 4/8	23 2/8	17 3/8	4	4	Hamilton County	OH	Jon Goldsberry	2005	32758
131 1/8	22 0/8	22 1/8	19 1/8	5	5	Westchester County	NY	Gus A. Congemi	2005	32758
*131 1/8	22 3/8	21 6/8	15 1/8	6	5	Clare County	MI	Ben Jones	2006	32758
131 1/8	23 3/8	22 1/8	17 1/8	4	4	Johnson County	IL	Charles Pate	2006	32758
*131 1/8	21 3/8	20 7/8	14 3/8	5	5	Miller County	MO	Will Patterson	2006	32758
131 1/8	23 4/8	22 6/8	17 2/8	5	5	Jackson County	WI	Douglas P. Rentschler	2006	32758
*131 1/8	22 5/8	25 5/8	18 0/8	5	5	Pendleton County	KY	Kathy Holland	2006	32758
131 1/8	19 7/8	20 2/8	16 5/8	5	5	Rawlins County	KS	Edward D. Porubsky	2006	32758
131 1/8	21 5/8	22 0/8	17 3/8	6	9	Green Lake County	WI	Robert N. Warren	2006	32758
131 1/8	20 7/8	22 4/8	15 5/8	4	4	Plymouth County	IA	Kyle Schlesser	2006	32758
131 1/8	23 0/8	22 5/8	18 7/8	5	5	Delaware County	IA	John T. Kuckler	2006	32758
*131 1/8	22 1/8	20 5/8	16 2/8	6	5	Douglas County	WI	Rodger B. Olby	2006	32758
*131 1/8	25 3/8	26 0/8	18 2/8	6	6	Hancock County	IL	Richard J. Ruta, Jr.	2006	32758
131 1/8	22 6/8	22 0/8	16 1/8	5	5	Johnson County	WY	Russell Bell	2007	32758
*131 1/8	22 3/8	22 7/8	16 7/8	6	5	Rock Island County	IL	C. Scott Kave	2007	32758
131 1/8	23 3/8	23 1/8	17 3/8	4	4	Labette County	KS	Ronnie McCorkell	2007	32758
131 1/8	22 0/8	22 7/8	15 5/8	4	4	Parke County	IN	Steve W. Buckallew	2007	32758
131 1/8	20 1/8	19 6/8	19 7/8	5	5	Douglas County	WI	Craig Golembiewski, Jr.	2007	32758
*131 1/8	20 2/8	20 1/8	13 3/8	5	5	Kinney County	TX	York Patterson	2007	32758
131 1/8	20 1/8	20 1/8	17 5/8	5	5	Trempealeau County	WI	Gary Jensen	2007	32758
131 1/8	23 0/8	23 4/8	19 2/8	6	7	Morgan County	OH	Richard L. Newson	2007	32758
131 1/8	20 1/8	20 7/8	16 7/8	4	4	Brown County	OH	David Montgomery	2007	32758
131 1/8	22 5/8	23 3/8	16 7/8	5	6	Henry County	IA	Taylor Buchholz	2007	32758
*131 1/8	24 3/8	23 5/8	18 5/8	4	4	Buffalo County	WI	Wayne Leeland	2007	32758
*131 1/8	21 1/8	22 0/8	13 3/8	5	6	Rock Island County	IL	Ronald F. Lax	2007	32758
*131 1/8	21 0/8	22 0/8	15 5/8	5	5	Dubois County	IN	Brian Partenheimer	2007	32758
*131 1/8	22 4/8	22 4/8	15 1/8	5	4	Lake County	IN	Tim Easton	2007	32758
131 1/8	24 2/8	23 1/8	16 7/8	6	5	Orangeburg County	SC	Lee Prickett	2008	32758
131 1/8	21 4/8	20 6/8	15 5/8	4	4	Grant County	WI	Scott LaBarge	2008	32758
*131 1/8	18 1/8	18 6/8	18 1/8	5	5	Somerset County	PA	Brian W. Hahl	2008	32758
*131 1/8	22 5/8	23 2/8	14 7/8	4	4	Ottawa County	OH	Mike Rosiak	2008	32758
131 1/8	21 6/8	21 3/8	17 4/8	7	6	Buffalo County	WI	Keith Michlig	2008	32758
131 1/8	24 4/8	24 2/8	19 5/8	4	5	Buffalo County	WI	Don J. Kane	2008	32758
131 1/8	23 0/8	21 3/8	15 2/8	6	6	Huntingdon County	PA	Terry Woodward	2008	32758
131 1/8	21 4/8	21 2/8	16 5/8	4	5	Morgan County	CO	Phil Lopez	2008	32758
*131 1/8	24 1/8	24 3/8	18 7/8	5	5	Steuben County	IN	Matt Hanna	2008	32758
131 1/8	22 0/8	21 4/8	18 1/8	4	4	Chester County	PA	Ryan Slopey	2008	32758
*131 1/8	21 0/8	19 6/8	16 1/8	4	4	Jewell County	KS	Angela K. Walk	2008	32758
131 1/8	20 7/8	21 7/8	15 7/8	4	5	Washington County	PA	Carl Jury	2008	32758
131 1/8	20 7/8	20 3/8	17 0/8	6	7	Custer County	SD	Chad P. Lehman	2008	32758
131 1/8	20 4/8	21 1/8	15 2/8	7	6	Bingham County	ID	Stephen J. Hammond	2009	32758
131 1/8	21 6/8	22 2/8	15 2/8	6	5	Allegany County	NY	Karen Gallmann	2009	32758
131 1/8	21 1/8	21 1/8	18 5/8	4	4	Cass County	ND	Jarrod Bogardus	2009	32758
*131 1/8	20 5/8	21 4/8	16 2/8	6	5	Pike County	IL	Barry Potteiger	2009	32758
*131 1/8	23 3/8	23 0/8	18 0/8	4	5	Henderson County	KY	Robert W. Tatro III	2009	32758
*131 1/8	20 5/8	20 2/8	16 1/8	5	5	Jefferson County	KS	Shane Crawford	2009	32758
*131 1/8	21 6/8	21 5/8	16 0/8	5	6	Washburn County	WI	Nate Steines	2009	32758
131 1/8	22 1/8	22 6/8	17 5/8	5	5	Menard County	IL	Douglas R. Lacross	2009	32758
131 1/8	20 0/8	19 1/8	17 4/8	6	6	Hot Springs County	WY	John Sarvis	2010	32758
131 1/8	25 4/8	25 3/8	18 5/8	5	5	Clearfield County	PA	Jeremiah Weber	2010	32758
131 0/8	23 7/8	23 4/8	17 6/8	6	4	Dodge County	MN	Joshua Thiemann	1995	33005
131 0/8	25 0/8	24 7/8	18 0/8	4	4	Berrien County	MI	Joseph P. Humphreys	1998	33005
131 0/8	23 0/8	22 2/8	19 2/8	5	6	Hardin County	IA	Chad D. Hagen	1999	33005
131 0/8	21 4/8	21 5/8	17 2/8	5	10	Clarion County	PA	David J. Seth	2002	33005
131 0/8	19 1/8	19 1/8	13 2/8	5	5	Nodaway County	MO	Dave Messner	2002	33005
131 0/8	22 3/8	23 0/8	15 0/8	7	6	Cowley County	KS	David M. Saleme	2003	33005
*131 0/8	23 5/8	22 7/8	17 5/8	7	5	Tama County	IA	Duane Bossman	2003	33005
131 0/8	22 2/8	21 6/8	15 1/8	5	4	Indiana County	PA	Eric Norberg	2003	33005
131 0/8	22 2/8	22 5/8	17 0/8	4	4	Plymouth County	MA	Ronald E. Carreau	2003	33005
131 0/8	22 0/8	22 0/8	17 4/8	5	4	Jackson County	IA	Jon E. Rath	2003	33005
*131 0/8	20 3/8	21 2/8	18 2/8	5	5	Allegheny County	PA	David P. Tirpak	2004	33005
131 0/8	24 4/8	22 3/8	16 0/8	4	4	Cattaraugus County	NY	Chris Gruka	2004	33005

586

WHITETAIL DEER (TYPICAL ANTLERS)

Minimum Score 125   Continued

SCORE	LENGTH OF R MAIN BEAM L	INSIDE SPREAD	NUMBER OF R POINTS L		AREA	STATE/ PROVINCE	HUNTER'S NAME	DATE	RANK
131 0/8	21 4/8	20 7/8	16 6/8	5	5	Marquette County	WI	John W. Steuck	2004	33005
131 0/8	19 6/8	19 6/8	15 6/8	6	5	Racine County	WI	Greg Hanson	2004	33005
131 0/8	23 6/8	23 5/8	17 0/8	4	4	Clermont County	OH	Fred Wilder	2004	33005
131 0/8	22 6/8	23 0/8	15 4/8	4	5	Ripley County	MO	Bruce Cole Newton	2004	33005
131 0/8	21 2/8	21 1/8	15 4/8	4	4	Montgomery County	KS	Jerry W. Laton	2004	33005
*131 0/8	22 4/8	22 6/8	17 2/8	4	5	Allegheny County	PA	Kevin Bush	2004	33005
131 0/8	20 6/8	21 5/8	18 4/8	5	6	Calhoun County	IL	David James	2004	33005
131 0/8	19 7/8	19 4/8	17 0/8	5	4	Logan County	WV	Michael Heath Roop	2004	33005
131 0/8	20 7/8	21 5/8	15 0/8	4	5	Fulton County	IL	Floyd Cunningham	2004	33005
*131 0/8	23 7/8	23 4/8	20 0/8	4	4	Wyandot County	OH	Scott Mouser	2004	33005
131 0/8	18 6/8	18 3/8	14 0/8	4	4	St. Louis County	MO	Chris Murphy	2004	33005
*131 0/8	23 2/8	23 2/8	22 0/8	4	4	Marathon County	WI	Stephen F. Riggle	2004	33005
131 0/8	23 0/8	23 5/8	19 4/8	4	4	Terrell County	TX	Jason Wrinkle	2004	33005
131 0/8	22 0/8	22 2/8	16 6/8	5	4	Buffalo County	WI	Stan Godfrey	2004	33005
131 0/8	22 0/8	22 2/8	17 3/8	6	6	Irion County	TX	Ronnie Parsons	2005	33005
131 0/8	20 4/8	20 6/8	16 2/8	5	5	Jumping Pound Creek	ALB	Dave Browne	2005	33005
131 0/8	24 1/8	23 3/8	17 0/8	4	4	Brown County	IL	Dana P. Dille	2005	33005
131 0/8	22 5/8	22 2/8	17 2/8	4	5	Tuscarawas County	OH	Steve Archer	2005	33005
131 0/8	21 6/8	22 1/8	18 0/8	4	4	Columbia County	WI	Paul W. Maguire	2005	33005
131 0/8	26 5/8	24 1/8	17 4/8	4	4	Licking County	OH	Todd McDonald	2005	33005
131 0/8	26 0/8	25 4/8	22 0/8	4	5	Dubuque County	IA	Paul D. Meissner	2005	33005
131 0/8	22 3/8	22 3/8	17 4/8	4	4	Mills County	IA	Brian Kehrli	2005	33005
*131 0/8	18 6/8	19 2/8	15 2/8	5	5	Macoupin County	IL	Christopher Gleason	2005	33005
*131 0/8	22 6/8	22 4/8	16 4/8	5	5	Harrison County	IA	Scott Tulenchik	2005	33005
131 0/8	24 2/8	23 4/8	17 6/8	4	4	Venango County	PA	Scott V. Salvo	2005	33005
*131 0/8	19 2/8	19 0/8	15 4/8	5	5	Cavalier County	ND	Michelle Logie	2005	33005
131 0/8	21 7/8	21 6/8	17 2/8	4	4	Rusk County	WI	Ryan Pagenkopf	2006	33005
*131 0/8	22 6/8	22 4/8	17 4/8	4	4	Washington County	PA	Gary J. Stiegel, Jr.	2006	33005
131 0/8	22 0/8	21 3/8	18 0/8	4	4	Allegheny County	PA	Matthew Spak	2006	33005
131 0/8	18 2/8	19 1/8	13 0/8	6	6	Keya Paha County	NE	Terry Marcukaitis	2006	33005
*131 0/8	22 5/8	22 3/8	16 4/8	4	4	Buffalo County	WI	Jason Anderson	2006	33005
131 0/8	22 0/8	22 1/8	14 6/8	5	5	Dearborn County	IN	James Sellers	2006	33005
*131 0/8	23 7/8	23 4/8	15 4/8	4	4	Kosciusko County	IN	Marc Andrews	2006	33005
131 0/8	23 4/8	24 0/8	17 0/8	6	8	Monroe County	MI	Mike Alen Heiden	2006	33005
*131 0/8	22 0/8	21 2/8	15 2/8	4	4	Jackson County	WI	Brian D. Lee	2006	33005
131 0/8	23 0/8	23 0/8	19 2/8	4	4	Barry County	MI	William M. Bivens	2006	33005
131 0/8	21 4/8	23 1/8	18 6/8	6	5	Portage County	OH	Jesse Withem	2006	33005
131 0/8	24 5/8	22 0/8	17 4/8	5	5	Geary County	KS	Gary A. Kepley	2006	33005
131 0/8	21 2/8	21 5/8	15 0/8	4	4	Stoddard County	MO	Lawson Metcalf	2007	33005
131 0/8	21 6/8	21 5/8	14 1/8	6	5	Cascade County	MT	Greg Grass	2007	33005
*131 0/8	22 2/8	21 4/8	17 0/8	4	4	De Kalb County	MO	Jim W. Martin	2007	33005
131 0/8	20 6/8	26 0/8	16 4/8	5	5	Dodge County	MN	Ed Pitzenberger	2007	33005
131 0/8	21 4/8	22 1/8	17 6/8	4	5	Price County	WI	Richard Kirchmeyer	2007	33005
*131 0/8	23 4/8	23 5/8	16 2/8	4	4	Pulaski County	AR	James Alexander Rogers III	2007	33005
131 0/8	24 3/8	24 4/8	17 2/8	4	5	Licking County	OH	Zach Thone	2007	33005
131 0/8	23 0/8	22 7/8	17 0/8	5	5	Adair County	MO	Mike Ploch	2007	33005
131 0/8	20 5/8	20 6/8	18 2/8	5	5	Cass County	IL	Edward Larson	2007	33005
*131 0/8	24 4/8	24 0/8	17 6/8	4	4	Butler County	OH	William P. Wurzelbacher	2007	33005
131 0/8	23 7/8	24 6/8	17 6/8	6	6	Anderson County	KS	Bob Morton	2007	33005
131 0/8	20 6/8	19 6/8	15 4/8	5	6	Grant County	ND	Matt Meidinger	2007	33005
131 0/8	23 0/8	22 4/8	15 5/8	6	5	Guthrie County	IA	Frank Moraco	2007	33005
*131 0/8	23 1/8	21 5/8	17 6/8	4	4	Greene County	IN	Tom Hudak	2007	33005
*131 0/8	22 5/8	21 4/8	17 6/8	4	3	Richardson County	NE	Jerry N. Roever	2007	33005
131 0/8	21 6/8	21 2/8	16 6/8	5	5	Noble County	OH	Jimmie D. Bates	2007	33005
131 0/8	25 1/8	24 2/8	17 4/8	5	4	Fulton County	GA	Bob Coombs	2007	33005
131 0/8	24 7/8	25 2/8	17 0/8	5	6	Mingo County	WV	Timothy D. Bailey	2007	33005
131 0/8	20 5/8	21 2/8	15 0/8	4	4	Walworth County	WI	Teric Taylor	2008	33005
*131 0/8	20 2/8	20 5/8	17 2/8	5	5	Sheridan County	NE	Darcie L. Thies	2008	33005
131 0/8	20 5/8	21 2/8	17 0/8	4	4	Steele County	MN	Daniel Simmons	2008	33005
131 0/8	19 1/8	19 3/8	15 0/8	5	5	Mingo County	WV	Wesley White	2008	33005
*131 0/8	23 1/8	22 4/8	17 4/8	4	4	Chester County	PA	Bret S. Neiman	2008	33005
*131 0/8	22 6/8	23 2/8	12 7/8	6	6	Brown County	IL	Thomas Spaulding	2008	33005
131 0/8	23 7/8	23 5/8	16 0/8	4	5	Sargent County	ND	Clay J. Evans	2008	33005
131 0/8	21 1/8	20 7/8	19 2/8	5	5	Miami County	IN	Zach Frey	2009	33005
*131 0/8	23 1/8	22 3/8	18 2/8	4	5	Dodge County	MN	Bill Archer	2009	33005
131 0/8	21 1/8	20 1/8	16 6/8	5	5	Antelope County	NE	Ralph J. Tichota	2009	33005
*131 0/8	23 2/8	24 6/8	17 0/8	5	5	Nelson County	KY	Barry "Hammer" Allgeier	2009	33005
*131 0/8	24 4/8	23 7/8	19 4/8	4	4	Cambria County	PA	Philip J. Bracken	2009	33005
*131 0/8	22 6/8	22 3/8	17 3/8	6	5	Dodge County	WI	Darwin Jacobs	2009	33005
131 0/8	22 2/8	22 0/8	18 0/8	4	5	Buffalo County	WI	Jeff Klieforth	2009	33005
*131 0/8	20 4/8	19 2/8	17 4/8	5	5	Greene County	IA	Chuck Kelly	2009	33005
*131 0/8	20 5/8	19 2/8	16 4/8	5	6	Carroll County	KY	Michael Stewart	2009	33005
131 0/8	24 4/8	24 5/8	17 6/8	4	4	Ingham County	MI	Bradley D. Blackmer	2009	33005
*131 0/8	22 3/8	20 6/8	18 2/8	6	6	Lyon County	KS	Mark A. Ferman	2009	33005
131 0/8	24 2/8	23 3/8	18 2/8	4	3	Hall County	GA	Scott Pruitt	2009	33005
*131 0/8	21 0/8	21 4/8	16 0/8	8	5	Ferry County	WA	Lonny Gabrio	2009	33005
131 0/8	20 4/8	20 6/8	14 6/8	5	5	Concordia Parish	LA	Marion Keith Almand	2010	33005
131 0/8	23 3/8	23 3/8	16 2/8	5	5	Sawyer County	WI	Bruce Beckwith	2010	33005
130 7/8	21 4/8	21 4/8	16 6/8	4	4	Sweet Grass County	MT	Dr. Dale Schlehuber	1996	33279
130 7/8	24 1/8	24 3/8	17 1/8	4	4	Lawrence County	IN	Allen Clark	2000	33279
130 7/8	20 1/8	20 2/8	17 2/8	5	6	Kendall County	IL	Eddie Spurlock	2001	33279
130 7/8	22 7/8	23 3/8	16 7/8	5	6	Dallas County	MO	Kevin Pinckney	2003	33279
*130 7/8	23 0/8	23 4/8	17 1/8	4	4	Hickory County	MO	Denny McLaughlin	2004	33279
130 7/8	21 2/8	21 3/8	16 7/8	4	4	Portage County	WI	Tyler Gawlik	2004	33279
130 7/8	21 5/8	21 7/8	17 0/8	4	4	McHenry County	IL	Mark W. Gullickson	2004	33279
130 7/8	22 2/8	21 4/8	15 5/8	4	5	Hudson Bay	SAS	Gary Roney	2004	33279
130 7/8	22 5/8	23 2/8	17 5/8	4	4	Rusk County	WI	Todd M. Collins	2004	33279
130 7/8	22 7/8	22 2/8	19 1/8	6	4	Preston County	WV	Charles Uphold	2004	33279
130 7/8	21 3/8	21 3/8	16 1/8	5	4	Lawrence County	IN	Jeff S. Armstrong	2004	33279
*130 7/8	23 2/8	22 2/8	19 0/8	4	6	McLean County	IL	Matt Cheever	2004	33279
130 7/8	23 5/8	22 6/8	20 2/8	6	5	Somerset County	NJ	Joseph Raio	2004	33279
130 7/8	22 5/8	23 0/8	16 1/8	4	4	Morgan County	IL	Donald E. Laidlaw	2004	33279
*130 7/8	22 3/8	21 1/8	17 7/8	4	4	Pike County	IL	Cliff Ritenour	2004	33279
130 7/8	21 4/8	21 7/8	16 6/8	5	4	Iowa County	IA	Kevin McDonald	2004	33279
130 7/8	23 0/8	23 7/8	17 7/8	4	4	Lawrence County	IL	Jerry Dunn	2004	33279

Deer entries below 141 0/8, that appeared in the 6th Edition, are not included here, but are included on the accompanying CD (see page 119), and also in the Club's Records Archives.

WHITETAIL DEER (TYPICAL ANTLERS)

Minimum Score 125   Continued

SCORE	LENGTH OF R MAIN BEAM L	INSIDE SPREAD	NUMBER OF R POINTS L	AREA	STATE/ PROVINCE	HUNTER'S NAME	DATE	RANK
130 7/8	22 0/8 23 0/8	16 7/8	4 4	McHenry County	ND	Scott Piton	2005	33279
130 7/8	22 5/8 23 1/8	16 5/8	5 5	Venango County	PA	Thomas A. McLaughlin	2005	33279
130 7/8	19 4/8 20 1/8	14 0/8	6 6	Cass County	IL	Brent Saranie	2005	33279
130 7/8	22 3/8 22 5/8	14 7/8	5 5	Macoupin County	IL	Tim Hasara	2005	33279
*130 7/8	22 7/8 22 7/8	16 1/8	5 4	Belmont County	OH	Robert Carnahan	2005	33279
*130 7/8	22 5/8 22 4/8	17 5/8	6 7	Jefferson County	WI	Dennis Ellis	2005	33279
130 7/8	20 1/8 20 2/8	17 1/8	5 5	Seneca County	NY	Randy Cottrell	2005	33279
130 7/8	21 6/8 22 0/8	15 7/8	6 5	Eau Claire County	WI	Jeffery L. Faanes	2005	33279
130 7/8	21 7/8 21 2/8	15 5/8	4 5	Eau Claire County	WI	Seth Torgerson	2005	33279
130 7/8	21 6/8 21 2/8	18 7/8	6 5	Buffalo County	WI	David Stuhr	2005	33279
*130 7/8	22 4/8 21 6/8	22 1/8	4 4	Wyandot County	OH	Robert E. Frey	2005	33279
*130 7/8	20 7/8 21 5/8	16 0/8	5 6	Jasper County	SC	Stanley Woo	2006	33279
130 7/8	21 4/8 20 6/8	14 4/8	5 6	Osage County	OK	Greg Pike	2006	33279
*130 7/8	22 4/8 23 3/8	15 1/8	5 5	Morgan County	OH	Stark Wilbor	2006	33279
*130 7/8	22 0/8 21 4/8	17 7/8	5 5	Allegheny County	PA	Michael Porter	2006	33279
130 7/8	19 3/8 19 5/8	13 5/8	5 6	Rusk County	WI	Robert Bush	2006	33279
*130 7/8	21 6/8 22 0/8	18 1/8	4 5	Carroll County	AR	Jay Middleton	2006	33279
130 7/8	20 5/8 21 4/8	17 5/8	5 6	Trempealeau County	WI	Frank G. Hood	2006	33279
*130 7/8	23 6/8 24 3/8	17 7/8	5 4	Adams County	IL	Edd Clack	2006	33279
*130 7/8	22 0/8 21 3/8	16 7/8	4 5	Audubon County	IA	Jerome Jensen	2006	33279
130 7/8	20 5/8 20 0/8	16 5/8	5 5	Oakland County	MI	Todd Hill	2006	33279
130 7/8	22 2/8 22 3/8	18 3/8	6 6	Warrick County	IN	Robert Hazlewood	2006	33279
130 7/8	24 1/8 25 0/8	17 3/8	4 4	Spotsylvania County	VA	Tony G. Oliver	2006	33279
*130 7/8	23 6/8 25 7/8	14 7/8	5 5	St. Louis County	MN	Phillip J. Peliska	2006	33279
130 7/8	21 7/8 21 7/8	16 3/8	4 5	Avoyelles Parish	LA	William C. Shockey	2006	33279
130 7/8	21 5/8 20 2/8	12 4/8	5 6	Park County	WY	Mike Graham	2007	33279
*130 7/8	21 1/8 19 7/8	15 3/8	5 6	Houston County	MN	Jason Sichler	2007	33279
130 7/8	22 0/8 22 7/8	18 1/8	5 5	Huntingdon County	PA	Joshua Jones	2007	33279
130 7/8	21 3/8 20 5/8	15 1/8	5 5	Marquette County	WI	Ryan McReath	2007	33279
*130 7/8	25 4/8 22 6/8	17 3/8	4 4	Fulton County	IN	Ryan Easterday	2007	33279
*130 7/8	19 5/8 20 2/8	14 3/8	5 5	Green County	WI	Ritch Miller	2007	33279
130 7/8	23 1/8 23 5/8	16 3/8	5 5	Iowa County	WI	Marc Bonin	2007	33279
130 7/8	23 3/8 24 1/8	15 1/8	5 5	Keya Paha County	NE	Sid Morrison	2007	33279
130 7/8	21 4/8 21 4/8	15 5/8	5 5	Trempealeau County	WI	Brad Sterry	2007	33279
130 7/8	22 3/8 21 0/8	16 7/8	4 5	Jackson County	WI	Ryan T. Braden	2007	33279
130 7/8	20 5/8 21 0/8	19 3/8	5 4	Sanilac County	MI	Eric Davis	2007	33279
130 7/8	25 2/8 23 6/8	17 4/8	6 6	Marion County	OH	David Ware	2007	33279
*130 7/8	23 1/8 21 3/8	17 1/8	5 6	Will County	IL	Bill Beaumont	2007	33279
130 7/8	22 5/8 23 2/8	16 1/8	5 6	Grenada County	MS	James Blaylock	2008	33279
*130 7/8	21 4/8 22 3/8	20 3/8	5 5	Randolph County	NC	Ryan Lackey	2008	33279
130 7/8	19 7/8 19 0/8	14 5/8	5 6	Dodge County	NE	Tom Henry	2008	33279
130 7/8	22 2/8 22 3/8	16 2/8	6 6	Jackson County	MI	Robert M. Craft	2008	33279
*130 7/8	24 0/8 24 3/8	17 4/8	4 6	Schuylkill County	PA	Jeremy L. Lupkin	2008	33279
130 7/8	22 7/8 23 2/8	17 7/8	5 7	Jersey County	IL	Rollin Matt Lewis	2008	33279
130 7/8	23 3/8 23 1/8	16 3/8	5 4	New Castle County	DE	Scott J. Swarter	2008	33279
130 7/8	23 1/8 23 2/8	19 2/8	5 7	Ashland County	OH	Randy Jordan	2008	33279
*130 7/8	24 3/8 24 2/8	20 1/8	4 3	Osage County	OK	Bryan White	2009	33279
130 7/8	21 4/8 21 2/8	19 2/8	5 5	Thurston County	NE	Larry L. Gilles	2009	33279
130 7/8	24 0/8 22 5/8	16 7/8	5 6	Sullivan County	NH	Matthew Hurd	2009	33279
*130 7/8	22 3/8 21 2/8	14 6/8	6 7	Whitley County	IN	Christopher LaRue	2009	33279
130 7/8	20 5/8 20 3/8	19 1/8	6 7	Monmouth County	NJ	Wayne Cecero	2009	33279
130 7/8	21 7/8 21 6/8	17 7/8	5 4	Marshall County	IN	Frank M. Yankovich	2009	33279
130 7/8	21 0/8 21 4/8	17 7/8	4 4	Monroe County	NY	Duane F. Briggs	2009	33279
*130 7/8	19 6/8 20 3/8	14 7/8	5 5	McCormick County	SC	Clifton M. Medlock, Jr.	2009	33279
*130 7/8	22 4/8 22 4/8	17 1/8	4 5	Jackson County	OH	Seth Newkirk	2009	33279
130 7/8	21 0/8 21 3/8	15 5/8	4 4	Vernon County	WI	Mark See	2009	33279
130 7/8	22 0/8 20 6/8	19 1/8	4 5	Hardin County	IA	Randall Martinson	2009	33279
*130 7/8	20 5/8 21 0/8	19 7/8	5 5	Indiana County	PA	Shawn T. Sambolich	2009	33279
130 7/8	20 7/8 20 7/8	15 3/8	5 5	Noble County	IN	Andrew J. L. Stump	2009	33279
130 7/8	22 6/8 22 1/8	16 5/8	4 4	Sauk County	WI	Jerehmy D. Griffiths	2009	33279
130 7/8	22 7/8 21 7/8	17 3/8	5 5	Buffalo County	WI	Barry Ollila	2009	33279
*130 7/8	21 0/8 20 7/8	16 0/8	6 6	Iowa County	WI	Dale Goytowski	2009	33279
*130 7/8	23 5/8 22 6/8	17 5/8	4 4	Keya Paha County	NE	Greg Coleman	2009	33279
130 7/8	22 1/8 21 5/8	16 4/8	6 5	Dane County	WI	David Cummings	2009	33279
130 7/8	23 2/8 23 4/8	18 4/8	5 7	Saline County	KS	Nelson S. Burnette	2009	33279
130 7/8	23 1/8 21 5/8	15 1/8	4 5	Barron County	WI	Trevor Herrman	2009	33279
*130 7/8	20 5/8 20 4/8	14 7/8	5 5	Custer County	SD	Joshua T. Morgan	2009	33279
*130 7/8	21 6/8 21 3/8	17 5/8	5 5	St. Croix County	WI	Scott Coddington	2009	33279
*130 7/8	22 2/8 22 0/8	15 5/8	4 4	Marathon County	WI	Chad Hoeppner	2010	33279
130 6/8	22 5/8 21 6/8	17 4/8	5 5	Martin County	IN	Bobby V. Hardwick	1994	33524
130 6/8	22 4/8 21 0/8	16 6/8	7 5	Saline County	IL	Darin DeNeal	1997	33524
130 6/8	22 5/8 22 2/8	16 0/8	4 4	Shawano County	WI	Shane N. Norder	1998	33524
130 6/8	23 5/8 25 4/8	18 2/8	4 4	Wagoner County	OK	Brandon Murray	1999	33524
130 6/8	19 3/8 18 1/8	15 0/8	5 5	Wells County	ND	Jeff Newman	2001	33524
130 6/8	22 2/8 21 3/8	15 2/8	4 5	Breckinridge County	KY	Josh Pierce	2002	33524
130 6/8	22 4/8 23 0/8	17 2/8	6 5	Sawyer County	WI	Robert M. Bay	2002	33524
*130 6/8	19 6/8 20 0/8	16 1/8	6 5	Langlade County	WI	Dennis H. Seis	2003	33524
130 6/8	23 3/8 23 1/8	19 4/8	4 5	Ross County	OH	Brian Sims	2003	33524
130 6/8	21 6/8 23 0/8	17 7/8	5 5	Warren County	IA	Randy Delaney	2003	33524
130 6/8	24 1/8 23 7/8	18 4/8	4 4	Dunn County	WI	David Waterhouse	2004	33524
130 6/8	19 3/8 21 0/8	15 2/8	5 5	Audubon County	IA	Mark Baier	2004	33524
130 6/8	20 4/8 20 2/8	16 0/8	5 5	Washington County	PA	Dennis Gondella	2004	33524
130 6/8	19 2/8 21 2/8	16 2/8	4 4	Columbia County	WI	Thomas C. Varner	2004	33524
130 6/8	20 0/8 19 5/8	15 6/8	6 5	Buffalo County	WI	Travis Malott	2004	33524
*130 6/8	25 3/8 23 3/8	18 0/8	5 4	Barron County	WI	Brad Knutson	2004	33524
*130 6/8	21 0/8 21 2/8	16 2/8	5 5	Kingman County	KS	Paul Styspeck	2004	33524
130 6/8	21 2/8 21 5/8	16 0/8	4 5	Chickasaw County	IA	Joel Betsinger	2004	33524
130 6/8	22 6/8 22 3/8	17 4/8	5 5	Henry County	KY	Jeremy Kelly	2004	33524
130 6/8	22 3/8 21 7/8	15 2/8	5 5	Pike County	IL	Charles Kozikowski, Jr.	2004	33524
130 6/8	22 4/8 22 3/8	16 6/8	4 4	Oldham County	KY	Dennis Magnusson	2004	33524
130 6/8	20 6/8 19 3/8	15 0/8	6 6	Dooly County	GA	John S. Lester	2004	33524
130 6/8	21 3/8 21 7/8	21 4/8	6 4	Love County	OK	William S. Duncan	2004	33524
130 6/8	22 4/8 21 2/8	21 0/8	4 4	Adams County	IL	Lou Evans	2004	33524
130 6/8	24 0/8 25 0/8	15 4/8	4 5	Waupaca County	WI	Brian Dey	2005	33524
130 6/8	21 5/8 20 5/8	15 0/8	5 5	Albany County	NY	Randy L. Edwards	2005	33524

WHITETAIL DEER (TYPICAL ANTLERS)

Minimum Score 125 — Continued

SCORE	R MAIN BEAM L	INSIDE SPREAD	R POINTS L		AREA	STATE/PROVINCE	HUNTER'S NAME	DATE	RANK
* 130 6/8	21 2/8 21 5/8	15 6/8	4	4	Allen County	KY	Craig Meador	2005	33524
130 6/8	20 7/8 21 2/8	17 4/8	5	5	Allegan County	MI	Chad A. Arens	2005	33524
130 6/8	22 4/8 23 3/8	15 2/8	5	4	Wayne County	IL	Todd M. Hewing	2005	33524
130 6/8	22 1/8 23 4/8	15 4/8	4	4	Fond du Lac County	WI	Nick Leonard	2005	33524
130 6/8	21 3/8 22 4/8	17 2/8	6	5	Pike County	IL	John Snoddy	2005	33524
130 6/8	21 4/8 21 7/8	14 6/8	5	5	Sedgwick County	KS	Bob Campbell	2005	33524
130 6/8	22 2/8 23 1/8	15 2/8	5	5	Washington County	IA	Kevin Rocca	2005	33524
130 6/8	21 6/8 22 2/8	15 7/8	6	5	Johnson County	KS	Jeff D. Fraka	2005	33524
130 6/8	20 0/8 20 6/8	16 0/8	5	5	McHenry County	ND	John Tuchscherer	2006	33524
130 6/8	18 5/8 18 6/8	15 4/8	5	5	Yellowstone County	MT	Austin Rogers	2006	33524
130 6/8	24 0/8 21 2/8	13 1/8	6	5	Shawnee County	KS	Shawn Harding	2006	33524
130 6/8	21 7/8 22 3/8	16 2/8	5	5	Tioga County	PA	Clay Rolinski	2006	33524
* 130 6/8	21 7/8 21 6/8	12 4/8	4	4	Shelby County	MO	Frederic E. Evens	2006	33524
130 6/8	21 3/8 20 7/8	16 2/8	5	5	Switzerland County	IN	John L. Cox	2006	33524
* 130 6/8	23 6/8 24 3/8	18 0/8	5	4	Sauk County	WI	Dennis V. Slaght	2006	33524
130 6/8	21 6/8 22 6/8	16 6/8	6	6	St. Croix County	WI	Tim J. Magee	2006	33524
* 130 6/8	21 6/8 22 0/8	17 0/8	4	4	Williamson County	IL	Roger Cantrell	2006	33524
130 6/8	22 6/8 21 5/8	16 1/8	6	5	Macon County	MO	Mike Mense	2006	33524
130 6/8	21 2/8 21 5/8	15 4/8	4	5	Green County	WI	Paul Ovadal	2006	33524
130 6/8	22 4/8 22 4/8	15 2/8	6	5	Graham County	KS	Mick Cheshire	2006	33524
130 6/8	21 6/8 21 4/8	18 2/8	7	6	Grant County	SD	Jim Cloos	2006	33524
* 130 6/8	23 0/8 22 5/8	15 6/8	4	6	Washington County	MD	Craig Higgins	2006	33524
130 6/8	21 5/8 21 5/8	18 3/8	5	6	Ferry County	WA	Margarito Guzman	2006	33524
130 6/8	23 0/8 23 0/8	15 0/8	4	4	Marion County	KS	Dennis N. Ballweg	2006	33524
130 6/8	25 2/8 23 6/8	21 6/8	3	4	Calhoun County	AL	Keith Fortenberry	2007	33524
130 6/8	22 6/8 19 3/8	16 6/8	6	6	Park County	WY	Jerry E. Dollard	2007	33524
130 6/8	18 0/8 18 3/8	16 2/8	5	5	Crook County	WY	Darin Holman	2007	33524
130 6/8	21 7/8 21 7/8	17 0/8	5	5	McCulloch County	TX	Phillip Zimmerhanzel	2007	33524
* 130 6/8	23 0/8 22 7/8	15 1/8	6	5	Lamoure County	ND	Tyler Triepke	2007	33524
130 6/8	23 1/8 23 0/8	18 4/8	4	5	Knox County	IL	Mel J. Johnson	2007	33524
130 6/8	22 2/8 21 0/8	18 0/8	5	5	Buffalo County	WI	Paul R. Olson	2007	33524
130 6/8	24 3/8 24 0/8	15 5/8	7	5	Brown County	IL	Donald P. Travis	2007	33524
* 130 6/8	20 5/8 21 4/8	15 0/8	4	5	Fountain County	IN	Warren Frazier	2007	33524
130 6/8	21 2/8 24 1/8	18 4/8	4	4	Whitley County	IN	Kyle Palan	2007	33524
130 6/8	21 2/8 22 2/8	19 2/8	5	5	Waukesha County	WI	Nicholas J. Klaas	2007	33524
130 6/8	21 7/8 21 0/8	17 6/8	5	5	Fairfield County	CT	John Mikolay	2008	33524
* 130 6/8	21 6/8 22 6/8	17 4/8	6	5	Columbia County	PA	Stephen Knorr	2008	33524
130 6/8	22 1/8 22 2/8	15 6/8	4	5	Kalamazoo County	MI	Scott R. Miller	2008	33524
130 6/8	21 3/8 21 2/8	14 6/8	4	4	Nemaha County	NE	Randall Rehmeier	2008	33524
130 6/8	21 4/8 24 4/8	18 6/8	4	5	Iowa County	WI	Randy Thompson	2008	33524
130 6/8	23 0/8 21 3/8	15 4/8	5	5	Walworth County	WI	Michael J. Wichser	2008	33524
* 130 6/8	20 0/8 19 6/8	14 4/8	5	5	Johnson County	NE	Chris Nielsen	2008	33524
* 130 6/8	21 2/8 21 6/8	15 0/8	5	5	Sherburne County	MN	Brian Gradin	2008	33524
130 6/8	22 4/8 22 3/8	18 5/8	5	5	Fulton County	IL	Greg Eudaley	2008	33524
130 6/8	20 5/8 20 2/8	15 0/8	4	5	Mason County	TX	Steve Watson	2008	33524
* 130 6/8	20 6/8 20 7/8	17 2/8	5	5	Lawrence County	OH	Rodney Ruggles	2008	33524
130 6/8	22 0/8 21 4/8	17 0/8	5	5	Jefferson County	WI	Brent Madden	2008	33524
130 6/8	20 6/8 20 5/8	16 1/8	5	6	Waupaca County	WI	Ryan Hemschel	2008	33524
* 130 6/8	21 7/8 21 6/8	23 1/8	5	8	Mercer County	NJ	Ronald Williams, Jr.	2009	33524
130 6/8	21 0/8 21 1/8	15 6/8	5	5	Buffalo County	WI	Daniel B. Wulff	2009	33524
130 6/8	26 4/8 26 1/8	16 6/8	5	8	Hall County	NE	Conor Ward	2009	33524
130 6/8	22 6/8 22 5/8	17 5/8	6	5	Buffalo County	WI	Joe Andreini	2009	33524
* 130 6/8	21 2/8 20 6/8	17 0/8	5	6	Seward County	NE	Steve Sisel	2009	33524
* 130 6/8	22 6/8 22 1/8	17 6/8	6	5	Tippecanoe County	IN	John W. Marks	2009	33524
* 130 6/8	21 6/8 22 1/8	17 4/8	4	4	Rice County	MN	Brandon Miller	2009	33524
130 6/8	21 7/8 21 3/8	17 2/8	4	4	Fulton County	IL	R. James Zehr	2010	33524
130 6/8	21 6/8 21 2/8	17 4/8	5	5	Claiborne County	MS	Kevin Knott	2010	33524
130 5/8	20 2/8 20 1/8	12 1/8	5	5	Manitowoc County	WI	David A. Ozarowicz, Sr.	1992	33789
130 5/8	23 0/8 23 1/8	15 5/8	5	5	Cass County	IN	Michael J. Moore	2001	33789
130 5/8	24 5/8 24 7/8	22 1/8	6	5	Fayette County	IA	Michael Judas	2001	33789
130 5/8	24 4/8 23 4/8	19 1/8	6	6	Carter County	MT	Jonathan Bartlett	2003	33789
* 130 5/8	24 6/8 23 6/8	16 7/8	4	5	Kosciusko County	IN	Tim Nussbaum	2003	33789
130 5/8	21 6/8 22 2/8	17 7/8	4	4	Hartford County	CT	Douglas A. Burton	2004	33789
130 5/8	22 3/8 21 4/8	19 1/8	5	7	Washington County	WI	Larry Lenling	2004	33789
130 5/8	23 0/8 23 0/8	17 3/8	4	4	Ripley County	MO	Daniel Moore	2004	33789
130 5/8	22 5/8 22 0/8	18 7/8	4	4	Clayton County	IA	Daniel Putz	2004	33789
* 130 5/8	21 2/8 21 5/8	19 2/8	7	5	Richland County	SC	Joseph L. Pratt	2004	33789
130 5/8	19 0/8 20 4/8	19 3/8	8	6	Indiana County	PA	Rick A. Elliott	2004	33789
130 5/8	19 4/8 21 2/8	14 1/8	5	5	Columbia County	WI	Matt Zuleger	2004	33789
130 5/8	21 0/8 22 2/8	16 5/8	4	5	Bayfield County	WI	Steven Burbach	2004	33789
* 130 5/8	21 5/8 21 0/8	16 5/8	4	5	Buffalo County	WI	Randall Wedde	2004	33789
130 5/8	21 6/8 22 1/8	18 5/8	6	6	Hennepin County	MN	Jeffrey L. Eggen	2004	33789
130 5/8	25 1/8 21 3/8	16 7/8	5	5	Adams County	IA	Dean Lammers	2004	33789
* 130 5/8	22 2/8 22 2/8	17 2/8	5	6	Washington County	NE	John Peterson	2005	33789
130 5/8	21 0/8 20 7/8	16 3/8	5	5	Northampton County	VA	Randy Tanner	2005	33789
130 5/8	20 6/8 22 1/8	18 4/8	5	4	Henry County	KY	Scott Tincher	2005	33789
* 130 5/8	22 2/8 23 1/8	19 1/8	5	6	Middlesex County	MA	Skip Burnham	2005	33789
130 5/8	21 7/8 20 2/8	17 5/8	4	5	Vigo County	IN	Ernest R. Woods II	2005	33789
130 5/8	20 0/8 20 4/8	14 1/8	5	5	Sheboygan County	WI	Chad Kienbaum	2005	33789
* 130 5/8	23 0/8 22 4/8	17 3/8	4	5	Dubuque County	IA	Todd Templen	2005	33789
130 5/8	21 4/8 22 2/8	17 3/8	4	4	Waukesha County	WI	Randall Cech	2005	33789
130 5/8	20 2/8 20 5/8	15 3/8	5	5	Buffalo County	WI	Clete L. Ziegler	2005	33789
* 130 5/8	22 0/8 22 1/8	17 7/8	4	4	Tom Green County	TX	Mark Harrington	2005	33789
130 5/8	22 6/8 21 3/8	18 5/8	4	4	Marquette County	WI	John W. Steuck	2005	33789
130 5/8	20 7/8 20 2/8	17 1/8	5	5	Otter Tail County	MN	Matt L. Olson	2006	33789
130 5/8	22 3/8 23 2/8	16 7/8	4	4	Green County	WI	Fred W. Cruse	2006	33789
130 5/8	19 7/8 20 5/8	15 5/8	6	6	Seneca County	NY	Scott M. Shumway	2006	33789
130 5/8	23 0/8 23 7/8	18 6/8	4	5	Pepin County	WI	Dominic Gruber	2006	33789
* 130 5/8	20 7/8 20 7/8	17 5/8	4	5	Marathon County	WI	Tim Riedel	2006	33789
* 130 5/8	25 6/8 24 5/8	17 1/8	6	7	Greenwood County	KS	Ronnie H. Hall	2006	33789
130 5/8	19 3/8 20 5/8	15 6/8	6	6	Adams County	IL	Dean Martin	2006	33789
130 5/8	23 4/8 22 3/8	16 7/8	5	4	Marathon County	WI	Brian Karau	2006	33789
* 130 5/8	18 6/8 18 5/8	15 5/8	5	6	Will County	IL	Scott Olthoff	2006	33789
130 5/8	24 7/8 24 4/8	16 3/8	4	4	St. Clair County	IL	Michael W. Reichling	2006	33789
130 5/8	21 3/8 22 1/8	20 5/8	4	4	Atchison County	MO	Patrick Athen	2007	33789

Deer entries below 141 0/8, that appeared in the 6th Edition, are not included here, but are included on the accompanying CD (see page 119), and also in the Club's Records Archives.

589

WHITETAIL DEER (TYPICAL ANTLERS)

Minimum Score 125   Continued

SCORE	LENGTH OF R MAIN BEAM L	INSIDE SPREAD	NUMBER OF R POINTS L	AREA	STATE/ PROVINCE	HUNTER'S NAME	DATE	RANK
130 5/8	19 0/8 18 7/8	14 5/8	5 5	Izard County	AR	Chance Battles	2007	33789
130 5/8	22 7/8 22 4/8	16 7/8	5 4	Marathon County	WI	Dan Parlier	2007	33789
130 5/8	23 0/8 22 0/8	18 1/8	4 4	Green County	WI	Dale Nafzger	2007	33789
130 5/8	18 2/8 20 4/8	16 3/8	6 6	Barber County	KS	Rich Grannis	2007	33789
*130 5/8	24 1/8 24 0/8	18 5/8	4 5	Monroe County	MI	H. Scott Kleinow	2007	33789
130 5/8	22 5/8 23 0/8	18 1/8	4 4	Richland County	OH	Ron Swanger	2007	33789
*130 5/8	23 2/8 22 1/8	16 3/8	4 4	La Porte County	IN	Chad A. Schau	2007	33789
130 5/8	21 1/8 21 3/8	16 1/8	5 5	Monroe County	IN	Michael J. Douthitt	2007	33789
130 5/8	20 4/8 19 5/8	17 0/8	6 6	Cass County	NE	Neil Chandler	2007	33789
130 5/8	18 7/8 19 6/8	15 1/8	6 5	Llano County	TX	Rick Schmidt	2007	33789
130 5/8	22 6/8 22 6/8	16 7/8	4 4	Sauk County	WI	David L. Gher	2007	33789
130 5/8	20 2/8 20 5/8	15 5/8	5 5	Barry County	MI	Jeff A. Nelson	2007	33789
130 5/8	20 0/8 20 0/8	15 1/8	5 5	Linn County	KS	Dennis M. Little	2007	33789
130 5/8	23 0/8 22 4/8	19 7/8	5 5	Jackson County	MO	Jerry Hibdon	2007	33789
*130 5/8	22 3/8 21 3/8	14 7/8	5 5	Vigo County	IN	Jeff Augustus	2007	33789
*130 5/8	22 4/8 22 6/8	15 3/8	4 5	Orange County	IN	Anthony J. Caudle	2007	33789
130 5/8	21 7/8 22 0/8	15 5/8	4 4	Mountrail County	ND	Craig Richardson	2007	33789
130 5/8	25 2/8 23 4/8	16 5/8	6 6	Jo Daviess County	IL	Jeffrey R. Fechner	2007	33789
130 5/8	19 5/8 20 2/8	14 7/8	5 5	Henry County	VA	Mike Weaver	2007	33789
130 5/8	22 5/8 23 3/8	18 3/8	4 4	Schuyler County	IL	Ashley Forbis	2008	33789
130 5/8	19 7/8 21 3/8	16 1/8	5 5	Clinton County	MI	Jeff Beebe	2008	33789
*130 5/8	23 2/8 22 2/8	16 4/8	8 6	Tom Green County	TX	Randall Curtis Witte	2008	33789
130 5/8	19 6/8 19 7/8	19 5/8	5 5	Coke County	TX	Tim Beggs	2008	33789
130 5/8	21 4/8 20 7/8	18 0/8	6 4	Morris County	NJ	Dr. Hans H. Stuting	2008	33789
130 5/8	22 1/8 21 6/8	16 3/8	4 4	Washington County	OK	Dwight S. Wolf	2008	33789
130 5/8	21 2/8 23 5/8	13 0/8	4 6	Comanche County	KS	Thomas J. Pluhar	2008	33789
*130 5/8	23 3/8 23 7/8	18 3/8	4 4	Olmsted County	MN	Ben Gerlsberger	2009	33789
*130 5/8	22 3/8 22 3/8	14 7/8	5 5	Kinney County	TX	Emmit Gueary	2009	33789
*130 5/8	19 0/8 18 0/8	16 1/8	5 6	Mountrail County	ND	Jake Smith	2009	33789
*130 5/8	21 4/8 21 5/8	16 5/8	5 7	Hardin County	KY	Michael Love	2009	33789
130 4/8	21 0/8 20 4/8	16 3/8	6 5	Spokane County	WA	John Schneider	1995	34027
130 4/8	23 4/8 22 2/8	16 0/8	5 4	Issaquena County	MS	Jim Williams	1997	34027
130 4/8	20 3/8 21 1/8	19 0/8	4 4	Essex County	NJ	Mark Spoto	2000	34027
130 4/8	24 5/8 23 0/8	18 2/8	5 4	Monroe County	WI	Allen Hart	2003	34027
*130 4/8	21 6/8 21 3/8	18 0/8	4 4	Monroe County	IL	John McMullan	2003	34027
*130 4/8	20 2/8 20 4/8	16 2/8	5 5	Victoria County	TX	Jimmy Bailey	2003	34027
130 4/8	21 4/8 22 2/8	16 6/8	5 5	Morris County	NJ	Stephen Olsson	2004	34027
130 4/8	22 1/8 21 6/8	15 2/8	5 5	Madison County	MT	J. Dudley Ottley, Sr.	2004	34027
130 4/8	21 3/8 21 5/8	15 2/8	5 5	Chautauqua County	NY	Kenneth R. Johnson	2004	34027
130 4/8	21 4/8 21 7/8	16 6/8	4 4	Brown County	TX	Keith Meisner	2004	34027
130 4/8	20 2/8 20 4/8	14 7/8	6 6	Houston County	MN	Dean Beneke	2004	34027
*130 4/8	21 0/8 21 2/8	16 2/8	5 5	Chippewa County	WI	Mitch Hilger	2004	34027
130 4/8	20 1/8 19 4/8	15 4/8	6 5	Livingston County	IL	Brad Kaisner	2004	34027
130 4/8	21 5/8 21 4/8	15 4/8	4 4	Dallas County	IA	Mark Lasnek	2004	34027
*130 4/8	20 1/8 21 3/8	16 6/8	7 5	Crawford County	WI	Brooks Volden	2004	34027
130 4/8	21 3/8 22 2/8	16 7/8	6 5	Zavala County	TX	Jay Dorman	2004	34027
130 4/8	24 3/8 23 1/8	18 1/8	4 4	Fulton County	IN	Jeffrey A. Martin	2004	34027
130 4/8	24 4/8 22 7/8	16 0/8	4 5	Richland County	WI	Glenn M. Crary	2004	34027
*130 4/8	23 5/8 23 2/8	17 1/8	4 4	Allegheny County	PA	Dennis M. Grimm	2004	34027
130 4/8	23 3/8 22 1/8	13 4/8	6 5	Alfalfa County	OK	Keith W. Kindle	2004	34027
130 4/8	23 2/8 22 5/8	15 2/8	5 5	Jefferson County	OH	Erik Betchker	2004	34027
130 4/8	21 0/8 21 1/8	18 0/8	4 4	Waupaca County	WI	Chris R. Nicklaus	2005	34027
130 4/8	21 0/8 20 5/8	16 4/8	5 5	Schleicher County	TX	Kent Bailey	2005	34027
130 4/8	21 5/8 21 0/8	16 4/8	5 5	Holt County	NE	Dennis Dale	2005	34027
*130 4/8	22 1/8 21 2/8	20 6/8	4 4	Ionia County	MI	Michael J. Klapmust	2005	34027
*130 4/8	23 1/8 24 0/8	18 0/8	4 4	Shelby County	MO	Nick Lange	2005	34027
130 4/8	22 2/8 21 5/8	14 6/8	5 5	Marquette County	WI	Robert L. Kampen	2005	34027
130 4/8	19 6/8 20 2/8	15 5/8	6 7	Baldwin County	GA	Hendley McLeod	2005	34027
130 4/8	21 1/8 22 3/8	17 2/8	5 5	Montgomery County	MO	Frank Schlanker	2005	34027
130 4/8	23 3/8 23 3/8	18 6/8	4 4	Knox County	MO	Tony Pulse	2005	34027
130 4/8	20 4/8 20 7/8	18 2/8	4 4	Lebanon County	PA	William D. Love	2005	34027
130 4/8	23 5/8 23 1/8	19 2/8	5 5	Licking County	OH	Michael Budd	2005	34027
*130 4/8	22 6/8 22 7/8	17 4/8	5 5	Ross County	OH	Sam Underhill	2005	34027
130 4/8	23 4/8 24 4/8	17 0/8	4 5	Livingston County	IL	Dana Coldren	2005	34027
*130 4/8	22 6/8 22 0/8	17 4/8	5 4	Jefferson County	MO	Glenn Frick	2005	34027
*130 4/8	21 2/8 20 4/8	16 4/8	4 5	Taylor County	WI	James A. Curtis	2005	34027
130 4/8	20 4/8 21 0/8	13 2/8	6 6	Kiowa County	KS	Shane Collier	2005	34027
130 4/8	23 2/8 18 3/8	19 5/8	8 6	Woodson County	KS	Joe Dewey	2005	34027
130 4/8	22 7/8 22 6/8	18 6/8	4 5	Steuben County	IN	M. Scott Penner	2006	34027
130 4/8	23 0/8 23 3/8	17 0/8	5 5	Will County	IL	Tom Mooi	2006	34027
130 4/8	23 1/8 22 4/8	18 2/8	5 5	Ross County	OH	Drew Zickafoose	2006	34027
130 4/8	20 7/8 20 2/8	15 6/8	5 5	Highlands County	FL	Lyman Holmes	2006	34027
130 4/8	23 3/8 22 6/8	17 4/8	5 5	Bolivar County	MS	Leland Speakes, Jr.	2006	34027
130 4/8	22 1/8 23 0/8	19 0/8	4 4	Ottawa County	OH	Robert Fleming	2006	34027
130 4/8	21 4/8 21 6/8	14 6/8	6 4	Brown County	IL	David R. Herschelman	2006	34027
130 4/8	23 0/8 21 1/8	18 0/8	4 4	Buffalo County	WI	Thad W. Henderson	2006	34027
*130 4/8	22 6/8 22 3/8	17 6/8	8 6	Dunn County	WI	Jason Hasse	2006	34027
*130 4/8	24 3/8 20 7/8	19 0/8	5 5	Brown County	IL	Windsor Barringer	2006	34027
130 4/8	24 0/8 24 1/8	17 6/8	5 4	Claiborne County	MS	Jennifer Jackson	2006	34027
*130 4/8	21 0/8 22 4/8	17 0/8	6 5	Pope County	IL	Chris McGuire	2006	34027
130 4/8	22 1/8 21 4/8	15 0/8	5 6	Hempstead County	AR	Aaron J. McDonnel	2006	34027
*130 4/8	22 2/8 22 0/8	13 4/8	6 5	Cass County	IL	Al Youman	2006	34027
130 4/8	23 7/8 24 5/8	17 2/8	5 4	Grand Forks County	ND	Richard Burt	2007	34027
*130 4/8	21 4/8 22 1/8	14 6/8	6 6	Cascade County	MT	Brian Walker	2007	34027
130 4/8	20 2/8 20 0/8	12 6/8	4 5	McCulloch County	TX	Larry Peterson, Jr.	2007	34027
130 4/8	21 0/8 20 1/8	15 0/8	6 6	Rusk County	WI	Jay Jay Colliver	2007	34027
130 4/8	20 6/8 21 1/8	16 6/8	4 5	Waushara County	WI	Mike Schwartz	2007	34027
130 4/8	20 5/8 21 3/8	16 5/8	5 5	Waupaca County	WI	Cody W. Kluth	2007	34027
*130 4/8	21 5/8 20 5/8	17 0/8	5 5	Beadle County	SD	Brett Boetel	2007	34027
130 4/8	21 7/8 22 1/8	19 4/8	6 6	Chippewa County	WI	Scott Zwiefelhofer	2007	34027
*130 4/8	22 2/8 21 3/8	17 0/8	6 4	Buffalo County	WI	Brian Stenseth	2007	34027
130 4/8	23 4/8 21 0/8	17 2/8	5 5	Fulton County	IL	Robert Bahr	2007	34027
130 4/8	25 3/8 25 6/8	19 4/8	5 4	Worcester County	MA	Paul Gosselin	2007	34027
*130 4/8	21 4/8 21 2/8	15 3/8	5 4	Appanoose County	IA	Ralph Lane	2007	34027
*130 4/8	20 5/8 21 2/8	15 4/8	5 5	Brown County	SD	Rick Lipp	2007	34027

590

WHITETAIL DEER (TYPICAL ANTLERS)

Minimum Score 125 — Continued

SCORE	LENGTH OF R MAIN BEAM L	INSIDE SPREAD	NUMBER OF R POINTS L	AREA	STATE/ PROVINCE	HUNTER'S NAME	DATE	RANK
130 4/8	22 0/8 20 6/8	16 0/8	4 4	Highland County	OH	Wilbur D. Greene	2007	34027
*130 4/8	21 6/8 21 4/8	17 7/8	6 5	Irion County	TX	Johnny A. Williams, Jr.	2007	34027
130 4/8	22 1/8 22 1/8	18 0/8	5 4	Powell County	MT	Ed Tomlin, Jr.	2008	34027
*130 4/8	22 0/8 22 5/8	15 0/8	5 5	Anoka County	MN	Richard Skibsted	2008	34027
*130 4/8	20 6/8 21 6/8	14 1/8	6 5	Brown County	WI	Jeff Kamps	2008	34027
130 4/8	23 0/8 21 6/8	17 4/8	5 5	McLean County	KY	Robert Rickard	2008	34027
130 4/8	21 6/8 21 7/8	17 2/8	4 4	Shiawassee County	MI	Benjamin R. Gulick	2008	34027
130 4/8	20 6/8 20 0/8	17 2/8	5 5	Chester County	PA	Nelson D. Hendrickson	2008	34027
130 4/8	21 1/8 21 5/8	13 6/8	5 5	Schuyler County	MO	Stephen Balee	2008	34027
*130 4/8	23 4/8 24 4/8	18 0/8	4 6	Red Willow County	NE	William Peck, Jr.	2008	34027
*130 4/8	20 6/8 20 2/8	19 4/8	5 5	Wirt County	WV	Brian L. Enoch	2008	34027
*130 4/8	22 4/8 21 2/8	14 4/8	4 4	Berkshire County	MA	Andy Boyne	2008	34027
*130 4/8	21 5/8 21 3/8	17 4/8	4 4	Jackson County	IA	Randy J. Weber	2008	34027
130 4/8	22 1/8 21 7/8	15 6/8	4 5	Juneau County	WI	Matt Lubinski	2008	34027
130 4/8	21 6/8 22 4/8	17 2/8	4 4	Hardeman County	TX	Rodney Alexander	2008	34027
*130 4/8	20 7/8 20 4/8	14 6/8	5 5	Highland County	OH	Jay Dotson	2009	34027
130 4/8	21 7/8 22 0/8	18 0/8	7 5	Sawyer County	WI	Joe Jalowitz	2009	34027
*130 4/8	22 0/8 22 1/8	18 0/8	4 5	Carroll County	OH	Michael R. Reiter	2009	34027
130 4/8	24 7/8 22 7/8	11 7/8	4 5	Turner County	GA	Ike Ellerbee	2009	34027
130 4/8	23 0/8 22 3/8	20 4/8	4 4	Gentry County	MO	Anthony Pierceall	2009	34027
130 4/8	23 5/8 22 0/8	16 4/8	7 5	Columbia County	WI	Tyler M. Lee	2009	34027
130 4/8	23 2/8 23 5/8	15 6/8	4 4	McLean County	KY	Jeremiah Baldwin	2009	34027
130 4/8	21 3/8 21 3/8	18 0/8	4 4	Vernon County	MO	Jeff Hubbard	2009	34027
*130 4/8	23 0/8 23 3/8	18 2/8	5 6	St. Louis County	MO	Scott G. Corley	2009	34027
130 4/8	23 2/8 22 5/8	18 5/8	6 4	Kewaunee County	WI	Kyle Hunsader	2009	34027
*130 4/8	21 3/8 20 7/8	19 2/8	4 4	Green Lake County	WI	Dave Knueppel	2009	34027
130 4/8	21 5/8 21 7/8	16 3/8	6 5	Washington County	NE	Ronald Stamper	2009	34027
130 4/8	18 6/8 19 5/8	15 6/8	5 5	Adams County	PA	Allen L. Smith	2009	34027
*130 4/8	22 3/8 22 1/8	16 5/8	6 6	Noble County	OH	Richard A. Blair	2009	34027
130 4/8	20 6/8 20 4/8	15 0/8	4 4	Ward County	ND	Don G. Scofield	2010	34027
130 3/8	21 1/8 20 6/8	17 5/8	5 5	Mahoning County	OH	Ron Osborne	1993	34302
130 3/8	21 0/8 19 7/8	14 7/8	5 5	Pembina County	ND	Randy Schuster	1998	34302
130 3/8	20 1/8 20 0/8	17 3/8	6 5	Jefferson County	WI	Kenneth Trinko	2001	34302
130 3/8	22 0/8 21 2/8	15 7/8	4 5	Richardson County	NE	Frank Jensen	2003	34302
130 3/8	18 6/8 19 3/8	18 5/8	4 4	Ripley County	MO	J. B. "Buddy" Newton	2004	34302
130 3/8	21 7/8 21 0/8	16 7/8	6 6	Fillmore County	MN	Wayne Volkart	2004	34302
130 3/8	21 5/8 22 1/8	16 1/8	5 5	Green Lake County	WI	Todd Standke	2004	34302
*130 3/8	23 3/8 23 1/8	18 7/8	4 4	Maverick County	TX	Bob Fleming	2004	34302
130 3/8	23 5/8 23 4/8	19 1/8	3 4	Barber County	KS	Mike Glanden	2004	34302
130 3/8	26 1/8 25 7/8	21 1/8	3 4	Pike County	IL	Dave G. Misner	2004	34302
130 3/8	20 3/8 21 2/8	17 1/8	5 4	Jefferson County	WI	Matthew Husting	2004	34302
*130 3/8	20 7/8 21 7/8	15 6/8	4 5	Cass County	IL	Charles F. Dick	2004	34302
130 3/8	22 0/8 22 1/8	16 1/8	5 6	Traill County	ND	Duane Dumas	2004	34302
130 3/8	21 4/8 21 4/8	15 7/8	5 5	Kewaunee County	WI	Bucky Ihlenfeldt	2004	34302
130 3/8	20 2/8 20 7/8	16 7/8	6 5	Trempealeau County	WI	Ray N. Andersen	2005	34302
*130 3/8	22 1/8 22 2/8	18 7/8	4 4	Jackson County	WI	Zane Flick	2005	34302
*130 3/8	25 4/8 24 5/8	15 5/8	5 5	Ocean County	NJ	Dean Hughes	2005	34302
130 3/8	23 0/8 21 5/8	15 1/8	5 6	Jersey County	IL	Frank Campione	2005	34302
130 3/8	20 4/8 21 5/8	15 5/8	5 5	Green County	WI	Paul Ovadal	2005	34302
*130 3/8	22 7/8 23 1/8	18 6/8	5 5	McHenry County	IL	Rich S. Pawelczyk	2005	34302
130 3/8	22 5/8 23 3/8	15 5/8	4 4	Knox County	MO	Martin Dixson	2005	34302
*130 3/8	22 0/8 22 5/8	17 4/8	6 5	Monroe County	PA	Fred D. Costanzi	2005	34302
130 3/8	20 2/8 20 6/8	15 7/8	5 5	Buffalo County	WI	Jason Meyers	2005	34302
130 3/8	23 0/8 24 1/8	21 5/8	4 4	Anne Arundel County	MD	Barry V. Appolin	2005	34302
130 3/8	20 7/8 20 1/8	16 5/8	5 5	Calhoun County	IL	Wade A. Hays	2005	34302
130 3/8	21 1/8 21 3/8	14 5/8	5 6	Clark County	WI	Billie Jo Brown	2005	34302
*130 3/8	21 5/8 21 4/8	18 3/8	4 4	Suffolk County	NY	John A. Griffin	2005	34302
130 3/8	22 6/8 22 0/8	12 7/8	5 5	Buffalo County	WI	Douglas A. Yapp	2006	34302
130 3/8	24 5/8 23 5/8	17 1/8	5 7	Anoka County	MN	Lenny B. Haberman	2006	34302
130 3/8	22 3/8 22 6/8	13 6/8	5 5	Cherokee County	TX	Sharon Reid	2006	34302
130 3/8	21 2/8 20 6/8	17 2/8	5 6	Oakland County	MI	Thomas J. Knight	2006	34302
130 3/8	22 2/8 23 2/8	15 5/8	5 5	Bracken County	KY	Gene Schadle	2006	34302
130 3/8	20 0/8 16 5/8	16 7/8	5 5	Trempealeau County	WI	Robert Frederick, Jr.	2006	34302
*130 3/8	21 0/8 21 0/8	18 7/8	5 5	Lafayette County	WI	Dave Johnson	2006	34302
130 3/8	21 5/8 20 6/8	16 1/8	4 5	Sauk County	WI	Ken Gher	2006	34302
*130 3/8	22 0/8 22 2/8	15 3/8	5 4	Allamakee County	IA	Patricia Burroughs	2006	34302
*130 3/8	22 5/8 23 2/8	16 5/8	6 5	Outagamie County	WI	Nicholas Kamba	2006	34302
*130 3/8	20 6/8 21 2/8	17 7/8	4 4	Fulton County	IL	Chris Rivers	2006	34302
*130 3/8	22 4/8 21 4/8	17 1/8	5 5	Trempealeau County	WI	Brian K. Lyngen	2006	34302
130 3/8	22 3/8 21 6/8	14 6/8	7 5	Ramsey County	MN	Mark LeMay	2006	34302
130 3/8	21 2/8 21 2/8	16 1/8	6 6	Lincoln County	WA	Bob Hall	2007	34302
*130 3/8	22 5/8 23 4/8	19 4/8	7 10	Sheridan County	WY	Rick Davidson	2007	34302
130 3/8	22 5/8 23 1/8	19 0/8	7 5	Buffalo County	WI	Dan Bernarde	2007	34302
130 3/8	24 0/8 24 2/8	16 5/8	6 7	Garland County	AR	Steven T. Tucker	2007	34302
130 3/8	22 6/8 21 7/8	15 7/8	7 6	Knox County	IL	Randy Bozarth	2007	34302
130 3/8	22 7/8 23 1/8	15 4/8	4 6	Marquette County	WI	Ken Fink, Jr.	2007	34302
*130 3/8	21 1/8 20 2/8	21 1/8	4 4	Cass County	MI	David Lee Knepple	2007	34302
130 3/8	25 0/8 23 2/8	18 5/8	5 4	Jefferson County	OH	Joel L. Rogers, Sr.	2007	34302
130 3/8	23 1/8 23 4/8	15 3/8	4 5	Rock County	WI	Ryan R. Arndt	2007	34302
*130 3/8	22 1/8 23 0/8	17 5/8	5 5	Buffalo County	WI	Paul Backes	2007	34302
130 3/8	21 3/8 21 3/8	17 5/8	5 5	Thayer County	NE	Earl V. Hillman, Jr.	2007	34302
130 3/8	23 0/8 21 6/8	18 4/8	4 6	Atchison County	MO	Jess Kucera	2007	34302
*130 3/8	22 7/8 24 7/8	14 5/8	4 5	McDowell County	WV	Christopher D. Lee	2007	34302
130 3/8	20 6/8 21 5/8	20 3/8	5 5	Outagamie County	WI	Jeff Gorenc	2007	34302
130 3/8	23 2/8 22 3/8	16 1/8	6 6	Martin County	IN	John R. Butcher	2007	34302
130 3/8	21 1/8 21 6/8	17 6/8	6 5	Huntingdon County	PA	Clair Traxler	2007	34302
130 3/8	22 3/8 21 3/8	15 5/8	5 5	Tift County	GA	Shawn K. Watson	2007	34302
*130 3/8	23 7/8 24 0/8	15 7/8	4 4	Washington County	AR	Jaysen Evans	2007	34302
130 3/8	19 4/8 21 3/8	14 1/8	5 5	Butler County	KS	Ron Partridge	2007	34302
130 3/8	21 0/8 21 1/8	18 7/8	5 5	Shawano County	WI	Douglas L. Below	2008	34302
*130 3/8	23 7/8 23 6/8	13 7/8	4 4	Norfolk County	MA	Dean P. Bogan	2008	34302
*130 3/8	22 4/8 22 3/8	16 7/8	5 5	Coshocton County	OH	Rick Kurz	2008	34302
*130 3/8	21 6/8 22 0/8	15 2/8	6 5	Des Moines County	IA	Allen Bradford	2008	34302
130 3/8	20 7/8 20 1/8	17 1/8	5 5	Mountrail County	ND	James Domaskin	2008	34302
*130 3/8	21 7/8 21 5/8	18 1/8	4 4	Lauderdale County	AL	Daniel Rose	2008	34302

Deer entries below 141 0/8, that appeared in the 6th Edition, are not included here, but are included on the accompanying CD (see page 119), and also in the Club's Records Archives.

591

WHITETAIL DEER (TYPICAL ANTLERS)

Minimum Score 125 — Continued

SCORE	LENGTH OF R MAIN BEAM L	INSIDE SPREAD	NUMBER OF R POINTS L		AREA	STATE/ PROVINCE	HUNTER'S NAME	DATE	RANK
130 3/8	22 5/8 22 1/8	14 3/8	5	5	Monroe County	MO	Lane Shortt	2008	34302
*130 3/8	20 0/8 21 6/8	12 1/8	5	5	Shiawassee County	MI	Daniel J. Malzahn	2008	34302
*130 3/8	20 4/8 21 4/8	18 0/8	5	6	Buffalo County	WI	Jerry Grueneberg	2008	34302
*130 3/8	21 1/8 21 4/8	14 5/8	5	5	Monroe County	WI	Jeffery Wessels	2008	34302
130 3/8	21 4/8 21 1/8	15 1/8	6	5	Darke County	OH	Rob Kaiser	2008	34302
130 3/8	20 0/8 21 6/8	18 0/8	6	6	Jackson County	MI	Douglas W. Christie	2009	34302
*130 3/8	21 5/8 22 2/8	17 0/8	5	4	Lycoming County	PA	Sam J. Fisher	2009	34302
*130 3/8	25 2/8 25 3/8	16 3/8	4	5	Berrien County	MI	Donald J. Mangold	2009	34302
130 3/8	22 3/8 22 4/8	16 3/8	5	4	Crawford County	WI	Norman Hare	2009	34302
130 3/8	20 2/8 19 6/8	18 7/8	5	5	Clark County	WI	Jack L. Rueth	2009	34302
130 3/8	23 0/8 22 6/8	15 1/8	4	4	Adams County	WI	Todd Poskey	2009	34302
*130 3/8	23 4/8 25 0/8	17 5/8	3	4	Lake County	IL	Mike Willand	2009	34302
130 3/8	22 6/8 22 7/8	17 6/8	4	5	La Grange County	IN	Ronald Vaughn	2009	34302
130 3/8	19 6/8 21 6/8	14 7/8	5	4	Burleigh County	ND	Scott Lang	2009	34302
130 3/8	21 6/8 21 3/8	15 3/8	5	5	Muskegon County	MI	Mike Wright	2010	34302
*130 3/8	21 6/8 21 5/8	14 7/8	4	5	Washtenaw County	MI	Terry W. Louth, Jr.	2010	34302
130 2/8	19 1/8 22 1/8	18 2/8	4	5	Sussex County	VA	Gary Wayne Adams	1993	34548
130 2/8	20 5/8 22 0/8	16 0/8	6	6	Pike County	MO	David W. Bentele	1995	34548
130 2/8	21 3/8 21 2/8	15 6/8	5	5	Pope County	AR	Christopher Aaron Baker	2001	34548
130 2/8	24 0/8 22 6/8	18 4/8	4	5	Vernon County	WI	Kelly R. Alexander	2002	34548
130 2/8	23 3/8 24 5/8	17 3/8	5	6	Champaign County	OH	Thomas Flohre	2002	34548
130 2/8	21 7/8 21 6/8	16 0/8	4	4	Fairfax County	VA	Fred R. Ansick, Jr.	2003	34548
130 2/8	25 1/8 23 6/8	16 6/8	4	5	DeKalb County	IL	Mark S. Swanson	2003	34548
130 2/8	21 0/8 20 5/8	15 5/8	5	6	Custer County	SD	Matt May	2003	34548
130 2/8	21 1/8 22 0/8	15 6/8	4	4	Highland County	OH	Roger Martin	2003	34548
*130 2/8	20 5/8 19 5/8	16 6/8	4	5	Toole County	MT	Chris McFadden	2004	34548
130 2/8	20 6/8 21 2/8	16 5/8	5	6	Pike County	IL	Steve M. Schuwerk	2004	34548
130 2/8	20 5/8 21 0/8	12 7/8	6	6	Meade County	SD	Tom Svendsen	2004	34548
130 2/8	22 0/8 23 0/8	20 4/8	5	5	White County	IL	Josh Butcher	2004	34548
130 2/8	21 3/8 21 6/8	16 0/8	5	5	Clarion County	PA	Amos E. Rudolph	2004	34548
130 2/8	22 4/8 21 5/8	19 2/8	4	4	Wabash County	IN	Steve Barton	2004	34548
130 2/8	22 5/8 21 5/8	15 7/8	7	6	Trigg County	KY	Troy Barley	2004	34548
130 2/8	23 7/8 24 0/8	17 0/8	4	5	Adams County	IL	Richard Fleischman	2004	34548
130 2/8	20 2/8 20 3/8	16 6/8	4	5	Buffalo County	WI	David A. O'Brien	2004	34548
130 2/8	23 0/8 23 1/8	17 1/8	7	6	Anderson County	KS	Jeff Smith	2004	34548
130 2/8	23 1/8 23 3/8	15 6/8	4	4	Grant County	OK	Roger Hulsey	2004	34548
130 2/8	20 4/8 20 4/8	14 0/8	6	5	York County	SC	Steven D. Godfrey	2004	34548
130 2/8	20 1/8 20 7/8	16 2/8	4	5	Jasper County	IL	Eric Sandschafer	2004	34548
130 2/8	21 7/8 21 2/8	18 0/8	5	6	Union County	IA	Shawn Majors	2004	34548
130 2/8	23 1/8 22 5/8	17 2/8	5	5	Delaware County	OH	Steve Byerly	2004	34548
130 2/8	24 3/8 24 0/8	17 1/8	4	5	Milwaukee County	WI	Billy Zimmermann	2004	34548
130 2/8	21 2/8 20 3/8	16 0/8	4	5	Mills County	IA	Henry Joslin III	2004	34548
130 2/8	23 0/8 22 5/8	19 1/8	6	4	Dickinson County	MI	Kurt Kramer	2004	34548
130 2/8	22 6/8 23 5/8	15 4/8	4	4	Lake County	IL	Donald W. Hansen, Jr.	2004	34548
130 2/8	24 6/8 24 6/8	18 6/8	4	4	Humphreys County	MS	Paul "Rivers Run" Korn	2004	34548
130 2/8	22 5/8 21 0/8	16 6/8	5	5	Chickasaw County	IA	Jareb Kellogg	2005	34548
130 2/8	20 5/8 21 1/8	14 7/8	5	6	Travis County	TX	Page J. McDaniel	2005	34548
*130 2/8	20 7/8 20 7/8	17 4/8	5	5	Richland County	ND	Dan Olsgaard	2005	34548
130 2/8	22 4/8 22 3/8	17 0/8	4	4	Macon County	MO	Mike Mense	2005	34548
130 2/8	22 7/8 24 0/8	15 2/8	5	6	Moniteau County	MO	Neil Gump	2005	34548
130 2/8	20 7/8 20 5/8	16 0/8	4	5	Delaware County	IA	Bruce Wohlers	2005	34548
130 2/8	23 0/8 23 1/8	18 4/8	4	4	Jackson County	WI	Robert A. Voss	2005	34548
130 2/8	24 1/8 25 5/8	19 3/8	6	7	Kent County	MD	Donald V. Forgan	2005	34548
130 2/8	24 1/8 22 3/8	18 6/8	4	4	Winnebago County	WI	Timothy R. Beck	2005	34548
130 2/8	23 1/8 22 3/8	15 0/8	5	5	Pike County	IL	Victor Pasquin	2005	34548
*130 2/8	23 3/8 21 2/8	20 0/8	4	4	Nicholas County	WV	Larry Phillips	2005	34548
130 2/8	21 4/8 20 6/8	18 2/8	5	5	Montgomery County	MD	Hank W. Voigt	2005	34548
130 2/8	24 3/8 25 3/8	19 4/8	7	5	Union County	SD	Greg Bolf	2005	34548
130 2/8	19 2/8 19 2/8	15 2/8	5	5	Union County	SD	Troy Van Roekel	2005	34548
130 2/8	24 0/8 23 5/8	18 2/8	4	5	Burleigh County	ND	Robert G. Doll	2005	34548
130 2/8	20 6/8 20 4/8	17 0/8	4	4	Mercer County	ND	Scott L. Johnson	2006	34548
130 2/8	22 4/8 22 1/8	15 5/8	6	6	Rainy River	ONT	Curtis Lanxton	2006	34548
130 2/8	24 4/8 25 2/8	19 0/8	5	5	Nelson County	KY	Kevin Barnette	2006	34548
130 2/8	21 3/8 21 1/8	18 6/8	5	5	Middlesex County	MA	Samuel Palmer III	2006	34548
130 2/8	21 0/8 21 5/8	17 6/8	4	4	Buffalo County	WI	Bryan Tamke	2006	34548
*130 2/8	19 5/8 21 2/8	18 2/8	5	5	Douglas County	WI	Timothy Larson	2006	34548
*130 2/8	20 0/8 19 5/8	14 4/8	5	5	Marshall County	SD	Scott Gangle	2006	34548
*130 2/8	22 6/8 23 7/8	14 7/8	5	5	Pierce County	WI	Eric Otto	2006	34548
130 2/8	20 7/8 20 0/8	15 7/8	7	5	Bayfield County	WI	Matt Casper	2006	34548
*130 2/8	22 2/8 20 0/8	14 6/8	5	5	Muskingum County	OH	Codey Elwood	2006	34548
130 2/8	21 2/8 21 5/8	15 6/8	4	5	Adams County	OH	Dave Gray	2006	34548
*130 2/8	23 4/8 24 5/8	20 6/8	5	6	Paulding County	GA	Jammie Newman	2006	34548
130 2/8	22 5/8 22 4/8	20 4/8	4	4	Carroll County	IL	Jim Carlson	2006	34548
130 2/8	22 3/8 23 4/8	17 6/8	5	4	Rusk County	WI	Daniel Sebold	2006	34548
*130 2/8	21 6/8 21 2/8	18 0/8	5	6	Westchester County	NY	Doug Erickson	2006	34548
*130 2/8	22 4/8 23 0/8	16 6/8	4	4	Pulaski County	KY	Ray Weddle	2006	34548
*130 2/8	22 6/8 22 5/8	16 0/8	4	4	Bath County	KY	Zachary McClurg	2007	34548
130 2/8	19 2/8 18 4/8	16 2/8	5	5	Traill County	ND	Duane Dumas	2007	34548
130 2/8	21 2/8 21 2/8	16 6/8	4	4	Independence County	AR	Carol Stephens	2007	34548
130 2/8	20 5/8 20 6/8	15 4/8	4	5	Custer County	SD	Jason Petik	2007	34548
130 2/8	21 5/8 23 1/8	17 1/8	6	5	Sutton County	TX	Dallas Young	2007	34548
*130 2/8	21 6/8 21 3/8	16 2/8	5	5	Marshall County	IN	David L. Thacker	2007	34548
*130 2/8	19 4/8 19 3/8	18 2/8	4	4	McLean County	IL	Lewis H. Arbuckle	2007	34548
*130 2/8	22 2/8 23 5/8	18 4/8	4	3	Lake County	IL	Kory Lang	2007	34548
*130 2/8	25 0/8 24 1/8	15 1/8	7	4	Bourbon County	KS	George Richison	2007	34548
130 2/8	21 4/8 21 3/8	15 4/8	4	4	Trempealeau County	WI	Charles A. Gauger	2007	34548
*130 2/8	21 4/8 21 7/8	17 0/8	4	4	McDonald County	MO	Rusty Johnson	2008	34548
130 2/8	22 2/8 21 6/8	15 3/8	5	4	Cavalier County	ND	Jocelyn Klein	2008	34548
*130 2/8	22 6/8 21 4/8	16 0/8	6	6	Eau Claire County	WI	Teresa K. Becker	2008	34548
130 2/8	24 0/8 22 7/8	16 5/8	6	5	Coffey County	KS	Eugene DuBois	2008	34548
*130 2/8	22 2/8 21 4/8	16 2/8	6	5	Richland County	WI	Steven Svacina	2008	34548
130 2/8	23 1/8 22 1/8	17 6/8	4	4	Eau Claire County	WI	Tony Hagedorn	2008	34548
*130 2/8	24 6/8 25 0/8	17 5/8	7	5	Van Buren County	IA	Scott Knauf	2008	34548
*130 2/8	24 4/8 22 6/8	17 0/8	4	4	Ionia County	MI	Jerry L. Selden	2008	34548
*130 2/8	22 5/8 22 1/8	16 0/8	4	5	Daviess County	IN	Allen Ray Graber	2008	34548

WHITETAIL DEER (TYPICAL ANTLERS)

Minimum Score 125
Continued

SCORE	LENGTH OF R MAIN BEAM L	INSIDE SPREAD	NUMBER OF R POINTS L		AREA	STATE/ PROVINCE	HUNTER'S NAME	DATE	RANK
*130 2/8	22 2/8 22 1/8	15 2/8	5	5	Jackson County	OH	Joshua Kelley	2008	34548
130 2/8	23 2/8 22 1/8	18 4/8	4	4	Maverick County	TX	Darren P. Cooper	2008	34548
130 2/8	21 6/8 21 6/8	17 2/8	5	5	Genesee County	MI	Jeffery L. Burkhardt	2008	34548
130 2/8	19 5/8 19 5/8	14 5/8	5	6	Barber County	KS	Mark Calkins	2009	34548
130 2/8	23 5/8 23 3/8	20 2/8	4	4	Buffalo County	WI	Joseph Kabus	2009	34548
*130 2/8	22 0/8 22 1/8	19 6/8	4	4	Kandiyohi County	MN	Larry Moore	2009	34548
130 2/8	20 6/8 21 0/8	19 0/8	4	5	Warren County	PA	Joe Kvortek	2009	34548
*130 2/8	21 7/8 21 4/8	18 0/8	4	4	Hamilton County	IL	Charles L. Wiggins III	2009	34548
130 2/8	19 7/8 19 6/8	16 6/8	5	6	Fayette County	PA	James Robert Sapp II	2009	34548
130 2/8	22 6/8 21 6/8	16 6/8	4	5	Shawano County	WI	Robert L. Olson	2009	34548
130 2/8	22 4/8 23 0/8	16 7/8	5	4	Niagara County	NY	Ken Swan, Jr.	2009	34548
*130 2/8	22 6/8 22 5/8	15 0/8	5	5	Elmore County	AL	Paul Bowden	2010	34548
130 1/8	24 0/8 23 4/8	18 3/8	4	5	Lyon County	MN	Bruce Grow	1972	34816
130 1/8	22 3/8 22 2/8	17 7/8	4	4	Stanly County	NC	Eric F. Efird	1998	34816
*130 1/8	22 7/8 21 6/8	16 5/8	5	5	Green Lake County	WI	Jennifer Kersting	2002	34816
130 1/8	22 2/8 20 6/8	15 7/8	4	4	Bourbon County	KS	Brian Eason	2003	34816
130 1/8	22 4/8 22 5/8	17 1/8	5	5	Broome County	NY	Neil Newkirk	2003	34816
130 1/8	21 3/8 21 2/8	15 1/8	5	5	McLean County	ND	Vance Tomlinson	2004	34816
130 1/8	20 5/8 21 0/8	17 7/8	4	4	Monmouth County	NJ	Brett Search	2004	34816
*130 1/8	21 4/8 21 7/8	13 3/8	5	5	White County	AR	Ed Mascarenas	2004	34816
130 1/8	23 7/8 22 0/8	19 5/8	5	5	Franklin County	PA	Terry L. Cline	2004	34816
130 1/8	21 2/8 22 0/8	14 5/8	7	6	Navarro County	TX	Marston Alexander	2004	34816
130 1/8	21 3/8 21 2/8	17 4/8	5	5	Howard County	IN	James Slaughter	2004	34816
130 1/8	20 4/8 15 4/8	18 3/8	6	5	Fulton County	IL	Jerry G. Heidel	2004	34816
130 1/8	23 6/8 23 7/8	17 5/8	4	4	Douglas County	MN	Glen L. Wink	2004	34816
130 1/8	22 4/8 21 5/8	17 2/8	7	7	Davis County	IA	Ron Friedman	2004	34816
130 1/8	22 6/8 21 7/8	21 3/8	4	4	Trempealeau County	WI	Bill J. Black	2004	34816
130 1/8	22 7/8 24 0/8	18 0/8	4	6	Rockingham County	NH	Richard Perreault	2004	34816
130 1/8	22 5/8 23 0/8	18 7/8	4	4	Douglas County	WI	Floyd E. Peters, Jr.	2004	34816
130 1/8	22 2/8 21 4/8	14 7/8	5	4	Mercer County	IL	Tony W. Duncan	2004	34816
130 1/8	22 4/8 21 6/8	15 5/8	5	5	Llano County	TX	Dan W. Kemp	2004	34816
130 1/8	20 3/8 20 1/8	15 5/8	5	5	Dodge County	MN	Jesse Stevenson	2005	34816
130 1/8	22 4/8 23 2/8	19 7/8	4	5	Traill County	ND	Josh Kritzberger	2005	34816
130 1/8	23 0/8 22 6/8	17 1/8	5	5	Sawyer County	WI	Sonja M. Dickerson	2005	34816
*130 1/8	21 0/8 20 7/8	13 5/8	4	4	Pike County	IL	Arthur Forman	2005	34816
*130 1/8	19 6/8 19 7/8	16 3/8	6	5	Allen County	IN	Lyle Felger	2005	34816
130 1/8	22 0/8 22 0/8	18 2/8	5	5	Mercer County	NJ	Salvatore Piazza, Jr.	2005	34816
130 1/8	24 6/8 23 4/8	17 3/8	7	4	Calhoun County	MI	Mark Reynolds	2005	34816
*130 1/8	24 0/8 23 2/8	19 3/8	4	4	La Crosse County	WI	Shawn Zellmer	2005	34816
130 1/8	19 7/8 21 2/8	19 1/8	4	4	Auglaize County	OH	Dave Slife	2005	34816
130 1/8	20 7/8 20 5/8	15 6/8	6	5	Buffalo County	WI	Dave Beeler	2005	34816
*130 1/8	23 2/8 23 0/8	17 5/8	5	5	Douglas County	WI	Kenneth J. Waldvogel	2005	34816
130 1/8	23 4/8 23 3/8	17 7/8	5	5	Adams County	IA	Dean Lammers	2005	34816
130 1/8	22 2/8 23 3/8	16 5/8	4	4	Crawford County	WI	John Yatzeck	2005	34816
130 1/8	22 2/8 22 2/8	17 4/8	6	5	Defiance County	OH	Gary Bendele	2005	34816
130 1/8	22 4/8 22 4/8	15 2/8	6	5	Spokane County	WA	John Schneider	2005	34816
130 1/8	22 6/8 22 1/8	18 7/8	4	4	Monmouth County	NJ	William Hyer	2005	34816
130 1/8	22 0/8 20 3/8	17 7/8	5	5	Kewaunee County	WI	Matthew J. Lensmire	2006	34816
*130 1/8	22 2/8 22 3/8	17 7/8	4	4	Waukesha County	WI	Scott Prucha	2006	34816
*130 1/8	19 6/8 20 1/8	18 3/8	5	5	Montgomery County	IN	Dan P. Yeager	2006	34816
*130 1/8	21 0/8 20 6/8	16 1/8	5	5	Ionia County	MI	Raymond K. Meyer	2006	34816
130 1/8	21 2/8 23 1/8	19 7/8	4	4	La Porte County	IN	Chad A. Schau	2006	34816
*130 1/8	21 4/8 21 2/8	18 3/8	6	5	Westmoreland County	PA	Jesse J. Orzehowski	2006	34816
130 1/8	24 4/8 24 1/8	18 3/8	5	6	Champaign County	IL	Doug McClure	2006	34816
130 1/8	22 4/8 22 4/8	16 3/8	4	4	Nodaway County	MO	Max Harden	2006	34816
130 1/8	23 7/8 24 0/8	16 3/8	4	4	Pike County	IL	Drew Lambert	2006	34816
130 1/8	23 5/8 24 2/8	17 1/8	6	4	Fayette County	IL	Scott Hunt	2006	34816
130 1/8	24 4/8 24 6/8	15 5/8	4	5	Bolivar County	MS	Henry Park Hiter, Jr.	2006	34816
130 1/8	22 4/8 23 2/8	19 0/8	5	5	Buffalo County	WI	Jim Wondzell	2006	34816
130 1/8	21 7/8 22 1/8	17 5/8	4	5	Bolivar County	MS	Lance Johnson	2006	34816
130 1/8	25 0/8 25 3/8	15 5/8	4	4	Fulton County	IL	Chuck Thome	2006	34816
*130 1/8	20 6/8 21 1/8	15 6/8	5	5	Crook County	WY	Lance Marshall	2007	34816
130 1/8	21 1/8 22 0/8	14 1/8	5	5	Henry County	IA	Bruce Krause	2007	34816
*130 1/8	21 7/8 21 4/8	14 7/8	4	4	Putnam County	FL	John R. Shaw III	2007	34816
*130 1/8	21 6/8 23 1/8	17 3/8	5	5	Marquette County	WI	Jim Poetter	2007	34816
130 1/8	20 1/8 20 3/8	14 5/8	5	5	Menard County	IL	George G. Bogie	2007	34816
130 1/8	23 0/8 22 4/8	12 4/8	5	6	Carroll County	MS	Butch Duvall	2007	34816
130 1/8	24 3/8 23 7/8	15 3/8	4	4	Linn County	KS	Douglas L. Below	2007	34816
130 1/8	23 3/8 22 7/8	17 5/8	6	4	Knox County	IL	Lee Lewis	2007	34816
*130 1/8	20 0/8 20 7/8	16 1/8	6	6	Marshall County	IN	Brent W. Ferman	2007	34816
130 1/8	23 1/8 23 6/8	18 7/8	4	4	Allamakee County	IA	Earl Goodman	2007	34816
130 1/8	23 0/8 21 4/8	17 1/8	5	5	Genesee County	NY	Richard Klein	2007	34816
130 1/8	19 5/8 20 1/8	15 0/8	5	6	Marion County	IL	Sid Tingen	2007	34816
130 1/8	21 0/8 20 5/8	14 7/8	5	5	Will County	IL	Charles Zandstra	2007	34816
130 1/8	19 7/8 18 7/8	13 3/8	5	5	Starke County	IN	Robert C. Compton	2007	34816
*130 1/8	25 5/8 24 2/8	21 5/8	7	5	Middlesex County	NJ	John Yaccarino	2007	34816
130 1/8	19 6/8 19 7/8	15 1/8	5	5	Campbell County	SD	Travis Hanson	2007	34816
130 1/8	24 7/8 24 4/8	16 3/8	4	4	Granville County	NC	Robert Anderson	2008	34816
130 1/8	21 6/8 21 3/8	15 3/8	5	5	Wells County	ND	Lydia Robarge	2008	34816
*130 1/8	23 0/8 23 1/8	19 3/8	5	4	Columbia County	WI	Keith Crawford	2008	34816
*130 1/8	22 2/8 22 3/8	14 5/8	6	4	Custer County	SD	Kevin Strand	2008	34816
130 1/8	20 3/8 21 0/8	15 5/8	5	5	Houston County	MN	Stephen A. Dougherty	2008	34816
*130 1/8	20 5/8 20 3/8	16 5/8	5	4	Hancock County	WV	Victor S. Holdren	2008	34816
*130 1/8	20 2/8 20 3/8	15 4/8	6	5	Grant County	WI	Chad Breuer	2008	34816
130 1/8	19 5/8 20 5/8	16 3/8	5	5	Archer County	TX	Jack Johnson	2008	34816
*130 1/8	24 7/8 24 3/8	17 2/8	5	4	Green Lake County	WI	Phillip Fisher	2009	34816
130 1/8	20 2/8 19 5/8	16 4/8	6	5	Dodge County	WI	Jesse R. Grew	2009	34816
130 1/8	20 5/8 20 5/8	15 1/8	8	6	Adams County	IL	Robert J. Riley	2009	34816
*130 1/8	19 3/8 18 2/8	15 1/8	5	5	Athens County	OH	David Iser	2009	34816
130 1/8	17 0/8 17 7/8	15 7/8	5	5	Buffalo County	SD	Jerri Ann Haak	2009	34816
130 1/8	22 6/8 22 0/8	14 7/8	6	4	Worth County	GA	Morris Brown Mitchell	2009	34816
*130 1/8	22 0/8 21 7/8	19 3/8	4	5	Obion County	TN	Tommy Stewart	2009	34816
130 0/8	22 2/8 22 3/8	16 1/8	5	5	Jefferson County	IN	Damon Broady	1992	35087
130 0/8	24 1/8 24 0/8	15 6/8	5	4	Rockingham County	NC	Richard B. Dyer	1997	35087
130 0/8	20 6/8 20 4/8	17 2/8	4	4	Weld County	CO	Timothy Bradley	1997	35087

Deer entries below 141 0/8, that appeared in the 6th Edition, are not included here, but are included on the accompanying CD (see page 119), and also in the Club's Records Archives.

593

WHITETAIL DEER (TYPICAL ANTLERS)

Minimum Score 125 — Continued

SCORE	LENGTH OF R MAIN BEAM L	INSIDE SPREAD	NUMBER OF R POINTS L		AREA	STATE/PROVINCE	HUNTER'S NAME	DATE	RANK
130 0/8	21 6/8	21 7/8	14 0/8	5	5	Pike County	IL	Joe P. Arbic	2000	35087
130 0/8	21 3/8	21 5/8	16 4/8	5	5	Ashland County	WI	Kenneth Meindl	2001	35087
130 0/8	19 2/8	19 5/8	17 0/8	4	4	Ward County	ND	John R. Plesuk	2002	35087
130 0/8	23 0/8	22 4/8	16 4/8	4	5	Livingston County	IL	Craig A. Greskoviak	2003	35087
130 0/8	22 7/8	22 6/8	17 4/8	4	5	Outagamie County	WI	Randy Vollmer	2003	35087
*130 0/8	22 4/8	21 5/8	15 1/8	5	6	Douglas County	MN	Jason Lybeck	2004	35087
130 0/8	20 6/8	20 1/8	17 4/8	5	5	Delaware County	IA	Kelly Salow	2004	35087
*130 0/8	22 0/8	22 7/8	16 0/8	4	4	Warren County	NJ	Jason Gardella	2004	35087
130 0/8	22 6/8	20 3/8	18 4/8	5	5	Will County	IL	Kenneth A. Zimny	2004	35087
*130 0/8	21 5/8	21 4/8	17 0/8	5	6	Allen County	OH	Chris Young	2004	35087
130 0/8	21 5/8	22 6/8	16 0/8	4	5	Mercer County	PA	Gene F. Schilling	2004	35087
130 0/8	23 0/8	22 6/8	16 4/8	5	5	Shelby County	IL	Jesse Wallin	2004	35087
130 0/8	21 6/8	22 0/8	15 0/8	5	5	Brown County	IL	Luke Stamerjohn	2004	35087
130 0/8	22 2/8	22 4/8	17 6/8	4	4	Steuben County	NY	David L. Fleet	2004	35087
130 0/8	20 3/8	20 4/8	17 0/8	5	6	Spokane County	WA	Hayden Symbol	2004	35087
130 0/8	22 6/8	21 6/8	18 4/8	5	5	Dimmit County	TX	Lawrence Demeuse	2004	35087
*130 0/8	22 3/8	23 2/8	19 2/8	4	4	San Saba County	TX	Lisa M. Ameen	2004	35087
130 0/8	20 6/8	20 7/8	13 4/8	5	6	Mingo County	WV	Greg Surber	2004	35087
130 0/8	23 2/8	23 5/8	19 2/8	4	4	Somerset County	NJ	Joseph Raio	2005	35087
*130 0/8	19 7/8	19 7/8	15 3/8	5	4	Goodlands	MAN	Glenn Allen	2005	35087
130 0/8	23 3/8	24 5/8	18 0/8	4	4	Calhoun County	MI	George I. Swan, Jr.	2005	35087
130 0/8	21 1/8	21 1/8	15 5/8	5	6	Van Buren County	MI	Jonathon Van Dam	2005	35087
*130 0/8	22 1/8	22 6/8	15 5/8	6	5	Oconto County	WI	Michael D. Peterson	2005	35087
130 0/8	20 5/8	20 4/8	18 2/8	5	5	Monongalia County	WV	Charles Uphold	2005	35087
130 0/8	18 7/8	18 6/8	15 6/8	6	6	Marathon County	WI	Mike Nelson	2005	35087
130 0/8	23 0/8	23 4/8	19 6/8	5	5	Trempealeau County	WI	Tom Kloss	2005	35087
*130 0/8	19 4/8	20 0/8	16 4/8	5	5	Brown County	SD	Shaun Opsahl	2005	35087
130 0/8	18 7/8	22 2/8	14 2/8	4	4	McLean County	IL	Bonnie Vance	2005	35087
130 0/8	22 1/8	22 2/8	18 0/8	4	5	Turtle Ford	SAS	Walter J. Palmer	2005	35087
*130 0/8	22 0/8	22 6/8	16 4/8	6	5	Pickens County	AL	Rodney King	2006	35087
*130 0/8	22 4/8	22 1/8	16 0/8	4	4	Cygnet Lake	ONT	Roger Schumacher	2006	35087
130 0/8	22 1/8	21 5/8	15 6/8	5	5	Jefferson County	OH	Ronald James Ault	2006	35087
130 0/8	20 7/8	20 3/8	16 0/8	5	5	Polk County	WI	Jason Cummings	2006	35087
130 0/8	19 0/8	19 2/8	18 6/8	5	5	Albany County	NY	Ron Bernhard	2006	35087
*130 0/8	19 6/8	19 3/8	16 4/8	5	5	Polk County	WI	Tom Steege	2006	35087
*130 0/8	21 5/8	20 4/8	17 6/8	4	4	Tippecanoe County	IN	James Beasley	2006	35087
130 0/8	21 5/8	21 2/8	15 6/8	5	4	Clay County	TX	Denver Cole	2006	35087
130 0/8	25 1/8	24 0/8	17 7/8	6	6	Licking County	OH	Joel Thone	2006	35087
*130 0/8	23 6/8	23 2/8	18 0/8	4	5	Lawrence County	IN	Justin Guarneri	2006	35087
130 0/8	23 2/8	24 1/8	16 4/8	4	4	Buffalo County	WI	Michael R. Senft	2006	35087
*130 0/8	18 2/8	19 0/8	15 2/8	4	4	Pulaski County	VA	Robert M. Crigger	2006	35087
130 0/8	20 6/8	19 7/8	17 6/8	5	5	Wyandot County	OH	James D. Herring	2006	35087
*130 0/8	22 4/8	21 6/8	17 3/8	7	6	Mitchell County	IA	Jason Wagner	2006	35087
130 0/8	19 7/8	20 0/8	16 4/8	5	5	Ontario County	NY	Jim Wicks	2006	35087
130 0/8	19 2/8	20 4/8	16 0/8	5	5	Harrison County	TX	Richard Kinas	2006	35087
130 0/8	21 2/8	20 7/8	16 7/8	5	5	Charles Mix County	SD	Robert Struck	2006	35087
130 0/8	20 4/8	20 0/8	15 0/8	5	5	Dane County	WI	James Mersberger	2006	35087
130 0/8	23 0/8	22 6/8	17 4/8	5	5	Christian County	KY	Brad Hodges	2006	35087
130 0/8	20 3/8	20 4/8	13 4/8	6	6	Lampasas County	TX	Kirk Worthington	2007	35087
130 0/8	21 3/8	21 2/8	19 6/8	5	6	Glasscock County	TX	Mark Dozier	2007	35087
130 0/8	18 2/8	20 7/8	19 4/8	4	4	Davis County	IA	Gary Biles	2007	35087
130 0/8	23 5/8	23 5/8	16 6/8	5	6	Grant County	NE	Travis Siddall	2007	35087
130 0/8	21 4/8	20 1/8	14 4/8	5	6	Richland County	WI	Harry Fischer	2007	35087
130 0/8	24 5/8	24 7/8	20 2/8	4	4	Montgomery County	AR	Donald Clark	2007	35087
130 0/8	22 0/8	23 1/8	18 6/8	4	4	Woodford County	IL	Jarod Reatherford	2007	35087
*130 0/8	20 4/8	20 5/8	16 2/8	5	5	Plymouth County	IA	Jeff Jurgensmeier	2007	35087
*130 0/8	21 1/8	20 4/8	14 6/8	4	4	Winnebago County	IL	Chris A. Herbig	2007	35087
130 0/8	22 2/8	21 6/8	17 0/8	4	4	Madison County	MS	Charles Wilson Boyer	2007	35087
130 0/8	24 1/8	24 5/8	17 6/8	7	5	Webb County	TX	John Fehlker	2007	35087
130 0/8	21 3/8	21 0/8	18 4/8	4	4	Hartford County	CT	David Hardy	2007	35087
130 0/8	21 6/8	21 1/8	18 0/8	7	7	Carroll County	TN	Tracy Coleman	2008	35087
130 0/8	24 0/8	22 5/8	18 2/8	5	5	Pike County	AR	Heath Van Camp	2008	35087
130 0/8	24 0/8	23 5/8	16 3/8	6	6	Eau Claire County	WI	Jeff Harvey	2008	35087
*130 0/8	23 6/8	23 4/8	19 2/8	4	4	McCook County	SD	LaTona Sandine	2008	35087
130 0/8	24 4/8	24 3/8	20 4/8	4	4	Guilford County	NC	Johnny Walser	2008	35087
130 0/8	22 4/8	21 6/8	17 2/8	4	4	Trempealeau County	WI	Rick Bryson	2008	35087
130 0/8	20 7/8	21 1/8	15 6/8	5	5	Sheboygan County	WI	Tim Weyker	2008	35087
130 0/8	22 3/8	21 5/8	16 2/8	5	5	Waushara County	WI	Jeremy Thull	2008	35087
*130 0/8	22 4/8	22 2/8	19 4/8	5	5	Pope County	AR	Ted Shinn	2008	35087
*130 0/8	23 3/8	23 1/8	16 0/8	5	6	Stoddard County	MO	Chad McGowan	2008	35087
*130 0/8	21 2/8	20 3/8	11 7/8	5	5	Ralls County	MO	Terry Oltman	2008	35087
130 0/8	21 7/8	21 4/8	18 1/8	4	5	Peoria County	IL	Steve Harenberg, Jr.	2008	35087
*130 0/8	23 4/8	23 6/8	16 3/8	6	5	Bureau County	IL	Douglas Gibson	2008	35087
*130 0/8	20 6/8	21 2/8	16 5/8	5	6	Henry County	IA	Gerald Allen	2008	35087
130 0/8	21 3/8	21 5/8	15 0/8	5	5	Clay County	MO	Philip Tiblow	2008	35087
130 0/8	23 7/8	22 7/8	14 6/8	5	4	Kewaunee County	WI	Tonya Delcore	2009	35087
130 0/8	22 0/8	21 7/8	14 4/8	5	4	Winnebago County	WI	Mathew R. Gollnick	2009	35087
130 0/8	19 4/8	19 3/8	14 4/8	5	5	Ripley County	MO	Bo Blackwell	2009	35087
*130 0/8	24 4/8	23 7/8	19 0/8	6	6	Woodbury County	IA	Russ R. Wauhob	2009	35087
*130 0/8	25 3/8	25 2/8	20 3/8	6	4	Bolivar County	MS	James Moore Bowen IV	2009	35087
130 0/8	21 1/8	21 2/8	15 4/8	5	5	McKenzie County	ND	Andy Grinde	2009	35087
*130 0/8	21 3/8	21 4/8	17 1/8	5	6	Pepin County	WI	Kyle R. Pinion	2009	35087
*130 0/8	20 6/8	21 4/8	14 6/8	5	5	Washington County	OH	Jacob S. D'Angelo	2009	35087
130 0/8	19 6/8	19 2/8	15 0/8	5	5	Berks County	PA	Jared S. Baer	2009	35087
*130 0/8	23 7/8	23 3/8	16 4/8	4	4	Dodge County	WI	Brian Held	2009	35087
*130 0/8	21 2/8	22 5/8	16 4/8	5	4	Labette County	KS	John Aguzzi	2009	35087
*130 0/8	24 6/8	24 7/8	19 0/8	4	4	Adams County	IL	Robert Osterman	2009	35087
*130 0/8	23 4/8	23 0/8	18 0/8	5	5	Gray County	TX	Matthew Krueger	2009	35087
129 7/8	21 0/8	21 0/8	17 5/8	4	4	White County	IN	Gordon L. Beck	1991	35370
129 7/8	22 2/8	22 5/8	20 2/8	4	6	Winnebago County	IL	Michael S. Kloster	1992	35370
129 7/8	22 4/8	21 4/8	20 6/8	6	6	Lebanon County	PA	James Carl Bomgardner	1992	35370
129 7/8	21 1/8	21 2/8	15 7/8	5	5	Tompkins County	NY	Merritt C. Compton	1998	35370
*129 7/8	22 2/8	23 4/8	15 7/8	4	4	Madison County	TN	Kenny Thompson	2002	35370
129 7/8	17 0/8	17 0/8	12 3/8	6	6	Kenedy County	TX	Clyde Miller	2002	35370
129 7/8	22 6/8	22 4/8	16 6/8	5	6	Buffalo County	WI	Jerry Rucinski	2003	35370

WHITETAIL DEER (TYPICAL ANTLERS)

Minimum Score 125 — Continued

SCORE	LENGTH OF MAIN BEAM R	L	INSIDE SPREAD	NUMBER OF POINTS R	L	AREA	STATE/ PROVINCE	HUNTER'S NAME	DATE	RANK
129 7/8	18 0/8	21 7/8	14 7/8	4	5	Crawford County	WI	Bud Rogers	2003	35370
129 7/8	25 6/8	26 4/8	21 7/8	4	4	Hunterdon County	NJ	Ira J. Deshields III	2004	35370
129 7/8	20 7/8	21 3/8	18 7/8	5	6	Portage County	WI	Jerome L. Kawski	2004	35370
*129 7/8	20 3/8	20 3/8	15 1/8	4	4	Dallas County	IA	Drew Love	2004	35370
129 7/8	21 7/8	21 6/8	15 3/8	5	5	Ripley County	IN	Scott Linkel	2004	35370
*129 7/8	21 5/8	21 6/8	15 7/8	4	5	Outagamie County	WI	Dennis Doro	2004	35370
129 7/8	21 2/8	21 2/8	14 7/8	6	7	Holt County	MO	Josie Hulser	2004	35370
129 7/8	22 0/8	21 0/8	15 7/8	6	8	Dunn County	WI	Troy Hollister	2004	35370
129 7/8	22 6/8	21 2/8	19 1/8	5	5	Anoka County	MN	Scott A. Berning	2004	35370
129 7/8	25 3/8	25 0/8	17 3/8	5	4	Sawyer County	WI	Bruce Beckwith	2005	35370
129 7/8	21 3/8	22 2/8	15 3/8	5	5	Buffalo County	WI	Jared Suckow	2005	35370
129 7/8	21 4/8	21 6/8	17 7/8	5	4	Manitowoc County	WI	Lucas Karls	2005	35370
129 7/8	23 1/8	22 5/8	16 5/8	4	4	Pike County	IL	Jim Dougherty	2005	35370
129 7/8	22 4/8	22 6/8	17 5/8	8	7	E. Feliciana Parish	LA	Guy Bergeron	2005	35370
129 7/8	23 6/8	23 0/8	17 2/8	5	5	Marquette County	WI	Lawrence D. Yaap	2005	35370
129 7/8	20 0/8	21 0/8	14 1/8	5	5	Vigo County	IN	Brian Crockett	2005	35370
129 7/8	21 3/8	22 2/8	15 5/8	4	5	Westmoreland County	PA	Ben Farmer	2005	35370
129 7/8	21 7/8	22 0/8	18 2/8	5	5	Brown County	WI	John "Bear" Van Straten	2005	35370
129 7/8	22 4/8	23 5/8	19 1/8	4	4	Shawano County	WI	Richard Pluger	2005	35370
129 7/8	20 6/8	21 2/8	17 3/8	4	5	Pike County	IL	Kim Bettinger	2005	35370
129 7/8	20 0/8	19 5/8	16 5/8	5	5	Ogle County	IL	Jeff Gustafson	2005	35370
129 7/8	25 0/8	24 4/8	19 6/8	5	4	Webster County	IA	Jeff P. Sweeney	2005	35370
*129 7/8	25 0/8	26 1/8	17 7/8	6	7	Greenup County	KY	William Frank Maddix, Jr.	2006	35370
129 7/8	21 4/8	20 1/8	15 5/8	5	5	Rock County	MN	Steve Petersen	2006	35370
129 7/8	21 6/8	21 1/8	12 5/8	6	5	Sauk County	WI	James E. Riphon	2006	35370
*129 7/8	21 4/8	22 0/8	17 3/8	4	5	Iroquois County	IL	Jason Brent Amato	2006	35370
129 7/8	20 3/8	21 4/8	15 3/8	5	5	Orange County	IN	James A. Hager	2006	35370
129 7/8	20 3/8	21 5/8	14 5/8	5	5	Butler County	IA	Klay Hoppenworth	2006	35370
*129 7/8	20 7/8	22 1/8	16 1/8	4	5	Clay County	SD	Casey J. Hatch	2006	35370
129 7/8	22 4/8	22 4/8	15 7/8	4	4	Athens County	OH	Richard B. Dyer	2006	35370
*129 7/8	22 5/8	22 3/8	16 7/8	4	4	Noble County	IN	Jared D. Shisler	2006	35370
*129 7/8	20 0/8	20 0/8	14 1/8	6	5	Harrison County	KY	Alex Lyons	2007	35370
129 7/8	22 5/8	22 4/8	17 7/8	4	4	Parke County	IN	Anthony Vore	2007	35370
129 7/8	21 2/8	19 5/8	17 0/8	5	6	Codington County	SD	Gary Brandsrud	2007	35370
129 7/8	24 3/8	23 2/8	20 1/8	6	7	Green County	WI	Steve Sawdey	2007	35370
129 7/8	22 3/8	23 4/8	16 2/8	6	5	Minaki	ONT	John Herrmann	2007	35370
*129 7/8	25 7/8	25 0/8	16 4/8	6	6	Muskingum County	OH	Codey Elwood	2007	35370
129 7/8	22 0/8	21 6/8	18 5/8	4	5	Washburn County	WI	Daniel Niehaus	2007	35370
129 7/8	21 6/8	22 4/8	19 3/8	4	4	Calhoun County	IL	Blaine W. Pazero	2007	35370
*129 7/8	22 2/8	22 6/8	17 5/8	8	7	Jennings County	IN	Troy Vance	2007	35370
*129 7/8	24 0/8	23 2/8	16 3/8	4	5	Washington County	MS	Dr. Larry Ennis	2007	35370
129 7/8	21 0/8	19 7/8	14 5/8	5	5	Steuben County	IN	Kevin Smith	2008	35370
129 7/8	20 2/8	20 5/8	16 0/8	5	6	Pike County	IL	Ray Spolarich	2008	35370
*129 7/8	20 7/8	21 3/8	15 5/8	4	4	Calumet County	WI	Ken Woelfel	2008	35370
*129 7/8	20 3/8	20 2/8	16 5/8	5	5	McHenry County	ND	Greg Newhouse	2008	35370
129 7/8	20 5/8	21 1/8	15 1/8	5	5	Adams County	IL	Carl Lattimer	2008	35370
129 7/8	23 5/8	21 5/8	14 2/8	5	4	Chautauqua County	KS	Dwight S. Wolf	2008	35370
129 7/8	22 1/8	21 7/8	16 5/8	4	5	Perry County	MO	Jeff Mattingly	2008	35370
129 7/8	23 3/8	23 3/8	18 5/8	4	4	Monroe County	WI	Carlton E. Peterson	2008	35370
*129 7/8	20 5/8	21 4/8	14 5/8	5	4	O'Brien County	IA	Marvin Anema	2008	35370
129 7/8	22 2/8	21 2/8	16 3/8	5	5	Madison County	IA	Robert Engle	2008	35370
*129 7/8	21 4/8	22 5/8	15 7/8	6	5	Christian County	KY	Donald Pittman, Jr.	2009	35370
*129 7/8	25 5/8	26 2/8	17 6/8	5	5	Lake County	IN	Mark Duff	2009	35370
129 7/8	21 4/8	21 0/8	18 3/8	3	5	Adams County	IL	Michael A. Shertzer	2009	35370
*129 7/8	19 1/8	19 3/8	14 3/8	5	5	Manitowoc County	WI	Sean Pritchard	2009	35370
*129 7/8	23 5/8	23 2/8	16 1/8	5	4	Burnett County	WI	Byron Hopke	2009	35370
*129 7/8	20 2/8	21 1/8	16 0/8	8	5	Vernon County	WI	Mike Kent	2009	35370
129 7/8	24 7/8	24 6/8	16 3/8	5	4	Massac County	IL	Kim Ralston	2009	35370
*129 7/8	19 0/8	20 1/8	13 5/8	5	5	Tuscola County	MI	James A. Pardo	2009	35370
*129 7/8	21 1/8	21 6/8	19 1/8	5	5	Gallatin County	IL	Gary Greenwood	2009	35370
129 7/8	22 3/8	21 4/8	16 2/8	5	4	Livingston County	MO	Roy Akerson	2009	35370
129 7/8	21 4/8	22 2/8	17 1/8	5	4	Pike County	IL	Dwight S. Wolf	2009	35370
129 7/8	22 3/8	22 4/8	16 5/8	5	4	Linn County	KS	Robert G. Skinner	2009	35370
129 7/8	22 5/8	22 7/8	15 3/8	4	5	Desha County	AR	Tucker Miller III	2009	35370
*129 6/8	22 1/8	22 1/8	15 5/8	5	5	St. Croix County	WI	Christopher Schone	2004	35614
129 6/8	22 6/8	22 2/8	16 0/8	4	4	Kingman County	KS	Patrick Kelleher	2004	35614
129 6/8	20 4/8	21 6/8	14 1/8	6	6	Wyandot County	OH	James A. Thiel	2004	35614
129 6/8	22 3/8	22 3/8	16 2/8	5	5	Pepin County	WI	Nicholas Strumness	2004	35614
*129 6/8	23 5/8	22 6/8	16 0/8	5	5	Eau Claire County	WI	Riley A. Fletschock	2004	35614
129 6/8	21 7/8	21 6/8	15 2/8	5	5	Price County	WI	Melvin Beth, Jr.	2004	35614
129 6/8	21 7/8	21 7/8	16 6/8	5	6	Jackson County	MN	Scott Sievert	2004	35614
129 6/8	21 5/8	21 4/8	16 4/8	4	5	Jo Daviess County	IL	James Bowden	2004	35614
129 6/8	20 6/8	20 3/8	16 0/8	5	5	Woodbury County	IA	Rod L. Buckholtz	2004	35614
129 6/8	23 0/8	22 4/8	16 6/8	5	4	Fillmore County	MN	Bill Rousu	2004	35614
129 6/8	18 6/8	18 6/8	16 6/8	6	6	Fond du Lac County	WI	Gerrad Kibbel	2004	35614
129 6/8	21 5/8	20 6/8	14 6/8	4	5	Washington County	KS	A. Scott Enloe	2004	35614
129 6/8	20 5/8	21 4/8	14 6/8	5	5	Buffalo County	WI	Aaron Nordby	2004	35614
129 6/8	22 5/8	21 5/8	18 0/8	5	5	Harrison County	OH	Rodney Stoner	2004	35614
129 6/8	22 2/8	21 5/8	15 0/8	4	4	Dearborn County	IN	Jeff Middendorf	2004	35614
129 6/8	19 2/8	18 6/8	15 0/8	6	5	Brown County	WI	Dennis R. Pieschek	2004	35614
129 6/8	24 0/8	24 5/8	17 4/8	4	4	Rock Island County	IL	Ken Yeater	2004	35614
129 6/8	18 4/8	18 4/8	16 2/8	5	5	Outagamie County	WI	Jeffrey L. Steede	2004	35614
129 6/8	21 6/8	22 3/8	13 0/8	4	6	Wilbarger County	TX	Rodney Alexander	2004	35614
*129 6/8	22 5/8	22 2/8	16 7/8	6	5	Cape Girardeau County	MO	Kenton Roth	2004	35614
129 6/8	19 7/8	19 4/8	16 0/8	5	5	Mineral County	MT	Bill Sansom	2005	35614
*129 6/8	19 4/8	19 7/8	14 6/8	5	5	Sauk County	WI	Marc J. Terry	2005	35614
129 6/8	24 4/8	24 6/8	16 5/8	4	6	Brookings County	SD	Zach Bartels	2005	35614
129 6/8	24 2/8	23 7/8	17 0/8	4	4	Chester County	PA	David M. Dry	2005	35614
*129 6/8	23 1/8	22 6/8	17 0/8	7	8	Richland County	IL	Jerry McVaigh	2005	35614
129 6/8	23 5/8	22 5/8	20 1/8	5	5	Delaware County	IA	John Osterhaus	2005	35614
129 6/8	19 5/8	19 5/8	15 6/8	5	5	Bon Homme County	SD	Corey Gall	2005	35614
*129 6/8	20 6/8	21 1/8	16 4/8	5	5	Kewaunee County	WI	Thomas C. Spiering	2005	35614
129 6/8	21 3/8	20 7/8	16 0/8	4	5	Shawano County	WI	Samuel Utke	2005	35614
129 6/8	22 3/8	22 1/8	17 0/8	4	4	Washington County	KS	Steve Line	2005	35614
129 6/8	23 2/8	23 0/8	18 6/8	5	4	Lamoure County	ND	Landyn Johnson	2005	35614

Deer entries below 141 0/8, that appeared in the 6th Edition, are not included here, but are included on the accompanying CD (see page 119), and also in the Club's Records Archives.

WHITETAIL DEER (TYPICAL ANTLERS)

Minimum Score 125   Continued

SCORE	LENGTH OF R MAIN BEAM L	INSIDE SPREAD	NUMBER OF R POINTS L	AREA	STATE/ PROVINCE	HUNTER'S NAME	DATE	RANK
*129 6/8	20 4/8 20 3/8	15 4/8	5 5	Tillman County	OK	Shane Smith	2005	35614
129 6/8	21 6/8 20 4/8	14 7/8	6 6	Webb County	TX	Mickey W. Hellickson	2005	35614
129 6/8	19 4/8 20 0/8	16 2/8	5 5	Renville County	ND	Brian C. Baska	2006	35614
129 6/8	22 3/8 22 6/8	18 2/8	4 5	La Crosse County	WI	Michael L. Marcou	2006	35614
129 6/8	20 0/8 20 0/8	15 2/8	6 6	Walsh County	ND	Shawn Cudmore	2006	35614
*129 6/8	21 0/8 20 3/8	17 1/8	6 4	Cass County	ND	Craig A. Wendt	2006	35614
129 6/8	23 5/8 22 6/8	15 7/8	5 4	Saline County	IL	Matthew Murray	2006	35614
129 6/8	22 4/8 22 5/8	15 6/8	4 4	Stearns County	MN	Mike Allen	2006	35614
*129 6/8	24 3/8 23 3/8	16 6/8	4 5	Scott County	IL	Gary Goldasich	2006	35614
129 6/8	22 0/8 22 7/8	16 6/8	4 4	Fillmore County	MN	Richard Dean	2006	35614
129 6/8	22 4/8 22 6/8	15 6/8	5 5	Cass County	NE	Roger G. Kuhn	2006	35614
*129 6/8	22 4/8 22 0/8	16 2/8	4 5	Granville County	NC	Robert Michael Ellington	2006	35614
*129 6/8	23 2/8 22 6/8	17 6/8	5 5	Kalamazoo County	MI	Joseph King	2006	35614
129 6/8	19 6/8 20 3/8	17 1/8	7 5	Johnson County	IA	Clint Larrison	2006	35614
129 6/8	21 1/8 21 4/8	14 4/8	4 4	Carbon County	PA	Earl Weller	2006	35614
*129 6/8	22 2/8 22 7/8	15 4/8	5 4	Sheboygan County	WI	Michael Budrecki	2006	35614
*129 6/8	21 4/8 21 6/8	16 1/8	5 4	Wabash County	IN	Donald R. Pulcifer	2006	35614
129 6/8	22 1/8 23 2/8	18 6/8	4 4	Franklin County	IL	Cedric L. Malone, Jr.	2006	35614
*129 6/8	22 5/8 21 1/8	18 4/8	4 4	Morgan County	IN	Chad M. Earlywine	2006	35614
129 6/8	23 0/8 22 4/8	17 0/8	4 4	Clark County	KS	Greg Pike	2006	35614
129 6/8	22 0/8 21 6/8	15 4/8	5 4	Branch County	MI	Mark David Routledge	2007	35614
*129 6/8	20 5/8 21 2/8	15 0/8	5 5	Hempstead County	AR	Steve Day	2007	35614
129 6/8	23 3/8 23 3/8	19 6/8	4 4	Allegan County	MI	Amber L. Tamer	2007	35614
*129 6/8	22 6/8 23 1/8	17 0/8	4 4	Wapello County	IA	Doug Meixner	2007	35614
129 6/8	20 0/8 20 1/8	15 4/8	6 5	Carlisle County	KY	Duane Rowe	2007	35614
*129 6/8	22 5/8 22 4/8	18 5/8	7 8	Lancaster County	NE	Brett Hillis	2007	35614
129 6/8	21 5/8 22 1/8	17 2/8	4 4	Rice County	MN	Dan Gillen	2007	35614
129 6/8	22 5/8 22 0/8	18 0/8	4 4	Portage County	WI	Al Wolloch	2007	35614
129 6/8	23 2/8 22 5/8	14 0/8	5 6	Highland County	OH	Tim Webb	2007	35614
129 6/8	22 7/8 22 7/8	18 2/8	4 4	Columbia County	WI	Peter J. McCormick	2007	35614
129 6/8	22 6/8 22 0/8	17 3/8	6 5	Sauk County	WI	Richard W. Krueger	2007	35614
*129 6/8	20 5/8 20 6/8	16 6/8	5 5	Crawford County	WI	Gary L. Birkholz	2007	35614
129 6/8	22 1/8 22 1/8	19 4/8	7 5	Vernon County	WI	Joseph J. Heckenkamp	2007	35614
*129 6/8	22 3/8 21 6/8	18 6/8	4 4	Outagamie County	WI	Richard Huettl	2007	35614
129 6/8	22 0/8 22 0/8	17 6/8	4 4	Defiance County	OH	Todd Twigg	2007	35614
*129 6/8	23 1/8 22 0/8	16 2/8	5 5	Knox County	OH	Dewey Rogers	2007	35614
*129 6/8	21 6/8 22 6/8	16 0/8	4 4	Darke County	OH	Todd J. Harter	2007	35614
129 6/8	21 4/8 22 0/8	17 2/8	4 4	Somerset County	NJ	James Dean Hartobey	2007	35614
129 6/8	21 0/8 20 5/8	14 2/8	5 5	Owen County	IN	Ty Hampe	2007	35614
129 6/8	21 7/8 22 3/8	15 6/8	5 4	Davis County	IA	Marc Rogers	2008	35614
*129 6/8	21 2/8 21 2/8	15 3/8	5 6	McKenzie County	ND	Patrick Hurt	2008	35614
*129 6/8	23 1/8 22 3/8	17 5/8	4 6	Tippecanoe County	IN	Phillip M. Hardy	2008	35614
129 6/8	18 1/8 18 5/8	13 7/8	6 6	Appanoose County	IA	Jerry Batzlaff	2008	35614
129 6/8	20 1/8 20 2/8	14 4/8	5 6	Marquette County	WI	David E. Wenzel	2008	35614
129 6/8	20 3/8 20 3/8	14 0/8	5 5	Marshall County	SD	Eric Marcoe	2008	35614
129 6/8	20 7/8 20 6/8	17 6/8	5 5	Schuylkill County	PA	Scott Schaffer	2008	35614
*129 6/8	20 3/8 19 5/8	19 0/8	5 5	Harlan County	NE	Roy K. Keefer	2008	35614
*129 6/8	19 6/8 20 6/8	16 4/8	5 5	Fremont County	IA	Rick Cardarelli	2008	35614
129 6/8	20 6/8 20 6/8	18 3/8	6 4	Grayson County	TX	Daniel Powell	2008	35614
129 6/8	22 3/8 21 1/8	20 0/8	4 4	Casey County	KY	James Humphrey	2008	35614
129 6/8	20 5/8 19 7/8	14 5/8	5 5	Platte County	MO	Dennis Ballweg	2009	35614
*129 6/8	21 4/8 21 3/8	14 4/8	4 5	Benson County	ND	Rod Wurgler	2009	35614
129 6/8	21 5/8 21 1/8	15 4/8	5 5	Morgan County	IL	Mike Jones	2009	35614
*129 6/8	21 6/8 22 3/8	18 6/8	6 5	Wabasha County	MN	Ianko Dimitrov Iankov	2009	35614
129 6/8	23 0/8 22 3/8	18 4/8	4 4	Erath County	TX	Justin Stafford	2009	35614
*129 6/8	22 5/8 21 1/8	15 4/8	5 5	Cattaraugus County	NY	Thomas Hazen	2009	35614
*129 6/8	23 4/8 22 2/8	19 6/8	5 6	Monmouth County	NJ	Jeff Paplin	2009	35614
129 6/8	22 4/8 21 0/8	14 0/8	5 5	Gratiot County	MI	Ralph Madden	2009	35614
129 5/8	22 2/8 22 4/8	15 7/8	5 6	Washington County	MN	Patrick Wilke	1991	35866
129 5/8	24 2/8 22 7/8	18 3/8	4 4	Allegan County	MI	Dennis J. Mulder	1995	35866
*129 5/8	22 1/8 22 1/8	14 3/8	4 4	Charles Mix County	SD	Gary D. DeJong	2001	35866
*129 5/8	20 1/8 19 4/8	15 1/8	5 5	Phillips County	AR	Chad Hill	2001	35866
129 5/8	22 5/8 22 1/8	15 7/8	4 4	Vernon County	WI	Craig R. Williams	2003	35866
129 5/8	20 7/8 21 3/8	19 5/8	4 4	Ashtabula County	OH	Rick Hildebrand	2003	35866
129 5/8	22 5/8 22 0/8	18 1/8	5 4	Macoupin County	IL	Randy Rutherford	2003	35866
129 5/8	22 2/8 23 3/8	15 1/8	6 6	Todd County	KY	Dwight Lehman	2004	35866
*129 5/8	19 6/8 20 3/8	15 7/8	5 5	Ward County	ND	Wayne Larcombe	2004	35866
129 5/8	24 4/8 23 6/8	18 6/8	6 5	Trempealeau County	WI	David A. Dornquast	2004	35866
129 5/8	22 7/8 22 3/8	16 1/8	4 4	Dodge County	WI	Randall L. Schmidt	2004	35866
129 5/8	22 4/8 22 0/8	15 0/8	6 4	Crawford County	PA	Michael Mioduszewski	2004	35866
129 5/8	19 0/8 19 5/8	12 7/8	5 5	Randolph County	MO	Terry Schnieders	2004	35866
129 5/8	21 4/8 20 4/8	15 7/8	4 4	Waupaca County	WI	Michael A. Meyers	2004	35866
129 5/8	23 5/8 22 6/8	17 1/8	4 4	Pike County	IL	Ivica Hrdjun	2004	35866
129 5/8	23 4/8 23 3/8	17 3/8	5 5	Montgomery County	OH	Anthony W. Simonson	2004	35866
*129 5/8	25 2/8 26 2/8	18 5/8	3 3	Schuyler County	IL	Brian K. Huston	2004	35866
129 5/8	21 2/8 20 5/8	14 6/8	6 6	Redwood County	MN	Jamie Jenniges	2004	35866
*129 5/8	21 2/8 21 3/8	17 1/8	5 5	Wilson County	TX	Paul Jarzombek	2004	35866
129 5/8	21 1/8 21 7/8	14 5/8	5 5	Henry County	KY	Jeremy Kelly	2005	35866
129 5/8	22 2/8 22 2/8	17 1/8	4 4	Fond du Lac County	WI	Stephen L. Klein	2005	35866
129 5/8	23 3/8 23 2/8	17 3/8	4 4	Winona County	MN	Mike Bronk	2005	35866
129 5/8	24 1/8 22 4/8	18 1/8	4 4	La Crosse County	WI	Brian Day	2005	35866
129 5/8	24 0/8 22 2/8	19 4/8	4 5	New Kent County	VA	Robert L. Highlander, Jr.	2005	35866
129 5/8	24 0/8 23 6/8	17 5/8	6 5	Jackson County	WI	Mike Labar	2005	35866
*129 5/8	21 4/8 22 0/8	19 7/8	4 5	Jersey County	IL	Justin Simpson	2005	35866
129 5/8	19 3/8 20 0/8	14 1/8	5 5	Lamar County	GA	Thomas McDaniel, Jr.	2006	35866
129 5/8	21 6/8 20 5/8	17 7/8	4 4	Marathon County	WI	Jon Shuda	2006	35866
*129 5/8	20 7/8 20 5/8	14 3/8	6 6	St. Clair County	MI	Steven Rickert	2006	35866
129 5/8	24 1/8 23 2/8	17 1/8	7 6	Lorain County	OH	Steven D. Reinhold	2006	35866
129 5/8	19 6/8 20 2/8	14 1/8	6 6	Knox County	NE	Duane Loecker	2006	35866
129 5/8	20 4/8 19 4/8	15 6/8	4 6	Claiborne County	MS	Mollie Van Devender	2006	35866
129 5/8	22 2/8 22 3/8	18 5/8	5 5	Clinton County	IA	Mark Schutt	2006	35866
129 5/8	20 6/8 20 0/8	16 1/8	4 4	Marshall County	KS	James L. Ungerer	2006	35866
129 5/8	21 4/8 21 2/8	18 1/8	4 4	Newaygo County	MI	Robert A. Niemiec	2006	35866
129 5/8	23 0/8 22 3/8	15 4/8	4 5	Fulton County	IL	David Courtright	2006	35866
*129 5/8	21 1/8 21 3/8	14 7/8	5 5	Scioto County	OH	Frank Queen	2006	35866

WHITETAIL DEER (TYPICAL ANTLERS)

Minimum Score 125 — Continued

SCORE	LENGTH OF R MAIN BEAM L	INSIDE SPREAD	NUMBER OF R POINTS L		AREA	STATE/ PROVINCE	HUNTER'S NAME	DATE	RANK
*129 5/8	23 0/8 23 0/8	15 5/8	3	4	Jefferson County	IN	Larry A. Phillips	2006	35866
129 5/8	20 4/8 20 3/8	17 5/8	5	5	Shawano County	WI	Karl Prien	2007	35866
129 5/8	22 7/8 22 5/8	14 3/8	4	5	Bradford County	PA	Kyle Sparling	2007	35866
*129 5/8	23 4/8 23 3/8	20 1/8	5	6	Vinton County	OH	Mario Bombardiere	2007	35866
129 5/8	24 0/8 22 3/8	16 3/8	4	5	Greene County	IN	Thomas L. Egnew	2007	35866
129 5/8	21 6/8 21 6/8	18 7/8	4	4	Carroll County	OH	Aaron Tourtillotte	2007	35866
129 5/8	21 1/8 22 1/8	20 1/8	4	4	Dubuque County	IA	Travis J. Boeckenstedt	2007	35866
129 5/8	24 0/8 21 7/8	14 1/8	4	4	Franklin County	KS	Warren D. Kennedy	2007	35866
*129 5/8	21 0/8 19 4/8	15 1/8	5	5	Ringgold County	IA	Greg Simon	2007	35866
129 5/8	23 5/8 24 0/8	18 5/8	4	4	Cayuga County	NY	Peter Drahms	2007	35866
129 5/8	18 1/8 20 1/8	11 1/8	5	5	Lincoln County	MO	Jesse Valdez	2007	35866
*129 5/8	20 2/8 21 0/8	15 7/8	5	5	Jennings County	IN	Melvin Robbins	2007	35866
*129 5/8	24 2/8 24 2/8	17 1/8	4	4	Chester County	PA	Jason B. Gibson	2008	35866
129 5/8	21 3/8 21 7/8	19 0/8	5	6	York County	PA	Kenneth Rocuskie	2008	35866
*129 5/8	21 3/8 20 0/8	13 6/8	5	6	Trempealeau County	WI	Steve Franck	2008	35866
129 5/8	22 0/8 22 1/8	17 7/8	5	5	Scott County	MN	Al Kasper	2008	35866
*129 5/8	20 1/8 19 2/8	16 7/8	4	5	Angelina County	TX	Taylor Haney	2008	35866
129 5/8	21 7/8 21 5/8	16 5/8	5	5	Rock County	WI	Michael J. Blaser, Jr.	2008	35866
*129 5/8	22 6/8 22 2/8	16 3/8	4	4	Parker County	TX	Jeff Mooney	2008	35866
129 5/8	21 5/8 21 4/8	17 1/8	4	5	Trempealeau County	WI	Tim Brandtner	2009	35866
*129 5/8	24 6/8 26 1/8	22 1/8	4	4	Somerset County	NJ	Fred Wistuba, Jr.	2009	35866
129 5/8	22 4/8 22 7/8	17 5/8	5	5	Marshall County	IA	Garry L. Brandenburg	2009	35866
129 5/8	19 7/8 21 0/8	15 6/8	6	6	Calhoun County	IL	Bert Mann	2009	35866
*129 5/8	23 0/8 22 4/8	17 5/8	4	4	Ontario County	NY	Ed Staten	2009	35866
*129 5/8	24 4/8 24 3/8	18 1/8	4	4	Chester County	PA	John Price, Jr.	2009	35866
129 5/8	23 1/8 23 3/8	18 3/8	6	4	Macon County	IL	John A. Michetti	2009	35866
129 5/8	22 1/8 22 3/8	16 5/8	6	5	McDonough County	IL	Richard L. Bothell	2009	35866
*129 5/8	20 3/8 19 3/8	15 5/8	6	5	Polk County	NE	Craig Lundstrom	2009	35866
*129 5/8	20 4/8 20 4/8	16 1/8	4	4	Schuyler County	IL	Daniel L. Cole	2009	35866
129 5/8	23 1/8 22 6/8	20 1/8	5	5	Ward County	ND	Robert S. Dohner	2009	35866
*129 5/8	23 0/8 23 3/8	19 0/8	5	7	Du Page County	IL	John P. Georgean	2010	35866
129 4/8	24 4/8 22 2/8	18 4/8	5	4	Allegan County	MI	Troy Spooner	1996	36092
129 4/8	21 6/8 21 4/8	16 0/8	5	4	Stephenson County	IL	Dana Wybourn	1996	36092
129 4/8	22 3/8 23 4/8	15 5/8	6	6	Bond County	IL	Larry Stockton	1998	36092
129 4/8	22 3/8 21 6/8	20 6/8	4	5	Montgomery County	PA	Phillip W. Feerrar	2001	36092
129 4/8	20 7/8 21 5/8	17 7/8	5	5	Berks County	PA	Jeff Young	2002	36092
129 4/8	21 2/8 22 2/8	17 0/8	4	4	Orange County	NY	Edward Finn	2002	36092
129 4/8	22 3/8 24 0/8	17 2/8	5	5	Allegheny County	PA	James S. Markovitz	2002	36092
129 4/8	21 6/8 22 3/8	16 2/8	4	5	Clinton County	IL	Todd Waymoth	2003	36092
129 4/8	21 1/8 21 2/8	17 3/8	4	5	Daviess County	MO	Garry Pierson	2003	36092
129 4/8	19 6/8 23 0/8	19 3/8	6	5	Holmes County	OH	Othello Croskey	2004	36092
129 4/8	23 2/8 22 6/8	15 6/8	4	4	Baltimore County	MD	George Cavelius	2004	36092
129 4/8	21 6/8 21 7/8	18 4/8	5	5	Chippewa County	WI	Rodney Gilles	2004	36092
129 4/8	19 0/8 21 3/8	15 7/8	6	5	Republic County	KS	Al Deems	2004	36092
*129 4/8	24 6/8 24 5/8	18 0/8	5	3	Jersey County	IL	Billy Bailey	2004	36092
129 4/8	20 7/8 22 3/8	13 2/8	4	4	St. Croix County	WI	Jesse F. Rose	2004	36092
129 4/8	22 4/8 22 3/8	16 7/8	4	5	Kankakee County	IL	Derek Larson	2004	36092
129 4/8	20 5/8 20 7/8	16 0/8	5	5	Ontario County	NY	William B. Switzer	2004	36092
129 4/8	20 3/8 20 2/8	15 0/8	6	6	Menard County	TX	Phil Harris	2004	36092
129 4/8	20 3/8 19 2/8	16 0/8	4	4	Tom Green County	TX	Mark Harrington	2004	36092
*129 4/8	21 6/8 19 7/8	16 7/8	6	5	Sarpy County	NE	Justin Hagge	2004	36092
129 4/8	22 7/8 22 3/8	19 2/8	4	4	Schleicher County	TX	John Harper	2005	36092
*129 4/8	23 2/8 21 7/8	13 2/8	4	4	Kerr County	TX	David Long	2005	36092
*129 4/8	21 4/8 22 1/8	18 0/8	4	4	Fayette County	IN	Darwin Templeton	2005	36092
129 4/8	20 3/8 20 5/8	16 0/8	6	5	Clayton County	IA	John R. Hochberger	2005	36092
129 4/8	23 7/8 22 5/8	16 6/8	5	5	Edgar County	IL	G. Douglas McPherson	2005	36092
*129 4/8	20 2/8 19 6/8	16 2/8	5	4	Mitchell County	IA	Alan Hoisington	2005	36092
129 4/8	19 0/8 19 6/8	13 3/8	6	5	Hardin County	IA	Randy Evans	2005	36092
129 4/8	23 3/8 23 4/8	19 7/8	5	5	Schuylkill County	PA	Frank P. Spleen	2005	36092
129 4/8	20 4/8 20 7/8	15 0/8	6	5	Waupaca County	WI	John W. Miller	2005	36092
129 4/8	24 2/8 24 0/8	17 4/8	4	4	Spencer County	KY	Harold Mudd	2005	36092
129 4/8	24 3/8 23 5/8	18 3/8	6	5	Wagoner County	OK	Steve Thomas	2005	36092
129 4/8	24 2/8 22 7/8	17 7/8	6	6	Franklin County	OH	Kevin M. Hall	2005	36092
129 4/8	22 3/8 23 1/8	14 4/8	5	6	Harris County	GA	Richard Kaigler	2006	36092
129 4/8	23 2/8 23 4/8	18 4/8	4	4	St. Louis County	MN	Nicholas Richards	2006	36092
*129 4/8	21 4/8 21 5/8	18 6/8	5	4	Harford County	MD	Joseph C. Glos	2006	36092
*129 4/8	24 0/8 23 3/8	17 6/8	3	6	Mercer County	PA	Douglas Melvin	2006	36092
129 4/8	19 0/8 18 6/8	15 6/8	5	5	Pueblo County	CO	Ivan Muzljakovich	2006	36092
*129 4/8	23 2/8 22 5/8	14 6/8	4	4	Adams County	IL	Vincent Martin	2006	36092
129 4/8	20 5/8 19 5/8	18 2/8	5	5	Walworth County	WI	Daniel France	2006	36092
*129 4/8	21 1/8 20 7/8	17 4/8	4	5	McHenry County	ND	David W. Bryant	2006	36092
129 4/8	21 3/8 21 5/8	16 0/8	4	5	Butte County	SD	Darin McIntosh	2006	36092
*129 4/8	26 2/8 25 6/8	19 2/8	5	6	Will County	IL	Andrew Manukas	2006	36092
129 4/8	24 2/8 24 0/8	13 2/8	4	4	Desha County	AR	Ben Bush	2006	36092
129 4/8	21 4/8 21 7/8	16 0/8	6	4	Spokane County	WA	Todd Greiner	2006	36092
129 4/8	24 5/8 24 5/8	22 6/8	4	5	Middlesex County	NJ	David A. Thomas	2006	36092
129 4/8	19 3/8 18 6/8	17 1/8	5	6	Leon County	TX	Brian Roberts	2007	36092
129 4/8	19 7/8 19 7/8	15 6/8	5	5	Greene County	IN	Tim L. Sherman	2007	36092
129 4/8	21 0/8 22 0/8	15 6/8	5	5	Woodford County	IL	Mike Theesfield	2007	36092
129 4/8	19 5/8 19 6/8	14 0/8	5	5	Sheboygan County	WI	Tim Weyker	2007	36092
129 4/8	22 2/8 22 0/8	17 5/8	5	5	Peoria County	IL	Troy Schlueter	2007	36092
*129 4/8	23 4/8 24 1/8	17 6/8	5	4	Charlotte County	VA	David Murray	2007	36092
129 4/8	21 0/8 21 0/8	13 0/8	4	6	Hamilton County	IL	David A. Lock	2007	36092
129 4/8	21 0/8 21 0/8	17 6/8	5	5	Buffalo County	WI	Greg Heiman	2007	36092
*129 4/8	21 1/8 21 4/8	16 4/8	4	4	Iowa County	WI	Keith Hasburgh	2007	36092
129 4/8	20 6/8 22 2/8	17 2/8	5	5	Licking County	OH	Eric P. Evers	2007	36092
129 4/8	20 0/8 21 1/8	15 0/8	7	6	Allamakee County	IA	Joe Lieb	2007	36092
129 4/8	22 3/8 22 3/8	16 6/8	4	4	Wabash County	IN	Tony Hoover	2008	36092
*129 4/8	21 2/8 20 2/8	17 0/8	5	5	Dubuque County	IA	Joshua Martyn	2008	36092
129 4/8	21 1/8 21 3/8	16 2/8	5	5	Daviess County	MO	M. Garry Pierson	2008	36092
129 4/8	25 1/8 22 4/8	17 4/8	5	5	Lafayette County	WI	Richard Saalsaa	2008	36092
*129 4/8	22 0/8 22 0/8	15 2/8	7	7	Schuylkill County	PA	John W. Mengle	2008	36092
129 4/8	20 2/8 19 7/8	15 2/8	6	5	Crawford County	IL	Dave Foreman	2008	36092
129 4/8	22 2/8 22 1/8	17 7/8	5	7	Eau Claire County	WI	Robert Mayer	2008	36092
129 4/8	23 1/8 22 2/8	17 6/8	4	4	Vernon County	WI	Kevin Magalsky	2008	36092

Deer entries below 141 0/8, that appeared in the 6th Edition, are not included here, but are included on the accompanying CD (see page 119), and also in the Club's Records Archives.

WHITETAIL DEER (TYPICAL ANTLERS)

Minimum Score 125 — Continued

SCORE	LENGTH OF R MAIN BEAM L	INSIDE SPREAD	NUMBER OF R POINTS L	AREA	STATE/ PROVINCE	HUNTER'S NAME	DATE	RANK
*129 4/8	22 4/8 21 7/8	18 5/8	5 5	Leavenworth County	KS	Michael R. Stephens	2008	36092
129 4/8	19 5/8 20 5/8	15 4/8	4 4	Johnson County	NE	Jerry Brinkman	2008	36092
129 4/8	20 3/8 22 3/8	19 2/8	5 5	Sarpy County	NE	Frank Krajicek, Jr.	2009	36092
*129 4/8	18 7/8 20 0/8	16 0/8	5 5	Columbia County	WI	Dutch H. Ladwig	2009	36092
129 4/8	23 6/8 24 0/8	16 6/8	5 4	Wyandot County	OH	James D. Herring	2009	36092
*129 4/8	21 2/8 22 1/8	16 6/8	4 5	Schuyler County	IL	James R. Wogsland	2009	36092
129 4/8	24 4/8 22 5/8	14 3/8	5 4	Yates County	NY	Eric C. Ryan	2009	36092
129 4/8	21 1/8 22 2/8	17 4/8	4 5	Armstrong County	PA	Floyd D. Claypoole	2009	36092
129 4/8	20 6/8 21 3/8	20 2/8	5 5	Kewaunee County	WI	Mark Koss	2009	36092
*129 4/8	24 3/8 22 3/8	15 5/8	6 4	Sedgwick County	KS	Scott A. Berger	2009	36092
*129 4/8	24 0/8 22 5/8	17 4/8	4 4	Fayette County	IL	Clint Elam	2009	36092
129 4/8	20 0/8 19 3/8	17 2/8	5 5	Sebastian County	AR	Stephen Cagle, Sr.	2009	36092
129 4/8	27 4/8 25 0/8	16 4/8	4 5	Marquette County	WI	Newell Easley	2009	36092
*129 4/8	19 7/8 19 2/8	13 0/8	5 5	Lake County	IN	S. Scott Evett	2009	36092
129 3/8	24 0/8 24 3/8	16 1/8	4 4	Morrison County	MN	Joe Pierce	1992	36347
129 3/8	23 0/8 23 1/8	16 1/8	4 4	Will County	IL	James E. Giese	1995	36347
129 3/8	23 4/8 22 6/8	13 6/8	6 6	Elliot County	KY	Dave Sturgill	2004	36347
129 3/8	19 6/8 20 5/8	15 3/8	5 5	Pushmataha County	OK	Tony Martin	2004	36347
*129 3/8	23 0/8 24 0/8	14 1/8	5 6	Delaware County	OH	Robert Boehm	2004	36347
129 3/8	21 4/8 22 1/8	19 3/8	5 4	Faulk County	SD	Michael J. Yost	2004	36347
129 3/8	21 0/8 20 2/8	16 4/8	5 4	Allegheny County	PA	Brad R. Robinson	2004	36347
129 3/8	22 1/8 19 5/8	17 6/8	4 5	Newton County	IN	Wayne E. Raper	2004	36347
129 3/8	22 4/8 22 7/8	17 3/8	4 4	Whiteside County	IL	Terry McKenna	2004	36347
129 3/8	21 5/8 22 6/8	14 7/8	5 5	Columbia County	WI	Mark N. Livingston	2004	36347
129 3/8	19 0/8 19 1/8	15 4/8	8 5	Sheboygan County	WI	Charles Schlessinger, Jr.	2004	36347
129 3/8	22 2/8 22 3/8	16 1/8	4 4	Marion County	KS	Dennis Ballweg	2004	36347
129 3/8	24 2/8 23 1/8	17 7/8	6 4	Kane County	IL	William Wayne Wishon, Jr.	2004	36347
129 3/8	22 2/8 22 2/8	17 7/8	4 5	Hancock County	OH	Shawn Garmong	2005	36347
129 3/8	19 3/8 19 4/8	15 1/8	6 6	Appanoose County	IA	Albert D. Sindt	2005	36347
*129 3/8	18 5/8 17 5/8	19 1/8	6 6	Westmoreland County	PA	Mark A. Marinchek	2005	36347
129 3/8	22 3/8 22 2/8	17 1/8	5 5	Botetourt County	VA	Matt Cooper	2005	36347
*129 3/8	21 6/8 21 3/8	14 7/8	5 5	Macoupin County	IL	Joe Miller	2005	36347
129 3/8	20 4/8 21 7/8	18 1/8	5 4	Pope County	IL	Lee Hodges	2005	36347
129 3/8	21 5/8 21 3/8	14 7/8	4 4	Richland County	WI	Michael B. Moore	2005	36347
129 3/8	20 4/8 19 5/8	16 7/8	5 5	Mason County	TX	Michele Cage	2005	36347
129 3/8	21 2/8 20 4/8	16 7/8	4 4	Trempealeau County	WI	Ray N. Andersen	2006	36347
129 3/8	21 4/8 20 0/8	17 3/8	4 5	Cambria County	PA	Sherry Jones	2006	36347
129 3/8	21 4/8 21 1/8	14 7/8	4 4	Marathon County	WI	Jeff Wendt	2006	36347
*129 3/8	24 3/8 24 1/8	17 1/8	4 4	Ontario County	NY	Richard W. Albaugh, Jr.	2006	36347
129 3/8	24 0/8 21 7/8	17 1/8	4 5	Shawano County	WI	Douglas L. Below	2006	36347
129 3/8	20 7/8 22 1/8	18 1/8	4 4	Pierce County	WI	Brian Nelson	2006	36347
129 3/8	21 2/8 24 5/8	14 4/8	4 8	Montgomery County	KS	Mark N. Jordan	2006	36347
129 3/8	23 6/8 23 0/8	18 1/8	4 4	Boone County	MO	Chad Grounds	2006	36347
*129 3/8	22 3/8 21 4/8	17 0/8	6 6	Washington County	MN	Mark Bergstrom	2006	36347
*129 3/8	19 3/8 19 1/8	14 4/8	6 5	Shelby County	KY	Christopher R. Morris	2007	36347
129 3/8	22 5/8 21 5/8	16 0/8	5 5	Sawyer County	WI	Barry Peterson	2007	36347
129 3/8	21 4/8 21 4/8	16 7/8	5 6	Gallatin County	MT	Tom Morton	2007	36347
*129 3/8	22 3/8 21 7/8	16 3/8	4 4	Lawrence County	SD	Daniel Axlund	2007	36347
129 3/8	22 4/8 22 4/8	15 4/8	6 4	Adams County	IA	Justin Archer	2007	36347
*129 3/8	22 1/8 21 1/8	15 3/8	5 5	Highland County	OH	Michael R. Cutler	2007	36347
129 3/8	22 0/8 20 7/8	17 3/8	5 5	Price County	WI	Roger G. Niewiadomski	2007	36347
129 3/8	21 4/8 21 4/8	17 1/8	5 5	Livingston County	IL	Jeff A. Hinshaw	2007	36347
129 3/8	24 0/8 22 4/8	16 1/8	4 4	Buffalo County	WI	Adam Pronschinske	2007	36347
129 3/8	23 4/8 21 0/8	17 2/8	5 5	Adams County	IL	Michael L. Brecht	2007	36347
129 3/8	20 2/8 20 4/8	16 3/8	6 5	Stephenson County	IL	Ron Kaderly	2007	36347
*129 3/8	22 3/8 22 1/8	16 3/8	5 6	Baltimore County	MD	Terry E. Grim	2007	36347
129 3/8	20 4/8 20 6/8	15 1/8	5 5	Hancock County	IL	Bradley J. Swanson	2007	36347
*129 3/8	22 4/8 22 5/8	17 6/8	6 4	Knox County	IL	Steve L. Larson	2007	36347
129 3/8	22 2/8 24 3/8	16 3/8	4 4	Comanche County	KS	Ron Rockwell	2007	36347
129 3/8	23 3/8 24 2/8	18 3/8	4 4	Buffalo County	WI	Randy Springborn	2007	36347
129 3/8	20 5/8 20 2/8	16 5/8	5 4	Jersey County	IL	Lawrence Thrash, Jr.	2007	36347
129 3/8	21 1/8 21 1/8	17 1/8	5 5	Ralls County	MO	Cory Romaker	2007	36347
129 3/8	21 6/8 21 7/8	16 1/8	4 4	Bolivar County	MS	Lance Johnson	2007	36347
*129 3/8	23 0/8 24 1/8	22 3/8	5 5	Logan County	CO	Demetrios Mellos	2007	36347
129 3/8	21 6/8 22 6/8	17 5/8	4 4	Saddle Hills	ALB	Mike Slocum	2008	36347
*129 3/8	23 3/8 24 0/8	20 6/8	7 6	Henderson County	KY	Steve Conrad	2008	36347
*129 3/8	21 2/8 21 5/8	17 3/8	5 4	Marion County	IN	Brett Hankins	2008	36347
129 3/8	23 0/8 22 3/8	15 0/8	6 6	Putnam County	WV	Gary L. Lacy	2008	36347
129 3/8	23 1/8 21 3/8	18 4/8	5 6	Cambria County	PA	Joey Hribar	2008	36347
129 3/8	21 3/8 21 3/8	16 3/8	5 5	Monongalia County	WV	Stacey Layton	2008	36347
129 3/8	23 2/8 24 0/8	18 1/8	4 4	Lucas County	IA	Bill Brown	2008	36347
129 3/8	21 0/8 20 7/8	16 4/8	4 6	Traill County	ND	Tyler Hanson	2008	36347
129 3/8	24 7/8 24 0/8	17 0/8	8 5	Chautauqua County	KS	Jeff McClelland	2008	36347
*129 3/8	20 6/8 21 5/8	17 5/8	5 5	Raleigh County	WV	Matthew King	2008	36347
129 3/8	20 0/8 21 6/8	15 1/8	5 5	Fairfield County	OH	Steve Justice	2008	36347
129 3/8	21 2/8 21 3/8	16 3/8	8 5	McCulloch County	TX	David W. Laxson	2008	36347
129 3/8	21 1/8 23 0/8	14 7/8	5 6	Sutton County	TX	Randy Watts	2008	36347
*129 3/8	20 6/8 21 1/8	15 7/8	5 5	Washington County	WI	Don Guerndt	2009	36347
129 3/8	20 4/8 20 3/8	18 2/8	6 5	Allegheny County	PA	Ronald A. Weigand, Jr.	2009	36347
129 3/8	21 7/8 22 7/8	17 6/8	5 5	Blanco County	TX	Walker Hubbard	2009	36347
*129 3/8	21 7/8 21 2/8	16 7/8	4 5	Macomb County	MI	James Lockemy	2009	36347
*129 3/8	21 3/8 21 1/8	16 1/8	4 5	Allegan County	MI	Bryon Pearson	2009	36347
129 3/8	21 4/8 21 2/8	17 2/8	6 5	Macon County	IL	Charlie DeBose	2009	36347
*129 3/8	24 1/8 22 2/8	15 0/8	5 7	Brown County	SD	Mike Hogg	2009	36347
129 3/8	22 3/8 22 3/8	17 5/8	5 4	Buffalo County	WI	Dallas Leo	2009	36347
129 3/8	23 4/8 21 3/8	17 0/8	5 5	Blue Earth County	MN	Blair Sonnek	2009	36347
*129 3/8	22 4/8 21 0/8	17 3/8	5 5	Marshall County	KS	Jason Westphal	2009	36347
129 3/8	22 0/8 21 5/8	17 7/8	4 4	Grant County	WI	Scott LaBarge	2009	36347
*129 3/8	20 1/8 21 3/8	16 5/8	4 4	Van Buren County	IA	Gus Myers	2009	36347
*129 3/8	21 5/8 20 7/8	21 3/8	4 4	Columbia County	PA	Jeremy Gehret	2009	36347
129 3/8	23 2/8 23 1/8	14 5/8	5 5	Okotoks	ALB	Jordan Cook	2009	36347
129 3/8	20 0/8 20 4/8	16 7/8	4 4	Erie County	NY	Joseph Nelson	2009	36347
*129 3/8	25 4/8 24 3/8	16 4/8	4 4	Fairfield County	CT	Larry Savo	2009	36347
*129 3/8	20 0/8 19 5/8	15 6/8	5 6	Black Hawk County	IA	Chris Thode	2010	36347
129 2/8	21 1/8 21 0/8	13 0/8	5 5	Sussex County	DE	Randall Johnson	1998	36587

WHITETAIL DEER (TYPICAL ANTLERS)

Minimum Score 125   Continued

SCORE	LENGTH OF R MAIN BEAM L	INSIDE SPREAD	NUMBER OF R POINTS L	AREA	STATE/ PROVINCE	HUNTER'S NAME	DATE	RANK
*129 2/8	20 0/8 20 7/8	16 6/8	5 5	Champaign County	OH	Eddie R. Dean, Sr.	2000	36587
129 2/8	23 4/8 25 0/8	18 6/8	4 4	Mayes County	OK	Norman Ancerson, Jr.	2001	36587
129 2/8	20 6/8 21 1/8	18 4/8	5 5	St. Louis County	MN	Duncan Puffer	2001	36587
129 2/8	23 4/8 22 6/8	15 6/8	4 4	Williamson County	TN	James Jones	2003	36587
129 2/8	19 5/8 20 6/8	17 0/8	6 5	St. Joseph County	MI	Daniel L. Farr	2003	36587
129 2/8	22 3/8 23 4/8	19 0/8	4 4	Morris County	NJ	Darren R. Da Costa	2004	36587
*129 2/8	20 0/8 20 4/8	14 6/8	5 5	Marathon County	WI	Dani Zimmerman	2004	36587
129 2/8	22 7/8 23 6/8	12 1/8	6 7	McKenzie County	ND	Shawn Staal	2004	36587
129 2/8	21 7/8 22 6/8	17 6/8	3 4	Pike County	IL	Daniel G. Wombles	2004	36587
129 2/8	21 7/8 21 4/8	16 6/8	4 4	La Porte County	IN	Shawn J. Dennis	2004	36587
129 2/8	22 0/8 21 3/8	17 0/8	4 5	Butler County	NE	Marty Masek	2004	36587
*129 2/8	22 5/8 21 6/8	16 2/8	4 4	Hartford County	CT	Shaun Glover	2004	36587
129 2/8	18 7/8 19 6/8	14 3/8	6 5	Jackson County	MI	Robert M. Craft	2004	36587
*129 2/8	21 5/8 21 4/8	16 6/8	4 4	Maverick County	TX	Mike Stegall	2005	36587
129 2/8	20 5/8 20 6/8	17 0/8	6 7	Schuyler County	MO	Matt Buechting	2005	36587
129 2/8	21 7/8 21 3/8	18 6/8	4 5	Houston County	MN	Cale Mensink	2005	36587
*129 2/8	21 5/8 23 3/8	17 2/8	4 5	Allegheny County	PA	Jody Miller	2005	36587
129 2/8	21 7/8 22 1/8	16 0/8	5 5	Trempealeau County	WI	Julianne Schaefer	2005	36587
129 2/8	23 1/8 23 0/8	16 4/8	5 4	La Crosse County	WI	Michael V. Hundt	2005	36587
*129 2/8	23 3/8 23 5/8	17 7/8	7 5	Licking County	OH	Brian Blankenship	2005	36587
129 2/8	23 3/8 23 0/8	16 4/8	5 5	Trempealeau County	WI	Robert Hinrichs	2005	36587
129 2/8	22 1/8 21 7/8	19 6/8	4 4	Douglas County	WI	Bob Gondek	2005	36587
129 2/8	19 6/8 19 4/8	15 6/8	5 5	Pike County	IL	Eric Yancey	2005	36587
129 2/8	20 5/8 20 2/8	15 6/8	5 5	Adams County	WI	Mark E. Zastrow	2005	36587
129 2/8	22 4/8 21 7/8	16 0/8	5 4	Douglas County	KS	Ronald F. Lax	2005	36587
129 2/8	21 4/8 21 2/8	17 0/8	4 4	Monroe County	NY	Cynthia A. Rolph	2005	36587
129 2/8	22 2/8 22 4/8	18 4/8	4 4	Butte County	SD	Brandan L. Lippert	2005	36587
129 2/8	19 4/8 20 1/8	13 6/8	5 6	Renville County	ND	Bruce S. Baska	2006	36587
*129 2/8	21 4/8 23 0/8	14 6/8	5 5	Portage County	WI	Corey W. Schilt	2006	36587
129 2/8	20 1/8 20 3/8	14 6/8	5 6	Merrick County	NE	Shawn Church	2006	36587
*129 2/8	21 2/8 21 6/8	16 4/8	4 4	Branch County	MI	Fred M. Jury	2006	36587
129 2/8	24 1/8 22 4/8	18 4/8	5 6	Fillmore County	MN	Jared Sagdalen	2006	36587
129 2/8	20 4/8 20 0/8	16 2/8	5 6	Douglas County	WI	Dan Mattson	2006	36587
129 2/8	21 7/8 22 4/8	20 4/8	5 5	Green County	WI	Paul Ovadal	2006	36587
129 2/8	22 1/8 22 0/8	18 0/8	5 4	Washtenaw County	MI	David L. Watson	2006	36587
*129 2/8	21 0/8 22 4/8	16 4/8	5 5	Gibson County	IN	Gilbert Scott King	2006	36587
*129 2/8	22 5/8 22 6/8	17 2/8	4 4	Elk County	PA	Randy Geci	2006	36587
129 2/8	23 0/8 23 0/8	15 3/8	4 5	Breckinridge County	KY	Robert E. Ebert	2006	36587
129 2/8	22 5/8 21 2/8	16 4/8	6 5	Guilford County	NC	Cabell "Trey" Early III	2006	36587
129 2/8	20 4/8 19 7/8	16 3/8	6 5	Sheridan County	WY	Tim D. Norton	2007	36587
129 2/8	23 2/8 21 1/8	16 0/8	4 4	Jasper County	IN	Tyler Downing	2007	36587
129 2/8	21 4/8 21 5/8	14 6/8	5 5	Concho County	TX	Phil Laquey	2007	36587
129 2/8	20 5/8 20 5/8	16 6/8	5 5	Venango County	PA	Chad T. Hoobler	2007	36587
129 2/8	19 0/8 18 5/8	17 1/8	5 6	Brown County	IL	Anthony J. DiMarzo	2007	36587
*129 2/8	21 2/8 20 1/8	14 6/8	5 5	Saline County	KS	Charles Werner	2007	36587
129 2/8	22 3/8 21 6/8	19 2/8	4 4	Washington County	OH	Chet Landis	2007	36587
129 2/8	23 6/8 23 0/8	18 6/8	5 5	Issaquena County	MS	Matt Riley	2007	36587
129 2/8	22 3/8 22 4/8	17 2/8	5 8	Athens County	OH	Mick Weller	2007	36587
*129 2/8	21 0/8 20 5/8	17 2/8	5 5	Menard County	IL	Chad Loy	2007	36587
129 2/8	22 1/8 21 6/8	17 3/8	5 6	Pittsburg County	OK	Robin L. Miller	2007	36587
129 2/8	21 6/8 20 6/8	13 6/8	5 5	Goodsoil	SAS	Robert Vogel	2008	36587
129 2/8	21 1/8 20 5/8	19 0/8	5 5	Licking County	OH	Hobert Payne	2008	36587
*129 2/8	21 6/8 20 7/8	14 6/8	4 4	Jumping Pound Creek	ALB	Dave Browne	2008	36587
129 2/8	24 3/8 25 0/8	19 3/8	8 6	Polk County	IA	Larry Grove	2008	36587
*129 2/8	21 2/8 21 2/8	20 0/8	5 4	Parkland	ALB	Cameron Johnson	2008	36587
*129 2/8	23 2/8 22 4/8	14 2/8	5 5	Coles County	IL	Charles Knox, Jr.	2008	36587
129 2/8	21 2/8 21 5/8	15 0/8	5 5	Sauk County	WI	William R. Brown	2009	36587
*129 2/8	22 1/8 22 5/8	18 2/8	4 5	Shawano County	WI	Leighon Pynenberg	2009	36587
*129 2/8	21 0/8 21 2/8	17 4/8	5 5	Sullivan County	IN	Brian A. McCammon	2009	36587
129 2/8	22 1/8 23 0/8	18 0/8	5 6	Jackson County	MI	Jon A. Colby	2009	36587
*129 2/8	22 7/8 21 6/8	15 6/8	6 5	Fairfield County	OH	Scott Lambert	2009	36587
129 2/8	20 7/8 21 0/8	15 0/8	4 5	Brown County	IL	Bruce Aldridge	2009	36587
*129 2/8	21 2/8 20 4/8	14 0/8	5 5	Putnam County	MO	Dusty Loveland	2009	36587
129 2/8	24 5/8 25 0/8	18 0/8	5 5	Albemarle County	VA	Rick Robertson	2009	36587
129 2/8	20 5/8 20 6/8	16 0/8	3 4	Ford County	KS	Bryan Harris	2009	36587
*129 2/8	22 5/8 25 0/8	20 0/8	4 5	Frederick County	MD	Charles B. Jones	2009	36587
129 1/8	22 2/8 20 4/8	17 6/8	7 8	Dodge County	MN	Jesse Stevenson	2000	36831
*129 1/8	22 2/8 21 1/8	14 2/8	5 7	Shiawassee County	MI	Richard M. Van Horn	2003	36831
*129 1/8	21 7/8 21 5/8	15 7/8	5 5	Ohio County	KY	Chris Johnson	2004	36831
129 1/8	19 7/8 19 4/8	14 4/8	5 6	Waukesha County	WI	Jeff Spott	2004	36831
129 1/8	19 7/8 20 3/8	15 0/8	6 5	Noble County	OH	Frank J. Dujanovic	2004	36831
129 1/8	20 2/8 21 2/8	16 7/8	4 4	Bucks County	PA	Jim Haus, Jr.	2004	36831
129 1/8	22 3/8 22 0/8	22 4/8	4 4	Dimmit County	TX	Eldon Knape, Jr.	2004	36831
*129 1/8	22 0/8 22 0/8	17 2/8	7 9	Hempstead County	AR	Joe Mac Raschke	2004	36831
129 1/8	22 0/8 23 0/8	17 6/8	7 5	Somerset County	NJ	Anthony Firrello	2004	36831
129 1/8	22 2/8 21 4/8	19 0/8	6 5	Boone County	MO	Mike Schanzmeyer	2004	36831
129 1/8	20 3/8 20 5/8	14 7/8	5 5	Carroll County	MS	Lee Hankins, Sr.	2004	36831
129 1/8	21 6/8 21 1/8	15 1/8	5 5	Winnebago County	IL	Jack L. Grabbert	2005	36831
129 1/8	22 4/8 21 4/8	19 2/8	5 6	Throckmorton County	TX	Joel Baze	2005	36831
*129 1/8	21 2/8 22 0/8	18 0/8	6 6	Buffalo County	WI	Chad Halama	2005	36831
129 1/8	21 4/8 22 1/8	14 3/8	6 5	Jefferson County	PA	Todd A. Meterko	2005	36831
*129 1/8	22 1/8 21 3/8	15 7/8	5 5	Greene County	IN	Bill Mullis	2005	36831
*129 1/8	23 0/8 22 2/8	16 7/8	5 5	Fulton County	PA	Wilmer Musser	2005	36831
129 1/8	22 6/8 23 0/8	14 5/8	4 5	Howard County	MO	J. Casey Roberts	2005	36831
129 1/8	21 2/8 21 4/8	19 5/8	4 5	Manitowoc County	WI	Eric D. Eichhorst	2005	36831
*129 1/8	22 3/8 26 2/8	17 4/8	5 7	Adams County	IL	James D. Dubuke	2005	36831
129 1/8	21 4/8 22 4/8	15 7/8	5 4	Morgan County	OH	Michael Todd Ware	2005	36831
129 1/8	19 4/8 20 5/8	17 3/8	5 5	Clark County	IL	Michael J. Karanovich	2005	36831
129 1/8	24 6/8 24 3/8	17 3/8	4 5	Onondaga County	NY	John "J.J." Rybinski	2005	36831
*129 1/8	21 7/8 22 4/8	16 0/8	5 4	Worcester County	MD	Gary L. Adkins	2005	36831
129 1/8	21 5/8 21 4/8	18 1/8	5 5	Talbot County	MD	Daniel D. Leonard	2005	36831
129 1/8	21 5/8 23 3/8	19 3/8	5 5	Monmouth County	NJ	Mark Kronyak	2006	36831
129 1/8	21 2/8 20 7/8	17 3/8	5 5	Vilas County	WI	Ronald F. Lax	2006	36831
129 1/8	20 4/8 21 5/8	17 6/8	5 6	Calumet County	WI	John P. Foress, Jr.	2006	36831
*129 1/8	23 2/8 23 2/8	14 3/8	4 4	Fayette County	IL	Troy Payne	2006	36831

Deer entries below 141 0/8, that appeared in the 6th Edition, are not included here, but are included on the accompanying CD (see page 119), and also in the Club's Records Archives.

WHITETAIL DEER (TYPICAL ANTLERS)

Minimum Score 125   Continued

Score	R Main Beam L	Inside Spread	R Points L	Area	State/Province	Hunter's Name	Date	Rank
129 1/8	22 6/8 20 3/8	14 5/8	4 4	Jefferson County	MS	Phillip Ray	2006	36831
*129 1/8	20 0/8 20 4/8	12 5/8	5 5	Jefferson County	WI	John Fonslow	2006	36831
*129 1/8	22 1/8 22 2/8	18 3/8	4 4	Jefferson County	OH	James R. Williamson	2006	36831
129 1/8	17 4/8 22 2/8	18 5/8	5 5	Langlade County	WI	Mark Lehrer	2006	36831
129 1/8	22 1/8 21 3/8	17 7/8	5 5	Jo Daviess County	IL	Bill Salzmann	2006	36831
*129 1/8	21 0/8 20 2/8	15 1/8	5 5	Stephens County	TX	Harvey G. Youngblood	2006	36831
*129 1/8	24 6/8 24 7/8	22 0/8	6 5	Shawano County	WI	Grant Bystol	2007	36831
129 1/8	19 0/8 18 4/8	16 7/8	6 9	Olmsted County	MN	Terry M. Flowers	2007	36831
*129 1/8	23 2/8 24 4/8	15 3/8	6 4	Osage County	MO	Ryan Lueckenhoff	2007	36831
*129 1/8	22 4/8 24 3/8	16 7/8	4 4	Patrick County	VA	Jackie Cole	2007	36831
*129 1/8	19 3/8 20 0/8	16 2/8	5 6	Edgar County	IL	Jerry David	2007	36831
*129 1/8	22 7/8 23 2/8	16 7/8	4 3	Clinton County	MI	Lonnie C. Buck	2007	36831
129 1/8	20 0/8 19 4/8	15 1/8	5 5	Lincoln County	MO	Brice Henry	2007	36831
129 1/8	20 5/8 20 2/8	13 5/8	5 5	White County	TN	Don R. Wagner	2007	36831
129 1/8	20 4/8 21 0/8	19 1/8	4 5	Jackson County	WI	John Schulte	2007	36831
129 1/8	23 7/8 23 4/8	18 7/8	5 5	Clayton County	IA	Tracy Bertch	2008	36831
129 1/8	22 7/8 22 0/8	19 0/8	6 4	Carver County	MN	Jesse R. Ramsburg	2008	36831
129 1/8	20 3/8 20 0/8	16 2/8	6 7	Decatur County	IA	Wendell B. Jackson	2008	36831
*129 1/8	22 1/8 20 7/8	16 6/8	5 5	Schuyler County	IL	Greg Smith	2008	36831
129 1/8	20 6/8 21 2/8	16 3/8	5 5	Macon County	MO	Sean Nephew	2008	36831
*129 1/8	20 4/8 21 3/8	15 0/8	6 5	Williams County	OH	Matt Hanna	2008	36831
*129 1/8	20 6/8 20 7/8	16 5/8	4 4	Lincoln County	MO	Scott G. Corley	2008	36831
129 1/8	25 4/8 24 2/8	18 5/8	4 4	Trempealeau County	WI	Frank G. Hood	2008	36831
*129 1/8	22 4/8 23 4/8	16 0/8	5 5	Jackson County	WI	Thomas Turks	2009	36831
*129 1/8	18 7/8 18 6/8	13 5/8	5 5	Houston County	MN	Derek Myers York	2009	36831
129 1/8	21 4/8 22 6/8	17 1/8	4 4	Phillips County	AR	Ryan Foster	2009	36831
129 1/8	22 7/8 22 6/8	18 0/8	6 5	McHenry County	IL	Mark Gullickson	2009	36831
*129 1/8	23 0/8 21 7/8	16 3/8	6 6	Trempealeau County	WI	Andrew J. Sheldon	2009	36831
129 1/8	21 1/8 20 4/8	16 3/8	4 5	Olmsted County	MN	Marc N. Shaft	2009	36831
129 1/8	23 0/8 23 0/8	16 4/8	7 5	Carrot River	SAS	Buck Horn	2009	36831
129 1/8	21 5/8 21 3/8	14 5/8	5 5	Crawford County	IN	Donald Shelton	2009	36831
129 1/8	19 1/8 19 4/8	16 1/8	5 5	Marinette County	WI	Curtis R. Theisen	2009	36831
129 1/8	21 6/8 21 5/8	13 2/8	6 4	Brown County	IL	Timothy W. Walker	2009	36831
*129 1/8	20 2/8 18 1/8	19 6/8	6 5	Polk County	WI	Charles Block	2009	36831
*129 1/8	22 6/8 21 1/8	16 0/8	7 7	Yuma County	CO	Kyle M. Meintzer	2009	36831
*129 1/8	22 3/8 22 5/8	18 3/8	5 6	Meigs County	OH	Beau J. Bailey	2009	36831
129 0/8	24 3/8 24 7/8	17 2/8	5 4	Dearborn County	IN	Abraham Hall	1991	37057
129 0/8	19 2/8 19 3/8	16 4/8	5 5	Rockland County	NY	Ben Risley	2003	37057
129 0/8	21 5/8 21 3/8	17 0/8	5 5	Isanti County	MN	Tim Dugas	2003	37057
129 0/8	19 5/8 20 1/8	14 2/8	5 5	Ashland County	WI	Jeffrey L. Steede	2003	37057
129 0/8	22 0/8 21 4/8	15 4/8	5 4	Eau Claire County	WI	Dave Stevens	2004	37057
*129 0/8	20 3/8 20 1/8	15 2/8	5 5	Roosevelt County	MT	Gary Dow	2004	37057
129 0/8	21 2/8 20 7/8	15 6/8	5 4	Adams County	OH	Dave Eskew	2004	37057
*129 0/8	22 0/8 19 4/8	13 4/8	5 9	Jefferson County	IN	B. Scott Cyrus	2004	37057
129 0/8	21 4/8 21 4/8	16 0/8	4 4	Scotland County	MO	Daniel Snyder	2004	37057
129 0/8	22 7/8 22 0/8	16 3/8	4 5	Jersey County	IL	Ryan Decker	2004	37057
129 0/8	21 0/8 22 6/8	18 4/8	4 4	Coles County	IL	Daniel Cohen	2004	37057
129 0/8	21 4/8 21 6/8	17 0/8	4 4	Jo Daviess County	IL	Gerry Ward	2004	37057
129 0/8	23 3/8 23 2/8	18 4/8	5 5	Wilson County	KS	Mike Lamade	2004	37057
129 0/8	21 4/8 21 4/8	16 0/8	4 4	Washburn County	WI	Ryan Furchtenicht	2004	37057
129 0/8	23 6/8 24 1/8	19 0/8	5 5	Providence County	RI	Stefano Soderi	2004	37057
129 0/8	20 3/8 20 1/8	16 6/8	4 4	Boone County	IL	Gary A. Noe	2004	37057
129 0/8	22 1/8 21 7/8	16 0/8	7 7	Spokane County	WA	Todd Greiner	2004	37057
129 0/8	19 7/8 19 7/8	15 0/8	5 5	Tom Green County	TX	Mark McDonald	2004	37057
*129 0/8	21 6/8 21 7/8	15 6/8	5 6	Crook County	WY	Jim Leqve	2005	37057
*129 0/8	21 6/8 22 2/8	20 6/8	4 4	Fairfax County	VA	Scott G. Schuler	2005	37057
129 0/8	21 6/8 21 5/8	14 2/8	4 5	Pike County	IL	Kevin Thorburn	2005	37057
129 0/8	25 0/8 24 1/8	19 2/8	4 4	Genesee County	NY	Randy Robb	2005	37057
129 0/8	20 1/8 20 1/8	14 3/8	6 5	Morrison County	MN	Kenneth Beckel	2005	37057
129 0/8	22 6/8 23 4/8	17 6/8	4 4	Delaware County	OH	Randy Rice	2005	37057
129 0/8	21 4/8 21 5/8	14 2/8	6 5	Ripley County	IN	Robert Hunger	2005	37057
129 0/8	20 6/8 21 0/8	15 2/8	6 5	Piatt County	IL	Charlie DeBose	2005	37057
129 0/8	22 6/8 22 1/8	19 0/8	4 4	Warren County	IN	Gary Williams	2005	37057
129 0/8	22 4/8 20 1/8	16 6/8	6 5	Pratt County	KS	Ronnie McCorkell	2005	37057
*129 0/8	23 6/8 23 3/8	16 6/8	6 6	Buffalo County	WI	Chad Sobottka	2005	37057
*129 0/8	22 0/8 20 3/8	19 3/8	6 6	Montgomery County	IL	Jesse R. Jones	2005	37057
129 0/8	22 0/8 23 2/8	20 6/8	5 4	Hampden County	MA	Gary Richard	2005	37057
*129 0/8	22 2/8 22 3/8	14 6/8	4 4	Muskingum County	OH	Doug Falter	2005	37057
*129 0/8	21 2/8 20 2/8	17 2/8	4 5	Shelby County	TN	Mark E. Jackson	2005	37057
129 0/8	22 4/8 23 0/8	17 5/8	7 8	Monmouth County	NJ	Richard Deickmann	2006	37057
*129 0/8	24 1/8 22 6/8	14 6/8	5 7	Pettis County	MO	Chris Smith	2006	37057
129 0/8	22 2/8 22 2/8	15 6/8	5 5	Green Lake County	WI	Bruce Zuehlke	2006	37057
129 0/8	21 3/8 20 3/8	15 4/8	4 5	Pike County	IL	Andy Trudell	2006	37057
129 0/8	24 5/8 23 0/8	20 7/8	5 5	Allamakee County	IA	Greg Gilbertson	2006	37057
129 0/8	22 7/8 24 2/8	16 0/8	4 4	Monroe County	OH	Barry J. Tatro	2006	37057
*129 0/8	24 7/8 25 7/8	21 2/8	3 3	Ontario County	NY	Mike Harvey	2006	37057
129 0/8	18 2/8 18 2/8	17 0/8	5 5	Jackson County	WI	Scott D. McBride	2006	37057
129 0/8	23 3/8 24 5/8	17 0/8	5 5	Buffalo County	WI	Wayne Olson	2006	37057
129 0/8	20 2/8 21 7/8	14 0/8	4 4	Wilcox County	AL	Jason Wilson	2006	37057
*129 0/8	20 6/8 20 2/8	16 0/8	5 5	Kanabec County	MN	Jason Ramthun	2007	37057
129 0/8	22 1/8 21 7/8	18 0/8	4 4	Woodbury County	IA	Mark D. Ricker	2007	37057
*129 0/8	22 6/8 22 2/8	17 6/8	5 5	Prince William County	VA	Mike Bowman	2007	37057
*129 0/8	19 2/8 20 5/8	14 4/8	5 5	Loudoun County	VA	Randy M. Hall, Jr.	2007	37057
129 0/8	23 6/8 21 7/8	14 2/8	4 4	Pike County	IL	Eric Mohrman	2007	37057
*129 0/8	23 1/8 22 5/8	15 2/8	4 4	Isle of Wight County	VA	Billy Handle	2007	37057
*129 0/8	22 6/8 22 6/8	15 4/8	4 4	Llano County	TX	Kenny Baxter	2007	37057
129 0/8	20 6/8 21 0/8	15 3/8	4 5	Cascade County	MT	Brandon Caldwell	2008	37057
129 0/8	19 3/8 19 1/8	15 2/8	5 5	Kaufman County	TX	David M. Upchurch	2008	37057
*129 0/8	22 4/8 23 4/8	19 0/8	4 5	Somerset County	PA	Jeffrey Marlin Gould	2008	37057
129 0/8	21 3/8 22 0/8	16 7/8	6 6	Fayette County	TX	Ryan Keith	2008	37057
129 0/8	21 0/8 21 2/8	16 0/8	5 5	Dane County	WI	Jeff Lange	2008	37057
*129 0/8	21 3/8 20 3/8	17 6/8	4 4	Niagara County	NY	Ryan Burns	2008	37057
129 0/8	22 6/8 22 3/8	19 0/8	5 5	Macon County	GA	David L. Sams	2008	37057
129 0/8	18 3/8 17 3/8	13 0/8	5 5	Mercer County	MO	Chase Milligan	2008	37057
129 0/8	21 7/8 22 5/8	14 4/8	4 5	Keya Paha County	NE	Joseph Edward Smisek	2008	37057

600

WHITETAIL DEER (TYPICAL ANTLERS)

Minimum Score 125 — Continued

SCORE	R MAIN BEAM L	INSIDE SPREAD	R POINTS L		AREA	STATE/PROVINCE	HUNTER'S NAME	DATE	RANK
129 0/8	22 3/8 · 22 3/8	21 0/8	4	4	Lehigh County	PA	Brian Glenn	2008	37057
129 0/8	23 3/8 · 22 6/8	15 4/8	5	4	Fayette County	IL	Michael Rucker	2008	37057
*129 0/8	22 1/8 · 22 2/8	17 0/8	5	5	Hancock County	OH	C. Michael Betts	2008	37057
129 0/8	21 0/8 · 23 0/8	18 0/8	4	5	Suffolk County	NY	Sam Heglund	2008	37057
*129 0/8	19 4/8 · 18 2/8	16 0/8	5	5	Lawrence County	IL	Greg Hance	2008	37057
129 0/8	22 0/8 · 22 1/8	14 0/8	6	6	Kewaunee County	WI	Justin Johnson	2009	37057
*129 0/8	23 0/8 · 22 7/8	14 6/8	4	4	Desha County	AR	Eddie Magness	2009	37057
129 0/8	21 4/8 · 21 6/8	21 2/8	6	6	Trempealeau County	WI	Allen LaRue	2009	37057
*129 0/8	22 1/8 · 21 3/8	16 4/8	4	4	Coshocton County	OH	Jeffrey L. Suter	2009	37057
129 0/8	21 6/8 · 22 7/8	15 7/8	4	5	Nevada County	AR	Dustin Cooley	2009	37057
129 0/8	21 5/8 · 21 6/8	17 0/8	5	5	Green Lake County	WI	Donald D. Hanson	2009	37057
*129 0/8	23 6/8 · 21 7/8	18 3/8	6	6	Noble County	IN	Brad S. Kissenger	2009	37057
129 0/8	21 1/8 · 21 1/8	16 4/8	5	5	Wayne County	NY	Glenn M. Romano	2009	37057
129 0/8	23 6/8 · 24 1/8	15 6/8	5	5	Logan County	OH	Greg McElroy	2009	37057
129 0/8	23 2/8 · 23 5/8	21 0/8	4	4	Cook County	IL	James E. Giese	2009	37057
128 7/8	22 4/8 · 23 2/8	15 1/8	4	4	Lafayette County	WI	James Bowden	1982	37325
128 7/8	20 0/8 · 19 5/8	15 2/8	7	7	Williams County	ND	David Tofte	1989	37325
128 7/8	23 0/8 · 23 3/8	18 6/8	5	4	Callaway County	MO	Marc Owen	1997	37325
128 7/8	21 2/8 · 21 2/8	17 5/8	5	5	Trempealeau County	WI	Matthew R. Andersen	2001	37325
128 7/8	19 6/8 · 19 7/8	12 7/8	5	5	Jackson County	MO	Sturg Cumberford	2002	37325
128 7/8	23 4/8 · 23 4/8	18 7/8	5	5	Nelson County	KY	Wayne Lewis	2002	37325
128 7/8	19 4/8 · 19 6/8	15 3/8	5	6	Monroe County	WI	Denis Haugrud	2003	37325
*128 7/8	23 5/8 · 23 5/8	16 7/8	4	4	Jefferson County	IL	Harlan Pierce	2003	37325
128 7/8	22 3/8 · 23 4/8	17 4/8	5	5	Yankton County	SD	Jeff Simonsen	2003	37325
128 7/8	21 1/8 · 20 4/8	15 1/8	5	5	Dakota County	NE	Danny Rager	2004	37325
128 7/8	25 7/8 · 25 2/8	21 0/8	6	5	Goochland County	VA	Jerry Lee Nixon, Jr.	2004	37325
128 7/8	22 2/8 · 20 7/8	15 6/8	5	5	Jefferson County	AL	Greg Sweeney	2004	37325
*128 7/8	23 5/8 · 22 0/8	16 1/8	4	4	Essex County	MA	Timothy Ropes	2004	37325
*128 7/8	21 2/8 · 21 1/8	16 1/8	4	4	Delaware County	PA	Kenneth G. Burton	2004	37325
128 7/8	22 4/8 · 22 6/8	16 1/8	7	7	Montcalm County	MI	Todd Andersen	2004	37325
128 7/8	22 3/8 · 22 3/8	17 5/8	4	4	Montgomery County	PA	Joseph D. Maddock	2004	37325
128 7/8	23 0/8 · 23 4/8	18 5/8	4	4	Clermont County	OH	Pat Dalton	2004	37325
128 7/8	21 0/8 · 20 7/8	13 1/8	5	5	McDonough County	IL	Troy W. Yingling	2004	37325
128 7/8	23 5/8 · 24 6/8	18 7/8	4	4	Lake County	IL	Greg Hanson	2004	37325
128 7/8	20 1/8 · 20 3/8	12 5/8	5	5	Waukesha County	WI	Alan Hermann	2005	37325
128 7/8	21 2/8 · 21 7/8	20 4/8	4	6	Windham County	CT	David R. Zadrozny	2005	37325
128 7/8	22 4/8 · 22 3/8	18 1/8	4	4	Lawrence County	PA	Art Jeffcoat, Jr.	2005	37325
128 7/8	22 0/8 · 23 1/8	15 0/8	5	5	La Grange County	IN	Aaron Gray	2005	37325
*128 7/8	20 7/8 · 21 3/8	13 7/8	5	5	Orange County	IN	Ryan Miller	2005	37325
*128 7/8	21 2/8 · 21 5/8	26 7/8	4	4	Cecil County	MD	Scott Wolfe	2005	37325
128 7/8	20 4/8 · 20 7/8	17 5/8	4	4	Jackson County	IA	Greg Kubitz	2005	37325
128 7/8	23 2/8 · 23 1/8	17 5/8	4	4	Lake County	IN	Michael Gudenschwager	2005	37325
128 7/8	21 1/8 · 21 5/8	16 7/8	6	6	McHenry County	IL	Ross S. Nelson	2005	37325
128 7/8	22 7/8 · 23 5/8	20 7/8	5	5	Orange County	NC	R. Lee Hayes, Jr.	2005	37325
128 7/8	20 1/8 · 21 1/8	13 3/8	4	5	Crockett County	TX	Bob Kahlden	2005	37325
128 7/8	22 1/8 · 22 7/8	17 3/8	4	4	San Saba County	TX	Aaron K. Flencher	2005	37325
*128 7/8	22 3/8 · 21 4/8	15 3/8	4	4	Madison County	AL	Patrick B. Lawler III	2006	37325
128 7/8	22 7/8 · 21 3/8	16 7/8	4	4	Shawano County	WI	Matthew Hietpas	2006	37325
*128 7/8	20 2/8 · 19 6/8	14 2/8	7	6	Albany County	WY	Ron Mason	2006	37325
*128 7/8	20 6/8 · 21 2/8	15 3/8	4	4	Scott County	IA	Robert Lytle	2006	37325
128 7/8	23 7/8 · 23 5/8	18 5/8	4	4	Sawyer County	WI	Lance M. Ewert	2006	37325
*128 7/8	22 7/8 · 24 3/8	16 7/8	4	6	Jefferson County	WV	Ron Garza	2006	37325
128 7/8	22 1/8 · 21 0/8	17 3/8	4	4	Iowa County	WI	Steve Segebrecht	2006	37325
128 7/8	23 0/8 · 23 3/8	17 5/8	4	4	Lawrence County	OH	Jim Downs	2006	37325
128 7/8	21 0/8 · 21 2/8	17 7/8	5	5	Bedford County	PA	David C. Stapleton	2006	37325
*128 7/8	20 0/8 · 20 6/8	13 1/8	6	7	Putnam County	MO	Chad Owens	2006	37325
128 7/8	20 0/8 · 20 2/8	15 7/8	5	5	Sarpy County	NE	Greg Mitchell	2006	37325
*128 7/8	20 5/8 · 21 0/8	15 0/8	7	5	Jackson County	IN	Doug Stickles	2006	37325
128 7/8	19 6/8 · 19 4/8	14 5/8	6	5	Yankton County	SD	John C. Smith	2006	37325
128 7/8	21 4/8 · 21 7/8	19 1/8	5	5	Meigs County	OH	Dean E. Weber	2006	37325
128 7/8	20 0/8 · 20 1/8	17 3/8	5	6	Wayne County	NY	Brian W. Neal	2006	37325
*128 7/8	23 2/8 · 23 5/8	17 1/8	4	4	Walker County	TX	Donald W. Odom	2006	37325
128 7/8	22 1/8 · 20 7/8	14 5/8	4	4	Tippecanoe County	IN	Brian Neer	2007	37325
128 7/8	21 3/8 · 22 2/8	18 5/8	6	5	Columbia County	WI	Lance Braaksma	2007	37325
128 7/8	20 6/8 · 20 4/8	18 3/8	4	4	Montague County	TX	James Willard	2007	37325
128 7/8	22 2/8 · 21 3/8	15 1/8	5	5	St. Croix County	WI	Joseph Edin	2007	37325
*128 7/8	21 4/8 · 21 6/8	17 3/8	5	4	Macoupin County	IL	Keith Judson Graham	2007	37325
128 7/8	21 0/8 · 21 0/8	16 1/8	5	5	Crawford County	IN	Chris Hart	2007	37325
*128 7/8	21 0/8 · 20 6/8	14 6/8	5	6	Buchanan County	MO	Jason Abbott	2007	37325
128 7/8	18 5/8 · 19 4/8	16 6/8	5	6	Trigg County	KY	Brannigan Free	2007	37325
128 7/8	21 2/8 · 22 0/8	17 1/8	5	5	Edgar County	IL	Larry Henson	2007	37325
*128 7/8	24 0/8 · 23 6/8	17 1/8	5	4	Putnam County	OH	Scott J. Osting	2007	37325
128 7/8	24 3/8 · 22 7/8	18 1/8	4	4	Fillmore County	MN	Joel Goodman	2007	37325
128 7/8	21 4/8 · 22 6/8	14 5/8	5	5	Grant County	OK	Scott Thompson	2007	37325
*128 7/8	23 1/8 · 23 3/8	15 3/8	5	5	Trempealeau County	WI	Brandon J. Lee	2007	37325
128 7/8	20 5/8 · 20 7/8	15 7/8	5	5	Spokane County	WA	John Schneider	2007	37325
128 7/8	22 0/8 · 22 3/8	16 1/8	5	5	Grenada County	MS	Gus Pieralisi, Jr.	2007	37325
128 7/8	21 7/8 · 23 4/8	14 5/8	4	4	Waupaca County	WI	Andrew M. Voss	2008	37325
*128 7/8	22 0/8 · 21 6/8	15 3/8	5	5	Kent County	RI	Robert Tedeschi	2008	37325
128 7/8	22 7/8 · 22 4/8	16 5/8	4	4	Leflore County	MS	Ben Bush	2008	37325
128 7/8	21 3/8 · 21 5/8	17 7/8	5	4	Pawnee County	NE	Bill J. Phillips	2008	37325
128 7/8	24 2/8 · 24 3/8	17 3/8	4	4	Stanly County	NC	Jonathan Smith	2008	37325
128 7/8	22 7/8 · 22 3/8	19 1/8	4	4	Buffalo County	WI	Rod Springborn	2008	37325
128 7/8	20 7/8 · 20 6/8	14 1/8	5	5	Waupaca County	WI	Chris Peterson	2008	37325
*128 7/8	22 6/8 · 24 0/8	21 0/8	5	5	Hardin County	OH	John Cummins	2008	37325
128 7/8	21 0/8 · 21 3/8	18 5/8	4	4	Clayton County	IA	Gabe Oldfather	2008	37325
*128 7/8	21 4/8 · 20 4/8	16 3/8	5	4	Adair County	OK	Hank Jenks	2008	37325
*128 7/8	20 4/8 · 24 7/8	17 0/8	8	4	Union County	OH	Ron Stephens	2008	37325
128 7/8	22 5/8 · 22 4/8	18 1/8	5	6	Indiana County	PA	Raymond Lancaster	2008	37325
128 7/8	22 1/8 · 24 7/8	14 3/8	8	4	Burlington County	NJ	Bill Bowers	2008	37325
*128 7/8	21 6/8 · 21 5/8	17 1/8	5	5	Wayne County	MI	Sean Logan	2008	37325
128 7/8	21 1/8 · 21 2/8	15 5/8	4	4	Buffalo County	WI	Jim Hjort	2009	37325
128 7/8	20 6/8 · 20 1/8	17 1/8	5	5	Oconto County	WI	Jeff Simpson	2009	37325
128 7/8	23 2/8 · 23 2/8	21 4/8	5	6	Wabasha County	MN	Ryan A. Sawinski	2009	37325
*128 7/8	21 7/8 · 21 7/8	15 1/8	4	5	Carroll County	MS	Keith Holmes	2009	37325

Deer entries below 141 0/8, that appeared in the 6th Edition, are not included here, but are included on the accompanying CD (see page 119), and also in the Club's Records Archives.

601

WHITETAIL DEER (TYPICAL ANTLERS)

Minimum Score 125 — Continued

SCORE	LENGTH OF R MAIN BEAM L	INSIDE SPREAD	NUMBER OF R POINTS L	AREA	STATE/ PROVINCE	HUNTER'S NAME	DATE	RANK
128 7/8	21 6/8 23 0/8	16 5/8	5 6	Sauk County	WI	Keith Peetz	2009	37325
128 7/8	18 7/8 19 0/8	16 5/8	5 5	Winnebago County	IL	Gary D. Kinne	2009	37325
*128 7/8	21 2/8 21 4/8	17 3/8	5 5	Manitowoc County	WI	Eric F. Nellis	2009	37325
128 7/8	21 6/8 21 2/8	18 3/8	4 6	Montcalm County	MI	Edwin L. DeYoung	2009	37325
128 7/8	21 7/8 20 6/8	15 7/8	5 5	Dodge County	WI	Douglas L. Sackett	2009	37325
*128 7/8	21 2/8 23 6/8	19 2/8	6 4	Nowata County	OK	Mark Mathews	2009	37325
*128 7/8	23 0/8 22 6/8	15 6/8	8 5	Linn County	KS	Greg Jones	2009	37325
*128 7/8	23 3/8 22 5/8	16 3/8	4 5	Stoddard County	MO	Lawson Metcalf	2009	37325
128 6/8	21 0/8 20 4/8	15 6/8	5 4	Elk County	KS	Matt Rosensweet	2000	37556
128 6/8	21 5/8 22 6/8	15 1/8	6 5	Essex County	NJ	Mark Spoto	2001	37556
128 6/8	25 3/8 25 7/8	17 0/8	5 5	Jersey County	IL	Dennis K. Johnson	2002	37556
128 6/8	19 3/8 19 4/8	15 6/8	5 5	Monroe County	OH	Tom Stant	2002	37556
128 6/8	21 2/8 21 1/8	18 2/8	4 4	Lorain County	OH	Steve Reinhold	2003	37556
128 6/8	21 2/8 21 5/8	17 6/8	5 5	Ransom County	ND	Mike Johnson	2004	37556
128 6/8	18 4/8 19 3/8	14 2/8	5 5	Ramsey County	ND	Dwight Logie	2004	37556
128 6/8	21 3/8 21 6/8	16 0/8	4 4	McHenry County	IL	Joe A. Florent	2004	37556
128 6/8	24 2/8 23 4/8	18 0/8	4 4	Salem County	NJ	Vincent Behrens	2004	37556
*128 6/8	20 5/8 21 3/8	17 0/8	5 5	Hillsdale County	MI	Shawn T. Mullaly	2004	37556
128 6/8	20 2/8 20 4/8	15 4/8	5 5	Oneida County	NY	Paul Rich	2004	37556
128 6/8	20 1/8 20 2/8	14 2/8	4 4	Cooper County	MO	Matt Kollmeyer	2004	37556
128 6/8	22 7/8 22 7/8	15 6/8	5 4	Adams County	WI	Paul Dellamuth	2004	37556
*128 6/8	22 1/8 22 2/8	16 6/8	4 4	Lewis County	MO	Kirk Nielsen	2004	37556
128 6/8	20 6/8 20 5/8	12 2/8	4 5	Erie County	NY	Christian J. Gerling	2004	37556
128 6/8	21 2/8 21 4/8	18 6/8	4 4	Washington County	MD	Jeffrey W. McAboy	2004	37556
*128 6/8	21 2/8 20 4/8	15 1/8	5 6	Outagamie County	WI	Michael J. Renier	2004	37556
128 6/8	20 0/8 20 4/8	16 2/8	5 5	Putnam County	WV	Scotty Gaylor	2004	37556
128 6/8	22 0/8 22 6/8	18 2/8	5 5	Ward County	ND	Clinton Crider	2005	37556
128 6/8	20 7/8 20 3/8	15 6/8	6 6	Buffalo County	WI	John W. Charles	2005	37556
*128 6/8	22 5/8 22 1/8	13 4/8	4 4	Benton County	TN	John H. Coleman	2005	37556
*128 6/8	21 3/8 21 4/8	19 2/8	4 5	Tazewell County	IL	Jerry Manning	2005	37556
128 6/8	21 0/8 20 0/8	14 4/8	5 5	Harvey County	KS	Dan Stahl	2005	37556
128 6/8	25 2/8 24 6/8	17 2/8	3 3	Stearns County	MN	Joe Gieske	2005	37556
128 6/8	23 1/8 22 1/8	18 0/8	4 5	Lawrence County	OH	Jim Brady	2005	37556
*128 6/8	22 3/8 22 4/8	15 6/8	4 4	Adams County	OH	Paul Rich	2005	37556
128 6/8	24 4/8 24 4/8	15 6/8	5 4	Adair County	IA	Rusty Ruble	2005	37556
128 6/8	21 5/8 21 5/8	16 0/8	4 5	Iowa County	WI	Doug Rule	2005	37556
*128 6/8	23 3/8 23 7/8	17 0/8	4 4	Story County	IA	Michael Augustin	2005	37556
128 6/8	21 6/8 21 0/8	16 0/8	5 5	Jefferson County	WI	Jerry Coy	2005	37556
128 6/8	22 6/8 25 2/8	22 0/8	4 5	Somerset County	NJ	Scott Parneg	2006	37556
128 6/8	21 6/8 21 6/8	15 6/8	5 5	Barron County	WI	Jeffrey Jay Lane	2006	37556
*128 6/8	24 7/8 23 4/8	19 0/8	5 4	Cameron County	PA	Hunter Bardo	2006	37556
128 6/8	22 2/8 22 1/8	15 2/8	6 6	Wabasha County	MN	Chad R. Collins	2006	37556
128 6/8	25 1/8 24 2/8	16 0/8	4 5	Union County	SD	Tyler Chicoine	2006	37556
128 6/8	21 2/8 22 3/8	17 0/8	4 4	Claiborne County	MS	Steve Rogers	2006	37556
128 6/8	20 5/8 18 6/8	16 0/8	6 5	Bottineau County	ND	Thomas Matz	2006	37556
128 6/8	23 3/8 22 1/8	15 4/8	5 5	Clark County	IL	Denny Mock	2006	37556
128 6/8	21 5/8 23 3/8	16 7/8	6 5	Monroe County	WI	Tom Nelson	2006	37556
128 6/8	22 2/8 22 1/8	15 4/8	4 5	Hand County	SD	Travis Sivertsen	2006	37556
*128 6/8	19 7/8 19 6/8	15 4/8	5 5	Marshall County	IN	Daniel J. Hubbard	2006	37556
128 6/8	21 5/8 23 0/8	16 2/8	4 4	Davis County	IA	Thor Johnson	2006	37556
128 6/8	18 2/8 20 7/8	18 4/8	6 6	Manistee County	MI	Andrew D. Krebill	2006	37556
128 6/8	23 5/8 23 4/8	20 2/8	5 5	Butler County	KS	Nancy Atwood	2006	37556
128 6/8	22 5/8 23 0/8	17 6/8	4 5	McCurtain County	OK	Joe Don Williams	2006	37556
128 6/8	23 2/8 23 6/8	18 0/8	4 4	Monmouth County	NJ	Nick Francisco	2006	37556
128 6/8	23 0/8 23 1/8	18 4/8	4 5	Sauk County	WI	Joseph J. Finnegan	2007	37556
*128 6/8	18 0/8 17 5/8	13 0/8	8 5	Moore County	TN	Greg Durm	2007	37556
*128 6/8	21 3/8 20 2/8	16 2/8	4 4	Jefferson County	OK	Dave Melchert	2007	37556
128 6/8	20 6/8 20 2/8	17 6/8	5 4	Jefferson County	KS	Dean Delk	2007	37556
128 6/8	21 4/8 22 4/8	13 6/8	5 6	Yazoo County	MS	Derek Gibbs	2007	37556
128 6/8	21 4/8 22 4/8	17 6/8	4 4	Coles County	IL	Charles Knox	2007	37556
128 6/8	24 0/8 23 2/8	17 2/8	4 5	Genesee County	NY	Christopher K. Leccese	2007	37556
128 6/8	23 2/8 24 0/8	18 2/8	4 4	Morrison County	MN	Kyle Rinke	2007	37556
128 6/8	20 7/8 21 4/8	18 6/8	6 5	Charlevoix County	MI	Zachary Ryan Scharenbroch	2007	37556
*128 6/8	20 7/8 20 0/8	15 6/8	4 5	Tuscarawas County	OH	Douglas Duff	2007	37556
128 6/8	21 0/8 21 0/8	15 3/8	6 6	Jackson County	WI	Jim Rindahl	2007	37556
128 6/8	22 6/8 21 3/8	17 2/8	5 5	Cuming County	NE	Tim Everett	2007	37556
128 6/8	22 0/8 21 1/8	14 2/8	5 5	Pittsburg County	OK	Jeremy Dean	2007	37556
*128 6/8	19 4/8 20 7/8	16 1/8	6 6	Brown County	IL	Gus Saucerman	2007	37556
*128 6/8	20 0/8 21 6/8	16 2/8	5 5	Appanoose County	IA	Jimmy Williams	2007	37556
128 6/8	21 6/8 22 2/8	22 2/8	4 4	Cass County	IA	Mark Armstrong	2007	37556
128 6/8	22 3/8 21 4/8	16 2/8	4 4	Early County	GA	Robert A. Edwards	2007	37556
*128 6/8	22 1/8 21 1/8	17 4/8	5 4	Pennington County	SD	Steven D. Schelske	2007	37556
128 6/8	21 0/8 21 5/8	17 4/8	4 5	San Saba County	TX	Kelby McCall	2008	37556
128 6/8	20 1/8 20 0/8	15 1/8	5 6	McKenzie County	ND	Corey Hugelen	2008	37556
128 6/8	21 2/8 20 6/8	14 2/8	6 5	Indiana County	PA	John Santoro	2008	37556
128 6/8	24 2/8 24 6/8	18 4/8	4 4	Wyandot County	OH	R. Gerald Ebert	2008	37556
128 6/8	20 3/8 18 0/8	13 2/8	5 6	Walsh County	ND	Chris Mattson	2008	37556
128 6/8	25 5/8 25 5/8	19 7/8	6 7	Allen County	IN	R. James Zehr	2008	37556
*128 6/8	21 2/8 21 3/8	16 6/8	4 4	Houston County	MN	Aaron Paul Bartsch	2008	37556
128 6/8	20 3/8 19 7/8	14 0/8	5 5	Olmsted County	MN	Brian Jorgenson	2008	37556
128 6/8	22 4/8 23 6/8	19 0/8	4 4	Clarion County	PA	Mark A. Miller	2008	37556
128 6/8	23 6/8 21 7/8	15 4/8	4 4	Ontario County	NY	Donald E. Bagshaw, Jr.	2008	37556
128 6/8	21 0/8 22 1/8	16 0/8	5 5	St. Marys County	MD	Michael A. Nyalko	2008	37556
128 6/8	22 1/8 21 4/8	17 2/8	5 5	Polk County	WI	Mike Ingham	2008	37556
*128 6/8	21 4/8 21 4/8	17 6/8	4 4	Sanborn County	SD	Scott Loecker	2008	37556
128 6/8	22 4/8 23 2/8	14 2/8	4 4	Vernon County	MO	Joseph Trey Payne	2008	37556
128 6/8	20 3/8 20 6/8	18 6/8	5 5	Westchester County	NY	Thomas J. Braig	2008	37556
*128 6/8	21 4/8 21 2/8	13 0/8	5 4	Phillips County	KS	Edward L. Berlier	2008	37556
128 6/8	22 7/8 24 0/8	17 1/8	6 4	Anderson County	KS	Hunter Edwards	2008	37556
*128 6/8	20 3/8 20 2/8	15 0/8	4 5	Van Buren County	IA	Levi Weaver, Jr.	2008	37556
128 6/8	22 0/8 23 0/8	18 0/8	5 4	Jackson County	WI	Bill Vollert	2009	37556
128 6/8	20 7/8 20 2/8	13 6/8	5 5	Stanly County	NC	James R. Bowers	2009	37556
128 6/8	21 1/8 21 4/8	16 0/8	5 5	Polk County	MN	Colter Dufault	2009	37556
128 6/8	20 7/8 23 5/8	19 0/8	5 5	Pierce County	NE	Robert J. Altwine	2009	37556
128 6/8	20 6/8 21 0/8	13 3/8	5 6	Elbert County	CO	David J. Barrow	2009	37556

602

WHITETAIL DEER (TYPICAL ANTLERS)

Minimum Score 125 Continued

SCORE	LENGTH OF R MAIN BEAM L	INSIDE SPREAD	NUMBER OF R POINTS L		AREA	STATE/ PROVINCE	HUNTER'S NAME	DATE	RANK
128 6/8	21 6/8	23 0/8	16 6/8	4	4	Columbia County	WI	Michael Johnson	2009	37556
*128 6/8	24 6/8	24 3/8	18 0/8	4	4	Anne Arundel County	MD	John K. McVicker	2009	37556
*128 6/8	21 7/8	21 5/8	16 2/8	4	4	Hillsdale County	MI	Justin M. Nichols	2009	37556
128 6/8	22 1/8	22 6/8	17 0/8	5	6	Marquette County	WI	Tim Koenen	2009	37556
128 6/8	20 3/8	19 4/8	16 4/8	5	5	Schuyler County	MO	J. T. Kreager	2009	37556
128 6/8	19 4/8	19 4/8	14 5/8	5	7	Cowley County	KS	David M. Saleme	2009	37556
*128 6/8	21 6/8	22 0/8	15 0/8	4	5	Meigs County	OH	Michael L. Parrish	2009	37556
128 6/8	23 4/8	21 4/8	17 0/8	4	4	Delaware County	OH	Ralph Tufts, Jr.	2009	37556
128 6/8	23 2/8	22 7/8	17 0/8	4	4	Bolivar County	MS	Brian Van Landingham	2009	37556
128 6/8	21 5/8	20 6/8	18 0/8	5	4	Crawford County	WI	Zachary Randall	2010	37556
128 5/8	23 2/8	24 1/8	16 7/8	4	4	Perry County	IL	Devon Daniels	1993	37824
128 5/8	22 0/8	23 1/8	17 3/8	4	4	Van Buren County	MI	Avon Lee Arbo	1996	37824
128 5/8	21 2/8	22 0/8	16 1/8	5	5	Berrien County	MI	Chad A. Schau	1998	37824
*128 5/8	24 6/8	20 4/8	19 1/8	4	5	Custer County	OK	Matthew R. Baker	2000	37824
128 5/8	21 0/8	21 1/8	15 3/8	5	5	Will County	IL	Tom Mooi	2001	37824
128 5/8	24 1/8	25 2/8	22 1/8	5	7	Suffolk County	NY	James Blamy	2001	37824
128 5/8	21 4/8	22 5/8	16 2/8	6	6	Calumet County	WI	Bryce D. Bodway	2002	37824
*128 5/8	22 6/8	21 5/8	15 0/8	4	5	Hillsdale County	MI	Mike Shores	2003	37824
128 5/8	20 6/8	22 6/8	13 7/8	4	5	Johnson County	IN	William Smith	2003	37824
*128 5/8	22 1/8	18 3/8	20 0/8	6	6	St. Croix County	WI	Brian Sturgul	2003	37824
128 5/8	21 6/8	22 1/8	17 1/8	6	4	Wright County	MO	Monty Swearengin	2004	37824
128 5/8	23 0/8	22 3/8	17 5/8	4	4	Tippecanoe County	IN	Jim R. Esposito	2004	37824
128 5/8	21 4/8	21 4/8	16 3/8	5	5	Johnson County	IN	Derek W. Litteral	2004	37824
128 5/8	20 0/8	20 3/8	15 3/8	5	4	Jackson County	MO	Clay Cumberford	2004	37824
128 5/8	20 5/8	20 1/8	16 1/8	5	5	Lafayette County	WI	Sonia Lien	2004	37824
128 5/8	20 0/8	20 0/8	15 7/8	5	4	Foster County	ND	Jody Davis	2004	37824
128 5/8	22 3/8	22 3/8	16 5/8	4	5	Portage County	WI	Jeff Rzentkowski	2004	37824
128 5/8	20 3/8	20 2/8	14 5/8	5	5	Prowers County	CO	Rick Hooley	2004	37824
128 5/8	22 2/8	22 3/8	13 6/8	6	4	Jefferson County	KS	Chris Gomel	2004	37824
128 5/8	20 2/8	20 6/8	18 7/8	5	4	Ferry County	WA	Tim Langstraat	2004	37824
128 5/8	20 1/8	19 3/8	15 3/8	5	7	Washburn County	WI	Paul A. Goering	2004	37824
128 5/8	24 1/8	23 1/8	18 2/8	5	4	Hughes County	OK	Tom Cartwright	2004	37824
128 5/8	20 3/8	20 7/8	17 1/8	4	4	Washington County	MS	Gus Pieralisi, Jr.	2004	37824
128 5/8	21 1/8	19 6/8	18 4/8	5	5	Nuevo Leon	MEX	John "Jack" C. Culpepper III	2005	37824
128 5/8	22 6/8	21 3/8	15 3/8	4	5	Beaverhead County	MT	Raymond Gross	2005	37824
*128 5/8	21 5/8	22 2/8	18 1/8	4	4	Gillespie County	TX	Chris Ottmers	2005	37824
*128 5/8	22 4/8	22 5/8	20 3/8	4	4	Middlesex County	CT	Andrew G. Walter	2005	37824
128 5/8	23 0/8	23 5/8	18 5/8	4	4	Trempealeau County	WI	Matt R. Andersen	2005	37824
128 5/8	22 1/8	22 7/8	19 1/8	5	7	Tompkins County	NY	David Salo	2005	37824
128 5/8	24 1/8	22 6/8	15 3/8	5	4	Dubois County	IN	Brandon Spears	2005	37824
128 5/8	21 1/8	22 6/8	14 7/8	5	5	Jackson County	MI	Bernard R. Belaire III	2005	37824
*128 5/8	21 2/8	20 6/8	15 3/8	5	6	Ashtabula County	OH	Richard T. Giffin, Sr.	2005	37824
128 5/8	22 4/8	21 4/8	15 4/8	6	5	Buffalo County	WI	Shane Stuhr	2005	37824
*128 5/8	21 2/8	20 5/8	16 3/8	5	5	Marinette County	WI	Ben Strobel	2005	37824
*128 5/8	22 6/8	23 4/8	17 5/8	4	5	Stafford County	KS	Clay Parrish	2005	37824
128 5/8	20 2/8	21 3/8	16 4/8	5	6	Spokane County	WA	Brandon Enevold	2006	37824
128 5/8	20 0/8	21 0/8	14 7/8	5	5	Redwood County	MN	Russ Dudgeon	2006	37824
128 5/8	20 6/8	22 0/8	16 7/8	6	5	Van Buren County	MI	Wayne R. Weisner	2006	37824
*128 5/8	22 0/8	22 4/8	13 3/8	5	5	Tom Green County	TX	Mark Harrington	2006	37824
128 5/8	23 3/8	21 7/8	18 7/8	4	5	Trempealeau County	WI	Matthew R. Andersen	2006	37824
*128 5/8	21 0/8	20 6/8	16 7/8	4	4	Kent County	MI	Don Ross, Jr.	2006	37824
*128 5/8	22 0/8	22 6/8	18 1/8	4	5	Trempealeau County	WI	David N. Andersen	2006	37824
128 5/8	23 1/8	22 2/8	18 1/8	4	4	Grant County	WI	Scott D. Philipps	2006	37824
128 5/8	24 0/8	23 2/8	18 7/8	4	4	Westchester County	NY	Anthony Drpich	2006	37824
*128 5/8	21 3/8	21 0/8	15 5/8	4	4	Dane County	WI	Stuart Smith	2006	37824
128 5/8	19 5/8	19 0/8	13 3/8	5	5	Cass County	NE	Neil Chandler	2006	37824
128 5/8	21 7/8	20 2/8	17 4/8	5	6	Clarion County	PA	John E. Royer IV	2006	37824
*128 5/8	19 4/8	20 4/8	16 1/8	4	4	Waushara County	WI	Jason Hupf	2006	37824
*128 5/8	19 4/8	21 0/8	14 7/8	4	4	Sullivan County	MO	Kyle D. Crigler	2006	37824
128 5/8	24 2/8	23 5/8	18 7/8	4	5	Kewaunee County	WI	Kyle Hunsader	2006	37824
128 5/8	21 3/8	22 3/8	16 3/8	4	4	Winnebago County	IL	Glenn R. Evans	2006	37824
*128 5/8	21 1/8	23 4/8	17 1/8	5	4	Onondaga County	NY	Cyrus Weichert	2006	37824
*128 5/8	21 0/8	18 3/8	16 3/8	5	5	Appanoose County	IA	Patrick A. Hudgens	2006	37824
128 5/8	21 4/8	21 4/8	16 3/8	5	4	Shannon County	MO	Dusty Smith	2007	37824
128 5/8	23 1/8	23 4/8	19 6/8	5	5	Sutton County	TX	Drake Shurley	2007	37824
*128 5/8	23 3/8	23 0/8	15 7/8	4	5	Adams County	WI	Charles A. Schweiger	2007	37824
128 5/8	21 0/8	20 6/8	14 5/8	5	5	Marinette County	WI	Jonathan P. Walber	2007	37824
*128 5/8	24 2/8	23 7/8	17 0/8	6	6	Allamakee County	IA	Tony Bonci	2007	37824
128 5/8	21 4/8	21 3/8	16 3/8	4	4	Guthrie County	IA	Harold "Bud" Osborne	2007	37824
128 5/8	23 0/8	23 3/8	16 3/8	4	4	Pike County	IL	Thomas J. Beissel	2007	37824
128 5/8	21 4/8	20 4/8	15 3/8	6	6	Sauk County	WI	Richard W. Krueger	2007	37824
*128 5/8	24 7/8	25 7/8	19 3/8	6	4	Casey County	KY	Jackey D. Wilson	2007	37824
128 5/8	22 5/8	22 6/8	18 1/8	4	4	Jo Daviess County	IL	John G. Baunach	2007	37824
*128 5/8	23 1/8	24 7/8	18 3/8	4	4	Marion County	OH	Kenneth Bell, Jr.	2007	37824
128 5/8	20 6/8	20 5/8	13 6/8	7	5	Ellis County	OK	Tom E. Quinton	2008	37824
*128 5/8	20 1/8	19 7/8	16 1/8	5	5	Trempealeau County	WI	Josh S. Sobczak	2008	37824
128 5/8	22 3/8	23 5/8	16 1/8	4	4	Anderson County	KS	Christopher W. Fechner	2008	37824
128 5/8	20 1/8	19 4/8	16 7/8	5	5	Taylor County	WI	Tim Pasek	2008	37824
128 5/8	22 4/8	22 0/8	19 3/8	4	4	Adams County	IN	Ryan Marbach	2008	37824
128 5/8	23 5/8	22 7/8	19 3/8	4	4	Schuylkill County	PA	Christopher R. Lawrence	2008	37824
128 5/8	21 6/8	20 5/8	13 3/8	4	5	Cottle County	TX	Mark Schauer	2008	37824
128 5/8	23 2/8	22 2/8	15 3/8	6	6	Dunn County	ND	Garth Olds	2008	37824
*128 5/8	23 7/8	23 1/8	17 5/8	4	4	Gallia County	OH	Jack L. Mathews	2008	37824
128 5/8	20 2/8	20 4/8	17 3/8	5	6	Meade County	SD	Scott Paramo	2008	37824
128 5/8	24 1/8	23 2/8	18 5/8	4	4	Lincoln County	AR	Warren Parker	2008	37824
128 5/8	21 2/8	21 7/8	18 7/8	5	4	La Grange County	IN	Ronald Vaughn	2008	37824
*128 5/8	22 1/8	22 3/8	17 4/8	6	5	Saline County	NE	Jason Busch	2009	37824
128 5/8	21 0/8	21 6/8	15 1/8	5	5	Butler County	PA	Cody H. Watterson	2009	37824
128 5/8	23 3/8	22 4/8	15 7/8	4	4	Oktibbeha County	MS	Jason Horner	2009	37824
*128 5/8	22 0/8	22 0/8	20 5/8	5	4	Cortland County	NY	Christopher Larkin	2009	37824
*128 5/8	21 7/8	21 2/8	16 1/8	5	5	Cowley County	KS	Jeremy M. Foster	2009	37824
128 5/8	18 6/8	19 3/8	16 1/8	5	5	Steuben County	IN	Alex Harris	2009	37824
128 5/8	23 2/8	22 0/8	18 1/8	5	4	Logan County	AR	Jimmy Fennell	2009	37824
128 5/8	20 4/8	19 3/8	13 7/8	5	5	Calhoun County	MI	Barry P. Katz	2009	37824
128 5/8	22 4/8	21 6/8	16 3/8	5	5	Fairfax County	VA	Gregg D. Brown	2009	37824

Deer entries below 141 0/8, that appeared in the 6th Edition, are not included here, but are included on the accompanying CD (see page 119), and also in the Club's Records Archives.

WHITETAIL DEER (TYPICAL ANTLERS)

Minimum Score 125 — Continued

SCORE	LENGTH OF R MAIN BEAM L	INSIDE SPREAD	NUMBER OF R POINTS L	AREA	STATE/ PROVINCE	HUNTER'S NAME	DATE	RANK
128 5/8	26 0/8 / 25 6/8	24 3/8	4 / 4	Portage County	WI	Tyler J. Herek	2009	37824
*128 5/8	25 2/8 / 25 0/8	18 0/8	6 / 4	De Kalb County	IN	Jeffrey R. Nickel	2009	37824
128 5/8	21 1/8 / 20 3/8	15 7/8	4 / 4	Gage County	NE	Brian Toalson	2009	37824
128 5/8	21 7/8 / 22 5/8	17 4/8	5 / 5	Scott County	IN	Jim H. Brown	2009	37824
128 5/8	22 7/8 / 23 2/8	16 5/8	4 / 4	Monroe County	WI	Ron Stayton	2009	37824
128 5/8	22 7/8 / 23 0/8	16 3/8	4 / 4	Jefferson County	OH	Walter R. Sutton	2009	37824
*128 5/8	22 4/8 / 21 6/8	13 5/8	6 / 4	De Soto County	MS	Paul Williams	2009	37824
*128 5/8	23 4/8 / 23 3/8	17 7/8	4 / 4	Trinity County	TX	Doyle Simons	2009	37824
128 5/8	21 0/8 / 20 6/8	16 1/8	5 / 4	St. Marys County	MD	Shawn W. Day	2009	37824
128 5/8	20 1/8 / 21 0/8	15 3/8	4 / 4	Morris County	NJ	Lou Cornine	2009	37824
128 5/8	22 7/8 / 22 0/8	21 5/8	5 / 5	Washington County	PA	Charles Trax	2009	37824
*128 5/8	22 0/8 / 21 0/8	15 1/8	4 / 4	Adair County	OK	Timothy Broughton	2010	37824
128 4/8	22 4/8 / 21 4/8	18 0/8	4 / 4	Westchester County	NY	Nicholas Corsi	1980	38080
128 4/8	22 7/8 / 22 1/8	17 5/8	7 / 5	Teton County	MT	Shanun Rammell	2001	38080
128 4/8	22 0/8 / 22 1/8	17 4/8	5 / 5	Berks County	PA	Tracey L. Jones	2001	38080
128 4/8	21 2/8 / 20 4/8	16 4/8	4 / 4	Hancock County	IL	Jeffrey Hummel	2001	38080
128 4/8	24 6/8 / 24 0/8	15 5/8	4 / 5	Mercer County	OH	W. Stevens, Jr.	2003	38080
*128 4/8	21 3/8 / 21 3/8	14 6/8	5 / 5	Claiborne County	MS	Mike Eubanks	2003	38080
128 4/8	22 0/8 / 20 4/8	17 3/8	5 / 6	Northumberland County	PA	David Comfort	2004	38080
128 4/8	22 5/8 / 22 5/8	17 2/8	5 / 5	Steuben County	NY	Michael J. Winters	2004	38080
128 4/8	22 0/8 / 21 6/8	19 0/8	5 / 5	Columbia County	WI	Bryan D. Terpstra	2004	38080
128 4/8	21 4/8 / 20 3/8	16 2/8	4 / 4	Buffalo County	WI	Mark Forster	2004	38080
128 4/8	21 2/8 / 20 5/8	15 6/8	4 / 6	Cottle County	TX	Mark Schauer	2004	38080
128 4/8	22 2/8 / 22 1/8	16 4/8	5 / 5	Bucks County	PA	Richard M. Slovich	2004	38080
128 4/8	21 1/8 / 20 5/8	15 6/8	5 / 5	Menard County	IL	Chad Loy	2004	38080
128 4/8	21 7/8 / 21 4/8	18 4/8	5 / 5	St. Joseph County	MI	J. Wade Robinson	2004	38080
*128 4/8	21 2/8 / 22 0/8	18 0/8	5 / 5	Fairfield County	CT	Dave Blersch	2005	38080
*128 4/8	23 0/8 / 22 6/8	18 4/8	4 / 4	Price County	WI	Bradley Dragovich	2005	38080
128 4/8	20 7/8 / 19 6/8	14 6/8	5 / 4	Jackson County	OH	Willy Saucerman	2005	38080
128 4/8	21 1/8 / 21 0/8	17 0/8	5 / 5	Calhoun County	MI	George Swan, Jr.	2005	38080
128 4/8	21 6/8 / 21 1/8	18 4/8	5 / 7	Pike County	IL	Todd Chapman	2005	38080
128 4/8	21 5/8 / 21 5/8	16 4/8	4 / 4	Juneau County	WI	Mark L. Meyer	2005	38080
128 4/8	21 6/8 / 21 5/8	17 4/8	5 / 5	Berrien County	MI	Carl D. Scurek	2005	38080
128 4/8	21 1/8 / 22 4/8	16 2/8	4 / 5	Fulton County	IL	Steve Peperis	2005	38080
128 4/8	21 3/8 / 22 4/8	16 4/8	5 / 5	Washington County	WI	Duane Mantz	2005	38080
128 4/8	20 6/8 / 21 1/8	20 2/8	6 / 7	Buffalo County	WI	Glenn Klomsten	2005	38080
128 4/8	20 5/8 / 22 0/8	23 1/8	4 / 4	Montgomery County	MD	Ken Hakes	2005	38080
128 4/8	20 6/8 / 20 6/8	18 2/8	5 / 5	Cortland County	NY	John E. Ryan, Jr.	2005	38080
128 4/8	21 4/8 / 21 6/8	19 2/8	5 / 5	Sauk County	WI	Tod R. Fleming	2005	38080
*128 4/8	20 4/8 / 21 4/8	16 2/8	5 / 6	Ross County	OH	Randy Johnson	2005	38080
128 4/8	21 6/8 / 19 5/8	20 0/8	5 / 5	Frio County	TX	Frank S. Noska IV	2005	38080
128 4/8	23 0/8 / 21 6/8	18 0/8	5 / 5	Adair County	MO	Vernon Woods	2005	38080
128 4/8	19 6/8 / 19 6/8	17 0/8	6 / 6	Dickson County	TN	Gary P. Jenkins	2006	38080
128 4/8	20 6/8 / 20 6/8	16 2/8	5 / 5	Madison County	MS	Ken Kugle	2006	38080
*128 4/8	21 5/8 / 21 2/8	16 4/8	4 / 4	Todd County	MN	Nathan P. Corder	2006	38080
128 4/8	20 5/8 / 21 1/8	17 6/8	5 / 5	St. Louis County	MN	Bret Ojala, Jr.	2006	38080
128 4/8	20 5/8 / 21 0/8	13 6/8	6 / 6	Green County	WI	Paul Ovadal	2006	38080
128 4/8	23 2/8 / 22 5/8	16 2/8	4 / 4	Grayson County	KY	Ronald E. Hines	2006	38080
128 4/8	22 3/8 / 23 1/8	16 4/8	4 / 4	Grant County	WI	Tod Herman	2006	38080
128 4/8	21 0/8 / 21 2/8	16 4/8	4 / 4	Tompkins County	NY	Tyler Alan Whittaker	2006	38080
128 4/8	21 6/8 / 21 7/8	21 4/8	7 / 6	Lehigh County	PA	Todd L. Schaffer	2006	38080
128 4/8	21 4/8 / 21 3/8	14 6/8	5 / 5	Buffalo County	WI	Craig Kjendle	2006	38080
128 4/8	22 4/8 / 22 2/8	17 0/8	4 / 4	Kent County	MD	Douglas Charles Wood	2006	38080
128 4/8	24 4/8 / 21 2/8	23 4/8	5 / 5	Pulaski County	GA	Chris Cornelius	2006	38080
128 4/8	21 6/8 / 22 1/8	17 6/8	4 / 4	Ontario County	NY	Edward Staten, Jr.	2006	38080
128 4/8	20 7/8 / 21 2/8	17 6/8	7 / 5	Green Lake County	WI	Jerry Isaac	2007	38080
128 4/8	20 4/8 / 22 7/8	17 0/8	6 / 6	Monmouth County	NJ	Garner Pruitt	2007	38080
*128 4/8	20 6/8 / 21 0/8	17 4/8	4 / 4	Putnam County	OH	Neil Dunlap	2007	38080
128 4/8	20 2/8 / 20 4/8	16 4/8	5 / 5	Henry County	OH	Scot C. Keck	2007	38080
128 4/8	20 4/8 / 20 5/8	15 4/8	5 / 5	Monroe County	WI	Ty Brey	2007	38080
128 4/8	24 4/8 / 25 4/8	22 0/8	5 / 6	Wyandot County	OH	James D. Herring	2007	38080
128 4/8	23 1/8 / 23 7/8	16 2/8	5 / 4	Monmouth County	NJ	Lou Cornine	2007	38080
128 4/8	22 6/8 / 22 4/8	17 0/8	4 / 5	Vernon County	WI	Steven Sidie	2007	38080
*128 4/8	22 0/8 / 21 4/8	16 0/8	4 / 4	Oklahoma County	OK	Eric Jones	2007	38080
128 4/8	20 7/8 / 21 3/8	16 0/8	4 / 5	Potter County	PA	George Lambert	2007	38080
128 4/8	20 4/8 / 22 6/8	16 6/8	5 / 5	Buffalo County	WI	David A. O'Brien	2007	38080
128 4/8	24 0/8 / 24 4/8	16 0/8	5 / 4	Coshocton County	OH	Charles S. Caley	2007	38080
*128 4/8	22 2/8 / 21 4/8	16 5/8	6 / 5	Switzerland County	IN	Allin D. Penfound	2007	38080
*128 4/8	23 4/8 / 24 1/8	17 2/8	4 / 4	Parkland	ALB	Troy Dzioba	2007	38080
128 4/8	22 1/8 / 21 4/8	14 6/8	5 / 5	Mason County	TX	Kent Bailey	2007	38080
*128 4/8	21 5/8 / 21 3/8	20 2/8	4 / 4	Fulton County	GA	Tony Wallace	2008	38080
128 4/8	21 5/8 / 21 6/8	15 2/8	5 / 5	Marshall County	WV	Shane Keller	2008	38080
128 4/8	23 5/8 / 22 6/8	15 2/8	6 / 6	Grayson County	TX	Joe Tom Cable	2008	38080
128 4/8	20 6/8 / 21 0/8	16 4/8	4 / 4	Matagorda County	TX	Doug Mathews	2008	38080
128 4/8	21 3/8 / 22 3/8	14 5/8	6 / 7	Otoe County	NE	Nate Keller	2008	38080
*128 4/8	22 5/8 / 22 4/8	15 2/8	8 / 7	Hancock County	IA	Darrell Hanks	2008	38080
128 4/8	20 7/8 / 21 3/8	15 2/8	5 / 4	Schuyler County	IL	Daniel L. Cole	2008	38080
128 4/8	20 6/8 / 20 7/8	14 6/8	5 / 5	Macoupin County	IL	Chad Garcia	2008	38080
*128 4/8	21 4/8 / 21 4/8	15 6/8	5 / 5	Adair County	MO	Brian Meyerhoff	2008	38080
128 4/8	19 7/8 / 19 3/8	15 5/8	6 / 5	Burnet County	TX	Richard Morrison	2008	38080
*128 4/8	20 6/8 / 19 2/8	16 1/8	6 / 6	Dane County	WI	Edward Neumann	2009	38080
*128 4/8	21 4/8 / 21 4/8	16 2/8	5 / 5	Todd County	SD	Michael Senft	2009	38080
128 4/8	20 5/8 / 20 4/8	18 0/8	6 / 6	Noble County	IN	John Rolison	2009	38080
128 4/8	22 6/8 / 22 6/8	17 0/8	4 / 4	Greene County	PA	R. Adrian Whipkey	2009	38080
*128 4/8	22 5/8 / 23 2/8	17 6/8	4 / 4	Green Lake County	WI	Dustin M. Jackowski	2009	38080
128 4/8	23 1/8 / 23 0/8	19 4/8	5 / 4	Polk County	TX	Justin Rowe	2009	38080
128 4/8	21 5/8 / 21 5/8	20 4/8	5 / 5	Clarion County	PA	Garett J. Holben	2009	38080
128 4/8	21 7/8 / 22 1/8	16 4/8	6 / 4	Shelby County	MO	George L. Muehlemann	2009	38080
*128 4/8	19 4/8 / 21 0/8	17 2/8	6 / 6	Jefferson County	OH	Victor S. Holdren	2009	38080
128 4/8	21 1/8 / 20 4/8	16 2/8	5 / 5	Andrew County	MO	Danny Westfall, Jr.	2009	38080
128 4/8	23 5/8 / 23 2/8	18 6/8	5 / 5	Alleghany County	NC	Marty Todd	2009	38080
*128 4/8	20 2/8 / 19 7/8	15 2/8	6 / 6	Marquette County	WI	Charles R. Walker	2009	38080
*128 4/8	22 6/8 / 23 2/8	15 3/8	5 / 5	Wood County	WV	Kim Cinglie	2009	38080
128 4/8	22 1/8 / 21 6/8	15 0/8	5 / 5	Somerset County	PA	Jordan Rehar	2009	38080
128 4/8	21 1/8 / 20 5/8	16 6/8	4 / 4	Union County	SD	Patsy Stark	2009	38080

604

WHITETAIL DEER (TYPICAL ANTLERS)

Minimum Score 125   Continued

SCORE	LENGTH OF R MAIN BEAM L	INSIDE SPREAD	NUMBER OF R POINTS L	AREA	STATE/ PROVINCE	HUNTER'S NAME	DATE	RANK
128 4/8	24 3/8 24 2/8	17 4/8	6 4	Osborne County	KS	Bob Snell	2009	38080
128 4/8	21 3/8 21 1/8	16 4/8	4 4	Redwood County	MN	Paul Gordon Grannes	2009	38080
*128 4/8	19 4/8 20 7/8	16 4/8	5 5	Cass County	MN	Timothy Hron	2010	38080
128 4/8	23 1/8 24 1/8	16 4/8	4 4	Mahoning County	OH	Mark W. Noel	2010	38080
128 3/8	23 2/8 23 1/8	20 1/8	5 5	Switzerland County	IN	Larry L. Bell	1981	38357
128 3/8	20 4/8 20 4/8	17 4/8	4 4	Hancock County	IL	Larry R. Kerr	2000	38357
128 3/8	22 5/8 21 3/8	14 4/8	7 4	Anne Arundel County	MD	James J. Fegan	2001	38357
128 3/8	20 0/8 20 0/8	16 7/8	5 5	White County	AR	Scott Eichhorn	2001	38357
*128 3/8	22 1/8 21 4/8	16 1/8	4 4	Somerset County	NJ	Joseph Raio	2003	38357
128 3/8	21 5/8 20 5/8	17 1/8	4 4	Eau Claire County	WI	Kevin J. Wahl	2004	38357
128 3/8	22 2/8 23 6/8	17 1/8	4 4	Le Flore County	OK	Russell Smith	2004	38357
128 3/8	23 1/8 22 4/8	16 7/8	4 4	Licking County	OH	Sam Lantz	2004	38357
128 3/8	21 2/8 21 3/8	22 7/8	4 5	Marshall County	IN	Cory L. Hollar	2004	38357
128 3/8	21 5/8 21 5/8	14 5/8	4 4	Knox County	IN	Jerry L. Hammelman	2004	38357
128 3/8	21 2/8 22 0/8	17 6/8	6 4	Barber County	KS	Dave Kenworthy	2004	38357
128 3/8	23 0/8 21 7/8	16 1/8	4 4	Union County	OH	Tim Cuthbert	2004	38357
128 3/8	20 5/8 21 0/8	15 5/8	5 5	Marquette County	WI	Josh A. Holliday	2004	38357
128 3/8	21 4/8 23 6/8	14 5/8	4 4	Bolivar County	MS	Lance Johnson	2004	38357
128 3/8	20 6/8 19 7/8	15 4/8	6 5	Fulton County	IN	Jason McClish	2005	38357
128 3/8	23 0/8 22 4/8	16 3/8	4 4	Tama County	IA	Kurt Chizek	2005	38357
*128 3/8	21 5/8 21 4/8	15 5/8	4 4	Parke County	IN	Luke Whitkanack	2005	38357
*128 3/8	19 4/8 19 6/8	17 4/8	5 6	Adair County	OK	Jack Wilbanks	2005	38357
128 3/8	21 0/8 20 5/8	14 7/8	4 5	Callaway County	MO	Jacob Riechers	2005	38357
128 3/8	21 2/8 20 1/8	14 7/8	5 6	Calhoun County	MI	Mark A. Collier	2005	38357
128 3/8	21 2/8 20 4/8	16 2/8	5 6	Lake County	IL	Greg Hanson	2005	38357
128 3/8	21 4/8 20 7/8	17 5/8	5 4	Greene County	PA	Dennis M. Blouir	2005	38357
128 3/8	21 6/8 22 0/8	18 3/8	5 4	White County	IL	Frank A. Paino, Jr.	2005	38357
128 3/8	22 7/8 22 4/8	18 1/8	5 4	Lake County	IL	John L. Szeliga	2005	38357
128 3/8	22 2/8 22 6/8	17 1/8	4 4	St-Joseph Madanaska	NBW	Sylvain Caron	2006	38357
*128 3/8	24 2/8 23 6/8	14 6/8	6 4	Morgan County	IL	James E. Deibert	2006	38357
128 3/8	22 3/8 22 6/8	15 2/8	6 4	Pike County	IL	Eric A. Mohrman	2006	38357
128 3/8	20 6/8 21 1/8	19 1/8	4 4	Randolph County	NC	Kevin Cox	2006	38357
128 3/8	21 6/8 22 2/8	18 5/8	4 4	Houston County	MN	Dylan Burrow	2006	38357
128 3/8	21 6/8 20 6/8	18 3/8	4 4	Foster County	ND	Lee Wahlurd	2006	38357
*128 3/8	22 4/8 23 3/8	23 6/8	5 5	Will County	IL	Tom Schiever	2006	38357
*128 3/8	22 6/8 22 6/8	16 1/8	4 4	Trumbull County	OH	William Gadd	2006	38357
*128 3/8	22 4/8 22 5/8	18 1/8	4 4	Allegan County	MI	Mitchell Wells	2006	38357
128 3/8	22 1/8 22 3/8	18 5/8	4 4	Lafayette County	WI	Robert N. Krueger	2006	38357
128 3/8	20 3/8 20 4/8	16 5/8	4 5	Decatur County	IA	Michael O. Sturm	2006	38357
*128 3/8	20 0/8 21 0/8	17 6/8	5 4	Republic County	KS	Robert M. "Mike" Young	2006	38357
128 3/8	23 2/8 23 3/8	17 7/8	4 4	Richland County	WI	Douglas Elliott	2006	38357
128 3/8	21 2/8 22 0/8	19 3/8	4 4	Washington County	RI	John T. Cragan	2006	38357
128 3/8	22 7/8 22 4/8	17 5/8	5 4	Greene County	OH	Douglas S. Cooney	2006	38357
*128 3/8	22 0/8 22 2/8	19 1/8	4 4	Strathcona	ALB	John Byrne	2007	38357
128 3/8	23 4/8 24 1/8	21 1/8	5 5	Litchfield County	CT	John Coniglio	2007	38357
128 3/8	21 4/8 21 7/8	15 7/8	5 5	Fayette County	IL	Mike Kistler	2007	38357
*128 3/8	19 2/8 19 4/8	15 5/8	5 5	Seward County	NE	Brock R. Henn	2007	38357
128 3/8	16 6/8 25 4/8	23 0/8	6 4	Fairfield County	OH	Roger Sisler, Jr.	2007	38357
128 3/8	20 2/8 19 6/8	15 0/8	6 5	Carroll County	KY	David Watts	2007	38357
128 3/8	19 2/8 19 6/8	14 5/8	5 5	Ramsey County	ND	Amber Logie	2007	38357
*128 3/8	19 6/8 19 4/8	15 1/8	5 4	Nemaha County	NE	Daniel Ross Williams	2007	38357
*128 3/8	23 0/8 22 6/8	16 7/8	4 4	Waukesha County	WI	James A. Schmidt	2007	38357
128 3/8	18 0/8 18 7/8	16 5/8	5 5	Rusk County	WI	John A. Bowers	2007	38357
*128 3/8	21 3/8 21 3/8	14 4/8	7 5	Yates County	NY	Paul D. English	2007	38357
*128 3/8	21 4/8 22 0/8	17 4/8	6 5	Oneida County	NY	Gregg C. Popple	2007	38357
*128 3/8	21 3/8 22 0/8	18 1/8	4 4	Dunn County	WI	Eric Torgerson	2007	38357
128 3/8	20 6/8 21 7/8	17 1/8	4 4	Spartanburg County	SC	Keith Troutman	2007	38357
128 3/8	20 0/8 20 1/8	14 5/8	5 5	Hopkins County	TX	Robert H. Daniel	2007	38357
128 3/8	21 2/8 20 6/8	15 5/8	5 5	Ste. Genevieve County	MO	Duane Schwent	2008	38357
128 3/8	24 1/8 23 3/8	17 7/8	4 5	Waupaca County	WI	Richard A. Hedtke	2008	38357
128 3/8	22 3/8 22 7/8	16 3/8	4 5	Morrison County	MN	Mike Sannan	2008	38357
128 3/8	23 5/8 22 6/8	17 7/8	4 4	Richland County	OH	John "Rosey" Roseland	2008	38357
128 3/8	21 3/8 21 6/8	17 3/8	4 4	Fayette County	TX	Rick Knape	2008	38357
*128 3/8	20 3/8 20 7/8	16 7/8	5 6	Rock County	WI	Ronald Vike, Jr.	2008	38357
*128 3/8	22 6/8 23 4/8	20 1/8	4 4	Essex	ONT	Rodney Shepley	2008	38357
128 3/8	22 3/8 23 5/8	16 5/8	4 4	Bourbon County	KS	Jerry J. Ruetten	2008	38357
128 3/8	22 7/8 24 0/8	17 5/8	6 6	Sumner County	KS	Clem Stroot	2008	38357
128 3/8	23 0/8 22 3/8	13 7/8	4 4	Hamilton County	IL	L. W. Miller	2008	38357
*128 3/8	20 6/8 22 3/8	16 5/8	5 5	Kosciusko County	IN	Ron L. Cornell	2009	38357
128 3/8	22 7/8 22 4/8	19 5/8	5 4	Marquette County	WI	Dennis E. Krueger	2009	38357
*128 3/8	23 7/8 21 7/8	16 5/8	6 6	Columbia County	WI	Kim S. Ades	2009	38357
128 3/8	22 2/8 22 0/8	19 7/8	5 5	Spencer County	IN	Mark Rahman	2009	38357
*128 3/8	22 6/8 22 3/8	17 1/8	4 4	Licking County	OH	Bob Wise	2009	38357
128 3/8	23 0/8 22 6/8	18 0/8	5 5	Calhoun County	MI	Mark M. Brankovich	2009	38357
*128 3/8	22 3/8 21 0/8	16 3/8	4 4	Outagamie County	WI	Rick Houterman, Jr.	2009	38357
*128 3/8	24 2/8 23 2/8	18 5/8	6 8	Knox County	IL	Richard Powles	2009	38357
128 3/8	20 3/8 21 6/8	15 7/8	5 6	Ringgold County	IA	Kelly Dougherty	2009	38357
128 3/8	20 5/8 20 2/8	13 7/8	5 5	Madison County	ID	Donny Kauer	2009	38357
*128 3/8	23 3/8 23 6/8	16 6/8	5 5	Daviess County	IN	Zachary Morris	2009	38357
128 3/8	23 5/8 24 2/8	15 7/8	4 4	Licking County	OH	Richard L. McCowen	2009	38357
*128 3/8	24 4/8 23 4/8	15 7/8	5 5	Lawrence County	IL	Greg Hance	2009	38357
*128 3/8	20 3/8 20 6/8	17 2/8	5 5	Comanche County	KS	Chris J. Hood	2009	38357
128 3/8	21 5/8 21 3/8	16 5/8	5 5	Nuevo Laredo	MEX	Gary Goodenow	2009	38357
*128 3/8	20 6/8 20 4/8	16 3/8	5 5	Greene County	PA	Raymond Kimmell	2010	38357
128 2/8	21 5/8 20 5/8	18 0/8	5 5	Madison Parish	LA	Gary D. Dobbs	1999	38609
128 2/8	22 7/8 24 0/8	15 4/8	4 4	Marathon County	WI	David Tuskowski	1999	38609
128 2/8	20 3/8 21 4/8	18 4/8	5 5	Wayne County	IA	Ben Grosz	2001	38609
128 2/8	22 3/8 22 1/8	19 2/8	4 4	Parke County	IN	Michael J. Fabyanic	2003	38609
128 2/8	21 1/8 21 4/8	15 2/8	6 6	Pike County	MO	Mike Colombo	2003	38609
128 2/8	23 5/8 23 3/8	19 6/8	4 4	Macon County	IL	Joe Pryor	2003	38609
128 2/8	22 6/8 23 3/8	21 5/8	5 5	Edwards County	IL	Todd Taylor	2003	38609
128 2/8	22 1/8 21 3/8	15 2/8	5 5	Jay County	IN	Todd A. Shaffer	2004	38609
128 2/8	22 2/8 22 0/8	19 4/8	5 4	St. Croix County	WI	Jason Prokop	2004	38609
128 2/8	22 3/8 24 2/8	18 0/8	6 4	Iroquois County	IL	Brian Weber	2004	38609
128 2/8	20 1/8 21 1/8	18 0/8	4 5	Portage County	WI	Joshua R. Ostrowski	2004	38609

Deer entries below 141 0/8, that appeared in the 6th Edition, are not included here, but are included on the accompanying CD (see page 119), and also in the Club's Records Archives.

605

WHITETAIL DEER (TYPICAL ANTLERS)

Minimum Score 125 — Continued

SCORE	LENGTH OF R MAIN BEAM L		INSIDE SPREAD	NUMBER OF R POINTS L		AREA	STATE/ PROVINCE	HUNTER'S NAME	DATE	RANK
128 2/8	21 4/8	21 4/8	16 6/8	4	4	Washington County	AR	Michael Poor	2004	38609
128 2/8	25 3/8	25 4/8	18 4/8	5	4	Highland County	OH	Dennis Egbert	2004	38609
128 2/8	20 4/8	21 6/8	15 6/8	6	6	Chickasaw County	IA	Kyle LaBarge	2004	38609
128 2/8	21 3/8	21 7/8	17 2/8	5	5	Macon County	IL	Chris Luttrell	2004	38609
*128 2/8	21 1/8	21 6/8	16 2/8	5	5	Anoka County	MN	Robert Jones, Jr.	2005	38609
128 2/8	21 5/8	21 2/8	19 0/8	6	6	Johnston County	OK	William C. Bowman	2005	38609
*128 2/8	22 6/8	21 7/8	17 4/8	5	5	Christian County	MO	Darrel Hogan	2005	38609
128 2/8	20 7/8	20 3/8	14 4/8	5	5	Jackson County	MO	George McPherson	2005	38609
128 2/8	23 1/8	24 0/8	18 0/8	4	5	Vinton County	OH	Clark Miller	2005	38609
*128 2/8	22 3/8	22 0/8	17 6/8	4	5	Douglas County	WI	Miika Otava	2005	38609
128 2/8	22 4/8	22 2/8	17 4/8	5	5	Suffolk County	NY	Rob Catalano	2005	38609
128 2/8	24 5/8	23 5/8	18 0/8	5	5	Stevens County	WA	Greg McCollough	2005	38609
128 2/8	20 7/8	20 4/8	14 4/8	5	5	Price County	WI	Kelly Kirchmeyer	2005	38609
128 2/8	24 0/8	23 2/8	19 6/8	4	4	Kent County	MI	Jon M. Brouwer	2006	38609
128 2/8	19 4/8	20 1/8	16 4/8	5	5	Mountrail County	ND	Daryl L. Belik	2006	38609
128 2/8	20 7/8	19 6/8	16 5/8	4	5	Miami County	IN	Robert Benzing	2006	38609
128 2/8	20 1/8	20 1/8	15 2/8	7	5	Garfield County	OK	Gordon Craig Nelson, Jr.	2006	38609
128 2/8	23 3/8	23 1/8	16 2/8	4	4	Jefferson County	WI	Larry Braatz	2006	38609
128 2/8	21 2/8	20 5/8	16 2/8	5	4	St. Joseph County	MI	J. Wade Robinson	2006	38609
128 2/8	21 2/8	20 6/8	13 6/8	5	5	Matagorda County	TX	Wesley R. Smolik, Jr.	2006	38609
128 2/8	21 1/8	21 0/8	13 6/8	5	5	Beadle County	SD	Gregory L. Weeldreyer	2006	38609
128 2/8	23 3/8	23 3/8	17 4/8	4	4	Jackson County	IA	Larry Galliart	2006	38609
*128 2/8	18 0/8	21 6/8	17 2/8	7	6	Harrison County	OH	Gerald L. Miller II	2006	38609
*128 2/8	22 7/8	22 5/8	15 5/8	6	6	Washington County	MN	Todd Clarkowski	2006	38609
128 2/8	20 7/8	21 1/8	15 0/8	5	5	Calhoun County	IL	Danny Moore	2006	38609
*128 2/8	20 6/8	22 2/8	18 0/8	4	5	Warren County	NJ	Peter Mancuso, Jr.	2006	38609
128 2/8	21 1/8	21 3/8	18 3/8	6	5	Seminole County	OK	Mike Villines	2006	38609
128 2/8	21 0/8	20 1/8	16 6/8	6	5	Fulton County	IN	Crystal J. Sipe	2007	38609
128 2/8	20 2/8	20 6/8	15 0/8	5	5	White County	AR	Steven Tucker	2007	38609
128 2/8	22 7/8	21 0/8	18 0/8	5	5	Kendall County	IL	Joe Onderisin	2007	38609
*128 2/8	20 5/8	20 6/8	17 0/8	5	5	Sheboygan County	WI	Michael Budrecki	2007	38609
128 2/8	21 0/8	20 5/8	14 2/8	5	4	Nemaha County	NE	Joseph Studebaker	2007	38609
128 2/8	23 1/8	23 1/8	21 0/8	4	4	Buffalo County	WI	James E. Turner	2007	38609
*128 2/8	20 6/8	20 7/8	16 0/8	5	5	Mitchell County	IA	Gerald Beaver	2007	38609
128 2/8	20 6/8	21 0/8	16 2/8	5	5	Henderson County	IL	Luke Patnesky	2007	38609
*128 2/8	23 4/8	23 4/8	16 4/8	4	4	McHenry County	ND	Jordan P. Vollmer	2007	38609
128 2/8	23 0/8	23 1/8	16 4/8	4	4	Chautauqua County	KS	James F. Watson	2007	38609
128 2/8	20 1/8	20 5/8	17 0/8	5	5	Woodbury County	IA	Russ R. Wauhob	2007	38609
*128 2/8	21 5/8	21 5/8	16 6/8	5	6	Chester County	PA	Shane Robinson	2008	38609
128 2/8	19 3/8	19 7/8	16 0/8	4	4	Trinity County	TX	Mark Wells	2008	38609
*128 2/8	20 2/8	21 5/8	18 2/8	6	5	Allegan County	MI	Dennis B. Dykhouse	2008	38609
128 2/8	23 3/8	23 2/8	17 6/8	4	4	Montcalm County	MI	Ann M. Smith	2008	38609
128 2/8	24 1/8	24 7/8	21 6/8	4	4	Hanover County	VA	Henri Lalik	2008	38609
*128 2/8	21 6/8	21 5/8	18 2/8	5	5	Carrot River	SAS	Jade Keeton	2008	38609
128 2/8	22 0/8	21 7/8	17 4/8	4	4	Osage County	MO	James W. Ferguson	2008	38609
*128 2/8	22 4/8	21 7/8	17 0/8	4	5	Beaver County	PA	Larry O'Neill	2008	38609
128 2/8	19 1/8	20 6/8	13 6/8	5	5	Pushmataha County	OK	Evan Sanders	2008	38609
128 2/8	22 3/8	24 0/8	15 1/8	7	7	Marshall County	KS	Samuel Ashley Rollans	2008	38609
128 2/8	20 6/8	21 2/8	17 2/8	5	5	Outagamie County	WI	Ryan Kettner	2008	38609
128 2/8	20 7/8	20 4/8	15 2/8	5	6	Waushara County	WI	Chad M. Casper	2008	38609
*128 2/8	23 1/8	23 4/8	18 0/8	4	5	Norton County	KS	Brian E. Berlier	2008	38609
*128 2/8	20 6/8	23 4/8	17 6/8	6	5	Logan County	KY	Lee Yoder	2009	38609
*128 2/8	21 4/8	21 4/8	16 2/8	4	4	Cass County	ND	Craig Wendt	2009	38609
*128 2/8	22 0/8	23 3/8	13 0/8	4	4	Alamance County	NC	C. J. Gantos	2009	38609
*128 2/8	22 0/8	22 4/8	16 4/8	4	4	Pierce County	WI	Jeffrey J. Holland	2009	38609
*128 2/8	21 3/8	20 4/8	14 2/8	5	5	Monona County	IA	Mathew L. Ritz	2009	38609
*128 2/8	20 6/8	19 6/8	14 2/8	5	5	Henry County	IL	Richard F. Orta	2009	38609
128 2/8	22 2/8	22 2/8	16 6/8	4	4	Lee County	GA	David M. Campbell	2009	38609
*128 2/8	22 7/8	22 5/8	18 0/8	4	4	Page County	IA	Randy Scheel	2009	38609
128 1/8	19 2/8	19 5/8	14 6/8	6	5	Bates County	MO	Bill Haas	2001	38860
128 1/8	23 4/8	23 4/8	14 5/8	5	5	Dodge County	WI	Eduardo I. Rodriguez Mayorga	2003	38860
128 1/8	21 2/8	21 3/8	20 0/8	5	6	Putnam County	OH	Michael Meyer	2004	38860
128 1/8	19 5/8	20 0/8	15 3/8	4	4	Monona County	IA	Kurt A. Becker	2004	38860
128 1/8	21 5/8	21 6/8	15 5/8	4	5	Cass County	MI	William B. Matthews	2004	38860
*128 1/8	21 4/8	21 0/8	19 1/8	5	5	Juneau County	WI	Robert Krantz	2004	38860
128 1/8	20 7/8	20 2/8	12 3/8	5	5	Pettis County	MO	Gary Brandes	2004	38860
128 1/8	21 1/8	21 0/8	15 1/8	4	4	Cedar County	MO	Kendall Gire	2004	38860
128 1/8	20 3/8	20 0/8	15 7/8	4	5	Ogle County	IL	Alan D. Schuler	2004	38860
128 1/8	22 6/8	21 7/8	16 2/8	4	5	Olmsted County	MN	Jim Leqve	2004	38860
128 1/8	21 2/8	23 2/8	16 3/8	5	5	Outagamie County	WI	Bruce Van Schyndel	2004	38860
128 1/8	21 4/8	21 2/8	17 1/8	4	5	Kane County	IL	Mike Bombardiere	2004	38860
*128 1/8	19 2/8	19 5/8	14 7/8	5	5	Grant County	WI	Richard Paul	2005	38860
128 1/8	21 5/8	20 3/8	14 5/8	4	5	Sheboygan County	WI	Ken Beckford	2005	38860
*128 1/8	22 1/8	22 1/8	17 3/8	4	5	Ramsey County	ND	Dean Fandrich, Jr.	2005	38860
128 1/8	20 5/8	20 5/8	16 3/8	6	5	Morgan County	IL	David W. Kelly	2005	38860
128 1/8	21 4/8	21 4/8	17 5/8	5	5	Trempealeau County	WI	Eric Arkowski	2005	38860
128 1/8	20 6/8	20 7/8	17 7/8	4	5	Woodbury County	IA	Russell J. Johnson	2005	38860
128 1/8	21 1/8	21 7/8	19 2/8	4	5	Adams County	OH	Robert Young	2005	38860
128 1/8	20 4/8	22 1/8	14 6/8	6	4	Prairie County	AR	Mark McDonnel	2005	38860
128 1/8	20 6/8	20 0/8	14 3/8	4	4	Sumner County	KS	Randy Hoffman	2005	38860
128 1/8	20 1/8	19 7/8	16 6/8	4	4	Lane County	KS	Tod Anthony	2005	38860
128 1/8	23 4/8	22 6/8	21 1/8	5	4	Wagoner County	OK	David Samples	2005	38860
128 1/8	20 7/8	19 1/8	17 0/8	7	4	Jasper County	IN	William B. Schoeneman	2005	38860
128 1/8	24 4/8	23 1/8	16 3/8	5	7	Riley County	KS	Scott T. King	2005	38860
128 1/8	20 3/8	20 5/8	15 3/8	4	4	Big Horn County	WY	David Moss	2005	38860
128 1/8	21 1/8	20 7/8	17 5/8	4	4	Cowley County	KS	Elwin E. Latham	2005	38860
128 1/8	22 2/8	22 0/8	16 7/8	4	4	Claiborne County	MS	Lance Stroud	2005	38860
128 1/8	21 2/8	20 7/8	16 3/8	6	6	Madison County	MT	Bill Woods	2006	38860
128 1/8	19 0/8	19 2/8	14 1/8	5	5	Ziebach County	SD	Ramon Birkeland	2006	38860
128 1/8	25 1/8	24 2/8	17 5/8	4	5	McHenry County	IL	William Snelgrove	2006	38860
*128 1/8	19 2/8	20 0/8	14 6/8	4	5	Johnson County	KS	James H. Schneider	2006	38860
*128 1/8	20 4/8	21 4/8	18 3/8	4	4	DeKalb County	IL	Joseph W. Shramovich	2006	38860
128 1/8	22 3/8	22 1/8	18 3/8	5	5	Knox County	OH	H. Todd McDonald	2006	38860
*128 1/8	21 0/8	20 1/8	12 3/8	4	4	McHenry County	ND	Craig Canaday	2006	38860
128 1/8	23 0/8	23 1/8	16 7/8	4	5	Sullivan County	IN	Doug Cassel	2006	38860

WHITETAIL DEER (TYPICAL ANTLERS)

Minimum Score 125 — Continued

SCORE	R MAIN BEAM L	INSIDE SPREAD	R POINTS L		AREA	STATE/PROVINCE	HUNTER'S NAME	DATE	RANK
128 1/8	22 1/8 22 0/8	16 5/8	4	4	Platte County	NE	Mike Becher	2006	38860
128 1/8	22 1/8 21 4/8	16 5/8	5	4	Chester County	PA	Thomas M. Delaney	2006	38860
128 1/8	19 6/8 20 2/8	15 1/8	5	5	Barron County	WI	Nathan Hubbard	2006	38860
128 1/8	22 0/8 22 2/8	14 6/8	7	7	Putnam County	MO	Dusty L. Loveland	2006	38860
*128 1/8	20 7/8 21 4/8	13 3/8	5	4	Nelson County	ND	Dan Ryba	2006	38860
128 1/8	22 1/8 22 4/8	16 1/8	4	4	Jefferson County	ID	Johnny Watson	2007	38860
128 1/8	17 2/8 20 5/8	17 7/8	6	5	Mercer County	NJ	Frank Prato	2007	38860
128 1/8	24 6/8 23 6/8	15 7/8	4	5	Knox County	IL	Randy Bozarth	2007	38860
*128 1/8	23 3/8 22 3/8	17 3/8	4	5	Woodruff County	AR	Frank C. Bombino	2007	38860
128 1/8	20 7/8 21 0/8	16 5/8	5	5	Olmsted County	MN	Rich Behne	2007	38860
128 1/8	21 1/8 21 3/8	15 7/8	4	5	Buffalo County	WI	Mark Phillips	2007	38860
*128 1/8	22 1/8 21 4/8	15 7/8	5	6	Beaver County	PA	Daniel Bobin	2007	38860
128 1/8	19 2/8 19 0/8	15 5/8	5	5	Cass County	MI	Daniel Scott Blaske	2007	38860
128 1/8	21 4/8 21 6/8	17 2/8	5	6	Marquette County	WI	Daniel L. Schultz	2007	38860
*128 1/8	19 5/8 20 2/8	16 3/8	5	5	Mitchell County	IA	Bob Spitz	2007	38860
*128 1/8	22 0/8 16 1/8	17 4/8	6	6	Decatur County	IA	Tom Waite	2007	38860
128 1/8	21 2/8 21 0/8	16 5/8	6	5	Livingston County	NY	Paul Luft	2007	38860
*128 1/8	20 4/8 20 5/8	16 3/8	4	4	Polk County	WI	Jeff Niemann	2007	38860
128 1/8	20 1/8 19 5/8	16 1/8	5	6	Strathcona	ALB	Scott D. Trelstad	2007	38860
*128 1/8	21 0/8 23 6/8	15 7/8	4	5	Dutchess County	NY	Jay Decker	2007	38860
128 1/8	20 0/8 21 4/8	16 1/8	4	4	Hall County	GA	Bob Schultz	2007	38860
128 1/8	21 6/8 20 2/8	16 4/8	5	5	Spokane County	WA	Steve Mitchell	2007	38860
*128 1/8	19 0/8 19 5/8	15 1/8	5	5	Anoka County	MN	Eric Nathe	2007	38860
*128 1/8	21 4/8 21 5/8	16 0/8	6	5	Fulton County	IN	Matthew L. Chupp	2008	38860
128 1/8	20 2/8 20 6/8	14 7/8	6	5	Cass County	MO	Mark Ackerson	2008	38860
128 1/8	19 5/8 20 0/8	17 0/8	5	6	Ontario County	NY	Thomas Giancursio	2008	38860
128 1/8	21 4/8 20 4/8	16 5/8	5	5	Logan County	AR	Will Beason	2008	38860
128 1/8	23 7/8 21 7/8	21 5/8	4	4	Sauk County	WI	Scott Oberst	2008	38860
128 1/8	19 4/8 19 4/8	14 5/8	5	5	Jackson County	MI	Chad Andrews	2008	38860
128 1/8	22 2/8 22 6/8	13 7/8	5	6	Switzerland County	IN	Brad Shephard	2008	38860
128 1/8	19 6/8 19 6/8	17 6/8	6	5	Buffalo County	WI	Aaron Dammen	2008	38860
*128 1/8	23 5/8 23 1/8	16 4/8	5	4	Steuben County	IN	Travis Goodwin	2008	38860
*128 1/8	19 2/8 19 0/8	14 3/8	5	6	Moultrie County	IL	Robert V. Mitchell	2008	38860
*128 1/8	23 2/8 23 5/8	17 3/8	4	4	Pike County	AR	Paul Kevin Gauthier	2008	38860
*128 1/8	21 6/8 21 5/8	15 3/8	5	5	Lewis County	WV	Timothy Bonnett	2008	38860
*128 1/8	21 7/8 22 0/8	18 5/8	5	5	Chippewa County	WI	Robert Jones	2008	38860
*128 1/8	21 6/8 19 7/8	16 5/8	4	4	Hamilton County	IL	Michael L. Ritter, Sr.	2008	38860
*128 1/8	23 5/8 22 6/8	15 3/8	4	4	Kingman County	KS	Michael Alan Cox, Jr.	2009	38860
128 1/8	21 5/8 20 5/8	13 3/8	5	5	Fulton County	AR	Bob Mils	2009	38860
*128 1/8	20 3/8 20 3/8	15 7/8	5	5	Barron County	WI	David Etlicher	2009	38860
*128 1/8	19 7/8 19 6/8	13 6/8	7	8	Brown County	IL	Ronald Hixson	2009	38860
128 1/8	21 0/8 20 2/8	13 5/8	5	6	Comanche County	KS	Pat Lefemine	2009	38860
128 1/8	21 2/8 20 7/8	15 2/8	5	6	Hudson Bay	SAS	Steve Hinton	2009	38860
*128 1/8	24 0/8 22 7/8	18 1/8	5	4	Escambia County	FL	Kenny Alford	2010	38860
128 0/8	20 1/8 20 6/8	14 2/8	6	5	Wilkinson County	MS	Patrick Kelleher	1999	39140
128 0/8	22 3/8 22 6/8	17 1/8	5	4	Oldham County	KY	Tom Woosley	2001	39140
128 0/8	23 1/8 22 3/8	14 4/8	5	6	Logan County	KY	J. Riley Watkins	2001	39140
128 0/8	20 1/8 20 7/8	17 0/8	5	5	Gladu Lake	ALB	Gunther Tondeleir	2002	39140
*128 0/8	19 4/8 20 2/8	16 0/8	5	5	Will County	IL	David A. McGinnis	2002	39140
128 0/8	21 6/8 21 1/8	20 6/8	5	5	Hunterdon County	NJ	Augie Matteo	2002	39140
128 0/8	25 5/8 25 3/8	17 4/8	6	5	Franklin County	PA	Robert R. Cramer	2004	39140
128 0/8	20 3/8 20 4/8	16 4/8	4	4	Orleans County	NY	Michael Plummer	2004	39140
128 0/8	20 7/8 20 4/8	15 4/8	6	5	Peoria County	IL	Larry T. Schmitt	2004	39140
128 0/8	23 3/8 22 5/8	15 6/8	4	4	Kent County	MD	Dave Schirmer	2004	39140
128 0/8	22 4/8 22 3/8	16 3/8	7	5	Dodge County	WI	Roy Zastrow	2004	39140
128 0/8	21 7/8 21 5/8	15 0/8	6	5	Dimmit County	TX	Clark O. Daniel, Jr.	2004	39140
*128 0/8	21 5/8 22 0/8	16 6/8	5	6	Portage County	WI	Brad Bastian	2004	39140
128 0/8	24 0/8 23 0/8	15 2/8	4	4	Cheatham County	TN	Jeff Rauschenberger	2004	39140
128 0/8	21 3/8 22 0/8	18 6/8	5	5	Adams County	WI	Wesley R. Redlin	2004	39140
*128 0/8	19 5/8 19 7/8	16 0/8	5	5	Vernon County	MO	James Newton	2004	39140
128 0/8	21 2/8 20 4/8	17 4/8	5	5	Tama County	IA	Scot Finke	2004	39140
128 0/8	22 4/8 22 3/8	17 0/8	5	4	Westchester County	NY	Doug Erickson	2004	39140
128 0/8	23 7/8 22 4/8	17 4/8	4	4	Hennepin County	MN	Matthew Daniel	2004	39140
*128 0/8	23 2/8 20 7/8	21 2/8	5	4	Schenectady County	NY	John Phillips	2004	39140
128 0/8	23 1/8 24 1/8	15 6/8	4	4	Guilford County	NC	Travis Vance	2005	39140
*128 0/8	23 1/8 20 2/8	16 2/8	4	6	Switzerland County	IN	Kenneth E. Lucero	2005	39140
*128 0/8	23 3/8 23 2/8	17 0/8	4	4	Chickasaw County	MS	Kerry Steven Vinson	2005	39140
128 0/8	23 6/8 22 4/8	16 2/8	4	5	Livingston County	MI	Tom Dorsey II	2005	39140
128 0/8	22 2/8 22 4/8	16 4/8	4	4	Hampshire County	MA	Tom Camilleri	2005	39140
128 0/8	17 5/8 17 4/8	15 0/8	5	5	Schleicher County	TX	Tony Mabe	2005	39140
128 0/8	18 4/8 19 0/8	18 0/8	5	5	La Salle County	IL	Don Westerhold	2005	39140
*128 0/8	21 7/8 21 1/8	17 6/8	5	5	Montgomery County	IA	William H. McClure	2005	39140
128 0/8	22 0/8 22 7/8	15 6/8	5	5	Morrow County	OH	Paul Burkhart	2005	39140
128 0/8	22 5/8 20 6/8	19 2/8	5	4	Waushara County	WI	Steve Swiatczak	2005	39140
128 0/8	21 6/8 22 2/8	17 0/8	5	4	Hocking County	OH	Trevor L. Steigerwalt	2005	39140
*128 0/8	20 4/8 21 2/8	17 0/8	5	5	Le Flore County	OK	Dennis W. Covey, Jr.	2005	39140
128 0/8	20 7/8 20 7/8	17 4/8	5	5	Trempealeau County	WI	Jeffrey Hruska	2005	39140
128 0/8	20 0/8 21 0/8	13 6/8	7	6	Pike County	AR	Robbie Crocker	2005	39140
*128 0/8	22 3/8 21 7/8	19 4/8	4	4	Fulton County	OH	Joe Hoffman	2005	39140
*128 0/8	20 5/8 20 4/8	15 3/8	6	6	Becker County	MN	Joe Skarie	2005	39140
128 0/8	24 4/8 23 6/8	19 6/8	4	5	Warren County	NY	Michael Sharp	2005	39140
128 0/8	22 4/8 22 2/8	20 0/8	4	4	Desha County	AR	Lee Walt	2005	39140
128 0/8	21 2/8 21 2/8	16 2/8	5	4	McKenzie County	ND	Corey Hugelen	2005	39140
128 0/8	21 6/8 22 0/8	14 6/8	5	4	Johnson County	KS	Lawrence H. Haake	2005	39140
*128 0/8	21 1/8 20 4/8	17 5/8	6	7	Buffalo County	WI	Chad Rebarchek	2006	39140
128 0/8	23 3/8 22 7/8	21 2/8	4	3	Bristol County	MA	Steven Rogers	2006	39140
128 0/8	22 1/8 22 2/8	15 7/8	5	6	Claiborne County	MS	Bob Lane	2006	39140
*128 0/8	22 0/8 22 0/8	16 0/8	4	5	Wood County	WV	Ronald Davis	2006	39140
128 0/8	23 1/8 22 6/8	15 4/8	5	5	Vernon County	WI	Jerry Willer	2006	39140
128 0/8	22 0/8 20 1/8	14 6/8	5	5	Columbia County	WI	Justin Berg	2006	39140
128 0/8	22 1/8 21 3/8	17 0/8	5	4	Clay County	IA	Marc Gustafson	2006	39140
*128 0/8	21 3/8 20 5/8	15 0/8	5	5	Trempealeau County	WI	Nathan Baer	2006	39140
128 0/8	21 3/8 22 0/8	14 2/8	5	5	Athens County	OH	Darren Ellingwood	2006	39140
128 0/8	23 0/8 22 3/8	18 2/8	5	6	Logan County	CO	Michael Dziekan	2006	39140
128 0/8	21 2/8 21 6/8	17 0/8	5	5	Jefferson County	WI	Mike Traub	2006	39140

Deer entries below 141 0/8, that appeared in the 6th Edition, are not included here, but are included on the accompanying CD (see page 119), and also in the Club's Records Archives.

WHITETAIL DEER (TYPICAL ANTLERS)

Minimum Score 125 — Continued

SCORE	LENGTH OF R MAIN BEAM L	INSIDE SPREAD	NUMBER OF R POINTS L	AREA	STATE/ PROVINCE	HUNTER'S NAME	DATE	RANK
128 0/8	21 5/8 22 1/8	14 5/8	6 7	La Porte County	IN	Linda K. Davis	2006	39140
*128 0/8	20 2/8 20 7/8	15 1/8	8 6	Dane County	WI	Ken Arndt	2006	39140
*128 0/8	23 0/8 23 4/8	17 0/8	4 4	Adair County	MO	Travis Bland	2006	39140
128 0/8	22 4/8 23 0/8	19 4/8	4 4	Appanoose County	IA	Rick Petersen	2007	39140
*128 0/8	21 7/8 22 2/8	16 4/8	5 4	Jasper County	GA	Mark Bradford	2007	39140
*128 0/8	21 2/8 20 5/8	17 2/8	5 4	Union County	IL	T. Kirk Hendershott	2007	39140
*128 0/8	20 3/8 21 4/8	13 6/8	4 4	Waupaca County	WI	Christopher Janke	2007	39140
128 0/8	21 7/8 21 7/8	13 7/8	7 5	Vernon County	WI	Mark See	2007	39140
128 0/8	20 4/8 21 5/8	17 2/8	5 5	Abbeville County	SC	Allen McKinney	2007	39140
128 0/8	20 6/8 20 4/8	15 2/8	5 5	Dane County	WI	Josh Mersberger	2007	39140
*128 0/8	20 0/8 21 5/8	14 1/8	6 5	Pike County	MO	Scott Corley	2007	39140
*128 0/8	22 6/8 22 3/8	16 4/8	4 4	Moniteau County	MO	Carlos Hoback	2007	39140
128 0/8	20 6/8 18 3/8	17 0/8	5 5	Pierce County	WI	Tom Place	2007	39140
128 0/8	21 6/8 22 0/8	16 6/8	5 5	Osborne County	KS	Gary Ozias	2007	39140
128 0/8	20 2/8 20 6/8	15 7/8	5 6	Spokane County	WA	Todd Greiner	2007	39140
128 0/8	20 7/8 21 2/8	15 4/8	4 4	Richland County	WI	Steven Henthorn	2007	39140
*128 0/8	18 5/8 21 6/8	17 0/8	4 4	St. Joseph County	IN	Michael L. Ritter, Jr.	2007	39140
128 0/8	26 5/8 24 0/8	17 4/8	4 5	Grenada County	MS	Al Hankins	2008	39140
128 0/8	22 1/8 22 2/8	16 0/8	4 4	Canwood	SAS	Shawn McCullough	2008	39140
*128 0/8	23 1/8 23 4/8	17 1/8	5 5	Alachua County	FL	Mark Hammond	2008	39140
*128 0/8	20 6/8 20 4/8	16 4/8	4 5	Pike County	IL	Casey Foster	2008	39140
128 0/8	24 0/8 23 5/8	14 6/8	5 4	Granville County	NC	Kenneth Hicks	2008	39140
128 0/8	19 7/8 19 7/8	13 7/8	5 6	Green Lake	SAS	Michael Wolff	2008	39140
128 0/8	21 6/8 22 4/8	15 6/8	5 4	Kiowa County	KS	Curt Slopey	2008	39140
*128 0/8	22 3/8 24 0/8	17 4/8	4 5	Cameron County	PA	Jeff Crawford	2008	39140
*128 0/8	22 6/8 21 5/8	18 4/8	4 4	Northumberland County	PA	Luther E. Haupt	2008	39140
128 0/8	20 3/8 19 0/8	14 4/8	5 5	Parke County	IN	Christine M. Wadkins	2008	39140
128 0/8	22 3/8 22 5/8	15 4/8	7 5	Buffalo County	WI	Trevor Bump	2008	39140
128 0/8	24 0/8 23 2/8	22 4/8	5 4	Peoria County	IL	Ross Edwards	2008	39140
128 0/8	23 2/8 22 4/8	16 4/8	5 5	Peoria County	IL	Troy Schlueter	2008	39140
128 0/8	22 4/8 22 1/8	19 0/8	5 4	Monroe County	NY	Colin Bachman	2008	39140
128 0/8	23 0/8 22 4/8	14 4/8	4 4	Ward County	ND	DuWayne Larson	2009	39140
*128 0/8	21 2/8 20 6/8	17 2/8	5 4	Northampton County	NC	William W. Whitley, Jr.	2009	39140
*128 0/8	20 3/8 19 7/8	14 6/8	5 5	Bayfield County	WI	Ann Altmann	2009	39140
128 0/8	21 2/8 23 1/8	18 0/8	5 5	Price County	WI	Roger G. Niewiadomski	2009	39140
*128 0/8	23 2/8 24 2/8	16 7/8	7 5	Creek County	OK	Brad D. Matherly	2009	39140
*128 0/8	25 2/8 23 7/8	20 6/8	5 5	Steuben County	IN	Tony Cope	2009	39140
128 0/8	20 4/8 20 3/8	19 2/8	4 4	Washburn County	WI	Joseph Martell	2009	39140
*128 0/8	23 4/8 23 4/8	17 2/8	4 4	Steuben County	IN	Jeremy M. Sassanella	2009	39140
128 0/8	22 3/8 21 6/8	16 0/8	4 4	Knox County	IL	Stan Parkerson	2009	39140
*128 0/8	23 0/8 21 7/8	16 4/8	4 4	Burke County	GA	Derik Still	2010	39140
*127 7/8	22 0/8 21 7/8	17 1/8	7 7	Monmouth County	NJ	Chris Errickson	1997	39418
*127 7/8	23 5/8 25 2/8	20 4/8	6 4	Henderson County	IL	Bruce Smith	2000	39418
127 7/8	19 6/8 21 7/8	15 2/8	5 6	Newton County	IN	Jeffrey Juergens	2000	39418
127 7/8	22 0/8 20 7/8	15 5/8	5 4	McMullen County	TX	Lannie B. Philley	2001	39418
127 7/8	22 7/8 22 2/8	17 3/8	4 5	Todd County	MN	Jon Arbogast	2001	39418
127 7/8	24 4/8 24 2/8	18 3/8	4 5	Oldham County	KY	W. Austin Musselman, Jr.	2001	39418
127 7/8	22 4/8 21 3/8	15 5/8	4 4	Hartford County	CT	Kerwin G. Gagne	2001	39418
127 7/8	20 5/8 20 1/8	15 1/8	6 7	Washington County	PA	Herbert M. Pratt	2002	39418
*127 7/8	22 1/8 22 0/8	18 7/8	6 6	Cass County	MI	Gary Gaskill	2003	39418
127 7/8	22 1/8 22 3/8	15 0/8	6 4	Seneca County	NY	Thomas P. Mitchell	2003	39418
127 7/8	23 0/8 23 3/8	15 7/8	7 5	Webb County	TX	Mickey W. Hellickson	2003	39418
127 7/8	19 5/8 19 2/8	16 6/8	5 6	Cascade County	MT	Mike Morgan	2004	39418
*127 7/8	21 6/8 21 6/8	17 5/8	4 4	Queen Annes County	MD	Peter S. Jayne	2004	39418
127 7/8	22 5/8 21 5/8	14 7/8	5 5	Outagamie County	WI	Marc Roesler	2004	39418
127 7/8	21 4/8 22 1/8	15 2/8	7 7	Allegheny County	PA	Stanley M. Hoover	2004	39418
127 7/8	21 1/8 22 2/8	14 2/8	4 6	Boone County	MO	Andrew Revelle	2004	39418
127 7/8	20 6/8 20 5/8	16 6/8	5 5	Polk County	WI	Ron Simmons	2004	39418
127 7/8	22 7/8 22 7/8	18 1/8	4 4	Lancaster County	PA	W. Scott Heidelbaugh	2004	39418
127 7/8	23 7/8 23 6/8	16 6/8	5 5	Sherwood Park	ALB	Troy Dzioba	2004	39418
127 7/8	20 5/8 20 2/8	15 3/8	5 6	Meade County	SD	Kevin R. Hvam	2004	39418
127 7/8	21 4/8 22 1/8	17 3/8	4 4	Polk County	IA	Jeff McCullough	2004	39418
127 7/8	21 2/8 21 7/8	20 3/8	4 4	Washington County	WI	Brad Robbins	2004	39418
127 7/8	23 1/8 22 6/8	16 4/8	5 6	Crow Wing County	MN	Jeff Hilgart	2004	39418
127 7/8	23 0/8 22 6/8	16 3/8	4 6	Madison County	KY	George Mateyoke	2005	39418
127 7/8	19 6/8 19 2/8	13 7/8	6 6	Woodbury County	IA	Lance H. Woodbury	2005	39418
*127 7/8	23 0/8 22 6/8	15 5/8	5 8	Clark County	WI	Philip Follen	2005	39418
127 7/8	22 2/8 21 7/8	17 5/8	5 5	Marshall County	AL	Jason Morrison	2005	39418
127 7/8	25 6/8 23 2/8	17 6/8	6 6	Washington County	WI	Rick Bertoni	2005	39418
127 7/8	22 5/8 21 6/8	14 5/8	5 4	Marquette County	WI	Robert L. Kampen	2005	39418
127 7/8	21 0/8 20 1/8	17 1/8	5 5	Fillmore County	MN	Joel Goodman	2005	39418
127 7/8	20 7/8 20 0/8	16 7/8	8 6	Van Buren County	IA	Ernie Merydith	2005	39418
127 7/8	23 6/8 23 6/8	16 3/8	4 5	Monmouth County	NJ	Michael Menzel	2005	39418
127 7/8	20 6/8 21 1/8	17 1/8	4 4	Buffalo County	WI	Jeff Wessels	2005	39418
127 7/8	22 1/8 22 5/8	18 7/8	4 4	Tompkins County	NY	David B. Nielsen	2005	39418
127 7/8	21 2/8 20 6/8	15 3/8	7 7	Shawano County	WI	Ronald N. Stuber	2005	39418
*127 7/8	20 2/8 20 6/8	16 3/8	5 5	Hardin County	IL	Regan James Robinson	2005	39418
127 7/8	18 2/8 18 3/8	12 7/8	5 5	Osage County	OK	Jim Bunnell	2005	39418
127 7/8	22 4/8 22 0/8	19 6/8	5 4	Washington County	MS	Carl E. Taylor	2006	39418
*127 7/8	23 5/8 24 4/8	17 4/8	5 6	Green Lake County	WI	Alex A. Preuss	2006	39418
*127 7/8	21 6/8 21 2/8	14 3/8	5 5	Frederick County	VA	Allen Pack	2006	39418
127 7/8	22 1/8 22 3/8	20 1/8	4 4	Mercer County	OH	Michael Aragon	2006	39418
127 7/8	19 4/8 20 3/8	14 5/8	5 5	Madison County	NE	Mike Wanke	2006	39418
*127 7/8	21 6/8 22 5/8	18 5/8	4 4	Fountain County	IN	Steven Edwards	2006	39418
127 7/8	22 5/8 23 3/8	18 5/8	4 4	Crawford County	WI	Christopher Anderson	2006	39418
127 7/8	21 7/8 21 3/8	17 5/8	4 4	Richland County	WI	Paul Henthorn	2006	39418
*127 7/8	22 2/8 22 7/8	18 5/8	4 4	Souris River	SAS	Jenn Leslie	2007	39418
127 7/8	20 5/8 19 7/8	13 3/8	6 4	Converse County	WY	Edwin DeYoung	2007	39418
127 7/8	19 7/8 20 1/8	13 3/8	5 5	Westmoreland County	PA	Charles W. Boggs	2007	39418
127 7/8	19 7/8 19 6/8	15 5/8	5 5	Labette County	KS	Rodney Kelly	2007	39418
*127 7/8	20 5/8 20 4/8	15 0/8	6 7	Scott County	IL	Chris Loeh	2007	39418
127 7/8	22 6/8 23 5/8	16 2/8	6 6	Shelby County	OH	Scott Rickert	2007	39418
*127 7/8	21 2/8 22 0/8	17 2/8	4 6	Sangamon County	IL	James Hicks	2007	39418
127 7/8	21 0/8 21 0/8	14 7/8	6 5	Calhoun County	IL	Brian Van Landingham	2007	39418
127 7/8	24 5/8 24 2/8	17 4/8	5 4	Guernsey County	OH	Daniel T. Townsend	2007	39418

608

WHITETAIL DEER (TYPICAL ANTLERS)

Minimum Score 125 — Continued

SCORE	R MAIN BEAM L	INSIDE SPREAD	R POINTS L	AREA	STATE/PROVINCE	HUNTER'S NAME	DATE	RANK
127 7/8	23 5/8 24 5/8	15 7/8	4 6	Rock County	WI	Dennis R. Koepp	2007	39418
*127 7/8	23 5/8 24 3/8	18 2/8	8 8	Muskingum County	OH	Michael J. Elliott	2007	39418
*127 7/8	24 0/8 21 7/8	18 7/8	4 5	Lake County	IL	Eric H. Wodek	2007	39418
127 7/8	22 1/8 21 3/8	16 3/8	5 6	St. Clair County	MO	Monty Hillsman	2007	39418
127 7/8	22 5/8 23 3/8	21 5/8	4 5	Drew County	AR	Tommy Bratton	2007	39418
127 7/8	21 6/8 20 5/8	17 3/8	4 4	Shelby County	MO	Rusty Hammond	2007	39418
127 7/8	22 3/8 21 3/8	16 7/8	5 4	Webb County	TX	Bob Gilbert	2008	39418
127 7/8	21 1/8 22 3/8	17 2/8	6 5	Lake County	MN	Randy Bowe	2008	39418
127 7/8	18 7/8 19 3/8	17 3/8	5 5	Olmsted County	MN	Jordan Paukert	2008	39418
*127 7/8	22 5/8 23 0/8	16 1/8	4 5	St. Louis County	MN	Alan Vorderbruggen	2008	39418
*127 7/8	18 7/8 20 2/8	14 3/8	5 5	Meadow Lake	SAS	Joshua D. Waskowitz	2008	39418
*127 7/8	19 3/8 18 3/8	12 3/8	6 6	St. Louis County	MO	Johnathan Robertson	2008	39418
127 7/8	22 1/8 20 4/8	16 5/8	4 5	Noble County	IN	Wayne R. Edwards	2008	39418
127 7/8	19 6/8 22 3/8	19 1/8	6 7	Tioga County	PA	Adam Smith	2008	39418
*127 7/8	21 2/8 20 6/8	15 3/8	5 5	Webster County	NE	Terence D. Wiley	2008	39418
127 7/8	22 0/8 22 5/8	14 0/8	4 6	Goodhue County	MN	Sue Cushing	2008	39418
*127 7/8	22 5/8 22 7/8	18 3/8	4 5	Jefferson County	OH	Brian Eagleton	2008	39418
127 7/8	21 4/8 21 3/8	16 1/8	4 4	Macon County	IL	Charlie DeBose	2008	39418
127 7/8	19 4/8 19 3/8	16 5/8	5 5	White County	IL	Thomas J. Drake	2008	39418
*127 7/8	22 6/8 23 3/8	17 7/8	4 4	Hill County	TX	Raymond Joe Hromadka III	2008	39418
127 7/8	20 6/8 21 1/8	16 3/8	5 5	Sheridan County	WY	Joseph E. Watson	2009	39418
127 7/8	22 7/8 23 4/8	17 5/8	4 4	Monmouth County	NJ	Bill Avon	2009	39418
127 7/8	20 1/8 20 0/8	14 5/8	4 4	Leavenworth County	KS	Kenneth L. Clayborn	2009	39418
127 7/8	21 4/8 21 6/8	18 7/8	5 6	Armstrong County	PA	George F. Verner, Jr.	2009	39418
127 7/8	23 6/8 23 1/8	17 0/8	5 7	Kimble County	TX	Dean R. Porter	2009	39418
127 7/8	24 0/8 23 2/8	16 0/8	5 6	De Soto County	MS	Scott Brunson	2009	39418
127 7/8	21 0/8 21 1/8	17 5/8	4 4	Schuylkill County	PA	Jason M. Hubiak	2009	39418
127 7/8	22 6/8 22 0/8	15 7/8	4 4	Delaware County	IN	Scott A. Conley	2009	39418
*127 7/8	22 0/8 21 7/8	14 3/8	5 4	Dunn County	WI	Carl Rabeneck	2009	39418
127 7/8	22 0/8 22 2/8	17 1/8	4 4	Calling Lake	ALB	Jesse Meyer	2009	39418
127 7/8	22 2/8 22 3/8	17 3/8	4 4	Barber County	KS	Lonnie Desmarais	2009	39418
*127 7/8	20 4/8 20 4/8	16 1/8	5 5	Buffalo County	WI	Brady Backes	2009	39418
*127 7/8	20 2/8 21 1/8	15 3/8	5 4	Antelope County	NE	Russ Vetick	2010	39418
127 6/8	22 2/8 22 6/8	19 4/8	5 5	La Salle County	TX	H. Mike Palmer	1993	39691
127 6/8	21 7/8 22 5/8	18 6/8	4 4	Linn County	IA	Matthew David Nezich	2001	39691
127 6/8	23 1/8 23 3/8	17 4/8	7 6	Dubuque County	IA	Jeff Hopkins	2002	39691
127 6/8	23 1/8 23 5/8	16 3/8	6 4	Bradford County	PA	Bob Rockwell	2003	39691
127 6/8	22 5/8 24 2/8	19 4/8	4 4	Elk County	KS	Mike Worrell	2003	39691
127 6/8	21 5/8 21 6/8	15 4/8	4 5	Shelby County	IL	Robert N. Stewart	2003	39691
127 6/8	23 3/8 23 2/8	14 6/8	4 4	Montgomery County	OH	Dean A. Stover	2004	39691
127 6/8	22 4/8 23 3/8	15 0/8	4 4	Lee County	GA	Jeff Fulford	2004	39691
*127 6/8	19 7/8 20 2/8	20 2/8	4 4	Prince Georges County	MD	Jonathan Aultman	2004	39691
*127 6/8	19 6/8 20 1/8	15 0/8	4 4	Wood County	WI	Robert A. Franz	2004	39691
127 6/8	20 5/8 19 6/8	13 4/8	5 5	Macoupin County	IL	Jack Behnke	2004	39691
127 6/8	21 6/8 20 7/8	15 2/8	4 5	Tuscarawas County	OH	Zachary Kaiser	2004	39691
*127 6/8	23 2/8 24 7/8	17 3/8	5 5	Winneshiek County	IA	Tim Everding	2004	39691
127 6/8	23 6/8 21 7/8	18 2/8	4 4	Hartford County	CT	Richard J. Langer	2004	39691
127 6/8	24 6/8 24 0/8	14 4/8	4 6	Woods County	OK	Worley L. Sewell III	2004	39691
*127 6/8	19 7/8 19 3/8	17 2/8	4 4	Calhoun County	IL	Theodore S. Westfall	2005	39691
127 6/8	24 2/8 22 1/8	18 0/8	4 4	Seneca County	OH	Jeff Ottney	2005	39691
127 6/8	22 5/8 22 0/8	16 6/8	5 5	Sullivan County	MO	Ray Haler	2005	39691
127 6/8	21 4/8 21 2/8	16 0/8	5 5	Lyon County	MN	Brent Kesteloot	2005	39691
*127 6/8	20 0/8 20 5/8	17 6/8	4 4	Monmouth County	NJ	Lou Grazioso	2005	39691
127 6/8	24 5/8 25 0/8	16 7/8	4 6	Seneca County	OH	Dave E. Cole	2005	39691
127 6/8	20 4/8 20 0/8	16 6/8	5 5	Rock County	WI	Rhett Precourt	2005	39691
127 6/8	19 1/8 18 0/8	14 2/8	5 5	Young County	TX	James Beadle	2005	39691
127 6/8	19 7/8 20 3/8	18 6/8	5 5	Kleberg County	TX	Rickey Phillips	2005	39691
127 6/8	20 3/8 21 2/8	17 0/8	4 4	Irion County	TX	Craig Horn	2005	39691
*127 6/8	22 2/8 22 6/8	15 7/8	8 5	Sussex County	DE	Israel L. Yoder	2005	39691
127 6/8	19 4/8 19 4/8	14 6/8	5 5	Wood County	WI	Joshua J. Haas	2005	39691
127 6/8	20 7/8 20 0/8	14 5/8	5 6	Tippecanoe County	IN	Owen P. Mason, Jr.	2005	39691
127 6/8	23 4/8 23 2/8	15 4/8	5 4	Waupaca County	WI	Steven Kluth	2005	39691
127 6/8	21 6/8 21 3/8	15 4/8	4 4	Douglas County	WI	Roger Chevrier	2005	39691
127 6/8	21 0/8 19 1/8	17 0/8	5 5	Livingston County	MI	Wesley L. Hatch	2005	39691
127 6/8	22 5/8 23 4/8	15 2/8	5 4	Jackson County	MO	Greg Caudle	2005	39691
*127 6/8	23 5/8 22 5/8	18 0/8	4 5	Athens County	OH	William Monroe	2005	39691
127 6/8	24 5/8 23 3/8	19 6/8	4 4	Anne Arundel County	MD	David Milway Wolf	2005	39691
*127 6/8	22 5/8 22 5/8	15 4/8	4 4	Oneida County	WI	Allan La Porte	2005	39691
127 6/8	22 4/8 21 6/8	18 0/8	4 4	Woodford County	IL	David Fultz	2005	39691
*127 6/8	20 6/8 20 7/8	16 7/8	6 5	Reno County	KS	Danny Gabbard, Sr.	2005	39691
127 6/8	25 4/8 25 4/8	20 6/8	4 4	Dane County	WI	Randy J. Langer	2005	39691
127 6/8	18 5/8 18 7/8	15 0/8	5 5	Refugio County	TX	Gary Hayek	2005	39691
*127 6/8	21 5/8 22 2/8	16 6/8	4 5	Marinette County	WI	Tom Kramer	2005	39691
127 6/8	19 0/8 18 4/8	15 0/8	5 5	Comanche County	KS	Pat Lefemine	2005	39691
*127 6/8	19 5/8 20 0/8	17 0/8	4 4	Erie County	NY	Bob Rosenswie	2006	39691
127 6/8	23 1/8 22 7/8	17 0/8	8 5	Gage County	NE	Keith Levendorf	2006	39691
127 6/8	20 1/8 20 5/8	14 4/8	5 5	Dunn County	WI	Joe Edin	2006	39691
*127 6/8	22 6/8 23 1/8	17 6/8	5 6	Pierce County	WI	Jerry Otto	2006	39691
*127 6/8	22 3/8 20 6/8	15 4/8	5 5	Erie County	NY	Dan Wagner	2006	39691
127 6/8	19 6/8 19 7/8	14 4/8	5 6	Pepin County	WI	Luke Tulip	2006	39691
127 6/8	20 7/8 21 0/8	16 6/8	4 4	Eau Claire County	WI	Steven Kopp	2006	39691
127 6/8	21 5/8 21 5/8	18 0/8	5 5	Buffalo County	WI	Jason Meyers	2006	39691
*127 6/8	21 1/8 20 1/8	19 6/8	5 6	Lake County	IN	Timothy G. Weaver	2006	39691
127 6/8	19 7/8 20 1/8	15 3/8	6 6	Baltimore County	MD	Tracy G. Groves	2006	39691
127 6/8	22 6/8 22 6/8	15 0/8	4 4	Allamakee County	IA	Tom Mueller	2006	39691
127 6/8	19 5/8 22 6/8	19 0/8	4 4	Mercer County	IL	Joe Turk	2006	39691
127 6/8	23 4/8 23 2/8	18 0/8	4 5	McCulloch County	TX	Roger Jonas	2006	39691
*127 6/8	21 3/8 20 7/8	16 2/8	5 5	Lawrence County	AR	Johnathan Robertson	2006	39691
127 6/8	19 5/8 19 3/8	17 5/8	5 6	Jim Hogg County	TX	Norman E. Speer	2006	39691
127 6/8	20 0/8 21 6/8	18 1/8	5 5	Edmonton	ALB	Andre Titley	2006	39691
*127 6/8	20 0/8 18 6/8	13 6/8	5 5	Coahuila	MEX	Jason Applebe	2006	39691
*127 6/8	20 6/8 21 4/8	17 6/8	5 5	Shawano County	WI	Kurt Prien	2007	39691
127 6/8	21 0/8 20 7/8	16 0/8	5 5	Nacogdoches County	TX	Lonnie Stone	2007	39691
127 6/8	20 5/8 20 3/8	15 4/8	4 4	Van Buren County	AR	Jeff McMullin	2007	39691
*127 6/8	21 6/8 20 5/8	16 1/8	4 5	Lucas County	IA	Tyson Irwin	2007	39691

Deer entries below 141 0/8, that appeared in the 6th Edition, are not included here, but are included on the accompanying CD (see page 119), and also in the Club's Records Archives.

WHITETAIL DEER (TYPICAL ANTLERS)

Minimum Score 125   Continued

SCORE	LENGTH OF R MAIN BEAM L	INSIDE SPREAD	NUMBER OF R POINTS L		AREA	STATE/ PROVINCE	HUNTER'S NAME	DATE	RANK
*127 6/8	20 4/8 22 3/8	21 4/8	4	4	Columbia County	WI	Daniel J. Reinke	2007	39691
127 6/8	21 0/8 20 7/8	16 0/8	5	5	Allamakee County	IA	Arlyn Meinders	2007	39691
127 6/8	23 2/8 23 0/8	15 3/8	6	4	Harrison County	OH	Cody Rodriguez	2007	39691
127 6/8	23 0/8 23 0/8	19 6/8	4	4	Monroe County	NY	Rich Greco	2007	39691
127 6/8	21 6/8 23 2/8	17 6/8	4	5	Ross County	OH	Gregory S. Spitzley	2007	39691
*127 6/8	20 4/8 22 3/8	14 2/8	4	4	Fairfax County	VA	Bogos Kaypaghian	2007	39691
127 6/8	19 7/8 20 3/8	13 2/8	5	5	Baltimore County	MD	Ross M. Fornaro	2008	39691
127 6/8	21 5/8 22 3/8	14 4/8	5	6	Redwood County	MN	Paul Gordon Grannes	2008	39691
127 6/8	20 1/8 20 1/8	18 2/8	4	4	Houston County	MN	Kyle J. Schweisthal	2008	39691
*127 6/8	21 2/8 22 6/8	19 4/8	4	4	Gallatin County	IL	Raymond B. Ellis	2008	39691
127 6/8	19 5/8 19 5/8	14 4/8	5	5	Dane County	WI	Dave Dilley	2008	39691
*127 6/8	21 7/8 21 4/8	16 0/8	5	4	Buffalo County	WI	Jon Weisenbeck	2008	39691
127 6/8	21 2/8 21 3/8	16 6/8	5	5	Allegheny County	PA	Zeke Martinkovich	2008	39691
*127 6/8	21 4/8 20 4/8	19 4/8	4	4	Cabarrus County	NC	Jason Kaufman	2008	39691
127 6/8	21 5/8 21 2/8	17 4/8	6	5	Allegheny County	PA	Jeff Danis	2008	39691
127 6/8	22 5/8 21 5/8	18 1/8	6	6	Clark County	KS	Jonah M. Stewart	2008	39691
127 6/8	19 5/8 20 1/8	15 0/8	5	5	Barton County	MO	Dwight S. Wolf	2008	39691
*127 6/8	22 0/8 22 4/8	16 0/8	4	4	Randolph County	AR	Jade Price	2008	39691
127 6/8	21 4/8 21 2/8	17 2/8	4	5	Richland County	ND	Paul Muscha	2009	39691
*127 6/8	21 5/8 21 7/8	14 4/8	5	4	Buncombe County	NC	Rocky Randall Deitz	2009	39691
127 6/8	19 6/8 23 3/8	17 4/8	5	6	Shawano County	WI	Scott Johnson	2009	39691
127 6/8	23 1/8 23 0/8	18 5/8	6	5	Gentry County	MO	John A. Martinelli, Sr.	2009	39691
*127 6/8	21 4/8 22 4/8	16 4/8	5	4	Iowa County	WI	Robert Aschliman	2009	39691
127 6/8	23 7/8 24 0/8	19 3/8	5	4	Saline County	NE	Michael A. Ellingson	2009	39691
127 6/8	24 7/8 22 2/8	21 0/8	4	4	Middlesex County	MA	Christopher Kearney	2009	39691
*127 6/8	22 2/8 21 0/8	17 6/8	4	4	Pushmataha County	OK	Justin D. Dampf	2009	39691
127 6/8	20 4/8 21 2/8	18 2/8	5	4	Grundy County	IL	David Both	2009	39691
127 6/8	20 4/8 19 6/8	16 2/8	5	5	Bingham County	ID	Vance Butler	2009	39691
*127 6/8	22 6/8 24 0/8	19 3/8	5	5	Bolivar County	MS	Walt Stubbs	2009	39691
127 6/8	25 7/8 22 6/8	17 4/8	4	4	Stevens County	WA	Greg McCollough	2009	39691
127 6/8	23 1/8 20 2/8	22 4/8	5	4	Northfield	ONT	Eric Mainville	2009	39691
127 6/8	20 6/8 21 7/8	13 6/8	6	5	Cavalier County	ND	Brenna Logie	2009	39691
127 6/8	21 5/8 21 4/8	14 6/8	5	5	Sawyer County	WI	Barry L. Peterson	2010	39691
127 6/8	22 2/8 22 6/8	17 0/8	5	6	Meigs County	OH	Jeremy Tucker	2010	39691
127 5/8	22 0/8 21 5/8	18 3/8	4	4	Adair County	OK	Timothy Broughton	1996	39989
127 5/8	19 4/8 19 7/8	17 1/8	5	5	Carroll County	IL	D. Scott Wolfe	1999	39989
127 5/8	21 2/8 22 4/8	19 7/8	5	4	Vinton County	OH	Mark Drotar	1999	39989
127 5/8	20 5/8 21 1/8	14 3/8	5	5	Marathon County	WI	Ralph Richmond	2002	39989
127 5/8	22 5/8 22 1/8	20 1/8	5	4	Oakland County	MI	Gary J. Staniec	2002	39989
127 5/8	21 0/8 17 6/8	16 1/8	5	5	Spirit Mtn.	SAS	Cameron R. Hanes	2003	39989
127 5/8	23 4/8 23 1/8	17 1/8	4	4	Hartford County	CT	Tim Hogan	2003	39989
127 5/8	19 6/8 19 2/8	14 3/8	5	5	Marquette County	WI	Ronald D. Bittner	2004	39989
127 5/8	19 5/8 19 7/8	16 5/8	5	5	Madison County	IA	John J. Nigl	2004	39989
*127 5/8	24 4/8 25 4/8	18 5/8	4	4	Worcester County	MA	Brian Ungerer	2004	39989
*127 5/8	22 0/8 21 6/8	18 1/8	5	4	Pulaski County	AR	Ryan M. Fitzgerald	2004	39989
127 5/8	18 1/8 18 7/8	18 2/8	6	6	Randolph County	IN	Kevin Small	2004	39989
127 5/8	21 2/8 21 5/8	17 3/8	5	5	Pushmataha County	OK	Michael D. Harrell, Jr.	2004	39989
127 5/8	21 2/8 22 3/8	16 1/8	4	4	Dakota County	MN	Patrick Hanson	2004	39989
127 5/8	21 4/8 21 4/8	15 3/8	4	4	McHenry County	ND	Jeff Jacobs	2004	39989
127 5/8	20 0/8 20 0/8	17 3/8	5	5	Maverick County	TX	Randy Cauthran	2004	39989
127 5/8	20 2/8 19 0/8	17 2/8	6	4	Kent County	RI	Tom Leavitt	2004	39989
*127 5/8	21 3/8 21 3/8	18 7/8	4	4	Johnson County	WY	Donald Bastian	2005	39989
*127 5/8	20 2/8 20 1/8	14 6/8	4	5	Sullivan County	IN	Brad Romine	2005	39989
127 5/8	22 4/8 22 4/8	15 7/8	4	4	Kent County	MI	Martin Perdok	2005	39989
127 5/8	24 6/8 23 0/8	14 1/8	5	5	Genesee County	NY	Bill Coons	2005	39989
127 5/8	21 3/8 21 6/8	17 5/8	5	4	Jefferson County	IN	Doug Ross	2005	39989
127 5/8	22 2/8 22 2/8	16 1/8	5	4	Sullivan County	IN	Brian McCammon	2005	39989
127 5/8	19 7/8 19 3/8	13 5/8	5	6	Monroe County	IN	Chris Harding	2005	39989
127 5/8	21 7/8 21 6/8	16 0/8	7	6	Norman County	MN	Tim Petry	2005	39989
127 5/8	22 5/8 23 0/8	18 5/8	5	5	Dubuque County	IA	Chad P. Brandel	2005	39989
*127 5/8	25 0/8 25 4/8	18 5/8	4	5	Buffalo County	WI	Todd Ness	2005	39989
127 5/8	21 6/8 22 2/8	16 7/8	4	4	Sauk County	WI	Aaron A. Feigl	2005	39989
*127 5/8	20 4/8 20 5/8	16 3/8	6	5	Schuyler County	IL	Bob Van Munster	2005	39989
127 5/8	22 3/8 19 5/8	16 1/8	5	4	Bartholomew County	IN	Travis Skinner	2005	39989
127 5/8	20 4/8 20 0/8	14 1/8	5	5	St. Louis County	MN	Bruce A. Fehringer	2005	39989
127 5/8	21 6/8 21 7/8	18 5/8	5	5	Ashland County	WI	Chris Beaudry	2005	39989
127 5/8	21 2/8 20 5/8	15 5/8	4	4	St. Charles County	MO	David Boschert	2005	39989
127 5/8	20 4/8 19 4/8	18 1/8	5	6	Maverick County	TX	H. Mike Palmer	2005	39989
127 5/8	21 3/8 22 2/8	16 0/8	4	9	Logan County	KY	Kevin Sears	2006	39989
*127 5/8	21 2/8 20 5/8	18 7/8	4	4	Trempealeau County	WI	Mike Beam	2006	39989
127 5/8	21 5/8 22 0/8	18 1/8	5	5	Prince Georges County	MD	Lawrence Doyle	2006	39989
*127 5/8	19 3/8 19 0/8	16 7/8	5	5	Walsh County	ND	Rodney Troftgruben	2006	39989
127 5/8	21 5/8 21 2/8	17 5/8	4	4	Cook County	IL	Michael Del Real	2006	39989
127 5/8	22 1/8 22 1/8	17 3/8	5	4	Wabasha County	MN	Christopher Stelling	2006	39989
127 5/8	22 5/8 23 0/8	17 7/8	4	5	Chester County	PA	Tom Buterbaugh	2006	39989
*127 5/8	23 6/8 22 1/8	19 0/8	6	5	Winnebago County	IL	Ron Kaderly	2006	39989
127 5/8	21 0/8 21 4/8	16 7/8	6	5	Hardin County	KY	Scott E. Meredith	2006	39989
127 5/8	20 0/8 20 4/8	15 1/8	5	6	Douglas County	WI	Keith Hammerbeck	2006	39989
127 5/8	21 3/8 22 4/8	16 5/8	5	5	Weld County	CO	Frank Piacentino	2006	39989
127 5/8	21 2/8 22 3/8	17 7/8	5	5	Clayton County	IA	Jim Vosberg	2006	39989
127 5/8	22 1/8 22 0/8	16 5/8	5	5	Sterling County	TX	Al Turner	2006	39989
127 5/8	21 0/8 21 0/8	19 3/8	4	4	Grand Forks County	ND	Darin Hart	2006	39989
*127 5/8	21 0/8 21 2/8	14 7/8	6	6	Rusk County	WI	Aaron Zahorski	2007	39989
127 5/8	22 3/8 22 0/8	14 4/8	5	5	Highland County	OH	Shawn Clark	2007	39989
*127 5/8	19 2/8 18 6/8	13 7/8	5	5	Howard County	MO	J. R. Royston	2007	39989
*127 5/8	22 7/8 22 3/8	17 3/8	5	5	Cortland County	NY	David A. Block	2007	39989
*127 5/8	22 0/8 21 0/8	15 5/8	5	5	Chester County	PA	Jonathan D. Graham	2007	39989
127 5/8	20 5/8 20 6/8	16 7/8	5	5	McKenzie County	ND	Milan Liesener	2007	39989
*127 5/8	21 2/8 20 4/8	15 5/8	4	4	Clinton County	MO	Dustin Mumm	2007	39989
127 5/8	22 2/8 24 0/8	17 1/8	5	6	Ottawa County	MI	Bob Vogteveen	2007	39989
*127 5/8	22 5/8 24 0/8	15 3/8	5	5	Middlesex County	MA	Dan O'Brien	2007	39989
*127 5/8	22 4/8 22 4/8	17 5/8	4	5	Lincoln County	WV	Steve Carper	2007	39989
*127 5/8	19 0/8 16 4/8	15 7/8	5	6	Cavalier County	ND	Michelle Logie	2007	39989
127 5/8	23 2/8 23 6/8	18 5/8	5	4	Hempstead County	AR	Derik Bain	2007	39989
127 5/8	22 5/8 23 3/8	18 5/8	4	5	Mountrail County	ND	James Domaskin	2007	39989

610

WHITETAIL DEER (TYPICAL ANTLERS)

Minimum Score 125   Continued

SCORE	LENGTH OF R MAIN BEAM L	INSIDE SPREAD	NUMBER OF R POINTS L		AREA	STATE/ PROVINCE	HUNTER'S NAME	DATE	RANK
*127 5/8	20 4/8 20 7/8	16 5/8	4	4	Marshall County	IL	Bob Dowdy	2007	39989
*127 5/8	21 0/8 20 6/8	18 3/8	5	5	Ebenezer	SAS	Cory Fransishyn	2008	39989
*127 5/8	22 3/8 22 7/8	17 5/8	4	5	Sherburne County	MN	Glen R. Senske	2008	39989
127 5/8	22 2/8 22 0/8	14 2/8	6	5	Randall County	TX	Brandon Ray	2008	39989
127 5/8	21 2/8 22 0/8	15 5/8	5	5	Buffalo County	WI	Marc N. Shaft	2008	39989
127 5/8	22 1/8 23 3/8	17 0/8	5	4	Jefferson County	WI	Kenneth Trinko	2008	39989
*127 5/8	24 0/8 24 4/8	16 7/8	4	4	Erie County	OH	Roger Brooks	2008	39989
*127 5/8	18 2/8 18 5/8	13 7/8	5	5	Cherokee County	KS	Mickey P. Zahn	2009	39989
*127 5/8	21 6/8 21 1/8	14 6/8	5	6	Carroll County	IA	Dan Anthcfer	2009	39989
127 5/8	21 5/8 21 2/8	17 1/8	6	5	Brown County	IL	Eric Yancey	2009	39989
*127 5/8	21 0/8 20 5/8	14 0/8	5	6	Owen County	IN	Andrew C. May	2009	39989
127 5/8	20 7/8 19 5/8	14 7/8	5	5	Coffey County	KS	Joseph D. Helget	2009	39989
127 5/8	23 2/8 23 0/8	16 3/8	4	4	Cumberland County	ME	Paul Willette	2009	39989
127 5/8	22 2/8 22 0/8	13 0/8	6	7	La Salle County	TX	Spencer Kunkel	2009	39989
127 5/8	19 0/8 20 2/8	19 3/8	5	5	Montgomery County	AR	Eugene Smith, Jr.	2009	39989
127 4/8	21 0/8 21 6/8	17 4/8	5	5	Washtenaw County	MI	Alan F. Schultz	2001	40239
127 4/8	22 0/8 21 0/8	16 3/8	6	7	Des Moines County	IA	Chad W. Clark	2002	40239
127 4/8	22 4/8 22 1/8	17 6/8	6	5	Brown County	OH	David Eskew	2003	40239
*127 4/8	20 3/8 20 6/8	18 4/8	5	5	Nodaway County	MO	Todd Gray	2003	40239
127 4/8	25 4/8 23 5/8	21 0/8	4	4	Delaware County	IA	Kelly Salow	2003	40239
127 4/8	20 1/8 20 7/8	17 0/8	5	6	Edmonson County	KY	Craig E. Browning	2004	40239
*127 4/8	22 4/8 22 6/8	17 5/8	5	6	Cherokee County	OK	Micco Charboneau	2004	40239
127 4/8	20 7/8 19 5/8	18 0/8	5	5	Meade County	SD	Robert L. Rohrbach	2004	40239
127 4/8	21 0/8 21 7/8	18 4/8	4	5	Clayton County	IA	Craig A. Bries	2004	40239
127 4/8	21 7/8 21 1/8	18 6/8	5	5	Kinney County	TX	Chuck Booth	2004	40239
127 4/8	20 1/8 20 6/8	16 2/8	5	5	Calhoun County	MI	Fermin Martinez	2004	40239
127 4/8	24 5/8 24 3/8	15 6/8	4	4	Northampton County	PA	Richard A. Hess	2004	40239
127 4/8	19 4/8 20 4/8	15 6/8	4	4	Camden County	MO	Jeff Wilson, Jr.	2004	40239
127 4/8	21 0/8 21 7/8	17 4/8	5	5	Polk County	WI	A. Roger Lehman	2004	40239
127 4/8	23 1/8 20 7/8	17 2/8	4	5	Wilson County	KS	Jeffrey J. Jolley	2004	40239
127 4/8	22 0/8 22 1/8	18 0/8	5	5	Buffalo County	WI	William R. Hedl	2004	40239
*127 4/8	22 2/8 22 0/8	15 4/8	5	4	Price County	WI	Craig Smith	2004	40239
127 4/8	21 7/8 21 4/8	17 4/8	8	5	Sauk County	WI	Ronald L. Kerska	2004	40239
127 4/8	20 2/8 21 2/8	17 2/8	5	5	Buffalo County	WI	Rodney W. Folz	2004	40239
127 4/8	22 4/8 22 0/8	14 6/8	4	5	Forest County	WI	Dean G. Van Epern	2004	40239
127 4/8	22 3/8 23 1/8	18 6/8	4	4	Ontario County	NY	Bill Lipnickey	2004	40239
127 4/8	20 1/8 20 1/8	14 6/8	5	5	Columbia County	WI	Scott N. Bartnick	2004	40239
127 4/8	19 6/8 20 4/8	15 0/8	5	5	Olmsted County	MN	Todd Pruismann	2004	40239
127 4/8	22 0/8 20 7/8	14 5/8	6	4	Appanoose County	IA	Rick Petersen	2004	40239
*127 4/8	21 1/8 21 0/8	16 0/8	4	4	Winnebago County	IL	Jeffrey S. Olsen	2004	40239
*127 4/8	23 1/8 22 4/8	15 6/8	4	4	Hemphill County	TX	Dean M. Peterson, Jr.	2004	40239
127 4/8	23 1/8 23 2/8	17 2/8	5	4	Meade County	KS	Bryan White	2004	40239
127 4/8	22 5/8 22 3/8	18 6/8	5	4	Montgomery County	IA	William Cmiel	2004	40239
127 4/8	16 6/8 18 2/8	15 0/8	5	5	Priddis	ALB	Lorne D. Rinkel	2004	40239
127 4/8	20 5/8 20 6/8	19 2/8	4	4	Fairfield County	CT	David A. Sanford	2004	40239
*127 4/8	22 2/8 22 1/8	17 6/8	5	5	La Salle County	TX	Ronnie Satterfield	2005	40239
127 4/8	21 6/8 22 3/8	15 4/8	4	4	Orange County	NC	Chad Meeks	2005	40239
127 4/8	20 4/8 20 6/8	15 6/8	5	5	Pontotoc County	OK	Scott Lynn Ward	2005	40239
127 4/8	21 0/8 20 5/8	17 2/8	5	5	Buffalo County	WI	Jeff Walcott	2005	40239
*127 4/8	23 1/8 22 4/8	18 6/8	5	5	Tillsonburg	ONT	Charlie Chilcott	2005	40239
*127 4/8	21 5/8 20 1/8	18 4/8	5	4	Litchfield County	CT	Scott W. Taylor	2005	40239
127 4/8	21 2/8 20 0/8	16 2/8	5	5	Jefferson County	WI	Kole L. Latsch	2005	40239
*127 4/8	23 2/8 22 5/8	16 0/8	7	6	Delaware County	PA	Michael Natale	2005	40239
127 4/8	23 2/8 21 7/8	17 2/8	5	5	Ashtabula County	OH	Doug A. Hummer	2005	40239
127 4/8	19 3/8 20 6/8	14 4/8	5	5	Sutton County	TX	W. C. Polster	2005	40239
127 4/8	22 1/8 22 1/8	14 5/8	6	4	Clarion County	PA	Justin Bell	2005	40239
127 4/8	21 3/8 21 6/8	15 2/8	5	5	Taylor County	IA	Jeff Justin	2005	40239
127 4/8	21 0/8 21 0/8	18 2/8	4	4	Schuyler County	IL	Darwin Sanno	2005	40239
127 4/8	22 5/8 22 1/8	17 6/8	5	5	Langlade County	WI	Richard L. Strebe	2005	40239
127 4/8	24 4/8 23 7/8	17 5/8	5	4	Woodford County	IL	Jim Curtis	2005	40239
127 4/8	22 3/8 23 1/8	16 2/8	5	5	Fayette County	WV	Paul Payne	2005	40239
127 4/8	22 3/8 23 5/8	16 2/8	4	4	Lake County	IL	William Snelgrove	2005	40239
127 4/8	20 6/8 20 6/8	16 2/8	4	4	Ferry County	WA	Brett Elizabeth Berry	2005	40239
*127 4/8	19 4/8 19 0/8	16 6/8	5	6	Madison County	MT	Robert Hind III	2006	40239
127 4/8	20 4/8 20 5/8	15 0/8	4	4	Carberry	MAN	Cris G. Kringel	2006	40239
*127 4/8	20 7/8 20 0/8	17 2/8	4	4	Charles Mix County	SD	Gary D. DeJong	2006	40239
127 4/8	21 1/8 21 0/8	14 1/8	5	5	Houston County	MN	Brent Parent	2006	40239
127 4/8	21 3/8 18 6/8	17 3/8	5	5	Kosciusko County	IN	Brett Anthony	2006	40239
*127 4/8	23 5/8 22 5/8	15 0/8	4	4	Barry County	MI	Al G. Perales	2006	40239
*127 4/8	21 1/8 21 5/8	18 1/8	6	5	Richland County	IL	Ed Beatty	2006	40239
127 4/8	23 1/8 23 7/8	17 2/8	4	5	Marion County	IN	William D. Golden, Jr.	2006	40239
127 4/8	20 4/8 20 3/8	17 2/8	5	5	Door County	WI	Matthew D. Stender	2006	40239
127 4/8	22 4/8 21 7/8	17 0/8	4	4	Hardin County	KY	Harold Eddie Whobrey	2006	40239
127 4/8	21 4/8 22 3/8	19 7/8	5	4	Allegheny County	PA	Gary Rodriguez	2006	40239
127 4/8	21 7/8 20 7/8	15 2/8	5	5	Monroe County	NY	Mark Thomas	2006	40239
*127 4/8	20 4/8 20 2/8	15 6/8	5	5	Tama County	IA	Rick Halverson	2006	40239
*127 4/8	25 1/8 24 3/8	19 4/8	4	4	Jefferson County	WI	Matthew Armstrong	2006	40239
127 4/8	22 6/8 23 0/8	20 0/8	4	4	Baltimore County	MD	Earle F. Yearsley	2006	40239
*127 4/8	22 4/8 22 6/8	15 2/8	4	4	Lumpkin County	GA	Jamie Ricketts	2007	40239
127 4/8	19 1/8 19 0/8	14 0/8	5	5	Bertie County	NC	Kelli W. Corbin	2007	40239
127 4/8	21 2/8 19 6/8	15 3/8	6	6	Madison County	AR	Heath Jones	2007	40239
127 4/8	25 0/8 25 2/8	20 1/8	6	5	Roseau County	MN	Mitch Haaby	2007	40239
127 4/8	22 4/8 22 6/8	14 6/8	6	5	Genesee County	NY	Kirk Newcomb	2007	40239
127 4/8	21 6/8 20 6/8	16 4/8	5	5	Guthrie County	IA	Frank Moraco	2007	40239
127 4/8	22 0/8 21 2/8	16 1/8	5	5	Van Wert County	OH	Harry Van Dalsen, Jr.	2007	40239
127 4/8	20 5/8 21 0/8	16 0/8	5	5	Licking County	OH	Mark Henshaw	2007	40239
*127 4/8	21 0/8 21 5/8	16 6/8	5	4	Crawford County	PA	Luke J. Hummer	2007	40239
*127 4/8	21 4/8 22 2/8	20 2/8	5	5	Buffalo County	WI	Steven E. Brueshaber	2007	40239
127 4/8	21 1/8 21 0/8	16 2/8	5	5	Haskell County	OK	Tim Burnett	2007	40239
*127 4/8	22 6/8 22 3/8	17 2/8	5	5	Calumet County	WI	Jesse Buechel	2007	40239
*127 4/8	21 4/8 21 4/8	16 6/8	5	5	Parke County	IN	Shawn Donnenhoffer	2007	40239
127 4/8	20 4/8 21 2/8	14 4/8	4	4	Peoria County	IL	Josh D. Youngren	2007	40239
127 4/8	23 6/8 22 2/8	16 0/8	4	5	Brown County	IL	Mike T. Willand	2007	40239
127 4/8	22 1/8 21 1/8	17 5/8	5	5	Baltimore County	MD	Stephen M. Talbott	2007	40239
127 4/8	22 5/8 22 1/8	16 0/8	4	4	San Saba County	TX	Kelby McCall	2007	40239

Deer entries below 141 0/8, that appeared in the 6th Edition, are not included here, but are included on the accompanying CD (see page 119), and also in the Club's Records Archives.

WHITETAIL DEER (TYPICAL ANTLERS)

Minimum Score 125 — Continued

SCORE	LENGTH OF R MAIN BEAM L	INSIDE SPREAD	NUMBER OF R POINTS L	AREA	STATE/PROVINCE	HUNTER'S NAME	DATE	RANK
127 4/8	21 7/8 23 1/8	16 2/8	5 5	Tippecanoe County	IN	Robert L. Whitus	2008	40239
*127 4/8	21 4/8 20 3/8	17 0/8	4 5	Dane County	WI	Jeff Lange	2008	40239
127 4/8	20 5/8 20 5/8	18 0/8	4 4	Stanton County	NE	Dave D. Beaudette	2008	40239
*127 4/8	21 0/8 19 7/8	14 4/8	4 4	Stephenson County	IL	Dana Wybourn	2008	40239
*127 4/8	20 1/8 19 7/8	17 2/8	5 6	Allen County	IN	Greg Parsenow	2008	40239
127 4/8	23 5/8 23 7/8	15 6/8	4 6	Parke County	IN	Joshua F. Carlson	2008	40239
127 4/8	23 4/8 22 7/8	19 0/8	4 4	McMullen County	TX	Steven M. Shedd	2008	40239
127 4/8	19 7/8 18 4/8	17 2/8	5 5	Shannon County	MO	Nicholas D. Galloup	2008	40239
127 4/8	22 4/8 21 4/8	16 1/8	6 5	Mayes County	OK	Casey Roberts	2008	40239
*127 4/8	23 0/8 22 0/8	18 4/8	5 5	La Grange County	IN	Steven Parker	2008	40239
*127 4/8	23 5/8 23 3/8	17 5/8	7 6	Armstrong County	PA	Neal Macurdy	2008	40239
127 4/8	20 0/8 19 2/8	17 4/8	4 4	Kalamazoo County	MI	Bob D. Graves	2008	40239
127 4/8	20 6/8 20 6/8	18 0/8	4 5	Allamakee County	IA	Mike Haut	2008	40239
*127 4/8	21 5/8 21 2/8	15 4/8	4 5	Rush County	IN	Ryan B. Miller	2008	40239
127 4/8	23 1/8 23 6/8	18 4/8	4 4	Jefferson County	MO	Stephen Balee	2008	40239
127 4/8	21 6/8 21 7/8	19 5/8	6 5	Marquette County	WI	Jay A. Severson	2008	40239
127 4/8	19 4/8 19 6/8	15 6/8	6 5	Caddo County	OK	Rocky Wilson	2009	40239
127 4/8	23 1/8 21 4/8	16 7/8	5 5	Shiawassee County	MI	Bob Elston	2009	40239
*127 4/8	24 4/8 26 0/8	17 4/8	5 6	Licking County	OH	Corey T. Derugen	2009	40239
*127 4/8	20 6/8 21 4/8	20 1/8	6 6	Custer County	NE	Steve Schnittker	2009	40239
127 4/8	19 3/8 19 3/8	18 2/8	5 5	Valley County	MT	Coltin Hurst	2009	40239
127 4/8	23 1/8 24 2/8	16 2/8	4 4	Hall County	GA	Jeb Bates	2009	40239
127 4/8	21 3/8 20 6/8	17 0/8	5 5	Polk County	WI	Brandon Kahl	2009	40239
127 4/8	20 5/8 20 0/8	17 4/8	5 5	Polk County	WI	David E. Johnson	2009	40239
*127 4/8	21 5/8 21 0/8	16 3/8	4 5	Adams County	IL	Chris Payne	2009	40239
127 4/8	21 3/8 21 2/8	20 4/8	6 4	Adams County	MS	Trey Finnegan	2009	40239
*127 4/8	21 0/8 21 2/8	16 0/8	5 5	Lewis County	MO	Forrest L. Mathias	2009	40239
*127 4/8	19 3/8 20 0/8	14 0/8	5 5	Kanawha County	WV	Nathanael Messinger	2009	40239
127 4/8	21 3/8 20 0/8	16 6/8	5 5	Dunn County	ND	James W. Casto, Jr.	2009	40239
127 4/8	22 3/8 22 4/8	15 2/8	5 5	Reno County	KS	Greg Sims	2009	40239
127 4/8	23 4/8 21 6/8	17 2/8	5 6	Crook County	WY	Faith Harvey	2010	40239
127 4/8	24 1/8 24 5/8	17 7/8	8 4	Crawford County	PA	William W. Sherrod	2010	40239
127 3/8	20 6/8 21 1/8	17 7/8	6 5	Douglas County	WI	Tom Vengrin	1995	40539
127 3/8	21 4/8 21 3/8	13 3/8	4 4	White County	IN	Glenn E. Miller	1998	40539
127 3/8	20 6/8 20 7/8	16 7/8	4 4	Brown County	SD	Robert Baker	1998	40539
127 3/8	21 3/8 21 5/8	16 1/8	4 4	Muhlenberg County	KY	Lewis R. Compton	1998	40539
127 3/8	22 1/8 20 6/8	17 1/8	5 5	Bureau County	IL	Steve Andrews	2000	40539
127 3/8	21 1/8 21 0/8	15 7/8	4 4	Ohio County	IN	John Dulworth	2002	40539
127 3/8	19 3/8 19 2/8	15 7/8	5 5	Switzerland County	IN	Alexander Kulik	2003	40539
127 3/8	21 6/8 21 1/8	17 1/8	5 5	Cobb County	GA	David Gilreath	2003	40539
127 3/8	23 7/8 23 2/8	14 5/8	4 5	Early County	GA	Charles Holmes	2003	40539
127 3/8	20 6/8 21 0/8	17 7/8	4 4	Webster County	IA	Dave Propst	2003	40539
127 3/8	20 5/8 22 0/8	18 5/8	5 5	Barber County	KS	Fred Johnston III	2003	40539
127 3/8	20 3/8 21 5/8	17 6/8	4 6	Jasper County	IL	Larry Hall	2003	40539
127 3/8	21 3/8 20 7/8	17 1/8	5 6	Green Lake County	WI	Brian L. Schulz	2003	40539
127 3/8	22 4/8 21 3/8	16 3/8	6 5	St. Louis County	MN	John Abdo	2004	40539
*127 3/8	20 2/8 19 2/8	14 4/8	6 6	Hunterdon County	NJ	Gerry L. DuMont	2004	40539
127 3/8	22 6/8 21 3/8	17 6/8	5 5	Coryell County	TX	Joshua Sears	2004	40539
127 3/8	18 2/8 19 2/8	15 1/8	5 5	Fulton County	IL	Chuck Thome	2004	40539
*127 3/8	21 4/8 22 4/8	17 5/8	4 5	Washington County	OH	Mark Keith Hall	2004	40539
127 3/8	22 4/8 23 0/8	16 0/8	7 5	Clayton County	IA	Barney Bennett	2004	40539
127 3/8	21 4/8 21 0/8	17 1/8	5 5	Erie County	PA	Jerome M. Laughlin	2004	40539
127 3/8	22 2/8 23 7/8	15 7/8	4 5	Massac County	IL	Ronald L. Wells	2004	40539
*127 3/8	21 4/8 21 1/8	15 1/8	4 4	Wayne County	IA	Randy Scheel	2004	40539
*127 3/8	20 5/8 20 4/8	16 1/8	5 5	Delaware County	OH	Tod Boger	2004	40539
*127 3/8	20 7/8 22 0/8	17 5/8	4 4	Monmouth County	NJ	Christopher Zduniak	2005	40539
127 3/8	23 4/8 24 3/8	18 1/8	4 4	Monroe County	WI	Scott Stintzi	2005	40539
127 3/8	22 4/8 23 4/8	15 7/8	4 4	Hunterdon County	NJ	Gerry L. Dumont	2005	40539
*127 3/8	21 4/8 22 3/8	15 7/8	4 4	Dane County	WI	Ken Arndt	2005	40539
127 3/8	22 5/8 21 4/8	17 1/8	4 4	Green County	WI	Garret J. Voegeli	2005	40539
127 3/8	22 6/8 22 4/8	19 3/8	5 5	Vernon County	WI	Ardie Schock	2005	40539
*127 3/8	20 0/8 20 6/8	15 5/8	5 5	Vigo County	IN	Greg Spurgeon	2005	40539
127 3/8	22 1/8 21 0/8	18 5/8	4 4	Passaic County	NJ	Robert Barone	2005	40539
127 3/8	21 2/8 23 6/8	19 1/8	5 4	Sauk County	WI	Randy Schmid	2005	40539
127 3/8	21 6/8 21 4/8	16 3/8	5 5	Chemung County	NY	David M. Donnelly	2005	40539
127 3/8	25 0/8 24 7/8	15 3/8	5 4	Southampton County	VA	Matt B. Glover	2005	40539
*127 3/8	22 6/8 22 2/8	13 5/8	4 4	Dane County	WI	Duane R. Schultz	2005	40539
127 3/8	22 4/8 21 2/8	16 7/8	5 4	Schuyler County	IL	John Andrews	2005	40539
127 3/8	21 0/8 21 0/8	18 7/8	4 4	Frio County	TX	Joe Keathley	2005	40539
*127 3/8	23 0/8 22 2/8	18 3/8	5 5	Delaware County	PA	Joseph D. Maddock	2005	40539
127 3/8	21 3/8 19 5/8	15 2/8	5 7	Marquette County	WI	Dana Kobs	2005	40539
127 3/8	23 4/8 21 5/8	19 5/8	4 4	Livingston County	MI	William Petzold	2006	40539
127 3/8	19 7/8 19 7/8	13 1/8	6 5	Burnett County	WI	Kent Bassett	2006	40539
127 3/8	21 3/8 21 4/8	16 7/8	4 4	Douglas County	WI	James R. Latvala	2006	40539
127 3/8	22 0/8 22 2/8	16 1/8	4 4	Boone County	IN	Steven Griffith	2006	40539
*127 3/8	22 6/8 23 0/8	15 6/8	6 5	Amelia County	VA	Dustin S. Gillespie	2006	40539
127 3/8	23 0/8 24 2/8	18 1/8	4 6	St. Clair County	IL	Dale McCain, Jr.	2006	40539
*127 3/8	25 0/8 26 3/8	16 6/8	4 3	St-Rosaire	QUE	Normand Nadeau	2006	40539
127 3/8	22 7/8 23 0/8	16 1/8	5 6	Putnam County	MO	Scott Buehrle	2006	40539
*127 3/8	21 4/8 21 3/8	18 1/8	4 4	Ozark County	MO	Dennis Coleman	2006	40539
127 3/8	22 4/8 23 2/8	17 3/8	4 4	Fayette County	IL	Steve Longhi	2006	40539
*127 3/8	22 5/8 21 6/8	17 7/8	4 4	Clark County	IN	Willy Ray Weatherford	2006	40539
127 3/8	20 4/8 20 2/8	14 3/8	5 5	Calhoun County	IL	Joshua Newton	2006	40539
127 3/8	24 4/8 24 4/8	22 5/8	4 4	Chenango County	NY	Joseph E. Storzinger	2006	40539
127 3/8	22 6/8 22 6/8	18 1/8	4 4	Carroll County	OH	Kevin Whitmore	2006	40539
127 3/8	21 5/8 21 5/8	16 7/8	4 5	Callahan County	TX	Bryan Archibald	2006	40539
127 3/8	22 3/8 23 0/8	17 5/8	5 5	Calumet County	WI	Jon Walber	2006	40539
127 3/8	24 4/8 21 7/8	17 1/8	4 4	Webster Parish	LA	Mike Pepper	2006	40539
*127 3/8	18 5/8 19 0/8	13 5/8	5 5	Powell County	MT	Paul R. Tremblay	2007	40539
127 3/8	22 5/8 23 6/8	18 5/8	6 5	Osage County	OK	Matt Roberts	2007	40539
*127 3/8	22 6/8 22 6/8	16 1/8	5 5	Monmouth County	NJ	Rick Going	2007	40539
127 3/8	20 3/8 19 0/8	15 3/8	5 5	Adams County	WI	Chris Gorenc	2007	40539
*127 3/8	19 0/8 19 0/8	16 5/8	4 4	Wabasha County	MN	Jody Wilson	2007	40539
*127 3/8	21 6/8 22 4/8	14 6/8	6 5	Poweshiek County	IA	Carrie Robison	2007	40539
127 3/8	24 2/8 24 4/8	17 5/8	4 5	Highland County	OH	Marty Lanier	2007	40539

WHITETAIL DEER (TYPICAL ANTLERS)

Minimum Score 125 — Continued

SCORE	LENGTH OF R MAIN BEAM L	INSIDE SPREAD	NUMBER OF R POINTS L	AREA	STATE/ PROVINCE	HUNTER'S NAME	DATE	RANK
*127 3/8	21 7/8 22 0/8	21 2/8	5 5	Logan County	OH	Scott Pflaumer	2007	40539
127 3/8	20 7/8 21 6/8	16 3/8	4 4	Outagamie County	WI	Randy Lemke	2007	40539
*127 3/8	18 4/8 18 3/8	16 3/8	5 5	Gonzales County	TX	Bert Reeves	2007	40539
127 3/8	18 6/8 19 7/8	14 7/8	5 5	McLean County	KY	Aaron James Henderson	2008	40539
*127 3/8	20 0/8 20 4/8	13 7/8	4 4	Becker County	MN	Ryan Nelson	2008	40539
127 3/8	20 4/8 20 1/8	19 1/8	4 4	Venango County	PA	Hunter Cory Ferris	2008	40539
127 3/8	19 7/8 20 0/8	16 6/8	6 6	Yankton County	SD	Reggie Hochstein	2008	40539
127 3/8	18 3/8 18 4/8	14 5/8	5 5	Franklin County	KS	Dayton Chapman	2008	40539
127 3/8	21 0/8 20 7/8	14 3/8	5 5	Fillmore County	MN	Tim Daul	2008	40539
127 3/8	21 3/8 21 0/8	16 5/8	5 5	Polk County	WI	David Johnson	2008	40539
*127 3/8	23 1/8 26 0/8	18 0/8	4 6	Cooper County	MO	Travis Layne	2008	40539
*127 3/8	19 6/8 19 7/8	14 1/8	5 6	Riley County	KS	Mark W. Goodrich	2008	40539
127 3/8	19 7/8 20 3/8	13 1/8	5 5	Benton County	AR	Travis Scantling	2008	40539
127 3/8	22 4/8 22 3/8	18 1/8	4 4	Plymouth County	MA	Hilston Ireland	2008	40539
127 3/8	20 0/8 20 7/8	17 5/8	5 6	Jefferson County	WI	Mike Brown	2008	40539
*127 3/8	22 0/8 21 6/8	17 3/8	4 4	Shelby County	KY	Lawrence E. Thomas, Jr.	2009	40539
*127 3/8	22 0/8 21 1/8	17 0/8	6 5	Alleghany County	NC	Micheal K. Crouch	2009	40539
127 3/8	25 0/8 24 7/8	19 0/8	4 6	Ellis County	OK	Tom Quinton	2009	40539
127 3/8	21 5/8 23 5/8	16 3/8	5 5	Jefferson County	PA	Jason J. Jacobson	2009	40539
127 3/8	22 0/8 22 4/8	14 7/8	4 4	Madison County	NY	William J. Snizek	2009	40539
*127 3/8	21 3/8 20 0/8	14 1/8	6 6	St. Joseph County	IN	Michael L. Ritter, Jr.	2009	40539
127 3/8	21 1/8 20 2/8	15 1/8	4 4	Andrew County	MO	Ron Browning	2009	40539
127 3/8	21 0/8 20 4/8	18 3/8	5 5	Washburn County	WI	Chuck Smith	2009	40539
*127 3/8	18 6/8 18 6/8	15 0/8	5 6	Cumberland County	PA	Michael P. Sanderson	2009	40539
*127 3/8	21 1/8 20 4/8	13 1/8	4 5	Montgomery County	PA	Matthew Musto	2009	40539
*127 3/8	22 2/8 23 4/8	15 5/8	5 5	Polk County	WI	Ted Carlson	2009	40539
127 3/8	21 4/8 20 3/8	15 7/8	4 4	E. Carroll Parish	LA	Jim Maddox	2009	40539
127 2/8	20 5/8 22 3/8	18 6/8	4 4	Grundy County	IL	Michael W. Marchio	1987	40797
127 2/8	21 6/8 22 1/8	15 6/8	4 4	St. Louis County	MN	Jeff Pederson	2001	40797
127 2/8	23 7/8 23 5/8	15 0/8	5 5	Litchfield County	CT	Richard Daris	2004	40797
127 2/8	19 5/8 21 0/8	17 2/8	7 7	Pembina County	ND	James Sonderland	2004	40797
*127 2/8	19 2/8 19 7/8	16 4/8	5 5	Pittsburg County	OK	Tim Suchy	2004	40797
127 2/8	20 0/8 19 0/8	18 4/8	4 4	Washington County	WI	Michael Veres	2004	40797
*127 2/8	20 2/8 19 4/8	15 5/8	6 5	Bedford County	PA	Trevor Young	2004	40797
127 2/8	24 5/8 24 7/8	18 2/8	4 4	Middlesex County	MA	Joe McGill	2004	40797
*127 2/8	21 6/8 20 7/8	18 2/8	5 5	Crawford County	PA	Scott J. Hoover	2004	40797
127 2/8	20 4/8 21 0/8	17 0/8	5 5	Adams County	PA	John Gumm	2004	40797
127 2/8	20 2/8 19 7/8	17 4/8	5 4	Vernon County	WI	Jason Grabbert	2004	40797
127 2/8	22 6/8 22 1/8	17 0/8	5 4	La Crosse County	WI	Timothy Kendall	2004	40797
127 2/8	21 6/8 22 2/8	16 0/8	5 5	Lancaster County	NE	Scott Mares	2004	40797
127 2/8	21 4/8 21 7/8	18 5/8	4 5	Dodge County	NE	Dennis Duckert	2004	40797
*127 2/8	20 0/8 21 0/8	16 0/8	5 5	Lawrence County	IN	Randall Roller	2004	40797
127 2/8	19 2/8 19 5/8	14 6/8	5 5	Madison County	ID	Alan Hall	2004	40797
*127 2/8	19 7/8 19 4/8	14 0/8	5 5	Vilas County	WI	Ronald F. Lax	2004	40797
127 2/8	21 3/8 20 7/8	16 2/8	4 4	Dunn County	WI	Luke Edin	2005	40797
127 2/8	23 1/8 23 7/8	17 0/8	4 5	Pierce County	WI	Rick A. Wilbur	2005	40797
127 2/8	22 3/8 21 5/8	15 2/8	4 4	Buffalo County	WI	Robert Harris	2005	40797
127 2/8	21 3/8 21 4/8	17 1/8	4 5	Decatur County	IA	Brad Blanchard	2005	40797
127 2/8	22 6/8 21 4/8	16 7/8	6 5	Will County	IL	Mark Shandro	2005	40797
*127 2/8	23 4/8 22 7/8	16 1/8	5 5	Schuyler County	IL	John Seabolt	2005	40797
127 2/8	20 2/8 20 0/8	16 4/8	5 5	Peoria County	IL	Ryan Lewis	2005	40797
127 2/8	22 2/8 21 2/8	19 6/8	4 4	Outagamie County	WI	Dennis Coenen, Jr.	2005	40797
127 2/8	22 3/8 22 1/8	18 0/8	4 5	Henderson County	IL	Dave Alberts	2005	40797
127 2/8	22 7/8 22 4/8	15 6/8	4 4	Hancock County	IL	David C. Casto	2005	40797
127 2/8	21 3/8 20 7/8	14 2/8	5 5	Spokane County	WA	Brandon Enevold	2005	40797
*127 2/8	22 6/8 23 2/8	17 7/8	5 5	Hunterdon County	NJ	Craig McLaughlin	2006	40797
127 2/8	20 5/8 21 5/8	17 4/8	4 5	Ionia County	MI	Jim W. Groesser	2006	40797
127 2/8	20 1/8 19 0/8	16 6/8	4 4	Brown County	SD	Carl Hanson	2006	40797
*127 2/8	24 4/8 25 4/8	18 7/8	6 6	Henry County	IA	Josh Mosman	2006	40797
127 2/8	20 5/8 20 5/8	17 2/8	4 4	Jefferson County	AR	Brandon Couch	2006	40797
127 2/8	25 0/8 23 3/8	17 6/8	4 4	Rockingham County	NC	Scooter Pegg	2006	40797
127 2/8	20 5/8 22 4/8	17 4/8	7 4	Marquette County	WI	Newell Easley	2006	40797
127 2/8	16 1/8 24 2/8	18 1/8	4 6	Dubuque County	IA	Michael J. Seipp	2006	40797
127 2/8	21 5/8 22 4/8	18 4/8	4 4	Bucks County	PA	John T. Fachet	2006	40797
*127 2/8	21 6/8 21 7/8	15 2/8	5 4	Adams County	IL	Kyle C. Miller	2006	40797
*127 2/8	21 5/8 22 0/8	17 6/8	4 4	Kit Carson County	CO	Joe Prinzi	2006	40797
*127 2/8	20 7/8 21 2/8	18 6/8	5 5	Monmouth County	NJ	George Duncan	2006	40797
*127 2/8	22 0/8 22 5/8	17 4/8	4 4	Morris County	NJ	Dennis George	2007	40797
*127 2/8	21 4/8 21 3/8	19 0/8	4 5	Crook County	WY	Mike Schmid	2007	40797
127 2/8	21 2/8 22 7/8	19 4/8	4 5	Lake County	IL	William Snelgrove	2007	40797
127 2/8	18 7/8 19 4/8	13 2/8	6 5	Wilbarger County	TX	Timothy Schur	2007	40797
127 2/8	20 2/8 20 5/8	16 4/8	4 4	Oconto County	WI	Travis Grady	2007	40797
127 2/8	23 3/8 23 6/8	16 3/8	5 4	Adams County	MS	Elijah Vincent	2007	40797
127 2/8	20 4/8 19 2/8	18 2/8	5 5	Monroe County	NY	Christopher L. Ruggieri	2007	40797
127 2/8	20 7/8 20 5/8	15 2/8	5 5	Dane County	WI	Jeff Lien	2007	40797
*127 2/8	21 2/8 21 6/8	18 2/8	4 4	Monroe County	WI	Tom Thurston	2007	40797
*127 2/8	20 7/8 22 2/8	15 6/8	5 5	Carter County	KY	Richard Drew Stockwell	2007	40797
*127 2/8	20 5/8 21 0/8	16 6/8	5 5	Washburn County	WI	Ky Terrill	2007	40797
*127 2/8	23 3/8 23 4/8	18 2/8	4 5	Sauk County	WI	Charles Arndt	2007	40797
127 2/8	23 3/8 23 6/8	17 3/8	6 5	Switzerland County	IN	Luke Z. Libby	2007	40797
127 2/8	23 1/8 24 0/8	16 3/8	5 5	Coffey County	KS	Joseph D. Helget	2007	40797
*127 2/8	22 2/8 22 2/8	17 4/8	5 5	Monroe County	MI	Mike Montri	2007	40797
127 2/8	19 7/8 21 6/8	17 0/8	5 5	Waupaca County	WI	Dennis Zietlow	2008	40797
127 2/8	20 0/8 19 7/8	17 2/8	4 4	Cascade County	MT	Stephen Tylinski	2008	40797
127 2/8	23 6/8 23 6/8	19 2/8	5 5	Sauk County	WI	Joshua M. Hammermeister	2008	40797
127 2/8	21 1/8 21 4/8	12 4/8	5 7	Ingham County	MI	Jerome H. Deaven	2008	40797
127 2/8	20 6/8 20 2/8	16 6/8	5 5	Hancock County	OH	Thomas Hansen II	2008	40797
*127 2/8	21 1/8 20 5/8	15 4/8	6 7	Sauk County	WI	Mike R. Harlock	2008	40797
127 2/8	20 4/8 19 4/8	14 0/8	5 5	St. Croix County	WI	Steven C. Beer	2008	40797
127 2/8	19 0/8 18 7/8	16 4/8	5 5	Dodge County	WI	Dallas J. Lasche	2008	40797
127 2/8	23 2/8 22 7/8	17 0/8	4 4	Wyandot County	OH	James D. Herring	2008	40797
127 2/8	21 1/8 22 2/8	17 6/8	4 4	Logan County	CO	Toby Garcia	2008	40797
*127 2/8	19 6/8 19 7/8	17 2/8	5 5	Richland County	WI	Bob Dye	2008	40797
127 2/8	24 0/8 22 7/8	16 2/8	4 4	La Crosse County	WI	Steven Schank	2008	40797
127 2/8	20 0/8 19 5/8	13 6/8	5 5	McKenzie County	ND	Ginger Brockman	2008	40797

Deer entries below 141 0/8, that appeared in the 6th Edition, are not included here, but are included on the accompanying CD (see page 119), and also in the Club's Records Archives.

WHITETAIL DEER (TYPICAL ANTLERS)

Minimum Score 125 — Continued

SCORE	LENGTH OF R MAIN BEAM L	INSIDE SPREAD	NUMBER OF R POINTS L	AREA	STATE/ PROVINCE	HUNTER'S NAME	DATE	RANK
127 2/8	19 7/8 19 7/8	16 6/8	4 4	Erie County	PA	Ben H. Green	2008	40797
127 2/8	23 4/8 23 1/8	18 3/8	5 4	Greene County	IL	Mike Wendel	2008	40797
*127 2/8	19 4/8 19 1/8	18 0/8	5 5	Cavalier County	ND	Travis Klein	2009	40797
127 2/8	24 7/8 23 7/8	16 4/8	4 5	Shelby County	OH	Craig Ambos	2009	40797
127 2/8	21 6/8 22 2/8	18 2/8	5 5	Trinity County	TX	Joseph F. Sinski III	2009	40797
*127 2/8	22 2/8 21 5/8	15 4/8	5 5	Davie County	NC	Craig Randall Reavis	2009	40797
*127 2/8	21 3/8 21 3/8	18 2/8	5 4	Saline County	MO	Hadley Wiskur	2009	40797
*127 2/8	22 7/8 22 5/8	16 4/8	4 4	Pike County	IL	Ken Rocha	2009	40797
127 2/8	21 3/8 21 4/8	20 0/8	4 4	Marquette County	WI	Jeffrey Frazer	2009	40797
*127 2/8	22 2/8 22 3/8	17 0/8	5 4	Cass County	IL	Brent Gregory	2009	40797
127 2/8	20 2/8 20 1/8	16 0/8	5 5	Buffalo County	WI	Tyler Heil	2009	40797
127 2/8	23 2/8 23 1/8	17 2/8	5 5	Marquette County	WI	Michael J. Redel	2009	40797
127 2/8	23 1/8 23 0/8	16 6/8	4 5	Kankakee County	IL	Timothy Haut	2009	40797
*127 2/8	20 5/8 19 1/8	18 0/8	4 4	Hunterdon County	NJ	Karl D. Zschack	2009	40797
127 2/8	23 1/8 21 6/8	17 6/8	4 4	Racine County	WI	Michael A. Lietke	2009	40797
*127 2/8	22 4/8 20 4/8	17 2/8	5 5	Cook County	IL	Scott Trodden	2009	40797
127 2/8	20 6/8 20 6/8	17 6/8	4 4	Belknap County	NH	David Thayer	2009	40797
127 1/8	22 1/8 23 5/8	19 3/8	5 6	Pike County	IN	Jack Denton	1998	41068
127 1/8	21 0/8 21 0/8	16 7/8	5 5	Dodge County	WI	Mark A. Ackerman	1999	41068
127 1/8	19 3/8 20 3/8	12 6/8	6 5	Lincoln County	SD	Jerry Ovre	2000	41068
127 1/8	22 5/8 23 1/8	16 3/8	5 6	Macoupin County	IL	Bill Morris	2003	41068
127 1/8	19 6/8 20 3/8	16 7/8	5 5	Stephenson County	IL	Terry L. Frint	2004	41068
127 1/8	21 4/8 20 4/8	18 1/8	5 5	Montcalm County	MI	Jim Weaver, Sr.	2004	41068
127 1/8	20 2/8 21 5/8	16 1/8	6 5	Kosciusko County	IN	Neil A. Likens	2004	41068
127 1/8	23 4/8 22 5/8	17 3/8	4 4	Edgar County	IL	Michael J. Karanovich	2004	41068
127 1/8	21 0/8 20 7/8	18 1/8	5 5	Winona County	MN	Darrel D. Schroeder	2004	41068
*127 1/8	22 5/8 22 5/8	15 3/8	4 5	Polk County	WI	Raymond Dueholm	2004	41068
127 1/8	21 7/8 22 3/8	15 3/8	4 6	Trigg County	KY	Mark Wayne Frost	2004	41068
127 1/8	19 7/8 20 1/8	16 0/8	6 5	Oneida County	NY	Kris Snyder	2004	41068
127 1/8	21 2/8 20 6/8	13 7/8	5 5	Jasper County	IL	Dave Fleming	2004	41068
*127 1/8	20 5/8 22 3/8	16 7/8	6 5	Stark County	ND	Greg Pruitt	2004	41068
127 1/8	23 4/8 22 0/8	19 1/8	4 5	Kankakee County	IL	Jeffery J. Schneider	2004	41068
127 1/8	20 3/8 20 6/8	18 3/8	4 4	Champaign County	OH	Jim Cremeans	2004	41068
127 1/8	21 2/8 22 2/8	16 4/8	6 5	Fulton County	IL	Tad Yetter	2004	41068
*127 1/8	21 5/8 21 0/8	16 3/8	4 4	Eau Claire County	WI	Teresa K. Becker	2005	41068
127 1/8	20 0/8 20 2/8	17 5/8	5 5	Douglas County	MN	Ryan Augeson	2005	41068
127 1/8	23 2/8 23 2/8	18 3/8	6 6	Concho County	TX	Steve Fegley	2005	41068
127 1/8	20 6/8 21 5/8	14 5/8	4 5	Woodbury County	IA	David A. Hesse	2005	41068
127 1/8	20 7/8 20 6/8	19 3/8	5 5	Ward County	ND	Blaine Huff	2005	41068
127 1/8	22 2/8 23 2/8	20 1/8	5 5	St. Louis County	MN	Randy S. Wendt	2005	41068
127 1/8	22 6/8 22 2/8	17 1/8	4 4	Eau Claire County	WI	John Ritsch	2005	41068
127 1/8	19 7/8 19 7/8	17 5/8	4 4	Wyandot County	OH	David Ware	2005	41068
*127 1/8	20 6/8 21 1/8	16 1/8	5 5	Dubuque County	IA	Tim Oberfoell	2005	41068
*127 1/8	19 2/8 24 3/8	16 3/8	4 4	Sanilac County	MI	David M. Doerr	2005	41068
127 1/8	24 0/8 23 5/8	18 7/8	4 4	Fayette County	IA	John J. Czerniakowski	2005	41068
127 1/8	21 3/8 21 4/8	15 5/8	5 5	Tioga County	NY	David A. Luther	2005	41068
*127 1/8	20 3/8 19 5/8	17 1/8	5 5	Jackson County	WI	George Laufenberg	2005	41068
127 1/8	22 3/8 23 0/8	20 2/8	5 7	Warren County	NJ	Nicholas Turano, Jr.	2005	41068
*127 1/8	19 5/8 20 3/8	15 3/8	5 5	Wyandot County	OH	Natalie Frey	2005	41068
127 1/8	19 3/8 19 1/8	13 4/8	6 5	Edwards County	TX	Michael F. Joseph	2005	41068
127 1/8	24 2/8 24 4/8	17 3/8	4 4	Fairfield County	CT	John Coniglio	2005	41068
127 1/8	21 6/8 23 2/8	16 2/8	5 5	Edmonson County	KY	Craig Browning	2006	41068
127 1/8	19 1/8 20 4/8	15 4/8	6 7	Bedford County	TN	Edwin Holt	2006	41068
*127 1/8	22 6/8 24 0/8	17 0/8	5 5	Lincoln County	TN	Ricky J. Smotherman	2006	41068
127 1/8	20 0/8 19 0/8	16 7/8	5 5	Hancock County	IL	James V. Thompson, Jr.	2006	41068
*127 1/8	20 7/8 22 5/8	16 0/8	4 6	Iroquois County	IL	Raymond J. Holohan	2006	41068
127 1/8	23 2/8 22 3/8	16 1/8	4 4	Sandusky County	OH	Fred Mollenhauer	2006	41068
127 1/8	23 3/8 22 7/8	16 5/8	5 5	Cortland County	NY	Robert A. Pendock, Jr.	2006	41068
127 1/8	19 4/8 20 7/8	16 7/8	5 5	Aitkin County	MN	Kenneth Beckel	2006	41068
*127 1/8	20 6/8 21 0/8	16 3/8	5 4	Floyd County	IA	Bob Spitz	2006	41068
127 1/8	24 7/8 21 7/8	18 7/8	4 5	La Crosse County	WI	Ronald Brown	2006	41068
127 1/8	21 1/8 21 0/8	17 1/8	5 5	Wilson County	KS	Dean Burgess	2006	41068
127 1/8	19 6/8 20 7/8	16 0/8	6 4	Cloud County	KS	Joseph D. Helget	2006	41068
127 1/8	21 5/8 21 0/8	15 2/8	4 5	Monona County	IA	Tim Grigerek	2006	41068
*127 1/8	21 3/8 21 3/8	15 3/8	4 4	Marathon County	WI	Tom Nowacki	2007	41068
127 1/8	22 6/8 22 3/8	17 5/8	4 4	Waupaca County	WI	Kyle Kolasinski	2007	41068
127 1/8	23 1/8 22 3/8	16 0/8	7 5	Washtenaw County	MI	Brian K. Smith	2007	41068
127 1/8	19 1/8 19 5/8	12 1/8	5 5	Nemaha County	NE	Randy Striggow	2007	41068
*127 1/8	22 2/8 21 5/8	17 1/8	5 4	Lancaster County	PA	Corey Sine	2007	41068
*127 1/8	23 6/8 23 5/8	20 1/8	8 6	De Witt County	IL	Bradley Miller	2007	41068
*127 1/8	20 1/8 20 7/8	19 5/8	5 4	Pepin County	WI	William Clark, Jr.	2007	41068
*127 1/8	20 4/8 21 2/8	17 2/8	7 6	Saunders County	NE	Ryan Miller	2007	41068
*127 1/8	21 0/8 22 3/8	17 3/8	5 4	Posey County	IN	Nathan Ponder	2007	41068
*127 1/8	23 0/8 23 1/8	16 7/8	4 4	Cayuga County	NY	Robert Napolitano	2007	41068
127 1/8	22 5/8 23 4/8	15 5/8	4 4	Morris County	NJ	William J. Jimeno	2007	41068
127 1/8	21 7/8 20 7/8	14 3/8	5 5	Wilson County	KS	Dean Burgess	2007	41068
127 1/8	19 1/8 19 1/8	17 5/8	5 5	Morgan County	GA	M. Keith Almand	2007	41068
127 1/8	21 0/8 20 5/8	15 7/8	6 5	Screven County	GA	Allen Pace	2007	41068
127 1/8	21 3/8 21 6/8	20 3/8	4 4	Stoddard County	MO	Terry Abner	2007	41068
127 1/8	20 4/8 18 6/8	14 7/8	5 5	Twiggs County	GA	Michael Lopez	2008	41068
*127 1/8	22 1/8 22 2/8	16 3/8	4 4	Price County	WI	Kevin Jensen	2008	41068
*127 1/8	22 1/8 21 7/8	15 3/8	5 5	Will County	IL	Darren Van Essen	2008	41068
*127 1/8	22 4/8 21 4/8	17 5/8	4 4	Monroe County	PA	Dan Mahn	2008	41068
127 1/8	22 5/8 21 5/8	17 3/8	4 4	Dallas County	IA	Joshua Benson	2008	41068
127 1/8	21 0/8 21 1/8	16 7/8	5 5	Perry County	PA	Ronald A. Rhoads, Jr.	2008	41068
127 1/8	22 3/8 22 7/8	17 7/8	5 4	St. Louis County	MN	Scott Schafer	2008	41068
*127 1/8	23 3/8 22 1/8	18 1/8	3 5	Houston County	MN	Rob Rebertus	2008	41068
127 1/8	21 4/8 21 4/8	16 3/8	4 4	Waupaca County	WI	William Peotter	2008	41068
127 1/8	21 0/8 20 6/8	16 5/8	5 5	Waupaca County	WI	David L. Seidl	2008	41068
127 1/8	19 5/8 19 7/8	17 7/8	6 6	Columbia County	WI	Kurt K. Southworth	2008	41068
*127 1/8	21 0/8 21 2/8	14 2/8	7 5	Fergus County	MT	Thad Kucera	2009	41068
*127 1/8	21 6/8 21 4/8	17 7/8	4 4	Weston County	WY	Lowell H. Boettcher	2009	41068
127 1/8	23 5/8 23 3/8	17 6/8	5 6	Cass County	IN	Neil Fowler	2009	41068
*127 1/8	22 1/8 21 6/8	14 5/8	6 7	Licking County	OH	Jason Grunkemeyer	2009	41068
*127 1/8	22 1/8 21 6/8	14 5/8	6 7	Cedar County	MO	Jeff Chambers	2009	41068

WHITETAIL DEER (TYPICAL ANTLERS)

Minimum Score 125   Continued

SCORE	LENGTH OF R MAIN BEAM L	INSIDE SPREAD	NUMBER OF R POINTS L	AREA	STATE/ PROVINCE	HUNTER'S NAME	DATE	RANK
*127 1/8	21 3/8 22 1/8	15 5/8	4 5	Buffalo County	WI	Gunnar Hagen	2009	41068
127 1/8	20 4/8 20 4/8	16 7/8	5 5	Jackson County	WV	Keith Holmes	2009	41068
127 1/8	22 4/8 22 6/8	14 4/8	5 4	Porter County	IN	Edward L. Dewes	2009	41068
*127 1/8	21 6/8 21 3/8	17 3/8	5 5	Burnett County	WI	Michael Olsen	2009	41068
*127 1/8	22 0/8 21 4/8	17 0/8	5 5	Steuben County	IN	Mark Hamlin	2009	41068
127 1/8	19 5/8 18 3/8	16 1/8	5 5	Caddo County	OK	Rocky Wilson	2009	41068
*127 1/8	23 2/8 23 2/8	16 7/8	4 4	Harrison County	IA	Ben Johnston	2009	41068
*127 1/8	21 2/8 20 6/8	16 5/8	5 5	Bingham County	ID	Joe Kaul	2009	41068
127 1/8	22 0/8 22 4/8	18 5/8	4 4	Ralls County	MO	Steve Hardy	2010	41068
*127 1/8	22 2/8 22 3/8	22 3/8	4 4	Monmouth County	NJ	Thomas Ulikowski	2010	41068
127 0/8	22 5/8 25 2/8	17 6/8	5 4	Dunn County	WI	Rodney Keenlyne	1990	41329
127 0/8	19 1/8 18 3/8	14 7/8	5 6	Forest County	WI	Joel LaRocque	1994	41329
127 0/8	22 1/8 23 1/8	16 2/8	4 7	Isle of Wight County	VA	Dwight S. Wolf	1994	41329
127 0/8	23 0/8 22 4/8	18 3/8	4 5	Bucks County	PA	Tod Fox	2003	41329
127 0/8	21 0/8 21 2/8	14 4/8	5 6	Licking County	OH	Hobert Payne	2003	41329
127 0/8	21 7/8 20 5/8	17 2/8	4 4	Calhoun County	MI	Mel R. Meck	2003	41329
*127 0/8	21 3/8 20 7/8	16 2/8	4 4	Anoka County	MN	Paul Contons	2003	41329
127 0/8	21 4/8 22 1/8	22 5/8	6 6	St. Louis County	MN	Mark Lewis	2003	41329
127 0/8	22 6/8 22 6/8	17 6/8	4 4	Lee County	NC	Dustin Wester	2004	41329
127 0/8	20 2/8 20 0/8	15 0/8	5 5	Mountrail County	ND	Glenn Schrempf	2004	41329
127 0/8	22 0/8 22 6/8	16 0/8	4 4	Marion County	WV	David Perkins	2004	41329
127 0/8	22 4/8 23 4/8	17 4/8	4 5	Dunn County	WI	Joseph Edin	2004	41329
127 0/8	21 7/8 21 7/8	20 4/8	5 5	Washington County	WI	Devan R. Faust	2004	41329
127 0/8	22 6/8 23 4/8	17 4/8	4 4	Bayfield County	WI	William Tuttle	2004	41329
127 0/8	20 4/8 20 2/8	15 4/8	4 4	Elkhart County	IN	Jon M. Stallman	2004	41329
127 0/8	21 2/8 22 0/8	18 4/8	6 5	Mifflin County	PA	Ken R. Snyder	2004	41329
127 0/8	22 0/8 20 5/8	18 2/8	4 4	Iowa County	WI	Marc W. Bonin	2004	41329
*127 0/8	20 3/8 20 7/8	15 0/8	4 4	Perry County	IL	Pete Drummond	2004	41329
*127 0/8	21 7/8 21 7/8	15 6/8	4 4	Delaware County	IA	Art Gourley	2004	41329
127 0/8	22 0/8 22 7/8	20 4/8	5 5	St. Louis County	MN	Duncan Puffer	2004	41329
*127 0/8	25 2/8 23 1/8	18 2/8	4 4	Duval County	TX	Brandon Ray	2005	41329
127 0/8	18 3/8 18 6/8	13 6/8	5 5	Washington County	WI	Keith Anderson	2005	41329
127 0/8	20 1/8 21 1/8	19 4/8	5 5	Shawano County	WI	Rickey L. Ashman	2005	41329
127 0/8	21 3/8 20 7/8	15 4/8	4 4	Lenawee County	MI	Martin I. Braddy	2005	41329
127 0/8	20 3/8 20 3/8	17 0/8	5 5	Dunn County	WI	Michael Benzel	2005	41329
127 0/8	21 3/8 22 3/8	16 4/8	5 5	Houston County	MN	Wayne J. Hood, Jr.	2005	41329
*127 0/8	20 1/8 20 2/8	16 4/8	6 6	Daviess County	IN	Matthew Gingerich	2005	41329
127 0/8	22 2/8 24 2/8	17 2/8	5 4	Westmoreland County	PA	Dalton L. Hogue	2005	41329
127 0/8	20 3/8 21 3/8	15 4/8	5 5	Sedgwick County	KS	Todd Wilson	2005	41329
*127 0/8	21 5/8 20 7/8	18 4/8	4 4	Tom Green County	TX	Mark Harrington	2005	41329
*127 0/8	20 0/8 20 6/8	16 2/8	4 5	Carroll County	IL	Ralph D. Malicki	2005	41329
127 0/8	20 7/8 21 0/8	14 4/8	4 5	Westchester County	NY	Hector DiLeo	2005	41329
127 0/8	21 6/8 21 0/8	18 2/8	4 4	Dodge County	WI	Keith S. Everson	2006	41329
*127 0/8	18 7/8 18 2/8	15 2/8	6 6	Menard County	TX	Steven Wayne Self, Sr.	2006	41329
127 0/8	21 7/8 21 7/8	16 2/8	4 4	Iowa County	WI	Justin Ganser	2006	41329
127 0/8	20 6/8 21 0/8	18 4/8	5 5	Wabash County	IN	Chris Pattee	2006	41329
*127 0/8	21 1/8 20 7/8	15 2/8	6 5	Cooper County	MO	Tim Taylor	2006	41329
127 0/8	22 3/8 22 5/8	18 6/8	6 6	Douglas County	WI	Brian C. Johnson	2006	41329
127 0/8	22 3/8 23 0/8	14 6/8	4 5	Ward County	ND	Dean Anhorn	2006	41329
*127 0/8	21 2/8 22 1/8	16 3/8	5 6	Calhoun County	IL	David N. Funk	2006	41329
127 0/8	22 6/8 22 2/8	15 2/8	4 4	Buffalo County	WI	Randal Shook	2006	41329
127 0/8	24 1/8 21 5/8	16 4/8	4 4	Carroll County	IL	Dick V. Lalowski	2006	41329
127 0/8	20 5/8 21 1/8	14 6/8	5 5	De Witt County	IL	Ryan Cook	2006	41329
*127 0/8	21 2/8 21 2/8	15 6/8	4 5	Macomb County	MI	Leonard Palys	2006	41329
*127 0/8	22 2/8 22 1/8	15 0/8	4 4	Columbia County	PA	Layne D. Bowes	2006	41329
127 0/8	21 4/8 21 3/8	16 2/8	4 4	Pope County	IL	Marty Buford	2006	41329
*127 0/8	20 0/8 21 2/8	15 0/8	5 5	Southampton County	VA	Kenneth J. Vick	2006	41329
127 0/8	25 3/8 25 2/8	19 6/8	3 3	Litchfield County	CT	Keith Miller	2006	41329
127 0/8	21 6/8 22 0/8	14 2/8	4 4	Llano County	TX	Dan Kemp	2006	41329
127 0/8	21 5/8 21 5/8	18 6/8	4 5	Price County	WI	Richard Kirchmeyer	2006	41329
*127 0/8	21 0/8 21 2/8	17 4/8	4 5	Griggs County	ND	Tera Tande	2007	41329
127 0/8	21 0/8 22 4/8	18 0/8	5 6	Livingston County	MI	Eric J. Stack	2007	41329
*127 0/8	20 7/8 21 6/8	16 6/8	6 6	Branch County	MI	Kurt Myers	2007	41329
127 0/8	23 1/8 22 6/8	16 0/8	4 4	Switzerland County	IN	Nathan Walker	2007	41329
127 0/8	21 4/8 20 6/8	15 6/8	4 4	Monroe County	WI	Steve Pfaff	2007	41329
127 0/8	19 3/8 24 2/8	15 6/8	5 5	Noble County	IN	Trenton Marsh	2007	41329
127 0/8	23 4/8 23 4/8	17 2/8	4 5	Chautauqua County	NY	Don Rankin	2007	41329
*127 0/8	23 0/8 19 0/8	17 1/8	6 7	Decatur County	IA	Jeffrey Dean Clark	2007	41329
*127 0/8	24 1/8 20 3/8	17 4/8	4 4	Jo Daviess County	IL	Andrew Robson	2007	41329
127 0/8	19 5/8 19 7/8	16 0/8	5 5	Adams County	IA	Kenneth M. Thompson	2007	41329
*127 0/8	25 0/8 23 7/8	18 2/8	5 4	Young County	TX	Jim Beadle	2007	41329
127 0/8	23 6/8 21 6/8	18 6/8	4 4	Montgomery County	OH	Eric Gildow	2007	41329
127 0/8	20 4/8 20 4/8	13 2/8	5 5	Trempealeau County	WI	Jayme Olson	2008	41329
127 0/8	18 2/8 20 4/8	14 0/8	5 5	Grant County	WI	Kevin S. Honahan	2008	41329
127 0/8	20 1/8 21 1/8	14 4/8	5 5	Lyon County	KY	Matt Colson	2008	41329
127 0/8	22 6/8 23 0/8	15 7/8	5 5	Suffolk County	VA	David T. Parrish	2008	41329
127 0/8	24 1/8 23 7/8	18 3/8	6 5	Fulton County	IL	David Geier	2008	41329
127 0/8	21 2/8 19 4/8	15 6/8	5 5	Manitowoc County	WI	Scott Bubolz	2008	41329
127 0/8	23 1/8 22 4/8	16 4/8	4 4	Kingman County	KS	Carl Litzenberger	2008	41329
*127 0/8	22 6/8 22 6/8	16 0/8	5 4	Saunders County	NE	Matt Donelan	2008	41329
127 0/8	22 4/8 22 5/8	17 7/8	4 8	Cass County	IA	Darren Miller	2008	41329
127 0/8	21 6/8 21 4/8	15 4/8	5 6	Athens County	OH	Phillip Jarvis	2008	41329
127 0/8	20 0/8 21 6/8	16 6/8	5 5	Norfolk County	MA	Lewis C. Melcher	2008	41329
127 0/8	20 1/8 20 1/8	17 6/8	5 5	Rusk County	WI	Joe Sandok	2009	41329
*127 0/8	21 7/8 21 2/8	14 4/8	4 4	Loudoun County	VA	Kenny Triplett	2009	41329
127 0/8	21 2/8 21 5/8	17 0/8	4 6	St. Brieux	SAS	Chad Rohel	2009	41329
127 0/8	25 5/8 24 4/8	18 0/8	5 4	Shawano County	WI	Raymond E. Creapeau, Jr.	2009	41329
127 0/8	19 7/8 20 1/8	16 5/8	6 7	Sutton County	TX	Drake Shurley	2009	41329
127 0/8	21 7/8 20 7/8	19 2/8	4 4	Steuben County	IN	Joseph M. Harris	2009	41329
*127 0/8	23 0/8 23 5/8	17 6/8	4 4	Spencer County	IN	Michael Kamuf	2009	41329
127 0/8	20 2/8 20 4/8	15 6/8	5 5	Oconto County	WI	Mark Uitenbroek	2009	41329
127 0/8	21 3/8 22 2/8	14 2/8	5 5	Brown County	IL	Michael Johnson	2009	41329
*127 0/8	22 5/8 22 3/8	19 4/8	5 5	Wyoming County	WV	Al Ferelli	2009	41329
127 0/8	21 1/8 21 4/8	16 0/8	5 5	Ottawa County	OK	Greggory S. Lamb	2009	41329
127 0/8	24 0/8 22 2/8	16 4/8	4 5	Perry County	OH	Guy Enfield	2009	41329

Deer entries below 141 0/8, that appeared in the 6th Edition, are not included here, but are included on the accompanying CD (see page 119), and also in the Club's Records Archives.

WHITETAIL DEER (TYPICAL ANTLERS)

Minimum Score 125   Continued

SCORE	LENGTH OF R MAIN BEAM L	INSIDE SPREAD	NUMBER OF R POINTS L	AREA	STATE/ PROVINCE	HUNTER'S NAME	DATE	RANK
127 0/8	19 6/8 19 6/8	15 0/8	4 4	McKenzie County	ND	Jody Smith	2009	41329
127 0/8	20 0/8 19 4/8	17 6/8	4 5	San Saba County	TX	Kelby McCall	2009	41329
*127 0/8	22 7/8 22 0/8	17 1/8	4 6	Meigs County	OH	Beau J. Bailey	2010	41329
*127 0/8	22 0/8 22 0/8	15 5/8	5 6	Red Deer County	ALB	Garrett Gow	2010	41329
126 7/8	20 0/8 20 4/8	18 3/8	6 4	Lorain County	OH	Steven D. Reinhold	1991	41596
126 7/8	23 2/8 23 4/8	16 7/8	4 4	Jefferson County	MS	Keith Stroud	2000	41596
126 7/8	20 6/8 21 3/8	16 5/8	4 4	Grant County	WI	Adam Kirschbaum	2001	41596
126 7/8	20 5/8 20 0/8	16 3/8	4 4	McHenry County	ND	Don Scofield	2001	41596
126 7/8	22 1/8 22 1/8	18 4/8	6 5	DeKalb County	IL	Donald R. Lalowski	2002	41596
*126 7/8	21 6/8 21 0/8	19 4/8	4 5	Calhoun County	IL	David Pohlman	2003	41596
126 7/8	19 3/8 19 3/8	17 5/8	4 4	Woodford County	IL	Larry Pisel, Jr.	2003	41596
126 7/8	21 4/8 22 2/8	18 1/8	4 4	Monmouth County	NJ	Nelson A. Roman	2003	41596
126 7/8	18 0/8 18 1/8	16 0/8	6 6	Cass County	NE	Levi Roeber	2004	41596
126 7/8	22 3/8 21 4/8	15 3/8	4 5	De Kalb County	GA	Lee Johnson	2004	41596
126 7/8	25 7/8 24 5/8	21 7/8	5 6	Montgomery County	PA	Francis J. Broskoskie, Jr.	2004	41596
126 7/8	22 6/8 22 3/8	15 3/8	5 5	Winona County	MN	Robert A. Micheel	2004	41596
*126 7/8	21 1/8 20 7/8	17 3/8	5 5	Crow Wing County	MN	Robert Wennerstrand	2004	41596
126 7/8	20 6/8 22 5/8	16 3/8	5 4	Union County	SD	Clint Ellis	2004	41596
*126 7/8	23 2/8 23 5/8	17 3/8	5 4	Hocking County	OH	Ed Zagurski	2004	41596
126 7/8	19 5/8 20 1/8	14 7/8	4 4	Columbia County	WI	Bruce F. Udell	2004	41596
126 7/8	26 2/8 26 2/8	20 5/8	5 3	Wayne County	IL	Dennis Vail	2004	41596
126 7/8	19 3/8 20 1/8	14 3/8	5 6	Hardin County	IL	Darrell Lott	2004	41596
126 7/8	21 2/8 21 6/8	16 7/8	5 5	La Crosse County	WI	Michael Marcou	2005	41596
126 7/8	19 7/8 18 6/8	16 6/8	5 8	St. Croix County	WI	Mike Johnson	2005	41596
126 7/8	21 0/8 20 2/8	15 6/8	6 6	Shawano County	WI	Alex Ostrowski	2005	41596
*126 7/8	22 5/8 21 6/8	17 2/8	7 4	Jefferson County	IN	Derek Buchanan	2005	41596
126 7/8	22 4/8 22 6/8	17 3/8	4 4	Todd County	MN	William H. Peterson	2005	41596
126 7/8	23 0/8 22 2/8	17 1/8	4 4	Grafton County	NH	Joe Hurley	2005	41596
126 7/8	22 3/8 21 4/8	19 3/8	4 4	Hunterdon County	NJ	Michael S. Kalinchock	2005	41596
126 7/8	22 1/8 22 0/8	14 5/8	5 5	Kewaunee County	WI	Ron Kinjerski	2005	41596
126 7/8	20 6/8 20 3/8	14 3/8	4 5	McHenry County	ND	Jeff Jacobs	2005	41596
126 7/8	21 2/8 21 7/8	16 1/8	4 4	Clinton County	OH	Scott Miller	2005	41596
*126 7/8	21 5/8 21 1/8	16 2/8	5 6	Fayette County	IN	Steve Mitchell	2005	41596
126 7/8	20 4/8 21 0/8	16 5/8	4 4	Newton County	MO	Melvin Ward	2005	41596
126 7/8	22 0/8 22 0/8	15 2/8	6 6	Door County	WI	Matthew C. Stender	2005	41596
126 7/8	24 1/8 25 4/8	18 5/8	4 4	Lemhi County	ID	Benjamin Fahnholz	2005	41596
126 7/8	20 4/8 20 7/8	16 1/8	4 4	Johnson County	TX	Derrick Payne	2005	41596
126 7/8	23 2/8 21 6/8	18 6/8	5 5	Spokane County	WA	Lon Lauber	2005	41596
126 7/8	21 4/8 21 4/8	16 1/8	4 4	Sutton County	TX	W. C. Polster	2005	41596
126 7/8	22 5/8 23 2/8	16 3/8	4 4	Russell County	AL	Gregory S. Young	2006	41596
126 7/8	21 7/8 20 5/8	15 0/8	5 6	Rice County	MN	Gary A. Kiekenapp-Higgins	2006	41596
126 7/8	23 0/8 23 5/8	15 7/8	4 4	Wabasha County	MN	Patti Welter	2006	41596
126 7/8	21 0/8 21 1/8	16 5/8	4 4	Washington County	WI	Richard E. Voigt	2006	41596
*126 7/8	22 1/8 21 2/8	18 5/8	5 5	Young County	TX	Angela S. Love	2006	41596
126 7/8	22 0/8 20 7/8	14 4/8	6 4	Roscommon County	MI	Marty Sheridan	2006	41596
126 7/8	21 1/8 21 1/8	15 7/8	4 4	Dorintosh	SAS	Robert Graham	2006	41596
126 7/8	20 5/8 20 5/8	16 1/8	4 4	Schuyler County	IL	Reece Whitley	2007	41596
*126 7/8	22 0/8 22 0/8	19 0/8	6 6	Fulton County	IL	Eric Wellauer	2007	41596
126 7/8	22 2/8 21 2/8	18 1/8	6 6	Tippecanoe County	IN	Tim Bundy	2007	41596
126 7/8	21 2/8 20 5/8	16 7/8	4 5	Okanogan County	WA	Randy Parker	2007	41596
126 7/8	22 7/8 25 6/8	18 0/8	7 4	Buffalo County	WI	Alex Skebba	2008	41596
126 7/8	21 0/8 20 4/8	13 6/8	7 7	Ramsey County	ND	Andrew Plaine	2008	41596
126 7/8	21 1/8 22 0/8	18 3/8	4 4	Madison County	IN	Chadney Hand	2008	41596
126 7/8	21 3/8 21 7/8	17 3/8	4 4	Isle of Wight County	VA	Ronald A. Edwards	2008	41596
126 7/8	21 1/8 20 5/8	16 3/8	5 5	Winnebago County	WI	Ronald A. Dercks	2008	41596
*126 7/8	20 5/8 21 2/8	15 3/8	5 5	Fayette County	TX	Allan G. Jurk	2008	41596
126 7/8	20 7/8 20 1/8	16 1/8	5 5	Sauk County	WI	Jim Riphon	2008	41596
*126 7/8	21 3/8 20 5/8	14 5/8	5 4	Jefferson County	OH	Victor S. Holdren	2008	41596
*126 7/8	22 2/8 23 2/8	18 5/8	5 5	Trempealeau County	WI	Mike Krajewski	2008	41596
*126 7/8	20 3/8 20 3/8	16 7/8	5 4	Jackson County	WI	Brooke Anderson	2008	41596
126 7/8	21 5/8 23 1/8	16 2/8	4 5	Lawrence County	OH	Christopher Ferguson	2008	41596
*126 7/8	23 7/8 23 1/8	19 5/8	4 4	Trempealeau County	WI	Ralph Lyon	2008	41596
*126 7/8	20 2/8 21 2/8	14 1/8	4 4	Houston County	TX	Doyle Ray	2008	41596
126 7/8	21 1/8 21 0/8	17 1/8	4 4	Missoula County	MT	Robert D. Mattie	2008	41596
126 7/8	23 0/8 22 2/8	16 2/8	5 6	Polk County	WI	David T. Borek	2009	41596
*126 7/8	19 6/8 20 2/8	16 5/8	5 5	Beaver County	PA	Larry O'Neill	2009	41596
*126 7/8	22 7/8 23 4/8	16 5/8	4 4	Yates County	NY	Jason A. Campbell	2009	41596
126 7/8	21 5/8 21 5/8	15 3/8	5 4	Columbia County	WI	Bill Faust	2009	41596
126 7/8	23 2/8 22 6/8	15 5/8	4 4	Susquehanna County	PA	Brian Reese	2009	41596
126 7/8	19 6/8 19 2/8	14 7/8	5 5	Waupaca County	WI	John W. Miller	2009	41596
*126 7/8	22 0/8 21 1/8	17 3/8	4 4	Broome County	NY	Shaun R. O'Connor	2009	41596
126 7/8	23 6/8 22 4/8	17 6/8	5 3	Lafayette County	WI	Craig McGinnis	2009	41596
126 7/8	19 5/8 20 2/8	14 1/8	5 4	Carroll County	MS	Lee J. Hankins	2009	41596
126 7/8	23 1/8 22 6/8	17 3/8	4 4	Atkinson County	GA	Ryan Solomon	2009	41596
126 7/8	26 0/8 24 1/8	16 3/8	5 5	Ottawa County	MI	Dave Ellis	2009	41596
*126 7/8	23 6/8 23 6/8	14 5/8	4 4	Lincoln County	WI	Dylan Detert	2010	41596
126 6/8	21 3/8 20 6/8	17 0/8	6 5	Rock Island County	IL	John Angel	1990	41838
126 6/8	22 3/8 21 2/8	14 6/8	4 4	Hall County	NE	Robert Gregg	1996	41838
126 6/8	21 4/8 22 3/8	19 0/8	4 5	Brown County	TX	Richard McCarty	1997	41838
126 6/8	22 0/8 21 7/8	17 4/8	4 5	Monmouth County	NJ	John McLaughlin	1998	41838
126 6/8	21 1/8 20 1/8	15 2/8	4 5	Montgomery County	OH	Andrew C. Evans	1999	41838
126 6/8	19 6/8 20 4/8	18 0/8	5 6	Isle of Wight County	VA	Dwight S. Wolf	2000	41838
*126 6/8	21 5/8 21 5/8	16 4/8	4 4	Nelson County	KY	Eric Culver	2001	41838
126 6/8	22 6/8 22 4/8	20 0/8	5 5	Green County	WI	Wade Strothman	2001	41838
126 6/8	21 7/8 21 2/8	18 2/8	5 4	Wood County	WI	James E. Frank	2002	41838
126 6/8	22 5/8 22 3/8	17 2/8	5 4	Green Lake County	WI	Joseph W. Minnema	2003	41838
126 6/8	22 2/8 21 3/8	13 4/8	6 6	Sullivan County	MO	Walter Eudaley	2003	41838
126 6/8	21 6/8 21 7/8	17 0/8	5 5	Highland County	OH	Richard Farkas	2003	41838
126 6/8	22 6/8 22 1/8	17 4/8	5 4	Cass County	MI	Andy W. Silverthorn	2003	41838
126 6/8	19 7/8 20 0/8	13 0/8	5 5	Valley County	MT	Richard M. Penn	2004	41838
126 6/8	20 4/8 20 0/8	16 2/8	5 5	Fulton County	AR	David Gibson	2004	41838
126 6/8	23 2/8 22 6/8	18 4/8	4 4	Venango County	PA	Steve Ferris	2004	41838
126 6/8	20 7/8 20 5/8	14 6/8	4 5	Vernon County	MO	Jeff Hubbard	2004	41838
126 6/8	24 0/8 23 7/8	17 6/8	5 5	Waupaca County	WI	Richard W. Pensis	2004	41838
126 6/8	22 2/8 22 0/8	14 0/8	6 6	Fayette County	PA	Joe Mellinger	2004	41838

WHITETAIL DEER (TYPICAL ANTLERS)

Minimum Score 125 — Continued

SCORE	LENGTH OF R MAIN BEAM L	INSIDE SPREAD	NUMBER OF R POINTS L	AREA	STATE/ PROVINCE	HUNTER'S NAME	DATE	RANK
126 6/8	23 1/8 22 4/8	15 0/8	4 5	Pinellas County	FL	James B. Nathe	2004	41838
126 6/8	20 3/8 20 4/8	18 4/8	4 4	Morris County	NJ	Kenneth Biss	2004	41838
126 6/8	19 2/8 20 0/8	15 6/8	5 5	Morgan County	KY	Seth Thomas	2004	41838
126 6/8	24 3/8 24 7/8	19 2/8	4 5	Chambers County	AL	Emory E. Lynn	2005	41838
*126 6/8	19 0/8 18 2/8	14 4/8	7 5	Brown County	WI	Timothy J. Renard	2005	41838
126 6/8	22 4/8 22 0/8	16 1/8	5 5	Langlade County	WI	Eric Bussiere	2005	41838
126 6/8	20 0/8 20 4/8	15 0/8	5 5	Columbia County	WI	Michael Paulcheck	2005	41838
126 6/8	21 6/8 21 4/8	16 1/8	7 6	La Grange County	IN	Edward A. Peters	2005	41838
126 6/8	20 0/8 19 1/8	15 0/8	4 4	Lenawee County	MI	Jason Lucas	2005	41838
126 6/8	22 7/8 22 4/8	17 7/8	4 5	Kent County	MI	Matthew McCauley	2005	41838
126 6/8	21 1/8 20 2/8	15 4/8	5 5	Green Lake County	WI	Michael A. Prachel	2005	41838
126 6/8	22 4/8 22 2/8	16 0/8	4 4	Allegheny County	PA	Jeff Rosak	2005	41838
126 6/8	23 3/8 23 0/8	20 0/8	5 4	McHenry County	IL	Donald E. Hoey	2005	41838
*126 6/8	21 1/8 20 2/8	16 2/8	4 5	Trempealeau County	WI	Brian K. Lyngen	2005	41838
126 6/8	20 4/8 21 2/8	14 0/8	4 4	Franklin County	IA	Larry Fanny	2005	41838
126 6/8	23 2/8 23 6/8	16 6/8	4 4	Peoria County	IL	Floyd Cunningham	2005	41838
126 6/8	21 4/8 21 2/8	17 3/8	4 6	Adams County	IL	Tres Childs	2005	41838
*126 6/8	19 5/8 19 7/8	17 2/8	5 5	Cedar County	NE	Eric Moore	2005	41838
126 6/8	20 4/8 21 1/8	16 4/8	5 5	Grand Forks County	ND	Ryan Svoboda	2006	41838
126 6/8	21 6/8 21 4/8	17 2/8	4 4	Tallahatchie County	MS	Clifton D. Steed	2006	41838
126 6/8	21 6/8 22 2/8	15 6/8	5 4	Crittenden County	KY	Don Head	2006	41838
*126 6/8	22 6/8 22 3/8	16 6/8	4 5	Chautauqua County	NY	Jason Tingue	2006	41838
*126 6/8	22 0/8 21 4/8	15 1/8	5 5	Franklin County	IN	Jeremy Isaacs	2006	41838
126 6/8	19 0/8 19 4/8	16 0/8	4 4	Lyon County	KS	Peter Dale	2006	41838
126 6/8	21 7/8 21 6/8	16 4/8	4 4	Houston County	MN	Kyle J. Schweisthal	2007	41838
126 6/8	20 6/8 20 7/8	15 6/8	5 5	Barrow County	GA	Shannon Vaeth	2007	41838
*126 6/8	22 1/8 22 6/8	15 4/8	6 7	Olmsted County	MN	Jay Rud	2007	41838
126 6/8	21 4/8 21 4/8	17 6/8	5 4	Lampasas County	TX	Daniel Sullivan	2007	41838
*126 6/8	21 6/8 20 7/8	19 0/8	4 5	Penobscot County	ME	Freeman B. Forbes, Jr.	2007	41838
*126 6/8	22 2/8 21 1/8	16 6/8	5 6	Hocking County	OH	Ralph C. Witte	2007	41838
*126 6/8	22 1/8 23 2/8	17 4/8	4 4	Tioga County	PA	Ward D. Slocum	2007	41838
126 6/8	22 4/8 22 7/8	17 4/8	4 5	Prairie River	SAS	Ken H. Taylor	2007	41838
126 6/8	21 7/8 22 3/8	17 6/8	4 4	Polk County	WI	Andrew D. Moris	2007	41838
126 6/8	21 0/8 21 0/8	17 2/8	4 4	Montgomery County	MD	Roger L. Noell	2007	41838
126 6/8	23 4/8 23 0/8	17 5/8	9 8	Red Willow County	NE	Greg Gans	2007	41838
126 6/8	22 4/8 22 3/8	13 3/8	5 4	Franklin County	IA	Mike Shell	2007	41838
*126 6/8	20 5/8 20 2/8	16 2/8	4 4	Hays County	TX	Ryan Seicers	2007	41838
126 6/8	20 7/8 21 4/8	17 0/8	4 5	Outagamie County	WI	Anthony K. Kraft	2007	41838
*126 6/8	20 0/8 21 0/8	17 2/8	4 4	Pierce County	WI	Scott A. Kruse	2007	41838
126 6/8	19 2/8 19 3/8	15 0/8	5 5	Putnam County	WV	Denny Painter	2007	41838
126 6/8	21 4/8 21 2/8	17 4/8	4 4	Wayne County	NY	Arthur M. Valletta	2007	41838
*126 6/8	23 1/8 21 4/8	18 0/8	4 4	Ramsey County	ND	Daniel Erickstad	2007	41838
126 6/8	20 1/8 19 5/8	17 7/8	5 6	Stevens County	WA	Scott Sorensen	2007	41838
*126 6/8	21 3/8 21 4/8	19 4/8	4 4	Grant County	WI	Joe Mulhern, Jr.	2008	41838
*126 6/8	21 4/8 21 5/8	16 2/8	4 5	Madison Parish	LA	John A. Lindigrin	2008	41838
126 6/8	21 1/8 21 2/8	15 2/8	4 5	Appanoose County	IA	Gary M. Grabowski	2008	41838
*126 6/8	20 7/8 20 0/8	14 6/8	5 6	Jefferson County	KS	Anthony W. Stein	2008	41838
126 6/8	21 1/8 21 1/8	14 1/8	7 7	Jackson County	OH	Gary G. Lackey	2008	41838
126 6/8	21 6/8 22 7/8	14 4/8	4 5	Portage County	WI	Erin Kalata	2008	41838
126 6/8	21 0/8 21 5/8	17 6/8	4 4	Vernon County	WI	Chris Dregne	2008	41838
126 6/8	20 0/8 20 0/8	16 2/8	5 5	Polk County	WI	Ray Little	2008	41838
*126 6/8	22 4/8 20 7/8	20 0/8	5 5	Randolph County	GA	Graham Lovett	2008	41838
126 6/8	21 6/8 18 4/8	18 4/8	4 4	McKenzie County	ND	Corey Hugelen	2008	41838
*126 6/8	23 3/8 22 5/8	17 3/8	4 5	Tensas Parish	LA	Martha D. Sumrall	2009	41838
126 6/8	20 3/8 20 6/8	16 2/8	5 5	Walsh County	ND	Philip Schanilec	2009	41838
126 6/8	20 0/8 20 5/8	15 0/8	5 4	Kimble County	TX	Stephen Longo	2009	41838
*126 6/8	21 6/8 21 6/8	16 6/8	5 5	Trempealeau County	WI	Chris J. Hood	2009	41838
126 6/8	22 5/8 22 3/8	17 2/8	4 4	Putnam County	MO	Bobby W. Hooven	2009	41838
*126 6/8	21 3/8 20 6/8	15 4/8	5 5	Mellette County	SD	Chad Mosteller	2009	41838
*126 6/8	21 2/8 21 2/8	15 6/8	4 4	Grant County	WI	Bob Johnson	2009	41838
126 6/8	20 4/8 21 7/8	17 0/8	5 5	Kosciusko County	IN	Rick Coburn	2009	41838
*126 6/8	18 7/8 20 0/8	17 0/8	5 5	Guernsey County	OH	Derek Davidson	2009	41838
126 6/8	21 2/8 23 4/8	14 2/8	5 5	Nodaway County	MO	Max Harden	2009	41838
126 6/8	20 7/8 21 2/8	15 2/8	5 5	Putnam County	MO	Trent J. Haley	2009	41838
126 6/8	21 2/8 20 2/8	17 6/8	5 5	Zapata County	TX	Charles Leon	2010	41838
126 6/8	20 5/8 20 1/8	15 0/8	4 4	Barron County	WI	Jon M. Fenske	2010	41838
126 5/8	22 3/8 22 3/8	18 5/8	4 4	Allegan County	MI	Dennis J. Mulder	1996	42109
126 5/8	19 4/8 19 6/8	17 3/8	7 5	Woodford County	KY	Andy R. Ingram	1999	42109
126 5/8	22 7/8 22 5/8	17 5/8	4 4	Pennington County	SD	Bret Hamm	1999	42109
126 5/8	24 1/8 22 5/8	16 1/8	5 4	Edmonton	ALB	Gunther Tondeleir	2001	42109
126 5/8	21 3/8 21 3/8	17 3/8	4 4	Kosciusko County	IN	Andrew D. Heckaman	2002	42109
126 5/8	21 1/8 21 3/8	15 0/8	6 4	Clark County	IL	Brad Keeney	2002	42109
126 5/8	21 7/8 21 6/8	17 5/8	5 5	Headingly	MAN	John E. Major	2003	42109
126 5/8	22 5/8 23 6/8	19 3/8	5 5	Crawford County	WI	Mike Simons	2003	42109
126 5/8	22 4/8 24 3/8	16 1/8	5 4	Clark County	IL	Michae J. Karanovich	2003	42109
*126 5/8	21 6/8 22 4/8	14 3/8	4 5	Cherokee County	OK	Dennis Covey, Jr.	2003	42109
126 5/8	21 4/8 20 5/8	18 5/8	4 5	Pawnee County	NE	James Aaron Parnell	2003	42109
126 5/8	21 1/8 20 7/8	16 1/8	5 5	Madison County	MT	Dyrk Eddie	2004	42109
126 5/8	22 0/8 21 6/8	13 3/8	4 5	Wright County	MN	Wayne Dearing	2004	42109
126 5/8	22 3/8 22 2/8	16 3/8	5 5	Buffalo County	WI	Dustin Mancl	2004	42109
126 5/8	22 2/8 21 2/8	18 5/8	4 4	Charles City County	VA	Paul H. Bendle	2004	42109
126 5/8	23 3/8 21 1/8	15 5/8	5 7	Warren County	MS	Peter Dale	2004	42109
*126 5/8	23 0/8 23 6/8	18 5/8	3 5	Clay County	MN	Shane Lee Swanson	2004	42109
126 5/8	23 0/8 21 2/8	15 1/8	4 4	Kent County	MI	Todd J Daily	2004	42109
*126 5/8	23 0/8 22 6/8	17 7/8	4 5	Lake County	IL	Rich S. Pawelczyk	2004	42109
126 5/8	24 2/8 24 5/8	15 3/8	4 5	Kent County	MI	Josef M. Huber	2004	42109
126 5/8	21 5/8 21 5/8	15 1/8	6 5	Hubbard County	MN	Bob Ness	2004	42109
*126 5/8	21 7/8 23 2/8	16 5/8	4 5	Lake County	IL	Larry DeRose	2004	42109
126 5/8	22 2/8 21 6/8	18 0/8	5 6	Carbon County	PA	Anthony A. Malaska	2004	42109
126 5/8	22 0/8 22 4/8	17 2/8	5 5	Clark County	KS	Greg Pike	2004	42109
*126 5/8	23 0/8 21 2/8	16 3/8	5 4	Audrain County	MO	Marvin Benskin	2004	42109
126 5/8	21 6/8 21 4/8	20 7/8	4 4	Montgomery County	PA	Lance F. Maleski	2005	42109
126 5/8	22 2/8 21 7/8	16 7/8	5 6	Butler County	KY	Brandon Miller	2005	42109
126 5/8	22 0/8 21 1/8	17 7/8	4 4	Hand County	SD	Travis Sivertsen	2005	42109
126 5/8	20 2/8 21 1/8	16 5/8	5 5	Lawrence County	PA	David Messner	2005	42109

Deer entries below 141 0/8, that appeared in the 6th Edition, are not included here, but are included on the accompanying CD (see page 119), and also in the Club's Records Archives.

617

WHITETAIL DEER (TYPICAL ANTLERS)

Minimum Score 125 — Continued

SCORE	R MAIN BEAM L	INSIDE SPREAD	R POINTS L	AREA	STATE/ PROVINCE	HUNTER'S NAME	DATE	RANK
126 5/8	23 1/8 23 0/8	16 1/8	5 5	Jackson County	WI	Paul Bilello	2005	42109
126 5/8	20 4/8 20 2/8	17 1/8	5 5	Clearfield County	PA	James Sinclair	2005	42109
*126 5/8	19 3/8 21 6/8	15 7/8	7 5	Christian County	KY	Tim Thomas	2005	42109
126 5/8	21 7/8 20 5/8	18 5/8	5 5	Jo Daviess County	IL	Dale Goytowski	2005	42109
126 5/8	19 1/8 19 1/8	15 0/8	6 7	Steuben County	IN	David Harris	2005	42109
126 5/8	21 2/8 21 2/8	17 5/8	5 5	Allegheny County	PA	Richard E. Kienzle	2005	42109
126 5/8	21 7/8 21 0/8	19 3/8	4 4	Suffolk County	NY	Michael Scavone	2005	42109
126 5/8	19 6/8 19 3/8	14 7/8	5 5	Juneau County	WI	Roger Balogh	2005	42109
126 5/8	22 4/8 24 0/8	18 1/8	5 4	Bartow County	GA	Jeff Hutcheson	2005	42109
126 5/8	21 3/8 22 4/8	15 1/8	5 4	Menard County	IL	Chad Loy	2005	42109
*126 5/8	21 7/8 21 5/8	17 0/8	8 6	Stevens County	WA	Wade Bogart, Sr.	2006	42109
126 5/8	21 1/8 20 5/8	14 5/8	5 5	Putnam County	WV	Robert Siders	2006	42109
*126 5/8	22 6/8 23 1/8	15 7/8	5 6	Oakland County	MI	Tom Schettling	2006	42109
126 5/8	19 7/8 18 7/8	15 1/8	5 5	Waupaca County	WI	Brian M. Wolfe	2006	42109
126 5/8	21 6/8 23 2/8	21 7/8	4 4	Lyon County	KS	Shawn Hugg	2006	42109
126 5/8	22 7/8 23 0/8	17 1/8	4 4	Buffalo County	WI	Randy Springborn	2006	42109
126 5/8	21 5/8 21 1/8	16 1/8	5 5	Portage County	WI	Steve Van Camp	2006	42109
126 5/8	22 3/8 22 6/8	16 5/8	4 4	Outagamie County	WI	Ed Verkuilen	2006	42109
126 5/8	23 0/8 23 2/8	18 5/8	4 4	Salem County	NJ	Tom Burns	2006	42109
*126 5/8	22 1/8 21 4/8	15 7/8	7 4	Webb County	TX	Richard H. Gross	2006	42109
126 5/8	20 2/8 19 2/8	15 0/8	6 7	Spokane County	WA	Lon E. Lauber	2006	42109
126 5/8	19 0/8 20 4/8	17 1/8	5 5	Lewis & Clark County	MT	Sonny Templeton	2007	42109
*126 5/8	19 7/8 18 2/8	15 1/8	4 5	Isanti County	MN	Jamie Freudenberg	2007	42109
*126 5/8	22 0/8 20 6/8	19 1/8	4 4	Washington County	WI	Todd Gillard	2007	42109
*126 5/8	23 7/8 23 4/8	19 1/8	4 4	Douglas County	NE	Travis Van Houten	2007	42109
126 5/8	23 0/8 23 6/8	19 3/8	5 4	Fond du Lac County	WI	Dave Sabel	2007	42109
*126 5/8	20 7/8 20 7/8	16 5/8	6 6	Young County	TX	Brad Hawpe	2007	42109
126 5/8	21 3/8 21 1/8	16 7/8	5 4	Buffalo County	WI	Macail Henderson	2007	42109
126 5/8	22 1/8 22 1/8	17 1/8	4 5	Callaway County	MO	Clarence F. Dains	2007	42109
*126 5/8	22 1/8 22 4/8	15 1/8	5 5	Laurens County	SC	Royce J. Carter	2007	42109
126 5/8	18 3/8 19 1/8	15 1/8	5 5	Elk County	KS	David Contreras	2007	42109
126 5/8	24 5/8 23 4/8	17 3/8	5 6	Hand County	SD	Bruce Briesemeister	2007	42109
126 5/8	21 4/8 22 7/8	17 7/8	6 4	Rice County	KS	Collen L. Steffen	2007	42109
*126 5/8	22 5/8 22 4/8	15 1/8	4 4	Harris County	GA	Blake Voltz	2007	42109
126 5/8	21 3/8 21 4/8	17 3/8	5 5	Kenedy County	TX	Bob Gilbert	2008	42109
126 5/8	21 1/8 20 5/8	16 4/8	9 8	Madison County	MT	Jim Kennedy	2008	42109
*126 5/8	21 3/8 21 0/8	16 3/8	5 4	Mitchell County	IA	Mike Betts	2008	42109
*126 5/8	22 5/8 22 3/8	16 1/8	4 4	Clay County	MO	John M. Lauderdale	2008	42109
126 5/8	22 7/8 23 6/8	15 1/8	4 4	Henry County	KY	Michael K. Lee	2008	42109
*126 5/8	21 4/8 21 4/8	16 7/8	6 4	Monroe County	WI	Rick Tully	2008	42109
126 5/8	20 1/8 19 5/8	13 5/8	5 5	Pike County	IL	Thomas J. Beissel	2008	42109
*126 5/8	21 5/8 21 0/8	17 5/8	5 5	Daviess County	IN	Kevin Dean Graber	2008	42109
*126 5/8	23 0/8 22 3/8	19 3/8	4 4	Schuylkill County	PA	Jeff V. Stahler	2008	42109
126 5/8	24 0/8 23 7/8	17 1/8	5 4	Comanche County	KS	Stephen Updegraff	2008	42109
*126 5/8	23 0/8 23 2/8	16 1/8	4 4	La Salle Parish	LA	Chuck Lucas	2008	42109
*126 5/8	20 1/8 20 0/8	14 7/8	4 4	Saline County	KS	Gary Nelson	2008	42109
*126 5/8	19 2/8 20 3/8	15 7/8	5 5	Sutton County	TX	Steve Osborne	2008	42109
*126 5/8	21 7/8 20 4/8	14 5/8	4 5	Kanabec County	MN	Fred Marsolek	2009	42109
126 5/8	20 2/8 22 6/8	17 1/8	5 4	Schuyler County	IL	Joe Riva	2009	42109
126 5/8	20 1/8 20 0/8	16 7/8	4 4	Columbia County	GA	Ralph Blackwelder	2009	42109
*126 5/8	21 4/8 20 7/8	15 3/8	6 6	Queen Annes County	MD	Jonathan Uyttewaal	2009	42109
126 5/8	22 5/8 21 3/8	16 1/8	5 4	Muskingum County	OH	William Badgley	2009	42109
126 5/8	21 7/8 22 1/8	15 3/8	6 5	Coahoma County	MS	Scott Flowers	2009	42109
126 5/8	21 4/8 22 2/8	16 7/8	4 5	Glasscock County	TX	Joey Pinard	2009	42109
126 4/8	21 1/8 21 1/8	16 6/8	4 4	Miami County	IN	Zachary Lawson	2001	42350
126 4/8	21 1/8 20 7/8	15 2/8	4 6	Brookings County	SD	Charles M. Lundin	2001	42350
*126 4/8	22 3/8 21 5/8	14 7/8	5 5	Coffey County	KS	Don Erbert	2002	42350
126 4/8	21 3/8 20 1/8	15 6/8	4 4	Green Lake County	WI	Douglas B. Werch	2002	42350
126 4/8	22 1/8 23 4/8	17 2/8	4 4	Hendricks County	IN	John Hasenauer	2002	42350
126 4/8	22 2/8 23 1/8	17 0/8	6 6	Columbia County	WI	Matthew B. Braaksma	2003	42350
*126 4/8	19 2/8 20 0/8	18 4/8	4 4	Sarpy County	NE	Jay Kocian	2004	42350
*126 4/8	21 1/8 22 7/8	18 0/8	8 7	Prairie County	AR	Jon B. Foster	2004	42350
*126 4/8	19 6/8 20 6/8	16 1/8	7 6	Sullivan County	IN	Wesley A. Forker	2004	42350
126 4/8	20 5/8 20 6/8	15 6/8	5 6	Montgomery County	IN	Tim Congleton	2004	42350
126 4/8	20 1/8 20 1/8	14 2/8	4 5	Colfax County	NE	Brian Kehrli	2004	42350
126 4/8	20 2/8 21 4/8	19 0/8	4 4	Marquette County	WI	Marty T. Clauson	2004	42350
*126 4/8	21 7/8 21 7/8	14 4/8	4 4	Sawyer County	WI	Troy Hafele	2004	42350
126 4/8	23 1/8 23 2/8	16 4/8	5 5	DeKalb County	IL	Jeffrey B. Johnson	2004	42350
126 4/8	22 4/8 22 4/8	16 6/8	4 4	Sussex County	DE	Thomas W. Rash III	2004	42350
126 4/8	23 2/8 24 0/8	18 6/8	4 5	Miami County	IN	Richard Eldridge	2004	42350
126 4/8	20 1/8 19 7/8	13 4/8	5 5	Pike County	IL	Kevin Thorburn	2004	42350
126 4/8	21 4/8 20 4/8	15 2/8	6 5	Chickasaw County	IA	Kirk Ackerson	2004	42350
126 4/8	19 5/8 19 7/8	15 0/8	5 5	McKenzie County	ND	Ronald K. Jackson II	2005	42350
126 4/8	22 0/8 21 3/8	15 4/8	4 4	Grant County	WI	Jeremy Hampton	2005	42350
*126 4/8	22 5/8 22 0/8	18 0/8	4 4	Rolette County	ND	Riley Zavada	2005	42350
*126 4/8	21 6/8 22 5/8	15 5/8	5 7	Day County	SD	Scott Gangle	2005	42350
*126 4/8	21 1/8 21 1/8	17 2/8	5 5	Marathon County	WI	Jason Richmond	2005	42350
126 4/8	19 7/8 20 4/8	15 6/8	5 4	Jackson County	MI	Susan R. Ziegler	2005	42350
126 4/8	21 3/8 22 2/8	18 2/8	4 5	Sarpy County	NE	Lon E. Lauber	2005	42350
126 4/8	20 6/8 20 2/8	14 4/8	5 5	Van Buren County	IA	Alan L. Francis	2005	42350
126 4/8	24 6/8 23 7/8	17 2/8	6 5	Will County	IL	Irv Lusk	2005	42350
*126 4/8	19 6/8 20 0/8	15 4/8	4 4	Comanche County	KS	Kyle M. Meintzer	2005	42350
126 4/8	18 6/8 21 1/8	16 2/8	5 6	Bond County	IL	Gary Netzler	2005	42350
126 4/8	18 3/8 17 4/8	13 4/8	5 5	Logan County	KY	Matthew R. Overholt	2005	42350
126 4/8	21 6/8 22 7/8	15 4/8	5 5	Buffalo County	WI	Gary Fleishauer	2005	42350
126 4/8	21 1/8 20 4/8	14 0/8	5 4	Otter Tail County	MN	Larry King	2006	42350
126 4/8	20 2/8 20 2/8	16 0/8	5 7	Brown County	WI	Jerry Morris	2006	42350
126 4/8	25 0/8 25 4/8	16 4/8	5 5	Frederick County	VA	Clay Harrison	2006	42350
126 4/8	20 5/8 20 6/8	16 2/8	4 5	Jefferson County	WI	Lyle Reich	2006	42350
126 4/8	22 7/8 23 5/8	17 6/8	4 4	Dunn County	WI	Josh Nave	2006	42350
126 4/8	19 5/8 20 1/8	12 5/8	5 5	Columbia County	WI	Dustin A. Hoffmann	2006	42350
*126 4/8	21 3/8 21 3/8	17 4/8	4 4	Pike County	IL	Clark Thorne	2006	42350
*126 4/8	21 0/8 20 5/8	14 2/8	4 5	Ross County	OH	Dustin A. Bethel	2006	42350
126 4/8	22 0/8 21 7/8	16 4/8	4 4	Armstrong County	PA	Allen Randal Smith	2006	42350
126 4/8	21 0/8 20 2/8	17 0/8	5 4	Orleans County	NY	Gerry Rightmyer	2006	42350

WHITETAIL DEER (TYPICAL ANTLERS)

Minimum Score 125 Continued

SCORE	LENGTH OF R MAIN BEAM L		INSIDE SPREAD	NUMBER OF R POINTS L		AREA	STATE/ PROVINCE	HUNTER'S NAME	DATE	RANK
*126 4/8	21 1/8	20 3/8	18 2/8	5	5	Tuscarawas County	OH	Kai Rieger	2006	42350
126 4/8	22 3/8	23 3/8	15 4/8	4	5	Genesee County	NY	William H. Williams III	2006	42350
*126 4/8	21 6/8	21 3/8	15 4/8	5	5	Jefferson County	IA	Douglas J. Kennedy	2006	42350
126 4/8	20 2/8	20 4/8	15 2/8	5	5	Buffalo County	WI	Michael F. Yira	2006	42350
126 4/8	20 0/8	20 1/8	16 2/8	5	5	St. Joseph County	MI	Douglas Houser	2006	42350
*126 4/8	21 4/8	20 2/8	16 0/8	5	4	Spencer County	IN	Chris Ewing	2006	42350
*126 4/8	19 1/8	20 4/8	16 4/8	4	4	Kingsbury County	SD	Mike Beyer	2006	42350
126 4/8	20 5/8	20 5/8	14 6/8	5	5	Rhea County	TN	Corwin W. Smith	2006	42350
126 4/8	21 3/8	21 5/8	15 2/8	5	4	Carroll County	MS	James William Wood, Jr.	2006	42350
126 4/8	22 2/8	24 0/8	16 2/8	5	5	Crittenden County	AR	Charles Pate	2006	42350
126 4/8	19 1/8	18 5/8	17 2/8	5	5	Fond du Lac County	WI	Patty Schmitz	2007	42350
*126 4/8	20 2/8	19 2/8	17 2/8	4	4	Morgan County	GA	Jason Simmons	2007	42350
*126 4/8	21 4/8	22 0/8	16 4/8	4	4	Morris County	NJ	Douglas F. Emann, Jr.	2007	42350
126 4/8	21 0/8	21 1/8	17 4/8	4	5	Roberts County	SD	Ryan Biel	2007	42350
126 4/8	22 5/8	22 4/8	17 4/8	5	5	Ripley County	MO	James Newton	2007	42350
126 4/8	22 7/8	22 2/8	19 6/8	4	4	Clark County	WI	Steven M. Kosmosky	2007	42350
*126 4/8	22 6/8	23 1/8	18 4/8	4	5	Shawano County	WI	James Snortum	2007	42350
126 4/8	21 2/8	20 5/8	16 0/8	4	4	Adams County	WI	Brandon Popp	2007	42350
126 4/8	22 0/8	23 2/8	18 2/8	6	4	Decatur County	IA	Steve Powles	2007	42350
126 4/8	22 4/8	22 7/8	18 0/8	4	4	Clarke County	VA	Alex C. Blackburn	2007	42350
*126 4/8	22 6/8	21 7/8	18 2/8	5	4	Pierce County	WI	Sean M. Riley	2007	42350
126 4/8	24 1/8	23 3/8	17 2/8	4	4	Livingston County	NY	Jacob Hughes	2007	42350
*126 4/8	19 4/8	19 6/8	13 0/8	5	5	Jackson County	MI	Andrew C. May	2007	42350
126 4/8	19 2/8	20 0/8	15 6/8	6	5	Rice County	MN	Christopher J. Cordes	2007	42350
126 4/8	22 1/8	22 3/8	15 6/8	5	4	Jackson County	OH	Jim Ridge	2007	42350
126 4/8	20 1/8	20 6/8	16 4/8	5	5	Denton County	TX	Jeremy Leger	2008	42350
*126 4/8	21 6/8	21 3/8	16 6/8	4	4	Guilford County	NC	Jeff Ferguson	2008	42350
126 4/8	22 0/8	21 1/8	16 2/8	7	7	Grant County	WI	David C. Underwood	2008	42350
126 4/8	20 0/8	21 1/8	17 4/8	4	4	Cedar County	NE	Reggie Hochstein	2008	42350
126 4/8	22 0/8	22 4/8	19 0/8	4	4	Potter County	PA	Bradley Hutzell	2008	42350
126 4/8	21 6/8	23 4/8	16 4/8	4	4	Henry County	IA	Bruce Krause	2008	42350
126 4/8	22 0/8	21 5/8	16 4/8	5	5	Anoka County	MN	Brian Chou	2008	42350
126 4/8	18 7/8	19 4/8	14 6/8	5	5	Douglas County	WI	Connie M. Ajer	2008	42350
126 4/8	21 4/8	22 7/8	15 5/8	4	5	Greene County	OH	Jeremy Short	2008	42350
126 4/8	23 1/8	22 5/8	17 3/8	7	8	Clay County	SD	Joe Martz	2008	42350
126 4/8	20 1/8	20 4/8	14 6/8	5	5	Jackson County	WI	Kris L. Bruley	2008	42350
126 4/8	20 0/8	19 7/8	18 3/8	5	6	Cowley County	KS	Frederick P. Hanson	2008	42350
126 4/8	24 0/8	23 5/8	13 5/8	4	6	Saline County	KS	Paul C. Powell	2008	42350
*126 4/8	21 6/8	21 4/8	20 6/8	4	4	Morris County	NJ	Daniel Koval	2009	42350
126 4/8	19 6/8	19 7/8	16 4/8	5	5	Buffalo County	WI	Cindy Metzger	2009	42350
*126 4/8	22 3/8	22 7/8	18 0/8	4	4	Marquette County	WI	Daniel E. Vogelsang	2009	42350
*126 4/8	21 4/8	22 4/8	18 6/8	5	4	Kent County	MI	Jeff Godfrey	2009	42350
*126 4/8	20 4/8	21 1/8	16 6/8	5	5	Harrison County	OH	Timm Cetts	2009	42350
126 4/8	22 1/8	22 5/8	17 2/8	3	4	Ferry County	WA	Chad Berry	2009	42350
126 4/8	21 4/8	21 2/8	17 2/8	5	5	Wilson Township	ONT	Ken Leppert	2009	42350
*126 4/8	22 2/8	22 0/8	17 4/8	5	6	Douglas County	WI	Joe Doskey	2009	42350
126 3/8	19 7/8	20 7/8	16 7/8	5	4	Winneshiek County	IA	Tim Everding	1993	42627
126 3/8	20 2/8	20 4/8	16 3/8	4	4	Winnebago County	IL	Marvin A. Longenecker	1994	42627
126 3/8	16 4/8	24 0/8	18 2/8	8	7	Cambria County	PA	Joseph V. Panczak	2002	42627
126 3/8	21 4/8	19 3/8	14 1/8	5	4	Van Buren County	MI	Scotty D. Goodwin	2002	42627
126 3/8	22 3/8	22 7/8	23 6/8	4	4	Marshall County	IL	Hubert Boatwright	2002	42627
126 3/8	19 1/8	20 5/8	16 5/8	5	5	Cedar County	NE	Kent Hochstein	2003	42627
126 3/8	20 5/8	21 2/8	16 7/8	5	5	De Kalb County	AL	Sammy Berry	2003	42627
126 3/8	22 4/8	22 0/8	17 3/8	5	4	Middlesex County	MA	Chad Bates	2003	42627
126 3/8	22 4/8	22 6/8	16 1/8	4	4	Hartford County	CT	Michael Slayton	2004	42627
126 3/8	22 1/8	22 1/8	16 3/8	5	4	Brooks County	TX	Travis Dreibelbis	2004	42627
126 3/8	20 6/8	21 4/8	17 5/8	5	5	Washburn County	WI	David Marker	2004	42627
126 3/8	19 6/8	20 0/8	14 5/8	5	6	McHenry County	ND	Jeff Jacobs	2004	42627
*126 3/8	25 5/8	21 2/8	20 2/8	4	5	Vermilion County	IL	Jack W. Toms, Jr.	2004	42627
*126 3/8	22 2/8	21 2/8	16 3/8	4	5	Muskegon County	MI	Brian Harwood	2004	42627
126 3/8	23 4/8	22 5/8	17 5/8	4	4	Clark County	WI	Tom Brown	2004	42627
126 3/8	21 6/8	21 7/8	17 3/8	6	4	Barber County	KS	Fernando Semiao	2004	42627
*126 3/8	22 3/8	22 2/8	19 4/8	4	6	Hancock County	WV	Steve Seminsky	2004	42627
126 3/8	21 2/8	22 5/8	16 6/8	4	4	Tyler County	TX	Michael Rubino	2004	42627
126 3/8	21 1/8	21 5/8	17 3/8	6	4	Cattaraugus County	NY	John Gemza	2004	42627
126 3/8	22 1/8	22 2/8	17 6/8	6	4	Tom Green County	TX	Brenton Leake	2004	42627
126 3/8	19 7/8	20 1/8	16 1/8	4	4	Lake County	IL	Sam Azarian	2005	42627
126 3/8	22 3/8	21 7/8	19 3/8	4	4	Morris County	NJ	Ken Biss	2005	42627
126 3/8	23 7/8	23 1/8	17 7/8	5	4	Vanderburgh County	IN	Nick Stratman	2005	42627
126 3/8	20 6/8	21 5/8	18 5/8	5	5	Kosciusko County	IN	Richard A. Wright	2005	42627
126 3/8	19 2/8	19 1/8	14 3/8	5	5	Mille Lacs County	MN	Stephanie Anderson	2005	42627
126 3/8	20 7/8	20 5/8	13 7/8	5	5	Lorain County	OH	Erick Swanson	2005	42627
126 3/8	21 6/8	21 3/8	14 7/8	5	5	Allegheny County	PA	Bruce Kovach	2005	42627
126 3/8	20 1/8	21 0/8	18 1/8	4	4	Dearborn County	IN	James H. Dell	2005	42627
126 3/8	21 6/8	21 5/8	15 3/8	4	4	Lenawee County	MI	James W. Lyons	2005	42627
126 3/8	20 7/8	20 2/8	16 7/8	4	4	Dundy County	NE	Ronald L. King	2005	42627
126 3/8	22 4/8	22 4/8	17 7/8	5	4	Buffalo County	WI	Rod Springborn	2005	42627
126 3/8	21 3/8	20 4/8	14 1/8	4	4	Alexander County	IL	Terry Kepley	2005	42627
126 3/8	19 6/8	20 0/8	14 3/8	5	5	Brown County	WI	Jim Diny	2005	42627
126 3/8	20 6/8	20 4/8	16 7/8	4	4	Niagara County	NY	Dan Albee	2005	42627
126 3/8	23 3/8	22 6/8	17 5/8	5	4	Meigs County	OH	Jack Satterfield, Jr.	2005	42627
126 3/8	23 1/8	22 6/8	19 7/8	4	4	Menard County	TX	Philip R. Harris	2005	42627
126 3/8	22 4/8	20 7/8	16 5/8	5	4	Pierce County	WI	Jens H. Loberg	2006	42627
126 3/8	20 7/8	19 4/8	14 3/8	5	6	Jackson County	MI	Bryon Keith Coppernoll	2006	42627
126 3/8	22 6/8	23 4/8	14 7/8	5	5	Poinsett County	AR	Jonathan Horst	2006	42627
126 3/8	21 5/8	21 7/8	17 5/8	4	4	Lincoln County	WV	John A. Simeral	2006	42627
*126 3/8	22 4/8	21 4/8	17 7/8	5	5	Douglas County	NE	Doug Schmidt	2006	42627
126 3/8	19 0/8	18 4/8	14 2/8	6	7	Miami County	IN	Jeff Harshman	2006	42627
126 3/8	21 3/8	22 3/8	18 7/8	6	9	Allegheny County	PA	Michael Turnell	2006	42627
*126 3/8	20 4/8	20 6/8	16 3/8	4	5	Coshocton County	OH	Justin S. Abbott	2006	42627
126 3/8	21 4/8	21 1/8	15 2/8	4	4	Warrick County	IN	Rance Carter	2006	42627
126 3/8	21 1/8	21 3/8	19 3/8	6	5	Athens County	OH	Philip R. King	2006	42627
126 3/8	22 2/8	24 2/8	16 5/8	5	6	Buffalo County	WI	Jason Leirmo	2006	42627
126 3/8	24 7/8	26 4/8	15 0/8	6	4	York County	PA	Gary Hostler	2006	42627
126 3/8	20 2/8	20 3/8	14 5/8	5	5	Pike County	AR	Michael A. Loy	2006	42627

Deer entries below 141 0/8, that appeared in the 6th Edition, are not included here, but are included on the accompanying CD (see page 119), and also in the Club's Records Archives.

WHITETAIL DEER (TYPICAL ANTLERS)

Minimum Score 125 — Continued

SCORE	R MAIN BEAM L	INSIDE SPREAD	R POINTS L	AREA	STATE/ PROVINCE	HUNTER'S NAME	DATE	RANK
126 3/8	20 6/8 22 1/8	18 5/8	4 4	Baltimore County	MD	Lee Haile	2006	42627
*126 3/8	23 0/8 23 1/8	12 5/8	4 4	Menard County	IL	Blake Henderson	2006	42627
126 3/8	20 2/8 20 3/8	18 3/8	5 5	Macoupin County	IL	Steven Dale	2006	42627
126 3/8	21 3/8 22 7/8	16 5/8	5 4	Polk County	IA	Travis Husted	2006	42627
126 3/8	25 1/8 20 7/8	17 5/8	6 5	Cook County	IL	Joseph F. Mack	2007	42627
126 3/8	22 2/8 22 1/8	12 5/8	5 5	Person County	NC	Gregory H. Rose	2007	42627
126 3/8	19 6/8 20 2/8	16 7/8	4 4	Monroe County	NY	Timothy M. Wahls	2007	42627
*126 3/8	19 3/8 19 6/8	14 3/8	5 5	Cerro Gordo County	IA	Christa Harms	2007	42627
126 3/8	22 0/8 21 7/8	17 7/8	4 4	Kosciusko County	IN	Jeremy Bowers	2007	42627
*126 3/8	20 6/8 21 0/8	16 1/8	4 5	Portage County	WI	Michael Maslinski	2007	42627
*126 3/8	19 0/8 19 1/8	14 5/8	5 5	Burleigh County	ND	Ken Clark	2007	42627
*126 3/8	22 1/8 23 6/8	15 3/8	5 6	Yancey County	NC	Joe Williams	2007	42627
126 3/8	18 7/8 19 0/8	15 5/8	5 5	Hughes County	OK	Tom Cartwright	2007	42627
126 3/8	19 7/8 20 2/8	19 3/8	4 4	Eau Claire County	WI	Johnny Onarheim	2007	42627
126 3/8	21 2/8 22 2/8	16 7/8	5 7	Park County	MT	George Kamps	2007	42627
126 3/8	23 2/8 23 4/8	15 3/8	4 4	Grant County	ND	Gregory S. Eider	2008	42627
*126 3/8	23 2/8 20 4/8	16 7/8	6 6	Linn County	MO	David Box	2008	42627
126 3/8	21 4/8 20 7/8	14 5/8	5 5	Wilkes County	NC	Anthony Blake Tilley	2008	42627
*126 3/8	22 4/8 22 0/8	17 7/8	5 5	Trempealeau County	WI	Gary Clark	2008	42627
126 3/8	22 4/8 22 2/8	18 1/8	4 4	Sangamon County	IL	Jerry Bugbee	2008	42627
126 3/8	19 1/8 19 0/8	15 5/8	5 5	Pottawatomie County	KS	Kevin J. Thorburn	2008	42627
*126 3/8	21 4/8 21 1/8	17 4/8	5 5	Brown County	WI	Tim Noe	2008	42627
*126 3/8	23 0/8 24 0/8	16 6/8	6 4	Lake County	IL	Trent Schneider	2008	42627
*126 3/8	21 6/8 22 4/8	14 3/8	4 4	Ramsey County	ND	Dan Erickstad	2008	42627
126 3/8	22 4/8 20 4/8	19 6/8	5 5	Polk County	WI	Larry L. Root	2009	42627
126 3/8	23 0/8 23 4/8	17 6/8	5 5	Chester County	PA	Roger Summers	2009	42627
*126 3/8	22 0/8 22 4/8	15 4/8	6 6	Pike County	IL	Lonnie Manalia	2009	42627
126 3/8	23 7/8 22 0/8	15 7/8	4 5	Clark County	IN	Stephen Morris	2009	42627
126 3/8	23 1/8 22 2/8	18 3/8	4 4	Grenada County	MS	Tom Lipe	2009	42627
126 3/8	24 4/8 24 2/8	20 1/8	5 4	Worcester County	MA	Jon Salisbury	2009	42627
*126 3/8	20 4/8 20 5/8	17 1/8	4 5	Barnes County	ND	Larry M. Wagner	2009	42627
*126 3/8	21 7/8 22 0/8	17 7/8	4 5	Lake County	IL	Mike Willand	2009	42627
*126 3/8	21 6/8 21 0/8	15 5/8	7 6	Carroll County	MO	Justin McMillan	2009	42627
126 3/8	19 6/8 19 6/8	15 6/8	6 9	Columbia County	WI	Eric L. Hamele	2010	42627
126 3/8	19 6/8 19 1/8	16 4/8	5 6	Meriwether County	GA	Drew Barnett	2010	42627
126 2/8	20 5/8 21 5/8	17 2/8	5 4	Butler County	MO	Tracy Crowley	1999	42893
126 2/8	21 6/8 20 3/8	16 0/8	5 5	Coahuila	MEX	Ernest "Kit" Alsop, MD	2000	42893
126 2/8	28 6/8 22 6/8	15 2/8	4 4	Allegheny County	PA	S. Andrew Wright	2002	42893
*126 2/8	22 6/8 21 5/8	18 4/8	5 5	Logan County	WV	Richard J. Prine	2002	42893
126 2/8	21 6/8 22 1/8	17 0/8	7 7	Marshall County	SD	Michael William Werner	2003	42893
126 2/8	22 7/8 23 4/8	16 6/8	4 4	Tazewell County	IL	Rich Kober	2003	42893
126 2/8	19 6/8 20 5/8	15 2/8	5 5	Roane County	TN	Tony Guinn	2004	42893
126 2/8	22 7/8 23 0/8	18 4/8	4 6	Columbiana County	OH	Larry Welton	2004	42893
126 2/8	20 0/8 20 7/8	16 6/8	5 6	Mercer County	PA	James Lakin	2004	42893
126 2/8	21 3/8 20 4/8	14 6/8	5 5	Adams County	WI	Michael R. Stadler	2004	42893
126 2/8	20 2/8 20 1/8	17 4/8	5 5	Houston County	MN	Robert Boland	2004	42893
126 2/8	22 5/8 23 0/8	17 2/8	4 5	Buffalo County	WI	Duane Dubiel	2004	42893
*126 2/8	18 3/8 19 0/8	15 6/8	4 4	Minnehaha County	SD	Dan Wheeler	2004	42893
126 2/8	21 6/8 21 4/8	16 4/8	5 4	Madison County	IL	Brent Barrows	2004	42893
*126 2/8	22 6/8 21 7/8	15 2/8	5 5	Pike County	IL	Richard Rheaume	2004	42893
126 2/8	18 5/8 19 5/8	16 7/8	5 6	Calhoun County	IL	Steve Hardy	2004	42893
126 2/8	24 4/8 23 1/8	19 0/8	5 6	Brown County	IL	Scott A. Knupp	2004	42893
*126 2/8	22 0/8 23 0/8	17 4/8	5 5	Trempealeau County	WI	Josh Rank	2005	42893
126 2/8	22 1/8 21 7/8	17 2/8	4 4	Hughes County	OK	Ray E. Combs	2005	42893
126 2/8	18 7/8 18 0/8	16 0/8	4 5	Norman County	MN	Matt Babler	2005	42893
126 2/8	22 6/8 21 2/8	20 4/8	4 4	Hennepin County	MN	Robert Wagoner	2005	42893
*126 2/8	20 2/8 20 0/8	14 6/8	5 5	Cayuga County	NY	Steven J. Sherman	2005	42893
126 2/8	21 7/8 20 4/8	18 4/8	4 4	Burnett County	WI	Dom Navarro	2005	42893
126 2/8	18 7/8 19 2/8	16 0/8	5 5	Columbia County	WI	Gary L. Carpenter	2005	42893
*126 2/8	18 4/8 18 4/8	11 6/8	5 5	Richardson County	NE	Jack D. Day, Sr.	2005	42893
126 2/8	21 6/8 21 4/8	16 2/8	4 5	Burnett County	WI	Tracy Schiebel	2005	42893
*126 2/8	22 5/8 22 5/8	14 3/8	6 6	Hubbard County	MN	John Haus	2005	42893
126 2/8	23 2/8 24 0/8	20 2/8	5 5	Mercer County	NJ	Antonio Prete	2005	42893
126 2/8	23 0/8 21 3/8	16 2/8	5 4	Wabash County	IL	Jason Poreda	2005	42893
126 2/8	22 0/8 22 7/8	17 6/8	5 4	Calumet County	WI	Michael G. Schwarz	2005	42893
126 2/8	23 4/8 25 2/8	18 3/8	4 5	Bourbon County	KS	Lawrence Cody Cutler	2006	42893
126 2/8	22 1/8 22 7/8	15 2/8	5 5	St. Louis County	MN	Robert T. Forrest	2006	42893
126 2/8	20 6/8 20 0/8	15 5/8	6 5	Sutton County	TX	Joe Tamburello III	2006	42893
126 2/8	23 2/8 22 4/8	18 6/8	4 4	Eaton County	MI	David R. Olmstead	2006	42893
*126 2/8	22 4/8 23 1/8	17 0/8	4 4	Seward County	NE	Travis Kittelson	2006	42893
126 2/8	21 4/8 21 4/8	13 0/8	5 5	Clay County	MN	Walter J. Palmer	2006	42893
126 2/8	25 6/8 26 1/8	21 6/8	5 4	Jefferson County	KS	Mutt Wilson	2006	42893
*126 2/8	20 6/8 20 6/8	15 0/8	5 5	Steuben County	NY	Clyde Sosnovik	2006	42893
126 2/8	22 5/8 22 5/8	15 6/8	4 4	Door County	WI	Greg Coulthurst	2006	42893
126 2/8	23 4/8 22 6/8	16 4/8	4 4	Prince William County	VA	Ted Williams	2006	42893
126 2/8	20 6/8 18 5/8	15 4/8	4 5	Morris County	NJ	Mark Spoto	2006	42893
126 2/8	21 0/8 21 0/8	16 2/8	4 5	Spokane County	WA	Greg McCollough	2007	42893
126 2/8	22 5/8 22 4/8	18 0/8	5 6	Monmouth County	NJ	Chris Schmidt	2007	42893
126 2/8	19 6/8 19 3/8	15 4/8	4 4	Mille Lacs County	MN	Randy L. Sundberg	2007	42893
126 2/8	23 3/8 21 0/8	16 6/8	5 7	Wyandot County	OH	Aaron Leightey	2007	42893
*126 2/8	23 3/8 22 6/8	21 0/8	4 4	Champaign County	OH	John May	2007	42893
*126 2/8	21 2/8 21 2/8	15 0/8	4 4	Hancock County	IL	Don Beveridge	2007	42893
126 2/8	23 6/8 23 0/8	17 6/8	6 5	Monroe County	NY	Shawn Thompson	2007	42893
126 2/8	19 2/8 19 4/8	12 7/8	6 5	Champaign County	IL	Barry A. Schlickman	2007	42893
126 2/8	22 1/8 20 7/8	16 0/8	5 5	Dawson County	NE	Shawn Church	2007	42893
126 2/8	21 1/8 22 2/8	17 2/8	5 4	Fulton County	IL	Michael J. Fazende	2007	42893
*126 2/8	22 7/8 21 7/8	20 0/8	4 6	Licking County	OH	Jeff Lee	2007	42893
126 2/8	19 5/8 19 5/8	14 2/8	6 5	Hamilton County	IL	Michael E. Tinsley	2007	42893
126 2/8	20 6/8 21 2/8	14 0/8	5 4	Johnson County	IA	Gary E. Rohret	2007	42893
*126 2/8	23 4/8 22 5/8	20 0/8	7 7	Washington County	MN	Patrick Ellias	2008	42893
126 2/8	20 5/8 20 0/8	16 2/8	5 4	Troup County	GA	David A. Lock	2008	42893
126 2/8	21 2/8 20 3/8	14 6/8	5 5	Martin County	IN	Paul D. Little	2008	42893
*126 2/8	21 0/8 20 7/8	16 5/8	5 5	Lafayette County	WI	Steven Lovell	2008	42893
126 2/8	21 1/8 21 3/8	17 6/8	5 6	Carroll County	IL	Marvin A. Longenecker	2008	42893
*126 2/8	22 7/8 22 2/8	17 4/8	4 4	Dixon County	NE	Matt Buresh	2008	42893

WHITETAIL DEER (TYPICAL ANTLERS)

Minimum Score 125   Continued

Score	R Main Beam L	Inside Spread	R Points L	Area	State/Province	Hunter's Name	Date	Rank
*126 2/8	22 0/8 22 0/8	16 2/8	5 5	Fountain County	IN	Joshua Clemence	2008	42893
126 2/8	23 6/8 22 7/8	17 6/8	4 4	Fulton County	IL	Robert A. Hammerich	2008	42893
*126 2/8	19 4/8 20 4/8	17 2/8	6 7	Fond du Lac County	WI	Greg R. Marshall	2008	42893
*126 2/8	19 7/8 18 7/8	14 2/8	5 5	Kanabec County	MN	David Shockman	2008	42893
126 2/8	21 0/8 20 6/8	15 6/8	7 6	Saunders County	NE	Travis Van Houten	2009	42893
*126 2/8	24 5/8 24 1/8	17 7/8	5 6	Cecil County	MD	Brent Pennell	2009	42893
126 2/8	21 4/8 21 7/8	14 6/8	4 4	Caldwell County	KY	Dan L. Jones	2009	42893
126 2/8	20 6/8 20 1/8	14 0/8	5 5	Schleicher County	TX	Jeffrey Philen	2009	42893
*126 2/8	21 5/8 21 6/8	12 6/8	5 5	Lake County	SD	Brandon Schardin	2009	42893
126 2/8	21 0/8 20 2/8	20 0/8	5 4	Elkhart County	IN	Chad W. Yotter	2009	42893
126 2/8	22 6/8 21 7/8	19 6/8	4 4	Chisago County	MN	Tom Kollodge	2009	42893
126 2/8	22 0/8 22 0/8	15 6/8	4 4	Buffalo County	WI	Chuck Baker	2009	42893
126 2/8	20 4/8 21 6/8	15 6/8	4 4	Manitowoc County	WI	Anthony J. Bonde	2009	42893
*126 2/8	21 4/8 22 0/8	14 6/8	8 6	Washington County	NE	Travis Furchert	2009	42893
126 2/8	19 7/8 19 4/8	14 5/8	5 6	Cherokee County	IA	Alan Bud Martin	2009	42893
126 2/8	21 5/8 23 0/8	16 0/8	4 5	Atlantic County	NJ	James Walker	2009	42893
*126 2/8	22 5/8 22 0/8	19 6/8	4 4	Madawaska	NBW	Sylvain Caron	2010	42893
126 1/8	23 4/8 23 7/8	18 4/8	5 5	Warren County	OH	Bill Thacker	1998	43194
126 1/8	20 3/8 20 2/8	14 7/8	6 5	Lake County	OH	Mark J. Schmelzer	1998	43194
*126 1/8	24 1/8 22 3/8	17 5/8	4 4	Shelby County	IL	William Shuemaker	2001	43194
126 1/8	19 4/8 20 4/8	16 3/8	5 5	Adams County	WI	Jana Waller	2003	43194
126 1/8	21 3/8 21 0/8	15 7/8	4 4	Kleberg County	TX	Johnnie R. Walters	2003	43194
126 1/8	21 4/8 20 7/8	15 0/8	6 4	Iowa County	WI	Randy K. Thompson	2003	43194
126 1/8	23 3/8 22 5/8	17 1/8	4 4	Vermilion County	IL	Jeff Toms	2003	43194
126 1/8	22 5/8 21 0/8	16 6/8	6 6	Phelps County	MO	Clifford Jadwin	2003	43194
*126 1/8	20 2/8 20 4/8	18 2/8	6 5	Coffey County	KS	Don Erbert	2003	43194
126 1/8	19 3/8 20 0/8	14 1/8	5 4	Columbia County	WI	Kraig M. Kalka	2004	43194
126 1/8	21 0/8 21 1/8	16 7/8	7 6	Brown County	WI	Gerald G. Van Dyn Hoven	2004	43194
*126 1/8	20 5/8 20 3/8	15 3/8	5 4	Schleicher County	TX	Randall Curtis Witte	2004	43194
126 1/8	24 1/8 22 7/8	13 3/8	5 6	Rock County	MN	Bobbie Boelman	2004	43194
126 1/8	22 4/8 22 2/8	17 5/8	7 9	Ohio County	IN	Casey Knigga	2004	43194
126 1/8	20 6/8 20 4/8	16 5/8	4 4	Pike County	IL	Richard P. Warner	2004	43194
*126 1/8	18 0/8 19 5/8	14 3/8	5 4	Richardson County	NE	Jack D. Day, Sr.	2004	43194
126 1/8	23 0/8 22 7/8	17 5/8	4 4	Brown County	IL	Jody Yancey	2004	43194
*126 1/8	21 0/8 21 0/8	18 5/8	4 5	Wyoming County	NY	Peter M. Rase	2004	43194
*126 1/8	22 2/8 21 5/8	14 2/8	5 4	Van Wert County	OH	Paul M. Carnes	2004	43194
126 1/8	27 1/8 25 5/8	19 3/8	4 5	Coos County	NH	Toby Owen	2004	43194
126 1/8	22 3/8 20 7/8	13 3/8	6 6	Marion County	IN	Robert A. Jones, Jr.	2004	43194
126 1/8	20 7/8 22 6/8	18 5/8	4 4	Luzerne County	PA	Gary Hoffacker	2005	43194
126 1/8	21 0/8 20 6/8	16 1/8	5 5	Polk County	TX	Joe D. Barringer	2005	43194
*126 1/8	23 6/8 22 3/8	18 3/8	4 5	Scott County	IN	Matt A. Smith	2005	43194
*126 1/8	23 4/8 22 2/8	16 4/8	5 6	Oldham County	KY	Phillip C. Bottorff	2005	43194
126 1/8	19 5/8 19 6/8	13 4/8	5 6	Johnson County	KS	Chris Lalik	2005	43194
*126 1/8	19 7/8 20 3/8	15 6/8	7 6	Trigg County	KY	Terry Bandy	2005	43194
126 1/8	22 4/8 22 1/8	14 3/8	5 5	Rusk County	WI	Brian Tessmann	2005	43194
126 1/8	22 4/8 22 1/8	14 5/8	4 4	Richardson County	NE	Chad Magnussen	2005	43194
*126 1/8	22 7/8 21 5/8	17 1/8	5 4	Houston County	MN	Richard Tenute	2005	43194
126 1/8	23 3/8 22 4/8	16 7/8	4 5	Washtenaw County	MI	Remie Joseph Reaume	2006	43194
126 1/8	22 0/8 21 4/8	17 3/8	4 4	Wirt County	WV	Bobby Lockhart	2006	43194
*126 1/8	22 5/8 22 5/8	16 5/8	4 4	Cerro Gordo County	IA	Travis Hunsaker	2006	43194
126 1/8	20 7/8 20 4/8	15 4/8	6 5	Erie County	NY	Steven Gubala	2006	43194
*126 1/8	23 3/8 23 4/8	18 4/8	4 6	Sheboygan County	WI	Ken Beckford	2006	43194
*126 1/8	19 6/8 19 7/8	17 3/8	5 5	Barron County	WI	Anthony Shelstad	2006	43194
126 1/8	21 1/8 22 1/8	14 7/8	7 6	Johnson County	NE	Paul Czekuc	2006	43194
126 1/8	20 7/8 20 7/8	18 1/8	4 4	Price County	WI	Michael Ullenbrauck	2006	43194
*126 1/8	22 6/8 20 6/8	16 3/8	4 4	Wayne County	IN	Jonathan C. Ferris	2006	43194
126 1/8	21 3/8 19 5/8	19 5/8	5 6	Brown County	WI	Michael Bruecker	2006	43194
*126 1/8	21 5/8 22 0/8	17 5/8	5 5	Adams County	IL	Jason A. Young	2006	43194
126 1/8	21 2/8 21 2/8	16 5/8	5 5	Steuben County	NY	Alan D. Strouse	2006	43194
126 1/8	22 3/8 22 6/8	18 3/8	5 6	Calumet County	WI	Joseph E. Wagner	2006	43194
*126 1/8	20 5/8 21 0/8	15 5/8	4 4	Mountrail County	ND	Richard E. LaFazia	2006	43194
126 1/8	19 2/8 19 2/8	13 5/8	5 5	Webb County	TX	Emily L. Fischer	2006	43194
126 1/8	20 4/8 20 7/8	18 1/8	5 5	Jefferson County	ID	Jakeob Maupin	2007	43194
*126 1/8	18 6/8 18 4/8	17 5/8	5 5	Marquette County	WI	Mark A. Baker	2007	43194
126 1/8	22 0/8 21 6/8	18 3/8	5 4	Venango County	PA	Jeff S. Feltenberger	2007	43194
*126 1/8	22 6/8 22 0/8	17 3/8	4 4	Brown County	IN	Nathan B. Atwood	2007	43194
126 1/8	21 7/8 21 5/8	14 1/8	4 4	Buffalo County	WI	Cody Henderson	2007	43194
126 1/8	21 0/8 20 1/8	16 7/8	5 4	Richland County	ND	Miranda J. Muscha	2007	43194
126 1/8	20 6/8 20 2/8	16 0/8	7 7	Lake County	IL	David G. Huntington	2007	43194
126 1/8	18 5/8 19 6/8	14 7/8	6 5	Pike County	IL	Brent Jones	2007	43194
*126 1/8	20 7/8 20 1/8	15 5/8	4 4	Marshall County	SD	Phil Mertens	2007	43194
126 1/8	23 5/8 23 6/8	16 5/8	4 5	Irwin County	GA	Neal J. Roberson	2008	43194
126 1/8	21 7/8 20 3/8	17 1/8	5 5	Foster County	ND	Jonathan J. Zieman	2008	43194
126 1/8	21 4/8 21 3/8	17 4/8	5 4	Davis County	IA	Grady Stevens	2008	43194
*126 1/8	22 7/8 22 1/8	17 3/8	5 5	Franklin County	IA	Ryan Conlon	2008	43194
126 1/8	22 0/8 19 6/8	14 6/8	6 6	Lyman County	SD	Kent Hochstein	2008	43194
126 1/8	21 7/8 22 0/8	16 2/8	5 5	McMullen County	TX	Benjamin Ty Po, Jr.	2008	43194
126 1/8	20 4/8 21 1/8	17 7/8	4 4	Dane County	WI	Dennis Carothers	2008	43194
*126 1/8	18 7/8 20 0/8	16 7/8	5 5	Clinton County	MI	Mark R. Buxton	2008	43194
126 1/8	22 6/8 21 4/8	20 5/8	5 5	Sullivan County	PA	Daniel L. Garman	2008	43194
*126 1/8	21 3/8 23 1/8	24 5/8	5 4	Berks County	PA	Ashley Riegel	2008	43194
126 1/8	23 3/8 23 2/8	20 1/8	4 5	McHenry County	IL	Mark W. Gullickson	2008	43194
*126 1/8	21 5/8 21 7/8	15 5/8	4 4	Jasper County	IN	Scott Olthoff	2008	43194
*126 1/8	21 3/8 21 4/8	16 7/8	4 4	Chester County	PA	Keith Arnold	2008	43194
126 1/8	23 2/8 22 3/8	19 1/8	4 5	Cape Girardeau County	MO	Jake Hindman	2008	43194
126 1/8	23 5/8 23 3/8	17 3/8	4 4	Butler County	KS	Matt Bump	2008	43194
*126 1/8	19 7/8 20 1/8	15 1/8	5 6	Matagorda County	TX	Les Bolton	2008	43194
126 1/8	23 4/8 22 1/8	16 7/8	5 4	Shawano County	WI	Andrew Eberhardt	2008	43194
126 1/8	24 3/8 23 3/8	17 7/8	4 5	Dougherty County	GA	Gerald L. Jones	2008	43194
126 1/8	19 5/8 20 0/8	17 3/8	6 6	Polk County	WI	William Rider	2009	43194
*126 1/8	21 4/8 20 7/8	16 1/8	4 4	Lorain County	OH	Lyle Bennett	2009	43194
126 1/8	22 2/8 22 5/8	17 7/8	4 4	Woodward County	OK	Cody B. Purviance	2009	43194
126 1/8	20 4/8 20 0/8	18 5/8	6 6	Wycliffe	BC	George Terpsma	2009	43194
126 1/8	23 3/8 20 3/8	19 2/8	6 6	Onondaga County	NY	Jim Gilkey	2009	43194
126 1/8	22 3/8 22 2/8	16 2/8	5 6	Polk County	WI	Andrew Roger Lehman	2009	43194

Deer entries below 141 0/8, that appeared in the 6th Edition, are not included here, but are included on the accompanying CD (see page 119), and also in the Club's Records Archives.

WHITETAIL DEER (TYPICAL ANTLERS)

Minimum Score 125 — Continued

SCORE	LENGTH OF MAIN BEAM R	L	INSIDE SPREAD	NUMBER OF POINTS R	L	AREA	STATE/PROVINCE	HUNTER'S NAME	DATE	RANK
*126 1/8	20 0/8	20 4/8	16 6/8	5	6	Morrison County	MN	Tyler Schmidt	2009	43194
126 1/8	22 3/8	23 6/8	18 7/8	5	4	Hocking County	OH	Gerry A. Lafreniere	2009	43194
126 1/8	20 7/8	20 5/8	17 5/8	5	4	Decatur County	IA	Ivan Muzljakovich	2009	43194
*126 1/8	19 7/8	20 5/8	18 2/8	6	6	Trigg County	KY	Terry Bandy	2009	43194
*126 1/8	20 6/8	19 6/8	16 7/8	5	5	Montgomery County	MD	Michael R. Deckelbaum	2009	43194
126 1/8	21 1/8	21 5/8	15 5/8	5	5	Monroe County	NY	Bill Daly	2010	43194
126 1/8	18 4/8	18 7/8	15 5/8	5	5	Eaton County	MI	Vern A. Walker	2010	43194
126 0/8	22 4/8	22 0/8	15 7/8	6	7	Chautauqua County	KS	Mark Klemm	1999	43460
126 0/8	22 7/8	21 4/8	16 0/8	5	7	Waupaca County	WI	Paul M. Schuelke	2000	43460
*126 0/8	20 1/8	20 4/8	17 6/8	4	5	Franklin County	MO	Todd Phillips	2001	43460
126 0/8	21 1/8	22 4/8	17 0/8	5	4	Trempealeau County	WI	Bobby Lince	2001	43460
126 0/8	22 6/8	22 7/8	20 4/8	4	4	Nicolet	QUE	Charles Henri Dorris	2001	43460
126 0/8	22 0/8	20 2/8	16 7/8	5	6	Murray County	MN	Pao Fue Yang	2002	43460
*126 0/8	23 2/8	22 5/8	19 6/8	4	4	Chippewa County	WI	Jacob M. North	2003	43460
*126 0/8	21 2/8	20 2/8	17 0/8	4	4	Schuyler County	IL	Daniel L. Cole	2003	43460
126 0/8	23 1/8	22 2/8	15 4/8	4	4	Van Buren County	MI	Benjamin D. Welsh	2003	43460
126 0/8	21 0/8	19 6/8	15 0/8	4	4	Vinton County	OH	Freeling M. Brundage	2003	43460
126 0/8	19 6/8	20 1/8	14 0/8	4	5	Madison County	GA	Robert P. Armour	2004	43460
*126 0/8	21 6/8	22 5/8	17 4/8	4	4	Juniata County	PA	Alex D. Stottle	2004	43460
126 0/8	22 6/8	22 1/8	15 7/8	5	5	Lucas County	IA	Wright Allen	2004	43460
126 0/8	21 2/8	21 2/8	13 2/8	4	4	Franklin County	MO	Mark Mitchell	2004	43460
126 0/8	21 5/8	20 3/8	15 5/8	5	6	Winnebago County	IL	Claude C. Yoakum	2004	43460
126 0/8	19 0/8	18 7/8	15 6/8	4	4	McHenry County	IL	William Wayne Wishon, Jr.	2004	43460
126 0/8	18 3/8	19 3/8	15 0/8	5	5	Carroll County	IN	Brian J. Curwick	2004	43460
*126 0/8	21 7/8	20 7/8	15 1/8	6	7	Fulton County	GA	Robert B. Coombs	2004	43460
126 0/8	21 7/8	21 7/8	16 0/8	5	4	Scotland County	MO	Bob Naucke	2004	43460
126 0/8	20 2/8	20 2/8	18 0/8	5	5	Hand County	SD	Dennis D. Lagge	2004	43460
126 0/8	20 5/8	21 6/8	17 2/8	5	5	Cayuga County	NY	Dominick J. Nicoletti	2004	43460
126 0/8	19 7/8	20 5/8	15 0/8	5	5	Karnes County	TX	Michael F. Joseph	2004	43460
126 0/8	20 2/8	21 0/8	17 0/8	7	5	Adams County	IL	Jim Moran	2004	43460
126 0/8	21 0/8	20 7/8	14 2/8	5	5	Bidwell	ONT	Ray Majerus	2005	43460
126 0/8	22 7/8	21 5/8	17 4/8	4	4	Lehigh County	PA	Glenn Weiss	2005	43460
126 0/8	17 6/8	21 2/8	18 0/8	5	5	Walworth County	WI	Michael R. Senft	2005	43460
126 0/8	21 7/8	22 3/8	18 6/8	5	5	Dane County	WI	Daniel L. Hellenbrand	2005	43460
*126 0/8	21 1/8	21 0/8	18 1/8	4	6	Hillsdale County	MI	Steven A. Bond	2005	43460
126 0/8	19 4/8	19 0/8	15 6/8	5	5	Allegan County	MI	Thomas MacDonald	2005	43460
126 0/8	24 5/8	23 7/8	18 3/8	7	7	Parke County	IN	Steve W. Buckallew	2005	43460
*126 0/8	20 5/8	20 0/8	16 4/8	5	5	Kewaunee County	WI	Jay Beyer	2005	43460
*126 0/8	21 5/8	21 4/8	16 0/8	5	4	Ashtabula County	OH	Matthew D. Smith	2005	43460
126 0/8	22 4/8	23 3/8	17 6/8	4	4	Elliot County	KY	Bill Ferguson	2006	43460
*126 0/8	19 4/8	20 1/8	16 4/8	4	4	Sebastian County	AR	Charlie Reames	2006	43460
126 0/8	20 0/8	18 5/8	16 7/8	5	6	Chautauqua County	NY	Leslie E. Seippel	2006	43460
126 0/8	22 6/8	20 5/8	18 1/8	4	5	Clark County	IL	John Bethea, Jr.	2006	43460
126 0/8	23 0/8	24 4/8	17 4/8	4	5	Kosciusko County	IN	Tracy Anderson	2006	43460
126 0/8	21 5/8	21 7/8	14 1/8	8	6	Grenada County	MS	Dean Savage	2006	43460
126 0/8	20 5/8	20 7/8	19 4/8	5	5	Tompkins County	NY	Andrew D. Vorhis	2006	43460
126 0/8	21 7/8	23 2/8	17 2/8	4	4	Desha County	AR	W. M. Gulledge, Jr.	2006	43460
126 0/8	22 0/8	20 2/8	16 6/8	5	5	St. Joseph County	MI	Troy Green	2006	43460
126 0/8	21 4/8	21 1/8	17 4/8	4	4	Marshall County	IL	Randall L. White	2006	43460
*126 0/8	25 6/8	25 4/8	20 6/8	6	5	Clark County	IL	Brett R. Hanlon	2006	43460
126 0/8	22 7/8	22 6/8	16 6/8	3	4	Worcester County	MD	Jason H. Malone	2006	43460
*126 0/8	20 4/8	20 2/8	18 0/8	5	5	Auglaize County	OH	Chris Breitigam	2006	43460
126 0/8	20 6/8	21 4/8	16 2/8	6	5	Big River	SAS	David A. Simmons	2006	43460
126 0/8	20 7/8	21 3/8	19 6/8	4	7	Fergus County	MT	John "Rosey" Roseland	2007	43460
126 0/8	22 6/8	22 4/8	16 6/8	4	4	Concho County	TX	David R. Toney	2007	43460
126 0/8	20 6/8	20 0/8	17 6/8	5	5	Anoka County	MN	Dan Super	2007	43460
126 0/8	20 5/8	20 0/8	15 4/8	5	5	Washtenaw County	MI	Steve Kowalchik	2007	43460
126 0/8	21 1/8	21 3/8	18 4/8	6	7	Westmoreland County	PA	Brent Harbert	2007	43460
126 0/8	23 7/8	23 4/8	20 4/8	5	5	Gasconade County	MO	Kurt Koch	2007	43460
*126 0/8	22 3/8	22 1/8	14 0/8	4	4	Berrien County	GA	Brad Everett Bennett	2007	43460
126 0/8	23 2/8	23 4/8	20 0/8	4	5	Chemung County	NY	Richard LaPierre	2007	43460
*126 0/8	18 7/8	19 4/8	17 2/8	4	4	Baxter County	AR	Lance Neal	2007	43460
126 0/8	18 4/8	18 4/8	12 6/8	5	5	Irwin County	GA	Neal J. Roberson	2007	43460
126 0/8	20 7/8	20 5/8	16 4/8	4	4	Sully County	SD	Dan McCormick	2007	43460
126 0/8	20 2/8	20 0/8	15 6/8	5	5	Jefferson County	AR	Brandon Couch	2007	43460
126 0/8	22 0/8	20 2/8	17 2/8	5	3	Tom Green County	TX	Eric Boley	2007	43460
126 0/8	22 2/8	21 5/8	15 2/8	4	4	Rogers County	OK	Corbin Rowe	2007	43460
126 0/8	22 2/8	21 6/8	19 0/8	3	4	Black Hawk County	IA	Mike Judas	2007	43460
126 0/8	21 5/8	22 1/8	15 3/8	6	6	Madison County	ID	Johnny Watson	2008	43460
*126 0/8	21 5/8	22 1/8	17 0/8	4	4	Butler County	NE	Austin Zeilinger	2008	43460
126 0/8	21 0/8	20 4/8	15 6/8	5	5	Vigo County	IN	Brian Crockett	2008	43460
*126 0/8	23 3/8	22 7/8	17 6/8	5	5	Ontario County	NY	Darik M. Jordan	2008	43460
126 0/8	20 5/8	20 4/8	16 0/8	6	5	Maverick County	TX	H. Mike Palmer	2008	43460
*126 0/8	23 5/8	23 4/8	17 4/8	4	4	New Haven County	CT	Chris Budris	2008	43460
*126 0/8	20 2/8	20 0/8	16 4/8	4	4	Wabasha County	MN	Matt Mangan	2008	43460
126 0/8	19 4/8	19 1/8	17 4/8	5	5	McCulloch County	TX	Austin T. Coble	2008	43460
126 0/8	20 4/8	20 4/8	15 0/8	5	6	Schuyler County	IL	Ashley D. Forbis	2008	43460
126 0/8	19 6/8	19 7/8	15 2/8	4	4	Pittsburg County	OK	Rodney Walker	2008	43460
*126 0/8	22 0/8	21 3/8	14 2/8	5	5	Saline County	NE	Mike Ellingson	2008	43460
126 0/8	20 6/8	21 6/8	15 6/8	4	4	Flathead County	MT	Chuck Williams	2008	43460
*126 0/8	21 7/8	20 7/8	17 6/8	6	4	Shawano County	WI	Sara Nellis	2009	43460
126 0/8	20 4/8	20 4/8	14 0/8	4	4	Richland County	WI	Dean A. Jewell	2009	43460
126 0/8	22 1/8	20 5/8	16 4/8	5	5	Jefferson County	OH	Ronald James Ault	2009	43460
126 0/8	22 3/8	23 4/8	19 6/8	4	4	Jackson County	MI	Robert Lee Haist	2009	43460
*126 0/8	22 7/8	22 7/8	18 6/8	4	4	Burnett County	WI	Steve Rossow	2009	43460
126 0/8	22 2/8	23 1/8	15 4/8	4	5	Chester County	PA	Robert C. Stanford	2009	43460
*126 0/8	21 6/8	22 2/8	15 1/8	6	8	Huntingdon County	PA	Brian E. Clark	2009	43460
126 0/8	21 1/8	20 7/8	16 0/8	4	4	Washtenaw County	MI	Brian F. Miller	2009	43460
*126 0/8	24 6/8	23 3/8	18 2/8	9	6	York County	PA	Robert J. Burns, Jr.	2009	43460
*126 0/8	20 3/8	21 0/8	17 0/8	4	4	Elkhart County	IN	Matthew M. Yoder	2009	43460
126 0/8	21 4/8	20 6/8	18 0/8	4	4	Buffalo County	WI	Jonas Nagle	2009	43460
*126 0/8	21 4/8	21 4/8	15 2/8	5	5	Jewell County	KS	James David Whitmire, Jr.	2009	43460
126 0/8	20 4/8	20 4/8	16 7/8	4	5	Marshall County	IN	Michael D. Miller	2010	43460
126 0/8	22 1/8	21 7/8	21 0/8	5	4	Jackson County	MI	Ronald R. Reardon	2010	43460
126 0/8	20 0/8	20 0/8	17 0/8	4	6	Sauk County	WI	Matt Allison	2010	43460

WHITETAIL DEER (TYPICAL ANTLERS)

Minimum Score 125   Continued

SCORE	LENGTH OF R MAIN BEAM L	INSIDE SPREAD	NUMBER OF R POINTS L	AREA	STATE/ PROVINCE	HUNTER'S NAME	DATE	RANK
125 7/8	21 6/8 21 4/8	16 5/8	5 7	Missoula County	MT	John T. Mandell	1999	43760
125 7/8	22 4/8 20 5/8	17 2/8	5 5	Hamlin County	SD	Scott Schamens	2000	43760
125 7/8	23 4/8 21 5/8	20 4/8	7 6	Tippecanoe County	IN	Sam Brooks II	2002	43760
125 7/8	22 3/8 22 2/8	16 5/8	4 5	Clark County	WI	Josh Opelt	2003	43760
*125 7/8	22 4/8 24 0/8	18 3/8	5 4	Champaign County	OH	Stephen R. Woolum	2003	43760
*125 7/8	18 4/8 19 3/8	16 5/8	5 5	Bayfield County	WI	John J. Dietrich	2004	43760
*125 7/8	21 1/8 21 3/8	15 3/8	4 5	Adams County	MS	Mark Cascio	2004	43760
125 7/8	21 4/8 18 6/8	15 3/8	5 6	Yazoo County	MS	Bill E. Scruggs	2004	43760
125 7/8	22 3/8 21 5/8	14 1/8	4 4	Angelina County	TX	Clint Teutsch	2004	43760
*125 7/8	19 4/8 19 3/8	18 5/8	5 5	Hughes County	SD	Mark V. Pecora	2004	43760
125 7/8	22 3/8 22 5/8	20 5/8	4 4	Berrien County	MI	Michael A. Holy	2004	43760
*125 7/8	21 4/8 21 7/8	16 7/8	4 4	Vinton County	OH	Hunter Young	2004	43760
125 7/8	21 4/8 19 6/8	18 3/8	5 6	Lucas County	IA	Jeffrey L. Howard	2004	43760
125 7/8	21 1/8 21 2/8	17 3/8	4 4	Buffalo County	WI	Robert J. Decker	2004	43760
125 7/8	20 7/8 21 2/8	18 1/8	5 4	Highland County	OH	Dan Sowders	2004	43760
*125 7/8	21 4/8 21 4/8	17 1/8	4 4	Lincoln County	TN	Brian Timberman	2004	43760
125 7/8	21 4/8 21 6/8	15 3/8	4 5	Waukesha County	WI	Mick Yorton	2004	43760
125 7/8	20 2/8 20 1/8	17 7/8	4 4	Mercer County	ND	James D. Felling	2005	43760
125 7/8	21 2/8 21 5/8	17 1/8	4 4	Polk County	WI	Craig A. Carlson	2005	43760
125 7/8	21 5/8 22 6/8	18 5/8	4 5	Buffalo County	WI	Patrick Barwick	2005	43760
*125 7/8	20 5/8 20 7/8	16 2/8	5 7	Marshall County	SD	Mitchell Geditz	2005	43760
*125 7/8	21 5/8 22 3/8	14 3/8	4 4	Allegany County	NY	Robert F. Riber	2005	43760
125 7/8	19 3/8 19 2/8	17 7/8	5 5	Keya Paha County	NE	Terry Marcukaitis	2005	43760
*125 7/8	22 0/8 22 2/8	18 5/8	4 6	Dunn County	WI	Michael Lauer	2005	43760
125 7/8	20 6/8 20 0/8	18 1/8	4 4	Grant County	WI	Ralph DiMartino, Sr.	2005	43760
*125 7/8	20 3/8 20 3/8	15 0/8	5 4	Kalamazoo County	MI	Mark Bommerscheim	2005	43760
125 7/8	22 4/8 21 6/8	18 1/8	4 4	Vinton County	OH	Jason Wackler	2005	43760
125 7/8	22 2/8 22 0/8	15 1/8	6 7	Callaway County	MO	Larry Molitor	2005	43760
125 7/8	21 4/8 21 7/8	17 7/8	4 4	Waupaca County	WI	Ronald M. Pohlman, Jr.	2005	43760
*125 7/8	22 2/8 21 1/8	13 6/8	6 6	Pottawatomie County	KS	Jared McJunkin	2005	43760
*125 7/8	22 3/8 22 4/8	16 0/8	5 5	Issaquena County	MS	Macky Myers	2005	43760
*125 7/8	22 7/8 22 3/8	18 0/8	5 5	Hunterdon County	NJ	William Gierman	2006	43760
125 7/8	21 4/8 22 7/8	18 5/8	5 6	Allen County	IN	R. James Zehr	2006	43760
125 7/8	20 5/8 19 2/8	16 7/8	6 6	Desha County	AR	Lee Walt	2006	43760
*125 7/8	23 3/8 21 4/8	22 1/8	6 8	Lac La Biche	ALB	Richard L. Drewry	2006	43760
125 7/8	23 0/8 22 6/8	16 1/8	5 5	Knox County	OH	Chris Thompson	2006	43760
125 7/8	19 0/8 19 0/8	16 4/8	5 6	Fond du Lac County	WI	Dean R. Krueger	2006	43760
*125 7/8	21 0/8 19 7/8	18 2/8	5 7	Adams County	IL	Andrew C. May	2006	43760
125 7/8	20 0/8 20 0/8	14 5/8	6 5	Jackson County	MI	Michael J. Zachary	2006	43760
125 7/8	22 2/8 21 5/8	15 1/8	6 5	Washtenaw County	MI	John Oliverio	2006	43760
*125 7/8	22 5/8 22 5/8	16 7/8	5 4	Bristol County	MA	Jim Rice	2006	43760
125 7/8	21 5/8 21 7/8	17 5/8	4 4	Boone County	MO	Chad Herwald	2006	43760
125 7/8	20 0/8 20 4/8	15 3/8	5 5	Hutchinson County	SD	Douglas Mercier	2006	43760
*125 7/8	22 3/8 22 3/8	15 1/8	4 4	Schley County	GA	Clint Strange	2006	43760
125 7/8	24 1/8 23 3/8	14 3/8	4 4	Bolivar County	MS	Lance Johnson	2006	43760
125 7/8	20 4/8 19 3/8	14 5/8	5 5	Fillmore County	MN	Scott Pierce	2007	43760
125 7/8	20 4/8 19 7/8	17 5/8	4 4	Independence County	AR	H. Ford Trotter	2007	43760
*125 7/8	19 5/8 21 0/8	17 1/8	5 5	Richland County	ND	Jeff Bommersbach	2007	43760
125 7/8	25 0/8 24 3/8	19 1/8	4 5	Dodge County	GA	Wright T. Harrell, Jr.	2007	43760
*125 7/8	23 4/8 22 4/8	17 3/8	6 5	Marinette County	WI	Ed McLernon	2007	43760
*125 7/8	22 0/8 21 2/8	15 5/8	4 4	Buffalo County	WI	Jeff Klieforth	2007	43760
125 7/8	21 4/8 21 3/8	14 3/8	7 7	Sauk County	WI	John F. Klus	2007	43760
125 7/8	20 5/8 20 6/8	18 5/8	4 4	Perry County	PA	Frank Boyer	2007	43760
*125 7/8	20 6/8 20 7/8	15 0/8	6 5	Washington County	PA	Joseph A. Horvath	2007	43760
125 7/8	19 7/8 20 4/8	16 3/8	5 5	McHenry County	IL	Larry J. Pfaffinger, Sr.	2007	43760
125 7/8	23 4/8 23 1/8	17 3/8	4 4	Fayette County	IA	Nick Judas	2007	43760
125 7/8	19 1/8 19 2/8	13 1/8	5 5	Estevan	SAS	Garry Leslie	2008	43760
125 7/8	19 7/8 19 7/8	16 3/8	5 5	Bosque County	TX	Jerry Bales	2008	43760
*125 7/8	21 0/8 21 2/8	13 4/8	5 6	Elmore County	AL	David McClinton	2008	43760
*125 7/8	20 6/8 20 0/8	17 1/8	5 5	Maries County	MO	Gary Voss	2008	43760
*125 7/8	21 3/8 21 0/8	16 5/8	5 5	Geauga County	OH	Douglas Nemeckay	2008	43760
125 7/8	20 6/8 20 3/8	13 7/8	5 5	Pike County	IL	Tim Webb	2008	43760
*125 7/8	20 1/8 19 7/8	14 3/8	5 5	Sheboygan County	WI	Jeremy J. Dekker	2008	43760
*125 7/8	21 1/8 21 7/8	17 5/8	4 4	Columbia County	WI	Brad A. Bauer	2008	43760
125 7/8	23 5/8 23 4/8	15 5/8	4 5	Vernon County	MO	Tony J. Mitchem	2008	43760
*125 7/8	21 1/8 22 2/8	18 6/8	7 4	Cayuga County	NY	Daniel E. Guzalak	2008	43760
125 7/8	19 6/8 19 3/8	14 1/8	5 5	Gallatin County	IL	Mike Willand	2008	43760
*125 7/8	22 0/8 22 2/8	19 1/8	4 4	Green County	WI	David Plath	2008	43760
*125 7/8	19 2/8 19 6/8	14 1/8	5 5	Walworth County	WI	Doug Scherer	2008	43760
*125 7/8	23 4/8 23 3/8	18 5/8	4 4	Perry County	IL	Joseph Swann	2008	43760
*125 7/8	21 5/8 22 2/8	15 3/8	6 5	Monroe County	WI	Randy Culpitt	2008	43760
125 7/8	23 4/8 23 6/8	16 7/8	4 4	Polk County	WI	Jon Leisch	2008	43760
*125 7/8	21 0/8 21 1/8	16 6/8	4 5	Trempealeau County	WI	Lee Matchey	2008	43760
125 7/8	19 5/8 19 4/8	13 7/8	5 5	Webb County	TX	A. Jay Burns, MD	2008	43760
*125 7/8	23 6/8 22 5/8	15 6/8	5 5	Adams County	OH	Bradley A. Bailey	2009	43760
*125 7/8	22 1/8 20 4/8	18 3/8	4 5	Southampton County	VA	Jason Wise	2009	43760
125 7/8	21 3/8 20 5/8	17 3/8	5 5	Dodge County	WI	Steve L. Rohn	2009	43760
125 7/8	21 2/8 22 0/8	14 7/8	5 5	Jackson County	WI	Michael Scaff	2009	43760
*125 7/8	21 0/8 20 6/8	14 5/8	5 5	Eau Claire County	WI	Bill Emery	2009	43760
*125 7/8	20 3/8 20 1/8	14 0/8	7 6	Onondaga County	NY	Robert A. Pendock, Jr.	2009	43760
*125 7/8	21 0/8 20 3/8	12 3/8	4 4	Vernon County	WI	Jeff Nelson	2009	43760
125 7/8	21 0/8 21 0/8	17 5/8	4 5	Price County	WI	Richard Kichmeyer	2009	43760
125 7/8	22 5/8 21 3/8	14 6/8	5 4	Stump Lake	SAS	Tysor Craney	2010	43760
125 7/8	18 5/8 17 4/8	17 5/8	5 6	Eaton County	MI	Dave Jolley	2010	43760
125 6/8	21 2/8 21 4/8	16 4/8	4 6	Lafayette County	WI	Dana Lawrence	1994	44012
125 6/8	21 0/8 21 2/8	19 2/8	4 4	Clark County	IL	Brad Keeney	1997	44012
125 6/8	19 3/8 19 7/8	14 6/8	5 5	Tensas Parish	LA	Todd Cerniglia	2001	44012
125 6/8	21 0/8 21 7/8	17 2/8	5 5	Traill County	ND	Richard L. Aamold	2001	44012
*125 6/8	20 6/8 20 6/8	17 0/8	4 4	Breckinridge County	KY	Daryl Adams	2002	44012
125 6/8	22 0/8 22 0/8	17 4/8	4 5	Shelby County	OH	Craig Ambos	2003	44012
125 6/8	21 0/8 20 3/8	14 2/8	5 5	Licking County	OH	Willard Jarvis	2003	44012
125 6/8	17 2/8 17 4/8	13 0/8	5 5	Johnson County	WY	Dana S. Redman	2004	44012
125 6/8	22 7/8 21 3/8	17 0/8	5 5	Polk County	WI	David T. Borek	2004	44012
125 6/8	22 6/8 22 4/8	18 6/8	5 7	Middlesex County	CT	David Pawloski	2004	44012
125 6/8	20 6/8 19 6/8	15 0/8	5 5	Boone County	MO	Jerry Barber	2004	44012

Deer entries below 141 0/8, that appeared in the 6th Edition, are not included here, but are included on the accompanying CD (see page 119), and also in the Club's Records Archives.

WHITETAIL DEER (TYPICAL ANTLERS)

Minimum Score 125 — Continued

SCORE	R MAIN BEAM L	INSIDE SPREAD	R POINTS L	AREA	STATE/PROVINCE	HUNTER'S NAME	DATE	RANK
125 6/8	21 5/8 21 2/8	16 6/8	5 5	Richland County	OH	Jared Dailey	2004	44012
*125 6/8	21 0/8 20 6/8	21 0/8	4 4	Kleberg County	TX	James Bass	2004	44012
125 6/8	22 3/8 21 5/8	16 0/8	5 4	Jackson County	MI	Gregory B. Pohl	2004	44012
125 6/8	23 6/8 23 5/8	17 0/8	4 4	York County	PA	Martin D. Wilt	2004	44012
125 6/8	21 0/8 21 7/8	17 4/8	5 5	Greenup County	KY	Jim Davis	2004	44012
125 6/8	22 6/8 22 1/8	17 6/8	5 4	Price County	WI	Michael Ullenbrauck	2004	44012
125 6/8	21 2/8 21 0/8	15 7/8	4 5	Licking County	OH	Travis Taylor	2004	44012
125 6/8	20 5/8 20 6/8	18 0/8	4 4	Buffalo County	WI	Thad Henderson	2004	44012
*125 6/8	19 4/8 22 4/8	17 0/8	7 5	Columbia County	WI	Mitchell J. Plautz	2004	44012
125 6/8	21 2/8 20 3/8	18 2/8	5 5	Oconto County	WI	Anthony "Tony" Janecek	2004	44012
125 6/8	20 2/8 20 0/8	14 4/8	4 4	Sutton County	TX	W. C. Polster	2004	44012
125 6/8	22 0/8 21 5/8	16 6/8	5 4	Dimmit County	TX	Mark Anders	2005	44012
125 6/8	23 2/8 25 3/8	15 4/8	5 8	Wichita County	TX	Shayde Hogue	2005	44012
125 6/8	21 0/8 21 0/8	16 2/8	5 6	Cheyenne County	KS	Philip D. Riley	2005	44012
125 6/8	21 7/8 21 7/8	16 0/8	5 5	Pepin County	WI	Chad I. Olson	2005	44012
*125 6/8	20 3/8 20 6/8	17 0/8	6 6	Bayfield County	WI	Thomas Binkowski	2005	44012
125 6/8	22 5/8 23 0/8	15 3/8	5 4	Kingman County	KS	Steve Utley	2005	44012
*125 6/8	19 4/8 20 3/8	14 6/8	5 5	Harris County	GA	Kenny Moore	2005	44012
*125 6/8	22 0/8 21 3/8	16 0/8	4 4	Madison County	NY	Carl Manner	2005	44012
*125 6/8	20 0/8 22 2/8	15 2/8	5 5	Bourbon County	KS	John Thomas	2005	44012
*125 6/8	21 7/8 21 7/8	16 6/8	5 5	Sutton County	TX	James Sowell, Jr.	2005	44012
125 6/8	20 2/8 19 7/8	15 4/8	6 5	Ramsey County	ND	Daniel Erickstad	2005	44012
125 6/8	21 4/8 22 3/8	16 4/8	4 4	Williamson County	IL	Ira J. Deshields	2005	44012
125 6/8	20 0/8 19 7/8	14 7/8	7 5	Schleicher County	TX	Tony Peyton	2005	44012
*125 6/8	20 5/8 20 7/8	17 2/8	4 5	Caldwell County	KY	Dan L. Jones	2006	44012
*125 6/8	19 6/8 19 7/8	13 2/8	5 5	Fillmore County	MN	Joe Magee	2006	44012
*125 6/8	23 5/8 20 5/8	15 6/8	4 4	St. Croix County	WI	Ben DeGross	2006	44012
125 6/8	19 4/8 19 2/8	16 5/8	7 5	Olmsted County	MN	Mick Herrli	2006	44012
125 6/8	21 6/8 21 3/8	16 6/8	7 7	Rolette County	ND	Justin Berg	2006	44012
125 6/8	20 6/8 21 3/8	16 0/8	4 4	Stewart County	TN	Zachery Crider	2006	44012
*125 6/8	23 1/8 23 5/8	17 4/8	5 5	Logan County	KY	Mark Alan Belcher	2006	44012
125 6/8	20 1/8 20 0/8	15 6/8	4 4	Hughes County	OK	James F. Griffith	2006	44012
125 6/8	20 0/8 19 0/8	13 2/8	4 4	Morris County	NJ	Dennis George	2006	44012
*125 6/8	20 6/8 20 4/8	14 7/8	5 5	Schuylkill County	PA	Kyle R. Essler	2006	44012
125 6/8	23 2/8 23 0/8	14 2/8	4 4	Harrison County	WV	Dan Suttle	2006	44012
125 6/8	22 4/8 23 4/8	15 0/8	5 8	Cass County	NE	Travis L. Brown	2006	44012
125 6/8	21 5/8 20 6/8	15 0/8	6 6	Lenawee County	MI	Mark A. Waldron	2006	44012
*125 6/8	23 3/8 22 4/8	17 6/8	4 4	Dunn County	WI	Steven Bowell	2006	44012
125 6/8	23 6/8 22 3/8	19 2/8	5 6	Lapeer County	MI	Peter Quinlan	2006	44012
*125 6/8	23 5/8 22 7/8	15 5/8	5 4	Kent County	MD	Michael Kaczor	2006	44012
125 6/8	19 1/8 19 3/8	15 0/8	5 5	Botetourt County	VA	Matt Cooper	2006	44012
125 6/8	22 4/8 23 0/8	17 3/8	6 6	Coles County	IL	Marilyn Saveley	2006	44012
125 6/8	21 6/8 21 1/8	16 6/8	6 5	Plymouth County	IA	Andy Kovarna	2007	44012
125 6/8	21 1/8 20 1/8	17 4/8	4 5	Chicot County	AR	Corey Melton	2007	44012
125 6/8	22 0/8 21 5/8	16 6/8	4 4	Sioux County	IA	Craig Van Den Berg	2007	44012
*125 6/8	20 7/8 21 5/8	13 6/8	5 6	Washtenaw County	MI	Brian F. Miller	2007	44012
*125 6/8	24 4/8 22 3/8	18 3/8	5 7	Mitchell County	IA	Kevin Krukow	2007	44012
*125 6/8	21 2/8 21 4/8	14 4/8	4 4	Athens County	OH	Chad Hale	2007	44012
*125 6/8	18 0/8 18 4/8	15 4/8	5 5	Burnett County	WI	Dennis Chell	2007	44012
*125 6/8	21 5/8 21 1/8	15 4/8	4 5	Fayette County	IL	Mike Rhodes	2007	44012
125 6/8	20 7/8 22 3/8	19 6/8	6 5	Lincoln County	WI	Michael Jones	2007	44012
125 6/8	21 2/8 21 4/8	18 7/8	5 5	Pierce County	WI	P. J. Hines	2008	44012
125 6/8	21 5/8 21 0/8	17 2/8	4 5	Kent County	MI	Eric Soucey	2008	44012
125 6/8	21 6/8 22 4/8	15 4/8	5 4	Jasper County	IL	Scotty Bensken	2008	44012
*125 6/8	20 6/8 20 4/8	16 4/8	4 4	Monmouth County	NJ	Tom Freiberger	2008	44012
*125 6/8	21 0/8 20 2/8	15 2/8	4 4	Somerset County	PA	Bruce Eller	2008	44012
125 6/8	19 5/8 19 0/8	14 4/8	5 6	Winnebago County	WI	Robert Krueger	2008	44012
125 6/8	20 7/8 17 3/8	18 2/8	6 5	Rusk County	WI	Joe Flater	2008	44012
125 6/8	19 5/8 20 1/8	14 4/8	6 7	Woodruff County	AR	Kenneth Medlock	2008	44012
125 6/8	22 1/8 22 2/8	16 0/8	5 4	Pike County	IL	Robert Brush	2008	44012
125 6/8	23 7/8 22 7/8	17 2/8	4 4	Onondaga County	NY	Donald V. Spencer, Jr.	2008	44012
125 6/8	21 7/8 22 0/8	16 4/8	4 6	Jackson County	IA	Kurt Rojemann	2008	44012
125 6/8	22 6/8 22 0/8	15 7/8	5 5	Plymouth County	MA	Ryan Nelligan	2008	44012
*125 6/8	22 0/8 21 2/8	16 2/8	4 4	Portage County	WI	Jeff Rzentkowski	2008	44012
125 6/8	23 0/8 22 5/8	14 6/8	6 6	Greenwood County	KS	Rodney Alexander	2008	44012
*125 6/8	21 3/8 21 7/8	15 6/8	4 4	Giles County	TN	Barney Heyward	2008	44012
*125 6/8	22 6/8 23 0/8	17 0/8	4 4	Worcester County	MA	Joseph F. Hall	2008	44012
125 6/8	22 4/8 22 4/8	14 4/8	5 5	Outagamie County	WI	Jeff L. Steede	2008	44012
*125 6/8	20 7/8 21 0/8	17 6/8	4 4	Taylor County	WI	Chad Klabon	2009	44012
*125 6/8	22 6/8 22 4/8	19 2/8	4 4	Dubuque County	IA	Paul Hill	2009	44012
125 6/8	20 1/8 20 6/8	18 2/8	5 5	Schuyler County	IL	David R. Herschelman	2009	44012
125 6/8	19 1/8 19 1/8	13 5/8	5 6	Williams County	ND	Mark Hughes	2009	44012
*125 6/8	20 5/8 20 5/8	17 2/8	4 5	Fond du Lac County	WI	Gregory R. Marshall	2009	44012
125 6/8	22 1/8 22 1/8	15 6/8	5 5	Hughes County	SD	Lance Peery	2009	44012
125 6/8	21 5/8 21 0/8	19 3/8	5 5	Grant County	WI	Joseph Hare	2009	44012
*125 6/8	21 2/8 21 0/8	15 5/8	6 6	Woodson County	KS	Lance Gainey	2009	44012
*125 6/8	21 7/8 20 2/8	17 0/8	4 5	Onondaga County	NY	Ralph P. Marzullo	2009	44012
125 6/8	22 0/8 22 1/8	18 6/8	5 5	St. Croix County	WI	Pete Midthun	2009	44012
125 6/8	21 7/8 22 2/8	13 1/8	5 4	Wilbarger County	TX	Rodney Alexander	2009	44012
125 6/8	18 0/8 18 1/8	14 0/8	5 5	Marwayne	ALB	Tonnie Elwood Davis	2010	44012
125 6/8	20 4/8 20 6/8	13 6/8	5 5	Traill County	ND	Eric Hoffer	2010	44012
125 6/8	20 2/8 20 7/8	15 0/8	4 4	Martin County	IN	Charles Waggoner	2010	44012
*125 6/8	21 5/8 21 6/8	14 6/8	4 5	Sullivan County	IN	Clarence Dawson	2010	44012
125 6/8	20 4/8 20 3/8	15 4/8	5 5	Berks County	PA	David L. Kocher	2010	44012
125 5/8	24 4/8 24 1/8	20 7/8	5 4	Westchester County	NY	Nicholas Corsi	1990	44305
125 5/8	20 0/8 21 1/8	18 1/8	4 6	Kane County	IL	Steven M. Sturtevant	1999	44305
125 5/8	21 2/8 21 5/8	13 1/8	4 5	Branch County	MI	Ben Warnimont	2000	44305
125 5/8	21 5/8 21 5/8	13 7/8	4 4	Ralls County	MO	Steve Hardy	2001	44305
125 5/8	21 5/8 21 1/8	14 3/8	4 4	Swift County	MN	Kurt Clitty	2001	44305
125 5/8	19 2/8 19 7/8	14 5/8	5 4	Lenawee County	MI	John Ferguson	2002	44305
125 5/8	19 6/8 19 6/8	17 6/8	6 7	Macon County	IL	James R. Wilson	2002	44305
125 5/8	20 3/8 20 4/8	16 7/8	5 5	Webb County	TX	Matthew Howard	2003	44305
125 5/8	24 0/8 23 2/8	18 3/8	4 4	White County	AR	Scott Eichhorn	2003	44305
125 5/8	19 7/8 20 6/8	19 3/8	4 5	Ward County	ND	Maureen Tomlinson	2004	44305
125 5/8	21 0/8 21 6/8	17 3/8	5 5	Portage County	WI	Dennis D. Kunst	2004	44305

WHITETAIL DEER (TYPICAL ANTLERS)

Minimum Score 125 — Continued

SCORE	LENGTH OF R MAIN BEAM L	INSIDE SPREAD	NUMBER OF R POINTS L	AREA	STATE/PROVINCE	HUNTER'S NAME	DATE	RANK
125 5/8	18 2/8 18 4/8	17 7/8	5 5	Livingston County	NY	Francis R. Camardo	2004	44305
*125 5/8	23 4/8 23 7/8	20 2/8	5 4	Strafford County	NH	Jamie Perron	2004	44305
*125 5/8	20 0/8 19 7/8	13 7/8	4 4	McCulloch County	TX	Les Hunter	2004	44305
*125 5/8	21 7/8 21 3/8	14 7/8	4 4	Clearfield County	PA	Arnie Bernard	2004	44305
125 5/8	24 3/8 21 7/8	14 3/8	5 5	Vinton County	OH	Robert Goldsberry	2004	44305
*125 5/8	21 4/8 20 6/8	13 4/8	7 7	Adams County	IL	Richard J. Krytus	2004	44305
125 5/8	20 2/8 21 1/8	14 3/8	4 4	Chatham County	NC	Jason Matthew Hayes	2004	44305
*125 5/8	21 1/8 21 3/8	17 3/8	4 5	Adams County	WI	Eric A. Frank	2004	44305
125 5/8	19 3/8 19 6/8	16 3/8	5 5	Columbia County	WI	Andrew R. Strachota	2004	44305
125 5/8	21 2/8 20 6/8	16 1/8	5 5	Lancaster County	NE	Anthony Perkins	2004	44305
*125 5/8	22 3/8 21 3/8	18 3/8	4 5	Orange County	NY	Steve Scarselli	2004	44305
*125 5/8	22 2/8 22 0/8	18 1/8	5 5	Zavala County	TX	Paul H. Abat	2004	44305
125 5/8	23 2/8 22 0/8	16 3/8	4 4	Trempealeau County	WI	Pete Koxlien	2005	44305
125 5/8	22 0/8 22 7/8	17 7/8	4 4	Isanti County	MN	Mackinzie Perry	2005	44305
125 5/8	19 7/8 19 6/8	16 1/8	5 5	Butler County	PA	Daniel L. Haney	2005	44305
125 5/8	21 1/8 21 7/8	16 5/8	4 5	Fountain County	IN	Tyler Ratcliff	2005	44305
125 5/8	21 4/8 20 7/8	17 7/8	4 4	Olmsted County	MN	Kevin Plank	2005	44305
*125 5/8	24 0/8 23 3/8	13 1/8	6 5	Cherokee County	KS	Guy Mullin	2005	44305
*125 5/8	22 7/8 22 7/8	16 1/8	5 5	Indiana County	PA	Gregory Cusimano	2005	44305
125 5/8	19 6/8 19 6/8	17 5/8	5 5	McHenry County	IL	James M. Schollhammer	2005	44305
125 5/8	22 0/8 22 3/8	17 2/8	6 5	Olmsted County	MN	Walter P. Krapohl	2005	44305
125 5/8	21 2/8 22 3/8	17 3/8	5 5	Ashtabula County	OH	Jonathan P. Triplett	2005	44305
125 5/8	22 7/8 22 5/8	17 0/8	7 8	Carroll County	OH	Dean Stebner	2005	44305
*125 5/8	23 3/8 23 7/8	17 3/8	3 5	Dane County	WI	Jason Juan Diaz	2005	44305
125 5/8	20 5/8 20 2/8	15 1/8	5 5	Allegan County	MI	Leonard Ruthven	2005	44305
125 5/8	22 4/8 24 1/8	23 0/8	6 6	Union County	SD	Bradley D. Mollet	2005	44305
125 5/8	18 0/8 20 0/8	18 4/8	6 5	Stutsman County	ND	Cory Robinson	2006	44305
*125 5/8	19 1/8 19 6/8	14 1/8	5 5	Cass County	MI	Andy W. Silverthorn	2006	44305
*125 5/8	19 7/8 20 5/8	14 7/8	5 4	Richland County	ND	Dan Olsgaard	2006	44305
125 5/8	21 1/8 21 5/8	18 7/8	4 5	Grant County	WI	Peter O'Brien	2006	44305
125 5/8	22 6/8 23 2/8	18 1/8	4 4	Passaic County	NJ	Walter D. Quirk	2006	44305
125 5/8	20 3/8 20 2/8	15 3/8	5 5	Shawano County	WI	Rob Van Offeren	2006	44305
125 5/8	22 6/8 22 4/8	18 3/8	5 5	Erie County	PA	Jeffrey L. Hoover	2006	44305
125 5/8	20 6/8 21 0/8	17 7/8	4 4	Sawyer County	WI	Thomas E. Carlson	2006	44305
125 5/8	21 3/8 21 5/8	16 7/8	4 7	McLean County	KY	Steve Conrad	2006	44305
125 5/8	22 0/8 22 4/8	18 3/8	4 5	Allegany County	NY	Charlie Kron	2006	44305
125 5/8	21 7/8 20 1/8	21 5/8	4 5	Hancock County	IL	Bradley J. Swanson	2006	44305
125 5/8	21 4/8 21 2/8	16 1/8	5 5	Lake County	IL	William Snelgrove	2006	44305
125 5/8	24 5/8 24 6/8	15 3/8	4 4	Greenwood County	KS	Rodney Alexander	2006	44305
*125 5/8	21 7/8 22 0/8	15 1/8	5 4	Mountrail County	ND	Gary Lonning	2006	44305
125 5/8	24 1/8 24 4/8	18 5/8	5 5	Douglas County	IL	Danny Cleland	2006	44305
125 5/8	20 4/8 20 2/8	15 5/8	5 5	Jackson County	IN	Keith Messel	2006	44305
125 5/8	22 0/8 21 3/8	14 3/8	4 4	Wayne County	NC	William David Lee, Jr.	2006	44305
125 5/8	21 2/8 21 1/8	16 7/8	4 4	Claiborne County	MS	Bob Lane	2007	44305
125 5/8	20 0/8 19 7/8	15 1/8	5 5	Outagamie County	WI	Joshua G. Snortum	2007	44305
125 5/8	20 1/8 20 4/8	14 1/8	5 5	Pawnee County	NE	Bill J. Phillips	2007	44305
*125 5/8	21 2/8 22 1/8	16 5/8	4 4	Marquette County	WI	Sheena M. Welke	2007	44305
125 5/8	22 3/8 20 4/8	14 3/8	6 6	Butler County	NE	Chris Pokorny	2007	44305
125 5/8	23 3/8 22 6/8	16 2/8	6 4	Columbia County	PA	Stephen Toczylousky	2007	44305
125 5/8	19 2/8 20 0/8	14 6/8	6 7	Warren County	IA	Bruce A. Sanburn	2007	44305
125 5/8	21 7/8 23 3/8	19 6/8	5 5	Pike County	IL	Kris J. Lescalleet	2007	44305
*125 5/8	20 1/8 21 0/8	16 5/8	5 4	Clark County	SD	Wyatt R. Skelton	2007	44305
125 5/8	20 6/8 21 0/8	16 5/8	5 5	Webb County	TX	Bob Gilbert	2007	44305
125 5/8	23 6/8 23 7/8	17 6/8	6 7	Love County	OK	Jason Christian	2007	44305
*125 5/8	22 2/8 21 6/8	17 3/8	4 4	Clark County	WI	Richard Rosemeyer	2008	44305
125 5/8	22 4/8 20 3/8	17 5/8	6 5	Stokes County	NC	Jeffrey Boyles	2008	44305
125 5/8	19 5/8 19 4/8	13 7/8	5 5	Harrison County	MO	Corey Melton	2008	44305
125 5/8	21 6/8 21 3/8	16 5/8	5 5	Washington County	PA	Kirk D. Munger	2008	44305
*125 5/8	22 2/8 22 6/8	16 4/8	5 4	Saline County	MO	Hadley Wiskur	2008	44305
125 5/8	22 6/8 21 6/8	19 3/8	4 4	Waukesha County	WI	Steve Grant	2008	44305
125 5/8	22 3/8 21 6/8	16 3/8	6 4	Wabasha County	MN	John Bazey	2008	44305
125 5/8	21 4/8 22 3/8	16 1/8	4 4	Muskingum County	OH	Ryan Berry	2008	44305
125 5/8	22 2/8 21 4/8	16 1/8	5 5	Valley County	MT	Eric Kuhlman	2008	44305
*125 5/8	20 1/8 19 5/8	13 5/8	4 5	Cochrane	ALB	Michael Serwa	2008	44305
125 5/8	21 3/8 21 6/8	19 1/8	4 4	Kanawha County	WV	Thomas McClure	2008	44305
125 5/8	22 7/8 22 7/8	16 7/8	4 4	Bolivar County	MS	Hunter Duke Palasini	2008	44305
125 5/8	21 3/8 21 5/8	15 7/8	4 5	Linn County	KS	Amanda Thornberry	2008	44305
125 5/8	20 4/8 20 2/8	14 7/8	5 4	Carroll County	MS	Al Hankins	2008	44305
125 5/8	19 0/8 19 2/8	16 1/8	5 5	Sterling County	TX	Randall Johnson	2009	44305
*125 5/8	24 2/8 21 3/8	16 3/8	5 4	Cass County	IN	John R. Byers	2009	44305
125 5/8	21 4/8 20 5/8	18 7/8	4 4	Monmouth County	NJ	Robert W. Taylor	2009	44305
*125 5/8	21 2/8 20 2/8	16 1/8	5 5	Worcester County	MA	Michael E. Stefanik	2009	44305
*125 5/8	22 0/8 22 1/8	14 7/8	4 4	Ionia County	MI	Jeff Ryan	2009	44305
*125 5/8	22 2/8 23 1/8	19 3/8	6 5	Winnebago County	IL	Earl Tamar	2009	44305
*125 5/8	19 3/8 19 5/8	15 1/8	6 5	McLean County	ND	Larry Rice	2009	44305
*125 5/8	21 1/8 20 1/8	16 3/8	5 4	Vermillion County	IN	Tyler N. Turchi	2009	44305
125 5/8	20 4/8 21 3/8	19 1/8	4 4	Iowa County	WI	Jason J. Munz	2009	44305
125 5/8	20 4/8 21 4/8	17 7/8	5 4	Buffalo County	WI	Jordan Dieckman	2009	44305
125 5/8	23 4/8 22 6/8	18 1/8	5 5	Columbia County	PA	Michael McCormick	2009	44305
*125 5/8	23 0/8 22 3/8	17 5/8	4 5	Goliad County	TX	Tanner Geiser	2009	44305
125 5/8	21 4/8 21 5/8	14 7/8	5 4	Linn County	KS	Amanda Thornberry	2009	44305
125 5/8	19 7/8 19 4/8	15 4/8	5 6	Muskingum County	OH	Ryan Berry	2009	44305
125 4/8	23 5/8 23 2/8	18 4/8	4 4	Isle of Wight County	VA	Dwight S. Wolf	2000	44591
*125 4/8	22 1/8 22 5/8	16 6/8	5 4	Breckinridge County	KY	Randy Tucker	2004	44591
125 4/8	21 7/8 23 2/8	16 3/8	7 5	Pulaski County	IN	Mark Narantic	2004	44591
*125 4/8	20 2/8 19 5/8	14 2/8	4 4	Woodson County	KS	Frank Pechacek	2004	44591
125 4/8	20 6/8 21 1/8	14 2/8	5 5	Delaware County	IA	J. Arend Gibson	2004	44591
125 4/8	21 0/8 21 3/8	18 6/8	4 4	Richland County	WI	Lee J. Keim	2004	44591
125 4/8	18 3/8 18 2/8	15 0/8	5 5	Hardin County	IA	Randy Evans	2004	44591
125 4/8	21 3/8 21 6/8	15 2/8	6 5	Clark County	SD	Mark Turner	2004	44591
125 4/8	23 0/8 22 2/8	17 0/8	5 6	Dane County	WI	Doug Johnson	2004	44591
125 4/8	20 0/8 19 7/8	13 6/8	5 5	De Witt County	TX	Bradly Balcar	2004	44591
*125 4/8	20 1/8 19 2/8	18 2/8	5 5	Bartow County	GA	Ronnie H. Hall	2005	44591
125 4/8	23 3/8 22 6/8	18 7/8	5 5	Gallia County	OH	Kent M. Trout	2005	44591
125 4/8	23 6/8 24 1/8	19 2/8	4 4	Miami County	OH	David Stacey	2005	44591

Deer entries below 141 0/8, that appeared in the 6th Edition, are not included here, but are included on the accompanying CD (see page 119), and also in the Club's Records Archives.

WHITETAIL DEER (TYPICAL ANTLERS)

Minimum Score 125 — Continued

SCORE	LENGTH OF MAIN BEAM R	L	INSIDE SPREAD	NUMBER OF POINTS R	L	AREA	STATE/ PROVINCE	HUNTER'S NAME	DATE	RANK
125 4/8	22 5/8	21 6/8	17 4/8	6	4	Pike County	IL	Darrell L. Nelson	2005	44591
125 4/8	19 3/8	20 2/8	13 4/8	5	5	Kosciusko County	IN	Chad W. Yotter	2005	44591
*125 4/8	22 6/8	23 3/8	17 0/8	4	4	Vigo County	IN	Tommy Terrell	2005	44591
125 4/8	17 6/8	17 1/8	15 6/8	5	5	Somervell County	TX	Dewey M. Dalton	2005	44591
*125 4/8	23 0/8	22 2/8	15 1/8	6	4	Jefferson County	IN	Andrew W. Pickett	2005	44591
125 4/8	21 0/8	20 5/8	14 4/8	4	4	Houston County	MN	Chanc L. Vogel	2005	44591
125 4/8	22 3/8	22 2/8	15 6/8	4	4	King and Queen County	VA	Jeffery G. Armistead	2005	44591
125 4/8	23 0/8	23 6/8	17 0/8	4	5	Waukesha County	WI	Michael Scaff	2005	44591
125 4/8	24 2/8	24 1/8	17 2/8	3	4	Tippecanoe County	IN	Bret A. Maxson	2005	44591
125 4/8	21 5/8	20 3/8	16 4/8	4	5	Brazos County	TX	Michael Laine	2005	44591
*125 4/8	22 4/8	22 0/8	17 0/8	4	4	Gibson County	IN	James S. Wright	2005	44591
125 4/8	22 1/8	21 6/8	16 2/8	4	4	Kenosha County	WI	David A. Wright	2005	44591
*125 4/8	21 1/8	20 1/8	16 4/8	5	5	Pierce County	WI	Adam T. Matzek	2005	44591
125 4/8	22 4/8	21 7/8	21 2/8	5	4	Jo Daviess County	IL	Dennis Heineman	2005	44591
125 4/8	22 4/8	21 7/8	18 4/8	4	4	Wapello County	IA	Shawn Kelly	2005	44591
125 4/8	20 2/8	19 3/8	16 6/8	5	5	Sheridan County	NE	Chad Stetson	2005	44591
125 4/8	20 1/8	19 5/8	15 2/8	8	5	Pike County	IL	Kenneth Woods	2005	44591
*125 4/8	20 2/8	20 6/8	14 6/8	5	4	Parke County	IN	Shawn E. Donnenhoffer	2005	44591
125 4/8	20 7/8	21 7/8	12 5/8	6	7	Rusk County	WI	Ryan Kopras	2005	44591
*125 4/8	22 5/8	21 2/8	15 4/8	4	5	Troup County	GA	Derick Staley	2005	44591
125 4/8	21 7/8	22 7/8	15 2/8	4	4	Cedar County	IA	David Orgeron	2005	44591
125 4/8	21 4/8	21 2/8	14 2/8	4	4	Ward County	ND	John R. Plesuk	2006	44591
*125 4/8	21 1/8	20 1/8	13 6/8	5	5	Irion County	TX	Craig Horn	2006	44591
125 4/8	20 4/8	22 2/8	16 0/8	4	5	Adams County	NE	Gary W. Bortis	2006	44591
125 4/8	20 6/8	20 7/8	16 2/8	4	4	Ogle County	IL	Brian M. Kean	2006	44591
125 4/8	24 6/8	25 4/8	16 4/8	4	4	Taylor County	IA	Todd Tobin	2006	44591
125 4/8	22 2/8	20 5/8	20 5/8	7	6	Cass County	IN	Timothy B. Hatfield	2006	44591
125 4/8	21 5/8	20 5/8	14 1/8	5	6	Saunders County	NE	Josh DePatie	2006	44591
125 4/8	21 2/8	21 0/8	18 0/8	4	4	Cass County	MI	Larry P. Spromberg	2006	44591
125 4/8	23 1/8	23 1/8	14 0/8	6	4	Miami County	IN	Mark Ross	2006	44591
125 4/8	19 3/8	21 4/8	18 4/8	5	5	Shawano County	WI	Randy Schenkoske	2006	44591
125 4/8	21 2/8	22 3/8	16 2/8	4	4	Barber County	KS	Rich Grannis	2006	44591
125 4/8	20 4/8	18 6/8	18 4/8	5	5	Fond du Lac County	WI	Matt Leonard	2006	44591
125 4/8	21 5/8	21 7/8	15 4/8	4	4	Jo Daviess County	IL	Paul P. Brescia	2006	44591
125 4/8	22 1/8	21 3/8	15 6/8	5	5	Huntingdon County	PA	Lloyd Weaver	2006	44591
*125 4/8	19 3/8	20 1/8	17 2/8	5	5	Vernon County	WI	Todd Suiter	2006	44591
*125 4/8	23 4/8	23 4/8	15 2/8	4	4	Coahoma County	MS	Eric Jennings	2006	44591
*125 4/8	21 0/8	21 0/8	15 2/8	5	5	Pike County	IL	David A. Brewer	2006	44591
125 4/8	22 2/8	24 1/8	19 6/8	5	4	Brown County	WI	Gerry Warden	2006	44591
*125 4/8	26 6/8	26 6/8	24 5/8	6	4	Comanche County	KS	Gregg J. Krikke	2006	44591
*125 4/8	23 4/8	22 2/8	16 4/8	4	4	Linn County	IA	James Hall	2006	44591
125 4/8	20 6/8	22 0/8	19 4/8	6	6	Logan County	KY	Shane Collier	2006	44591
125 4/8	23 1/8	22 1/8	14 4/8	5	4	Pickaway County	OH	Roger Hopkins	2006	44591
*125 4/8	22 4/8	21 3/8	17 3/8	4	5	Nelson County	KY	Eric Culver	2007	44591
125 4/8	20 4/8	21 4/8	17 0/8	7	5	Pepin County	WI	Brent King	2007	44591
125 4/8	21 7/8	21 6/8	16 5/8	6	6	Grundy County	MO	Aaron Griffin	2007	44591
125 4/8	20 1/8	19 5/8	16 4/8	4	4	Johnston County	OK	Gary Higgins	2007	44591
125 4/8	21 4/8	18 6/8	13 4/8	5	5	Val Verde County	TX	Kenny Powell	2007	44591
125 4/8	20 4/8	21 3/8	18 4/8	5	5	Dane County	WI	Dylan Way	2007	44591
125 4/8	19 3/8	19 1/8	17 2/8	5	5	Dane County	WI	Miles Weaver	2007	44591
125 4/8	22 4/8	22 5/8	16 4/8	5	4	Clarion County	PA	John E. Royer IV	2007	44591
125 4/8	21 7/8	20 6/8	16 6/8	5	5	Jefferson County	OH	Fred P. Bowen	2007	44591
*125 4/8	22 0/8	22 0/8	17 6/8	4	4	Cayuga County	NY	Dennis Johnson	2007	44591
125 4/8	20 0/8	21 0/8	13 7/8	6	5	Crawford County	WI	Chris Dregne	2007	44591
125 4/8	22 0/8	22 5/8	18 4/8	5	3	Vernon County	WI	Casey Blum	2007	44591
*125 4/8	21 3/8	22 5/8	16 6/8	4	4	Vigo County	IN	Eli Hendricks	2007	44591
125 4/8	22 1/8	23 2/8	18 4/8	4	4	Allegany County	NY	Walter Yacus	2007	44591
125 4/8	21 3/8	22 2/8	15 2/8	4	4	Pope County	IL	Lee Weldon	2007	44591
125 4/8	18 6/8	20 0/8	15 6/8	5	4	Adams County	IA	Mark Armstrong	2007	44591
125 4/8	21 6/8	21 3/8	17 7/8	5	6	Irion County	TX	Ronnie Parsons	2008	44591
*125 4/8	21 4/8	20 3/8	19 3/8	4	5	Licking County	OH	Garrett Tucker	2008	44591
*125 4/8	22 6/8	23 3/8	18 3/8	5	5	Douglas County	IL	Keith Findley	2008	44591
125 4/8	20 2/8	20 2/8	17 2/8	4	4	Columbia County	WI	James J. Van Erem, Jr.	2008	44591
*125 4/8	19 6/8	20 1/8	12 2/8	4	4	Sussex County	VA	Bryan Cockrell	2008	44591
*125 4/8	19 2/8	20 3/8	16 4/8	5	5	Oakland County	MI	William Lee Hienz	2008	44591
*125 4/8	21 0/8	20 6/8	17 2/8	5	4	Brown County	WI	Nick Van Lanen	2008	44591
125 4/8	21 0/8	21 6/8	15 6/8	5	5	Polk County	WI	Freddie D. Lay	2008	44591
125 4/8	22 1/8	22 4/8	15 2/8	4	4	Grant County	WI	Warren DeSmidt	2008	44591
125 4/8	21 6/8	22 4/8	16 6/8	4	4	Screven County	GA	Ryan Beasley	2008	44591
125 4/8	21 1/8	20 4/8	16 2/8	5	5	Sullivan County	MO	Jeff Johnson	2008	44591
125 4/8	21 5/8	21 4/8	16 2/8	5	4	Breckinridge County	KY	John Smedley	2008	44591
125 4/8	21 4/8	22 3/8	16 2/8	4	5	Parker County	TX	Robert L. Moss	2008	44591
*125 4/8	20 4/8	21 3/8	19 0/8	4	4	Winnebago County	WI	Todd Stecker	2009	44591
125 4/8	20 3/8	20 7/8	15 0/8	4	5	Martin County	IN	Christopher G. Collins	2009	44591
*125 4/8	22 4/8	23 1/8	19 0/8	4	4	Monmouth County	NJ	Michael Popek	2009	44591
125 4/8	21 2/8	21 5/8	19 0/8	5	4	Gallatin County	IL	Paul Morgan	2009	44591
*125 4/8	21 5/8	21 6/8	16 4/8	4	4	Dunn County	WI	Tom Forster	2009	44591
125 4/8	20 2/8	19 5/8	12 3/8	7	4	Marquette County	WI	Todd Grota	2009	44591
125 4/8	20 6/8	19 7/8	14 6/8	6	7	Aitkin County	MN	Ben J. Johnson	2009	44591
125 4/8	20 7/8	20 7/8	15 4/8	7	5	Appanoose County	IA	Bruce Humphrey	2009	44591
125 4/8	21 7/8	22 5/8	16 4/8	4	4	Jefferson County	OH	Nate Felton	2009	44591
125 4/8	23 7/8	24 3/8	15 0/8	4	4	Clark County	WI	Gregory A. Artac	2009	44591
*125 4/8	21 4/8	22 1/8	17 0/8	5	5	Belmont County	OH	Donald Simpson	2009	44591
125 3/8	24 0/8	24 0/8	16 1/8	4	4	Harrison County	IN	Glenn Huber	1992	44901
125 3/8	21 5/8	21 6/8	17 5/8	5	5	Winnebago County	WI	Jim Wesenberg	1997	44901
125 3/8	19 0/8	20 2/8	18 3/8	5	5	Ogle County	IL	Marvin A. Longenecker	2000	44901
125 3/8	20 0/8	20 5/8	16 1/8	5	4	Winnebago County	WI	Deno Loukidis	2002	44901
125 3/8	20 6/8	20 6/8	15 1/8	5	5	Nodaway County	MO	Chris A. Burns	2002	44901
125 3/8	25 7/8	25 5/8	22 1/8	4	3	Comanche County	KS	Ted K. Jaycox	2002	44901
125 3/8	20 1/8	20 6/8	14 3/8	5	5	Iowa County	IA	Kevin McDonald	2003	44901
125 3/8	24 0/8	24 4/8	17 3/8	5	4	Jo Daviess County	IL	Chris Holden	2003	44901
125 3/8	16 5/8	17 0/8	16 0/8	7	7	Lyon County	KY	Ricky J. Smotherman	2003	44901
125 3/8	22 4/8	22 6/8	18 3/8	5	4	Mercer County	NJ	Salvatore Piazza, Jr.	2004	44901
125 3/8	20 1/8	21 0/8	16 0/8	5	7	Anoka County	MN	Daniel Iacarella	2004	44901
125 3/8	22 6/8	22 3/8	16 1/8	4	4	Montgomery County	TN	Christopher N. Bryant	2004	44901

WHITETAIL DEER (TYPICAL ANTLERS)

Minimum Score 125   Continued

SCORE	LENGTH OF R MAIN BEAM L	INSIDE SPREAD	NUMBER OF R POINTS L	AREA	STATE/ PROVINCE	HUNTER'S NAME	DATE	RANK
125 3/8	22 7/8 22 4/8	16 3/8	4 5	New Kent County	VA	James M. Adams	2004	44901
*125 3/8	21 4/8 20 6/8	17 5/8	4 5	Wabasha County	MN	Craig Bloom	2004	44901
125 3/8	19 5/8 20 4/8	15 1/8	4 4	Pike County	IL	J. J. Judd	2004	44901
125 3/8	21 5/8 22 0/8	17 5/8	4 4	Buffalo County	WI	Rob Hasse	2004	44901
125 3/8	23 1/8 23 1/8	19 3/8	5 6	Cass County	IL	Mark Livingston	2004	44901
125 3/8	22 0/8 22 0/8	14 7/8	5 5	Yankton County	SD	Jeff Simonsen	2004	44901
125 3/8	19 1/8 17 7/8	15 3/8	5 5	Richland County	WI	Michael D. Alexander	2004	44901
125 3/8	21 4/8 21 1/8	19 1/8	5 5	Meigs County	OH	Eric E. Lawson	2004	44901
125 3/8	19 0/8 20 1/8	15 1/8	5 5	Dubuque County	IA	John Duggan	2004	44901
125 3/8	22 5/8 21 7/8	12 5/8	5 7	Troup County	GA	Steve Pollard	2004	44901
125 3/8	20 2/8 19 5/8	14 7/8	5 5	Spokane County	WA	Steve Mitchell	2004	44901
125 3/8	23 0/8 22 4/8	15 3/8	5 4	Runnels County	TX	Austin Terry	2004	44901
*125 3/8	21 7/8 21 4/8	16 7/8	5 5	Jefferson County	IN	Andrew W. Pickett	2005	44901
125 3/8	20 6/8 21 6/8	17 5/8	4 4	Roberts County	SD	Wesley Koehler	2005	44901
125 3/8	22 2/8 21 7/8	14 5/8	4 4	Putnam County	TN	Jerry Williams	2005	44901
125 3/8	21 0/8 20 3/8	14 7/8	6 5	Licking County	OH	Robert M. Osgood, Jr.	2005	44901
125 3/8	22 6/8 22 3/8	21 4/8	4 5	Newport News County	VA	Dwight S. Wolf	2005	44901
125 3/8	24 5/8 24 2/8	19 2/8	5 5	Somerset County	NJ	Charlie Keri	2005	44901
125 3/8	22 2/8 21 6/8	15 5/8	5 4	Somerset County	NJ	John J. Mascellino, Sr.	2005	44901
125 3/8	19 3/8 20 4/8	15 7/8	5 5	Jackson County	MI	Robert M. Watson	2005	44901
125 3/8	20 0/8 20 2/8	16 7/8	5 5	Mecosta County	MI	Brian Moore	2005	44901
125 3/8	21 6/8 22 0/8	17 5/8	5 5	Jefferson County	WV	Joseph Proctor	2005	44901
125 3/8	21 0/8 21 6/8	16 2/8	4 5	Sioux County	IA	Lyle Schut	2005	44901
125 3/8	20 6/8 21 2/8	19 2/8	4 5	Delaware County	IN	Scott A. Conley	2005	44901
125 3/8	22 4/8 22 5/8	14 5/8	4 4	Richland County	WI	Chanc L. Vogel	2005	44901
125 3/8	19 5/8 20 4/8	19 7/8	6 5	Ashtabula County	OH	Ray A. Youngs	2005	44901
125 3/8	22 0/8 22 0/8	15 1/8	4 4	Jefferson County	WI	Dennis Jones	2005	44901
*125 3/8	21 0/8 20 7/8	16 1/8	5 5	Washington County	OH	Mark Keith Hall	2005	44901
125 3/8	21 3/8 20 3/8	17 3/8	5 5	Polk County	WI	Joseph J. Kahl	2005	44901
125 3/8	20 5/8 20 4/8	17 1/8	5 5	Rockland County	NY	Ben Risley	2005	44901
*125 3/8	21 6/8 22 0/8	14 5/8	4 5	Shelby County	KY	Daniel Quire	2006	44901
125 3/8	22 3/8 22 3/8	15 7/8	4 4	Dodge County	MN	Jesse Stevenson	2006	44901
*125 3/8	21 4/8 22 1/8	13 3/8	4 4	Hickman County	TN	Richard Boehms	2006	44901
125 3/8	20 7/8 19 5/8	15 4/8	5 5	Shawano County	WI	Mark Redman	2006	44901
125 3/8	21 5/8 21 3/8	15 7/8	4 5	Ashe County	NC	Scott Hurley	2006	44901
125 3/8	21 6/8 21 4/8	16 5/8	4 4	Allegheny County	PA	Nick Denobile	2006	44901
125 3/8	21 2/8 20 3/8	16 5/8	5 5	Jackson County	MI	Thomas P. Bloomfield	2006	44901
125 3/8	20 5/8 20 6/8	16 7/8	4 5	Franklin County	KS	Kent Bailey	2006	44901
*125 3/8	22 3/8 21 5/8	18 5/8	4 4	York County	PA	Brad A. Hirneisen	2006	44901
125 3/8	21 6/8 20 2/8	14 5/8	4 4	Washington County	OH	Hobert Payne	2006	44901
125 3/8	20 6/8 20 1/8	16 6/8	5 6	Kewaunee County	WI	Thomas C. Spiering	2006	44901
*125 3/8	24 7/8 24 5/8	17 5/8	5 5	Norfolk County	MA	David J. Robertson	2006	44901
*125 3/8	18 4/8 23 1/8	17 7/8	4 4	Griggs County	ND	Al Messner	2006	44901
*125 3/8	19 2/8 20 4/8	16 3/8	5 5	Green Lake County	WI	Rodney Busse	2006	44901
125 3/8	21 5/8 22 0/8	17 7/8	4 5	Madison County	MS	Ken Pugh	2007	44901
125 3/8	19 5/8 20 2/8	15 7/8	4 4	Marathon County	WI	Scott Bessette	2007	44901
125 3/8	19 2/8 20 2/8	19 1/8	5 5	Athens County	OH	Travis Q. Crook	2007	44901
*125 3/8	21 3/8 22 3/8	15 7/8	5 6	Sutton County	TX	Raymond Joe Hromadka III	2007	44901
*125 3/8	24 3/8 22 5/8	18 6/8	5 5	Marion County	OH	James L. Rowland	2007	44901
125 3/8	21 3/8 21 4/8	15 7/8	4 4	Butler County	MO	Terry Abner	2007	44901
125 3/8	20 6/8 21 5/8	15 7/8	4 4	Guthrie County	IA	Tracy G. Groves	2007	44901
*125 3/8	20 6/8 19 0/8	14 5/8	5 4	Cass County	ND	Roy Aafedt	2007	44901
*125 3/8	20 6/8 20 3/8	17 1/8	4 5	Mason County	TX	David McWilliams	2007	44901
125 3/8	21 3/8 22 6/8	15 1/8	4 4	Adams County	IL	William M. Roach	2007	44901
125 3/8	20 4/8 19 2/8	15 5/8	5 5	Adams County	WI	Todd Calverley	2007	44901
125 3/8	20 4/8 18 6/8	14 4/8	5 6	Waukesha County	WI	Tom J. Gorski	2007	44901
*125 3/8	21 0/8 21 7/8	15 7/8	4 4	Cayuga County	NY	Marvin Russell	2007	44901
*125 3/8	20 6/8 20 7/8	16 3/8	6 5	Madison Parish	LA	John Robert Gaumnitz	2007	44901
*125 3/8	22 0/8 22 0/8	18 2/8	4 5	Lincoln County	TN	Jason Reed McCormick	2007	44901
125 3/8	21 3/8 20 6/8	16 7/8	5 5	Edwards County	IL	Eli Landingham	2008	44901
125 3/8	19 6/8 20 0/8	16 5/8	5 4	Marshall County	IN	Michael A. Splix	2008	44901
125 3/8	22 5/8 22 1/8	17 2/8	5 4	Pepin County	WI	Jim Clark	2008	44901
125 3/8	18 7/8 20 1/8	16 3/8	4 5	Oakland County	MI	Gary J. Johnson	2008	44901
125 3/8	22 3/8 23 0/8	18 2/8	5 4	La Crosse County	WI	Lee J. Keim	2008	44901
*125 3/8	22 2/8 21 0/8	17 3/8	5 5	Will County	IL	David A. McGinnis	2008	44901
125 3/8	21 2/8 20 0/8	15 5/8	5 5	Hancock County	IL	Josh Adkins	2008	44901
*125 3/8	23 7/8 25 7/8	16 4/8	5 5	Madison County	MS	Harvey Bozeman	2009	44901
*125 3/8	22 0/8 21 5/8	16 2/8	4 5	Seward County	NE	Keith Sedlak	2009	44901
125 3/8	22 4/8 21 4/8	15 3/8	5 5	Henry County	GA	Greg Wiggins	2009	44901
125 3/8	21 1/8 21 2/8	16 1/8	4 4	Carroll County	MS	Chris Reed	2009	44901
125 3/8	22 5/8 22 2/8	20 3/8	4 4	Centre County	PA	Curtis W. Smith	2009	44901
*125 3/8	23 0/8 22 2/8	15 7/8	4 5	St. Clair County	MI	Daniel I. Delor	2009	44901
125 3/8	21 3/8 21 0/8	15 6/8	5 4	Will County	IL	Jeff Pals	2009	44901
125 3/8	21 3/8 21 7/8	17 1/8	4 4	Steuben County	IN	Jeremy Antrup	2009	44901
*125 3/8	22 2/8 21 2/8	15 3/8	4 5	Dunn County	WI	Matthew C. Benrud	2009	44901
*125 3/8	19 3/8 20 3/8	19 3/8	5 5	Washburn County	WI	Mike Schuster	2009	44901
125 3/8	22 5/8 23 6/8	15 0/8	4 5	Washington County	PA	Dale Robison	2009	44901
125 3/8	22 6/8 22 4/8	15 3/8	4 4	Mower County	MN	Cameron Landherr	2009	44901
125 3/8	20 1/8 21 1/8	16 7/8	4 4	Cavalier County	ND	Brenna Logie	2010	44901
125 3/8	23 4/8 23 0/8	17 4/8	5 5	Barron County	WI	Travis Newhouse	2010	44901
125 3/8	18 7/8 18 5/8	14 3/8	4 4	Liberty County	TX	Mark Campbell	2010	44901
*125 3/8	24 5/8 24 7/8	14 3/8	5 6	Kent County	MI	Thomas Dean	2010	44901
125 2/8	19 5/8 19 3/8	15 6/8	5 5	Butler County	PA	Allen K. Frye	1996	45199
125 2/8	22 3/8 23 6/8	18 0/8	5 5	Brown County	TX	Lindy McCarty	1998	45199
125 2/8	21 1/8 20 4/8	17 2/8	5 4	Clarion County	PA	Michael T. Hamilton	1998	45199
*125 2/8	20 2/8 21 6/8	15 0/8	5 5	Sullivan County	IN	Bo Eikelman	2002	45199
125 2/8	22 6/8 22 2/8	14 6/8	4 4	Kent County	MI	Jerry Ouderkirk	2003	45199
125 2/8	20 7/8 20 0/8	17 4/8	4 4	Kane County	IL	Fred Lehman	2003	45199
125 2/8	19 0/8 20 1/8	13 6/8	6 6	Manitowoc County	WI	Davic A. Ozarowicz, Sr.	2004	45199
125 2/8	19 5/8 18 7/8	16 4/8	4 4	Nuckolls County	NE	John D. Price	2004	45199
125 2/8	22 0/8 21 3/8	16 4/8	4 4	Lawrence County	IN	Michael J. Bartlett	2004	45199
125 2/8	22 4/8 21 0/8	15 4/8	4 5	Cecil County	MD	Penny Grove	2004	45199
125 2/8	21 5/8 21 3/8	15 6/8	6 5	Marquette County	WI	Jay A. Severson	2004	45199
125 2/8	22 4/8 22 2/8	15 0/8	4 4	Pawnee County	NE	Julie D. Thornburg	2004	45199
*125 2/8	18 3/8 18 3/8	15 6/8	6 6	Wabasha County	MN	John Corfits	2004	45199

Deer entries below 141 0/8, that appeared in the 6th Edition, are not included here, but are included on the accompanying CD (see page 119), and also in the Club's Records Archives.

WHITETAIL DEER (TYPICAL ANTLERS)

Minimum Score 125 — Continued

SCORE	LENGTH OF R MAIN BEAM L	INSIDE SPREAD	NUMBER OF R POINTS L		AREA	STATE/ PROVINCE	HUNTER'S NAME	DATE	RANK
125 2/8	22 1/8	22 5/8	16 0/8	5	6	Raleigh County	WV	Eric VanGilder	2004	45199
125 2/8	21 4/8	20 3/8	16 6/8	5	6	Carrot River	SAS	Tom Nelson	2004	45199
*125 2/8	25 7/8	23 5/8	15 7/8	5	4	Brown County	IL	John Fulkerth	2004	45199
125 2/8	22 1/8	21 0/8	18 4/8	7	7	Bremer County	IA	Ryan Reiter	2004	45199
*125 2/8	22 0/8	22 3/8	17 4/8	4	5	Pulaski County	KY	Marty Flynn	2004	45199
125 2/8	21 6/8	21 0/8	16 4/8	4	4	Lucas County	IA	Kent Brigham	2004	45199
125 2/8	22 0/8	21 0/8	16 0/8	4	4	Jackson County	WI	Terry J. Aide	2004	45199
125 2/8	22 1/8	22 5/8	18 5/8	5	8	Washington County	IL	Brad Sanders	2004	45199
125 2/8	18 4/8	18 4/8	14 0/8	4	4	Hocking County	OH	Charles Torson	2004	45199
125 2/8	22 0/8	16 3/8	16 4/8	6	5	Anoka County	MN	Kraig Garmaker	2004	45199
125 2/8	21 1/8	21 6/8	18 2/8	4	4	Hamilton County	KS	Tim Cuthriell	2004	45199
125 2/8	21 0/8	20 5/8	16 6/8	4	4	Burlington County	NJ	Wilford Staley	2004	45199
125 2/8	20 2/8	21 2/8	15 6/8	4	4	Cass County	IL	Gregg Krikke	2004	45199
125 2/8	19 7/8	19 7/8	14 4/8	4	4	Sheridan County	WY	Mark Buehrer	2005	45199
125 2/8	19 4/8	19 3/8	16 2/8	6	5	Spokane County	WA	Joel R. Enevold	2005	45199
125 2/8	18 6/8	20 5/8	17 4/8	4	4	Hancock County	GA	Clay Lumsden	2005	45199
*125 2/8	21 0/8	22 3/8	13 2/8	4	5	Jefferson County	IN	Kenneth D. Routh	2005	45199
125 2/8	22 1/8	22 7/8	18 4/8	4	4	Brown County	OH	Harold E. Uhl	2005	45199
*125 2/8	19 5/8	20 3/8	16 6/8	4	4	Waukesha County	WI	Barry Grimm	2005	45199
125 2/8	22 0/8	21 3/8	16 2/8	4	5	Guilford County	NC	Ty Anderson	2005	45199
*125 2/8	21 7/8	20 5/8	16 6/8	4	4	Beaver County	PA	Jared Kramer	2005	45199
125 2/8	20 6/8	21 2/8	15 4/8	5	5	Buffalo County	WI	Curt Rotering	2005	45199
125 2/8	22 0/8	21 7/8	15 4/8	5	5	Morgan County	IN	James M. McBride	2005	45199
125 2/8	21 3/8	21 1/8	13 2/8	4	4	Mercer County	MO	David W. Grindley	2005	45199
125 2/8	21 7/8	20 6/8	19 0/8	5	4	Pittsburg County	OK	James L. Fowler	2005	45199
125 2/8	23 6/8	21 4/8	20 3/8	5	8	Mercer County	PA	Jeff Burncheck	2005	45199
125 2/8	21 1/8	21 4/8	16 2/8	5	5	Leelanau County	MI	Noel J. Flohe	2005	45199
125 2/8	18 7/8	19 3/8	12 6/8	6	5	Davis County	IA	Jeremy Sickles	2005	45199
125 2/8	18 5/8	19 2/8	16 4/8	5	5	Bradford County	PA	Christopher B. Muller	2005	45199
125 2/8	23 3/8	22 4/8	16 2/8	4	4	New Haven County	CT	John Harrison	2005	45199
125 2/8	21 5/8	21 5/8	15 6/8	4	4	Missoula County	MT	Marlon Clapham	2005	45199
*125 2/8	21 0/8	20 7/8	17 3/8	6	5	Huron County	OH	Rob Crouse	2005	45199
*125 2/8	22 3/8	22 4/8	18 6/8	4	4	Tom Green County	TX	Austin Terry	2005	45199
125 2/8	21 2/8	21 2/8	16 4/8	4	4	Burnett County	WI	Dean Anderson	2006	45199
125 2/8	23 0/8	23 2/8	16 6/8	5	4	Marathon County	WI	Shawn Cychosz	2006	45199
125 2/8	20 4/8	21 0/8	13 4/8	5	5	Eddy County	ND	Jason Stafford	2006	45199
*125 2/8	22 7/8	21 7/8	13 4/8	4	4	Daviess County	IN	Cory Swartzentruber	2006	45199
125 2/8	22 0/8	22 4/8	18 2/8	4	4	Bucks County	PA	Stephen Kollar	2006	45199
125 2/8	21 6/8	22 1/8	16 4/8	4	6	Allegany County	NY	Roger Gross	2006	45199
125 2/8	21 6/8	19 7/8	17 5/8	5	6	Butler County	OH	Matthew J. Dillon	2006	45199
125 2/8	23 5/8	22 2/8	19 1/8	5	5	Jack County	TX	J. W. Lindsey, Jr.	2006	45199
*125 2/8	19 0/8	19 2/8	14 6/8	6	5	Lucas County	IA	Thomas Novak	2006	45199
125 2/8	19 4/8	20 1/8	16 2/8	5	5	Vernon County	WI	Greg A. Miller	2006	45199
*125 2/8	21 0/8	22 0/8	17 6/8	5	5	Boone County	MO	L. Stephen Claypool	2006	45199
125 2/8	22 3/8	21 2/8	15 6/8	5	5	McHenry County	ND	Rodney "Spud" Walker	2006	45199
125 2/8	21 7/8	21 1/8	17 7/8	5	6	Kingsbury County	SD	Reginald E. Faber, Jr.	2006	45199
*125 2/8	22 3/8	23 3/8	19 4/8	5	5	Linn County	IA	Mary Benion	2006	45199
125 2/8	19 3/8	19 7/8	14 2/8	5	5	Kimble County	TX	Spencer Jerome Smith	2007	45199
125 2/8	21 7/8	19 7/8	19 0/8	4	4	Muskegon County	MI	Matt Wurm	2007	45199
125 2/8	22 0/8	21 6/8	13 2/8	4	5	Gregory County	SD	Bill Porter	2007	45199
*125 2/8	19 2/8	19 4/8	14 3/8	6	6	Cavalier County	ND	Dwight Logie	2007	45199
125 2/8	20 5/8	21 6/8	16 2/8	5	5	Ontario County	NY	Christopher J. Kunes	2007	45199
*125 2/8	21 3/8	20 7/8	16 6/8	5	4	Brown County	KS	Kirk Clark	2007	45199
125 2/8	19 6/8	19 5/8	15 1/8	5	6	Adams County	IL	Rob Hyland	2007	45199
*125 2/8	20 0/8	20 0/8	15 2/8	6	6	Barber County	KS	Keith Geasey	2007	45199
*125 2/8	19 7/8	19 7/8	13 6/8	5	5	Fayette County	IL	Derek Rigdon	2007	45199
*125 2/8	20 7/8	18 5/8	19 0/8	4	5	Fountain County	IN	Matthew Hanna	2007	45199
125 2/8	20 5/8	20 5/8	14 4/8	4	4	Nemaha County	NE	Randall L. Rehmeier	2007	45199
*125 2/8	21 6/8	20 6/8	14 2/8	5	5	Cooper County	MO	Dayton Jones	2007	45199
125 2/8	21 2/8	21 2/8	17 1/8	5	5	Buffalo County	WI	Ronald Williams	2007	45199
125 2/8	21 2/8	20 7/8	14 2/8	4	5	Hubbard County	MN	Marvin H. Walter	2007	45199
125 2/8	23 1/8	22 1/8	14 0/8	5	5	Henderson County	IL	Michael A. Chauvet	2007	45199
125 2/8	22 2/8	23 0/8	17 6/8	4	4	Richland County	OH	Bill Boggs	2007	45199
125 2/8	20 2/8	18 7/8	14 0/8	6	5	Wyoming County	WV	Joseph Ratliff	2007	45199
125 2/8	25 6/8	25 2/8	15 6/8	4	4	Surry County	VA	Dwight S. Wolf	2007	45199
*125 2/8	21 6/8	21 6/8	20 0/8	5	5	Douglas County	WI	Brian Raygor	2007	45199
125 2/8	20 0/8	20 6/8	17 4/8	4	4	Shackelford County	TX	Brandon Ray	2008	45199
125 2/8	20 4/8	20 0/8	13 6/8	5	5	Clark County	WI	Dawn Gregorich	2008	45199
*125 2/8	19 6/8	19 3/8	14 6/8	4	4	Allamakee County	IA	Wayne A. Buckley	2008	45199
*125 2/8	20 7/8	21 3/8	16 6/8	4	5	Cayuga County	NY	William F. Walker	2008	45199
125 2/8	20 6/8	21 1/8	18 0/8	4	5	Colorado County	TX	Jon Stephens, Jr.	2008	45199
125 2/8	21 4/8	21 5/8	15 3/8	4	6	Saline County	AR	Mike Mobley	2008	45199
125 2/8	20 2/8	21 1/8	14 2/8	4	5	Wyandot County	OH	Jeremy Mouser	2008	45199
*125 2/8	20 7/8	20 7/8	18 4/8	4	4	Licking County	OH	Corey Enders	2008	45199
125 2/8	20 1/8	21 1/8	16 2/8	5	4	Lincoln County	KS	Larry R. Morris	2008	45199
125 2/8	22 0/8	23 0/8	15 0/8	4	6	Coweta County	GA	Ken Yearta	2008	45199
125 2/8	22 2/8	22 0/8	16 2/8	5	5	Sheboygan County	WI	Jeremy S. Groeschl	2008	45199
125 2/8	20 4/8	20 7/8	14 1/8	6	6	Van Buren County	IA	Chris McAfee	2008	45199
*125 2/8	20 5/8	20 5/8	15 6/8	5	5	Bucks County	PA	Jack E. Titlow	2008	45199
125 2/8	22 0/8	22 2/8	15 4/8	4	4	Zavala County	TX	Ronald Wardell	2008	45199
125 2/8	22 0/8	21 3/8	16 2/8	4	4	Love County	OK	Ted Taylor	2008	45199
125 2/8	20 4/8	19 6/8	17 6/8	5	5	Chisago County	MN	Dan Husnik	2009	45199
*125 2/8	24 0/8	24 0/8	17 6/8	7	7	Green Lake County	WI	John T. Quade	2009	45199
*125 2/8	19 3/8	19 3/8	13 0/8	5	5	Monroe County	PA	Michael J. Russo, Jr.	2009	45199
125 2/8	20 6/8	21 2/8	18 4/8	5	5	Livingston County	NY	Herb Ellis	2009	45199
*125 2/8	22 3/8	21 6/8	17 3/8	7	4	Ontario County	NY	Gerard E. Brzezinski	2009	45199
*125 2/8	21 4/8	20 4/8	18 6/8	5	5	Baltimore County	MD	Brian Russell	2009	45199
125 2/8	21 5/8	21 0/8	16 0/8	4	5	Cayuga County	NY	Robert VanWie	2009	45199
125 2/8	23 1/8	23 0/8	17 0/8	4	5	Vermillion County	IN	Ernest Hurst	2009	45199
125 1/8	22 1/8	21 6/8	13 7/8	5	5	Buffalo County	WI	Todd Suiter	1987	45547
125 1/8	21 5/8	22 4/8	14 7/8	4	5	Kerr County	TX	Ronald G. Ralston	1994	45547
125 1/8	23 0/8	24 0/8	17 5/8	4	4	Martin County	IN	Brian Huber	1996	45547
125 1/8	20 5/8	19 3/8	16 5/8	5	5	Chautauqua County	KS	Tim Williams	1998	45547
125 1/8	21 2/8	20 7/8	16 3/8	4	4	Monroe County	WI	James Amundson	1998	45547
*125 1/8	19 0/8	19 3/8	17 1/8	5	5	Woodford County	KY	Joe Lacefield	2001	45547

WHITETAIL DEER (TYPICAL ANTLERS)

Minimum Score 125   Continued

SCORE	LENGTH OF R MAIN BEAM L	INSIDE SPREAD	NUMBER OF R POINTS L		AREA	STATE/ PROVINCE	HUNTER'S NAME	DATE	RANK
*125 1/8	21 7/8 21 3/8	17 4/8	5	5	Cass County	MI	Patrick D. Kleppert	2002	45547
*125 1/8	22 4/8 22 2/8	16 6/8	6	6	Muskingum County	OH	Jeff Lee	2003	45547
125 1/8	22 1/8 21 5/8	17 3/8	4	5	Fayette County	IL	Rob Shuff	2003	45547
125 1/8	20 1/8 22 0/8	16 0/8	6	4	Grant County	WI	Thomas J. Hinman	2003	45547
*125 1/8	21 6/8 21 3/8	15 7/8	4	4	Guernsey County	OH	Bryan Wentzel	2003	45547
125 1/8	21 7/8 21 6/8	16 6/8	4	5	Lake County	IL	Joseph J. Legat	2003	45547
125 1/8	22 3/8 23 3/8	17 1/8	4	4	Fairfield County	CT	David A. Sanford	2004	45547
125 1/8	23 1/8 23 2/8	18 1/8	4	4	Forest County	WI	Clifford Folkers	2004	45547
125 1/8	22 4/8 22 5/8	19 7/8	6	6	Marquette County	WI	Ty Stafford	2004	45547
125 1/8	21 3/8 21 1/8	17 3/8	7	8	Lake County	IL	Ken Wodek III	2004	45547
125 1/8	19 3/8 18 7/8	14 5/8	5	5	Dearborn County	IN	Daniel R. Smith	2004	45547
125 1/8	23 3/8 23 3/8	19 4/8	5	4	Bayfield County	WI	Ronald Hornstein	2004	45547
125 1/8	22 1/8 22 4/8	13 7/8	4	4	Tom Green County	TX	Justin Duyck	2004	45547
125 1/8	21 1/8 22 0/8	16 4/8	6	8	Licking County	OH	Hobert Payne	2004	45547
125 1/8	19 2/8 20 1/8	15 7/8	5	5	Stutsman County	ND	Jon Sjostrom	2004	45547
*125 1/8	21 3/8 22 4/8	18 7/8	4	4	Buffalo County	WI	Josh Chelf	2005	45547
125 1/8	19 6/8 19 7/8	14 3/8	4	4	Washburn County	WI	Douglas R. Schlattman	2005	45547
*125 1/8	20 5/8 20 6/8	14 7/8	4	5	Clinton County	MI	Jim Dunigan	2005	45547
125 1/8	21 0/8 20 6/8	15 7/8	4	4	Dewey County	OK	Sean Holt	2005	45547
125 1/8	22 6/8 24 4/8	17 3/8	7	5	Jefferson County	WI	Dan Gottschalk	2005	45547
125 1/8	22 5/8 23 0/8	18 5/8	4	4	Lehigh County	PA	James E. Weiss	2005	45547
*125 1/8	20 4/8 20 6/8	15 7/8	4	4	Belmont County	OH	Rick Goode	2005	45547
*125 1/8	21 5/8 20 5/8	16 1/8	4	4	Kent County	MI	Sam Cooley, Jr.	2005	45547
125 1/8	23 5/8 23 4/8	20 1/8	4	4	St. Louis County	MO	Bill Hutchens	2005	45547
125 1/8	25 2/8 25 0/8	16 1/8	5	3	La Crosse County	WI	Jordan P. Gerardy	2005	45547
125 1/8	19 0/8 19 2/8	16 6/8	7	6	Pulaski County	MO	Ken Morgan	2005	45547
*125 1/8	22 4/8 22 2/8	17 0/8	5	4	Trempealeau County	WI	Keith Schaefer	2005	45547
125 1/8	19 7/8 20 1/8	16 3/8	4	4	Logan County	WV	Edward Humphreys	2005	45547
*125 1/8	20 5/8 21 3/8	16 1/8	5	6	Ontario County	NY	Fred N. Wesley	2005	45547
125 1/8	22 0/8 23 0/8	19 3/8	4	4	Middlesex County	MA	Ed Crowley	2005	45547
125 1/8	21 6/8 21 5/8	16 6/8	7	5	Howard County	IA	John Koschmeder	2005	45547
125 1/8	21 5/8 22 0/8	15 1/8	4	4	Woodford County	IL	John Wesley Zerby	2005	45547
125 1/8	20 6/8 21 0/8	17 1/8	5	6	Nuevo Leon	MEX	Spencer Smith	2005	45547
125 1/8	20 5/8 21 0/8	17 4/8	5	4	Monmouth County	NJ	Anthony Cona	2006	45547
*125 1/8	20 7/8 20 7/8	13 1/8	7	7	Polk County	WI	Robert E. Benjamin	2006	45547
*125 1/8	23 0/8 22 1/8	18 5/8	4	5	Greene County	PA	Dewey L. Stillwagon	2006	45547
125 1/8	19 3/8 19 6/8	17 1/8	4	4	Keith County	NE	Michael Montgomery	2006	45547
125 1/8	20 7/8 21 0/8	12 7/8	5	4	Orange County	IN	Sam Schroeder	2006	45547
125 1/8	21 0/8 21 0/8	19 1/8	5	5	McHenry County	ND	Jeff Jacob	2006	45547
*125 1/8	20 0/8 20 5/8	18 1/8	5	5	Manitowoc County	WI	Tony Thelen	2006	45547
125 1/8	23 7/8 24 0/8	18 7/8	4	5	Kosciusko County	IN	Daniel J. List	2006	45547
*125 1/8	22 1/8 21 5/8	15 3/8	4	4	Coles County	IL	Anthony Chrisagis	2006	45547
125 1/8	19 5/8 19 4/8	16 5/8	5	5	Knox County	IL	Randy Bozarth	2006	45547
125 1/8	21 0/8 20 2/8	16 5/8	4	4	Jackson County	WI	Carl B. Ward, Jr.	2006	45547
125 1/8	22 2/8 22 4/8	17 5/8	5	4	Buffalo County	WI	Jerry Rucinski	2006	45547
125 1/8	21 7/8 21 6/8	15 1/8	4	5	Jackson County	WI	Dave Schilling	2006	45547
125 1/8	21 1/8 21 2/8	14 3/8	5	4	Maries County	MO	Sean Travis	2006	45547
125 1/8	24 3/8 24 5/8	18 7/8	3	3	Oconto County	WI	Patrick John Gauthier	2006	45547
*125 1/8	21 4/8 20 6/8	19 1/8	5	5	Rock Island County	IL	Ronald F. Lax	2006	45547
125 1/8	20 5/8 21 2/8	16 3/8	5	5	Otero County	CO	Peter J. Bodette	2006	45547
125 1/8	18 6/8 17 4/8	15 3/8	5	5	Monroe County	IA	Gary Martin	2006	45547
125 1/8	23 3/8 23 6/8	18 3/8	4	4	Pierce County	WI	Lance J. Olson	2006	45547
*125 1/8	21 0/8 20 7/8	17 6/8	5	6	Chautauqua County	KS	Timothy Broughton	2006	45547
*125 1/8	20 4/8 20 6/8	19 1/8	4	4	Hunterdon County	NJ	Karl D. Zschack	2007	45547
125 1/8	19 3/8 21 7/8	17 5/8	5	5	St. Clair County	MI	Mike Lavens	2007	45547
*125 1/8	21 1/8 21 1/8	15 7/8	5	5	Putnam County	GA	Jeff Hegwood	2007	45547
*125 1/8	20 2/8 21 1/8	16 1/8	5	4	Putnam County	WV	Holden Eads	2007	45547
*125 1/8	19 4/8 19 4/8	13 3/8	5	5	Washington County	PA	John Konwick	2007	45547
125 1/8	20 3/8 20 1/8	16 1/8	4	4	Coshocton County	OH	H. Dewey Thompson	2007	45547
125 1/8	21 4/8 21 5/8	17 3/8	4	4	Dane County	WI	Lewton D. Peterson	2007	45547
*125 1/8	22 2/8 22 0/8	16 5/8	5	5	Shelby County	KY	Greg Wethington	2007	45547
*125 1/8	22 7/8 22 6/8	17 3/8	5	6	Spink County	SD	Randy Dewald	2007	45547
*125 1/8	20 0/8 20 1/8	17 1/8	4	4	Berks County	PA	Michael P. Follweiler	2007	45547
125 1/8	20 6/8 20 6/8	16 3/8	4	4	Houghton County	MI	Dennis L. Hodge	2007	45547
125 1/8	20 5/8 19 6/8	15 3/8	5	5	Dimmit County	TX	Clark Daniel	2007	45547
*125 1/8	23 7/8 22 5/8	15 7/8	4	4	Berrien County	MI	Chad A. Schau	2007	45547
125 1/8	20 3/8 21 3/8	17 3/8	4	5	Outagamie County	WI	Frank Pierri	2007	45547
125 1/8	20 3/8 21 0/8	15 4/8	4	6	Caley County	KS	Terri Ferrell	2007	45547
125 1/8	23 2/8 21 5/8	19 1/8	4	4	Coffey County	KS	Darrell Shaw	2007	45547
125 1/8	20 0/8 20 5/8	18 1/8	5	5	Powell County	MT	Kurt J. Wilkinson	2007	45547
125 1/8	22 4/8 21 5/8	16 5/8	5	5	Jefferson County	ID	David Chappell	2007	45547
125 1/8	22 1/8 22 1/8	20 3/8	4	4	Forest County	PA	Lee Eric Estes	2007	45547
125 1/8	19 5/8 19 5/8	16 3/8	5	5	Bureau County	IL	Greg Bowers	2007	45547
125 1/8	20 6/8 20 6/8	19 3/8	4	4	Clay County	MN	John Schaffer	2008	45547
125 1/8	19 7/8 19 7/8	16 7/8	4	4	Fergus County	MT	John "Rosey" Roseland	2008	45547
*125 1/8	21 5/8 22 3/8	16 4/8	5	6	Lake County	IL	Peter H. Sarbacker	2008	45547
125 1/8	21 7/8 22 0/8	16 5/8	4	5	Steuben County	IN	Grant Schimmele	2008	45547
*125 1/8	20 4/8 20 1/8	17 7/8	5	5	Muskingum County	OH	Charles D. Martin	2008	45547
125 1/8	20 2/8 20 1/8	16 7/8	5	5	Shawano County	WI	Steve Van Camp	2008	45547
*125 1/8	20 0/8 18 7/8	15 1/8	4	4	Dane County	WI	Jeffrey Lange	2008	45547
*125 1/8	20 1/8 20 4/8	16 3/8	4	4	Allamakee County	IA	Ken G. Raffik	2008	45547
125 1/8	23 0/8 21 2/8	14 3/8	4	4	Cowley County	KS	Stephen O. Van Hoose	2008	45547
125 1/8	21 6/8 22 5/8	17 3/8	4	4	Schuyler County	MO	Joseph Balee	2008	45547
125 1/8	21 3/8 20 4/8	14 1/8	6	5	Russell County	AL	Warner Neal	2008	45547
*125 1/8	20 1/8 19 5/8	14 7/8	5	5	Hancock County	IL	Terry A. Megee	2008	45547
125 1/8	24 4/8 24 5/8	16 3/8	4	5	Hancock County	OH	Jason Osting	2008	45547
125 1/8	21 7/8 21 3/8	17 5/8	5	4	McDonough County	IL	William R. Brown	2008	45547
125 1/8	20 5/8 20 4/8	16 5/8	5	5	Lafayette County	WI	Keith Droessler	2008	45547
125 1/8	21 6/8 22 1/8	14 7/8	4	4	Bond County	IL	William T. Rench	2008	45547
125 1/8	19 0/8 19 5/8	15 3/8	6	5	Queen Annes County	MD	Joseph H. Apple	2008	45547
*125 1/8	20 4/8 20 5/8	15 7/8	5	7	Jasper County	IA	Terry Weltz	2008	45547
125 1/8	23 2/8 22 4/8	17 7/8	4	5	Henry County	VA	Mike Weaver	2008	45547
125 1/8	23 3/8 24 3/8	17 1/8	5	5	Shelby County	KY	Joseph C. Fehribach	2009	45547
*125 1/8	20 0/8 20 5/8	18 3/8	5	4	Fayette County	PA	Steve Younkin	2009	45547
125 1/8	21 5/8 21 6/8	15 5/8	6	6	Athens County	OH	Mike Van Fossen	2009	45547

Deer entries below 141 0/8, that appeared in the 6th Edition, are not included here, but are included on the accompanying CD (see page 119), and also in the Club's Records Archives.

WHITETAIL DEER (TYPICAL ANTLERS)

Minimum Score 125   Continued

SCORE	LENGTH OF R MAIN BEAM L	INSIDE SPREAD	NUMBER OF R POINTS L		AREA	STATE/ PROVINCE	HUNTER'S NAME	DATE	RANK
*125 1/8	22 5/8 22 3/8	14 5/8	4	5	Bristol County	MA	Daniel J. Furtado	2009	45547
125 1/8	21 0/8 21 4/8	17 1/8	4	4	Trempealeau County	WI	Daniel Schriener	2009	45547
*125 1/8	23 2/8 22 3/8	18 1/8	4	5	Broome County	NY	Gordon L. Sprague	2009	45547
125 1/8	20 6/8 19 4/8	16 5/8	6	6	Antelope County	NE	Martin Vetick	2009	45547
*125 1/8	24 7/8 24 1/8	18 5/8	5	5	Linn County	KS	F. David Thornberry	2009	45547
*125 1/8	23 3/8 23 3/8	15 7/8	4	4	Cowley County	KS	Scott M. Bowman	2009	45547
125 1/8	21 6/8 22 6/8	14 1/8	4	4	Grenada County	MS	Al Hankins	2009	45547
125 1/8	21 4/8 21 3/8	16 3/8	4	4	Caddo County	OK	Rocky Wilson	2009	45547
125 0/8	22 5/8 23 0/8	18 7/8	6	6	Wright County	MN	Dan Socher	1989	45925
125 0/8	20 2/8 19 4/8	13 6/8	5	5	Alcona County	MI	Argene Miracle, Jr.	1990	45925
*125 0/8	19 2/8 20 2/8	16 4/8	5	5	Winona County	MN	Dennis Hengel	1997	45925
125 0/8	22 1/8 21 3/8	15 4/8	4	4	Blaine County	MT	Michael Maurer	1998	45925
125 0/8	20 6/8 21 1/8	16 6/8	5	5	Lyon County	IA	Michael Judas	1998	45925
125 0/8	18 2/8 18 2/8	14 6/8	5	5	Howard County	IA	Lynn Scheidel	2001	45925
125 0/8	22 4/8 21 3/8	17 0/8	4	4	Licking County	OH	Ron Spence	2001	45925
125 0/8	22 4/8 22 5/8	18 6/8	4	5	Lorain County	OH	Steven Reinhold	2001	45925
125 0/8	21 1/8 21 0/8	15 0/8	4	4	Davis County	IA	Randy Templeton	2001	45925
125 0/8	20 3/8 21 2/8	18 2/8	4	6	Adams County	IL	Toby Schrock	2002	45925
*125 0/8	22 4/8 21 3/8	16 4/8	5	4	Clark County	WI	Todd A. Schmutzler	2003	45925
125 0/8	18 5/8 17 4/8	17 0/8	5	5	Pike County	AL	Richard Albright	2004	45925
125 0/8	23 7/8 23 1/8	18 1/8	5	4	Douglas County	IL	Steve Vandeventer	2004	45925
125 0/8	21 3/8 21 0/8	17 6/8	4	4	Licking County	OH	David P. Chrisman	2004	45925
125 0/8	21 2/8 20 5/8	15 4/8	4	4	Grant County	WI	Jeremy Hampton	2004	45925
125 0/8	22 5/8 21 3/8	15 0/8	4	6	Columbia County	WI	Chad M. Theis	2004	45925
125 0/8	23 0/8 24 2/8	13 4/8	6	6	Gage County	NE	Dustin S. Rasmussen	2004	45925
125 0/8	22 3/8 22 5/8	18 2/8	5	5	Randolph County	IN	Jerry L. Hale	2004	45925
125 0/8	19 4/8 20 1/8	17 0/8	4	4	Buffalo County	WI	Jeff Walcott	2004	45925
125 0/8	22 4/8 21 7/8	18 4/8	5	5	Delaware County	OH	David A. Wilson	2004	45925
125 0/8	21 4/8 21 7/8	17 2/8	4	4	Clay County	IA	Brad Jones	2004	45925
125 0/8	21 5/8 21 4/8	18 0/8	4	4	Worth County	MO	Keith E. Arnold	2004	45925
125 0/8	21 6/8 21 2/8	15 4/8	5	4	Ramsey County	MN	Paul Erickson	2004	45925
125 0/8	21 2/8 20 7/8	16 0/8	5	5	Price County	WI	Chad Zieher	2004	45925
125 0/8	20 6/8 20 2/8	15 0/8	6	5	Claiborne County	MS	Lance Stroud	2004	45925
125 0/8	21 4/8 21 0/8	17 2/8	5	5	Tom Green County	TX	Eric H. Boley	2004	45925
125 0/8	23 1/8 23 4/8	17 2/8	5	4	Jackson County	IA	John E. Combs	2004	45925
*125 0/8	21 2/8 20 7/8	18 0/8	6	5	Kinney County	TX	Jim Dillard	2004	45925
125 0/8	21 0/8 20 1/8	13 5/8	5	5	Phillips County	AR	Chad Hill	2004	45925
125 0/8	17 7/8 18 6/8	16 4/8	5	5	Iowa County	WI	Chad Vivian	2005	45925
125 0/8	19 0/8 20 0/8	15 5/8	6	5	Brown County	WI	Marty Bruecker	2005	45925
125 0/8	20 1/8 21 1/8	15 5/8	5	5	Irion County	TX	David Rogers	2005	45925
*125 0/8	20 0/8 20 4/8	14 6/8	5	5	Vermillion County	IN	Brannon V. Fowler	2005	45925
*125 0/8	21 6/8 22 3/8	18 0/8	4	4	Suffolk County	NY	Donald E. Cook	2005	45925
125 0/8	21 2/8 20 7/8	19 2/8	5	5	Newton County	IN	George G. Bogie	2005	45925
125 0/8	20 2/8 21 3/8	14 2/8	5	5	Ozaukee County	WI	Adam Poull	2005	45925
125 0/8	23 2/8 23 0/8	17 6/8	4	4	Macomb County	MI	Earl N. Riske	2005	45925
125 0/8	21 3/8 18 4/8	16 2/8	5	5	Shawano County	WI	Ken Alft	2005	45925
125 0/8	20 0/8 21 6/8	17 6/8	5	5	St. Croix County	WI	Nathen Prokop	2005	45925
125 0/8	19 3/8 18 6/8	14 6/8	5	5	Jo Daviess County	IL	Jim Collachia	2005	45925
125 0/8	21 0/8 21 2/8	16 0/8	5	5	Clark County	WI	Lonnie Damewood	2005	45925
125 0/8	19 6/8 19 3/8	16 2/8	4	4	Coles County	IL	Rick Boyer	2005	45925
*125 0/8	22 5/8 22 6/8	16 0/8	5	5	Pulaski County	IL	Jonathan Leonard Featherstone	2005	45925
125 0/8	20 6/8 21 0/8	15 6/8	4	5	Hughes County	OK	Tom Cartwright	2005	45925
125 0/8	20 3/8 20 3/8	15 0/8	5	5	Stillwater County	MT	Wendy Scott	2006	45925
125 0/8	22 1/8 22 4/8	18 6/8	5	4	Columbia County	WI	Mitchell J. Plautz	2006	45925
125 0/8	21 3/8 22 3/8	18 0/8	4	4	New Haven County	CT	Joseph Russo	2006	45925
125 0/8	17 2/8 17 3/8	15 4/8	7	6	Linn County	KS	Jason Yosick	2006	45925
125 0/8	22 6/8 22 3/8	21 2/8	4	4	Lawrence County	PA	James S. Medvit	2006	45925
*125 0/8	20 6/8 20 1/8	14 0/8	5	5	Dane County	WI	Dennis Carothers, Jr.	2006	45925
125 0/8	23 6/8 22 5/8	16 6/8	5	4	Prince Georges County	MD	Roger E. Harris	2006	45925
125 0/8	20 3/8 20 6/8	15 6/8	5	5	Warren County	PA	Gail Bidwell	2006	45925
125 0/8	22 1/8 22 1/8	13 5/8	4	5	Clay County	SD	Jeffrey J. Olson	2006	45925
*125 0/8	20 4/8 22 0/8	15 4/8	5	5	Marquette County	WI	Timothy J. O'Leary	2007	45925
125 0/8	23 3/8 24 0/8	17 5/8	4	7	Kent County	DE	Shawn L. Radis	2007	45925
125 0/8	21 6/8 21 2/8	16 2/8	5	5	Portage County	WI	Shawn Domaszek	2007	45925
*125 0/8	18 2/8 17 7/8	12 4/8	6	6	Berrien County	MI	Nathan Smith	2007	45925
125 0/8	20 7/8 20 2/8	17 2/8	5	5	Trempealeau County	WI	William W. Wishon, Jr.	2007	45925
125 0/8	22 4/8 21 0/8	15 4/8	5	5	Jefferson County	OH	Steve Peperis	2007	45925
125 0/8	26 2/8 24 3/8	18 1/8	4	5	Delaware County	IA	Bev Dempster	2007	45925
125 0/8	24 6/8 24 4/8	21 2/8	5	4	Boone County	IA	Clint Christensen	2007	45925
125 0/8	21 4/8 21 1/8	16 0/8	4	5	Allegany County	NY	Roger Gross	2007	45925
*125 0/8	21 7/8 22 5/8	16 4/8	5	5	Allegheny County	PA	David M. Guiste	2007	45925
125 0/8	20 4/8 20 6/8	14 2/8	5	5	Franklin County	IL	Cedric L. Malone, Jr.	2007	45925
125 0/8	22 7/8 22 2/8	19 3/8	4	5	Dakota County	MN	Peter D. Fasbender	2007	45925
125 0/8	22 3/8 18 7/8	19 6/8	4	5	Peoria County	IL	Ross Edwards	2007	45925
125 0/8	20 5/8 20 4/8	18 2/8	4	5	Lewis & Clark County	MT	Stephen Riley West	2007	45925
125 0/8	20 6/8 20 6/8	18 2/8	5	4	Powell County	MT	John "Rosey" Roseland	2007	45925
*125 0/8	21 6/8 21 5/8	17 4/8	5	5	Queen Annes County	MD	Larry Reese	2007	45925
125 0/8	22 1/8 24 6/8	17 2/8	4	3	Kane County	IL	Richard C. Wise	2007	45925
125 0/8	21 5/8 20 7/8	19 4/8	4	5	McLennan County	TX	Lee H. Bristow	2007	45925
*125 0/8	21 0/8 21 6/8	18 0/8	4	5	La Salle County	TX	Ted McMillion	2007	45925
125 0/8	21 1/8 20 2/8	19 3/8	5	5	Woodford County	KY	Joe Lacefield	2008	45925
125 0/8	18 6/8 18 6/8	17 2/8	5	5	Morton County	ND	Joe Ness	2008	45925
*125 0/8	21 5/8 21 1/8	18 2/8	4	4	Charleston County	SC	Hunter S. Nash	2008	45925
125 0/8	23 2/8 21 3/8	17 6/8	5	4	Gratiot County	MI	Joe L. Fleisher	2008	45925
*125 0/8	24 0/8 20 1/8	19 6/8	4	5	Columbia County	WI	Larry Lee Prochnow	2008	45925
125 0/8	21 0/8 22 1/8	17 0/8	4	4	Vernon County	WI	Jacob Halverson	2008	45925
125 0/8	24 2/8 23 5/8	19 6/8	6	7	Johnson County	IL	Charles Pate	2008	45925
125 0/8	19 3/8 19 6/8	17 2/8	6	6	Blue Earth County	MN	Lucas Cornish	2008	45925
125 0/8	24 0/8 23 1/8	14 6/8	5	5	Tuscarawas County	OH	Charles S. Caley	2008	45925
125 0/8	23 1/8 22 7/8	17 4/8	4	4	Calumet County	WI	Pauly Paul	2008	45925
*125 0/8	21 0/8 21 6/8	15 2/8	4	4	Fayette County	IL	Chad Zumwalt	2008	45925
*125 0/8	19 5/8 20 7/8	15 2/8	4	4	Clayton County	IA	Josh Holzapfel	2008	45925
*125 0/8	21 4/8 21 1/8	16 6/8	6	5	Tioga County	PA	Gary D. Krieger	2008	45925
125 0/8	20 0/8 19 7/8	14 4/8	5	5	Adams County	OH	Brian Demma	2008	45925
125 0/8	21 2/8 21 1/8	16 4/8	5	4	Brown County	IL	Michael V. Cheek	2008	45925

WHITETAIL DEER (TYPICAL ANTLERS)

Minimum Score 125

SCORE	LENGTH OF R MAIN BEAM L		INSIDE SPREAD	NUMBER OF R POINTS L		AREA	STATE/ PROVINCE	HUNTER'S NAME	DATE	RANK
125 0/8	20 5/8	21 2/8	15 3/8	5	7	Dakota County	MN	Brian LeMay	2008	45925
*125 0/8	21 4/8	22 1/8	18 2/8	4	5	Henderson County	KY	Darrin Eaton	2009	45925
125 0/8	23 7/8	20 1/8	15 6/8	6	5	Williamson County	TN	Erich C. Graeflin	2009	45925
125 0/8	23 6/8	23 6/8	19 5/8	5	8	Montgomery County	PA	Robert Nagy	2009	45925
*125 0/8	21 2/8	21 4/8	15 2/8	4	6	Carroll County	MS	Chris Thomas	2009	45925
125 0/8	23 4/8	23 6/8	16 3/8	5	4	Montgomery County	IN	Derrick W. Kidd	2009	45925
*125 0/8	20 4/8	20 7/8	16 5/8	5	6	Buffalo County	WI	Cory Krogman	2009	45925
125 0/8	19 5/8	21 0/8	15 2/8	4	4	Grant County	WI	Leo Jewett	2009	45925
*125 0/8	22 2/8	22 2/8	14 4/8	4	4	New London County	CT	David A. Miller	2009	45925
125 0/8	24 1/8	21 4/8	17 4/8	4	5	Garfield County	OK	John Cannon	2009	45925
*125 0/8	22 5/8	22 6/8	16 0/8	4	5	Hampshire County	MA	Michael Horton	2009	45925
125 0/8	18 4/8	18 5/8	15 4/8	5	5	Regina	SAS	John Rajczakowski	2010	45925
*125 0/8	22 2/8	22 2/8	22 3/8	4	4	Jackson County	MI	Daniel L. Knevel	2010	45925

Deer entries below 141 0/8, that appeared in the 6th Edition, are not included here, but are included on the accompanying CD (see page 119), and also in the Club's Records Archives.

WHITETAIL DEER (TYPICAL VELVET ANTLERS)

Minimum Score 125

SCORE	LENGTH OF R MAIN BEAM L		INSIDE SPREAD	NUMBER OF R POINTS L		AREA	STATE/ PROVINCE	HUNTER'S NAME	DATE	RANK
*178 4/8	25 6/8	25 3/8	23 6/8	8	8	Debolt	ALB	Jason House	2009	*
170 1/8	25 3/8	25 4/8	18 3/8	5	5	Towner County	ND	Chad Haberstroh	2009	*
*170 0/8	27 1/8	26 2/8	17 1/8	7	7	Cumberland County	KY	Pat Smith	2010	*
168 4/8	28 3/8	27 2/8	19 3/8	6	9	Warren County	OH	Kevin Woods	2008	*
167 6/8	27 2/8	27 0/8	17 6/8	5	4	Todd County	KY	Bubba Lynch	2010	*
*166 6/8	23 6/8	24 2/8	18 6/8	6	5	Kidder County	ND	Lance Larson	2008	*
162 4/8	27 2/8	27 1/8	20 6/8	5	4	Russell County	KY	Darren Day	2006	*
*162 1/8	22 7/8	23 6/8	14 5/8	7	8	Monroe County	IA	Chris Rivers	2008	*
161 0/8	26 3/8	25 5/8	17 3/8	6	6	Rosebud County	MT	Ed Bukoskey	1995	*
160 6/8	26 5/8	26 0/8	18 0/8	7	6	New London County	CT	Sean M. Coffey	2005	*
160 1/8	24 3/8	24 2/8	15 7/8	5	5	Todd County	KY	Michael Skipworth	2007	*
*160 0/8	25 1/8	24 1/8	15 1/8	6	7	Rosebud County	MT	Frank M. Moody	2008	*
158 5/8	24 0/8	23 7/8	19 4/8	7	6	Ramsey County	ND	Larry Brodina	2008	*
*158 3/8	24 0/8	23 5/8	16 5/8	6	9	Powder River County	MT	George Finck	2006	*
*158 3/8	24 0/8	23 2/8	17 7/8	7	6	Ohio County	KY	Gregory Lee Gill	2009	*
156 5/8	24 4/8	23 3/8	21 3/8	5	5	Lee County	GA	David Byrd	2006	*
156 3/8	25 0/8	24 5/8	16 2/8	5	6	Swift Current	SAS	Stacy Bolton	2007	*
156 1/8	22 2/8	22 2/8	17 2/8	6	7	Cavalier County	ND	Terry Lund	2008	*
*156 0/8	23 4/8	23 1/8	17 4/8	5	5	Pulaski County	KY	Billy F. Barnett	2007	*
*155 3/8	22 0/8	22 6/8	17 5/8	6	6	Kidder County	ND	Jason Devore	2008	*
155 1/8	23 5/8	24 7/8	18 3/8	5	5	Sturgeon River	SAS	Bradley Arabsky	2005	*
*154 6/8	24 4/8	25 5/8	17 4/8	9	9	Pendleton County	KY	Colin Shane Allgyer	2010	*
*154 4/8	22 6/8	25 0/8	20 3/8	5	6	Kenton County	KY	Mike S. Wagner	2007	*
*152 5/8	23 6/8	23 5/8	16 1/8	5	5	Marion County	KY	Scott Osbourne	2005	*
152 5/8	22 1/8	22 6/8	15 3/8	5	5	Natrona County	WY	Ryan Kuharski	2005	*
*152 4/8	22 7/8	22 7/8	18 4/8	6	5	Oldham County	KY	Josh Riordan	2009	*
152 2/8	25 7/8	25 1/8	18 6/8	5	6	Tippecanoe County	IN	Tom McIntyre	2005	*
151 7/8	22 3/8	22 5/8	18 0/8	5	8	Johnson County	WY	Pax Harness	2004	*
151 4/8	22 3/8	21 7/8	14 4/8	7	6	Burleigh County	ND	Justin H. Jones	2004	*
*151 1/8	26 0/8	25 6/8	20 6/8	6	4	Scott County	KY	Rich Springer	2007	*
*151 1/8	24 1/8	24 4/8	20 1/8	4	4	Leg Lake	ALB	Raymond Melom	2009	*
150 5/8	23 6/8	23 4/8	16 5/8	5	6	Ramsey County	ND	Jason B. Ramberg	2008	*
150 4/8	20 2/8	19 4/8	14 0/8	5	5	Madison County	MT	Thomas Sadler	2006	*
*150 0/8	22 4/8	23 6/8	18 4/8	6	6	Bottineau County	ND	Darren Foss	2007	*
149 0/8	20 3/8	20 3/8	17 2/8	7	5	Lac La Biche	ALB	Matthew Nezich	2002	*
149 0/8	24 2/8	23 3/8	17 0/8	4	4	Bracken County	KY	Gene Schadle	2005	*
149 0/8	23 1/8	23 0/8	16 4/8	5	5	Keg Lake	SAS	Teana Buchanan	2008	*
148 5/8	26 2/8	26 4/8	18 1/8	5	5	Grayson County	KY	Pat Harris	2007	*
148 4/8	23 1/8	22 6/8	20 4/8	5	5	Caldwell County	KY	Aaron Kirk	2007	*
148 1/8	23 5/8	24 2/8	19 1/8	7	5	Cavalier County	ND	Danny Mostad	1983	*
146 7/8	21 3/8	22 0/8	16 7/8	5	5	Madison County	MT	Dyrk Eddie	2006	*
146 7/8	24 6/8	23 5/8	18 5/8	4	4	Allen County	KY	Jamie Towe	2006	*
146 6/8	21 7/8	23 5/8	16 6/8	5	6	Burleigh County	ND	Robert L. Hanson	2008	*
146 3/8	21 6/8	22 2/8	17 5/8	5	5	Ramsey County	ND	Josh Worley	2008	*
146 3/8	20 7/8	20 0/8	16 5/8	5	5	Stevens County	WA	Chris Van Kempen	2009	*
146 1/8	26 0/8	25 1/8	17 3/8	4	4	Henry County	KY	Arthur Logan	2006	*
145 5/8	25 1/8	24 3/8	18 1/8	4	4	Dougherty County	GA	Garrett Jones	2007	*
145 4/8	24 3/8	24 1/8	15 5/8	5	6	Crooked Creek	ALB	Rick Martin	2004	*
145 4/8	23 6/8	24 4/8	18 6/8	4	4	Thunder Bay	ONT	Dan Fadyshen	2007	*
145 1/8	23 3/8	23 5/8	16 7/8	6	5	Buffalo County	NE	Chad Sinnema	2007	*
145 0/8	22 6/8	23 2/8	15 3/8	5	6	Dunn County	ND	Bill J. Haase	2007	*
144 6/8	22 2/8	21 6/8	18 2/8	6	8	Mercer County	KY	Brian Lay	2007	*
*144 5/8	22 5/8	21 1/8	14 7/8	5	5	Sussex County	DE	Brian R. Wilson	2006	*
*144 3/8	24 5/8	25 6/8	19 3/8	5	4	Lewis County	KY	Jeremy Ruckel	2007	*
144 1/8	22 4/8	22 5/8	15 1/8	5	6	Dougherty County	GA	Jacob Paschal	2007	*
144 1/8	23 3/8	22 2/8	18 1/8	6	6	Trempealeau County	WI	Matt Andersen	2010	*
143 2/8	23 2/8	23 2/8	18 4/8	5	5	Jackson County	KY	Darren Day	2007	*
*143 0/8	21 2/8	20 1/8	17 6/8	5	5	Cold Lake	ALB	Martin Belisle	2008	*
*142 6/8	20 2/8	21 1/8	15 0/8	5	5	Estill County	KY	Jason Freeman	2008	*
142 5/8	23 4/8	23 6/8	18 5/8	6	5	Boundary County	ID	Ryan Farrens	2007	*
*142 5/8	23 7/8	24 1/8	17 3/8	4	4	St. Louis County	MO	Ron Arnold	2008	*
142 4/8	26 1/8	26 7/8	19 6/8	4	5	Decatur County	GA	Robert E. Meredith	2009	*
*142 3/8	22 5/8	22 0/8	15 5/8	4	4	Dickey County	ND	Matthew D. Handt	2010	*
*142 2/8	23 2/8	24 2/8	17 2/8	5	6	Anderson County	KY	Jefferey W. Bennett	2007	*
*142 0/8	23 4/8	23 3/8	16 4/8	4	4	Barnes County	ND	William Berntson	2007	*
*142 0/8	23 4/8	23 0/8	15 5/8	7	6	Bear Lake	ALB	Derek Bruce	2009	*
*141 7/8	22 4/8	22 3/8	16 5/8	5	5	Dougherty County	GA	Garrett Jones	2008	*
*141 6/8	20 7/8	22 4/8	16 2/8	6	5	Oldham County	KY	Larry Truman	2005	*
141 5/8	22 0/8	21 7/8	21 3/8	7	5	Oldham County	KY	Titus Riner	2005	*
141 3/8	21 4/8	22 7/8	17 1/8	4	4	St. Brieux	SAS	Pamela Rohel	2003	*
141 3/8	22 5/8	23 1/8	18 7/8	6	6	Boundary County	ID	Clark M. Halverson	2003	*
141 2/8	23 1/8	22 6/8	15 2/8	5	5	Adams County	MS	Patrick Kelleher	2003	*
141 0/8	22 2/8	21 7/8	17 4/8	7	7	Jefferson County	MT	Bruce Barrie	2003	*
*141 0/8	25 0/8	24 5/8	16 2/8	5	5	Lincoln County	TN	Jason P. Rozar	2007	*
140 7/8	22 3/8	21 7/8	18 1/8	5	6	Woodford County	KY	Jackson Roberts	2007	*
140 1/8	23 1/8	23 1/8	15 5/8	5	4	Dougherty County	GA	Glenn Paschal	2009	*
139 2/8	22 6/8	23 6/8	15 4/8	5	6	Crisp County	GA	James E. Ellis	2003	*
*139 2/8	24 7/8	25 4/8	16 0/8	6	7	Good Spirit Lake	SAS	Shawn Frankfurt	2009	*
139 1/8	22 4/8	22 0/8	16 3/8	5	5	Winona County	MN	Shawn Clough	2009	*
139 0/8	22 1/8	21 3/8	17 0/8	5	5	Cavalier County	ND	Kim Elsperger	2007	*
*139 0/8	21 1/8	21 1/8	16 4/8	6	7	Crook County	WY	Jon Sanborn	2007	*
*138 7/8	22 2/8	23 3/8	18 1/8	5	5	Holmes County	MS	Andrew K. Howorth	2010	*
138 6/8	27 4/8	25 6/8	21 2/8	6	6	Ohio County	KY	Ralph Porter, Jr.	2006	*
138 4/8	21 5/8	21 1/8	16 2/8	4	4	Ohio County	KY	Nicolaus Hall	2006	*
*137 6/8	23 5/8	22 4/8	18 4/8	4	5	Clay County	TX	Kenneth Sherrell	2009	*
137 2/8	22 2/8	23 1/8	16 7/8	6	5	Madison County	ID	Todd Kauer	2000	*
*137 2/8	20 4/8	20 1/8	16 0/8	6	6	Emmons County	ND	Troy Hanson	2008	*
137 1/8	23 0/8	21 2/8	15 4/8	6	7	Carroll County	KY	Thomas E. Hale, Jr.	2007	*
*137 1/8	22 7/8	22 6/8	20 3/8	4	5	New Castle County	DE	Michael Schauber	2008	*
137 0/8	22 4/8	23 6/8	16 4/8	4	4	Shelby County	KY	Robert Wheeler	2004	*
136 4/8	22 0/8	21 0/8	16 2/8	5	5	Chatham County	NC	Aaron Horton	2007	*
136 3/8	23 5/8	23 4/8	18 1/8	4	5	Shelby County	KY	Neil Raizor	2008	*
136 3/8	24 6/8	24 0/8	18 6/8	5	4	Dougherty County	GA	Jacob Paschal	2005	*
*136 2/8	20 7/8	20 5/8	14 2/8	5	5	Bamberg County	SC	Alex S. Boykin, Jr.	2009	*
136 1/8	21 3/8	21 4/8	17 1/8	5	5	Crook County	WY	Tom Sundeen	2010	*

WHITETAIL DEER (TYPICAL VELVET ANTLERS)

Minimum Score 125 — Continued

SCORE	LENGTH OF R MAIN BEAM L	INSIDE SPREAD	NUMBER OF R POINTS L		AREA	STATE/PROVINCE	HUNTER'S NAME	DATE	RANK
*135 7/8	21 6/8 21 6/8	15 4/8	6	4	Cass County	ND	Chad Zaun	2008	*
135 5/8	22 7/8 21 4/8	17 7/8	4	5	Okanogan	BC	Lorenzo Bortolotto	2007	*
*135 5/8	20 4/8 20 2/8	15 3/8	7	5	Taylor County	GA	Troy Harrison	2007	*
135 4/8	24 0/8 23 5/8	18 4/8	4	5	Burleigh County	ND	Mark L. Wonders	2006	*
*135 3/8	23 0/8 23 6/8	15 7/8	5	5	Butler County	KY	Tim Holland	2004	*
*135 3/8	21 0/8 22 0/8	17 5/8	4	4	Wells County	ND	Jeff Newman	2006	*
135 0/8	19 4/8 19 7/8	17 4/8	6	5	Towner County	ND	Dylan Holien	2005	*
135 0/8	21 5/8 20 5/8	17 0/8	6	7	Jessamine County	KY	Sam Hughes	2007	*
*135 0/8	20 4/8 20 5/8	16 2/8	4	4	McHenry County	ND	Shane Collier	2008	*
*134 7/8	21 2/8 22 2/8	15 1/8	5	5	High Level	ALB	Rick Ruzzamenti	2007	*
*134 7/8	23 2/8 23 0/8	17 3/8	5	5	Knox County	KY	Steve Smith	2008	*
134 6/8	21 5/8 22 0/8	17 6/8	5	5	Edmonson County	KY	Chad Lashley	2004	*
134 6/8	22 4/8 23 2/8	18 0/8	4	5	Casey County	KY	Derek Stephens	2007	*
134 3/8	23 0/8 22 6/8	16 2/8	6	7	Bullitt County	KY	Sam Satori	2006	*
134 3/8	21 2/8 21 5/8	16 1/8	5	5	Souris	MAN	Bryan Klein	2008	*
134 2/8	24 1/8 24 7/8	16 0/8	5	4	Nelson County	KY	Kory Lang	2008	*
133 7/8	21 7/8 21 5/8	15 3/8	5	5	Butler County	KY	Phillip T. Murphy	2004	*
133 5/8	21 7/8 22 5/8	15 3/8	4	4	Ward County	ND	Thomas J. Lake	2009	*
133 4/8	21 6/8 21 4/8	19 4/8	6	4	Edmonson County	KY	Joey Decker	2006	*
133 3/8	27 3/8 25 3/8	16 5/8	4	4	Transylvania County	NC	Randall L. Gant	2007	*
133 0/8	23 2/8 22 3/8	18 3/8	6	6	Mercer County	ND	Jesse R. Carter	2006	*
132 7/8	23 7/8 22 6/8	16 1/8	5	4	Chippewa County	WI	Rob White	2003	*
*132 6/8	20 5/8 20 0/8	12 3/8	6	5	Barnes County	ND	Craig Schroeder	2006	*
132 5/8	22 7/8 23 6/8	17 3/8	4	5	Edmonson County	KY	Harold Eddie Whobrey	2006	*
*132 5/8	20 4/8 22 0/8	15 0/8	6	5	Walsh County	ND	Larry Brodina	2007	*
*132 3/8	22 2/8 22 7/8	16 5/8	4	4	Ward County	ND	Greg DeSaye	2004	*
*132 0/8	20 4/8 20 6/8	17 4/8	5	5	Allen County	KY	Garrett Tucker	2007	*
131 7/8	23 0/8 22 3/8	16 3/8	5	4	Ransom County	ND	Terry A. Anderson	2004	*
*131 7/8	23 1/8 24 1/8	17 7/8	4	5	Wake County	NC	Jamie Dean	2007	*
131 4/8	23 0/8 22 1/8	18 0/8	7	6	Madison County	MT	Robert Reed	2005	*
131 3/8	22 3/8 22 3/8	14 7/8	4	4	Kent County	DE	Leonard R. Hobbs	1995	*
131 2/8	21 3/8 18 2/8	18 3/8	6	5	Manitowoc County	WI	Scott J. Stelzer	2005	*
131 2/8	20 5/8 21 1/8	15 4/8	4	4	Ramsey County	ND	Lee Myklebust	2006	*
131 2/8	23 4/8 22 2/8	15 2/8	5	5	Dougherty County	GA	Chris Vance	2007	*
131 2/8	22 6/8 23 4/8	17 4/8	5	4	Litchfield County	CT	Chris Nichols	2008	*
130 7/8	18 6/8 19 5/8	15 7/8	5	5	Renville County	ND	Bob Demers	2004	*
*130 7/8	23 0/8 23 1/8	15 4/8	5	5	Flathead County	MT	Jarred R. Krueger	2005	*
130 7/8	21 7/8 21 5/8	17 1/8	4	4	Todd County	KY	Dwight Brock	2006	*
130 5/8	21 1/8 22 4/8	13 3/8	5	5	Barnwell County	SC	Kenneth K. Kearse	1997	*
*129 6/8	22 3/8 22 3/8	14 6/8	4	4	Ohio County	KY	Chris Johnson	2006	*
*129 6/8	19 4/8 19 6/8	15 0/8	5	5	Ramsey County	ND	Vickie Erickstad	2009	*
*129 5/8	25 1/8 23 6/8	18 2/8	5	4	Hopkins County	KY	Travis Littlepage	2003	*
129 5/8	22 1/8 23 1/8	14 7/8	7	7	Harrison County	KY	Aaron Howard	2007	*
129 5/8	24 4/8 22 2/8	14 5/8	6	6	Hart County	KY	Michael Sloan	2008	*
129 1/8	24 6/8 26 0/8	18 1/8	5	4	Butler County	KY	Edwin Craft	2007	*
129 1/8	22 1/8 22 5/8	15 1/8	4	5	Dougherty County	GA	Billy Pate	2007	*
129 0/8	21 7/8 20 2/8	19 2/8	7	6	Dane County	WI	Jim Krawczyk	2006	*
129 0/8	20 0/8 19 4/8	16 2/8	5	5	Scott County	KY	Robert Sageser	2008	*
*128 6/8	23 2/8 22 5/8	15 6/8	4	4	Adair County	MO	Jody Sullivan	2007	*
128 5/8	21 4/8 21 0/8	17 5/8	4	4	Lincoln County	MT	Paul Torres	2005	*
128 5/8	23 6/8 25 5/8	17 1/8	5	5	Woodford County	KY	Andy R. Ingram	2006	*
128 5/8	20 1/8 20 7/8	14 5/8	4	4	Scott County	KY	Robert Sageser	2007	*
128 2/8	21 2/8 21 7/8	15 0/8	5	5	Ohio County	KY	Samuel Edward Hagan	2007	*
128 1/8	22 2/8 20 7/8	18 3/8	4	4	Gallatin County	KY	Jody Beck	2005	*
*128 0/8	20 7/8 21 7/8	16 1/8	6	5	Kent County	DE	C. Melvin Wyatt, Jr.	2009	*
127 7/8	22 5/8 23 1/8	16 1/8	4	4	Sussex County	DE	Phil Ranalli	2003	*
127 7/8	21 3/8 21 0/8	15 0/8	5	9	Cabri Lake	SAS	Tyson Craney	2006	*
127 6/8	21 1/8 21 3/8	15 6/8	4	4	Lewis & Clark County	MT	Kyle Carlson	2006	*
*127 6/8	20 6/8 19 1/8	15 0/8	5	5	Cavalier County	ND	Jeff Furstenau	2008	*
127 4/8	21 4/8 21 1/8	16 2/8	7	6	Saskatoon Mtn.	ALB	Brent Watson	2006	*
127 4/8	21 1/8 20 6/8	17 0/8	5	5	Wells County	ND	Aaron Opdahl	2006	*
127 4/8	21 0/8 20 7/8	16 5/8	4	5	Buffalo County	WI	Kim Ganz	2008	*
127 2/8	20 6/8 18 6/8	14 6/8	5	5	Cascade County	MT	Ben Orsua	2007	*
*127 2/8	21 0/8 20 4/8	16 0/8	5	5	Casey County	KY	James McAninch	2007	*
127 2/8	20 4/8 20 4/8	16 2/8	4	4	Big Horn County	WY	Chas Arthur	2010	*
127 1/8	23 1/8 22 7/8	15 1/8	4	4	Lee County	GA	David Byrd	2010	*
*126 6/8	20 6/8 20 0/8	12 6/8	5	5	Nelson County	KY	Eric Culver	2005	*
126 6/8	20 2/8 19 3/8	15 4/8	4	4	Houston County	TX	Kevin R. Wisener	2009	*
*126 1/8	21 1/8 20 5/8	12 3/8	4	4	Ocean County	NJ	Joseph Raio	2007	*
126 0/8	20 2/8 19 2/8	16 2/8	5	4	Pembina County	ND	Roger Furstenau	2003	*
126 0/8	20 4/8 20 5/8	14 6/8	4	6	Park County	WY	Justin Dollard	2009	*
125 6/8	21 6/8 22 3/8	16 4/8	5	4	Gallatin County	MT	Sara Koelzer	2005	*
*125 6/8	21 1/8 20 6/8	17 0/8	4	4	Lyon County	KY	Matt Colson	2006	*
125 5/8	24 1/8 23 5/8	14 5/8	4	4	Wake County	NC	Frank McCabe	2005	*
125 5/8	21 1/8 19 6/8	15 7/8	6	6	Grand Forks County	ND	Travis Eastman	2007	*
*125 4/8	23 7/8 23 7/8	17 3/8	5	5	Edmonson County	KY	Craig Board	2007	*
125 3/8	22 4/8 22 5/8	16 5/8	4	5	Dougherty County	GA	Glenn Paschal	2005	*
125 2/8	21 3/8 20 0/8	15 4/8	4	5	Towner County	ND	Zack Kennedy	2006	*
*125 2/8	21 1/8 22 0/8	15 0/8	4	4	Calgary	ALB	Dennis Budgen	2007	*
125 1/8	21 2/8 20 7/8	14 7/8	5	4	Cavalier County	ND	Chase Furstenau	2007	*

WORLD RECORD WHITETAIL DEER
Non-Typical Antlers
Score: 294 0/8
Location: Greene County, Ohio
Date: 2000
Hunter: Michael Beatty

Non-Typical Whitetail Deer

by Michael Beatty

When I moved to western Ohio from Pennsylvania years ago, my brother-in-law told me I was taking up residence in an area where the bucks get really big. On November 8, 2000, I learned just how right he was.

I arrived at around 4pm that day. It was in the mid-50s with a light breeze and misting rain, great for pre-rut activity. After some time went by, I turned a can call over a couple times. A few minutes later a deer was behind me working a scrape at roughly 40 yards. It was a high, wide eight pointer that my son and I had been watching all summer. The big eight pointer stopped working the scrape and started down the edge of the corn right for my stand. Everything seemed to be falling right into place, until the buck stopped 15 yards from my stand behind a tree, turned and simply walked away. Go figure, a deer of a lifetime was right there with no shot opportunity, and all I could do was watch him walk away.

With the adrenaline rush just about gone, I tried to gather myself. I grunt called and rattled a few times trying to draw the buck back out of the cornfield. After waiting a few minutes, with nothing happening, I gave three more calls on the can call. Within moments a deer appeared, standing behind me with his head up in a long hanging tree working a lick branch. Thinking it was the same buck I'd seen earlier, I stood up, grabbed my bow and got ready. As the deer got closer I could see it was not the same buck. This rack was darker and had a lot more mass, but at 40 yards and with wet corn stalks behind his rack, it was tough to make out what he really was. I could just tell he was a big buck. At that point, I positioned myself so that the tree I was in was between his head and mine. The buck got to the same spot where the 8 point turned but instead of turning he ducked under a low hanging branch, as I drew my bow for the second time that day. Focus just focus, I told myself as I stood there at full draw, trying desperately to maintain what was left of my composure.

I watched the buck stop at just 12 yards and my arrow was gone. After waiting for what seemed to be an eternity, I went in search of the buck. After following the blood trail about 250 yards I heard a deer blow at me so I turned off the light thinking it could be the buck I had shot. I slowly backed out and waited until morning. Man, what a sleepless night! Returning with my son, we cut across a cow pasture to where I last found blood the night before. As my son and I were cutting across the pasture he tugged one my jacket. "Dad there he is!" he said pointing ahead. The buck had died only 30 yards from where I had stopped looking the night before. I have no greater memory of hunting than sharing that special moment with my son, Andrew.

Being very fortunate to be in the right spot at the right time and having the opportunity to arrow one of the biggest bucks in history, I'm still living just about every hunter's dream.

WHITETAIL DEER (NON-TYPICAL ANTLERS)

Minimum Score 155

Odocoileus hemionus and certain related subspecies

SCORE	LENGTH OF R MAIN BEAM L	INSIDE SPREAD	NUMBER OF R POINTS L	AREA	STATE/ PROVINCE	HUNTER'S NAME	DATE	RANK
*294 0/8	25 7/8 25 6/8	26 0/8	18 21	Greene County	OH	Michael Beatty	2000	1
279 7/8	27 7/8 28 1/8	21 3/8	21 18	Hall County	NE	Del Austin	1962	2
269 7/8	26 7/8 27 2/8	20 3/8	17 16	Pike County	MO	Randy Simonitch	2000	3
267 1/8	25 7/8 27 4/8	18 2/8	16 21	Mason County	IL	David H. Jones	2003	4
*264 6/8	26 0/8 26 6/8	23 3/8	13 14	Jackson County	IA	Kyle Simmons	2008	5
264 1/8	29 6/8 31 0/8	24 2/8	14 17	Pottawatomie County	KS	Dale R. Larson	1998	6
*261 5/8	24 6/8 25 1/8	21 6/8	20 16	Kendall County	IL	Christopher G. Kiernan	2009	7
257 0/8	27 1/8 25 7/8	18 6/8	12 11	Reno County	KS	Kenneth B. Fowler	1988	8
255 6/8	26 7/8 24 4/8	17 2/8	14 16	Leavenworth County	KS	Ronald F. Ewert, Jr.	2004	9
253 1/8	30 1/8 27 3/8	20 4/8	8 18	Buchanan County	IA	Brian Andrews	2003	10
250 6/8	29 4/8 26 7/8	24 0/8	12 12	Miami County	KS	Kenneth R. Cartwright	1994	11
*250 6/8	26 0/8 27 0/8	20 2/8	12 12	Macoupin County	IL	Jess Gilpin	2008	12
250 4/8	29 6/8 29 7/8	20 5/8	13 9	Alexander County	IL	Andrew French III	2000	13
249 6/8	28 0/8 27 7/8	20 2/8	8 10	Greenwood County	KS	Clifford Pickell	1968	14
247 1/8	23 0/8 23 1/8	15 4/8	14 14	Barry County	MO	Scott Odenbrett	2010	15
246 3/8	27 7/8 26 1/8	29 3/8	9 14	Anderson County	KS	Richard Stahl	1992	16
246 2/8	26 0/8 27 5/8	19 0/8	18 13	De Kalb County	MO	Jerald D. Utt	2007	17
245 5/8	29 4/8 29 3/8	20 3/8	16 15	Vermilion County	IL	Robert E. Chestnut	1981	18
245 4/8	28 5/8 28 4/8	19 1/8	18 12	Chase County	KS	Douglas A. Siebert	1988	19
243 6/8	26 5/8 27 1/8	20 5/8	14 15	Fond du Lac County	WI	Wayne Schumacher	2009	27
243 4/8	22 2/8 24 2/8	20 7/8	18 15	Harrison County	IA	Tim Waldron	2005	22
242 0/8	27 1/8 27 1/8	18 1/8	13 13	Decatur County	IA	Steven R. Binkley	2008	23
241 3/8	23 5/8 23 2/8	20 7/8	13 8	Putnam County	IL	Michael Ublish	2001	24
241 2/8	25 4/8 26 3/8	18 2/8	19 20	Cochrane	ALB	Dean Dwernuchuk	1984	25
240 0/8	28 5/8 27 5/8	17 0/8	10 11	Allen County	KS	Douglas Whitcomb	1987	26
*240 0/8	23 3/8 22 4/8	19 4/8	13 19	Lucas County	IA	Travis L. Hamilton	2009	26
*240 0/8	26 7/8 25 1/8	18 3/8	11 13	Ross County	OH	Jason McClintic	2009	26
239 4/8	26 7/8 27 0/8	19 1/8	13 15	Jasper County	IL	Kevin Radke	2007	28
238 6/8	22 6/8 22 2/8	18 3/8	18 15	Mahoning County	OH	Ronald K. Osborne	1986	29
238 0/8	23 7/8 26 1/8	17 5/8	10 11	Meade County	KS	Kevin Wright	1994	30
237 6/8	26 3/8 26 4/8	25 0/8	9 13	Des Moines County	IA	Harlan Swehla	2002	31
237 5/8	22 4/8 25 4/8	16 5/8	13 12	Wilson County	KS	Gilbert Boss	1986	32
237 3/8	24 7/8 24 6/8	16 3/8	13 10	Monroe County	IA	Larry V. Zach	2000	33
*237 1/8	21 3/8 20 4/8	12 3/8	20 14	Jackson County	KS	Darren Jenson	2008	34
*237 0/8	28 4/8 28 4/8	24 2/8	9 9	Fulton County	IL	Shawn R. Bennett	2009	35
236 1/8	22 0/8 25 2/8	17 6/8	16 8	Adams County	MS	Tracy Laird	2003	36
234 5/8	27 0/8 28 3/8	25 3/8	12 17	Parkland	ALB	Frank J. Caza	2002	37
234 4/8	27 1/8 26 3/8	24 2/8	14 11	Knox County	IL	Jim Hensley	2000	38
234 1/8	26 1/8 26 4/8	21 1/8	11 14	Hamilton County	IL	Mark A. Potts	1995	39
233 7/8	28 4/8 27 1/8	22 0/8	17 16	Greenwood County	KS	Randy Young	1989	40
233 2/8	27 7/8 26 6/8	20 2/8	8 8	Buffalo County	WI	Robert J. Decker	2008	41
233 1/8	27 4/8 26 0/8	20 5/8	13 14	Allamakee County	IA	Dave Gordon	2000	42
233 1/8	27 6/8 26 4/8	19 6/8	12 10	Allamakee County	IA	Harvey Dirks	2003	42
232 7/8	26 0/8 25 3/8	20 6/8	12 10	Kiowa County	KS	Royce E. Frazier	1987	44
232 4/8	25 5/8 25 0/8	18 0/8	14 10	Pushmataha County	OK	Brett Brame	2000	45
231 7/8	25 5/8 26 1/8	18 1/8	9 12	Windham County	CT	Paul Seremet	1994	46
231 7/8	27 0/8 26 3/8	24 7/8	11 10	Dallas County	IA	Russ Clarken	1994	46
231 5/8	28 1/8 26 5/8	19 2/8	11 11	Dane County	WI	Dennis Shanks	1979	48
231 4/8	26 0/8 25 6/8	18 3/8	11 10	Iroquois County	IL	Sam G. Townsend	1986	49
231 0/8	25 2/8 26 2/8	22 4/8	16 12	Phillips County	KS	Virgil Henry	1987	50
230 6/8	26 1/8 27 6/8	19 5/8	11 11	Peoria County	IL	Tophil L. Simon	1984	51
*230 6/8	25 2/8 26 3/8	20 1/8	15 12	Weld County	CO	Ron Kammerzell	2001	51
230 2/8	26 7/8 28 1/8	18 5/8	10 11	Madison County	IA	Ryan Hobart	2009	53
229 7/8	25 2/8 25 6/8	19 1/8	12 15	Yuma County	CO	David "Jake" Powell	1986	54
229 5/8	26 5/8 26 7/8	18 6/8	10 11	Madison County	IA	Mike Hobart	1993	55
229 4/8	27 5/8 26 2/8	21 3/8	13 9	Polk County	IA	Terry M. Long	1995	56
229 2/8	29 0/8 29 0/8	17 5/8	16 11	Crawford County	KS	Dennis D. Jameson	2003	57
*229 2/8	25 0/8 24 6/8	18 6/8	12 11	Buffalo County	WI	Brian G. Stenseth	2004	57
*229 2/8	21 5/8 23 0/8	16 6/8	17 11	McLean County	IL	Brent F. Van Hoveln	2005	57
229 1/8	27 4/8 25 6/8	20 0/8	12 15	Phillips County	KS	Russ Van Zoeren	2006	60
229 0/8	27 1/8 27 4/8	16 2/8	8 9	Lake County	IL	Rodney Rasmussen	1995	61
*228 5/8	20 6/8 24 5/8	17 5/8	14 12	McDonough County	IL	Nate R. Campbell	2009	62
227 6/8	25 5/8 25 4/8	20 6/8	13 20	Fulton County	IL	Richard Keener	1977	63
227 5/8	23 6/8 24 4/8	15 2/8	10 10	Pike County	IL	Gavin Risley	2002	64
227 3/8	27 2/8 26 5/8	17 1/8	7 10	Madison County	IA	Jerry L. Wells	2001	65
*227 3/8	25 4/8 25 0/8	19 7/8	14 13	Morrison County	MN	Scott O'Konek	2009	65
227 0/8	29 4/8 30 1/8	26 3/8	11 11	Dominion City	MAN	Terry S. Pearse	1994	67
227 0/8	29 4/8 30 4/8	23 1/8	10 11	Decatur County	IA	Jack Jr. Schuler, Jr.	1995	67
*226 7/8	26 6/8 27 4/8	20 0/8	14 14	Adams County	IL	Steve DeWitt	2006	69
226 6/8	27 3/8 27 2/8	21 2/8	10 9	Piatt County	IL	Mark Wimpy	2000	70
226 3/8	26 6/8 26 7/8	23 7/8	12 12	Linn County	IA	Matt Yamilkoski	2006	71
226 3/8	26 5/8 26 5/8	23 4/8	12 11	Houston County	MN	Ben W. Spanjers	2008	71
225 7/8	22 5/8 19 4/8	17 4/8	13 13	Grayson County	TX	Jeffery L. Duncan	2001	73
225 7/8	24 5/8 24 3/8	18 0/8	10 8	Linn County	KS	Douglas L. Below	2001	73
225 1/8	29 4/8 28 4/8	23 1/8	9 12	Walworth County	WI	F. Dan Dinelli	1992	75
224 7/8	24 5/8 22 6/8	16 7/8	12 12	Buffalo County	WI	Paul Hofer	2003	76
224 3/8	28 5/8 27 1/8	23 0/8	9 10	Stevens County	WA	J. C. Baker	1987	77
*224 2/8	27 4/8 27 3/8	20 2/8	11 12	Schuyler County	IL	Don Mummert	2007	78
224 0/8	23 1/8 21 6/8	17 3/8	13 14	La Salle County	IL	Ronald R. Lahman, Sr.	1989	79
*223 5/8	25 5/8 25 3/8	22 0/8	8 11	Jefferson County	MO	Eugene Gill	2004	80
223 0/8	29 0/8 28 2/8	21 1/8	10 12	Lancaster County	NE	Jeff Moody	2003	81
222 7/8	27 5/8 28 1/8	18 6/8	9 7	Coles County	IL	Kim L. Boes	1989	82
222 7/8	21 6/8 22 6/8	26 1/8	9 10	Van Buren County	IA	Gene Wensel	2004	82
*222 6/8	20 1/8 22 4/8	21 1/8	11 16	Lawrence County	AL	Randy Coffey	2000	84
222 5/8	27 3/8 27 0/8	20 0/8	10 12	Todd County	MN	Gary Martin	1992	85
222 3/8	26 6/8 26 2/8	21 2/8	12 10	Linn County	IA	Travis Hanf	2003	86
222 2/8	24 5/8 23 6/8	20 3/8	15 9	Ramsey County	MN	Debra J. Luzinski	2006	87
222 1/8	26 7/8 25 6/8	17 5/8	15 12	Hancock County	IA	J. M. Monson	1977	88
222 0/8	26 2/8 25 7/8	20 6/8	8 8	Marion County	KS	Claude Allen	1989	89
222 0/8	24 3/8 24 7/8	20 2/8	14 11	Riley County	KS	Larry Fronce	1997	89
221 7/8	27 3/8 27 1/8	21 0/8	10 10	Jefferson County	IA	Jared L. Rebling	2000	91
221 4/8	23 2/8 25 0/8	21 1/8	11 11	Winneshiek County	IA	Brian Keith La Rue	2005	92
221 2/8	27 3/8 25 6/8	31 4/8	11 13	Logan County	IL	Donald D. Stiner	1993	93
221 0/8	25 7/8 29 0/8	17 0/8	12 9	Warren County	IN	Robert C. Philips, Jr.	1993	94
220 7/8	26 1/8 25 1/8	25 2/8	9 11	Gove County	KS	Mike Shull	1986	95

WHITETAIL DEER (NON-TYPICAL ANTLERS)

Minimum Score 155   Continued

SCORE	LENGTH OF R MAIN BEAM L	INSIDE SPREAD	NUMBER OF R POINTS L	AREA	STATE/ PROVINCE	HUNTER'S NAME	DATE	RANK
220 7/8	17 1/8 27 6/8	16 5/8	15 11	Scotland County	MO	Glen Young	1996	95
*220 7/8	27 3/8 26 6/8	18 2/8	10 11	Osceola County	IA	Troy J. Vandehoef	2005	95
220 6/8	24 6/8 25 2/8	17 6/8	18 16	Rock Island County	IL	John L. Angel	1979	98
220 3/8	25 3/8 24 4/8	18 3/8	13 9	Riley County	KS	Melvin D. Padgett	1989	99
*220 3/8	20 1/8 22 3/8	13 4/8	21 14	Chautauqua County	KS	David A. Myers	2008	99
219 7/8	26 5/8 26 0/8	19 3/8	10 13	Bent County	CO	Sandi Hansen	2006	101
219 6/8	24 6/8 26 0/8	21 2/8	12 11	Cass County	MI	Bruce Heslet II	2000	102
*219 6/8	25 4/8 27 0/8	19 5/8	12 12	Hocking County	OH	Aaron J. Ireland	2004	102
219 5/8	24 3/8 25 4/8	22 0/8	11 11	Guernsey County	OH	Tim R. King	2005	104
219 3/8	28 1/8 27 5/8	20 5/8	12 17	Webster County	IA	David Propst	1987	105
219 2/8	25 5/8 25 2/8	22 4/8	11 11	Maverick County	TX	Thomas D. Friedkin	2006	106
219 1/8	26 2/8 26 4/8	18 3/8	8 10	Schuyler County	IL	James R. Lehman	2000	107
219 1/8	29 3/8 29 4/8	18 0/8	13 9	McPherson County	KS	Randy Bercume	2006	107
219 0/8	27 3/8 27 0/8	17 6/8	8 11	Morrison County	MN	Michael R. Langin	1992	109
219 0/8	28 1/8 28 1/8	18 5/8	11 10	Neosho County	KS	Joshua Root	2009	109
218 4/8	24 5/8 26 4/8	23 5/8	8 11	Pike County	IL	Scott Jones	2004	111
218 4/8	28 4/8 28 3/8	21 6/8	9 6	Will County	IL	Troy A. Shoaf	2009	111
218 1/8	26 2/8 25 6/8	17 3/8	10 9	Clay County	IA	Blaine R. Salzkorn	1970	113
217 7/8	25 6/8 25 1/8	16 4/8	13 7	Jefferson County	IL	Steve Gum	2002	114
*217 7/8	24 1/8 24 0/8	18 6/8	11 11	Fremont County	IA	Andy Sheldon	2008	114
217 5/8	24 5/8 23 0/8	19 7/8	14 9	Morrison County	MN	Allan D. Yager	1993	116
*217 5/8	26 1/8 25 6/8	19 3/8	12 11	Marshall County	IA	Jeff Manzer	2003	116
217 3/8	26 1/8 26 0/8	19 4/8	11 9	Fulton County	IL	Parrish Brown	2006	118
217 0/8	28 2/8 23 3/8	16 7/8	13 13	Wilson County	KS	John Bowser	2002	119
216 6/8	25 0/8 25 0/8	18 0/8	13 14	Menard County	IL	Randy Boyle	1995	120
216 4/8	29 2/8 27 1/8	17 5/8	8 10	Jersey County	IL	Walter L. Baker	1998	121
216 3/8	29 3/8 29 1/8	22 2/8	6 9	Waukesha County	WI	David Klermund	2003	122
216 3/8	28 2/8 25 5/8	20 1/8	9 11	Delaware County	IN	Jeffery J. Harty	2009	122
216 1/8	23 0/8 23 1/8	18 4/8	15 19	Dunn County	ND	James W. Casto, Jr.	2006	124
216 0/8	20 4/8 23 6/8	15 0/8	12 12	Calhoun County	IA	Scott E. Benz	2004	125
*216 0/8	26 0/8 26 3/8	17 0/8	13 7	Huron County	OH	Rodney Stumbo	2009	125
216 0/8	25 1/8 26 4/8	20 0/8	11 11	Eau Claire County	WI	Cole Johnson	2009	125
215 6/8	27 4/8 28 7/8	18 6/8	11 14	Meeker County	MN	Steve Turck	1982	128
215 5/8	24 2/8 27 0/8	22 2/8	11 7	Wayne County	IA	Chris Hackney	1983	129
*215 5/8	26 0/8 25 5/8	17 6/8	14 11	Linn County	KS	Jason Hodge	2003	129
215 2/8	25 5/8 24 6/8	19 6/8	11 15	Monroe County	IA	Bill Kirkpatrick	2009	131
215 0/8	30 3/8 30 0/8	22 7/8	10 8	Allen County	KS	Jim Baker	1992	132
215 0/8	24 4/8 23 3/8	22 2/8	8 10	Caldwell County	KY	C. J. Brummett	1998	132
*214 7/8	22 0/8 20 2/8	15 3/8	11 21	Pottawatomie County	OK	Shane D. Dockrey	2009	134
214 6/8	27 4/8 25 2/8	22 4/8	10 11	Shawano County	WI	Boyd L. Dallmann	2007	135
214 6/8	22 2/8 28 4/8	19 3/8	12 7	Grundy County	IL	Joel Carpenter	2008	135
214 4/8	20 5/8 20 6/8	15 7/8	16 15	Parker County	TX	George C. Courtney	1991	137
214 4/8	23 4/8 20 7/8	28 6/8	15 12	De Witt County	IL	Kelly Riggs	1996	137
*214 4/8	26 7/8 26 6/8	26 6/8	11 15	Payne County	OK	Chad Hane	2003	137
*214 4/8	26 6/8 25 3/8	21 1/8	8 12	Jasper County	IL	Brock Tarr	2008	137
214 2/8	23 7/8 26 2/8	15 6/8	13 9	Lyon County	KS	Gary Dall, Jr.	1992	141
214 2/8	27 1/8 27 1/8	20 6/8	6 9	Buffalo County	WI	Paul R. Borowick	1996	141
*214 2/8	25 3/8 24 3/8	21 3/8	10 13	Schuyler County	IL	Norman Gorsuch	2006	141
*214 1/8	23 5/8 23 3/8	19 4/8	9 14	Union County	IA	Jerad Dreeszen	2009	144
214 0/8	23 5/8 23 1/8	16 1/8	11 12	Douglas County	WI	Larry Kline	2004	145
214 0/8	27 0/8 28 3/8	20 5/8	11 8	Boone County	IA	Casey Moorman	2006	145
213 7/8	25 6/8 27 5/8	20 7/8	7 9	Pope County	IL	Jason B. Potts	1995	147
213 6/8	27 6/8 26 0/8	20 0/8	10 10	Switzerland County	IN	J. Chris Robbins	2006	148
213 5/8	24 7/8 25 6/8	19 7/8	12 13	Ogle County	IL	Jerome F. Bruns	1994	149
213 4/8	24 1/8 25 3/8	19 0/8	10 13	Madison County	IA	Merle Allen	1998	150
*213 4/8	20 5/8 22 0/8	20 5/8	11 7	Fulton County	GA	Jay Maxwell	2007	150
213 2/8	24 0/8 24 4/8	16 4/8	11 8	Washington County	KS	Lance D. Black	2002	152
*213 2/8	26 6/8 26 2/8	25 4/8	9 14	Ashburn	ONT	Alex MacCulloch	2008	152
*213 0/8	25 3/8 25 1/8	18 4/8	15 11	Miami County	KS	Jerry Pape	2006	154
*213 0/8	26 7/8 24 4/8	20 0/8	11 8	Morgan County	OH	Eric Morrow	2009	154
*212 7/8	24 7/8 25 1/8	18 1/8	12 10	Warren County	IL	Robert Rice	2009	156
212 6/8	26 3/8 27 2/8	22 6/8	12 12	Audrain County	MO	Jeff Arens	2005	157
212 5/8	23 5/8 25 5/8	20 1/8	8 7	Allamakee County	IA	George A. Smith	1991	158
212 5/8	27 2/8 27 4/8	20 3/8	12 8	Licking County	OH	Chris Lepley	2001	158
212 5/8	25 5/8 24 7/8	22 5/8	9 6	McHenry County	IL	Paul G. Picard, Jr.	2004	158
212 5/8	27 4/8 27 2/8	21 6/8	10 9	Lancaster County	NE	Jon Allen	2007	158
212 5/8	25 1/8 26 2/8	17 0/8	14 13	Hancock County	IL	Ohne Raasch	2007	158
212 3/8	23 4/8 23 3/8	19 1/8	11 9	Martin County	IN	David D. Foote	1988	163
212 3/8	28 0/8 27 6/8	22 2/8	10 9	Thurston County	NE	Ronald E. Kelly	1995	163
212 2/8	27 3/8 26 3/8	18 3/8	15 6	Williams County	OH	Michael A. Bowling	1993	165
212 0/8	25 4/8 27 1/8	17 2/8	9 8	Dodge County	WI	John "Jack" Hoey	1955	166
212 0/8	26 0/8 24 5/8	17 7/8	12 7	Barber County	KS	Dennis L. Rule	1992	166
212 0/8	26 4/8 25 7/8	22 6/8	11 11	Kankakee County	IL	Thomas Miller	2002	166
211 7/8	29 3/8 29 3/8	20 0/8	11 6	Hancock County	IL	Bob Zalkus	2004	169
211 6/8	26 4/8 26 5/8	18 3/8	10 8	Green County	WI	Kevin Bouers	1999	170
211 4/8	26 2/8 26 2/8	20 2/8	9 11	Schuyler County	IL	Greg J. Edwards	2002	171
211 2/8	25 4/8 25 6/8	18 0/8	8 6	Allamakee County	IA	Jason J. Johnson	2003	172
211 2/8	25 4/8 24 7/8	18 2/8	10 11	Washington County	IL	Jeff Powell	2007	172
211 1/8	26 1/8 25 7/8	16 3/8	11 12	McHenry County	IL	Chadd Hartwig	2003	174
*211 1/8	24 1/8 23 7/8	15 5/8	8 9	Henderson County	IL	Ross Bigger	2009	174
211 0/8	27 0/8 26 4/8	19 3/8	9 10	Lenawee County	MI	Paul Kintner	1996	176
210 7/8	23 1/8 23 2/8	18 6/8	9 9	Teton County	MT	Todd Jensen	1986	177
210 6/8	25 5/8 24 5/8	19 4/8	9 8	Marion County	KS	Bruce Schroeder	1985	178
210 6/8	27 2/8 27 6/8	19 2/8	9 6	Shelby County	IL	Jack Jansen	2009	178
210 5/8	25 7/8 27 1/8	20 3/8	7 7	Waukesha County	WI	Gerald J. Roethle, Jr.	1991	180
210 5/8	26 6/8 27 2/8	22 1/8	9 8	Ogle County	IL	Dan Pierce	1994	180
210 3/8	27 2/8 28 4/8	19 1/8	12 6	Lac qui Parle County	MN	Steven J. Karels	1974	182
210 2/8	26 2/8 26 2/8	19 3/8	9 7	Pottawatomie County	KS	Lacy Shomaker	2009	183
210 0/8	22 0/8 24 0/8	13 5/8	10 8	Jefferson County	IA	Jared Rebling	1998	184
210 0/8	25 3/8 25 7/8	19 2/8	14 8	Ramsey County	MN	Frank M. Frattalone	2006	184
209 7/8	30 0/8 30 0/8	22 3/8	10 12	Richardson County	NE	Albert W. Montgomery	1989	186
209 7/8	25 7/8 27 0/8	21 1/8	12 8	Adams County	IA	Greg Andrews	1998	186
209 7/8	25 1/8 22 2/8	22 3/8	10 9	Randolph County	IL	Mike C. Umbdenstock	2006	186
209 6/8	25 4/8 25 0/8	19 5/8	14 18	Pulaski County	KY	Alan Sidwell	1988	189
209 6/8	26 5/8 27 5/8	20 7/8	9 8	Sangamon County	IL	Mark A. Rademaker	1994	189

637

WHITETAIL DEER (NON-TYPICAL ANTLERS)

Minimum Score 155 — Continued

SCORE	LENGTH OF R MAIN BEAM L	INSIDE SPREAD	NUMBER OF R POINTS L		AREA	STATE/ PROVINCE	HUNTER'S NAME	DATE	RANK
209 5/8	24 4/8 25 3/8	21 0/8	10	10	Livingston County	MI	Michel LaFountain	2000	191
209 3/8	24 6/8 26 6/8	20 1/8	10	9	Racine County	WI	Lon Swatek	1994	192
209 3/8	25 4/8 26 2/8	21 2/8	13	11	Highland County	OH	Jeff Groth	1996	192
209 3/8	24 5/8 24 3/8	19 6/8	8	6	Macon County	MO	Bryan Dickbernd	2002	192
*209 3/8	25 5/8 24 6/8	18 3/8	12	9	Cumberland County	IL	Bob Green	2006	192
*209 3/8	25 3/8 25 3/8	17 5/8	12	13	Allen County	KS	Kortney McGraw	2009	192
209 3/8	26 5/8 27 6/8	21 4/8	10	10	McPherson County	KS	Lonnie Ensminger	1968	197
209 2/8	25 6/8 22 2/8	20 4/8	9	11	De Witt County	IL	Ron L. Willmore	1997	197
*209 2/8	30 1/8 30 5/8	20 0/8	11	7	Chautauqua County	KS	Dwight S. Wolf	2007	197
209 1/8	23 4/8 22 7/8	17 3/8	10	12	Riley County	KS	Jerry McIntyre	1994	200
209 1/8	24 1/8 24 0/8	17 3/8	9	17	Waupaca County	WI	Vince "Chip" Burns II	1999	200
209 1/8	23 7/8 23 4/8	17 0/8	15	21	Allegheny County	PA	Gerald R. Simkonis	2007	200
209 1/8	26 0/8 24 7/8	22 7/8	11	10	Knox County	IL	Troy Huffman	2007	200
208 5/8	26 2/8 26 4/8	22 3/8	9	9	Buffalo County	NE	Carl Clements	1985	204
*208 5/8	29 3/8 28 5/8	16 6/8	11	13	Hamilton County	IL	Adam Brookshire	2008	204
*208 5/8	25 2/8 25 4/8	18 4/8	8	11	Dallas County	IA	Kenny Head	2008	204
208 3/8	29 4/8 26 5/8	21 2/8	8	6	La Salle County	IL	Timothy E. Hawley	2004	207
208 2/8	28 4/8 29 1/8	22 6/8	10	12	Saline County	IL	Mark Sheldon	1999	208
208 2/8	27 1/8 25 4/8	23 4/8	7	13	Rockingham County	NH	Glenn R. Townsend	2000	208
208 1/8	26 6/8 26 5/8	18 3/8	11	9	Brown County	IL	Mark V. Piazza	1989	210
208 0/8	23 5/8 24 2/8	16 0/8	11	11	Marshall County	KS	Tim Wanklyn	1994	211
208 0/8	25 0/8 25 1/8	22 2/8	10	9	Calhoun County	IL	Bobby R. Woods	2001	211
*208 0/8	25 6/8 24 0/8	17 5/8	7	6	Morgan County	IL	Jared Blimling	2009	211
207 7/8	28 3/8 27 5/8	19 0/8	8	10	Otter Tail County	MN	Patrick Millard	1986	214
207 7/8	26 0/8 23 4/8	20 0/8	6	13	Butler County	KS	Matt Powe	2001	214
*207 5/8	28 4/8 30 2/8	24 0/8	12	4	Hamilton County	IA	Brent Johnson	2007	216
*207 4/8	27 5/8 26 2/8	18 4/8	9	11	Osage County	OK	Aaron Scott Vaught	2009	217
207 1/8	24 3/8 25 6/8	18 6/8	9	10	Macoupin County	IL	Kurt A. Bohl	1996	218
207 1/8	29 3/8 28 4/8	25 4/8	8	7	Page County	IA	Jeremy Williams	1997	218
207 1/8	27 6/8 27 3/8	25 1/8	9	9	Leavenworth County	KS	Bart Cox	2002	218
207 1/8	24 2/8 25 0/8	17 3/8	10	12	Clermont County	OH	Kelly Kerkhoff	2003	218
207 1/8	28 0/8 28 0/8	22 1/8	10	7	Macon County	IL	Shannon Babb	2004	218
*207 1/8	26 7/8 25 3/8	20 6/8	13	13	Brown County	IL	William R. Sowell	2009	218
207 0/8	27 7/8 28 1/8	17 7/8	9	11	Noble County	IN	Joesph A. Fulford	1987	224
206 7/8	27 2/8 24 3/8	20 6/8	8	8	Smoky River	ALB	Kirby Smith	1991	225
206 7/8	30 5/8 29 3/8	21 6/8	8	9	McPherson County	KS	Dennis G. Bordner	1994	225
206 7/8	26 3/8 25 0/8	17 2/8	11	8	Hamilton County	OH	Mickey E. Lotz	1995	225
*206 7/8	22 3/8 19 3/8	16 1/8	8	11	Nojack	ALB	John Homik	2004	225
*206 7/8	27 4/8 28 0/8	24 5/8	11	9	Mills County	IA	Scott Warren	2006	225
206 7/8	27 2/8 26 5/8	20 4/8	9	11	Lee County	IL	Matthew C. Rehor	2008	225
206 7/8	27 2/8 27 3/8	18 0/8	9	8	Decatur County	IA	Jeff Gale	2009	225
206 6/8	26 7/8 27 0/8	20 1/8	7	10	Buffalo County	WI	Monte R. Nichols	1996	232
206 6/8	25 6/8 25 7/8	19 5/8	13	9	Greene County	OH	Robert M. Gerleman	2003	232
206 6/8	23 5/8 26 2/8	18 2/8	15	7	Barber County	KS	Rob Grannis	2003	232
*206 6/8	27 0/8 25 0/8	20 4/8	8	14	Tippecanoe County	IN	Chad A. Compton	2006	232
206 2/8	26 2/8 25 2/8	21 1/8	10	8	Monona County	IA	Robert J. Humpal	1994	236
206 2/8	26 2/8 26 5/8	19 0/8	9	13	Pike County	IN	William J. Goepner	2003	236
*206 2/8	27 5/8 26 5/8	20 6/8	7	10	Lancaster County	NE	Robert Findley	2005	236
*206 1/8	24 6/8 25 3/8	18 2/8	9	11	Van Buren County	MI	Robert A. Reits	2007	239
*206 1/8	27 5/8 26 4/8	20 7/8	9	9	Henry County	IA	Phil Coffin	2008	239
206 0/8	22 3/8 24 1/8	17 4/8	9	11	Saunders County	NE	Nordean E. Bade	1964	241
*206 0/8	22 4/8 26 5/8	16 4/8	11	11	Warren County	MO	Bob Reese	2006	241
205 7/8	21 5/8 23 3/8	19 4/8	9	14	Valley County	MT	Richard Blank	1995	243
205 7/8	25 0/8 25 6/8	21 6/8	8	9	Greene County	IL	Ronald R. Okonek	1998	243
205 6/8	25 7/8 25 4/8	21 3/8	14	9	Cottonwood County	MN	Larry Gravely	1975	245
*205 6/8	22 4/8 23 3/8	17 2/8	13	15	Davis County	IA	Joe Bedell	2006	245
205 5/8	29 3/8 28 3/8	26 5/8	8	6	Chase County	KS	Kent Wartick	2008	247
*205 5/8	29 7/8 30 3/8	19 7/8	6	7	Vermillion County	IN	Sean M. Lagacy	2009	247
205 4/8	27 0/8 26 7/8	24 6/8	7	9	Seward County	KS	Lynn Leonard	1988	249
205 4/8	26 6/8 26 4/8	19 6/8	11	8	Dodge County	WI	John Steckling	1998	249
205 3/8	25 1/8 24 0/8	15 0/8	8	12	Beltrami County	MN	Matt Stone	1990	251
205 2/8	29 0/8 29 2/8	19 4/8	7	8	Washington County	IA	Ed Lash	1999	252
205 2/8	25 6/8 25 1/8	19 7/8	8	8	Morgan County	IL	Shawn R. Keegan	2000	252
*205 2/8	17 4/8 18 6/8	17 6/8	18	13	Kaufman County	TX	Eric C. Minter	2009	252
205 1/8	28 7/8 29 0/8	24 1/8	9	8	Erie County	NY	Mark Surdi	1996	255
205 1/8	28 3/8 24 1/8	19 0/8	8	9	Henry County	IL	Mark Burgess	2001	255
205 1/8	25 5/8 26 0/8	19 2/8	9	11	Marion County	MO	Danny Sawyer	2004	255
205 1/8	27 5/8 27 3/8	19 0/8	12	13	Schuyler County	MO	Tracy Boetsma	2009	255
205 0/8	25 4/8 25 4/8	18 7/8	12	10	Marathon County	WI	Joshua J. Erdman	1994	259
205 0/8	25 6/8 25 0/8	18 3/8	8	8	Pike County	IL	Jason Lewis Barnwell	2000	259
204 7/8	26 3/8 26 4/8	18 5/8	9	12	Yankton County	SD	Dan Rederick	1998	261
*204 7/8	24 2/8 24 1/8	22 0/8	9	12	Outagamie County	WI	Randy L. Kabble	2005	261
204 7/8	26 2/8 26 4/8	18 4/8	9	10	Brown County	IL	Michael Postema	2006	261
204 7/8	23 4/8 18 3/8	15 3/8	14	22	Dodge County	WI	Casey Heine	2007	261
204 6/8	28 0/8 28 2/8	21 7/8	8	8	Marathon County	WI	Travis Timothy Behnke	2003	265
*204 6/8	26 0/8 23 0/8	19 3/8	6	11	Hancock County	IL	Mike Nelson	2006	265
204 5/8	27 1/8 25 7/8	21 6/8	6	11	Spruce Grove	ALB	Darryl Legge	1999	267
204 5/8	29 5/8 30 4/8	20 3/8	7	6	Calhoun County	IL	Chad Strickland	1999	267
*204 4/8	26 0/8 25 7/8	18 4/8	8	8	Vermilion County	IL	John Little	2005	269
204 4/8	24 2/8 24 2/8	22 6/8	10	10	Grant County	WI	Mark Rikli	2006	269
*204 4/8	23 6/8 25 4/8	18 1/8	8	9	Jewell County	KS	Mike Pebeck	2009	269
204 2/8	28 3/8 28 1/8	18 4/8	11	11	Grant County	WI	Michael M. White	2001	272
204 2/8	30 0/8 29 1/8	22 5/8	7	7	Morrow County	OH	Lonnie J. Brake	2003	272
204 2/8	26 0/8 25 0/8	18 6/8	10	11	Greenwood County	KS	Charles Schlotterbeck	2006	272
204 1/8	26 5/8 26 2/8	22 0/8	7	9	Dubuque County	IA	Joe Rettenmeier	1987	275
204 1/8	26 0/8 25 4/8	19 7/8	9	11	Jefferson County	OH	Ronald J. Ault	2002	275
204 1/8	20 4/8 25 0/8	16 6/8	14	12	Chase County	KS	Stephen J. Stivaly	2003	275
204 1/8	25 2/8 22 0/8	18 1/8	7	14	Wells County	IN	Jeffrey S. Gordon	2009	275
*204 1/8	22 2/8 22 5/8	17 0/8	14	11	Sully County	SD	Justin Joachim	2009	275
204 0/8	27 1/8 25 2/8	16 6/8	14	12	Webster County	MS	Denver Eshee	1996	280
204 0/8	26 2/8 26 4/8	22 6/8	12	8	Warren County	IA	Jack J. Schuler, Jr.	1997	280
204 0/8	25 2/8 25 5/8	20 5/8	6	8	Cuyahoga County	OH	James J. Gazso	2004	280
203 7/8	25 7/8 25 1/8	20 2/8	11	9	Union County	OR	Joe Mengore	1982	283
203 7/8	24 5/8 25 7/8	17 1/8	15	13	Cloud County	KS	Patrick E. Helget	2009	283
203 6/8	23 6/8 24 6/8	19 6/8	10	8	Washtenaw County	MI	Ronald "Rick" Chabot	1996	285

638

WHITETAIL DEER (NON-TYPICAL ANTLERS)

Minimum Score 155   Continued

SCORE	LENGTH OF MAIN BEAM R / L	INSIDE SPREAD	NUMBER OF POINTS R / L	AREA	STATE/PROVINCE	HUNTER'S NAME	DATE	RANK
203 5/8	25 1/8 / 25 1/8	17 5/8	9 / 11	Warren County	IA	Ted Miller	1986	286
203 5/8	26 2/8 / 25 6/8	17 3/8	10 / 13	Benton County	IA	Rick Gibson	2004	286
*203 5/8	26 0/8 / 25 5/8	19 0/8	9 / 12	Pike County	IL	Chuck "Doc" Conner	2005	286
203 5/8	21 6/8 / 23 4/8	23 0/8	7 / 9	Delaware County	OH	Colin Harman	2009	286
*203 5/8	27 1/8 / 25 2/8	19 2/8	12 / 9	Pottawattamie County	IA	Derrick Sudmann	2009	286
203 4/8	26 6/8 / 27 6/8	17 0/8	7 / 13	Dodge County	MN	Lawrence Sowieja	1955	291
203 3/8	25 0/8 / 24 2/8	19 0/8	10 / 13	Marquette County	WI	Joseph E. Bell	1969	292
203 3/8	24 3/8 / 24 5/8	20 5/8	10 / 9	Adams County	IL	Elroy Little	1981	292
203 3/8	24 3/8 / 25 3/8	20 4/8	12 / 10	Lehigh County	PA	Craig E. Krisher	1988	292
203 3/8	22 3/8 / 21 2/8	18 2/8	10 / 13	Cumberland County	NJ	Darrell T. Capps	2000	292
203 3/8	22 3/8 / 24 1/8	17 5/8	11 / 10	Monroe County	WI	Darrell G. Schultz	2001	292
203 3/8	25 6/8 / 24 4/8	17 7/8	10 / 9	Wabaunsee County	KS	Brandon Blue	2004	292
203 3/8	23 1/8 / 23 6/8	20 4/8	9 / 8	Rock County	WI	Bryan S. Hanthorn	2006	292
203 3/8	26 6/8 / 26 5/8	20 6/8	9 / 10	Kane County	IL	Brian A. Haberkamp	2009	292
203 2/8	26 0/8 / 27 2/8	21 5/8	12 / 13	Decatur County	IA	Kenneth R. Jones	1995	300
203 2/8	22 2/8 / 21 3/8	15 4/8	9 / 10	Pike County	IL	J. Brett Evans	2001	300
*203 2/8	26 5/8 / 26 3/8	20 3/8	7 / 11	Wabash County	IN	Jeff Dale	2007	300
203 2/8	23 7/8 / 24 3/8	17 4/8	11 / 9	Hutchinson County	SD	Matt Weiss	2009	300
203 1/8	24 5/8 / 26 1/8	24 0/8	10 / 7	Bureau County	IL	Jack Davis	2001	304
203 1/8	22 2/8 / 28 3/8	12 0/8	16 / 9	Warren County	IA	Tim C. Deskin	2006	304
203 0/8	25 0/8 / 25 4/8	19 3/8	12 / 10	Geauga County	OH	Rudy Grecar	1969	306
203 0/8	25 6/8 / 26 2/8	21 2/8	7 / 10	Du Page County	IL	Kevin J. Moran	1995	306
202 7/8	25 3/8 / 26 7/8	20 1/8	11 / 12	Decatur County	IA	Kevin J. Anderson	1992	308
202 7/8	27 2/8 / 28 3/8	22 6/8	10 / 8	Brown County	IL	Slyvan Purcell, Jr.	1992	308
202 7/8	21 5/8 / 23 0/8	21 0/8	11 / 9	Stony Plain	ALB	Jeff Lutz	2008	308
*202 6/8	24 0/8 / 24 0/8	18 3/8	9 / 11	Sheridan County	ND	Darnell Arndt	2008	311
202 5/8	23 7/8 / 23 7/8	16 0/8	12 / 12	Jefferson County	KS	Kurt R. Grimmett	1998	312
202 5/8	28 6/8 / 27 2/8	19 4/8	10 / 8	Menard County	IL	Andrae D'Acquisto	2007	312
202 4/8	25 3/8 / 25 2/8	24 2/8	10 / 8	Bremer County	IA	Howard Schmitz	1998	314
*202 4/8	29 5/8 / 28 0/8	20 0/8	8 / 12	La Crosse County	WI	Jed Allen Domke	2007	314
202 3/8	28 5/8 / 26 4/8	20 3/8	9 / 9	Cook County	IL	Joseph Licatesi	1998	316
202 3/8	25 0/8 / 25 3/8	17 4/8	8 / 10	Jefferson County	KS	Brad Christman	2004	316
202 3/8	22 5/8 / 23 5/8	17 4/8	10 / 8	Neosho County	KS	Curt Janssen	2006	316
202 2/8	23 3/8 / 25 6/8	19 6/8	12 / 9	Clay County	SD	Patrick Hudson	1969	319
202 1/8	29 3/8 / 28 0/8	25 0/8	9 / 10	Wood County	OH	Wynn A. Brinker	2001	320
202 0/8	29 0/8 / 27 1/8	22 6/8	9 / 8	Clark County	KS	Dennis Rule	1982	321
*202 0/8	28 0/8 / 28 6/8	22 0/8	7 / 9	Tippecanoe County	IN	Sam D. Brooks II	2005	321
202 0/8	26 0/8 / 26 1/8	17 3/8	12 / 12	Tuscola County	MI	John Benedict	2009	321
201 7/8	22 1/8 / 22 0/8	20 4/8	11 / 11	Davis County	IA	Kevin Scott	2003	324
201 7/8	25 1/8 / 26 5/8	21 3/8	7 / 7	Clark County	IL	Troy Biddle	2005	324
201 6/8	27 2/8 / 27 4/8	20 1/8	10 / 10	Fulton County	IL	Darren Gardner	1994	326
201 5/8	24 2/8 / 24 6/8	16 6/8	15 / 9	Kane County	IL	Keith Kampert	1991	327
201 5/8	25 6/8 / 26 2/8	19 7/8	13 / 8	Sheboygan County	WI	Darren Winter	1995	327
201 5/8	26 3/8 / 25 7/8	16 2/8	9 / 13	Tama County	IA	Rod Waschkat	2001	327
201 4/8	23 3/8 / 22 6/8	25 5/8	10 / 10	Rock Island County	IL	Jeff Maier	1989	330
201 4/8	27 0/8 / 24 5/8	20 0/8	11 / 12	Monona County	IA	Allen Yanke	2007	330
201 4/8	22 5/8 / 23 6/8	19 6/8	6 / 11	Marion County	IL	Benjamin Tate	2008	330
201 3/8	24 4/8 / 25 3/8	20 2/8	14 / 12	Grayson County	TX	Donnie M. Brewer	1995	333
201 3/8	22 7/8 / 21 1/8	18 4/8	10 / 11	Iowa County	IA	Jerry Foubert	2001	333
201 3/8	25 7/8 / 27 4/8	22 0/8	11 / 9	Harvey County	KS	Dennis Pugh	2004	333
201 3/8	27 5/8 / 25 2/8	24 4/8	10 / 8	Trempealeau County	WI	Michael D. George	2006	333
*201 3/8	25 3/8 / 24 0/8	19 0/8	7 / 8	Clark County	KS	Darin Seacat	2007	333
201 2/8	23 7/8 / 24 5/8	20 0/8	13 / 8	Stearns County	MN	Richard D. Berens	1991	338
201 2/8	25 6/8 / 24 1/8	21 2/8	9 / 9	Garden County	NE	Gayle Verbeck	1995	338
201 2/8	24 5/8 / 25 4/8	19 0/8	10 / 9	Hancock County	IN	Christopher L. Kendal	2006	338
*201 2/8	27 4/8 / 27 0/8	22 5/8	11 / 13	Grayson County	TX	Brock Benson	2007	338
201 1/8	28 0/8 / 27 2/8	20 6/8	8 / 10	Carroll County	IL	Mel Landwehr	1991	342
201 1/8	27 5/8 / 25 5/8	21 5/8	7 / 9	Coffey County	KS	Lance W. Jacob	2000	342
201 1/8	25 5/8 / 25 2/8	24 1/8	8 / 8	Grundy County	IL	Earl L. Immormino	2005	342
201 1/8	24 0/8 / 19 0/8	16 1/8	10 / 13	Bracken County	KY	Dennis Sharp	2007	342
201 1/8	24 4/8 / 23 3/8	20 0/8	14 / 14	Grayson County	TX	Donnie Herod	2007	342
*201 1/8	26 0/8 / 26 0/8	18 6/8	9 / 11	Waupaca County	WI	Earl H. Clement	2009	342
*201 0/8	27 6/8 / 20 3/8	20 5/8	10 / 7	Oakland County	MI	Will Werner	2004	348
201 0/8	23 7/8 / 24 2/8	16 4/8	12 / 9	Jennings County	IN	Derik J. Vance	2007	348
200 7/8	25 3/8 / 25 1/8	20 0/8	10 / 12	Morgan County	KY	Greg Powers	1989	350
200 7/8	28 2/8 / 28 1/8	18 7/8	6 / 9	Washington County	KS	Ronald Montague	1990	350
200 7/8	25 6/8 / 26 4/8	23 0/8	10 / 9	Sundre	ALB	Ken R. Madsen	2001	350
200 7/8	28 0/8 / 29 7/8	19 0/8	11 / 9	Cochrane	ALB	Terry L. Raymond	2001	350
200 7/8	23 3/8 / 24 3/8	16 7/8	8 / 10	Riley County	KS	George Nasif	2006	350
200 6/8	29 2/8 / 28 7/8	20 3/8	9 / 6	Medina County	OH	Kenneth Anderson	2001	355
200 6/8	26 3/8 / 27 4/8	18 5/8	8 / 9	Riley County	KS	Jim Fox	2002	355
200 6/8	25 6/8 / 26 5/8	20 7/8	9 / 12	Iroquois County	IL	John Nichols	2006	355
*200 6/8	26 7/8 / 27 2/8	16 6/8	10 / 8	Jefferson County	MO	Jacob D. DeRousse	2009	355
200 5/8	25 1/8 / 27 0/8	18 7/8	7 / 7	Clayton County	IA	Dorrance Arnold	1977	359
200 5/8	26 2/8 / 25 2/8	18 3/8	8 / 9	Madison County	IA	Steve Marsh	1994	359
200 5/8	23 4/8 / 24 1/8	18 4/8	11 / 8	Grayson County	TX	Forrest L. Robertson	1995	359
*200 5/8	23 7/8 / 22 6/8	19 2/8	11 / 9	Cole County	MO	Andy Groose	2007	359
200 5/8	31 1/8 / 29 1/8	23 5/8	9 / 11	Bureau County	IL	Eugene Headings	2010	359
*200 5/8	28 3/8 / 27 1/8	21 2/8	7 / 9	Pottawatomie County	KS	Dave Dreiling	2010	359
200 4/8	25 4/8 / 22 5/8	18 4/8	7 / 9	Macon County	MO	Brad Hudelson	1982	365
200 4/8	27 4/8 / 28 0/8	21 1/8	9 / 6	Sawyer County	WI	Gary Haus	2000	365
200 4/8	30 0/8 / 30 1/8	22 4/8	5 / 8	Lyon County	KS	Blair D. Ogleby	2005	365
200 3/8	25 6/8 / 25 7/8	20 3/8	8 / 8	Branch County	MI	Mitchell S. Brock	1995	368
*200 3/8	24 7/8 / 25 7/8	19 3/8	7 / 7	Washington County	NE	Elton Jones	2002	368
200 3/8	23 6/8 / 22 1/8	18 5/8	9 / 10	Sauk County	WI	Rob Horton	2003	368
200 3/8	27 7/8 / 28 5/8	23 1/8	7 / 10	Douglas County	WI	Christopher Breister	2003	368
200 3/8	27 2/8 / 21 7/8	20 4/8	7 / 10	Sangamon County	IL	Dan Hupp	2004	368
200 2/8	26 2/8 / 25 1/8	20 3/8	11 / 7	Will County	IL	Tom Gawczynski	1993	373
200 2/8	22 5/8 / 23 6/8	19 6/8	12 / 10	Mills County	IA	Randy D. Gearhart	1998	373
200 1/8	28 5/8 / 27 0/8	19 3/8	12 / 7	Ogle County	IL	Theodore H. Hysell	1993	375
200 1/8	26 4/8 / 24 3/8	20 4/8	12 / 10	Riley County	KS	Bryan Glaser	1997	375
200 1/8	24 3/8 / 24 3/8	19 5/8	8 / 11	Marion County	IA	Boyd Mathes	2002	375
200 1/8	27 5/8 / 25 0/8	18 2/8	6 / 8	Knox County	IL	Dennis Easley	2006	375
200 1/8	23 3/8 / 23 6/8	19 5/8	11 / 9	Dakota County	MN	Dean Basch	2006	375
*200 1/8	24 2/8 / 25 6/8	16 2/8	10 / 17	Marion County	IL	Rodney Armstrong	2008	375

WHITETAIL DEER (NON-TYPICAL ANTLERS)

Minimum Score 155 — Continued

SCORE	LENGTH OF R MAIN BEAM L	INSIDE SPREAD	NUMBER OF R POINTS L	AREA	STATE/PROVINCE	HUNTER'S NAME	DATE	RANK
200 0/8	27 1/8 — 27 7/8	22 5/8	8 — 10	Lake County	IN	John E. Quinlan	2002	381
199 7/8	25 4/8 — 27 2/8	22 5/8	7 — 9	Bureau County	IL	Darryl F. Tucker	2003	382
199 7/8	27 1/8 — 27 1/8	20 4/8	8 — 10	Will County	IL	Bill Dyer	2003	382
*199 7/8	26 3/8 — 25 3/8	18 5/8	8 — 10	Riley County	KS	Ken Burnette	2007	382
199 6/8	28 3/8 — 28 4/8	18 2/8	8 — 16	Jackson County	MO	Jack Hollingsworth	1989	385
199 6/8	24 2/8 — 26 2/8	20 2/8	11 — 9	Crawford County	WI	John M. Kane	1996	385
199 6/8	23 7/8 — 22 6/8	22 3/8	10 — 9	Iroquois County	IL	Timothy S. Roach	2003	385
199 5/8	25 7/8 — 24 4/8	21 6/8	10 — 9	Ellsworth County	KS	Paul Gerlach	2007	388
199 4/8	24 6/8 — 24 3/8	19 4/8	10 — 9	Jackson County	IN	J. Anthony Ray	1992	389
199 4/8	26 3/8 — 27 0/8	21 7/8	8 — 10	Jefferson County	IL	James A. Hart	2004	389
199 4/8	29 2/8 — 28 6/8	19 7/8	7 — 8	Butler County	OH	Donald Ehling	2007	389
199 3/8	24 3/8 — 23 4/8	22 2/8	12 — 11	Atchison County	KS	Kirby A. Clifton	1973	392
199 3/8	24 3/8 — 23 1/8	17 6/8	8 — 8	Comanche County	KS	Phillip L. Kirkland	1981	392
199 3/8	24 7/8 — 24 4/8	21 4/8	16 — 12	Eau Claire County	WI	Steven J. Schmitt	2003	392
199 3/8	24 6/8 — 24 3/8	18 2/8	11 — 9	Beadle County	SD	Jason Meyer	2006	392
199 2/8	26 1/8 — 26 3/8	18 1/8	11 — 11	Washtenaw County	MI	Donnie Bollinger	1998	396
199 2/8	20 7/8 — 20 7/8	19 2/8	9 — 10	Sauk County	WI	Daniel G. Kruchten	2006	396
*199 1/8	26 6/8 — 22 4/8	17 1/8	7 — 9	Milwaukee County	WI	Kim Acker	2010	398
199 0/8	29 6/8 — 28 4/8	20 0/8	8 — 10	Lake County	IL	Steven Hysell	1994	399
199 0/8	27 7/8 — 27 2/8	18 4/8	7 — 7	Macoupin County	IL	Jon DeNeef	1995	399
199 0/8	23 3/8 — 23 7/8	20 5/8	9 — 8	Trempealeau County	WI	Germaine Marsolek	1999	399
198 7/8	27 0/8 — 26 7/8	17 7/8	11 — 13	Logan County	KY	Oscar Howard	1989	402
198 7/8	25 2/8 — 23 5/8	18 7/8	14 — 13	Harrison County	IA	Kody Wohlers	1998	402
198 7/8	25 2/8 — 25 1/8	17 2/8	7 — 7	Pike County	IL	James Kruczynski	1998	402
198 7/8	29 3/8 — 28 5/8	20 7/8	14 — 13	Van Buren County	IA	Ivan Muzljakovich	2008	402
198 6/8	22 5/8 — 24 5/8	15 0/8	11 — 11	Peoria County	IL	Roger Woodcock	1989	406
198 6/8	23 7/8 — 25 4/8	19 6/8	10 — 7	Randolph County	IL	John Brown	1992	406
198 6/8	28 0/8 — 28 0/8	15 4/8	8 — 11	Menard County	IL	Ron J. Wadsworth	2004	406
198 6/8	27 4/8 — 27 7/8	19 6/8	8 — 9	Ottawa County	KS	Christopher S. Hicks	2006	406
198 6/8	26 4/8 — 26 5/8	17 3/8	8 — 8	Licking County	OH	Robert Wingeier	2008	406
198 5/8	26 2/8 — 25 0/8	22 6/8	5 — 5	Douglas County	NE	Ivan Mascher	1961	411
198 5/8	27 2/8 — 29 5/8	19 4/8	6 — 9	Montgomery County	IL	Earl W. Law, Jr.	1989	411
198 5/8	26 6/8 — 27 6/8	20 4/8	10 — 8	Des Moines County	IA	Craig R. Belknap	1998	411
*198 5/8	25 0/8 — 25 6/8	17 7/8	7 — 7	Montgomery County	IL	Cody DeWitt	2009	411
*198 4/8	27 3/8 — 27 1/8	19 4/8	11 — 6	Ross County	OH	Nicole Wolf	2005	415
198 4/8	23 2/8 — 23 4/8	16 0/8	12 — 9	Steuben County	NY	Rex Taft	2005	415
*198 4/8	28 5/8 — 27 6/8	22 1/8	6 — 8	Washington County	MN	Michael Versland	2009	415
198 3/8	24 3/8 — 24 3/8	20 7/8	10 — 10	Lyon County	MN	Edward Matthys	1966	418
198 3/8	27 2/8 — 26 6/8	18 6/8	10 — 7	Reno County	KS	Greig Sims	1987	418
198 3/8	23 6/8 — 23 3/8	19 7/8	9 — 7	Pottawattamie County	IA	Rodney P. Stahlnecker	1991	418
198 3/8	28 2/8 — 30 1/8	20 0/8	8 — 9	Pike County	OH	Lenny Downs	1999	418
198 3/8	23 3/8 — 22 7/8	19 4/8	18 — 16	Butler County	KS	Caiden Bump	2004	418
198 2/8	27 5/8 — 27 2/8	19 5/8	7 — 9	Fulton County	IL	Mike Massingale	1991	423
*198 2/8	25 1/8 — 23 0/8	21 2/8	10 — 10	Pawnee County	OK	David Nance	2008	423
198 1/8	27 0/8 — 26 3/8	20 2/8	10 — 7	Hocking County	OH	Hugh Cox	1964	425
198 1/8	24 1/8 — 23 6/8	17 2/8	8 — 7	DeKalb County	IL	Donald R. Lalowski	2006	425
198 0/8	26 7/8 — 28 0/8	19 0/8	9 — 10	Union County	OH	Michael Amsbaugh	2000	427
198 0/8	26 5/8 — 26 5/8	19 4/8	12 — 8	Meigs County	OH	Jack Satterfield, Jr.	2000	427
198 0/8	25 5/8 — 27 5/8	18 7/8	8 — 9	Jackson County	IA	Jesse Smith	2001	427
198 0/8	25 4/8 — 23 3/8	22 2/8	9 — 8	Cooper County	MO	Eddie Hoff	2010	427
197 7/8	22 2/8 — 23 0/8	19 2/8	8 — 12	Latah County	ID	Dean Weyen	1992	431
197 7/8	25 2/8 — 25 2/8	20 0/8	12 — 11	Richardson County	NE	Bob Campbell	1996	431
197 7/8	24 6/8 — 24 5/8	19 4/8	8 — 7	Walworth County	WI	Frank F. Gerke, Jr.	2001	431
197 6/8	23 6/8 — 22 4/8	17 4/8	8 — 11	Pratt County	KS	Mike Patton	1987	434
197 6/8	27 3/8 — 28 0/8	20 4/8	6 — 10	Preble County	OH	Larry E. Hickman	1999	434
197 5/8	25 2/8 — 25 2/8	18 7/8	10 — 10	Preble County	OH	Mike McCabe	1995	436
197 5/8	26 5/8 — 27 1/8	17 1/8	9 — 10	McDonough County	IL	Thad Powell	1998	436
197 5/8	21 4/8 — 21 2/8	14 3/8	10 — 6	Monmouth County	NJ	Gene DeMeter II	2005	436
197 5/8	23 5/8 — 21 2/8	15 1/8	13 — 12	Harper County	KS	Adam Thomas	2007	436
197 4/8	25 0/8 — 23 7/8	22 2/8	7 — 7	Johnson County	IA	Dennis R. Ballard	1971	440
197 4/8	25 3/8 — 26 3/8	16 7/8	6 — 8	Lyon County	KS	John R. Clifton	1984	440
197 4/8	25 4/8 — 26 6/8	19 2/8	8 — 6	Franklin County	KS	Lyle Henry Wierenga	2002	440
197 4/8	25 2/8 — 26 1/8	16 2/8	6 — 5	Crittenden County	KY	Sean Shuecraft	2005	440
*197 4/8	28 0/8 — 27 5/8	21 6/8	7 — 9	Finney County	KS	Randall Miller	2005	440
*197 4/8	23 4/8 — 22 7/8	15 6/8	11 — 12	Chickasaw County	IA	Greg Richards	2007	440
197 4/8	24 4/8 — 25 4/8	19 3/8	10 — 8	Fairfield County	OH	Richard Hutchison	2008	440
197 3/8	27 3/8 — 26 3/8	20 4/8	8 — 9	Faribault County	MN	Randy Lee Sandt	1982	447
197 3/8	23 7/8 — 21 7/8	24 0/8	7 — 10	Gallia County	OH	Jim W. Brumfield	1992	447
197 3/8	24 3/8 — 24 4/8	20 1/8	8 — 7	Clark County	SD	Steve Frank	1995	447
197 3/8	27 4/8 — 28 4/8	19 2/8	8 — 8	Lanark	ONT	Dave Glithero	2001	447
197 3/8	28 5/8 — 27 6/8	21 6/8	16 — 14	Suffolk County	NY	John E. Hansen	2001	447
197 3/8	23 4/8 — 24 0/8	18 7/8	10 — 7	Schuyler County	IL	Gregory A. Runkle	2003	447
197 3/8	24 3/8 — 25 0/8	21 0/8	9 — 8	Des Moines County	IA	Stan Yocius, Jr.	2005	447
197 3/8	27 2/8 — 27 4/8	19 7/8	10 — 12	Henry County	VA	Anthony Hodges	2006	447
*197 3/8	26 0/8 — 25 4/8	18 6/8	7 — 11	Union County	IL	Mark Andrew Bundren	2008	447
197 2/8	27 3/8 — 27 6/8	19 1/8	9 — 10	Nemaha County	KS	D. Jay Hartter	1990	456
*197 2/8	24 0/8 — 24 2/8	20 2/8	9 — 13	Linn County	MO	Eric Meyer	2004	456
197 2/8	26 0/8 — 26 6/8	19 0/8	11 — 8	Piatt County	IL	Scott D. Johnson	2004	456
197 2/8	24 7/8 — 24 2/8	20 3/8	10 — 8	Licking County	OH	David Nichols	2007	456
197 1/8	26 4/8 — 24 2/8	18 5/8	9 — 12	Linn County	IA	Marsha Fairbanks	1974	460
197 1/8	26 1/8 — 26 3/8	17 3/8	8 — 7	Jackson County	MO	Jim Martin	1984	460
197 1/8	16 4/8 — 18 3/8	18 0/8	10 — 10	Bullock County	AL	Ronnie Everett	1990	460
197 1/8	24 0/8 — 25 2/8	17 5/8	7 — 7	Bourbon County	KS	David Cox	1997	460
197 1/8	25 4/8 — 25 2/8	25 4/8	9 — 8	Butler County	IA	Tom Demro	2009	460
197 0/8	26 1/8 — 26 4/8	21 5/8	8 — 9	Marshall County	IL	Larry Rowe	1975	465
197 0/8	21 5/8 — 22 2/8	21 0/8	9 — 7	Woodford County	KY	Daniel E. Jackson II	1994	465
197 0/8	26 4/8 — 26 4/8	21 0/8	8 — 9	La Salle County	IL	Kenneth Sparks	2002	465
*197 0/8	25 0/8 — 25 5/8	23 0/8	7 — 8	Poinsett County	AR	Kevin Owens	2003	465
197 0/8	25 4/8 — 25 0/8	20 2/8	10 — 9	Mahaska County	IA	Larry Vander Linden	2004	465
197 0/8	24 7/8 — 25 2/8	18 4/8	7 — 8	La Crosse County	WI	Nathan Tucker	2005	465
196 7/8	30 1/8 — 26 5/8	21 0/8	9 — 7	Lake County	IL	Kory Lang	1991	471
196 7/8	25 1/8 — 25 1/8	18 5/8	11 — 11	Jackson County	MI	Herbert C. Miller, Jr.	1993	471
196 7/8	21 6/8 — 25 5/8	17 6/8	8 — 10	Linn County	IA	James L. Newman	1996	471
196 7/8	28 0/8 — 28 2/8	22 0/8	7 — 11	Winneshiek County	IA	David G. Baumler	1997	471
*196 7/8	26 4/8 — 24 7/8	24 7/8	8 — 7	Jackson County	KS	Steven K. Parker	2009	471

WHITETAIL DEER (NON-TYPICAL ANTLERS)

Minimum Score 155   Continued

SCORE	LENGTH OF R MAIN BEAM L	INSIDE SPREAD	NUMBER OF R POINTS L	AREA	STATE/ PROVINCE	HUNTER'S NAME	DATE	RANK
196 6/8	24 5/8 25 1/8	23 6/8	6 8	Lawrence County	IN	John E. Johnson	1987	476
196 6/8	25 1/8 26 4/8	18 2/8	6 11	Crawford County	IL	Scott Schackmann	2003	476
*196 6/8	24 3/8 25 4/8	18 6/8	8 7	Putnam County	MO	David A. Brown	2004	476
*196 6/8	26 4/8 27 3/8	20 5/8	7 7	Clayton County	IA	Jeff E. Palmer	2008	476
*196 6/8	27 6/8 25 1/8	18 7/8	7 10	Gage County	NE	Ben Vilda	2009	476
196 5/8	27 7/8 27 5/8	20 6/8	9 9	Dufferin	ONT	James P. Baird	2000	481
196 5/8	29 2/8 28 5/8	19 1/8	7 9	Pinawa	MAN	Mark Ilijanic	2000	481
196 5/8	24 4/8 23 2/8	17 1/8	9 9	Bourbon County	KS	Tony Starr	2003	481
*196 5/8	25 4/8 25 4/8	22 5/8	8 6	Schuyler County	IL	Justin D. Ketterman	2004	481
196 5/8	25 7/8 26 4/8	16 4/8	7 8	Worcester County	MD	John W. Bromley III	2005	481
196 5/8	28 2/8 26 6/8	18 2/8	8 7	Tuscarawas County	OH	Troy Wrather	2005	481
196 4/8	27 2/8 26 6/8	20 1/8	8 7	Warren County	IL	Shawn Guyer	2007	487
196 3/8	22 3/8 27 2/8	18 6/8	9 7	Butler County	IA	Bret Moore	2006	488
196 2/8	24 7/8 24 6/8	18 4/8	8 7	Louisa County	IA	Tony Thomas	1995	489
*196 2/8	23 2/8 26 3/8	20 2/8	10 12	Suffolk County	NY	Richard S. Gates	2006	489
196 1/8	27 5/8 26 2/8	20 2/8	7 8	Edgar County	IL	Jerry R. David	1988	491
196 0/8	26 6/8 23 3/8	15 5/8	9 9	Cumberland County	IL	Jeff Light	1997	492
196 0/8	25 1/8 25 6/8	24 6/8	9 9	Lucas County	IA	Brian Bailey	1998	492
196 0/8	24 4/8 25 6/8	19 7/8	9 7	Franklin County	IN	John D. Burkhart	2002	492
196 0/8	25 5/8 25 0/8	19 5/8	10 11	Coles County	IL	John Bailey	2004	492
196 0/8	21 6/8 22 6/8	19 5/8	11 12	St. Louis County	MN	Richard Van Valkenburg	2007	492
195 7/8	25 3/8 26 0/8	22 0/8	15 15	Wayne County	OH	Gary L. Fowler	2005	497
195 7/8	25 0/8 23 5/8	17 5/8	9 11	Woodford County	IL	Marc Anthony	2005	497
195 7/8	25 1/8 25 2/8	16 1/8	9 9	Boone County	KY	Jim Litmer	2006	497
*195 7/8	28 0/8 28 7/8	19 3/8	11 10	Champaign County	IL	Ben Self	2007	497
*195 7/8	27 5/8 27 7/8	24 5/8	11 7	Houston County	MN	Nathan L. Ulmen	2010	497
195 6/8	27 1/8 26 6/8	21 5/8	7 6	Dubuque County	IA	Jim H. Dougherty	1985	502
195 6/8	29 1/8 29 0/8	21 3/8	7 8	Pierce County	WI	Jody M. Anderson	1998	502
195 6/8	25 5/8 24 1/8	16 4/8	9 13	Story County	IA	Jarod Pedersen	1999	502
195 6/8	24 1/8 24 3/8	22 4/8	7 8	Scotland County	MO	Doug Sorter	2003	502
195 5/8	28 6/8 28 2/8	20 2/8	9 10	Martin County	MN	Ben Johnson	1973	506
195 5/8	24 1/8 24 2/8	19 0/8	9 7	Waushara County	WI	Randy Chamberlain	1984	506
195 5/8	27 3/8 27 3/8	19 7/8	9 10	Allamakee County	IA	Gary L. Mezera	1994	506
195 5/8	24 1/8 23 5/8	21 7/8	12 11	Livingston County	MI	Patrick Harris	1995	506
195 5/8	24 3/8 24 0/8	18 3/8	7 7	Madison County	MS	Damon Saik	2001	506
*195 5/8	30 3/8 29 3/8	21 1/8	7 7	Champaign County	OH	Robert Wilson	2009	506
195 4/8	27 2/8 28 1/8	18 2/8	9 7	Putnam County	IN	Chris M. Tanner	1982	512
195 4/8	25 2/8 26 2/8	19 7/8	6 7	Crawford County	IA	Larry Sparks	1985	512
195 4/8	21 4/8 23 4/8	15 2/8	11 8	Jessamine County	KY	Tony W Drury	1991	512
195 4/8	25 6/8 24 0/8	15 3/8	11 9	Allegan County	MI	Jason A. Newman	1994	512
195 4/8	26 3/8 27 3/8	18 1/8	8 10	Morris County	KS	Craig Johnson	1994	512
195 4/8	24 4/8 23 4/8	18 3/8	11 10	Owen County	IN	Tony Harris	1998	512
195 4/8	24 2/8 24 1/8	18 4/8	10 9	Door County	WI	Robert Meingast	2002	512
195 3/8	22 2/8 19 5/8	16 1/8	15 11	Pope County	IL	Dennis Boaz	1993	519
195 3/8	26 4/8 27 5/8	21 0/8	8 8	Dallas County	IA	Darrell Langworthy	1997	519
*195 3/8	26 1/8 27 5/8	19 3/8	6 10	Preble County	OH	Mark Bassler	2006	519
195 3/8	25 6/8 27 2/8	20 4/8	9 9	Jo Daviess County	IL	Craig James Olson	2007	519
195 3/8	21 3/8 21 0/8	17 0/8	10 10	Clinton County	IA	Lee J. Schultz	2009	519
195 2/8	24 7/8 25 5/8	20 0/8	8 9	Dakota County	MN	Mark LeMay	1993	524
195 2/8	26 3/8 25 5/8	19 2/8	9 7	Richland County	WI	James Torrez	2005	524
*195 2/8	26 1/8 26 0/8	18 3/8	9 10	Burke County	ND	Jeff Bohl	2006	524
195 2/8	21 6/8 23 3/8	22 1/8	12 9	Grayson County	TX	Robert Keith Kimberlin	2006	524
195 2/8	26 6/8 26 4/8	17 1/8	7 6	Greene County	OH	Scott Burton	2008	524
195 2/8	25 3/8 25 4/8	21 2/8	6 10	Fulton County	IL	Jeff Souza	2009	524
195 1/8	27 0/8 25 7/8	15 5/8	9 9	Cecil County	MD	Chuck Crouse	1995	530
195 1/8	27 5/8 29 0/8	21 5/8	6 4	Clinton County	IA	Steve Wagner	1995	530
195 1/8	26 7/8 26 0/8	24 0/8	7 8	Washington County	IL	Leo Suchomski	2002	530
195 1/8	24 0/8 24 5/8	19 1/8	11 10	Montgomery County	IN	James A. Rogers, Jr.	2005	530
195 1/8	24 6/8 24 2/8	17 3/8	8 11	Buchanan County	IA	Kevin Peterson	2005	530
195 0/8	26 6/8 25 0/8	16 3/8	9 13	Juneau County	WI	Maurice Sterba	1955	535
195 0/8	27 4/8 27 7/8	20 2/8	9 10	Jersey County	IL	Glenn Wilson	1994	535
195 0/8	25 6/8 27 2/8	20 1/8	11 9	Westmoreland County	PA	Eugene W. Livingston	1995	535
195 0/8	25 4/8 26 1/8	22 0/8	8 9	McLean County	IL	Frank Bartels	1996	535
195 0/8	27 3/8 27 0/8	18 5/8	7 9	Guthrie County	IA	Chad Laabs	1996	535
195 0/8	26 0/8 26 0/8	19 4/8	10 7	Marion County	IA	Brian Moore	2000	535
195 0/8	26 4/8 26 1/8	15 2/8	7 7	Dubuque County	IA	Adam W. Anglin	2001	535
*195 0/8	29 5/8 23 7/8	19 1/8	10 9	Parke County	IN	Brian K. Berrisford	2004	535
195 0/8	26 7/8 25 6/8	21 7/8	9 8	Stephenson County	IL	James E. Farmer	2005	535
*195 0/8	24 5/8 23 7/8	19 4/8	9 8	Lyon County	KS	Ryan Alexander	2007	535
195 0/8	24 4/8 24 1/8	18 7/8	7 10	Crow Wing County	MN	Lance Wasniewski	2007	535
*195 0/8	23 0/8 22 3/8	20 0/8	12 6	Iroquois County	IL	Josh Sparling	2008	535
*195 0/8	25 3/8 25 4/8	17 7/8	6 7	Linn County	IA	John Eaton	2008	535
195 0/8	25 3/8 23 4/8	18 3/8	9 9	Waushara County	WI	Eric J. Haag	2010	535
195 0/8	25 5/8 26 2/8	22 2/8	7 11	Ogle County	IL	Julie Page	2010	535
194 7/8	27 7/8 26 1/8	19 0/8	11 10	Warren County	MO	Dennis Jones	1982	550
194 7/8	25 5/8 24 6/8	18 6/8	11 9	Davis County	IA	Richard Flink	2004	550
194 5/8	26 3/8 24 7/8	20 7/8	7 8	Guernsey County	OH	Dick Bayer	1985	552
194 5/8	26 2/8 24 0/8	23 7/8	6 7	Lake County	IL	Paul H. Woit	1991	552
194 5/8	27 6/8 28 3/8	20 1/8	7 10	Walworth County	WI	Michael Senft	2000	552
194 5/8	26 2/8 25 6/8	18 0/8	10 10	Fond du Lac County	WI	Tim Johnson	2009	552
194 4/8	28 1/8 26 2/8	18 4/8	8 7	Miami County	KS	Alfred E. Smith	1990	556
194 4/8	26 7/8 27 0/8	24 2/8	9 8	Polk County	IA	Paul Beesley	1990	556
*194 4/8	24 7/8 25 2/8	21 3/8	8 9	Marion County	OH	Martin E. Hamm, Jr.	2007	556
194 3/8	27 5/8 28 0/8	22 4/8	7 7	Fulton County	IL	Dwayne Etter	1994	559
194 3/8	22 7/8 22 5/8	16 7/8	7 7	Clay County	IA	Shane Wade Helmich	1998	559
194 3/8	26 2/8 26 1/8	18 5/8	12 11	Shawnee County	KS	Larry Walters	2001	559
*194 3/8	22 5/8 25 2/8	19 6/8	11 9	Parke County	IN	Fred Prewitt, Sr.	2005	559
194 3/8	25 2/8 27 1/8	18 1/8	8 8	Cass County	IL	Timothy Hinz	2005	559
*194 3/8	28 6/8 27 1/8	21 7/8	9 8	Comanche County	KS	Joseph D. Simpson	2009	559
194 2/8	27 1/8 26 0/8	23 5/8	9 6	Pike County	MO	William E. Knowles	1980	565
194 2/8	24 3/8 23 6/8	14 1/8	12 10	Pulaski County	VA	Roger N. White	1996	565
194 2/8	23 1/8 23 1/8	18 5/8	6 7	Brown County	IL	Les Davenport	2002	565
194 2/8	26 3/8 27 1/8	18 3/8	10 11	Clermont County	OH	Charles Combs	2003	565
*194 2/8	23 4/8 26 4/8	20 2/8	9 10	Posey County	IN	Brart Lamm	2007	565
194 2/8	24 6/8 24 6/8	16 0/8	8 7	Jefferson County	NE	Jon Novotny	2008	565

641

WHITETAIL DEER (NON-TYPICAL ANTLERS)

Minimum Score 155 — Continued

SCORE	LENGTH OF MAIN BEAM R	L	INSIDE SPREAD	NUMBER OF POINTS R	L	AREA	STATE/PROVINCE	HUNTER'S NAME	DATE	RANK
194 1/8	25 7/8	25 4/8	20 2/8	9	8	Jackson County	KS	Fred Dunn	1996	571
194 1/8	25 2/8	25 4/8	18 4/8	8	8	Whiteside County	IL	Scott Klingenberg	2004	571
194 1/8	23 3/8	24 2/8	17 7/8	8	7	Clayton County	IA	Brian Beck	2007	571
194 0/8	24 5/8	24 4/8	18 5/8	9	11	Cass County	NE	Sean Platt	1996	574
194 0/8	26 5/8	26 0/8	21 1/8	10	8	Louisa County	IA	Jerry Bixby	2000	574
194 0/8	26 0/8	24 3/8	22 0/8	9	8	Fremont County	IA	Mark Armstrong	2000	574
194 0/8	26 7/8	26 3/8	20 6/8	6	7	Bureau County	IL	Jared Piacenti	2003	574
194 0/8	23 3/8	24 3/8	21 0/8	11	7	Warren County	IL	Dan T. Nordstrom	2004	574
193 7/8	25 1/8	27 2/8	18 0/8	11	11	Blaine County	MT	Gene Wensel	1981	579
193 7/8	27 6/8	26 3/8	21 1/8	9	9	Eau Claire County	WI	Greg Miller	1990	579
193 6/8	29 6/8	28 0/8	20 2/8	9	9	Lake County	IN	Walter Sobczak	1979	581
193 6/8	23 7/8	24 4/8	19 6/8	8	6	Moody County	SD	Matt Plummer	2005	581
*193 6/8	25 2/8	24 7/8	20 0/8	7	10	Simcoe	ONT	Bob Dutton	2007	581
*193 6/8	24 6/8	25 1/8	16 2/8	6	9	Buffalo County	WI	James D. Jacobson	2008	581
193 5/8	25 7/8	25 5/8	15 4/8	8	9	La Crosse County	WI	Fred G. Baures	2007	585
193 4/8	26 1/8	27 4/8	18 5/8	9	8	Clarke County	IA	Don Mealey	1993	586
193 4/8	28 0/8	27 7/8	21 2/8	11	8	Parke County	IN	James H. Griggs	1996	586
193 4/8	24 6/8	25 2/8	16 0/8	14	12	Warren County	IN	Bill D. Wadkins	1999	586
*193 4/8	25 4/8	26 2/8	18 3/8	10	7	Lenawee County	MI	Jeremy Collingsworth	2009	586
193 3/8	24 3/8	25 3/8	19 3/8	16	9	Roanoke County	VA	Randy Brookshier	1983	590
193 3/8	27 4/8	24 0/8	21 3/8	9	9	McHenry County	IL	Mike Kaufmann	1999	590
193 3/8	25 4/8	25 6/8	16 2/8	12	7	Clay County	MO	Rod Owen	2003	590
*193 3/8	25 4/8	27 1/8	24 0/8	7	8	Madison County	IL	Terry Jenkins	2006	590
193 3/8	28 7/8	28 6/8	19 5/8	8	7	Marquette County	WI	Bobby Ziarek	2008	590
193 3/8	21 1/8	25 1/8	14 5/8	10	6	Decatur County	IA	Sid Tingen	2009	590
193 3/8	23 7/8	24 7/8	20 3/8	7	9	Fremont County	IA	Aaron McCormick	2009	590
193 2/8	25 0/8	24 3/8	19 6/8	8	7	Pottawatomie County	KS	Dale R. Larson	1997	597
193 2/8	25 2/8	23 6/8	18 5/8	7	8	Fulton County	IL	James Crane	1997	597
193 2/8	27 0/8	24 5/8	18 5/8	8	11	Clark County	IN	Mike West	1998	597
193 2/8	24 4/8	26 4/8	17 3/8	12	12	Pike County	IL	Bill Gregory	2001	597
193 2/8	27 3/8	25 4/8	19 0/8	7	8	Noble County	IN	Chris Addison	2004	597
*193 2/8	23 5/8	22 6/8	16 3/8	8	9	Lyon County	KS	Jim Bohrer	2006	597
193 2/8	28 5/8	26 0/8	21 0/8	11	10	Polk County	IA	Matt Buttz	2007	597
193 2/8	29 3/8	29 3/8	20 2/8	7	7	Champaign County	OH	Bill Coe	2008	597
*193 2/8	21 7/8	22 2/8	17 4/8	11	9	Hyde County	SD	Rick Hanson	2009	597
*193 1/8	24 7/8	24 7/8	22 1/8	7	8	Marion County	MO	David Moss	2001	606
193 1/8	23 2/8	22 6/8	14 4/8	13	7	Doniphan County	KS	Brian Hickman	2002	606
193 1/8	25 4/8	24 6/8	16 6/8	11	12	Wood County	WV	Howard D. Powell III	2009	606
193 0/8	27 4/8	27 1/8	19 7/8	8	7	Lake County	IL	Steven Derkson	1989	609
193 0/8	24 1/8	22 7/8	20 0/8	6	7	Outagamie County	WI	James C. Snortum	2001	609
193 0/8	25 3/8	23 5/8	19 2/8	9	9	McHenry County	IL	Nevin R. Salvino	2005	609
*193 0/8	26 1/8	26 4/8	18 2/8	8	10	Schuyler County	IL	Melissa Bachman	2007	609
192 7/8	20 6/8	19 5/8	14 3/8	9	11	Charles County	MD	Fred Hoffman	1991	613
192 7/8	26 0/8	26 5/8	18 2/8	7	8	Morrison County	MN	Brent M. Beimert	2001	613
192 7/8	21 3/8	24 4/8	22 3/8	10	14	St. Francis County	AR	Jay Wright	2001	613
192 7/8	26 1/8	27 2/8	22 0/8	10	8	Parke County	IN	Michael S. Jones	2005	613
*192 7/8	23 5/8	26 0/8	16 6/8	15	9	Oldham County	KY	Mike LeClair	2008	613
*192 7/8	19 4/8	20 3/8	16 0/8	10	10	Vernon County	WI	James E. Wiltinger	2009	613
192 6/8	27 0/8	27 7/8	21 7/8	8	6	Washington County	KS	Jim Snyder	1986	619
192 6/8	27 3/8	26 2/8	17 7/8	9	7	Vermilion County	IL	Ed Gudgel	1988	619
192 6/8	24 1/8	23 4/8	18 5/8	10	9	Clay County	IN	Gordon Eldridge	1994	619
192 6/8	26 4/8	26 5/8	17 1/8	10	8	Nemaha County	KS	Tyran L. Hartter	1996	619
192 6/8	24 2/8	23 0/8	17 2/8	6	11	Anderson County	KS	Raymond Yoder	1997	619
192 6/8	24 3/8	25 5/8	22 3/8	8	7	Piatt County	IL	Wesley Eckart	2001	619
*192 6/8	26 6/8	28 0/8	20 0/8	6	7	Mingo County	WV	Dennis H. Hall	2003	619
192 5/8	25 0/8	27 0/8	22 1/8	6	8	Republic County	KS	Don Dejmal	1983	626
192 5/8	27 5/8	27 5/8	20 7/8	9	8	Putnam County	MO	Timothy W. Murchison	1995	626
192 5/8	21 6/8	21 4/8	17 0/8	12	10	Dubuque County	IA	Greg Wille	2002	626
192 5/8	22 2/8	22 4/8	18 1/8	10	12	Fairfield County	OH	Matt DeFazio	2003	626
192 5/8	24 4/8	25 1/8	18 3/8	8	9	Macoupin County	IL	Dale Fritzche	2007	626
192 4/8	21 4/8	20 5/8	15 4/8	11	10	Redwood County	MN	Mark A. Steinle	1973	631
192 4/8	25 5/8	25 1/8	22 2/8	9	8	Edmonton	ALB	Jon Okonek	1997	631
192 4/8	27 5/8	27 2/8	22 5/8	7	7	Adams County	OH	Chris Eldridge	2003	631
192 4/8	26 3/8	27 4/8	20 3/8	11	8	Stafford County	KS	Chad Milligan	2005	631
192 4/8	24 3/8	25 4/8	15 0/8	14	8	Warren County	KY	Paul Campbell	2006	631
*192 4/8	25 6/8	27 1/8	18 6/8	9	10	Scioto County	OH	Joshua A. Banard	2010	631
192 3/8	25 4/8	25 6/8	20 1/8	9	7	Pickaway County	OH	Gerald E. Dunn	1992	637
192 3/8	19 1/8	17 3/8	11 3/8	17	14	James City County	VA	Chuck R. Handle	1994	637
192 3/8	25 2/8	27 4/8	22 3/8	10	6	Edgar County	IL	Brad Davis	1996	637
192 3/8	25 6/8	25 7/8	21 7/8	7	6	Warren County	IA	Randy Messer	1997	637
192 3/8	19 4/8	23 7/8	18 5/8	8	8	Kankakee County	IL	Jeffery J. Schneider	2000	637
192 3/8	22 5/8	24 6/8	18 6/8	7	10	Allen County	IN	Wayne Leazier, Jr.	2005	637
192 2/8	25 1/8	27 0/8	20 5/8	6	9	Jasper County	IL	Dan Flach	1994	643
192 2/8	24 6/8	25 0/8	17 2/8	9	7	Monmouth County	NJ	Joseph J. Meglio	1999	643
*192 2/8	23 7/8	23 6/8	18 6/8	7	9	Queen Annes County	MD	Hunter Trae Lockwood	2004	643
192 1/8	24 3/8	21 1/8	17 3/8	11	10	Gray County	KS	Randall Koehn	1985	646
192 1/8	28 2/8	27 0/8	19 5/8	10	9	Brown County	OH	Paul R. Durbin	1992	646
192 1/8	25 1/8	26 1/8	18 0/8	7	7	Somerset County	MD	Archie East	1993	646
192 1/8	28 6/8	27 6/8	20 4/8	10	7	Knox County	IL	Dan Hicks	2003	646
192 1/8	26 1/8	26 1/8	20 2/8	8	8	Taylor County	IA	Todd Tobin	2009	646
192 0/8	26 2/8	25 6/8	25 6/8	7	10	Day County	SD	Doug Rumpca	1985	651
192 0/8	25 4/8	26 0/8	20 1/8	9	10	Fulton County	IL	Richard Luton	2004	651
192 0/8	25 0/8	25 7/8	20 6/8	7	11	Bremer County	IA	James A. Harris	2006	651
*192 0/8	28 5/8	27 0/8	21 5/8	10	9	Union County	OH	Isaac Heyne	2007	651
191 7/8	21 3/8	21 4/8	15 4/8	9	9	Du Page County	IL	Pete Heliotis	1986	655
191 7/8	25 0/8	24 1/8	18 6/8	7	8	Calhoun County	MI	Daniel B. Farmer	2005	655
*191 7/8	24 6/8	24 3/8	19 3/8	7	8	Barton County	KS	Mark E. Johnson	2005	655
191 7/8	23 3/8	22 7/8	20 3/8	7	14	Oklahoma County	OK	George Moore	2010	655
191 6/8	23 2/8	20 7/8	16 5/8	6	15	Murray County	MN	Delbert Peck	1956	659
191 6/8	28 5/8	28 6/8	16 4/8	7	6	Preble County	OH	Claude Adkins	1989	659
191 6/8	25 0/8	24 7/8	18 2/8	9	11	Dodge County	MN	Corey Chick	1997	659
191 6/8	27 4/8	28 1/8	16 5/8	9	8	Jefferson County	IL	Kenny L. Ferguson	1998	659
191 6/8	25 4/8	25 6/8	20 3/8	8	8	Woodford County	IL	Gunnar R. Darnall	2001	659
191 6/8	26 7/8	27 4/8	17 2/8	9	10	Yankton County	SD	Brad R. Jones	2002	659
191 6/8	23 4/8	22 2/8	22 3/8	13	11	Buffalo County	WI	Scott Wnuk	2005	659

WHITETAIL DEER (NON-TYPICAL ANTLERS)

Minimum Score 155 — Continued

SCORE	LENGTH OF R MAIN BEAM L	INSIDE SPREAD	NUMBER OF R POINTS L	AREA	STATE/PROVINCE	HUNTER'S NAME	DATE	RANK
191 6/8	25 1/8 27 2/8	16 6/8	10 11	Taylor County	WI	Cory Halida	2009	659
191 6/8	23 0/8 24 1/8	20 5/8	10 8	Brown County	OH	James Schulz	2009	659
191 5/8	27 1/8 25 7/8	18 2/8	8 8	Riley County	KS	Larry Larson	1994	668
191 5/8	28 6/8 28 3/8	19 2/8	7 6	Greenwood County	KS	Bill D. Holcomb	1999	668
*191 5/8	25 6/8 24 3/8	21 0/8	7 9	Saline County	KS	Jason Buschbom	2009	668
191 4/8	23 3/8 25 1/8	18 3/8	10 7	Tippecanoe County	IN	Jim Foster	1993	671
191 4/8	24 4/8 25 1/8	20 5/8	8 8	Otero County	CO	Levi C. Hansen	2000	671
*191 4/8	26 5/8 26 6/8	23 5/8	10 10	Reno County	KS	Terry L. Yoder	2004	671
*191 4/8	27 6/8 27 1/8	23 1/8	9 8	Harvey County	KS	Tyson L. Koehn	2007	671
191 3/8	22 1/8 22 5/8	20 1/8	9 9	St. Joseph County	IN	Daniel T. Karaszewski	1979	675
191 3/8	26 3/8 25 2/8	17 4/8	9 8	Ozaukee County	WI	Brad Kernats	1998	675
191 3/8	27 4/8 27 7/8	20 2/8	10 8	Lawrence County	IL	Paul Devin, Jr.	1999	675
191 3/8	22 6/8 23 4/8	18 2/8	7 6	Calhoun County	IL	Eric Friedel	2002	675
191 3/8	25 5/8 26 3/8	17 0/8	6 9	Jackson County	OH	Frank Banks	2007	675
*191 3/8	23 7/8 25 5/8	19 0/8	8 10	Marion County	IA	Dwight Kelderman	2009	675
191 2/8	24 6/8 24 2/8	17 3/8	11 10	Boone County	IA	Paul Whitmore	1980	681
191 2/8	25 7/8 25 0/8	22 3/8	8 9	Westchester County	NY	Nick Rigano	1987	681
191 2/8	27 2/8 27 1/8	18 5/8	7 9	Pike County	IL	Timothy M. Fulmer	1991	681
191 2/8	25 0/8 25 5/8	20 6/8	8 7	Pottawattamie County	IA	Buddy Simons	1997	681
*191 2/8	24 3/8 26 0/8	18 2/8	8 6	Wyoming County	WV	Christopher Clark	2003	681
*191 2/8	28 1/8 26 5/8	17 6/8	8 8	Adams County	IL	Bradley Caro	2006	681
191 2/8	25 0/8 26 2/8	20 2/8	8 9	La Salle County	IL	Robert Myers	2007	681
*191 2/8	27 1/8 28 5/8	21 7/8	9 9	Washington County	IL	Scott Juenger	2009	681
*191 2/8	22 6/8 23 0/8	21 2/8	10 9	Pierce County	WI	Adam Webster	2010	681
191 1/8	26 2/8 26 2/8	21 0/8	7 6	Crawford County	OH	Michael B. Hoffman	1988	690
191 1/8	21 5/8 21 5/8	15 2/8	10 11	St. Louis County	MO	Gene Werges	1996	690
191 0/8	23 5/8 24 1/8	20 6/8	13 11	Pope County	MN	Ron Johnson	1985	692
191 0/8	25 5/8 26 1/8	21 2/8	6 9	Greenwood County	KS	Don Copley	1992	692
191 0/8	25 7/8 26 7/8	20 0/8	9 8	Fayette County	OH	Scott A. Boyer	2000	692
191 0/8	20 7/8 20 6/8	16 2/8	10 8	Osage County	KS	Carl Metter	2005	692
*191 0/8	26 1/8 26 2/8	17 5/8	6 11	Floyd County	IA	Mike Zelenak	2006	692
191 0/8	24 2/8 23 5/8	20 0/8	7 14	Moultrie County	IL	Joe Matheson	2007	692
190 7/8	25 0/8 18 4/8	15 1/8	11 13	Douglas County	KS	Leon J. Bidinger	1983	698
190 7/8	25 4/8 25 0/8	20 6/8	8 7	Nemaha County	KS	Larry Burdiek	1995	698
190 7/8	27 1/8 27 4/8	18 5/8	10 6	Davis County	IA	Nathan Byrn	2004	698
190 7/8	26 3/8 26 3/8	19 3/8	9 7	Rice County	MN	Joe DeGrood	2009	698
190 6/8	24 6/8 25 7/8	19 4/8	12 11	Lake County	IL	Donald Linnean	1992	702
190 6/8	23 3/8 23 1/8	18 4/8	11 10	Waukesha County	WI	Frank J. Murphy	1998	702
190 6/8	26 3/8 25 5/8	15 7/8	12 7	Anne Arundel County	MD	Paul S. Macey, Jr.	2000	702
190 6/8	24 6/8 24 4/8	20 4/8	7 9	Jefferson County	IL	Greg McCoy	2001	702
190 6/8	25 0/8 25 1/8	15 6/8	11 8	Page County	IA	Brian Barkey	2002	702
190 6/8	25 5/8 24 7/8	17 0/8	8 10	Bond County	IL	Jimmy Revisky	2002	702
190 6/8	24 1/8 23 6/8	19 4/8	8 9	Muskingum County	OH	Clint N. Morrow, Jr.	2003	702
*190 6/8	25 6/8 26 1/8	25 4/8	10 7	Grundy County	MO	Justin Moore	2007	702
*190 6/8	24 6/8 24 3/8	20 7/8	8 8	Schuyler County	IL	John C. Miner	2007	702
*190 6/8	24 0/8 23 0/8	15 1/8	9 8	Highland County	OH	Gregory Malpass	2009	702
190 6/8	24 4/8 25 0/8	15 2/8	9 7	Boone County	KY	Tyler DeWalt	2010	702
190 5/8	23 5/8 22 3/8	21 1/8	13 11	Lee County	IA	Tim D gnan	1981	713
190 5/8	21 2/8 21 1/8	14 2/8	11 11	Johnston County	OK	Kevin Lovett	1993	713
190 5/8	26 2/8 27 3/8	21 3/8	9 7	Doniphan County	KS	Dave Harrison	2002	713
190 5/8	28 0/8 27 1/8	22 1/8	7 6	Des Moines County	IA	Dave Hackett	2002	713
190 5/8	25 1/8 25 7/8	18 7/8	9 12	Dallas County	IA	John Esdohr	2005	713
190 5/8	19 2/8 22 7/8	22 6/8	9 8	Butler County	KS	Jim Vaught	2005	713
190 5/8	24 7/8 24 6/8	15 7/8	9 10	Rogers County	OK	Jeremy Spencer	2009	713
190 4/8	29 2/8 28 0/8	18 6/8	8 8	Licking County	OH	John McGee	1982	720
190 4/8	22 4/8 25 3/8	16 3/8	11 7	Lake County	IL	Kirk J. Preti	1989	720
190 4/8	25 4/8 24 7/8	22 3/8	7 6	Douglas County	MN	Rodney McClellan	1992	720
190 4/8	25 5/8 25 6/8	20 2/8	9 9	Dane County	WI	Dean Goecks	1995	720
190 4/8	25 3/8 25 1/8	23 2/8	9 9	Allegheny County	PA	Pat Capatolla	2001	720
190 4/8	20 1/8 21 3/8	22 0/8	11 13	Warren County	IA	Kelly Grandstaff	2003	720
*190 4/8	26 4/8 27 6/8	18 5/8	7 7	Jasper County	IL	John Zumbahlen	2006	720
190 4/8	21 4/8 23 1/8	19 1/8	8 7	Richland County	WI	Gerard P. Braun	2006	720
190 3/8	25 4/8 24 1/8	16 5/8	9 9	Saginaw County	MI	Robert T. Morey	1975	728
190 3/8	24 6/8 24 5/8	18 6/8	7 8	Howard County	IN	Michael T. Downing	1999	728
190 3/8	25 5/8 26 2/8	19 0/8	11 11	Lac La Biche	ALB	Todd Thompson	2002	728
190 3/8	24 5/8 24 5/8	17 3/8	12 9	Mercer County	MO	Larry L. Darnell	2004	728
*190 3/8	23 7/8 24 0/8	18 6/8	10 12	Union County	IA	Ryan Osgood	2009	728
190 3/8	26 0/8 26 3/8	18 0/8	8 9	Kosciusko County	IN	Robert H. Eccles	2009	728
190 2/8	20 0/8 23 4/8	19 7/8	8 9	Isanti County	MN	Johnny J. Williams	1982	734
190 2/8	27 5/8 29 2/8	20 2/8	12 8	Montgomery County	PA	David S. Krempasky	1985	734
190 2/8	23 5/8 24 1/8	17 1/8	8 8	Butler County	KS	Mike Schweigert	1998	734
190 2/8	26 3/8 26 1/8	19 2/8	8 8	Woodbury County	IA	Lewis Byers	1998	734
190 2/8	26 2/8 26 5/8	19 3/8	6 6	Appanoose County	IA	Jim Lindsey	2000	734
190 2/8	24 2/8 23 7/8	19 0/8	8 9	Buffalo County	WI	Todd Nelson	2002	734
190 2/8	25 7/8 26 5/8	18 5/8	10 10	Marinette County	WI	Ed Flemel	2006	734
190 2/8	27 0/8 26 6/8	16 6/8	8 7	Saline County	KS	Clint Spitler	2006	734
*190 2/8	24 4/8 24 5/8	19 0/8	10 8	Lucas County	IA	Rich Watson	2008	734
*190 2/8	25 3/8 24 6/8	15 6/8	12 8	Webster County	IA	Jeff Sweeney	2009	734
190 1/8	28 4/8 25 6/8	21 3/8	8 7	Cook County	IL	Rusy Mitcheff III	1995	744
190 1/8	25 4/8 26 1/8	21 0/8	9 6	Page County	IA	Dave Messner	2001	744
190 1/8	25 0/8 26 5/8	21 4/8	8 8	Will County	IL	Blair Konczal	2002	744
*190 1/8	24 7/8 24 5/8	18 5/8	5 9	Washington County	IN	Jason A. Coffman	2009	744
190 0/8	24 3/8 24 6/8	18 0/8	8 8	Douglas County	KS	Dan Norris	1977	748
190 0/8	24 4/8 25 2/8	19 1/8	7 8	McHenry County	IL	Edward Schultz	1984	748
190 0/8	27 0/8 25 7/8	18 6/8	9 6	Tippecanoe County	IN	Mitchell R. Tuinstra	1994	748
190 0/8	26 1/8 26 2/8	26 4/8	7 7	Pottawatomie County	KS	Dale R. Larson	1996	748
190 0/8	21 7/8 21 3/8	17 4/8	10 9	Glendon	ALB	Phil Kozak	2001	748
190 0/8	26 1/8 25 3/8	20 2/8	9 7	Van Buren County	IA	Brian Grove	2004	748
190 0/8	23 2/8 22 5/8	18 6/8	7 8	Buffalo County	WI	Cory Mielke	2006	748
189 7/8	26 1/8 26 3/8	24 3/8	7 7	Logan County	OH	Larry Pooler	1989	755
189 7/8	26 1/8 25 0/8	18 2/8	10 11	Benton County	MO	Steve Nichols	1996	755
189 7/8	23 0/8 23 1/8	18 2/8	7 7	Effingham County	IL	Jeff Bailey	1999	755
189 7/8	27 0/8 25 4/8	23 2/8	8 7	Piatt County	IL	Mike Bily	1999	755
189 7/8	25 2/8 25 5/8	20 3/8	11 8	Morrison County	MN	William B. Crooker	2002	755
*189 7/8	22 7/8 22 4/8	19 4/8	9 9	Callaway County	MO	Devon Daniels	2004	755

643

WHITETAIL DEER (NON-TYPICAL ANTLERS)

Minimum Score 155   Continued

SCORE	LENGTH OF R MAIN BEAM L	INSIDE SPREAD	NUMBER OF R POINTS L	AREA	STATE/PROVINCE	HUNTER'S NAME	DATE	RANK
*189 7/8	29 2/8 27 3/8	17 0/8	11 9	Randolph County	IL	Jay Roudabush	2007	755
189 6/8	24 4/8 23 3/8	16 3/8	9 7	Chisago County	MN	Reinhold L. Lind	1956	762
189 6/8	25 4/8 25 3/8	18 3/8	10 9	Jefferson County	OH	Ed Gates	1993	762
189 6/8	24 6/8 25 0/8	19 7/8	8 7	Schuyler County	IL	Jason A. Floyd	2000	762
189 5/8	21 1/8 22 4/8	15 5/8	14 10	Stearns County	MN	Nathan Batzel	1991	765
*189 5/8	24 3/8 26 5/8	23 2/8	9 7	Ellsworth County	KS	Ronald J. Meier	1994	765
189 5/8	25 4/8 17 6/8	18 1/8	9 6	Monroe County	IA	Tom O'Brien	1994	765
*189 5/8	24 0/8 22 7/8	16 0/8	8 11	Canadian County	OK	Zach Birdsong	2004	765
189 5/8	23 5/8 23 4/8	15 7/8	8 10	Goodhue County	MN	Kathy Jilk	2006	765
189 4/8	23 7/8 23 6/8	17 2/8	7 9	Cass County	IL	Ronald L. McClure	1994	770
189 4/8	27 5/8 27 5/8	20 0/8	6 11	Iron County	WI	Bryan "Lynn" Bellows	1994	770
189 4/8	23 4/8 24 2/8	19 5/8	10 9	Houston County	MN	Chad Burroughs	1996	770
189 4/8	25 0/8 24 5/8	19 3/8	10 8	Goodhue County	MN	Kyle M. Halvorson	2002	770
*189 4/8	24 4/8 22 4/8	21 6/8	6 9	Pike County	IL	Paul Roeber	2006	770
189 4/8	24 3/8 24 5/8	15 4/8	9 10	Schuyler County	IL	Thomas E. Pinyan, Jr.	2006	770
189 3/8	24 0/8 23 7/8	17 2/8	9 8	Buffalo County	WI	Stuart Hagen	2002	776
189 3/8	27 2/8 28 0/8	22 1/8	8 9	Lincoln County	SD	Gaylon Lems	2007	776
*189 3/8	27 3/8 26 3/8	20 7/8	6 7	Prince Edward County	ONT	Jamie Branscombe	2008	776
189 2/8	21 4/8 23 1/8	21 3/8	10 8	Clayton County	IA	Jim Monat	1981	779
189 2/8	23 1/8 23 0/8	20 0/8	6 7	Buffalo County	WI	Roger Comero	1987	779
189 2/8	26 0/8 26 4/8	21 6/8	9 10	Franklin County	KS	John E. Taylor	2003	779
189 2/8	28 0/8 27 1/8	19 6/8	5 7	Winneshiek County	IA	Gerald Folstad	2004	779
*189 2/8	25 3/8 23 0/8	21 2/8	9 8	Orleans County	NY	Michael Biernacki	2009	779
189 1/8	21 5/8 24 2/8	17 3/8	13 7	Graham County	KS	Don Berry	1970	784
189 1/8	23 5/8 25 0/8	19 4/8	8 6	McDowell County	WV	Lonnie Wolfe	1991	784
189 1/8	24 4/8 22 1/8	16 6/8	11 8	Hodgeman County	KS	Gary Tenbrink	1997	784
189 1/8	24 7/8 24 3/8	18 6/8	7 10	Harrison County	IA	Lane Ostendorf	1997	784
189 1/8	25 0/8 23 5/8	14 4/8	7 10	Knox County	MO	Terry Morrow	1999	784
*189 1/8	26 4/8 25 3/8	19 1/8	8 10	Grant County	IN	John R. Neargardner	2005	784
189 1/8	24 1/8 24 6/8	18 7/8	11 10	Livingston County	NY	Kenneth Arner	2005	784
*189 1/8	25 6/8 25 0/8	17 2/8	8 12	Cass County	MI	Todd A. Seiler	2009	784
189 1/8	24 3/8 25 0/8	18 4/8	7 9	Winnebago County	WI	Stuart C. Miller	2009	784
189 0/8	22 4/8 21 7/8	22 4/8	10 9	Scott County	MN	Chris Rivers	1987	793
189 0/8	25 3/8 25 3/8	20 0/8	7 8	Grant County	WI	Chad Tracy	1995	793
189 0/8	25 1/8 24 7/8	17 7/8	8 9	Knox County	OH	Chad Christopher	1998	793
*189 0/8	25 3/8 24 6/8	17 4/8	9 8	Waushara County	WI	Tony O'Kon	1999	793
189 0/8	27 7/8 28 2/8	22 0/8	8 8	Ogle County	IL	Russell Young	2000	793
189 0/8	24 1/8 26 4/8	23 2/8	6 7	Cowley County	KS	Joe Carder	2003	793
*189 0/8	24 6/8 23 4/8	16 1/8	11 11	Washington County	NE	Darold "Toby" Fitz	2006	793
189 0/8	24 0/8 25 6/8	19 1/8	13 7	Edgar County	IL	Tony Dawson	2007	793
189 0/8	25 0/8 24 5/8	17 2/8	9 6	Dunn County	WI	Neil Bygd	2010	793
188 7/8	27 4/8 28 1/8	18 3/8	11 9	Marinette County	WI	James Spielvogel	1981	802
188 7/8	26 5/8 27 1/8	17 6/8	8 8	Preble County	OH	Jim Lipps	1994	802
188 7/8	23 7/8 23 7/8	21 7/8	8 6	Harper County	KS	Kevin Albright	1994	802
188 7/8	27 6/8 27 2/8	19 5/8	9 11	Mercer County	IL	Dana Pace, Jr.	1997	802
188 7/8	24 5/8 25 1/8	19 7/8	8 9	Clayton County	IA	Jeff Loeffelholz	1999	802
188 7/8	23 6/8 23 0/8	17 4/8	6 7	Bucks County	PA	Francis Cole	2000	802
*188 7/8	25 1/8 25 6/8	16 6/8	8 7	Hamilton County	OH	Don Clements	2004	802
188 7/8	27 2/8 25 1/8	22 1/8	5 7	Jefferson County	WI	Chad Montalbano	2006	802
*188 7/8	29 6/8 28 7/8	18 5/8	8 7	Champaign County	IL	Martin R. Cloud	2006	802
188 7/8	25 4/8 24 4/8	19 0/8	8 10	Macon County	MO	Matt Meisner	2007	802
*188 7/8	24 6/8 25 4/8	18 1/8	7 9	Knox County	IL	Hall H. Ratcliffe III	2007	802
188 6/8	23 5/8 22 6/8	19 1/8	8 10	Adair County	MO	David C. Reid	1991	813
188 6/8	24 6/8 25 0/8	24 0/8	8 5	Will County	IL	Ray Smith	2003	813
*188 6/8	23 2/8 24 3/8	19 2/8	9 8	Effingham County	IL	Aaron McManaway	2005	813
188 6/8	24 6/8 23 6/8	19 7/8	7 9	Conmee	ONT	Dan Fadyshen	2009	813
188 5/8	27 3/8 27 0/8	18 6/8	7 5	Ross County	OH	Dan Seymour	1987	817
188 5/8	23 5/8 22 7/8	20 6/8	8 7	Portage County	OH	William Collins, Jr.	2004	817
*188 5/8	25 2/8 27 6/8	21 3/8	9 5	Lafayette County	WI	William C. Broge	2004	817
*188 5/8	24 7/8 25 4/8	17 4/8	8 5	Fulton County	IL	Todd Steven Earnhardt	2005	817
188 4/8	28 0/8 27 5/8	21 0/8	8 8	Edgar County	IL	Bruce Huey Lankster	1992	821
188 4/8	27 1/8 25 2/8	19 0/8	10 7	Pike County	IL	Scott W. Riley	1998	821
188 3/8	24 0/8 24 4/8	18 4/8	9 7	Benton County	IA	Lyle Miller	1977	823
188 3/8	26 0/8 26 7/8	19 0/8	6 9	Rock County	WI	Steven J. Shull	1988	823
188 3/8	25 3/8 27 3/8	20 3/8	10 7	Washington County	KS	William B. Wilgers	1994	823
188 3/8	25 2/8 24 1/8	16 4/8	12 8	Payne County	OK	Robert L. Lochmiller	1995	823
188 3/8	25 2/8 26 3/8	17 1/8	7 9	New Haven County	CT	Christopher Krista	1998	823
188 3/8	20 1/8 21 1/8	22 6/8	10 9	Knox County	OH	Bradley D. Schaaf	2000	823
188 3/8	25 7/8 26 7/8	19 7/8	6 10	Sherburne County	MN	Matt Bentzin	2002	823
*188 3/8	26 3/8 28 4/8	24 7/8	8 10	Lucas County	IA	Jason Nicolino	2007	823
188 3/8	26 1/8 25 1/8	19 3/8	7 7	Lee County	IL	Matthew C. Rehor	2008	823
188 3/8	27 1/8 26 3/8	17 0/8	11 7	Jessamine County	KY	Andrew Stachon	2010	823
188 2/8	25 4/8 28 0/8	19 3/8	8 9	Story County	IA	Matt Okland	2001	833
188 2/8	23 1/8 24 0/8	20 6/8	8 6	Fayette County	IL	Jeff Hoffman	2003	833
188 2/8	23 4/8 24 0/8	19 7/8	9 7	Montgomery County	VA	Jerry W. Chrisley, Sr.	2005	833
188 2/8	27 2/8 25 0/8	19 4/8	6 8	Warren County	IA	Steve Sieloff	2005	833
188 1/8	26 5/8 26 0/8	19 4/8	7 10	Barnes County	ND	William Cruff	1961	837
188 1/8	26 3/8 26 0/8	19 5/8	10 7	Dane County	WI	Bill Needham	1983	837
188 1/8	23 1/8 23 0/8	23 4/8	8 7	La Salle County	IL	James E. Giese	2002	837
*188 1/8	28 0/8 28 0/8	19 3/8	10 4	Fulton County	IL	Ferenc Davidovics	2004	837
188 1/8	26 2/8 27 3/8	14 0/8	10 13	Wilson County	KS	Sean Wallace	2007	837
188 1/8	24 0/8 23 7/8	19 2/8	9 9	Clarion County	PA	Eric J. Dobrowski	2007	837
188 0/8	23 2/8 22 3/8	17 3/8	8 8	La Salle County	IL	Gary Tabor	1983	843
188 0/8	24 5/8 25 5/8	16 2/8	8 11	Buffalo County	WI	Russell G. Goldsmith	1991	843
188 0/8	26 7/8 26 4/8	18 4/8	12 7	Licking County	OH	Eric Ashcraft	2000	843
188 0/8	26 6/8 26 7/8	17 3/8	6 8	Polk County	IA	Michael E. Hall	2001	843
188 0/8	23 3/8 24 2/8	18 0/8	10 10	Fairfield County	OH	Allen Anderson	2001	843
*188 0/8	25 7/8 25 5/8	19 7/8	7 13	Winnebago County	IA	Douglas L. Aasland	2003	843
188 0/8	25 2/8 23 6/8	16 3/8	10 10	Ford County	IL	Jeremiah Brandon	2004	843
188 0/8	24 0/8 24 0/8	15 4/8	9 8	Monroe County	IA	Dean G. Elbe	2004	843
*188 0/8	25 6/8 25 4/8	19 1/8	7 7	Montmorency County	MI	Larry Chastain	2006	843
188 0/8	23 6/8 23 2/8	19 3/8	7 9	Ramsey County	MN	Michael J. Schuett	2007	843
188 0/8	27 2/8 26 1/8	20 4/8	8 6	Cole County	MO	Marvin Phillips	2008	843
187 7/8	24 4/8 24 7/8	20 3/8	8 8	Shiawassee County	MI	Joseph S. Lunkas	1978	854
187 7/8	25 3/8 24 6/8	19 1/8	7 9	Sedgwick County	KS	Phil Mohr	1992	854

WHITETAIL DEER (NON-TYPICAL ANTLERS)

Minimum Score 155 — Continued

SCORE	LENGTH OF R MAIN BEAM L	INSIDE SPREAD	NUMBER OF R POINTS L	AREA	STATE/PROVINCE	HUNTER'S NAME	DATE	RANK
187 7/8	28 2/8 27 4/8	22 0/8	8 9	Chisago County	MN	Chris Johnson	1998	854
*187 7/8	25 3/8 26 2/8	18 1/8	9 7	Walworth County	WI	Brad Wilson	2005	854
187 7/8	21 6/8 22 0/8	19 5/8	10 10	Riley County	KS	Robert Bletscher	2006	854
187 7/8	29 5/8 27 6/8	20 6/8	8 7	Marion County	IA	James Wallace	2009	854
187 6/8	22 7/8 25 0/8	19 1/8	7 7	Hitchcock County	NE	Tom Chance	1986	860
187 6/8	23 1/8 24 0/8	16 7/8	10 7	Bent County	CO	Chris Malden	1991	860
187 6/8	27 0/8 27 1/8	25 0/8	6 7	Peoria County	IL	Christopher J. Karl	1997	860
187 6/8	25 6/8 25 5/8	18 5/8	7 8	Gage County	NE	Terry Charf	1997	860
187 6/8	26 0/8 27 0/8	21 3/8	8 5	Peoria County	IL	Stan Hayes	2000	860
187 6/8	24 0/8 25 4/8	22 6/8	8 6	Clayton County	IA	Virgil High	2002	860
187 6/8	21 0/8 20 6/8	15 1/8	10 8	Johnson County	KS	Ron Shanks	2003	860
*187 6/8	22 5/8 22 2/8	15 5/8	10 9	Atoka County	OK	Michael Rector	2004	860
187 6/8	30 1/8 29 0/8	17 5/8	7 10	Pepin County	WI	Thomas J. Lee	2005	860
*187 6/8	26 6/8 26 3/8	19 6/8	10 8	Hocking County	OH	Robert Westhoven	2006	860
187 6/8	23 4/8 24 3/8	17 2/8	10 7	Monroe County	IA	Richard Miller	2007	860
*187 6/8	25 5/8 26 2/8	19 2/8	10 11	Warren County	OH	Chad Grote	2008	860
*187 6/8	25 5/8 25 0/8	20 0/8	9 10	Berrien County	MI	Mark Kelly	2009	860
187 5/8	27 6/8 25 2/8	18 0/8	8 6	Monroe County	IA	Cecil Dicks	1961	873
187 5/8	26 0/8 26 0/8	17 4/8	11 9	Washburn County	WI	Russell Worman	1988	873
187 5/8	24 6/8 24 5/8	15 7/8	9 7	Barrhead	ALB	J. J. Handel	1993	873
187 5/8	25 6/8 27 1/8	17 7/8	6 10	Butler County	OH	Ken Russell	1998	873
187 5/8	26 2/8 27 2/8	21 7/8	7 8	Logan County	WV	Scotty Workman	2002	873
187 5/8	24 7/8 23 6/8	18 2/8	7 8	Clark County	IL	Steven Parr	2005	873
*187 5/8	27 7/8 27 3/8	17 2/8	8 8	Rock County	WI	Keith W. Hackett	2007	873
187 5/8	25 3/8 26 1/8	20 3/8	10 12	Portage County	WI	John Kurszewski	2008	873
*187 5/8	24 5/8 25 1/8	17 6/8	10 9	Boone County	KY	Chris White	2009	873
187 4/8	26 2/8 26 0/8	18 0/8	8 7	Juneau County	WI	George "Butch" Sterbenz	1947	882
187 4/8	25 6/8 26 4/8	17 7/8	10 6	Monroe County	IL	Travis Gilliam	1998	882
187 4/8	23 5/8 24 1/8	16 5/8	8 10	Pike County	IL	Scott Kelley	2001	882
187 4/8	24 3/8 24 7/8	15 7/8	8 7	Jefferson County	MO	Dan Crawford	2002	882
*187 4/8	21 7/8 23 2/8	22 3/8	9 8	Wilson County	KS	Curtis Cleaveland	2006	882
187 4/8	24 3/8 26 6/8	19 4/8	9 9	Republic County	KS	P. C. "Bo" Aughtry III	2007	882
187 4/8	25 2/8 27 2/8	17 7/8	14 11	Linn County	KS	John W. Ferguson, Jr.	2008	882
*187 4/8	25 3/8 23 4/8	15 0/8	10 8	De Kalb County	GA	Rusty Osborne	2008	882
187 4/8	24 5/8 24 5/8	19 7/8	7 10	Marquette County	WI	Joseph P. Steuck	2010	882
187 3/8	23 2/8 23 1/8	17 1/8	11 10	Vernon County	WI	Darrell A. Bendel	1986	891
187 3/8	26 3/8 25 5/8	20 4/8	6 6	Vermilion County	IL	Ronald D. Nunn	1996	891
187 3/8	30 0/8 23 1/8	19 2/8	9 8	Adams County	OH	Pete Detro	1997	891
187 3/8	25 4/8 26 5/8	15 3/8	7 7	Stoddard County	MO	Jeffrey Hale	2005	891
187 3/8	25 6/8 25 6/8	24 0/8	7 8	Washington County	MS	Angus Catchot	2007	891
187 2/8	25 3/8 23 6/8	21 0/8	7 9	Morrill County	NE	Glenn Schmidt	1975	896
187 2/8	27 1/8 26 1/8	16 6/8	7 7	Waupaca County	WI	Timothy J. Dercks	1991	896
187 2/8	26 4/8 29 2/8	20 6/8	7 6	Monroe County	MI	John L. Benedict	2003	896
187 2/8	26 0/8 24 2/8	19 5/8	9 10	Shelby County	IA	John Petsche	2006	896
187 2/8	24 6/8 25 1/8	16 4/8	9 9	Allamakee County	IA	Darrel Moose	2007	896
*187 2/8	21 5/8 23 1/8	18 4/8	13 11	Auglaize County	OH	Jason Vanderhorst	2009	896
187 1/8	22 7/8 23 3/8	14 2/8	9 9	Palo Pinto County	TX	Scott Layne	1994	902
187 1/8	25 2/8 24 6/8	16 1/8	9 7	Clark County	IL	Myron S. Johnson	1995	902
187 1/8	29 3/8 28 7/8	22 5/8	8 7	Lycoming County	PA	Steven Craig	2002	902
187 1/8	24 4/8 25 6/8	20 3/8	8 10	Carter County	OK	Mike Hope	2007	902
187 1/8	23 0/8 23 7/8	22 3/8	12 7	Monroe County	IA	Bill Kirkpatrick	2007	902
187 0/8	27 5/8 28 5/8	21 2/8	8 10	Clayton County	IA	Rick Felder	1994	907
187 0/8	24 4/8 24 1/8	17 7/8	9 9	Buffalo County	WI	Travis L. Althoff	1995	907
187 0/8	26 0/8 25 7/8	22 0/8	8 7	Sangamon County	IL	Kurt R. Hulse	2002	907
*187 0/8	26 4/8 26 0/8	22 6/8	7 10	Barron County	WI	David R. Kuffel	2005	907
187 0/8	28 0/8 27 5/8	20 3/8	8 7	Winnebago County	IL	David T. Marske	2007	907
186 7/8	26 6/8 25 4/8	20 2/8	9 9	Du Page County	IL	James A. Wetmore	1997	912
186 7/8	26 5/8 26 2/8	19 1/8	7 7	Clinton County	IL	Charles Wes Cummins	2001	912
186 7/8	26 6/8 25 0/8	19 7/8	5 9	Clarke County	IA	Mike Ogbourne	2002	912
*186 7/8	24 6/8 25 3/8	20 2/8	10 6	Forsyth County	GA	Brian R. Stephens	2007	912
186 7/8	28 5/8 28 7/8	21 5/8	8 8	Monroe County	WI	Dave Scharping	2007	912
186 7/8	25 7/8 24 2/8	19 6/8	9 3	Kingman County	KS	Jeremy Adams	2008	912
*186 7/8	22 3/8 23 2/8	19 1/8	8 6	Arkansas County	AR	Dean Davis	2009	912
186 6/8	24 2/8 25 1/8	19 3/8	9 10	Traverse County	MN	Roland L. Hausmann	1964	919
186 6/8	24 6/8 23 6/8	18 3/8	10 10	Mackinac County	MI	Steve Gorsuch	1989	919
186 6/8	25 3/8 25 5/8	17 6/8	8 6	Coles County	IL	Philip H. Blaase	1994	919
186 6/8	25 5/8 25 3/8	21 1/8	8 8	Harrow	ONT	Rodney Shepley	2000	919
186 6/8	23 4/8 24 3/8	17 2/8	7 7	McDonough County	IL	Jack Laverdiere	2003	919
186 6/8	23 2/8 24 4/8	20 7/8	7 6	Shelby County	KY	Kevin Raleigh	2007	919
*186 6/8	23 7/8 23 7/8	17 1/8	9 7	Harper County	KS	Buddy Bass	2009	919
186 5/8	25 3/8 25 0/8	20 7/8	7 9	Scotland County	MO	Charles Lee Smith	1984	926
186 5/8	25 7/8 24 5/8	18 2/8	6 6	Stafford County	KS	Robert G. Williams	1997	926
186 5/8	26 4/8 25 4/8	21 3/8	9 8	Fulton County	IL	Howard Van Houten	1998	926
186 5/8	26 3/8 27 2/8	21 5/8	9 9	Wayne County	IN	Donald Sean Sylvester	1998	926
186 5/8	25 5/8 25 4/8	17 4/8	5 9	Golden Valley County	ND	Darin Opel	2001	926
186 5/8	24 4/8 24 3/8	16 6/8	9 10	Comanche County	OK	Brian Roberts	2004	926
*186 5/8	19 7/8 21 0/8	15 4/8	14 13	Montague County	TX	Andre C. Bonvillian	2005	926
*186 5/8	27 2/8 27 3/8	20 0/8	6 9	Chickasaw County	IA	Casey Cajthaml	2007	926
186 5/8	25 4/8 26 2/8	14 3/8	7 10	Washington County	MN	Douglas A. Schultze	2008	926
186 4/8	22 3/8 24 6/8	14 7/8	10 7	Montgomery County	IL	Brett Goldsmith	2003	935
186 4/8	23 7/8 23 5/8	17 1/8	9 9	Brown County	IL	Kevin E. Wort	2005	935
*186 4/8	21 7/8 24 4/8	15 6/8	7 5	Macon County	MO	Mickey "Michael" Greer	2006	935
186 3/8	22 0/8 23 4/8	20 0/8	9 8	Perry County	IL	Scott Kreger	1996	938
186 3/8	27 2/8 25 6/8	18 2/8	10 10	Kiowa County	KS	George Martinez	1996	938
186 3/8	27 6/8 27 6/8	21 7/8	6 7	La Salle County	IL	Kevin Gibson	1997	938
186 3/8	23 7/8 24 6/8	17 0/8	10 8	Daviess County	MO	Michael Earl Cross	1998	938
186 3/8	21 1/8 21 3/8	15 4/8	11 9	Wells County	ND	Dustin Willey	2003	938
186 3/8	24 5/8 25 0/8	19 0/8	8 7	Vigo County	IN	Jason Pearman	2005	938
186 3/8	26 0/8 26 6/8	18 0/8	6 10	Geary County	KS	William "Bill" Collins	2009	938
186 2/8	23 1/8 22 5/8	18 6/8	9 9	Otter Tail County	MN	D. F. Vraspir	1959	945
186 2/8	23 1/8 23 2/8	14 6/8	8 8	Coles County	IL	Bob Baker	2002	945
*186 2/8	27 6/8 25 4/8	21 1/8	8 7	Iowa County	WI	Robert Yarnell	2003	945
*186 2/8	28 5/8 27 1/8	19 6/8	13 9	Fulton County	IL	Ron Dixon	2004	945
186 2/8	25 3/8 25 3/8	19 0/8	7 7	Buffalo County	WI	Pat Pelikan	2006	945
*186 2/8	23 7/8 25 1/8	20 4/8	7 8	Coshocton County	OH	Doug Akins	2006	945

645

WHITETAIL DEER (NON-TYPICAL ANTLERS)

Minimum Score 155   Continued

SCORE	LENGTH OF R MAIN BEAM L	INSIDE SPREAD	NUMBER OF R POINTS L	AREA	STATE/ PROVINCE	HUNTER'S NAME	DATE	RANK
186 2/8	23 4/8 23 0/8	18 2/8	15 12	Jefferson County	NE	Vernon D. Hampton	2007	945
*186 2/8	26 2/8 27 1/8	19 3/8	7 6	Jefferson County	MO	Dennis Kobermann	2007	945
186 2/8	25 4/8 25 5/8	20 0/8	7 9	St. Brieux	SAS	Jeff Thorlakson	2009	945
186 2/8	28 2/8 28 6/8	20 7/8	7 7	Coshocton County	OH	Bob Lux	2009	945
186 2/8	26 2/8 25 4/8	17 5/8	6 8	Polk County	IA	Gary D. Kilcollins, Jr.	2010	945
186 1/8	25 3/8 26 2/8	18 0/8	8 9	Lake County	IL	Alan F. Benson	1990	956
186 1/8	23 0/8 24 4/8	17 7/8	8 9	Lyon County	KS	Edward Bess	1991	956
186 1/8	24 0/8 23 7/8	16 2/8	11 10	Stevens County	WA	John Wantulok	1992	956
186 1/8	25 6/8 25 6/8	18 7/8	7 10	St. Joseph County	IN	Mike Ritter, Jr.	1992	956
186 1/8	26 7/8 26 5/8	19 0/8	7 9	Cowley County	KS	Justin Crawford	2000	956
*186 1/8	25 6/8 24 6/8	18 7/8	12 10	Warren County	KY	Stephen M. Young	2000	956
186 1/8	23 1/8 22 4/8	18 2/8	7 8	Hand County	SD	Dennis D. Lagge	2001	956
186 1/8	26 5/8 27 4/8	21 6/8	9 8	Washington County	WI	Steven J. Biksadski	2005	956
*186 1/8	24 0/8 22 0/8	16 4/8	10 8	Dodge County	WI	Jamie Nickerson	2007	956
186 1/8	26 2/8 26 3/8	17 5/8	8 7	St. Joseph County	MI	Nick J. Perry	2009	956
186 0/8	25 6/8 22 4/8	23 6/8	8 9	Jefferson County	KS	Bob George	1991	966
186 0/8	25 0/8 24 4/8	16 4/8	10 7	Washington County	AR	Gary Powell	1994	966
186 0/8	26 7/8 25 4/8	17 5/8	8 8	Indiana County	PA	Frank R. Lecorchick	1996	966
186 0/8	22 7/8 22 6/8	19 2/8	10 12	Calhoun County	IL	Mark D. Grommet	2001	966
186 0/8	26 4/8 25 5/8	18 4/8	9 11	Bath County	VA	Michael B. Renzi	2002	966
186 0/8	27 4/8 27 4/8	19 4/8	6 5	Wayne County	MI	Kevin H. Olson	2002	966
*186 0/8	23 3/8 22 0/8	19 0/8	6 11	Decatur County	IA	Mike Adrianse	2003	966
186 0/8	26 1/8 28 0/8	21 2/8	6 6	St. Charles County	MO	Paul Gragg	2003	966
186 0/8	21 6/8 21 5/8	16 3/8	12 8	Kent County	MI	Drew Doornbos	2004	966
186 0/8	22 7/8 24 0/8	21 1/8	9 9	Columbia County	WI	Jennifer Baerwolf	2005	966
186 0/8	27 0/8 26 4/8	18 5/8	9 10	Delaware County	IA	Brendon Dempster	2007	966
*186 0/8	22 4/8 23 1/8	23 7/8	9 7	Reno County	KS	Jason Applebe	2008	966
186 0/8	26 5/8 26 5/8	16 6/8	7 7	Pulaski County	KY	Hurley Ray Combs, Jr.	2009	966
185 7/8	24 7/8 22 2/8	18 0/8	6 10	Jones County	GA	Wallace Reeves, Jr.	1973	979
185 7/8	25 6/8 27 6/8	21 2/8	8 11	Cass County	MO	Mike Wheeler	1989	979
185 7/8	26 3/8 28 0/8	18 3/8	8 6	Todd County	KY	Alan Mansfield	1998	979
185 7/8	25 1/8 24 4/8	18 3/8	9 8	Becker County	MN	Anthony Donner	1998	979
185 7/8	26 7/8 26 2/8	18 6/8	6 8	Cook County	IL	Timothy L. Harkness	2000	979
185 7/8	25 4/8 24 3/8	23 2/8	8 6	Crawford County	WI	Aaron J. Richter	2003	979
*185 7/8	24 5/8 23 6/8	19 1/8	7 6	Clark County	IL	Jerry Ramsey	2005	979
*185 7/8	24 5/8 24 5/8	17 0/8	7 6	Alfalfa County	OK	James R. Hillaker II	2005	979
185 6/8	26 1/8 26 0/8	25 0/8	7 6	Christian County	IL	Donald D. Stiner	1990	987
185 6/8	27 1/8 22 4/8	22 6/8	7 9	Charles County	MD	Thomas M. Maddox	1999	987
185 6/8	23 6/8 25 2/8	18 0/8	9 10	Sharp County	AR	Witt Stephens	2001	987
185 6/8	23 0/8 23 7/8	16 4/8	6 7	Cass County	ND	Denny Hansen	2001	987
185 6/8	23 2/8 23 5/8	17 3/8	11 8	Allegheny County	PA	Dale Pinto, Jr.	2006	987
185 6/8	24 5/8 24 1/8	14 0/8	11 12	Ripley County	IN	Jason P. Caudill	2008	987
*185 6/8	27 0/8 24 2/8	17 7/8	9 10	St. Marys County	MD	Brian Long	2010	987
185 5/8	27 0/8 25 3/8	18 6/8	11 12	Anderson County	KS	Wayne Hanna	1991	994
185 5/8	25 2/8 26 6/8	18 4/8	8 8	Henry County	MO	Lance E. Wagoner	1999	994
185 5/8	26 2/8 28 4/8	18 6/8	13 7	Hancock County	IL	Tracy Longenecker	2000	994
185 5/8	26 5/8 26 1/8	22 1/8	11 7	Clark County	IL	Jay Tarble	2004	994
185 4/8	29 2/8 28 0/8	22 1/8	8 8	Pickaway County	OH	Jerry R. Forson	1979	998
185 4/8	22 4/8 23 6/8	18 6/8	7 6	Grant County	WI	Jeff Hochhausen	1994	998
185 4/8	24 7/8 24 6/8	19 0/8	6 8	Grand Forks County	ND	Tom Lunski	1994	998
185 4/8	26 4/8 26 5/8	20 3/8	8 9	Jefferson County	KS	Mark Dennis	1994	998
185 4/8	28 2/8 27 2/8	19 2/8	10 6	Greene County	IA	Dennis Matthews	1994	998
*185 4/8	26 0/8 24 7/8	21 2/8	7 8	Lake County	IN	John G. Blanchard	2007	998
185 3/8	27 6/8 27 4/8	23 5/8	8 8	Allamakee County	IA	LeRoy B. Spiker	1968	1004
185 3/8	27 3/8 26 7/8	20 7/8	6 6	Rice County	MN	Wayne Jahnke	1975	1004
185 3/8	27 2/8 27 3/8	20 4/8	8 10	Lyon County	KS	Jim Black	1991	1004
185 3/8	25 6/8 26 0/8	20 4/8	8 7	Wayne County	IL	Randy Sawyer	1991	1004
185 3/8	26 2/8 26 5/8	21 1/8	7 6	Beaumont	ALB	Glen Pettinger	1997	1004
185 3/8	25 7/8 24 4/8	15 4/8	9 10	Madison County	IA	Dwayne Bechtol	1999	1004
185 3/8	25 3/8 24 3/8	20 0/8	9 12	Stephenson County	IL	Ron Kaderly	2002	1004
185 3/8	27 0/8 26 3/8	16 3/8	8 10	Logan County	IL	Brad Beggs	2005	1004
185 2/8	26 1/8 25 0/8	16 6/8	9 8	Sedgwick County	KS	Alfred Weaver	1965	1012
185 2/8	23 6/8 24 3/8	19 2/8	9 6	Winneshiek County	IA	Steve Herold	1994	1012
185 2/8	25 0/8 25 0/8	17 3/8	8 9	Buffalo County	WI	Gale Zich	1995	1012
185 2/8	25 6/8 25 6/8	20 5/8	9 8	Suffolk County	NY	Paul Davidson	1996	1012
185 2/8	23 0/8 24 0/8	16 4/8	11 9	Fulton County	IL	Robert Bear	2000	1012
185 2/8	24 6/8 26 2/8	18 4/8	8 6	Henderson County	IL	Lee Fields	2002	1012
185 2/8	26 5/8 27 0/8	21 0/8	8 7	Davis County	IA	Greg Sims	2005	1012
185 2/8	24 0/8 23 6/8	19 6/8	11 8	Buffalo County	WI	Jacob Reich	2008	1012
*185 2/8	27 7/8 27 2/8	17 3/8	8 9	Marshall County	KS	Ricky Barrett	2008	1012
185 1/8	27 3/8 26 7/8	18 0/8	9 9	Lewis County	KY	Jeremie Lee Bretz	1992	1021
185 1/8	23 5/8 23 1/8	20 7/8	7 8	Calhoun County	IL	Mike Bucher	1995	1021
185 1/8	22 5/8 22 3/8	18 7/8	8 8	Kent County	MD	W. Ralph Fleegle	2001	1021
185 1/8	26 2/8 26 7/8	20 4/8	9 8	Henderson County	KY	Morris Lee	2002	1021
*185 1/8	25 3/8 26 5/8	18 4/8	8 7	Oconto County	WI	Dawn Janousky	2003	1021
185 1/8	23 1/8 22 2/8	16 4/8	12 11	Jasper County	IN	John M. Babe	2005	1021
185 1/8	24 6/8 24 7/8	21 4/8	7 8	Saline County	NE	Michael S. Theis	2009	1021
*185 1/8	27 0/8 26 1/8	21 2/8	7 9	Lawrence County	IL	Mick Montcalm	2009	1021
*185 1/8	23 6/8 24 2/8	17 0/8	9 10	Monroe County	IA	Bill E. Bridges	2009	1021
185 0/8	25 1/8 25 5/8	17 1/8	9 12	Christian County	KY	John Blakeley	2001	1030
185 0/8	24 5/8 25 0/8	22 1/8	8 7	Marion County	IN	Jason S. Losee	2001	1030
185 0/8	27 0/8 27 3/8	19 4/8	9 9	Clay County	IN	Murray Paul Harbour	2002	1030
185 0/8	27 2/8 27 3/8	18 1/8	9 5	Sarpy County	NE	Brian Dickinson	2003	1030
185 0/8	24 3/8 24 0/8	17 5/8	10 8	Coffey County	KS	Edward L. Cloud	2007	1030
*185 0/8	24 0/8 24 3/8	17 4/8	8 8	Morgan County	OH	Terry B. Lindenmuth	2007	1030
184 7/8	25 0/8 25 4/8	25 2/8	7 9	Monona County	IA	Patrick Salmen	1989	1036
184 7/8	26 2/8 24 4/8	18 6/8	10 7	St. Agathe	MAN	Maurice A. Trudeau	1995	1036
184 7/8	24 0/8 23 4/8	19 5/8	7 7	New Haven County	CT	Alan P. Tracy	1995	1036
184 7/8	26 6/8 26 2/8	19 0/8	6 8	St. Louis County	MO	Scott Van Gennip	1999	1036
184 7/8	25 4/8 26 0/8	18 4/8	8 7	Warren County	IA	Richard Stanton	1999	1036
*184 7/8	26 5/8 24 4/8	23 4/8	7 7	Johnson County	IA	Seth Bartlett	2006	1036
184 7/8	26 4/8 25 2/8	18 1/8	9 7	Jackson County	IA	Eric C. Proshuto	2007	1036
*184 7/8	25 3/8 23 1/8	15 3/8	6 11	Franklin County	KS	Burke L. Sink	2008	1036
184 6/8	30 4/8 28 0/8	22 2/8	8 7	Scioto County	OH	Ryan Darnell	1990	1044
184 6/8	22 6/8 23 6/8	19 0/8	9 6	Nemaha County	KS	Monty G. Noland	1996	1044

646

WHITETAIL DEER (NON-TYPICAL ANTLERS)

Minimum Score 155   Continued

SCORE	LENGTH OF R MAIN BEAM L	INSIDE SPREAD	NUMBER OF R POINTS L	AREA	STATE/ PROVINCE	HUNTER'S NAME	DATE	RANK
184 6/8	19 1/8 22 1/8	15 1/8	13 11	Jasper County	IN	Mike T. Stowers	1996	1044
184 6/8	24 4/8 24 0/8	20 3/8	12 11	Jackson County	IL	Ron Pyron	1999	1044
*184 6/8	24 3/8 24 0/8	16 3/8	9 8	Vernon County	WI	Jeff DeGarmo	2009	1044
184 6/8	26 1/8 24 7/8	20 4/8	10 11	Vinton County	OH	Dan Davis	1985	1049
184 5/8	23 7/8 22 6/8	19 1/8	7 11	Calhoun County	IL	Chris Baker	1992	1049
184 5/8	24 1/8 23 5/8	18 6/8	9 9	Waushara County	WI	Jeffrey Van Zeeland	1995	1049
184 5/8	28 1/8 27 7/8	19 2/8	9 7	Cass County	IL	Gary Holbrook	1996	1049
184 5/8	25 2/8 25 3/8	20 6/8	8 9	Delaware County	IN	Joseph A. Hirst	2004	1049
184 5/8	25 2/8 25 6/8	20 2/8	10 8	Linn County	IA	Bert Carmer	2007	1049
184 5/8	24 5/8 25 7/8	16 0/8	9 6	Douglas County	KS	Gary Lee Murphree	2007	1049
184 5/8	24 1/8 24 5/8	17 4/8	6 7	Sumner County	KS	Adam Swiler	2009	1049
184 4/8	26 3/8 26 6/8	23 0/8	8 6	Washington County	MN	Ron Schleusner	1994	1057
184 4/8	23 2/8 23 4/8	18 4/8	7 7	Cerro Gordo County	IA	Ed Adamski	1997	1057
184 4/8	21 7/8 22 4/8	14 7/8	11 7	Adams County	IL	Steve Cingano	2006	1057
184 4/8	25 7/8 26 3/8	17 2/8	6 6	Monroe County	IA	Robert Smith	2007	1057
184 4/8	25 3/8 26 2/8	17 6/8	7 6	McDonough County	IL	Jeffrey P. Fountain	2007	1057
184 4/8	24 7/8 25 5/8	24 4/8	8 6	Dakota County	MN	Jason Fox	2009	1057
184 3/8	22 7/8 22 6/8	17 6/8	8 11	Texas County	OK	William E. Miller	1983	1063
184 3/8	23 2/8 23 3/8	21 5/8	10 8	Black Hawk County	IA	Paul Hughson	1985	1063
184 3/8	23 1/8 26 0/8	17 4/8	10 7	St. Louis County	MN	Jim Ceglar	1994	1063
184 3/8	26 5/8 26 6/8	18 2/8	7 7	McLean County	IL	Michael F. Bily	1997	1063
184 3/8	24 5/8 26 2/8	18 4/8	5 9	Rock County	WI	David D. Shultz	1999	1063
184 3/8	22 3/8 23 0/8	16 1/8	7 6	Menard County	IL	Don Bacon	2002	1063
184 3/8	22 2/8 21 4/8	18 3/8	10 8	Will County	IL	Charles E. Reavis	2003	1063
184 3/8	26 7/8 26 0/8	14 4/8	13 8	Riley County	KS	Wade T. Keltner	2006	1063
*184 3/8	26 3/8 26 1/8	18 2/8	8 10	Lorain County	OH	Steven Reinhold	2008	1063
184 2/8	25 2/8 24 5/8	19 0/8	9 9	Linn County	KS	Mike R. Wheeler	1994	1072
184 2/8	28 6/8 30 7/8	23 7/8	5 9	Hamilton County	OH	Dan Misali	1997	1072
184 2/8	26 5/8 27 0/8	20 5/8	5 6	Washington County	NE	Russ Campbell	1997	1072
184 2/8	28 3/8 26 5/8	22 0/8	6 7	Morgan County	IL	Paul Mueller	2001	1072
184 2/8	20 5/8 21 4/8	15 1/8	9 9	Tom Green County	TX	Billy D. Whitley	2005	1072
184 2/8	23 5/8 23 5/8	16 6/8	10 10	Hamilton County	IN	Todd M. Becker	2007	1072
*184 2/8	25 6/8 25 3/8	19 7/8	9 6	Hillsdale County	MI	Andrew J. Paulsen	2008	1072
184 1/8	25 1/8 26 3/8	21 3/8	7 6	St. Charles County	MO	Larry D. Stelzer	1962	1079
184 1/8	24 3/8 26 5/8	19 1/8	8 9	Waushara County	WI	Dwight A. Olson	1979	1079
184 1/8	22 0/8 22 7/8	17 0/8	7 10	Jasper County	IA	Dan Ingle	1993	1079
184 1/8	28 7/8 26 5/8	21 3/8	7 7	Pulaski County	IL	Donny Drew	1993	1079
184 1/8	24 0/8 25 1/8	21 0/8	7 6	Prince Georges County	MD	Clarence Parsons	1996	1079
184 1/8	22 7/8 24 0/8	19 6/8	11 9	Rowan County	KY	Ted W. Sivert	1999	1079
*184 1/8	23 0/8 22 1/8	19 2/8	7 8	Nicollet County	MN	Sid Denzer	2003	1079
184 1/8	24 7/8 24 2/8	18 2/8	8 11	Jefferson County	KS	Andy Petesch	2003	1079
184 1/8	25 4/8 25 5/8	17 3/8	7 7	Miami County	KS	Dennis Doherty	2006	1079
184 1/8	23 3/8 23 0/8	17 7/8	8 10	Jefferson County	WI	John Britzke	2006	1079
184 0/8	22 5/8 22 7/8	16 7/8	7 8	Buffalo County	WI	Jeff Owen	1996	1089
184 0/8	26 2/8 25 5/8	16 3/8	8 8	Switzerland County	IN	Michael R. Harner	2002	1089
*184 0/8	23 4/8 23 6/8	17 7/8	8 6	Lancaster County	NE	Kelly Sieckmeyer	2004	1089
*184 0/8	24 6/8 26 6/8	19 7/8	7 8	Effingham County	IL	Neil Ruholl	2005	1089
184 0/8	22 7/8 23 0/8	17 0/8	8 7	Spokane County	WA	Dr. Ross Simonds	2005	1089
184 0/8	27 5/8 28 0/8	19 4/8	11 7	Jersey County	IL	Rollin M. Lewis	2007	1089
*184 0/8	23 5/8 25 5/8	16 0/8	11 10	Richland County	IL	Scott Prosser	2008	1089
183 7/8	19 3/8 22 0/8	15 4/8	9 9	Williamson County	IL	Lowell D. Mausey	1992	1096
183 7/8	24 7/8 24 2/8	18 4/8	8 9	Cross County	AR	Randal Harris	1993	1096
183 7/8	24 2/8 26 1/8	13 6/8	8 9	Brown County	WI	Jeff Gajeski	1996	1096
183 7/8	26 2/8 27 0/8	18 4/8	7 6	Edwards County	IL	Gary Gifford	1997	1096
183 7/8	25 0/8 25 2/8	18 5/8	7 9	Jasper County	IL	Bryan Cramer	1999	1096
183 7/8	24 0/8 24 4/8	16 2/8	6 7	Oconto County	WI	John D. Block	2001	1096
183 7/8	26 3/8 26 7/8	18 5/8	8 8	Ottawa County	KS	Scott Bill	2005	1096
183 7/8	25 7/8 28 6/8	20 2/8	10 8	Clermont County	OH	Wayne Smith	2006	1096
*183 7/8	24 5/8 26 1/8	16 3/8	7 7	Woodson County	KS	Richard Stone, Jr.	2008	1096
183 6/8	25 3/8 25 4/8	18 2/8	7 10	Lake County	MN	Christopher Harristhal	1990	1105
*183 6/8	25 3/8 26 5/8	18 2/8	11 12	Lucas County	IA	Jason Nicolino	2004	1105
183 6/8	25 6/8 24 6/8	17 7/8	11 6	Phelps County	MO	Heath House	2006	1105
*183 6/8	22 3/8 22 2/8	16 0/8	8 7	Minnehaha County	SD	Jay Schleuter	2006	1105
183 6/8	25 4/8 25 5/8	18 1/8	10 6	McLeod County	MN	Kevin Schuette	2008	1105
183 6/8	24 5/8 25 0/8	18 1/8	8 10	Pepin County	WI	Dale Anderson	2009	1105
183 5/8	25 1/8 25 0/8	17 7/8	10 10	Lincoln County	SD	Mervin Sterk	1985	1111
183 5/8	28 0/8 28 0/8	21 5/8	6 6	Polk County	IA	Chris Olson	1993	1111
183 5/8	26 0/8 25 3/8	21 2/8	10 8	Polk County	WI	Ron R. Fehlen	1995	1111
183 5/8	24 0/8 24 0/8	18 1/8	6 10	Douglas County	WI	Frank Fudally	1997	1111
183 5/8	21 7/8 21 0/8	15 4/8	9 12	Portage County	OH	Donald E. Vargo	1997	1111
183 5/8	26 5/8 26 2/8	19 4/8	8 7	Sherburne County	MN	Greg Newhouse	1997	1111
183 5/8	28 0/8 27 0/8	17 3/8	7 9	Marion County	OH	Jeff Mitchell	2000	1111
*183 5/8	23 0/8 21 5/8	16 7/8	10 8	Monroe County	IA	Michael L. Friedland	2005	1111
183 5/8	26 5/8 26 4/8	19 1/8	7 7	Johnson County	IA	Robert Havlicek	2005	1111
*183 5/8	25 4/8 26 2/8	17 2/8	9 8	Osage County	KS	Carl Metter	2009	1111
183 4/8	26 2/8 24 7/8	18 1/8	10 8	Stark County	OH	Richard M. Cratty	1993	1121
183 4/8	22 6/8 22 7/8	17 0/8	9 8	Benton County	IA	Matt Wildman	1996	1121
183 4/8	24 2/8 26 2/8	18 7/8	6 9	Du Page County	IL	Bruno Parzych, Jr.	2000	1121
183 4/8	24 7/8 24 2/8	15 0/8	6 10	Washington County	WI	Michael J. Crass	2000	1121
183 4/8	24 3/8 25 0/8	18 4/8	7 8	Clearwater County	MN	Scott Ambuehl	2004	1121
183 4/8	23 3/8 23 1/8	16 0/8	10 8	Appanoose County	IA	Ryan Rogers	2005	1121
183 4/8	25 4/8 26 3/8	19 7/8	7 8	Berks County	PA	Matt Lytle	2006	1121
183 4/8	23 5/8 25 1/8	16 3/8	7 8	Wayne County	IL	William N. Reed	2006	1121
183 4/8	20 7/8 20 6/8	14 6/8	8 10	Clark County	IL	Fred Dodrill	2008	1121
183 3/8	24 3/8 25 2/8	19 0/8	11 10	Morrison County	MN	Ralph Hakel	1974	1130
183 3/8	24 4/8 25 5/8	16 5/8	8 9	Fillmore County	MN	Michael M. Gehrking	1985	1130
*183 3/8	24 0/8 24 3/8	20 0/8	10 11	Trempealeau County	WI	Dave Blaha	2008	1130
183 2/8	27 3/8 24 5/8	21 7/8	6 9	Holt County	NE	Lyle Ruff	1967	1133
183 2/8	28 4/8 26 6/8	16 4/8	10 9	Christian County	MO	Roger J. Newell	1984	1133
183 2/8	27 4/8 26 4/8	20 7/8	7 7	Riley County	KS	Larry Larson	1985	1133
183 2/8	24 0/8 25 3/8	20 3/8	10 8	Washburn County	WI	Jerry J. Genson	1989	1133
183 2/8	23 0/8 24 5/8	19 5/8	6 7	Monona County	IA	Joe Biggerstaff	1998	1133
183 2/8	24 6/8 25 3/8	17 5/8	9 8	La Salle County	IL	John E. Quinlan	2002	1133
183 2/8	25 3/8 24 7/8	19 0/8	7 9	Henry County	IA	William A. Peebler	2003	1133
183 2/8	27 2/8 26 3/8	22 6/8	7 8	Chariton County	MO	Kent Ratliff	2003	1133

647

WHITETAIL DEER (NON-TYPICAL ANTLERS)

Minimum Score 155 — Continued

SCORE	LENGTH OF R MAIN BEAM L	INSIDE SPREAD	NUMBER OF R POINTS L		AREA	STATE/ PROVINCE	HUNTER'S NAME	DATE	RANK
*183 2/8	26 1/8 25 2/8	18 6/8	7	8	Cowley County	KS	Jesse Sample	2008	1133
183 1/8	26 7/8 26 0/8	18 0/8	7	6	Grayson County	TX	Wayne Tarpley	1998	1142
183 1/8	24 1/8 25 6/8	18 0/8	8	7	Clarion County	PA	Mark G. Minnicks	1999	1142
183 1/8	24 7/8 24 3/8	16 3/8	7	11	Boone County	MO	Dave Marlett	2004	1142
183 1/8	25 5/8 26 5/8	20 7/8	7	8	Fulton County	IL	David Geier	2004	1142
183 1/8	25 0/8 26 1/8	16 5/8	10	8	St. Louis County	MN	Gene R. Smith	2005	1142
*183 1/8	22 1/8 23 2/8	17 6/8	7	8	Seward County	NE	Leon Leapaldt	2006	1142
*183 1/8	25 0/8 24 6/8	16 1/8	6	10	Owen County	IN	Danny J. Schulz	2008	1142
183 1/8	24 4/8 25 1/8	20 6/8	8	9	Pope County	MN	Kavin J. Bailey	2010	1142
183 0/8	23 1/8 23 2/8	18 7/8	7	6	Buffalo County	WI	Joel Torkilsen	2000	1150
183 0/8	23 7/8 21 1/8	19 0/8	11	7	Franklin County	IA	Michael L. Lauffer	2000	1150
183 0/8	24 2/8 24 3/8	18 1/8	9	9	Sullivan County	IN	Clint House	2001	1150
183 0/8	24 5/8 26 0/8	22 0/8	8	8	Lemhi County	ID	Gary C. Gapp	2002	1150
183 0/8	22 4/8 22 6/8	17 3/8	10	9	Cowley County	KS	Marion Scott	2003	1150
182 7/8	24 2/8 25 5/8	19 2/8	9	7	Arkansas County	AR	Tommy Horton	1971	1155
182 7/8	24 3/8 25 2/8	18 0/8	11	5	Olmsted County	MN	Dan Matheson	1973	1155
182 7/8	24 4/8 25 0/8	20 5/8	6	8	Dane County	WI	Clayton Bodoh, Jr.	1997	1155
*182 7/8	22 3/8 23 1/8	17 7/8	6	9	Dubuque County	IA	David Doerr	2004	1155
182 7/8	25 6/8 26 1/8	17 5/8	9	6	La Salle County	IL	Gary N. Blanco	2005	1155
182 7/8	26 1/8 26 0/8	20 4/8	9	7	Woodbury County	IA	Daniel J. Myers	2007	1155
*182 7/8	19 5/8 21 0/8	15 3/8	11	11	Worth County	MO	Jeremiah Stephens	2009	1155
182 6/8	26 1/8 28 7/8	21 1/8	8	8	Jefferson County	NE	Robert W. Peperkorn	1997	1162
182 6/8	25 1/8 24 0/8	18 4/8	12	8	Henry County	GA	Wyman Brooks	1999	1162
*182 6/8	23 5/8 23 4/8	13 1/8	6	7	Linn County	KS	F. David Thornberry	2008	1162
182 5/8	24 5/8 23 2/8	13 7/8	10	10	Union County	IL	Tracy D. Hawes	1994	1165
182 5/8	23 7/8 23 6/8	18 4/8	8	8	Osage County	MO	Ronnie Lee Tyree	1995	1165
182 5/8	25 6/8 24 2/8	19 0/8	5	6	Washington County	KS	Scott A. Wilkens	1997	1165
182 5/8	25 0/8 25 5/8	18 1/8	7	8	Anoka County	MN	John Pregler	2000	1165
182 5/8	27 4/8 25 2/8	19 5/8	9	5	Arapahoe County	CO	David L. Brandon	2000	1165
182 5/8	25 5/8 24 5/8	20 0/8	9	11	Harrison County	OH	Shane A. Stine	2004	1165
182 5/8	24 4/8 25 2/8	19 1/8	8	7	Labette County	KS	Jaret Drummond	2004	1165
182 5/8	28 4/8 26 5/8	20 3/8	6	9	Chippewa County	WI	Curtis Benson	2010	1165
182 4/8	19 5/8 26 7/8	17 2/8	11	11	Will County	IL	Richard Heintz	1971	1173
182 4/8	25 7/8 25 5/8	19 0/8	9	9	Macoupin County	IL	John Tevini	1991	1173
182 4/8	24 3/8 23 5/8	18 3/8	6	8	Wapello County	IA	Arnold E. Vest	1993	1173
182 4/8	26 6/8 26 7/8	18 1/8	10	9	Walton County	GA	Michael Thomas	1996	1173
182 4/8	24 1/8 25 2/8	18 1/8	6	6	Adams County	IL	Kevin Huner	2000	1173
182 4/8	28 3/8 27 6/8	21 2/8	7	8	Racine County	WI	Brian Schmalfeldt	2000	1173
182 4/8	25 0/8 24 7/8	22 6/8	9	8	Des Moines County	IA	Bob Andresen	2003	1173
182 4/8	22 4/8 23 3/8	16 0/8	8	13	Wagoner County	OK	Darrin Hargrove	2007	1173
*182 4/8	22 2/8 24 6/8	16 4/8	10	5	Yankton County	SD	Matt Bertsch	2009	1173
182 3/8	29 3/8 27 7/8	20 5/8	6	8	Goodhue County	MN	Jim Danielson	1984	1182
182 3/8	25 5/8 25 5/8	19 5/8	6	8	Warren County	IN	Gregory S. Zak	1990	1182
182 3/8	24 6/8 25 4/8	20 6/8	8	6	Pike County	IL	William R. Graham	1997	1182
182 3/8	25 3/8 25 4/8	19 4/8	8	7	Macoupin County	IL	Michael Kuhar	1998	1182
182 3/8	22 3/8 22 3/8	16 1/8	9	8	Washington County	WI	Benjamin Krebs	2001	1182
182 3/8	25 5/8 26 3/8	19 3/8	8	6	Caddo County	OK	Todd Wilson	2004	1182
182 3/8	27 0/8 20 2/8	19 5/8	7	9	Des Moines County	IA	Robin Schneider	2005	1182
182 3/8	20 7/8 23 7/8	19 1/8	14	6	Pottawatomie County	OK	Miles Jones	2006	1182
182 3/8	23 3/8 22 7/8	14 4/8	6	9	Ellsworth County	KS	Rob Upchurch	2007	1182
*182 3/8	24 3/8 24 0/8	16 7/8	8	8	Decatur County	IA	Jeffrey Lindsey	2009	1182
182 2/8	27 2/8 26 2/8	18 1/8	11	7	Pike County	IL	Dennis Kendall	1990	1192
182 2/8	24 2/8 24 6/8	18 0/8	9	10	Macoupin County	IL	Les Rhodes	1994	1192
182 2/8	26 5/8 26 6/8	22 2/8	8	8	Waukesha County	WI	J. Bradley Bence	1995	1192
182 2/8	21 4/8 22 3/8	15 5/8	8	7	Logan County	IL	Rick Redfairn	1995	1192
182 2/8	26 5/8 26 3/8	20 3/8	7	9	Pike County	IL	Paul Schmidt	1997	1192
182 2/8	27 0/8 25 3/8	22 1/8	10	7	Moultrie County	IL	Joe Matheson	2002	1192
182 2/8	23 3/8 23 4/8	16 7/8	7	8	Wyandot County	OH	James D. Herring	2005	1192
182 1/8	22 4/8 22 4/8	17 1/8	10	9	Brown County	KS	Bill Butrick	1985	1199
182 1/8	26 0/8 26 4/8	17 1/8	8	7	Barber County	KS	Tom Langford	1996	1199
182 1/8	24 6/8 24 4/8	16 6/8	6	9	Wright County	MN	Walter Halberg	2000	1199
182 1/8	23 3/8 23 2/8	17 1/8	7	12	Barber County	KS	Shane Patterson	2003	1199
*182 1/8	22 7/8 22 3/8	18 3/8	12	9	Will County	IL	Richard L. Carlson	2004	1199
182 1/8	22 0/8 21 6/8	15 2/8	11	10	Lawrence County	IN	Dale Waldbieser	2004	1199
*182 1/8	25 4/8 25 5/8	22 6/8	6	9	Barron County	WI	Greg Nelson	2008	1199
*182 1/8	23 6/8 24 0/8	17 6/8	9	10	Marion County	IN	Ryan Kimble	2009	1199
182 0/8	24 3/8 24 5/8	17 1/8	6	7	Albemarle County	VA	Richard A. Shifflett	1989	1207
182 0/8	25 2/8 25 1/8	15 6/8	7	9	Sawyer County	WI	Joel McVinnie	1995	1207
182 0/8	26 5/8 26 3/8	19 6/8	7	8	Winnebago County	IL	John R. Prenot	2000	1207
182 0/8	27 1/8 26 5/8	21 0/8	6	8	Green Lake County	WI	James L. Pretz	2001	1207
*182 0/8	25 1/8 27 1/8	22 3/8	7	8	Delaware County	OH	Andrew A. Yant	2003	1207
182 0/8	24 4/8 23 3/8	15 6/8	8	7	Henry County	KY	Brian Matthew Silvers	2005	1207
182 0/8	27 4/8 27 0/8	19 6/8	7	8	Brown County	OH	Thomas L. Luck	2005	1207
*182 0/8	23 7/8 23 3/8	19 5/8	8	8	Coshocton County	OH	David M. Mumaw	2007	1207
181 7/8	24 4/8 24 4/8	18 6/8	7	10	Marion County	IA	Roger DeMoss	1990	1215
181 7/8	24 0/8 23 6/8	18 6/8	9	8	El Paso County	CO	Kyle Schomaker	1992	1215
181 7/8	24 3/8 26 4/8	18 4/8	8	6	Whiteside County	IL	Kyle A. Kennedy	1996	1215
181 7/8	26 6/8 26 4/8	19 2/8	8	7	Chester County	PA	Robert E. Ferguson, Jr.	1998	1215
181 7/8	26 5/8 27 2/8	22 4/8	8	8	Des Moines County	IA	Henry Roberts	2001	1215
181 7/8	23 7/8 23 0/8	20 5/8	11	12	Franklin County	IL	Jim Ford	2002	1215
181 7/8	23 1/8 22 7/8	17 1/8	8	10	St. Marys County	MD	Mark Dominiak	2004	1215
181 7/8	26 4/8 26 3/8	21 3/8	5	9	Scott County	IL	Curt Vincent	2005	1215
181 7/8	23 0/8 22 0/8	17 5/8	9	9	Winnebago County	IL	Roger G. Garrie	2008	1215
181 6/8	23 2/8 22 6/8	20 1/8	8	7	Adams County	IL	Festal McCarty	1967	1224
181 6/8	25 4/8 25 0/8	18 1/8	7	11	Kiowa County	KS	Royce E. Frazier	1985	1224
181 6/8	24 1/8 23 1/8	17 7/8	8	10	Cross County	AR	Britt Johnson	1995	1224
181 6/8	22 1/8 22 7/8	21 4/8	9	7	St. Charles County	MO	Tony Oxford	1995	1224
181 6/8	24 3/8 24 5/8	17 4/8	7	9	Kane County	IL	Ed Saloga	1996	1224
181 6/8	23 0/8 23 1/8	16 4/8	6	9	Macoupin County	IL	Kurt A. Bohl	1997	1224
181 6/8	22 6/8 24 5/8	19 3/8	8	8	Johnson County	IA	Craig Goetz	1997	1224
181 6/8	24 3/8 24 5/8	17 4/8	7	9	Monroe County	IA	Shawn Bagley	2003	1224
*181 6/8	20 4/8 21 7/8	17 3/8	13	13	Pottawatomie County	KS	Rick Anderson	2004	1224
181 6/8	23 5/8 22 6/8	16 5/8	8	7	Adams County	IL	Brian Duesterhaus	2006	1224
181 6/8	22 0/8 24 2/8	22 0/8	8	6	Ashland County	OH	Mark McCracken	2007	1224
181 6/8	23 2/8 23 5/8	18 4/8	8	9	Washington County	MN	Willie Petersen	2008	1224

WHITETAIL DEER (NON-TYPICAL ANTLERS)

Minimum Score 155   Continued

SCORE	LENGTH OF R MAIN BEAM L	INSIDE SPREAD	NUMBER OF R POINTS L		AREA	STATE/ PROVINCE	HUNTER'S NAME	DATE	RANK
181 5/8	21 3/8	23 5/8	19 7/8	9	6	Bureau County	IL	Louis J. Guerrini	1990	1236
181 5/8	25 5/8	26 7/8	18 6/8	9	8	Pike County	IL	Steven R. Tice	1991	1236
181 5/8	24 5/8	25 5/8	20 5/8	7	6	Okanagon	BC	Richard Kirkvold	1994	1236
181 5/8	25 0/8	24 4/8	17 4/8	9	9	Las Animas County	CO	Daniel E. Reif	1995	1236
181 5/8	23 7/8	23 0/8	17 3/8	10	9	Bedford County	PA	Stacey L. Steele	2004	1236
181 5/8	22 7/8	23 0/8	17 0/8	11	7	Douglas County	WI	Adam W. Claussen	2004	1236
181 5/8	27 3/8	26 3/8	23 2/8	7	7	Jo Daviess County	IL	Brian Pekarek	2004	1236
*181 5/8	26 1/8	26 6/8	20 1/8	8	8	Adams County	IA	Keelan Woods	2006	1236
*181 5/8	25 2/8	24 1/8	18 5/8	7	8	Sangamon County	IL	Terry M. Dixon	2008	1236
181 4/8	26 1/8	26 0/8	21 0/8	10	9	Morrison County	MN	Peter De Chaine	1984	1245
181 4/8	25 6/8	26 0/8	19 7/8	9	8	Wyoming County	WV	Bobby Smith	1985	1245
181 4/8	20 6/8	23 0/8	19 1/8	8	14	Edgar County	IL	Dennis Gosnell	1991	1245
181 4/8	22 1/8	22 4/8	17 4/8	7	6	Howard County	IA	Rod Ellingson	1993	1245
181 4/8	24 0/8	26 4/8	19 2/8	7	6	Alexander County	IL	Terry L. Kepley	1996	1245
181 4/8	24 3/8	23 1/8	18 0/8	6	9	Lake County	IL	Dan Trudeau	2003	1245
181 4/8	26 6/8	27 1/8	20 2/8	8	7	Fulton County	IL	William T. Geist	2003	1245
181 4/8	26 4/8	26 3/8	26 4/8	5	8	Clark County	IL	Rusty Johnson	2003	1245
*181 4/8	22 4/8	21 0/8	19 4/8	8	10	Hennepin County	MN	Doug Kurkowski	2007	1245
181 4/8	25 4/8	24 4/8	18 4/8	8	8	Middlesex County	CT	Joseph M. Armenia	2008	1245
181 3/8	28 0/8	28 0/8	20 5/8	11	6	Hardin County	IA	Howard Nelson	1963	1255
181 3/8	26 2/8	24 3/8	16 6/8	9	8	Sawyer County	WI	Bill "Red" Gilbert	1989	1255
181 3/8	27 6/8	23 2/8	18 7/8	8	6	Muskingum County	OH	Donnie Ledbetter	1996	1255
181 3/8	24 0/8	26 6/8	15 1/8	13	8	Crawford County	IL	Robert Loveall	1996	1255
181 3/8	25 2/8	25 0/8	22 2/8	10	8	Anne Arundel County	MD	John E. Ambrose, Jr.	1997	1255
181 3/8	26 5/8	25 1/8	16 4/8	7	8	Iowa County	WI	Leo Doescher	1998	1255
181 3/8	23 5/8	22 7/8	17 3/8	11	9	Pike County	IL	Jim C. Cooper	1998	1255
181 3/8	23 5/8	24 2/8	16 3/8	7	8	Champaign County	OH	Curt Roberts	1999	1255
181 3/8	25 5/8	26 0/8	20 1/8	9	8	Waupaca County	WI	Steve Henriksen	1999	1255
181 3/8	20 7/8	26 5/8	19 2/8	12	7	Appanoose County	IA	Steven M. Smith	2001	1255
181 3/8	22 4/8	23 7/8	18 2/8	8	7	Rawlins County	KS	Danny Carmen	2002	1255
181 3/8	23 1/8	22 6/8	18 7/8	7	9	Johnson County	KS	Kevin Hansen	2003	1255
181 3/8	22 1/8	25 4/8	14 4/8	7	9	Osage County	KS	Richard McCarty	2004	1255
*181 3/8	24 7/8	24 6/8	17 5/8	6	10	Otthon	SAS	Bryon Priebe	2010	1255
181 2/8	22 1/8	24 5/8	19 0/8	12	8	Desha County	AR	John T. Greer	1962	1269
181 2/8	26 1/8	25 4/8	25 0/8	12	9	Darke County	OH	Dean P. Neff	1979	1269
181 2/8	24 5/8	22 3/8	20 6/8	9	7	Clark County	IA	Larry Bear	1991	1269
181 2/8	27 3/8	27 0/8	22 3/8	8	7	Madison County	IL	Michael N. Doles	1994	1269
181 2/8	22 2/8	23 6/8	15 2/8	9	8	Brown County	OH	William Rowland	2002	1269
181 2/8	23 6/8	22 7/8	14 2/8	7	9	Pike County	IL	Thomas Beissel	2003	1269
*181 2/8	25 0/8	24 4/8	19 0/8	11	8	Fulton County	IL	Joe Cochrane	2004	1269
181 2/8	25 2/8	24 3/8	14 5/8	5	11	Kingman County	KS	Shawn Baker	2005	1269
181 2/8	24 1/8	23 4/8	18 5/8	9	7	Marquette County	WI	Russell D. Puterbaugh	2006	1269
181 2/8	22 7/8	21 2/8	16 5/8	8	10	Steele County	ND	Derrick Rygg	2009	1269
181 1/8	24 1/8	24 1/8	17 6/8	9	6	Coles County	IL	Gerald L. Davis	1973	1279
181 1/8	24 2/8	25 5/8	17 7/8	7	8	Tazewell County	IL	Gerald Sweckard	1994	1279
181 1/8	24 7/8	23 4/8	18 1/8	11	8	Warren County	OH	Bobby Clark	1995	1279
181 1/8	23 6/8	25 6/8	18 3/8	6	9	Randolph County	MO	Donnie Lee Palmatory	1996	1279
181 1/8	25 3/8	24 0/8	17 4/8	11	11	Harrison County	IA	John W. Shumate	1996	1279
181 1/8	23 6/8	22 6/8	18 4/8	11	9	Kane County	IL	Clayton Johnson	1998	1279
181 1/8	25 6/8	25 0/8	18 1/8	6	6	Buffalo County	WI	Dan Prissel	2000	1279
181 1/8	25 2/8	25 1/8	17 1/8	8	7	Butler County	KS	Phillip Fiene	2002	1279
181 1/8	24 6/8	25 7/8	20 4/8	7	7	Dubuque County	IA	Gregory J. Kuhlmann	2004	1279
181 1/8	25 5/8	27 7/8	20 0/8	10	7	Jefferson County	KS	Michael Adkins, Sr.	2004	1279
181 1/8	22 4/8	25 1/8	16 2/8	8	6	Bureau County	IL	Scott Maupin	2005	1279
181 1/8	26 6/8	25 1/8	18 1/8	7	8	La Crosse County	WI	Paul W. Balmer	2005	1279
*181 1/8	23 7/8	23 4/8	14 2/8	9	11	Buchanan County	MO	Seth McCray	2006	1279
*181 1/8	23 0/8	22 5/8	16 7/8	9	9	Hot Springs County	WY	Flint Smith	2009	1279
181 0/8	24 6/8	25 4/8	19 6/8	11	8	Knox County	OH	Don Quick	1984	1293
181 0/8	23 7/8	23 5/8	19 1/8	12	9	Pittsburg County	OK	Harold Jones	1986	1293
181 0/8	23 4/8	24 1/8	17 2/8	8	9	Clark County	IL	Harold A. Funk	1991	1293
181 0/8	25 0/8	23 3/8	18 3/8	8	7	Holt County	MO	Jim Zawodny	1992	1293
181 0/8	28 3/8	26 3/8	18 4/8	11	8	Massac County	IL	Gilbert McNichols	1995	1293
181 0/8	25 5/8	25 2/8	18 0/8	7	7	Houston County	MN	Tom Murray	1997	1293
181 0/8	24 5/8	24 6/8	18 5/8	8	6	Grundy County	MO	Paul F. Duffner	2000	1293
181 0/8	24 7/8	24 4/8	23 1/8	8	7	Charles County	MD	Lance F. Knight	2002	1293
*181 0/8	27 4/8	25 3/8	20 0/8	12	9	Phillips County	KS	Sean VanKooten	2009	1293
180 7/8	28 2/8	24 2/8	21 6/8	10	9	Hamilton County	OH	David Beard	1994	1302
180 7/8	24 4/8	25 3/8	20 0/8	6	5	Sangamon County	IL	Harold Myers	2000	1302
180 7/8	24 4/8	23 6/8	22 4/8	7	10	Tuscarawas County	OH	Steve Couts	2000	1302
180 7/8	20 6/8	21 4/8	18 3/8	6	10	Brown County	IL	Joseph W. Conrad	2002	1302
*180 7/8	24 5/8	24 5/8	14 4/8	5	9	Olmsted County	MN	Bill Clink	2004	1302
180 7/8	21 0/8	26 0/8	22 4/8	6	8	Madison County	IA	Jack Theiler	2004	1302
180 7/8	22 5/8	23 0/8	16 6/8	8	9	Marion County	IA	Joel R. Earls	2005	1302
180 7/8	25 6/8	25 3/8	17 0/8	8	7	St. Croix County	WI	Marty W. Powers	2009	1302
180 6/8	22 3/8	24 1/8	17 3/8	8	7	Pope County	AR	Johnny Reed	1983	1310
180 6/8	23 4/8	23 6/8	16 6/8	6	9	Lee County	IA	Matthew A. Trexel	1994	1310
180 6/8	22 7/8	24 0/8	17 3/8	8	8	Fall River County	SD	Brad S. Thomsen	1999	1310
180 6/8	24 2/8	24 4/8	19 3/8	11	9	Clay County	IL	Kevin Roley	2006	1310
180 6/8	23 3/8	23 0/8	16 4/8	7	11	Brown County	KS	Dan Hershey	2006	1310
180 6/8	21 0/8	24 6/8	18 5/8	6	6	Van Buren County	IA	Brian D. Smith	2007	1310
*180 6/8	24 5/8	23 2/8	16 5/8	7	9	Butler County	OH	Keith Fenrich	2008	1310
180 6/8	22 5/8	22 5/8	20 7/8	7	11	Warren County	IA	Rick Hawxby	2008	1310
180 5/8	28 5/8	28 6/8	24 5/8	7	7	Preble County	OH	James R. Whittaker	1978	1318
180 5/8	27 5/8	26 3/8	21 1/8	9	6	Linn County	IA	Craig Shepard	1980	1318
180 5/8	27 0/8	28 0/8	18 6/8	6	9	Delaware County	OH	John P. Stark	1994	1318
180 5/8	24 1/8	23 5/8	16 2/8	11	11	Cherokee County	KS	Gene R. Hamilton	1996	1318
180 5/8	25 5/8	25 3/8	18 0/8	7	9	Franklin County	MO	Dave Linders	2001	1318
180 5/8	23 5/8	23 6/8	18 3/8	8	9	Woodford County	KY	Kelly C. Ison	2003	1318
180 5/8	26 4/8	24 3/8	21 5/8	5	7	Adams County	IL	Bo Davis	2003	1318
180 5/8	23 2/8	22 6/8	15 4/8	8	9	Buffalo County	WI	Randy Hollister	2006	1318
*180 5/8	23 2/8	22 2/8	17 7/8	6	9	Kane County	IL	Ted W. Diangikes	2006	1318
*180 5/8	22 7/8	23 6/8	15 7/8	9	8	Pulaski County	IN	Bryan D. Busse	2008	1318
180 4/8	23 0/8	23 0/8	16 3/8	7	8	Teton County	MT	James Dean	1981	1328
180 4/8	26 7/8	27 3/8	21 1/8	7	6	Buffalo County	WI	John L. Smith	1988	1328
180 4/8	24 7/8	25 4/8	21 2/8	8	6	Butler County	KS	John Parsons	1989	1328

649

WHITETAIL DEER (NON-TYPICAL ANTLERS)

Minimum Score 155 — Continued

SCORE	LENGTH OF R MAIN BEAM L	INSIDE SPREAD	NUMBER OF R POINTS L	AREA	STATE/ PROVINCE	HUNTER'S NAME	DATE	RANK
180 4/8	23 6/8 24 2/8	15 2/8	10 7	Osage County	OK	James H. Farmer	1991	1328
180 4/8	24 6/8 24 7/8	19 1/8	8 7	Jewell County	KS	Bruce Meyer	1991	1328
180 4/8	25 7/8 26 1/8	17 6/8	10 8	Price County	WI	John Michalski	1991	1328
180 4/8	25 4/8 26 1/8	17 5/8	8 7	Gage County	NE	Gary L. Stohs	1994	1328
180 4/8	25 4/8 25 2/8	18 6/8	7 7	Grundy County	IL	Mike Ceranski	1998	1328
180 4/8	25 6/8 25 0/8	19 0/8	7 6	Dallas County	IA	Mitch Hosler	2000	1328
180 4/8	23 3/8 22 3/8	18 1/8	8 10	Big River	SAS	Randy Peck	2006	1328
180 4/8	22 3/8 22 1/8	17 4/8	12 10	Livingston County	NY	Marvin Yamonaco	2007	1328
*180 4/8	24 3/8 22 3/8	16 0/8	9 12	Porter County	IN	Ed B. McMullin	2007	1328
180 3/8	23 5/8 23 5/8	16 1/8	9 11	Edgar County	IL	Timothy W. Kirby	1993	1340
180 3/8	24 2/8 24 6/8	17 4/8	8 6	Monroe County	WI	Craig C. Tormoen	1996	1340
180 3/8	27 0/8 28 1/8	18 5/8	5 5	Knox County	IL	Bryan E. DeJaynes	1997	1340
180 3/8	30 5/8 29 6/8	20 3/8	7 7	Jackson County	MO	Randy J. Lappe	1998	1340
*180 3/8	23 0/8 22 5/8	13 0/8	15 7	Hardin County	KY	Woody Noe	2008	1340
*180 3/8	27 4/8 26 3/8	21 0/8	7 6	Allen County	IN	Randy R. Rorick	2009	1340
180 2/8	25 4/8 25 3/8	18 7/8	10 8	Woodford County	KY	Gary Hatton	1993	1346
180 2/8	26 1/8 25 4/8	20 5/8	6 7	Kleberg County	TX	Mike Lemker	1995	1346
180 2/8	23 1/8 24 4/8	19 6/8	7 7	McKenzie County	ND	Rodney Fretland	1998	1346
180 2/8	23 2/8 23 1/8	19 4/8	9 8	Will County	IL	Jon Gall	1998	1346
180 2/8	23 2/8 23 6/8	18 0/8	7 7	Jasper County	IA	Doni Rowan	1999	1346
*180 2/8	25 2/8 25 5/8	18 3/8	6 9	La Crosse County	WI	David Ganschow	2005	1346
180 2/8	23 1/8 23 1/8	16 0/8	6 6	Calumet County	WI	Gary Schmidt	2006	1346
*180 2/8	24 5/8 24 0/8	17 6/8	9 7	Wayne County	IA	Cody L. McIntire	2007	1346
180 1/8	24 2/8 23 4/8	18 5/8	10 8	Winnebago County	IA	Jim Orthel	1983	1354
180 1/8	26 5/8 26 6/8	20 0/8	8 8	McLean County	IL	Tim Kaufman	1995	1354
180 1/8	24 6/8 24 5/8	18 5/8	7 9	Cook County	IL	Roger Kleinfelder	1996	1354
180 1/8	23 5/8 24 7/8	19 6/8	8 7	Mercer County	MO	John D. Green	1996	1354
180 1/8	26 0/8 27 2/8	22 2/8	7 9	Ogle County	IL	John Kaltenbach	1997	1354
180 1/8	25 5/8 24 2/8	17 5/8	8 9	Buffalo County	WI	Paul B. Doenier	1998	1354
180 1/8	25 0/8 24 4/8	18 0/8	6 6	Washington County	IN	Kevin Lee Kramer	2001	1354
180 1/8	25 3/8 25 0/8	21 1/8	6 7	Knox County	IL	Dale Graves	2005	1354
*180 1/8	24 2/8 21 4/8	13 4/8	9 8	Talbot County	MD	Curt Monath	2006	1354
180 1/8	27 7/8 24 7/8	21 6/8	7 9	Montgomery County	IN	John W. Foster	2006	1354
180 1/8	22 7/8 23 7/8	18 0/8	7 9	Fulton County	IL	Raymond Dela Bruere	2007	1354
180 1/8	24 7/8 25 2/8	15 4/8	7 7	Trempealeau County	WI	Matt R. Andersen	2010	1354
180 0/8	26 0/8 23 3/8	18 5/8	6 9	Madison County	IL	Pat Devine	1990	1366
180 0/8	26 4/8 25 1/8	19 6/8	6 6	Buchanan County	IA	Robert R. Parker	1996	1366
180 0/8	23 7/8 24 3/8	20 5/8	7 6	Saline County	KS	Jack Goates	1997	1366
180 0/8	24 6/8 23 4/8	19 6/8	7 8	Langlade County	WI	Michael Kaster	1998	1366
180 0/8	29 0/8 29 0/8	21 3/8	5 5	Jefferson County	KS	Stuart G. Hazard III	1998	1366
*180 0/8	23 4/8 26 4/8	20 5/8	8 7	Kane County	IL	Ron Tazelaar	2000	1366
180 0/8	25 3/8 25 1/8	20 1/8	7 6	St. Louis County	MN	John L. King	2001	1366
180 0/8	25 6/8 25 5/8	17 2/8	6 8	Butler County	KS	David R. Rogers	2005	1366
*180 0/8	16 0/8 22 6/8	16 3/8	10 8	Comanche County	KS	Tom Hoffman	2008	1366
180 0/8	26 0/8 25 7/8	15 3/8	6 5	Henderson County	KY	David Conely	2009	1366
179 7/8	26 4/8 26 5/8	23 1/8	7 7	Cass County	IL	Jeffrey A. Williams	1995	1376
179 7/8	24 0/8 24 6/8	19 7/8	7 6	Washington County	MN	Mike Haines	1996	1376
179 7/8	22 1/8 22 5/8	17 5/8	7 8	Grant County	WI	Larry J. Oldenburg	1999	1376
179 7/8	24 2/8 22 7/8	18 1/8	8 10	Harper County	KS	Paul J. Chackan	2001	1376
*179 7/8	23 2/8 23 2/8	19 2/8	9 8	Polk County	WI	Joseph L. Marek	2003	1376
179 7/8	23 3/8 23 4/8	18 4/8	11 8	Worth County	IA	Larry Porter	2005	1376
179 7/8	23 0/8 22 7/8	15 6/8	8 11	Callaway County	MO	Don Johnson	2005	1376
179 7/8	25 1/8 25 1/8	16 5/8	6 7	Washington County	WI	Karl Scheife	2005	1376
*179 7/8	24 5/8 24 6/8	22 2/8	8 9	Wabasha County	MN	Josh Wolf	2008	1376
179 7/8	25 5/8 24 7/8	18 2/8	7 6	Edmonton	ALB	Brad Huempfner	2008	1376
179 6/8	24 4/8 24 2/8	21 0/8	7 8	Creek County	OK	Marion Lewis	1975	1386
179 6/8	24 7/8 25 7/8	22 0/8	6 7	Hamilton County	OH	Lawrence Ashbrook	1981	1386
179 6/8	25 1/8 22 5/8	17 4/8	8 11	Licking County	OH	Tony Johnson	1992	1386
179 6/8	23 4/8 24 2/8	17 4/8	7 8	Sauk County	WI	Reg Acker	1994	1386
179 6/8	25 4/8 27 1/8	17 7/8	7 8	Adams County	IL	Jim Favreau	2001	1386
179 6/8	23 5/8 23 4/8	17 2/8	8 10	Kane County	IL	David C. Gibbons	2005	1386
179 6/8	23 7/8 22 1/8	19 0/8	13 11	Washington County	IA	L. W. Miller	2007	1386
179 6/8	24 4/8 24 6/8	16 2/8	10 8	Elk County	KS	Jeff Fitts	2008	1386
179 5/8	24 4/8 25 6/8	19 5/8	9 11	Fillmore County	MN	Wayne Pfremmer	1972	1394
179 5/8	29 4/8 25 7/8	20 1/8	5 8	Dane County	WI	Kip Kalscheur	1989	1394
179 5/8	23 7/8 25 0/8	19 7/8	8 7	Allegheny County	PA	Anthony Vecenie, Jr.	1995	1394
179 5/8	24 0/8 23 7/8	16 3/8	10 7	Pottawattamie County	IA	Murray Stewart	1996	1394
179 5/8	24 6/8 26 5/8	21 6/8	8 6	Waukesha County	WI	Paul Kolbeck	1998	1394
179 5/8	22 0/8 22 3/8	20 4/8	10 13	Van Buren County	MI	George M. Pleyte, Sr.	2001	1394
179 5/8	21 7/8 23 7/8	19 0/8	8 8	Edmonton	ALB	Tony Zambon	2002	1394
179 5/8	22 3/8 24 7/8	19 1/8	9 11	Menard County	IL	Ron Wadsworth	2003	1394
179 5/8	23 3/8 23 4/8	16 1/8	11 12	Greene County	OH	Lance Kerr	2004	1394
179 5/8	20 5/8 18 4/8	14 0/8	8 11	Fountain County	IN	Dale E. Davis	2009	1394
179 4/8	26 3/8 26 1/8	20 1/8	7 7	Sawyer County	WI	Wesley A. Marcsis	1996	1404
179 4/8	28 7/8 27 6/8	22 0/8	9 9	Des Moines County	IA	Mark Thomson	1996	1404
179 4/8	23 0/8 20 4/8	12 5/8	9 19	Murray County	OK	J. Scott Stedman	2003	1404
179 4/8	24 6/8 24 5/8	22 3/8	6 8	La Salle County	IL	Donald Greathouse	2004	1404
179 4/8	24 0/8 23 2/8	15 4/8	9 7	Mercer County	PA	Scott Franks	2004	1404
179 4/8	23 0/8 20 4/8	21 6/8	10 9	La Salle County	IL	Don Greathouse	2008	1404
179 4/8	25 0/8 25 2/8	19 1/8	7 8	Rooks County	KS	Mark Westhusin	2008	1404
179 4/8	18 5/8 21 5/8	18 3/8	9 8	Grant County	SD	Mark Gunnufson	2009	1404
179 3/8	26 3/8 26 4/8	19 5/8	6 6	Cass County	IL	Craig Myers	1994	1412
179 3/8	23 0/8 24 2/8	20 4/8	8 10	Licking County	OH	Tom Lott	1998	1412
179 3/8	22 2/8 22 5/8	16 7/8	10 7	Champaign County	IL	Dana Reynolds	2001	1412
179 3/8	23 2/8 24 0/8	16 3/8	6 7	Jackson County	WI	Mike Labar	2001	1412
179 3/8	25 7/8 27 7/8	16 1/8	6 6	Montgomery County	OH	Mike Barnett	2006	1412
179 3/8	22 6/8 26 1/8	16 4/8	8 7	Portage County	OH	Daniel H. Knippenberg	2006	1412
179 3/8	24 4/8 24 5/8	21 0/8	9 7	Columbia County	WI	James R. Leystra	2009	1412
179 2/8	25 4/8 23 2/8	23 0/8	12 7	Marion County	IA	Roger DeMoss	1982	1419
179 2/8	24 7/8 25 7/8	21 5/8	8 7	Chippewa County	WI	Kip Knez	1986	1419
179 2/8	21 6/8 23 2/8	14 0/8	8 13	Sangamon County	IL	Guy H. Hinrichs	1993	1419
179 2/8	21 1/8 19 3/8	15 7/8	8 9	Oneida County	WI	Kathy Fancher	1993	1419
179 2/8	24 1/8 23 5/8	16 0/8	9 6	Iron County	WI	Gerhard Frank	1996	1419
179 2/8	25 5/8 24 2/8	21 3/8	6 9	Louisa County	IA	Everett Rickheim, Jr.	1998	1419
179 2/8	25 5/8 24 2/8	20 7/8	7 10	Cass County	IN	James Bubb	2000	1419

650

WHITETAIL DEER (NON-TYPICAL ANTLERS)

Minimum Score 155 Continued

SCORE	R MAIN BEAM L	INSIDE SPREAD	R POINTS L		AREA	STATE/ PROVINCE	HUNTER'S NAME	DATE	RANK
179 2/8	25 3/8 24 5/8	19 1/8	7	7	Pierce County	WI	David L. Monett	2001	1419
179 2/8	25 0/8 26 1/8	21 2/8	8	10	Eagle Hill	ALB	Dallas Kaiser	2004	1419
179 2/8	22 7/8 22 2/8	16 6/8	7	8	Bayfield County	WI	Dale T. Nixon	2004	1419
179 2/8	23 7/8 24 5/8	18 3/8	8	8	Ross County	OH	Paul Leroy Tull	2008	1419
179 1/8	26 0/8 26 3/8	20 1/8	6	8	Will County	IL	Michael Suggs	1990	1430
179 1/8	24 0/8 24 1/8	19 0/8	9	13	Wayne County	NY	John Regis, Jr.	1998	1430
179 1/8	24 1/8 23 4/8	17 2/8	6	7	St. Charles County	MO	Martin F. Meier	1999	1430
179 1/8	24 1/8 23 6/8	20 5/8	7	6	Chester County	PA	Richard Hash	2002	1430
*179 1/8	22 1/8 22 1/8	19 3/8	9	11	Scotland County	MO	Terry Bereitschaft	2004	1430
*179 1/8	24 1/8 23 0/8	17 6/8	6	10	Cass County	IL	Keith E. Holley	2004	1430
179 1/8	26 2/8 25 4/8	21 4/8	8	8	Clark County	KS	Dennis F. Craft	2004	1430
*179 1/8	23 2/8 22 5/8	18 1/8	10	8	Outagamie County	WI	Ross Schmidt	2006	1430
*179 1/8	26 0/8 25 6/8	18 1/8	7	7	Clark County	IL	Woody Bomgaars	2007	1430
179 1/8	23 2/8 21 4/8	16 3/8	5	10	Clay County	IA	Terry Betz	2008	1430
179 0/8	25 6/8 26 1/8	19 4/8	7	6	Brown County	IL	Larry Grant	1992	1440
179 0/8	24 0/8 23 5/8	20 0/8	6	7	Bearspaw	ALB	Rick Eliuk	1994	1440
179 0/8	23 7/8 24 3/8	17 6/8	8	6	Anoka County	MN	Jeff Schultz	1995	1440
179 0/8	24 4/8 20 7/8	20 4/8	4	11	Tazewell County	IL	Jeremy Crew	2002	1440
179 0/8	24 6/8 25 5/8	19 5/8	8	8	Rice County	KS	Aaron L. Horne	2003	1440
179 0/8	23 4/8 22 5/8	17 5/8	6	10	Hughes County	OK	Jason Tedder	2005	1440
178 7/8	21 7/8 24 1/8	16 0/8	8	7	Big Stone County	MN	Jerry Lundgren	1992	1446
178 7/8	26 1/8 25 3/8	20 0/8	9	7	Warren County	IA	Larry Hyler	1993	1446
178 7/8	27 4/8 26 4/8	23 6/8	9	10	Bayfield County	WI	Max Karl	1994	1446
178 7/8	23 5/8 23 7/8	19 4/8	7	6	Des Moines County	IA	Tim Wallin	2000	1446
178 7/8	26 2/8 25 4/8	20 5/8	6	6	Ripley County	IN	Ted McClintic	2002	1446
178 7/8	24 1/8 24 2/8	19 2/8	9	7	Douglas County	NE	Phil Kneifl	2003	1446
178 7/8	25 4/8 24 0/8	18 1/8	9	6	La Grange County	IN	Randy L. Bolen	2004	1446
*178 7/8	22 7/8 21 1/8	17 0/8	6	8	Bureau County	IL	Jerry Golgin	2005	1446
178 7/8	22 0/8 21 6/8	20 2/8	11	8	Somerset County	NJ	Robert Staudt, Jr.	2006	1446
178 7/8	29 6/8 29 4/8	17 6/8	8	10	Carroll County	OH	John M. Shockey	2008	1446
178 6/8	21 2/8 25 3/8	20 5/8	9	8	Lincoln County	SD	H. L. Tuggle	1975	1456
178 6/8	22 2/8 23 1/8	13 4/8	10	9	Madison County	IL	Michael B. Fenton	1984	1456
178 6/8	24 2/8 25 5/8	18 2/8	10	6	Clark County	OH	Jerry B. Sowards	1994	1456
178 6/8	23 0/8 22 3/8	19 1/8	8	10	Pike County	IL	Blake McCann	1995	1456
178 6/8	25 1/8 23 7/8	16 1/8	7	6	Plymouth County	IA	Jayson A. Gunn	2002	1456
178 6/8	20 6/8 21 3/8	17 0/8	11	15	Day County	SD	Gary A. Kuecker	2002	1456
*178 6/8	23 1/8 23 4/8	16 6/8	6	6	Buffalo County	WI	Joe Braun	2004	1456
178 6/8	26 3/8 26 1/8	17 7/8	7	7	Marion County	KS	John Dykes	2004	1456
*178 6/8	23 0/8 23 7/8	18 5/8	8	9	Waushara County	WI	Danny M. Duket	2005	1456
178 6/8	23 1/8 23 0/8	16 3/8	8	7	Pike County	IL	Joseph Tanis, Jr.	2007	1456
178 6/8	25 7/8 26 7/8	18 5/8	10	7	Delaware County	IN	Charles E. Boggs	2007	1456
178 6/8	23 6/8 20 6/8	20 4/8	10	9	Madison County	IL	Pat Cox	2007	1456
178 5/8	24 5/8 25 3/8	16 0/8	8	7	Clay County	IN	Jim Tracy	1989	1468
178 5/8	24 4/8 23 6/8	17 6/8	6	9	Ozaukee County	WI	Robert A. Wallock	1989	1468
178 5/8	25 0/8 26 3/8	17 3/8	10	9	Ozaukee County	WI	Gerald Berres	1991	1468
178 5/8	19 2/8 18 3/8	15 7/8	10	11	Erath County	TX	Michae D. Hendrick	1998	1468
178 5/8	24 6/8 25 2/8	17 0/8	9	7	Pendleton County	KY	Chris A. Niehaus	2003	1468
178 5/8	25 3/8 26 2/8	20 5/8	7	6	McHenry County	IL	Harold E. Wiese	2004	1468
178 5/8	25 3/8 25 1/8	18 4/8	9	6	Vigo County	IN	John Isbell	2004	1468
178 5/8	24 7/8 25 2/8	18 7/8	7	6	Washington County	OH	David Wallace	2004	1468
178 5/8	27 7/8 22 2/8	20 0/8	8	11	Harvey County	KS	Bill J. Zerger	2006	1468
*178 5/8	25 4/8 24 4/8	18 3/8	7	7	Johnson County	IA	Shane Bowers	2008	1468
178 4/8	22 1/8 23 6/8	17 0/8	12	11	Keokuk County	IA	Ron Turner	1983	1478
178 4/8	26 2/8 25 2/8	18 2/8	8	6	St. Croix County	WI	James Walsh	1988	1478
178 4/8	26 0/8 20 3/8	16 3/8	8	11	Tama County	IA	Duane Bossman	1997	1478
178 4/8	24 0/8 24 5/8	17 7/8	10	7	La Salle County	IL	Sean Thompson	2002	1478
178 4/8	25 0/8 25 1/8	19 1/8	10	9	Sumner County	KS	Brett L. Wiley	2005	1478
178 4/8	25 4/8 26 0/8	18 5/8	8	8	Holmes County	MS	Wynn Diggs	2006	1478
*178 4/8	24 3/8 23 6/8	18 7/8	10	8	Noble County	IN	Jason D. Hile	2008	1478
178 4/8	21 3/8 21 1/8	19 1/8	8	8	Livingston County	IL	Blake Bushman	2009	1478
*178 4/8	24 4/8 23 7/8	17 6/8	8	7	Anderson County	KS	Jon Holloway	2009	1478
*178 4/8	22 7/8 23 3/8	15 2/8	9	12	Woodson County	KS	Earl Stubblefield	2009	1478
178 3/8	23 3/8 22 7/8	19 6/8	8	8	Traverse County	MN	Roland L. Hausmann	1953	1488
178 3/8	25 1/8 24 4/8	19 6/8	8	10	Mineral County	MT	Gene Wensel	1981	1488
178 3/8	22 6/8 24 7/8	17 0/8	11	10	Finney County	KS	Randy Miller	1984	1488
178 3/8	25 6/8 24 6/8	21 6/8	7	7	Jefferson County	IL	Bill Kesler	1992	1488
178 3/8	27 0/8 27 4/8	19 3/8	7	7	Oconto County	WI	Ronald Thomson	1996	1488
178 3/8	24 2/8 23 6/8	17 3/8	10	10	Clay County	IA	Dennis D. Somers	2001	1488
178 3/8	25 0/8 24 5/8	18 0/8	6	11	Richland County	WI	Glenn M. Crary	2003	1488
178 3/8	23 4/8 23 0/8	17 7/8	8	9	Oconto County	WI	Todd Pszanka	2004	1488
*178 3/8	23 4/8 23 2/8	14 6/8	10	11	Pike County	IL	Scott W. Riley	2009	1488
178 3/8	21 5/8 22 0/8	17 4/8	7	10	St. Croix County	WI	Jason E. Nilssen	2010	1488
178 2/8	25 2/8 24 3/8	22 7/8	11	6	Clinton County	OH	Kenneth Pickard	2004	1498
178 2/8	23 7/8 25 0/8	15 2/8	9	7	Juneau County	WI	Scott Haske	2005	1498
*178 2/8	24 6/8 26 1/8	17 4/8	8	7	Peoria County	IL	Tim Shoff	2005	1498
178 2/8	26 0/8 25 6/8	16 6/8	5	9	Cherokee County	GA	Chad McCook	2007	1498
178 1/8	24 7/8 25 4/8	19 0/8	11	9	Montgomery County	OH	Jack B. Odum	1990	1502
178 1/8	22 7/8 21 3/8	15 0/8	9	10	Douglas County	WI	Greg A. Kaczmarski	1994	1502
178 1/8	25 5/8 26 4/8	20 3/8	7	9	Adams County	OH	David B. Hill	1998	1502
178 1/8	26 2/8 25 1/8	26 7/8	7	7	Brown County	OH	Kenneth J. Herbert	2002	1502
178 1/8	24 2/8 24 0/8	18 6/8	8	7	Wayne County	IL	Jay D. Harrison	2005	1502
178 1/8	23 1/8 24 7/8	15 4/8	6	9	Pepin County	WI	Brennan Fayerweather	2007	1502
178 1/8	22 0/8 22 4/8	19 2/8	7	7	Washington County	WI	Robert S. Loduha, Jr.	2007	1502
*178 1/8	25 3/8 25 2/8	23 2/8	7	7	Clark County	OH	Shane Farnsworth	2009	1502
178 0/8	24 1/8 25 4/8	19 0/8	8	6	Jefferson County	WI	Mike Leslie	1988	1510
178 0/8	24 7/8 25 3/8	14 0/8	9	8	Kenedy County	TX	Miguel Mireles	1991	1510
178 0/8	25 7/8 25 3/8	18 7/8	9	7	Jefferson County	KY	Arson Thornsbury, Sr.	1992	1510
178 0/8	25 6/8 24 2/8	18 3/8	7	9	Morgan County	CO	Douglas Nagle	1994	1510
178 0/8	25 6/8 28 1/8	21 3/8	6	7	Pottawattamie County	IA	Mike Feeney	1995	1510
*178 0/8	23 7/8 23 4/8	17 3/8	7	8	Cumberland County	ME	Bill Gardner	2005	1510
178 0/8	25 0/8 25 2/8	23 5/8	7	7	Vernon County	MO	Chad Butler	2006	1510
178 0/8	23 6/8 24 0/8	17 6/8	10	9	Johnson County	IA	James Cheney	2007	1510
*178 0/8	25 4/8 25 6/8	18 1/8	10	8	Sarpy County	NE	Chris Woodman	2007	1510
178 0/8	23 2/8 22 2/8	19 5/8	7	8	Brown County	OH	David W. Feck	2007	1510
177 7/8	28 2/8 27 0/8	18 3/8	6	6	Ross County	OH	Robert L. Elliott	1981	1520

651

WHITETAIL DEER (NON-TYPICAL ANTLERS)

Minimum Score 155 — Continued

SCORE	LENGTH OF MAIN BEAM R	L	INSIDE SPREAD	NUMBER OF POINTS R	L	AREA	STATE/PROVINCE	HUNTER'S NAME	DATE	RANK
177 7/8	26 5/8	25 2/8	18 2/8	8	7	Pottawatomie County	KS	Loyd C. Flowers	1983	1520
177 7/8	26 3/8	27 4/8	23 0/8	8	5	Shelby County	IL	Joe E. Carnahan, Jr.	1996	1520
177 7/8	24 0/8	25 5/8	25 3/8	7	6	Grayson County	TX	Mike Corzine	1999	1520
177 7/8	22 4/8	23 0/8	16 7/8	11	10	Bayfield County	WI	Michelle LaFon	2002	1520
*177 7/8	23 1/8	23 5/8	15 3/8	10	7	Parke County	IN	Steve Lancaster	2005	1520
*177 7/8	24 1/8	23 0/8	19 0/8	6	8	Comanche County	KS	John Hunsucker	2005	1520
177 7/8	23 5/8	25 0/8	21 7/8	8	7	E. Carroll Parish	LA	Louis Lambiotte	2006	1520
*177 7/8	24 2/8	24 0/8	15 2/8	8	10	Van Buren County	MI	John L. Franks	2008	1520
177 6/8	21 4/8	22 2/8	18 1/8	10	9	Pope County	MN	Roger Tollefson	1977	1529
177 6/8	23 0/8	21 2/8	16 0/8	6	13	Delaware County	OH	Ronald Eugene Murphy	1983	1529
177 6/8	22 0/8	22 4/8	20 4/8	9	8	Des Moines County	IA	Dave Bremhorst	1994	1529
177 6/8	20 7/8	20 3/8	18 1/8	10	11	St. Louis County	MO	Keith Gunn	1994	1529
177 6/8	24 0/8	23 4/8	18 0/8	7	7	St. Croix County	WI	Charles T. Hutera	1997	1529
177 6/8	22 1/8	20 3/8	17 7/8	10	5	Minnehaha County	SD	William J. Horner	1999	1529
177 6/8	21 6/8	21 7/8	15 5/8	11	11	Waupaca County	WI	Dennis Haase	2000	1529
177 6/8	23 6/8	23 4/8	16 6/8	6	9	Chase County	KS	Les Julian	2002	1529
177 6/8	22 5/8	22 7/8	16 6/8	9	7	Butler County	PA	Harold Watterson	2002	1529
177 6/8	25 4/8	25 5/8	20 0/8	7	6	Leavenworth County	KS	Chad Fortner	2002	1529
*177 6/8	24 5/8	23 1/8	19 5/8	11	6	Barber County	KS	Sandra Simpson	2007	1529
177 6/8	23 4/8	26 2/8	16 2/8	9	5	Wicomico County	MD	Glenn Steele	2008	1529
*177 6/8	26 0/8	24 5/8	19 1/8	7	6	Ford County	KS	Heath Hill	2009	1529
*177 6/8	26 2/8	26 1/8	17 4/8	8	6	Buffalo County	WI	Barry J. Orne	2009	1529
177 5/8	24 4/8	23 6/8	21 0/8	8	9	Menard County	IL	Donald Alwerdt	1993	1543
177 5/8	25 0/8	24 2/8	17 4/8	5	6	McLean County	IL	Scott Darnall	2001	1543
177 5/8	23 1/8	24 0/8	18 2/8	8	6	Dane County	WI	James A. Zbigniewicz	2002	1543
177 5/8	26 3/8	25 0/8	17 4/8	9	7	Schuyler County	IL	Timothy Barnes	2005	1543
*177 5/8	20 3/8	20 7/8	13 4/8	9	13	St. Louis County	MO	Lou Salamone	2005	1543
*177 5/8	23 4/8	24 5/8	18 5/8	10	9	Holmes County	MS	Adam McCurdy	2005	1543
177 5/8	25 2/8	23 5/8	17 6/8	8	11	Buffalo County	WI	Eugene Mancl	2006	1543
177 5/8	23 2/8	24 2/8	17 2/8	10	6	Johnson County	IA	Mike McGowan	2006	1543
177 5/8	25 7/8	24 7/8	19 2/8	8	8	St. Joseph County	IN	Daniel L. Shoop	2009	1543
177 5/8	23 0/8	22 6/8	16 1/8	7	12	Linn County	IA	Allen Stueck	2009	1543
177 4/8	23 4/8	22 6/8	18 1/8	7	8	Flathead County	MT	Jerry Karsky	1972	1553
177 4/8	26 1/8	25 2/8	18 7/8	8	6	Butler County	OH	Michael Rumpler	1994	1553
177 4/8	19 6/8	22 0/8	15 6/8	14	7	Beaumont	ALB	Jake Goodwin	1998	1553
177 4/8	25 6/8	25 0/8	18 3/8	10	5	Todd County	KY	Mark A. Shanklin	1999	1553
177 4/8	26 6/8	26 5/8	16 6/8	8	5	Woodbury County	IA	Chris L. Groves	2000	1553
177 4/8	25 6/8	24 2/8	18 3/8	8	6	Riley County	KS	Christopher Thurlow	2000	1553
177 4/8	24 6/8	24 6/8	17 2/8	8	8	Cass County	IL	Chet B. Hollar	2003	1553
177 4/8	24 6/8	24 0/8	21 0/8	6	8	Winnebago County	IL	James R. Petersen	2003	1553
177 4/8	25 0/8	25 3/8	18 6/8	8	9	McHenry County	IL	George G. Gilpin	2004	1553
*177 4/8	25 5/8	24 4/8	13 5/8	8	8	Warren County	KY	Brad Cowles	2005	1553
*177 4/8	21 5/8	22 2/8	21 7/8	8	6	Guthrie County	IA	Billy Davis	2005	1553
177 3/8	25 2/8	22 7/8	16 1/8	15	19	Pike County	IL	Daniel Doran	1992	1564
177 3/8	23 2/8	24 2/8	18 4/8	10	10	Marengo County	AL	David Darnell	1997	1564
177 3/8	25 0/8	19 1/8	19 1/8	5	9	Washington County	NE	Keith Southworth	2002	1564
177 3/8	24 3/8	24 2/8	15 4/8	9	5	Camden County	MO	Andy J. Hawsey	2004	1564
177 3/8	23 0/8	22 5/8	16 7/8	7	7	Charles Mix County	SD	Charles Zacharias	2006	1564
*177 3/8	24 4/8	24 5/8	21 1/8	10	7	Parkland	ALB	Troy Dzioba	2006	1564
177 3/8	25 2/8	24 4/8	20 5/8	7	8	Jefferson County	NE	Marvin L. Stelling	2007	1564
177 2/8	23 4/8	25 2/8	16 1/8	7	9	Pierce County	WI	Jason Holt	2003	1571
177 2/8	24 5/8	25 5/8	16 1/8	7	9	McHenry County	IL	Michael R. Neri	2006	1571
177 1/8	23 0/8	22 6/8	18 6/8	7	12	Pope County	MN	Doyle Anderson	1988	1573
177 1/8	25 0/8	27 1/8	19 6/8	8	9	Delaware County	OH	Jeff Miller	1993	1573
177 1/8	22 6/8	22 4/8	14 5/8	8	9	Warren County	IA	Randy Manuel	1998	1573
177 1/8	25 0/8	23 6/8	21 0/8	9	9	Allamakee County	IA	Robert Billings	1998	1573
177 1/8	24 2/8	24 0/8	17 3/8	6	7	Linn County	IA	Mark Fencl	1999	1573
177 1/8	26 4/8	25 7/8	20 6/8	8	9	Sawyer County	WI	Brad Beise	2000	1573
177 1/8	24 5/8	26 2/8	18 5/8	6	9	Johnston County	OK	Casey Estep	2001	1573
177 1/8	22 4/8	22 7/8	21 6/8	7	7	Brown County	SD	Mark White	2001	1573
*177 1/8	24 2/8	23 3/8	19 3/8	10	9	Missoula County	MT	Daniel Westberg	2007	1573
*177 1/8	22 6/8	21 0/8	22 3/8	9	10	Saunders County	NE	Frank Jirovsky	2007	1573
177 1/8	22 7/8	22 2/8	17 3/8	10	12	Canadian County	OK	Dale Miller	2008	1573
*177 1/8	25 4/8	25 4/8	20 1/8	7	7	Wyandot County	OH	James A. Thiel	2009	1573
177 0/8	25 2/8	25 6/8	18 6/8	7	9	Rock County	WI	Kirk C. Douglas	1987	1585
177 0/8	24 3/8	22 6/8	17 6/8	7	9	Boone County	IA	Robert J. Van Roekel	1989	1585
177 0/8	24 0/8	24 3/8	16 0/8	7	7	Olmsted County	MN	Leo Kuisle	1991	1585
177 0/8	20 4/8	21 4/8	16 2/8	9	8	Buffalo County	WI	Steve Bautch	2001	1585
177 0/8	22 3/8	20 2/8	21 5/8	11	11	Grayson County	TX	Dale K. Moses	2002	1585
177 0/8	25 5/8	24 0/8	20 1/8	8	7	Morrow County	OH	Kevin Squires	2003	1585
*177 0/8	23 2/8	24 0/8	15 4/8	7	7	Trempealeau County	WI	Jon Peters	2003	1585
177 0/8	27 3/8	28 4/8	23 2/8	6	8	Schuyler County	IL	Mike Smith	2003	1585
176 7/8	24 2/8	23 7/8	20 7/8	8	8	Suffolk County	NY	James Matuszewski	1994	1593
176 7/8	25 6/8	24 4/8	20 4/8	9	8	Johnson County	IA	Gary E. Rohret	2000	1593
176 7/8	25 1/8	24 5/8	16 7/8	7	6	Wayne County	OH	Jason E. Taylor	2002	1593
176 7/8	22 7/8	22 2/8	16 4/8	8	9	Ogle County	IL	Michael O'Malley	2003	1593
176 7/8	20 3/8	22 0/8	19 6/8	12	9	Halifax County	NC	Jonathan Brent Mabrey	2005	1593
*176 7/8	23 2/8	22 3/8	17 0/8	9	11	Tippecanoe County	IN	Zach Frey	2007	1593
*176 7/8	24 0/8	23 4/8	21 5/8	8	8	Allegheny County	PA	Glenn E. Smith	2008	1593
*176 7/8	23 3/8	23 4/8	16 2/8	8	8	Crosby County	TX	R. W. Chisum	2010	1593
176 6/8	28 4/8	28 2/8	19 4/8	8	9	Dodge County	WI	Erwin C. Koehler	1957	1601
176 6/8	29 0/8	26 3/8	22 3/8	7	5	Allamakee County	IA	Jim Dyer	1993	1601
176 6/8	25 7/8	25 7/8	20 0/8	7	7	Loudon County	TN	Charles R. Brewster, Sr.	2001	1601
176 6/8	22 4/8	23 2/8	18 2/8	7	10	Pawnee County	KS	Robert O. Faris II	2002	1601
176 6/8	25 0/8	25 6/8	19 0/8	7	6	Stark County	OH	Tom Kovacik II	2003	1601
176 6/8	26 3/8	26 7/8	17 5/8	6	6	Crawford County	WI	Joshua J. Selck	2005	1601
176 6/8	24 0/8	23 3/8	16 4/8	7	7	Wood County	WI	jason L. Lang	2005	1601
*176 6/8	27 2/8	27 2/8	19 4/8	6	7	Scott County	IA	Doug Buchanan	2005	1601
176 6/8	23 6/8	23 4/8	16 0/8	8	5	Dane County	WI	Casey Preimesberger	2006	1601
176 5/8	22 2/8	21 3/8	16 4/8	10	7	Day County	SD	Lonnie L. Heuer	1987	1610
176 5/8	24 1/8	24 0/8	19 4/8	8	8	Polk County	WI	Jesse Tonn	1991	1610
176 5/8	25 1/8	24 6/8	18 7/8	6	9	Pickaway County	OH	Jerry L. Rhoades	1992	1610
176 5/8	27 2/8	26 3/8	18 5/8	7	6	Parke County	IN	Shain A. Loveland	2000	1610
176 5/8	24 0/8	24 0/8	17 5/8	6	7	Chickasaw County	IA	Randy Fisher	2002	1610
176 5/8	25 7/8	24 7/8	16 2/8	7	7	Mercer County	MO	Scott Ferguson	2002	1610

652

WHITETAIL DEER (NON-TYPICAL ANTLERS)

Minimum Score 155   Continued

SCORE	LENGTH OF R MAIN BEAM L	INSIDE SPREAD	NUMBER OF R POINTS L	AREA	STATE/ PROVINCE	HUNTER'S NAME	DATE	RANK
176 5/8	30 2/8	30 3/8	21 0/8	6	5	Johnson County	NE	Robbie Pride	2004	1610
176 5/8	25 7/8	27 3/8	18 2/8	9	7	Logan County	WV	Patrick Donahue	2008	1610
176 4/8	23 2/8	21 7/8	17 1/8	9	8	Macon County	IL	Dave Elliot	1997	1618
176 4/8	25 3/8	25 3/8	16 2/8	9	7	Coles County	IL	Thomas Dobbs	2003	1618
176 4/8	23 6/8	22 6/8	15 5/8	10	7	Page County	IA	Chris Barton	2004	1618
176 3/8	24 6/8	25 4/8	20 3/8	8	8	Greene County	OH	Leroy M. Thompson	1982	1621
176 3/8	25 6/8	26 2/8	17 6/8	6	9	Berrien County	MI	Ron Dahms	1999	1621
176 3/8	20 7/8	22 4/8	15 5/8	8	6	Ogle County	IL	Marvin A. Longenecke	1999	1621
176 3/8	20 3/8	21 3/8	18 0/8	7	6	Fulton County	IL	Ronald Potteiger	2000	1621
*176 3/8	22 7/8	22 7/8	18 2/8	6	8	Buffalo County	WI	Jerry Riley	2006	1621
*176 3/8	22 6/8	22 5/8	15 5/8	7	7	Floyd County	IA	Chris Hohenfield	2007	1621
*176 3/8	23 0/8	24 6/8	15 4/8	8	8	Scotland County	MO	Jade Price	2007	1621
176 2/8	22 2/8	22 5/8	15 2/8	7	8	Winnebago County	WI	Todd A. Pitsch	1994	1628
176 2/8	24 3/8	24 4/8	21 1/8	6	11	Calhoun County	IL	Paul Quirk	2003	1628
*176 2/8	24 1/8	24 1/8	20 0/8	7	6	Barber County	KS	Jason R. Reed	2008	1628
176 1/8	22 0/8	23 3/8	21 4/8	7	6	Brandon	MAN	Larry J. Pollock	1980	1631
176 1/8	27 0/8	27 6/8	20 4/8	4	7	Pike County	OH	Jim Widdig	1997	1631
176 1/8	22 2/8	25 4/8	17 4/8	10	8	Marshall County	IL	William J. Starry	1997	1631
176 1/8	25 2/8	25 5/8	17 5/8	7	10	Grayson County	TX	John A. Evans	2000	1631
176 1/8	23 3/8	23 4/8	15 0/8	11	8	Mingo County	WV	Charles Wallace	2004	1631
176 1/8	24 7/8	25 0/8	19 0/8	8	5	Greene County	IN	Tim Neal	2005	1631
*176 1/8	20 4/8	21 1/8	14 4/8	10	7	Hand County	SD	Dylan Deuter	2009	1631
176 0/8	22 6/8	22 3/8	21 7/8	6	7	Todd County	MN	Richard L. Boelter	1993	1638
176 0/8	26 0/8	27 1/8	24 4/8	9	9	Linn County	KS	Tipton Cook	1993	1638
176 0/8	23 2/8	24 2/8	20 1/8	8	9	DeKalb County	IL	Kevin M. Grivetti	1995	1638
176 0/8	23 4/8	21 0/8	21 7/8	8	8	Dane County	WI	Randy Schmid	1999	1638
176 0/8	27 6/8	28 3/8	23 0/8	9	6	Warren County	IL	Glenn W. Hickok	2001	1638
176 0/8	26 4/8	26 5/8	19 4/8	5	6	Allamakee County	IA	Joe Kriener	2005	1638
*176 0/8	26 4/8	25 4/8	20 6/8	7	9	Page County	IA	Don H. Mabry	2007	1638
*176 0/8	22 7/8	22 6/8	17 7/8	9	7	Adams County	IL	Michael Hunter	2008	1638
176 0/8	23 0/8	26 6/8	20 3/8	6	5	Iowa County	WI	Brian Pete	2008	1638
176 0/8	21 1/8	21 4/8	18 1/8	6	7	Effingham County	IL	Dennis Mason	2009	1638
175 7/8	27 4/8	28 1/8	23 3/8	8	7	Guernsey County	OH	Jack L. Milligan	1971	1648
175 7/8	24 3/8	25 1/8	17 4/8	9	8	Freeborn County	MN	Douglas Swank	1979	1648
175 7/8	23 3/8	22 2/8	17 1/8	7	7	Clark County	IL	Alan Lee	1995	1648
175 7/8	23 6/8	24 7/8	19 6/8	5	6	Yankton County	SD	Dan Rederick	1997	1648
175 7/8	25 4/8	26 4/8	18 3/8	7	8	Greene County	IL	Wendell W. Koontz	2003	1648
175 7/8	23 4/8	23 1/8	18 7/8	7	7	La Salle County	IL	Francis A. Kelley	2004	1648
175 7/8	23 4/8	22 2/8	18 1/8	7	9	Polk County	IA	Jerald W. Osborne, Jr.	2005	1648
175 7/8	24 6/8	24 3/8	18 5/8	9	9	Buffalo County	WI	Jeff Keogh	2006	1648
175 7/8	24 0/8	23 3/8	17 4/8	8	8	Adams County	IA	Cheyenne Foote	2008	1648
175 6/8	22 4/8	22 2/8	19 2/8	5	7	Rush County	IN	Kent D. Clark	1991	1657
175 6/8	25 1/8	24 7/8	17 5/8	9	9	Sangamon County	IL	Brian Bergmann	1994	1657
175 6/8	25 7/8	25 5/8	19 2/8	10	5	Orange County	IN	Mark Verble	1995	1657
175 6/8	26 3/8	25 7/8	21 6/8	6	8	Fond du Lac County	WI	Willard Nolan	1997	1657
*175 6/8	23 7/8	22 7/8	18 4/8	7	7	Dunn County	WI	Adam Kopras	2003	1657
*175 6/8	27 4/8	28 2/8	17 5/8	8	8	Graves County	KY	Jason Burchard	2003	1657
175 6/8	26 1/8	23 7/8	18 0/8	6	7	Clark County	IL	Brad Conine	2004	1657
175 6/8	22 0/8	23 0/8	18 7/8	7	11	Olmsted County	MN	Bryan King	2009	1657
175 6/8	25 2/8	24 5/8	19 1/8	6	7	Dane County	WI	Joshua Huberd	2009	1657
175 5/8	29 7/8	30 4/8	21 2/8	6	4	Sarpy County	NE	Steve Houston	1985	1666
175 5/8	22 4/8	24 2/8	19 2/8	8	8	Greene County	IL	Josh Davis	2000	1666
175 5/8	27 2/8	26 7/8	18 5/8	5	5	Jay County	IN	Jeremy L. Davis	2001	1666
175 5/8	23 5/8	24 7/8	16 5/8	6	8	Johnson County	KS	Kevin Hansen	2002	1666
175 5/8	28 1/8	28 0/8	21 4/8	7	7	Buffalo County	WI	Dave Beeler	2004	1666
175 5/8	21 6/8	20 5/8	18 7/8	5	9	Lawrence County	IL	John Barrick	2004	1666
*175 5/8	23 3/8	23 4/8	18 5/8	7	8	Richmond County	GA	William Claude Goodwin, Jr.	2005	1666
175 5/8	21 5/8	22 0/8	13 5/8	12	13	Highland County	VA	Ricky Moats	2006	1666
*175 5/8	22 3/8	22 7/8	16 5/8	9	10	Trempealeau County	WI	Dan Puls	2007	1666
175 5/8	24 2/8	24 0/8	18 5/8	6	7	Trempealeau County	WI	Randy Symicek	2007	1666
*175 5/8	22 5/8	23 1/8	18 5/8	7	8	Schuyler County	MO	Michael Popek	2008	1666
175 4/8	22 4/8	22 7/8	19 2/8	10	10	Woodbury County	IA	Everett Gothier	1962	1677
175 4/8	28 4/8	27 5/8	20 6/8	7	7	Belmont County	OH	Dan Clutter	1985	1677
175 4/8	26 6/8	25 4/8	23 2/8	13	7	Fairfield County	OH	Ron Perdew	1992	1677
175 4/8	23 0/8	22 2/8	18 1/8	6	10	Linn County	IA	Ken Miller	2001	1677
175 4/8	26 7/8	25 3/8	19 1/8	6	7	Kane County	IL	Michael J. Hanratty	2002	1677
*175 4/8	25 6/8	25 2/8	18 3/8	9	9	Dickey County	ND	Justin Oss	2006	1677
175 4/8	26 6/8	28 3/8	18 6/8	9	10	Fulton County	IL	John Pliska	2006	1677
*175 4/8	23 7/8	22 7/8	21 4/8	8	8	Todd County	MN	Levi Kneisl	2008	1677
175 4/8	25 3/8	24 2/8	19 2/8	11	4	Waukesha County	WI	John Paul Mesching	2008	1677
175 3/8	24 5/8	23 7/8	20 1/8	8	7	Grant County	MN	Lee Offerdahl	1972	1686
175 3/8	26 2/8	25 3/8	14 4/8	8	11	Buffalo County	WI	Timothy L. Brommer	1984	1686
175 3/8	23 4/8	24 3/8	19 6/8	7	9	Salem County	NJ	Richard Wendt	1985	1686
175 3/8	25 4/8	23 2/8	16 5/8	8	8	Hennepin County	MN	Robert R. Herman	1993	1686
175 3/8	24 6/8	23 5/8	19 7/8	6	8	Schoolcraft County	MI	Jim Hedglen	1995	1686
175 3/8	24 2/8	23 3/8	18 4/8	6	6	Elk County	KS	Gary Fritzler	1997	1686
175 3/8	24 5/8	24 6/8	20 0/8	8	8	Sarpy County	NE	Kevin Indra	2000	1686
175 3/8	25 5/8	26 2/8	19 0/8	8	6	Forest County	WI	Walter E. Freeman	2001	1686
175 3/8	24 3/8	23 4/8	19 5/8	10	8	Ward County	ND	Todd Aberle	2001	1686
175 3/8	22 5/8	23 1/8	17 2/8	8	8	Yorkton	SAS	Ron Vandermeulen	2001	1686
*175 3/8	24 5/8	24 5/8	18 7/8	7	9	Marquette County	WI	Daniel L. Thome	2002	1686
175 3/8	26 4/8	25 4/8	23 2/8	8	6	Will County	IL	Kenneth Capps	2004	1686
175 3/8	25 5/8	25 0/8	17 6/8	7	8	Refugio County	TX	Brent A. Tucker	2005	1686
175 3/8	27 5/8	28 0/8	23 2/8	5	7	Meade County	KS	John Garinger	2005	1686
175 3/8	27 4/8	27 3/8	20 2/8	7	6	Edgar County	IL	Gene A. Anderson	2006	1686
175 2/8	26 1/8	26 0/8	17 1/8	9	7	McHenry County	IL	Richard G. Hickey	1988	1701
175 2/8	22 0/8	21 6/8	21 1/8	9	9	Jackson County	MI	Scott A. Weaver	1996	1701
175 2/8	28 3/8	28 0/8	22 1/8	5	8	Howard County	MD	Robert W. Evans	1998	1701
175 2/8	21 2/8	23 1/8	20 1/8	7	5	Marquette County	WI	Newell Easley	1999	1701
175 2/8	25 0/8	25 6/8	18 2/8	8	8	Lee County	IL	Mark H. Swegle	1999	1701
175 2/8	20 5/8	15 7/8	18 5/8	6	15	Douglas County	WI	Dr. Michael R. Lawler	2003	1701
*175 2/8	25 0/8	26 3/8	20 7/8	7	8	Miami County	OH	Richard Hunt	2003	1701
*175 2/8	27 6/8	26 1/8	23 1/8	6	6	Labette County	KS	Jaret J. Drummond	2003	1701
*175 2/8	25 5/8	26 7/8	21 4/8	8	6	Hendricks County	IN	William Walters	2008	1701
175 2/8	26 6/8	26 4/8	19 0/8	11	8	Marion County	KY	Chris Hensley	2009	1701

653

WHITETAIL DEER (NON-TYPICAL ANTLERS)

Minimum Score 155   Continued

SCORE	LENGTH OF R MAIN BEAM L	INSIDE SPREAD	NUMBER OF R POINTS L	AREA	STATE/ PROVINCE	HUNTER'S NAME	DATE	RANK
175 2/8	26 4/8 24 6/8	16 5/8	6 5	Stephenson County	IL	Ron Kaderly	2009	1701
175 1/8	26 4/8 25 1/8	20 0/8	6 7	Dubuque County	IA	Gregory Klein	1983	1712
175 1/8	24 4/8 23 3/8	17 2/8	9 10	Cherokee County	KS	Darren Collins	1988	1712
175 1/8	25 7/8 25 2/8	18 3/8	6 8	Franklin County	KS	Dennis N. Ballweg	1988	1712
175 1/8	24 6/8 24 5/8	18 6/8	7 9	Wayne County	MO	Jesse Whittley, Jr.	1988	1712
175 1/8	25 6/8 26 5/8	19 0/8	6 6	Chase County	KS	Greg Windler	1988	1712
175 1/8	23 3/8 15 6/8	23 1/8	9 9	Clinton County	IA	Mark Schutt	1993	1712
175 1/8	23 7/8 23 2/8	16 4/8	7 8	Roseau County	MN	Ernest Janousek	1994	1712
175 1/8	24 3/8 25 6/8	18 4/8	13 9	Jersey County	IL	Terry Dale	1994	1712
175 1/8	24 4/8 26 3/8	16 3/8	9 6	Dane County	WI	Kevin Tennant	1998	1712
175 1/8	27 3/8 26 7/8	20 3/8	5 5	McHenry County	IL	Don Hansen	1999	1712
175 1/8	25 3/8 25 4/8	22 3/8	7 7	Union County	IA	Marc Olson	2001	1712
175 1/8	24 6/8 24 4/8	18 3/8	6 7	Manitowoc County	WI	Douglas Buchholz	2002	1712
175 1/8	26 4/8 28 5/8	21 4/8	7 7	Bullitt County	KY	Gary W. Gilliatt	2003	1712
*175 1/8	23 7/8 24 0/8	17 2/8	9 6	Lincoln County	MO	Ron Burr	2003	1712
175 1/8	25 5/8 30 3/8	17 4/8	10 7	Jackson County	IL	Tim Cobin	2003	1712
*175 1/8	22 3/8 21 3/8	17 5/8	9 7	Winona County	MN	Derek Bosteter	2004	1712
175 1/8	22 4/8 24 0/8	17 4/8	9 5	Schuyler County	IL	Gaylen Michael	2004	1712
*175 1/8	23 5/8 23 2/8	17 0/8	6 8	Lyon County	IA	Gerald Jason Lems	2006	1712
175 1/8	21 3/8 22 1/8	14 5/8	8 9	Jackson County	WI	Peter Koxlien	2007	1712
175 0/8	26 2/8 28 3/8	21 2/8	5 6	Jersey County	IL	Judy Kovar	1988	1731
175 0/8	23 2/8 23 5/8	18 4/8	7 6	Pottawatomie County	KS	Tod Edwin Anthony	1993	1731
175 0/8	21 3/8 21 3/8	14 2/8	8 7	Roane County	WV	Carroll Rogers	1994	1731
175 0/8	23 2/8 24 0/8	19 5/8	7 5	Outagamie County	WI	Ted Louis Peterson	2004	1731
*175 0/8	25 7/8 25 0/8	17 6/8	7 8	Scott County	IA	Jerrod Clark	2004	1731
*175 0/8	24 4/8 25 4/8	17 3/8	8 9	Putnam County	MO	Drew Voss	2005	1731
*175 0/8	24 3/8 25 5/8	19 3/8	8 7	Dane County	WI	Darryl Ford	2006	1731
*175 0/8	25 2/8 22 5/8	20 5/8	8 11	Ramsey County	MN	Marlene Odahlen-Hinz	2006	1731
175 0/8	28 1/8 28 3/8	19 6/8	6 5	Allamakee County	IA	Lee J. Keim	2007	1731
175 0/8	25 2/8 25 5/8	17 4/8	5 7	Sheboygan County	WI	Michael Gregoire	2009	1731
174 7/8	26 6/8 25 3/8	19 7/8	9 9	Waseca County	MN	Robert Barrie	1974	1741
174 7/8	25 5/8 27 3/8	19 2/8	10 6	Des Moines County	IA	Tom Lappe	1985	1741
174 7/8	23 7/8 22 1/8	16 4/8	7 11	Branch County	MI	Roy D. Grigsby	1994	1741
174 7/8	22 5/8 22 5/8	20 0/8	6 7	Goliad County	TX	Mark Thompson	1995	1741
174 7/8	22 4/8 22 1/8	16 0/8	9 8	Spokane County	WA	Gustav Daniel Wittenberg	2003	1741
174 7/8	22 6/8 22 2/8	17 1/8	6 8	Jefferson County	IN	Art Moystner	2003	1741
174 7/8	23 5/8 23 0/8	18 6/8	6 8	Wright County	MN	Jerry Goodale	2003	1741
174 7/8	25 1/8 26 0/8	18 1/8	6 10	De Kalb County	GA	Taylor McCann	2004	1741
*174 7/8	24 1/8 23 5/8	17 4/8	8 8	Washington County	KS	Craig Kochenderfer	2008	1741
*174 7/8	25 1/8 23 4/8	18 7/8	8 11	Mitchell County	KS	Curtis Keller	2008	1741
*174 7/8	24 5/8 25 2/8	17 6/8	8 8	Marshall County	IN	John M. Bellman	2009	1741
174 6/8	22 2/8 21 5/8	19 0/8	7 7	Columbia County	WI	Robert L. Lex	1992	1752
174 6/8	22 0/8 22 2/8	18 2/8	13 9	Carroll County	MO	Danny Davies	1994	1752
174 6/8	24 0/8 23 3/8	21 0/8	7 8	Pulaski County	VA	Gary Blackwell	1997	1752
174 6/8	25 6/8 26 3/8	20 4/8	6 6	Menard County	IL	Ron Wadsworth	1998	1752
174 6/8	25 4/8 24 7/8	19 2/8	8 7	Jackson County	IL	Lewis W. Henry, Jr.	1998	1752
174 6/8	24 6/8 25 5/8	17 5/8	8 7	Geary County	KS	Don Herter	2004	1752
174 6/8	23 2/8 22 4/8	18 2/8	6 9	Douglas County	MN	Rodney McClellan	2005	1752
174 6/8	23 1/8 24 5/8	26 5/8	7 7	Jefferson County	OH	Kenneth W. Day	2006	1752
174 6/8	23 6/8 23 4/8	18 5/8	7 8	Madison County	IA	Ronald D. Falke	2008	1752
174 6/8	26 3/8 24 5/8	19 0/8	6 8	Trempealeau County	WI	Douglas Terpstra	2009	1752
174 6/8	26 2/8 26 2/8	22 3/8	8 7	Graham County	KS	Anita Kerbaugh	2009	1752
174 5/8	23 3/8 21 6/8	16 0/8	9 9	Harvey County	KS	Richard Krehbiel	1995	1763
174 5/8	24 4/8 25 5/8	20 1/8	7 6	St. Marys County	MD	Robert Anthony Martin	2000	1763
174 5/8	21 0/8 23 6/8	19 4/8	9 5	Hennepin County	MN	Dan Burns	2003	1763
174 5/8	25 2/8 25 6/8	16 3/8	5 5	Madison County	MO	Doug Rehkop	2004	1763
*174 5/8	23 0/8 21 7/8	17 0/8	9 11	Spink County	SD	John Soost	2006	1763
*174 5/8	26 2/8 25 0/8	17 4/8	9 9	Muskingum County	OH	James Gregory	2009	1763
174 4/8	24 0/8 25 4/8	22 5/8	5 6	Otter Tail County	MN	Don Oelschlager	1976	1769
174 4/8	22 1/8 22 3/8	16 4/8	8 8	Benson County	ND	Curtis A. Ehnert	1977	1769
174 4/8	21 1/8 21 0/8	17 2/8	8 9	Brown County	IL	Angela Vogel	1988	1769
174 4/8	24 4/8 23 3/8	18 0/8	7 9	Dodge County	WI	Cory Ewert	2004	1769
174 4/8	22 7/8 22 7/8	17 7/8	6 8	Marinette County	WI	Chuck Druckrey	2004	1769
174 4/8	26 1/8 26 3/8	18 6/8	7 7	Prowers County	CO	Newell Easley	2005	1769
174 4/8	25 2/8 22 6/8	21 4/8	8 9	Carroll County	IL	Tony Smith	2005	1769
*174 4/8	23 3/8 22 5/8	15 7/8	12 9	Vermillion County	IN	Chad Garzolini	2007	1769
174 4/8	23 1/8 24 2/8	18 2/8	5 10	De Kalb County	GA	Kyle Ellis	2007	1769
174 4/8	24 3/8 24 5/8	18 4/8	9 6	Jackson County	IA	Matt Herrig	2008	1769
*174 4/8	25 5/8 25 4/8	28 5/8	6 8	Christian County	KY	Kevin E. Testement	2009	1769
174 3/8	26 0/8 25 7/8	18 2/8	9 7	Vinton County	OH	Jack McConnell	1982	1780
174 3/8	21 3/8 22 4/8	17 2/8	7 9	Franklin County	KY	Michael W. Wilson	1985	1780
174 3/8	28 4/8 28 3/8	22 2/8	6 8	Winnebago County	IL	Dave Fisher	1986	1780
174 3/8	22 1/8 21 7/8	18 2/8	8 9	Marshall County	MN	Barry Liimatainen	1993	1780
174 3/8	25 4/8 24 3/8	16 1/8	9 7	Sauk County	WI	John Skau, Jr.	1995	1780
174 3/8	29 0/8 28 1/8	22 6/8	7 5	Scott County	MN	Joshua Gross	1996	1780
174 3/8	25 0/8 25 4/8	21 5/8	9 8	Love County	OK	G. C. Flanagan	1999	1780
174 3/8	25 0/8 25 2/8	17 0/8	7 9	Knox County	OH	Craig Campbell	2000	1780
174 3/8	23 1/8 24 4/8	21 2/8	12 9	Pike County	IL	Rodney W. Staake	2004	1780
174 3/8	23 6/8 24 5/8	16 0/8	10 10	Fulton County	GA	Brian M. Taylor	2008	1780
*174 3/8	26 2/8 25 5/8	18 4/8	8 7	Barber County	KS	Sal Collemi	2009	1780
174 3/8	23 7/8 24 7/8	17 0/8	7 8	Randall County	TX	Brandon Ray	2009	1780
174 3/8	25 4/8 22 3/8	19 1/8	5 9	Hartford County	CT	Michael Roberts	2010	1780
174 2/8	26 6/8 25 1/8	19 7/8	9 6	Clay County	IA	Darrell Magnussen	1962	1793
174 2/8	22 3/8 24 0/8	16 0/8	10 9	Rawlins County	KS	Curtis Walston	1991	1793
174 2/8	22 3/8 22 4/8	16 1/8	6 7	Greene County	MO	Norm Nothnagel	1993	1793
174 2/8	22 0/8 22 2/8	19 3/8	6 8	Spokane County	WA	Eric Choker	1996	1793
174 2/8	25 2/8 24 3/8	24 3/8	7 8	Monroe County	NY	Scott Laney	2000	1793
174 2/8	23 7/8 23 5/8	20 2/8	9 8	Rock County	WI	Dan Pann	2001	1793
174 2/8	23 4/8 23 3/8	19 0/8	6 7	Knox County	MO	Aaron Parrish	2002	1793
174 2/8	24 1/8 24 2/8	17 6/8	6 7	Clarke County	IA	Raymond Leo Showers II	2002	1793
174 2/8	24 6/8 26 2/8	19 7/8	9 9	Miami County	OH	Steve Thokey	2003	1793
174 2/8	27 0/8 26 2/8	17 6/8	8 6	Litchfield County	CT	Alex L. Simko	2003	1793
*174 2/8	23 7/8 23 4/8	20 1/8	8 7	Washington County	IL	Coty Frieman	2004	1793
174 2/8	24 2/8 25 2/8	17 1/8	6 7	Howard County	IA	Craig P. Fencl	2004	1793
174 2/8	27 3/8 26 1/8	19 0/8	7 6	Marathon County	WI	John Gorman	2005	1793

WHITETAIL DEER (NON-TYPICAL ANTLERS)

Minimum Score 155 — Continued

SCORE	LENGTH OF R MAIN BEAM L	INSIDE SPREAD	NUMBER OF R POINTS L		AREA	STATE/PROVINCE	HUNTER'S NAME	DATE	RANK
174 2/8	23 6/8	24 1/8	18 5/8	7	6	Tippecanoe County	IN	Ryan Mounts	2005	1793
*174 2/8	23 3/8	23 2/8	15 0/8	10	12	Ramsey County	MN	Keith Ericson	2009	1793
174 1/8	26 1/8	25 7/8	26 2/8	7	8	Charles County	MD	Robert H. Jones, Sr.	1971	1808
174 1/8	25 5/8	27 1/8	18 4/8	9	6	Henderson County	IL	Ron De May	1997	1808
174 1/8	24 6/8	24 4/8	16 6/8	6	7	Collingsworth County	TX	Brad Casal	1997	1808
174 1/8	22 4/8	22 3/8	19 1/8	8	7	Franklin County	KY	Michael Riddle	1998	1808
174 1/8	26 6/8	25 7/8	19 1/8	5	8	Delaware County	IA	Jason N. Nolz	2000	1808
174 1/8	23 7/8	24 3/8	15 4/8	7	9	Stewart County	TN	Stephen R. Campbell	2001	1808
174 1/8	25 1/8	25 7/8	21 0/8	7	10	Adams County	IL	Alan Harvey	2003	1808
174 1/8	24 3/8	24 3/8	20 6/8	6	8	Rock County	WI	Brian Ducss	2004	1808
174 1/8	24 6/8	23 5/8	17 4/8	10	10	Richardson County	NE	Daniel J. Jones	2004	1808
*174 1/8	24 6/8	25 7/8	18 5/8	9	9	Barber County	KS	Matt Jones	2004	1808
174 1/8	26 5/8	25 0/8	20 4/8	10	10	Weld County	CO	Roger D. Bechler	2009	1808
174 0/8	26 0/8	27 6/8	26 6/8	7	6	Delaware County	OH	Michael H. Seamster	1983	1819
174 0/8	22 7/8	21 3/8	20 2/8	7	7	Coles County	IL	Fred Hartbank	1994	1819
174 0/8	26 0/8	26 6/8	18 4/8	8	6	E. Carroll Parish	LA	Gary D. Carr	1996	1819
174 0/8	25 4/8	26 5/8	16 2/8	7	8	Bucks County	PA	Clifford Saxby	2000	1819
174 0/8	25 4/8	25 0/8	20 6/8	7	6	Henry County	IL	Bruce Farmer	2002	1819
174 0/8	22 4/8	23 2/8	17 0/8	8	6	Tom Green County	TX	Jason Alley	2004	1819
174 0/8	25 0/8	22 1/8	18 6/8	5	8	Slave Lake	ALB	Thomas J. Nitterour	2005	1819
174 0/8	24 6/8	24 6/8	19 2/8	8	8	Sauk County	WI	Lee J. Keim	2005	1819
174 0/8	23 6/8	24 3/8	17 1/8	9	6	Burnett County	WI	Byron Hopke	2006	1819
173 7/8	27 5/8	26 0/8	18 0/8	10	7	Marshall County	KS	Michael J. Krogman	1984	1828
173 7/8	24 4/8	23 3/8	19 7/8	7	7	Anne Arundel County	MD	David R. McMullen, Sr.	1992	1828
173 7/8	24 6/8	25 0/8	17 3/8	9	7	Morrison County	MN	Mike Sannan	1993	1828
173 7/8	22 6/8	22 5/8	19 1/8	9	9	Dane County	WI	Eric L. Hamele	1993	1828
173 7/8	25 0/8	25 2/8	20 3/8	7	6	Richland County	WI	Mathew D. Omernik	1994	1828
173 7/8	24 0/8	25 6/8	19 6/8	8	6	Washtenaw County	MI	Timothy L. Clary	1995	1828
173 7/8	25 7/8	25 4/8	22 2/8	6	7	Sauk County	WI	Timothy J. Terbilcox	1998	1828
173 7/8	26 7/8	26 7/8	20 0/8	7	6	Washington County	OH	Rod Williams	1999	1828
173 7/8	24 7/8	24 5/8	19 5/8	6	7	La Crosse County	WI	Daniel Koenen	2000	1828
173 7/8	25 3/8	26 1/8	20 3/8	6	9	Carroll County	IL	Mel Landwehr	2000	1828
173 6/8	25 4/8	25 2/8	22 0/8	8	9	Spink County	SD	Milton Haag	1959	1838
173 6/8	19 3/8	19 5/8	17 1/8	9	9	Douglas County	MN	John Duberowski	1980	1838
173 6/8	25 3/8	24 5/8	17 6/8	7	7	Cass County	MI	James Akey	1995	1838
173 6/8	26 4/8	20 7/8	21 6/8	11	11	Norton County	KS	Jeff Dold	1997	1838
173 6/8	23 6/8	23 5/8	18 4/8	10	9	Genesee County	NY	Marc Mueller	1998	1838
173 6/8	25 3/8	25 3/8	21 4/8	7	6	Lincoln County	MO	Kevin Guss	1999	1838
173 6/8	25 3/8	25 5/8	18 0/8	7	10	Adams County	MS	Jimmy Riley	2000	1838
173 6/8	23 6/8	23 4/8	16 0/8	6	7	Platte County	MO	Michael Auman	2001	1838
173 6/8	24 6/8	24 2/8	20 0/8	8	6	Peoria County	IL	Paula DeWeese	2002	1838
173 6/8	23 2/8	22 2/8	18 3/8	8	8	Clay County	MN	Lee Engebretson	2002	1838
*173 6/8	25 5/8	25 5/8	19 0/8	6	10	Waupaca County	WI	Paul Keller	2003	1838
173 6/8	25 4/8	25 5/8	19 6/8	7	10	Jefferson County	NE	John E. Waldrep	2003	1838
173 6/8	21 3/8	20 3/8	16 5/8	7	10	Dodge County	WI	Tim Loomans	2003	1838
173 6/8	24 5/8	24 1/8	20 3/8	8	7	Maverick County	TX	Ryan Friedkin	2004	1838
173 6/8	24 4/8	23 6/8	17 4/8	7	5	Louisa County	IA	Jerry Lee	2007	1838
*173 6/8	24 6/8	27 7/8	19 1/8	11	7	Wayne County	OH	David W. Wyckoff	2007	1838
173 6/8	20 3/8	20 4/8	16 3/8	8	10	Warren County	IA	Norman Hutchinson, Jr.	2009	1838
*173 6/8	19 0/8	25 4/8	17 6/8	7	6	Morgan County	CO	Martin W. Thiel	2009	1838
173 5/8	25 4/8	24 3/8	18 1/8	7	6	Gray County	KS	Allen D. Bailey	1982	1856
173 5/8	22 7/8	23 2/8	18 4/8	8	6	Pepin County	WI	Don Linse	1988	1856
173 5/8	23 1/8	22 3/8	17 2/8	11	7	St. Louis County	MO	Michael M. Branson	1989	1856
173 5/8	29 1/8	28 4/8	17 4/8	11	9	Chippewa County	WI	George A. Olson	1991	1856
173 5/8	26 7/8	27 1/8	18 7/8	7	7	Pope County	IL	Doug Casey	1995	1856
173 5/8	22 5/8	24 4/8	17 7/8	8	8	Christian County	IL	Dave L. Gross	1996	1856
173 5/8	23 5/8	25 6/8	20 3/8	7	8	Richland County	OH	Andrew F. Moncayo	1999	1856
173 5/8	26 7/8	26 6/8	20 7/8	8	7	New Haven County	CT	Steven Rich	2000	1856
173 5/8	24 3/8	23 2/8	17 4/8	8	10	Franklin County	MO	Keith Sappington	2001	1856
173 5/8	25 0/8	25 0/8	19 5/8	6	8	Dallas County	IA	John Cavanaugh	2002	1856
*173 5/8	21 5/8	22 5/8	17 1/8	13	11	Ramsey County	ND	Victor Pintar	2003	1856
*173 5/8	24 3/8	23 0/8	17 2/8	6	6	Lucas County	IA	Roy Palmer	2003	1856
173 5/8	25 1/8	24 5/8	15 7/8	9	7	Rusk County	WI	Mark Deraitus	2007	1856
173 5/8	21 4/8	22 6/8	18 2/8	8	7	Greenwood County	KS	Matt Jones	2007	1856
*173 5/8	23 5/8	24 2/8	18 2/8	8	7	Kossuth County	IA	Charles Loeschen	2008	1856
173 4/8	24 7/8	25 5/8	21 6/8	6	6	Barton County	KS	Norman Kimber	1967	1871
173 4/8	22 4/8	23 7/8	14 1/8	6	8	Trumbull County	OH	Peter Bradley	1969	1871
173 4/8	26 1/8	21 7/8	16 7/8	7	10	Renville County	MN	Larry Godejahn	1973	1871
173 4/8	25 1/8	25 4/8	17 6/8	7	8	Scott County	KY	Joey Lusby	1995	1871
173 4/8	24 3/8	23 6/8	16 1/8	10	6	Cass County	MO	Jerrol Walton	1996	1871
173 4/8	27 2/8	25 6/8	19 6/8	6	5	Walworth County	WI	Charles G. Palmer	1996	1871
173 4/8	23 0/8	23 3/8	18 1/8	6	8	Pike County	IL	Shawn Baker	1997	1871
173 4/8	24 3/8	21 4/8	15 6/8	11	11	Graves County	KY	Mitchell Knight	1999	1871
173 4/8	26 0/8	25 4/8	20 1/8	6	6	Dunn County	WI	Ryan J. Loomis	1999	1871
173 4/8	23 2/8	23 3/8	17 3/8	8	9	Dunn County	WI	Jerold R. Olson	1999	1871
173 4/8	24 0/8	24 5/8	19 0/8	13	6	Cass County	IN	Daniel L. Ridlen	2003	1871
173 4/8	24 0/8	23 7/8	17 1/8	7	8	Outagamie County	WI	Chris A. Bettin	2004	1871
*173 4/8	21 6/8	19 0/8	20 2/8	5	11	Jo Daviess County	IL	Owen V. Enke	2006	1871
173 4/8	21 3/8	22 6/8	16 3/8	10	8	Marion County	IA	Bill Wold	2007	1871
173 4/8	22 2/8	22 1/8	17 2/8	8	8	Pike County	IL	Mark Blakely	2008	1871
173 4/8	23 0/8	23 4/8	18 7/8	8	7	Washington County	MS	Gus Pieralisi, Jr.	2010	1871
*173 4/8	24 4/8	24 7/8	21 1/8	6	9	Dunn County	WI	Kyle Knops	2010	1871
173 3/8	26 4/8	26 2/8	19 5/8	8	7	Pike County	IL	Ronnie Bauer	1988	1888
173 3/8	24 4/8	24 4/8	20 5/8	6	8	DeKalb County	IL	Tom Kane	1995	1888
173 3/8	26 3/8	23 7/8	21 4/8	7	8	Barber County	KS	Bruce Swartley	1995	1888
173 3/8	25 3/8	25 5/8	19 2/8	8	7	Dane County	WI	David D. Hilgers	1997	1888
173 3/8	26 2/8	26 1/8	20 6/8	9	7	Prince Georges County	MD	Phil Harris	1997	1888
173 3/8	25 3/8	24 0/8	19 1/8	8	6	Door County	WI	Kim Starr	2000	1888
173 3/8	25 4/8	26 0/8	20 5/8	6	6	Brown County	IL	Ryan Wenninger	2001	1888
173 3/8	20 2/8	20 0/8	17 6/8	12	11	Le Flore County	OK	Kelly Jones	2003	1888
173 3/8	22 4/8	24 5/8	19 0/8	9	6	Rooks County	KS	Donald S. Dvoroznak	2003	1888
173 3/8	21 1/8	22 7/8	18 2/8	8	8	Ontario County	NY	Jon Aldrich	2008	1888
173 3/8	26 5/8	27 3/8	18 7/8	6	9	Berrien County	MI	Steven P. Spenner	2009	1888
173 2/8	27 4/8	27 0/8	20 6/8	7	9	Ross County	OH	Glen A. Cummings	1991	1899
173 2/8	25 2/8	25 4/8	20 1/8	6	7	Jefferson County	IA	James Steele	1992	1899

655

WHITETAIL DEER (NON-TYPICAL ANTLERS)

Minimum Score 155   Continued

SCORE	LENGTH OF R MAIN BEAM L	INSIDE SPREAD	NUMBER OF R POINTS L		AREA	STATE/ PROVINCE	HUNTER'S NAME	DATE	RANK
173 2/8	24 4/8 24 6/8	14 7/8	6	10	Marion County	KY	J. W. Witt	1993	1899
173 2/8	20 4/8 21 0/8	18 5/8	8	8	Brown County	SD	Barry J. Smith	1995	1899
173 2/8	24 0/8 23 4/8	17 7/8	6	6	Lyon County	IA	Michael Judas	1996	1899
173 2/8	21 6/8 22 4/8	16 4/8	8	10	Sauk County	WI	Dean Judd	1998	1899
173 2/8	20 2/8 21 0/8	14 0/8	9	9	Kingman County	KS	Len Dalmas	2000	1899
173 2/8	24 3/8 23 2/8	21 0/8	10	8	Millarville	ALB	Jeff Ensor	2002	1899
173 2/8	23 6/8 23 4/8	16 2/8	6	7	Woodson County	KS	Danny Linnebur	2002	1899
173 2/8	17 5/8 21 5/8	15 0/8	11	8	Trempealeau County	WI	Matt R. Andersen	2003	1899
*173 2/8	27 0/8 24 3/8	22 0/8	5	10	Martin County	IN	Wade Roark	2003	1899
173 2/8	24 6/8 24 7/8	21 0/8	6	6	Mercer County	MO	Robert Baker	2004	1899
173 2/8	25 3/8 24 0/8	15 5/8	11	8	Niagara County	NY	Ron Wolf, Jr.	2006	1899
*173 2/8	26 2/8 25 4/8	18 1/8	10	11	Adams County	IL	Ben Lause	2008	1899
173 1/8	24 6/8 24 6/8	18 1/8	8	9	Lee County	IA	Dan Enger	1992	1913
173 1/8	23 4/8 22 5/8	16 6/8	8	8	Waukesha County	WI	David J. Timm	1994	1913
173 1/8	24 4/8 24 6/8	18 3/8	7	8	Lake County	IL	Brian D. Berg	1999	1913
173 1/8	25 3/8 26 2/8	16 2/8	5	10	Howard County	MO	Bruce Hackman	2003	1913
*173 1/8	27 0/8 26 1/8	17 2/8	7	6	Adams County	WI	Paul Dellamuth	2007	1913
173 0/8	22 4/8 21 5/8	16 6/8	7	8	Lincoln County	KS	Scott Kingery	1988	1918
173 0/8	24 0/8 24 2/8	17 6/8	6	9	Champaign County	IL	Greg Burr	1994	1918
173 0/8	22 7/8 23 4/8	18 0/8	9	10	Boyd County	NE	Lora Cline	1997	1918
173 0/8	22 3/8 23 5/8	25 0/8	10	8	Eastland County	TX	Jonray E. Childers	1999	1918
173 0/8	23 6/8 24 2/8	18 3/8	7	7	La Salle County	IL	John G. Sykes	1999	1918
173 0/8	25 5/8 25 3/8	17 7/8	5	9	Goodhue County	MN	John "Jack" Cordes	2000	1918
173 0/8	23 2/8 22 2/8	15 5/8	8	11	Jefferson County	NE	Bill Hays	2001	1918
173 0/8	26 1/8 27 0/8	15 0/8	7	6	Belmont County	OH	Brian Herrin	2004	1918
173 0/8	21 0/8 21 2/8	17 0/8	7	7	Johnson County	IN	Dan Pennington	2004	1918
173 0/8	21 0/8 21 2/8	18 4/8	9	7	Bucks County	PA	Francis A. Zydzik	2009	1918
173 0/8	20 4/8 20 0/8	15 1/8	10	12	Olmsted County	MN	Gavin Sawyer	2010	1918
172 7/8	24 0/8 21 4/8	14 4/8	10	10	McIntosh County	OK	Clark Utley	1976	1929
172 7/8	23 6/8 24 1/8	16 7/8	9	9	Morrison County	MN	Harlan Grams	1988	1929
172 7/8	22 5/8 23 7/8	19 3/8	8	8	Sedgwick County	KS	Cary Renner	1989	1929
172 7/8	23 3/8 24 2/8	19 2/8	6	10	Barton County	KS	Alan D. Bullard	1994	1929
172 7/8	26 1/8 25 0/8	21 4/8	6	7	Zavala County	TX	Joe Little	1997	1929
172 7/8	23 7/8 23 3/8	18 4/8	5	7	Kleberg County	TX	W. Scott Brandon	2000	1929
172 7/8	23 5/8 23 3/8	23 0/8	6	6	Chemung County	NY	John W. Hunter	2002	1929
172 7/8	26 0/8 24 5/8	19 2/8	6	6	Plymouth County	IA	Tim Sanow	2003	1929
172 7/8	24 4/8 25 2/8	20 2/8	8	8	Fillmore County	MN	Chad Boehmke	2005	1929
172 7/8	24 4/8 24 2/8	18 3/8	7	6	Dodge County	WI	John R. Puetz	2005	1929
172 7/8	25 2/8 24 0/8	18 5/8	8	6	Monroe County	WI	Marvin Pitkin	2006	1929
172 7/8	27 5/8 24 0/8	19 5/8	4	8	Chase County	KS	Roger Peery	2009	1929
172 6/8	22 2/8 22 6/8	16 2/8	9	11	Washburn County	WI	Clint Atkinson	1986	1941
172 6/8	25 5/8 25 1/8	15 5/8	7	5	Wyoming County	WV	Teddy Mills	1999	1941
172 6/8	25 7/8 27 3/8	17 2/8	8	6	Schuyler County	IL	Rick Park	2000	1941
172 6/8	25 6/8 25 1/8	17 6/8	14	10	Barber County	KS	Stephen Kotz	2002	1941
172 6/8	25 3/8 24 7/8	19 2/8	8	7	Allegheny County	PA	Raymond R. Drabicki	2003	1941
172 6/8	23 2/8 23 1/8	17 3/8	10	7	Blaine County	OK	Tony Lucero	2004	1941
172 6/8	24 4/8 24 1/8	17 3/8	7	11	Jay County	IN	Jerry L. Reynard	2004	1941
172 6/8	21 7/8 21 2/8	18 4/8	7	7	Ogle County	IL	Clayton Wehmhoefer	2005	1941
172 6/8	24 0/8 23 2/8	19 7/8	6	7	Cerro Gordo County	IA	Richard Honsey	2005	1941
172 6/8	22 6/8 22 2/8	17 1/8	6	11	Athens County	OH	Mick Weller	2006	1941
*172 6/8	25 7/8 25 3/8	21 1/8	8	7	Dunn County	WI	Aaron Paulson	2006	1941
172 6/8	24 6/8 24 1/8	17 2/8	5	7	Wayne County	IA	Steve Peperis	2007	1941
172 5/8	24 2/8 25 2/8	17 6/8	11	7	Trumbull County	OH	Dick Keagy	1989	1953
172 5/8	26 3/8 24 7/8	17 2/8	8	9	Brown County	SD	Craig Papke	1995	1953
172 5/8	24 2/8 24 2/8	18 2/8	6	7	Harper County	KS	Brian Chackan	2000	1953
*172 5/8	22 7/8 22 4/8	18 7/8	8	7	Story County	IA	Mike Augustin	2001	1953
*172 5/8	24 4/8 24 3/8	17 5/8	9	5	Cedar County	IA	Scott Walker	2007	1953
*172 5/8	22 7/8 23 1/8	16 6/8	8	9	Lycoming County	PA	Reuben K. Fisher	2008	1953
172 4/8	18 0/8 25 2/8	19 0/8	14	7	Marshall County	MN	James C. Pederson	1992	1959
172 4/8	27 7/8 28 0/8	18 3/8	7	6	Jefferson County	IN	Dwight Rines	2000	1959
172 4/8	24 0/8 25 3/8	19 2/8	9	8	Essex	ONT	Gary Caba	2000	1959
*172 4/8	24 0/8 24 4/8	20 4/8	7	5	Sarpy County	NE	Thomas Kelly	2004	1959
*172 4/8	24 5/8 23 7/8	18 6/8	8	10	Livingston County	MO	Keith R. Forsyth	2007	1959
172 3/8	23 6/8 23 0/8	18 4/8	7	8	Mississippi County	AR	Dennis Perkins	1990	1964
172 3/8	23 2/8 24 5/8	18 6/8	9	5	Chariton County	MO	Dennis W. Meyers	1991	1964
172 3/8	28 0/8 27 3/8	15 4/8	5	7	Cass County	MI	Patrick G. Dowling	1999	1964
172 3/8	24 6/8 25 6/8	18 1/8	6	7	Sedgwick County	KS	Tim Hommertzheim	2000	1964
*172 3/8	23 5/8 24 2/8	23 5/8	11	7	Reynolds County	MO	Steven W. Watson	2004	1964
172 3/8	25 4/8 25 2/8	20 4/8	5	8	Mingo County	WV	John C. Felix	2004	1964
172 3/8	22 6/8 24 0/8	19 7/8	7	7	Barron County	WI	Doug Severude	2006	1964
172 3/8	25 2/8 24 2/8	20 0/8	7	6	Pike County	IL	Kim Bettinger	2007	1964
*172 3/8	20 6/8 19 7/8	17 6/8	11	10	Tensas Parish	LA	Vicki Husted	2008	1964
172 2/8	24 5/8 23 6/8	15 4/8	9	10	Calhoun County	MI	Roger W. Hanselman	1989	1973
172 2/8	22 3/8 23 5/8	18 2/8	7	7	Cadogan	ALB	Howard Schreiber	1991	1973
172 2/8	25 0/8 25 2/8	25 6/8	9	8	Cass County	MO	Jerrol Walton	1992	1973
172 2/8	27 0/8 25 2/8	21 3/8	7	9	Henderson County	IL	Darren E. Blakley	1993	1973
172 2/8	26 0/8 26 0/8	17 6/8	8	8	Tazewell County	VA	Michael L. Sawyers	1995	1973
172 2/8	25 6/8 27 0/8	18 1/8	6	5	Jersey County	IL	Tim Hellrung	1998	1973
172 2/8	22 3/8 23 1/8	16 7/8	6	6	Callaway County	MO	Dale Brondel	1999	1973
172 2/8	26 3/8 25 7/8	22 4/8	6	6	Macon County	IL	Dave Elliott	2002	1973
172 2/8	26 0/8 25 3/8	17 3/8	7	7	Crawford County	PA	Andy Mullett	2003	1973
*172 2/8	25 7/8 24 4/8	19 6/8	6	6	Cass County	IL	Lance Hemken	2004	1973
172 2/8	21 3/8 21 5/8	17 4/8	7	9	Wilkinson County	MS	Clifford Welch	2008	1973
172 2/8	24 6/8 23 4/8	22 5/8	6	8	Marshall County	OK	Preston Mullings	2009	1973
172 1/8	22 6/8 23 2/8	24 7/8	8	7	Green County	WI	Dean Dilly	1974	1985
172 1/8	25 0/8 25 4/8	18 0/8	9	7	Chippewa County	MN	Sheldon Holzheimer	1993	1985
172 1/8	23 2/8 23 2/8	19 4/8	6	7	Kanawha County	WV	Billy Lamb	1995	1985
172 1/8	21 3/8 19 6/8	16 7/8	8	6	Wyandotte County	KS	Billy Gardner	2000	1985
172 1/8	23 7/8 20 2/8	20 4/8	6	10	Benewah County	ID	Joe H. Ochsner	2001	1985
172 1/8	23 3/8 22 5/8	18 6/8	7	7	Hardin County	IA	Stan Caldwell	2002	1985
*172 1/8	22 1/8 22 2/8	16 3/8	7	7	Monmouth County	NJ	Mike Castro	2006	1985
172 1/8	22 6/8 23 7/8	18 2/8	6	5	Cumberland County	IL	Gabe Shafer	2006	1985
172 1/8	23 3/8 23 0/8	15 0/8	9	9	Bartholomew County	IN	Ronnie Tempest	2007	1985
172 0/8	24 4/8 25 4/8	17 4/8	7	7	Warren County	IA	Dennis R. Jacobe	1988	1994
172 0/8	21 6/8 21 6/8	21 6/8	7	9	Jo Daviess County	IL	John C. Sanborn	1990	1994

WHITETAIL DEER (NON-TYPICAL ANTLERS)

Minimum Score 155 — Continued

SCORE	LENGTH OF R MAIN BEAM L	INSIDE SPREAD	NUMBER OF R POINTS L		AREA	STATE/ PROVINCE	HUNTER'S NAME	DATE	RANK
172 0/8	23 5/8 23 5/8	17 2/8	5	8	Onaway	ALB	Edward Toelken	1994	1994
172 0/8	21 5/8 22 2/8	18 2/8	11	10	Charles County	MD	Harold J. Welch	1997	1994
172 0/8	23 6/8 24 3/8	17 4/8	7	10	Wood County	WI	Richard D. Schaetz	2000	1994
172 0/8	25 1/8 22 6/8	18 3/8	10	6	St. Clair County	IL	Jason Shacy	2001	1994
172 0/8	26 2/8 25 0/8	16 0/8	11	10	Dodge County	WI	Steven J. Buchholz	2003	1994
172 0/8	23 4/8 23 5/8	18 1/8	5	7	Crawford County	WI	James E. Irwin	2003	1994
172 0/8	27 0/8 21 2/8	18 4/8	8	6	Geauga County	OH	Darrin D. Sotera	2004	1994
172 0/8	24 5/8 24 2/8	21 2/8	11	8	Jasper County	IL	Richard Goss	2004	1994
*172 0/8	24 0/8 24 7/8	17 0/8	7	7	Montgomery County	IL	Dennis Whitley	2004	1994
172 0/8	25 1/8 24 1/8	16 6/8	9	7	Greenwood County	KS	Don Copley	2005	1994
*172 0/8	25 5/8 24 7/8	17 3/8	7	7	Iroquois County	IL	Matt McCullough	2006	1994
172 0/8	23 0/8 22 6/8	20 0/8	8	9	Barry County	MI	Michael E. Emmons	2007	1994
*172 0/8	22 7/8 25 2/8	19 7/8	6	7	Tensas Parish	LA	Billy Husted	2008	1994
*172 0/8	22 5/8 21 5/8	16 4/8	6	10	Scotland County	MO	Christopher W. Emily	2009	1994
171 7/8	22 4/8 22 3/8	19 6/8	11	9	Will County	IL	James Giese	1987	2010
171 7/8	22 7/8 23 7/8	19 2/8	8	8	Calgary	ALB	James Sheret	1990	2010
171 7/8	23 4/8 23 6/8	19 7/8	8	9	Brown County	MN	Chad Freiderick	1995	2010
171 7/8	23 4/8 23 4/8	18 0/8	11	8	Harrison County	IA	Ken Butler	1997	2010
171 7/8	24 0/8 23 6/8	18 4/8	9	11	Pike County	OH	Marcus Hoholick	1997	2010
171 7/8	24 2/8 25 2/8	18 5/8	10	9	Humboldt County	IA	Jeff Meyer	1999	2010
171 7/8	24 0/8 24 1/8	19 7/8	6	9	Wayne County	OH	Gary Maxwell	2003	2010
171 7/8	25 1/8 23 0/8	18 6/8	5	10	Saline County	IL	David Morris	2003	2010
171 7/8	23 0/8 22 6/8	17 4/8	9	7	Macoupin County	IL	Augie Reznicek	2003	2010
*171 7/8	25 4/8 24 0/8	17 1/8	8	6	Whiteside County	IL	Mat Newman	2004	2010
*171 7/8	25 0/8 25 0/8	20 1/8	7	7	Jo Daviess County	IL	Alexander K. Phillips	2005	2010
171 7/8	25 1/8 23 6/8	18 3/8	7	10	Wilson County	KS	Dennis Wilson	2005	2010
*171 7/8	23 7/8 22 6/8	19 2/8	7	6	Pulaski County	KY	Gary Bullock	2006	2010
171 7/8	26 0/8 24 7/8	19 7/8	5	7	Washington County	IL	Dave Burke	2006	2010
171 7/8	26 1/8 25 7/8	18 6/8	7	10	Scott County	IL	Michael Postema	2006	2010
171 6/8	22 3/8 21 5/8	20 5/8	8	9	Dubuque County	IA	Dick Theis	1975	2025
171 6/8	24 1/8 25 3/8	15 5/8	8	6	Montgomery County	IA	James Baker	1982	2025
171 6/8	26 0/8 26 7/8	19 6/8	9	7	Vermilion County	IL	Gene Maier	1984	2025
171 6/8	23 7/8 18 3/8	18 0/8	7	10	Leavenworth County	KS	Albert Lyle Karl	1987	2025
171 6/8	23 0/8 23 5/8	15 6/8	7	7	Montgomery County	TN	Dennis Morris	1991	2025
171 6/8	25 7/8 25 5/8	18 6/8	9	8	McLean County	IL	Kenneth Kolakowski	1993	2025
171 6/8	25 0/8 25 1/8	21 2/8	4	7	Sangamon County	IL	Robert Churchill	1995	2025
171 6/8	21 3/8 21 1/8	17 5/8	8	6	McHenry County	IL	Frank Oakley	1997	2025
171 6/8	23 0/8 25 3/8	16 4/8	10	9	Wayne County	OH	Michael L. Butler	2001	2025
171 6/8	23 3/8 24 4/8	14 0/8	9	7	Union County	IA	Jay Herter	2003	2025
171 6/8	24 3/8 23 0/8	14 3/8	7	11	Morgan County	GA	Loy H. Banks	2005	2025
171 6/8	21 7/8 22 6/8	19 3/8	7	7	Greene County	IN	Peter Rogers	2005	2025
*171 6/8	25 6/8 22 6/8	22 7/8	6	7	Vermilion County	IL	Jon Kepling	2006	2025
171 6/8	24 2/8 24 2/8	19 4/8	8	8	Warren County	IA	Jonathan Wallenburg	2006	2025
171 5/8	22 7/8 24 1/8	16 4/8	7	7	Wapello County	IA	Rex Jones	1983	2039
171 5/8	26 1/8 21 4/8	24 0/8	6	8	Iroquois County	IL	Frank Snow	1987	2039
171 5/8	24 0/8 23 0/8	19 2/8	6	9	Muskingum County	OH	Dan Jennings	1991	2039
171 5/8	22 3/8 22 3/8	18 0/8	7	6	Monona County	IA	Eric J. Tweet	1999	2039
171 5/8	23 7/8 24 2/8	22 5/8	7	7	Fulton County	IL	Denver L. Ford, Sr.	1999	2039
171 5/8	26 3/8 25 6/8	15 1/8	10	9	Lake County	IL	Terry Nelson	1999	2039
171 5/8	26 5/8 27 3/8	18 7/8	6	6	McPherson County	KS	Bill Zerger	1999	2039
171 5/8	26 4/8 25 4/8	21 1/8	7	7	Jackson County	IA	Branden A. Post	2001	2039
171 5/8	25 6/8 26 4/8	21 5/8	6	6	Clayton County	IA	Keith A. Lewis	2003	2039
171 5/8	23 5/8 23 0/8	20 2/8	8	10	Estill County	KY	Roger D. Haney	2006	2039
171 5/8	26 2/8 24 5/8	20 7/8	7	6	Edgar County	IL	Virgil Haynes	2007	2039
171 4/8	24 5/8 24 5/8	19 1/8	7	7	Butler County	KS	Jeff Stevens	1982	2050
171 4/8	23 2/8 24 3/8	17 7/8	9	6	Monona County	IA	Kevin M. Rittenhouse	1994	2050
171 4/8	27 6/8 27 1/8	18 6/8	8	10	Pike County	IL	Fred Coleman	1998	2050
171 4/8	21 3/8 22 1/8	16 3/8	9	7	Orleans County	NY	Robert Fulwell	2000	2050
171 4/8	25 0/8 25 0/8	17 2/8	7	9	Barber County	KS	Steve Cray	2000	2050
*171 4/8	24 6/8 23 0/8	21 3/8	8	9	Crawford County	PA	Ron King	2004	2050
171 4/8	22 0/8 22 7/8	19 6/8	8	6	Trempealeau County	WI	Jeff Larson	2004	2050
171 4/8	24 5/8 24 6/8	25 3/8	9	9	Clark County	IL	Dennis E. Mock, Jr.	2005	2050
171 4/8	23 2/8 23 4/8	18 7/8	6	7	Taylor County	WI	Kenneth Hemmer	2005	2050
171 4/8	23 5/8 23 5/8	15 7/8	9	9	Butler County	KS	David R. Rogers	2007	2050
171 4/8	23 0/8 23 4/8	16 2/8	9	6	Onoway	ALB	Chris Crispin	2010	2050
171 3/8	20 4/8 23 7/8	19 4/8	8	10	Logan County	OK	Billy Wayne McBride	1989	2061
171 3/8	18 2/8 18 3/8	11 4/8	9	9	Chariton County	MO	Jeff Brand	1991	2061
171 3/8	24 1/8 21 7/8	19 5/8	6	8	Kane County	IL	Matthew Peterson	1991	2061
171 3/8	26 0/8 25 0/8	17 3/8	7	5	Delaware County	IA	Parker Fransen	1997	2061
171 3/8	27 1/8 24 5/8	13 7/8	8	7	Wayne County	IA	Andy C. Decker	1998	2061
171 3/8	25 4/8 24 1/8	19 3/8	7	6	Butler County	OH	Ken Fox	1999	2061
171 3/8	25 1/8 25 7/8	16 4/8	6	5	Warren County	IA	Randy Brandt	2001	2061
171 3/8	26 0/8 26 2/8	21 4/8	8	6	Hancock County	IL	Larry E. Teel	2003	2061
*171 3/8	25 7/8 24 3/8	18 0/8	6	8	Pike County	IL	Michael E. Summers	2004	2061
171 3/8	19 6/8 20 6/8	16 0/8	7	8	Pike County	IL	Thomas Dustyn Gordon	2004	2061
171 3/8	27 3/8 26 3/8	24 4/8	5	5	Buffalo County	WI	Cory Mielke	2005	2061
*171 3/8	23 5/8 23 0/8	16 1/8	7	8	Tarrant County	TX	David Wilson	2007	2061
171 3/8	22 6/8 22 1/8	14 7/8	7	9	Poweshiek County	IA	Dean Roth	2007	2061
*171 3/8	24 6/8 26 0/8	21 5/8	7	10	Jefferson County	WI	Darin Schultz	2008	2061
171 3/8	25 5/8 25 5/8	17 1/8	11	7	Clermont County	OH	Kevin Tindle	2008	2061
171 2/8	27 0/8 27 0/8	18 5/8	4	5	Van Buren County	MI	David Anderson	1979	2076
171 2/8	23 5/8 24 7/8	14 4/8	6	6	Scotts Bluff County	NE	Doug Hauser	1984	2076
171 2/8	25 4/8 25 4/8	17 3/8	7	6	Trempealeau County	WI	Steven W. Franck	1995	2076
171 2/8	25 2/8 25 3/8	18 5/8	6	9	Ozaukee County	WI	Jamie Langerman	1998	2076
171 2/8	23 0/8 23 2/8	18 7/8	6	6	Pike County	IL	Brad Stamp	1999	2076
171 2/8	24 0/8 24 0/8	17 5/8	8	7	Waukesha County	WI	Barry Rohde	2001	2076
171 2/8	25 5/8 25 2/8	18 2/8	7	8	Douglas County	WI	Brian Sislo	2002	2076
171 2/8	24 3/8 24 3/8	17 7/8	5	6	De Witt County	IL	Daan Dunn	2003	2076
171 2/8	25 5/8 25 2/8	17 0/8	8	7	Clayton County	IA	Jason Gillihan	2004	2076
171 2/8	27 6/8 26 5/8	18 6/8	8	6	Johnson County	IL	Dwayne Dreyer	2005	2076
171 2/8	22 4/8 21 7/8	17 6/8	10	8	Creek County	OK	Drew Hardridge	2005	2076
171 2/8	24 2/8 24 0/8	15 5/8	9	8	Pottawattamie County	IA	Daryl Schnoes	2007	2076
171 2/8	25 2/8 25 0/8	23 4/8	6	8	Mitchell County	KS	Jerry Gotz	2009	2076
*171 2/8	26 1/8 25 5/8	17 1/8	7	7	Green Lake County	WI	Matt Mertens	2009	2076
171 1/8	23 4/8 24 0/8	20 2/8	8	6	Jackson County	MI	Shawn R. Surque	1985	2090

657

WHITETAIL DEER (NON-TYPICAL ANTLERS)

Minimum Score 155   Continued

SCORE	LENGTH OF R MAIN BEAM L	INSIDE SPREAD	NUMBER OF R POINTS L	AREA	STATE/ PROVINCE	HUNTER'S NAME	DATE	RANK
171 1/8	25 4/8 25 4/8	18 6/8	6 8	Birds Hill	MAN	Daniel Kowalchuk	1991	2090
171 1/8	26 7/8 26 0/8	19 7/8	7 8	Coffey County	KS	Kevin Parks	1992	2090
171 1/8	23 0/8 24 2/8	16 1/8	10 8	Bayfield County	WI	Eric Carlson	1995	2090
171 1/8	26 0/8 27 1/8	20 7/8	6 7	Oakland County	MI	Tim Fralick	2004	2090
171 1/8	21 7/8 22 0/8	15 5/8	11 6	Polk County	WI	Jeff Niemann	2005	2090
171 1/8	22 4/8 23 5/8	14 6/8	9 6	Knox County	IL	Richard M. Stinson, Jr.	2005	2090
171 1/8	23 3/8 25 2/8	19 4/8	7 9	Allegheny County	PA	Zeke Martinkovich	2007	2090
171 0/8	24 0/8 24 4/8	18 1/8	7 7	Dodge County	WI	Dallas Johnson	1955	2098
171 0/8	26 3/8 22 6/8	22 4/8	4 10	Lee County	IA	Gary Frost	1967	2098
171 0/8	25 7/8 26 0/8	26 0/8	6 5	Clark County	KS	William A. Rule	1993	2098
171 0/8	26 2/8 23 5/8	17 1/8	5 6	Greene County	IL	Clayton Whitlock	1999	2098
171 0/8	22 6/8 22 7/8	19 2/8	7 9	Middlesex County	CT	Stephen Kiback III	2004	2098
*171 0/8	22 2/8 23 6/8	17 5/8	7 8	Warren County	IA	Brian Murillo	2005	2098
171 0/8	25 1/8 24 7/8	21 3/8	7 7	Parkland	ALB	Troy Dzioba	2005	2098
171 0/8	25 2/8 24 0/8	16 6/8	7 11	Hutchinson County	SD	John Kleeberg	2006	2098
171 0/8	23 2/8 23 2/8	18 1/8	7 8	Grayson County	TX	Rick Cantu	2007	2098
171 0/8	24 4/8 24 0/8	15 4/8	9 6	Schuyler County	IL	Donald K. Curless	2008	2098
171 0/8	20 6/8 19 1/8	17 5/8	7 11	Delaware County	IA	Ryan D. Davis	2009	2098
*171 0/8	24 7/8 25 4/8	20 3/8	7 9	Wright County	MN	Matthew Schlink	2010	2098
170 7/8	24 5/8 25 2/8	15 3/8	6 6	Redwood County	MN	Todd G. Gilb	1982	2110
170 7/8	21 6/8 23 2/8	14 6/8	10 12	Kleberg County	TX	Bradley Peltier	1989	2110
170 7/8	23 6/8 24 1/8	16 5/8	9 9	Cook County	IL	Kenneth S. Koeneman	1997	2110
170 7/8	21 7/8 21 6/8	16 4/8	7 8	Brandon	MAN	Clifford L. Joynt	2000	2110
170 7/8	27 4/8 28 0/8	20 0/8	7 7	Fayette County	IA	Beau Myers	2000	2110
170 7/8	23 5/8 24 3/8	20 5/8	6 6	Washington County	WI	Mark A. Gonzales	2003	2110
170 7/8	21 7/8 19 6/8	17 0/8	8 9	Warren County	OH	Joe Vires	2006	2110
*170 7/8	25 2/8 23 3/8	22 4/8	7 9	St. Marys County	MD	William Lyon, Jr.	2007	2110
170 7/8	24 4/8 24 2/8	18 5/8	7 7	La Salle County	IL	Jeffery Middleton	2008	2110
170 6/8	24 3/8 23 6/8	17 2/8	9 8	Nobles County	MN	David Janssen	1973	2119
170 6/8	23 7/8 23 6/8	18 2/8	6 12	Washtenaw County	MI	Dennis D. Clarke	1989	2119
170 6/8	22 0/8 20 7/8	14 5/8	9 7	Anoka County	MN	Wayne Nicholson	1991	2119
170 6/8	23 5/8 22 6/8	16 4/8	10 8	St. Charles County	MO	Jack A. Jones	1992	2119
170 6/8	27 5/8 26 0/8	20 2/8	5 5	Dakota County	MN	Craig Adams	1994	2119
170 6/8	22 2/8 22 7/8	17 2/8	8 7	Adams County	IL	Steve M. Giesing	1995	2119
170 6/8	25 1/8 25 2/8	19 0/8	7 6	Linn County	IA	James L. Corkery	1996	2119
170 6/8	26 0/8 25 1/8	25 5/8	7 11	Henderson County	IL	Terry L. Cook	1997	2119
170 6/8	25 2/8 24 7/8	26 5/8	6 7	Ogle County	IL	Dr. Todd M. Anderson	1999	2119
170 6/8	27 0/8 28 1/8	17 0/8	9 4	McDowell County	WV	Jeffrey Ellison	2001	2119
170 6/8	20 7/8 21 0/8	13 4/8	10 10	Trempealeau County	WI	Scott N. Arenz	2006	2119
170 5/8	18 1/8 26 2/8	21 7/8	10 6	Oklahoma County	OK	Tim R. Reid	1990	2130
170 5/8	22 6/8 24 6/8	19 0/8	8 6	Fulton County	IL	Mike Foster	1994	2130
170 5/8	25 4/8 22 7/8	17 4/8	6 9	Warren County	IA	David Wolfkill	1994	2130
170 5/8	26 2/8 25 3/8	19 2/8	8 6	Winnebago County	IA	Terry L. Hammond	1995	2130
170 5/8	27 1/8 26 2/8	21 1/8	6 4	Dane County	WI	Keith Green	1996	2130
170 5/8	27 5/8 27 3/8	22 2/8	8 6	Adams County	WI	Matthew S. Czerkas	1998	2130
170 5/8	23 6/8 25 0/8	17 5/8	12 8	Larue County	KY	Joseph Blando	1998	2130
170 5/8	23 7/8 23 2/8	20 3/8	5 5	Clay County	KS	Tom E. Bowman	1999	2130
170 5/8	23 6/8 23 0/8	15 6/8	8 6	Johnston County	OK	Michael Grace	2003	2130
170 5/8	25 1/8 24 2/8	14 7/8	7 9	Adams County	IL	Timothy J. Ryan	2004	2130
*170 5/8	22 6/8 23 7/8	18 2/8	7 9	Union County	SD	Bradley K. Kjose	2006	2130
*170 5/8	25 2/8 25 6/8	18 3/8	7 9	Iroquois County	IL	Raymond Holohan	2007	2130
*170 5/8	21 7/8 22 2/8	15 2/8	8 8	Monroe County	IN	Gregory R. Sowder	2007	2130
170 5/8	23 0/8 23 1/8	15 2/8	10 12	Sauk County	WI	John F. Albert	2007	2130
170 4/8	26 3/8 26 1/8	20 5/8	7 7	Tazewell County	IL	Bret Hamilton	1982	2144
170 4/8	25 4/8 25 4/8	19 2/8	7 6	Sauk County	WI	Del R. Hisel	1994	2144
170 4/8	27 7/8 26 4/8	17 7/8	8 5	Guthrie County	IA	Larry Bryan	1995	2144
170 4/8	23 1/8 22 6/8	17 4/8	7 6	Adair County	KY	Gary Feese	2002	2144
170 4/8	21 3/8 21 3/8	15 6/8	7 7	Edwards County	IL	Mike Walters	2002	2144
170 4/8	25 3/8 25 6/8	18 0/8	9 10	Vernon County	WI	James J. Folcey	2003	2144
170 4/8	21 6/8 22 1/8	14 3/8	9 9	Marion County	IL	Jimmie Storey	2005	2144
170 4/8	25 0/8 23 6/8	22 2/8	11 8	Crawford County	IL	Justin R. Childress	2005	2144
170 4/8	25 7/8 26 3/8	20 1/8	8 6	Columbia County	WI	Willis Schmidt	2006	2144
*170 4/8	26 6/8 18 5/8	17 6/8	7 6	Warren County	MO	Mark J. Potthast	2006	2144
*170 4/8	23 0/8 21 0/8	19 7/8	7 12	Randolph County	MO	Philip Doolittle, Jr.	2008	2144
*170 4/8	22 1/8 22 0/8	18 6/8	10 10	Clarke County	IA	Adam J. Urich	2008	2144
170 4/8	24 3/8 25 1/8	16 6/8	6 7	McLean County	IL	Gunnar Darnall	2008	2144
*170 4/8	20 5/8 23 5/8	14 6/8	10 12	Douglas County	KS	Tom Gray	2009	2144
170 3/8	24 1/8 22 7/8	21 1/8	6 8	Fairfield County	OH	Brian Morrison	1987	2158
170 3/8	22 6/8 23 5/8	17 2/8	7 9	Logan County	NE	John Croghan	1994	2158
170 3/8	23 4/8 23 4/8	21 6/8	8 8	Webster County	IA	Edward E. Ulicki	1996	2158
170 3/8	23 6/8 23 3/8	16 5/8	5 8	Oneida County	WI	Deborah K. Goldsworthy	1998	2158
170 3/8	28 4/8 27 1/8	20 0/8	7 6	Rockingham County	NH	Dan Parks	2000	2158
170 3/8	22 3/8 21 2/8	13 6/8	9 7	Minnehaha County	SD	Bruce Vander Waal	2000	2158
170 3/8	26 7/8 25 6/8	19 6/8	9 10	Pike County	IN	Bill Daugherty	2000	2158
170 3/8	24 1/8 24 1/8	19 2/8	7 6	Reno County	KS	L. W. Miller	2002	2158
170 3/8	26 2/8 26 6/8	19 6/8	6 6	Jo Daviess County	IL	Brian L. Sherman	2004	2158
170 3/8	21 3/8 20 5/8	16 0/8	13 15	Logan County	KY	David Yoder	2006	2158
170 3/8	25 0/8 24 4/8	18 0/8	8 7	Mahnomen County	MN	Jared Schafer	2006	2158
*170 3/8	24 6/8 24 6/8	20 0/8	7 7	Madison County	MS	Roger Glenn Tankesly, Jr.	2007	2158
*170 3/8	25 5/8 21 4/8	16 5/8	5 9	Highland County	OH	Billy Hester	2008	2158
*170 3/8	24 0/8 23 3/8	17 2/8	6 8	Stony Plain	ALB	Alexander W. Ruddock	2009	2158
170 3/8	23 2/8 22 2/8	17 6/8	6 7	Hardin County	OH	Lee Fensler	2009	2158
170 2/8	24 7/8 25 5/8	17 6/8	11 9	Callaway County	MO	Larry Murphy	1988	2173
170 2/8	26 4/8 26 2/8	18 7/8	7 6	Stephenson County	IL	James Heiler	1988	2173
170 2/8	22 1/8 23 6/8	19 0/8	7 9	Warren County	IA	Grant A. Poindexter	1991	2173
170 2/8	20 7/8 21 2/8	20 0/8	12 9	Penobscot County	ME	Joe Valley	1998	2173
170 2/8	24 7/8 24 0/8	19 1/8	7 6	Schuyler County	IL	Jay D. Van Voorhis	1998	2173
170 2/8	25 4/8 25 0/8	19 0/8	8 7	Russell County	KY	Richard Stephens	1999	2173
170 2/8	24 4/8 23 4/8	16 3/8	7 9	Jasper County	IL	Jerry A. Martin	2000	2173
170 2/8	23 7/8 23 4/8	20 6/8	8 7	Vermillion County	IN	Jack D. Fields II	2002	2173
*170 2/8	25 6/8 25 0/8	16 6/8	7 5	St. Louis County	MO	Scott Boain	2003	2173
170 2/8	25 1/8 23 0/8	19 7/8	7 6	Schuyler County	IL	Robert Paveletz	2004	2173
170 2/8	25 0/8 25 5/8	19 4/8	6 9	Richland County	IL	Keith Craig	2005	2173
170 2/8	22 3/8 23 2/8	18 2/8	7 7	Kleberg County	TX	Robert Nichols	2006	2173
*170 2/8	22 3/8 24 2/8	16 4/8	9 10	Adams County	IL	Ronald D. Carlson, Jr.	2009	2173

658

WHITETAIL DEER (NON-TYPICAL ANTLERS)

Minimum Score 155   Continued

SCORE	LENGTH OF R MAIN BEAM L	INSIDE SPREAD	NUMBER OF R POINTS L	AREA	STATE/PROVINCE	HUNTER'S NAME	DATE	RANK
170 1/8	24 1/8 22 3/8	17 6/8	7 9	Lyon County	KS	Russell Reed	1986	2186
170 1/8	22 6/8 23 0/8	17 2/8	9 8	Cowley County	KS	Aaron Chaplin	1990	2186
170 1/8	21 1/8 22 0/8	16 1/8	7 8	Grayson County	TX	Freddie Gowin	1992	2186
170 1/8	23 0/8 24 3/8	17 7/8	10 11	Washington County	KS	Bruce A. Eickmann	1994	2186
170 1/8	22 4/8 25 2/8	19 3/8	8 7	Trempealeau County	WI	Don Baardseth	1997	2186
170 1/8	25 0/8 24 0/8	21 2/8	8 7	Logan County	IL	Doug Knox	1997	2186
170 1/8	25 4/8 27 5/8	19 1/8	7 11	Henderson County	KY	Taylor N. Tompkins	2001	2186
170 1/8	24 1/8 24 7/8	19 5/8	7 6	Sawyer County	WI	Alan Meyers	2001	2186
170 1/8	22 5/8 21 7/8	19 5/8	6 6	Comanche County	KS	Ken Beck	2001	2186
170 1/8	23 0/8 22 4/8	23 6/8	7 7	Vernon County	WI	Michael Kyser	2002	2186
170 1/8	24 3/8 24 7/8	18 7/8	7 8	Bond County	IL	Rande Hediger	2002	2186
170 1/8	25 1/8 24 5/8	19 1/8	6 7	La Porte County	IN	Gene Davis	2002	2186
170 1/8	21 0/8 20 5/8	16 4/8	7 8	Suffolk County	NY	Mark T. Butta	2002	2186
170 1/8	23 0/8 24 3/8	15 4/8	6 6	Pike County	IL	Tom Goldasich	2004	2186
*170 1/8	25 2/8 25 1/8	21 2/8	5 5	Guthrie County	IA	Mike Ayres	2004	2186
170 1/8	21 2/8 20 7/8	16 4/8	9 8	Waupaca County	WI	Wesley Beyersdorf	2005	2186
*170 1/8	22 7/8 22 7/8	21 2/8	9 8	Charles County	MD	Jason C. Easterling	2005	2186
170 1/8	23 0/8 23 7/8	15 0/8	7 7	Walsh County	ND	Lynn Campbell	2009	2186
170 0/8	25 1/8 21 6/8	19 5/8	9 12	Van Buren County	IA	Gary W. Schutt	1987	2204
170 0/8	23 5/8 23 1/8	18 5/8	4 11	Lawrence County	IL	Steven M. Blinn	1995	2204
170 0/8	22 4/8 22 1/8	17 6/8	6 6	Fremont County	IA	Leeland Harvey	1998	2204
170 0/8	22 5/8 23 2/8	17 0/8	9 4	Beaverhead County	MT	Dennis Rehse	1999	2204
170 0/8	23 7/8 24 5/8	18 5/8	12 8	Greene County	IL	Clinton M. Thompson	2002	2204
170 0/8	23 3/8 23 5/8	18 2/8	8 8	Jones County	IA	Mark Stanlberg	2002	2204
170 0/8	22 7/8 24 6/8	20 2/8	7 5	Houston County	MN	Bill Clink	2002	2204
170 0/8	23 6/8 22 6/8	23 1/8	7 7	Barton County	KS	Mathew Wharton	2002	2204
170 0/8	26 2/8 27 2/8	18 4/8	5 8	Wayne County	KY	Michael Dobbs	2003	2204
170 0/8	22 1/8 22 4/8	16 0/8	8 9	Meriwether County	GA	Bill Keith	2003	2204
170 0/8	25 7/8 26 3/8	20 5/8	7 7	Wapello County	IA	Greg J. Riley	2003	2204
170 0/8	24 0/8 24 3/8	19 0/8	8 6	McDonough County	IL	Dustin Freeman	2006	2204
170 0/8	24 1/8 25 2/8	19 0/8	8 9	Clark County	IN	Ronald D. Knox	2009	2204
169 7/8	25 2/8 23 4/8	21 3/8	10 12	Marion County	IA	Gerald T. Dowell	1994	2217
169 7/8	25 2/8 26 4/8	21 6/8	5 7	Will County	IL	Dwane G. Young	1995	2217
169 7/8	24 3/8 24 3/8	18 6/8	9 7	Dodge County	NE	Erik Palle	1997	2217
169 7/8	26 6/8 27 1/8	19 7/8	6 10	Harper County	KS	Brian Chackan	2001	2217
169 7/8	21 5/8 22 2/8	18 2/8	7 8	Fayette County	IL	Terry L. Jones	2003	2217
*169 7/8	21 3/8 21 4/8	16 4/8	6 9	Wyandotte County	KS	Johno F. Marks	2003	2217
169 7/8	25 6/8 24 4/8	16 4/8	7 7	St. Charles County	MO	Frank Quesenberry	2005	2217
169 7/8	21 6/8 22 3/8	15 0/8	8 6	Beaverhead County	MT	Dennis Rehse	2007	2217
*169 7/8	23 4/8 23 5/8	17 7/8	6 8	Warren County	IA	Gary Albertson	2007	2217
169 7/8	26 1/8 24 6/8	17 2/8	6 7	Dallas County	IA	Steve A. Marsh	2008	2217
*169 7/8	23 3/8 26 3/8	16 5/8	7 5	Morrison County	MN	Kurt Da quist	2009	2217
169 6/8	24 4/8 25 1/8	17 7/8	6 6	Carter County	KY	Timothy Carter	1974	2228
169 6/8	26 2/8 27 2/8	20 7/8	8 5	Oldham County	KY	Dewane Shepherd	2000	2228
169 6/8	24 6/8 24 4/8	19 5/8	5 7	Piatt County	IL	Jason Walker	2000	2228
169 6/8	25 3/8 25 1/8	17 0/8	8 6	Hamilton County	IL	Mark A. Miller	2002	2228
169 6/8	21 5/8 19 7/8	15 4/8	7 9	Ray County	MO	Brett Gryder	2004	2228
169 6/8	21 6/8 21 0/8	16 2/8	7 6	Howard County	MO	Gary Davis	2005	2228
169 6/8	21 6/8 24 0/8	17 0/8	9 9	Carter County	MO	Greg Meyer	2006	2228
*169 6/8	26 3/8 26 1/8	18 0/8	9 6	Muscatine County	IA	Marty Radtke	2007	2228
*169 6/8	27 2/8 25 5/8	21 2/8	6 7	Grant County	WI	John Borzick	2007	2228
*169 6/8	26 5/8 25 0/8	20 2/8	5 6	Tippecanoe County	IN	Don Pickell	2007	2228
169 6/8	21 5/8 22 2/8	18 3/8	7 9	Nemaha County	NE	Gus D. Smith	2008	2228
169 5/8	26 5/8 27 6/8	22 0/8	7 7	Dodge County	MN	Lawrence Sowieja	1973	2239
169 5/8	22 7/8 20 4/8	20 0/8	7 8	Pike County	MO	Marlin E. Foree	1988	2239
169 5/8	22 6/8 22 4/8	17 7/8	7 8	Clark County	IL	Dennis Snow	1998	2239
169 5/8	22 2/8 21 3/8	15 3/8	7 6	Oconto County	WI	Anthony Janecek	2000	2239
169 5/8	20 6/8 22 0/8	17 1/8	7 8	Pike County	IL	Brent Smith	2002	2239
*169 5/8	22 7/8 22 4/8	16 6/8	7 7	Dearborn County	IN	Charlie Amberger	2003	2239
169 5/8	23 5/8 25 0/8	18 1/8	6 6	Crawford County	WI	Jeffrey Heisz	2004	2239
*169 5/8	23 4/8 23 5/8	8 0/8	10 10	Montgomery County	KS	Jason Snellbaker	2004	2239
169 5/8	27 2/8 27 6/8	23 1/8	8 6	Barber County	KS	Dan Wolf	2007	2239
169 5/8	25 6/8 23 7/8	19 6/8	6 7	Madison County	IL	Todd Johnessee	2007	2239
169 5/8	21 0/8 24 1/8	21 7/8	10 9	Barron County	WI	Shelby Fox	2009	2239
169 4/8	25 5/8 24 2/8	23 0/8	6 8	Branch County	MI	Roy D. Grigsby	1988	2250
169 4/8	25 2/8 25 4/8	21 0/8	6 7	Price County	WI	James E. Johnson	1990	2250
169 4/8	21 4/8 21 3/8	14 0/8	8 8	Adams County	IL	Sal Carlomagno	1996	2250
169 4/8	24 1/8 22 2/8	15 4/8	7 8	Pawnee County	OK	Virgil Cunningham	1999	2250
169 4/8	26 0/8 25 5/8	17 3/8	9 6	Henry County	IN	Charles D. Moore	2000	2250
169 4/8	24 4/8 23 6/8	18 1/8	8 7	La Porte County	IN	Chad A. Schau	2004	2250
*169 4/8	22 1/8 18 3/8	17 3/8	6 8	Lucas County	IA	Bryan Rabb	2006	2250
169 4/8	26 4/8 27 1/8	20 1/8	8 8	Lafayette County	WI	Peter A. Whitcomb	2007	2250
169 4/8	24 2/8 23 3/8	17 4/8	6 8	Kewaunee County	WI	Christine Romuald	2009	2250
169 3/8	25 6/8 25 0/8	18 6/8	8 6	Emmet County	IA	Paul Love	1992	2259
169 3/8	25 5/8 25 1/8	17 5/8	6 5	Jo Daviess County	IL	Thomas M. Bradbury	1998	2259
169 3/8	26 6/8 24 0/8	18 1/8	8 9	Crawford County	WI	Brian M. Johannes	1998	2259
169 3/8	23 0/8 22 4/8	20 0/8	7 8	Jackson County	MI	Robert M. Craft	1999	2259
169 3/8	21 6/8 21 0/8	15 2/8	7 9	Clark County	KS	Arthur Trey Brown	2001	2259
169 3/8	23 0/8 23 7/8	17 1/8	9 8	McLean County	IL	Chad Davis	2003	2259
169 3/8	23 0/8 21 6/8	17 1/8	9 7	Dallas County	IA	Jimmy Mikesell	2004	2259
*169 3/8	25 7/8 25 6/8	21 0/8	8 6	Linn County	IA	Paul Yamilkoski	2004	2259
169 3/8	23 4/8 24 2/8	18 0/8	9 6	Brown County	IL	Kenneth Garls	2004	2259
*169 3/8	22 0/8 22 4/8	19 0/8	10 8	Jefferson County	IL	Derrick Cunningham	2005	2259
169 3/8	22 0/8 22 0/8	15 7/8	8 8	New Castle County	DE	Kevin P. Cuff	2006	2259
*169 3/8	23 2/8 23 0/8	17 1/8	6 8	Madison County	IA	Brian Allen Gray	2006	2259
*169 3/8	17 6/8 20 5/8	14 2/8	15 6	Harlan County	NE	Dennis Duckert	2008	2259
169 2/8	23 4/8 23 7/8	18 5/8	6 8	Rice County	MN	Vernon J. Kleve	1972	2272
169 2/8	25 4/8 26 2/8	19 4/8	7 8	Schuyler County	IL	Robert J. Logsdon	1981	2272
169 2/8	23 2/8 23 6/8	17 4/8	7 8	Washington County	WI	Tony Snow	1991	2272
169 2/8	24 0/8 23 4/8	18 4/8	8 7	La Crosse County	WI	Ronald E. Anderson	1995	2272
169 2/8	22 1/8 22 6/8	17 1/8	8 9	Saginaw County	MI	Dawn M. Adlen	1998	2272
169 2/8	24 5/8 25 5/8	18 0/8	8 7	Sumner County	KS	Terry DuPree	1998	2272
169 2/8	23 3/8 23 3/8	17 2/8	7 7	Vermilion County	IL	Jeff Parkerson	2000	2272
169 2/8	24 6/8 23 3/8	17 7/8	6 8	Jefferson County	KS	James A. Baker	2003	2272
169 2/8	22 5/8 22 7/8	15 3/8	9 9	Douglas County	WI	Bryan D. Score	2005	2272

659

WHITETAIL DEER (NON-TYPICAL ANTLERS)

Minimum Score 155

Continued

SCORE	LENGTH OF R MAIN BEAM L	INSIDE SPREAD	NUMBER OF R POINTS L	AREA	STATE/ PROVINCE	HUNTER'S NAME	DATE	RANK
*169 2/8	25 1/8 24 4/8	16 2/8	5 10	Jackson County	IA	Allen Roling	2005	2272
*169 2/8	26 0/8 26 0/8	19 3/8	8 9	Clark County	IL	Greg A. Gonder	2007	2272
169 1/8	22 2/8 22 2/8	15 5/8	9 10	Lincoln County	NE	Michael Scott Chase	1994	2283
169 1/8	21 7/8 22 6/8	18 5/8	9 6	Wapello County	IA	Arnold E. Vest	2002	2283
169 1/8	21 4/8 21 0/8	16 7/8	8 8	Frederick County	VA	Neil P. Bartles	2003	2283
169 1/8	24 1/8 23 4/8	16 5/8	8 8	Adams County	IL	Brad L. Voth	2003	2283
169 1/8	25 4/8 26 2/8	18 2/8	5 5	Kay County	OK	Casey Weant	2003	2283
169 1/8	23 3/8 23 7/8	17 1/8	8 6	Sarpy County	NE	Arthur Estes	2003	2283
169 1/8	25 6/8 25 4/8	20 0/8	9 10	Venango County	PA	Randy E. Miller II	2004	2283
169 1/8	23 2/8 22 7/8	18 6/8	7 8	Greene County	PA	David M. O'Hara	2005	2283
169 1/8	23 5/8 24 2/8	21 4/8	8 8	Erie County	NY	Todd Anderson	2006	2283
169 1/8	22 5/8 21 4/8	20 1/8	5 8	Bureau County	IL	Josef K. Rud	2006	2283
169 1/8	29 1/8 27 5/8	22 4/8	9 4	Coles County	IL	Jim Eveland	2008	2283
169 0/8	23 5/8 22 6/8	22 6/8	11 9	Suffolk County	NY	John Bennett	1991	2294
169 0/8	23 4/8 22 1/8	16 4/8	6 6	Vilas County	WI	Dan Herson	1992	2294
169 0/8	24 1/8 19 7/8	17 4/8	5 11	Fond du Lac County	WI	Steven Beer	1998	2294
169 0/8	25 2/8 25 2/8	19 1/8	9 6	Logan County	KY	David Lynn Yoder	1998	2294
169 0/8	21 1/8 22 5/8	17 1/8	7 7	Wilson County	KS	Lanny Forsythe	1998	2294
169 0/8	23 3/8 22 4/8	19 7/8	7 6	Chippewa County	WI	Steven Telisczak, Sr.	1999	2294
169 0/8	25 4/8 24 6/8	16 1/8	5 7	Dane County	WI	Steven R. Miller	1999	2294
169 0/8	23 2/8 23 6/8	19 2/8	9 6	Carroll County	MO	Richard Cunningham	2000	2294
169 0/8	26 0/8 25 0/8	17 7/8	7 9	Barber County	KS	Donald Moulton	2002	2294
169 0/8	24 5/8 24 0/8	19 2/8	5 7	Stafford County	KS	Bill J. Zerger	2004	2294
169 0/8	24 6/8 22 0/8	19 5/8	11 8	Ward County	ND	Kevin P. Nelson	2005	2294
169 0/8	26 0/8 25 3/8	22 3/8	5 6	Alexander County	IL	Marc Sheffer	2005	2294
*169 0/8	29 0/8 27 7/8	21 6/8	5 10	Fayette County	IN	Dan Scott	2007	2294
169 0/8	25 0/8 24 2/8	20 7/8	8 6	Chisago County	MN	Brady Sinn	2009	2294
168 7/8	22 4/8 21 6/8	19 4/8	7 8	Meeker County	MN	Ralph Hakel	1964	2308
168 7/8	25 5/8 23 5/8	19 7/8	6 6	Otoe County	NE	Roberto Z. Duran	1990	2308
168 7/8	26 7/8 26 3/8	19 5/8	7 6	Dane County	WI	Craig Lunaas	1997	2308
168 7/8	24 7/8 24 7/8	22 4/8	6 7	McLean County	IL	James B. Smith	1998	2308
*168 7/8	23 6/8 24 1/8	16 5/8	7 7	Elk County	KS	Clinton Hromek	2003	2308
168 7/8	24 6/8 24 4/8	17 2/8	6 7	Switzerland County	IN	Jeff Bennett	2004	2308
*168 7/8	28 5/8 27 4/8	22 5/8	7 7	Crawford County	WI	Jeff Bald	2005	2308
168 7/8	24 0/8 23 7/8	19 6/8	6 7	De Kalb County	IN	N. Dallas Frye	2005	2308
168 6/8	24 1/8 25 1/8	20 3/8	9 8	Olmsted County	MN	Jeff Meyer	1974	2316
168 6/8	23 6/8 24 6/8	23 5/8	6 8	Saunders County	NE	Joe Crnkovich	1991	2316
168 6/8	21 3/8 21 2/8	15 3/8	11 9	Alfalfa County	OK	William D. Yirka	1991	2316
168 6/8	25 2/8 25 1/8	16 6/8	8 6	La Salle County	IL	David J. Kinczewski	1995	2316
168 6/8	26 2/8 26 1/8	19 2/8	6 9	Elgin	ONT	Steve Marcinkiewicz	1995	2316
168 6/8	23 1/8 21 3/8	15 3/8	8 8	Olmsted County	MN	Aaron Stevens	1998	2316
168 6/8	27 2/8 26 2/8	17 0/8	7 8	McDonough County	IL	Greg A. Breeden	2000	2316
168 6/8	26 4/8 25 2/8	18 0/8	8 7	Woodbury County	IA	Wendell Van Beek	2005	2316
168 6/8	22 4/8 24 2/8	16 5/8	7 6	Riley County	KS	Richard L. Frye	2006	2316
*168 6/8	24 1/8 22 1/8	19 0/8	9 6	Schuyler County	MO	Richard E. St. Pierre	2008	2316
168 5/8	21 0/8 19 4/8	13 7/8	7 7	Lyon County	KS	Russell Reed	1984	2326
168 5/8	25 0/8 23 6/8	17 7/8	8 8	Grundy County	IL	Ed Vitko, Jr.	1989	2326
168 5/8	23 6/8 23 6/8	17 5/8	7 10	Waukesha County	WI	Jeff Stanton	1991	2326
168 5/8	27 6/8 26 4/8	19 5/8	7 7	Prince Georges County	MD	Mark Andrew DeVaughn	1997	2326
168 5/8	22 6/8 23 5/8	16 6/8	6 6	St. Louis County	MO	Craig R. Dew	2000	2326
168 5/8	21 6/8 22 3/8	19 1/8	8 9	La Salle County	IL	Joseph N. Arkins	2000	2326
*168 5/8	25 0/8 25 5/8	20 3/8	8 4	White County	IL	Ashley McCreary	2003	2326
168 5/8	22 5/8 21 5/8	18 3/8	7 7	Wapello County	IA	Ron Scherer	2004	2326
168 5/8	21 3/8 21 4/8	14 5/8	7 8	Greene County	IL	Robert E. Brush	2005	2326
*168 5/8	21 7/8 22 5/8	16 6/8	7 7	Charles Mix County	SD	Dave Tolliver	2009	2326
168 5/8	22 7/8 23 1/8	18 3/8	7 7	Isabella County	MI	Daniel J. Betts	2009	2326
168 4/8	24 5/8 23 5/8	16 1/8	5 7	Stearns County	MN	Robert Opatz	1987	2337
168 4/8	24 4/8 24 4/8	18 1/8	7 6	Fulton County	IN	Dennis L. Kamp	1988	2337
168 4/8	19 7/8 21 1/8	13 0/8	8 6	Pend Oreille County	WA	Aaron Coleman	1991	2337
168 4/8	23 3/8 23 2/8	20 3/8	8 8	Kleberg County	TX	Johnnie R. Walters	1997	2337
168 4/8	25 7/8 25 0/8	18 0/8	6 7	Wyandotte County	KS	Brent Chapman	2000	2337
168 4/8	25 6/8 26 0/8	19 3/8	5 6	Buffalo County	WI	Ron Schreiber	2000	2337
168 4/8	24 1/8 22 4/8	20 6/8	7 8	Allegheny County	PA	Scott L. Madey	2001	2337
168 4/8	24 0/8 23 3/8	17 4/8	7 7	Decatur County	IA	Steve Snow	2002	2337
168 4/8	26 3/8 27 5/8	17 6/8	7 6	Van Buren County	IA	Don Davidson	2002	2337
168 4/8	25 1/8 24 2/8	17 5/8	6 6	Williamson County	IL	Kevin Pyatt	2003	2337
168 4/8	25 2/8 25 2/8	16 7/8	7 7	Wichita County	TX	John Kelly	2007	2337
168 4/8	22 1/8 22 1/8	16 3/8	9 7	Gentry County	MO	Rob Teschner	2009	2337
*168 4/8	23 2/8 24 5/8	18 6/8	9 7	Pike County	IL	Don Patsy, Jr.	2009	2337
168 3/8	23 1/8 22 7/8	18 7/8	6 8	Jefferson County	IN	Michael Abston	1987	2350
168 3/8	22 2/8 22 0/8	15 7/8	8 7	Winona County	MN	Dan Hengel	1992	2350
168 3/8	25 1/8 25 4/8	15 1/8	7 7	Knox County	IL	Frank Thomas Cain	1994	2350
168 3/8	25 4/8 26 4/8	20 0/8	6 6	Lee County	IL	Gordon Gabelmann	1995	2350
168 3/8	24 4/8 24 4/8	20 6/8	6 7	Morgan County	IL	Roger Hedgpeth	1997	2350
168 3/8	24 4/8 24 3/8	16 2/8	11 12	Edmonson County	KY	Robert Cena	1998	2350
168 3/8	23 2/8 23 6/8	21 7/8	10 7	Dearborn County	IN	Mark Ginder	1998	2350
168 3/8	23 1/8 23 3/8	17 5/8	7 7	Brown County	SD	Mark White	2000	2350
168 3/8	21 7/8 21 6/8	17 2/8	8 9	Kleberg County	TX	Robert Nichols	2002	2350
168 3/8	20 6/8 22 2/8	24 7/8	8 9	Crawford County	IL	Michael L. Hardiek	2002	2350
*168 3/8	20 0/8 20 2/8	16 0/8	7 7	Waupaca County	WI	Nick Roberts	2008	2350
168 2/8	20 6/8 19 7/8	23 1/8	7 8	Washington County	OH	Mike Ferrell	1982	2361
168 2/8	25 6/8 26 4/8	18 5/8	5 9	Madison County	IA	Sam Greer	1995	2361
168 2/8	22 6/8 22 4/8	16 5/8	7 8	Burleigh County	ND	Jeff Schulz	1996	2361
168 2/8	20 6/8 22 0/8	17 1/8	8 8	Winneshiek County	IA	Bob Le Cocq	1997	2361
168 2/8	21 1/8 20 3/8	16 5/8	8 7	Fulton County	GA	Nesbit Bedingfield	1999	2361
168 2/8	22 6/8 23 3/8	16 3/8	10 9	Kent County	MD	Steve Demchyk	2002	2361
168 2/8	27 0/8 28 7/8	20 1/8	6 5	Saginaw County	MI	David R. Kiefer	2006	2361
*168 2/8	24 1/8 23 2/8	18 7/8	10 6	Schuyler County	IL	Kevin M. Garrett	2006	2361
168 2/8	20 2/8 19 0/8	19 2/8	11 14	Cooke County	TX	Brent McGee	2007	2361
*168 2/8	24 1/8 24 4/8	19 4/8	10 10	Warren County	IA	Bruce Hupke	2007	2361
*168 2/8	23 1/8 23 2/8	18 2/8	6 6	Wapello County	IA	Steve Baskett	2008	2361
168 2/8	26 7/8 25 7/8	19 2/8	7 7	Buffalo County	WI	Michael C. Kreibich	2008	2361
168 1/8	22 3/8 23 0/8	18 3/8	6 7	Ozaukee County	WI	Joe Spata	1991	2373
168 1/8	23 6/8 24 1/8	18 3/8	7 8	Cedar County	IA	Dan Burnette	1997	2373
168 1/8	19 4/8 20 7/8	19 7/8	10 7	Houston County	MN	Donald Woodhouse	1998	2373

660

WHITETAIL DEER (NON-TYPICAL ANTLERS)

Minimum Score 155 — Continued

SCORE	R MAIN BEAM L	INSIDE SPREAD	R POINTS L	AREA	STATE/ PROVINCE	HUNTER'S NAME	DATE	RANK
168 1/8	25 0/8 25 2/8	17 4/8	8 6	Marion County	IA	Chad Johnston	1998	2373
168 1/8	24 0/8 24 0/8	15 6/8	7 7	Black Hawk County	IA	Kevin Brustkern	1998	2373
168 1/8	22 1/8 22 4/8	20 4/8	6 8	Sauk County	WI	Steven Feiner	1999	2373
*168 1/8	24 6/8 24 0/8	14 1/8	8 9	Green Lake County	WI	Brian L. Schulz	2005	2373
168 1/8	22 5/8 21 7/8	19 0/8	8 8	Woodford County	KY	Jimmy Rhodus	2007	2373
*168 1/8	22 3/8 21 5/8	17 0/8	6 7	Phillips County	KS	Todd Schacknies	2007	2373
168 1/8	23 1/8 24 0/8	21 5/8	8 10	Waukesha County	WI	Daniel J. Bauer	2007	2373
168 1/8	22 1/8 23 6/8	14 5/8	10 6	Leavenworth County	KS	Doug Porter	2008	2373
168 0/8	21 3/8 21 2/8	15 6/8	7 9	Martin County	MN	Charles Sutphin	1974	2384
168 0/8	23 6/8 23 5/8	18 0/8	8 6	Jackson County	OH	Larry Carter	1996	2384
168 0/8	19 0/8 18 7/8	16 5/8	7 7	Sheboygan County	WI	Kevin K. Blanke	1998	2384
168 0/8	21 3/8 21 2/8	15 1/8	10 9	Comanche County	KS	Dan McClure	2000	2384
168 0/8	20 2/8 21 4/8	16 3/8	6 6	Doniphan County	KS	Ronald K. McConnell	2000	2384
168 0/8	25 4/8 26 0/8	15 5/8	7 7	Linn County	KS	Don Sherpy	2000	2384
168 0/8	24 0/8 23 5/8	20 0/8	6 7	McDonough County	IL	Wayne Tupper	2001	2384
168 0/8	23 0/8 23 0/8	19 2/8	6 9	Clark County	WI	Eric R. Naedler	2003	2384
168 0/8	23 1/8 23 5/8	13 7/8	11 10	Mason County	TX	Mike Cage	2005	2384
168 0/8	24 2/8 20 3/8	16 3/8	5 7	Vermillion County	IN	Steve Todd	2007	2384
*168 0/8	23 5/8 23 2/8	16 4/8	7 9	Waukesha County	WI	Mike Szalanski	2007	2384
168 0/8	24 1/8 23 3/8	23 4/8	5 7	Carroll County	IL	Scott Hartman	2007	2384
*168 0/8	24 1/8 24 2/8	16 3/8	11 6	Caldwell County	KY	Adam Peterson	2008	2384
*168 0/8	24 0/8 24 4/8	13 6/8	8 7	Marshall County	KS	Ronald C. Neill	2008	2384
168 0/8	23 3/8 24 7/8	19 3/8	7 7	Mitchell County	IA	Brandon Pajer	2009	2384
167 7/8	23 4/8 26 6/8	20 0/8	8 5	Trempealeau County	WI	Tom Reedy	1984	2399
167 7/8	22 2/8 22 2/8	19 7/8	6 8	Cypress River	MAN	Harvey Gagne	1987	2399
167 7/8	27 6/8 26 1/8	18 2/8	5 6	Greenwood County	KS	Danny Linnebur	1991	2399
167 7/8	22 4/8 21 7/8	20 4/8	7 9	Oldham County	KY	Michael G. Jeffries	1993	2399
167 7/8	22 4/8 23 0/8	17 6/8	9 9	Ferry County	WA	Tim Jerald	1994	2399
167 7/8	25 0/8 25 2/8	20 4/8	7 7	St. Clair County	IL	Bryan J. Apostol	1995	2399
167 7/8	24 0/8 24 1/8	19 6/8	9 6	Kalamazoo County	MI	Michael E. Malek	1999	2399
167 7/8	24 7/8 23 6/8	18 0/8	6 9	Erie County	PA	Ronald J. Hedlund	2000	2399
*167 7/8	22 5/8 22 7/8	15 5/8	8 6	Hancock County	IL	Diane Hurt	2003	2399
*167 7/8	23 0/8 23 6/8	19 0/8	7 8	Warren County	IN	Michael Justice	2005	2399
*167 7/8	24 4/8 24 5/8	19 7/8	5 8	Dunn County	ND	Shawn Kukowski	2005	2399
*167 7/8	21 2/8 20 5/8	12 7/8	7 9	Clay County	SD	Clint Ellis	2006	2399
*167 7/8	25 3/8 25 5/8	23 2/8	6 5	Putnam County	IL	Brad Kays	2006	2399
167 6/8	24 3/8 24 3/8	19 7/8	9 7	Scott County	IA	Gordon Vrana	1967	2412
167 6/8	24 7/8 23 7/8	19 5/8	5 8	Huntington County	IN	Scott Smith	1990	2412
167 6/8	21 7/8 24 1/8	17 4/8	5 6	Adair County	MO	Rick L. Oster	1990	2412
167 6/8	21 7/8 23 3/8	14 5/8	8 8	Barton County	KS	Lance Hockett	1990	2412
167 6/8	26 1/8 26 4/8	18 5/8	10 6	Calhoun County	MI	Joseph D. Tallent	1995	2412
167 6/8	22 2/8 22 7/8	15 1/8	7 8	Bremer County	IA	Larry Burman	1997	2412
167 6/8	21 7/8 22 2/8	17 2/8	8 6	Carroll County	IL	Carl Spaeth	1998	2412
167 6/8	25 7/8 24 5/8	23 2/8	7 7	St. Croix County	WI	Luke Seiler	2000	2412
167 6/8	24 5/8 25 0/8	18 6/8	7 6	Warren County	IA	Brad Vonk	2000	2412
167 6/8	26 3/8 25 0/8	16 2/8	6 7	Queen Annes County	MD	Peter Jayne	2002	2412
167 6/8	26 5/8 25 7/8	20 0/8	6 7	Lake County	IL	Don Kelton	2003	2412
*167 6/8	23 4/8 24 1/8	20 0/8	7 5	La Crosse County	WI	Jason W. Hess	2003	2412
167 6/8	21 4/8 21 1/8	15 2/8	9 12	Ingham County	MI	Kenneth M. Thompson	2006	2412
167 5/8	23 7/8 21 0/8	19 4/8	5 8	Frederick County	MD	Kenneth T. Ward	1991	2425
167 5/8	26 1/8 25 1/8	21 1/8	8 8	Harrison County	IA	Curt Van Lith	1992	2425
167 5/8	27 3/8 26 6/8	21 3/8	6 9	Washington County	KS	Bob Funke	1997	2425
167 5/8	23 5/8 23 3/8	20 6/8	9 8	Johnson County	IA	Mike Borwig	1997	2425
167 5/8	22 5/8 23 0/8	16 2/8	8 5	Lake County	IL	Dennis Dewar	1999	2425
167 5/8	22 2/8 22 4/8	19 6/8	8 8	Lee County	IA	Tad J. Boeding	2001	2425
167 5/8	21 6/8 19 5/8	14 5/8	10 10	Ross County	OH	Bryan L. Robson	2001	2425
167 5/8	24 4/8 26 0/8	22 0/8	9 6	Powell County	MT	Greg Carley	2004	2425
167 5/8	25 1/8 25 3/8	19 3/8	7 7	Clark County	IL	J. Scott McIlvoy	2004	2425
167 5/8	22 5/8 20 6/8	18 6/8	7 8	Dubuque County	IA	Joseph C. Hinderman	2006	2425
167 5/8	24 5/8 23 5/8	17 2/8	9 7	Cold Lake	ALB	Jeff Knowlton	2007	2425
167 5/8	21 5/8 21 5/8	14 6/8	7 9	Grant County	MN	Roger Derby	2007	2425
167 5/8	23 6/8 23 7/8	18 0/8	11 8	Pipestone	ALB	Brad Tourett	2008	2425
167 4/8	24 1/8 23 6/8	16 0/8	9 10	Iroquois County	IL	Al Weissbohn	1986	2438
167 4/8	22 1/8 22 7/8	16 5/8	8 8	Olmsted County	MN	Jay R. Flicker	1997	2438
167 4/8	25 1/8 25 0/8	20 1/8	7 5	Trempealeau County	WI	Steve Stenberg	1999	2438
167 4/8	26 6/8 26 4/8	19 6/8	6 5	Clarke County	IA	Jeff Jorgensen	1999	2438
167 4/8	23 6/8 24 2/8	18 1/8	6 6	Dane County	WI	Mike Hughes	2000	2438
167 4/8	23 3/8 23 4/8	17 2/8	9 7	Meigs County	OH	Dave Wandling	2000	2438
167 4/8	22 4/8 23 1/8	15 7/8	6 6	Hardin County	IA	Jason Jedele	2002	2438
167 4/8	21 0/8 20 6/8	14 0/8	5 8	Davis County	IA	Arvid Goettsche	2004	2438
167 4/8	21 6/8 23 1/8	20 3/8	12 6	Muscatine County	IA	Larry James Parker	2004	2438
167 4/8	22 5/8 21 4/8	16 5/8	7 10	Sauk County	WI	Mark Davis	2004	2438
167 4/8	23 5/8 26 0/8	17 2/8	6 7	Clay County	KS	Lenny Swaim	2004	2438
167 4/8	23 6/8 25 1/8	17 7/8	6 10	Will County	IL	Nicholas Macak	2005	2438
*167 4/8	25 5/8 25 5/8	19 6/8	9 6	Jewell County	KS	Stan McGuigan	2005	2438
167 4/8	22 2/8 23 1/8	14 2/8	6 9	Callaway County	MO	Tommy Thomas	2006	2438
167 4/8	20 2/8 20 6/8	19 0/8	5 8	Tippecanoe County	IN	Matt Herndon	2006	2438
167 4/8	23 1/8 23 2/8	19 0/8	8 7	Armstrong County	PA	David D. Campbell	2007	2438
167 4/8	20 2/8 22 3/8	18 1/8	8 7	Monroe County	IA	Jim Keller	2008	2438
*167 4/8	25 7/8 25 6/8	21 0/8	6 6	Boyd County	NE	Matt Alford	2009	2438
167 3/8	24 0/8 25 1/8	21 2/8	7 5	Greene County	AR	Michael Lanier	1992	2456
167 3/8	23 5/8 24 4/8	18 7/8	6 9	Vigo County	IN	Darren Scott	1994	2456
167 3/8	23 6/8 22 4/8	17 7/8	6 8	La Salle County	IL	Donald K. Greathouse	2000	2456
*167 3/8	23 6/8 24 4/8	16 3/8	9 9	Pope County	AR	Brardon Hunt	2003	2456
167 3/8	25 4/8 23 1/8	18 6/8	7 6	Steuben County	IN	Denny E. Cobb	2003	2456
167 3/8	22 5/8 23 3/8	18 5/8	7 6	Kankakee County	IL	Thomas J. Campbell	2003	2456
167 3/8	24 3/8 24 2/8	16 4/8	5 9	Clinton County	IA	Zach Summers	2006	2456
167 2/8	24 0/8 24 3/8	17 1/8	7 6	Sauk County	WI	Charles Davenport	1969	2463
167 2/8	24 5/8 26 1/8	20 3/8	9 6	Lee County	IL	Glenn L. Whitehouse	1994	2463
167 2/8	23 0/8 22 4/8	17 3/8	6 6	Buffalo County	WI	Steven B. Schroeder	1998	2463
167 2/8	22 1/8 22 0/8	19 5/8	6 6	Pike County	IL	Paul C. Morgan	1998	2463
167 2/8	23 7/8 23 4/8	17 5/8	8 9	Williamson County	IL	Jamie Ashley	1998	2463
167 2/8	25 5/8 25 4/8	19 1/8	9 7	Taylor County	WI	Brian Bucki	1998	2463
167 2/8	22 0/8 21 0/8	16 7/8	6 8	Anderson County	TX	Donnie Harris	1999	2463
167 2/8	24 0/8 23 3/8	18 0/8	7 9	Grayson County	TX	Alan Fleming	1999	2463

WHITETAIL DEER (NON-TYPICAL ANTLERS)

Minimum Score 155 — Continued

SCORE	R MAIN BEAM L	INSIDE SPREAD	R POINTS L	AREA	STATE/PROVINCE	HUNTER'S NAME	DATE	RANK
167 2/8	26 0/8 24 3/8	17 7/8	4 9	Ralls County	MO	Mike Ames	2000	2463
167 2/8	23 2/8 25 2/8	22 4/8	8 7	Bent County	CO	Harold Martine	2000	2463
*167 2/8	21 7/8 25 5/8	22 1/8	8 5	Green Lake County	WI	Ross Hausmann	2003	2463
167 2/8	20 5/8 23 0/8	22 4/8	5 6	Clark County	IL	Gerald "Gabe" Shaffner	2004	2463
167 2/8	26 5/8 26 1/8	18 3/8	6 6	La Crosse County	WI	Jim Finn	2005	2463
167 2/8	21 5/8 21 7/8	15 7/8	9 8	Door County	WI	Eric N. Johnson	2005	2463
167 2/8	20 2/8 22 3/8	17 4/8	7 10	Cass County	IN	Joseph G. Baker	2008	2463
167 2/8	20 5/8 21 2/8	18 0/8	10 7	Fulton County	GA	Greg Chesnut	2009	2463
*167 2/8	25 0/8 25 6/8	18 1/8	6 7	Jackson County	IN	Trevor Wiggam	2009	2463
*167 2/8	25 4/8 25 2/8	18 3/8	7 8	Venango County	PA	Jason Seifert	2009	2463
167 1/8	26 0/8 24 2/8	22 0/8	5 7	Macoupin County	IL	Dennis Austin	1987	2481
167 1/8	23 1/8 22 0/8	21 6/8	7 9	Floyd County	IA	Patrick E. Barrett	1990	2481
167 1/8	23 4/8 23 4/8	18 4/8	8 10	Licking County	OH	Mike Stevens	1994	2481
167 1/8	20 5/8 19 6/8	14 5/8	6 7	Hillsdale County	MI	Michael Leshkevich	1994	2481
167 1/8	20 3/8 20 3/8	17 1/8	9 7	Brown County	KS	Mike Liberty	1999	2481
167 1/8	21 0/8 21 0/8	19 6/8	6 6	Mitchell County	IA	Steven G. Johnson	2002	2481
167 1/8	27 1/8 25 2/8	14 1/8	8 6	Shawano County	WI	Raymond E. Creapeau, Jr.	2003	2481
167 1/8	20 7/8 20 6/8	20 2/8	10 7	Atoka County	OK	Duane Bodette	2004	2481
*167 1/8	26 0/8 26 2/8	19 3/8	5 7	Webster County	KY	Manny Alexander	2005	2481
167 1/8	23 5/8 23 0/8	17 5/8	8 6	Madison County	IA	Randy Andreini	2006	2481
167 1/8	26 2/8 25 2/8	20 4/8	8 8	Spokane County	WA	John Schneider	2008	2481
167 1/8	21 2/8 22 4/8	18 0/8	7 10	Miller County	MO	Dalton Helmig	2009	2481
*167 1/8	22 4/8 25 5/8	16 7/8	6 7	Door County	WI	Scott Kolstad	2009	2481
167 1/8	22 1/8 20 2/8	14 0/8	4 8	Wayne County	NE	Mark C. Hawkins	2009	2481
167 1/8	24 3/8 23 5/8	18 6/8	6 9	Ferry County	WA	George Webster	2009	2481
167 1/8	22 0/8 22 4/8	16 4/8	6 8	Bureau County	IL	Jim F. Entwistle	2009	2481
167 0/8	22 2/8 22 1/8	18 3/8	8 5	Wright County	IA	Robert Filbrandt	1974	2497
167 0/8	24 7/8 24 0/8	19 0/8	7 9	Pawnee County	NE	Ed Baburek	1987	2497
167 0/8	21 3/8 22 0/8	14 4/8	5 6	Jackson County	WI	Craig R. Johnson	1993	2497
167 0/8	23 6/8 23 7/8	18 1/8	8 6	Juneau County	WI	Darren M. Green, Sr.	1994	2497
167 0/8	21 5/8 24 2/8	18 1/8	7 6	Amherst County	VA	Anthony Olswfski	1996	2497
167 0/8	25 6/8 25 0/8	21 6/8	6 6	Kane County	IL	Jason Dempsay	2001	2497
167 0/8	23 6/8 21 6/8	19 3/8	7 6	Washtenaw County	MI	David G. Noack	2001	2497
167 0/8	22 1/8 22 2/8	17 4/8	7 5	Adams County	IL	Edward D. Benson III	2002	2497
167 0/8	24 3/8 25 4/8	17 0/8	10 7	Warren County	IA	Bruce Hupke	2005	2497
167 0/8	21 4/8 21 4/8	18 6/8	6 8	Grant County	SD	Arnie Veen	2006	2497
166 7/8	25 3/8 25 6/8	18 2/8	6 6	Hubbard County	MN	Jack Smythe	1973	2507
166 7/8	19 3/8 20 2/8	16 2/8	8 6	Buffalo County	WI	Alan Gleiter	1998	2507
166 7/8	24 0/8 24 2/8	17 0/8	8 6	Columbia County	WI	Doug Unser	1998	2507
166 7/8	24 2/8 24 7/8	18 0/8	7 9	Callaway County	MO	Mark Dodge	1999	2507
166 7/8	22 5/8 23 4/8	14 3/8	9 8	Adams County	IL	Tracy Hanlin	2002	2507
166 7/8	26 1/8 24 3/8	18 2/8	10 8	Linn County	IA	Christopher J. Swanke	2003	2507
166 7/8	19 2/8 24 0/8	13 5/8	10 6	Chester County	PA	Dave Hill	2003	2507
166 7/8	23 4/8 24 0/8	20 3/8	8 7	Livingston County	IL	Richard Friedman	2004	2507
166 7/8	22 6/8 24 1/8	18 6/8	7 7	Monroe County	IL	Ben Neff	2004	2507
166 7/8	23 5/8 22 7/8	17 2/8	5 7	Harrison County	IA	D. Scott Jochims	2004	2507
166 7/8	24 1/8 24 4/8	17 7/8	7 7	Worcester County	MA	Larry Berestka	2005	2507
*166 7/8	22 2/8 21 2/8	15 6/8	6 8	Johnson County	IA	Jeremy Hotz	2005	2507
166 7/8	22 7/8 22 5/8	16 4/8	9 8	Union County	SD	Chad Anema	2007	2507
*166 7/8	24 2/8 23 6/8	18 1/8	6 10	Emmons County	ND	Troy Hanson	2007	2507
*166 7/8	25 3/8 25 1/8	20 0/8	4 7	Pike County	IL	Jarrod Dwight Ring	2007	2507
*166 7/8	25 5/8 24 4/8	14 7/8	6 8	Taylor County	WI	Jeramie Duellman	2008	2507
*166 7/8	23 3/8 24 6/8	17 7/8	7 9	Dunn County	WI	Del Shay	2008	2507
*166 7/8	20 0/8 17 1/8	19 5/8	15 6	Good Spirit Lake	SAS	Kevin Kohlert	2010	2507
166 6/8	25 1/8 24 5/8	17 7/8	7 7	Kenedy County	TX	Steve Ray Dollar	1990	2525
166 6/8	27 4/8 26 6/8	20 6/8	5 7	Berrien County	MI	Larry Lewis	1998	2525
166 6/8	21 4/8 24 5/8	21 3/8	6 8	McHenry County	IL	Brent Smith	2001	2525
166 6/8	23 2/8 23 2/8	19 5/8	7 7	Buffalo County	WI	Kurt Sleighter	2002	2525
*166 6/8	24 6/8 23 6/8	22 3/8	7 6	Muskingum County	OH	Greg Gohring	2003	2525
*166 6/8	21 7/8 22 4/8	19 6/8	7 6	Suffolk County	NY	Mario Curra	2003	2525
166 6/8	25 3/8 25 5/8	14 5/8	6 7	Knox County	IL	Brent Lindsey	2003	2525
*166 6/8	24 2/8 25 7/8	17 2/8	5 6	Clayton County	IA	Dennis Ulbrich	2004	2525
166 6/8	23 0/8 22 6/8	19 0/8	5 7	Trempealeau County	WI	Greg Korpal	2009	2525
166 5/8	28 3/8 26 6/8	15 1/8	8 9	Shelby County	IA	Billy Custer	1968	2534
166 5/8	22 7/8 21 7/8	20 5/8	7 7	Wabaunsee County	KS	Charles Bisnette	1991	2534
166 5/8	23 4/8 25 1/8	19 4/8	6 7	E. Carroll Parish	LA	Tim Harrell	1997	2534
166 5/8	23 1/8 23 7/8	15 7/8	9 8	Franklin County	KS	Tim Berry	1998	2534
166 5/8	23 2/8 25 0/8	21 7/8	8 9	Fairfax County	VA	David Phillip Conrad	1999	2534
166 5/8	24 3/8 22 7/8	19 6/8	6 7	Gogebic County	MI	Wayne A. Stanz	2000	2534
166 5/8	22 0/8 23 0/8	17 0/8	6 5	Marathon County	WI	Kevin Fischer	2004	2534
*166 5/8	21 4/8 22 0/8	15 2/8	7 8	Fond du Lac County	WI	Tim Lamonska	2006	2534
166 5/8	26 3/8 20 4/8	19 7/8	5 7	Chippewa County	WI	Brent Conrad	2008	2534
*166 5/8	22 0/8 22 5/8	15 3/8	7 6	Pottawatomie County	KS	Arnie Camire	2008	2534
*166 5/8	25 7/8 25 0/8	20 4/8	8 5	Brown County	IL	Timothy L. Wyrick	2009	2534
166 4/8	22 0/8 23 3/8	14 5/8	9 5	Midland County	MI	Michael D. Pretzer	1987	2545
166 4/8	26 4/8 25 4/8	17 6/8	10 7	Trempealeau County	WI	Jason J. Molis	2001	2545
166 4/8	22 0/8 22 1/8	20 3/8	6 6	McDonough County	IL	Les Twidwell	2003	2545
166 4/8	23 4/8 24 6/8	13 3/8	8 9	Randolph County	IL	Bret Heckenberger	2003	2545
*166 4/8	20 6/8 23 5/8	18 4/8	7 7	Knox County	IL	Kurt Vanderostyne	2004	2545
166 4/8	25 6/8 26 0/8	19 6/8	4 9	Iowa County	WI	Kevin Peterson	2007	2545
166 4/8	22 7/8 22 1/8	15 6/8	8 8	Monona County	IA	Michael E. Long	2007	2545
166 4/8	24 0/8 23 7/8	17 3/8	8 9	Cumberland County	IL	Glen Waldhoff	2008	2545
166 3/8	24 5/8 24 5/8	16 2/8	6 6	Brown County	SD	Frank Bauer	1974	2553
166 3/8	21 6/8 20 3/8	17 3/8	7 7	Okotoks	ALB	Darren Dale	1980	2553
166 3/8	21 7/8 24 5/8	18 4/8	9 7	Seminole County	OK	Aliene Turner	1994	2553
166 3/8	22 5/8 23 1/8	21 3/8	8 8	Waupaca County	WI	Terry A. Butterfield	1998	2553
166 3/8	21 5/8 21 3/8	14 1/8	7 11	Outagamie County	WI	John R. Friebel	1998	2553
166 3/8	20 6/8 23 6/8	15 2/8	9 8	Iron County	WI	Joseph Hahn	2001	2553
*166 3/8	17 3/8 17 0/8	16 4/8	8 8	Wise County	TX	Delk Batson	2005	2553
166 3/8	24 0/8 24 4/8	16 6/8	8 8	Buffalo County	WI	Donald Gorichanaz	2005	2553
166 3/8	23 7/8 24 5/8	20 7/8	8 7	Dunn County	WI	Paul L. Behling	2005	2553
*166 3/8	21 1/8 20 3/8	11 6/8	6 6	St. Louis County	MN	Darrin Severance	2008	2553
166 2/8	23 2/8 23 2/8	18 0/8	7 9	Linn County	IA	Guy D. Williams, Jr.	1986	2563
166 2/8	27 0/8 25 3/8	21 3/8	6 10	Cecil County	MD	John E. Kostic	1991	2563
166 2/8	22 6/8 22 4/8	19 4/8	9 8	Washington County	WI	William R. Mahnke	1995	2563

WHITETAIL DEER (NON-TYPICAL ANTLERS)

Minimum Score 155   Continued

SCORE	LENGTH OF R MAIN BEAM L	INSIDE SPREAD	NUMBER OF R POINTS L	AREA	STATE/ PROVINCE	HUNTER'S NAME	DATE	RANK
166 2/8	21 6/8	26 2/8	23 3/8	9	8	Clark County	OH	James A. Boyd	1999	2563
166 2/8	24 0/8	25 4/8	23 4/8	7	7	Clark County	SD	Nordean Froke	2001	2563
166 2/8	22 1/8	21 6/8	16 3/8	7	9	Sumner County	KS	Brian K. Strickland	2002	2563
166 2/8	28 5/8	27 1/8	19 1/8	8	9	Waupaca County	WI	Steven A. Hauk	2005	2563
*166 2/8	21 1/8	21 2/8	15 0/8	7	7	Warren County	IL	Chris Bies	2006	2563
*166 2/8	19 7/8	19 7/8	15 4/8	9	7	Monona County	IA	Tom Sorenson	2009	2563
166 1/8	22 5/8	23 1/8	17 3/8	7	7	Reagan County	TX	James E. Borron	1997	2572
166 1/8	24 7/8	23 6/8	16 1/8	9	10	Suffolk County	NY	Anthony Alesi	1997	2572
166 1/8	27 2/8	26 4/8	17 3/8	9	5	Forsyth County	NC	Bill Froelich	1998	2572
166 1/8	22 2/8	23 4/8	17 3/8	7	11	Marshall County	KS	Travis Prockish	1999	2572
166 1/8	21 3/8	23 2/8	21 2/8	7	7	Belmont County	OH	Loring Ramsay	2000	2572
166 1/8	24 7/8	25 3/8	18 5/8	6	7	Washington County	PA	Timothy G. Hickle, Jr.	2002	2572
166 1/8	24 4/8	24 4/8	18 7/8	7	6	Clark County	IL	Tommy Thornton	2002	2572
*166 1/8	23 7/8	23 7/8	18 5/8	7	7	Polk County	WI	Tim Hutton	2004	2572
*166 1/8	23 1/8	23 2/8	16 5/8	8	6	Brown County	IL	Patrick Eberhardt	2004	2572
*166 1/8	25 5/8	24 0/8	20 1/8	8	6	Suffolk County	NY	Michael Tessitore	2004	2572
166 1/8	22 7/8	20 6/8	13 6/8	8	7	Sheboygan County	WI	Randy Kolpin	2007	2572
166 1/8	27 5/8	25 5/8	18 5/8	7	7	Union County	IA	Mickey W. Hellickson	2008	2572
166 0/8	23 0/8	27 0/8	20 1/8	8	7	Ross County	OH	Randy Johnson	1981	2584
166 0/8	21 5/8	20 2/8	15 3/8	8	8	Pope County	AR	Donald Alan Barnett	1983	2584
166 0/8	24 4/8	22 5/8	18 1/8	7	8	Talbot County	MD	Ritchy Eason	1987	2584
166 0/8	25 5/8	26 1/8	18 4/8	8	8	Winnebago County	IA	Greg Beaver	1996	2584
166 0/8	25 2/8	24 7/8	17 3/8	10	6	Clinton County	MO	Chris Thomas	1996	2584
166 0/8	25 6/8	26 2/8	18 3/8	6	8	Madison County	IA	Gary Knoll	1997	2584
166 0/8	26 3/8	26 3/8	19 7/8	6	9	Mills County	IA	Allen Bruce	1997	2584
166 0/8	26 2/8	26 1/8	19 1/8	6	7	Marquette County	WI	Tim Landolt	1999	2584
166 0/8	26 2/8	24 6/8	18 4/8	5	7	Defiance County	OH	William Riley	2002	2584
*166 0/8	24 4/8	25 3/8	17 4/8	6	8	Fillmore County	MN	Tyler Benson	2005	2584
166 0/8	21 5/8	21 4/8	16 1/8	5	7	Clarke County	IA	Brad Northway	2007	2584
166 0/8	22 2/8	22 7/8	16 7/8	7	11	Pottawatomie County	KS	Drew Forster	2008	2584
*166 0/8	26 1/8	26 5/8	14 6/8	9	6	Marion County	IL	Clifford E. Phillips	2008	2584
165 7/8	24 2/8	22 2/8	17 3/8	6	6	Arkansas County	AR	Bruce Wiggins	1959	2597
165 7/8	21 1/8	25 2/8	19 3/8	8	8	Gallatin County	KY	John C. Vetter	1977	2597
165 7/8	23 0/8	22 7/8	19 4/8	6	6	Brown County	IL	Angela Vogel	1983	2597
165 7/8	25 4/8	25 1/8	16 3/8	6	8	Carroll County	MD	John F. Brunnett	1986	2597
165 7/8	20 3/8	21 6/8	14 5/8	8	9	Sedgwick County	KS	Gary Raney	1988	2597
165 7/8	24 0/8	23 6/8	16 4/8	9	6	Hardin County	KY	Dale Roberson	1995	2597
165 7/8	21 2/8	23 0/8	17 2/8	7	9	Kleberg County	TX	Johnnie R. Walters	1995	2597
165 7/8	23 3/8	23 0/8	17 4/8	5	8	Pike County	MO	Paul Wickerham	1997	2597
165 7/8	23 2/8	22 0/8	17 1/8	9	8	Fort Assiniboine	ALB	William Lee Farr, Jr.	2005	2597
165 7/8	23 5/8	24 1/8	17 5/8	7	5	Monroe County	IA	Duane A. Harthoorn	2005	2597
*165 7/8	27 1/8	26 1/8	17 5/8	7	8	Jefferson County	NE	Dave Bedlan	2005	2597
165 7/8	25 6/8	24 3/8	19 2/8	7	5	Edwards County	IL	Donnie Goldman	2005	2597
165 7/8	24 1/8	23 6/8	17 1/8	7	7	Jefferson County	OH	Luke Hoobler	2006	2597
165 7/8	22 4/8	22 4/8	13 3/8	8	9	Webb County	TX	James D. Bailey	2007	2597
165 6/8	23 0/8	25 0/8	19 5/8	8	6	Bureau County	IL	Timothy J. Ellis	1992	2611
165 6/8	19 0/8	26 6/8	20 0/8	6	5	Brown County	IL	Jeff Richardson	1993	2611
165 6/8	23 1/8	23 4/8	18 2/8	7	6	Vermilion County	IL	John D. Brassard, Sr.	1995	2611
165 6/8	25 3/8	23 5/8	17 0/8	9	6	Morris County	NJ	Russell Davidson	1995	2611
165 6/8	22 0/8	22 4/8	14 3/8	8	8	Gibson County	IN	Bruce Matsel	1996	2611
165 6/8	23 5/8	22 0/8	16 1/8	6	7	Polk County	IA	Todd Doering	1996	2611
165 6/8	21 4/8	22 0/8	18 4/8	7	10	Lincoln County	NE	Ronnie Bordelon	2000	2611
165 6/8	22 6/8	21 6/8	14 6/8	7	8	Jefferson County	OH	Kevin Butler	2001	2611
165 6/8	21 7/8	22 1/8	19 4/8	6	8	Grayson County	TX	Eric Burnett	2002	2611
165 6/8	20 3/8	19 2/8	17 4/8	8	7	Adams County	IL	Bill Blanchard	2003	2611
165 6/8	22 7/8	23 6/8	15 5/8	7	7	Priddis	ALB	Lorne D. Rinkel	2006	2611
165 5/8	25 0/8	24 5/8	20 4/8	11	8	Washington County	MS	James Goss, Jr.	1987	2622
165 5/8	22 3/8	21 5/8	18 6/8	8	7	Delaware County	OH	Brent Forman	1992	2622
165 5/8	23 6/8	24 4/8	13 5/8	9	7	Clark County	IL	Michael L. Ealy	1994	2622
165 5/8	24 6/8	25 5/8	18 7/8	9	9	Outagamie County	WI	Mark Lamers	1995	2622
165 5/8	22 7/8	22 5/8	19 2/8	6	8	Waupaca County	WI	Charlie Diestler	1997	2622
165 5/8	25 2/8	24 6/8	18 7/8	5	7	White Fox	SAS	Edward Toelken	1998	2622
165 5/8	20 4/8	23 0/8	17 5/8	7	8	Grundy County	IL	Larry Turner	2000	2622
165 5/8	26 1/8	25 5/8	17 0/8	6	8	Hancock County	OH	Stoney King	2001	2622
165 5/8	25 5/8	24 4/8	22 4/8	9	5	Pike County	PA	Gregory S. Guerrieri	2002	2622
165 5/8	23 6/8	23 4/8	17 7/8	6	6	Andrew County	MO	Gene Kelly	2002	2622
165 5/8	23 2/8	22 4/8	17 3/8	7	9	Clark County	MO	Troy Gregory	2003	2622
*165 5/8	24 2/8	24 6/8	17 1/8	6	7	Grand Forks County	ND	Don Wurzbacher	2004	2622
165 5/8	22 5/8	24 3/8	17 4/8	6	6	Columbia County	WI	Mark Preuss	2006	2622
165 5/8	22 4/8	23 3/8	17 3/8	6	8	Fulton County	IL	Michael Vaka	2006	2622
*165 5/8	24 5/8	25 4/8	15 7/8	9	5	Hand County	SD	Kevin Bertsch	2007	2622
165 5/8	22 6/8	22 4/8	15 4/8	6	9	Venango County	PA	Randy E. Miller II	2008	2622
165 4/8	23 5/8	22 2/8	16 2/8	5	8	Boundary County	ID	Gary Stueve	1991	2638
165 4/8	25 3/8	26 5/8	19 4/8	6	6	Lake County	IL	Daniel H. Goff	1995	2638
165 4/8	23 0/8	24 0/8	17 6/8	6	6	Stevens County	WA	Glen Berry	1995	2638
165 4/8	23 6/8	23 0/8	18 0/8	7	8	Dodge County	WI	Mike Pawelka	1996	2638
165 4/8	23 0/8	23 0/8	20 4/8	6	8	Effingham County	IL	Rollir C. Wilson	1999	2638
165 4/8	23 0/8	24 0/8	17 6/8	9	6	St. Croix County	WI	John F. Carroccio	2000	2638
165 4/8	26 4/8	25 7/8	22 3/8	5	6	Menard County	IL	Jim Elliott	2001	2638
165 4/8	25 5/8	25 4/8	17 5/8	6	9	Washington County	IL	James Lohman	2004	2638
165 4/8	21 6/8	22 6/8	14 7/8	7	7	Peoria County	IL	Lee Lewis	2005	2638
*165 4/8	23 0/8	23 4/8	17 1/8	8	6	Adams County	WI	Robert Bertzyk	2005	2638
*165 4/8	24 2/8	22 7/8	17 2/8	8	9	Monmouth County	NJ	John McLaughlin	2005	2638
165 4/8	23 3/8	23 5/8	15 7/8	7	9	Langlade County	WI	Beau Below	2006	2638
*165 4/8	22 2/8	23 2/8	14 0/8	10	6	Comanche County	KS	Zachary Koehn	2007	2638
*165 4/8	26 2/8	23 4/8	18 1/8	9	7	Orleans County	NY	Jared Reger	2008	2638
165 4/8	22 4/8	21 5/8	16 3/8	5	8	Waukesha County	WI	William R. Hinz	2009	2638
*165 4/8	23 5/8	22 4/8	16 6/8	7	10	Fulton County	IL	Roger Childers	2009	2638
165 3/8	25 0/8	25 0/8	14 7/8	9	8	Barber County	KS	Mike Zipp	1998	2654
165 3/8	22 7/8	22 4/8	17 6/8	8	11	Will County	IL	Cohlyn Dupes	2005	2654
*165 3/8	20 6/8	21 7/8	20 1/8	8	7	Lafayette County	WI	Brian Zimmerman	2009	2654
*165 3/8	22 6/8	22 2/8	15 0/8	6	7	Macoupin County	IL	Tony Gucciardo	2009	2654
165 2/8	20 3/8	21 0/8	15 2/8	8	10	Lee County	IA	Gary Frost	1991	2658
165 2/8	25 0/8	24 7/8	21 0/8	6	6	McHenry County	IL	William Weiss	1996	2658
165 2/8	23 6/8	23 0/8	18 6/8	6	6	Washington County	WI	Mike Reckner	1996	2658

663

WHITETAIL DEER (NON-TYPICAL ANTLERS)

Minimum Score 155 — Continued

SCORE	R MAIN BEAM	L MAIN BEAM	INSIDE SPREAD	R POINTS	L POINTS	AREA	STATE/PROVINCE	HUNTER'S NAME	DATE	RANK
165 2/8	25 5/8	24 4/8	19 5/8	6	7	Jo Daviess County	IL	Michael J. Pitzen	2001	2658
165 2/8	25 0/8	24 3/8	18 4/8	8	6	St. Croix County	WI	Melroy Gess	2003	2658
165 2/8	23 0/8	25 5/8	20 5/8	7	6	Talbot County	MD	Steven Zornak	2004	2658
165 2/8	23 3/8	24 0/8	16 7/8	8	5	Sangamon County	IL	Jess Gilpin	2004	2658
165 2/8	23 7/8	24 0/8	18 4/8	5	9	Pittsburg County	OK	Justin Ammons	2004	2658
165 2/8	23 5/8	24 3/8	18 0/8	6	7	Delaware County	IA	Brendon Dempster	2005	2658
*165 2/8	21 7/8	20 5/8	17 6/8	7	6	Shelby County	MO	Christopher Murphy	2006	2658
*165 2/8	21 2/8	21 2/8	17 2/8	7	6	Licking County	OH	Kenneth Brian Blankenship	2007	2658
165 2/8	23 5/8	23 2/8	17 0/8	8	10	Johnson County	IL	Bennie Adams	2009	2658
165 1/8	21 1/8	23 4/8	17 0/8	7	8	Creek County	OK	Gary Roberson	1991	2670
165 1/8	24 4/8	23 6/8	20 3/8	9	7	Brooks County	GA	Charles E. Mullins	1992	2670
165 1/8	21 4/8	23 0/8	20 3/8	7	6	Suffolk County	NY	Jim Matuszewski	1992	2670
165 1/8	22 4/8	23 0/8	18 5/8	11	8	Summit County	OH	Robert M. Wysocki	1993	2670
165 1/8	21 4/8	20 3/8	16 4/8	8	10	Grant County	WI	Eugene Willkomm	1994	2670
165 1/8	25 1/8	24 2/8	19 0/8	8	6	Vermilion County	IL	Jim Melton	1997	2670
165 1/8	23 6/8	23 6/8	15 6/8	7	5	Hendricks County	IN	Scott L. First	1997	2670
165 1/8	23 4/8	23 6/8	17 7/8	10	6	Wilson County	KS	Edward Dombal	1998	2670
165 1/8	24 0/8	24 0/8	18 1/8	7	7	Calhoun County	IL	Ben Robertson	2001	2670
165 1/8	23 2/8	23 2/8	17 2/8	8	5	Polk County	IA	Ron Mongar	2002	2670
165 1/8	25 2/8	23 6/8	17 2/8	6	7	Guilford County	NC	Shane R. Nelson	2003	2670
165 1/8	26 5/8	24 7/8	21 6/8	5	6	Eau Claire County	WI	Gale E. Zich	2003	2670
165 1/8	24 6/8	24 0/8	23 4/8	8	9	Charles County	MD	Ron Fansler	2004	2670
165 1/8	25 0/8	23 2/8	24 0/8	7	5	Will County	IL	Anthony J. Katauskas	2004	2670
*165 1/8	25 0/8	24 1/8	19 4/8	7	7	Vermilion County	IL	Robert Dave Mitchell	2004	2670
165 1/8	21 5/8	21 1/8	17 7/8	8	10	Ward County	ND	Rob Reiner	2005	2670
*165 1/8	24 5/8	23 7/8	16 5/8	8	7	Clay County	IN	Rick Ganly	2007	2670
165 1/8	24 4/8	24 0/8	19 1/8	6	8	Ashtabula County	OH	Doug A. Hummer	2008	2670
*165 1/8	23 6/8	23 1/8	14 5/8	8	8	Hubbard County	MN	Max Hoefs	2009	2670
*165 1/8	23 4/8	23 4/8	19 4/8	7	9	Fulton County	IL	Dennis I. Martin	2009	2670
165 0/8	24 3/8	24 3/8	19 0/8	9	9	Columbia County	WI	Daniel L. Golz	1987	2690
165 0/8	22 3/8	22 1/8	15 0/8	7	8	Wabaunsee County	KS	Ron Phillips	1991	2690
165 0/8	23 3/8	23 7/8	17 7/8	7	5	Buffalo County	WI	Thomas H. Schultz	1994	2690
165 0/8	22 7/8	23 0/8	14 6/8	6	7	Madison County	TX	Robert G. Skinner	1995	2690
165 0/8	23 1/8	21 6/8	17 0/8	8	5	Bureau County	IL	Dan Nordstrom	2005	2690
*165 0/8	23 1/8	25 6/8	20 2/8	6	7	Vernon County	WI	Jeff Nelson	2006	2690
165 0/8	23 2/8	23 6/8	21 6/8	8	6	Fayette County	IA	Mike Judas	2007	2690
*165 0/8	24 2/8	22 3/8	20 2/8	6	7	Vernon County	WI	Todd Suiter	2009	2690
*165 0/8	20 3/8	20 6/8	17 0/8	7	8	Marathon County	WI	Michael Schlund	2010	2690
164 7/8	20 1/8	22 4/8	16 4/8	7	6	Murray County	MN	Lanny Engler	1975	2699
164 7/8	23 2/8	23 7/8	17 2/8	9	8	Beltrami County	MN	Kelly O'Brien	1986	2699
164 7/8	20 1/8	20 4/8	19 3/8	6	9	Bentley	ALB	Gary Bruns	1990	2699
164 7/8	22 3/8	22 2/8	17 2/8	9	9	Plymouth County	IA	Dale E. Brock	1990	2699
164 7/8	22 1/8	21 5/8	18 3/8	8	8	Cerro Gordo County	IA	David Hoffman	1999	2699
164 7/8	24 5/8	25 0/8	20 3/8	8	6	Calhoun County	IL	Dan Gibbons	2003	2699
164 7/8	25 3/8	25 0/8	16 1/8	7	8	Waukesha County	WI	Noah Lange	2004	2699
164 7/8	25 6/8	27 2/8	19 1/8	9	5	Tazewell County	IL	Mark Davis	2005	2699
*164 7/8	23 7/8	23 4/8	18 4/8	6	6	Door County	WI	Scott A. Richard	2005	2699
164 7/8	22 5/8	22 1/8	18 7/8	6	6	Buffalo County	WI	Luke Ellens	2010	2699
164 6/8	18 0/8	20 4/8	16 1/8	9	9	Chippewa County	MN	Steven P. Ellingson	1975	2709
164 6/8	21 4/8	20 3/8	17 4/8	7	10	Will County	IL	Gene R. Francisco	1988	2709
164 6/8	18 3/8	22 4/8	18 3/8	12	8	Piatt County	IL	Boomer Dolbert	1990	2709
164 6/8	23 3/8	22 6/8	16 4/8	7	7	Fairfield County	CT	Charles R. Stahl	1997	2709
164 6/8	24 5/8	24 5/8	20 0/8	8	6	Fayette County	IA	Gary Pavlovec	2000	2709
164 6/8	21 1/8	20 3/8	16 3/8	7	10	Guilford County	NC	Neal Stanfield	2001	2709
164 6/8	21 7/8	23 1/8	17 1/8	8	9	Wilson County	KS	Billy S. Worthy	2004	2709
*164 6/8	27 2/8	26 0/8	17 5/8	4	7	Scott County	IA	Sam Lee Carlson, Jr.	2005	2709
164 5/8	23 5/8	22 0/8	18 6/8	6	8	Fulton County	IL	Jeff Parsons	1992	2717
164 5/8	20 0/8	18 5/8	15 6/8	9	8	Fremont County	IA	Phillip M. Revering	1995	2717
164 5/8	20 1/8	20 5/8	15 6/8	7	7	Waukesha County	WI	Richard A. Riehle, Jr.	1995	2717
164 5/8	23 4/8	23 0/8	16 4/8	8	5	Columbia County	WI	Mark Preuss	1997	2717
164 5/8	23 4/8	23 5/8	14 1/8	8	8	Columbia County	WI	Kim D. Standke	1997	2717
164 5/8	23 6/8	22 2/8	20 0/8	6	8	Reno County	KS	Gene Kane	2000	2717
164 5/8	20 6/8	21 7/8	17 0/8	7	7	Gasconade County	MO	Darrin Danuser	2001	2717
164 5/8	23 0/8	23 0/8	18 1/8	6	8	Monroe County	NY	Mark Freemesser	2001	2717
164 5/8	20 7/8	20 6/8	16 1/8	6	8	Clay County	MN	Gregory L. Landa	2004	2717
164 5/8	27 0/8	27 1/8	25 0/8	5	6	Fulton County	IL	Michael C. Vaka	2005	2717
164 5/8	20 2/8	20 2/8	15 3/8	7	5	Dundurn	SAS	Lindsey Paterson	2005	2717
164 5/8	23 5/8	24 4/8	18 7/8	13	9	McHenry County	ND	Steve Marklevitz	2006	2717
164 4/8	23 4/8	23 4/8	19 0/8	7	10	Iowa County	IA	Bob Moenk	1994	2729
164 4/8	25 5/8	25 2/8	19 6/8	8	7	Harrison County	MO	Richard Pemberton	1996	2729
164 4/8	22 4/8	23 2/8	20 2/8	6	6	Seward County	KS	Lynn Leonard	2002	2729
164 4/8	23 0/8	22 3/8	18 0/8	6	6	Johnson County	MO	Gary Moore	2002	2729
164 4/8	21 2/8	22 2/8	17 0/8	9	6	Dane County	WI	Wayne Schlimgen	2007	2729
164 3/8	24 1/8	22 5/8	17 2/8	7	6	Lake County	IL	Steven Hysell	1995	2734
164 3/8	25 1/8	26 1/8	18 4/8	7	5	Lafayette County	WI	Tim Palzkill	1998	2734
164 3/8	23 0/8	23 2/8	16 3/8	5	9	Ferry County	WA	Jeff Anderson	2001	2734
*164 3/8	23 6/8	24 1/8	18 5/8	7	6	Crawford County	WI	Randy Nash	2003	2734
164 3/8	26 3/8	26 2/8	19 1/8	8	4	Adams County	OH	Randy Lewis	2003	2734
164 3/8	23 0/8	24 2/8	18 1/8	9	7	Jackson County	WI	Kevin Gilbertson	2004	2734
*164 3/8	22 3/8	21 4/8	15 4/8	6	11	Brown County	OH	Brandon Becraft	2007	2734
164 2/8	22 1/8	23 4/8	14 2/8	10	6	Rush County	KS	Shawn McHaley	1988	2741
164 2/8	26 2/8	25 5/8	19 7/8	4	7	Lawrence County	OH	Pete G. McCloud	1990	2741
164 2/8	24 3/8	25 2/8	18 0/8	8	7	Laclede County	MO	Jerry Goans	1996	2741
164 2/8	26 2/8	25 1/8	19 5/8	6	7	Ross County	OH	Daniel Rawlings	1997	2741
164 2/8	23 4/8	23 3/8	16 2/8	6	8	Lake County	MT	Frank Dykstra, Jr.	2000	2741
164 2/8	25 5/8	26 1/8	17 1/8	8	8	Maverick County	TX	Rex Dacus	2003	2741
164 2/8	23 0/8	23 4/8	18 6/8	6	6	Lorain County	OH	Lawrence L. Lanenga, Jr.	2007	2741
*164 2/8	20 1/8	20 4/8	18 0/8	9	9	Trempealeau County	WI	Michael Price	2007	2741
164 1/8	23 5/8	22 1/8	18 5/8	9	8	Winona County	MN	Charles W. Benson	1974	2749
164 1/8	23 4/8	23 6/8	20 5/8	5	6	Seward County	KS	Lynn Leonard	1984	2749
164 1/8	28 0/8	27 2/8	20 4/8	5	5	Christian County	KY	Thomas A. Patterson	1989	2749
164 1/8	20 6/8	22 3/8	16 3/8	7	9	Meeker County	MN	Mike Rollinger	1989	2749
164 1/8	27 0/8	26 5/8	18 7/8	8	13	Wyandot County	OH	James D. Herring	1995	2749
164 1/8	26 3/8	25 7/8	18 4/8	7	7	Oakland County	MI	Paul W. Vachon	1998	2749
164 1/8	22 1/8	21 0/8	15 6/8	8	8	Kleberg County	TX	Robert Nichols	1998	2749

WHITETAIL DEER (NON-TYPICAL ANTLERS)

Minimum Score 155   Continued

SCORE	LENGTH OF R MAIN BEAM L	INSIDE SPREAD	NUMBER OF R POINTS L	AREA	STATE/ PROVINCE	HUNTER'S NAME	DATE	RANK
164 1/8	22 1/8 23 2/8	15 6/8	7 7	Buffalo County	WI	Scott W. Doenier	1999	2749
164 1/8	23 6/8 23 6/8	17 1/8	5 6	Tazewell County	IL	Kent E. Wiker	2000	2749
164 1/8	22 5/8 22 4/8	17 7/8	6 9	Kleberg County	TX	Robert Nichols	2001	2749
164 1/8	24 4/8 24 6/8	16 7/8	6 6	Coles County	IL	John Clough	2002	2749
164 1/8	24 0/8 24 2/8	18 0/8	7 6	Calhoun County	IL	Frank Greenlee	2003	2749
164 1/8	22 4/8 22 2/8	16 2/8	7 7	Crooked Creek	ALB	Chad Lenz	2007	2749
164 1/8	18 2/8 19 4/8	16 1/8	9 7	Franklin County	KY	Shane Clemons	2007	2749
*164 1/8	22 0/8 20 6/8	17 2/8	9 6	Green Lake County	WI	Mark P. Strelow	2007	2749
*164 1/8	20 2/8 20 2/8	18 5/8	7 6	Garfield County	OK	Ryan A. Ross	2008	2749
164 0/8	20 6/8 21 7/8	15 0/8	7 7	Guthrie County	IA	Dick Rote	1980	2765
164 0/8	27 0/8 27 3/8	23 3/8	5 5	Fairfax County	VA	Larry C. Sherertz	1987	2765
164 0/8	22 0/8 22 3/8	17 6/8	6 6	Lake County	IL	Ted Hysell	1990	2765
164 0/8	23 6/8 23 4/8	16 0/8	7 6	Randolph County	IL	Scott Oathout	1991	2765
164 0/8	23 6/8 23 0/8	17 6/8	5 7	Coshocton County	OH	Lee Cooper	1993	2765
164 0/8	21 6/8 21 3/8	15 7/8	7 9	Boone County	IN	Gary R. Barb	1995	2765
164 0/8	23 5/8 22 4/8	18 0/8	7 6	Kleberg County	TX	Johnnie R. Walters	1996	2765
164 0/8	23 2/8 23 0/8	19 2/8	8 7	Pike County	IL	Ben Beine	1996	2765
164 0/8	24 7/8 24 0/8	17 4/8	8 11	Hickory County	MO	Jimmy Bilyeu	1998	2765
164 0/8	24 6/8 24 6/8	16 4/8	7 6	Wapello County	IA	Dennis Bradley	1998	2765
164 0/8	24 1/8 21 4/8	18 0/8	7 6	Dane County	WI	G.W. E. Buckeridge	1999	2765
164 0/8	25 1/8 25 0/8	19 2/8	7 6	Jones County	IA	Kyle Claussen	2001	2765
164 0/8	22 2/8 21 7/8	17 3/8	8 6	Allegheny County	PA	Bill Cramer	2003	2765
164 0/8	21 6/8 23 1/8	18 4/8	6 9	Linn County	IA	Stuart Slaymaker	2004	2765
*164 0/8	24 7/8 23 7/8	18 6/8	7 6	Ross County	OH	Jacob M. Gray	2004	2765
164 0/8	25 1/8 22 6/8	18 0/8	7 7	Henry County	KY	Tim Greener	2007	2765
*164 0/8	22 5/8 23 2/8	14 6/8	7 10	Douglas County	KS	Joe Vojtko	2007	2765
163 7/8	27 1/8 25 1/8	20 5/8	6 6	Dickinson County	IA	Eldon L. Kraninger	1969	2782
163 7/8	27 1/8 28 7/8	24 5/8	5 7	Grundy County	IL	Ed Vitko, Jr.	1974	2782
163 7/8	20 3/8 22 5/8	22 4/8	8 8	Sumner County	KS	Kelly Seal	1998	2782
163 7/8	21 1/8 20 4/8	19 7/8	9 9	Coles County	IL	Terry Waggoner	2002	2782
*163 7/8	23 2/8 23 3/8	18 1/8	8 8	Wright County	IA	Nolan L. Ysker	2005	2782
*163 7/8	22 6/8 21 2/8	15 6/8	9 11	Pottawattamie County	IA	Gary Matters	2006	2782
163 7/8	21 6/8 21 6/8	15 0/8	10 7	Jo Daviess County	IL	Gerry D. Ward	2006	2782
163 7/8	22 7/8 22 0/8	19 1/8	7 8	Bureau County	IL	Mark Leonard	2009	2782
163 6/8	22 0/8 20 6/8	18 7/8	8 7	Kenedy County	TX	Miguel Mireles	1987	2790
163 6/8	24 2/8 23 4/8	18 5/8	6 7	Buffalo County	WI	Dave Fredrickson	1994	2790
163 6/8	24 4/8 25 5/8	18 0/8	6 7	Burt County	NE	Brian Keith Schultz	2001	2790
163 6/8	19 6/8 20 2/8	13 6/8	8 6	Franklin County	IN	Mike DiBease	2001	2790
163 6/8	22 3/8 21 5/8	16 1/8	6 6	Vigo County	IN	Cindy Rothrock	2004	2790
163 6/8	27 0/8 28 1/8	27 0/8	6 4	Kent County	DE	Rob Rockemann	2005	2790
*163 6/8	25 6/8 24 6/8	18 6/8	8 6	Coshocton County	OH	William T. Randles	2009	2790
163 5/8	23 4/8 20 7/8	17 6/8	7 8	Pepin County	WI	Mike J. Breitung	1988	2797
163 5/8	23 5/8 24 1/8	14 5/8	6 8	McDonough County	IL	Troy Shirrell	1999	2797
163 5/8	26 6/8 26 4/8	20 2/8	6 4	Vermilion County	IL	Charlie Heidrick	1999	2797
163 5/8	25 0/8 24 4/8	15 3/8	9 8	Sarpy County	NE	Jake Gable	2001	2797
163 5/8	25 4/8 25 6/8	21 4/8	6 5	Guernsey County	OH	Kent Austin	2002	2797
163 5/8	21 3/8 23 3/8	18 7/8	8 5	Pike County	IL	Brian Jennings	2003	2797
163 5/8	21 1/8 22 3/8	19 3/8	8 8	Dunn County	WI	Kevin Lechner	2003	2797
*163 5/8	21 4/8 22 3/8	18 6/8	9 7	Wood County	WI	Randy Schmick	2005	2797
163 5/8	26 7/8 26 7/8	20 2/8	5 6	Greene County	MO	Fred Martinez	2005	2797
*163 5/8	22 1/8 22 2/8	14 5/8	5 6	Warren County	KY	Mike Sale	2007	2797
163 5/8	21 2/8 21 7/8	15 0/8	8 8	Columbia County	WI	William Buckley	2008	2797
163 5/8	25 4/8 23 0/8	16 6/8	5 7	Marathon County	WI	Craig Bunkelman	2010	2797
163 4/8	25 1/8 25 1/8	18 4/8	6 5	Hancock County	ME	Daniel D. Hardy	1990	2809
*163 4/8	26 1/8 24 5/8	17 2/8	8 10	Muskingum County	OH	Ross Lykins	2003	2809
163 4/8	25 0/8 25 0/8	18 1/8	6 7	Manitowoc County	WI	Tim D. Malay	2003	2809
163 4/8	21 5/8 22 0/8	18 7/8	5 6	Mercer County	ND	Jesse D. Schumaker	2004	2809
163 4/8	25 5/8 24 6/8	20 0/8	7 9	Knox County	OH	Gary Campbell	2004	2809
*163 4/8	26 4/8 25 7/8	20 2/8	5 7	Washington County	WI	Robert M. Shilts	2006	2809
163 4/8	21 5/8 22 1/8	15 4/8	8 8	Logan County	OK	Ronald Swanson	2009	2809
*163 4/8	22 1/8 23 1/8	19 2/8	11 9	Owen County	IN	Joshua J. Thomas	2009	2809
*163 4/8	22 5/8 24 0/8	15 2/8	8 8	Otoe County	NE	Keith Nolda	2009	2809
*163 4/8	21 2/8 22 2/8	17 2/8	7 9	St. Joseph County	IN	Charles D. Sims	2010	2809
163 3/8	21 2/8 23 5/8	15 5/8	9 5	Wapello County	IA	Rick Grooms	1990	2819
163 3/8	19 4/8 20 4/8	18 5/8	6 7	Kane County	IL	Paul Neidhardt	1992	2819
163 3/8	24 4/8 24 1/8	21 2/8	7 8	Will County	IL	Alton Miller	1994	2819
163 3/8	23 3/8 21 2/8	21 6/8	7 10	Hancock County	WV	William Gary Rusinovich	1995	2819
163 3/8	24 4/8 25 7/8	16 3/8	4 6	St. Louis County	MO	David Shelton	1999	2819
163 3/8	25 4/8 25 4/8	17 4/8	5 4	Williams County	OH	Raymond A. McMullen	2001	2819
163 3/8	21 1/8 22 2/8	19 5/8	8 8	Buffalo County	WI	Kim L. Ganz	2002	2819
163 3/8	21 0/8 21 0/8	15 3/8	9 7	Butler County	PA	Joshua Baron	2002	2819
163 3/8	22 7/8 22 0/8	18 5/8	8 7	Grayson County	TX	Rick Cantu	2003	2819
163 3/8	24 0/8 24 1/8	20 0/8	7 7	Lake County	IL	Paul D. Hein	2008	2819
163 2/8	23 2/8 24 5/8	20 3/8	7 5	Warren County	IA	Arthur Henry Newell	1995	2829
163 2/8	22 7/8 23 5/8	17 2/8	7 9	Elkhart County	IN	Karl E. Miller	1997	2829
163 2/8	23 0/8 22 7/8	17 0/8	12 7	Hazelwood	SAS	Mark Dube	2005	2829
163 2/8	25 6/8 24 6/8	15 2/8	5 8	Grant County	WI	Paul Trudeau	2005	2829
*163 2/8	22 4/8 23 1/8	22 5/8	7 7	Buffalo County	WI	Joe Jilot	2005	2829
163 2/8	22 4/8 22 1/8	14 2/8	8 9	Hubbard County	MN	Bernard Hasse	2006	2829
163 2/8	25 5/8 26 2/8	17 0/8	7 7	La Crosse County	WI	Chris A. Colburn	2006	2829
163 2/8	22 1/8 22 5/8	18 6/8	7 8	Mahaska County	IA	Larry Vander Linden	2006	2829
*163 2/8	24 2/8 24 6/8	20 2/8	6 6	Leake County	MS	Rich Nichols	2008	2829
163 2/8	23 7/8 23 1/8	16 6/8	8 7	Pike County	IL	Turner Sibley	2008	2829
163 1/8	21 6/8 22 0/8	16 7/8	7 7	Cherry County	NE	Walter Cady	1975	2839
163 1/8	20 5/8 20 2/8	17 1/8	7 7	Burke County	GA	John A. "Andy" Tisdale	1989	2839
163 1/8	21 5/8 22 4/8	18 7/8	8 7	Sac County	IA	Lee C. Green	1991	2839
163 1/8	24 5/8 24 7/8	17 3/8	6 5	Walworth County	WI	Steven Johnson	1994	2839
163 1/8	22 4/8 24 2/8	15 5/8	8 7	Prince Georges County	MD	Paul Brocht	1995	2839
163 1/8	25 6/8 25 7/8	17 2/8	6 7	Clarke County	IA	Mike Veigulis	1996	2839
163 1/8	24 7/8 24 5/8	17 7/8	8 6	Chautauqua County	KS	Steve Stoltz	1996	2839
163 1/8	21 1/8 23 7/8	18 5/8	8 5	Allamakee County	IA	Thomas E. Peters	1998	2839
163 1/8	24 0/8 26 0/8	21 0/8	7 5	Marion County	IA	Roy Ver Woert	2001	2839
163 1/8	23 1/8 24 2/8	18 6/8	5 8	Woodbury County	IA	Tony C. Flesjer, Jr.	2002	2839
163 1/8	22 4/8 23 1/8	19 2/8	6 5	Morgan County	OH	Todd Kidd	2003	2839
163 1/8	26 1/8 25 5/8	15 2/8	8 7	Richardson County	NE	John Duggan	2004	2839

665

WHITETAIL DEER (NON-TYPICAL ANTLERS)

Minimum Score 155 — Continued

SCORE	LENGTH OF R MAIN BEAM L	INSIDE SPREAD	NUMBER OF R POINTS L	AREA	STATE/ PROVINCE	HUNTER'S NAME	DATE	RANK
*163 1/8	25 5/8 23 4/8	17 0/8	7 7	Ralls County	MO	Brad Smith	2006	2839
*163 1/8	26 6/8 26 2/8	18 1/8	7 7	Suffolk County	NY	Edward J. Korf	2007	2839
163 0/8	20 6/8 21 1/8	17 0/8	10 11	Caddo County	OK	Donald Boling	1975	2853
163 0/8	25 5/8 24 6/8	16 6/8	5 6	Richland County	WI	Katherine A. Ellenbolt	1994	2853
163 0/8	25 0/8 26 1/8	21 0/8	7 5	Scott County	IA	Mike Groenwoldt	1999	2853
163 0/8	21 5/8 21 6/8	15 6/8	8 7	Randolph County	IL	Gene Jewell	2002	2853
163 0/8	22 5/8 22 4/8	15 6/8	5 5	Monroe County	IA	Tom O'Brien	2002	2853
163 0/8	21 0/8 24 7/8	20 4/8	8 6	St. Joseph County	IN	Anthony B. Weaver	2005	2853
163 0/8	23 2/8 24 0/8	17 7/8	7 7	Wichita County	TX	John Kelly	2005	2853
163 0/8	23 6/8 24 4/8	21 2/8	10 9	Buffalo County	WI	Jeff Meinen	2008	2853
163 0/8	23 7/8 26 5/8	17 2/8	7 6	Wyandot County	OH	Adam J. Thiel	2008	2853
*163 0/8	25 0/8 24 2/8	20 6/8	9 9	Osage County	OK	Bryan Wright	2009	2853
162 7/8	20 5/8 20 4/8	17 3/8	7 8	Walsh County	ND	Randy Schuster	1985	2863
162 7/8	21 0/8 20 4/8	15 6/8	6 9	Pike County	IL	Robert E. O'Donnell	1997	2863
162 7/8	25 0/8 25 0/8	17 7/8	5 6	Calhoun County	IL	Donny Landry	2000	2863
162 7/8	25 0/8 24 2/8	18 6/8	6 6	Buffalo County	WI	Terry Skebba	2000	2863
162 7/8	19 6/8 21 1/8	15 4/8	6 9	Erie County	PA	Ronald J. Hedlund	2001	2863
162 7/8	22 3/8 21 7/8	15 0/8	6 6	Linn County	IA	Christopher J. Swanke	2001	2863
162 7/8	26 6/8 25 5/8	20 0/8	6 5	Weld County	CO	Frank Piacentino	2001	2863
162 7/8	27 3/8 27 2/8	19 6/8	5 6	Middlesex County	CT	Tom Manente	2003	2863
*162 7/8	25 5/8 26 4/8	16 3/8	8 8	Hancock County	IL	Harry Brackenbury	2004	2863
162 7/8	23 0/8 23 2/8	15 6/8	8 8	Pike County	IN	Richard A. Pflanz	2006	2863
162 6/8	23 4/8 24 3/8	22 4/8	9 7	Webb County	TX	James Richter, Jr.	1977	2873
162 6/8	26 7/8 26 3/8	20 0/8	6 9	Crawford County	IL	Charlie Guyer	1987	2873
162 6/8	23 2/8 22 4/8	11 3/8	7 6	Franklin County	OH	Randy Kelley	1991	2873
162 6/8	23 2/8 19 3/8	19 3/8	6 6	Buffalo County	WI	Dave Parker	1994	2873
162 6/8	23 2/8 23 6/8	15 4/8	7 7	Crook County	WY	Heron H. Head	1995	2873
162 6/8	24 2/8 23 6/8	17 5/8	5 6	Morrison County	MN	James J. Willard	1995	2873
162 6/8	26 0/8 27 1/8	18 5/8	9 8	Lake County	IL	Art Olson	1996	2873
162 6/8	23 1/8 23 1/8	18 5/8	6 9	Suffolk County	NY	Robert Lee III	1996	2873
162 6/8	26 0/8 27 1/8	17 1/8	7 5	Fulton County	IN	John J. Ingram	2000	2873
162 6/8	23 4/8 22 2/8	17 0/8	7 6	Hillsdale County	MI	Ronald W. Riddle	2002	2873
*162 6/8	23 0/8 24 5/8	18 0/8	8 11	St. Louis County	MO	Kien Ton	2003	2873
162 6/8	24 2/8 22 3/8	18 4/8	7 7	Mingo County	WV	Shane Dillon	2003	2873
*162 6/8	22 1/8 23 5/8	17 5/8	7 7	Lucas County	OH	Bradley D. Robinson	2004	2873
162 6/8	20 0/8 20 6/8	17 6/8	8 6	White County	IL	Josh Butcher	2005	2873
162 5/8	25 2/8 24 1/8	19 1/8	7 5	Burnett County	WI	Scott L. Treague	1989	2887
162 5/8	22 1/8 22 1/8	18 7/8	7 8	Columbia County	PA	Paul Weisser, Jr.	1989	2887
162 5/8	25 0/8 22 7/8	16 3/8	6 9	Iroquois County	IL	James Albricht	1991	2887
162 5/8	24 4/8 21 7/8	16 4/8	6 6	Coshocton County	OH	Bill Randles	1995	2887
162 5/8	19 2/8 22 2/8	20 1/8	8 6	Calvert County	MD	Troy T. Naylor	1996	2887
162 5/8	23 1/8 25 0/8	17 0/8	8 8	Hardin County	IA	Chad D. Hagen	1997	2887
162 5/8	20 0/8 21 1/8	14 4/8	10 7	Cass County	MN	Rex Kinsey	1998	2887
162 5/8	23 7/8 23 1/8	19 7/8	7 7	Geauga County	OH	Blaine Davidson	1998	2887
162 5/8	24 2/8 23 5/8	15 3/8	5 7	Anne Arundel County	MD	Glen H. Jones	1998	2887
162 5/8	24 6/8 27 0/8	17 6/8	9 8	St. Charles County	MO	Bret Martin	1999	2887
162 5/8	24 7/8 26 6/8	22 1/8	8 4	Montgomery County	PA	Joseph D. Maddock	2001	2887
162 5/8	23 4/8 22 1/8	18 0/8	7 6	Jersey County	IL	Robert Parker	2001	2887
162 5/8	23 5/8 24 4/8	19 5/8	6 7	Greenwood County	KS	Jeffery A. Girls	2001	2887
162 5/8	24 1/8 22 4/8	24 0/8	6 8	Cloud County	KS	Greg Dockins	2003	2887
162 5/8	25 6/8 24 6/8	19 7/8	7 5	Coffey County	KS	Craig Giancola	2003	2887
162 5/8	24 1/8 25 0/8	19 2/8	6 6	St. Joseph County	IN	Keith M. McMahan	2009	2887
*162 5/8	25 2/8 24 3/8	17 4/8	8 7	Hamilton County	TN	Richard H. Britt	2009	2887
162 4/8	22 3/8 23 2/8	13 2/8	8 7	Douglas County	OR	Hugh C. Bennett	1958	2904
162 4/8	25 7/8 26 5/8	18 3/8	6 9	Houston County	MN	Russell Craig Kruse	1991	2904
162 4/8	24 2/8 25 5/8	15 5/8	7 5	Jasper County	MO	Douglas H. Roberts	1991	2904
162 4/8	23 7/8 23 5/8	16 7/8	7 6	Clayton County	IA	Mark M. Muir	1992	2904
162 4/8	23 0/8 23 4/8	19 6/8	10 7	Taylor County	WI	Tony Caramanidis	1995	2904
162 4/8	24 2/8 24 4/8	19 1/8	5 6	Lake County	IL	Trent J. Schneider	1996	2904
162 4/8	24 2/8 24 7/8	19 5/8	7 6	Columbia County	WI	Rick A. Knutson	1998	2904
162 4/8	22 2/8 22 1/8	15 7/8	8 7	Cowley County	KS	Mike Peters	1998	2904
162 4/8	25 2/8 28 1/8	18 7/8	7 7	Polk County	WI	Douglas Emerson	2000	2904
162 4/8	22 2/8 24 4/8	19 1/8	8 6	Taylor County	IA	Patrick Jennings	2000	2904
162 4/8	23 7/8 23 4/8	21 0/8	7 6	Jefferson County	WI	Kenneth Mauer	2001	2904
162 4/8	23 2/8 23 2/8	15 4/8	11 8	La Porte County	IN	Don E. Ferrell	2002	2904
162 4/8	23 1/8 22 0/8	17 5/8	8 10	Suffolk County	NY	Richard S. Gates	2002	2904
162 4/8	21 7/8 23 1/8	17 4/8	9 8	Montgomery County	IL	Rodney Manning	2002	2904
162 4/8	21 5/8 21 2/8	16 7/8	7 7	Fayette County	PA	Robert J. Schroyer	2002	2904
162 4/8	20 4/8 24 3/8	16 2/8	9 6	Buffalo County	WI	Ronald A. Walski	2005	2904
162 4/8	22 2/8 24 4/8	18 3/8	6 6	Jo Daviess County	IL	Richard P. Geyer	2005	2904
162 4/8	23 4/8 22 5/8	15 5/8	10 6	Dodge County	WI	Dallas J. Lasche	2006	2904
162 4/8	24 2/8 23 2/8	17 3/8	7 8	Sheboygan County	WI	Tim Weyker	2009	2904
162 3/8	22 0/8 22 7/8	19 0/8	6 6	Cold Lake	ALB	Eric Rauhanen	1994	2923
162 3/8	19 6/8 19 6/8	14 6/8	10 8	Pike County	IL	Gary Tyranski	2000	2923
162 3/8	23 7/8 22 5/8	17 0/8	7 9	Greenwood County	KS	Curtis Fletcher	2000	2923
162 3/8	25 3/8 25 0/8	16 0/8	7 7	Monroe County	PA	Joel Beers	2001	2923
162 3/8	25 6/8 26 1/8	21 0/8	6 8	Caledon	ONT	Carl Whittier	2002	2923
*162 3/8	21 2/8 23 1/8	18 4/8	10 10	Anderson County	KS	Tom Brandt	2003	2923
162 3/8	23 7/8 24 3/8	19 1/8	7 8	Grant County	WI	Casey J. Sweet	2003	2923
162 3/8	23 1/8 24 1/8	14 2/8	7 7	Licking County	OH	Andy Rollins	2005	2923
*162 3/8	21 5/8 22 4/8	20 1/8	7 6	Washington County	WI	Darin J. Gordon	2008	2923
162 3/8	22 3/8 21 4/8	16 6/8	9 11	Pope County	AR	Kelly Davis	2009	2923
*162 3/8	25 5/8 23 4/8	16 3/8	11 7	Chautauqua County	KS	Paulia Hubert	2009	2923
162 2/8	24 6/8 25 0/8	20 7/8	6 7	Elma	MAN	Wendell Schatkowsky	1990	2934
162 2/8	22 1/8 23 0/8	17 7/8	6 6	Pike County	IL	Robert Sacher	1994	2934
162 2/8	25 0/8 24 7/8	17 5/8	6 9	Clark County	IL	Gerald "Gabe" Shaffner	1998	2934
162 2/8	23 6/8 24 6/8	18 1/8	6 5	Clinton County	IA	Craig R. Black	2000	2934
162 2/8	24 0/8 23 7/8	16 6/8	6 5	Lancaster County	NE	Robin Burianek	2001	2934
162 2/8	24 1/8 23 5/8	16 0/8	6 5	Franklin County	IN	Steve Morris	2001	2934
162 2/8	22 7/8 22 4/8	15 2/8	7 8	Hart County	KY	Terry W. Avery	2002	2934
162 2/8	23 1/8 26 6/8	16 4/8	6 7	Clark County	KS	James R. "Ron" Barnett	2003	2934
162 2/8	22 5/8 24 1/8	15 5/8	7 7	Muskingum County	OH	Jerry Johnson	2004	2934
162 2/8	18 7/8 18 7/8	16 2/8	8 8	Desha County	AR	William Jones	2005	2934
*162 2/8	23 7/8 24 0/8	17 4/8	6 9	Brown County	IL	Chad Dobson	2005	2934
*162 2/8	20 1/8 20 5/8	14 7/8	7 8	Buffalo County	WI	Peter Theoharis	2006	2934

666

WHITETAIL DEER (NON-TYPICAL ANTLERS)

Minimum Score 155 — Continued

SCORE	R MAIN BEAM L	INSIDE SPREAD	R POINTS L		AREA	STATE/PROVINCE	HUNTER'S NAME	DATE	RANK
*162 2/8	20 5/8 21 2/8	18 3/8	12	6	Kalamazoo County	MI	Jake Coville	2006	2934
*162 2/8	22 6/8 22 3/8	16 3/8	7	8	Houston County	TX	Woody Bloxom	2007	2934
162 1/8	25 4/8 23 6/8	18 2/8	7	11	Jackson County	IA	Larry R. Zirkelbach	1990	2948
162 1/8	22 2/8 21 7/8	20 1/8	8	8	Chippewa County	WI	Jeffrey T. Miller	1995	2948
162 1/8	22 0/8 21 7/8	18 7/8	8	11	Portage County	WI	Timothy J. Kitowski	1997	2948
162 1/8	23 0/8 22 6/8	18 3/8	8	7	Johnson County	IA	John Fields	2000	2948
162 1/8	22 4/8 22 7/8	17 6/8	5	7	Pike County	IL	John Aspinall	2001	2948
162 1/8	26 1/8 25 6/8	18 2/8	6	6	Columbia County	WI	Kevin Dickman	2001	2948
162 1/8	20 5/8 17 7/8	13 5/8	5	9	Chickasaw County	IA	Greg Richards	2002	2948
162 1/8	23 3/8 25 4/8	18 1/8	9	6	Fayette County	IL	Ryan McHenry	2004	2948
162 1/8	24 3/8 24 6/8	17 1/8	5	6	Houston County	MN	Chris Moon	2004	2948
162 1/8	24 1/8 25 1/8	19 0/8	6	6	Van Buren County	IA	Richard Penn	2006	2948
*162 1/8	23 6/8 23 5/8	14 4/8	7	7	Shelby County	IL	Michael Mitchell	2006	2948
162 1/8	24 0/8 24 2/8	19 4/8	8	5	Monmouth County	NJ	Art Fariello	2007	2948
162 1/8	21 2/8 23 1/8	16 2/8	11	7	Logan County	IL	Stewart Riedle	2007	2948
162 1/8	22 1/8 23 5/8	15 5/8	7	5	Jones County	IA	Kraig Hansen	2007	2948
162 0/8	23 4/8 24 6/8	16 6/8	8	8	Coshocton County	OH	Richard Morgan	1987	2962
162 0/8	25 3/8 25 0/8	17 7/8	7	7	Montgomery County	IA	Dick R. Paul	1990	2962
162 0/8	22 3/8 22 2/8	16 7/8	7	6	Becker County	MN	Ronald Hendrickson	1993	2962
162 0/8	23 5/8 24 7/8	20 5/8	5	10	Ontario County	NY	Lee Beaton	1995	2962
162 0/8	26 0/8 25 3/8	18 0/8	6	6	Muskingum County	OH	Arnold Schlater	1995	2962
162 0/8	23 5/8 23 5/8	20 5/8	6	6	Macoupin County	IL	Chris Loeh	2000	2962
162 0/8	26 0/8 25 2/8	18 0/8	5	7	Green County	WI	Jeff McArdle	2001	2962
162 0/8	23 7/8 23 6/8	20 0/8	6	6	Decatur County	IA	Courtland W. Smith	2001	2962
162 0/8	24 2/8 26 2/8	16 4/8	7	7	Edmonson County	KY	Kevin T. Ray	2002	2962
162 0/8	21 4/8 21 0/8	14 2/8	7	7	Williams County	ND	Richard Liesener	2002	2962
162 0/8	22 6/8 24 0/8	18 4/8	6	7	Kane County	IL	William W. Wishon, Jr.	2003	2962
162 0/8	24 1/8 22 7/8	19 1/8	5	6	Polk County	WI	Brian L. Pedersen	2005	2962
162 0/8	21 4/8 22 2/8	15 0/8	11	6	Scotland County	MO	Carl Litzenberger	2007	2962
161 7/8	24 7/8 25 5/8	22 0/8	7	9	Cascade County	MT	Kits Smith	1980	2975
161 7/8	24 4/8 28 4/8	17 3/8	6	11	Warren County	IA	Bob R. Branchcomb	1988	2975
161 7/8	21 7/8 22 6/8	16 2/8	8	7	Gorlitz	SAS	Greg Landstad	1994	2975
161 7/8	23 0/8 22 5/8	17 4/8	6	9	Kenosha County	WI	Kevin Meyers	1994	2975
161 7/8	21 2/8 23 4/8	19 6/8	9	8	Ogle County	IL	Marvin E. Stewart	1997	2975
161 7/8	26 3/8 26 2/8	15 7/8	8	5	Kingman County	KS	George Schuttler	1998	2975
161 7/8	24 3/8 23 5/8	22 4/8	11	10	Chautauqua County	NY	Ronald Ferry	2001	2975
161 7/8	23 3/8 23 2/8	18 0/8	6	6	Jo Daviess County	IL	Mike Feldermann	2001	2975
161 7/8	24 2/8 24 0/8	22 6/8	6	10	Des Moines County	IA	Craig R. Belknap	2002	2975
*161 7/8	21 5/8 21 2/8	17 2/8	8	7	Cumberland County	IL	Chris A. Phillips	2004	2975
161 7/8	23 3/8 23 7/8	18 2/8	7	6	Perry County	IL	Donald G. Robinson	2005	2975
*161 7/8	22 4/8 20 3/8	17 3/8	9	5	Tama County	IA	Tim Van Hamme	2005	2975
*161 7/8	23 3/8 23 6/8	18 7/8	6	6	Pope County	IL	Robby Briggs	2005	2975
161 6/8	23 2/8 24 3/8	19 6/8	6	6	Cass County	IL	Donald B. Coufal	1989	2988
161 6/8	22 7/8 23 3/8	20 3/8	7	6	Vernon County	WI	Jeff M. Fish	1992	2988
161 6/8	22 0/8 22 2/8	16 1/8	7	8	St. Marys County	MD	Richard Gooding	1996	2988
161 6/8	23 2/8 25 5/8	21 3/8	7	7	McHenry County	IL	James C. Mass	1999	2988
161 6/8	23 1/8 22 4/8	17 0/8	6	7	Marinette County	WI	Matthew Olson	1999	2988
161 6/8	23 5/8 23 5/8	19 1/8	7	8	Hughes County	SD	Carl R. Chambers	2000	2988
161 6/8	24 2/8 25 0/8	18 5/8	8	6	Putnam County	MO	Scott Whitlock	2000	2988
161 6/8	17 4/8 24 2/8	18 0/8	8	6	Wells County	IN	Eric Behr	2001	2988
161 6/8	23 5/8 25 1/8	19 2/8	6	8	Bremer County	IA	Howard Schmitz	2001	2988
161 6/8	22 3/8 22 4/8	17 3/8	6	7	Marathon County	WI	James M. Krueger, Jr.	2002	2988
*161 6/8	23 5/8 23 4/8	19 7/8	6	6	Berks County	PA	Randy J. Collins	2003	2988
161 6/8	23 0/8 22 1/8	17 5/8	7	6	Clark County	IL	Gerald "Gabe" Shaffrer	2003	2988
161 6/8	26 3/8 24 2/8	17 1/8	5	9	Olmsted County	MN	Jim Leqve	2003	2988
161 6/8	23 6/8 24 1/8	18 7/8	6	7	Dunn County	WI	Aaron Knutson	2004	2988
*161 6/8	18 0/8 14 0/8	12 5/8	9	11	Pike County	IL	Paul Peacock	2008	2988
161 5/8	21 6/8 21 0/8	15 6/8	8	9	White Fox	SAS	Edward Toelken	1995	3003
161 5/8	21 3/8 22 5/8	19 5/8	6	8	Winneshiek County	IA	Marvin Folstad	1997	3003
161 5/8	22 2/8 21 0/8	21 5/8	7	8	Aurora County	SD	Mark D. Hanten	1998	3003
161 5/8	27 2/8 25 2/8	16 4/8	6	6	Sauk County	WI	John B. Lamb	2000	3003
161 5/8	23 3/8 23 1/8	18 2/8	6	6	Fayette County	IA	Rick Taylor	2000	3003
161 5/8	23 0/8 23 2/8	15 0/8	6	8	Sherburne County	MN	Earl Huffman	2003	3003
161 5/8	24 3/8 22 2/8	20 7/8	5	6	Maverick County	TX	Randy Couthran	2003	3003
161 5/8	24 3/8 26 2/8	20 7/8	5	7	Polk County	IA	Adam Sieren	2004	3003
*161 5/8	21 6/8 22 1/8	15 2/8	7	6	Wood County	WV	Kent Dean	2005	3003
161 5/8	25 5/8 23 2/8	19 6/8	6	7	Anoka County	MN	Jim Jarvi	2005	3003
161 5/8	25 2/8 19 4/8	16 5/8	6	7	Barber County	KS	Patrick J. McGlaflin	2005	3003
161 4/8	22 3/8 23 4/8	15 4/8	9	9	Butler County	KS	Dave Rogers	1989	3014
161 4/8	23 1/8 24 0/8	16 2/8	7	6	Woodbury County	IA	Matt Van Meter	1995	3014
161 4/8	25 0/8 24 5/8	15 1/8	7	7	Cole County	MO	Luke Markway	1999	3014
161 4/8	27 0/8 26 1/8	20 7/8	6	6	Luzerne County	PA	Richard M. Stanek	2001	3014
161 4/8	26 2/8 25 2/8	19 7/8	7	6	Marquette County	WI	Jay Severson	2002	3014
161 4/8	22 1/8 22 1/8	18 0/8	7	8	Monmouth County	NJ	Edward H. McCay, Jr.	2002	3014
161 4/8	21 7/8 23 2/8	18 5/8	6	7	Kleberg County	TX	Peeler G. Lacey, MD	2004	3014
161 4/8	22 2/8 23 0/8	17 2/8	6	5	Newaygo County	MI	Marc C. Schooley	2005	3014
161 4/8	25 3/8 25 3/8	17 5/8	7	6	Anne Arundel County	MD	Joe Malecki	2006	3014
*161 4/8	23 1/8 22 6/8	17 4/8	6	5	Scott County	MN	Cloid John Green	2007	3014
161 4/8	24 4/8 25 1/8	20 1/8	6	6	Baltimore County	MD	Ulysses David Perry	2008	3014
161 3/8	23 5/8 22 2/8	18 0/8	5	7	Tippecanoe County	IN	Brian Blankenship	1994	3025
161 3/8	20 4/8 20 5/8	16 0/8	8	8	Burt County	NE	Mike Olson	1995	3025
161 3/8	25 4/8 26 3/8	17 3/8	7	6	Mason County	KY	Brian P. Maynard	1995	3025
161 3/8	23 2/8 24 0/8	16 4/8	5	8	Leavenworth County	KS	Tommy Harrington	1999	3025
*161 3/8	24 4/8 24 5/8	18 1/8	7	6	Trempealeau County	WI	Cory D. Holiday	2000	3025
161 3/8	23 5/8 23 0/8	20 2/8	5	5	Washington County	NE	Jason Griffis	2001	3025
161 3/8	24 7/8 24 4/8	19 2/8	8	6	Edgar County	IL	Michael J. Karanovich	2001	3025
161 3/8	23 4/8 22 7/8	19 1/8	9	9	Pierce County	WI	Brent Schuler	2002	3025
161 3/8	22 2/8 23 6/8	15 7/8	5	9	St. Louis County	MO	Jim Holdenried	2002	3025
161 3/8	23 1/8 22 2/8	19 4/8	6	9	Vinton County	OH	Martin E. Cain	2004	3025
161 3/8	22 3/8 22 2/8	15 2/8	6	6	Brown County	IL	Noah S. McGhee	2005	3025
161 3/8	23 2/8 23 2/8	17 5/8	6	6	Lee County	IL	Gordon C. Gabelman	2005	3025
161 3/8	23 2/8 23 2/8	18 2/8	8	7	St. Clair County	MI	Derek L. Newberry	2006	3025
161 3/8	23 4/8 24 0/8	18 5/8	8	5	Johnson County	NE	Sam Baacke	2007	3025
161 3/8	24 7/8 24 4/8	17 3/8	7	7	Wells County	IN	Gary T. Powers	2007	3025
*161 3/8	25 1/8 25 7/8	17 4/8	8	8	Franklin County	NC	David Schnack	2009	3025

667

WHITETAIL DEER (NON-TYPICAL ANTLERS)

Minimum Score 155   Continued

SCORE	LENGTH OF R MAIN BEAM L	INSIDE SPREAD	NUMBER OF R POINTS L	AREA	STATE/ PROVINCE	HUNTER'S NAME	DATE	RANK
*161 3/8	23 4/8 24 7/8	17 3/8	8 7	Whitley County	IN	Kit Goldwood	2009	3025
161 2/8	25 2/8 28 4/8	20 1/8	5 9	Des Moines County	IA	Whitey Johnson	1987	3042
161 2/8	25 7/8 24 6/8	23 0/8	7 6	Edmonton	ALB	Roger F. Carpenter	1998	3042
161 2/8	22 0/8 22 1/8	15 3/8	12 8	Sullivan County	IN	Chad House	1998	3042
161 2/8	20 7/8 20 5/8	11 7/8	7 6	Duval County	TX	Robert Moseley	1999	3042
161 2/8	23 6/8 21 6/8	19 4/8	8 6	Racine County	WI	Dennis F. Burrows	1999	3042
161 2/8	20 5/8 24 2/8	22 1/8	8 6	Vigo County	IN	George Custer	2001	3042
161 2/8	24 5/8 24 5/8	17 2/8	9 5	Chautauqua County	KS	Rick D. Olmstead	2004	3042
161 2/8	23 1/8 22 7/8	17 3/8	6 5	Henry County	IA	Ben Moore	2005	3042
161 2/8	21 5/8 21 5/8	18 1/8	7 9	Matagorda County	TX	Dick Kubecka	2005	3042
161 2/8	23 4/8 23 1/8	17 1/8	8 8	Jackson County	MO	Lynn Behm	2005	3042
161 2/8	25 5/8 25 3/8	18 6/8	5 5	Highland County	OH	Jim Sluss	2006	3042
*161 2/8	21 3/8 22 0/8	14 5/8	8 10	Jackson County	KS	Benjy Cranford	2008	3042
161 1/8	22 2/8 24 4/8	17 3/8	9 8	Marshall County	MN	Richard Hoff	1983	3054
161 1/8	22 4/8 23 3/8	21 7/8	8 7	Sauk County	WI	Pat Reed	1993	3054
161 1/8	23 0/8 23 0/8	17 5/8	7 7	Elkhart County	IN	David G. Sanders	1995	3054
161 1/8	24 2/8 25 0/8	14 6/8	7 8	Orange County	NC	Ron Honrine	1998	3054
161 1/8	25 6/8 24 2/8	20 7/8	7 5	Union County	IL	Dennis Long	1999	3054
161 1/8	25 4/8 22 0/8	16 4/8	5 9	Marathon County	WI	Craig Olson	2000	3054
161 1/8	27 0/8 21 2/8	17 0/8	7 5	Branch County	MI	Jamie Stewart Collert	2000	3054
161 1/8	22 6/8 22 6/8	12 6/8	7 9	Shawnee County	KS	Brad Sparks	2002	3054
161 1/8	27 5/8 25 3/8	20 5/8	6 5	Williams County	OH	Cory L. Wickerham	2003	3054
161 1/8	22 7/8 22 0/8	18 2/8	6 7	Calhoun County	IL	Herman W. Kovar, Sr.	2003	3054
161 1/8	23 2/8 24 2/8	16 3/8	7 8	Andrew County	MO	Terry Waltemath	2005	3054
*161 1/8	23 2/8 23 4/8	17 4/8	6 6	McLean County	KY	Hugh C. Dickens	2006	3054
161 1/8	16 0/8 17 6/8	17 3/8	11 7	Oakland County	MI	Gary Jordan	2007	3054
*161 1/8	21 1/8 23 3/8	17 3/8	5 6	Delaware County	IA	Kevin Lamphier	2007	3054
161 0/8	22 6/8 23 4/8	21 2/8	7 6	Douglas County	NE	Ivan Mascher	1969	3068
161 0/8	24 4/8 23 3/8	17 6/8	5 8	Johnson County	NE	Stan Pfingsten	1988	3068
161 0/8	20 3/8 21 1/8	15 4/8	6 7	Kleberg County	TX	Jarred W. Peeples	1993	3068
161 0/8	25 2/8 25 2/8	17 7/8	5 6	Broadwater County	MT	Jason L. Benner	1995	3068
161 0/8	22 2/8 22 3/8	13 3/8	7 7	Dane County	WI	William "Bruce" Webb	1995	3068
161 0/8	24 5/8 24 4/8	28 3/8	5 6	Will County	IL	Brian Kirkpatrick	1996	3068
161 0/8	21 4/8 21 0/8	17 4/8	7 8	Dakota County	MN	Glen J. Tischler	1997	3068
161 0/8	21 0/8 23 6/8	20 0/8	9 7	Monroe County	IN	Eddie Lake, Jr.	1998	3068
161 0/8	23 3/8 25 5/8	15 0/8	6 6	Butler County	KS	David Kuttler, Jr.	1998	3068
161 0/8	22 4/8 22 7/8	16 5/8	6 5	Kent County	MI	John R. Cooper	1999	3068
161 0/8	25 3/8 23 7/8	17 6/8	6 7	Columbus County	NC	Reubin Greene	2001	3068
161 0/8	21 7/8 23 5/8	17 2/8	8 8	Winona County	MN	Dale L. Schulz	2001	3068
161 0/8	22 1/8 23 0/8	15 3/8	8 9	Greene County	OH	Dr. Larry Hall	2001	3068
161 0/8	22 4/8 21 7/8	17 4/8	8 7	Kosciusko County	IN	Dean E. Bickel	2001	3068
161 0/8	22 4/8 22 2/8	21 6/8	6 4	Columbia County	WI	Wayne A. Buckley	2003	3068
161 0/8	20 5/8 22 6/8	18 0/8	7 6	Montgomery County	PA	Donald C. Marin	2004	3068
161 0/8	24 0/8 24 7/8	20 0/8	6 4	Montcalm County	MI	Thomas J. Kok	2005	3068
161 0/8	23 3/8 23 5/8	15 5/8	11 7	Oakland County	MI	Gary Jordan	2006	3068
161 0/8	22 2/8 21 4/8	13 4/8	6 6	Sedgwick County	KS	Todd A. Wilson	2008	3068
160 7/8	22 6/8 23 4/8	19 4/8	7 6	Saginaw County	MI	Marty Massa	1986	3087
160 7/8	23 5/8 26 7/8	17 3/8	8 8	Roane County	TN	Rodney Maynard	1986	3087
160 7/8	23 0/8 23 0/8	16 1/8	7 5	Jefferson County	WI	Robert G. Magnussen	1996	3087
160 7/8	23 7/8 23 7/8	19 0/8	6 7	Butler County	IA	Ron Brown	1998	3087
160 7/8	23 4/8 22 7/8	14 5/8	8 7	Macon County	GA	David Campbell	2003	3087
160 7/8	22 7/8 22 2/8	17 2/8	7 6	Hancock County	IL	Mark D. Haling	2003	3087
*160 7/8	23 4/8 24 0/8	16 5/8	8 8	Miami County	IN	Terry Brantley	2004	3087
160 7/8	25 0/8 25 7/8	17 1/8	7 5	Hancock County	KY	Jeffrey R. Goddard	2005	3087
160 7/8	23 4/8 21 5/8	18 2/8	10 8	Mountrail County	ND	John G. Warberg	2007	3087
*160 7/8	23 1/8 22 6/8	17 4/8	6 5	Anderson County	KY	John McAnelly	2007	3087
160 7/8	22 7/8 22 1/8	17 7/8	10 7	Hamilton County	OH	Richard Robins	2007	3087
*160 7/8	21 3/8 21 5/8	14 3/8	7 9	Clay County	NE	James Hamik	2008	3087
160 6/8	20 4/8 21 4/8	18 4/8	7 5	Bremer County	IA	Steven Sims	1983	3099
160 6/8	25 4/8 23 4/8	17 0/8	8 8	Columbiana County	OH	David Tice	1987	3099
160 6/8	24 6/8 25 2/8	18 1/8	6 6	Neosho County	KS	William E. Louvier	1992	3099
160 6/8	25 6/8 24 1/8	17 6/8	6 7	Nemaha County	KS	Mike Hiltibrand	1993	3099
160 6/8	23 2/8 24 0/8	19 2/8	7 7	Tazewell County	IL	John P. Condis	1993	3099
160 6/8	23 0/8 24 2/8	17 7/8	5 5	Jo Daviess County	IL	Gerry Ward	2001	3099
160 6/8	22 7/8 23 3/8	21 0/8	7 7	Knox County	OH	Randy Frazee	2002	3099
160 6/8	23 4/8 26 2/8	21 0/8	11 7	Polk County	WI	Scott Soderman	2003	3099
160 6/8	23 3/8 22 2/8	19 2/8	7 6	Guthrie County	IA	Kevin L. Smith	2003	3099
160 6/8	23 4/8 24 4/8	16 4/8	8 6	Stearns County	MN	Steven Zaczkowski	2007	3099
160 5/8	19 6/8 21 4/8	17 0/8	11 9	Adams County	IL	Ray Gedaminski	1967	3109
160 5/8	22 2/8 23 4/8	18 4/8	5 9	Rice County	KS	Carl Gillespie	1990	3109
160 5/8	21 5/8 22 5/8	18 3/8	7 6	Dane County	WI	Roger Taylor	1995	3109
160 5/8	25 0/8 24 1/8	18 3/8	7 7	St. Joseph County	IN	Al Lusk	1997	3109
160 5/8	25 1/8 24 7/8	19 5/8	6 7	Belmont County	OH	Aaron R. Wiley	1999	3109
160 5/8	22 6/8 23 4/8	14 6/8	10 8	Osage County	OK	Larry L. Armstrong, Jr.	2001	3109
160 5/8	24 5/8 24 1/8	16 5/8	6 5	Dubuque County	IA	Ray Nicks	2002	3109
160 5/8	24 7/8 25 6/8	17 0/8	7 7	Athens County	OH	K. Mike Johnson	2003	3109
160 5/8	24 1/8 24 5/8	19 4/8	5 6	Fond du Lac County	WI	Robert G. Pater	2005	3109
160 5/8	21 6/8 20 2/8	18 5/8	6 8	Allegheny County	PA	Stephen R. Wolota	2005	3109
160 5/8	26 4/8 25 2/8	22 6/8	8 6	Jackson County	MI	Jason F. Engle	2007	3109
*160 5/8	22 3/8 22 7/8	16 3/8	5 7	Montgomery County	IL	Matt Hofstetter	2008	3109
*160 5/8	22 3/8 21 5/8	16 4/8	9 7	Chippewa County	MN	Chris Wenisch	2009	3109
160 4/8	22 1/8 24 7/8	21 6/8	8 10	McDonough County	IL	David S. Irwin	1987	3122
160 4/8	21 4/8 21 2/8	17 1/8	9 8	Nemaha County	NE	William M. Johnson	1999	3122
160 4/8	24 0/8 25 0/8	18 4/8	6 6	Ralls County	MO	Kevin Damron	2003	3122
160 4/8	24 3/8 25 7/8	23 1/8	6 7	Portage County	OH	Darren Werab	2003	3122
160 4/8	22 2/8 19 7/8	17 6/8	7 8	Macoupin County	IL	D. J. Kroeschel	2005	3122
*160 4/8	21 1/8 21 6/8	14 5/8	6 7	Monroe County	OH	Billy Austin	2008	3122
160 4/8	19 5/8 20 7/8	22 6/8	9 6	Jo Daviess County	IL	Raymond Tesmer	2009	3122
160 4/8	24 4/8 23 2/8	17 2/8	7 6	Vigo County	IN	Brian Crockett	2009	3122
160 3/8	23 1/8 23 1/8	16 1/8	8 13	Winnebago County	WI	John M. Duchatschek	1980	3130
160 3/8	22 0/8 23 5/8	16 7/8	7 7	Jackson County	MO	Wendell Hood	1991	3130
160 3/8	21 7/8 21 5/8	16 5/8	8 6	Brown County	IL	Steven B. Schroeder	1994	3130
160 3/8	23 6/8 24 7/8	16 6/8	8 8	Pulaski County	MO	Rich Sphar	1996	3130
160 3/8	23 2/8 24 0/8	17 1/8	7 6	Kenedy County	TX	Rich Kimball	1996	3130
160 3/8	24 3/8 24 3/8	18 7/8	9 11	Greene County	IL	Kyle D. Turner	1998	3130

668

WHITETAIL DEER (NON-TYPICAL ANTLERS)

Minimum Score 155   Continued

SCORE	LENGTH OF R MAIN BEAM L	INSIDE SPREAD	NUMBER OF R POINTS L		AREA	STATE/PROVINCE	HUNTER'S NAME	DATE	RANK
160 3/8	25 4/8 24 2/8	13 5/8	8	6	Buffalo County	WI	Kyle R. Stay	2000	3130
160 3/8	24 2/8 25 0/8	19 5/8	7	6	Goodhue County	MN	David L. Holtorf	2000	3130
160 3/8	25 4/8 26 2/8	23 1/8	12	9	Jackson County	WI	Tracy T. Parr	2002	3130
160 3/8	23 0/8 22 7/8	16 0/8	7	6	St. Louis County	MO	Mike Manion	2003	3130
160 3/8	18 5/8 20 5/8	17 5/8	9	5	Custer County	MT	Larry Murphy	2004	3130
*160 3/8	24 4/8 23 5/8	17 1/8	6	8	Mills County	IA	Eric Johnson	2005	3130
160 3/8	23 1/8 21 3/8	18 2/8	7	9	Winona County	MN	Kevin Winkelman	2006	3130
*160 3/8	21 2/8 20 7/8	16 6/8	6	8	Jasper County	IN	Paul G. Anthony, Jr.	2006	3130
*160 3/8	25 2/8 24 4/8	23 4/8	5	6	Columbiana County	OH	Paul E. Drotar	2006	3130
*160 3/8	23 2/8 23 3/8	16 7/8	7	10	Jackson County	IN	Trevor L. Wiggam	2008	3130
160 2/8	23 1/8 23 1/8	15 3/8	6	7	Lawrence County	IL	Mike Deckard	1978	3146
160 2/8	21 3/8 21 3/8	15 7/8	7	6	Scott County	IA	Jeffrey R. Coonts	1989	3146
160 2/8	21 4/8 23 4/8	17 4/8	7	9	Waukesha County	WI	Kyle Kaltz	1994	3146
160 2/8	25 6/8 26 5/8	20 3/8	6	7	Pike County	IL	Brandon Shoults	2000	3146
160 2/8	23 1/8 21 2/8	18 4/8	7	5	McCurtain County	OK	Tim Moyer	2001	3146
160 2/8	21 4/8 22 4/8	16 3/8	7	6	Lafayette County	MO	Richard Vochatzer	2002	3146
*160 2/8	23 6/8 27 7/8	23 0/8	6	6	Harlan County	NE	Michael Henry	2003	3146
160 2/8	23 2/8 24 0/8	19 3/8	7	5	McMullen County	TX	Kathleen P. Countiss	2003	3146
160 2/8	22 7/8 23 5/8	21 7/8	7	8	Ogle County	IL	Tom Campbell	2006	3146
*160 2/8	23 7/8 22 0/8	18 0/8	7	5	Pierce County	WI	Jared P. Fern	2007	3146
160 2/8	20 1/8 23 2/8	17 7/8	6	11	Jefferson County	KY	Charles Newman	2009	3146
*160 2/8	25 6/8 25 2/8	16 7/8	6	7	Wabash County	IN	Seth C. McKinney	2009	3146
160 1/8	19 7/8 23 0/8	19 1/8	8	6	Kenedy County	TX	Johnnie R. Walters	1994	3158
160 1/8	20 5/8 20 4/8	13 5/8	7	6	Woods County	OK	Vaughn Rader	2000	3158
160 1/8	23 5/8 25 6/8	20 0/8	8	10	Livingston County	MI	Norman Nielsen	2001	3158
160 1/8	21 5/8 22 6/8	17 5/8	6	7	Kendall County	IL	Carol Scholl	2003	3158
160 1/8	25 6/8 22 0/8	19 0/8	10	8	Calhoun County	IL	Bobby Wagner	2003	3158
160 1/8	22 3/8 21 4/8	17 6/8	12	8	Pottawattamie County	IA	Keith Mehlin	2004	3158
160 1/8	23 5/8 23 2/8	20 0/8	8	6	Delaware County	OH	David Rathje	2005	3158
160 1/8	21 1/8 23 0/8	17 3/8	7	7	Kent County	MI	Matthew McCauley	2006	3158
160 1/8	19 2/8 19 5/8	16 2/8	9	9	Logan County	CO	Larry Harnois	2009	3158
160 0/8	27 4/8 26 6/8	18 0/8	7	6	Gallatin County	KY	William J. Epeards	1980	3167
160 0/8	19 0/8 20 2/8	17 2/8	7	9	Rockingham County	NC	Michael R. Chrismon	1987	3167
160 0/8	23 6/8 23 5/8	22 1/8	7	8	DeKalb County	IL	Jeffery M. Peterson	1993	3167
160 0/8	21 1/8 23 3/8	18 5/8	6	7	Cedar County	IA	Jack J. Sines	1994	3167
160 0/8	23 1/8 23 0/8	22 3/8	8	11	Edgar County	IL	Russell Guthrie	1995	3167
160 0/8	23 5/8 23 0/8	15 5/8	9	6	Harper County	KS	Darren Boden	1997	3167
160 0/8	23 1/8 22 2/8	19 2/8	6	7	Smith County	KS	Tim Paymal	1999	3167
160 0/8	21 3/8 21 5/8	24 3/8	7	8	Knox County	OH	Antonio "Nito" Mortera II	1999	3167
160 0/8	25 0/8 23 6/8	17 0/8	5	6	Wood County	WI	Ryan Becker	2003	3167
160 0/8	19 6/8 18 4/8	14 2/8	8	8	White County	IL	Frank Paino, Jr.	2004	3167
*160 0/8	22 5/8 23 1/8	20 6/8	9	9	Allegheny County	PA	Daniel Derbish	2009	3167
159 7/8	22 1/8 24 4/8	19 2/8	9	8	Edmonton	ALB	Brian Bruce	1981	3178
159 7/8	23 2/8 24 1/8	18 2/8	5	6	Huron County	OH	Donald W. Howard	1984	3178
159 7/8	21 4/8 20 2/8	16 2/8	6	6	Huron County	OH	John R. Gockstetter	1984	3178
159 7/8	23 2/8 23 1/8	17 4/8	6	7	Columbia County	WI	Neil D. Miller	1995	3178
159 7/8	25 5/8 25 3/8	22 7/8	8	7	Polk County	IA	Reenie Doornenbal	1996	3178
159 7/8	24 7/8 24 4/8	22 3/8	6	6	Hunterdon County	NJ	Ernie Hofer	2000	3178
159 7/8	24 2/8 25 1/8	16 7/8	8	7	Blaine County	MT	Bernard R. Belaire III	2000	3178
159 7/8	24 0/8 23 6/8	20 3/8	6	8	Ontario County	NY	Rick A. Cascarano	2001	3178
159 7/8	21 7/8 21 5/8	17 5/8	7	7	Harper County	KS	Jeremy Sickles	2002	3178
159 7/8	23 4/8 23 6/8	18 1/8	7	6	Jefferson County	KS	Jason Tarwater	2002	3178
159 7/8	26 0/8 24 2/8	18 1/8	7	8	Black Hawk County	IA	Randy Marvets	2004	3178
*159 7/8	24 5/8 22 7/8	15 3/8	7	7	Waupaca County	WI	Ronald Stock	2007	3178
159 7/8	23 3/8 23 7/8	16 1/8	5	8	Atchison County	MO	Tom Nauman	2008	3178
159 7/8	20 6/8 25 3/8	15 0/8	7	6	New Castle County	DE	David L. Foraker, Jr.	2009	3178
159 6/8	21 6/8 26 5/8	15 6/8	10	7	Greene County	AR	Randy Ladd	1985	3192
159 6/8	20 5/8 21 5/8	17 0/8	11	8	Dane County	WI	Karl J. Ketelboeter	1993	3192
159 6/8	22 7/8 21 5/8	16 7/8	7	7	Cass County	NE	Duane Denton	1995	3192
159 6/8	23 0/8 21 4/8	15 4/8	7	8	Vernon County	WI	Tom Henry	1998	3192
159 6/8	19 6/8 23 1/8	18 0/8	5	6	Hardin County	IA	Ronald S. Allen	1999	3192
159 6/8	22 5/8 22 0/8	15 5/8	7	5	Butler County	KS	Darrell Allen	2000	3192
159 6/8	23 0/8 23 1/8	15 6/8	5	8	Brooks County	TX	Ronnie Howard	2000	3192
159 6/8	24 5/8 25 4/8	18 2/8	8	5	St. Louis County	MN	Kent Voelkner	2001	3192
159 6/8	23 0/8 23 0/8	17 1/8	6	6	Dodge County	MN	Allen Iverson	2002	3192
159 6/8	21 7/8 22 7/8	18 5/8	7	9	Jones County	IA	Milo F. Brown, Jr.	2002	3192
159 6/8	22 5/8 23 5/8	15 6/8	6	6	Kleberg County	TX	Jan Seski	2003	3192
159 6/8	20 4/8 22 0/8	15 3/8	10	7	Reno County	KS	Caley J. Ediger	2003	3192
159 6/8	23 1/8 22 4/8	18 1/8	6	9	Bayfield County	WI	Jon Bloch	2004	3192
159 6/8	24 3/8 24 3/8	15 2/8	6	6	Breckinridge County	KY	Michael D. Oliver	2008	3192
*159 6/8	21 4/8 21 2/8	17 1/8	7	7	Pawnee County	OK	Mark B. Armstrong	2008	3192
*159 6/8	21 5/8 21 7/8	14 5/8	7	7	Crawford County	WI	Joshua Straka	2009	3192
159 5/8	20 1/8 21 0/8	15 2/8	7	8	Stephenson County	IL	Ron Kaderly	1998	3208
159 5/8	24 0/8 24 6/8	14 7/8	8	8	Henry County	IL	Mike Angel	1999	3208
159 5/8	27 6/8 25 6/8	25 0/8	8	5	Stony Plain	ALB	Dennis Forchic	2000	3208
159 5/8	28 6/8 27 7/8	20 1/8	7	6	Allen County	OH	James A. Schneider	2001	3208
159 5/8	24 1/8 25 0/8	17 3/8	6	9	Spencer County	IN	Christopher Wood	2002	3208
159 5/8	20 6/8 18 2/8	20 2/8	5	9	Callahan County	TX	Elvan Goode	2007	3208
159 5/8	22 0/8 23 0/8	19 1/8	7	6	Green Lake County	WI	Jerold L. Zamzow	2007	3208
159 5/8	22 5/8 19 1/8	18 6/8	6	9	Keya Paha County	NE	R. Kirk Sharp	2009	3208
159 5/8	22 6/8 22 3/8	16 0/8	7	8	Stephens County	OK	Jimmy Bigham	2009	3208
159 4/8	20 7/8 20 5/8	15 4/8	6	6	McPherson County	KS	Kenneth L. Vogts	1979	3217
159 4/8	23 3/8 25 6/8	17 5/8	7	6	Davis County	IA	Douglas E. Miller	1997	3217
159 4/8	24 6/8 25 6/8	16 1/8	6	6	Iowa County	IA	Scott Wedemeier	1999	3217
159 4/8	23 4/8 23 4/8	21 5/8	7	7	Suffolk County	NY	Derek Matuszewski	2002	3217
159 4/8	26 6/8 20 7/8	24 4/8	5	8	Calvert County	MD	Steve Keithley	2003	3217
159 4/8	21 1/8 22 5/8	15 0/8	7	6	Adams County	IL	Darin A. Kent	2004	3217
*159 4/8	24 2/8 25 7/8	17 6/8	5	7	Clark County	IL	Brett R. Hanlon	2004	3217
*159 4/8	21 4/8 22 1/8	17 4/8	6	6	Macoupin County	IL	Larry Frensko	2005	3217
159 4/8	24 7/8 21 0/8	16 2/8	7	10	Madison County	MT	Jim Kennedy	2006	3217
*159 4/8	22 0/8 21 5/8	17 7/8	8	10	Fillmore County	MN	Beau Jensen	2006	3217
159 4/8	21 6/8 20 3/8	14 7/8	6	5	Dane County	WI	Dave Dilley	2006	3217
*159 4/8	23 2/8 24 3/8	15 7/8	6	6	Pike County	IL	Mark A. Towers	2008	3217
159 4/8	21 7/8 25 3/8	21 2/8	7	8	Warren County	IN	Codie S. Brewer	2008	3217
159 3/8	25 2/8 25 3/8	16 1/8	10	6	Vernon County	WI	Daniel F. Malin	1986	3230

669

WHITETAIL DEER (NON-TYPICAL ANTLERS)

Minimum Score 155 — Continued

SCORE	LENGTH OF R MAIN BEAM L	INSIDE SPREAD	NUMBER OF R POINTS L	AREA	STATE/PROVINCE	HUNTER'S NAME	DATE	RANK
159 3/8	22 6/8 22 2/8	18 5/8	7 8	Brown County	IL	Angela Vogel	1987	3230
159 3/8	23 1/8 23 0/8	15 3/8	6 7	Cherokee County	OK	Jeff Matlock	1995	3230
159 3/8	23 3/8 25 3/8	19 7/8	5 9	Edgar County	IL	William M. Liffick	1996	3230
159 3/8	25 3/8 25 3/8	20 0/8	8 7	Delaware County	OH	Ralph Aisel	2001	3230
159 3/8	24 2/8 25 2/8	18 1/8	7 10	Brown County	IL	Mike Cheek	2002	3230
159 3/8	21 2/8 22 0/8	17 6/8	6 6	Kane County	IL	Clem Acitelli, Sr.	2003	3230
*159 3/8	23 3/8 22 7/8	18 5/8	7 7	De Kalb County	IN	Troy Shuman	2007	3230
159 2/8	21 3/8 20 3/8	16 2/8	7 10	Knox County	OH	Dennis Campbell	1992	3238
159 2/8	22 1/8 21 7/8	15 4/8	7 8	Kenedy County	TX	Grayson Lacey	1993	3238
159 2/8	23 0/8 22 5/8	17 3/8	7 9	Buffalo County	WI	Daniel G. Motszko	1994	3238
159 2/8	22 6/8 23 2/8	19 2/8	8 5	Clarke County	IA	Don Mealey	1994	3238
159 2/8	23 3/8 23 3/8	18 2/8	7 6	Outagamie County	WI	Randy Lemke	1995	3238
159 2/8	23 1/8 24 1/8	21 3/8	7 6	Bedford County	VA	John P. Dowdy	1995	3238
159 2/8	22 7/8 22 3/8	16 1/8	5 6	Jefferson County	NE	Lennie Eubanks	1999	3238
159 2/8	25 0/8 25 1/8	15 5/8	7 7	Gratiot County	MI	Kent A. Whitford	2000	3238
159 2/8	26 0/8 21 3/8	19 2/8	9 7	Jefferson County	WI	Rick Schroeder	2000	3238
159 2/8	23 7/8 24 3/8	21 0/8	7 6	Suffolk County	NY	Martin R. Hagerott	2000	3238
159 2/8	23 3/8 24 2/8	17 0/8	6 6	Tazewell County	IL	Eric Hove	2001	3238
159 2/8	25 1/8 23 0/8	20 4/8	5 7	Meigs County	OH	Dennis Grooms	2004	3238
*159 2/8	23 0/8 21 5/8	17 6/8	5 8	Allamakee County	IA	Kevin A. Juedes	2005	3238
159 2/8	22 7/8 22 1/8	14 4/8	8 7	Clermont County	OH	Chris Zerhusen	2007	3238
159 2/8	24 1/8 23 2/8	20 0/8	6 7	Athens County	OH	James R. Harper II	2009	3238
*159 2/8	23 3/8 23 1/8	19 3/8	6 6	Montgomery County	MD	Jordan C. Cissel	2009	3238
*159 2/8	22 6/8 22 7/8	14 4/8	8 8	Wyandotte County	KS	Cris J. Powell	2009	3238
159 2/8	23 3/8 19 5/8	18 7/8	8 11	Eckville	ALB	Brad Janzen	2010	3238
159 1/8	21 0/8 21 6/8	13 3/8	8 10	Scott County	KY	Vic Morrison	1972	3256
159 1/8	21 0/8 21 3/8	16 6/8	6 9	Columbia County	WI	Scott M. Hazard	1980	3256
159 1/8	22 3/8 21 4/8	14 2/8	6 8	Price County	WI	Ernie P. Jablonsky, Jr.	1995	3256
159 1/8	22 2/8 21 5/8	21 3/8	5 11	Garvin County	OK	Lindell R. Armstrong	1995	3256
159 1/8	25 6/8 24 7/8	21 3/8	6 8	Rice County	KS	Chris Baldwin	2000	3256
159 1/8	24 1/8 24 7/8	20 2/8	6 6	Crockett County	TN	Walter Wilkerson, Jr.	2003	3256
159 1/8	24 3/8 24 4/8	15 7/8	7 6	Richland County	OH	Ron Swanger	2005	3256
*159 1/8	22 7/8 22 6/8	20 4/8	5 6	Butler County	PA	John J. Szymanowski	2006	3256
159 1/8	18 1/8 20 2/8	15 7/8	8 7	Union County	SD	Kenny Van Ballegooyen	2006	3256
159 1/8	23 0/8 22 6/8	16 1/8	7 8	Scotland County	MO	George Shirk	2009	3256
159 0/8	24 0/8 24 4/8	17 3/8	7 5	Lake County	IL	Robert H. Fugett	1976	3266
159 0/8	22 5/8 21 5/8	21 1/8	6 8	Sullivan County	IN	Steve Hobbs	1980	3266
159 0/8	22 6/8 23 6/8	17 7/8	7 6	Winnebago County	IL	Gordon Bates	1994	3266
159 0/8	18 4/8 19 2/8	14 6/8	7 8	Lafayette County	WI	Richard Ames	1997	3266
159 0/8	25 5/8 25 0/8	14 3/8	6 7	Sauk County	WI	Tanner J. Zimmerman	2000	3266
159 0/8	23 2/8 25 3/8	18 0/8	6 7	Van Buren County	IA	Joe Coleman	2000	3266
159 0/8	21 4/8 22 1/8	18 3/8	9 6	Beaverhead County	MT	Dennis Rehse	2002	3266
159 0/8	25 0/8 25 5/8	17 6/8	7 6	Anson County	NC	Matthew J. Luck	2003	3266
159 0/8	22 1/8 22 7/8	17 3/8	7 5	Henry County	IL	Tennie Weaver	2003	3266
159 0/8	22 4/8 20 3/8	18 1/8	10 6	Elkhart County	IN	Brian Hite	2009	3266
158 7/8	27 1/8 25 1/8	22 7/8	5 6	Buffalo County	WI	Ted Bauer	1984	3276
158 7/8	25 4/8 25 1/8	15 4/8	7 7	Washtenaw County	MI	Larry R. Lange	1984	3276
158 7/8	25 5/8 25 3/8	16 5/8	7 7	Monroe County	IL	Wayne Doerr	1987	3276
158 7/8	24 4/8 24 5/8	21 3/8	8 6	Clark County	IL	Eric Montgomery	1994	3276
158 7/8	23 5/8 22 7/8	19 4/8	6 5	Haskell County	KS	Neal Heaton	1996	3276
158 7/8	23 7/8 24 4/8	19 2/8	5 9	Kleberg County	TX	Johnnie R. Walters	1999	3276
158 7/8	22 3/8 19 6/8	21 2/8	8 7	Kane County	IL	Dean V. Ashton	2000	3276
158 7/8	21 4/8 22 3/8	15 7/8	6 7	Portage County	WI	Jeffrey P. Zelinski	2002	3276
158 7/8	22 1/8 21 3/8	15 2/8	7 9	Logan County	KY	David L. Yoder	2003	3276
*158 7/8	24 0/8 23 6/8	17 1/8	4 7	Powell County	MT	Gerald Bakey	2005	3276
158 7/8	22 2/8 23 3/8	17 7/8	8 7	La Porte County	IN	Scott J. Shaffer	2005	3276
*158 7/8	21 5/8 23 3/8	18 0/8	5 7	Vernon County	MO	George Richison	2009	3276
158 6/8	25 0/8 25 1/8	20 4/8	8 6	Osborne County	KS	Robert Grabast	1981	3288
158 6/8	23 2/8 21 2/8	17 7/8	7 7	Jo Daviess County	IL	Gerald J. Dupasquier	1987	3288
158 6/8	25 0/8 26 1/8	20 0/8	9 4	Licking County	OH	Scott Popplewell	1997	3288
158 6/8	22 2/8 23 5/8	16 6/8	6 9	Lenawee County	MI	Steve Spangler	1999	3288
158 6/8	22 2/8 22 2/8	16 4/8	6 6	Tazewell County	IL	Andrew E. Payne	2002	3288
158 6/8	25 4/8 25 3/8	14 1/8	7 7	Callaway County	MO	Kevin Pinckney	2005	3288
158 6/8	21 5/8 20 3/8	17 6/8	7 8	McLean County	ND	Brady Norland	2006	3288
158 6/8	21 4/8 22 1/8	17 1/8	8 5	Douglas County	KS	Rickey Beach	2006	3288
158 6/8	26 0/8 24 2/8	19 3/8	6 6	Fulton County	IL	Trent Painter	2008	3288
*158 6/8	22 1/8 22 6/8	19 4/8	6 7	Fort Macleod	ALB	Shane Marsh	2009	3288
158 6/8	22 0/8 20 3/8	16 1/8	8 6	White County	AR	Jeffery Brimer	2009	3288
158 5/8	21 2/8 21 1/8	14 5/8	6 7	Sullivan County	IN	John P. Hale	1986	3299
158 5/8	23 3/8 24 0/8	16 1/8	7 8	Elk County	KS	Jason Beem	1995	3299
158 5/8	22 6/8 22 0/8	15 5/8	5 6	Brown County	SD	Eric J. Voss	1995	3299
158 5/8	18 6/8 24 2/8	14 4/8	9 10	Carroll County	OH	Martin V. Joliat	1996	3299
158 5/8	22 1/8 22 3/8	18 3/8	7 7	Peoria County	IL	Ross A. Edwards	1997	3299
158 5/8	25 3/8 25 6/8	17 5/8	8 5	Bent County	CO	Kurt W. Keskimaki	1998	3299
158 5/8	20 4/8 23 2/8	18 7/8	8 7	Clayton County	IA	Mike Reittinger	1998	3299
158 5/8	24 1/8 24 1/8	16 4/8	6 7	Orange County	NC	Joseph Matthews	2000	3299
158 5/8	22 5/8 23 7/8	16 5/8	6 7	Wandering River	ALB	Darrin West	2000	3299
158 5/8	21 0/8 23 5/8	15 6/8	8 9	Mississippi County	AR	Barry Annalora	2000	3299
158 5/8	22 2/8 21 2/8	23 2/8	4 7	Lorain County	OH	Steven D. Reinhold	2002	3299
158 5/8	24 1/8 23 4/8	15 3/8	6 7	Switzerland County	IN	Bill Martin	2002	3299
158 5/8	23 7/8 24 1/8	18 3/8	7 8	Cowley County	KS	Justin Crawford	2003	3299
158 5/8	26 6/8 26 5/8	18 4/8	4 6	Riley County	KS	Ryan D. Hubbard	2005	3299
158 5/8	23 3/8 23 6/8	14 2/8	6 6	Dane County	WI	Jeremy Plautz	2009	3299
158 4/8	22 4/8 24 1/8	19 4/8	7 4	Winona County	MN	Randy SuPalla	1985	3314
158 4/8	23 6/8 22 6/8	16 4/8	7 7	Winnebago County	WI	Michael S. Henschel	1993	3314
158 4/8	25 7/8 23 4/8	15 2/8	7 9	Bent County	CO	Bob Renner	1995	3314
158 4/8	25 2/8 26 2/8	19 6/8	7 7	Ross County	OH	Terry Bridenbaugh	1998	3314
158 4/8	22 7/8 21 7/8	19 0/8	7 6	Sarpy County	NE	Scott Warren	2000	3314
158 4/8	23 3/8 23 7/8	17 3/8	7 9	Missoula County	MT	Doug Stout	2003	3314
158 4/8	24 6/8 25 2/8	13 4/8	6 6	Barber County	KS	James C. Wilson	2003	3314
158 4/8	22 2/8 22 4/8	16 5/8	6 6	Montgomery County	IA	Dick Paul	2003	3314
158 4/8	21 4/8 21 1/8	16 7/8	5 7	Fulton County	IL	Carson Herrman	2004	3314
158 4/8	25 0/8 23 4/8	12 6/8	5 9	Macoupin County	IL	Wayne Hadley	2004	3314
158 4/8	23 0/8 22 6/8	17 7/8	7 8	Reno County	KS	Gene Kane	2004	3314
158 4/8	24 4/8 22 1/8	18 1/8	6 9	Seward County	KS	Lynn Leonard	2004	3314

WHITETAIL DEER (NON-TYPICAL ANTLERS)

Minimum Score 155 — Continued

SCORE	LENGTH OF R MAIN BEAM L	INSIDE SPREAD	NUMBER OF R POINTS L		AREA	STATE/PROVINCE	HUNTER'S NAME	DATE	RANK
158 4/8	27 6/8	27 7/8	18 7/8	6	7	Eau Claire County	WI	Ryan L. Empey	2005	3314
158 4/8	23 0/8	22 5/8	16 7/8	8	8	Dubuque County	IA	Jeffrey J. Schwartz	2005	3314
158 4/8	23 4/8	23 1/8	14 2/8	5	6	Sauk County	WI	Lee J. Keim	2005	3314
158 4/8	19 7/8	20 6/8	19 7/8	7	10	Randolph County	IL	Ben Giddens	2007	3314
*158 4/8	21 2/8	21 3/8	16 5/8	8	8	Walsh County	ND	Robert Langerud	2009	3314
158 3/8	24 7/8	24 0/8	16 2/8	8	6	Morrison County	MN	Duane Rodine	1987	3331
158 3/8	22 0/8	22 0/8	19 4/8	8	8	Suffolk County	NY	Joseph LaRue	1998	3331
158 3/8	22 0/8	20 7/8	20 5/8	8	8	Woodson County	KS	Mark Seel	1999	3331
158 3/8	19 7/8	21 1/8	15 2/8	7	7	Powder River County	MT	Arthur Perleberg	2000	3331
158 3/8	22 3/8	22 3/8	18 4/8	7	8	Hennepin County	MN	Dean Balzum	2000	3331
158 3/8	24 4/8	23 0/8	19 3/8	7	5	Jones County	IA	Tracy Meyers	2001	3331
158 3/8	23 2/8	23 0/8	19 4/8	7	7	Uvalde County	TX	Randy Couthran	2002	3331
158 3/8	20 7/8	21 6/8	17 3/8	9	7	Columbia County	WI	Clint R. Dornfeld	2003	3331
*158 3/8	24 2/8	24 0/8	18 7/8	4	10	Pickaway County	OH	DeShane Rose	2003	3331
158 3/8	25 2/8	24 2/8	19 3/8	6	8	Pike County	IL	Brian Johnson	2004	3331
*158 3/8	24 1/8	25 5/8	19 1/8	9	7	Washington County	IL	Kim Houser	2004	3331
158 3/8	21 5/8	21 6/8	18 1/8	8	7	Linn County	IA	Scott D. Moon	2005	3331
158 3/8	22 6/8	23 2/8	14 3/8	7	6	Oglethorpe County	GA	John Seginak	2007	3331
158 2/8	23 0/8	23 1/8	21 0/8	7	6	La Salle County	IL	John Thomas	1988	3344
158 2/8	23 4/8	23 5/8	14 2/8	7	6	Dubuque County	IA	Joe Lieb	1996	3344
158 2/8	22 1/8	21 4/8	16 6/8	8	6	Greene County	PA	Donald Angott	1998	3344
158 2/8	25 3/8	26 4/8	20 2/8	6	4	Hancock County	OH	Jamie Pratt	1999	3344
158 2/8	23 5/8	23 1/8	17 7/8	8	6	Butler County	KS	Jack A. Pedersen	2000	3344
158 2/8	22 4/8	24 1/8	15 7/8	8	7	Kenedy County	TX	Mickey W. Hellickson	2001	3344
158 2/8	23 4/8	23 0/8	21 6/8	6	10	Beaver County	PA	Michael Patterson	2002	3344
158 2/8	23 4/8	22 2/8	18 5/8	8	6	Bureau County	IL	Jared Piacenti	2003	3344
158 2/8	24 4/8	23 0/8	18 5/8	7	6	Clay County	MO	Tim Bushart	2004	3344
*158 2/8	25 4/8	25 3/8	18 1/8	6	6	Fayette County	IL	Zac Pittman	2005	3344
158 2/8	22 4/8	21 7/8	19 2/8	6	9	Butler County	KS	Gary Merriman	2005	3344
158 2/8	24 3/8	22 0/8	17 5/8	7	8	Stearns County	MN	Jim Baker	2006	3344
*158 2/8	22 7/8	22 3/8	19 2/8	6	6	Chickasaw County	IA	Joel Betsinger	2008	3344
158 1/8	19 2/8	21 0/8	17 1/8	6	8	Jackson County	MI	Kim H. Whittman	1982	3357
158 1/8	22 0/8	20 4/8	14 5/8	6	7	Hughes County	OK	Trent Hodgins	1993	3357
158 1/8	19 0/8	19 5/8	14 7/8	8	6	Barron County	WI	Daryl K. Dostal	1999	3357
158 1/8	23 5/8	23 4/8	19 4/8	7	6	Jessamine County	KY	Jay Richardson	2001	3357
158 1/8	24 0/8	25 5/8	15 7/8	5	6	Livingston County	MI	Keith L. Solomon	2001	3357
158 1/8	23 2/8	23 4/8	18 0/8	8	8	Buffalo County	WI	Kory A. Rud	2003	3357
158 1/8	25 3/8	24 4/8	17 6/8	7	8	Alfalfa County	OK	Terrence Horan	2004	3357
158 1/8	24 2/8	23 3/8	16 2/8	7	8	Clay County	MO	John Stephen Smith	2004	3357
158 1/8	22 0/8	22 0/8	18 4/8	5	6	Barron County	WI	Christopher R. Sonterre	2005	3357
158 1/8	23 1/8	23 4/8	16 5/8	8	5	Douglas County	IL	Scott Crist	2006	3357
*158 1/8	24 2/8	24 3/8	20 3/8	8	6	Webster County	KY	Michael Morris	2007	3357
158 0/8	24 3/8	23 4/8	18 2/8	6	6	Peoria County	IL	E. Scott Phillips	1994	3368
158 0/8	20 7/8	22 0/8	17 4/8	8	11	Gwinnett County	GA	Stephen Patrick Finn	1995	3368
158 0/8	23 6/8	24 1/8	22 4/8	7	5	Suffolk County	NY	Paul Sharpe	1995	3368
158 0/8	23 0/8	23 0/8	22 5/8	6	6	Kleberg County	TX	Johnnie R. Walters	1996	3368
158 0/8	23 5/8	21 7/8	15 3/8	7	7	Greene County	OH	Neil D. Preibisch	1996	3368
158 0/8	20 4/8	19 6/8	15 1/8	6	6	Thurston County	NE	Kelly S. Buske	1997	3368
158 0/8	25 3/8	23 7/8	16 0/8	7	7	Waukesha County	WI	James Rossi	1997	3368
158 0/8	23 1/8	22 6/8	18 6/8	6	9	Carter County	OK	Rick Orr	1998	3368
158 0/8	21 5/8	21 1/8	13 3/8	7	6	Ralls County	MO	Bradley Smith	2000	3368
158 0/8	24 7/8	23 0/8	19 5/8	5	8	Schoharie County	NY	Shawn Bevins	2004	3368
158 0/8	22 6/8	20 0/8	15 6/8	6	8	Gentry County	MO	Rob Teschner	2007	3368
157 7/8	22 6/8	23 2/8	16 7/8	10	8	Dane County	WI	Donald W. Pache	1982	3379
157 7/8	25 1/8	21 4/8	18 0/8	8	5	Macoupin County	IL	Floyd Wiltshire	1987	3379
157 7/8	24 5/8	24 6/8	21 2/8	5	6	Suffolk County	NY	Glen Thorne	1996	3379
157 7/8	21 7/8	22 6/8	18 2/8	7	7	Montgomery County	IL	Toby Hicks	1997	3379
157 7/8	25 6/8	26 0/8	18 6/8	5	8	Johnson County	IA	Richard Milder	2001	3379
157 7/8	25 7/8	25 1/8	19 0/8	6	9	Edgar County	IL	Jack D. Hoffman	2003	3379
157 7/8	26 2/8	23 5/8	18 1/8	5	6	Doniphan County	KS	Mark Jacobson	2003	3379
157 7/8	23 3/8	22 5/8	16 4/8	6	6	McKenzie County	ND	Corey Hugelen	2004	3379
*157 7/8	21 7/8	20 5/8	15 5/8	8	6	Carberry	MAN	Dennis Kalar	2004	3379
157 7/8	27 0/8	26 4/8	20 7/8	4	6	Delaware County	IA	Kevin D. Dempster	2004	3379
*157 7/8	21 1/8	21 3/8	17 1/8	9	7	Aurora County	SD	Eric Steichen	2006	3379
157 7/8	22 2/8	20 4/8	20 0/8	7	6	Walsh County	ND	Doug Davis	2007	3379
*157 7/8	20 6/8	21 3/8	19 3/8	13	7	Chautauqua County	KS	Jeff Davis	2008	3379
157 6/8	23 7/8	22 7/8	17 4/8	7	7	Lincoln County	SD	Mac Butler	1987	3392
157 6/8	21 6/8	21 4/8	17 0/8	8	7	Saunders County	NE	Joseph S. Loomis	1993	3392
157 6/8	23 1/8	22 4/8	19 5/8	7	7	Oneida County	WI	Randy W. Michael	1993	3392
157 6/8	22 3/8	21 7/8	18 4/8	5	6	Jackson County	MO	Jeff Stahl	1994	3392
157 6/8	21 0/8	22 1/8	16 2/8	10	9	Morris County	KS	Shawn Younts	1996	3392
157 6/8	24 2/8	24 1/8	17 2/8	5	6	Jefferson County	IL	Lynn Wollerman	2001	3392
*157 6/8	22 2/8	21 7/8	15 2/8	6	7	Union County	SD	Eugene Kjose	2003	3392
157 6/8	24 0/8	24 2/8	15 5/8	7	6	Iowa County	WI	Ryan Lipska	2006	3392
*157 6/8	26 3/8	26 0/8	18 5/8	5	7	Meigs County	OH	Joseph H. Pursley	2006	3392
*157 6/8	20 2/8	24 5/8	17 3/8	7	8	Jackson County	KS	Kevin Beam	2008	3392
157 6/8	20 5/8	16 1/8	15 2/8	9	10	Adams County	IL	Chuck I. Elliston	2009	3392
157 5/8	25 3/8	25 1/8	17 5/8	8	8	Black Hawk County	IA	Darrell Zacharias	1976	3403
157 5/8	21 6/8	21 6/8	13 4/8	8	9	Menard County	IL	Barry D. Sampson	1992	3403
157 5/8	21 0/8	21 4/8	16 1/8	6	9	Adams County	WI	Tim Hickey	1995	3403
157 5/8	21 0/8	21 0/8	18 6/8	6	7	Rock County	WI	Cory Mielke	1999	3403
157 5/8	26 6/8	26 1/8	21 6/8	6	6	Richardson County	NE	Bob Cline	1999	3403
*157 5/8	27 5/8	22 3/8	16 5/8	5	9	Jackson County	MO	Travis Schoenberger	2002	3403
157 5/8	20 7/8	20 5/8	13 3/8	7	6	Outagamie County	WI	Jim Ernst	2004	3403
157 5/8	24 0/8	22 4/8	21 3/8	7	7	Schoharie County	NY	Arnold V. Porach	2004	3403
157 5/8	20 4/8	21 2/8	15 0/8	8	7	Pontotoc County	OK	Ed Rutherford	2004	3403
*157 5/8	22 2/8	21 7/8	17 3/8	7	10	Scotland County	MO	David R. Mahue	2004	3403
157 5/8	24 3/8	23 1/8	19 4/8	5	8	Somerset County	MD	Tom Daniels	2005	3403
*157 5/8	23 3/8	24 3/8	18 0/8	10	9	Shackelford County	TX	Brandon Ray	2007	3403
*157 5/8	22 3/8	24 1/8	21 3/8	6	4	Fountain County	IN	Steve A. Winstead	2008	3403
157 5/8	20 3/8	23 4/8	16 2/8	7	6	St. Croix County	WI	Michael A. Kieckhoefer	2008	3403
157 5/8	23 1/8	24 0/8	18 2/8	5	6	Douglas County	NE	Scott Feldhacker	2009	3403
157 4/8	23 4/8	22 6/8	17 5/8	6	5	Cass County	MI	Michael A. Tulley	1996	3418
157 4/8	22 3/8	22 2/8	12 5/8	6	7	Lawrence County	MO	Darren Deal	1999	3418
157 4/8	22 7/8	23 3/8	14 6/8	7	5	Nemaha County	NE	Perry Oates	2003	3418

WHITETAIL DEER (NON-TYPICAL ANTLERS)

Minimum Score 155 — Continued

SCORE	R MAIN BEAM L	INSIDE SPREAD	R POINTS L	AREA	STATE/PROVINCE	HUNTER'S NAME	DATE	RANK
*157 4/8	23 1/8 23 4/8	19 1/8	6 5	Dakota County	MN	Paul Eckman	2003	3418
157 4/8	25 5/8 23 1/8	17 6/8	6 10	Dunn County	WI	Matt Wheeler	2005	3418
*157 4/8	26 4/8 25 6/8	16 4/8	4 7	Sandusky County	OH	Adam Dymond	2006	3418
157 4/8	22 3/8 20 7/8	18 3/8	7 8	Coal County	OK	Scott Walker	2010	3418
157 3/8	20 3/8 24 2/8	18 1/8	7 6	Guernsey County	OH	Robert T. Fedorke, Jr.	1993	3425
157 3/8	23 5/8 24 4/8	14 2/8	6 6	Washington County	MN	Craig Osterkamp	1997	3425
157 3/8	23 0/8 24 2/8	17 2/8	7 7	Green Lake County	WI	Rodney R. Sommer	1998	3425
157 3/8	25 4/8 24 6/8	16 3/8	5 7	Throckmorton County	TX	Bryan W. Rambo	1999	3425
157 3/8	26 0/8 25 3/8	22 3/8	4 5	La Salle County	IL	Larry Longbons	1999	3425
157 3/8	20 7/8 20 6/8	18 1/8	6 8	Columbia County	WI	Dustin A. Hoffmann	2003	3425
*157 3/8	21 3/8 20 1/8	16 1/8	8 12	Washington County	AR	Clay Newcomb	2007	3425
157 2/8	22 4/8 19 6/8	22 4/8	6 6	Crawford County	IA	Scott Pelino	1990	3432
157 2/8	23 4/8 25 3/8	19 1/8	8 7	Montgomery County	IL	Charles O. Herman III	1991	3432
157 2/8	26 4/8 26 6/8	18 1/8	6 7	Raleigh County	WV	Jackie Davis	1997	3432
157 2/8	25 1/8 23 0/8	27 4/8	5 7	Arkansas County	AR	Joe O'Dell	1998	3432
157 2/8	23 6/8 22 5/8	18 6/8	5 9	Eau Claire County	WI	Mike Pritchard	1998	3432
157 2/8	24 1/8 25 7/8	21 5/8	5 7	Suffolk County	NY	John B. Ward, Jr.	2000	3432
157 2/8	21 4/8 21 6/8	16 4/8	6 8	Jefferson County	WI	Tim Gallitz	2003	3432
157 2/8	24 4/8 23 7/8	18 2/8	7 6	Crawford County	KS	Patrick B. Arkeketa	2003	3432
157 2/8	20 7/8 22 7/8	17 3/8	9 7	Cass County	NE	Chad Zimmerman	2007	3432
157 2/8	22 4/8 23 0/8	19 4/8	6 7	Tippecanoe County	IN	Cody Spitznagle	2007	3432
157 2/8	20 2/8 19 3/8	18 3/8	8 6	Becker County	MN	Randy Tate	2008	3432
*157 2/8	21 7/8 23 5/8	14 4/8	11 7	Linn County	IA	Whitney Woods	2009	3432
157 1/8	23 1/8 22 7/8	16 4/8	8 6	Rock County	WI	Daniel T. Steinke	1982	3444
157 1/8	24 3/8 22 4/8	16 7/8	7 7	Genesee County	NY	John Michalak	2000	3444
157 1/8	24 4/8 24 2/8	20 0/8	7 6	Pepin County	WI	Tom P. Weiss, Jr.	2002	3444
157 1/8	22 3/8 22 6/8	16 3/8	6 8	Macon County	MO	Mike Trumper	2002	3444
157 1/8	21 5/8 22 2/8	19 0/8	7 7	Pottawattamie County	IA	Bernard Klindt	2004	3444
157 1/8	23 4/8 25 4/8	20 1/8	8 7	Lincoln County	OK	Carl Leabo	2005	3444
157 1/8	23 3/8 25 0/8	20 3/8	8 5	Holt County	MO	Craig A. Barrett	2005	3444
157 1/8	24 6/8 25 0/8	22 0/8	7 5	Shiawassee County	MI	Chris Reed	2005	3444
157 1/8	24 6/8 24 5/8	20 0/8	4 5	Vernon County	WI	Adam Highman	2005	3444
157 1/8	22 0/8 22 1/8	17 7/8	8 7	Stearns County	MN	Darren Kiffmeyer	2006	3444
157 1/8	25 4/8 25 4/8	18 5/8	6 5	Seneca County	NY	Thomas P. Mitchell, Jr.	2007	3444
157 0/8	25 4/8 24 5/8	19 6/8	6 6	Allen County	IN	Denny Emrich	1993	3455
157 0/8	22 4/8 23 0/8	16 5/8	6 5	Worth County	IA	Larry B. Porter	1997	3455
157 0/8	26 2/8 26 1/8	18 0/8	6 5	Richardson County	NE	Todd A. Baker	2001	3455
157 0/8	22 2/8 21 6/8	16 2/8	8 6	Allen County	KY	Billy Joe Miller	2002	3455
157 0/8	25 5/8 24 4/8	19 1/8	7 7	St. Clair County	MO	Steven A. Smith	2003	3455
157 0/8	21 5/8 22 7/8	17 7/8	9 7	Jefferson County	IL	Branden W. Schrader	2006	3455
156 7/8	23 2/8 22 2/8	16 2/8	8 9	Suffolk County	NY	Neal Heaton	1994	3461
156 7/8	22 6/8 22 1/8	18 1/8	6 6	Menard County	IL	Ron Wadsworth	1996	3461
156 7/8	25 4/8 22 6/8	23 4/8	5 6	Lake County	IL	Kris Wilson	1997	3461
156 7/8	23 6/8 24 0/8	15 4/8	6 6	Columbia County	WI	Craig L. Schreiber	1998	3461
156 7/8	23 1/8 22 4/8	15 5/8	8 8	Pike County	IL	Steven D. Wright	1999	3461
156 7/8	20 5/8 19 0/8	16 4/8	8 7	Thurston County	NE	Kelly Jones	2002	3461
156 7/8	25 6/8 25 5/8	17 7/8	4 6	Morris County	NJ	Ronald Ireland	2002	3461
*156 7/8	20 5/8 20 2/8	17 4/8	6 9	Monroe County	MO	Mike Boylan	2003	3461
156 7/8	23 5/8 25 2/8	16 5/8	5 5	Yankton County	SD	Gary Sejnoha	2003	3461
*156 7/8	24 4/8 25 4/8	18 4/8	5 9	Clark County	IL	Greg Finney	2004	3461
156 7/8	25 5/8 25 6/8	19 2/8	7 7	St. Louis County	MN	Aaron Hildebrant	2005	3461
156 7/8	20 1/8 20 5/8	15 0/8	5 8	Victoria County	TX	Monroe Schroeder	2006	3461
156 6/8	26 7/8 24 7/8	18 4/8	9 7	Prince Georges County	MD	Anthony C. Malpasso	1979	3473
156 6/8	23 4/8 23 4/8	16 5/8	8 5	Buffalo County	WI	Pat Slaby	1986	3473
156 6/8	22 1/8 22 2/8	18 1/8	8 9	Jackson County	MO	Daniel L. Johnson	1986	3473
156 6/8	21 5/8 21 0/8	16 6/8	7 7	Green Lake County	WI	Douglas L. Jenkins	1995	3473
156 6/8	21 5/8 21 0/8	12 1/8	5 8	Montgomery County	MO	Jon Leonard	1998	3473
156 6/8	17 5/8 22 1/8	18 3/8	10 6	Washington County	RI	Stephen Tyrrell	1998	3473
156 6/8	22 6/8 21 6/8	21 0/8	8 8	Brown County	SD	David Severson	2002	3473
156 6/8	21 3/8 22 2/8	17 0/8	7 8	Dubois County	IN	Drew J. Schmitt	2003	3473
156 6/8	19 7/8 19 5/8	16 5/8	8 8	Platte County	MO	Alan Graves	2003	3473
*156 6/8	21 6/8 21 4/8	18 6/8	6 6	Woodford County	IL	Bill Ullrich	2003	3473
*156 6/8	26 2/8 25 5/8	18 6/8	6 7	Iroquois County	IL	Ray Holohan	2004	3473
*156 6/8	25 5/8 26 2/8	18 0/8	6 6	St. Louis County	MN	Jeffrey A. Mitchell	2005	3473
*156 6/8	20 4/8 20 6/8	14 7/8	8 8	Steuben County	IN	Michael Klavinski	2006	3473
*156 6/8	21 4/8 20 4/8	17 5/8	8 8	Marathon County	WI	Jerry Check	2006	3473
156 5/8	23 7/8 24 3/8	20 1/8	8 7	Highland County	OH	Samuel D. Chinn	1993	3487
156 5/8	19 4/8 21 2/8	13 7/8	9 7	Lake County	IL	Aaron J. Jecevicus	1994	3487
156 5/8	25 2/8 25 1/8	13 6/8	6 4	Greenwood County	KS	Mike Holland	1996	3487
156 5/8	22 3/8 22 4/8	15 1/8	8 6	Kleberg County	TX	Mickey W. Hellickson	1999	3487
156 5/8	21 6/8 24 0/8	14 6/8	6 7	Schuyler County	IL	Richard P. Barnes	2002	3487
156 5/8	26 0/8 24 2/8	18 5/8	7 7	Van Buren County	IA	Joe Coleman	2004	3487
156 5/8	22 2/8 25 4/8	17 5/8	9 6	Kiowa County	KS	Drue Scull	2004	3487
156 5/8	24 2/8 23 7/8	17 4/8	6 5	Gallatin County	IL	Tim Justus	2004	3487
*156 5/8	25 5/8 22 5/8	17 0/8	6 8	Effingham County	IL	Richard Doolittle	2006	3487
156 4/8	24 3/8 25 0/8	20 1/8	7 8	Lyon County	MN	Harold G. Halfmann	1972	3496
156 4/8	24 6/8 23 3/8	20 2/8	7 9	Winnebago County	IL	Jim Dorney	1975	3496
156 4/8	21 2/8 22 0/8	18 1/8	7 6	Monroe County	NY	David Stymus	1991	3496
156 4/8	19 5/8 21 3/8	16 2/8	6 8	Clay County	MN	Joe Lahlum	1991	3496
156 4/8	19 2/8 18 7/8	15 0/8	8 6	Valley County	MT	Michael J. Sandy	1992	3496
156 4/8	23 4/8 25 2/8	19 7/8	5 5	Sedgwick County	KS	Louis E. Turner	1994	3496
156 4/8	23 6/8 23 5/8	18 6/8	5 5	Columbia County	WI	Jotham E. Pease	1998	3496
156 4/8	24 4/8 25 3/8	19 6/8	5 6	Bucks County	PA	Eric Miller	1998	3496
156 4/8	24 4/8 23 0/8	15 5/8	6 7	Upson County	GA	Robert Kleinschmidt	1998	3496
156 4/8	24 4/8 23 0/8	15 4/8	6 5	Grayson County	KY	Daniel Oller	1999	3496
156 4/8	22 2/8 22 0/8	20 0/8	4 8	Roger Mills County	OK	Tammy Frost	2001	3496
156 4/8	24 3/8 24 3/8	21 3/8	7 8	Jay County	IN	Jim Vaughn	2002	3496
156 4/8	22 5/8 21 6/8	18 5/8	5 7	Des Moines County	IA	Craig R. Belknap	2003	3496
156 4/8	23 3/8 23 5/8	17 0/8	5 7	Elk County	KS	Jim Frey	2005	3496
156 3/8	21 4/8 21 2/8	20 2/8	7 6	Washington County	KS	Doug Kruse	1993	3510
156 3/8	21 4/8 21 4/8	21 4/8	9 8	Suffolk County	NY	James Matuszewski	1995	3510
156 3/8	24 6/8 24 3/8	18 1/8	5 5	Jefferson County	WI	Robert Simoneau	1998	3510
156 3/8	22 3/8 23 0/8	21 7/8	5 8	Kleberg County	TX	Johnnie R. Walters	1998	3510
156 3/8	23 0/8 21 2/8	17 4/8	6 9	Edmonton	ALB	Dale Johnson	1999	3510
156 3/8	24 3/8 23 4/8	16 3/8	5 6	Erie County	NY	Nicholas A. Schmitt	2000	3510

WHITETAIL DEER (NON-TYPICAL ANTLERS)

Minimum Score 155 — Continued

SCORE	LENGTH OF R MAIN BEAM L	INSIDE SPREAD	NUMBER OF R POINTS L		AREA	STATE/ PROVINCE	HUNTER'S NAME	DATE	RANK
156 3/8	23 6/8 26 6/8	20 6/8	8	5	Coshocton County	OH	Joseph P. Kent	2001	3510
156 3/8	25 4/8 24 5/8	15 4/8	6	5	Vernon County	MO	Roger L. Hensley	2002	3510
156 3/8	20 7/8 21 5/8	18 3/8	8	6	Holland	MAN	Ronald W. Lapan II	2003	3510
156 3/8	24 0/8 24 2/8	17 1/8	5	7	Sauk County	WI	Michael E. Cole	2004	3510
156 3/8	19 0/8 22 3/8	16 3/8	7	5	Pope County	MN	Clark Hagemeyer	2004	3510
156 3/8	25 3/8 25 6/8	18 3/8	6	5	Fountain County	IN	Art Brannon	2004	3510
156 3/8	22 4/8 22 3/8	15 1/8	6	7	Spink County	SD	Mark Grote	2005	3510
*156 3/8	22 3/8 22 6/8	13 3/8	7	9	Gove County	KS	Matt Palmquist	2007	3510
*156 3/8	26 2/8 26 7/8	16 5/8	7	5	Lauderdale County	TN	Nolan B. Graham	2007	3510
156 2/8	23 2/8 20 0/8	16 4/8	8	5	Holt County	NE	Darrell Clyde	1963	3525
156 2/8	21 5/8 22 4/8	17 2/8	7	5	Meriwether County	GA	William Clark Brown	1990	3525
156 2/8	20 1/8 20 6/8	16 4/8	8	6	Buffalo County	WI	Randy C. Reidt	1993	3525
156 2/8	26 7/8 26 4/8	20 4/8	6	6	Delaware County	IA	Dean Dempster	1995	3525
156 2/8	24 1/8 24 5/8	18 4/8	8	4	Dubuque County	IA	Michael D. Wolter	1995	3525
156 2/8	24 0/8 23 7/8	21 2/8	7	4	Springbank	ALB	Archie J. Nesbitt	1999	3525
156 2/8	24 0/8 24 6/8	16 1/8	7	7	Osage County	KS	Ronald Olson	1999	3525
156 2/8	23 5/8 24 0/8	18 2/8	6	6	Brown County	IL	Marty Chester	2001	3525
156 2/8	21 2/8 22 6/8	18 5/8	8	6	Wythe County	VA	Michael S. Shipwash	2002	3525
*156 2/8	22 6/8 21 1/8	18 3/8	8	6	Portage County	OH	Justin Makin	2003	3525
156 2/8	24 4/8 25 3/8	18 4/8	9	5	Grayson County	TX	James R. Willis, Jr.	2003	3525
156 2/8	22 2/8 22 2/8	18 2/8	6	7	Osborne County	KS	Gary Ozias	2004	3525
156 2/8	22 7/8 23 1/8	18 3/8	8	7	Harper County	KS	Walter P. Wood	2005	3525
156 2/8	22 0/8 21 1/8	17 6/8	5	8	Waupaca County	WI	Travis Jorgensen	2006	3525
*156 2/8	21 2/8 20 3/8	15 3/8	8	8	Tom Green County	TX	Mark Harrington	2008	3525
156 1/8	24 4/8 27 7/8	23 3/8	8	9	Cottonwood County	MN	Joe Earl	1959	3540
156 1/8	24 5/8 25 5/8	20 3/8	5	5	Lake County	IL	Mike Mitten	1984	3540
156 1/8	23 4/8 23 0/8	20 6/8	6	7	Walworth County	WI	Al Lehman	1988	3540
156 1/8	24 4/8 23 4/8	18 6/8	9	8	McHenry County	IL	Donald Kerns	1998	3540
156 1/8	23 1/8 22 4/8	17 3/8	8	6	Polk County	WI	Tom P. Moore	1999	3540
156 1/8	24 5/8 23 6/8	16 6/8	6	7	Sauk County	WI	Ronald L. Van Swol	1999	3540
156 1/8	21 2/8 20 2/8	12 4/8	9	6	Greenwood County	KS	James E. Samia	1999	3540
156 1/8	22 2/8 23 3/8	20 1/8	8	4	Jackson County	IA	Chip Pregler	2000	3540
156 1/8	22 7/8 19 3/8	18 4/8	7	7	Jackson County	IL	Timothy J. Cobin	2001	3540
156 1/8	21 2/8 20 6/8	14 4/8	6	5	Buffalo County	WI	Tom Schooley	2003	3540
*156 1/8	25 6/8 23 2/8	18 7/8	5	5	Kewaunee County	WI	Scott Van Remortel	2005	3540
156 1/8	22 7/8 23 2/8	18 7/8	5	6	Schuyler County	IL	Robert A. Patterson, Jr.	2007	3540
156 0/8	25 3/8 24 0/8	15 7/8	8	6	Stewart County	TN	Ronald M. Widner	1974	3552
156 0/8	21 0/8 22 0/8	18 5/8	7	7	Lake County	SD	Lonnie Iverson	1987	3552
156 0/8	24 4/8 23 4/8	15 6/8	8	6	Poinsett County	AR	Wallace G. Perkins	1994	3552
156 0/8	22 6/8 23 2/8	16 1/8	6	6	Uvalde County	TX	John T. Halbert	1997	3552
156 0/8	24 5/8 24 1/8	17 0/8	10	7	Cass County	MI	Wilbur Seager, Jr.	1997	3552
156 0/8	20 3/8 20 7/8	17 3/8	6	7	Davidson County	TN	Will Jones	1999	3552
156 0/8	18 5/8 25 0/8	7 2/8	12	8	Saline County	NE	Travis Schnell	2000	3552
156 0/8	21 7/8 22 1/8	17 7/8	7	9	Montgomery County	IA	Allen Bruce	2001	3552
156 0/8	19 6/8 20 2/8	17 4/8	8	7	Jewell County	KS	Daniel Novovesky	2009	3552
155 7/8	27 4/8 27 0/8	21 4/8	6	6	Bureau County	IL	Lester Behrends	1992	3561
155 7/8	22 0/8 23 2/8	15 5/8	7	7	Pulaski County	KY	Billy Taylor	1994	3561
155 7/8	23 4/8 22 4/8	16 1/8	7	6	Jefferson County	MO	Richard G. Dow	1998	3561
155 7/8	22 6/8 23 2/8	17 3/8	6	7	Iowa County	IA	Kevin L. McDonald	1998	3561
155 7/8	19 3/8 26 0/8	16 7/8	8	6	Jasper County	IN	Scott Lockard, Sr.	2000	3561
155 7/8	22 1/8 21 4/8	16 2/8	7	6	McDonald County	MO	Thomas E. Bradford	2002	3561
155 7/8	23 4/8 22 4/8	19 4/8	6	7	Dodge County	WI	David Chatos	2002	3561
155 6/8	23 2/8 23 7/8	20 2/8	6	6	Sedgwick County	KS	Keith Jopp	1987	3568
155 6/8	21 6/8 21 7/8	16 5/8	6	7	Grundy County	IL	Wesley Holm	1988	3568
155 6/8	22 0/8 22 3/8	15 5/8	8	7	Cadogan	ALB	Vernon C. Smedley	1994	3568
155 6/8	22 4/8 21 2/8	16 0/8	7	7	Jo Daviess County	IL	Tim Koester	1997	3568
155 6/8	23 1/8 21 2/8	19 2/8	4	8	Monroe County	OH	Dave Gomish	1997	3568
155 6/8	24 6/8 16 2/8	17 5/8	4	11	Iowa County	WI	Rick Bilkey	2000	3568
155 6/8	29 4/8 26 3/8	19 0/8	8	6	Miami County	OH	Patrick Adams	2001	3568
155 6/8	23 5/8 23 7/8	17 5/8	7	5	Knox County	IL	George D. Reed, Jr.	2002	3568
155 6/8	21 5/8 21 2/8	16 2/8	6	5	Douglas County	NE	Bryon Miller	2004	3568
155 6/8	21 4/8 20 1/8	17 2/8	7	9	Randolph County	IL	Danny Wahl	2006	3568
155 5/8	25 3/8 24 1/8	18 6/8	6	5	Chickasaw County	IA	David J. Kerkove	1995	3578
155 5/8	20 4/8 18 7/8	16 4/8	8	10	Ravalli County	MT	James A. Schott	1996	3578
155 5/8	22 2/8 22 3/8	19 0/8	6	6	Waukesha County	WI	James A. Hitchcock	1997	3578
155 5/8	24 2/8 24 2/8	16 1/8	6	7	Kosciusko County	IN	Jeffrey A. Feldman	1997	3578
155 5/8	24 2/8 25 2/8	14 2/8	4	7	Morgan County	CO	Arnie Potter	1998	3578
155 5/8	21 3/8 21 3/8	14 7/8	9	8	Marshall County	WV	Scot Goodnight	2002	3578
155 5/8	21 7/8 22 6/8	14 3/8	9	7	Pittsburg County	OK	Chris Victory	2003	3578
155 5/8	21 5/8 21 7/8	15 6/8	6	7	Macon County	MO	Dennis Brand	2005	3578
*155 5/8	23 6/8 25 2/8	17 5/8	7	6	Ohio County	KY	Jerry Young	2006	3578
155 4/8	25 1/8 25 1/8	16 3/8	9	9	Pottawatomie County	KS	Richard L. Ruetti	1970	3587
155 4/8	23 0/8 21 0/8	19 4/8	6	8	Douglas County	MN	Al Ratajesak	1986	3587
155 4/8	21 5/8 23 0/8	17 3/8	6	6	Fayette County	IA	James E. Smith	1991	3587
155 4/8	23 6/8 23 2/8	22 0/8	6	6	Logan County	WV	Raymond Snyder	1995	3587
155 4/8	23 6/8 20 4/8	18 6/8	5	8	Scott County	IA	David Paulsen	1997	3587
*155 4/8	25 3/8 26 1/8	17 1/8	7	6	Belknap County	NH	Roland R. Poulin	2003	3587
155 4/8	22 7/8 21 2/8	15 5/8	7	7	Greene County	IL	Bill Henneman	2003	3587
*155 4/8	23 3/8 22 6/8	19 2/8	6	7	Jo Daviess County	IL	Jack Lickes	2004	3587
*155 4/8	21 3/8 21 3/8	17 3/8	6	7	Buchanan County	IA	Rev. David Q. Street	2006	3587
155 4/8	20 6/8 21 1/8	18 0/8	13	12	Denton County	TX	Bill Costin	2006	3587
155 4/8	23 1/8 22 6/8	18 6/8	6	6	Suffolk County	NY	Richard Gutman	2007	3587
155 4/8	25 5/8 23 5/8	17 3/8	6	6	Dane County	WI	Troy Schroeder	2007	3587
*155 4/8	25 5/8 25 1/8	17 3/8	8	5	Pike County	OH	Bryan Wafford	2007	3587
155 3/8	21 2/8 21 3/8	17 1/8	6	8	Lyon County	MN	Daryl Miller	1968	3600
155 3/8	21 2/8 21 3/8	16 5/8	12	8	Winona County	MN	John W. Zahrte	1974	3600
155 3/8	24 2/8 23 3/8	17 6/8	7	8	Morton County	ND	Dennis Simenson	1981	3600
155 3/8	22 0/8 22 4/8	15 2/8	6	6	Vigo County	IN	Lowell Leturgez	1991	3600
155 3/8	23 2/8 23 5/8	16 7/8	7	5	Warren County	OH	Sam Y. Perone	1993	3600
155 3/8	20 6/8 19 0/8	12 5/8	7	8	Shawnee County	KS	Richard Hochanadel	1993	3600
155 3/8	19 7/8 22 0/8	16 5/8	9	6	Waushara County	WI	Steven Heuser	1998	3600
155 3/8	22 6/8 22 4/8	16 5/8	7	7	Monroe County	NY	Rob Patterson	1999	3600
155 3/8	24 6/8 24 1/8	17 4/8	8	8	Lincoln County	WI	Gregory L. Brandenburg	2000	3600
155 3/8	24 5/8 24 0/8	18 4/8	7	8	Bullock County	AL	Tyler Walker	2000	3600
155 3/8	23 1/8 23 1/8	17 5/8	6	6	Howard County	IA	John Koschmeder	2003	3600

673

WHITETAIL DEER (NON-TYPICAL ANTLERS)

Minimum Score 155 — Continued

SCORE	R MAIN BEAM	L MAIN BEAM	INSIDE SPREAD	R POINTS	L POINTS	AREA	STATE/PROVINCE	HUNTER'S NAME	DATE	RANK
155 3/8	19 0/8	19 7/8	17 1/8	7	9	Marshall County	IN	Doug L. Workman	2005	3600
*155 3/8	21 7/8	22 2/8	16 4/8	7	7	Pike County	MO	Devon Daniels	2006	3600
155 2/8	23 3/8	23 7/8	18 6/8	7	7	Missoula County	MT	Dino Fanelli	1994	3613
155 2/8	22 0/8	22 4/8	17 0/8	9	7	Washington County	OH	Tulsa Lee Green	1995	3613
155 2/8	22 3/8	22 6/8	20 0/8	5	8	Rogers County	OK	Brian J. Potter	1998	3613
155 2/8	23 3/8	24 3/8	15 7/8	8	6	Webb County	TX	David Waclawczyk	2000	3613
155 2/8	20 2/8	21 3/8	16 5/8	7	7	Warren County	IA	Bob Mezera	2000	3613
155 2/8	24 0/8	20 7/8	17 3/8	7	7	Portage County	WI	Matthew P. Tepp	2001	3613
*155 2/8	23 4/8	23 6/8	20 4/8	7	6	Branch County	MI	Richard L. Angerer	2001	3613
155 2/8	23 1/8	22 4/8	15 6/8	7	6	Linn County	KS	Douglas L. Below	2002	3613
155 2/8	22 6/8	21 5/8	17 4/8	5	5	Bradford County	PA	Andrew Fanaras	2003	3613
155 2/8	22 1/8	21 6/8	17 4/8	7	5	Woodbury County	IA	Randy Hammond	2003	3613
155 2/8	21 6/8	21 6/8	15 2/8	8	8	Crawford County	WI	Robert McCann	2004	3613
155 2/8	22 7/8	22 3/8	16 2/8	12	6	Audrain County	MO	Kelly Sells	2005	3613
155 2/8	21 2/8	19 7/8	14 3/8	8	8	Mitchell County	IA	Jordan Schwarck	2005	3613
155 2/8	23 0/8	22 6/8	17 1/8	8	6	Ward County	ND	Jack Sorum	2005	3613
*155 2/8	20 1/8	20 3/8	13 3/8	8	8	Waupaca County	WI	Roger Ver Voort	2006	3613
*155 2/8	21 6/8	21 2/8	16 1/8	6	6	Grand Forks County	ND	Ryan Svoboda	2009	3613
155 1/8	25 5/8	22 5/8	20 3/8	4	6	Jo Daviess County	IL	James Boop	1991	3629
155 1/8	26 2/8	24 2/8	21 3/8	7	4	Ashtabula County	OH	James D. Bunce, Jr.	1994	3629
155 1/8	22 6/8	22 1/8	15 1/8	6	7	Buffalo County	WI	Tony Heil	1995	3629
155 1/8	20 4/8	21 2/8	16 6/8	6	7	Rock County	WI	Terry Saunders	1997	3629
155 1/8	22 3/8	23 7/8	16 7/8	4	6	Fulton County	IL	Mark C. Durner	1998	3629
155 1/8	21 4/8	21 4/8	19 4/8	6	5	Miami County	OH	Timothy A. Anderson	1999	3629
155 1/8	23 2/8	23 3/8	18 2/8	6	8	White County	IL	Donald H. Keck	1999	3629
155 1/8	24 3/8	24 5/8	19 7/8	7	6	Montgomery County	MD	Mike Flaxcomb	2000	3629
155 1/8	22 4/8	23 0/8	15 0/8	7	7	Woodford County	IL	Dale Ragan	2001	3629
155 1/8	22 6/8	22 3/8	20 3/8	5	6	Rusk County	WI	Rich Varsho	2003	3629
*155 1/8	22 3/8	22 0/8	17 1/8	9	8	Jackson County	MI	Ronald A. Kerr	2005	3629
*155 1/8	20 2/8	22 1/8	14 7/8	7	7	Polk County	WI	Mike Funk	2008	3629
155 0/8	24 4/8	23 7/8	17 2/8	8	5	McCreary County	KY	Eddie Howard	1985	3641
155 0/8	23 5/8	23 4/8	16 5/8	7	8	Buffalo County	WI	Robert P. Jansen	1994	3641
155 0/8	24 2/8	24 0/8	22 4/8	6	6	Delaware County	OH	Maurice Rice	1994	3641
155 0/8	26 0/8	25 6/8	14 4/8	6	4	Winona County	MN	David R. Olson	1995	3641
155 0/8	25 1/8	24 3/8	16 0/8	5	7	Waukesha County	WI	Dan Bauman	1996	3641
155 0/8	22 2/8	22 2/8	17 1/8	7	7	Coshocton County	OH	Dennis Haverstock	1998	3641
155 0/8	23 6/8	23 2/8	19 6/8	9	7	Todd County	MN	Don Lisson	1998	3641
155 0/8	22 4/8	21 7/8	16 6/8	7	8	Sauk County	WI	Dave Merkes	1999	3641
155 0/8	24 7/8	20 7/8	18 2/8	7	7	Buffalo County	WI	Travis L. Althoff	2000	3641
155 0/8	21 3/8	21 4/8	18 0/8	5	7	Polk County	WI	Jerry Lunde	2000	3641
155 0/8	18 2/8	21 3/8	20 0/8	11	10	Kent County	MI	Rick Hayes	2002	3641
155 0/8	22 1/8	22 2/8	14 5/8	9	8	Pike County	IL	Russell Greer II	2002	3641
155 0/8	25 7/8	24 7/8	19 2/8	8	4	Dubuque County	IA	John Williams	2002	3641
155 0/8	23 0/8	21 3/8	15 3/8	7	7	Shawnee County	KS	Steve Meggison	2002	3641
155 0/8	23 3/8	23 1/8	17 6/8	6	5	Delaware County	IA	Daniel Putz	2002	3641
155 0/8	23 6/8	24 5/8	13 5/8	5	6	Washington County	KS	Mike Hansen	2004	3641
155 0/8	22 0/8	22 0/8	14 5/8	8	8	Branch County	MI	Anthony W. Fisher	2004	3641
155 0/8	29 1/8	26 6/8	17 5/8	6	8	Van Buren County	IA	Eric Bussiere	2006	3641
155 0/8	24 0/8	24 2/8	15 1/8	6	5	Dubuque County	IA	Tob Patzner	2006	3641
155 0/8	25 6/8	27 1/8	20 5/8	7	4	Jay County	IN	Clifton Joe Holloway	2007	3641
*155 0/8	25 4/8	23 6/8	17 5/8	8	8	Lancaster County	NE	Steve Woitaszewski	2008	3641
*155 0/8	25 6/8	26 0/8	20 3/8	4	4	Lee County	IL	Ray Jasper	2009	3641

WHITETAIL DEER (NON-TYPICAL VELVET ANTLERS)

Minimum Score 155

SCORE	LENGTH OF R MAIN BEAM L		INSIDE SPREAD	NUMBER OF R POINTS L		AREA	STATE/ PROVINCE	HUNTER'S NAME	DATE	RANK
*228 2/8	26 3/8	24 5/8	16 6/8	15	13	Wells County	ND	Tom Miller	2005	*
*219 1/8	25 7/8	20 5/8	18 6/8	7	11	Tensas Parish	LA	Billy Husted	2007	*
*205 6/8	26 7/8	26 5/8	18 1/8	9	9	Casey County	KY	Hurley Ray Combs, Jr.	2007	*
*204 0/8	21 5/8	22 6/8	18 3/8	10	10	Alder Flats	ALB	Darcy Wedlund	2007	*
185 1/8	27 0/8	27 0/8	17 6/8	8	9	Grayson County	KY	Randy Bradley	2008	*
*184 2/8	22 2/8	23 0/8	15 4/8	9	6	Yorkton	SAS	Josh Laycock	2009	*
183 6/8	24 1/8	25 2/8	16 5/8	6	8	Spokane County	WA	Kerry Warren	2009	*
*181 6/8	22 0/8	23 4/8	20 3/8	10	7	Franklin County	IL	Mike D. McKinney	2008	*
174 5/8	26 5/8	26 1/8	20 7/8	6	10	St. Louis County	MO	Paul C. Gragg	2006	*
*172 3/8	26 1/8	26 5/8	14 7/8	4	8	Hamilton County	TN	Eric Cabrera	2007	*
*172 2/8	26 2/8	25 2/8	18 5/8	7	7	Knox County	KY	Robert Dunaway	2007	*
*172 1/8	23 1/8	22 5/8	20 5/8	7	6	Teton County	MT	Bruce L. Selin	2006	*
170 4/8	24 2/8	23 5/8	15 4/8	10	8	Allen County	KY	Terry Driver	2009	*
170 1/8	24 3/8	25 2/8	16 1/8	8	8	Spokane County	WA	LaFawn Sutton	2010	*
168 1/8	21 3/8	19 1/8	20 3/8	7	14	Fillmore County	MN	Tracey Maxon	2009	*
165 4/8	23 4/8	23 4/8	20 0/8	7	6	Sturgis	SAS	Cory Babiuk	2006	*
163 6/8	22 2/8	22 6/8	18 5/8	7	9	Yellowhead	ALB	Dean Kirkeby	2005	*
161 6/8	20 1/8	20 5/8	11 3/8	7	6	Cascade County	MT	Truitt J. Kinna	2005	*
160 5/8	19 2/8	21 4/8	13 3/8	13	7	Cascade County	MT	Ray Goff	2006	*
158 4/8	21 5/8	20 2/8	18 5/8	6	6	Bottineau County	ND	Jocelyn Audet	2008	*

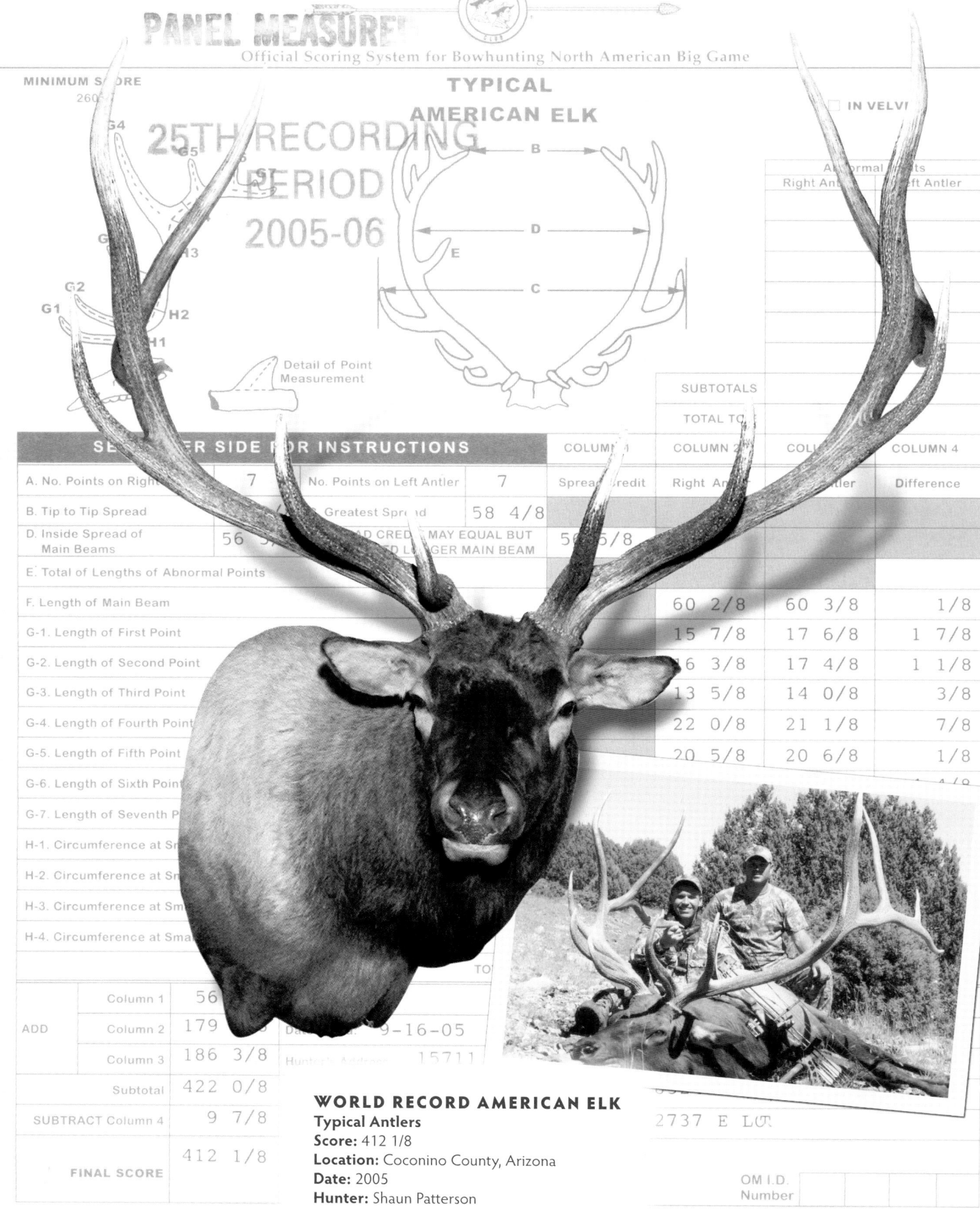

WORLD RECORD AMERICAN ELK
Typical Antlers
Score: 412 1/8
Location: Coconino County, Arizona
Date: 2005
Hunter: Shaun Patterson

WORLD RECORD
Typical American Elk

by Shaun Patterson

The night before opening morning, David won the coin toss and promptly chose to hunt the biggest bull we had seen while scouting. My guide, Levi, and I would pursue some seven other bulls to the north. With so many big bulls in the area I wasn't going to complain. After a sleepless night, opening morning finally arrived with all the anticipation, excitement and uncertainty it holds.

Starting to hike up a long narrow ridge, three bugles greeted our eager ears. A short deep guttural bugle got our blood boiling and was the obvious choice. We made a beeline in his direction as a frenzy of bugles filled the dawn. We pursued our bull for a mile when we walked right in the midst of a battle of the clashing bulls.

Alternating from being completely pinned down, to spooking off small satellite bulls, we gradually advanced towards the big moving bull. Levi led the charge as we closed the gap to 100yds. I set-up by a juniper tree as Levi blew a serenade on his cow call. My guts twisted into knots waiting to see if he would be persuaded by the call. My eyes were locked in his direction when all suddenly there he was. I was mesmerized by the swaying of ivory tips as he moved closer and closer.

Suddenly there was movement to my right. It was the rag-horn we bumped earlier. He walked around a small tree only 10yds away and busted us. A creepy silence fell over the mountain as the bugling bulls fell silent with all the commotion. We picked up the big bull's tracks and followed them for another 400 to 500 yards calling occasionally with no response. We soon lost his tracks in the rocks. We looked around and found ourselves in the middle of the thickest nastiest juniper forest ever, with no idea as to where our bull had disappeared. Suddenly, we heard the most beautiful sound in the world, the unmistakable deep low growl of our bull only 150yds to our left. "That's him!" Then, a second bull to his left bellowed a response, allowing us to advance closer.

As I entered into a small clearing about 15yards wide, I saw antlers moving through the branches of a tree just 30yards to my left. Instead of skirting along the tree as he had been doing and holding at 30yards, he angled down-hill gaining another ten. I had no time to adjust. The split second it took him to enter the lane would mean he could disappear just as quickly. I tried to adjust as the arrow was sent on its mission. The fletching spun in mid-air and then buried deep into the side of the biggest bull I had ever seen. He lunged forward then tore down-hill disappearing over a small rise.

Silence, silence and more silence. No crash, no sound of pounding hooves, no breaking of branches as he made his escape, nothing at all but silence. I looked at Levi with disgust written all over my face. "I blew it," I thought to myself.

We sat there listening for any sound from our bull but only more silence greeted our ears. With nothing to go on we decided to ease out of the area.

Joined by David and his guide, we decided to go back to find the arrow, a blood trail and at least get the direction he had headed. We held little hope of finding him dead, but we needed to get a direction none-the-less. At the scene of the shot, I prepared myself for a long afternoon on my hands and knees searching every pebble for sign of his passing. I showed everyone where I made the shot and the direction my bull went. David stepped forward a few steps and about jumped out of his skin. "He's down, he's down, right there, can you see him? He's down," David yelled at the top of his lungs.

We raced down the hill to the trophy of a lifetime. Levi had been right; the bull went down hill, stopped and turned to see what had spooked him. As he stood there he had quickly bled out and quietly died. I thank God for allowing me to harvest one of his beautiful creations, and I thank the McClendon's for all of their hard work and incredible skill.

On a side note, when we processed the meat we found an archer's broadhead imbedded in the ridge of the spine. If the arrow had fallen just two inches lower he would have been harvested a year earlier. If you recognize the rack I would love to hear from the person who placed it there.

AMERICAN ELK (TYPICAL ANTLERS)

Minimum Score 260
Cervus elaphus nelsoni and certain related subspecies

SCORE	LENGTH OF R MAIN BEAM L	INSIDE SPREAD	NUMBER OF R POINTS L	AREA	STATE/ PROVINCE	HUNTER'S NAME	DATE	RANK
*412 1/8	60 2/8 60 3/8	56 5/8	7 7	Coconino County	AZ	Shaun Patterson	2005	1
409 2/8	55 5/8 56 6/8	52 2/8	6 7	Rosebud County	MT	Chuck Adams	2000	2
404 0/8	56 4/8 57 1/8	44 0/8	7 7	Coconino County	AZ	William Wright	1992	3
402 5/8	52 2/8 52 3/8	36 6/8	8 7	Athabasca	ALB	Will Huppertz	2004	4
400 4/8	58 0/8 60 4/8	43 0/8	6 6	Coconino County	AZ	Larry C. Fischer	1998	5
399 1/8	60 0/8 61 5/8	51 1/8	6 6	Rosebud County	MT	Chuck Adams	2003	6
398 7/8	53 0/8 53 2/8	40 1/8	7 7	Rio Arriba County	NM	Robert North	2004	7
398 3/8	60 3/8 65 4/8	50 5/8	7 8	Navajo County	AZ	Marvin W. Wuertz	1993	8
396 2/8	58 2/8 57 6/8	39 0/8	6 6	Socorro County	NM	Bill Clark	2006	9
395 3/8	56 6/8 53 5/8	47 1/8	6 6	Rosebud County	MT	Jeff Larson	2007	10
395 0/8	56 4/8 54 3/8	39 4/8	7 6	Child's Lake	MAN	Irvin Funk	1998	11
395 0/8	61 3/8 61 3/8	45 4/8	6 6	Coconino County	AZ	Stan Durkalec	2001	11
394 4/8	60 4/8 59 5/8	51 0/8	6 6	Catron County	NM	Bruce R. Heare	1998	13
394 2/8	59 3/8 58 4/8	42 6/8	6 7	Yavapai County	AZ	Randy Ulmer	2009	14
393 6/8	54 7/8 53 5/8	40 0/8	6 6	Greenlee County	AZ	Alan Pennington	1999	15
393 2/8	57 6/8 57 6/8	43 7/8	7 7	Coconino County	AZ	Chad J. Connor	1995	16
393 1/8	61 5/8 63 0/8	43 7/8	7 9	Montrose County	CO	Wayne Bradley	1986	17
393 0/8	57 7/8 55 2/8	44 1/8	6 7	Rosebud County	MT	Jeramy Ohmstede	2009	18
392 6/8	55 7/8 57 1/8	40 6/8	7 7	Yellowstone County	MT	Walter Tate	2006	20
*392 5/8	58 0/8 56 2/8	46 5/8	6 6	Garfield County	UT	Richard L. Crawford, Jr.	2009	21
392 1/8	53 1/8 52 4/8	38 5/8	7 9	Blaine County	MT	Matt True	2005	22
*391 6/8	53 5/8 57 4/8	45 6/8	6 6	Catron County	NM	Mike Andrews	2005	23
391 6/8	56 1/8 55 3/8	36 2/8	7 7	Big Horn County	MT	Salvatore Blancato	2008	23
391 4/8	55 2/8 55 4/8	43 2/8	6 6	Catron County	NM	Bob Miller	1997	25
391 0/8	56 6/8 58 2/8	48 2/8	6 7	Beaver County	UT	Aaron W. Cox	2006	26
390 7/8	55 3/8 55 1/8	36 5/8	6 6	Duck Mtns.	MAN	Melvin J. Podaima	1991	27
390 7/8	57 5/8 60 2/8	42 7/8	9 8	Grant County	NM	David L. Morgan	1992	27
390 4/8	53 6/8 54 2/8	40 0/8	6 7	Garfield County	UT	Kurt DeLucero	2004	29
390 0/8	54 1/8 53 1/8	49 4/8	6 6	Johnson County	WY	Duffy Brown	2001	30
389 7/8	61 0/8 58 3/8	38 5/8	6 8	Apache County	AZ	Chase Clonts	2007	31
*389 7/8	56 4/8 58 4/8	50 5/8	6 6	Powder River County	MT	Jerry McPherson	2010	31
*389 3/8	60 2/8 53 5/8	52 6/8	6 7	Coconino County	AZ	Dave Ledbetter	2009	33
389 2/8	63 6/8 63 0/8	42 1/8	7 7	Coconino County	AZ	Jay Elmer	1980	34
389 1/8	59 7/8 58 5/8	41 6/8	8 7	Catron County	NM	Kim E. Womer	1998	35
388 4/8	57 2/8 55 4/8	47 2/8	6 7	Elko County	NV	John Hildebrand	2004	36
388 1/8	54 4/8 54 6/8	40 3/8	6 7	Meagher County	MT	D. "Mitch" Kottas	1994	37
388 0/8	54 6/8 54 0/8	41 6/8	7 6	Beaver County	UT	Daniel Carter	1998	38
387 6/8	52 5/8 54 5/8	34 3/8	8 6	Gila County	AZ	Michael Scott Park	2009	39
387 3/8	54 7/8 57 6/8	51 5/8	6 7	Catron County	NM	Brad Miller	1995	40
386 5/8	53 5/8 53 6/8	41 2/8	8 7	Madison County	MT	Allan Mintken	1986	41
*386 5/8	55 3/8 49 7/8	49 7/8	7 6	Goshen County	WY	David A. Stenson	2005	41
386 4/8	56 4/8 55 0/8	51 4/8	7 6	Larimer County	CO	David McCormick	1997	42
386 3/8	57 1/8 52 0/8	52 5/8	6 6	Catron County	NM	L. Wayne Carlton	2008	43
386 2/8	54 3/8 54 2/8	48 6/8	6 6	White Pine County	NV	Edward Michael Neilsen	2005	44
386 2/8	58 2/8 56 7/8	50 4/8	7 8	Lincoln County	NV	Dan Evans	2005	44
386 1/8	64 3/8 61 7/8	41 7/8	6 6	Sweet Grass County	MT	Buck Duncan	2004	46
386 0/8	61 2/8 59 6/8	37 2/8	8 8	Coconino County	AZ	Randy Elmer	1988	47
385 7/8	54 3/8 55 4/8	41 7/8	6 7	Coconino County	AZ	Danny Moore	2005	48
385 6/8	55 3/8 55 6/8	50 0/8	7 7	Beaverhead County	MT	Ray Ford	1998	49
385 2/8	55 5/8 56 5/8	40 4/8	6 6	Catron County	NM	Tracy G. Hardy	1993	50
385 2/8	58 6/8 59 3/8	47 4/8	6 6	San Juan County	UT	Karl Hirst	2005	50
*385 2/8	51 4/8 54 3/8	39 6/8	7 7	Rosebud County	MT	Tim W. Hite	2007	50
385 0/8	52 6/8 53 5/8	43 2/8	7 7	Catron County	NM	Larry A. Green	1997	53
385 0/8	57 0/8 53 4/8	57 5/8	7 6	Gila County	AZ	Frisco Tsosie	2005	53
384 6/8	55 2/8 53 4/8	44 2/8	6 7	Coconino County	AZ	Jay Elmer	1979	55
384 6/8	52 2/8 51 0/8	43 4/8	6 6	Converse County	WY	Dustin Pexton	2005	55
384 4/8	53 4/8 54 6/8	45 4/8	7 7	Meagher County	MT	David Snyder	1981	57
384 2/8	58 0/8 58 0/8	43 0/8	6 6	Catron County	NM	Robert John Seeds	1996	58
384 1/8	57 6/8 62 6/8	47 7/8	6 7	Coconino County	AZ	Mike Taylor	1985	59
384 1/8	50 5/8 50 4/8	41 1/8	6 6	Coconino County	AZ	Dave Pierce	1997	59
*384 1/8	56 7/8 58 0/8	43 1/8	6 6	Big Horn County	MT	Ken Carter	2009	59
384 0/8	53 5/8 51 1/8	38 2/8	6 6	Tooele County	UT	Kurt Erickson	2004	62
*383 7/8	52 6/8 54 4/8	39 3/8	6 6	Catron County	NM	William M. Kain	2003	63
383 4/8	56 7/8 55 5/8	38 6/8	7 6	Coconino County	AZ	Gilbert Romero	1992	64
383 4/8	51 3/8 52 1/8	40 6/8	6 6	Garfield County	UT	Jeff Albrecht	2007	64
383 3/8	65 0/8 61 7/8	48 5/8	6 6	Catron County	NM	Rudy O. Duran	1988	66
382 6/8	58 7/8 56 4/8	40 6/8	7 7	Coconino County	AZ	Patrick J. Loescher	1997	67
*382 4/8	58 1/8 58 7/8	41 4/8	6 6	White Pine County	NV	Karl J. Garcia	2010	68
382 2/8	60 0/8 60 0/8	47 2/8	6 6	Coconino County	AZ	Don R. Newton, Jr.	1985	69
382 2/8	51 7/8 52 5/8	39 6/8	7 7	Fergus County	MT	Leroy Sabe	1996	69
382 2/8	53 3/8 54 1/8	37 4/8	6 6	Phillips County	MT	Ryan Werner	2008	69
381 7/8	56 1/8 55 5/8	42 7/8	7 7	Coconino County	AZ	Keith D. Argyle	2005	72
*381 5/8	52 1/8 52 0/8	38 5/8	6 6	Stillwater County	MT	Jim Bailey	2006	73
381 3/8	56 4/8 56 6/8	34 7/8	6 6	Catron County	NM	Gary Jamieson	1993	74
381 1/8	55 5/8 54 6/8	35 7/8	6 7	Idaho County	ID	Rod Cullip	2007	75
380 7/8	60 0/8 60 1/8	43 5/8	6 6	Elko County	NV	Tracy R. Mitton	2005	76
380 6/8	56 7/8 55 5/8	48 0/8	6 7	Socorro County	NM	Michael S. Weldon	1992	77
380 6/8	57 0/8 54 3/8	47 2/8	7 7	Coconino County	AZ	John C. McClendon	1995	77
380 5/8	56 0/8 56 0/8	43 0/8	8 8	Apache County	AZ	Mike Aleff	1995	79
*380 5/8	63 0/8 65 0/8	49 3/8	6 6	Custer County	CO	Eric Reckentine	2009	79
380 4/8	53 4/8 53 2/8	51 7/8	7 7	Rich County	UT	Fahy S. Robinson, Jr.	1988	81
380 3/8	56 3/8 58 0/8	44 1/8	7 6	Catron County	NM	Don Parks, Jr.	1988	81
380 2/8	56 2/8 54 1/8	45 0/8	6 6	Coconino County	AZ	Doug Kittredge	1975	83
380 2/8	53 3/8 53 0/8	39 2/8	6 6	Sierra County	NM	John Harris	1998	83
380 1/8	55 3/8 56 2/8	40 5/8	6 6	Coconino County	AZ	Paul R. Titus	1995	85
380 0/8	53 1/8 54 0/8	43 6/8	6 6	Blaine County	ID	Howard W. Holmes	2001	86
379 7/8	57 7/8 56 5/8	47 6/8	6 6	Coconino County	AZ	Gregory K. Scott	1986	87
379 5/8	48 1/8 51 1/8	40 3/8	7 9	Benito	MAN	Dean Randell	1998	88
379 4/8	44 6/8 44 3/8	40 6/8	7 7	Las Animas County	CO	Peter A. Davis II	2004	89
379 3/8	53 4/8 56 0/8	42 7/8	7 8	Coconino County	AZ	Jeff Elmer	1984	90
379 3/8	55 5/8 56 5/8	36 3/8	6 7	Catron County	NM	Mark Nelson	1995	90
379 2/8	54 5/8 53 5/8	41 2/8	6 6	Millard County	UT	Timothy D. Park	1996	92
378 7/8	52 2/8 52 2/8	45 7/8	7 7	Coconino County	AZ	James G. Wells	1995	93
*378 7/8	55 3/8 55 1/8	42 7/8	6 7	Coconino County	AZ	Mike Crimmins	2010	93
378 6/8	57 6/8 58 2/8	39 4/8	7 7	Umatilla County	OR	Colby Lundstrom	2006	95

AMERICAN ELK (TYPICAL ANTLERS)

Minimum Score 260   Continued

SCORE	LENGTH OF R MAIN BEAM L	INSIDE SPREAD	NUMBER OF R POINTS L	AREA	STATE/ PROVINCE	HUNTER'S NAME	DATE	RANK
378 5/8	60 4/8 59 3/8	41 7/8	6 6	Coconino County	AZ	Robb G. Evans	1997	96
378 1/8	58 3/8 56 0/8	39 1/8	6 6	Greenlee County	AZ	Roger Soderberg	2004	97
378 0/8	53 4/8 54 2/8	47 2/8	7 6	White Pine County	NV	Nathan Conk	2003	98
377 7/8	56 6/8 53 3/8	39 7/8	6 6	Coconino County	AZ	Dennis Lee Manuell	1997	99
377 6/8	50 6/8 50 6/8	50 4/8	6 6	Valley County	MT	Greg Knaff	2008	100
*377 6/8	55 0/8 55 6/8	45 4/8	6 7	Mesa County	CO	Harlan J. Allman	2009	100
377 4/8	56 6/8 56 1/8	42 4/8	7 7	Big Horn County	MT	Craig Overman	2009	102
*377 1/8	47 6/8 47 2/8	38 0/8	8 7	Petroleum County	MT	Ralph M. Brown, Sr.	2003	103
377 0/8	59 2/8 57 1/8	39 4/8	6 6	Coconino County	AZ	Jack Frazier	1981	104
377 0/8	56 1/8 51 1/8	40 3/8	7 8	Coconino County	AZ	Larry Thomas	1985	104
377 0/8	56 7/8 55 2/8	42 0/8	6 6	Park County	WY	Brad K. Wagler	2007	104
376 6/8	47 2/8 50 3/8	39 2/8	6 7	Adams County	ID	Jack D. Sheppard	1966	107
376 6/8	59 3/8 60 6/8	49 0/8	6 5	Lincoln County	NV	Eric Merritt	2006	107
376 5/8	49 7/8 51 1/8	40 5/8	6 6	Catron County	NM	Debra Jameson	2007	109
376 4/8	52 6/8 47 2/8	40 0/8	8 7	Douglas County	CO	Glen Summers	2004	110
376 4/8	59 4/8 57 7/8	43 2/8	6 6	Garfield County	UT	Jesse Hatch	2005	110
376 3/8	60 1/8 59 1/8	40 3/8	6 7	Catron County	NM	Wayne K. Curtis	1986	112
376 3/8	56 2/8 56 2/8	39 7/8	6 6	Lincoln County	NV	Alfred R. Barnson	2002	112
*376 2/8	53 3/8 54 7/8	44 1/8	6 7	Catron County	NM	Steve Borden	2007	114
376 2/8	56 0/8 55 4/8	39 2/8	6 6	Cache County	UT	Tyler J. Hubble	2010	114
376 1/8	48 1/8 47 7/8	52 6/8	6 7	Johnson County	WY	Tom Roush	1993	116
376 0/8	56 6/8 56 4/8	50 2/8	6 8	Elko County	NV	Dan Evans	2006	117
375 7/8	53 2/8 53 0/8	45 7/8	6 6	Flathead County	MT	Jeb Casazza	2001	118
375 7/8	53 5/8 53 0/8	44 7/8	6 6	Sweetwater County	WY	Clay J. Evans	2010	118
375 6/8	56 5/8 53 4/8	47 2/8	6 6	Coconino County	AZ	Randy Ulmer	1997	120
*375 6/8	57 3/8 55 4/8	43 0/8	7 6	White Pine County	NV	Brett L. Foster	2010	120
375 5/8	55 7/8 54 1/8	37 7/8	6 6	Catron County	NM	Steve Ortiz	1992	122
375 5/8	47 1/8 51 1/8	47 7/8	6 6	Socorro County	NM	David R. Aikin	1993	122
375 4/8	54 2/8 55 3/8	46 6/8	6 6	Fergus County	MT	Randy Ulmer	2004	124
*375 4/8	51 7/8 54 4/8	45 1/8	6 9	White Pine County	NV	Cachu Melendez	2009	124
*375 3/8	51 7/8 50 2/8	51 3/8	6 6	Sevier County	UT	Brandon T. Wicks	2008	126
375 2/8	56 0/8 55 0/8	38 0/8	6 6	Converse County	WY	Don Stewart	1981	127
375 2/8	54 4/8 54 0/8	47 2/8	6 6	Multnomah County	OR	Chuck Feldhacker	2001	127
375 2/8	54 7/8 55 0/8	41 6/8	6 6	Socorro County	NM	Jan H. Ohlander	2003	127
375 1/8	53 5/8 55 7/8	46 7/8	6 6	Jackson County	CO	Vincent Kvidera	1976	130
375 1/8	53 4/8 55 1/8	37 5/8	7 8	Socorro County	NM	Robert Bryant	2003	130
375 0/8	52 3/8 53 7/8	39 1/8	6 7	Sierra County	NM	Jim Wagner	1986	132
375 0/8	55 6/8 53 1/8	41 2/8	6 6	Catron County	NM	Ed Sautier	1991	132
375 0/8	57 7/8 57 5/8	49 4/8	6 6	Coconino County	AZ	Arthur Ortiz	1993	132
375 0/8	59 4/8 58 0/8	42 0/8	8 7	Cibola County	NM	Archie J. Nesbitt	1997	132
375 0/8	57 7/8 56 5/8	43 6/8	8 7	Millard County	UT	Ryan T. Wood	2005	132
*375 0/8	56 2/8 51 5/8	47 6/8	6 6	Golden Valley County	MT	Brendan V. Burns	2008	132
*375 0/8	56 3/8 55 6/8	48 2/8	6 7	Apache County	AZ	Les Rainey	2009	132
374 7/8	52 2/8 50 7/8	44 0/8	8 6	Catron County	NM	David A. Hughes	1996	139
374 5/8	58 1/8 60 4/8	39 1/8	6 6	Coconino County	AZ	Ramey Thomas	2009	140
374 4/8	51 2/8 51 1/8	41 4/8	6 6	Sevier County	UT	Frank Janiszewski	2004	141
374 3/8	53 5/8 53 7/8	41 1/8	6 6	Grant County	NM	Jesse O. Ogas	1990	142
374 3/8	53 4/8 52 6/8	44 1/8	7 7	Caribou County	ID	Greg Agpawa	2003	142
374 1/8	57 6/8 51 2/8	48 0/8	7 9	Catron County	NM	Martin D. Huggins	1992	144
374 1/8	52 0/8 59 1/8	41 3/8	7 7	Cibola County	NM	Dennis C. Kerr	2003	144
373 6/8	56 5/8 54 7/8	37 4/8	7 8	Cibola County	NM	Lance Lippert	2000	146
373 6/8	55 3/8 55 1/8	41 4/8	6 6	Yellowstone County	MT	Richard Damerau	2004	146
373 6/8	59 5/8 58 7/8	52 6/8	6 7	Jefferson County	CO	Alan Hannasch	2005	146
373 5/8	57 2/8 57 3/8	53 1/8	6 6	Chouteau County	MT	Stephen Tylinski	2005	149
373 4/8	59 2/8 56 6/8	40 0/8	7 6	Coconino County	AZ	John A. Lovrin	2005	150
373 3/8	50 5/8 51 7/8	50 5/8	6 6	Otero County	NM	Rick Hullum	2003	151
373 1/8	57 5/8 57 6/8	41 5/8	6 6	Crook County	OR	Jeffrey E. Hale	1988	152
373 1/8	49 1/8 48 4/8	41 7/8	7 6	Albany County	WY	Wes Walton	1990	152
373 1/8	49 4/8 51 4/8	50 6/8	6 7	Albany County	WY	Jeff Lundahl	2004	152
373 0/8	56 2/8 54 6/8	42 6/8	6 6	Socorro County	NM	Tom Alvin	2001	155
373 0/8	55 4/8 53 7/8	44 6/8	7 7	Kittitas County	WA	Eric Johnson	2005	155
372 7/8	55 5/8 56 0/8	40 5/8	6 6	Otero County	NM	Ivan Hochstetler	2004	157
372 7/8	50 1/8 50 6/8	38 1/8	6 6	Catron County	NM	Lance Johnson	2010	157
372 6/8	53 0/8 55 0/8	43 6/8	6 6	Socorro County	NM	Douglas H. Sharp	2002	159
372 5/8	57 2/8 55 1/8	39 3/8	6 6	White Pine County	NV	Art Phillips	2006	160
372 3/8	50 7/8 49 1/8	39 7/8	6 6	Minitonas	MAN	Brian Brownlie	1989	161
372 0/8	52 2/8 52 2/8	44 0/8	7 6	Lincoln County	MT	Jerry Regh	1986	162
371 7/8	52 3/8 53 0/8	46 5/8	6 6	Mineral County	MT	Scott J. Stern	1983	163
371 7/8	59 3/8 57 2/8	42 7/8	6 6	Coconino County	AZ	George Flournoy	1986	163
371 6/8	55 4/8 55 2/8	46 0/8	6 6	Gallatin County	MT	William Elfland	2005	165
371 6/8	54 6/8 51 1/8	42 4/8	6 6	Cibola County	NM	David Kaden	2007	165
371 6/8	53 5/8 51 6/8	37 2/8	7 6	Columbia County	WA	Rick Stinson	2009	165
371 5/8	54 0/8 52 6/8	43 4/8	7 6	Johnson County	WY	John Atter	1998	168
371 5/8	59 3/8 61 6/8	39 1/8	7 6	Cibola County	NM	Don Button	2003	168
371 5/8	55 4/8 55 5/8	39 1/8	7 6	Coconino County	AZ	Dan Guzek	2004	168
371 3/8	53 4/8 51 5/8	38 1/8	7 6	Powder River County	MT	Ron Evans	2008	171
371 2/8	55 1/8 53 7/8	42 2/8	6 6	Skamania County	WA	Kevin Schmid	1990	172
371 2/8	51 6/8 50 3/8	40 5/8	6 7	Musselshell County	MT	Mike Renn II	2000	172
*371 1/8	55 1/8 54 6/8	50 3/8	6 6	Elko County	NV	Zach Hastie	2009	174
371 0/8	58 6/8 60 0/8	39 2/8	6 6	Coconino County	AZ	Judson J. Brown, Jr.	1993	175
371 0/8	47 1/8 49 2/8	50 0/8	6 7	Campbell County	WY	Kurt A. Bohl	1996	175
*371 0/8	53 1/8 53 3/8	40 0/8	6 6	Coconino County	AZ	William L. Bruggeman III	2008	175
370 7/8	56 0/8 58 0/8	42 5/8	6 6	Coconino County	AZ	Mike Moulton	1987	178
*370 7/8	52 0/8 52 5/8	41 5/8	6 6	Elko County	NV	Dan Evans	2008	178
370 6/8	52 3/8 52 5/8	47 2/8	6 6	Campbell County	WY	Steve Lauer	1998	180
*370 6/8	47 0/8 49 6/8	47 2/8	6 6	Navajo County	AZ	Raymond M. Ramirez	2003	180
370 5/8	49 5/8 49 5/8	38 1/8	6 6	Spruce Woods	MAN	Peter Sawatzky	1992	182
370 5/8	54 3/8 54 0/8	37 3/8	6 6	Catron County	NM	Dan Evans	1997	182
370 4/8	49 1/8 54 4/8	38 2/8	6 7	Garfield County	MT	D. Mitch Kottas	1999	184
370 3/8	56 3/8 56 3/8	42 3/8	6 6	Sheridan County	WY	Ron Johnson	1991	185
370 3/8	60 7/8 59 0/8	43 5/8	7 7	Coconino County	AZ	Michael S. Weldon	1992	185
370 3/8	56 0/8 56 2/8	33 6/8	7 6	Madison County	MT	Lee Poole	1992	185
370 3/8	49 3/8 51 3/8	41 4/8	6 7	Millard County	UT	Mitchell Bastian	2003	185
370 2/8	54 3/8 52 0/8	41 6/8	6 6	Millard County	UT	Brandon Peterson	2009	189
370 1/8	51 5/8 50 7/8	41 5/8	6 6	Petroleum County	MT	G. L. 'Buck' Damone	1985	190

679

AMERICAN ELK (TYPICAL ANTLERS)

Minimum Score 260 — Continued

SCORE	LENGTH OF R MAIN BEAM L	INSIDE SPREAD	NUMBER OF R POINTS L		AREA	STATE/ PROVINCE	HUNTER'S NAME	DATE	RANK
370 0/8	52 0/8 51 1/8	40 0/8	6	6	Catron County	NM	Len Abernathy	1994	191
370 0/8	52 2/8 52 5/8	49 0/8	6	7	Catron County	NM	Marty Reddell	1996	191
370 0/8	59 6/8 58 3/8	38 0/8	6	6	Coconino County	AZ	Bill Drake	2006	191
369 6/8	54 6/8 53 0/8	47 6/8	6	6	Greenlee County	AZ	Clifford White	1986	194
369 5/8	59 7/8 58 6/8	44 7/8	6	6	Coconino County	AZ	Jeff Schorey	1992	195
*369 5/8	50 6/8 51 3/8	42 7/8	6	6	Teller County	CO	Bradley Eicher	2008	195
369 4/8	53 2/8 51 2/8	39 4/8	7	7	Bonner County	ID	Steve Noort	1986	197
369 4/8	53 0/8 53 0/8	42 4/8	6	7	Catron County	NM	Frank A. Hayes	1986	197
369 4/8	53 0/8 56 6/8	43 7/8	7	7	Sheridan County	WY	Mike Barrett	1998	197
369 4/8	52 6/8 51 5/8	42 5/8	6	7	Wallowa County	OR	David L. Greenwalt	1999	197
369 4/8	57 3/8 56 1/8	42 4/8	6	7	Albany County	WY	Joseph J. Iribarren	2009	197
369 3/8	56 0/8 50 6/8	48 7/8	6	7	Big Horn County	MT	Jason Watson	2000	202
369 3/8	50 1/8 51 4/8	43 0/8	7	6	Greenlee County	AZ	Andrew W. Taylor	2001	202
369 3/8	50 5/8 49 5/8	51 5/8	6	7	Park County	WY	Kurt E. Larson	2002	202
369 3/8	57 5/8 56 7/8	42 5/8	6	6	Juab County	UT	Jason Worwood	2003	202
369 2/8	51 0/8 55 4/8	48 4/8	6	6	Madison County	MT	Jeff Engler	1977	206
369 1/8	51 6/8 54 4/8	34 1/8	6	6	Coconino County	AZ	Todd Smith	2004	207
369 0/8	57 2/8 56 4/8	38 2/8	7	6	Coconino County	AZ	Tom Hinson	1987	208
369 0/8	51 3/8 52 0/8	48 0/8	6	6	Sevier County	UT	Gerald Laurino	2007	208
368 7/8	54 1/8 56 3/8	43 4/8	6	7	Sweet Grass County	MT	Frank Frampton	1995	210
368 7/8	51 4/8 50 7/8	42 6/8	7	6	Duck Mtns.	MAN	William Watkinson	1999	210
368 6/8	52 1/8 51 0/8	39 6/8	6	6	Coconino County	AZ	John V. Beaufeaux	1990	212
368 6/8	57 1/8 56 0/8	47 0/8	6	6	Cibola County	NM	Archie J. Nesbitt	1998	212
368 6/8	48 6/8 45 4/8	37 4/8	6	6	Wasatch County	UT	Roy Hampton	2003	212
368 6/8	54 4/8 54 4/8	47 0/8	6	6	Coconino County	AZ	Cathy Grgas	2005	212
368 6/8	56 1/8 54 5/8	47 4/8	7	6	Big Horn County	WY	Terry Blazek	2007	212
368 5/8	54 4/8 55 4/8	42 1/8	6	6	Huerfano County	CO	David Montano	1999	217
368 4/8	55 1/8 56 3/8	46 4/8	6	6	Apache County	AZ	Kevin Robinson	2000	218
368 4/8	54 0/8 53 0/8	46 2/8	6	6	Rosebud County	MT	Chuck Adams	2002	218
368 4/8	57 2/8 57 1/8	42 6/8	6	6	White Pine County	NV	Kevin D. Peterson	2008	218
368 3/8	46 4/8 53 4/8	48 4/8	6	7	Moffat County	CO	John Freed	2004	221
368 3/8	54 4/8 53 4/8	51 7/8	7	7	Park County	WY	Jack L. Morey, Jr.	2008	221
368 2/8	53 0/8 53 1/8	40 2/8	7	7	Kittitas County	WA	Robert Carl Sater	1987	223
368 2/8	50 5/8 50 3/8	46 0/8	6	6	Costilla County	CO	Kenneth Scott Brown	2003	223
368 1/8	55 4/8 56 6/8	52 0/8	6	7	Apache County	AZ	Darren Peek	2003	225
368 0/8	52 7/8 52 3/8	44 4/8	6	6	Grant County	OR	Greg E. Willmore	1988	226
367 7/8	58 7/8 53 2/8	43 3/8	7	6	Coconino County	AZ	Gary Hanson	1993	227
367 7/8	55 3/8 55 4/8	39 5/8	6	6	Catron County	NM	Patrick L. McMaster	1995	227
367 7/8	49 5/8 49 6/8	50 2/8	6	7	Rosebud County	MT	Chuck Adams	2001	227
367 7/8	58 1/8 57 3/8	38 7/8	7	8	Kittitas County	WA	Tom J. Little	2005	227
367 6/8	50 7/8 51 0/8	36 2/8	6	6	Teton County	MT	Gene Ward	1994	231
367 3/8	47 7/8 49 3/8	45 1/8	8	7	Larimer County	CO	H. Troxell/B. Alexander	1970	232
367 3/8	54 1/8 51 7/8	43 2/8	8	8	Gila County	AZ	Patrick Kirby	1992	232
367 2/8	55 4/8 57 7/8	46 0/8	6	6	Lemhi County	ID	Ben Fahnholz	1982	234
367 2/8	55 4/8 54 3/8	42 4/8	6	6	Rio Arriba County	NM	David O. Conrad	1990	234
367 2/8	57 6/8 53 0/8	42 0/8	6	6	Catron County	NM	John R. Quarrell	1998	234
367 2/8	59 6/8 60 1/8	32 4/8	7	6	Socorro County	NM	Clyde O. Booth	2001	234
367 2/8	52 6/8 52 7/8	38 6/8	7	7	Rosebud County	MT	Gary Dickhaut	2003	234
367 2/8	55 5/8 57 0/8	35 6/8	6	6	Coconino County	AZ	John G. Padilla	2008	234
367 1/8	50 1/8 51 7/8	45 1/8	6	6	Albany County	WY	David Denny	1999	240
367 0/8	54 3/8 54 4/8	33 6/8	6	7	Coconino County	AZ	Brian Drake	2005	241
367 0/8	51 5/8 52 1/8	40 4/8	6	6	Laramie County	WY	Todd Longgood	2006	241
*367 0/8	53 6/8 57 6/8	45 0/8	6	8	Missoula County	MT	Steven C. Walker	2010	241
366 7/8	53 2/8 52 1/8	40 4/8	7	7	Mineral County	MT	Gerry Lamarre	1977	244
366 6/8	58 6/8 57 4/8	40 4/8	6	6	Coconino County	AZ	Karl Ahto Raudsepp	2003	245
366 6/8	53 1/8 53 1/8	40 2/8	6	6	Custer County	ID	Tim Malone	2005	245
366 5/8	53 0/8 53 2/8	45 3/8	7	7	Shoshone County	ID	D. A. Johnson	1962	247
366 5/8	46 1/8 47 1/8	35 6/8	6	7	Phillips County	MT	Ronnie Molstad	1983	247
366 5/8	50 4/8 52 4/8	45 5/8	6	6	Valencia County	NM	Dean Dunaway	1991	247
366 5/8	56 6/8 54 7/8	45 1/8	6	6	Apache County	AZ	Luke Grover	2005	247
366 4/8	49 7/8 55 1/8	39 6/8	6	6	Duck Mtns.	MAN	Brian W. Brownlie	1992	251
366 4/8	52 3/8 53 4/8	43 2/8	7	7	Coconino County	AZ	Lloyd H. Farr	1994	251
366 4/8	58 2/8 56 3/8	44 2/8	6	6	Navajo County	AZ	Michael J. McEntee	2005	251
366 3/8	52 5/8 50 7/8	41 7/8	6	6	Fergus County	MT	J. Douglas Krings	1980	254
366 3/8	55 5/8 57 6/8	40 5/8	6	6	Catron County	NM	J. W. Young	1990	254
366 2/8	54 4/8 51 1/8	45 6/8	6	6	Catron County	NM	Michael C. Dean	1994	256
366 1/8	52 3/8 51 0/8	43 7/8	6	6	Berland River	ALB	Brad Sidebottom	1986	257
366 1/8	55 5/8 55 4/8	45 7/8	6	7	Catron County	NM	Danny Ray	1992	257
366 1/8	53 1/8 51 5/8	39 6/8	6	6	Catron County	NM	Stephen L. Penrod	1994	257
365 7/8	49 5/8 52 4/8	37 5/8	7	6	Fergus County	MT	Nicholas Econom	2000	260
*365 6/8	51 4/8 51 7/8	45 2/8	6	6	Larimer County	CO	Douglas W. Rampy	2008	261
365 5/8	52 4/8 50 1/8	38 7/8	6	6	Rio Blanco County	CO	Jay Verzuh	1995	262
365 4/8	55 3/8 56 4/8	39 3/8	6	6	Greenlee County	AZ	Bill Bishop, Sr.	2008	262
365 4/8	54 7/8 54 5/8	41 4/8	6	7	Columbia County	WA	Scott Baysinger	2007	264
365 3/8	46 6/8 47 3/8	31 2/8	7	7	Garfield County	MT	Pat Murphy	2000	265
365 3/8	54 3/8 52 1/8	37 5/8	6	6	Grant County	NM	Paul J. Speth	2003	265
365 3/8	58 7/8 57 5/8	47 3/8	6	6	Cibola County	NM	Nicholas D. Gonzales	2005	265
365 3/8	53 3/8 53 3/8	44 3/8	6	6	Washington County	UT	Cal Bauer	2009	265
*365 2/8	53 3/8 56 0/8	38 6/8	7	6	Coconino County	AZ	Travis Slater	2010	269
365 1/8	51 4/8 51 2/8	38 5/8	6	6	Sandoval County	NM	John C. McClendon	1985	270
365 1/8	60 0/8 57 1/8	43 5/8	6	6	Johnson County	WY	Rod M. Odenbach	1999	270
365 1/8	57 4/8 56 3/8	41 3/8	7	7	Fergus County	MT	Joshua Bunch	2009	270
365 0/8	60 6/8 61 4/8	50 2/8	6	6	Fergus County	MT	John Jeide	1983	273
365 0/8	57 0/8 55 5/8	41 0/8	6	6	Garfield County	UT	Brady G. Daybell	2007	273
364 7/8	55 1/8 53 5/8	40 7/8	6	6	Catron County	NM	Todd Hewing	2001	275
364 6/8	50 3/8 46 2/8	39 2/8	6	6	Grant County	OR	William C. Sanowski	1976	276
364 5/8	50 7/8 50 0/8	39 3/8	6	6	Rossburn	MAN	Fred Hay	1993	277
364 4/8	51 0/8 50 4/8	43 0/8	6	6	Jefferson County	CO	Ron Roderick	2001	278
364 4/8	54 0/8 53 7/8	40 2/8	6	7	Tooele County	UT	Scott Barrus	2005	278
*364 4/8	52 6/8 49 7/8	37 4/8	6	7	Mesa County	CO	Jim Prock	2006	278
364 3/8	57 2/8 51 6/8	37 3/8	8	7	Kootenai County	ID	Curtis Yanzick	1990	281
*364 2/8	54 5/8 53 7/8	45 0/8	6	6	Stillwater County	MT	Dan Mayland	2007	282
364 1/8	54 4/8 56 5/8	46 3/8	6	6	Catron County	NM	Lee Hetrick	1991	283
364 0/8	52 7/8 52 7/8	40 4/8	6	7	Catron County	NM	Paul J. Butler	1988	284
363 7/8	50 5/8 47 0/8	41 4/8	7	8	Converse County	WY	David P. Lindman	1986	285

680

AMERICAN ELK (TYPICAL ANTLERS)

Minimum Score 260   Continued

SCORE	LENGTH OF R MAIN BEAM L	INSIDE SPREAD	NUMBER OF R POINTS L	AREA	STATE/ PROVINCE	HUNTER'S NAME	DATE	RANK
363 6/8	55 1/8 54 0/8	43 2/8	7 6	Yavapai County	AZ	Rod Laubach	2001	286
363 5/8	56 3/8 54 7/8	43 1/8	6 6	Graham County	AZ	Steve M. Titla	1988	287
363 5/8	56 5/8 59 6/8	42 5/8	6 6	Catron County	NM	W. Glenn Wood, Jr.	1992	287
363 5/8	50 6/8 52 5/8	38 4/8	8 7	Catron County	NM	Paul D. Payne II	1994	287
363 5/8	54 5/8 55 0/8	43 1/8	6 7	Sierra County	NM	Roy L. Walk	2000	287
363 4/8	53 0/8 52 0/8	38 2/8	6 6	Garfield County	UT	L. Todd Becker	2007	291
363 3/8	58 6/8 56 6/8	43 1/8	6 6	White Pine County	NV	John T. Caviglia	2000	292
363 3/8	54 4/8 52 1/8	45 3/8	6 6	Grant County	OR	Cliff Garrett, Jr.	2005	292
363 2/8	50 5/8 51 2/8	37 0/8	6 6	Coconino County	AZ	Robert E. Reed	1994	294
363 2/8	54 7/8 55 4/8	46 6/8	6 6	Park County	WY	Michael Till	2000	294
363 2/8	53 7/8 54 0/8	46 6/8	6 6	Catron County	NM	Lowry W. Hunt III	2003	294
363 2/8	55 3/8 54 4/8	39 4/8	7 7	Cibola County	NM	Steve Douglas Mitchell	2004	294
363 2/8	52 7/8 53 5/8	38 2/8	7 7	Fergus County	MT	Ronald A. Peterson	2004	294
363 1/8	56 0/8 57 7/8	43 1/8	7 6	Catron County	NM	Jimmy Kruckenberg	1994	299
363 0/8	57 1/8 58 0/8	42 0/8	6 6	Coconino County	AZ	Dan Heasley	1995	300
363 0/8	50 3/8 50 0/8	42 2/8	6 6	Judith Basin County	MT	Phil Allen	2000	300
*363 0/8	53 3/8 53 4/8	41 2/8	6 7	Flathead County	MT	Roy Berkhahn	2009	300
362 6/8	50 5/8 53 2/8	37 4/8	6 7	Catron County	NM	Ray Cloud	1993	303
*362 6/8	55 4/8 50 6/8	44 0/8	7 7	Eagle County	CO	Tim LaRose	2006	303
362 5/8	48 7/8 50 3/8	41 3/8	6 6	Cibola County	NM	Scott Paramo	2009	305
362 4/8	51 3/8 50 6/8	37 6/8	6 6	Cibola County	NM	Dave Gentile	2000	306
*362 4/8	54 2/8 52 6/8	39 4/8	6 6	Catron County	NM	Robert R. Scaife	2004	306
362 4/8	47 3/8 47 7/8	36 4/8	7 6	Jefferson County	MT	Brian Robbins	2005	306
*362 4/8	54 1/8 56 6/8	37 4/8	7 6	Gila County	AZ	Terry Ray Chapman	2010	306
362 2/8	50 2/8 49 4/8	46 2/8	7 7	Jackson County	CO	Alfred H. O'Brien	1972	310
362 2/8	54 5/8 55 0/8	40 6/8	6 6	Yavapai County	AZ	Chris J. Dunn	2007	310
*362 1/8	52 0/8 49 5/8	39 5/8	6 6	Eagle County	CO	Russell T. Winder	2005	312
362 0/8	48 4/8 53 5/8	42 4/8	6 7	Coconino County	AZ	Frank Robert Ortiz	1993	313
361 7/8	47 7/8 48 2/8	35 1/8	6 6	Park County	WY	John R. Buche	2001	314
*361 7/8	52 3/8 54 4/8	44 7/8	7 6	Park County	MT	David R. Day	2008	314
361 7/8	54 5/8 55 5/8	41 3/8	6 6	San Juan County	UT	Bret K. Lowe	2008	314
361 7/8	48 7/8 49 6/8	41 5/8	6 6	Garfield County	UT	Chance Nelson	2009	314
361 6/8	54 1/8 55 2/8	36 6/8	6 7	Oneida County	ID	David "Dusty" Goulding	2010	318
361 5/8	52 0/8 57 4/8	45 3/8	7 6	Catron County	NM	Robert A. Oines	1997	319
361 5/8	52 2/8 52 7/8	38 7/8	6 6	Musselshell County	MT	Poncho McCoy	1997	319
361 5/8	49 3/8 47 6/8	40 1/8	6 6	Moffat County	CO	Tim Hamilton	2000	319
361 5/8	52 1/8 51 4/8	39 3/8	8 7	Washington County	ID	Perk Rose	2002	319
361 4/8	51 5/8 54 0/8	48 0/8	6 6	Fergus County	MT	D. Mitch Kottas	1992	323
361 3/8	54 3/8 51 0/8	47 3/8	6 6	Coconino County	AZ	Dean Dunaway	1990	324
361 3/8	57 2/8 58 5/8	45 1/8	6 6	Coconino County	AZ	Andrew Grannan	2000	324
*361 3/8	53 6/8 55 2/8	38 1/8	7 6	Johnson County	WY	Tammy Severeide	2004	324
361 3/8	55 3/8 56 5/8	43 1/8	7 7	San Miguel County	CO	Preston Gardner	2005	324
361 2/8	58 4/8 56 4/8	37 0/8	6 6	Coconino County	AZ	Tom Phelps	1986	328
361 2/8	52 3/8 52 1/8	41 6/8	7 7	Garfield County	MT	Bryant Shermoe	2001	328
361 2/8	57 2/8 57 5/8	34 6/8	6 6	Coconino County	AZ	James L. Herwick	2005	328
361 2/8	50 6/8 49 7/8	37 6/8	7 7	Coconino County	AZ	Joseph Whitmer	2005	328
361 2/8	54 2/8 53 2/8	43 4/8	6 7	Jefferson County	OR	Candi Wood	2006	328
361 2/8	53 5/8 56 2/8	41 6/8	7 8	Meagher County	MT	Don Ellingsen	2006	328
361 2/8	48 2/8 48 0/8	47 2/8	6 7	Coconino County	AZ	Gary Furman	2007	328
361 1/8	55 2/8 54 6/8	49 6/8	7 6	Garfield County	UT	Brent M. Rowley	2004	335
361 1/8	51 4/8 49 4/8	42 7/8	6 6	Petroleum County	MT	D. "Mitch" Kottas	2009	335
361 0/8	54 0/8 55 0/8	44 4/8	6 6	Coconino County	AZ	Laura Wuertz	1986	337
361 0/8	51 7/8 49 2/8	34 6/8	7 6	Gila County	AZ	Dick Gephard	1990	337
361 0/8	52 6/8 52 3/8	39 0/8	7 6	Lincoln County	WY	Steve Merritt	2004	337
361 0/8	53 1/8 54 6/8	40 0/8	6 8	Gilpin County	CO	Nathan T. Bloomingdale	2005	337
*361 0/8	49 6/8 51 4/8	42 0/8	6 6	Rich County	UT	Oren S. Gatten	2010	337
360 7/8	54 7/8 56 1/8	41 7/8	7 6	Lemhi County	ID	Tony Latham	1983	342
360 7/8	52 1/8 52 1/8	37 5/8	6 6	White Pine County	NV	Darcy Tate	1993	342
360 7/8	52 0/8 51 0/8	46 1/8	6 6	Catron County	NM	Mark Jacobson	1997	342
*360 7/8	56 0/8 54 4/8	48 3/8	6 6	Socorro County	NM	James P. Bredy	2005	342
360 6/8	51 1/8 49 7/8	37 0/8	6 6	Petroleum County	MT	Kerby A. Durbin	1987	346
360 6/8	53 6/8 53 4/8	48 0/8	6 7	Garfield County	UT	Michael Radford	2007	346
360 4/8	61 7/8 57 3/8	43 5/8	8 7	White Pine County	NV	Thomas Enewold	1990	348
360 4/8	54 2/8 54 4/8	42 6/8	8 7	Catron County	NM	Blaine Underwood	1991	348
360 4/8	55 7/8 56 3/8	40 2/8	7 7	Albany County	WY	Kevin Christopherson	1996	348
360 4/8	52 7/8 51 0/8	39 4/8	6 6	Elko County	NV	Anthony R. Bauer	2009	348
360 3/8	57 5/8 53 2/8	48 7/8	7 6	Socorro County	NM	James A. Trujillo	1987	352
360 3/8	46 0/8 47 3/8	39 1/8	6 6	Catron County	NM	Glenn W. Isler	1994	352
360 3/8	53 5/8 54 3/8	38 5/8	6 6	Garfield County	UT	Martin R. Kilen	2002	352
360 3/8	51 3/8 51 7/8	43 3/8	6 6	Park County	MT	William Bradley	2007	352
360 3/8	57 2/8 58 3/8	42 5/8	6 6	Lassen County	CA	Thad Wallace	2010	352
360 2/8	54 5/8 55 0/8	46 4/8	8 6	Clark County	ID	Tim Thomas	1996	357
*360 2/8	53 6/8 51 6/8	41 0/8	6 6	Petroleum County	MT	Chuck Carrell	2010	357
360 1/8	49 3/8 49 3/8	37 5/8	6 6	Sandoval County	NM	Robert Seeds	1995	359
*360 1/8	52 5/8 53 4/8	42 5/8	6 7	Carbon County	UT	Jayson Harvey	2010	359
360 0/8	47 1/8 44 4/8	42 4/8	7 6	Las Animas County	CO	Rob Lucero	1992	361
360 0/8	56 0/8 61 2/8	43 2/8	6 6	Socorro County	NM	Doug Aikin	2001	361
360 0/8	55 1/8 53 1/8	35 2/8	7 6	Rio Arriba County	NM	Eudane Vicenti	2003	361
360 0/8	51 6/8 54 6/8	39 6/8	6 6	Garfield County	MT	Lynn Moeller	2004	361
360 0/8	52 5/8 53 4/8	38 2/8	7 6	Catron County	NM	Marc P. LeBrun	2005	361
359 6/8	54 1/8 55 2/8	38 6/8	7 7	Catron County	NM	George Pieros, Jr.	1994	366
359 6/8	51 6/8 50 1/8	37 4/8	6 7	Boundary County	ID	Daniel Jay Carter	1999	366
*359 6/8	51 3/8 53 6/8	48 2/8	6 6	Musselshell County	MT	Phil Perry	2005	366
359 6/8	53 1/8 52 6/8	42 4/8	6 6	Sevier County	UT	Bob Ballantyne	2006	366
359 5/8	50 4/8 52 0/8	47 1/8	6 6	Pierce County	WA	Doug Nearhood	1985	370
359 5/8	50 5/8 42 5/8	36 1/8	6 6	Powder River County	MT	Randy Trucano	1994	370
359 5/8	51 5/8 50 1/8	42 3/8	6 6	Edgerton	ALB	Archie Day	1997	370
359 5/8	52 6/8 52 6/8	43 1/8	6 6	Lewis & Clark County	MT	Stephen C. Zabransky	2003	370
359 4/8	48 4/8 52 3/8	44 4/8	7 6	Fergus County	MT	Jerry Knerr	1999	374
359 4/8	43 5/8 45 5/8	36 2/8	6 6	Elko County	NV	Wes Talbert	2002	374
359 3/8	48 1/8 49 2/8	48 1/8	6 6	Mesa County	CO	David W. Christopherson	1978	376
359 2/8	51 0/8 52 5/8	42 0/8	6 9	Coconino County	AZ	Robert Cecrle	1972	377
359 2/8	58 2/8 56 7/8	42 0/8	6 6	Coconino County	AZ	Jim David	1974	377
359 2/8	56 3/8 53 7/8	40 0/8	7 6	Greenlee County	AZ	N. Richard McMullan	1992	377
359 2/8	50 6/8 52 7/8	42 2/8	6 6	Morgan County	UT	Hugh H. Hogle	1993	377

AMERICAN ELK (TYPICAL ANTLERS)

Minimum Score 260 — Continued

SCORE	LENGTH OF MAIN BEAM R	L	INSIDE SPREAD	NUMBER OF POINTS R	L	AREA	STATE/PROVINCE	HUNTER'S NAME	DATE	RANK
359 2/8	53 4/8	54 1/8	50 0/8	7	6	Garfield County	UT	Kurt Gale	1997	377
359 2/8	56 1/8	57 4/8	42 4/8	7	6	Elko County	NV	Phillip R. Steiner, Jr.	2005	377
*359 2/8	54 1/8	57 0/8	44 4/8	6	6	Garfield County	UT	Dan Heath	2006	377
359 1/8	49 0/8	52 4/8	36 0/8	7	6	Coconino County	AZ	Frank J. Mayorga	1987	384
359 1/8	57 1/8	53 6/8	39 7/8	8	6	Lincoln County	NV	Jim Wakeling	2006	384
359 0/8	56 4/8	57 2/8	36 4/8	6	6	Coconino County	AZ	Michael J. Proulx	1986	386
359 0/8	50 4/8	50 0/8	47 6/8	7	6	Baca County	CO	Randy Bacon/Rich Pianalto	1994	386
359 0/8	55 0/8	53 5/8	43 0/8	6	6	Park County	WY	Bob Whisonant	1998	386
359 0/8	54 2/8	51 4/8	46 0/8	6	6	Coconino County	AZ	Michael L. Wolfe	1998	386
359 0/8	55 4/8	54 4/8	35 4/8	6	6	Jefferson County	CO	Jerry L. Grueneberg	2005	386
358 7/8	55 5/8	54 5/8	40 7/8	6	6	Coconino County	AZ	Gary Bills	1986	391
358 6/8	51 7/8	55 0/8	47 6/8	6	6	Sheridan County	WY	Mike Barrett	1986	392
358 6/8	51 2/8	46 2/8	42 0/8	6	6	Park County	WY	Ron Niziolek	2006	392
*358 6/8	53 3/8	53 6/8	44 2/8	6	6	Park County	CO	Chuck Fetterly	2007	392
358 5/8	53 0/8	49 7/8	38 3/8	6	6	Cibola County	NM	Moises Perea	1980	395
358 5/8	48 6/8	48 5/8	47 1/8	6	6	Coconino County	AZ	Tom Crabill	1998	395
358 5/8	49 4/8	49 4/8	33 3/8	6	6	Albany County	WY	Jeromy Herrick	2000	395
358 5/8	56 4/8	54 6/8	37 5/8	6	7	Carbon County	WY	Lloyd M. Hettick	2007	395
358 5/8	55 5/8	53 2/8	41 1/8	7	7	Mesa County	CO	Chuck Thompson	2008	395
358 4/8	58 1/8	57 4/8	40 2/8	6	6	Sierra County	NM	Steve J. Koscher	1993	400
358 4/8	52 3/8	52 0/8	39 0/8	7	7	Cibola County	NM	Thomas R. Grabowski	1997	400
358 4/8	52 5/8	54 6/8	37 3/8	7	7	Greenlee County	AZ	Bill Madison	1997	400
358 4/8	57 4/8	55 3/8	44 4/8	6	6	Albany County	WY	David E. Hulshizer, Jr.	1999	400
358 4/8	50 7/8	52 1/8	39 0/8	6	6	Catron County	NM	Mark Gerrald	2004	400
358 4/8	53 3/8	53 5/8	45 4/8	6	6	Converse County	WY	Colton J. Bowers	2005	400
358 3/8	52 3/8	52 5/8	39 5/8	6	6	Sanders County	MT	Eugene Roesler	1986	406
358 3/8	55 6/8	55 6/8	31 5/8	6	6	Catron County	NM	Steve D. Lozano	1992	406
358 2/8	54 1/8	51 4/8	47 0/8	6	6	Crook County	OR	Oliver Weger	1983	408
358 2/8	58 6/8	54 3/8	42 0/8	6	6	Catron County	NM	David G. Anderson	1993	408
358 2/8	55 0/8	54 2/8	38 0/8	6	7	Coconino County	AZ	Harvey G. Ward, Jr.	2004	408
358 2/8	53 4/8	53 1/8	44 0/8	6	6	Eddy County	NM	John M. McCarville	2007	408
358 1/8	56 2/8	60 2/8	42 7/8	6	6	Catron County	NM	Robert E. Duke	1991	412
358 1/8	50 4/8	49 4/8	40 1/8	7	6	Otero County	NM	Pete R. Silva	2001	412
358 0/8	52 3/8	54 3/8	40 4/8	6	8	Grant County	NM	David O. Smith	1997	414
358 0/8	48 5/8	47 4/8	32 4/8	7	6	White Pine County	NV	Reese Hoy	2002	414
358 0/8	55 0/8	55 0/8	39 6/8	6	6	Musselshell County	MT	Troy M. Hill	2003	414
358 0/8	52 5/8	52 4/8	41 6/8	7	7	Custer County	ID	John Wells	2004	414
357 7/8	54 2/8	54 6/8	45 1/8	7	7	Coconino County	AZ	Mark Clammer	1987	418
357 7/8	54 6/8	57 3/8	45 5/8	6	6	Albany County	WY	Richard L. Andre	1990	418
357 7/8	54 0/8	53 3/8	42 7/8	6	6	Catron County	NM	Mike Moore	1990	418
357 7/8	54 1/8	50 7/8	37 7/8	6	6	Sierra County	NM	David Swisher	1992	418
357 6/8	50 2/8	50 6/8	40 4/8	6	6	Park County	CO	Donald R. Looper	1975	422
357 6/8	53 4/8	56 3/8	46 4/8	6	6	Apache County	AZ	John B. Bowman	1991	422
357 6/8	56 3/8	51 3/8	44 3/8	8	7	Fergus County	MT	James Dover	2000	422
*357 5/8	52 3/8	53 4/8	36 5/8	6	6	Coconino County	AZ	John Gittus	2009	425
357 4/8	52 5/8	55 0/8	37 6/8	7	6	Fergus County	MT	Michael B. Hedrick	1981	426
357 4/8	52 1/8	52 5/8	46 6/8	7	7	Bonneville County	ID	Gregg Allen Youngerman	1996	426
357 4/8	54 7/8	55 2/8	41 0/8	6	6	Rosebud County	MT	Chuck Adams	1999	426
357 3/8	56 2/8	49 2/8	37 1/8	6	6	Meagher County	MT	David G. Snyder	1978	429
357 3/8	50 4/8	50 4/8	34 5/8	6	6	Swan River	MAN	Kelly Shykitka	1986	429
357 3/8	55 6/8	54 0/8	37 7/8	6	6	Moffat County	CO	Kurt W. Keskimaki	1987	429
357 3/8	55 0/8	53 7/8	41 5/8	7	7	Missoula County	MT	Andrew J. Kelly	1990	429
357 3/8	54 4/8	53 1/8	42 5/8	7	7	Catron County	NM	Linda Strong	1994	429
357 3/8	54 1/8	53 1/8	46 1/8	6	7	Idaho County	ID	Dan McClure	2002	429
357 2/8	49 1/8	50 3/8	34 6/8	7	7	Crook County	WY	Paul J. Harris	2003	435
*357 2/8	51 2/8	49 1/8	49 2/8	7	7	Coconino County	AZ	Grant E. Miller	2008	435
*357 1/8	50 5/8	50 1/8	53 2/8	6	6	Montrose County	CO	Roy Runnestrand	2009	437
357 0/8	54 2/8	56 0/8	41 0/8	6	6	Caribou County	ID	Howard E. Johnson	1968	438
357 0/8	56 5/8	56 7/8	46 6/8	6	6	Gila County	AZ	David L. Crockett	1973	438
357 0/8	53 5/8	53 6/8	43 2/8	6	6	Strawberry Lake	CO	Frank Fraser	1977	438
357 0/8	50 5/8	49 5/8	44 4/8	6	6	Garfield County	UT	William B. McGuire	2002	438
*357 0/8	54 5/8	52 2/8	40 2/8	6	6	Catron County	NM	Ryan Paulk	2004	438
356 7/8	54 1/8	53 6/8	53 7/8	6	7	Park County	MT	Charles Alkire	1964	443
356 7/8	49 6/8	51 0/8	46 3/8	7	6	Flathead County	MT	Terry Krogstad	1984	443
356 7/8	54 4/8	54 7/8	44 7/8	7	7	Custer County	ID	Tim Malone	2002	443
356 7/8	52 1/8	51 2/8	34 3/8	6	6	Douglas County	CO	Andrew Baker	2006	443
356 7/8	54 4/8	53 4/8	35 3/8	7	7	Coconino County	AZ	William Donahue	2009	443
356 6/8	51 0/8	50 2/8	41 2/8	6	6	Grant County	OR	James M. Carter	1988	448
356 6/8	52 5/8	52 2/8	40 6/8	6	6	Coconino County	AZ	Ralph E. Anderson	1993	448
356 6/8	49 7/8	50 6/8	39 0/8	7	7	Catron County	NM	Bear Brewer	1995	448
356 6/8	52 2/8	51 0/8	42 0/8	7	7	Catron County	NM	Kyle M. Meintzer	1998	448
356 6/8	52 6/8	51 3/8	43 2/8	6	6	Rosebud County	MT	Chad P. Lehman	2005	448
*356 6/8	54 0/8	53 2/8	38 6/8	6	6	Piute County	UT	Stephen W. Speer	2008	448
356 6/8	58 4/8	56 0/8	40 2/8	6	6	San Juan County	UT	Bobby Winn	2009	448
356 5/8	50 4/8	50 7/8	39 3/8	7	7	Lewis & Clark County	MT	Patrick Hover	1999	455
356 4/8	57 3/8	53 1/8	46 4/8	6	6	Catron County	NM	Bill Elmer	1986	456
356 4/8	54 5/8	56 0/8	40 2/8	6	6	Coconino County	AZ	Blaine "Bub" Mathews	1990	456
356 3/8	52 4/8	48 6/8	36 1/8	6	7	Fergus County	MT	Leonard L. Weeks	1984	458
356 2/8	53 1/8	48 0/8	46 0/8	6	7	Camas County	ID	Jeff Baker	2006	459
356 2/8	45 4/8	45 5/8	41 4/8	6	7	Jackson County	CO	Tom Kelley	2010	459
356 2/8	50 3/8	50 4/8	43 6/8	6	6	Greenlee County	AZ	Mike Kovach	2010	459
356 1/8	54 3/8	53 0/8	39 3/8	6	8	Catron County	NM	Edward Eskew	1990	462
356 1/8	54 4/8	54 3/8	39 3/8	6	6	Apache County	AZ	Andy Terry	1998	462
356 1/8	55 3/8	54 0/8	33 3/8	7	7	Fergus County	MT	Shannon Smith	2009	462
356 0/8	52 1/8	50 1/8	36 4/8	7	6	Linn County	OR	David E. Renoud	1983	465
356 0/8	61 2/8	60 2/8	51 0/8	6	6	Coconino County	AZ	Kent G. Frei	1990	465
356 0/8	56 2/8	59 0/8	40 0/8	7	6	Coconino County	AZ	John Mertz	1995	465
356 0/8	48 0/8	48 6/8	54 0/8	6	6	Coconino County	AZ	Chad Heuser	2009	465
355 6/8	53 5/8	58 2/8	34 2/8	6	6	Larimer County	CO	Shawn Greathouse	1993	469
355 6/8	53 4/8	51 6/8	56 4/8	8	6	Natrona County	WY	Shane Pitkin	2005	469
355 5/8	49 7/8	46 7/8	41 0/8	8	6	Catron County	NM	Doug Aikin	1987	471
355 5/8	53 5/8	55 3/8	47 3/8	6	6	Cibola County	NM	Steven M. Prince	1997	471
355 5/8	53 6/8	52 6/8	36 3/8	7	8	Fergus County	MT	D. Mitch Kottas	2004	471
355 5/8	49 3/8	51 6/8	39 3/8	6	6	Yavapai County	AZ	Robert E. Brown	2008	471
355 4/8	54 7/8	56 5/8	42 6/8	6	6	Beaverhead County	MT	Robert B. McKay	1973	475

682

AMERICAN ELK (TYPICAL ANTLERS)

Minimum Score 260 — Continued

SCORE	R MAIN BEAM L	INSIDE SPREAD	R POINTS L	AREA	STATE/PROVINCE	HUNTER'S NAME	DATE	RANK
355 4/8	52 4/8 50 5/8	45 4/8	6 6	Catron County	NM	Phil Kirkland	1991	475
355 4/8	53 1/8 52 1/8	40 4/8	6 6	Musselshell County	MT	Joseph Karls	1996	475
355 4/8	51 7/8 52 0/8	38 4/8	6 7	Fergus County	MT	James A. "Rusty" South	2001	475
355 4/8	46 7/8 47 2/8	46 0/8	7 7	Gilpin County	CO	Thomas G. Bloomingdale	2003	475
355 4/8	48 5/8 49 3/8	38 2/8	6 6	Wasatch County	UT	Les C. Goodwin	2006	475
*355 4/8	55 6/8 54 7/8	39 2/8	6 6	Valley County	MT	Kris Keller	2010	475
355 3/8	48 7/8 48 6/8	40 3/8	6 6	Jumping Pound Creek	ALB	Archie J. Nesbitt	1997	482
355 3/8	48 1/8 49 5/8	38 3/8	6 6	Summit County	UT	Bridger Bolinder	1998	482
355 2/8	52 1/8 51 5/8	35 2/8	6 6	Otero County	NM	Jimmy King	1989	484
355 2/8	50 3/8 57 1/8	37 0/8	6 6	Rio Arriba County	NM	Nelson Martinez, Jr.	1997	484
355 1/8	50 6/8 50 2/8	35 5/8	6 6	Fergus County	MT	Rusten L. Barnes	1995	486
355 1/8	50 5/8 48 5/8	39 5/8	6 6	Coconino County	AZ	Tim Godwin	2001	486
355 1/8	50 2/8 50 4/8	40 1/8	7 6	Sheep Creek	ALB	Paul S. Unger	2005	486
355 0/8	50 1/8 50 1/8	38 0/8	6 6	Shoshone County	ID	Vern Clary/Ed Oliver	1978	489
355 0/8	53 6/8 53 7/8	45 2/8	6 6	Park County	CO	Mark Martin	1996	489
355 0/8	52 1/8 52 7/8	34 0/8	6 6	Phillips County	MT	Kyle J. Koschmeder	2005	489
355 0/8	50 2/8 52 1/8	52 1/8	7 7	Jackson County	CO	Jack K. Dodge	2008	489
354 7/8	51 4/8 51 0/8	41 6/8	6 7	Greenlee County	AZ	David Dickson	1986	493
354 7/8	56 3/8 56 4/8	43 5/8	6 6	Coconino County	AZ	Noel Harris	1991	493
354 7/8	48 6/8 48 2/8	43 1/8	7 7	Wheeler County	OR	Dan R. Kinder	1996	493
354 7/8	55 5/8 54 0/8	48 1/8	7 6	Apache County	AZ	Mark E. Clonts	2005	493
354 6/8	54 0/8 53 7/8	36 6/8	6 6	Valley County	MT	Kenneth R. Johnson	1986	497
354 6/8	56 5/8 56 4/8	44 3/8	7 8	Custer County	ID	Wayne VanVechten	1987	497
354 6/8	53 5/8 54 4/8	40 4/8	6 6	Beaver County	UT	Jake Bess	2003	497
354 6/8	54 6/8 55 3/8	41 2/8	6 6	Coconino County	AZ	Eric Pierce	2003	497
354 6/8	49 4/8 48 2/8	41 4/8	6 6	Albany County	WY	Ron Mason	2003	497
354 6/8	52 7/8 52 4/8	40 6/8	7 7	Crook County	WY	Morgan Ellsbury	2004	497
354 6/8	45 0/8 47 0/8	42 2/8	7 7	Catron County	NM	Edmund L. DeFrank	2005	497
354 5/8	55 6/8 56 6/8	37 7/8	6 6	Catron County	NM	Duane "Corky" Richardson	1991	504
354 5/8	49 2/8 50 2/8	42 3/8	7 7	Millard County	UT	Adam Park	1999	504
354 4/8	49 1/8 50 4/8	38 6/8	6 6	Coconino County	AZ	Ron Scherer	1980	506
354 4/8	53 6/8 53 2/8	42 6/8	6 6	Navajo County	AZ	Erik M. Thorsrud	1994	506
354 4/8	55 3/8 58 3/8	40 0/8	6 6	Coconino County	AZ	James Peoble	1998	506
354 3/8	56 0/8 55 3/8	39 1/8	6 7	Converse County	WY	Edward Coy	1972	509
354 3/8	53 2/8 58 3/8	46 1/8	6 6	Coconino County	AZ	James M. Frey	1980	509
354 3/8	52 5/8 52 7/8	45 2/8	6 6	Valley County	MT	Gregg Pauley	1985	509
354 3/8	51 3/8 53 1/8	39 7/8	6 6	Lincoln County	MT	Keith Krumbeck	1986	509
354 3/8	54 1/8 54 2/8	37 5/8	7 7	Park County	WY	Mike Graham	2002	509
354 2/8	48 0/8 44 2/8	50 4/8	6 6	Morgan County	UT	Dennis Shirley	1987	514
354 2/8	52 3/8 51 4/8	42 0/8	6 6	Catron County	NM	E. Lance Whary	1997	514
354 1/8	49 5/8 47 4/8	40 5/8	6 6	Sheridan County	WY	Shane Evans	2006	516
354 0/8	60 4/8 61 2/8	34 4/8	7 6	Coconino County	AZ	Jack Cahill	1982	517
354 0/8	53 0/8 51 1/8	41 0/8	6 6	Duck Mtns.	MAN	Bob Ginther	1992	517
354 0/8	52 1/8 52 6/8	39 2/8	7 7	Judith Basin County	MT	Kyle Schmitt	2001	517
353 7/8	54 0/8 54 2/8	40 7/8	6 7	Catron County	NM	Joe Pruett	1998	520
353 7/8	50 0/8 53 2/8	43 1/8	6 6	Gallatin County	MT	Lance DeHaan	2001	520
353 7/8	55 2/8 56 4/8	41 1/8	6 7	White Pine County	NV	Randy E. Buffington	2002	520
353 7/8	52 0/8 52 1/8	39 1/8	8 8	Fergus County	MT	John Niebur	2010	520
353 6/8	53 5/8 50 2/8	44 2/8	6 6	Coconino County	AZ	Rodney Robinson	1987	524
353 6/8	53 4/8 55 5/8	44 2/8	7 6	Catron County	NM	C. H. Anderson	1992	524
353 6/8	46 5/8 46 7/8	36 4/8	6 7	Utah County	UT	Richard B. Coles	2003	524
353 6/8	53 1/8 53 4/8	36 2/8	7 7	Otero County	NM	David A. McDonald	2005	524
353 5/8	50 5/8 51 0/8	40 5/8	6 6	Sheridan County	WY	Ron Johnson	1990	528
353 5/8	47 4/8 51 2/8	41 7/8	6 7	Catron County	NM	Fred M. Fox	1995	528
353 5/8	54 7/8 56 4/8	40 7/8	6 6	White Pine County	NV	Richard F. Rowley	1999	528
353 5/8	50 7/8 53 2/8	40 1/8	6 6	Sevier County	UT	Seth Neuenschwander	2000	528
353 5/8	54 3/8 53 3/8	35 5/8	7 6	Johnson County	WY	Chris H. Apel	2004	528
353 5/8	48 3/8 48 2/8	46 5/8	6 6	Mesa County	CO	Robert E. Goodson III	2009	528
353 5/8	51 4/8 49 6/8	40 7/8	6 6	Adams County	ID	Mike Storz	2010	528
353 4/8	54 3/8 54 3/8	43 0/8	6 6	Flathead County	MT	Cory Lamb	1989	535
353 4/8	52 3/8 54 1/8	36 4/8	7 7	Valley County	MT	Travis W. Scott	1999	535
353 4/8	52 0/8 50 1/8	38 6/8	6 6	Park County	CO	Thomas P. Newton	2007	535
353 3/8	56 6/8 56 6/8	34 5/8	6 6	Otero County	NM	Bill Stage	1993	538
353 3/8	50 4/8 49 4/8	41 3/8	6 6	Washakie County	WY	Rod Gleason	2005	538
353 3/8	55 1/8 55 2/8	41 1/8	6 6	Fergus County	MT	Mark Schwomeyer	2007	538
353 2/8	56 5/8 54 4/8	33 4/8	6 6	Gallatin County	MT	J. D. Hartman	2005	541
353 2/8	54 6/8 54 5/8	41 2/8	6 6	Converse County	WY	Vicki Thiel	2007	541
353 1/8	59 6/8 60 4/8	40 1/8	7 6	Coconino County	AZ	Richard S. Jones	1991	543
353 1/8	48 0/8 50 2/8	41 1/8	6 8	Converse County	WY	Glen Mark Gates	1991	543
353 1/8	53 2/8 52 6/8	36 7/8	6 6	White Pine County	NV	Joseph G. DeAngelis	2002	543
353 0/8	50 4/8 49 6/8	43 2/8	6 6	Coconino County	AZ	Richard M. Larsen	1980	546
353 0/8	47 2/8 46 1/8	38 0/8	6 7	Grant County	OR	Kenneth Mills	1983	546
353 0/8	53 3/8 53 1/8	46 2/8	6 6	Coconino County	AZ	Bob Dawson	1992	546
352 7/8	54 4/8 53 4/8	42 0/8	6 7	Teton County	MT	Jack Howard	1972	549
352 7/8	51 6/8 52 1/8	41 7/8	6 6	Sandoval County	NM	John W. Rose	1981	549
*352 7/8	52 6/8 51 7/8	40 7/8	6 6	Catron County	NM	William Gurley	2006	549
352 7/8	52 1/8 53 3/8	39 1/8	6 6	Johnson County	WY	Jeff Schomer	2008	549
352 6/8	53 4/8 50 5/8	40 6/8	6 6	Catron County	NM	Francis D. Elias	1993	553
352 6/8	50 6/8 50 2/8	42 6/8	7 6	Petroleum County	MT	Tim Kunes	2003	553
352 6/8	54 4/8 53 3/8	38 6/8	6 6	Sheridan County	WY	Chad Reed	2003	553
352 5/8	50 1/8 50 0/8	37 5/8	6 6	Woody Ridge	AZ	Oscar Dale Porter	1982	556
352 5/8	58 0/8 59 0/8	42 3/8	6 6	King County	WA	Ed Pressley	2003	556
352 5/8	53 7/8 49 7/8	39 7/8	6 6	Elko County	NV	Casey Jones	2004	556
*352 5/8	51 4/8 54 0/8	40 7/8	6 7	Navajo County	AZ	Erich Schmidbauer	2007	556
352 5/8	49 6/8 51 6/8	37 7/8	6 6	Navajo County	AZ	Scott McGill	2007	556
352 4/8	54 2/8 52 1/8	37 2/8	6 6	Coconino County	AZ	John F. Gurasich	1988	561
*352 4/8	51 6/8 50 2/8	33 4/8	7 6	Catron County	NM	Brian Brochu	2005	561
352 3/8	48 6/8 48 5/8	34 7/8	6 6	Garfield County	MT	Ernie Jablonsky	2001	563
352 3/8	49 7/8 49 1/8	37 3/8	6 7	Natrona County	WY	Derek Amadio	2001	563
352 3/8	47 5/8 47 5/8	34 1/8	7 7	Delta County	CO	Brad Spence	2004	563
352 2/8	51 5/8 50 5/8	37 6/8	6 6	Johnson County	WY	Russell Elrod	2001	566
352 2/8	48 1/8 51 6/8	35 0/8	6 6	Socorro County	NM	Trevor L. Esparza	2001	566
352 2/8	48 0/8 45 4/8	39 2/8	7 6	Larimer County	CO	Clay Cushman	2004	566
352 2/8	55 0/8 58 4/8	39 0/8	6 6	Sevier County	UT	Mark Alger	2008	566
352 2/8	55 2/8 52 2/8	47 2/8	7 8	Powder River County	MT	Gary D. Sumwalt	2008	566

683

AMERICAN ELK (TYPICAL ANTLERS)

Minimum Score 260 — Continued

SCORE	LENGTH OF R MAIN BEAM L	INSIDE SPREAD	NUMBER OF R POINTS L		AREA	STATE/ PROVINCE	HUNTER'S NAME	DATE	RANK
352 1/8	53 2/8 53 1/8	36 3/8	6	6	Petroleum County	MT	Gorm Scarpholt	1987	571
352 1/8	54 1/8 54 0/8	47 1/8	7	6	Catron County	NM	James F. Welles	1993	571
352 1/8	50 4/8 48 7/8	34 3/8	6	6	Garfield County	MT	Robert A. Lee	2002	571
352 0/8	51 4/8 53 0/8	38 5/8	6	7	Coconino County	AZ	Bill Elmer	1981	574
352 0/8	51 3/8 51 2/8	43 6/8	6	6	Powell County	MT	Philip L. Karper	1987	574
352 0/8	49 4/8 51 0/8	44 3/8	8	7	Catron County	NM	Tom Hoffman	1991	574
352 0/8	51 4/8 51 4/8	44 4/8	6	6	Kootenai County	ID	Mark Gerber	1997	574
352 0/8	56 3/8 56 0/8	42 0/8	6	6	Musselshell County	MT	Mark L. Goitein	2000	574
352 0/8	50 3/8 50 3/8	41 4/8	6	6	Wheeler County	OR	Dave Heather	2000	574
352 0/8	51 1/8 49 3/8	37 6/8	8	6	Petroleum County	MT	Robert Saykally	2003	574
352 0/8	48 3/8 46 6/8	37 4/8	6	6	Catron County	NM	Jon Preston	2006	574
352 0/8	48 2/8 48 5/8	42 0/8	6	6	Garfield County	UT	John L. Davies IV	2007	574
*352 0/8	50 1/8 49 6/8	44 6/8	6	6	Lawrence County	SD	Tyson Gunn	2009	574
351 7/8	50 6/8 50 2/8	40 4/8	7	6	Crook County	OR	Curtis Demaris	1983	584
351 7/8	46 4/8 46 4/8	39 5/8	7	7	Park County	MT	Randy F. Petrich	1991	584
351 7/8	54 2/8 54 5/8	39 7/8	8	8	Catron County	NM	George T. Basabilvazo	1998	584
351 7/8	49 6/8 50 4/8	35 7/8	6	6	Eagle County	CO	Donald Kotecki	2002	584
351 7/8	54 0/8 50 6/8	40 4/8	6	8	Chouteau County	MT	Steve Yancey	2002	584
351 6/8	49 4/8 50 6/8	39 6/8	6	8	Coconino County	AZ	Joseph A. Lorenz	1999	589
351 5/8	54 7/8 56 0/8	48 5/8	6	7	Coconino County	AZ	James West	2004	590
351 5/8	53 7/8 52 7/8	36 7/8	6	6	White Pine County	NV	L. Grant Foster	2006	590
351 4/8	51 7/8 51 2/8	39 4/8	7	7	Coconino County	AZ	Marvin L. Slaughter	1979	592
351 4/8	50 6/8 49 7/8	40 0/8	6	6	Grant County	OR	Curtis Demaris	1980	592
351 4/8	56 5/8 56 0/8	46 4/8	6	6	Coconino County	AZ	John F. Gurasich	1986	592
351 4/8	43 7/8 45 3/8	40 0/8	6	6	Lincoln County	NM	Terry Arnim	1986	592
351 4/8	51 6/8 56 5/8	37 2/8	7	7	Flathead County	MT	Paul Cosman	1989	592
351 4/8	50 4/8 49 2/8	38 0/8	6	6	Garfield County	UT	Chris Beck	2007	592
351 3/8	49 6/8 54 2/8	48 2/8	8	7	Grant County	OR	Bob Lindsay	1981	598
351 3/8	50 3/8 50 4/8	39 1/8	6	6	Millarville	ALB	Barry Pocha	1991	598
351 3/8	53 6/8 55 0/8	40 3/8	6	6	Greenlee County	AZ	Dennis Jensen	1991	598
351 3/8	56 0/8 57 4/8	44 3/8	7	7	Ferry County	WA	Brett Black	1997	598
351 3/8	50 2/8 47 2/8	41 7/8	7	6	Fremont County	WY	Tom K. Dunlap	2001	598
*351 3/8	48 2/8 50 1/8	36 2/8	9	6	Lincoln County	NV	Slade Faught	2004	598
351 2/8	55 6/8 53 5/8	41 6/8	6	6	Coconino County	AZ	Jay Elmer	1977	604
351 2/8	51 5/8 50 3/8	34 0/8	7	7	Missoula County	MT	James P. Loughran	1986	604
351 2/8	52 1/8 49 1/8	40 4/8	6	6	Morgan County	UT	Dr. Peter E. Paulos	1994	604
351 2/8	48 5/8 50 4/8	37 6/8	6	6	Socorro County	NM	Doug Aikin	1995	604
351 2/8	47 4/8 51 6/8	45 0/8	7	6	Wasco County	OR	Sheldon D. Ayres	1995	604
351 2/8	58 2/8 57 4/8	45 4/8	6	5	Coconino County	AZ	Mark Penninger	2003	604
351 2/8	55 6/8 56 1/8	36 6/8	6	6	Broadwater County	MT	Mike McLeod	2003	604
*351 2/8	57 3/8 55 3/8	34 6/8	7	7	Millard County	UT	John W. Bateman	2009	604
351 1/8	54 0/8 52 3/8	40 3/8	6	6	Lincoln County	NM	Frank Scott	1989	612
351 1/8	54 2/8 53 2/8	40 3/8	7	7	Mineral County	CO	Dwight S. Wolf	1999	612
*351 1/8	48 7/8 48 3/8	43 1/8	6	6	Chaffee County	CO	Kenneth Dionne	2009	612
*351 1/8	56 3/8 56 7/8	39 3/8	6	6	Grand County	CO	Melissa Johnson	2009	612
351 0/8	54 6/8 51 3/8	36 0/8	6	6	Greenlee County	AZ	Jim Coleman	1987	616
351 0/8	51 7/8 51 6/8	38 2/8	6	6	Canmore	ALB	Gunter Lemke	1987	616
351 0/8	51 4/8 50 7/8	42 0/8	7	6	Coconino County	AZ	Robert Bejarano	1998	616
351 0/8	52 0/8 52 5/8	53 0/8	7	6	Laramie County	WY	Dennis Magnusson	2003	616
351 0/8	53 3/8 52 1/8	40 2/8	7	8	Washakie County	WY	Bruce Briesemeister	2004	616
350 7/8	49 7/8 50 1/8	46 7/8	6	6	Child's Lake	MAN	Maurice Martel	2002	621
350 7/8	54 4/8 52 6/8	41 7/8	6	6	Tooele County	UT	Kollin Garfield	2005	621
350 7/8	57 4/8 59 3/8	43 1/8	6	6	Catron County	NM	Paul L. Allison	2005	621
350 6/8	49 2/8 51 1/8	37 7/8	6	6	Bear Lake County	ID	Kay Parker	2008	621
350 6/8	53 2/8 53 0/8	40 2/8	6	6	Sheridan County	WY	Kurt M. Baughman	1980	625
350 6/8	48 7/8 49 6/8	37 2/8	6	6	Catron County	NM	Al Hankins	1998	625
350 6/8	56 2/8 54 6/8	44 4/8	6	6	Summit County	CO	Greg Bradley	2007	625
350 5/8	49 7/8 49 5/8	40 6/8	7	6	Catron County	NM	Cary Cuba	1987	628
350 5/8	53 4/8 52 6/8	39 3/8	6	6	Catron County	NM	Billy R. Leach	1992	628
350 5/8	57 2/8 54 7/8	44 1/8	6	8	Coconino County	AZ	Arthur R. M. Ramirez, Jr.	2007	628
350 4/8	49 0/8 49 0/8	38 2/8	6	6	Teton County	WY	Jerry Bodar	2001	631
350 4/8	51 4/8 50 5/8	39 2/8	7	6	Carbon County	WY	Rhett Heflin	2001	631
*350 4/8	46 7/8 46 0/8	40 6/8	7	6	Coconino County	AZ	Thomas J. McClain	2006	631
350 3/8	48 7/8 48 5/8	41 7/8	8	7	Fergus County	MT	G. L. 'Buck' Damone	1981	634
350 3/8	53 5/8 53 7/8	41 1/8	6	6	Catron County	NM	George Richardson	1993	634
350 3/8	51 2/8 51 3/8	37 5/8	6	6	Johnson County	WY	John Lindell	2006	634
350 3/8	53 1/8 53 2/8	37 5/8	7	6	Coconino County	AZ	Debra Sieloff	2007	634
350 2/8	51 6/8 48 7/8	40 2/8	6	6	Routt County	CO	Mark L. Houslet	1977	638
350 2/8	53 4/8 53 1/8	41 2/8	6	6	Sandoval County	NM	Jose Montalvo	1981	638
350 2/8	54 1/8 53 3/8	39 2/8	6	6	Catron County	NM	Bobby Elkins	1993	638
350 2/8	46 3/8 45 6/8	39 2/8	6	6	Mohave County	AZ	Rodney W. Bump	2002	638
*350 2/8	55 7/8 56 0/8	41 4/8	6	6	La Plata County	CO	Mike Wing	2009	638
350 2/8	53 1/8 52 0/8	39 2/8	6	6	Montrose County	CO	Adam James Lynch	2009	638
350 1/8	50 2/8 52 5/8	37 7/8	6	6	Cibola County	NM	Ted Shinn	1987	644
350 1/8	54 7/8 52 5/8	44 7/8	6	7	Summit County	CO	Jeffrey J. Granowsky	1987	644
350 1/8	52 2/8 52 1/8	37 1/8	6	6	Petroleum County	MT	Dennis Bergan	1994	644
350 1/8	54 7/8 53 4/8	34 5/8	6	6	Navajo County	AZ	Don Parks, Jr.	1995	644
350 1/8	47 5/8 47 0/8	36 2/8	7	6	Catron County	NM	John P. Carlton	1998	644
350 1/8	52 0/8 52 2/8	43 3/8	6	6	Yavapai County	AZ	Bill Armstrong III	2001	644
350 1/8	47 0/8 47 4/8	38 3/8	6	6	Fergus County	MT	Fridolin H. Rud	2004	644
350 1/8	54 7/8 53 2/8	37 7/8	6	6	Navajo County	AZ	Steve Osminski	2005	644
*350 1/8	50 2/8 47 5/8	37 1/8	7	7	Fergus County	MT	Matt Moen	2007	644
350 1/8	52 5/8 51 7/8	40 5/8	6	6	Garfield County	MT	Beau Hensen	2008	644
350 0/8	53 1/8 51 5/8	38 6/8	6	6	Sandoval County	NM	Tom David	1984	654
350 0/8	51 6/8 50 2/8	33 6/8	6	6	Catron County	NM	Philip G. McClelland	1988	654
350 0/8	51 2/8 53 6/8	41 4/8	6	6	Catron County	NM	Eddie Claypool	1990	654
350 0/8	55 0/8 52 0/8	43 0/8	6	7	Navajo County	AZ	Alan C. Ellsworth	1994	654
350 0/8	49 4/8 50 1/8	39 6/8	7	7	Washington County	ID	Joe Shearer	2004	654
350 0/8	51 2/8 54 7/8	39 6/8	6	6	Washakie County	WY	Justin Pivik	2007	654
350 0/8	49 4/8 50 0/8	40 4/8	6	6	Grand County	CO	Robert Stietz	2008	654
*350 0/8	56 4/8 53 7/8	43 4/8	6	8	Musselshell County	MT	Robert R. Moline	2008	654
349 7/8	50 1/8 51 1/8	48 5/8	6	6	Crook County	OR	Dale Shiery	1984	662
349 7/8	43 6/8 46 0/8	38 1/8	6	6	Catron County	NM	Kenny T. Rhodes	1991	662
349 6/8	53 0/8 52 6/8	41 6/8	6	6	Wheeler County	OR	Dale Shiery	1983	664
349 6/8	57 4/8 56 4/8	40 4/8	6	7	Coconino County	AZ	Gary A. Linendoll	1991	664

684

AMERICAN ELK (TYPICAL ANTLERS)

Minimum Score 260   Continued

SCORE	LENGTH OF R MAIN BEAM L	INSIDE SPREAD	NUMBER OF R POINTS L	AREA	STATE/ PROVINCE	HUNTER'S NAME	DATE	RANK
349 6/8	53 6/8 55 0/8	39 6/8	6 6	Idaho County	ID	Louis Wasniewski	1996	664
349 5/8	46 0/8 44 4/8	37 1/8	6 6	Huerfano County	CO	Richard L. Doman	1972	667
349 5/8	51 4/8 52 2/8	40 4/8	8 7	Coconino County	AZ	Cindi J. Richardson	1991	667
349 5/8	50 5/8 49 7/8	33 7/8	6 7	Taos County	NM	Michael R. Deschamps	1992	667
349 5/8	52 1/8 51 4/8	40 4/8	6 7	Albany County	WY	Mark Adamson	1998	667
*349 5/8	50 5/8 47 3/8	39 3/8	6 6	Larimer County	CO	Clay Cushman	2009	667
349 4/8	58 0/8 58 6/8	43 6/8	7 6	Idaho County	ID	Jim Robbins	1996	672
349 4/8	53 2/8 53 3/8	36 5/8	6 8	Catron County	NM	Paul R. Bovee	1997	672
349 4/8	52 7/8 53 0/8	42 6/8	6 6	Catron County	NM	Daniel R. Strickland	1999	672
349 4/8	46 5/8 52 4/8	36 0/8	6 6	Duck Mtn.	MAN	Chris Dushanek	2002	672
349 4/8	54 0/8 53 6/8	46 6/8	6 6	Garfield County	UT	Jon Reynolds	2006	672
349 3/8	52 2/8 51 7/8	36 7/8	6 6	Fergus County	MT	Charles R. Bowman	1966	677
349 3/8	50 4/8 45 4/8	46 1/8	6 6	Park County	CO	Gary Jones	1984	677
349 3/8	53 3/8 54 6/8	43 1/8	6 6	Apache County	AZ	David Sullivan	1986	677
349 2/8	50 6/8 51 0/8	39 4/8	7 6	Clackamas County	OR	Paul Smith	1984	680
349 2/8	53 0/8 54 0/8	35 0/8	6 7	Albany County	WY	Mark Stiller	1993	680
349 2/8	54 1/8 51 3/8	35 6/8	7 7	Sierra County	NM	Joe H. Campbell	1994	680
349 2/8	51 5/8 52 4/8	40 6/8	6 6	Catron County	NM	Andrew Brown	1998	680
349 2/8	50 5/8 50 6/8	45 2/8	6 6	Wasatch County	UT	Steve Millard	2007	680
349 2/8	49 3/8 49 7/8	40 6/8	6 6	Granite County	MT	August Barany	2009	680
349 1/8	56 4/8 60 2/8	45 3/8	6 7	Coconino County	AZ	Alan R. Miller	1975	686
349 1/8	59 4/8 58 6/8	45 5/8	6 6	San Miguel County	NM	James L. Maves	1991	686
349 1/8	53 5/8 50 1/8	40 2/8	7 8	White Pine County	NV	Lew Webb	2001	686
349 1/8	53 0/8 52 1/8	35 3/8	6 6	Custer County	SD	Merle Twedt	2003	686
*349 1/8	51 0/8 50 2/8	37 0/8	7 6	Sheridan County	WY	Daniel Sexton	2009	686
349 0/8	51 1/8 47 6/8	39 2/8	6 6	Los Alamos County	NM	Chuck Adams	1982	691
349 0/8	59 7/8 59 6/8	46 0/8	6 7	Catron County	NM	William C. Davis	1993	691
349 0/8	52 5/8 51 6/8	47 6/8	6 6	Coconino County	AZ	Claud F. Adams	1994	691
349 0/8	51 0/8 51 2/8	38 5/8	7 8	Catron County	NM	David L. Workman	1997	691
349 0/8	53 7/8 52 4/8	39 4/8	6 6	Garfield County	MT	Tony J. Swiontek	2003	691
348 6/8	56 2/8 55 1/8	43 5/8	6 6	Coconino County	AZ	Jason Manuell	2001	696
348 6/8	50 1/8 50 2/8	37 0/8	6 6	Phillips County	MT	Ron Bachmeier	1990	697
348 6/8	52 1/8 53 0/8	42 0/8	6 6	Apache County	AZ	Mace D. Cochran	1995	697
348 6/8	50 2/8 52 7/8	41 4/8	7 6	Mesa County	CO	Jimmy Wayne Birchfield	2002	697
348 6/8	54 2/8 52 1/8	38 6/8	6 8	Gila County	AZ	Ray Potter	2003	697
348 5/8	52 2/8 53 5/8	46 3/8	6 6	Caribou County	ID	Kenneth P. Kelley	1991	701
348 5/8	50 4/8 49 0/8	36 5/8	7 6	Grand County	CO	Gary Williamson	1994	701
*348 5/8	42 4/8 44 4/8	36 7/8	7 7	Otero County	NM	Wesley Gipson	2005	701
*348 5/8	47 4/8 50 0/8	36 0/8	8 6	Montrose County	CO	Davin Kropf	2007	701
348 4/8	55 0/8 55 0/8	43 6/8	6 6	Coconino County	AZ	Bob Jensen	1981	705
348 4/8	45 3/8 44 4/8	41 6/8	6 6	Bonneville County	ID	Ronald L. Mueller	1982	705
348 4/8	54 1/8 54 4/8	42 2/8	6 6	Caribou County	ID	Raymond Bruderer	2003	705
348 3/8	50 0/8 51 7/8	34 4/8	7 7	Pierce County	WA	John Lyday	1984	708
348 3/8	50 3/8 48 1/8	37 3/8	6 6	Duchesne County	UT	Victor J. Fossat	1995	708
348 3/8	51 6/8 51 6/8	37 2/8	7 7	Grant County	NM	Justin Lick	2001	708
348 3/8	48 2/8 46 2/8	33 3/8	6 6	Umatilla County	OR	Tony McKague	2003	708
*348 3/8	54 5/8 53 1/8	34 3/8	7 7	Larimer County	CO	Clay Cushman	2006	708
348 3/8	53 1/8 53 1/8	40 1/8	6 6	Stevens County	WA	Dusty Rieckers	2006	708
348 2/8	30 7/8 47 3/8	34 4/8	6 7	Rio Blanco County	CO	Clark Gallup	1976	714
348 2/8	50 0/8 50 4/8	41 6/8	6 7	Carbon County	UT	Rick G. Huempfner	1989	714
348 2/8	47 7/8 48 2/8	39 2/8	6 6	Sanders County	MT	Glen Haas	1991	714
348 2/8	51 1/8 51 0/8	39 6/8	7 7	Judith Basin County	MT	Thomas Cook	1997	714
348 1/8	52 3/8 56 0/8	40 1/8	6 6	Garfield County	UT	Robert A. Lee	2005	718
348 1/8	48 4/8 47 4/8	42 3/8	7 6	Park County	WY	Randy J. Merritt	2006	718
348 1/8	57 5/8 57 0/8	41 3/8	6 6	Madison County	MT	Branden L. Van Dyken	2008	718
348 1/8	55 6/8 55 4/8	40 7/8	6 6	Greenlee County	AZ	William M. Hornbeck	2009	718
348 0/8	53 4/8 53 6/8	43 6/8	6 6	Sheridan County	WY	Mark S. Hutchins	1992	722
348 0/8	50 7/8 48 5/8	41 1/8	7 8	Adams County	ID	Darwin DeCroo	1996	722
348 0/8	51 5/8 50 1/8	41 6/8	7 7	Millard County	UT	Greg S. Herbert	2000	722
348 0/8	57 0/8 57 0/8	32 4/8	6 6	Coconino County	AZ	Todd Zeuske	2000	722
348 0/8	51 0/8 49 3/8	33 0/8	6 6	Taos County	NM	Dennis Howell	2004	722
348 0/8	51 7/8 52 1/8	35 7/8	7 7	Coconino County	AZ	Clark Unruh	2004	722
348 0/8	53 4/8 49 7/8	36 2/8	6 6	Catron County	NM	Debra Dixon	2007	722
347 7/8	49 2/8 47 2/8	36 5/8	6 6	Swan River	MAN	Carl Robblee	1988	729
347 7/8	53 0/8 54 0/8	30 1/8	8 6	Broadwater County	MT	Kris C. Rains	2004	729
347 6/8	51 4/8 47 6/8	38 0/8	6 6	Valley County	MT	Greg Zahn	1981	731
347 6/8	49 6/8 52 1/8	38 6/8	6 6	Phillips County	MT	Craig Hall	1986	731
347 6/8	54 6/8 53 6/8	42 4/8	6 6	Coconino County	AZ	Jack W. Adams	2003	731
347 6/8	54 3/8 53 3/8	37 4/8	6 7	Saguache County	CO	Amberlyn Lake	2009	731
347 5/8	54 4/8 54 1/8	41 3/8	6 6	Coconino County	AZ	Allen L. King II	1992	735
347 5/8	53 3/8 53 4/8	46 1/8	6 6	Butte County	ID	Paul L. Nelson	2005	735
347 5/8	52 3/8 53 0/8	46 7/8	6 6	Mesa County	CO	Cody A. Leach	2009	735
347 4/8	50 2/8 49 5/8	45 6/8	7 6	Fremont County	ID	Bob Baird	1961	738
347 4/8	48 2/8 48 5/8	38 0/8	6 6	Fergus County	MT	Mark DeBoo	1988	738
347 4/8	51 7/8 53 5/8	45 0/8	6 6	Larimer County	CO	Rick Heaton	2003	738
347 4/8	54 7/8 55 5/8	39 4/8	6 7	Apache County	AZ	Rob Harms	2004	738
347 4/8	51 7/8 51 3/8	38 0/8	6 6	Fergus County	MT	Dois R. Chesshir	2007	738
347 3/8	50 0/8 50 2/8	40 5/8	6 6	Columbia County	WA	Ronald C. Schutz	2000	743
347 3/8	53 2/8 55 1/8	41 3/8	6 7	Custer County	MT	Glenn Bornhoft	2004	743
347 3/8	52 7/8 52 0/8	38 3/8	6 6	Socorro County	NM	Buck Siler	2004	743
*347 3/8	53 0/8 52 3/8	39 0/8	6 7	Fergus County	MT	Charles Doll	2007	743
347 2/8	46 2/8 51 0/8	41 0/8	6 6	Socorro County	NM	Donald H. Paul	1992	747
347 2/8	50 3/8 50 5/8	38 4/8	6 6	Navajo County	AZ	Henry Roberts	1994	747
347 2/8	58 0/8 56 7/8	43 6/8	6 6	Catron County	NM	Hector Aguirre	1998	747
347 2/8	53 5/8 53 7/8	42 2/8	6 6	Gallatin County	MT	Rory Edwards	2001	747
347 2/8	45 0/8 46 0/8	45 2/8	6 6	Salt Lake County	UT	Jason A. Gammell	2003	747
347 1/8	54 1/8 53 2/8	37 3/8	6 6	Clackamas County	OR	Bill Lancaster	1986	752
347 1/8	53 3/8 55 0/8	35 7/8	6 6	Colfax County	NM	John J. Teahan	1999	752
347 1/8	52 0/8 52 6/8	41 3/8	7 7	Umatilla County	OR	Martin Romero	1999	752
347 1/8	55 6/8 53 3/8	38 3/8	6 6	Carbon County	WY	Evan Reish	2003	752
347 1/8	52 3/8 53 1/8	42 7/8	6 6	Juab County	UT	Travis N. Gates	2010	752
347 0/8	49 1/8 51 2/8	36 0/8	7 8	Apache County	AZ	Jesus T. Guerena	1988	757
347 0/8	50 5/8 54 3/8	43 0/8	7 6	Shoshone County	ID	Max A. Jones	2005	757
346 7/8	54 1/8 51 4/8	35 5/8	7 7	Lake County	MT	Scott Ganz	1984	759
346 7/8	50 7/8 51 7/8	37 5/8	6 6	Mora County	NM	James L. Romero	1987	759

685

AMERICAN ELK (TYPICAL ANTLERS)

Minimum Score 260 Continued

SCORE	LENGTH OF R MAIN BEAM L	INSIDE SPREAD	NUMBER OF R POINTS L		AREA	STATE/PROVINCE	HUNTER'S NAME	DATE	RANK
346 7/8	50 5/8 48 3/8	36 3/8	6	6	Fergus County	MT	D. Mitch Kottas	1998	759
346 7/8	53 4/8 54 6/8	42 5/8	7	6	Sheridan County	WY	Daniel K. Doke	1998	759
346 7/8	51 2/8 50 7/8	39 3/8	7	7	Fergus County	MT	Brad Tank	1998	759
346 7/8	52 3/8 53 2/8	39 7/8	7	7	Garfield County	MT	Ernie Jablonsky	2002	759
346 7/8	50 0/8 51 4/8	41 5/8	6	6	Rosebud County	MT	Gary Dickhaut	2005	759
346 6/8	44 2/8 45 4/8	41 0/8	6	6	Bighorn Mtns.	WY	John Yeager	1980	766
346 6/8	49 6/8 51 2/8	40 4/8	6	6	Catron County	NM	Gardner Rowell	2000	766
*346 6/8	54 6/8 55 5/8	38 0/8	6	6	Boulder County	CO	Dave Lind	2004	766
346 6/8	48 7/8 50 3/8	35 0/8	6	7	Fergus County	MT	Wade Sommer	2005	766
*346 6/8	56 0/8 55 5/8	42 2/8	7	7	Custer County	SD	Gabe J. Ellerton	2007	766
*346 6/8	47 2/8 56 4/8	42 0/8	6	6	Gila County	AZ	Francis Cameron	2008	766
*346 6/8	53 2/8 53 0/8	37 0/8	6	6	Routt County	CO	Oren Diehl	2009	766
346 5/8	52 6/8 53 6/8	44 5/8	7	6	San Miguel County	NM	Frank C. Sciorilli	1977	773
346 5/8	55 0/8 53 2/8	39 3/8	7	6	Coconino County	AZ	Rodney L. Miskin	1994	773
346 5/8	52 1/8 51 5/8	39 7/8	6	6	Powder River County	MT	Mark Rost	2005	773
*346 5/8	54 0/8 54 7/8	36 1/8	6	6	Sheridan County	WY	Darrel A. Mann	2009	773
346 4/8	51 4/8 51 1/8	42 5/8	7	6	Coconino County	AZ	Brett Kendall	1990	777
346 4/8	54 2/8 54 1/8	40 2/8	6	6	Catron County	NM	Michael J. Nielsen	1994	777
346 4/8	60 2/8 60 0/8	40 2/8	6	6	Sierra County	NM	Deone Johnson	1997	777
346 4/8	50 2/8 54 5/8	41 2/8	6	6	Sanders County	MT	George Clark	2001	777
346 4/8	53 3/8 51 4/8	39 6/8	6	6	Phillips County	MT	Kyle Koschmeder	2006	777
346 4/8	53 0/8 52 2/8	41 6/8	6	6	Columbia County	WA	Tyson Chambers	2009	777
346 3/8	47 7/8 47 6/8	43 1/8	6	7	Navajo County	AZ	Joseph Wade Kauffman	2000	783
346 3/8	52 7/8 52 5/8	40 5/8	6	6	Moffat County	CO	Larry Gene Robidoux	2001	783
346 3/8	49 4/8 49 6/8	44 5/8	7	7	Fremont County	ID	Thomas Wolcott	2004	783
346 3/8	51 4/8 51 6/8	39 5/8	6	6	Lawrence County	SD	Rod Ruen	2006	783
346 3/8	50 4/8 49 5/8	40 7/8	6	6	Garfield County	UT	Jerry Woodland	2008	783
346 3/8	49 1/8 48 1/8	40 7/8	6	6	Catron County	NM	James Willard	2009	783
346 2/8	52 4/8 51 4/8	36 6/8	6	6	Garfield County	UT	Bob Ehle	2004	789
346 2/8	52 3/8 52 3/8	38 2/8	6	6	Garfield County	UT	Craig P. Mitton	2005	789
346 2/8	56 6/8 54 7/8	33 0/8	7	7	Columbia County	WA	Matthew Vucelick	2008	789
346 1/8	50 7/8 50 0/8	40 7/8	7	8	White Pine County	NV	James R. Puryear	1988	792
346 1/8	56 2/8 51 3/8	39 5/8	6	6	Catron County	NM	Teddy Orr	1992	792
346 1/8	50 2/8 50 3/8	41 3/8	6	7	Linn County	OR	Jeff Baker	1995	792
*346 1/8	52 3/8 51 4/8	41 3/8	6	6	Laramie County	WY	Alton J. Krenzelok	2005	792
*346 1/8	47 4/8 45 6/8	40 7/8	6	6	Lincoln County	NV	Clayton Larsen	2007	792
346 0/8	49 5/8 45 2/8	35 4/8	6	6	Coconino County	AZ	Chris Kengla	1993	797
346 0/8	55 0/8 54 4/8	37 4/8	6	6	Catron County	NM	Rudy Apodala	2004	797
346 0/8	55 1/8 55 7/8	43 0/8	7	7	Catron County	NM	Mike Garretson	2005	797
346 0/8	50 6/8 52 1/8	42 4/8	6	6	Garfield County	UT	Chance Platt	2006	797
*346 0/8	46 1/8 45 4/8	36 2/8	6	6	Garfield County	UT	Joe Hughes	2008	797
*346 0/8	57 4/8 56 5/8	46 4/8	6	6	Mesa County	CO	Joseph Lambert	2009	797
345 7/8	52 5/8 52 0/8	41 5/8	7	6	Blaine County	ID	Danny F. Watson	1977	803
345 7/8	47 6/8 47 4/8	36 1/8	6	7	White Pine County	NV	Gregg Tanner	1989	803
345 7/8	59 1/8 57 4/8	35 5/8	6	6	Catron County	NM	A. E. McCaskill	1991	803
345 7/8	52 6/8 52 2/8	42 3/8	6	6	Phillips County	MT	Michael J. McFate	1992	803
345 7/8	48 2/8 48 5/8	42 7/8	6	6	Catron County	NM	Ricky Adams	1996	803
345 7/8	54 3/8 54 3/8	47 6/8	6	8	Catron County	NM	Tommy Roach	1998	803
345 7/8	51 1/8 50 4/8	51 6/8	6	6	Albany County	WY	Aaron G. Madsen	1998	803
345 7/8	57 5/8 58 3/8	33 1/8	6	6	Coconino County	AZ	Jack Chastain	2001	803
345 7/8	53 3/8 54 5/8	38 1/8	7	6	Catron County	NM	Mark D. Morris	2004	803
345 7/8	52 2/8 52 5/8	41 1/8	6	6	Coconino County	AZ	Bruce Barrie	2005	803
345 6/8	54 0/8 55 6/8	40 0/8	6	6	Graham County	AZ	Steve M. Titla	1987	813
345 6/8	51 5/8 54 2/8	36 4/8	6	6	Summit County	UT	Monty Dyke	1992	813
345 6/8	52 6/8 52 6/8	43 0/8	6	6	Lemhi County	ID	Elmer Hamilton	1995	813
345 6/8	53 2/8 52 4/8	44 4/8	6	6	Musselshell County	MT	James S. Nelson IV	1998	813
345 6/8	49 6/8 52 4/8	37 2/8	6	6	Coconino County	AZ	Carl Guilliams	2001	813
345 6/8	52 1/8 53 6/8	35 6/8	6	8	Coconino County	AZ	Darren Hanson	2004	813
345 6/8	49 7/8 50 5/8	40 4/8	7	7	Gila County	AZ	Gary Mehaffey	2007	813
345 6/8	54 0/8 53 7/8	41 4/8	6	6	Coconino County	AZ	Barry R. Sopher	2008	813
345 6/8	52 3/8 49 5/8	36 0/8	6	6	Moffat County	CO	Christopher M. Roe	2009	813
345 5/8	50 3/8 51 0/8	36 7/8	6	6	Socorro County	NM	Frederick V. Brown	1995	822
345 5/8	54 6/8 54 1/8	38 7/8	6	6	Catron County	NM	Elmer R. Luce, Jr.	1995	822
345 5/8	53 7/8 54 6/8	30 7/8	7	7	Coconino County	AZ	Stephen Frost	1998	822
345 5/8	51 3/8 53 6/8	37 1/8	6	6	Garfield County	MT	Todd B. Jensen	2009	822
345 4/8	52 1/8 52 3/8	37 4/8	7	7	Ravalli County	MT	Howard Nichols	1983	826
*345 4/8	53 4/8 51 6/8	40 2/8	6	6	Fergus County	MT	Don Moen	2005	826
345 4/8	49 1/8 48 4/8	39 0/8	6	6	Catron County	NM	Sam Davidson	2007	826
345 4/8	53 2/8 52 5/8	43 2/8	6	6	San Juan County	UT	Donald A. Newman, MD	2008	826
345 3/8	54 0/8 53 3/8	42 1/8	6	7	Coconino County	AZ	Pete Foti	1999	830
345 3/8	51 4/8 52 1/8	47 3/8	7	7	Owyhee County	ID	Bill Stutzman	2002	830
345 3/8	50 3/8 49 6/8	42 3/8	6	6	Utah County	UT	Bryan Olsen	2003	830
345 3/8	51 6/8 50 6/8	43 3/8	7	7	Sevier County	UT	Tyler D. Torgerson	2003	830
345 3/8	55 4/8 57 7/8	44 5/8	6	6	Garfield County	UT	Chad Glauser	2004	830
345 2/8	54 3/8 53 4/8	41 4/8	7	6	Coconino County	AZ	Jim P. Harris	1995	835
345 2/8	56 2/8 57 0/8	40 4/8	8	6	Coconino County	AZ	Keith R. Hubbard	2003	835
345 2/8	47 4/8 47 0/8	35 4/8	8	6	Catron County	NM	Christopher C. Kengla	2004	835
345 2/8	52 3/8 49 4/8	36 0/8	8	6	Coconino County	AZ	Justin M. Leitner	2004	835
*345 2/8	47 7/8 50 7/8	39 4/8	7	7	Phillips County	MT	Chris Cernohous	2004	835
345 2/8	51 7/8 50 6/8	41 4/8	6	6	Petroleum County	MT	Jeffrey P. Ebiner	2009	835
345 2/8	51 5/8 51 4/8	37 4/8	6	6	Carbon County	WY	George F. Kamps	2009	835
*345 2/8	49 6/8 49 0/8	42 0/8	6	6	Yellowstone County	MT	Paul J. Meyers	2010	835
*345 2/8	49 4/8 49 2/8	44 5/8	7	7	Catron County	NM	Troy Gibbs	2010	835
345 1/8	49 2/8 51 7/8	43 7/8	6	6	Catron County	NM	Ron Adam	1987	844
345 1/8	52 3/8 51 5/8	45 5/8	6	6	Crook County	OR	Chuck Reed	1999	844
345 1/8	45 6/8 46 3/8	46 3/8	6	6	Garfield County	UT	John Caruso	2002	844
345 1/8	52 6/8 53 3/8	42 1/8	6	6	Las Animas County	CO	Donald Travis	2006	844
345 0/8	52 3/8 55 0/8	37 4/8	6	7	Archuleta County	CO	Val M. Koeberlein	1989	848
345 0/8	51 6/8 52 2/8	51 6/8	7	6	Fremont County	ID	Mark J. Sherick	2001	848
*345 0/8	49 5/8 48 4/8	35 4/8	6	6	Teton County	WY	Eric Lippincott	2006	848
345 0/8	52 2/8 52 1/8	37 4/8	7	7	Big Horn County	WY	Randy Burtis	2008	848
345 0/8	49 7/8 47 3/8	36 2/8	6	6	Powder River County	MT	Mike Barrett	2009	848
344 7/8	50 2/8 49 4/8	40 7/8	7	7	Coconino County	AZ	Jody Davis	2004	853
344 6/8	53 2/8 55 0/8	41 0/8	8	7	Coconino County	AZ	Les Shelton	1979	854
344 6/8	50 7/8 49 3/8	38 6/8	7	7	Coconino County	AZ	Mark R. Harvey	1986	854

686

AMERICAN ELK (TYPICAL ANTLERS)

Minimum Score 260   Continued

SCORE	LENGTH OF R MAIN BEAM L	INSIDE SPREAD	NUMBER OF R POINTS L	AREA	STATE/ PROVINCE	HUNTER'S NAME	DATE	RANK
344 6/8	53 4/8 52 7/8	34 0/8	7 7	King County	WA	Robin F. Buck	1989	854
344 6/8	49 0/8 47 3/8	34 6/8	5 6	Catron County	NM	Brent Meadors	2001	854
344 5/8	53 4/8 53 3/8	37 1/8	7 7	Mohave County	AZ	Jim Machac	1998	858
344 3/8	52 0/8 52 6/8	45 1/8	6 6	Lincoln County	MT	Lance Sink	1984	859
344 3/8	50 0/8 49 7/8	36 3/8	7 7	Petroleum County	MT	Dennis R. Thompson	1985	859
344 3/8	50 4/8 54 7/8	40 7/8	6 6	Catron County	NM	Christopher D. Walp	1992	859
344 3/8	51 6/8 46 0/8	42 5/8	6 6	Moffat County	CO	Dean Carey	1996	859
344 3/8	48 0/8 48 4/8	42 3/8	9 7	Valley County	MT	Ernie Freebury	2003	859
344 3/8	51 6/8 53 3/8	36 7/8	6 7	Phillips County	MT	Andy Van Den Heuvel	2005	859
*344 3/8	43 7/8 43 7/8	36 0/8	7 8	Fergus County	MT	Robert Holtz	2007	859
344 2/8	49 0/8 48 4/8	38 4/8	6 6	Ravalli County	MT	Steven Welty	1987	866
344 2/8	52 1/8 50 6/8	39 4/8	6 6	Catron County	NM	J. B. Lemon	1995	866
344 2/8	55 3/8 56 2/8	36 2/8	7 7	Yakima County	WA	Ryan Lampers	2005	866
344 2/8	53 0/8 53 7/8	43 2/8	6 6	Sevier County	UT	Kelly Erickson	2006	866
*344 2/8	51 0/8 51 4/8	44 1/8	7 7	Fergus County	MT	Brett L. Foster	2009	866
*344 2/8	53 1/8 56 2/8	44 2/8	5 6	Ravalli County	MT	Teah-Rae J. Hinson	2010	866
344 1/8	49 0/8 50 6/8	36 5/8	6 6	Mesa County	CO	Dick Steele	1994	872
344 1/8	50 4/8 51 4/8	37 5/8	7 6	Petroleum County	MT	Arthur S. Kelsey III	2003	872
344 1/8	51 1/8 47 7/8	46 1/8	6 7	Catron County	NM	Mike Miller	2007	872
344 1/8	53 0/8 52 4/8	40 5/8	6 6	Greenlee County	AZ	Robert Samson	2007	872
344 0/8	49 7/8 52 7/8	41 4/8	6 7	Catron County	NM	Wayne Ludington	1985	876
344 0/8	57 0/8 53 3/8	38 6/8	6 6	Modoc County	CA	Jeremy Austin	2004	876
344 0/8	53 7/8 52 5/8	41 0/8	7 7	Cochise County	AZ	Richard Krug	2005	876
344 0/8	44 5/8 47 7/8	41 2/8	6 6	Mesa County	CO	Hunter Wayne Birchfield	2008	876
344 0/8	54 6/8 54 6/8	40 4/8	6 7	Hinsdale County	CO	Russ A. Moldenhauer	2010	876
344 0/8	54 0/8 55 1/8	35 0/8	6 6	Columbia County	WA	Daniel Dengate	2010	876
*344 0/8	52 5/8 52 1/8	38 0/8	6 6	Sheridan County	WY	Lance Baker	2010	876
343 7/8	49 0/8 49 4/8	42 3/8	6 6	Union County	OR	Craig Gorham	1983	883
343 7/8	50 7/8 50 2/8	36 5/8	6 6	Grant County	NM	Randall Madding	1991	883
343 7/8	52 0/8 51 2/8	41 5/8	6 6	Catron County	NM	Tim Friday	1995	883
343 7/8	51 3/8 51 0/8	35 1/8	8 7	Catron County	NM	David M. Podany, Sr.	2004	883
343 7/8	53 0/8 52 7/8	41 1/8	7 7	Musselshell County	MT	Jerry E. Dollard	2005	883
343 6/8	45 6/8 46 2/8	45 2/8	6 6	Catron County	NM	Russell Gash	1990	888
343 6/8	50 2/8 48 4/8	41 6/8	6 7	Cascade County	MT	Leighton Dresch	1996	888
343 6/8	54 6/8 55 4/8	38 2/8	6 6	Coconino County	AZ	Daniel P. Cartwright	1997	888
343 6/8	47 0/8 49 4/8	37 4/8	6 7	Daggett County	UT	Steven Tyler Fuller	2000	888
*343 6/8	41 4/8 43 4/8	41 4/8	7 7	Rich County	UT	Tres Childs	2005	888
343 6/8	54 0/8 53 5/8	35 0/8	6 6	Albany County	WY	Dan Bryant	2010	888
343 5/8	52 4/8 55 3/8	38 7/8	6 7	Coconino County	AZ	J. R. Wilhelmy	1976	894
343 5/8	48 5/8 53 0/8	39 3/8	6 6	Catron County	NM	Ralph "Abe" Meline	1992	894
343 5/8	55 3/8 57 7/8	37 1/8	6 7	Grant County	NM	Toby B. Rascon	1993	894
343 5/8	43 0/8 42 3/8	32 3/8	8 8	Lewis & Clark County	MT	Dennis Perkins	1993	894
343 5/8	54 4/8 53 6/8	33 7/8	6 6	Navajo County	AZ	Randy Ulmer	1995	894
343 5/8	50 4/8 52 4/8	41 7/8	6 6	Lemhi County	ID	Gabriel R. Gibbons	1998	894
343 5/8	45 7/8 43 7/8	33 0/8	6 8	Lawrence County	SD	Bill Rentz	2000	894
343 5/8	51 6/8 52 3/8	42 7/8	6 6	Mineral County	MT	Vayeeleng K. Moua	2000	894
343 5/8	50 0/8 51 2/8	37 1/8	6 6	Fergus County	MT	Josef K. Rud	2002	894
343 5/8	53 0/8 50 5/8	36 1/8	6 6	Hot Springs County	WY	Kregg L. Thomassen	2004	894
343 4/8	49 2/8 46 6/8	49 5/8	6 6	Grand County	CO	Leon Lambert	1981	904
343 4/8	49 2/8 47 0/8	37 6/8	6 6	Lemhi County	ID	Roger Brockhoff	1985	904
343 4/8	51 4/8 52 1/8	38 4/8	6 7	Socorro County	NM	Richard Dewey	1986	904
343 4/8	53 7/8 52 4/8	44 6/8	6 6	Sierra County	NM	Robert A. Maurin III	1992	904
343 4/8	52 3/8 51 1/8	44 0/8	6 6	Grant County	OR	Donald R. Hardman	2001	904
343 4/8	52 3/8 50 7/8	44 4/8	6 6	Valley County	ID	Ronald E. Pontius	2003	904
343 3/8	58 5/8 59 5/8	40 7/8	6 7	Mesa County	CO	Don Boyles	1990	910
343 3/8	48 3/8 46 7/8	39 7/8	7 7	Sublette County	WY	John C. Prince	1994	910
343 3/8	48 6/8 49 2/8	39 1/8	6 6	Meagher County	MT	Dennis Rehse	2003	910
343 3/8	49 1/8 49 7/8	40 7/8	6 6	Beaverhead County	MT	Bill Fuller	2005	910
343 3/8	52 4/8 52 3/8	38 1/8	6 6	Sanpete County	UT	Jason M. Eldredge	2008	910
343 2/8	52 2/8 51 2/8	40 0/8	6 6	Idaho County	ID	Mike Schlegel	1978	915
343 2/8	51 7/8 52 7/8	42 3/8	7 7	Morgan County	UT	Warren Strickland	1993	915
343 2/8	49 2/8 46 1/8	40 2/8	8 6	Yellowstone County	MT	Richard D. Cunningham	1997	915
343 2/8	56 6/8 55 6/8	53 2/8	7 6	Beaver County	UT	Kasey Willden	1998	915
343 2/8	52 6/8 55 0/8	36 6/8	6 7	Chouteau County	MT	Ron Sperl	1998	915
*343 2/8	51 0/8 52 4/8	45 6/8	6 6	Garfield County	UT	Chad C. Nelson	2009	915
343 1/8	50 3/8 54 3/8	42 5/8	7 6	Coconino County	AZ	Jeff Currey	1997	921
343 1/8	48 5/8 46 3/8	40 3/8	6 6	Catron County	NM	Dicky Massey	1999	921
343 1/8	48 7/8 48 6/8	42 1/8	6 6	Wallowa County	OR	Pat Niemi	2002	921
343 1/8	51 3/8 53 2/8	45 3/8	6 6	Gem County	ID	Scott E. McGann	2005	921
343 1/8	46 3/8 45 1/8	42 1/8	6 6	Skamania County	WA	Roy Ostroski	2007	921
343 1/8	53 2/8 52 4/8	37 5/8	7 6	Coconino County	AZ	Jenn Rose	2007	921
343 0/8	54 4/8 52 7/8	38 2/8	6 6	Fergus County	MT	Doug Sereday	1993	927
343 0/8	55 0/8 50 2/8	43 6/8	8 9	Coconino County	AZ	Tom Jensen	1994	927
343 0/8	57 2/8 52 0/8	42 0/8	6 6	Socorro County	NM	Anthony J. Turrietta	1995	927
343 0/8	51 2/8 53 3/8	40 2/8	7 7	Catron County	NM	Charles M. "Chip" Caravati	2001	927
342 7/8	54 3/8 54 3/8	42 2/8	8 8	Grand County	CO	G. Fred Asbell	1980	931
342 7/8	56 3/8 56 1/8	43 0/8	7 6	Catron County	NM	Bill Elmer	1991	931
342 7/8	54 6/8 56 3/8	44 1/8	6 6	Coconino County	AZ	Rusty K. Kappel	1992	931
342 7/8	56 4/8 56 5/8	37 7/8	6 6	Petroleum County	MT	James C. Miller	1998	931
342 7/8	55 0/8 52 6/8	41 7/8	6 6	Coconino County	AZ	John Webster	1998	931
342 7/8	52 2/8 52 2/8	49 5/8	6 6	Coconino County	AZ	Brian Bejarano	1998	931
342 7/8	51 1/8 50 4/8	38 7/8	6 7	Fremont County	ID	David H. Jones	2000	931
342 7/8	54 4/8 55 0/8	31 1/8	7 7	Fergus County	MT	Walter H. Rud	2000	931
342 7/8	52 6/8 50 0/8	41 7/8	6 6	Millard County	UT	Doug Noland	2001	931
342 7/8	51 4/8 53 4/8	47 7/8	6 6	Lincoln County	WY	Bill Swett	2001	931
342 7/8	52 0/8 51 2/8	42 4/8	6 6	Grand County	CO	Kevin J. Gee	2009	931
342 6/8	48 5/8 49 4/8	46 0/8	5 6	Catron County	NM	Carlton Armstrong	1990	942
342 6/8	51 4/8 52 6/8	41 4/8	6 6	Catron County	NM	Glenn W. Isler	1992	942
342 6/8	50 6/8 50 4/8	40 4/8	6 6	Colfax County	NM	Robert Torstenson	1995	942
342 6/8	53 3/8 51 0/8	38 3/8	6 7	Valencia County	NM	Paul H. Becraft	2002	942
342 6/8	51 5/8 50 3/8	43 0/8	7 6	Wallowa County	OR	Stanley E. Grove	2007	942
342 6/8	51 0/8 50 4/8	51 7/8	6 6	Garfield County	UT	Merritt C. Compton	2009	942
342 6/8	48 4/8 46 6/8	38 3/8	6 6	Routt County	CO	Brad Jones	1987	948
342 5/8	53 2/8 49 4/8	36 1/8	6 6	Coconino County	AZ	Victor Lee	1991	948
342 5/8	58 0/8 58 7/8	42 1/8	6 7	Coconino County	AZ	Mark G. Worischeck	2003	948

687

AMERICAN ELK (TYPICAL ANTLERS)

Minimum Score 260 Continued

SCORE	LENGTH OF R MAIN BEAM L	INSIDE SPREAD	NUMBER OF R POINTS L		AREA	STATE/ PROVINCE	HUNTER'S NAME	DATE	RANK
342 4/8	55 4/8	55 0/8	42 0/8	6	6	Morgan County	UT	Hugh H. Hogle	1990	951
342 4/8	50 0/8	49 3/8	37 3/8	7	7	Archuleta County	CO	M. R. James	1996	951
342 4/8	50 5/8	50 7/8	35 2/8	6	6	Catron County	NM	Gary Wisdom	1997	951
342 4/8	50 0/8	47 0/8	42 0/8	7	7	White Pine County	NV	Daniel J. Martter	2001	951
342 4/8	52 1/8	53 6/8	39 0/8	7	6	Catron County	NM	Lon E. Lauber	2004	951
342 4/8	52 0/8	48 5/8	43 2/8	6	6	Catron County	NM	Richard Crombie	2004	951
342 4/8	53 7/8	53 3/8	47 2/8	7	6	Gallatin County	MT	Cass Bolton	2009	951
342 3/8	54 7/8	53 7/8	42 5/8	6	6	Flathead County	MT	Eric Schmidt	1994	958
342 3/8	46 1/8	46 0/8	48 3/8	7	7	Garfield County	MT	Steve Rehak	1998	958
342 3/8	51 6/8	50 7/8	45 3/8	6	7	Douglas County	CO	Tony Burmester	1998	958
*342 3/8	48 1/8	49 7/8	43 1/8	6	6	Shoshone County	ID	Clint Helvey	2009	958
342 3/8	50 6/8	51 7/8	47 1/8	7	7	Musselshell County	MT	Kevin W. Weed	2009	958
342 2/8	49 7/8	49 2/8	37 2/8	6	6	Grant County	NM	Larry M. Sellers	1985	963
342 2/8	49 2/8	48 6/8	35 1/8	6	7	Uintah County	UT	Charles "Smiley" Denver	1988	963
342 2/8	49 6/8	48 4/8	35 6/8	8	7	Coconino County	AZ	Gary Steinmann	1991	963
342 2/8	56 6/8	56 4/8	35 4/8	7	7	Catron County	NM	David H. Boland	1992	963
342 2/8	50 6/8	50 4/8	40 6/8	6	6	Petroleum County	MT	Michael R. Johnson	1994	963
342 2/8	49 6/8	51 5/8	40 4/8	6	6	Fergus County	MT	John Kryfka	1998	963
342 2/8	54 6/8	54 1/8	38 4/8	6	6	Coconino County	AZ	Jerry Fails	2003	963
*342 2/8	48 0/8	45 5/8	35 4/8	7	7	Beaverlodge	ALB	Derek Olson	2009	963
342 1/8	52 3/8	52 4/8	45 1/8	6	6	Routt County	CO	Jerry A. Krueger	1981	971
342 1/8	53 7/8	50 4/8	34 7/8	6	7	Jackson County	OR	J. T. Tepper	1986	971
342 1/8	47 0/8	48 6/8	34 5/8	6	6	Coconino County	AZ	Lynn M. Johnson	1994	971
342 1/8	49 5/8	48 4/8	41 3/8	6	6	Coconino County	AZ	George Richardson	1995	971
342 1/8	49 1/8	51 1/8	38 5/8	7	7	Coconino County	AZ	Steve Porter	1999	971
342 1/8	47 5/8	45 5/8	40 3/8	6	7	Petroleum County	MT	Derek Taylor	2002	971
342 1/8	55 6/8	53 1/8	38 5/8	8	7	Cibola County	NM	Chuck Polzin	2004	971
*342 1/8	52 2/8	50 6/8	45 2/8	7	7	Boulder County	CO	Edward Ivkov	2005	971
342 1/8	51 6/8	53 0/8	44 5/8	6	6	Madison County	MT	Leo E. Evans	2009	971
342 1/8	57 2/8	55 3/8	37 1/8	6	6	Ferry County	WA	Kyle Pomrankey	2010	971
342 0/8	58 6/8	59 0/8	46 6/8	6	6	Cibola County	NM	Dois R. Chesshir	1986	981
342 0/8	56 1/8	55 7/8	40 0/8	6	7	Socorro County	NM	Tom Alvin	1992	981
342 0/8	52 4/8	54 5/8	40 6/8	6	8	Socorro County	NM	Randall C. Barnes	1996	981
342 0/8	48 6/8	49 1/8	35 4/8	6	6	Mineral County	CO	Kenneth L. Ryan	1996	981
342 0/8	53 4/8	53 0/8	45 4/8	6	6	Clark County	ID	Dale Goytowski	2001	981
342 0/8	48 0/8	50 7/8	34 0/8	6	6	Gila County	AZ	Kevin Harms	2002	981
342 0/8	51 7/8	46 3/8	40 0/8	6	6	Park County	WY	Tom Buller	2005	981
341 7/8	49 5/8	50 2/8	37 4/8	7	8	Fergus County	MT	Keith Meckling	1992	988
341 7/8	50 6/8	50 6/8	44 1/8	6	6	Umatilla County	OR	Don Sturm	1997	988
341 7/8	59 3/8	55 2/8	47 5/8	7	6	Kittitas County	WA	Brad Goodwin	2003	988
341 6/8	54 7/8	53 1/8	44 2/8	6	6	Greenlee County	AZ	Pete Shepley	1983	991
341 6/8	55 3/8	53 3/8	45 6/8	6	6	Garfield County	CO	Gary Frauenkron	1983	991
341 6/8	55 3/8	55 0/8	33 5/8	7	7	Catron County	NM	Mike Hillis	1988	991
341 6/8	51 4/8	50 1/8	38 3/8	7	7	Grant County	NM	Dick Stoll	1989	991
341 6/8	50 3/8	52 0/8	48 0/8	6	6	Kittitas County	WA	Cindy Coker	1993	991
341 6/8	49 1/8	48 7/8	39 4/8	6	6	Socorro County	NM	Don Carpenter	1998	991
341 6/8	53 3/8	50 4/8	43 0/8	6	6	Broadwater County	MT	Jeremiah J. Theys	2002	991
341 6/8	46 3/8	46 0/8	35 2/8	6	6	Grande Prairie	ALB	Rock Weeks	2005	991
341 5/8	54 4/8	56 2/8	44 3/8	6	6	Socorro County	NM	Ross Johnson	1982	999
341 5/8	54 1/8	52 2/8	45 1/8	6	6	Garfield County	MT	Darryl Turner	1985	999
341 5/8	47 0/8	47 2/8	39 3/8	6	6	Clackamas County	OR	Paul Smith	1987	999
341 5/8	48 7/8	46 5/8	33 7/8	6	6	Navajo County	AZ	Leon W. Smith	1989	999
341 5/8	51 0/8	51 2/8	36 5/8	6	6	Petroleum County	MT	Randy Jonjak	1992	999
341 4/8	45 6/8	47 5/8	37 4/8	6	6	Las Animas County	CO	Douglas F. Murray	1974	1004
341 4/8	53 4/8	54 6/8	36 6/8	6	6	Pitkin County	CO	Nelson Harrington	1977	1004
341 4/8	50 5/8	48 5/8	39 4/8	6	6	Adams County	ID	Emery Meeks	1982	1004
341 4/8	52 3/8	51 7/8	46 0/8	7	7	Routt County	CO	Todd Bandemer	1991	1004
341 4/8	51 6/8	52 0/8	31 2/8	6	6	Jefferson County	CO	Mickey Wirth	1992	1004
341 4/8	51 4/8	52 4/8	40 2/8	7	6	Lake County	OR	Jody E. Ward	2001	1004
*341 4/8	55 1/8	53 5/8	44 6/8	6	6	Elko County	NV	Gordon G. Smith	2006	1004
341 4/8	45 3/8	45 1/8	29 0/8	6	6	Petroleum County	MT	Ryan Rusley	2009	1004
341 3/8	47 7/8	48 1/8	44 5/8	6	6	Chaffee County	CO	Tom E. Bowman	1979	1012
341 3/8	54 0/8	52 3/8	37 7/8	9	7	Missoula County	MT	Ted Miller	1984	1012
341 3/8	54 1/8	51 6/8	42 3/8	6	6	McKinley County	NM	Glenn W. Isler	1988	1012
341 3/8	49 7/8	50 4/8	46 2/8	7	7	Canmore	ALB	Lee Oshust	1989	1012
341 3/8	55 6/8	53 4/8	35 3/8	7	7	Klickitat County	WA	Bill "Razz" Philley, Jr.	1991	1012
341 3/8	51 0/8	48 4/8	38 7/8	6	6	Catron County	NM	Robert A. Williams	1993	1012
341 3/8	52 6/8	51 4/8	38 1/8	6	6	Navajo County	AZ	Francis J. Meyers	1998	1012
341 3/8	50 3/8	50 1/8	35 7/8	6	6	Power County	ID	Dave R. Burget	2001	1012
*341 3/8	51 5/8	49 6/8	39 3/8	6	6	Las Animas County	CO	Cameron R. Hanes	2005	1012
341 2/8	53 0/8	54 6/8	44 6/8	6	7	Coconino County	AZ	Dean Dunaway	1991	1021
341 2/8	51 7/8	51 0/8	38 4/8	7	7	Umatilla County	OR	Tim Guild	1996	1021
341 1/8	55 5/8	55 4/8	33 1/8	6	6	Crook County	OR	Lynn Pettit	1983	1023
341 1/8	55 5/8	53 2/8	37 5/8	6	6	Fergus County	MT	Dan Johnson	1999	1023
341 1/8	47 0/8	47 4/8	39 5/8	7	7	Fergus County	MT	Lynn Bowman	2010	1023
341 0/8	53 0/8	53 0/8	42 6/8	6	6	Custer County	ID	John R. Sample	1986	1026
341 0/8	54 2/8	54 1/8	40 6/8	6	6	Catron County	NM	Ronnie Coburn	1986	1026
341 0/8	55 5/8	54 4/8	40 4/8	6	6	White Pine County	NV	Justin T. Williams	1994	1026
341 0/8	53 0/8	53 5/8	39 4/8	6	7	Catron County	NM	Brian Harrington	1998	1026
341 0/8	51 7/8	52 4/8	46 3/8	6	8	Wasatch County	UT	Preston Muir	2003	1026
341 0/8	51 3/8	52 5/8	41 4/8	6	6	Custer County	ID	Cory A. Beverly	2003	1026
341 0/8	51 1/8	51 6/8	35 2/8	6	6	Coconino County	AZ	Gary Martin	2003	1026
341 0/8	51 2/8	53 2/8	43 0/8	6	6	Albany County	WY	Eric Otero	2004	1026
341 0/8	55 0/8	55 5/8	43 7/8	7	6	White Pine County	NV	Kenneth A. Zimny	2006	1026
340 7/8	54 7/8	54 5/8	35 7/8	7	7	Boise County	ID	George A. Foote	1962	1035
340 7/8	48 1/8	47 4/8	37 5/8	6	6	Carbon County	WY	Roger Swensen	1977	1035
340 7/8	56 3/8	56 4/8	39 5/8	7	7	Yakima County	WA	Randy Kaech	1986	1035
340 7/8	54 7/8	52 7/8	40 0/8	6	7	Coconino County	AZ	Kevin B. Call	1994	1035
340 7/8	46 2/8	42 3/8	41 3/8	6	6	Washakie County	WY	Scott Long	1997	1035
340 7/8	50 4/8	50 1/8	49 1/8	6	6	Boise County	ID	Kenneth Hyde	1998	1035
340 7/8	50 7/8	49 4/8	42 3/8	6	6	Las Animas County	CO	Pat Powell	2000	1035
340 7/8	53 2/8	54 2/8	37 1/8	6	7	Clearwater County	ID	Pat Garrett	2004	1035
340 7/8	55 5/8	52 6/8	40 3/8	6	6	White Pine County	NV	James Davis	2007	1035
340 6/8	56 2/8	59 5/8	33 6/8	6	6	Coconino County	AZ	Earnest E. Milton	1976	1044
340 6/8	54 0/8	51 7/8	41 2/8	7	6	Petroleum County	MT	John 'Rosey' Roseland	1983	1044

688

AMERICAN ELK (TYPICAL ANTLERS)

Minimum Score 260

Continued

SCORE	LENGTH OF R MAIN BEAM L	INSIDE SPREAD	NUMBER OF R POINTS L		AREA	STATE/ PROVINCE	HUNTER'S NAME	DATE	RANK
340 6/8	46 0/8 46 4/8	40 2/8	6	6	Granite County	MT	Tom Adams	1991	1044
340 6/8	48 2/8 46 4/8	40 2/8	6	6	Larimer County	CO	Arnold Hale	1992	1044
340 6/8	52 5/8 52 0/8	46 2/8	6	6	Lemhi County	ID	David Tande	1994	1044
340 6/8	51 6/8 49 6/8	35 2/8	6	6	Coconino County	AZ	John D. Audsley	1997	1044
340 6/8	54 0/8 52 4/8	44 0/8	6	7	Garfield County	MT	Rick L. Stauffer	1999	1044
340 6/8	55 0/8 52 2/8	40 4/8	6	6	Navajo County	AZ	Chuck McDonald	1999	1044
*340 6/8	52 7/8 53 5/8	39 0/8	7	6	Socorro County	NM	Tom Alvin	2006	1044
340 6/8	55 5/8 54 6/8	43 6/8	6	6	Coconino County	AZ	Robert Gerlak	2006	1044
340 6/8	52 1/8 49 6/8	46 6/8	6	6	Maugher County	MT	Jim Kennedy	2008	1044
*340 6/8	54 2/8 53 7/8	38 6/8	6	6	Larimer County	CO	Don Stachowiak	2010	1044
340 5/8	47 3/8 48 6/8	33 1/8	6	6	Nordegg	ALB	Thaddaus Fenske	1978	1056
340 5/8	54 5/8 53 2/8	39 1/8	6	6	Coconino County	AZ	Gregory S. Wood	1990	1056
340 5/8	52 4/8 54 6/8	41 3/8	6	6	Sierra County	NM	Dr. Hamid Massiha	1991	1056
340 5/8	54 2/8 53 7/8	40 7/8	6	7	Coconino County	AZ	Paul Hicks	1991	1056
340 5/8	58 3/8 55 5/8	42 4/8	6	7	Catron County	NM	Walter Palmer	1994	1056
340 5/8	51 2/8 52 1/8	38 4/8	7	7	Shoshone County	ID	Matt Capka	1998	1056
340 5/8	52 3/8 50 1/8	40 3/8	7	7	Las Animas County	CO	Donald Travis	2002	1056
340 5/8	47 0/8 47 1/8	35 3/8	7	8	Park County	MT	Fred Regenfuss	2005	1056
340 5/8	52 4/8 51 1/8	33 6/8	7	8	Park County	WY	Bryan McKenzie	2006	1056
340 4/8	51 5/8 49 1/8	41 2/8	6	6	Sanders County	MT	Walt Borgmann	1983	1065
340 4/8	51 0/8 52 4/8	42 0/8	6	7	Catron County	NM	Brice McWethy	1985	1065
340 4/8	50 6/8 50 5/8	39 2/8	6	7	Sierra County	NM	Tony L. Jones	1988	1065
340 4/8	53 2/8 54 6/8	44 6/8	6	6	Morgan County	UT	Patrick Hogle	1994	1065
340 4/8	53 3/8 53 3/8	35 2/8	6	6	Piute County	UT	Kelly Parry	1999	1065
340 3/8	51 0/8 51 1/8	38 1/8	6	6	Crook County	OR	Curtis Edwards	1989	1070
340 3/8	51 1/8 48 4/8	33 5/8	7	6	Catron County	NM	Manuel Baeza	1998	1070
*340 3/8	53 0/8 51 4/8	43 5/8	6	6	Edson	ALB	Gary Meropoulis	2003	1070
340 3/8	51 1/8 53 7/8	43 1/8	6	6	White Pine County	NV	Rick Lund	2004	1070
*340 3/8	51 7/8 53 0/8	36 5/8	7	7	Otero County	NM	W. Bruce Brown	2005	1070
340 3/8	50 3/8 50 7/8	34 3/8	6	6	Catron County	NM	Glenn Hubman	2005	1070
340 2/8	53 3/8 54 2/8	40 4/8	6	6	Missoula County	MT	David M. Anderson	1978	1076
340 2/8	50 4/8 51 3/8	36 7/8	7	6	Socorro County	NM	Randy B. Furr	1983	1076
340 2/8	54 4/8 56 2/8	43 2/8	6	7	Catron County	NM	John Fehrenbacher	1986	1076
340 2/8	50 6/8 50 7/8	37 4/8	6	6	Lincoln County	NM	Tony L. Najar	1993	1076
340 2/8	51 1/8 50 7/8	45 4/8	6	6	Hudson Bay	SAS	Kenneth Baker	1994	1076
340 2/8	55 4/8 57 1/8	38 2/8	6	6	Coconino County	AZ	Duane A. Wilson, Jr.	1994	1076
340 2/8	54 5/8 55 6/8	41 2/8	6	6	Flathead County	MT	Erik Wenum	1994	1076
340 2/8	51 1/8 49 0/8	43 2/8	6	7	Umatilla County	OR	Andrew N. Mentzer	2000	1076
340 2/8	48 0/8 47 7/8	39 4/8	7	6	Farrell Creek	BC	Ron Miller	2001	1076
340 2/8	52 5/8 51 1/8	35 6/8	6	6	Coconino County	AZ	Danny Howard	2004	1076
340 1/8	52 2/8 52 6/8	46 7/8	6	6	Coconino County	AZ	Richard H. Wetnight	1984	1086
340 1/8	52 1/8 50 5/8	43 7/8	6	6	Judith Basin County	MT	Jeffrey M. Smith	1998	1086
340 1/8	51 2/8 49 7/8	44 3/8	8	6	San Juan County	UT	J. Scott Krahenbuhl	2002	1086
*340 1/8	51 7/8 50 6/8	42 5/8	6	6	Mesa County	CO	Ronald Dotson	2006	1086
340 0/8	49 2/8 50 7/8	37 4/8	7	7	Flathead County	MT	Henry Herman	1984	1090
340 0/8	53 4/8 53 3/8	42 4/8	6	6	Converse County	WY	Russell Brines	1999	1090
340 0/8	52 1/8 52 2/8	43 6/8	8	7	Ravalli County	MT	Steve Kamps	2002	1090
340 0/8	52 7/8 51 5/8	33 2/8	7	6	Navajo County	AZ	Thomas Groves	2003	1090
*340 0/8	54 1/8 52 7/8	45 0/8	7	6	Musselshell County	MT	Dale Godfrey	2009	1090
339 7/8	52 6/8 53 3/8	38 1/8	6	6	Yavapai County	AZ	Gene Barcak	1991	1095
339 6/8	47 7/8 46 7/8	41 4/8	6	6	Lewis & Clark County	MT	Doug J. Powell	1983	1096
339 6/8	51 4/8 51 4/8	46 4/8	6	6	Otero County	NM	Bonnie A. Allen	1987	1096
339 6/8	50 5/8 50 6/8	42 6/8	6	6	Beaver County	UT	Calvin Dalke	1995	1096
339 6/8	51 6/8 52 1/8	35 0/8	6	6	Niton Junction	ALB	Ron Sargent	1996	1096
339 6/8	51 0/8 50 3/8	45 0/8	7	6	Taos County	NM	Mike Wolff	1999	1096
*339 6/8	54 3/8 55 1/8	38 6/8	6	6	Costilla County	CO	Jeremiah Johnson	2006	1096
339 6/8	52 4/8 51 3/8	50 2/8	6	6	Apache County	AZ	Roger Soderberg	2006	1096
*339 6/8	57 6/8 59 1/8	42 2/8	5	6	Larimer County	CO	Dale Nixon	2010	1096
339 5/8	51 6/8 53 5/8	47 1/8	6	6	Coconino County	AZ	Bruce D. Ludeke	1977	1104
339 5/8	45 2/8 43 3/8	44 7/8	6	7	Bighorn Mtns.	WY	Edward F. Hanlon	1979	1104
339 5/8	45 4/8 45 5/8	39 1/8	6	6	Sanders County	MT	Robert A. Sieloff	1994	1104
339 5/8	48 6/8 54 7/8	45 1/8	7	7	Catron County	NM	Ray Hammond	1999	1104
339 5/8	50 0/8 46 6/8	48 2/8	6	7	Apache County	AZ	J. Agustin Ballesteros	2003	1104
339 4/8	49 0/8 48 7/8	38 0/8	7	7	Grant County	OR	Dan Dorn	1986	1109
339 4/8	51 3/8 50 5/8	39 2/8	6	6	Mineral County	MT	Tom Porter	1986	1109
339 4/8	51 0/8 51 2/8	38 0/8	6	7	Colfax County	NM	Christopher Green	1990	1109
339 4/8	51 0/8 50 5/8	40 6/8	6	6	Rio Arriba County	NM	Brit Bower	2000	1109
*339 4/8	52 1/8 49 0/8	39 2/8	6	6	Gallatin County	MT	Chris Beilke	2004	1109
339 4/8	53 0/8 51 3/8	41 0/8	6	6	Park County	MT	Dustin Burns	2006	1109
339 4/8	50 5/8 48 7/8	42 4/8	6	6	Sierra County	NM	David L. Keith	2007	1109
339 4/8	49 7/8 52 5/8	41 6/8	6	6	Powder River County	MT	Jerry Klemm	2010	1109
339 3/8	48 4/8 49 5/8	42 1/8	6	6	Cibola County	NM	Delbert Mariano	1980	1117
339 3/8	47 4/8 44 7/8	43 6/8	6	7	Petroleum County	MT	Steven A. Barstow	1989	1117
339 3/8	51 5/8 52 3/8	40 7/8	6	7	Catron County	NM	David Rodriguez	1999	1117
339 3/8	50 0/8 50 5/8	40 1/8	6	6	Madison County	ID	Rick W. Elliott	2000	1117
339 2/8	51 7/8 51 0/8	40 6/8	7	6	Fremont County	ID	Gary Skoy	1981	1121
339 2/8	50 1/8 49 2/8	46 0/8	6	7	Iron County	UT	Luke Carter	2004	1121
*339 2/8	54 4/8 53 3/8	37 2/8	6	6	Caribou County	ID	Colt Johnson	2010	1121
339 1/8	50 5/8 49 5/8	42 6/8	6	7	Coconino County	AZ	Stretch Penberthy	1987	1124
339 1/8	56 0/8 52 7/8	39 3/8	6	6	Sublette County	WY	Tony Burchett	1988	1124
339 1/8	52 2/8 52 2/8	42 1/8	6	8	Grant County	OR	Brad Miller	1988	1124
339 1/8	47 5/8 46 3/8	40 3/8	9	8	Catron County	NM	Danny V. Bennett	1990	1124
339 1/8	44 1/8 44 4/8	34 4/8	7	7	Bonner County	ID	H. Dale Stone	1990	1124
339 1/8	54 4/8 54 4/8	48 1/8	6	6	Navajo County	AZ	Larry D. Jones	1993	1124
339 1/8	51 0/8 54 3/8	39 7/8	6	6	Coconino County	AZ	William C. Bolt, Jr.	1995	1124
339 1/8	50 3/8 50 2/8	42 7/8	6	7	Millarville	ALB	Stuart Sinclair-Smith	1995	1124
339 1/8	54 6/8 52 2/8	40 4/8	6	6	Catron County	NM	Kim E. Womer	1997	1124
339 1/8	54 6/8 54 3/8	41 5/8	6	6	Lemhi County	ID	Justin Freeman	1998	1124
339 0/8	50 6/8 51 2/8	45 4/8	6	6	Powell County	MT	Kenneth M. Darr	1996	1134
339 0/8	49 0/8 50 1/8	44 0/8	6	6	Catron County	NM	Gerard Pugliese	1997	1134
339 0/8	47 0/8 46 6/8	40 0/8	6	6	Gallatin County	MT	Kurt D. Rued	2000	1134
339 0/8	45 2/8 45 2/8	34 3/8	6	7	Carberry	MAN	Mark Fisk	2001	1134
339 0/8	53 4/8 54 7/8	39 0/8	6	6	Socorro County	NM	Doug Aikin	2005	1134
339 0/8	50 3/8 49 2/8	33 5/8	7	6	Fergus County	MT	Dennis Seyfert	2008	1134
338 7/8	55 6/8 54 2/8	38 1/8	6	6	Catron County	NM	Stan Maynes	1999	1140

689

AMERICAN ELK (TYPICAL ANTLERS)

Minimum Score 260   Continued

SCORE	LENGTH OF MAIN BEAM R	L	INSIDE SPREAD	NUMBER OF POINTS R	L	AREA	STATE/ PROVINCE	HUNTER'S NAME	DATE	RANK
338 7/8	55 1/8	55 1/8	42 1/8	6	5	Mesa County	CO	Robert Mansell	2001	1140
338 7/8	47 0/8	45 6/8	44 7/8	6	6	Madison County	MT	Shane Shima	2002	1140
338 7/8	52 0/8	50 3/8	40 5/8	6	6	Park County	WY	Steven B. Pitsch	2004	1140
338 7/8	52 0/8	50 3/8	40 5/8	6	6	Petroleum County	MT	Tim Wood	2004	1140
*338 7/8	48 3/8	47 4/8	42 1/8	6	6	Petroleum County	MT	Tim Wood	2004	1140
338 6/8	45 6/8	45 6/8	43 0/8	6	7	Greenlee County	AZ	Jed Dahar	1989	1145
338 6/8	47 4/8	45 6/8	44 0/8	7	6	Beaverhead County	MT	Gene Loder	1991	1145
338 6/8	51 6/8	50 5/8	40 6/8	7	7	Grant County	NM	Lance Maloney	1997	1145
338 6/8	49 7/8	48 4/8	38 4/8	6	6	Coconino County	AZ	Frank T. Sandstedt	1997	1145
338 6/8	53 4/8	54 4/8	45 2/8	6	6	Park County	WY	Tim Raubinger	2000	1145
338 5/8	50 4/8	53 4/8	42 1/8	6	6	Rio Arriba County	NM	Lee Braudt	1983	1150
338 5/8	49 2/8	48 4/8	36 5/8	6	6	Lincoln County	WY	Doug Jenkins	1986	1150
338 5/8	53 7/8	55 0/8	39 3/8	5	6	Fremont County	ID	James R. Foote	1995	1150
338 5/8	50 7/8	49 5/8	42 3/8	6	7	Lemhi County	ID	Robert Reed	1996	1150
338 5/8	55 2/8	55 5/8	34 7/8	6	7	Idaho County	ID	Robert Maves	1998	1150
338 5/8	48 4/8	47 4/8	41 7/8	6	6	Utah County	UT	P. C. "Bo" Aughtry III	2008	1150
*338 5/8	46 3/8	46 7/8	40 5/8	6	7	Larimer County	CO	Pat Lefemine	2010	1150
338 4/8	49 2/8	49 6/8	29 2/8	6	6	Catron County	NM	Eugene Arndt	1993	1157
338 4/8	50 4/8	50 4/8	41 6/8	6	6	Smoky River	ALB	Norris Bates	1995	1157
338 4/8	51 1/8	51 5/8	37 0/8	6	6	Fergus County	MT	Karl J. Rud	2002	1157
*338 4/8	54 1/8	54 1/8	38 2/8	6	6	Dolores County	CO	Trent Danes	2007	1157
*338 4/8	54 7/8	55 2/8	34 2/8	7	6	Lawrence County	SD	Dean E. Mahaffy	2007	1157
338 3/8	55 5/8	54 0/8	36 7/8	6	6	Sheridan County	WY	Mike Barrett	1981	1162
338 3/8	50 4/8	52 1/8	34 1/8	6	6	Coconino County	AZ	Jeff Kammerzell	1999	1162
338 3/8	53 1/8	53 6/8	44 3/8	6	6	Park County	WY	Carol Niziolek	2002	1162
338 3/8	48 4/8	48 5/8	40 7/8	7	7	Yakima County	WA	Kevin Lane	2004	1162
338 3/8	49 4/8	48 2/8	39 5/8	6	6	Coconino County	AZ	Tom Eichorst	2008	1162
338 3/8	55 2/8	58 0/8	39 5/8	6	7	Musselshell County	MT	Pete Gierke	2008	1162
338 2/8	48 1/8	52 2/8	38 3/8	7	7	Garfield County	MT	Richard R. Chamberlin	1989	1168
338 2/8	47 7/8	47 4/8	36 2/8	7	6	Catron County	NM	Nick Arnett	1990	1168
338 2/8	49 0/8	51 0/8	39 6/8	7	7	Deer Lodge County	MT	Stephen Herrera	1990	1168
338 2/8	49 7/8	50 2/8	36 6/8	7	7	Natrona County	WY	Kevin Christopherson	1997	1168
338 2/8	51 1/8	48 2/8	41 6/8	6	6	Sanders County	MT	Darrell "Speed" Tessier	1998	1168
338 2/8	50 2/8	49 2/8	50 4/8	6	6	Kittitas County	WA	Bruce Hedlund	2002	1168
338 2/8	51 1/8	49 6/8	41 0/8	7	6	Taos County	NM	Sean D. Kelly	2004	1168
338 2/8	51 6/8	51 3/8	38 2/8	7	6	Johnson County	WY	Dawson D. Powers	2010	1168
338 1/8	50 4/8	50 5/8	37 1/8	7	7	Lincoln County	NM	Kurt Hollis	1987	1176
338 1/8	47 0/8	50 7/8	39 3/8	5	6	Lincoln County	WY	Gary L. Sims	1991	1176
*338 1/8	50 1/8	49 4/8	43 7/8	6	6	Lewis & Clark County	MT	John W. Meyer	2003	1176
338 1/8	50 4/8	50 5/8	37 5/8	6	6	Coconino County	AZ	Phillip C. Dalrymple	2006	1176
338 1/8	52 0/8	52 3/8	41 1/8	6	6	King County	WA	Cory P. McDonough	2009	1176
338 0/8	47 4/8	46 6/8	45 5/8	6	7	Caribou County	ID	Jim L. Fowler	1987	1181
338 0/8	53 5/8	54 7/8	41 6/8	6	7	Catron County	NM	James Baumgardner	1990	1181
338 0/8	51 4/8	52 5/8	41 0/8	6	6	Coconino County	AZ	Mike Leach	1991	1181
338 0/8	44 7/8	46 1/8	35 3/8	8	8	Apache County	AZ	Frank P. Martinez	1992	1181
338 0/8	55 4/8	53 3/8	40 0/8	6	6	Mesa County	CO	David G. Anderson	1994	1181
338 0/8	51 1/8	50 5/8	40 6/8	6	7	Umatilla County	OR	Donald W. Mittag	2003	1181
338 0/8	51 6/8	48 2/8	34 4/8	6	6	White Pine County	NV	Russell J. Draper	2005	1181
337 7/8	47 3/8	51 2/8	46 3/8	6	6	Sheridan County	WY	Mike Barrett	2001	1188
*337 7/8	48 2/8	47 1/8	44 7/8	7	6	Columbia County	WA	Tony Kunch	2010	1188
337 7/8	54 7/8	51 4/8	37 1/8	7	6	Latah County	ID	Isaac O. Reilly	2010	1188
337 6/8	45 0/8	46 0/8	37 4/8	6	7	Boulder County	CO	Roger Schuett	1977	1191
337 6/8	55 2/8	55 2/8	45 6/8	5	5	Socorro County	NM	Wesley Henderson	1986	1191
337 6/8	51 1/8	50 3/8	38 4/8	7	6	Coconino County	AZ	Robert Dishmon	1991	1191
337 6/8	47 6/8	49 0/8	42 0/8	7	7	Washakie County	WY	Roger Peabody	1991	1191
337 6/8	48 2/8	47 4/8	43 2/8	6	6	Otero County	NM	Allen Dalton	1991	1191
337 6/8	51 6/8	50 1/8	45 6/8	7	6	Converse County	WY	James M. Wolff	2000	1191
337 6/8	49 0/8	48 0/8	33 0/8	6	6	Greenlee County	AZ	Dennis Howell	2004	1191
*337 6/8	47 0/8	46 5/8	30 2/8	7	6	Petroleum County	MT	John Ilgenfritz	2008	1191
337 5/8	49 1/8	49 6/8	39 1/8	6	6	Granite County	MT	George E. Wood	1978	1199
337 5/8	52 1/8	52 6/8	37 3/8	6	6	Missoula County	MT	Mel Nyman, Jr.	1983	1199
337 5/8	49 3/8	51 2/8	36 1/8	6	6	Coconino County	AZ	Danny Eloy Martinez	1985	1199
337 5/8	53 1/8	53 2/8	34 4/8	7	6	Sierra County	NM	Jason Wenrick	2000	1199
337 5/8	48 2/8	49 7/8	36 5/8	6	7	Judith Basin County	MT	Neil Hamm	2000	1199
337 5/8	52 0/8	51 6/8	34 3/8	6	6	Jefferson County	CO	Robert B. Nicklow, Jr.	2001	1199
337 5/8	47 7/8	49 2/8	38 1/8	7	6	Fergus County	MT	Pete Gierke	2003	1199
337 5/8	49 1/8	50 4/8	29 1/8	7	7	Petroleum County	MT	Levi Johnson	2004	1199
337 5/8	50 5/8	50 4/8	41 7/8	6	6	Catron County	NM	Jeffrey Carl	2004	1199
337 4/8	52 3/8	54 5/8	41 4/8	7	6	Coconino County	AZ	Alan Blanchard	1972	1208
337 4/8	63 6/8	62 3/8	42 0/8	6	6	Coconino County	AZ	Gregory B. Minton	1992	1208
337 4/8	51 6/8	52 0/8	56 0/8	6	6	Converse County	WY	Mike Hammond	1998	1208
337 4/8	49 3/8	50 4/8	40 0/8	6	6	Moffat County	CO	Scott C. Wanstedt	1999	1208
337 4/8	56 4/8	54 5/8	41 4/8	7	6	Grant County	OR	Nate Simmons	2001	1208
337 4/8	46 6/8	45 6/8	40 2/8	6	7	Albany County	WY	Craig Koger	2002	1208
337 4/8	48 0/8	48 5/8	44 0/8	6	6	Catron County	NM	Holly L. Tow	2005	1208
337 4/8	49 7/8	50 0/8	36 6/8	7	6	Chouteau County	MT	Ray Gamradt	2005	1208
337 3/8	53 0/8	49 2/8	42 1/8	6	5	Mesa County	CO	Mike Flores	1970	1216
337 3/8	46 4/8	45 7/8	34 5/8	6	7	Rio Blanco County	CO	Jay Verzuh	1990	1216
337 3/8	55 2/8	50 0/8	35 5/8	6	6	Coconino County	AZ	Cindi Richardson	1995	1216
337 3/8	47 0/8	46 5/8	39 7/8	6	6	Las Animas County	CO	Peter Clifton Swenson	2000	1216
337 3/8	47 5/8	47 1/8	39 7/8	6	6	Converse County	WY	Mark Harris	2006	1216
337 2/8	48 2/8	49 4/8	41 6/8	6	8	Beaverhead County	MT	Theodore T. Ralls, Sr.	1990	1221
337 2/8	50 4/8	53 3/8	44 4/8	6	6	Coconino County	AZ	Henry L. Roberts	1990	1221
337 2/8	51 5/8	50 5/8	48 4/8	6	6	Lincoln County	NM	Wayne McMakin	1992	1221
337 2/8	51 0/8	50 2/8	39 2/8	6	6	Shoshone County	ID	Danny W. Scammel	1998	1221
337 2/8	46 0/8	47 4/8	35 6/8	6	6	Coconino County	AZ	Robert Hanneman	2004	1221
337 2/8	51 0/8	51 2/8	42 6/8	6	6	Catron County	NM	Gordon Green	2005	1221
337 2/8	53 2/8	52 2/8	41 0/8	6	6	Flathead County	MT	Steven Barta	2006	1221
337 1/8	51 3/8	50 0/8	37 3/8	6	6	Catron County	NM	Larry Evanson	1992	1228
337 1/8	51 1/8	51 2/8	42 1/8	6	6	Mesa County	CO	Don Boyles	1993	1228
337 1/8	51 4/8	50 0/8	37 7/8	6	7	Catron County	NM	Bill L. Marek	1998	1228
337 1/8	49 4/8	49 0/8	37 7/8	6	6	Wallowa County	OR	Joseph F. Mitchell	2005	1228
*337 1/8	51 5/8	50 3/8	43 2/8	7	6	Apache County	AZ	Scott Keetch	2009	1228
337 0/8	52 4/8	51 4/8	38 2/8	6	6	Socorro County	NM	Ron White	1976	1233
337 0/8	57 6/8	57 6/8	36 2/8	7	7	Lewis County	WA	Terry I LaFrance	1984	1233
337 0/8	50 3/8	50 3/8	41 6/8	6	6	Albany County	WY	Gordon Wigdahl	1997	1233

690

AMERICAN ELK (TYPICAL ANTLERS)

Minimum Score 260   Continued

SCORE	LENGTH OF R MAIN BEAM L	INSIDE SPREAD	NUMBER OF R POINTS L	AREA	STATE/ PROVINCE	HUNTER'S NAME	DATE	RANK
337 0/8	48 1/8 50 3/8	41 1/8	6 7	White Pine County	NV	Marvin Rowley	2003	1233
337 0/8	52 4/8 54 5/8	33 0/8	6 7	Broadwater County	MT	Brock A. Thomas	2006	1233
*337 0/8	53 0/8 51 0/8	38 4/8	6 6	Musselshell County	MT	Steve Ness	2006	1233
337 0/8	55 6/8 56 1/8	34 4/8	6 6	San Juan County	UT	Bryan Cowley	2009	1233
336 7/8	49 3/8 48 0/8	43 1/8	7 7	Apache County	AZ	Eric Penrod	1982	1240
336 7/8	53 1/8 53 1/8	37 5/8	6 6	Missoula County	MT	Pao K. Moua	1996	1240
336 7/8	55 7/8 55 4/8	36 7/8	6 6	Johnson County	WY	Warren L. March, Jr.	1999	1240
336 7/8	52 5/8 51 2/8	40 4/8	7 6	Apache County	AZ	Brad Wedding	2002	1240
336 7/8	51 0/8 47 2/8	47 4/8	7 7	Otero County	NM	John W. Sword	2003	1240
336 7/8	50 2/8 51 2/8	39 2/8	7 6	Washakie County	WY	Luke Roush	2006	1240
336 7/8	47 2/8 49 2/8	42 1/8	7 7	Columbia County	WA	Daren Dahlman	2007	1240
336 7/8	50 3/8 50 6/8	42 1/8	7 7	Pend Oreille County	WA	Gary Lakey	2007	1240
*336 7/8	52 7/8 52 5/8	45 3/8	7 6	Petroleum County	MT	Mark Gregorich	2007	1240
336 7/8	48 4/8 50 4/8	36 1/8	6 6	Tooele County	UT	Russell Johnson	2010	1240
336 6/8	50 7/8 51 3/8	34 6/8	6 7	Uintah County	UT	Everett Burson	1981	1250
336 6/8	53 5/8 53 3/8	39 4/8	6 6	Taos County	NM	Jeff Lampe	1992	1250
336 6/8	53 5/8 51 0/8	32 6/8	6 6	Catron County	NM	Glen P. Gerhart	1992	1250
336 6/8	48 1/8 48 6/8	50 4/8	6 6	Beaverhead County	MT	Corey W. Murray	1993	1250
336 6/8	50 3/8 50 1/8	39 2/8	6 6	Park County	WY	William Manske	1994	1250
336 6/8	46 6/8 48 6/8	41 6/8	6 7	Fremont County	ID	Kendon H. Jensen	1998	1250
336 6/8	50 2/8 50 2/8	43 2/8	6 6	Caribou County	ID	Tim J. Solberg	2002	1250
336 6/8	51 4/8 49 0/8	37 0/8	6 6	Garfield County	UT	Mark M. Munson, Jr.	2004	1250
336 6/8	52 6/8 53 6/8	35 6/8	5 6	Catron County	NM	Richard W. Wahl	2005	1250
336 5/8	46 7/8 48 2/8	36 1/8	6 6	Lincoln County	WY	Len Merritt	1994	1259
336 5/8	53 5/8 52 7/8	47 3/8	5 6	Socorro County	NM	Dr. Mark J. Yurchisin	1998	1259
336 5/8	50 5/8 50 2/8	40 3/8	7 7	Yakima County	WA	Douglas J. Charles	1999	1259
336 5/8	54 7/8 52 6/8	36 1/8	9 8	Granite County	MT	Dwight S. Wolf	2004	1259
336 4/8	56 2/8 55 6/8	36 6/8	6 7	Coconino County	AZ	David M. Geiger	1990	1263
336 4/8	50 7/8 50 1/8	41 4/8	7 6	Meagher County	MT	George O. Johnson	1991	1263
336 4/8	51 2/8 48 7/8	43 7/8	6 6	Big Horn County	WY	Lance Crawford	1992	1263
336 4/8	49 0/8 49 2/8	37 0/8	7 7	White Pine County	NV	Robert McDonald	1993	1263
336 4/8	51 3/8 49 0/8	40 0/8	6 6	Beaverhead County	MT	Lee Murphree	1994	1263
336 4/8	53 1/8 52 0/8	37 2/8	6 6	Catron County	NM	Delbert Capps	1995	1263
336 4/8	48 7/8 50 0/8	46 2/8	6 6	Rio Blanco County	CO	Mark J. Crossett	1999	1263
336 4/8	52 6/8 52 5/8	39 4/8	7 7	Natrona County	WY	Gage Wollerman	2002	1263
336 4/8	58 1/8 58 0/8	40 2/8	6 6	Musselshell County	MT	Dale Godfrey	2004	1263
*336 4/8	49 2/8 48 4/8	37 6/8	7 7	Summit County	CO	Bryan Murdock	2006	1263
336 3/8	47 2/8 48 2/8	34 1/8	6 6	Meagher County	MT	Ronald K. Granneman	1973	1273
336 3/8	56 0/8 54 5/8	41 3/8	6 6	Custer County	ID	Gregg Welch	1984	1273
336 3/8	49 2/8 52 1/8	43 5/8	6 6	Lincoln County	MT	James J. Parkins	2001	1273
336 3/8	49 4/8 47 6/8	38 1/8	6 6	Granite County	MT	John Cuddy	2006	1273
*336 3/8	52 5/8 54 4/8	43 5/8	6 6	Garfield County	CO	Jeff Ryel	2009	1273
336 2/8	52 4/8 50 6/8	33 2/8	6 6	Lewis & Clark County	MT	Ronald K. Granneman	1979	1278
336 2/8	52 4/8 51 5/8	40 2/8	6 6	Coconino County	AZ	Jeremy Harness	1993	1278
336 2/8	55 5/8 56 5/8	42 2/8	6 6	Catron County	NM	Mike H. Farwell	1994	1278
336 2/8	51 6/8 51 7/8	38 0/8	7 6	Malheur County	OR	Raymond R. Kappell	1994	1278
336 2/8	51 4/8 50 6/8	36 6/8	6 6	Bonneville County	ID	Samuel Zitlau	2005	1278
336 1/8	54 6/8 52 1/8	40 2/8	7 6	Catron County	NM	R. Grant Clawson	1986	1283
336 1/8	48 0/8 48 2/8	34 6/8	6 7	Fergus County	MT	Randall L. Zeman	1991	1283
336 1/8	48 4/8 47 2/8	41 1/8	6 6	Archuleta County	CO	Lester Hawkins, Jr.	1998	1283
336 1/8	49 3/8 49 0/8	37 1/8	7 7	Phillips County	MT	Jason Radinovich	2003	1283
336 1/8	50 6/8 51 6/8	42 5/8	6 6	Bonneville County	ID	Donald Dombrowski	2003	1283
336 1/8	49 6/8 49 2/8	31 5/8	7 6	Grand County	CO	Stephen D. Monacelli	2007	1283
*336 1/8	53 4/8 54 2/8	33 3/8	7 7	Navajo County	AZ	Mike Aleff	2008	1283
336 0/8	50 0/8 50 1/8	42 4/8	6 6	Granite County	MT	Tom Storm	1982	1290
336 0/8	50 3/8 50 6/8	40 4/8	5 7	White Pine County	NV	Don Snodgrass	1989	1290
336 0/8	51 2/8 52 5/8	47 0/8	6 6	Coconino County	AZ	Darell Lee Christensen	1997	1290
336 0/8	55 3/8 56 6/8	33 0/8	6 6	White Pine County	NV	John David Stanley, Jr.	1997	1290
*336 0/8	49 7/8 50 2/8	38 6/8	6 6	Chouteau County	MT	Ray Gamradt	2006	1290
336 0/8	49 4/8 49 1/8	41 3/8	6 7	Rich County	UT	Ricky J. Long	2006	1290
336 0/8	51 6/8 52 7/8	35 4/8	6 6	Washington County	ID	Jon Lindsey	2010	1290
335 7/8	54 0/8 53 3/8	40 1/8	6 6	Coconino County	AZ	David R. Nelson	1997	1297
335 7/8	53 3/8 51 6/8	44 3/8	6 6	Garfield County	MT	Greg Hensen	2003	1297
335 7/8	53 7/8 55 4/8	38 2/8	7 7	Lewis & Clark County	MT	Forest Brown	2004	1297
*335 7/8	48 1/8 46 6/8	39 6/8	7 7	Fergus County	MT	Jim Tillman	2009	1297
335 6/8	53 4/8 53 1/8	37 6/8	7 8	Phillips County	MT	John 'Rosey' Roseland	1977	1301
335 6/8	51 2/8 53 6/8	39 2/8	6 6	Shoshone County	ID	Ernest W. Clanton	1983	1301
335 6/8	51 3/8 51 6/8	40 0/8	8 7	Fergus County	MT	Larry L. Schweitzer	1985	1301
335 6/8	49 1/8 50 0/8	41 6/8	6 6	Spray Lakes	ALB	Danny Moore	1987	1301
335 6/8	53 2/8 53 0/8	51 4/8	6 6	Catron County	NM	Scot P. McClelland	1988	1301
335 6/8	51 2/8 49 4/8	41 4/8	7 6	Coconino County	AZ	James Whitaker	1989	1301
335 6/8	53 4/8 52 3/8	41 2/8	6 7	Powell County	MT	Theodore J. Poper	1991	1301
335 6/8	51 6/8 48 7/8	41 2/8	6 6	Sanpete County	UT	Shane Spader	2005	1301
335 6/8	49 1/8 50 2/8	45 0/8	6 6	Sevier County	UT	Darren Peterson	2007	1301
335 5/8	52 6/8 50 7/8	43 3/8	6 6	Catron County	NM	Barrett L. Lemmon	1991	1310
335 5/8	43 5/8 46 4/8	38 3/8	8 7	Phillips County	MT	David E. Snowden, Jr.	1995	1310
335 5/8	52 0/8 51 4/8	40 1/8	6 6	Larimer County	CO	Jim Botner	1996	1310
335 5/8	45 5/8 46 6/8	35 3/8	6 6	Phillips County	MT	Dan VanderPloeg	1996	1310
335 4/8	47 4/8 48 6/8	49 0/8	6 6	Clearwater County	ID	Robert J. Kreisher	1958	1314
335 4/8	52 0/8 52 6/8	45 4/8	7 7	Skamania County	WA	Ted Jaycox	1985	1314
335 4/8	45 2/8 47 2/8	64 5/8	6 6	Lincoln County	MT	R. C. Peters	1985	1314
335 4/8	49 6/8 49 2/8	38 0/8	6 6	Fergus County	MT	Bucky Lindstrand	2000	1314
335 4/8	58 7/8 57 0/8	34 6/8	6 6	Sierra County	NM	James C. Blanchard	2005	1314
335 4/8	52 1/8 51 1/8	33 6/8	7 7	Boise County	ID	James Champion	2005	1314
335 4/8	54 1/8 50 2/8	33 4/8	6 6	Fremont County	ID	Jack Williams	2007	1314
335 3/8	56 4/8 57 0/8	40 4/8	6 8	Yakima County	WA	Tony Fitzgerald	2006	1321
*335 3/8	54 0/8 54 6/8	35 7/8	6 6	Grant County	CO	Tyler Triepke	2007	1321
335 2/8	52 1/8 51 4/8	37 4/8	6 6	Millard County	UT	Raymond M. Loveless	1993	1323
335 2/8	50 4/8 50 7/8	38 2/8	6 6	Jackson County	CO	Karl Kagelmann	1999	1323
335 2/8	56 1/8 55 2/8	36 6/8	6 6	Carbon County	WY	Dave Mundorf	2001	1323
335 2/8	52 0/8 52 4/8	42 6/8	6 7	Fergus County	MT	John Chaput	2003	1323
335 2/8	47 3/8 48 1/8	39 6/8	6 6	Idaho County	ID	Adam Haarberg	2003	1323
335 2/8	56 3/8 53 3/8	42 6/8	6 6	Gila County	AZ	Rodney Ronnebaum	2005	1323
335 2/8	53 0/8 53 0/8	39 2/8	6 6	Lemhi County	ID	John Wells	2007	1323
335 1/8	46 4/8 46 2/8	38 1/8	6 6	Camas County	ID	Derek Trent	1991	1330

AMERICAN ELK (TYPICAL ANTLERS)

Minimum Score 260 — Continued

Score	R Main Beam L	Inside Spread	R Points L	Area	State/Province	Hunter's Name	Date	Rank
335 1/8	51 6/8 50 7/8	40 3/8	6 6	Coconino County	AZ	David J. Martin	1992	1330
335 1/8	50 6/8 51 5/8	40 3/8	6 6	Phillips County	MT	Tom S. Crabill	1992	1330
335 1/8	48 6/8 44 7/8	36 5/8	6 6	Catron County	NM	Randy Springborn	2005	1330
335 1/8	52 3/8 52 4/8	40 6/8	6 7	Garfield County	MT	Jim P. Anthony	2006	1330
*335 1/8	45 6/8 46 3/8	31 1/8	6 7	Pueblo County	CO	Donald Griggs	2010	1330
335 0/8	50 7/8 50 5/8	40 0/8	6 6	Caribou County	ID	Charles Humphreys	1977	1336
335 0/8	53 3/8 52 0/8	39 4/8	6 6	Sanders County	MT	Gil Gilbertson	1984	1336
335 0/8	51 0/8 53 0/8	40 2/8	7 7	Grant County	NM	Johnny W. Morris	1991	1336
335 0/8	50 6/8 49 1/8	34 2/8	8 7	Petroleum County	MT	Craig Wagner	1992	1336
335 0/8	48 0/8 48 3/8	38 4/8	7 7	Harney County	OR	Joel R. Griffin	1993	1336
335 0/8	49 5/8 48 3/8	35 2/8	7 6	Grant County	OR	Charlie A. Gannon	1996	1336
335 0/8	53 0/8 54 4/8	39 3/8	6 7	Catron County	NM	Dyrk Eddie	1996	1336
335 0/8	50 3/8 48 5/8	37 2/8	6 6	Catron County	NM	Tony Cutbirth	1998	1336
335 0/8	54 2/8 55 1/8	40 2/8	6 7	Madison County	MT	Scott L. Koelzer	1999	1336
335 0/8	49 6/8 47 3/8	41 4/8	6 6	Gem County	ID	Shawn L. Kelley	2000	1336
335 0/8	52 6/8 53 7/8	41 4/8	6 6	Custer County	ID	Boone Peterson	2005	1336
335 0/8	52 5/8 51 0/8	44 6/8	7 6	Powell County	MT	Troy Volbrecht	2005	1336
*335 0/8	53 3/8 53 0/8	40 3/8	7 6	Navajo County	AZ	Mitchell A. Atkinson	2007	1336
*335 0/8	52 2/8 52 6/8	39 4/8	6 6	Park County	MT	Steve Jones	2007	1336
335 0/8	50 6/8 49 7/8	45 6/8	6 6	Teller County	CO	Jeffrey Forest Rushay	2008	1336
334 7/8	46 0/8 46 0/8	34 2/8	7 6	Union County	NM	Jeffrey L. Clevenger	2004	1351
*334 7/8	49 5/8 48 6/8	41 5/8	6 6	Bonneville County	ID	Joseph Brick	2007	1351
*334 7/8	55 5/8 55 4/8	40 5/8	6 6	Gallatin County	MT	Donald M. Dolph, Sr.	2009	1351
334 6/8	51 4/8 51 7/8	44 6/8	6 6	Summit County	CO	Michael Beckwith	1976	1354
334 6/8	52 0/8 52 2/8	43 0/8	6 6	Custer County	ID	Hal J. Dillashaw	1991	1354
334 6/8	54 3/8 52 4/8	36 0/8	6 7	White Pine County	NV	Gene A. Jones	1992	1354
334 6/8	49 4/8 49 7/8	44 2/8	6 6	Catron County	NM	Richard Gage	1996	1354
334 6/8	51 4/8 50 7/8	43 0/8	6 7	White Pine County	NV	Richard Sandoz	1998	1354
334 6/8	53 3/8 51 5/8	42 0/8	6 6	Boulder County	CO	Jamie J. Seyler	2002	1354
334 6/8	49 2/8 49 2/8	42 6/8	6 6	Teller County	CO	Patrick Adams	2002	1354
334 6/8	48 3/8 52 6/8	35 1/8	8 7	Montrose County	CO	Patrick Kelleher	2005	1354
334 5/8	50 0/8 49 5/8	34 1/8	7 7	Garfield County	CO	Darren Mack	1989	1362
334 5/8	50 3/8 49 1/8	38 5/8	6 6	Navajo County	AZ	Tod Thornton	1994	1362
334 5/8	53 1/8 51 2/8	33 0/8	6 8	Petroleum County	MT	Mutt Wilson	1995	1362
334 5/8	53 0/8 51 5/8	40 5/8	6 7	Sevier County	UT	Rick Farnsworth	2003	1362
334 5/8	51 7/8 50 1/8	40 7/8	6 6	Meagher County	MT	Terry Carlson	2005	1362
334 5/8	53 3/8 51 1/8	44 4/8	6 7	Mesa County	CO	Gary Angell	2010	1362
334 4/8	49 7/8 48 5/8	46 4/8	6 6	Gunnison County	CO	Roy M. Goodwin	1988	1368
334 4/8	48 3/8 48 2/8	40 7/8	6 7	Apache County	AZ	George Harms	2004	1368
334 3/8	53 3/8 52 5/8	38 5/8	6 6	Coconino County	AZ	Stephen Jon McGaughey	1988	1370
334 3/8	54 4/8 54 1/8	40 3/8	6 6	Catron County	NM	Dave Holt	1995	1370
334 3/8	49 0/8 50 0/8	37 7/8	6 6	Socorro County	NM	Ron Madsen	1996	1370
334 3/8	49 6/8 50 4/8	41 7/8	6 6	Sierra County	NM	Betty J. Kutchey	2000	1370
334 2/8	52 5/8 49 0/8	38 4/8	6 6	Sweetwater County	WY	Lawrence Branson	1984	1374
334 2/8	47 7/8 46 4/8	44 0/8	6 6	Albany County	WY	Thomas Bradach	1988	1374
334 2/8	50 3/8 49 7/8	32 6/8	6 6	White Pine County	NV	Richard A. Hanson	1992	1374
334 2/8	50 4/8 51 2/8	40 4/8	6 6	Petroleum County	MT	Michael Thomas	1995	1374
334 2/8	49 7/8 48 6/8	44 4/8	6 6	Shoshone County	ID	Joel Larsen	2003	1374
*334 2/8	46 4/8 47 3/8	37 4/8	6 6	Wasatch County	UT	Roy Hampton	2004	1374
334 1/8	48 3/8 51 0/8	39 5/8	6 6	Madison County	MT	John Aalto	1979	1380
334 1/8	46 2/8 49 2/8	43 5/8	6 6	Boulder County	CO	Billy E. Corley	1991	1380
334 1/8	54 2/8 54 2/8	40 7/8	6 6	Madison County	MT	Bruce A. Traucht	1992	1380
334 1/8	52 5/8 50 2/8	42 3/8	7 6	Fremont County	ID	Cecil F. Crow	1994	1380
334 1/8	49 6/8 50 2/8	40 3/8	6 6	Catron County	NM	James A. Trujillo	1995	1380
334 1/8	44 7/8 44 4/8	37 5/8	6 7	Valhalla Centre	ALB	Roger D. VanEerden	1996	1380
334 1/8	47 0/8 47 3/8	37 3/8	6 6	White Pine County	NV	William J. Ricci	2000	1380
334 1/8	48 0/8 50 1/8	36 4/8	8 6	Garfield County	MT	John Rhodes	2003	1380
334 1/8	52 6/8 51 2/8	38 5/8	6 6	Kittitas County	WA	Tom Zimmerman	2003	1380
334 1/8	45 2/8 46 5/8	35 3/8	7 7	Coconino County	AZ	Nicholas Harrison	2004	1380
334 1/8	55 6/8 54 6/8	35 4/8	7 6	San Juan County	UT	Ralph Wolfe	2005	1380
334 1/8	49 2/8 49 2/8	36 7/8	6 7	Fremont County	ID	Matt Dyche	2006	1380
334 1/8	57 0/8 56 0/8	40 5/8	6 6	White Pine County	NV	Larry D. Draper	2007	1380
334 1/8	51 0/8 51 7/8	45 1/8	7 6	Sanders County	MT	Greg Hertel	2009	1380
334 0/8	45 5/8 47 6/8	41 2/8	7 6	Boulder County	CO	Gus Roe	1984	1394
334 0/8	50 2/8 50 4/8	43 4/8	6 6	Pennington County	SD	Stuart A. Jacobsen	1996	1394
334 0/8	52 2/8 51 7/8	34 4/8	6 6	Petroleum County	MT	Jerry Clawson	1999	1394
334 0/8	51 3/8 52 1/8	36 2/8	7 6	Flagstaff	ALB	Brent Kuntz	2003	1394
333 7/8	51 6/8 49 0/8	34 6/8	7 7	Fergus County	MT	Edwin Evans	1983	1398
333 7/8	48 2/8 47 4/8	46 5/8	6 6	Fremont County	ID	Mark J. Sherick	2000	1398
333 7/8	45 4/8 46 6/8	35 1/8	6 6	Phillips County	MT	Brad Eide	2001	1398
333 7/8	56 5/8 54 1/8	39 5/8	6 6	Gallatin County	MT	Dan Talbert	2004	1398
333 7/8	46 5/8 45 5/8	37 1/8	7 6	Phillips County	MT	Jason Fuhrman	2005	1398
*333 7/8	55 3/8 57 0/8	38 3/8	6 6	Otero County	NM	James Steinmetz	2005	1398
*333 7/8	52 5/8 51 3/8	33 7/8	6 6	Lewis & Clark County	MT	Joe Kapphan	2006	1398
*333 7/8	49 6/8 50 5/8	40 3/8	6 6	Beaver County	UT	Mike Juretich	2009	1398
333 6/8	49 4/8 49 4/8	45 0/8	6 6	Baker County	OR	Russell B. Jones	1946	1406
333 6/8	53 4/8 52 2/8	44 2/8	7 6	Sheridan County	WY	Chuck McKenzie	1976	1406
333 6/8	46 5/8 47 1/8	38 6/8	6 6	Otero County	NM	Richard D. Burton	1997	1406
333 6/8	50 6/8 50 7/8	41 0/8	6 6	Sevier County	UT	David L. Karren	2001	1406
333 6/8	46 2/8 45 4/8	32 4/8	7 6	Gunnison County	CO	Johnny Martin	2004	1406
*333 6/8	54 5/8 52 4/8	41 6/8	6 6	Apache County	AZ	Roger W. Fowler	2006	1406
*333 6/8	48 4/8 50 0/8	34 4/8	6 6	Coconino County	AZ	Charles R. Gordon	2007	1406
333 6/8	50 0/8 49 0/8	42 4/8	6 6	Moffat County	CO	Marty Ruggles	2007	1406
333 6/8	53 7/8 51 2/8	44 2/8	6 6	Elko County	NV	Tim Bottari	2008	1406
333 6/8	49 5/8 53 0/8	43 4/8	6 6	Coconino County	AZ	Donald R. Jenkins	2008	1406
333 5/8	53 1/8 52 4/8	40 3/8	6 6	Taos County	NM	Robert K. Marshall	1999	1416
333 5/8	57 0/8 58 3/8	43 3/8	6 6	Park County	WY	Robert C. Coble	2005	1416
333 5/8	46 0/8 44 3/8	38 6/8	8 6	Socorro County	NM	Bob Bartoshesky	2007	1416
*333 5/8	55 5/8 55 6/8	41 7/8	6 6	Greenlee County	AZ	Michael W. Goodyear	2009	1416
*333 5/8	48 3/8 50 0/8	35 5/8	6 6	Teller County	CO	Macky Myers	2009	1416
333 4/8	47 2/8 47 0/8	35 0/8	6 6	Waterton Park	ALB	Barry Linklater	1987	1421
333 4/8	49 1/8 48 0/8	39 6/8	7 7	Canmore	ALB	Jordon Ohrn	1988	1421
333 4/8	51 4/8 52 4/8	46 0/8	6 6	Fergus County	MT	Kennie Williams	2001	1421
333 4/8	53 3/8 53 4/8	43 0/8	6 6	Wallowa County	OR	Kirk Skovlin	2003	1421
333 4/8	44 6/8 45 6/8	38 4/8	7 7	Sublette County	WY	Bryson Thomason	2004	1421

AMERICAN ELK (TYPICAL ANTLERS)

Minimum Score 260
Continued

SCORE	LENGTH OF R MAIN BEAM L	INSIDE SPREAD	NUMBER OF R POINTS L	AREA	STATE/ PROVINCE	HUNTER'S NAME	DATE	RANK
333 4/8	52 3/8 53 7/8	37 6/8	6 6	Navajo County	AZ	Les Floyd	2004	1421
*333 4/8	53 3/8 52 2/8	38 2/8	6 6	Sanders County	MT	Steven W. Fairbank	2010	1421
333 3/8	45 6/8 47 4/8	39 7/8	6 6	Catron County	NM	Gary A Littauer	1984	1428
333 3/8	46 0/8 46 0/8	34 3/8	7 6	Union County	OR	Mark Simmons	1985	1428
333 3/8	54 7/8 55 3/8	43 2/8	6 7	Canmore	ALB	Brian Francis	1986	1428
333 3/8	50 6/8 50 6/8	43 7/8	6 7	Wheatland County	MT	Tim Klosterman	1996	1428
333 3/8	49 0/8 49 0/8	41 1/8	6 6	Beaverhead County	MT	Colleen Rose	1996	1428
333 3/8	49 0/8 55 4/8	41 5/8	6 6	Albany County	WY	Don Maston	1997	1428
333 3/8	51 4/8 53 4/8	39 1/8	6 6	Apache County	AZ	Shane Howard	1997	1428
333 3/8	46 0/8 46 5/8	45 4/8	7 6	Catron County	NM	William E. Pipes III	2004	1428
333 3/8	47 6/8 49 0/8	31 1/8	6 6	Washington County	ID	Michael R. Buchanan	2009	1428
*333 3/8	55 2/8 50 3/8	38 7/8	6 6	La Plata County	CO	Paul Moschler	2009	1428
333 2/8	47 0/8 48 4/8	39 4/8	6 6	Jefferson County	CO	Jerry Gruenberg	1988	1438
333 2/8	52 6/8 54 0/8	38 0/8	7 6	Teton County	WY	Jerry W. Lashuay	1988	1438
333 2/8	47 1/8 46 5/8	41 4/8	6 6	Carbon County	UT	Tom Paluso	1989	1438
333 2/8	50 0/8 50 2/8	37 6/8	6 6	Catron County	NM	Bill Powell	1991	1438
333 2/8	48 5/8 49 1/8	35 0/8	6 7	Ravalli County	MT	Ray Joy	1993	1438
333 2/8	49 2/8 48 6/8	33 2/8	6 6	San Juan County	UT	Robert Winder	2000	1438
333 2/8	49 7/8 49 5/8	34 6/8	6 6	Utah County	UT	Steve Gren	2003	1438
333 2/8	52 3/8 52 4/8	38 6/8	6 6	Lincoln County	NV	Frank S. Noska IV	2003	1438
333 2/8	53 7/8 51 6/8	39 4/8	6 6	Park County	MT	Steve Kamps	2005	1438
333 2/8	47 3/8 49 1/8	38 4/8	6 6	Powder River County	MT	Lewis R. Showalter	2006	1438
*333 2/8	46 1/8 46 6/8	45 4/8	7 6	Fremont County	ID	Heath Dowers	2007	1438
333 2/8	52 2/8 56 6/8	43 6/8	7 6	Albany County	WY	Corey Hamrick	2007	1438
*333 2/8	57 0/8 55 7/8	43 4/8	6 5	Yavapai County	AZ	Skip Rimsza	2008	1438
333 2/8	50 6/8 52 5/8	43 0/8	6 6	Socorro County	NM	John Megel	2008	1438
333 2/8	52 5/8 52 7/8	37 4/8	6 7	Eagle County	CO	James B. Versailles	2009	1438
*333 2/8	50 5/8 51 1/8	29 4/8	6 6	Navajo County	AZ	Brett L. Foster	2010	1438
333 1/8	41 3/8 46 2/8	41 3/8	6 6	Grand County	CO	Dennis Wehling	1981	1454
333 1/8	49 0/8 49 0/8	40 3/8	6 6	Natrona County	WY	Mike Urlacher	1993	1454
333 1/8	51 0/8 50 1/8	43 5/8	6 6	Judith Basin County	MT	Jerry Tabacco	1996	1454
333 1/8	48 4/8 47 7/8	44 3/8	6 6	Glacier County	MT	Thomas Gervais	2005	1454
333 1/8	53 6/8 54 0/8	42 3/8	6 6	Baker County	OR	Zachary Boehm	2009	1454
333 0/8	45 7/8 47 1/8	37 0/8	6 6	Catron County	NM	J. B. Lemon	1993	1459
333 0/8	56 3/8 53 7/8	31 0/8	7 7	Coconino County	AZ	Stephen C. Christensen	1997	1459
333 0/8	52 1/8 50 2/8	41 4/8	6 6	Catron County	NM	Bill Brown	1997	1459
333 0/8	53 3/8 48 5/8	44 5/8	7 6	Coconino County	AZ	John Kovac	1997	1459
333 0/8	53 7/8 53 1/8	40 4/8	6 6	Coconino County	AZ	Kenneth Lobnow	2000	1459
333 0/8	48 2/8 50 1/8	41 2/8	7 7	Valley County	ID	Kevin Gaither	2003	1459
333 0/8	48 2/8 48 3/8	37 2/8	6 6	Boyd County	NE	Marty Neilan	2004	1459
333 0/8	53 0/8 50 0/8	37 6/8	6 6	White Pine County	NV	Robert Hanneman	2006	1459
333 0/8	45 7/8 45 5/8	38 6/8	7 6	Athabasca	ALB	Will Huppertz	2006	1459
333 0/8	56 0/8 54 0/8	40 4/8	6 6	Apache County	AZ	Rico M. Acevedo	2007	1459
333 0/8	49 0/8 49 2/8	43 4/8	6 6	Carbon County	WY	Rob Sherman	2008	1459
*333 0/8	52 1/8 52 6/8	40 2/8	6 6	Sandoval County	NM	Jed E. Jones	2009	1459
333 0/8	50 7/8 50 6/8	39 6/8	6 6	Cibola County	NM	Garrett I. Chavez	2009	1459
332 7/8	48 4/8 49 3/8	41 3/8	7 7	Grant County	OR	Neil Hinton	1985	1472
332 7/8	52 1/8 49 6/8	36 1/8	6 6	Phillips County	MT	Todd A. Erickson	1989	1472
332 7/8	51 3/8 53 7/8	40 1/8	6 6	Catron County	NM	Marvin H. Walter	1992	1472
332 7/8	48 1/8 47 3/8	41 7/8	7 7	Valley County	ID	Tracy Hunt	1992	1472
332 7/8	55 0/8 53 6/8	43 7/8	6 6	Catron County	NM	Kevin L. Reid	1998	1472
*332 7/8	54 6/8 52 6/8	38 5/8	7 6	Elko County	NV	David C. Hong	2003	1472
332 6/8	53 7/8 51 6/8	43 2/8	6 6	Albany County	WY	Pat McAteer	1981	1478
332 6/8	52 0/8 49 2/8	37 0/8	6 6	Catron County	NM	John Howard	1984	1478
332 6/8	51 1/8 51 7/8	32 0/8	7 6	King County	WA	Curtis H. Fowler	1987	1478
332 6/8	51 6/8 50 4/8	40 4/8	6 6	Carbon County	UT	Dan Summers	1989	1478
332 6/8	48 7/8 51 2/8	33 6/8	7 6	Fergus County	MT	Jess Knerr	1998	1478
332 6/8	49 6/8 50 3/8	40 4/8	7 8	Union County	OR	Donnie J. Allen	2000	1478
332 6/8	51 2/8 52 3/8	38 4/8	6 6	Elko County	NV	Thomas D. Pearson	2003	1478
332 6/8	44 2/8 45 4/8	44 4/8	6 6	Garfield County	CO	Bruce Hendy	2003	1478
332 6/8	55 6/8 56 5/8	40 0/8	6 6	Coconino County	AZ	Susan Sandoz	2004	1478
*332 6/8	51 3/8 53 0/8	40 6/8	6 6	Uintah County	UT	Ron Brunson	2007	1478
332 5/8	50 7/8 49 7/8	45 3/8	6 6	Teton County	MT	Wayne Lawrence	1995	1488
332 5/8	48 6/8 47 0/8	34 5/8	6 6	Lincoln County	NV	Larry Pabst	1997	1488
332 5/8	52 4/8 51 4/8	37 5/8	6 6	Elko County	NV	Sean Shea	1999	1488
332 5/8	46 0/8 46 3/8	43 7/8	7 7	Catron County	NM	Jaime G. Chavez	2001	1488
332 5/8	47 2/8 48 7/8	34 1/8	6 6	Navajo County	AZ	L. Grant Foster	2007	1488
332 4/8	54 4/8 53 2/8	41 6/8	7 7	Apache County	AZ	Steve Schaufer	1989	1493
332 4/8	47 2/8 47 0/8	45 1/8	6 7	Coconino County	AZ	Gregory B. Minton	1991	1493
332 4/8	51 4/8 50 0/8	42 2/8	6 6	Apache County	AZ	George Pieros	2001	1493
332 4/8	45 2/8 48 5/8	34 0/8	5 5	Cache County	UT	Jason Martin	2005	1493
332 4/8	56 4/8 56 4/8	43 2/8	6 6	Sandoval County	NM	Jeff Taylor	2007	1493
*332 4/8	52 0/8 49 0/8	38 2/8	6 6	Powder River County	MT	Matthew Nelson	2008	1493
332 3/8	54 4/8 52 0/8	33 7/8	7 6	Apache County	AZ	Charles G. Dawe	1986	1499
332 3/8	49 4/8 49 4/8	42 7/8	6 6	Coconino County	AZ	Jerry Vogel	1990	1499
332 3/8	52 4/8 52 5/8	37 2/8	6 7	Lewis & Clark County	MT	Michael DalSoglio	2000	1499
332 3/8	49 0/8 49 3/8	36 5/8	6 6	Navajo County	AZ	Gary Banken	2001	1499
*332 3/8	49 3/8 51 6/8	39 3/8	6 6	Morgan County	UT	P. C. "Bo" Aughtry III	2005	1499
332 3/8	51 1/8 52 2/8	38 7/8	6 6	White Pine County	NV	Justin Alanis	2009	1499
332 2/8	50 6/8 49 0/8	42 2/8	6 6	Natrona County	WY	Justin Frick	2000	1505
332 2/8	51 7/8 52 7/8	46 4/8	6 6	Judith Basin County	MT	Richard Lamere	2000	1505
332 2/8	53 7/8 51 5/8	35 4/8	7 6	Musselshell County	MT	Art Smith	2000	1505
332 2/8	52 0/8 49 4/8	40 0/8	6 6	Las Animas County	CO	Eugene Palumbo	2001	1505
332 2/8	47 0/8 47 0/8	40 4/8	6 6	Catron County	NM	Russell J. Wendorf	2004	1505
332 2/8	57 2/8 56 4/8	42 0/8	7 7	Navajo County	AZ	Dean E. Lippert	2007	1505
332 1/8	53 4/8 54 6/8	36 7/8	6 6	Coconino County	AZ	James R. Moore	1980	1511
332 1/8	47 0/8 50 4/8	40 1/8	6 6	Sublette County	WY	Danny E. Williams	1995	1511
332 1/8	47 2/8 46 6/8	31 7/8	6 6	Jumping Pound Creek	ALB	Archie Nesbitt	1996	1511
332 1/8	50 5/8 53 6/8	46 1/8	6 6	Lawrence County	SD	Mike Jass	2000	1511
332 1/8	50 7/8 49 3/8	38 5/8	6 6	White Pine County	NV	Anthony J. Muscato	2005	1511
332 1/8	48 1/8 49 1/8	37 7/8	7 6	Jefferson County	MT	Kirt Daken	2007	1511
332 1/8	48 7/8 44 1/8	35 3/8	7 6	Morrill County	NE	Kent Hochstein	2009	1511
332 1/8	47 0/8 47 0/8	36 1/8	7 6	Petroleum County	MT	James D. Ellington	2010	1511
332 0/8	49 2/8 50 5/8	38 2/8	6 7	Caribou County	ID	Joseph M. Hulse	1967	1519
332 0/8	52 0/8 51 6/8	42 0/8	7 6	Clearwater County	ID	Don West	1983	1519

693

AMERICAN ELK (TYPICAL ANTLERS)

Minimum Score 260   Continued

SCORE	LENGTH OF R MAIN BEAM L	INSIDE SPREAD	NUMBER OF R POINTS L	AREA	STATE/ PROVINCE	HUNTER'S NAME	DATE	RANK
332 0/8	51 3/8 50 6/8	37 2/8	6 6	Custer County	ID	Delos G. Robinson	1987	1519
332 0/8	49 5/8 49 0/8	37 0/8	6 6	Catron County	NM	Christopher Green	1990	1519
332 0/8	47 1/8 46 1/8	38 4/8	6 6	Clearwater County	ID	Richard L. Sandusky	1990	1519
332 0/8	52 3/8 51 0/8	56 1/8	6 7	Coconino County	AZ	Andrew L. Grannan	1991	1519
332 0/8	50 3/8 49 6/8	37 2/8	6 6	Grant County	OR	Robert Reed	1992	1519
332 0/8	50 2/8 48 3/8	39 4/8	6 6	Catron County	NM	Carl McGlothlin	1994	1519
332 0/8	51 7/8 51 6/8	37 6/8	6 6	Taos County	NM	Steve R. Rivera	1994	1519
332 0/8	48 2/8 51 5/8	48 7/8	7 6	Catron County	NM	William E. Fleshman	1995	1519
332 0/8	49 6/8 55 2/8	36 6/8	6 6	Greenlee County	AZ	Justin W. Serr	2000	1519
332 0/8	51 2/8 50 6/8	38 6/8	6 7	Johnson County	WY	Scott Petrie	2001	1519
332 0/8	49 6/8 51 6/8	39 6/8	6 6	Musselshell County	MT	Jim Borgreen	2006	1519
332 0/8	46 4/8 47 3/8	34 4/8	6 6	Wasatch County	UT	Mike McGee	2007	1519
*332 0/8	49 4/8 58 2/8	44 4/8	5 6	Moffat County	CO	Chris Schiller	2009	1519
331 7/8	53 3/8 50 4/8	36 7/8	6 7	Los Alamos County	NM	Robert Barrie	1986	1534
331 7/8	50 0/8 50 5/8	41 3/8	6 6	Catron County	NM	Thomas Blaeser	1991	1534
331 7/8	45 2/8 45 0/8	31 4/8	6 6	Catron County	NM	Carl D. Bradford	1993	1534
331 7/8	53 7/8 52 1/8	43 7/8	6 6	Ravalli County	MT	Eddie Polich	1994	1534
331 7/8	48 5/8 48 1/8	35 3/8	7 7	Coconino County	AZ	Garrett Haupt	2000	1534
331 7/8	47 1/8 46 3/8	40 4/8	8 7	Park County	MT	Steve Kamps	2000	1534
331 7/8	46 4/8 44 7/8	34 1/8	6 6	Park County	WY	Robert M. Stroupe	2001	1534
331 7/8	50 7/8 50 4/8	37 1/8	6 6	Catron County	NM	Ardon Lee	2001	1534
331 7/8	53 2/8 53 1/8	40 3/8	6 6	Coconino County	AZ	James F. Watson	2003	1534
331 7/8	51 7/8 47 5/8	56 2/8	6 7	Petroleum County	MT	Lee Murphree	2003	1534
331 7/8	50 7/8 50 5/8	35 3/8	7 7	Phillips County	MT	Mark D. Dauenhauer	2004	1534
331 7/8	46 5/8 47 6/8	38 3/8	6 6	Yakima County	WA	Ryan Banks	2006	1534
331 7/8	43 5/8 45 0/8	44 3/8	7 6	Summit County	CO	Michael R. Rohr	2007	1534
*331 7/8	52 2/8 50 5/8	37 3/8	6 6	Fergus County	MT	Don Moen	2007	1534
*331 7/8	50 5/8 51 4/8	37 5/8	6 6	Petroleum County	MT	Paul Goetsch	2009	1534
331 6/8	48 0/8 49 6/8	45 7/8	7 6	Canmore	ALB	Ken Madsen	1985	1549
331 6/8	48 0/8 50 4/8	37 2/8	6 6	Catron County	NM	Randall S. Madding	1988	1549
331 6/8	49 4/8 50 2/8	37 2/8	6 6	Jefferson County	OR	Gary Naugher	1996	1549
331 6/8	54 0/8 54 3/8	42 0/8	6 6	Garfield County	MT	Dave Gins	1997	1549
331 6/8	48 3/8 50 7/8	32 6/8	6 6	Clark County	ID	Glen Berry	1999	1549
331 6/8	51 2/8 50 3/8	43 0/8	6 6	Garfield County	UT	Troy Bennett	2002	1549
331 6/8	54 3/8 55 0/8	37 5/8	6 7	Emery County	UT	Victor J. Fossat	2004	1549
331 6/8	50 1/8 48 3/8	41 2/8	6 6	Carbon County	WY	Cody Duhon	2006	1549
331 6/8	50 4/8 49 0/8	37 2/8	6 6	Sublette County	WY	Eric Andersen	2006	1549
*331 6/8	50 4/8 50 5/8	37 2/8	6 6	Catron County	NM	Steven G. Eason	2010	1549
331 5/8	51 3/8 48 6/8	43 7/8	6 6	Sublette County	WY	Rod Knight	1983	1559
331 5/8	49 0/8 47 4/8	41 5/8	6 6	Fremont County	ID	Rick Harris	1986	1559
331 5/8	48 0/8 46 5/8	35 1/8	6 7	Flathead County	MT	David L. Thompson	1991	1559
331 5/8	51 2/8 50 4/8	39 5/8	6 6	Custer County	ID	Garry L. Bolinder	1993	1559
331 5/8	49 1/8 49 0/8	41 1/8	6 6	Petroleum County	MT	Chuck Adams	1994	1559
331 5/8	50 0/8 47 5/8	45 1/8	6 7	Park County	WY	Dan Hart	1998	1559
331 5/8	48 0/8 47 1/8	40 1/8	6 7	Umatilla County	OR	Doug Kinser	2000	1559
331 5/8	50 6/8 51 2/8	39 7/8	7 6	Johnson County	WY	Duffy Brown	2002	1559
331 5/8	51 7/8 50 6/8	43 2/8	7 6	Grand County	CO	Isaac D. Cullum	2003	1559
331 5/8	54 1/8 55 3/8	40 3/8	6 7	Navajo County	AZ	George Quinif	2005	1559
331 5/8	46 3/8 46 6/8	42 1/8	6 6	Grand County	CO	Jeffrey S. Besaw	2006	1559
331 5/8	49 3/8 49 5/8	37 5/8	6 6	Natrona County	WY	Mike Lewis	2007	1559
331 5/8	53 2/8 53 2/8	38 7/8	6 6	Millard County	UT	Clark A. Moss	2008	1559
331 4/8	47 1/8 48 5/8	40 6/8	6 6	Shoshone County	ID	John C. Dawson II	1990	1572
331 4/8	53 0/8 54 7/8	42 6/8	6 7	Coconino County	AZ	Mike Norman Oliver	1990	1572
331 4/8	54 0/8 53 5/8	39 4/8	6 6	Boulder County	CO	Ron Readmond	1991	1572
331 4/8	51 2/8 49 3/8	38 4/8	6 8	Coconino County	AZ	Kevin Forsman	1992	1572
331 4/8	49 7/8 50 6/8	39 0/8	6 6	Beaverhead County	MT	Gerald DeBoar	1992	1572
331 4/8	50 3/8 50 6/8	41 0/8	6 6	Navajo County	AZ	Randy L. Hill	1995	1572
331 4/8	51 5/8 50 0/8	40 0/8	7 7	Beaverhead County	MT	Jeremy Liedtka	1996	1572
331 4/8	51 1/8 50 4/8	37 4/8	6 6	Judith Basin County	MT	Kelly Norskog	1997	1572
331 4/8	46 5/8 46 5/8	39 4/8	6 6	White Pine County	NV	Bryan Milano	2000	1572
*331 4/8	51 7/8 50 2/8	34 2/8	6 6	Catron County	NM	Michael J. McNarney	2001	1572
331 4/8	50 5/8 50 0/8	36 6/8	6 6	Petroleum County	MT	Toby Richardson	2002	1572
331 4/8	47 7/8 47 4/8	33 0/8	6 6	Lincoln County	MT	Paul Tisher	2003	1572
331 4/8	46 4/8 46 1/8	51 6/8	6 6	Catron County	NM	L. Wayne Carlton	2007	1572
331 3/8	49 2/8 50 6/8	36 3/8	7 7	Big Horn County	WY	Kendel Cheatham	1983	1585
331 3/8	55 6/8 54 1/8	40 7/8	6 6	Lemhi County	ID	James A. Spinti	1994	1585
331 3/8	52 0/8 51 1/8	41 1/8	6 7	King County	WA	David Wayne Bentley	1995	1585
331 3/8	50 2/8 52 0/8	44 3/8	6 6	Madison County	MT	Kurt D. Rued	1997	1585
331 3/8	43 7/8 46 0/8	41 5/8	6 6	Catron County	NM	Steve Murphy	1998	1585
331 3/8	56 2/8 56 1/8	46 5/8	6 6	Socorro County	NM	Dwayne Strength	2001	1585
331 3/8	52 0/8 49 0/8	50 0/8	7 7	Coconino County	AZ	Aaron J. McDonnel	2005	1585
331 3/8	48 2/8 48 3/8	38 6/8	8 7	Park County	MT	Robert J. Hoekstra	2007	1585
*331 3/8	48 4/8 47 5/8	37 1/8	6 6	Catron County	NM	Mark D. Thomson	2008	1585
331 2/8	52 3/8 47 4/8	43 0/8	7 6	Catron County	NM	Monte Green	1993	1594
331 2/8	48 5/8 49 0/8	37 2/8	6 6	Los Alamos County	NM	Jeffrey Severson	1998	1594
331 2/8	54 5/8 53 6/8	44 2/8	7 7	Navajo County	AZ	Alan C. Ellsworth	1999	1594
331 2/8	50 6/8 52 0/8	40 0/8	6 7	Bonneville County	ID	Arlynn Jacobson	2000	1594
331 2/8	50 1/8 49 3/8	43 3/8	6 7	Bear Lake County	ID	Albert J. Behrman	2000	1594
331 2/8	50 7/8 50 5/8	33 6/8	6 6	Elko County	NV	Simone Zaga	2001	1594
331 2/8	50 1/8 49 3/8	41 5/8	6 7	Wallowa County	OR	Matt R. Rinard	2001	1594
331 2/8	48 1/8 47 1/8	46 0/8	6 7	Malheur County	OR	Kenneth Remmer	2002	1594
331 2/8	48 6/8 48 1/8	37 2/8	6 6	Park County	WY	Jason Stafford	2002	1594
331 2/8	48 7/8 50 5/8	39 4/8	6 6	Fergus County	MT	John Sarvis	2004	1594
331 2/8	51 7/8 52 1/8	41 4/8	6 7	Petroleum County	MT	D. "Mitch" Kottas	2008	1594
331 2/8	45 5/8 45 6/8	42 2/8	6 6	Jackson County	CO	T. J. Thrasher	2009	1594
331 2/8	51 6/8 48 5/8	39 2/8	6 6	Cibola County	NM	Anthony J. Jerulle	2009	1594
331 2/8	52 4/8 52 3/8	41 4/8	7 6	Gilpin County	CO	Scott Powers	2009	1594
331 1/8	48 3/8 48 1/8	38 3/8	6 6	Sheridan County	WY	Mike Barrett	1984	1608
331 1/8	46 7/8 47 0/8	40 5/8	6 6	Apache County	AZ	Blaine C. Mullenaux	1993	1608
331 1/8	46 4/8 45 7/8	39 1/8	6 6	Pitkin County	CO	James L. Behn	1997	1608
331 1/8	52 1/8 49 0/8	41 7/8	6 6	Park County	WY	Vince Philipps	1998	1608
331 1/8	55 5/8 56 4/8	45 1/8	6 6	Apache County	AZ	Ryan C. Langner	1999	1608
331 1/8	49 2/8 52 5/8	39 5/8	7 6	Coconino County	AZ	Mike Blanchard	2001	1608
331 1/8	46 7/8 47 3/8	36 6/8	7 8	Catron County	NM	Jay Smith	2004	1608
331 1/8	52 4/8 52 3/8	35 5/8	6 6	Archuleta County	CO	Milton H. Sherman, Jr.	2008	1608

694

AMERICAN ELK (TYPICAL ANTLERS)

Minimum Score 260

SCORE	LENGTH OF R MAIN BEAM L	INSIDE SPREAD	NUMBER OF R POINTS L	AREA	STATE/ PROVINCE	HUNTER'S NAME	DATE	RANK
*331 1/8	47 4/8 50 2/8	38 7/8	6 6	Custer County	MT	Dylan Deuter	2009	1608
331 0/8	51 5/8 52 5/8	45 2/8	7 6	Sublette County	WY	Clair Adams	1987	1617
331 0/8	50 6/8 49 6/8	40 2/8	6 6	Catron County	NM	Randal E. Probst	1993	1617
331 0/8	44 1/8 46 3/8	45 4/8	7 7	Catron County	NM	Robert A. Oines	2002	1617
331 0/8	55 1/8 53 5/8	37 2/8	6 6	El Paso County	CO	William R. Hull	2007	1617
331 0/8	50 3/8 50 2/8	38 4/8	7 7	Johnson County	WY	Ryan Hochstein	2009	1617
330 7/8	53 5/8 50 4/8	39 5/8	6 6	Coconino County	AZ	Jeff W. Elmer	1985	1622
330 7/8	50 2/8 50 0/8	41 1/8	6 6	Catron County	NM	J. D. Mills	1988	1622
330 7/8	52 1/8 51 6/8	38 7/8	7 7	Coconino County	AZ	Douglas W. Koepsel	1992	1622
330 7/8	52 4/8 51 4/8	35 1/8	6 6	Fergus County	MT	John P. Hartman	2007	1622
330 6/8	47 0/8 46 3/8	37 4/8	6 6	Jackson County	CO	Marshall F. Whitsel, Jr.	1996	1626
330 6/8	53 7/8 54 4/8	41 6/8	6 6	Ravalli County	MT	Steve Kamps	2001	1626
330 6/8	56 2/8 54 0/8	40 4/8	6 7	Utah County	UT	Clay M. Carter	2003	1626
330 6/8	46 6/8 46 0/8	42 4/8	6 6	Valencia County	NM	Michael McCormick	2009	1626
330 5/8	49 1/8 51 5/8	38 1/8	6 6	Otero County	NM	Timothy K. Richards	1992	1630
330 5/8	52 4/8 54 4/8	35 7/8	6 6	Catron County	NM	Eugene Smith	1993	1630
330 5/8	52 0/8 51 3/8	37 1/8	6 6	White Pine County	NV	Patty Cornejo	1994	1630
330 5/8	49 7/8 50 2/8	40 5/8	6 6	Union County	OR	Steven Wayne Brooks	1997	1630
330 5/8	48 0/8 46 7/8	47 1/8	6 6	Coconino County	AZ	Brian Beamer	1999	1630
330 5/8	51 3/8 52 1/8	41 5/8	6 6	Ravalli County	MT	H. Earl Butler	2000	1630
330 5/8	52 4/8 52 1/8	33 7/8	5 5	Nye County	NV	Brady Shippy	2001	1630
330 5/8	50 2/8 49 0/8	41 3/8	7 7	Mora County	NM	Bobby Watkins	2002	1630
330 5/8	55 1/8 52 7/8	36 3/8	6 6	Sheridan County	WY	Michael Turner	2003	1630
330 5/8	51 3/8 51 6/8	40 1/8	6 6	Apache County	AZ	Kevin Harms	2004	1630
330 5/8	50 6/8 50 2/8	41 0/8	6 7	Sandoval County	NM	C. Michael Morrow	2007	1630
*330 5/8	46 4/8 46 3/8	37 4/8	6 7	White Pine County	NV	Jason Richards	2009	1630
330 4/8	44 6/8 46 4/8	38 1/8	6 6	Latah County	ID	John K. Pell	1964	1642
330 4/8	54 7/8 54 3/8	34 0/8	7 6	Shoshone County	ID	Kelly Thompson	1986	1642
330 4/8	55 3/8 55 4/8	38 0/8	6 6	Coconino County	AZ	Larry Moore	1991	1642
330 4/8	44 1/8 45 3/8	45 0/8	6 6	Petroleum County	MT	Chuck Eldredge	1998	1642
330 4/8	49 1/8 50 6/8	37 0/8	6 6	Johnson County	WY	James M. Barnes, Jr.	2002	1642
330 4/8	50 0/8 50 2/8	39 0/8	6 6	Grand County	CO	Kevin Vecchiarelli	2004	1642
330 4/8	54 1/8 55 0/8	42 0/8	7 6	Coconino County	AZ	Duane "Corky" Richardson	2004	1642
330 4/8	48 1/8 46 1/8	38 0/8	6 6	Big Horn County	WY	Jack Satterfield, Jr.	2007	1642
330 4/8	50 0/8 47 4/8	46 4/8	6 6	Albany County	WY	David Fleig	2009	1642
330 3/8	50 6/8 49 1/8	38 5/8	6 6	Madison County	MT	Tom Koelzer	1975	1651
330 3/8	53 6/8 52 1/8	39 5/8	8 10	Coconino County	AZ	James L. Ludrigson	1985	1651
330 3/8	48 6/8 48 5/8	38 7/8	6 6	Grant County	NM	Jack W. Hooper	1989	1651
330 3/8	53 1/8 54 3/8	38 5/8	7 6	Coconino County	AZ	Dave Pierce, Jr.	1993	1651
330 3/8	50 3/8 50 1/8	37 1/8	7 6	Catron County	NM	Eddie Claypool	1997	1651
330 3/8	56 3/8 53 6/8	46 7/8	6 5	Catron County	NM	Tim Canalito	1998	1651
330 3/8	47 3/8 50 1/8	34 3/8	6 6	Eagle Lake	SAS	Floyd Forster	1998	1651
330 3/8	53 7/8 50 5/8	41 7/8	6 6	Moffat County	CO	Don Bradley	2004	1651
330 3/8	53 3/8 54 3/8	45 7/8	6 6	Coconino County	AZ	Jeremy Podborny	2007	1651
330 3/8	53 1/8 53 7/8	42 1/8	6 6	Ravalli County	MT	Nou Yang	2010	1651
330 2/8	52 1/8 49 4/8	40 4/8	6 6	Larimer County	CO	Carl Spina	2002	1661
330 2/8	52 3/8 51 5/8	39 0/8	6 6	Big Horn County	WY	Tim Kindred	2005	1661
*330 2/8	51 0/8 51 3/8	36 6/8	6 6	Mineral County	MT	Randy Cote	2007	1661
330 2/8	52 3/8 48 0/8	36 2/8	7 6	Sheridan County	WY	Randy Burtis	2010	1661
330 1/8	50 1/8 50 0/8	42 7/8	6 6	Grant County	OR	James M. Carter	1986	1665
330 1/8	46 5/8 47 4/8	43 7/8	6 6	Larimer County	CO	Danny M. Holt	1996	1665
330 1/8	48 0/8 46 7/8	35 6/8	8 7	Bonneville County	ID	Myron T. Custer	1997	1665
330 1/8	49 1/8 52 0/8	39 1/8	6 6	Valley County	ID	Scott L. Stevens	1999	1665
330 1/8	49 6/8 52 1/8	32 3/8	6 6	Coconino County	AZ	Ken Stieh	1999	1665
330 1/8	48 3/8 49 3/8	47 5/8	6 6	Petroleum County	MT	Steve Wharton	2002	1665
330 1/8	45 7/8 48 2/8	41 4/8	6 7	Butte County	ID	Douglas Howell	2003	1665
330 0/8	53 2/8 53 5/8	45 0/8	6 6	Socorro County	NM	Ron White	1977	1672
330 0/8	48 7/8 49 0/8	37 0/8	7 7	Sanders County	MT	Steve Larson	1981	1672
330 0/8	52 7/8 50 4/8	33 4/8	6 6	Petroleum County	MT	John Fleharty	1985	1672
330 0/8	46 7/8 49 7/8	43 6/8	6 6	Albany County	WY	Paul Ayotte	1985	1672
330 0/8	52 5/8 52 6/8	41 2/8	6 6	Catron County	NM	Russell Arndt	1998	1672
330 0/8	42 4/8 42 7/8	37 2/8	6 6	Petroleum County	MT	Craig Enervold	1999	1672
330 0/8	51 0/8 49 5/8	41 2/8	6 7	Caribou County	ID	Robert L. Rigby	1999	1672
330 0/8	47 1/8 48 3/8	37 6/8	6 6	Mohave County	AZ	Kevin M. Calmes	1999	1672
330 0/8	53 2/8 52 2/8	36 2/8	6 6	Coconino County	AZ	Roy E. Grace	1999	1672
330 0/8	50 5/8 49 5/8	46 2/8	6 6	Chouteau County	MT	Thomas D. Willson	1999	1672
330 0/8	47 4/8 41 4/8	39 4/8	6 6	Toad River	BC	Roy Baird	2001	1672
330 0/8	48 7/8 49 2/8	39 4/8	7 6	Jefferson County	OR	Patrick McCaffrey	2003	1672
330 0/8	52 6/8 52 2/8	34 2/8	6 6	Coconino County	AZ	Richard Barkley	2005	1672
330 0/8	53 4/8 53 6/8	42 0/8	6 6	Coconino County	AZ	Michael A. Pfander	2005	1672
*330 0/8	49 7/8 49 5/8	39 1/8	7 7	Cibola County	NM	Thomas R. Hicks	2008	1672
329 7/8	46 1/8 45 1/8	36 7/8	6 6	Eagle County	CO	Jeffrey A. Duckworth	1981	1687
329 7/8	51 4/8 48 6/8	39 3/8	6 6	Powell County	MT	Marlon J. Clapham	1986	1687
329 7/8	47 2/8 49 2/8	34 3/8	6 6	Crook County	OR	Terry Luther	1991	1687
329 7/8	50 3/8 49 1/8	37 5/8	7 7	Catron County	NM	Donald M. Graves	1991	1687
329 7/8	47 4/8 46 5/8	33 1/8	6 6	Phillips County	MT	Rick Miller	1992	1687
329 7/8	47 4/8 49 4/8	39 5/8	6 7	Shoshone County	ID	Kenny M. Nelson	1996	1687
329 7/8	52 0/8 53 7/8	44 3/8	7 6	Coconino County	AZ	Gary Dyer	1997	1687
329 7/8	56 0/8 56 4/8	38 3/8	6 6	Moffat County	CO	Jeff Lampe	1999	1687
329 7/8	52 6/8 51 7/8	35 3/8	6 6	Lemhi County	ID	Joe C. Klink	2001	1687
*329 7/8	48 6/8 48 3/8	35 5/8	6 6	Petroleum County	MT	Justin Raber	2003	1687
329 6/8	49 1/8 49 0/8	37 4/8	6 6	Rio Blanco County	CO	Myles Keller	1974	1697
329 6/8	48 1/8 47 6/8	38 0/8	6 6	Coconino County	AZ	Mike Moulton	1983	1697
329 6/8	53 0/8 51 0/8	34 4/8	6 6	Phillips County	MT	Gregg Pauley	1987	1697
329 6/8	44 0/8 47 0/8	36 6/8	6 6	Catron County	NM	Eddie Claypool	1991	1697
329 6/8	57 2/8 58 0/8	50 0/8	6 6	Cibola County	NM	Johnny M. Perea	1991	1697
329 6/8	54 1/8 54 2/8	49 0/8	6 6	Larimer County	CO	Billy E. Corley	1993	1697
329 6/8	53 5/8 54 1/8	35 2/8	7 6	Latah County	ID	James H. Weatherford	1998	1697
329 6/8	52 4/8 50 1/8	41 2/8	6 7	Wallowa County	OR	Jared L. Rogers	2003	1697
329 6/8	48 0/8 47 3/8	35 4/8	6 6	Washington County	ID	Richard A. Young	2005	1697
329 6/8	52 3/8 52 2/8	37 3/8	7 7	Mesa County	CO	Jody Green	2007	1697
329 6/8	52 6/8 50 1/8	34 6/8	6 6	Moffat County	CO	Preston H. Parker	2007	1697
329 6/8	53 1/8 52 4/8	39 2/8	6 6	Montrose County	CO	Tony Lee Schell	2008	1697
329 5/8	42 1/8 44 7/8	34 2/8	6 7	Adams County	ID	Curtis Lemon	1978	1709
329 5/8	54 6/8 52 7/8	40 5/8	6 7	Silver Bow County	MT	William E. Bullock	1981	1709

695

AMERICAN ELK (TYPICAL ANTLERS)

Minimum Score 260   Continued

SCORE	LENGTH OF R MAIN BEAM L	INSIDE SPREAD	NUMBER OF R POINTS L	AREA	STATE/ PROVINCE	HUNTER'S NAME	DATE	RANK
329 5/8	52 1/8 49 0/8	40 1/8	7 6	Washington County	ID	Kevin Tams	1994	1709
329 5/8	52 2/8 53 6/8	45 1/8	6 6	Moffat County	CO	Frank S. Noska IV	2001	1709
329 5/8	53 5/8 53 0/8	42 6/8	6 8	Coconino County	AZ	Jerry D. Lees	2002	1709
329 5/8	52 1/8 53 7/8	41 5/8	6 6	Sandoval County	NM	John Solomon	2007	1709
329 4/8	47 4/8 47 3/8	43 2/8	6 6	Custer County	ID	Gary Kimball	1979	1715
329 4/8	48 2/8 48 4/8	35 2/8	6 6	Catron County	NM	Donald W. Duewall	1982	1715
329 4/8	49 2/8 51 4/8	45 0/8	6 8	Phillips County	MT	Dennis R. King	1989	1715
329 4/8	47 2/8 48 2/8	38 2/8	6 6	Coconino County	AZ	Lynn M. Johnson	1995	1715
329 4/8	51 5/8 52 1/8	39 6/8	6 6	Beaverhead County	MT	Todd P. Green	1998	1715
329 4/8	50 5/8 49 0/8	33 0/8	6 6	Petroleum County	MT	Eric Hoggarth	2004	1715
329 4/8	50 1/8 52 2/8	39 0/8	6 7	Iron County	UT	Dustin Orton	2006	1715
329 4/8	50 4/8 50 1/8	41 2/8	6 6	Johnson County	WY	Joe Baird	2008	1715
329 3/8	55 4/8 51 1/8	37 2/8	7 6	Catron County	NM	James Scarbrough	1986	1723
329 3/8	50 0/8 49 7/8	39 1/8	6 6	Gallatin County	MT	Mark Hanshue	1987	1723
329 3/8	52 7/8 53 1/8	37 2/8	6 7	Lincoln County	NM	Henry Vega	1988	1723
*329 3/8	48 6/8 48 6/8	41 1/8	6 6	Park County	WY	Gary Joseph	2003	1723
329 3/8	49 2/8 50 0/8	39 3/8	6 6	Duchesne County	UT	Kris Weaver	2008	1723
329 3/8	53 4/8 52 6/8	36 7/8	6 6	Wallowa County	OR	Dave Chapman	2008	1723
329 2/8	52 3/8 52 4/8	44 4/8	6 6	Valley County	ID	B. C. Cunningham	1969	1729
329 2/8	50 1/8 52 4/8	35 6/8	6 6	Valley County	MT	Thomas L. Solem	1981	1729
329 2/8	48 6/8 51 1/8	38 2/8	7 6	Bonneville County	ID	Paul H. Laver	1981	1729
329 2/8	50 0/8 53 2/8	38 2/8	7 6	Sanders County	MT	Glenn Nerby	1991	1729
329 2/8	45 5/8 46 1/8	37 6/8	6 6	Duck Mtns.	MAN	Mark Kobelka	2000	1729
*329 2/8	49 1/8 48 5/8	41 4/8	6 6	Garfield County	MT	Kenneth F. Hammond, Jr.	2004	1729
329 2/8	51 5/8 51 6/8	43 2/8	6 7	Garfield County	MT	Tony Swiontek	2004	1729
329 2/8	52 6/8 52 3/8	39 2/8	6 7	Custer County	SD	Aaron Thompson	2004	1729
329 2/8	48 1/8 49 1/8	42 4/8	6 6	Caribou County	ID	Mick McCullough	2009	1729
329 2/8	52 1/8 54 2/8	37 6/8	6 6	Meagher County	MT	Jim Kennedy	2009	1729
329 1/8	47 7/8 49 4/8	40 1/8	6 6	Adams County	ID	Curt Lemmons	1965	1739
329 1/8	51 5/8 53 7/8	44 3/8	7 7	Moffat County	CO	Glenn W. Pritchard	1972	1739
329 1/8	44 6/8 44 2/8	37 0/8	6 6	Rio Blanco County	CO	Harold Boyack	1976	1739
329 1/8	45 4/8 46 1/8	39 7/8	6 6	Mineral County	MT	Gary A. Hudson	1988	1739
329 1/8	54 6/8 53 5/8	40 1/8	6 6	Erickson	MAN	Kim Meger	1996	1739
329 1/8	53 5/8 54 0/8	39 4/8	6 7	Clark County	NV	Ron Reed	1997	1739
329 1/8	51 4/8 50 3/8	37 7/8	6 7	Judith Basin County	MT	Shawn P. Price	1997	1739
329 1/8	53 1/8 54 4/8	40 5/8	6 6	Ouray County	CO	Mike Masker	1997	1739
329 1/8	52 4/8 53 6/8	44 7/8	6 6	Sevier County	UT	Steve Ulibarri	1998	1739
329 1/8	50 5/8 50 6/8	47 1/8	6 6	Sevier County	UT	Albert Blair	2001	1739
329 1/8	52 5/8 53 5/8	41 7/8	6 7	Big Horn County	MT	Duffy Brown	2003	1739
329 1/8	52 1/8 51 3/8	36 7/8	6 6	Sevier County	UT	Shawn Kendall	2004	1739
*329 1/8	52 2/8 50 4/8	35 7/8	7 7	Fergus County	MT	David Corrigan	2005	1739
329 1/8	55 2/8 58 7/8	40 7/8	7 7	Coconino County	AZ	David F. Depler	2005	1739
*329 1/8	48 4/8 49 2/8	38 7/8	6 6	Coconino County	AZ	Arnie Crum	2006	1739
329 1/8	49 3/8 48 5/8	44 1/8	6 6	Jefferson County	MT	Steve J. Joyner	2009	1739
*329 1/8	44 2/8 45 6/8	41 7/8	8 6	Taos County	NM	R. Kirk Sharp	2010	1739
329 0/8	56 0/8 54 3/8	40 2/8	8 6	Yakima County	WA	Jerry Harris	1963	1756
329 0/8	48 1/8 48 5/8	38 6/8	6 7	Sanders County	MT	Fred Mensik	1983	1756
329 0/8	49 3/8 48 5/8	37 2/8	6 6	Garfield County	CO	Vance A. Fairhurst	1993	1756
329 0/8	50 5/8 54 0/8	39 4/8	6 6	Catron County	NM	Joseph A. Lorenz	1995	1756
329 0/8	56 1/8 56 0/8	40 6/8	6 6	Coconino County	AZ	Brandon Wynn	2001	1756
329 0/8	50 7/8 50 3/8	42 2/8	6 6	Grand County	CO	Scott Kellogg	2003	1756
329 0/8	46 0/8 47 5/8	36 6/8	7 7	Catron County	NM	Tim R. Dawson	2005	1756
329 0/8	47 7/8 49 5/8	35 0/8	6 6	Petroleum County	MT	Brad Seyfert	2006	1756
329 0/8	48 7/8 47 1/8	34 4/8	6 6	Wayne County	UT	Jason Ekker	2007	1756
328 7/8	47 5/8 50 4/8	43 5/8	6 7	Catron County	NM	Gil Holland	1995	1765
328 7/8	50 3/8 50 5/8	40 1/8	6 7	Siskiyou County	CA	Michael J. Dangler	2003	1765
328 7/8	54 6/8 55 4/8	36 1/8	6 7	Umatilla County	OR	Tim Cooper	2005	1765
328 7/8	47 1/8 46 1/8	37 5/8	6 6	Sheridan County	WY	James Caron	2005	1765
328 7/8	51 0/8 51 2/8	41 5/8	6 7	Umatilla County	OR	Darrell S. Primmer	2005	1765
328 7/8	53 2/8 50 0/8	37 5/8	6 6	Lane County	OR	Avel Salgado	2009	1765
328 6/8	48 5/8 49 0/8	43 6/8	6 6	Crook County	OR	Gary Kiepert	1983	1771
328 6/8	46 1/8 47 1/8	38 6/8	6 6	Colfax County	NM	Robert Torstenson	1996	1771
328 6/8	50 2/8 49 6/8	38 2/8	6 7	Lake County	CO	Kirk Mulkin	2000	1771
328 6/8	53 5/8 53 4/8	42 2/8	6 6	Coconino County	AZ	Blake Walker	2004	1771
328 6/8	50 4/8 53 1/8	41 4/8	6 8	Lincoln County	NV	G. Lowe Morrison	2008	1771
*328 6/8	51 4/8 49 2/8	34 4/8	6 6	Moffat County	CO	Kurt W. Keskimaki	2009	1771
328 6/8	56 0/8 53 4/8	34 0/8	6 6	Graham County	AZ	Joel J. Dingeldien	2009	1771
328 6/8	48 6/8 48 3/8	44 2/8	6 6	Moffat County	CO	Mike Dziekan	2010	1771
*328 6/8	49 4/8 49 4/8	47 4/8	6 6	Utah County	UT	Todd Grossenbach	2010	1771
328 5/8	52 7/8 54 0/8	34 3/8	7 7	Catron County	NM	George F. Corriher	1991	1780
328 5/8	45 3/8 43 5/8	39 7/8	6 7	Valley County	ID	Curt L. Giese	2000	1780
328 5/8	51 7/8 54 0/8	40 1/8	6 6	Coconino County	AZ	Gerry Backhaus	2003	1780
328 4/8	50 1/8 47 6/8	39 0/8	6 6	Sanders County	MT	Kenneth B. Neubauer	1983	1783
328 4/8	49 5/8 50 0/8	47 0/8	6 6	Rio Arriba County	NM	Schuyler B. Marshall	1994	1783
328 4/8	55 2/8 52 3/8	35 0/8	6 6	Apache County	AZ	Bryan R. Yorksmith	1997	1783
328 4/8	55 7/8 53 7/8	45 2/8	6 6	Catron County	NM	John W. Ellas	1998	1783
328 4/8	46 6/8 49 0/8	37 2/8	6 6	Apache County	AZ	Ralph B. Harris	2001	1783
328 4/8	51 2/8 52 6/8	39 2/8	6 6	Butte County	ID	Douglas Howell	2001	1783
328 4/8	50 0/8 50 6/8	39 0/8	6 6	Albany County	WY	Hub Lenz	2003	1783
328 3/8	47 6/8 48 3/8	40 1/8	7 8	Kittitas County	WA	Gary W. Fletcher	1993	1790
328 3/8	54 5/8 55 7/8	29 1/8	7 6	Coconino County	AZ	Cary Jellison	1995	1790
328 3/8	48 0/8 50 0/8	37 1/8	6 6	Lemhi County	ID	Mike Dunn	1996	1790
328 3/8	47 4/8 48 7/8	39 7/8	7 6	Umatilla County	OR	Chris Neufeld	1997	1790
328 3/8	51 1/8 50 6/8	45 1/8	6 6	Custer County	ID	Jeff A. Buck	2000	1790
328 3/8	46 7/8 47 2/8	42 5/8	6 6	Idaho County	ID	Stephen Garwick	2002	1790
328 3/8	46 4/8 47 0/8	33 1/8	6 6	Elko County	NV	Kevin G. Peterson	2003	1790
328 3/8	52 1/8 52 5/8	41 7/8	6 6	Garfield County	UT	Michael J. Trujillo	2004	1790
*328 3/8	44 0/8 45 3/8	40 3/8	6 7	Union County	OR	Karlton Perkins	2009	1790
328 2/8	48 4/8 49 4/8	40 4/8	6 7	Crook County	OR	Scott Reed	1984	1799
328 2/8	52 3/8 50 6/8	43 4/8	6 7	Adams County	ID	Ted Cutler/Craig Keyser	1985	1799
328 2/8	52 0/8 52 6/8	37 2/8	6 6	Coconino County	AZ	Richard D. Tone	1989	1799
328 2/8	50 7/8 53 2/8	44 2/8	6 6	Union County	OR	Steven Nichols	1996	1799
328 2/8	51 3/8 51 5/8	40 6/8	6 6	Coconino County	AZ	H. Thomas Jensen	1998	1799
328 2/8	48 0/8 50 5/8	40 4/8	6 6	Catron County	NM	Douglas W. Rampy	2001	1799
328 2/8	48 2/8 50 2/8	38 2/8	6 6	Douglas County	OR	Spencer Black	2005	1799

AMERICAN ELK (TYPICAL ANTLERS)

Minimum Score 260 — Continued

SCORE	LENGTH OF R MAIN BEAM L	INSIDE SPREAD	NUMBER OF R POINTS L	AREA	STATE/ PROVINCE	HUNTER'S NAME	DATE	RANK
328 2/8	47 2/8 49 4/8	45 4/8	7 6	Socorro County	NM	Doug Aikin	2006	1799
328 2/8	47 1/8 49 3/8	34 2/8	6 7	Petroleum County	MT	D. "Mitch" Kottas	2006	1799
328 2/8	50 0/8 50 7/8	37 0/8	6 7	Catron County	NM	Blake Bender	2008	1799
328 1/8	44 7/8 44 3/8	41 3/8	6 6	Lewis County	WA	Larry F. Smith	1986	1809
328 1/8	45 6/8 47 5/8	37 1/8	6 7	Albany County	WY	Brian L. Biel	1986	1809
328 1/8	46 7/8 46 3/8	40 5/8	7 6	Catron County	NM	William Holdman	1993	1809
328 1/8	46 2/8 50 6/8	39 7/8	6 6	Coconino County	AZ	Joe Bruscato	2005	1809
328 1/8	44 3/8 46 0/8	38 7/8	6 6	Rio Blanco County	CO	Daniel E. Rudy	2007	1809
328 1/8	49 0/8 52 0/8	40 1/8	6 6	Sweetwater County	WY	Robert C. Brinkerhoff	2007	1809
328 1/8	45 4/8 46 6/8	35 3/8	6 6	Garfield County	UT	Michael C. Hirschi	2008	1809
*328 1/8	45 2/8 44 3/8	35 1/8	6 6	Apache County	AZ	Cody L. Gifford	2008	1809
*328 1/8	49 5/8 51 2/8	46 0/8	7 6	Montrose County	CO	Brett H. Queen	2010	1809
328 0/8	54 1/8 51 3/8	40 0/8	6 7	Coconino County	AZ	James L. Hyde	1977	1818
328 0/8	44 2/8 44 3/8	39 6/8	6 6	Larimer County	CO	J. G. Hamblet, Jr.	1979	1818
328 0/8	50 6/8 52 0/8	39 6/8	6 7	Coconino County	AZ	Clay Stazenski	1991	1818
328 0/8	50 7/8 50 4/8	45 6/8	6 6	Madison County	MT	Joseph K. Stokes	1993	1818
328 0/8	45 0/8 45 5/8	34 0/8	6 6	Teton County	WY	Jerry Bodar	1999	1818
328 0/8	48 4/8 51 7/8	44 6/8	6 6	Carbon County	WY	Allen Frude	2004	1818
328 0/8	47 4/8 46 0/8	37 6/8	6 7	Coconino County	AZ	John Erdody IV	2007	1818
328 0/8	50 2/8 49 4/8	32 6/8	6 6	Petroleum County	MT	D. "Mitch" Kottas	2007	1818
328 0/8	49 3/8 48 6/8	42 2/8	6 6	Coconino County	AZ	Wendy D. Winn	2007	1818
327 7/8	48 1/8 46 2/8	46 3/8	6 6	Lewis & Clark County	MT	Darrell J. Archey	1984	1827
327 7/8	48 0/8 48 4/8	43 5/8	5 6	Cochrane	ALB	Rod Newsham	1986	1827
327 7/8	46 1/8 47 2/8	36 5/8	6 6	Coconino County	AZ	Drazen Baricevic	1996	1827
327 7/8	48 6/8 46 6/8	34 7/8	6 6	Park County	CO	Howard D. Drummond, Sr.	1999	1827
327 7/8	50 6/8 51 4/8	38 5/8	6 6	Mesa County	CO	Eric Peterson	2001	1827
327 7/8	49 4/8 50 4/8	39 2/8	6 7	Yavapai County	AZ	Kevin L. Wolfe	2001	1827
327 7/8	52 6/8 54 5/8	37 1/8	6 6	Mineral County	MT	Sou Thao	2005	1827
*327 7/8	50 3/8 50 1/8	39 1/8	6 6	Meagher County	MT	Michael T. Reardon	2006	1827
327 7/8	50 2/8 51 1/8	36 5/8	6 6	Johnson County	WY	Tippy H. Clark	2007	1827
327 6/8	51 6/8 53 1/8	36 2/8	6 6	Coconino County	AZ	Jim Parker	1989	1836
327 6/8	50 7/8 52 6/8	40 0/8	6 6	Mesa County	CO	Brian Karsten	1991	1836
327 6/8	50 5/8 51 5/8	38 6/8	7 6	Gallatin County	MT	Scott L. Koelzer	1993	1836
327 6/8	49 0/8 47 7/8	47 4/8	6 6	Lemhi County	ID	Robert A. Johnson	1998	1836
327 6/8	52 7/8 50 2/8	37 6/8	6 6	Catron County	NM	Steve R. Dunlap	1999	1836
327 6/8	50 5/8 49 6/8	37 6/8	6 6	Park County	WY	Greg L. Deatsman	2001	1836
327 6/8	52 3/8 46 7/8	41 6/8	6 6	Larimer County	CO	Russ Rohloff	2002	1836
*327 6/8	47 3/8 47 1/8	41 0/8	6 6	Garfield County	CO	Mike K. Thompson	2004	1836
327 6/8	48 6/8 50 5/8	39 4/8	6 6	Gallatin County	MT	Lawrence R. Jones	2004	1836
327 6/8	62 6/8 59 5/8	38 2/8	6 6	Klickitat County	WA	Kurt Goesch	2005	1836
327 6/8	53 0/8 54 4/8	41 0/8	6 6	Coconino County	AZ	Linda M. Hutchinson	2006	1836
327 6/8	47 1/8 45 1/8	33 0/8	6 7	Sweetwater County	WY	Kreston J. Cross	2007	1836
*327 6/8	52 0/8 53 2/8	32 2/8	6 6	Socorro County	NM	Tamara Bredy	2007	1836
*327 6/8	47 0/8 47 4/8	38 4/8	6 6	Fergus County	MT	L. Grant Foster	2009	1836
327 5/8	48 5/8 49 4/8	38 3/8	6 6	Lincoln County	WY	Kirby Booth	1990	1850
327 5/8	49 3/8 49 4/8	37 1/8	6 6	Lincoln County	WY	Brett R. Ure	1995	1850
327 5/8	50 7/8 52 0/8	44 1/8	6 6	Coconino County	AZ	Patrick F. Connelly	1995	1850
327 5/8	53 0/8 53 2/8	39 1/8	6 6	Lemhi County	ID	Mike Virgin	1996	1850
327 5/8	54 3/8 54 4/8	39 3/8	6 6	Coconino County	AZ	Jason Dishmon	1998	1850
327 5/8	46 1/8 46 1/8	35 7/8	6 7	Jefferson County	CO	Jerry Grueneberg	2002	1850
327 5/8	48 4/8 47 4/8	37 1/8	6 6	Idaho County	ID	Craig Friedrich	2009	1850
327 4/8	48 4/8 46 4/8	43 6/8	6 6	Beaverhead County	MT	Dave Knudsen	1974	1857
327 4/8	49 4/8 47 4/8	40 4/8	6 6	Lewis & Clark County	MT	Richard J. Kornick	1980	1857
327 4/8	49 6/8 48 0/8	39 0/8	6 6	Beaverhead County	MT	Roy F. Bach	1984	1857
327 4/8	51 7/8 48 2/8	34 6/8	6 7	Mesa County	CO	Dr. John R. Thodos	1987	1857
327 4/8	49 5/8 48 5/8	37 6/8	6 6	Yakima County	WA	Jim Rathbun	1989	1857
327 4/8	55 6/8 56 4/8	48 2/8	6 6	Apache County	AZ	Paul J. Grube	2003	1857
327 4/8	49 6/8 50 3/8	39 2/8	6 6	Iron County	UT	Terry R. Price	2004	1857
*327 4/8	52 0/8 56 2/8	37 0/8	6 6	Coconino County	AZ	Jerry Fuller	2008	1857
327 3/8	47 4/8 47 0/8	34 3/8	7 7	Coconino County	AZ	Richard D. Tone	1991	1865
327 3/8	49 6/8 48 2/8	41 5/8	6 6	Phillips County	MT	Ervin Langseth	1992	1865
327 3/8	50 1/8 49 6/8	39 7/8	6 6	Fergus County	MT	Jeffrey Stockhill	2002	1865
327 3/8	50 3/8 49 5/8	33 7/8	6 6	Colfax County	NM	Bob Ameen	2003	1865
327 3/8	46 4/8 46 1/8	40 1/8	6 6	Rich County	UT	Robert G. Petersen	2005	1865
327 3/8	49 7/8 48 6/8	42 3/8	6 5	Coconino County	AZ	Dale Christensen	2006	1865
327 3/8	51 0/8 51 1/8	41 0/8	7 8	Lincoln County	NM	Kurtis Carman	2009	1865
327 3/8	51 0/8 50 7/8	38 1/8	7 7	Douglas County	OR	Jared Moffitt	2010	1865
327 2/8	49 5/8 50 6/8	36 2/8	6 6	Clackamas County	OR	Jeff Youngberg	1993	1873
327 2/8	49 5/8 49 1/8	35 0/8	6 6	Boulder County	CO	Steve Nichols	1996	1873
327 2/8	51 1/8 51 0/8	37 4/8	6 6	Rio Arriba County	NM	Larson Panzy	2000	1873
*327 2/8	48 1/8 48 4/8	44 2/8	6 6	Lewis County	WA	Lonny Gabrio	2007	1873
327 2/8	52 0/8 51 1/8	39 4/8	6 6	White Pine County	NV	Ron Caldwell	2007	1873
327 2/8	50 3/8 50 3/8	36 4/8	6 6	Catron County	NM	Dagen Haymore	2007	1873
*327 2/8	46 7/8 45 7/8	35 2/8	6 6	Utah County	UT	Trinton Thomas	2009	1873
327 1/8	50 3/8 48 2/8	43 3/8	6 6	Park County	MT	Dale Alt	1968	1880
327 1/8	49 7/8 49 4/8	41 7/8	6 6	Lincoln County	WA	David C. Hubbard	2001	1880
327 1/8	50 0/8 49 1/8	39 4/8	7 6	Comanche County	OK	Hunter D. Cook	2002	1880
*327 1/8	49 5/8 50 2/8	35 4/8	7 7	Utah County	UT	Troy Olson	2004	1880
327 1/8	50 0/8 51 6/8	41 1/8	6 6	Uintah County	UT	Daniel R. Strickland	2005	1880
327 1/8	55 6/8 57 5/8	39 1/8	7 7	Park County	WY	Darrell Wright	2005	1880
327 1/8	50 2/8 52 2/8	43 7/8	7 7	Coconino County	AZ	Don C. Giblin, Sr.	2006	1880
327 1/8	50 5/8 48 5/8	35 1/8	7 7	Apache County	AZ	Kevin Mitchell	2008	1880
327 0/8	50 6/8 51 7/8	40 4/8	6 6	Clearwater County	ID	C. Randall Byers	1976	1888
327 0/8	48 0/8 48 2/8	39 4/8	6 6	Catron County	NM	David Chavez	1981	1888
327 0/8	50 0/8 50 2/8	36 0/8	6 7	Rossburn	MAN	Glen J. White	1986	1888
327 0/8	48 7/8 47 0/8	37 4/8	7 6	Sandoval County	NM	Freddie Barber	1989	1888
327 0/8	44 7/8 44 1/8	33 2/8	6 6	Meagher County	MT	Robert L. Crafts	1991	1888
327 0/8	47 7/8 47 2/8	39 2/8	6 6	Park County	MT	Richard Backes	1996	1888
327 0/8	45 6/8 46 5/8	34 0/8	7 6	Otero County	NM	Scott Scarborough	2004	1888
327 0/8	50 7/8 51 2/8	35 4/8	6 7	Garfield County	WA	Shane Broeske	2005	1888
327 0/8	48 2/8 48 3/8	40 4/8	7 6	Wallowa County	OR	Brian S. Bergstrom	2005	1888
327 0/8	52 1/8 51 7/8	36 2/8	6 6	Union County	OR	Lee V. Pearce	2006	1888
*327 0/8	48 7/8 48 6/8	39 2/8	7 6	Fergus County	MT	Chad W. Martin	2006	1888
*327 0/8	52 0/8 53 0/8	40 0/8	6 6	Yavapai County	AZ	Vince Hart	2006	1888
326 7/8	48 6/8 47 4/8	38 1/8	6 6	Custer County	CO	Rohn L. Garnhart	1990	1900

697

AMERICAN ELK (TYPICAL ANTLERS)

Minimum Score 260 Continued

SCORE	LENGTH OF R MAIN BEAM L	INSIDE SPREAD	NUMBER OF R POINTS L	AREA	STATE/ PROVINCE	HUNTER'S NAME	DATE	RANK
326 7/8	55 4/8 57 3/8	40 3/8	6 6	Grant County	NM	Toby B. Rascon	1995	1900
326 7/8	47 0/8 47 6/8	40 1/8	6 6	Petroleum County	MT	Dennis Trapp	1997	1900
326 7/8	50 6/8 49 5/8	44 1/8	6 6	Clear Creek County	CO	Jeff Mees	2001	1900
326 7/8	47 7/8 44 4/8	33 3/8	6 7	Pennington County	SD	Jarrod Rayhill	2003	1900
326 7/8	49 6/8 51 3/8	42 1/8	6 6	San Juan County	UT	Kenny E. Leo	2009	1900
*326 7/8	46 7/8 47 7/8	38 5/8	6 6	Socorro County	NM	Steven Jones	2010	1900
326 7/8	48 0/8 49 0/8	42 7/8	6 6	Grand County	CO	Kevin E. Vecchiarelli	2010	1900
326 6/8	48 5/8 50 3/8	43 0/8	7 6	Bighorn Mtns.	WY	Rick Mitchell	1981	1908
326 6/8	50 4/8 47 4/8	48 2/8	6 7	Larimer County	CO	Tom Duncan	1983	1908
326 6/8	46 6/8 46 4/8	39 4/8	6 6	Colfax County	NM	John L. Chapman	1984	1908
326 6/8	52 1/8 51 5/8	35 6/8	6 6	Rio Arriba County	NM	Vincent R. Vicenti	1989	1908
326 6/8	50 6/8 53 0/8	34 1/8	9 6	Catron County	NM	Ron Rhodes	1993	1908
326 6/8	51 2/8 51 6/8	45 2/8	6 6	Blaine County	ID	John Wells	1995	1908
326 6/8	50 3/8 49 6/8	39 2/8	6 6	Greenlee County	AZ	Jeffrey S. Black	1998	1908
326 6/8	51 3/8 51 7/8	35 0/8	7 7	Apache County	AZ	Norman Low	2001	1908
326 6/8	49 2/8 45 0/8	37 2/8	6 7	Shoshone County	ID	Steve Williams	2003	1908
326 6/8	45 6/8 45 2/8	35 0/8	6 7	Bonneville County	ID	Richard D. Houck	2006	1908
326 5/8	52 1/8 53 5/8	42 1/8	6 7	Coconino County	AZ	Larry Glasson	1975	1918
326 5/8	48 3/8 50 2/8	40 7/8	6 6	Clackamas County	OR	William E. Lancaster	1987	1918
326 5/8	47 2/8 47 3/8	39 1/8	6 6	Wallowa County	OR	Dusty Powers	1988	1918
326 5/8	48 6/8 46 3/8	43 7/8	6 6	King County	WA	Eric Johnson	1993	1918
326 5/8	49 0/8 49 6/8	33 1/8	6 6	Garfield County	MT	David M. Borzick	1998	1918
326 5/8	51 4/8 49 2/8	37 7/8	6 6	Caribou County	ID	Scott Craig	2001	1918
326 5/8	54 4/8 52 1/8	38 7/8	6 6	Shoshone County	ID	Todd Standke	2005	1918
326 4/8	51 5/8 51 0/8	37 6/8	6 6	King County	WA	Leonard L Stolen	1984	1925
326 4/8	53 1/8 52 1/8	36 0/8	6 6	Coconino County	AZ	John Coffman	1990	1925
326 4/8	56 1/8 51 5/8	38 0/8	7 6	Fergus County	MT	Ronald Nelson	1992	1925
326 4/8	55 3/8 58 3/8	39 2/8	6 7	Dolores County	CO	Phillip Kibel	2003	1925
326 4/8	46 1/8 46 6/8	41 4/8	7 6	Johnson County	WY	Ron Apel	2003	1925
326 4/8	51 3/8 50 4/8	42 0/8	7 6	White Pine County	NV	Paul J. Harris	2006	1925
*326 4/8	46 0/8 46 3/8	41 6/8	7 7	Baker County	OR	John Bond	2007	1925
326 3/8	51 3/8 51 1/8	47 1/8	5 6	Socorro County	NM	Billy R. Spears	1976	1932
326 3/8	55 0/8 55 4/8	39 3/8	6 6	Flathead County	MT	Phil Von Bargen	1976	1932
326 3/8	51 6/8 51 6/8	32 3/8	6 7	White Pine County	NV	David E. Provost	1994	1932
326 3/8	51 1/8 52 6/8	41 1/8	6 6	Otero County	NM	Donald E. Westerbur	1994	1932
326 3/8	49 4/8 51 3/8	36 5/8	6 6	Custer County	ID	Tony Jerulle	1995	1932
326 3/8	46 5/8 46 5/8	36 1/8	6 6	Sublette County	WY	Campbell K. Kreps	2004	1932
*326 3/8	48 6/8 51 2/8	35 4/8	6 7	Phillips County	MT	Mike Mattis	2005	1932
326 3/8	46 6/8 45 5/8	32 5/8	7 7	Lincoln County	MT	Ray Sobiek	2006	1932
326 2/8	48 3/8 53 3/8	38 0/8	7 7	Carbon County	UT	Scott Wilkins	1989	1940
326 2/8	46 5/8 48 3/8	35 2/8	6 6	Fergus County	MT	Michael F. Otto	1997	1940
326 2/8	56 5/8 54 7/8	39 4/8	7 7	Wheatland County	MT	Timothy E. Klosterman	1998	1940
326 2/8	48 5/8 52 1/8	35 1/8	7 6	White Pine County	NV	Paul Wilmot	2000	1940
326 2/8	49 4/8 49 6/8	37 0/8	6 6	Apache County	AZ	Kenneth A. Zimny	2002	1940
326 2/8	51 1/8 46 4/8	36 2/8	8 7	Quay County	NM	Howard S. Harris	2004	1940
326 1/8	44 6/8 46 6/8	35 5/8	6 6	Lemhi County	ID	Ray Torrey	1967	1946
326 1/8	54 2/8 54 6/8	37 5/8	6 6	Grand County	CO	Paul Adams	1977	1946
326 1/8	49 5/8 48 6/8	34 1/8	6 7	Converse County	WY	Kevin Conway	1992	1946
326 1/8	49 7/8 51 7/8	43 1/8	6 6	Idaho County	ID	Ron Perry	1997	1946
326 1/8	53 2/8 52 7/8	34 5/8	7 6	Teton County	WY	William E. Schultz, DVM	1998	1946
326 1/8	49 4/8 48 5/8	38 3/8	6 6	Moffat County	CO	Tim Cuthriell	1998	1946
326 1/8	48 7/8 50 5/8	38 3/8	6 7	Apache County	AZ	Angelina Gina Chavez	2000	1946
326 1/8	48 4/8 48 0/8	42 0/8	6 7	Catron County	NM	Thomas J. Jakusz	2001	1946
*326 1/8	52 0/8 54 0/8	37 5/8	6 6	Catron County	NM	Mike Connett	2001	1946
326 1/8	51 2/8 50 1/8	40 1/8	6 6	Ravalli County	MT	Terran W. Lohman	2002	1946
326 1/8	50 1/8 49 2/8	31 1/8	6 6	Catron County	NM	Brady K. McGee	2009	1946
326 0/8	51 1/8 50 6/8	46 2/8	7 6	Boulder County	CO	Duke Prentup	1977	1957
326 0/8	51 4/8 51 3/8	38 4/8	6 6	Beaverhead County	MT	Scott P. Swan	1978	1957
326 0/8	49 3/8 47 4/8	36 4/8	6 6	Catron County	NM	Randall Cooley	1984	1957
326 0/8	53 1/8 49 2/8	39 6/8	6 6	Socorro County	NM	Ray Hatfield	1984	1957
326 0/8	46 2/8 46 7/8	36 6/8	6 6	Lemhi County	ID	John Bennett	1992	1957
326 0/8	51 0/8 52 2/8	36 4/8	7 6	Custer County	ID	Judd Mackintosh	1994	1957
326 0/8	50 4/8 50 4/8	45 0/8	6 6	Catron County	NM	Dean G. Martin	1996	1957
326 0/8	53 2/8 50 7/8	39 6/8	6 6	Pembina River	ALB	Kevin Nicol	1996	1957
326 0/8	50 0/8 49 2/8	35 2/8	6 7	Petroleum County	MT	Randy S. Bowler	2003	1957
326 0/8	49 6/8 49 3/8	36 4/8	6 6	Fremont County	WY	Thomas K. Dunlap	2004	1957
*326 0/8	45 5/8 45 3/8	30 2/8	6 6	Phillips County	MT	Bill Groesch	2007	1957
326 0/8	51 0/8 53 2/8	32 2/8	7 7	Coconino County	AZ	Mark Ovitt	2010	1957
325 7/8	50 7/8 47 1/8	35 4/8	7 7	Idaho County	ID	Robert C. Mitchell	1978	1969
325 7/8	45 3/8 45 1/8	34 5/8	6 6	Canmore	ALB	Douglas A. Parker	1984	1969
325 7/8	47 6/8 47 4/8	36 5/8	6 6	Catron County	NM	James Willard	1997	1969
325 7/8	52 4/8 50 2/8	39 3/8	6 6	Hinton	ALB	Jason Spenst	1997	1969
325 7/8	45 1/8 44 2/8	37 7/8	6 6	Catron County	NM	Paul Ludwig	1998	1969
325 7/8	52 7/8 54 0/8	42 1/8	6 7	Grant County	NM	James D. Schulz	2000	1969
325 7/8	51 0/8 51 1/8	36 4/8	6 7	Utah County	UT	Rod Akers	2002	1969
*325 7/8	49 1/8 51 4/8	34 1/8	6 6	Carter County	MT	Victor J. Ronder	2003	1969
325 7/8	52 0/8 53 2/8	40 7/8	5 6	Phillips County	MT	Patrick E. Wheeler	2004	1969
*325 7/8	46 5/8 46 6/8	45 7/8	6 6	Sierra County	NM	Ronald B. Duchac	2005	1969
325 6/8	49 1/8 51 5/8	43 6/8	6 6	Beaverhead County	MT	Bob Helming	1980	1979
325 6/8	46 7/8 46 5/8	40 0/8	6 6	Marion County	OR	Ron Bergeron	1983	1979
325 6/8	47 4/8 45 4/8	40 2/8	6 6	Otero County	NM	Jessie Cheramie	1993	1979
325 6/8	45 7/8 47 2/8	39 2/8	6 6	Caribou County	ID	William Trainor, Jr.	1995	1979
325 6/8	53 1/8 53 2/8	41 2/8	6 6	Catron County	NM	Patrick Kirby	1995	1979
325 6/8	49 2/8 51 4/8	41 0/8	6 6	Platte County	WY	Pat Souza	1996	1979
325 6/8	50 2/8 48 1/8	36 0/8	6 6	Catron County	NM	Zeb Kern	1998	1979
325 6/8	53 2/8 51 1/8	40 6/8	6 6	White Pine County	NV	Jerry E. McGuire	1998	1979
325 6/8	51 7/8 51 6/8	51 6/8	5 6	Cibola County	NM	Michael D. Furry	2000	1979
325 6/8	50 4/8 51 1/8	39 0/8	6 6	Johnson County	WY	Bonnie S. Anderson	2004	1979
325 5/8	43 6/8 45 0/8	39 1/8	7 7	Beaverhead County	MT	Danny Moore	1983	1989
325 5/8	51 2/8 52 3/8	41 5/8	6 6	Wheeler County	OR	Robert V. Martin	1986	1989
325 5/8	51 2/8 50 2/8	37 5/8	6 6	Deschutes County	OR	Royce D. Nelson	1992	1989
325 5/8	51 0/8 49 2/8	38 1/8	7 6	Washakie County	WY	Alan Grzybowski	1997	1989
325 5/8	50 6/8 50 2/8	38 3/8	6 6	Fergus County	MT	Robert Guenther	1999	1989
325 5/8	47 5/8 46 2/8	38 1/8	6 6	Phillips County	MT	Tim Taylor	2001	1989
325 5/8	50 4/8 49 3/8	40 5/8	8 7	Park County	WY	Ron Niziolek	2002	1989

698

AMERICAN ELK (TYPICAL ANTLERS)

Minimum Score 260

Continued

SCORE	LENGTH OF R MAIN BEAM L	INSIDE SPREAD	NUMBER OF R POINTS L	AREA	STATE/ PROVINCE	HUNTER'S NAME	DATE	RANK
325 5/8	51 4/8 52 6/8	36 7/8	6 6	Grant County	OR	Kyle Buschelman	2002	1989
325 5/8	50 1/8 48 6/8	39 5/8	6 6	Summit County	UT	Frank Staropoli	2004	1989
325 5/8	48 1/8 49 4/8	39 7/8	7 7	Wallowa County	OR	Tom Schmid	2004	1989
325 5/8	51 2/8 49 1/8	32 1/8	6 7	Chelan County	WA	Mark Gregory Yaple	2007	1989
325 5/8	48 2/8 50 1/8	37 0/8	6 7	Crook County	OR	Paul Askew	2008	1989
325 4/8	49 6/8 50 3/8	40 4/8	6 6	Montrose County	CO	Carol Cassidy	1973	2001
325 4/8	45 4/8 45 5/8	38 6/8	6 6	Larimer County	CO	Arnold Hale	1989	2001
325 4/8	48 1/8 51 2/8	38 0/8	6 6	Catron County	NM	Steve Van Zile	1991	2001
325 4/8	48 4/8 49 6/8	42 0/8	6 6	Fremont County	WY	Rene Suda	1995	2001
325 4/8	51 5/8 50 4/8	36 0/8	6 6	Saguache County	CO	Tony Heil	1998	2001
325 4/8	47 7/8 48 2/8	43 4/8	6 6	Gallatin County	MT	Larry Jent	1998	2001
325 4/8	48 0/8 49 5/8	36 4/8	7 6	Catron County	NM	Chad Birrenkott	1999	2001
325 4/8	48 7/8 49 7/8	39 4/8	6 6	Butte County	ID	Steve F. Keller	2000	2001
325 4/8	46 6/8 46 5/8	36 4/8	6 6	Utah County	UT	Craig Hill	2003	2001
325 4/8	51 2/8 51 5/8	43 4/8	6 6	King County	WA	Ronald Goff	2006	2001
325 4/8	53 2/8 53 0/8	38 4/8	6 6	San Miguel County	CO	Jade Huskey	2007	2001
325 3/8	47 3/8 45 2/8	33 3/8	7 6	Benewah County	ID	Tim Chandler	1984	2012
325 3/8	51 0/8 51 4/8	40 3/8	6 7	Coconino County	AZ	Les Shelton	1989	2012
325 3/8	50 2/8 51 5/8	40 7/8	6 6	Coconino County	AZ	Gary D. Bills	1991	2012
325 3/8	51 0/8 51 2/8	41 5/8	6 6	Apache County	AZ	Igor E. Ivanoff	1992	2012
325 3/8	50 1/8 50 0/8	38 7/8	6 6	Caribou County	ID	Paul L. Arnold	2002	2012
325 2/8	49 0/8 49 0/8	36 6/8	6 6	Caribou County	ID	Doug Foss	1986	2017
325 2/8	49 1/8 49 3/8	39 6/8	6 6	Lemhi County	ID	Mike Benton	1989	2017
325 2/8	50 3/8 49 2/8	42 6/8	6 7	Coconino County	AZ	Jerry L. Stewart	1992	2017
325 2/8	48 1/8 46 2/8	36 6/8	6 6	Gilpin County	CO	Joseph W. Mourray	1996	2017
325 2/8	51 1/8 50 6/8	36 2/8	6 6	Phillips County	MT	Jack Sorum	2004	2017
325 2/8	45 6/8 47 4/8	44 4/8	6 6	Idaho County	ID	Adam Haarberg	2005	2017
*325 2/8	45 7/8 47 5/8	38 2/8	6 6	Uinta County	WY	Mark Sambrailo	2007	2017
325 2/8	52 6/8 51 7/8	40 0/8	7 6	Catron County	NM	Sarah D. Miller	2008	2017
325 2/8	49 7/8 48 6/8	38 0/8	6 6	Park County	CO	Larry Clark	2008	2017
325 2/8	48 4/8 48 3/8	35 4/8	6 6	Park County	CO	Larry Clark	2009	2017
325 1/8	48 3/8 49 3/8	39 5/8	6 6	Lincoln County	NM	John D. Fitzgibbon	1991	2027
325 1/8	49 4/8 49 0/8	44 3/8	6 6	Caribou County	ID	Dennis Nelson	1994	2027
325 1/8	52 6/8 51 5/8	40 5/8	6 6	Apache County	AZ	R. Christopher Ellis	1997	2027
325 1/8	50 5/8 51 4/8	40 3/8	6 7	Umatilla County	OR	Merritt E. Tuttle	1998	2027
325 1/8	46 6/8 49 7/8	36 4/8	6 7	Idaho County	ID	Patrick Coop	2000	2027
325 1/8	49 1/8 49 0/8	37 5/8	6 6	Albany County	WY	Tim Wahe	2003	2027
325 1/8	51 6/8 51 2/8	37 6/8	6 7	Delta County	CO	Steve D. Martinez	2003	2027
*325 1/8	49 1/8 48 7/8	39 2/8	6 7	Catron County	NM	Mark Kayser	2005	2027
*325 1/8	48 1/8 49 4/8	39 5/8	6 6	White Pine County	NV	Don Waechtler	2007	2027
325 1/8	46 6/8 47 1/8	40 5/8	6 6	Catron County	NM	Jade Keeton	2007	2027
325 0/8	47 1/8 47 3/8	35 6/8	7 7	Silver Bow County	MT	Bob Gossack	1977	2037
325 0/8	52 4/8 49 5/8	39 4/8	6 6	Catron County	NM	Courtney King	1985	2037
325 0/8	44 7/8 51 0/8	45 2/8	6 6	Catron County	NM	Steve McCoy	1988	2037
325 0/8	49 7/8 51 1/8	41 0/8	7 7	Rio Arriba County	NM	Gene White	1990	2037
325 0/8	50 4/8 50 5/8	46 0/8	6 6	Valley County	ID	Will Grasmick	1998	2037
325 0/8	50 4/8 50 1/8	37 4/8	6 7	Catron County	NM	Alan Graves	1999	2037
325 0/8	53 4/8 52 2/8	35 0/8	6 6	Clark County	ID	Glen Berry	2000	2037
325 0/8	46 5/8 46 4/8	32 2/8	6 6	Bonneville County	ID	Ron Sherwood	2000	2037
325 0/8	51 5/8 53 2/8	37 6/8	6 6	Fergus County	MT	Robert O. Engum	2001	2037
325 0/8	47 3/8 50 4/8	39 6/8	6 7	Eagle County	CO	Nathan Flowers	2003	2037
325 0/8	50 6/8 48 0/8	35 0/8	7 7	Camas County	ID	Mark Cox	2003	2037
325 0/8	52 4/8 51 5/8	44 4/8	6 6	Gunnison County	CO	Christopher E. Cluley	2005	2037
*325 0/8	52 0/8 52 5/8	45 0/8	6 6	Yavapai County	AZ	Roy K. Keefer	2009	2037
324 7/8	52 4/8 47 1/8	36 7/8	6 6	Coconino County	AZ	William V. West	1995	2050
324 7/8	50 0/8 49 6/8	29 5/8	6 6	Caribou County	ID	Mark D. Siciliano	2001	2050
324 7/8	55 0/8 53 3/8	39 1/8	6 6	Phillips County	MT	Matt Strozewski	2002	2050
324 7/8	52 7/8 52 4/8	35 1/8	6 6	Wheatland County	MT	John Raty	2004	2050
324 7/8	52 6/8 51 7/8	39 1/8	6 8	Apache County	AZ	Rick Curley	2004	2050
324 7/8	53 4/8 50 5/8	41 5/8	6 6	Catron County	NM	Greg Lewis	2006	2050
*324 7/8	48 3/8 50 6/8	29 5/8	6 6	Washakie County	WY	Rod A. Salzman	2010	2050
324 6/8	47 1/8 46 2/8	42 0/8	7 6	Coconino County	AZ	William S. Acheson	1979	2057
324 6/8	45 7/8 45 2/8	37 0/8	6 6	Beaverhead County	MT	Tyler Robinson	1983	2057
324 6/8	46 4/8 46 0/8	42 0/8	6 6	Flathead County	MT	James Norvell	1995	2057
324 6/8	53 7/8 53 5/8	34 0/8	6 6	Coconino County	AZ	Jeff Adams	1999	2057
324 6/8	47 2/8 47 7/8	45 2/8	7 6	Gallatin County	MT	James S. Robinson	1999	2057
324 6/8	51 6/8 51 0/8	36 0/8	6 6	Johnson County	WY	Jerry Landrey	2003	2057
324 6/8	54 2/8 55 0/8	41 4/8	7 7	Park County	MT	Gabriel M. St. Pierre	2005	2057
324 6/8	48 2/8 48 6/8	39 4/8	6 6	Rich County	UT	Glen O. Hallows	2009	2057
324 5/8	46 0/8 47 4/8	32 1/8	6 8	Moffat County	CO	Glenn W. Pritchard	1986	2065
324 5/8	51 2/8 51 4/8	40 1/8	6 6	Coconino County	AZ	Gerald E. Hunter	2005	2065
324 5/8	51 0/8 50 0/8	39 1/8	6 6	Catron County	NM	David Hall	2006	2065
324 4/8	49 3/8 48 7/8	40 6/8	6 6	Grant County	OR	Chuck Boatman	1982	2068
324 4/8	48 3/8 49 2/8	34 6/8	6 6	Petroleum County	MT	Gary Damuth	1986	2068
324 4/8	50 1/8 50 2/8	46 7/8	7 8	Musselshell County	MT	Ted Steinke	1988	2068
324 4/8	50 6/8 50 3/8	34 0/8	7 7	Catron County	NM	Richard V. Gray	1998	2068
324 4/8	47 7/8 48 6/8	42 2/8	6 6	Wallowa County	OR	Glen G. Miller	2000	2068
324 4/8	58 2/8 58 0/8	36 2/8	6 6	Kittitas County	WA	Luke Oberhansly	2003	2068
324 4/8	50 6/8 50 4/8	34 0/8	6 6	Kane County	UT	LeGrande Tracy	2004	2068
*324 4/8	47 2/8 47 5/8	34 2/8	6 6	Garfield County	CO	Bruce Street	2005	2068
324 4/8	51 4/8 51 7/8	40 6/8	6 6	Yakima County	WA	Dan Apodaca	2006	2068
324 4/8	48 6/8 50 3/8	41 7/8	7 6	Idaho County	ID	Gary Gapp	2006	2068
324 4/8	49 6/8 49 1/8	39 2/8	7 6	Teller County	CO	Steve Mach	2008	2068
*324 4/8	48 4/8 48 6/8	36 2/8	7 7	Clearwater County	ID	Brandon S. Blackwell	2009	2068
*324 4/8	49 6/8 50 5/8	40 0/8	7 6	Navajo County	AZ	Austin A. Atkinson	2009	2068
324 3/8	53 2/8 54 2/8	33 7/8	7 6	Summit County	CO	Gordon R. Horn	1986	2081
324 3/8	54 1/8 53 1/8	40 7/8	6 7	Elmore County	ID	Robert Rhoads, Jr.	1992	2081
324 3/8	50 7/8 48 2/8	42 5/8	5 5	Washington County	UT	Richard D. Van Ausdal	2002	2081
324 3/8	48 2/8 50 4/8	42 1/8	6 6	Socorro County	NM	Steve McCluskey	2005	2081
324 3/8	51 5/8 51 4/8	39 0/8	7 7	Lewis County	WA	Matt Rich	2009	2081
324 2/8	47 5/8 47 4/8	31 0/8	6 6	Hodgson	MAN	Barry Bird	1982	2086
324 2/8	52 0/8 51 1/8	37 5/8	6 7	Catron County	NM	Thomas Drumme	1990	2086
324 2/8	46 5/8 49 2/8	43 6/8	5 5	Socorro County	NM	Daniel T. Webb	1996	2086
324 2/8	45 2/8 45 5/8	40 4/8	6 7	Wallowa County	OR	Ron Williams	1996	2086
324 2/8	46 6/8 46 6/8	36 2/8	6 6	Endeavour	SAS	Les Lesinszki	2003	2086

AMERICAN ELK (TYPICAL ANTLERS)

Minimum Score 260   Continued

SCORE	LENGTH OF R MAIN BEAM L	INSIDE SPREAD	NUMBER OF R POINTS L	AREA	STATE/ PROVINCE	HUNTER'S NAME	DATE	RANK
324 2/8	52 6/8 52 4/8	41 6/8	6 6	Cascade County	MT	Dan Lencioni	2005	2086
324 2/8	46 7/8 49 0/8	34 2/8	7 6	Socorro County	NM	Ryan Beasley	2007	2086
324 2/8	47 1/8 47 4/8	33 2/8	6 6	Grand County	CO	Chuck Revak	2007	2086
324 2/8	54 4/8 53 4/8	35 2/8	6 8	Coconino County	AZ	Carl E. McFarland	2008	2086
324 1/8	47 7/8 48 6/8	46 7/8	6 7	Rio Arriba County	NM	Richard Manwell	1986	2095
324 1/8	54 2/8 53 3/8	44 1/8	6 7	Apache County	AZ	Rick Mazol	1989	2095
324 1/8	53 5/8 55 5/8	34 1/8	6 6	Coconino County	AZ	Phillip C. Dalrymple	1990	2095
324 1/8	47 5/8 48 6/8	43 1/8	7 7	Shoshone County	ID	Jerry D. Ely	1991	2095
324 1/8	53 1/8 52 2/8	32 7/8	6 7	Sanders County	MT	John Boger	1992	2095
324 1/8	46 4/8 44 7/8	35 7/8	6 7	Harney County	OR	Jeff Nichols	1994	2095
324 1/8	48 0/8 49 2/8	40 1/8	6 6	Jackson County	CO	Tom G. Kelley	1998	2095
324 1/8	54 7/8 52 6/8	43 1/8	6 7	Custer County	SD	Mark Kayser	2003	2095
324 1/8	46 3/8 45 1/8	39 3/8	6 6	Pueblo County	CO	Alan Blair	2007	2095
324 1/8	45 6/8 47 7/8	34 7/8	8 6	Sanpete County	UT	Brad Rochell	2009	2095
*324 1/8	51 3/8 49 2/8	42 5/8	6 6	Elko County	NV	Myles Nance	2010	2095
324 0/8	45 2/8 44 4/8	46 1/8	6 7	Madison County	MT	Alan Noack	1991	2106
324 0/8	52 0/8 50 0/8	41 4/8	7 6	Catron County	NM	Dave Scott	1991	2106
324 0/8	51 5/8 51 5/8	36 4/8	6 6	Catron County	NM	John Ruppert	1994	2106
324 0/8	44 7/8 43 7/8	42 2/8	6 6	Catron County	NM	Duane "Corky" Richardson	1997	2106
324 0/8	47 3/8 44 4/8	39 6/8	6 6	Sweetwater County	WY	Jim Race	2001	2106
324 0/8	51 5/8 50 7/8	38 2/8	6 6	Coconino County	AZ	Mike Blanchard	2003	2106
*324 0/8	52 0/8 51 1/8	37 6/8	6 6	Gunnison County	CO	Shawn Farnsworth	2009	2106
323 7/8	48 7/8 47 2/8	37 1/8	6 6	Granite County	MT	Clint Carlson	1983	2113
323 7/8	50 7/8 52 0/8	43 3/8	6 6	Coconino County	AZ	John Stigsell	1987	2113
323 7/8	45 1/8 46 2/8	37 3/8	6 6	Phillips County	MT	Todd A. Erickson	1991	2113
323 7/8	53 6/8 51 3/8	39 3/8	7 7	Coconino County	AZ	Joseph O. Fogleman	1992	2113
323 7/8	53 5/8 53 3/8	37 5/8	6 6	Sierra County	NM	Dennis D. Johnson	1998	2113
323 7/8	48 6/8 50 1/8	38 5/8	6 6	Huerfano County	CO	Craig Baudino	1999	2113
323 7/8	48 3/8 51 2/8	34 5/8	7 7	Union County	OR	Bob Comer	2003	2113
323 7/8	52 6/8 51 4/8	41 5/8	6 6	Grant County	OR	Craig Baker	2004	2113
*323 7/8	51 2/8 49 5/8	40 1/8	6 7	Park County	CO	Justin Davis	2006	2113
323 6/8	48 2/8 51 1/8	43 6/8	6 7	Valley County	ID	Rodney Bremer	1983	2122
323 6/8	51 0/8 49 6/8	38 2/8	6 6	Sandoval County	NM	Johnny Zoetjes	1996	2122
323 6/8	48 1/8 49 0/8	38 4/8	6 6	Converse County	WY	Jim Van Norman	1999	2122
323 6/8	52 0/8 52 4/8	37 0/8	6 6	Catron County	NM	Steven C. Johnson	2004	2122
323 6/8	49 0/8 49 6/8	38 4/8	6 6	Natrona County	WY	Tom Bradach	2004	2122
323 6/8	47 1/8 47 4/8	36 0/8	6 8	Cibola County	NM	Kirk Mills	2006	2122
323 6/8	48 6/8 50 5/8	38 0/8	7 8	Cascade County	MT	Don Davidson, Jr.	2009	2122
323 5/8	46 6/8 46 3/8	40 3/8	7 6	Teton County	MT	Ron Granneman	1978	2129
323 5/8	52 0/8 53 7/8	42 4/8	6 8	Cascade County	MT	Bill Tesinsky	1983	2129
323 5/8	47 4/8 48 7/8	35 5/8	6 7	Custer County	ID	John R. Sample	1983	2129
323 5/8	48 0/8 47 6/8	36 7/8	6 6	Taos County	NM	Jeffrey D. Butts	1987	2129
323 5/8	50 5/8 51 1/8	37 3/8	7 7	Flathead County	MT	John Hale	1990	2129
323 5/8	47 1/8 47 7/8	34 5/8	6 6	Taos County	NM	Chris T. Sanner	1991	2129
323 5/8	49 6/8 49 3/8	35 3/8	6 6	Catron County	NM	John Sielicki	1993	2129
323 5/8	54 7/8 53 3/8	34 5/8	6 6	Sevier County	UT	David Hughes	1995	2129
323 5/8	47 1/8 44 4/8	36 7/8	6 6	Navajo County	AZ	Gayland Jones	1995	2129
323 5/8	50 3/8 49 5/8	35 4/8	6 7	Mesa County	CO	James Snortum	1996	2129
323 5/8	45 6/8 47 2/8	38 1/8	6 6	Skamania County	WA	Cory Schmid	1998	2129
323 5/8	46 5/8 46 5/8	41 1/8	6 6	Union County	OR	Richard M. Bellisario	2000	2129
323 5/8	57 2/8 54 2/8	41 1/8	6 5	Johnson County	WY	Travis Howard	2004	2129
*323 5/8	51 4/8 48 6/8	35 7/8	6 6	Custer County	SD	Michael P. Twedt	2005	2129
323 4/8	40 7/8 41 2/8	35 6/8	6 6	Phillips County	MT	Buzz Beto	1983	2143
323 4/8	49 4/8 48 6/8	37 6/8	6 6	Missoula County	MT	John W. Zahrte	1987	2143
323 4/8	51 5/8 52 0/8	35 0/8	6 6	Spirit River	ALB	Gerald Desjardins	1990	2143
323 4/8	44 2/8 47 3/8	37 2/8	6 6	Catron County	NM	Abe Dimas	1992	2143
323 4/8	50 4/8 53 4/8	43 4/8	5 6	Socorro County	NM	Tom Alvin	1996	2143
323 4/8	49 1/8 52 7/8	42 0/8	6 6	Mora County	NM	Robert Snell	2002	2143
323 4/8	51 6/8 51 6/8	41 0/8	8 8	Lewis & Clark County	MT	Randy Kottke	2003	2143
*323 4/8	47 0/8 49 3/8	37 6/8	6 6	Petroleum County	MT	Rick Breitenbach	2004	2143
*323 4/8	47 1/8 47 2/8	32 4/8	7 6	McKenzie County	ND	Shawn Staal	2006	2143
323 4/8	56 0/8 55 4/8	40 6/8	6 6	Coconino County	AZ	Kevin L. Beckwith	2007	2143
*323 4/8	47 5/8 47 0/8	45 7/8	6 6	Socorro County	NM	Barry Brownhill	2008	2143
323 3/8	50 6/8 50 1/8	37 7/8	7 6	Gallatin County	MT	Rick Jones	1977	2154
323 3/8	50 1/8 51 1/8	38 3/8	6 6	Catron County	NM	Roy L. Hall	1991	2154
323 3/8	52 0/8 51 7/8	40 1/8	7 6	Archuleta County	CO	Matthew T. Old	1994	2154
323 3/8	52 3/8 52 1/8	38 5/8	7 7	Fergus County	MT	Tod Rector	1998	2154
323 3/8	53 1/8 53 2/8	35 7/8	7 6	Coconino County	AZ	Timothy P. Martin	2004	2154
323 2/8	55 7/8 53 5/8	44 2/8	6 6	Grant County	OR	Andy Day	1982	2159
323 2/8	46 7/8 46 4/8	38 7/8	7 8	Catron County	NM	Thomas R. Sansom	1984	2159
323 2/8	50 6/8 49 0/8	40 2/8	6 6	Adams County	ID	Stacy V. LaFay	1993	2159
323 2/8	51 2/8 50 5/8	41 2/8	6 6	Rio Arriba County	NM	Allen J. Martinez	1996	2159
323 2/8	50 5/8 52 3/8	46 0/8	6 6	Washington County	ID	C. Craig Boll	2000	2159
323 2/8	51 6/8 48 5/8	43 0/8	6 7	Socorro County	NM	Dana K. Wilson	2001	2159
323 2/8	50 0/8 52 3/8	39 4/8	6 6	Bear Lake County	ID	Ryan Hartley	2001	2159
*323 2/8	47 5/8 47 5/8	39 6/8	6 6	Coconino County	AZ	Chris Wagner	2003	2159
323 2/8	54 7/8 53 7/8	35 4/8	7 7	Fall River County	SD	Michael J. Jarding	2004	2159
323 2/8	54 4/8 53 6/8	38 0/8	7 6	Big Horn County	WY	Tim Smith	2004	2159
*323 2/8	48 4/8 48 2/8	33 4/8	6 6	Las Animas County	CO	Chris M. Barnett	2009	2159
323 1/8	49 6/8 49 5/8	42 3/8	6 6	Blaine County	ID	Larry Whittaker	1988	2170
323 1/8	50 6/8 51 0/8	36 5/8	6 6	Flathead County	MT	Don Mills	1992	2170
323 1/8	50 3/8 46 7/8	35 3/8	6 6	Catron County	NM	David A. Chester	1997	2170
323 1/8	48 4/8 48 0/8	37 7/8	6 6	Grande Prairie	ALB	David Pitman	2000	2170
323 1/8	53 4/8 52 3/8	41 1/8	6 6	Catron County	NM	Steve Borden	2001	2170
323 0/8	52 5/8 50 1/8	39 0/8	6 6	Blaine County	ID	Ted Chu	1977	2175
323 0/8	47 4/8 48 3/8	40 0/8	6 6	Grand County	CO	Russell Gross	1985	2175
323 0/8	50 4/8 51 0/8	40 0/8	6 6	White Pine County	NV	Paul D. Patterson	1987	2175
323 0/8	50 7/8 51 4/8	39 2/8	6 6	Morgan County	UT	Hugh H. Hogle	1991	2175
323 0/8	51 3/8 50 3/8	43 4/8	6 6	Nye County	NV	Ken Longballa	1993	2175
323 0/8	54 3/8 51 0/8	40 4/8	6 6	Coconino County	AZ	Glen D. Whited	1993	2175
323 0/8	47 4/8 48 2/8	30 0/8	6 6	Meagher County	MT	D. (Mitch) Kottas	1993	2175
323 0/8	51 0/8 48 0/8	35 4/8	6 6	Beaverhead County	MT	Shaun P. Twardoski	1995	2175
323 0/8	47 0/8 47 2/8	34 2/8	6 6	Adams County	ID	Michael A. Bledsoe	1995	2175
323 0/8	43 3/8 43 3/8	37 2/8	6 6	Las Animas County	CO	Steve Barnhill	1996	2175
*323 0/8	52 7/8 53 4/8	40 2/8	6 6	Rosebud County	MT	Jeffrey R. Lee	2008	2175

700

AMERICAN ELK (TYPICAL ANTLERS)

Minimum Score 260 — Continued

SCORE	LENGTH OF R MAIN BEAM L	INSIDE SPREAD	NUMBER OF R POINTS L		AREA	STATE/ PROVINCE	HUNTER'S NAME	DATE	RANK
*323 0/8	47 3/8 45 7/8	37 6/8	8	8	Socorro County	NM	John B. Bowman	2008	2175
322 7/8	50 6/8 51 0/8	44 3/8	6	7	Phillips County	MT	Ray Hoveskeland	1967	2187
322 7/8	48 5/8 46 5/8	36 5/8	6	6	Deer Lodge County	MT	Eddie McGreevey	1977	2187
322 7/8	51 3/8 52 2/8	41 4/8	7	7	Coconino County	AZ	Darrell Christensen	1979	2187
322 7/8	47 4/8 47 5/8	36 1/8	6	6	Canmore	ALB	David R. Coupland	1982	2187
322 7/8	48 6/8 50 4/8	38 7/8	7	6	Coconino County	AZ	Dave Holt	1994	2187
322 7/8	50 1/8 49 1/8	32 5/8	6	6	Coconino County	AZ	Phillip C. Dalrymple	1998	2187
322 7/8	46 1/8 45 3/8	43 4/8	7	6	Camas County	ID	Mark E. Cox	2002	2187
322 7/8	52 1/8 51 1/8	45 2/8	6	6	Elko County	NV	Brandon Fordin	2003	2187
322 7/8	49 3/8 49 3/8	34 3/8	6	6	Fergus County	MT	Don Jackson	2009	2187
322 6/8	49 2/8 48 5/8	36 4/8	6	6	Rio Arriba County	NM	Santos E. Corriz	1982	2196
322 6/8	46 6/8 46 1/8	44 0/8	7	5	McKinley County	NM	Dennis L. Stettler	1995	2196
322 6/8	46 4/8 44 5/8	47 7/8	6	6	Jefferson County	MT	Chet Graham	1997	2196
322 6/8	44 5/8 46 6/8	37 0/8	6	6	Clark County	ID	Brad Foster	1998	2196
322 6/8	45 5/8 45 2/8	36 6/8	6	6	Umatilla County	OR	Tyson E. Armstrong	1998	2196
322 6/8	52 7/8 52 4/8	46 2/8	6	6	Multnomah County	OR	Marc B. Caldwell	2000	2196
322 6/8	54 6/8 52 5/8	40 6/8	6	7	Elko County	NV	Gary Sampley	2005	2196
322 6/8	51 6/8 53 5/8	38 4/8	6	6	Routt County	CO	David Bishop	2007	2196
322 6/8	49 7/8 51 6/8	42 4/8	6	6	Utah County	UT	Nathan Smith	2010	2196
*322 6/8	48 4/8 50 2/8	44 0/8	6	6	Johnson County	WY	Robert Thome	2010	2196
322 5/8	49 4/8 47 1/8	37 7/8	6	6	Taos County	NM	Jason Kent	1991	2206
322 5/8	54 4/8 55 1/8	37 0/8	6	8	Gila County	AZ	Jason Johnson	2001	2206
322 5/8	50 5/8 47 1/8	37 1/8	6	6	Otero County	NM	David Rutherford	2002	2206
322 5/8	49 1/8 49 6/8	35 3/8	6	6	Sierra County	NM	Brett Bynum	2004	2206
322 5/8	48 7/8 49 1/8	37 5/8	6	6	Platte County	WY	Benjamin Michelena	2006	2206
322 4/8	51 3/8 48 7/8	40 0/8	6	7	Lewis & Clark County	MT	Jerry Biresch	1970	2211
322 4/8	48 6/8 49 1/8	36 4/8	6	6	Sublette County	WY	Charles T. Moore II	1988	2211
322 4/8	46 6/8 48 2/8	41 2/8	6	6	Coconino County	AZ	Lee J. Sorcinelli	1997	2211
322 4/8	49 2/8 49 4/8	34 4/8	6	6	Fremont County	ID	Brian Frickey	1999	2211
322 4/8	52 0/8 51 7/8	37 2/8	8	6	Umatilla County	OR	Kurt Rosenberg	1999	2211
322 4/8	48 3/8 48 5/8	45 6/8	6	6	Gallatin County	MT	Corey McDonald	2002	2211
322 4/8	51 2/8 50 1/8	35 2/8	6	6	Park County	MT	Paul B. Bradley	2003	2211
322 4/8	52 1/8 54 2/8	41 4/8	5	6	Albany County	WY	Eric Hunter	2008	2211
*322 4/8	51 0/8 50 2/8	44 2/8	6	6	Coconino County	AZ	Donley Schuld	2008	2211
*322 4/8	48 7/8 48 6/8	34 2/8	6	6	Summit County	CO	Doug Scott	2009	2211
322 4/8	49 3/8 49 2/8	35 4/8	6	6	Shoshone County	ID	Fred L. Smith	2009	2211
*322 4/8	52 2/8 49 7/8	35 2/8	6	6	Rio Blanco County	CO	Bob Beverwyk	2009	2211
322 3/8	46 7/8 44 3/8	40 1/8	6	6	Coconino County	AZ	Salvatore J. Carlomagno	1991	2223
322 3/8	51 2/8 48 2/8	38 3/8	6	8	Catron County	NM	Stoney Jeff Black	1993	2223
322 3/8	50 0/8 51 4/8	41 7/8	6	6	Beaverhead County	MT	Russell Swindall	1996	2223
322 3/8	44 6/8 43 5/8	35 7/8	6	6	Yavapai County	AZ	James Benigar	1997	2223
322 3/8	51 4/8 49 5/8	38 5/8	6	6	Rio Arriba County	NM	Larson E. Panzy	1999	2223
322 3/8	48 2/8 49 2/8	36 3/8	6	6	Duchesne County	UT	Max L. Healy	2000	2223
322 3/8	46 2/8 47 5/8	39 1/8	6	6	Petroleum County	MT	Kristopher Cummings	2002	2223
322 3/8	50 6/8 50 4/8	38 7/8	6	6	Coconino County	AZ	Peter Rembisz	2005	2223
322 3/8	48 2/8 48 3/8	42 7/8	6	7	Granite County	MT	Kurt Jones	2009	2223
*322 3/8	48 2/8 54 0/8	37 5/8	6	6	Fergus County	MT	Brock H. Steingruber	2009	2223
322 2/8	51 5/8 53 1/8	33 0/8	6	6	Colfax County	NM	Tom L. Handy	1986	2233
322 2/8	52 4/8 49 7/8	38 2/8	6	6	Catron County	NM	Sam Chavez	1990	2233
322 2/8	47 5/8 46 4/8	41 2/8	6	6	Catron County	NM	Gino Giannetti	1993	2233
322 2/8	50 0/8 49 4/8	37 4/8	6	6	Albany County	WY	Scott Woolsey	1997	2233
322 2/8	50 7/8 51 0/8	39 4/8	6	6	Apache County	AZ	Ricky Dean Miller	1998	2233
322 2/8	51 4/8 53 5/8	40 2/8	6	6	Coconino County	AZ	Randall L. Perkins	2000	2233
322 2/8	53 5/8 53 6/8	39 0/8	6	6	Apache County	AZ	Ryan Mangum	2000	2233
322 2/8	49 5/8 50 6/8	34 6/8	6	6	Klickitat County	WA	Kurt E. Goesch	2002	2233
322 2/8	49 1/8 48 7/8	36 2/8	7	7	Powell County	MT	Ryan Nelson	2004	2233
322 2/8	46 1/8 47 4/8	38 6/8	6	6	Natrona County	WY	Justin Putzier	2005	2233
322 1/8	50 4/8 50 6/8	37 3/8	6	6	Coconino County	AZ	John F. Schultz	1978	2243
322 1/8	50 5/8 50 4/8	37 3/8	6	6	Powell County	MT	Gene Coughlin	1982	2243
322 1/8	45 6/8 44 3/8	34 3/8	7	8	Fergus County	MT	Ben Starburg	1985	2243
322 1/8	47 0/8 47 2/8	40 3/8	6	6	Beaverhead County	MT	Ric Twardoski	1987	2243
322 1/8	47 5/8 49 5/8	43 3/8	7	7	Coconino County	AZ	Roger O. Iveson	1990	2243
322 1/8	53 1/8 51 5/8	42 2/8	6	8	Rio Arriba County	NM	Michael Herrera	1991	2243
322 1/8	49 7/8 50 5/8	37 3/8	6	6	Coconino County	AZ	David L. Schwartz, Sr.	1992	2243
322 1/8	54 4/8 56 4/8	37 7/8	6	6	Rio Arriba County	NM	Aaron Jones	1998	2243
322 1/8	50 7/8 50 6/8	37 7/8	6	7	Teton County	WY	Joe Martinez	2000	2243
322 1/8	49 6/8 50 3/8	35 1/8	6	6	Apache County	AZ	George Harms	2000	2243
322 1/8	48 0/8 49 3/8	37 3/8	6	6	Otero County	NM	Alan Cain	2007	2243
322 0/8	50 3/8 50 6/8	36 2/8	7	8	Coconino County	AZ	Dick Hensley	1979	2254
322 0/8	46 3/8 48 0/8	36 2/8	6	6	Sandoval County	NM	John McClendon	1983	2254
322 0/8	52 6/8 53 0/8	35 0/8	6	6	Moffat County	CO	Guy Love	1984	2254
322 0/8	47 2/8 49 0/8	40 6/8	6	6	Pierce County	WA	Dale Kistenmacher	1985	2254
322 0/8	48 4/8 49 0/8	34 4/8	6	7	Boggy Creek	MAN	Tom Nebbs	1986	2254
322 0/8	52 6/8 53 1/8	41 2/8	6	7	Caribou County	ID	Brian D. Bailey	1991	2254
322 0/8	50 3/8 50 0/8	41 6/8	6	6	Coconino County	AZ	Daniel P. Cartwright	1995	2254
322 0/8	53 5/8 52 7/8	40 2/8	6	6	Wallowa County	OR	Jared C. Rogers	1996	2254
322 0/8	52 2/8 52 7/8	36 0/8	6	7	Navajo County	AZ	Wayne Riley	1997	2254
322 0/8	46 0/8 46 1/8	34 4/8	6	6	Umatilla County	OR	Doug A. Holland	1997	2254
322 0/8	49 1/8 49 1/8	39 4/8	6	6	Park County	WY	Jim Coyle	2000	2254
322 0/8	52 6/8 52 1/8	40 0/8	6	6	Coconino County	AZ	David Wolf	2003	2254
322 0/8	50 0/8 51 3/8	45 0/8	6	6	Madison County	MT	John D. "Jack" Frost	2008	2254
322 0/8	51 1/8 49 6/8	40 4/8	6	6	Huerfano County	CO	Shawn Rowe	2008	2254
*322 0/8	48 4/8 50 3/8	38 2/8	6	6	Grand County	CO	Benjamin D. Monday	2009	2254
321 7/8	47 7/8 43 6/8	41 7/8	6	6	Taos County	NM	Dr. Dean A. Henbest	1971	2269
321 7/8	49 3/8 53 2/8	34 1/8	6	6	Coconino County	AZ	Mike Burm	1981	2269
321 7/8	51 0/8 50 5/8	37 7/8	6	6	Teller County	CO	Harry Rathke	1983	2269
321 7/8	47 2/8 49 1/8	36 5/8	6	6	Flathead County	MT	Pat Fleming	1992	2269
321 7/8	57 1/8 57 5/8	35 3/8	6	6	Coconino County	AZ	Rick Strain	2000	2269
321 7/8	49 3/8 50 0/8	35 7/8	6	6	Utah County	UT	William Jensen	2003	2269
321 7/8	47 2/8 48 7/8	40 1/8	6	6	Harney County	OR	R. A. Daniels, Sr.	2004	2269
321 7/8	48 5/8 50 2/8	42 5/8	6	7	Johnson County	WY	Shawn Dorr	2007	2269
321 6/8	50 6/8 52 5/8	38 6/8	6	6	Fergus County	MT	Jake Damone	1991	2277
321 6/8	49 1/8 47 7/8	40 2/8	6	7	Grant County	OR	Randy Walz	1995	2277
321 6/8	49 2/8 49 4/8	40 4/8	6	6	Fergus County	MT	Rolly Nelson	1998	2277
321 6/8	52 5/8 50 5/8	36 2/8	6	6	Catron County	NM	Donnie Sultan	1998	2277

701

AMERICAN ELK (TYPICAL ANTLERS)

Minimum Score 260 — Continued

SCORE	LENGTH OF R MAIN BEAM L	INSIDE SPREAD	NUMBER OF R POINTS L	AREA	STATE/ PROVINCE	HUNTER'S NAME	DATE	RANK
321 6/8	47 6/8 49 0/8	40 0/8	8 8	Las Animas County	CO	Blake Patton	2001	2277
321 6/8	52 3/8 48 2/8	48 0/8	5 5	Nye County	NV	Danny Moore	2005	2277
*321 6/8	44 0/8 47 3/8	34 6/8	6 7	Morgan County	UT	P. C. "Bo" Aughtry III	2006	2277
321 6/8	49 1/8 48 5/8	43 0/8	6 6	Stevens County	WA	Dean R. Bennetch	2009	2277
321 5/8	49 6/8 49 0/8	38 1/8	6 6	Carbon County	WY	David S. Nacey, Jr.	2000	2285
321 5/8	50 5/8 51 7/8	38 5/8	6 6	Coconino County	AZ	Carl Guilliams	2002	2285
321 5/8	46 7/8 44 5/8	42 1/8	6 6	Petroleum County	MT	Darwin J. Roberts	2003	2285
321 5/8	47 2/8 45 0/8	33 7/8	7 7	Petroleum County	MT	Bart T. Duray	2005	2285
321 5/8	58 4/8 58 3/8	35 0/8	8 6	King County	WA	Kurt Goesch	2006	2285
*321 5/8	46 7/8 45 4/8	37 5/8	6 6	Carbon County	WY	Mike Ginther	2010	2285
*321 5/8	44 4/8 43 5/8	36 1/8	6 6	Phillips County	MT	Dawn Baumgartner	2010	2285
321 4/8	45 2/8 56 2/8	39 2/8	5 6	Apache County	AZ	John D. 'Jack' Frost	1986	2292
321 4/8	48 4/8 48 3/8	40 0/8	6 6	Petroleum County	MT	David Mitchell	1994	2292
321 4/8	48 6/8 49 0/8	38 4/8	7 7	Petroleum County	MT	Jay Kintzing	1995	2292
321 4/8	59 6/8 46 7/8	41 2/8	6 6	Coconino County	AZ	John Kimball	2001	2292
321 4/8	46 6/8 46 4/8	41 0/8	6 6	Butte County	ID	Douglas B. Howell	2002	2292
*321 4/8	51 1/8 51 4/8	40 6/8	6 6	Converse County	WY	Matt Nordwald	2003	2292
321 4/8	51 6/8 51 1/8	38 4/8	7 9	Garfield County	CO	Terry Day	2006	2292
321 3/8	45 6/8 45 6/8	43 3/8	6 6	Gallatin County	MT	Ed Tertelgte	1975	2299
321 3/8	44 2/8 46 6/8	44 5/8	6 6	Sibbald Flats	ALB	Archie J. Nesbitt	1998	2299
321 3/8	44 1/8 47 2/8	40 2/8	7 6	St. Walburg	SAS	Merle Janish	2000	2299
321 3/8	48 5/8 47 4/8	36 3/8	6 6	Makwa Lake	SAS	Barry Rogers	2000	2299
321 3/8	48 3/8 49 2/8	33 5/8	7 6	Lincoln County	NM	Wayne Carter	2003	2299
321 3/8	53 0/8 54 1/8	36 1/8	7 7	Albany County	WY	Willard Woods	2005	2299
321 3/8	47 2/8 47 4/8	35 5/8	6 6	Big Horn County	WY	Rayneal McKim	2006	2299
*321 3/8	50 5/8 49 6/8	44 3/8	6 6	Grant County	OR	Kevin Lee Backes	2009	2299
321 2/8	46 1/8 48 4/8	40 0/8	6 6	Larimer County	CO	Tom Tietz	1981	2307
321 2/8	50 6/8 50 5/8	35 6/8	6 6	Elmore County	ID	Robert M. Egusquiza	1991	2307
321 2/8	53 1/8 53 5/8	41 6/8	6 7	Camas County	ID	Steve Wiedmeier	1992	2307
321 2/8	46 7/8 46 2/8	35 6/8	6 6	Gallatin County	MT	Lee Poole	1998	2307
321 2/8	47 0/8 47 4/8	40 4/8	7 6	Chouteau County	MT	Tom Willson	2000	2307
321 2/8	51 6/8 50 3/8	46 0/8	6 6	Fergus County	MT	Dave McLendon	2001	2307
321 2/8	51 1/8 51 0/8	38 5/8	7 6	Colfax County	NM	Jeff Johnson	2002	2307
*321 2/8	49 2/8 49 7/8	40 2/8	6 6	Chaffee County	CO	Lance Maynard	2010	2307
321 1/8	48 6/8 50 2/8	38 1/8	6 6	Lincoln County	NM	Jay H. Henley, Sr.	1985	2315
321 1/8	43 0/8 45 3/8	36 1/8	8 8	Idaho County	ID	Randy J. Demro	1989	2315
321 1/8	46 3/8 46 7/8	34 3/8	6 6	Pierce County	WA	Joe H. Frields	1990	2315
321 1/8	49 6/8 51 0/8	38 3/8	6 6	Park County	MT	Brian D. Stoner	1994	2315
321 1/8	48 6/8 48 0/8	40 1/8	6 6	Gallatin County	MT	Robert Louis Bratton	1996	2315
321 1/8	53 4/8 54 7/8	41 3/8	6 6	Lemhi County	ID	Michael S. Forga	1998	2315
321 1/8	46 0/8 44 5/8	37 5/8	6 6	Musselshell County	MT	Keith Hice	2005	2315
321 0/8	46 4/8 46 7/8	46 4/8	7 7	Lincoln County	MT	Steve A. Kluver	1986	2322
321 0/8	51 7/8 49 4/8	42 4/8	6 6	Shoshone County	ID	Chax Peterson	1991	2322
321 0/8	50 2/8 50 6/8	41 2/8	6 6	Carbon County	WY	Keith Hansen	1994	2322
321 0/8	47 4/8 47 4/8	37 0/8	6 6	Catron County	NM	Jeffrey C. Utter	1998	2322
321 0/8	47 7/8 48 1/8	42 2/8	6 6	Bear Lake County	ID	Rod Compton	2001	2322
321 0/8	46 5/8 45 1/8	38 0/8	8 6	Sheridan County	WY	Luke Sherman	2002	2322
321 0/8	49 7/8 50 2/8	41 4/8	6 6	Gila County	AZ	James A. Rimsza	2008	2322
320 7/8	49 2/8 52 0/8	45 5/8	6 6	Jefferson County	OR	Steve C. Yeoman	1991	2329
320 7/8	54 5/8 49 5/8	39 1/8	6 6	Catron County	NM	Robert L. Bryant	1993	2329
320 7/8	50 0/8 49 4/8	41 5/8	6 6	Teton County	WY	Donald R. Hoard	1994	2329
320 7/8	51 6/8 51 2/8	41 1/8	6 6	Crook County	OR	Bob Hayes	1995	2329
320 7/8	46 7/8 46 2/8	38 7/8	6 7	Utah County	UT	Dave Cushing	2004	2329
*320 7/8	52 1/8 52 0/8	47 3/8	6 6	Custer County	SD	Kevin Miller	2005	2329
320 7/8	51 0/8 53 4/8	35 7/8	6 6	Rio Blanco County	CO	Frank Ciminalro	2005	2329
320 7/8	47 6/8 50 2/8	33 1/8	6 6	Petroleum County	MT	Jody Martin	2005	2329
320 6/8	56 2/8 55 4/8	41 2/8	5 6	Coconino County	AZ	Michael P. Hendrix	1995	2337
320 6/8	49 6/8 48 7/8	35 4/8	6 6	Grant County	OR	Larry L. Wagoner	1995	2337
320 6/8	53 0/8 53 0/8	43 4/8	6 6	Sheridan County	WY	Duane E. McClure, Jr.	1997	2337
320 6/8	54 4/8 51 7/8	40 0/8	6 6	Grant County	NM	Lance Maloney	2000	2337
320 6/8	49 1/8 48 2/8	44 0/8	7 7	Kootenai County	ID	Ken Snyder	2003	2337
320 6/8	58 1/8 54 2/8	35 0/8	7 7	Moffat County	CO	Kevin McDonough	2007	2337
*320 6/8	49 7/8 51 3/8	38 6/8	6 6	Eagle County	CO	Mark Hershberger	2008	2337
320 5/8	46 3/8 46 4/8	38 3/8	6 6	Phillips County	MT	Richard R. Gardner	1992	2344
320 5/8	48 5/8 47 5/8	38 7/8	7 7	Madison County	MT	Richard King	1993	2344
320 5/8	47 1/8 46 0/8	37 1/8	7 6	Fergus County	MT	Eric C. Abbott	1995	2344
320 5/8	45 7/8 48 2/8	43 5/8	5 6	Pennington County	SD	Tim E. Weber	1996	2344
320 5/8	44 5/8 47 1/8	42 3/8	6 6	Rich County	UT	Edwin L. DeYoung	1998	2344
320 5/8	51 0/8 50 2/8	39 5/8	6 8	Lewis County	WA	Mitchel J. Hausserman	1999	2344
*320 5/8	53 2/8 53 7/8	47 3/8	6 7	Apache County	AZ	Larry Weigel	2005	2344
*320 5/8	50 7/8 50 0/8	44 7/8	6 6	Flathead County	MT	Douglas D. Rogers	2009	2344
320 5/8	48 1/8 49 0/8	39 5/8	7 7	Garfield County	CO	Gary Lemery	2009	2344
320 4/8	53 2/8 51 4/8	42 2/8	6 6	Catron County	NM	Ray Francingues III	1996	2353
320 4/8	52 0/8 49 0/8	36 0/8	6 6	Mesa County	CO	Jeffery Lynn Birchfield	1997	2353
320 4/8	50 1/8 51 2/8	38 6/8	6 6	Catron County	NM	Dale Jenkins	1998	2353
320 4/8	50 4/8 49 2/8	35 4/8	6 6	Powell County	MT	Jeff Weer	1999	2353
320 4/8	48 3/8 48 3/8	40 6/8	6 6	Moffat County	CO	Troy Willardson	2002	2353
320 4/8	54 5/8 53 4/8	36 0/8	6 6	Meagher County	MT	Jim Kennedy	2005	2353
320 4/8	47 4/8 49 1/8	31 6/8	7 7	Fergus County	MT	Kelly Norskog	2009	2353
*320 4/8	54 0/8 54 5/8	35 6/8	6 6	Big Horn County	WY	Mike McCalla	2009	2353
320 3/8	46 1/8 46 6/8	39 3/8	6 6	Rio Grande County	CO	Bing Kemp	1966	2361
320 3/8	49 3/8 50 7/8	36 5/8	7 6	Catron County	NM	Randall S. Madding	1986	2361
320 3/8	53 0/8 53 0/8	34 7/8	6 6	Greenlee County	AZ	Dean L. Staub	1999	2361
320 3/8	46 4/8 46 2/8	39 3/8	7 6	Natrona County	WY	Brock R. Wollerman	2001	2361
320 3/8	47 3/8 47 0/8	41 1/8	6 6	Summit County	CO	Michael Lauterbach	2001	2361
320 3/8	50 1/8 49 6/8	41 7/8	6 6	Albany County	WY	Randy Bomar	2003	2361
*320 3/8	48 0/8 48 3/8	32 1/8	7 6	Navajo County	AZ	Carl Bryant	2006	2361
320 3/8	57 2/8 56 3/8	30 6/8	8 8	Catron County	NM	Scott Kohrs	2007	2361
320 3/8	51 7/8 52 5/8	40 3/8	6 6	Montezuma County	CO	Ronnie W. Hurst	2007	2361
320 2/8	52 0/8 50 6/8	36 0/8	6 6	Meagher County	MT	Ted Hysell	1983	2370
320 2/8	49 4/8 49 6/8	47 6/8	6 6	Shoshone County	ID	Tom J. O'Grady	1986	2370
320 2/8	45 1/8 44 2/8	30 6/8	6 6	Garfield County	CO	Jason Adamson	1990	2370
320 2/8	47 6/8 45 5/8	44 6/8	6 6	Beaverhead County	MT	Raymond Cote	1991	2370
320 2/8	48 2/8 50 5/8	38 3/8	7 6	Catron County	NM	Dean Dunaway	1993	2370
320 2/8	46 4/8 44 3/8	44 6/8	7 6	Shoshone County	ID	Ron Long	1996	2370

702

AMERICAN ELK (TYPICAL ANTLERS)

Minimum Score 260 Continued

SCORE	LENGTH OF R MAIN BEAM L	INSIDE SPREAD	NUMBER OF R POINTS L	AREA	STATE/ PROVINCE	HUNTER'S NAME	DATE	RANK
320 2/8	49 2/8 49 2/8	38 2/8	6 6	Albany County	WY	Richard A. Strickland	1998	2370
320 2/8	48 2/8 50 6/8	42 2/8	6 6	Larimer County	CO	Steve Stumbo	2001	2370
320 2/8	44 6/8 44 6/8	32 0/8	6 6	Moffat County	CO	Jim Brooks	2001	2370
320 2/8	50 0/8 49 0/8	32 0/8	6 6	Treasure County	MT	Tom Cushing	2006	2370
320 2/8	53 2/8 52 3/8	38 2/8	6 6	Lewis & Clark County	MT	Mike Hartnett	2006	2370
320 1/8	46 2/8 47 7/8	41 3/8	6 6	Madison County	MT	Lee J. Poole	1976	2381
320 1/8	48 6/8 48 7/8	38 7/8	6 6	Fergus County	MT	J. Douglas Krings	1979	2381
320 1/8	48 1/8 45 1/8	44 3/8	6 7	Albany County	WY	Doug Pope	1979	2381
320 1/8	50 1/8 48 4/8	37 1/8	6 6	Lemhi County	ID	Joe Fraser	1980	2381
320 1/8	52 6/8 51 1/8	41 1/8	6 6	Yellowstone County	MT	Robert M. Labert	1986	2381
320 1/8	50 5/8 49 1/8	46 7/8	6 6	Cibola County	NM	Howard Schreiber	1992	2381
320 1/8	52 6/8 53 7/8	39 1/8	6 6	Catron County	NM	Bruce Fair	1995	2381
320 1/8	53 3/8 53 5/8	41 7/8	6 6	Harney County	OR	William "Bill" L. Sherrill	1997	2381
320 1/8	47 1/8 53 0/8	42 3/8	6 6	Wallowa County	OR	Tim Wright	2001	2381
320 1/8	51 3/8 51 4/8	51 3/8	5 5	Otero County	NM	Neal Snyder	2003	2381
320 1/8	46 2/8 44 2/8	34 7/8	6 6	Fergus County	MT	Jimmy Simmons	2003	2381
*320 1/8	48 7/8 47 7/8	38 1/8	6 6	Petroleum County	MT	Tom Bender	2004	2381
*320 1/8	53 1/8 48 5/8	34 7/8	6 6	Sanders County	MT	Sam Phillips	2005	2381
*320 1/8	46 7/8 47 2/8	35 7/8	6 6	Rio Arriba County	NM	Jack Nobles	2006	2381
*320 1/8	50 0/8 51 0/8	36 5/8	6 6	Otero County	NM	Luci V. Gonzalez	2006	2381
320 0/8	50 6/8 53 1/8	39 6/8	6 6	Mineral County	MT	Michael Ruhkala	1980	2396
320 0/8	51 4/8 50 5/8	36 6/8	6 6	Huerfano County	CO	Mike Culwell	1984	2396
320 0/8	48 7/8 48 1/8	41 0/8	7 6	Grant County	OR	James M. Carter	1985	2396
320 0/8	48 1/8 50 0/8	37 0/8	6 6	Catron County	NM	Henry Montoya	1992	2396
320 0/8	49 6/8 48 2/8	35 0/8	6 6	Fergus County	MT	Rick A. Martin	1993	2396
320 0/8	50 7/8 48 6/8	39 2/8	6 6	Catron County	NM	Alan C. Ellsworth	1994	2396
320 0/8	51 1/8 50 4/8	34 2/8	7 7	Coconino County	AZ	Jim Van Lieu	1996	2396
320 0/8	50 2/8 51 7/8	35 2/8	6 6	Petroleum County	MT	Colby Loudon	2000	2396
320 0/8	50 5/8 48 0/8	42 0/8	6 6	Lincoln County	NM	Mark E. Chavez	2004	2396
320 0/8	49 5/8 49 2/8	38 2/8	6 6	Union County	OR	Brian Clark	2007	2396
319 7/8	51 7/8 50 2/8	38 1/8	7 8	Socorro County	NM	David Ryles	1977	2406
319 7/8	51 7/8 52 2/8	40 5/8	6 6	Hinton	ALB	Blair D. Crites	1979	2406
319 7/8	46 3/8 47 6/8	39 7/8	7 6	Otero County	NM	Simon L. Gomez	1986	2406
319 7/8	50 5/8 50 4/8	43 1/8	6 6	Sandoval County	NM	James E. Montgomery	1992	2406
319 7/8	51 6/8 52 2/8	44 3/8	7 6	Fergus County	MT	Richard Dilling	1993	2406
319 7/8	48 7/8 47 6/8	42 3/8	6 5	Garfield County	CO	Paul J. Chackan	1997	2406
319 7/8	46 3/8 45 7/8	30 7/8	6 6	Jefferson County	CO	Ed Kuehster	1998	2406
319 7/8	50 2/8 49 6/8	36 5/8	6 6	Park County	CO	Ramsey L. Knowles	2007	2406
319 7/8	51 3/8 50 4/8	40 5/8	8 6	Coconino County	AZ	Robert B. Elam	2007	2406
*319 7/8	52 5/8 53 4/8	37 0/8	7 6	Mesa County	CO	Rex Crawford	2008	2406
319 7/8	47 4/8 47 0/8	43 3/8	6 7	Valley County	ID	Jack C. Nave	2009	2406
319 7/8	49 3/8 48 7/8	33 3/8	6 6	Coconino County	AZ	Paul H. English	2010	2406
319 6/8	46 3/8 44 7/8	34 0/8	6 7	Larimer County	CO	Jeremy Oberlander	1995	2418
319 6/8	53 2/8 49 2/8	34 6/8	6 6	Jefferson County	CO	Scott Stordahl	2001	2418
319 6/8	48 5/8 48 5/8	36 6/8	6 6	McKenzie County	ND	Ryan Hugelen	2005	2418
319 6/8	49 4/8 52 3/8	35 4/8	6 6	Washakie County	WY	Sidney Kelly	2005	2418
319 6/8	49 1/8 48 5/8	37 4/8	6 6	Salt Lake County	UT	Darin N. Miller	2006	2418
*319 6/8	53 7/8 51 6/8	37 0/8	6 6	Millard County	UT	Shane Shaw	2010	2418
319 5/8	48 3/8 50 7/8	39 0/8	7 6	Catron County	NM	Roy L. Walk	1993	2424
319 5/8	45 3/8 47 0/8	36 5/8	6 6	Morgan County	UT	James A. Martin, MD	1956	2424
319 5/8	47 6/8 47 3/8	38 5/8	6 6	Edgerton	ALB	Trevor Thorpe	1997	2424
319 5/8	49 7/8 49 3/8	38 3/8	6 6	Clackamas County	OR	Paul M. Bender	2004	2424
319 5/8	47 0/8 48 0/8	33 7/8	6 6	Lincoln County	MT	Jodi Williams	2005	2424
*319 5/8	51 7/8 51 7/8	34 3/8	6 7	Catron County	NM	Keith Dixon	2008	2424
319 5/8	53 1/8 53 6/8	37 7/8	7 6	Lewis & Clark County	MT	Cody P. Voermans	2009	2424
319 4/8	48 4/8 49 0/8	40 2/8	6 6	Pitkin County	CO	Bob Gulman	1975	2431
319 4/8	49 5/8 49 6/8	36 4/8	7 6	Clearwater County	ID	Audie Powers	1979	2431
319 4/8	50 6/8 52 0/8	41 2/8	6 6	Caribou County	ID	Mark Hill	1980	2431
319 4/8	47 1/8 47 6/8	47 1/8	7 6	Madison County	MT	Robert Koons	2000	2431
319 4/8	57 0/8 56 7/8	44 2/8	6 6	Custer County	ID	Bryan Tilly	2003	2431
*319 4/8	44 7/8 48 3/8	39 2/8	7 6	Catron County	NM	Nick J. Vanecek	2007	2431
319 4/8	47 4/8 44 5/8	43 5/8	6 6	Clark County	ID	Bruce R. Horton	2008	2431
319 4/8	47 5/8 51 0/8	36 0/8	6 6	Catron County	NM	James Jones, Jr.	2008	2431
319 4/8	51 6/8 52 0/8	37 6/8	6 6	Montrose County	CO	Don H. Brumley	2009	2431
*319 4/8	55 5/8 52 0/8	41 0/8	6 6	Meade County	SD	Reed Vandervoort	2009	2431
319 3/8	44 2/8 43 2/8	35 4/8	7 7	Crook County	OR	Jeff Carver	1985	2441
319 3/8	52 6/8 54 1/8	42 2/8	6 6	Catron County	NM	Travis Gillentine	1987	2441
319 3/8	47 5/8 47 1/8	37 1/8	6 6	Fergus County	MT	Edwin Evans	1990	2441
319 3/8	47 3/8 48 2/8	39 7/8	6 6	Sublette County	WY	Douglas Weir/ Glenn Socia	1990	2441
319 3/8	47 4/8 50 0/8	46 7/8	6 6	Garfield County	UT	Brett Emett	2005	2441
319 3/8	48 5/8 48 4/8	33 7/8	6 6	Albany County	WY	Matt Geis	2005	2441
319 3/8	49 6/8 48 6/8	41 0/8	6 7	Fergus County	MT	Pete Gierke	2007	2441
*319 3/8	48 0/8 51 1/8	39 2/8	6 7	Caribou County	ID	Chad Collins	2009	2441
319 2/8	45 2/8 46 1/8	35 0/8	6 6	Morgan County	UT	C. Keith Maynes	1987	2449
319 2/8	48 6/8 50 0/8	36 0/8	6 6	Granite County	MT	Bob Clouse	1991	2449
319 2/8	51 4/8 50 6/8	43 6/8	6 6	Catron County	NM	Joel Hobson III	1996	2449
319 2/8	50 3/8 43 5/8	47 2/8	6 6	Garfield County	UT	Clifford R. Goytowski	2001	2449
319 2/8	52 7/8 53 2/8	40 4/8	6 6	Coconino County	AZ	Michael P. Hendrix	2005	2449
319 2/8	55 0/8 51 5/8	41 6/8	6 7	Coconino County	AZ	Dean P. Hofman	2005	2449
319 2/8	48 7/8 51 1/8	34 0/8	7 6	Phillips County	MT	Patrick E. Wheeler	2007	2449
319 2/8	49 6/8 50 5/8	41 2/8	6 7	Wallowa County	OR	Glenn Hanna	2008	2449
319 2/8	55 0/8 55 0/8	35 6/8	6 6	Douglas County	CO	Rick Duggan	2010	2449
319 1/8	45 2/8 45 0/8	36 3/8	7 7	Rio Arriba County	NM	Dr. O. D. Brown	1986	2458
319 1/8	52 1/8 50 5/8	37 1/8	6 6	Fremont County	ID	Steve W. Sherick	1994	2458
319 1/8	49 1/8 51 5/8	40 3/8	6 6	Coconino County	AZ	Tom Pasley	1995	2458
319 1/8	47 5/8 48 7/8	34 2/8	8 7	Clearwater County	ID	William R. Freytag	2000	2458
319 1/8	42 2/8 42 0/8	33 3/8	8 7	Cameron County	PA	Todd R. Yoder	2001	2458
319 1/8	48 1/8 49 3/8	37 5/8	5 6	Albany County	WY	Ron Mason	2004	2458
319 1/8	50 0/8 48 5/8	39 2/8	6 6	Adams County	ID	Kurt Stieglitz	2005	2458
319 1/8	48 3/8 46 1/8	39 3/8	6 6	Jefferson County	CO	Greg S. Jones	2006	2458
319 1/8	47 1/8 47 2/8	37 1/8	6 6	Greenlee County	AZ	R. G. Soderberg III	2006	2458
*319 1/8	50 0/8 47 5/8	28 5/8	7 6	Washington County	ID	Troy Thomas	2007	2458
*319 1/8	51 4/8 53 3/8	43 4/8	7 7	Rich County	UT	Ted Hallows	2007	2458
319 1/8	50 2/8 49 2/8	35 7/8	6 6	Grant County	OR	Rick A. Anderson	2008	2458
319 0/8	48 7/8 53 2/8	39 6/8	5 6	Catron County	NM	Eddie Howard	1983	2470

AMERICAN ELK (TYPICAL ANTLERS)

Minimum Score 260 Continued

SCORE	LENGTH OF R MAIN BEAM L	INSIDE SPREAD	NUMBER OF R POINTS L	AREA	STATE/PROVINCE	HUNTER'S NAME	DATE	RANK
319 0/8	53 3/8 55 0/8	35 4/8	6 6	McKinley County	NM	David M. Richards	1993	2470
319 0/8	49 7/8 49 3/8	44 6/8	7 6	Clearwater County	ID	Burgess Blevins	1993	2470
319 0/8	49 0/8 46 7/8	37 6/8	6 6	Catron County	NM	Brad Bridgewater	1995	2470
319 0/8	47 2/8 47 1/8	35 6/8	6 6	Kakwa River	ALB	Paul L. Holtz	1996	2470
319 0/8	48 7/8 44 6/8	39 6/8	6 6	Washington County	ID	Donald Garrison	2000	2470
319 0/8	50 6/8 50 4/8	39 0/8	6 6	Coconino County	AZ	Stuart D. Keil	2000	2470
319 0/8	47 1/8 47 4/8	38 2/8	5 6	Otero County	NM	Leigh Livermore	2001	2470
319 0/8	51 4/8 49 1/8	38 0/8	6 6	Catron County	NM	Owen Keeton, Jr.	2005	2470
319 0/8	53 6/8 52 7/8	40 0/8	6 6	Stevens County	WA	Ger Vang	2006	2470
319 0/8	50 3/8 49 5/8	36 0/8	6 6	Catron County	NM	Patrick B. Patridge	2007	2470
319 0/8	44 1/8 42 7/8	38 2/8	6 6	Las Animas County	CO	Ronald W. Gallina	2008	2470
319 0/8	51 6/8 51 1/8	38 0/8	6 6	Valley County	ID	Mark Mathews	2008	2470
*319 0/8	48 6/8 47 6/8	38 4/8	8 6	Phillips County	MT	Steven Patrick Gammons	2008	2470
*319 0/8	47 0/8 45 6/8	38 6/8	6 6	Glacier County	MT	Arlen Sharp	2009	2470
318 7/8	44 3/8 47 5/8	31 3/8	6 7	Valley County	MT	Don G. Scofield	1979	2485
318 7/8	45 4/8 45 4/8	37 1/8	7 6	Fergus County	MT	Donald R. Hecht	1984	2485
318 7/8	48 0/8 49 6/8	41 5/8	6 6	Carbon County	UT	Sam Raby	1989	2485
318 7/8	48 4/8 49 4/8	34 1/8	6 6	Coconino County	AZ	Eugene E. Hafen	1990	2485
318 7/8	46 0/8 46 2/8	43 5/8	7 7	Lemhi County	ID	Jim Pekola	1994	2485
318 7/8	43 3/8 43 4/8	36 5/8	7 7	Lincoln County	MT	Terry V. Crooks	1997	2485
318 7/8	46 1/8 45 0/8	42 0/8	8 6	Kittitas County	WA	Ralph "Buddy" Klinkers IV	2009	2485
318 7/8	44 4/8 46 1/8	38 1/8	6 6	Utah County	UT	Jason Yates	2009	2485
318 7/8	49 0/8 50 4/8	37 7/8	7 6	Fergus County	MT	Ollie Urick	2009	2485
318 6/8	48 5/8 48 1/8	42 2/8	6 7	Larimer County	CO	Tony Seahorn	1972	2494
318 6/8	52 1/8 51 1/8	39 2/8	7 6	Niobrara County	WY	Donald L. Smith	1973	2494
318 6/8	50 1/8 53 6/8	45 0/8	7 6	Coconino County	AZ	Tom Dalrymple	1980	2494
318 6/8	47 4/8 47 4/8	39 4/8	6 6	Sanders County	MT	Wayne L. Haines	1982	2494
318 6/8	44 3/8 44 2/8	35 2/8	6 6	Bow Valley	ALB	Pat Leiser	1986	2494
318 6/8	48 6/8 46 2/8	31 2/8	6 6	Morgan County	UT	Hugh H. Hogle	1988	2494
318 6/8	46 6/8 47 5/8	43 2/8	6 6	Converse County	WY	Chris D. Yeoman	1990	2494
318 6/8	54 7/8 53 3/8	37 6/8	6 6	Coconino County	AZ	Eldon L. Helm	1995	2494
318 6/8	44 2/8 44 3/8	39 6/8	6 6	Albany County	WY	Robert A. Robbins	1999	2494
318 6/8	46 0/8 46 6/8	35 2/8	6 6	Sanders County	MT	Tony Bierwagen	1999	2494
318 6/8	48 2/8 44 5/8	35 0/8	6 6	Golden Valley County	MT	Michael R. Cameron	2003	2494
318 6/8	52 6/8 53 4/8	41 4/8	7 6	Mora County	NM	Zane Streater	2004	2494
318 6/8	49 2/8 48 5/8	38 4/8	6 6	Coconino County	AZ	Ted Spradling	2004	2494
318 6/8	54 1/8 53 1/8	41 2/8	6 6	Navajo County	AZ	Gary W. Crowe	2006	2494
318 6/8	48 4/8 46 4/8	45 6/8	6 6	Gallatin County	MT	William Elfland	2006	2494
318 6/8	59 5/8 51 6/8	31 6/8	7 6	Gila County	AZ	Cory Worischeck	2007	2494
318 6/8	52 5/8 51 3/8	38 4/8	6 7	Coconino County	AZ	David Gamertsfelder	2007	2494
318 5/8	44 4/8 44 4/8	34 6/8	6 6	Mineral County	CO	David Powell	1969	2511
318 5/8	54 0/8 55 7/8	39 7/8	6 6	Beaverhead County	MT	Greg L. Munther	1981	2511
318 5/8	49 3/8 49 7/8	37 7/8	6 6	Missoula County	MT	J. Scott Graham	1982	2511
318 5/8	47 7/8 49 6/8	43 1/8	6 6	Lincoln County	WY	Randy Ulmer	1990	2511
318 5/8	46 7/8 46 7/8	44 3/8	6 7	Sweetwater County	WY	Mark Hamilton	1990	2511
318 5/8	49 0/8 50 3/8	43 3/8	6 6	Morgan County	UT	Bob Frank	1991	2511
318 5/8	42 1/8 43 1/8	30 5/8	6 6	Mesa County	CO	John W. Franklin	2004	2511
318 4/8	43 7/8 42 6/8	39 4/8	6 6	Bighorn Mtns.	WY	Ron Johnson	1975	2518
318 4/8	51 1/8 49 4/8	43 0/8	6 6	Shoshone County	ID	Michael R. Whaley	1989	2518
318 4/8	46 4/8 48 2/8	47 0/8	6 6	Apache County	AZ	Dave Mortimer	1989	2518
318 4/8	42 2/8 45 5/8	40 0/8	7 6	Catron County	NM	Tracy G. Hardy	1992	2518
318 4/8	51 4/8 50 6/8	38 4/8	7 7	Flathead County	MT	Jeffrey M. Benda	1992	2518
318 4/8	44 3/8 44 1/8	35 6/8	6 6	Park County	WY	Paul Bormes	1993	2518
318 4/8	45 2/8 44 6/8	41 2/8	6 6	Saguache County	CO	Charlie VanTreese	1996	2518
318 4/8	46 5/8 48 5/8	37 0/8	6 6	Grant County	NM	D. Kyle Brown	1996	2518
318 4/8	52 3/8 54 2/8	38 0/8	6 6	Fergus County	MT	Jeffrey M. Stockhill	1997	2518
318 4/8	46 6/8 46 6/8	44 0/8	6 6	Sublette County	WY	John Gedroez	2003	2518
318 4/8	53 7/8 51 3/8	38 6/8	6 6	Crook County	OR	Brian D. Bottoms	2006	2518
318 4/8	51 4/8 51 4/8	37 0/8	6 6	Lewis & Clark County	MT	John F. Hamrick	2006	2518
318 4/8	50 6/8 46 6/8	40 0/8	6 5	Tooele County	UT	William H. Bryant	2006	2518
318 4/8	52 1/8 49 1/8	37 0/8	6 6	Coconino County	AZ	David E. Stonestreet	2006	2518
318 4/8	47 2/8 49 7/8	48 6/8	6 6	Rio Arriba County	NM	David Gelatt, Jr.	2008	2518
318 3/8	51 4/8 49 7/8	33 3/8	6 6	Mineral County	MT	Farrell Cooper	1975	2533
318 3/8	52 4/8 51 5/8	41 0/8	7 6	Deer Lodge County	MT	Dennis Neitzke	1980	2533
318 3/8	48 1/8 48 1/8	36 5/8	6 6	Sierra County	NM	Jim Ryan	1988	2533
318 3/8	51 0/8 51 6/8	34 3/8	6 6	Catron County	NM	Dr. Dale Mansfield	1992	2533
318 3/8	52 3/8 49 4/8	37 7/8	6 6	Coconino County	AZ	Marvin N. Zieser	1999	2533
318 3/8	44 6/8 45 2/8	43 3/8	6 7	Petroleum County	MT	Michael C. Hunter	2002	2533
318 3/8	49 5/8 49 2/8	34 5/8	7 7	Yavapai County	AZ	Roy Hampton	2003	2533
318 3/8	45 0/8 46 4/8	35 5/8	6 6	Park County	WY	Keith Toone	2003	2533
318 3/8	47 5/8 53 6/8	38 3/8	7 6	Apache County	AZ	Mark Abrams	2004	2533
318 3/8	44 0/8 46 3/8	39 7/8	6 6	Adams County	ID	Ray Simpson	2006	2533
318 3/8	46 2/8 46 4/8	40 5/8	6 6	Gallatin County	MT	Cory Craver	2007	2533
318 3/8	51 2/8 51 5/8	41 7/8	6 7	Union County	OR	Jim E. Bolender	2007	2533
318 3/8	42 3/8 43 0/8	34 1/8	7 7	Phillips County	MT	James D. Herring	2009	2533
318 3/8	49 4/8 46 2/8	35 7/8	6 6	Beaverhead County	MT	Chad Schulz	2009	2533
*318 3/8	54 1/8 52 0/8	46 0/8	8 6	Garfield County	UT	L. Grant Foster	2010	2533
318 2/8	45 1/8 45 4/8	36 0/8	6 6	Gunnison County	CO	Brian Newton	1989	2548
318 2/8	53 0/8 52 4/8	41 0/8	6 6	Catron County	NM	Ray Francingues III	1992	2548
318 2/8	45 7/8 46 1/8	38 4/8	6 6	Fergus County	MT	Bob Allen	1992	2548
318 2/8	49 4/8 48 4/8	34 0/8	6 6	Beaverhead County	MT	Skip G. Mathewson	1994	2548
318 2/8	51 0/8 50 0/8	34 4/8	6 6	Lemhi County	ID	John David Stuart	1997	2548
318 2/8	48 2/8 45 7/8	38 6/8	6 6	Sheridan County	WY	Shane J. Shannon	1998	2548
318 2/8	42 2/8 41 0/8	38 4/8	7 7	Rimbey	ALB	Bruno Greco	1998	2548
318 2/8	51 7/8 51 5/8	37 6/8	6 6	Catron County	NM	Robert Michael Inman	1999	2548
318 2/8	54 3/8 51 5/8	48 2/8	6 6	Broadwater County	MT	Vincent Gordon	1999	2548
318 2/8	44 6/8 45 7/8	39 0/8	6 6	Catron County	NM	Patrick J. Pascarelli	2002	2548
318 2/8	51 0/8 51 4/8	37 4/8	6 6	Sierra County	NM	Matt Plitt	2004	2548
318 2/8	46 6/8 46 4/8	33 4/8	7 6	Catron County	NM	John Connaughty	2004	2548
318 2/8	50 6/8 48 6/8	40 4/8	6 6	Park County	MT	David Hreha	2009	2548
318 1/8	48 4/8 47 0/8	34 2/8	7 7	Ravalli County	MT	Rick Twardoski	1984	2561
318 1/8	49 3/8 47 1/8	36 7/8	6 6	Uintah County	UT	Everett Burson	1986	2561
318 1/8	48 7/8 51 2/8	41 1/8	6 6	Catron County	NM	Delbert Holley	1987	2561
318 1/8	52 0/8 52 2/8	35 7/8	7 8	Baker County	OR	John Buck	1987	2561
318 1/8	52 7/8 52 4/8	36 3/8	6 6	Fergus County	MT	John Benes	1992	2561

AMERICAN ELK (TYPICAL ANTLERS)

Minimum Score 260 — Continued

SCORE	LENGTH OF MAIN BEAM R	L	INSIDE SPREAD	NUMBER OF POINTS R	L	AREA	STATE/ PROVINCE	HUNTER'S NAME	DATE	RANK
318 1/8	49 1/8	48 4/8	38 3/8	6	6	Rio Arriba County	NM	Jerry R. McManus, Jr.	1994	2561
318 1/8	46 6/8	46 3/8	34 5/8	6	6	Fergus County	MT	James Sproul	1996	2561
318 1/8	47 5/8	48 0/8	36 4/8	6	7	Petroleum County	MT	Chris G. Sanford	1997	2561
318 1/8	51 7/8	50 5/8	37 3/8	6	6	Colfax County	NM	Robert H. Torstenson	1999	2561
318 1/8	48 3/8	48 0/8	34 1/8	6	6	Apache County	AZ	Stephan Waltz	2004	2561
318 1/8	47 7/8	48 0/8	38 7/8	6	6	Navajo County	AZ	Logan Bouwman	2010	2561
318 0/8	45 6/8	45 2/8	44 4/8	7	8	Bighorn Mtns.	WY	Henry 'Hank' Frey	1977	2572
318 0/8	45 6/8	48 4/8	46 6/8	6	6	Carbon County	WY	James Blocker	1980	2572
318 0/8	50 1/8	48 6/8	34 6/8	7	6	Fergus County	MT	Don Davidson	1995	2572
318 0/8	46 6/8	49 2/8	36 6/8	6	6	Rich County	UT	John Harding	2003	2572
318 0/8	51 3/8	51 1/8	36 6/8	6	6	Fergus County	MT	Dois Chesshir	2004	2572
318 0/8	47 5/8	49 3/8	41 2/8	7	7	Lewis & Clark County	MT	Kenneth M. Sharp	2005	2572
318 0/8	49 1/8	50 1/8	37 4/8	6	6	Phillips County	MT	Phillip Jarvis	2007	2572
318 0/8	49 6/8	51 0/8	38 0/8	6	6	Utah County	UT	Bart Thompson	2008	2572
318 0/8	51 4/8	49 4/8	38 7/8	6	7	Grant County	OR	Melissa Randall	2010	2572
317 7/8	45 6/8	45 4/8	45 1/8	6	6	Teton County	MT	Ronald K. Granneman	1974	2581
317 7/8	47 6/8	43 3/8	38 5/8	6	6	Park County	WY	Wesley D. Engleman	1983	2581
317 7/8	53 0/8	53 7/8	42 5/8	6	6	Flathead County	MT	James Norvell	1986	2581
317 7/8	46 2/8	45 4/8	44 1/8	6	6	Clackamas County	OR	Gerald L. Egbert	1987	2581
317 7/8	50 6/8	50 1/8	35 5/8	6	6	White Pine County	NV	Michael Scott Laity	1989	2581
317 7/8	44 6/8	45 6/8	34 7/8	6	6	Fergus County	MT	James Schneider	1993	2581
317 7/8	43 1/8	42 5/8	39 1/8	6	6	Custer County	SD	Ryan Baker	1998	2581
317 7/8	44 1/8	44 4/8	37 1/8	6	6	Lincoln County	MT	Kurt Spencer	2006	2581
317 6/8	47 3/8	48 0/8	44 6/8	6	6	Valley County	ID	William R. Stephenson	1983	2589
317 6/8	55 2/8	55 2/8	41 0/8	6	7	Coconino County	AZ	Pete Foti	1990	2589
317 6/8	44 3/8	44 1/8	35 4/8	6	6	Lincoln County	MT	Ron Halvorson	1991	2589
317 6/8	44 1/8	44 5/8	35 6/8	6	6	Albany County	WY	Kenneth T. Tingo	1997	2589
317 6/8	50 6/8	51 2/8	35 2/8	6	6	Madison County	MT	Jeffrey J. Moris	2002	2589
317 6/8	44 5/8	45 7/8	41 0/8	6	6	Riley County	KS	Trevor Haddix	2002	2589
317 6/8	46 1/8	45 0/8	40 6/8	7	6	Wasatch County	UT	Jarred B. Olsen	2003	2589
317 6/8	49 3/8	51 7/8	39 6/8	6	6	Blaine County	ID	Benny Davis	2003	2589
*317 6/8	46 0/8	45 4/8	40 6/8	6	6	Colfax County	NM	Kirk Sharp	2006	2589
317 6/8	52 6/8	55 2/8	37 4/8	6	6	Idaho County	ID	Mark Knudson	2008	2589
317 6/8	47 1/8	47 6/8	34 4/8	6	6	Petroleum County	MT	Scott Retzlaff	2008	2589
317 5/8	47 6/8	47 7/8	42 3/8	6	6	Lemhi County	ID	Lewis Zane Abbott	1981	2600
317 5/8	56 6/8	55 5/8	35 3/8	6	6	Grant County	NM	Jimmy Head	1988	2600
317 5/8	48 3/8	45 4/8	42 1/8	6	6	Pincher Creek	ALB	John Jacoby	1989	2600
317 5/8	49 6/8	49 5/8	40 5/8	6	6	Beaverhead County	MT	Jim Muzynoski	1990	2600
317 5/8	43 0/8	43 0/8	37 5/8	6	6	Jackson County	CO	Hal Rogers	1991	2600
317 5/8	55 7/8	52 1/8	43 1/8	7	7	Grant County	OR	Larry McWilliams	1991	2600
317 5/8	50 0/8	49 3/8	36 1/8	6	6	Coconino County	AZ	Randy S. Wagner	1992	2600
317 5/8	55 0/8	52 3/8	48 1/8	5	5	McKinley County	NM	Ken Coleman	1997	2600
317 5/8	47 1/8	48 0/8	40 1/8	6	6	Cascade County	MT	Charles J. Marlen, MD	1998	2600
317 5/8	49 2/8	49 1/8	41 1/8	7	7	Meagher County	MT	Buzz Marvin	1999	2600
317 5/8	53 0/8	53 0/8	35 5/8	6	5	San Juan County	UT	Wade Lish	2003	2600
317 5/8	48 2/8	48 4/8	38 7/8	6	6	Catron County	NM	Billie R. James III	2005	2600
317 5/8	51 7/8	52 0/8	32 5/8	6	6	Mesa County	CO	Erik Watts	2010	2600
317 4/8	52 0/8	52 3/8	40 2/8	6	6	Custer County	ID	Ed McIntosh	1989	2613
317 4/8	52 4/8	53 0/8	38 4/8	5	6	Catron County	NM	C. Eric Wickman	1995	2613
317 4/8	49 1/8	47 5/8	39 0/8	6	6	Park County	CO	Mark DeFurio	1996	2613
317 4/8	49 7/8	49 1/8	42 0/8	7	6	Blaine County	ID	David Doxey	1997	2613
317 4/8	49 5/8	51 2/8	35 0/8	6	6	Coconino County	AZ	Gerald Wachob	1997	2613
317 4/8	51 1/8	50 4/8	39 2/8	6	7	Catron County	NM	Scott Posner	2001	2613
317 4/8	50 3/8	50 2/8	35 4/8	6	6	Carbon County	UT	Dennis Gibson	2004	2613
317 4/8	47 6/8	48 2/8	37 2/8	6	6	Catron County	NM	Ray Francingues III	2006	2613
*317 4/8	48 2/8	48 7/8	35 0/8	6	6	Idaho County	ID	Ryan Williams	2010	2613
317 3/8	49 0/8	48 3/8	40 7/8	6	6	Fremont County	ID	Donald M. Sherick	1982	2622
317 3/8	45 1/8	47 1/8	36 4/8	7	7	Boundary County	ID	Walt Dinning	1987	2622
317 3/8	51 2/8	49 5/8	44 1/8	7	5	Crook County	OR	Edward Laite	1988	2622
317 3/8	51 3/8	50 0/8	37 1/8	6	6	Coconino County	AZ	Jim Norris	1991	2622
317 3/8	47 1/8	48 1/8	44 6/8	9	6	Fergus County	MT	Jess Knerr	1992	2622
317 3/8	51 4/8	52 2/8	41 2/8	6	6	Park County	WY	Melanie DeBusk	1999	2622
317 3/8	49 5/8	50 0/8	37 6/8	6	7	Catron County	NM	Jim Wagner	2003	2622
317 3/8	51 4/8	51 4/8	41 5/8	5	5	Catron County	NM	Mikel T. Vance	2003	2622
317 3/8	49 4/8	48 7/8	44 4/8	6	7	Catron County	NM	David C. Cluck	2005	2622
317 3/8	48 5/8	48 0/8	36 1/8	6	6	Costilla County	CO	M. Blake Patton	2005	2622
317 3/8	52 2/8	49 5/8	40 5/8	6	6	Custer County	ID	Nevin Herr	2005	2622
317 3/8	49 7/8	53 0/8	39 5/8	6	6	Mesa County	CO	Thoran Martinez	2006	2622
317 3/8	46 7/8	46 3/8	34 7/8	6	6	Grand County	UT	Bill McCunn	2007	2622
*317 3/8	51 2/8	52 6/8	34 7/8	6	6	Mesa County	CO	Matt Reetz	2008	2622
317 2/8	51 4/8	52 6/8	36 4/8	6	6	Coconino County	AZ	Blaine "Bub" Mathews	1991	2636
317 2/8	53 2/8	53 1/8	35 0/8	6	6	Coconino County	AZ	Michael Ellena	1992	2636
317 2/8	47 7/8	47 7/8	40 2/8	5	5	Pennington County	SD	Dan Hotchkiss	1992	2636
317 2/8	51 4/8	50 4/8	42 2/8	6	6	Petroleum County	MT	Bryant Shermoe	1992	2636
317 2/8	47 4/8	47 7/8	48 1/8	7	7	Coconino County	AZ	Brian Beamer	1997	2636
317 2/8	46 0/8	45 7/8	34 4/8	6	6	Carbon County	WY	Rhett Heflin	1999	2636
317 2/8	48 6/8	50 2/8	47 0/8	6	6	Valley County	ID	G. Dan Feighner	2001	2636
317 2/8	51 5/8	51 6/8	42 0/8	6	7	Yakima County	WA	Richard Brock	2003	2636
*317 2/8	48 6/8	48 7/8	37 7/8	7	7	Washakie County	WY	Rod Gleason	2010	2636
317 1/8	49 0/8	47 0/8	39 7/8	6	6	Catron County	NM	Eddie Claypool	1989	2645
317 1/8	49 1/8	47 7/8	35 5/8	6	6	Catron County	NM	Robert Haymaker	1990	2645
317 1/8	47 5/8	47 0/8	47 7/8	6	6	Catron County	NM	Rick L. Chukas	1990	2645
317 1/8	47 2/8	47 5/8	39 5/8	6	6	Colfax County	NM	Mike Wiley	1990	2645
317 1/8	49 1/8	53 0/8	38 7/8	6	7	Coconino County	AZ	Bill Grahlherr	1991	2645
317 1/8	47 6/8	48 0/8	36 7/8	6	6	Wallowa County	OR	Russ Hultberg	1996	2645
317 1/8	47 6/8	48 2/8	40 1/8	6	6	Valley County	MT	D. J. Elletson	1996	2645
317 1/8	51 0/8	48 7/8	36 7/8	6	6	Sandoval County	NM	Mark D. Bauder	1998	2645
317 1/8	50 2/8	48 4/8	31 7/8	6	6	Coconino County	AZ	Wally Schwartz	1999	2645
317 1/8	50 6/8	51 1/8	38 0/8	7	7	Big Horn County	WY	David L. McCullough	2002	2645
317 1/8	45 4/8	45 2/8	38 3/8	6	6	Granite County	MT	John Podebradsky	2002	2645
317 1/8	50 4/8	44 6/8	43 5/8	6	6	Baker County	OR	Michael S. Chandler	2003	2645
317 1/8	48 1/8	49 2/8	39 7/8	6	7	Gallatin County	MT	Edward Leritz	2003	2645
317 1/8	47 1/8	44 2/8	40 1/8	6	6	Teller County	CO	David D. Stratton	2005	2645
317 1/8	48 0/8	45 3/8	40 3/8	6	6	Coconino County	AZ	Bill Forbes	2005	2645
317 1/8	44 5/8	45 3/8	34 1/8	6	6	Las Animas County	CO	Ronnie Hall	2007	2645

705

AMERICAN ELK (TYPICAL ANTLERS)

Minimum Score 260   Continued

SCORE	LENGTH OF R MAIN BEAM L	INSIDE SPREAD	NUMBER OF R POINTS L		AREA	STATE/ PROVINCE	HUNTER'S NAME	DATE	RANK
*317 1/8	49 7/8 48 2/8	31 3/8	6	8	Petroleum County	MT	Paul Marchese	2009	2645
317 1/8	51 0/8 57 0/8	34 5/8	7	6	Coconino County	AZ	Jerry Douthit	2010	2645
317 0/8	46 5/8 47 0/8	42 2/8	6	7	Apache County	AZ	Robert H. Warren	1975	2663
317 0/8	51 3/8 51 7/8	39 4/8	6	6	Rio Arriba County	NM	Alfred Vigil	1984	2663
317 0/8	48 4/8 43 3/8	41 4/8	6	6	Mineral County	MT	S. Howie Henrikson	1987	2663
317 0/8	49 3/8 51 1/8	37 0/8	6	6	Catron County	NM	Lars E. Winquist	1991	2663
317 0/8	46 0/8 44 5/8	37 4/8	6	6	Albany County	WY	Paul Jakovac	1994	2663
317 0/8	52 4/8 53 0/8	37 6/8	7	6	Coconino County	AZ	Dan Allred	1999	2663
317 0/8	45 4/8 44 1/8	37 0/8	6	6	Umatilla County	OR	Tom Nieradka	2004	2663
317 0/8	48 7/8 52 2/8	46 0/8	6	6	Coconino County	AZ	Dyrk Eddie	2004	2663
317 0/8	51 5/8 51 6/8	35 4/8	6	6	Phillips County	MT	Adam Pronschinske	2005	2663
*317 0/8	50 6/8 50 6/8	44 2/8	6	6	Caribou County	ID	Jeff Martinsen	2008	2663
317 0/8	49 0/8 38 6/8	40 2/8	7	6	Fergus County	MT	Lynn Bowman	2009	2663
316 7/8	52 7/8 51 6/8	41 5/8	6	6	Converse County	WY	Troy Wickman	1993	2674
316 7/8	47 6/8 48 2/8	38 5/8	6	6	Catron County	NM	Tony Cutbirth	2001	2674
316 7/8	47 0/8 46 7/8	32 7/8	6	6	Phillips County	MT	Jason Radinovich	2007	2674
*316 7/8	48 3/8 50 6/8	35 5/8	6	6	Archuleta County	CO	Floyd Martinez	2009	2674
316 6/8	49 3/8 49 5/8	35 6/8	6	6	Lodgepole	ALB	Lynn M. Kasper	1991	2678
316 6/8	47 6/8 48 5/8	35 2/8	6	6	Coconino County	AZ	Joseph O. Fogleman	1991	2678
316 6/8	46 7/8 48 2/8	39 0/8	6	6	Otero County	NM	Marvin Samford, Jr.	1993	2678
316 6/8	50 5/8 49 5/8	45 4/8	6	6	Catron County	NM	Bill Shaw	1993	2678
316 6/8	49 1/8 50 3/8	37 2/8	6	6	Valley County	MT	Larry Ochsner	1993	2678
316 6/8	47 2/8 47 0/8	35 6/8	6	6	Coconino County	AZ	Greg Godbehere	1998	2678
316 6/8	52 0/8 51 1/8	39 0/8	6	6	Musselshell County	MT	Chuck Adams	1998	2678
316 6/8	47 6/8 49 1/8	45 6/8	7	6	Park County	WY	Tom Buller	2003	2678
316 6/8	50 0/8 48 4/8	40 7/8	7	6	Fergus County	MT	Rusten Barnes	2005	2678
*316 6/8	50 2/8 50 0/8	41 4/8	6	6	Rio Arriba County	NM	Austin Garcia	2005	2678
316 6/8	47 5/8 47 0/8	38 2/8	6	6	Valley County	ID	Brandon Petross	2005	2678
316 6/8	48 6/8 50 1/8	42 6/8	7	6	Garfield County	MT	Richard Kuckelman	2006	2678
*316 6/8	49 7/8 51 2/8	33 2/8	6	6	Las Animas County	CO	Mitchell Butler	2008	2678
316 6/8	57 1/8 54 6/8	40 4/8	6	6	Moffat County	CO	R. Scott Stewart, Jr.	2009	2678
316 5/8	46 1/8 49 3/8	37 5/8	6	7	Morrow County	OR	Bob Lindsay	1989	2692
316 5/8	48 7/8 46 5/8	39 7/8	7	7	Coconino County	AZ	John Gurasich	1989	2692
316 5/8	54 4/8 53 4/8	41 0/8	7	6	Garfield County	MT	David Cochell	1997	2692
316 5/8	48 2/8 49 1/8	44 5/8	6	6	Lincoln County	MT	Jerry Lees	1999	2692
316 5/8	50 2/8 46 7/8	32 7/8	6	7	Carbon County	WY	J. T. "Mick" McClure	2000	2692
316 5/8	48 2/8 45 0/8	39 7/8	7	7	Coconino County	AZ	Kevin B. Call	2000	2692
316 5/8	47 5/8 47 2/8	48 0/8	6	6	Baker County	OR	Anthony VanCleave	2003	2692
316 5/8	50 4/8 49 4/8	36 5/8	6	6	Judith Basin County	MT	Tom Trevathan	2003	2692
*316 5/8	55 7/8 47 5/8	46 1/8	6	6	Coconino County	AZ	Mike Aleff	2004	2692
316 5/8	50 0/8 50 3/8	36 7/8	6	7	Park County	CO	Troy Koldenhoven	2005	2692
316 5/8	48 6/8 46 5/8	41 1/8	7	6	Petroleum County	MT	Matthew Sutton	2006	2692
*316 5/8	43 5/8 41 7/8	34 3/8	6	7	Las Animas County	CO	Robert McGehee	2010	2692
316 4/8	49 2/8 48 5/8	39 4/8	6	6	Grant County	OR	A. Corey Heath	1984	2704
316 4/8	54 0/8 56 6/8	40 2/8	7	6	Kootenai County	ID	Theodore Costo	1991	2704
316 4/8	49 3/8 53 2/8	38 6/8	6	6	Catron County	NM	John Sielicki	1994	2704
316 4/8	44 2/8 44 6/8	34 0/8	6	6	Coconino County	AZ	Rick Forrest	1998	2704
316 4/8	56 0/8 51 0/8	33 6/8	7	7	Catron County	NM	Larry Olmstead	1998	2704
316 4/8	54 2/8 54 4/8	46 6/8	6	6	Garfield County	UT	Peter Schaber	2003	2704
316 4/8	48 4/8 50 0/8	45 2/8	6	7	Linn County	OR	James Gutierrez II	2003	2704
316 4/8	41 3/8 44 5/8	43 7/8	6	6	Grant County	OR	Joel Youngerman	2004	2704
316 3/8	51 0/8 51 0/8	40 5/8	6	6	Missoula County	MT	Ben L. Jennings	1984	2712
316 3/8	52 3/8 51 1/8	38 5/8	6	6	Lewis County	WA	Leonard L. Stolen	1986	2712
316 3/8	50 1/8 48 4/8	39 1/8	6	6	Coconino County	AZ	Joseph D. Ehmann	1992	2712
316 3/8	50 6/8 48 5/8	37 7/8	6	6	Yavapai County	AZ	Jack Seckington	1994	2712
316 3/8	46 0/8 45 6/8	36 7/8	6	6	Catron County	NM	Cindi Richardson	1996	2712
316 3/8	53 0/8 52 6/8	40 1/8	6	6	McKinley County	NM	Stephen M. Milano	1997	2712
316 3/8	49 4/8 48 7/8	36 7/8	6	6	Coconino County	AZ	Troy A. Graziadei	1998	2712
316 3/8	51 0/8 51 3/8	45 5/8	6	6	Broadwater County	MT	Robert J. Bossi, Sr.	2000	2712
316 3/8	49 6/8 44 4/8	34 7/8	7	7	Coconino County	AZ	Henry Thornhill	2003	2712
316 3/8	44 2/8 43 2/8	43 3/8	6	6	Wasatch County	UT	Burkely Gerhardt	2007	2712
316 3/8	45 4/8 47 4/8	44 5/8	6	6	Moffat County	CO	Robert Lowers, Jr.	2008	2712
316 2/8	48 2/8 48 2/8	34 6/8	7	7	Coconino County	AZ	William M. Lanese	1981	2723
316 2/8	49 5/8 49 1/8	39 4/8	6	6	Canmore	ALB	Glenn Derovin	1990	2723
316 2/8	52 7/8 51 3/8	42 6/8	6	6	Shoshone County	ID	Randy Lee Collecchi	1995	2723
316 2/8	49 4/8 48 1/8	38 6/8	6	6	Coconino County	AZ	Darr Colburn	1995	2723
316 2/8	43 4/8 44 0/8	40 0/8	6	5	Eureka County	NV	Ken Mallory	1996	2723
316 2/8	50 3/8 48 1/8	36 6/8	6	6	Lewis & Clark County	MT	Dave Jaraczeski	1997	2723
316 2/8	51 0/8 51 7/8	37 2/8	6	6	Albany County	WY	Adam Uthlaut	2004	2723
316 1/8	54 0/8 51 0/8	37 7/8	6	6	Valley County	MT	Dan Sturgis	1981	2730
316 1/8	44 1/8 47 4/8	39 3/8	6	6	Rio Blanco County	CO	Darrell S. Jones	1987	2730
316 1/8	48 1/8 48 6/8	43 1/8	6	6	Fergus County	MT	Joe Rud	1995	2730
316 1/8	48 1/8 48 1/8	41 7/8	6	6	Caribou County	ID	Chad Gentry	2001	2730
316 1/8	47 5/8 48 3/8	42 7/8	7	6	Meagher County	MT	Jason Crawford	2002	2730
316 1/8	51 0/8 52 7/8	38 5/8	6	6	Beaverhead County	MT	Neal Davis	2002	2730
316 1/8	43 5/8 43 3/8	40 3/8	6	7	Bonner County	ID	Eric Weisz	2003	2730
316 1/8	50 4/8 49 6/8	35 7/8	6	6	Coconino County	AZ	Bryan Wheeler	2008	2730
*316 1/8	48 1/8 47 5/8	37 5/8	6	6	Highwood River	ALB	Jason Hjelsvold	2008	2730
316 1/8	48 1/8 50 0/8	41 1/8	6	6	Kern County	CA	Doug Meeks	2009	2730
316 0/8	48 4/8 46 0/8	52 7/8	7	6	Deer Lodge County	MT	Bob Gossack	1976	2740
316 0/8	46 4/8 48 2/8	40 0/8	6	6	Archuleta County	CO	Loren Hofeldt	1981	2740
316 0/8	54 3/8 52 1/8	38 0/8	6	6	Sweet Grass County	MT	Marlin F. Dunlap	1983	2740
316 0/8	45 1/8 43 7/8	43 2/8	6	6	Rich County	UT	Robert G. Petersen	1988	2740
316 0/8	48 3/8 49 0/8	39 4/8	7	7	Apache County	AZ	Melvin E. Norris	1989	2740
316 0/8	44 0/8 45 4/8	36 0/8	6	6	Coconino County	AZ	Earnest D. Stanley	1991	2740
316 0/8	45 6/8 48 0/8	35 0/8	6	6	Lincoln County	NV	Kevin Paintner	1995	2740
316 0/8	50 5/8 48 7/8	38 2/8	6	6	Colfax County	NM	Gudrun M. Richardson	1996	2740
316 0/8	48 7/8 50 4/8	35 4/8	6	6	Lemhi County	ID	Gary Triplett	1997	2740
316 0/8	47 6/8 46 1/8	37 0/8	6	6	Johnson County	WY	Derek Thompson	1998	2740
316 0/8	49 2/8 46 5/8	39 0/8	6	6	Park County	WY	John Morlang	1998	2740
316 0/8	45 0/8 45 3/8	33 6/8	6	6	Sheridan County	WY	Dave Moss	1999	2740
316 0/8	46 4/8 49 0/8	41 4/8	5	5	Socorro County	NM	Bruce J. Church	2001	2740
316 0/8	48 4/8 48 1/8	39 6/8	6	6	Bonneville County	ID	Jim Pratt	2002	2740
316 0/8	47 4/8 46 5/8	37 4/8	7	7	Salt Lake County	UT	Todd Saxey	2006	2740
315 7/8	51 2/8 51 4/8	43 3/8	6	6	Wasco County	OR	Ivan Duncan	1982	2755

706

AMERICAN ELK (TYPICAL ANTLERS)

Minimum Score 260
Continued

SCORE	LENGTH OF MAIN BEAM R	L	INSIDE SPREAD	NUMBER OF POINTS R	L	AREA	STATE/ PROVINCE	HUNTER'S NAME	DATE	RANK
315 7/8	51 7/8	51 0/8	34 5/8	6	6	Sheridan County	WY	Dan Doke	1990	2755
315 7/8	54 1/8	54 0/8	51 1/8	6	6	Cibola County	NM	Wayne A. Nicholson	1994	2755
315 7/8	49 4/8	49 0/8	42 5/8	6	6	Coconino County	AZ	John Strippelman	1995	2755
315 7/8	47 4/8	46 1/8	37 1/8	6	6	Colfax County	NM	Donald Travis	1999	2755
315 7/8	54 5/8	53 5/8	36 7/8	6	6	Bonneville County	ID	Ron Sherwood	1999	2755
315 7/8	48 6/8	48 5/8	40 3/8	6	6	Huerfano County	CO	Jim Mitchell, Jr.	1999	2755
315 7/8	45 4/8	45 4/8	32 7/8	6	7	Judith Basin County	MT	Jeffrey Evans	2001	2755
315 7/8	48 3/8	46 4/8	40 3/8	6	5	Garfield County	CO	Stan Ryan	2001	2755
315 7/8	48 0/8	48 4/8	39 7/8	6	7	Garfield County	MT	DuWayne M. Larson	2002	2755
315 7/8	44 5/8	44 2/8	31 5/8	7	6	Catron County	NM	George Polachak	2002	2755
315 7/8	54 4/8	53 5/8	39 1/8	6	6	Carbon County	UT	Don R. Logston	2005	2755
315 7/8	47 7/8	47 6/8	34 3/8	6	7	Phillips County	MT	Jack Sorum	2005	2755
*315 7/8	50 1/8	52 2/8	40 5/8	7	7	Yavapai County	AZ	Kirk MacDonald	2005	2755
315 7/8	51 6/8	51 5/8	37 1/8	6	6	Coconino County	AZ	Andrew Grannan	2005	2755
*315 7/8	47 3/8	46 4/8	35 5/8	7	6	Park County	MT	David Hackney	2007	2755
315 6/8	47 7/8	48 5/8	38 0/8	6	6	Nez Perce County	ID	Alfred J. Gemrich	1984	2771
315 6/8	48 4/8	47 2/8	34 2/8	6	6	Converse County	WY	Arthur Rubel	1987	2771
315 6/8	49 1/8	50 5/8	41 4/8	7	8	Converse County	WY	Frank Moore	1989	2771
315 6/8	40 0/8	47 7/8	42 4/8	6	6	Caribou County	ID	Coby Tigert	1990	2771
315 6/8	49 5/8	56 0/8	31 6/8	6	6	Catron County	NM	John S. Patterson	1992	2771
315 6/8	46 6/8	48 4/8	32 4/8	6	6	Catron County	NM	Jorge Garcia-Segovia	1992	2771
315 6/8	50 1/8	50 7/8	41 0/8	7	7	Larimer County	CO	Anthony Artessa	1995	2771
315 6/8	48 4/8	45 7/8	41 6/8	6	6	Sierra County	NM	Deone Johnson	1998	2771
315 6/8	48 6/8	47 0/8	34 6/8	6	6	White Pine County	NV	Mike Collie	2002	2771
315 6/8	47 5/8	46 1/8	40 3/8	6	7	Fremont County	ID	Forrest W. Carter	2004	2771
315 5/8	48 6/8	47 6/8	36 3/8	6	6	Gallatin National Forest	MT	Rocky Miller	1981	2781
315 5/8	47 0/8	46 3/8	45 1/8	6	6	Lemhi County	ID	Jeffrey T. Shaffer	1990	2781
315 5/8	55 2/8	54 1/8	39 4/8	8	6	Coconino County	AZ	David C. Fretz	1992	2781
315 5/8	47 3/8	47 4/8	35 5/8	6	6	Montrose County	CO	Zach Parker	2000	2781
315 5/8	46 7/8	45 0/8	35 7/8	7	6	Sanders County	MT	Dean J. Stahl	2000	2781
315 5/8	52 2/8	51 1/8	34 1/8	6	6	Apache County	AZ	Robert A. Shelley	2004	2781
315 5/8	46 0/8	47 0/8	36 7/8	7	6	Coconino County	AZ	Cindi Richardson	2004	2781
315 5/8	47 0/8	47 2/8	34 2/8	7	8	Mesa County	CO	Mark Livingston	2005	2781
315 5/8	50 2/8	48 5/8	43 5/8	6	6	Powell County	MT	Thomas Nelson	2008	2781
315 5/8	49 1/8	49 3/8	33 5/8	6	6	Albany County	WY	Craig Oceanak	2009	2781
315 4/8	51 7/8	49 0/8	42 6/8	6	6	Wallowa County	OR	Dr. Russell A. Colgan	1976	2791
315 4/8	45 2/8	46 3/8	44 4/8	7	6	Harney County	OR	"Ray" L. D. Reimers	1989	2791
315 4/8	48 2/8	48 2/8	34 2/8	7	6	Coconino County	AZ	Gregg Thurston	1994	2791
315 4/8	43 2/8	44 1/8	40 2/8	6	6	Teton County	WY	John I. Ritter	2001	2791
315 4/8	45 5/8	45 4/8	37 2/8	6	6	Moffat County	CO	Chad A. Filener	2001	2791
315 4/8	44 3/8	44 3/8	41 0/8	6	6	Gallatin County	MT	Derrick Christensen	2003	2791
315 4/8	43 0/8	42 1/8	41 0/8	6	6	Fording River	BC	Walter Conibear	2006	2791
*315 4/8	46 4/8	48 2/8	35 2/8	5	5	Coconino County	AZ	John Douglas Vivian	2009	2791
315 3/8	53 0/8	50 7/8	37 3/8	6	6	Clear Creek County	CO	Gary Christoffersen	1982	2799
315 3/8	51 3/8	50 4/8	37 3/8	6	6	Judith Basin County	MT	David Decker	1992	2799
315 3/8	51 3/8	51 4/8	39 3/8	6	6	Coconino County	AZ	Jim Wheeler	1997	2799
315 3/8	50 3/8	51 3/8	40 1/8	6	6	Granite County	MT	William Boyd Kurtz Gilbert	2000	2799
315 3/8	49 1/8	50 3/8	40 7/8	6	6	Harney County	OR	Joel R. Griffin	2002	2799
315 3/8	47 0/8	46 4/8	40 1/8	6	6	Washington County	ID	Patrick E. Wheeler	2003	2799
315 3/8	46 5/8	43 1/8	36 3/8	6	6	Catron County	NM	Lawrence S. Nichols III	2004	2799
315 3/8	50 5/8	50 4/8	33 3/8	6	6	Valley County	ID	Michael Doherty	2005	2799
*315 3/8	51 4/8	51 1/8	42 3/8	6	6	Mesa County	CO	Daniel Salazar	2008	2799
315 2/8	51 0/8	51 1/8	41 2/8	6	6	Teton County	MT	Ronald K. Granneman	1976	2808
315 2/8	50 4/8	52 0/8	40 2/8	6	6	Clark County	ID	Ken Vander Linden	1986	2808
315 2/8	46 6/8	45 6/8	41 4/8	6	6	Canmore	ALB	Dennis Francis	1986	2808
315 2/8	45 7/8	45 6/8	40 0/8	5	6	Custer County	ID	Edward Allen Mack	1987	2808
315 2/8	45 0/8	44 3/8	33 6/8	6	6	Catron County	NM	Christopher D. Walp	1994	2808
315 2/8	53 0/8	53 4/8	42 0/8	6	6	Garfield County	UT	Randy Jackson	1998	2808
315 2/8	50 3/8	50 6/8	36 0/8	6	6	Socorro County	NM	Mark C. Schwei	2001	2808
315 2/8	46 6/8	47 0/8	39 0/8	6	6	Garfield County	MT	Glenn DeLabarre	2001	2808
*315 2/8	51 0/8	51 0/8	36 4/8	5	6	San Miguel County	CO	Anthony Pierino	2006	2808
315 2/8	51 4/8	50 3/8	34 6/8	6	6	Meagher County	MT	Jim Kennedy	2006	2808
315 2/8	47 3/8	45 3/8	40 2/8	6	6	Gallatin County	MT	Shawn Morgan	2007	2808
315 2/8	51 4/8	50 7/8	36 4/8	6	6	Meagher County	MT	Jim Kennedy	2007	2808
*315 2/8	47 0/8	49 4/8	41 2/8	6	7	Costilla County	CO	Elof Eriksson	2007	2808
315 1/8	42 4/8	43 4/8	38 3/8	6	6	Grant County	OR	Rod Curtis	1988	2821
315 1/8	50 0/8	47 1/8	43 5/8	6	6	Bear Lake County	ID	Jerry B. Tueller	1991	2821
315 1/8	47 1/8	48 2/8	37 3/8	6	6	Butte County	ID	Kirk W. Reese	1995	2821
315 1/8	46 4/8	43 5/8	39 1/8	6	6	Phillips County	MT	Joey Ardrey	1996	2821
315 1/8	49 3/8	48 2/8	35 7/8	6	6	Montrose County	CO	Stanley Van	1997	2821
315 1/8	50 7/8	49 0/8	34 1/8	6	6	Grand County	UT	Ron Barngrover	2003	2821
315 1/8	54 0/8	54 2/8	35 7/8	6	6	Park County	CO	Charles Metz, Jr.	2008	2821
*315 1/8	49 6/8	49 3/8	38 3/8	6	6	Custer County	CO	Steve D. Powers	2009	2821
*315 1/8	46 2/8	43 2/8	37 1/8	6	6	Big Horn County	WY	David M. Bufkin	2009	2821
315 0/8	52 3/8	50 0/8	38 6/8	6	6	Grant County	OR	Bryan Kue	1994	2830
315 0/8	50 0/8	48 7/8	38 6/8	6	6	Apache County	AZ	Larry R. Marin	1997	2830
315 0/8	53 1/8	53 1/8	40 2/8	6	6	Lemhi County	ID	Daniel Breissinger	1998	2830
315 0/8	47 4/8	43 3/8	40 0/8	6	6	Clearwater County	ID	Kendall J. Bauer	2000	2830
315 0/8	47 6/8	46 4/8	29 6/8	6	6	Taos County	NM	Andy Milam	2000	2830
315 0/8	49 1/8	50 2/8	40 6/8	6	6	Elko County	NV	Susan Sandoz	2003	2830
315 0/8	47 2/8	41 1/8	36 5/8	6	7	Powell County	MT	Stan Alexander	2004	2830
315 0/8	49 4/8	48 3/8	39 2/8	6	6	Park County	WY	Tyler L. Henry	2005	2830
315 0/8	54 6/8	51 1/8	43 2/8	7	7	Phillips County	MT	Ron Kukus	2005	2830
315 0/8	49 6/8	52 0/8	39 2/8	7	7	Coconino County	AZ	Larry O. Hutchinson, Jr.	2006	2830
314 7/8	51 5/8	48 5/8	38 3/8	6	6	Catron County	NM	Dale R. Larson	1996	2840
314 7/8	50 1/8	50 3/8	31 7/8	6	6	Caribou County	ID	Chad Gentry	2000	2840
314 7/8	43 4/8	44 1/8	37 1/8	6	6	Caribou County	ID	Brody Gibson	2002	2840
314 7/8	49 0/8	51 1/8	40 0/8	6	6	Rio Blanco County	CO	Kurt Hall	2009	2840
314 7/8	48 5/8	49 7/8	35 3/8	6	6	Petroleum County	MT	Ron Kilgore	2010	2840
314 6/8	50 0/8	51 3/8	40 0/8	6	6	Catron County	NM	Wayne K. Curtis	1984	2845
314 6/8	46 7/8	45 6/8	42 2/8	6	6	Catron County	NM	Dennis Curtis	1986	2845
314 6/8	48 3/8	48 1/8	31 0/8	6	6	Mesa County	CO	Parker Leon	1989	2845
314 6/8	44 4/8	46 0/8	34 6/8	6	7	Catron County	NM	Marvis Meyer	1992	2845
314 6/8	45 1/8	46 5/8	36 2/8	6	6	Lemhi County	ID	Shawn M. West	1997	2845
314 6/8	51 3/8	45 1/8	36 4/8	6	6	Colfax County	NM	Ralph Edward Johnson, Jr.	1999	2845

707

AMERICAN ELK (TYPICAL ANTLERS)

Minimum Score 260 Continued

SCORE	LENGTH OF R MAIN BEAM L	INSIDE SPREAD	NUMBER OF R POINTS L		AREA	STATE/ PROVINCE	HUNTER'S NAME	DATE	RANK
314 6/8	43 4/8	42 7/8	37 2/8	6	6	Socorro County	NM	David C. Wade	2000	2845
314 6/8	48 3/8	49 6/8	35 6/8	6	6	Yakima County	WA	John Neudorfer	2004	2845
314 6/8	44 6/8	43 3/8	39 4/8	6	6	Albany County	WY	Ken Harder	2005	2845
314 6/8	47 4/8	45 6/8	35 6/8	6	6	Mineral County	MT	Chia Yang	2005	2845
314 6/8	47 1/8	49 6/8	42 6/8	5	5	Teton County	WY	Stanley Richards	2005	2845
314 6/8	49 0/8	50 6/8	45 2/8	6	6	Sierra County	NM	Matt Plitt	2006	2845
314 5/8	50 6/8	52 7/8	35 3/8	7	7	Hinsdale County	CO	Leon Shreve, Jr.	1995	2857
314 5/8	41 6/8	49 1/8	38 3/8	6	6	Catron County	NM	Dr. Charles W. Hendricks	1997	2857
314 5/8	52 7/8	53 0/8	39 3/8	6	5	Coconino County	AZ	John D. Beers	1997	2857
314 5/8	45 2/8	44 2/8	33 6/8	6	7	Sierra County	NM	Billy W. Barger	1999	2857
314 5/8	47 1/8	45 2/8	43 1/8	6	6	Park County	WY	Larry Hicks	1999	2857
*314 5/8	43 1/8	45 6/8	44 7/8	6	7	Sierra County	NM	James W. Murphy, Jr.	2004	2857
314 4/8	48 0/8	48 2/8	39 4/8	6	6	Caribou County	ID	Alan E. Christiansen	1982	2863
314 4/8	47 7/8	47 6/8	36 0/8	6	6	Moffat County	CO	Dave Holt	1985	2863
314 4/8	47 0/8	48 5/8	35 6/8	6	6	Big Horn County	WY	Steve Schulz	1998	2863
314 4/8	42 7/8	43 5/8	36 6/8	6	6	Fremont County	WY	Jim Allington	2001	2863
314 4/8	46 7/8	45 5/8	40 0/8	6	6	Routt County	CO	Mark Crain	2003	2863
314 4/8	52 6/8	51 3/8	37 6/8	7	6	Coconino County	AZ	Jason Mark Florell	2007	2863
314 4/8	46 4/8	46 1/8	40 6/8	6	6	Pennington County	SD	Gene M. Hove	2008	2863
314 4/8	51 3/8	49 7/8	40 4/8	6	6	Valley County	ID	Ryan McBarron	2009	2863
314 3/8	48 4/8	46 1/8	41 3/8	6	6	Caribou County	ID	Bruce N. Moss	1980	2871
314 3/8	48 4/8	52 3/8	35 3/8	6	6	Grant County	NM	Ronald L. Pack, Sr.	1988	2871
314 3/8	45 5/8	45 4/8	42 3/8	6	6	Catron County	NM	Bruce Carlisle	1989	2871
314 3/8	51 1/8	50 1/8	40 5/8	6	6	Caribou County	ID	Dennis Dursteler	2001	2871
314 3/8	46 6/8	46 6/8	42 1/8	6	6	Beaverhead County	MT	Gary Lampkins	2004	2871
314 3/8	46 7/8	44 7/8	42 1/8	6	6	Valley County	ID	Sean Cook	2005	2871
314 3/8	48 1/8	47 7/8	31 1/8	7	6	White Pine County	NV	L. Grant Foster	2005	2871
*314 3/8	52 7/8	53 4/8	41 7/8	6	6	Apache County	AZ	John Hoffman	2005	2871
*314 3/8	46 2/8	46 5/8	38 7/8	6	6	San Miguel County	NM	Alfred Heras, Jr.	2009	2871
314 2/8	48 6/8	45 3/8	47 0/8	6	6	Coconino County	AZ	Michael Faherty	1986	2880
314 2/8	44 6/8	44 4/8	36 6/8	6	6	Coconino County	AZ	Ron Kirk	1989	2880
314 2/8	50 2/8	51 2/8	35 4/8	6	6	Uintah County	UT	J. Brad Denver	1995	2880
314 2/8	50 5/8	51 7/8	36 6/8	6	6	Gilpin County	CO	John Arnesen	1997	2880
314 2/8	46 2/8	48 0/8	39 0/8	6	6	Catron County	NM	Kevin Robinson	2000	2880
314 2/8	46 4/8	48 4/8	37 0/8	6	6	Beaverhead County	MT	Rory E. Indreland	2001	2880
314 2/8	47 0/8	43 6/8	27 0/8	6	6	Catron County	NM	Dan Kimmel	2004	2880
314 2/8	50 3/8	48 4/8	39 2/8	6	6	Martin County	KY	Michael Duncan	2006	2880
*314 2/8	48 0/8	48 4/8	29 0/8	6	6	Phillips County	MT	Adam Pronschinske	2008	2880
314 1/8	51 0/8	51 2/8	41 5/8	6	6	Gallatin County	MT	C. W. Smith	1974	2889
314 1/8	49 1/8	49 7/8	35 1/8	6	6	Custer County	ID	Ken Mallory	1994	2889
314 1/8	52 0/8	51 2/8	39 5/8	6	6	Rio Arriba County	NM	John Greaney	2001	2889
314 1/8	44 6/8	46 3/8	33 5/8	8	7	Musselshell County	MT	James E. Kirby	2003	2889
314 1/8	48 0/8	47 0/8	37 3/8	6	6	Albany County	WY	James M. Dahl	2003	2889
314 1/8	47 5/8	51 5/8	39 5/8	5	5	Coconino County	AZ	Mark E. Chavez	2006	2889
*314 1/8	54 2/8	53 6/8	39 5/8	8	7	Coconino County	AZ	Marc Twidwell	2008	2889
314 1/8	50 5/8	51 2/8	46 7/8	6	6	Catron County	NM	Ronald W. Dendy	2009	2889
314 1/8	45 1/8	46 5/8	35 7/8	6	6	Fergus County	MT	Chance Norskog	2009	2889
314 0/8	47 7/8	48 2/8	44 0/8	6	6	Fremont County	ID	Tom Savage	1981	2898
314 0/8	46 1/8	45 5/8	36 4/8	6	7	Phillips County	MT	Mark D. Hughes	1982	2898
314 0/8	50 3/8	50 1/8	40 4/8	6	6	Catron County	NM	Randall F. Cooley	1983	2898
314 0/8	54 3/8	54 4/8	37 0/8	6	5	Coconino County	AZ	James R. Dreves	1985	2898
314 0/8	45 6/8	46 4/8	42 4/8	7	7	Big Horn County	WY	Mike Belcourt	1986	2898
314 0/8	49 5/8	49 2/8	42 6/8	6	6	Flathead County	MT	Jim Hawkins	1986	2898
314 0/8	44 4/8	44 4/8	35 2/8	6	6	Lemhi County	ID	Frank L. Dumbeck	1991	2898
314 0/8	45 2/8	46 0/8	47 5/8	6	6	Fremont County	ID	Donald M. Sherick	1995	2898
314 0/8	45 5/8	45 5/8	52 3/8	7	7	Gallatin County	MT	Rex Rogers	1995	2898
314 0/8	47 4/8	48 4/8	32 2/8	6	6	Catron County	NM	Gregory G. Clark	1996	2898
314 0/8	47 5/8	47 1/8	37 4/8	6	6	Montrose County	CO	Jim Holdenried	1996	2898
314 0/8	46 7/8	45 4/8	38 0/8	6	6	Washington County	ID	Joe D. Olivas	1999	2898
314 0/8	47 5/8	47 6/8	36 1/8	6	7	Lemhi County	ID	Jason T. Leishman	1999	2898
314 0/8	49 7/8	51 5/8	42 4/8	6	6	Rich County	UT	Jonathan Edwards	2001	2898
314 0/8	43 4/8	42 5/8	36 2/8	6	6	Bingham County	ID	Jared M. Winterbottom	2002	2898
314 0/8	47 5/8	47 6/8	39 6/8	7	6	Grant County	OR	Curt Thompson	2003	2898
314 0/8	46 0/8	47 4/8	31 6/8	6	6	Skamania County	WA	George A. Barnes	2004	2898
314 0/8	49 7/8	50 3/8	33 6/8	6	6	Catron County	NM	Mike Giles	2007	2898
313 7/8	49 2/8	47 3/8	44 2/8	7	6	Coconino County	AZ	Don R. Newton	1980	2916
313 7/8	47 5/8	44 7/8	33 3/8	7	7	Porcupine Hills	ALB	John Archibald	1980	2916
313 7/8	44 4/8	44 3/8	34 1/8	6	6	Apache County	AZ	Doug Kleck	1986	2916
313 7/8	49 0/8	52 5/8	41 1/8	6	6	Rich County	UT	C. Keith Maynes	1990	2916
313 7/8	49 6/8	51 1/8	46 1/8	6	6	Johnson County	WY	Gary D. Hughes	1992	2916
313 7/8	49 4/8	45 7/8	34 1/8	7	7	Albany County	WY	Bill Gorman	1992	2916
313 7/8	53 0/8	51 2/8	35 7/8	6	6	Los Alamos County	NM	Kevin Peterson	1995	2916
313 7/8	52 4/8	48 6/8	35 1/8	6	6	Idaho County	ID	Mike Estrada	1996	2916
313 7/8	44 3/8	44 3/8	35 1/8	6	6	Fergus County	MT	Josef K. Rud	1996	2916
313 7/8	45 2/8	45 2/8	38 1/8	7	7	Catron County	NM	Jimmy W. Stafford	1998	2916
313 7/8	50 0/8	50 2/8	36 1/8	6	6	Albany County	WY	Mark Anderson	1999	2916
313 7/8	49 1/8	50 5/8	33 7/8	7	6	Park County	WY	Danny Ilkich	2004	2916
*313 7/8	47 1/8	44 6/8	34 7/8	6	6	Coconino County	AZ	Chip Beiner	2004	2916
*313 7/8	50 4/8	52 0/8	33 5/8	6	6	Jefferson County	CO	Rick Schaffhauser	2005	2916
313 7/8	48 7/8	49 2/8	36 5/8	6	6	Broadwater County	MT	Matthew J. Ottusch	2007	2916
313 6/8	47 7/8	47 7/8	36 2/8	6	6	Otero County	NM	Lynn Saxon	1987	2931
313 6/8	44 4/8	45 2/8	48 0/8	6	5	Moffat County	CO	Mike Wallers	1991	2931
313 6/8	51 1/8	50 7/8	42 4/8	7	7	Sublette County	WY	Ron Couture	1993	2931
313 6/8	46 3/8	48 4/8	33 4/8	7	6	Washington County	ID	Jorden Doggett	1997	2931
313 6/8	45 4/8	47 1/8	38 2/8	6	6	Idaho County	ID	Dean M. Miller	1999	2931
313 6/8	50 3/8	50 5/8	39 0/8	7	6	Ravalli County	MT	E. A. McCracken, Jr.	1999	2931
313 6/8	52 1/8	50 0/8	39 4/8	6	6	Moffat County	CO	Scott N. Bartnick	2003	2931
313 6/8	48 7/8	49 7/8	37 4/8	6	6	Fremont County	ID	Bradley Roker	2004	2931
*313 6/8	44 6/8	43 4/8	34 4/8	6	6	Eagle County	CO	Cody Doig	2008	2931
313 5/8	53 3/8	53 2/8	31 4/8	6	7	Coconino County	AZ	Michael John Bylina	1988	2940
313 5/8	47 5/8	46 7/8	37 1/8	6	6	Valley County	ID	Kevin Primrose	1996	2940
313 5/8	52 3/8	50 3/8	38 7/8	6	6	Sweetwater County	WY	Patrick J. Malone	1997	2940
313 5/8	48 6/8	47 1/8	41 1/8	6	6	Ravalli County	MT	Dan Wiedigri	2005	2940
313 5/8	49 2/8	48 0/8	35 1/8	6	6	Summit County	CO	Brian P. Egging	2009	2940
313 5/8	44 4/8	44 7/8	47 3/8	6	6	Gallatin County	MT	David Anderson	2009	2940

708

AMERICAN ELK (TYPICAL ANTLERS)

Minimum Score 260   Continued

SCORE	LENGTH OF R MAIN BEAM L	INSIDE SPREAD	NUMBER OF R POINTS L		AREA	STATE/ PROVINCE	HUNTER'S NAME	DATE	RANK
313 5/8	51 3/8	47 6/8	37 1/8	6	6	Coconino County	AZ	Andrew J. Assereto	2009	2940
*313 5/8	49 5/8	46 4/8	37 7/8	6	6	Jefferson County	CO	John G. Whitten	2010	2940
313 4/8	45 0/8	43 4/8	41 4/8	6	6	Jefferson County	CO	Charles Cater	1976	2948
313 4/8	50 5/8	51 0/8	43 4/8	6	6	Grant County	OR	Andy Day	1980	2948
313 4/8	51 2/8	52 4/8	45 2/8	6	6	Catron County	NM	Mike Moore	1988	2948
313 4/8	47 6/8	46 1/8	40 6/8	6	6	Coconino County	AZ	Troy Dagenhart	1995	2948
313 4/8	44 4/8	45 2/8	40 4/8	6	6	Albany County	WY	Mark E. Adamson	1997	2948
313 4/8	50 6/8	50 4/8	37 2/8	6	6	Duchesne County	UT	Matthew Lowe	1999	2948
313 4/8	48 5/8	48 6/8	42 0/8	6	6	Custer County	SD	Mike LaCuran	1999	2948
313 4/8	54 1/8	52 3/8	37 2/8	7	7	Lewis County	WA	Ryan Davenport	2002	2948
313 4/8	46 2/8	43 1/8	43 0/8	6	6	Socorro County	NM	Robert Nowakowski	2002	2948
313 4/8	51 4/8	48 1/8	39 0/8	6	6	Moffat County	CO	Michael D. Haden	2003	2948
*313 4/8	46 5/8	45 6/8	36 4/8	6	7	Blaine County	MT	David Christianson	2007	2948
313 3/8	42 7/8	42 4/8	34 1/8	6	6	Apache County	AZ	Ronald Mellick	1990	2959
313 3/8	47 2/8	47 2/8	37 5/8	6	7	Harney County	OR	Robert M. Choate	1990	2959
313 3/8	55 5/8	54 2/8	36 3/8	6	6	Rio Arriba County	NM	Eudane Vicenti	1995	2959
313 3/8	49 2/8	48 6/8	35 5/8	6	6	Rio Arriba County	NM	Eudane Vicenti	1997	2959
313 3/8	45 6/8	44 1/8	32 1/8	6	6	Garfield County	MT	Ron Borgeson	1997	2959
313 3/8	51 3/8	50 4/8	43 1/8	6	6	Rich County	UT	Rick Wilson	1999	2959
313 3/8	58 3/8	55 0/8	40 3/8	6	6	Lawrence County	SD	Lonny Kracht	2008	2959
313 2/8	49 2/8	46 0/8	44 2/8	6	6	Albany County	WY	Jerry Bowen	1979	2966
313 2/8	43 4/8	44 1/8	30 4/8	7	7	Park County	MT	Robert Wennerstrom	1985	2966
313 2/8	51 2/8	51 2/8	39 6/8	6	6	Bonneville County	ID	Ron Mueller	1986	2966
313 2/8	51 4/8	50 7/8	45 4/8	6	6	Idaho County	ID	William E. Dean	1994	2966
313 2/8	48 2/8	47 4/8	39 6/8	6	5	Coconino County	AZ	Todd Smith	1994	2966
313 2/8	47 1/8	46 5/8	39 0/8	7	7	Lincoln County	MT	Tony Bierwagen	1996	2966
313 2/8	48 3/8	49 4/8	37 0/8	6	6	Archuleta County	CO	Jerome C. Haverda	1997	2966
313 2/8	55 0/8	50 6/8	41 0/8	6	6	Carbon County	WY	Sonny Jaramillo	1998	2966
313 2/8	49 2/8	51 4/8	31 0/8	6	7	Catron County	NM	Fredrick D. Speechly II	1999	2966
313 2/8	52 0/8	50 6/8	40 6/8	6	6	Fergus County	MT	Mike Bentler	2001	2966
313 2/8	45 0/8	44 7/8	34 6/8	6	6	Judith Basin County	MT	John W. Nation	2004	2966
313 2/8	51 3/8	51 5/8	37 2/8	6	6	Sublette County	WY	Joe Gillis	2004	2966
313 2/8	49 5/8	47 6/8	34 0/8	6	6	Fergus County	MT	Glen Berry	2004	2966
313 2/8	47 3/8	47 5/8	32 6/8	7	7	Sublette County	WY	George Chase, Jr.	2005	2966
313 2/8	46 7/8	45 7/8	39 4/8	6	6	Caribou County	ID	Jerome D. Larson	2007	2966
*313 2/8	48 5/8	48 2/8	38 4/8	6	6	Sanders County	MT	Chad Carter	2008	2966
313 1/8	46 1/8	49 3/8	34 0/8	8	7	Chaffee County	CO	Rick D. Montgomery	1986	2982
313 1/8	49 5/8	49 1/8	42 4/8	7	6	Glacier County	MT	Rick R. Winkowitsch	1989	2982
313 1/8	51 2/8	50 6/8	35 3/8	6	6	Albany County	WY	Mark Stiller	1992	2982
313 1/8	47 6/8	48 7/8	38 7/8	6	6	Shoshone County	ID	David Keith Robertson	1992	2982
313 1/8	49 3/8	49 6/8	34 3/8	6	6	Beaverhead County	MT	Michael John Smith	1994	2982
313 1/8	52 0/8	49 5/8	36 3/8	6	6	Albany County	WY	Jerry Bowen	1995	2982
313 1/8	43 6/8	42 5/8	32 7/8	6	6	Sublette County	WY	Tony Crnkovich	1996	2982
313 1/8	50 6/8	50 0/8	40 7/8	6	6	Idaho County	ID	Donald W. Hansen, Jr.	2001	2982
313 1/8	48 6/8	49 2/8	34 7/8	7	7	Washington County	ID	Tom Alford	2006	2982
*313 1/8	46 3/8	49 2/8	35 1/8	6	7	Colfax County	NM	Thomas C. Atwood	2007	2982
313 0/8	48 4/8	47 3/8	46 2/8	6	6	Park County	MT	Charles Milner	1973	2992
313 0/8	48 3/8	47 3/8	31 4/8	6	6	Catron County	NM	Steven J. Vittetow	1987	2992
313 0/8	56 5/8	55 4/8	39 4/8	6	6	Coconino County	AZ	Vince Dimiceli	1989	2992
313 0/8	47 2/8	46 2/8	35 6/8	7	6	Greenlee County	AZ	Charles Steven Williams	1990	2992
313 0/8	49 5/8	50 1/8	35 6/8	7	6	Sierra County	NM	Gerald Lambert Lopez	1991	2992
313 0/8	46 2/8	46 2/8	39 2/8	6	7	Sanders County	MT	Doug Van Tassell	1995	2992
313 0/8	50 1/8	50 5/8	40 0/8	6	6	Judith Basin County	MT	Kelly Norskog	1996	2992
313 0/8	53 3/8	52 6/8	39 4/8	5	6	Blaine County	ID	Tom Daquino	1996	2992
313 0/8	47 5/8	46 7/8	42 0/8	6	6	Blaine County	ID	M. Wayne Carey	1997	2992
313 0/8	49 1/8	49 0/8	36 2/8	6	6	Adams County	ID	Tom Gerdau, Jr.	2000	2992
313 0/8	51 5/8	52 7/8	34 4/8	6	6	Natrona County	WY	Gregg R. Bohlig	2003	2992
313 0/8	45 7/8	43 6/8	28 6/8	6	6	Beaver County	UT	Allan S. Dangerfield	2004	2992
313 0/8	45 0/8	46 4/8	38 0/8	6	6	Mesa County	CO	Steve Welch	2004	2992
313 0/8	48 4/8	46 0/8	36 4/8	6	6	Apache County	AZ	Dave Van Ooteghem	2005	2992
*313 0/8	49 5/8	46 5/8	48 4/8	6	7	Moffat County	CO	David Iverson	2009	2992
312 7/8	46 7/8	50 1/8	43 7/8	6	6	Shoshone County	ID	Harry Barker	1962	3007
312 7/8	49 6/8	50 0/8	41 6/8	6	7	Catron County	NM	Lee Braudt	1988	3007
312 7/8	45 7/8	46 1/8	31 5/8	7	7	Alder Flats	ALB	John Miller	1990	3007
312 7/8	44 4/8	45 3/8	38 3/8	6	6	Valley County	MT	Kenneth Smoker, Jr.	1990	3007
312 7/8	50 0/8	52 4/8	36 7/8	6	6	Moffat County	CO	Glenn W. Pritchard	1991	3007
312 7/8	50 1/8	50 2/8	37 1/8	6	6	Catron County	NM	Randall S. Ulmer	1991	3007
312 7/8	47 6/8	49 1/8	32 3/8	7	7	Catron County	NM	Robin Klemme	1997	3007
312 7/8	44 5/8	46 7/8	36 3/8	6	6	Greenlee County	AZ	Mark A. Vallejo	1998	3007
312 7/8	47 5/8	48 2/8	48 1/8	5	6	Caribou County	ID	Wayne W. Cutler	1998	3007
312 7/8	47 6/8	49 2/8	39 3/8	6	6	Park County	WY	David D. Darwin	2003	3007
312 7/8	46 4/8	49 5/8	42 1/8	6	6	Gallatin County	MT	Mark E. Pangle	2008	3007
*312 7/8	49 4/8	47 4/8	32 7/8	6	6	Beaverhead County	MT	Kevin L. Hadley	2010	3007
312 6/8	44 3/8	46 1/8	33 4/8	7	6	Clearwater County	ID	Doyle Anderegg	1975	3019
312 6/8	55 2/8	54 0/8	40 4/8	5	5	Cibola County	NM	Mark Webber	1982	3019
312 6/8	53 5/8	53 6/8	39 4/8	6	6	Greenlee County	AZ	Dick Hall	1986	3019
312 6/8	46 7/8	45 4/8	39 4/8	6	6	Rio Arriba County	NM	Dave Cook	2002	3019
312 6/8	45 4/8	46 6/8	39 2/8	6	6	Pierce County	WA	Glenn Broadwell	2003	3019
312 6/8	46 4/8	46 5/8	39 0/8	6	6	San Juan County	UT	David B. Nielsen	2004	3019
*312 6/8	49 4/8	47 4/8	28 6/8	6	6	White Pine County	NV	Mark Jones	2006	3019
312 6/8	52 0/8	50 4/8	39 4/8	6	6	White Pine County	NV	James F. Watson	2009	3019
312 5/8	47 0/8	47 3/8	39 5/8	6	6	Caribou County	ID	Dean Humphreys	1962	3027
312 5/8	50 4/8	54 4/8	41 7/8	6	6	Fremont County	ID	Blair R. Jones	1987	3027
312 5/8	46 7/8	47 6/8	32 3/8	6	6	Park County	CO	William Elfland	1991	3027
312 5/8	43 6/8	43 4/8	39 1/8	6	6	Clark County	ID	Eugene Bennett	2000	3027
312 5/8	46 5/8	47 5/8	34 6/8	6	7	Ravalli County	MT	Phillip Hopcroft	2005	3027
312 5/8	48 4/8	48 3/8	43 3/8	6	6	Park County	WY	Stephen Koerner	2006	3027
312 5/8	56 0/8	52 2/8	37 3/8	6	6	Sheridan County	WY	Anthony Spiegelberg	2007	3027
*312 5/8	49 7/8	46 5/8	34 5/8	6	6	Crook County	WY	Justin Larsen	2009	3027
312 4/8	51 0/8	51 6/8	42 3/8	9	7	Sanders County	MT	Ron Halvorson	1980	3035
312 4/8	46 4/8	49 5/8	40 2/8	6	6	Clearwater County	ID	Steven E. Baxter	1984	3035
312 4/8	48 0/8	46 6/8	37 2/8	6	6	Coconino County	AZ	Tony W. Zimbaro	1989	3035
312 4/8	51 6/8	51 4/8	38 6/8	6	7	Grant County	OR	James M. Carter	1991	3035
312 4/8	53 3/8	51 4/8	35 5/8	6	7	Catron County	NM	Johnny C. Parsons	1992	3035
312 4/8	49 4/8	48 3/8	35 0/8	7	6	Phillips County	MT	Jerry Parsons	1995	3035

709

AMERICAN ELK (TYPICAL ANTLERS)

Minimum Score 260 — Continued

SCORE	LENGTH OF MAIN BEAM R	L	INSIDE SPREAD	NUMBER OF POINTS R	L	AREA	STATE/ PROVINCE	HUNTER'S NAME	DATE	RANK
312 4/8	46 7/8	47 6/8	39 2/8	6	6	Big Horn County	WY	Steve Schulz	1997	3035
312 4/8	51 6/8	49 5/8	41 6/8	6	7	Lawrence County	SD	Lance Carter	2001	3035
312 4/8	52 2/8	52 2/8	35 5/8	6	7	Kane County	UT	Andy Peterson	2002	3035
312 4/8	51 2/8	48 0/8	41 4/8	6	6	Meagher County	MT	Tim Fisk	2003	3035
312 4/8	50 7/8	49 0/8	41 2/8	6	6	Klamath County	OR	Ron Willis	2004	3035
312 4/8	48 6/8	48 4/8	38 6/8	6	6	Garfield County	MT	Corey Green	2004	3035
*312 4/8	45 7/8	48 4/8	44 0/8	7	6	Teton County	WY	Bradley Rhodes	2004	3035
312 4/8	47 4/8	48 1/8	34 4/8	6	6	Catron County	NM	Joseph M. Taglialegami	2005	3035
312 3/8	53 5/8	52 0/8	36 1/8	6	6	Socorro County	NM	James C. Hayes	1992	3049
312 3/8	52 1/8	51 4/8	40 7/8	5	7	Moffat County	CO	Gary A. Gray	2003	3049
312 2/8	44 6/8	44 7/8	38 2/8	6	6	Eagle County	CO	Gary D. Allen	1974	3051
312 2/8	48 1/8	48 4/8	36 4/8	6	6	Larimer County	CO	Steve Stumbo	1975	3051
312 2/8	50 0/8	49 0/8	35 5/8	7	8	Butte County	ID	Floyd L. Collins, Jr.	1982	3051
312 2/8	46 4/8	46 2/8	35 0/8	6	7	Catron County	NM	Billy E. Gourley	1984	3051
312 2/8	49 4/8	50 3/8	38 4/8	7	6	Grant County	NM	Gregory M. Theisen	2000	3051
312 2/8	44 5/8	43 0/8	31 6/8	6	6	Routt County	CO	Randal Hensley	2003	3051
312 2/8	47 1/8	50 2/8	36 4/8	6	6	Golden Valley County	MT	Kevin Larson	2005	3051
*312 2/8	47 5/8	46 7/8	41 2/8	6	6	Saguache County	CO	John Matous	2008	3051
312 2/8	51 3/8	50 4/8	37 6/8	6	6	Morrow County	OR	Kip Read	2008	3051
312 2/8	44 6/8	50 2/8	39 2/8	6	6	Eagle County	CO	Bernard J. Krueger	2010	3051
312 1/8	45 5/8	45 3/8	33 3/8	6	6	Garfield County	UT	Russell Peterson	1984	3061
312 1/8	45 2/8	44 4/8	35 3/8	6	6	Catron County	NM	Randy Williams	1985	3061
312 1/8	50 2/8	50 4/8	34 7/8	6	6	Lemhi County	ID	Mike S. Szekely	1986	3061
312 1/8	48 4/8	47 6/8	36 1/8	6	6	Musselshell County	MT	Bill Krenz	1992	3061
312 1/8	45 5/8	46 3/8	42 1/8	6	6	Catron County	NM	James D. Powless	1996	3061
312 1/8	46 7/8	46 2/8	39 3/8	7	6	Fergus County	MT	Rob Miller	1999	3061
312 1/8	51 5/8	51 5/8	41 3/8	6	6	Millard County	UT	Kevin Higley	2003	3061
312 1/8	49 3/8	50 7/8	40 7/8	6	5	Lincoln County	NV	Jerry Leair	2004	3061
312 1/8	45 4/8	47 3/8	43 3/8	7	7	Grant County	OR	Keenan C. Roberts	2008	3061
312 0/8	48 2/8	48 6/8	37 7/8	6	6	Montrose County	CO	Stanley R. Godfrey	1978	3070
312 0/8	49 7/8	49 7/8	39 0/8	6	6	Rio Blanco County	CO	John Richardson	1990	3070
312 0/8	49 0/8	48 6/8	36 6/8	6	7	Clackamas County	OR	Jeromy F. Adamson	1992	3070
312 0/8	45 3/8	46 7/8	38 1/8	8	6	Navajo County	AZ	David A. Niemann	1994	3070
312 0/8	41 7/8	43 1/8	34 4/8	6	6	Otero County	NM	Mark S. Hahn	1997	3070
312 0/8	51 3/8	51 6/8	45 2/8	6	6	Larimer County	CO	Steven W. Stumbo	1997	3070
312 0/8	49 3/8	46 4/8	39 4/8	6	6	Carbon County	WY	Cris McWilliams	1998	3070
*312 0/8	48 1/8	49 0/8	35 2/8	6	6	Rio Arriba County	NM	Ruben R. Balli	2004	3070
312 0/8	47 1/8	48 1/8	39 4/8	6	7	Wallowa County	OR	Timothy Tilander	2004	3070
312 0/8	50 0/8	48 5/8	37 2/8	6	6	Garfield County	CO	Shannon Fink	2005	3070
*312 0/8	49 3/8	49 4/8	32 0/8	6	6	Moffat County	CO	D. Lee Guyton, Jr.	2007	3070
*312 0/8	47 7/8	47 4/8	43 0/8	6	6	Adams County	ID	Tim Craft	2008	3070
*312 0/8	48 4/8	45 2/8	39 0/8	6	6	Pierce County	WA	Cody D. Peterson	2008	3070
312 0/8	45 2/8	47 3/8	34 6/8	6	6	Wallowa County	OR	Richard "Brent" Morris	2009	3070
311 7/8	46 4/8	48 0/8	34 1/8	6	6	Socorro County	NM	J. Dale Hale	1996	3084
311 7/8	46 4/8	49 1/8	36 1/8	6	6	Cibola County	NM	Dustin Earl Arp	2000	3084
311 7/8	51 7/8	52 3/8	35 2/8	7	7	Caribou County	ID	Bret F. Davis	2001	3084
311 7/8	45 5/8	48 3/8	33 7/8	6	6	Ravalli County	MT	Saxon Holbrook	2006	3084
*311 7/8	53 3/8	55 3/8	37 3/8	6	6	Garfield County	UT	Jeremy Bone	2010	3084
311 6/8	47 6/8	47 1/8	37 6/8	6	8	Lewis & Clark County	MT	Douglas L. Conrady	1980	3089
311 6/8	51 5/8	52 1/8	38 4/8	6	6	Deschutes County	OR	Gary Scroggins	1988	3089
311 6/8	49 7/8	48 6/8	35 2/8	6	6	White Pine County	NV	Sherri Pinnock	1993	3089
311 6/8	50 2/8	48 5/8	41 2/8	6	6	Beaverhead County	MT	Pete Zemljak	1995	3089
311 6/8	52 7/8	51 5/8	42 4/8	6	6	Butte County	ID	John Whipple	1996	3089
311 6/8	48 0/8	48 0/8	40 0/8	6	6	Park County	WY	Carlo Bonomi	1998	3089
311 6/8	46 4/8	48 1/8	39 4/8	6	6	Petroleum County	MT	Jerry Wandler	1998	3089
311 6/8	48 6/8	49 3/8	44 0/8	6	7	Valley County	ID	Rob Marz	2000	3089
311 6/8	50 0/8	51 2/8	33 0/8	7	6	Gallatin County	MT	William Elfland	2002	3089
311 6/8	48 3/8	47 4/8	38 2/8	6	6	Deer Lodge County	MT	Jarred Behm	2003	3089
311 6/8	47 6/8	46 7/8	36 0/8	7	6	Hill County	MT	Stephen Tylinski	2004	3089
*311 6/8	51 3/8	50 3/8	44 4/8	6	6	Costilla County	CO	M. Blake Patton	2008	3089
311 6/8	44 5/8	44 7/8	35 2/8	6	6	Catron County	NM	Harry E. Shawver	2008	3089
311 5/8	47 0/8	48 7/8	35 1/8	7	7	Larimer County	CO	Roger J. Kabage	1992	3102
311 5/8	48 0/8	48 4/8	34 1/8	6	6	Catron County	NM	George D. Cain	1993	3102
311 5/8	46 2/8	47 4/8	33 5/8	6	6	Park County	WY	Langdon G. Smith, Jr.	1994	3102
311 5/8	47 1/8	47 3/8	39 6/8	7	6	Grant County	OR	Dan Guzek	1998	3102
311 5/8	48 5/8	47 4/8	39 1/8	6	6	Albany County	WY	Clay A. Kelly	2003	3102
311 5/8	51 5/8	51 5/8	34 5/8	6	6	Willow River	BC	Mark Christofferson	2004	3102
311 5/8	52 1/8	52 7/8	33 4/8	7	7	Fergus County	MT	Joe K. Rud	2007	3102
311 5/8	44 6/8	47 0/8	44 5/8	6	6	Catron County	NM	David Hall	2007	3102
311 4/8	52 3/8	51 6/8	39 4/8	6	6	Coconino County	AZ	Richard Foss	1977	3110
311 4/8	48 7/8	45 7/8	37 2/8	6	6	Bonneville County	ID	Gene H. Dressen	1978	3110
311 4/8	46 2/8	45 4/8	38 0/8	6	6	Rio Blanco County	CO	Jack Lambert	1980	3110
311 4/8	55 6/8	54 4/8	37 4/8	6	6	Archuleta County	CO	Tim Chavez	1983	3110
311 4/8	44 6/8	44 2/8	37 2/8	6	6	Cypress River	MAN	Perry Fleet	1986	3110
311 4/8	48 2/8	48 1/8	38 4/8	6	6	Idaho County	ID	Stan Myers	1988	3110
311 4/8	48 0/8	49 2/8	34 4/8	6	6	Greenlee County	AZ	Carl L. Plasterer	1990	3110
311 4/8	51 0/8	50 7/8	41 0/8	7	7	Coconino County	AZ	John Mullins	1994	3110
311 4/8	48 0/8	47 7/8	38 0/8	6	6	Coconino County	AZ	Daniel Tone	1998	3110
311 4/8	49 1/8	50 2/8	46 4/8	6	7	Broadwater County	MT	Bill Hangas	2006	3110
311 4/8	44 1/8	47 0/8	34 2/8	6	7	Baker County	OR	Wayne Bailey	2007	3110
*311 4/8	48 6/8	49 6/8	45 4/8	6	6	Catron County	NM	Michael J. Weber	2010	3110
311 3/8	48 4/8	46 5/8	37 3/8	7	7	Sanders County	MT	Rus Willis	1981	3122
311 3/8	49 3/8	48 5/8	39 7/8	6	6	Coconino County	AZ	Greg Winn	1991	3122
311 3/8	48 2/8	47 5/8	44 3/8	6	8	Catron County	NM	Duane "Corky" Richardson	1992	3122
311 3/8	54 4/8	53 0/8	35 3/8	6	6	Park County	WY	Joe Thomas	1998	3122
311 3/8	48 2/8	48 7/8	35 3/8	6	6	Colfax County	NM	Judy A. Terry	1998	3122
311 3/8	51 5/8	47 5/8	39 1/8	6	6	Lincoln County	NV	B. J. Almberg	2000	3122
*311 3/8	49 7/8	49 6/8	40 0/8	6	8	Pend Oreille County	WA	Tyler Johnson	2007	3122
311 3/8	46 7/8	46 7/8	36 1/8	6	6	Skookumchuck	BC	George Terpsma	2010	3122
311 3/8	49 6/8	48 4/8	35 1/8	6	7	Coconino County	AZ	Jim Messner	2010	3122
311 2/8	44 5/8	46 2/8	33 6/8	6	6	Park County	CO	Lynn Campbell	1981	3131
311 2/8	48 3/8	48 5/8	37 0/8	6	6	Clackamas County	OR	Bill Hensley	1984	3131
311 2/8	47 7/8	49 3/8	32 2/8	6	7	Madison County	MT	Jacob Baine	1991	3131
311 2/8	50 0/8	49 1/8	35 0/8	6	6	Socorro County	NM	Frank Sanders	1991	3131
311 2/8	49 3/8	49 1/8	34 6/8	6	6	Mesa County	CO	David Parker Leon	1996	3131

AMERICAN ELK (TYPICAL ANTLERS)

Minimum Score 260
Continued

SCORE	LENGTH OF R MAIN BEAM L	INSIDE SPREAD	NUMBER OF R POINTS L	AREA	STATE/ PROVINCE	HUNTER'S NAME	DATE	RANK
311 2/8	43 1/8 42 6/8	36 0/8	7 8	Lemhi County	ID	Thomas E. Lingenfelter	1998	3131
311 2/8	46 5/8 48 2/8	41 2/8	6 6	Fremont County	CO	Rick M. Young	2003	3131
311 2/8	48 1/8 49 0/8	43 4/8	6 7	Coconino County	AZ	Phillip C. Dalrymple	2005	3131
311 1/8	51 2/8 50 0/8	40 7/8	6 6	Ravalli County	MT	Gary J. Hartman	1989	3139
311 1/8	48 6/8 47 6/8	34 5/8	6 6	Flathead County	MT	Ron Krueger	1989	3139
311 1/8	42 2/8 44 3/8	42 1/8	6 6	Coconino County	AZ	Todd Walsh	1994	3139
311 1/8	43 5/8 44 0/8	43 1/8	6 6	Gallatin County	MT	Lawrance F. Blucher	1999	3139
311 1/8	48 2/8 47 1/8	33 5/8	6 6	Catron County	NM	John A. Standefer, Jr.	1999	3139
311 1/8	46 6/8 48 4/8	33 7/8	6 6	Bonneville County	ID	Randy Taylor	2003	3139
*311 1/8	53 2/8 48 6/8	34 4/8	7 6	Coconino County	AZ	Gregory B. Carmichael	2005	3139
*311 1/8	49 4/8 50 7/8	35 7/8	6 6	Saguache County	CO	Greg Dix	2008	3139
311 0/8	51 6/8 50 0/8	41 6/8	6 6	Teton County	WY	Fred Bear	1953	3147
311 0/8	51 1/8 49 5/8	47 2/8	8 6	Larimer County	CO	H. Mike Palmer	1983	3147
311 0/8	47 3/8 47 4/8	43 6/8	6 6	Beaverhead County	MT	Jerry Strodtman	1985	3147
311 0/8	46 0/8 46 0/8	41 0/8	6 6	Mineral County	MT	Robert F. Erickson	1988	3147
311 0/8	49 1/8 49 0/8	38 2/8	6 6	Sanders County	MT	Rick Dieterich	1990	3147
311 0/8	46 3/8 48 2/8	41 6/8	6 6	Coconino County	AZ	Eddy Broderick	1992	3147
311 0/8	48 3/8 46 0/8	37 6/8	6 6	Phillips County	MT	William K. Stephens	1995	3147
311 0/8	48 7/8 48 1/8	44 4/8	7 6	Valley County	ID	Timothy Hill	1998	3147
311 0/8	51 4/8 49 0/8	39 2/8	6 6	Coconino County	AZ	Kristine Wright	1998	3147
311 0/8	44 5/8 44 1/8	39 0/8	5 6	Colfax County	NM	Gene E. Ohmstede	1999	3147
311 0/8	46 0/8 44 4/8	37 4/8	7 6	Fergus County	MT	Justin Deacon	1999	3147
*311 0/8	47 7/8 47 5/8	38 4/8	6 6	Harney County	OR	Gary Grossen	2009	3147
311 0/8	50 5/8 50 3/8	42 0/8	6 7	Bonneville County	ID	Casey Bame	2009	3147
310 7/8	55 2/8 53 6/8	53 1/8	6 6	Pitkin County	CO	Bob Gulman	1973	3160
310 7/8	45 6/8 45 0/8	36 3/8	6 6	Flathead County	MT	Scott Halama	1986	3160
310 7/8	48 4/8 47 1/8	36 5/8	6 6	Uintah County	UT	J. Brad Denver	1994	3160
310 7/8	43 7/8 43 2/8	35 1/8	6 6	Catron County	NM	Keith Vanderburg	1996	3160
310 7/8	51 4/8 51 2/8	41 1/8	6 6	Catron County	NM	James D. Bradley	2003	3160
310 7/8	47 4/8 46 5/8	34 6/8	7 7	Mineral County	MT	Vayeeleng Moua	2004	3160
310 7/8	51 6/8 48 6/8	34 7/8	8 6	Granite County	MT	Vayeeleng K. Moua	2005	3160
*310 7/8	53 3/8 52 0/8	35 3/8	7 6	Delta County	CO	Justin Towe	2007	3160
310 6/8	49 5/8 51 2/8	43 4/8	6 6	Lemhi County	ID	Joe Hollifield	1977	3168
310 6/8	45 5/8 46 2/8	35 0/8	7 8	Fergus County	MT	Steven J. Nelson	1977	3168
310 6/8	45 6/8 47 0/8	36 2/8	6 7	Ravalli County	MT	Alan Lear	1988	3168
310 6/8	44 6/8 42 2/8	39 6/8	6 6	Fergus County	MT	Billy E. Martin	1993	3168
310 6/8	48 4/8 48 4/8	37 2/8	6 6	Flathead County	MT	Justin D. Lasater	1995	3168
310 6/8	43 6/8 44 3/8	34 4/8	7 7	Fergus County	MT	Scott Abrams	1995	3168
310 6/8	44 3/8 43 2/8	36 6/8	6 6	Rio Arriba County	NM	Brian Lambie	2000	3168
310 6/8	46 6/8 47 0/8	49 1/8	6 6	Apache County	AZ	Dave Holt	2001	3168
310 6/8	48 1/8 46 3/8	38 6/8	6 7	Park County	MT	Thomas A. Stock	2002	3168
310 6/8	47 0/8 48 0/8	33 2/8	6 6	Coconino County	AZ	Dagen Haymore	2004	3168
310 6/8	46 6/8 46 5/8	40 0/8	7 7	Sevier County	UT	Judd Kendall	2006	3168
*310 6/8	52 5/8 52 6/8	33 0/8	6 6	Montrose County	CO	Mark Williams	2006	3168
310 6/8	47 7/8 47 1/8	41 6/8	6 6	Hinsdale County	CO	Larry Rodolph	2007	3168
*310 6/8	45 0/8 43 7/8	42 6/8	6 6	Lincoln County	NM	Joseph L. Hall	2010	3168
310 5/8	51 3/8 51 2/8	38 3/8	6 6	Little Belt Mtns.	MT	Jim Ekness	1978	3182
310 5/8	47 1/8 44 6/8	39 3/8	7 6	Coconino County	AZ	Rick Brewer	1984	3182
310 5/8	49 5/8 50 7/8	49 5/8	5 6	Granite County	MT	Shaun Twardoski	1992	3182
310 5/8	55 2/8 53 2/8	42 1/8	6 6	Coconino County	AZ	Gary S. Kessinger	1992	3182
310 5/8	50 2/8 50 2/8	37 3/8	6 6	Yellowstone County	MT	Monte Meredith	1997	3182
310 5/8	47 0/8 46 4/8	40 1/8	6 6	Adams County	ID	Daniel Wisner	1997	3182
310 5/8	51 5/8 52 5/8	35 7/8	6 6	Musselshell County	MT	Steve Ness	2001	3182
310 5/8	51 6/8 49 2/8	40 3/8	8 7	Catron County	NM	Steve McCluskey	2001	3182
310 5/8	47 6/8 48 5/8	48 5/8	7 7	Park County	CO	Jason Roe	2003	3182
310 5/8	47 3/8 48 3/8	31 7/8	6 6	Carter County	MT	William L. Hansen	2009	3182
310 4/8	49 0/8 49 0/8	43 6/8	6 6	La Plata County	CO	Tom Price	1967	3192
310 4/8	43 2/8 43 6/8	38 2/8	6 6	Baker County	OR	Billy J. Cruise	1970	3192
310 4/8	46 7/8 46 6/8	37 4/8	6 6	Clearwater County	ID	Rory Roby	1981	3192
310 4/8	46 1/8 46 3/8	41 0/8	6 6	Valley County	ID	Ron Phillips	1983	3192
310 4/8	53 3/8 51 1/8	37 0/8	6 6	Converse County	WY	Dennis Spawn	1986	3192
310 4/8	52 2/8 51 2/8	33 2/8	6 7	Apache County	AZ	Steve McInelly	1986	3192
310 4/8	45 2/8 45 7/8	42 6/8	6 6	Grant County	OR	Dean P. Pasche	1990	3192
310 4/8	50 1/8 48 7/8	44 0/8	6 6	McKinley County	NM	David Westmoreland	1997	3192
310 4/8	42 0/8 37 5/8	31 4/8	6 6	Moffat County	CO	John C. Steger	2003	3192
310 4/8	54 6/8 50 7/8	36 5/8	6 7	Rio Arriba County	NM	John E. Harper	2003	3192
310 4/8	46 4/8 46 4/8	39 4/8	6 6	Blaine County	MT	Danny Moore	2004	3192
310 4/8	49 2/8 47 5/8	35 0/8	6 6	Moffat County	CO	Alex Hermosillo	2005	3192
310 4/8	49 1/8 45 3/8	40 1/8	6 7	Albany County	WY	Ralph D. Hayes	2007	3192
*310 4/8	46 4/8 46 7/8	43 6/8	6 6	Fergus County	MT	Austin Phillips	2009	3192
310 3/8	49 0/8 51 0/8	39 2/8	8 6	Caribou County	ID	Patrick G. Selfridge	1980	3206
310 3/8	43 7/8 46 0/8	36 1/8	6 6	Santa Fe County	NM	Bennie "Buddy" Rhodes, Jr.	1990	3206
310 3/8	55 0/8 48 7/8	37 4/8	7 9	Catron County	NM	Steven J. Niedzielski	1993	3206
310 3/8	53 5/8 52 7/8	42 1/8	6 6	Larimer County	CO	Michael Raymer	1993	3206
310 3/8	48 4/8 47 4/8	42 5/8	6 6	Boise County	ID	Neil J. Russell	1994	3206
310 3/8	49 7/8 50 1/8	35 7/8	6 6	Coconino County	AZ	James Dale Casady	1996	3206
310 3/8	49 4/8 49 6/8	38 3/8	6 6	Grant County	OR	Rodger C. Scott	1998	3206
310 3/8	44 7/8 47 0/8	37 5/8	6 6	Meagher County	MT	Stephen Tylinski	1999	3206
310 3/8	51 5/8 51 6/8	37 3/8	6 7	Kittitas County	WA	Jim Bogesvang	2004	3206
310 3/8	46 4/8 46 3/8	42 7/8	6 6	Skamania County	WA	Tracy Gillis	2006	3206
310 3/8	50 0/8 46 1/8	34 7/8	6 6	Lincoln County	NM	John R. Wilmesher	2007	3206
310 3/8	45 3/8 45 6/8	38 3/8	6 7	Las Animas County	CO	Ronnie Hall	2009	3206
310 2/8	49 4/8 50 0/8	30 0/8	6 6	Phillips County	MT	Daniel Tollefson	1981	3218
310 2/8	45 0/8 45 4/8	33 4/8	6 6	Canmore	ALB	Cam Wilson	1984	3218
310 2/8	48 2/8 49 7/8	34 6/8	6 6	Coconino County	AZ	Russ Warner	1984	3218
310 2/8	45 1/8 43 4/8	39 0/8	6 6	Gallatin County	MT	David Burtch	1986	3218
310 2/8	45 3/8 47 6/8	46 6/8	6 6	Coconino County	AZ	Alan H. Timonen	1992	3218
310 2/8	45 7/8 45 7/8	35 2/8	6 6	Phillips County	MT	David L. Skiff	1996	3218
310 2/8	47 3/8 48 3/8	32 6/8	6 6	Archuleta County	CO	C. Cheyenne Fuchs	2006	3218
310 2/8	49 1/8 48 1/8	34 4/8	6 7	Jefferson County	CO	Gregg Richter	2009	3218
310 1/8	50 3/8 50 4/8	48 3/8	8 5	Idaho County	ID	Roy S. Lathen	1988	3226
310 1/8	51 4/8 52 7/8	40 3/8	5 5	Rio Arriba County	NM	Isaac Julian, Sr.	1989	3226
310 1/8	50 7/8 50 4/8	41 3/8	7 6	Lincoln County	WY	Scott C. Nielsen	2001	3226
310 1/8	44 3/8 45 2/8	39 1/8	6 6	Iron County	UT	Thomas Day	2005	3226
310 0/8	51 2/8 50 3/8	38 0/8	6 6	Ravalli County	MT	Bob Sappenfield	1978	3230

711

AMERICAN ELK (TYPICAL ANTLERS)

Minimum Score 260 Continued

SCORE	LENGTH OF MAIN BEAM R L	INSIDE SPREAD	NUMBER OF POINTS R L	AREA	STATE/ PROVINCE	HUNTER'S NAME	DATE	RANK
310 0/8	46 5/8 49 1/8	37 2/8	5 6	Grant County	OR	Andy Day	1987	3230
310 0/8	47 1/8 48 7/8	33 2/8	6 8	Clearwater County	ID	Jim Lashly	1990	3230
310 0/8	48 6/8 48 7/8	44 2/8	6 7	Grant County	OR	Darin C. Jenison	1992	3230
310 0/8	47 4/8 49 6/8	40 0/8	6 6	Coconino County	AZ	Rodman Ward	1993	3230
310 0/8	47 2/8 45 5/8	36 2/8	7 7	Skamania County	WA	Cory Michael Anderson	1998	3230
310 0/8	47 6/8 47 3/8	33 6/8	6 6	Gallatin County	MT	Olaf Smith	2000	3230
310 0/8	48 3/8 49 5/8	38 6/8	7 7	Arran	SAS	Kevin Yaremko	2003	3230
310 0/8	46 6/8 46 0/8	38 4/8	6 6	San Miguel County	CO	Brian Lewis	2006	3230
310 0/8	43 5/8 45 3/8	32 2/8	6 6	Grant County	OR	Steve Paulsen	2007	3230
310 0/8	48 7/8 46 0/8	42 0/8	6 6	Catron County	NM	Jim Kent	2008	3230
309 7/8	47 2/8 47 3/8	37 3/8	6 7	Baker County	OR	James D. Ward	1983	3241
309 7/8	47 0/8 44 7/8	42 1/8	7 7	Creston	BC	Derek Vance	1993	3241
309 7/8	48 5/8 49 7/8	38 1/8	7 6	Lemhi County	ID	Dick McKeown	1996	3241
309 7/8	48 0/8 48 3/8	36 3/8	6 6	Fremont County	WY	Larry Orr	1996	3241
309 7/8	50 7/8 49 3/8	44 5/8	7 6	San Juan County	NM	Jim Herrick	1997	3241
309 7/8	50 0/8 50 1/8	35 3/8	6 6	Phillips County	MT	Grant Christopher	1998	3241
309 7/8	44 2/8 45 1/8	32 7/8	8 7	Sierra County	NM	Bob Quillen	2001	3241
309 7/8	51 2/8 51 4/8	36 1/8	6 6	Madison County	MT	Danny H. Lewis	2001	3241
309 7/8	45 5/8 46 3/8	39 3/8	8 6	Pierce County	WA	Peter Laney	2002	3241
309 7/8	49 4/8 50 4/8	30 7/8	6 6	Mesa County	CO	Randy West	2002	3241
309 7/8	47 0/8 45 5/8	40 5/8	6 6	Rio Arriba County	NM	Scott Pope	2004	3241
*309 7/8	55 2/8 53 4/8	42 7/8	7 7	Coconino County	AZ	David Logan	2005	3241
309 7/8	46 3/8 45 1/8	40 5/8	6 7	Flathead County	MT	Rob Goodman	2007	3241
309 7/8	48 7/8 48 2/8	36 7/8	6 6	Gila County	AZ	Rodney L. Ronnebaum	2007	3241
309 6/8	43 1/8 43 3/8	35 0/8	6 6	Routt County	CO	Steve Gorr	1971	3255
309 6/8	50 6/8 51 0/8	40 0/8	7 6	Sanders County	MT	Brad Borden	1984	3255
309 6/8	48 6/8 50 6/8	43 2/8	6 6	Coconino County	AZ	Robert L. Smith	1986	3255
309 6/8	48 3/8 46 5/8	37 0/8	6 6	Park County	MT	Steve Kamps	1987	3255
309 6/8	46 2/8 49 2/8	42 3/8	7 6	Yavapai County	AZ	Mark A. Rucker	1991	3255
309 6/8	46 7/8 45 7/8	43 0/8	6 6	Dolores County	CO	Rev Charles Brannon	1992	3255
309 6/8	43 7/8 43 4/8	37 4/8	7 6	Las Animas County	CO	Sal Petrolino	1998	3255
309 6/8	53 4/8 52 2/8	35 2/8	6 6	Catron County	NM	Frank Robert Stehr	2001	3255
309 6/8	45 5/8 47 3/8	33 6/8	7 7	Catron County	NM	Eric W. Kelsh	2001	3255
309 6/8	46 5/8 45 5/8	38 0/8	6 6	Millard County	UT	Blaine Jensen	2003	3255
309 6/8	48 4/8 51 1/8	47 0/8	6 6	Lemhi County	ID	Luke Cranney	2003	3255
309 6/8	51 2/8 51 2/8	37 6/8	6 6	Jefferson County	MT	Randy Rowe	2004	3255
309 6/8	44 6/8 44 0/8	33 2/8	6 6	Sublette County	WY	John Freed	2004	3255
309 6/8	52 0/8 50 6/8	36 6/8	7 7	Yakima County	WA	John Foster	2006	3255
309 6/8	51 0/8 49 4/8	35 6/8	6 6	Harney County	OR	George Monroe	2006	3255
309 6/8	51 0/8 50 6/8	39 7/8	6 6	Flathead County	MT	Paul Roney	1976	3270
309 5/8	46 2/8 44 7/8	37 1/8	6 6	Lincoln County	MT	Mike Billingsley	1990	3270
309 5/8	50 0/8 47 1/8	36 1/8	6 6	Garfield County	CO	Andy Jeanjaquet	1994	3270
309 5/8	47 1/8 47 5/8	35 7/8	6 6	Coconino County	AZ	Daniel Omner Ward	1997	3270
309 5/8	45 3/8 45 3/8	37 1/8	6 6	Colfax County	NM	Witt Stephens, Jr.	1998	3270
309 5/8	53 0/8 51 4/8	47 1/8	7 6	Socorro County	NM	Robert H. Torstenson	2001	3270
309 5/8	51 7/8 51 7/8	37 5/8	7 7	Petroleum County	MT	Mark Oliveira	2001	3270
309 5/8	51 5/8 51 0/8	35 1/8	7 7	Chelan County	WA	Jason Michael	2003	3270
309 5/8	53 7/8 53 6/8	40 5/8	6 6	Ravalli County	MT	Lukas Judd Omlid	2003	3270
309 5/8	46 7/8 46 5/8	35 5/8	7 6	Otero County	NM	Bruce A. Barna	2004	3270
*309 5/8	45 1/8 44 4/8	31 3/8	6 6	Coconino County	AZ	Gary Hensley	2005	3270
*309 5/8	49 6/8 49 7/8	42 3/8	6 6	Coconino County	AZ	Tom Alvin	2005	3270
309 5/8	44 4/8 44 3/8	38 1/8	6 6	Caribou County	ID	Don Jenkins	2005	3270
309 4/8	44 3/8 44 4/8	30 0/8	6 6	Valley County	MT	Charles Seiler	1976	3283
309 4/8	42 6/8 41 7/8	32 6/8	6 6	Lincoln County	MT	Lee S. Lampton	1992	3283
309 4/8	52 3/8 53 4/8	39 6/8	6 6	Catron County	NM	Bill Horvath	1997	3283
309 4/8	46 1/8 48 1/8	34 6/8	7 6	Sanders County	MT	Harold E. Watford	2000	3283
309 4/8	56 5/8 54 1/8	37 0/8	6 6	Coconino County	AZ	John B. Tuttle	2004	3283
*309 4/8	49 3/8 46 4/8	40 6/8	6 6	Umatilla County	OR	Rich A. Thurman	2008	3283
309 3/8	44 0/8 42 4/8	41 1/8	7 6	Crook County	OR	Hank Baxter	1996	3289
309 3/8	49 6/8 50 0/8	40 7/8	6 6	Socorro County	NM	Jimmy Donahoo	1996	3289
309 3/8	52 4/8 52 6/8	32 7/8	6 6	Coconino County	AZ	Roy Jimenez	2000	3289
309 3/8	44 7/8 45 1/8	34 3/8	6 6	Big Horn County	MT	John Nelson, Jr.	2001	3289
*309 3/8	47 2/8 48 6/8	40 3/8	6 6	Coconino County	AZ	Justin Gabler	2007	3289
309 2/8	44 6/8 47 4/8	44 4/8	5 6	Fremont County	ID	Larry Bauer	1960	3294
309 2/8	45 0/8 45 7/8	34 4/8	6 6	Union County	OR	Ron Angell	1981	3294
309 2/8	48 0/8 47 6/8	42 2/8	6 6	Sheridan County	WY	George Rogers	1988	3294
309 2/8	48 2/8 47 4/8	41 4/8	6 6	Uintah County	UT	Justin Arrowchis	1990	3294
309 2/8	45 0/8 44 4/8	44 2/8	5 6	Rio Arriba County	NM	Dr. Leo A. Lucas	1990	3294
309 2/8	51 1/8 51 2/8	38 6/8	7 7	Garfield County	CO	Harry Earl Temple	1990	3294
309 2/8	44 0/8 43 0/8	39 2/8	6 6	Phillips County	MT	Randy S. Bowler	1994	3294
309 2/8	48 0/8 47 4/8	35 4/8	6 7	Union County	OR	Robert H. Deibel	1994	3294
309 2/8	49 7/8 50 2/8	45 4/8	6 6	Coconino County	AZ	Henry Robert Garcia, Sr.	1995	3294
309 2/8	48 6/8 47 0/8	40 2/8	6 6	Socorro County	NM	Richard Berger	1996	3294
309 2/8	43 5/8 44 6/8	40 5/8	9 7	Park County	MT	Paul Meyers	1997	3294
309 2/8	44 3/8 43 0/8	45 7/8	6 6	Coconino County	AZ	Charles David Gallinger IV	1998	3294
309 2/8	44 5/8 44 2/8	43 6/8	6 6	Baker County	OR	Randy S. White	1999	3294
309 2/8	42 1/8 42 2/8	34 2/8	6 6	Ravalli County	MT	Bee K. Moua	2006	3294
*309 2/8	45 5/8 41 6/8	35 6/8	7 7	Fergus County	MT	Rusten Barnes	2007	3294
309 1/8	44 4/8 46 4/8	34 5/8	6 6	Coconino County	AZ	Les Butters	1981	3309
309 1/8	48 0/8 46 4/8	39 7/8	6 6	Missoula County	MT	Chad Spicknall	1984	3309
309 1/8	49 5/8 50 0/8	37 5/8	6 6	Mora County	NM	Randy Ries	1990	3309
309 1/8	45 6/8 45 5/8	37 1/8	6 6	Toad River	BC	Peter Swenson	1991	3309
309 1/8	48 5/8 50 1/8	41 1/8	6 6	Sandoval County	NM	Chuck Adams	1991	3309
309 1/8	50 5/8 48 2/8	42 1/8	6 6	Coconino County	AZ	John Woodruff	1992	3309
309 1/8	48 0/8 45 4/8	37 1/8	6 6	Fergus County	MT	Donny Roy	1996	3309
309 1/8	43 4/8 43 5/8	31 1/8	6 6	Catron County	NM	Darren Pickard	2004	3309
309 1/8	48 4/8 47 0/8	37 5/8	6 6	Montrose County	CO	Tyler L. Mousner	2008	3309
*309 1/8	46 6/8 47 7/8	34 7/8	6 6	Lawrence County	SD	Gary C. Velder	2009	3309
309 1/8	46 5/8 47 1/8	36 1/8	6 6	Daggett County	UT	Mark DeCoursey	2010	3309
309 0/8	46 3/8 45 5/8	38 6/8	6 6	Boise County	ID	Steve Groff	1989	3320
309 0/8	47 0/8 48 6/8	38 6/8	6 6	Archuleta County	CO	Darla Bramwell	1997	3320
309 0/8	43 3/8 42 6/8	39 6/8	7 7	Coconino County	AZ	Richard D. Tone	1998	3320
309 0/8	49 6/8 49 4/8	36 0/8	6 6	Valley County	ID	William F. Sheel	2000	3320
309 0/8	49 0/8 45 4/8	36 2/8	6 6	Wallowa County	OR	Rick L. Hardy	2001	3320
309 0/8	46 5/8 46 0/8	40 0/8	6 6	Lemhi County	ID	Brent McBride	2001	3320

712

AMERICAN ELK (TYPICAL ANTLERS)

Minimum Score 260 — Continued

SCORE	LENGTH OF R MAIN BEAM L	INSIDE SPREAD	NUMBER OF R POINTS L	AREA	STATE/ PROVINCE	HUNTER'S NAME	DATE	RANK
*309 0/8	43 5/8 50 7/8	38 5/8	8 6	Johnson County	WY	Jack L. Morey, Jr.	2006	3320
*309 0/8	53 2/8 54 0/8	40 4/8	6 5	Rio Arriba County	NM	Larry Nicholson	2007	3320
309 0/8	47 7/8 48 4/8	38 0/8	6 6	Lincoln County	NM	Fred Sprague	2008	3320
308 7/8	47 4/8 47 4/8	37 7/8	6 7	Wallowa County	OR	Greg Bogh	1997	3329
308 7/8	54 5/8 53 1/8	47 7/8	6 5	Albany County	WY	Jeremy Artery	2004	3329
308 6/8	44 6/8 45 0/8	36 6/8	7 6	Lincoln County	MT	Steve Kluver	1987	3331
308 6/8	52 0/8 50 6/8	32 0/8	8 7	Caribou County	ID	Ron Harrod	1999	3331
308 6/8	49 3/8 49 4/8	40 6/8	6 6	Boulder County	CO	Jamie Seyler	1999	3331
308 6/8	50 3/8 49 0/8	37 6/8	6 6	Mineral County	MT	David M. Bufkin	2007	3331
308 5/8	47 5/8 46 3/8	40 1/8	7 6	Wasco County	OR	Gary Paugh	1984	3335
308 5/8	50 2/8 51 2/8	37 5/8	6 6	Taos County	NM	Nicholas J Rowley	1985	3335
308 5/8	45 6/8 44 1/8	31 7/8	6 6	Fergus County	MT	Lawrence B. Benedict	1992	3335
308 5/8	42 0/8 42 5/8	37 5/8	6 6	Huerfano County	CO	Ken Beck	1998	3335
308 5/8	47 4/8 49 2/8	33 1/8	6 6	Gander Creek	BC	Richard Kirkvold	2002	3335
308 5/8	49 3/8 49 4/8	39 1/8	6 6	Klickitat County	WA	Kurt E. Goesch	2004	3335
*308 5/8	47 7/8 47 4/8	45 7/8	7 6	Park County	MT	Richard Backes	2007	3335
*308 5/8	46 2/8 46 0/8	37 4/8	6 8	Catron County	NM	Jason Ramaker	2008	3335
308 5/8	52 2/8 51 3/8	32 7/8	6 6	Albany County	WY	Kris Brown	2009	3335
308 4/8	47 7/8 47 7/8	41 2/8	7 6	Socorro County	NM	Jack W. Bruton	1985	3344
308 4/8	48 0/8 48 2/8	39 0/8	6 6	Catron County	NM	Bob A. Gourley	1986	3344
308 4/8	45 1/8 47 4/8	40 4/8	6 6	Elmore County	ID	Matt March, Jr.	1987	3344
308 4/8	47 6/8 46 6/8	37 7/8	7 7	Elmore County	ID	Anthony L. Mudd	1992	3344
308 4/8	45 3/8 44 6/8	37 2/8	6 6	Custer County	ID	Clayton Nielson	1995	3344
308 4/8	50 2/8 51 1/8	41 0/8	6 6	Lincoln County	MT	Brian Wilkins	1995	3344
308 4/8	48 6/8 48 0/8	40 2/8	6 6	Valley County	ID	David W. Rickert II	1998	3344
308 4/8	49 7/8 46 5/8	35 2/8	6 6	Rich County	UT	Raymond L. Howell, Sr.	2000	3344
308 4/8	48 4/8 47 4/8	35 0/8	6 6	Bonneville County	ID	Chris G. Sant	2002	3344
308 4/8	44 6/8 44 4/8	31 2/8	6 6	Dolores County	CO	Clint Proffitt	2004	3344
308 4/8	43 1/8 44 4/8	36 6/8	6 6	La Plata County	CO	Jim Hastings	2005	3344
308 4/8	44 2/8 43 3/8	38 4/8	6 6	Catron County	NM	Mike Acheson	2007	3344
*308 4/8	49 0/8 47 2/8	37 7/8	7 6	Coconino County	AZ	Lawrence A. Bettendorf	2009	3344
308 3/8	49 0/8 50 4/8	38 5/8	7 6	Idaho County	ID	Bill G. Davis	1989	3357
308 3/8	48 3/8 47 3/8	37 1/8	6 6	Lincoln County	MT	John C. McDivitt	1992	3357
308 3/8	49 5/8 48 4/8	33 3/8	7 7	Missoula County	MT	Joseph J. Simone, Jr.	1992	3357
308 3/8	46 0/8 46 0/8	34 5/8	6 6	Lemhi County	ID	Nancy Atwood	1993	3357
308 3/8	46 1/8 37 4/8	34 1/8	6 6	Petroleum County	MT	Rob Miller	1997	3357
308 3/8	44 2/8 45 7/8	41 1/8	7 6	Grant County	OR	Jamie Lee	2000	3357
308 3/8	45 3/8 44 6/8	37 7/8	7 6	Gallatin County	MT	Curtis Dykstra	2002	3357
308 3/8	47 0/8 46 5/8	36 7/8	6 6	Fergus County	MT	Kelly Norskog	2002	3357
308 3/8	48 6/8 47 2/8	40 3/8	7 6	Catron County	NM	Tim Cuthriell	2004	3357
*308 3/8	44 2/8 45 6/8	36 7/8	6 7	Jackson County	CO	Ben Ratzlaff	2006	3357
308 3/8	45 5/8 45 0/8	35 6/8	7 6	Bissett Creek	BC	Wayne Chmelyk	2008	3357
*308 3/8	47 7/8 48 7/8	45 1/8	6 6	Moffat County	CO	James M. Ergler	2009	3357
308 3/8	45 0/8 44 6/8	34 3/8	6 6	Garfield County	CO	Dennis R. Tice	2009	3357
308 2/8	42 4/8 44 0/8	42 4/8	6 6	Kane County	UT	Ron Simmers	1991	3370
308 2/8	44 4/8 44 4/8	38 4/8	6 6	Lincoln County	WY	Tom A. Daughetee	1991	3370
308 2/8	51 2/8 50 3/8	43 0/8	6 7	Rich County	UT	Hugh H. Hogle	1992	3370
308 2/8	46 6/8 47 1/8	37 4/8	6 6	Jefferson County	OR	Jay T. Roth	1997	3370
308 2/8	51 6/8 51 1/8	38 0/8	6 6	Sublette County	WY	Campbell K. Kreps	2001	3370
308 2/8	44 6/8 43 4/8	33 7/8	6 7	Ravalli County	MT	Cletus Wandler	2002	3370
308 2/8	47 7/8 47 6/8	40 2/8	6 6	Bannock County	ID	Jerry Giovannoni	2004	3370
308 2/8	48 3/8 48 4/8	39 0/8	6 6	Fergus County	MT	Lynn Bowman	2007	3370
308 1/8	51 1/8 50 6/8	42 7/8	6 5	Crook County	OR	Jim Hodson	1983	3378
308 1/8	48 3/8 49 4/8	39 1/8	6 6	Coconino County	AZ	Richard D. Tone	1987	3378
308 1/8	49 3/8 49 7/8	40 1/8	6 7	Missoula County	MT	Kevin P. Grenier	1990	3378
308 1/8	48 0/8 47 7/8	42 4/8	6 7	Sevier County	UT	Jim Madsen	1996	3378
308 1/8	52 1/8 51 5/8	40 1/8	6 6	Coconino County	AZ	Gene Witt	1999	3378
308 1/8	50 3/8 52 1/8	39 3/8	6 6	Petroleum County	MT	Gerald C. Miller	2005	3378
308 1/8	49 2/8 49 1/8	38 1/8	6 6	Apache County	AZ	Kimberly B. McCann	2007	3378
308 1/8	45 0/8 46 3/8	38 3/8	5 5	Lincoln County	WY	Erik S. Youngberg	2008	3378
308 1/8	46 0/8 45 2/8	37 1/8	6 6	San Miguel County	CO	Kevin D. Hall	2010	3378
308 0/8	43 4/8 48 0/8	32 6/8	6 6	Shoshone County	ID	Randy Hammond	1983	3387
308 0/8	50 2/8 48 3/8	36 6/8	6 7	Kane County	UT	Clay Carter	1999	3387
308 0/8	45 1/8 48 6/8	34 2/8	6 6	Park County	WY	Johnny Keymon	2001	3387
*308 0/8	45 6/8 46 0/8	34 6/8	6 6	Mineral County	MT	Randy Cote	2008	3387
*308 0/8	48 2/8 47 5/8	39 4/8	6 6	Lawrence County	SD	Craig W. Knapp	2008	3387
*308 0/8	51 2/8 50 0/8	32 0/8	6 6	Las Animas County	CO	Jeff Evans	2009	3387
307 7/8	46 5/8 46 3/8	37 5/8	6 6	Ravalli County	MT	Ray Tlamka	1984	3393
307 7/8	47 3/8 48 6/8	36 3/8	6 5	Baca County	CO	Max Crocker	1989	3393
307 7/8	47 4/8 46 4/8	43 1/8	6 6	Carbon County	WY	Brenda Sapp	1998	3393
307 7/8	47 0/8 46 6/8	35 5/8	6 6	Catron County	NM	Mike Lely	1999	3393
307 7/8	48 5/8 48 0/8	41 5/8	8 6	Idaho County	ID	Peter Pernsteiner	2001	3393
307 7/8	47 2/8 48 5/8	37 3/8	7 6	Sanders County	MT	Bernard Jacob Stender	2006	3393
307 7/8	44 4/8 43 7/8	33 5/8	6 6	Phillips County	MT	Robert L. Bailey	2009	3393
307 7/8	51 4/8 50 3/8	42 7/8	6 6	Rio Arriba County	NM	Eudane Vicenti	2010	3393
307 6/8	47 0/8 47 1/8	40 2/8	6 6	Valley County	ID	Neil Thagard	1991	3401
307 6/8	49 0/8 51 4/8	35 4/8	6 6	Graham County	AZ	Steven Monroe	1992	3401
307 6/8	44 7/8 46 2/8	49 2/8	6 6	Madison County	MT	Everett W. Ayers, Sr.	1992	3401
307 6/8	45 5/8 45 1/8	41 4/8	6 6	Fergus County	MT	Jerry Knerr	1993	3401
307 6/8	46 4/8 43 7/8	35 0/8	6 6	San Juan County	NM	Terry L. Lewis	1994	3401
307 6/8	49 6/8 48 6/8	39 0/8	6 6	Fergus County	MT	Darwin Reynolds	2001	3401
307 6/8	50 5/8 50 5/8	38 4/8	6 6	Coconino County	AZ	Jeffery M. Barrick	2003	3401
*307 6/8	47 5/8 49 4/8	38 6/8	6 6	Meagher County	MT	Kevin Sensenig	2009	3401
307 5/8	48 5/8 50 3/8	35 1/8	6 6	San Juan County	UT	Christopher M. Beck	1997	3409
307 5/8	46 3/8 47 3/8	36 7/8	6 6	Custer County	ID	Jared R. Frothinger	2001	3409
*307 5/8	53 4/8 50 6/8	34 5/8	6 6	Coconino County	AZ	Cliff Winn	2004	3409
307 5/8	45 1/8 45 2/8	41 1/8	6 6	Catron County	NM	James "Ron" Dellinger	2006	3409
*307 5/8	47 7/8 46 6/8	32 1/8	6 6	Coconino County	AZ	Joseph M. Duffalo	2008	3409
307 4/8	45 5/8 42 7/8	37 4/8	7 7	Huerfano County	CO	Wilbur F. Lay, Jr.	1974	3414
307 4/8	47 7/8 48 0/8	40 4/8	5 6	Caribou County	ID	Charlie Humphreys	1979	3414
307 4/8	54 6/8 54 6/8	46 3/8	7 7	Apache County	AZ	Tom David	1985	3414
307 4/8	44 0/8 43 7/8	40 4/8	6 5	Gallatin County	MT	Don Syvrud	1985	3414
307 4/8	46 7/8 47 1/8	37 2/8	6 6	Teller County	CO	James M. Strampe	1985	3414
307 4/8	44 4/8 43 7/8	33 6/8	6 6	Valley County	ID	Brian Hunter Heck	1990	3414
307 4/8	47 1/8 48 0/8	34 4/8	6 6	Beaverhead County	MT	Gary Dudden	1991	3414

713

AMERICAN ELK (TYPICAL ANTLERS)

Minimum Score 260 — Continued

SCORE	LENGTH OF R MAIN BEAM L	INSIDE SPREAD	NUMBER OF R POINTS L		AREA	STATE/ PROVINCE	HUNTER'S NAME	DATE	RANK
307 4/8	51 2/8 49 6/8	37 6/8	6	6	Archuleta County	CO	Lester D. Hawkins, Jr.	1992	3414
307 4/8	47 4/8 47 0/8	35 2/8	6	6	Grant County	OR	Steve L. Paulsen	1998	3414
307 4/8	47 3/8 45 7/8	34 2/8	6	6	Petroleum County	MT	Thomas J. Madden	2001	3414
307 4/8	47 0/8 47 2/8	36 6/8	6	6	La Plata County	CO	Darrell Lynn	2002	3414
307 4/8	52 6/8 52 6/8	37 6/8	6	6	Phillips County	MT	Joey Ardrey	2006	3414
*307 4/8	47 3/8 46 7/8	37 4/8	6	6	Las Animas County	CO	Wright T. Harrell, Jr.	2007	3414
*307 4/8	44 7/8 44 6/8	35 2/8	6	7	Mineral County	MT	Clem Stroot	2009	3414
307 4/8	48 0/8 48 0/8	40 3/8	6	8	Adams County	ID	Jerry L. Wischmeier	2009	3414
307 3/8	46 2/8 36 4/8	33 3/8	6	6	Garfield County	MT	Jerry L. Molstad	1986	3429
307 3/8	48 2/8 47 4/8	36 1/8	6	6	Lemhi County	ID	George C. Engelhardt	1988	3429
307 3/8	46 5/8 47 0/8	37 7/8	7	6	Greenlee County	AZ	Clifford White	1989	3429
307 3/8	42 4/8 43 3/8	51 7/8	7	7	Park County	CO	Marko Green	1989	3429
307 3/8	50 4/8 47 4/8	34 7/8	6	6	Coconino County	AZ	Jim Beaumier	1992	3429
307 3/8	43 3/8 43 5/8	40 5/8	6	6	Delta County	CO	Cliff Beaver	1995	3429
307 3/8	47 4/8 48 4/8	46 5/8	6	6	Harney County	OR	Joel Haslett	2005	3429
*307 3/8	48 4/8 52 0/8	36 3/8	6	6	Boulder County	CO	Joseph C. Marcotte	2009	3429
*307 3/8	45 4/8 46 4/8	42 3/8	6	6	Las Animas County	CO	Mike Raley	2009	3429
307 2/8	49 5/8 50 4/8	35 6/8	6	6	Coconino County	AZ	Larry Hines	1981	3438
307 2/8	48 6/8 46 1/8	35 1/8	7	7	Bonner County	ID	Brian T. Farley	1982	3438
307 2/8	52 5/8 47 0/8	38 1/8	7	8	Idaho County	ID	John Moehrle	1987	3438
307 2/8	44 6/8 46 0/8	38 2/8	6	6	Grand County	CO	Gary W. Billiet	1993	3438
307 2/8	51 3/8 48 3/8	38 2/8	6	6	Coconino County	AZ	Dale Houston	1997	3438
307 2/8	50 2/8 49 4/8	34 7/8	6	7	Phillips County	MT	David T. Borek	1997	3438
307 2/8	49 3/8 49 5/8	41 0/8	7	7	Lewis & Clark County	MT	Tres Childs	2003	3438
307 2/8	43 5/8 43 5/8	41 6/8	6	6	Phillips County	MT	David J. Slade	2003	3438
307 2/8	47 4/8 46 7/8	38 4/8	6	6	Gallatin County	MT	Amos H. Crowley III	2009	3438
307 2/8	48 4/8 46 7/8	33 4/8	6	6	Park County	WY	Jason Stafford	2009	3438
307 1/8	54 4/8 52 4/8	40 3/8	6	6	Park County	MT	David Thiry	1981	3448
307 1/8	47 0/8 47 5/8	43 1/8	6	6	Grant County	OR	George Schiedler	1983	3448
307 1/8	50 4/8 51 0/8	42 3/8	6	6	Park County	MT	Robert Ward	1983	3448
307 1/8	47 1/8 46 6/8	33 3/8	6	6	Navajo County	AZ	Warren A. Adams	1992	3448
307 1/8	48 5/8 45 4/8	33 1/8	6	6	Missoula County	MT	Tou Lee	1992	3448
307 1/8	47 5/8 49 6/8	40 7/8	6	6	Coconino County	AZ	Duane "Corky" Richardson	1995	3448
307 1/8	54 2/8 54 5/8	35 5/8	6	6	Jefferson County	CO	Bill Ramsey	1997	3448
307 1/8	45 0/8 47 4/8	46 7/8	6	6	Grant County	OR	Jon Simonson	1997	3448
307 1/8	48 4/8 45 7/8	37 7/8	6	6	Cibola County	NM	Rick U. Rensch	1997	3448
307 1/8	47 4/8 47 4/8	36 1/8	6	7	Wainwright	ALB	Dale Johnson	1998	3448
307 1/8	46 0/8 44 7/8	36 1/8	6	6	Clearwater County	ID	Nou Yang	2007	3448
307 1/8	49 4/8 48 5/8	38 1/8	6	6	Bonneville County	ID	Craig Muehleip	2007	3448
307 0/8	51 5/8 50 2/8	35 6/8	6	6	Judith Basin County	MT	Mark A. Petroni	1982	3460
307 0/8	49 3/8 50 6/8	37 0/8	6	6	Apache County	AZ	Melvin Edward Norris	1986	3460
307 0/8	53 1/8 52 0/8	38 6/8	6	7	Clearwater County	ID	Ralph L. Albright	1986	3460
307 0/8	48 6/8 48 0/8	36 2/8	6	6	Sheridan County	WY	Jerome D. Larson	1997	3460
307 0/8	43 4/8 43 2/8	35 0/8	6	6	Costilla County	CO	Jeff Geiser	2000	3460
307 0/8	47 7/8 47 7/8	38 4/8	6	6	Moffat County	CO	Ron Faust	2001	3460
307 0/8	45 1/8 45 0/8	41 6/8	6	6	Garfield County	UT	Jerry Woodland	2001	3460
307 0/8	54 3/8 51 2/8	36 6/8	6	6	Valley County	MT	Dennis Bense	2002	3460
*307 0/8	47 1/8 46 5/8	34 0/8	6	6	Huerfano County	CO	Roger A. Boushley	2003	3460
*307 0/8	47 4/8 48 5/8	40 2/8	6	6	Montrose County	CO	Jerry Check	2006	3460
*307 0/8	48 6/8 47 1/8	39 2/8	6	7	Pierce County	WA	Kurt Kominski	2007	3460
*307 0/8	44 2/8 45 5/8	42 4/8	6	6	Catron County	NM	James E. Willard	2008	3460
*307 0/8	53 2/8 52 6/8	42 2/8	7	6	Mesa County	CO	Thomas M. Santomauro	2009	3460
306 7/8	46 0/8 44 0/8	42 5/8	6	6	Sandoval County	NM	Rett Kelly	1991	3473
306 7/8	41 2/8 42 5/8	41 1/8	6	6	Boundary County	ID	Roger N. Myers	1994	3473
306 7/8	43 7/8 44 4/8	40 7/8	7	7	Grant County	NM	James Schulz	1997	3473
306 7/8	49 3/8 49 1/8	41 3/8	7	7	Custer County	ID	Patrick Corcoran	1997	3473
306 7/8	44 6/8 46 6/8	31 1/8	6	6	Shoshone County	ID	Edward J. Wagner	1998	3473
306 7/8	48 5/8 49 5/8	40 5/8	6	6	Catron County	NM	Gip Friesen	1998	3473
306 7/8	48 1/8 46 5/8	40 3/8	6	6	Granite County	MT	Eric Urban	1999	3473
306 7/8	44 0/8 43 5/8	40 5/8	6	6	Teton County	WY	Jerry Bodar	2005	3473
*306 7/8	45 4/8 45 4/8	34 3/8	6	6	Broadwater County	MT	John Hoyle	2005	3473
*306 7/8	45 4/8 47 3/8	34 4/8	7	6	Moffat County	CO	Dale Finkler	2007	3473
306 7/8	46 7/8 47 4/8	40 7/8	6	6	Albany County	WY	Slade H. Taylor	2009	3473
306 6/8	50 5/8 43 7/8	35 6/8	6	6	Coconino County	AZ	Philip M. Rippey	1988	3484
306 6/8	44 7/8 46 0/8	30 2/8	8	6	Fergus County	MT	Roland E. Sanford, Jr.	1988	3484
306 6/8	43 0/8 42 5/8	32 4/8	6	6	Sanders County	MT	Jeffrey M. Myny	1991	3484
306 6/8	50 2/8 50 2/8	35 6/8	6	6	Millard County	UT	Ross J. Madsen	1993	3484
306 6/8	43 3/8 45 4/8	34 6/8	6	6	Johnson County	WY	Brett Burditt	1994	3484
306 6/8	39 7/8 40 7/8	35 2/8	6	6	Crook County	OR	Jeff Wingert	1996	3484
306 6/8	50 3/8 49 3/8	37 6/8	6	7	Pueblo County	CO	James L. Smith	1996	3484
306 6/8	48 3/8 50 5/8	38 2/8	7	6	Ravalli County	MT	Thomas Kresnak	2002	3484
306 6/8	43 1/8 44 6/8	34 2/8	6	6	Teton County	WY	Jerry Bodar	2003	3484
306 6/8	49 6/8 45 0/8	40 0/8	7	5	Rosebud County	MT	Michael J. Jarding	2005	3484
306 6/8	51 2/8 48 2/8	40 2/8	6	6	Powell County	MT	Chris Dahl	2005	3484
*306 6/8	45 1/8 42 1/8	41 0/8	6	6	Beaverhead County	MT	Tommy M. Anderson	2005	3484
*306 6/8	43 6/8 45 1/8	32 2/8	6	7	Moffat County	CO	Wally Schaub	2009	3484
306 5/8	50 2/8 49 1/8	39 7/8	5	5	Granite County	MT	J. Greg Jones	1983	3497
306 5/8	47 5/8 46 4/8	31 7/8	7	6	White Pine County	NV	Jerry A. Manges	1992	3497
306 5/8	47 5/8 47 3/8	37 5/8	8	6	Mora County	NM	Kenneth Morga	1993	3497
306 5/8	47 4/8 46 5/8	33 7/8	7	7	Phillips County	MT	Bob H. Paine	1994	3497
306 5/8	49 5/8 49 2/8	38 7/8	6	6	Judith Basin County	MT	Brandon Johns	1997	3497
306 5/8	45 6/8 45 7/8	37 1/8	6	6	Larimer County	CO	Mike Kelly	1998	3497
306 5/8	46 5/8 48 5/8	34 7/8	6	6	Phillips County	MT	Joe Aldworth	2001	3497
*306 5/8	47 1/8 45 2/8	35 3/8	6	6	Montrose County	CO	Jeffrey A. Good	2006	3497
*306 5/8	49 1/8 49 6/8	29 3/8	6	6	White Pine County	NV	Chris Crookshanks	2008	3497
306 5/8	47 4/8 47 1/8	33 7/8	6	6	Grant County	OR	James Moss	2010	3497
306 4/8	42 7/8 43 2/8	43 4/8	5	5	Lemhi County	ID	A. LaVerne Hokanson	1974	3507
306 4/8	43 4/8 44 5/8	40 0/8	6	6	Clearwater County	ID	Kim J. Vander Sys	1977	3507
306 4/8	46 4/8 47 2/8	37 4/8	6	6	Blaine County	ID	Tom Goicoechea	1982	3507
306 4/8	45 4/8 46 3/8	33 6/8	6	6	Valley County	ID	Bob Shaw	1991	3507
306 4/8	51 2/8 49 4/8	43 2/8	6	6	McKinley County	NM	Ben W. Gibson	1992	3507
306 4/8	47 4/8 47 4/8	40 4/8	6	6	Crook County	OR	Jack Robertson	1992	3507
306 4/8	45 1/8 45 3/8	34 4/8	6	6	Phillips County	MT	Roger Conaway	2003	3507
306 4/8	52 2/8 51 5/8	41 6/8	5	6	Albany County	WY	Jerry Bowen	2005	3507
*306 4/8	47 7/8 47 4/8	40 6/8	6	6	Uinta County	WY	Todd Hoover	2005	3507

AMERICAN ELK (TYPICAL ANTLERS)

Minimum Score 260 — Continued

SCORE	LENGTH OF R MAIN BEAM L	INSIDE SPREAD	NUMBER OF R POINTS L		AREA	STATE/ PROVINCE	HUNTER'S NAME	DATE	RANK
306 4/8	46 2/8 47 4/8	32 2/8	6	6	Rio Blanco County	CO	Patrick Harm	2007	3507
306 3/8	48 4/8 48 5/8	40 6/8	7	6	Summit County	UT	Clifton B. Johnson	1978	3517
306 3/8	45 3/8 47 1/8	32 7/8	6	6	Catron County	NM	Jim R. Wood	1992	3517
306 3/8	48 4/8 47 6/8	37 1/8	6	6	Cibola County	NM	Gerald Skees	1999	3517
306 3/8	50 2/8 51 3/8	38 5/8	5	6	Moffat County	CO	Glen A. Filener	2001	3517
306 3/8	44 1/8 47 4/8	38 7/8	6	6	Coconino County	AZ	Bill West	2003	3517
*306 3/8	50 3/8 49 6/8	39 7/8	6	6	Converse County	WY	Jeffrey Green	2004	3517
306 3/8	53 3/8 51 6/8	32 7/8	6	6	Montrose County	CO	Euel Gene Beach	2007	3517
306 3/8	53 0/8 52 0/8	40 3/8	6	6	Wallowa County	OR	Mike Kraner	2008	3517
306 3/8	43 4/8 44 3/8	36 1/8	6	6	Sierra County	NM	Martin Kilen	2008	3517
306 2/8	49 3/8 48 3/8	40 2/8	6	6	Garfield County	UT	Bruce E. Carlisle	1985	3526
306 2/8	46 2/8 45 7/8	37 3/8	7	6	Catron County	NM	Sonny Turner	1991	3526
306 2/8	45 4/8 48 4/8	41 5/8	7	7	Coconino County	AZ	William Shaler	1997	3526
306 2/8	50 6/8 50 7/8	42 4/8	6	6	Larimer County	CO	Bill Harvey	1997	3526
306 2/8	45 2/8 43 1/8	41 6/8	6	6	Garfield County	WA	Lee Campbell	1997	3526
306 2/8	44 4/8 43 4/8	36 4/8	6	6	Jackson County	CO	Craig Willard	2000	3526
306 2/8	47 0/8 48 3/8	37 2/8	6	6	Rio Arriba County	NM	Jon T. Stephens	2000	3526
306 2/8	51 0/8 48 7/8	37 4/8	7	7	Bonner County	ID	Matthew Burrows	2003	3526
306 2/8	46 0/8 43 3/8	32 4/8	6	6	Fergus County	MT	John P. Hartman	2003	3526
306 2/8	45 6/8 47 3/8	35 6/8	6	6	La Plata County	CO	Michael J. Walker	2003	3526
306 2/8	46 5/8 44 6/8	33 4/8	6	6	Sublette County	WY	Rick Laframboise	2008	3526
*306 2/8	48 0/8 49 0/8	40 0/8	6	6	Park County	MT	Wes Kellogg	2008	3526
*306 2/8	43 3/8 42 4/8	41 3/8	7	7	Teton County	ID	James Gullickson	2008	3526
306 1/8	48 6/8 46 0/8	34 1/8	6	7	Beaverhead County	MT	Kenneth M. Carlson	1983	3539
306 1/8	49 5/8 47 2/8	39 5/8	6	6	Catron County	NM	Martin Plugge	1991	3539
306 1/8	52 0/8 52 0/8	34 5/8	6	6	Sheridan County	WY	Ron Johnson	1993	3539
306 1/8	48 0/8 47 4/8	32 5/8	6	6	Sublette County	WY	Casey Saxton	1997	3539
306 1/8	50 2/8 51 5/8	39 4/8	6	7	Phillips County	MT	Michael J. Domeika	1999	3539
306 1/8	51 4/8 52 1/8	39 7/8	6	6	Pennington County	SD	Larry A. Johnson	2002	3539
306 1/8	47 5/8 46 6/8	33 5/8	6	6	Eagle County	CO	Bryan Tinsley	2005	3539
306 1/8	45 0/8 45 7/8	39 5/8	6	6	Adams County	ID	P. Anthony Collins	2006	3539
306 1/8	44 4/8 46 0/8	40 1/8	6	6	Big Horn County	WY	Rick Yeske	2006	3539
*306 1/8	54 2/8 52 2/8	36 5/8	6	6	Montrose County	CO	Ben Brown	2007	3539
306 1/8	44 1/8 44 6/8	37 7/8	7	6	Park County	WY	Dave Justmann	2007	3539
306 0/8	45 0/8 44 3/8	36 6/8	6	6	Eagle County	CO	Walt Williams	1979	3550
306 0/8	49 2/8 48 7/8	34 2/8	6	6	Catron County	NM	William C. Davis	1986	3550
306 0/8	53 2/8 53 2/8	39 4/8	6	6	Ravalli County	MT	Dave L. Fretz	1987	3550
306 0/8	48 7/8 48 1/8	39 3/8	7	6	Phillips County	MT	Dave Farnsworth	1991	3550
306 0/8	49 5/8 50 0/8	35 1/8	6	7	Mora County	NM	Larry A. Claar	1993	3550
306 0/8	44 3/8 44 2/8	39 0/8	7	7	Garfield County	MT	Darren J. Moulthrop	1995	3550
306 0/8	49 2/8 46 2/8	45 4/8	6	6	Coconino County	AZ	Lee Evans	1998	3550
306 0/8	43 0/8 42 3/8	36 7/8	7	7	Rio Arriba County	NM	Eudane Vicenti	2001	3550
306 0/8	49 6/8 51 0/8	42 2/8	7	6	Madison County	MT	Ann White	2002	3550
*306 0/8	50 0/8 48 0/8	38 6/8	6	6	Grand County	CO	Rodney Doogs	2003	3550
306 0/8	46 4/8 45 5/8	42 0/8	6	6	Lincoln County	WY	Shawn Witte	2003	3550
306 0/8	49 0/8 46 4/8	33 1/8	6	7	Lincoln County	MT	Kevin Rousseau	2003	3550
306 0/8	45 0/8 47 0/8	35 4/8	6	6	Park County	WY	Jason Stafford	2004	3550
306 0/8	48 4/8 48 4/8	42 4/8	6	6	Iron County	UT	Wayne Hansen	2005	3550
306 0/8	46 2/8 46 0/8	36 6/8	7	7	Bonneville County	ID	Mike Burbank	2009	3550
305 7/8	46 5/8 46 6/8	37 7/8	6	6	Grant County	OR	Gregory Stathos	1987	3565
305 7/8	46 0/8 46 2/8	39 1/8	7	6	Sheridan County	WY	Randy Lee Reece	1990	3565
305 7/8	49 3/8 51 2/8	41 7/8	5	6	Catron County	NM	Jerry Romero	1993	3565
305 7/8	48 1/8 39 6/8	36 3/8	6	6	Lincoln County	NM	Harold Dean Britt	1996	3565
305 7/8	48 5/8 48 5/8	37 0/8	7	7	Grant County	NM	Paul R. Bovee	1996	3565
305 7/8	47 3/8 47 7/8	41 7/8	6	6	Baker County	OR	Heath Hansen	2004	3565
*305 7/8	49 4/8 51 6/8	46 5/8	6	6	San Miguel County	CO	Tripp Hise	2005	3565
305 6/8	46 7/8 47 7/8	34 0/8	6	6	Larimer County	CO	Steve Stumbo	1980	3572
305 6/8	45 2/8 46 4/8	38 6/8	6	6	Kootenai County	ID	Brent K. Jacobson	1982	3572
305 6/8	47 6/8 47 2/8	33 4/8	6	6	Catron County	NM	Randall S. Madding	1984	3572
305 6/8	40 1/8 42 0/8	36 4/8	7	6	Gilpin County	CO	Dennis Myer	1985	3572
305 6/8	44 5/8 46 1/8	38 2/8	6	6	Lincoln County	WY	Steven J. Vanlerberghe	1987	3572
305 6/8	52 7/8 52 7/8	37 0/8	5	5	Catron County	NM	Russell Hull	1989	3572
305 6/8	37 1/8 44 0/8	37 2/8	6	6	Santa Fe County	NM	Anthony J. Turrietta	1993	3572
305 6/8	46 3/8 46 3/8	33 3/8	6	7	Phillips County	MT	John R. Koschmeder	1994	3572
305 6/8	44 3/8 45 7/8	40 0/8	7	6	Sanders County	MT	Stephen E. Quinn	1995	3572
305 6/8	46 5/8 46 1/8	47 5/8	6	7	Ravalli County	MT	Bill Sullivan	1995	3572
305 6/8	47 2/8 45 7/8	37 5/8	7	7	Catron County	NM	David E. Serbonich	1999	3572
305 6/8	46 0/8 44 3/8	34 6/8	6	6	Wallowa County	OR	Zackery J. Grover	1999	3572
305 6/8	45 7/8 45 7/8	33 2/8	6	6	Kootenai County	ID	Matt Fuller	2002	3572
*305 6/8	46 1/8 46 0/8	37 2/8	6	6	Rio Blanco County	CO	Ernest F. Wheeler	2004	3572
*305 6/8	46 7/8 46 7/8	39 4/8	6	6	Dolores County	CO	Larry F. Davis	2005	3572
305 6/8	45 5/8 45 0/8	37 0/8	6	6	Umatilla County	OR	Daniel Dauenhauer	2005	3572
305 6/8	41 0/8 41 3/8	35 6/8	6	6	Idaho County	ID	William E. Dean	2006	3572
305 6/8	46 0/8 45 2/8	34 6/8	6	6	Lincoln County	NM	Joseph Strasser	2007	3572
305 6/8	49 1/8 49 0/8	38 6/8	6	6	Sheridan County	WY	Bruce Murray	2009	3572
305 6/8	48 6/8 49 0/8	38 2/8	6	7	Catron County	NM	Tracy Hawks	2009	3572
305 5/8	48 6/8 49 6/8	36 3/8	6	6	Archuleta County	CO	Lester Hawkins, Jr.	1989	3592
305 5/8	43 7/8 45 3/8	33 5/8	6	6	Catron County	NM	M. Richard Warner	1993	3592
305 5/8	46 1/8 46 5/8	38 5/8	6	6	Rio Arriba County	NM	James C. Slack	1994	3592
305 5/8	49 6/8 47 4/8	36 1/8	6	6	Jefferson County	CO	Brad Lenz	1997	3592
305 5/8	47 4/8 48 0/8	37 5/8	7	6	Catron County	NM	Frank J. Vilsmeier	1999	3592
305 5/8	45 7/8 45 1/8	42 5/8	6	6	Beaverhead County	MT	Christopher L. Costello	2000	3592
305 5/8	43 3/8 48 3/8	37 5/8	8	6	Clark County	ID	Jason McConeghy	2002	3592
305 5/8	43 0/8 44 0/8	38 1/8	6	6	Yavapai County	AZ	Kevin Bryan	2003	3592
305 5/8	46 4/8 46 6/8	30 7/8	6	6	Park County	WY	William O. Merrill	2007	3592
305 5/8	50 0/8 49 0/8	35 1/8	6	6	Fergus County	MT	Lynn Bowman	2008	3592
305 5/8	45 2/8 42 5/8	37 2/8	6	7	Coconino County	AZ	Chris D. Krueger	2008	3592
305 4/8	46 7/8 47 5/8	43 6/8	5	6	Clackamas County	OR	Bill Lancaster	1981	3603
305 4/8	47 4/8 47 5/8	40 2/8	6	6	Catron County	NM	Stan Rauch	1985	3603
305 4/8	50 1/8 52 1/8	40 4/8	7	6	Mesa County	CO	Don Boyles	1987	3603
305 4/8	48 0/8 48 6/8	37 2/8	6	6	Coconino County	AZ	Wayne Miller	1988	3603
305 4/8	44 1/8 48 4/8	41 0/8	5	6	Morgan County	UT	Tim J. Misewicz	1995	3603
305 4/8	47 2/8 47 2/8	40 6/8	7	7	Catron County	NM	David Rodriguez	1995	3603
305 4/8	52 0/8 48 6/8	44 5/8	7	7	Fremont County	ID	Brad Foster	1996	3603
305 4/8	46 4/8 47 6/8	41 2/8	5	5	Catron County	NM	E. Lance Whary	1996	3603

715

AMERICAN ELK (TYPICAL ANTLERS)

Minimum Score 260 — Continued

SCORE	LENGTH OF R MAIN BEAM L	INSIDE SPREAD	NUMBER OF R POINTS L		AREA	STATE/PROVINCE	HUNTER'S NAME	DATE	RANK
*305 4/8	46 3/8 46 3/8	40 0/8	6	6	Las Animas County	CO	Gordon Markle, Jr.	2003	3603
305 4/8	47 5/8 49 5/8	35 0/8	6	6	Rio Blanco County	CO	John W. Ellas	2005	3603
305 4/8	52 1/8 53 6/8	42 4/8	6	6	Custer County	ID	Edward D. Koch	2005	3603
*305 4/8	46 2/8 47 2/8	47 0/8	8	6	Catron County	NM	Leslie Kent Jackson	2008	3603
*305 4/8	45 1/8 43 0/8	43 0/8	7	7	Pitkin County	CO	Randy Wagner	2008	3603
*305 4/8	50 5/8 49 3/8	40 4/8	6	6	Otero County	NM	Mark Michalsky	2008	3603
305 4/8	46 6/8 44 2/8	31 2/8	6	6	Garfield County	CO	Duane Domaszek	2008	3603
305 4/8	44 7/8 43 7/8	37 6/8	6	6	Shoshone County	ID	Bryan D. Ward	2009	3603
305 4/8	51 2/8 50 0/8	36 4/8	6	7	Big Horn County	WY	Steve Schulz	2009	3603
305 4/8	46 4/8 45 5/8	34 4/8	6	6	Lincoln County	WY	Jared Hamp	2010	3603
*305 4/8	49 2/8 48 7/8	42 4/8	6	6	Salt Lake County	UT	Kenneth Oetker	2010	3603
305 3/8	47 3/8 43 6/8	34 7/8	6	6	Caribou County	ID	Russ W. Arman	1992	3622
305 3/8	44 5/8 46 2/8	38 5/8	6	6	Morgan County	UT	Poncho McCoy	1993	3622
305 3/8	47 4/8 48 0/8	29 3/8	6	7	Mohave County	AZ	Deb Fuller	1993	3622
305 3/8	55 2/8 54 4/8	31 5/8	6	6	Greenlee County	AZ	Kevin H. Johnson	1993	3622
305 3/8	48 5/8 48 4/8	34 1/8	6	6	Yavapai County	AZ	Robert W. Ledbetter	1993	3622
305 3/8	49 3/8 48 3/8	46 3/8	7	7	Coconino County	AZ	Eddy Broderick	1995	3622
305 3/8	45 2/8 45 0/8	35 1/8	7	6	Beaverhead County	MT	Danny Moore	1997	3622
305 3/8	51 3/8 50 4/8	40 1/8	6	6	Archuleta County	CO	Drew McCartney	1997	3622
305 3/8	49 4/8 48 5/8	34 3/8	6	6	Millarville	ALB	Kyle Sinclair-Smith	2003	3622
*305 3/8	45 6/8 45 0/8	40 1/8	6	7	Summit County	CO	Kurt Keskimaki	2005	3622
305 3/8	49 2/8 51 0/8	39 5/8	6	6	Pitkin County	CO	Michael Tornes	2005	3622
*305 3/8	45 4/8 45 7/8	36 7/8	6	6	Jefferson County	CO	Randy D. Stolba	2005	3622
305 2/8	50 2/8 51 2/8	39 4/8	6	6	Larimer County	CO	Craig Nelson	1968	3634
305 2/8	48 7/8 48 6/8	38 0/8	6	6	Catron County	NM	Glen L. Dillehay	1984	3634
305 2/8	47 0/8 45 2/8	38 1/8	7	6	Lincoln County	NM	Henry Vega	1987	3634
305 2/8	49 4/8 48 5/8	36 0/8	6	6	Lincoln County	NM	Johnny King	1988	3634
305 2/8	48 6/8 49 5/8	40 2/8	6	6	Grant County	OR	Randy Burgess	1990	3634
305 2/8	47 6/8 46 5/8	33 5/8	7	6	Granite County	MT	Jeremy J. Sandoz	1992	3634
305 2/8	46 6/8 46 3/8	37 0/8	6	6	Beaverhead County	MT	Gene Loder	1993	3634
305 2/8	51 6/8 51 7/8	40 2/8	6	6	Madison County	MT	David K. Naibert, Jr.	1993	3634
305 2/8	47 5/8 46 7/8	33 6/8	6	6	Garfield County	WA	Dan Spanner	1993	3634
305 2/8	50 0/8 49 3/8	39 6/8	5	6	Skamania County	WA	Bob Morehouse	1993	3634
305 2/8	47 1/8 46 5/8	33 3/8	8	7	Shoshone County	ID	David B. Cobb	1994	3634
305 2/8	48 3/8 48 2/8	37 2/8	7	6	Beaverhead County	MT	Mike Davis	1995	3634
305 2/8	52 5/8 51 7/8	32 4/8	6	6	Coconino County	AZ	Bret Lee Meacham	1995	3634
305 2/8	46 0/8 46 1/8	36 4/8	6	6	Petroleum County	MT	Chuck Adams	1996	3634
305 2/8	43 2/8 45 3/8	43 6/8	7	7	Sanders County	MT	Steve Potts	1998	3634
305 2/8	44 5/8 44 5/8	39 6/8	6	6	Ravalli County	MT	John Sain	1998	3634
305 2/8	44 7/8 44 7/8	36 0/8	6	6	Cascade County	MT	Tory E. Ewing	1998	3634
305 2/8	41 6/8 43 1/8	34 4/8	6	6	Bear Lake County	ID	Lance Swinney	2002	3634
305 2/8	41 5/8 43 1/8	34 2/8	6	6	Petroleum County	MT	Cory K. Roberts	2002	3634
305 2/8	47 6/8 44 6/8	42 0/8	6	6	Park County	WY	Kurt E. Larson	2003	3634
305 2/8	49 4/8 51 3/8	35 0/8	5	6	Garfield County	MT	Michael D. Gingrich	2003	3634
305 2/8	54 3/8 51 4/8	38 6/8	6	7	Laramie County	WY	Dennis Magnusson	2004	3634
*305 2/8	52 0/8 51 3/8	38 2/8	5	5	Las Animas County	CO	Dan Schlabach	2007	3634
305 2/8	45 6/8 44 0/8	45 6/8	6	6	Clearwater County	ID	Lance R. Rea	2008	3634
305 1/8	45 1/8 45 5/8	38 4/8	7	7	Fergus County	MT	Gary O. Stewart	1986	3658
305 1/8	47 1/8 45 1/8	34 3/8	6	6	Meagher County	MT	Jim Bouchard	1995	3658
305 1/8	48 1/8 45 2/8	30 4/8	7	8	Phillips County	MT	Bill Connors	1995	3658
305 1/8	46 7/8 47 2/8	33 3/8	6	7	N. Saskatchewan River	ALB	Darrin Petrie	1997	3658
305 1/8	49 6/8 48 1/8	35 5/8	6	6	Clark County	ID	Ken Loporto	2001	3658
305 1/8	46 7/8 48 6/8	45 5/8	6	6	Montrose County	CO	Darby Bender, Jr.	2003	3658
305 1/8	47 2/8 45 2/8	37 5/8	7	7	Caribou County	ID	Chad Gentry	2003	3658
305 1/8	50 2/8 47 6/8	29 1/8	7	6	Catron County	NM	Bill Bishop, Sr.	2004	3658
305 1/8	46 1/8 45 0/8	47 7/8	6	6	Clark County	ID	Ken Loporto	2006	3658
305 1/8	46 7/8 44 6/8	42 7/8	6	6	Harney County	OR	Alex Baron	2010	3658
*305 1/8	47 6/8 49 2/8	38 1/8	6	6	Blaine County	MT	Courtney Tyree	2010	3658
305 0/8	44 6/8 43 5/8	37 6/8	6	6	Morgan County	UT	Hugh Hogle	1987	3669
305 0/8	47 4/8 47 1/8	36 4/8	6	6	Mountain View	ALB	Randy Bernier	1994	3669
305 0/8	44 4/8 45 0/8	47 3/8	5	6	Catron County	NM	Leonard Scarborough	1994	3669
305 0/8	44 2/8 43 4/8	38 6/8	6	6	Sweetwater County	WY	Michael D. Haden	1995	3669
305 0/8	45 7/8 45 6/8	37 6/8	6	6	La Plata County	CO	Sean Stafford	1999	3669
305 0/8	51 2/8 50 7/8	34 7/8	7	8	Yakima County	WA	Richard Siekawitch	1999	3669
305 0/8	56 2/8 54 4/8	30 4/8	6	9	Mesa County	CO	Don Boyles	1999	3669
305 0/8	46 5/8 47 3/8	43 2/8	6	6	Park County	WY	Dave Ellis	2000	3669
*305 0/8	48 6/8 50 0/8	30 0/8	6	7	Petroleum County	MT	Sam Hubbard	2005	3669
305 0/8	51 1/8 49 5/8	36 2/8	6	6	Catron County	NM	Kyle S. Mathews	2008	3669
304 7/8	47 4/8 47 2/8	37 1/8	7	7	Garfield County	MT	Todd O. Kletke	1995	3679
304 7/8	47 0/8 46 4/8	31 1/8	6	6	Mineral County	CO	Brian K. Strickland	2002	3679
304 7/8	52 1/8 53 1/8	36 1/8	6	5	Park County	WY	Gary Yates	2005	3679
304 6/8	42 4/8 45 0/8	45 6/8	6	6	Coconino County	AZ	Art Potter	1976	3682
304 6/8	49 5/8 50 2/8	43 2/8	7	6	Coconino County	AZ	Jerry Carpenter	1979	3682
304 6/8	46 6/8 46 7/8	37 6/8	6	6	Madison County	MT	Fred B. McCullar	1993	3682
304 6/8	48 3/8 50 1/8	41 0/8	7	7	Etolin Island	AK	Jack Hicks	2000	3682
304 6/8	44 2/8 42 2/8	36 2/8	6	6	Teton County	MT	Greg Feroglia	2002	3682
*304 6/8	51 0/8 50 7/8	35 2/8	6	6	Yavapai County	AZ	Leo Armenta	2005	3682
304 6/8	49 6/8 51 1/8	36 0/8	7	6	Coconino County	AZ	Roy E. Grace	2005	3682
304 6/8	47 4/8 51 2/8	35 0/8	7	6	Stillwater County	MT	Charlie W. Green	2007	3682
*304 6/8	46 7/8 46 3/8	34 4/8	6	6	Rio Grande County	CO	Raul Quesada	2007	3682
*304 6/8	47 2/8 45 4/8	35 4/8	7	7	Catron County	NM	Gary Kohler	2010	3682
304 5/8	51 1/8 49 6/8	37 5/8	6	6	Catron County	NM	A. Jerry McBride	1991	3692
304 5/8	46 0/8 49 6/8	27 1/8	6	7	Park County	WY	Marion O. DeBusk	1992	3692
304 5/8	46 2/8 46 1/8	39 1/8	6	6	Uintah County	UT	Jim Arrant	1994	3692
304 5/8	47 2/8 49 0/8	37 3/8	7	6	Fergus County	MT	Michael R. Hassinger	1995	3692
304 5/8	42 3/8 42 4/8	37 7/8	6	6	Fremont County	ID	Glen Berry	1996	3692
304 5/8	52 3/8 51 2/8	39 6/8	6	5	Graham County	AZ	Brian Jay Winans	2001	3692
304 5/8	44 3/8 47 0/8	32 5/8	6	6	Lincoln County	NM	Leroy Lavender	2003	3692
*304 5/8	49 4/8 47 5/8	33 3/8	6	6	Larimer County	CO	Alfred C. Groth	2004	3692
304 5/8	47 2/8 46 4/8	41 5/8	6	6	Moffat County	CO	Michael Paulcheck	2005	3692
*304 5/8	44 5/8 43 1/8	37 1/8	6	6	Rich County	UT	Ted Hallows	2005	3692
304 5/8	48 0/8 48 4/8	35 3/8	6	6	Valley County	ID	Kevin A. Sullivan	2005	3692
*304 5/8	47 6/8 48 7/8	33 3/8	6	7	Ouray County	CO	Scott Stedman	2009	3692
304 5/8	51 7/8 52 0/8	36 5/8	6	6	Coconino County	AZ	Ryan Nogosek	2009	3692
*304 5/8	43 7/8 43 5/8	38 5/8	6	6	Delta County	CO	Todd Ray	2010	3692

716

AMERICAN ELK (TYPICAL ANTLERS)

Minimum Score 260 Continued

SCORE	LENGTH OF R MAIN BEAM L	INSIDE SPREAD	NUMBER OF R POINTS L		AREA	STATE/ PROVINCE	HUNTER'S NAME	DATE	RANK
*304 5/8	49 4/8 49 4/8	38 3/8	6	6	Colfax County	NM	Kenneth Fusilier	2010	3692
304 4/8	46 7/8 45 4/8	45 2/8	6	6	Grant County	OR	Clayton Severin	1982	3707
304 4/8	52 1/8 52 7/8	39 4/8	6	6	Catron County	NM	Robert W. Chilcutt	1986	3707
304 4/8	45 7/8 45 7/8	35 0/8	6	6	Missoula County	MT	Byron Schurg	1989	3707
304 4/8	48 7/8 46 0/8	35 0/8	6	6	Coconino County	AZ	David Rabellino	1995	3707
304 4/8	47 1/8 45 5/8	35 6/8	6	5	Petroleum County	MT	Chuck Adams	1995	3707
304 4/8	45 4/8 46 3/8	35 6/8	7	7	Uintah County	UT	Derk Murray	2002	3707
304 4/8	46 4/8 46 2/8	31 2/8	6	6	Socorro County	NM	Thomas J. Perrett, Jr.	2003	3707
304 4/8	44 5/8 44 3/8	40 0/8	6	6	Montrose County	CO	Joel Hunt	2006	3707
304 3/8	50 6/8 48 1/8	44 1/8	6	6	McKinley County	NM	Rick Collard	1987	3715
304 3/8	44 4/8 45 4/8	34 5/8	6	6	Lincoln County	WY	Lee Lesmeister	1998	3715
304 3/8	48 0/8 48 5/8	36 6/8	6	7	Larimer County	CO	Robert H. Miller	2002	3715
304 3/8	48 1/8 50 0/8	43 1/8	6	6	Beaverhead County	MT	Pete Brion	2003	3715
304 3/8	46 1/8 46 5/8	40 3/8	7	6	Los Alamos County	NM	Charles R. Shubert, Sr.	2005	3715
*304 3/8	49 4/8 46 0/8	43 5/8	6	6	Umatilla County	OR	Ryan L. Cramer	2007	3715
304 3/8	48 6/8 49 2/8	37 1/8	7	6	Kittitas County	WA	Daniel B. Christiansen	2007	3715
304 3/8	53 0/8 50 3/8	36 4/8	6	7	Elko County	NV	Dan Schaller	2009	3715
304 2/8	46 6/8 49 0/8	36 4/8	6	6	Flathead County	MT	Steven C. Street	1980	3723
304 2/8	49 5/8 49 6/8	34 4/8	6	6	Sanders County	MT	Ray J. Baenen	1982	3723
304 2/8	48 2/8 47 3/8	40 6/8	6	6	Cibola County	NM	Jim Pepper	1983	3723
304 2/8	45 2/8 45 5/8	33 4/8	6	6	Douglas County	CO	James Phelps	1990	3723
304 2/8	49 7/8 49 6/8	34 2/8	6	5	Routt County	CO	Craig Greenheck	1990	3723
304 2/8	45 1/8 43 5/8	35 0/8	6	6	Otero County	NM	James E. Borron	1990	3723
304 2/8	55 2/8 53 3/8	32 4/8	6	6	Greenlee County	AZ	Lonnie R. Lashley	1991	3723
304 2/8	45 4/8 42 0/8	35 2/8	6	6	Mesa County	CO	Baree Weber	1995	3723
304 2/8	47 1/8 45 1/8	34 4/8	6	6	Petroleum County	MT	George Klaysmat	1996	3723
304 2/8	47 4/8 50 2/8	37 0/8	6	6	Cibola County	NM	Mark Siedschlag	1998	3723
304 2/8	50 1/8 49 4/8	34 2/8	6	6	Catron County	NM	Richard Van Valkenburg	1998	3723
304 2/8	51 4/8 49 6/8	37 6/8	6	6	Grant County	OR	Randy Carter	1998	3723
304 2/8	48 5/8 48 5/8	31 0/8	6	6	Harney County	OR	Jason L. Radinovich	1998	3723
304 2/8	47 1/8 47 2/8	40 6/8	6	6	Grand County	CO	Jeff P. Zelinski	1999	3723
304 2/8	46 6/8 48 4/8	48 7/8	7	8	Gunnison County	CO	Joseph Paul Kitko	2000	3723
304 2/8	50 7/8 50 1/8	37 6/8	6	6	Coconino County	AZ	Ronnie Parsons	2004	3723
304 2/8	47 5/8 47 1/8	33 4/8	6	6	Fergus County	MT	Walter Rud	2006	3723
304 2/8	46 2/8 45 2/8	39 2/8	6	6	Coconino County	AZ	Gene Carmickle	2009	3723
304 1/8	46 6/8 47 0/8	42 7/8	6	6	Coconino County	AZ	Dyrk Eddie	1994	3741
304 1/8	50 7/8 49 7/8	37 3/8	6	6	San Juan County	UT	Shad D. Schmidt	1996	3741
304 1/8	51 0/8 50 4/8	43 7/8	6	6	Lewis County	WA	Ray Schliesser	2003	3741
304 1/8	50 2/8 51 0/8	38 7/8	7	6	Catron County	NM	Myron Hershberger	2003	3741
304 1/8	45 7/8 44 7/8	33 6/8	8	7	Phillips County	MT	Patrick E. Wheeler	2005	3741
*304 1/8	47 7/8 48 7/8	38 1/8	6	6	Fremont County	WY	Kurt N. Johnson	2006	3741
304 1/8	50 5/8 49 5/8	38 1/8	6	6	Lincoln County	NM	Kelby McCall	2008	3741
304 0/8	50 1/8 48 4/8	37 0/8	5	5	Park County	CO	Ronald King	1981	3748
304 0/8	47 5/8 46 6/8	39 6/8	6	6	Grant County	OR	James E. Hodson	1981	3748
304 0/8	49 3/8 53 4/8	44 2/8	6	6	Cibola County	NM	Wayne L. Mathews	1986	3748
304 0/8	48 5/8 48 7/8	37 2/8	6	6	Chouteau County	MT	K. C. Palagi	1986	3748
304 0/8	43 5/8 42 5/8	32 4/8	6	6	Harney County	OR	Patrick E. Wheeler	1993	3748
304 0/8	50 6/8 52 5/8	36 2/8	6	6	Grant County	NM	Marlin A. Olson	1995	3748
304 0/8	45 2/8 44 3/8	32 6/8	6	6	Lemhi County	ID	Dan Laboone	1996	3748
304 0/8	49 2/8 49 6/8	39 6/8	6	7	Sanders County	MT	Joseph A. Cunningham	1998	3748
*304 0/8	50 5/8 52 2/8	39 0/8	6	6	Rio Blanco County	CO	Scott Allen	2005	3748
*304 0/8	46 3/8 46 6/8	41 4/8	6	6	Broadwater County	MT	Jerry Otto	2008	3748
304 0/8	47 3/8 45 7/8	35 6/8	6	7	Beaverhead County	MT	Nate Pelkey	2010	3748
303 7/8	48 6/8 46 0/8	41 7/8	6	6	Pitkin County	CO	Joseph Mendozza	1980	3759
303 7/8	43 3/8 43 4/8	41 3/8	6	6	Fergus County	MT	Carson J. Rife	1984	3759
303 7/8	46 3/8 44 4/8	37 5/8	6	6	Flathead County	MT	Doug Bronson	1987	3759
303 7/8	42 4/8 44 7/8	41 1/8	6	8	Apache County	AZ	Jim Scholes	1991	3759
303 7/8	46 1/8 39 6/8	37 1/8	6	6	Shoshone County	ID	Richard Enck	1995	3759
303 7/8	52 4/8 51 0/8	43 3/8	6	6	Larimer County	CO	Thomas Coseo	2002	3759
*303 7/8	43 4/8 44 0/8	39 5/8	6	7	Sheridan County	WY	Dave Strehlo	2004	3759
303 7/8	52 5/8 50 6/8	35 5/8	6	6	Huerfano County	CO	Travis Samuel	2005	3759
303 7/8	43 5/8 49 5/8	43 7/8	6	7	Lewis & Clark County	MT	Gary Pershall	2006	3759
303 6/8	46 2/8 47 7/8	36 2/8	6	6	Eagle County	CO	Tim W. Hulce	1981	3768
303 6/8	44 4/8 44 4/8	38 2/8	6	6	Benewah County	ID	Eugene Lewis	1989	3768
303 6/8	46 0/8 44 4/8	36 0/8	6	6	Coconino County	AZ	David S. Stone	1990	3768
303 6/8	47 2/8 47 4/8	36 6/8	6	6	Linn County	OR	Jeff Baker	1997	3768
303 6/8	47 0/8 38 7/8	40 2/8	7	7	Carbon County	WY	Sherrod W. France	1997	3768
303 6/8	44 5/8 44 2/8	41 0/8	6	6	Montrose County	CO	Dennis E. Lerum	1997	3768
303 6/8	50 4/8 49 1/8	34 0/8	6	6	Valley County	ID	Art Ingram	2003	3768
303 6/8	47 0/8 48 2/8	31 2/8	6	6	Lincoln County	NV	Herbert Holtam	2005	3768
303 6/8	43 4/8 42 2/8	42 1/8	6	7	Costilla County	CO	Jim Kennedy	2005	3768
303 6/8	47 7/8 48 1/8	36 0/8	6	6	Grand County	UT	Tony Perri	2006	3768
*303 6/8	47 0/8 46 2/8	42 0/8	6	6	Coconino County	AZ	Roger Dodt	2008	3768
303 5/8	51 7/8 51 0/8	36 3/8	6	6	Grant County	OR	James M. Carter	1987	3779
303 5/8	52 1/8 54 2/8	39 3/8	7	6	Pierce County	WA	Joe Harrison Frields	1987	3779
303 5/8	49 3/8 48 2/8	35 2/8	6	6	Sandoval County	NM	Gerald Schullo	1988	3779
303 5/8	49 7/8 49 5/8	38 1/8	6	6	Catron County	NM	A. Jerry McBride	1988	3779
303 5/8	50 0/8 50 0/8	39 3/8	6	6	Custer County	ID	Jeremy A. Lormis	2001	3779
*303 5/8	49 5/8 48 5/8	36 1/8	6	6	Costilla County	CO	Blake Barnett	2010	3779
303 4/8	49 1/8 42 1/8	41 0/8	6	6	Grand County	CO	Jim Cleland	1977	3785
303 4/8	44 6/8 45 3/8	36 2/8	6	6	Sierra County	NM	Chuck Wagner	1986	3785
303 4/8	48 0/8 47 4/8	38 4/8	6	6	Sheridan County	WY	Dan G. Powers	1991	3785
303 4/8	44 2/8 43 4/8	43 6/8	6	6	Idaho County	ID	Glen Burney	1991	3785
303 4/8	48 3/8 48 7/8	39 6/8	6	6	Coconino County	AZ	Patrick Fillman	1991	3785
303 4/8	43 5/8 43 5/8	40 0/8	6	6	Rio Arriba County	NM	Gene Bishop	1992	3785
303 4/8	45 0/8 45 4/8	41 1/8	6	7	Park County	WY	John Kilgore	1994	3785
303 4/8	46 5/8 46 0/8	40 6/8	6	6	Broadwater County	MT	James Gelhaus	1994	3785
303 4/8	48 3/8 47 4/8	39 2/8	6	6	Catron County	NM	Kenneth M. Thompson	1998	3785
303 4/8	49 4/8 48 5/8	35 2/8	6	6	Jackson County	OR	Toby Womack	2000	3785
303 4/8	51 6/8 51 7/8	36 2/8	6	6	Wallowa County	OR	Darren Lee	2001	3785
303 4/8	48 0/8 48 5/8	32 2/8	6	6	Lincoln County	WY	Layne Foxley	2001	3785
303 4/8	48 0/8 48 3/8	36 2/8	8	7	Petroleum County	MT	Joseph M. Mucka	2001	3785
303 4/8	50 5/8 46 2/8	39 0/8	6	6	Larimer County	CO	Todd Stuart	2003	3785
303 4/8	46 6/8 47 1/8	41 0/8	7	7	Clearwater County	ID	Paul Hammond	2003	3785
303 4/8	45 1/8 45 7/8	34 0/8	6	6	Shoshone County	ID	William Freytag	2005	3785

717

AMERICAN ELK (TYPICAL ANTLERS)

Minimum Score 260 — Continued

SCORE	LENGTH OF R MAIN BEAM L	INSIDE SPREAD	NUMBER OF R POINTS L	AREA	STATE/ PROVINCE	HUNTER'S NAME	DATE	RANK
303 4/8	47 1/8 47 6/8	35 6/8	6 6	Sanders County	MT	Elizabeth A. Wormwood	2009	3785
303 4/8	46 2/8 44 2/8	40 0/8	6 7	Eagle County	CO	B. J. Connaway	2009	3785
303 3/8	44 0/8 43 0/8	42 7/8	5 6	Adams County	ID	Rick Mason	1984	3803
303 3/8	45 4/8 45 4/8	42 2/8	6 7	Park County	MT	Bryon D. Long	1989	3803
303 3/8	47 1/8 48 1/8	38 5/8	6 6	Flathead County	MT	Kenneth M. Sharp	1992	3803
303 3/8	45 4/8 45 4/8	37 5/8	7 6	Platte County	WY	Willard Woods	1994	3803
303 3/8	46 3/8 45 5/8	34 5/8	6 6	Rio Arriba County	NM	Eugene R. Lujan	1995	3803
303 3/8	47 0/8 46 1/8	38 5/8	6 6	Ravalli County	MT	David Bradt	1995	3803
303 3/8	50 5/8 50 5/8	38 1/8	6 6	Canmore	ALB	J. Raymond Temchuk	1996	3803
303 3/8	47 7/8 49 5/8	38 7/8	5 6	Coconino County	AZ	Greg Buckler	2005	3803
303 3/8	44 6/8 43 6/8	40 1/8	6 6	Idaho County	ID	Robert Virgil Baden II	2005	3803
303 3/8	46 4/8 47 1/8	30 7/8	6 7	Natrona County	WY	Chad Lewis	2005	3803
303 3/8	50 4/8 53 2/8	38 3/8	6 6	Moffat County	CO	T. J. Thrasher	2007	3803
303 3/8	44 6/8 43 6/8	40 3/8	6 6	Phillips County	MT	Stephen Roehm	2008	3803
303 2/8	47 4/8 45 6/8	38 4/8	6 6	Garfield County	CO	Alan Harbin	1980	3815
303 2/8	47 1/8 47 0/8	35 4/8	6 6	Park County	WY	James Dinkins	1983	3815
303 2/8	49 0/8 50 4/8	34 2/8	6 7	Grant County	OR	James M. Carter	1989	3815
303 2/8	46 6/8 46 0/8	38 0/8	6 8	Millard County	UT	Bryon M. Griffiths	1990	3815
303 2/8	56 7/8 51 5/8	42 4/8	6 6	Custer County	ID	John W. Heimes	1991	3815
303 2/8	47 4/8 48 0/8	35 4/8	6 6	Greenlee County	AZ	Tim E. Downs	1991	3815
303 2/8	46 0/8 48 1/8	35 2/8	6 6	Catron County	NM	Ron Madsen	1992	3815
303 2/8	45 4/8 44 2/8	31 6/8	6 6	Catron County	NM	Joseph A. Lorenz	1992	3815
303 2/8	50 0/8 49 7/8	42 2/8	6 6	Catron County	NM	Jerry A. Davis	1997	3815
303 2/8	46 3/8 46 6/8	38 4/8	6 6	Albany County	WY	Chuck Anderson	1999	3815
303 2/8	39 6/8 40 5/8	40 2/8	6 6	Clark County	ID	Michael Sherick	1999	3815
303 2/8	46 7/8 47 0/8	42 4/8	6 6	Valley County	ID	Bryan E. Cramer	2002	3815
303 2/8	46 3/8 47 2/8	37 2/8	6 6	Petroleum County	MT	Daryl Parker	2005	3815
303 2/8	42 5/8 42 2/8	34 0/8	7 7	Camas County	ID	Rick Palmer	2006	3815
303 2/8	49 7/8 48 2/8	39 6/8	5 6	Park County	WY	William Gartland	2007	3815
303 2/8	46 3/8 46 3/8	37 2/8	6 6	Phillips County	MT	Danny Moore	2010	3815
303 2/8	49 4/8 49 1/8	45 4/8	6 6	Greenlee County	AZ	Clarence Jellema	2010	3815
303 1/8	45 7/8 46 7/8	35 7/8	6 6	Jackson County	OR	Armone Foulon	1990	3832
303 1/8	49 4/8 50 3/8	33 1/8	6 7	Navajo County	AZ	Randy Ulmer	1993	3832
303 1/8	44 4/8 44 0/8	41 1/8	6 6	Fremont County	ID	Brett Ball	1993	3832
303 1/8	45 3/8 47 0/8	35 5/8	6 7	Socorro County	NM	Ronald F. Pierce	2001	3832
303 1/8	49 1/8 47 2/8	32 5/8	7 7	Clark County	ID	Brian G. Edgerton	2006	3832
303 1/8	47 1/8 48 2/8	36 1/8	6 6	Routt County	CO	Craig Thrasher	2009	3832
303 1/8	47 2/8 44 6/8	38 5/8	6 6	Apache County	AZ	James A. Milligan	2009	3832
303 0/8	48 7/8 47 6/8	41 0/8	5 6	Las Animas County	CO	David L. Brady	1983	3839
303 0/8	48 0/8 50 7/8	35 2/8	6 6	Fergus County	MT	Mark Robbins	1990	3839
303 0/8	48 2/8 50 1/8	37 6/8	8 9	Catron County	NM	L. David Hubler, MD	1990	3839
303 0/8	47 4/8 48 6/8	36 6/8	7 6	Sandoval County	NM	George McGoldrick	2001	3839
303 0/8	40 7/8 43 0/8	35 0/8	7 7	Gallatin County	MT	Kurt D. Rued	2002	3839
303 0/8	44 7/8 41 2/8	33 2/8	6 6	Apache County	AZ	Stuart Hazard III	2003	3839
303 0/8	49 0/8 47 3/8	36 2/8	6 6	Big Horn County	WY	Paul S. Warren	2005	3839
*303 0/8	47 4/8 49 2/8	41 2/8	6 6	Rio Blanco County	CO	Bruce R. Mabrey	2007	3839
303 0/8	50 4/8 49 3/8	37 0/8	6 6	Rio Arriba County	NM	Greg Vigil	2008	3839
303 0/8	45 6/8 45 4/8	35 4/8	6 6	Montezuma County	CO	Bruce Freshcorn	2009	3839
302 7/8	44 6/8 45 4/8	38 5/8	6 6	Swan River	MT	Joe Lawrence	1969	3849
302 7/8	46 0/8 44 5/8	39 5/8	6 6	Beaverhead County	MT	John L. Palmer, Sr.	1985	3849
302 7/8	43 3/8 45 0/8	41 7/8	7 6	Grant County	OR	Jim Richardson	1990	3849
302 7/8	41 1/8 41 1/8	41 5/8	6 6	Valley County	ID	Gary Christensen	1997	3849
302 7/8	45 1/8 46 7/8	47 4/8	6 6	Harney County	OR	Jerry Mills	1997	3849
302 7/8	45 2/8 45 7/8	31 5/8	6 6	Navajo County	AZ	Michael Hunter McCarey	1997	3849
302 7/8	43 7/8 43 6/8	32 1/8	7 6	Catron County	NM	Mark A. Nagelkirk	2001	3849
*302 7/8	42 5/8 45 2/8	35 5/8	6 6	Saguache County	CO	Robert Johnston	2006	3849
*302 7/8	48 7/8 49 3/8	39 5/8	6 6	Fergus County	MT	Logan Miller	2010	3849
302 6/8	49 4/8 47 4/8	43 0/8	5 6	Apache County	AZ	Gary Preston	1981	3858
302 6/8	49 1/8 47 0/8	34 0/8	7 7	Converse County	WY	Fred Romero	1992	3858
302 6/8	52 2/8 50 4/8	41 6/8	6 6	Catron County	NM	Stephen Herrera	1994	3858
302 6/8	46 6/8 45 3/8	41 3/8	6 7	Catron County	NM	Lawrence B. Dickson, Jr.	1994	3858
302 6/8	42 3/8 47 2/8	43 0/8	6 6	Coconino County	AZ	Roy R. Clark	1994	3858
302 6/8	49 6/8 50 3/8	34 0/8	7 6	Petroleum County	MT	Brian Sinclair	1999	3858
302 6/8	50 0/8 50 3/8	39 0/8	6 6	Coconino County	AZ	Matt Reetz	2001	3858
302 6/8	48 1/8 46 6/8	44 4/8	6 6	Catron County	NM	Michael D. Moore	2002	3858
302 6/8	48 1/8 46 2/8	39 6/8	6 7	Santa Fe County	NM	Burton R. Thompson, Jr.	2004	3858
302 6/8	43 2/8 44 5/8	34 4/8	7 6	Apache County	AZ	Vincent G. Amendolare	2004	3858
302 6/8	45 0/8 45 0/8	40 0/8	6 6	Idaho County	ID	Mike Bonugli	2005	3858
302 6/8	45 3/8 46 5/8	40 4/8	6 6	Park County	CO	Danny Stotler	2007	3858
302 6/8	44 3/8 43 1/8	37 6/8	6 6	Lincoln County	WY	Ronell Skinner	2010	3858
302 5/8	45 0/8 46 0/8	42 3/8	6 6	Clear Creek County	CO	Billy E. Corley	1987	3871
302 5/8	49 2/8 48 7/8	38 7/8	6 6	Beaverhead County	MT	Jack Brilz	1990	3871
302 5/8	39 2/8 41 3/8	40 3/8	6 6	Socorro County	NM	Tom Alvin	1991	3871
302 5/8	48 2/8 48 1/8	38 3/8	6 6	Lemhi County	ID	Tim Thomas	1993	3871
302 5/8	46 7/8 47 4/8	35 1/8	6 7	Shoshone County	ID	Erin Sacksteder	1996	3871
302 5/8	46 4/8 45 6/8	35 3/8	6 6	Idaho County	ID	Scott Hurd	1997	3871
302 5/8	46 5/8 47 2/8	35 5/8	6 6	Jefferson County	MT	Eugene Damron	1999	3871
302 5/8	48 0/8 48 0/8	37 4/8	7 7	Wallowa County	OR	Adrion Rimbey	2000	3871
302 5/8	47 5/8 47 1/8	39 5/8	6 6	Lawrence County	SD	Douglas A. Goehring	2001	3871
*302 5/8	46 3/8 47 1/8	33 1/8	6 6	Shoshone County	ID	Dustin Brodina	2005	3871
302 5/8	48 6/8 47 0/8	48 5/8	6 6	Wasatch County	UT	Judd Olsen	2008	3871
*302 5/8	46 3/8 47 2/8	30 3/8	6 6	Catron County	NM	Michael L. Ritter, Sr.	2009	3871
302 4/8	47 7/8 47 2/8	38 5/8	6 6	Eagle County	CO	Roger Rothhaar	1974	3883
302 4/8	46 4/8 46 2/8	37 0/8	6 6	Beaverhead County	MT	Dennis Rehse	1982	3883
302 4/8	50 3/8 48 5/8	38 4/8	6 5	Johnson County	WY	Zachary A. Rust	1993	3883
302 4/8	47 4/8 50 1/8	39 6/8	7 6	Sublette County	WY	Bill Pickett	1994	3883
302 4/8	45 6/8 44 4/8	36 6/8	5 5	Adams County	ID	Wayne Crownover	1997	3883
302 4/8	51 3/8 49 0/8	35 7/8	7 7	Catron County	NM	Gary Swinson	1998	3883
302 4/8	47 0/8 44 5/8	37 4/8	6 6	Park County	WY	Jim Van Stensel, Jr.	2000	3883
302 4/8	51 3/8 50 1/8	40 2/8	6 5	Blaine County	MT	Roman Cirignani	2001	3883
302 4/8	45 2/8 46 1/8	38 6/8	6 6	Coconino County	AZ	Sheffield Sabin Jordan	2003	3883
302 4/8	46 5/8 43 5/8	33 4/8	6 6	Fergus County	MT	John "Rosey" Roseland	2003	3883
302 4/8	50 6/8 48 4/8	41 0/8	6 6	Washington County	ID	Richard A. Young	2009	3883
302 3/8	44 0/8 45 4/8	35 3/8	6 6	Routt County	CO	Mike Newman	1989	3894
302 3/8	47 6/8 49 6/8	37 5/8	6 6	Rio Arriba County	NM	John Lucero	1992	3894

718

AMERICAN ELK (TYPICAL ANTLERS)

Minimum Score 260 — Continued

SCORE	LENGTH OF MAIN BEAM R	L	INSIDE SPREAD	NUMBER OF POINTS R	L	AREA	STATE/ PROVINCE	HUNTER'S NAME	DATE	RANK
302 3/8	49 2/8	44 3/8	30 7/8	6	6	Coconino County	AZ	Jeffery Duane Hines	1992	3894
302 3/8	49 7/8	49 4/8	34 7/8	6	6	Coconino County	AZ	Michael Campbell	1992	3894
302 3/8	44 1/8	45 4/8	39 1/8	5	5	Catron County	NM	Wayne "Audie" Gowens	1996	3894
302 3/8	46 4/8	45 4/8	38 3/8	7	6	Rio Grande County	CO	Stephen Teague	1997	3894
302 3/8	53 6/8	52 0/8	41 4/8	6	7	Idaho County	ID	Lonnie L. Jenkins	1998	3894
302 3/8	47 6/8	47 1/8	37 3/8	7	6	Petroleum County	MT	Joe Sevart	1999	3894
302 3/8	50 2/8	49 3/8	40 7/8	6	6	Rio Blanco County	CO	Dewey J. Cameron	1999	3894
302 3/8	45 2/8	46 5/8	34 5/8	6	6	Beaverhead County	MT	Ray Ford	2005	3894
302 3/8	45 6/8	45 0/8	34 7/8	6	7	Teton County	WY	Tom Rumney	2006	3894
302 3/8	46 3/8	47 0/8	37 3/8	6	5	Rossburn	MAN	Tim Yaremchuk	2007	3894
302 2/8	48 7/8	48 7/8	39 0/8	6	6	Grant County	OR	Randy Bonner	1983	3906
302 2/8	53 3/8	50 3/8	39 4/8	6	6	Coconino County	AZ	G. Henry Strohm	1986	3906
302 2/8	45 6/8	45 4/8	36 6/8	7	7	Cascade County	MT	Jay Sherley	1993	3906
302 2/8	49 6/8	48 2/8	35 4/8	6	6	Catron County	NM	Richard V. Gray	1994	3906
302 2/8	49 3/8	49 4/8	38 0/8	7	7	Catron County	NM	Jeffrey Tate	1994	3906
302 2/8	48 1/8	46 7/8	43 4/8	6	7	Park County	WY	Brian L. Wagner	1994	3906
302 2/8	46 6/8	46 0/8	36 4/8	6	6	Fremont County	WY	Joel Nirider	1996	3906
302 2/8	45 3/8	45 1/8	38 6/8	6	6	Sanders County	MT	Jeff Kirkland	1998	3906
302 2/8	45 6/8	45 3/8	43 4/8	6	6	Park County	WY	Robert C. Gregory, DVM	1998	3906
302 2/8	42 5/8	44 2/8	36 2/8	6	6	Petroleum County	MT	Gerry Brusletten	1998	3906
302 2/8	47 2/8	45 7/8	37 6/8	5	5	Garfield County	UT	Lance Brown	2000	3906
302 2/8	47 1/8	47 4/8	35 4/8	6	6	Powder River County	MT	Mark Kayser	2000	3906
302 2/8	46 6/8	45 7/8	35 6/8	6	6	Ravalli County	MT	George Kamps	2001	3906
302 2/8	46 7/8	48 3/8	38 4/8	6	6	Apache County	AZ	Roy Jimenez	2002	3906
302 2/8	49 3/8	48 5/8	42 0/8	6	6	Garfield County	CO	Nathan Sandburg	2004	3906
302 1/8	51 1/8	49 4/8	37 7/8	6	6	Canmore	ALB	David R. Coupland	1984	3921
302 1/8	44 1/8	44 1/8	35 1/8	6	6	Greenlee County	AZ	Timothy Hall	1985	3921
302 1/8	48 1/8	46 7/8	37 3/8	6	6	Valley County	ID	Michael S. Moore	1987	3921
302 1/8	51 2/8	51 3/8	39 5/8	8	6	Catron County	NM	Jay J. Sopiwnik	1988	3921
302 1/8	46 6/8	47 0/8	40 1/8	6	7	Beaverhead County	MT	Fred C. Church	1991	3921
302 1/8	44 5/8	44 7/8	42 1/8	6	6	Routt County	CO	Tim Oestmann	1992	3921
302 1/8	45 7/8	47 4/8	38 1/8	6	6	Okotoks	ALB	Brent Brown	1994	3921
302 1/8	48 1/8	50 2/8	26 2/8	7	7	Catron County	NM	Duane "Corky" Richardson	1995	3921
302 1/8	40 2/8	40 3/8	38 5/8	6	6	Big Horn County	WY	Mark Masamori	1996	3921
302 1/8	52 0/8	51 0/8	38 1/8	6	6	Navajo County	AZ	Frank S. Noska IV	2000	3921
302 1/8	48 6/8	48 6/8	44 5/8	6	6	Johnson County	WY	Brian Schick	2001	3921
302 1/8	45 4/8	46 6/8	46 6/8	7	6	Columbia County	WA	David E. Fisk	2003	3921
302 1/8	50 4/8	51 1/8	43 3/8	6	6	Jefferson County	OR	Alan Nelson	2006	3921
*302 1/8	47 0/8	45 1/8	32 3/8	6	6	Montezuma County	CO	Gregory J. Miller	2007	3921
302 0/8	45 0/8	46 6/8	40 0/8	6	6	Archuleta County	CO	Billy Ellis	1977	3935
302 0/8	50 4/8	49 6/8	38 6/8	6	6	Eagle County	CO	John Schell	1980	3935
302 0/8	42 3/8	41 6/8	31 0/8	6	6	Routt County	CO	Kevin Stailey	1981	3935
302 0/8	47 6/8	48 0/8	35 4/8	6	7	Missoula County	MT	Richard W. Talbert	1986	3935
302 0/8	44 0/8	43 7/8	37 4/8	6	6	Fremont County	WY	Edward A. Dykstra	1988	3935
302 0/8	44 6/8	45 2/8	34 0/8	6	6	Lemhi County	ID	Buster Williams	1990	3935
302 0/8	51 3/8	53 0/8	36 6/8	6	6	Taos County	NM	Jeffrey D. Butts	1995	3935
302 0/8	47 0/8	47 7/8	36 6/8	5	5	Laramie County	WY	Robert Allen Robbins	1996	3935
302 0/8	48 0/8	47 5/8	35 6/8	6	6	Coconino County	AZ	Daniel C. Parks	1998	3935
302 0/8	49 3/8	48 7/8	40 2/8	6	6	Apache County	AZ	Aaron J. Scott	1999	3935
302 0/8	49 1/8	47 7/8	37 4/8	6	6	Lewis & Clark County	MT	Lance A. Lott	2000	3935
302 0/8	46 0/8	47 0/8	40 2/8	6	6	Montrose County	CO	Joshua A. Boyd	2009	3935
*302 0/8	44 7/8	43 0/8	34 2/8	6	6	Pitkin County	CO	Joel Franks	2010	3935
301 7/8	44 2/8	44 2/8	38 3/8	6	6	Larimer County	CO	Adrian H. Farmer, Jr.	1984	3948
301 7/8	53 3/8	54 4/8	38 1/8	6	6	Coconino County	AZ	Michael N. Miller	1998	3948
301 7/8	49 4/8	49 0/8	40 7/8	6	6	Socorro County	NM	Mark R. Miller	1999	3948
301 7/8	44 6/8	44 7/8	34 3/8	6	6	Converse County	WY	Jeff Turpin	2003	3948
301 7/8	44 5/8	47 3/8	35 1/8	6	6	Lincoln County	NM	Terrence Horan	2005	3948
301 7/8	41 5/8	42 4/8	38 1/8	6	7	Gunnison County	CO	Scott Alan Marschke	2009	3948
301 6/8	47 2/8	46 2/8	36 0/8	6	6	Missoula County	MT	Guy Leibenguth	1976	3954
301 6/8	40 6/8	40 5/8	33 6/8	6	6	Yakima County	WA	James Garner	1989	3954
301 6/8	55 7/8	55 2/8	41 0/8	6	6	Millard County	UT	Chad J. Hall	1995	3954
301 6/8	51 0/8	49 4/8	33 4/8	6	6	Mesa County	CO	Alan Barrett	2000	3954
301 6/8	46 0/8	46 0/8	38 4/8	6	6	Costilla County	CO	Michael Benrud	2003	3954
301 6/8	43 7/8	45 3/8	33 0/8	6	5	Sheridan County	WY	Brian Morgan	2005	3954
301 6/8	47 1/8	47 3/8	31 4/8	6	6	Moffat County	CO	Jerry Dietz	2005	3954
301 6/8	48 1/8	49 3/8	29 2/8	5	6	Fremont County	WY	Douglas P. Rentschler	2009	3954
301 6/8	47 3/8	51 1/8	45 0/8	7	6	Mora County	NM	Craig Lawrence	2010	3954
301 5/8	44 1/8	42 2/8	39 2/8	7	7	Ravalli County	MT	Dick Kerr	1977	3963
301 5/8	44 0/8	41 2/8	31 5/8	7	6	Grant County	NM	Raymond Albertina	1991	3963
301 5/8	49 2/8	50 1/8	38 7/8	6	7	Ravalli County	MT	Ned Coorough	1992	3963
301 5/8	47 3/8	45 2/8	42 5/8	6	6	Coconino County	AZ	Ron Eckerman	1995	3963
301 5/8	46 4/8	47 3/8	36 7/8	6	6	Rich County	UT	Glen O. Hallows	1996	3963
301 5/8	46 2/8	47 4/8	40 6/8	7	8	Kootenai County	ID	D. V. Moyer	1996	3963
301 5/8	50 0/8	50 0/8	39 5/8	5	6	Bonner County	ID	Ron Britton	1997	3963
301 5/8	55 6/8	52 3/8	42 7/8	6	6	Socorro County	NM	Vernon C. Smedley	1997	3963
301 5/8	47 7/8	48 7/8	37 5/8	6	6	Sierra County	NM	Dave Holt	1998	3963
301 5/8	48 3/8	49 3/8	36 3/8	6	6	Catron County	NM	Jim Jones	1999	3963
301 5/8	46 3/8	46 2/8	43 7/8	6	6	Greenlee County	AZ	Roy L. Wyatt	2000	3963
301 5/8	43 5/8	43 5/8	44 0/8	6	6	Park County	WY	David G. Misner	2002	3963
301 5/8	44 0/8	43 2/8	44 0/8	8	7	Catron County	NM	Neal Barron	2003	3963
301 5/8	44 0/8	44 5/8	45 1/8	6	6	Albany County	WY	W. Scott Brandon	2004	3963
301 5/8	49 4/8	50 0/8	37 5/8	6	6	Coconino County	AZ	Douglas E. Callies	2005	3963
301 4/8	45 1/8	44 6/8	37 0/8	6	6	Lewis & Clark County	MT	Doug Conrady	1979	3978
301 4/8	47 3/8	44 5/8	41 1/8	6	7	Park County	MT	Donald Lee Ferguson	1988	3978
301 4/8	45 5/8	44 2/8	42 0/8	6	6	Madison County	MT	Vaughn Ballard	1989	3978
301 4/8	43 3/8	42 4/8	33 1/8	6	9	Wallowa County	OR	Tim Andrew Collins	1990	3978
301 4/8	46 0/8	47 0/8	40 2/8	6	6	McKinley County	NM	Ben Gibson	1991	3978
301 4/8	48 0/8	43 5/8	36 4/8	8	7	Yakima County	WA	Mark Wilcox	2000	3978
301 4/8	46 5/8	47 3/8	34 6/8	6	6	Idaho County	ID	Jacob Deberg	2002	3978
301 4/8	49 5/8	48 1/8	41 0/8	6	6	Jefferson County	CO	Gerry Leibfried	2003	3978
301 4/8	44 5/8	43 1/8	28 1/8	6	7	Garfield County	MT	Richard Rankka	2005	3978
301 3/8	47 1/8	48 4/8	35 5/8	5	6	Catron County	NM	Timothy C. Junior	1992	3987
301 3/8	46 2/8	45 2/8	40 0/8	6	6	Clearwater County	ID	David Thorkildsen	1996	3987
301 3/8	44 0/8	44 5/8	36 3/8	6	6	Coconino County	AZ	Paul Fritzinger	1997	3987
301 3/8	45 3/8	45 1/8	35 1/8	6	6	Montrose County	CO	Michael Dudzinski	2000	3987

719

AMERICAN ELK (TYPICAL ANTLERS)

Minimum Score 260   Continued

SCORE	LENGTH OF R MAIN BEAM L	INSIDE SPREAD	NUMBER OF R POINTS L		AREA	STATE/ PROVINCE	HUNTER'S NAME	DATE	RANK
301 3/8	46 2/8 46 4/8	38 7/8	6	6	Latah County	ID	Jacob L. Vowels	2003	3987
301 3/8	45 0/8 47 2/8	40 7/8	7	6	Converse County	WY	Ken Ball	2004	3987
301 3/8	46 5/8 47 2/8	33 3/8	6	6	Lemhi County	ID	Tyler Moore	2004	3987
301 3/8	51 3/8 49 4/8	43 7/8	6	6	Sandoval County	NM	Michael A. Lee	2005	3987
301 3/8	42 4/8 43 6/8	31 2/8	7	6	Saguache County	CO	Aaron Polkowske	2006	3987
301 2/8	47 6/8 47 5/8	39 4/8	6	6	Catron County	NM	Dale Mansfield	1995	3996
301 2/8	50 2/8 49 4/8	38 4/8	6	6	Narraway River	ALB	Rick Martin	1996	3996
301 2/8	52 0/8 53 0/8	37 3/8	6	6	McKinley County	NM	Billy Gordon	1997	3996
301 2/8	45 1/8 45 3/8	38 2/8	6	6	Coconino County	AZ	James Cook	2004	3996
301 2/8	51 1/8 50 0/8	32 4/8	7	7	Catron County	NM	Gordon Dixon	2007	3996
301 2/8	44 0/8 45 0/8	38 0/8	6	6	Fergus County	MT	Steven V. Jenkins	2008	3996
301 2/8	49 2/8 50 0/8	40 2/8	6	6	Garfield County	CO	Gary Devereaux	2009	3996
*301 2/8	52 2/8 53 2/8	35 0/8	6	5	Rio Blanco County	CO	Tony M. Wiegel	2009	3996
301 2/8	50 6/8 49 2/8	35 0/8	6	6	Archuleta County	CO	Geoffrey Hesslink	2009	3996
301 2/8	46 5/8 48 2/8	31 6/8	6	6	Valley County	MT	Gordon Severude	2009	3996
301 1/8	45 0/8 41 2/8	38 4/8	7	6	Teton County	WY	Craig Sorenson	1979	4006
301 1/8	43 7/8 44 1/8	32 1/8	6	6	Clearwater County	ID	Jim Walters	1981	4006
301 1/8	47 3/8 45 7/8	37 7/8	6	6	Lincoln County	MT	Paul Buti	1984	4006
301 1/8	46 6/8 47 7/8	36 3/8	6	6	Larimer County	CO	Randy A. Reeves	1993	4006
301 1/8	45 0/8 45 0/8	38 5/8	6	6	Rio Arriba County	NM	Steve Boham	2002	4006
301 1/8	44 0/8 45 1/8	39 5/8	7	6	Jumping Pound Creek	ALB	Archie J. Nesbitt	2002	4006
301 1/8	55 4/8 53 7/8	40 7/8	6	6	Cascade County	MT	Brian McCoy	2003	4006
301 1/8	48 2/8 46 3/8	34 7/8	6	6	Union County	OR	Dale Boyd	2003	4006
301 1/8	45 4/8 45 4/8	40 1/8	7	6	Caribou County	ID	Bryce Thurgood	2004	4006
301 1/8	45 7/8 47 2/8	41 3/8	7	7	Catron County	NM	Buck Horn	2005	4006
301 1/8	44 5/8 45 4/8	35 3/8	6	6	Big Horn County	WY	Randy Burtis	2009	4006
301 1/8	44 6/8 46 2/8	37 3/8	6	6	Mesa County	CO	Don Clark	2009	4006
301 0/8	46 2/8 49 6/8	38 4/8	5	6	Sandoval County	NM	Fred J. McDonald	1985	4018
301 0/8	48 7/8 48 3/8	36 6/8	6	6	Coconino County	AZ	Roy E. Grace	1993	4018
301 0/8	47 0/8 43 7/8	37 7/8	7	7	Larimer County	CO	Brad Riley	1999	4018
301 0/8	46 6/8 45 6/8	40 2/8	6	6	Valley County	ID	Candess L. Pirnie	2000	4018
301 0/8	44 7/8 46 3/8	35 4/8	6	6	Mesa County	CO	Mike Bates	2001	4018
301 0/8	43 4/8 45 1/8	35 4/8	6	6	Catron County	NM	James E. Willard	2003	4018
301 0/8	48 7/8 47 0/8	42 2/8	6	6	Catron County	NM	Marvin Harding	2003	4018
*301 0/8	44 4/3 46 2/8	37 0/8	6	6	Rich County	UT	Tres Childs	2004	4018
301 0/8	47 0/8 45 0/8	34 2/8	6	6	White Pine County	NV	Thomas Scoggin	2004	4018
*301 0/8	49 6/8 47 7/8	34 2/8	6	6	Greenlee County	AZ	Sean C. Regan	2005	4018
301 0/8	45 7/8 45 1/8	42 4/8	6	6	Albany County	WY	Brady Balzan	2009	4018
300 7/8	45 6/8 44 5/8	39 1/8	6	5	Teton County	MT	Bill Schenck	1979	4029
300 7/8	48 2/8 51 6/8	34 3/8	6	6	Converse County	WY	Kevin Christopherson	1995	4029
300 7/8	42 1/8 43 2/8	33 5/8	6	7	Park County	CO	Mark Martin	1995	4029
300 7/8	44 2/8 45 3/8	45 6/8	6	6	Boise County	ID	Jason L. Angell	1996	4029
300 7/8	46 4/8 49 5/8	34 1/8	6	6	Rio Blanco County	CO	Jim Dougherty	1996	4029
300 7/8	50 0/8 50 6/8	35 3/8	6	6	Garfield County	MT	D. Mitch Kottas	1997	4029
300 7/8	52 0/8 52 7/8	37 5/8	5	5	Apache County	AZ	Jim Scott	1999	4029
300 7/8	46 6/8 48 0/8	39 7/8	6	6	Camas County	ID	Robert L. Rhoads, Jr.	2001	4029
300 7/8	48 1/8 48 5/8	36 1/8	6	6	Park County	WY	Dave Justmann	2001	4029
*300 7/8	46 2/8 45 3/8	29 5/8	6	6	Coconino County	AZ	Jim Riggle	2009	4029
300 7/8	46 6/8 47 2/8	42 1/8	6	6	Sandoval County	NM	Lloyd Wood	2010	4029
300 6/8	42 1/8 43 7/8	36 4/8	6	6	Sheridan County	WY	Kerry Struckman	1992	4040
300 6/8	47 6/8 48 5/8	35 1/8	8	8	Bonneville County	ID	Danel R. Thomas	1996	4040
300 6/8	49 1/8 48 0/8	36 0/8	6	6	Blaine County	ID	Tim W. Chadwick	1997	4040
300 6/8	42 7/8 42 2/8	35 4/8	6	6	Cutbank River	ALB	Brent Watson	1998	4040
300 6/8	46 7/8 49 6/8	36 4/8	6	7	Petroleum County	MT	Joseph M. Mucka	2002	4040
300 6/8	48 0/8 48 2/8	40 4/8	6	6	Baker County	OR	Glenn Goergen	2005	4040
*300 6/8	44 5/8 44 5/8	35 3/8	7	7	Coconino County	AZ	Brian Anton Rimsza	2005	4040
300 6/8	48 4/8 47 0/8	35 2/8	6	6	Lewis & Clark County	MT	Lee Fleming	2005	4040
300 6/8	47 7/8 46 5/8	33 4/8	7	6	Clackamas County	OR	James Ball	2006	4040
300 6/8	42 3/8 42 6/8	39 0/8	5	5	Deschutes County	OR	Robert Allen McDaniel	2006	4040
*300 6/8	48 0/8 47 5/8	37 0/8	6	6	Meade County	SD	Dale D. Johnson	2008	4040
300 5/8	44 3/8 44 5/8	44 6/8	6	6	Beaverhead County	MT	Monty Moravec	1989	4051
300 5/8	46 3/8 44 0/8	33 3/8	7	6	Benewah County	ID	Joel L. Emerson	1991	4051
300 5/8	46 5/8 46 6/8	38 1/8	6	6	Lemhi County	ID	Brad White	1996	4051
300 5/8	47 1/8 43 5/8	43 3/8	6	6	Apache County	AZ	Bryan R. Yorksmith	2001	4051
300 5/8	43 4/8 42 5/8	30 5/8	6	6	Rosebud County	MT	Craig Compher, Sr.	2002	4051
*300 5/8	46 2/8 47 0/8	33 0/8	7	7	Sanders County	MT	Christopher J. Nothstein	2005	4051
*300 5/8	45 5/8 46 7/8	39 7/8	7	7	Garfield County	MT	Delbert J. Auker	2006	4051
300 5/8	42 4/8 43 7/8	38 5/8	6	6	Gunnison County	CO	David T. Crigler	2007	4051
300 4/8	42 2/8 44 4/8	38 6/8	6	6	Boundary County	ID	John Thomas	1992	4059
300 4/8	44 1/8 47 1/8	43 4/8	6	6	Lewis & Clark County	MT	Dr. David Baldridge	1993	4059
300 4/8	45 3/8 45 4/8	38 6/8	6	6	Lincoln County	MT	Ron Halvorson	1994	4059
300 4/8	45 7/8 45 2/8	36 4/8	6	6	Boise County	ID	Ralph L. Albright	1995	4059
300 4/8	51 7/8 51 0/8	36 6/8	6	6	Columbia County	WA	Michael W. Isdell	1996	4059
300 4/8	50 1/8 49 2/8	43 6/8	6	7	Sublette County	WY	Raymond Kennedy	1996	4059
300 4/8	47 6/8 47 5/8	47 0/8	6	6	Fremont County	WY	David Stepp	1997	4059
300 4/8	50 6/8 47 5/8	38 0/8	6	7	Idaho County	ID	Michael K. DeSantis	2000	4059
300 4/8	52 0/8 52 7/8	31 0/8	6	6	Coconino County	AZ	Dr. Steven L. Lysenko	2001	4059
300 4/8	45 5/8 44 2/8	41 1/8	7	6	Socorro County	NM	Doug Aikin	2002	4059
300 4/8	44 0/8 43 7/8	34 2/8	6	6	Valley County	ID	Mike Joelson	2006	4059
300 4/8	53 5/8 55 5/8	35 6/8	7	7	Yavapai County	AZ	Bryce DeForest	2008	4059
300 3/8	41 5/8 40 0/8	36 1/8	6	6	Fergus County	MT	Randy Cook	1981	4071
300 3/8	46 5/8 44 5/8	44 0/8	7	7	Marion County	OR	Ron Bergeron	1986	4071
300 3/8	47 3/8 48 4/8	30 5/8	6	6	Madison County	MT	Gary Moris	1992	4071
300 3/8	47 4/8 45 3/8	37 3/8	6	6	Dolores County	CO	Todd Giles	1992	4071
300 3/8	45 7/8 45 3/8	40 3/8	6	6	Madison County	MT	Lee Poole	1993	4071
300 3/8	51 0/8 50 0/8	40 5/8	6	6	La Plata County	CO	Walter G. Sievers	1994	4071
300 3/8	44 7/8 45 1/8	29 3/8	6	7	Phillips County	MT	Stephen T. Musser	1995	4071
300 3/8	50 7/8 50 4/8	32 3/8	6	6	El Paso County	CO	James W. Holder	2000	4071
300 3/8	50 2/8 48 2/8	33 3/8	6	6	Petroleum County	MT	Glen Berry	2001	4071
300 3/8	46 6/8 46 0/8	40 1/8	6	6	Meagher County	MT	Kerry Robertson	2003	4071
*300 3/8	47 6/8 46 4/8	41 5/8	6	6	Routt County	CO	Cedar Beauregard	2007	4071
300 2/8	46 2/8 45 3/8	41 0/8	6	6	McKinley County	NM	Mark Sauters	1987	4082
300 2/8	45 7/8 46 6/8	38 2/8	5	6	Coconino County	AZ	Bradley Mitchell Irish	1990	4082
300 2/8	41 0/8 41 2/8	38 2/8	6	6	Petroleum County	MT	Ron Kukus	1991	4082
300 2/8	49 4/8 47 6/8	33 4/8	6	6	Garfield County	CO	Judson Smith	1997	4082

720

AMERICAN ELK (TYPICAL ANTLERS)

Minimum Score 260   Continued

SCORE	LENGTH OF R MAIN BEAM L	INSIDE SPREAD	NUMBER OF R POINTS L	AREA	STATE/ PROVINCE	HUNTER'S NAME	DATE	RANK
300 2/8	47 5/8 51 1/8	49 2/8	6 6	Duchesne County	UT	Rodney Bump	2003	4082
300 2/8	46 0/8 46 3/8	39 0/8	6 6	Hinsdale County	CO	L. Wayne Bell	2003	4082
300 2/8	46 3/8 47 2/8	35 2/8	6 6	Sanpete County	UT	Jerl Savage	2004	4082
300 2/8	44 2/8 48 4/8	47 0/8	6 6	Linn County	OR	Gerald D. Coulter	2004	4082
300 2/8	51 2/8 51 3/8	41 0/8	6 6	Idaho County	ID	Mike S. Ihnat	2004	4082
300 2/8	42 7/8 42 4/8	38 0/8	6 6	Park County	MT	David Hreha	2006	4082
300 2/8	43 1/8 44 7/8	36 6/8	6 6	Park County	WY	Jason Stafford	2006	4082
*300 2/8	53 3/8 52 0/8	36 2/8	6 5	Carbon County	WY	Fred Heizler	2007	4082
300 2/8	51 7/8 49 4/8	36 4/8	6 6	Mora County	NM	Bobby Watkins	2008	4082
300 2/8	46 2/8 43 5/8	43 6/8	6 6	Garfield County	UT	L. Kevin Wright	2009	4082
300 2/8	48 7/8 46 4/8	40 0/8	6 6	Mineral County	CO	Richard Orchard	2010	4082
300 1/8	45 4/8 47 4/8	39 7/8	6 6	San Miguel County	NM	Lawrence Stiscak	1977	4097
300 1/8	46 3/8 44 2/8	35 7/8	6 6	Clearwater County	ID	Danny Moore	1985	4097
300 1/8	46 3/8 44 7/8	36 1/8	6 6	Sandoval County	NM	Bob Young	1990	4097
300 1/8	43 3/8 44 6/8	38 3/8	6 6	La Plata County	CO	Bob E. Wren	1992	4097
300 1/8	44 6/8 44 5/8	41 3/8	6 6	Fremont County	ID	James K. Nash	1996	4097
300 1/8	49 5/8 51 3/8	36 7/8	6 6	Socorro County	NM	Marvin H. Walter	1997	4097
300 1/8	44 3/8 45 3/8	40 3/8	6 6	Park County	MT	Fred Regenfuss	1999	4097
300 1/8	48 5/8 47 4/8	37 5/8	6 6	Wallowa County	OR	Robert L. Morton	2003	4097
*300 1/8	44 0/8 44 0/8	32 1/8	6 6	Park County	CO	Robert J. Hammers	2004	4097
300 1/8	47 1/8 43 3/8	35 1/8	6 6	Powell County	MT	Steven Blessing	2005	4097
*300 1/8	42 4/8 43 6/8	36 5/8	6 6	Teton County	WY	Derek Smith	2006	4097
300 1/8	49 2/8 49 3/8	35 5/8	6 5	Wasatch County	UT	Chad W. Doyle	2007	4097
300 1/8	46 6/8 47 4/8	34 3/8	6 6	Beaver County	UT	Danny Moore	2009	4097
300 0/8	43 0/8 44 2/8	43 2/8	6 6	Albany County	WY	Jerry Bowen	1980	4110
300 0/8	45 2/8 44 5/8	47 3/8	6 6	Beaverhead County	MT	Greg L. Munther	1980	4110
300 0/8	39 5/8 42 0/8	37 4/8	7 6	Coconino County	AZ	Mike Kentera	1985	4110
300 0/8	47 4/8 46 0/8	40 0/8	6 6	Missoula County	MT	Anthony K Nease	1985	4110
300 0/8	48 5/8 48 4/8	38 4/8	6 6	Adams County	ID	Robert Dowen	1985	4110
300 0/8	41 4/8 42 6/8	34 6/8	6 6	Catron County	NM	Ned Smith	1991	4110
300 0/8	45 4/8 46 7/8	38 1/8	6 7	Catron County	NM	Rafael Espino	1994	4110
300 0/8	52 0/8 50 6/8	35 2/8	6 6	Lemhi County	ID	Kody L. Harrison	1995	4110
300 0/8	43 4/8 44 2/8	33 2/8	6 6	Natrona County	WY	Keith Frick	1995	4110
300 0/8	45 4/8 44 7/8	35 2/8	7 6	Union County	OR	Randy Carter	1997	4110
300 0/8	51 4/8 51 2/8	44 4/8	6 6	Garfield County	UT	Richard D. Lowe	1999	4110
300 0/8	51 2/8 49 6/8	34 0/8	6 7	Phillips County	MT	Donald F. Holz	1999	4110
300 0/8	49 6/8 49 3/8	53 4/8	5 5	Mora County	NM	Andy Kent	2000	4110
300 0/8	43 4/8 44 0/8	36 4/8	6 6	Routt County	CO	Darrell J. Prielipp	2000	4110
300 0/8	42 2/8 45 0/8	40 2/8	6 6	Fergus County	MT	Lynn Bowman	2000	4110
300 0/8	44 2/8 54 2/8	37 6/8	6 6	Coconino County	AZ	Lew Webb	2003	4110
*300 0/8	48 4/8 46 4/8	47 0/8	6 6	Ouray County	CO	John Pannell	2004	4110
*300 0/8	48 6/8 45 1/8	41 6/8	6 6	Sierra County	NM	James P. Murphy	2004	4110
*300 0/8	48 3/8 50 1/8	32 4/8	5 6	Fergus County	MT	James Overholt	2007	4110
300 0/8	50 3/8 49 6/8	41 2/8	6 6	Missoula County	MT	Amber Alexander	2010	4110
299 7/8	51 0/8 54 0/8	41 0/8	6 7	Fergus County	MT	Charles R. Bowman	1966	4130
299 7/8	44 4/8 44 0/8	36 3/8	5 5	Routt County	CO	Mark Wuerthele	1987	4130
299 7/8	47 4/8 43 6/8	36 3/8	6 6	Rio Blanco County	CO	Mike Zech	1995	4130
299 7/8	44 7/8 45 3/8	41 5/8	6 7	Beaverhead County	MT	Larry Gerlach	1995	4130
299 7/8	49 1/8 47 3/8	35 7/8	6 6	Catron County	NM	Sam Y. Perone	1998	4130
299 7/8	48 3/8 46 4/8	39 7/8	5 5	Greenlee County	AZ	Jon Buseman	1998	4130
299 7/8	49 4/8 50 1/8	34 7/8	6 6	Shoshone County	ID	Kerry "Bama" Fann	2001	4130
299 7/8	45 7/8 45 7/8	38 7/8	6 6	Petroleum County	MT	Randy Bowler	2001	4130
299 7/8	46 2/8 47 3/8	48 4/8	7 6	Custer County	ID	Mike Zavadlov	2002	4130
299 7/8	47 6/8 46 3/8	44 7/8	6 6	Wayne County	UT	Andy Low	2004	4130
299 7/8	47 7/8 49 5/8	37 1/8	6 6	Sanders County	MT	Josh Conat	2004	4130
299 7/8	44 0/8 42 6/8	38 1/8	6 6	Catron County	NM	Stephen A. Dougherty	2009	4130
299 6/8	50 6/8 48 1/8	37 0/8	6 6	Albany County	WY	Jerry Bowen	1982	4142
299 6/8	41 4/8 42 1/8	37 0/8	6 6	Shoshone County	ID	Glen Berry	1987	4142
299 6/8	53 2/8 53 7/8	44 6/8	6 6	Coconino County	AZ	Michael L. Campbell	1987	4142
299 6/8	50 4/8 49 2/8	35 6/8	6 6	Flathead County	MT	Ken White	1989	4142
299 6/8	43 1/8 44 6/8	37 0/8	6 6	Caribou County	ID	Steven J. Slaton	1994	4142
299 6/8	44 6/8 46 1/8	32 6/8	6 6	Lemhi County	ID	John McCarthy	1996	4142
299 6/8	49 0/8 49 3/8	34 2/8	6 6	Custer County	ID	Robin Glantz	1997	4142
299 6/8	48 4/8 52 5/8	40 0/8	6 6	Coconino County	AZ	Donna L. Telles	1998	4142
299 6/8	51 4/8 52 2/8	33 2/8	6 6	Clark County	ID	Chad Berry	1998	4142
299 6/8	47 1/8 47 0/8	41 4/8	6 6	Pierce County	WA	Dan Zimmer	1999	4142
299 6/8	47 4/8 46 3/8	40 6/8	6 6	Kittitas County	WA	Tom J. Little	2002	4142
*299 6/8	48 1/8 49 6/8	31 7/8	7 6	Moffat County	CO	Dave Holt	2004	4142
299 6/8	48 6/8 50 3/8	36 2/8	5 6	Montrose County	CO	William Wade	2005	4142
299 6/8	48 3/8 48 0/8	29 4/8	6 6	Coconino County	AZ	Greg A. Schweppe	2005	4142
*299 6/8	49 0/8 51 1/8	37 4/8	6 6	San Juan County	CO	Bret Ackerman	2006	4142
299 6/8	47 7/8 49 3/8	39 4/8	6 6	Park County	WY	Greg Paris	2006	4142
299 6/8	45 6/8 46 7/8	39 0/8	6 6	Baker County	OR	Jevon A. Struve	2007	4142
*299 6/8	48 0/8 47 3/8	30 2/8	5 6	Catron County	NM	Steven W. Cotten	2009	4142
299 5/8	48 0/8 48 6/8	34 1/8	5 6	Taos County	NM	Bubba Finstad	1987	4160
299 5/8	45 2/8 44 7/8	43 5/8	6 7	Klamath County	OR	Ron Botsford	1991	4160
299 5/8	48 2/8 49 2/8	32 1/8	6 6	Mohave County	AZ	Greg Carmichael	1992	4160
299 5/8	50 5/8 50 3/8	40 2/8	7 6	King County	WA	David C. Andress	1993	4160
299 5/8	46 2/8 47 7/8	37 1/8	7 7	Dolores County	CO	Gaylen Schaugaard	1995	4160
299 5/8	45 7/8 44 1/8	35 5/8	6 6	Valencia County	NM	Paul H. Becraft	1998	4160
299 5/8	47 5/8 45 5/8	41 7/8	6 6	Larimer County	CO	Bill Harvey	1999	4160
299 5/8	45 2/8 42 2/8	37 7/8	7 6	Coconino County	AZ	Lonnie Crabtree	1999	4160
299 5/8	44 3/8 47 3/8	37 3/8	6 6	Fergus County	MT	Lewis Clark Tennant	2003	4160
299 5/8	48 0/8 48 0/8	38 7/8	6 6	La Plata County	CO	Daniel E. Parkinson	2006	4160
299 4/8	44 2/8 45 7/8	34 0/8	6 6	White Pine County	NV	Audrey Hanson	1998	4170
299 4/8	47 5/8 46 4/8	38 2/8	6 7	Caribou County	ID	Thomas L. Hulme	2000	4170
299 4/8	44 5/8 44 2/8	37 2/8	6 6	Swan River	MAN	Brad J. Parker	2000	4170
299 4/8	39 6/8 42 0/8	46 0/8	5 5	Lincoln County	NM	Michael Gorman	2001	4170
299 4/8	47 7/8 47 1/8	38 6/8	6 6	Phillips County	MT	Jason Brenden	2002	4170
299 4/8	47 4/8 47 2/8	39 6/8	6 7	Marion County	OR	Kelly Witham	2003	4170
299 4/8	46 0/8 45 7/8	36 1/8	7 6	Garfield County	MT	Mark L. Meyer	2004	4170
299 4/8	50 7/8 49 2/8	41 4/8	6 6	Lewis & Clark County	MT	Ron Gibson	2004	4170
299 4/8	41 0/8 39 6/8	40 4/8	6 6	Petroleum County	MT	Todd Kidd	2005	4170
299 4/8	49 5/8 50 7/8	41 0/8	6 6	Greenlee County	AZ	Jose S. Montano, Jr.	2005	4170
299 3/8	45 2/8 46 2/8	38 3/8	6 6	Gunnison County	CO	Gene Chastain	1985	4180

AMERICAN ELK (TYPICAL ANTLERS)

Minimum Score 260   Continued

SCORE	LENGTH OF R MAIN BEAM L		INSIDE SPREAD	NUMBER OF R POINTS L		AREA	STATE/ PROVINCE	HUNTER'S NAME	DATE	RANK
299 3/8	42 1/8	42 3/8	42 4/8	6	8	Coconino County	AZ	Tony W. Zimbaro	1992	4180
299 3/8	51 3/8	54 0/8	38 3/8	6	6	Harney County	OR	Patrick E. Wheeler	1995	4180
299 3/8	43 7/8	43 7/8	36 7/8	6	6	Routt County	CO	Steve B. Cooper	1997	4180
299 3/8	43 1/8	46 1/8	27 7/8	7	6	Catron County	NM	Glen R. Cousins	2001	4180
299 3/8	48 5/8	49 3/8	39 5/8	7	7	Custer County	ID	Nate Simmons	2001	4180
*299 3/8	49 0/8	48 4/8	33 7/8	6	6	Garfield County	MT	David W. Bentele	2005	4180
299 2/8	47 2/8	46 1/8	34 4/8	6	6	Caribou County	ID	Tex Wolfley	1979	4187
299 2/8	51 4/8	49 7/8	37 2/8	6	6	Coconino County	AZ	Larry VanLiew	1983	4187
299 2/8	46 6/8	43 3/8	32 2/8	6	7	Idaho County	ID	Neal Forrester	1989	4187
299 2/8	47 2/8	48 1/8	39 0/8	6	6	Custer County	ID	Robert Ward	1995	4187
299 2/8	46 7/8	46 3/8	34 4/8	6	5	McKinley County	NM	Ronald Hanna	1997	4187
299 2/8	39 5/8	46 2/8	33 4/8	6	6	Johnson County	WY	David S. Harness	2000	4187
299 2/8	52 6/8	49 4/8	39 4/8	6	6	Lincoln County	NM	Tony Wilson	2002	4187
299 2/8	43 0/8	41 4/8	41 4/8	6	6	Wasatch County	UT	Stuart Gehrke	2004	4187
*299 2/8	48 3/8	50 6/8	38 0/8	6	6	Fergus County	MT	Mark Gregorich	2005	4187
*299 2/8	42 6/8	41 0/8	36 4/8	7	6	Granite County	MT	Blane Dale	2009	4187
299 1/8	44 2/8	41 2/8	32 5/8	6	6	Lincoln County	WY	Richard Peart	1980	4197
299 1/8	47 0/8	48 1/8	39 5/8	6	6	Madison County	MT	Royce A. Carroll	1988	4197
299 1/8	51 4/8	50 1/8	38 6/8	7	8	Catron County	NM	Thomas Merritt	1990	4197
299 1/8	45 2/8	47 6/8	34 1/8	6	7	Catron County	NM	Jules Pacheco	1990	4197
299 1/8	46 5/8	45 2/8	36 2/8	7	7	Boundary County	ID	Roger N. Myers	1992	4197
299 1/8	48 2/8	49 7/8	41 7/8	6	7	Sandoval County	NM	Melvin Sloan	1992	4197
299 1/8	45 6/8	46 6/8	39 4/8	7	8	Lemhi County	ID	David Tande	1993	4197
299 1/8	51 4/8	50 6/8	37 3/8	6	6	Petroleum County	MT	Mark Hegge	1996	4197
299 1/8	48 4/8	49 2/8	38 3/8	6	6	Coconino County	AZ	Michael D. Wall	1998	4197
299 1/8	44 0/8	43 6/8	33 7/8	6	6	Big Horn County	WY	Deven David	2000	4197
299 1/8	41 5/8	41 5/8	37 3/8	6	6	Caribou County	ID	Cary Jellison	2000	4197
299 1/8	46 6/8	45 2/8	34 1/8	7	7	Grand County	UT	Josh Whittaker	2004	4197
299 1/8	50 7/8	49 7/8	36 3/8	7	7	Musselshell County	MT	Brad Walker	2006	4197
299 1/8	48 3/8	48 6/8	36 5/8	6	6	Rio Arriba County	NM	Wendy Christensen Senk	2006	4197
299 0/8	42 3/8	43 1/8	33 0/8	6	6	Mineral County	CO	Gary Oden	1976	4211
299 0/8	45 5/8	46 4/8	37 2/8	6	6	Powell County	MT	Paul Brunner	1979	4211
299 0/8	46 1/8	47 3/8	42 0/8	6	6	Park County	MT	Joe Skaggs	1988	4211
299 0/8	45 0/8	46 3/8	40 4/8	6	6	Clearwater County	ID	James L. Tucker	1992	4211
299 0/8	49 2/8	51 2/8	39 4/8	6	6	Klamath County	OR	Gene Hamilton	1997	4211
299 0/8	44 5/8	46 4/8	31 7/8	8	7	Phillips County	MT	Layton W. Foltyn	1997	4211
299 0/8	44 6/8	44 0/8	35 0/8	6	6	Petroleum County	MT	Eddie McGreevey	1998	4211
299 0/8	49 7/8	48 1/8	39 3/8	7	7	Kootenai County	ID	Jon C. Schnider	1998	4211
*299 0/8	45 3/8	46 6/8	37 4/8	7	7	Catron County	NM	Mike Bordovsky	2001	4211
299 0/8	45 0/8	46 1/8	37 0/8	6	6	Gallatin County	MT	Thomas A. Tiedemann	2001	4211
299 0/8	46 0/8	42 0/8	38 0/8	6	6	Socorro County	NM	Todd M. Hewing	2003	4211
299 0/8	48 6/8	50 0/8	35 1/8	7	6	Apache County	AZ	Robert A. Oines	2003	4211
299 0/8	46 6/8	45 7/8	35 4/8	6	7	Idaho County	ID	Richard C. McCormick	2003	4211
299 0/8	46 7/8	47 4/8	35 6/8	7	7	Lane County	OR	Fred B. Harp	2004	4211
299 0/8	46 0/8	44 4/8	38 2/8	6	6	Sheridan County	WY	Ronald E. Olson	2004	4211
298 7/8	45 5/8	46 1/8	39 7/8	6	6	Jefferson County	CO	Jerry Grueneberg	1989	4226
298 7/8	45 5/8	46 4/8	35 3/8	6	6	Coconino County	AZ	Craig Dunlap	1993	4226
298 7/8	52 6/8	50 3/8	36 1/8	6	6	Platte County	WY	Jeff Murray	1994	4226
298 7/8	51 5/8	51 4/8	35 5/8	6	6	Coconino County	AZ	Phil Villamor	1997	4226
298 7/8	49 3/8	49 2/8	36 1/8	6	6	Catron County	NM	Lynn Saxon	1998	4226
298 7/8	48 3/8	47 6/8	40 3/8	6	5	Sublette County	WY	Rene J. Suda	2001	4226
298 7/8	43 7/8	42 4/8	38 5/8	6	6	Natrona County	WY	Steve Hilde	2006	4226
*298 7/8	48 3/8	46 4/8	29 7/8	6	6	Carbon County	WY	Terry J. Beaver	2008	4226
*298 7/8	46 3/8	48 2/8	33 3/8	6	6	Las Animas County	CO	Lannie B. Philley	2008	4226
298 6/8	46 3/8	46 3/8	31 5/8	6	7	Mineral County	MT	James Kingsley	1983	4235
298 6/8	44 2/8	45 5/8	38 0/8	6	6	Gallatin County	MT	Steven P Hopkins	1984	4235
298 6/8	50 6/8	52 2/8	37 2/8	6	6	Catron County	NM	Wayne Keehart	1986	4235
298 6/8	48 1/8	48 4/8	33 0/8	6	6	Sheridan County	WY	Robert H. Bookman	1992	4235
298 6/8	49 5/8	48 0/8	35 6/8	6	6	Missoula County	MT	Lykou Lee	1995	4235
298 6/8	48 4/8	48 4/8	37 0/8	6	6	Archuleta County	CO	John M. Pringle	1996	4235
*298 6/8	38 1/8	38 0/8	37 4/8	6	7	Fremont County	CO	Robert Baker	1998	4235
298 6/8	50 2/8	49 6/8	38 0/8	6	6	Greenlee County	AZ	Bill Bishop, Sr.	1999	4235
298 6/8	40 4/8	42 2/8	39 4/8	6	6	Larimer County	CO	Merle R. Foster	2001	4235
298 6/8	48 7/8	47 7/8	38 4/8	6	6	Wallowa County	OR	Josh R. Rinard	2001	4235
298 6/8	46 0/8	46 7/8	37 6/8	6	6	Kootenai County	ID	Chester A. Sergo	2004	4235
*298 6/8	47 3/8	46 2/8	36 4/8	7	6	Phillips County	MT	Drew Slade	2004	4235
298 6/8	50 3/8	49 1/8	39 4/8	7	6	Apache County	AZ	Ernest Acevedo	2007	4235
298 6/8	49 1/8	51 3/8	33 2/8	7	8	Montrose County	CO	Jeff Profera	2007	4235
*298 6/8	50 1/8	50 3/8	40 0/8	6	6	Harney County	OR	Thomas K. Powell	2010	4235
298 5/8	55 0/8	56 5/8	38 3/8	5	6	Coconino County	AZ	Kevin Cox	1979	4250
298 5/8	46 0/8	47 5/8	41 7/8	6	6	Coconino County	AZ	Pete Shepley	1986	4250
298 5/8	43 3/8	40 0/8	48 6/8	6	6	Gem County	ID	Ron Williams	1988	4250
298 5/8	42 2/8	42 5/8	44 5/8	6	6	Sandoval County	NM	Robert Woeck	1991	4250
298 5/8	45 3/8	44 2/8	40 1/8	6	7	Catron County	NM	Sam Thompson	1992	4250
298 5/8	49 0/8	48 7/8	33 1/8	7	6	Colfax County	NM	Kim Sevitts	1995	4250
298 5/8	53 2/8	51 5/8	38 3/8	6	6	Mesa County	CO	Jimmy Wayne Birchfield	1996	4250
298 5/8	45 3/8	44 4/8	41 3/8	6	6	Gallatin County	MT	Eric N. Nunberg	2001	4250
298 5/8	44 1/8	44 0/8	33 7/8	7	6	Grant County	OR	Eddy Howard	2002	4250
298 5/8	47 3/8	46 3/8	37 1/8	6	6	Union County	OR	Darrell Miller	2003	4250
298 5/8	49 1/8	47 7/8	35 7/8	6	6	Utah County	UT	Joe Bruscato	2003	4250
298 5/8	53 1/8	50 0/8	38 1/8	7	6	Park County	MT	Dave Bash	2004	4250
298 5/8	47 5/8	49 4/8	39 7/8	6	6	Fergus County	MT	Stephen LePage	2005	4250
*298 5/8	45 2/8	47 5/8	35 1/8	7	6	Valley County	ID	Shane Meredith	2007	4250
298 5/8	45 0/8	42 4/8	38 5/8	6	6	Jackson County	CO	Wesley Fisher	2009	4250
298 4/8	44 5/8	46 1/8	42 6/8	6	7	Coconino County	AZ	Les Shelton	1991	4265
298 4/8	48 4/8	46 6/8	36 6/8	6	6	Catron County	NM	Steve Mastagni	1992	4265
298 4/8	47 7/8	48 7/8	42 5/8	6	7	Coconino County	AZ	Tony Leverty	1992	4265
298 4/8	49 4/8	49 2/8	32 0/8	8	5	Sheridan County	WY	Paul Schaumburg	1994	4265
298 4/8	56 2/8	52 0/8	36 4/8	6	6	Sweetwater County	WY	Gordon M. Tattersall	1995	4265
298 4/8	45 1/8	44 5/8	34 5/8	7	6	Caribou County	ID	Daniel J. Pritzl	1997	4265
298 4/8	52 6/8	52 2/8	34 2/8	6	8	Converse County	WY	Frank N. Moore	1997	4265
298 4/8	46 7/8	44 4/8	36 4/8	6	6	Moffat County	CO	Gary Kohler	1998	4265
298 4/8	48 0/8	49 4/8	34 6/8	6	6	Caribou County	ID	Dan Pritzl	2000	4265
298 4/8	46 7/8	46 6/8	38 4/8	6	6	Butte County	ID	Mike O'Toole	2003	4265
298 4/8	47 3/8	47 6/8	40 6/8	6	7	Park County	MT	Michael A. Hudzick	2003	4265

AMERICAN ELK (TYPICAL ANTLERS)

Minimum Score 260

Continued

SCORE	LENGTH OF R MAIN BEAM L	INSIDE SPREAD	NUMBER OF R POINTS L	AREA	STATE/ PROVINCE	HUNTER'S NAME	DATE	RANK
298 4/8	49 1/8 48 2/8	37 4/8	6 6	Alamosa County	CO	Mark Calkins	2004	4265
298 4/8	51 4/8 50 4/8	35 4/8	6 6	Sheridan County	WY	Anthony Piccinno	2005	4265
298 4/8	48 2/8 47 6/8	35 4/8	6 6	Lemhi County	ID	Rick Riemer	2006	4265
298 4/8	43 6/8 43 2/8	44 5/8	6 6	Custer County	SD	Stacey Bork	2007	4265
298 4/8	51 0/8 46 4/8	39 4/8	6 6	Greenlee County	AZ	Danny Crain	2007	4265
298 3/8	44 0/8 45 6/8	49 4/8	7 7	Navajo County	AZ	Stan Hacker	1993	4281
298 3/8	43 1/8 45 0/8	31 1/8	6 6	Phillips County	MT	Larry I. Nordlund	1993	4281
298 3/8	51 6/8 50 7/8	32 3/8	6 6	Costilla County	CO	David L. Bushnell	1999	4281
298 3/8	47 3/8 49 0/8	44 5/8	6 6	Catron County	NM	Robert A. Williams	2000	4281
298 3/8	48 3/8 46 3/8	33 3/8	6 6	Garfield County	MT	Rick Thomas	2001	4281
298 3/8	47 7/8 50 4/8	39 4/8	7 7	Rio Arriba County	NM	Larson Panzy	2003	4281
298 3/8	43 6/8 43 2/8	31 1/8	7 7	Phillips County	MT	Tim Pierson	2005	4281
298 2/8	48 6/8 46 6/8	35 6/8	6 6	Fremont County	ID	Tad Parke	1994	4288
298 2/8	48 1/8 48 3/8	40 4/8	6 6	Catron County	NM	Quentin Fisher	1994	4288
298 2/8	51 4/8 52 3/8	37 0/8	5 6	Grant County	OR	Ted Turano	2001	4288
298 2/8	44 5/8 43 0/8	43 0/8	6 6	Saguache County	CO	James M. Gustin, Sr.	2006	4288
298 2/8	45 3/8 47 1/8	36 6/8	6 6	La Plata County	CO	Kevin Brill	2009	4288
298 1/8	49 7/8 48 0/8	33 1/8	6 6	Park County	WY	Bruce K. Fauskee	1986	4293
298 1/8	46 2/8 47 1/8	33 3/8	6 6	Iron County	UT	Brad Robinson	1992	4293
298 1/8	46 6/8 48 2/8	40 7/8	8 6	Mora County	NM	Kenneth J. Morga	1995	4293
298 1/8	48 2/8 48 1/8	36 7/8	6 6	Catron County	NM	Dale Hoekstra	1995	4293
298 1/8	41 7/8 41 4/8	32 3/8	6 6	Las Animas County	CO	Larry Vander Linden	1999	4293
298 1/8	45 0/8 41 6/8	34 5/8	6 6	Petroleum County	MT	Carlton DeFoor	2001	4293
*298 1/8	42 7/8 43 2/8	38 0/8	7 6	Phillips County	MT	Lynn Fliger	2003	4293
*298 1/8	48 1/8 46 2/8	39 5/8	6 6	Larimer County	CO	Steven W. Lutz, Jr.	2004	4293
298 1/8	53 4/8 53 1/8	39 5/8	6 6	Jefferson County	MT	Tim Gies	2007	4293
298 1/8	46 0/8 47 1/8	36 5/8	6 6	Beaverhead County	MT	Dexter Tart	2007	4293
298 1/8	46 1/8 48 3/8	36 1/8	6 6	Routt County	CO	Dan Adsit	2008	4293
298 1/8	45 3/8 44 2/8	34 3/8	6 6	Union County	OR	Ralph N. Snyder	2009	4293
*298 1/8	48 6/8 47 0/8	37 5/8	6 6	Coconino County	AZ	Eric Frazier	2009	4293
298 1/8	44 1/8 43 6/8	37 7/8	6 6	Gunnison County	CO	Andrew J. Logan	2009	4293
298 0/8	45 6/8 46 4/8	37 0/8	6 6	Caribou County	ID	Dean Monson	1982	4307
298 0/8	48 6/8 47 2/8	38 6/8	6 6	Delta County	CO	Todd B. Roberts	1992	4307
298 0/8	40 0/8 41 2/8	42 0/8	6 6	Yakima County	WA	Troy Goben	1992	4307
298 0/8	45 6/8 46 6/8	35 0/8	6 6	Beaverhead County	MT	Cliff Smith	1996	4307
298 0/8	49 5/8 49 0/8	35 4/8	6 6	Grant County	OR	Scott H. Stewart	1998	4307
298 0/8	45 5/8 45 2/8	32 2/8	6 6	Crook County	OR	Stacy L. Williams	1998	4307
298 0/8	46 4/8 46 5/8	37 6/8	6 6	Jackson County	OR	Tony Stanfield	2001	4307
298 0/8	46 4/8 47 4/8	39 0/8	7 6	Custer County	CO	Richard Madison	2003	4307
298 0/8	46 0/8 49 1/8	38 2/8	6 6	Apache County	AZ	Blaine "Bub" Mathews	2003	4307
298 0/8	53 0/8 51 2/8	43 0/8	6 6	Gila County	AZ	Dallas Fleagle	2003	4307
298 0/8	47 2/8 47 0/8	33 2/8	6 6	Lincoln County	NM	Rocky Wilson	2008	4307
*298 0/8	47 5/8 49 1/8	40 6/8	6 6	Clark County	NV	Shelby M. Keefer	2010	4307
297 7/8	44 5/8 46 7/8	31 1/8	7 8	Coconino County	AZ	Mark Vancas	1980	4319
297 7/8	46 4/8 47 0/8	33 5/8	6 6	Lincoln County	MT	Darryl Lien	1985	4319
297 7/8	45 4/8 44 2/8	37 7/8	6 6	Clear Creek County	CO	Paul Ray	1988	4319
297 7/8	46 3/8 45 0/8	37 5/8	6 6	Catron County	NM	Gale A. Hedges	1989	4319
297 7/8	44 6/8 40 4/8	40 4/8	6 7	Idaho County	ID	Kenneth Kirkeby	1994	4319
297 7/8	45 1/8 47 4/8	40 5/8	5 6	Otero County	NM	Tony Heil	1995	4319
297 7/8	43 4/8 42 0/8	39 2/8	7 7	Sanders County	MT	Tony Bierwagen	1995	4319
297 7/8	43 7/8 44 5/8	39 3/8	6 6	Coconino County	AZ	Jeff Persenaire	1996	4319
297 7/8	50 4/8 53 2/8	39 1/8	6 5	Coconino County	AZ	Brandt M. Lewis	2000	4319
297 7/8	48 6/8 47 3/8	31 5/8	7 7	Idaho County	ID	J. Kenneth Bowman	2000	4319
297 7/8	51 3/8 49 2/8	36 3/8	6 6	Park County	MT	Richard Backes	2001	4319
297 7/8	52 1/8 50 7/8	39 7/8	6 6	Washington County	ID	Paul Rose	2002	4319
297 7/8	50 2/8 49 6/8	32 5/8	6 6	Umatilla County	OR	Richard Thomas	2004	4319
297 6/8	46 4/8 46 5/8	41 4/8	6 6	Boulder County	CO	Steve Gorr	1969	4332
297 6/8	48 6/8 50 0/8	38 6/8	6 7	Caribou County	ID	Doug Cushman, Jr.	1981	4332
297 6/8	45 6/8 43 6/8	37 6/8	6 6	Apache County	AZ	Donata P. Montgomery	1990	4332
297 6/8	42 7/8 43 1/8	34 2/8	6 6	Meagher County	MT	Stephen Tylinski	1998	4332
297 6/8	51 0/8 52 0/8	32 0/8	6 6	Coconino County	AZ	Richard Mason	2004	4332
297 6/8	46 2/8 48 3/8	43 2/8	6 6	Park County	WY	Greg Paris	2005	4332
297 6/8	44 1/8 45 2/8	40 0/8	6 6	Lemhi County	ID	Dean Leshousky	2005	4332
297 5/8	45 4/8 44 2/8	37 5/8	6 6	Caribou County	ID	Tom M. Carter	1990	4339
297 5/8	46 2/8 47 5/8	34 5/8	6 6	Coconino County	AZ	Wayne A. Nicholson	1997	4339
297 5/8	45 2/8 44 4/8	39 3/8	6 6	Valley County	ID	Bill McCarthy	2000	4339
297 5/8	48 7/8 48 3/8	41 5/8	6 6	Catron County	NM	Kevin Brothers	2001	4339
297 5/8	49 0/8 48 5/8	31 1/8	6 6	Archuleta County	CO	Bruce Sears	2002	4339
297 5/8	44 3/8 44 4/8	39 1/8	6 6	Converse County	WY	Wayne Neumiller	2007	4339
297 4/8	45 1/8 41 6/8	43 0/8	6 7	King County	WA	Larry L. Sheward	1984	4345
297 4/8	47 2/8 48 6/8	39 2/8	6 6	Lewis & Clark County	MT	Mike McDaniel	1992	4345
297 4/8	41 3/8 42 2/8	34 6/8	6 7	Huerfano County	CO	Esco R. Billings III	1992	4345
297 4/8	44 5/8 46 1/8	29 3/8	6 7	Catron County	NM	Robert Lepard	1997	4345
297 4/8	47 3/8 48 7/8	35 0/8	6 6	Coconino County	AZ	Bob Kyhn	1997	4345
297 4/8	45 5/8 44 5/8	35 6/8	6 6	Fergus County	MT	Don Davidson	2003	4345
297 4/8	47 1/8 45 6/8	36 6/8	6 6	Taos County	NM	Joseph Landon Bell	2007	4345
297 3/8	46 1/8 45 2/8	42 3/8	5 7	Fremont County	ID	Thomas W. Savage	1982	4352
297 3/8	50 2/8 53 2/8	39 7/8	6 6	Taos County	NM	Randal Church	1989	4352
297 3/8	48 3/8 47 5/8	37 3/8	6 7	Moffat County	CO	Glenn Pritchard	1990	4352
297 3/8	46 5/8 47 0/8	35 5/8	6 6	Wheeler County	OR	James Deyo	1998	4352
297 3/8	45 6/8 49 0/8	37 7/8	6 6	Valley County	ID	Richard Buskirk	1998	4352
297 3/8	43 4/8 50 4/8	36 1/8	6 7	Rio Arriba County	NM	Stephen J. Stovall	2000	4352
297 3/8	43 1/8 45 0/8	38 5/8	6 6	Fremont County	WY	Chancy Brown	2001	4352
297 3/8	45 5/8 46 7/8	37 7/8	7 7	Fergus County	MT	D. Mitch Kottas	2002	4352
297 3/8	47 6/8 50 5/8	34 3/8	6 6	Wheeler County	OR	Joe L. Ford	2005	4352
297 3/8	44 1/8 42 0/8	32 3/8	6 6	Ashern	MAN	Peter Heppner	2006	4352
*297 3/8	45 2/8 42 5/8	39 3/8	5 5	Routt County	CO	Chris Francis	2007	4352
297 3/8	43 1/8 46 1/8	52 0/8	6 6	Albany County	WY	Mark Nelson	2007	4352
297 3/8	45 4/8 45 7/8	37 1/8	6 6	Routt County	CO	Tomas O. Paiz	2008	4352
297 2/8	50 0/8 47 5/8	30 6/8	6 6	Grant County	OR	Joe Copeland	1986	4365
297 2/8	47 2/8 49 4/8	50 6/8	6 7	Musselshell County	MT	John A. Dallas	1995	4365
297 2/8	43 2/8 47 0/8	43 4/8	6 5	Caribou County	ID	Rick Dunn	1996	4365
297 2/8	44 0/8 45 4/8	40 6/8	6 6	Meade County	SD	Brynolf Wanhanen	1996	4365
297 2/8	45 4/8 44 6/8	38 2/8	7 6	Catron County	NM	David Samuel	2000	4365
297 2/8	42 4/8 44 6/8	35 6/8	6 6	Baker County	OR	Michael S. Chandler	2002	4365

723

AMERICAN ELK (TYPICAL ANTLERS)

Minimum Score 260 — Continued

SCORE	LENGTH OF MAIN BEAM R	L	INSIDE SPREAD	NUMBER OF POINTS R	L	AREA	STATE/PROVINCE	HUNTER'S NAME	DATE	RANK
297 2/8	48 6/8	48 3/8	35 0/8	6	7	Garfield County	UT	Jeffery M. Barrick	2006	4365
*297 2/8	49 2/8	51 0/8	38 4/8	6	6	Mesa County	CO	Brian McBride	2007	4365
297 2/8	45 5/8	47 6/8	43 6/8	6	6	Beaverhead County	MT	Ray Gross	2007	4365
297 2/8	44 2/8	43 3/8	39 2/8	6	6	Eagle County	CO	Mike Dziekan	2008	4365
297 2/8	47 2/8	39 2/8	31 2/8	6	6	White Pine County	NV	Paul Podborny	2008	4365
297 2/8	47 6/8	49 5/8	45 6/8	6	6	Lincoln County	NM	Stephen A. Dougherty	2008	4365
297 2/8	43 2/8	44 1/8	36 6/8	6	6	Johnson County	WY	Jeff Donner	2009	4365
297 1/8	46 1/8	44 2/8	42 3/8	6	8	Missoula County	MT	David E. Torrey, Jr.	1977	4378
297 1/8	46 0/8	48 0/8	40 6/8	7	8	Coconino County	AZ	Dave Baker	1979	4378
297 1/8	43 0/8	42 3/8	39 3/8	6	6	Wainwright	ALB	Norman Hookes	1982	4378
297 1/8	45 0/8	45 3/8	38 3/8	6	6	Granite County	MT	Ralph W. Phillips	1992	4378
297 1/8	49 0/8	45 7/8	41 7/8	6	6	Bear Lake County	ID	Randy K. Guinn	1993	4378
297 1/8	48 0/8	46 4/8	36 5/8	6	6	Adams County	ID	Lee Jenkerson	1995	4378
297 1/8	43 7/8	43 7/8	38 3/8	5	6	Fergus County	MT	Edwin Evans	1995	4378
297 1/8	44 7/8	44 7/8	46 6/8	6	6	Beaverhead County	MT	Greg L. Munther	1996	4378
297 1/8	48 2/8	49 0/8	38 7/8	6	6	Grant County	OR	Gary Saylor	2002	4378
297 1/8	51 2/8	51 2/8	37 7/8	6	6	Grant County	OR	Robert Fitzsimmons, Jr.	2002	4378
297 1/8	47 1/8	47 3/8	38 5/8	6	7	Wheeler County	OR	Bill Swoyer	2007	4378
297 1/8	44 0/8	42 1/8	37 1/8	6	7	Park County	WY	Greg Paris	2009	4378
297 1/8	49 5/8	48 0/8	43 4/8	7	6	Grand County	CO	Darrin J. Zempko	2009	4378
297 0/8	46 4/8	46 0/8	36 2/8	6	6	Wallowa County	OR	Martha J. Soeth	1985	4391
297 0/8	44 4/8	44 3/8	34 0/8	6	6	Rich County	UT	Hugh H. Hogle	1986	4391
297 0/8	41 6/8	46 5/8	37 2/8	6	6	Rio Arriba County	NM	Patrick Smith	1988	4391
297 0/8	43 2/8	42 0/8	36 2/8	6	6	Coconino County	AZ	Gary Linendoll	1990	4391
297 0/8	50 1/8	45 3/8	43 2/8	7	6	Park County	WY	John Morlang	1993	4391
297 0/8	44 6/8	42 0/8	34 6/8	6	6	Catron County	NM	Walter Troy Slape	1993	4391
297 0/8	51 7/8	51 3/8	38 2/8	6	6	Sanders County	MT	Thomas B. Cramer III	1993	4391
297 0/8	41 7/8	42 7/8	40 6/8	6	6	Big Horn County	WY	Jerome Larson	1993	4391
297 0/8	47 0/8	43 4/8	31 0/8	6	6	Socorro County	NM	Edward C. Robinson	1998	4391
297 0/8	49 7/8	50 0/8	40 4/8	5	5	Montrose County	CO	Phillip Fidel Crespin	1999	4391
297 0/8	43 4/8	43 2/8	30 0/8	6	6	Creston	BC	John Shannon	1999	4391
297 0/8	38 7/8	49 3/8	39 2/8	6	6	Gilpin County	CO	Kim Herzfeldt	1999	4391
297 0/8	46 3/8	47 0/8	45 0/8	6	6	Mineral County	MT	Kelly B. McAllister	2000	4391
297 0/8	47 0/8	45 4/8	40 5/8	7	6	Caribou County	ID	Gary Brogan	2001	4391
297 0/8	43 3/8	48 7/8	43 4/8	4	4	Navajo County	AZ	Tom Walker	2004	4391
297 0/8	46 0/8	46 2/8	36 6/8	7	6	Salt Lake County	UT	Kelly Bingham	2007	4391
297 0/8	45 1/8	45 7/8	41 0/8	6	6	Coconino County	AZ	Chris Hannah	2007	4391
297 0/8	44 6/8	45 3/8	41 2/8	6	6	Otero County	NM	Joel Edin	2009	4391
297 0/8	47 0/8	46 5/8	36 0/8	6	6	Clearwater County	ID	Ian J. Meinke	2009	4391
296 7/8	45 2/8	45 4/8	43 3/8	6	6	Lemhi County	ID	Jim Frazier	1995	4410
296 7/8	46 4/8	46 4/8	36 3/8	6	6	Lemhi County	ID	DelRay Layton	1996	4410
296 7/8	44 7/8	44 3/8	38 5/8	6	6	Catron County	NM	Chris L. Skinner	1998	4410
296 7/8	51 0/8	52 1/8	37 1/8	6	6	Apache County	AZ	Rusty J. Sherman	1998	4410
296 7/8	46 7/8	45 2/8	35 1/8	6	6	Umatilla County	OR	David L. Roberts	1999	4410
296 7/8	48 1/8	48 2/8	33 5/8	6	6	Lane County	OR	Robert J. Halbert	2002	4410
296 7/8	51 5/8	51 2/8	49 3/8	6	5	Johnson County	WY	Brett Brenden	2002	4410
296 7/8	43 7/8	46 6/8	35 2/8	7	6	Benewah County	ID	Chuck Kiser	2004	4410
296 7/8	45 0/8	45 0/8	30 3/8	6	6	Saddle Hills	ALB	Brandon Brown	2005	4410
296 7/8	48 2/8	48 6/8	36 3/8	6	6	Lincoln County	MT	Terry G. Peterson, Jr.	2006	4410
296 6/8	47 4/8	46 4/8	35 6/8	6	6	Idaho County	ID	Gerald B. Jameson	1987	4420
296 6/8	50 7/8	51 6/8	40 6/8	6	6	Coconino County	AZ	Jerry W. Lilly	1992	4420
296 6/8	46 0/8	42 6/8	42 0/8	6	6	Shoshone County	ID	Dan Payne	1994	4420
296 6/8	44 3/8	47 0/8	41 4/8	5	5	Greenlee County	AZ	Ben Montgomery	1994	4420
296 6/8	55 5/8	52 4/8	37 2/8	6	6	Albany County	WY	Randy Bomar	1996	4420
296 6/8	43 2/8	42 4/8	39 4/8	6	7	Valley County	ID	George S. Holomshek	1999	4420
296 6/8	47 3/8	49 5/8	41 2/8	6	6	Blaine County	MT	Richard Koschak	2001	4420
296 6/8	49 0/8	47 3/8	45 2/8	6	5	Union County	OR	Kurt Zimmerman	2003	4420
*296 6/8	46 0/8	47 2/8	38 4/8	6	6	La Plata County	CO	David Henley	2004	4420
296 6/8	46 7/8	46 6/8	38 4/8	6	6	Fergus County	MT	Chris G. Sanford	2004	4420
296 6/8	48 4/8	49 7/8	33 4/8	6	6	Fergus County	MT	Wayne Godfrey	2007	4420
296 6/8	42 3/8	43 3/8	33 6/8	6	6	Caribou County	ID	Joe Burgoyne	2007	4420
296 6/8	42 0/8	43 4/8	28 2/8	6	6	Grant County	NM	Eddie Martinez	2009	4420
296 5/8	46 6/8	44 6/8	32 6/8	6	7	Kakwa River	ALB	Wilf Lehners	1990	4433
296 5/8	48 2/8	52 1/8	44 7/8	6	7	Greenlee County	AZ	Bill Golden	1992	4433
296 5/8	46 0/8	45 1/8	33 5/8	6	6	Moffat County	CO	Jim Willems	1994	4433
296 5/8	48 4/8	50 0/8	37 7/8	6	6	Catron County	NM	W. J. Sellars	1997	4433
296 5/8	42 2/8	43 0/8	35 7/8	6	6	Montrose County	CO	Jim Holdenried	1997	4433
296 5/8	50 6/8	52 0/8	35 3/8	8	7	Catron County	NM	Christopher D. Matthews	1998	4433
296 5/8	45 1/8	42 4/8	29 3/8	6	7	Catron County	NM	Ken Grosslight	1998	4433
296 5/8	51 0/8	49 0/8	31 1/8	6	6	Catron County	NM	Joseph A. Salisz	2001	4433
296 5/8	50 3/8	51 1/8	38 1/8	6	6	Fremont County	WY	Bradley D. Pate	2002	4433
296 4/8	45 1/8	46 7/8	35 4/8	6	6	Catron County	NM	Randall N. Bostick	1988	4442
296 4/8	46 5/8	46 0/8	31 2/8	6	6	Harney County	OR	Wayne Rogers	1997	4442
296 4/8	51 4/8	52 4/8	40 4/8	6	6	Archuleta County	CO	William D. Burch, DDS	1997	4442
296 4/8	50 1/8	50 5/8	35 2/8	6	6	Sweet Grass County	MT	Fred Holbert	1997	4442
296 4/8	45 3/8	46 3/8	33 2/8	6	7	Cibola County	NM	Charles D. Harzke	1998	4442
296 4/8	44 7/8	46 0/8	32 6/8	5	5	Big Horn County	MT	Richard Cunningham	1998	4442
296 4/8	52 0/8	47 7/8	40 6/8	6	6	Utah County	UT	Lance Brown	2003	4442
296 3/8	40 5/8	40 4/8	32 7/8	6	6	Teton County	MT	Myron E. Moore	1976	4449
296 3/8	41 7/8	44 2/8	39 3/8	6	6	Idaho County	ID	Jerry Vega	1985	4449
296 3/8	39 3/8	39 1/8	42 7/8	6	6	Sheridan County	WY	Richard M. Young, Jr.	1988	4449
296 3/8	41 3/8	44 3/8	35 5/8	6	6	Socorro County	NM	Thomas J. Leach	1997	4449
296 3/8	47 5/8	48 6/8	34 5/8	6	6	Catron County	NM	Syverson Homer	1997	4449
296 3/8	46 4/8	46 7/8	45 3/8	6	6	Duchesne County	UT	Craig Webb	2001	4449
296 3/8	48 4/8	48 0/8	34 1/8	6	6	Greenlee County	AZ	Barry R. Sopher	2001	4449
*296 3/8	43 3/8	43 6/8	32 7/8	7	6	Grant County	NM	Vincent M. Leonard	2004	4449
*296 3/8	42 1/8	43 6/8	35 5/8	6	7	Big Horn County	WY	David DeLapp	2004	4449
296 3/8	40 3/8	39 7/8	37 7/8	6	6	Lincoln County	MT	Patrick Flanagan	2005	4449
296 3/8	43 1/8	41 2/8	36 7/8	6	6	Las Animas County	CO	Fred Eichler	2006	4449
*296 3/8	47 0/8	48 4/8	33 7/8	6	6	Carbon County	UT	Mark Bailey	2008	4449
*296 3/8	46 4/8	47 4/8	37 5/8	6	6	Carbon County	UT	Mike King	2009	4449
296 2/8	45 7/8	44 6/8	37 0/8	6	7	Clackamas County	OR	Bill Lancaster	1984	4462
296 2/8	44 6/8	44 2/8	36 0/8	6	6	Crook County	OR	Rod Curtis	1984	4462
296 2/8	48 7/8	45 3/8	37 6/8	6	6	Moffat County	CO	Robert L Syvertson, Jr.	1984	4462
296 2/8	48 4/8	48 0/8	40 2/8	6	6	Catron County	NM	Pete Raynor	1989	4462

724

AMERICAN ELK (TYPICAL ANTLERS)

Minimum Score 260   Continued

SCORE	LENGTH OF R MAIN BEAM L	INSIDE SPREAD	NUMBER OF R POINTS L	AREA	STATE/ PROVINCE	HUNTER'S NAME	DATE	RANK
296 2/8	49 2/8 49 1/8	35 2/8	6 6	Canal Flats	BC	Glenn Dreger	1990	4462
296 2/8	49 4/8 48 1/8	37 2/8	7 6	Coconino County	AZ	Charles Urban	1992	4462
296 2/8	40 7/8 43 1/8	34 4/8	6 6	Catron County	NM	Jim Eppler	1994	4462
296 2/8	46 3/8 45 7/8	39 1/8	6 8	Baca County	CO	Robert D. Downs	1995	4462
296 2/8	46 6/8 46 4/8	41 6/8	6 6	Caribou County	ID	Todd R. Burgin	1997	4462
296 2/8	48 5/8 48 4/8	33 0/8	6 6	Gila County	AZ	Brett W. Bostian	1997	4462
296 2/8	44 1/8 42 6/8	24 0/8	7 7	Phillips County	MT	Mike Liane	1998	4462
296 2/8	53 4/8 50 4/8	37 0/8	6 6	Coconino County	AZ	Edwin J. Smith	1999	4462
296 2/8	50 3/8 50 2/8	35 2/8	6 6	Yakima County	WA	Ken Doyle	2002	4462
296 2/8	41 7/8 43 0/8	34 6/8	6 5	Fergus County	MT	John P. Hartman	2002	4462
296 2/8	41 6/8 42 2/8	45 2/8	6 6	Las Animas County	CO	M. Blake Patton	2006	4462
296 2/8	46 6/8 51 7/8	39 2/8	6 6	Catron County	NM	Mark Nedelco	2007	4462
296 2/8	50 2/8 47 7/8	33 6/8	6 6	Socorro County	NM	Doug Aikin	2007	4462
*296 2/8	44 0/8 41 1/8	32 3/8	6 7	Garfield County	CO	Mike Scott	2010	4462
296 1/8	43 2/8 45 3/8	43 1/8	6 6	Sheridan County	WY	Mike Barrett	1982	4480
296 1/8	44 3/8 44 3/8	32 1/8	6 6	Wolverine Creek	ALB	Dave Bathke	1990	4480
296 1/8	46 4/8 45 2/8	40 1/8	6 6	Valley County	ID	Jeff D. Dursteler	1997	4480
296 1/8	42 5/8 43 5/8	38 5/8	6 6	Grand County	CO	Perry Wright	1998	4480
296 1/8	43 5/8 42 5/8	34 5/8	6 6	Shoshone County	ID	Robert Kruger	1999	4480
296 1/8	45 6/8 46 0/8	30 7/8	6 6	Caribou County	ID	William T. Trainor, Jr.	2000	4480
296 1/8	51 4/8 53 0/8	37 1/8	6 6	Blaine County	ID	Mark E. Cox	2001	4480
296 1/8	44 1/8 43 7/8	37 1/8	6 6	Sibbald Flats	ALB	Archie J. Nesbitt	2001	4480
296 1/8	46 6/8 47 5/8	34 5/8	6 6	Gallatin County	MT	Steve Hardy	2002	4480
296 1/8	40 6/8 43 3/8	37 1/8	6 6	Otero County	NM	Morgan Ellis	2003	4480
296 1/8	55 1/8 55 0/8	38 1/8	5 6	Coconino County	AZ	Robert V. Mitchell	2004	4480
296 1/8	43 1/8 46 6/8	45 1/8	6 6	Coconino County	AZ	Jay B. Wyatt	2005	4480
296 1/8	48 7/8 48 0/8	37 5/8	6 6	Coconino County	AZ	Jerry Satterfield	2005	4480
296 1/8	51 1/8 52 1/8	43 5/8	6 6	Mineral County	CO	Rick Gaccetta	2009	4480
296 0/8	44 2/8 45 0/8	39 4/8	6 6	Gallatin County	MT	Bob Savage	1968	4494
296 0/8	48 7/8 46 6/8	37 6/8	6 6	Bighorn Mtns.	WY	Dean Fudge	1979	4494
296 0/8	40 7/8 41 7/8	28 4/8	8 6	Spruce Woods	MAN	Brian Morash	1981	4494
296 0/8	44 5/8 44 0/8	33 4/8	6 6	Flathead County	MT	Mark Fopp	1987	4494
296 0/8	48 7/8 50 6/8	40 2/8	6 5	Lemhi County	ID	David C. Manca	1991	4494
296 0/8	47 2/8 52 0/8	41 4/8	5 6	Phillips County	MT	Ronald S. Kline	1991	4494
296 0/8	45 6/8 45 6/8	38 6/8	6 6	Montrose County	CO	Bobby David Tipping	1992	4494
296 0/8	50 0/8 48 5/8	35 0/8	6 6	Albany County	WY	Merle Vowers	1995	4494
296 0/8	48 7/8 49 1/8	39 2/8	6 6	Ravalli County	MT	Evelio Elledias, Jr.	1996	4494
296 0/8	46 1/8 46 6/8	33 2/8	6 6	Lincoln County	NM	Harold Dean Britt	1998	4494
296 0/8	43 2/8 43 3/8	30 6/8	6 6	Coconino County	AZ	Will Pick	1998	4494
296 0/8	53 4/8 55 2/8	33 0/8	6 6	Coconino County	AZ	Merlin Dahlke	1999	4494
296 0/8	45 5/8 47 7/8	41 0/8	6 6	Greenlee County	AZ	Barry R. Sopher	2000	4494
*296 0/8	50 7/8 51 2/8	44 6/8	5 6	Big Horn County	WY	F. Matt Lentsch	2001	4494
*296 0/8	46 6/8 47 4/8	37 4/8	6 6	Fergus County	MT	Anthony Eash	2005	4494
*296 0/8	49 2/8 49 1/8	39 4/8	6 6	Mineral County	MT	Lue Yang	2009	4494
295 7/8	42 5/8 40 5/8	38 2/8	6 7	Larimer County	CO	Ben Alexander	1972	4510
295 7/8	44 4/8 43 7/8	38 1/8	6 7	Madison County	MT	Kevin Fogal	1985	4510
295 7/8	58 5/8 58 7/8	41 5/8	5 6	Shoshone County	ID	Randy Neal	1994	4510
295 7/8	46 7/8 48 2/8	33 5/8	6 6	Union County	OR	Andy Mickelson	1994	4510
295 7/8	48 7/8 50 2/8	35 1/8	6 6	Cascade County	MT	Philip Ladner	1997	4510
295 7/8	51 2/8 50 0/8	39 3/8	5 6	Coconino County	AZ	Phillip J. Petrore	1999	4510
295 7/8	42 6/8 42 5/8	33 1/8	6 6	Lemhi County	ID	Joseph C. Klink	2003	4510
295 7/8	42 1/8 42 2/8	36 7/8	6 6	Lewis & Clark County	MT	Craig J. Marr	2005	4510
295 6/8	49 6/8 50 0/8	38 4/8	6 6	Bonneville County	ID	Jim Cox	1976	4518
295 6/8	43 7/8 44 6/8	32 6/8	6 6	Powell County	MT	Bryan C. Anderson	1985	4518
295 6/8	42 0/8 46 0/8	40 2/8	6 6	Boulder County	CO	Jerry Bryan	1986	4518
295 6/8	45 5/8 45 3/8	41 0/8	6 6	Gallatin County	MT	H. C. Tysinger, Jr.	1986	4518
295 6/8	46 0/8 45 3/8	38 0/8	6 6	Socorro County	NM	Don Koester	1991	4518
295 6/8	43 2/8 44 5/8	38 0/8	6 6	Mesa County	CO	James Stover	1992	4518
295 6/8	44 1/8 42 4/8	35 4/8	7 7	Granite County	MT	Chris Pileski	1996	4518
295 6/8	47 0/8 48 5/8	37 4/8	6 6	Sheridan County	WY	Dave Moss	1997	4518
295 6/8	45 0/8 45 0/8	35 6/8	6 6	Fergus County	MT	John Fleharty	1999	4518
295 6/8	42 7/8 43 3/8	42 4/8	6 6	Otero County	NM	Doug Felton	1999	4518
295 6/8	42 6/8 42 6/8	41 6/8	6 6	Meagher County	MT	Jim Kennedy	2000	4518
295 6/8	51 7/8 52 6/8	35 4/8	5 6	Washakie County	WY	Marvin Harding	2001	4518
295 6/8	45 3/8 46 2/8	35 6/8	6 6	Petroleum County	MT	Robert Brooke	2002	4518
295 6/8	47 6/8 46 4/8	36 4/8	6 6	Fergus County	MT	Josef K. Rud	2003	4518
*295 6/8	39 2/8 43 4/8	28 0/8	6 6	Otero County	NM	Lynn Saxon	2005	4518
295 6/8	48 0/8 48 0/8	39 0/8	7 7	Yavapai County	AZ	Ryan Nogosek	2008	4518
*295 6/8	50 4/8 50 2/8	51 5/8	5 6	Coconino County	AZ	Gerry Berkel	2008	4518
295 5/8	52 2/8 48 4/8	37 5/8	6 6	Los Alamos County	NM	Gary Haus	2002	4535
295 5/8	52 4/8 51 1/8	35 3/8	6 6	Powder River County	MT	Jim Wilkins	2002	4535
*295 5/8	42 2/8 46 4/8	33 3/8	6 6	Phillips County	MT	Bradley F. Nei	2003	4535
295 5/8	49 6/8 54 0/8	35 3/8	7 7	Modoc County	CA	Ed Austin	2004	4535
295 4/8	48 0/8 47 1/8	37 0/8	6 6	Custer County	ID	A. Lynn Burton	1982	4539
295 4/8	46 4/8 45 3/8	42 0/8	6 6	Clearwater County	ID	Jerry Weverka	1988	4539
295 4/8	46 1/8 45 0/8	39 4/8	6 6	Clackamas County	OR	David L. Winters	1989	4539
295 4/8	47 6/8 47 5/8	37 0/8	6 6	Colfax County	NM	Charles H. Morrisette, Jr.	1992	4539
295 4/8	50 1/8 50 3/8	33 3/8	6 6	Navajo County	AZ	Joe D. Insall	1993	4539
295 4/8	45 5/8 46 2/8	34 0/8	6 6	Navajo County	AZ	Stephen Hoblick	1998	4539
295 4/8	46 6/8 45 3/8	38 6/8	6 6	Lincoln County	MT	Brent Kvapil	2000	4539
295 4/8	43 3/8 43 1/8	41 6/8	6 6	Petroleum County	MT	Scott Schultz	2001	4539
295 4/8	47 6/8 45 6/8	37 2/8	5 5	Shasta County	CA	Steve Eskridge	2002	4539
295 4/8	45 2/8 43 6/8	40 4/8	6 6	Beaver County	UT	Eldon Richter	2004	4539
295 4/8	53 0/8 53 2/8	36 4/8	6 6	Montezuma County	CO	Mark R. Bertram	2007	4539
295 4/8	45 4/8 46 6/8	39 0/8	6 6	Wallowa County	OR	Chad Zirkle	2008	4539
*295 4/8	47 6/8 47 2/8	34 6/8	6 6	Lake County	CO	Steven Gauvin	2009	4539
295 3/8	45 2/8 43 6/8	37 1/8	6 6	Catron County	NM	Ricardo Unzueta	1992	4552
295 3/8	44 3/8 43 0/8	36 5/8	8 6	Weber County	UT	David R. Drysdale/K. Taylor	1992	4552
295 3/8	47 5/8 47 7/8	33 7/8	6 6	Socorro County	NM	Doug Aikin	1992	4552
295 3/8	46 4/8 47 5/8	38 7/8	7 7	Mineral County	MT	Denny Morkert	1992	4552
295 3/8	50 0/8 48 7/8	39 1/8	6 6	Phillips County	MT	Lynn Paris	1995	4552
295 3/8	47 4/8 47 2/8	37 1/8	6 6	Chouteau County	MT	David M. Campbell	2006	4552
*295 3/8	52 0/8 50 2/8	39 5/8	6 6	Sandoval County	NM	Jed E. Jones	2006	4552
295 3/8	48 4/8 47 7/8	41 5/8	5 6	Union County	OR	Jason N. Schacher	2008	4552
295 3/8	42 4/8 42 2/8	31 3/8	6 6	Park County	WY	Dave Justmann	2010	4552

725

AMERICAN ELK (TYPICAL ANTLERS)

Minimum Score 260   Continued

SCORE	LENGTH OF R MAIN BEAM L	INSIDE SPREAD	NUMBER OF R POINTS L	AREA	STATE/ PROVINCE	HUNTER'S NAME	DATE	RANK
295 2/8	45 0/8 46 4/8	38 4/8	6 6	Lincoln County	NM	Bart J. Gillan III	1984	4561
295 2/8	51 3/8 51 3/8	37 0/8	7 6	Kittitas County	WA	Kirk Cresto	1984	4561
295 2/8	48 4/8 48 4/8	40 6/8	6 6	Catron County	NM	Gary Burnett	1986	4561
295 2/8	43 4/8 48 4/8	39 6/8	6 5	Catron County	NM	Spencer O. Moore III	1986	4561
295 2/8	42 5/8 42 0/8	41 4/8	6 6	Clearwater County	ID	Rudy Marmelo, Jr.	1988	4561
295 2/8	44 4/8 44 1/8	51 1/8	6 6	Pueblo County	CO	Steve Willsey	1991	4561
295 2/8	45 3/8 44 6/8	38 2/8	7 6	Sanders County	MT	Barry L. Dore	1995	4561
295 2/8	46 6/8 47 1/8	39 1/8	7 6	Latah County	ID	Mick Weinmann	1999	4561
295 2/8	42 0/8 42 1/8	35 3/8	6 7	Park County	WY	Vaughn Wright	2000	4561
295 2/8	45 6/8 45 0/8	36 0/8	6 6	Rio Blanco County	CO	David Williams	2005	4561
*295 2/8	45 2/8 44 4/8	34 4/8	6 6	Broadwater County	MT	Steven M. Washkuhn	2006	4561
295 2/8	45 4/8 45 2/8	35 4/8	6 6	Cibola County	NM	Nicholas A. Gonzales	2006	4561
295 2/8	43 5/8 46 3/8	39 4/8	7 6	Baker County	OR	Jeffrey Mishler	2006	4561
295 2/8	40 7/8 43 4/8	28 2/8	6 6	Grand County	CO	Brian Gustke	2007	4561
295 1/8	43 1/8 42 0/8	39 1/8	6 6	Gallatin County	MT	Tom L. Miller	1986	4575
295 1/8	42 4/8 44 0/8	36 3/8	6 6	Sublette County	WY	Ronald A. Noble	1989	4575
295 1/8	48 0/8 49 4/8	38 3/8	6 6	Catron County	NM	Craig Chilson	1994	4575
295 1/8	47 0/8 46 2/8	38 1/8	6 7	Garfield County	MT	Steve Kreitinger	1997	4575
295 1/8	44 4/8 44 4/8	32 7/8	6 6	Phillips County	MT	Mark Meyer	1997	4575
295 1/8	49 4/8 48 5/8	30 5/8	6 6	Las Animas County	CO	Robert Hicks	1998	4575
295 1/8	48 5/8 46 5/8	35 7/8	6 6	Catron County	NM	Kyle J. Wildschut	2001	4575
295 1/8	45 1/8 45 7/8	37 7/8	6 6	Las Animas County	CO	David Wildenstein	2002	4575
*295 1/8	45 7/8 48 1/8	47 3/8	5 6	Iron County	UT	Tyler Truman	2004	4575
295 0/8	51 2/8 49 7/8	38 5/8	7 6	Crook County	OR	Michael Hawkins	1983	4584
295 0/8	43 7/8 42 7/8	36 6/8	6 6	Catron County	NM	Loyd Street	1988	4584
295 0/8	46 5/8 46 5/8	32 2/8	6 6	Greenlee County	AZ	Robert Cisneros	1991	4584
295 0/8	46 4/8 47 6/8	37 2/8	6 6	Lincoln County	WY	Dale Williams	1992	4584
295 0/8	47 2/8 46 0/8	39 4/8	6 6	Park County	MT	Steve Kamps	1993	4584
295 0/8	45 6/8 45 0/8	35 6/8	5 5	Otero County	NM	Gary Garcia	1996	4584
295 0/8	47 0/8 45 4/8	39 4/8	7 8	Pueblo County	CO	Dan Wyberg	1998	4584
295 0/8	45 0/8 46 7/8	32 4/8	6 6	La Plata County	CO	Andrew McCoy	2001	4584
295 0/8	45 3/8 45 1/8	32 0/8	6 6	Phillips County	MT	Steve Pfaff	2007	4584
*295 0/8	47 7/8 45 6/8	32 2/8	6 6	Coconino County	AZ	William Anderson	2007	4584
*295 0/8	51 2/8 52 0/8	43 2/8	6 6	Mora County	NM	Thomas McCabe	2009	4584
*295 0/8	46 7/8 45 6/8	38 6/8	6 6	Clearwater County	ID	Brett Urness	2009	4584
294 7/8	42 1/8 41 0/8	46 3/8	6 6	Catron County	NM	John McClendon	1987	4596
294 7/8	48 4/8 44 5/8	44 3/8	6 6	Coconino County	AZ	Michael Weldon	1988	4596
294 7/8	41 1/8 40 6/8	38 7/8	6 6	Priddis Creek	ALB	Roger Meyer	1991	4596
294 7/8	48 6/8 48 6/8	37 3/8	6 6	Coconino County	AZ	Ralph B. Harris	1991	4596
294 7/8	43 0/8 42 6/8	38 3/8	6 6	Valley County	ID	Rick Van Leuven	1998	4596
294 7/8	44 3/8 44 2/8	34 3/8	6 6	Garfield County	MT	Kenneth Bykonen	1999	4596
294 7/8	41 6/8 42 0/8	37 3/8	6 6	Colfax County	NM	Ronnie Howard	1999	4596
294 7/8	44 7/8 45 1/8	36 7/8	6 6	Beaverhead County	MT	Bob Fivey, Jr.	1999	4596
294 7/8	47 7/8 45 6/8	38 5/8	6 6	Navajo County	AZ	Blake Isaacson	2001	4596
294 7/8	43 1/8 42 6/8	45 6/8	6 6	Grant County	OR	James D. Ramming	2003	4596
294 7/8	45 4/8 47 3/8	44 5/8	6 6	Gunnison County	CO	Andrew L. Bohm	2005	4596
294 6/8	47 1/8 48 2/8	35 2/8	6 7	Crook County	OR	John F. Nelson	1994	4607
294 6/8	46 7/8 48 5/8	37 2/8	6 6	Archuleta County	CO	Wayne Peeples	1997	4607
294 6/8	42 4/8 42 4/8	35 6/8	6 6	Lemhi County	ID	Richard F. Skinner	1998	4607
294 6/8	42 7/8 43 6/8	41 2/8	6 6	Gallatin County	MT	Vince Galli	1998	4607
294 6/8	43 7/8 44 3/8	42 2/8	6 6	Yellowstone County	MT	Chris Beilke	2001	4607
294 6/8	40 5/8 43 0/8	35 2/8	6 6	Morgan County	UT	Walt Phillips	2002	4607
294 6/8	44 0/8 43 0/8	34 2/8	6 6	Rio Blanco County	CO	Derek Nichols	2002	4607
294 6/8	43 0/8 44 2/8	32 6/8	6 6	Park County	WY	Abraham Hall	2003	4607
*294 6/8	44 2/8 44 1/8	37 0/8	6 6	Grand County	CO	Bob Amstadt	2006	4607
294 5/8	41 2/8 39 7/8	38 7/8	6 6	Fremont County	CO	William Bowlby	1984	4616
294 5/8	52 3/8 49 0/8	38 7/8	5 6	Sanders County	MT	Ralph W. Flockerzi	1987	4616
294 5/8	50 0/8 47 2/8	35 5/8	6 6	Sandoval County	NM	Robert K. Woeck	1992	4616
294 5/8	46 3/8 46 6/8	39 1/8	6 6	Catron County	NM	Wayne Eskew	1992	4616
294 5/8	45 7/8 51 7/8	37 1/8	5 6	Lincoln County	WY	Brian K. Jones	2001	4616
294 5/8	43 4/8 44 2/8	34 7/8	6 6	Umatilla County	OR	Kurt Rosenberg	2001	4616
294 5/8	44 3/8 47 1/8	41 3/8	6 6	Caribou County	ID	Eric Lawrence	2001	4616
294 5/8	44 0/8 45 0/8	32 1/8	6 6	Petroleum County	MT	Randy Bowler	2002	4616
294 5/8	43 3/8 43 2/8	34 5/8	6 6	Umatilla County	OR	Kenneth Cochell, Jr.	2003	4616
294 5/8	43 6/8 44 0/8	31 3/8	6 6	Cascade County	MT	Kenneth Bean	2003	4616
294 5/8	43 7/8 45 2/8	29 3/8	6 6	Caribou County	ID	Jeff Martinsen	2004	4616
294 5/8	49 0/8 49 3/8	39 5/8	6 6	Lincoln County	MT	Ben Cook	2007	4616
294 4/8	46 0/8 45 2/8	40 2/8	6 6	Deer Lodge County	MT	Dale J. Goytowski	1986	4628
294 4/8	48 3/8 50 0/8	46 4/8	6 6	McKinley County	NM	Eugene Duran	1987	4628
294 4/8	45 2/8 47 1/8	32 4/8	6 6	Coconino County	AZ	Jesse Smith	1988	4628
294 4/8	45 2/8 41 5/8	41 6/8	6 7	Grant County	OR	James M. Carter	1990	4628
294 4/8	46 4/8 45 6/8	39 0/8	6 6	Shoshone County	ID	David V. Wait	1992	4628
294 4/8	46 1/8 44 7/8	38 6/8	6 6	Otero County	NM	Lewis Green	1998	4628
294 4/8	48 6/8 48 0/8	34 0/8	6 6	Grand County	UT	David Gassen	2000	4628
294 4/8	43 6/8 43 1/8	35 2/8	6 6	Routt County	CO	Larry Chapman	2000	4628
294 4/8	47 3/8 47 0/8	36 6/8	6 6	Idaho County	ID	Steve Hickman	2001	4628
294 4/8	39 6/8 38 6/8	47 5/8	6 7	Teton County	WY	Daniel Jay Wolfe	2003	4628
294 4/8	43 4/8 42 1/8	32 5/8	6 7	Petroleum County	MT	James Lewis	2003	4628
294 4/8	47 4/8 46 0/8	36 2/8	6 6	Converse County	WY	Dan Gregg	2004	4628
294 4/8	46 3/8 43 7/8	36 4/8	7 7	Valley County	ID	Bill Kenney	2004	4628
*294 4/8	42 1/8 41 5/8	39 4/8	6 6	Montrose County	CO	James A. Steckel	2006	4628
*294 4/8	51 3/8 53 2/8	32 0/8	6 6	Phillips County	MT	Jason Wise	2006	4628
*294 4/8	44 3/8 45 7/8	43 0/8	5 5	Cibola County	NM	Jerry Groth	2006	4628
294 3/8	45 0/8 48 4/8	37 1/8	5 7	Saguache County	CO	David A. Larson	1978	4644
294 3/8	45 1/8 46 0/8	35 1/8	6 6	Socorro County	NM	Eddie Claypool	1988	4644
294 3/8	45 7/8 44 1/8	44 7/8	6 6	Granite County	MT	Scott A. Breum	1992	4644
294 3/8	43 2/8 44 4/8	36 7/8	6 6	Lincoln County	WY	Steven B. Julander	1992	4644
294 3/8	47 6/8 46 1/8	43 5/8	6 6	Coconino County	AZ	George J. Alvarez	1996	4644
294 3/8	53 5/8 51 5/8	47 1/8	6 6	Park County	MT	Steven B. Kamps	1998	4644
294 3/8	45 5/8 44 6/8	42 3/8	6 6	Mesa County	CO	Jerome C. Affholder	2000	4644
294 3/8	50 2/8 49 2/8	36 5/8	7 7	Blaine County	ID	M. Wayne Carey	2001	4644
294 3/8	40 3/8 42 2/8	29 5/8	6 6	Garfield County	CO	William Krout	2003	4644
*294 3/8	45 5/8 47 3/8	37 1/8	6 6	Mesa County	CO	Tyson Pinnt	2007	4644
*294 3/8	56 0/8 51 4/8	36 3/8	6 5	San Juan County	UT	Brayden Richmond	2008	4644
*294 3/8	43 1/8 43 2/8	30 7/8	6 6	Sheridan County	WY	Jason Mann	2009	4644

726

AMERICAN ELK (TYPICAL ANTLERS)

Minimum Score 260
Continued

SCORE	LENGTH OF R MAIN BEAM L	INSIDE SPREAD	NUMBER OF R POINTS L		AREA	STATE/ PROVINCE	HUNTER'S NAME	DATE	RANK
294 2/8	50 2/8 45 6/8	37 0/8	7	6	La Plata County	CO	J. Barry Dyar	1983	4656
294 2/8	43 5/8 45 4/8	40 2/8	7	6	Apache County	AZ	Fred Clifford	1985	4656
294 2/8	42 5/8 46 2/8	42 0/8	6	6	Catron County	NM	Billy Barber	1986	4656
294 2/8	43 7/8 40 7/8	35 2/8	6	6	Otero County	NM	Bruce Bonnet	1990	4656
294 2/8	48 4/8 48 2/8	38 1/8	7	6	Grand County	CO	Mike Brown	1992	4656
294 2/8	48 7/8 48 3/8	36 0/8	6	6	Coconino County	AZ	Randy McKusick	1993	4656
294 2/8	46 6/8 46 6/8	33 0/8	6	6	Fergus County	MT	Douglas C. McWilliams	1994	4656
294 2/8	49 2/8 45 6/8	44 1/8	8	5	Rio Blanco County	CO	Larry McCarty	1994	4656
294 2/8	48 1/8 46 7/8	35 2/8	6	6	Wallowa County	OR	Carl Anderson	1999	4656
294 2/8	44 6/8 46 5/8	38 6/8	6	6	Adams County	ID	Pete Reil	1999	4656
294 2/8	43 4/8 44 0/8	35 0/8	7	6	Chouteau County	MT	Eric Bachofner	2003	4656
294 2/8	40 6/8 41 4/8	37 0/8	6	6	Albany County	WY	Gary Shear	2004	4656
* 294 2/8	41 2/8 38 6/8	37 4/8	6	6	Costilla County	CO	Nicholas Dexter	2005	4656
294 2/8	45 2/8 43 4/8	40 4/8	7	6	Lincoln County	MT	Ron Goodman	2006	4656
294 2/8	43 4/8 42 2/8	29 0/8	6	6	Rio Blanco County	CO	Alan Craig Milbreath	2007	4656
294 2/8	43 2/8 42 7/8	33 2/8	6	6	Catron County	NM	Steven "Blair" Gardner	2007	4656
294 2/8	43 6/8 45 3/8	41 4/8	6	6	Carbon County	WY	Joe Gillespie	2009	4656
* 294 2/8	44 2/8 44 1/8	37 2/8	6	6	Archuleta County	CO	Ed Boldt, Jr. DVM	2009	4656
294 2/8	46 0/8 46 4/8	31 6/8	6	6	Fremont County	ID	Drake R. Atwood	2010	4656
294 1/8	41 6/8 42 3/8	39 3/8	6	6	Lincoln County	WY	Bill Swett	1997	4675
294 1/8	49 1/8 49 2/8	39 1/8	6	6	Grant County	OR	Dwight E. Sturn	1998	4675
294 1/8	47 1/8 45 4/8	39 3/8	6	6	Rio Arriba County	NM	Steve T. Hinken	2000	4675
294 1/8	42 0/8 42 0/8	34 5/8	6	6	Park County	WY	Mike Holden	2001	4675
294 1/8	48 2/8 47 5/8	45 5/8	6	7	Sheridan County	WY	Kendel Cheatham	2002	4675
* 294 1/8	43 4/8 44 6/8	41 7/8	6	6	Pennington County	SD	Mark E. Ellerton	2005	4675
294 1/8	49 3/8 49 1/8	34 5/8	6	6	Lewis & Clark County	MT	Kyle Carlson	2008	4675
294 1/8	47 4/8 46 0/8	36 3/8	6	6	Albany County	WY	Miles Bundy	2008	4675
294 0/8	41 1/8 42 5/8	33 0/8	6	6	Clearwater County	ID	Don Kubasch	1981	4683
294 0/8	44 7/8 44 5/8	31 4/8	6	6	Big Horn County	WY	Dave Moss	1988	4683
294 0/8	46 7/8 46 4/8	36 2/8	6	6	Coconino County	AZ	Jerry Bradshaw	1997	4683
294 0/8	48 1/8 48 5/8	43 2/8	6	6	Lemhi County	ID	Brian Lane	2003	4683
294 0/8	46 1/8 45 3/8	37 2/8	6	6	La Plata County	CO	Greg Betzing	2005	4683
* 294 0/8	46 4/8 47 3/8	40 4/8	5	5	Catron County	NM	Jake Hutson	2006	4683
294 0/8	47 2/8 48 0/8	36 2/8	6	7	Coconino County	AZ	La Rue Parr	2007	4683
294 0/8	43 4/8 44 6/8	34 2/8	6	6	Park County	MT	Adam Larson	2007	4683
294 0/8	45 7/8 46 4/8	39 6/8	6	6	Daggett County	UT	Burkely Gerhardt	2008	4683
* 294 0/8	46 2/8 44 0/8	37 2/8	6	6	Mineral County	MT	Randy Cote	2009	4683
293 7/8	46 3/8 48 0/8	40 5/8	6	6	Gunnison County	CO	Robert C. Goodman	1974	4693
293 7/8	42 6/8 44 4/8	34 5/8	6	5	Graham County	AZ	Clifford White	1982	4693
293 7/8	50 4/8 47 5/8	33 5/8	6	6	Phillips County	MT	Mike Mjelstad	1987	4693
293 7/8	45 5/8 45 4/8	39 5/8	5	5	Idaho County	ID	Michael J. Collins	1990	4693
293 7/8	48 0/8 48 6/8	37 3/8	6	6	Custer County	ID	Tom Szurgot	1990	4693
293 7/8	48 3/8 48 3/8	33 3/8	6	6	Missoula County	MT	Pao K. Moua	1990	4693
293 7/8	40 0/8 51 6/8	30 1/8	6	6	Sierra County	NM	Don Draper	1993	4693
293 7/8	43 2/8 43 3/8	35 5/8	6	6	Valencia County	NM	A. M. Oakes, Jr.	1993	4693
293 7/8	44 4/8 44 4/8	41 7/8	6	7	Klickitat County	WA	Bill Campbell	1998	4693
293 7/8	42 6/8 41 7/8	41 5/8	7	7	Crook County	OR	Randy Baker	1998	4693
293 7/8	45 5/8 43 3/8	33 5/8	6	6	Klamath County	OR	Greg Chakarun	2005	4693
293 7/8	48 7/8 48 5/8	39 3/8	6	6	Wallowa County	OR	R. S. Boggan	2005	4693
* 293 7/8	46 0/8 45 0/8	37 6/8	6	6	Gunnison County	CO	Dominic Danni	2008	4693
293 7/8	54 4/8 50 0/8	36 7/8	6	6	Coconino County	AZ	Joel Webster	2008	4693
293 6/8	47 0/8 45 4/8	37 0/8	6	6	Archuleta County	CO	Eddie Claypool	1985	4707
293 6/8	43 1/8 46 0/8	46 6/8	6	6	Lemhi County	ID	Ben L. Fahnholz	1987	4707
293 6/8	49 3/8 48 0/8	38 6/8	6	6	Sheridan County	WY	Gary T. Laya	1988	4707
293 6/8	50 4/8 52 2/8	31 0/8	6	6	Rio Arriba County	NM	Paul Locey	1990	4707
293 6/8	48 3/8 47 0/8	45 0/8	6	7	Grant County	OR	Tim L. Hayward	1991	4707
293 6/8	42 2/8 43 0/8	42 0/8	6	6	Pitkin County	CO	Norman Shawn Hopkins	1992	4707
293 6/8	45 1/8 46 1/8	42 2/8	6	6	Judith Basin County	MT	Ken Schmidt	1993	4707
293 6/8	50 7/8 50 6/8	39 6/8	6	6	Caribou County	ID	Tyler Stiens	2002	4707
293 6/8	43 0/8 43 7/8	40 4/8	6	6	Clearwater County	ID	Mel Goodrich	2003	4707
293 6/8	44 2/8 44 7/8	33 2/8	6	6	Lemhi County	ID	Clayton Moore	2004	4707
293 6/8	43 0/8 46 0/8	43 4/8	6	6	King County	WA	John Grosvenor	2005	4707
* 293 6/8	45 7/8 46 1/8	34 6/8	6	6	Beaverhead County	MT	Padraig Hagan	2007	4707
293 6/8	46 6/8 45 1/8	36 0/8	6	6	Catron County	NM	Joey G. Columb	2007	4707
293 6/8	48 6/8 48 7/8	39 0/8	6	6	Kittitas County	WA	Steve Link	2007	4707
293 5/8	42 6/8 43 3/8	39 7/8	6	6	West	MT	Raymond Alt	1962	4721
293 5/8	46 2/8 47 7/8	38 5/8	6	6	Larimer County	CO	Wayne R. Haas	1996	4721
293 5/8	49 4/8 46 6/8	40 1/8	6	7	Taos County	NM	Matthew Howard	1998	4721
293 5/8	46 0/8 46 7/8	34 5/8	6	6	Petroleum County	MT	Kent A. Bender	2000	4721
293 4/8	49 5/8 50 2/8	42 2/8	6	5	Sheridan County	WY	Mike Barrett	1980	4725
293 4/8	47 4/8 46 6/8	34 6/8	6	6	Beaverhead County	MT	Dennis Rehse	1981	4725
293 4/8	50 0/8 46 4/8	33 6/8	6	6	Catron County	NM	Bob Gourley	1984	4725
293 4/8	44 1/8 44 0/8	37 4/8	6	6	Idaho County	ID	Gary Knoles	1993	4725
293 4/8	45 3/8 44 7/8	38 2/8	5	5	Grand County	CO	Carlis Stephens	1996	4725
293 4/8	46 2/8 44 1/8	30 4/8	6	6	Greenlee County	AZ	John Olvey	1998	4725
293 4/8	48 5/8 49 0/8	38 2/8	6	6	Sheridan County	WY	Randy Burtis	2004	4725
293 4/8	46 4/8 46 4/8	34 0/8	6	6	Jefferson County	OR	Dale K. Thornton	2005	4725
293 4/8	42 6/8 42 0/8	35 4/8	6	6	Flathead County	MT	Richard Cowley	2006	4725
293 3/8	46 0/8 45 5/8	37 5/8	6	6	Boise County	ID	David Hale	1983	4734
293 3/8	46 0/8 45 5/8	30 5/8	6	7	Lemhi County	ID	William C. Shuster	1986	4734
293 3/8	46 6/8 47 4/8	32 5/8	6	6	Gallatin County	MT	Michael Groulx	1990	4734
293 3/8	45 1/8 43 0/8	40 1/8	5	6	Morgan County	UT	Poncho McCoy	1992	4734
293 3/8	46 6/8 46 5/8	36 5/8	6	6	Lewis County	WA	Scott Murray	1992	4734
293 3/8	44 6/8 45 4/8	42 7/8	6	6	Lemhi County	ID	Bryce K. DeForest	1999	4734
293 3/8	47 2/8 45 1/8	37 3/8	6	6	Sevier County	UT	Scott Dalebout	2000	4734
293 3/8	47 1/8 49 7/8	31 3/8	6	6	Crook County	OR	Robert J. Schriever	2000	4734
293 3/8	39 6/8 40 3/8	37 1/8	7	8	Benewah County	ID	Jason Brebner	2003	4734
293 3/8	47 5/8 49 5/8	28 5/8	6	6	Mineral County	MT	Clements L. Stroot	2004	4734
293 2/8	47 2/8 47 6/8	39 2/8	6	6	Musselshell County	MT	Dan Acord	1986	4744
293 2/8	42 2/8 42 6/8	32 4/8	6	6	Flathead County	MT	Larry O. Hadley	1987	4744
293 2/8	46 6/8 46 6/8	35 6/8	6	6	Navajo County	AZ	Corky Richardson	1990	4744
293 2/8	47 7/8 47 7/8	36 6/8	6	6	Los Alamos County	NM	Jeffrey M. Bradley	1992	4744
293 2/8	46 6/8 47 6/8	35 0/8	6	6	Platte County	WY	Willard Woods	1993	4744
293 2/8	54 5/8 53 6/8	40 0/8	6	8	Chouteau County	MT	Gus Smith	1995	4744
293 2/8	48 5/8 49 1/8	35 6/8	6	6	Carbon County	WY	Larry J. Thoney	1997	4744

AMERICAN ELK (TYPICAL ANTLERS)

Minimum Score 260 Continued

SCORE	LENGTH OF R MAIN BEAM L	INSIDE SPREAD	NUMBER OF R POINTS L	AREA	STATE/PROVINCE	HUNTER'S NAME	DATE	RANK
293 2/8	42 3/8 41 5/8	35 0/8	7 6	San Juan County	CO	Greg A. Frisch	2000	4744
293 2/8	50 0/8 49 2/8	36 0/8	6 6	Butte County	ID	Don Glenn, Jr.	2000	4744
293 2/8	42 0/8 41 4/8	36 6/8	6 6	Stillwater County	MT	Norman R. Colbert, Jr.	2002	4744
293 2/8	48 0/8 47 3/8	43 2/8	6 6	Meagher County	MT	Chris Howell	2004	4744
293 2/8	43 0/8 43 7/8	38 6/8	6 6	Pennington County	SD	Steve Hansen	2005	4744
293 2/8	44 2/8 45 1/8	40 6/8	6 6	Madison County	MT	John Shane Shima	2006	4744
*293 2/8	46 4/8 44 0/8	31 3/8	6 7	Pembina County	ND	Tom Lehar	2008	4744
293 1/8	44 6/8 39 1/8	32 1/8	6 6	Clearwater County	ID	T. LeRoy West	1981	4758
293 1/8	42 6/8 39 6/8	35 1/8	6 6	Catron County	NM	Butch Allen	1990	4758
293 1/8	47 1/8 45 6/8	45 0/8	6 7	Rio Blanco County	CO	Mike Wallers	1993	4758
293 1/8	45 5/8 45 2/8	36 6/8	6 6	Gallatin County	MT	Craig P. Henrikson	2003	4758
*293 1/8	43 3/8 44 5/8	38 7/8	6 6	Grand County	UT	John A. Anthony	2006	4758
293 1/8	47 0/8 46 5/8	43 5/8	6 7	Rio Blanco County	CO	Ed Hartman	2007	4758
293 0/8	49 0/8 48 4/8	32 4/8	6 6	Beaverhead County	MT	Martin L. Sapp	1988	4764
293 0/8	42 7/8 44 2/8	40 4/8	6 6	Sandoval County	NM	John Clarence Rector	1990	4764
293 0/8	42 6/8 45 4/8	40 2/8	8 7	Wallowa County	OR	Dwight Huffman	1990	4764
293 0/8	44 0/8 44 1/8	38 6/8	6 6	Catron County	NM	Leonard Rohlik	1991	4764
293 0/8	47 6/8 44 3/8	43 4/8	6 6	Otero County	NM	Jim Howard	1997	4764
293 0/8	41 7/8 42 4/8	34 4/8	6 6	Archuleta County	CO	Thomas A. Medary	1998	4764
293 0/8	48 6/8 47 7/8	33 4/8	6 7	Carbon County	WY	Miles Bundy	2000	4764
293 0/8	48 2/8 49 5/8	34 2/8	6 6	Union County	OR	Joe Neer	2002	4764
293 0/8	46 3/8 45 0/8	35 2/8	6 7	Phillips County	MT	Ray Gamradt	2002	4764
293 0/8	57 6/8 55 6/8	28 6/8	6 6	Siskiyou County	CA	Michael J. McEntee	2007	4764
293 0/8	45 6/8 46 1/8	40 4/8	6 7	Grant County	OR	Tracey Lindsey	2008	4764
292 7/8	48 0/8 52 4/8	38 5/8	6 6	Sweet Grass County	MT	Dr. Dale Schlehuber	1986	4775
292 7/8	46 7/8 46 4/8	40 5/8	6 6	Lincoln County	MT	Dan Bundrock	1989	4775
292 7/8	41 4/8 41 3/8	38 5/8	6 6	Boulder County	CO	Ron Readmond	1990	4775
292 7/8	45 5/8 44 1/8	36 1/8	6 6	Petroleum County	MT	Don Davidson	1992	4775
292 6/8	42 3/8 44 5/8	34 0/8	6 6	Chouteau County	MT	Tom Brady	1987	4779
292 6/8	44 5/8 45 4/8	36 2/8	6 6	Carbon County	UT	David J. Hansen	1993	4779
292 6/8	46 4/8 47 2/8	35 0/8	6 6	Jackson County	CO	William R. Aycock	1995	4779
292 6/8	43 0/8 43 4/8	40 0/8	6 6	Catron County	NM	Mike Holland	1996	4779
292 6/8	41 6/8 41 3/8	34 0/8	6 6	Cascade County	MT	Edward Keltgen	1997	4779
292 6/8	47 1/8 48 0/8	32 6/8	6 6	Umatilla County	OR	Jim White	1998	4779
292 6/8	46 2/8 46 3/8	33 4/8	6 6	Rio Blanco County	CO	Kevin L. Vaught	2001	4779
*292 6/8	48 1/8 51 3/8	39 6/8	6 6	Coconino County	AZ	Robert L. Burns	2004	4779
292 5/8	43 6/8 42 1/8	34 1/8	7 6	Rio Blanco County	CO	James Raetz	1976	4787
292 5/8	45 2/8 42 6/8	35 1/8	6 6	Catron County	NM	John Stanley	1987	4787
292 5/8	41 1/8 41 1/8	33 5/8	6 6	Albany County	WY	Michael Lancaster	1990	4787
292 5/8	39 2/8 38 5/8	39 7/8	6 7	Colfax County	NM	Dave Holt	1990	4787
292 5/8	44 0/8 44 6/8	38 1/8	6 6	Larimer County	CO	Todd K. Johnson	1993	4787
292 5/8	44 7/8 43 7/8	36 7/8	6 6	Crook County	OR	Jason Simpson	1995	4787
292 5/8	43 5/8 46 7/8	37 5/8	6 6	Coconino County	AZ	Stephen Herrera	1997	4787
292 5/8	42 2/8 45 7/8	42 0/8	7 7	Sanders County	MT	Glen A. Drexler	1998	4787
292 5/8	44 5/8 43 4/8	42 1/8	6 6	Montrose County	CO	Jerald Sebesta	2001	4787
292 5/8	44 3/8 47 7/8	35 2/8	6 7	Gila County	AZ	George Harms	2002	4787
292 5/8	50 2/8 50 3/8	30 5/8	6 6	Coconino County	AZ	Gary N. Island	2005	4787
292 4/8	48 0/8 50 4/8	33 4/8	6 6	Sanders County	MT	Doug Gunderson	1978	4798
292 4/8	43 0/8 43 6/8	40 2/8	6 6	Jackson County	CO	Daniel H. Chaney	1981	4798
292 4/8	43 1/8 42 1/8	30 0/8	6 6	Strathcona	ALB	Jack Kempf	1984	4798
292 4/8	46 6/8 46 2/8	34 4/8	6 6	Grant County	OR	Terry J. Caster	1990	4798
292 4/8	42 4/8 42 0/8	37 0/8	6 6	Morgan County	UT	Brad T. Francis	1991	4798
292 4/8	46 4/8 47 4/8	38 4/8	5 6	Mesa County	CO	Victor Zugibe	1995	4798
292 4/8	41 6/8 41 2/8	35 6/8	6 6	Garfield County	MT	Lynn A. Reed	1998	4798
292 4/8	42 1/8 43 7/8	32 2/8	6 6	Routt County	CO	T. J. Thrasher	1999	4798
292 4/8	46 2/8 48 4/8	38 3/8	7 6	Radium	BC	Ron Klassen	2001	4798
292 4/8	47 0/8 46 6/8	34 6/8	6 6	Clark County	ID	Steven Craig Talbot	2003	4798
292 4/8	45 0/8 45 4/8	40 0/8	6 7	Rich County	UT	Glen O. Hallows	2004	4798
292 4/8	50 1/8 48 2/8	40 2/8	6 6	Umatilla County	OR	Jerry Dale Tower	2008	4798
292 4/8	42 3/8 42 1/8	39 0/8	6 6	Grant County	OR	Nels Toftdahl	2009	4798
292 4/8	48 4/8 49 2/8	33 6/8	7 8	Clackamas County	OR	Andy Warren	2009	4798
292 3/8	44 6/8 40 4/8	35 1/8	6 6	Idaho County	ID	Robert C. Mitchell	1979	4812
292 3/8	44 6/8 44 2/8	36 3/8	6 6	Ravalli County	MT	Paul Hamilton	1984	4812
292 3/8	44 3/8 43 0/8	40 1/8	6 6	Ravalli County	MT	Pao K. Moua	1998	4812
292 3/8	46 3/8 43 3/8	38 3/8	6 6	Coconino County	AZ	Gary R. Williams	1999	4812
292 3/8	52 6/8 54 5/8	41 7/8	6 6	Blaine County	ID	John F. Burke	2006	4812
292 2/8	41 2/8 44 4/8	39 6/8	6 6	Idaho County	ID	Richard C. Nichols	1975	4817
292 2/8	47 5/8 46 1/8	31 4/8	6 6	Mineral County	MT	Kenneth D. Verley	1981	4817
292 2/8	45 2/8 49 1/8	33 4/8	6 6	Grant County	OR	Robert R. Gedlick	1983	4817
292 2/8	42 5/8 41 3/8	35 2/8	6 6	Clark County	ID	Billy Burbank III	1988	4817
292 2/8	47 5/8 50 0/8	35 2/8	6 7	Missoula County	MT	Jeffrey G. Winter	1993	4817
292 2/8	43 5/8 42 4/8	34 0/8	6 6	Sheridan County	WY	Mike Barrett	1996	4817
292 2/8	48 5/8 46 0/8	37 0/8	5 5	Nose Mtn.	ALB	Les Baird	1997	4817
292 2/8	48 5/8 47 1/8	36 6/8	6 6	Sevier County	UT	Darren Peterson	1997	4817
292 2/8	46 6/8 46 0/8	43 4/8	6 6	Blaine County	ID	Jim Wentworth	1998	4817
292 2/8	46 3/8 45 0/8	40 0/8	6 6	Flathead County	MT	Shawn Price	1999	4817
292 2/8	45 2/8 45 5/8	41 4/8	7 7	Grant County	OR	Nate Simmons	2000	4817
292 2/8	44 6/8 41 0/8	44 6/8	6 6	Colfax County	NM	John E. Dell	2001	4817
292 2/8	43 0/8 42 5/8	36 6/8	6 6	Washington County	ID	Jim Lambrecht	2007	4817
*292 2/8	46 2/8 46 1/8	40 4/8	7 7	Bonneville County	ID	James O. Reardon	2008	4817
292 1/8	44 7/8 47 0/8	34 3/8	6 6	Powell County	MT	Richard W. Malone	1976	4831
292 1/8	47 5/8 47 0/8	46 7/8	6 6	Coconino County	AZ	Bryant McGee	1980	4831
292 1/8	49 4/8 48 2/8	39 5/8	6 6	Custer County	ID	James Schrader	1991	4831
292 1/8	40 3/8 38 4/8	41 4/8	6 6	Park County	WY	Scott Moore	1991	4831
292 1/8	44 4/8 48 4/8	43 3/8	6 6	Socorro County	NM	Manfred Quentel	1996	4831
292 1/8	46 4/8 44 0/8	37 3/8	6 6	Otero County	NM	Brad A. King	1997	4831
292 1/8	45 5/8 45 6/8	38 5/8	6 6	Catron County	NM	Robin Johnson	2001	4831
292 1/8	52 3/8 48 6/8	38 3/8	7 6	Ravalli County	MT	Pao K. Moua	2001	4831
292 1/8	44 3/8 43 7/8	40 7/8	6 6	Apache County	AZ	Bryant Shermoe	2003	4831
292 1/8	49 5/8 47 1/8	33 3/8	6 6	Creston	BC	Jason Wall	2004	4831
*292 1/8	45 0/8 44 4/8	32 1/8	6 6	Petroleum County	MT	Tim Lundmark	2005	4831
292 1/8	43 3/8 44 1/8	40 5/8	6 6	Converse County	WY	Mike Lowe	2005	4831
292 1/8	45 7/8 46 2/8	36 7/8	6 6	Teller County	CO	Scott Leeling	2008	4831
292 1/8	47 4/8 48 5/8	35 3/8	6 6	Lincoln County	WY	Randy Benish	2009	4831
292 0/8	36 2/8 37 6/8	33 4/8	6 6	Lincoln County	NM	Terence A. Wahlgren	1985	4845

AMERICAN ELK (TYPICAL ANTLERS)

Minimum Score 260

SCORE	LENGTH OF R MAIN BEAM L	INSIDE SPREAD	NUMBER OF R POINTS L	AREA	STATE/ PROVINCE	HUNTER'S NAME	DATE	RANK
292 0/8	46 0/8 45 0/8	34 0/8	6 6	Catron County	NM	Brad Blanchard	1989	4845
292 0/8	43 7/8 43 0/8	36 2/8	6 7	Uintah County	UT	Smiley Arrowchis	1989	4845
292 0/8	44 6/8 44 6/8	39 0/8	6 6	Coconino County	AZ	Mark J. Dominguez	1991	4845
292 0/8	48 1/8 49 2/8	36 6/8	6 6	Apache County	AZ	Aaron J. Scott	1994	4845
292 0/8	44 1/8 44 5/8	36 0/8	6 6	Park County	WY	Beau Beck	1998	4845
292 0/8	49 0/8 48 3/8	44 0/8	8 7	Park County	MT	Fred Regenfuss	2000	4845
292 0/8	48 3/8 48 1/8	42 4/8	6 6	Routt County	CO	John A. Bloom	2002	4845
292 0/8	43 4/8 44 7/8	33 6/8	6 6	Harney County	OR	Rolly Hoyt	2004	4845
292 0/8	51 4/8 43 7/8	46 0/8	7 7	Coconino County	AZ	Kenny J. Hutchinson	2004	4845
292 0/8	40 6/8 44 2/8	36 4/8	6 7	Custer County	SD	Brian Heidbrink	2007	4845
291 7/8	45 7/8 45 0/8	46 2/8	6 6	Coconino County	AZ	Dick & Gary Mendenhall	1974	4856
291 7/8	45 5/8 45 2/8	38 5/8	6 6	Chaffee County	CO	Douglas E. Wilson	1982	4856
291 7/8	52 7/8 51 5/8	46 1/8	5 6	King County	WA	Ty Martin	1984	4856
291 7/8	44 2/8 44 0/8	35 7/8	6 6	Saguache County	CO	Dario J. Archuleta	1991	4856
291 7/8	46 6/8 43 2/8	39 1/8	5 5	Fremont County	WY	Nelson Scherrer	1991	4856
291 7/8	44 6/8 46 0/8	35 4/8	7 6	Coconino County	AZ	Roy Jimenez	1994	4856
291 7/8	49 0/8 48 1/8	37 5/8	6 6	Malheur County	OR	Landel M. McBride	1995	4856
291 7/8	39 6/8 44 1/8	34 1/8	8 6	Nojack	ALB	Calvin Briggs	1998	4856
291 7/8	48 2/8 47 3/8	35 5/8	6 6	Sierra County	NM	Ev Tarrell	2003	4856
291 6/8	45 2/8 45 5/8	41 0/8	6 6	Summit County	CO	Howard Moser	1972	4865
291 6/8	45 4/8 45 1/8	40 0/8	6 6	Gem County	ID	Larry Holmquist	1986	4865
291 6/8	47 0/8 47 1/8	31 4/8	6 6	Wapiti River	ALB	Ted Brown	1993	4865
291 6/8	49 6/8 49 2/8	32 4/8	6 6	Lane County	OR	James Phelps	1994	4865
291 6/8	42 4/8 44 3/8	39 2/8	6 5	Mineral County	MT	Don Leedham	1998	4865
291 6/8	47 3/8 48 3/8	34 0/8	6 6	Mineral County	CO	Jon M. Britton	2001	4865
291 6/8	47 7/8 48 1/8	36 0/8	6 6	Dolores County	CO	Tom Watts	2003	4865
291 6/8	46 6/8 44 2/8	34 6/8	6 6	Routt County	CO	Thane Anderson	2004	4865
291 5/8	53 2/8 54 6/8	34 7/8	7 7	Coconino County	AZ	Bruce Ludeke	1989	4873
291 5/8	43 1/8 44 3/8	36 1/8	6 6	Catron County	NM	Timothy J. Duffney	1993	4873
291 5/8	45 0/8 47 4/8	34 3/8	6 6	Columbia County	WA	James Stenersen	1995	4873
291 5/8	44 5/8 46 2/8	33 7/8	6 6	Shoshone County	ID	Linda Leake	1996	4873
291 5/8	50 3/8 51 6/8	34 5/8	6 6	Beaverhead County	MT	Jerry T. Arch	1996	4873
291 5/8	42 2/8 42 7/8	35 6/8	7 7	Rio Arriba County	NM	Lannie S. McGaughey	1997	4873
291 5/8	41 3/8 46 7/8	39 3/8	6 6	Grant County	OR	A. Duane Drewett	1997	4873
291 5/8	50 2/8 50 7/8	39 1/8	6 6	Judith Basin County	MT	Scott B. Duncan	2000	4873
291 5/8	43 7/8 43 2/8	36 1/8	6 6	Grant County	OR	Glenn Moodenbaugh	2001	4873
291 5/8	45 3/8 45 6/8	34 3/8	6 6	Bonneville County	ID	Joe Lewis	2001	4873
291 5/8	47 3/8 44 4/8	35 1/8	6 6	Union County	OR	Douglas L. Jennings	2004	4873
*291 5/8	42 7/8 45 5/8	37 7/8	7 6	Carbon County	WY	Jared J. Graham	2007	4873
*291 5/8	47 7/8 49 0/8	31 7/8	6 5	Lemhi County	ID	Bryan Geisel	2008	4873
291 5/8	43 2/8 40 6/8	30 7/8	7 7	Garfield County	MT	John Warberg	2009	4873
*291 5/8	42 7/8 42 2/8	38 1/8	6 6	Sanders County	MT	Bradley T. Dunkin	2009	4873
291 4/8	45 4/8 43 7/8	38 4/8	6 6	Dolores County	CO	William W. Gurley	1977	4888
291 4/8	42 2/8 43 4/8	35 2/8	7 6	Garfield County	MT	Gaylord Johnson	1983	4888
291 4/8	44 2/8 44 6/8	34 4/8	6 6	Sanders County	MT	Matthew J. Dorenkamper	1992	4888
291 4/8	44 0/8 42 5/8	31 4/8	6 6	Routt County	CO	Mark Upson	1994	4888
291 4/8	46 7/8 45 3/8	36 4/8	6 6	Catron County	NM	Chris Skinner	1997	4888
291 4/8	51 4/8 52 7/8	35 6/8	6 6	Judith Basin County	MT	Shawn Price	1998	4888
291 4/8	46 7/8 47 6/8	39 2/8	6 6	Valley County	ID	Jeff Dursteler	2001	4888
291 4/8	41 6/8 41 7/8	30 6/8	7 6	Baker County	OR	Brandon Palmer	2003	4888
291 4/8	44 5/8 43 4/8	34 0/8	6 6	Beaverhead County	MT	Dale A. Larson	2003	4888
291 4/8	46 2/8 45 1/8	33 6/8	6 6	Eagle County	CO	Kevin Wagner	2004	4888
291 4/8	46 2/8 46 6/8	32 2/8	6 6	Moffat County	CO	Mike Dziekan	2004	4888
291 4/8	44 1/8 43 3/8	37 4/8	6 6	Catron County	NM	Chris L. Skinner	2004	4888
*291 4/8	46 6/8 45 0/8	36 6/8	6 6	Park County	WY	Bruce Hildebrand	2004	4888
291 4/8	45 2/8 44 7/8	36 0/8	6 6	Routt County	CO	T. J. Thrasher	2005	4888
291 4/8	50 3/8 51 3/8	42 0/8	6 6	Dolores County	CO	Robert J. Jones	2006	4888
291 4/8	51 3/8 49 5/8	38 6/8	5 6	Beaverhead County	MT	Bruce Fuller	2007	4888
291 3/8	44 6/8 46 1/8	42 1/8	6 5	Idaho County	ID	Dr. Brian M. Howard	1987	4904
291 3/8	45 4/8 46 2/8	36 3/8	7 6	Grant County	OR	Terry Harling	1994	4904
291 3/8	40 2/8 40 2/8	37 1/8	6 6	Caribou County	ID	Darryl D. Lamoreaux	1997	4904
291 3/8	44 5/8 44 1/8	43 3/8	6 6	Adams County	ID	Larry Hoff	2003	4904
291 3/8	45 1/8 45 6/8	36 7/8	6 6	Fremont County	ID	Gary Niblock	2003	4904
291 3/8	49 0/8 48 4/8	37 1/8	6 6	Sublette County	WY	John Gedroez	2004	4904
*291 3/8	44 6/8 46 6/8	37 3/8	6 6	Rio Arriba County	NM	Frank A. Goodwin, Jr.	2005	4904
291 3/8	49 2/8 49 0/8	27 3/8	6 6	Mesa County	CO	Erik Watts	2009	4904
291 2/8	44 1/8 48 1/8	27 0/8	6 6	Phillips County	MT	Scott L. Augustine	1980	4912
291 2/8	47 5/8 45 0/8	36 6/8	6 6	Albany County	WY	Oliver P. Williamson	1982	4912
291 2/8	43 7/8 44 6/8	46 5/8	6 7	Clearwater County	ID	Scott Rabe	1984	4912
291 2/8	43 6/8 46 7/8	31 4/8	7 6	Gilpin County	CO	Lee L. Florian	1986	4912
291 2/8	52 1/8 51 4/8	35 4/8	6 6	Clearwater County	ID	Jim Horneck	1987	4912
291 2/8	42 4/8 41 6/8	34 4/8	6 6	Lincoln County	WY	George Walker	1993	4912
291 2/8	45 0/8 47 2/8	36 2/8	6 6	Fremont County	WY	Dale D. Gettel	1993	4912
291 2/8	48 1/8 48 0/8	36 2/8	8 6	Musselshell County	MT	Shawn Lar	1996	4912
291 2/8	46 4/8 45 2/8	37 4/8	5 6	Otero County	NM	Richard D. Burton	1998	4912
291 2/8	43 3/8 45 2/8	41 4/8	6 6	Uintah County	UT	Bernard P. Streily, Jr.	2000	4912
291 2/8	45 2/8 46 3/8	35 2/8	6 7	Washakie County	WY	Roger Peabody	2003	4912
291 2/8	45 3/8 44 6/8	42 6/8	6 6	Valley County	MT	Kerry L. Beechie	2006	4912
291 2/8	39 4/8 39 5/8	35 4/8	6 6	Cache County	UT	Scott Winters	2008	4912
*291 2/8	46 4/8 46 0/8	36 2/8	6 6	Catron County	NM	Gordon D. Markle, Jr.	2009	4912
291 2/8	44 3/8 41 6/8	35 0/8	6 6	Johnson County	WY	Darryl Amason	2010	4912
291 1/8	43 4/8 41 1/8	35 3/8	7 6	Coconino County	AZ	Tom Jensen	1989	4927
291 1/8	48 1/8 47 6/8	39 5/8	6 6	Grant County	OR	Dennis McClelland	1991	4927
291 1/8	46 7/8 47 2/8	30 5/8	6 6	Montrose County	CO	Lannie Ellis	1991	4927
291 1/8	46 6/8 46 7/8	36 3/8	6 6	Fremont County	CO	Michael Miller	1998	4927
291 1/8	42 1/8 47 4/8	33 0/8	7 8	Las Animas County	CO	Jim Hamill	2003	4927
291 1/8	47 2/8 47 5/8	35 3/8	6 6	Rio Arriba County	NM	Richie Bland	2004	4927
291 1/8	44 7/8 41 0/8	36 3/8	6 6	Madison County	MT	Vaughan Hodges	2005	4927
291 0/8	48 4/8 49 4/8	40 4/8	6 6	Custer County	CO	Douglas R. Jones	1970	4934
291 0/8	50 2/8 49 1/8	35 0/8	6 6	Elmore County	ID	Gary Briggs	1986	4934
291 0/8	47 2/8 47 0/8	38 4/8	6 5	Skamania County	WA	Terry Kern	1987	4934
291 0/8	44 2/8 41 4/8	37 0/8	6 6	Park County	WY	Paul W. McClelland, Jr.	1995	4934
291 0/8	49 6/8 49 7/8	33 6/8	6 6	Garfield County	MT	Bryant Shermoe	1995	4934
291 0/8	46 0/8 48 6/8	38 4/8	6 6	Shoshone County	ID	Neil Kimberling	1996	4934
291 0/8	44 4/8 47 6/8	29 6/8	7 8	Phillips County	MT	James G. Albrecht	1999	4934

AMERICAN ELK (TYPICAL ANTLERS)

Minimum Score 260   Continued

SCORE	LENGTH OF R MAIN BEAM L	INSIDE SPREAD	NUMBER OF R POINTS L	AREA	STATE/ PROVINCE	HUNTER'S NAME	DATE	RANK
291 0/8	41 4/8 41 5/8	28 4/8	6 6	Catron County	NM	David Wells	2001	4934
291 0/8	46 0/8 45 3/8	41 6/8	6 6	Johnson County	WY	Pax Harness	2001	4934
291 0/8	45 0/8 45 3/8	33 1/8	6 7	Nye County	NV	David Powning	2002	4934
291 0/8	59 0/8 55 2/8	35 2/8	6 6	Coconino County	AZ	Lynn Pomeroy	2003	4934
*291 0/8	46 2/8 46 1/8	34 0/8	6 6	Jefferson County	CO	John Stodola	2009	4934
*291 0/8	48 0/8 49 6/8	38 4/8	6 6	Otero County	NM	Bruce Barna	2009	4934
290 7/8	44 6/8 42 6/8	38 5/8	6 6	Ravalli County	MT	Sheldon M. Jones	1991	4947
290 7/8	49 5/8 45 7/8	35 5/8	6 6	Converse County	WY	John Fanto	1995	4947
290 7/8	45 6/8 44 0/8	32 7/8	6 6	Archuleta County	CO	Johnnie R. Walters	1997	4947
290 7/8	46 7/8 46 0/8	41 3/8	6 6	Elko County	NV	John Thayer	2002	4947
290 7/8	45 6/8 46 7/8	35 7/8	7 6	Catron County	NM	Larry Longenette	2003	4947
290 7/8	43 7/8 40 7/8	42 2/8	6 7	Las Animas County	CO	Donald P. Travis	2009	4947
290 6/8	42 4/8 43 0/8	35 6/8	6 6	Park County	WY	William P. Mastrangel	1955	4953
290 6/8	42 6/8 43 6/8	36 2/8	5 5	Larimer County	CO	Tom Tietz	1979	4953
290 6/8	41 5/8 41 3/8	38 0/8	6 6	Rio Arriba County	NM	Craig Barrows	1990	4953
290 6/8	46 2/8 46 5/8	38 6/8	6 7	Coconino County	AZ	Duane "Corky" Richardson	1991	4953
290 6/8	42 4/8 43 6/8	38 2/8	6 6	Madison County	MT	Randy Brown	1991	4953
290 6/8	46 3/8 43 4/8	35 2/8	6 6	Otero County	NM	Ronnie L. Elswick	1994	4953
290 6/8	46 0/8 50 2/8	37 0/8	6 6	Rio Arriba County	NM	Gordon Lee	1997	4953
290 6/8	45 5/8 45 4/8	38 4/8	6 6	Juab County	UT	Jason Jarrett	1999	4953
290 6/8	44 7/8 44 6/8	34 0/8	6 6	Idaho County	ID	Ryan Tyler	2002	4953
290 6/8	43 0/8 45 5/8	37 4/8	6 6	Johnson County	WY	Dave Harness	2003	4953
290 6/8	41 6/8 41 1/8	37 4/8	6 6	Millard County	UT	David D. Adams	2003	4953
*290 6/8	48 2/8 46 1/8	36 0/8	6 6	La Plata County	CO	Paul A. Moschler	2008	4953
*290 6/8	45 2/8 42 2/8	31 0/8	6 6	Catron County	NM	Terry Boyles	2009	4953
290 6/8	42 4/8 43 3/8	38 0/8	6 6	St. Brieux	SAS	Chad Rohel	2009	4953
290 5/8	45 2/8 46 6/8	36 7/8	8 8	Greenlee County	AZ	Sonny Turner	1986	4967
290 5/8	51 7/8 50 0/8	30 3/8	6 7	Coconino County	AZ	John Alfred Musgrove	1989	4967
290 5/8	41 2/8 41 4/8	35 4/8	7 6	Larimer County	CO	Steve W. Stumbo	1995	4967
290 5/8	51 5/8 52 4/8	37 7/8	6 6	Moffat County	CO	Rob Syvertson	1995	4967
290 5/8	44 5/8 45 1/8	37 5/8	6 6	Lemhi County	ID	Kevin L. Kenney	1996	4967
290 5/8	46 5/8 46 5/8	38 1/8	6 6	Granite County	MT	Frank H. Wilmot	1996	4967
290 5/8	45 5/8 47 1/8	31 3/8	6 6	Mineral County	MT	William B. Ross	1996	4967
290 5/8	40 0/8 39 3/8	36 5/8	6 6	Lincoln County	NM	Paul Vidrine	2000	4967
290 5/8	50 1/8 49 4/8	36 1/8	6 6	Elmore County	ID	Randy Lawson	2000	4967
290 5/8	49 6/8 46 1/8	34 1/8	6 6	Beaverhead County	MT	Skip Mathewson	2001	4967
290 5/8	46 0/8 46 6/8	34 5/8	6 6	Swan River	MAN	Jim A. Parker	2001	4967
290 5/8	46 2/8 45 0/8	36 7/8	6 7	Treasure County	MT	Mark T. Jacobson	2003	4967
290 5/8	44 7/8 43 6/8	44 3/8	6 6	Grant County	OR	Steven A. Evans	2003	4967
*290 5/8	46 4/8 45 7/8	35 5/8	6 6	Custer County	CO	Terry Lowe	2008	4967
*290 5/8	45 2/8 44 3/8	35 5/8	5 5	Cibola County	NM	Tom Nelson	2010	4967
290 4/8	48 3/8 51 3/8	34 2/8	5 6	Garfield County	CO	John W. Ellas	1998	4982
290 4/8	50 0/8 49 0/8	31 4/8	6 6	Caribou County	ID	Ed Ulicki	1999	4982
290 4/8	46 4/8 50 0/8	42 4/8	7 6	Camas County	ID	Blake Mitchell	1999	4982
290 4/8	48 6/8 51 2/8	38 6/8	6 6	Coconino County	AZ	Lyle Nils Bjelde	2001	4982
290 4/8	44 3/8 46 4/8	35 0/8	6 6	Dolores County	CO	Karl Schreck	2003	4982
*290 4/8	44 4/8 44 4/8	39 4/8	5 6	Grant County	OR	Jason Tarrant	2007	4982
*290 4/8	50 2/8 48 6/8	36 6/8	6 6	Montrose County	CO	Jeff Redfern	2008	4982
*290 4/8	48 4/8 47 0/8	37 4/8	6 6	Park County	UT	Jeff Furstenau	2009	4982
290 3/8	49 4/8 48 7/8	36 7/8	6 6	Custer County	ID	Tom Jarvis	1984	4990
290 3/8	49 2/8 49 2/8	39 5/8	6 6	Sublette County	WY	Joey Gomes	1989	4990
290 3/8	46 6/8 45 0/8	32 1/8	6 6	Idaho County	ID	Stanley L. Rider	1993	4990
290 3/8	42 6/8 41 6/8	31 5/8	6 6	Catron County	NM	Jim Talak	1994	4990
290 3/8	48 6/8 51 2/8	34 5/8	6 7	Coconino County	AZ	Randy H. Sifford	1996	4990
290 3/8	44 7/8 43 7/8	38 1/8	6 6	Valley County	ID	Brian Stroschein	2003	4990
290 3/8	43 7/8 43 7/8	39 3/8	6 6	Pierce County	WA	David Sundance Pierce	2007	4990
290 2/8	45 7/8 46 4/8	41 4/8	6 6	Gunnison County	CO	Jack Allen Rasmusson	1982	4997
290 2/8	42 6/8 44 5/8	40 0/8	6 6	Granite County	MT	Dennis Neitzke	1985	4997
290 2/8	42 1/8 40 3/8	34 6/8	6 6	Gallatin County	MT	Chris Cey	1991	4997
290 2/8	50 4/8 53 4/8	42 4/8	5 6	Cibola County	NM	Brandon Wynn	1992	4997
290 2/8	43 4/8 46 0/8	42 6/8	6 6	Jefferson County	CO	Gene Swanson	1992	4997
290 2/8	45 6/8 44 4/8	44 4/8	6 6	Jackson County	CO	Randy Chase	1999	4997
290 2/8	41 0/8 43 3/8	33 0/8	6 6	Huerfano County	CO	Anthony Verno, Jr.	2003	4997
290 2/8	41 5/8 38 4/8	30 4/8	6 6	Eagle County	CO	Joseph Mucilli	2004	4997
290 2/8	47 0/8 46 5/8	34 4/8	6 6	Gunnison County	CO	David R. Allison	2004	4997
290 2/8	46 2/8 46 3/8	31 2/8	7 7	Converse County	WY	Jason Swanson	2004	4997
290 2/8	45 3/8 44 4/8	31 4/8	6 6	Idaho County	ID	David Briggs	2006	4997
290 2/8	47 0/8 46 2/8	38 2/8	6 6	Grant County	OR	Bryan Summers	2007	4997
290 2/8	43 5/8 44 4/8	33 6/8	6 6	Las Animas County	CO	Mike Broadwell	2009	4997
*290 2/8	45 1/8 48 4/8	37 2/8	6 6	Las Animas County	CO	Brent A. Tamburelli	2009	4997
290 2/8	45 2/8 43 2/8	38 6/8	5 5	Salt Lake County	UT	Kipp D. Jamison	2010	4997
290 1/8	45 6/8 44 7/8	38 3/8	6 6	Grant County	OR	James M. Carter	1984	5012
290 1/8	49 4/8 49 4/8	40 7/8	6 6	McKinley County	NM	Larry Dwyer	1989	5012
290 1/8	43 0/8 45 6/8	40 1/8	6 6	Colfax County	NM	Robert Torstenson	1997	5012
290 1/8	43 2/8 45 2/8	38 7/8	6 6	Lincoln County	NM	Joseph Allen Tobey	2003	5012
290 1/8	46 6/8 46 7/8	37 5/8	6 6	Navajo County	AZ	Darold Randa	2003	5012
290 1/8	43 4/8 44 3/8	33 7/8	6 6	Otero County	NM	Wayne Schneider	2009	5012
290 0/8	47 2/8 46 4/8	39 0/8	6 6	Phillips County	MT	Cecil I. Tharp	1978	5018
290 0/8	41 6/8 43 5/8	43 5/8	6 7	Canmore	ALB	David R. Coupland	1980	5018
290 0/8	45 7/8 42 2/8	35 6/8	6 6	Shoshone County	ID	Larry Rose	1988	5018
290 0/8	47 7/8 44 0/8	34 7/8	7 6	Sandoval County	NM	Robert L. Pagel	1989	5018
290 0/8	43 4/8 45 1/8	38 2/8	8 6	Coconino County	AZ	Greg Buckler	1999	5018
290 0/8	58 3/8 52 6/8	43 0/8	5 5	Sublette County	WY	Steven L. Despain	2001	5018
290 0/8	45 4/8 45 2/8	38 0/8	6 6	Gunnison County	CO	Randy Hoffman	2003	5018
290 0/8	47 2/8 46 5/8	35 0/8	6 6	Gallatin County	MT	Matt Weiler	2004	5018
290 0/8	45 0/8 45 3/8	36 2/8	6 6	Colfax County	NM	Robert Ameen	2005	5018
289 7/8	43 0/8 41 0/8	40 3/8	6 6	Boulder County	CO	John Powell	1983	5027
289 7/8	47 7/8 47 4/8	36 5/8	6 6	Missoula County	MT	Bill Spicknall	1984	5027
289 7/8	41 5/8 46 3/8	40 4/8	6 6	Mesa County	CO	George P. Sofronas	1986	5027
289 7/8	44 6/8 45 0/8	39 3/8	6 6	Sandoval County	NM	William F. Gorman	1996	5027
289 7/8	42 1/8 43 6/8	40 5/8	6 6	Adams County	ID	Greg Richardson	1997	5027
289 7/8	44 3/8 41 0/8	28 7/8	6 6	Caribou County	ID	Anthony Robinson	1997	5027
289 7/8	47 5/8 47 4/8	36 5/8	6 6	Linn County	OR	Dean Mintken	2001	5027
289 7/8	46 2/8 47 0/8	33 1/8	6 6	Yellowhead	ALB	Dwayne Huggins	2001	5027
289 7/8	47 0/8 47 0/8	33 7/8	6 6	Petroleum County	MT	Guy Hinrichs	2002	5027

730

AMERICAN ELK (TYPICAL ANTLERS)

Minimum Score 260

Continued

SCORE	LENGTH OF R MAIN BEAM L	INSIDE SPREAD	NUMBER OF R POINTS L	AREA	STATE/ PROVINCE	HUNTER'S NAME	DATE	RANK
289 7/8	45 7/8 45 7/8	40 2/8	5 7	Shoshone County	ID	Wayne Lynn	2003	5027
289 7/8	41 2/8 40 5/8	39 1/8	7 6	Catron County	NM	Fernando Semiao	2007	5027
289 6/8	45 3/8 45 0/8	35 6/8	6 6	Ravalli County	MT	Dan Smith	1980	5038
289 6/8	42 3/8 41 6/8	33 0/8	5 6	Rich County	UT	Raymond E. Goff	1989	5038
289 6/8	45 4/8 45 6/8	42 6/8	6 6	Los Alamos County	NM	Bruce Barrie	1989	5038
289 6/8	46 3/8 46 4/8	36 2/8	6 6	Coconino County	AZ	Tom H. Sissom	1995	5038
289 6/8	42 7/8 41 2/8	36 2/8	7 7	Cowlitz County	WA	Larry Bryan Skaar	1997	5038
289 6/8	45 3/8 44 5/8	39 2/8	6 6	Beaverhead County	MT	Dag Jenshus	1998	5038
289 6/8	46 6/8 44 2/8	37 0/8	6 6	Grand County	UT	John Caruso	2005	5038
289 6/8	44 0/8 47 5/8	35 2/8	6 6	Park County	WY	Ron Niziolek	2005	5038
289 6/8	43 4/8 44 0/8	34 2/8	6 6	Grand County	CO	Rob Kohlwey	2006	5038
289 6/8	43 6/8 44 5/8	39 2/8	6 6	Fergus County	MT	Jared Wichman	2009	5038
289 5/8	42 2/8 42 2/8	38 3/8	6 6	Ravalli County	MT	Michael S. Mitchell	1985	5048
289 5/8	49 0/8 49 3/8	40 1/8	6 6	Johnson County	WY	Gary Peterson	1999	5048
289 5/8	46 1/8 50 4/8	36 3/8	6 6	Clearwater County	ID	Doug Brady	2004	5048
289 4/8	48 0/8 50 3/8	33 2/8	6 6	Clearwater County	ID	LeRoy West	1983	5051
289 4/8	48 0/8 46 4/8	41 0/8	6 6	Coconino County	AZ	Fred Searle	1985	5051
289 4/8	44 5/8 42 0/8	39 2/8	7 7	Grant County	OR	Ray Martin	1988	5051
289 4/8	45 5/8 43 6/8	38 2/8	6 5	Ravalli County	MT	Shaun Twardoski	1993	5051
289 4/8	44 4/8 44 3/8	38 0/8	6 6	Flathead County	MT	Douglas E. Skoczek	1996	5051
289 4/8	48 0/8 47 0/8	40 0/8	8 6	Coconino County	AZ	Steve Christensen	1996	5051
289 4/8	41 7/8 42 3/8	40 4/8	6 6	Grant County	OR	Kevin P. Scanlan	1997	5051
289 4/8	51 5/8 51 1/8	39 4/8	6 6	La Plata County	CO	J. T. Kreager	1998	5051
289 4/8	47 6/8 48 4/8	37 0/8	6 6	Flathead County	MT	Steve Herman	1999	5051
289 4/8	50 1/8 45 5/8	32 0/8	6 6	Catron County	NM	Michael A. Frank	1999	5051
289 4/8	46 2/8 46 6/8	35 4/8	6 6	Park County	CO	Jason Roe	2004	5051
289 4/8	48 1/8 40 0/8	36 0/8	6 6	Larimer County	CO	Robert Devore	2006	5051
289 4/8	42 7/8 41 7/8	37 2/8	6 6	Crook County	OR	Gary O'Grady	2007	5051
289 3/8	43 1/8 43 4/8	38 7/8	5 5	Lewis County	WA	Douglas H. Brandt	1986	5064
289 3/8	40 4/8 42 0/8	37 3/8	6 7	Valley County	MT	Erik E. Scarpholt	1986	5064
289 3/8	41 7/8 44 5/8	38 7/8	6 6	Hinsdale County	CO	Kevin W. Bauman	1989	5064
289 3/8	46 1/8 46 1/8	44 1/8	6 6	Sandoval County	NM	Randy Erickson	1992	5064
289 3/8	44 1/8 44 0/8	35 5/8	6 6	Larimer County	CO	Gary Greathouse	1993	5064
289 3/8	41 6/8 44 5/8	39 7/8	6 6	Lincoln County	WY	Lyle S. Bainbridge	1994	5064
289 3/8	43 7/8 44 7/8	33 3/8	6 6	Columbia County	WA	Douglas Eaton	2000	5064
289 3/8	47 2/8 44 0/8	37 3/8	6 6	Albany County	WY	Bruce R. Cotherman	2004	5064
289 3/8	41 7/8 42 7/8	35 5/8	6 6	Coconino County	AZ	Nick Rowley II	2004	5064
*289 3/8	43 4/8 41 0/8	39 2/8	8 7	Big Horn County	WY	David Heberling	2005	5064
289 3/8	47 2/8 47 6/8	38 5/8	6 5	Sheridan County	WY	Daniel K. Doke	2008	5064
289 2/8	43 7/8 45 3/8	33 0/8	6 6	Converse County	WY	Darin L. Geringer	1989	5075
289 2/8	48 0/8 50 0/8	34 2/8	6 6	Sandoval County	NM	Danny Lee Reed	1989	5075
289 2/8	49 2/8 48 0/8	41 4/8	6 6	Pitkin County	CO	James L. Behn	1990	5075
289 2/8	54 7/8 55 4/8	38 0/8	7 7	Grant County	NM	Adam Jimenez, Jr.	1991	5075
289 2/8	39 0/8 41 2/8	37 0/8	6 6	Clark County	ID	John C. Miller	1994	5075
289 2/8	43 6/8 43 4/8	39 2/8	6 6	Clark County	ID	Tony L. Rossi	1995	5075
289 2/8	46 1/8 46 0/8	46 0/8	5 5	Elmore County	ID	George T. Peter, Jr.	1995	5075
289 2/8	43 7/8 46 1/8	34 2/8	6 6	Ravalli County	MT	Ric Twardoski	1996	5075
289 2/8	52 4/8 52 5/8	35 4/8	6 6	Jackson County	OR	David Shanklin	1998	5075
289 2/8	44 3/8 44 1/8	31 2/8	6 6	Montezuma County	CO	Nate T. Hicks	2000	5075
289 2/8	45 1/8 46 2/8	36 0/8	8 7	Asotin County	WA	Richard D. Howell	2001	5075
289 2/8	45 5/8 47 2/8	36 6/8	6 6	Coconino County	AZ	Dan Howe	2001	5075
289 2/8	51 4/8 49 6/8	33 2/8	6 6	Musselshell County	MT	Kelly Bingham	2005	5075
289 2/8	44 6/8 46 0/8	35 0/8	6 6	Custer County	ID	Katherine Boren	2007	5075
289 1/8	46 0/8 46 1/8	35 1/8	6 6	Catron County	NM	Paul D. Payne	1986	5089
289 1/8	46 5/8 45 7/8	38 3/8	6 6	Flathead County	MT	Bill Love	1987	5089
289 1/8	43 4/8 48 1/8	35 7/8	6 6	Lemhi County	ID	Danny Moore	1988	5089
289 1/8	45 4/8 47 0/8	37 5/8	6 6	Johnson County	WY	Donald Janoff, DDS	1993	5089
289 1/8	47 7/8 49 3/8	36 6/8	7 7	Catron County	NM	Chris Trujillo	1995	5089
289 1/8	45 7/8 43 7/8	32 1/8	6 6	Teller County	CO	Ron Largent	1996	5089
289 1/8	44 3/8 44 5/8	38 3/8	6 6	Idaho County	ID	Mike Marano	1996	5089
289 1/8	42 5/8 43 4/8	35 7/8	6 6	Rio Arriba County	NM	Ryan Panzy	2002	5089
289 1/8	48 5/8 49 6/8	39 3/8	5 5	Garfield County	CO	James E. Godfrey	2004	5089
289 1/8	44 2/8 44 1/8	38 7/8	6 6	Rio Arriba County	NM	Richie Bland	2005	5089
289 1/8	46 7/8 46 0/8	34 1/8	6 6	Rosebud County	MT	Chad P. Lehman	2007	5089
289 1/8	56 6/8 56 6/8	30 4/8	6 7	Lewis & Clark County	MT	Ray Pape	2008	5089
*289 1/8	42 7/8 42 7/8	41 3/8	6 6	Fremont County	CO	Nick Vindivich, Jr.	2008	5089
289 0/8	51 6/8 50 0/8	38 6/8	6 6	Socorro County	NM	Will Eckelhoff	1991	5102
289 0/8	48 1/8 47 7/8	33 6/8	7 7	Flathead County	MT	Mason Gray Riley II	1995	5102
289 0/8	41 0/8 40 6/8	35 6/8	6 6	Baker County	OR	Francis Tyler	1997	5102
289 0/8	37 2/8 36 6/8	33 6/8	6 6	Greenwater Lake	SAS	Cory Sawchuk	2003	5102
289 0/8	44 2/8 42 1/8	31 2/8	6 6	Sevier County	UT	David J. Hansen	2004	5102
289 0/8	46 5/8 49 2/8	38 6/8	6 6	Montezuma County	CO	Ken Schenkenberger	2004	5102
*289 0/8	45 1/8 45 6/8	29 6/8	6 6	Montrose County	CO	Fred King	2005	5102
289 0/8	42 6/8 41 0/8	35 0/8	6 6	Rio Blanco County	CO	Walt Krom	2008	5102
289 0/8	49 0/8 48 2/8	42 6/8	5 6	Yakima County	WA	Christopher E. Rankin	2008	5102
*289 0/8	43 3/8 46 0/8	40 6/8	5 6	Sheridan County	WY	Julie Nickel	2009	5102
289 0/8	49 3/8 50 3/8	45 0/8	6 6	Powell County	MT	Tim Harris	2009	5102
289 0/8	46 3/8 46 1/8	31 4/8	6 6	Granite County	MT	Duane D. DuFresne	2009	5102
*289 0/8	44 2/8 43 5/8	39 6/8	6 6	Lincoln County	WY	Alexander Noam Teutsch	2009	5102
288 7/8	47 6/8 46 3/8	38 1/8	6 6	Linn County	OR	Richard D. Howell	1986	5115
288 7/8	44 6/8 45 4/8	38 6/8	6 7	Ravalli County	MT	David Harris Stalling	1992	5115
288 7/8	44 6/8 43 6/8	33 7/8	6 6	Coconino County	AZ	Dale Milton	1994	5115
288 7/8	48 6/8 49 4/8	42 5/8	6 6	Granite County	MT	Randy L. Cloak	1996	5115
288 7/8	45 5/8 45 4/8	33 3/8	6 6	Jackson County	CO	Patrick M. Jolly	2005	5115
288 7/8	48 0/8 48 2/8	31 5/8	6 6	Phillips County	MT	Scott T. Smith	2005	5115
288 6/8	53 1/8 52 2/8	34 2/8	5 6	Lane County	OR	Ken Abraham	1986	5121
288 6/8	43 3/8 44 0/8	31 2/8	6 6	Teton County	MT	Brad Stewart	1992	5121
288 6/8	50 3/8 49 2/8	31 2/8	6 6	Umatilla County	OR	Mike Billman	1998	5121
288 6/8	46 2/8 45 6/8	37 2/8	6 5	Apache County	AZ	Ron Jay Aschenbach	2000	5121
288 6/8	50 4/8 53 4/8	36 6/8	6 6	Catron County	NM	Lawrence S. Nichols	2001	5121
288 6/8	41 3/8 47 1/8	39 4/8	7 6	Breathitt County	KY	Craig Wheeler	2002	5121
288 6/8	49 6/8 52 7/8	40 6/8	6 7	Coconino County	AZ	David Harrison	2004	5121
288 6/8	44 2/8 44 5/8	31 2/8	6 6	Garfield County	MT	Martin R. Kilen	2004	5121
288 6/8	46 3/8 46 0/8	37 0/8	6 6	Rio Blanco County	CO	Daniel E. Rudy	2005	5121
288 6/8	41 2/8 41 5/8	40 6/8	5 6	Delta County	CO	Timothy C. Funnell	2008	5121

731

AMERICAN ELK (TYPICAL ANTLERS)

Minimum Score 260 Continued

SCORE	LENGTH OF R MAIN BEAM L	INSIDE SPREAD	NUMBER OF R POINTS L		AREA	STATE/ PROVINCE	HUNTER'S NAME	DATE	RANK
288 6/8	43 0/8	43 5/8	31 4/8	6	6	Garfield County	CO	Forest Keith	2008	5121
288 6/8	50 4/8	51 4/8	36 0/8	6	6	Wheeler County	OR	Jason A. Crafton	2008	5121
*288 6/8	46 2/8	45 4/8	46 3/8	5	5	Grant County	OR	Jason Tarrant	2008	5121
*288 6/8	45 5/8	45 3/8	49 0/8	7	9	Gilpin County	CO	Topher Donahue	2009	5121
288 6/8	45 0/8	46 0/8	40 0/8	6	6	Lawrence County	SD	John A. Meyen	2009	5121
*288 6/8	51 4/8	51 4/8	35 4/8	5	6	Mineral County	CO	David T. Holden	2009	5121
288 5/8	46 5/8	44 6/8	39 1/8	6	6	Rio Arriba County	NM	Keith Cheatham	1988	5137
288 5/8	43 0/8	45 4/8	37 5/8	6	6	Adams County	ID	Randal R. Siemens	1990	5137
288 5/8	49 6/8	48 5/8	38 3/8	6	6	Sierra County	NM	Bill Elmer	1990	5137
288 5/8	47 3/8	44 2/8	35 3/8	6	6	Coconino County	AZ	David C. Fretz	1991	5137
288 5/8	47 3/8	46 6/8	42 0/8	7	6	Sierra County	NM	Olaf R. Lundquist	1995	5137
288 5/8	40 3/8	45 1/8	38 1/8	6	6	Rio Arriba County	NM	Ken A. Olson	2000	5137
288 5/8	44 3/8	42 7/8	33 3/8	6	6	Clark County	ID	Chad Berry	2001	5137
288 5/8	47 3/8	46 3/8	37 7/8	6	6	Fergus County	MT	Robert J. Tyndall	2002	5137
288 5/8	44 4/8	45 1/8	39 3/8	6	6	Valley County	ID	Shane Miller	2003	5137
288 5/8	47 4/8	47 5/8	35 3/8	6	6	La Plata County	CO	Clinton Wilson	2004	5137
288 5/8	47 5/8	47 0/8	35 5/8	5	5	Crook County	OR	Gregg T. Embree	2005	5137
*288 5/8	41 6/8	42 5/8	34 7/8	6	6	Jefferson County	CO	Randy Stolba	2007	5137
288 4/8	50 2/8	49 2/8	34 4/8	6	6	Lemhi County	ID	Ben L. Fahnholz	1984	5149
288 4/8	44 5/8	48 3/8	39 4/8	5	6	San Miguel County	NM	Robert B. Lewis	1987	5149
288 4/8	40 6/8	41 5/8	38 6/8	6	6	Sandoval County	NM	Peter C. Swenson	1990	5149
288 4/8	44 0/8	45 0/8	44 0/8	6	6	Klickitat County	WA	Tom Gaul	1991	5149
288 4/8	47 6/8	49 3/8	40 4/8	6	6	Rio Arriba County	NM	Scott Miller	1992	5149
288 4/8	47 5/8	46 5/8	36 0/8	6	7	Fergus County	MT	Josef Rud	1993	5149
288 4/8	51 5/8	52 3/8	33 0/8	6	6	Catron County	NM	Kurt D. Rued	1999	5149
288 4/8	45 5/8	47 3/8	37 6/8	6	6	Wheeler County	OR	Steven T. Jones	2003	5149
288 4/8	42 4/8	43 4/8	43 6/8	5	5	Otero County	NM	Gene Majchrzak	2005	5149
288 4/8	44 4/8	50 5/8	35 6/8	6	6	Fergus County	MT	Josef K. Rud	2006	5149
*288 4/8	44 1/8	43 0/8	37 2/8	6	6	Gunnison County	CO	Jerry V. Miller	2010	5149
288 3/8	43 2/8	44 4/8	34 7/8	6	6	Marion County	OR	Daniel Smith	1989	5160
288 3/8	46 5/8	46 5/8	34 1/8	6	6	Park County	WY	Michael Turner	1993	5160
288 3/8	42 6/8	44 5/8	37 7/8	6	6	Navajo County	AZ	Kevin D. Hatfield	1993	5160
288 3/8	48 4/8	46 7/8	38 1/8	6	6	Baker County	OR	David J. Freske	1994	5160
288 3/8	39 2/8	40 2/8	38 5/8	6	6	Sandoval County	NM	Michael G. Morton	1996	5160
288 3/8	44 7/8	45 5/8	42 5/8	6	6	Shoshone County	ID	Tony A. Hartman	1998	5160
288 3/8	43 4/8	43 3/8	29 2/8	6	7	Sanders County	MT	Elizabeth A. Stender	2003	5160
288 3/8	44 2/8	41 6/8	35 5/8	6	6	Catron County	NM	Bruce Carleton Kelly	2004	5160
288 3/8	49 0/8	51 0/8	36 7/8	6	6	Gila County	AZ	Gary H. Mehaffey	2009	5160
288 2/8	50 6/8	48 3/8	39 2/8	6	6	Lincoln County	MT	Robert L. Burk	1976	5169
288 2/8	46 2/8	45 0/8	39 6/8	6	6	Lemhi County	ID	John A. McCarthy	1984	5169
288 2/8	44 5/8	44 1/8	32 7/8	7	6	Greenlee County	AZ	John C. Jackson	1987	5169
288 2/8	48 0/8	48 2/8	30 6/8	6	6	Madison County	MT	Ben Manor	1990	5169
288 2/8	45 2/8	45 6/8	35 4/8	6	6	Apache County	AZ	James L. Crampton	1992	5169
288 2/8	45 7/8	46 0/8	43 4/8	6	5	Beaverhead County	MT	Danny Moore	1995	5169
288 2/8	44 0/8	42 6/8	35 6/8	6	6	Garfield County	MT	Bryant Shermoe	1996	5169
288 2/8	44 1/8	44 0/8	33 0/8	6	6	Idaho County	ID	Stanley L. Rider	1997	5169
288 2/8	46 0/8	45 7/8	36 4/8	6	6	Phillips County	MT	Joe K. Aldworth	1998	5169
288 2/8	50 0/8	44 5/8	37 0/8	6	6	Catron County	NM	Justin Kipp	2001	5169
288 2/8	52 2/8	55 3/8	43 4/8	5	6	La Plata County	CO	Kenny Bell	2003	5169
288 2/8	48 1/8	47 4/8	38 6/8	6	6	Grant County	NM	Richard E. Hewett	2006	5169
288 2/8	46 6/8	46 6/8	38 0/8	5	5	Grant County	OR	Chad Marmolejo	2007	5169
288 1/8	48 4/8	48 5/8	37 5/8	7	6	Fergus County	MT	Craig Leslie Osborne	1993	5182
288 1/8	50 2/8	48 4/8	35 7/8	6	6	Catron County	NM	David LeClaire	1995	5182
288 1/8	41 5/8	43 1/8	39 7/8	6	6	Valley County	ID	Andy D. Anderson	1996	5182
288 1/8	47 4/8	44 2/8	32 1/8	6	6	Socorro County	NM	Marvin H. Walter	1996	5182
288 1/8	43 3/8	40 3/8	46 2/8	5	5	Custer County	ID	Daryl Pilarski	1997	5182
288 1/8	47 4/8	51 4/8	36 5/8	5	5	Fremont County	ID	Gene Dobbs	1999	5182
288 1/8	45 2/8	44 4/8	42 1/8	6	6	Cache County	UT	John "Jake" Peterson	2001	5182
288 1/8	46 6/8	46 1/8	34 5/8	6	6	Weston County	WY	Craig Overman	2003	5182
288 1/8	42 2/8	45 2/8	36 1/8	6	6	Flathead County	MT	Charles Avery	2003	5182
288 1/8	48 4/8	48 6/8	40 1/8	7	6	Catron County	NM	Greg S. Hartung	2004	5182
288 1/8	46 6/8	46 5/8	33 5/8	6	6	La Plata County	CO	Tom W. Jones	2005	5182
288 0/8	46 4/8	44 4/8	35 0/8	6	6	Albany County	WY	Dan Kolb	1981	5193
288 0/8	49 2/8	47 7/8	36 0/8	5	6	Carbon County	UT	David A. Justmann	1989	5193
288 0/8	44 3/8	45 6/8	44 0/8	6	6	Yakima County	WA	Gaylen Bierman	1990	5193
288 0/8	46 0/8	47 3/8	36 6/8	6	6	Coconino County	AZ	Randall Madding	1992	5193
288 0/8	40 0/8	41 0/8	34 4/8	6	6	Fergus County	MT	Kelly Norskog	1993	5193
288 0/8	39 3/8	39 3/8	31 2/8	6	6	Clark County	ID	Brian McIlnay	1994	5193
288 0/8	47 0/8	45 0/8	33 6/8	6	6	Jefferson County	CO	Rob Sparks	2004	5193
288 0/8	43 2/8	46 5/8	35 4/8	6	6	Coconino County	AZ	Lee Mitchell	2004	5193
288 0/8	42 6/8	44 0/8	45 0/8	6	6	Bonner County	ID	Jim E. Bolender	2005	5193
287 7/8	38 1/8	38 4/8	34 7/8	6	6	Garfield County	CO	Michael J. Reid	1981	5202
287 7/8	47 1/8	48 1/8	38 7/8	6	6	Granite County	MT	Stephen F. Culp	1991	5202
287 7/8	44 4/8	44 7/8	33 3/8	6	6	Park County	WY	Robert J. Horner	1992	5202
287 7/8	41 5/8	44 4/8	34 6/8	7	6	Fergus County	MT	Mike T. Dellwo	1994	5202
287 7/8	43 1/8	46 1/8	35 3/8	6	6	Caribou County	ID	Tom Norris	1995	5202
287 7/8	46 0/8	44 4/8	38 5/8	6	6	Colfax County	NM	Richard Albright	1999	5202
*287 7/8	46 6/8	45 2/8	36 7/8	6	6	Grant County	OR	Jason C. Tarrant	2009	5202
287 6/8	44 0/8	44 0/8	35 4/8	6	6	Idaho County	ID	Ronald Ward	1984	5209
287 6/8	38 7/8	38 7/8	30 2/8	6	6	Cypress Hills	ALB	Clayton Knutson	1993	5209
287 6/8	41 2/8	42 5/8	39 4/8	6	6	Grant County	OR	Richard S. Hadley	1997	5209
287 6/8	46 1/8	45 2/8	39 2/8	6	6	Lemhi County	ID	Heath Nicholls	2001	5209
287 6/8	46 0/8	45 6/8	41 4/8	6	5	La Plata County	CO	Michael Hinson	2007	5209
287 5/8	50 4/8	48 5/8	38 1/8	6	7	Park County	MT	George Kamps	1987	5214
287 5/8	42 5/8	43 0/8	34 3/8	6	6	Catron County	NM	Danny Burgess	1994	5214
287 5/8	42 0/8	45 1/8	37 3/8	6	6	Greenlee County	AZ	Steve Rainey	1995	5214
287 5/8	45 6/8	46 5/8	42 3/8	7	6	Lemhi County	ID	Bob Johnson	1996	5214
287 5/8	40 7/8	40 3/8	37 1/8	6	6	Las Animas County	CO	Lannie B. Philley	1997	5214
287 5/8	46 0/8	46 1/8	35 3/8	6	6	Linn County	OR	Todd A. Walsh	1998	5214
287 5/8	45 5/8	43 4/8	32 5/8	6	6	Valley County	ID	Dennis Crew	1998	5214
287 5/8	47 2/8	46 3/8	33 1/8	6	6	Clackamas County	OR	Tim Metzger	1999	5214
287 5/8	47 7/8	45 6/8	31 7/8	6	6	Coconino County	AZ	Scott Prucha	2003	5214
287 5/8	49 3/8	48 6/8	38 5/8	6	7	Teton County	WY	Eric Moore	2005	5214
*287 5/8	44 4/8	43 7/8	27 7/8	6	6	Colfax County	NM	Lisa Ameen	2005	5214
287 4/8	44 4/8	45 0/8	38 2/8	6	6	Adams County	ID	Gary Kinney	1986	5225

732

AMERICAN ELK (TYPICAL ANTLERS)

Minimum Score 260

Continued

SCORE	LENGTH OF R MAIN BEAM L	INSIDE SPREAD	NUMBER OF R POINTS L	AREA	STATE/ PROVINCE	HUNTER'S NAME	DATE	RANK
287 4/8	45 2/8 44 0/8	39 0/8	6 6	Baker County	OR	Larry D. Jones	1987	5225
287 4/8	43 1/8 41 6/8	36 1/8	6 7	Morgan County	UT	Hal Stauff	1987	5225
287 4/8	45 4/8 44 5/8	35 6/8	6 6	Phillips County	MT	William P. Kirkman	1987	5225
287 4/8	42 0/8 41 0/8	37 2/8	6 6	Phillips County	MT	Kenneth E. Ruzicka	1988	5225
287 4/8	46 2/8 46 2/8	39 0/8	7 7	Rio Grande County	CO	Chris Hale	1997	5225
287 4/8	43 6/8 49 1/8	34 4/8	6 6	Coconino County	AZ	Glen Dillehay	1997	5225
287 4/8	44 7/8 48 6/8	40 0/8	6 6	Jefferson County	CO	Jim Shoening	1999	5225
287 4/8	42 0/8 42 4/8	36 2/8	6 6	Routt County	CO	Ronald Breitsprecher	2000	5225
287 4/8	42 5/8 43 0/8	32 0/8	6 6	Catron County	NM	John Sarvis	2001	5225
287 4/8	45 2/8 46 0/8	39 0/8	6 6	Shoshone County	ID	Peter D. "Beau" Durham	2004	5225
287 4/8	46 1/8 45 7/8	42 4/8	6 6	Caribou County	ID	David J. Hanson	2005	5225
*287 4/8	44 6/8 44 4/8	38 0/8	6 6	Catron County	NM	Kevin Brown	2009	5225
287 4/8	49 5/8 48 6/8	39 2/8	6 6	Catron County	NM	Ambrose Calles	2010	5225
287 3/8	45 2/8 43 2/8	29 3/8	6 7	Bighorn Mtns.	WY	Don Dvoroznak	1977	5239
287 3/8	49 7/8 50 4/8	35 4/8	7 7	Coconino County	AZ	William P. Pate	1979	5239
287 3/8	51 3/8 50 0/8	44 1/8	7 7	Beaverhead County	MT	Ronnie Everett	1982	5239
287 3/8	50 7/8 50 1/8	39 3/8	6 6	Lane County	OR	Charles M. Reich	1991	5239
287 3/8	50 2/8 50 6/8	37 3/8	6 6	Coconino County	AZ	Steven G. Rickner	1993	5239
287 3/8	43 5/8 43 5/8	37 3/8	6 6	Otero County	NM	Terry Morrow	1995	5239
287 3/8	47 7/8 47 1/8	34 5/8	6 6	Rio Arriba County	NM	Dr. Gary E. Palmer, D.C.	1997	5239
287 3/8	47 4/8 49 5/8	34 3/8	6 7	Caribou County	ID	Robert L. Rigby	1998	5239
287 3/8	44 4/8 44 7/8	37 1/8	6 6	Douglas County	OR	Wayne H. Beattie	1998	5239
287 3/8	40 7/8 39 3/8	43 7/8	6 6	Albany County	WY	Jerry Bowen	1998	5239
287 3/8	46 4/8 46 2/8	31 5/8	6 6	Lewis County	WA	Boyd W. Dart	2000	5239
287 3/8	37 6/8 45 0/8	36 5/8	6 6	Catron County	NM	Michael Knepp	2001	5239
287 3/8	41 6/8 42 2/8	38 5/8	6 6	Wheatland County	MT	John Clough	2002	5239
287 3/8	43 3/8 43 4/8	31 3/8	6 6	Routt County	CO	Don Schultz	2005	5239
287 3/8	48 3/8 47 0/8	38 3/8	6 6	Jackson County	OR	Dustin Govenor	2006	5239
287 2/8	41 4/8 41 4/8	29 2/8	6 6	San Isabel National Forest	CO	Richard L. Doman	1977	5254
287 2/8	50 0/8 50 6/8	35 4/8	6 6	Grand County	CO	Robert Pitt	1978	5254
287 2/8	42 6/8 41 6/8	32 0/8	6 6	Flathead County	MT	Rod Hickle	1982	5254
287 2/8	45 6/8 46 7/8	35 6/8	6 6	Sublette County	WY	Ron A. Noble	1987	5254
287 2/8	40 0/8 41 6/8	36 4/8	7 6	Larimer County	CO	Brent Byram	1989	5254
287 2/8	46 4/8 46 5/8	32 4/8	5 6	Catron County	NM	Glenn Isler	1991	5254
287 2/8	42 0/8 41 2/8	38 0/8	6 6	La Plata County	CO	Brook Jobes	1991	5254
287 2/8	41 6/8 43 6/8	38 6/8	6 6	San Juan County	CO	William J. Farrell	1991	5254
287 2/8	44 1/8 45 6/8	34 0/8	6 6	Sandoval County	NM	Joe H. Campbell	1992	5254
287 2/8	43 2/8 43 2/8	36 1/8	7 6	Shoshone County	ID	Charles Gerhard	1992	5254
287 2/8	42 3/8 43 0/8	33 2/8	6 7	Canmore	ALB	John Visscher	1995	5254
287 2/8	45 5/8 46 0/8	32 2/8	5 5	White Pine County	NV	Felton Hickman	2003	5254
287 2/8	49 0/8 47 6/8	34 0/8	6 6	Grant County	OR	Forrest Denison	2004	5254
287 2/8	44 2/8 44 2/8	41 6/8	6 6	Coconino County	AZ	Gary Zimmerer	2005	5254
287 1/8	46 0/8 45 5/8	37 3/8	6 7	Valley County	ID	L. Lombard/C. Rukkala	1980	5268
287 1/8	44 1/8 44 0/8	32 7/8	6 6	Apache County	AZ	John A. Holcomb	1981	5268
287 1/8	44 7/8 43 6/8	37 3/8	7 7	Sheridan County	WY	Richard Miller	1987	5268
287 1/8	48 0/8 49 0/8	37 5/8	6 6	Washakie County	WY	Terry Kuhnert	1991	5268
287 1/8	44 1/8 44 3/8	41 1/8	6 6	Uinta County	WY	Jason Rooney	1992	5268
287 1/8	45 4/8 50 1/8	30 5/8	5 7	Coconino County	AZ	Jack W. Starnes	1993	5268
287 1/8	44 3/8 45 0/8	37 3/8	6 6	Little Elbow River	ALB	Roger E. Meyer	1996	5268
287 1/8	46 1/8 46 1/8	36 1/8	6 6	Union County	OR	Keith A. Reber	1998	5268
287 1/8	45 4/8 44 7/8	31 5/8	6 6	Larimer County	CO	Richard M. Cordova	1999	5268
287 1/8	44 6/8 44 6/8	34 3/8	6 6	Beaverhead County	MT	Bruce R. Barrett	1999	5268
287 1/8	46 2/8 47 6/8	38 3/8	6 6	Rich County	UT	Glen O. Hallows	2000	5268
287 1/8	43 1/8 44 7/8	35 2/8	7 6	Catron County	NM	Randall Johnson	2001	5268
*287 1/8	47 6/8 44 4/8	36 7/8	7 6	Coconino County	AZ	Toby Barnett	2006	5268
*287 1/8	39 4/8 38 5/8	36 5/8	6 6	Otero County	NM	Marcus J. Cramer	2008	5268
287 1/8	46 1/8 46 4/8	33 7/8	5 6	Routt County	CO	Chad Dufresne	2008	5268
287 0/8	46 2/8 47 2/8	42 6/8	6 5	Three Sisters Mtn.	ALB	David R. Coupland	1986	5283
287 0/8	45 4/8 46 0/8	31 6/8	6 6	Custer County	ID	Tracy Daves	2000	5283
287 0/8	45 0/8 45 6/8	35 6/8	6 6	Clark County	ID	Terry L. Laufenberg	2002	5283
*287 0/8	42 3/8 41 0/8	45 6/8	7 7	Rich County	UT	Ted Hallows	2004	5283
287 0/8	43 1/8 43 5/8	36 0/8	6 6	Catron County	NM	Alan D. Baxter	2008	5283
*287 0/8	47 1/8 47 4/8	37 6/8	6 6	Ouray County	CO	Brett H. Queen	2009	5283
286 7/8	42 4/8 42 0/8	40 5/8	6 6	Lewis & Clark County	MT	Stephen Tylinski	1979	5289
286 7/8	48 2/8 46 4/8	36 6/8	6 6	Valley County	MT	Jim Seiler	1986	5289
286 7/8	43 0/8 42 6/8	39 1/8	6 7	Fergus County	MT	Robert L. Little, Jr.	1989	5289
286 7/8	49 2/8 48 0/8	33 7/8	7 6	Coconino County	AZ	Van Clark	1989	5289
286 7/8	45 2/8 46 1/8	31 5/8	5 5	Park County	MT	George Kamps	1991	5289
286 7/8	41 4/8 42 1/8	32 3/8	6 6	Rio Blanco County	CO	Roxie Kelly	1994	5289
286 7/8	52 1/8 49 1/8	37 5/8	6 6	Catron County	NM	Ted Winchester	1995	5289
286 7/8	48 5/8 48 2/8	35 5/8	6 6	Petroleum County	MT	Lee Moore	1996	5289
286 7/8	45 1/8 45 2/8	40 3/8	6 6	Park County	MT	Paul Backes	1997	5289
286 7/8	45 1/8 44 0/8	32 5/8	6 6	Madison County	MT	Jeff Klein	2000	5289
286 7/8	46 4/8 46 7/8	33 7/8	6 6	Custer County	SD	Charles Zacharias	2003	5289
*286 7/8	45 7/8 46 1/8	38 6/8	6 6	Apache County	AZ	Kevin Rowan	2008	5289
286 7/8	44 2/8 43 4/8	32 3/8	6 5	Larimer County	CO	Todd Wagner	2009	5289
286 6/8	46 5/8 47 0/8	36 2/8	6 6	Valley County	ID	Phil VonBargen	1982	5302
286 6/8	49 7/8 47 2/8	35 2/8	6 6	Sandoval County	NM	Wilbern Glenn Hitt	1985	5302
286 6/8	43 7/8 45 4/8	38 2/8	6 6	Mesa County	CO	Brad R. Davidson	1988	5302
286 6/8	44 0/8 44 6/8	32 4/8	6 5	Petroleum County	MT	Scott Ballem	1992	5302
286 6/8	45 3/8 43 3/8	35 0/8	6 6	Adams County	ID	Paul Kinberg	1996	5302
286 6/8	47 3/8 44 2/8	34 0/8	6 6	Crook County	OR	Seth R. Michel	1997	5302
286 6/8	44 1/8 44 0/8	35 6/8	6 6	Coconino County	AZ	Perry V. Dunn	1999	5302
286 6/8	46 1/8 46 1/8	31 2/8	7 6	Rio Arriba County	NM	Ted W. Douglass, Jr.	2001	5302
286 6/8	50 0/8 46 4/8	35 2/8	6 6	Lane County	OR	Joshua B. Mannier	2003	5302
286 6/8	43 0/8 42 7/8	38 2/8	6 6	Park County	WY	Mike Holden	2006	5302
286 6/8	43 3/8 44 2/8	29 2/8	6 6	Washakie County	WY	Bruce Briesemeister	2006	5302
286 6/8	48 2/8 49 4/8	33 4/8	7 5	Park County	WY	Larry Pulkrabek	2007	5302
*286 6/8	45 3/8 48 1/8	39 6/8	6 6	Garfield County	CO	Robert J. Clement	2008	5302
286 6/8	43 5/8 41 1/8	42 2/8	5 6	Adams County	ID	Brad Farner	2008	5302
286 6/8	46 6/8 47 0/8	36 2/8	6 6	Lemhi County	ID	Jack Gunsallus	2010	5302
286 5/8	42 1/8 42 0/8	39 3/8	6 6	Gallatin County	MT	Arnold Marolf	1977	5317
286 5/8	43 4/8 42 4/8	39 5/8	6 6	Routt County	CO	Floyd Montgomery	1994	5317
286 5/8	46 4/8 45 4/8	33 1/8	6 6	Otero County	NM	Todd Tschirhart	1996	5317
286 5/8	45 1/8 41 3/8	33 3/8	6 6	Wallowa County	OR	Dale M. Primmer	1999	5317

733

AMERICAN ELK (TYPICAL ANTLERS)

Minimum Score 260 Continued

SCORE	LENGTH OF R MAIN BEAM L	INSIDE SPREAD	NUMBER OF R POINTS L		AREA	STATE/ PROVINCE	HUNTER'S NAME	DATE	RANK
286 5/8	41 1/8 40 1/8	30 3/8	6	6	Caribou County	ID	Rick Dunn	1999	5317
286 5/8	40 2/8 41 3/8	35 3/8	6	6	Caribou County	ID	Raymond Bruderer	2004	5317
286 5/8	42 2/8 42 0/8	31 7/8	6	6	Grand County	CO	Jerry Garrigan	2005	5317
286 5/8	40 4/8 40 1/8	35 5/8	6	6	Boundary County	ID	Brent Piehl	2006	5317
286 4/8	43 1/8 44 1/8	39 4/8	6	6	Shoshone County	ID	Donald A. Young	1979	5325
286 4/8	41 4/8 43 6/8	39 4/8	6	6	Clackamas County	OR	Larry D. Jones	1983	5325
286 4/8	49 0/8 52 2/8	30 6/8	6	6	Coconino County	AZ	Bob Dooley	1984	5325
286 4/8	44 0/8 44 2/8	36 0/8	6	6	Morgan County	UT	Robert G. Petersen	1987	5325
286 4/8	40 5/8 40 5/8	35 6/8	6	6	Ravalli County	MT	Rod Osburn	1989	5325
286 4/8	47 2/8 46 6/8	34 2/8	6	6	Boise County	ID	Todd Kane	1990	5325
286 4/8	47 0/8 46 7/8	40 4/8	6	6	Phillips County	MT	Mark Meyer	1994	5325
286 4/8	43 7/8 45 0/8	36 2/8	6	6	Idaho County	ID	David P. Lewis	1997	5325
286 4/8	46 6/8 46 1/8	31 2/8	6	6	Elko County	NV	Jerry E. McNabb	2000	5325
286 4/8	47 0/8 45 5/8	36 2/8	6	6	Coconino County	AZ	John L. Chase	2000	5325
286 4/8	44 0/8 44 4/8	32 0/8	6	6	San Juan County	CO	Derek Voss	2003	5325
*286 4/8	43 5/8 46 3/8	39 4/8	6	6	Cache County	UT	Jeremy Volt	2005	5325
286 4/8	46 7/8 47 3/8	44 2/8	6	6	Klickitat County	WA	Mike Stickney	2006	5325
286 4/8	44 4/8 44 0/8	40 0/8	6	6	Wasatch County	UT	Mike Blair	2007	5325
286 4/8	44 0/8 43 4/8	33 6/8	6	6	Clearwater County	ID	Brad S. Fulmer	2008	5325
286 3/8	42 2/8 41 7/8	38 7/8	6	6	Rio Arriba County	NM	Jim Dougherty	1989	5340
286 3/8	46 5/8 46 3/8	39 1/8	6	6	San Miguel County	NM	Jerry Hands	1996	5340
286 3/8	44 1/8 44 5/8	35 3/8	6	6	Wheeler County	OR	Mark Winslow	1998	5340
286 3/8	47 3/8 45 2/8	36 7/8	6	6	Grand County	CO	Scott Zoromski	1999	5340
286 3/8	38 4/8 40 5/8	41 0/8	6	6	Larimer County	CO	Eric Vance	2001	5340
286 3/8	40 2/8 45 3/8	42 2/8	7	6	Grant County	NM	Joe Coleman	2001	5340
286 3/8	45 4/8 45 2/8	38 0/8	7	6	Lincoln County	MT	Gary Halvorson	2002	5340
286 3/8	49 3/8 46 6/8	34 7/8	6	6	Clear Creek County	CO	Troy A. Cunningham	2004	5340
*286 3/8	43 7/8 43 5/8	39 7/8	6	6	Johnson County	WY	Robert Anticoli	2005	5340
286 3/8	48 2/8 47 2/8	36 5/8	6	7	Bad Heart	ALB	Moe Timmerman	2010	5340
286 2/8	44 6/8 47 2/8	43 6/8	6	6	Uintah County	UT	Larry L. Parker	1990	5350
286 2/8	44 6/8 44 2/8	38 0/8	6	6	La Plata County	CO	David A. Crom	1991	5350
286 2/8	48 2/8 51 5/8	40 4/8	6	6	Rio Arriba County	NM	Eudane Vicenti	1993	5350
286 2/8	45 3/8 46 2/8	34 6/8	7	6	Umatilla County	OR	Kurt Rosenberg	1994	5350
286 2/8	44 4/8 49 0/8	36 0/8	6	6	Coconino County	AZ	Michael Harrell	1994	5350
286 2/8	48 2/8 48 4/8	43 2/8	6	6	Fergus County	MT	Don Davidson, Jr.	1994	5350
286 2/8	49 5/8 50 2/8	34 4/8	6	7	Crook County	OR	Eric Shawn Haney	1995	5350
286 2/8	49 3/8 48 5/8	32 0/8	6	6	Johnson County	WY	Charles H. Sagner	1998	5350
*286 2/8	42 2/8 42 7/8	34 6/8	6	6	Garfield County	MT	Gregory R. Ward	2005	5350
286 2/8	42 4/8 41 6/8	33 2/8	6	6	Klickitat County	WA	Smokey Crews	2006	5350
286 2/8	41 0/8 39 5/8	37 2/8	6	6	Beaverhead County	MT	Travis B. Horton	2008	5350
286 1/8	44 6/8 44 6/8	41 7/8	6	6	Mineral County	MT	Ken Drake	1981	5361
286 1/8	46 6/8 49 5/8	38 3/8	6	6	Yakima County	WA	Raymond Gimlin	1984	5361
286 1/8	41 7/8 41 5/8	40 0/8	6	7	Beaverhead County	MT	Shaun Twardoski	1987	5361
286 1/8	48 2/8 49 4/8	33 1/8	6	6	Catron County	NM	Michael Travis	1992	5361
286 1/8	47 2/8 46 0/8	37 3/8	6	6	Custer County	ID	Clayton L. Nielson	1996	5361
286 1/8	42 4/8 42 4/8	38 4/8	6	7	Cypress Hills	ALB	Gary Weiss	1997	5361
286 1/8	46 4/8 46 0/8	35 7/8	6	6	Harney County	OR	Rolly Hoyt	2001	5361
286 1/8	47 4/8 45 3/8	37 1/8	6	6	Douglas County	OR	Richard Pickering	2003	5361
*286 1/8	43 5/8 43 5/8	33 7/8	6	6	Johnson County	WY	Dave Strehlo	2007	5361
*286 1/8	49 1/8 52 1/8	35 3/8	6	7	Navajo County	AZ	David G. Paullin	2009	5361
286 0/8	45 3/8 45 0/8	35 2/8	6	6	Lemhi County	ID	Steve Vetrhus	1990	5371
286 0/8	45 4/8 45 5/8	31 6/8	6	6	Fergus County	MT	Tom Madden	1991	5371
286 0/8	43 0/8 42 0/8	44 2/8	6	6	Catron County	NM	Ken C. Taylor	1995	5371
286 0/8	43 1/8 44 2/8	40 0/8	7	6	Fremont County	WY	Dwight Sempert	1996	5371
286 0/8	41 4/8 44 4/8	43 6/8	6	6	Coconino County	AZ	Kenneth E. Gallinger	1999	5371
286 0/8	44 4/8 46 5/8	36 0/8	6	6	Custer County	ID	Mike Rolling	2000	5371
286 0/8	45 6/8 44 6/8	45 2/8	6	6	Custer County	ID	Lynn M. Gregorash	2002	5371
*286 0/8	47 2/8 46 6/8	34 0/8	6	6	Cibola County	NM	John G. Sutter	2007	5371
285 7/8	45 7/8 46 0/8	42 3/8	6	6	Beaverhead County	MT	Lawrence J. Young	1996	5379
285 7/8	43 0/8 44 1/8	41 5/8	6	7	Valley County	ID	Charles Powell	2000	5379
*285 7/8	44 4/8 44 2/8	43 5/8	6	6	Sevier County	UT	David Mitchell	2005	5379
*285 7/8	46 6/8 46 4/8	40 7/8	7	6	Meagher County	MT	Keegan Hill	2005	5379
285 7/8	42 6/8 43 7/8	42 7/8	6	6	Caribou County	ID	Chad Collins	2005	5379
285 7/8	39 5/8 41 0/8	36 1/8	6	6	Fergus County	MT	Todd Krasselt	2008	5379
*285 7/8	44 7/8 41 5/8	39 5/8	6	7	Colfax County	NM	R. Kirk Sharp	2009	5379
*285 7/8	43 2/8 42 5/8	33 5/8	6	6	Costilla County	CO	Chris M. Barnett	2010	5379
285 6/8	46 1/8 47 4/8	30 6/8	6	6	Blaine County	ID	Andy Moore	1985	5387
285 6/8	41 4/8 41 3/8	41 0/8	6	6	Crook County	OR	Scott Stomps	1988	5387
285 6/8	40 0/8 39 5/8	35 2/8	5	5	Morgan County	UT	Rick C. Wilson	1996	5387
285 6/8	45 4/8 41 5/8	38 6/8	6	6	Park County	MT	Greg Service	1998	5387
285 6/8	40 4/8 42 2/8	32 4/8	6	7	Fergus County	MT	Donny Roy	1998	5387
285 6/8	45 5/8 45 4/8	33 2/8	6	6	Las Animas County	CO	Ashley Dickson	2003	5387
*285 6/8	42 4/8 44 1/8	36 0/8	6	6	Gunnison County	CO	Terry Morgan	2004	5387
285 6/8	47 1/8 47 1/8	32 2/8	5	5	Rio Blanco County	CO	David M. Wannamaker	2007	5387
*285 6/8	42 0/8 40 2/8	33 2/8	6	6	Huerfano County	CO	Shawn Rowe	2007	5387
285 5/8	47 3/8 48 2/8	45 3/8	6	6	Lemhi County	ID	Dennis DesJardins	1969	5396
285 5/8	42 7/8 39 6/8	44 3/8	6	6	Lemhi County	ID	Larry Cross	1981	5396
285 5/8	45 3/8 45 1/8	37 3/8	6	7	Missoula County	MT	Paul Pasquariello	1982	5396
285 5/8	44 4/8 43 6/8	34 3/8	6	6	Taos County	NM	Randal Church	1987	5396
285 5/8	45 6/8 46 4/8	41 5/8	6	6	Coconino County	AZ	Robert V. Ruiz	1988	5396
285 5/8	42 1/8 41 1/8	38 3/8	6	6	Larimer County	CO	George Banderia	1989	5396
285 5/8	42 0/8 42 7/8	38 5/8	6	6	Lake County	OR	Jonathan Dale Armstrong	2000	5396
285 5/8	45 7/8 45 3/8	36 3/8	6	6	Morrow County	OR	Scott Kluempke	2002	5396
*285 5/8	43 5/8 46 0/8	33 1/8	6	6	Gila County	AZ	John Hoffman	2003	5396
285 5/8	52 2/8 50 0/8	31 6/8	6	7	Coconino County	AZ	Joseph Lainson	2004	5396
*285 5/8	48 1/8 49 1/8	38 7/8	6	6	Rio Arriba County	NM	Ken Richardson	2005	5396
285 5/8	45 4/8 46 4/8	36 7/8	6	6	Sublette County	WY	Ronell Skinner	2005	5396
285 5/8	43 6/8 42 2/8	36 7/8	6	6	Wasatch County	UT	Tarey Everill	2006	5396
285 5/8	44 4/8 45 2/8	37 7/8	6	6	Missoula County	MT	Darwin Frison	2007	5396
285 4/8	42 2/8 38 1/8	40 4/8	6	5	Catron County	NM	Eddie Collins	1986	5410
285 4/8	43 3/8 44 4/8	41 2/8	6	6	Beaverhead County	MT	Mike Davis	1989	5410
285 4/8	42 6/8 43 3/8	36 0/8	7	6	Catron County	NM	Les Norman	1990	5410
285 4/8	46 1/8 45 3/8	40 4/8	7	6	Socorro County	NM	Gilbert Apodaca	1990	5410
285 4/8	49 4/8 48 4/8	36 4/8	6	5	Coconino County	AZ	Harold L. Gibbons	1992	5410
285 4/8	43 7/8 43 3/8	36 4/8	6	6	Jackson County	OR	Mike Kaiser	1993	5410

AMERICAN ELK (TYPICAL ANTLERS)

Minimum Score 260

Continued

SCORE	LENGTH OF R MAIN BEAM L	INSIDE SPREAD	NUMBER OF R POINTS L		AREA	STATE/ PROVINCE	HUNTER'S NAME	DATE	RANK
285 4/8	43 4/8 44 4/8	31 2/8	6	6	Musselshell County	MT	Chris A. Hipple	1996	5410
285 4/8	41 7/8 41 0/8	31 4/8	6	7	King County	WA	John R. Olson	1997	5410
285 4/8	54 0/8 54 2/8	41 2/8	6	6	Musselshell County	MT	David W. Smith	1997	5410
285 4/8	40 4/8 47 1/8	37 1/8	7	7	Clackamas County	OR	Ben A. Munoz	1998	5410
285 4/8	48 1/8 48 3/8	37 4/8	6	6	Beaverhead County	MT	Harry Clay Cuthbertson	1998	5410
285 4/8	45 3/8 44 5/8	32 4/8	6	6	Routt County	CO	Dan Ergler	2000	5410
285 4/8	40 2/8 40 4/8	30 6/8	6	6	St. Brieux	SAS	Chad Rohel	2000	5410
285 4/8	45 2/8 45 0/8	32 4/8	6	6	Caribou County	ID	Chad Gentry	2000	5410
285 4/8	43 2/8 43 1/8	34 4/8	6	6	Garfield County	CO	Jim Kokott	2002	5410
285 4/8	45 3/8 47 0/8	36 4/8	6	7	Morgan County	UT	P. C. Aughtry III	2002	5410
285 4/8	36 0/8 44 5/8	36 0/8	6	6	Sweetwater County	WY	Jay A. Keeler	2003	5410
285 4/8	46 2/8 48 0/8	37 1/8	7	7	Lewis County	WA	Vince Selway	2005	5410
*285 4/8	43 7/8 44 2/8	32 0/8	6	6	Cochrane	ALB	Gary Gillett	2008	5410
285 3/8	45 4/8 45 7/8	36 1/8	6	6	Umatilla County	OR	Bob Burggraff	1982	5429
285 3/8	46 5/8 38 4/8	32 5/8	6	6	Caribou County	ID	Craig Hill	1988	5429
285 3/8	46 3/8 45 5/8	37 1/8	6	6	Mineral County	CO	Douglas A. Ducote, Jr.	1990	5429
285 3/8	43 2/8 45 4/8	35 5/8	6	6	Grant County	OR	Dean Pasche	1991	5429
285 3/8	42 3/8 43 0/8	34 1/8	6	6	Lemhi County	ID	Bob Johnson	1997	5429
285 3/8	45 6/8 46 0/8	31 2/8	7	7	Catron County	NM	William N. Thompson	1997	5429
285 3/8	43 3/8 45 2/8	39 7/8	6	6	Harney County	OR	Deren R. /Kerry D. Williams	2004	5429
285 3/8	43 6/8 45 4/8	35 3/8	7	8	Teller County	CO	Steve Voss	2004	5429
285 3/8	50 0/8 48 4/8	34 7/8	7	6	Coconino County	AZ	Michael J. Bylina	2005	5429
*285 3/8	45 3/8 45 0/8	32 3/8	6	6	Garfield County	CO	Chuck Latta	2008	5429
285 2/8	43 2/8 41 5/8	52 0/8	6	6	Albany County	WY	Douglas Cringan	1991	5439
285 2/8	46 0/8 45 7/8	31 0/8	6	6	Caribou County	ID	John C. Miller	1991	5439
285 2/8	46 6/8 47 5/8	42 2/8	6	6	Madison County	MT	Marvin J. Holt	1996	5439
285 2/8	47 4/8 45 7/8	40 2/8	8	7	Catron County	NM	Eddie Claypool	2000	5439
285 2/8	41 4/8 44 3/8	27 4/8	6	6	Colfax County	NM	Robert Gruenberg	2003	5439
285 2/8	47 0/8 49 6/8	40 6/8	6	6	Grand County	UT	Christopher Montaque	2005	5439
285 2/8	46 0/8 45 1/8	41 0/8	6	6	Moffat County	CO	Bob Sanders	2005	5439
*285 2/8	46 0/8 47 7/8	37 2/8	7	6	Teton County	WY	Michael W. Kozak	2008	5439
285 1/8	44 6/8 46 0/8	45 4/8	7	6	Sanders County	MT	Conrad Anderson	1983	5447
285 1/8	46 6/8 46 7/8	34 3/8	6	5	Gallatin County	MT	Mark Heckel	1993	5447
285 1/8	43 3/8 45 0/8	33 7/8	6	6	Missoula County	MT	Kirt Alan Tanner	1995	5447
285 1/8	37 5/8 40 7/8	29 1/8	6	6	Fergus County	MT	Edwin Evans	2003	5447
*285 1/8	38 7/8 40 4/8	33 5/8	6	6	Eagle County	CO	John T. Baumstark	2009	5447
285 0/8	45 4/8 45 2/8	33 4/8	6	6	Fergus County	MT	James Southworth	1980	5452
285 0/8	40 3/8 44 6/8	33 4/8	6	6	Umatilla County	OR	Ray A. Warren	1982	5452
285 0/8	47 7/8 47 4/8	37 2/8	5	6	Sandoval County	NM	Robert L. Pagel	1987	5452
285 0/8	51 3/8 49 7/8	33 0/8	6	6	Besa River	BC	Chris Barker	1993	5452
285 0/8	42 2/8 43 3/8	42 4/8	5	5	Catron County	NM	Charles G. Collier, Jr.	1996	5452
285 0/8	49 0/8 47 1/8	40 6/8	6	6	Johnson County	WY	Warren March, Jr.	1998	5452
285 0/8	44 1/8 44 6/8	43 0/8	6	6	Lemhi County	ID	R. Bart Summers	1998	5452
285 0/8	48 6/8 47 7/8	34 4/8	6	6	Crook County	OR	Robert R. Stamp	2000	5452
285 0/8	47 1/8 46 6/8	38 4/8	6	6	Rio Arriba County	NM	Russell Vigil	2001	5452
*285 0/8	42 5/8 42 0/8	28 4/8	6	6	Colfax County	NM	Bob Shearman	2004	5452
285 0/8	42 3/8 40 0/8	30 6/8	6	6	Fergus County	MT	Lynn Bowman	2006	5452
284 7/8	44 2/8 44 7/8	35 7/8	6	6	Lewis & Clark County	MT	Ron Granneman	1977	5463
284 7/8	43 3/8 42 4/8	44 1/8	6	6	Malheur County	OR	Kent Kemble	1982	5463
284 7/8	43 0/8 44 1/8	35 1/8	6	7	Catron County	NM	Dean Hamilton	1986	5463
284 7/8	44 2/8 43 4/8	32 3/8	6	6	Sanders County	MT	Jim Regh, Jr.	1986	5463
284 7/8	49 4/8 48 0/8	34 3/8	6	6	Judith Basin County	MT	Fred Reed	1995	5463
284 7/8	44 5/8 44 0/8	41 3/8	6	6	Summit County	UT	Michael V. Arrant	1996	5463
284 7/8	45 0/8 45 6/8	35 3/8	6	6	Moffat County	CO	Parley Dale Tewalt	1997	5463
*284 7/8	52 1/8 50 2/8	35 5/8	6	6	Custer County	ID	Richard L. Krug	2006	5463
284 7/8	47 5/8 47 7/8	33 1/8	6	6	Mineral County	MT	Cha Yang	2006	5463
284 7/8	49 1/8 47 6/8	33 3/8	6	6	San Juan County	UT	Brandon Fails	2008	5463
284 7/8	46 3/8 47 1/8	36 7/8	6	6	Archuleta County	CO	E. Fred Richter, Jr.	2008	5463
284 6/8	47 5/8 47 7/8	37 4/8	6	6	Marion County	OR	Jack Smith	1984	5474
284 6/8	46 4/8 45 4/8	39 6/8	6	5	Coconino County	AZ	Dan Howe	1990	5474
284 6/8	43 2/8 43 6/8	43 0/8	6	6	Socorro County	NM	Kenneth M. Thompson	1991	5474
284 6/8	45 0/8 45 0/8	38 6/8	6	6	Grand County	CO	Carlis Stephens	1993	5474
284 6/8	46 1/8 47 1/8	41 4/8	6	5	Rio Arriba County	NM	Kermit Evans	1993	5474
284 6/8	47 7/8 47 6/8	33 4/8	6	6	Gallatin County	MT	William Elfland	1998	5474
284 6/8	44 6/8 45 7/8	33 0/8	6	6	Catron County	NM	Ed Lovett	2000	5474
284 6/8	42 6/8 43 0/8	35 0/8	6	6	Ravalli County	MT	Greg Munther	2000	5474
284 6/8	43 7/8 42 7/8	38 0/8	6	6	Phillips County	MT	Mike Blanchard	2001	5474
284 6/8	44 7/8 44 6/8	31 4/8	6	6	Larimer County	CO	Brad Baldwin	2002	5474
284 6/8	52 7/8 51 7/8	40 6/8	6	5	Cochise County	AZ	Cindy Seitz-Krug	2005	5474
284 6/8	41 1/8 41 2/8	34 2/8	6	6	Shoshone County	ID	Shawn Price	2006	5474
284 6/8	48 2/8 47 3/8	39 0/8	6	6	Gila County	AZ	Dallas Fleagle	2006	5474
284 6/8	47 7/8 49 0/8	35 4/8	6	5	Lewis County	WA	Dean Rockwood	2007	5474
284 5/8	44 0/8 45 0/8	33 7/8	5	7	Eagle County	CO	Stan Hunt	1981	5488
284 5/8	41 1/8 40 6/8	37 3/8	6	6	Fergus County	MT	Frank R. Thompson	1991	5488
284 5/8	42 0/8 40 2/8	37 7/8	6	6	Boundary County	ID	Steve Kamps	1994	5488
284 5/8	49 6/8 48 0/8	36 1/8	6	6	Beaverhead County	MT	E. Lance Whary	1995	5488
284 5/8	45 6/8 44 3/8	35 5/8	7	8	Albany County	WY	Willard Woods	2001	5488
284 5/8	49 4/8 47 6/8	36 7/8	5	5	Coconino County	AZ	David J. Hofman	2003	5488
284 5/8	44 6/8 46 5/8	35 3/8	6	6	Clearwater County	ID	Michael Reitler	2003	5488
*284 5/8	40 7/8 40 4/8	35 3/8	6	6	Washakie County	WY	Bryan T. Reinhardt	2009	5488
284 4/8	46 4/8 40 0/8	40 2/8	6	7	Gallatin National Forest	MT	Dennis Fishbaugher	1981	5496
284 4/8	38 0/8 40 0/8	38 4/8	6	6	Garfield County	CO	Bruce Easterly	1985	5496
284 4/8	47 6/8 50 0/8	36 6/8	6	6	Sheridan County	WY	Dave Moss	1995	5496
284 4/8	44 7/8 44 3/8	38 2/8	6	6	King County	WA	Robert Wilber	1996	5496
284 4/8	45 7/8 45 0/8	32 0/8	6	6	Wallowa County	OR	Dustin Boyd Rorden	2000	5496
284 4/8	40 6/8 41 6/8	32 2/8	6	6	Carbon County	WY	Dan Miner	2003	5496
284 4/8	45 5/8 48 0/8	39 3/8	7	8	Apache County	AZ	Andrew Lopez	2003	5496
284 4/8	48 5/8 48 6/8	37 0/8	6	6	Valley County	ID	Troy Miller	2005	5496
284 4/8	42 5/8 42 6/8	33 2/8	6	6	Bonner County	ID	Clayton R. Bowman	2006	5496
284 4/8	41 5/8 41 5/8	32 0/8	6	6	Las Animas County	CO	Thomas Wade Patteson	2006	5496
284 4/8	47 0/8 47 0/8	37 4/8	6	6	Rio Arriba County	NM	Richard Penn	2006	5496
284 4/8	45 2/8 42 2/8	35 2/8	6	6	Park County	WY	Jason Stafford	2007	5496
284 4/8	48 7/8 47 2/8	37 0/8	5	5	Hinsdale County	CO	John Stubbs	2007	5496
284 4/8	46 0/8 47 4/8	37 2/8	6	6	Coconino County	AZ	John Thayer	2009	5496
*284 4/8	38 0/8 38 0/8	37 0/8	6	6	Fergus County	MT	Matt Moen	2010	5496

AMERICAN ELK (TYPICAL ANTLERS)

Minimum Score 260 — Continued

SCORE	LENGTH OF MAIN BEAM R	L	INSIDE SPREAD	NUMBER OF POINTS R	L	AREA	STATE/PROVINCE	HUNTER'S NAME	DATE	RANK
284 3/8	44 1/8	43 6/8	46 4/8	7	6	Clearwater County	ID	Neil Hinton	1983	5511
284 3/8	44 0/8	41 2/8	35 7/8	6	6	Sierra County	NM	Gerald Lambert Lopez	1990	5511
284 3/8	46 3/8	47 4/8	33 3/8	7	6	Coconino County	AZ	George Toot, Jr.	1990	5511
284 3/8	46 7/8	45 0/8	36 5/8	6	6	Petroleum County	MT	Dale Herritz	1993	5511
284 3/8	47 1/8	46 3/8	38 7/8	6	6	Harney County	OR	Bob Choate	2000	5511
284 3/8	46 1/8	45 4/8	36 5/8	5	6	Garfield County	CO	Kurt Wood	2005	5511
284 3/8	46 2/8	46 2/8	34 7/8	6	6	Washakie County	WY	Bruce Briesemeister	2008	5511
284 2/8	47 7/8	46 3/8	34 4/8	6	6	Apache County	AZ	Ronald King	1985	5518
284 2/8	49 3/8	48 0/8	37 2/8	6	6	Coconino County	AZ	John Toot	1990	5518
284 2/8	48 3/8	47 6/8	37 0/8	6	6	Moffat County	CO	Frank Harper	1995	5518
284 2/8	45 6/8	44 6/8	39 4/8	6	6	Wallowa County	OR	Robert Shane Boggan	1999	5518
284 2/8	45 0/8	47 0/8	37 6/8	6	6	Valley County	ID	Curt Giese	2004	5518
284 2/8	43 5/8	45 1/8	40 3/8	6	7	Park County	MT	James Harner	2005	5518
284 2/8	45 1/8	46 2/8	35 6/8	6	6	Teller County	CO	Robert T. Houck	2008	5518
*284 2/8	38 6/8	37 2/8	41 2/8	6	6	Las Animas County	CO	Verle Schlabach	2008	5518
284 1/8	50 4/8	49 3/8	37 7/8	5	6	Clear Creek County	CO	Gary Christoffersen	1980	5526
284 1/8	44 1/8	43 1/8	31 1/8	6	6	Sandoval County	NM	Steve Alderete	1986	5526
284 1/8	48 2/8	47 2/8	34 5/8	7	6	Apache County	AZ	David N. Brilhart	1989	5526
284 1/8	44 5/8	44 4/8	37 1/8	7	6	Fergus County	MT	Tom Madden	1990	5526
284 1/8	50 0/8	44 7/8	45 3/8	7	7	Catron County	NM	Wayne W. Franzen	1992	5526
284 1/8	47 7/8	45 2/8	32 7/8	6	6	Coconino County	AZ	Gerardo Saldivar	1995	5526
284 1/8	44 0/8	43 6/8	43 3/8	6	6	Conejos County	CO	Brian R. Luers	1999	5526
284 1/8	43 6/8	44 3/8	32 7/8	6	6	Chain Lakes	ALB	Misty Grasza	2002	5526
284 1/8	46 4/8	51 5/8	31 7/8	6	6	Sandoval County	NM	Kevin J. Liedel	2003	5526
284 0/8	49 4/8	46 7/8	42 2/8	6	6	Grant County	OR	Robert Gedlick	1981	5535
284 0/8	41 3/8	43 6/8	39 4/8	6	7	Clearwater County	ID	Steve Richards	1986	5535
284 0/8	49 6/8	48 4/8	37 2/8	6	6	Colfax County	NM	John L. Chapman	1989	5535
284 0/8	45 7/8	48 4/8	34 6/8	6	6	Phillips County	MT	Henry J. Mischel	1990	5535
284 0/8	46 5/8	45 6/8	33 7/8	7	6	Missoula County	MT	James W. Kelly	1994	5535
284 0/8	43 0/8	43 5/8	39 6/8	6	6	Rio Blanco County	CO	Steve N. Wilson	1995	5535
284 0/8	41 7/8	42 2/8	38 2/8	6	6	Catron County	NM	Doug Turner	1995	5535
284 0/8	41 1/8	40 4/8	40 4/8	6	6	Coconino County	AZ	Chad Loy	1997	5535
284 0/8	46 5/8	45 4/8	39 0/8	6	6	Idaho County	ID	Kenneth C. Prince	1998	5535
284 0/8	47 4/8	45 5/8	32 6/8	6	6	Musselshell County	MT	Joseph M. Lahr	1998	5535
284 0/8	48 3/8	49 6/8	37 2/8	6	6	Apache County	AZ	Steven E. Paige	2003	5535
284 0/8	46 6/8	46 6/8	32 0/8	6	6	Catron County	NM	Richard Baca	2005	5535
283 7/8	47 5/8	47 2/8	33 3/8	6	6	Phillips County	MT	Doug Quilling	1979	5547
283 7/8	42 6/8	43 5/8	33 5/8	6	6	Adams County	ID	Richard Fletcher	1987	5547
283 7/8	44 2/8	45 0/8	31 7/8	6	6	Harney County	OR	Craig D. Hawkins	1991	5547
283 7/8	49 3/8	49 2/8	43 7/8	6	7	Shoshone County	ID	Dennis Doyle	1993	5547
283 7/8	45 1/8	44 0/8	33 5/8	6	6	Catron County	NM	William E. Fleshman	1996	5547
283 7/8	42 0/8	42 2/8	41 7/8	6	6	Fremont County	WY	Dana Richardson	1996	5547
283 7/8	48 5/8	48 7/8	36 1/8	7	7	Lemhi County	ID	Dave Batterton	1997	5547
283 7/8	45 6/8	44 2/8	32 3/8	6	6	Gallatin County	MT	Kurt D. Rued	1998	5547
283 7/8	43 5/8	43 6/8	33 7/8	6	6	Catron County	NM	Robert Duke	1998	5547
283 7/8	45 4/8	46 0/8	33 1/8	6	6	Phillips County	MT	Michael H. Smith	1998	5547
283 7/8	44 4/8	41 3/8	34 5/8	6	6	Costilla County	CO	Stephen R. Boster	1999	5547
283 7/8	42 3/8	43 5/8	39 4/8	7	7	Adams County	ID	Casey Mitchell	1999	5547
*283 7/8	44 4/8	43 4/8	49 0/8	6	6	Gunnison County	CO	Jason D. Wade	2004	5547
*283 7/8	41 3/8	41 0/8	33 5/8	6	6	Crook County	WY	Ed Heeb	2008	5547
283 7/8	39 0/8	38 7/8	36 5/8	6	5	Huerfano County	CO	Gregory Burton	2010	5547
283 6/8	46 0/8	45 4/8	40 6/8	6	6	Conejos County	CO	Arthur M. Davis	1974	5562
283 6/8	47 3/8	49 0/8	36 6/8	6	6	Custer County	ID	Donald Johnson	1986	5562
283 6/8	43 6/8	43 1/8	44 2/8	6	6	Mesa County	CO	Lawrence Clark	1987	5562
283 6/8	46 2/8	45 1/8	39 0/8	6	6	Eagle County	CO	Keith Scheitzer	1990	5562
283 6/8	48 2/8	48 6/8	35 4/8	6	6	Deschutes County	OR	Royce D. Nelson	1994	5562
283 6/8	44 0/8	41 4/8	32 0/8	6	7	Petroleum County	MT	Tim Stiles	1999	5562
283 6/8	47 1/8	46 1/8	38 6/8	7	7	Clearwater County	ID	Mark Kuechenmeister	2000	5562
283 6/8	45 3/8	43 4/8	38 0/8	6	6	Adams County	ID	Duane Van Leuven	2000	5562
283 6/8	45 3/8	47 4/8	37 4/8	6	6	Summit County	CO	Mark Osborne	2001	5562
283 6/8	42 4/8	43 5/8	39 6/8	6	5	Catron County	NM	Don J. Papczynski	2002	5562
283 6/8	43 3/8	42 0/8	32 2/8	6	6	Garfield County	MT	Michael Bowman	2003	5562
283 6/8	44 4/8	44 2/8	40 6/8	6	6	Fergus County	MT	P. J. Londo	2004	5562
283 6/8	47 6/8	48 2/8	32 6/8	6	6	Montrose County	CO	Keith Creel	2008	5562
283 6/8	44 1/8	44 3/8	37 4/8	6	6	Carbon County	MT	Dick Dubell	2008	5562
*283 6/8	42 1/8	43 4/8	40 4/8	6	6	Grand County	CO	Marcus Casano	2010	5562
283 5/8	46 6/8	45 6/8	33 7/8	6	6	Hinsdale County	CO	Dennis Pistole	1990	5577
283 5/8	43 5/8	44 5/8	36 3/8	6	6	Blaine County	ID	Doug Ramsey	2000	5577
283 5/8	43 3/8	43 3/8	35 5/8	5	6	Lincoln County	WY	John Dunivin	2001	5577
283 5/8	46 1/8	46 1/8	36 5/8	6	6	Wheeler County	OR	Gladstone Butch Jones	2003	5577
283 5/8	49 1/8	50 3/8	40 5/8	5	6	Lewis & Clark County	MT	Ron Gibson	2007	5577
283 5/8	45 3/8	44 4/8	36 7/8	6	6	Lake County	CO	Derick Holmes	2009	5577
283 4/8	40 3/8	40 2/8	39 6/8	6	6	Apache County	AZ	Sonny Turner	1985	5583
283 4/8	49 3/8	47 7/8	39 2/8	6	6	Rio Arriba County	NM	Ray Milligan	1987	5583
283 4/8	46 6/8	44 7/8	35 2/8	6	6	Park County	MT	Jon Okonek	1990	5583
283 4/8	55 1/8	51 2/8	36 4/8	4	6	Gallatin County	MT	Rourk Price	1994	5583
283 4/8	43 3/8	43 5/8	43 0/8	6	6	Douglas County	OR	Kevin Pearce	1997	5583
283 4/8	45 0/8	45 3/8	35 6/8	6	6	Petroleum County	MT	Roy D. Tinkey, Jr.	2007	5583
283 4/8	51 1/8	50 1/8	34 4/8	6	5	Umatilla County	OR	Alex Tanner	2007	5583
283 3/8	42 0/8	44 4/8	31 7/8	6	6	Routt County	CO	Kevin Cole	1990	5590
283 3/8	44 1/8	44 4/8	31 5/8	7	6	Routt County	CO	Randy Kendrick	1996	5590
283 3/8	43 2/8	42 2/8	36 3/8	6	6	Franklin County	ID	Rick Jones	2002	5590
283 3/8	49 1/8	48 0/8	40 1/8	6	6	Lake County	CO	Kevin Brothers	2003	5590
283 3/8	46 0/8	44 4/8	39 5/8	6	6	Coconino County	AZ	Tom McEntire	2004	5590
283 3/8	44 7/8	47 2/8	35 5/8	6	6	Lemhi County	ID	Cedric Meeks	2004	5590
283 3/8	43 7/8	44 1/8	35 7/8	6	6	Catron County	NM	Buck Horn	2006	5590
283 3/8	40 4/8	41 4/8	35 5/8	6	6	Consort	ALB	Gary E. Whalen	2008	5590
283 3/8	42 0/8	47 2/8	39 1/8	6	6	Mesa County	CO	Nathan P. Leuallen	2010	5590
283 2/8	44 6/8	40 5/8	32 6/8	6	6	Clearwater County	ID	Jay Deones	1983	5599
283 2/8	44 6/8	46 0/8	45 4/8	7	6	Lincoln County	NM	Steve Morgan	1986	5599
283 2/8	37 4/8	38 0/8	43 2/8	6	6	Sandoval County	NM	Gary F. Bogner	1994	5599
283 2/8	45 2/8	42 4/8	42 4/8	6	5	Mineral County	MT	William E. Sansom	1995	5599
283 2/8	46 7/8	44 0/8	42 2/8	7	6	Douglas County	OR	Tobin J. Howell	1998	5599
283 2/8	49 2/8	47 2/8	40 0/8	6	6	Custer County	ID	Nevin Herr	2001	5599
283 2/8	44 5/8	44 1/8	30 2/8	6	6	Garfield County	CO	Joey Bartgis	2001	5599

736

AMERICAN ELK (TYPICAL ANTLERS)

Minimum Score 260
Continued

SCORE	LENGTH OF R MAIN BEAM L	INSIDE SPREAD	NUMBER OF R POINTS L		AREA	STATE/ PROVINCE	HUNTER'S NAME	DATE	RANK
*283 2/8	49 7/8 51 4/8	37 6/8	6	5	Mesa County	CO	Gary Sherrell	2008	5599
*283 2/8	43 4/8 42 5/8	41 2/8	6	6	Elk County	PA	Brian J. Nolan	2008	5599
283 1/8	50 3/8 48 1/8	31 6/8	6	7	Bighorn Mtns.	WY	David Shoop	1979	5608
283 1/8	41 2/8 40 6/8	38 7/8	6	7	Bergen	ALB	Sandy Watt	1991	5608
283 1/8	41 6/8 40 7/8	32 1/8	7	7	Lincoln County	MT	Scott Westlund	1994	5608
283 1/8	43 6/8 42 7/8	35 7/8	6	6	Sheridan County	WY	Dale Stahl	1995	5608
283 1/8	44 3/8 46 6/8	38 1/8	6	6	Catron County	NM	Gary Rowles	1995	5608
283 1/8	43 2/8 42 5/8	36 2/8	7	6	Catron County	NM	Gary D. Martinez	1996	5608
283 1/8	47 3/8 47 0/8	37 1/8	6	5	Clark County	ID	Glen Berry	1998	5608
283 1/8	49 1/8 45 0/8	45 3/8	6	6	Catron County	NM	Troy J. Lane	2000	5608
283 1/8	42 5/8 41 4/8	34 5/8	6	6	Montrose County	CO	Brian Zuhse	2000	5608
283 1/8	43 1/8 43 1/8	34 3/8	6	6	Mesa County	CO	Art Rayner	2000	5608
283 1/8	52 5/8 51 6/8	37 5/8	5	6	Washakie County	WY	Jerry Simmons	2008	5608
283 0/8	42 7/8 44 5/8	41 0/8	6	6	Baker County	OR	Don Rajnus	1962	5619
283 0/8	45 1/8 47 5/8	43 2/8	6	6	Grand County	CO	G. Fred Asbell	1973	5619
283 0/8	48 4/8 46 4/8	36 2/8	6	6	Crook County	OR	Rick V. Herbst	1985	5619
283 0/8	43 6/8 44 3/8	33 0/8	6	6	La Plata County	CO	David R. Hall	1985	5619
283 0/8	42 2/8 43 3/8	35 5/8	7	6	Bear Lake County	ID	Barry James Shelton	1989	5619
283 0/8	39 5/8 39 3/8	34 0/8	6	6	Fergus County	MT	Matthew McWilliams	1994	5619
283 0/8	43 2/8 44 2/8	33 0/8	6	6	Catron County	NM	Rick L. Morley	1997	5619
283 0/8	44 5/8 46 4/8	35 4/8	6	6	Rio Arriba County	NM	Jay Ewing	2000	5619
283 0/8	45 0/8 43 5/8	35 0/8	6	6	Park County	MT	Richard Backes	2000	5619
283 0/8	46 2/8 46 3/8	32 4/8	6	6	Greenlee County	AZ	Scott Daniel Overall, Sr.	2001	5619
*283 0/8	49 0/8 47 1/8	36 6/8	6	6	Dolores County	CO	Jason Cassady	2003	5619
283 0/8	43 4/8 43 2/8	33 2/8	6	6	Mesa County	CO	Gabe Lucero	2004	5619
*283 0/8	43 6/8 44 1/8	39 2/8	6	6	Skamania County	WA	Jonathan W. Gabrio	2007	5619
283 0/8	45 5/8 46 3/8	35 2/8	6	7	Caribou County	ID	Zaren Adams	2008	5619
283 0/8	42 6/8 43 6/8	33 4/8	7	6	Colfax County	NM	Larry Dwyer	2009	5619
*283 0/8	43 0/8 41 0/8	38 4/8	6	6	White Pine County	NV	Brett L. Foster	2010	5619
282 7/8	41 7/8 41 4/8	38 7/8	6	6	Wallowa County	OR	Steven R. Zollman	1986	5635
282 7/8	47 3/8 47 4/8	37 7/8	7	6	Albany County	WY	Doug Cringan	1993	5635
282 7/8	40 0/8 40 1/8	43 5/8	6	6	Pueblo County	CO	Steven Belport	1996	5635
282 7/8	48 7/8 49 1/8	44 1/8	5	5	Apache County	AZ	Donald W. Williams	1996	5635
282 7/8	45 1/8 42 2/8	37 1/8	5	5	Coconino County	AZ	Perry Lee Dawson	2002	5635
282 7/8	42 5/8 42 1/8	33 1/8	6	6	Wasatch County	UT	Mike McGee	2003	5635
282 7/8	41 5/8 43 7/8	34 3/8	6	6	Caroline	ALB	Eric Kalberg	2005	5635
*282 7/8	44 2/8 43 1/8	35 5/8	6	6	Jackson County	CO	Todd Ellgren	2007	5635
282 7/8	43 4/8 44 0/8	31 3/8	6	6	Lawrence County	SD	Doug R. Eichler	2009	5635
282 6/8	39 7/8 40 2/8	42 3/8	6	6	Gallatin County	MT	Gregg L. Welch	1982	5644
282 6/8	46 4/8 47 3/8	31 0/8	6	6	Colfax County	NM	Melvin Sloan	1990	5644
282 6/8	45 4/8 45 1/8	31 4/8	6	6	Larimer County	CO	Thomas Langer	1991	5644
282 6/8	39 3/8 42 7/8	35 6/8	6	6	Jumping Pound Creek	ALB	Archie Nesbitt	1992	5644
282 6/8	50 7/8 49 5/8	33 6/8	7	6	Coconino County	AZ	Sheffield Jordan	1995	5644
282 6/8	41 6/8 42 0/8	34 6/8	6	6	Beaverhead County	MT	Gary Dudden	1996	5644
282 6/8	44 3/8 44 0/8	36 0/8	6	6	Otero County	NM	James T. Summers	1996	5644
282 6/8	45 7/8 44 6/8	37 2/8	6	6	Petroleum County	MT	Chuck Adams	1997	5644
282 6/8	44 5/8 44 0/8	36 4/8	6	6	Blaine County	ID	Sean R. Haggerty	2001	5644
282 6/8	40 5/8 43 3/8	39 4/8	7	6	Lane County	OR	Damian Hensley	2002	5644
282 6/8	47 4/8 48 4/8	37 0/8	6	6	Mineral County	MT	Vayesleng K. Moua	2008	5644
*282 6/8	48 7/8 51 6/8	43 6/8	6	6	Beaverhead County	MT	Reese A. Hadley	2010	5644
*282 6/8	46 0/8 46 6/8	30 4/8	6	6	Jefferson County	CO	James L. Price	2010	5644
282 5/8	50 0/8 47 2/8	42 1/8	7	6	Gallatin County	MT	Scott L. Koelzer	1979	5657
282 5/8	47 1/8 44 7/8	39 7/8	6	6	Meagher County	MT	Pete Ecker	1980	5657
282 5/8	39 2/8 43 7/8	33 3/8	5	6	Valley County	ID	Dennis Gratton	1983	5657
282 5/8	42 6/8 43 0/8	42 7/8	6	6	Dolores County	CO	Mike Zion	1985	5657
282 5/8	41 2/8 41 6/8	35 5/8	6	6	Mesa County	CO	Jeffrey Price	1989	5657
282 5/8	47 0/8 43 4/8	24 3/8	6	6	Sheridan County	WY	Mike Barrett	1990	5657
282 5/8	44 4/8 48 1/8	33 0/8	7	7	Catron County	NM	Bill Harmon	1992	5657
282 5/8	42 7/8 40 3/8	35 7/8	6	6	Sanders County	MT	John H. Reynolds	1994	5657
282 5/8	45 2/8 43 2/8	29 2/8	7	5	Catron County	NM	Mike W. Leonard	1995	5657
282 5/8	46 7/8 44 5/8	28 5/8	6	6	Carbon County	UT	Brady R. Cox	1998	5657
282 5/8	49 4/8 50 5/8	39 6/8	7	6	Lane County	OR	Aaron P. Fielden	1999	5657
282 5/8	43 6/8 44 6/8	36 3/8	6	6	Moffat County	CO	Scott George	2000	5657
282 5/8	46 5/8 45 4/8	35 3/8	5	6	Fergus County	MT	Kelly Norskog	2001	5657
282 5/8	43 2/8 44 0/8	34 7/8	6	5	Granite County	MT	Paul Korn	2002	5657
282 5/8	40 6/8 40 7/8	41 3/8	6	6	Colfax County	NM	Robert S. Bartoshesky	2002	5657
*282 5/8	40 7/8 51 5/8	42 1/8	5	6	Rich County	UT	Brian Campbell	2003	5657
*282 5/8	41 0/8 41 0/8	36 1/8	6	6	Rio Blanco County	CO	Daniel L. Wilber	2003	5657
282 5/8	44 4/8 44 7/8	52 4/8	5	6	Flathead County	MT	Paul Martin	2006	5657
282 5/8	42 6/8 42 4/8	37 7/8	6	6	Garfield County	MT	Corey Green	2007	5657
*282 5/8	43 7/8 45 4/8	38 3/8	6	7	Navajo County	AZ	William Lahr	2008	5657
282 5/8	47 4/8 45 7/8	34 5/8	5	6	Elko County	NV	John "Gundy" Gunderson	2009	5657
282 4/8	32 6/8 39 2/8	36 4/8	6	6	Judith Basin County	MT	Jerome R. Parsons	1981	5678
282 4/8	46 0/8 45 7/8	42 4/8	7	6	Custer County	ID	Joel C. Lenz	1986	5678
282 4/8	40 7/8 40 7/8	37 0/8	6	6	Lemhi County	ID	Dan Hooper	1996	5678
282 4/8	45 0/8 46 2/8	35 5/8	7	6	Douglas County	OR	George Decker	1996	5678
282 4/8	39 0/8 41 4/8	37 0/8	6	6	Granite County	MT	Gene Meisner	1997	5678
282 4/8	46 1/8 45 6/8	35 2/8	5	5	Caribou County	ID	Michael Bradeen	1999	5678
282 4/8	51 3/8 49 4/8	31 0/8	6	6	Mesa County	CO	Richard J. Bombard	1999	5678
282 4/8	46 4/8 45 3/8	40 4/8	6	6	Beaverhead County	MT	Joe J. Stolarczyk	1999	5678
282 4/8	47 0/8 47 2/8	35 6/8	6	6	Fergus County	MT	John P. Hartman	2001	5678
282 4/8	41 2/8 40 4/8	46 2/8	6	7	Greenlee County	AZ	Scott D. Overall, Jr.	2001	5678
282 4/8	40 6/8 40 1/8	33 6/8	6	6	Garfield County	MT	Mark L. Meyer	2002	5678
282 4/8	46 1/8 45 6/8	34 4/8	6	6	La Plata County	CO	Andy Oliver	2004	5678
282 4/8	46 6/8 44 5/8	34 4/8	6	6	Catron County	NM	Mike Cottingham	2005	5678
282 3/8	44 2/8 41 0/8	38 1/8	6	6	Larimer County	CO	Dale E. Wenger	1981	5691
282 3/8	44 4/8 46 2/8	34 3/8	7	6	Catron County	NM	Todd Zeuske	1987	5691
282 3/8	46 1/8 45 2/8	43 3/8	6	6	Clearwater County	ID	Rich L. Rounds	1992	5691
282 3/8	44 4/8 44 4/8	35 1/8	6	6	Clearwater County	ID	Jerry Long	1994	5691
282 3/8	41 7/8 42 5/8	39 5/8	6	6	Pierce County	WA	Mike Rumpza	1996	5691
282 3/8	44 4/8 43 3/8	35 5/8	6	6	Moffat County	CO	Gary Hinaman	1998	5691
282 3/8	42 4/8 44 4/8	33 3/8	6	6	Ravalli County	MT	Cory Johnson	1998	5691
282 3/8	44 7/8 45 6/8	41 1/8	6	6	Grant County	OR	Pat Niemi	2003	5691
282 3/8	39 3/8 40 7/8	33 5/8	6	6	Line Creek	BC	Allan Latka	2005	5691
*282 3/8	41 6/8 43 2/8	33 3/8	6	6	Fremont County	WY	Joseph A. Moody	2009	5691

737

AMERICAN ELK (TYPICAL ANTLERS)

Minimum Score 260   Continued

SCORE	LENGTH OF R MAIN BEAM L		INSIDE SPREAD	NUMBER OF R POINTS L		AREA	STATE/ PROVINCE	HUNTER'S NAME	DATE	RANK
282 3/8	46 3/8	44 0/8	35 7/8	6	7	Clearwater County	ID	Daryl Pilarski	2009	5691
282 2/8	42 6/8	43 1/8	39 2/8	6	6	Wallowa County	OR	Neil Summers	1986	5702
282 2/8	44 6/8	43 3/8	30 6/8	6	6	Harney County	OR	Steven J. Christensen	1990	5702
282 2/8	39 4/8	38 4/8	34 6/8	6	6	Routt County	CO	Marion A. Heintz	1991	5702
282 2/8	38 6/8	39 4/8	38 2/8	6	6	Petroleum County	MT	John Wooldridge	1996	5702
282 2/8	41 4/8	42 1/8	41 0/8	6	5	Garfield County	UT	John Caruso	2003	5702
282 2/8	43 5/8	43 1/8	39 2/8	6	6	Grant County	OR	Stan J. Payne	2004	5702
282 2/8	39 0/8	41 6/8	39 0/8	6	6	Montezuma County	CO	David Acree	2005	5702
282 2/8	46 5/8	42 4/8	34 2/8	6	6	Coconino County	AZ	John B. Kasper	2005	5702
282 2/8	42 3/8	45 0/8	31 0/8	6	6	Teller County	CO	Steven Coyne	2008	5702
282 2/8	43 1/8	44 0/8	34 0/8	6	6	Flathead County	MT	Christopher K. Salminen	2010	5702
281 4/8	45 4/8	44 7/8	44 7/8	5	6	Wallowa County	OR	Dale F. Story	1967	5712
282 1/8	43 7/8	43 4/8	33 3/8	6	6	Teton County	MT	James Dean	1977	5712
282 1/8	43 3/8	44 2/8	32 3/8	6	6	Sheridan County	WY	Mike Barrett	1983	5712
282 1/8	45 4/8	42 5/8	35 1/8	6	6	Coconino County	AZ	Ronald G. Scherer	1990	5712
282 1/8	43 6/8	41 0/8	32 5/8	6	6	Coconino County	AZ	Brett W. Bostian	1993	5712
282 1/8	41 6/8	42 4/8	36 5/8	6	6	Valley County	ID	Darren W. Robbins	1993	5712
282 1/8	45 2/8	47 3/8	37 1/8	6	6	Cibola County	NM	Robert H. Ennis	1995	5712
282 1/8	41 2/8	42 2/8	38 1/8	6	6	Mesa County	CO	Al Ceprano	1997	5712
282 1/8	45 3/8	43 3/8	36 5/8	6	7	Klamath County	OR	Terry Maddock	1999	5712
282 1/8	46 5/8	50 1/8	44 5/8	5	6	Sheridan County	WY	Mel Dutton	2002	5712
282 1/8	45 1/8	45 1/8	33 5/8	6	6	Union County	OR	Todd M. Lyon	2002	5712
282 1/8	48 5/8	46 7/8	38 3/8	7	6	Gallatin County	MT	David James	2007	5712
282 1/8	42 6/8	42 4/8	39 5/8	6	6	Navajo County	AZ	Darin Holman	2010	5712
282 0/8	53 7/8	53 5/8	34 0/8	6	6	Moffat County	CO	Clark Stokes	1985	5725
282 0/8	44 0/8	45 0/8	37 0/8	6	6	Otero County	NM	John Bowman	1991	5725
282 0/8	41 5/8	41 5/8	32 2/8	6	6	Lincoln County	NM	Gary E. Wright	1995	5725
282 0/8	44 7/8	42 1/8	33 7/8	6	7	Garfield County	MT	Bob Smith	2000	5725
282 0/8	48 5/8	49 6/8	39 6/8	6	6	Valley County	ID	Jacob Buskirk	2001	5725
282 0/8	45 4/8	45 0/8	39 2/8	6	6	Shoshone County	ID	James G. Spinelli	2001	5725
282 0/8	44 6/8	43 4/8	40 4/8	6	5	Otero County	NM	John W. Sword	2002	5725
*282 0/8	47 5/8	43 5/8	42 2/8	6	6	Coconino County	AZ	Ryan Nogosek	2006	5725
282 0/8	45 3/8	45 7/8	33 6/8	6	6	Mineral County	CO	Robert Den Bleyker, Jr.	2007	5725
282 0/8	42 6/8	42 0/8	32 2/8	6	6	Grant County	OR	Spencer Heard	2008	5725
282 0/8	47 3/8	47 6/8	36 4/8	5	5	San Juan County	UT	Paul R. Weyand	2009	5725
*282 0/8	47 2/8	47 3/8	38 1/8	6	7	Alamosa County	CO	Ted Arnold	2009	5725
282 0/8	47 1/8	49 7/8	37 1/8	6	8	Wallowa County	OR	Arthur Scott Bryant	2010	5725
281 7/8	49 3/8	48 7/8	33 5/8	6	6	Costilla County	CO	Nathan Jones	1995	5738
281 7/8	49 1/8	48 5/8	30 3/8	6	6	Coconino County	AZ	Steve Thurmon	1995	5738
281 7/8	41 2/8	42 4/8	34 5/8	6	7	Catron County	NM	Robert A. Williams	1996	5738
281 7/8	42 1/8	40 0/8	34 1/8	6	6	Catron County	NM	Daniel J. Loucks	1996	5738
281 7/8	49 1/8	49 3/8	38 4/8	7	6	Coconino County	AZ	Eric Loeffler	1998	5738
281 7/8	47 5/8	47 3/8	38 5/8	6	6	Clark County	ID	Glen Berry	2002	5738
*281 7/8	45 4/8	44 2/8	37 7/8	6	6	Park County	WY	David D. Darwin	2004	5738
281 7/8	46 1/8	45 4/8	41 1/8	6	6	Yavapai County	AZ	Ryan Moses	2005	5738
*281 7/8	50 6/8	51 2/8	29 3/8	6	6	Caribou County	ID	John Berndt	2007	5738
*281 7/8	43 2/8	43 2/8	32 3/8	7	7	Powder River County	MT	Mary L. Gruntzel	2008	5738
*281 7/8	46 6/8	47 0/8	34 7/8	6	6	Crook County	WY	Kevin Bertsch	2008	5738
281 6/8	38 4/8	39 3/8	32 5/8	7	6	Powell County	MT	James L. Tillotson	1980	5749
281 6/8	40 7/8	42 2/8	42 5/8	6	6	Missoula County	MT	Charles E. Hansen	1982	5749
281 6/8	41 7/8	42 4/8	37 0/8	7	7	Lincoln County	MT	Mark Wachsman	1982	5749
281 6/8	43 4/8	45 0/8	38 6/8	6	6	Custer County	ID	Vito Palazzolo	1983	5749
281 6/8	43 7/8	44 3/8	36 0/8	6	6	Mesa County	CO	Don Boyles	1986	5749
281 6/8	48 2/8	47 4/8	38 0/8	6	5	Greenlee County	AZ	Joseph Barry	1986	5749
281 6/8	46 0/8	46 4/8	38 4/8	6	7	San Miguel County	CO	Tony Thomas	1988	5749
281 6/8	35 3/8	48 0/8	41 5/8	5	7	Mesa County	CO	Don Boyles	1989	5749
281 6/8	45 3/8	42 3/8	39 5/8	7	6	Wheeler County	OR	Roetta Williams	1990	5749
281 6/8	53 6/8	52 6/8	42 1/8	6	7	Coconino County	AZ	Dean Willette	2001	5749
281 6/8	45 7/8	48 2/8	26 0/8	6	6	Wapiti River	ALB	Terry Hagman	2001	5749
281 6/8	47 1/8	45 2/8	37 2/8	6	6	Carbon County	WY	Dan Myron	2004	5749
281 6/8	42 0/8	42 6/8	40 2/8	6	6	Adams County	ID	Larry Hoff	2005	5749
281 6/8	44 6/8	46 0/8	32 2/8	6	6	Petroleum County	MT	Bruce W. Weyh	2007	5749
*281 6/8	45 0/8	43 1/8	37 4/8	6	6	Custer County	SD	Reginald E. Faber, Jr.	2009	5749
281 6/8	43 3/8	49 3/8	33 4/8	7	6	White Pine County	NV	Jason R. Pierson	2010	5749
281 5/8	44 6/8	45 6/8	39 3/8	6	6	Phillips County	MT	Robert Monhollon	1986	5765
281 5/8	50 3/8	49 7/8	44 1/8	5	6	Latah County	ID	Mark Gottschalk	1992	5765
281 5/8	42 4/8	42 0/8	36 1/8	6	6	Mesa County	CO	Ron M. O'Dell	1995	5765
281 5/8	45 3/8	45 4/8	36 1/8	6	6	Lemhi County	ID	Rodger L. Willett, Jr.	2003	5765
281 5/8	45 4/8	45 5/8	33 5/8	6	6	Coconino County	AZ	Tom Vanasche	2003	5765
281 5/8	46 3/8	46 3/8	36 3/8	6	6	Fergus County	MT	Darrell Bates	2003	5765
281 5/8	45 3/8	45 4/8	40 7/8	6	6	Coconino County	AZ	Jacob L. Bowden	2004	5765
281 5/8	44 1/8	43 7/8	33 3/8	6	6	Dolores County	CO	Aaron J. McDonnel	2004	5765
281 4/8	43 1/8	42 4/8	36 0/8	6	6	Sandoval County	NM	Robert L. Pagel	1988	5773
281 4/8	47 4/8	48 3/8	40 0/8	6	6	Catron County	NM	Randy Lockhart	1991	5773
281 4/8	48 6/8	49 6/8	30 0/8	6	6	Colfax County	NM	Howard L. Samit	1991	5773
281 4/8	47 7/8	48 0/8	34 2/8	6	6	Crook County	OR	Hank Baxter	1998	5773
281 4/8	44 1/8	44 7/8	37 6/8	5	6	Phillips County	MT	Danny Moore	2002	5773
281 4/8	44 0/8	41 7/8	31 2/8	6	6	Bonneville County	ID	Kirt Schwieder	2003	5773
281 4/8	47 3/8	46 1/8	37 6/8	6	6	Bernalillo County	NM	Rick Grubbs	2004	5773
*281 4/8	45 4/8	45 0/8	37 2/8	6	6	McKinley County	NM	James Sowell, Jr.	2005	5773
281 4/8	47 3/8	49 0/8	36 2/8	6	6	Madison County	MT	Steve Droogsma	2006	5773
281 4/8	44 0/8	44 6/8	42 6/8	6	5	Glacier County	MT	Gabe Grant	2007	5773
*281 4/8	45 6/8	46 0/8	39 6/8	6	6	Union County	OR	Tuan Myles	2008	5773
*281 4/8	44 1/8	44 4/8	35 3/8	7	6	Jefferson County	CO	John Stodola	2010	5773
281 3/8	45 1/8	45 4/8	36 3/8	6	6	Coconino County	AZ	Judy Shelton	1991	5785
281 3/8	37 5/8	37 0/8	36 1/8	6	6	Gunnison County	CO	Doug McCauley	1992	5785
281 3/8	42 1/8	41 1/8	37 5/8	6	6	Madison County	MT	Kurt D. Rued	1996	5785
281 3/8	47 3/8	48 1/8	33 1/8	6	6	Coconino County	AZ	Donald C. Azlin	1997	5785
281 3/8	45 1/8	45 5/8	31 3/8	6	6	Harney County	OR	Bob Daniels	1997	5785
281 3/8	42 1/8	40 6/8	38 5/8	6	6	Larimer County	CO	John C. Beckett, Jr.	2004	5785
281 2/8	43 4/8	44 1/8	35 2/8	6	6	Powell County	MT	John Bottman	1986	5791
281 2/8	47 5/8	46 4/8	34 6/8	6	6	Sublette County	WY	Shawn Witte	1993	5791
281 2/8	41 6/8	41 3/8	34 0/8	6	6	Montezuma County	CO	Darrell Knierihm	1997	5791
281 2/8	41 0/8	43 6/8	35 7/8	7	6	Pierce County	WA	Allen Williams	2000	5791
281 2/8	45 6/8	45 7/8	30 2/8	6	6	Fergus County	MT	Bruce A. Erickson	2003	5791

738

AMERICAN ELK (TYPICAL ANTLERS)

Minimum Score 260

Continued

SCORE	LENGTH OF R MAIN BEAM L	INSIDE SPREAD	NUMBER OF R POINTS L		AREA	STATE/ PROVINCE	HUNTER'S NAME	DATE	RANK
281 2/8	42 7/8 40 7/8	39 4/8	6	6	Garfield County	CO	Gary Devereaux	2007	5791
281 2/8	42 4/8 40 7/8	28 7/8	7	6	Mineral County	MT	Justin Downing	2007	5791
*281 2/8	40 2/8 39 6/8	36 2/8	7	7	Routt County	CO	Matthew J. Williams	2007	5791
281 2/8	45 0/8 46 2/8	33 6/8	6	6	Grand County	CO	Jared Cooper	2009	5791
281 1/8	42 4/8 44 1/8	35 6/8	6	6	Larimer County	CO	Gary Galloway	1984	5800
281 1/8	44 0/8 44 7/8	39 3/8	6	6	Shoshone County	ID	Dean C. Weyen	1988	5800
281 1/8	41 3/8 42 4/8	37 5/8	7	7	Fergus County	MT	Tom Madden	1989	5800
281 1/8	45 6/8 43 2/8	41 1/8	5	6	Malheur County	OR	Dennis H. Slagle	1992	5800
281 1/8	44 4/8 45 0/8	36 3/8	6	6	Coconino County	AZ	Ron Warring	1994	5800
281 1/8	47 2/8 46 5/8	34 3/8	6	6	Coconino County	AZ	Brandt Lewis	1998	5800
281 1/8	42 0/8 42 7/8	35 1/8	6	6	Idaho County	ID	Michael A. Radko	1999	5800
*281 1/8	46 0/8 45 4/8	41 7/8	7	6	Rio Blanco County	CO	Arthur W. Wheless	2005	5800
281 1/8	47 2/8 47 0/8	38 3/8	6	6	Conejos County	CO	T. J. Neal	2005	5800
281 1/8	43 3/8 43 5/8	35 7/8	6	6	Otero County	NM	Brad M. Jackson	2007	5800
281 1/8	45 5/8 45 4/8	40 5/8	6	6	Big Horn County	WY	Ryan Schulz	2009	5800
281 0/8	43 2/8 43 4/8	38 0/8	6	6	Lemhi County	ID	A. Marc Whisler	1980	5811
281 0/8	47 0/8 45 5/8	37 0/8	6	6	Baker County	OR	Robert L. Unruh	1982	5811
281 0/8	44 4/8 49 0/8	36 6/8	6	6	Moffat County	CO	Lonny Vanatta	1984	5811
281 0/8	42 6/8 42 1/8	34 2/8	6	6	Sublette County	WY	George E. Hall	1984	5811
281 0/8	42 5/8 41 3/8	39 2/8	6	6	Lemhi County	ID	William Bullock, Sr.	1984	5811
281 0/8	51 3/8 52 1/8	37 0/8	5	6	Apache County	AZ	Kendall R. Adair	1991	5811
281 0/8	39 4/8 41 1/8	41 0/8	6	6	Lincoln County	WY	Tim Isaacson	1995	5811
281 0/8	47 1/8 45 3/8	32 0/8	6	6	Clark County	NV	Dan Klebenow	1995	5811
281 0/8	45 7/8 48 0/8	36 4/8	6	6	Catron County	NM	Steve Garner	1996	5811
281 0/8	50 2/8 48 2/8	44 6/8	5	6	Custer County	ID	Lucien Rouse	1998	5811
281 0/8	41 0/8 41 7/8	32 6/8	6	7	Coconino County	AZ	Greg Morris	2005	5811
281 0/8	44 1/8 43 4/8	31 4/8	6	6	Albany County	WY	Rick Parish	2008	5811
*281 0/8	43 4/8 47 5/8	37 0/8	6	6	Custer County	MT	Jeffery R. Hillman	2008	5811
280 7/8	43 1/8 42 3/8	32 7/8	6	6	Johnson County	WY	Paul S. Warren	1979	5824
280 7/8	45 7/8 41 0/8	38 1/8	6	6	Jefferson County	CO	David A. Graham	1991	5824
280 7/8	42 7/8 43 1/8	33 3/8	6	6	Shoshone County	ID	Harold L. Sterner, Jr.	1991	5824
280 7/8	46 3/8 44 0/8	34 3/8	6	6	Lemhi County	ID	M. G. Reynolds	1992	5824
280 7/8	50 5/8 50 2/8	45 3/8	5	6	Apache County	AZ	Fred Clifford	1995	5824
280 7/8	44 6/8 45 2/8	31 7/8	6	6	Pierce County	WA	William H. Wakeley	1997	5824
280 7/8	43 2/8 45 0/8	41 3/8	6	6	Fergus County	MT	Brad Tank	1999	5824
280 7/8	49 0/8 43 4/8	43 0/8	7	6	Otero County	NM	Scot Lambert	2002	5824
280 7/8	48 5/8 44 0/8	33 1/8	6	6	Union County	OR	Ryan Justus	2002	5824
280 7/8	45 7/8 45 6/8	36 2/8	8	6	Wallowa County	OR	Tom Vanasche	2005	5824
280 7/8	41 0/8 42 2/8	38 7/8	6	5	Larimer County	CO	Dale Nixon	2006	5824
280 7/8	45 5/8 45 6/8	41 1/8	6	6	Wallowa County	OR	Rodney Smallen	2009	5824
280 6/8	48 5/8 47 0/8	38 2/8	6	6	Summit County	UT	John B. Rice, Jr.	1986	5836
280 6/8	44 6/8 44 1/8	35 6/8	6	6	Yakima County	WA	Kevin Spencer	1989	5836
280 6/8	40 7/8 45 4/8	43 4/8	6	6	Socorro County	NM	Eugene Flick	1994	5836
280 6/8	42 4/8 42 6/8	36 2/8	6	6	Idaho County	ID	C. R. Wenger	1998	5836
280 6/8	39 4/8 39 6/8	37 6/8	6	6	Millard County	UT	Ronald K. Adams	2003	5836
280 6/8	48 0/8 45 3/8	35 4/8	6	6	Costilla County	CO	Casey A. Blum	2003	5836
280 6/8	48 0/8 49 2/8	39 6/8	6	6	Pennington County	SD	Dwight D. Pochant	2005	5836
280 6/8	39 2/8 38 1/8	29 0/8	6	6	Petroleum County	MT	Randy S. Bowler	2005	5836
280 6/8	43 5/8 42 0/8	37 0/8	6	6	Meagher County	MT	Steven J. Halama	2006	5836
*280 6/8	45 6/8 44 7/8	38 3/8	6	8	La Plata County	CO	Russ Dufva	2007	5836
280 6/8	44 2/8 41 4/8	39 3/8	6	6	Coconino County	AZ	Randall S. MacMillan	1990	5846
280 5/8	42 0/8 40 4/8	33 7/8	7	7	Rocky Mountain House	ALB	Terry Brew	1991	5846
280 5/8	44 5/8 44 7/8	36 3/8	7	6	Catron County	NM	Eddie Claypool	1992	5846
280 5/8	43 3/8 42 5/8	42 7/8	6	6	Bear Lake County	ID	Bryce W. Crane	1998	5846
280 5/8	44 1/8 45 0/8	36 7/8	6	6	Lemhi County	ID	Nathan Voss	2002	5846
280 5/8	41 1/8 40 4/8	45 6/8	6	6	Coconino County	AZ	Jerry Francoeur	2003	5846
280 5/8	48 1/8 46 5/8	35 3/8	6	6	Butte County	ID	Westley S. Portwood	2005	5846
280 5/8	46 6/8 46 0/8	32 5/8	6	6	Lewis & Clark County	MT	Don Roberson	2006	5846
280 4/8	43 3/8 41 5/8	33 6/8	6	6	Garfield County	CO	Perry Trujillo	1989	5854
280 4/8	46 3/8 44 6/8	34 2/8	6	6	Boise County	ID	Robert D. Dowen	1991	5854
280 4/8	44 5/8 43 4/8	35 6/8	6	6	Catron County	NM	Bob "Jake" Jacobsen	1992	5854
280 4/8	41 4/8 43 0/8	30 2/8	6	6	Phillips County	MT	Jim Edmundson	1994	5854
280 4/8	45 3/8 44 0/8	33 3/8	7	7	Catron County	NM	George Pharis	2000	5854
*280 4/8	46 0/8 47 6/8	32 4/8	6	6	Moffat County	CO	Ted McMillion	2006	5854
280 4/8	53 5/8 53 0/8	36 4/8	6	6	Stevens County	WA	Dean R. Bannetch	2007	5854
280 4/8	45 7/8 44 6/8	32 4/8	6	6	Butte County	ID	Jerry Simmons	2007	5854
280 4/8	46 0/8 47 0/8	29 2/8	6	6	Phillips County	MT	Jeffrey M. Smith	2007	5854
280 3/8	49 7/8 49 1/8	37 5/8	5	5	Rocky Mountain House	ALB	Eugene Lopushinsky	1981	5863
280 3/8	47 0/8 46 2/8	36 3/8	6	6	Clearwater County	ID	Tony Hyde	1986	5863
280 3/8	50 4/8 53 5/8	37 7/8	6	6	Coconino County	AZ	David H. Scott	1995	5863
280 3/8	45 0/8 43 7/8	37 3/8	6	6	Beaverhead County	MT	Matthew White	1999	5863
280 3/8	44 5/8 44 7/8	40 1/8	6	6	Lemhi County	ID	Rodger Willett, Jr.	2000	5863
280 3/8	41 7/8 40 0/8	36 5/8	6	6	Fergus County	MT	Mike Bentler	2004	5863
280 3/8	43 2/8 44 3/8	33 5/8	5	6	Crook County	WY	Kenneth J. Morga	2004	5863
280 3/8	46 6/8 45 7/8	35 5/8	6	6	Harney County	OR	Dewayne Conley	2005	5863
280 3/8	45 0/8 43 5/8	36 7/8	5	5	Otero County	NM	Jody A. Bartnick	2006	5863
280 2/8	39 2/8 37 3/8	33 6/8	6	5	Routt County	CO	D. F. Holt	1981	5872
280 2/8	42 4/8 42 1/8	34 2/8	6	6	Beaverhead County	MT	Danny Moore	1987	5872
280 2/8	44 5/8 43 2/8	36 2/8	6	6	La Plata County	CO	Jeff Tusing	1996	5872
280 2/8	44 4/8 43 6/8	36 6/8	6	6	Valley County	ID	Shane D. Miller	1998	5872
280 2/8	47 2/8 45 7/8	33 4/8	6	7	Latah County	ID	Terry Proctor	1998	5872
280 2/8	51 5/8 49 5/8	37 6/8	6	5	Catron County	NM	Albert F. Haas	1999	5872
280 2/8	45 6/8 45 3/8	35 6/8	6	6	Lake County	CO	Robin A. Musser	1999	5872
280 2/8	43 2/8 44 1/8	33 0/8	6	6	Rio Arriba County	NM	James Knoke	2000	5872
280 2/8	40 5/8 43 0/8	36 0/8	6	6	Larimer County	CO	Clay Cushman	2001	5872
280 2/8	40 1/8 40 1/8	47 4/8	5	7	Navajo County	AZ	Karl R. Allen	2003	5872
280 2/8	47 2/8 47 0/8	33 4/8	6	6	Douglas County	OR	Jon Havens	2004	5872
280 2/8	41 5/8 42 2/8	32 6/8	6	6	Saguache County	CO	Adam Johnson	2004	5872
*280 2/8	40 6/8 40 6/8	32 4/8	6	6	Garfield County	CO	Cindy Seitz-Krug	2006	5872
280 2/8	45 2/8 44 5/8	36 2/8	6	6	Navajo County	AZ	Jerry Dean Thorson	2006	5872
*280 2/8	49 3/8 47 7/8	39 0/8	5	5	Coconino County	AZ	Matt Curry	2008	5872
280 1/8	44 0/8 40 2/8	38 7/8	6	7	Coconino County	AZ	Scott Kellner	1983	5887
280 1/8	39 3/8 40 0/8	29 7/8	6	6	Phillips County	MT	Thomas R. Herman	1987	5887
280 1/8	51 4/8 48 0/8	40 5/8	6	6	Coconino County	AZ	Todd Hinkins	1989	5887
280 1/8	42 6/8 45 7/8	36 3/8	7	6	Adams County	ID	Jerome E. Arledge	1990	5887

AMERICAN ELK (TYPICAL ANTLERS)

Minimum Score 260   Continued

SCORE	LENGTH OF MAIN BEAM R / L	INSIDE SPREAD	NUMBER OF POINTS R / L	AREA	STATE/PROVINCE	HUNTER'S NAME	DATE	RANK
280 1/8	44 5/8 / 39 0/8	34 0/8	6 / 7	Sanders County	MT	Gerry Mercer	1992	5887
280 1/8	46 2/8 / 46 3/8	40 1/8	6 / 6	Wasco County	OR	Ben Munoz	1994	5887
280 1/8	45 5/8 / 45 0/8	39 3/8	6 / 6	Johnson County	WY	Mark W. Robinson	1998	5887
280 1/8	44 6/8 / 45 0/8	33 7/8	6 / 6	Kevisville	ALB	Dallas Kaiser	1998	5887
280 1/8	47 5/8 / 50 1/8	29 5/8	6 / 6	Coconino County	AZ	Darren Edward Burke	1998	5887
280 1/8	48 0/8 / 46 1/8	42 3/8	6 / 6	Baker County	OR	Tana Thompson	1998	5887
280 1/8	48 7/8 / 48 5/8	38 5/8	5 / 6	Larimer County	CO	John Westers	2003	5887
280 1/8	49 1/8 / 49 2/8	31 3/8	7 / 7	Larimer County	CO	Clint Siddons	2008	5887
*280 1/8	49 1/8 / 49 2/8	31 3/8	7 / 7	Larimer County	CO	Clint Siddons	2008	5887
280 0/8	45 4/8 / 45 3/8	33 6/8	6 / 6	Rio Blanco County	CO	Rolland M. Esterline	1969	5899
280 0/8	47 3/8 / 45 5/8	32 5/8	6 / 7	Judith Basin County	MT	Ronald Ozbun	1987	5899
280 0/8	45 6/8 / 45 0/8	27 4/8	6 / 6	King County	WA	George Dan Feighner	1987	5899
280 0/8	43 0/8 / 42 6/8	41 4/8	6 / 6	Washington County	ID	Randy Wilkins	1989	5899
280 0/8	45 3/8 / 46 4/8	35 0/8	6 / 6	Park County	WY	David C. Ruhl	1992	5899
280 0/8	47 7/8 / 49 7/8	35 6/8	6 / 6	Catron County	NM	Glen L. Dillehay	1993	5899
280 0/8	44 5/8 / 44 3/8	33 6/8	6 / 6	Moffat County	CO	Matt Potts	2001	5899
280 0/8	40 6/8 / 40 1/8	31 0/8	6 / 6	Meagher County	MT	Jim Kennedy	2002	5899
280 0/8	39 7/8 / 38 3/8	28 6/8	6 / 6	Fremont County	CO	Matt Tellock	2006	5899
279 7/8	43 6/8 / 44 0/8	40 2/8	7 / 6	Valley County	ID	Kenneth A Hyde	1983	5908
279 7/8	40 1/8 / 37 6/8	32 6/8	7 / 9	Umatilla County	OR	Kurt Rosenberg	1995	5908
279 7/8	43 1/8 / 45 6/8	32 5/8	6 / 6	Larimer County	CO	Thomas Coseo	2004	5908
279 7/8	45 3/8 / 46 6/8	37 3/8	6 / 6	Grant County	OR	Robert Wennerstrom	2006	5908
279 6/8	45 7/8 / 44 2/8	33 0/8	6 / 6	Valley County	ID	Phil Barton	1989	5912
279 6/8	44 6/8 / 43 2/8	34 0/8	6 / 6	Catron County	NM	Abe Dimas, Jr.	1993	5912
279 6/8	40 6/8 / 40 3/8	40 0/8	5 / 5	Colfax County	NM	David C. Lighty	1996	5912
279 6/8	43 6/8 / 42 7/8	39 0/8	6 / 6	Archuleta County	CO	Dr. Vernon Ray	1996	5912
279 6/8	44 1/8 / 44 1/8	31 6/8	6 / 6	Valley County	MT	Christian Duane Gartner	1997	5912
279 6/8	43 7/8 / 44 0/8	41 0/8	6 / 6	Blaine County	ID	Don Torbert, Sr.	1998	5912
279 6/8	42 6/8 / 48 0/8	32 0/8	5 / 6	Navajo County	AZ	John A. North	1998	5912
279 6/8	44 0/8 / 45 7/8	32 2/8	6 / 6	Catron County	NM	Dr. Charles W. Hendricks	1999	5912
279 6/8	38 4/8 / 39 6/8	41 1/8	5 / 5	Gallatin County	MT	Mike Lely	1999	5912
279 6/8	45 2/8 / 43 0/8	42 4/8	7 / 6	Broadwater County	MT	Steve Latimer	2002	5912
279 6/8	42 1/8 / 44 4/8	37 0/8	6 / 6	Union County	OR	Dennis T. Mascher	2003	5912
279 6/8	43 3/8 / 43 5/8	39 2/8	6 / 6	Jackson County	CO	Richard Vail	2007	5912
*279 6/8	42 2/8 / 42 3/8	31 4/8	8 / 7	Pitkin County	CO	Josh Gustad	2009	5912
279 5/8	41 2/8 / 42 5/8	41 1/8	6 / 6	Sheridan County	WY	Mike Barrett	1987	5925
279 5/8	43 4/8 / 45 4/8	33 7/8	6 / 6	Catron County	NM	John Wirth, Jr.	1991	5925
279 5/8	41 5/8 / 41 5/8	39 5/8	6 / 6	Sublette County	WY	Dale L. White	1995	5925
279 5/8	43 1/8 / 43 0/8	38 1/8	6 / 6	Fremont County	WY	Dean P. Simmons	1996	5925
279 5/8	46 5/8 / 45 6/8	42 7/8	6 / 6	Custer County	ID	Lars L. Colberg	1998	5925
279 4/8	41 2/8 / 39 0/8	33 0/8	6 / 6	Wallowa County	OR	James R. Brackenbury	1970	5930
279 4/8	46 5/8 / 45 0/8	40 4/8	6 / 5	Idaho County	ID	Richard C. Nichols	1973	5930
279 4/8	41 6/8 / 40 6/8	33 2/8	6 / 6	Clearwater County	ID	John Burns, Sr.	1982	5930
279 4/8	41 7/8 / 41 5/8	38 0/8	5 / 5	Duck Mtns.	MAN	Harvey Gagne	1995	5930
279 4/8	40 4/8 / 41 4/8	37 0/8	6 / 6	Petroleum County	MT	Carlton DeFoor	1997	5930
279 4/8	41 1/8 / 40 4/8	37 2/8	6 / 6	Summit County	CO	Bill Easterly	2005	5930
279 3/8	45 6/8 / 45 1/8	39 1/8	6 / 6	Phillips County	MT	Dave Zimmer	1983	5936
279 3/8	49 2/8 / 49 4/8	36 3/8	6 / 6	Park County	WY	Allen J. Fike	2000	5936
279 3/8	51 6/8 / 49 4/8	34 5/8	6 / 6	Gila County	AZ	Wayne Carter	2003	5936
*279 3/8	45 1/8 / 44 7/8	37 1/8	6 / 6	Lawrence County	SD	Jerrold J. Vaughn	2005	5936
279 3/8	42 6/8 / 43 6/8	32 5/8	6 / 6	Phillips County	MT	Danny Moore	2005	5936
*279 3/8	47 2/8 / 44 6/8	36 3/8	6 / 6	Navajo County	AZ	Bob LeCocq	2008	5936
279 2/8	45 2/8 / 46 0/8	34 0/8	6 / 6	Clearwater County	ID	Don West	1981	5942
279 2/8	48 7/8 / 46 5/8	33 6/8	6 / 5	Clear Creek County	CO	Ken Shelton	1986	5942
279 2/8	46 2/8 / 45 6/8	28 4/8	6 / 6	Phillips County	MT	Bill Rackley	1986	5942
279 2/8	42 1/8 / 46 5/8	29 2/8	6 / 7	Missoula County	MT	Jim B. Bradford	1987	5942
279 2/8	42 1/8 / 40 7/8	31 6/8	6 / 6	Grant County	NM	David H. Walske	1991	5942
279 2/8	41 3/8 / 43 0/8	38 0/8	5 / 5	Custer County	ID	Bruce Miller	1994	5942
279 2/8	47 0/8 / 48 2/8	33 0/8	6 / 6	Mesa County	CO	Yvonne Simmons	2007	5942
*279 2/8	47 7/8 / 51 3/8	40 2/8	6 / 6	Coconino County	AZ	Mike Lanoue	2008	5942
*279 2/8	46 6/8 / 48 0/8	38 4/8	7 / 6	Apache County	AZ	David Piccinini	2008	5942
279 1/8	45 2/8 / 44 6/8	35 5/8	6 / 6	Coconino County	AZ	Todd B. Rice	1990	5951
279 1/8	48 2/8 / 45 2/8	45 5/8	5 / 6	Elko County	NV	Jerry Vega	1998	5951
279 1/8	49 6/8 / 49 5/8	40 1/8	6 / 6	Summit County	CO	Brad Ham	1998	5951
279 1/8	46 4/8 / 48 0/8	36 3/8	6 / 6	Coconino County	AZ	Gary Palmer	2001	5951
279 1/8	45 6/8 / 48 3/8	30 5/8	6 / 6	Las Animas County	CO	Peter Swenson	2002	5951
*279 1/8	45 7/8 / 45 2/8	39 7/8	6 / 6	Coconino County	AZ	Richard W. Wahl	2009	5951
279 0/8	44 6/8 / 44 5/8	32 4/8	7 / 6	Las Animas County	CO	Ray Ramirez	1976	5957
279 0/8	41 1/8 / 39 5/8	36 6/8	6 / 6	Caribou County	ID	Randy J. Stephens	1979	5957
279 0/8	43 2/8 / 40 4/8	40 4/8	6 / 6	Cascade County	MT	Rick Holzheimer	1991	5957
279 0/8	47 1/8 / 46 0/8	35 4/8	6 / 6	Coconino County	AZ	Russ Pearson	1991	5957
279 0/8	45 4/8 / 44 0/8	40 6/8	6 / 6	Granite County	MT	Garret Decker	1991	5957
279 0/8	44 3/8 / 44 7/8	38 5/8	7 / 7	Custer County	ID	Jeff A. Buck	1993	5957
279 0/8	42 6/8 / 43 6/8	37 4/8	6 / 6	Sheridan County	WY	Mike Barrett	1994	5957
279 0/8	44 3/8 / 43 4/8	44 2/8	5 / 6	Park County	MT	George Kamps	1996	5957
279 0/8	46 6/8 / 46 1/8	31 4/8	6 / 6	Wallowa County	OR	Cameron R. Hanes	1997	5957
279 0/8	42 4/8 / 45 1/8	33 2/8	8 / 7	Catron County	NM	Richard L. Peterson, Jr.	1997	5957
279 0/8	43 4/8 / 43 4/8	41 5/8	7 / 6	Valley County	ID	Frank B. Gettig	1998	5957
279 0/8	39 2/8 / 40 6/8	32 6/8	6 / 6	Garfield County	MT	Anthony Swiontek	2001	5957
279 0/8	42 2/8 / 42 6/8	36 2/8	6 / 6	Shoshone County	ID	Daniel H. Yoder	2003	5957
*279 0/8	43 7/8 / 43 3/8	33 4/8	6 / 6	Petroleum County	MT	Scott M. Kamrath	2005	5957
279 0/8	46 6/8 / 45 1/8	33 4/8	6 / 5	Larimer County	CO	Bruce Mitzel	2005	5957
279 0/8	43 6/8 / 44 7/8	35 0/8	6 / 6	Meagher County	MT	Don Davidson, Jr.	2008	5957
278 7/8	45 7/8 / 45 6/8	33 3/8	6 / 6	Apache County	AZ	Marvin W. Wuertz	1989	5973
278 7/8	42 5/8 / 40 1/8	44 7/8	5 / 6	Los Alamos County	NM	Stevan R. Weekly	1997	5973
278 7/8	48 7/8 / 46 1/8	34 5/8	6 / 7	Petroleum County	MT	Scott J. Strese	1997	5973
278 7/8	43 0/8 / 42 4/8	37 5/8	6 / 6	Lincoln County	NM	Darrell Bozarth	2000	5973
278 7/8	37 1/8 / 37 6/8	34 5/8	7 / 7	Catron County	NM	Ned Greer	2001	5973
278 7/8	39 6/8 / 42 0/8	39 3/8	6 / 6	Platte County	WY	Willard Woods	2002	5973
278 7/8	47 4/8 / 46 4/8	36 3/8	5 / 6	Hinsdale County	CO	John T. Been	2003	5973
278 7/8	43 2/8 / 43 7/8	29 0/8	7 / 7	Coconino County	AZ	Earnest E. Milton	2003	5973
278 7/8	43 1/8 / 48 1/8	32 7/8	7 / 6	Idaho County	ID	Kent Rotchy	2006	5973
*278 7/8	43 4/8 / 42 0/8	30 2/8	7 / 7	Carbon County	WY	Joe Sestak, Jr.	2007	5973
*278 7/8	44 5/8 / 43 1/8	33 7/8	6 / 6	Garfield County	CO	Bill Heller	2009	5973
278 6/8	43 5/8 / 43 7/8	35 2/8	6 / 6	Cascade County	MT	Norman T. Frusti	1979	5984
278 6/8	42 3/8 / 39 0/8	36 4/8	6 / 6	Park County	MT	George Kamps	1984	5984

740

AMERICAN ELK (TYPICAL ANTLERS)

Minimum Score 260   Continued

SCORE	LENGTH OF R MAIN BEAM L	INSIDE SPREAD	NUMBER OF R POINTS L	AREA	STATE/ PROVINCE	HUNTER'S NAME	DATE	RANK
278 6/8	44 0/8 44 6/8	33 2/8	6 6	Sevier County	UT	Dall Dimick	1987	5984
278 6/8	40 4/8 43 0/8	35 0/8	6 6	Grant County	OR	Dennis Marshall	1989	5984
278 6/8	46 7/8 45 3/8	38 2/8	6 6	Clearwater County	ID	Bryan Ohlms	1990	5984
278 6/8	41 2/8 43 6/8	42 6/8	6 6	Coconino County	AZ	Dale Tasa	1991	5984
278 6/8	38 6/8 39 4/8	35 2/8	7 7	Phillips County	MT	Lee D. Laeupple	1992	5984
278 6/8	48 5/8 48 2/8	37 4/8	6 6	Caribou County	ID	Cory R. Kosek	2002	5984
278 6/8	41 4/8 41 1/8	43 2/8	6 7	Lake County	CO	Lynn F. Engle	2003	5984
278 6/8	41 2/8 41 7/8	31 0/8	6 6	Fergus County	MT	Steve Lourenco	2003	5984
278 6/8	43 4/8 42 4/8	39 4/8	6 6	Meagher County	MT	Jim Kennedy	2004	5984
278 6/8	45 2/8 46 4/8	36 6/8	6 6	Moffat County	CO	Michael Paulcheck	2004	5984
278 5/8	48 1/8 48 2/8	41 3/8	6 6	King County	WA	Brian Kannas	1985	5996
278 5/8	46 0/8 46 5/8	34 7/8	6 6	Rio Arriba County	NM	Michael J. Cullen	1987	5996
278 5/8	45 4/8 50 5/8	42 5/8	6 6	Sierra County	NM	David Swisher	1991	5996
278 5/8	46 0/8 44 1/8	36 3/8	6 6	Idaho County	ID	Greg Walter	1995	5996
278 5/8	40 3/8 44 2/8	34 7/8	6 6	Garfield County	MT	Greg L. Barstow	2005	5996
278 5/8	41 4/8 40 6/8	35 3/8	7 6	Garfield County	CO	Kevin Barnett	2006	5996
278 5/8	41 2/8 50 4/8	34 1/8	6 7	Petroleum County	MT	Dan Belanger	2007	5996
*278 5/8	41 3/8 38 3/8	42 6/8	6 6	Fergus County	MT	Todd Rothrock	2007	5996
278 4/8	45 4/8 43 4/8	31 4/8	6 6	Cascade County	MT	David Holloway	1983	6004
278 4/8	42 5/8 42 0/8	38 6/8	6 6	Socorro County	NM	Randall McAfee	1989	6004
278 4/8	51 2/8 51 1/8	32 4/8	6 7	Navajo County	AZ	William R."Randy" Vaughn	1990	6004
278 4/8	46 3/8 45 5/8	33 0/8	6 6	Valley County	MT	Myran Gartner	1991	6004
278 4/8	44 5/8 41 5/8	35 0/8	6 6	Catron County	NM	David L. Willis	1992	6004
278 4/8	43 2/8 44 2/8	33 4/8	6 6	Rio Arriba County	NM	Alfred Vigil	1993	6004
278 4/8	48 7/8 49 3/8	38 6/8	6 6	Missoula County	MT	Andrew J. Kelly	1993	6004
278 4/8	43 6/8 44 1/8	32 0/8	6 6	Grant County	OR	Robert J. Schriever	1997	6004
278 4/8	43 0/8 41 3/8	36 2/8	6 6	Baker County	OR	Mike Raney	1998	6004
278 4/8	41 4/8 40 3/8	34 4/8	6 6	Harney County	OR	Greg Keller	2001	6004
278 4/8	42 7/8 41 4/8	36 6/8	6 6	Idaho County	ID	Eric D. Swanson	2002	6004
278 4/8	45 2/8 46 2/8	39 6/8	6 6	Grant County	OR	Matt Rinard	2002	6004
278 4/8	44 5/8 44 1/8	30 6/8	6 6	Power County	ID	Dave R. Burget	2003	6004
278 4/8	42 6/8 43 0/8	30 4/8	6 6	Chouteau County	MT	Philipe Bachofner	2003	6004
278 4/8	50 6/8 44 7/8	38 4/8	6 6	Coconino County	AZ	Pete Bazan	2004	6004
*278 4/8	42 2/8 42 4/8	35 2/8	6 6	Sheridan County	WY	Dave Lieffort	2008	6004
278 4/8	44 2/8 43 0/8	34 4/8	6 6	Dolores County	CO	Cory Riehl	2008	6004
278 4/8	42 3/8 42 5/8	37 0/8	6 6	Grant County	NM	Henry Moore	2009	6004
278 3/8	48 7/8 44 0/8	35 7/8	6 6	Madison County	MT	Jerome E. Skinner, Jr.	1992	6022
278 3/8	51 0/8 51 0/8	39 3/8	6 6	Moffat County	CO	Paul E. Miller	1994	6022
278 3/8	41 7/8 44 3/8	30 1/8	6 6	Phillips County	MT	Darwin J. Roberts	1998	6022
278 3/8	42 2/8 40 4/8	36 5/8	6 6	La Plata County	CO	Alan J. Andrews	2000	6022
278 3/8	39 5/8 39 4/8	41 5/8	7 6	Sublette County	WY	George E. Chase, Jr.	2001	6022
*278 3/8	46 7/8 46 3/8	34 1/8	6 6	Cibola County	NM	Chuck Hogan	2005	6022
278 3/8	41 4/8 41 5/8	32 7/8	6 6	Jackson County	CO	Mark Minta	2009	6022
278 2/8	46 5/8 46 0/8	33 0/8	6 6	Blaine County	ID	Larry R. Newton	1993	6029
278 2/8	42 6/8 42 3/8	39 6/8	6 6	Camas County	ID	Russell R. Scharman	1996	6029
278 2/8	40 4/8 39 4/8	36 0/8	6 6	Mora County	NM	Mike Landmesser	1997	6029
278 2/8	41 5/8 41 6/8	40 4/8	6 6	Idaho County	ID	Mike Nowaczyk	1998	6029
278 2/8	43 6/8 46 5/8	35 6/8	7 6	Mineral County	MT	Ber Yang	2006	6029
278 1/8	42 3/8 43 0/8	38 3/8	6 6	Ravalli County	MT	Michael J. Nielsen	1992	6034
278 1/8	44 7/8 44 2/8	39 5/8	6 6	Beaverhead County	MT	Danny L. Moore	1993	6034
278 1/8	42 4/8 42 2/8	32 1/8	6 6	Coconino County	AZ	Robert J. "Bob" Cates	1996	6034
278 1/8	42 1/8 42 4/8	31 5/8	6 6	Converse County	WY	David Moore	1998	6034
278 1/8	44 1/8 44 6/8	27 3/8	6 6	Medicine Lake	ALB	Glen William Miller	1998	6034
278 1/8	43 2/8 44 2/8	37 1/8	6 6	Beaverhead County	MT	Richard A. Sater	2001	6034
278 1/8	44 3/8 41 3/8	38 3/8	6 6	Phillips County	MT	Ronald W. Vanden Brink	2002	6034
*278 1/8	39 4/8 39 6/8	35 3/8	6 6	Rich County	UT	Ted Hallows	2003	6034
278 1/8	41 5/8 42 6/8	29 1/8	6 6	Gallatin County	MT	Robert W. Moos	2004	6034
278 1/8	50 3/8 47 3/8	34 4/8	6 6	Coconino County	AZ	Shane Faulkner	2004	6034
*278 1/8	45 4/8 44 6/8	32 1/8	6 6	Montrose County	CO	Russel H. Rudy	2007	6034
*278 1/8	44 3/8 43 6/8	32 7/8	6 6	Mesa County	CO	Stuart Russell	2007	6034
*278 1/8	41 5/8 46 0/8	40 1/8	5 6	Rosebud County	MT	Rick Hanson	2009	6034
278 0/8	48 2/8 44 3/8	47 0/8	6 6	Lincoln County	MT	Bud Journey	1978	6047
278 0/8	41 2/8 43 1/8	37 2/8	6 6	Grant County	OR	Clayton Severin	1984	6047
278 0/8	46 1/8 46 5/8	37 4/8	5 6	Rio Arriba County	NM	Fred Vigil	1994	6047
278 0/8	45 3/8 45 6/8	37 6/8	6 6	Coconino County	AZ	Ricardo Saldivar	1994	6047
278 0/8	46 2/8 49 1/8	35 2/8	6 6	Grant County	NM	Scott Maloney	1996	6047
278 0/8	47 3/8 46 3/8	36 4/8	6 6	McKinley County	NM	Jim Gresham	1996	6047
278 0/8	41 5/8 40 4/8	39 6/8	6 6	Custer County	ID	Steve Higgins	1999	6047
278 0/8	47 6/8 46 5/8	34 0/8	6 6	Tuchodi River	BC	Brian Williams	2004	6047
*278 0/8	44 5/8 43 4/8	37 4/8	6 6	Laramie County	WY	Mark Kayser	2008	6047
278 0/8	39 4/8 38 2/8	34 4/8	6 7	East Kootenay	BC	Jim Thurow	2009	6047
*278 0/8	41 3/8 43 0/8	33 2/8	6 6	Meagher County	MT	Mark Stinebrink	2009	6047
278 0/8	45 6/8 46 0/8	42 4/8	6 6	Malheur County	OR	Bob Hayes	2009	6047
277 7/8	42 2/8 41 7/8	36 3/8	6 6	Beaverhead County	MT	Gary Palmer	1990	6059
277 7/8	45 5/8 45 4/8	36 7/8	6 6	Caribou County	ID	Tyler Martinsen	1994	6059
277 7/8	47 6/8 45 5/8	37 7/8	6 6	Beaverhead County	MT	John Hefferman	1998	6059
277 7/8	44 1/8 45 6/8	33 3/8	6 6	Lemhi County	ID	Eric J. Dexter	2000	6059
277 7/8	43 6/8 43 2/8	37 1/8	6 6	Big Horn County	WY	Brett Burditt	2000	6059
277 7/8	46 2/8 45 5/8	37 7/8	6 6	Coconino County	AZ	Viron Barbay	2000	6059
277 7/8	45 5/8 42 7/8	36 3/8	6 6	Washington County	ID	Lawson J. Struve	2004	6059
277 7/8	46 3/8 45 2/8	37 7/8	6 6	Sheridan County	WY	Brian Mutch	2005	6059
*277 7/8	43 5/8 43 0/8	32 1/8	6 6	Coconino County	AZ	Troy McGinnis	2008	6059
277 6/8	39 0/8 38 6/8	37 0/8	7 7	High River	ALB	Andrew Schrock	1987	6068
277 6/8	47 2/8 47 6/8	34 4/8	6 6	Big Horn County	WY	Robert Partridge	1992	6068
277 6/8	48 0/8 45 5/8	33 4/8	6 7	Fremont County	WY	Guy LeMonnier, Jr.	1993	6068
277 6/8	45 7/8 46 7/8	39 6/8	6 6	Catron County	NM	Jeff Persenaire	1998	6068
277 6/8	39 5/8 44 1/8	38 6/8	6 6	Routt County	CO	Bob Sanders	2003	6068
277 6/8	47 7/8 46 7/8	35 6/8	6 6	Lincoln County	MT	Hansel Lee Moore, Jr.	2003	6068
277 6/8	43 2/8 44 7/8	35 2/8	6 6	Lemhi County	ID	Ryan J. Leszczynski	2007	6068
277 6/8	45 0/8 45 1/8	40 6/8	6 6	Carbon County	WY	Kyle Cook	2009	6068
*277 6/8	48 0/8 54 0/8	40 2/8	5 6	Catron County	NM	Larry Dwyer	2010	6068
277 5/8	47 1/8 45 6/8	38 1/8	6 6	Sandoval County	NM	David V. Collis	1983	6077
277 5/8	45 7/8 44 4/8	33 5/8	6 7	Catron County	NM	Donny Guest	1992	6077
277 5/8	44 1/8 44 0/8	30 1/8	6 6	Archuleta County	CO	Ed DeYoung	1995	6077
*277 5/8	40 5/8 40 0/8	30 3/8	6 6	Park County	CO	Earl R. Kaufman	2006	6077

741

AMERICAN ELK (TYPICAL ANTLERS)

Minimum Score 260   Continued

SCORE	LENGTH OF R MAIN BEAM L	INSIDE SPREAD	NUMBER OF R POINTS L	AREA	STATE/ PROVINCE	HUNTER'S NAME	DATE	RANK
*277 5/8	44 4/8 45 1/8	39 1/8	6 6	Harney County	OR	Robert L. Conley	2009	6077
277 4/8	45 2/8 47 4/8	38 0/8	6 6	La Plata County	CO	Andy White	1980	6082
277 4/8	43 4/8 45 2/8	37 0/8	6 6	Larimer County	CO	Bruce Bowman	1985	6082
277 4/8	44 3/8 43 3/8	30 0/8	7 7	Caribou County	ID	Royce Brown	1986	6082
277 4/8	42 4/8 41 1/8	36 4/8	6 6	Clearwater County	ID	Fred Gill	1994	6082
277 4/8	43 0/8 41 3/8	34 6/8	6 6	Lawrence County	SD	Larry J. Hannan	1996	6082
277 4/8	43 3/8 46 1/8	38 6/8	6 6	Fremont County	ID	Wayne M. Jensen	1998	6082
277 4/8	44 3/8 40 2/8	31 4/8	6 6	Washington County	ID	Richard Lewis Hansen	1999	6082
277 4/8	41 4/8 41 2/8	36 6/8	6 6	Swan River	MAN	Richard J. Klima	2000	6082
277 4/8	43 0/8 42 2/8	36 4/8	6 6	Rio Blanco County	CO	David M. Wannamaker	2001	6082
277 4/8	43 1/8 45 0/8	32 2/8	6 6	Boise County	ID	William Weiss	2001	6082
277 4/8	45 1/8 44 6/8	32 0/8	6 6	Catron County	NM	Stephen A. Dougherty	2003	6082
277 4/8	48 5/8 48 6/8	34 2/8	6 5	Montrose County	CO	Troy R. Lamb	2004	6082
277 4/8	47 1/8 44 1/8	35 2/8	6 6	Fremont County	WY	Marty Ruggles	2004	6082
*277 4/8	49 2/8 47 3/8	33 4/8	6 6	Johnson County	WY	David Bilotti	2006	6082
277 4/8	43 2/8 44 6/8	35 4/8	6 6	Powell County	MT	Alvise P. Pedrali	2007	6082
*277 4/8	37 1/8 38 3/8	27 4/8	6 6	Golden Valley County	MT	Brad Seyfert	2008	6082
*277 4/8	46 7/8 46 2/8	39 2/8	5 5	Gallatin County	MT	Aaron Scharf	2009	6082
277 3/8	37 7/8 39 2/8	37 3/8	6 6	Greenlee County	AZ	Clifford White	1984	6099
277 3/8	42 1/8 43 0/8	38 1/8	6 6	Larimer County	CO	Forrest McMichael	1987	6099
277 3/8	44 0/8 44 5/8	33 2/8	7 6	Lodgepole	ALB	Marvin Dusterhoft	1990	6099
277 3/8	39 5/8 39 5/8	40 3/8	6 6	Shoshone County	ID	Russell A. Keaton	1993	6099
277 3/8	43 7/8 43 0/8	33 7/8	6 6	Fremont County	WY	Kyle H. Frandsen	1994	6099
277 3/8	43 4/8 42 0/8	39 1/8	6 6	Catron County	NM	Frank S. Noska IV	1998	6099
277 3/8	46 4/8 47 4/8	38 5/8	6 6	Jefferson County	OR	Dale K. Thornton	1998	6099
277 3/8	46 3/8 43 1/8	31 3/8	6 6	Clearwater County	ID	Lucas Payne	2001	6099
277 3/8	47 3/8 48 1/8	38 1/8	6 6	Park County	CO	Richard A. Devrous, Jr.	2003	6099
277 3/8	42 2/8 45 3/8	36 5/8	6 6	Grant County	OR	Jerry Simmons	2009	6099
*277 3/8	48 5/8 54 0/8	40 3/8	5 6	Moffat County	CO	John Stubecki	2010	6099
277 2/8	47 0/8 47 3/8	40 2/8	6 6	Bonneville County	ID	Jerry Clark	1979	6110
277 2/8	41 1/8 39 7/8	40 2/8	6 7	Fergus County	MT	Ray Lundin	1982	6110
277 2/8	38 6/8 38 6/8	38 2/8	6 6	Colfax County	NM	Kenny Brice Poulson	1988	6110
277 2/8	39 4/8 37 3/8	34 0/8	5 6	Clearwater County	ID	Thomas Storr	1989	6110
277 2/8	42 4/8 43 3/8	37 0/8	6 6	Granite County	MT	Christian L. Frank	1992	6110
277 2/8	43 5/8 44 6/8	31 2/8	6 6	Coconino County	AZ	Gregg Tanner	1994	6110
277 2/8	41 2/8 42 7/8	34 0/8	6 6	Phillips County	MT	Casey Lyle Prell	1998	6110
277 2/8	45 6/8 45 2/8	30 4/8	7 7	Navajo County	AZ	Gene Milton	2001	6110
277 2/8	43 0/8 40 4/8	37 0/8	6 6	Custer County	ID	Troy Daves	2001	6110
277 2/8	48 0/8 48 6/8	36 4/8	6 6	Gallatin County	MT	Bob Morton	2003	6110
*277 2/8	42 5/8 43 2/8	33 6/8	6 6	Uintah County	UT	Evelyn Johnson	2004	6110
277 2/8	44 3/8 44 3/8	36 4/8	6 6	Adams County	ID	Derry Hawker	2004	6110
277 2/8	46 6/8 45 7/8	32 6/8	6 6	Apache County	AZ	Daniel W. Peloso	2007	6110
277 1/8	41 7/8 39 3/8	42 5/8	6 6	Clearwater County	ID	Jon Skinner	1988	6123
277 1/8	48 4/8 48 6/8	37 7/8	6 6	Valley County	ID	Brian Holbrook	1993	6123
277 1/8	44 1/8 42 1/8	34 5/8	6 6	Columbia County	WA	Shane Broeske	1997	6123
277 1/8	46 0/8 43 3/8	34 5/8	6 6	Valley County	ID	Erik I. Jacobs	1998	6123
277 1/8	39 5/8 40 6/8	39 5/8	6 6	Fremont County	ID	Merrill Huntsman	1998	6123
*277 1/8	42 2/8 42 3/8	31 2/8	6 7	Petroleum County	MT	Samuel Joe Balgaard	2007	6123
277 1/8	43 6/8 45 6/8	34 0/8	8 8	Adams County	ID	Jim Lambrecht	2008	6123
277 0/8	43 0/8 43 0/8	31 6/8	6 6	Grant County	OR	Andy Day	1981	6130
277 0/8	40 4/8 40 3/8	32 0/8	6 6	Cascade County	MT	David Yaeger	1983	6130
277 0/8	39 0/8 40 3/8	35 4/8	6 6	Flathead County	MT	Jerry L. Wootan	1984	6130
277 0/8	43 1/8 42 4/8	36 0/8	6 6	Sanders County	MT	Chuck Adams	1985	6130
277 0/8	45 6/8 46 4/8	44 4/8	5 5	Coconino County	AZ	Steve Neuberger	1993	6130
277 0/8	40 3/8 40 1/8	39 4/8	6 6	Pierce County	WA	Joe Lilley	1994	6130
277 0/8	47 0/8 47 0/8	39 6/8	6 6	Custer County	ID	Shawn Perry	1996	6130
277 0/8	43 3/8 42 6/8	30 4/8	6 6	Catron County	NM	Thomas Guetzke	1998	6130
277 0/8	37 7/8 41 2/8	37 6/8	6 6	Pitkin County	CO	George F. Reel	2004	6130
*277 0/8	40 3/8 41 3/8	35 6/8	6 6	Lincoln County	WY	Eric Hardgrave	2005	6130
277 0/8	44 2/8 43 4/8	33 4/8	6 6	Coconino County	AZ	Shane Faulkner	2006	6130
277 0/8	42 0/8 42 4/8	33 6/8	6 6	Fergus County	MT	Logan G. Miller	2009	6130
276 7/8	46 4/8 46 1/8	38 1/8	6 7	Pitkin County	CO	Byron S. Donahue	1981	6142
276 7/8	47 6/8 47 2/8	26 5/8	7 6	Rio Arriba County	NM	Michael G. Fierro	1982	6142
276 7/8	42 2/8 41 3/8	37 1/8	6 6	Benewah County	ID	Greg DesLaurier	1984	6142
276 7/8	46 1/8 45 4/8	33 5/8	6 6	Grant County	OR	Gary Nyden	1984	6142
276 7/8	49 0/8 46 4/8	33 5/8	6 6	Idaho County	ID	Charles Edward Steve	1995	6142
*276 7/8	45 0/8 46 2/8	37 3/8	5 6	Madison County	MT	Benjamin Walker	2004	6142
276 7/8	43 1/8 40 7/8	41 4/8	6 8	Eagle County	CO	Pat Shambow	2004	6142
*276 7/8	42 3/8 42 0/8	32 3/8	6 6	Jefferson County	CO	John T. Stodola	2006	6142
276 7/8	42 4/8 44 0/8	34 7/8	6 6	Custer County	SD	Bruce Briesemeister	2007	6142
276 7/8	43 7/8 43 3/8	36 6/8	6 7	Natrona County	WY	Jim Hinson	2008	6142
276 6/8	45 0/8 44 1/8	34 4/8	6 6	Lincoln County	MT	Jerry Brown	1982	6152
276 6/8	45 2/8 45 0/8	36 2/8	6 6	Taos County	NM	Calvin Farner	1986	6152
276 6/8	42 0/8 45 0/8	35 0/8	6 6	Carbon County	UT	Kenneth D. Evans	1989	6152
276 6/8	40 7/8 38 0/8	31 4/8	6 6	Larimer County	CO	Todd Johnson	1990	6152
276 6/8	44 5/8 45 3/8	32 4/8	6 6	Archuleta County	CO	Don Myers	1995	6152
276 6/8	43 1/8 42 7/8	38 0/8	5 5	Socorro County	NM	Steven J. Bone	1995	6152
276 6/8	42 6/8 43 4/8	29 6/8	6 6	Colfax County	NM	Jack Dell	1996	6152
276 6/8	41 2/8 45 5/8	39 4/8	6 6	Skamania County	WA	Melody R. Newman	1998	6152
276 6/8	46 3/8 45 4/8	41 2/8	6 6	Gila County	AZ	Dana Eric Slack	1998	6152
276 6/8	43 2/8 43 7/8	36 2/8	6 6	Custer County	ID	Stephen W. Smith	2005	6152
*276 6/8	43 3/8 43 4/8	42 4/8	6 6	Custer County	SD	Thomas B. May	2006	6152
276 6/8	47 2/8 47 3/8	37 0/8	7 7	Washington County	ID	Ray L. Shirts	2007	6152
276 6/8	44 0/8 44 3/8	32 6/8	6 6	Teton County	ID	Kimberly Mills	2009	6152
276 5/8	45 7/8 45 1/8	32 5/8	6 6	Belmont Creek	MT	Max G. Bauer, Jr.	1980	6165
276 5/8	46 6/8 45 5/8	35 1/8	6 6	Teton County	MT	William McRae	1982	6165
276 5/8	44 4/8 43 4/8	36 5/8	6 6	Bear Lake County	ID	Troy Hymas	1984	6165
276 5/8	39 6/8 37 2/8	31 3/8	6 6	Custer County	ID	Donald Brydon	1994	6165
276 5/8	43 0/8 41 7/8	34 5/8	6 6	Beaverhead County	MT	Mark J. Sherick	1994	6165
276 5/8	43 7/8 46 2/8	31 1/8	6 6	Catron County	NM	Neal Childers	1998	6165
276 5/8	39 4/8 41 4/8	36 1/8	6 6	Catron County	NM	Joe Moore	2000	6165
276 4/8	41 1/8 40 2/8	35 0/8	6 6	Rio Blanco County	CO	Tom O. Milligan	1976	6172
276 4/8	42 3/8 42 2/8	34 0/8	6 6	Gallatin County	MT	George Kamps	1981	6172
276 4/8	46 6/8 50 1/8	38 4/8	6 5	Clearwater County	ID	Marvin J. Gerking	1983	6172
276 4/8	43 0/8 42 4/8	33 4/8	6 6	Shoshone County	ID	Stephen P. Rapier	1983	6172

AMERICAN ELK (TYPICAL ANTLERS)

Minimum Score 260   Continued

SCORE	LENGTH OF R MAIN BEAM L	INSIDE SPREAD	NUMBER OF R POINTS L	AREA	STATE/ PROVINCE	HUNTER'S NAME	DATE	RANK
276 4/8	47 2/8 44 3/8	36 0/8	6 6	Navajo County	AZ	Randy L. Hill	1991	6172
276 4/8	39 1/8 37 5/8	36 2/8	6 6	Morgan County	UT	Rob Helfrich	1992	6172
276 4/8	44 5/8 41 3/8	36 6/8	7 6	Marion County	OR	Jack T. Hinkle	1994	6172
276 4/8	45 0/8 45 4/8	34 4/8	6 6	Jackson County	CO	Tom Kelley	1995	6172
276 4/8	44 2/8 44 5/8	36 0/8	6 6	Park County	WY	Paul Pearson	1996	6172
276 4/8	45 6/8 46 2/8	33 6/8	6 6	Flathead County	MT	Stephan Secrest	1997	6172
276 4/8	42 6/8 42 1/8	36 2/8	6 6	Gallatin County	MT	William M. Elfland	1999	6172
276 4/8	46 0/8 45 0/8	40 2/8	6 7	Beaverhead County	MT	Ronald Miller	2000	6172
276 4/8	45 6/8 46 2/8	29 6/8	5 5	Lincoln County	MT	Hansel Lee Moore, Jr.	2001	6172
276 4/8	41 4/8 44 0/8	37 6/8	6 6	Otero County	NM	Jeff G. Nelson	2001	6172
276 4/8	45 3/8 44 5/8	34 4/8	6 6	Park County	MT	Rhett Delaney	2004	6172
276 4/8	38 4/8 38 2/8	40 0/8	6 6	Phillips County	MT	David W. Wyckoff	2004	6172
276 3/8	45 6/8 47 2/8	33 1/8	5 5	McKinley County	NM	Shawn R. Bloom	1993	6188
276 3/8	42 5/8 42 6/8	35 1/8	6 6	Carbon County	WY	David S. Christman	1997	6188
276 3/8	46 6/8 46 1/8	36 7/8	6 6	Crook County	OR	Ken West	1999	6188
276 3/8	40 4/8 41 3/8	40 5/8	6 7	Hinsdale County	CO	Jontie Aldrich	2001	6188
276 3/8	44 0/8 44 3/8	36 3/8	6 6	Routt County	CO	Dan Anello	2009	6188
276 2/8	50 4/8 44 2/8	40 6/8	6 7	Fremont County	ID	Rene' Harrop	1981	6193
276 2/8	43 5/8 44 2/8	38 4/8	5 6	Sandoval County	NM	Rett Kelly	1987	6193
276 2/8	45 6/8 45 7/8	35 5/8	6 5	Park County	WY	Mike Hamra	1993	6193
276 2/8	41 2/8 41 1/8	33 2/8	6 7	Archuleta County	CO	Bruce Morris	1995	6193
276 2/8	46 4/8 47 2/8	31 2/8	6 6	Coconino County	AZ	Bob Dawson	1995	6193
276 2/8	43 5/8 46 0/8	37 0/8	6 6	Coconino County	AZ	Kimball Taylor	1998	6193
276 2/8	44 2/8 45 2/8	32 2/8	6 6	Lincoln County	WY	Tim Hare	2003	6193
276 2/8	48 2/8 50 3/8	37 5/8	7 7	Lincoln County	WY	Randy S. Mixon	2003	6193
276 2/8	43 4/8 41 5/8	32 6/8	6 6	Las Animas County	CO	Donald Travis	2004	6193
276 2/8	41 1/8 39 6/8	38 6/8	7 7	Colfax County	NM	R. Kirk Sharp	2008	6193
276 1/8	42 3/8 38 7/8	41 7/8	6 6	Saguache County	CO	Jerry Woodland	1977	6203
276 1/8	44 4/8 45 7/8	33 1/8	7 6	Caribou County	ID	Irv Wanlass	1981	6203
276 1/8	47 2/8 47 6/8	39 3/8	6 7	Greenlee County	AZ	Joel W. Hampton	1993	6203
*276 1/8	47 0/8 48 2/8	34 4/8	6 6	Beaverhead County	MT	Doug Anibas	2007	6203
276 1/8	45 2/8 47 2/8	34 3/8	6 6	Albany County	WY	John Sarvis	2007	6203
276 0/8	42 2/8 44 4/8	33 4/8	6 6	Teller County	CO	Dr. David B. Johnson	1983	6208
276 0/8	42 5/8 42 6/8	33 2/8	6 6	Morgan County	UT	Hugh H. Hogle	1989	6208
276 0/8	41 7/8 41 0/8	30 6/8	6 6	Lincoln County	WY	Rodney L. Dehart	1991	6208
276 0/8	40 4/8 41 1/8	32 4/8	6 6	Routt County	CO	Charles DeLong	1991	6208
276 0/8	49 2/8 46 2/8	42 2/8	6 6	Wasco County	OR	Alvin Meyers	1992	6208
276 0/8	45 6/8 45 6/8	38 3/8	6 5	Sheridan County	WY	Fred P. Rybarz, Sr.	1993	6208
276 0/8	39 4/8 39 7/8	31 7/8	7 6	Archuleta County	CO	Dr. Robert Speegle	1993	6208
276 0/8	42 1/8 42 4/8	44 6/8	5 5	Catron County	NM	Kenny E. Leo	1994	6208
*276 0/8	47 4/8 45 5/8	45 2/8	6 5	Sevier County	UT	Dale Goytowski	2008	6208
275 7/8	47 1/8 46 5/8	39 1/8	6 6	Madison County	MT	Edward Wright	1990	6217
275 7/8	39 4/8 41 2/8	38 5/8	6 6	Rio Arriba County	NM	Troy Wagner	1998	6217
275 7/8	43 6/8 43 7/8	36 7/8	6 7	Caribou County	ID	Scott Draves	2000	6217
275 7/8	44 1/8 44 5/8	36 5/8	6 6	Albany County	WY	Randy Bomar	2000	6217
275 7/8	39 6/8 41 1/8	39 4/8	6 6	Lawrence County	SD	Robert C. Koski	2002	6217
275 7/8	48 5/8 49 2/8	38 5/8	6 5	Wheeler County	OR	Ron Miller	2004	6217
275 7/8	42 6/8 42 7/8	34 5/8	6 6	Albany County	WY	Norman K. Epler	2005	6217
275 7/8	42 7/8 43 6/8	36 7/8	6 7	Archuleta County	CO	Michael A. Hudzick	2009	6217
275 6/8	45 6/8 44 2/8	34 0/8	6 6	Valley County	ID	David G. Nagelmann	1986	6225
275 6/8	48 4/8 48 3/8	36 4/8	6 7	Teton County	MT	Keith Aune	1988	6225
275 6/8	44 7/8 43 5/8	30 4/8	6 6	Idaho County	ID	Jerry Vega	1989	6225
275 6/8	49 2/8 50 4/8	36 2/8	6 5	Phillips County	MT	Mark L. Meyer	1993	6225
275 6/8	40 6/8 42 2/8	36 6/8	6 6	Catron County	NM	John D. Lowe	1995	6225
275 6/8	42 7/8 40 1/8	37 2/8	6 6	Lemhi County	ID	Paul Gritton	1998	6225
275 6/8	44 5/8 44 4/8	38 4/8	6 6	Lawrence County	SD	Scott Guffey	1998	6225
275 6/8	50 4/8 51 0/8	36 2/8	6 6	Garfield County	MT	Stewart P. Kline	1999	6225
275 6/8	51 0/8 53 3/8	29 2/8	6 7	Catron County	NM	Eric Kuhlman	2005	6225
275 6/8	47 1/8 47 4/8	34 6/8	6 6	Jefferson County	CO	James S. Downie	2006	6225
275 6/8	41 0/8 39 7/8	40 0/8	6 6	Las Animas County	CO	Ronnie Hall	2010	6225
275 5/8	42 1/8 43 6/8	38 7/8	6 6	Ravalli County	MT	Rod Osburn	1980	6236
275 5/8	45 4/8 44 4/8	34 7/8	6 6	Moffat County	CO	Glenn Pritchard	1988	6236
275 5/8	46 2/8 45 1/8	35 4/8	6 6	Sheridan County	WY	Ron Niziolek	1990	6236
275 5/8	46 4/8 44 2/8	33 1/8	6 6	Coconino County	AZ	Allen Farnsworth	1990	6236
275 5/8	45 4/8 45 1/8	32 2/8	7 6	Adams County	ID	Joey Van Leuven	1997	6236
275 5/8	40 3/8 38 3/8	36 1/8	6 6	Kelvington	SAS	Cory Sawchuk	2000	6236
275 5/8	44 3/8 46 5/8	41 5/8	6 5	Park County	MT	Jennifer L. Hanson-McCollim	2001	6236
275 5/8	41 3/8 42 4/8	41 5/8	6 6	Grant County	OR	Dale Stutevoss	2004	6236
275 5/8	45 0/8 47 7/8	39 0/8	6 6	Archuleta County	CO	William J. Langer	2005	6236
*275 5/8	41 6/8 43 4/8	36 7/8	6 6	Judith Basin County	MT	Shane Rutledge	2007	6236
275 4/8	35 6/8 40 2/8	33 6/8	6 6	Valley County	MT	Andy Hicks	1983	6246
275 4/8	48 5/8 48 7/8	34 2/8	6 6	Clackamas County	OR	Rip H. Caswell	1986	6246
275 4/8	43 6/8 42 4/8	33 2/8	6 6	Catron County	NM	James E. Willard	1994	6246
275 4/8	40 7/8 38 4/8	39 2/8	6 7	Catron County	NM	Bob Bruss	1994	6246
275 4/8	42 6/8 42 7/8	29 4/8	6 6	Douglas County	CO	Sam E. Holst	2003	6246
275 4/8	42 0/8 40 0/8	32 2/8	6 6	Bonneville County	ID	Mark Soetenga	2004	6246
275 4/8	46 0/8 51 1/8	50 0/8	7 7	Coconino County	AZ	Fred V. Smith	2005	6246
275 4/8	46 0/8 42 1/8	38 2/8	6 6	Rich County	UT	Robert Dotson	2008	6246
*275 4/8	42 2/8 41 3/8	42 4/8	6 6	Coconino County	AZ	Robert Ohlund	2009	6246
275 3/8	47 0/8 46 5/8	34 1/8	5 6	Carbon County	WY	James T. Luxem	1992	6255
275 3/8	44 2/8 46 4/8	30 1/8	5 6	Rich County	UT	Rick Wilson	1993	6255
275 3/8	47 1/8 47 0/8	39 7/8	6 6	Union County	OR	Wayne Brown	2001	6255
275 3/8	44 1/8 45 2/8	33 5/8	6 8	Fergus County	MT	Jim Roth	2001	6255
275 3/8	41 6/8 41 0/8	40 5/8	6 6	Rich County	UT	Glen O. Hallows	2005	6255
275 3/8	42 2/8 43 4/8	38 3/8	6 6	Idaho County	ID	William E. Dean	2008	6255
275 3/8	44 7/8 44 6/8	35 7/8	5 5	Clear Creek County	CO	Kyle M. Ouzts	2009	6255
275 2/8	44 0/8 44 3/8	30 6/8	6 6	Missoula County	MT	John A. Reiter	1990	6262
275 2/8	43 5/8 44 5/8	37 6/8	6 6	Grant County	OR	Tim Hall	1990	6262
275 2/8	50 3/8 49 5/8	40 0/8	6 6	Wheeler County	OR	Anthony DiMaggio	1995	6262
275 2/8	41 6/8 42 3/8	35 6/8	6 6	Clearwater County	ID	Mark E. Kuechenmeister	1996	6262
275 2/8	40 7/8 43 1/8	28 0/8	6 6	Colfax County	NM	Ralph E. Johnson, Jr.	1997	6262
275 2/8	40 7/8 41 0/8	40 6/8	6 6	Petroleum County	MT	Thomas J. Madden	1998	6262
275 2/8	42 0/8 41 7/8	32 6/8	6 6	Catron County	NM	Tom Kooistra	2001	6262
275 2/8	45 3/8 43 7/8	38 0/8	6 6	Lewis County	WA	Grant L. Giacomazzi	2003	6262
275 2/8	43 4/8 43 0/8	36 2/8	6 6	Fording River	BC	Dale Webber	2003	6262

743

AMERICAN ELK (TYPICAL ANTLERS)

Minimum Score 260 Continued

SCORE	LENGTH OF R MAIN BEAM L	INSIDE SPREAD	NUMBER OF R POINTS L	AREA	STATE/ PROVINCE	HUNTER'S NAME	DATE	RANK
275 2/8	44 6/8 42 5/8	34 4/8	6 7	Douglas County	CO	Dale Stolba	2009	6262
275 2/8	44 0/8 42 0/8	45 3/8	6 6	Clay County	KY	Brian Griffin	2009	6262
275 2/8	46 4/8 44 7/8	36 2/8	6 5	Archuleta County	CO	Devon Brueckner	2010	6262
275 1/8	42 6/8 39 6/8	39 7/8	6 6	Bonner County	ID	Ren Hone	1980	6274
275 1/8	46 6/8 44 6/8	28 7/8	6 6	Idaho County	ID	Hollis Sapp, Jr.	1986	6274
275 1/8	44 4/8 45 6/8	34 7/8	6 6	Jefferson County	MT	Ron Scharf	1986	6274
275 1/8	38 1/8 39 1/8	35 6/8	6 7	San Juan County	NM	Gerry J. Johnson	1988	6274
275 1/8	45 5/8 44 2/8	28 1/8	6 6	Rio Arriba County	NM	Terry Karl	1989	6274
275 1/8	46 0/8 47 0/8	39 5/8	5 6	Socorro County	NM	Randall C. Barnes	1990	6274
275 1/8	42 6/8 43 1/8	39 1/8	7 6	Jackson County	CO	Kevin Primrose	1992	6274
275 1/8	44 4/8 45 2/8	41 5/8	6 6	Wallowa County	OR	Sam Shuh	1992	6274
275 1/8	42 2/8 41 4/8	34 5/8	6 6	Union County	OR	Kenneth R. Holmes	2000	6274
275 1/8	40 4/8 41 3/8	36 3/8	6 6	Routt County	CO	Dan Ergler	2001	6274
275 1/8	45 3/8 44 6/8	34 1/8	7 8	Klickitat County	WA	Noe Rodriguez, Sr.	2001	6274
275 1/8	42 1/8 41 7/8	37 6/8	6 7	Catron County	NM	Larry T. Orr	2003	6274
275 1/8	45 6/8 46 7/8	35 1/8	6 6	Douglas County	OR	Jim Caddock	2003	6274
275 1/8	42 3/8 44 6/8	36 1/8	6 6	Valley County	ID	Russell E. Guttu	2007	6274
275 1/8	42 6/8 42 3/8	37 5/8	6 6	Umatilla County	OR	Zach A. Ritter	2009	6274
275 1/8	41 3/8 40 5/8	36 3/8	6 6	Mineral County	MT	Vayeeleng K. Moua	2009	6274
275 0/8	43 1/8 44 6/8	33 0/8	7 6	Garfield County	MT	Frank Kasten	1982	6290
275 0/8	45 1/8 42 3/8	33 4/8	6 6	Conejos County	CO	Dewey Brown	1982	6290
275 0/8	45 3/8 45 5/8	38 3/8	6 7	Madison County	ID	Shayne L. Ard	1982	6290
275 0/8	45 2/8 44 6/8	36 6/8	6 6	Missoula County	MT	Terry See	1985	6290
275 0/8	44 4/8 42 2/8	36 0/8	6 6	Eagle County	CO	Kevin Scott	1994	6290
275 0/8	44 0/8 44 6/8	32 0/8	6 6	Pennington County	SD	Dave Hicks	1997	6290
275 0/8	41 6/8 40 6/8	32 6/8	6 6	Routt County	CO	Keith A. Trout	1998	6290
275 0/8	44 1/8 40 6/8	39 4/8	6 6	Clearwater County	ID	Nicholas Lapp	1998	6290
275 0/8	44 4/8 43 6/8	40 6/8	6 6	Lincoln County	WY	Paul Bilski	1999	6290
275 0/8	39 3/8 42 7/8	36 6/8	5 6	Chaffee County	CO	John E. Axelson	2000	6290
275 0/8	41 5/8 39 4/8	34 2/8	6 6	Nye County	NV	Todd Bresemann	2005	6290
275 0/8	38 4/8 37 1/8	36 2/8	6 6	Garfield County	CO	Greg Easton	2005	6290
*275 0/8	38 0/8 37 6/8	43 5/8	6 5	Park County	WY	Dan Hart	2009	6290
274 7/8	43 5/8 43 4/8	37 1/8	6 6	Flathead County	MT	Dean F. Cole	1985	6303
274 7/8	43 7/8 42 7/8	35 5/8	6 6	Fremont County	ID	Shawn Allgood	1995	6303
274 7/8	45 4/8 43 2/8	36 7/8	5 5	Coconino County	AZ	Tony Opheim	1995	6303
274 7/8	48 7/8 49 3/8	36 7/8	6 6	Catron County	NM	William B. Crum, Jr.	1996	6303
274 7/8	44 2/8 45 3/8	32 1/8	6 6	Eagle County	CO	Mark Martin	1997	6303
274 7/8	46 2/8 45 1/8	42 5/8	7 6	Lincoln County	NM	Donald Thompson	1999	6303
274 7/8	45 7/8 46 3/8	41 5/8	7 6	Powell County	MT	Rusten Barnes	2000	6303
274 7/8	43 3/8 43 1/8	40 3/8	6 6	Big Horn County	MT	Shannon McClure	2001	6303
274 7/8	45 6/8 43 4/8	31 7/8	6 6	Apache County	AZ	Roy D. Wyatt	2002	6303
274 7/8	46 1/8 39 7/8	35 3/8	5 6	Musselshell County	MT	Robert R. Larsen	2002	6303
274 7/8	41 4/8 40 7/8	35 5/8	6 6	Union County	OR	Wayne C. Green	2007	6303
*274 7/8	42 7/8 44 1/8	29 3/8	5 5	Garfield County	MT	Scott Gudowicz	2009	6303
274 7/8	39 0/8 41 3/8	39 1/8	6 6	Lewis & Clark County	MT	Jay Roberson	2009	6303
274 6/8	42 4/8 41 1/8	29 7/8	7 7	Rimbey	ALB	Clifford Hill	1984	6316
274 6/8	44 0/8 39 6/8	41 4/8	5 5	Navajo County	AZ	Troy Eiffert	1988	6316
274 6/8	44 0/8 44 3/8	32 4/8	6 6	Union County	OR	Gene Macomb	1990	6316
274 6/8	35 0/8 42 2/8	35 2/8	5 6	Larimer County	CO	Troy Freed	1993	6316
274 6/8	39 3/8 35 7/8	33 0/8	6 6	Morgan County	UT	Poncho McCoy	1996	6316
274 6/8	47 6/8 43 2/8	31 6/8	6 6	Lewis County	WA	Jay E. Franklin	1998	6316
274 6/8	45 0/8 42 3/8	31 0/8	6 6	Las Animas County	CO	Christopher Roe	1999	6316
274 6/8	40 6/8 42 6/8	40 1/8	7 7	Garfield County	UT	Richie Bland	2000	6316
274 6/8	42 3/8 40 7/8	34 0/8	7 8	Sanders County	MT	Anthony Caturano	2004	6316
*274 6/8	40 4/8 45 0/8	35 4/8	6 6	Lincoln County	WY	Brett Ritter	2009	6316
274 5/8	39 6/8 40 1/8	35 7/8	6 6	Coconino County	AZ	Paul E. Wells	1992	6326
274 5/8	44 1/8 43 3/8	36 1/8	6 6	Mesa County	CO	Ron Stanley	1993	6326
274 5/8	39 6/8 38 6/8	37 7/8	6 6	Jackson County	CO	John Fuller	1994	6326
274 5/8	51 6/8 52 7/8	38 7/8	6 6	Coconino County	AZ	James E. Richards III	1995	6326
274 5/8	42 7/8 42 7/8	31 3/8	7 6	Custer County	ID	John Wells, Jr.	1996	6326
274 5/8	45 0/8 44 0/8	40 3/8	6 5	Yavapai County	AZ	Danny Womack	1996	6326
274 5/8	44 3/8 43 6/8	32 7/8	6 6	Sandoval County	NM	Jeffrey L. Weisberger	1999	6326
274 5/8	41 2/8 41 5/8	35 5/8	6 6	Grant County	OR	Chris Blamer	1999	6326
274 5/8	43 2/8 40 6/8	35 7/8	6 6	Conejos County	CO	Tom Hooker	2000	6326
274 5/8	41 7/8 44 0/8	34 7/8	6 6	Catron County	NM	Dennis Rieck	2001	6326
274 5/8	44 1/8 45 5/8	44 1/8	5 6	Custer County	ID	Joe Klink	2002	6326
274 4/8	44 1/8 43 5/8	37 2/8	5 5	Sandoval County	NM	Dave McInroy	1988	6337
274 4/8	46 1/8 51 3/8	34 0/8	6 6	Stevens County	WA	Dusty N. Rieckers	1992	6337
274 4/8	46 2/8 46 0/8	34 2/8	6 6	Fergus County	MT	Dr. Daniel F. Alderman	1997	6337
274 4/8	42 7/8 46 3/8	37 6/8	6 6	Mora County	NM	James "Tommy" Jordan	1999	6337
274 4/8	40 3/8 40 2/8	33 0/8	6 6	Eagle County	CO	John Duggan	2004	6337
*274 4/8	42 0/8 42 2/8	35 0/8	6 6	Grant County	OR	Rick Waters	2006	6337
274 4/8	43 1/8 44 5/8	31 0/8	6 6	Crook County	OR	Tim Wattman	2008	6337
274 4/8	45 2/8 43 4/8	29 2/8	6 6	Mineral County	MT	Tom Moua	2008	6337
*274 4/8	42 1/8 43 6/8	33 0/8	6 6	La Plata County	CO	John T. Myer	2010	6337
274 3/8	41 3/8 42 0/8	31 1/8	6 6	Saguache County	CO	Jerry Woodland	1973	6346
274 3/8	47 1/8 44 2/8	28 7/8	6 6	Sanders County	MT	Gayle A. Voisine	1992	6346
274 3/8	43 3/8 44 2/8	38 7/8	7 6	Apache County	AZ	Michael W. Goodyear	1992	6346
274 3/8	45 4/8 45 0/8	36 3/8	6 6	El Paso County	CO	William R. Hull	1997	6346
274 3/8	44 4/8 44 6/8	33 5/8	6 6	Wallowa County	OR	Pat Niemi	1998	6346
274 3/8	45 0/8 45 2/8	35 3/8	6 6	Santa Fe County	NM	Charles "Chuck" Gahagan	1999	6346
274 3/8	47 3/8 49 1/8	38 6/8	6 6	White Pine County	NV	Marcus D. Dunn	2003	6346
274 3/8	49 0/8 50 4/8	35 7/8	6 5	Rio Arriba County	NM	Jaymes R. Panzy	2003	6346
274 3/8	43 4/8 43 7/8	33 3/8	6 6	Big Horn County	WY	Rick Paasch	2004	6346
274 3/8	42 1/8 47 1/8	41 7/8	6 6	Apache County	AZ	Michael W. McKenna	2005	6346
274 3/8	46 1/8 44 3/8	31 1/8	6 6	Fremont County	WY	Bill Wilson	2010	6346
274 2/8	42 4/8 42 3/8	40 0/8	6 6	Fremont County	ID	Clarence A. Frickey	1981	6357
274 2/8	46 4/8 46 6/8	35 6/8	6 6	Blaine County	ID	Larry Newton	1987	6357
274 2/8	50 3/8 53 6/8	40 4/8	6 5	McKinley County	NM	Malcolm D. Snyder	1991	6357
274 2/8	45 6/8 43 3/8	35 0/8	6 6	Phillips County	MT	Mark L. Meyer	1992	6357
274 2/8	48 0/8 49 0/8	37 0/8	7 6	Garfield County	CO	Bruce Hendy	1995	6357
274 2/8	44 6/8 44 2/8	33 2/8	6 6	Larimer County	CO	William E. Peck, Jr.	1997	6357
274 2/8	48 3/8 46 6/8	42 0/8	6 6	Sandoval County	NM	Bob Hubbard	1998	6357
274 2/8	43 2/8 45 2/8	34 0/8	6 6	Sevier County	UT	Lamar Potts	2004	6357
*274 2/8	42 0/8 40 3/8	33 6/8	6 6	Tanglefoot Creek	BC	Darrin Brown	2004	6357

744

AMERICAN ELK (TYPICAL ANTLERS)

Minimum Score 260
Continued

SCORE	LENGTH OF R MAIN BEAM L	INSIDE SPREAD	NUMBER OF R POINTS L	AREA	STATE/ PROVINCE	HUNTER'S NAME	DATE	RANK
274 2/8	47 7/8 48 2/8	37 4/8	6 6	Umatilla County	OR	Darrell S. Primmer	2004	6357
274 2/8	43 2/8 43 1/8	36 0/8	6 6	Otero County	NM	David J. Cramer	2005	6357
274 1/8	42 2/8 43 7/8	38 0/8	7 6	Gallatin County	MT	David F. Gibson	1974	6368
274 1/8	48 3/8 48 3/8	34 5/8	6 6	Converse County	WY	Jeffrey Rieker	1979	6368
274 1/8	49 5/8 41 3/8	31 3/8	6 5	Dunn County	ND	Craig Richardson	1989	6368
274 1/8	46 3/8 46 3/8	34 1/8	6 7	Catron County	NM	Tommy C. Jones	1992	6368
274 1/8	41 5/8 43 4/8	36 3/8	6 6	Clearwater County	ID	Carl F. Conklin	1993	6368
274 1/8	44 5/8 44 7/8	36 3/8	6 6	Custer County	CO	Mark Wuerthele	1995	6368
274 1/8	41 5/8 40 7/8	34 1/8	6 6	Routt County	CO	Cedar Beauregard	1997	6368
274 1/8	38 7/8 39 7/8	46 4/8	6 6	Park County	WY	Larry Hicks	1997	6368
274 1/8	43 5/8 42 6/8	39 1/8	6 6	Rio Blanco County	CO	Troy Johnson	1998	6368
274 1/8	41 4/8 47 2/8	33 5/8	6 6	Crook County	OR	Tim Wattman	2004	6368
274 1/8	40 7/8 43 4/8	37 5/8	5 5	Phillips County	MT	Chris Sanford	2009	6368
274 0/8	43 3/8 43 4/8	31 2/8	6 6	Clearwater County	ID	Jay Deones	1984	6379
274 0/8	43 0/8 41 4/8	36 0/8	6 6	Grant County	OR	Robert D. Coffey	1986	6379
274 0/8	41 3/8 41 6/8	31 2/8	7 6	Delta County	CO	Ronnie Steve Hall	1992	6379
274 0/8	38 4/8 38 3/8	37 2/8	6 6	Colfax County	NM	Howard Gallegos	1993	6379
274 0/8	49 4/8 48 0/8	33 6/8	6 6	Gallatin County	MT	Gordon Strachan II	1994	6379
274 0/8	44 0/8 43 5/8	34 6/8	6 6	Missoula County	MT	Tou Lee	1996	6379
274 0/8	44 4/8 45 3/8	31 6/8	6 7	Idaho County	ID	Dean C. Weyen	2000	6379
274 0/8	44 5/8 42 6/8	33 2/8	6 6	Fremont County	WY	Paul Jakovac	2001	6379
274 0/8	41 2/8 41 1/8	30 2/8	7 7	Clearwater County	ID	James G. Spinelli	2004	6379
274 0/8	41 2/8 41 4/8	33 4/8	7 6	Powell County	MT	Jeffrey H. Towill	2005	6379
*274 0/8	41 4/8 41 4/8	31 2/8	6 6	Carbon County	WY	Terry J. Beaver	2009	6379
273 7/8	45 7/8 45 1/8	36 5/8	6 6	Custer County	ID	Scott A. Wondergem	1993	6390
273 7/8	42 1/8 41 4/8	36 7/8	6 6	Linn County	OR	Ben McKillop	1994	6390
273 7/8	46 2/8 47 2/8	37 3/8	6 6	Routt County	CO	Joe Wilhelm	1995	6390
273 7/8	43 4/8 43 1/8	31 7/8	6 6	Colfax County	NM	Jack Dell	1997	6390
273 7/8	44 4/8 45 2/8	29 7/8	6 6	Adams County	ID	Darwin DeCroo	2001	6390
*273 7/8	46 0/8 45 3/8	26 5/8	6 6	Eagle County	CO	Mark Wilson	2004	6390
*273 7/8	44 5/8 45 3/8	36 7/8	6 6	La Plata County	CO	Joseph W. Antinucci	2009	6390
273 6/8	48 4/8 49 0/8	33 6/8	6 6	Lemhi County	ID	Greg Munther	1963	6397
273 6/8	42 1/8 43 3/8	33 0/8	6 6	Broadwater County	MT	Don Lovely	1978	6397
273 6/8	39 3/8 37 6/8	37 6/8	6 6	Grant County	OR	John Bridgewater	1983	6397
273 6/8	44 5/8 43 6/8	40 6/8	6 6	Valley County	ID	Tom Scoggin	1990	6397
273 6/8	47 5/8 46 5/8	32 2/8	6 6	Sandoval County	NM	Robert K. Woeck	1993	6397
273 6/8	44 6/8 42 7/8	36 0/8	6 6	Coconino County	AZ	Daniel P. Spatchek	1994	6397
273 6/8	45 3/8 46 7/8	34 0/8	6 6	Coconino County	AZ	Dawn J. Butterfield	1998	6397
273 6/8	39 3/8 38 2/8	34 0/8	6 6	Catron County	NM	Gordon B. Brown	2000	6397
273 6/8	44 0/8 45 1/8	40 2/8	6 7	Sublette County	WY	Clint Condos	2003	6397
273 6/8	43 2/8 40 4/8	31 6/8	6 6	Fergus County	MT	Frank J. Mancuso	2003	6397
273 6/8	52 2/8 51 0/8	36 0/8	6 6	Navajo County	AZ	Thomas M. Ault	2004	6397
273 6/8	41 1/8 43 6/8	35 6/8	6 6	La Plata County	CO	Larry D. Burcz	2009	6397
273 5/8	48 0/8 47 6/8	40 5/8	6 7	Sublette County	WY	Lyndon W. Henri	1987	6409
273 5/8	44 6/8 43 1/8	29 5/8	6 6	Beaverhead County	MT	Danny Moore	1988	6409
273 5/8	41 4/8 39 5/8	35 2/8	6 7	Shoshone County	ID	Orrin R. Cox	1995	6409
273 5/8	41 3/8 44 0/8	38 1/8	6 6	Larimer County	CO	Chris F. Seiler	1997	6409
273 5/8	40 0/8 41 4/8	31 7/8	6 6	Endeavour	SAS	Cory Babiuk	1998	6409
273 5/8	42 4/8 42 4/8	37 7/8	6 6	Idaho County	ID	Matthew J. Dunn	2001	6409
273 5/8	42 5/8 42 1/8	35 3/8	6 6	Ravalli County	MT	Jerry Johnson	2003	6409
273 5/8	40 4/8 43 3/8	36 5/8	6 6	Butte County	ID	Scott Esterholdt	2004	6409
*273 5/8	43 7/8 46 1/8	46 1/8	5 6	Jackson County	CO	Roger Stankowski	2010	6409
273 4/8	43 1/8 43 3/8	32 6/8	6 6	Archuleta County	CO	J.D. "Chip" Davis, Jr.	1990	6418
273 4/8	44 4/8 42 6/8	31 1/8	8 7	Douglas County	OR	Ken French	1990	6418
273 4/8	36 1/8 38 0/8	38 2/8	6 6	Mesa County	CO	John J. Ferrara	1990	6418
273 4/8	41 1/8 42 6/8	39 0/8	6 6	Fremont County	WY	Ken Davis	1991	6418
273 4/8	40 5/8 42 0/8	40 4/8	6 6	Skamania County	WA	Michael Culbertson	2003	6418
273 4/8	47 5/8 47 0/8	39 4/8	6 6	Wallowa County	OR	Jesse D. Grace	2003	6418
273 4/8	42 6/8 37 2/8	43 0/8	6 6	Lemhi County	ID	Dick Galbraith	2003	6418
273 4/8	38 7/8 40 4/8	33 2/8	6 6	Valley County	ID	Nick Harold	2004	6418
273 3/8	44 4/8 44 2/8	35 3/8	6 7	Sanders County	MT	Douglas Weber	1992	6426
273 3/8	43 1/8 42 6/8	38 5/8	6 5	Grant County	NM	Patrick Sughroue	1996	6426
273 3/8	50 7/8 52 7/8	41 7/8	6 6	Mesa County	CO	Michael Conn	1997	6426
273 3/8	49 2/8 47 4/8	40 1/8	6 6	Wallowa County	OR	Randy Hess	1997	6426
273 3/8	43 4/8 43 5/8	29 3/8	6 6	Ravalli County	MT	Gary Palmer	1998	6426
273 3/8	42 2/8 42 7/8	35 3/8	6 6	Beaverhead County	MT	Mark Miller	1998	6426
273 3/8	40 3/8 41 6/8	37 1/8	6 6	Socorro County	NM	Mickey Ormseth	1998	6426
273 3/8	46 3/8 46 4/8	31 1/8	6 6	Catron County	NM	Buck Horn	1999	6426
273 2/8	46 5/8 47 5/8	31 6/8	6 6	Phillips County	MT	Buddy Lundstrom	1981	6434
273 2/8	45 5/8 44 3/8	37 6/8	6 6	Coconino County	AZ	Tony W. Zimbaro	1986	6434
273 2/8	35 1/8 34 4/8	34 4/8	6 6	Elmore County	ID	George Law	1988	6434
273 2/8	40 0/8 37 3/8	39 4/8	6 6	Custer County	ID	Jerry L. Bowhay	1990	6434
273 2/8	47 3/8 44 0/8	35 0/8	6 6	Sandoval County	NM	Steve E. Lynch	1991	6434
273 2/8	44 4/8 43 3/8	32 6/8	6 6	Lane County	OR	Rick Willhite	1992	6434
273 2/8	42 4/8 44 3/8	36 2/8	6 6	Lemhi County	ID	Robert Merrill	1995	6434
273 2/8	44 2/8 42 7/8	39 0/8	5 5	Taos County	NM	John Skibber	1998	6434
273 2/8	44 6/8 43 2/8	33 4/8	6 6	Gila County	AZ	Thomas J. Pluhar	1998	6434
273 2/8	45 5/8 45 0/8	38 6/8	5 5	Yakima County	WA	Mark S. Golder	2001	6434
273 2/8	46 2/8 48 6/8	42 4/8	6 6	Grant County	OR	Dennis Swanson	2001	6434
273 2/8	45 5/8 46 5/8	32 2/8	6 6	Meagher County	MT	Tim Fisk	2002	6434
*273 2/8	43 7/8 42 7/8	33 4/8	6 6	Fremont County	WY	Joseph Moody	2010	6434
273 1/8	42 3/8 41 7/8	39 3/8	6 6	Mora County	NM	Michael J. Maes	1986	6447
273 1/8	48 1/8 48 6/8	31 3/8	6 6	Duchesne County	UT	Bob Dawson	1990	6447
273 1/8	44 2/8 44 4/8	33 7/8	6 6	Apache County	AZ	Edward Cummings	1998	6447
273 1/8	44 7/8 43 6/8	34 5/8	6 6	Park County	MT	David A. Voigt	2001	6447
273 1/8	43 3/8 44 5/8	35 3/8	6 6	Powell County	MT	Jeff O'Rourke	2001	6447
273 1/8	44 7/8 42 7/8	33 4/8	7 7	Coconino County	AZ	Cal Carlson	2007	6447
*273 1/8	42 7/8 42 0/8	43 7/8	6 6	Coconino County	AZ	Robert Forrest	2007	6447
273 0/8	42 2/8 42 1/8	32 6/8	6 6	Sandoval County	NM	George Bennett, Jr.	1984	6454
273 0/8	41 1/8 40 7/8	37 2/8	6 6	Grant County	OR	Coby Moulton	1987	6454
273 0/8	48 1/8 46 0/8	34 4/8	6 6	Custer County	ID	Randy Guinn	1987	6454
273 0/8	47 0/8 46 2/8	37 2/8	6 6	Teton County	MT	Jerry Bianchi	1988	6454
273 0/8	40 0/8 40 2/8	37 1/8	7 6	Apache County	AZ	John F. Richards	1990	6454
273 0/8	44 6/8 42 2/8	36 0/8	6 6	Carbon County	WY	Rodney C. Hill	1990	6454
273 0/8	47 3/8 44 7/8	36 6/8	6 5	Coconino County	AZ	Wiley Burnett	1990	6454

AMERICAN ELK (TYPICAL ANTLERS)

Minimum Score 260 — Continued

SCORE	LENGTH OF R MAIN BEAM L	INSIDE SPREAD	NUMBER OF R POINTS L		AREA	STATE/PROVINCE	HUNTER'S NAME	DATE	RANK
273 0/8	41 7/8 42 4/8	31 0/8	6	6	Red Deer Lake	ALB	Dennis Smith	1992	6454
273 0/8	44 3/8 44 6/8	36 2/8	6	6	Jackson County	CO	Hal Rogers	1994	6454
273 0/8	41 3/8 42 3/8	31 4/8	6	6	Gallatin County	MT	Jerry Karsky	1998	6454
273 0/8	40 4/8 39 6/8	35 2/8	5	6	Fergus County	MT	Dennis Clodi	2002	6454
273 0/8	43 4/8 44 4/8	37 0/8	5	6	Coconino County	AZ	Bob Rimsza	2003	6454
273 0/8	50 5/8 50 2/8	33 4/8	5	5	Yakima County	WA	Eric Nyberg	2005	6454
273 0/8	43 7/8 44 0/8	35 4/8	6	6	La Plata County	CO	Alan Sawyer	2009	6454
272 7/8	39 6/8 40 0/8	37 7/8	6	6	Clackamas County	OR	Ed Bensel	1959	6468
272 7/8	37 1/8 37 1/8	36 0/8	6	6	Rio Blanco County	CO	Dr. Charles Leidheiser	1973	6468
272 7/8	44 7/8 44 2/8	41 5/8	5	6	Sanders County	MT	Donald R. Read	1991	6468
272 7/8	42 7/8 42 6/8	30 7/8	6	6	Carbon County	WY	Steven Perkins	1995	6468
272 7/8	40 7/8 41 2/8	37 3/8	6	6	Coconino County	AZ	Barry Louis Defer	1995	6468
272 7/8	42 0/8 41 2/8	34 5/8	6	6	Coconino County	AZ	Lee Evans	1997	6468
272 7/8	42 0/8 43 0/8	39 1/8	6	6	Lemhi County	ID	Vernon Taylor	1999	6468
272 7/8	44 5/8 44 1/8	34 3/8	6	6	Lincoln County	WY	Shawn Witte	2002	6468
272 7/8	50 5/8 49 2/8	39 7/8	6	6	Fergus County	MT	Lynn Bowman	2004	6468
272 7/8	44 7/8 45 1/8	32 5/8	6	6	Moffat County	CO	Doug Feist	2006	6468
272 7/8	47 5/8 45 2/8	42 1/8	6	5	Garfield County	MT	Mark L. Meyer	2006	6468
272 6/8	51 6/8 48 3/8	31 6/8	7	6	Beaverhead County	MT	Ms. Charlie I. White	1988	6479
272 6/8	47 0/8 44 6/8	38 0/8	6	6	Catron County	NM	Rick Mann	1991	6479
272 6/8	41 2/8 42 1/8	39 2/8	6	6	Gallatin County	MT	Eddie Claypool	1996	6479
272 6/8	44 0/8 41 1/8	32 2/8	6	6	Madison County	MT	Erik Hoar	1998	6479
272 6/8	44 0/8 43 3/8	34 2/8	6	6	Lincoln County	WY	Danny Irland	2007	6479
272 6/8	45 4/8 44 1/8	35 4/8	6	5	Coconino County	AZ	Robert Rimsza	2008	6479
272 6/8	44 2/8 40 4/8	32 0/8	8	6	Union County	NM	Ronald Ghighi	2009	6479
272 5/8	44 7/8 42 1/8	36 3/8	6	6	Pitkin County	CO	Robert F. Cutting	1975	6486
272 5/8	44 0/8 45 1/8	35 7/8	6	6	Baker County	OR	Lloyd V. Christensen	1987	6486
272 5/8	44 4/8 44 4/8	35 1/8	6	6	Sublette County	WY	John B. Rice, Jr.	1990	6486
272 5/8	40 5/8 39 4/8	42 5/8	6	6	Greenlee County	AZ	Craig Marietta	1990	6486
272 5/8	42 7/8 42 4/8	32 5/8	6	5	Coconino County	AZ	Michael Fabritz	1995	6486
272 5/8	45 0/8 47 6/8	33 3/8	6	6	Clark County	ID	Brian S. McIlnay	1998	6486
272 5/8	39 7/8 38 5/8	37 7/8	5	6	Bonneville County	ID	Lendul David Tanney	1999	6486
272 5/8	36 6/8 36 5/8	30 7/8	6	6	Lincoln County	NM	Michael L. Ritter	2004	6486
272 5/8	42 0/8 42 2/8	31 3/8	6	6	Blaine County	MT	Danny Moore	2006	6486
*272 5/8	43 2/8 43 3/8	36 5/8	6	6	Eagle County	CO	John T. Baumstark	2008	6486
272 5/8	43 2/8 43 5/8	30 5/8	6	6	Colfax County	NM	Tyson C. Phillips	2009	6486
272 4/8	42 5/8 43 7/8	35 6/8	6	6	Grant County	OR	Dean P. Pasche	1981	6497
272 4/8	42 7/8 41 5/8	33 4/8	6	6	Lincoln County	WY	Peggy Barcak	1987	6497
272 4/8	40 6/8 39 6/8	36 4/8	6	7	Lincoln County	WY	David McKae	1987	6497
272 4/8	39 4/8 39 3/8	38 2/8	7	6	Sibbald Flats	ALB	Archie Nesbitt	1989	6497
272 4/8	40 6/8 39 3/8	36 4/8	6	6	Garfield County	CO	Frank Spartano	1995	6497
272 4/8	40 2/8 41 5/8	40 0/8	6	6	Lincoln County	WY	James J. Doherty, Jr.	1996	6497
272 4/8	39 1/8 40 3/8	37 0/8	6	6	Lemhi County	ID	Tom Heltemes	1997	6497
272 4/8	39 6/8 40 6/8	45 2/8	6	6	East Kootenay	BC	Dave Davidow	2000	6497
272 4/8	43 6/8 43 5/8	36 2/8	6	6	Fremont County	ID	Thomas G. Tuchscherer	2001	6497
272 3/8	41 7/8 39 5/8	35 3/8	6	6	Skagit County	WA	Steve Gorr	1982	6506
272 3/8	38 0/8 39 6/8	38 5/8	7	6	Teller County	CO	Rick K. Campbell	1987	6506
272 3/8	44 1/8 42 2/8	40 1/8	6	6	Harney County	OR	Doug Foster	1989	6506
272 3/8	37 2/8 38 5/8	38 6/8	6	6	Catron County	NM	James F. Welles	1991	6506
272 3/8	42 5/8 42 5/8	36 5/8	6	5	Mist Creek	ALB	Shawn D. Hillstead	1996	6506
272 3/8	38 6/8 41 6/8	35 7/8	6	6	Otero County	NM	Tex Welch	1997	6506
272 3/8	40 4/8 43 5/8	35 7/8	7	6	Pima County	AZ	Jeff Newbold	1997	6506
272 3/8	42 0/8 45 2/8	39 3/8	6	6	Catron County	NM	William R. Brown	2003	6506
272 3/8	42 6/8 44 5/8	41 1/8	6	5	Albany County	WY	Shane Woods	2008	6506
272 2/8	38 6/8 39 5/8	34 4/8	6	6	Idaho County	ID	Stanley D. Miles	1976	6515
272 2/8	48 0/8 46 5/8	37 2/8	5	5	Saguache County	CO	Kenneth A. Wollermann	1986	6515
272 2/8	45 2/8 39 3/8	39 6/8	6	5	Morgan County	UT	Don Keady	1992	6515
272 2/8	45 6/8 44 0/8	34 4/8	6	6	Valley County	MT	Dan E. Sturgis	1995	6515
272 2/8	47 0/8 47 7/8	37 2/8	5	6	Clear Creek County	CO	Clint E. O'Hotto	1997	6515
272 2/8	39 7/8 40 4/8	40 0/8	6	6	Madison County	MT	Thomas Anzalone	1999	6515
272 2/8	41 3/8 41 1/8	33 0/8	6	6	Park County	CO	Jeff Mekelburg	2003	6515
272 2/8	37 6/8 38 0/8	40 0/8	6	6	Johnson County	WY	Daniel E. Oakes	2003	6515
272 2/8	43 0/8 43 1/8	38 6/8	6	6	Coconino County	AZ	Mark R. Thompson	2004	6515
272 1/8	43 0/8 41 0/8	33 5/8	6	6	Garfield County	CO	Kevin L. Sheets	1998	6524
272 1/8	42 0/8 42 6/8	37 3/8	6	6	Park County	CO	Jason Roe	2002	6524
272 1/8	41 7/8 40 7/8	39 5/8	6	5	Rio Arriba County	NM	Larson Panzy	2002	6524
272 1/8	44 5/8 46 1/8	40 3/8	5	6	Custer County	ID	Jim Thomas	2002	6524
272 1/8	44 5/8 45 4/8	27 1/8	6	6	Montezuma County	CO	Darren R. Mitchell	2004	6524
*272 1/8	43 7/8 43 0/8	33 3/8	6	6	Lewis & Clark County	MT	Ken Parquette	2005	6524
272 0/8	43 7/8 44 4/8	38 0/8	6	6	Saguache County	CO	Buster Mize	1968	6530
272 0/8	45 5/8 45 0/8	37 4/8	6	6	Idaho County	ID	Donald M. Martin	1978	6530
272 0/8	44 2/8 43 4/8	37 6/8	6	6	Clear Creek County	CO	Matt Burrows	1994	6530
272 0/8	39 7/8 40 3/8	33 6/8	6	6	Umatilla County	OR	Mike Agidius	1999	6530
272 0/8	45 5/8 45 1/8	32 2/8	6	6	Coconino County	AZ	Joel Patterson	2000	6530
272 0/8	40 2/8 40 2/8	41 0/8	6	6	Boise County	ID	Steven Wells	2002	6530
272 0/8	44 1/8 42 3/8	43 4/8	6	6	Broadwater County	MT	Bill Hangas	2005	6530
*272 0/8	47 2/8 48 5/8	36 6/8	9	7	Jefferson County	CO	Rob Sparks	2005	6530
272 0/8	44 2/8 43 4/8	32 0/8	6	6	Phillips County	MT	Mutt Wilson	2007	6530
*272 0/8	52 6/8 49 7/8	33 0/8	5	6	Catron County	NM	Brian Brochu	2008	6530
271 7/8	47 4/8 49 1/8	32 5/8	6	6	Chelan County	WA	Claude E. Gates	1973	6540
271 7/8	40 7/8 38 7/8	31 3/8	6	6	Lincoln County	WY	Doug Plumstead	1995	6540
271 7/8	41 4/8 41 4/8	32 1/8	6	6	Washington County	ID	Kay J. Moore	1999	6540
271 7/8	46 0/8 46 0/8	33 5/8	6	6	Rio Arriba County	NM	Jeff Trumble	2000	6540
*271 7/8	47 2/8 45 5/8	32 7/8	6	6	Petroleum County	MT	Troy Erickson	2003	6540
*271 7/8	38 7/8 37 7/8	31 5/8	6	6	Garfield County	CO	Jay F. Shell	2004	6540
271 7/8	46 3/8 47 4/8	37 7/8	6	6	Lemhi County	ID	Dave R. Burget	2005	6540
271 7/8	49 2/8 48 6/8	34 1/8	6	5	Larimer County	CO	George Perreault	2008	6540
271 7/8	40 2/8 40 1/8	34 5/8	6	6	Chaffee County	CO	Brian T. Pollack	2009	6540
271 6/8	46 4/8 46 5/8	33 6/8	6	6	Sheridan County	WY	Mike Barrett	1985	6549
271 6/8	41 7/8 43 7/8	32 6/8	6	6	Catron County	NM	Mark D. Barboa	1990	6549
271 6/8	41 1/8 40 7/8	38 0/8	6	6	Phillips County	MT	Kevin Bertsch	1992	6549
271 6/8	39 4/8 42 1/8	40 2/8	6	6	Sheridan County	WY	Ron Apel	1996	6549
271 6/8	41 3/8 40 4/8	33 2/8	6	6	Adams County	ID	Larry Hoff	1998	6549
271 6/8	43 1/8 39 7/8	36 4/8	6	6	Clearwater County	ID	Daryl L. Holland	2000	6549
271 6/8	47 1/8 44 6/8	39 4/8	6	6	Park County	WY	Robert C. Gregory	2000	6549

746

AMERICAN ELK (TYPICAL ANTLERS)

Minimum Score 260   Continued

SCORE	LENGTH OF R MAIN BEAM L	INSIDE SPREAD	NUMBER OF R POINTS L	AREA	STATE/ PROVINCE	HUNTER'S NAME	DATE	RANK
271 6/8	42 0/8 41 5/8	30 0/8	5 5	Duchesne County	UT	Victor J. Fossat	2003	6549
271 6/8	42 5/8 42 6/8	33 4/8	6 6	Union County	OR	Jerry Simmons	2003	6549
271 6/8	44 5/8 42 3/8	32 6/8	6 6	Montrose County	CO	Jeremy Sickles	2006	6549
271 6/8	43 0/8 43 4/8	38 2/8	5 6	Sandoval County	NM	Raymond Lance Chapman	2007	6549
271 5/8	43 1/8 43 6/8	36 1/8	5 6	Park County	MT	Dennis Vance	1975	6560
271 5/8	38 5/8 39 5/8	36 1/8	6 6	Larimer County	CO	Kenneth D. Allen	1981	6560
271 5/8	43 5/8 44 4/8	32 7/8	6 6	Lewis County	WA	Keith Heldreth	1985	6560
271 5/8	38 6/8 41 2/8	40 5/8	6 6	Natrona County	WY	Brian L. Wagner	1996	6560
271 5/8	44 6/8 44 6/8	38 3/8	6 6	Lemhi County	ID	Mike Studt	1997	6560
271 5/8	43 5/8 43 3/8	34 7/8	6 6	Valley County	ID	Ron R. Sisson	1998	6560
271 5/8	38 6/8 40 2/8	34 5/8	5 6	Rosebud County	MT	Mike Cadwell	2002	6560
271 5/8	41 3/8 41 1/8	37 7/8	6 6	Delta County	CO	Larry Stephen Johns	2004	6560
*271 5/8	41 4/8 44 4/8	30 5/8	6 6	Mesa County	CO	Daniel Powell	2007	6560
271 5/8	44 3/8 45 4/8	34 7/8	6 6	Coconino County	AZ	Ryan Nogosek	2007	6560
271 5/8	43 4/8 43 7/8	35 5/8	6 6	Phillips County	MT	Jerry Strese	2007	6560
271 4/8	38 4/8 40 6/8	34 2/8	6 6	Mud Creek	ID	Jr. Barnett	1977	6571
271 4/8	44 4/8 45 6/8	43 0/8	6 5	Caribou County	ID	Preston Phelps	1980	571
271 4/8	46 3/8 47 2/8	36 2/8	6 6	Sweetwater County	WY	Vaughn Cross	1981	o571
271 4/8	45 2/8 46 3/8	36 0/8	6 5	Flathead County	MT	Rick Meyer	1987	6571
271 4/8	38 5/8 38 7/8	37 4/8	7 7	King County	WA	G. Dan Feighner	1989	6571
271 4/8	42 5/8 41 0/8	29 0/8	6 8	Shoshone County	ID	Roy A. Clanton	1992	6571
271 4/8	41 5/8 41 6/8	34 4/8	6 6	Beaverhead County	MT	Gary Lampkins	1997	6571
271 4/8	46 2/8 47 3/8	35 0/8	6 5	Cibola County	NM	Kirby Hunter Wynn	1997	6571
271 4/8	39 0/8 40 2/8	34 6/8	6 6	Carbon County	WY	Ken Fluck	1999	6571
271 4/8	43 4/8 42 4/8	44 5/8	6 6	Madison County	MT	Fred B. McCullar, DVM	2006	6571
*271 4/8	47 1/8 46 1/8	38 0/8	5 7	Weston County	WY	Ronald F. Lax	2008	6571
271 3/8	42 7/8 42 5/8	39 7/8	6 6	Rio Arriba County	NM	Bryan Adair	1984	6582
271 3/8	40 4/8 41 3/8	36 3/8	7 6	Idaho County	ID	Dan Hollibush	1994	6582
271 3/8	44 5/8 46 3/8	38 6/8	7 7	Coconino County	AZ	Wayne Smith	1997	6582
271 3/8	40 5/8 40 7/8	37 2/8	7 7	Jackson County	CO	David C. Lueker	2002	6582
271 3/8	42 5/8 42 0/8	33 7/8	6 6	Catron County	NM	Jeffrey D. Eddy	2002	6582
271 3/8	37 4/8 37 3/8	30 5/8	6 6	Rio Blanco County	CO	Derrick J. Kinsey	2004	6582
271 2/8	44 2/8 45 7/8	27 0/8	6 6	Gunnison County	CO	Jeff Helming	1984	6588
271 2/8	39 5/8 39 5/8	32 2/8	6 6	Rio Arriba County	NM	Lee Braudt	1985	6588
271 2/8	42 1/8 43 4/8	39 4/8	6 5	Grant County	OR	Don D. Litts	1986	6588
271 2/8	41 0/8 39 3/8	34 4/8	7 7	Rio Arriba County	NM	Greg Harmsen	1986	6588
271 2/8	38 6/8 38 3/8	39 5/8	6 6	Sanders County	MT	Z. Kent Sullivan	1988	6588
271 2/8	38 6/8 40 6/8	39 6/8	6 6	Lemhi County	ID	Glen Berry	1989	6588
271 2/8	39 6/8 39 1/8	34 4/8	6 6	Socorro County	NM	Ted A. Shinn	1990	6588
271 2/8	44 4/8 46 1/8	32 0/8	6 6	Sandoval County	NM	Robert L. Pagel	1990	6588
271 2/8	51 5/8 45 5/8	34 2/8	6 5	Otero County	NM	Rocky Abney	1991	6588
271 2/8	45 4/8 46 3/8	35 6/8	5 6	Grand County	CO	Dave Rayfield	1992	6588
271 2/8	40 1/8 40 5/8	37 6/8	6 6	Lemhi County	ID	Michael Studt	1998	6588
271 2/8	46 1/8 45 1/8	38 4/8	6 6	Bonneville County	ID	Donald E. Dombrowski	2002	6588
271 2/8	46 4/8 43 0/8	47 2/8	6 6	Coconino County	AZ	Jeff Kartheiser	2005	6588
*271 2/8	44 3/8 44 6/8	35 4/8	6 6	Mesa County	CO	Erik Watts	2008	6588
271 1/8	43 3/8 43 3/8	33 3/8	6 6	Washington County	ID	Wade C. Davis	1982	6602
271 1/8	45 1/8 45 6/8	31 3/8	6 6	Rio Arriba County	NM	James A. Waters	1988	6602
271 1/8	43 3/8 43 4/8	38 3/8	6 6	Lemhi County	ID	David A. Bronson	1991	6602
271 1/8	49 3/8 48 6/8	35 1/8	6 6	Rio Arriba County	NM	Owen Phone	1994	6602
271 1/8	40 1/8 39 5/8	36 1/8	6 6	Las Animas County	CO	Paul Strong	1996	6602
271 1/8	41 6/8 41 6/8	39 3/8	5 5	McKinley County	NM	David Westmoreland	1996	6602
271 1/8	38 0/8 42 5/8	43 4/8	7 6	Grant County	OR	Boyd Guthrie	1999	6602
271 1/8	44 5/8 44 4/8	32 7/8	5 6	Petroleum County	MT	Charles "Perky" Rother	2000	6602
271 1/8	43 4/8 42 6/8	32 3/8	6 6	Teton County	WY	John Schriever	2004	6602
271 1/8	40 6/8 42 2/8	34 3/8	5 5	Coconino County	AZ	John Horn	2007	6602
271 0/8	48 0/8 47 7/8	34 2/8	6 5	Park County	CO	Victor B. Hines	1981	6612
271 0/8	41 2/8 41 3/8	33 4/8	6 6	Routt County	CO	Starlene Clayson	1991	6612
271 0/8	40 6/8 41 0/8	33 0/8	6 6	Las Animas County	CO	Jason Crockett Pettigrew	1992	6612
271 0/8	36 7/8 41 2/8	43 0/8	5 6	Coconino County	AZ	Louie S. Herrera	1993	6612
271 0/8	46 2/8 48 5/8	35 6/8	6 6	Archuleta County	CO	Jose A. Morales	1995	6612
271 0/8	48 5/8 57 1/8	45 4/8	5 5	Catron County	NM	Bob "Jake" Jacobsen	1995	6612
271 0/8	38 2/8 37 6/8	34 4/8	6 6	Custer County	CO	Brad S. Kissinger	1996	6612
271 0/8	43 6/8 45 5/8	31 2/8	6 5	Navajo County	AZ	Brian Goble	1998	6612
271 0/8	42 2/8 42 4/8	39 6/8	6 6	Jefferson County	MT	Kent A. Bender	1999	6612
271 0/8	44 3/8 44 0/8	35 0/8	7 6	Cascade County	MT	Bert Vandiver III	2002	6612
271 0/8	42 0/8 40 2/8	32 0/8	5 6	Lewis County	WA	Jerry Montgomery	2004	6612
*271 0/8	41 4/8 39 2/8	34 6/8	6 6	Albany County	WY	Thierry Mahon	2007	6612
270 7/8	38 5/8 38 4/8	34 5/8	6 6	Gallatin National Forest	MT	Steve D. Wing	1979	6624
270 7/8	37 1/8 42 6/8	31 3/8	6 6	Morgan County	UT	Hugh H. Hogle	1983	6624
270 7/8	40 5/8 38 5/8	38 5/8	5 5	King County	WA	Ken Gettman	1987	6624
270 7/8	42 4/8 43 5/8	30 3/8	6 6	Petroleum County	MT	Bryant Shermoe	1989	6624
270 7/8	42 0/8 41 5/8	35 3/8	6 6	Natrona County	WY	Jeff Kovalick	1990	6624
270 7/8	42 0/8 43 7/8	32 3/8	6 6	Shoshone County	ID	Glen Berry	1990	6624
270 7/8	43 1/8 41 6/8	32 3/8	6 6	Mineral County	CO	Larry M. Moore	1996	6624
270 7/8	42 1/8 40 4/8	39 3/8	6 6	Caribou County	ID	Mark L. Olson	1997	6624
270 7/8	45 5/8 46 2/8	34 5/8	6 6	Wasatch County	UT	Colton Jones	2004	6624
*270 7/8	43 0/8 46 6/8	38 1/8	6 6	Garfield County	CO	Travis Layne	2007	6624
270 7/8	43 4/8 45 3/8	35 5/8	6 6	Sheridan County	WY	Lucas Giesey	2009	6624
*270 7/8	40 1/8 37 4/8	36 1/8	6 6	Warner	ALB	Tom Foss	2010	6624
270 6/8	44 3/8 45 0/8	35 0/8	6 6	Custer County	ID	Scott Mackintosh	1994	6636
270 6/8	46 0/8 45 7/8	37 6/8	6 6	Beaverhead County	MT	Fred C. Church	1996	6636
270 6/8	45 0/8 42 0/8	32 2/8	6 6	Hinsdale County	CO	Scott Hargrove	2000	6636
270 6/8	44 7/8 41 1/8	34 2/8	6 6	Beaverhead County	MT	Jeffery Gagnon	2001	6636
270 6/8	46 2/8 48 7/8	34 2/8	6 5	Taos County	NM	Harold "Daniel" Romero	2002	6636
270 6/8	50 5/8 47 2/8	37 2/8	5 5	Navajo County	AZ	Mark Greving	2005	6636
*270 6/8	43 4/8 41 1/8	39 6/8	5 5	Catron County	NM	Brian Rimsza	2006	6636
270 6/8	43 5/8 44 4/8	36 4/8	6 6	Baker County	OR	Trace Moorhead	2009	6636
*270 6/8	46 3/8 43 0/8	37 2/8	6 6	Connor Creek	ALB	Kevin Daase	2010	6636
270 5/8	38 1/8 39 2/8	36 3/8	6 6	Routt County	CO	Jake Hoeschler	1977	6645
270 5/8	45 7/8 45 5/8	35 5/8	6 6	Granite County	MT	Michael J. Nielsen	1988	6645
270 5/8	45 3/8 45 3/8	38 1/8	6 6	Judith Basin County	MT	Jeff Jackson	1995	6645
270 5/8	42 1/8 42 3/8	36 7/8	6 6	Park County	WY	Winston G. Irvin, Jr.	1995	6645
270 5/8	43 3/8 43 7/8	31 1/8	6 6	Catron County	NM	Rapheal Kukowski	1999	6645
270 5/8	42 0/8 42 7/8	32 3/8	6 6	Catron County	NM	Joseph C. Krejci	2001	6645

747

AMERICAN ELK (TYPICAL ANTLERS)

Minimum Score 260

SCORE	LENGTH OF R MAIN BEAM L	INSIDE SPREAD	NUMBER OF R POINTS L	AREA	STATE/ PROVINCE	HUNTER'S NAME	DATE	RANK
270 5/8	42 6/8 44 5/8	35 2/8	7 6	Findlay Creek	BC	George Terpsma	2002	6645
270 5/8	44 3/8 45 2/8	32 1/8	6 6	Powell County	MT	Julian Proctor	2004	6645
270 5/8	38 2/8 38 5/8	39 2/8	6 6	Wheatland County	MT	Ricky Umstead, Jr.	2005	6645
270 5/8	51 2/8 44 6/8	34 0/8	6 9	Johnson County	WY	Kent Hochstein	2008	6645
270 4/8	50 5/8 48 6/8	42 0/8	5 5	King County	WA	Jon Fuller	1985	6655
270 4/8	44 1/8 45 3/8	35 4/8	6 6	Rio Blanco County	CO	Perry Smith	1989	6655
270 4/8	42 5/8 41 0/8	30 4/8	6 6	Clearwater County	ID	Bob Moenk	1992	6655
270 4/8	46 2/8 48 1/8	35 2/8	6 6	Ouray County	CO	Joseph Testerman	1993	6655
270 4/8	41 3/8 43 0/8	31 6/8	5 6	Sheridan County	WY	Ron Niziolek	1995	6655
270 4/8	42 7/8 42 6/8	37 0/8	6 6	Blaine County	ID	Aaron J. Fortune	1996	6655
270 4/8	40 4/8 41 3/8	37 6/8	6 6	Idaho County	ID	Chris Buchta	2003	6655
270 4/8	43 5/8 43 4/8	33 0/8	6 6	Colfax County	NM	Doug Ciccarello	2004	6655
*270 4/8	44 2/8 42 7/8	35 0/8	6 6	Sheridan County	WY	John Rogers II	2005	6655
270 4/8	44 0/8 42 2/8	36 2/8	6 6	Carbon County	WY	Joe Gillespie	2008	6655
270 3/8	40 6/8 40 4/8	36 5/8	6 6	Ravalli County	MT	Wayne Buhler	1982	6665
270 3/8	46 0/8 46 4/8	36 7/8	6 6	Grant County	OR	Dennis G. Marshall	1986	6665
270 3/8	43 5/8 42 6/8	34 7/8	6 6	Catron County	NM	Bill Clink	1989	6665
270 3/8	47 4/8 46 0/8	30 1/8	6 6	Rio Arriba County	NM	C. Randall Byers	1994	6665
270 3/8	42 1/8 42 3/8	32 5/8	6 6	Converse County	WY	Randy Bomar	1999	6665
270 3/8	39 3/8 37 2/8	33 5/8	7 6	Park County	MT	George Kamps	1999	6665
270 3/8	39 7/8 39 7/8	35 3/8	6 6	Idaho County	ID	Amanda Sisson	2004	6665
*270 3/8	43 5/8 41 5/8	37 5/8	6 6	Garfield County	CO	Daniel R. Barth	2005	6665
*270 3/8	43 0/8 41 7/8	33 5/8	6 6	Beaverhead County	MT	Thomas E. Frisk	2008	6665
270 2/8	42 6/8 41 6/8	36 2/8	6 6	Montezuma County	CO	Dwight V. English	1976	6674
270 2/8	38 6/8 37 0/8	32 2/8	6 6	Blaine County	ID	John Turner	1977	6674
270 2/8	42 7/8 44 4/8	43 6/8	5 5	Shoshone County	ID	Roy Meyer	1979	6674
270 2/8	41 0/8 40 4/8	35 4/8	5 6	Simonette River	ALB	Gerald Rogers	1990	6674
270 2/8	41 6/8 43 2/8	39 4/8	6 6	Coconino County	AZ	James Dale Casady	1993	6674
270 2/8	42 6/8 41 2/8	39 4/8	6 7	Mineral County	MT	Kou F. Thao	1999	6674
270 2/8	42 5/8 43 3/8	38 2/8	6 6	Lemhi County	ID	Brad Anderson	2002	6674
270 2/8	45 6/8 44 0/8	39 6/8	6 6	Park County	WY	David D. Darwin	2002	6674
270 2/8	40 2/8 43 6/8	34 0/8	5 5	Beaverhead County	MT	Jim Sausen	2009	6674
270 1/8	38 1/8 39 1/8	35 5/8	6 6	Powell County	MT	E. Kits Smith	1976	6683
270 1/8	36 3/8 36 7/8	42 0/8	6 6	Albany County	WY	Jerry Bowen	1984	6683
270 1/8	41 2/8 42 5/8	28 5/8	6 6	Petroleum County	MT	Ken Rustad	1991	6683
270 1/8	42 7/8 43 1/8	36 1/8	6 5	Catron County	NM	George Morris	1991	6683
270 1/8	43 6/8 43 6/8	27 7/8	6 6	Conejos County	CO	Jack A. Gardner	1991	6683
270 1/8	41 0/8 42 6/8	36 5/8	6 6	Big Horn County	WY	Dave Moss	1992	6683
270 1/8	42 7/8 40 4/8	43 6/8	6 6	Wasco County	OR	Jeffrey M. Kortge	1995	6683
270 1/8	44 1/8 45 0/8	32 1/8	6 6	Lemhi County	ID	Douglas Schulze	1997	6683
270 1/8	43 7/8 42 4/8	33 3/8	6 6	Routt County	CO	Jacob K. Marsden	2004	6683
270 1/8	48 2/8 47 5/8	35 3/8	6 6	Grant County	NM	Bill Golla	2006	6683
270 1/8	43 0/8 43 4/8	35 5/8	6 6	Converse County	WY	Jason A. Swanson	2008	6683
270 0/8	45 6/8 46 5/8	31 2/8	6 6	Coconino County	AZ	James H. Hansen	1981	6694
270 0/8	48 6/8 47 5/8	32 4/8	6 6	Coconino County	AZ	Wade L. Carstens	1983	6694
270 0/8	46 0/8 48 5/8	41 5/8	6 5	Umatilla County	OR	Steven Hemrich	1994	6694
270 0/8	41 1/8 40 4/8	32 4/8	6 6	Custer County	SD	Jon D. Heck	1998	6694
270 0/8	43 6/8 40 1/8	34 2/8	6 6	Catron County	NM	Todd Hewing	1999	6694
270 0/8	45 1/8 45 3/8	36 2/8	6 7	Flagstaff	ALB	Brent Kuntz	2004	6694
270 0/8	40 5/8 40 6/8	35 2/8	6 6	Cowlitz County	WA	Billy R. Greer	2005	6694
270 0/8	42 1/8 45 2/8	45 6/8	5 5	Montezuma County	CO	Foy Chandler	2006	6694
270 0/8	42 7/8 43 7/8	37 4/8	6 6	Mineral County	MT	Chia Yang	2007	6694
*270 0/8	40 1/8 42 2/8	43 6/8	6 6	Lawrence County	SD	Jesse Larson	2008	6694
269 7/8	38 2/8 36 6/8	28 1/8	6 6	Bear Lake County	ID	Dennis Burdick	1969	6704
269 7/8	45 4/8 45 4/8	38 5/8	6 5	Park County	MT	Jay Bosma	1984	6704
269 7/8	36 2/8 39 4/8	33 3/8	5 6	Rio Blanco County	CO	Brad Murray	1990	6704
269 7/8	43 3/8 39 0/8	37 4/8	6 7	Daggett County	UT	Michiel D. Watts	1991	6704
269 7/8	46 7/8 45 4/8	35 1/8	6 6	Madison County	MT	Joseph Kahl	2004	6704
*269 7/8	42 4/8 41 6/8	31 1/8	6 6	Teller County	CO	Brad D. Cooper	2005	6704
*269 7/8	44 3/8 44 4/8	36 1/8	6 6	Routt County	CO	John Stubecki	2005	6704
269 7/8	44 3/8 44 2/8	34 7/8	6 6	Coconino County	AZ	Jack L. Watson	2010	6704
269 7/8	41 4/8 39 7/8	40 1/8	6 6	Sheridan County	WY	Bruce Burr	2010	6704
269 7/8	42 2/8 45 3/8	38 7/8	6 6	Coconino County	AZ	Gene Fleming	2010	6704
269 6/8	47 4/8 47 5/8	46 2/8	6 5	Idaho County	ID	Edward Keeton	1985	6714
269 6/8	44 4/8 46 5/8	36 4/8	6 6	Malheur County	OR	Jim Hodson	1986	6714
269 6/8	38 4/8 39 4/8	32 4/8	6 6	Ravalli County	MT	Mark Hoseltion	1987	6714
269 6/8	43 1/8 45 3/8	35 6/8	6 6	Archuleta County	CO	Floyd Earl Fralish	1990	6714
269 6/8	40 4/8 38 0/8	41 0/8	6 6	Fremont County	WY	Justin Dvergsdal	1996	6714
269 6/8	39 0/8 38 2/8	37 0/8	6 6	Lemhi County	ID	James R. Giovanelli	1997	6714
269 6/8	46 1/8 44 0/8	37 6/8	6 6	Granite County	MT	Mark S. Golder	1997	6714
269 6/8	44 5/8 44 7/8	31 0/8	6 6	Shoshone County	ID	Linda Leake	1998	6714
269 6/8	41 5/8 39 7/8	38 4/8	5 5	Catron County	NM	Blake W. Pazero	2006	6714
269 6/8	42 7/8 43 2/8	31 7/8	6 7	Catron County	NM	Frank DeCleene	2006	6714
269 6/8	41 4/8 41 4/8	41 4/8	7 6	Garfield County	CO	Billy Dinkel	2008	6714
*269 6/8	39 3/8 39 4/8	33 0/8	6 6	Lemhi County	ID	Landon Johnson	2008	6714
*269 6/8	41 6/8 39 7/8	36 2/8	6 6	Colfax County	NM	Rob Crawford	2009	6714
269 5/8	41 6/8 42 3/8	35 5/8	6 6	Bonneville County	ID	Mike Taylor	1980	6727
269 5/8	42 0/8 41 1/8	36 1/8	6 6	Caribou County	ID	Chet Hopkins	1985	6727
269 5/8	44 4/8 44 1/8	33 1/8	6 6	Park County	MT	George Kamps	1986	6727
269 5/8	44 3/8 44 7/8	32 1/8	6 6	Lewis County	WA	Grant L. Giacomazzi	1999	6727
269 5/8	40 5/8 40 0/8	35 7/8	6 6	Jackson County	CO	Louis Phillippe	1999	6727
269 5/8	43 6/8 46 6/8	33 1/8	6 6	Gila County	AZ	Thomas Grantham	2005	6727
269 5/8	42 1/8 43 0/8	38 6/8	9 8	Camas County	ID	Brady Jones	2006	6727
*269 5/8	44 3/8 40 2/8	38 1/8	6 6	Meagher County	MT	Michael S. Reed	2007	6727
*269 5/8	42 2/8 41 1/8	37 1/8	6 6	Clearwater River	ALB	Brett Mason	2009	6727
269 4/8	42 7/8 42 4/8	35 4/8	6 7	Pinal County	AZ	Larry P. Matthews	1985	6736
269 4/8	45 1/8 45 0/8	40 3/8	7 5	Custer County	ID	Bryan R. Sword	1988	6736
269 4/8	42 5/8 40 7/8	35 6/8	6 6	Park County	WY	John R. Buche	1989	6736
269 4/8	44 4/8 44 2/8	33 7/8	6 7	Huerfano County	CO	Danny Ray	1992	6736
269 4/8	41 6/8 41 7/8	30 3/8	7 6	Powell County	MT	Douglas J. Peters	1996	6736
269 4/8	41 3/8 44 4/8	34 4/8	6 6	Meagher County	MT	James Michael Meadows	1998	6736
269 4/8	44 0/8 43 1/8	36 6/8	6 6	Idaho County	ID	Richard J. McEwen	2000	6736
269 4/8	40 7/8 41 7/8	33 2/8	6 6	Montezuma County	CO	John Gross	2003	6736
269 4/8	48 2/8 49 3/8	40 7/8	7 6	Multnomah County	OR	David J. Emerson	2005	6736
269 3/8	46 1/8 47 2/8	36 5/8	5 6	Cibola County	NM	Deryl Moore	1986	6745

AMERICAN ELK (TYPICAL ANTLERS)

Minimum Score 260   Continued

SCORE	LENGTH OF R MAIN BEAM L	INSIDE SPREAD	NUMBER OF R POINTS L	AREA	STATE/ PROVINCE	HUNTER'S NAME	DATE	RANK
*269 3/8	45 0/8 43 6/8	39 3/8	6 6	Garfield County	CO	Charles Crumbly	2009	6745
269 3/8	41 2/8 42 1/8	39 3/8	6 6	Routt County	CO	Keng S. Lee	2010	6745
269 2/8	44 0/8 43 4/8	34 2/8	6 6	Grant County	NM	Joe F. Apodaca	1990	6748
269 2/8	42 1/8 44 5/8	39 2/8	6 6	Catron County	NM	Gerry W. Carstens	1995	6748
269 2/8	42 2/8 43 3/8	38 6/8	7 7	Larimer County	CO	Gary Kelley	1996	6748
269 2/8	41 4/8 41 4/8	41 2/8	6 6	Custer County	ID	Don Glenn, Jr.	1998	6748
269 2/8	40 0/8 43 4/8	35 0/8	6 6	Fremont County	WY	Timothy Hugh Wahe	1999	6748
269 2/8	44 2/8 42 2/8	36 2/8	6 6	Grant County	OR	Monte Wade Hack	1999	6748
269 2/8	45 6/8 40 6/8	33 2/8	6 6	Baker County	OR	John Angus	2001	6748
269 2/8	40 4/8 40 3/8	33 0/8	5 5	Catron County	NM	Chris Skinner	2002	6748
269 2/8	50 0/8 46 6/8	29 6/8	6 6	Coconino County	AZ	Clinton Piper	2004	6748
*269 2/8	52 0/8 52 0/8	36 2/8	6 5	Sanders County	MT	Dennis P. Turin	2008	6748
269 1/8	41 7/8 42 5/8	34 1/8	6 6	Archuleta County	CO	George Eubank	1989	6758
269 1/8	42 1/8 42 0/8	33 1/8	6 6	Rio Arriba County	NM	Robert Nichols	1993	6758
269 1/8	41 4/8 42 2/8	37 5/8	6 6	Hinsdale County	CO	Arland N. Rininger	1994	6758
269 1/8	42 4/8 43 1/8	33 1/8	6 6	Yellowhead	ALB	Dale Grimstead	2003	6758
269 0/8	48 5/8 44 6/8	39 6/8	5 6	Bighorn Mtns.	WY	Dennis A. Phaneuf	1980	6762
269 0/8	41 3/8 40 5/8	35 6/8	6 6	Idaho County	ID	Larry A. Youngdell	1980	6762
269 0/8	39 2/8 40 6/8	37 2/8	6 6	Lewis & Clark County	MT	Steven E. Miller	1982	6762
269 0/8	42 7/8 41 1/8	33 4/8	6 6	Converse County	WY	Jim Young	1982	6762
269 0/8	35 5/8 35 5/8	33 2/8	6 6	Park County	CO	Jarold Allen Shriver	1988	6762
269 0/8	39 2/8 38 2/8	39 0/8	7 6	Boise County	ID	Jeffrey S. Stevens	1988	6762
269 0/8	41 6/8 45 0/8	33 2/8	6 6	Teton County	MT	Don Davidson	1990	6762
269 0/8	44 4/8 45 4/8	37 6/8	6 7	Lane County	OR	Jeff Bell	1998	6762
269 0/8	38 0/8 37 2/8	33 6/8	6 6	Umatilla County	OR	Richard S. Campbell	1998	6762
269 0/8	43 7/8 44 4/8	36 2/8	6 6	Fort Nelson	BC	Kevin Peterson	1999	6762
269 0/8	41 7/8 40 3/8	36 4/8	6 6	Rich County	UT	Glen O. Hallows	2003	6762
269 0/8	41 3/8 42 6/8	38 0/8	6 6	Pitkin County	CO	Roger D. Coombs	2003	6762
269 0/8	38 2/8 38 7/8	33 6/8	6 6	Grand County	CO	Steve Strickland	2008	6762
268 7/8	44 0/8 43 4/8	34 7/8	6 6	Judith Basin County	MT	Dan Hassel	1985	6775
268 7/8	41 6/8 42 2/8	34 3/8	6 6	Sanders County	MT	Craig R. Johnson	1986	6775
268 7/8	41 0/8 41 0/8	36 7/8	6 6	Grand County	CO	Neal Morse	1995	6775
268 7/8	40 6/8 39 0/8	36 5/8	7 6	Gallatin County	MT	Kelly D. Johnson	1995	6775
268 7/8	45 0/8 40 4/8	40 1/8	6 5	Catron County	NM	Sam Sowders	1996	6775
268 7/8	41 1/8 42 1/8	30 3/8	6 6	Petroleum County	MT	Gene Smith	1999	6775
268 7/8	38 4/8 39 0/8	31 7/8	6 6	Phillips County	MT	Joey Ardrey	2004	6775
268 7/8	46 2/8 44 4/8	31 0/8	7 6	Boundary County	ID	Garrett Hull	2006	6775
268 7/8	43 4/8 42 3/8	35 7/8	6 6	Fergus County	MT	John P. Hartman	2006	6775
268 7/8	44 6/8 42 5/8	31 1/8	6 6	Sublette County	WY	Craig Germond	2009	6775
*268 7/8	40 5/8 41 7/8	33 3/8	6 6	Alamosa County	CO	Michael Rossi	2009	6775
268 6/8	41 3/8 42 5/8	39 4/8	6 6	Park County	CO	Wayne Helming	1983	6786
268 6/8	44 7/8 43 4/8	35 0/8	6 7	Huerfano County	CO	Lee Moore	1985	6786
268 6/8	48 2/8 47 7/8	34 0/8	6 6	Ouray County	CO	Keith Peeples	1990	6786
268 6/8	43 5/8 44 6/8	31 4/8	6 7	San Miguel County	CO	Jeff Keehfuss	1995	6786
268 6/8	41 5/8 43 2/8	31 0/8	6 5	Mesa County	CO	Bob Boarman	1996	6786
268 6/8	46 7/8 45 1/8	35 4/8	6 6	Mesa County	CO	Wesley Jackson	1999	6786
268 6/8	40 5/8 42 5/8	33 0/8	6 6	Catron County	NM	Angela K. Walk	2000	6786
268 6/8	42 3/8 41 2/8	32 6/8	6 6	Catron County	NM	Dave P. Lange	2002	6786
268 6/8	42 6/8 42 0/8	38 6/8	6 6	Grant County	OR	Pat Niemi	2004	6786
268 6/8	46 3/8 46 4/8	35 0/8	6 6	Fergus County	MT	Lynn Bowman	2005	6786
268 6/8	40 7/8 41 1/8	28 0/8	6 7	Czar	ALB	Brad Rieland	2007	6786
268 5/8	41 7/8 43 1/8	32 2/8	6 6	Hinsdale County	CO	Billy R. Spears	1973	6797
268 5/8	39 1/8 40 4/8	38 3/8	6 6	Catron County	NM	Scott Miltenberger	1990	6797
268 5/8	46 1/8 43 3/8	30 1/8	6 6	Coconino County	AZ	Paul M. Rogers	1991	6797
268 5/8	39 7/8 38 6/8	38 0/8	7 5	Lincoln County	MT	Jerry Brown	1996	6797
268 5/8	43 3/8 42 6/8	32 5/8	6 6	Custer County	ID	Jeff A. Buck	1998	6797
268 5/8	44 3/8 43 1/8	36 7/8	6 6	Blaine County	ID	Gary Verhasselt	2000	6797
268 5/8	44 2/8 44 0/8	33 1/8	7 6	Boise County	ID	Steven J. Wells	2001	6797
268 5/8	41 0/8 40 3/8	31 7/8	6 6	Petroleum County	MT	Joseph M. Mucka	2003	6797
268 5/8	42 0/8 42 3/8	34 5/8	7 6	Mineral County	MT	Ko Moua	2006	6797
268 5/8	42 4/8 43 4/8	34 5/8	6 6	Clearwater County	ID	Shane Mussey	2006	6797
268 4/8	43 6/8 43 4/8	32 4/8	5 6	Coconino County	AZ	Charles R. Haverin	1984	6807
268 4/8	49 1/8 48 0/8	33 2/8	5 5	Sandoval County	NM	Roby Grossheim	1988	6807
268 4/8	46 2/8 46 0/8	36 0/8	5 5	Shoshone County	ID	Steven Rinaldi	1991	6807
268 4/8	41 4/8 42 0/8	32 4/8	6 6	Lemhi County	ID	Kevin Walsh	1995	6807
268 4/8	46 4/8 46 6/8	29 2/8	6 5	Catron County	NM	Mark A. Lutz	1997	6807
268 4/8	46 4/8 46 6/8	34 4/8	6 6	Rio Blanco County	CO	Philip R. Webb	2004	6807
268 4/8	44 0/8 43 5/8	31 2/8	6 6	Albany County	WY	Khery Otero	2004	6807
268 4/8	42 2/8 43 0/8	33 4/8	6 6	Lincoln County	MT	Douglas G. Butts	2005	6807
*268 4/8	38 2/8 38 1/8	32 6/8	6 6	Garfield County	CO	Todd LaLonde	2007	6807
268 3/8	41 1/8 40 4/8	29 5/8	6 6	Harney County	OR	Robert M. Choate	1996	6816
268 3/8	39 7/8 41 2/8	31 3/8	6 6	Sherman County	OR	Ron Wold	1999	6816
268 3/8	42 0/8 45 6/8	43 3/8	6 6	Baker County	OR	Dwayne Powell	2000	6816
*268 3/8	42 2/8 41 6/8	29 1/8	6 6	Moffat County	CO	Chris A. Benson	2005	6816
268 3/8	39 2/8 38 4/8	29 7/8	6 6	Musselshell County	MT	Cheryl L. Weed	2009	6816
268 2/8	45 6/8 42 6/8	35 2/8	6 6	Navajo County	AZ	Julius Fortuna	1983	6821
268 2/8	43 3/8 43 7/8	39 0/8	6 6	Caribou County	ID	Edward E. Ulicki	2004	6821
268 2/8	43 7/8 45 0/8	34 6/8	6 6	Lemhi County	ID	Ben L. Fahnholz	2004	6821
*268 2/8	43 3/8 43 2/8	36 2/8	5 6	Montrose County	CO	Rob Crawford	2006	6821
*268 2/8	42 4/8 41 5/8	33 2/8	6 6	Dolores County	CO	Craig N. Johnson	2006	6821
*268 2/8	41 7/8 43 2/8	39 6/8	6 6	Lemhi County	ID	Jim Havens	2007	6821
268 2/8	41 4/8 41 6/8	40 6/8	6 6	Meagher County	MT	Tanner Ozburn	2007	6821
268 2/8	45 3/8 47 0/8	32 2/8	6 5	Otero County	NM	Joe Edin	2009	6821
268 1/8	39 0/8 40 3/8	30 0/8	7 6	Lincoln County	WY	Troy Miller	1973	6829
268 1/8	45 2/8 46 0/8	36 5/8	5 6	Gallatin County	MT	William L. Anderson	1982	6829
268 1/8	44 3/8 44 5/8	34 1/8	6 6	Silver Bow County	MT	Andrew Kuchtyn	1982	6829
268 1/8	44 4/8 44 2/8	35 1/8	6 6	Grant County	OR	Gary Persinger	1983	6829
268 1/8	42 5/8 41 0/8	33 7/8	6 6	Caribou County	ID	Max F. Park	1990	6829
268 1/8	39 6/8 39 0/8	31 1/8	6 6	Mesa County	CO	Rich Grannis	1993	6829
268 1/8	43 3/8 42 2/8	44 1/8	5 5	Idaho County	ID	Richard J. McEwen	1996	6829
268 1/8	42 2/8 41 4/8	37 3/8	6 6	Union County	OR	Joe Cunha IV	2000	6829
268 0/8	42 3/8 40 5/8	32 6/8	6 5	Baker County	OR	Les Thoreby	1963	6837
268 0/8	41 7/8 42 2/8	33 3/8	7 6	Idaho County	ID	Richard C. Nichols	1974	6837
268 0/8	41 0/8 40 7/8	35 2/8	6 6	Colfax County	NM	Peter J. Santi	1991	6837
268 0/8	42 0/8 43 3/8	34 6/8	6 6	Gallatin County	MT	Matt Rognlie	1998	6837

749

AMERICAN ELK (TYPICAL ANTLERS)

Minimum Score 260 — Continued

SCORE	LENGTH OF R MAIN BEAM L	INSIDE SPREAD	NUMBER OF R POINTS L		AREA	STATE/ PROVINCE	HUNTER'S NAME	DATE	RANK
268 0/8	46 4/8 46 5/8	37 6/8	6	6	Granite County	MT	Dennis E. Gordon	1999	6837
268 0/8	44 6/8 43 3/8	42 4/8	6	6	Park County	MT	Jim Caspers	2003	6837
268 0/8	43 5/8 45 7/8	38 0/8	6	6	Madison County	MT	Scott Lemieux	2007	6837
268 0/8	36 7/8 36 6/8	32 2/8	6	6	Sheridan County	WY	Susan Barrett	2009	6837
*268 0/8	43 0/8 42 5/8	35 2/8	7	6	Fergus County	MT	Don Moen	2010	6837
267 7/8	45 2/8 43 5/8	41 3/8	6	6	Valley County	ID	Jack St. Germain	1981	6846
267 7/8	44 2/8 43 6/8	32 7/8	6	6	Los Alamos County	NM	Doug Aikin	1983	6846
267 7/8	41 4/8 42 0/8	29 4/8	7	6	Phillips County	MT	Dr. Richard L. Lopez	1987	6846
267 7/8	46 5/8 44 7/8	47 7/8	6	5	Coconino County	AZ	Kenneth Wilson	1989	6846
267 7/8	40 3/8 39 0/8	41 0/8	6	6	Silver Bow County	MT	Steve Petroni	1990	6846
267 7/8	40 5/8 40 7/8	35 7/8	6	6	Harney County	OR	Wayne Dorey	2000	6846
267 7/8	38 1/8 37 6/8	37 3/8	6	6	Garfield County	MT	Donald E. Dombrowski	2001	6846
267 7/8	48 5/8 48 7/8	41 1/8	6	5	Custer County	ID	L. Grant Foster	2001	6846
267 7/8	46 1/8 42 4/8	35 5/8	6	6	Beaverhead County	MT	Alan W. Smith	2010	6846
267 6/8	43 3/8 47 0/8	39 6/8	6	6	Caribou County	ID	Jerry Baird	1976	6855
267 6/8	47 3/8 46 2/8	33 2/8	5	5	Rich County	UT	C. Keith Maynes	1989	6855
267 6/8	40 1/8 39 4/8	31 4/8	7	7	Catron County	NM	Ronald R. Johnson	1990	6855
267 6/8	46 0/8 45 2/8	41 2/8	6	6	Coconino County	AZ	Denzil Hackathorn	1993	6855
267 6/8	48 1/8 46 1/8	36 2/8	6	6	Moffat County	CO	Michael Hackett	1995	6855
267 6/8	42 5/8 44 2/8	38 2/8	6	6	Hinsdale County	CO	William D. Seaman, Jr.	1998	6855
267 6/8	41 6/8 41 2/8	37 0/8	5	5	Otero County	NM	Terry N. Morrow	1998	6855
*267 6/8	46 4/8 48 2/8	39 0/8	6	6	Bingham County	ID	Michael P. Tate	2008	6855
267 5/8	42 2/8 42 4/8	33 3/8	6	6	Larimer County	CO	Dennis Worrell	1979	6863
267 5/8	40 0/8 39 6/8	33 7/8	6	6	Chaffee County	CO	Bruce Long	1985	6863
267 5/8	35 4/8 36 1/8	39 6/8	6	6	Wallowa County	OR	Peter E. Palmer	1989	6863
267 5/8	47 5/8 46 2/8	33 5/8	8	6	Coconino County	AZ	Steven Takajo	1992	6863
267 5/8	42 2/8 42 2/8	37 1/8	6	6	Meagher County	MT	James F. Wright	1994	6863
267 5/8	42 4/8 42 1/8	33 1/8	6	6	Grant County	OR	Douglas Lee Smith	2001	6863
267 5/8	42 6/8 43 4/8	33 7/8	6	6	Grant County	OR	Jason Tarrant	2002	6863
267 5/8	43 3/8 43 2/8	31 3/8	7	6	Valley County	MT	Duane Nelson	2003	6863
267 5/8	44 0/8 41 5/8	33 1/8	6	6	Pitkin County	CO	Rex Crawford	2003	6863
267 5/8	43 3/8 43 5/8	37 1/8	6	6	Meagher County	MT	Warren Werp	2008	6863
*267 5/8	42 2/8 40 7/8	33 7/8	6	6	Summit County	UT	Adam Rametta	2009	6863
267 4/8	42 2/8 44 4/8	31 6/8	6	6	Gallatin County	MT	Jim Wondzell	1990	6874
267 4/8	42 7/8 52 1/8	36 2/8	5	6	Mesa County	CO	Don Boyles	1991	6874
267 4/8	43 7/8 43 4/8	41 3/8	5	6	Grant County	OR	Jerry W. Simmons	1992	6874
267 4/8	44 2/8 47 5/8	40 4/8	7	6	Archuleta County	CO	Eddie Claypool	1995	6874
267 4/8	41 4/8 39 4/8	32 4/8	6	6	Butte County	ID	Brent L. McMillan	1996	6874
267 4/8	42 3/8 41 5/8	35 4/8	6	6	Catron County	NM	John H. Trewern	1997	6874
267 4/8	40 7/8 38 6/8	31 6/8	6	6	Routt County	CO	Thomas E. Garrett	1998	6874
267 4/8	40 5/8 41 6/8	26 2/8	6	6	Fergus County	MT	Bruce A. Erickson	2002	6874
267 4/8	44 3/8 45 0/8	38 4/8	6	6	Coconino County	AZ	Scott Wills	2003	6874
*267 4/8	46 6/8 46 6/8	32 6/8	6	6	La Plata County	CO	Darren H. Ferrell	2005	6874
*267 4/8	40 6/8 40 4/8	34 4/8	6	7	Petroleum County	MT	Charles Gifford	2008	6874
267 3/8	40 4/8 39 3/8	30 3/8	6	6	Ravalli County	MT	Harold Wilson	1977	6885
267 3/8	38 2/8 47 4/8	33 1/8	5	6	Coconino County	AZ	John C. McClendon	1980	6885
267 3/8	43 6/8 45 6/8	35 5/8	6	6	Linn County	OR	Michael Hawkins	1982	6885
267 3/8	40 6/8 42 3/8	36 7/8	5	7	Greenlee County	AZ	Robert B. Miller	1992	6885
267 3/8	40 6/8 41 7/8	38 7/8	7	6	Jackson County	OR	Zach W. Badley	1998	6885
267 3/8	43 7/8 43 6/8	29 5/8	6	6	Fergus County	MT	Brent Milliron	2001	6885
267 3/8	41 6/8 41 6/8	39 5/8	6	6	Sanders County	MT	William C. King	2005	6885
*267 3/8	41 4/8 40 4/8	31 7/8	6	7	Catron County	NM	John Add Benson	2008	6885
267 2/8	44 4/8 47 4/8	35 2/8	5	5	Grand County	CO	David C. Goble	1994	6893
267 2/8	40 6/8 40 0/8	29 4/8	6	6	Pennington County	SD	Delana D. Nelson	1994	6893
267 2/8	46 3/8 48 2/8	34 4/8	6	5	Shoshone County	ID	Ernest W. Clanton	1995	6893
267 2/8	43 1/8 43 5/8	28 4/8	6	6	Catron County	NM	Gip Friesen	1997	6893
267 2/8	46 5/8 48 0/8	38 6/8	5	6	Otero County	NM	Morgan Ellis	2000	6893
267 2/8	41 0/8 40 2/8	35 0/8	6	6	Cascade County	MT	John Schaffer	2001	6893
*267 2/8	43 2/8 41 4/8	39 2/8	6	6	Ravalli County	MT	Todd Kleen	2005	6893
*267 2/8	44 0/8 42 3/8	36 0/8	6	6	Albany County	WY	Ronald Le Beaumont	2007	6893
267 1/8	42 3/8 42 4/8	33 3/8	6	6	Beaverhead County	MT	Neal Davis	1987	6901
267 1/8	39 4/8 40 4/8	38 3/8	6	6	Albany County	WY	Jerry Bowen	1988	6901
267 1/8	41 2/8 42 3/8	36 1/8	6	6	Lincoln County	NM	Gregory A. Lompart	1993	6901
267 1/8	42 7/8 42 6/8	30 3/8	6	6	Archuleta County	CO	Richard Robbins	1994	6901
267 1/8	46 3/8 44 4/8	36 6/8	6	6	Petroleum County	MT	Dustin B. Sturm	1997	6901
267 1/8	41 7/8 41 7/8	38 1/8	6	6	Archuleta County	CO	Gene Hopkins	2000	6901
267 1/8	44 0/8 44 2/8	37 1/8	6	6	Baker County	OR	Michael S. Chandler	2000	6901
267 1/8	41 4/8 40 6/8	30 5/8	6	6	Jefferson County	MT	Brian Trachsel	2003	6901
267 1/8	40 2/8 40 2/8	29 3/8	6	6	Grand County	CO	Mitch Winther	2003	6901
*267 1/8	47 4/8 49 0/8	37 3/8	6	7	Petroleum County	MT	Richard D. Riemer	2005	6901
*267 1/8	41 4/8 41 6/8	36 7/8	6	6	Gunnison County	CO	Hillary A. Buscovick	2008	6901
267 0/8	43 2/8 37 7/8	36 1/8	7	6	Teton County	WY	James Yager	1990	6912
267 0/8	42 2/8 39 3/8	31 0/8	6	6	Coconino County	AZ	Russell C. Horst	1992	6912
267 0/8	39 6/8 38 5/8	37 2/8	6	6	Garfield County	MT	Jeff Fisher	1995	6912
267 0/8	45 3/8 45 0/8	36 0/8	6	6	Adams County	ID	Smokey Crews	1997	6912
266 7/8	36 2/8 39 7/8	40 0/8	6	6	Carbon County	WY	Merle M. Vowers	1992	6916
266 7/8	42 3/8 42 0/8	31 3/8	6	6	Larimer County	CO	Wayne Haas	1998	6916
266 7/8	42 1/8 43 0/8	37 5/8	6	6	Judith Basin County	MT	Shawn Price	2000	6916
266 6/8	41 0/8 40 4/8	32 6/8	6	6	Lemhi County	ID	Scott Spaeth	1978	6919
266 6/8	45 5/8 43 2/8	37 4/8	6	6	Apache County	AZ	Tom David	1980	6919
266 6/8	43 7/8 44 6/8	39 2/8	6	6	Caribou County	ID	Max Park	1981	6919
266 6/8	42 5/8 42 7/8	29 0/8	6	6	Rio Blanco County	CO	Bill McMahan	1989	6919
266 6/8	41 6/8 41 6/8	33 1/8	6	7	Catron County	NM	Jack Dykstra	1991	6919
266 6/8	42 3/8 41 4/8	32 7/8	7	9	Big Horn County	WY	Scott White	1993	6919
266 6/8	49 1/8 50 3/8	40 2/8	6	6	Missoula County	MT	Lucas Osellame	1994	6919
266 6/8	44 7/8 44 0/8	34 6/8	6	6	Fremont County	WY	Matthew L. Wheeler	1997	6919
266 6/8	36 5/8 36 4/8	29 4/8	6	6	Lewis & Clark County	MT	Mark D. Reller	1999	6919
266 6/8	37 1/8 49 5/8	36 7/8	5	7	Albany County	WY	Jerry Bowen	2002	6919
266 6/8	42 7/8 43 6/8	41 2/8	5	5	Routt County	CO	Cedar Beauregard	2003	6919
266 6/8	41 5/8 45 5/8	37 0/8	6	6	Crook County	OR	Todd C. Horne	2005	6919
266 6/8	44 2/8 43 4/8	30 4/8	6	6	Eagle County	CO	Laurence W. Trotter II	2009	6919
266 5/8	42 1/8 43 7/8	29 5/8	6	6	Chaffee County	CO	Frank A. Morminello	1977	6932
266 5/8	48 1/8 45 0/8	42 5/8	6	6	Caribou County	ID	Max Park	1982	6932
266 5/8	43 2/8 43 2/8	31 7/8	6	6	Phillips County	MT	Steve Baeth	1985	6932
266 5/8	47 0/8 43 2/8	29 7/8	6	5	White Pine County	NV	Gary Wright	1989	6932

AMERICAN ELK (TYPICAL ANTLERS)

Minimum Score 260   Continued

SCORE	LENGTH OF R MAIN BEAM L	INSIDE SPREAD	NUMBER OF R POINTS L	AREA	STATE/ PROVINCE	HUNTER'S NAME	DATE	RANK
266 5/8	42 7/8 40 7/8	39 1/8	6 6	Sandoval County	NM	Peter F. Woeck II	1991	6932
266 5/8	44 6/8 42 0/8	36 4/8	6 6	Routt County	CO	Craig Thrasher	1991	6932
266 5/8	41 2/8 41 5/8	33 3/8	6 6	Mesa County	CO	Jimmy Wayne Birchfield	1991	6932
266 5/8	47 0/8 42 5/8	33 7/8	6 6	Jefferson County	OR	David G. Sonnenburg	1994	6932
266 5/8	46 4/8 44 6/8	32 1/8	6 6	Ravalli County	MT	Russell Byrne	1997	6932
266 5/8	46 0/8 43 3/8	36 5/8	6 6	Crook County	OR	Robert A. Rosales	1998	6932
266 5/8	39 2/8 37 7/8	35 7/8	5 5	Custer County	ID	Michael Scott Park	1998	6932
*266 5/8	44 1/8 42 2/8	42 5/8	6 6	Pennington County	SD	Kent B. White	2003	6932
*266 5/8	40 2/8 40 0/8	30 3/8	6 6	Sublette County	WY	Darrick Carney	2008	6932
*266 5/8	39 6/8 40 7/8	38 5/8	6 6	Carbon County	WY	Robert Sherman	2010	6932
266 4/8	36 7/8 37 0/8	30 4/8	6 6	Lewis & Clark County	MT	Laurence F. Crim	1977	6946
266 4/8	41 7/8 43 1/8	35 2/8	6 6	Gem County	ID	Randy L. Wilkins	1985	6946
266 4/8	41 5/8 42 2/8	39 4/8	6 6	Missoula County	MT	Steve Byerly	1988	6946
266 4/8	44 6/8 49 6/8	35 0/8	6 6	Coconino County	AZ	Rick Betten	1992	6946
266 4/8	42 3/8 42 6/8	41 0/8	7 7	Rio Arriba County	NM	Dave Conrad	1992	6946
266 4/8	40 0/8 41 1/8	41 0/8	6 5	Lane County	OR	Michael Kreiling	1992	6946
266 4/8	46 0/8 43 0/8	38 4/8	6 5	Coconino County	AZ	Michael Chamberlain	1992	6946
266 4/8	44 1/8 43 0/8	37 4/8	6 6	Lemhi County	ID	Frederick J. Gimbel	1993	6946
266 4/8	44 4/8 42 6/8	30 4/8	6 6	Los Alamos County	NM	M. R. James	1994	6946
266 4/8	46 3/8 47 0/8	34 4/8	6 5	Boundary County	ID	Roger N. Myers	1995	6946
266 4/8	44 3/8 46 7/8	38 2/8	6 6	Rio Arriba County	NM	Mark Patrick Seraly, MD	1995	6946
266 4/8	46 2/8 44 2/8	30 0/8	6 6	Yavapai County	AZ	Chance H. Cheatham	1997	6946
266 4/8	39 4/8 37 7/8	39 2/8	6 7	Douglas County	OR	Louie Thompson	2002	6946
266 4/8	40 6/8 40 4/8	30 4/8	6 6	Garfield County	MT	Kevin Brewer	2003	6946
266 4/8	46 5/8 47 4/8	37 0/8	6 5	Grand County	CO	Ed Moyer	2004	6946
266 4/8	42 5/8 42 3/8	36 2/8	6 6	Uintah County	UT	Christian Gerling	2006	6946
266 4/8	42 5/8 46 0/8	36 2/8	6 6	Coconino County	AZ	Richard Barkley	2008	6946
266 3/8	45 1/8 45 3/8	31 7/8	6 6	Archuleta County	CO	Mark Lowery	1989	6963
266 3/8	42 2/8 42 6/8	31 7/8	5 6	Sandoval County	NM	Greg Strait	1989	6963
266 3/8	41 1/8 43 1/8	36 3/8	5 6	Teller County	CO	James Wolfe	1990	6963
266 3/8	40 4/8 41 4/8	33 1/8	6 6	Park County	MT	Paul Backes	1999	6963
266 3/8	45 4/8 44 3/8	40 5/8	6 6	Idaho County	ID	Ron Kollar	2000	6963
266 3/8	38 2/8 39 6/8	36 5/8	6 5	Mesa County	CO	Steve Welch	2003	6963
266 3/8	38 7/8 36 7/8	31 3/8	6 6	Navajo County	AZ	Jeff Koznek	2005	6963
266 3/8	44 0/8 44 7/8	31 3/8	7 7	Huerfano County	CO	Ross W. Billings	2006	6963
266 3/8	40 1/8 41 2/8	35 7/8	6 6	Garfield County	CO	Jonathan Ellis	2007	6963
266 2/8	47 3/8 45 6/8	36 4/8	5 6	La Plata County	CO	Charlie Chrane	1977	6972
266 2/8	45 7/8 46 6/8	41 2/8	6 6	McKinley County	NM	Robert Stearns	1987	6972
266 2/8	39 4/8 40 6/8	30 6/8	6 6	Fremont County	ID	Gary Detwiler	1995	6972
266 2/8	40 4/8 40 2/8	30 4/8	6 6	Muskwa River	BC	Jim Nowakowski	1995	6972
266 2/8	39 1/8 38 4/8	31 2/8	6 6	Colfax County	NM	Pete Pieper	1997	6972
266 2/8	44 6/8 47 0/8	36 6/8	6 6	Wallowa County	OR	Steven M. Stoneking	1997	6972
266 2/8	46 6/8 45 2/8	40 2/8	6 7	Catron County	NM	Angelo Bacalocostantis	1999	6972
266 2/8	42 3/8 43 2/8	39 4/8	6 6	Coconino County	AZ	David R. Radatz	2001	6972
266 2/8	40 6/8 44 5/8	39 0/8	6 6	Garfield County	UT	Race Wells Wentz	2003	6972
266 2/8	43 4/8 44 6/8	29 4/8	6 6	Park County	WY	Kelly J. Brower	2004	6972
266 2/8	39 6/8 38 7/8	35 4/8	6 6	Grand County	CO	James Ven Huizen	2008	6972
266 2/8	42 1/8 41 7/8	40 0/8	5 5	Salt Lake County	UT	Mike Mayhew	2010	6972
266 1/8	42 6/8 43 6/8	32 3/8	6 6	Skamania County	WA	James S. Newman	1986	6984
266 1/8	41 2/8 42 1/8	36 5/8	6 6	Idaho County	ID	Charles E. Groft	1988	6984
266 1/8	45 6/8 47 0/8	34 7/8	6 6	Otero County	NM	Bruce Barrie	1998	6984
266 1/8	41 6/8 46 4/8	34 7/8	6 6	Uintah County	UT	Guy Mills	2000	6984
266 1/8	43 2/8 46 4/8	33 5/8	6 5	Petroleum County	MT	Troy Erickson	2001	6984
266 1/8	41 0/8 40 6/8	32 3/8	7 7	Blaine County	ID	Eddie Long	2001	6984
266 1/8	42 0/8 41 2/8	31 5/8	6 6	Lincoln County	NM	Mark E. Chavez	2003	6984
266 0/8	47 1/8 45 7/8	38 6/8	6 6	Sandoval County	NM	Lloyd Baird	1984	6991
266 0/8	48 5/8 47 5/8	31 0/8	5 6	Douglas County	CO	James Robert Phelps	1986	6991
266 0/8	38 4/8 39 6/8	34 2/8	6 6	Sublette County	WY	Michael D. Haden	1992	6991
266 0/8	41 3/8 41 7/8	35 4/8	6 6	Mesa County	CO	Kim A. Nail	1998	6991
266 0/8	40 2/8 39 5/8	39 2/8	6 5	McKinley County	NM	Neil J. Patrone	1998	6991
266 0/8	38 4/8 40 4/8	29 1/8	6 7	Valley County	MT	Charles J. Schultz	1998	6991
266 0/8	40 4/8 40 0/8	36 6/8	6 6	Garfield County	CO	Doug Hazzard	2000	6991
266 0/8	37 3/8 39 7/8	35 4/8	6 6	Catron County	NM	John Lober	2001	6991
266 0/8	41 0/8 41 1/8	38 0/8	6 6	Routt County	CO	Brad Odle	2001	6991
266 0/8	42 4/8 44 0/8	35 6/8	6 6	Pitkin County	CO	Bernard Hasse	2004	6991
266 0/8	44 5/8 46 4/8	38 0/8	6 6	Jackson County	CO	Del R. Jolly	2005	6991
265 7/8	40 1/8 40 5/8	36 5/8	6 7	San Miguel County	CO	Bubba Schmidt	1988	7002
265 7/8	42 4/8 45 0/8	37 7/8	6 6	Coconino County	AZ	Prentiss Chanceller	1988	7002
265 7/8	43 7/8 47 0/8	30 7/8	6 6	Coconino County	AZ	Cy Hershey	1990	7002
265 7/8	39 5/8 38 4/8	43 5/8	6 6	Elkford	BC	Dale Webber	1997	7002
265 7/8	41 3/8 43 3/8	38 1/8	6 6	Sanders County	MT	Zarach H. Epperson	2004	7002
265 7/8	44 5/8 45 4/8	34 7/8	5 6	Hood River County	OR	John P. Fitzgerald	2005	7002
*265 7/8	43 3/8 42 5/8	31 5/8	6 6	Yavapai County	AZ	John Mallin	2009	7002
265 6/8	41 2/8 40 6/8	36 0/8	6 6	Wallowa County	OR	Grainger Hunt	1987	7009
265 6/8	39 2/8 40 6/8	32 2/8	6 6	Madison County	MT	Richard Ballard	1987	7009
265 6/8	40 4/8 39 6/8	40 2/8	6 6	Sheridan County	WY	Skip Reilly	1988	7009
265 6/8	49 4/8 50 3/8	40 4/8	5 5	Boise County	ID	John E. Smith	1988	7009
265 6/8	39 2/8 39 0/8	28 2/8	6 6	Lincoln County	WY	Donlee L. Jackson	1990	7009
265 6/8	40 1/8 40 6/8	37 0/8	6 6	Colfax County	NM	Scott Walker	1996	7009
265 6/8	39 2/8 40 6/8	39 0/8	6 5	Coconino County	AZ	John Brooks	1996	7009
265 6/8	41 0/8 41 7/8	37 4/8	6 5	Rich County	UT	Glen Hallows	1997	7009
265 6/8	39 3/8 40 1/8	33 4/8	6 6	Garfield County	CO	Jay F. Shell	2002	7009
265 6/8	43 0/8 42 1/8	31 4/8	6 6	Archuleta County	CO	Michael B. Renzi	2003	7009
265 6/8	41 1/8 41 6/8	35 4/8	6 6	Sheridan County	WY	Barry L. Sweigart	2003	7009
*265 6/8	46 4/8 45 6/8	39 4/8	6 5	Socorro County	NM	Brantney Cox	2005	7009
265 6/8	40 4/8 40 7/8	37 0/8	6 6	Albany County	WY	Brad Crocco	2005	7009
265 6/8	40 7/8 39 7/8	33 2/8	5 6	Lamb Creek	BC	Richard Kirkvold	2005	7009
265 5/8	41 6/8 42 1/8	40 1/8	5 6	Rio Blanco County	CO	Jerry Bowen	1974	7023
265 5/8	37 2/8 38 4/8	29 1/8	6 6	Shoshone County	ID	Jeff Jackson	1987	7023
265 5/8	44 0/8 44 4/8	31 1/8	6 6	Huerfano County	CO	Steve Jeans	1988	7023
265 5/8	43 4/8 43 4/8	33 3/8	5 5	Mineral County	CO	Greg Ogle	1988	7023
265 5/8	44 4/8 43 2/8	39 3/8	6 6	Wallowa County	OR	Rick Turner	1990	7023
265 5/8	45 4/8 44 4/8	29 5/8	6 6	Columbia County	WA	Jess Mings	1992	7023
265 5/8	42 4/8 42 2/8	35 5/8	6 7	Teton County	ID	Shane Albertson	1997	7023
265 5/8	44 1/8 40 6/8	38 3/8	6 6	Union County	OR	Christopher J. Broderson	2001	7023

751

AMERICAN ELK (TYPICAL ANTLERS)

Minimum Score 260   Continued

Score	Length of Main Beam R	L	Inside Spread	Number of Points R	L	Area	State/Province	Hunter's Name	Date	Rank
265 5/8	40 2/8	40 7/8	37 3/8	6	6	Otero County	NM	Scott T. King	2008	7023
*265 5/8	39 2/8	38 7/8	29 2/8	7	7	Carbon County	WY	Lisa Cameron	2009	7023
265 4/8	43 2/8	42 7/8	32 6/8	6	6	Delta County	CO	Emil C. Frein	1973	7033
265 4/8	49 4/8	45 5/8	31 6/8	6	6	Dolores County	CO	Scott Roberts	1975	7033
265 4/8	37 6/8	35 3/8	39 5/8	6	6	Catron County	NM	John D. Smith	1989	7033
265 4/8	43 6/8	43 2/8	38 6/8	5	5	Jumping Pound Creek	ALB	Archie Nesbitt	1993	7033
265 4/8	45 4/8	44 1/8	31 2/8	6	6	Meagher County	MT	Theodore H. Hysell	1994	7033
265 4/8	46 0/8	47 0/8	36 2/8	6	6	Ouray County	CO	Michael D. Riley	1994	7033
265 4/8	44 3/8	44 1/8	33 4/8	6	6	Rio Arriba County	NM	Brian T. Christman	1995	7033
265 4/8	38 7/8	40 3/8	39 2/8	7	7	Coconino County	AZ	David DuBois O'Brien	2001	7033
*265 4/8	38 4/8	37 6/8	37 0/8	6	6	Catron County	NM	Brett Williams	2003	7033
265 4/8	44 2/8	44 2/8	41 6/8	6	6	Park County	MT	Paul Backes	2006	7033
265 3/8	39 7/8	38 5/8	34 3/8	6	6	Mineral County	CO	Will Pick	1993	7043
265 3/8	43 5/8	44 0/8	33 5/8	6	6	Beaverhead County	MT	K. F. Allworden	1998	7043
265 3/8	47 4/8	44 7/8	37 1/8	6	6	Navajo County	AZ	Tracy Lindsay	2005	7043
265 2/8	40 1/8	40 6/8	28 4/8	6	6	Mesa County	CO	Randy Page	1998	7046
265 2/8	35 4/8	36 5/8	36 0/8	6	6	Chaffee County	CO	Mike Nelson	2007	7046
265 2/8	43 0/8	42 1/8	35 2/8	6	6	Douglas County	CO	Matthew A. Boschert	2009	7046
265 2/8	42 1/8	42 2/8	35 6/8	6	6	Phillips County	MT	Justin Burt	2009	7046
265 1/8	41 2/8	39 2/8	29 1/8	6	7	Mineral County	CO	Rod Wintz	1968	7050
265 1/8	44 2/8	43 5/8	31 3/8	6	6	Huerfano County	CO	Duane Raspotnik	1989	7050
265 1/8	40 4/8	40 6/8	39 1/8	5	5	Catron County	NM	Jeffrey Aycock	1990	7050
265 1/8	42 4/8	44 4/8	28 5/8	6	6	Navajo County	AZ	Steve Johnston	1991	7050
265 1/8	45 0/8	42 7/8	34 5/8	6	6	Caribou County	ID	Richard Fletcher	1991	7050
265 1/8	46 3/8	45 5/8	36 1/8	6	6	Boise County	ID	Jeffrey Stevens	1993	7050
265 1/8	35 6/8	40 3/8	44 0/8	7	6	Catron County	NM	Matt Burrows	1994	7050
265 1/8	38 6/8	38 7/8	38 1/8	6	6	Eagle County	CO	Randy Chastain	1996	7050
265 1/8	44 5/8	44 3/8	31 5/8	6	6	Catron County	NM	G. Merrill Jones	2001	7050
265 1/8	42 0/8	41 0/8	35 5/8	6	6	Weeks	SAS	Lynn Hrywkiw	2003	7050
265 1/8	38 3/8	38 2/8	29 1/8	6	6	Cranbrook	BC	Les Kisner	2004	7050
265 1/8	38 3/8	37 6/8	39 0/8	6	6	Garfield County	CO	Michael D. Owens	2005	7050
265 1/8	44 6/8	46 1/8	37 6/8	6	6	Sublette County	WY	Craig Germond	2007	7050
265 0/8	44 5/8	43 2/8	30 0/8	6	6	Kittitas County	WA	Eric Seim	1991	7063
265 0/8	43 0/8	42 1/8	34 4/8	6	6	Petroleum County	MT	Mark Rigotti	1992	7063
265 0/8	40 7/8	40 1/8	37 4/8	6	6	Madison County	MT	Raymond Gross	1999	7063
265 0/8	42 3/8	42 2/8	37 0/8	6	6	Yakima County	WA	Todd Phetteplace	2000	7063
265 0/8	39 7/8	37 6/8	37 0/8	6	6	El Paso County	CO	Craig E. Kimball	2004	7063
*265 0/8	42 2/8	45 0/8	30 0/8	6	6	Sanders County	MT	Wade Prasil	2009	7063
264 7/8	42 5/8	45 5/8	33 1/8	6	6	Coconino County	AZ	Dennis Newman	1973	7069
264 7/8	39 1/8	42 2/8	33 5/8	6	6	Huerfano County	CO	Michael J. Eutsler	1986	7069
264 7/8	40 0/8	38 2/8	39 7/8	6	6	Union County	OR	Ellis E. Speer	1986	7069
264 7/8	42 6/8	42 0/8	35 5/8	5	6	Sandoval County	NM	Pat Lovato	1993	7069
264 7/8	45 0/8	45 3/8	36 3/8	5	6	Garfield County	MT	Richard Hjort	1993	7069
264 7/8	38 7/8	39 2/8	33 3/8	6	6	Luna County	NM	Jim DeVries	2001	7069
264 7/8	41 3/8	39 6/8	30 3/8	6	6	Lane County	OR	Ron Kimble	2003	7069
264 7/8	42 5/8	43 6/8	38 7/8	6	6	Broadwater County	MT	Nancy Terry	2004	7069
*264 7/8	43 1/8	43 6/8	32 3/8	6	6	Lewis & Clark County	MT	Dean E. Eisenhart	2004	7069
264 7/8	40 0/8	37 0/8	34 7/8	6	6	Duchesne County	UT	Sean P. Davis	2008	7069
*264 7/8	43 0/8	42 1/8	36 1/8	5	5	DeWinton	ALB	Giuseppe Valente	2009	7069
264 6/8	38 5/8	37 4/8	32 2/8	6	6	Teton County	WY	Paul Birkholz	1966	7080
264 6/8	43 0/8	44 1/8	36 0/8	5	5	Meagher County	MT	Gary H. Thompson	1981	7080
264 6/8	41 4/8	40 5/8	35 4/8	6	6	Pitkin County	CO	Donald Hanford	1981	7080
264 6/8	41 3/8	41 0/8	36 4/8	6	6	Meagher County	MT	Gene Clark	1982	7080
264 6/8	39 3/8	39 2/8	32 6/8	6	6	Duchesne County	UT	Russel McClellan	1994	7080
264 6/8	44 1/8	44 2/8	39 2/8	6	5	Lemhi County	ID	John Hanowski	1995	7080
264 6/8	41 7/8	44 3/8	30 3/8	7	7	Petroleum County	MT	Timothy W. Mitchell	1998	7080
264 6/8	41 5/8	43 3/8	36 6/8	6	6	Grand County	CO	Chuck Cullum	2002	7080
264 6/8	43 1/8	42 3/8	31 6/8	6	6	Valley County	ID	Tim Baldwin	2003	7080
264 6/8	44 2/8	45 4/8	36 2/8	5	5	Larimer County	CO	Gary Becwar, Jr.	2004	7080
264 6/8	45 4/8	45 1/8	34 6/8	6	6	Ouray County	CO	Lance Hockett	2004	7080
264 6/8	44 0/8	43 3/8	41 2/8	6	6	Adams County	ID	Larry Hoff	2004	7080
264 6/8	41 1/8	42 1/8	38 6/8	5	5	Sandoval County	NM	Mitchell Lee Chapman	2006	7080
264 6/8	41 2/8	41 6/8	36 4/8	5	5	Lincoln County	MT	David B. Snipes, Sr.	2006	7080
*264 6/8	41 0/8	42 0/8	30 2/8	6	6	Jefferson County	CO	Michael Mandell	2007	7080
264 6/8	40 0/8	39 5/8	36 6/8	6	6	Sheridan County	WY	Jason A. Swanson	2007	7080
264 5/8	43 2/8	43 7/8	29 7/8	6	5	Ouray County	CO	Mark Timken	2000	7096
264 5/8	43 1/8	44 3/8	34 5/8	5	5	Clark County	NV	Robin D. Dunn	2000	7096
264 5/8	40 6/8	40 1/8	31 1/8	6	6	Wheeler County	OR	Joe Bruscato	2001	7096
264 5/8	40 7/8	41 3/8	32 5/8	6	6	Coconino County	AZ	Skip Rimsza	2003	7096
264 5/8	44 6/8	45 6/8	31 1/8	6	6	Bonneville County	ID	Hayden E. Long	2004	7096
264 5/8	43 0/8	42 0/8	35 5/8	6	6	Musselshell County	MT	Russell W. Guthrie	2005	7096
*264 5/8	44 1/8	43 7/8	36 5/8	6	7	Meagher County	MT	Donald L. Yingling, Jr.	2008	7096
264 4/8	44 6/8	45 7/8	34 4/8	7	7	Boise County	ID	Robert Hiller	1969	7103
264 4/8	38 6/8	39 2/8	33 6/8	6	6	Jefferson County	CO	Darrell Kitzman	1986	7103
264 4/8	42 3/8	42 1/8	37 0/8	6	6	Lincoln County	NM	Jim Tyler	1988	7103
264 4/8	46 3/8	49 6/8	39 2/8	6	6	Sierra County	NM	Guy D. Pointer	1988	7103
264 4/8	42 4/8	43 7/8	36 4/8	5	6	Catron County	NM	Adam Jimenez, Jr.	1989	7103
264 4/8	42 4/8	42 3/8	30 2/8	6	6	Saguache County	CO	Arthur D. Johnson	1991	7103
264 4/8	42 7/8	41 6/8	37 6/8	6	6	Powell County	MT	Dan J. Burns	1995	7103
264 4/8	45 5/8	46 5/8	36 2/8	6	5	Valley County	ID	David W. Rickert II	2002	7103
264 4/8	41 3/8	44 1/8	35 6/8	6	6	Valley County	ID	Ralph L. Albright	2003	7103
264 4/8	49 6/8	40 6/8	25 0/8	6	5	Gallatin County	MT	Richard Daniotti, Jr.	2003	7103
264 4/8	38 2/8	40 0/8	36 2/8	6	6	Park County	MT	George Kamps	2003	7103
264 4/8	39 1/8	38 7/8	38 2/8	6	6	Albany County	WY	Greg Bokash	2006	7103
*264 4/8	44 1/8	44 0/8	37 0/8	6	5	Fergus County	MT	Don Moen	2006	7103
264 4/8	39 1/8	39 4/8	35 2/8	6	6	Lewis County	WA	Chad Taylor	2007	7103
264 4/8	45 0/8	43 1/8	31 6/8	6	6	Sheridan County	WY	Daniel Doke	2007	7103
264 3/8	44 2/8	44 4/8	30 7/8	6	6	Coconino County	AZ	Joel R. Youngblood III	1990	7118
264 3/8	39 4/8	40 1/8	33 5/8	6	6	Huerfano County	CO	Esco R. Billings, III	1991	7118
264 3/8	40 7/8	41 0/8	38 1/8	6	6	Meagher County	MT	Donovan A. Khalar	1995	7118
264 3/8	44 1/8	43 2/8	29 5/8	5	6	Rio Arriba County	NM	Bert A. McJimsey	2003	7118
264 3/8	42 5/8	42 3/8	29 1/8	6	6	Lewis County	WA	Chad Taylor	2008	7118
264 2/8	41 4/8	43 5/8	27 6/8	6	6	Coconino County	AZ	Randy Breland	1984	7123
264 2/8	39 7/8	39 3/8	39 6/8	5	5	Catron County	NM	Adam Jimenez Jr.	1986	7123
264 2/8	43 5/8	43 4/8	38 6/8	6	5	Gunnison County	CO	Mark Asplund	1987	7123

AMERICAN ELK (TYPICAL ANTLERS)

Minimum Score 260 — Continued

SCORE	LENGTH OF R MAIN BEAM L	INSIDE SPREAD	NUMBER OF R POINTS L	AREA	STATE/PROVINCE	HUNTER'S NAME	DATE	RANK
264 2/8	39 6/8 40 1/8	27 2/8	6 6	Sheridan County	WY	Richard E. Jones	1992	7123
264 2/8	47 1/8 44 4/8	32 2/8	6 6	Ravalli County	MT	Scott Wilke	1994	7123
264 2/8	41 1/8 41 4/8	34 2/8	6 7	Larimer County	CO	Jack Shinogle	2000	7123
264 2/8	42 0/8 42 3/8	38 6/8	6 6	Garfield County	UT	Richie Bland	2001	7123
264 2/8	43 5/8 45 7/8	36 2/8	6 6	Lincoln County	MT	Dan Halvorson	2004	7123
*264 2/8	42 0/8 40 4/8	33 6/8	6 6	Rio Arriba County	NM	Lou Evans	2006	7123
264 2/8	43 2/8 44 5/8	22 2/8	6 6	Petroleum County	MT	Ryan Rusley	2007	7123
264 2/8	49 0/8 53 3/8	36 0/8	6 6	Johnson County	WY	Jamie Becker	2007	7123
264 1/8	40 4/8 39 0/8	39 7/8	5 5	Larimer County	CO	Eric Peterson	1982	7134
264 1/8	39 7/8 38 7/8	31 3/8	6 6	Taos County	NM	Ronald Corvin	1990	7134
264 1/8	41 3/8 41 3/8	36 1/8	6 6	Valencia County	NM	Chett Britton	1994	7134
264 1/8	40 0/8 38 2/8	32 3/8	6 6	Park County	WY	Ron Niziolek	2001	7134
264 1/8	40 3/8 42 4/8	29 1/8	6 6	Musselshell County	MT	Kenneth A. Sharp	2005	7134
*264 1/8	39 2/8 38 6/8	29 7/8	6 6	Carbon County	WY	Bradley Dragovich	2007	7134
264 0/8	40 1/8 40 5/8	37 0/8	6 6	Valley County	ID	Brian Crook	1989	7140
264 0/8	49 1/8 48 5/8	37 6/8	6 6	Montrose County	CO	Gary Chambliss	1995	7140
264 0/8	36 4/8 36 0/8	39 6/8	5 5	Catron County	NM	Vicki L. Leonard	1996	7140
264 0/8	39 2/8 39 6/8	29 5/8	7 6	Jackson County	CO	Gerald W. White	2000	7140
264 0/8	39 6/8 39 2/8	33 6/8	6 6	Uintah County	UT	Joseph F. Schipani	2001	7140
264 0/8	37 2/8 35 2/8	30 4/8	6 6	Larimer County	CO	Dale T. Nixon	2005	7140
*264 0/8	42 7/8 44 1/8	39 6/8	6 6	Pennington County	SD	Craig A. Zoss	2009	7140
263 7/8	46 4/8 46 7/8	39 7/8	6 5	Boise County	ID	Jack Brennan	1964	7147
263 7/8	41 2/8 40 4/8	35 1/8	6 6	Valley County	MT	Myron Gartner	1976	7147
263 7/8	38 4/8 41 5/8	35 3/8	6 6	Garfield County	MT	Gary Andler	1998	7147
263 7/8	41 3/8 43 2/8	40 6/8	7 6	Garfield County	CO	Andrew Bair	2003	7147
263 7/8	40 5/8 39 6/8	28 3/8	6 5	Sierra County	NM	Robert Clancy	2005	7147
263 7/8	39 2/8 37 2/8	34 1/8	6 6	Albany County	WY	Miles Bundy	2007	7147
263 6/8	43 7/8 43 5/8	34 2/8	6 6	Phillips County	MT	Bill Connors	1994	7153
263 6/8	38 3/8 38 6/8	36 0/8	6 6	Sandoval County	NM	Michael G. Morton	1995	7153
263 6/8	38 4/8 36 1/8	35 2/8	6 6	Meagher County	MT	John Roberts	1995	7153
263 6/8	40 5/8 41 6/8	38 2/8	6 6	Larimer County	CO	Ron Wahl	1998	7153
263 6/8	46 0/8 45 0/8	39 4/8	6 5	Rio Blanco County	CO	Mark Muller	1998	7153
263 6/8	40 1/8 40 3/8	33 2/8	5 5	Carbon County	WY	Patrick Malone	1999	7153
263 6/8	39 4/8 38 4/8	40 6/8	5 6	Pend Oreille County	WA	Joe Kiefer	2005	7153
*263 6/8	39 5/8 39 7/8	38 0/8	6 6	Carbon County	WY	James J. Campbell	2010	7153
263 5/8	40 5/8 39 6/8	34 3/8	6 6	Ouray County	CO	Doug McCauley	1982	7161
263 5/8	35 2/8 37 7/8	32 1/8	6 6	Petroleum County	MT	Greg Deutsch	1993	7161
263 5/8	39 7/8 39 3/8	33 0/8	7 6	Mesa County	CO	Mark Crain	1997	7161
263 5/8	41 6/8 41 4/8	32 3/8	6 6	Jefferson County	MT	Paul E. Galuska	2002	7161
263 5/8	41 5/8 39 4/8	36 3/8	6 6	Valley County	MT	Kerry L. Beechie	2002	7161
*263 5/8	46 1/8 42 4/8	32 5/8	5 6	Garfield County	MT	Ernie Jablonsky	2004	7161
263 4/8	41 5/8 41 4/8	37 4/8	6 6	Caribou County	ID	Wade Dursteler	1988	7167
263 4/8	42 2/8 43 0/8	37 2/8	6 6	Lemhi County	ID	Rob Valnoski	1994	7167
263 4/8	39 6/8 42 1/8	29 4/8	6 6	Lemhi County	ID	Gary R. Heward	1997	7167
263 4/8	40 6/8 39 6/8	34 6/8	6 6	Carbon County	WY	Tracy Villwok	2008	7167
263 3/8	38 7/8 38 4/8	33 5/8	6 6	Idaho County	ID	John C. Mitchell	1985	7171
263 3/8	40 1/8 39 2/8	38 2/8	6 7	Larimer County	CO	B.D. Ramsey	1988	7171
263 3/8	37 7/8 43 0/8	34 7/8	7 6	Las Animas County	CO	Lowell Thomas	1989	7171
263 3/8	51 3/8 49 2/8	36 4/8	6 6	Rio Blanco County	CO	Brad Murray	1992	7171
263 3/8	42 0/8 40 1/8	33 5/8	6 6	Beaverhead County	MT	Steve Rigby	1996	7171
263 3/8	44 6/8 45 3/8	29 5/8	6 6	Garfield County	CO	Wayne A. Buckley	2004	7171
263 2/8	40 7/8 43 1/8	32 5/8	6 7	Coconino County	AZ	Michael H. Bingham	1982	7177
263 2/8	45 3/8 43 5/8	34 2/8	6 6	Gallatin County	MT	Bob Fromme	1983	7177
263 2/8	43 7/8 43 6/8	35 4/8	6 6	Fremont County	WY	Guy LeMonnier, Jr.	1989	7177
263 2/8	39 2/8 40 7/8	36 0/8	6 6	Ouray County	CO	Dexter G. Efird	1990	7177
263 2/8	39 4/8 40 4/8	28 2/8	7 7	Petroleum County	MT	Ken Rustad	1990	7177
263 2/8	38 3/8 41 1/8	35 6/8	6 6	Pitkin County	CO	Rocky Dan Tschappat	1994	7177
263 2/8	42 2/8 42 0/8	35 4/8	6 6	Fremont County	ID	Chad Berry	1995	7177
263 2/8	37 5/8 37 3/8	36 2/8	6 6	Huerfano County	CO	Jack L. Sciacca	1996	7177
263 2/8	47 0/8 45 5/8	36 0/8	6 6	Smoky River	ALB	Kirby Smith	1996	7177
263 2/8	40 6/8 47 3/8	41 1/8	6 6	Catron County	NM	Philip J. Guarino, Jr.	1999	7177
263 2/8	39 7/8 39 5/8	34 4/8	6 7	Adams County	ID	Scott McGann	2001	7177
263 2/8	42 4/8 41 0/8	32 2/8	6 6	Coconino County	AZ	Alex Rendon	2001	7177
263 2/8	41 0/8 40 2/8	38 2/8	6 6	Routt County	CO	Tom E. James	2003	7177
263 2/8	41 7/8 41 3/8	34 6/8	6 6	Cibola County	NM	Bill T. Dimercurio	2005	7177
263 2/8	33 6/8 36 4/8	44 6/8	5 5	Meagher County	MT	Geoffrey Gelhaus	2005	7177
263 1/8	43 5/8 42 6/8	35 5/8	6 5	Lewis County	WA	Keith Heldreth	1984	7192
263 1/8	44 6/8 42 6/8	36 3/8	6 6	Socorro County	NM	Joe Caskey	1986	7192
263 1/8	44 2/8 46 0/8	30 3/8	7 7	Blaine County	ID	James B. Thompson	1992	7192
263 1/8	40 5/8 39 4/8	32 1/8	6 6	Jefferson County	CO	Jerry Grueneberg	1998	7192
263 1/8	40 7/8 41 7/8	41 2/8	7 5	Musselshell County	MT	Dwight M. Corle	1999	7192
263 1/8	39 0/8 39 4/8	33 5/8	6 6	Catron County	NM	R. Mark Bailey	2004	7192
263 1/8	40 4/8 41 5/8	31 3/8	6 6	Garfield County	CO	Tammy Wagner	2006	7192
263 0/8	41 0/8 41 3/8	36 2/8	6 6	Clear Creek County	CO	Don Bording	1982	7199
263 0/8	41 7/8 42 6/8	35 2/8	6 6	Los Alamos County	NM	Doug Aikin	1984	7199
263 0/8	38 7/8 39 4/8	38 6/8	6 6	Grant County	OR	Phillip Koep	1991	7199
263 0/8	42 2/8 43 7/8	33 4/8	5 6	Silver Bow County	MT	Victor Romano	1992	7199
263 0/8	45 2/8 42 2/8	37 0/8	5 5	Hinsdale County	CO	Mark J. Wollert	1995	7199
263 0/8	41 3/8 44 2/8	30 4/8	6 6	Catron County	NM	Mike W. Leonard	1996	7199
263 0/8	40 7/8 42 5/8	38 4/8	6 6	Caribou County	ID	Chad Jones	2003	7199
263 0/8	40 4/8 40 7/8	33 1/8	7 7	Huerfano County	CO	Rick Rice	2004	7199
263 0/8	39 0/8 38 4/8	38 6/8	6 6	Camas County	ID	James Herrett	2005	7199
*263 0/8	40 5/8 38 7/8	32 2/8	6 6	Harney County	OR	John L. Conley	2008	7199
263 0/8	42 3/8 43 3/8	30 0/8	5 6	Iron County	UT	Kurt Gale	2008	7199
262 7/8	37 7/8 36 7/8	34 3/8	6 6	Garfield County	CO	Clifford White	1977	7210
262 7/8	43 3/8 44 0/8	36 5/8	7 6	Coconino County	AZ	Dr. Van Bennett	1985	7210
262 7/8	45 7/8 45 5/8	38 1/8	6 6	Teton County	WY	Bret R. Cary	2004	7210
262 7/8	40 2/8 40 5/8	37 5/8	5 5	Otero County	NM	Justin S. Olk	2006	7210
262 6/8	40 5/8 42 2/8	31 6/8	6 6	Archuleta County	CO	David W. Cather	1984	7214
262 6/8	41 3/8 39 6/8	40 7/8	7 7	Catron County	NM	Robert Barrie	1995	7214
262 6/8	39 5/8 41 2/8	37 6/8	6 6	Lemhi County	ID	Thomas N. Thiel	1996	7214
262 6/8	42 4/8 41 1/8	39 4/8	6 6	Caribou County	ID	William T. Trainor	1997	7214
262 6/8	38 4/8 43 0/8	37 3/8	8 6	Meagher County	MT	James C. Kennedy	1999	7214
262 6/8	38 2/8 39 2/8	37 2/8	6 6	Gila County	AZ	Dennis L. Brown	2001	7214
262 6/8	43 3/8 43 5/8	35 4/8	6 5	Granite County	MT	Rodney Diemer	2002	7214

AMERICAN ELK (TYPICAL ANTLERS)

Minimum Score 260 Continued

SCORE	LENGTH OF R MAIN BEAM L	INSIDE SPREAD	NUMBER OF R POINTS L	AREA	STATE/ PROVINCE	HUNTER'S NAME	DATE	RANK
262 6/8	44 1/8 · 43 4/8	39 6/8	5 · 6	Flathead County	MT	David Fortenberry	2004	7214
262 6/8	45 4/8 · 47 4/8	42 7/8	6 · 7	Otero County	NM	Eugene Majchrzak	2007	7214
262 6/8	39 6/8 · 39 7/8	30 4/8	6 · 6	Clearwater County	ID	Rev. Joseph F. Classen	2007	7214
262 6/8	44 7/8 · 44 6/8	32 1/8	7 · 6	Lincoln County	NM	Michael Serwa	2009	7214
*262 6/8	44 7/8 · 44 6/8	32 1/8	7 · 6	Lincoln County	NM	Michael Serwa	2009	7214
262 5/8	39 5/8 · 39 4/8	36 7/8	6 · 6	Pierce County	WA	David T. Robertson	1985	7225
262 5/8	41 5/8 · 39 3/8	34 7/8	6 · 6	Custer County	ID	Brent McBride	1987	7225
262 5/8	47 5/8 · 46 0/8	30 1/8	6 · 6	Routt County	CO	John Pershing Lundberg	1990	7225
262 5/8	41 6/8 · 45 2/8	29 5/8	6 · 6	Rio Arriba County	NM	Mike Cherner	2005	7225
262 4/8	39 4/8 · 40 0/8	31 6/8	6 · 7	Coconino County	AZ	Donald L. Kennedy	1977	7229
262 4/8	42 6/8 · 43 4/8	38 4/8	6 · 6	Flathead County	MT	Chester Fessum	1983	7229
262 4/8	42 7/8 · 43 2/8	30 2/8	5 · 6	Pierce County	WA	Andy Bales	1989	7229
262 4/8	40 5/8 · 41 1/8	39 6/8	6 · 6	Montezuma County	CO	Ron Laird	1991	7229
262 4/8	38 4/8 · 38 0/8	39 0/8	6 · 6	Chaffee County	CO	Joel D. Morgan	1991	7229
262 4/8	40 3/8 · 42 4/8	38 2/8	6 · 7	Catron County	NM	Zeb Kern	1997	7229
262 4/8	38 0/8 · 38 7/8	35 6/8	6 · 6	Yakima County	WA	Mark Golder	2000	7229
262 4/8	42 4/8 · 43 4/8	35 4/8	5 · 5	Colfax County	NM	John E. Dell	2000	7229
262 4/8	39 1/8 · 38 0/8	41 2/8	7 · 7	Rio Blanco County	CO	Dewey J. Cameron	2003	7229
*262 4/8	41 0/8 · 41 0/8	39 6/8	5 · 6	Mesa County	CO	R. Kirk Sharp	2005	7229
262 4/8	39 1/8 · 40 3/8	32 6/8	6 · 6	Park County	CO	Timothy Grzesiak	2007	7229
262 4/8	39 5/8 · 39 1/8	36 0/8	6 · 6	Sheridan County	WY	Mike Barrett	2009	7229
262 4/8	50 0/8 · 43 3/8	36 6/8	6 · 6	Carbon County	WY	Toby Merritt	2009	7229
262 3/8	46 1/8 · 44 5/8	32 6/8	7 · 6	Rio Arriba County	NM	Ronnie Williams	1986	7242
262 3/8	43 3/8 · 43 3/8	32 0/8	7 · 6	Kakwa River	ALB	Wilf Lehners	1991	7242
262 3/8	43 0/8 · 42 0/8	34 7/8	6 · 5	Clearwater County	ID	Mark E. Kuechenmeister	1994	7242
262 3/8	39 1/8 · 39 1/8	35 5/8	6 · 6	Fergus County	MT	Gary "Grizz" Hoffer	1995	7242
262 3/8	40 3/8 · 42 6/8	30 5/8	6 · 6	Fremont County	ID	Johnny R. Watson	2000	7242
262 3/8	46 2/8 · 45 3/8	31 1/8	6 · 6	Eagle County	CO	Brian Trachsel	2004	7242
262 3/8	33 7/8 · 39 0/8	35 3/8	6 · 6	Clark County	ID	David Campbell	2004	7242
262 2/8	45 0/8 · 45 3/8	32 6/8	5 · 5	Grand County	CO	G. Fred Asbell	1979	7249
262 2/8	41 4/8 · 40 2/8	37 0/8	5 · 5	Crook County	OR	Terry A. Luther	1981	7249
262 2/8	46 1/8 · 43 5/8	38 4/8	6 · 6	Saguache County	CO	Burton R. Thompson, Jr.	1995	7249
262 2/8	46 1/8 · 47 6/8	38 6/8	6 · 6	Coconino County	AZ	Donald A. Karcher	1995	7249
262 2/8	38 6/8 · 39 2/8	41 1/8	6 · 6	Douglas County	CO	Michael Manning	1997	7249
262 2/8	40 4/8 · 40 4/8	38 4/8	6 · 6	Grant County	OR	Eric Kuiken	2003	7249
262 2/8	47 2/8 · 49 0/8	37 2/8	6 · 5	Coconino County	AZ	Douglas Parch	2004	7249
262 2/8	38 5/8 · 37 2/8	30 0/8	6 · 6	Routt County	CO	Randy Kendrick	2005	7249
*262 2/8	41 7/8 · 41 5/8	38 4/8	6 · 6	Larimer County	CO	V. Bruce Clark	2006	7249
262 1/8	43 7/8 · 44 2/8	31 7/8	6 · 6	Blaine County	ID	Bruce Anderson	1996	7258
262 1/8	43 5/8 · 41 4/8	31 1/8	6 · 6	Pierce County	WA	Brant J. Williams	2000	7258
262 1/8	40 5/8 · 39 5/8	34 5/8	6 · 6	Garfield County	CO	Jason Umsted	2009	7258
262 0/8	43 4/8 · 43 6/8	35 4/8	6 · 6	Chaffee County	CO	Ray Nelson	1981	7261
262 0/8	42 4/8 · 42 1/8	37 4/8	6 · 6	Deer Lodge County	MT	Todd R. Zeuske	1982	7261
262 0/8	38 5/8 · 41 4/8	34 2/8	6 · 6	Catron County	NM	Bob "Jake" Jacobsen	1993	7261
262 0/8	38 2/8 · 39 0/8	29 6/8	6 · 6	Montrose County	CO	Ted Winchester	1993	7261
262 0/8	44 4/8 · 42 5/8	38 6/8	6 · 6	Catron County	NM	Robert J. Martin	1996	7261
262 0/8	43 6/8 · 42 7/8	31 2/8	6 · 6	Montrose County	CO	Steven M. Grantham	1997	7261
262 0/8	42 6/8 · 46 5/8	32 0/8	6 · 6	Eagle County	CO	Christopher R. Beck	1998	7261
262 0/8	43 2/8 · 42 3/8	34 1/8	7 · 6	Rio Arriba County	NM	Wilson McKibben	2001	7261
262 0/8	43 4/8 · 42 4/8	33 4/8	6 · 6	Ravalli County	MT	Lena Wiediger	2004	7261
262 0/8	37 7/8 · 38 4/8	35 6/8	6 · 6	Douglas County	OR	Kelly A. Hallenbeck	2006	7261
262 0/8	44 5/8 · 45 5/8	35 2/8	6 · 6	Moffat County	CO	Thomas E. Powell	2007	7261
*262 0/8	45 1/8 · 45 2/8	42 3/8	5 · 6	Jackson County	CO	Mark Johnson	2008	7261
262 0/8	38 4/8 · 37 1/8	34 2/8	6 · 6	Garfield County	MT	Pao K. Moua	2009	7261
262 0/8	40 7/8 · 40 4/8	33 1/8	5 · 5	Otero County	NM	John M. Cogswell	2010	7261
261 7/8	36 6/8 · 41 3/8	34 7/8	6 · 6	Coconino County	AZ	Charles Stevenson	1980	7275
261 7/8	41 1/8 · 41 0/8	35 7/8	6 · 6	Clearwater County	ID	Jim Prudhomme	1990	7275
261 7/8	42 5/8 · 41 3/8	34 3/8	6 · 6	Montezuma County	CO	Gene Benavidez	1998	7275
261 6/8	38 0/8 · 40 0/8	37 6/8	6 · 5	Taos County	NM	Dr. D. A. Henbest	1972	7278
261 6/8	39 4/8 · 40 2/8	32 4/8	6 · 6	Delta County	CO	John C. Lamont	1989	7278
261 6/8	44 6/8 · 44 0/8	36 0/8	7 · 6	Coconino County	AZ	Gary Hanson	1992	7278
261 6/8	47 6/8 · 46 5/8	32 4/8	6 · 5	Albany County	WY	Doug Cringan	1992	7278
261 6/8	41 5/8 · 42 4/8	42 4/8	6 · 6	Clear Creek County	CO	Mark Turner	1993	7278
261 6/8	40 4/8 · 41 4/8	45 4/8	6 · 6	Coconino County	AZ	Robert F. Plew	1994	7278
261 6/8	36 3/8 · 40 2/8	33 6/8	6 · 6	Otero County	NM	Ronald Friesner	1995	7278
261 6/8	41 4/8 · 42 0/8	34 6/8	6 · 6	Teller County	CO	Jose C. Simoes	1998	7278
*261 6/8	37 1/8 · 37 2/8	39 2/8	6 · 6	Sanders County	MT	Tom Venezia	2009	7278
261 5/8	40 0/8 · 37 2/8	33 5/8	6 · 6	Rio Blanco County	CO	H. V. McFarland, Jr.	1974	7287
261 5/8	37 1/8 · 36 1/8	37 6/8	6 · 6	Flathead County	MT	Dr. Brad Black	1981	7287
261 5/8	35 6/8 · 35 4/8	34 5/8	6 · 6	Fremont County	ID	Todd J. Frickey	1987	7287
261 5/8	43 1/8 · 43 2/8	37 5/8	5 · 6	Garfield County	CO	Francis J. Dehner	1989	7287
261 5/8	39 1/8 · 40 2/8	34 1/8	6 · 6	Beaverhead County	MT	Eduard Hale	1990	7287
261 5/8	36 5/8 · 35 0/8	36 6/8	6 · 6	Missoula County	MT	Vinnie Pisani	1993	7287
261 5/8	39 0/8 · 41 1/8	38 6/8	6 · 6	Comanche County	OK	Richard J. Warren	1993	7287
261 5/8	43 7/8 · 44 0/8	36 1/8	6 · 6	Archuleta County	CO	Keith Sherrill	1997	7287
261 5/8	37 4/8 · 36 6/8	32 5/8	6 · 6	Rio Blanco County	CO	Jimmy N. Brown	1998	7287
261 5/8	41 4/8 · 41 0/8	32 3/8	6 · 6	Sheridan County	WY	Dave Moss	2002	7287
261 5/8	36 5/8 · 46 1/8	36 7/8	5 · 6	Douglas County	OR	Kody Kellom	2003	7287
261 5/8	38 4/8 · 40 4/8	31 7/8	6 · 6	Johnson County	WY	Douglas E. Callies	2003	7287
261 5/8	45 1/8 · 47 1/8	35 7/8	6 · 6	Lemhi County	ID	Mark L. Hamele	2010	7287
261 4/8	43 0/8 · 43 2/8	35 0/8	6 · 6	Caribou County	ID	Randy K. Guinn	1986	7300
261 4/8	42 0/8 · 39 3/8	31 6/8	6 · 6	Madison County	MT	Robert J. Kleinhans	1992	7300
261 4/8	51 2/8 · 50 0/8	40 0/8	5 · 6	Granite County	MT	D. Neitzke/M. Nielsen	1998	7300
261 4/8	41 4/8 · 40 6/8	43 0/8	6 · 6	Mesa County	CO	Don Morris	2000	7300
261 4/8	40 6/8 · 41 3/8	32 2/8	6 · 6	Coconino County	AZ	Darryl Coe	2004	7300
261 3/8	41 6/8 · 41 3/8	31 1/8	6 · 6	Fremont County	ID	Gary Owens	1980	7305
261 3/8	39 0/8 · 40 1/8	34 7/8	6 · 6	Gallatin County	MT	Paul D. Amdahl	1993	7305
261 3/8	38 6/8 · 38 7/8	31 1/8	6 · 6	Lincoln County	WY	Gerald Henrickson	1994	7305
261 3/8	43 2/8 · 42 6/8	40 1/8	5 · 5	Wallowa County	OR	Sidney R. Marks	1996	7305
261 3/8	43 5/8 · 43 6/8	35 7/8	6 · 6	Valley County	ID	Alan R. Bentley	1997	7305
261 3/8	40 5/8 · 39 6/8	32 7/8	6 · 6	Baker County	OR	Lon Raney	2007	7305
261 3/8	43 0/8 · 43 0/8	34 7/8	6 · 6	Conejos County	CO	Garett Pfeffenbach	2009	7305
261 2/8	42 5/8 · 42 4/8	31 0/8	5 · 5	Rio Arriba County	NM	Donald N. Lehman	1983	7312
261 2/8	42 4/8 · 41 3/8	33 4/8	6 · 6	Costilla County	CO	Timothy L. Walters	1985	7312
261 2/8	44 6/8 · 44 1/8	34 0/8	5 · 5	Cibola County	NM	Duane T. Corley	1986	7312
261 2/8	46 2/8 · 44 3/8	37 6/8	6 · 6	Sheridan County	WY	Mike Barrett	1988	7312

754

AMERICAN ELK (TYPICAL ANTLERS)

Minimum Score 260
Continued

SCORE	LENGTH OF R MAIN BEAM L		INSIDE SPREAD	NUMBER OF R POINTS L		AREA	STATE/ PROVINCE	HUNTER'S NAME	DATE	RANK
261 2/8	41 4/8	41 4/8	29 0/8	6	6	Colfax County	NM	Ronald Ralston	1994	7312
261 2/8	42 2/8	42 1/8	39 4/8	5	5	Butte County	ID	George L. Decker	1999	7312
261 2/8	38 5/8	41 2/8	36 4/8	6	6	Colfax County	NM	Mike Jurica	2003	7312
261 2/8	45 7/8	43 3/8	33 0/8	5	7	Fergus County	MT	Gary Bishop	2003	7312
261 1/8	37 7/8	36 2/8	37 7/8	6	6	Jackson County	CO	Knut A. Paulsen	1975	7320
261 1/8	44 1/8	43 1/8	36 7/8	6	7	Caribou County	ID	Richard T. Vance	1975	7320
261 1/8	41 1/8	42 6/8	35 5/8	6	6	Clearwater County	ID	Steve Eiede	1988	7320
261 1/8	41 5/8	40 6/8	40 2/8	6	7	Lewis & Clark County	MT	Sonny Templeton	1991	7320
261 1/8	41 3/8	43 4/8	40 5/8	5	6	Catron County	NM	Robert J. Castle	2000	7320
261 0/8	46 6/8	45 6/8	32 4/8	6	5	Saguache County	CO	Irene M. Blaskowski	1990	7325
261 0/8	46 0/8	45 1/8	36 2/8	6	6	Clearwater County	ID	Don Leedham	1991	7325
261 0/8	44 2/8	42 6/8	38 6/8	5	5	Sublette County	WY	Kim A. Glasgow	1991	7325
261 0/8	47 7/8	40 6/8	37 1/8	7	6	Taos County	NM	David Muzny	1994	7325
261 0/8	37 0/8	37 2/8	35 0/8	6	6	Tuchodi River	BC	Scott Ebert	1994	7325
261 0/8	39 3/8	38 4/8	33 2/8	6	6	Grand County	CO	Raymond C. Reading	1998	7325
261 0/8	42 6/8	43 1/8	35 4/8	6	7	Rio Blanco County	CO	Larry Dominguez	2000	7325
261 0/8	39 5/8	39 4/8	37 4/8	6	6	Boulder County	CO	Rockie Bliss	2002	7325
261 0/8	39 0/8	38 4/8	41 0/8	6	6	Lincoln County	MT	Jerry Brown	2004	7325
261 0/8	41 3/8	42 7/8	33 0/8	6	6	Bear Lake County	ID	Eric Hansen	2004	7325
*261 0/8	42 5/8	42 5/8	37 2/8	6	6	Montrose County	CO	Edward McQuillan	2005	7325
261 0/8	41 1/8	43 2/8	33 0/8	6	6	Gunnison County	CO	Dave Hatch	2006	7325
261 0/8	41 6/8	42 0/8	30 6/8	6	6	Grant County	OR	Rick Herron	2007	7325
*261 0/8	43 5/8	43 7/8	36 4/8	6	6	La Plata County	CO	Terry Grimes	2007	7325
*261 0/8	36 6/8	41 6/8	36 0/8	6	6	Douglas County	OR	Graham Payer	2008	7325
261 0/8	40 2/8	40 3/8	36 6/8	6	6	Jackson County	CO	Freddie D. Lay	2009	7325
260 7/8	37 6/8	37 6/8	34 3/8	6	6	Grant County	OR	Colby Moulton	1986	7341
260 7/8	41 7/8	42 0/8	38 7/8	6	6	Pitkin County	CO	Jim Plett	1987	7341
260 7/8	41 2/8	41 1/8	31 3/8	6	6	Madison County	MT	Chester Graham	1992	7341
260 7/8	38 0/8	38 1/8	42 5/8	6	6	San Miguel County	CO	Wayne Carlton	1993	7341
260 7/8	44 3/8	45 0/8	35 1/8	6	6	Dolores County	CO	Scott Hawthorne	1994	7341
260 7/8	36 7/8	37 7/8	38 3/8	7	8	Franklin County	ID	James R. Keller	1995	7341
260 7/8	40 2/8	39 6/8	35 1/8	5	5	Grant County	NM	Harold L. Sides	1996	7341
260 7/8	44 0/8	41 2/8	36 1/8	6	6	Park County	MT	Richard Backes	2006	7341
260 7/8	40 7/8	39 2/8	34 1/8	6	7	Musselshell County	MT	Troy Danielson	2008	7341
260 7/8	44 5/8	43 7/8	36 3/8	6	6	Crook County	WY	Gordon L. Doyle	2010	7341
260 6/8	40 4/8	44 6/8	30 2/8	7	7	Coconino County	AZ	James Casady	1978	7351
260 6/8	38 0/8	37 3/8	34 0/8	6	6	Converse County	WY	Russell Burghart	1983	7351
260 6/8	38 0/8	37 5/8	34 2/8	6	6	Clearwater County	ID	Chuck Lynde	1988	7351
260 6/8	40 2/8	40 2/8	35 6/8	6	6	Beaverhead County	MT	Marvin Hearon	1992	7351
260 6/8	42 7/8	41 6/8	33 6/8	6	6	Gallatin County	MT	Edd L. Clack	1993	7351
260 6/8	42 7/8	43 1/8	36 4/8	5	5	Lewis & Clark County	MT	James Gravatt	1993	7351
260 6/8	48 2/8	48 0/8	39 4/8	5	6	Linn County	OR	Joe Etter II	1994	7351
260 6/8	40 7/8	39 7/8	36 4/8	6	6	Park County	MT	Barry S. Schultz	1994	7351
260 6/8	47 2/8	45 4/8	32 2/8	5	6	Archuleta County	CO	Darla Bramwell	1996	7351
260 6/8	43 6/8	41 4/8	36 6/8	6	6	Rio Arriba County	NM	Bob Hubbard	1997	7351
260 6/8	40 7/8	40 4/8	30 4/8	6	6	Grant County	OR	Thomas E. Sutherland	2001	7351
260 6/8	40 6/8	38 5/8	32 6/8	5	6	Coconino County	AZ	Mike Hansen	2002	7351
260 6/8	37 7/8	38 0/8	31 6/8	6	6	Yakima County	WA	Eric Nyberg	2003	7351
*260 6/8	37 0/8	37 1/8	30 1/8	7	6	Reserve	SAS	Jonas Prysliak	2008	7351
*260 6/8	44 4/8	44 7/8	30 6/8	6	6	Phillips County	MT	Robert Hohmann	2008	7351
260 5/8	40 5/8	42 0/8	34 7/8	6	6	Kimberley	BC	Rick Hammond	1986	7366
260 5/8	38 1/8	38 4/8	38 1/8	6	6	Catron County	NM	Michael J. Bradeen	1990	7366
260 5/8	40 6/8	40 4/8	34 3/8	6	6	Mineral County	MT	Chris W. Dix	1992	7366
260 5/8	36 2/8	37 2/8	34 0/8	7	7	Phillips County	MT	Mark Meyer	1995	7366
260 5/8	45 0/8	44 2/8	36 1/8	6	5	Catron County	NM	David M. Bufkin	1996	7366
260 5/8	38 6/8	37 5/8	36 5/8	6	6	Franklin County	ID	William L. Watters	2000	7366
260 5/8	42 5/8	43 2/8	30 5/8	6	7	Wallowa County	OR	Greg Osburn	2001	7366
260 5/8	42 7/8	41 3/8	37 7/8	6	6	Catron County	NM	Jerry Giovannoni	2003	7366
*260 5/8	41 6/8	42 3/8	38 5/8	6	6	Custer County	SD	Chris Vanwormer	2005	7366
*260 5/8	40 5/8	44 1/8	33 1/8	5	5	Valhalla Centre	ALB	Jim Foshee	2006	7366
260 5/8	41 3/8	40 6/8	46 3/8	6	6	Park County	WY	Toni L. Bell	2010	7366
260 4/8	40 4/8	40 7/8	38 0/8	6	6	Blaine County	ID	Wesley Moore	1986	7377
260 4/8	40 6/8	40 1/8	34 0/8	6	7	Fergus County	MT	Jerry Knerr	1987	7377
260 4/8	40 2/8	37 4/8	34 0/8	6	6	Elmore County	ID	Roger W. Atwood	1988	7377
260 4/8	46 2/8	44 7/8	34 5/8	6	7	Montrose County	CO	David Henkie	1989	7377
260 4/8	38 6/8	38 5/8	33 6/8	6	6	Catron County	NM	Jerry G. Roberts	1992	7377
260 4/8	40 6/8	44 4/8	32 4/8	6	6	Coconino County	AZ	Patrick Donald Dufek	1992	7377
260 4/8	43 1/8	43 1/8	36 2/8	5	6	Sandoval County	NM	Mitchell Lee Chapman	1993	7377
260 4/8	41 1/8	42 5/8	35 7/8	7	6	Boulder County	CO	Bill J. Buck	1995	7377
260 4/8	37 2/8	38 5/8	35 4/8	6	5	Catron County	NM	Charlie Schlosser	1998	7377
260 4/8	41 5/8	39 2/8	33 3/8	6	6	Lincoln County	WY	James Michel Clark	2000	7377
260 4/8	46 5/8	48 1/8	33 4/8	6	6	Chouteau County	MT	David Campbell	2002	7377
260 4/8	40 7/8	41 1/8	32 0/8	5	6	Montrose County	CO	Jack Satterfield, Jr.	2004	7377
260 4/8	39 4/8	38 6/8	34 4/8	6	6	Eagle County	CO	Glenn Thurston	2004	7377
*260 4/8	37 6/8	37 4/8	30 2/8	6	6	Carbon County	WY	Terry J. Beaver	2005	7377
260 4/8	47 2/8	46 6/8	40 2/8	6	6	Lemhi County	ID	Benjamin C. Fahnholz	2006	7377
260 4/8	41 5/8	43 1/8	34 4/8	6	6	Park County	WY	James H. Langlois	2007	7377
260 3/8	38 4/8	38 7/8	30 7/8	6	6	Madison County	ID	Paul L. Beesley	1979	7393
260 3/8	42 2/8	41 5/8	32 7/8	6	6	Archuleta County	CO	Lester D. Hawkins, Jr.	1988	7393
260 3/8	37 5/8	40 0/8	37 7/8	6	6	Lewis & Clark County	MT	Jeff Jackson	1992	7393
260 3/8	42 0/8	40 5/8	39 1/8	6	6	Carbon County	UT	Kit Critchlow	1993	7393
260 3/8	42 5/8	47 6/8	36 0/8	8	6	Coconino County	AZ	Tony W. Zimbaro	1993	7393
260 3/8	46 2/8	46 3/8	33 3/8	6	5	Grant County	OR	Jerry W. Simmons	1995	7393
260 3/8	37 4/8	39 4/8	35 3/8	6	6	Catron County	NM	Kenneth Brongo	1998	7393
260 3/8	41 3/8	41 5/8	35 1/8	6	6	Ravalli County	MT	Joseph P. Ferraro	2001	7393
260 3/8	40 5/8	40 3/8	32 1/8	6	6	Otero County	NM	Duane Hopland	2002	7393
260 3/8	39 3/8	38 4/8	35 3/8	6	6	Caribou County	ID	Richard L. Phillippie	2002	7393
*260 3/8	42 2/8	42 5/8	33 3/8	6	5	Rio Arriba County	NM	Larry D. Sylvester	2005	7393
260 3/8	39 0/8	38 7/8	28 3/8	6	6	Albany County	WY	Ryan Johnson	2005	7393
*260 3/8	43 2/8	43 6/8	29 3/8	6	6	Park County	WY	Thomas Frieberger	2007	7393
260 3/8	36 1/8	39 2/8	30 3/8	6	6	Grand County	CO	Kevin J. Gee	2007	7393
260 2/8	41 2/8	41 4/8	37 0/8	6	6	Pitkin County	CO	Wayne MacDonnell	1987	7407
260 2/8	37 0/8	38 0/8	35 0/8	6	6	Rio Blanco County	CO	Charles R. Clark	1991	7407
260 2/8	46 1/8	46 2/8	35 4/8	5	6	Cibola County	NM	Reid S. Christopher, M.D.	1997	7407
260 2/8	39 6/8	39 4/8	38 4/8	6	6	Fremont County	WY	Patrick Sutter	2001	7407

AMERICAN ELK (TYPICAL ANTLERS)

Minimum Score 260

SCORE	R MAIN BEAM L	INSIDE SPREAD	R POINTS L	AREA	STATE/PROVINCE	HUNTER'S NAME	DATE	RANK
260 2/8	45 7/8 43 3/8	34 2/8	6 6	Taos County	NM	Tom Miranda	2004	7407
260 2/8	40 1/8 39 4/8	33 4/8	6 6	Larimer County	CO	Frank W. Harner, Jr.	2006	7407
260 2/8	40 5/8 41 1/8	34 4/8	6 6	Ravalli County	MT	Kirt Hoffmann	2006	7407
260 2/8	42 6/8 41 7/8	33 0/8	6 6	Rio Grande County	CO	Donald Stidman	2007	7407
260 1/8	44 1/8 43 2/8	37 5/8	6 6	Catron County	NM	Bob "Jake" Jacobsen	1989	7415
260 1/8	41 0/8 44 3/8	36 3/8	5 5	Catron County	NM	Jim Eppler	1990	7415
260 1/8	42 4/8 44 1/8	35 5/8	5 5	Idaho County	ID	Steven L. DeBauche	1992	7415
260 1/8	44 6/8 44 5/8	37 7/8	5 6	Rio Arriba County	NM	Thomas A. Hornby	1995	7415
260 1/8	47 1/8 46 2/8	35 6/8	5 7	Meagher County	MT	Robert Davison	1996	7415
260 1/8	39 3/8 39 3/8	34 7/8	6 7	Pembina County	ND	George E. Walker III	1997	7415
260 1/8	39 2/8 39 6/8	34 5/8	6 6	Valley County	MT	Dan Sturgis	1998	7415
260 1/8	39 7/8 39 4/8	33 3/8	6 6	Rio Arriba County	NM	Michael D. Brown	2000	7415
260 1/8	55 6/8 45 0/8	42 2/8	6 5	Coconino County	AZ	Steven E. Sheehy	2001	7415
*260 1/8	42 6/8 39 3/8	32 1/8	6 6	Montrose County	CO	Nicolas DiSanto	2006	7415
*260 1/8	37 6/8 38 1/8	34 7/8	6 6	Huerfano County	CO	James Wilhelm	2006	7415
260 1/8	40 5/8 43 0/8	36 5/8	5 6	Summit County	CO	Edward Pinckney	2007	7415
260 0/8	36 4/8 36 4/8	39 5/8	6 6	Grand County	CO	Kevin O'Connell	1981	7427
260 0/8	44 7/8 44 3/8	35 4/8	6 6	Catron County	NM	Duane "Corky" Richardson	1996	7427
260 0/8	38 7/8 39 3/8	38 4/8	5 6	Carbon County	UT	James L. Stowe	1998	7427
260 0/8	44 6/8 45 0/8	33 2/8	6 6	Caribou County	ID	Lyle E. Nygren, Jr.	1999	7427
260 0/8	39 6/8 41 1/8	32 6/8	6 6	Mineral County	CO	Pat Boudreau	2002	7427
*260 0/8	43 3/8 44 6/8	36 6/8	7 6	Rio Blanco County	CO	Michael A. Harenchar	2004	7427
260 0/8	41 1/8 40 4/8	31 4/8	6 6	Catron County	NM	Stephen Brecq	2004	7427
260 0/8	34 5/8 35 0/8	29 4/8	6 7	Catron County	NM	Brian Green	2005	7427
260 0/8	33 2/8 47 4/8	41 6/8	5 6	Routt County	CO	Robert W. Unger, Jr.	2005	7427

AMERICAN ELK (TYPICAL VELVET ANTLERS)

Minimum Score 260

SCORE	LENGTH OF MAIN BEAM R / L	INSIDE SPREAD	NUMBER OF POINTS R / L	AREA	STATE/ PROVINCE	HUNTER'S NAME	DATE	RANK
*349 5/8	52 2/8 / 51 0/8	40 5/8	6 / 6	Carbon County	UT	Calvin Grogan	2008	*

POPE & YOUNG CLUB

442 0/8

PANEL MEASURED

Official Scoring System for Bowhunting North American Big Game

NON-TYPICAL AMERICAN ELK

MINIMUM SCORE 335

☐ IN VELVET

24TH RECORDING PERIOD 2003-0...

Abnormal Points	Right Antler	Left Antler
	2 4/8	1 5/8
	13 3/8	3 6/8
	7 5/8	11 2/8
		2 0/8
SUBTOTALS	4/8	1 5/8
E. TOTAL	42 1/8	

				COLUMN 1	COLUMN 2	COLUMN 3	COLUMN 4
	SEE OTHER SIDE FOR INSTRUCTIONS			Spread Credit	Right Antler	Left Antler	Difference
A. No. Points on Right Antler	9	No. Points Left Antler	10				
B. Tip to Tip Spread	58 0/8	C. Greatest Spread	5 0/				
D. Inside Spread of Main Beams	54 1/8	SPREAD CREDIT MAY NOT EXCEED LONGER		54 1/8			
F. Length of Main Beam					55		1 6/8
G-1. Length of First Point					/8	16 6/8	2 0/8
G-2. Length of Second Point					1/8	20 0/8	2 7/8
G-3. Length of Third Point					/8	17 7/8	1 7/8
G-4. Length of Fourth Point					/8	22 5/8	1 0/8
G-5. Length of Fifth Point						18 6/8	2 2/8
G-6. Length of Sixth Point, If Present							
G-7. Length of Seventh Point, If Present							
H-1. Circumference at Smallest Place Be...							
H-2. Circumference at Smallest Place Bet...							
H-3. Circumference at Smallest Place Bet...							
H-4. Circumference at Smallest Place Bet...							

ADD	Column 1	54 1/8
	Column 2	177 2/8
	Column 3	181 3/8
	Subtotal	412 6/8
SUBTRACT Column 4		12 7/8
	Subtotal	399 7/8
Add Line E Total		42 1/8
FINAL SCORE		**442 0/8**

WORLD RECORD AMERICAN ELK
Non-Typical Antlers
Score: 442 0/8
Location: Coconino County, Arizona
Date: 2003
Hunter: Nick Franklin

Non-Typical American Elk

by Nick Franklin

I just received the news I had been drawn for one of the toughest units to get a tag in the Arizona draw. Then started the sleepless nights dreaming of big bulls screaming and rutting.

I started my scouting by going out every weekend and any other chance I had to slip up to my unit. My brother Charlie and I gathered as much information about the area as we could. No big bulls materialized during my scouting but, as the season got closer, they started to rut and become more visible. I could tell from the horn growth on even the young bulls that this was going to be a great year to have a tag. I guess it was meant to be.

The season started uneventful. I was seeing nice bulls everyday but had no good shots at anything I thought was worth taking so early in the season. Then, about a week into the hunt, my friend Travis joined me. He arrived in camp during the middle of the night and planned to skip the morning hunt to get some rest. Something changed his mind, though, and we both headed out.

Getting out to our area about an hour before daylight, we sat down and heard only one faint bugle. We decided to move up the ridge, where I had patterned the elk crossing each morning. As the dark turned to gray we heard a distant bugle. We each pointed in opposite directions, so decided to "split the difference" and off we went. As it started to get light, we heard the bull bugle several more times, helping us to pin down the direction. We knew we had to get there before they started to feed off, so our speed increased. Just as we stopped to catch our breath, Travis said "did you hear that?" We crouched down just in time to let two satellite bulls walk right by at a short distance. As we started to get closer we saw very fresh sign. Travis picked it up and wiped it on both of us…this was getting real serious, real fast! Just then we caught movement and another satellite bull walked within fifteen yards of us. As we moved up, we started to see some cows and heard two bulls crashing and fighting. Then Travis whispered "Oh my gosh! It's huge! I'm counting ten or twelve points!" Just then another bull bugled behind us. This worked to our advantage (I guess it was meant to be). That bugle brought the huge bull around to our side of the cows. At about 80 yards he started to rake some trees. Each time he raked a tree, I moved up a little closer, until I was within range. Everything was perfect. He had his head down as I drew and released. Everything stood still and the bull just turned and looked the other way at the arrow bouncing into the trees behind him. I removed another arrow from the quiver just as the bull started to run. Travis cow called and the bull collapsed 40 yards away. The first arrow had done its job. Travis starting hugging me, as I stood there in shock. It was like it was meant to be!

AMERICAN ELK (NON-TYPICAL ANTLERS)

Minimum Score 300

Cervus elaphus nelsoni and certain related subspecies

SCORE	LENGTH OF MAIN BEAM R	L	INSIDE SPREAD	NUMBER OF POINTS R	L	AREA	STATE/ PROVINCE	HUNTER'S NAME	DATE	RANK
442 0/8	55 1/8	53 3/8	54 1/8	9	10	Coconino County	AZ	Nick Franklin	2003	1
422 6/8	49 2/8	50 2/8	40 5/8	9	9	Navajo County	AZ	Clay R. Heuett	2003	2
420 7/8	52 6/8	52 4/8	37 7/8	8	6	Millard County	UT	Jimmie R. Ryan	2007	3
420 5/8	57 5/8	58 1/8	39 2/8	9	8	Shoshone County	ID	Steven W. Mullin	1981	4
419 5/8	53 1/8	51 6/8	39 4/8	8	10	Coconino County	AZ	James L. Ludvigson	1985	5
417 0/8	56 0/8	56 1/8	51 7/8	8	7	Coconino County	AZ	Brady J. Dupke	1993	6
414 7/8	50 7/8	50 0/8	42 5/8	8	8	Iron County	UT	Troy Ence	2007	7
414 5/8	54 3/8	56 2/8	39 4/8	7	8	Flagstaff	ALB	Brent Kuntz	2002	8
412 4/8	55 1/8	54 0/8	47 7/8	8	9	Kittitas County	WA	Jeffery G. Thorpe	2003	9
411 2/8	56 5/8	57 5/8	45 1/8	8	7	Coconino County	AZ	Mike Drake	2005	10
*410 0/8	58 0/8	56 7/8	42 1/8	7	7	Gila County	AZ	Philip Brailsford	2008	11
409 7/8	50 1/8	50 1/8	46 4/8	7	8	White Pine County	NV	Randy Ulmer	2003	12
409 2/8	55 2/8	56 4/8	48 6/8	8	8	Coconino County	AZ	Robert Duane Hartwig	2004	13
409 0/8	54 7/8	53 5/8	40 4/8	8	7	Lincoln County	MT	Terry V. Crooks	1996	14
*407 7/8	50 4/8	48 7/8	50 2/8	8	8	White Pine County	NV	Quentin Jones	2010	15
405 6/8	47 7/8	52 3/8	45 1/8	6	8	Hill County	MT	Brendan V. Burns	2000	17
405 5/8	57 2/8	54 3/8	50 5/8	7	6	Catron County	NM	Dusty Mathis	2004	18
*404 0/8	51 6/8	47 2/8	40 7/8	8	9	Cibola County	NM	Lacy Harber	2005	19
403 7/8	59 4/8	58 1/8	33 6/8	7	7	Catron County	NM	Charles "Jeff" Sillivent	2006	20
403 6/8	56 4/8	57 4/8	54 4/8	7	7	Mora County	NM	Zane T. Streater	2008	21
403 0/8	49 0/8	50 2/8	39 0/8	8	9	Powell County	MT	Donald Roberson	1987	22
402 6/8	51 2/8	52 2/8	42 3/8	7	7	Coconino County	AZ	Dion M. Laney	2007	23
402 5/8	48 7/8	48 2/8	42 1/8	8	8	Sierra County	NM	Joey L. Lange	1999	24
401 1/8	52 3/8	52 2/8	47 5/8	7	7	Carbon County	UT	Dan Green	2004	25
*401 0/8	54 4/8	57 4/8	34 3/8	7	8	Gila County	AZ	Preston Mercer	2008	26
398 1/8	53 4/8	52 2/8	42 5/8	8	8	White Pine County	NV	Brian Harwood	1998	27
*398 0/8	48 2/8	52 2/8	43 1/8	8	7	Cassia County	ID	K. C. Ramsey	2008	28
397 5/8	47 7/8	56 4/8	37 0/8	8	8	Sierra County	NM	Neil Lawson	2005	29
*397 3/8	51 0/8	54 5/8	36 2/8	6	8	Cache County	UT	Cory Meacham	2007	30
*397 2/8	49 1/8	45 6/8	39 6/8	14	12	Columbia County	WA	Patrick Naumann	2010	31
396 6/8	55 6/8	56 1/8	39 2/8	7	7	Coconino County	AZ	Dustin Loftis	2004	32
396 5/8	52 0/8	50 6/8	54 3/8	7	7	Petroleum County	MT	D. "Mitch" Kottas	2005	33
395 3/8	55 7/8	55 7/8	49 7/8	6	7	Yavapai County	AZ	Don Waggoner	2000	34
394 4/8	46 0/8	47 2/8	35 1/8	9	9	Sandridge	MAN	Joel Kayer	2003	35
394 2/8	54 3/8	55 4/8	34 6/8	7	7	Natrona County	WY	Steven Lamb	2006	36
391 7/8	40 5/8	40 1/8	34 3/8	13	11	Camp Hughs	MAN	Brent Maxwell	1991	37
391 4/8	50 1/8	53 4/8	35 1/8	9	7	Garfield County	MT	D. Mitch Kottas	1995	38
391 1/8	49 4/8	49 5/8	46 3/8	8	7	Fergus County	MT	Matthew McWilliams	2001	39
*391 0/8	49 2/8	52 3/8	40 1/8	6	8	Graham County	AZ	Jay Scott	2006	40
389 5/8	52 4/8	54 0/8	35 6/8	7	7	Douglas County	CO	Mark Martin	1998	41
389 1/8	53 0/8	52 5/8	56 4/8	8	6	Garfield County	UT	Kyle Bone	2008	42
388 6/8	50 5/8	48 1/8	45 0/8	7	7	Shoshone County	ID	Roger R. Davis	1978	43
388 4/8	50 2/8	50 5/8	42 0/8	7	6	Saguache County	CO	Tony Heil	2000	44
387 7/8	52 4/8	49 3/8	48 6/8	7	7	Owyhee County	ID	Gregory Ryan Pimentel	2006	45
387 6/8	55 0/8	54 7/8	41 6/8	8	8	Clackamas County	OR	Kris Baillie	2010	46
*387 5/8	59 6/8	57 6/8	39 1/8	7	8	Navajo County	AZ	Ron Carpenter	2008	47
387 4/8	53 0/8	52 5/8	38 4/8	6	9	Lincoln County	NV	Cory Lytle	1998	48
387 2/8	48 6/8	48 3/8	37 3/8	7	7	Catron County	NM	Robert J. Brooks	1992	49
386 7/8	45 2/8	42 6/8	37 2/8	7	11	Comanche County	OK	Patrick Sanden	2007	50
386 6/8	52 6/8	50 7/8	38 4/8	7	7	White Pine County	NV	Garth K. Carter	2008	51
386 5/8	48 2/8	48 5/8	38 0/8	8	8	Albany County	WY	Don Fischer	1998	52
386 2/8	49 6/8	51 4/8	44 2/8	6	8	Socorro County	NM	William H. Williams III	2005	53
385 5/8	50 4/8	49 7/8	35 4/8	8	7	Petroleum County	MT	Gregory A. Herrin	1997	54
385 4/8	52 2/8	53 3/8	45 2/8	8	7	Garfield County	UT	Dallen M. Baugh	2004	55
385 3/8	56 2/8	53 3/8	43 0/8	8	7	Kittitas County	WA	Douglas Burnett	2004	56
385 2/8	59 6/8	53 1/8	45 1/8	8	9	Siskiyou County	CA	Gary Turner, Jr.	2004	57
384 7/8	60 3/8	55 4/8	36 3/8	7	8	Fergus County	MT	James "Rusty" South	1999	58
384 2/8	52 6/8	49 3/8	41 4/8	8	6	Chouteau County	MT	Bill Strong	2001	59
384 1/8	46 7/8	45 2/8	43 0/8	8	8	Garfield County	MT	Bill Waigle	2006	60
384 0/8	52 3/8	52 4/8	37 7/8	7	7	Albany County	WY	Justin Schwartzkopf	2004	61
*382 4/8	54 1/8	54 4/8	40 1/8	7	7	Catron County	NM	Tony Cutbirth	2005	62
381 7/8	54 2/8	54 1/8	42 2/8	7	7	Coconino County	AZ	Dick Kirby	1992	63
381 7/8	53 6/8	54 1/8	44 5/8	8	8	Catron County	NM	Anthony J. Berardis, Jr.	1997	63
381 3/8	52 7/8	51 5/8	41 5/8	7	8	Coconino County	AZ	David A. Niemann	1990	64
381 3/8	49 0/8	49 6/8	39 1/8	9	7	Garfield County	UT	Scott McClintic	2003	64
381 2/8	50 1/8	46 4/8	35 0/8	10	8	Navajo County	AZ	Robert J. Rush	2005	66
381 2/8	55 7/8	55 6/8	37 2/8	8	7	Garfield County	UT	Jacob Love	2007	66
381 1/8	55 2/8	60 1/8	55 0/8	8	7	Catron County	NM	Steve Borden	2005	68
*381 0/8	50 1/8	50 5/8	42 1/8	8	9	Catron County	NM	Jim Knief	2005	69
380 6/8	51 0/8	51 0/8	39 7/8	8	6	Catron County	NM	Mike Garretson	1996	70
380 4/8	55 1/8	53 7/8	58 6/8	7	9	Gallatin County	MT	Jeff Cook	2005	71
380 3/8	54 2/8	54 5/8	43 2/8	8	7	Socorro County	NM	George Rude	1994	72
378 3/8	58 5/8	56 0/8	43 2/8	6	8	Coconino County	AZ	Scott Schuff	1998	73
377 7/8	46 7/8	45 0/8	50 1/8	7	8	Park County	CO	Jess David Hargrave	2007	74
377 3/8	50 7/8	51 1/8	32 6/8	9	8	Huerfano County	CO	Brett Wyka	1996	75
*376 7/8	51 6/8	54 1/8	40 6/8	7	7	Garfield County	UT	Gary Felice	2007	76
376 0/8	48 0/8	49 3/8	57 0/8	7	7	Catron County	NM	Shaun D. Finch	1995	77
376 0/8	54 3/8	58 4/8	36 6/8	7	8	Gila County	AZ	Ray Potter	2001	77
*375 7/8	60 0/8	57 0/8	36 6/8	9	7	Greenlee County	AZ	Jerry Hathcock	2008	79
375 5/8	53 6/8	49 4/8	40 5/8	7	6	Catron County	NM	Mike R. Scorsella	2004	80
*375 4/8	52 4/8	53 0/8	35 4/8	7	6	Apache County	AZ	Jeff Wentworth	2008	81
375 3/8	55 1/8	52 2/8	41 5/8	7	7	Navajo County	AZ	Bob Dawson	2001	82
374 5/8	52 1/8	52 2/8	44 4/8	8	9	Catron County	NM	William C. King III	1997	83
374 3/8	51 6/8	49 5/8	52 3/8	7	8	Fergus County	MT	Kim Latterell	1999	84
374 3/8	52 2/8	54 7/8	43 4/8	8	6	Elko County	NV	Tim Iveson	2001	84
374 0/8	50 6/8	49 5/8	42 0/8	6	7	Lewis & Clark County	MT	Jay Roberson	2001	86
373 4/8	53 0/8	50 6/8	43 3/8	7	7	Johnson County	WY	Cenny Burnell	2003	87
373 4/8	49 7/8	50 7/8	37 6/8	6	8	Big Horn County	MT	Duane Heitzman	2004	87
373 2/8	47 1/8	47 6/8	41 2/8	8	8	Lincoln County	MT	Larry M. Monroe	1992	89
373 0/8	53 5/8	52 7/8	43 5/8	6	8	Navajo County	AZ	Randy Ulmer	1994	90
372 3/8	49 1/8	52 5/8	49 0/8	6	7	Navajo County	AZ	Paul Allen	1997	91
372 3/8	53 4/8	49 6/8	37 2/8	8	9	Pueblo County	CO	Ron R. Minton	2009	91
371 5/8	52 6/8	53 4/8	42 4/8	10	9	White Pine County	NV	Anthony L. Mudd	2004	93
371 1/8	53 0/8	49 5/8	48 0/8	9	9	Sierra County	NM	Kevin L. Keyes	1989	94
371 1/8	50 0/8	49 2/8	42 5/8	7	7	Catron County	NM	Eddie Collins	1991	94

AMERICAN ELK (NON-TYPICAL ANTLERS)

Minimum Score 300
Continued

SCORE	LENGTH OF R MAIN BEAM L	INSIDE SPREAD	NUMBER OF R POINTS L	AREA	STATE/PROVINCE	HUNTER'S NAME	DATE	RANK
371 0/8	48 1/8 50 4/8	48 5/8	7 6	Mora County	NM	George P. Mann	1990	96
370 7/8	51 6/8 52 6/8	40 6/8	8 8	Millard County	UT	Jeff Mitchell	1997	97
370 3/8	53 0/8 54 0/8	47 3/8	8 9	Gila County	AZ	John Bush	1989	98
370 3/8	50 4/8 51 0/8	43 7/8	7 7	Carbon County	WY	Lee Ford	2005	98
370 1/8	52 4/8 52 5/8	33 7/8	7 7	Navajo County	AZ	Adam Moro	1999	100
369 4/8	51 6/8 53 7/8	44 4/8	7 7	Otero County	NM	Leland Wood	1997	101
369 4/8	56 7/8 55 4/8	47 1/8	8 7	San Juan County	UT	Dennis Doherty	2005	101
*369 3/8	52 4/8 52 6/8	32 2/8	7 8	Phillips County	MT	Scott Henning	2005	103
369 1/8	50 0/8 48 5/8	40 6/8	8 8	Fergus County	MT	Pete Walter	1998	104
368 7/8	54 7/8 52 1/8	40 6/8	9 10	Jefferson County	MT	Leroy Ballard	2000	105
368 3/8	54 1/8 56 4/8	39 7/8	8 6	Custer County	ID	Scott Griggs	1992	106
368 2/8	49 3/8 48 3/8	37 7/8	7 8	Catron County	NM	Craig J. Cooper	1997	107
367 7/8	53 1/8 53 0/8	41 3/8	7 10	Catron County	NM	Steve Mathis	1997	108
367 2/8	51 1/8 50 4/8	40 0/8	7 6	White Pine County	NV	George H. Fujii	1998	109
*367 1/8	58 3/8 54 4/8	37 3/8	8 7	Catron County	NM	Michael Fischer	2000	110
367 0/8	55 6/8 55 1/8	38 5/8	7 7	Catron County	NM	Shayne Franzoy	1994	111
366 6/8	50 3/8 51 3/8	42 6/8	7 7	Yavapai County	AZ	Jason Danielson	2004	112
366 3/8	54 2/8 51 3/8	48 2/8	7 7	Garfield County	UT	Kurt Fisher	2001	113
366 1/8	46 2/8 45 4/8	44 1/8	6 7	Catron County	NM	Craig C. Sanchez	1997	114
365 5/8	51 0/8 48 6/8	38 6/8	6 7	Fergus County	MT	Donny Roy	1999	115
365 2/8	49 6/8 49 6/8	39 5/8	8 8	Fergus County	MT	Brent Sudduth	2003	116
365 2/8	48 2/8 45 2/8	34 6/8	8 11	Coconino County	AZ	Lance E. Swinney	2007	116
365 0/8	44 3/8 44 0/8	41 6/8	7 8	Lincoln County	NM	Kurt Hollis	1992	118
364 7/8	50 4/8 50 5/8	36 1/8	7 6	Lane County	OR	Jack Stewart	2006	119
364 6/8	54 7/8 53 1/8	42 5/8	6 7	Fergus County	MT	Jerry Knerr	1997	120
364 6/8	53 0/8 51 7/8	33 3/8	8 10	King County	WA	Don Goodin	1998	120
364 4/8	53 1/8 53 5/8	36 0/8	8 8	Coconino County	AZ	David Ferrario	1994	122
364 3/8	50 1/8 50 0/8	29 2/8	6 8	Catron County	NM	Wayne K. Curtis	1988	123
364 0/8	53 7/8 56 3/8	37 4/8	7 7	Cibola County	NM	Mike Worrell	1998	124
363 6/8	49 4/8 52 0/8	41 7/8	8 8	Coconino County	AZ	Dean Dunaway	1993	125
363 6/8	54 6/8 52 6/8	38 7/8	8 8	Navajo County	AZ	Chad Jasperson	1997	125
363 6/8	53 1/8 53 6/8	40 5/8	8 8	Columbia County	WA	Travis A. Smith	2008	125
362 6/8	52 0/8 50 1/8	40 1/8	7 8	Teton County	WY	Frank J. Cina	1999	128
362 6/8	50 6/8 52 2/8	41 4/8	7 6	Gallatin County	MT	Kurt D. Rued	2001	128
362 0/8	46 1/8 47 5/8	33 0/8	7 7	Catron County	NM	Dave Holt	1997	130
*361 7/8	47 6/8 44 2/8	35 2/8	8 7	Alamosa County	CO	Ivan Johnson	2003	131
361 3/8	45 6/8 45 1/8	39 5/8	8 8	Nez Perce County	ID	Randy Hollibaugh	1989	132
361 3/8	47 1/8 48 3/8	35 4/8	8 7	Apache County	AZ	Tom Ensman	1995	132
361 2/8	49 2/8 49 3/8	33 4/8	7 7	White Pine County	NV	James Ronald Woodford	2003	134
361 0/8	48 6/8 47 2/8	41 2/8	8 7	Flathead County	MT	Chester G. Fossum, Jr.	1992	135
*360 6/8	47 6/8 43 7/8	32 1/8	8 8	Rio Blanco County	CO	Mike Strawbridge	2009	136
360 1/8	51 1/8 52 0/8	47 5/8	7 7	Tooele County	UT	James Smith	2003	137
*359 6/8	52 2/8 52 1/8	46 5/8	7 7	Coconino County	AZ	Keith Bessent	2004	138
*359 5/8	49 6/8 49 4/8	43 4/8	6 9	Lincoln County	NV	Jerry Menesini	2003	139
359 5/8	46 6/8 45 7/8	41 4/8	7 9	Elko County	NV	Jim Buonamici	2005	139
359 3/8	51 1/8 44 4/8	37 2/8	8 7	Catron County	NM	Ronald M. Gerdes	1992	141
358 5/8	48 4/8 47 1/8	36 3/8	7 8	Rich County	UT	Paul L. Bowden	1998	142
356 2/8	50 2/8 50 3/8	37 5/8	8 8	Madison County	MT	Scott Covey	2007	143
356 1/8	55 5/8 49 7/8	35 2/8	8 7	Greenlee County	AZ	Robert M. Dryden	1995	144
356 1/8	52 0/8 51 0/8	50 2/8	7 6	Jefferson County	CO	Corey I. Guildner	2008	144
356 0/8	51 2/8 52 4/8	44 3/8	7 6	Garfield County	UT	Jerry Simmons	2005	146
355 6/8	47 2/8 46 1/8	39 0/8	7 8	Umatilla County	OR	Guy P. Hurlbert	1998	147
354 5/8	46 4/8 46 6/8	46 2/8	6 8	Catron County	NM	David L. Story	2005	148
354 2/8	47 6/8 50 3/8	37 7/8	7 7	Duchesne County	UT	Sean P. Davis	2004	149
354 1/8	54 1/8 51 1/8	34 5/8	7 7	Wallowa County	OR	Woody Ehrhart	2009	150
353 5/8	50 0/8 48 4/8	37 4/8	7 6	Coconino County	AZ	Russell Richardson	1995	151
353 5/8	50 0/8 51 4/8	36 1/8	7 6	Wasatch County	UT	Jeff Cummings	2003	151
352 4/8	44 4/8 46 7/8	33 1/8	9 8	Flathead County	MT	Mark J. Holderbaum	2000	153
351 6/8	51 0/8 47 7/8	45 1/8	7 7	Lake County	OR	Jack Hodnett	1998	154
351 2/8	46 0/8 47 7/8	38 6/8	7 6	Fergus County	MT	D. Mitch Kottas	2003	155
350 4/8	48 1/8 49 0/8	31 3/8	6 7	Socorro County	NM	Marvin H. Walter	1998	156
350 4/8	50 1/8 49 6/8	35 3/8	8 8	Lake County	CO	Ray Douglas	2008	156
350 3/8	53 4/8 49 0/8	42 2/8	7 7	Coconino County	AZ	James D. Hamberlin	2001	158
350 0/8	40 3/8 39 0/8	40 2/8	7 7	Meagher County	MT	Steven W. Prunty	1996	159
349 4/8	49 5/8 51 1/8	38 6/8	7 8	Sweet Grass County	MT	Mark Mager	2001	160
349 2/8	45 4/8 45 0/8	42 1/8	7 8	Garfield County	MT	D. Mitch Kottas	1996	161
349 2/8	37 5/8 34 6/8	35 6/8	7 9	Clackamas County	OR	James A. Walls	2005	161
348 4/8	49 7/8 48 2/8	42 0/8	7 8	Gunnison County	CO	Terry "The Hawk" Cramer	2000	163
348 0/8	53 1/8 60 1/8	43 2/8	6 7	Fergus County	MT	D. Mitch Kottas	2000	164
347 3/8	53 1/8 53 4/8	42 5/8	7 7	Fergus County	MT	John Fleharty	1992	165
346 5/8	50 0/8 49 5/8	40 1/8	7 8	Fergus County	MT	Jess Knerr	1999	166
346 3/8	50 2/8 49 5/8	44 1/8	7 7	Garfield County	UT	Eric R. Nielsen	2000	167
346 2/8	48 7/8 49 4/8	39 3/8	7 7	Shoshone County	ID	Dan Payne	1995	168
346 2/8	54 2/8 57 1/8	38 0/8	7 9	Catron County	NM	Jerry Leair	1999	168
346 1/8	51 6/8 52 1/8	39 2/8	8 8	Union County	OR	Randy L. Egelhoff	2004	170
346 0/8	54 0/8 57 3/8	45 1/8	5 7	Socorro County	NM	Doug Aikin	1997	171
345 7/8	47 2/8 47 5/8	50 4/8	8 9	Valley County	ID	Julian Salutregui	1998	172
345 6/8	50 0/8 50 5/8	45 2/8	8 6	Coconino County	AZ	Ken Kea	1999	173
345 4/8	48 0/8 49 4/8	31 6/8	7 7	Coconino County	AZ	Barry Stonehouse	1992	174
345 2/8	44 2/8 45 2/8	46 6/8	8 8	Catron County	NM	Jerry Leair	1998	175
345 1/8	49 0/8 49 4/8	41 7/8	8 6	Lewis & Clark County	MT	Ray Lee	2002	175
345 0/8	48 4/8 51 0/8	30 4/8	7 8	Grant County	NM	Charles T. Wood	1998	177
344 5/8	42 0/8 41 7/8	34 4/8	7 10	Catron County	NM	Glenn Isler	1993	178
344 3/8	51 2/8 48 1/8	33 7/8	8 7	Elko County	NV	Kent Arrien	1996	179
344 0/8	44 7/8 47 7/8	38 1/8	6 7	White Pine County	NV	Mark Kyle	2002	180
*343 2/8	52 2/8 50 5/8	37 6/8	8 7	Sandoval County	NM	Brandon Wynn	2004	181
342 7/8	52 7/8 51 4/8	38 7/8	7 7	Greenlee County	AZ	Bill Golden	1990	182
342 7/8	49 7/8 49 0/8	35 0/8	6 7	Phillips County	MT	Lynn Paris	2000	183
342 7/8	49 2/8 49 4/8	35 7/8	7 6	Carbon County	UT	Jeff Cisneros	2005	183
342 5/8	50 4/8 53 2/8	34 2/8	7 7	Washakie County	WY	Derrik Ducheneau	2005	185
342 1/8	48 3/8 55 1/8	40 3/8	8 6	San Juan County	UT	Mark B. Anderson	2003	186
342 1/8	45 1/8 46 7/8	40 2/8	6 7	Greenlee County	AZ	Bill Bishop, Sr.	2003	186
342 0/8	47 3/8 45 6/8	38 3/8	7 7	Mineral County	MT	Sou A. Thao	2001	188
341 2/8	44 7/8 45 0/8	35 2/8	7 7	Franklin County	ID	Benton Christensen	1999	189
340 6/8	48 1/8 48 4/8	38 2/8	7 7	Catron County	NM	Vito Andriano	2003	190

AMERICAN ELK (NON-TYPICAL ANTLERS)

Minimum Score 300 — Continued

SCORE	LENGTH OF R MAIN BEAM L		INSIDE SPREAD	NUMBER OF R POINTS L		AREA	STATE/ PROVINCE	HUNTER'S NAME	DATE	RANK
340 5/8	53 3/8	53 3/8	39 4/8	8	7	Sweetwater County	WY	Clay J. Evans	2008	191
340 4/8	49 7/8	50 6/8	36 6/8	7	7	Navajo County	AZ	Stan H. Hacker	1996	192
340 4/8	47 4/8	47 1/8	37 5/8	7	7	Alder Flats	ALB	Graydon Bishop	2000	192
340 1/8	53 2/8	53 2/8	41 6/8	7	8	Valley County	ID	Curt Giese	1998	194
*340 0/8	46 7/8	47 6/8	29 0/8	7	8	Catron County	NM	Larry D. Clark	2004	195
339 4/8	49 1/8	48 1/8	34 3/8	6	7	Meagher County	MT	Brian Stremcha	2004	196
339 1/8	43 6/8	41 3/8	40 4/8	8	7	Benewah County	ID	Jerry Ely	2003	197
338 6/8	42 2/8	44 5/8	37 4/8	7	7	Fremont County	ID	Claude Riglemon	2000	198
336 0/8	47 0/8	46 3/8	38 4/8	8	6	Lincoln County	MT	Salvatore Montiagnino	2003	199
335 5/8	45 5/8	42 6/8	40 0/8	8	7	Catron County	NM	Paul T. Horne	1990	200
335 4/8	46 1/8	48 0/8	34 0/8	8	8	Moffat County	CO	Tom Walker	1996	201

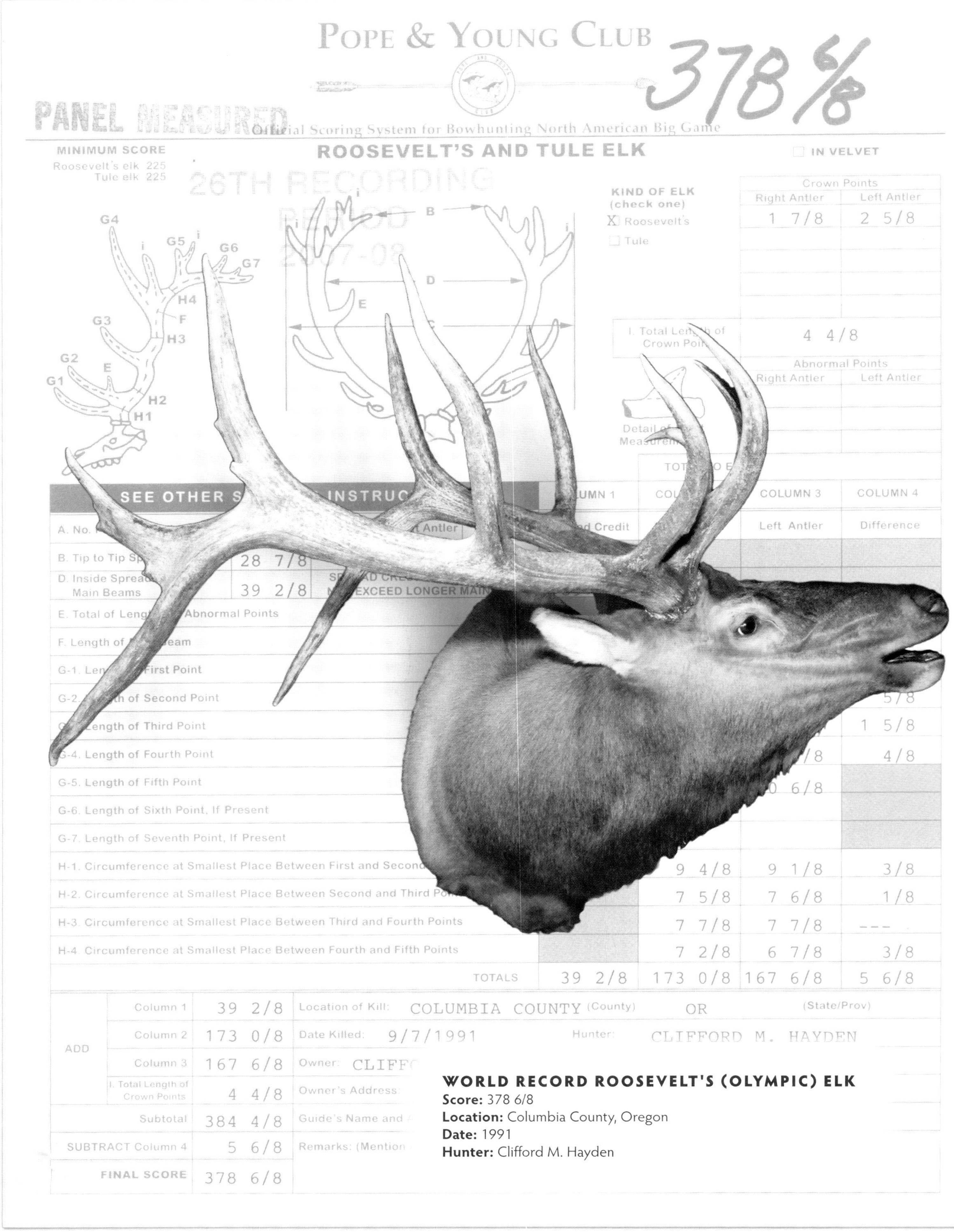

POPE & YOUNG CLUB

Official Scoring System for Bowhunting North American Big Game

378 6/8

PANEL MEASURED

ROOSEVELT'S AND TULE ELK

☐ IN VELVET

MINIMUM SCORE
Roosevelt's elk 225
Tule elk 225

26TH RECORDING PERIOD 2007-08

KIND OF ELK (check one)
[X] Roosevelt's
☐ Tule

	Crown Points	
	Right Antler	Left Antler
	1 7/8	2 5/8

I. Total Length of Crown Points	4 4/8

	Abnormal Points	
	Right Antler	Left Antler

	Column 1	Column 2	Column 3	Column 4
		Right Antler	Left Antler	Difference
A. No. of Points				
B. Tip to Tip Spread	28 7/8			
D. Inside Spread Main Beams	39 2/8	SPREAD CREDIT MAY EQUAL BUT NOT EXCEED LONGER MAIN BEAM		
E. Total of Lengths of Abnormal Points				
F. Length of Main Beam				
G-1. Length of First Point				
G-2. Length of Second Point				5/8
G-3. Length of Third Point				1 5/8
G-4. Length of Fourth Point			/8	4/8
G-5. Length of Fifth Point			0 6/8	
G-6. Length of Sixth Point, If Present				
G-7. Length of Seventh Point, If Present				
H-1. Circumference at Smallest Place Between First and Second		9 4/8	9 1/8	3/8
H-2. Circumference at Smallest Place Between Second and Third Points		7 5/8	7 6/8	1/8
H-3. Circumference at Smallest Place Between Third and Fourth Points		7 7/8	7 7/8	---
H-4. Circumference at Smallest Place Between Fourth and Fifth Points		7 2/8	6 7/8	3/8
TOTALS	39 2/8	173 0/8	167 6/8	5 6/8

ADD	Column 1	39 2/8
	Column 2	173 0/8
	Column 3	167 6/8
	I. Total Length of Crown Points	4 4/8
	Subtotal	384 4/8
SUBTRACT	Column 4	5 6/8
	FINAL SCORE	378 6/8

Location of Kill: COLUMBIA COUNTY (County) OR (State/Prov)
Date Killed: 9/7/1991 Hunter: CLIFFORD M. HAYDEN
Owner: CLIFFORD
Owner's Address:
Guide's Name and
Remarks: (Mention

WORLD RECORD ROOSEVELT'S (OLYMPIC) ELK
Score: 378 6/8
Location: Columbia County, Oregon
Date: 1991
Hunter: Clifford M. Hayden

Roosevelt's (Olympic) Elk

by Clifford M. Hayden

I've been hunting elk and deer for more than fifty years. This bull came from an area I had been hunting which is locked up to motorized traffic...walk-in only. I first saw this elk two years prior to the harvest. That year I had two opportunities to see him, but never got within range either time.

When I finally got the shot, the arrow ricocheted off a small vine maple branch. I was very lucky that the arrow still connected and I found this great elk some 150 yards later.

I hope this great animal left his mark on this earth before he met me. I've named him Ramses II, after the great Egyptian pharaoh. The amount of time that I spent after this bull was huge. My wife told me many times to give up. Of course, I didn't.

I'm a disabled, mature hunter and tell all mature hunters I meet that "you can do it!"

ROOSEVELT'S (OLYMPIC) ELK

Minimum Score 225

Cervus elaphus roosevelti

SCORE	LENGTH OF R MAIN BEAM L	INSIDE SPREAD	NUMBER OF R POINTS L	AREA	STATE/ PROVINCE	HUNTER'S NAME	DATE	RANK
378 6/8	54 2/8 52 7/8	39 2/8	7 7	Columbia County	OR	Clifford M. Hayden	1991	1
367 3/8	43 5/8 45 6/8	40 0/8	7 8	Tillamook County	OR	D. Baumgartner / K. Sisco	1985	2
353 7/8	52 3/8 53 4/8	40 1/8	7 8	Josephine County	OR	Johnny Costello	2004	3
353 3/8	51 6/8 53 1/8	38 2/8	7 7	Columbia County	OR	Ken R. Adamson	1985	4
352 0/8	46 5/8 46 6/8	41 2/8	7 8	Tillamook County	OR	Scott McKibbin	2009	5
343 6/8	54 7/8 56 0/8	39 5/8	7 7	Curry County	OR	Kendal Smith	1986	6
343 5/8	49 3/8 48 5/8	44 1/8	6 6	Jefferson County	WA	Robert Bailey	2001	7
343 3/8	51 4/8 52 3/8	31 5/8	7 7	Clatsop County	OR	Jim Pekola	1995	8
343 2/8	48 4/8 49 5/8	38 6/8	8 7	Lewis County	WA	Keith Heldreth	1988	9
339 6/8	47 4/8 48 1/8	35 6/8	7 7	Union Bay	BC	Thomas J. Hoffman	1995	10
338 3/8	45 6/8 45 4/8	40 3/8	6 7	Jefferson County	WA	Kevin Baretich	2002	11
337 5/8	51 2/8 47 6/8	37 1/8	6 6	Clatsop County	OR	Paul Clavette	1996	12
336 3/8	51 3/8 52 0/8	41 2/8	6 6	Vancouver Island	BC	Tom Foss	2007	13
336 0/8	53 7/8 48 7/8	36 0/8	7 7	Coos County	OR	Rich L. Rounds	2004	14
336 0/8	40 1/8 43 4/8	34 7/8	8 8	Union Bay	BC	Chipper Dippel	2008	14
334 7/8	45 7/8 46 3/8	37 6/8	7 9	Campbell River	BC	Rick Duggan	2004	16
333 0/8	51 4/8 52 1/8	38 0/8	6 8	Polk County	OR	Britt Richard Madison	2005	17
332 4/8	54 0/8 52 2/8	36 0/8	7 7	Curry County	OR	Mark J. Becker	2009	18
331 4/8	47 2/8 44 1/8	39 2/8	7 9	Washer Creek	BC	Archie J. Nesbitt	1997	19
330 0/8	52 0/8 49 0/8	40 4/8	6 7	Lincoln County	OR	Randy Storaasli	2004	20
328 5/8	48 3/8 47 7/8	37 7/8	8 8	Washington County	OR	Rene Ramos	2010	21
*324 5/8	44 3/8 44 7/8	39 5/8	7 7	Columbia County	OR	Jonathan Kernutt	2008	22
324 4/8	45 3/8 44 6/8	44 6/8	7 7	Jefferson County	WA	Larry Haddock	1988	23
323 5/8	55 7/8 55 0/8	36 6/8	7 7	Humboldt County	CA	Walter J. Palmer	2010	24
322 7/8	53 0/8 51 5/8	42 5/8	8 6	Curry County	OR	Dallas E. Ettinger	1993	25
322 1/8	48 7/8 49 0/8	41 4/8	7 6	Grays Harbor County	WA	Clifford S. Foss	1998	26
321 4/8	42 4/8 44 0/8	37 5/8	8 8	Polk County	OR	Larry L. Foster, Jr.	2005	27
321 3/8	42 3/8 44 7/8	38 1/8	7 7	Grays Harbor County	WA	Jim Pekola	2004	28
321 2/8	51 6/8 52 4/8	39 7/8	6 7	Jefferson County	WA	Russ Poppe	2003	29
319 2/8	51 1/8 48 5/8	38 4/8	8 8	Conuma River	BC	Jason Hird	2000	30
318 6/8	45 7/8 44 5/8	37 0/8	6 6	Jefferson County	WA	David J. Miller	1986	31
318 5/8	50 2/8 53 1/8	41 0/8	6 7	Douglas County	OR	Shane Kronberger	1996	32
318 4/8	51 1/8 48 0/8	38 5/8	6 7	Vancouver Island	BC	Ed Kellow	1993	33
318 4/8	49 1/8 48 0/8	33 2/8	8 8	Coos County	OR	Todd Freitag	2003	33
317 2/8	44 5/8 44 4/8	41 7/8	8 6	Washington County	OR	Matt Schmidlin	2006	35
316 4/8	42 6/8 41 2/8	35 5/8	7 7	Lincoln County	OR	Jake Murray	2010	36
316 1/8	48 1/8 46 3/8	35 6/8	6 7	Benton County	OR	Stacy Sherman	2001	37
*315 6/8	52 0/8 49 2/8	43 0/8	6 6	King County	WA	Charles D. Jones	2008	38
315 2/8	41 6/8 43 0/8	39 6/8	7 7	Columbia County	OR	David Evenson	1998	39
314 1/8	48 0/8 49 0/8	37 0/8	7 7	Jefferson County	WA	George W. Powers	2001	40
313 1/8	46 2/8 45 4/8	36 6/8	6 7	Douglas County	OR	Ray Argo	2001	41
313 1/8	43 5/8 44 1/8	50 1/8	6 7	Yamhill County	OR	Britt Madison	2002	41
312 7/8	40 3/8 42 4/8	37 0/8	9 6	Yamhill County	OR	Dale R. Thornton	2010	43
312 4/8	52 1/8 49 5/8	36 2/8	6 6	Coos County	OR	Robert Dean Dunson	1982	44
312 1/8	48 5/8 46 5/8	34 3/8	6 7	Clallam County	WA	Michael L. Fisher	1993	45
310 4/8	49 7/8 48 2/8	42 0/8	7 7	Curry County	OR	R. Scott Knox	2004	46
309 6/8	48 6/8 48 0/8	38 2/8	6 7	Clallam County	WA	Jon Blank	1997	47
309 5/8	50 3/8 50 6/8	34 2/8	6 7	Linn County	OR	Todd Stoffel	2000	48
309 1/8	47 3/8 40 6/8	40 7/8	7 7	Jefferson County	WA	Walter L. Campbell	1987	49
309 0/8	47 2/8 48 2/8	38 6/8	7 6	Douglas County	OR	Bert Petit	1984	50
308 7/8	46 3/8 46 2/8	36 2/8	9 7	Tillamook County	OR	Ed Flinter	1998	51
308 4/8	44 3/8 44 6/8	39 0/8	7 6	Douglas County	OR	Christopher Tipton	2007	52
308 1/8	48 4/8 48 4/8	42 3/8	6 7	Coos County	OR	Dean Dunson	1986	53
307 5/8	45 5/8 41 2/8	42 0/8	6 8	Clatsop County	OR	Brett E. Doyle	1998	54
307 3/8	51 4/8 51 0/8	41 2/8	6 6	Jefferson County	WA	David Sanford	1997	55
307 3/8	47 3/8 49 0/8	41 3/8	6 5	Grays Harbor County	WA	Todd Hubble	2001	55
306 6/8	50 2/8 50 4/8	38 6/8	6 6	Polk County	OR	James Wallen	1980	57
306 5/8	42 4/8 45 6/8	37 3/8	6 6	Grays Harbor County	WA	Jim Pekola	2001	58
306 4/8	49 6/8 50 6/8	37 3/8	6 6	Douglas County	OR	Mitch Rhodes	2005	59
306 2/8	48 5/8 48 3/8	38 2/8	6 6	Jefferson County	WA	Chong Pak	1992	60
306 1/8	49 2/8 45 4/8	40 4/8	7 6	Jefferson County	WA	Monte Dahlstrom	1987	61
306 1/8	49 5/8 46 0/8	41 0/8	6 6	Clallam County	WA	Arnold J. La Gambina	2005	61
306 1/8	44 7/8 47 1/8	40 7/8	7 6	Lincoln County	OR	Raymond J. Kosydar	2008	61
304 4/8	44 2/8 42 0/8	47 2/8	6 6	Grays Harbor County	WA	Jim Pekola	1992	64
304 2/8	45 0/8 42 3/8	36 4/8	7 7	Lane County	OR	Ted Spencer	2009	65
303 1/8	47 3/8 45 1/8	39 0/8	6 6	Jefferson County	WA	Ray Capp	1997	66
303 1/8	45 4/8 44 4/8	35 2/8	6 6	Polk County	OR	Bryon Davidson	2005	66
*303 0/8	48 0/8 50 5/8	35 5/8	8 7	Tillamook County	OR	Ryan Vandecoevering	2010	68
302 3/8	43 4/8 45 2/8	39 0/8	7 6	Jefferson County	WA	Jim Pekola	1994	69
302 2/8	48 5/8 49 2/8	40 0/8	6 6	Clatsop County	OR	Mike D. Moore	1999	70
302 2/8	41 6/8 44 7/8	38 0/8	6 6	Tillamook County	OR	Shawn L. Woods	2006	70
302 2/8	42 4/8 42 6/8	36 2/8	7 7	Tillamook County	OR	Joe Phillips	2007	70
301 5/8	51 2/8 45 6/8	44 3/8	6 5	Grays Harbor County	WA	Fred M. Gordon	1985	73
301 5/8	44 3/8 48 2/8	37 2/8	6 7	Grays Harbor County	WA	Frank Stinchfield	2001	73
301 0/8	45 0/8 47 3/8	37 1/8	8 8	Washington County	OR	Jon King	1987	75
301 0/8	47 0/8 46 6/8	42 7/8	6 6	Jefferson County	WA	Russ Poppe	1994	75
301 0/8	43 0/8 43 6/8	36 3/8	6 6	Powell River	BC	Ron Klassen	2002	75
300 5/8	48 7/8 47 1/8	42 0/8	6 6	Curry County	OR	Allen Boice	1998	78
300 1/8	41 3/8 43 1/8	33 3/8	7 7	Columbia County	OR	Cody Wade Ogle	2006	79
299 6/8	46 4/8 43 2/8	36 3/8	8 7	Columbia County	OR	Kelley Lungberg	1993	80
299 5/8	42 6/8 42 4/8	35 7/8	8 7	Clatsop County	OR	David T. Bogh	2002	81
299 4/8	44 4/8 44 4/8	36 1/8	8 8	Yamhill County	OR	Julian Hernandez	2001	82
298 7/8	46 3/8 46 5/8	41 6/8	6 6	Jefferson County	WA	Wayne McReynolds	1990	83
298 6/8	48 3/8 49 3/8	33 6/8	5 6	Lane County	OR	Joe Waite	1981	84
298 6/8	45 5/8 45 2/8	32 0/8	6 7	Jefferson County	WA	Robert C. Allan	1993	84
298 6/8	44 6/8 45 0/8	33 1/8	6 7	Conuma River	BC	Monty Klein	1998	84
298 6/8	46 4/8 47 1/8	33 4/8	7 7	Lewis County	WA	Glenn Lee	2001	84
298 5/8	45 4/8 47 4/8	40 2/8	7 6	Grays Harbor County	WA	Jim Pekola	1999	88
298 0/8	44 3/8 46 2/8	38 6/8	8 8	Washington County	OR	Ron Adamson	1992	89
297 6/8	48 0/8 49 1/8	37 6/8	6 5	Sechelt	BC	Kevin Harms	2004	90
297 6/8	46 7/8 47 0/8	44 6/8	5 5	Grays Harbor County	WA	Clifford S. Foss	2001	91
*297 6/8	45 1/8 44 4/8	36 1/8	6 6	Coos County	OR	Cameron Hanes	2010	91
297 3/8	41 5/8 41 1/8	38 1/8	7 7	Jefferson County	WA	Doug Smith	1989	93
297 3/8	38 3/8 40 2/8	29 5/8	7 7	Wahkiakum County	WA	Monte Henry Longtain	2005	93
297 2/8	46 0/8 45 7/8	42 2/8	6 6	Clallam County	WA	Arnold LaGambina	1988	95

ROOSEVELT'S (OLYMPIC) ELK

Minimum Score 225   Continued

SCORE	LENGTH OF R MAIN BEAM L	INSIDE SPREAD	NUMBER OF R POINTS L	AREA	STATE/ PROVINCE	HUNTER'S NAME	DATE	RANK
297 1/8	47 4/8 48 4/8	41 5/8	6 6	Pacific County	WA	Warren M. Hazen	2002	96
296 6/8	40 3/8 41 2/8	39 3/8	6 7	Clatsop County	OR	Edwin J. Thompson	1987	97
296 6/8	43 0/8 43 5/8	41 4/8	6 6	Jefferson County	WA	Kurt Goesch	1989	97
296 4/8	46 6/8 47 0/8	41 3/8	7 7	Pacific County	WA	Jess Martin, Jr.	1971	99
296 1/8	46 5/8 47 1/8	31 5/8	6 6	Coos County	OR	Jared Reeves	2006	100
296 0/8	40 1/8 37 2/8	35 3/8	7 8	Grays Harbor County	WA	Kelvin Brogan	2008	101
295 6/8	43 2/8 43 3/8	41 1/8	6 7	Clatsop County	OR	Brian Stanley	1992	102
295 6/8	43 7/8 45 1/8	34 7/8	7 7	Coos County	OR	Wes Plummer	2001	102
295 5/8	47 4/8 49 0/8	37 7/8	7 7	Jefferson County	WA	Bill Weidman	1982	104
295 3/8	50 4/8 47 0/8	36 5/8	7 6	Humboldt County	CA	James Ron Jarvis	2009	105
295 0/8	45 6/8 45 4/8	39 0/8	8 7	Columbia County	OR	Smokey Crews	1987	106
294 7/8	46 7/8 49 0/8	41 6/8	6 6	Jefferson County	WA	Bob Rosie	1990	107
294 7/8	48 3/8 48 5/8	38 6/8	6 6	Benton County	OR	Corey Putney	1992	107
294 6/8	44 2/8 41 3/8	42 2/8	7 6	Coos County	OR	Steven C. Humbert	2007	109
294 0/8	44 2/8 46 0/8	41 2/8	6 6	Jefferson County	WA	Sam Windle	1993	110
294 0/8	39 2/8 41 2/8	33 0/8	6 6	Lewis County	WA	Aaron Evans	2004	110
293 6/8	50 3/8 47 5/8	37 6/8	5 6	Jefferson County	WA	Ronald E. Ihrig	1984	112
293 6/8	42 7/8 46 4/8	34 3/8	9 7	Yamhill County	OR	Dean A. McMullen	1993	112
293 6/8	46 2/8 47 1/8	39 5/8	6 6	Lincoln County	OR	Ted Gibson	1996	112
292 6/8	47 0/8 45 7/8	34 6/8	6 6	Douglas County	OR	Robert Huselton	2003	115
292 4/8	42 7/8 43 3/8	43 3/8	7 7	Coos County	OR	Samuel Wayne Lillie	2002	116
*292 4/8	47 2/8 47 5/8	37 2/8	6 5	Clatsop County	OR	Slade H. Taylor	2007	116
292 1/8	42 3/8 44 0/8	40 0/8	6 6	Lane County	OR	Thomas A. Whitaker	1988	118
291 4/8	41 0/8 43 1/8	33 5/8	6 7	Pacific County	WA	Dan Free	1983	119
291 3/8	43 5/8 43 7/8	37 3/8	6 7	Washington County	OR	Matt Schmidlin	2001	120
291 2/8	41 1/8 42 1/8	41 4/8	6 6	Clallam County	WA	Russ Spaulding	1985	121
291 1/8	42 3/8 44 1/8	40 0/8	6 7	Curry County	OR	James Atherton	1985	122
291 0/8	42 1/8 42 1/8	37 0/8	7 7	Lincoln County	OR	Terry W. Smith	1997	123
291 0/8	42 4/8 41 4/8	39 2/8	5 6	Jefferson County	WA	Craig Baar	2003	123
290 7/8	39 5/8 39 5/8	32 4/8	8 7	Columbia County	OR	Mike Pense	2007	125
290 5/8	43 7/8 43 2/8	34 3/8	7 8	Clatsop County	OR	Jim Thrower	1998	126
290 2/8	45 2/8 45 6/8	37 6/8	5 5	Jefferson County	WA	Jim Pekola	1993	127
*290 2/8	47 2/8 48 0/8	32 6/8	6 6	Clallam County	WA	William Templin	2010	127
289 2/8	44 7/8 44 7/8	32 4/8	6 5	Pacific County	WA	Dan Free	1980	129
289 0/8	44 1/8 44 4/8	34 0/8	7 7	Columbia County	OR	Andrew Morris	2004	130
289 0/8	47 1/8 46 7/8	38 7/8	7 6	Douglas County	OR	Tadd Moore	2005	130
288 3/8	43 2/8 45 3/8	36 7/8	6 6	Lewis County	WA	Glenn Lee	1980	132
287 5/8	42 4/8 42 4/8	38 2/8	6 6	Douglas County	OR	Dean Bright	2002	133
287 2/8	41 3/8 40 3/8	31 4/8	6 9	Clatsop County	OR	Robert A. Hanthorn	2002	134
286 7/8	42 0/8 43 1/8	27 4/8	8 7	Coos County	OR	Mark Johnston	1999	135
286 4/8	43 4/8 42 4/8	34 1/8	7 8	Tillamook County	OR	Ben Owens	2005	136
285 7/8	40 2/8 37 6/8	42 2/8	6 6	Coos County	OR	Mark Klepetka	2002	137
285 3/8	41 2/8 40 4/8	34 3/8	6 7	Douglas County	OR	Christopher Tipton	2002	138
285 3/8	39 3/8 39 5/8	36 0/8	7 7	Jefferson County	WA	Calvin L. Rowan	2003	139
285 1/8	47 3/8 48 1/8	37 1/8	6 6	Clackamas County	OR	Randy W. Kubitz	1986	140
285 0/8	44 6/8 46 2/8	34 1/8	6 6	Douglas County	OR	Tim Wattman	1999	141
284 7/8	42 0/8 41 5/8	31 7/8	7 9	Tillamook County	OR	Timothy Tilander	2002	142
284 0/8	42 1/8 43 3/8	40 1/8	8 7	Jefferson County	WA	Daniel J. Siegner	1991	143
283 5/8	47 4/8 48 0/8	40 7/8	6 6	Jefferson County	WA	Robert J. Rosie	1990	144
283 3/8	46 0/8 42 7/8	29 7/8	6 5	Skamania County	WA	Jerry L. Carter	1973	145
283 3/8	46 0/8 47 1/8	30 5/8	6 6	Polk County	OR	Terry W. Smith	1991	145
283 3/8	43 0/8 41 7/8	44 0/8	6 6	Jefferson County	WA	Paul Szumlanski	1991	145
283 2/8	45 3/8 45 3/8	34 4/8	6 6	Pacific County	WA	Jerry Webster	1979	148
283 2/8	43 4/8 41 1/8	38 6/8	6 7	Clallam County	WA	Wayne Haag	1982	148
282 5/8	42 6/8 45 2/8	38 6/8	6 6	Jefferson County	WA	Gary M. Douthit	1986	150
282 4/8	44 6/8 44 1/8	38 7/8	7 6	Afognak Island	AK	Edward L. Russell	1980	151
282 0/8	45 0/8 43 6/8	42 0/8	6 6	Jefferson County	WA	Dave Robertson	1970	152
282 0/8	45 2/8 44 7/8	35 6/8	7 7	Jefferson County	WA	Michael C. Giardino	1992	152
282 0/8	40 1/8 39 3/8	34 0/8	7 7	Tillamook County	OR	Kenneth R. Hurliman	2006	152
281 7/8	47 4/8 49 0/8	34 2/8	6 6	Jefferson County	WA	Kurt Goesch	1995	155
281 6/8	44 4/8 45 4/8	34 7/8	6 6	Clatsop County	OR	Larry W. Atkins	1996	156
281 3/8	44 5/8 45 1/8	32 2/8	6 6	Lincoln County	OR	Kevin Gassner	2008	157
281 1/8	44 3/8 44 7/8	33 6/8	6 8	Lincoln County	OR	Kevin Dean Zook	1996	158
281 1/8	44 2/8 42 0/8	37 7/8	8 8	Tillamook County	OR	Robert E. Smith	2006	158
281 0/8	41 6/8 40 7/8	34 4/8	6 6	Jefferson County	WA	Talmadge Dobbs	1989	160
281 0/8	46 4/8 47 1/8	31 1/8	6 6	Yamhill County	OR	Dale R. Thornton	1997	160
280 6/8	45 6/8 44 1/8	38 1/8	6 6	Jefferson County	WA	Donald N. Morey	1978	162
280 6/8	41 4/8 42 1/8	36 1/8	6 7	Clatsop County	OR	Frank Twardoch	2007	162
280 4/8	43 2/8 43 0/8	33 0/8	6 6	Lane County	OR	Jeff Sindt	1982	164
280 2/8	42 0/8 43 0/8	39 2/8	6 5	Jefferson County	WA	Wayne McReynolds	1984	165
279 7/8	47 4/8 47 2/8	37 2/8	5 6	Grays Harbor County	WA	G. A. "Toby" Hart	1986	166
279 7/8	44 1/8 46 6/8	34 6/8	5 6	Jefferson County	WA	Jim Pekola	1990	166
279 5/8	39 4/8 41 7/8	35 0/8	7 6	Pacific County	WA	Victor "Tor" Larson	2000	168
279 3/8	42 0/8 42 3/8	37 5/8	6 5	Pender Harbour	BC	George Harms	2006	169
278 3/8	48 1/8 50 7/8	34 1/8	5 6	Jefferson County	WA	Jim Pekola	2009	170
278 1/8	44 7/8 44 2/8	37 3/8	5 5	Jefferson County	WA	Kevin Baretich	2005	171
278 1/8	44 3/8 40 2/8	41 5/8	6 6	Grays Harbor County	WA	Bob Mayton	2008	171
278 0/8	39 6/8 41 6/8	41 6/8	6 6	Douglas County	OR	Daryll Southwick	2007	173
277 4/8	41 1/8 40 0/8	43 0/8	6 6	Jefferson County	WA	Robert C. Allan	1996	174
277 4/8	44 0/8 43 2/8	29 1/8	6 6	Jefferson County	WA	Chris Moore	2001	174
277 2/8	43 5/8 48 6/8	41 0/8	6 6	Jefferson County	WA	Merl Reed	2003	176
277 2/8	47 3/8 45 5/8	36 6/8	6 6	Klamath County	OR	Brian Foy	2005	176
276 7/8	45 5/8 44 1/8	35 5/8	5 5	Tillamook County	OR	Steve Weeks	1994	178
276 6/8	40 4/8 40 1/8	39 7/8	6 6	Clallam County	WA	Clyde E. Graham	1985	179
276 3/8	41 3/8 41 6/8	36 6/8	6 5	Jefferson County	WA	Kevin Barber	1995	180
276 1/8	40 1/8 43 3/8	41 5/8	5 5	Clallam County	WA	Scott Williams	2003	181
275 6/8	42 0/8 41 4/8	39 2/8	6 6	Polk County	OR	Jed McMullen	2006	182
275 5/8	48 4/8 45 1/8	38 3/8	5 5	Jefferson County	WA	Jerry Childs	1991	183
275 3/8	37 0/8 37 4/8	36 1/8	7 7	Tillamook County	OR	Alan Richardson	1980	184
275 3/8	44 0/8 43 1/8	35 3/8	6 6	Tillamook County	OR	Jody Cyr	2003	184
275 2/8	41 2/8 38 3/8	36 0/8	7 7	Jefferson County	WA	Jon E. Nelson	1986	186
275 1/8	45 7/8 46 4/8	39 7/8	6 6	Grays Harbor County	WA	Bob Mayton	2003	187
275 0/8	43 5/8 45 0/8	33 7/8	6 6	Douglas County	OR	Frank Michels II	2001	188
274 7/8	42 5/8 40 4/8	35 0/8	7 7	Columbia County	OR	Greg S. Osburn	2000	189
274 6/8	42 3/8 44 0/8	39 4/8	5 5	Columbia County	OR	Steve Cox	1989	190

ROOSEVELT'S (OLYMPIC) ELK

Minimum Score 225   Continued

SCORE	LENGTH OF R MAIN BEAM L	INSIDE SPREAD	NUMBER OF R POINTS L		AREA	STATE/ PROVINCE	HUNTER'S NAME	DATE	RANK
274 4/8	46 5/8	44 7/8	37 5/8	6	6	Jefferson County	WA	Ron Brockavich	2000	191
274 3/8	47 6/8	47 5/8	36 0/8	8	5	Jefferson County	WA	Eric Olson	1985	192
274 2/8	48 4/8	47 7/8	36 6/8	5	5	Grays Harbor County	WA	Jim Pekola	1995	193
273 7/8	42 4/8	42 4/8	32 5/8	7	7	Jefferson County	WA	Dave Dasher	1989	194
273 4/8	44 6/8	45 1/8	38 3/8	6	6	Pacific County	WA	Glen Watland	1980	195
273 4/8	42 1/8	42 4/8	35 6/8	6	7	Jefferson County	WA	George Walker	1994	195
273 0/8	44 2/8	44 0/8	35 0/8	5	5	Jefferson County	WA	Ken Chamberlin	1987	197
273 0/8	42 7/8	41 4/8	31 6/8	6	6	Lincoln County	OR	Larry Beggs, Jr.	2000	197
272 7/8	39 5/8	38 5/8	37 4/8	6	7	Clatsop County	OR	Lester "Skip" Croft, Jr.	1993	199
272 7/8	42 0/8	41 2/8	36 5/8	6	6	Pacific County	WA	Paul A. Zaveruha	1999	199
272 7/8	42 6/8	43 2/8	36 2/8	7	6	Grays Harbor County	WA	Frank Stinchfield	2010	199
272 5/8	46 4/8	45 1/8	36 1/8	5	5	Jefferson County	WA	Bryan Mittge	1986	202
272 2/8	42 6/8	44 6/8	39 5/8	7	6	Polk County	OR	Tom Krauthoefer	1994	203
272 1/8	39 4/8	40 6/8	33 5/8	5	5	Wahkiakum County	WA	Russ Poppe	1982	204
272 1/8	39 6/8	41 0/8	41 6/8	6	6	Clatsop County	OR	Josh Luttrell	2009	204
271 6/8	48 3/8	49 1/8	36 0/8	5	5	Clallam County	WA	Michael J. Hill	2003	206
271 5/8	43 5/8	40 3/8	40 7/8	6	6	Lincoln County	OR	Brandon D. Weston	2007	207
271 4/8	41 3/8	42 0/8	37 2/8	6	6	Douglas County	OR	Kenneth A. French	1995	208
271 4/8	44 6/8	42 1/8	37 3/8	6	6	Columbia County	OR	Dan B. Howard	2006	208
271 3/8	44 3/8	44 3/8	38 0/8	6	5	Grays Harbor County	WA	Scott Bergen	1985	210
271 3/8	43 6/8	42 6/8	38 0/8	6	6	Columbia County	OR	Robert Shetler	2006	210
271 2/8	40 2/8	40 2/8	33 4/8	6	6	Cowlitz County	WA	Kelly King	1991	212
271 1/8	46 0/8	45 3/8	33 3/8	6	6	Afognak Island	AK	David Harper	1970	213
270 6/8	40 1/8	37 4/8	36 0/8	5	6	Curry County	OR	Will L. Merritt IV	1999	214
270 4/8	43 2/8	42 4/8	38 0/8	7	7	Coos County	OR	David Fritz	2002	215
270 3/8	38 2/8	39 5/8	36 4/8	8	6	Clatsop County	OR	James L. Friesz	1981	216
270 3/8	40 5/8	42 4/8	37 4/8	6	6	Grays Harbor County	WA	Brian Mitchell	1990	216
270 2/8	44 6/8	44 1/8	44 4/8	4	5	Grays Harbor County	WA	Bill Brown	1959	218
270 2/8	43 2/8	44 2/8	40 3/8	6	5	Jefferson County	WA	Patrick Stoddard	1993	218
270 0/8	41 1/8	42 1/8	36 0/8	5	5	Clallam County	WA	Arne Swanson	1990	220
270 0/8	42 5/8	44 1/8	31 5/8	6	6	Tillamook County	OR	Tom Harrison	2001	220
269 7/8	36 5/8	37 1/8	33 7/8	6	6	Jefferson County	WA	Jim Pekola	1988	222
*269 7/8	40 1/8	41 5/8	38 3/8	7	5	Douglas County	OR	Ty Stubblefield	2008	222
269 6/8	37 3/8	39 6/8	36 4/8	6	6	Columbia County	OR	Richard Heiberg	2003	224
269 6/8	41 2/8	41 3/8	31 2/8	6	6	Washington County	OR	Frank Scott Bailey	2005	224
269 4/8	39 3/8	40 6/8	39 0/8	5	5	Clallam County	WA	George McDonald	1985	226
269 4/8	43 3/8	43 6/8	34 0/8	10	6	Columbia County	OR	Matt Schmidlin	1998	226
269 3/8	43 7/8	43 1/8	32 6/8	6	7	Columbia County	OR	Andrew C. Morris	2003	228
269 2/8	45 6/8	45 0/8	33 1/8	6	6	Jefferson County	WA	Ray Capp	1987	229
269 2/8	42 0/8	42 7/8	34 5/8	6	6	Washington County	OR	Jim Richter	1994	229
269 2/8	43 4/8	43 4/8	31 3/8	6	6	Tillamook County	OR	Daniel A. Fleming	1995	229
269 1/8	40 5/8	41 5/8	35 3/8	6	6	Clatsop County	OR	David M. Jones	1982	232
268 7/8	40 5/8	41 1/8	34 1/8	5	7	Coos County	OR	Thomas E. Tipton	1986	233
268 7/8	39 4/8	40 1/8	33 0/8	7	7	Coos County	OR	Terry Lee Bird	2000	233
268 7/8	44 1/8	40 4/8	38 2/8	9	7	Douglas County	OR	Tim Tollett	2009	233
268 4/8	42 4/8	43 1/8	34 1/8	6	6	Coos County	OR	Tim Stallard	2003	236
268 2/8	43 7/8	43 7/8	41 0/8	5	5	Grays Harbor County	WA	Terry Plato	1984	237
268 1/8	38 0/8	39 2/8	37 3/8	6	6	Clatsop County	OR	Ed Beisley	1967	238
267 7/8	44 7/8	44 1/8	33 6/8	6	5	Jefferson County	WA	L. Scot Jenkins	1998	239
267 6/8	46 6/8	45 6/8	39 1/8	6	6	Douglas County	OR	John E. Nunn	2004	240
267 6/8	40 3/8	39 2/8	41 1/8	6	6	Tillamook County	OR	Rodney W. Breazile	2005	240
267 4/8	38 5/8	36 1/8	35 2/8	8	7	Lincoln County	OR	Timothy J. Edwards	1996	242
267 4/8	43 6/8	43 2/8	36 3/8	6	6	Coos County	OR	Jeff Fletcher	2006	242
267 3/8	37 0/8	36 3/8	34 3/8	6	6	Clatsop County	OR	Douglas W. Hamilton	1982	244
267 2/8	43 3/8	42 4/8	40 2/8	5	5	Jefferson County	WA	Dave Mirka	1987	245
266 5/8	37 3/8	38 1/8	35 5/8	5	5	Clallam County	WA	George McDonald	1989	246
266 5/8	41 7/8	40 6/8	39 3/8	6	6	Conuma Valley	BC	Lance Grubisich	1997	246
266 5/8	41 1/8	39 0/8	36 6/8	6	6	Pender Harbour	BC	Calvin Higano	2003	246
266 4/8	41 3/8	41 5/8	31 4/8	6	6	Pacific County	WA	Brandon Metcalf	2010	249
266 3/8	46 2/8	41 6/8	45 0/8	5	6	Grays Harbor County	WA	Mark R. Nieznalski	1984	250
265 6/8	42 2/8	45 7/8	32 3/8	6	6	Columbia County	OR	Kent Moeller	1995	251
265 4/8	39 7/8	40 0/8	35 6/8	5	6	Clallam County	WA	George McDonald	1990	252
265 3/8	39 3/8	37 4/8	44 5/8	5	5	Clallam County	WA	Ray Capp	1989	253
265 1/8	40 1/8	37 6/8	34 7/8	8	7	Tillamook County	OR	Lynn C. Reddekopp	1998	254
264 5/8	38 2/8	36 1/8	33 1/8	5	5	Douglas County	OR	Steve Simpson	1993	255
264 3/8	42 5/8	42 7/8	33 0/8	6	6	Clatsop County	OR	Ryan Roe	2007	256
264 2/8	38 0/8	42 2/8	37 2/8	6	6	Vancouver Island	BC	Gary F. Bogner	1993	257
264 1/8	44 6/8	43 2/8	43 7/8	6	6	Lincoln County	OR	Pat Chanley	2009	258
263 6/8	37 2/8	35 7/8	30 5/8	7	7	Washington County	OR	Gregory Dean Lueptow	2010	259
263 5/8	42 5/8	42 1/8	34 4/8	6	6	Lincoln County	OR	Malcam Moberly	1988	260
263 5/8	39 5/8	38 5/8	33 0/8	7	5	Curry County	OR	Joshua J. Rodriguez	2004	260
263 3/8	41 2/8	42 6/8	29 2/8	6	6	Lane County	OR	Max Lee	1980	262
263 1/8	36 3/8	36 2/8	36 6/8	6	7	Douglas County	OR	Robert J. Huselton	1998	263
262 7/8	40 1/8	40 0/8	34 0/8	6	6	Coos County	OR	Larry Frost	1985	264
262 7/8	44 5/8	45 0/8	32 3/8	6	6	Clatsop County	OR	James A. Davis, Jr.	1997	264
262 4/8	42 1/8	42 3/8	30 6/8	5	5	Clatsop County	OR	Anthony H. White	1998	266
262 3/8	44 6/8	44 4/8	33 7/8	5	5	Clallam County	WA	Arnold LaGambina	1991	267
262 2/8	45 4/8	45 5/8	28 6/8	6	6	Douglas County	OR	Dennis Olson	1984	268
262 2/8	38 2/8	38 3/8	33 2/8	5	5	Grays Harbor County	WA	Jim Pekola	1997	268
262 0/8	39 6/8	40 2/8	41 0/8	5	5	Coos County	OR	Tom Tipton	1991	270
262 0/8	42 0/8	42 3/8	39 6/8	6	6	Lincoln County	OR	Robert E. Duran	2004	270
*262 0/8	42 4/8	40 2/8	33 0/8	5	6	Coos County	OR	Jason M. Warner	2008	270
261 6/8	43 0/8	43 3/8	38 3/8	6	6	Jefferson County	WA	Robert C. Allan	1988	273
261 5/8	40 7/8	41 2/8	38 7/8	5	5	Jefferson County	WA	Mark J. Tupper	1986	274
261 5/8	40 0/8	40 0/8	36 3/8	6	6	Clatsop County	OR	William H. Stevens	1991	274
*261 5/8	41 6/8	41 3/8	35 4/8	6	6	Tillamook County	OR	Thomas K. Powell	2005	274
261 4/8	41 1/8	41 3/8	36 1/8	6	6	Columbia County	OR	Dale Buxton	1995	277
261 2/8	41 3/8	42 2/8	36 4/8	6	7	Jefferson County	WA	Kevin Baretich	2008	278
261 1/8	46 2/8	45 6/8	38 0/8	6	5	Tillamook County	OR	Scott McKibbin	1995	279
260 5/8	41 2/8	40 0/8	37 4/8	6	7	Jefferson County	WA	Gaillard R. Graham	1990	280
260 4/8	41 4/8	41 1/8	34 4/8	6	5	Douglas County	OR	J. B. Hollander	1984	281
260 3/8	45 0/8	44 2/8	35 1/8	6	5	Benton County	OR	Timothy Pearson	1989	282
260 3/8	39 2/8	40 4/8	36 0/8	8	7	Clatsop County	OR	Daniel D. Thompson	2000	282
260 3/8	40 7/8	41 0/8	32 6/8	7	7	Wahkiakum County	WA	Kenneth R. Arveson, Jr.	2005	282
260 0/8	40 1/8	38 6/8	38 7/8	6	6	Columbia County	OR	Smokey Crews	1988	285

ROOSEVELT'S (OLYMPIC) ELK

Minimum Score 225 — Continued

SCORE	LENGTH OF MAIN BEAM R	L	INSIDE SPREAD	NUMBER OF POINTS R	L	AREA	STATE/PROVINCE	HUNTER'S NAME	DATE	RANK
259 6/8	43 1/8	42 1/8	37 6/8	6	6	Columbia County	OR	Don Malloy	1988	286
259 2/8	42 3/8	42 4/8	37 0/8	5	5	Coos County	OR	James M. Speelman	1974	287
259 1/8	42 1/8	40 2/8	34 2/8	6	6	Clallam County	WA	Frank LaGambina	1980	288
259 1/8	41 2/8	40 2/8	35 2/8	6	6	Lane County	OR	Eric Strickler	2000	288
258 5/8	40 3/8	38 4/8	32 6/8	7	7	Columbia County	OR	Larry W. Fox	1987	290
258 5/8	40 3/8	38 2/8	31 6/8	6	6	Lane County	OR	Todd L. Wilkinson	1996	290
258 2/8	39 0/8	39 7/8	31 4/8	7	7	Coos County	OR	John D. "Jack" Frost	2004	292
258 0/8	44 0/8	44 3/8	37 1/8	6	5	Pacific County	WA	Carson M. Kemmer	2004	293
257 6/8	37 7/8	38 4/8	33 0/8	6	6	Clatsop County	OR	Gerald T. Bogh	1993	294
257 6/8	40 4/8	40 1/8	32 4/8	5	6	Douglas County	OR	John W. Dickenson	1995	294
257 6/8	42 3/8	41 3/8	35 4/8	6	7	Yamhill County	OR	Stanley M. Varuska	2005	294
257 2/8	43 3/8	43 0/8	38 7/8	5	6	Douglas County	OR	Larry D. Jones	2004	297
257 1/8	40 4/8	40 0/8	43 1/8	6	6	Columbia County	OR	Randy Jennings	1985	298
257 1/8	41 4/8	42 4/8	30 3/8	6	5	Benton County	OR	Corky Wray	2001	298
256 5/8	35 7/8	35 2/8	26 4/8	7	7	Clatsop County	OR	Ray Kelton	1999	300
256 4/8	35 0/8	40 1/8	36 1/8	6	6	Coos County	OR	Mike Fisher	2004	301
256 3/8	44 5/8	45 3/8	30 4/8	6	6	Polk County	OR	Gregg Allen Youngerman	1996	302
255 5/8	36 7/8	36 7/8	38 2/8	7	6	Tillamook County	OR	Parry M. Hurliman	1994	303
255 2/8	41 4/8	42 3/8	38 6/8	5	5	Jefferson County	WA	Daniel Siegner	1993	304
*255 1/8	40 3/8	42 2/8	38 5/8	5	5	Jefferson County	WA	Jeff McLaughlin	2005	305
255 1/8	39 2/8	41 5/8	40 0/8	6	6	Tillamook County	OR	Peter Chetney	2007	305
255 0/8	37 2/8	38 5/8	29 0/8	7	5	Coos County	OR	Jeff Franson/Mark Johnston	1992	307
254 4/8	40 4/8	37 7/8	30 7/8	5	6	Benton County	OR	Stanley D. Miles	2005	308
254 3/8	37 0/8	37 0/8	37 4/8	6	7	Clatsop County	OR	Gary Jacobson	2006	309
253 7/8	45 2/8	43 5/8	29 5/8	5	7	Yamhill County	OR	Jerry S. Bailey	1986	310
253 4/8	39 3/8	39 2/8	28 6/8	7	7	Coos County	OR	Craig Matson	1980	311
253 2/8	43 6/8	44 4/8	33 6/8	6	6	Lincoln County	OR	E. J. Howard	2004	312
253 1/8	43 1/8	42 0/8	33 6/8	5	6	Pacific County	WA	Bill Egner	1977	313
253 0/8	35 1/8	36 4/8	36 1/8	6	5	Clatsop County	OR	John C. Bernards	1985	314
253 0/8	39 6/8	38 1/8	31 0/8	6	6	Clatsop County	OR	Bob Bingham	1994	314
252 7/8	40 7/8	42 1/8	31 3/8	6	6	Pacific County	WA	John Wall	1979	316
252 6/8	39 0/8	38 4/8	39 3/8	5	5	Jefferson County	WA	Ed Kim	2000	317
252 2/8	41 2/8	42 0/8	35 6/8	5	5	Tillamook County	OR	Chad Brooks	2003	318
251 5/8	41 4/8	36 2/8	40 6/8	6	6	Jefferson County	WA	Sanford Windle	1972	319
251 2/8	39 1/8	40 4/8	33 2/8	6	6	Jefferson County	WA	Bill Pudell	1982	320
251 1/8	37 2/8	35 2/8	35 0/8	6	6	Coos County	OR	Robon Evans	1993	321
*251 1/8	38 6/8	38 6/8	31 6/8	6	6	Jefferson County	WA	Ron Humerickhouse	2006	321
250 7/8	38 7/8	39 4/8	34 7/8	6	6	Polk County	OR	Terry W. Smith	1996	323
250 4/8	35 6/8	35 5/8	30 0/8	6	7	Clatsop County	OR	Jim Pekola	1997	324
250 3/8	37 5/8	37 3/8	31 4/8	7	6	Lane County	OR	John Buss	2004	325
250 2/8	36 3/8	39 0/8	34 0/8	6	6	Lane County	OR	Dave Allen	1999	326
250 1/8	39 7/8	38 1/8	30 6/8	7	5	Clatsop County	OR	Rodney Watson	2003	327
250 0/8	40 5/8	39 1/8	35 5/8	6	7	Douglas County	OR	Dean Bright	2001	328
249 5/8	43 2/8	44 6/8	30 3/8	6	6	Tillamook County	OR	Steve Pieren	1982	329
249 4/8	45 3/8	45 7/8	32 6/8	6	6	Polk County	OR	Kevin Dean Zook	1992	330
249 4/8	40 2/8	38 7/8	33 7/8	6	6	Lane County	OR	Michael Strickler	2004	330
249 3/8	41 1/8	39 3/8	32 4/8	6	6	Clatsop County	OR	Charles Lee Smith	1990	332
248 7/8	41 2/8	41 7/8	31 3/8	5	5	Lane County	OR	Steven L. Allen	1996	333
248 4/8	40 0/8	39 3/8	43 1/8	5	5	Jefferson County	WA	Chris Krueger	1987	334
248 4/8	41 7/8	43 4/8	32 2/8	7	5	Jefferson County	WA	Mike Sturman	1991	334
248 3/8	39 1/8	40 2/8	35 3/8	5	5	Jefferson County	WA	Larry Haddock	1987	336
248 2/8	42 6/8	43 0/8	40 2/8	5	5	Jefferson County	WA	Robert J. Rosie	1992	337
*248 0/8	37 1/8	36 5/8	31 0/8	7	7	Tillamook County	OR	Greg Blankenship	2009	338
247 6/8	34 4/8	36 6/8	37 1/8	5	5	Grays Harbor County	WA	Wayne McReynolds	1981	339
247 6/8	45 2/8	44 2/8	38 7/8	6	6	Coos County	OR	Mark E. Cox	1990	339
247 4/8	39 6/8	42 7/8	37 6/8	5	5	Columbia County	OR	Brandon Kent	2004	341
247 3/8	37 6/8	39 7/8	36 0/8	7	7	Tillamook County	OR	David Hopkes	2004	342
247 2/8	38 0/8	39 2/8	30 0/8	5	5	Grays Harbor County	WA	Jim Pekola	2005	343
247 0/8	39 6/8	38 4/8	39 6/8	5	5	Olympic Peninsula	WA	Lloyd Beebe	1951	344
247 0/8	37 4/8	42 5/8	32 7/8	6	5	Clatsop County	OR	Garland D. Shipley	2003	344
246 6/8	39 5/8	37 3/8	34 0/8	6	6	Jefferson County	WA	Eugene Wells	1960	346
246 5/8	37 6/8	40 7/8	33 2/8	8	7	Columbia County	OR	Keith Jones	2003	347
246 3/8	39 0/8	38 2/8	35 4/8	6	6	Tillamook County	OR	Scott A. Westlund	2010	348
246 2/8	35 3/8	37 5/8	34 4/8	6	5	Clatsop County	OR	Voyle E. "Bo" Armstrong	2004	349
246 0/8	38 0/8	38 3/8	37 2/8	7	6	Coos County	OR	Frank S. Noska IV	2006	350
245 7/8	39 6/8	39 0/8	31 2/8	6	6	Clallam County	WA	Arnold LaGambina	1990	351
245 7/8	37 3/8	39 5/8	35 1/8	6	5	Clallam County	WA	Arnold LaGambina	2006	351
245 5/8	41 3/8	41 0/8	28 5/8	5	5	Pacific County	WA	Jeff Nissell	1999	353
245 3/8	39 1/8	38 6/8	31 6/8	5	7	Cowlitz County	WA	Harold Gibson	2002	354
245 1/8	38 3/8	37 5/8	34 7/8	7	5	Columbia County	OR	Leroy E. Lewis	1989	355
244 4/8	36 5/8	36 2/8	35 7/8	7	7	Clallam County	WA	Arnold La Gambina	1989	356
244 1/8	39 2/8	39 5/8	34 5/8	6	6	Clatsop County	OR	Tom Seimears	2002	357
*243 7/8	40 3/8	39 5/8	35 5/8	5	5	Jefferson County	WA	Bill Robinson	2008	358
243 6/8	43 4/8	41 4/8	33 0/8	5	5	Clallam County	WA	Glenn St. Charles	1952	359
243 6/8	34 2/8	33 3/8	34 2/8	6	6	Lincoln County	OR	Randy Smith II	1998	359
243 5/8	37 4/8	38 4/8	36 3/8	5	5	Josephine County	OR	Peter J. Tibbits	1999	361
243 5/8	35 3/8	34 6/8	30 6/8	6	7	Lewis County	WA	David Dupree	2000	361
243 4/8	39 2/8	39 2/8	37 2/8	5	5	Jefferson County	WA	Ron Humerickhouse	2005	363
243 1/8	38 4/8	41 0/8	31 7/8	6	5	Coos County	OR	Trent Fisher	2007	364
243 0/8	45 0/8	44 0/8	40 2/8	5	5	Jefferson County	WA	James M. Stark	1977	365
242 4/8	38 4/8	39 4/8	31 0/8	6	7	Lincoln County	OR	Terry W. Smith	2006	366
242 3/8	34 5/8	33 0/8	38 7/8	7	7	Douglas County	OR	Chad T. Montgomery	1993	367
242 2/8	36 2/8	36 5/8	32 4/8	7	6	Washington County	OR	Jack Mickel	2003	368
242 2/8	38 6/8	37 7/8	32 1/8	6	6	Lincoln County	OR	Terry W. Smith	2007	368
242 0/8	37 4/8	37 1/8	35 6/8	6	6	Jefferson County	WA	Kurt Goesch	1996	370
241 7/8	39 7/8	39 1/8	34 6/8	6	6	Clatsop County	OR	David Lawrence	1982	371
241 6/8	39 5/8	38 2/8	39 4/8	5	5	Clallam County	WA	Arnold LaGambina	1986	371
241 5/8	37 1/8	37 1/8	36 1/8	5	5	Washington County	OR	Douglas Rick Clark	1991	373
241 4/8	36 5/8	37 5/8	33 2/8	5	5	Coos County	OR	Colby Stemmerman	2003	374
241 3/8	38 2/8	39 0/8	33 3/8	6	5	Jefferson County	WA	Jim Pekola	2000	375
241 2/8	36 0/8	36 2/8	27 3/8	6	7	Clatsop County	OR	Robert G. Mucken	1989	376
*241 1/8	40 2/8	36 2/8	33 6/8	5	6	Coos County	OR	Phil Luschen	2008	377
240 7/8	36 7/8	36 3/8	36 6/8	5	5	Douglas County	OR	Richard J. Huselton	1992	378
240 6/8	39 4/8	40 0/8	35 2/8	5	5	Washington County	OR	Mark Plummer	2001	379
240 4/8	38 4/8	36 3/8	28 3/8	6	7	Lewis County	WA	Jeffrey D. Husted	2005	380

ROOSEVELT'S (OLYMPIC) ELK

Minimum Score 225 — Continued

SCORE	LENGTH OF R MAIN BEAM L	INSIDE SPREAD	NUMBER OF R POINTS L		AREA	STATE/ PROVINCE	HUNTER'S NAME	DATE	RANK
240 4/8	38 3/8	38 2/8	28 6/8	6	6	Coos County	OR	Jeff Weigel	2007	380
240 4/8	36 1/8	35 6/8	32 2/8	6	6	Grays Harbor County	WA	Bob Mayton	2010	380
*240 1/8	38 0/8	37 1/8	33 5/8	6	6	Jefferson County	WA	Jeff McLaughlin	2009	383
239 6/8	42 1/8	41 6/8	30 4/8	7	5	Tillamook County	OR	Parry M. Hurliman	2005	384
239 4/8	36 0/8	39 0/8	36 5/8	5	5	Pacific County	WA	Ronald J. Olsen	2000	385
239 0/8	39 2/8	37 0/8	36 4/8	6	6	Benton County	OR	Patrick Privatsky	1999	386
239 0/8	38 4/8	39 4/8	33 6/8	6	7	Coos County	OR	Lon E. Lauber	2007	386
238 7/8	40 7/8	41 0/8	36 1/8	6	8	Curry County	OR	Andy Johnson	2004	388
238 6/8	36 5/8	37 6/8	38 0/8	5	6	Grays Harbor County	WA	Richard Mazzei	1984	389
238 6/8	40 3/8	39 3/8	32 4/8	6	6	Lincoln County	OR	Warren Lynch	1986	389
238 6/8	39 6/8	38 5/8	32 4/8	6	6	Grays Harbor County	WA	Neil Mefford	2003	389
238 5/8	40 3/8	40 0/8	38 3/8	5	5	Benton County	OR	Donald E. Zuhlke	1989	392
238 4/8	40 7/8	40 3/8	34 2/8	5	5	Tillamook County	OR	Glen Link	2008	393
238 2/8	46 2/8	45 1/8	39 6/8	5	4	Pacific County	WA	John R. Martin	1978	394
238 2/8	39 4/8	37 3/8	37 0/8	5	5	Grays Harbor County	WA	Jack McDougall	1986	394
238 0/8	39 7/8	40 4/8	34 2/8	5	5	Jefferson County	WA	Larry Jensen	1985	396
238 0/8	40 0/8	39 7/8	34 6/8	5	6	Lincoln County	OR	Travis L. Robison	1998	396
237 6/8	36 0/8	36 6/8	33 4/8	7	6	Lincoln County	OR	Teddy Kosydar	1989	398
237 4/8	36 4/8	38 6/8	30 6/8	7	6	Coos County	OR	Derik Ford	2009	399
237 2/8	32 4/8	33 1/8	36 2/8	6	6	Clatsop County	OR	Robert J. Wilkie	1984	400
237 0/8	39 0/8	37 4/8	35 6/8	5	5	Jefferson County	WA	James A. Crain	2006	401
236 6/8	39 0/8	37 3/8	31 3/8	6	6	Jefferson County	WA	Mathew Hayvaz	1984	402
236 6/8	39 5/8	41 5/8	30 7/8	6	6	Lane County	OR	Steven T. Jones	1994	402
236 3/8	36 0/8	34 4/8	27 7/8	5	6	Coos County	OR	James T. Russ	1997	404
236 2/8	39 2/8	38 2/8	50 0/8	6	6	Douglas County	OR	Sam Wagner	2003	405
236 1/8	37 1/8	38 4/8	32 6/8	6	5	Washington County	OR	Joe Rutledge	1993	406
236 1/8	33 4/8	33 4/8	36 1/8	6	7	Grays Harbor County	WA	Jeff Loree	1999	406
236 1/8	36 6/8	37 4/8	36 5/8	5	6	Tillamook County	OR	Ron Sisson	2001	406
235 7/8	37 1/8	37 0/8	35 4/8	6	6	Polk County	OR	Joseph K. Saboe	1990	409
235 2/8	38 0/8	39 1/8	34 0/8	5	5	Tillamook County	OR	Smokey Crews	1983	410
235 2/8	37 4/8	38 5/8	33 7/8	5	6	Clallam County	WA	Daniel Siegner	1986	410
235 2/8	40 7/8	41 7/8	38 5/8	6	5	Jefferson County	WA	Kyle A. Winton	2001	410
235 0/8	39 1/8	39 2/8	31 2/8	6	5	Josephine County	OR	Joel Robertson	1982	413
235 0/8	36 2/8	34 1/8	38 0/8	6	6	Tillamook County	OR	Parry M. Hurliman	1995	413
234 7/8	37 6/8	35 6/8	35 7/8	7	7	Clatsop County	OR	Clint W. Heinz	2005	415
234 4/8	36 6/8	34 7/8	34 6/8	5	6	Coos County	OR	Bruce B. Stamp	1993	416
234 4/8	37 7/8	37 4/8	25 7/8	6	7	Tillamook County	OR	Ron Sisson	2004	416
234 4/8	40 1/8	38 3/8	35 0/8	5	5	Clatsop County	OR	Dusty McGrorty	2006	416
234 2/8	39 5/8	38 4/8	33 6/8	5	5	Clallam County	WA	Dean R. Swerin	1985	419
233 4/8	40 2/8	40 6/8	28 6/8	5	5	Grays Harbor County	WA	John J. Durst	1987	420
233 4/8	36 1/8	37 4/8	33 0/8	6	6	Tillamook County	OR	Joe Hulburt	1992	420
233 1/8	41 4/8	40 3/8	30 0/8	5	6	Curry County	OR	Kendal Smith	1982	422
233 0/8	35 6/8	37 1/8	28 0/8	5	5	Pacific County	WA	Parry Bagley	1991	423
233 0/8	36 5/8	35 2/8	36 6/8	5	6	Coos County	OR	Michael Fisher	2003	423
232 1/8	40 4/8	41 3/8	33 5/8	5	5	Columbia County	OR	Mitch Elliott	1993	425
231 7/8	35 5/8	37 4/8	32 3/8	5	5	Clallam County	WA	Frank LaGambina	1979	426
231 6/8	38 4/8	40 3/8	32 4/8	5	5	Columbia County	OR	Kirc Mattinen	2003	427
231 5/8	40 3/8	39 4/8	40 7/8	5	5	Grays Harbor County	WA	Todd Plato	1992	428
231 5/8	35 5/8	34 5/8	36 2/8	6	6	Tillamook County	OR	Glenn M. Link	2000	428
231 4/8	41 0/8	38 3/8	31 6/8	5	5	Washington County	OR	Jim Richter	1996	430
231 4/8	33 4/8	37 4/8	30 2/8	5	5	Grays Harbor County	WA	Jim Pekola	1996	430
231 3/8	35 3/8	33 5/8	30 6/8	6	6	Washington County	OR	Gregory D. Lueptow	1990	432
231 3/8	38 4/8	36 3/8	35 5/8	5	5	Coos County	OR	Chris Metzgus	2005	432
231 1/8	37 3/8	38 0/8	29 7/8	5	5	Yamhill County	OR	Curtis C. Altman	1983	434
231 0/8	34 2/8	34 6/8	40 0/8	5	6	Clatsop County	OR	Ronald Ray Noel	1989	435
230 6/8	35 2/8	34 4/8	32 2/8	6	6	Clallam County	WA	Wayne Haag	1980	436
230 5/8	34 4/8	34 2/8	33 2/8	6	6	Clatsop County	OR	Ted Perreard	1999	437
230 3/8	35 1/8	37 3/8	36 7/8	5	5	Wahkiakum County	WA	Westly Oatfield	2008	438
230 2/8	38 5/8	36 4/8	38 0/8	5	5	Coos County	OR	Thomas Tipton	1984	439
230 1/8	37 6/8	35 2/8	36 1/8	5	5	Tillamook County	OR	Lynn C. Reddekopp	1981	440
230 1/8	39 5/8	39 6/8	24 6/8	6	7	Douglas County	OR	Lee R. Hutsell	1996	440
230 0/8	35 6/8	34 7/8	34 0/8	6	6	Yamhill County	OR	Doug Bain	1994	442
229 0/8	44 3/8	44 3/8	35 6/8	5	4	Clallam County	WA	Pete J. Germeau	1982	443
228 7/8	36 7/8	37 2/8	29 5/8	6	6	Tillamook County	OR	Ed Flinter	2002	444
228 4/8	38 0/8	39 1/8	31 2/8	5	5	Jefferson County	WA	Blake Turner	2007	445
228 2/8	38 5/8	37 6/8	30 4/8	6	6	Tillamook County	OR	Rich Jensen	2002	446
228 1/8	36 7/8	34 7/8	34 1/8	5	5	Columbia County	OR	Mitch Elliott	1987	447
228 0/8	36 2/8	36 0/8	32 1/8	6	6	Curry County	OR	Ken French	1988	448
227 5/8	40 3/8	38 1/8	34 2/8	6	7	Clatsop County	OR	Ray C Nelson	1985	449
227 5/8	41 3/8	38 5/8	34 5/8	5	4	Clallam County	WA	Arnold LaGambina	1987	449
227 2/8	37 5/8	40 4/8	29 4/8	5	6	Benton County	OR	Felix Alan Lafond	1986	451
227 0/8	37 0/8	35 4/8	32 6/8	5	5	Columbia County	OR	Doug Guisinger	2001	451
227 1/8	36 2/8	31 0/8	29 5/8	5	7	Clatsop County	OR	Randy Jennings	1980	453
227 1/8	42 1/8	40 6/8	28 3/8	6	5	Clatsop County	OR	David Braem	1982	453
227 1/8	39 2/8	39 2/8	31 6/8	6	6	Columbia County	OR	Randy Jennings	2001	453
227 0/8	38 1/8	36 3/8	35 1/8	6	6	Lincoln County	OR	Richard Smith	1989	456
227 0/8	37 4/8	37 4/8	30 5/8	5	6	Clatsop County	OR	Roy R. Stevens	1992	456
227 0/8	34 0/8	33 5/8	35 0/8	6	6	Tillamook County	OR	Melody Sisson	2007	456
226 5/8	39 7/8	39 4/8	31 7/8	5	5	Columbia County	OR	Matt Schmidlin	2000	459
226 3/8	42 0/8	40 6/8	26 5/8	5	5	Clatsop County	OR	Jim Pekola	1993	460
226 3/8	37 6/8	38 6/8	34 3/8	6	6	Tillamook County	OR	Dallas Ash	2000	460
226 1/8	39 1/8	38 5/8	29 5/8	5	5	Yamhill County	OR	Patrick L. McGanty	1993	462
226 0/8	39 6/8	40 3/8	34 6/8	5	5	Clatsop County	OR	Johnny R. Holbrook	2001	463
225 7/8	36 2/8	37 0/8	32 1/8	5	5	Polk County	OR	Jerry Bailey	1991	464
225 4/8	37 0/8	35 4/8	35 2/8	5	5	Jefferson County	WA	Rodger Squirrel	1984	465
225 3/8	33 0/8	32 7/8	33 3/8	6	7	Polk County	OR	Gary Freuler	1988	466
225 0/8	37 1/8	34 0/8	36 4/8	5	5	Columbia County	OR	Robin Anderson	2000	467

Pope & Young Club

312 5/8

Official Scoring System for Bowhunting North American Big Game

ROOSEVELT'S ELK — Tule Elk

MINIMUM SCORE: 225

PANEL MEASURED

Crown Points	Right Antler	Left Antler
	4 2/8	2 1/8
	4 3/8	3 5/8

I. Total Length of Crown Points: 14 3/8

Abnormal Points	Right Antler	Left Antler
	13 3/8	

TOTAL TO E: 13 3/8

	COLUMN 1 Spread Credit	COLUMN 2	COLUMN 3 Left Antler	COLUMN 4 Difference
A. No. Points on Right Antler	9			
B. Tip to Tip Spread		44 6/8		
D. Inside Spread of Main Beams				
E. Total of Lengths of Abnormal				13 3/8
F. Length of Main Beam			40 4/8	3 1/8
G-1. Length of First Point			4/8	1 1/8
G-2. Length of Second Point			0/8	1 0/8
G-3. Length of Third Point				2 3/8
G-4. Length of Fourth Point				1 0/8
H-1.		8 0/8	8 2/8	2/8
H-2.		5 4/8	6 2/8	6/8
H-3.		9 1/8	6 2/8	2 7/8
H-4.		9 0/8	7 6/8	1 2/8
TOTALS	42 4/8	145 5/8	137 2/8	27 1/8

County: SOLANO   State/Prov: CA
Date: /1/90
Hunter: AUDREY GOODNIGHT

SUBTRACT Column 4: 27 1/8
FINAL SCORE: 312 5/8

WORLD RECORD TULE ELK
Score: 312 5/8
Location: Solano County, California
Date: 1990
Hunter: Audrey Goodnight

Tule Elk

by Audrey Goodnight

In 1990, my husband Rob and I applied for tags to hunt Tule Elk at Grizzly Island in Solano, California, which hadn't been hunted for many years. We later found out that I had been drawn to hunt September 1st through 4th; the fourth of five hunt periods.

We arrived at the island the day before opening day, scouted the area one final time and attended a mandatory hunter orientation meeting. At the meeting, we met our fellow hunters and were issued DFG blaze orange vests for obvious safety reasons (the other five hunters were using rifles) and so that law enforcement personnel could distinguish between hunters and possible "saboteurs" who were expected to show up to interfere with the hunt. During the previous three hunt periods, 29 protesters had been arrested and numerous citations had been issued for trespassing.

Spotting a herd far off, we began our stalk. At one point about half way there, one bull began bugling and rubbing his antlers on a telephone pole while the other bull moved behind a curve in the levee and out of sight. We stopped frequently to look over the levee and finally, about 150 yards from the pole, we spotted the bull, a large animal with a beautiful rack, lying 120 yards out from and 150 yards down the levee with his back to us! Crouching very low, we kept moving toward the telephone pole and, after what seemed an eternity, reached it. Now the bull was just over the short levee and about 120 yards away.

When Rob & I peeked over the levee, we saw directly in front of us a small one-and-a-half-foot deep drainage ditch running from the foot of the levee straight out to within 20 yards of the sleeping bull. Between the quiet pickle weed and the soft dirt in the bottom this low ditch, I couldn't have asked for better cover. And since the wind was blowing into our faces, the situation was perfect.

While Rob stayed behind, I crept over the levee and into the ditch and slowly and very carefully crawled to within 40 yards from the bull. Looking back, I saw Rob motioning to move closer to the bull and I crawled another ten yards. At that point, I noticed that if I got any closer, my shot would be blocked by a pole near where the bull was sleeping. I nocked an arrow, slowly stood, drew my 50-lb. Carroll bow and released the arrow, hitting the bull just behind the left shoulder. I quickly knelt down and nocked another arrow as he jumped up, trotted to my left and stopped broadside to me after running only 15 yards. Unfortunately, my second arrow missed completely, just under his chest.

I quietly snapped another arrow on my string as Rob began bugling from the levee behind me. The bull turned to look toward him and I put my head down, covered my face with the top limb of my bow and froze. After a moment, Rob stopped calling and several long seconds later, the bull turned to the right and stood broadside to me again. I shot my third arrow from a kneeling position and made a perfect lung shot.

I watched in amazement when the bull ran, stumbled and went down only 50 yards from where he had been hit. I couldn't believe it was over so quickly. I had taken my first bull elk on my first elk hunt, on opening day with a 50-lb. bow in an area with little or no cover. And what a bull! He weighted 625 lbs. and had a massive 9x9 rack with heavy webbing at the crown points. I will never forget this wonderful, once-in-a-lifetime experience!

TULE ELK

Minimum Score 225
Cervus elaphus nannodes

SCORE	LENGTH OF MAIN BEAM R	L	INSIDE SPREAD	NUMBER OF POINTS R	L	AREA	STATE/ PROVINCE	HUNTER'S NAME	DATE	RANK
312 5/8	43 5/8	40 4/8	42 4/8	9	8	Solano County	CA	Audrey Goodnight	1990	1
311 4/8	40 3/8	40 1/8	43 4/8	8	9	Solano County	CA	Walter J. Palmer	2009	2
311 1/8	46 1/8	45 2/8	40 7/8	7	8	Inyo County	CA	Mike McCall	2006	3
309 7/8	40 1/8	41 2/8	40 7/8	7	6	Monterey County	CA	Chuck Adams	1990	4
304 4/8	43 1/8	43 1/8	39 4/8	7	7	Inyo County	CA	Ed Fanchin	2005	5
303 0/8	44 2/8	43 7/8	45 5/8	7	7	Mendocino County	CA	Rick Duggan	2010	6
292 3/8	46 5/8	47 6/8	42 5/8	6	6	Mendocino County	CA	Chipper Dippel	2009	7
*291 1/8	41 7/8	42 0/8	42 6/8	7	9	Inyo County	CA	Cindy Krug	2008	8
*286 1/8	41 6/8	42 1/8	44 4/8	7	6	Monterey County	CA	Tim Sharpe	2005	9
*285 1/8	39 1/8	42 6/8	42 3/8	7	7	Inyo County	CA	Travis Schwartz	2008	10
275 3/8	42 0/8	43 1/8	36 0/8	7	7	Inyo County	CA	George Engelmann	2009	11
273 0/8	39 5/8	40 5/8	38 6/8	6	7	San Luis Obispo County	CA	Gary F. Bogner	1997	12
266 2/8	35 2/8	35 6/8	34 2/8	6	6	Kern County	CA	Richie Bland	2000	13
263 5/8	39 2/8	41 2/8	39 3/8	7	7	Inyo County	CA	Eric Jensen	2007	14
*263 1/8	40 3/8	39 4/8	34 5/8	7	7	Monterey County	CA	David W. Kiper	2004	15
*261 1/8	37 0/8	35 3/8	34 5/8	6	7	Inyo County	CA	Gary Roney	2007	16
*257 5/8	35 4/8	38 7/8	37 3/8	6	6	Mendocino County	CA	George Harms	2010	17
256 2/8	38 3/8	38 6/8	44 4/8	7	6	Inyo County	CA	Jim Walton	2007	18
255 3/8	39 4/8	39 2/8	37 1/8	6	6	Santa Clara County	CA	John D. "Jack" Frost	2008	19
248 3/8	38 1/8	37 1/8	40 4/8	6	7	Inyo County	CA	Chad Meadors	2008	20
247 6/8	39 6/8	38 4/8	40 2/8	6	7	Monterey County	CA	Todd Carminati	2006	21
244 1/8	39 1/8	38 4/8	41 0/8	5	7	Monterey County	CA	Ty Pelfrey	2009	22
243 4/8	36 1/8	33 3/8	45 3/8	7	7	Mendocino County	CA	Edwin L. DeYoung	2008	23
241 6/8	36 3/8	36 5/8	34 5/8	6	6	San Joaquin County	CA	Jeffrey D. Husted	2004	24
240 7/8	39 1/8	39 5/8	38 2/8	6	6	Inyo County	CA	John C. Martin	2010	25
240 6/8	33 3/8	33 3/8	35 7/8	7	6	Inyo County	CA	Richard Eckenburg	2005	26
237 4/8	35 4/8	34 6/8	39 3/8	6	6	San Luis Obispo County	CA	Gary M. Martin	2010	27
*233 4/8	36 3/8	37 0/8	36 6/8	6	6	Inyo County	CA	Shaun Ayers	2007	28
232 1/8	39 0/8	41 6/8	31 6/8	5	7	Inyo County	CA	Dave Semple	2006	29

WORLD RECORD ALASKA-YUKON MOOSE
Score: 249 1/8
Location: Earn Lake, Yukon Territory
Date: 2008
Hunter: Real Langlois

ALASKA-YUKON MOOSE

Minimum Score 170

Alces alces gigas

SCORE	INSIDE SPREAD	WIDTH OF R PALM L	NUMBER OF R POINTS L	AREA	STATE/ PROVINCE	HUNTER'S NAME	DATE	RANK
249 1/8	75 5/8	20 0/8 17 4/8	14 13	Earn Lake	YUK	Real Langlois	2008	1
248 0/8	74 0/8	18 6/8 19 2/8	11 11	Bear Creek	AK	Dr. Michael L. Cusack	1973	2
240 4/8	70 0/8	16 2/8 15 6/8	12 12	Galena	AK	Sam Smith	1995	3
229 6/8	63 4/8	17 2/8 17 3/8	11 13	Stewart River	YUK	Tim Butts	2007	4
229 1/8	70 1/8	15 0/8 14 7/8	11 11	Doghouse Creek	AK	Rick Schikora	2002	5
229 1/8	63 1/8	15 2/8 15 0/8	13 14	King Salmon	AK	Thomas E. Monacelli	2005	5
227 7/8	68 3/8	18 2/8 16 3/8	14 13	Earn Lake	YUK	Ted Brown	1995	7
227 6/8	60 0/8	17 1/8 16 1/8	13 12	Koyukuk River	AK	Larry Oppe	1998	8
227 2/8	72 2/8	15 6/8 17 5/8	9 11	Salmon River	AK	Ryan Hoerner	2002	9
226 1/8	66 7/8	18 6/8 16 7/8	9 15	Kenai Peninsula	AK	Randy Ulmer	2002	10
224 6/8	67 6/8	19 7/8 16 4/8	12 14	Koyukuk River	AK	Larry D. Jones	2000	11
224 3/8	59 5/8	17 0/8 16 4/8	15 13	Iliamna Lake	AK	George Faerber	1974	12
224 1/8	67 4/8	19 0/8 14 5/8	10 12	Mosquito Flats	AK	William C. Shuster	1998	13
224 0/8	65 4/8	15 0/8 14 2/8	12 12	Iliamna Lake	AK	Zane Streater	1995	14
224 0/8	65 0/8	15 0/8 14 1/8	12 13	Dulbi River	AK	Rick Boullion	1995	14
223 7/8	73 7/8	14 2/8 16 0/8	12 11	Kugruk River	AK	Rocky Tope	1978	16
223 2/8	68 0/8	14 3/8 16 2/8	11 14	Innoko River	AK	Roger Stewart	1993	17
223 1/8	62 5/8	13 3/8 14 2/8	11 11	Sugarloaf Mtn.	AK	James C. Walters	1990	18
222 1/8	67 1/8	20 0/8 15 4/8	13 12	Lower Susitna River	AK	Steve McCalmant	1981	19
221 6/8	64 2/8	16 0/8 16 0/8	9 9	Moose John River	AK	Michael S. Pasztor	1993	20
221 6/8	60 2/8	16 1/8 14 7/8	14 17	Mac Millan River	YUK	Dr. Warren Strickland	1998	20
221 4/8	64 2/8	15 5/8 15 2/8	11 12	Koyukuk River	AK	Windell Arnold	1995	22
221 3/8	54 7/8	16 6/8 15 2/8	14 13	Hart Lake	YUK	M. Robert DeLaney	2001	23
220 3/8	57 3/8	16 0/8 16 2/8	12 11	Little Delta River	AK	William Wright	1959	24
220 2/8	64 2/8	14 4/8 15 0/8	14 12	Koyukuk River	AK	Craig Pfent	1998	25
219 7/8	65 5/8	14 4/8 14 5/8	16 14	Hart River	YUK	Kim S. Hussong	1994	26
219 7/8	64 7/8	13 2/8 14 0/8	12 12	Kuskokwim River	AK	A. "ROBNHD" Domas III	2004	26
219 0/8	61 0/8	14 4/8 8 0/8	13 12	Kichatna River	AK	Ronald N. Kolpin	1974	28
*218 3/8	65 3/8	13 2/8 17 4/8	11 14	Ambler River	AK	George Semple	2005	29
218 2/8	69 0/8	15 7/8 17 4/8	10 8	Galena	AK	Lon E. Lauber	1993	30
*218 2/8	55 0/8	20 2/8 18 3/8	13 13	Redstone River	AK	Lonny Traweek	2008	30
217 4/8	71 2/8	13 2/8 12 6/8	10 12	Ugashik River	AK	Gary Hoffer	1986	32
217 4/8	63 6/8	18 4/8 18 3/8	14 11	Grayling Creek	AK	Carl Spaeth	1995	32
217 3/8	64 1/8	17 0/8 15 0/8	14 15	Moose John River	AK	Mike Parsons	1991	34
217 0/8	59 6/8	15 1/8 15 4/8	10 10	Selawik River	AK	James Matuszewski	1997	35
216 4/8	57 6/8	16 1/8 18 1/8	13 13	Jim River	AK	James A. Todhunter	1996	36
216 1/8	57 1/8	16 7/8 16 1/8	11 12	Cheeneetnuk River	AK	Rocky D. Tschappat	1995	37
215 7/8	63 3/8	13 2/8 12 1/8	15 14	Koyukuk River	AK	Rickie D. Snell	1990	38
215 7/8	63 1/8	16 2/8 17 1/8	12 13	Stony River	AK	Thomas R. Johnson	1997	38
215 4/8	68 0/8	14 0/8 19 2/8	12 10	Cinder River	AK	D. Kevin Moore, DDS	1997	40
215 4/8	60 4/8	13 6/8 13 3/8	12 12	Tanana	AK	Eric Whaley	1999	40
215 3/8	71 7/8	13 5/8 12 7/8	11 11	Boston Creek	AK	Charles Harrison	1992	42
215 0/8	56 2/8	14 0/8 13 2/8	13 17	Koyukuk River	AK	Patricio Sada	1998	43
214 4/8	63 4/8	15 2/8 17 2/8	8 11	Mac Millan River	YUK	Robert W. Harris	1996	44
214 3/8	62 3/8	11 1/8 10 6/8	10 13	Beluga River	AK	Tony Dawson	2004	45
214 2/8	57 2/8	14 5/8 17 2/8	11 16	Cheeneetnuk River	AK	Dean Layman	1988	46
214 2/8	63 0/8	16 6/8 15 1/8	9 10	Hogatza River	AK	Dennis Burnett	2000	46
213 3/8	70 5/8	15 7/8 14 1/8	7 8	Two Peat Mtn.	YUK	Mark Zimmerman	1998	48
213 2/8	62 4/8	18 4/8 15 6/8	9 10	Rainy Pass	AK	Rick Tollison	1978	49
213 1/8	59 7/8	17 3/8 18 1/8	13 12	Mulchatna River	AK	Peter Weatherford	1988	50
213 1/8	64 7/8	13 5/8 14 2/8	12 12	Dishna River	AK	Michael Turner	1999	50
213 0/8	55 6/8	14 0/8 14 3/8	13 13	Kobuk River	AK	Joe Ellsworth	1998	52
212 7/8	65 7/8	13 0/8 17 6/8	9 10	Mulchatna River	AK	Jay Massey	1973	53
212 7/8	65 5/8	12 4/8 15 5/8	12 14	Tetlin River	AK	Mike Kistler	1997	53
212 6/8	61 4/8	18 5/8 16 3/8	10 10	Tay River	YUK	Johnnie Walters	2000	55
212 5/8	69 3/8	11 5/8 13 3/8	12 13	Kenai	AK	Charles Palmer	1993	56
212 4/8	68 4/8	17 7/8 14 7/8	10 13	Tagagawik River	AK	Ronell Skinner	2001	57
212 3/8	60 7/8	14 7/8 15 7/8	13 9	Moose Lake	YUK	Greg Wadsworth	2005	58
212 2/8	62 6/8	14 2/8 15 0/8	12 13	Koyukuk River	AK	Joe Caswell	1991	59
212 1/8	58 3/8	15 4/8 14 6/8	16 15	Brooks Range	AK	Roger Stewart	1985	60
212 1/8	60 1/8	14 1/8 15 2/8	12 13	Mac Millan River	YUK	Jerry Seyller	1998	60
212 1/8	66 7/8	15 4/8 11 7/8	11 10	Koliganek	AK	James Retzer	2003	60
211 2/8	66 6/8	15 0/8 14 4/8	9 9	Anchorage	AK	Dr. Rex Hancock	1961	63
211 2/8	66 6/8	21 3/8 16 0/8	7 9	Meshik River	AK	Art Kragness	1970	63
211 1/8	55 1/8	16 2/8 13 0/8	11 10	Mac Millan River	YUK	David Emken	1994	65
211 0/8	59 4/8	12 0/8 13 0/8	14 13	Galena	AK	John C. Fisher	1996	66
210 6/8	60 0/8	12 7/8 13 1/8	13 13	New Stuyahok	AK	Thomas Clevenger	1988	67
210 6/8	64 6/8	15 3/8 12 6/8	13 11	Mystery Creek	AK	Kevin M. Krause	1997	67
210 5/8	60 1/8	15 0/8 15 6/8	13 10	Kichatna River	AK	Frank Leonardo	1996	69
210 5/8	61 3/8	15 3/8 15 3/8	10 11	Mac Millan River	YUK	Don Lind	1998	69
210 4/8	55 4/8	14 5/8 15 2/8	15 16	Dulbi River	AK	Ray L. Bunney	2003	71
210 2/8	64 5/8	14 1/8 13 6/8	8 9	Nabesna	AK	Bill Ellis	1965	72
209 7/8	60 5/8	13 2/8 11 3/8	14 14	Koyukuk River	AK	Gerald Weeks	1990	73
209 6/8	69 0/8	13 0/8 14 4/8	9 9	Port Heiden	AK	Margaret Cooley	1966	74
209 6/8	63 4/8	16 2/8 13 3/8	11 11	Toklat	AK	Craig R. Crawford	2009	74
209 4/8	59 4/8	11 1/8 12 5/8	11 11	Healy	AK	Jack P. Lohrenz	1996	75
209 4/8	56 4/8	14 6/8 15 2/8	12 13	Coal River	YUK	Vance Mitchell	2002	75
209 3/8	63 3/8	15 3/8 14 3/8	11 13	Mac Millan River	YUK	David Harris	1995	77
*209 2/8	63 4/8	14 4/8 13 4/8	9 7	Becharof Lake	AK	Timothy R. Holt	2005	78
209 1/8	62 7/8	14 6/8 19 4/8	8 9	Susitna River	AK	John D. 'Jack' Frost	1981	79
209 1/8	64 7/8	15 0/8 16 0/8	9 10	Tagagawik River	AK	Bill Grahlherr	1984	79
209 1/8	63 1/8	15 0/8 14 1/8	13 13	Mac Millan River	YUK	David Baldwin	1989	79
208 6/8	63 0/8	13 3/8 13 7/8	9 9	Galena	AK	James McCloskey	1988	82
208 6/8	64 2/8	11 4/8 12 6/8	11 14	Koyukuk River	AK	David Emken	1998	82
208 4/8	65 2/8	14 2/8 13 3/8	12 12	Kemuk Mtn.	AK	L. Grant Foster	1997	84
208 1/8	59 7/8	13 5/8 15 2/8	13 13	Brooks Range	AK	Ted Grover	1985	85
208 0/8	65 4/8	13 0/8 12 0/8	9 7	Alaska Peninsula	AK	Jack Niles	1970	86
207 5/8	59 1/8	14 3/8 14 2/8	14 15	Coleen River	AK	Lyle Willmarth	1990	87
207 2/8	60 4/8	12 1/8 16 6/8	10 10	Yenlo Mtns.	AK	John F. Sumrall	1979	88
207 0/8	63 2/8	16 5/8 15 7/8	12 10	Dawson City	YUK	Buck Siler	2008	89
206 5/8	62 1/8	12 2/8 13 2/8	12 13	Kotzebue	AK	Bruce A. Moe	1980	90
206 3/8	69 3/8	12 0/8 9 4/8	7 9	Alaska Peninsula	AK	Dr. Charles R. Leidheiser	1974	91
206 2/8	59 4/8	12 5/8 15 2/8	15 14	Kuparuk River	AK	Kurt Lepping	1987	92
206 2/8	50 6/8	16 5/8 16 2/8	13 17	Mac Millan River	YUK	T. Sanford Roberts	1990	92
206 0/8	65 0/8	12 1/8 14 0/8	12 11	Chulitna River	AK	Rodney Bremer	1988	94

777

ALASKA-YUKON MOOSE

Minimum Score 170   Continued

SCORE	INSIDE SPREAD	WIDTH OF PALM R L	NUMBER OF POINTS R L	AREA	STATE/ PROVINCE	HUNTER'S NAME	DATE	RANK
206 0/8	57 6/8	13 2/8 16 7/8	15 10	Grayling Creek	AK	Karl R. Spaeth	1997	94
205 7/8	55 1/8	13 1/8 14 0/8	12 10	Innoko River	AK	Jack Smythe	1974	96
205 6/8	70 0/8	15 7/8 13 3/8	9 9	Alaska Peninsula	AK	Dr. Howard Schneider	1982	97
205 6/8	67 6/8	11 6/8 12 0/8	12 9	Kuskokwim River	AK	Jimmy Harkins	1986	97
205 6/8	59 4/8	11 3/8 12 6/8	12 16	Koyukuk River	AK	Richard W. Main	1998	97
205 5/8	52 5/8	13 4/8 15 1/8	15 14	Koyukuk River	AK	R. Eric Shields	2003	100
205 4/8	57 6/8	13 4/8 13 3/8	11 13	Horsetrail Lake	AK	Donald Poole	1979	101
205 4/8	54 4/8	15 6/8 12 4/8	13 12	Willow	AK	Dwight E. Guynn	2001	101
205 3/8	68 3/8	12 0/8 14 5/8	13 14	Bearpaw River	AK	Mark C. Booth	2006	103
205 2/8	64 0/8	14 0/8 12 7/8	8 12	Alaska Peninsula	AK	Donald B. McIntosh	1969	104
205 1/8	57 7/8	14 2/8 12 4/8	15 13	Telaquana	AK	Mike Mitten	1988	105
205 1/8	63 3/8	15 1/8 14 3/8	13 14	Mac Millan River	YUK	David M. Richards	1996	105
*205 1/8	62 5/8	15 2/8 11 6/8	14 10	Noatak River	AK	Randy Goza	2006	105
204 7/8	60 3/8	14 5/8 15 6/8	10 11	Paxon	AK	Alan Perry	1972	108
204 7/8	68 3/8	14 7/8 14 6/8	7 11	Black Lake	AK	Stanley Winslow	1973	108
204 7/8	58 1/8	15 1/8 15 4/8	12 11	Jim River	AK	Eldon Holm	1990	108
204 4/8	58 0/8	12 6/8 13 0/8	11 11	Chilikadrotna River	AK	Peter Thomas Weatherford	1987	111
204 2/8	61 4/8	13 4/8 12 5/8	10 11	Fairbanks	AK	Keith Jensen	1986	112
204 2/8	56 6/8	14 1/8 14 3/8	14 12	Deer Hunting Slough	AK	Ted K. Jaycox	1995	112
204 2/8	54 0/8	12 4/8 11 7/8	12 13	Mac Millan River	YUK	Edward Pylman	2001	112
204 1/8	57 3/8	14 1/8 15 5/8	15 10	Cooper Creek	AK	Joe W. Harrison	1993	115
203 7/8	55 7/8	14 4/8 13 3/8	14 13	Grayling Creek	AK	Carl Spaeth	2001	116
203 6/8	66 0/8	11 5/8 12 7/8	13 11	Port Heiden	AK	Jim Dougherty	1968	117
203 6/8	62 2/8	14 1/8 14 3/8	11 14	Dadina River	AK	Mike Mitten	2002	117
203 5/8	51 1/8	13 4/8 16 1/8	14 19	Tobally Lake	YUK	Tom Lester	2005	119
203 3/8	66 7/8	11 0/8 11 7/8	13 12	Seven Mile Lake	AK	Dr. William J. Young, Jr.	1980	120
203 3/8	66 5/8	15 2/8 17 5/8	11 13	Dulbi River	AK	Kenneth E. Gordon	1998	120
203 3/8	54 5/8	14 2/8 15 7/8	16 15	Toobally Lake	YUK	Steve Rider	2004	120
203 1/8	59 1/8	18 3/8 17 7/8	10 11	Earn Lake	YUK	Kevin M. Fisher	1999	124
203 1/8	55 1/8	16 5/8 17 2/8	12 11	Poison Lake	YUK	Derrill Herman	2004	124
202 7/8	58 1/8	12 6/8 13 4/8	15 13	Earn Lake	YUK	Dr. R. D. Keeler	1986	126
202 7/8	66 3/8	13 2/8 12 4/8	8 14	Susitna River	AK	David Bieganski	1997	126
202 4/8	49 6/8	14 2/8 14 4/8	10 12	Brooks Range	AK	Brent Chapman	1978	128
202 4/8	58 2/8	15 2/8 14 1/8	13 12	Chulitna River	AK	Rickie D. Snell	1982	128
202 3/8	67 1/8	14 7/8 13 7/8	12 8	Lower MacMillan River	YUK	Doug Hutchinson	2004	130
202 2/8	62 6/8	12 5/8 13 4/8	9 10	Toolik River	AK	George P. Mann	1987	131
202 0/8	63 1/8	14 2/8 13 5/8	10 8	Moose John River	AK	Kent Brigham	1985	132
202 0/8	61 2/8	12 2/8 13 2/8	13 13	Yukon River	AK	Tom Skripps	1994	132
202 0/8	51 2/8	15 0/8 17 0/8	14 13	Tay River	YUK	William L. Cox	1999	132
202 0/8	57 6/8	12 7/8 13 0/8	12 14	Salcha River	AK	Dirk Stolz/Jane Stolz	2000	132
202 0/8	62 0/8	12 0/8 12 4/8	12 14	Worm Lake	YUK	Tom Hoffman	2002	132
201 7/8	62 1/8	17 0/8 20 1/8	8 12	Mac Millan River	YUK	Michael J. Windemuller	2001	137
201 6/8	59 0/8	11 7/8 13 0/8	13 12	Brooks Range	AK	Mike Rosetti	1985	138
201 5/8	58 1/8	12 0/8 12 3/8	13 13	Natla River	NWT	Will Pick	2003	139
201 4/8	61 4/8	10 2/8 13 3/8	7 10	Ogilvie Mtns.	YUK	Camp Newton	2008	140
201 2/8	62 4/8	14 1/8 13 2/8	10 10	Rackla Lake	YUK	Paul Hight	1991	142
201 2/8	63 6/8	14 7/8 14 7/8	14 13	Brooks Range	AK	James L. Behn	1991	142
201 1/8	60 1/8	13 5/8 10 6/8	10 14	Wood River	AK	Kyle Koschmeder	2002	144
200 7/8	58 5/8	12 5/8 15 0/8	13 13	Wrangell Mtns.	AK	Robert Warpack	1988	145
200 4/8	64 0/8	14 4/8 14 0/8	10 11	Dog Salmon River	AK	Robert C. Keadle	1972	146
200 2/8	62 2/8	13 1/8 12 7/8	12 12	King Salmon	AK	Ken Slaght	1982	146
200 2/8	60 4/8	13 6/8 11 0/8	12 12	Skwentna River	AK	David Bailey	1983	146
200 2/8	56 4/8	14 0/8 14 2/8	13 14	Hogatza River	AK	Bob Ameen	2000	146
200 0/8	65 2/8	12 2/8 15 1/8	9 12	Galena	AK	Sam Smith	1993	150
199 7/8	50 1/8	14 5/8 13 6/8	13 13	Bonnet Plume Lake	YUK	Rick Stockburger	2000	151
199 7/8	58 5/8	12 3/8 13 5/8	12 12	Copper River	AK	Jeffrey Amerson	2008	151
199 6/8	52 0/8	12 5/8 12 2/8	10 11	Timberline Lk. Kenai Peninsula	AK	DeWayne Benton	1984	153
199 5/8	61 3/8	15 2/8 14 2/8	13 14	Koyukuk River	AK	Dan Waelbrock	1989	154
199 5/8	59 5/8	12 6/8 12 2/8	13 11	Kalzas Lake	YUK	Robert Krasinski	1996	154
199 3/8	56 1/8	11 2/8 11 2/8	9 9	Nelchina	AK	Henry Wichers	1962	156
199 2/8	58 4/8	14 4/8 14 7/8	12 10	Koyukuk River	AK	Joe Caswell	1990	157
199 2/8	62 0/8	12 5/8 14 4/8	9 13	Hogatza River	AK	Dean Ashton	2004	157
198 7/8	63 7/8	11 1/8 13 0/8	8 10	Gulkana Basin	AK	Thomas L. A. Pucci	1970	159
198 7/8	64 1/8	15 3/8 15 6/8	7 8	Tagagawik River	AK	Thomas E. Rothrock	1991	159
198 7/8	62 5/8	13 0/8 11 6/8	12 10	Koyukuk River	AK	M. R. James	2000	159
198 7/8	64 5/8	14 2/8 14 2/8	11 11	Tsiu River	AK	Jim Gianladis	2005	159
198 6/8	56 2/8	12 4/8 14 0/8	12 14	Ogilvie River	YUK	Rick Duggan	2004	163
198 5/8	54 5/8	15 6/8 17 1/8	10 11	Stokes Lake	YUK	Raymond L. Howell, Sr.	1997	164
198 4/8	60 2/8	16 0/8 15 4/8	9 10	Arctic Wildlife Refuge	AK	William Gardner Rowell	1981	165
198 4/8	64 4/8	14 3/8 13 6/8	10 7	Koyukuk River	AK	Michael W. Carroll	1998	165
198 4/8	60 4/8	13 3/8 14 3/8	14 12	Koyukuk River	AK	Mark C. Petersen	2001	165
198 2/8	52 2/8	17 0/8 13 4/8	8 10	Nenana River	AK	Dr. Harley Scholz	1973	168
198 1/8	63 5/8	11 3/8 11 6/8	10 12	Rainy Pass	AK	Dr. Henry C. McDonald	1970	169
198 1/8	53 5/8	14 3/8 15 2/8	12 9	Grayling Creek	AK	James C. Carlson	1995	169
198 0/8	61 2/8	17 3/8 14 5/8	10 12	Yantarni Bay	AK	Mark "Gutz" Gutsmiedl	2001	171
197 6/8	64 0/8	11 4/8 11 2/8	12 11	King Salmon	AK	Gary L. Petty	1976	172
197 6/8	63 2/8	13 2/8 12 1/8	8 9	Susitna	AK	Mark S Bode	1989	172
197 6/8	54 4/8	15 4/8 13 4/8	6 8	Mac Millan River	YUK	Alan Schroeder	1995	172
197 6/8	58 0/8	14 2/8 14 6/8	8 8	Yellow River	AK	Dave Christofferson	2000	172
197 6/8	63 2/8	12 7/8 13 7/8	7 9	Wind River	AK	Mark Buehrer	2009	172
197 5/8	59 5/8	12 7/8 12 5/8	9 9	Galena	AK	George Ollert	1988	176
197 5/8	55 1/8	14 3/8 12 0/8	12 12	Mac Millan River	YUK	Bill Bolin	2007	176
197 4/8	65 4/8	13 0/8 14 5/8	6 9	Ugashik River	AK	Robert Borland	1972	178
197 4/8	61 4/8	10 6/8 12 1/8	8 11	Ugashik Lake	AK	John Wallace	1974	178
197 4/8	59 2/8	11 4/8 15 2/8	12 12	Chulitna River	AK	Rickie D. Snell	1983	178
197 4/8	62 6/8	16 5/8 19 3/8	6 11	Mac Millan River	YUK	Robert H. Torstenson	1998	178
197 2/8	64 2/8	12 3/8 14 4/8	8 8	Sugar Loaf Mtn.	AK	Jeffrey S. Stevens	1988	182
197 1/8	62 1/8	14 4/8 11 1/8	12 10	Susitna River	AK	Jake Sonnentag	1969	183
197 1/8	59 3/8	19 1/8 13 5/8	11 8	Mac Millan River	YUK	Bob Fromme	1991	183
197 1/8	64 7/8	12 6/8 17 1/8	10 11	Mount Gillis	YUK	Rick Martin	1999	183
197 0/8	62 6/8	12 0/8 12 3/8	8 11	King Salmon	AK	Brian L. Heise	1977	186
197 0/8	64 0/8	16 2/8 15 4/8	11 7	Deer Hunting Slough	AK	Ronnie Everett	1995	186
197 0/8	56 6/8	14 2/8 14 4/8	13 12	Dury Lake	YUK	Darlene J. Stansfield	2005	186
197 0/8	62 2/8	12 4/8 12 2/8	8 10	Hogatza River	AK	Dick Driscol	2005	186
197 0/8	59 4/8	12 5/8 12 1/8	8 10	North Lake	YUK	F. David Thornberry	2005	186

778

ALASKA-YUKON MOOSE

Minimum Score 170

Continued

SCORE	INSIDE SPREAD	WIDTH OF PALM R / L	NUMBER OF POINTS R / L	AREA	STATE/ PROVINCE	HUNTER'S NAME	DATE	RANK
*196 7/8	55 5/8	13 2/8 / 13 7/8	8 / 11	Tonsina River	AK	Scott Smith	2010	191
196 6/8	63 6/8	13 2/8 / 16 4/8	6 / 6	Alaska Peninsula	AK	Phillip Durr	1969	192
196 6/8	62 4/8	10 7/8 / 11 2/8	8 / 8	Becharof Lake	AK	Tom Behunin	1999	192
196 5/8	58 3/8	15 2/8 / 14 1/8	9 / 10	Kaktovik	AK	Judy Grooms	1987	194
196 5/8	59 7/8	11 4/8 / 12 5/8	12 / 9	Cheeneetnuk River	AK	Dan J. Ryle, Jr.	2002	194
196 5/8	57 3/8	12 6/8 / 13 4/8	10 / 10	Wrangell Mtns.	AK	Stephen A. Kenesie	2009	194
196 4/8	63 0/8	11 1/8 / 11 1/8	10 / 10	Chilikadrotna River	AK	Patrick J. Lefemine	1991	197
196 4/8	55 0/8	13 1/8 / 14 1/8	10 / 11	Koyukuk River	AK	Mike Misch	1994	197
*196 3/8	57 7/8	11 3/8 / 11 1/8	12 / 13	Fort Richardson	AK	Marc Taylor	2008	199
196 2/8	58 0/8	11 0/8 / 11 5/8	8 / 9	Mulchatna River	AK	Kurt M. Zurawski	1989	200
196 1/8	59 5/8	13 2/8 / 15 7/8	9 / 8	Selawik River	AK	Todd Bandemer	2003	201
195 7/8	55 5/8	13 3/8 / 12 2/8	13 / 14	June Lake	NWT	Chuck Adams	1993	202
195 7/8	61 7/8	12 0/8 / 12 4/8	10 / 10	Galena	AK	Dan Ermatinger	2002	202
195 6/8	55 2/8	10 1/8 / 11 3/8	13 / 11	Koyukuk River	AK	Mark Hanson	1990	204
195 6/8	56 6/8	11 4/8 / 11 6/8	14 / 14	Kuskokwim River	AK	Brian Brockette	1996	204
195 5/8	52 5/8	11 4/8 / 11 0/8	12 / 12	Fairbanks	AK	Rocky Chisholm	1988	206
195 4/8	55 6/8	12 6/8 / 13 6/8	10 / 10	Bonnet Plume Lake	YUK	Billy Ellis	1981	207
195 4/8	54 4/8	13 5/8 / 13 3/8	10 / 9	Hart River	YUK	Brett R. DeGraaf	2007	207
195 1/8	53 5/8	14 2/8 / 13 2/8	10 / 9	Artic Red River	NWT	Raymond E. Stongle	1995	209
195 1/8	60 5/8	13 5/8 / 11 0/8	12 / 11	Dicer Creek	YUK	Jordan Engelsma	2000	209
195 1/8	58 1/8	11 3/8 / 13 2/8	11 / 13	Mac Millan River	YUK	Bruce Hall	2007	209
195 0/8	68 2/8	14 0/8 / 12 6/8	7 / 7	Iliamna Lake	AK	Rex William Maurer	1987	212
195 0/8	52 0/8	14 0/8 / 14 0/8	11 / 10	Hess River	YUK	Anthony "Del" DelMastro	2005	212
194 7/8	53 1/8	11 7/8 / 12 4/8	13 / 14	Tustumena Lake	AK	Lavern Davidhizar	1980	214
194 6/8	56 6/8	12 2/8 / 12 3/8	9 / 9	Juniper Creek	AK	David L. Stull	1991	215
194 4/8	64 0/8	17 5/8 / 15 3/8	11 / 7	Alaska Peninsula	AK	Jim Dougherty	1962	216
194 4/8	61 0/8	11 6/8 / 11 0/8	12 / 11	Faro	YUK	Dennis Forchic	2002	216
194 4/8	52 6/8	13 4/8 / 13 6/8	11 / 13	Bonasila River	AK	Walter J. Palmer	2002	216
194 4/8	64 2/8	12 5/8 / 13 5/8	12 / 12	Mac Millan River	YUK	Mike Wampold	2004	216
194 3/8	57 5/8	11 4/8 / 15 5/8	11 / 12	Mystery Creek	AK	Joe Kelly	1989	220
194 2/8	61 6/8	12 7/8 / 13 7/8	7 / 12	Koyukuk River	AK	Thomas J. Hentrick	1984	221
194 2/8	59 4/8	12 5/8 / 13 0/8	11 / 10	Ladue River	AK	Larry Daly	1999	221
194 0/8	58 6/8	13 6/8 / 12 2/8	8 / 9	Lake Clark	AK	Dr. Gary G. Sauer	1987	223
194 0/8	59 6/8	11 4/8 / 12 2/8	12 / 13	Kotzebue	AK	Mark D. Mishinski	1990	223
193 5/8	60 3/8	10 7/8 / 12 5/8	8 / 9	Beluga Mtn.	AK	Dennis A. Lundine	1984	225
193 5/8	59 3/8	11 4/8 / 12 2/8	12 / 11	Dishna River	AK	Luther L.N. Trower, Jr.	1999	225
193 5/8	58 3/8	10 0/8 / 11 3/8	7 / 9	Iowa Ridge	AK	Fred P. Biasiello	2008	225
193 4/8	57 0/8	14 4/8 / 14 2/8	10 / 10	Pilot Point	AK	Lucien Rouse	1997	228
193 4/8	60 0/8	14 2/8 / 17 2/8	8 / 11	Kotzebue	AK	Frank S. Noska IV	2007	228
193 3/8	53 7/8	11 6/8 / 11 6/8	10 / 10	Kenai Peninsula	AK	Robert LaFollette	1962	230
193 2/8	56 2/8	13 6/8 / 13 4/8	10 / 13	Can Creek	AK	Dale Dye	2000	231
193 0/8	52 6/8	13 5/8 / 12 3/8	8 / 10	Kateel River	AK	Dennis Tol	1987	232
193 0/8	53 2/8	12 2/8 / 12 4/8	10 / 12	Galena	AK	Greg Campbell	1996	232
193 0/8	62 4/8	10 4/8 / 9 5/8	12 / 12	Koyukuk River	AK	Jeff Wingard	2003	232
192 7/8	56 3/8	13 7/8 / 12 7/8	9 / 10	Little Tok River	AK	Dennis L. Lattery	1977	235
192 6/8	57 0/8	11 6/8 / 11 7/8	12 / 13	Old Steese Hwy.	AK	Michael R. Chadwick	1994	236
192 5/8	55 1/8	10 5/8 / 12 5/8	11 / 13	Wrangell Mtns.	AK	Loren Willey	1973	237
192 5/8	60 1/8	13 1/8 / 12 4/8	11 / 11	Iditarod River	AK	Raymond P. Mozes	2007	237
192 4/8	60 6/8	14 2/8 / 12 4/8	7 / 9	Kluane Lake	YUK	Eugene A. Tieman	1973	239
192 4/8	51 0/8	10 6/8 / 9 2/8	14 / 12	Fort Richardson	AK	Donald D. Roberts	1984	239
192 4/8	61 4/8	11 3/8 / 12 0/8	8 / 10	Kuparuk River	AK	Robert Barrie	1987	239
192 3/8	55 7/8	11 6/8 / 12 0/8	11 / 11	Eklutna Lake	AK	Ron C. Harvey	1989	242
192 3/8	60 5/8	15 6/8 / 12 2/8	12 / 10	Wood River	AK	David A. Van Dyke	1996	242
192 2/8	63 4/8	12 0/8 / 12 4/8	13 / 8	Fish Creek	AK	Jack Hightower	1999	244
192 1/8	51 3/8	12 0/8 / 13 0/8	12 / 12	Koyukuk River	AK	Jeffery R. Barnett	1997	245
192 0/8	52 6/8	14 2/8 / 16 2/8	8 / 10	Clarence Lake	AK	John Schoenike	1966	246
192 0/8	69 6/8	10 6/8 / 13 4/8	7 / 9	Wood River	AK	Doug Strecker	1981	246
192 0/8	56 4/8	14 0/8 / 13 3/8	8 / 9	Koyukuk River	AK	Joe Caswell	1989	246
192 0/8	56 6/8	14 4/8 / 11 1/8	11 / 12	Kilik River	AK	John S. Borg	1991	246
192 0/8	59 6/8	11 6/8 / 12 6/8	9 / 9	Mac Millan River	YUK	Rick Morley	1993	246
191 7/8	57 7/8	16 3/8 / 14 7/8	8 / 10	Rainy Pass	AK	Rick Tollison	1977	251
191 7/8	67 7/8	10 5/8 / 10 4/8	8 / 7	Fish Creek	AK	Richard D. Clemons	1998	251
191 7/8	59 7/8	12 2/8 / 13 1/8	11 / 11	Mac Millan River	YUK	Larry Ellis	2010	251
191 6/8	54 6/8	12 3/8 / 12 2/8	9 / 12	Brooks Range	AK	Joseph Stanevich	1986	254
191 5/8	59 5/8	11 6/8 / 12 5/8	11 / 12	Mac Millan River	YUK	Mike Craig	1996	255
191 3/8	57 3/8	14 0/8 / 14 5/8	8 / 11	Whitefish Lake	AK	Jim Hoss	1975	256
191 3/8	61 1/8	16 4/8 / 11 7/8	10 / 9	Koyukuk River	AK	Gary Olsen	1992	256
*191 3/8	63 3/8	13 4/8 / 12 6/8	9 / 10	Mac Millan River	YUK	Pat Powell	2009	256
191 1/8	58 5/8	13 2/8 / 14 2/8	11 / 9	Galena	AK	Frank Prata	1988	259
191 0/8	56 0/8	14 4/8 / 15 6/8	10 / 13	Anaktuvuk River	AK	Frank S. Noska IV	2008	260
190 7/8	59 1/8	11 4/8 / 10 4/8	8 / 10	Innoko River	AK	Samuel D. Adams	1997	261
190 7/8	56 7/8	14 0/8 / 13 7/8	8 / 11	Farewell Station	AK	Jim Horneck	1998	261
190 6/8	52 4/8	11 3/8 / 10 3/8	10 / 11	Ugashik Lake	AK	Dr. William Schultz	1987	263
190 5/8	57 3/8	8 4/8 / 9 2/8	11 / 10	Kotzebue	AK	Raymond Lengyel	1990	264
190 5/8	60 3/8	13 1/8 / 12 7/8	12 / 13	Kotzebue	AK	Larry Welchlen	1995	264
190 5/8	54 1/8	13 6/8 / 13 5/8	13 / 12	Coldfoot	AK	Max Buck	2004	264
190 4/8	63 6/8	11 0/8 / 11 1/8	7 / 7	Mother Goose Lake	AK	Cecil Jarvis	1987	267
190 3/8	57 3/8	13 0/8 / 13 0/8	12 / 12	Teslin Lake	YUK	Paul Schafer	1977	268
190 3/8	62 3/8	13 6/8 / 15 1/8	11 / 12	Derby Creek	AK	Greg Kempf	1991	268
190 2/8	58 4/8	14 0/8 / 13 2/8	9 / 14	Yentna River	AK	Dan Hollingsworth	1978	270
190 2/8	57 0/8	11 6/8 / 13 2/8	13 / 12	Anchorage	AK	Paul Persano	1981	270
190 2/8	53 2/8	13 5/8 / 14 5/8	8 / 11	Moose John River	AK	Monty Moravec	1992	270
190 2/8	58 2/8	14 4/8 / 13 0/8	7 / 9	Judd Lake	AK	Dr. Steve Edwards	2000	270
190 1/8	60 5/8	11 2/8 / 10 6/8	10 / 12	Alaska Peninsula	AK	Rick W. Simpson	1979	274
190 0/8	57 4/8	12 4/8 / 15 1/8	11 / 11	Lime Village	AK	Jerad Dittrich	1976	275
190 0/8	56 2/8	12 2/8 / 11 7/8	9 / 13	Mackenzie Mtns.	NWT	Robert A. Hermann	1992	275
190 0/8	59 6/8	12 3/8 / 13 0/8	8 / 9	Coal River	YUK	Joe Logan	2008	275
189 6/8	57 2/8	15 4/8 / 13 4/8	4 / 9	Iliamna	AK	Thomas R. Grabowski	1994	278
189 6/8	57 4/8	13 1/8 / 14 4/8	12 / 9	Mulchatna River	AK	John M. Milender	2007	278
189 4/8	53 2/8	11 1/8 / 9 4/8	8 / 7	Stony River	AK	Douglas P. Reichel	1993	280
189 4/8	59 4/8	13 3/8 / 12 0/8	8 / 7	Cold Bay	AK	William K. McNeil	2000	280
189 3/8	59 3/8	11 4/8 / 10 3/8	11 / 10	Kogoluktuk River	AK	Tony Casagrande	2005	282
189 2/8	61 0/8	12 0/8 / 10 5/8	10 / 10	Kateel River	AK	Jack Boullion	1995	283
189 1/8	57 1/8	11 0/8 / 8 5/8	11 / 12	Wood River	AK	David Van Dyke	1994	284
189 0/8	53 6/8	13 1/8 / 13 1/8	9 / 13	Alaska Peninsula	AK	Richard T. Vance	1972	285

779

ALASKA-YUKON MOOSE

Minimum Score 170 — Continued

SCORE	INSIDE SPREAD	WIDTH OF PALM R	WIDTH OF PALM L	NUMBER OF POINTS R	NUMBER OF POINTS L	AREA	STATE/PROVINCE	HUNTER'S NAME	DATE	RANK
189 0/8	55 0/8	13 0/8	14 2/8	11	11	Latna River	AK	Ed Wentzler	1995	285
188 7/8	57 7/8	11 1/8	12 5/8	13	10	Sagavanirktok River	AK	Robert G. Chouinard	1980	287
188 7/8	59 1/8	14 3/8	14 3/8	10	9	Cantwell	AK	John W. Williams	1983	287
188 5/8	60 3/8	12 5/8	13 6/8	8	7	Lake Clark	AK	David Westmoreland	1995	289
188 5/8	57 1/8	16 0/8	15 0/8	10	9	Faro	YUK	Darryl Kublik	2005	289
188 4/8	63 0/8	11 5/8	12 3/8	8	8	Kenai Peninsula	AK	Dale L. Lofstedt	1969	291
188 4/8	55 6/8	12 5/8	12 2/8	10	11	Koidern Mtn.	YUK	D. Kirk Brown, MD	1997	291
*188 4/8	55 6/8	10 5/8	11 4/8	10	11	Willow Handle Lake	NWT	Roy Ruiz	2007	291
188 3/8	58 5/8	13 1/8	10 4/8	12	10	Selawik River	AK	Mike McCabe	1998	294
188 2/8	61 2/8	12 3/8	11 0/8	10	9	Upper Dog Salmon River	AK	Robert T. Morgan	1983	295
188 2/8	61 0/8	14 2/8	15 3/8	7	8	Hoholitna River	AK	Russ Strong/Scott Strong	2001	295
*188 2/8	62 0/8	11 5/8	11 0/8	8	9	Godlin River	NWT	M. Blake Patton	2010	295
188 1/8	53 7/8	12 5/8	13 2/8	11	13	Alaska Range	AK	Richard Moran	1991	298
188 1/8	55 5/8	13 0/8	12 1/8	10	10	Kichatna River	AK	Douglas W. Hill	1994	298
188 1/8	59 7/8	14 5/8	8 5/8	9	11	Hodzana River	AK	Bruce Bartenfelder	2001	298
187 7/8	67 7/8	11 4/8	13 4/8	10	11	Jim River	AK	Ernie Dempsey	1981	301
187 7/8	48 1/8	14 4/8	14 4/8	10	13	Watson Lake	YUK	Pete Shepley	1985	301
187 7/8	56 1/8	13 1/8	13 0/8	8	9	Koyukuk River	AK	Mike O'Connor	1996	301
187 7/8	59 7/8	12 5/8	11 5/8	9	8	Yantarni Bay	AK	Tony Swiontek	2002	301
187 5/8	60 7/8	12 5/8	11 6/8	12	12	Innoko River	AK	Ron Madsen	1989	305
187 4/8	60 4/8	13 6/8	12 0/8	9	13	Koyuk River	AK	V. Randy Liljenquist	1994	306
187 4/8	56 4/8	11 6/8	13 0/8	12	11	Tanana Flats	AK	Jerry Lees	1999	306
187 3/8	56 3/8	12 1/8	12 4/8	9	10	Stony River	AK	Bob Ameen	1993	308
187 3/8	56 7/8	13 0/8	14 6/8	9	11	Selawik River	AK	Bruce R. Walker	2003	308
187 3/8	63 1/8	12 2/8	11 0/8	6	7	Dick Creek	AK	Mark Wayne Smith	2010	308
187 2/8	60 2/8	13 5/8	13 0/8	9	8	Lone Wolf River	YUK	George Harms	2001	311
187 1/8	55 1/8	10 6/8	11 2/8	10	11	Mac Millan River	YUK	Richard I. Albright	1998	312
187 1/8	62 1/8	10 2/8	11 4/8	10	11	Cordova	AK	Archie J. Nesbitt	2001	312
187 1/8	60 7/8	11 6/8	10 4/8	11	11	Wood River	AK	David A. Van Dyke	2007	312
186 6/8	53 6/8	12 2/8	15 4/8	13	10	Campbell Creek	AK	Raymond H. Tucker	1983	315
186 6/8	62 0/8	12 1/8	12 2/8	7	6	Ugashik Lake	AK	Richard King	1988	315
186 6/8	56 6/8	12 1/8	12 5/8	12	12	Tsiu River	AK	Dean F. Stebner	1997	315
186 6/8	53 4/8	11 3/8	11 5/8	7	9	Flat River	NWT	Lew Webb	2004	315
186 5/8	53 1/8	12 0/8	12 7/8	10	10	Squirrel River	AK	Randy Martin	1992	319
186 5/8	59 1/8	13 1/8	10 7/8	11	12	Eklutna River	AK	Larry M. Moore	2002	319
186 4/8	50 4/8	12 5/8	13 7/8	13	13	Fox Mtn.	YUK	Steve Crooks	1991	321
186 4/8	52 4/8	11 7/8	13 4/8	11	12	Dennison River	AK	Bronk Jorgensen	1993	321
186 3/8	52 5/8	13 5/8	14 0/8	10	10	Middle Fork	AK	Glen Williams	1969	323
186 3/8	50 7/8	12 4/8	12 7/8	11	12	Hess River	YUK	Russell Thornberry	1987	323
186 3/8	56 7/8	11 1/8	11 3/8	10	10	Mackenzie Mtns.	NWT	Chuck Adams	1990	323
186 2/8	56 2/8	11 2/8	12 4/8	8	8	Cook Inlet	AK	George Moerlein	1961	326
186 2/8	62 2/8	13 2/8	12 2/8	9	9	Kejulik River	AK	John Crump	1981	326
186 1/8	61 5/8	10 6/8	10 7/8	10	9	Cinder River	AK	Glenn Hisey	1976	328
186 1/8	56 5/8	13 1/8	13 2/8	12	9	Salcha River	AK	Chris G. Sanford	1996	328
186 0/8	52 0/8	13 0/8	12 2/8	11	11	Bonanza Creek	AK	Bart Colledge	1999	330
186 0/8	47 0/8	12 4/8	13 0/8	12	10	Nabesna River	AK	Mike Slinkard	2000	330
185 7/8	56 5/8	11 2/8	10 7/8	8	9	Susitna River	AK	Dan J. Tobin	1984	332
185 7/8	55 1/8	12 2/8	11 0/8	11	11	Kanuti River	AK	Scott R. Nordin	1989	332
185 7/8	60 7/8	11 4/8	11 0/8	10	9	Upper Ugashik Lake	AK	Gene Moore	2001	332
185 5/8	56 3/8	14 0/8	14 3/8	7	6	Cantwell	AK	John Eilertson	1983	335
185 5/8	48 1/8	15 5/8	13 2/8	11	13	Fort Richardson	AK	Kyle Metcalf	2008	335
185 4/8	56 4/8	12 0/8	9 4/8	12	11	Fort Richardson	AK	David Dodds	1991	337
185 3/8	57 5/8	10 0/8	9 6/8	10	11	King Salmon	AK	Paul Persano	1982	338
185 3/8	56 1/8	12 5/8	12 4/8	12	10	Ambler River	AK	Don Owen	2004	338
185 2/8	60 2/8	12 7/8	13 3/8	6	12	Birch Creek	AK	Michael Evans	2005	340
185 0/8	56 0/8	10 6/8	11 6/8	10	11	Squirrel River	AK	James Borron	1992	341
185 0/8	61 6/8	11 6/8	13 6/8	10	10	Galena	AK	Kendall Harling	2002	341
184 7/8	59 7/8	13 1/8	11 5/8	12	10	Susitna River	AK	Dan J. Tobin	1988	343
184 6/8	55 5/8	11 3/8	12 4/8	5	10	Cinder River	AK	Francis Hosch	1965	344
184 6/8	59 4/8	15 4/8	13 3/8	7	8	Anaktuvuk Pass	AK	Rod Van DeGraaf	1990	344
184 6/8	57 0/8	11 6/8	14 4/8	10	12	Yentna River	AK	Herman J. Griese	1997	344
184 4/8	55 0/8	12 1/8	12 0/8	10	9	Port Heiden	AK	Frank 'Rit' Heller	1974	347
184 4/8	59 6/8	12 0/8	12 2/8	9	15	Eklutna Lake	AK	Steve J. Latz	1986	347
184 3/8	53 5/8	9 4/8	13 4/8	12	13	Palmer	AK	A. H. Stange, Jr.	1962	349
184 3/8	63 3/8	12 4/8	11 0/8	12	8	Mishik Creek	AK	George Wright	1969	349
184 3/8	56 5/8	12 5/8	14 1/8	11	10	Mac Millan River	YUK	Larry Oppe	1994	349
184 3/8	51 7/8	13 1/8	13 1/8	7	9	Koyukuk River	AK	Gunnar Darnall	2002	349
184 3/8	52 5/8	12 5/8	13 6/8	11	9	Chain Lakes	YUK	Eric E. Moore	2009	349
184 2/8	67 4/8	12 4/8	12 7/8	5	11	Nushagak River	AK	David C. Ferrario	1997	354
184 1/8	59 7/8	11 1/8	13 0/8	10	10	Brooks Range	AK	Kent Devine	1988	355
184 1/8	50 3/8	9 3/8	12 0/8	11	12	Swift River	AK	J. Dale Hale	1993	355
184 1/8	55 3/8	13 3/8	12 3/8	8	9	Fort Richardson	AK	Daniel S. Osborn	1995	355
184 0/8	59 6/8	11 0/8	10 6/8	6	7	Whitefish Lake	AK	George A. Mohr	1982	358
184 0/8	56 0/8	14 4/8	12 2/8	12	14	Natla River	NWT	Michael R. Traub	2003	358
183 6/8	50 4/8	12 5/8	12 1/8	8	8	Nabesna	AK	George Moerlein	1962	360
183 6/8	59 2/8	14 4/8	11 3/8	7	9	Minto Flats	AK	John A. Miller	1999	360
183 3/8	51 7/8	14 4/8	13 4/8	9	10	Tutna Lake	AK	Michael Dziekan	2002	362
183 3/8	53 5/8	12 5/8	12 5/8	10	9	Nahanni Butte	NWT	Roy M. Goodwin	1990	363
183 2/8	53 4/8	11 4/8	11 7/8	7	7	Brooks Range	AK	Matt Jones	1990	364
183 1/8	62 1/8	10 4/8	9 7/8	10	9	Fortymile River	AK	William E. Dean	2005	365
183 0/8	54 6/8	11 1/8	11 2/8	10	10	Alaska Peninsula	AK	Jerry Putnam	1973	366
183 0/8	61 0/8	10 1/8	11 1/8	7	7	Kelly River	AK	Doug Burgard	1994	366
183 0/8	57 0/8	12 0/8	14 1/8	13	9	Koyukuk River	AK	Mark Buehrer	2000	366
183 0/8	56 4/8	12 4/8	13 2/8	7	9	Kansas Creek	AK	Clifford Skaggs	2008	366
182 7/8	55 1/8	11 0/8	12 0/8	11	11	Eklutna Lake	AK	K. Edward Atwood	1986	370
182 7/8	52 1/8	12 3/8	11 7/8	8	10	Ivishak River	AK	Ed Strayhorn	1987	370
182 7/8	55 1/8	12 0/8	11 2/8	11	13	Pat Creek	AK	Kelly Collins	1998	370
182 6/8	55 0/8	13 3/8	13 2/8	11	11	Nowitna River	AK	Alan Winger	1988	373
182 6/8	52 4/8	10 4/8	9 0/8	11	11	Kahiltna River	AK	Ronald R. Hull	1998	373
182 5/8	57 5/8	11 2/8	16 1/8	10	10	Little Delta River	AK	Keith R. Clemmons	1957	375
182 5/8	54 5/8	13 5/8	13 2/8	9	8	Juniper River	AK	Dennis Faulkenberry	1986	375
182 5/8	59 1/8	12 5/8	15 0/8	5	12	Koyukuk River	AK	Troy A. Graziadei	1993	375
182 5/8	56 7/8	13 5/8	13 2/8	7	10	Koyukuk River	AK	Jeff Barnett	1993	375
182 4/8	56 0/8	12 0/8	12 0/8	6	7	Fort Richardson	AK	Mark Wojtalik	1988	379
182 4/8	60 2/8	10 6/8	11 2/8	11	10	Kogoluktuk River	AK	Dennis "Poncho" McCoy	2008	379

780

ALASKA-YUKON MOOSE

Minimum Score 170 Continued

SCORE	INSIDE SPREAD	WIDTH OF PALM R	WIDTH OF PALM L	NUMBER OF POINTS R	NUMBER OF POINTS L	AREA	STATE/ PROVINCE	HUNTER'S NAME	DATE	RANK
182 3/8	50 5/8	13 2/8	12 5/8	13	13	Witna River	AK	Stan Parkerson	1993	381
182 3/8	54 1/8	12 1/8	11 6/8	10	7	Talkeetna River	AK	Rick Hayley	1997	381
182 2/8	57 4/8	12 2/8	12 6/8	7	8	Nome	AK	Erv Plotz	1979	383
182 2/8	57 4/8	11 5/8	10 5/8	12	12	Innoko River	AK	Jim Fitzgerald	1993	383
182 1/8	56 5/8	9 7/8	12 0/8	7	9	Toolik River	AK	Reggie Spiegelberg	1986	385
182 1/8	56 5/8	9 7/8	11 1/8	12	12	Colville River	AK	Kurt Lepping	1990	385
182 1/8	54 7/8	12 6/8	12 5/8	7	8	Wrench Creek	AK	Kirk Westervelt	1993	385
182 0/8	59 0/8	12 0/8	11 4/8	10	10	Slope Mtn.	AK	Roger Wheelock	1980	388
182 0/8	56 0/8	14 2/8	14 0/8	6	7	Wulik River	AK	Al Boehne	2000	388
181 7/8	56 1/8	13 0/8	14 0/8	7	7	Arctic Wildlife Refuge	AK	Thomas J. Hoffman	1996	390
181 6/8	56 0/8	11 4/8	12 6/8	10	12	Moose Creek	AK	Bill Brown	1991	391
181 5/8	53 5/8	12 6/8	12 4/8	11	14	Koyukuk River	AK	Greg L. Munther	1995	392
181 5/8	56 5/8	11 1/8	12 3/8	10	12	Southfork River	YUK	Rob Harms	2003	392
181 4/8	57 2/8	14 3/8	16 6/8	7	9	Port Heiden	AK	Bill L. Carlos	1970	394
181 4/8	55 4/8	12 4/8	12 6/8	6	10	Fort Yukon	AK	Ron Rockwell	1985	394
181 4/8	52 4/8	13 0/8	12 0/8	11	9	Koliganek	AK	Dan Helton	2003	394
181 3/8	58 3/8	11 4/8	12 1/8	8	8	Nicuhuna Lake	AK	Benny R. Reed	1993	397
181 3/8	56 5/8	9 6/8	10 0/8	13	10	White River	YUK	Ray F. Daniels	1994	397
181 1/8	57 7/8	9 7/8	10 0/8	10	11	Ugashik Lake	AK	Scott Showalter	1972	399
181 1/8	54 1/8	8 6/8	10 2/8	8	10	King Salmon	AK	Joe Fogleman	1982	399
181 1/8	55 7/8	12 6/8	9 4/8	9	10	Nikolai Creek	AK	Lewis Ledlow	1999	399
181 0/8	56 6/8	13 3/8	12 3/8	7	6	Colville River	AK	Kurt Lepping	1986	402
180 7/8	54 1/8	10 6/8	10 3/8	9	11	Earn Lake	YUK	Glen R. Cousins	1978	403
180 7/8	48 7/8	12 6/8	12 3/8	10	11	Coal River	YUK	M. Richard Warner	1996	403
180 6/8	54 6/8	12 4/8	13 1/8	8	8	Toobally Lake	YUK	Michael D. Moore	2005	405
180 5/8	51 3/8	11 1/8	11 2/8	8	9	Port Heiden	AK	Art Heinze	1973	406
180 4/8	57 6/8	12 7/8	11 3/8	10	8	Middle Fork	AK	Norm Goodwin	1969	407
180 4/8	52 0/8	15 1/8	15 3/8	8	10	Sheenjek River	AK	David W. Doran	1992	407
180 3/8	59 1/8	12 4/8	10 1/8	10	13	Watson Lake	YUK	Peter L. Page	2003	409
180 2/8	61 4/8	11 6/8	10 2/8	7	10	Alaska Peninsula	AK	Keith Pilz	1976	410
180 2/8	53 6/8	11 0/8	12 1/8	8	10	Lake Clark	AK	Paul L. Fischer	1988	410
180 2/8	55 6/8	11 3/8	12 1/8	10	10	Koyukuk River	AK	Doug Whitehead	1999	410
179 7/8	56 1/8	11 3/8	11 2/8	9	9	Sugar Loaf Mtn.	AK	James White	1988	413
179 7/8	46 3/8	10 5/8	10 5/8	8	9	Noatak River	AK	Rob Swanson	1995	413
179 6/8	59 2/8	9 3/8	12 3/8	8	7	Susitna River	AK	Robert Pitt	1968	415
179 6/8	54 2/8	14 3/8	12 8/8	9	9	Tagagawik River	AK	Scott Privette	1986	415
179 6/8	54 6/8	13 2/8	11 0/8	10	10	Wrangell Mtns.	AK	Bret T. Walker	1991	415
179 5/8	53 3/8	11 0/8	11 2/8	11	12	Berry Creek	AK	Larry Jones	1962	418
179 5/8	53 1/8	9 4/8	13 3/8	10	13	Kenai Peninsula	AK	George Moerlein	1969	418
179 4/8	48 2/8	11 0/8	11 2/8	12	12	Kotzebue	AK	Stephen Kotz	1990	420
179 4/8	59 0/8	11 4/8	16 4/8	6	6	Mac Millan River	YUK	Ed DeYoung	1993	420
179 3/8	56 3/8	9 7/8	9 6/8	8	9	Stony River	AK	Bob Ameen	1986	422
179 3/8	47 1/8	12 4/8	14 0/8	11	12	Coal River	YUK	Gip Friesen	1996	422
179 3/8	54 3/8	12 0/8	13 5/8	10	8	Dietrich River	AK	Kevin T. Schaus, Jr.	2006	422
179 2/8	57 0/8	11 4/8	11 6/8	8	10	Brooks Range	AK	Kurt W. Keskimaki	1989	425
179 1/8	55 7/8	13 1/8	12 0/8	6	7	Fort Yukon	AK	Barry J. Smith	1985	426
179 1/8	49 5/8	13 4/8	12 5/8	9	11	Koyukuk River	AK	Fredrick D. Speechly II	2000	426
*179 1/8	48 3/8	10 1/8	9 2/8	8	9	Tok	AK	Kevin Jacobson	2009	426
179 0/8	53 0/8	13 6/8	13 3/8	8	10	Fort Richardson	AK	Earl G. Brown	1984	429
178 6/8	49 2/8	13 0/8	12 3/8	10	11	Earn Lake	YUK	Greg Wadsworth	1995	430
178 5/8	52 5/8	10 5/8	11 3/8	12	12	Koyukuk River	AK	Steven M. Stroka	1991	431
178 4/8	55 4/8	13 0/8	11 5/8	10	9	Kuskokwim River	AK	Bill Stonebraker	1980	432
178 4/8	53 2/8	12 7/8	11 0/8	11	13	Koyukuk River	AK	Mark Reyher	1997	432
178 3/8	53 7/8	9 6/8	7 2/8	13	9	Tustumena Lake	AK	Lowell Thomas	1973	434
178 3/8	58 3/8	14 2/8	11 3/8	8	7	Lone Wolf River	YUK	Kevin Harms	2001	434
178 2/8	52 2/8	11 0/8	10 3/8	8	10	Mac Millan River	YUK	Mike Lutt	1994	436
178 1/8	59 1/8	10 1/8	9 5/8	9	7	Cheeneetnuk River	AK	H. R. 'Rusty' Neely	1982	437
178 0/8	47 4/8	10 7/8	12 5/8	10	8	Mac Millan River	YUK	Robert H. Torstenson	1998	438
178 0/8	59 0/8	12 1/8	11 1/8	6	6	Nushagak River	AK	Robert L. Migliore	2001	438
177 5/8	58 1/8	13 2/8	12 5/8	7	8	Babble River	AK	Rick Karbowski	1995	440
177 4/8	57 0/8	11 2/8	9 5/8	8	7	American River	AK	Paul Van Dongen	1995	441
177 3/8	61 1/8	10 4/8	10 5/8	6	12	Iliamna	AK	Thad Barnes	1989	442
177 3/8	58 7/8	12 1/8	12 3/8	8	9	Coldfoot	AK	Butch A. Todd	1990	442
177 3/8	58 7/8	11 0/8	11 4/8	11	12	Galena	AK	Larry Spiva	1992	442
177 2/8	51 6/8	12 4/8	12 0/8	9	9	Kenai Peninsula	AK	Alan Perry	1971	445
177 2/8	55 0/8	13 7/8	12 1/8	7	12	Whitehorse	YUK	Scott Koelzer	1977	445
177 2/8	60 0/8	10 1/8	10 0/8	8	7	Juniper River	AK	Boyd Holley	1986	445
177 2/8	61 0/8	11 0/8	14 7/8	9	13	Noatak River	AK	Guy M. Leibenguth	1995	445
177 1/8	53 7/8	12 3/8	15 0/8	10	11	Fox Mtn.	YUK	Todd R. Zeuske	1995	449
177 1/8	52 1/8	11 4/8	11 6/8	11	10	Nowitna River	AK	David C. Manca	1998	449
*177 1/8	50 1/8	12 2/8	12 0/8	13	9	Birchwood	AK	Kenneth E. Bailey	2004	449
177 0/8	62 0/8	9 0/8	9 2/8	5	7	Port Heiden	AK	James R. Scott	1966	452
176 6/8	56 6/8	10 4/8	11 4/8	11	11	Brooks Range	AK	Steve Weekly	1990	453
176 6/8	51 4/8	12 7/8	11 6/8	10	10	Alagnak River	AK	Gene Moore	1998	453
176 6/8	46 4/8	12 0/8	13 0/8	14	12	Hess River	YUK	Rod McGrath	2001	453
176 5/8	57 3/8	10 1/8	11 0/8	11	10	Crow Pass	AK	Michael J. Schneider	1982	456
176 4/8	50 0/8	11 6/8	9 3/8	8	8	Jim River	AK	Patrick A. Campanella	1997	457
176 2/8	54 0/8	10 2/8	10 1/8	11	8	Chugiak	AK	Jerry D. Fletcher	1990	458
176 2/8	55 4/8	9 3/8	9 7/8	9	8	Eklutna Lake	AK	Thomas J. Rutz	1991	458
176 2/8	48 0/8	11 3/8	11 2/8	10	12	Kuskokwim River	AK	Terry Hanson	1996	458
176 2/8	49 4/8	11 4/8	11 0/8	9	9	Flat River	NWT	Richie Bland	2005	458
176 1/8	54 3/8	12 4/8	13 5/8	6	9	Iliamna	AK	Jim Jensen	1994	462
176 1/8	56 3/8	10 7/8	11 3/8	7	9	Innoko River	AK	John McCullough	1998	462
175 6/8	48 2/8	10 0/8	9 0/8	11	11	Anvil Mtns.	YUK	James V. Barwick	1994	464
*175 5/8	50 3/8	12 4/8	12 2/8	10	10	Nenana River	AK	Paul E. Korn	2005	465
175 5/8	52 7/8	11 4/8	11 1/8	8	10	Murray Lake	YUK	Brian D. Campbell	2005	465
175 4/8	60 4/8	11 6/8	10 0/8	7	8	Susitna River	AK	David A. Drover	1971	467
175 4/8	50 6/8	11 4/8	11 3/8	9	9	Kuparuk River	AK	Bill Krenz	1984	467
175 4/8	54 0/8	10 4/8	11 2/8	12	11	Mountain River	NWT	Dale Selby	2000	467
175 3/8	46 3/8	11 3/8	13 1/8	11	15	Kaktovik	AK	Grant Poindexter	1987	470
175 2/8	56 6/8	11 7/8	11 1/8	4	5	Brooks Range	AK	Thomas T. King	1989	471
175 1/8	51 3/8	11 2/8	12 1/8	9	10	Healy	AK	Vic Killian	1991	472
174 6/8	58 6/8	8 0/8	9 6/8	8	8	McCarty Creek	AK	Stanley J. Rogers, Jr.	1972	473
174 6/8	55 2/8	11 1/8	11 4/8	9	9	Hogatza River	AK	Jon Wren	1999	473
174 5/8	58 1/8	13 3/8	12 2/8	8	8	Koyukuk River	AK	Gerald L. Weeks	1991	475

781

ALASKA-YUKON MOOSE

Minimum Score 170

SCORE	INSIDE SPREAD	WIDTH OF R PALM L	NUMBER OF R POINTS L	AREA	STATE/ PROVINCE	HUNTER'S NAME	DATE	RANK
174 5/8	59 3/8	11 0/8 · 10 7/8	7 · 8	Mac Millan River	YUK	Brent Noel	2008	475
174 3/8	57 5/8	12 5/8 · 12 0/8	13 · 8	Tustumena Lake	AK	Gary Wall	1974	477
174 3/8	52 1/8	11 3/8 · 12 3/8	9 · 10	Koyukuk River	AK	Roger Stewart	1982	477
174 3/8	53 5/8	11 0/8 · 10 1/8	8 · 8	Wrench Creek	AK	Alan Harris	1993	477
174 2/8	54 6/8	10 0/8 · 10 0/8	12 · 9	Delta River	AK	Dr. R. Congdon	1960	480
174 2/8	58 0/8	11 3/8 · 11 6/8	11 · 9	Kejulik River	AK	Mike Hedrick	1984	480
174 2/8	56 2/8	9 0/8 · 9 0/8	9 · 9	Stony River	AK	Bob Ameen	1991	480
174 2/8	54 0/8	8 0/8 · 10 1/8	11 · 9	Lake Telequana	AK	Greg S. Fields	1992	480
174 2/8	47 0/8	12 0/8 · 11 1/8	11 · 6	Mac Millan River	YUK	Wayne Nicholson	1999	480
174 1/8	57 3/8	11 6/8 · 11 0/8	6 · 10	Kelly River	AK	Richard L. Westervelt	1994	485
174 0/8	51 2/8	12 5/8 · 13 4/8	7 · 9	Koyukuk River	AK	Gary M. Martin	2001	486
174 0/8	45 6/8	12 3/8 · 13 6/8	8 · 9	Toobally Lake	YUK	Dennis C. Kerr	2003	486
173 6/8	49 0/8	9 2/8 · 10 7/8	10 · 11	Chistochina River	AK	Larry L. Schweitzer	1982	488
173 6/8	53 6/8	10 6/8 · 10 4/8	7 · 6	Colville River	AK	Bob Gulman	1984	488
173 5/8	57 5/8	12 5/8 · 11 4/8	12 · 10	Northway	AK	Chuck Adams	1978	490
173 5/8	55 1/8	12 7/8 · 12 4/8	8 · 8	Juniper River	AK	Dr. F. D. Elias	1986	490
173 4/8	54 4/8	11 6/8 · 9 4/8	10 · 8	Elmendorf AFB	AK	Sidney Parris	1997	492
*173 3/8	60 5/8	9 7/8 · 10 5/8	7 · 9	Mac Millan River	YUK	Jeff Furstenau	2007	493
173 1/8	47 1/8	11 4/8 · 11 2/8	13 · 12	Toobally Lake	YUK	Lee Jernigan	2007	494
173 0/8	50 4/8	10 1/8 · 10 4/8	12 · 12	Koyukuk River	AK	William E. Lee	1984	495
173 0/8	58 2/8	11 2/8 · 10 4/8	11 · 10	Koksetna River	AK	Ron Hopkins	1987	495
172 7/8	49 3/8	14 0/8 · 12 6/8	12 · 12	Coldfoot	AK	Danny F. Watson	1988	497
172 7/8	51 5/8	12 4/8 · 10 6/8	7 · 7	Nahanni River	NWT	James A. Schneider	2002	497
172 5/8	47 1/8	11 0/8 · 12 0/8	7 · 7	Brooks Range	AK	John Ribic	1983	499
172 5/8	53 5/8	9 5/8 · 10 3/8	10 · 11	Lake Chauekuktuli	AK	David R. Aikin	2000	499
172 1/8	55 1/8	12 4/8 · 10 3/8	11 · 9	Stony River	AK	Bob Ameen	1992	501
172 0/8	50 4/8	11 0/8 · 9 5/8	11 · 11	Black Stone River	YUK	Rick Duggan	2002	502
171 7/8	60 5/8	9 2/8 · 7 5/8	13 · 10	Brooks Range	AK	Bruce R. Schoeneweis	1989	503
171 5/8	57 3/8	10 6/8 · 9 0/8	13 · 7	Hayes Creek	AK	Keith R. Clemmons	1962	504
171 4/8	49 4/8	10 2/8 · 10 6/8	12 · 9	Delta River	AK	Richard R. Cooper	1959	505
171 4/8	57 0/8	10 2/8 · 10 0/8	10 · 12	Fish Creek	AK	Doug Keller	1990	505
171 4/8	52 0/8	13 4/8 · 10 6/8	10 · 9	Fortymile River	AK	Kent Rotchy	2005	505
171 2/8	59 0/8	12 0/8 · 10 1/8	11 · 9	Big River Flats	AK	Lonnie Rumley	1988	508
171 2/8	58 6/8	10 2/8 · 13 2/8	6 · 9	Rohn Roadhouse	AK	Fred Eichler	1994	508
171 2/8	52 2/8	7 6/8 · 10 2/8	8 · 10	Earn Lake	YUK	Wayne Greene	1996	508
171 2/8	59 0/8	9 5/8 · 10 3/8	7 · 9	Dulbi River	AK	Glen Klomsten	2005	508
171 1/8	53 3/8	10 4/8 · 10 2/8	10 · 12	Tillei Lake	YUK	Roger M. Tyler	1989	512
171 1/8	50 1/8	14 3/8 · 13 7/8	6 · 8	Alaska Peninsula	AK	Jack Dykstra	1993	512
171 0/8	48 2/8	12 0/8 · 11 4/8	7 · 8	Brooks Range	AK	Edward Keltgen	1986	514
171 0/8	45 2/8	11 1/8 · 8 4/8	8 · 7	Bonnet Plume Lake	YUK	Stan Rauch	1989	514
170 7/8	58 1/8	12 0/8 · 10 6/8	8 · 5	Port Heiden	AK	John E. Lawson	1970	516
170 7/8	48 5/8	11 0/8 · 9 2/8	9 · 10	King Salmon River	AK	Bob Sweisthal	1986	516
170 7/8	62 7/8	10 1/8 · 11 4/8	6 · 9	Ugashik Lake	AK	Dennis Statham	1989	516
170 6/8	56 0/8	10 0/8 · 12 1/8	9 · 8	Ugashik Lake	AK	Dr. Von A. Mitton	1978	519
170 6/8	44 6/8	12 3/8 · 12 3/8	12 · 10	Moose John River	AK	Mike Pasztor	1996	519
170 4/8	52 6/8	12 1/8 · 11 4/8	10 · 9	Unit 13D	AK	Dayle Paulson	1969	521
*170 4/8	50 4/8	10 0/8 · 10 4/8	12 · 12	Stewart River	YUK	Derek Gentile	2009	521
170 1/8	50 1/8	10 3/8 · 11 2/8	9 · 9	Fort Richardson	AK	Harry Gordon Evans	1989	523
170 0/8	58 2/8	12 2/8 · 11 5/8	9 · 10	Zone 4	YUK	Keith Baker	1988	524
170 0/8	48 2/8	13 0/8 · 11 5/8	15 · 13	Tsiu River	AK	Gary F. Bogner	1998	524
170 0/8	50 0/8	13 4/8 · 12 0/8	8 · 10	Mac Millan River	YUK	Joel A. Johnson	1999	524

ALASKA-YUKON MOOSE (VELVET ANTLERS)
Minimum Score 170

SCORE	INSIDE SPREAD	WIDTH OF PALM R / L	NUMBER OF POINTS R / L	AREA	STATE/ PROVINCE	HUNTER'S NAME	DATE	RANK
171 7/8	56 1/8	8 5/8 / 9 3/8	9 / 10	Shungnak	AK	Eric F. Efird	2000	*

POPE & YOUNG CLUB
NORTH AMERICAN BIG GAME TROPHY SCORING FORM
BOWHUNTING
BIG GAME — RECORDS

222 1/8

PANEL MEASURED

MOOSE

KIND OF MOOSE: Canada

	Column 1		Column 4
A. Greatest Spread	66 1/8		Difference
B. Number of...			
C. Number of Normal...			
D. Width of Palm			1/8
E. Length of Palm			4/8
F. Circumference of Beam		3/8	3 5/8

Locality where killed (County) Cap-Chat (State) QUE
Date killed 10/8/88 By whom killed Charles Roy
Present owner Same

ADD	Column 1	
	Column 2	
	Column 3	19 3/8
Total		225 6/8
SUBTRACT Column 4		3 5/8
FINAL SCORE		222 1/8

REMARKS: (Mention any abnormalities)

I certify that I have measured the above trophy on _____ 19 93
at (address) Panel Measuring City Hudson
State WI Zip Code _____ and that these measurements and data are, to the best of my knowledge and belief, made in accordance with the instructions given.
Witness: _____
(To Measurer's Signature)

WORLD RECORD CANADA MOOSE
Score: 222 1/8
Location: Cap-Chat, Quebec
Date: 1988
Hunter: Charles Roy

Canada Moose

by Charles Roy

Eight days into the 1988 season, we were greeted with twelve inches of fresh snow. Archery season on the Gaspe Peninsula takes place during the moose rutting season. Therefore, tree stand hunting, coupled with calling, was a method of choice.

We left early that morning to head to our stands. Along the way we crossed several fresh sets of tracks, making us very optimistic. The woods were very quiet as my father began to make a low cow call. Within minutes we heard a bull answer…repeatedly. At twenty second intervals, his calls kept getting louder and louder. We knew he was coming in to meet the female.

After a few minutes, he appeared. But when he stopped, his chest was behind a tree. My arrow was knocked and ready. Everything seemed frozen, except for my heart which I could hear clearly beating. Suddenly, the bull took a couple of steps forward and stopped again. That was what I was waiting for and sent the arrow flying. He disappeared into the dense cover of spruces. My father and I agreed that I had a good hit, so we waited a few minutes. It was an easy tracking job in the fresh snow.

I will never forget our shock when we found him and saw the size of his antlers.

CANADA MOOSE

Minimum Score 135

Alces alces americana and *Alces alces andersoni*

SCORE	INSIDE SPREAD	WIDTH OF PALM R	L	NUMBER OF POINTS R	L	AREA	STATE/ PROVINCE	HUNTER'S NAME	DATE	RANK
222 1/8	66 1/8	16 1/8	14 7/8	16	15	Cap-Chat	QUE	Charles Roy	1988	1
218 1/8	64 3/8	13 0/8	13 4/8	13	14	Dease Lake	BC	Randy V. Liljenquist	2001	2
217 0/8	56 0/8	14 4/8	14 6/8	12	11	Birch Mtn.	ALB	Fredrick J. Gimbel	1994	3
214 3/8	55 7/8	14 1/8	14 4/8	16	17	Chevis Creek	BC	Wayne Carlton	1988	4
214 0/8	57 4/8	18 7/8	17 2/8	14	16	Dixie Lake	BC	Dennis Odian	1997	5
210 7/8	58 5/8	14 3/8	15 4/8	13	12	Churchill River	MAN	Duane Carroll	2003	6
202 1/8	61 3/8	13 3/8	13 2/8	12	11	Tatsamenie Lake	BC	Tom Close	1997	7
201 4/8	55 2/8	12 4/8	11 4/8	12	12	Mt. Lady Laurier	BC	Peter Halbig	1968	8
201 2/8	60 4/8	11 1/8	11 1/8	12	11	Hutt Township	ONT	Fred Robinson	1986	9
200 5/8	59 1/8	12 6/8	13 1/8	8	12	Cindy Lake	BC	Brian Koelzer	2003	10
200 0/8	50 4/8	13 5/8	15 0/8	15	17	Disella Lake	BC	T. J. Conrads	2001	11
*200 0/8	57 2/8	12 2/8	14 2/8	13	13	Nanton	ALB	Joe Arnt	2005	11
*199 4/8	54 4/8	12 7/8	13 3/8	13	11	Red Lake	ONT	Dale Tucker	2009	13
199 3/8	55 7/8	15 0/8	14 5/8	8	11	Turtle Mtn.	MAN	Jan Collins	1994	14
199 0/8	56 0/8	12 6/8	14 5/8	11	11	Redwillow River	BC	Steven W. Hiebert	1992	15
199 0/8	57 4/8	14 0/8	13 2/8	10	10	Teslin River	BC	Scott L. Koelzer	1996	15
198 6/8	56 6/8	16 3/8	16 7/8	15	13	Toad River	BC	Dirk V. Lawyer	1984	17
198 0/8	59 4/8	15 4/8	14 0/8	14	12	Thunder Bay	ONT	Steve Shore	2004	18
197 0/8	58 6/8	16 4/8	13 5/8	9	7	Cold Fish Lake	BC	Steve Gorr	1975	19
196 7/8	52 3/8	17 3/8	14 6/8	16	15	Dryden	ONT	Murray Macquarrie	1990	20
196 6/8	48 5/8	16 4/8	15 2/8	12	13	Besa River	BC	Edward Flowerdew	1976	21
196 2/8	59 5/8	14 4/8	13 7/8	10	13	Skeena	BC	Larry Garoutte	1972	22
196 2/8	53 6/8	12 3/8	15 4/8	13	12	Nacht Creek	BC	Scott L. Koelzer	1991	22
195 7/8	56 7/8	11 6/8	11 6/8	6	7	Hurkett	ONT	David L. Keith	2002	24
195 7/8	59 3/8	14 2/8	15 2/8	10	10	Peace River	ALB	Jeff Morris	2008	24
195 4/8	59 2/8	13 2/8	13 6/8	12	17	Teslin Lake	BC	Kent Michie	1993	26
195 0/8	55 0/8	10 5/8	10 6/8	11	12	Liard River	BC	Richie Bland	2004	27
194 6/8	61 0/8	12 4/8	11 2/8	11	11	Lake Leroy	BC	Lee Poole	1998	28
194 4/8	55 6/8	13 4/8	14 2/8	11	13	Thunder Bay	ONT	Bob Toderash	1987	29
194 4/8	56 4/8	12 6/8	12 5/8	13	15	Wainwright	ALB	Gary Kenna	2003	29
193 6/8	56 2/8	17 2/8	15 4/8	10	13	Heiss Lake	ONT	Bob Toderash	1993	31
193 5/8	52 1/8	13 7/8	14 2/8	12	12	Thunder Bay	ONT	Paul Ward	2005	32
193 3/8	49 7/8	15 4/8	16 1/8	11	14	Choiceland	SAS	Jeff Smith	2003	33
193 1/8	47 5/8	14 1/8	13 6/8	14	12	Rabbit Creek	BC	Scott Jankowski	2010	34
192 7/8	55 3/8	14 4/8	15 2/8	12	13	Algoma	ONT	Larry Pilon	1989	35
192 6/8	56 6/8	11 5/8	10 5/8	12	13	Cassiar Mtns.	BC	Thomas B. Frye	1978	36
192 3/8	61 1/8	12 3/8	13 6/8	7	8	Thunder Bay	ONT	Ron Mahler	1992	37
192 3/8	61 7/8	10 1/8	9 6/8	11	12	Taku River	BC	Whitley Stephenson	2001	37
192 3/8	56 3/8	11 3/8	11 5/8	12	12	Tees	ALB	Keith Rowley	2002	37
191 6/8	53 6/8	12 2/8	12 0/8	8	8	Lake Discella	BC	Sid Morrison	1995	40
191 2/8	51 4/8	13 0/8	12 6/8	12	14	Duck Mtns.	MAN	M. Dale Robins	1992	41
191 0/8	67 0/8	12 7/8	12 0/8	10	12	Dease Lake	BC	Adrian Erickson	1989	42
190 2/8	55 2/8	15 4/8	16 0/8	9	6	Lake Nipigon	ONT	Ohne Raasch	1991	43
190 2/8	49 6/8	12 5/8	11 6/8	10	11	Fouch Lake	ONT	Camille Hache	1995	43
190 2/8	56 6/8	14 7/8	12 5/8	9	9	McLennan	ALB	Hugh Dougherty	2001	43
190 1/8	53 5/8	13 1/8	13 2/8	9	9	Ignace	ONT	Michael Barkac	1993	46
190 0/8	60 4/8	14 1/8	12 6/8	13	12	Nakina River	BC	Ricardo L. Garza	1997	47
*189 7/8	58 3/8	13 0/8	9 6/8	11	9	Terrace Bay	ONT	Samuel H. Schmidt	2005	48
189 1/8	60 3/8	13 3/8	11 2/8	12	11	Sultan	ONT	Michael Wiseman	1989	49
189 2/8	52 4/8	13 6/8	13 2/8	11	12	McNalley Lake	ALB	Dewayne Mullins	1995	50
188 7/8	47 3/8	15 3/8	12 6/8	11	14	Stikine River	BC	Will Pick	1997	51
188 6/8	53 4/8	11 2/8	11 6/8	11	11	Devon	ONT	Lorne Davis	1993	52
188 5/8	52 5/8	10 0/8	10 6/8	8	8	Sultan	ONT	Mike R. Nowaczyk	1986	53
188 0/8	57 0/8	12 3/8	13 2/8	12	10	Thunder Bay	ONT	David Nuttall	1993	54
187 6/8	54 4/8	13 2/8	11 4/8	10	8	Dease Lake	BC	Peter McKeen	2002	55
187 6/8	58 4/8	11 0/8	12 1/8	12	10	Perrault Falls	ONT	Greg Wierzba	2009	55
187 5/8	57 0/8	13 3/8	12 1/8	11	13	Turnagin River	BC	Glenn Hisey	1978	57
187 3/8	50 7/8	11 1/8	11 7/8	11	13	Muskwa River	BC	Kevin J. Kansky	1997	58
187 0/8	50 6/8	12 6/8	11 5/8	13	13	Dibble Lake	ONT	Bruce Zuehlke	1992	59
187 0/8	54 0/8	13 6/8	11 4/8	10	9	Ear Falls	ONT	Robert Scott Ellery	1995	59
187 0/8	49 2/8	13 4/8	13 5/8	11	8	Kechika River	BC	Scott Neil	1998	59
186 7/8	57 1/8	13 2/8	13 1/8	8	12	Klastline River	BC	Gregory White	1992	62
*186 7/8	56 7/8	13 5/8	11 2/8	8	8	Rob Lake	BC	Mike Rossi	2008	62
186 3/8	53 7/8	12 7/8	12 6/8	12	12	Wawa	ONT	William D. Brooks	1994	64
186 3/8	48 7/8	12 1/8	12 0/8	13	13	Turnagin River	BC	Scott Ebert	1995	64
186 3/8	59 5/8	12 4/8	11 3/8	8	9	Lecoure Township	ONT	Richard Bordin	2004	64
186 2/8	54 0/8	11 2/8	11 2/8	10	11	Ash Mtn.	BC	Pink Atkins	1984	67
186 2/8	57 6/8	12 0/8	11 2/8	8	9	Grassy Narrows	ONT	Jason North	2000	67
186 1/8	53 1/8	14 1/8	13 2/8	11	12	Pitman Lake	BC	Kevin Schmid	1990	69
186 0/8	62 0/8	10 5/8	10 4/8	10	13	St. Gilles	QUE	Michel Aubert	1986	70
186 0/8	53 0/8	10 5/8	9 5/8	14	13	Ardrossan	ALB	Brian Burrows	1994	70
*186 0/8	62 0/8	13 5/8	14 3/8	5	6	Sand Ridge Lake	ONT	Michael J. Staelgraeve	2006	70
185 7/8	56 7/8	13 3/8	11 2/8	11	10	Nakina Lake	BC	Ken Stieh	2002	73
185 5/8	54 4/8	11 2/8	12 2/8	11	12	Atikokan	ONT	Jim Gianladis	2003	74
185 3/8	54 3/8	11 4/8	11 3/8	13	11	Mossy River	SAS	Jerome J. Huseby	1966	75
185 2/8	53 0/8	10 5/8	11 6/8	12	11	Buffalo Creek	ALB	Philip Ramish	1998	76
184 7/8	58 7/8	11 3/8	11 4/8	9	9	Goat Creek	BC	Atley Lovelace	1974	77
184 7/8	57 3/8	11 0/8	11 0/8	10	11	Trapper Lake	BC	David E. Stepp	1998	77
184 7/8	52 5/8	12 2/8	13 2/8	12	14	Notre-Dame-des-Bois	QUE	Michel Hebert	2001	77
184 6/8	55 7/8	11 7/8	11 5/8	13	8	Blanchard Creek	BC	Ron Johnson	1974	80
184 6/8	51 6/8	11 2/8	12 7/8	9	9	Pinto Creek	ALB	Brent Watson	2004	80
*184 4/8	57 6/8	11 5/8	13 3/8	11	11	Wintering Lake	ONT	Richard Byard	2008	82
184 2/8	49 0/8	12 5/8	13 2/8	11	11	St. Gilles	QUE	Michel Aubert	1985	83
183 5/8	51 1/8	11 7/8	12 5/8	13	11	Rabbit River	BC	Rick Young	2002	84
183 4/8	60 6/8	10 4/8	11 5/8	10	9	Terminus Valley	BC	Paul P. Schafer	1975	85
183 2/8	54 0/8	14 4/8	13 2/8	10	8	Skinny Lake	BC	Brian Koelzer	2006	86
182 7/8	52 5/8	13 6/8	12 2/8	11	6	Christian Falls	BC	Mike Ryan	1990	87
182 7/8	50 7/8	13 2/8	16 2/8	10	9	Upsala	ONT	Mark Berringer	1992	87
182 4/8	58 4/8	14 6/8	14 3/8	8	9	East Hereford	QUE	Daniel Fecteau	1990	89
182 3/8	49 3/8	14 3/8	13 0/8	11	11	Bonnie Lake	BC	Dale Karch	2004	90
182 1/8	50 5/8	11 3/8	11 1/8	10	10	Stanley Creek	BC	Donald L. Pahl	1973	91
182 1/8	51 5/8	12 4/8	12 0/8	11	12	Atlin	BC	Tom Nelson	2001	91
181 4/8	54 2/8	11 5/8	10 6/8	11	11	Muncho Lake	BC	Gary Martin	1995	93
181 4/8	52 4/8	10 5/8	11 1/8	11	11	Klastline River	BC	James Gabrick	2003	93
181 1/8	51 5/8	12 0/8	11 5/8	12	13	Halfway River	BC	Duane L. Scroggins	1977	95

786

CANADA MOOSE

Minimum Score 135   Continued

Score	Inside Spread	Width of Palm R	Width of Palm L	Number of Points R	Number of Points L	Area	State/Province	Hunter's Name	Date	Rank
181 1/8	47 5/8	14 3/8	17 7/8	11	13	Lake Nipigon	ONT	Raymond J. Seguin	1994	95
181 0/8	56 6/8	14 6/8	12 6/8	11	11	Ear Falls	ONT	Dell Mercey	1995	96
180 4/8	51 2/8	14 2/8	13 3/8	8	8	Halfway River	BC	Mark "Gutz" Gutsmiedl	2007	97
180 3/8	54 7/8	11 7/8	11 0/8	8	9	Cristina Falls	BC	Fred Ray Woods	1994	100
180 3/8	51 1/8	14 0/8	13 4/8	8	11	Hooch Lake	ONT	Tom Nebbs	2001	100
180 3/8	53 7/8	10 1/8	9 6/8	10	10	Wadlon Lake	ALB	Bruce W. Weyh	2003	100
180 2/8	44 6/8	12 4/8	11 4/8	13	14	Lake Lac Seul	ONT	Josef K. Rud	1989	103
180 2/8	46 6/8	13 4/8	11 4/8	13	10	Steamboat Mtn.	BC	Wayne Norris	1994	103
180 2/8	49 0/8	12 6/8	10 0/8	12	11	Keily Creek	BC	Thomas M. Taylor	2001	103
180 1/8	47 3/8	11 6/8	11 1/8	12	13	Unit 23	ONT	Paul F. J. Petrie	1985	107
180 0/8	55 4/8	12 0/8	13 0/8	9	10	Algoma	ONT	Larry Pilon	1988	108
179 6/8	50 6/8	11 5/8	13 2/8	11	12	Dease Lake	BC	Robert G. Petersen	1985	109
179 6/8	59 2/8	9 3/8	11 7/8	9	12	Penobscot County	ME	Scott E. Phillips	1998	109
179 4/8	49 4/8	11 2/8	12 1/8	12	14	Taku River	BC	Richard A. Smith	2001	111
179 4/8	54 6/8	11 2/8	13 4/8	8	12	Hurkett	ONT	Larry C. Holcomb	2008	111
179 3/8	53 5/8	11 5/8	11 4/8	8	8	Atlin	BC	Tim R. Dawson	2009	113
179 1/8	56 3/8	11 0/8	10 0/8	11	9	Atikokan	ONT	Russ Martin	1987	114
179 0/8	47 2/8	14 5/8	14 2/8	12	12	Alliance	ALB	Chad O'Hagan	1996	115
179 0/8	52 4/8	12 0/8	12 2/8	13	12	Runway Lake	ONT	Thomas Lange	1999	115
179 0/8	50 6/8	12 3/8	11 6/8	12	12	Jennings River	BC	Jim Horneck	2005	115
179 0/8	54 4/8	12 3/8	12 6/8	10	11	Sesseganaga Lake	ONT	Eric L. Hamele	2010	115
178 5/8	51 2/8	11 1/8	12 6/8	10	10	Kechika River	BC	Scott L. Koelzer	1976	119
178 5/8	57 5/8	12 3/8	11 6/8	8	11	Kawdy Plateau	BC	Gary F. Bogner	1996	119
178 5/8	46 3/8	12 3/8	11 6/8	13	14	Muskwa River	BC	Jim Boyer	1997	119
178 4/8	50 4/8	11 6/8	12 6/8	8	7	Worsley	ALB	Mike Scott	1993	122
178 4/8	56 2/8	11 4/8	12 2/8	10	10	Lake County	MN	Dave Mitteness	2009	122
178 3/8	43 7/8	11 3/8	10 6/8	12	12	Peace River	ALB	Kenneth B. Jenkins	2006	124
178 2/8	49 0/8	9 0/8	9 0/8	13	11	Battle River	ALB	Wayne Mihalicz	2006	125
*178 2/8	55 0/8	13 0/8	11 7/8	7	6	Geraldton	ONT	Kristy Parsons	2009	125
178 0/8	46 6/8	11 2/8	11 1/8	10	12	Ketchika Valley	BC	Edd Clack	1991	127
177 6/8	46 4/8	14 5/8	12 6/8	12	13	Gourlay Lake	ONT	William Keiper	2006	128
*177 6/8	52 4/8	11 2/8	11 3/8	11	12	Perrault Falls	ONT	Robert Lee Hamm	2008	128
*177 6/8	50 2/8	13 2/8	12 4/8	12	11	Nipigon	ONT	Tom Kirvin	2009	128
177 2/8	52 2/8	10 7/8	9 0/8	10	8	Thrimble Lake	BC	Chester Schardt	1966	131
177 2/8	43 6/8	14 6/8	14 2/8	14	15	Herod	ONT	Bill McQuillen	1995	131
*177 2/8	55 0/8	11 7/8	12 7/8	11	8	White River	ONT	Michael R. Lesiow	2007	131
177 1/8	56 7/8	12 7/8	12 4/8	7	8	Heyson Township	ONT	R. S. Illingworth	1986	134
177 1/8	53 7/8	10 5/8	10 0/8	10	10	Ignace	ONT	Roland Matte	1996	134
177 1/8	56 1/8	13 5/8	12 2/8	13	10	Gridiron Lake	ONT	Jim Caspers	2004	134
176 7/8	53 1/8	12 2/8	12 3/8	10	11	Beardmore	ONT	Randy Hopkins	2004	137
176 6/8	52 0/8	12 5/8	12 2/8	9	13	Majuba Lake	BC	Glenn Dreger	1990	138
176 5/8	51 5/8	10 4/8	10 0/8	11	11	Mine Centre	ONT	Charles Harb	1997	139
176 4/8	58 4/8	11 6/8	11 4/8	8	6	McNalley Lake	ALB	Judd Cooney	1993	140
176 4/8	54 0/8	11 1/8	11 7/8	10	12	Algoma	ONT	Larry Pilon	1996	140
176 4/8	46 4/8	13 7/8	13 7/8	9	13	Nordegg	ALB	Melanie DeBusk	2003	140
*176 4/8	47 6/8	10 6/8	12 5/8	8	7	Gamble Lake	ONT	Perry Cuddeback	2010	140
176 4/8	51 6/8	15 4/8	13 5/8	9	10	Meteionga Lake	ONT	Larry Sumner	2010	140
176 3/8	47 7/8	11 2/8	10 4/8	10	10	Algoma	ONT	Edward Broderick	1989	144
176 3/8	52 1/8	12 0/8	11 4/8	8	8	Ignace	ONT	Bruce R.S. Turner	1996	144
176 2/8	57 6/8	9 4/8	10 4/8	9	9	Fallon Township	ONT	Frank J. Julling	1987	146
176 1/8	48 3/8	11 2/8	12 1/8	11	13	Hyland Lake	BC	Randall S. Smith	1998	147
176 1/8	55 1/8	10 6/8	12 4/8	11	10	Minto	MAN	Russell Glover	2001	147
176 1/8	49 3/8	12 5/8	13 2/8	12	8	Ignace	ONT	Thomas M. Stepanek	2001	147
176 0/8	55 0/8	13 6/8	14 2/8	9	14	Long Range Mtns.	NFL	Waldemar D. Maya	1965	150
176 0/8	58 2/8	9 5/8	9 0/8	9	9	Algoma	ONT	Larry Pilon	1987	150
175 6/8	59 4/8	12 7/8	14 4/8	4	5	Kenora	ONT	Franlin Mullen	1992	152
*175 5/8	49 7/8	10 6/8	9 2/8	10	11	Geraldton	ONT	Nathan Ullmer	2006	153
175 4/8	50 6/8	11 2/8	9 6/8	10	10	Moose Lake	BC	Dan Martin	1986	154
175 4/8	53 0/8	10 5/8	10 5/8	9	12	Swan River	MAN	Kirk Mulkin	1999	154
175 3/8	51 7/8	11 4/8	11 7/8	8	9	Dease Lake	BC	Bill Coburn	1979	156
175 3/8	54 7/8	10 3/8	11 4/8	9	9	Harmmer Creek	BC	Richard Podrasky	2006	156
175 2/8	50 2/8	12 1/8	13 2/8	7	8	Highland Lake	BC	Timothy B. Fisk	1999	158
175 2/8	65 4/8	10 4/8	12 3/8	5	7	Aroostook County	ME	Craig A. Warren	2009	158
175 1/8	47 5/8	10 4/8	11 4/8	11	13	Lake Nipigon	ONT	Raymond J. Seguin	1986	160
175 1/8	50 3/8	12 0/8	11 6/8	10	11	Northern Light Lake	ONT	Ian Robinson	1991	160
175 1/8	53 1/8	12 4/8	14 2/8	9	12	John Lake	ALB	M. R. James	1999	160
175 0/8	52 0/8	10 1/8	10 7/8	10	9	Central	BC	Ronald Lauretti	1973	163
175 0/8	53 4/8	10 4/8	12 0/8	8	10	Kechika River	BC	Paul F. Schafer	1974	163
175 0/8	50 6/8	13 6/8	14 1/8	12	10	Hyland Lake	BC	Gene A. Welle	1997	163
*175 0/8	56 0/8	11 3/8	11 4/8	11	10	Grovedale	ALB	Michael Grundmann	2008	163
174 6/8	54 6/8	13 4/8	9 4/8	11	11	Algoma	ONT	Larry Pilon	1990	167
174 6/8	49 4/8	13 3/8	12 6/8	8	9	Pink Mtn.	BC	Adam Foss	2003	167
174 5/8	50 5/8	11 3/8	10 7/8	12	11	McConnell Range	BC	Dave Young	1976	169
174 4/8	42 2/8	11 4/8	11 1/8	10	9	Sikanni Chief River	BC	Bob W. Ehle	1996	170
174 3/8	56 1/8	13 0/8	10 2/8	10	7	Algoma District	ONT	Paul Kovich	1981	171
174 2/8	51 4/8	12 1/8	12 2/8	9	8	Atikokan	ONT	David Williams	1992	172
174 2/8	50 4/8	12 1/8	12 0/8	14	13	Nipigon	ONT	Carl Whittier	2007	172
174 0/8	48 2/8	10 7/8	11 0/8	12	11	Taku Plateau	BC	Walter J. Palmer	1995	174
174 0/8	57 0/8	13 5/8	13 0/8	8	9	Savant Lake	ONT	Cliff "Buck" Sturdevant	2000	174
*173 6/8	54 4/8	10 5/8	8 3/8	11	12	Donalda	ALB	Roy K. Keefer	2009	176
173 5/8	52 1/8	9 4/8	11 1/8	10	10	Lake Lac Seul	ONT	Josef K. Rud	1990	177
173 4/8	50 6/8	10 6/8	14 5/8	12	12	Rainy River	ONT	Robert White	1998	178
173 2/8	52 6/8	10 6/8	12 3/8	12	10	Red Deer Lake	ALB	Terry Lane	1988	179
173 2/8	55 2/8	11 3/8	9 4/8	10	8	Churchill River	MAN	Kirk Wermager	1997	179
173 1/8	52 5/8	11 5/8	12 4/8	8	9	Red Lake	ONT	James Rus	2004	181
173 0/8	56 6/8	9 4/8	10 5/8	9	8	Somerset County	ME	Richard Bjornson	1996	182
172 4/8	53 2/8	9 0/8	10 4/8	11	12	Besa River	BC	Mark H. Freeman	1979	183
172 4/8	59 2/8	10 4/8	9 4/8	11	9	Piscataquis County	ME	Frank White	1989	183
*172 3/8	52 5/8	10 3/8	12 2/8	8	10	Bath Lake	ONT	Thomas M. Fauser	2006	185
172 3/8	54 4/8	9 5/8	11 2/8	10	9	Donalda	ALB	John Paul Schaffer	2010	185
172 2/8	61 4/8	10 2/8	9 5/8	9	8	Lake County	MN	Chuck Schultz	1987	187
172 2/8	57 4/8	10 2/8	11 3/8	8	11	Thurston Lake	ALB	Garry G. Schalla	1997	187
172 0/8	50 4/8	11 4/8	10 2/8	10	10	Thutade Lake	BC	Larry Nirk	1975	189
172 0/8	53 0/8	11 2/8	10 2/8	9	7	Timmins	ONT	Carl Doerner	1976	189
172 0/8	48 6/8	11 4/8	11 3/8	11	10	Magone Township	ONT	John L. Burket	1986	189

787

CANADA MOOSE

Minimum Score 135 — Continued

SCORE	INSIDE SPREAD	WIDTH OF PALM R	L	NUMBER OF POINTS R	L	AREA	STATE/ PROVINCE	HUNTER'S NAME	DATE	RANK
172 0/8	50 0/8	12 2/8	10 7/8	11	9	Ignace	ONT	Paul A. Strong	1993	189
171 6/8	48 4/8	10 4/8	12 2/8	12	11	South Branch	NFL	Paul Erdbrink	1966	193
171 5/8	44 1/8	15 5/8	13 1/8	13	11	Cape Anquille Mtns.	NFL	Terrance Estes	1966	194
171 4/8	50 6/8	10 5/8	10 4/8	7	9	Algoma	ONT	David Reinke	1991	195
171 4/8	49 6/8	11 6/8	12 0/8	9	12	Beardmore	ONT	Randy Hopkins	2006	195
*171 4/8	44 4/8	12 0/8	11 2/8	12	10	Berlin River	ALB	Ryan King	2009	195
171 2/8	53 2/8	12 6/8	12 6/8	9	13	Atikokan	ONT	Mark C. Johnson	1987	198
171 2/8	45 4/8	10 2/8	10 3/8	9	12	County of Woodlands	ALB	Blaine Trigg	1998	198
171 0/8	53 4/8	8 3/8	8 5/8	9	8	Gaspe'	QUE	Claude St'Amour	1989	200
*171 0/8	47 2/8	12 6/8	13 4/8	11	13	White River	ONT	James Thibodeau	2004	200
170 7/8	49 3/8	10 2/8	10 6/8	9	9	Graham River	BC	Dr. James Shubert	1979	202
170 6/8	55 4/8	12 2/8	11 2/8	8	11	Perrault Falls	ONT	Terry A. Zarr	1993	203
170 6/8	51 4/8	10 6/8	11 7/8	10	10	Kingman	ALB	Brian Green	1996	203
170 5/8	47 1/8	10 2/8	10 4/8	9	10	Sesseganaga Lake	ONT	Eric L. Hamele	2008	205
170 4/8	44 4/8	10 7/8	12 4/8	13	12	Quibell	ONT	Fred Bear	1945	206
170 3/8	54 7/8	12 2/8	15 0/8	8	10	Nipigon Bay	ONT	Bryant Shermoe	2003	207
170 2/8	52 0/8	11 3/8	10 0/8	7	10	Tua Lake	BC	Jeff Koelzer	1991	208
170 2/8	51 0/8	11 6/8	11 1/8	7	7	Moose Lake	BC	Dan Hurd	2003	208
170 1/8	47 1/8	11 0/8	12 1/8	10	10	Misehkow River	ONT	Gary C. Schwartz	1998	210
170 0/8	55 2/8	13 0/8	12 3/8	8	7	Aroostook County	ME	Cory Mattson	1996	211
*169 6/8	47 0/8	13 1/8	13 0/8	13	11	Red Lake	ONT	Dale Nerby	2005	212
169 5/8	56 3/8	11 1/8	11 6/8	6	5	Vermilion	ONT	Matthew D. Lorge	2007	213
169 4/8	52 4/8	8 0/8	9 6/8	10	13	Two Lakes	ALB	Rick Martin	2004	214
169 3/8	48 5/8	11 1/8	12 0/8	8	10	Geraldton	ONT	Cello Milani	1996	215
169 2/8	50 0/8	11 4/8	11 4/8	11	10	Somerset County	ME	Diane Brochu/Brian Brochu	1994	216
169 1/8	50 7/8	12 5/8	12 2/8	9	11	Stikine River	BC	Dave Brousseau	1979	217
169 1/8	56 7/8	9 2/8	10 3/8	10	6	Somerset County	ME	Ron Helling	1998	217
*169 1/8	61 3/8	11 3/8	12 1/8	7	10	Wawa	ONT	Michael L. Ritter, Jr.	2009	217
169 0/8	51 4/8	9 0/8	9 6/8	10	9	Yellowhead	ALB	Dale Grimstead	2007	219
168 6/8	50 2/8	10 5/8	10 5/8	8	11	Blind Man River	ALB	David Golem	2005	220
168 5/8	54 7/8	14 2/8	11 3/8	11	10	Terrace Bay	ONT	Otto Ten Hoeve	1996	221
168 2/8	51 2/8	11 5/8	10 2/8	8	5	Atlin	BC	Camp Newton	2006	222
168 1/8	45 7/8	12 5/8	11 1/8	13	10	Fort St. John	BC	Duane Hicks	1981	223
168 1/8	48 1/8	11 1/8	10 6/8	5	6	Stone Lake	ONT	D. E. "Babe" Winkelman	1991	223
168 1/8	44 7/8	9 5/8	10 6/8	12	9	Nose Mtn.	ALB	Ted Brown	1998	223
168 0/8	46 4/8	10 3/8	11 0/8	10	12	Kechika River	BC	Dave Seidelman	1989	226
168 0/8	51 2/8	11 4/8	11 5/8	10	10	Wabigoon River	ONT	Peter Simon	2004	226
168 0/8	51 6/8	10 7/8	13 6/8	7	10	Fort Nelson	BC	Michael J. Davis	2004	226
167 7/8	48 3/8	11 7/8	10 7/8	10	12	Fort Francis	ONT	Jeffrey Baumgartner	2001	229
167 6/8	50 6/8	10 2/8	11 0/8	6	6	Chevis Creek	BC	Wayne Carlton	1989	230
*167 5/8	53 5/8	10 1/8	8 7/8	9	9	Reserve Rimouski	QUE	Guy Sauve	2007	231
167 4/8	55 0/8	15 1/8	10 3/8	11	7	Pink Mtn.	BC	Tom Foss	2003	232
167 4/8	52 0/8	11 1/8	12 1/8	10	11	Chase Lake	ONT	Ryan C. Cronk	2006	232
167 3/8	49 3/8	13 5/8	13 0/8	11	8	Thunder Bay	ONT	Rob Remus	1994	234
167 0/8	58 4/8	10 7/8	10 7/8	11	11	Argenteuil	QUE	Richard K. Clark	1983	235
166 7/8	51 1/8	12 2/8	11 4/8	10	10	Stikine River	BC	Scott Golike	1998	236
166 6/8	48 4/8	9 4/8	9 4/8	9	10	Nipisi Lake	ALB	Lee Hamilton	1991	237
166 6/8	54 2/8	11 0/8	9 5/8	7	11	Dease Lake	BC	Don Davidson	1993	237
166 6/8	49 6/8	10 6/8	10 5/8	10	11	Disella Lake	BC	John D. "Jack" Frost	1996	237
166 6/8	45 2/8	11 4/8	9 5/8	11	12	Athabasca	ALB	Thomas C. Johnson	1998	237
166 6/8	48 4/8	12 6/8	12 4/8	6	7	Otter Lake	MAN	Warren Johnson	1998	237
166 4/8	46 4/8	12 0/8	12 0/8	12	10	Atikokan	ONT	David Wolf	1995	242
166 4/8	52 2/8	10 2/8	11 1/8	9	9	Leland Lake	ALB	Richard Orich/Ken Madsen	1995	242
*166 2/8	44 0/8	11 3/8	12 6/8	9	10	Smoky Lake	ALB	Vince G. Halisky	2009	244
166 0/8	54 6/8	8 0/8	8 4/8	8	8	Lake Nipigon	ONT	Raymond J. Seguin	1991	245
166 0/8	50 0/8	11 2/8	10 4/8	10	9	Muncho Lake	BC	Frank S. Noska IV	2008	245
165 7/8	49 3/8	9 3/8	10 0/8	10	8	Halfway River	BC	Eldon Hagen	2003	247
*165 7/8	54 1/8	8 6/8	11 5/8	8	9	Piscataquis County	ME	David Wildenstein	2008	247
165 6/8	40 4/8	10 6/8	11 0/8	11	10	Buckinghorse Lake	BC	Lloyd Benedict	1993	249
165 6/8	56 1/8	15 6/8	12 7/8	7	11	Whiskey Den Brook	NS	Chris Tobin	1999	250
165 4/8	57 0/8	7 3/8	10 1/8	7	9	Coos County	NH	Marty V. Cairns	2004	251
165 2/8	50 0/8	14 0/8	12 5/8	5	7	Cottonwood River	BC	Scott L. Koelzer	1995	252
164 6/8	50 4/8	9 0/8	9 1/8	9	8	Zec Casault	QUE	Yves Leblanc	1989	253
164 6/8	49 2/8	10 1/8	9 1/8	9	10	Somerset County	ME	Phil Austin, Jr.	2001	253
164 6/8	55 0/8	8 1/8	9 6/8	6	7	Matane	QUE	Roger Gelinas	2003	253
164 6/8	45 4/8	12 0/8	12 5/8	10	9	Ignace	ONT	Mark Esser	2003	253
*164 6/8	46 4/8	9 2/8	9 0/8	8	10	Fawnie Creek	BC	Gary Mulligan	2008	253
164 5/8	44 5/8	12 4/8	12 2/8	10	7	Rice Lake	ONT	Bill Snelgrove	2000	258
164 5/8	48 7/8	11 5/8	12 7/8	9	10	Rainy River	ONT	Ian Brooks	2002	258
164 4/8	46 4/8	10 3/8	10 3/8	10	9	Woman River	ONT	Jim C. Dehoey	1991	260
164 4/8	46 0/8	10 0/8	10 3/8	13	11	Hudson Hope	BC	Mark Scott	1997	260
164 4/8	48 2/8	9 4/8	9 4/8	10	9	Sikanni Chief River	BC	Joel M. Riotto	1998	260
164 4/8	45 0/8	10 4/8	10 7/8	9	10	Prairie River	BC	Matthew Liljenquist	2006	260
164 4/8	50 4/8	12 1/8	11 2/8	11	9	Wawa	ONT	Thomas P. Kanalas	2007	260
164 3/8	47 7/8	10 2/8	10 3/8	9	12	Fort St. John	BC	Chuck Adams	1976	265
*164 3/8	47 3/8	10 5/8	11 4/8	10	10	Hayter	ALB	Nathan Gregory	2009	265
164 2/8	44 4/8	10 6/8	10 1/8	9	11	Muskwa River	BC	G. Lowe Morrison	2001	267
164 1/8	49 3/8	12 5/8	11 2/8	12	10	Tweedsmuir Park	BC	Glenn St. Charles	1954	268
164 1/8	49 3/8	9 7/8	10 2/8	8	9	Conne River	NFL	Alan Anglyn	2008	268
164 0/8	48 5/8	12 6/8	11 6/8	7	9	Atlin	BC	Thomas J. Hoffman	1997	270
163 7/8	49 7/8	9 6/8	11 4/8	8	10	Ignace	ONT	Wayne Yocum, Jr.	1996	271
163 6/8	47 6/8	10 4/8	10 2/8	11	9	Pink Mtn.	BC	Gerald R. Dishion	1987	272
163 6/8	46 4/8	11 4/8	11 4/8	11	12	Gundahoo River	BC	Dyrk Eddie	2009	272
163 5/8	47 7/8	11 7/8	12 3/8	8	9	Wegg	ONT	Scott Pelino	1991	274
163 4/8	48 2/8	10 0/8	10 2/8	9	9	Cadomin Creek	ALB	Darrell Bozarth	2002	275
163 4/8	52 0/8	9 5/8	10 2/8	9	9	Wine Lake	ONT	Jerry Huber	2003	275
163 3/8	45 1/8	11 1/8	10 2/8	10	10	McKeough Township	ONT	Larry Pilon	1991	277
163 3/8	50 1/8	9 2/8	9 1/8	10	9	Wawa	ONT	William D. Brooks	1994	277
163 3/8	53 3/8	11 2/8	10 2/8	10	8	Ignace	ONT	Paul Strong	1996	277
163 3/8	52 5/8	10 3/8	16 7/8	9	12	Teslin River	BC	Randy D. Oleson	2002	277
163 2/8	45 2/8	9 4/8	10 2/8	9	9	Cassiar Mtns.	BC	Harold Boyack	1978	281
163 2/8	46 2/8	10 3/8	10 0/8	10	9	Ear Falls	ONT	James C. Gates	2001	281
163 1/8	50 3/8	10 6/8	10 4/8	9	9	Edmonton	ALB	Pat Marek	1989	283
163 1/8	52 1/8	9 3/8	10 0/8	13	9	Okotoks	ALB	Stuart Sinclair-Smith	1996	283
163 1/8	51 7/8	11 3/8	12 3/8	8	8	Cook County	MN	Kirk D. Grupa	1997	283

788

CANADA MOOSE

Minimum Score 135
Continued

SCORE	INSIDE SPREAD	WIDTH OF PALM R	L	NUMBER OF POINTS R	L	AREA	STATE/ PROVINCE	HUNTER'S NAME	DATE	RANK
163 1/8	47 7/8	11 3/8	11 1/8	8	10	Battle River	ALB	J. P. McDonald	2008	283
163 0/8	50 4/8	10 1/8	11 2/8	6	6	Nakanok Lake	BC	Phil Forte	1984	287
163 0/8	54 6/8	9 0/8	8 0/8	10	8	Algoma	ONT	Larry Pilon	1986	287
163 0/8	54 0/8	9 1/8	9 0/8	8	8	Sudbury	ONT	Vite Chomicki	1986	287
163 0/8	51 6/8	12 1/8	12 6/8	7	10	Turtle Mtn.	MAN	Daryl Fisher	1987	287
162 7/8	46 5/8	10 5/8	9 7/8	11	11	Pink Mtn.	BC	Allyn Ladd	2009	291
162 6/8	47 0/8	10 5/8	11 2/8	6	7	Kenora	ONT	John P. Hartman	1991	292
*162 6/8	48 0/8	11 4/8	11 0/8	10	9	Sioux Lookout	ONT	Mike Horan	2006	292
*162 6/8	45 0/8	9 4/8	10 0/8	8	9	Fawnie Creek	BC	Gary Mulligan	2009	292
162 4/8	48 0/8	9 0/8	9 0/8	10	11	Kapuskasing	ONT	Ron Alguire	1963	295
162 4/8	50 0/8	8 2/8	8 0/8	10	13	Andrew Lake	ALB	Warren Witherspoon	1994	295
162 3/8	47 5/8	10 6/8	11 2/8	9	11	Bottineau County	ND	Curtis Michaelson	1994	297
162 2/8	50 0/8	12 7/8	11 5/8	9	8	Nakina Lake	BC	Dee C. Steinheiser	1986	298
162 2/8	44 6/8	10 6/8	11 1/8	9	11	Dryden	ONT	Ronald Hintz/Gary Hintz	1995	298
162 2/8	46 6/8	10 4/8	10 0/8	12	12	Edmonton	ALB	Lowdell Taylor	2000	298
162 1/8	48 3/8	11 6/8	11 6/8	11	8	Cook County	MN	Terry Krahn	1994	301
162 1/8	49 7/8	10 4/8	10 6/8	10	11	Hearst	ONT	Jim Jones	1997	301
*162 1/8	44 7/8	11 7/8	10 1/8	11	12	Burnt Lake	BC	George Harms	2009	301
162 0/8	47 2/8	9 4/8	10 7/8	11	11	Steamboat	BC	Chris Partridge	2002	304
161 6/8	48 0/8	11 6/8	11 6/8	8	10	Somerset County	ME	George A. Vinal	1994	305
161 6/8	39 4/8	9 4/8	9 1/8	8	9	Clear Hills	ALB	Geordie Lund	1996	305
161 6/8	48 2/8	10 0/8	11 4/8	9	8	Sikanni Chief River	BC	Brad S. Fulmer	2004	305
161 5/8	51 1/8	10 0/8	10 4/8	10	10	Ramsey County	ND	Boone Liane	1998	308
161 5/8	50 7/8	10 0/8	7 5/8	7	8	Wine Lake	ONT	Jeff Johnson	2003	308
161 4/8	50 0/8	6 4/8	9 5/8	7	7	Tatla Lake	BC	Bill Nickerson	1985	310
161 4/8	51 4/8	10 4/8	11 1/8	10	8	Sand Ridge Lake	ONT	David Baker	2005	310
161 3/8	49 1/8	10 0/8	9 2/8	8	8	Dease Lake	BC	Gene Welle	1995	312
161 3/8	47 3/8	13 6/8	11 4/8	9	6	Mine Centre	ONT	Norman R. Drefcinski	1996	312
161 2/8	46 6/8	10 0/8	10 1/8	9	9	Schalze River	BC	Dale Snyder	1983	314
161 2/8	40 2/8	10 0/8	9 2/8	11	10	Nakina Lake	BC	Dean Stebner	1988	314
161 2/8	42 6/8	13 0/8	13 3/8	10	9	Obonga Lake	ONT	Carl Tallon	1999	314
161 2/8	37 4/8	12 0/8	12 6/8	10	11	Bay d' Espoir	NFL	Alan H. Anglyn	2004	314
161 2/8	47 2/8	10 0/8	9 6/8	9	10	Ignace	ONT	Joseph M. Lemerond	2005	314
161 1/8	45 5/8	10 5/8	11 6/8	11	11	Lloyds River	NFL	Harold A. Hill	1966	319
161 0/8	47 4/8	9 3/8	10 1/8	10	10	Toad River	BC	Archie Nesbitt	1994	320
161 0/8	50 6/8	11 6/8	11 4/8	13	10	Ear Falls	ONT	Josh Miller	2002	320
160 7/8	51 1/8	9 3/8	9 0/8	8	8	Metagama	ONT	Kerry Koning/Andy Weisgerber	1994	322
160 7/8	51 5/8	11 0/8	11 4/8	10	10	Thunder Bay	ONT	Drew Good	2001	322
160 7/8	47 1/8	10 6/8	10 4/8	10	6	Grande Cache	ALB	Tim Rice	2005	322
*160 6/8	54 2/8	10 4/8	9 4/8	10	9	Wawa	ONT	Judy Black	2010	325
160 4/8	46 0/8	10 4/8	10 4/8	10	9	Muskwa River	BC	W. Jay Boynton III	1970	326
160 4/8	41 0/8	13 1/8	11 7/8	8	9	Cook County	MN	Kevin Walsh	1993	326
160 2/8	52 0/8	10 4/8	9 3/8	9	9	Saskatoon Mtn.	ALB	Terry Hagman	2009	328
160 1/8	50 7/8	10 0/8	9 5/8	9	8	Toad River	BC	Jerry Leair	1986	329
160 1/8	43 5/8	10 0/8	11 6/8	6	7	Lilly Lake	ONT	Fern Duquette	1996	329
160 0/8	49 2/8	10 0/8	9 6/8	8	9	Matane	QUE	Claude St' Amour	1990	331
160 0/8	47 0/8	11 4/8	11 7/8	10	9	Machion	ONT	Michael J. Goza	1991	331
159 7/8	47 5/8	9 3/8	8 7/8	10	10	Mameigwess Lake	ONT	Mick Borowitz	2002	333
*159 7/8	55 1/8	10 2/8	8 3/8	6	6	Wawa	ONT	Michael L. Ritter, Sr.	2010	333
159 6/8	52 2/8	11 1/8	10 2/8	8	9	Aroostook County	ME	Dennis Wojcik	1998	335
159 5/8	49 5/8	15 2/8	12 2/8	6	6	Moose Lake	BC	Michael Delfino, Sr.	1988	336
159 4/8	48 0/8	11 2/8	9 6/8	9	10	Chic-Chocs	QUE	Ken H. Taylor	2005	337
159 3/8	53 5/8	9 4/8	6 5/8	8	8	Josephburg	ALB	Doug Long	1996	338
159 3/8	42 5/8	12 0/8	10 7/8	10	9	Fort Nelson	BC	Alan Harris	2004	338
159 1/8	51 7/8	9 5/8	8 7/8	9	8	Gogama	ONT	Jack Richard	1984	340
159 1/8	47 3/8	12 1/8	10 1/8	8	13	Hancock County	ME	Roger Avery	2001	340
159 0/8	45 6/8	10 3/8	9 6/8	10	10	Bath Lake	ONT	Stuart Hazard	2005	342
159 0/8	49 0/8	8 4/8	9 4/8	8	7	Aroostook County	ME	Scott H. Pelletier	2005	342
158 7/8	50 7/8	12 1/8	11 7/8	13	11	Kirkland Lake	ONT	Luther Gordon	1963	344
158 6/8	50 4/8	12 0/8	12 1/8	8	10	Dryden	ONT	Dean J. Smaney	1990	345
158 6/8	48 0/8	8 5/8	9 0/8	8	8	Odin Lake	ONT	Bob Page	1996	345
158 6/8	52 4/8	8 5/8	9 6/8	7	11	Aroostook County	ME	Richard J. Langer	2001	345
158 5/8	47 1/8	8 4/8	9 7/8	10	9	Hillsport	ONT	Mark Stephenson	1996	348
158 4/8	46 2/8	12 4/8	11 7/8	7	8	Millarville	ALB	Stuart Sinclair-Smith	1993	349
158 3/8	52 5/8	9 0/8	10 4/8	10	11	Lake County	MN	Glenn Thompson	2006	350
158 2/8	62 6/8	9 3/8	9 7/8	5	7	Taku River	BC	Roy L. Walk	2006	351
158 0/8	49 0/8	8 0/8	8 5/8	7	8	Williams Lake	BC	Gary Swan	1968	352
158 0/8	47 6/8	10 2/8	9 7/8	11	13	Strathcona	ALB	Darrell Stiles	1985	352
157 7/8	47 7/8	9 5/8	9 7/8	9	10	Longlac	ONT	Dennis E. Klaiber	2006	354
157 6/8	47 4/8	10 4/8	9 5/8	7	8	Thunder Bay	ONT	Bill Stringer	1991	355
157 6/8	46 6/8	9 4/8	8 4/8	10	10	Mossy River	SAS	John Ross	1997	355
157 6/8	46 2/8	9 5/8	8 3/8	10	8	Clear Hills	ALB	Les Baird	1998	355
157 6/8	46 6/8	10 1/8	11 2/8	8	8	Ignace	ONT	James C. Forsyth	1999	355
157 5/8	45 7/8	10 1/8	10 1/8	8	8	Groat Creek	ALB	Justin Michalski	2009	359
157 5/8	47 7/8	8 0/8	10 0/8	8	11	Basin Lake	SAS	Kevin Wehage	2009	359
157 4/8	46 0/8	11 4/8	10 7/8	9	10	Rocky Mtn. House	ALB	Dennis Meyer	1988	361
157 4/8	51 2/8	9 5/8	8 3/8	10	7	Edmonton	ALB	Ryk Visscher	2000	361
157 3/8	47 3/8	11 6/8	9 2/8	11	9	St. Louis County	MN	Gus Maxfield	1987	363
157 3/8	45 7/8	9 6/8	10 7/8	8	10	Perrault Falls	ONT	Scott A. Cisewski	1997	363
157 1/8	46 7/8	11 2/8	12 5/8	9	11	Ear Falls	ONT	Chad Crowley	1995	365
157 1/8	45 5/8	8 2/8	9 4/8	11	8	Wildcat Hills	SAS	Floyd Brausen	1999	365
*157 1/8	54 3/8	10 6/8	10 1/8	7	6	Geraldton	ONT	Cori Bangs	2008	365
156 7/8	46 5/8	10 7/8	9 7/8	11	12	Eagle Hill	ALB	Dallas Kaiser	2000	368
156 6/8	51 0/8	8 5/8	8 5/8	8	8	Blue Lake	BC	Rick Duggan	2005	369
156 6/8	46 4/8	11 5/8	11 4/8	5	8	Beardmore	ONT	Randy Hopkins	2005	369
156 5/8	46 5/8	10 2/8	12 0/8	8	8	Main Brook	NFL	Scott Langston	2000	371
156 4/8	48 2/8	10 6/8	9 0/8	8	11	Tsayta Lake	BC	Bob Duncan	1986	372
156 4/8	50 2/8	9 7/8	9 6/8	4	4	Phair Lake	ONT	Teijo Wall	1987	372
156 4/8	50 4/8	8 4/8	9 5/8	5	6	Kluachesi Lake	BC	Jerry R. Stutt	1987	372
156 4/8	42 0/8	9 3/8	10 0/8	11	10	Westward Ho	ALB	Danny Moore	1993	372
156 4/8	40 4/8	10 2/8	9 0/8	11	9	Triangle Lake	BC	Bob Ameen	2006	372
156 3/8	50 3/8	8 6/8	8 0/8	9	9	Loganberry Lake	ONT	Mike Werner	2005	377
156 2/8	42 0/8	9 6/8	9 5/8	9	9	AK Hwy. Milepost 163	BC	John Zahrte	1978	378
156 2/8	49 0/8	10 3/8	10 4/8	7	8	Canton De Kondiaronk	QUE	Wayne J. Martin	1991	378
156 2/8	47 6/8	10 5/8	10 6/8	8	7	Pasqua Hills	SAS	Brian F. Tarnowski	2001	378

CANADA MOOSE

Minimum Score 135 Continued

SCORE	INSIDE SPREAD	WIDTH OF PALM R	L	NUMBER OF POINTS R	L	AREA	STATE/ PROVINCE	HUNTER'S NAME	DATE	RANK
*156 2/8	44 4/8	12 5/8	12 7/8	12	11	Coal Creek	BC	Dan Fediuk	2004	378
*156 2/8	49 4/8	10 1/8	9 4/8	10	8	Halfway River	BC	Joe Thomas	2007	378
156 1/8	46 1/8	10 1/8	9 2/8	10	10	Muskwa River	BC	Steve D. Munier	1995	383
156 1/8	50 1/8	10 6/8	11 0/8	10	8	Red Lake	ONT	Kevin D. Springman	2002	383
156 0/8	46 0/8	9 4/8	8 2/8	9	8	Fort Nelson	BC	Kevin Peterson	1999	385
156 0/8	49 4/8	9 6/8	10 0/8	10	10	Pink Mtn.	BC	Pam Baird	2009	385
*155 7/8	45 5/8	8 7/8	10 2/8	12	11	Amisk Lake	ALB	Gary Dexter	2006	387
155 6/8	48 6/8	9 5/8	8 7/8	7	9	Maniwaki	QUE	Jay Pitha	1983	388
155 6/8	46 2/8	10 5/8	10 5/8	9	9	Sioux Lookout	ONT	Ross Lehne	1994	388
155 5/8	46 3/8	10 7/8	12 4/8	9	12	Nestor Falls	ONT	Laurence R. Howland	1999	390
155 5/8	43 3/8	9 6/8	9 5/8	11	10	Sheep River	ALB	Dennis C. Kerr	2000	390
155 3/8	34 2/8	8 0/8	10 0/8	8	10	Smithers	BC	Chris VanderHorst	1974	392
155 3/8	48 7/8	8 7/8	9 2/8	9	11	Kapuskasing	ONT	Tom Nowakowski	1980	392
155 2/8	44 0/8	8 2/8	8 2/8	8	6	Algoma	ONT	Dan Bertalan	1991	394
155 2/8	41 4/8	10 0/8	11 0/8	8	8	Valleyview	ALB	Ted K. Jaycox	2002	394
*155 2/8	48 2/8	9 6/8	8 6/8	9	10	Pierceland	SAS	Curtis Lee	2003	394
155 2/8	46 0/8	8 6/8	9 6/8	9	8	Toad River	BC	Peter C. Swenson	2005	394
155 1/8	51 5/8	10 3/8	10 4/8	8	9	Algoma District	ONT	Carol Wert	1963	398
155 1/8	52 3/8	9 0/8	9 0/8	7	9	LeLuv Township	ONT	David Lawson	1994	398
155 1/8	40 1/8	11 2/8	11 2/8	8	11	Lamb Creek	BC	Joe Romeo, Jr.	2006	398
155 0/8	49 6/8	9 1/8	9 3/8	9	8	Perrault Falls	ONT	Leighton J. Trice	2006	401
155 0/8	49 2/8	9 2/8	8 1/8	9	12	Ministik	ALB	Keith Crawford	2006	401
154 7/8	49 7/8	10 3/8	11 4/8	8	11	Saddler Pond	NFL	Paul Locey	1982	403
154 7/8	44 3/8	9 5/8	9 4/8	9	9	Duffield Creek	BC	Wayne Johnson	1990	403
154 7/8	49 3/8	9 6/8	9 7/8	8	9	Ignace	ONT	Dave Shumway	2008	403
154 6/8	46 0/8	8 6/8	9 4/8	9	8	Hyland Lake	BC	Dennis Dunn	1999	406
*154 6/8	48 0/8	9 0/8	10 4/8	7	11	Aroostook County	ME	Michael Hebert	2009	406
154 4/8	48 6/8	12 1/8	11 4/8	10	9	Turtle Mtn.	MAN	Jack Barrows	1992	408
154 3/8	41 7/8	11 0/8	11 2/8	11	11	Eaglehead Lake	ONT	Carl J. Johnson	2004	409
154 1/8	44 3/8	9 7/8	9 7/8	8	11	Thutade Lake	BC	Donald N. Lehman	1973	410
154 1/8	45 7/8	13 4/8	11 5/8	10	8	Pink Mtn.	BC	William Newman	2009	410
154 0/8	49 2/8	10 0/8	10 3/8	9	9	Jackfish Creek	ONT	Darryl Miller	1987	412
154 0/8	46 4/8	9 1/8	9 1/8	9	8	Phillips Lake	ONT	Mark D. Stephenson	1992	412
*154 0/8	43 6/8	10 3/8	10 0/8	10	7	Nipigon	ONT	Don Morris	2009	412
153 6/8	49 2/8	10 0/8	10 2/8	5	6	Main Brook	NFL	Don Rozema	2002	415
153 5/8	45 3/8	10 6/8	11 2/8	7	12	Lloyds River	NFL	Harold A. Hill	1964	416
153 4/8	45 2/8	9 0/8	7 2/8	8	8		QUE	Bruce R. Wilson	1983	417
153 4/8	44 0/8	10 2/8	9 3/8	13	9	Meadow Lake	SAS	Mark Dietz	2001	417
*153 3/8	46 7/8	10 2/8	9 0/8	8	7	Williams County	ND	Jason Brevik	2009	419
153 2/8	40 4/8	11 1/8	9 6/8	10	8	Gathto River	BC	Richard Davis	2003	420
153 1/8	38 1/8	9 3/8	9 7/8	10	10	Johnny Lake	BC	Jerry A. Davis	1998	421
153 1/8	50 3/8	9 7/8	9 0/8	8	12	Aroostook County	ME	James W. Heffernan	2001	421
*153 1/8	46 3/8	9 2/8	9 5/8	6	6	Fernie	BC	Tim Richardson	2007	421
152 7/8	42 7/8	9 1/8	9 7/8	10	10	Zone 1	NFL	Harold A. Hill	1961	424
152 7/8	47 1/8	8 4/8	10 1/8	8	8	Trout Lake	ONT	Mike Brees	1998	424
152 6/8	45 2/8	10 0/8	9 4/8	6	6	Tetsa River	BC	Mark Calkins	1993	426
152 6/8	42 0/8	10 7/8	11 1/8	10	10	Lake County	MN	Cody Lane Detzel	1994	426
152 6/8	45 6/8	10 1/8	9 5/8	10	9	Atikokan	ONT	Scott Manford	1998	426
*152 5/8	42 5/8	12 0/8	13 3/8	9	11	Towner County	ND	Lance Larson	2005	429
152 4/8	49 0/8	8 0/8	8 3/8	6	6	Gilbault Creek	BC	David V. Collis	1977	430
152 4/8	54 2/8	7 7/8	8 1/8	9	8	McKeough Township	ONT	Larry Pilon	1992	430
152 4/8	52 4/8	9 4/8	12 4/8	6	13	Wawa	ONT	William D. Brooks	1996	430
152 4/8	41 4/8	9 2/8	7 5/8	10	8	Grand-Remous	QUE	Bruno Martel	1997	430
152 4/8	51 4/8	11 0/8	8 1/8	10	8	Delburne	ALB	Dennis D. Johnson	2001	430
*152 3/8	53 3/8	10 0/8	11 7/8	9	7	McKenzie County	ND	Stuart McDaniel	2010	435
152 2/8	49 6/8	11 2/8	10 6/8	5	6	Nakina Lake	BC	Guy Anttila	1982	436
152 2/8	47 0/8	9 5/8	8 7/8	9	10	Rossburn	MAN	Tim Yaremchuk	2007	436
152 1/8	48 7/8	8 3/8	10 0/8	9	11	Thutade Lake	BC	Rodney Lee Wilt	1991	438
152 1/8	47 1/8	9 3/8	9 2/8	7	9	Atikokan	ONT	David Wolf	1993	438
152 0/8	49 2/8	10 7/8	9 7/8	8	6	Devon Township	ONT	Lorne Davis	1991	440
152 0/8	45 6/8	9 0/8	8 4/8	8	8	Nakina	ONT	Richard Denes	1997	440
*152 0/8	45 6/8	7 6/8	8 5/8	9	9	Fallen Timber Creek	ALB	Jon Quiring	2008	440
151 6/8	47 6/8	11 5/8	9 6/8	9	10		NFL	Bill Hirst	1960	443
151 6/8	44 0/8	10 6/8	9 4/8	9	9	Duti Lake	BC	Walter J. Sawicki	1972	443
151 6/8	47 0/8	8 4/8	8 4/8	8	8	Chinchaga River	ALB	Dwayne Huggins	1998	443
151 6/8	44 6/8	10 3/8	10 1/8	6	8	Blueberry Hill	ALB	Rodney M. Alexander	2000	443
151 6/8	45 2/8	10 3/8	9 1/8	7	8	Clearwater	ALB	Grant Petersen	2002	443
*151 6/8	47 0/8	8 2/8	8 2/8	8	8	Ewin Creek	BC	Kent Fraser	2005	443
151 5/8	53 3/8	8 7/8	9 6/8	8	6	Stikine River	BC	James A. Farnsworth	1973	449
151 5/8	41 3/8	9 5/8	10 4/8	7	7	Gathto River	BC	Richard E. Davis	2005	449
151 4/8	51 4/8	9 2/8	9 2/8	7	12	Muncho Lake	BC	Chad Lenz	1994	451
151 3/8	53 7/8	9 1/8	8 6/8	9	8	Frantz Township	ONT	Marv Ries	2003	452
151 2/8	42 2/8	8 2/8	9 4/8	9	9	Josephburg	ALB	Darwin Hunter	1990	453
151 2/8	42 4/8	9 2/8	9 3/8	8	8	Wabigoon River	ONT	Daniel L. Yff	2003	453
151 0/8	46 2/8	5 7/8	10 2/8	7	9	Fort St. John	BC	Larry C. Holcomb	2002	455
150 7/8	43 7/8	8 1/8	8 2/8	8	9	Gander River	NFL	David Lamoreaux	1997	456
150 6/8	43 4/8	11 0/8	10 2/8	9	5	Serpentine River	NFL	John Wietecha	1997	457
150 6/8	50 0/8	10 0/8	9 4/8	9	8	Nakina	ONT	Joel A. Hyma	2000	457
150 6/8	40 0/8	10 4/8	10 0/8	7	9	Snowshoe Lake	ONT	Chuck Gahagan	2001	457
150 5/8	52 7/8	9 6/8	8 2/8	10	7	Atlin	BC	Tim R. Dawson	2006	460
150 4/8	41 0/8	10 4/8	11 2/8	10	7	Red Lake	ONT	Joseph B. Burgess	1993	461
150 3/8	45 3/8	11 0/8	10 6/8	8	7	Jumbo Lake	ALB	Derek Nichols	2000	462
150 2/8	42 2/8	9 1/8	8 4/8	9	11	Dumbell Lake	ONT	Gregory D. Keeton	1998	463
150 2/8	47 4/8	10 4/8	9 3/8	8	8	East Kootenay	BC	Christian Therrien	2007	463
150 1/8	48 3/8	8 2/8	10 4/8	8	10	Thunder Bay	ONT	Carl Whittier	1990	465
150 1/8	47 7/8	7 6/8	7 5/8	9	7	Fort McMurray	ALB	Bruce Hendy	1992	465
150 0/8	45 2/8	9 6/8	9 0/8	8	7	Atikokan	ONT	Albert Clement	1991	467
150 0/8	51 0/8	8 6/8	10 2/8	8	9	Black Bay Peninsula	ONT	Carl Whittier	2001	467
150 0/8	46 4/8	9 0/8	8 4/8	6	8	Drayton Valley	ALB	Dale Fournier	2004	467
*150 0/8	41 2/8	10 4/8	11 4/8	10	4	Hylean Lake	BC	Rich Snapper	2005	467
150 0/8	45 6/8	11 1/8	11 4/8	8	7	Aroostook County	ME	John M. Cogswell	2006	467
150 0/8	44 2/8	8 5/8	8 1/8	7	8	Weary Creek	BC	Allan Latka	2008	467
149 6/8	46 2/8	8 5/8	9 3/8	7	7	Little Johnny Lake	BC	Larry D. Jones	1988	473
149 6/8	46 6/8	10 0/8	10 7/8	8	9	Gaspie Peninsula	QUE	Cecil A. Stanley	1997	473
149 5/8	52 1/8	11 5/8	11 0/8	9	9	Manitouwadge	ONT	David W. Sturrus	1992	475

CANADA MOOSE

Minimum Score 135

Continued

SCORE	INSIDE SPREAD	WIDTH OF PALM R	WIDTH OF PALM L	NUMBER OF POINTS R	NUMBER OF POINTS L	AREA	STATE/ PROVINCE	HUNTER'S NAME	DATE	RANK
149 5/8	46 3/8	10 6/8	10 0/8	9	6	Lake Borel	ONT	Paul E. Holcomb	2000	475
149 4/8	39 4/8	9 5/8	8 2/8	11	7	Pinto Creek	ALB	Douglas Erickson	2004	477
149 3/8	49 5/8	9 2/8	10 7/8	6	6	Grey River	NFL	Tim W. Schenk	2006	478
149 2/8	44 2/8	9 4/8	9 4/8	9	9	Muskwa River	BC	Evan Steinhorst	1995	479
149 2/8	41 6/8	8 0/8	7 1/8	5	7	Mameigwees Lake	ONT	John "Bear" Van Straten	2002	479
149 0/8	51 0/8	5 6/8	6 0/8	7	7	Ministik	ALB	Robert D. Barnes	2001	481
149 0/8	40 6/8	7 6/8	9 3/8	7	7	Monashee Mtn.	BC	Thomas M. Basch	2002	481
148 7/8	49 5/8	7 2/8	7 4/8	7	6	Caledonia County	VT	Todd Rainville	1999	483
*148 7/8	54 1/8	7 2/8	8 3/8	9	10	Strathcona	ALB	Gord Nuttall	2010	483
148 6/8	43 6/8	9 3/8	8 1/8	9	9	Edmonton	ALB	Doug Long	1995	485
148 6/8	41 6/8	10 0/8	10 6/8	7	9	Highland Lake	BC	Renee Welle	1996	485
148 3/8	42 1/8	9 2/8	9 2/8	10	10	South Branch	NFL	W. P. Hirst	1964	487
*148 3/8	43 5/8	10 7/8	10 5/8	9	8	Bigknife Creek	ALB	Tom Foss	2010	487
148 2/8	40 4/8	9 7/8	9 7/8	10	8	Hearst	ONT	Jim Jones, Jr.	1996	489
148 2/8	48 2/8	7 4/8	7 4/8	7	7	Sutton	QUE	Guy Turcotte	2002	489
148 0/8	47 6/8	9 0/8	9 1/8	9	11	Spray Lakes	ALB	Yves Blanchette	1991	491
148 0/8	48 0/8	10 4/8	10 2/8	3	7	Coos County	NH	Stephen C. Van Hoose	1997	491
147 6/8	49 6/8	9 7/8	10 6/8	10	9	Millarville	ALB	Blaine Southgate	1997	493
*147 5/8	47 1/8	10 0/8	10 0/8	9	8	Grande Cache	ALB	Vern Maerz	2005	494
147 5/8	44 7/8	9 4/8	10 4/8	7	5	Willow Lake	BC	Bob Gilbert	2008	494
147 2/8	48 2/8	8 2/8	7 4/8	9	8	Kenora	ONT	John P. Hartman	1990	496
147 0/8	41 2/8	8 2/8	8 2/8	6	5	Owl Pond	NFL	Michael J. Kennedy	2000	497
146 6/8	39 4/8	8 1/8	9 5/8	8	10	King George IV Lake	NFL	Bill Hirst	1966	498
146 6/8	50 6/8	8 6/8	8 0/8	8	7	Penobscot County	ME	Scott E. Phillips	1999	498
146 6/8	44 4/8	8 4/8	8 2/8	8	8	Rivercourse	ALB	Talen J. Lakusta	2008	498
146 5/8	45 5/8	11 2/8	11 6/8	10	12	Prophet River	BC	Brian P. Williams	1994	501
146 4/8	43 0/8	9 1/8	9 5/8	9	8	Akie River	BC	David L. Butler	1999	502
146 3/8	45 3/8	9 2/8	10 2/8	6	9	Ardrossan	ALB	John Visscher	1987	503
146 3/8	45 7/8	8 4/8	10 2/8	8	9	Caramat	ONT	L. Reed Breight	1988	503
146 2/8	38 4/8	11 1/8	9 4/8	10	12	Pelican Lake	MAN	Craig Kozak	2000	505
146 1/8	42 5/8	8 5/8	8 2/8	10	9	Toad River	BC	Glen Berry	1991	506
146 0/8	46 0/8	8 4/8	8 0/8	9	8	Tarnezell Lake	BC	Dr. Rex Hancock	1960	507
146 0/8	40 2/8	7 5/8	8 4/8	9	9	Algoma	ONT	Mauri Uusitalo	1993	507
145 7/8	47 5/8	8 5/8	10 0/8	6	6	Kitchener Lake	BC	Randy E. Doyle	1979	509
145 7/8	45 1/8	8 6/8	7 3/8	9	10	Atikokan	ONT	Loran M. Marceau	1993	509
145 7/8	48 5/8	8 2/8	7 7/8	8	10	Vermilion	ALB	Greg Lumley	2007	509
145 6/8	47 4/8	8 3/8	8 4/8	9	8	Princess Lake	NFL	John Iannuzzo	1967	512
145 5/8	41 1/8	9 2/8	7 6/8	8	8	Fort McMurray	ALB	Jim Miller, Jr.	1993	513
145 4/8	45 4/8	9 1/8	8 3/8	9	8	Tatlatui Lake	BC	G. Fred Asbell	1975	514
145 4/8	47 2/8	9 1/8	7 4/8	8	7	Pierceland	SAS	George C. Swanson	1998	514
145 4/8	45 2/8	7 5/8	9 4/8	9	11	Edmonton	ALB	H. Mike Palmer	2005	514
145 3/8	48 5/8	9 0/8	8 6/8	9	9	Duck Mtns.	MAN	Richard Hay	1986	517
*145 3/8	41 3/8	8 3/8	9 2/8	9	9	Dry Creek	BC	Sebastien Therrien	2007	517
145 3/8	49 5/8	11 1/8	9 0/8	9	7	Wabigoon River	ONT	Douglas A. Yff	2008	517
145 2/8	45 0/8	10 0/8	9 4/8	10	8	Morton	MAN	Dennis Olischefski	1988	520
145 2/8	45 6/8	10 1/8	12 4/8	7	11	Lewisporte	NFL	Francis Ogden	1995	520
145 2/8	45 4/8	10 3/8	11 2/8	8	10	Bottineau County	ND	Dennis Bense	2000	520
145 1/8	46 3/8	12 4/8	9 5/8	7	8	Trapnarrows Lake	ONT	John A. Schmidt	1985	523
145 1/8	45 1/8	8 4/8	10 2/8	5	7	Muskwa River	BC	K-Tal Johnson	1995	523
*145 1/8	41 5/8	8 5/8	7 2/8	8	7	Burlington	NFL	Charles W. Rehor	2010	523
144 6/8	41 6/8	9 4/8	11 0/8	9	11	Dease Lake	BC	Dave Ramsay	1981	526
144 6/8	46 2/8	7 3/8	8 7/8	6	8	Newbrook	ALB	Ernest Larocque	1997	526
144 6/8	49 6/8	11 0/8	8 2/8	8	9	Fraserdale	ONT	A. Michael Matala, Jr.	1997	526
144 6/8	49 0/8	10 3/8	7 4/8	8	10	Grande Cache	ALB	Bruce R. Cifelli	2000	526
*144 6/8	43 2/8	11 5/8	10 0/8	9	9	Cecil Lake	ONT	Randy Stankowski	2004	526
144 6/8	40 4/8	10 2/8	9 6/8	8	8	Hudson Bay	SAS	Albert Olmstead	2010	526
*144 4/8	42 3/8	9 3/8	10 0/8	9	8	Nechako River	BC	Rod Aspden	2008	532
144 3/8	48 3/8	8 4/8	10 5/8	6	9	Vermilion Bay	ONT	Robert Scott Ellery	1994	533
144 3/8	44 5/8	9 1/8	9 7/8	6	8	Prince George	BC	Gary Gapp	2001	533
*144 3/8	47 7/8	8 3/8	10 0/8	4	4	Athabasca	ALB	Jeff Steinke	2010	533
144 2/8	50 2/8	8 5/8	10 3/8	8	9	Raith	ONT	Gerald D. Young	1983	536
144 1/8	44 3/8	8 0/8	7 0/8	7	6	Charlotte Lake	BC	Stanley D. Moore	1996	537
144 1/8	42 5/8	9 2/8	9 3/8	8	8	Trout River	ONT	James C. Gates	1998	537
144 0/8	47 2/8	10 1/8	10 0/8	8	9	Besa River	BC	Chris Barker	1991	539
144 0/8	47 2/8	9 5/8	10 7/8	8	9	Ear Falls	ONT	Kenneth Graber	2002	539
143 6/8	44 0/8	10 0/8	11 1/8	7	6	Lake Nipigon	ONT	Ohne Raasch	1992	541
143 6/8	44 0/8	9 0/8	10 3/8	10	12	Nipigon	ONT	Don Mealey	2006	541
143 3/8	45 7/8	9 5/8	8 7/8	9	7	Thunder Bay	ONT	David Nuttall	2007	543
143 2/8	41 0/8	11 1/8	12 1/8	8	11	Devils Lake	BC	R. Eric Shields	1999	544
143 2/8	44 2/8	10 7/8	10 4/8	9	9	Conne River	NFL	Alan Anglyn	2009	544
143 1/8	44 3/8	9 0/8	8 3/8	9	9	Algoma	ONT	Larry Pilon	1985	546
143 1/8	52 3/8	9 6/8	12 5/8	9	7	Oak Lake	ONT	James F. Knickmeyer	1998	546
143 1/8	40 1/8	9 7/8	10 0/8	10	8	Tweedsmuir Park	BC	Lawrence Michalchuk	2000	546
143 1/8	44 3/8	9 4/8	9 0/8	7	7	Myrnam	ALB	Dave Browne	2003	546
142 7/8	45 2/8	10 3/8	8 7/8	9	8	Nakina	ONT	Cammeron Bauer	2000	550
142 7/8	43 5/8	10 2/8	10 3/8	9	8	Cumberland House	SAS	Ken Brandl	2003	550
142 7/8	48 3/8	7 0/8	7 0/8	6	5	Kootenay River	BC	William Fiore	2005	550
142 5/8	46 7/8	7 2/8	10 4/8	8	8	Edmonton	ALB	William Riley	2003	553
*142 5/8	49 5/8	7 7/8	9 3/8	6	7	Causapscal	QUE	Dominique Girard	2003	553
142 4/8	47 0/8	10 2/8	7 7/8	7	9	Myrnam	ALB	Orest Popil	1995	555
142 3/8	42 5/8	8 6/8	8 1/8	8	8	Hurdman Lake	QUE	Bill Dunn	1987	556
142 2/8	42 2/8	10 3/8	9 2/8	8	8	Lake Discella	BC	Ken Grosslight	1995	557
142 2/8	41 6/8	9 7/8	9 5/8	10	12	Aroostook County	ME	Val De Santis, Jr.	2002	557
142 1/8	47 7/8	12 5/8	9 3/8	9	7	Oak Lake	ONT	William W. Knickmeyer	1998	559
142 0/8	49 4/8	8 4/8	8 6/8	9	8	Zec St. Patrice	QUE	Henry P. Bouchard	1993	560
142 0/8	46 2/8	8 6/8	9 4/8	6	10	Thunder Bay	ONT	Steve Shore	2002	560
142 0/8	44 6/8	10 2/8	6 5/8	10	7	Bow Lake	ONT	Steven Hearne	2006	560
141 7/8	43 5/8	9 2/8	9 5/8	10	9	Spruce View	ALB	Glen Cunningham	1998	563
141 6/8	41 2/8	11 4/8	9 5/8	6	9	Sheba Township	ONT	Jerry Boudreault	1987	564
*141 6/8	45 0/8	8 4/8	8 1/8	7	9	Hornepayne	ONT	Jonathan Koon	2007	564
141 4/8	44 0/8	8 3/8	8 3/8	7	6	Keily Creek	BC	Tom Vanasche	1998	566
141 4/8	49 0/8	6 0/8	6 4/8	7	8	Pakwash Lake	ONT	John Flies	1998	566
141 3/8	44 5/8	12 1/8	13 0/8	6	4	Penobscot County	ME	Gregory A. Bonecutter, Sr.	1991	568
141 3/8	41 1/8	10 2/8	10 6/8	8	6	Sesseganaga Lake	ONT	Eric L. Hamele	2000	568
141 3/8	50 1/8	8 3/8	7 4/8	8	6	Reed Lake	ONT	Joe Manuszak	2002	568

791

CANADA MOOSE

Minimum Score 135 — Continued

SCORE	INSIDE SPREAD	WIDTH OF PALM R	WIDTH OF PALM L	NUMBER OF POINTS R	NUMBER OF POINTS L	AREA	STATE/PROVINCE	HUNTER'S NAME	DATE	RANK
*141 3/8	51 1/8	6 0/8	8 4/8	5	7	North Bay	ONT	Larry Ferguson	2009	568
141 2/8	42 6/8	8 2/8	8 5/8	7	10	Lamont	ALB	William Como	1996	572
141 2/8	44 4/8	9 0/8	9 1/8	8	9	Numakoos Lake	MAN	Leonard G. Ahlen	1998	572
*141 2/8	51 0/8	8 4/8	9 1/8	7	6	French Township	ONT	John Horner	2008	572
141 1/8	45 5/8	10 4/8	8 4/8	9	8	Thunder Bay	ONT	Greg Peters	1994	575
140 7/8	43 1/8	9 0/8	9 0/8	6	6	Strathcona	ALB	Pat Marek	1985	576
140 7/8	46 1/8	10 6/8	10 1/8	9	9	Smoky Lake	ALB	Vince Halisky	2006	576
*140 6/8	46 2/8	9 0/8	9 5/8	5	5	Oak Lake	ONT	Jerry Roberts	2008	578
140 4/8	42 2/8	9 7/8	8 5/8	10	13	Pink Mtn.	BC	Douglas M. Stuart	2001	579
140 3/8	38 5/8	11 4/8	11 4/8	8	11	Atikokan	ONT	Norm R. Drefcinski	1999	580
140 3/8	42 1/8	9 2/8	10 6/8	9	8	Stork Lake	ONT	Shawn Sand	2006	580
140 2/8	48 2/8	7 0/8	7 2/8	7	7	Princess Lake	NFL	John Musacchia	1966	582
140 1/8	39 5/8	12 0/8	11 3/8	13	8	Neebing	ONT	David Nuttall	2000	583
140 1/8	46 3/8	9 2/8	9 4/8	8	6	Aroostook County	ME	Reginald Rouse	2005	583
140 0/8	39 0/8	9 3/8	9 6/8	8	9	Sturgeon Lake	ONT	Terry Hanson	1990	585
140 0/8	50 2/8	7 7/8	6 4/8	7	6	Gogama	ONT	Roger Sheppard	1998	585
139 7/8	40 5/8	8 2/8	9 0/8	10	10	Edmonton	ALB	Wes Pietz	1991	587
139 7/8	38 3/8	10 2/8	10 5/8	10	9	Saskatoon Mtn.	ALB	Wilf Lehners	1995	587
139 6/8	42 2/8	10 2/8	13 4/8	6	12	Sikanni Chief River	BC	Stacy Hoeme	1998	589
139 6/8	44 0/8	9 5/8	9 2/8	3	3	Main Brook	NFL	Fred A. Schuman	2000	589
139 6/8	39 4/8	9 1/8	9 3/8	6	8	Tweedsmuir Peak	BC	George S. Walker	2003	589
139 5/8	40 7/8	8 0/8	9 0/8	8	8	Fort St. John	BC	Michael R. Traub	1981	592
139 5/8	39 5/8	10 2/8	9 2/8	10	10	Saskatoon Mtn.	ALB	Terry Hagman	2003	592
139 4/8	38 0/8	8 5/8	7 4/8	8	9	Edmonton	ALB	Kevin Jeffrey	1991	594
139 4/8	44 2/8	8 0/8	6 5/8	7	5	Jellicoe	ONT	Scott Britton	2004	594
139 4/8	43 6/8	7 7/8	7 7/8	9	7	Longlac	ONT	Dennis E. Klaiber	2005	594
*139 3/8	39 1/8	8 6/8	8 2/8	6	9	Strathcona	ALB	Gord Nuttall	2008	597
139 2/8	38 4/8	8 5/8	8 6/8	10	10	Spruce Grove	ALB	John Nagtegaal	1998	598
139 2/8	48 4/8	8 2/8	10 0/8	8	12	Cooking Lake	ALB	Steve Grue	1999	598
139 1/8	49 5/8	6 3/8	4 7/8	6	6	Aroostook County	ME	William G. Miller II	1994	600
139 1/8	45 7/8	9 0/8	7 7/8	8	8	Smithers	BC	Joseph M. Clevinger	1997	600
139 0/8	46 6/8	8 3/8	11 1/8	8	9	Caribus Lake	ONT	Scott Munro	2003	602
*139 0/8	47 0/8	6 1/8	4 7/8	6	5	Findlay Creek	BC	Ross Aigner	2009	602
138 7/8	48 1/8	8 1/8	7 6/8	8	9	Lodgepole	ALB	Randy Ewen	1997	604
138 4/8	46 2/8	8 4/8	8 2/8	6	6	Ministik	ALB	Chris Crawford	2004	605
138 2/8	44 4/8	9 0/8	9 0/8	7	9	Chapleau	ONT	Gary Riedke	1992	606
138 2/8	46 0/8	7 2/8	8 2/8	5	7	Red Lake	ONT	Frank Rus	2001	606
138 0/8	34 4/8	11 2/8	10 5/8	8	10	St. George Lake	NFL	Bill Carlos	1968	608
138 0/8	38 6/8	11 4/8	10 4/8	5	11	Bear Lake	ONT	Ralph H. Torbeck	2007	608
137 7/8	41 5/8	8 1/8	10 6/8	7	8	Princess Lake	NFL	Ken Rapp	1966	610
137 7/8	44 1/8	11 1/8	10 7/8	7	9	Nipigon Bay	ONT	Tony Giesige	2005	610
137 6/8	48 0/8	7 0/8	7 4/8	8	7	Algoma	ONT	Edward K. Broderick	1987	612
137 6/8	42 0/8	12 5/8	10 3/8	6	7	Rolette County	ND	Robert J. Benth	1991	612
137 6/8	42 6/8	8 4/8	10 3/8	5	7	Belby Pond	NFL	Michael J. Kennedy	1997	612
137 5/8	44 7/8	7 7/8	7 0/8	8	9	Thutade Lake	BC	Kim S Ades	1984	615
137 4/8	43 4/8	9 4/8	9 0/8	7	5	Duck Mtn.	SAS	James D. Hacking	1999	616
137 2/8	44 4/8	8 2/8	8 6/8	8	7	Caroline	ALB	Edwin DeYoung	2007	617
137 1/8	44 7/8	8 0/8	8 4/8	9	9	Gowganda	ONT	James Kelley	1993	618
137 1/8	40 3/8	10 4/8	9 4/8	9	11	Temagami	ONT	Jim Krech	2001	618
137 0/8	43 4/8	7 7/8	8 2/8	9	7	McLaughlin	ALB	Rod Bouck	1999	620
136 6/8	54 0/8	10 0/8	12 6/8	3	5	Dryden	ONT	Mark Mussey	1996	621
136 5/8	41 7/8	8 7/8	10 4/8	9	8	Pants Lake	BC	William Bos	1994	622
*136 4/8	42 2/8	8 1/8	9 0/8	6	8	Van Creek	BC	Jordan Smith	2005	623
136 2/8	46 4/8	7 2/8	7 4/8	6	6	Aroostook County	ME	Dennis M. Hayden	1993	624
136 2/8	44 2/8	9 4/8	12 1/8	7	10	Saskatoon Mtn.	ALB	Duane Hagman	2005	624
136 1/8	43 7/8	5 5/8	5 0/8	6	6	Cassiar Mtns.	BC	Jeff Fitts	1996	626
136 1/8	39 3/8	8 2/8	9 4/8	6	9	Buchans Plateau	NFL	Lesley Bartus	1998	626
136 0/8	45 0/8	6 7/8	10 4/8	7	8	Vermilion Bay	ONT	Todd Miller	2002	628
136 0/8	48 4/8	8 4/8	8 3/8	6	8	Manion Lake	ONT	Roger A. Hazelton	2004	628
135 7/8	43 3/8	7 4/8	7 2/8	7	6	Sangudo	ALB	Allan C. Doell	1983	630
135 7/8	45 5/8	8 2/8	9 4/8	7	10	Timmins	ONT	Gerald Daniel Conrad	2002	630
135 6/8	40 2/8	8 7/8	8 5/8	6	7	Blue Bell Mtn.	BC	Dr. Chuck Leidheiser	1996	632
135 6/8	41 4/8	7 5/8	9 4/8	8	10	Bottineau County	ND	Dale Mowder	1997	632
135 6/8	44 4/8	8 4/8	9 7/8	8	6	Cynthia	ALB	Randy Tellier	1998	632
135 4/8	47 2/8	8 3/8	9 0/8	4	7	Sheerway Lake	QUE	Richard A. Sawyer	1985	635
135 4/8	47 0/8	8 2/8	6 4/8	9	6	Kananaskis	ALB	John Visscher	1992	635
135 4/8	46 2/8	9 1/8	7 6/8	8	7	South Flanders	ONT	Corey Hayes	1996	635
135 4/8	37 6/8	10 1/8	10 1/8	5	5	Toad River	BC	Peter C. Swenson	1999	635
135 4/8	38 2/8	9 3/8	9 5/8	8	6	Maylrthorpe	ALB	Troy Dzioba	2002	635
*135 4/8	41 0/8	8 3/8	8 4/8	6	6	Kootenay	BC	Dwayne Zarr	2006	635
*135 3/8	43 3/8	8 1/8	7 6/8	7	7	Wawa	ONT	Michael L. Ritter	2008	641
135 2/8	41 2/8	11 0/8	12 3/8	9	4	Boissevain	MAN	Hellar Nakonechny	1987	642
135 2/8	42 2/8	8 3/8	8 4/8	9	8	Cumberland House	SAS	Ken Brandl	1998	642
135 2/8	39 2/8	8 3/8	8 2/8	10	10	Swan Lake	ALB	Derrill Herman	1999	642
135 1/8	41 3/8	8 3/8	8 6/8	8	9	Endeavour	SAS	Ronald W. Porter	2001	645
*135 0/8	39 0/8	9 6/8	10 1/8	8	10	Williams Lake	BC	Lee Jackman	2010	646

CANADA MOOSE (VELVET ANTLERS)

Minimum Score 135

SCORE	INSIDE SPREAD	WIDTH OF PALM R L	NUMBER OF POINTS R L	AREA	STATE/ PROVINCE	HUNTER'S NAME	DATE	RANK
142 2/8	44 0/8	7 5/8 7 4/8	6 4	St. Anthony	NFL	William G. Mason	2000	*
156 6/8	47 2/8	9 0/8 9 6/8	8 8	McKenzie County	ND	Jason D. Rockswold	2010	*

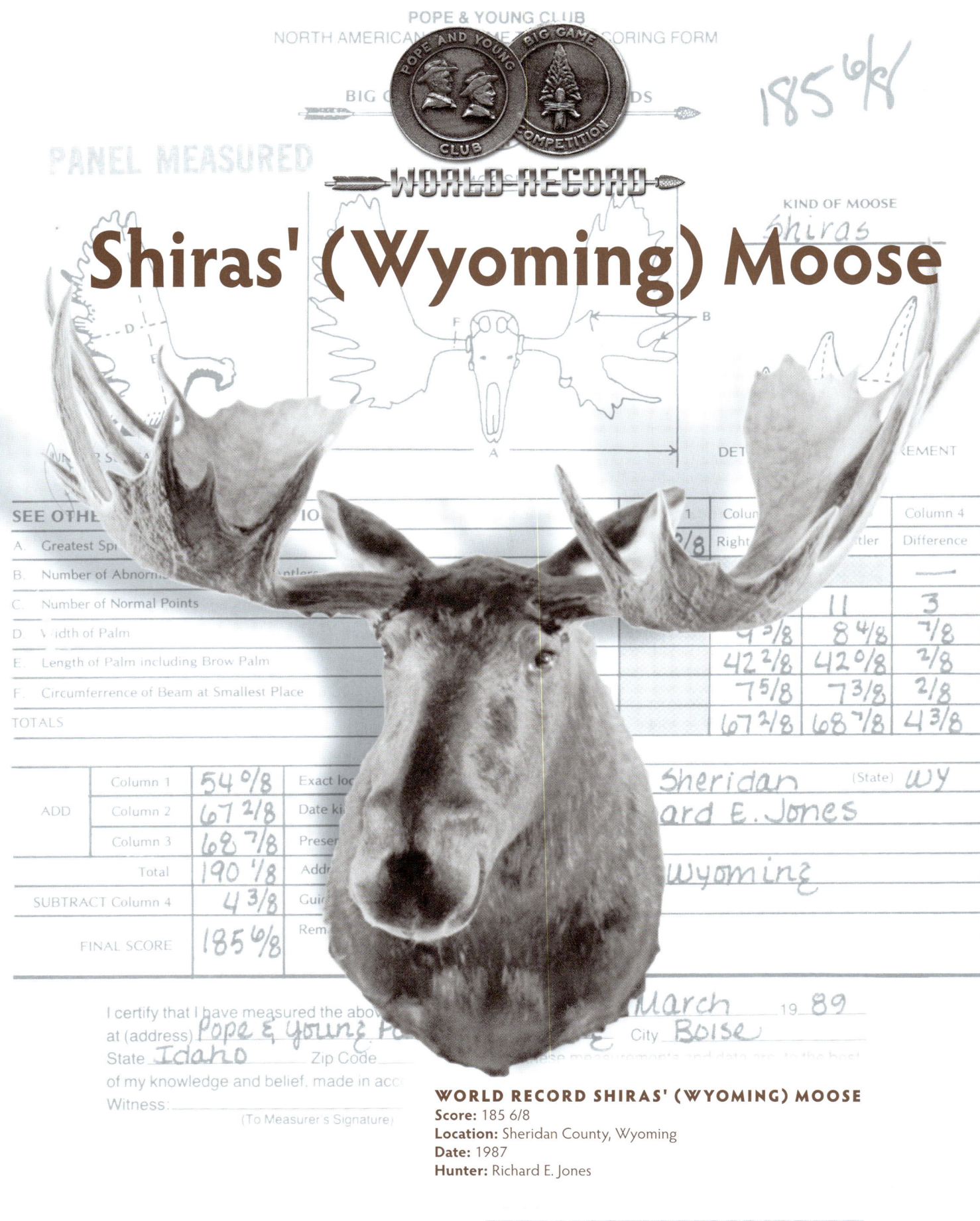

WORLD RECORD SHIRAS' (WYOMING) MOOSE
Score: 185 6/8
Location: Sheridan County, Wyoming
Date: 1987
Hunter: Richard E. Jones

SHIRAS' (WYOMING) MOOSE

Minimum Score 125

Alces alces shirasi

SCORE	INSIDE SPREAD	WIDTH OF R PALM L	NUMBER OF R POINTS L	AREA	STATE/ PROVINCE	HUNTER'S NAME	DATE	RANK
185 6/8	54 0/8	9 3/8 8 4/8	8 11	Sheridan County	WY	Richard E. Jones	1987	1
185 5/8	50 1/8	13 1/8 12 4/8	11 11	Big Horn County	WY	John Harvey	1996	2
183 7/8	49 7/8	13 3/8 14 4/8	12 10	Johnson County	WY	Scott A. Wodahl	2002	3
180 3/8	48 1/8	10 4/8 11 0/8	10 10	Fremont County	ID	Kenneth K. Fordyce	1983	4
177 5/8	43 3/8	11 5/8 10 0/8	10 12	Madison County	ID	Gerald Madsen	1998	5
177 1/8	43 1/8	15 6/8 13 3/8	13 14	Bingham County	ID	David Cederberg	1995	6
*176 3/8	48 1/8	11 1/8 13 5/8	14 15	Grand County	CO	Weldon W. Flaharty	2009	7
176 1/8	54 5/8	11 6/8 12 0/8	12 10	Johnson County	WY	Benjamin L. Michelena	2001	8
174 5/8	45 1/8	11 5/8 13 5/8	15 13	Caribou County	ID	James Keller	1992	9
174 3/8	48 1/8	13 0/8 15 2/8	14 12	Bonneville County	ID	David C. Cole	1987	10
174 2/8	55 2/8	11 4/8 9 5/8	11 11	Idaho County	ID	Larry Hoff	1991	11
174 2/8	47 4/8	13 7/8 15 1/8	9 10	Caribou County	ID	Brian L. Paulsen	2000	11
173 6/8	47 4/8	9 2/8 8 3/8	12 13	Teton County	ID	Van W. Shotzman	1988	14
173 6/8	46 6/8	11 4/8 11 6/8	9 11	Larimer County	CO	Ed Wick	2005	14
172 0/8	46 6/8	10 4/8 10 0/8	12 11	Madison County	ID	Trent Wood	1983	16
170 2/8	47 2/8	8 6/8 11 4/8	9 10	Madison County	ID	Ron Stacey	1988	17
170 1/8	51 7/8	12 6/8 9 6/8	10 10	Clearwater County	ID	Ken Radach	2004	18
169 7/8	51 5/8	12 3/8 8 6/8	13 11	Sheridan County	WY	James L. Nealey	1990	19
169 3/8	51 1/8	9 7/8 11 5/8	11 9	Sheridan County	WY	Mark Policky	2002	20
169 2/8	53 0/8	10 7/8 11 7/8	9 12	Park County	MT	Sam A. Terakedis	1995	21
168 7/8	52 5/8	10 4/8 11 0/8	10 10	Salt Lake County	UT	Michael Christensen	2007	22
168 6/8	49 2/8	11 3/8 10 5/8	13 13	Salt Lake County	UT	Rob Dixon	2009	23
168 3/8	50 5/8	12 3/8 10 3/8	11 10	Larimer County	CO	Dale Rush	2008	24
167 7/8	46 3/8	12 1/8 13 0/8	11 7	Teton County	WY	Jon S. Fossel	1998	25
167 2/8	49 2/8	8 6/8 11 1/8	10 12	Sheridan County	WY	Mark B. Steffen	2003	26
166 7/8	39 1/8	12 7/8 14 6/8	9 11	Jackson County	CO	Randal W. Chase	2002	27
166 7/8	47 5/8	9 7/8 12 0/8	9 10	Johnson County	WY	Walter Palmer	2006	27
166 5/8	50 1/8	10 1/8 11 0/8	11 10	Madison County	ID	Dale Johnson	1987	29
166 4/8	45 4/8	10 6/8 13 2/8	9 11	Sheridan County	WY	Don Groskopf	1986	30
166 3/8	44 5/8	9 2/8 12 2/8	9 14	Sheridan County	WY	Rob Marosok	1993	31
166 1/8	53 3/8	10 1/8 10 6/8	10 11	Madison County	ID	Roger K. Wood	1995	32
165 7/8	43 3/8	10 6/8 11 4/8	10 11	Sheridan County	WY	Dave Ackerman	2001	33
165 5/8	47 7/8	10 1/8 8 7/8	11 11	Gallatin County	MT	Albert D. Williams	1986	34
165 5/8	44 7/8	12 1/8 12 3/8	9 11	Larimer County	CO	Jon E. Hoyt	2004	34
165 4/8	47 4/8	10 4/8 10 4/8	9 8	Utah County	UT	Chad J. Hall	1997	36
164 7/8	49 3/8	8 6/8 9 6/8	9 10	Idaho County	ID	Oliver E. Robinett	1980	37
164 7/8	50 1/8	10 3/8 11 0/8	8 12	Park County	WY	Dennis F. Bost	2000	37
164 3/8	48 5/8	10 3/8 13 0/8	10 11	Cache County	UT	Bob "Jake" Jacobsen	1994	39
164 1/8	41 3/8	13 4/8 13 2/8	14 12	Gallatin County	MT	Larry Schweitzer	1984	40
164 1/8	55 3/8	7 2/8 9 0/8	9 9	Teton County	WY	Rick Parish	1996	40
163 7/8	53 5/8	9 2/8 8 2/8	10 8	Lincoln County	WY	Brad Hugh Jacobs	1990	42
163 7/8	50 1/8	9 4/8 11 2/8	8 12	Summit County	UT	Wade Wilde	2001	42
163 6/8	44 6/8	13 1/8 13 4/8	12 10	Lincoln County	WY	Walter Walbridge	1980	44
163 6/8	60 0/8	10 6/8 10 3/8	10 8	Carbon County	WY	Rodney B. Weinman	2000	44
163 3/8	44 7/8	9 6/8 11 4/8	12 12	Morgan County	UT	Archie Nesbitt	1987	46
163 1/8	48 1/8	11 3/8 10 6/8	11 11	Weber County	UT	Randy K. Allen	1992	47
162 3/8	48 1/8	12 1/8 10 2/8	11 11	Teton County	ID	Howard W. Beins	1994	48
162 1/8	50 5/8	11 3/8 10 7/8	11 10	Gallatin County	MT	Jerry D. Johnson	1994	49
162 0/8	51 4/8	8 3/8 9 4/8	8 11	Sheridan County	WY	Dan Hart	1996	50
161 7/8	50 7/8	10 1/8 10 1/8	8 9	Jackson County	CO	Kirt Krieger	1992	51
161 7/8	47 1/8	9 7/8 13 2/8	10 10	Carbon County	MT	Stephen Tylinski	2001	51
161 6/8	47 0/8	11 3/8 11 0/8	9 10	Sheridan County	WY	John D. "Jack" Frost	1988	53
*161 6/8	48 0/8	12 7/8 10 4/8	13 8	Larimer County	CO	Chipper L. Clark	2008	53
161 4/8	44 2/8	15 2/8 12 4/8	12 11	Bonneville County	ID	Michael Magalsky	2009	55
161 3/8	40 3/8	11 2/8 12 5/8	10 14	Morgan County	UT	Jon P. Miller	2004	56
161 1/8	42 3/8	10 3/8 12 6/8	9 8	Big Horn County	WY	Mike Lutt	2003	57
160 6/8	51 6/8	9 3/8 8 0/8	10 8	Bonneville County	ID	Marty George	1986	58
160 4/8	47 0/8	9 3/8 10 0/8	12 9	Weber County	UT	Hugh H. Hogle	1989	59
160 4/8	50 4/8	11 0/8 9 5/8	10 10	Jackson County	CO	Ron Madsen	1996	59
*160 1/8	50 3/8	9 4/8 10 1/8	8 10	Carbon County	WY	Paul Parke	2009	61
159 6/8	43 0/8	15 4/8 12 0/8	6 7	Teton County	WY	Daniel B. White	1978	62
159 6/8	45 6/8	9 0/8 9 3/8	11 11	Sweetwater County	WY	Mike Deaton	1992	62
159 2/8	47 4/8	9 0/8 9 4/8	12 10	Boundary County	ID	John Thomas	2000	64
159 1/8	49 5/8	12 7/8 10 7/8	8 10	Gallatin County	MT	Keith Wheat	1960	65
159 1/8	48 3/8	9 2/8 7 6/8	9 9	Grand County	CO	Rick Karbowski	1998	65
159 0/8	48 0/8	9 4/8 9 5/8	10 8	Sheridan County	WY	Bradley Carl Wichman	1990	67
158 7/8	47 1/8	9 2/8 10 3/8	7 9	Larimer County	CO	Scott Wilson	2006	68
158 6/8	50 2/8	10 6/8 11 0/8	11 11	Lincoln County	WY	Mike Smith	1976	69
158 6/8	45 6/8	10 4/8 10 4/8	10 11	Boundary County	ID	Richard M. Penn	2005	69
158 5/8	49 7/8	11 0/8 11 4/8	6 8	Albany County	WY	Lenard Brashier	2008	71
158 4/8	51 0/8	7 4/8 10 5/8	8 10	Ravalli County	MT	Stan Billingsley	1998	72
158 3/8	44 3/8	10 4/8 10 2/8	12 13	Sublette County	WY	Steve Gosar	1996	73
158 1/8	45 5/8	9 1/8 10 5/8	10 10	Wasatch County	UT	Todd Lemley	1992	74
158 0/8	49 0/8	10 6/8 10 2/8	7 9	Madison County	MT	Paul Anthony Pernak	2001	75
*157 7/8	48 5/8	8 0/8 9 3/8	5 6	Sheridan County	WY	Brian Brochu	2007	76
157 1/8	45 3/8	11 6/8 12 1/8	8 8	Bighorn Mtns.	WY	Jeffrey L. Welsh	1980	77
157 0/8	47 6/8	12 5/8 10 5/8	10 10	Summit County	UT	Mike T. Schneider	2004	78
156 5/8	53 1/8	11 4/8 11 3/8	8 9	Jackson County	CO	Frank S. Noska IV	2002	79
*156 4/8	40 2/8	9 3/8 9 2/8	9 8	Sublette County	WY	Mike Schmid	2007	80
155 7/8	47 7/8	10 0/8 10 0/8	9 8	Morgan County	UT	James A. Pickering	2010	81
155 5/8	47 5/8	10 1/8 10 0/8	9 9	Lemhi County	ID	Bob Johnson	1991	82
155 5/8	45 5/8	12 4/8 10 6/8	12 9	Bannock County	ID	Geoff Hogander	1997	82
155 5/8	52 3/8	12 0/8 14 3/8	8 6	Grand County	CO	Kevin McDonough	2010	82
155 2/8	49 6/8	10 1/8 10 3/8	9 11	Morgan County	UT	Jeff Husted	2002	85
155 1/8	44 4/8	10 1/8 10 0/8	7 9	Summit County	UT	Wayne Hansen	2001	86
155 0/8	50 0/8	11 5/8 8 6/8	9 9	Salt Lake County	UT	Gary T. Albert	2004	86
154 6/8	45 4/8	11 0/8 10 5/8	8 9	Sheridan County	WY	Jerry Bailey	1992	88
154 6/8	40 2/8	10 2/8 9 6/8	11 9	Hot Springs County	WY	Luke R. Mead	2000	88
154 5/8	44 1/8	12 1/8 7 6/8	10 13	Caribou County	ID	James F. Dougherty	1992	90
154 4/8	41 4/8	10 0/8 10 6/8	9 9	Cache County	UT	Kirk Peterson	1992	91
154 3/8	45 7/8	9 6/8 10 0/8	10 9	Gallatin County	MT	Greg Flaherty	1998	92
154 2/8	48 4/8	10 1/8 9 3/8	8 9	Wasatch County	UT	Shayne Thompson	2005	93
154 0/8	49 4/8	9 1/8 8 7/8	8 9	Flathead County	MT	C. P. Mendenhall	1960	94
154 0/8	45 2/8	9 2/8 9 2/8	10 11	Caribou County	ID	Brett Dee Hymas	1986	94
153 7/8	43 5/8	8 0/8 9 4/8	7 8	Clearwater County	ID	Ray Matson	1993	96

795

SHIRAS' (WYOMING) MOOSE

Minimum Score 125 — Continued

SCORE	INSIDE SPREAD	WIDTH OF PALM R	L	NUMBER OF POINTS R	L	AREA	STATE/ PROVINCE	HUNTER'S NAME	DATE	RANK
153 6/8	42 0/8	11 7/8	11 0/8	13	11	Bonneville County	ID	Lonnie Pickens	1988	97
153 5/8	48 3/8	7 7/8	10 4/8	9	11	Teton County	WY	M. R. James	1992	98
153 5/8	50 1/8	9 5/8	10 2/8	7	9	Sublette County	WY	Richard Glasgow	1999	98
153 4/8	45 4/8	10 0/8	12 6/8	9	11	Deer Lodge County	MT	Terry L. Button	1986	100
153 4/8	45 0/8	8 7/8	8 7/8	8	8	Jackson County	CO	Scott Koester	1996	100
153 2/8	45 6/8	9 2/8	10 1/8	9	10	Uintah County	WY	Glen O. Hallows	2005	102
153 1/8	45 7/8	10 5/8	12 4/8	8	8	Sheridan County	WY	William Ludwig	1994	103
152 7/8	46 5/8	10 6/8	9 5/8	10	9	Lincoln County	WY	Franklin W. Sheets	1989	104
152 5/8	51 1/8	9 6/8	9 1/8	8	8	Johnson County	WY	Robert N. Rust	2004	105
152 4/8	39 6/8	13 2/8	12 2/8	9	10	Sweetwater County	WY	Patti Pollard	1990	106
*152 4/8	39 6/8	10 3/8	9 4/8	9	10	Missoula County	MT	Bridger Stratford	2005	106
152 4/8	44 2/8	9 2/8	8 4/8	9	8	Grand County	CO	Greg Sinn	2010	106
152 1/8	45 1/8	10 4/8	9 0/8	9	7	Clearwater County	ID	Louis W. Wasniewski	2009	109
152 0/8	41 2/8	9 5/8	8 4/8	11	11	Washakie County	WY	John Crump	2010	110
151 6/8	43 4/8	10 3/8	8 2/8	12	6	Morgan County	UT	Len Cardinale	1987	111
151 6/8	46 0/8	10 5/8	10 4/8	10	9	Lincoln County	WY	Kenneth M. Thompson	1997	111
151 5/8	40 5/8	8 5/8	8 5/8	10	9	Sanders County	MT	Jim Ryan	1989	113
151 5/8	41 3/8	10 3/8	11 4/8	9	9	Caribou County	ID	Scott Godfrey	2006	113
151 3/8	47 1/8	12 4/8	10 4/8	12	9	Rich County	UT	Mike Poynor	1990	115
151 3/8	45 7/8	8 2/8	7 3/8	7	8	Sheridan County	WY	Troy Carnes	2003	115
151 2/8	44 0/8	9 2/8	9 0/8	9	8	Johnson County	WY	Nicolette Hanson	1998	117
151 0/8	49 4/8	10 4/8	10 1/8	8	8	Bonneville County	ID	Alan L. Hall	1998	118
150 7/8	42 3/8	10 7/8	9 7/8	10	10	Clark County	ID	Joseph E. Packer	1981	119
150 6/8	39 4/8	9 4/8	11 2/8	10	11	Sublette County	WY	Bryan Radakovich	1990	120
150 4/8	48 6/8	9 3/8	8 7/8	9	10	Rich County	UT	Blake Poppleton	1987	121
150 4/8	49 4/8	8 4/8	8 3/8	7	8	Sheridan County	WY	Darrell Cook	1991	121
150 4/8	42 6/8	9 3/8	11 0/8	9	10	Bonneville County	ID	Dr. Tom W. Dorrell, Jr.	1996	121
150 4/8	41 2/8	9 3/8	10 5/8	10	11	Teton County	WY	Jerry Bodar	2000	121
150 0/8	48 4/8	8 6/8	8 2/8	8	8	Bannock County	ID	Virgil Burget	1998	125
149 6/8	45 6/8	11 0/8	12 3/8	4	5	Idaho County	ID	Larry Hoff	2007	126
149 2/8	37 4/8	9 2/8	10 2/8	9	11	Park County	WY	Marion J. De Busk	1994	127
149 2/8	41 4/8	8 6/8	9 3/8	9	8	Lincoln County	WY	Dustin C. Hays	1998	127
149 1/8	46 1/8	9 2/8	10 0/8	8	10	Clark County	ID	Spence Settles	1990	129
149 1/8	49 7/8	9 6/8	9 4/8	7	7	Lincoln County	WY	Ken Hoehn	1994	129
149 0/8	47 4/8	10 7/8	9 3/8	10	8	Bonneville County	ID	Boyd Bowman	1998	131
*149 0/8	41 2/8	10 7/8	12 0/8	11	6	Albany County	WY	Rick Wydoski	2008	131
148 4/8	44 4/8	9 6/8	9 4/8	6	8	Cache County	UT	R. Dale Drilling	2002	133
148 4/8	43 6/8	9 3/8	10 4/8	6	8	Sublette County	WY	James P. Graf	2006	133
148 3/8	49 3/8	7 6/8	7 2/8	6	6	Lincoln County	MT	Jeffrey A. Hintz	1998	135
148 3/8	45 3/8	9 5/8	10 6/8	9	10	Sublette County	WY	Bernie Weisgerber	1999	135
148 3/8	39 5/8	10 4/8	10 0/8	9	9	Big Horn County	WY	Mark L. Preston	2003	135
148 2/8	43 0/8	9 7/8	10 2/8	7	10	Sublette County	WY	Carol Niziolek	1996	138
148 0/8	41 2/8	10 5/8	10 6/8	8	9	Larimer County	CO	Bill Harvey	2002	139
148 0/8	38 2/8	12 6/8	10 4/8	10	12	Park County	WY	Dan S. Webber	2006	139
147 7/8	47 5/8	8 7/8	9 1/8	11	7	Weber County	UT	Michael L. Pope	1997	141
147 7/8	49 7/8	9 4/8	8 3/8	10	8	Weber County	UT	Daniel E. Harris	1999	141
147 6/8	46 4/8	10 0/8	10 2/8	8	9	Uinta County	WY	Vernon M. Poynor	1989	143
*147 6/8	36 4/8	9 0/8	10 1/8	11	12	Lincoln County	WY	Brett I. Ritter	2007	143
147 5/8	45 3/8	9 4/8	9 0/8	7	9	Bonneville County	ID	Steven R. Eldredge	1993	145
147 4/8	41 2/8	10 0/8	11 3/8	8	10	Sublette County	WY	Michael Beckwith	1985	146
147 4/8	41 0/8	8 4/8	11 4/8	9	10	Jackson County	CO	Dan Pfannenstiel	1993	146
147 3/8	47 7/8	10 7/8	9 1/8	10	8	Salt Lake County	UT	R. Todd Inman	1997	148
147 2/8	41 6/8	10 6/8	10 2/8	5	8	Madison County	ID	Randy Lee Davison	1987	149
147 2/8	42 4/8	7 7/8	8 3/8	7	5	Sheridan County	WY	Larry Katz	1992	149
147 1/8	43 3/8	7 5/8	8 3/8	8	9	Summit County	UT	Jerry Cross	1979	151
147 1/8	46 3/8	10 1/8	9 6/8	10	9	Lincoln County	WY	Gary Gale	1988	151
147 1/8	43 7/8	8 5/8	9 4/8	8	9	Big Horn County	WY	George Harms	2004	151
147 0/8	45 0/8	11 3/8	9 6/8	9	8	Teton County	WY	Jerry Bowen	1982	154
147 0/8	46 2/8	6 1/8	11 1/8	8	13	Weber County	UT	Matthew G. Hogle	1990	154
*146 5/8	39 1/8	8 0/8	8 7/8	8	8	Lincoln County	WY	David E. Evanow	2009	156
146 4/8	44 4/8	7 3/8	7 5/8	6	6	Park County	MT	Randy Cook	1982	157
146 4/8	42 4/8	11 0/8	9 2/8	10	6	Spokane County	WA	Lance B. Cussons	1991	157
146 4/8	45 2/8	7 6/8	8 3/8	8	8	Teton County	WY	Ronell Skinner	1999	157
146 4/8	40 4/8	11 1/8	9 4/8	11	11	Sublette County	WY	Kurt W. Krech	2005	157
146 3/8	45 1/8	9 1/8	9 1/8	8	7	Sheridan County	WY	Cecil Benner	1990	161
146 3/8	43 3/8	10 5/8	10 0/8	10	11	Jackson County	CO	Dave Hughes	1993	161
146 2/8	47 6/8	8 6/8	11 6/8	7	8	Boundary County	ID	Randy Neal	2001	163
*146 2/8	45 0/8	8 3/8	8 6/8	8	10	Washakie County	WY	F. Matt Lentsch	2005	163
146 1/8	40 2/8	10 4/8	8 4/8	9	9	Sheridan County	WY	Dan Barngrover	1989	165
146 0/8	47 6/8	9 1/8	8 5/8	7	7	Idaho County	ID	Dave Loos	2006	166
146 0/8	43 4/8	9 5/8	13 3/8	9	9	Sublette County	WY	Jim Summerall	2006	166
145 7/8	44 5/8	10 5/8	9 1/8	10	9	Sheridan County	WY	Tom Pindell	2004	168
145 5/8	52 1/8	7 2/8	7 6/8	6	6	Flathead County	MT	Paul Albertoni	1996	169
145 4/8	41 2/8	10 5/8	10 3/8	7	6	Meagher County	MT	Kenny Roy	1997	170
145 1/8	45 2/8	9 4/8	8 2/8	5	6	Beaverhead County	MT	Greg L. Munther	1982	171
144 7/8	39 5/8	9 3/8	10 7/8	10	9	Sheridan County	WY	Clay Beard	2005	172
144 6/8	56 0/8	5 5/8	7 4/8	6	8	Summit County	UT	Ryan R. Anderson	1993	173
144 6/8	34 2/8	11 2/8	11 6/8	7	8	Sublette County	WY	Bill G. Davis	1994	173
144 6/8	42 6/8	9 4/8	12 4/8	8	7	Grand County	CO	Doug J. Carlton	2010	173
144 5/8	40 7/8	8 5/8	9 2/8	8	8	Pend Oreille County	WA	Douglas D. Kikendall	2002	176
*144 5/8	43 5/8	9 0/8	8 5/8	10	9	Bingham County	ID	Travis Hess	2008	176
144 4/8	43 0/8	11 0/8	10 7/8	9	8	Sublette County	WY	Boyd Andersen	1988	178
144 3/8	47 3/8	8 5/8	10 4/8	9	8	Weber County	UT	Chuck Adams	1987	179
143 7/8	45 1/8	8 4/8	7 7/8	10	8	Laramie County	WY	Rene Suda	2007	180
143 6/8	38 2/8	10 0/8	8 2/8	8	9	Bonneville County	ID	Chris R. Tripp	1994	181
143 4/8	44 4/8	11 0/8	10 0/8	7	9	Jackson County	CO	Rory E. Ciepiela	2000	182
143 4/8	41 0/8	9 4/8	9 5/8	7	9	Lincoln County	WY	John I. Ritter	2009	182
143 3/8	43 7/8	10 2/8	10 2/8	10	10	Silver Bow County	MT	J. Ray Haffey	1994	184
143 2/8	47 4/8	9 3/8	10 0/8	9	7	Idaho County	ID	Stanley Leake	1979	185
143 1/8	44 1/8	8 6/8	8 1/8	4	6	Jackson County	CO	Kevin M. Ayers	2002	186
143 1/8	42 3/8	9 6/8	8 1/8	9	10	Weber County	UT	Randy E. Dalton	2004	186
143 1/8	41 3/8	9 4/8	10 0/8	9	10	Lincoln County	WY	Jerry Bowen	2004	186
143 0/8	47 4/8	13 3/8	8 4/8	9	8	Clark County	ID	Alton Howell	1987	189
143 0/8	47 0/8	8 7/8	8 2/8	7	7	Sheridan County	WY	Ronald Jay Buisman	1996	189
*142 7/8	39 3/8	10 5/8	11 4/8	9	9	Lincoln County	MT	Doug Tu	2005	191

796

SHIRAS' (WYOMING) MOOSE

Minimum Score 125

Continued

SCORE	INSIDE SPREAD	WIDTH OF PALM R / L	NUMBER OF POINTS R / L	AREA	STATE/PROVINCE	HUNTER'S NAME	DATE	RANK
142 6/8	40 6/8	9 4/8 / 9 4/8	8 / 7	Gallatin County	MT	Stuart J. Georgitis	1986	192
142 6/8	39 0/8	9 3/8 / 9 6/8	10 / 12	Uinta County	WY	Kevin Earl	1996	192
142 5/8	39 5/8	10 2/8 / 11 0/8	9 / 10	Lincoln County	WY	Clayton "Karl" Knudsen	1992	194
142 4/8	40 4/8	9 6/8 / 10 1/8	7 / 10	Granite County	MT	Vince Van Witbeck	2005	195
142 3/8	45 3/8	8 4/8 / 10 4/8	9 / 10	Weber County	UT	Ken C. Taylor	1995	196
142 3/8	45 1/8	6 1/8 / 6 5/8	7 / 7	Fremont County	ID	Jon A. Lammle	2001	196
142 2/8	46 4/8	9 0/8 / 10 3/8	10 / 8	Hot Springs County	WY	William L. Robing	1997	198
142 2/8	42 0/8	9 7/8 / 8 0/8	10 / 9	Sheridan County	WY	Earl Lee McClure	2000	198
142 2/8	37 2/8	10 3/8 / 9 6/8	9 / 8	Johnson County	WY	Michel C. Sullivan	2004	198
142 2/8	47 2/8	8 2/8 / 7 4/8	7 / 7	Franklin County	ID	Amber Christensen	2008	198
142 0/8	43 2/8	8 4/8 / 8 3/8	9 / 9	Sheridan County	WY	Thomas Ostrander	1995	202
142 0/8	47 2/8	7 1/8 / 7 2/8	8 / 8	Wasatch County	UT	Dennis Howell	2004	202
*142 0/8	45 6/8	8 5/8 / 7 5/8	10 / 9	Grand County	CO	Chas McConnell	2009	202
141 6/8	41 0/8	8 4/8 / 8 4/8	6 / 10	Flathead County	MT	Gregory Louden	2008	205
141 5/8	46 7/8	11 1/8 / 9 0/8	4 / 4	Fremont County	WY	Craig J. Engelhard	1996	206
141 4/8	40 4/8	12 2/8 / 11 1/8	9 / 9	Lincoln County	WY	Von K. Merritt	1992	207
141 3/8	42 1/8	9 5/8 / 8 2/8	10 / 8	Summit County	UT	Richie Bland	1998	208
141 2/8	44 2/8	9 3/8 / 9 6/8	7 / 9	Caribou County	ID	Steve Chikato	1992	209
141 1/8	40 5/8	11 5/8 / 10 5/8	8 / 9	Granite County	MT	Robert G. Felts	1996	210
141 1/8	42 1/8	9 6/8 / 11 2/8	7 / 8	Johnson County	WY	Russell Schoonover	2005	210
141 1/8	43 5/8	7 2/8 / 8 4/8	7 / 8	Pend Oreille County	WA	Larry Mitchem	2005	210
141 0/8	41 1/8	9 5/8 / 9 4/8	8 / 7	Lincoln County	WY	V. Kay Bangerter	1978	213
140 6/8	42 6/8	10 1/8 / 11 0/8	11 / 6	Sublette County	WY	Jerry Harding	1993	214
140 4/8	44 2/8	11 5/8 / 12 3/8	8 / 5	Morgan County	UT	Bruce Carlisle	1988	215
140 3/8	46 3/8	9 3/8 / 10 5/8	9 / 10	Lincoln County	WY	Charles W. Gilgore	1992	216
140 2/8	42 2/8	10 5/8 / 10 6/8	9 / 6	Lincoln County	WY	Keith Dana	1977	217
139 7/8	42 5/8	9 5/8 / 9 7/8	10 / 11	Bear Lake County	ID	Robby Taylor	1996	218
139 7/8	44 7/8	9 3/8 / 8 7/8	8 / 9	Bannock County	ID	Quinn Poll	1999	218
139 6/8	42 4/8	11 1/8 / 11 5/8	9 / 9	Johnson County	WY	Jay Opp	2005	220
139 5/8	41 3/8	10 4/8 / 13 6/8	9 / 11	Big Horn County	WY	Richard Lewallen	2005	221
139 5/8	43 1/8	8 1/8 / 7 7/8	8 / 7	Johnson County	WY	Paul Starkey	2008	221
139 3/8	42 1/8	8 4/8 / 7 6/8	5 / 7	Idaho County	ID	Ray Torrey	1968	223
139 2/8	37 0/8	7 4/8 / 8 4/8	10 / 10	Big Horn County	WY	Kevin Bertsch	2006	224
139 0/8	46 4/8	7 4/8 / 7 7/8	8 / 8	Sheridan County	WY	Tom Hlinka	1986	225
139 0/8	42 2/8	9 0/8 / 9 6/8	9 / 11	Weber County	UT	Mike Steckel	1991	225
138 5/8	41 3/8	8 0/8 / 10 1/8	8 / 9	Sublette County	WY	R. Mark LeFaivre	2004	227
138 4/8	40 6/8	11 4/8 / 13 2/8	6 / 7	Teton County	WY	Jerry A. Bodar	1990	228
138 4/8	41 0/8	8 3/8 / 8 6/8	10 / 11	Teton County	WY	Gary F. Bogner	1994	228
138 4/8	41 0/8	9 4/8 / 12 0/8	9 / 10	Salt Lake County	UT	Kurt Wood	2003	228
138 4/8	39 2/8	8 4/8 / 7 5/8	9 / 9	Sublette County	WY	William S. Trapp	2006	228
138 2/8	42 0/8	9 6/8 / 7 6/8	9 / 7	Lincoln County	MT	Thomas A. DeShazer	1965	232
138 0/8	46 4/8	6 0/8 / 8 5/8	6 / 9	Salt Lake County	UT	Neil T. Phillips	2008	233
137 7/8	47 1/8	9 2/8 / 11 3/8	7 / 9	Sublette County	WY	R. H. Siegert	1969	234
137 7/8	49 5/8	7 1/8 / 6 5/8	8 / 7	Madison County	ID	Paul Beesley	1993	234
137 7/8	36 3/8	10 3/8 / 9 2/8	9 / 8	Teton County	WY	Kevin Anderson	1998	234
137 7/8	40 3/8	8 6/8 / 9 7/8	7 / 10	Johnson County	WY	Tom Taylor	2003	234
*137 7/8	46 5/8	9 0/8 / 8 5/8	7 / 7	Lincoln County	MT	Eric Bachofner	2009	234
137 6/8	43 0/8	7 2/8 / 7 3/8	9 / 10	Park County	WY	Chuck Hassler	1995	239
137 5/8	44 1/8	9 0/8 / 9 1/8	8 / 9	Grand County	CO	Keith Johnson	2000	240
137 2/8	42 4/8	10 4/8 / 9 0/8	8 / 11	Lincoln County	WY	Robert K. Robinson	1978	241
137 2/8	41 0/8	10 0/8 / 11 0/8	10 / 8	Weber County	UT	Kory C. Boekweg	2000	241
137 2/8	41 0/8	9 0/8 / 9 1/8	9 / 8	Morgan County	UT	Camp Newton	2003	241
137 2/8	35 4/8	9 6/8 / 9 3/8	9 / 9	Teton County	WY	Jason Stafford	2008	241
136 7/8	42 1/8	6 5/8 / 9 6/8	8 / 10	Cache County	UT	Larry Cross	1986	245
136 7/8	43 1/8	6 3/8 / 5 5/8	7 / 8	Clark County	ID	Gayland Gilson	1987	245
136 7/8	38 5/8	7 7/8 / 7 3/8	7 / 7	Ravalli County	MT	Steve Powers	1999	245
136 4/8	36 4/8	9 2/8 / 10 0/8	11 / 9	Caribou County	ID	Kevin Akers	2002	248
136 2/8	36 0/8	9 5/8 / 10 5/8	8 / 9	Bonneville County	ID	Ken Bielenberg	2000	249
136 2/8	39 4/8	10 0/8 / 11 4/8	7 / 8	Sheridan County	WY	Dave Holt	2002	249
136 1/8	46 3/8	11 4/8 / 7 7/8	8 / 7	Sheridan County	WY	Mike Traub	1993	251
136 0/8	43 2/8	8 6/8 / 8 2/8	7 / 7	Sublette County	WY	August S. Gray	1991	252
136 0/8	40 4/8	10 2/8 / 8 6/8	10 / 9	Bear Lake County	ID	Kenneth Van Darlin	1998	252
135 7/8	44 7/8	8 4/8 / 7 3/8	7 / 8	Park County	WY	Mike Yonker	1987	254
135 7/8	45 1/8	8 4/8 / 8 2/8	7 / 5	Cache County	UT	Chris Brunker	2006	254
*135 6/8	43 6/8	7 4/8 / 8 7/8	7 / 9	Sublette County	WY	Terry W. Krohn	2004	256
135 6/8	47 6/8	8 5/8 / 8 6/8	7 / 6	Albany County	WY	Mike Perez	2005	256
135 4/8	44 2/8	8 2/8 / 8 0/8	7 / 7	Lincoln County	WY	James M. Machac	1999	258
135 4/8	41 4/8	9 4/8 / 8 7/8	10 / 7	Beaverhead County	MT	Raymond L. Gross, Jr.	2000	258
135 3/8	46 1/8	9 4/8 / 8 4/8	8 / 8	Sublette County	WY	Dave Funderburk	1978	260
135 3/8	42 7/8	8 4/8 / 9 2/8	6 / 6	Idaho County	ID	Ronald Smith	1986	260
135 3/8	44 1/8	6 3/8 / 5 0/8	7 / 6	Lincoln County	WY	Earl Keysaw	2002	260
135 3/8	41 3/8	10 1/8 / 9 5/8	10 / 6	Weber County	UT	Dennis Dunn	2006	260
135 3/8	42 1/8	8 0/8 / 10 5/8	6 / 8	Grand County	CO	Doug Schelhaas	2008	260
135 2/8	40 2/8	8 4/8 / 10 4/8	9 / 8	Fremont County	ID	Shayne Ard	1998	265
135 1/8	33 3/8	8 2/8 / 8 0/8	8 / 8	Lincoln County	MT	Mel Siefke	2005	266
135 0/8	43 2/8	8 2/8 / 9 0/8	8 / 7	Teton County	WY	Greg Perkins	1997	267
134 7/8	40 5/8	8 0/8 / 10 2/8	6 / 8	Lincoln County	MT	Jerry Brown	1982	268
134 6/8	44 4/8	9 2/8 / 8 2/8	9 / 7	Jackson County	CO	Preston Parker	2002	269
134 5/8	38 1/8	8 2/8 / 10 1/8	7 / 9	Bonneville County	ID	David Crane	2004	270
134 4/8	38 6/8	8 1/8 / 7 5/8	8 / 9	Lincoln County	MT	Don Davidson	1989	271
134 1/8	40 1/8	10 4/8 / 8 6/8	10 / 8	Caribou County	ID	Mark Olson	1998	272
*134 0/8	36 2/8	10 4/8 / 11 2/8	4 / 5	Weber County	UT	Kelly R. Moore	2008	273
133 7/8	41 7/8	9 7/8 / 7 7/8	9 / 7	Sublette County	WY	Guy M. Leibenguth	2001	274
133 6/8	43 0/8	9 3/8 / 6 7/8	8 / 8	Teton County	WY	Dr. Joel J. Bickler	1996	275
133 6/8	41 6/8	8 1/8 / 10 2/8	7 / 9	Madison County	MT	Leo Christensen	2000	275
133 6/8	47 2/8	9 2/8 / 8 7/8	10 / 7	Weber County	UT	Glen R. Hampton	2000	275
133 6/8	46 4/8	6 6/8 / 8 0/8	6 / 9	Pend Oreille County	WA	Ray L. Bunney	2008	275
*133 6/8	38 4/8	10 7/8 / 10 4/8	9 / 9	Salt Lake County	UT	Dale L. Hansen	2009	275
133 5/8	44 3/8	8 0/8 / 9 1/8	7 / 7	Sheridan County	WY	Duff De Lon	1989	280
133 4/8	44 2/8	10 1/8 / 8 7/8	9 / 9	Bonneville County	ID	Bruce E. Fuller	2000	281
133 3/8	45 5/8	10 3/8 / 7 5/8	9 / 7	Lincoln County	WY	Mike Johnston	1988	282
133 1/8	40 7/8	8 2/8 / 9 1/8	8 / 8	Jackson County	CO	Mike Brezonick	1993	283
133 0/8	41 6/8	8 6/8 / 7 4/8	10 / 9	Teton County	WY	Bob Dawson	1988	284
*133 0/8	44 2/8	8 0/8 / 7 1/8	9 / 7	Sheridan County	WY	James R. Kiser II	2006	284
132 7/8	43 3/8	8 4/8 / 9 3/8	8 / 6	Weber County	UT	Brian Ferebee	1998	286

SHIRAS' (WYOMING) MOOSE

Minimum Score 125 — Continued

SCORE	INSIDE SPREAD	WIDTH OF R PALM L	NUMBER OF R POINTS L	AREA	STATE/PROVINCE	HUNTER'S NAME	DATE	RANK
*132 7/8	40 3/8	9 7/8 9 4/8	8 9	Teton County	WY	Clark A. Schmitz	2009	286
132 6/8	42 2/8	8 5/8 9 0/8	9 9	Jefferson County	ID	Ray L. Kagel, Jr.	2004	288
132 4/8	43 0/8	8 0/8 8 1/8	8 8	Salt Lake County	UT	M. Tim McIntyre	1999	289
132 4/8	41 0/8	8 0/8 8 1/8	6 8	Utah County	UT	William C. Bolt, Jr.	1999	289
132 4/8	48 2/8	12 0/8 8 0/8	8 7	Morgan County	UT	Dr. David E. Samuel	2002	289
132 2/8	37 6/8	10 3/8 10 6/8	11 9	Lincoln County	WY	Dennis L. Shirley	1988	292
132 1/8	42 2/8	8 5/8 9 1/8	8 8	Lincoln County	WY	Lee Challinor	1982	293
132 1/8	38 3/8	7 5/8 11 5/8	8 9	Lincoln County	WY	Bennett L. McMillian	1997	293
132 1/8	43 1/8	8 2/8 10 0/8	9 10	Weber County	UT	Craig P. Mitton	1998	293
*131 7/8	42 3/8	9 2/8 10 4/8	9 9	Stevens County	WA	Chris A. Howell	2007	296
131 6/8	44 0/8	7 6/8 7 7/8	7 7	Lincoln County	WY	Kevin Jackson	1980	297
131 6/8	40 4/8	8 6/8 10 3/8	9 9	Morgan County	UT	Larry Mathis	1989	297
131 6/8	42 0/8	8 1/8 8 5/8	4 7	Sheridan County	WY	Daniel Henthorn	1995	297
131 6/8	45 0/8	8 5/8 6 0/8	7 7	Caribou County	ID	Mark L. Mansfield	1995	297
131 5/8	34 7/8	11 0/8 11 1/8	4 4	Madison County	ID	William E. Dean	1996	301
131 4/8	47 0/8	8 1/8 8 7/8	7 7	Gallatin County	MT	Scott L. Koelzer	1992	302
131 4/8	41 0/8	8 0/8 10 1/8	8 6	Sublette County	WY	Bruce Peery	2001	302
131 4/8	43 6/8	7 6/8 8 3/8	6 5	Big Horn County	WY	Kendel Cheatham	2008	302
131 3/8	43 5/8	8 5/8 8 3/8	7 8	Sublette County	WY	Kenneth R. Keierleber	1992	305
131 2/8	34 4/8	10 6/8 11 0/8	8 8	Bonneville County	ID	Edward Keller	1986	306
131 2/8	43 6/8	9 5/8 7 7/8	9 8	Uinta County	WY	Larry Lee Francis, Jr.	1991	306
131 1/8	39 7/8	7 4/8 6 2/8	8 7	Sheridan County	WY	Susan K. Barrett	2002	308
*131 1/8	36 5/8	11 3/8 10 4/8	7 8	Johnson County	WY	Andrew Tkach	2006	308
131 1/8	44 5/8	6 4/8 8 1/8	6 9	Sheridan County	WY	Mike Barrett	2008	308
131 0/8	40 6/8	6 7/8 8 2/8	8 8	Beaverhead County	MT	Will R. Schott	2002	311
130 7/8	39 5/8	8 6/8 9 1/8	9 8	Lincoln County	WY	Dave Cordes	1982	312
130 6/8	46 2/8	7 2/8 7 5/8	6 6	Lincoln County	WY	Ken Allen	1986	313
130 6/8	37 4/8	10 2/8 13 6/8	9 10	Lincoln County	WY	Brian L. Wagner	1987	313
130 6/8	48 2/8	8 0/8 7 6/8	7 9	Bear Lake County	ID	Steve Douglas	2006	313
130 5/8	38 3/8	8 4/8 8 3/8	7 11	Park County	WY	Greg Deatsman	1985	316
130 5/8	36 7/8	7 4/8 9 3/8	8 7	Beaverhead County	MT	Robert Rooney	1991	316
130 4/8	36 0/8	9 0/8 8 4/8	9 9	Caribou County	ID	Jerry W. Giles	2000	318
130 4/8	40 2/8	10 3/8 8 5/8	8 5	Bonner County	ID	John Wells	2009	318
130 3/8	36 5/8	9 2/8 9 2/8	7 7	Morgan County	UT	Richard L. Phillippie	2001	320
130 3/8	47 3/8	9 6/8 8 1/8	4 7	Grand County	CO	Brandon Powell	2010	320
130 1/8	38 1/8	9 6/8 9 0/8	10 10	Clark County	ID	William Gardner	1985	322
130 1/8	34 7/8	13 3/8 10 6/8	10 8	Jefferson County	ID	Larry R. Hundley	1999	322
*130 1/8	38 3/8	8 0/8 7 4/8	8 8	Weber County	UT	Bridger D. Gerhardt	2008	322
130 0/8	36 4/8	9 3/8 9 2/8	7 7	Park County	WY	Melanie DeBusk	1998	325
129 7/8	39 1/8	8 2/8 10 2/8	9 11	Lincoln County	WY	Bob Tynsky	1987	326
129 7/8	37 1/8	7 0/8 9 7/8	7 9	Sheridan County	WY	Michael L. Graham	1988	326
129 7/8	38 7/8	8 0/8 8 6/8	7 7	Sublette County	WY	Kevin Cross	1989	326
129 6/8	38 6/8	10 1/8 9 0/8	7 7	Sublette County	WY	Tim Thompson	1998	329
129 6/8	41 2/8	7 0/8 7 0/8	8 6	Jackson County	CO	Russell Overton	2009	329
129 5/8	44 5/8	9 0/8 8 5/8	7 7	Weber County	UT	Jamie Roper	1991	331
129 5/8	43 1/8	8 2/8 8 2/8	7 7	Grand County	CO	Rick Duggan	1999	331
129 5/8	37 7/8	8 6/8 8 5/8	7 8	Big Horn County	WY	Dyrk Eddie	2001	331
129 3/8	42 7/8	7 6/8 9 0/8	7 9	Lincoln County	MT	Jerry Brown	1990	334
129 3/8	40 5/8	9 2/8 8 0/8	9 9	Lincoln County	MT	Kevin Hadley	1997	334
129 2/8	37 2/8	8 6/8 8 5/8	8 8	Sublette County	WY	Jerrold M. Judkins	1979	336
129 0/8	39 4/8	7 4/8 8 0/8	9 8	Flathead County	MT	Dyrk Eddie	1991	337
129 0/8	45 0/8	8 4/8 6 6/8	7 8	Morgan County	UT	Robert G. Petersen	1992	337
128 6/8	39 2/8	7 1/8 7 0/8	9 8	Lincoln County	WY	Jim S. Vilos	2005	339
128 6/8	38 0/8	9 5/8 8 4/8	9 9	Spokane County	WA	Kim M. Thomas	2007	339
128 5/8	39 5/8	7 2/8 5 2/8	7 5	Sublette County	WY	Kyle M. Meintzer	2001	341
128 5/8	42 1/8	7 0/8 6 5/8	6 6	Sheridan County	WY	Paul W. Gale	2004	341
128 4/8	40 0/8	13 0/8 8 4/8	7 9	Sheridan County	WY	Robert R. Long	1994	343
128 1/8	40 5/8	6 4/8 6 0/8	6 6	Teton County	WY	Keith Frick	1984	344
128 0/8	39 0/8	7 6/8 9 4/8	6 8	Fremont County	WY	Gary M. Oksuita	1997	345
128 0/8	40 6/8	8 3/8 9 6/8	6 11	Sublette County	WY	Donald J. Propson	1997	345
128 0/8	37 0/8	8 5/8 9 6/8	6 5	Johnson County	WY	Allen Pehringer	2003	345
128 0/8	38 4/8	11 2/8 11 6/8	8 7	Sublette County	WY	Jim Willems	2006	345
127 6/8	46 4/8	7 4/8 7 0/8	6 6	Shoshone County	ID	David D. Duthie, Jr.	2005	349
127 6/8	36 4/8	10 2/8 8 4/8	11 9	Madison County	ID	Colby Hyde	2006	349
127 5/8	38 1/8	6 6/8 6 6/8	7 7	Jefferson County	ID	David Brizendine	2007	351
127 4/8	35 0/8	9 6/8 12 0/8	8 8	Lincoln County	WY	Al Bitker	1982	352
127 4/8	36 6/8	7 0/8 7 4/8	7 7	Idaho County	ID	Brad Johnson	1985	352
127 3/8	42 5/8	8 2/8 8 2/8	6 7	Fremont County	WY	Richard J. Tokarski	1997	354
127 2/8	41 2/8	6 4/8 6 4/8	9 8	Missoula County	MT	Richard Schaub	1997	355
127 2/8	34 4/8	8 1/8 10 2/8	8 9	Morgan County	UT	Scott T. Christensen	2005	355
127 0/8	42 2/8	7 0/8 7 2/8	7 7	Sublette County	WY	Ron Madsen	1999	357
126 7/8	44 7/8	5 2/8 6 2/8	6 8	Summit County	UT	Kenneth D. Evans	1996	358
126 5/8	41 3/8	8 6/8 9 3/8	6 6	Gallatin County	MT	Jim Winjum	2003	359
126 2/8	43 3/8	8 6/8 9 1/8	7 7	Idaho County	ID	Robert Jackson	1990	360
126 2/8	44 0/8	6 4/8 6 4/8	5 6	Shoshone County	ID	Duane E. Hughes	1999	360
126 1/8	44 5/8	6 7/8 5 1/8	7 7	Beaverhead County	MT	Donny Kaneshiro	2005	362
125 6/8	45 0/8	8 6/8 8 2/8	5 7	Lincoln County	WY	Dawn J. Traub	2002	363
125 5/8	49 3/8	8 2/8 7 7/8	8 7	Weber County	UT	Clark Stokes	1986	364
125 4/8	39 4/8	9 4/8 9 4/8	8 8	Lemhi County	ID	Lewis Zane Abbott	1992	365
125 4/8	41 2/8	7 7/8 6 0/8	10 7	Duchesne County	UT	Jonny C. Parsons	1994	365
125 4/8	41 2/8	8 6/8 8 0/8	5 7	Sublette County	WY	William T. Bos	2001	365
125 2/8	38 2/8	7 4/8 7 3/8	6 6	Sheridan County	WY	Mark Jost	2003	368
125 2/8	39 0/8	8 3/8 9 0/8	8 9	Broadwater County	MT	Dennis Willson	2005	368
125 2/8	37 4/8	8 2/8 9 1/8	7 7	Lincoln County	WY	Robert R. Sherman	2009	368
125 0/8	34 4/8	9 5/8 8 6/8	9 9	Morgan County	UT	C. Danny Butler	1991	371
125 0/8	37 6/8	7 3/8 9 1/8	8 9	Weber County	UT	Frank L. Fackovec	1993	371
125 0/8	40 6/8	8 4/8 8 0/8	8 7	Lincoln County	WY	Al Haines	2002	371
125 0/8	42 0/8	7 7/8 9 5/8	8 11	Big Horn County	WY	Bradley Wichman	2006	371

798

SHIRAS' (WYOMING) MOOSE (VELVET ANTLERS)
Minimum Score 125

SCORE	INSIDE SPREAD	WIDTH OF R PALM L	NUMBER OF R POINTS L	AREA	STATE/ PROVINCE	HUNTER'S NAME	DATE	RANK
*169 2/8	45 6/8	11 1/8 11 4/8	12 12	Teton County	WY	Donald R. Hoard	2005	*
161 6/8	42 0/8	11 1/8 11 5/8	8 8	Teton County	WY	Brenda Bergquist	2006	*
150 5/8	46 7/8	9 5/8 10 0/8	8 10	Teton County	WY	Claude Rauch	2009	*
*150 0/8	46 0/8	6 7/8 7 3/8	6 6	Sublette County	WY	Michael Short	2010	*
142 0/8	41 2/8	9 2/8 8 5/8	8 8	Caribou County	ID	Doug Rueth	2009	*

WORLD RECORD MUSKOX (TIE)
Score: 127 2/8
Location: Coppermine, Nunavut
Date: 1996
Hunter: Bob Black

Muskox

by Bob Black

I arrived at Coppermine on March 25, 1996, and met Frank, my Inuit guide for the hunt. My equipment and I were placed on a snowmobile sled, and we set off for base camp. On the first day, 100 miles from Coppermine, we saw a herd of sixty five muskox, but decided it would be very hard to stalk a herd that large with little or no cover. On the second day we left early to go scouting and, after several hours, we spotted a group of fifteen, including two nice bulls. Prior to beginning the stalk, we watched the herd to see what direction they were grazing. Fortunately a small snowbank separated us from the herd, providing the only cover for miles.

As the herd moved slowly toward me, I prepared for the shot. The bull was broadside at 40 yards when I removed my hands from the mittens and drew my bow. My point of aim was just to the right of the bull's left shoulder. I made my shot, just like I had practiced except for one small detail. With the adrenaline pumping, my natural instincts took over and I failed to bend my wrist to compensate for the additional clothing. Consequently, the bow string hit my coat, causing the arrow to strike seven inches to the left, resulting in impact directly at his left shoulder joint. The broadhead shattered the shoulder joint of this huge animal; however, the arrow only penetrated through the joint. I immediately nocked another arrow and started to draw my bow. If you have ever been really, really cold and tried to draw a bow, you will understand my embarrassment when I could not get the bow drawn! This is one of those times when you have a very brief, intense talk with yourself and try again. I drew and again I hit exactly seven inches left of where I was aiming. This time the broadhead completely penetrated the animal. The whole herd, minus one huge bull, left the scene. The bull did not go over twenty feet and collapsed. We quickly skinned and quartered him and, by the time we had the meat loaded on the sled, a good portion of it was already frozen. It was 50 degrees below zero! I was surprised to see how massive his head was. The skull cap and horns alone weighed sixty pounds.

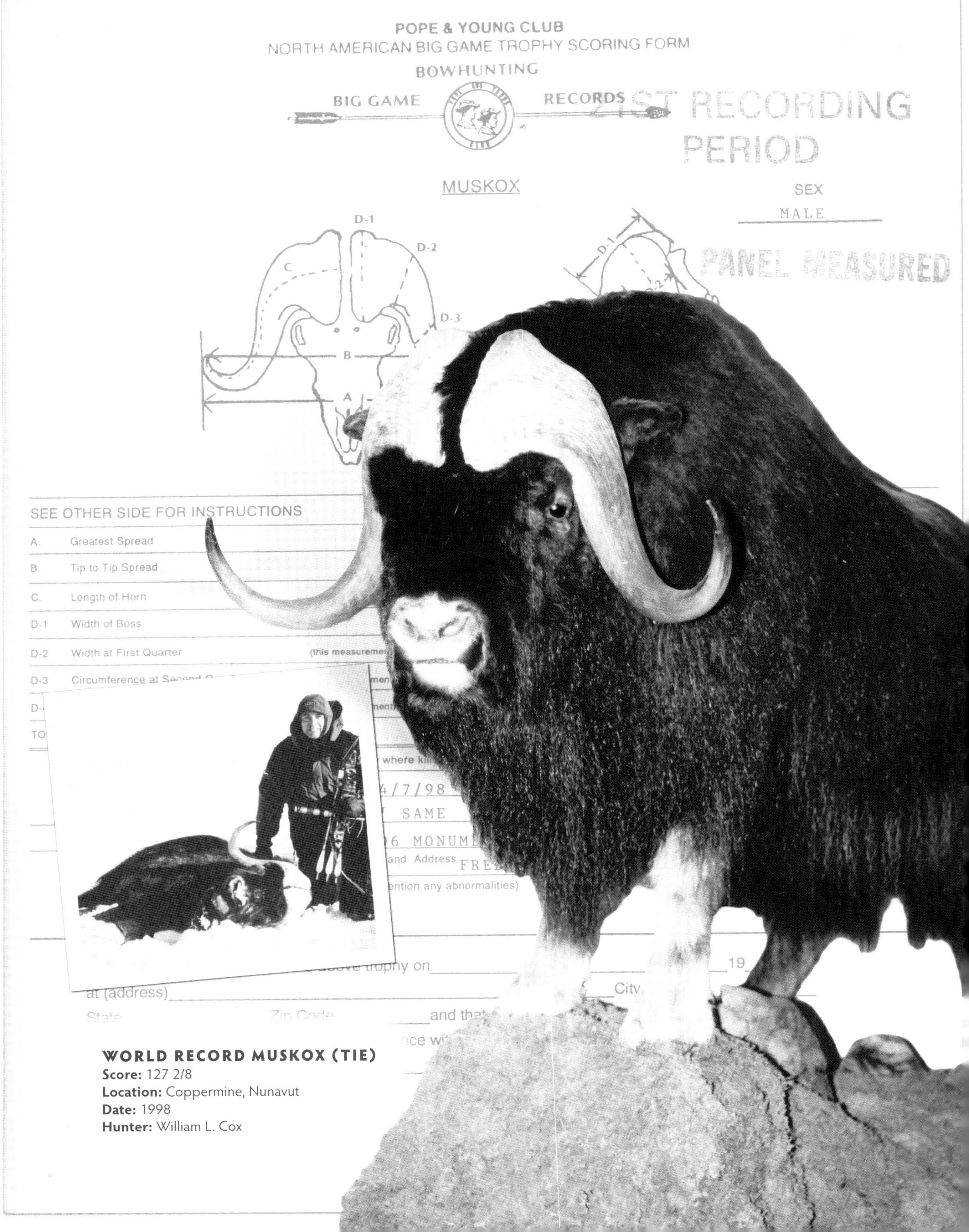

WORLD RECORD MUSKOX (TIE)
Score: 127 2/8
Location: Coppermine, Nunavut
Date: 1998
Hunter: William L. Cox

Muskox

by William L. Cox

I'm not sure why…and I'm only vaguely aware of when…my fantasy of stalking muskox on the frozen tundra congealed into an all-out obsession. But it was an obsession that smoldered for many years. I simply could not get away from work during those months. Then one of those neat twists in life occurred. My job was no more. It produced the freedom I needed and plans for an arctic journey were in the works.

I landed in Kugluktuk at noon and was sliding east on the Coronation Gulf by three that afternoon. Travel was "interesting." A snowmobile pulling a wooden sled with no shocks produced my first lesson---after almost biting your tongue in half, you learn to keep your mouth shut.

We camped twenty miles east and the morning would start the hunt. It was cold, clear and serene. You felt you could see forever. The only noise was your own. Framed in frigid clear sunshine, the first group of muskox was an unforgettable sight, running with a rocking motion that is their own. The trip had paid for itself in just the first few moments.

It was afternoon when we found the bull I was looking for. Strangely, he had separated himself from the herd. There was no ambush. There was no cover. And, there was no fear in that bull's demeanor. But for I, there was trepidation as I moved slowly forward. I did not relish the thought that, in an instant, my role could switch from predator to matador.

The thirty-seven yard shot was clean and the bull was down. As we later made our way towards camp, we saw caribou on a ridge framed by the setting sun. I felt a smile emerge as adventure, serenity, danger and excitement all fused together to become one of those memories that stays vivid with the passing years.

MUSKOX

Minimum Score 90 · *Ovibos moschatus* and certain related subspecies

SCORE	LENGTH OF R HORN L	WIDTH R OF BOSS L	GREATEST SPREAD	AREA	STATE/ PROVINCE	HUNTER'S NAME	DATE	RANK
127 2/8	30 1/8 30 1/8	10 1/8 10 2/8	31 0/8	Coppermine	NUN	Bob Black	1996	1
127 2/8	29 1/8 29 0/8	11 4/8 11 5/8	29 3/8	Coppermine	NUN	William L. Cox	1998	1
126 3/8	29 3/8 29 3/8	11 1/8 11 2/8	28 4/8	Coppermine	NUN	Fred P. Gonzales	1996	3
126 2/8	29 2/8 29 4/8	10 5/8 11 0/8	27 7/8	Coppermine	NUN	M. R. James	2000	4
123 0/8	29 1/8 28 7/8	10 2/8 10 3/8	28 2/8	Kent Peninsula	NUN	Raymond L. Howell, Sr.	2000	5
122 6/8	29 1/8 28 3/8	11 3/8 11 1/8	28 7/8	Kugluktuk	NUN	M. Blake Patton	2008	6
122 4/8	28 6/8 30 4/8	10 3/8 10 1/8	28 0/8	Coppermine	NUN	Michael J. Davis	2003	7
121 6/8	27 6/8 29 0/8	11 1/8 11 0/8	28 4/8	Coppermine	NUN	Jay Clayson	1995	8
121 0/8	29 1/8 28 2/8	10 3/8 10 2/8	29 4/8	Coppermine	NUN	Raymond Young	1996	9
120 4/8	28 0/8 28 4/8	10 0/8 9 6/8	27 4/8	Coppermine	NUN	Bob Ehle	2000	10
118 6/8	29 0/8 27 2/8	10 6/8 11 0/8	28 2/8	Coppermine	NUN	David A. Bower	1995	11
118 6/8	27 6/8 26 4/8	11 0/8 10 5/8	29 0/8	Coppermine	NUN	Alan Harris	2003	11
118 4/8	28 4/8 28 7/8	9 5/8 9 5/8	29 6/8	Coppermine River	NUN	Frank S. Noska IV	2003	13
117 6/8	27 4/8 27 0/8	10 2/8 10 2/8	28 3/8	Coppermine	NUN	Robert Edward Speegle, MD	1997	14
117 4/8	27 6/8 28 1/8	9 0/8 9 2/8	31 0/8	Kugluktuk	NUN	David Harris	2001	15
116 2/8	28 2/8 27 2/8	10 1/8 10 2/8	27 7/8	Paulatuk	NWT	Steve Reedy	2001	16
116 0/8	27 0/8 27 1/8	10 1/8 10 2/8	27 4/8	Kugluktuk	NUN	Randy Oleson	2007	17
115 4/8	27 2/8 29 7/8	10 4/8 10 2/8	27 6/8	Coppermine	NUN	David G. Anderson	1996	18
115 2/8	27 0/8 28 0/8	9 3/8 9 4/8	24 4/8	Horton River	NWT	John R. Wilson	1996	19
115 0/8	27 7/8 26 6/8	10 4/8 10 3/8	26 7/8	Kugluktuk	NUN	Patrick C. Allen	2005	20
114 6/8	27 0/8 27 0/8	10 3/8 10 3/8	25 7/8	Horton River	NWT	Phil Muller	2000	21
114 6/8	26 1/8 26 6/8	10 3/8 10 6/8	27 6/8	Paulatuk	NWT	William T. Bos	2004	21
114 2/8	29 1/8 28 0/8	9 0/8 9 3/8	28 7/8	Ellice River	NUN	Steve Munier	1988	23
114 0/8	27 4/8 27 6/8	9 0/8 8 7/8	30 6/8	Perry Island	NUN	J. T. Smith	1988	24
114 0/8	27 1/8 25 5/8	10 4/8 10 7/8	26 0/8	Coppermine	NUN	William Snelgrove	2007	24
113 2/8	25 2/8 25 6/8	9 5/8 9 5/8	28 1/8	Kent Peninsula	NUN	Archie Nesbitt	1989	26
113 0/8	27 1/8 28 3/8	9 5/8 9 4/8	27 7/8	Anderson River	NWT	Jack Leggo	1995	27
112 6/8	28 0/8 27 4/8	8 5/8 8 4/8	27 6/8	Garfield Creek	AK	Mark W Smith/Howard Appel	2002	28
*112 4/8	25 1/8 26 1/8	10 1/8 10 1/8	28 0/8	Asialca River	NUN	Dan Hurd	2007	29
112 2/8	27 7/8 27 3/8	9 1/8 9 1/8	27 4/8	Rendez-vous Lake	NWT	Mike E. Kuglitsch	1994	30
112 2/8	25 7/8 25 6/8	8 6/8 9 0/8	30 4/8	Kugluktuk	NUN	Robert Miller	2003	30
112 0/8	24 3/8 23 7/8	10 0/8 10 0/8	25 3/8	Banks Island	NWT	Bill Lancaster	1995	32
111 4/8	26 3/8 26 0/8	9 5/8 9 5/8	25 5/8	Banks Island	NWT	David V. Collis	1985	33
111 4/8	26 3/8 26 0/8	9 4/8 9 2/8	31 2/8	Umingmaktok	NUN	R. Eric Shields	2002	33
111 0/8	26 1/8 26 0/8	8 6/8 8 6/8	26 4/8	Rendez-vous Lake	NWT	Mike Morgan	1995	35
110 6/8	27 1/8 27 2/8	8 5/8 8 4/8	26 3/8	Nunivak Island	AK	Todd A. Sneesby	1988	37
110 6/8	26 6/8 26 0/8	8 7/8 8 7/8	28 5/8	McLoughlin River	NUN	Archie J. Nesbitt	1990	37
110 4/8	27 0/8 27 3/8	9 2/8 9 3/8	26 1/8	Banks Island	NWT	Robert L. Jacobsen	1987	39
110 4/8	25 2/8 25 2/8	8 6/8 8 5/8	28 4/8	Nome	AK	Mark Wayne Smith	2001	39
110 4/8	26 7/8 26 6/8	9 4/8 9 7/8	26 5/8	Norwegian Bay	NUN	Al Hankins	2008	39
110 2/8	26 1/8 26 7/8	10 0/8 9 5/8	28 2/8	Rendez-vous Lake	NWT	Craig Adams	1995	42
110 2/8	27 2/8 26 0/8	8 5/8 8 5/8	28 0/8	Nuluk River	AK	Al Grierson	1998	42
110 2/8	26 2/8 26 6/8	9 1/8 8 7/8	28 7/8	Cambridge Bay	NUN	Mark Berrie	2002	42
110 0/8	28 0/8 27 2/8	8 3/8 8 5/8	26 7/8	Nunivak Island	AK	Richard Moran	1988	45
110 0/8	26 2/8 26 2/8	8 6/8 9 1/8	26 2/8	Wilburn Island	NUN	Randy Liljenquist	2000	45
109 6/8	30 1/8 28 4/8	9 0/8 9 5/8	24 4/8	Banks Island	NWT	Colin McRae	2000	47
*109 6/8	27 1/8 28 7/8	9 2/8 9 1/8	31 6/8	Umingmaktok	NUN	Tom Nebbs	2008	47
109 6/8	26 3/8 26 2/8	8 2/8 8 1/8	27 7/8	Shishmaref	AK	Frank S. Noska IV	2010	47
109 4/8	26 2/8 26 5/8	9 5/8 9 5/8	26 7/8	Banks Island	NWT	Roger Anderson	1986	50
109 4/8	26 1/8 26 0/8	9 4/8 9 5/8	25 5/8	Banks Island	NWT	Larry Hoff	1986	50
109 4/8	25 6/8 25 6/8	9 7/8 9 6/8	25 5/8	Banks Island	NWT	Jim Ryan	1989	50
109 2/8	26 3/8 27 2/8	9 0/8 8 5/8	26 7/8	Nunivak Island	AK	Craig Scarbrough	1988	53
109 2/8	25 4/8 25 4/8	9 2/8 9 2/8	25 6/8	Victoria Island	NWT	Larry Barton	1991	53
109 2/8	26 0/8 26 5/8	9 5/8 9 1/8	28 4/8	Caribou Creek	AK	Mark Wayne Smith	2009	53
109 0/8	27 3/8 27 2/8	9 4/8 9 2/8	26 3/8	McNaughton Lake	NUN	Rick Stockburger	2004	56
109 0/8	26 5/8 28 3/8	9 0/8 8 5/8	27 6/8	Coyote Creek	AK	Allyn Ladd	2005	56
109 0/8	27 5/8 27 1/8	8 7/8 9 0/8	26 3/8	Nunivak Island	AK	William "Scott" Duncan	2009	56
108 4/8	26 3/8 28 2/8	9 5/8 9 6/8	27 0/8	Paulatuk	NWT	Ron Kolpin	1981	59
108 4/8	25 0/8 25 2/8	8 4/8 8 3/8	26 0/8	Kougarok River	AK	Mark Wayne Smith	2005	59
108 2/8	26 4/8 26 6/8	8 7/8 8 2/8	24 5/8	Bluenose Lake	NUN	George P. Mann	1990	61
108 2/8	26 6/8 28 5/8	8 6/8 8 4/8	27 6/8	Nelson Island	AK	Dexter Lemon	1994	61
108 2/8	26 2/8 27 0/8	9 0/8 9 0/8	26 7/8	Gjoa Haven	NUN	Chuck Adams	2002	61
108 0/8	27 5/8 28 5/8	8 4/8 8 4/8	25 4/8	Nelson Island	AK	Dexter Lemon	1986	64
108 0/8	26 0/8 25 3/8	9 3/8 9 4/8	26 1/8	Perry Island	NUN	Theodore Dzienis	1986	64
108 0/8	26 0/8 26 0/8	9 2/8 9 3/8	25 2/8	Sachs Harbour	NWT	K-Tal Johnson	1997	64
107 6/8	25 1/8 27 3/8	9 6/8 9 5/8	27 3/8	Banks Island	NWT	Rusty Neely	1987	67
107 6/8	25 1/8 25 5/8	8 7/8 9 0/8	25 3/8	Coppermine	NUN	Glenn Thurman	1993	67
107 6/8	25 1/8 25 3/8	8 3/8 8 2/8	26 0/8	Nuluk River	AK	Al Grierson	1997	67
107 6/8	25 6/8 25 3/8	8 3/8 8 3/8	26 3/8	Mekoryuk	AK	Ken Charron	2006	67
107 6/8	26 7/8 27 1/8	8 4/8 8 4/8	25 7/8	Kougarok River	AK	Mark Wayne Smith	2007	67
107 4/8	26 3/8 26 0/8	9 5/8 10 0/8	25 7/8	Banks Island	NWT	John McAteer	1986	72
107 4/8	25 0/8 25 1/8	8 1/8 8 1/8	26 3/8	Nunivak Island	AK	Timothy A. Gleason	1992	72
107 4/8	26 2/8 25 5/8	8 3/8 8 4/8	27 1/8	Nunivak Island	AK	Merle R. Frank	1997	72
107 4/8	25 5/8 26 1/8	9 0/8 9 0/8	25 6/8	Paulatuk	NWT	Kevin Dahm	2001	72
107 2/8	24 6/8 25 3/8	10 0/8 10 1/8	26 7/8	Victoria Island	NWT	Ray Keenan	1987	76
107 2/8	26 2/8 26 4/8	9 0/8 9 1/8	24 6/8	Banks Island	NWT	Karen K. Jacobsen	1987	76
107 2/8	26 2/8 26 6/8	9 0/8 9 1/8	27 0/8	Victoria Island	NWT	Johnnie R. Walters	1993	76
107 2/8	25 6/8 27 3/8	9 7/8 9 6/8	26 6/8	Bay Chimo	NUN	Dyrk Eddie	1998	76
107 2/8	27 4/8 25 0/8	10 1/8 10 1/8	28 6/8	Cambridge Bay	NUN	George E. Mann	2001	76
107 2/8	25 4/8 24 7/8	8 6/8 8 6/8	26 4/8	Nunivak Island	AK	Smoky LeFebvre	2008	76
*107 2/8	26 2/8 27 3/8	9 4/8 9 3/8	25 6/8	Tuktoyatuk	NUN	Ron Stoller	2010	76
107 0/8	28 2/8 26 3/8	9 3/8 9 4/8	26 7/8	Banks Island	NWT	Dennis Kamstra	1987	83
107 0/8	25 4/8 25 5/8	8 5/8 9 1/8	26 2/8	Nunivak Island	AK	Ken Radach	2004	83
107 0/8	26 1/8 26 2/8	8 4/8 8 5/8	27 6/8	Shishmaref	AK	Richard H. Dykema	2006	83
106 6/8	25 5/8 26 2/8	8 5/8 9 0/8	27 6/8	Banks Island	NWT	Billy Ellis	1982	86
106 6/8	25 5/8 25 6/8	8 6/8 8 2/8	27 6/8	Nelson Island	AK	Dexter Lemon	1985	86
106 6/8	28 6/8 27 3/8	8 5/8 8 4/8	28 1/8	Nunivak Island	AK	Ernest J. Emmi	1991	86
106 6/8	26 0/8 27 3/8	9 5/8 9 5/8	27 3/8	Banks Island	NWT	Jim Gall	1995	86
106 6/8	25 6/8 25 1/8	9 3/8 9 2/8	26 7/8	Beyaingayolehok Lake	NWT	Dave Justmann	1997	86
106 6/8	25 5/8 25 4/8	8 3/8 8 3/8	25 4/8	Nunivak Island	AK	Doug Baily	2005	86
106 6/8	25 1/8 26 1/8	8 4/8 8 2/8	24 6/8	Shishmaref	AK	Randy St. Ores	2009	86
106 4/8	24 3/8 24 5/8	8 3/8 8 4/8	27 3/8	Nunivak Island	AK	Joseph O. Fogleman	1976	92
106 4/8	26 7/8 27 3/8	8 0/8 8 0/8	27 4/8	Nunivak Island	AK	John D. 'Jack' Frost	1986	92
106 4/8	26 5/8 27 2/8	8 5/8 8 3/8	26 2/8	Nelson Island	AK	Dexter Lemon	1990	92
106 4/8	25 7/8 25 3/8	9 2/8 9 3/8	25 1/8	Paulatuk	NWT	Tom Taylor	1994	92

MUSKOX

Minimum Score 90 — Continued

SCORE	LENGTH OF R HORN L	WIDTH R OF BOSS L	GREATEST SPREAD	AREA	STATE/ PROVINCE	HUNTER'S NAME	DATE	RANK
106 4/8	27 3/8 26 2/8	9 0/8 8 6/8	29 0/8	Umingmaktok	NUN	Joe Coleman	2002	92
106 4/8	26 0/8 26 1/8	8 2/8 8 2/8	28 1/8	Nunivak Island	AK	Roy Whitford	2008	92
106 4/8	21 0/8 22 3/8	8 6/8 8 5/8	21 6/8	Kuzitrin River	AK	Bob Ameen	2009	92
106 2/8	25 4/8 25 5/8	8 2/8 8 2/8	27 5/8	Kaktovik	AK	Herman Griese	1984	99
106 2/8	26 4/8 25 7/8	7 6/8 8 1/8	27 6/8	Perry River	NUN	Jack Downing	1988	99
106 2/8	25 0/8 24 6/8	9 5/8 9 7/8	24 4/8	Holman	NWT	Stephen Kotz	2000	99
106 2/8	26 6/8 25 5/8	9 6/8 9 7/8	25 4/8	Holman	NWT	Frederick Johnston III	2000	99
106 2/8	25 3/8 24 5/8	7 6/8 7 5/8	26 0/8	Granet Lake	NWT	Richie Bland	2003	99
*106 2/8	28 4/8 27 0/8	8 3/8 8 6/8	28 1/8	Nunivak Island	AK	Jerry Soukup	2008	99
106 2/8	22 7/8 23 0/8	8 4/8 8 6/8	26 5/8	Mason River	NWT	Terry Ermel	2009	99
106 2/8	25 6/8 26 4/8	8 6/8 9 0/8	27 0/8	Camp Creek	AK	Mac Burrell	2009	99
106 0/8	26 0/8 26 2/8	9 0/8 8 6/8	29 1/8	Nunivak Island	AK	Raymond S. George	2001	107
106 0/8	25 1/8 25 3/8	8 2/8 8 3/8	26 5/8	Nunivak Island	AK	Todd Vorisek	2003	107
106 0/8	25 6/8 26 1/8	8 5/8 8 5/8	27 2/8	Nunivak Island	AK	David Benitz	2007	107
106 0/8	26 3/8 26 6/8	9 0/8 9 1/8	26 4/8	Cambridge Bay	NUN	Oscar Garcia	2007	107
105 6/8	25 1/8 25 1/8	9 2/8 9 2/8	26 0/8	Banks Island	NWT	Kirk Westervelt	1986	111
105 6/8	24 2/8 25 1/8	9 1/8 9 1/8	27 2/8	Coppermine	NUN	Leo F. Neuls	1991	111
105 6/8	26 7/8 26 6/8	9 1/8 8 7/8	25 4/8	Victoria Island	NWT	J. Dale Hale	2003	111
105 4/8	26 0/8 25 2/8	8 7/8 8 5/8	28 5/8	Perry Island	NUN	Ronald E. Sanders	1988	114
105 4/8	25 5/8 24 2/8	9 0/8 9 0/8	26 5/8	Sachs Harbour	NWT	David G. Sonnenburg	1994	114
105 2/8	25 6/8 26 2/8	8 6/8 9 2/8	27 4/8	Victoria Island	NWT	Len Cardinale	1987	116
105 2/8	25 0/8 25 4/8	9 4/8 9 0/8	29 3/8	Umingmaktok	NUN	Robert Hancock, Jr.	2005	116
105 2/8	25 1/8 24 6/8	9 5/8 9 3/8	28 3/8	Ellice River	NUN	Gary Netzer	2005	116
105 0/8	25 1/8 26 4/8	8 7/8 8 6/8	26 2/8	Kaktovik	AK	Bill Petrovish	1984	119
105 0/8	27 2/8 26 4/8	8 2/8 9 0/8	28 0/8	Nunivak Island	AK	Harvey A. Kolberg	1991	119
105 0/8	25 3/8 25 4/8	8 7/8 8 6/8	29 3/8	Melbourne Island	NUN	Richard E. Davis	2001	119
105 0/8	25 5/8 27 7/8	9 2/8 8 5/8	26 6/8	Nome	AK	Mark Wayne Smith	2003	119
105 0/8	23 5/8 25 6/8	9 6/8 9 5/8	26 2/8	Tuktoyaktuk	NWT	Jim Horneck	2008	119
104 6/8	24 5/8 25 0/8	9 4/8 9 2/8	25 0/8	Banks Island	NWT	Susan D. Sherer	1986	124
104 6/8	24 6/8 24 1/8	8 2/8 8 4/8	27 3/8	Combo Lake	NWT	Nathan L. Andersohn	1997	124
104 6/8	25 4/8 27 4/8	8 6/8 8 1/8	24 2/8	Caribou Creek	AK	Mark Wayne Smith	2010	124
104 4/8	27 2/8 25 4/8	9 2/8 9 0/8	27 2/8	Banks Island	NWT	Dr. Howard Schneider	1985	127
104 4/8	25 4/8 25 2/8	9 0/8 9 1/8	25 4/8	Banks Island	NWT	Ronald L. Sherer	1986	127
104 4/8	24 6/8 25 0/8	9 2/8 9 2/8	26 0/8	Banks Island	NWT	Richard L. Westervelt	1986	127
104 4/8	25 1/8 26 1/8	9 5/8 9 2/8	25 7/8	West Victoria Island	NWT	John Janelli	1987	127
104 4/8	24 1/8 24 2/8	9 3/8 9 3/8	26 4/8	Banks Island	NWT	James R. Gabrick	1997	127
104 4/8	27 0/8 25 0/8	9 2/8 9 1/8	27 0/8	Paulatuk	NWT	Aaron W. Barsamian	2003	127
104 4/8	25 6/8 25 0/8	7 7/8 8 0/8	29 0/8	Kougarok River	AK	Mark Wayne Smith	2004	127
104 4/8	25 2/8 26 4/8	8 6/8 8 7/8	29 0/8	Baldy Dome	AK	Mark Wayne Smith	2006	127
104 4/8	26 4/8 25 2/8	9 2/8 9 3/8	25 7/8	Seward Peninsula	AK	Steve Hohensee	2009	127
104 2/8	26 6/8 28 1/8	9 1/8 9 1/8	25 1/8	Cambridge Bay	NUN	Dave Dusthimer	2000	136
104 0/8	24 3/8 24 6/8	9 6/8 9 5/8	24 4/8	Banks Island	NWT	Larry Hoff	1986	137
104 0/8	24 6/8 25 4/8	8 4/8 8 3/8	26 6/8	Perry River	NUN	Bruce R. Schoeneweis	1990	137
104 0/8	24 4/8 24 4/8	8 4/8 9 0/8	25 0/8	Banks Island	NWT	Mark F. Vancas	1998	137
104 0/8	25 3/8 24 5/8	9 5/8 9 5/8	25 5/8	Holman	NWT	Ryk Visscher	1998	137
104 0/8	25 4/8 25 5/8	8 6/8 8 3/8	25 4/8	Tuktoyaktuk	NWT	Steve Tennant	1999	137
104 0/8	24 3/8 24 0/8	8 2/8 8 6/8	26 0/8	Sagavanirktok River	AK	Paul E. Werder	1999	137
103 6/8	26 0/8 26 4/8	8 1/8 8 1/8	27 3/8	Nunivak Island	AK	Carl E. Brent	1993	143
103 6/8	25 2/8 25 2/8	9 4/8 9 2/8	25 1/8	Banks Island	NWT	Phil Bertellotti	1999	143
103 6/8	24 7/8 25 2/8	8 7/8 8 6/8	26 0/8	Holman	NWT	Steven A. Rider	2004	143
103 6/8	26 4/8 25 7/8	8 3/8 8 2/8	25 1/8	Nunivak Island	AK	Travis Peterson	2005	143
103 4/8	25 4/8 26 0/8	8 6/8 8 7/8	27 0/8	Banks Island	NWT	Jeffrey A. Lute	1999	147
103 2/8	27 0/8 27 0/8	8 1/8 8 2/8	25 5/8	Paulatuk	NWT	Erv Plotz	1980	148
103 2/8	26 6/8 26 0/8	9 1/8 9 0/8	25 0/8	Holman	NWT	Scott Trelstad	1997	148
103 2/8	24 4/8 23 6/8	8 5/8 8 5/8	26 0/8	Paulatuk	NWT	Mike A. Janicki, Jr.	2003	148
103 2/8	26 2/8 25 7/8	9 1/8 9 3/8	23 3/8	Holman	NWT	Bryce Olson	2009	148
103 0/8	22 6/8 23 5/8	8 5/8 8 4/8	26 7/8	Nunivak Island	AK	P.J. Londo	1977	152
103 0/8	25 1/8 24 7/8	9 1/8 9 1/8	24 7/8	Holman	NWT	Ronald Regan	1992	152
103 0/8	25 6/8 25 3/8	9 0/8 9 1/8	25 2/8	Holman	NWT	James Matuszewski	2000	152
102 6/8	25 0/8 27 0/8	8 7/8 8 3/8	29 0/8	Nunivak Island	AK	Jim Voeller	1978	155
102 6/8	24 4/8 24 6/8	9 3/8 9 2/8	26 0/8	Banks Island	NWT	Frank C. Eifert	1987	155
102 6/8	25 4/8 23 7/8	9 3/8 9 1/8	27 5/8	Victoria Island	NWT	Jerry R. Westcott	1997	155
102 4/8	25 4/8 27 1/8	8 7/8 9 0/8	25 0/8	Holman Bay	NWT	Benny White	1992	158
102 4/8	25 2/8 26 1/8	9 1/8 8 6/8	25 5/8	Nunivak Island	AK	David A. Widby	1993	158
102 4/8	25 1/8 25 5/8	9 3/8 9 3/8	24 7/8	Holman	NWT	Warren Witherspoon	1997	158
102 4/8	25 6/8 25 0/8	9 1/8 9 1/8	23 7/8	Holman	NWT	Walter J. Palmer	1998	158
102 2/8	24 4/8 25 0/8	8 5/8 8 6/8	26 5/8	Nunivak Island	AK	Raymond C. Bahma, Jr.	1994	162
102 2/8	25 0/8 25 0/8	9 0/8 9 0/8	23 3/8	Holman	NWT	Richard A. Smith	2001	162
102 0/8	24 5/8 27 3/8	8 7/8 8 6/8	27 5/8	Nome	AK	Mark Wayne Smith	2000	164
101 6/8	24 3/8 24 5/8	7 7/8 7 7/8	27 3/8	Nunivak Island	AK	Tim Moerlein	1990	165
101 6/8	23 7/8 24 0/8	8 1/8 8 0/8	26 2/8	Nunivak Island	AK	Rick D. Snell	1994	165
101 6/8	25 4/8 24 6/8	8 2/8 8 1/8	23 7/8	Banks Island	NWT	James R. Gabrick	1997	165
101 6/8	23 5/8 24 0/8	8 1/8 8 0/8	26 0/8	Nunivak Island	AK	Tom Chadwick	1999	165
101 6/8	24 5/8 24 4/8	7 5/8 7 6/8	25 2/8	Coyote Creek	AK	Allyn Ladd	2007	165
101 4/8	24 6/8 25 2/8	8 6/8 8 6/8	27 6/8	Nunivak Island	AK	David A. Widby	1983	170
101 4/8	26 1/8 25 1/8	8 3/8 8 6/8	26 3/8	Nunivak Island	AK	Lon E. Lauber	1991	170
101 4/8	24 4/8 24 4/8	8 3/8 8 3/8	25 3/8	Nunivak Island	AK	Larry Daly	1994	170
101 4/8	25 3/8 26 2/8	9 2/8 9 6/8	24 5/8	Holman	NWT	Anthony "Del" DelMastro	1995	170
101 4/8	23 0/8 22 5/8	8 4/8 8 3/8	25 3/8	Banks Island	NWT	Dean Grommet	1995	170
101 4/8	23 7/8 26 0/8	8 7/8 9 5/8	29 0/8	Ellice River	NUN	Frank L. Fackovec	2001	170
101 4/8	25 6/8 24 6/8	8 0/8 8 1/8	24 5/8	Moon Mtns.	AK	Allyn Ladd	2004	170
101 2/8	24 4/8 25 2/8	9 4/8 9 3/8	26 0/8	Banks Island	NWT	James C. Hicks	1995	177
101 2/8	25 4/8 24 4/8	9 0/8 8 5/8	24 6/8	Ellice River	NUN	Ralph F. Merkley	1995	177
101 2/8	24 1/8 24 5/8	9 1/8 9 0/8	22 7/8	Holman	NWT	Anthony "Del" DelMastro	1995	177
101 0/8	25 1/8 25 0/8	8 0/8 8 2/8	26 2/8	Nunivak Island	AK	Edward L. Russell	1984	180
101 0/8	24 7/8 26 4/8	8 0/8 8 2/8	26 0/8	Nunivak Island	AK	Michael J. Lettis	1989	180
101 0/8	23 6/8 22 7/8	8 7/8 9 2/8	33 1/8	Banks Island	NWT	Jim Gall	1997	180
*101 0/8	25 1/8 24 3/8	8 2/8 8 2/8	24 4/8	Holman	NWT	Larry Welchlen	2008	180
100 6/8	24 1/8 25 1/8	7 7/8 7 7/8	24 1/8	Nunivak Island	AK	Dr. Von A. Mitton	1978	184
100 6/8	24 1/8 25 0/8	8 6/8 8 6/8	26 3/8	Victoria Island	NWT	David Richey	1988	184
100 6/8	26 4/8 25 2/8	8 3/8 8 3/8	25 7/8	Nunivak Island	AK	Maxallen D. Jackson	1991	184
100 6/8	26 2/8 25 0/8	8 5/8 8 3/8	25 0/8	Cambridge Bay	NUN	James B. Walter, Jr.	2001	184
100 4/8	25 2/8 26 2/8	7 7/8 7 6/8	28 1/8	Nunivak Island	AK	Bruce J. Werba	1977	188
100 4/8	24 5/8 26 4/8	10 2/8 10 1/8	27 2/8	Banks Island	NWT	Dr. Howard Schneider	1985	188
100 4/8	24 1/8 24 7/8	9 2/8 8 7/8	26 0/8	Nunivak Island	AK	Rick Schikora	1993	188

MUSKOX

Minimum Score 90 — Continued

SCORE	LENGTH OF R HORN L	WIDTH R OF BOSS L	GREATEST SPREAD	AREA	STATE/ PROVINCE	HUNTER'S NAME	DATE	RANK
100 4/8	24 3/8 24 3/8	8 5/8 8 3/8	27 4/8	Nunivak Island	AK	Ron C. Harvey	1994	188
100 4/8	25 4/8 26 2/8	8 2/8 8 3/8	27 1/8	Nunivak Island	AK	Kurt M. Burroughs	1995	188
100 4/8	25 2/8 25 6/8	9 4/8 9 2/8	24 1/8	Holman	NWT	John Watson, Sr.	2000	188
100 4/8	24 0/8 24 2/8	8 5/8 8 2/8	27 7/8	Nunivak Island	AK	Jeffrey A. Carlson	2003	188
100 4/8	24 5/8 25 0/8	9 4/8 9 0/8	26 0/8	Sachs Harbour	NWT	Timothy Otis	2004	188
100 4/8	24 4/8 24 4/8	8 3/8 9 2/8	23 7/8	Resolute Bay	NUN	Camp Newton	2005	188
100 4/8	25 2/8 25 2/8	7 5/8 7 6/8	23 1/8	Creswell Bay	NUN	Stacee Frost	2005	188
100 2/8	24 5/8 25 5/8	8 3/8 7 7/8	24 0/8	Nunivak Island	AK	Curt Lynn	1984	198
100 2/8	25 3/8 24 4/8	8 2/8 8 3/8	27 3/8	Nunivak Island	AK	Rex Wright	1992	198
100 2/8	25 2/8 25 0/8	8 4/8 8 4/8	25 0/8	Victoria Island	NWT	Mark Buehrer	1997	198
100 2/8	25 3/8 25 7/8	8 3/8 8 0/8	23 0/8	Combo Lake	NWT	Thomas J. Hoffman	1997	198
100 2/8	25 1/8 25 2/8	8 6/8 8 4/8	26 2/8	Cambridge Bay	NUN	Ronald G. Ralston	2002	198
100 2/8	24 7/8 24 3/8	9 3/8 9 6/8	24 1/8	Banks Island	NWT	Marc N. Shaft	2004	198
100 2/8	24 2/8 25 6/8	9 2/8 9 0/8	25 3/8	Banks Island	NWT	Matt R. Andersen	2005	198
100 2/8	22 6/8 24 2/8	8 6/8 8 4/8	25 0/8	Cape Peel	NUN	Robert Snell	2005	198
100 0/8	25 0/8 26 4/8	8 4/8 8 3/8	25 1/8	Nunivak Island	AK	Max C. Lyon, Jr.	1991	206
100 0/8	24 4/8 26 3/8	8 7/8 8 7/8	27 1/8	Paulatuk	NWT	Roy Goodwin	1994	206
100 0/8	24 5/8 25 6/8	7 6/8 7 7/8	27 4/8	Nunivak Island	AK	Ted Nugent	1996	206
100 0/8	25 0/8 24 4/8	9 4/8 9 0/8	24 4/8	Cambridge Bay	NUN	Steve Neuberger	2000	206
100 0/8	26 2/8 24 3/8	8 1/8 8 2/8	24 4/8	Nome	AK	Allyn Ladd	2003	206
100 0/8	22 2/8 25 0/8	8 7/8 9 1/8	28 2/8	Umingmaktok	NUN	Bryan W. Miller	2004	206
100 0/8	23 3/8 24 2/8	9 1/8 9 2/8	29 1/8	Victoria Island	NWT	Joel A. Johnson	2004	206
100 0/8	25 2/8 26 0/8	8 7/8 9 0/8	23 2/8	Merkley Lake	NUN	David Corley	2009	206
99 6/8	24 0/8 23 6/8	8 5/8 8 2/8	26 0/8	Nunivak Island	AK	David A. Widby	1996	214
99 6/8	23 4/8 24 7/8	8 1/8 8 2/8	24 7/8	Sagavanirktok River	AK	Raymond A. White	2000	214
99 6/8	25 6/8 25 2/8	7 5/8 7 4/8	25 2/8	Ellesmere Island	NUN	K-Tal Johnson	2001	214
99 6/8	25 6/8 24 4/8	9 0/8 8 7/8	25 0/8	Cambridge Bay	NUN	Steff Stefanovich	2005	214
99 6/8	24 6/8 27 0/8	8 7/8 8 5/8	25 4/8	Holman	NWT	Leonard Rinke	2005	214
*99 6/8	24 7/8 24 3/8	9 1/8 9 0/8	25 6/8	Cambridge Bay	NUN	Robert L. Migliore	2007	214
99 4/8	24 6/8 22 7/8	9 3/8 9 0/8	25 1/8	Cambridge Bay	NUN	Ricardo Longoria	1998	220
99 4/8	24 2/8 26 0/8	9 1/8 9 2/8	28 7/8	Banks Island	NWT	Jim Dunigan	1999	220
99 4/8	26 0/8 26 6/8	8 2/8 7 7/8	24 4/8	Cambridge Bay	NUN	Ronald G. Ralston	2002	220
99 4/8	24 7/8 25 0/8	8 6/8 8 7/8	27 5/8	Sachs Harbour	NWT	Dale Selby	2002	220
99 4/8	23 7/8 24 3/8	9 4/8 9 2/8	24 0/8	Paulatuk	NWT	Martin E. Cain	2006	220
*99 4/8	25 2/8 25 6/8	8 4/8 8 1/8	25 0/8	Nunivak Island	AK	John Burick	2009	220
99 2/8	25 4/8 25 6/8	8 5/8 8 5/8	25 3/8	Banks Island	NWT	Jim Gall	1995	226
99 2/8	25 2/8 25 2/8	8 6/8 8 4/8	22 1/8	Holman	NWT	Tom Nelson	1997	226
99 2/8	24 7/8 23 3/8	8 3/8 8 4/8	24 7/8	Paulatuk	NWT	Tom Foss	1997	226
99 2/8	25 2/8 23 6/8	9 0/8 9 1/8	23 5/8	Holman	NWT	James Matuszewski	2000	226
99 0/8	24 4/8 26 1/8	9 0/8 9 0/8	26 4/8	Banks Island	NWT	Gary Martin	1996	230
99 0/8	23 4/8 23 3/8	8 4/8 8 4/8	22 4/8	Creswell Bay	NUN	Mike Wilson	2005	230
98 6/8	23 6/8 24 6/8	9 2/8 9 0/8	25 7/8	Holman	NWT	Wayne E. Meyers	1994	232
98 6/8	25 3/8 26 4/8	8 1/8 7 5/8	25 7/8	Nunivak Island	AK	Gary R. Crawford	1998	232
98 6/8	24 2/8 25 3/8	8 6/8 8 4/8	24 1/8	Holman	NWT	Larry Streiff	1998	232
98 6/8	23 7/8 26 0/8	8 4/8 7 5/8	26 7/8	Cape Mendenhall	AK	Stan Parkerson	1999	232
98 6/8	23 2/8 24 0/8	8 6/8 8 5/8	25 4/8	Banks Island	NWT	Michael L. Ritter	2000	232
98 6/8	24 0/8 24 1/8	7 4/8 7 3/8	25 4/8	Nunivak Island	AK	Richard W. Stewart	2006	232
*98 6/8	24 3/8 24 3/8	8 6/8 9 0/8	24 4/8	Somerset Island	NUN	Mark "Gutz" Gutsmiedl	2006	232
*98 6/8	23 1/8 24 4/8	9 3/8 9 0/8	23 5/8	Victoria Island	NWT	C. Scott Forst	2006	232
98 4/8	23 4/8 24 1/8	9 0/8 8 5/8	25 7/8	Sachs Harbour	NWT	Dwight Pfeiffer	1989	240
98 4/8	23 5/8 24 1/8	8 0/8 8 0/8	25 0/8	Holman	NWT	Duane Hicks	1997	240
98 4/8	23 6/8 23 4/8	9 0/8 8 7/8	23 7/8	Banks Island	NWT	Michael L. Ritter, Jr.	2000	240
98 4/8	24 1/8 25 2/8	9 5/8 9 6/8	24 6/8	Holman	NWT	Ron Hagen	2009	240
98 2/8	23 5/8 24 1/8	7 3/8 7 5/8	28 3/8	Nunivak Island	AK	Tony Russ	1990	244
98 2/8	25 1/8 24 4/8	8 6/8 8 6/8	26 3/8	Victoria Island	NWT	Ronald Sallman	1993	244
98 2/8	22 7/8 22 3/8	8 0/8 8 0/8	26 2/8	Nunivak Island	AK	Bob Ameen	2002	244
98 2/8	24 5/8 24 1/8	8 7/8 8 4/8	26 0/8	Sachs Harbour	NWT	John F. Cedarberg IV	2005	244
*98 2/8	24 0/8 22 7/8	8 7/8 9 4/8	26 1/8	Somerset Island	NUN	Mark Beeler	2008	244
98 0/8	23 7/8 23 4/8	8 5/8 8 7/8	24 4/8	Banks Island	NWT	Scott Zoellick	1995	249
98 0/8	23 4/8 22 5/8	9 1/8 9 2/8	22 7/8	Sachs Harbour	NWT	Val Koeberlein	2003	249
98 0/8	23 2/8 23 3/8	9 3/8 9 1/8	23 4/8	Cambridge Bay	NUN	Dr. David Samuel	2004	249
*98 0/8	24 1/8 25 2/8	7 5/8 7 7/8	27 1/8	Tuktoyatuk	NUN	Neil Mefford	2010	249
97 6/8	22 4/8 24 6/8	8 6/8 8 5/8	29 0/8	Nunivak Island	AK	Charles A. Eisenhower	1999	253
97 6/8	26 7/8 25 3/8	9 5/8 9 4/8	24 0/8	Caperon Lake	NWT	Peter L. Bucklin	1999	253
97 6/8	23 0/8 24 0/8	9 1/8 8 7/8	25 4/8	Resolute Bay	NUN	Robert M. Daggett	2003	253
97 6/8	24 2/8 25 5/8	8 7/8 8 7/8	25 7/8	Cape Peel	NUN	Lee Jernigan	2003	253
97 6/8	24 1/8 24 3/8	9 1/8 8 7/8	24 1/8	Victoria Island	NUN	Ross Stokes	2005	253
97 6/8	23 4/8 24 2/8	8 1/8 7 7/8	26 4/8	Nunivak Island	AK	Robert Floyd, Jr.	2007	253
97 4/8	24 7/8 24 2/8	7 0/8 7 1/8	25 0/8	Paulatuk	NWT	Richard Gerhart	2000	259
97 2/8	24 3/8 25 2/8	8 5/8 8 5/8	24 7/8	Sachs Harbour	NWT	George Engelhardt	1995	260
97 2/8	23 0/8 24 2/8	9 6/8 9 4/8	26 6/8	Holman	NWT	Joseph E. Watson	2000	260
*97 2/8	24 4/8 24 7/8	8 2/8 8 2/8	25 1/8	Banks Island	NWT	Joe Arnt	2000	260
97 2/8	24 1/8 23 2/8	9 1/8 9 4/8	26 2/8	Banks Island	NWT	Ray N. Andersen	2005	260
97 2/8	24 2/8 26 3/8	9 5/8 9 2/8	27 0/8	Surrey Lake	NUN	Ron Klassen	2008	260
97 0/8	24 4/8 24 1/8	8 3/8 8 4/8	28 0/8	Nunivak Island	AK	Michael J. Schneider	1983	265
97 0/8	23 7/8 24 0/8	9 3/8 9 2/8	25 3/8	Banks Island	NWT	Michael Teff	1997	265
97 0/8	23 5/8 24 0/8	8 4/8 8 2/8	24 1/8	Cambridge Bay	NUN	Archie J. Nesbitt	2002	265
97 0/8	24 1/8 23 7/8	8 0/8 8 3/8	25 2/8	Caperon Lake	NWT	Angus M. Brown	2004	265
*97 0/8	24 2/8 24 6/8	8 4/8 8 6/8	24 4/8	Victoria Island	NUN	Donald H. Corey	2004	265
97 0/8	24 3/8 24 5/8	8 2/8 8 0/8	24 2/8	Cambridge Bay	NUN	Rick Wilson	2007	265
97 0/8	24 3/8 24 4/8	7 7/8 8 0/8	24 6/8	Holman	NWT	Rocco Verelli	2008	265
96 6/8	22 5/8 24 0/8	8 2/8 8 0/8	26 2/8	Nunivak Island	AK	Bob Hammond	1988	272
96 6/8	24 2/8 25 3/8	8 4/8 8 3/8	28 3/8	Nunivak Island	AK	Matt Jones	1992	272
96 6/8	24 4/8 26 2/8	8 2/8 8 2/8	24 3/8	Nunivak Island	AK	Paul Ritz	1997	272
96 6/8	25 2/8 25 6/8	7 4/8 8 0/8	22 2/8	Victoria Island	NWT	Robert G. Barden	2003	272
96 6/8	22 2/8 22 2/8	8 2/8 8 6/8	23 2/8	Creswell Bay	NUN	Greg Bokash	2005	272
96 4/8	25 1/8 24 1/8	8 0/8 8 2/8	26 0/8	Victoria Island	NWT	Charles G. Schibler	1992	277
96 4/8	23 1/8 24 3/8	9 0/8 8 6/8	23 0/8	Banks Island	NWT	Jim Dunigan	1999	277
96 4/8	23 0/8 23 5/8	9 5/8 9 5/8	26 2/8	Victoria Island	NWT	Paul Korn	2001	277
96 4/8	23 7/8 23 4/8	8 4/8 8 1/8	24 2/8	Victoria Island	NWT	J. Dale Hale	2003	277
96 4/8	25 4/8 23 4/8	8 0/8 8 3/8	24 4/8	Holman	NWT	Bill Shuster	2003	277
96 4/8	22 5/8 23 0/8	8 2/8 8 2/8	26 5/8	Cambridge Bay	NUN	Dennis McCoy	2007	277
96 2/8	23 1/8 25 1/8	9 0/8 9 0/8	25 4/8	Victoria Island	NWT	Martin Glover	1997	283
96 2/8	23 0/8 24 4/8	9 2/8 9 2/8	28 0/8	Cambridge Bay	NUN	Dennis M. Hayden	2001	283
96 2/8	22 7/8 22 7/8	9 0/8 9 3/8	24 5/8	Sachs Harbour	NWT	Dale Selby	2002	283

806

MUSKOX

Minimum Score 90
Continued

SCORE	LENGTH OF R HORN L	WIDTH R OF BOSS L	GREATEST SPREAD	AREA	STATE/ PROVINCE	HUNTER'S NAME	DATE	RANK
96 2/8	22 5/8 23 5/8	9 2/8 9 2/8	26 2/8	Banks Island	NWT	David N. Andersen	2005	283
96 2/8	23 4/8 22 3/8	8 1/8 8 7/8	23 5/8	Somerset Island	NUN	Tim Walters	2008	283
96 0/8	23 2/8 23 4/8	8 6/8 9 2/8	23 1/8	Banks Island	NWT	Dennis Dunn	2001	288
96 0/8	23 1/8 23 1/8	7 1/8 7 1/8	24 0/8	Granet Lake	NWT	Richie Bland	2003	288
95 6/8	25 0/8 23 2/8	8 7/8 9 1/8	25 0/8	Sachs Harbour	NWT	K-Tal Johnson	1997	290
95 6/8	24 1/8 26 1/8	9 3/8 9 2/8	25 1/8	Holman Mtn.	NWT	Beard Hobbs	2005	290
95 6/8	24 2/8 23 2/8	8 4/8 9 1/8	22 6/8	Holman	NWT	Rocco Verelli	2008	290
95 6/8	23 4/8 23 4/8	6 6/8 6 5/8	26 4/8	Bella Creek	AK	Mark Wayne Smith	2008	290
95 4/8	21 0/8 20 6/8	8 0/8 8 2/8	26 2/8	Nunivak Island	AK	Dick Gulman	1978	294
95 4/8	26 6/8 24 7/8	8 0/8 8 2/8	27 6/8	Nunivak Island	AK	Ken Vorisek	1995	294
95 4/8	23 7/8 23 5/8	8 7/8 8 6/8	24 2/8	Sachs Harbour	NWT	Alan E. Schroeder	1998	294
95 4/8	22 6/8 24 2/8	9 1/8 9 1/8	25 1/8	Cambridge Bay	NUN	Robert J. Amaral	2002	294
95 4/8	24 1/8 24 7/8	8 2/8 8 1/8	24 7/8	Cambridge Bay	NUN	Marlin Hoch	2003	294
95 4/8	24 1/8 24 0/8	8 1/8 7 6/8	25 5/8	Cambridge Bay	NUN	Mark Calkins	2008	294
95 2/8	25 4/8 24 2/8	8 6/8 9 1/8	26 7/8	Banks Island	NWT	Jonathan S. Warke	2002	300
95 2/8	24 6/8 24 1/8	8 5/8 9 2/8	24 1/8	Banks Island	NWT	Roger Wintle	2003	300
95 2/8	23 1/8 24 1/8	8 5/8 8 5/8	23 5/8	Cambridge Bay	NUN	Steve Crooks	2006	300
95 2/8	23 2/8 24 0/8	8 5/8 8 6/8	22 5/8	Cambridge Bay	NUN	Garth Olds	2006	300
95 2/8	25 2/8 24 0/8	8 2/8 8 7/8	24 1/8	Victoria Island	NUN	Michael Dziekan	2006	300
95 2/8	23 2/8 24 1/8	8 4/8 8 3/8	25 0/8	Nunivak Island	AK	Joe Romano	2007	300
94 6/8	25 0/8 23 2/8	8 3/8 8 3/8	25 6/8	Nunivak Island	AK	Jeff Eichholz	1997	306
94 6/8	22 5/8 22 4/8	8 3/8 8 4/8	26 4/8	Banks Island	NWT	Marc N. Shaft	2004	306
*94 6/8	22 7/8 23 6/8	9 0/8 9 0/8	24 2/8	Sachs Harbour	NWT	Dan Kingma	2004	306
94 6/8	23 1/8 23 4/8	8 2/8 8 5/8	24 2/8	Victoria Island	NUN	Dale Karch	2005	306
94 6/8	23 7/8 23 7/8	8 6/8 8 4/8	24 0/8	Cambridge Bay	NUN	Pat Garrett	2009	306
94 4/8	24 5/8 23 6/8	6 6/8 6 6/8	26 7/8	Nunivak Island	AK	C. Vernon Humble	1976	311
94 4/8	21 0/8 22 7/8	9 2/8 9 2/8	25 1/8	Gjoa Haven	NUN	Gary Bogner	1991	311
94 4/8	23 2/8 25 0/8	9 3/8 9 1/8	25 7/8	Holman	NWT	Stephen Haufsk	2000	311
94 4/8	23 2/8 24 7/8	8 4/8 8 4/8	26 4/8	Victoria Island	NWT	Thomas M. Basch	2003	311
94 4/8	22 5/8 23 0/8	8 6/8 8 7/8	21 2/8	Cambridge Bay	NUN	Edwin DeYoung	2007	311
94 2/8	23 2/8 24 3/8	8 6/8 8 3/8	24 3/8	Victoria Island	NWT	Rick Kroll	1993	316
94 2/8	24 4/8 23 6/8	8 1/8 7 6/8	24 2/8	Banks Island	NWT	Jay Deones	2001	316
94 0/8	23 4/8 23 2/8	6 0/8 6 0/8	25 4/8	Paulatuk	NWT	Doug Burgard	1995	318
94 0/8	22 0/8 22 7/8	8 6/8 8 7/8	23 2/8	Caperon Lake	NWT	L. Scot Jenkins	1996	318
94 0/8	24 0/8 23 4/8	8 5/8 8 2/8	27 7/8	Victoria Island	NWT	Mark Connor	1997	318
*94 0/8	23 3/8 24 7/8	8 5/8 8 2/8	24 1/8	Cambridge Bay	NUN	Randy Carey	2006	318
94 0/8	23 6/8 24 0/8	8 5/8 8 4/8	24 2/8	Wellington Bay	NUN	Carol Kindred	2008	318
93 6/8	23 0/8 22 5/8	7 6/8 8 4/8	24 6/8	Grise Fiord	NUN	Joseph Testerman	1993	323
93 4/8	24 5/8 24 2/8	7 5/8 7 2/8	20 1/8	Paulatuk	NWT	Tom Foss	1997	324
93 4/8	22 6/8 20 5/8	9 4/8 9 4/8	24 6/8	Banks Island	NWT	Dennis Dunn	2001	324
93 4/8	21 3/8 21 4/8	8 3/8 8 3/8	26 4/8	Cambridge Bay	NUN	Tom Miranda	2005	324
93 4/8	23 2/8 23 2/8	8 4/8 8 2/8	26 6/8	Holman	NWT	Rick Duggan	2006	324
93 2/8	24 4/8 24 0/8	8 2/8 8 5/8	24 7/8	Holman	NWT	Todd J. Rider	2000	328
93 2/8	22 5/8 24 3/8	8 3/8 8 4/8	26 1/8	Victoria Island	NWT	Bernie Weisgerber	2003	328
93 2/8	24 2/8 23 0/8	9 4/8 9 5/8	24 0/8	Caperon Lake	NWT	Angus M. Brown	2004	328
92 6/8	24 6/8 22 7/8	7 4/8 7 6/8	24 4/8	Holman	NWT	Jim Wondzell	2006	331
92 4/8	23 1/8 23 4/8	8 4/8 8 5/8	23 0/8	Cambridge Bay	NUN	Dale Slama	1993	332
92 4/8	23 6/8 23 5/8	7 4/8 7 3/8	24 4/8	Holman	NWT	Todd J. Rider	2000	332
92 2/8	23 4/8 25 2/8	8 6/8 8 5/8	23 2/8	Wellington Bay	NUN	Lou Kindred	2008	334
92 0/8	21 6/8 22 7/8	8 3/8 8 2/8	24 1/8	Sachs Harbour	NWT	John F. Cedarberg IV	2005	335
91 4/8	23 6/8 24 5/8	8 3/8 8 3/8	21 7/8	Cambridge Bay	NUN	Joseph D. Maddock	1998	336
91 4/8	22 4/8 23 7/8	9 0/8 9 0/8	24 6/8	Holman	NWT	Ralph Hernandez	2005	336
91 0/8	23 2/8 21 0/8	8 7/8 8 5/8	23 1/8	Victoria Island	NWT	Joel A. Johnson	2004	338
90 6/8	21 6/8 20 5/8	8 4/8 8 5/8	22 3/8	Holman	NWT	Craig Mitton	2006	339
90 4/8	22 2/8 24 6/8	9 0/8 8 7/8	25 7/8	Victoria Island	NUN	Robert Catelli	2004	340
90 4/8	21 4/8 23 1/8	8 6/8 8 5/8	23 1/8	Ulukhaktok	NWT	Gene Fleming	2010	340
90 2/8	24 6/8 24 1/8	7 2/8 7 1/8	25 4/8	Resolute Bay	NUN	Rodney M. Brush	2005	342
90 0/8	23 2/8 22 2/8	9 1/8 9 0/8	24 1/8	Holman	NWT	Johnny R. Watson	2000	343

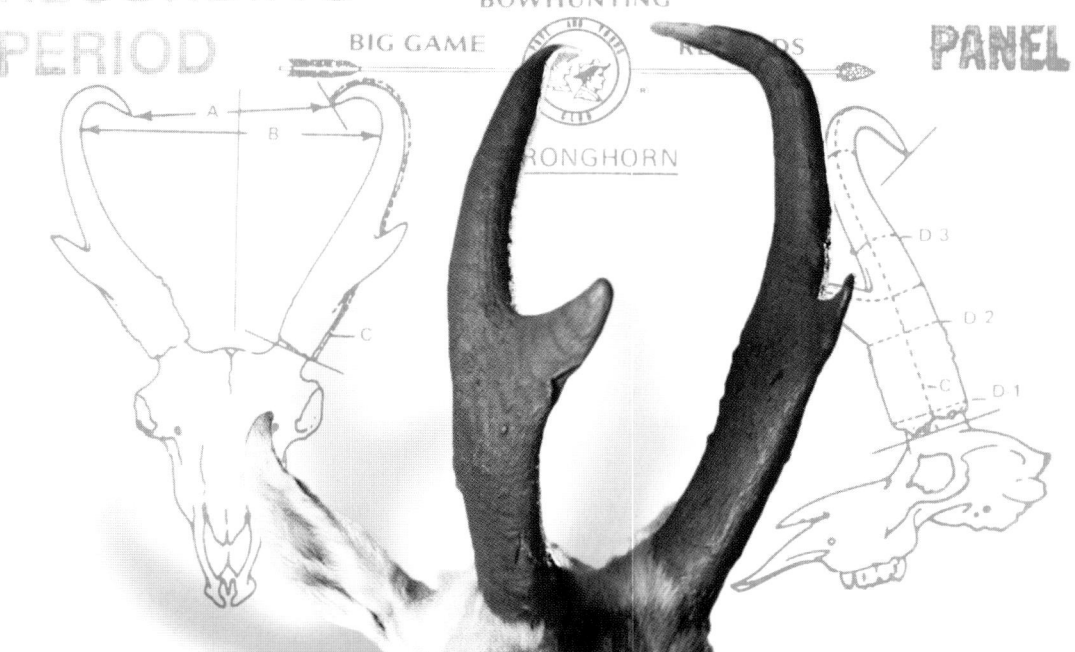
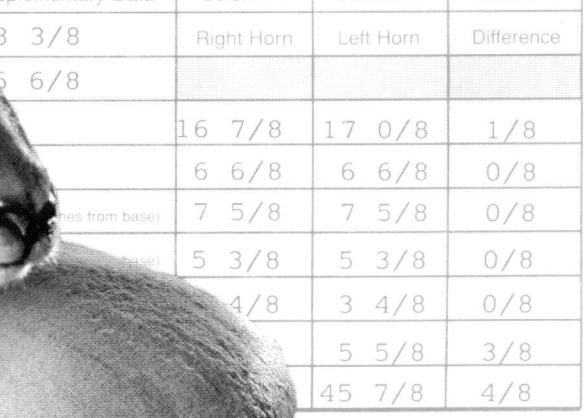

WORLD RECORD PRONGHORN
Score: 91 4/8
Location: Yavapai County, Arizona
Date: 1995
Hunter: Marvin N. Zieser

Pronghorn

by Marvin N. Zieser

After taking an 80 4/8 buck in 1993, I was excited to locate two huge bucks in the same area in 1995. "Slant" had the most massive horns I had ever seen, but they were oddly tilted with little curve making him difficult to judge. The tallest buck I had ever seen I named "Criss-Cross," for his cross-tipped horns would surely exceed 19 inches. I was positive that he would be the new world record with a bow….. if I could take him.

I located water being used by both bucks, and decided to leave my formerly successful methods of decoying, pit blinds and stalking and use a blind so I could videotape the hunt. I salivated over the photos and videos I took before the season, feeling I had a very legitimate chance at a world record.

I caught glimpses of the bucks the first two days of the hunt, but never within range. Day three was sizzling inside the stuffy blind. An exceptionally wide buck, "Flair", finally broke up the scorching afternoon by feeding nearby. Suddenly realizing that Slant and his harem were approaching, I knew I couldn't pass up a buck of this caliber, even though I had my heart set on Criss-Cross.

I had little time to make a choice as he passed my shooting window, forcing me to twist and shoot through the four-inch opening above the camera. Cattle and a fawn made my shot timing more difficult. He slowed, offering me a momentarily clear shot as my bow sent the arrow entirely through the buck's chest at 30 yards.

Camp measurements proved the buck taller and even more massive than I had thought. Due to his horns' odd shape and unbelievable mass, he had been difficult to judge. I then realized I might have taken a new world record after all! While I knew he was exceptional, I had been so taken by Criss-Cross that I had not recognized the importance exceptional mass would be to his score. Ironically, my Criss-Cross obsession likely helped me stay calm for the shot on Slant! The thought that I had even considered letting him pass, now made me slightly faint.

PRONGHORN

Minimum Score 67 — *Autilocapra americana americana* and related subspecies

SCORE	LENGTH OF R HORN L	CIRCUMFERENCE R OF BASE L	INSIDE SPREAD	AREA	STATE/ PROVINCE	HUNTER'S NAME	DATE	RANK
91 4/8	16 7/8 17 0/8	6 6/8 6 6/8	6 6/8	Yavapai County	AZ	Marvin N. Zieser	1995	1
90 6/8	17 0/8 17 0/8	7 0/8 6 7/8	9 3/8	Coconino County	AZ	Les Shelton	1998	2
90 2/8	20 6/8 20 6/8	6 4/8 6 0/8	11 2/8	Yavapai County	AZ	Duane "Corky" Richardson	1999	3
90 0/8	16 3/8 17 3/8	7 1/8 7 2/8	11 4/8	Lake County	OR	Roger W. Clarno	1993	4
89 0/8	17 0/8 16 7/8	6 3/8 6 3/8	9 1/8	Yavapai County	AZ	Kevin Robinson	1996	5
88 6/8	15 6/8 15 7/8	7 2/8 7 0/8	14 2/8	Grant County	ND	Archie Malm	1958	6
88 4/8	15 2/8 15 1/8	7 7/8 7 6/8	12 0/8	Big Horn County	WY	Jeremiah Fauver	2009	7
88 2/8	16 2/8 16 4/8	6 7/8 6 7/8	14 2/8	Yavapai County	AZ	Eric Gardner	2006	8
*88 0/8	18 4/8 17 7/8	7 1/8 7 0/8	7 3/8	Catron County	NM	Cade Salopek	2006	9
87 4/8	18 1/8 17 7/8	6 3/8 6 3/8	11 5/8	Kit Carson County	CO	Nathan Jones	2004	10
87 0/8	16 6/8 16 5/8	6 3/8 6 4/8	12 4/8	Yavapai County	AZ	Garnet Kingsland	1995	11
*87 0/8	16 6/8 16 4/8	7 0/8 7 0/8	10 4/8	Humboldt County	NV	Norman Beach	2008	11
86 6/8	16 0/8 15 7/8	6 6/8 6 6/8	8 6/8	Maple Creek	SAS	Jerry Bien	1990	13
86 6/8	16 0/8 16 0/8	7 1/8 7 1/8	12 0/8	Yavapai County	AZ	Jim Machac	1993	13
86 6/8	15 4/8 15 4/8	7 3/8 7 3/8	9 6/8	Yavapai County	AZ	Jim Machac	1998	13
86 4/8	16 0/8 16 1/8	6 7/8 6 6/8	9 5/8	Converse County	WY	Jordan Hypes	2006	16
86 2/8	18 3/8 18 4/8	6 3/8 6 2/8	12 4/8	Yavapai County	AZ	Perry Schaal	1994	17
86 2/8	15 2/8 15 4/8	7 4/8 7 4/8	10 5/8	Carbon County	WY	Robert E. Bergquist	2000	17
86 2/8	14 5/8 15 2/8	7 0/8 7 0/8	9 0/8	Big Horn County	WY	Kendel D. Cheatham	2010	17
86 0/8	18 0/8 17 7/8	6 2/8 6 1/8	11 4/8	Lea County	NM	Jon E. Hoff	1999	21
86 0/8	15 4/8 15 4/8	7 2/8 7 3/8	10 3/8	Carbon County	WY	Zachary Weber	2004	21
86 0/8	16 6/8 16 6/8	7 0/8 7 0/8	10 3/8	Socorro County	NM	Doug Aikin	2006	21
*86 0/8	17 0/8 17 0/8	6 6/8 6 6/8	8 4/8	Yavapai County	AZ	Marvin N. Zieser	2008	21
86 0/8	16 0/8 15 4/8	7 2/8 7 2/8	11 6/8	Lewis & Clark County	MT	Kody J. Baker	2010	21
85 6/8	16 2/8 15 4/8	6 6/8 6 7/8	13 2/8	Coconino County	AZ	Kevin Rector	1996	26
85 6/8	15 7/8 15 7/8	6 7/8 6 6/8	10 0/8	Sweetwater County	WY	Bradley J. Profaizer	2000	26
85 6/8	16 0/8 16 1/8	7 0/8 7 1/8	10 5/8	Natrona County	WY	Alfred Gemrich	2004	26
85 6/8	14 4/8 14 4/8	7 4/8 7 3/8	12 7/8	Carbon County	WY	Martinez Miguel	2006	26
85 6/8	17 0/8 16 6/8	7 1/8 7 1/8	16 0/8	Humboldt County	NV	Tom Scoggin	2007	26
*85 4/8	17 0/8 16 6/8	6 4/8 6 3/8	12 3/8	Sioux County	NE	Kerry Keane	2010	32
85 4/8	17 0/8 16 4/8	6 4/8 6 3/8	9 4/8	Lake County	OR	David Miller	2010	32
85 2/8	16 1/8 16 4/8	6 5/8 6 5/8	13 1/8	Carbon County	WY	Lonny Curtis	1990	34
85 2/8	16 4/8 16 3/8	6 4/8 6 4/8	10 0/8	Coconino County	AZ	Les R. Shelton	1995	34
85 2/8	17 0/8 16 7/8	6 6/8 6 5/8	10 3/8	Pershing County	NV	John Sarvis	2004	34
85 0/8	17 2/8 17 1/8	6 4/8 6 4/8	10 3/8	Moffat County	CO	Judd Cooney	1983	37
85 0/8	16 7/8 16 6/8	6 1/8 6 1/8	10 1/8	Malheur County	OR	Kenneth L. Barstad	1994	37
85 0/8	16 1/8 16 1/8	7 1/8 7 1/8	13 0/8	Natrona County	WY	Mark B. Steffen	1997	37
85 0/8	15 7/8 16 0/8	6 5/8 6 5/8	10 1/8	Mora County	NM	Benjamin L. Ingwerson	2007	37
84 6/8	16 2/8 16 6/8	6 6/8 6 6/8	8 0/8	Otero County	CO	Larry C. Hansen	1992	41
84 6/8	16 3/8 16 3/8	6 5/8 6 5/8	9 6/8	Humboldt County	NV	Ken Longballa	1999	41
84 6/8	16 2/8 16 2/8	7 0/8 7 0/8	11 1/8	Converse County	WY	Charles DeLong	2001	41
84 6/8	16 1/8 16 0/8	6 6/8 6 6/8	10 6/8	Big Horn County	WY	Brett Tippets	2007	41
84 4/8	17 0/8 16 7/8	6 4/8 6 4/8	11 4/8	White Pine County	NV	Harold R. "Bud" Kirk	1988	45
84 4/8	15 2/8 16 2/8	7 1/8 7 0/8	12 0/8	Catron County	NM	Martin Silva	1997	45
84 4/8	16 5/8 16 3/8	7 1/8 7 0/8	9 6/8	Brooks	ALB	Shaun Steidel	2002	45
84 4/8	15 3/8 15 1/8	7 3/8 7 3/8	9 7/8	Owyhee County	ID	Randy "Rann" Haight	2005	45
84 4/8	16 2/8 15 6/8	7 3/8 7 4/8	8 4/8	Siskiyou County	CA	Brent Miller	2008	45
84 2/8	16 0/8 15 7/8	6 3/8 6 3/8	10 0/8	Garfield County	MT	Ron J. Hoaglund	1989	50
84 2/8	15 7/8 15 7/8	7 1/8 7 0/8	9 3/8	Sweetwater County	WY	Kurt D. Olson	1990	50
84 2/8	16 3/8 16 2/8	6 4/8 6 2/8	13 4/8	Goshen County	WY	Gary Korell	1992	50
84 2/8	15 2/8 15 3/8	7 4/8 7 5/8	11 6/8	Sweetwater County	WY	Jared Mason	1995	50
84 2/8	15 3/8 15 5/8	7 1/8 7 1/8	8 1/8	Moffat County	CO	Kenneth M. Appelgren	1999	50
84 2/8	16 3/8 16 0/8	6 6/8 6 6/8	10 0/8	Yavapai County	AZ	Tracy G. Hardy	2000	50
84 2/8	16 7/8 16 6/8	6 2/8 6 3/8	13 2/8	Meade County	SD	William J. Bushong	2005	50
*84 2/8	15 6/8 16 1/8	6 6/8 6 6/8	9 4/8	Lea County	NM	Brandon Ray	2007	50
84 0/8	16 2/8 15 5/8	6 7/8 6 7/8	11 6/8	Perkins County	SD	Spike Jorgensen	1964	58
84 0/8	16 6/8 16 3/8	6 4/8 6 4/8	11 0/8	Catron County	NM	Perry Harper	1991	58
84 0/8	17 1/8 17 1/8	6 5/8 6 5/8	10 6/8	Campbell County	WY	Loy Dean Peters	1992	58
84 0/8	16 0/8 16 1/8	6 7/8 6 5/8	14 1/8	Youngstown	ALB	Kevin D. Parker	1994	58
84 0/8	15 7/8 16 4/8	6 7/8 7 0/8	11 6/8	Socorro County	NM	Patrick Snyder	1996	58
84 0/8	15 2/8 15 3/8	6 7/8 6 6/8	10 2/8	Yavapai County	AZ	Perry Schaal	1996	58
*84 0/8	17 6/8 17 5/8	6 5/8 6 3/8	6 3/8	Perkins County	SD	Ryan Sieveke	2007	58
84 0/8	16 2/8 16 5/8	6 7/8 6 6/8	7 5/8	Iron County	UT	Kody Orton	2009	58
83 6/8	15 4/8 15 2/8	7 3/8 7 3/8	15 2/8	Washoe County	NV	Fred Church	1978	66
83 6/8	15 2/8 15 6/8	6 3/8 6 4/8	11 6/8	Nye County	NV	Rich Sauer	1985	66
83 6/8	16 3/8 16 3/8	7 0/8 7 1/8	10 2/8	Harney County	OR	John S. Hansen	1990	66
83 6/8	15 7/8 15 7/8	6 3/8 6 2/8	11 5/8	Yavapai County	AZ	Roland J. Chooljian	1991	66
83 6/8	17 0/8 17 0/8	6 3/8 6 2/8	8 4/8	Sioux County	NE	Daniel F. Hejl	1991	66
83 6/8	15 2/8 15 3/8	6 4/8 6 4/8	9 6/8	Catron County	NM	Dave Fulson	1994	66
83 6/8	15 4/8 16 0/8	6 1/8 6 2/8	13 7/8	Coconino County	AZ	Steven Winiecki	1995	66
83 6/8	15 7/8 16 4/8	6 6/8 6 6/8	10 0/8	Minidoka County	ID	Eric Miller	2001	66
83 6/8	16 0/8 16 7/8	6 4/8 6 4/8	7 2/8	Colfax County	NM	Charlie Schlosser	2004	66
83 6/8	16 0/8 16 7/8	6 4/8 6 4/8	7 2/8	Colfax County	NM	Charlie Schlosser	2004	66
83 6/8	16 4/8 16 4/8	6 4/8 6 4/8	9 6/8	Pershing County	NV	Chad D. Bliss	2005	66
83 6/8	15 4/8 15 6/8	7 0/8 7 0/8	9 2/8	Rosebud County	MT	Jim E. Bolender	2005	66
*83 6/8	16 1/8 16 0/8	6 5/8 6 5/8	10 6/8	Billings County	ND	Shawn Kukowski	2005	66
83 4/8	16 1/8 16 1/8	6 2/8 6 2/8	10 7/8	Yavapai County	AZ	Richard S. Jones	1987	79
83 4/8	15 2/8 15 2/8	6 7/8 6 7/8	9 3/8	Campbell County	WY	James N. Monat	1990	79
83 4/8	15 4/8 15 4/8	6 6/8 6 7/8	9 2/8	Moffat County	CO	L. Dale Adkins	1992	79
83 4/8	14 5/8 15 0/8	7 0/8 7 0/8	9 4/8	Sweetwater County	WY	Keith Dana	1994	79
83 4/8	15 1/8 15 0/8	7 7/8 7 6/8	11 7/8	Emery County	UT	Rick Stockburger	1997	79
83 2/8	15 3/8 15 7/8	6 6/8 6 5/8	8 5/8	Natrona County	WY	Gary L. Miller	1990	84
83 2/8	16 4/8 16 3/8	6 3/8 6 2/8	9 1/8	Catron County	NM	James F. Welles	1991	84
83 2/8	15 3/8 15 4/8	6 6/8 6 6/8	10 6/8	Baca County	CO	Earl Leon Hollenback	1993	84
83 2/8	15 3/8 15 4/8	6 3/8 6 2/8	11 2/8	Rio Grande County	CO	Mark Thonhoff	2001	84
*83 2/8	15 2/8 15 2/8	7 0/8 7 2/8	7 6/8	Sherman County	KS	Matthew R. Bain	2006	84
83 2/8	16 2/8 16 5/8	6 7/8 6 5/8	10 6/8	Natrona County	WY	Dorian Gilbert	2010	84
83 0/8	17 0/8 17 0/8	6 0/8 6 0/8	12 3/8	Eddy County	NM	Jim Stell	1984	90
83 0/8	16 6/8 16 6/8	6 1/8 6 0/8	13 6/8	Coconino County	AZ	William P Pate	1985	90
83 0/8	16 4/8 16 4/8	6 5/8 6 4/8	15 7/8	Moffat County	CO	Mike Wallers	1989	90
83 0/8	15 6/8 15 5/8	7 2/8 6 7/8	14 5/8	Washoe County	NV	Daniel R. Brown	1990	90
83 0/8	15 4/8 15 6/8	6 6/8 6 5/8	13 6/8	Socorro County	NM	Tad Jones	1998	90
83 0/8	18 1/8 18 4/8	6 3/8 6 2/8	11 4/8	Lake County	OR	Ed Jones	2001	90
83 0/8	16 0/8 15 6/8	6 5/8 6 4/8	15 0/8	Natrona County	WY	Paul Narloch	2003	90
*83 0/8	14 7/8 15 3/8	7 1/8 7 1/8	11 0/8	Las Animas County	CO	Steve Fernandez	2010	90

810

PRONGHORN

Minimum Score 67 Continued

SCORE	LENGTH OF R HORN L	CIRCUMFERENCE R OF BASE L	INSIDE SPREAD	AREA	STATE/ PROVINCE	HUNTER'S NAME	DATE	RANK
82 6/8	16 4/8 16 3/8	6 2/8 6 3/8	8 5/8	Sublette County	WY	Michael D. Towne	1987	98
82 6/8	16 1/8 15 5/8	6 6/8 6 4/8	12 6/8	Coconino County	AZ	Kenneth C. Fulk	1988	98
82 6/8	16 2/8 16 1/8	6 5/8 6 4/8	9 0/8	Juab County	UT	David B. Nielsen	1992	98
82 6/8	16 2/8 16 1/8	6 5/8 6 6/8	12 0/8	Yavapai County	AZ	Larry Kindred	1994	98
82 6/8	16 0/8 16 1/8	6 3/8 6 2/8	8 5/8	Yavapai County	AZ	Paul S. Keltner	1997	98
82 6/8	16 6/8 16 4/8	6 3/8 6 2/8	9 1/8	Eureka County	NV	Mike Holt	2002	98
82 6/8	16 2/8 15 7/8	6 3/8 6 4/8	11 0/8	Sweetwater County	WY	Bob Wyant	2002	98
82 6/8	16 6/8 16 6/8	6 3/8 6 4/8	18 1/8	Rosebud County	MT	Kurt D. Rued	2003	98
82 6/8	15 3/8 15 3/8	6 3/8 6 2/8	10 4/8	Yavapai County	AZ	Robert Griego	2006	98
*82 6/8	15 6/8 15 7/8	6 5/8 6 4/8	10 7/8	Meade County	SD	Joe R. Gunderson	2007	98
82 4/8	15 1/8 16 0/8	6 5/8 6 3/8	6 3/8	McLean County	ND	Edward J. Weigel	1966	108
82 4/8	17 1/8 15 4/8	6 4/8 6 4/8	8 5/8	Yavapai County	AZ	Chris Skoczylas	1988	108
82 4/8	15 6/8 15 6/8	6 2/8 6 4/8	9 2/8	Graham County	AZ	Daniel C Hicks	1989	108
82 4/8	16 7/8 16 5/8	6 3/8 6 2/8	17 0/8	Luna County	NM	Ed Lowry	1990	108
82 4/8	14 2/8 14 1/8	7 0/8 6 7/8	10 1/8	Elko County	NV	Paul M. Adams	1994	108
82 4/8	17 1/8 17 4/8	6 4/8 6 5/8	16 6/8	Coconino County	AZ	Ken Patrick	1996	108
82 4/8	16 3/8 16 4/8	6 1/8 6 1/8	8 2/8	Santa Cruz County	AZ	Stan Haag	1996	108
82 4/8	15 2/8 15 1/8	6 6/8 6 6/8	10 6/8	Moffat County	CO	Kim Steven Hussong	1996	108
82 4/8	17 1/8 17 1/8	6 0/8 6 0/8	8 2/8	Yavapai County	AZ	Mike Brogdon	1997	108
82 4/8	15 7/8 15 6/8	6 4/8 6 3/8	10 3/8	Yavapai County	AZ	Paul Fritzinger	1998	108
82 4/8	14 7/8 14 6/8	6 7/8 6 7/8	7 2/8	Campbell County	WY	Richard E. LaCrone	1998	108
82 4/8	15 5/8 15 4/8	6 6/8 6 6/8	12 5/8	Harney County	OR	Corky Wray	2002	108
*82 4/8	15 0/8 15 0/8	7 2/8 7 2/8	7 3/8	Lewis & Clark County	MT	Eric Urban	2007	108
*82 4/8	16 3/8 16 6/8	6 2/8 6 1/8	9 3/8	Yavapai County	AZ	Jim Machac	2008	108
82 4/8	15 3/8 15 7/8	6 5/8 6 4/8	9 3/8	Moffat County	CO	Clay J. Evans	2009	108
82 2/8	15 7/8 15 6/8	7 0/8 6 6/8	12 1/8	Elko County	NV	Monte D. Fuller	1987	123
82 2/8	16 5/8 16 1/8	6 3/8 6 4/8	14 1/8	Dunn County	ND	Peter Braun	1990	123
82 2/8	14 6/8 14 5/8	6 5/8 6 4/8	8 0/8	Washoe County	NV	Mark Mannens	1994	123
82 2/8	15 5/8 16 0/8	6 3/8 6 4/8	13 2/8	Catron County	NM	Jimmy Cotant	1995	123
82 2/8	16 0/8 16 0/8	6 6/8 6 5/8	10 1/8	Fergus County	MT	Brad Burney	1998	123
82 2/8	15 5/8 15 3/8	7 0/8 6 7/8	9 6/8	Sheridan County	NE	Fred Kober	2000	123
82 2/8	15 6/8 15 7/8	6 6/8 6 5/8	9 2/8	Owyhee County	ID	Matthew B. Grant	2001	123
82 2/8	16 0/8 16 2/8	7 0/8 6 6/8	14 1/8	Coconino County	AZ	Robert M. "Mike" Young	2002	123
82 2/8	15 1/8 14 6/8	6 6/8 6 6/8	10 0/8	Lewis & Clark County	MT	Rhett Styren Young	2004	123
*82 2/8	15 4/8 15 5/8	7 4/8 7 3/8	9 7/8	Carter County	MT	Todd L. Kanavel	2005	123
82 2/8	15 7/8 15 6/8	6 4/8 6 4/8	11 6/8	Sioux County	NE	Ryan Hochstein	2008	123
*82 2/8	13 2/8 13 6/8	6 7/8 6 6/8	9 4/8	Albany County	WY	Chad Hoefs	2009	123
82 2/8	15 3/8 15 5/8	6 5/8 6 5/8	12 6/8	Natrona County	WY	Shawn L. Wagner	2009	123
82 0/8	17 4/8 18 2/8	6 6/8 6 2/8	15 6/8	Guadalupe County	NM	C. E. Foster, Jr.	1961	136
82 0/8	16 3/8 16 2/8	6 3/8 6 4/8	9 6/8	Coconino County	AZ	Fred W. Fernow, Jr.	1981	136
82 0/8	16 4/8 17 0/8	7 0/8 7 0/8	14 4/8	Billings County	ND	Kenneth E. Ruzicka	1987	136
82 0/8	16 0/8 16 0/8	6 3/8 6 2/8	15 0/8	Coconino County	AZ	Mike Kentera	1988	136
82 0/8	16 4/8 16 3/8	6 3/8 6 3/8	13 0/8	Cochise County	AZ	Dan Larkin	1992	136
82 0/8	14 6/8 14 6/8	6 2/8 6 2/8	6 3/8	Navajo County	AZ	Shane Koury	1993	136
82 0/8	15 0/8 15 1/8	6 3/8 6 3/8	12 5/8	Las Animas County	CO	Gary L. Cleaver	1994	136
82 0/8	16 1/8 16 5/8	6 3/8 6 3/8	8 7/8	Moffat County	CO	Marv Clyncke	1998	136
82 0/8	16 3/8 16 3/8	6 6/8 6 5/8	9 5/8	Socorro County	NM	Alan W. Krause	1998	136
82 0/8	17 5/8 17 3/8	6 1/8 6 3/8	9 3/8	Tilley	ALB	Dale Heinz	2000	136
82 0/8	14 2/8 14 7/8	7 0/8 6 7/8	9 4/8	Big Horn County	WY	George Kamps	2001	136
82 0/8	14 7/8 15 4/8	6 4/8 6 3/8	10 4/8	Johnson County	WY	J. Scott McIlvoy	2006	136
82 0/8	14 7/8 15 1/8	6 4/8 6 4/8	9 3/8	Carbon County	WY	Robert Bergquist	2007	136
82 0/8	15 4/8 15 3/8	6 7/8 6 4/8	8 4/8	Great Sand Hills	SAS	Chris Garland	2008	136
82 0/8	15 4/8 16 0/8	6 1/8 6 0/8	9 3/8	Blaine County	MT	Adam Wherley	2008	136
81 6/8	15 0/8 15 3/8	6 4/8 6 4/8	11 0/8	Coconino County	AZ	Noel Harris	1988	151
81 6/8	16 2/8 16 3/8	6 3/8 6 2/8	7 5/8	Yavapai County	AZ	Philip Rippey	2001	151
*81 6/8	15 4/8 15 3/8	6 2/8 6 2/8	14 2/8	Jackson County	CO	Cheryl Ray	2003	151
81 6/8	17 0/8 17 2/8	6 5/8 6 5/8	8 7/8	Perkins County	SD	Aaron Boe Ambur	2004	151
*81 6/8	15 2/8 15 6/8	6 2/8 6 1/8	10 3/8	Millard County	UT	Greg Dalton	2008	151
81 4/8	15 4/8 15 1/8	7 0/8 6 7/8	13 1/8	Washoe County	NV	Owen K. Mercer, Jr.	1981	156
81 4/8	16 3/8 16 6/8	6 6/8 5 7/8	13 6/8	Yellowstone County	MT	Robert M. Labert	1984	156
81 4/8	16 4/8 16 4/8	6 6/8 6 6/8	17 2/8	Jackson County	CO	Steve Jackson	1985	156
81 4/8	16 5/8 16 5/8	6 2/8 6 2/8	11 3/8	Yavapai County	AZ	James C. Roth	1990	156
81 4/8	15 2/8 15 3/8	6 5/8 6 4/8	10 6/8	Lake County	OR	Jeff Eder	1990	156
81 4/8	13 7/8 14 0/8	7 1/8 7 0/8	12 3/8	Natrona County	WY	Brian L. Wagner	1991	156
81 4/8	16 3/8 16 3/8	6 1/8 6 1/8	8 7/8	Lea County	NM	Mike Cowger	1992	156
81 4/8	16 2/8 15 4/8	5 7/8 6 1/8	12 4/8	Custer County	ID	Rick Day	1996	156
81 4/8	17 4/8 17 2/8	6 0/8 6 2/8	10 0/8	Coconino County	AZ	Patrick Loescher	1997	156
81 4/8	15 6/8 15 6/8	7 4/8 7 2/8	9 0/8	Big Horn County	WY	Zack Thorington	1999	156
81 4/8	14 7/8 14 7/8	6 6/8 6 5/8	11 7/8	Sweetwater County	WY	Daniel A. Gregg	2000	156
81 4/8	15 7/8 16 0/8	7 0/8 6 6/8	11 2/8	Rio Blanco County	CO	Tyler A. Pratt	2002	156
81 4/8	15 2/8 15 1/8	6 1/8 6 1/8	8 5/8	Big Horn County	WY	George Kamps	2004	156
*81 4/8	14 3/8 13 7/8	7 3/8 7 2/8	13 2/8	Deuel County	NE	Justin Misegadis	2007	156
81 4/8	13 7/8 13 5/8	7 1/8 7 0/8	10 7/8	Chouteau County	MT	Kirk Pederson	2009	156
81 2/8	15 4/8 15 3/8	7 1/8 7 1/8	6 6/8	Sweetwater County	WY	Clifford Rockhold	1985	171
81 2/8	16 2/8 16 3/8	6 1/8 5 7/8	17 3/8	Coconino County	AZ	Les Shelton	1985	171
81 2/8	15 2/8 15 1/8	6 2/8 6 3/8	10 4/8	Sublette County	WY	Ronald J. Clark	1986	171
81 2/8	15 5/8 15 4/8	6 7/8 6 6/8	10 0/8	Jefferson County	ID	Scott Griggs	1987	171
81 2/8	17 0/8 17 1/8	6 3/8 6 2/8	22 2/8	Yavapai County	AZ	Rick Anderson	1987	171
81 2/8	15 7/8 15 2/8	6 2/8 6 1/8	11 7/8	Yavapai County	AZ	Marty Cowie	1988	171
81 2/8	14 6/8 15 0/8	6 5/8 6 5/8	7 4/8	Etzikom	ALB	Rick Livingston	1988	171
81 2/8	16 2/8 16 4/8	6 5/8 6 5/8	13 1/8	Coconino County	AZ	Bob Gourley	1990	171
81 2/8	16 0/8 15 7/8	6 7/8 6 5/8	10 6/8	Catron County	NM	Jim Machac	1992	171
81 2/8	15 7/8 15 7/8	6 3/8 6 1/8	13 1/8	Coconino County	AZ	Glenn David Myrick	1992	171
81 2/8	16 4/8 16 5/8	6 3/8 6 1/8	10 1/8	Fergus County	MT	Jess Knerr	1993	171
81 2/8	15 3/8 15 4/8	6 4/8 6 5/8	8 0/8	Natrona County	WY	Wayne E. Brensinger	1995	171
81 2/8	16 4/8 16 2/8	6 2/8 6 2/8	12 4/8	Millard County	UT	Bob J. McGill	1996	171
81 2/8	16 7/8 16 7/8	6 2/8 6 2/8	11 6/8	Washoe County	NV	Patrick F. Ryle	1997	171
81 2/8	15 6/8 15 4/8	6 7/8 6 6/8	10 0/8	Big Horn County	WY	Brian P. Voss	1998	171
81 2/8	16 5/8 16 4/8	6 5/8 6 6/8	17 1/8	Cheyenne County	NE	Ev Tarrell	1999	171
81 2/8	15 5/8 15 3/8	7 0/8 7 0/8	11 2/8	Big Horn County	WY	Dave Moss	2000	171
81 2/8	15 5/8 15 4/8	6 7/8 6 6/8	10 5/8	Converse County	WY	Jeff Ensor	2000	171
81 2/8	16 0/8 15 4/8	6 1/8 6 2/8	10 7/8	Moffat County	CO	Frank S. Noska IV	2001	171
81 2/8	16 4/8 16 1/8	6 6/8 6 5/8	10 3/8	Natrona County	WY	Dave McFarlin	2004	171
81 2/8	16 2/8 16 2/8	5 4/8 5 4/8	11 0/8	Coconino County	AZ	Gary M. Howell	2004	171
81 2/8	15 2/8 15 0/8	6 5/8 6 6/8	11 1/8	Niobrara County	WY	Tom Bruegger	2005	171

PRONGHORN

Minimum Score 67 — Continued

Score	R Horn	L Horn	R Base	L Base	Inside Spread	Area	State/Province	Hunter's Name	Date	Rank
81 2/8	16 3/8	15 7/8	6 3/8	6 2/8	7 7/8	Jones County	SD	Clayton Miller	2006	171
81 2/8	15 0/8	15 0/8	7 0/8	6 6/8	13 7/8	Carbon County	WY	Shawn Wagner	2007	171
81 2/8	15 5/8	15 5/8	6 4/8	6 4/8	11 0/8	Las Animas County	CO	Barry J. Smith	2009	171
81 0/8	15 7/8	15 6/8	6 7/8	6 6/8	10 7/8	McLean County	ND	James Lahman	1971	196
81 0/8	15 3/8	15 4/8	7 0/8	6 6/8	12 0/8	Converse County	WY	Richard L. Huber	1978	196
81 0/8	15 4/8	15 4/8	6 6/8	6 6/8	11 6/8	Elko County	NV	Darcy W. Tate	1979	196
81 0/8	14 6/8	16 4/8	6 3/8	6 4/8	10 0/8	Coconino County	AZ	Jim Scott	1984	196
81 0/8	15 5/8	16 6/8	6 3/8	6 3/8	9 2/8	Yavapai County	AZ	Dan Robbins	1986	196
81 0/8	15 2/8	15 1/8	6 4/8	6 4/8	8 3/8	Lassen County	CA	Brian McCoslin	1990	196
81 0/8	16 4/8	16 3/8	6 3/8	6 3/8	8 5/8	Coconino County	AZ	John Lund	1990	196
81 0/8	15 7/8	15 4/8	6 3/8	6 3/8	9 6/8	Orion	ALB	Dan Kilborn	1990	196
81 0/8	16 7/8	17 1/8	6 2/8	6 1/8	6 4/8	Yavapai County	AZ	Walter J. Kellner, Jr.	1991	196
81 0/8	14 6/8	14 6/8	6 4/8	6 6/8	10 5/8	Humboldt County	NV	Scott Tilzey	1992	196
81 0/8	15 1/8	15 1/8	6 3/8	6 4/8	8 0/8	Yavapai County	AZ	Ben Gibson	1992	196
81 0/8	15 7/8	14 4/8	6 1/8	5 7/8	8 4/8	Hartley County	TX	Todd Hodnett	1992	196
81 0/8	14 2/8	13 7/8	7 2/8	7 2/8	13 3/8	Larimer County	CO	Allen Muirhead	1993	196
81 0/8	16 1/8	15 7/8	6 2/8	6 2/8	10 6/8	Yavapai County	AZ	Gene Lucas	1994	196
81 0/8	15 4/8	15 4/8	6 2/8	6 1/8	10 7/8	Saguache County	CO	Thomas Torrez	1996	196
81 0/8	14 5/8	14 1/8	6 7/8	6 7/8	11 0/8	Sweetwater County	WY	Harold Stinchcomb	1999	196
81 0/8	16 6/8	16 7/8	5 5/8	5 6/8	13 5/8	Park County	CO	Guy Pierce	2001	196
81 0/8	15 3/8	15 2/8	6 4/8	6 4/8	7 1/8	Teton County	MT	Scott M. Hayes	2003	196
*81 0/8	15 0/8	15 3/8	6 5/8	6 6/8	10 5/8	Converse County	WY	Jim Steele	2004	196
81 0/8	16 0/8	15 6/8	6 5/8	6 6/8	11 0/8	Humboldt County	NV	Duane F. Butler	2006	196
*81 0/8	15 2/8	15 3/8	6 6/8	6 3/8	7 7/8	Campbell County	WY	Durand Wagner	2006	196
*81 0/8	15 4/8	15 4/8	6 7/8	6 7/8	11 6/8	Rosebud County	MT	Mark DeCock	2008	196
81 0/8	16 3/8	16 1/8	6 4/8	6 4/8	12 1/8	Fergus County	MT	Chad Chord	2008	196
*81 0/8	15 6/8	15 7/8	6 6/8	6 4/8	11 4/8	Washakie County	WY	Rod Gleason	2010	196
80 6/8	15 5/8	15 5/8	6 3/8	6 2/8	11 6/8	Lincoln County	NM	Robert W. Davis	1959	220
80 6/8	16 0/8	15 4/8	5 7/8	5 7/8	10 1/8	Converse County	WY	Greg Winters	1989	220
80 6/8	16 0/8	16 0/8	6 1/8	6 2/8	8 4/8	Harney County	OR	Russell Jacobs	1990	220
80 6/8	14 2/8	14 3/8	6 7/8	6 7/8	8 2/8	Albany County	WY	John Buxton	1990	220
80 6/8	15 6/8	15 6/8	7 0/8	7 1/8	10 3/8	Washoe County	NV	Dave Holt	1992	220
80 6/8	16 2/8	15 7/8	6 0/8	6 2/8	6 4/8	Dawes County	NE	Ron Amack	1992	220
80 6/8	15 0/8	15 1/8	6 6/8	6 6/8	12 2/8	Rosebud County	MT	Mike Cummings	1992	220
80 6/8	16 0/8	16 1/8	6 4/8	6 4/8	11 6/8	Thomas County	NE	Andrew L. Glidden	1993	220
80 6/8	14 4/8	14 3/8	6 6/8	6 6/8	11 1/8	Deuel County	NE	Ev Tarrell	1993	220
80 6/8	16 6/8	16 6/8	6 1/8	6 1/8	10 0/8	Yavapai County	AZ	Henry Robert Garcia, Sr.	1994	220
80 6/8	15 3/8	15 6/8	7 4/8	7 3/8	9 4/8	Lake County	OR	Brian Day	1994	220
80 6/8	16 1/8	16 2/8	6 5/8	6 5/8	13 1/8	Lake County	OR	Jerry Donovan	1997	220
80 6/8	15 1/8	15 0/8	6 6/8	6 6/8	9 0/8	Big Horn County	WY	Tim Kindred	1998	220
80 6/8	14 7/8	15 0/8	6 5/8	6 5/8	9 2/8	Moffat County	CO	Tim Trehearne	1999	220
80 6/8	15 4/8	15 2/8	6 2/8	6 1/8	12 3/8	Brooks	ALB	Dave Samuel	2001	220
80 6/8	15 7/8	16 3/8	6 0/8	6 0/8	8 0/8	Brooks	ALB	Ozzie Schalm	2001	220
80 6/8	16 1/8	16 0/8	6 2/8	6 2/8	9 2/8	Perkins County	SD	Jerrod M. Hoff	2002	220
80 6/8	15 7/8	15 7/8	6 4/8	6 4/8	8 2/8	Cherry County	NE	Robert J. Hardy	2005	220
*80 6/8	14 3/8	14 7/8	6 6/8	6 7/8	11 2/8	Lea County	NM	Luci V. Gonzalez	2006	220
*80 6/8	14 7/8	15 0/8	6 1/8	6 0/8	6 5/8	Madison County	MT	Dan Mayland	2007	220
80 6/8	16 0/8	16 0/8	6 2/8	6 2/8	13 0/8	Harding County	SD	Jerry Notch	2008	220
*80 6/8	16 2/8	16 1/8	6 2/8	6 2/8	10 6/8	Nye County	NV	Justin Rozich	2010	220
80 4/8	16 5/8	17 0/8	5 5/8	5 6/8	10 3/8	Humboldt County	NV	Shane E. Evans	1984	242
80 4/8	15 0/8	15 0/8	6 4/8	6 4/8	9 7/8	Sweetwater County	WY	Christopher J. Cordes	1986	242
80 4/8	16 3/8	16 0/8	6 3/8	6 2/8	9 0/8	Sweetwater County	WY	Gene McFadden	1987	242
80 4/8	15 3/8	15 3/8	6 6/8	6 6/8	9 2/8	Owyhee County	ID	Shane Gehring	1991	242
80 4/8	16 0/8	15 4/8	7 0/8	7 0/8	8 5/8	Dawes County	NE	Roger Westemeier	1992	242
80 4/8	16 6/8	16 4/8	6 1/8	6 0/8	12 2/8	Yavapai County	AZ	Marvin N. Zieser	1993	242
80 4/8	15 2/8	15 0/8	6 6/8	6 6/8	7 7/8	Yuma County	CO	Randy Wilkins	1993	242
80 4/8	15 6/8	15 6/8	6 1/8	6 0/8	11 6/8	Wallace County	KS	Danny Pfaff	1996	242
80 4/8	14 6/8	14 4/8	6 3/8	6 2/8	8 5/8	Sweetwater County	WY	Mark Preston	1999	242
80 4/8	15 5/8	15 6/8	6 0/8	5 7/8	11 5/8	Converse County	WY	William R. Horn, Jr.	1999	242
80 4/8	15 1/8	14 7/8	6 3/8	6 3/8	10 2/8	Lake County	OR	Mike Jackson	2001	242
80 4/8	14 7/8	15 0/8	6 6/8	6 5/8	9 1/8	Elmore County	ID	Mike Potucek	2003	242
80 4/8	15 4/8	15 5/8	6 4/8	6 4/8	11 4/8	Golden Prairie	SAS	Kevin Paslawski	2005	242
*80 4/8	14 5/8	14 5/8	6 6/8	6 6/8	14 4/8	Converse County	WY	Craig S. Talbot	2006	242
80 2/8	14 5/8	14 5/8	7 1/8	7 3/8	8 6/8	Natrona County	WY	Dr. J. A. Martin	1964	256
80 2/8	14 1/8	13 7/8	7 3/8	7 3/8	10 6/8	Butte County	ID	Danny Owens	1974	256
80 2/8	15 4/8	15 3/8	6 6/8	6 6/8	8 7/8	Modoc County	CA	Ed Dowling	1982	256
80 2/8	14 5/8	14 7/8	6 6/8	6 7/8	10 4/8	Yuma County	CO	Mark Sievers	1982	256
80 2/8	15 7/8	15 6/8	6 4/8	6 4/8	8 4/8	Yavapai County	AZ	Jim Machac	1988	256
80 2/8	15 7/8	15 7/8	6 6/8	6 6/8	13 0/8	Natrona County	WY	Brian L. Wagner	1989	256
80 2/8	16 3/8	14 4/8	6 6/8	6 6/8	11 3/8	Lassen County	CA	Greg Morris	1990	256
80 2/8	15 4/8	15 5/8	6 6/8	6 6/8	11 0/8	Mora County	NM	George P. Mann	1991	256
80 2/8	15 2/8	14 7/8	6 4/8	6 4/8	10 4/8	Rio Blanco County	CO	Don Collier	1993	256
80 2/8	15 6/8	15 7/8	6 6/8	6 4/8	11 2/8	Rio Blanco County	CO	Gary L. Hinaman	1993	256
80 2/8	13 4/8	13 6/8	6 4/8	6 2/8	12 0/8	Coconino County	AZ	Chris Tabor	1994	256
80 2/8	13 5/8	13 5/8	6 3/8	6 3/8	8 0/8	Dundy County	NE	Matt Gideon	1995	256
80 2/8	17 0/8	17 3/8	6 3/8	6 1/8	13 0/8	Campbell County	WY	David Westmoreland	1995	256
80 2/8	15 3/8	15 2/8	6 3/8	6 4/8	9 3/8	Humboldt County	NV	Ivan Brown	1998	256
80 2/8	15 5/8	15 6/8	6 2/8	6 1/8	9 4/8	Yavapai County	AZ	David A. Niemann	1998	256
80 2/8	14 5/8	14 6/8	6 7/8	6 7/8	8 1/8	Moffat County	CO	Dewayne Mullins	1999	256
80 2/8	16 3/8	16 2/8	6 3/8	6 2/8	13 2/8	Navajo County	AZ	Stephen C. Christensen	2000	256
80 2/8	16 0/8	15 7/8	6 2/8	6 1/8	9 0/8	Natrona County	WY	Shawn Wagner	2002	256
80 2/8	15 0/8	14 7/8	6 4/8	6 5/8	8 5/8	Carbon County	UT	Kirk E. Mascaro	2003	256
80 2/8	14 0/8	15 3/8	6 7/8	6 7/8	8 7/8	Humboldt County	NV	Duane F. Butler	2005	256
*80 2/8	15 0/8	15 4/8	6 3/8	6 1/8	14 6/8	Carter County	MT	Colby Moellenberndt	2005	256
80 2/8	15 2/8	15 1/8	6 7/8	6 6/8	9 4/8	Natrona County	WY	Wayne Wirrenga	2007	256
80 2/8	15 5/8	15 0/8	6 3/8	6 2/8	10 6/8	Converse County	WY	Troy Thompson	2007	256
80 2/8	15 7/8	15 6/8	6 2/8	6 2/8	9 7/8	Liberty County	MT	Lewis Johnson	2010	256
80 0/8	16 6/8	16 5/8	6 1/8	6 1/8	13 6/8	Albany County	WY	Dave A. Current	1969	280
80 0/8	16 0/8	16 0/8	6 3/8	6 3/8	10 7/8	Washoe County	NV	Kevin S. Wheeler	1983	280
80 0/8	16 4/8	16 2/8	6 4/8	6 4/8	13 0/8	McKinley County	NM	Steve Yearout	1985	280
80 0/8	15 6/8	15 6/8	6 0/8	6 2/8	8 5/8	Coconino County	AZ	Jim Felt	1987	280
80 0/8	15 7/8	16 4/8	6 5/8	6 4/8	14 0/8	Coconino County	AZ	David Bushell	1988	280
80 0/8	16 1/8	15 5/8	6 4/8	6 3/8	9 7/8	Rosebud County	MT	Everett M. Morris	1988	280
80 0/8	14 6/8	15 0/8	7 0/8	7 0/8	8 5/8	Humboldt County	NV	James Puryear	1990	280
80 0/8	14 7/8	14 7/8	6 5/8	6 4/8	13 0/8	Cibola County	NM	Shaun Finch	1990	280

812

PRONGHORN

Minimum Score 67 — Continued

SCORE	LENGTH OF R HORN L	CIRCUMFERENCE R OF BASE L	INSIDE SPREAD	AREA	STATE/ PROVINCE	HUNTER'S NAME	DATE	RANK
80 0/8	16 3/8 16 3/8	6 1/8 6 1/8	11 0/8	McKenzie County	ND	Travis Wollan	1990	280
80 0/8	15 4/8 14 4/8	6 4/8 6 5/8	6 6/8	Moffat County	CO	Breck Johnson	1992	280
80 0/8	15 0/8 15 3/8	6 5/8 6 4/8	11 2/8	Natrona County	WY	Jeff Laub	1992	280
80 0/8	14 6/8 14 6/8	6 4/8 6 6/8	12 3/8	Converse County	WY	Kevin Louis Stier	1992	280
80 0/8	16 4/8 16 4/8	6 1/8 6 0/8	11 4/8	Millard County	UT	John Tuttle	1995	280
80 0/8	15 0/8 15 3/8	6 5/8 6 4/8	7 6/8	Weld County	CO	Rick Parish	1995	280
80 0/8	15 4/8 16 0/8	6 3/8 6 2/8	10 2/8	Sweetwater County	WY	Ken McFarland	1998	280
80 0/8	15 1/8 15 2/8	6 4/8 6 2/8	9 0/8	Campbell County	WY	Josh Coleman	2000	280
80 0/8	14 0/8 14 0/8	7 4/8 7 7/8	13 0/8	Converse County	WY	Randy Hopp	2000	280
80 0/8	15 6/8 15 5/8	6 2/8 6 1/8	10 3/8	Sierra County	NM	Lacy Harber	2001	280
80 0/8	15 7/8 15 5/8	6 5/8 6 4/8	8 0/8	Natrona County	WY	Brian Wagner	2002	280
80 0/8	15 3/8 14 7/8	6 2/8 6 2/8	12 4/8	Sierra County	NM	Joe Keathley	2003	280
*80 0/8	15 6/8 15 6/8	6 1/8 6 1/8	9 7/8	Converse County	WY	Steve McCoy	2004	280
80 0/8	15 5/8 15 0/8	7 1/8 7 1/8	6 4/8	Humboldt County	NV	David Hoid	2005	280
*80 0/8	15 0/8 14 5/8	6 6/8 6 6/8	11 2/8	Toole County	MT	Shane Overbey	2007	280
*80 0/8	15 6/8 15 5/8	6 4/8 6 4/8	11 5/8	Yavapai County	AZ	Robert W. Alanis	2007	280
80 0/8	14 6/8 15 1/8	6 5/8 6 5/8	9 7/8	Albany County	WY	Jerry Bowen	2007	280
80 0/8	15 2/8 14 4/8	6 4/8 6 5/8	7 4/8	Carbon County	WY	Clay J. Evans	2009	280
80 0/8	14 2/8 14 3/8	7 0/8 6 7/8	13 3/8	Natrona County	WY	Michael Lopez	2009	280
80 0/8	15 6/8 15 4/8	6 0/8 6 0/8	8 2/8	Lincoln County	WY	Heath Eddins	2009	280
*80 0/8	15 6/8 15 6/8	6 1/8 6 0/8	9 1/8	Cimarron County	OK	David Harley Coleman	2009	280
*80 0/8	15 7/8 16 1/8	6 1/8 6 0/8	8 3/8	Coconino County	AZ	Bill Ferguson	2010	280
79 6/8	15 4/8 14 6/8	7 1/8 7 3/8	9 3/8	Mellette County	SD	John Anderson	1970	310
79 6/8	15 4/8 15 4/8	6 0/8 6 0/8	10 5/8	Washoe County	NV	Mike J. Ellena	1983	310
79 6/8	13 7/8 13 6/8	6 5/8 6 4/8	11 5/8	Modoc County	CA	Dave Masamori	1990	310
79 6/8	15 2/8 15 3/8	6 4/8 6 4/8	12 2/8	Converse County	WY	Roger J. Reynolds	1990	310
79 6/8	16 0/8 15 7/8	6 1/8 6 1/8	14 4/8	McKenzie County	ND	Kevin Caroline	1990	310
79 6/8	15 4/8 15 3/8	6 4/8 6 4/8	11 0/8	Sweetwater County	WY	Keith Dana	1991	310
79 6/8	16 0/8 15 6/8	6 4/8 6 4/8	11 4/8	Dunn County	ND	Vance Vaagen	1991	310
79 6/8	15 7/8 16 0/8	6 6/8 6 4/8	17 1/8	Washoe County	NV	James P. Mason	1992	310
79 6/8	15 3/8 15 2/8	6 5/8 6 5/8	13 5/8	Yavapai County	AZ	Patrick Kirby	1992	310
79 6/8	15 5/8 15 6/8	6 3/8 6 3/8	10 0/8	Weld County	CO	Erik J. Smith	1993	310
79 6/8	15 5/8 15 5/8	6 7/8 6 5/8	9 4/8	Rosebud County	MT	Jeff Mitchell	1993	310
79 6/8	16 2/8 15 7/8	6 2/8 6 1/8	12 0/8	Campbell County	WY	Brian Tweeden	1993	310
79 6/8	15 6/8 15 6/8	6 3/8 6 2/8	13 4/8	Coconino County	AZ	Robert Y. Childers	1995	310
79 6/8	14 7/8 14 4/8	6 0/8 5 7/8	12 1/8	Yavapai County	AZ	John Bute	1996	310
79 6/8	16 4/8 16 2/8	6 2/8 6 1/8	11 2/8	Yavapai County	AZ	Jacob M. Underwood	1998	310
79 6/8	16 7/8 16 5/8	6 1/8 6 0/8	10 6/8	Chouteau County	MT	Joe Byers	2000	310
79 6/8	15 2/8 15 0/8	6 4/8 6 5/8	9 3/8	Yavapai County	AZ	Joseph Wayne Rippey	2001	310
79 6/8	15 1/8 15 1/8	7 0/8 7 4/8	18 0/8	Garfield County	MT	Kurt D. Rued	2002	310
79 6/8	15 3/8 15 1/8	6 0/8 6 0/8	11 6/8	Golden Valley County	ND	Terry Buechler	2004	310
*79 6/8	14 1/8 14 0/8	6 4/8 6 3/8	9 3/8	Converse County	WY	Dennis Arnold	2005	310
79 6/8	15 1/8 15 1/8	6 2/8 6 2/8	9 7/8	Weld County	CO	Tim Bradley	2006	310
*79 6/8	15 3/8 15 3/8	6 3/8 6 3/8	9 3/8	Pershing County	NV	Darrell Gogert	2007	310
79 6/8	14 5/8 15 0/8	7 2/8 7 1/8	9 5/8	Carter County	MT	Michael Moose	2008	310
79 6/8	15 2/8 15 1/8	6 0/8 5 7/8	8 6/8	Albany County	WY	Dana Robertson	2008	310
79 6/8	14 3/8 14 3/8	7 0/8 6 7/8	7 6/8	Owyhee County	ID	Jeremy R. Willis	2009	310
79 4/8	14 3/8 14 4/8	5 7/8 5 6/8	11 6/8	Mountrail County	ND	Bill Kurry	1976	335
79 4/8	16 4/8 16 0/8	6 3/8 6 4/8	9 0/8	Klamath County	OR	Harold Benson	1977	335
79 4/8	14 4/8 14 4/8	6 3/8 6 3/8	7 5/8	Converse County	WY	Russ Guerndt, Jr.	1985	335
79 4/8	14 1/8 14 0/8	7 2/8 7 2/8	9 2/8	Carbon County	WY	Michael L. Cone	1986	335
79 4/8	15 1/8 15 0/8	6 1/8 6 2/8	12 5/8	Dundy County	NE	Bradley Wiese	1987	335
79 4/8	16 0/8 16 0/8	6 2/8 6 2/8	13 3/8	Dunn County	ND	Terry Buechler	1990	335
79 4/8	15 5/8 15 5/8	6 1/8 6 2/8	10 6/8	Juab County	UT	Julie Robertson	1992	335
79 4/8	15 0/8 15 6/8	6 3/8 6 7/8	10 5/8	Socorro County	NM	Gerald Chavez	1993	335
79 4/8	15 3/8 15 3/8	6 6/8 6 6/8	10 6/8	Uintah County	UT	David A. Young	1993	335
79 4/8	16 0/8 16 2/8	6 0/8 6 0/8	11 4/8	Washoe County	NV	Lee McKenzie	1995	335
79 4/8	14 3/8 14 2/8	6 3/8 6 2/8	11 0/8	Natrona County	WY	Alfred J. Gemrich	2001	335
79 4/8	15 5/8 15 4/8	6 2/8 6 2/8	7 3/8	Dunn County	ND	Myles Fisher	2002	335
79 4/8	15 5/8 15 4/8	6 4/8 6 4/8	12 4/8	Sheridan County	WY	Luke Roush	2003	335
79 4/8	16 4/8 16 3/8	6 1/8 6 1/8	11 6/8	Lewis & Clark County	MT	Boudie Schneider	2003	335
79 4/8	15 2/8 15 2/8	6 2/8 6 2/8	11 5/8	Campbell County	WY	Edwin H. Gehringer	2005	335
79 4/8	15 3/8 15 6/8	6 2/8 6 1/8	8 0/8	Sweetwater County	WY	Duane F. Butler	2006	335
79 4/8	14 7/8 15 0/8	6 1/8 6 0/8	11 6/8	Emery County	UT	Darius Simons	2007	335
79 4/8	16 2/8 16 1/8	6 3/8 6 2/8	11 3/8	Hatton	SAS	Sam Peterson	2007	335
*79 4/8	14 4/8 14 6/8	6 3/8 6 2/8	8 6/8	Stanley County	SD	Derek Schiefelbein	2008	335
*79 4/8	15 2/8 15 3/8	6 5/8 6 5/8	12 4/8	Sweetwater County	WY	Joshua Barnes	2009	335
*79 4/8	15 5/8 15 5/8	6 3/8 6 3/8	10 6/8	Perkins County	SD	Chad Mosteller	2009	335
79 4/8	14 5/8 14 5/8	6 3/8 6 4/8	13 7/8	Albany County	WY	Jerry Bowen	2009	335
*79 4/8	16 2/8 16 3/8	6 4/8 6 2/8	9 5/8	Richland County	MT	Derek Werner	2010	335
79 2/8	14 3/8 14 5/8	6 4/8 6 2/8	9 2/8	Musselshell County	MT	Jon Kowalski	1982	358
79 2/8	15 5/8 15 3/8	6 6/8 6 4/8	9 4/8	Moffat County	CO	Alan Martellaro	1986	358
79 2/8	15 5/8 15 4/8	6 5/8 6 4/8	10 6/8	Washoe County	NV	Kenneth J. Wilkinson	1987	358
79 2/8	15 2/8 15 0/8	6 2/8 6 1/8	8 4/8	Lincoln County	WY	LeRoy Moulding	1987	358
79 2/8	16 1/8 15 5/8	6 2/8 6 1/8	13 6/8	Eddy County	NM	Carl D. Bradford	1987	358
79 2/8	15 0/8 15 4/8	6 5/8 6 5/8	10 4/8	Sublette County	WY	Steven Hill	1990	358
79 2/8	15 3/8 15 2/8	6 6/8 6 6/8	10 7/8	Colfax County	NM	Delbert T. Vigil	1991	358
79 2/8	16 1/8 16 3/8	6 3/8 6 3/8	12 5/8	Washoe County	NV	A. H. "Wilk" Wilkerson	1992	358
79 2/8	15 3/8 15 4/8	6 7/8 7 0/8	11 2/8	Weld County	CO	Kevin Waller	1992	358
79 2/8	16 3/8 15 7/8	6 2/8 6 4/8	11 1/8	Lincoln County	WY	C. R. (Bob) Bolton	1992	358
79 2/8	14 1/8 13 7/8	6 6/8 6 7/8	8 6/8	Moffat County	CO	Steven Vittetow	1992	358
79 2/8	13 5/8 13 6/8	7 0/8 6 5/8	11 0/8	Twin Falls County	ID	Brent L. Compton	1992	358
79 2/8	13 6/8 14 0/8	7 1/8 7 2/8	10 4/8	Moffat County	CO	Mike Kiser	1997	358
79 2/8	14 6/8 14 6/8	6 2/8 6 2/8	11 6/8	Lincoln County	NM	Robert John Seeds	1997	358
79 2/8	15 1/8 15 3/8	6 7/8 6 7/8	14 4/8	Weld County	CO	Neil Chandler	1998	358
79 2/8	16 2/8 16 4/8	6 0/8 6 1/8	10 2/8	Big Horn County	WY	Randy Whyte	1999	358
79 2/8	15 7/8 15 7/8	6 4/8 6 3/8	9 5/8	Brooks	ALB	Mark Nelson	2000	358
79 2/8	15 2/8 15 2/8	6 2/8 6 2/8	13 3/8	Brooks	ALB	Brandon Ray	2000	358
79 2/8	15 3/8 15 5/8	6 3/8 6 2/8	10 3/8	Yavapai County	AZ	Kevin Kay McCall	2001	358
*79 2/8	16 1/8 16 1/8	5 7/8 5 6/8	10 5/8	El Paso County	CO	Larry Dale Heavner	2002	358
79 2/8	15 1/8 15 1/8	6 6/8 6 4/8	12 5/8	Lake County	OR	John Hensley	2004	358
*79 2/8	15 3/8 15 4/8	6 4/8 6 3/8	10 7/8	Moffat County	CO	Julie Cuthriell	2004	358
79 2/8	15 0/8 14 7/8	6 2/8 6 4/8	10 6/8	Millard County	UT	Robert Adam Warnock	2004	358
*79 2/8	14 5/8 14 5/8	6 5/8 6 6/8	14 4/8	Weld County	CO	Mike Kattawar, Jr.	2005	358
79 2/8	15 4/8 15 5/8	6 6/8 6 7/8	9 4/8	Carbon County	WY	Bert Herrera	2005	358

813

PRONGHORN

Minimum Score 67 — Continued

SCORE	LENGTH OF HORN R	L	CIRCUMFERENCE OF BASE R	L	INSIDE SPREAD	AREA	STATE/ PROVINCE	HUNTER'S NAME	DATE	RANK
79 2/8	15 5/8	15 5/8	5 7/8	6 0/8	10 0/8	Las Animas County	CO	Justin Barajas	2005	358
79 2/8	15 0/8	15 2/8	6 4/8	6 4/8	6 3/8	Natrona County	WY	Morgan T. Young	2006	358
79 2/8	15 0/8	15 0/8	6 2/8	5 7/8	9 0/8	Albany County	WY	Dennis Magnusson	2006	358
*79 2/8	16 0/8	16 0/8	6 2/8	6 1/8	12 2/8	Harding County	SD	Kent Lewis	2007	358
79 2/8	15 1/8	15 2/8	6 2/8	6 2/8	10 4/8	Custer County	MT	James Bornman	2007	358
*79 2/8	14 1/8	13 7/8	6 5/8	6 4/8	9 4/8	Milk River	ALB	M. Blake Patton	2009	358
79 0/8	15 0/8	15 3/8	6 3/8	6 3/8	11 5/8	Washoe County	NV	Tom Thompson	1979	389
79 0/8	15 7/8	15 6/8	6 2/8	6 2/8	12 6/8	Carbon County	WY	Michael Ambur	1982	389
79 0/8	14 4/8	14 6/8	6 6/8	6 6/8	15 3/8	Moffat County	CO	Steven J. Lepic	1983	389
79 0/8	14 7/8	15 0/8	6 3/8	6 2/8	8 5/8	Carbon County	WY	Kim Cooper	1983	389
79 0/8	14 6/8	14 5/8	7 2/8	7 3/8	7 0/8	Sweetwater County	WY	Steve Rueck	1985	389
79 0/8	14 1/8	14 4/8	6 3/8	6 2/8	11 5/8	Millard County	UT	Keith Dana	1988	389
79 0/8	14 6/8	15 0/8	6 5/8	6 4/8	9 4/8	Sweetwater County	WY	Gerry Wolfe	1988	389
79 0/8	15 7/8	15 7/8	6 0/8	6 1/8	9 4/8	Harney County	OR	Jim Nielsen	1990	389
79 0/8	15 0/8	15 0/8	7 4/8	7 3/8	11 2/8	Campbell County	WY	Mike "Pie" Piaskowski	1990	389
79 0/8	16 4/8	17 1/8	6 1/8	6 0/8	8 7/8	Yavapai County	AZ	T. J. Baehre	1991	389
79 0/8	15 0/8	13 6/8	6 6/8	7 1/8	12 2/8	Bennett County	SD	Wayne Johnson	1991	389
79 0/8	14 6/8	14 7/8	6 2/8	6 3/8	10 7/8	Luna County	NM	Ray Trejo	1993	389
79 0/8	15 5/8	15 2/8	6 3/8	6 3/8	9 2/8	Quay County	NM	Kenneth McKinney	1993	389
79 0/8	15 2/8	15 1/8	6 2/8	6 1/8	12 7/8	Clark County	ID	Fred H. Hanks	1994	389
79 0/8	15 1/8	15 1/8	6 7/8	6 7/8	11 3/8	Weld County	CO	Fred Eichler	1995	389
79 0/8	15 1/8	15 2/8	6 5/8	6 5/8	15 2/8	Colfax County	NM	Stephen Nilsen	1995	389
79 0/8	14 7/8	14 7/8	6 6/8	6 5/8	10 3/8	Campbell County	WY	Ronald T. Morgan	1995	389
79 0/8	15 1/8	15 0/8	6 2/8	6 2/8	9 6/8	Saguache County	CO	Alan R. Palmer	1995	389
*79 0/8	14 2/8	15 1/8	6 3/8	6 2/8	10 4/8	Forty Mile	ALB	R. Keith O'Neal	2001	389
79 0/8	15 4/8	15 6/8	6 4/8	6 3/8	11 4/8	Brooks	ALB	Leo F. Romano	2001	389
79 0/8	15 5/8	16 2/8	6 3/8	6 2/8	11 4/8	Phillips County	MT	F. Drew Henry	2002	389
79 0/8	14 2/8	14 3/8	6 5/8	6 5/8	13 6/8	Garfield County	MT	Jerry Locati	2003	389
79 0/8	14 6/8	14 3/8	6 5/8	6 6/8	9 5/8	Powder River County	MT	Brian Williams	2004	389
79 0/8	14 6/8	14 4/8	6 4/8	6 4/8	13 1/8	Natrona County	WY	Ed Reish	2005	389
79 0/8	15 3/8	15 1/8	7 1/8	7 1/8	13 7/8	Owyhee County	ID	Sheldon William Doughty	2005	389
*79 0/8	15 0/8	15 0/8	6 5/8	6 4/8	10 4/8	Converse County	WY	Mark Kayser	2008	389
79 0/8	15 1/8	15 1/8	6 3/8	6 3/8	12 0/8	Brooks	ALB	Chris Barker	2008	389
*79 0/8	16 4/8	16 2/8	6 5/8	6 3/8	14 7/8	Morton County	ND	Chad Miller	2008	389
*79 0/8	15 0/8	15 1/8	6 0/8	5 6/8	7 1/8	Logan County	KS	Chris Wolkensdorfer	2008	389
79 0/8	15 1/8	15 1/8	6 3/8	6 2/8	13 2/8	Tide Lake	ALB	Victor Dyck	2009	389
79 0/8	16 0/8	15 7/8	6 0/8	6 1/8	8 7/8	Natrona County	WY	Jerry Simmons	2010	389
78 6/8	14 2/8	14 4/8	7 1/8	7 1/8	12 2/8	Johnson County	WY	Steve Winkey	1982	420
78 6/8	16 5/8	16 2/8	6 4/8	6 2/8	7 4/8	Sweetwater County	WY	Mike Holmes	1982	420
78 6/8	16 1/8	16 3/8	6 3/8	6 3/8	15 4/8	Clark County	ID	Dennis R Marshall	1985	420
78 6/8	15 5/8	15 7/8	6 2/8	6 2/8	9 7/8	Converse County	WY	Tom Glendinning	1988	420
78 6/8	15 6/8	15 7/8	6 2/8	6 1/8	10 1/8	Catron County	NM	Steve Frazier	1991	420
78 6/8	13 4/8	14 0/8	7 0/8	6 7/8	10 5/8	Natrona County	WY	Timothy D. Baer	1991	420
78 6/8	15 7/8	15 7/8	6 2/8	6 1/8	11 0/8	Hudspeth County	TX	Craig B. Baird	1991	420
78 6/8	15 5/8	16 0/8	6 2/8	6 2/8	12 5/8	Humboldt County	NV	Carl W. Rose	1992	420
78 6/8	14 0/8	14 0/8	6 4/8	6 4/8	9 3/8	Sweetwater County	WY	Mark L. Preston	1992	420
78 6/8	14 5/8	14 6/8	6 3/8	6 3/8	10 2/8	Sweetwater County	WY	Mike Barrett	1992	420
78 6/8	15 3/8	15 6/8	6 3/8	6 2/8	10 0/8	McKenzie County	ND	Travis Wollan	1992	420
78 6/8	16 0/8	15 4/8	6 1/8	6 0/8	9 4/8	Wallace County	KS	Loren Goss	1993	420
78 6/8	13 4/8	13 6/8	6 6/8	6 6/8	8 4/8	Sublette County	WY	Stephen Kotz	1994	420
78 6/8	15 5/8	15 2/8	6 3/8	6 3/8	8 3/8	Campbell County	WY	Danny D. Brown	1995	420
78 6/8	14 0/8	14 5/8	6 4/8	6 4/8	11 2/8	Yavapai County	AZ	George A. Ovalle	1995	420
78 6/8	15 2/8	15 2/8	6 3/8	6 3/8	11 2/8	Nye County	NV	Todd Bresemann	1996	420
78 6/8	14 0/8	14 1/8	6 5/8	6 3/8	10 0/8	Elko County	NV	Beau M. Nyrehn	1998	420
78 6/8	15 1/8	17 7/8	6 1/8	6 2/8	8 7/8	Socorro County	NM	Elton Warriner	1998	420
78 6/8	15 0/8	15 0/8	6 2/8	6 3/8	12 0/8	Big Horn County	WY	John Michael Gams	1998	420
78 6/8	14 3/8	14 5/8	6 7/8	7 0/8	9 0/8	Sublette County	WY	Darren Davison	2000	420
78 6/8	14 0/8	14 1/8	6 5/8	6 4/8	8 1/8	Natrona County	WY	Roy Keefer	2000	420
78 6/8	15 4/8	16 1/8	6 1/8	6 1/8	7 4/8	Jenner	ALB	Bradley Sankey	2000	420
78 6/8	15 1/8	15 4/8	6 6/8	6 6/8	10 5/8	Valley County	MT	Brad Faber	2000	420
78 6/8	14 3/8	14 3/8	6 5/8	6 5/8	7 5/8	Moffat County	CO	Mike Dziekan	2003	420
78 6/8	15 4/8	15 3/8	6 3/8	6 3/8	13 0/8	Sierra County	NM	Dyrk Eddie	2003	420
78 6/8	14 4/8	14 4/8	6 3/8	6 2/8	12 3/8	Navajo County	AZ	Todd Smith	2003	420
78 6/8	13 6/8	13 6/8	6 6/8	6 6/8	12 0/8	Washoe County	NV	David Kirkwood	2004	420
78 6/8	14 6/8	15 0/8	6 4/8	6 1/8	11 5/8	Sweetwater County	WY	Deidra Homann	2004	420
78 6/8	14 2/8	14 0/8	6 5/8	6 6/8	7 7/8	Niobrara County	WY	Tim L. Donnelly	2004	420
78 6/8	14 4/8	14 2/8	7 0/8	6 7/8	11 4/8	Lake County	OR	Mike Jackson	2004	420
78 6/8	14 5/8	14 6/8	6 7/8	6 6/8	12 6/8	Crook County	WY	Jeff Jacobs	2004	420
78 6/8	14 2/8	13 4/8	6 4/8	6 4/8	10 7/8	Sweetwater County	WY	Jim Bob Brundidge	2006	420
*78 6/8	15 7/8	15 7/8	6 3/8	6 1/8	7 2/8	Chouteau County	MT	Jared Vielleux	2006	420
78 6/8	15 5/8	15 7/8	6 1/8	6 3/8	11 4/8	Meade County	SD	Chris L. Cammack	2006	420
78 6/8	14 7/8	14 7/8	6 5/8	6 4/8	11 3/8	Routt County	CO	Mark S. Peffer	2007	420
78 6/8	14 7/8	14 6/8	6 3/8	6 3/8	9 1/8	Humboldt County	NV	G. Todd Brooks	2008	420
*78 6/8	14 7/8	15 1/8	6 6/8	6 5/8	9 6/8	Chouteau County	MT	Don Dvoroznak	2009	420
78 4/8	16 0/8	15 7/8	6 0/8	6 2/8	11 4/8	Chaves County	NM	Dr. D. A. Henbest	1957	457
78 4/8	15 1/8	14 7/8	6 5/8	6 5/8	10 0/8	Mountrail County	ND	Bennie J. Burtts	1967	457
78 4/8	14 4/8	14 1/8	6 3/8	6 2/8	10 6/8	Klamath County	OR	Paul D. Lewis	1976	457
78 4/8	13 7/8	14 0/8	6 4/8	6 2/8	8 2/8	Moffat County	CO	Mike Brezonick	1986	457
78 4/8	15 7/8	16 0/8	6 0/8	6 1/8	13 2/8	Coconino County	AZ	Randy McKusick	1988	457
78 4/8	14 1/8	14 6/8	7 0/8	7 1/8	10 2/8	Big Horn County	MT	Ron Johnson	1988	457
78 4/8	15 2/8	15 1/8	6 2/8	6 2/8	9 1/8	Lassen County	CA	Eddie L. Boyd	1989	457
78 4/8	15 0/8	15 2/8	6 3/8	6 2/8	11 0/8	Sweetwater County	WY	Kenneth Stinchcomb	1989	457
78 4/8	14 3/8	14 3/8	7 0/8	6 6/8	7 6/8	Sweetwater County	WY	Mark L. Preston	1989	457
78 4/8	15 3/8	15 0/8	6 2/8	6 4/8	10 3/8	Catron County	NM	Wade Finch	1990	457
78 4/8	16 2/8	16 3/8	5 6/8	5 6/8	14 5/8	Lea County	NM	Jim King	1990	457
78 4/8	15 3/8	15 1/8	6 4/8	6 4/8	9 5/8	Petroleum County	MT	Clark Jenner	1990	457
78 4/8	14 2/8	14 4/8	6 1/8	6 0/8	10 2/8	Medicine Hat	ALB	Dale Fournier	1990	457
78 4/8	14 5/8	14 5/8	7 1/8	7 3/8	11 0/8	Klamath County	OR	Chuck Woolley	1991	457
78 4/8	15 0/8	14 7/8	6 2/8	6 2/8	10 0/8	Millard County	UT	Nathan Lucas	1992	457
78 4/8	17 6/8	18 0/8	6 3/8	6 2/8	6 6/8	Las Animas County	CO	Darren Peacock	1992	457
78 4/8	13 7/8	13 7/8	6 7/8	7 0/8	10 1/8	Converse County	WY	Ronald D. Stoynoff	1992	457
78 4/8	15 4/8	15 0/8	6 3/8	6 3/8	14 6/8	Converse County	WY	Gary Lynn Fischer	1993	457
78 4/8	16 2/8	16 2/8	6 1/8	6 0/8	15 1/8	Moffat County	CO	Tim R. Hamilton	1993	457
78 4/8	15 0/8	15 0/8	5 4/8	5 4/8	9 6/8	Grant County	NM	Art Ramirez	1994	457
78 4/8	14 1/8	14 4/8	6 2/8	6 1/8	9 6/8	Custer County	SD	Jon Hardesty	1994	457

PRONGHORN

Minimum Score 67 | Continued

SCORE	LENGTH OF R HORN L	CIRCUMFERENCE R OF BASE L	INSIDE SPREAD	AREA	STATE/ PROVINCE	HUNTER'S NAME	DATE	RANK
78 4/8	15 0/8 14 7/8	6 7/8 6 6/8	9 3/8	Albany County	WY	Todd Fugate	1995	457
78 4/8	15 3/8 15 6/8	6 3/8 6 2/8	14 0/8	Colfax County	NM	James F. Welles	1995	457
78 4/8	15 1/8 14 7/8	6 3/8 6 3/8	11 6/8	Carbon County	WY	Peeler G. Lacey, MD	1995	457
78 4/8	14 2/8 14 4/8	6 4/8 6 3/8	8 2/8	Campbell County	WY	Randy Springborn	1995	457
78 4/8	15 4/8 15 7/8	6 1/8 6 2/8	11 2/8	Socorro County	NM	William Schultz	1996	457
78 4/8	15 6/8 15 6/8	6 0/8 6 0/8	8 7/8	Socorro County	NM	Archie J. Nesbitt	1997	457
78 4/8	16 2/8 16 3/8	6 2/8 6 2/8	10 4/8	Blaine County	MT	Corey Halvorson	2000	457
78 4/8	14 0/8 14 0/8	6 4/8 6 4/8	12 3/8	Big Horn County	WY	Dave Justmann	2000	457
78 4/8	15 0/8 15 0/8	6 2/8 6 2/8	8 0/8	Lake County	OR	Robert A. Rosales	2000	457
78 4/8	15 0/8 15 0/8	6 1/8 6 3/8	12 0/8	Sweetwater County	WY	Paul D. Kauchich	2001	457
78 4/8	15 2/8 15 2/8	6 2/8 6 3/8	15 0/8	Sweetwater County	WY	Wade Ferguson	2001	457
78 4/8	14 7/8 14 6/8	6 5/8 6 4/8	13 7/8	Big Horn County	WY	Dave Moss	2001	457
78 4/8	15 6/8 15 1/8	6 5/8 6 5/8	10 6/8	Fremont County	WY	Walter Phillips	2004	457
78 4/8	15 0/8 15 0/8	7 0/8 6 7/8	11 2/8	Perkins County	SD	Troy Hanson	2004	457
78 4/8	14 6/8 15 0/8	6 1/8 6 1/8	9 5/8	Coconino County	AZ	Kyle Wells	2005	457
*78 4/8	14 5/8 14 5/8	6 4/8 6 1/8	9 7/8	Campbell County	WY	Michael Peddie	2005	457
*78 4/8	14 4/8 14 6/8	6 6/8 6 5/8	8 4/8	Dawson County	MT	Wade Brilz	2005	457
78 4/8	15 0/8 14 7/8	6 3/8 6 5/8	7 5/8	Owyhee County	ID	Erik Jacobs	2006	457
78 4/8	14 2/8 13 7/8	7 0/8 7 1/8	9 4/8	Carbon County	WY	Zach Herold	2006	457
78 4/8	14 4/8 15 0/8	6 5/8 6 6/8	10 3/8	Campbell County	WY	Jeff A. Bennett	2006	457
*78 4/8	15 1/8 16 0/8	6 1/8 6 1/8	11 4/8	Moffat County	CO	David Iverson	2007	457
78 4/8	15 3/8 15 1/8	6 1/8 6 2/8	13 7/8	Socorro County	NM	Russ Richardson	2007	457
78 4/8	15 6/8 16 2/8	6 0/8 6 4/8	10 0/8	Jackson County	CO	Eugene Ray	2008	457
78 4/8	15 1/8 15 1/8	6 0/8 6 1/8	10 1/8	Carbon County	WY	Solomon Griffith	2008	457
*78 4/8	14 5/8 14 5/8	6 4/8 6 2/8	13 2/8	Washakie County	WY	Jose L. Sanchez	2008	457
78 4/8	14 5/8 14 5/8	6 2/8 6 1/8	12 3/8	Beaver County	UT	Jay C. Hansen	2009	457
78 2/8	17 3/8 17 1/8	5 5/8 5 6/8	14 6/8	Guadalupe County	NM	James L. Henry	1961	504
78 2/8	15 2/8 15 0/8	6 2/8 6 1/8	10 6/8	Wheatland County	MT	Phil Reno	1981	504
78 2/8	16 1/8 16 1/8	6 2/8 6 1/8	6 2/8	Moffat County	CO	Dan Liccardi	1982	504
78 2/8	15 2/8 15 7/8	5 7/8 5 7/8	7 3/8	Moffat County	CO	Ralph L. Albright	1985	504
78 2/8	14 3/8 14 4/8	6 1/8 6 1/8	11 3/8	Cochise County	AZ	Michael John Bylina	1985	504
78 2/8	13 7/8 14 0/8	6 2/8 6 2/8	12 6/8	Sweetwater County	WY	Tom Domson	1986	504
78 2/8	15 7/8 15 7/8	5 7/8 5 6/8	12 2/8	Washoe County	NV	Robert Jenney	1988	504
78 2/8	16 0/8 16 4/8	6 1/8 6 1/8	5 0/8	Klamath County	OR	Chuck Warner	1989	504
78 2/8	16 1/8 15 7/8	6 2/8 6 2/8	13 1/8	Coconino County	AZ	Randy McKusick	1989	504
78 2/8	15 0/8 15 2/8	6 0/8 6 0/8	10 2/8	Socorro County	NM	Glenn W. Isler	1990	504
78 2/8	14 0/8 14 1/8	6 2/8 6 1/8	9 0/8	Socorro County	NM	Mike Van Wormer	1990	504
78 2/8	13 6/8 13 7/8	6 5/8 6 4/8	8 7/8	Natrona County	WY	Jack Conner	1990	504
78 2/8	16 2/8 15 2/8	6 7/8 6 6/8	11 0/8	Sweetwater County	WY	Mark Olson	1991	504
78 2/8	15 6/8 15 5/8	5 7/8 6 0/8	13 5/8	Wayne County	UT	Shane Daley	1991	504
78 2/8	15 0/8 15 2/8	6 7/8 6 7/8	9 2/8	Natrona County	WY	Rene Suda	1991	504
78 2/8	15 0/8 15 3/8	6 1/8 6 0/8	11 2/8	Yavapai County	AZ	Van M. Clark	1992	504
78 2/8	15 1/8 15 2/8	6 3/8 6 3/8	10 2/8	Converse County	WY	Kevin W. Schmieg	1992	504
78 2/8	16 7/8 16 4/8	6 5/8 6 5/8	9 1/8	Box Butte County	NE	Michael L. Dietrich	1993	504
78 2/8	16 1/8 16 0/8	6 2/8 6 3/8	6 7/8	Rio Grande County	CO	Todd R. Slade	1995	504
78 2/8	15 2/8 15 2/8	6 3/8 6 3/8	10 0/8	Yavapai County	AZ	Kendall R. Adair	1995	504
78 2/8	14 5/8 14 4/8	6 0/8 6 0/8	11 0/8	Natrona County	WY	Don Meyer	1996	504
78 2/8	14 5/8 14 4/8	6 3/8 6 3/8	8 4/8	Twin Falls County	ID	Louis W. Wasniewski	1997	504
78 2/8	13 0/8 13 1/8	7 1/8 7 4/8	9 5/8	Moffat County	CO	David L. Skiff	1997	504
78 2/8	16 2/8 16 2/8	5 6/8 5 6/8	8 0/8	Yavapai County	AZ	Cindi Richardson	1997	504
78 2/8	14 4/8 16 3/8	6 2/8 6 3/8	9 2/8	Socorro County	NM	David A. Little	1998	504
78 2/8	15 4/8 15 4/8	6 1/8 6 0/8	8 1/8	Moffat County	CO	Randal Poundstone	1998	504
78 2/8	15 5/8 15 4/8	6 3/8 6 4/8	8 4/8	Uintah County	UT	Cory Callahan	1999	504
78 2/8	15 3/8 15 3/8	6 3/8 6 3/8	12 5/8	Lewis & Clark County	MT	Clinton Brown	2000	504
78 2/8	14 6/8 14 6/8	6 2/8 6 3/8	9 5/8	Jenner	ALB	James Worth	2000	504
78 2/8	15 7/8 16 1/8	6 0/8 6 0/8	8 7/8	Nye County	NV	Robert McKinnis	2001	504
78 2/8	14 1/8 14 0/8	6 5/8 6 4/8	11 5/8	Converse County	WY	Tim Donnelly	2001	504
78 2/8	15 4/8 15 4/8	6 1/8 6 0/8	10 5/8	Pershing County	NV	Joe L. Maslach	2002	504
78 2/8	15 3/8 15 5/8	5 6/8 5 6/8	12 6/8	Carbon County	WY	Eugene T. Fleming	2003	504
78 2/8	14 7/8 15 0/8	6 4/8 6 5/8	10 3/8	Rosebud County	MT	Neil Hamilton	2003	504
78 2/8	14 0/8 14 0/8	6 6/8 6 6/8	9 5/8	Humboldt County	NV	Bill Diehl	2004	504
78 2/8	14 5/8 14 4/8	6 3/8 6 1/8	11 2/8	Las Animas County	CO	Scott Burns	2004	504
*78 2/8	15 0/8 14 7/8	6 6/8 6 5/8	10 5/8	Harding County	SD	Don Massa	2005	504
78 2/8	15 3/8 15 5/8	6 4/8 6 2/8	12 0/8	Crook County	WY	Don Scofield	2005	504
78 2/8	15 4/8 15 4/8	6 0/8 5 7/8	9 6/8	Fallon County	MT	Joe Ness	2006	504
*78 2/8	15 3/8 14 4/8	6 6/8 6 6/8	10 6/8	Washoe County	NV	David Hoover	2007	504
78 2/8	14 0/8 13 5/8	6 2/8 6 2/8	7 3/8	Custer County	MT	Jeffrey M. Benjamin	2008	504
78 2/8	15 2/8 15 2/8	6 5/8 6 5/8	12 7/8	Las Animas County	CO	Jennifer C. Baudino	2009	504
78 0/8	15 5/8 15 1/8	6 2/8 6 2/8	18 2/8	Sweetwater County	WY	Don Dvoroznak	1976	546
78 0/8	15 0/8 14 7/8	6 3/8 6 2/8	11 5/8	Lemhi County	ID	Eugene J. Ottonello	1980	546
78 0/8	15 3/8 15 2/8	6 5/8 6 4/8	13 7/8	Moffat County	CO	Tony Seahorn	1980	546
78 0/8	15 1/8 15 2/8	6 2/8 6 1/8	11 3/8	Stanley County	SD	Rick Ray	1980	546
78 0/8	14 4/8 14 5/8	5 7/8 6 0/8	12 4/8	Stanley County	SD	George Hipple	1982	546
78 0/8	14 7/8 14 4/8	6 5/8 6 3/8	7 5/8	Fremont County	WY	Joe E. Nelson	1983	546
78 0/8	16 0/8 16 0/8	6 0/8 6 0/8	12 2/8	Washoe County	NV	Gregg Tanner	1986	546
78 0/8	14 1/8 14 2/8	6 5/8 6 5/8	13 2/8	Moffat County	CO	Calvin Farner	1986	546
78 0/8	14 5/8 14 4/8	5 6/8 6 0/8	10 1/8	Coconino County	AZ	Les Shelton	1990	546
78 0/8	14 6/8 14 1/8	6 7/8 7 1/8	11 6/8	Lincoln County	WY	Marlin Batista	1991	546
78 0/8	15 4/8 15 3/8	6 1/8 6 1/8	12 3/8	Saguache County	CO	Dan Bertalan	1991	546
78 0/8	14 3/8 14 4/8	6 3/8 6 3/8	14 3/8	Campbell County	WY	Mark A. Hoffman	1992	546
78 0/8	13 7/8 15 3/8	6 7/8 6 6/8	11 6/8	Yavapai County	AZ	Rick Kimball	1994	546
78 0/8	14 4/8 14 5/8	6 3/8 6 3/8	8 3/8	Converse County	WY	Rick L. Morley	1995	546
78 0/8	14 7/8 15 0/8	7 0/8 7 0/8	12 4/8	Baker County	OR	Michael D. Towne	1997	546
78 0/8	15 7/8 15 3/8	6 2/8 6 2/8	7 6/8	Yavapai County	AZ	Duane Russell Richardson	1997	546
78 0/8	15 0/8 15 0/8	6 4/8 6 4/8	9 6/8	Moffat County	CO	Bob Black	1997	546
78 0/8	14 6/8 14 6/8	6 1/8 6 0/8	8 6/8	Lassen County	CA	Ray Bailey	1997	546
78 0/8	13 2/8 13 2/8	6 6/8 6 6/8	10 3/8	Big Horn County	WY	Charlotte Moss	1998	546
78 0/8	15 4/8 15 5/8	6 2/8 6 2/8	11 2/8	Jeff Davis County	TX	Whit Smith	1999	546
78 0/8	14 5/8 14 5/8	6 3/8 6 3/8	11 3/8	Rio Blanco County	CO	Jeffrey D. McDonald	2000	546
78 0/8	13 4/8 13 4/8	6 3/8 6 3/8	12 5/8	Sweetwater County	WY	Harold F. Stinchcomb	2000	546
78 0/8	15 1/8 15 3/8	6 4/8 6 5/8	9 5/8	Yavapai County	AZ	Phillip C. Dalrymple	2000	546
78 0/8	14 5/8 15 0/8	6 2/8 6 2/8	11 7/8	Wheatland County	MT	Phil Kendall	2000	546
78 0/8	14 1/8 14 1/8	6 4/8 6 3/8	11 2/8	Tide Lake	ALB	Kevin Stewart	2001	546
78 0/8	15 6/8 15 7/8	7 0/8 6 6/8	11 2/8	Klamath County	OR	John Mackey	2002	546
78 0/8	14 7/8 15 7/8	6 2/8 6 1/8	10 1/8	Meade County	SD	William J. Bushong	2002	546

815

PRONGHORN

Minimum Score 67 — Continued

SCORE	LENGTH OF R HORN L	CIRCUMFERENCE R OF BASE L	INSIDE SPREAD	AREA	STATE/ PROVINCE	HUNTER'S NAME	DATE	RANK
78 0/8	15 3/8 15 3/8	6 2/8 6 2/8	9 7/8	Lake County	OR	Bill Wheat	2004	546
78 0/8	14 2/8 14 4/8	6 4/8 6 2/8	9 3/8	Modoc County	CA	Craig C. Fritz	2004	546
78 0/8	14 2/8 14 2/8	6 0/8 6 1/8	7 1/8	Powder River County	MT	Rick Simonson	2004	546
78 0/8	14 4/8 13 7/8	6 6/8 6 6/8	10 4/8	Colfax County	NM	David L. Skiff	2005	546
78 0/8	15 1/8 15 1/8	6 2/8 6 1/8	8 3/8	Tooele County	UT	Robby Weber	2005	546
78 0/8	14 1/8 14 0/8	6 2/8 6 2/8	7 5/8	Powder River County	MT	Terry Krahn	2005	546
78 0/8	14 2/8 14 3/8	6 6/8 6 7/8	10 2/8	Natrona County	WY	Thomas G. Nelson	2005	546
78 0/8	14 4/8 14 6/8	6 4/8 6 5/8	11 6/8	Rosebud County	MT	Kevin Brewer	2006	546
78 0/8	13 4/8 13 5/8	6 4/8 6 3/8	6 0/8	Hudspeth County	TX	Marc Bartoskewitz	2006	546
*78 0/8	15 4/8 15 7/8	5 7/8 6 0/8	13 1/8	Humboldt County	NV	Richard Genseal	2007	546
78 0/8	14 0/8 14 1/8	6 3/8 6 4/8	10 5/8	Guadalupe County	NM	Juaquin B. Sanchez	2007	546
78 0/8	15 3/8 15 2/8	5 7/8 6 1/8	9 5/8	Moffat County	CO	Dean W. Burke	2007	546
78 0/8	15 3/8 14 4/8	6 3/8 6 2/8	9 4/8	Converse County	WY	Thompson Bruegger	2007	546
78 0/8	15 1/8 14 6/8	6 2/8 6 2/8	12 3/8	Converse County	WY	Kevin Kaczmarek	2007	546
78 0/8	15 4/8 15 3/8	6 2/8 6 0/8	16 0/8	Cherry County	NE	Reggie Hochstein	2007	546
*78 0/8	14 5/8 14 6/8	6 2/8 6 1/8	8 7/8	Johnson County	WY	Gary Bessler	2008	546
78 0/8	14 1/8 14 0/8	6 6/8 6 6/8	11 4/8	Humboldt County	NV	Carla Pierson	2009	546
*78 0/8	15 0/8 15 1/8	6 3/8 6 2/8	9 2/8	Millard County	UT	Jeremy Black	2009	546
*78 0/8	14 2/8 14 2/8	6 2/8 6 1/8	10 0/8	Converse County	WY	Thomas E. Day	2009	546
78 0/8	15 6/8 15 6/8	6 2/8 6 2/8	9 2/8	Moffat County	CO	Glenn Thurston	2010	546
*78 0/8	14 7/8 14 2/8	6 7/8 6 7/8	9 2/8	Campbell County	WY	Shaun R. Ehrhard	2010	546
77 6/8	15 4/8 15 4/8	6 2/8 6 1/8	11 5/8	McKinley County	NM	Lee Burnett	1975	594
77 6/8	15 7/8 15 0/8	6 0/8 5 6/8	10 4/8	Lincoln County	CO	Steve Winkelman	1978	594
77 6/8	14 3/8 14 1/8	6 5/8 6 5/8	6 0/8	Moffat County	CO	Phil Hughes	1983	594
77 6/8	14 5/8 15 0/8	6 4/8 6 5/8	9 0/8	Converse County	WY	Ed Toelken	1988	594
77 6/8	14 0/8 14 0/8	7 0/8 6 5/8	12 1/8	Navajo County	AZ	Pat Nichols	1989	594
77 6/8	15 6/8 15 6/8	5 7/8 5 6/8	13 2/8	Powder River County	MT	Bob Carlson	1989	594
77 6/8	14 1/8 14 5/8	7 1/8 7 1/8	12 5/8	Musselshell County	MT	Wayne Muth	1990	594
77 6/8	14 7/8 14 7/8	6 1/8 6 1/8	10 2/8	Williams County	ND	Jeff Syverson	1990	594
77 6/8	13 1/8 13 4/8	6 6/8 6 7/8	7 5/8	Big Horn County	WY	Terry A. Long	1990	594
77 6/8	15 0/8 15 0/8	6 2/8 6 1/8	8 5/8	Fremont County	WY	Gary Laya	1991	594
77 6/8	15 7/8 15 6/8	6 2/8 6 2/8	12 7/8	Harney County	OR	Michael J. Kaiser	1991	594
77 6/8	14 7/8 15 0/8	6 1/8 6 1/8	10 7/8	Millard County	UT	Dave Scott	1992	594
77 6/8	14 7/8 14 6/8	5 7/8 5 6/8	11 6/8	Millard County	UT	Jeanie Clements	1992	594
77 6/8	14 0/8 14 0/8	6 5/8 6 3/8	9 0/8	Hot Springs County	WY	Larry Dickerson	1992	594
77 6/8	14 3/8 14 3/8	6 4/8 6 3/8	8 2/8	McKenzie County	ND	Don G. Scofield	1992	594
77 6/8	14 6/8 14 3/8	6 2/8 6 2/8	13 3/8	Yavapai County	AZ	Josiah Scott	1994	594
77 6/8	14 3/8 14 4/8	6 1/8 6 1/8	9 7/8	Billings County	ND	Jeff Lafferre	1994	594
77 6/8	15 2/8 15 3/8	5 7/8 5 7/8	13 2/8	Medicine Hat	ALB	Paul Unger	1994	594
77 6/8	15 7/8 14 7/8	5 6/8 5 6/8	7 5/8	Hudspeth County	TX	Ernest M. Elbert, Jr.	1994	594
77 6/8	14 7/8 14 7/8	6 3/8 6 3/8	12 7/8	Rio Blanco County	CO	Ray Richardson	1997	594
77 6/8	14 7/8 15 2/8	6 5/8 6 5/8	10 7/8	Golden Valley County	MT	John Ohmer	1997	594
77 6/8	14 1/8 14 2/8	6 5/8 6 5/8	10 1/8	Harding County	SD	Henry Loving	1997	594
77 6/8	16 0/8 16 2/8	5 6/8 5 6/8	10 0/8	Yavapai County	AZ	Gregg Murray	1998	594
77 6/8	15 3/8 15 1/8	6 6/8 6 6/8	10 1/8	Daggett County	UT	Louis W. Wasniewski	2000	594
77 6/8	15 3/8 15 5/8	6 0/8 6 0/8	9 5/8	Sweetwater County	WY	Randy Downs	2000	594
77 6/8	15 0/8 15 1/8	6 2/8 6 2/8	11 3/8	Duchesne County	UT	Chris Moore	2000	594
77 6/8	14 2/8 16 2/8	6 2/8 6 2/8	8 3/8	Rio Blanco County	CO	Loyd D. Pinckard	2001	594
77 6/8	16 1/8 16 3/8	6 2/8 6 1/8	13 1/8	Washakie County	WY	R. Cade Powell	2001	594
77 6/8	15 2/8 14 7/8	6 5/8 6 5/8	10 1/8	Uintah County	UT	Monte Mecham	2001	594
77 6/8	15 5/8 15 5/8	5 7/8 5 7/8	8 3/8	Campbell County	WY	Eric F. Efird	2001	594
77 6/8	15 0/8 14 6/8	6 4/8 6 2/8	11 7/8	Converse County	WY	Jeff Fitts	2001	594
77 6/8	14 4/8 14 4/8	6 4/8 6 3/8	11 1/8	Chouteau County	MT	Steve Herman	2001	594
77 6/8	16 1/8 16 1/8	6 0/8 6 0/8	9 3/8	Hanna	ALB	Douglas Erickson	2001	594
77 6/8	15 1/8 15 0/8	6 2/8 5 7/8	7 6/8	Jackson County	CO	Mark Johnson	2002	594
77 6/8	13 5/8 13 5/8	6 0/8 5 7/8	8 0/8	Rosebud County	MT	Tim Clarin	2002	594
77 6/8	14 0/8 14 2/8	6 6/8 6 4/8	9 3/8	Washoe County	NV	Tom Enewold	2003	594
77 6/8	15 0/8 14 6/8	6 2/8 6 2/8	7 1/8	Humboldt County	NV	Bart Williams	2003	594
77 6/8	15 5/8 15 4/8	5 7/8 6 0/8	10 6/8	Elko County	NV	Joan Holland	2003	594
77 6/8	15 7/8 16 3/8	6 1/8 6 0/8	12 2/8	Socorro County	NM	Wayne Ortland	2005	594
77 6/8	15 0/8 15 2/8	6 5/8 6 4/8	12 2/8	Powder River County	MT	Jeff Gavne	2005	594
77 6/8	14 2/8 15 0/8	6 0/8 6 0/8	9 2/8	Meade County	SD	Kim Magnussen	2005	594
77 6/8	15 0/8 14 6/8	6 3/8 6 2/8	13 2/8	Campbell County	WY	Kellen Smith	2005	594
77 6/8	15 0/8 15 0/8	6 3/8 6 0/8	9 3/8	Sweetwater County	WY	Neil Thagard	2006	594
77 6/8	14 7/8 15 0/8	6 4/8 6 4/8	6 4/8	Fremont County	WY	Gary Laya	2006	594
77 6/8	12 6/8 13 0/8	6 2/8 6 3/8	11 0/8	Twin Falls County	ID	Storm McKague	2006	594
77 6/8	14 0/8 13 7/8	6 4/8 6 2/8	11 4/8	Natrona County	WY	Gus Congemi	2008	594
77 6/8	14 5/8 14 5/8	6 2/8 6 2/8	10 3/8	Natrona County	WY	Steve Schulz	2008	594
77 6/8	14 3/8 14 0/8	7 2/8 7 1/8	9 1/8	Natrona County	WY	N. Guy Eastman	2010	594
77 4/8	15 1/8 15 1/8	6 0/8 6 0/8	8 3/8	Washoe County	NV	Christian J. Coleman	1979	642
77 4/8	15 1/8 15 1/8	6 1/8 6 2/8	13 6/8	Butte County	ID	Ron Johnson	1979	642
77 4/8	15 7/8 16 1/8	5 7/8 5 7/8	12 0/8	Carbon County	WY	Doug Cringan	1983	642
77 4/8	14 7/8 14 5/8	6 1/8 6 2/8	9 2/8	Graham County	AZ	Scott Kellner	1984	642
77 4/8	16 0/8 16 0/8	6 4/8 6 2/8	12 5/8	Washoe County	NV	James Mason	1985	642
77 4/8	14 0/8 14 4/8	6 2/8 6 2/8	11 5/8	Sweetwater County	WY	Dean Simmons	1987	642
77 4/8	15 4/8 15 1/8	6 1/8 6 1/8	12 4/8	McKenzie County	ND	Scott Borchert	1987	642
77 4/8	14 5/8 14 5/8	6 4/8 6 3/8	8 1/8	Moffat County	CO	Robert W. Wilkerson	1988	642
77 4/8	16 6/8 16 0/8	6 2/8 6 3/8	13 1/8	Yavapai County	AZ	Jay Dee Shaw	1988	642
77 4/8	14 7/8 14 7/8	6 2/8 6 2/8	10 6/8	Golden Valley County	ND	Terry Buechler	1988	642
77 4/8	15 4/8 15 2/8	6 4/8 6 3/8	9 6/8	Yavapai County	AZ	Robert M. Dryden	1989	642
77 4/8	14 3/8 14 4/8	6 3/8 6 3/8	15 0/8	Campbell County	WY	Michael H. Albers	1989	642
77 4/8	16 0/8 16 5/8	6 0/8 6 0/8	10 1/8	Sioux County	NE	Lane Ostendorf	1990	642
77 4/8	14 7/8 14 6/8	6 4/8 6 4/8	8 7/8	Moffat County	CO	Tim Atwater	1991	642
77 4/8	16 2/8 15 4/8	6 3/8 6 3/8	9 2/8	Fremont County	WY	Gary L. Hinaman	1992	642
77 4/8	14 7/8 15 4/8	6 3/8 6 3/8	10 6/8	Duchesne County	UT	Cindy Labrum	1992	642
77 4/8	15 6/8 15 6/8	6 1/8 6 0/8	14 1/8	Lincoln County	WY	Allen D. Sellers	1992	642
77 4/8	16 4/8 15 5/8	6 3/8 6 1/8	10 0/8	Carbon County	WY	Zack Koch	1993	642
77 4/8	13 7/8 14 1/8	6 5/8 6 5/8	12 6/8	Lake County	OR	Raymon L. Johnson	1993	642
77 4/8	14 0/8 14 2/8	6 3/8 6 2/8	10 5/8	Chaves County	NM	Brandon Griffith	1994	642
77 4/8	15 1/8 15 2/8	6 1/8 6 1/8	9 4/8	Lincoln County	WY	Rocky Rollins	1994	642
77 4/8	13 7/8 13 7/8	7 1/8 7 0/8	10 6/8	Moffat County	CO	Michael Schirer	1995	642
77 4/8	14 5/8 14 4/8	6 2/8 6 2/8	8 7/8	Malheur County	OR	Ken Barstad	1995	642
77 4/8	15 2/8 15 1/8	6 2/8 6 2/8	11 6/8	Lincoln County	NM	Rick Pope	1996	642
77 4/8	15 3/8 14 0/8	6 3/8 6 3/8	11 4/8	Yavapai County	AZ	Daniel A. Kasprzyk	1996	642
77 4/8	14 6/8 14 4/8	6 6/8 6 6/8	12 0/8	Big Horn County	WY	Tim Kindred	1996	642

PRONGHORN

Minimum Score 67 — Continued

SCORE	LENGTH OF R HORN L	CIRCUMFERENCE R OF BASE L	INSIDE SPREAD	AREA	STATE/ PROVINCE	HUNTER'S NAME	DATE	RANK
77 4/8	14 3/8 14 3/8	6 5/8 6 5/8	10 7/8	Rosebud County	MT	David William Bieber	1997	642
77 4/8	16 0/8 16 0/8	6 0/8 6 0/8	10 3/8	Billings County	ND	Harold Hugelen	1999	642
77 4/8	15 4/8 15 5/8	6 0/8 6 4/8	5 4/8	Manyberries	ALB	Gary Gillett	2000	642
77 4/8	13 6/8 14 1/8	6 1/8 6 2/8	8 6/8	Platte County	WY	Josh Albers	2002	642
77 4/8	14 5/8 14 7/8	6 1/8 6 1/8	10 5/8	Jenner	ALB	Kyle Sinclair-Smith	2003	642
77 4/8	16 4/8 16 4/8	6 2/8 6 2/8	8 1/8	Fergus County	MT	Jerry Knerr	2003	642
77 4/8	13 7/8 13 5/8	6 4/8 6 5/8	14 4/8	Laramie County	WY	Patrick J. Buscher	2003	642
77 4/8	15 2/8 15 6/8	6 2/8 6 2/8	9 2/8	Carbon County	WY	Dwight Crump	2004	642
77 4/8	14 3/8 14 4/8	6 5/8 6 5/8	12 2/8	Haakon County	SD	Kent Lewis	2004	642
77 4/8	14 4/8 14 4/8	6 5/8 6 5/8	7 6/8	Campbell County	WY	Nathan Perleberg	2004	642
77 4/8	14 7/8 14 5/8	6 4/8 6 3/8	10 3/8	Brooks	ALB	William Tittle	2004	642
77 4/8	15 3/8 15 1/8	5 7/8 5 5/8	12 0/8	Sweetwater County	WY	Margaret L. Brundidge	2006	642
77 4/8	16 0/8 15 7/8	5 7/8 5 7/8	8 5/8	Lea County	NM	Brandon Ray	2006	642
77 4/8	15 3/8 15 2/8	6 4/8 6 2/8	10 2/8	Milk River	ALB	Wade Aebli	2007	642
77 4/8	13 5/8 13 1/8	7 1/8 6 7/8	9 6/8	Chouteau County	MT	Jason Widaman	2008	642
77 4/8	15 2/8 15 2/8	6 0/8 6 0/8	12 5/8	Sweetwater County	WY	Shawn Yeager	2008	642
77 4/8	14 7/8 14 7/8	6 1/8 6 1/8	9 0/8	Brooks	ALB	Doug Field	2008	642
*77 4/8	16 2/8 15 7/8	6 0/8 5 6/8	10 1/8	Emery County	UT	Steven E. Sheehy	2009	642
*77 4/8	14 6/8 14 4/8	5 6/8 5 5/8	11 4/8	Carbon County	WY	Doug Aikin	2009	642
77 4/8	13 6/8 13 6/8	6 3/8 6 2/8	12 2/8	Sublette County	WY	RaShea Simmons	2009	642
*77 4/8	14 0/8 14 1/8	6 4/8 6 4/8	11 3/8	Park County	CO	Robert Feeney	2010	642
77 4/8	15 7/8 15 7/8	5 7/8 5 6/8	10 7/8	Yavapai County	AZ	Rocky Gange	2010	642
77 2/8	16 3/8 16 4/8	6 0/8 6 0/8	10 0/8	Lincoln County	NM	Charles L. Hughes	1960	690
77 2/8	15 0/8 15 1/8	5 7/8 5 7/8	9 0/8	Treasure County	MT	Tom Grunhuvd	1975	690
77 2/8	15 4/8 15 2/8	6 1/8 5 1/8	10 4/8	Yavapai County	AZ	Tim Pender	1978	690
77 2/8	14 6/8 15 1/8	6 2/8 6 0/8	12 1/8	Sweetwater County	WY	William Dolenc	1978	690
77 2/8	15 1/8 15 1/8	6 5/8 6 3/8	8 7/8	Moffat County	CO	Tom States	1981	690
77 2/8	15 6/8 15 4/8	6 1/8 6 0/8	14 4/8	Moffat County	CO	Mike Brust	1982	690
77 2/8	14 0/8 14 2/8	6 7/8 6 6/8	14 0/8	Sweetwater County	WY	David L. Price	1983	690
77 2/8	14 4/8 14 3/8	6 0/8 6 0/8	8 7/8	Mesa County	CO	Bob Black	1983	690
77 2/8	16 3/8 16 3/8	6 3/8 6 3/8	14 1/8	Bowman County	ND	Donald C. Hestekin	1983	690
77 2/8	14 4/8 14 4/8	6 3/8 6 1/8	10 6/8	Custer County	MT	Joe Good	1984	690
77 2/8	14 0/8 14 0/8	6 0/8 6 0/8	14 6/8	Garfield County	MT	Paul Schafer	1984	690
77 2/8	14 5/8 14 5/8	6 1/8 6 1/8	10 3/8	Moffat County	CO	David Gunning	1987	690
77 2/8	15 5/8 15 3/8	6 2/8 6 1/8	9 3/8	Rosebud County	MT	Dr. Dale Schlehuber	1987	690
77 2/8	15 0/8 15 2/8	6 1/8 6 0/8	11 1/8	Rosebud County	MT	Gene Welle	1988	690
77 2/8	16 0/8 16 4/8	5 5/8 5 5/8	7 7/8	Humboldt County	NV	Clayton Keister	1989	690
77 2/8	15 7/8 16 0/8	6 2/8 6 1/8	8 6/8	Natrona County	WY	Kenneth D. Sundquist	1989	690
77 2/8	15 0/8 15 0/8	6 2/8 6 3/8	10 7/8	Golden Valley County	ND	Terry Buechler	1989	690
77 2/8	14 0/8 14 0/8	6 6/8 6 5/8	10 6/8	Lassen County	CA	Danny Westerberg	1990	690
77 2/8	15 1/8 15 1/8	5 6/8 5 5/8	8 6/8	Harney County	OR	Donald R. Paulsen	1990	690
77 2/8	15 6/8 15 0/8	6 3/8 6 2/8	10 4/8	Yavapai County	AZ	James N. Schmidt	1991	690
77 2/8	14 2/8 14 2/8	6 1/8 6 0/8	10 2/8	Harney County	OR	Ralph Burt	1991	690
77 2/8	14 5/8 14 5/8	7 2/8 7 2/8	10 3/8	Radville	SAS	Ken Paslawski	1991	690
77 2/8	14 2/8 14 2/8	6 5/8 6 6/8	11 3/8	Sweetwater County	WY	Brad Hugh Jacobs	1992	690
77 2/8	15 2/8 14 7/8	6 1/8 6 1/8	9 4/8	Uintah County	UT	Daniel B. Hammons	1993	690
77 2/8	14 3/8 14 3/8	6 2/8 6 1/8	9 6/8	Powder River County	MT	John Martinson	1993	690
77 2/8	15 2/8 15 2/8	6 5/8 6 4/8	10 2/8	Sweetwater County	WY	Mike Barrett	1994	690
77 2/8	12 2/8 12 5/8	6 5/8 6 4/8	8 2/8	Box Elder County	UT	Verl Hanchett	1994	690
77 2/8	13 7/8 14 0/8	6 2/8 6 3/8	10 7/8	Custer County	ID	Jim Marek	1994	690
77 2/8	15 3/8 15 1/8	6 2/8 6 3/8	13 0/8	Converse County	WY	Dan Schneewind	1994	690
77 2/8	15 2/8 15 3/8	6 2/8 6 2/8	12 0/8	Coconino County	AZ	Bob Kyhn	1995	690
77 2/8	14 6/8 14 5/8	6 2/8 5 7/8	7 6/8	Saguache County	CO	Lance Thonhoff	1999	690
77 2/8	14 4/8 14 4/8	6 1/8 6 1/8	14 2/8	Sweetwater County	WY	Larry Cross	1999	690
77 2/8	15 3/8 15 4/8	6 0/8 6 0/8	10 6/8	Washoe County	NV	Tim Naveran	2000	690
77 2/8	16 4/8 16 1/8	5 6/8 5 6/8	9 4/8	Yavapai County	AZ	Daniel H. Esteves	2001	690
77 2/8	15 1/8 15 2/8	6 0/8 5 6/8	9 1/8	Blaine County	MT	Tom M. Benson	2002	690
77 2/8	15 0/8 14 5/8	6 7/8 6 5/8	11 5/8	Fergus County	MT	Dave McLendon	2002	690
77 2/8	15 2/8 15 1/8	6 5/8 6 5/8	10 3/8	Crook County	WY	Derek Matuszewski	2003	690
77 2/8	15 0/8 15 2/8	6 0/8 5 7/8	8 5/8	Park County	WY	Jason Stafford	2003	690
77 2/8	15 3/8 15 2/8	6 7/8 6 6/8	9 6/8	Converse County	WY	Pete Woeck	2004	690
77 2/8	15 3/8 15 3/8	5 6/8 5 5/8	12 7/8	Carbon County	WY	Clay J. Evans	2005	690
77 2/8	15 6/8 16 2/8	6 1/8 6 0/8	8 0/8	Johnson County	WY	Craig Grant	2005	690
77 2/8	14 3/8 14 7/8	6 1/8 6 0/8	7 7/8	Navajo County	AZ	George Ovalle	2005	690
77 2/8	14 4/8 14 3/8	6 3/8 6 4/8	11 3/8	Routt County	CO	Mark S. Peffer	2006	690
77 2/8	14 4/8 14 7/8	6 1/8 6 1/8	9 5/8	Twin Falls County	ID	Doug Ramsey	2006	690
77 2/8	15 4/8 15 3/8	6 2/8 6 0/8	9 1/8	Slope County	ND	Joey Wadeson	2006	690
77 2/8	14 7/8 14 5/8	6 0/8 5 7/8	10 7/8	Carbon County	WY	Jason A. Swanson	2007	690
77 2/8	15 6/8 15 5/8	6 3/8 6 0/8	13 0/8	Converse County	WY	Jordan Hypes	2007	690
*77 2/8	16 2/8 16 0/8	5 6/8 5 6/8	7 2/8	McCone County	MT	Derek Werner	2008	690
77 2/8	15 1/8 15 0/8	6 4/8 6 3/8	9 1/8	Harding County	SD	Craig Schmidt	2008	690
*77 2/8	14 5/8 14 4/8	6 3/8 6 4/8	6 0/8	Carbon County	UT	Kelle M. Adams	2008	690
*77 2/8	14 0/8 13 7/8	6 5/8 6 4/8	10 6/8	Mohave County	AZ	Eduardo Esteves	2009	690
*77 2/8	13 3/8 15 4/8	6 5/8 6 4/8	9 7/8	Carbon County	WY	Todd Gentzler	2009	690
*77 2/8	14 3/8 14 1/8	6 3/8 6 3/8	16 1/8	Golden Valley County	ND	Patrick Hurt	2009	690
77 0/8	15 4/8 15 4/8	5 5/8 5 5/8	16 7/8	Dunn County	ND	Allan Lynch	1975	743
77 0/8	14 1/8 15 2/8	6 2/8 6 0/8	9 4/8	Billings County	ND	Jonathan Zieman	1984	743
77 0/8	14 4/8 14 5/8	6 2/8 6 1/8	11 1/8	Rosebud County	MT	Steve Cutright	1987	743
77 0/8	15 2/8 15 1/8	6 0/8 6 0/8	10 5/8	Garfield County	MT	Daryl P. Hinther	1987	743
77 0/8	14 7/8 14 7/8	6 0/8 6 1/8	7 3/8	Sweetwater County	WY	Rod Schmidt	1988	743
77 0/8	15 2/8 15 0/8	6 1/8 6 2/8	8 5/8	Moffat County	CO	Louis Dodaro	1988	743
77 0/8	14 0/8 14 0/8	6 3/8 6 2/8	11 0/8	Cochise County	AZ	Brian Davis	1988	743
77 0/8	14 4/8 15 1/8	5 7/8 5 7/8	11 3/8	Park County	WY	Rocky Deromedi	1988	743
77 0/8	14 3/8 14 3/8	5 7/8 5 7/8	8 0/8	Bare Creek	ALB	Paul Ronald Goodberry	1988	743
77 0/8	15 1/8 14 6/8	5 7/8 5 6/8	11 4/8	Washoe County	NV	Jeffrey L. Dodge	1990	743
77 0/8	14 4/8 14 2/8	6 0/8 6 1/8	10 1/8	Mesa County	CO	Darren K. Peacock	1990	743
77 0/8	15 6/8 15 4/8	6 1/8 6 1/8	16 4/8	Coconino County	AZ	Kevin Shackleford	1990	743
77 0/8	14 7/8 15 2/8	6 0/8 5 7/8	10 6/8	Millard County	UT	Vee F. Hanks	1990	743
77 0/8	14 4/8 14 4/8	6 3/8 6 3/8	8 4/8	Humboldt County	NV	Mike Fillmore	1992	743
77 0/8	14 7/8 14 4/8	6 0/8 5 7/8	7 4/8	Carbon County	WY	Scott Penman	1992	743
77 0/8	15 0/8 14 7/8	6 2/8 6 2/8	9 3/8	Carbon County	WY	Rod Schmidt	1992	743
77 0/8	15 1/8 15 5/8	6 4/8 6 2/8	10 1/8	Box Butte County	NE	Tim Christophersen	1992	743
77 0/8	15 1/8 15 1/8	6 2/8 6 1/8	9 6/8	Hudspeth County	TX	William R. Fair	1992	743
77 0/8	16 1/8 16 4/8	5 4/8 5 5/8	10 4/8	Socorro County	NM	Ronald C. Zengerly	1993	743
77 0/8	14 2/8 14 2/8	6 1/8 6 0/8	12 2/8	Converse County	WY	John S. Miller	1993	743

817

PRONGHORN

Minimum Score 67 — Continued

SCORE	LENGTH OF R HORN L	CIRCUMFERENCE R OF BASE L	INSIDE SPREAD	AREA	STATE/ PROVINCE	HUNTER'S NAME	DATE	RANK
77 0/8	14 3/8 14 6/8	6 1/8 6 4/8	7 7/8	Washoe County	NV	Randy Tognoni	1994	743
77 0/8	15 0/8 15 2/8	5 7/8 5 6/8	11 1/8	Millard County	UT	Don Bates	1995	743
77 0/8	14 7/8 15 1/8	6 1/8 6 1/8	10 3/8	Larimer County	CO	Fred M. Velasquez	1995	743
77 0/8	14 4/8 14 4/8	5 6/8 5 6/8	9 5/8	Catron County	NM	Carl D. Bradford	1995	743
77 0/8	15 0/8 15 1/8	6 6/8 6 6/8	10 4/8	Campbell County	WY	Mark D. Sesvold	1995	743
77 0/8	13 7/8 14 0/8	6 6/8 6 4/8	8 7/8	Millard County	UT	Cory S. Christensen	1996	743
77 0/8	14 5/8 15 0/8	6 0/8 6 0/8	11 0/8	Lincoln County	WY	Harold "Buck" Wood	1997	743
77 0/8	14 5/8 14 5/8	6 5/8 6 5/8	11 5/8	Converse County	WY	Ron Grant	1997	743
77 0/8	15 4/8 15 7/8	6 0/8 6 0/8	10 5/8	Tooele County	UT	Russell J. Draper	1999	743
77 0/8	13 1/8 13 4/8	6 5/8 6 5/8	7 3/8	Weld County	CO	H. Mike Palmer	1999	743
77 0/8	17 0/8 16 5/8	6 0/8 6 0/8	8 2/8	Humboldt County	NV	Rick Lund	2001	743
77 0/8	15 7/8 16 4/8	5 7/8 5 6/8	9 6/8	Washington County	CO	Matt Wagner	2001	743
77 0/8	15 3/8 14 6/8	6 4/8 6 3/8	12 3/8	Phillips County	MT	Chris Clevenger	2001	743
77 0/8	16 2/8 17 0/8	6 0/8 6 6/8	14 1/8	Perkins County	SD	Aaron Ambur	2002	743
77 0/8	15 4/8 15 4/8	5 6/8 5 5/8	7 3/8	Buffalo	ALB	John Soderberg	2003	743
77 0/8	15 0/8 15 0/8	6 4/8 6 4/8	13 1/8	Coconino County	AZ	Woody Kazlo	2004	743
77 0/8	14 0/8 13 5/8	6 2/8 6 1/8	10 2/8	Petroleum County	MT	Dylan Tripp	2004	743
77 0/8	15 1/8 15 0/8	6 2/8 6 3/8	10 5/8	Natrona County	WY	Jason A. Swanson	2005	743
77 0/8	15 5/8 15 4/8	5 7/8 6 0/8	9 1/8	Harding County	SD	Bruce A. Sanburn	2005	743
77 0/8	14 1/8 14 1/8	6 2/8 6 2/8	10 1/8	Jones County	SD	Jade Frederick	2006	743
77 0/8	15 0/8 15 1/8	6 2/8 6 1/8	7 4/8	Pershing County	NV	Dyrk Eddie	2007	743
77 0/8	14 0/8 13 6/8	6 7/8 7 0/8	8 1/8	Blaine County	ID	Craig Phillips	2007	743
77 0/8	14 2/8 14 2/8	6 3/8 6 3/8	11 5/8	Sweetwater County	WY	William Jensen	2007	743
77 0/8	14 1/8 15 2/8	5 7/8 5 6/8	10 1/8	Meade County	SD	Ron Schauer	2007	743
77 0/8	15 0/8 15 2/8	6 4/8 6 3/8	13 6/8	Natrona County	WY	Steve Schulz	2007	743
77 0/8	14 5/8 14 5/8	5 6/8 5 6/8	9 3/8	Madison County	MT	Eric Huff	2008	743
77 0/8	14 6/8 14 6/8	6 5/8 6 5/8	4 6/8	Coconino County	AZ	Perry V. Dunn	2008	743
*77 0/8	14 3/8 14 0/8	6 5/8 6 5/8	10 3/8	Brooks	ALB	George R. Garman	2008	743
*77 0/8	13 2/8 13 3/8	7 0/8 6 7/8	9 6/8	Natrona County	WY	Tom Ossa	2008	743
77 0/8	15 0/8 15 0/8	6 2/8 6 2/8	10 7/8	Butte County	SD	Mark D. Schuh	2008	743
77 0/8	15 7/8 15 4/8	6 2/8 6 0/8	8 7/8	Juab County	UT	Bryan Durfee	2009	743
77 0/8	15 3/8 15 6/8	6 4/8 6 3/8	10 1/8	Elko County	NV	Jack Smith	2010	743
76 6/8	14 1/8 14 5/8	6 2/8 6 2/8	14 2/8	Fremont County	WY	Jim Puthoff	1969	795
76 6/8	14 6/8 14 6/8	6 2/8 6 3/8	10 5/8	Fremont County	WY	Ron D. Evitt	1982	795
76 6/8	14 6/8 14 6/8	6 1/8 6 1/8	8 6/8	Converse County	WY	Vito Palazzolo	1984	795
76 6/8	14 2/8 14 2/8	6 1/8 6 0/8	12 4/8	Campbell County	WY	Tony Janssen	1984	795
76 6/8	15 5/8 15 7/8	5 7/8 5 7/8	10 2/8	Butte County	ID	Champ Church	1986	795
76 6/8	14 0/8 13 6/8	5 5/8 5 6/8	13 4/8	San Miguel County	CO	Stuart Howard	1986	795
76 6/8	16 7/8 17 1/8	5 7/8 6 0/8	10 6/8	Humboldt County	NV	Lance R. Wodke	1987	795
76 6/8	15 0/8 15 0/8	6 1/8 6 0/8	10 3/8	Dunn County	ND	Ron Bachmeier	1987	795
76 6/8	15 5/8 15 5/8	6 3/8 6 4/8	9 2/8	Fremont County	WY	Dan Chappell	1990	795
76 6/8	14 1/8 14 0/8	7 0/8 6 7/8	14 1/8	Natrona County	WY	Brian L. Wagner	1990	795
76 6/8	14 3/8 13 6/8	6 0/8 6 1/8	13 7/8	Jackson County	CO	Dominic Florian	1990	795
76 6/8	16 2/8 15 7/8	5 7/8 5 7/8	10 7/8	Santa Cruz County	AZ	Jerry A. Clarno	1990	795
76 6/8	15 1/8 14 5/8	6 2/8 6 1/8	8 2/8	Moffat County	CO	Roderick E. Nutter	1991	795
76 6/8	13 5/8 14 1/8	6 5/8 6 5/8	8 3/8	Natrona County	WY	Gary L. Miller	1991	795
76 6/8	14 5/8 15 2/8	6 0/8 6 0/8	10 4/8	Carbon County	WY	Marc D. Hallowell	1991	795
76 6/8	15 1/8 15 1/8	6 5/8 6 4/8	11 7/8	Grant County	NM	John Trewern	1992	795
76 6/8	15 6/8 15 6/8	5 5/8 5 5/8	12 3/8	Park County	CO	William E. Karnish, Jr.	1992	795
76 6/8	14 0/8 14 0/8	6 4/8 6 3/8	9 4/8	Moffat County	CO	Doy K. Curtis	1993	795
76 6/8	12 4/8 12 2/8	6 7/8 6 6/8	9 1/8	Moffat County	CO	James L. Tatro	1993	795
76 6/8	14 3/8 14 3/8	5 7/8 5 7/8	6 7/8	Converse County	WY	James C. Gates	1993	795
76 6/8	15 4/8 15 4/8	5 4/8 5 6/8	11 0/8	Washoe County	NV	Ed Madsen	1994	795
76 6/8	15 3/8 15 0/8	6 2/8 6 4/8	7 4/8	Twin Falls County	ID	Cory Brodine	1994	795
76 6/8	15 4/8 14 3/8	7 0/8 6 7/8	10 2/8	Weld County	CO	Alan J. Douthit	1995	795
76 6/8	14 4/8 14 7/8	6 3/8 6 1/8	14 4/8	Jackson County	CO	Matt Archuleta	1996	795
76 6/8	16 2/8 16 0/8	6 5/8 6 5/8	7 2/8	Socorro County	NM	Doug Aikin	1996	795
76 6/8	14 3/8 14 6/8	6 5/8 6 3/8	10 1/8	Campbell County	WY	Dennis D. Klemick	1996	795
76 6/8	14 5/8 14 6/8	6 7/8 6 6/8	11 4/8	Elmore County	ID	Steven B. Alderman	1996	795
76 6/8	14 4/8 14 2/8	6 1/8 6 0/8	8 6/8	Goshen County	WY	Rodney L. Garringer	1999	795
76 6/8	14 6/8 15 0/8	5 7/8 5 7/8	7 6/8	Coconino County	AZ	Gary Dyer	1999	795
76 6/8	14 2/8 14 4/8	6 5/8 6 3/8	9 1/8	Carbon County	WY	Ty Crawford	2002	795
76 6/8	13 6/8 13 5/8	6 3/8 6 3/8	9 3/8	Weld County	CO	Casey S. Lauer	2002	795
76 6/8	15 1/8 14 7/8	6 4/8 6 4/8	10 1/8	Custer County	MT	Eric Siegfried	2003	795
76 6/8	15 6/8 16 2/8	6 0/8 5 7/8	14 3/8	Owyhee County	ID	Dee Desaro	2004	795
76 6/8	13 0/8 13 4/8	6 5/8 6 6/8	11 0/8	Carbon County	WY	Shawn Wagner	2004	795
76 6/8	14 3/8 14 2/8	6 2/8 6 1/8	11 2/8	Weston County	WY	Jeremy P. Terhune	2004	795
*76 6/8	13 2/8 13 4/8	6 5/8 6 4/8	18 2/8	Fremont County	WY	Jacob Arima	2005	795
76 6/8	13 6/8 13 3/8	6 2/8 6 3/8	8 2/8	Elmore County	ID	Carl W. Claycomb	2005	795
76 6/8	13 6/8 14 0/8	7 0/8 7 0/8	9 6/8	Johnson County	WY	Don Mealey	2005	795
76 6/8	13 2/8 13 4/8	6 5/8 6 5/8	11 5/8	Powder River County	MT	Kerry A. White	2006	795
76 6/8	14 6/8 14 5/8	6 2/8 6 2/8	5 1/8	Powder River County	MT	Susan K. Barrett	2006	795
76 6/8	14 5/8 14 5/8	6 3/8 6 2/8	14 1/8	Sweetwater County	WY	William Haines	2006	795
76 6/8	15 2/8 15 3/8	6 2/8 6 2/8	9 5/8	Moffat County	CO	T. J. Thrasher	2007	795
*76 6/8	14 2/8 14 4/8	5 6/8 5 6/8	6 0/8	Weld County	CO	Mike Kattawar, Jr.	2007	795
76 6/8	14 2/8 14 3/8	6 3/8 6 2/8	8 4/8	Yavapai County	AZ	Chip Leivas	2007	795
76 6/8	15 4/8 15 6/8	6 6/8 6 5/8	8 5/8	Twin Falls County	ID	Doug Hughes	2007	795
76 6/8	13 6/8 14 0/8	6 4/8 6 4/8	10 5/8	Sioux County	NE	Daniel Hejl	2007	795
*76 6/8	14 1/8 13 7/8	6 6/8 6 4/8	8 4/8	Lemhi County	ID	Rockie L. Walker	2008	795
*76 6/8	15 5/8 15 2/8	6 1/8 6 2/8	10 4/8	Meade County	SD	Lance Steiger	2008	795
76 6/8	14 3/8 14 4/8	6 7/8 7 0/8	9 0/8	Converse County	WY	Gary L. Fischer	2010	795
76 6/8	15 6/8 15 7/8	6 1/8 6 1/8	12 0/8	Brooks	ALB	Joel A. Johnson	2010	795
76 4/8	14 5/8 14 6/8	5 6/8 5 7/8	10 3/8	Lemhi County	ID	Roger W. Atwood	1977	845
76 4/8	14 6/8 14 6/8	6 1/8 6 1/8	12 3/8	Custer County	ID	Juilan Salutregui	1983	845
76 4/8	14 1/8 14 1/8	6 0/8 6 0/8	7 4/8	Converse County	WY	Scott Ames	1983	845
76 4/8	16 0/8 15 7/8	6 2/8 6 2/8	9 2/8	McKinley County	NM	Patrick J. Sharp	1984	845
76 4/8	15 1/8 14 6/8	6 0/8 6 0/8	11 3/8	Carter County	MT	Jamie Byrne	1984	845
76 4/8	13 6/8 13 6/8	6 6/8 6 6/8	10 3/8	Carbon County	WY	Jerry DeCroo	1985	845
76 4/8	15 2/8 15 2/8	6 1/8 6 1/8	12 1/8	Washoe County	NV	Ken Tavener	1986	845
76 4/8	15 4/8 15 4/8	6 2/8 6 3/8	12 6/8	Coconino County	AZ	Gary D. Davis	1986	845
76 4/8	15 2/8 15 3/8	6 0/8 6 0/8	8 1/8	Clark County	SD	Scott Lindgren	1988	845
76 4/8	13 2/8 12 7/8	6 0/8 6 0/8	11 3/8	Sceptre	SAS	Ron Todd	1988	845
76 4/8	16 0/8 16 1/8	6 0/8 6 0/8	14 4/8	Humboldt County	NV	Dwight Schuh	1989	845
76 4/8	14 1/8 13 7/8	6 3/8 6 7/8	9 5/8	Coconino County	AZ	Dennis Pugh	1990	845
76 4/8	14 2/8 14 7/8	6 1/8 6 2/8	13 5/8	Yavapai County	AZ	Josiah Scott	1990	845

818

PRONGHORN

Minimum Score 67   Continued

SCORE	LENGTH OF R HORN L	CIRCUMFERENCE R OF BASE L	INSIDE SPREAD	AREA	STATE/ PROVINCE	HUNTER'S NAME	DATE	RANK
76 4/8	14 2/8 14 4/8	5 7/8 6 0/8	10 2/8	Carter County	MT	Donald Travis	1990	845
76 4/8	15 1/8 15 0/8	6 1/8 6 1/8	10 4/8	Fergus County	MT	Dwight Martin	1990	845
76 4/8	15 5/8 15 5/8	6 0/8 6 0/8	8 2/8	Beaverhead County	MT	Neil L. Jacobson	1990	845
76 4/8	15 0/8 15 1/8	6 4/8 6 3/8	11 7/8	Thomas County	NE	Andrew L. Glidden	1990	845
76 4/8	15 4/8 15 4/8	6 0/8 5 7/8	11 0/8	Delta County	CO	Donald E. Liddell	1991	845
76 4/8	14 3/8 14 3/8	6 4/8 6 3/8	11 5/8	Sweetwater County	WY	Randy Downs	1991	845
76 4/8	14 7/8 14 7/8	6 1/8 6 1/8	11 6/8	Fremont County	WY	Gary Laya	1992	845
76 4/8	13 5/8 13 3/8	5 7/8 5 7/8	9 0/8	Converse County	WY	G. Allen Sink	1992	845
76 4/8	14 1/8 14 1/8	6 3/8 6 3/8	10 6/8	Humboldt County	NV	Kyle Swanson	1993	845
76 4/8	15 3/8 15 1/8	5 7/8 5 7/8	15 6/8	Yavapai County	AZ	Patrick M. Kirby	1993	845
76 4/8	14 5/8 14 6/8	6 3/8 6 1/8	8 6/8	Stanley County	SD	Chris Hipple	1993	845
76 4/8	14 0/8 13 6/8	6 2/8 6 0/8	7 6/8	Converse County	WY	Dan Baker	1993	845
76 4/8	14 2/8 14 4/8	6 6/8 6 2/8	10 2/8	Wallace County	KS	Kent Hensley	1993	845
76 4/8	15 3/8 15 5/8	5 6/8 5 6/8	13 2/8	Socorro County	NM	Glenn W. Isler	1994	845
76 4/8	14 5/8 14 3/8	6 6/8 6 6/8	10 6/8	Meagher County	MT	D. "Mitch" Kottas	1994	845
76 4/8	14 0/8 14 1/8	6 3/8 6 3/8	8 2/8	Albany County	WY	Leonard Sheaffer	1994	845
76 4/8	15 4/8 15 1/8	6 1/8 6 2/8	8 7/8	Coconino County	AZ	David Shiflet	1994	845
76 4/8	15 0/8 14 5/8	6 1/8 6 1/8	10 5/8	Larimer County	CO	Mark N. Johnson	1995	845
76 4/8	13 3/8 13 3/8	6 5/8 6 5/8	12 5/8	Big Horn County	WY	Dan Moss	1995	845
76 4/8	15 2/8 14 7/8	6 2/8 6 0/8	8 7/8	Bernalillo County	NM	Brian D. Shaw	1995	845
76 4/8	13 5/8 13 5/8	6 5/8 6 6/8	13 1/8	Colfax County	NM	Patrick Lovato	1995	845
76 4/8	14 3/8 14 0/8	5 7/8 5 7/8	10 4/8	Jackson County	CO	Bruce Ayers	1995	845
76 4/8	15 6/8 16 0/8	6 0/8 5 7/8	9 6/8	Rosebud County	MT	Jack Ferguson	1996	845
76 4/8	14 6/8 15 0/8	6 2/8 6 2/8	10 3/8	Roosevelt County	NM	Justin Jackson	1997	845
76 4/8	15 6/8 15 3/8	5 6/8 6 0/8	8 0/8	Moffat County	CO	Robert G. Ronsse	1997	845
76 4/8	15 3/8 15 3/8	5 7/8 5 7/8	11 7/8	Catron County	NM	William King	1998	845
76 4/8	15 0/8 14 7/8	6 5/8 6 5/8	10 2/8	Weld County	CO	Cindy Rothrock	1998	845
76 4/8	14 0/8 14 0/8	6 3/8 6 3/8	12 6/8	Moffat County	CO	Jim Leqve	1999	845
76 4/8	14 0/8 14 0/8	6 4/8 6 2/8	10 5/8	Moffat County	CO	Doug Gilley	1999	845
76 4/8	14 3/8 14 2/8	6 7/8 6 6/8	9 5/8	Crook County	OR	Tony Partipilo	1999	845
76 4/8	13 4/8 15 5/8	6 5/8 6 7/8	9 7/8	Toole County	MT	Jay Hould	2000	845
76 4/8	15 5/8 15 7/8	5 6/8 6 0/8	11 6/8	Brooks	ALB	Joseph C. Krejci	2001	845
76 4/8	14 0/8 14 0/8	6 1/8 6 1/8	12 7/8	Grant County	NM	Greg Schleusner	2002	845
76 4/8	14 0/8 14 1/8	6 5/8 6 5/8	9 4/8	Perkins County	SD	Troy Hanson	2002	845
76 4/8	15 3/8 15 1/8	6 3/8 6 4/8	8 0/8	Hyde County	SD	Dillon Baloun	2002	845
76 4/8	14 5/8 14 5/8	6 4/8 6 7/8	12 3/8	Sweetwater County	WY	Clay M. Carter	2003	845
76 4/8	14 3/8 14 5/8	5 7/8 5 7/8	9 7/8	Sierra County	NM	John D. "Jack" Frost	2003	845
76 4/8	14 1/8 14 2/8	6 3/8 6 4/8	9 4/8	Big Horn County	WY	Mike Barrett	2004	845
76 4/8	14 4/8 14 4/8	6 2/8 6 2/8	11 2/8	Campbell County	WY	Robert Long	2004	845
76 4/8	14 5/8 14 4/8	6 0/8 6 0/8	9 5/8	Harding County	SD	James D. Herring	2005	845
76 4/8	15 2/8 15 1/8	6 0/8 6 0/8	10 4/8	Albany County	WY	Mike Yancey	2006	845
76 4/8	13 5/8 13 2/8	6 5/8 6 5/8	8 2/8	Natrona County	WY	Steve Schulz	2006	845
76 4/8	14 3/8 14 2/8	6 5/8 6 5/8	13 0/8	Gunnison County	CO	Dean Derby	2007	845
76 4/8	15 3/8 15 4/8	5 4/8 5 5/8	11 4/8	Cherry County	NE	Kyle Hochstein	2007	845
*76 4/8	15 2/8 15 2/8	6 1/8 6 3/8	13 2/8	Natrona County	WY	Scott Lopez	2007	845
76 4/8	14 4/8 14 4/8	6 2/8 6 2/8	10 7/8	Meade County	SD	Bill Bushong	2007	845
76 4/8	14 1/8 14 1/8	6 5/8 6 5/8	8 5/8	Powder River County	MT	Carl Fritz	2007	845
*76 4/8	15 1/8 15 1/8	6 1/8 6 2/8	12 6/8	Sheridan County	WY	Curtis Walters	2007	845
76 4/8	14 4/8 14 5/8	5 7/8 5 7/8	11 5/8	Gallatin County	MT	Bob Morton	2007	845
76 4/8	13 7/8 13 6/8	6 0/8 6 0/8	10 0/8	Natrona County	WY	Eric Anderson	2008	845
76 4/8	15 3/8 15 0/8	6 6/8 6 4/8	12 0/8	Weld County	CO	Frank Piacentino	2008	845
*76 4/8	14 7/8 14 6/8	6 4/8 6 4/8	8 2/8	Lincoln County	WY	Brett Ritter	2008	845
76 4/8	14 0/8 14 1/8	6 6/8 6 6/8	13 0/8	Johnson County	WY	Robert Swank	2008	845
76 4/8	15 6/8 15 5/8	6 1/8 6 0/8	12 0/8	Moffat County	CO	Eddie Maddox	2009	845
76 2/8	14 5/8 14 1/8	6 1/8 6 1/8	10 3/8	Citten	ND	Richard R. Chandler	1972	912
76 2/8	16 3/8 16 1/8	6 0/8 6 1/8	8 5/8	Weston County	WY	David M. Nahrgang	1980	912
76 2/8	14 7/8 14 6/8	5 5/8 5 6/8	8 6/8	Blaine County	ID	Champ Church	1980	912
76 2/8	14 1/8 14 2/8	6 4/8 6 2/8	10 6/8	Converse County	WY	Jack Cassidy	1980	912
76 2/8	13 6/8 14 1/8	6 2/8 6 2/8	8 5/8	Converse County	WY	Chris Cassidy	1980	912
76 2/8	14 3/8 14 3/8	5 6/8 5 7/8	9 2/8	Converse County	WY	Robert R. Vance	1981	912
76 2/8	16 0/8 15 6/8	5 7/8 6 1/8	11 4/8	Converse County	WY	Jack M. Conner	1981	912
76 2/8	14 6/8 14 6/8	6 3/8 6 3/8	11 1/8	Moffat County	CO	James Bowerman	1982	912
76 2/8	14 4/8 14 5/8	6 2/8 6 2/8	10 5/8	Sweetwater County	WY	Darrell H. Nations	1982	912
76 2/8	14 4/8 14 5/8	6 0/8 6 0/8	10 2/8	Taos County	NM	Galen G. Roumpf	1983	912
76 2/8	13 4/8 13 7/8	6 4/8 6 2/8	10 6/8	Wallace County	KS	Steve Rugg	1983	912
76 2/8	14 6/8 14 7/8	6 5/8 6 3/8	7 7/8	Sweetwater County	WY	Steve L. Rueck	1984	912
76 2/8	14 6/8 14 7/8	5 7/8 5 6/8	10 6/8	Eddy County	NM	Derek A. Tierney	1986	912
76 2/8	14 0/8 13 6/8	6 2/8 6 1/8	9 1/8	Converse County	WY	David Kugler	1987	912
76 2/8	15 2/8 15 2/8	6 4/8 6 4/8	10 4/8	Hettinger County	ND	Bill Clink	1988	912
76 2/8	14 3/8 14 7/8	6 5/8 6 4/8	11 2/8	Bowman County	ND	Craig Egeland	1988	912
76 2/8	15 2/8 15 2/8	5 7/8 5 7/8	11 3/8	Empress	ALB	Kenneth John Akkermans	1988	912
76 2/8	16 0/8 16 3/8	5 7/8 5 7/8	12 1/8	Lassen County	CA	Gary Bagnaschi	1989	912
76 2/8	15 0/8 15 0/8	5 7/8 5 7/8	11 1/8	Moffat County	CO	Robert M. Fromme	1990	912
76 2/8	13 4/8 13 6/8	7 3/8 7 2/8	9 3/8	Mountrail County	ND	Lonny G. Waggoner	1990	912
76 2/8	15 0/8 15 0/8	6 2/8 6 3/8	13 4/8	Harney County	OR	Trevin Webster	1990	912
76 2/8	15 2/8 15 1/8	6 0/8 6 0/8	9 5/8	Catron County	NM	Cary Cuba	1991	912
76 2/8	15 0/8 15 0/8	6 3/8 6 2/8	10 1/8	Sweetwater County	WY	William Metz	1991	912
76 2/8	13 5/8 13 5/8	6 5/8 6 5/8	8 4/8	Converse County	WY	William L. Randles	1991	912
76 2/8	14 7/8 14 4/8	6 1/8 6 2/8	9 2/8	Johnson County	WY	Joseph L. Ravis	1991	912
76 2/8	15 0/8 14 6/8	6 4/8 6 3/8	10 4/8	Box Butte County	NE	Myron R. Drumheller	1991	912
76 2/8	16 5/8 16 5/8	6 3/8 6 1/8	14 2/8	Lake County	OR	Robert Gentry	1992	912
76 2/8	15 0/8 15 1/8	6 2/8 6 2/8	9 3/8	Saguache County	CO	Gary W. Bohochik	1992	912
76 2/8	14 6/8 15 0/8	6 3/8 6 2/8	11 3/8	Weld County	CO	Mike Brooks	1994	912
76 2/8	15 6/8 15 4/8	6 1/8 6 1/8	10 1/8	Rio Blanco County	CO	Dave Holt	1994	912
76 2/8	15 6/8 14 5/8	6 3/8 6 2/8	9 4/8	Yavapai County	AZ	Henry Redondo Garcia	1994	912
76 2/8	14 6/8 14 4/8	6 0/8 6 1/8	9 6/8	Jackson County	CO	Bob Sanders	1994	912
76 2/8	16 1/8 16 4/8	5 5/8 5 5/8	8 0/8	White Pine County	NV	Denis Joiner	1995	912
76 2/8	15 3/8 15 2/8	6 2/8 6 2/8	11 7/8	Coconino County	AZ	Michael L. Campbell	1995	912
76 2/8	14 6/8 14 5/8	5 6/8 5 6/8	10 3/8	Petroleum County	MT	Craig Richardson	1995	912
76 2/8	15 5/8 16 2/8	6 1/8 6 0/8	11 7/8	Medicine Hat	ALB	Jim Osinchuk	1995	912
76 2/8	14 6/8 14 2/8	5 7/8 5 6/8	11 0/8	Routt County	CO	Cedar Beauregard	1996	912
76 2/8	14 6/8 14 7/8	6 2/8 6 1/8	7 6/8	Platte County	WY	Derek Long II	1998	912
76 2/8	14 6/8 15 0/8	5 6/8 5 6/8	9 5/8	Millard County	UT	Ron Christensen	2000	912
76 2/8	14 6/8 14 2/8	6 0/8 6 0/8	14 5/8	Coconino County	AZ	Scott Seeley	2000	912
76 2/8	15 1/8 15 1/8	6 1/8 6 1/8	8 7/8	Washakie County	WY	Brock Greek	2002	912

819

PRONGHORN

Minimum Score 67 Continued

SCORE	LENGTH OF R HORN L	CIRCUMFERENCE R OF BASE L	INSIDE SPREAD	AREA	STATE/ PROVINCE	HUNTER'S NAME	DATE	RANK
76 2/8	15 5/8 15 4/8	6 0/8 6 1/8	10 5/8	Yavapai County	AZ	Michael D. Wall	2002	912
76 2/8	15 7/8 15 6/8	6 1/8 6 2/8	9 1/8	Uintah County	UT	Jerry Reynolds	2003	912
*76 2/8	14 5/8 14 6/8	6 3/8 6 1/8	10 5/8	Moffat County	CO	Andrew P. Jacobi	2003	912
76 2/8	16 4/8 16 3/8	5 7/8 5 6/8	12 2/8	Elmore County	ID	Harry Knox	2003	912
76 2/8	15 0/8 14 5/8	6 2/8 6 0/8	13 6/8	Rio Blanco County	CO	Tim Stanosheck	2004	912
76 2/8	14 6/8 14 4/8	6 1/8 6 1/8	11 6/8	Las Animas County	CO	Fred Eichler	2004	912
76 2/8	14 3/8 14 3/8	6 2/8 6 2/8	8 7/8	Johnson County	WY	Pax Harness	2004	912
76 2/8	14 2/8 14 2/8	6 1/8 6 1/8	9 3/8	Niobrara County	WY	Rick Thaden	2004	912
76 2/8	15 3/8 15 5/8	6 4/8 6 4/8	8 0/8	Lemhi County	ID	Gary Gapp	2005	912
*76 2/8	14 4/8 14 4/8	5 4/8 5 5/8	11 0/8	Las Animas County	CO	Thomas Ruggles	2005	912
*76 2/8	15 3/8 15 1/8	6 4/8 6 1/8	10 2/8	Dawson County	MT	Heath Werner	2005	912
*76 2/8	15 6/8 15 4/8	6 1/8 6 1/8	15 4/8	Washakie County	WY	Rodney A. Salzman	2006	912
*76 2/8	15 4/8 15 2/8	6 0/8 6 0/8	9 2/8	Natrona County	WY	Jason Hamrick	2006	912
*76 2/8	15 0/8 15 0/8	5 5/8 5 6/8	10 7/8	Wayne County	UT	David E. Mitchell	2006	912
*76 2/8	14 3/8 14 2/8	6 0/8 6 1/8	7 1/8	Emery County	UT	Carl Sitterud	2006	912
76 2/8	16 5/8 16 2/8	6 5/8 6 3/8	10 2/8	Owyhee County	ID	Cody Cameron	2006	912
76 2/8	14 5/8 14 6/8	6 0/8 5 7/8	7 7/8	Beaverhead County	MT	Benjamin L. Ingwerson	2006	912
76 2/8	14 1/8 14 1/8	6 1/8 6 2/8	6 2/8	El Paso County	CO	John Quillen	2007	912
76 2/8	13 6/8 14 0/8	6 7/8 6 6/8	9 4/8	Carbon County	WY	Clay J. Evans	2007	912
*76 2/8	14 3/8 14 3/8	6 4/8 6 3/8	11 0/8	Powder River County	MT	Timothy Howell	2007	912
76 2/8	14 1/8 14 1/8	5 7/8 5 7/8	9 2/8	Goshen County	WY	Roland L. Kauffman	2007	912
*76 2/8	15 4/8 15 0/8	5 7/8 5 7/8	11 6/8	Sioux County	NE	Kerry Keane	2008	912
76 2/8	13 2/8 13 2/8	6 6/8 6 6/8	6 4/8	Natrona County	WY	Steve Schulz	2008	912
76 2/8	14 5/8 14 7/8	6 3/8 6 1/8	9 2/8	Perkins County	SD	Tony Nogy	2008	912
*76 2/8	13 5/8 14 0/8	6 2/8 6 1/8	8 1/8	Campbell County	WY	Clint Weier	2008	912
76 2/8	16 1/8 16 0/8	6 0/8 6 1/8	10 2/8	Converse County	WY	Sam Boyles	2009	912
76 2/8	15 2/8 15 2/8	6 0/8 6 0/8	7 4/8	Sweetwater County	WY	Gordon Tattersall	2009	912
76 2/8	15 7/8 16 0/8	6 1/8 6 1/8	15 1/8	Albany County	WY	Michael Kerckaert	2009	912
76 2/8	15 4/8 15 3/8	6 0/8 6 0/8	7 6/8	Kit Carson County	CO	Joshua Moberly	2009	912
76 2/8	14 5/8 14 6/8	6 2/8 6 3/8	10 1/8	Natrona County	WY	Don G. Scofield	2010	912
76 0/8	15 0/8 14 7/8	6 0/8 6 0/8	14 6/8	Mountrail County	ND	Wayne A. Metcalf	1972	983
76 0/8	14 5/8 14 5/8	6 2/8 6 4/8	13 4/8	Clark County	ID	Kerry Hillman	1977	983
76 0/8	14 7/8 14 3/8	5 6/8 6 1/8	10 0/8	Sweetwater County	WY	John Grady Lee	1983	983
76 0/8	14 2/8 14 2/8	6 1/8 6 1/8	9 3/8	Converse County	WY	Richard Rabe, Jr.	1985	983
76 0/8	14 4/8 14 3/8	6 0/8 6 1/8	9 7/8	Nye County	NV	Paul Campos	1988	983
76 0/8	14 0/8 14 1/8	6 0/8 6 0/8	8 7/8	Yavapai County	AZ	T. J. Baehre	1989	983
76 0/8	14 6/8 14 7/8	6 4/8 6 5/8	19 1/8	Colfax County	NM	Ron Serwa	1990	983
76 0/8	14 6/8 14 3/8	6 5/8 6 4/8	10 4/8	Sweetwater County	WY	Lori Kay Stinchcomb	1990	983
76 0/8	14 2/8 13 6/8	6 3/8 6 3/8	11 2/8	Campbell County	WY	James K. Keim	1990	983
76 0/8	15 4/8 15 2/8	6 0/8 5 7/8	12 2/8	Quay County	NM	Tommy C. Jones	1991	983
76 0/8	15 4/8 15 5/8	6 3/8 6 2/8	8 7/8	Milk River	ALB	Daniel Harder	1991	983
76 0/8	15 2/8 15 2/8	6 0/8 6 0/8	12 1/8	Morton County	ND	Gary Hanson	1991	983
76 0/8	14 2/8 14 1/8	6 3/8 6 2/8	9 5/8	Campbell County	WY	Doy K. Curtis	1991	983
76 0/8	15 4/8 15 6/8	5 4/8 5 3/8	13 7/8	Lake County	OR	Donald R. Pritchett	1992	983
76 0/8	13 5/8 13 5/8	6 5/8 6 4/8	9 6/8	Sweetwater County	WY	Justin Miller	1992	983
76 0/8	13 6/8 13 5/8	6 5/8 6 5/8	10 1/8	Converse County	WY	Melvin Wells	1992	983
76 0/8	15 0/8 15 1/8	5 7/8 5 4/8	9 7/8	Sioux County	NE	Jack F. Buckley	1992	983
76 0/8	14 3/8 14 4/8	6 0/8 6 0/8	8 2/8	Lincoln County	NV	Gary F. Bogner	1993	983
76 0/8	14 6/8 14 5/8	6 3/8 6 3/8	10 1/8	Moffat County	CO	David Buell	1993	983
76 0/8	13 5/8 13 3/8	6 4/8 6 2/8	8 3/8	Jefferson County	OR	Clinton J. Hall	1993	983
76 0/8	13 4/8 13 4/8	7 0/8 6 7/8	14 2/8	Big Horn County	WY	Jason Doumitt	1994	983
76 0/8	14 6/8 14 6/8	6 1/8 6 1/8	13 2/8	Moffat County	CO	Kelly Semple	1996	983
76 0/8	15 1/8 15 2/8	6 3/8 6 1/8	8 6/8	Natrona County	WY	Bradley Chamberlain	1996	983
76 0/8	15 6/8 15 4/8	5 6/8 5 5/8	11 1/8	Toole County	MT	Keith Miller	1996	983
76 0/8	13 1/8 13 0/8	6 4/8 6 5/8	9 3/8	Platte County	WY	Jerry Bowen	1996	983
76 0/8	15 0/8 15 0/8	6 1/8 6 0/8	12 7/8	Catron County	NM	Frank Argo	1997	983
76 0/8	13 7/8 14 0/8	6 4/8 6 5/8	11 1/8	Natrona County	WY	Richard Manchur	1997	983
76 0/8	14 6/8 14 5/8	6 5/8 6 4/8	10 4/8	Rosebud County	MT	Chuck Adams	1997	983
76 0/8	15 6/8 15 5/8	5 4/8 5 4/8	9 0/8	Yellowstone County	MT	Gary Lee Murphree	1999	983
76 0/8	15 5/8 15 4/8	5 7/8 6 0/8	9 5/8	Fergus County	MT	Jerry Knerr	1999	983
76 0/8	14 0/8 14 1/8	6 3/8 6 3/8	7 3/8	Natrona County	WY	Richard A. Hanson	1999	983
76 0/8	14 4/8 14 2/8	6 2/8 6 2/8	10 5/8	Catron County	NM	Mark McFarland	2000	983
76 0/8	14 3/8 14 4/8	6 2/8 6 2/8	8 7/8	Rio Blanco County	CO	Brent Armbruster	2001	983
76 0/8	15 1/8 15 1/8	6 1/8 6 0/8	10 1/8	Campbell County	WY	Ray N. Andersen	2001	983
76 0/8	15 3/8 15 2/8	6 3/8 6 1/8	9 2/8	Las Animas County	CO	Anthony B. Whiting III	2002	983
76 0/8	14 0/8 13 7/8	5 5/8 5 5/8	9 4/8	Apache County	AZ	Jess Burns	2002	983
76 0/8	15 1/8 15 1/8	6 2/8 6 2/8	9 7/8	Natrona County	WY	Alfred J. Gemrich	2002	983
*76 0/8	13 6/8 14 5/8	6 3/8 6 3/8	11 6/8	Moffat County	CO	Dave Holt	2003	983
76 0/8	15 4/8 15 4/8	5 6/8 5 6/8	9 1/8	Socorro County	NM	Anthony Caliger	2003	983
76 0/8	12 6/8 13 6/8	6 4/8 6 2/8	9 1/8	Sioux County	NE	Richard W. Waller	2003	983
76 0/8	14 5/8 14 5/8	6 4/8 6 3/8	12 5/8	Converse County	WY	Gene Mathias	2003	983
*76 0/8	14 2/8 14 4/8	5 6/8 5 6/8	8 4/8	Catron County	NM	Chris Green	2004	983
76 0/8	15 1/8 15 1/8	6 0/8 6 1/8	9 1/8	Redcliff	ALB	Leonard Verbaas	2004	983
76 0/8	15 1/8 15 0/8	5 7/8 5 7/8	9 2/8	Larimer County	CO	Brady Bradford	2005	983
76 0/8	15 0/8 15 0/8	6 1/8 6 1/8	8 0/8	Butte County	SD	Scott G. Ewest	2005	983
76 0/8	13 3/8 13 3/8	6 3/8 6 3/8	10 4/8	Powder River County	MT	Gary L. Magnus	2006	983
*76 0/8	16 1/8 15 7/8	6 0/8 5 7/8	10 4/8	Beaverhead County	MT	Gary D. Becker	2006	983
76 0/8	14 4/8 14 5/8	6 1/8 6 2/8	14 4/8	Deschutes County	OR	Paul Fiedorek	2006	983
76 0/8	14 0/8 14 7/8	6 3/8 6 3/8	6 3/8	Powder River County	MT	Sharon F. Noble	2006	983
76 0/8	15 1/8 14 5/8	6 4/8 6 2/8	10 7/8	Owyhee County	ID	Erik Jacobs	2007	983
76 0/8	13 1/8 13 1/8	7 2/8 7 2/8	9 2/8	Rio Blanco County	CO	Joe Richardson	2007	983
76 0/8	15 3/8 15 2/8	6 1/8 6 0/8	8 0/8	Bingham County	ID	Timothy A. Hyde	2007	983
76 0/8	15 0/8 15 4/8	5 6/8 5 6/8	11 1/8	Potter County	SD	Brandon Schardin	2007	983
76 0/8	16 2/8 16 0/8	6 1/8 6 1/8	7 2/8	Rosebud County	MT	Kris O'Bleness	2008	983
*76 0/8	14 4/8 14 1/8	6 1/8 5 7/8	9 3/8	Fremont County	WY	Nate Peckinpaugh	2009	983
76 0/8	14 3/8 14 4/8	6 5/8 6 3/8	10 2/8	Natrona County	WY	Dan Reeve	2009	983
76 0/8	13 6/8 13 5/8	6 2/8 6 2/8	9 5/8	Converse County	WY	Gary Tarver	2010	983
75 6/8	14 0/8 14 0/8	6 1/8 6 1/8	12 4/8	Sweetwater County	WY	Gene McFadden	1982	1040
75 6/8	15 2/8 14 6/8	5 7/8 5 7/8	11 1/8	Moffat County	CO	Judd Cooney	1982	1040
75 6/8	14 4/8 14 5/8	6 1/8 6 1/8	10 0/8	Natrona County	WY	Jack M. Conner	1982	1040
75 6/8	15 1/8 15 1/8	6 2/8 6 2/8	10 3/8	Converse County	WY	Lonny G. Herrick	1983	1040
75 6/8	15 0/8 15 0/8	5 7/8 5 6/8	14 2/8	Sweetwater County	WY	Marty Martin	1986	1040
75 6/8	14 1/8 14 0/8	6 2/8 6 2/8	10 4/8	Moffat County	CO	Tom Foss	1987	1040
75 6/8	14 2/8 15 2/8	6 6/8 6 6/8	15 2/8	Moffat County	CO	Randy Major/Frank Major	1988	1040
75 6/8	13 5/8 14 0/8	6 4/8 6 3/8	6 3/8	Carbon County	WY	David Wiltse	1988	1040

820

PRONGHORN

Minimum Score 67 — Continued

SCORE	LENGTH OF R HORN L	CIRCUMFERENCE R OF BASE L	INSIDE SPREAD	AREA	STATE/ PROVINCE	HUNTER'S NAME	DATE	RANK
75 6/8	15 0/8 15 1/8	5 5/8 5 5/8	9 1/8	Sublette County	WY	Ronell Skinner	1988	1040
75 6/8	15 7/8 15 4/8	6 1/8 6 1/8	9 7/8	Moffat County	CO	Brad Fort	1988	1040
75 6/8	13 5/8 13 5/8	6 0/8 6 1/8	11 7/8	Coconino County	AZ	Noel Harris	1989	1040
75 6/8	13 4/8 13 4/8	5 6/8 5 6/8	10 7/8	Converse County	WY	Kevin Peterson	1989	1040
75 6/8	14 6/8 14 5/8	6 0/8 5 7/8	9 2/8	Moffat County	CO	Joseph Schwartz	1990	1040
75 6/8	15 6/8 15 2/8	6 0/8 5 6/8	10 4/8	Elko County	NV	Paul J. Vietti	1990	1040
75 6/8	14 2/8 14 3/8	5 6/8 6 1/8	6 5/8	Carbon County	WY	Clarence E. Faber	1990	1040
75 6/8	13 6/8 13 3/8	6 1/8 6 0/8	12 4/8	Sublette County	WY	Mike Lamade	1990	1040
75 6/8	15 1/8 15 2/8	5 7/8 5 7/8	9 4/8	Millard County	UT	Dennis L. Shirley	1990	1040
75 6/8	15 2/8 15 3/8	6 1/8 6 1/8	12 4/8	Harney County	OR	Gary Nyden	1990	1040
75 6/8	13 6/8 13 7/8	6 3/8 6 4/8	10 4/8	Converse County	WY	Wayne Sanders	1990	1040
75 6/8	12 6/8 12 5/8	6 3/8 6 6/8	7 6/8	Harney County	OR	Eugene F. Martin	1990	1040
75 6/8	14 6/8 15 1/8	5 6/8 5 6/8	8 1/8	Lemhi County	ID	Ben Fahnholz	1991	1040
75 6/8	15 1/8 15 3/8	6 0/8 6 0/8	10 7/8	Yavapai County	AZ	Paul Fritzinger	1991	1040
75 6/8	15 4/8 15 4/8	5 7/8 5 6/8	10 1/8	Socorro County	NM	Mike Van Wormer	1992	1040
75 6/8	15 7/8 16 2/8	6 0/8 6 0/8	6 2/8	Carbon County	WY	Jeff Martin	1992	1040
75 6/8	14 0/8 13 7/8	6 6/8 6 5/8	10 4/8	Jenner	ALB	Carter Calliou	1992	1040
75 6/8	14 3/8 14 3/8	6 4/8 6 3/8	9 5/8	Fremont County	WY	Gary L. Hinaman	1993	1040
75 6/8	14 3/8 14 5/8	6 3/8 6 4/8	10 5/8	Hot Springs County	WY	Greg Lompart	1993	1040
75 6/8	14 7/8 14 7/8	6 2/8 6 3/8	11 0/8	Cheyenne County	NE	Matt Highby	1994	1040
75 6/8	14 7/8 15 2/8	6 4/8 6 4/8	8 5/8	Lake County	OR	Glen Bridgmon	1994	1040
75 6/8	14 6/8 14 3/8	6 2/8 6 2/8	11 0/8	Yavapai County	AZ	Herb Fisher	1995	1040
75 6/8	13 7/8 13 4/8	6 3/8 6 3/8	12 0/8	Campbell County	WY	Dave Hinton	1995	1040
75 6/8	13 3/8 13 3/8	6 5/8 6 4/8	8 2/8	Sweetwater County	WY	Roger Wintle	1996	1040
75 6/8	14 4/8 14 6/8	5 6/8 6 0/8	14 3/8	Weld County	CO	Kaylan Shaffer	1996	1040
75 6/8	13 1/8 13 2/8	6 4/8 6 6/8	7 4/8	Moffat County	CO	Timothy J. Schneider	1997	1040
75 6/8	14 6/8 14 5/8	5 4/8 5 4/8	8 2/8	Converse County	WY	Tim Connaughty	1997	1040
75 6/8	14 6/8 14 5/8	6 2/8 6 2/8	9 5/8	Campbell County	WY	Jim Dunigan	1998	1040
75 6/8	14 3/8 14 1/8	6 4/8 6 4/8	10 0/8	Natrona County	WY	Steven Zignorski	1999	1040
75 6/8	13 4/8 13 5/8	6 3/8 6 3/8	10 0/8	Converse County	WY	Lee Waltman	1999	1040
75 6/8	15 0/8 14 4/8	6 0/8 6 1/8	8 4/8	Lake County	OR	Kevin R. Irelan	2000	1040
75 6/8	14 3/8 14 4/8	6 1/8 6 2/8	9 2/8	Pershing County	NV	Andy Allen	2000	1040
75 6/8	13 3/8 13 6/8	6 6/8 6 6/8	11 4/8	Natrona County	WY	Gus Congemi	2000	1040
75 6/8	13 3/8 13 3/8	6 3/8 6 3/8	11 5/8	Musselshell County	MT	Richard M. Penn	2000	1040
75 6/8	15 2/8 15 2/8	5 5/8 5 5/8	10 6/8	Lake County	OR	Brian Charkowicz	2000	1040
75 6/8	15 7/8 15 7/8	5 3/8 5 2/8	12 5/8	Moffat County	CO	Gary Christoffersen	2000	1040
75 6/8	15 2/8 15 5/8	6 0/8 5 7/8	12 3/8	Manyberries	ALB	Tom Manley	2000	1040
75 6/8	13 3/8 13 5/8	6 2/8 6 1/8	10 7/8	Manyberries	ALB	Aaron Arnell	2000	1040
75 6/8	14 6/8 14 6/8	7 0/8 6 7/8	9 6/8	Washoe County	NV	Anthony L. Mudd	2002	1040
75 6/8	14 1/8 14 2/8	6 2/8 6 4/8	11 2/8	Lake County	OR	Mark Quant	2002	1040
75 6/8	15 0/8 15 0/8	6 3/8 6 0/8	7 3/8	Owyhee County	ID	Dave Heck	2002	1040
75 6/8	15 0/8 15 4/8	6 1/8 6 1/8	8 4/8	Weld County	CO	Christopher S. Gomes	2003	1040
75 6/8	15 2/8 15 2/8	6 1/8 6 0/8	11 5/8	Eddy County	NM	Scot Lambert	2003	1040
75 6/8	14 4/8 14 0/8	7 0/8 6 6/8	4 1/8	Big Horn County	WY	George Kamps	2003	1040
75 6/8	13 7/8 14 2/8	6 4/8 6 4/8	10 1/8	Crook County	WY	Don Scofield	2004	1040
75 6/8	15 1/8 14 7/8	6 1/8 6 0/8	10 7/8	Harding County	SD	Timothy J. Gallagher	2004	1040
75 6/8	14 1/8 14 0/8	6 1/8 6 0/8	10 4/8	Thomas County	KS	Gary Niblock	2005	1040
*75 6/8	13 0/8 13 0/8	6 5/8 6 4/8	13 0/8	Converse County	WY	Ty Foster	2006	1040
75 6/8	14 5/8 14 6/8	6 5/8 6 4/8	11 7/8	Rosebud County	MT	Thomas Jacobs	2006	1040
75 6/8	14 3/8 15 0/8	6 2/8 6 1/8	8 2/8	Converse County	WY	Jason P. Flies	2006	1040
*75 6/8	14 5/8 14 6/8	6 1/8 6 3/8	8 6/8	Johnson County	WY	David Bilotti	2006	1040
75 6/8	14 2/8 14 1/8	6 0/8 6 0/8	10 0/8	Natrona County	WY	Rich Kimball	2007	1040
75 6/8	15 3/8 15 3/8	6 1/8 6 2/8	10 2/8	Harding County	SD	Mark R. Hill	2007	1040
75 6/8	15 4/8 15 3/8	6 2/8 6 1/8	11 5/8	Golden Valley County	ND	Tom Schillo	2007	1040
75 6/8	14 0/8 14 2/8	6 1/8 6 1/8	6 7/8	Yavapai County	AZ	Blake Lanoue	2008	1040
75 6/8	12 7/8 13 4/8	6 3/8 6 5/8	10 0/8	Carbon County	WY	Jason A. Swanson	2008	1040
75 6/8	14 1/8 14 1/8	6 1/8 6 3/8	8 1/8	Owyhee County	ID	Erik I. Jacobs	2008	1040
75 6/8	14 3/8 14 3/8	6 3/8 6 2/8	11 4/8	Humboldt County	NV	Jason Pierson	2010	1040
75 4/8	12 1/8 12 2/8	5 7/8 6 0/8	8 2/8	Campbell County	WY	Dr. R. F. Helzerman	1960	1106
75 4/8	17 2/8 16 4/8	6 0/8 5 6/8	15 0/8	Guadalupe County	NM	M. K. Vance	1962	1106
75 4/8	14 3/8 14 2/8	6 0/8 6 2/8	12 6/8	McLean County	ND	Don Sorge	1970	1106
75 4/8	14 7/8 14 7/8	6 0/8 6 0/8	12 0/8	Williams County	ND	Terry L. Halgrimson	1970	1106
75 4/8	13 3/8 13 4/8	6 6/8 6 7/8	11 6/8	Converse County	WY	Richard L. Huber	1979	1106
75 4/8	15 3/8 15 2/8	5 6/8 5 6/8	12 5/8	Fergus County	MT	Don Davidson	1981	1106
75 4/8	14 5/8 14 7/8	6 2/8 6 2/8	9 6/8	Klamath County	OR	Larry E. Jones	1982	1106
75 4/8	16 0/8 16 0/8	6 0/8 5 7/8	11 0/8	Moffat County	CO	John R. Morris II	1983	1106
75 4/8	14 4/8 14 4/8	6 4/8 6 4/8	11 6/8	Coconino County	AZ	Gary Warnica	1983	1106
75 4/8	14 0/8 14 0/8	6 2/8 6 2/8	10 0/8	Powder River County	MT	Raleigh D. Buckmaster	1983	1106
75 4/8	16 2/8 16 2/8	6 0/8 6 0/8	12 0/8	Coconino County	AZ	Harry M. Weeks	1984	1106
75 4/8	14 4/8 14 0/8	6 4/8 6 4/8	12 1/8	Weld County	CO	Lorn Barnica	1984	1106
75 4/8	14 6/8 14 6/8	6 0/8 6 0/8	11 1/8	Lassen County	CA	Pete Becker	1985	1106
75 4/8	15 1/8 15 2/8	6 0/8 5 7/8	9 3/8	Meagher County	MT	Don Babcock	1986	1106
75 4/8	15 0/8 14 4/8	5 6/8 5 7/8	6 7/8	Washoe County	NV	Conrad Stitser	1987	1106
75 4/8	14 3/8 14 5/8	5 5/8 5 7/8	12 0/8	Coconino County	AZ	Bill Kerr	1987	1106
75 4/8	14 7/8 15 1/8	6 1/8 6 2/8	10 3/8	Cochise County	AZ	Jerry Clarno	1987	1106
75 4/8	14 0/8 14 1/8	6 6/8 6 4/8	8 1/8	Moffat County	CO	Tracy L. Gulliksen	1987	1106
75 4/8	15 6/8 15 3/8	6 1/8 6 2/8	12 3/8	Humboldt County	NV	G. Todd Brooks	1988	1106
75 4/8	15 3/8 15 1/8	6 7/8 6 7/8	7 4/8	Custer County	ID	Matt March	1990	1106
75 4/8	13 6/8 13 6/8	6 0/8 6 0/8	10 0/8	Coconino County	AZ	Rick Betten	1991	1106
75 4/8	14 4/8 14 0/8	6 0/8 6 0/8	12 7/8	Campbell County	WY	Gene Bremmer	1991	1106
75 4/8	14 5/8 14 5/8	6 0/8 6 0/8	10 5/8	Sweetwater County	WY	Harvey L. Dalton	1992	1106
75 4/8	14 1/8 14 1/8	6 2/8 6 1/8	10 1/8	Yavapai County	AZ	Jeffrey W. Adams	1992	1106
75 4/8	14 2/8 14 2/8	5 7/8 5 6/8	10 2/8	Stanley County	SD	Robert G. Barden	1992	1106
75 4/8	13 6/8 13 6/8	6 5/8 6 3/8	9 6/8	Carbon County	WY	Larry Cross	1992	1106
75 4/8	14 5/8 14 5/8	5 5/8 5 5/8	8 4/8	Catron County	NM	Carl D. Bradford	1993	1106
75 4/8	12 6/8 12 6/8	6 7/8 6 6/8	9 7/8	Box Elder County	UT	Wayne Payne	1993	1106
75 4/8	15 6/8 15 6/8	6 1/8 6 1/8	11 6/8	Chaves County	NM	Matt Hentrick	1994	1106
75 4/8	15 3/8 15 2/8	5 7/8 6 0/8	10 7/8	Owyhee County	ID	Neil Thagard	1995	1106
75 4/8	14 5/8 15 1/8	5 6/8 5 5/8	11 1/8	Moffat County	CO	Jordan T. Smith	1995	1106
75 4/8	14 7/8 15 1/8	6 3/8 6 3/8	9 2/8	Colfax County	NM	Robert L. Pagel, Sr.	1995	1106
75 4/8	15 6/8 15 6/8	6 0/8 6 0/8	7 3/8	Yavapai County	AZ	James C. Roth	1995	1106
75 4/8	15 1/8 15 2/8	6 1/8 6 0/8	14 7/8	Owyhee County	ID	Gary Angell	1996	1106
75 4/8	14 3/8 14 0/8	5 7/8 5 7/8	11 0/8	Yavapai County	AZ	Erik Pedersen	1996	1106
75 4/8	14 5/8 15 1/8	6 0/8 6 0/8	9 3/8	Sheridan County	WY	Jack Hayes	1996	1106
75 4/8	14 4/8 14 3/8	6 1/8 6 2/8	11 5/8	Saguache County	CO	Robert E. Schwanke	1997	1106

821

PRONGHORN

Minimum Score 67 — Continued

SCORE	LENGTH OF R HORN L	CIRCUMFERENCE R OF BASE L	INSIDE SPREAD	AREA	STATE/ PROVINCE	HUNTER'S NAME	DATE	RANK
75 4/8	14 3/8 14 4/8	6 2/8 6 2/8	10 7/8	Moffat County	CO	Tim Cuthriell	1997	1106
75 4/8	14 7/8 15 0/8	5 7/8 6 0/8	11 7/8	Socorro County	NM	Boone Fisher	1997	1106
75 4/8	14 2/8 14 2/8	6 1/8 6 1/8	12 7/8	Powder River County	MT	Bob Yeakel	1997	1106
75 4/8	15 4/8 15 4/8	5 7/8 5 7/8	9 6/8	Elko County	NV	Phil Kendall	1998	1106
75 4/8	14 2/8 14 2/8	6 0/8 5 6/8	7 4/8	Albany County	WY	Jerry Bowen	1998	1106
75 4/8	14 5/8 14 5/8	5 7/8 6 2/8	10 1/8	Weld County	CO	Kenneth E. Barnett	1999	1106
75 4/8	14 1/8 14 1/8	6 0/8 6 0/8	8 2/8	Mellette County	SD	Jim Kieler	1999	1106
75 4/8	13 5/8 13 5/8	6 0/8 6 0/8	10 5/8	Minidoka County	ID	Bret Bott	2000	1106
75 4/8	15 0/8 15 0/8	6 1/8 6 0/8	10 4/8	Rio Blanco County	CO	Don Collier	2000	1106
75 4/8	14 1/8 14 1/8	6 0/8 5 7/8	9 6/8	Billings County	ND	Troy A. Miller	2000	1106
75 4/8	12 6/8 12 4/8	6 5/8 6 5/8	8 2/8	Sweetwater County	WY	Frank S. Noska IV	2000	1106
75 4/8	14 5/8 14 7/8	6 2/8 6 2/8	12 0/8	Elko County	NV	Jim Cooney	2001	1106
75 4/8	15 1/8 15 1/8	5 6/8 5 7/8	11 1/8	Lake County	OR	William K. Graves	2001	1106
75 4/8	13 4/8 13 4/8	6 2/8 6 1/8	9 5/8	Park County	WY	Tyler Henry	2001	1106
75 4/8	15 3/8 15 2/8	6 1/8 6 2/8	10 0/8	Rosebud County	MT	Gene A. Welle	2001	1106
75 4/8	14 0/8 14 1/8	5 7/8 6 0/8	8 6/8	Campbell County	WY	Bruce Hudalla	2001	1106
75 4/8	14 7/8 15 2/8	6 0/8 5 7/8	11 0/8	Fergus County	MT	D. Mitch Kottas	2001	1106
75 4/8	15 2/8 15 1/8	5 7/8 5 7/8	9 1/8	Albany County	WY	Jerry Bowen	2002	1106
75 4/8	14 1/8 14 1/8	6 1/8 6 0/8	8 1/8	Lincoln County	WY	Warren Hatcher	2002	1106
75 4/8	14 0/8 14 0/8	6 0/8 5 5/8	10 2/8	Lincoln County	WY	Ronald R. Alexander	2002	1106
75 4/8	14 6/8 14 7/8	5 6/8 5 6/8	8 0/8	Yavapai County	AZ	Phillip C. Dalrymple	2002	1106
75 4/8	14 5/8 14 3/8	6 2/8 6 2/8	12 3/8	Elmore County	ID	Chris Ogle	2002	1106
75 4/8	16 4/8 16 2/8	5 6/8 5 6/8	10 7/8	Socorro County	NM	Frank Vallejos	2003	1106
75 4/8	14 2/8 14 2/8	6 3/8 6 2/8	10 4/8	Campbell County	WY	Tippy H. Clark	2003	1106
75 4/8	15 1/8 15 0/8	5 7/8 5 6/8	11 4/8	Lake County	OR	Chris Bedsaul	2004	1106
*75 4/8	14 6/8 14 5/8	6 1/8 6 1/8	17 0/8	Broadwater County	MT	Forrest Fawthrop	2005	1106
75 4/8	15 4/8 15 3/8	5 6/8 5 7/8	11 4/8	Johnson County	WY	Ron Maguire	2005	1106
75 4/8	14 6/8 14 7/8	6 0/8 6 0/8	10 3/8	Campbell County	WY	David Caskey	2005	1106
75 4/8	14 4/8 14 2/8	6 3/8 6 4/8	12 4/8	Humboldt County	NV	Ryan Garaventa	2006	1106
75 4/8	13 4/8 13 4/8	6 7/8 6 6/8	11 1/8	Las Animas County	CO	Andrew C. Bair	2006	1106
*75 4/8	12 7/8 13 0/8	6 5/8 6 5/8	12 4/8	Rosebud County	MT	Dave Fredrickson	2006	1106
75 4/8	16 2/8 16 1/8	5 7/8 5 7/8	11 3/8	Rosebud County	MT	Richard Gustafson	2006	1106
75 4/8	15 2/8 15 1/8	5 7/8 5 7/8	9 1/8	Liberty County	MT	Brant Borden	2006	1106
*75 4/8	14 7/8 14 6/8	5 7/8 5 6/8	7 5/8	Fergus County	MT	Matt Moen	2007	1106
75 4/8	14 4/8 14 2/8	6 5/8 6 4/8	9 1/8	Lea County	NM	Brandon Ray	2008	1106
75 4/8	14 4/8 14 3/8	6 0/8 6 0/8	9 2/8	Moffat County	CO	Marvin Clyncke	2008	1106
75 4/8	14 2/8 14 2/8	6 5/8 6 4/8	10 5/8	Carter County	MT	Jody Ketterling	2008	1106
75 4/8	14 1/8 14 4/8	5 7/8 5 7/8	13 1/8	Millard County	UT	Karen H. Gorringe	2009	1106
75 4/8	15 0/8 15 2/8	6 3/8 6 3/8	12 4/8	Converse County	WY	Clint Janson	2009	1106
75 4/8	15 2/8 15 0/8	6 4/8 6 2/8	9 7/8	Fergus County	MT	D. "Mitch" Kottas	2009	1106
75 4/8	14 0/8 14 0/8	6 4/8 6 4/8	8 1/8	Park County	WY	Jason Housel	2010	1106
75 4/8	14 3/8 14 5/8	6 0/8 6 0/8	11 1/8	Goshen County	WY	Douglas N. Bremer	2010	1106
*75 4/8	14 5/8 14 6/8	6 2/8 6 2/8	13 0/8	Catron County	NM	Troy Holley	2010	1106
75 2/8	15 4/8 15 3/8	5 7/8 5 7/8	8 6/8	Burke County	ND	Richard R. Chandler	1971	1186
75 2/8	16 1/8 16 6/8	5 6/8 5 5/8	11 2/8	Klamath County	OR	Steve H. Bell	1973	1186
75 2/8	14 5/8 14 5/8	6 2/8 6 2/8	10 2/8	Musselshell County	MT	John Crump	1980	1186
75 2/8	14 3/8 14 5/8	6 3/8 6 4/8	9 2/8	Carbon County	WY	Duane Caudle	1980	1186
75 2/8	13 0/8 13 0/8	7 0/8 7 1/8	10 6/8	Sweetwater County	WY	Charlene Shaw	1985	1186
75 2/8	15 0/8 14 4/8	7 0/8 6 6/8	9 2/8	Sweetwater County	WY	Marlene Bowen	1986	1186
75 2/8	14 0/8 14 5/8	6 0/8 6 0/8	12 0/8	Coconino County	AZ	David L. Wolf	1986	1186
75 2/8	13 7/8 14 0/8	6 5/8 6 4/8	12 5/8	Dunn County	ND	Jeff J. Kostelecky	1987	1186
75 2/8	14 1/8 14 0/8	6 2/8 6 2/8	8 5/8	Lea County	NM	Lynn Sims	1987	1186
75 2/8	15 2/8 15 2/8	6 0/8 5 7/8	8 4/8	Klamath County	OR	Lynn Pettit	1988	1186
75 2/8	13 7/8 13 6/8	6 4/8 6 5/8	11 2/8	Coconino County	AZ	Johnny Rooker	1988	1186
75 2/8	15 6/8 16 0/8	6 3/8 6 2/8	10 7/8	Phillips County	MT	Don Andrews	1988	1186
75 2/8	14 4/8 14 4/8	6 3/8 6 3/8	12 3/8	Presidio County	TX	Tommy Culbertson	1988	1186
75 2/8	15 0/8 14 5/8	6 2/8 6 3/8	8 7/8	Sweetwater County	WY	Norman Bradley	1989	1186
75 2/8	13 7/8 14 0/8	6 0/8 5 7/8	7 1/8	Moffat County	CO	Rickey Phillips	1989	1186
75 2/8	13 7/8 14 0/8	6 1/8 6 2/8	12 5/8	Sweetwater County	WY	Harv Dalton	1989	1186
75 2/8	15 3/8 15 4/8	5 6/8 5 6/8	11 3/8	Eddy County	NM	Dennis L. Howell	1989	1186
75 2/8	14 4/8 14 5/8	6 1/8 6 2/8	9 0/8	Washoe County	NV	Cory Pengelly	1990	1186
75 2/8	14 2/8 14 1/8	6 2/8 6 2/8	7 3/8	Sweetwater County	WY	Edward Ferebee	1990	1186
75 2/8	15 7/8 15 4/8	5 5/8 5 5/8	6 5/8	Sweetwater County	WY	Ron Serwa	1990	1186
75 2/8	14 4/8 14 5/8	6 1/8 6 0/8	12 2/8	Moffat County	CO	Ronald King	1990	1186
75 2/8	15 4/8 16 1/8	5 7/8 5 5/8	9 1/8	Harney County	OR	Stanley Miles	1990	1186
75 2/8	14 3/8 14 1/8	5 6/8 5 6/8	9 0/8	Billings County	ND	Mark Sowieja	1990	1186
75 2/8	14 2/8 14 0/8	6 1/8 6 3/8	9 3/8	Wallace County	KS	Daniel P. Carmen	1990	1186
75 2/8	14 3/8 14 4/8	6 3/8 6 3/8	14 4/8	Moffat County	CO	Bud Boker	1991	1186
75 2/8	14 3/8 14 3/8	6 1/8 6 0/8	11 3/8	Carbon County	WY	Greg Bonetti	1991	1186
75 2/8	13 2/8 13 4/8	6 5/8 6 4/8	12 0/8	Garfield County	MT	Kim Tatman	1991	1186
75 2/8	15 1/8 15 0/8	6 6/8 6 5/8	11 1/8	Sioux County	NE	Steve Woitaszewski	1991	1186
75 2/8	14 6/8 14 5/8	5 6/8 5 6/8	10 2/8	Catron County	NM	Patrick Kirk	1992	1186
75 2/8	13 5/8 13 7/8	6 7/8 6 6/8	8 0/8	Twin Falls County	ID	Gary Painter	1992	1186
75 2/8	13 7/8 15 0/8	6 2/8 6 2/8	10 1/8	Yavapai County	AZ	Roland J. Chooljian	1992	1186
75 2/8	15 6/8 15 4/8	6 0/8 6 0/8	9 7/8	Yavapai County	AZ	Don Parks, Jr.	1992	1186
75 2/8	14 0/8 14 0/8	5 6/8 5 7/8	8 4/8	Yavapai County	AZ	Keith A. Robinson	1993	1186
75 2/8	15 0/8 14 7/8	5 4/8 5 4/8	11 3/8	Juab County	UT	Bruce Carlisle	1993	1186
75 2/8	13 7/8 14 0/8	6 0/8 6 0/8	9 4/8	Clark County	SD	Jared Mason	1993	1186
75 2/8	13 2/8 13 2/8	7 0/8 6 4/8	11 1/8	Campbell County	WY	Michael J. Kennedy	1993	1186
75 2/8	13 5/8 13 7/8	6 0/8 6 0/8	8 0/8	Platte County	WY	John M. Dobish	1993	1186
75 2/8	13 3/8 13 4/8	6 0/8 6 1/8	10 6/8	Converse County	WY	Ralph Inverso	1993	1186
75 2/8	15 4/8 16 2/8	6 0/8 6 0/8	8 5/8	Sioux County	NE	John J. Schaffer	1993	1186
75 2/8	13 6/8 13 7/8	6 4/8 6 6/8	10 1/8	Rio Blanco County	CO	Richard Muller	1994	1186
75 2/8	14 7/8 14 5/8	6 0/8 5 7/8	8 5/8	Jenner	ALB	Tim Sailer	1994	1186
75 2/8	14 4/8 15 2/8	6 0/8 6 2/8	8 2/8	Hot Springs County	WY	Dale "Chuck" Cornella	1994	1186
75 2/8	13 3/8 13 2/8	6 4/8 6 3/8	9 3/8	Big Horn County	WY	Charlotte Moss	1995	1186
75 2/8	15 3/8 15 4/8	6 0/8 6 0/8	12 4/8	Juab County	UT	Paul R. Quayle	1995	1186
75 2/8	13 4/8 13 4/8	6 5/8 6 5/8	8 1/8	Weld County	CO	David L. Skiff	1995	1186
75 2/8	15 1/8 15 2/8	6 1/8 6 1/8	11 1/8	Rosebud County	MT	Charles E. Speck	1995	1186
75 2/8	14 3/8 14 3/8	6 0/8 5 5/8	10 5/8	Millard County	UT	Brandon Snell	1996	1186
75 2/8	13 2/8 13 2/8	6 3/8 6 2/8	6 3/8	Haakon County	SD	Aaron Doolittle	1997	1186
75 2/8	13 6/8 13 2/8	6 3/8 6 3/8	11 4/8	Sweetwater County	WY	Vic R. Dana	1998	1186
75 2/8	15 4/8 15 6/8	6 0/8 6 0/8	14 2/8	Campbell County	WY	Jim Stroud	1998	1186
75 2/8	15 4/8 15 4/8	5 6/8 5 7/8	15 0/8	Socorro County	NM	Delbert R. Miller	1999	1186
75 2/8	14 4/8 14 3/8	6 2/8 6 2/8	9 3/8	Albany County	WY	Jerry Bowen	1999	1186

822

PRONGHORN

Minimum Score 67   Continued

SCORE	LENGTH OF R HORN L	CIRCUMFERENCE R OF BASE L	INSIDE SPREAD	AREA	STATE/ PROVINCE	HUNTER'S NAME	DATE	RANK
75 2/8	14 7/8 14 6/8	5 6/8 6 0/8	9 3/8	Coconino County	AZ	Derrick English	1999	1186
75 2/8	14 0/8 13 6/8	6 1/8 6 2/8	11 3/8	Carter County	MT	Cameron W. Hayden	2001	1186
*75 2/8	15 5/8 15 5/8	5 4/8 5 4/8	11 4/8	Lincoln County	NM	Justin Jackson	2002	1186
75 2/8	14 4/8 14 3/8	6 2/8 6 2/8	10 6/8	Petroleum County	MT	Levi Johnson	2002	1186
75 2/8	14 3/8 14 2/8	6 3/8 6 5/8	7 2/8	Rosebud County	MT	Kevin J. Westerberg	2002	1186
75 2/8	15 1/8 15 0/8	6 1/8 6 1/8	13 4/8	Humboldt County	NV	J. A. Tyburczy	2003	1186
75 2/8	14 6/8 15 2/8	6 1/8 6 0/8	13 4/8	Carbon County	WY	Donald Wales	2003	1186
75 2/8	15 3/8 15 3/8	5 7/8 5 6/8	6 6/8	Powder River County	MT	Robert Dowen	2003	1186
75 2/8	16 3/8 16 2/8	5 3/8 5 2/8	8 4/8	Mercer County	ND	Gregory S. Passa	2003	1186
75 2/8	15 0/8 15 0/8	5 6/8 5 6/8	7 5/8	Campbell County	WY	Calvin Taylor	2003	1186
75 2/8	14 5/8 14 3/8	6 5/8 6 5/8	14 6/8	Perkins County	SD	Jerrod M. Hoff	2003	1186
75 2/8	15 3/8 15 0/8	6 2/8 6 3/8	10 4/8	Campbell County	WY	Dwayne Hunt	2003	1186
*75 2/8	13 5/8 13 4/8	6 0/8 6 2/8	12 3/8	Las Animas County	CO	Russel C. Harris	2004	1186
75 2/8	14 5/8 13 7/8	6 0/8 6 1/8	8 5/8	Elmore County	ID	Eric G. Prentice	2004	1186
*75 2/8	13 3/8 13 4/8	6 3/8 6 2/8	9 1/8	Natrona County	WY	Gary Joseph	2004	1186
75 2/8	14 3/8 15 0/8	5 7/8 5 7/8	11 6/8	Broadwater County	MT	Jason Brenden	2004	1186
75 2/8	14 0/8 13 3/8	6 2/8 6 0/8	8 7/8	Crook County	WY	Jeff Jacobs	2005	1186
75 2/8	13 7/8 13 7/8	6 3/8 6 2/8	10 6/8	Weld County	CO	Richard A. Devrous, Jr.	2006	1186
75 2/8	15 4/8 15 0/8	6 0/8 6 0/8	6 6/8	Humboldt County	NV	Michael Doherty	2006	1186
75 2/8	14 6/8 14 5/8	6 0/8 5 7/8	12 0/8	Sublette County	WY	Dale Feagler	2006	1186
75 2/8	14 0/8 13 7/8	6 7/8 6 6/8	12 5/8	Lincoln County	WY	Eric H. Boley	2006	1186
*75 2/8	15 0/8 14 6/8	6 4/8 6 4/8	11 6/8	Moffat County	CO	Randy Kendrick	2007	1186
75 2/8	15 4/8 15 2/8	6 7/8 6 4/8	8 6/8	Lemhi County	ID	Gary Gapp	2007	1186
75 2/8	14 1/8 14 1/8	6 0/8 6 0/8	8 7/8	White Pine County	NV	Tim Murphy	2008	1186
75 2/8	13 4/8 13 2/8	6 0/8 6 1/8	7 4/8	Converse County	WY	Gary L. Fischer	2008	1186
*75 2/8	14 3/8 14 5/8	6 0/8 5 7/8	8 2/8	Moffat County	CO	Doug Field	2008	1186
75 2/8	14 3/8 14 1/8	6 1/8 6 1/8	9 3/8	Las Animas County	CO	Michele Eichler	2008	1186
*75 2/8	14 6/8 14 7/8	5 7/8 5 6/8	10 1/8	Hot Springs County	WY	Bryce C. Harvey	2008	1186
75 2/8	13 6/8 13 6/8	6 6/8 6 6/8	10 1/8	Moffat County	CO	Travis Simplot	2008	1186
75 2/8	15 2/8 15 2/8	6 1/8 6 0/8	10 7/8	Yavapai County	AZ	Rodney L. Ronnebaum	2009	1186
75 2/8	14 1/8 14 0/8	5 7/8 5 7/8	8 5/8	Lea County	NM	Ronnie Parsons	2009	1186
75 2/8	14 0/8 14 3/8	6 0/8 6 0/8	12 4/8	Lea County	NM	Brandon Ray	2009	1186
75 2/8	13 7/8 13 7/8	6 2/8 6 0/8	8 4/8	Lewis & Clark County	MT	Larry Fischer	2009	1186
*75 2/8	14 6/8 14 4/8	6 3/8 6 1/8	12 0/8	McKenzie County	ND	Anthony Von Ruden	2009	1186
75 2/8	15 7/8 15 0/8	6 3/8 6 2/8	9 4/8	Carbon County	WY	Dustin Baird	2010	1186
75 0/8	14 2/8 14 2/8	6 3/8 6 1/8	10 2/8	Butte County	ID	Ross M. Conlin	1971	1273
75 0/8	14 0/8 13 6/8	7 4/8 7 4/8	11 6/8	Sheridan County	ND	Dave Baumiller	1973	1273
75 0/8	13 4/8 13 5/8	6 5/8 6 3/8	10 2/8	Campbell County	WY	Mick Larson	1975	1273
75 0/8	13 6/8 14 0/8	6 2/8 6 2/8	8 6/8	Sweetwater County	WY	Mike Ward	1976	1273
75 0/8	14 5/8 14 4/8	6 2/8 6 1/8	8 7/8	Humboldt County	NV	Robert Mathews	1977	1273
75 0/8	14 0/8 14 0/8	5 5/8 5 6/8	9 7/8	Moffat County	CO	Ronald C. Halpin	1980	1273
75 0/8	14 0/8 14 0/8	6 1/8 6 0/8	12 6/8	Wheatland County	MT	Phil Reno	1980	1273
75 0/8	14 2/8 14 1/8	6 3/8 6 3/8	10 1/8	Sweetwater County	WY	Earl Frye	1980	1273
75 0/8	13 5/8 14 6/8	6 0/8 6 0/8	13 0/8	Moffat County	CO	Carl Smith	1981	1273
75 0/8	15 0/8 14 7/8	6 2/8 6 2/8	9 0/8	Natrona County	WY	Richard A. Schreiber	1982	1273
75 0/8	14 5/8 14 5/8	6 0/8 6 0/8	12 1/8	Meagher County	MT	Gene Clark	1984	1273
75 0/8	15 5/8 15 3/8	6 0/8 6 0/8	11 6/8	Coconino County	AZ	Jim Scott	1986	1273
75 0/8	14 4/8 14 4/8	5 5/8 5 5/8	10 4/8	Converse County	WY	William G. Mason	1986	1273
75 0/8	14 4/8 14 4/8	5 6/8 5 6/8	13 5/8	Sweetwater County	WY	Steve Bellis	1988	1273
75 0/8	14 6/8 14 6/8	5 6/8 5 6/8	11 2/8	Pueblo County	CO	Freeman Howard	1989	1273
75 0/8	14 3/8 14 4/8	6 1/8 6 2/8	9 2/8	Custer County	MT	Marty Penrod	1989	1273
75 0/8	12 0/8 12 1/8	6 2/8 6 2/8	9 4/8	Campbell County	WY	Richard Reeb	1990	1273
75 0/8	14 4/8 13 6/8	6 0/8 6 0/8	11 2/8	Grant County	NM	Brandon Jones	1991	1273
75 0/8	13 6/8 13 5/8	6 2/8 6 1/8	11 7/8	Carbon County	WY	Heather E. Haines	1991	1273
75 0/8	13 7/8 13 7/8	6 4/8 6 5/8	12 7/8	Carbon County	WY	Kenneth J. Kahler	1991	1273
75 0/8	14 5/8 14 5/8	6 2/8 6 4/8	9 2/8	Fremont County	WY	Joel Nirider	1991	1273
75 0/8	13 5/8 13 7/8	6 1/8 6 2/8	12 2/8	Mercer County	ND	Leland A. Mehlhoff	1991	1273
75 0/8	15 3/8 15 3/8	5 3/8 5 2/8	9 0/8	Converse County	WY	Robert Brenneman	1991	1273
75 0/8	14 1/8 13 7/8	6 3/8 6 3/8	8 6/8	Sweetwater County	WY	James B. White	1992	1273
75 0/8	14 3/8 14 3/8	6 1/8 6 1/8	10 2/8	Sweetwater County	WY	Donald Ace Morgan	1992	1273
75 0/8	15 0/8 15 0/8	6 2/8 6 1/8	8 3/8	Butte County	ID	L. D. Green	1992	1273
75 0/8	15 3/8 15 4/8	6 1/8 6 0/8	9 6/8	Millard County	UT	Terry Costa	1992	1273
75 0/8	13 6/8 14 0/8	6 1/8 6 1/8	9 0/8	Sweetwater County	WY	Jonathan M. Kautt	1992	1273
75 0/8	13 6/8 14 3/8	6 7/8 7 1/8	12 4/8	Moffat County	CO	Glenn W. Pritchard	1992	1273
75 0/8	14 4/8 14 2/8	6 3/8 6 3/8	9 5/8	Moffat County	CO	Jim Leqve	1993	1273
75 0/8	15 1/8 15 5/8	6 0/8 5 6/8	11 5/8	Washoe County	NV	Gilbert Hernandez	1993	1273
75 0/8	13 6/8 13 1/8	6 1/8 6 1/8	11 2/8	Weld County	CO	B. Duane Kropf	1993	1273
75 0/8	14 6/8 14 6/8	6 2/8 6 1/8	7 5/8	Natrona County	WY	Brian L. Wagner	1993	1273
75 0/8	15 0/8 14 6/8	6 3/8 6 2/8	9 1/8	Yavapai County	AZ	Steve Rawlins	1993	1273
75 0/8	15 2/8 15 2/8	6 2/8 6 2/8	11 6/8	Manyberries	ALB	Doug Erickson	1993	1273
75 0/8	15 4/8 15 2/8	6 0/8 6 0/8	9 3/8	Yellowstone County	MT	Gary R. Petty	1993	1273
75 0/8	14 4/8 15 1/8	5 6/8 6 0/8	10 1/8	San Miguel County	NM	Marty Martinez	1994	1273
75 0/8	12 6/8 13 2/8	6 4/8 6 4/8	12 1/8	Graham County	AZ	John C. Rhodes	1994	1273
75 0/8	14 4/8 14 6/8	5 7/8 5 7/8	16 1/8	Harney County	OR	John Jaques	1994	1273
75 0/8	13 5/8 13 6/8	7 2/8 7 0/8	10 0/8	Mankota	SAS	Kelly Johnson	1994	1273
75 0/8	14 5/8 14 7/8	6 1/8 6 1/8	10 1/8	Hanna	ALB	Glen Hutton	1994	1273
75 0/8	14 1/8 14 0/8	5 7/8 5 7/8	6 5/8	Campbell County	WY	Bruce Witte	1994	1273
75 0/8	13 7/8 13 4/8	6 0/8 5 7/8	10 3/8	Hudspeth County	TX	Paul Thurman	1994	1273
75 0/8	14 2/8 14 2/8	7 0/8 7 0/8	13 1/8	Weld County	CO	Stuart Stevens	1995	1273
75 0/8	15 5/8 15 2/8	6 2/8 6 4/8	6 4/8	Custer County	ID	George Versis	1995	1273
75 0/8	14 4/8 14 3/8	6 5/8 6 3/8	10 4/8	Buffalo County	SD	Ed Werdel	1995	1273
75 0/8	12 4/8 12 4/8	6 5/8 6 5/8	8 6/8	Hot Springs County	WY	Micheal H. Eastman	1995	1273
75 0/8	14 3/8 14 2/8	6 4/8 6 4/8	8 7/8	Moffat County	CO	Paul M. Martin	1996	1273
75 0/8	14 4/8 14 6/8	6 3/8 6 1/8	9 6/8	Yavapai County	AZ	Archie J. Nesbitt	1997	1273
75 0/8	14 2/8 14 2/8	6 0/8 5 7/8	11 5/8	Carbon County	UT	McCade Mascaro	1997	1273
75 0/8	14 0/8 13 7/8	6 5/8 6 5/8	8 6/8	Toole County	MT	Keith Miller	1997	1273
75 0/8	14 0/8 14 0/8	6 1/8 6 0/8	11 7/8	Big Horn County	WY	Dave Moss	1998	1273
75 0/8	15 6/8 15 2/8	6 3/8 6 2/8	12 2/8	Catron County	NM	John Flores	1998	1273
75 0/8	16 5/8 16 2/8	5 4/8 5 4/8	9 0/8	Lemhi County	ID	Scott Bridges	1998	1273
75 0/8	15 1/8 15 0/8	5 7/8 5 7/8	9 5/8	Elko County	NV	Andrew W. Elam	1999	1273
75 0/8	14 2/8 14 0/8	5 6/8 5 5/8	8 6/8	Logan County	CO	Scott Withrow	1999	1273
75 0/8	14 3/8 14 0/8	6 0/8 6 1/8	7 4/8	Uintah County	UT	Peggy Aplanalp	1999	1273
75 0/8	15 0/8 15 0/8	6 0/8 6 0/8	9 1/8	Converse County	WY	Mark Giese	1999	1273
75 0/8	15 0/8 13 3/8	6 5/8 6 4/8	9 7/8	Pershing County	NV	Victor E. Gierhart	2000	1273
75 0/8	14 4/8 14 5/8	6 0/8 6 0/8	8 1/8	Tooele County	UT	Russell Johnson	2000	1273

823

PRONGHORN

Minimum Score 67 — Continued

SCORE	LENGTH OF HORN R	L	CIRCUMFERENCE OF BASE R	L	INSIDE SPREAD	AREA	STATE/ PROVINCE	HUNTER'S NAME	DATE	RANK
75 0/8	13 3/8	12 7/8	6 3/8	6 3/8	12 3/8	Converse County	WY	J. Michael Umbaugh	2000	1273
75 0/8	15 4/8	16 0/8	5 6/8	5 7/8	9 1/8	Fergus County	MT	Jerry Knerr	2001	1273
75 0/8	14 4/8	14 6/8	6 2/8	6 2/8	11 7/8	Yavapai County	AZ	Marty V. Cairns	2002	1273
75 0/8	15 7/8	15 4/8	5 3/8	5 3/8	12 1/8	Eddy County	NM	Donald G. Atkins	2002	1273
75 0/8	15 2/8	15 2/8	6 1/8	6 1/8	10 3/8	Perkins County	SD	Roger Darling	2003	1273
75 0/8	15 0/8	14 6/8	5 5/8	5 6/8	6 3/8	Laramie County	WY	Jim Collins	2004	1273
75 0/8	14 1/8	14 0/8	6 2/8	6 2/8	10 4/8	Converse County	WY	James W. Casto III	2004	1273
75 0/8	13 7/8	13 5/8	6 5/8	6 3/8	11 0/8	Converse County	WY	Kenneth Sorg	2005	1273
75 0/8	15 0/8	14 7/8	6 1/8	6 1/8	12 1/8	Lake County	OR	Donald R. Pritchett	2005	1273
75 0/8	13 4/8	13 1/8	6 4/8	6 4/8	8 2/8	Powder River County	MT	Jeffrey A. Noble	2005	1273
75 0/8	14 6/8	14 6/8	6 1/8	6 0/8	7 2/8	Campbell County	WY	Bob Balk	2005	1273
*75 0/8	15 5/8	15 7/8	5 3/8	5 3/8	8 0/8	Brooks	ALB	Gary Joseph	2005	1273
75 0/8	13 4/8	13 5/8	6 4/8	6 4/8	10 5/8	Powder River County	MT	Adam Gronning	2006	1273
*75 0/8	15 0/8	15 1/8	5 6/8	5 7/8	11 6/8	Campbell County	WY	David M. Bufkin	2006	1273
75 0/8	15 3/8	15 1/8	6 0/8	5 7/8	9 5/8	Campbell County	WY	Robert W. Miller	2006	1273
*75 0/8	13 7/8	13 4/8	6 4/8	6 2/8	7 0/8	Carbon County	WY	Rodney A. Lindsten	2006	1273
*75 0/8	14 1/8	14 2/8	6 4/8	6 3/8	10 3/8	Moffat County	CO	Christopher C. Robertson	2007	1273
*75 0/8	14 1/8	14 2/8	6 4/8	6 4/8	10 0/8	Sweetwater County	WY	Teno Trujillo	2007	1273
*75 0/8	14 1/8	14 5/8	5 6/8	5 6/8	11 4/8	Niobrara County	WY	Jess Kucera	2008	1273
*75 0/8	14 6/8	14 4/8	6 2/8	6 0/8	11 2/8	Sweetwater County	WY	Dave R. Burget	2009	1273
75 0/8	14 0/8	14 0/8	5 7/8	5 7/8	7 3/8	Weston County	WY	Chris Sanford	2009	1273
75 0/8	15 1/8	15 0/8	6 0/8	6 1/8	10 4/8	Lake County	OR	Pete Gray	2009	1273
*75 0/8	13 2/8	13 1/8	6 4/8	6 3/8	13 1/8	McKenzie County	ND	Anthony Von Ruden	2009	1273
75 0/8	15 0/8	14 7/8	5 5/8	5 5/8	11 1/8	Brooks	ALB	Ricardo Longoria	2009	1273
75 0/8	14 5/8	14 5/8	6 0/8	6 1/8	11 1/8	Medicine Hat	ALB	Dean G. Elbe	2009	1273
*75 0/8	14 4/8	13 3/8	6 3/8	6 3/8	8 6/8	Carter County	MT	Jim Pyfer	2009	1273
75 0/8	14 0/8	14 3/8	6 6/8	6 6/8	8 3/8	Lincoln County	WY	Josh Backman	2010	1273
75 0/8	15 2/8	14 6/8	6 2/8	6 2/8	9 5/8	Converse County	WY	Donald Gibson	2010	1273
74 6/8	14 3/8	14 3/8	5 5/8	5 5/8	9 5/8	Lemhi County	ID	Kent Merrill	1979	1361
74 6/8	13 5/8	13 2/8	7 4/8	7 5/8	11 2/8	Converse County	WY	George A. Zanoni	1980	1361
74 6/8	14 3/8	14 3/8	5 6/8	5 6/8	10 1/8	Fremont County	WY	James R. Mecca	1981	1361
74 6/8	14 4/8	14 5/8	6 3/8	6 1/8	7 0/8	Converse County	WY	Norm Goodwin	1981	1361
74 6/8	14 2/8	14 2/8	6 1/8	6 1/8	9 1/8	Sweetwater County	WY	Pete J Cintorino	1982	1361
74 6/8	14 7/8	14 1/8	6 2/8	6 1/8	12 1/8	Moffat County	CO	Richard K. Hess	1982	1361
74 6/8	14 1/8	14 1/8	6 0/8	5 7/8	5 7/8	Converse County	WY	Thomas Fleming	1982	1361
74 6/8	14 4/8	14 5/8	6 0/8	6 1/8	9 6/8	Converse County	WY	Steve Gorr	1982	1361
74 6/8	14 3/8	14 3/8	6 2/8	6 2/8	8 6/8	Sweetwater County	WY	Mike Denney	1982	1361
74 6/8	13 7/8	14 0/8	5 7/8	6 1/8	12 4/8	Carbon County	WY	Len Cardinale	1982	1361
74 6/8	14 7/8	14 7/8	6 0/8	6 0/8	8 7/8	Humboldt County	NV	Ken Mallory	1983	1361
74 6/8	14 0/8	14 1/8	6 0/8	5 7/8	10 3/8	Moffat County	CO	Wallace Hobby	1983	1361
74 6/8	14 5/8	14 6/8	6 2/8	6 2/8	9 7/8	Campbell County	WY	Arthur Geltz	1984	1361
74 6/8	14 4/8	14 4/8	6 2/8	6 2/8	10 3/8	Moffat County	CO	Susan Bingham Syvertson	1985	1361
74 6/8	15 3/8	15 4/8	5 7/8	5 6/8	8 0/8	Fremont County	WY	Joe E. Nelson	1985	1361
74 6/8	14 1/8	14 1/8	6 1/8	6 0/8	7 3/8	Sweetwater County	WY	Dennis L. Shirley	1986	1361
74 6/8	14 2/8	14 1/8	6 4/8	6 3/8	9 6/8	Sweetwater County	WY	Michael Chaffin	1986	1361
74 6/8	14 7/8	15 6/8	6 0/8	6 0/8	11 0/8	Yavapai County	AZ	Jody Krueger	1987	1361
74 6/8	14 3/8	14 7/8	6 1/8	6 0/8	10 5/8	Carbon County	WY	Robert L. Hudman	1988	1361
74 6/8	14 5/8	14 6/8	5 7/8	5 7/8	10 7/8	Billings County	ND	Pam Baird	1988	1361
74 6/8	14 3/8	14 3/8	5 7/8	5 7/8	8 3/8	Converse County	WY	James Erickson	1988	1361
74 6/8	13 4/8	13 3/8	6 3/8	6 3/8	11 0/8	Humboldt County	NV	David Stoker	1991	1361
74 6/8	14 3/8	14 5/8	6 1/8	6 1/8	11 7/8	Perkins County	SD	Darin Allen Manthie	1991	1361
74 6/8	14 7/8	14 6/8	5 7/8	6 0/8	7 2/8	Washoe County	NV	Jim Bradley	1992	1361
74 6/8	15 2/8	14 7/8	5 7/8	5 7/8	7 4/8	Washoe County	NV	Charlie Powning	1992	1361
74 6/8	14 6/8	14 5/8	6 2/8	6 1/8	10 6/8	Sweetwater County	WY	Dwight Brown, Jr.	1992	1361
74 6/8	13 7/8	14 0/8	6 6/8	6 6/8	7 7/8	Sweetwater County	WY	Robert G. Petersen	1992	1361
74 6/8	13 4/8	13 2/8	6 6/8	7 0/8	8 7/8	Natrona County	WY	Russ Weakland	1992	1361
74 6/8	13 4/8	13 4/8	5 7/8	6 0/8	8 0/8	Converse County	WY	Russell A. Nichols	1992	1361
74 6/8	14 6/8	14 5/8	5 7/8	5 7/8	11 1/8	Natrona County	WY	Elmer R. Luce, Jr.	1992	1361
74 6/8	14 7/8	14 7/8	6 1/8	6 1/8	6 1/8	Lemhi County	ID	Pat McFadden	1993	1361
74 6/8	14 2/8	14 5/8	6 1/8	6 2/8	11 4/8	Johnson County	WY	James E. Taylor	1993	1361
74 6/8	14 3/8	14 1/8	6 2/8	6 2/8	12 2/8	Twin Falls County	ID	John Stevens	1994	1361
74 6/8	15 1/8	15 4/8	6 0/8	6 1/8	10 3/8	Fergus County	MT	Jerry Knerr	1994	1361
74 6/8	14 4/8	13 6/8	6 3/8	6 2/8	9 2/8	Rosebud County	MT	Kyle Zimmerman	1994	1361
74 6/8	14 5/8	14 5/8	5 6/8	5 6/8	9 4/8	Owyhee County	ID	Mark K. Rackowitz	1994	1361
74 6/8	14 3/8	14 3/8	6 0/8	5 7/8	7 6/8	Broadwater County	MT	Neil Larson	1994	1361
74 6/8	14 7/8	14 7/8	6 0/8	6 1/8	12 5/8	Colfax County	NM	Pat Lovato	1995	1361
74 6/8	14 4/8	14 5/8	6 0/8	6 0/8	12 6/8	Mercer County	ND	Jim Helling	1995	1361
74 6/8	13 4/8	13 3/8	6 2/8	6 0/8	8 2/8	Lincoln County	NV	Michael Zech	1996	1361
74 6/8	13 1/8	13 4/8	6 5/8	6 3/8	7 5/8	Weld County	CO	Guy Pierce	1996	1361
74 6/8	13 5/8	13 7/8	6 4/8	6 4/8	8 5/8	Campbell County	WY	Dennis W. Klemick	1996	1361
74 6/8	14 3/8	14 0/8	6 6/8	6 4/8	12 2/8	Weld County	CO	Guy Pierce	1997	1361
74 6/8	14 1/8	14 6/8	6 0/8	6 0/8	10 0/8	Moffat County	CO	Steven R. Hickok	1997	1361
74 6/8	13 4/8	13 4/8	6 2/8	6 1/8	11 6/8	Malheur County	OR	Ricky D. Stratton	1997	1361
74 6/8	14 5/8	14 6/8	6 4/8	6 4/8	12 1/8	Moffat County	CO	Jerry Douthit	1997	1361
74 6/8	14 1/8	14 2/8	6 2/8	6 2/8	8 5/8	Sweetwater County	WY	Paul R. Quayle	1997	1361
74 6/8	16 4/8	15 7/8	5 3/8	5 2/8	7 1/8	Yavapai County	AZ	Bruce Felker	1997	1361
74 6/8	14 3/8	14 1/8	6 4/8	6 3/8	5 5/8	Carbon County	WY	Steve Torok	1998	1361
74 6/8	13 4/8	14 1/8	6 5/8	6 5/8	12 3/8	Converse County	WY	Steve Williams	1998	1361
74 6/8	15 3/8	15 3/8	5 5/8	5 6/8	12 2/8	Big Horn County	MT	Pete Gierke	1998	1361
74 6/8	14 1/8	13 6/8	6 1/8	6 1/8	10 4/8	Musselshell County	MT	Paul S. Black	1998	1361
74 6/8	15 1/8	15 3/8	5 4/8	5 4/8	10 4/8	Campbell County	WY	Kenneth Morga	1998	1361
74 6/8	14 3/8	14 6/8	6 1/8	6 1/8	10 4/8	Moffat County	CO	Lonny Vanatta	1999	1361
74 6/8	14 0/8	14 0/8	6 0/8	6 0/8	8 2/8	Twin Falls County	ID	Dan Carrico	1999	1361
74 6/8	15 4/8	15 1/8	5 6/8	5 6/8	10 3/8	Rosebud County	MT	Ronald D. May	1999	1361
74 6/8	14 0/8	14 2/8	6 2/8	6 1/8	6 4/8	Iron County	UT	LeGrande Tracy	2000	1361
74 6/8	15 1/8	15 0/8	6 0/8	6 0/8	10 7/8	Lake County	OR	Sheldon Doughty	2000	1361
74 6/8	14 1/8	14 2/8	6 6/8	6 4/8	10 4/8	Humboldt County	NV	Chris Gonfiantini	2002	1361
74 6/8	13 6/8	13 2/8	6 4/8	6 3/8	7 5/8	Elko County	NV	John V. Bottari	2002	1361
74 6/8	13 7/8	13 3/8	5 7/8	5 7/8	9 6/8	Natrona County	WY	Grant Pozarnsky	2002	1361
74 6/8	14 4/8	14 6/8	6 2/8	6 2/8	9 3/8	Butte County	SD	Rick Richards	2002	1361
74 6/8	13 0/8	13 2/8	6 3/8	6 0/8	7 6/8	Sweetwater County	WY	Jodell M. Hefley	2003	1361
74 6/8	14 4/8	15 6/8	6 2/8	6 2/8	7 6/8	Campbell County	WY	Drew McCartney	2003	1361
74 6/8	14 5/8	14 5/8	6 2/8	6 1/8	11 5/8	Johnson County	WY	Dave Harness	2003	1361
74 6/8	14 4/8	14 3/8	6 0/8	6 0/8	10 3/8	Rio Blanco County	CO	Chris Richardson	2004	1361
74 6/8	15 7/8	15 2/8	6 0/8	5 7/8	9 6/8	Converse County	WY	Scott Wilson	2004	1361

PRONGHORN

Minimum Score 67
Continued

SCORE	LENGTH OF R HORN L	CIRCUMFERENCE R OF BASE L	INSIDE SPREAD	AREA	STATE/ PROVINCE	HUNTER'S NAME	DATE	RANK
*74 6/8	14 5/8 14 5/8	6 2/8 5 7/8	11 1/8	Johnson County	WY	Roy L. Walk	2004	1361
74 6/8	13 6/8 13 7/8	5 7/8 5 6/8	8 1/8	Gunnison County	CO	Pat Reilly	2005	1361
74 6/8	14 2/8 14 4/8	6 6/8 6 7/8	9 5/8	Moffat County	CO	Richard Bray	2005	1361
*74 6/8	14 4/8 14 6/8	6 0/8 6 0/8	11 4/8	Campbell County	WY	Joe McDaniel	2005	1361
74 6/8	15 7/8 16 1/8	6 2/8 6 2/8	15 6/8	Fallon County	MT	Kevin Lech	2006	1361
74 6/8	15 0/8 14 7/8	5 7/8 5 7/8	7 4/8	Washoe County	NV	Matt Brown	2007	1361
74 6/8	13 2/8 14 3/8	6 1/8 6 2/8	9 3/8	Clark County	ID	Dave R. Burget	2007	1361
74 6/8	14 6/8 15 1/8	5 5/8 5 5/8	9 7/8	Sioux County	NE	John P. Filsinger	2007	1361
74 6/8	14 4/8 15 0/8	6 0/8 5 7/8	8 2/8	Moffat County	CO	Clay J. Evans	2007	1361
74 6/8	14 1/8 13 7/8	6 0/8 5 7/8	10 0/8	Mora County	NM	Gus Congemi	2008	1361
74 6/8	12 4/8 12 3/8	5 6/8 5 6/8	12 1/8	Big Horn County	WY	Charlotte Moss	2008	1361
74 1/8	14 1/8 14 2/8	6 2/8 5 7/8	7 4/8	Wayne County	UT	Roy Hampton	2008	1361
74 6/8	14 5/8 14 6/8	6 1/8 6 1/8	10 6/8	Converse County	WY	James Holtgrewe	2008	1361
74 6/8	13 7/8 14 0/8	6 1/8 6 1/8	8 1/8	Washakie County	WY	David Gluyas	2008	1361
74 6/8	15 3/8 15 3/8	5 7/8 5 7/8	8 5/8	Custer County	SD	Chad P. Lehman	2008	1361
74 6/8	14 4/8 14 6/8	5 6/8 5 6/8	11 6/8	Catron County	NM	John Hoffman	2009	1361
*74 6/8	14 1/8 13 7/8	6 1/8 6 1/8	7 0/8	Garfield County	UT	Alan Kendall	2009	1361
74 6/8	14 4/8 14 4/8	6 3/8 6 3/8	12 5/8	Lincoln County	WY	Eric Boley	2009	1361
74 6/8	15 0/8 14 6/8	5 6/8 5 6/8	9 0/8	Lincoln County	WY	David R. Ellis	2009	1361
*74 6/8	14 4/8 14 4/8	5 7/8 5 7/8	12 6/8	Cimarron County	OK	Rollie L. Lunsford	2009	1361
74 4/8	14 6/8 14 4/8	6 2/8 6 2/8	12 3/8	Campbell County	WY	William P. Mastrangel	1957	1448
74 4/8	15 3/8 15 3/8	6 3/8 6 2/8	11 2/8	Lincoln County	NM	Harvey May	1960	1448
74 4/8	14 2/8 14 6/8	6 0/8 6 1/8	12 0/8	Ward County	ND	Bennie Burtts	1964	1448
74 4/8	14 1/8 14 0/8	6 6/8 6 5/8	8 7/8	Wheeler County	NE	Lynn M. Briggs	1965	1448
74 4/8	13 4/8 13 6/8	7 1/8 7 2/8	8 5/8	Sioux County	NE	Bill Carlos	1969	1448
74 4/8	14 0/8 14 2/8	6 4/8 6 4/8	11 5/8	Lyman County	SD	Loran Hills	1970	1448
74 4/8	15 4/8 15 2/8	5 6/8 5 6/8	9 7/8	Sweetwater County	WY	Clifford White	1977	1448
74 4/8	14 4/8 14 4/8	6 0/8 5 6/8	7 2/8	Logan County	KS	Calvin Henry	1980	1448
74 4/8	13 3/8 13 3/8	6 1/8 6 0/8	9 0/8	Moffat County	CO	George Griffiths	1981	1448
74 4/8	12 5/8 12 7/8	6 4/8 6 4/8	10 5/8	Arapahoe County	CO	Sid Strzok	1982	1448
74 4/8	14 2/8 14 2/8	6 4/8 6 4/8	10 0/8	Baca County	CO	Bill McEndree	1982	1448
74 4/8	13 5/8 13 2/8	6 3/8 6 3/8	12 1/8	Moffat County	CO	Dale Drilling	1985	1448
74 4/8	14 1/8 14 5/8	6 1/8 6 2/8	14 4/8	Modoc County	CA	George Taylor	1985	1448
74 4/8	14 1/8 13 7/8	5 0/8 5 0/8	9 4/8	Converse County	WY	Ronald M. Cook	1985	1448
74 4/8	13 3/8 13 3/8	6 5/8 6 5/8	10 0/8	Sweetwater County	WY	Bill Clink	1986	1448
74 4/8	13 3/8 13 3/8	6 4/8 6 4/8	7 4/8	Sweetwater County	WY	Glenn E. Hisey	1986	1448
74 4/8	14 3/8 12 7/8	6 4/8 6 4/8	10 2/8	Carbon County	UT	Don R. Logston	1986	1448
74 4/8	14 2/8 14 4/8	6 4/8 6 3/8	15 7/8	Rosebud County	MT	Wayne Pearson	1986	1448
74 4/8	15 3/8 15 4/8	6 0/8 6 0/8	8 4/8	Washoe County	NV	Timothy P. Wooley	1987	1448
74 4/8	14 4/8 14 4/8	6 0/8 6 0/8	10 2/8	Natrona County	WY	James R. McCain	1988	1448
74 4/8	14 4/8 14 4/8	6 4/8 6 3/8	8 6/8	Moffat County	CO	Doy K. Curtis	1988	1448
74 4/8	15 0/8 14 6/8	5 7/8 5 7/8	6 5/8	Nye County	NV	Jim Loncar	1989	1448
74 4/8	14 0/8 13 7/8	5 7/8 5 7/8	8 1/8	Tooele County	UT	Paul H. Laver	1989	1448
74 4/8	14 4/8 15 1/8	6 1/8 6 1/8	14 1/8	Washoe County	NV	Darrel Reed	1990	1448
74 4/8	13 5/8 14 0/8	6 7/8 6 7/8	11 4/8	Washoe County	NV	Rick Lund	1990	1448
74 4/8	14 2/8 14 1/8	5 7/8 6 0/8	8 1/8	Carbon County	WY	Dennis Bader	1990	1448
74 4/8	13 4/8 13 3/8	6 2/8 6 1/8	10 4/8	Yavapai County	AZ	Van Clark	1990	1448
74 4/8	15 1/8 15 1/8	5 5/8 5 5/8	13 3/8	Millard County	UT	Tom Stephenson	1991	1448
74 4/8	14 1/8 14 3/8	6 2/8 6 2/8	6 7/8	Rosebud County	MT	Rick Miller	1991	1448
74 4/8	14 2/8 14 2/8	6 2/8 6 2/8	14 5/8	Toole County	MT	Ryan Winkowitsch	1991	1448
74 4/8	13 5/8 13 3/8	6 7/8 6 2/8	9 0/8	Butte County	SD	Gary English	1992	1448
74 4/8	13 3/8 13 3/8	6 6/8 6 7/8	10 3/8	Uinta County	WY	Clifford Rockhold	1992	1448
74 4/8	15 0/8 15 2/8	6 0/8 6 0/8	10 4/8	Carbon County	WY	Robert E. Bergquist	1992	1448
74 4/8	15 0/8 15 0/8	6 0/8 6 1/8	12 3/8	Converse County	WY	A. M. Oakes, Jr.	1992	1448
74 4/8	14 2/8 14 0/8	6 3/8 6 3/8	9 7/8	Kimball County	NE	Kevin Matthews	1993	1448
74 4/8	14 1/8 14 3/8	6 2/8 6 2/8	8 3/8	Carbon County	WY	Willis Duhon	1993	1448
74 4/8	15 7/8 15 4/8	5 5/8 5 4/8	11 0/8	Hudspeth County	TX	Randy Martin	1993	1448
74 4/8	14 6/8 13 7/8	6 4/8 6 4/8	18 1/8	Yavapai County	AZ	Patrick Kirby	1994	1448
74 4/8	14 4/8 14 4/8	6 2/8 6 2/8	7 6/8	Grand County	UT	Melinda Schmidt	1994	1448
74 4/8	13 3/8 13 3/8	6 1/8 6 0/8	9 5/8	Campbell County	WY	Lee Seeley	1994	1448
74 4/8	13 7/8 13 5/8	6 1/8 6 1/8	9 1/8	Moffat County	CO	Michael L. Cone	1995	1448
74 4/8	14 6/8 14 7/8	5 6/8 5 6/8	11 0/8	Golden Valley County	ND	Terry Buechler	1995	1448
74 4/8	13 7/8 14 0/8	6 2/8 6 2/8	9 7/8	Petroleum County	MT	Mark D. Hughes	1995	1448
74 4/8	14 3/8 14 2/8	6 7/8 6 4/8	10 4/8	Huerfano County	CO	George S. Smith III	1995	1448
74 4/8	14 2/8 14 0/8	6 1/8 6 1/8	8 1/8	Natrona County	WY	Dale A. Storey	1995	1448
74 4/8	14 6/8 14 3/8	6 1/8 6 1/8	12 4/8	Sweetwater County	WY	Paul D. Kauchich	1996	1448
74 4/8	13 2/8 13 2/8	6 4/8 6 4/8	9 0/8	Weld County	CO	Neil Chandler	1997	1448
74 4/8	14 0/8 14 1/8	5 6/8 5 6/8	11 3/8	Albany County	WY	John J. Brooks	1999	1448
74 4/8	14 6/8 14 5/8	5 6/8 5 6/8	9 6/8	Carbon County	WY	Steven J. Torok	1999	1448
74 4/8	13 5/8 13 7/8	6 2/8 6 2/8	10 3/8	Moffat County	CO	Tom Hoffman	2000	1448
74 4/8	14 4/8 14 6/8	6 2/8 6 2/8	16 0/8	Lincoln County	NM	David J. Fuller	2000	1448
74 4/8	14 5/8 14 5/8	5 5/8 5 5/8	10 2/8	Rio Grande County	CO	Manuel A. Banderas	2000	1448
74 4/8	14 5/8 14 6/8	5 6/8 5 4/8	15 6/8	Johnson County	WY	Paul Chaffee	2000	1448
74 4/8	15 3/8 15 3/8	6 1/8 6 1/8	14 0/8	Garfield County	MT	Mike Backes	2001	1448
74 4/8	13 6/8 14 1/8	6 2/8 6 1/8	8 7/8	Harding County	SD	Jack Volk	2001	1448
74 4/8	14 6/8 14 5/8	6 0/8 6 0/8	11 3/8	Campbell County	WY	Skip Valentine	2001	1448
74 4/8	13 2/8 13 4/8	6 4/8 6 3/8	9 4/8	Natrona County	WY	Justin Wollerman	2002	1448
74 4/8	13 2/8 14 2/8	5 7/8 6 0/8	9 0/8	Las Animas County	CO	Eldon J. Jandreau	2002	1448
74 4/8	13 6/8 13 7/8	6 0/8 6 0/8	8 2/8	Tooele County	UT	Bill Plowman	2002	1448
74 4/8	13 4/8 13 6/8	6 4/8 6 4/8	8 6/8	Natrona County	WY	Shawn Wagner	2003	1448
74 4/8	14 1/8 14 1/8	6 0/8 6 0/8	8 3/8	Madison County	MT	Bruce Ryan	2003	1448
74 4/8	14 6/8 14 6/8	6 3/8 6 3/8	9 2/8	Perkins County	SD	Troy Hanson	2003	1448
74 4/8	15 4/8 15 2/8	6 3/8 6 0/8	10 1/8	Washakie County	WY	Tom Buller	2003	1448
*74 4/8	15 2/8 15 0/8	5 6/8 5 6/8	10 4/8	Weld County	CO	Jordan Tarbett	2004	1448
*74 4/8	14 4/8 14 2/8	6 0/8 6 0/8	8 6/8	Humboldt County	NV	Mark Jones	2004	1448
74 4/8	13 3/8 13 1/8	7 0/8 7 0/8	11 3/8	Rosebud County	MT	Gene A. Welle	2004	1448
74 4/8	14 2/8 14 4/8	5 4/8 5 4/8	14 5/8	Converse County	WY	Jeff Thomas	2004	1448
74 4/8	13 1/8 13 2/8	6 4/8 6 4/8	10 2/8	Converse County	WY	Ben Lauer	2004	1448
74 4/8	14 2/8 14 4/8	5 7/8 5 7/8	10 4/8	Clark County	ID	Virgil Burget	2005	1448
74 4/8	13 1/8 12 4/8	6 6/8 6 6/8	10 2/8	Rosebud County	MT	Doug Spieker	2006	1448
*74 4/8	15 0/8 15 1/8	5 6/8 6 1/8	7 3/8	Johnson County	WY	Brian Thomas	2006	1448
*74 4/8	14 0/8 14 2/8	6 4/8 6 6/8	12 2/8	Medicine Hat	ALB	David L. Sipple	2006	1448
*74 4/8	13 6/8 13 2/8	6 6/8 6 4/8	9 0/8	Sioux County	NE	Steve Anderson	2006	1448
74 4/8	14 0/8 14 2/8	6 2/8 6 2/8	12 5/8	Millard County	UT	LaMar K. Cox	2007	1448
*74 4/8	13 2/8 13 3/8	6 3/8 6 3/8	10 0/8	Madison County	MT	John P. Branger	2007	1448

825

PRONGHORN
Continued

Minimum Score 67

SCORE	LENGTH OF R HORN L	CIRCUMFERENCE R OF BASE L	INSIDE SPREAD	AREA	STATE/ PROVINCE	HUNTER'S NAME	DATE	RANK
74 4/8	13 0/8 13 1/8	6 2/8 6 2/8	9 0/8	Carbon County	WY	Clay J. Evans	2008	1448
74 4/8	13 4/8 13 4/8	6 2/8 6 2/8	10 3/8	Moffat County	CO	Cory Collins	2008	1448
74 4/8	15 2/8 15 1/8	6 0/8 5 7/8	7 2/8	Hanna	ALB	Tracey Erickson	2008	1448
74 4/8	14 3/8 14 3/8	5 4/8 5 3/8	6 7/8	Lewis & Clark County	MT	Steve Tennant	2008	1448
*74 4/8	13 7/8 13 5/8	6 1/8 6 1/8	11 0/8	Blindloss	ALB	Dan Hartley	2008	1448
74 4/8	15 4/8 15 3/8	5 4/8 5 4/8	18 4/8	Ziebach County	SD	Wesley Koehler	2008	1448
74 4/8	14 4/8 14 4/8	6 4/8 6 4/8	7 5/8	Crook County	WY	Don G. Scofield	2008	1448
*74 4/8	14 2/8 14 2/8	5 6/8 5 5/8	10 2/8	Humboldt County	NV	Nelson Holman	2009	1448
74 4/8	15 2/8 14 7/8	6 0/8 5 7/8	7 1/8	Lake County	OR	Rick Herron	2009	1448
74 4/8	14 1/8 14 5/8	6 2/8 6 1/8	7 7/8	Natrona County	WY	Benjamin A. Minks	2009	1448
74 4/8	14 3/8 14 3/8	5 6/8 5 6/8	7 5/8	Las Animas County	CO	Jason Baudino	2009	1448
74 4/8	13 2/8 13 2/8	6 6/8 6 6/8	12 7/8	Cherry County	NE	Kyle Hochstein	2009	1448
74 4/8	16 0/8 15 6/8	5 7/8 6 0/8	10 2/8	Weston County	WY	Ronald E. Bruce	2009	1448
*74 4/8	13 3/8 13 3/8	6 5/8 6 3/8	8 7/8	Natrona County	WY	Bill Clink	2010	1448
74 4/8	14 1/8 14 0/8	6 1/8 6 1/8	9 1/8	Converse County	WY	Dane Shryock	2010	1448
74 4/8	14 6/8 15 0/8	5 3/8 5 1/8	10 4/8	Moffat County	CO	Craig A. Bries	2010	1448
74 2/8	13 4/8 13 7/8	5 5/8 5 5/8	8 1/8	Sweet Grass County	MT	Charles Alkire	1964	1539
74 2/8	14 5/8 14 6/8	6 3/8 6 2/8	10 3/8	Sioux County	NE	Wayne Scherbarth	1969	1539
74 2/8	13 2/8 13 2/8	6 7/8 6 7/8	10 2/8	Converse County	WY	Arnie Roytek	1981	1539
74 2/8	14 0/8 14 0/8	6 1/8 6 1/8	11 4/8	Carbon County	WY	Scott A. Smith	1981	1539
74 2/8	14 1/8 14 0/8	6 0/8 6 0/8	9 2/8	Moffat County	CO	Bret Thomas Atkins	1981	1539
74 2/8	14 6/8 14 4/8	6 0/8 6 1/8	14 7/8	Moffat County	CO	Dennis Heitz	1982	1539
74 2/8	14 2/8 14 2/8	5 3/8 5 3/8	8 5/8	Moffat County	CO	Rich Padula	1982	1539
74 2/8	13 1/8 13 0/8	6 2/8 6 2/8	7 6/8	Sweetwater County	WY	Keith Dana	1983	1539
74 2/8	14 6/8 14 7/8	6 0/8 5 7/8	9 1/8	Graham County	AZ	Jeran E Montierth	1983	1539
74 2/8	14 4/8 14 3/8	5 7/8 5 7/8	9 5/8	Union County	NM	Keith Cheatham	1983	1539
74 2/8	13 3/8 13 5/8	6 1/8 6 0/8	11 7/8	Converse County	WY	John Ellas	1983	1539
74 2/8	12 6/8 14 4/8	6 4/8 6 4/8	12 7/8	Crook County	OR	Garry Rodakowski	1986	1539
74 2/8	13 4/8 13 4/8	6 1/8 6 1/8	12 2/8	Moffat County	CO	Tim Decker	1987	1539
74 2/8	14 6/8 14 7/8	6 0/8 6 0/8	13 1/8	Sweetwater County	WY	Marty Talbott	1987	1539
74 2/8	14 5/8 14 4/8	5 6/8 5 7/8	10 0/8	Cochise County	AZ	Jim Tomlin	1987	1539
74 2/8	15 3/8 15 4/8	6 5/8 6 6/8	13 0/8	Rosebud County	MT	Ricky L. Miller	1987	1539
74 2/8	15 4/8 15 6/8	5 7/8 5 7/8	10 4/8	Eddy County	NM	Jimmy King	1987	1539
74 2/8	13 4/8 13 5/8	6 4/8 6 4/8	9 0/8	Sweetwater County	WY	Brenda Hatcher	1988	1539
74 2/8	15 4/8 14 7/8	6 1/8 6 3/8	13 0/8	Natrona County	WY	George A. Fenton	1988	1539
74 2/8	14 4/8 14 7/8	6 0/8 6 0/8	9 3/8	Natrona County	WY	Gerry C. Stinski	1988	1539
74 2/8	13 5/8 13 5/8	5 7/8 5 6/8	8 3/8	Coconino County	AZ	Jim Wheeler	1989	1539
74 2/8	13 6/8 13 6/8	6 1/8 6 1/8	11 0/8	Sweetwater County	WY	Quince Hale	1989	1539
74 2/8	14 4/8 14 6/8	6 2/8 6 0/8	11 2/8	Washoe County	NV	Robert D. Jeffers	1990	1539
74 2/8	14 4/8 14 6/8	6 2/8 6 3/8	8 7/8	Rich County	UT	Patrick Hogle	1990	1539
74 2/8	14 6/8 15 0/8	5 6/8 5 5/8	9 2/8	Laramie County	WY	Steve Bellis	1990	1539
74 2/8	15 0/8 15 0/8	6 0/8 6 0/8	10 0/8	Billings County	ND	Todd Winczewski	1990	1539
74 2/8	15 0/8 15 0/8	5 7/8 5 6/8	7 7/8	Natrona County	WY	Paul A. Anderson	1990	1539
74 2/8	14 0/8 13 5/8	6 3/8 6 3/8	7 6/8	Rich County	UT	Robert G. Petersen	1990	1539
74 2/8	12 7/8 12 7/8	6 0/8 6 0/8	12 2/8	Johnson County	WY	Gerald V. Shields	1990	1539
74 2/8	14 4/8 14 3/8	5 4/8 5 4/8	8 5/8	Carter County	MT	Jamie Byrne	1990	1539
74 2/8	14 2/8 14 5/8	6 2/8 6 0/8	8 2/8	Moffat County	CO	John L. Gardner	1991	1539
74 2/8	14 0/8 14 0/8	6 2/8 6 3/8	10 0/8	Moffat County	CO	Michael Dziekan	1991	1539
74 2/8	14 1/8 13 6/8	6 3/8 6 3/8	11 6/8	Moffat County	CO	Cary Laman	1991	1539
74 2/8	13 7/8 14 0/8	6 4/8 6 2/8	8 2/8	Carbon County	WY	Daniel H. House, Jr.	1991	1539
74 2/8	14 0/8 14 1/8	6 2/8 6 2/8	11 0/8	Moffat County	CO	Bruno Ammann	1991	1539
74 2/8	14 2/8 14 2/8	5 5/8 5 5/8	9 5/8	Converse County	WY	Gene Mathias	1991	1539
74 2/8	15 1/8 15 4/8	5 6/8 5 6/8	16 1/8	Hettinger County	ND	Scott Wiseman	1991	1539
74 2/8	15 0/8 14 7/8	5 6/8 5 6/8	7 3/8	Natrona County	WY	Ronald Dean Nelson	1991	1539
74 2/8	13 3/8 13 2/8	6 3/8 6 3/8	9 7/8	Laramie County	WY	Jim Krawczyk	1992	1539
74 2/8	14 2/8 14 3/8	6 7/8 6 6/8	10 0/8	Natrona County	WY	Gary Morse	1992	1539
74 2/8	13 1/8 13 1/8	6 5/8 6 4/8	9 3/8	Weld County	CO	Michael J. McArtor	1992	1539
74 2/8	15 3/8 15 3/8	5 3/8 5 2/8	10 0/8	Socorro County	NM	John J. Hayes	1993	1539
74 2/8	14 3/8 14 3/8	5 7/8 5 6/8	13 1/8	Moffat County	CO	K-Tal G. Johnson	1993	1539
74 2/8	15 0/8 15 1/8	6 0/8 6 3/8	12 2/8	Owyhee County	ID	Jay D. King	1993	1539
74 2/8	14 2/8 13 6/8	5 6/8 5 6/8	10 2/8	Nemiscam	ALB	Murray T. Campbell	1993	1539
74 2/8	13 2/8 13 3/8	6 0/8 6 0/8	9 0/8	Box Butte County	NE	Richard E. Placzek	1994	1539
74 2/8	13 6/8 13 6/8	6 3/8 6 3/8	8 5/8	Campbell County	WY	Dave Justmann	1994	1539
74 2/8	14 1/8 14 2/8	5 7/8 5 6/8	10 1/8	Owyhee County	ID	Jason L. Angell	1996	1539
74 2/8	16 0/8 16 2/8	5 0/8 4 6/8	8 3/8	Yavapai County	AZ	Mickey Clancy	1996	1539
74 2/8	14 0/8 14 2/8	6 4/8 6 4/8	9 5/8	Moffat County	CO	Casey Oliver	1996	1539
74 2/8	12 1/8 12 3/8	6 4/8 6 5/8	12 5/8	Lyman County	SD	Kirk C. Graham	1996	1539
74 2/8	14 0/8 14 2/8	6 3/8 6 2/8	9 0/8	Moffat County	CO	David L. Butler	1996	1539
74 2/8	14 1/8 14 3/8	6 1/8 6 1/8	9 0/8	Moffat County	CO	Scott George	1996	1539
74 2/8	15 3/8 15 3/8	5 4/8 5 4/8	10 5/8	Pima County	AZ	Michael John Bylina	1997	1539
74 2/8	14 6/8 14 7/8	6 0/8 6 0/8	7 7/8	Natrona County	WY	Joel Goodman	1997	1539
74 2/8	14 6/8 14 5/8	6 1/8 6 1/8	9 6/8	Moffat County	CO	Brandon Ray	1998	1539
74 2/8	14 4/8 14 3/8	5 7/8 6 1/8	10 1/8	Lassen County	CA	Jeff Rose	1998	1539
74 2/8	14 3/8 14 4/8	6 3/8 6 2/8	10 3/8	Albany County	WY	Mark J. Anderson	1998	1539
74 2/8	14 1/8 14 0/8	5 7/8 5 7/8	12 2/8	Grant County	NM	John H. Trewern	1998	1539
74 2/8	13 7/8 14 0/8	5 6/8 5 6/8	8 7/8	Malheur County	OR	Rick Martin	1998	1539
74 2/8	15 0/8 15 0/8	6 0/8 6 0/8	7 3/8	Moffat County	CO	Steve Sheehy	1999	1539
74 2/8	14 1/8 14 1/8	6 5/8 6 5/8	12 1/8	Moffat County	CO	Michael P. McCarty	1999	1539
74 2/8	14 1/8 14 0/8	6 1/8 6 1/8	12 3/8	Natrona County	WY	Gus Congemi	1999	1539
74 2/8	14 4/8 14 4/8	6 0/8 5 7/8	8 2/8	Rosebud County	MT	Chuck Adams	2000	1539
74 2/8	14 1/8 14 2/8	4 5/8 5 0/8	12 2/8	Campbell County	WY	Kenneth Morga	2000	1539
74 2/8	15 4/8 14 7/8	6 2/8 6 1/8	4 4/8	Weld County	CO	Jacob Chandler	2001	1539
74 2/8	13 6/8 13 4/8	5 5/8 5 5/8	13 4/8	Park County	CO	Spencer Esch	2002	1539
74 2/8	13 2/8 15 2/8	6 4/8 6 3/8	12 4/8	Uintah County	UT	Jake Gardiner	2002	1539
74 2/8	14 4/8 14 4/8	5 7/8 6 0/8	11 3/8	Washakie County	WY	Luke Roush	2002	1539
74 2/8	14 0/8 13 7/8	6 1/8 6 1/8	9 4/8	Ziebach County	SD	Tom Svendsen	2002	1539
74 2/8	15 3/8 15 4/8	6 0/8 5 7/8	11 4/8	Powder River County	MT	Don G. Scofield	2002	1539
74 2/8	14 6/8 14 5/8	5 6/8 5 5/8	11 6/8	Albany County	WY	Jerry Bowen	2003	1539
74 2/8	13 5/8 13 6/8	6 4/8 6 3/8	9 2/8	Converse County	WY	Joseph R. Russo	2003	1539
74 2/8	15 1/8 15 2/8	6 2/8 6 0/8	10 4/8	Campbell County	WY	Rick Petersen	2003	1539
*74 2/8	14 3/8 13 7/8	5 5/8 5 5/8	9 0/8	Las Animas County	CO	Michael Yeary	2004	1539
74 2/8	13 6/8 14 0/8	6 0/8 6 0/8	14 0/8	Gunnison County	CO	Jon Boyd	2004	1539
74 2/8	14 0/8 13 7/8	6 0/8 6 0/8	11 2/8	Campbell County	WY	Eric F. Efird	2004	1539
74 2/8	13 5/8 13 1/8	6 7/8 6 6/8	9 4/8	Converse County	WY	Bob Gilbert	2004	1539
*74 2/8	14 2/8 14 2/8	6 4/8 6 4/8	6 2/8	Uinta County	WY	Jerry Brunow	2005	1539

826

PRONGHORN

Minimum Score 67 — Continued

SCORE	LENGTH OF R HORN L	CIRCUMFERENCE R OF BASE L	INSIDE SPREAD	AREA	STATE/ PROVINCE	HUNTER'S NAME	DATE	RANK
74 2/8	13 7/8 13 5/8	5 6/8 5 7/8	10 4/8	Custer County	ID	Matt Douthit	2005	1539
74 2/8	14 6/8 14 5/8	6 3/8 6 2/8	9 6/8	Owyhee County	ID	Mike Moore	2005	1539
*74 2/8	12 5/8 12 4/8	6 4/8 6 2/8	5 0/8	Pueblo County	CO	Jerry Viera	2006	1539
74 2/8	14 4/8 14 3/8	6 1/8 6 1/8	10 5/8	Blaine County	MT	Tom M. Benson	2006	1539
74 2/8	14 1/8 13 7/8	6 5/8 6 5/8	9 1/8	Crook County	WY	Bruce Ryan	2006	1539
74 2/8	13 2/8 13 2/8	6 4/8 6 4/8	12 6/8	Berry Creek	ALB	Russell Hillis	2008	1539
*74 2/8	15 2/8 15 2/8	5 7/8 5 7/8	9 2/8	Crook County	WY	Robert C. Smith	2008	1539
74 2/8	14 1/8 14 3/8	6 4/8 6 4/8	4 6/8	Weld County	CO	Rudy E. Maestas, Jr.	2009	1539
74 2/8	14 1/8 13 6/8	6 2/8 6 3/8	10 7/8	Fremont County	WY	Garland Nelson	2009	1539
*74 2/8	14 0/8 14 5/8	6 3/8 6 2/8	12 2/8	Jackson County	CO	Marlan D. Hanson	2009	1539
74 2/8	13 0/8 13 0/8	6 5/8 6 4/8	10 4/8	Natrona County	WY	Jeff Jacob	2009	1539
74 2/8	14 7/8 14 7/8	5 7/8 5 7/8	14 3/8	Jackson County	CO	Tom Kelley	2009	1539
*74 2/8	14 7/8 15 4/8	6 1/8 6 1/8	8 7/8	Johnson County	WY	Tom Nelson	2010	1539
74 2/8	14 0/8 14 0/8	6 0/8 6 0/8	12 1/8	Moffat County	CO	Todd Clyncke	2010	1539
74 2/8	13 3/8 13 3/8	6 1/8 5 7/8	12 1/8	Beaver County	UT	Wayne Hansen	2010	1539
74 2/8	14 4/8 14 3/8	6 0/8 5 7/8	12 4/8	Albany County	WY	Jerry Bowen	2010	1539
74 0/8	14 1/8 13 7/8	6 2/8 6 2/8	9 5/8	Carbon County	WY	James N. Willcox	1977	1634
74 0/8	15 2/8 15 5/8	6 2/8 6 3/8	11 4/8	McKinley County	NM	Alfred J. Herrera	1979	1634
74 0/8	14 3/8 14 0/8	6 3/8 6 1/8	11 3/8	Jefferson County	ID	Earl Peterson	1980	1634
74 0/8	15 0/8 15 1/8	5 5/8 5 5/8	10 5/8	Wallace County	KS	Mike Gilbert	1980	1634
74 0/8	16 0/8 15 4/8	5 6/8 5 4/8	8 6/8	Converse County	WY	Frank Moore	1981	1634
74 0/8	13 7/8 13 7/8	6 1/8 6 2/8	10 1/8	Moffat County	CO	Randy Sanburg	1981	1634
74 0/8	14 5/8 14 4/8	6 4/8 6 2/8	8 6/8	Valley County	MT	Tom Devlin	1984	1634
74 0/8	13 4/8 13 3/8	5 7/8 5 6/8	10 4/8	Sweetwater County	WY	Herb Voyles	1985	1634
74 0/8	15 1/8 14 6/8	6 1/8 6 1/8	8 4/8	Moffat County	CO	John Cottrell	1986	1634
74 0/8	14 1/8 14 0/8	6 4/8 6 4/8	11 7/8	Billings County	ND	Greg Schafer	1986	1634
74 0/8	14 2/8 14 3/8	6 2/8 6 0/8	8 7/8	Klamath County	OR	Randall T. Drabandt	1987	1634
74 0/8	14 3/8 14 1/8	6 0/8 5 7/8	8 3/8	Moffat County	CO	Bob Bain	1987	1634
74 0/8	15 1/8 15 3/8	6 2/8 6 2/8	10 6/8	Sweetwater County	WY	Jackie Simmons	1988	1634
74 0/8	14 0/8 13 6/8	5 6/8 5 5/8	11 3/8	Millard County	UT	John G. Homatas	1988	1634
74 0/8	15 0/8 14 4/8	6 4/8 6 4/8	8 7/8	Sweetwater County	WY	Norman Lee Bradley	1990	1634
74 0/8	14 1/8 13 5/8	6 6/8 6 4/8	12 1/8	Carbon County	WY	Rod Schmidt	1990	1634
74 0/8	15 0/8 14 5/8	5 3/8 5 3/8	8 3/8	Moffat County	CO	Glenn Pritchard	1990	1634
74 0/8	14 2/8 14 7/8	5 7/8 5 5/8	8 0/8	Carter County	MT	Mark Frank	1990	1634
74 0/8	13 1/8 13 2/8	6 4/8 6 3/8	8 5/8	County of 40 Mile	ALB	Brent Van Maarion	1990	1634
74 0/8	14 1/8 14 1/8	6 3/8 6 2/8	12 3/8	Sierra County	NM	Peter La Scala	1991	1634
74 0/8	14 5/8 14 7/8	6 5/8 6 5/8	9 5/8	Morgan County	UT	Dallas Smith	1991	1634
74 0/8	13 1/8 13 4/8	6 5/8 6 4/8	9 3/8	Niobrara County	WY	Tom J. Bruegger	1991	1634
74 0/8	13 4/8 13 4/8	6 1/8 6 1/8	7 2/8	Millard County	UT	Craig Bonham	1992	1634
74 0/8	14 3/8 13 6/8	6 1/8 6 2/8	10 7/8	Lake County	OR	Rick Breckel	1992	1634
74 0/8	14 2/8 14 0/8	6 2/8 6 1/8	10 2/8	Johnson County	WY	Gary L. Miller	1992	1634
74 0/8	14 1/8 14 3/8	5 7/8 5 7/8	11 1/8	Converse County	WY	Louis Cinquegrano	1992	1634
74 0/8	13 3/8 13 3/8	6 5/8 6 4/8	10 2/8	Sioux County	NE	Roger DeKok	1993	1634
74 0/8	14 7/8 15 1/8	5 7/8 5 6/8	9 5/8	Sweetwater County	WY	Bill Clink	1993	1634
74 0/8	13 4/8 13 4/8	6 3/8 6 4/8	9 6/8	Johnson County	WY	Gary G. Olson	1993	1634
74 0/8	13 6/8 14 0/8	5 7/8 5 7/8	9 1/8	Uintah County	UT	Ron Williams	1994	1634
74 0/8	12 6/8 13 1/8	6 6/8 6 6/8	10 2/8	Wallace County	KS	Dale R. Larson	1994	1634
74 0/8	13 4/8 13 4/8	6 6/8 6 5/8	7 6/8	Converse County	WY	David L. Miller	1994	1634
74 0/8	13 4/8 13 7/8	5 7/8 5 6/8	13 6/8	Converse County	WY	John S. Miller	1994	1634
74 0/8	15 4/8 15 6/8	5 5/8 5 5/8	9 7/8	Lincoln County	NM	Ed Whitten	1995	1634
74 0/8	15 0/8 14 5/8	6 0/8 6 0/8	13 1/8	Lemhi County	ID	Ben Fahnholz	1995	1634
74 0/8	14 0/8 14 3/8	6 0/8 5 7/8	12 0/8	Campbell County	WY	Ryan J. Dorak	1995	1634
74 0/8	13 2/8 13 3/8	6 1/8 6 0/8	5 6/8	Moffat County	CO	E. Damon Handley	1996	1634
74 0/8	13 4/8 13 4/8	6 4/8 6 4/8	10 5/8	Moffat County	CO	Jim Halbritter	1996	1634
74 0/8	15 5/8 15 2/8	5 6/8 5 6/8	8 2/8	Colfax County	NM	Robert L. Pagel, Jr.	1996	1634
74 0/8	13 4/8 15 1/8	6 0/8 6 0/8	11 0/8	Coconino County	AZ	Mark Purcell	1996	1634
74 0/8	14 4/8 14 6/8	5 7/8 6 0/8	10 6/8	Moffat County	CO	Dan Hedgecoke	1996	1634
74 0/8	14 2/8 14 1/8	5 7/8 5 7/8	9 0/8	Natrona County	WY	Richard Manchur	1996	1634
74 0/8	13 3/8 13 3/8	7 1/8 7 1/8	11 5/8	Natrona County	WY	Todd C. Braschler	1996	1634
74 0/8	13 0/8 13 3/8	6 4/8 6 3/8	10 7/8	Moffat County	CO	Chuck Adams	1997	1634
74 0/8	14 5/8 14 0/8	6 1/8 6 1/8	14 6/8	Lea County	NM	John A. Barnes	1997	1634
74 0/8	15 4/8 15 3/8	5 7/8 5 6/8	8 4/8	Yavapai County	AZ	Michael Aleff	1997	1634
74 0/8	14 6/8 15 4/8	5 7/8 5 7/8	10 1/8	Campbell County	WY	Michael King	1997	1634
74 0/8	13 7/8 13 6/8	6 4/8 6 4/8	11 3/8	Sweetwater County	WY	Rick Schack	1997	1634
74 0/8	14 1/8 14 3/8	5 6/8 5 6/8	9 3/8	Humboldt County	NV	Ben E. Clark	1998	1634
74 0/8	13 3/8 13 2/8	6 1/8 6 0/8	9 7/8	Natrona County	WY	Alex Gemrich	1998	1634
74 0/8	13 6/8 13 5/8	6 2/8 6 2/8	12 6/8	Moffat County	CO	Joel D. Morgan	1999	1634
74 0/8	14 4/8 14 2/8	6 1/8 6 0/8	9 6/8	Natrona County	WY	Dave McFarlin	1999	1634
74 0/8	13 2/8 15 0/8	6 1/8 5 7/8	8 3/8	Yavapai County	AZ	Randy J. Stalcup	1999	1634
74 0/8	14 2/8 14 1/8	5 7/8 5 7/8	9 0/8	Natrona County	WY	Richard Manchur	1999	1634
74 0/8	14 2/8 13 6/8	6 3/8 6 4/8	8 7/8	Uintah County	UT	Jed Brown	2001	1634
74 0/8	17 0/8 17 1/8	5 4/8 5 5/8	10 0/8	Lincoln County	NM	Rudy Apodala	2001	1634
74 0/8	13 1/8 13 1/8	6 4/8 6 4/8	9 6/8	Blaine County	MT	Kirk Perszyk	2001	1634
74 0/8	14 0/8 13 5/8	6 4/8 6 3/8	8 6/8	Moffat County	CO	Michael Adkins, Sr.	2001	1634
74 0/8	14 7/8 15 1/8	5 4/8 5 3/8	9 7/8	Chouteau County	MT	Richard Pierce	2001	1634
74 0/8	14 1/8 14 1/8	6 0/8 6 0/8	10 4/8	Albany County	WY	Roger L. Garrett	2002	1634
74 0/8	13 7/8 14 0/8	6 1/8 6 0/8	10 5/8	Larimer County	CO	Chad Lee Andrews	2002	1634
74 0/8	14 5/8 15 1/8	6 0/8 6 0/8	9 4/8	Lincoln County	WY	Heath Eddins	2003	1634
74 0/8	13 6/8 14 4/8	5 7/8 5 7/8	9 2/8	Campbell County	WY	Richard Kent	2003	1634
74 0/8	13 1/8 13 1/8	6 2/8 6 1/8	9 0/8	Garfield County	MT	DuWayne Larson	2004	1634
*74 0/8	14 2/8 14 3/8	5 7/8 5 7/8	12 2/8	Medicine Hat	ALB	Jim Hillstead	2004	1634
74 0/8	13 2/8 12 7/8	6 3/8 6 4/8	9 2/8	Powder River County	MT	Jim Bradford	2005	1634
74 0/8	15 4/8 15 2/8	5 5/8 5 5/8	8 5/8	Crook County	WY	Don Scofield	2005	1634
*74 0/8	14 3/8 14 5/8	6 3/8 6 3/8	12 0/8	Powder River County	MT	Denny South	2006	1634
74 0/8	15 1/8 15 3/8	6 0/8 6 0/8	9 5/8	Owyhee County	ID	Paul Pierce	2006	1634
*74 0/8	13 5/8 13 7/8	6 3/8 6 1/8	8 6/8	Natrona County	WY	Darren Douglas	2006	1634
74 0/8	14 6/8 14 6/8	5 5/8 5 5/8	9 6/8	Powder River County	MT	Robert Dowen	2006	1634
*74 0/8	14 0/8 14 0/8	5 4/8 5 5/8	12 0/8	Campbell County	WY	Joe McDaniel	2006	1634
74 0/8	15 0/8 14 1/8	6 4/8 6 2/8	12 6/8	Converse County	WY	Peter Woeck	2006	1634
74 0/8	13 1/8 13 6/8	6 1/8 6 0/8	8 4/8	Big Horn County	WY	Jeff Gavne	2007	1634
74 0/8	14 1/8 14 1/8	6 2/8 6 1/8	7 4/8	Carbon County	WY	Brent Jensen	2007	1634
74 0/8	15 1/8 14 7/8	5 6/8 5 4/8	7 4/8	Garfield County	UT	Joseph T. Allman	2007	1634
74 0/8	14 7/8 14 6/8	6 0/8 5 7/8	6 0/8	Uinta County	WY	Amy C. Jasso	2007	1634
*74 0/8	15 1/8 14 2/8	5 5/8 5 6/8	8 7/8	Huerfano County	CO	Rafael Mendoza, Jr.	2008	1634
*74 0/8	13 5/8 14 0/8	6 0/8 6 0/8	11 0/8	Natrona County	WY	Charles Denny	2008	1634

PRONGHORN

Minimum Score 67 — Continued

SCORE	LENGTH OF R HORN L	CIRCUMFERENCE R OF BASE L	INSIDE SPREAD	AREA	STATE/ PROVINCE	HUNTER'S NAME	DATE	RANK
74 0/8	13 4/8 13 5/8	6 1/8 6 0/8	11 7/8	Converse County	WY	Mike Swartz	2008	1634
74 0/8	14 2/8 14 2/8	6 2/8 6 0/8	9 6/8	White Pine County	NV	Denise Edwards	2009	1634
*74 0/8	14 0/8 13 6/8	5 6/8 5 4/8	10 3/8	Las Animas County	CO	Nate Treadwell	2009	1634
*74 0/8	14 4/8 14 4/8	6 0/8 5 7/8	11 4/8	Campbell County	WY	Mike Schmidt	2009	1634
74 0/8	15 4/8 15 4/8	5 4/8 5 4/8	7 5/8	Campbell County	WY	Mike B. Ryan	2009	1634
74 0/8	13 5/8 13 4/8	6 0/8 6 1/8	10 1/8	Sweetwater County	WY	Michael Hagar	2009	1634
74 0/8	14 5/8 14 3/8	5 7/8 5 7/8	9 4/8	Park County	MT	Edward Lamb	2009	1634
*74 0/8	14 2/8 14 4/8	5 5/8 5 5/8	12 4/8	Coconino County	AZ	Geoffrey Walker	2009	1634
73 6/8	14 0/8 14 0/8	6 1/8 6 2/8	13 7/8	Williams County	ND	Robert Halseth	1967	1721
73 6/8	14 2/8 14 0/8	6 2/8 6 2/8	10 4/8	Sweetwater County	WY	Dan Winder	1973	1721
73 6/8	13 4/8 13 3/8	5 6/8 5 6/8	10 5/8	Sweetwater County	WY	Ellen Lewis	1978	1721
73 6/8	14 4/8 15 0/8	6 0/8 6 0/8	10 0/8	Sweetwater County	WY	Clifford White	1978	1721
73 6/8	14 2/8 14 1/8	6 1/8 6 0/8	7 7/8	Converse County	WY	Charles Stephens	1980	1721
73 6/8	14 2/8 14 1/8	6 5/8 6 4/8	8 5/8	Converse County	WY	Don Schram	1982	1721
73 6/8	13 4/8 13 4/8	6 2/8 6 2/8	12 2/8	Carbon County	WY	Willis P. Duhon, Jr.	1983	1721
73 6/8	14 4/8 14 7/8	6 0/8 5 7/8	9 3/8	Sweetwater County	WY	Larry J. Aksamit	1983	1721
73 6/8	13 3/8 13 4/8	6 3/8 6 1/8	10 1/8	Natrona County	WY	John Priday	1983	1721
73 6/8	12 7/8 12 7/8	7 0/8 6 7/8	10 7/8	Natrona County	WY	Pat McAteer	1984	1721
73 6/8	14 7/8 15 0/8	5 6/8 5 6/8	14 0/8	Custer County	MT	Marty Penrod	1984	1721
73 6/8	15 1/8 15 0/8	5 7/8 5 7/8	10 3/8	Moffat County	CO	Lonny Vanatta	1985	1721
73 6/8	14 6/8 14 4/8	6 0/8 6 0/8	10 6/8	Moffat County	CO	Kurt Keskimaki	1986	1721
73 6/8	13 3/8 13 6/8	6 0/8 6 1/8	8 5/8	Sweetwater County	WY	Ryan Roark	1986	1721
73 6/8	14 1/8 13 6/8	6 3/8 6 3/8	10 7/8	McKinley County	NM	Terry L. Sanders	1986	1721
73 6/8	14 3/8 14 2/8	6 2/8 6 3/8	8 6/8	Lemhi County	ID	Ben Fahnholz	1987	1721
73 6/8	15 4/8 15 1/8	6 0/8 6 1/8	11 1/8	Divide County	ND	Kenneth Engelhart	1987	1721
73 6/8	14 2/8 14 1/8	6 1/8 6 1/8	10 6/8	Campbell County	WY	Tamas M. Raday	1988	1721
73 6/8	14 7/8 14 6/8	6 2/8 6 2/8	10 4/8	Converse County	WY	Bruce Warburg	1988	1721
73 6/8	13 7/8 13 6/8	6 0/8 6 1/8	9 6/8	Campbell County	WY	Nick Hengel	1988	1721
73 6/8	14 2/8 14 2/8	5 7/8 5 6/8	11 6/8	Moffat County	CO	Ron Rockwell	1988	1721
73 6/8	13 7/8 13 7/8	6 0/8 6 0/8	11 4/8	Converse County	WY	Gary De Smidt	1988	1721
73 6/8	14 5/8 15 0/8	6 0/8 6 0/8	11 0/8	Carbon County	WY	Rod Schmidt	1989	1721
73 6/8	14 3/8 14 2/8	6 2/8 6 2/8	8 1/8	Washoe County	NV	Gregory G. Koehl	1990	1721
73 6/8	14 3/8 14 4/8	6 4/8 6 4/8	8 0/8	Natrona County	WY	Ron Niziolek	1990	1721
73 6/8	13 6/8 14 1/8	6 2/8 6 0/8	10 3/8	Moffat County	CO	Ron Serwa	1990	1721
73 6/8	14 2/8 14 4/8	5 7/8 5 6/8	9 4/8	Cascade County	MT	Dan Holskey	1990	1721
73 6/8	14 1/8 14 1/8	5 6/8 5 7/8	10 3/8	Moffat County	CO	Robert L. Syvertson, Jr.	1991	1721
73 6/8	13 7/8 13 7/8	6 2/8 6 1/8	9 3/8	Las Animas County	CO	J. Austin Warfield	1991	1721
73 6/8	14 7/8 14 5/8	5 5/8 5 5/8	11 2/8	Campbell County	WY	Russ Miller	1991	1721
73 6/8	13 7/8 13 7/8	6 1/8 6 1/8	10 7/8	Converse County	WY	Jerry Worley	1991	1721
73 6/8	14 1/8 14 1/8	6 1/8 6 0/8	13 2/8	Harney County	OR	Donald R. Paulsen	1991	1721
73 6/8	14 6/8 15 0/8	6 1/8 5 7/8	8 1/8	Madison County	MT	Doug Stonebraker	1991	1721
73 6/8	14 3/8 14 3/8	5 6/8 5 4/8	10 2/8	Campbell County	WY	Bruce Hudalla	1991	1721
73 6/8	15 4/8 15 2/8	5 5/8 5 6/8	8 7/8	Rosebud County	MT	Michael J. Kemp	1991	1721
73 6/8	13 4/8 13 4/8	6 1/8 6 1/8	9 0/8	Sheridan County	WY	Gerhard Eimer	1991	1721
73 6/8	14 1/8 14 0/8	6 1/8 6 1/8	9 6/8	Uinta County	WY	Joseph D. Maddock	1992	1721
73 6/8	14 2/8 13 7/8	6 4/8 6 2/8	7 7/8	Manyberries	ALB	Dale Farn	1992	1721
73 6/8	14 6/8 15 4/8	6 4/8 6 4/8	14 4/8	Yavapai County	AZ	Curtis Gregory	1993	1721
73 6/8	13 6/8 13 7/8	6 1/8 6 1/8	12 7/8	Jackson County	CO	Richard Bellows	1993	1721
73 6/8	13 0/8 13 0/8	6 0/8 6 0/8	10 3/8	Cypress	ALB	Dan David	1993	1721
73 6/8	13 5/8 13 2/8	6 2/8 6 3/8	10 3/8	Sweetwater County	WY	Renee A. Dana	1994	1721
73 6/8	14 5/8 14 5/8	6 1/8 6 1/8	9 3/8	Custer County	ID	David A. Faike	1994	1721
73 6/8	15 6/8 15 7/8	5 5/8 5 4/8	12 2/8	Harding County	SD	Al Kuntz	1994	1721
73 6/8	14 0/8 14 0/8	6 4/8 6 3/8	9 4/8	Crook County	WY	Mike Galles	1994	1721
73 6/8	14 3/8 14 1/8	5 7/8 5 6/8	10 0/8	Carbon County	WY	Larry Cross	1995	1721
73 6/8	13 7/8 13 7/8	6 1/8 6 1/8	12 2/8	Weld County	CO	Jim Tatro	1995	1721
73 6/8	15 3/8 15 0/8	5 5/8 5 4/8	7 3/8	Jenner	ALB	Melvin Barr	1995	1721
73 6/8	14 5/8 14 5/8	6 3/8 6 1/8	10 0/8	Platte County	WY	Dennis Crew	1995	1721
73 6/8	13 7/8 13 4/8	5 6/8 5 6/8	10 6/8	White Pine County	NV	Robert McDonald	1996	1721
73 6/8	14 4/8 14 4/8	6 0/8 6 0/8	9 2/8	Elko County	NV	Chief Nutting	1996	1721
73 6/8	13 4/8 13 2/8	6 3/8 6 2/8	11 2/8	Moffat County	CO	Jeff LaBaw	1996	1721
73 6/8	14 1/8 13 7/8	5 5/8 5 5/8	8 7/8	Converse County	WY	Jeff Haltom	1996	1721
73 6/8	13 2/8 13 2/8	5 7/8 5 7/8	7 6/8	Moffat County	CO	Warren Strickland	1997	1721
73 6/8	14 6/8 14 3/8	6 3/8 6 4/8	8 0/8	Hot Springs County	WY	Nathan Messenger	1997	1721
73 6/8	14 4/8 14 5/8	5 4/8 5 4/8	8 6/8	Uintah County	UT	Jerry Dee Slaugh	1998	1721
73 6/8	14 7/8 14 5/8	5 6/8 5 5/8	8 5/8	Millard County	UT	Greg S. Dalton	1998	1721
73 6/8	14 3/8 14 4/8	6 0/8 6 0/8	10 6/8	Weld County	CO	Wesley Peterson	1998	1721
73 6/8	15 0/8 14 6/8	6 5/8 6 2/8	11 7/8	Natrona County	WY	Beth Nelson	1998	1721
73 6/8	14 1/8 14 0/8	6 0/8 5 6/8	8 2/8	Johnson County	WY	Andy Stanco	1998	1721
73 6/8	13 6/8 14 1/8	6 3/8 6 3/8	9 3/8	Big Horn County	WY	H. Mike Palmer	1999	1721
73 6/8	15 0/8 14 0/8	6 3/8 6 3/8	8 7/8	Weld County	CO	Neil Chandler	1999	1721
73 6/8	14 6/8 14 6/8	6 1/8 5 7/8	11 4/8	Weld County	CO	Aaron Fite	2000	1721
73 6/8	14 7/8 15 0/8	5 6/8 5 6/8	9 3/8	McKenzie County	ND	Jack Sorum	2000	1721
73 6/8	14 7/8 14 5/8	6 3/8 6 2/8	11 5/8	Laramie County	WY	Greg Bokash	2004	1721
73 6/8	14 1/8 14 0/8	5 7/8 5 6/8	10 0/8	Elko County	NV	Jesse Buckner	2004	1721
73 6/8	13 7/8 14 0/8	6 3/8 6 4/8	11 3/8	Natrona County	WY	Jason Swanson	2004	1721
73 6/8	13 7/8 13 7/8	6 3/8 6 3/8	9 1/8	Albany County	WY	Jerry Bowen	2004	1721
73 6/8	13 6/8 13 3/8	6 0/8 6 0/8	10 7/8	Rosebud County	MT	Kris Obleness	2005	1721
73 6/8	15 1/8 15 4/8	5 6/8 5 6/8	9 5/8	Garfield County	UT	Mark E. Nentwich	2005	1721
73 6/8	13 5/8 13 5/8	6 2/8 6 0/8	9 5/8	Petroleum County	MT	Mike Huff	2005	1721
73 6/8	15 1/8 13 3/8	6 2/8 6 2/8	6 1/8	Rio Blanco County	CO	Scott Jankowski	2005	1721
73 6/8	12 6/8 13 1/8	6 5/8 6 6/8	10 6/8	Crook County	WY	Chris Kifer	2005	1721
73 6/8	14 0/8 14 2/8	6 2/8 6 2/8	10 4/8	Perkins County	SD	David L. Delsoldato	2005	1721
*73 6/8	12 5/8 12 5/8	6 1/8 6 2/8	7 2/8	Converse County	WY	Greg Flynn	2005	1721
73 6/8	13 4/8 13 4/8	6 2/8 6 2/8	16 3/8	Sweetwater County	WY	Dave R. Burget	2006	1721
73 6/8	14 4/8 14 4/8	5 6/8 5 6/8	9 2/8	Rosebud County	MT	Pier Brewer	2006	1721
73 6/8	13 7/8 13 7/8	6 0/8 5 6/8	7 6/8	Albany County	WY	Chad Hoefs	2006	1721
73 6/8	14 2/8 14 4/8	6 0/8 6 1/8	11 2/8	Moffat County	CO	John Sarvis	2006	1721
*73 6/8	14 1/8 13 4/8	5 7/8 5 6/8	7 4/8	Sublette County	WY	David L. Brady	2006	1721
73 6/8	13 2/8 13 3/8	6 2/8 6 0/8	11 4/8	Converse County	WY	Mike Stover	2006	1721
73 6/8	14 2/8 14 5/8	6 3/8 6 2/8	7 3/8	Malheur County	OR	Dusty Bourasa	2006	1721
*73 6/8	14 4/8 14 6/8	6 7/8 6 7/8	10 1/8	Natrona County	WY	Darren Douglas	2007	1721
*73 6/8	12 7/8 13 0/8	6 5/8 6 5/8	9 2/8	Lewis & Clark County	MT	Beau Parisi	2007	1721
*73 6/8	14 3/8 14 1/8	5 6/8 5 6/8	7 4/8	Harding County	SD	Jack Volk	2007	1721
73 6/8	14 5/8 14 6/8	5 6/8 5 5/8	11 0/8	Niobrara County	WY	Mike Kucera	2007	1721
73 6/8	13 7/8 13 7/8	6 4/8 6 5/8	11 7/8	Converse County	WY	Michael Clevinger	2008	1721

PRONGHORN

Minimum Score 67
Continued

SCORE	LENGTH OF R HORN L	CIRCUMFERENCE R OF BASE L	INSIDE SPREAD	AREA	STATE/ PROVINCE	HUNTER'S NAME	DATE	RANK
73 6/8	13 3/8 13 4/8	6 1/8 6 1/8	9 3/8	Johnson County	WY	Mike Kistler	2008	1721
73 6/8	14 2/8 14 2/8	6 2/8 6 2/8	12 0/8	Fergus County	MT	D. "Mitch" Kottas	2008	1721
73 6/8	14 0/8 14 1/8	6 1/8 6 2/8	11 0/8	Las Animas County	CO	Mandie Hill	2008	1721
*73 6/8	13 2/8 13 4/8	6 1/8 6 1/8	7 1/8	Sheridan County	WY	Jim W. Martin	2009	1721
73 6/8	13 3/8 14 0/8	6 0/8 6 0/8	9 6/8	Converse County	WY	Alan Brock	2009	1721
*73 6/8	13 6/8 14 0/8	6 2/8 6 3/8	16 1/8	Suffield	ALB	Steven J. Kullman	2009	1721
73 6/8	13 4/8 13 2/8	6 2/8 6 2/8	10 5/8	Converse County	WY	Stephen P. Satterlund	2009	1721
73 6/8	14 7/8 14 4/8	6 0/8 5 7/8	7 3/8	Johnson County	WY	Jody L. Ketterling	2010	1721
73 6/8	13 6/8 13 4/8	7 0/8 7 1/8	9 5/8	Powder River County	MT	Robert Dowen	2010	1721
73 4/8	15 4/8 15 1/8	5 6/8 5 7/8	8 3/8	Moffat County	CO	Henry Wichers	1957	1817
73 4/8	16 0/8 16 4/8	5 6/8 5 6/8	15 6/8	Guadalupe County	NM	Jack McCaw	1961	1817
73 4/8	15 7/8 16 0/8	5 7/8 5 6/8	10 5/8	Coconino County	AZ	Charles Meriwether	1968	1817
73 4/8	13 0/8 12 6/8	6 1/8 6 6/8	10 7/8	McLean County	ND	Roy O. Yunker	1971	1817
73 4/8	13 0/8 12 5/8	6 1/8 6 2/8	9 4/8	Carbon County	WY	John Marolt III	1971	1817
73 4/8	13 2/8 13 2/8	6 7/8 6 6/8	10 0/8	Moffat County	CO	Curtis Lynn	1972	1817
73 4/8	15 4/8 15 4/8	5 3/8 5 3/8	12 4/8	Natrona County	WY	Mel Johnson	1981	1817
73 4/8	13 0/8 13 4/8	6 3/8 6 3/8	10 6/8	Sublette County	WY	Terry Reach	1982	1817
73 4/8	14 4/8 14 6/8	6 2/8 6 3/8	8 3/8	Natrona County	WY	Kim S. Ades	1982	1817
73 4/8	15 0/8 15 2/8	5 6/8 5 7/8	8 4/8	Val Marie	SAS	Allan Sykes	1982	1817
73 4/8	15 4/8 15 4/8	6 0/8 6 1/8	13 2/8	Fremont County	WY	Dan Lookingbill	1983	1817
73 4/8	14 0/8 13 7/8	6 3/8 6 2/8	9 6/8	Weston County	WY	Dick Kinder	1983	1817
73 4/8	13 7/8 14 1/8	6 2/8 6 3/8	8 6/8	Sweetwater County	WY	Jim Dougherty	1983	1817
73 4/8	15 2/8 15 3/8	5 3/8 5 3/8	9 4/8	Prowers County	CO	Lloyd M. Brown	1984	1817
73 4/8	15 1/8 15 0/8	5 4/8 5 4/8	9 0/8	Coconino County	AZ	Richard Ball	1985	1817
73 4/8	13 7/8 14 2/8	6 1/8 6 0/8	9 7/8	Converse County	WY	Leland E. Scott	1985	1817
73 4/8	15 2/8 15 4/8	5 4/8 5 3/8	12 6/8	Lassen County	CA	Richard K. Hoppis	1986	1817
73 4/8	14 7/8 14 4/8	6 2/8 6 3/8	12 4/8	Garfield County	MT	John Fleharty	1986	1817
73 4/8	14 1/8 14 5/8	6 2/8 6 1/8	7 7/8	Moffat County	CO	Roger Gipple	1986	1817
73 4/8	13 6/8 14 2/8	6 0/8 6 0/8	8 3/8	Carbon County	WY	Rod Schmidt	1987	1817
73 4/8	14 2/8 14 6/8	6 0/8 6 0/8	7 3/8	Jefferson County	ID	Lonnie Gilson	1988	1817
73 4/8	14 4/8 14 1/8	6 1/8 6 0/8	9 1/8	Fremont County	WY	Jim Thieme	1988	1817
73 4/8	15 0/8 14 7/8	6 1/8 6 0/8	7 4/8	Campbell County	WY	Jim Keim	1988	1817
73 4/8	13 6/8 13 5/8	6 0/8 5 7/8	9 2/8	Carbon County	WY	Larry N. Perkins	1990	1817
73 4/8	14 2/8 14 1/8	6 1/8 6 1/8	8 1/8	Moffat County	CO	Michael LaVan	1990	1817
73 4/8	15 0/8 14 5/8	6 4/8 6 4/8	10 4/8	Millard County	UT	Robert Quayle	1990	1817
73 4/8	14 6/8 14 6/8	6 2/8 6 1/8	13 3/8	White Pine County	NV	Patrick Fillman	1991	1817
73 4/8	12 5/8 12 6/8	6 7/8 6 7/8	8 1/8	Campbell County	WY	Elroy Thorson	1991	1817
73 4/8	13 3/8 13 3/8	6 1/8 6 0/8	9 7/8	Niobrara County	WY	Rodney W. Rowe	1991	1817
73 4/8	13 1/8 13 4/8	6 0/8 6 2/8	12 0/8	Dunn County	ND	Keith Kaste	1991	1817
73 4/8	15 4/8 15 4/8	6 0/8 5 7/8	14 2/8	Harney County	OR	Charles L. Boatman	1991	1817
73 4/8	14 6/8 14 6/8	5 6/8 5 6/8	12 5/8	Harney County	OR	Roger Bersin	1991	1817
73 4/8	14 2/8 14 2/8	6 0/8 5 7/8	7 5/8	Platte County	WY	John Stienmetz	1991	1817
73 4/8	15 2/8 15 3/8	6 0/8 6 0/8	15 7/8	Washoe County	NV	Gregg Tanner	1992	1817
73 4/8	15 7/8 15 6/8	5 6/8 5 6/8	12 1/8	Mora County	NM	Doug Aikin	1992	1817
73 4/8	14 3/8 14 3/8	6 4/8 6 4/8	7 6/8	Washoe County	NV	Trinidad Guillen	1992	1817
73 4/8	13 6/8 13 5/8	6 3/8 6 3/8	12 6/8	Grant County	NM	Senovid Perea	1992	1817
73 4/8	13 6/8 13 7/8	6 3/8 6 3/8	8 7/8	Lincoln County	WY	Darrell Hansen	1992	1817
73 4/8	15 0/8 15 0/8	5 4/8 5 3/8	10 7/8	Millard County	UT	Steven Jackson	1992	1817
73 4/8	13 2/8 13 6/8	5 7/8 6 0/8	9 1/8	Malheur County	OR	Fredrick Johnson	1992	1817
73 4/8	13 2/8 13 2/8	6 1/8 6 1/8	9 1/8	Natrona County	WY	Gregory A. Lompart	1992	1817
73 4/8	14 3/8 14 2/8	5 7/8 6 2/8	8 3/8	Fremont County	WY	Gerald S. O'Dean	1992	1817
73 4/8	14 2/8 14 6/8	6 0/8 6 0/8	8 6/8	Campbell County	WY	Phillip M. Revering	1992	1817
73 4/8	14 6/8 14 5/8	6 0/8 5 5/8	10 0/8	Moffat County	CO	Scott Nelson	1993	1817
73 4/8	13 1/8 13 4/8	6 7/8 6 7/8	10 2/8	Moffat County	CO	Rett Kelly	1993	1817
73 4/8	14 1/8 14 0/8	6 2/8 6 2/8	11 1/8	Rosebud County	MT	Val Dierks	1993	1817
73 4/8	15 6/8 16 0/8	6 1/8 6 2/8	10 6/8	Wallace County	KS	Russell Hull	1993	1817
73 4/8	14 7/8 12 0/8	7 0/8 6 6/8	7 4/8	Rich County	UT	Hugh H. Hogle	1993	1817
73 4/8	14 3/8 15 1/8	6 2/8 6 0/8	10 6/8	Klamath County	OR	Patrick E. Wheeler	1994	1817
73 4/8	14 7/8 15 3/8	6 2/8 6 1/8	9 2/8	Weld County	CO	David L. Skiff	1994	1817
73 4/8	13 7/8 13 4/8	6 2/8 6 2/8	7 1/8	Converse County	WY	Bock Low	1994	1817
73 4/8	14 2/8 14 3/8	6 3/8 6 2/8	7 5/8	Clark County	ID	Max Heberling	1995	1817
73 4/8	14 5/8 14 5/8	6 0/8 6 0/8	12 0/8	Sweetwater County	WY	Ken Lumpkin	1996	1817
73 4/8	14 0/8 13 5/8	6 2/8 6 3/8	10 6/8	Moffat County	CO	Gary Stampka	1996	1817
73 4/8	14 1/8 13 7/8	6 3/8 6 3/8	8 5/8	Big Horn County	WY	Rob J. Westby	1996	1817
73 4/8	15 2/8 15 1/8	6 0/8 6 0/8	8 6/8	Moffat County	CO	Dave Accashian	1997	1817
73 4/8	14 1/8 14 1/8	5 7/8 5 7/8	11 1/8	Grand County	UT	Timothy D. Park	1997	1817
73 4/8	14 4/8 14 0/8	5 7/8 5 6/8	10 3/8	Lake County	OR	Donald W. Smith	1997	1817
73 4/8	13 4/8 13 4/8	6 1/8 6 1/8	11 5/8	Weld County	CO	Dennis Conran	1997	1817
73 4/8	14 1/8 14 0/8	7 2/8 7 0/8	10 7/8	Sweetwater County	WY	Clifford W. Rockhold	1998	1817
73 4/8	14 3/8 13 4/8	6 2/8 5 6/8	9 0/8	Campbell County	WY	Curtis C. Stull	1998	1817
73 4/8	13 5/8 13 5/8	6 4/8 6 5/8	11 7/8	Converse County	WY	Jason Abel	1998	1817
73 4/8	14 6/8 14 5/8	6 0/8 5 7/8	10 6/8	Moffat County	CO	Rob Crawford	1999	1817
73 4/8	14 2/8 14 2/8	6 0/8 6 1/8	11 4/8	Moffat County	CO	Mark D. Thomson	2000	1817
73 4/8	14 2/8 14 3/8	6 2/8 6 0/8	9 3/8	Garfield County	MT	Gary Panasuk	2000	1817
73 4/8	13 0/8 13 7/8	6 1/8 6 1/8	8 2/8	Cascade County	MT	Travis Almos	2000	1817
73 4/8	14 7/8 15 1/8	6 0/8 6 0/8	11 0/8	Converse County	WY	Jim Engle	2001	1817
73 4/8	14 5/8 13 5/8	6 0/8 6 0/8	9 0/8	Adams County	CO	Timothy L. Wagner	2002	1817
73 4/8	14 2/8 14 2/8	6 1/8 6 1/8	10 5/8	Blaine County	MT	Tom M. Benson	2003	1817
73 4/8	13 4/8 13 4/8	5 0/8 5 0/8	13 2/8	Converse County	WY	Frank S. Noska IV	2003	1817
73 4/8	13 5/8 13 4/8	6 6/8 6 5/8	9 1/8	Carter County	MT	Scott G. Hettinger	2003	1817
73 4/8	14 5/8 14 4/8	6 0/8 5 6/8	14 5/8	Meade County	SD	William J. Bushong	2003	1817
73 4/8	14 6/8 14 7/8	6 0/8 5 7/8	10 5/8	Powder River County	MT	Rick Hicks	2004	1817
73 4/8	13 2/8 13 3/8	6 3/8 6 4/8	9 6/8	Butte County	SD	Earl R. Smith	2004	1817
73 4/8	15 3/8 15 1/8	5 5/8 5 7/8	12 1/8	Sierra County	NM	Cole Eddie	2004	1817
73 4/8	13 4/8 13 6/8	6 1/8 6 0/8	7 4/8	Platte County	WY	Pat Covert	2004	1817
73 4/8	13 6/8 13 6/8	6 0/8 6 0/8	7 5/8	Apache County	AZ	Larry R. Marin	2004	1817
73 4/8	14 5/8 14 3/8	5 7/8 5 6/8	12 1/8	Converse County	WY	Gary Kautz	2004	1817
73 4/8	14 7/8 15 1/8	5 5/8 5 5/8	9 0/8	Powder River County	MT	Shane Johnson	2004	1817
73 4/8	13 4/8 13 4/8	6 1/8 6 1/8	12 4/8	Albany County	WY	Mike Yancey	2005	1817
73 4/8	14 1/8 14 2/8	6 2/8 6 5/8	8 5/8	Lake County	OR	Sheldon William Doughty	2005	1817
73 4/8	13 6/8 14 0/8	6 0/8 5 7/8	12 6/8	Carter County	MT	Kerry Bodeker	2005	1817
*73 4/8	15 0/8 15 2/8	6 0/8 6 2/8	9 5/8	Dawson County	MT	Gary Kreiman	2005	1817
73 4/8	12 6/8 12 6/8	6 1/8 6 0/8	6 5/8	Nye County	NV	Kyle Gray	2006	1817
73 4/8	15 0/8 14 7/8	5 4/8 5 5/8	13 0/8	Yavapai County	AZ	David D. O'Brien	2006	1817
*73 4/8	14 1/8 14 1/8	5 7/8 5 5/8	10 4/8	Campbell County	WY	Stephen P. Satterlund	2006	1817

829

PRONGHORN

Minimum Score 67 — Continued

SCORE	LENGTH OF R HORN L	CIRCUMFERENCE R OF BASE L	INSIDE SPREAD	AREA	STATE/ PROVINCE	HUNTER'S NAME	DATE	RANK
*73 4/8	13 1/8 — 13 3/8	6 4/8 — 6 3/8	8 2/8	Crook County	WY	DuWayne Larson	2006	1817
73 4/8	13 7/8 — 14 0/8	5 6/8 — 5 6/8	8 6/8	Elmore County	ID	Eric G. Prentice	2006	1817
73 4/8	13 7/8 — 14 4/8	6 1/8 — 6 0/8	10 7/8	Natrona County	WY	Gus Congemi	2006	1817
73 4/8	14 6/8 — 14 5/8	5 4/8 — 5 3/8	10 2/8	Albany County	WY	Greg Bokash	2006	1817
73 4/8	14 7/8 — 14 6/8	5 5/8 — 5 5/8	8 7/8	Lemhi County	ID	Brandon L. Fahnholz	2007	1817
73 4/8	15 0/8 — 14 6/8	6 3/8 — 6 4/8	11 3/8	Moffat County	CO	Ann Forster	2007	1817
73 4/8	14 0/8 — 14 2/8	6 1/8 — 6 2/8	10 0/8	Natrona County	WY	Chris Mautino	2007	1817
*73 4/8	14 4/8 — 14 4/8	6 1/8 — 6 2/8	9 5/8	Cavendish	ALB	Bryce Dillabough	2007	1817
73 4/8	15 1/8 — 14 6/8	5 7/8 — 5 7/8	8 0/8	Brooks	ALB	Doug Field	2007	1817
*73 4/8	13 7/8 — 14 0/8	6 1/8 — 6 2/8	12 4/8	Hidalgo County	NM	Marcy Harris	2008	1817
73 4/8	14 3/8 — 14 3/8	5 6/8 — 5 7/8	9 6/8	Converse County	WY	Sam Morello	2008	1817
73 4/8	13 3/8 — 13 1/8	6 0/8 — 6 0/8	9 3/8	Converse County	WY	Patrick Ferrie	2008	1817
*73 4/8	15 2/8 — 15 0/8	6 0/8 — 5 4/8	10 5/8	Grant County	ND	Steve L. Winkler	2008	1817
73 4/8	13 4/8 — 13 3/8	6 3/8 — 6 2/8	10 3/8	Sioux County	NE	Ross Nantkes	2008	1817
73 4/8	13 7/8 — 14 0/8	6 1/8 — 5 7/8	12 4/8	Converse County	WY	Edwin L. DeYoung	2008	1817
*73 4/8	14 6/8 — 14 4/8	6 3/8 — 6 1/8	10 0/8	Carbon County	WY	Mike Schmid	2009	1817
*73 4/8	13 1/8 — 13 2/8	6 0/8 — 6 0/8	8 4/8	Natrona County	WY	Bill Clink	2009	1817
*73 4/8	14 2/8 — 14 1/8	5 5/8 — 5 5/8	9 5/8	Converse County	WY	Thomas E. Day	2009	1817
73 4/8	14 0/8 — 14 2/8	6 2/8 — 6 0/8	8 6/8	Carbon County	WY	Clay J. Evans	2010	1817
73 4/8	13 4/8 — 13 4/8	6 2/8 — 6 0/8	11 5/8	Moffat County	CO	Clay J. Evans	2010	1817
73 2/8	13 0/8 — 13 1/8	6 6/8 — 6 4/8	11 3/8	Fremont County	WY	Chuck Kroll	1952	1923
73 2/8	11 3/8 — 11 7/8	6 3/8 — 6 3/8	11 1/8	Carter County	MT	Benny F. Padden	1960	1923
73 2/8	14 2/8 — 14 2/8	5 2/8 — 5 2/8	7 5/8	Fergus County	MT	Wayne Miller	1962	1923
73 2/8	14 6/8 — 14 3/8	6 0/8 — 6 0/8	9 2/8	Garfield County	MT	Paul Brunner	1976	1923
73 2/8	13 5/8 — 13 3/8	6 2/8 — 6 1/8	9 5/8	Converse County	WY	Abe White	1980	1923
73 2/8	13 0/8 — 13 0/8	6 4/8 — 6 5/8	9 6/8	Natrona County	WY	Robert F. Naumann	1981	1923
73 2/8	15 2/8 — 15 2/8	5 5/8 — 5 5/8	8 3/8	Sweetwater County	WY	Randy Gamble	1982	1923
73 2/8	15 2/8 — 15 0/8	5 4/8 — 5 5/8	9 4/8	Santa Cruz County	AZ	Tracy G. Hardy	1982	1923
73 2/8	13 3/8 — 13 5/8	6 2/8 — 6 2/8	13 3/8	Fremont County	WY	Bill Lookingbill	1982	1923
73 2/8	13 6/8 — 13 3/8	6 0/8 — 6 0/8	12 5/8	Musselshell County	MT	Daniel A. Nielsen	1982	1923
73 2/8	13 6/8 — 13 5/8	6 0/8 — 5 7/8	9 6/8	Natrona County	WY	James I. Shipley, Jr.	1982	1923
73 2/8	11 5/8 — 11 5/8	7 3/8 — 7 1/8	7 3/8	Siskiyou County	CA	Mike Domeyer	1982	1923
73 2/8	12 7/8 — 13 2/8	5 7/8 — 6 0/8	11 0/8	Moffat County	CO	Jack Cassidy	1983	1923
73 2/8	12 3/8 — 13 3/8	6 3/8 — 6 2/8	9 3/8	Moffat County	CO	John W. Rose	1983	1923
73 2/8	14 2/8 — 14 4/8	6 1/8 — 6 1/8	12 1/8	Moffat County	CO	Paul Locey	1983	1923
73 2/8	15 4/8 — 17 0/8	6 1/8 — 6 0/8	9 6/8	Coconino County	AZ	Randy Fix	1983	1923
73 2/8	13 4/8 — 14 0/8	5 7/8 — 6 1/8	10 4/8	Moffat County	CO	Charles B. Lanzarone	1983	1923
73 2/8	13 7/8 — 14 0/8	6 2/8 — 6 2/8	13 4/8	Fremont County	WY	John Priday	1984	1923
73 2/8	14 4/8 — 14 3/8	6 4/8 — 6 3/8	8 7/8	Converse County	WY	Lee Jernigan	1984	1923
73 2/8	14 2/8 — 14 4/8	6 1/8 — 6 1/8	10 0/8	Rosebud County	MT	Greg Munther	1986	1923
73 2/8	13 4/8 — 13 6/8	6 3/8 — 6 3/8	12 2/8	Moffat County	CO	Evans V. Brewster	1986	1923
73 2/8	14 5/8 — 15 0/8	6 1/8 — 6 0/8	15 1/8	Sweetwater County	WY	Harvey L. Dalton	1988	1923
73 2/8	14 1/8 — 14 5/8	5 7/8 — 5 7/8	9 2/8	Natrona County	WY	Robert F. Naumann	1988	1923
73 2/8	14 3/8 — 14 3/8	5 7/8 — 5 7/8	8 2/8	Converse County	WY	Ron Rockwell	1988	1923
73 2/8	14 3/8 — 15 0/8	5 7/8 — 5 7/8	10 5/8	Washoe County	NV	Larry Burchard	1990	1923
73 2/8	14 4/8 — 14 2/8	6 2/8 — 6 1/8	7 7/8	Abbey	SAS	Clarence Hughes	1990	1923
73 2/8	14 6/8 — 14 4/8	6 1/8 — 6 0/8	11 7/8	Fergus County	MT	Jess Knerr	1990	1923
73 2/8	13 1/8 — 13 2/8	6 1/8 — 6 0/8	9 7/8	Mountrail County	ND	Don Scofield	1990	1923
73 2/8	14 4/8 — 14 3/8	5 6/8 — 5 6/8	10 3/8	Buffalo	ALB	Roger Meyer	1990	1923
73 2/8	13 2/8 — 13 5/8	6 2/8 — 6 2/8	10 5/8	Campbell County	WY	Russell Guerndt	1990	1923
73 2/8	13 3/8 — 12 7/8	6 2/8 — 6 1/8	9 3/8	Musselshell County	MT	Michael James Songer	1990	1923
73 2/8	14 0/8 — 13 7/8	6 0/8 — 5 7/8	11 1/8	Sweetwater County	WY	Norman Lee Bradley	1991	1923
73 2/8	13 0/8 — 13 0/8	7 2/8 — 6 6/8	9 1/8	Converse County	WY	Russ Weakland	1991	1923
73 2/8	15 1/8 — 15 2/8	5 7/8 — 5 7/8	11 4/8	McKenzie County	ND	John H. Holt	1991	1923
73 2/8	14 4/8 — 14 6/8	5 6/8 — 5 7/8	10 2/8	Val Marie	SAS	Steve Von Hagen	1991	1923
73 2/8	15 3/8 — 15 1/8	5 7/8 — 5 6/8	11 6/8	Musselshell County	MT	Keith W. Hice	1991	1923
73 2/8	13 1/8 — 13 0/8	6 4/8 — 6 5/8	11 3/8	Sweetwater County	WY	Jeff Castagna	1992	1923
73 2/8	13 6/8 — 13 6/8	6 1/8 — 6 1/8	12 0/8	Sweetwater County	WY	Fred R. Trujillo	1992	1923
73 2/8	14 7/8 — 14 2/8	5 7/8 — 5 7/8	8 0/8	Moffat County	CO	Anthony Harrison	1992	1923
73 2/8	15 2/8 — 15 1/8	6 4/8 — 6 4/8	7 1/8	Butte County	ID	Troy Dale Green	1992	1923
73 2/8	13 7/8 — 14 0/8	6 1/8 — 6 1/8	11 3/8	Sweetwater County	WY	Richard L. Gasser	1992	1923
73 2/8	14 0/8 — 14 4/8	6 4/8 — 6 4/8	9 6/8	Laramie County	WY	Larry C. Bramich, Jr.	1992	1923
73 2/8	14 7/8 — 15 0/8	6 0/8 — 5 6/8	11 7/8	Jerome County	ID	John Wells	1992	1923
73 2/8	16 0/8 — 15 5/8	5 7/8 — 5 7/8	10 4/8	Sioux County	NE	Orville J. DeVoss	1992	1923
73 2/8	13 1/8 — 13 0/8	6 2/8 — 6 2/8	9 4/8	Rosebud County	MT	Michael J. Kemp	1992	1923
73 2/8	15 0/8 — 15 1/8	5 7/8 — 5 7/8	8 3/8	Converse County	WY	Donna M. Johnson	1992	1923
73 2/8	15 0/8 — 15 2/8	5 4/8 — 5 4/8	13 7/8	Eddy County	NM	Adam T. Wortley	1993	1923
73 2/8	13 6/8 — 13 6/8	6 0/8 — 5 7/8	8 5/8	Moffat County	CO	Kenneth M. Appelgren	1993	1923
73 2/8	12 7/8 — 13 0/8	6 2/8 — 6 2/8	11 2/8	Converse County	WY	Stephen C. Kremp	1993	1923
73 2/8	14 2/8 — 14 5/8	6 1/8 — 6 1/8	10 0/8	Converse County	WY	Mark Zastrow	1993	1923
73 2/8	14 2/8 — 14 2/8	6 0/8 — 5 7/8	11 2/8	Jenner	ALB	Kevin Stewart	1993	1923
73 2/8	13 4/8 — 13 2/8	6 3/8 — 6 3/8	10 0/8	Butte County	ID	Troy Green	1994	1923
73 2/8	14 4/8 — 14 2/8	5 6/8 — 5 6/8	12 0/8	Coconino County	AZ	Paul T. Carter	1994	1923
73 2/8	14 2/8 — 14 2/8	6 0/8 — 6 0/8	9 2/8	Lake County	OR	Mike Jackson	1994	1923
73 2/8	15 4/8 — 14 7/8	6 1/8 — 6 1/8	11 2/8	Lake County	OR	Jeffrey A. Eder	1994	1923
73 2/8	14 5/8 — 14 4/8	6 0/8 — 6 0/8	8 4/8	Campbell County	WY	Richard Lee Collins	1994	1923
73 2/8	14 2/8 — 14 1/8	5 7/8 — 5 7/8	10 3/8	Converse County	WY	Herbert F. Mielke	1994	1923
73 2/8	13 7/8 — 14 4/8	6 3/8 — 6 2/8	9 2/8	Jenner	ALB	Kevin Stewart	1994	1923
73 2/8	14 3/8 — 14 2/8	6 0/8 — 6 2/8	12 1/8	Deuel County	NE	Everett Tarrell	1994	1923
73 2/8	13 6/8 — 13 5/8	6 0/8 — 6 2/8	11 6/8	Beaverhead County	MT	Justin B. Quilling	1994	1923
73 2/8	14 1/8 — 13 6/8	6 2/8 — 6 1/8	7 4/8	Rio Blanco County	CO	Wade Shults	1995	1923
73 2/8	13 4/8 — 13 5/8	6 1/8 — 6 2/8	7 3/8	Twin Falls County	ID	Darrell Nunez	1995	1923
73 2/8	13 5/8 — 13 7/8	6 0/8 — 5 6/8	9 7/8	Fergus County	MT	Chris G. Sanford	1995	1923
73 2/8	13 6/8 — 14 0/8	6 1/8 — 5 6/8	8 0/8	Campbell County	WY	Derek J. Green	1995	1923
73 2/8	14 5/8 — 15 1/8	5 7/8 — 6 0/8	7 5/8	Sheridan County	WY	Thomas Ostrander	1995	1923
73 2/8	14 1/8 — 13 5/8	6 1/8 — 6 0/8	7 6/8	Converse County	WY	Don Miller	1995	1923
73 2/8	14 6/8 — 13 7/8	6 1/8 — 6 0/8	12 4/8	Carter County	MT	Scott Garner	1995	1923
73 2/8	14 0/8 — 13 7/8	6 1/8 — 6 2/8	10 2/8	Moffat County	CO	Bud Boker	1996	1923
73 2/8	14 7/8 — 15 0/8	5 5/8 — 5 6/8	12 1/8	Gunnison County	CO	George H. Bock	1996	1923
73 2/8	13 6/8 — 13 7/8	6 7/8 — 6 5/8	9 7/8	Converse County	WY	Ralph M. Inverso	1996	1923
73 2/8	13 5/8 — 13 6/8	6 1/8 — 5 7/8	10 0/8	Moffat County	CO	Bob Gulliksen	1997	1923
73 2/8	14 5/8 — 15 0/8	6 3/8 — 6 3/8	10 1/8	Moffat County	CO	Ron Lightley	1997	1923
73 2/8	13 5/8 — 13 3/8	6 4/8 — 6 4/8	12 3/8	Weld County	CO	Lynn Reese	1997	1923
73 2/8	14 3/8 — 14 1/8	6 3/8 — 6 2/8	12 1/8	Campbell County	WY	John A. Meyen	1997	1923
73 2/8	16 0/8 — 15 1/8	6 0/8 — 5 6/8	9 0/8	Yavapai County	AZ	Nathan Shane Garcia	1998	1923

PRONGHORN

Minimum Score 67 — Continued

SCORE	LENGTH OF R HORN L	CIRCUMFERENCE R OF BASE L	INSIDE SPREAD	AREA	STATE/PROVINCE	HUNTER'S NAME	DATE	RANK
73 2/8	14 4/8 14 3/8	6 3/8 6 2/8	13 3/8	Brown County	NE	Wade Luther	1998	1923
73 2/8	14 5/8 15 0/8	6 1/8 6 0/8	10 7/8	El Paso County	CO	Gene Pask	1998	1923
73 2/8	13 1/8 13 1/8	6 6/8 6 6/8	12 3/8	Weld County	CO	David L. Skiff	1998	1923
73 2/8	15 4/8 15 3/8	5 7/8 6 0/8	11 4/8	Musselshell County	MT	Joseph F. Petti	1999	1923
73 2/8	14 6/8 14 1/8	6 0/8 6 1/8	8 7/8	Elko County	NV	John Cooper	2000	1923
73 2/8	14 2/8 14 0/8	5 7/8 5 5/8	11 4/8	Weld County	CO	Matt Wagner	2000	1923
73 2/8	13 6/8 14 0/8	6 0/8 5 6/8	9 3/8	Blaine County	MT	Tom Benson	2000	1923
73 2/8	14 4/8 14 5/8	6 0/8 5 7/8	8 6/8	Las Animas County	CO	Andrew Bair	2001	1923
73 2/8	13 4/8 13 6/8	6 5/8 6 4/8	8 7/8	Gallatin County	MT	Bob Morton	2001	1923
73 2/8	14 7/8 14 6/8	6 3/8 6 0/8	8 2/8	Albany County	WY	David Rouge	2002	1923
73 2/8	15 0/8 14 4/8	6 0/8 6 0/8	11 1/8	Humboldt County	NV	Kevin D. Peterson	2003	1923
73 2/8	13 3/8 13 4/8	6 2/8 6 2/8	14 0/8	Washakie County	WY	Randy Burtis	2003	1923
73 2/8	13 0/8 13 5/8	6 3/8 6 5/8	8 2/8	Sweetwater County	WY	Mark Petersen	2003	1923
73 2/8	15 0/8 14 4/8	5 7/8 6 0/8	11 7/8	Butte County	SD	Nathan Jones	2003	1923
73 2/8	12 5/8 12 6/8	6 7/8 6 6/8	9 5/8	Big Horn County	WY	Susan K. Barrett	2004	1923
73 2/8	14 3/8 14 3/8	6 2/8 6 1/8	12 7/8	Perkins County	SD	Dale Penning	2004	1923
73 2/8	14 2/8 14 1/8	5 5/8 5 5/8	10 0/8	Garfield County	UT	McLain B. Mecham	2005	1923
73 2/8	14 0/8 14 2/8	6 0/8 6 0/8	10 7/8	Carbon County	UT	Tod Tabone	2005	1923
73 2/8	12 7/8 13 6/8	6 5/8 6 2/8	10 3/8	Beaverhead County	MT	Raymond Gross	2005	1923
73 2/8	12 0/8 12 0/8	7 1/8 6 6/8	10 7/8	Big Horn County	WY	George Kamps	2006	1923
*73 2/8	14 4/8 14 4/8	5 6/8 5 7/8	10 3/8	Carbon County	WY	Richard F. Katchuk	2006	1923
73 2/8	14 2/8 14 4/8	6 0/8 6 0/8	9 5/8	Johnson County	WY	Dallas F. Loney	2007	1923
73 2/8	13 4/8 14 2/8	6 1/8 6 1/8	7 3/8	Lewis & Clark County	MT	Larry Fischer	2008	1923
73 2/8	14 2/8 14 2/8	5 7/8 5 6/8	11 2/8	Las Animas County	CO	Barry J. Smith	2008	1923
73 2/8	14 2/8 14 5/8	5 7/8 5 7/8	7 5/8	Sheridan County	WY	Todd Richins	2008	1923
73 2/8	12 7/8 12 7/8	6 3/8 6 3/8	7 4/8	Campbell County	WY	Corey Hugelen	2008	1923
*73 2/8	14 0/8 13 6/8	6 5/8 6 4/8	9 1/8	Converse County	WY	Roy K. Keefer	2009	1923
*73 2/8	15 3/8 14 5/8	6 0/8 6 0/8	7 4/8	Powder River County	MT	Rick Arendsen	2009	1923
73 2/8	14 6/8 14 3/8	5 7/8 6 0/8	7 7/8	Campbell County	WY	Shawn Terry	2010	1923
*73 2/8	14 6/8 14 5/8	6 1/8 5 7/8	7 3/8	Las Animas County	CO	David Samuel	2010	1923
73 2/8	13 6/8 13 4/8	5 4/8 5 4/8	10 1/8	Moffat County	CO	Mark Turner	2010	1923
73 2/8	13 7/8 14 0/8	6 0/8 6 1/8	8 3/8	Natrona County	WY	Jason Stafford	2010	1923
73 2/8	14 5/8 14 5/8	6 0/8 5 7/8	9 2/8	Keith County	NE	Pete Luth	2010	1923
73 0/8	13 5/8 13 5/8	5 3/8 5 3/8	9 6/8	Harding County	SD	Ted G. Carter	1961	2031
73 0/8	12 7/8 12 6/8	6 2/8 6 3/8	11 7/8	Stark County	ND	Ronald D. Hauck	1970	2031
73 0/8	15 1/8 14 6/8	6 1/8 6 1/8	7 1/8	Converse County	WY	Ed Coy	1976	2031
73 0/8	14 0/8 14 2/8	5 4/8 5 4/8	11 6/8	Moffat County	CO	Fred Cornish	1980	2031
73 0/8	14 4/8 13 5/8	6 0/8 5 7/8	8 4/8	Klamath County	OR	Tom Tipton	1981	2031
73 0/8	13 7/8 13 7/8	6 3/8 6 2/8	11 0/8	Rosebud County	MT	Dan Helm	1982	2031
73 0/8	14 1/8 13 2/8	6 5/8 6 5/8	9 1/8	Sioux County	NE	Dick Kohles	1983	2031
73 0/8	13 5/8 13 7/8	5 6/8 5 6/8	7 6/8	Converse County	WY	Edward Oswald	1983	2031
73 0/8	13 4/8 13 4/8	6 1/8 6 0/8	11 2/8	Sweetwater County	WY	Marty Stubstad	1985	2031
73 0/8	14 1/8 13 7/8	5 5/8 5 5/8	9 6/8	Yavapai County	AZ	Christopher R. Jackson	1985	2031
73 0/8	14 7/8 12 6/8	6 0/8 10 1/8	9 1/8	Coconino County	AZ	Todd Rice	1987	2031
73 0/8	15 3/8 15 2/8	5 4/8 5 4/8	8 2/8	Blaine County	ID	Bruce McStay	1988	2031
73 0/8	13 2/8 13 4/8	6 4/8 6 2/8	10 6/8	Moffat County	CO	Garret Decker	1988	2031
73 0/8	16 0/8 16 0/8	5 3/8 5 5/8	12 0/8	Coconino County	AZ	Gary Steinmann	1988	2031
73 0/8	15 0/8 15 2/8	5 4/8 5 4/8	11 2/8	Converse County	WY	James Gates	1988	2031
73 0/8	14 1/8 14 2/8	6 0/8 6 0/8	10 6/8	Sargent County	ND	Dennis Wheeler	1988	2031
73 0/8	14 2/8 14 4/8	6 1/8 5 7/8	11 7/8	Washoe County	NV	Daryl Salley	1989	2031
73 0/8	13 5/8 13 7/8	5 7/8 5 7/8	8 6/8	Moffat County	CO	James Phelps	1989	2031
73 0/8	14 0/8 13 6/8	6 1/8 6 1/8	8 1/8	Sweetwater County	WY	David Urasky	1989	2031
73 0/8	15 0/8 15 1/8	5 6/8 5 6/8	12 0/8	Sublette County	WY	David Seaver	1989	2031
73 0/8	14 6/8 14 1/8	6 0/8 6 2/8	10 5/8	Sioux County	NE	David Clancy	1989	2031
73 0/8	15 4/8 15 0/8	5 5/8 5 5/8	14 7/8	Washoe County	NV	Jeffrey M. Kovac	1990	2031
73 0/8	13 3/8 13 5/8	6 4/8 6 5/8	9 5/8	Fremont County	WY	Gary Laya	1990	2031
73 0/8	13 1/8 13 3/8	5 7/8 6 1/8	8 2/8	Millard County	UT	Michael Pietropaolo	1990	2031
73 0/8	13 5/8 13 4/8	5 6/8 5 6/8	7 1/8	Lake County	OR	Rodney W. Ferry	1990	2031
73 0/8	14 0/8 13 5/8	5 7/8 5 7/8	7 6/8	Natrona County	WY	Greg Downs	1990	2031
73 0/8	14 1/8 14 4/8	6 2/8 6 2/8	13 4/8	Lassen County	CA	Stan Xavier	1991	2031
73 0/8	15 1/8 15 1/8	6 0/8 6 0/8	9 2/8	Rich County	UT	Hugh H. Hogle	1991	2031
73 0/8	13 0/8 13 0/8	6 2/8 6 2/8	8 6/8	Converse County	WY	Wayne Nicholson	1991	2031
73 0/8	15 0/8 15 1/8	5 7/8 5 6/8	7 2/8	Sioux County	NE	Dave Wray	1991	2031
73 0/8	14 1/8 14 2/8	6 6/8 6 5/8	8 1/8	Owyhee County	ID	Sam Wells	1992	2031
73 0/8	14 6/8 14 4/8	6 4/8 6 4/8	6 5/8	Twin Falls County	ID	Derek Trent	1992	2031
73 0/8	13 4/8 13 4/8	6 5/8 6 6/8	11 2/8	Sweetwater County	WY	Neil E. Hanson	1992	2031
73 0/8	15 2/8 15 0/8	5 5/8 5 5/8	11 3/8	Converse County	WY	Florentino G. Escobedo	1992	2031
73 0/8	13 4/8 13 2/8	6 2/8 6 3/8	9 3/8	Converse County	WY	Jon Brockfeld	1992	2031
73 0/8	13 1/8 13 2/8	6 1/8 6 1/8	8 0/8	Carbon County	WY	Joe Parziale	1993	2031
73 0/8	14 1/8 14 1/8	6 2/8 6 0/8	12 6/8	Sweetwater County	WY	Mike Barrett	1993	2031
73 0/8	13 7/8 13 7/8	5 6/8 5 6/8	11 1/8	Billings County	ND	Ron Feland	1993	2031
73 0/8	15 6/8 13 5/8	5 7/8 5 7/8	12 6/8	Hudspeth County	TX	Craig Baird	1993	2031
73 0/8	14 1/8 14 1/8	5 6/8 5 7/8	9 2/8	Klamath County	OR	Jason Townsend	1994	2031
73 0/8	13 3/8 13 3/8	6 4/8 6 4/8	8 7/8	Converse County	WY	George A. Zanoni	1994	2031
73 0/8	14 0/8 14 1/8	5 6/8 5 6/8	8 2/8	Medicine Hat	ALB	David W. Stuhr	1994	2031
73 0/8	14 7/8 13 4/8	6 4/8 6 4/8	7 6/8	Campbell County	WY	Kathy M. Patrone	1994	2031
73 0/8	13 1/8 13 4/8	6 1/8 6 0/8	9 6/8	Moffat County	CO	Bob Hoaglin, Jr.	1995	2031
73 0/8	14 4/8 14 3/8	5 6/8 5 6/8	10 1/8	Albany County	WY	Stuart Hazard	1995	2031
73 0/8	13 4/8 13 2/8	6 6/8 6 5/8	12 4/8	Converse County	WY	Frank S. Noska IV	1995	2031
73 0/8	13 4/8 13 0/8	5 7/8 6 0/8	9 2/8	Wallace County	KS	Kent Hensley	1995	2031
73 0/8	13 6/8 13 6/8	6 1/8 6 1/8	9 2/8	Lincoln County	WY	Doug Jenkins	1996	2031
73 0/8	14 2/8 14 4/8	6 0/8 6 0/8	12 4/8	Coconino County	AZ	Glen Whited	1996	2031
73 0/8	14 3/8 14 2/8	6 0/8 6 0/8	9 6/8	Natrona County	WY	Brian L. Wagner	1996	2031
73 0/8	14 1/8 14 3/8	6 4/8 6 3/8	9 6/8	Campbell County	WY	Dan W. Collins	1996	2031
73 0/8	13 7/8 14 1/8	6 0/8 6 0/8	10 1/8	Dunn County	ND	Troy A. Morris	1996	2031
73 0/8	15 1/8 15 0/8	6 0/8 6 0/8	9 1/8	Socorro County	NM	Lucas Robbins	1997	2031
73 0/8	14 2/8 14 0/8	6 1/8 6 0/8	8 7/8	Yavapai County	AZ	Duane "Corky" Richardson	1997	2031
73 0/8	13 2/8 13 2/8	6 5/8 6 3/8	10 5/8	Saguache County	CO	Alan R. Palmer	1997	2031
73 0/8	15 2/8 15 1/8	5 4/8 5 4/8	8 7/8	Yavapai County	AZ	Charles D. Lee	1998	2031
73 0/8	13 6/8 13 7/8	6 2/8 6 1/8	11 3/8	Beaverhead County	MT	Colleen Rose	1998	2031
73 0/8	13 6/8 13 7/8	5 7/8 5 6/8	14 3/8	Albany County	WY	Richard A. Walker	1999	2031
73 0/8	14 7/8 15 1/8	6 1/8 6 0/8	10 4/8	Converse County	WY	Jim Wondzell	1999	2031
73 0/8	13 0/8 13 4/8	6 4/8 6 3/8	12 4/8	Moffat County	CO	Dewayne Mullins	2000	2031
73 0/8	13 7/8 13 7/8	6 3/8 6 2/8	7 6/8	Moffat County	CO	Richard Bray	2000	2031
73 0/8	14 6/8 14 3/8	5 6/8 5 6/8	12 7/8	Lincoln County	WY	Greg Munther	2000	2031

831

PRONGHORN

Minimum Score 67   Continued

SCORE	LENGTH OF HORN R	L	CIRCUMFERENCE OF BASE R	L	INSIDE SPREAD	AREA	STATE/PROVINCE	HUNTER'S NAME	DATE	RANK
73 0/8	13 7/8	13 6/8	5 6/8	5 6/8	9 2/8	Sweetwater County	WY	James L. Steiss	2000	2031
73 0/8	14 1/8	14 1/8	5 7/8	5 6/8	7 5/8	Uintah County	UT	Cameron Woffinden	2000	2031
73 0/8	14 2/8	14 3/8	6 2/8	6 6/8	10 0/8	Powder River County	MT	Don G. Scofield	2000	2031
73 0/8	15 0/8	15 0/8	5 5/8	5 3/8	8 1/8	Park County	CO	Gary Fischer	2000	2031
73 0/8	13 4/8	13 2/8	5 6/8	6 4/8	11 0/8	Natrona County	WY	Richard Manchur	2001	2031
73 0/8	16 1/8	15 6/8	5 6/8	5 5/8	14 5/8	Garfield County	MT	John Sherwood	2001	2031
73 0/8	14 2/8	14 0/8	6 1/8	6 2/8	7 7/8	Fremont County	WY	Carlos Jasso	2001	2031
73 0/8	14 3/8	14 2/8	5 7/8	5 6/8	9 0/8	Owyhee County	ID	Doug Hawker	2002	2031
73 0/8	14 7/8	14 7/8	5 6/8	5 5/8	9 6/8	Las Animas County	CO	Stephen R. Haufsk	2002	2031
73 0/8	14 0/8	13 6/8	6 0/8	5 7/8	10 7/8	Emery County	UT	Jud D. Jensen	2002	2031
73 0/8	13 3/8	13 1/8	5 6/8	5 6/8	11 2/8	Converse County	WY	Michael L. Ritter	2002	2031
73 0/8	13 3/8	13 4/8	6 0/8	6 0/8	11 7/8	Gunnison County	CO	George H. Bock	2002	2031
73 0/8	14 2/8	13 6/8	6 1/8	6 1/8	11 3/8	Fergus County	MT	D. Mitch Kottas	2002	2031
73 0/8	14 0/8	13 6/8	5 7/8	6 1/8	14 0/8	Sublette County	WY	Dave R. Burget	2003	2031
73 0/8	13 4/8	13 3/8	6 3/8	6 6/8	9 2/8	Campbell County	WY	Bob Davis	2003	2031
73 0/8	14 2/8	14 2/8	5 6/8	5 6/8	8 7/8	Converse County	WY	Leonard Scarborough	2003	2031
73 0/8	15 1/8	15 0/8	6 0/8	5 6/8	12 2/8	Converse County	WY	Bruce E. Thompson	2003	2031
73 0/8	14 0/8	14 0/8	6 0/8	6 0/8	7 0/8	Hill County	MT	Ronald John Zurek	2003	2031
73 0/8	13 6/8	13 2/8	6 2/8	6 1/8	8 7/8	Meade County	SD	Mike Garrow	2003	2031
*73 0/8	14 2/8	14 4/8	6 2/8	6 2/8	11 6/8	Johnson County	WY	Angela K. Walk	2004	2031
73 0/8	14 1/8	13 7/8	6 0/8	5 6/8	13 7/8	Converse County	WY	Myron Jochmann	2004	2031
73 0/8	14 0/8	13 7/8	6 0/8	6 0/8	7 7/8	Washoe County	NV	Ernesto M. Santana	2005	2031
73 0/8	15 0/8	14 6/8	6 2/8	5 4/8	10 5/8	Campbell County	WY	Bruce Ryan	2005	2031
73 0/8	14 1/8	14 4/8	5 6/8	5 6/8	9 7/8	Sweetwater County	WY	Mike Beck	2006	2031
73 0/8	14 4/8	14 3/8	5 6/8	5 6/8	7 6/8	Park County	MT	George Kamps	2006	2031
*73 0/8	13 2/8	13 2/8	5 7/8	5 7/8	13 0/8	Campbell County	WY	Milton G. Wagner	2006	2031
73 0/8	14 5/8	14 6/8	5 5/8	5 5/8	8 3/8	Lea County	NM	Ronnie Parsons	2007	2031
*73 0/8	14 5/8	14 6/8	5 6/8	5 6/8	9 6/8	Buffalo County	SD	John P. Stallone	2007	2031
*73 0/8	13 4/8	13 6/8	6 1/8	6 0/8	11 7/8	Navajo County	AZ	Trent Penrod	2007	2031
73 0/8	14 1/8	14 2/8	5 7/8	6 0/8	9 3/8	Converse County	WY	Lee Jernigan	2007	2031
73 0/8	15 1/8	15 0/8	5 7/8	5 7/8	12 7/8	Carter County	MT	Robert E. Ebert	2007	2031
73 0/8	14 1/8	14 0/8	6 3/8	6 2/8	12 4/8	Laramie County	WY	Pat J. Buscher	2007	2031
73 0/8	13 1/8	13 0/8	6 0/8	6 1/8	10 0/8	Beaverhead County	MT	Ray Gross	2008	2031
73 0/8	13 1/8	13 1/8	6 3/8	6 3/8	10 2/8	Cherry County	NE	Kyle Hochstein	2008	2031
73 0/8	15 0/8	14 4/8	6 2/8	6 0/8	8 2/8	Moffat County	CO	Javen Gumber	2009	2031
73 0/8	13 4/8	13 2/8	6 2/8	6 1/8	10 7/8	Powder River County	MT	Jason S. Campbell	2009	2031
*73 0/8	13 5/8	13 5/8	6 0/8	6 0/8	9 6/8	Johnson County	WY	Seth McCormick	2009	2031
73 0/8	14 3/8	14 3/8	5 7/8	5 6/8	10 2/8	Albany County	WY	Mike Yancey	2009	2031
73 0/8	13 0/8	12 7/8	6 6/8	6 5/8	10 0/8	Rosebud County	MT	Gene A. Welle	2009	2031
73 0/8	14 2/8	14 1/8	6 0/8	6 0/8	8 6/8	Weld County	CO	Michael A. Lee	2009	2031
*73 0/8	13 4/8	13 5/8	5 5/8	5 6/8	9 1/8	Pennant	SAS	Justin Paramzchuk	2009	2031
73 0/8	14 5/8	15 0/8	6 0/8	6 0/8	8 5/8	Meade County	SD	Thaine Strom	2009	2031
73 0/8	13 3/8	13 6/8	6 1/8	6 0/8	7 0/8	Campbell County	WY	Daniel Gleason	2009	2031
*73 0/8	13 7/8	14 0/8	6 3/8	6 2/8	7 4/8	Carbon County	WY	Greg Newhouse	2010	2031
72 6/8	14 3/8	14 2/8	6 0/8	6 0/8	8 0/8	Washoe County	NV	Lawrence Heward	1973	2137
72 6/8	12 1/8	12 1/8	6 6/8	6 6/8	10 6/8	Natrona County	WY	Dennis Spawn	1974	2137
72 6/8	15 1/8	14 6/8	5 6/8	5 7/8	9 2/8	Carbon County	WY	I. C. Benjamin	1976	2137
72 6/8	14 0/8	14 1/8	5 6/8	5 7/8	10 7/8	Washoe County	NV	Ritchard E. Golden	1977	2137
72 6/8	12 1/8	11 6/8	6 7/8	6 7/8	9 1/8	Moffat County	CO	Dwight D. Greenwell	1980	2137
72 6/8	13 5/8	13 2/8	5 6/8	5 4/8	7 1/8	Moffat County	CO	Lyle Willmarth	1981	2137
72 6/8	14 0/8	14 0/8	5 6/8	5 6/8	14 6/8	Converse County	WY	Jack Cassidy	1981	2137
72 6/8	13 2/8	13 2/8	6 2/8	6 3/8	12 4/8	Moffat County	CO	Albert Ahlrich	1981	2137
72 6/8	13 3/8	13 4/8	6 3/8	6 2/8	11 3/8	Moffat County	CO	Thomas H. States	1982	2137
72 6/8	14 5/8	14 5/8	5 7/8	5 5/8	8 0/8	Washoe County	NV	Gary Furman	1982	2137
72 6/8	13 4/8	13 6/8	5 7/8	5 7/8	9 5/8	Hettinger County	ND	Jeff Watne	1983	2137
72 6/8	14 0/8	13 6/8	6 0/8	6 0/8	7 0/8	Moffat County	CO	Jim Dougherty	1983	2137
72 6/8	14 0/8	14 0/8	6 2/8	6 1/8	9 0/8	Converse County	WY	Willis Chapman	1983	2137
72 6/8	14 6/8	15 1/8	5 6/8	5 6/8	9 0/8	Duchesne County	UT	Delos W. 'Sonny' Kempton	1984	2137
72 6/8	14 0/8	14 1/8	5 7/8	5 7/8	7 1/8	Natrona County	WY	Dorian Gilbert	1985	2137
72 6/8	13 7/8	13 7/8	5 7/8	6 0/8	13 5/8	Yavapai County	AZ	Richard S. Jones	1985	2137
72 6/8	13 6/8	13 7/8	6 1/8	6 0/8	11 7/8	Washington County	CO	Randy Fassler	1986	2137
72 6/8	14 1/8	14 2/8	6 4/8	6 3/8	10 5/8	Fergus County	MT	Daniel R. Vogl	1986	2137
72 6/8	12 7/8	12 7/8	6 1/8	6 0/8	10 1/8	Coconino County	AZ	Phillip K. Hugh	1987	2137
72 6/8	13 5/8	14 0/8	5 6/8	5 5/8	14 7/8	Bernalillo County	NM	Timothy C. Ozmun	1988	2137
72 6/8	14 0/8	14 0/8	5 4/8	5 3/8	8 4/8	Wheatland County	MT	Bob Radocy	1988	2137
72 6/8	15 0/8	15 0/8	5 7/8	5 6/8	9 2/8	Mountrail County	ND	Todd Boechler	1988	2137
72 6/8	14 4/8	15 3/8	6 0/8	6 0/8	10 3/8	Sublette County	WY	Steven Hill	1989	2137
72 6/8	14 5/8	14 2/8	6 0/8	6 0/8	8 3/8	Meagher County	MT	D. Mitch Kottas	1989	2137
72 6/8	13 7/8	13 7/8	5 7/8	5 6/8	11 0/8	Moffat County	CO	Ralph Compton	1990	2137
72 6/8	12 3/8	12 4/8	5 6/8	5 6/8	11 3/8	Moffat County	CO	Gary Biles	1990	2137
72 6/8	14 4/8	14 0/8	6 0/8	6 0/8	9 2/8	Moffat County	CO	Dave Palonis	1990	2137
72 6/8	13 2/8	13 3/8	6 0/8	6 0/8	13 0/8	Moffat County	CO	Pat Grogan	1990	2137
72 6/8	13 7/8	14 0/8	6 0/8	6 1/8	11 7/8	Moffat County	CO	Ron Rockwell	1990	2137
72 6/8	14 3/8	14 0/8	5 7/8	5 6/8	6 2/8	Campbell County	WY	Gary DeSmidt	1990	2137
72 6/8	13 3/8	13 3/8	6 2/8	6 1/8	12 4/8	Sweet Grass County	MT	Dr. Dale Schlehuber	1990	2137
72 6/8	14 0/8	13 3/8	5 7/8	5 6/8	9 2/8	Natrona County	WY	Kim Cooper	1990	2137
72 6/8	15 3/8	15 2/8	5 6/8	5 6/8	11 6/8	Elko County	NV	Jimmie Rebich	1991	2137
72 6/8	15 1/8	15 0/8	5 5/8	5 4/8	13 1/8	Box Elder County	UT	Henry O. Davies	1991	2137
72 6/8	13 6/8	13 6/8	6 0/8	6 0/8	8 0/8	Campbell County	WY	Mark Yelken	1991	2137
72 6/8	14 0/8	14 4/8	6 2/8	6 3/8	8 7/8	Sheridan County	WY	Michael Briganti	1991	2137
72 6/8	14 2/8	14 3/8	6 6/8	6 5/8	7 5/8	Beaverhead County	MT	Neal Davis	1991	2137
72 6/8	14 0/8	14 0/8	5 7/8	6 0/8	9 7/8	Crook County	WY	John A. Bogucki	1991	2137
72 6/8	13 3/8	13 3/8	6 1/8	6 0/8	11 2/8	Humboldt County	NV	Tim Iveson	1992	2137
72 6/8	13 2/8	13 1/8	6 5/8	6 7/8	13 0/8	Sweetwater County	WY	Clayton "Karl" Knudsen	1992	2137
72 6/8	13 7/8	13 3/8	5 7/8	5 7/8	10 6/8	Laramie County	WY	Wayne Mackey	1992	2137
72 6/8	13 5/8	13 5/8	5 6/8	5 6/8	9 6/8	Weld County	CO	James L. Tatro	1992	2137
72 6/8	14 3/8	14 5/8	5 5/8	5 5/8	8 1/8	Crook County	WY	Chuck Mead	1992	2137
72 6/8	12 5/8	12 4/8	5 7/8	5 6/8	8 7/8	Fall River County	SD	Bill Lynch	1992	2137
72 6/8	13 4/8	13 6/8	6 0/8	6 1/8	11 5/8	Converse County	WY	Donald Paul Charpentier	1992	2137
72 6/8	13 6/8	13 6/8	6 2/8	6 1/8	8 6/8	Converse County	WY	John W. Flies	1992	2137
72 6/8	13 2/8	13 2/8	6 6/8	6 6/8	11 1/8	Rosebud County	MT	Walter J. Palmer	1992	2137
72 6/8	14 3/8	14 4/8	6 2/8	6 2/8	8 6/8	Slope County	ND	Rick A. Schaeffer	1992	2137
72 6/8	14 3/8	14 3/8	5 6/8	5 6/8	9 5/8	Albany County	WY	Jack Satterfield, Jr.	1992	2137
72 6/8	12 2/8	13 0/8	6 7/8	6 7/8	8 1/8	Yellowstone County	MT	Tom Wulfekuhle	1992	2137
72 6/8	12 2/8	13 0/8	6 7/8	6 7/8	8 1/8	Campbell County	WY	Suzy Smith	1992	2137

PRONGHORN

Minimum Score 67 — Continued

SCORE	LENGTH OF R HORN L	CIRCUMFERENCE R OF BASE L	INSIDE SPREAD	AREA	STATE/PROVINCE	HUNTER'S NAME	DATE	RANK
72 6/8	14 0/8 14 4/8	5 6/8 5 6/8	10 5/8	Moffat County	CO	Daniel G. Willems	1993	2137
72 6/8	13 0/8 12 4/8	6 6/8 6 6/8	8 4/8	Fremont County	WY	Chris Ruys	1993	2137
72 6/8	13 2/8 13 1/8	6 3/8 6 3/8	10 4/8	Campbell County	WY	John S. Shields	1993	2137
72 6/8	15 3/8 15 7/8	5 6/8 5 6/8	8 6/8	Estevan	SAS	Garry Leslie	1993	2137
72 6/8	14 2/8 14 2/8	6 3/8 6 2/8	8 7/8	Albany County	WY	Ron Books, Sr.	1994	2137
72 6/8	13 0/8 13 0/8	6 5/8 6 6/8	10 3/8	Moffat County	CO	Jasen Decker	1994	2137
72 6/8	13 0/8 13 1/8	6 4/8 6 3/8	10 1/8	Moffat County	CO	Eugene Ray, Sr.	1994	2137
72 6/8	13 6/8 13 7/8	6 0/8 6 0/8	11 2/8	Moffat County	CO	Joel A. Anderson	1994	2137
72 6/8	15 4/8 15 2/8	5 4/8 5 4/8	14 0/8	Chaves County	NM	John B. Bright	1994	2137
72 6/8	13 7/8 14 0/8	6 2/8 6 1/8	10 3/8	Campbell County	WY	Grant Telleri	1994	2137
72 6/8	13 3/8 13 3/8	6 1/8 6 1/8	11 5/8	Powder River County	MT	Don G. Scofield	1994	2137
72 6/8	13 3/8 13 5/8	5 5/8 5 6/8	8 1/8	Converse County	WY	Kevin Schmieg	1994	2137
72 6/8	12 5/8 12 6/8	6 2/8 6 0/8	11 4/8	Cheyenne County	NE	Michael McCallister	1994	2137
72 6/8	14 4/8 14 5/8	5 7/8 5 7/8	7 6/8	Rio Arriba County	NM	Len Cardinale	1995	2137
72 6/8	14 6/8 14 6/8	5 4/8 5 5/8	10 3/8	Platte County	WY	Tim Millikin	1995	2137
72 6/8	13 3/8 13 3/8	5 7/8 6 0/8	11 6/8	Moffat County	CO	Dean Gribble	1997	2137
72 6/8	15 0/8 15 2/8	5 4/8 5 2/8	10 5/8	Chaves County	NM	Douglas R. Johnson	1997	2137
72 6/8	14 0/8 14 2/8	6 3/8 6 1/8	8 2/8	Moffat County	CO	Brad Herman	1997	2137
72 6/8	14 1/8 14 2/8	6 2/8 6 1/8	10 1/8	Yavapai County	AZ	Dan Kasprzyk	1997	2137
72 6/8	13 5/8 14 0/8	6 1/8 6 1/8	14 4/8	Navajo County	AZ	William C. Bolt, Jr.	1997	2137
72 6/8	13 4/8 13 2/8	5 7/8 5 7/8	9 7/8	Moffat County	CO	Brad Suitts	1997	2137
72 6/8	13 3/8 13 6/8	6 3/8 6 0/8	12 4/8	Converse County	WY	Douglas Edward Colle	1997	2137
72 6/8	13 2/8 13 4/8	5 6/8 5 5/8	9 7/8	Malheur County	OR	Randy Ashcraft	1997	2137
72 6/8	14 6/8 14 5/8	5 7/8 6 0/8	8 6/8	Crook County	WY	Terry Gordon	1997	2137
72 6/8	12 4/8 12 4/8	6 3/8 6 2/8	7 7/8	Big Horn County	WY	Don Davidson, Jr.	1998	2137
72 6/8	12 4/8 12 3/8	6 1/8 6 1/8	7 5/8	Grand County	UT	Cori L. McClellan	1998	2137
72 6/8	14 2/8 14 3/8	6 3/8 6 2/8	11 1/8	Petroleum County	MT	Mark D. Hughes	1998	2137
72 6/8	15 3/8 15 1/8	5 2/8 5 2/8	12 2/8	Guadalupe County	NM	Matthew A. C. DeBaca	1999	2137
72 6/8	14 0/8 13 7/8	6 4/8 6 3/8	11 7/8	Chaves County	NM	Andy Milam	2000	2137
72 6/8	15 0/8 15 3/8	6 1/8 5 7/8	7 4/8	McKenzie County	ND	Troy Cooper	2000	2137
72 6/8	14 0/8 13 7/8	6 1/8 6 0/8	13 5/8	Converse County	WY	Alton Darling, Jr.	2000	2137
72 6/8	13 3/8 13 4/8	6 1/8 6 1/8	11 6/8	Moffat County	CO	Richard A. Schreiber	2001	2137
72 6/8	12 7/8 12 5/8	6 5/8 6 5/8	9 4/8	Converse County	WY	Steve McCoy	2001	2137
72 6/8	14 6/8 14 4/8	5 5/8 5 5/8	12 2/8	Elkwater	ALB	Christian D. Pagenkopf	2001	2137
72 6/8	14 4/8 14 7/8	5 5/8 5 4/8	8 3/8	Navajo County	AZ	Chris T. Salyer	2002	2137
72 6/8	13 2/8 13 4/8	6 3/8 6 3/8	12 1/8	Campbell County	WY	Ron Hise	2003	2137
72 6/8	14 3/8 14 4/8	5 6/8 5 6/8	8 6/8	Powder River County	MT	Bob Schlesser	2003	2137
72 6/8	14 2/8 14 1/8	6 0/8 6 0/8	8 7/8	Fergus County	MT	John Fleharty	2003	2137
72 6/8	13 6/8 13 6/8	6 2/8 6 1/8	6 2/8	Buffalo	ALB	Andre Titley	2003	2137
*72 6/8	13 5/8 13 6/8	6 4/8 6 2/8	12 4/8	Sweetwater County	WY	Stephen Foster	2004	2137
72 6/8	14 0/8 13 6/8	6 1/8 6 2/8	7 7/8	Blaine County	ID	Darrell Nunez	2004	2137
72 6/8	14 7/8 15 0/8	5 4/8 5 4/8	8 0/8	Campbell County	WY	Steven J. Draisey	2004	2137
72 6/8	14 1/8 14 7/8	6 2/8 5 7/8	8 5/8	Powder River County	MT	Louie Kitcoff	2004	2137
72 6/8	14 2/8 14 0/8	5 6/8 5 5/8	11 0/8	Mercer County	ND	Greg Passa	2004	2137
72 6/8	14 2/8 14 0/8	5 7/8 5 7/8	9 4/8	Campbell County	WY	Thomas J. Peterson	2004	2137
72 6/8	15 1/8 15 6/8	5 4/8 5 4/8	9 3/8	Washoe County	NV	Randy Long	2005	2137
72 6/8	13 4/8 13 2/8	5 5/8 5 6/8	9 3/8	Apache County	AZ	Dan Mattausch	2005	2137
72 6/8	14 5/8 14 7/8	5 5/8 5 6/8	8 5/8	Lemhi County	ID	Bryce K. DeForest	2005	2137
*72 6/8	14 0/8 14 0/8	6 1/8 5 7/8	10 0/8	Natrona County	WY	Craig Talbot	2005	2137
72 6/8	12 0/8 12 1/8	7 7/8 7 7/8	9 0/8	Natrona County	WY	Glen E. VanGuilder	2005	2137
72 6/8	14 3/8 14 0/8	5 6/8 6 0/8	8 5/8	Owyhee County	ID	Todd Wells	2005	2137
72 6/8	14 6/8 15 0/8	6 0/8 6 0/8	8 4/8	Sweetwater County	WY	Ronald A. Noble	2006	2137
72 6/8	14 1/8 14 6/8	6 3/8 6 4/8	13 2/8	Sweetwater County	WY	Garrett Bradley	2006	2137
72 6/8	12 7/8 12 4/8	6 5/8 6 4/8	9 5/8	Owyhee County	ID	Shain Zenor	2006	2137
72 6/8	13 5/8 13 5/8	6 0/8 5 6/8	10 0/8	Johnson County	WY	Joseph W. Snider	2006	2137
72 6/8	13 5/8 13 6/8	5 6/8 5 6/8	9 0/8	Crook County	WY	Don Scofield	2006	2137
72 6/8	12 5/8 12 6/8	6 0/8 6 0/8	11 6/8	Wallace County	KS	Paul Babcock	2006	2137
72 6/8	14 6/8 14 5/8	5 5/8 5 6/8	12 3/8	White Pine County	NV	Austin J. Sheehy	2007	2137
72 6/8	13 7/8 14 0/8	6 1/8 6 1/8	8 3/8	Las Animas County	CO	Bruce Wilson	2007	2137
*72 6/8	14 4/8 14 1/8	5 4/8 5 6/8	8 3/8	Converse County	WY	James Thibodeau	2007	2137
72 6/8	14 0/8 14 0/8	5 6/8 5 7/8	8 3/8	Moffat County	CO	Richard N. King	2007	2137
72 6/8	13 4/8 13 4/8	6 2/8 6 2/8	9 5/8	Campbell County	WY	Tippy H. Clark	2007	2137
72 6/8	13 4/8 13 3/8	5 5/8 5 4/8	8 7/8	Campbell County	WY	Tippy H. Clark	2007	2137
72 6/8	14 0/8 14 2/8	7 0/8 6 7/8	10 6/8	Sweetwater County	WY	Eric H. Boley	2007	2137
*72 6/8	14 4/8 14 4/8	5 2/8 5 3/8	10 5/8	Moffat County	CO	Kurt W. Keskimaki	2008	2137
72 6/8	14 2/8 14 4/8	6 0/8 5 7/8	9 5/8	Sublette County	WY	Virgil R. Burget	2008	2137
72 6/8	13 2/8 14 2/8	6 0/8 6 0/8	11 3/8	Rich County	UT	Matthew Thomson	2008	2137
72 6/8	13 6/8 13 3/8	5 6/8 5 6/8	9 0/8	Converse County	WY	Steve Osminski	2008	2137
*72 6/8	14 1/8 14 1/8	6 0/8 6 1/8	8 4/8	El Paso County	CO	Jeremiah D. Johns	2008	2137
*72 6/8	14 0/8 13 7/8	6 3/8 6 2/8	9 1/8	Campbell County	WY	Steve V. Shelton	2008	2137
72 6/8	14 1/8 14 1/8	6 0/8 5 7/8	11 1/8	Carbon County	WY	Jason Yates	2008	2137
72 6/8	13 4/8 13 4/8	5 4/8 5 4/8	10 4/8	Natrona County	WY	Steve Hamilton	2008	2137
*72 6/8	14 0/8 14 2/8	6 0/8 6 0/8	9 4/8	Petroleum County	MT	Joseph Rydman	2008	2137
*72 6/8	15 5/8 13 5/8	6 4/8 5 7/8	10 6/8	Millard County	UT	Jason Black	2009	2137
*72 6/8	13 7/8 13 7/8	5 7/8 6 0/8	7 5/8	Clark County	ID	Dave R. Burget	2009	2137
*72 6/8	14 1/8 14 0/8	6 3/8 6 4/8	8 4/8	Powder River County	MT	Shawn Wahl	2009	2137
72 6/8	15 6/8 16 1/8	5 6/8 5 6/8	7 4/8	Powder River County	MT	Tony Dawson	2009	2137
72 6/8	13 1/8 13 2/8	6 3/8 6 4/8	11 0/8	Butte County	ID	William E. Dean	2010	2137
72 6/8	14 4/8 14 2/8	5 6/8 5 6/8	11 7/8	Johnson County	WY	Stacee Frost	2010	2137
72 6/8	13 5/8 13 3/8	6 2/8 6 5/8	11 1/8	Park County	WY	Patrick Allen	2010	2137
72 4/8	13 6/8 13 5/8	7 0/8 7 3/8	9 4/8	Meade County	SD	Wallace C. Neville	1977	2268
72 4/8	14 3/8 14 2/8	6 0/8 6 0/8	8 4/8	Jefferson County	ID	Kenny Peterson	1980	2268
72 4/8	15 4/8 15 4/8	5 5/8 5 2/8	9 0/8	Converse County	WY	Joseph F. Scheuerman	1982	2268
72 4/8	13 6/8 13 3/8	5 7/8 5 7/8	8 1/8	Natrona County	WY	Gilbert Clement	1983	2268
72 4/8	13 2/8 13 3/8	6 4/8 6 4/8	11 5/8	Natrona County	WY	Tony Lanzarone	1983	2268
72 4/8	13 7/8 13 6/8	5 5/8 5 4/8	10 4/8	Carbon County	WY	Jerome Deaven	1983	2268
72 4/8	14 0/8 14 0/8	5 7/8 5 6/8	8 3/8	Converse County	WY	Lee Jernigan	1983	2268
72 4/8	13 1/8 13 1/8	6 0/8 5 7/8	8 2/8	Moffat County	CO	Holt Dougherty	1984	2268
72 4/8	15 2/8 14 0/8	6 1/8 6 1/8	11 3/8	Modoc County	CA	Tim Sayer	1986	2268
72 4/8	14 6/8 14 3/8	5 7/8 5 7/8	8 2/8	Sweetwater County	WY	Kirby Warnock	1986	2268
72 4/8	12 7/8 12 3/8	6 4/8 6 2/8	10 5/8	Lemhi County	ID	Matt March, Jr.	1986	2268
72 4/8	14 3/8 13 3/8	6 0/8 6 0/8	9 3/8	Fremont County	WY	John Lemke	1986	2268
72 4/8	13 5/8 13 5/8	6 3/8 6 2/8	7 5/8	Moffat County	CO	Terry Weimer	1987	2268
72 4/8	13 7/8 13 7/8	6 2/8 6 1/8	9 4/8	Moffat County	CO	Judd Cooney	1987	2268
72 4/8	13 6/8 13 4/8	5 7/8 5 7/8	9 5/8	Sweetwater County	WY	Stan Godfrey	1987	2268

833

PRONGHORN

Minimum Score 67   Continued

SCORE	LENGTH OF R HORN L	CIRCUMFERENCE R OF BASE L	INSIDE SPREAD	AREA	STATE/ PROVINCE	HUNTER'S NAME	DATE	RANK
72 4/8	14 1/8 13 1/8	6 3/8 6 3/8	6 3/8	Rosebud County	MT	Vic Riggs	1987	2268
72 4/8	14 3/8 14 6/8	5 7/8 6 1/8	12 6/8	Petroleum County	MT	D. Mitch Kottas	1987	2268
72 4/8	14 3/8 14 0/8	5 3/8 5 7/8	16 0/8	Clark County	ID	Shane Bird	1988	2268
72 4/8	15 6/8 15 4/8	6 2/8 6 1/8	15 6/8	Converse County	WY	Frank Moore	1988	2268
72 4/8	13 4/8 13 2/8	5 5/8 5 4/8	7 4/8	Navajo County	AZ	Mike D. Meyer	1989	2268
72 4/8	14 6/8 14 6/8	6 1/8 6 1/8	10 0/8	Stewart Valley	SAS	Sean Ferguson	1989	2268
72 4/8	14 3/8 14 1/8	5 3/8 5 3/8	9 6/8	Yavapai County	AZ	Daniel J. Hellman	1989	2268
72 4/8	14 6/8 14 5/8	5 3/8 5 3/8	12 5/8	Las Animas County	CO	Bill Swift	1989	2268
72 4/8	15 5/8 15 3/8	5 5/8 5 5/8	8 6/8	Natrona County	WY	Michael Ryan	1989	2268
72 4/8	14 0/8 13 6/8	5 7/8 5 6/8	11 0/8	Sweetwater County	WY	Bryan Radakovich	1990	2268
72 4/8	14 1/8 13 3/8	6 4/8 6 3/8	10 7/8	Sweetwater County	WY	Ted Williams	1990	2268
72 4/8	14 4/8 13 4/8	5 6/8 5 5/8	10 2/8	Natrona County	WY	John Comstock, Jr.	1990	2268
72 4/8	14 0/8 14 1/8	5 7/8 6 0/8	5 5/8	Washoe County	NV	Terrie Powning	1991	2268
72 4/8	13 5/8 14 2/8	6 3/8 6 3/8	12 2/8	Sweetwater County	WY	George R. Koebel	1991	2268
72 4/8	13 1/8 12 7/8	5 6/8 5 6/8	9 4/8	Weld County	CO	Bruce Butterworth	1991	2268
72 4/8	14 2/8 14 0/8	5 7/8 5 7/8	11 4/8	Campbell County	WY	Jim Reints	1991	2268
72 4/8	14 0/8 14 2/8	6 0/8 5 7/8	10 1/8	Natrona County	WY	Gerald Gay	1991	2268
72 4/8	13 7/8 14 1/8	5 2/8 5 3/8	8 4/8	Converse County	WY	Bruce R. Schoeneweis	1991	2268
72 4/8	15 0/8 15 0/8	5 3/8 5 2/8	6 5/8	Converse County	WY	Kenneth D. Musgrove	1991	2268
72 4/8	14 3/8 14 3/8	5 7/8 5 6/8	9 4/8	Sioux County	NE	Steve Leichleiter	1991	2268
72 4/8	14 5/8 15 0/8	5 7/8 5 7/8	10 0/8	Rosebud County	MT	Gene A. Welle	1991	2268
72 4/8	13 7/8 13 6/8	6 2/8 6 2/8	13 4/8	Fremont County	WY	Richard C. Hampe	1991	2268
72 4/8	14 0/8 14 4/8	5 6/8 5 6/8	10 6/8	Stark County	ND	Randy A. Heitz	1991	2268
72 4/8	12 6/8 12 7/8	6 2/8 6 4/8	9 3/8	Sioux County	NE	Lyle Prell	1991	2268
72 4/8	13 3/8 12 6/8	6 7/8 6 7/8	11 5/8	Rich County	UT	Hal Stauff	1991	2268
72 4/8	14 1/8 13 7/8	5 7/8 5 7/8	14 7/8	Humboldt County	NV	Tony Reinolds	1992	2268
72 4/8	13 7/8 13 7/8	5 5/8 5 5/8	9 3/8	Elko County	NV	Jeremy Loncar	1992	2268
72 4/8	13 2/8 13 0/8	6 3/8 6 2/8	10 0/8	Weld County	CO	Scott Butterworth	1992	2268
72 4/8	13 3/8 13 3/8	6 7/8 6 5/8	9 6/8	Twin Falls County	ID	Ron Klimes	1992	2268
72 4/8	13 4/8 13 3/8	6 3/8 6 2/8	7 6/8	Moffat County	CO	Chuck Adams	1993	2268
72 4/8	12 6/8 13 0/8	5 7/8 6 0/8	7 6/8	Box Elder County	UT	Scott Payne	1993	2268
72 4/8	15 2/8 14 7/8	6 1/8 6 0/8	8 6/8	Coconino County	AZ	Dan Turner	1993	2268
72 4/8	13 4/8 13 6/8	6 3/8 6 4/8	9 0/8	Hot Springs County	WY	Richard Wormington	1993	2268
72 4/8	14 4/8 14 5/8	6 0/8 6 0/8	8 1/8	Johnson County	WY	Charles H. Sagner	1993	2268
72 4/8	13 3/8 13 3/8	6 0/8 6 0/8	9 2/8	Moffat County	CO	Roger Stewart	1994	2268
72 4/8	14 1/8 14 1/8	6 2/8 6 1/8	9 5/8	Jackson County	CO	Paul Martin	1994	2268
72 4/8	13 0/8 13 0/8	6 2/8 6 0/8	10 3/8	Campbell County	WY	Ritch A. Stolpe	1994	2268
72 4/8	14 3/8 14 3/8	5 5/8 5 5/8	10 0/8	Converse County	WY	Dale A. Storey	1994	2268
72 4/8	14 2/8 14 2/8	6 2/8 6 2/8	6 2/8	Laramie County	WY	Dave Gregory	1994	2268
72 4/8	13 2/8 13 1/8	6 3/8 6 2/8	11 2/8	Sweetwater County	WY	Roger Wintle	1995	2268
72 4/8	14 1/8 14 0/8	5 2/8 5 2/8	11 2/8	Socorro County	NM	Joel R. Mills	1995	2268
72 4/8	13 1/8 13 2/8	6 5/8 6 3/8	9 4/8	Lincoln County	WY	Scott Hesterly	1995	2268
72 4/8	14 0/8 14 2/8	5 4/8 5 5/8	6 7/8	Lake County	OR	Troy Garrison	1995	2268
72 4/8	13 7/8 14 0/8	6 0/8 5 7/8	11 0/8	Moffat County	CO	Richard A. Smith	1996	2268
72 4/8	14 2/8 14 1/8	5 5/8 5 5/8	12 1/8	Grand County	UT	Mark Sheets	1996	2268
72 4/8	14 4/8 14 4/8	6 0/8 5 7/8	9 3/8	Moffat County	CO	Rocky Tschappat	1996	2268
72 4/8	14 2/8 13 4/8	6 2/8 6 2/8	12 6/8	Rosebud County	MT	Kevin Brewer	1996	2268
72 4/8	13 1/8 13 1/8	6 4/8 6 3/8	8 6/8	Moffat County	CO	Clifford R. Neville, Sr.	1997	2268
72 4/8	14 2/8 14 2/8	6 2/8 6 1/8	10 0/8	Yavapai County	AZ	Dawn J. Butterfield	1997	2268
72 4/8	13 7/8 14 0/8	5 6/8 5 6/8	8 2/8	Converse County	WY	Robert Kutz	1997	2268
72 4/8	13 3/8 13 4/8	6 0/8 5 7/8	12 2/8	Kimball County	NE	Duane Loecker	1997	2268
72 4/8	13 7/8 13 6/8	6 2/8 6 2/8	9 2/8	Rosebud County	MT	Craig Richardson	1998	2268
72 4/8	13 4/8 13 3/8	6 3/8 6 3/8	10 4/8	Converse County	WY	Jeffrey A. Sansburry	1998	2268
72 4/8	14 0/8 14 1/8	6 0/8 5 7/8	13 2/8	Campbell County	WY	Larry J. Bunnell, Jr.	1999	2268
72 4/8	12 5/8 12 5/8	6 1/8 6 1/8	16 7/8	Converse County	WY	Mark Keith Hall	1999	2268
72 4/8	13 1/8 13 5/8	5 6/8 5 6/8	10 1/8	Converse County	WY	Robert D. Helmer	1999	2268
72 4/8	15 4/8 15 6/8	5 4/8 5 4/8	11 0/8	Yavapai County	AZ	Mike Jones	2001	2268
72 4/8	14 6/8 14 4/8	5 4/8 5 4/8	8 0/8	Eddy County	NM	David Rutherford	2002	2268
72 4/8	12 5/8 13 2/8	6 4/8 6 4/8	10 3/8	Campbell County	WY	Gregory T. Bolf	2002	2268
72 4/8	12 0/8 12 0/8	5 7/8 5 7/8	8 4/8	Stanley County	SD	Derek Schiefelbein	2003	2268
72 4/8	14 1/8 14 1/8	6 0/8 5 7/8	15 4/8	Gem	ALB	Ron Murphy	2003	2268
72 4/8	13 4/8 12 6/8	5 7/8 5 7/8	10 1/8	Lassen County	CA	Harold R. Berton	2004	2268
72 4/8	14 3/8 14 4/8	5 6/8 5 6/8	10 6/8	Owyhee County	ID	Mike Barningham	2004	2268
72 4/8	16 0/8 15 3/8	5 3/8 5 2/8	7 1/8	Owyhee County	ID	Steven E. Peeples	2004	2268
72 4/8	13 6/8 13 7/8	6 0/8 6 0/8	13 0/8	Carbon County	WY	Alicia Viskoe	2004	2268
72 4/8	14 7/8 14 2/8	6 0/8 6 0/8	10 1/8	Klamath County	OR	Allan Sanford	2005	2268
72 4/8	13 4/8 13 3/8	5 7/8 6 0/8	8 4/8	Las Animas County	CO	Raymond Boone	2005	2268
72 4/8	13 6/8 13 7/8	6 0/8 6 1/8	11 0/8	Natrona County	WY	Gus A. Congemi	2005	2268
72 4/8	13 4/8 13 4/8	6 4/8 6 4/8	9 7/8	Harding County	SD	Troy Hanson	2005	2268
*72 4/8	13 5/8 13 6/8	5 6/8 6 1/8	9 5/8	Niobrara County	WY	Jess Kucera	2005	2268
72 4/8	14 2/8 14 4/8	6 0/8 6 1/8	11 6/8	Washakie County	WY	Tom Buller	2005	2268
*72 4/8	13 7/8 13 7/8	5 6/8 5 5/8	10 6/8	Yavapai County	AZ	Jeremy Human	2006	2268
72 4/8	14 2/8 14 2/8	6 2/8 6 2/8	11 3/8	Rosebud County	MT	Steve Rehak	2006	2268
72 4/8	14 1/8 14 1/8	5 7/8 5 7/8	13 3/8	Sublette County	WY	Ronell Skinner	2006	2268
72 4/8	12 6/8 12 6/8	6 1/8 6 1/8	10 7/8	Clark County	ID	Dave R. Burget	2006	2268
*72 4/8	13 5/8 15 2/8	6 2/8 6 2/8	10 6/8	Pennington County	SD	Cory J. Dodds	2006	2268
72 4/8	13 4/8 13 2/8	6 2/8 6 3/8	8 2/8	Converse County	WY	Mike Wilson	2006	2268
*72 4/8	13 3/8 13 4/8	6 2/8 6 1/8	10 3/8	Harding County	SD	Chris Hofer	2006	2268
*72 4/8	13 7/8 14 0/8	5 7/8 5 7/8	10 1/8	Moffat County	CO	Wally Schaub	2007	2268
72 4/8	15 5/8 15 2/8	5 3/8 5 3/8	7 7/8	Sioux County	NE	Ryan Hochstein	2007	2268
*72 4/8	14 3/8 14 2/8	6 2/8 6 0/8	9 5/8	Carter County	MT	Scott A. Olthoff	2007	2268
72 4/8	14 1/8 14 0/8	6 0/8 5 7/8	9 2/8	Meagher County	MT	Todd McIntyre	2007	2268
*72 4/8	14 4/8 14 3/8	5 6/8 5 5/8	11 3/8	Butte County	SD	Brett P. Burke	2007	2268
72 4/8	14 1/8 14 2/8	6 0/8 6 0/8	9 4/8	Laramie County	WY	Scott Benz	2007	2268
*72 4/8	13 3/8 13 3/8	5 5/8 5 5/8	10 5/8	Custer County	MT	Larry E. Rezin	2007	2268
72 4/8	12 6/8 12 6/8	5 7/8 5 7/8	9 4/8	Converse County	WY	Thomas Morang	2008	2268
72 4/8	13 6/8 13 6/8	6 2/8 6 0/8	10 5/8	Niobrara County	WY	Dennis Ballweg	2008	2268
72 4/8	14 1/8 14 2/8	5 6/8 5 5/8	8 2/8	Carter County	MT	Robert Soares	2008	2268
72 4/8	14 2/8 14 7/8	6 0/8 5 6/8	7 0/8	Sheridan County	WY	Roy L. Walk	2008	2268
72 4/8	14 0/8 13 5/8	6 0/8 6 1/8	8 1/8	Las Animas County	CO	Barbara Musacchia	2008	2268
*72 4/8	13 7/8 14 0/8	6 0/8 6 0/8	10 6/8	Harding County	SD	Mike Van Essen	2008	2268
72 4/8	15 0/8 15 0/8	5 4/8 5 3/8	10 7/8	Powder River County	MT	Tony Dawson	2008	2268
*72 4/8	15 5/8 15 6/8	5 3/8 5 4/8	7 7/8	Campbell County	WY	Nate Cina	2008	2268
*72 4/8	14 1/8 14 1/8	5 4/8 5 4/8	9 7/8	Elko County	NV	Myles Nance	2009	2268
*72 4/8	13 3/8 13 1/8	6 7/8 6 7/8	13 2/8	Natrona County	WY	Michael E. Allman	2009	2268

PRONGHORN

Minimum Score 67 Continued

SCORE	LENGTH OF R HORN L	CIRCUMFERENCE R OF BASE L	INSIDE SPREAD	AREA	STATE/ PROVINCE	HUNTER'S NAME	DATE	RANK
72 4/8	13 6/8 14 2/8	5 5/8 5 5/8	9 2/8	Cibola County	NM	Bill Van Buskirk	2009	2268
72 4/8	14 3/8 14 6/8	6 1/8 6 1/8	11 5/8	Carbon County	WY	John C. Baird	2009	2268
72 4/8	14 0/8 13 7/8	5 6/8 5 6/8	8 7/8	Cascade County	MT	Michael Iten	2009	2268
*72 4/8	14 2/8 14 1/8	6 0/8 5 6/8	11 2/8	Campbell County	WY	Nate Cina	2009	2268
72 4/8	14 1/8 13 6/8	6 0/8 6 2/8	11 3/8	Converse County	WY	Randy R. Mabe	2009	2268
72 4/8	13 2/8 13 5/8	5 6/8 5 6/8	7 4/8	Moffat County	CO	Todd A. Brickel	2009	2268
*72 4/8	14 2/8 14 2/8	6 1/8 6 2/8	10 3/8	Johnson County	WY	Quint M. Gonzales	2009	2268
72 4/8	13 5/8 13 6/8	5 7/8 5 7/8	7 5/8	Rosebud County	MT	Kevin Davis	2009	2268
72 2/8	13 5/8 13 5/8	6 2/8 6 1/8	11 1/8	Carbon County	WY	William Scoggin	1953	2386
72 2/8	14 0/8 14 0/8	6 0/8 5 7/8	10 4/8	Campbell County	WY	K. K. Knickerbocker	1954	2386
72 2/8	13 1/8 13 2/8	6 1/8 6 1/8	7 3/8	Campbell County	WY	Carol Wert	1966	2386
72 2/8	13 4/8 13 5/8	5 7/8 5 7/8	10 5/8	Carbon County	WY	Harold Boyack	1972	2386
72 2/8	15 1/8 14 7/8	5 5/8 5 4/8	8 6/8	Meade County	SD	John S. Anderson	1973	2386
72 2/8	14 3/8 14 3/8	6 0/8 5 7/8	9 5/8	Valley County	MT	Wayne Anderson	1975	2386
72 2/8	14 1/8 14 0/8	6 2/8 6 3/8	8 5/8	Moffat County	CO	Glenn Pritchard	1977	2386
72 2/8	13 7/8 13 6/8	6 1/8 5 7/8	8 0/8	Carbon County	WY	Arthur Heinze	1977	2386
72 2/8	13 7/8 13 6/8	6 0/8 6 0/8	7 2/8	Butte County	ID	Dennis A. Gratton	1978	2386
72 2/8	14 3/8 14 4/8	6 1/8 6 0/8	12 3/8	Moffat County	CO	Glenn Pritchard	1979	2386
72 2/8	11 3/8 11 3/8	6 3/8 6 3/8	10 4/8	Humboldt County	NV	Verlyn Owens	1981	2386
72 2/8	14 3/8 14 6/8	5 4/8 5 4/8	13 0/8	Coconino County	AZ	Terry E. Hansen	1981	2386
72 2/8	17 0/8 15 5/8	5 4/8 5 5/8	9 0/8	Klamath County	OR	Richard Howell	1981	2386
72 2/8	13 3/8 13 2/8	6 1/8 6 1/8	7 3/8	Moffat County	CO	Wayne A. Jensen	1982	2386
72 2/8	13 0/8 12 7/8	6 1/8 6 1/8	6 6/8	Converse County	WY	Thomas Brannagan	1982	2386
72 2/8	14 4/8 14 5/8	6 0/8 6 2/8	6 6/8	Carbon County	WY	Kim Cooper	1982	2386
72 2/8	14 0/8 13 7/8	6 0/8 6 0/8	7 6/8	Morgan County	CO	Barry Smith	1983	2386
72 2/8	13 5/8 13 4/8	5 6/8 5 6/8	8 2/8	Moffat County	CO	Dan Liccardi	1983	2386
72 2/8	12 7/8 12 7/8	6 3/8 6 1/8	8 0/8	Converse County	WY	Tim Cassidy	1983	2386
72 2/8	13 2/8 13 6/8	6 0/8 5 7/8	10 5/8	Carbon County	WY	Paul Persano	1983	2386
72 2/8	13 1/8 13 2/8	6 0/8 6 2/8	10 3/8	Carbon County	WY	Larry Hayes	1983	2386
72 2/8	13 6/8 13 4/8	6 4/8 6 4/8	14 2/8	Converse County	WY	James B. Evans, Jr.	1983	2386
72 2/8	13 5/8 13 7/8	5 6/8 5 5/8	11 5/8	Valley County	MT	David Tofte	1983	2386
72 2/8	13 0/8 13 0/8	6 1/8 6 2/8	9 3/8	Carbon County	WY	Robert L. Hudman	1984	2386
72 2/8	14 7/8 15 0/8	6 0/8 5 7/8	14 1/8	Campbell County	WY	Mike Ballard	1985	2386
72 2/8	15 2/8 15 0/8	6 0/8 6 1/8	16 3/8	Modoc County	CA	Richard Wormington	1986	2386
72 2/8	14 3/8 14 1/8	6 4/8 6 1/8	10 4/8	Lemhi County	ID	Peter Cintorino	1986	2386
72 2/8	13 4/8 13 4/8	6 1/8 6 2/8	10 5/8	Natrona County	WY	J. Bruce Ashcroft	1986	2386
72 2/8	14 0/8 14 0/8	5 7/8 6 0/8	11 1/8	Sweetwater County	WY	Dale Hill	1987	2386
72 2/8	13 0/8 13 2/8	6 3/8 6 3/8	8 7/8	Jackson County	CO	Bruce Ayers	1987	2386
72 2/8	15 0/8 14 6/8	5 4/8 5 4/8	8 2/8	Sweetwater County	WY	Michael Chaffin	1987	2386
72 2/8	13 1/8 13 2/8	6 0/8 6 0/8	11 0/8	Carter County	MT	Robert Keith Hacker	1987	2386
72 2/8	14 4/8 14 0/8	6 0/8 6 2/8	12 4/8	Moffat County	CO	Richard King	1987	2386
72 2/8	14 0/8 14 0/8	5 6/8 5 4/8	11 1/8	Carbon County	WY	Paul M. Kniss	1988	2386
72 2/8	12 5/8 12 7/8	6 3/8 6 3/8	12 2/8	Fremont County	WY	Kevin Anderson	1989	2386
72 2/8	14 3/8 14 3/8	5 5/8 5 3/8	14 2/8	Yavapai County	AZ	Richard Anderson	1989	2386
72 2/8	14 4/8 14 6/8	5 2/8 5 2/8	7 5/8	Rio Grande County	CO	James A. Phillips	1989	2386
72 2/8	13 7/8 13 6/8	6 3/8 6 4/8	8 4/8	Moffat County	CO	Scott A. Wilson	1990	2386
72 2/8	14 3/8 13 6/8	6 0/8 6 0/8	8 6/8	Billings County	ND	William R. Metzger	1990	2386
72 2/8	13 2/8 13 6/8	6 7/8 6 4/8	14 5/8	Converse County	WY	Tommy L. Mackey	1990	2386
72 2/8	15 4/8 16 0/8	6 1/8 6 0/8	16 3/8	Washoe County	NV	Gene A. Jones	1991	2386
72 2/8	13 3/8 13 6/8	6 0/8 5 7/8	11 4/8	Catron County	NM	Clifford Armstrong	1991	2386
72 2/8	14 0/8 13 7/8	6 4/8 6 2/8	9 5/8	Fremont County	WY	Troy Stone	1991	2386
72 2/8	15 0/8 15 3/8	5 5/8 5 6/8	9 5/8	Fox Valley	SAS	Floyd Forster	1991	2386
72 2/8	14 2/8 14 2/8	5 7/8 5 6/8	7 1/8	Converse County	WY	Kevin Stier	1991	2386
72 2/8	14 3/8 14 3/8	5 6/8 5 7/8	11 0/8	Rosebud County	MT	Robert L. Fraley	1991	2386
72 2/8	13 4/8 13 5/8	6 3/8 6 5/8	11 0/8	Moffat County	CO	Wayne Depperschmidt	1992	2386
72 2/8	14 2/8 14 0/8	6 4/8 6 3/8	10 3/8	Moffat County	CO	J. Keith Chastain	1992	2386
72 2/8	13 2/8 13 2/8	6 3/8 6 1/8	8 2/8	Moffat County	CO	Janet George	1992	2386
72 2/8	13 4/8 13 3/8	6 3/8 6 3/8	13 7/8	Manyberries	ALB	Terry Ermel	1992	2386
72 2/8	15 2/8 15 4/8	5 7/8 5 4/8	11 3/8	Hill County	MT	Lon Waid	1992	2386
72 2/8	14 6/8 14 7/8	5 6/8 5 6/8	10 0/8	Campbell County	WY	David Vomela	1992	2386
72 2/8	14 4/8 15 0/8	5 4/8 5 5/8	13 0/8	Park County	CO	Joe Kruczynski	1992	2386
72 2/8	13 1/8 12 4/8	6 0/8 5 7/8	12 1/8	Garfield County	MT	Christopher Downs	1992	2386
72 2/8	14 0/8 14 1/8	5 2/8 5 2/8	11 6/8	Chaves County	NM	Bill Daniel	1993	2386
72 2/8	13 0/8 13 3/8	6 3/8 6 2/8	11 2/8	Box Elder County	UT	Brett Payne	1993	2386
72 2/8	14 1/8 14 2/8	5 4/8 5 4/8	10 6/8	Moffat County	CO	Steve Murphy	1993	2386
72 2/8	14 1/8 14 2/8	5 4/8 5 5/8	9 3/8	Wayne County	UT	Johnny C. Parsons	1993	2386
72 2/8	13 5/8 13 7/8	5 7/8 5 7/8	15 1/8	Sublette County	WY	T. J. Dupee	1993	2386
72 2/8	13 0/8 13 0/8	6 0/8 6 0/8	12 3/8	Garfield County	MT	L. "Andy" Anderson	1993	2386
72 2/8	15 1/8 14 7/8	5 7/8 5 7/8	10 2/8	Hudspeth County	TX	Bruce Baird	1993	2386
72 2/8	13 7/8 14 0/8	5 7/8 5 7/8	10 0/8	Sweetwater County	WY	Shaneon Lance	1994	2386
72 2/8	14 0/8 14 1/8	6 0/8 6 1/8	11 6/8	Carbon County	UT	Kooper Pierce	1994	2386
72 2/8	13 4/8 13 3/8	5 5/8 5 5/8	8 5/8	Butte County	ID	L. D. Green	1994	2386
72 2/8	14 4/8 14 6/8	5 5/8 5 5/8	8 3/8	Millard County	UT	Jeremy Harness	1994	2386
72 2/8	13 4/8 13 3/8	5 7/8 5 7/8	12 0/8	Campbell County	WY	Jim Hengel	1994	2386
72 2/8	14 3/8 14 4/8	5 5/8 5 4/8	12 1/8	Hilda	ALB	Steve MacKenzie	1994	2386
72 2/8	14 0/8 14 0/8	5 7/8 5 7/8	9 5/8	Phillips County	MT	Brad Walker	1994	2386
72 2/8	15 4/8 15 7/8	5 4/8 5 4/8	10 2/8	Nye County	NV	James F. Watson	1995	2386
72 2/8	13 5/8 14 3/8	6 2/8 6 2/8	12 3/8	Modoc County	CA	Gerald W. Smith	1995	2386
72 2/8	14 6/8 14 4/8	5 6/8 5 6/8	7 4/8	Rio Grande County	CO	David R. Hall	1995	2386
72 2/8	13 1/8 13 1/8	5 6/8 6 0/8	8 7/8	Weld County	CO	Jason Rhodes	1995	2386
72 2/8	15 0/8 15 0/8	5 7/8 5 7/8	10 3/8	Larimer County	CO	Mark A. Germonprez	1995	2386
72 2/8	13 4/8 13 1/8	6 0/8 6 0/8	9 7/8	Moffat County	CO	Jim Brewer	1995	2386
72 2/8	13 4/8 13 6/8	6 2/8 6 2/8	13 0/8	Converse County	WY	Ralph Inverso	1995	2386
72 2/8	15 0/8 15 0/8	5 6/8 5 6/8	9 6/8	Navajo County	AZ	Amy Holladay	1995	2386
72 2/8	13 2/8 13 3/8	6 3/8 6 3/8	8 6/8	Campbell County	WY	Jeffrey A. Hoover	1995	2386
72 2/8	15 0/8 14 6/8	6 0/8 6 0/8	9 5/8	Duchesne County	UT	William T. Burbridge	1996	2386
72 2/8	14 1/8 14 1/8	5 6/8 5 6/8	9 5/8	Millard County	UT	David Anderson	1996	2386
72 2/8	13 3/8 13 0/8	6 0/8 6 0/8	8 5/8	Converse County	WY	Tim Angelo	1996	2386
72 2/8	12 6/8 12 4/8	5 7/8 5 6/8	9 0/8	Converse County	WY	Marlin Stapleton, Jr.	1996	2386
72 2/8	13 2/8 13 2/8	5 7/8 5 7/8	8 6/8	Rosebud County	MT	Richard M. Penn	1996	2386
72 2/8	14 7/8 14 4/8	6 2/8 6 2/8	10 0/8	Sierra County	NM	Audie F. Click	1997	2386
72 2/8	14 1/8 14 1/8	5 7/8 5 7/8	8 7/8	Weld County	CO	Rodney E. Perrine	1997	2386
72 2/8	13 1/8 13 3/8	5 6/8 5 6/8	11 4/8	Custer County	CO	Phillip Gaines	1997	2386
72 2/8	13 1/8 13 1/8	6 3/8 6 1/8	11 1/8	Moffat County	CO	Mark C. Gardner	1998	2386
72 2/8	13 0/8 13 0/8	7 0/8 7 0/8	10 7/8	Custer County	MT	Lyle R. Prell	1998	2386

835

PRONGHORN

Minimum Score 67 — Continued

SCORE	LENGTH OF R HORN L	CIRCUMFERENCE R OF BASE L	INSIDE SPREAD	AREA	STATE/ PROVINCE	HUNTER'S NAME	DATE	RANK
72 2/8	13 6/8 13 7/8	5 6/8 5 5/8	8 1/8	Valley County	MT	Scott Lysenko	1998	2386
72 2/8	14 5/8 14 3/8	6 0/8 5 6/8	9 5/8	Twin Falls County	ID	Steven Vining	1999	2386
72 2/8	14 1/8 13 2/8	7 1/8 7 2/8	13 2/8	Big Horn County	WY	Jerome D. Larson	1999	2386
72 2/8	13 5/8 13 5/8	6 0/8 5 7/8	9 7/8	Converse County	WY	Frank S. Noska IV	1999	2386
72 2/8	14 1/8 14 1/8	5 6/8 5 6/8	9 6/8	Manyberries	ALB	Mark McQueen	1999	2386
72 2/8	15 0/8 14 6/8	6 3/8 6 1/8	9 6/8	Blaine County	MT	Tom M. Benson	1999	2386
72 2/8	13 4/8 13 2/8	6 1/8 6 1/8	9 3/8	Lincoln County	NM	Steve Farrell	1999	2386
72 2/8	13 6/8 13 6/8	5 6/8 5 6/8	10 4/8	Albany County	WY	Chris Krueger	1999	2386
72 2/8	13 7/8 13 6/8	6 3/8 6 2/8	8 6/8	Moffat County	CO	David B. Green	2000	2386
72 2/8	15 7/8 15 3/8	5 5/8 5 5/8	12 4/8	Brooks	ALB	Jerry Oldfield	2000	2386
72 2/8	14 0/8 13 5/8	6 2/8 6 1/8	13 4/8	Lincoln County	NV	Jim Holden	2001	2386
72 2/8	13 4/8 13 1/8	6 0/8 6 0/8	9 7/8	Wayne County	UT	Jim Horneck	2001	2386
72 2/8	13 2/8 13 2/8	5 6/8 5 6/8	9 3/8	Campbell County	WY	Wayne Peeples	2001	2386
72 2/8	13 2/8 13 6/8	6 0/8 5 7/8	9 4/8	Tide Lake	ALB	W. E. Stewart	2001	2386
72 2/8	13 6/8 13 6/8	6 1/8 6 0/8	8 0/8	Las Animas County	CO	Rodney Kelly	2002	2386
72 2/8	14 1/8 13 7/8	6 0/8 5 5/8	10 2/8	Larimer County	CO	Doug Baumer	2003	2386
72 2/8	13 6/8 15 2/8	6 3/8 6 1/8	8 0/8	Rosebud County	MT	Warren Buss	2003	2386
72 2/8	15 4/8 15 1/8	5 3/8 5 2/8	7 5/8	Powder River County	MT	Royce DeCook	2003	2386
72 2/8	14 1/8 14 0/8	5 7/8 6 0/8	9 1/8	Wibaux County	MT	Gary Nunberg	2003	2386
72 2/8	13 0/8 13 4/8	6 2/8 6 3/8	10 0/8	Weld County	CO	Randy Ries	2004	2386
72 2/8	13 4/8 13 4/8	6 0/8 6 0/8	11 2/8	Powder River County	MT	Don Scofield	2004	2386
72 2/8	13 3/8 13 6/8	6 4/8 6 3/8	8 2/8	Perkins County	SD	Tony Nogy	2004	2386
72 2/8	14 1/8 14 2/8	6 2/8 6 3/8	8 3/8	Lake County	OR	Robert A. Rosales	2004	2386
72 2/8	12 4/8 12 1/8	6 2/8 6 2/8	10 3/8	Natrona County	WY	Todd Collins	2005	2386
72 2/8	14 7/8 14 6/8	5 5/8 5 5/8	9 4/8	Albany County	WY	Jerry Bowen	2005	2386
72 2/8	14 0/8 14 2/8	5 7/8 5 7/8	11 2/8	Converse County	WY	Lee Jernigan	2005	2386
72 2/8	14 0/8 13 7/8	6 0/8 5 6/8	16 5/8	Converse County	WY	John Hoinowski	2005	2386
72 2/8	14 4/8 14 0/8	6 0/8 6 0/8	10 7/8	Weld County	CO	Michael McArtor	2005	2386
72 2/8	14 0/8 14 0/8	6 3/8 6 2/8	12 0/8	Moffat County	CO	Tim R. Hamilton	2005	2386
*72 2/8	13 5/8 13 2/8	6 3/8 6 2/8	11 4/8	Powder River County	MT	Mark R. Anderson	2006	2386
72 2/8	13 3/8 13 4/8	6 2/8 6 3/8	9 4/8	Converse County	WY	Forrest Boone	2006	2386
*72 2/8	13 1/8 13 1/8	6 3/8 6 2/8	8 1/8	Sheridan County	WY	Darrell Wright	2006	2386
72 2/8	14 5/8 14 3/8	6 6/8 6 4/8	12 7/8	Campbell County	WY	Jon E. Silks	2006	2386
72 2/8	13 6/8 13 6/8	5 7/8 6 0/8	8 1/8	Campbell County	WY	Randall J. Brandt	2006	2386
72 2/8	14 5/8 14 4/8	5 7/8 5 5/8	8 7/8	Harding County	SD	Ricky J. Guy	2006	2386
*72 2/8	14 6/8 14 5/8	5 6/8 5 6/8	10 0/8	Wayne County	UT	Cory Elmer	2007	2386
72 2/8	14 1/8 14 4/8	6 5/8 6 6/8	9 4/8	Gallatin County	MT	Tom Morton	2007	2386
*72 2/8	13 3/8 13 3/8	6 0/8 6 0/8	9 6/8	Las Animas County	CO	Tom Smith	2007	2386
72 2/8	14 0/8 14 0/8	5 4/8 5 4/8	11 7/8	Lincoln County	NV	Herbert Holtam	2007	2386
72 2/8	14 3/8 14 3/8	6 0/8 6 0/8	6 6/8	Moffat County	CO	Lyle A. Hall	2007	2386
72 2/8	14 5/8 14 6/8	6 1/8 6 0/8	10 4/8	Socorro County	NM	Duane "Corky" Richardson	2007	2386
*72 2/8	14 2/8 14 0/8	6 2/8 6 1/8	12 2/8	Tooele County	UT	Garth Jacklin	2007	2386
*72 2/8	15 3/8 15 2/8	5 6/8 5 4/8	9 6/8	Powder River County	MT	David N. Sabel	2007	2386
72 2/8	14 0/8 13 7/8	6 0/8 6 1/8	9 5/8	Converse County	WY	Ben Maier	2007	2386
72 2/8	14 2/8 14 4/8	5 7/8 5 7/8	11 4/8	Harding County	SD	Mark P. Butler	2007	2386
*72 2/8	14 7/8 15 1/8	5 7/8 5 6/8	10 3/8	Converse County	WY	Bryce Luth	2007	2386
*72 2/8	14 0/8 14 2/8	5 4/8 5 5/8	7 7/8	Elko County	NV	Chassy Fry	2008	2386
72 2/8	13 4/8 13 6/8	6 2/8 6 2/8	9 4/8	Campbell County	WY	Craig Overman	2008	2386
72 2/8	15 5/8 15 2/8	5 6/8 6 0/8	11 0/8	Millard County	UT	Stan Smith	2008	2386
72 2/8	14 2/8 14 0/8	6 0/8 6 0/8	11 2/8	Coconino County	AZ	David L. Barber	2008	2386
72 2/8	13 4/8 13 5/8	6 2/8 6 4/8	9 2/8	Larimer County	CO	Mark E. Gonyo	2008	2386
*72 2/8	14 2/8 14 5/8	5 5/8 5 6/8	12 6/8	Perkins County	SD	Tom Donovan	2008	2386
72 2/8	14 3/8 14 2/8	5 6/8 5 6/8	10 3/8	Lassen County	CA	Blake Marsters	2009	2386
72 2/8	14 1/8 14 1/8	6 0/8 5 7/8	10 2/8	Converse County	WY	James L. Holtgrewe	2009	2386
72 2/8	12 5/8 12 5/8	6 5/8 6 3/8	10 6/8	Moffat County	CO	Jason Yates	2009	2386
72 2/8	13 2/8 13 6/8	6 1/8 6 0/8	12 2/8	Powder River County	MT	Garry L. Brandenburg	2009	2386
72 2/8	13 7/8 14 2/8	6 1/8 6 2/8	11 6/8	Rich County	UT	Brian Brown	2010	2386
72 2/8	14 5/8 15 0/8	5 5/8 5 5/8	8 4/8	Rio Blanco County	CO	Toby Garcia	2010	2386
72 2/8	14 3/8 14 0/8	5 6/8 5 5/8	7 2/8	Johnson County	WY	Pat Rowland	2010	2386
72 0/8	13 4/8 13 5/8	5 6/8 5 7/8	9 4/8	Perkins County	SD	Ben Clark	1974	2532
72 0/8	13 3/8 13 3/8	5 6/8 6 0/8	11 2/8	Sioux County	NE	Richard Koons	1974	2532
72 0/8	12 7/8 12 4/8	6 7/8 6 7/8	10 1/8	Bennett County	SD	Donald Pierce	1978	2532
72 0/8	13 3/8 13 1/8	5 7/8 5 7/8	10 5/8	Butte County	ID	Mike Ellis	1980	2532
72 0/8	14 1/8 14 3/8	5 7/8 5 6/8	14 5/8	Custer County	ID	Gene Nelson	1981	2532
72 0/8	13 3/8 13 2/8	6 1/8 6 0/8	6 2/8	Klamath County	OR	Harold McCraven	1981	2532
72 0/8	13 3/8 13 1/8	6 0/8 6 0/8	11 0/8	Natrona County	WY	E. W. Onken	1981	2532
72 0/8	13 3/8 13 3/8	5 7/8 5 7/8	10 4/8	Moffat County	CO	Gary Smith	1981	2532
72 0/8	13 4/8 14 0/8	6 3/8 6 3/8	9 3/8	Carbon County	WY	Charles A. Vande Hei	1982	2532
72 0/8	13 7/8 14 1/8	5 6/8 5 7/8	11 2/8	Carbon County	WY	Michael Beckwith	1982	2532
72 0/8	14 3/8 14 2/8	5 5/8 5 5/8	8 6/8	Moffat County	CO	Augie Nicolas	1983	2532
72 0/8	13 1/8 13 1/8	6 1/8 6 1/8	8 2/8	Converse County	WY	Tom Flemming	1983	2532
72 0/8	14 1/8 13 6/8	5 7/8 5 6/8	12 3/8	McCone County	MT	Gary Rueh	1983	2532
72 0/8	14 2/8 14 1/8	5 6/8 5 7/8	10 2/8	Carter County	MT	Dean Irwin	1983	2532
72 0/8	14 6/8 14 6/8	5 3/8 5 3/8	10 6/8	Tide Lake	ALB	Adrian Erickson	1983	2532
72 0/8	14 3/8 14 6/8	5 5/8 5 5/8	10 4/8	Washoe County	NV	C. J. Coleman	1984	2532
72 0/8	13 2/8 13 1/8	6 0/8 6 0/8	8 7/8	Moffat County	CO	Lynn Pariso	1985	2532
72 0/8	13 6/8 13 3/8	6 2/8 6 2/8	8 1/8	Carbon County	UT	Kenny E. Leo	1986	2532
72 0/8	14 5/8 15 0/8	5 5/8 5 5/8	11 6/8	Moffat County	CO	Roger Gipple	1987	2532
72 0/8	13 4/8 13 2/8	6 4/8 6 3/8	11 4/8	Box Elder County	UT	Gary E. Craner	1987	2532
72 0/8	13 6/8 13 5/8	6 0/8 6 1/8	13 5/8	Rosebud County	MT	Dr. Kevin Brewer	1987	2532
72 0/8	14 2/8 14 3/8	5 6/8 5 6/8	7 2/8	Humboldt County	NV	Carl J. Corey	1988	2532
72 0/8	14 2/8 14 3/8	5 6/8 5 7/8	12 1/8	Moffat County	CO	Tom Bartholomew	1988	2532
72 0/8	13 2/8 13 0/8	6 1/8 6 2/8	8 6/8	Carbon County	WY	Darrus D. Martin	1988	2532
72 0/8	13 7/8 14 2/8	5 2/8 5 2/8	9 2/8	Moffat County	CO	M. R. James	1988	2532
72 0/8	13 2/8 13 4/8	6 0/8 6 0/8	10 1/8	Grant County	ND	Mark Bogert	1988	2532
72 0/8	12 5/8 12 5/8	5 7/8 5 7/8	8 2/8	Wallace County	KS	Roger Potter	1988	2532
72 0/8	13 0/8 12 7/8	6 2/8 6 2/8	10 0/8	Klamath County	OR	Bob Baley	1989	2532
72 0/8	14 0/8 13 7/8	6 1/8 6 1/8	9 5/8	Campbell County	WY	Dave Vomela	1989	2532
72 0/8	13 7/8 13 7/8	5 4/8 5 4/8	8 2/8	Carbon County	WY	Raymond R. Robison	1989	2532
72 0/8	13 5/8 13 4/8	6 1/8 6 2/8	7 6/8	Uinta County	WY	Drew Dockstader	1989	2532
72 0/8	13 7/8 13 3/8	6 3/8 6 2/8	9 6/8	Uinta County	WY	Scott Dockstader	1989	2532
72 0/8	14 4/8 14 3/8	5 7/8 6 0/8	9 1/8	Moffat County	CO	Keith Hensel	1989	2532
72 0/8	12 1/8 12 2/8	6 4/8 6 3/8	8 6/8	Carbon County	WY	Dean Stebner	1990	2532
72 0/8	12 7/8 12 7/8	6 2/8 6 0/8	10 6/8	Converse County	WY	Kelvin W. Lancaster	1990	2532
72 0/8	12 5/8 13 0/8	7 0/8 7 0/8	11 4/8	Rosebud County	MT	Gary C. Wolf	1990	2532

836

PRONGHORN

Minimum Score 67 — Continued

SCORE	LENGTH OF R HORN L	CIRCUMFERENCE R OF BASE L	INSIDE SPREAD	AREA	STATE/ PROVINCE	HUNTER'S NAME	DATE	RANK
72 0/8	14 0/8 14 0/8	5 3/8 5 3/8	11 4/8	Converse County	WY	Roy W. Mackey	1990	2532
72 0/8	14 7/8 14 5/8	5 6/8 5 6/8	9 6/8	Elko County	NV	Jimmy Cooney	1991	2532
72 0/8	13 2/8 13 2/8	5 6/8 6 0/8	8 6/8	Park County	WY	Craig Childress	1991	2532
72 0/8	13 7/8 13 7/8	5 7/8 5 6/8	9 5/8	Sweetwater County	WY	R. E. "Bud" Watson	1991	2532
72 0/8	13 7/8 13 7/8	5 5/8 5 5/8	11 4/8	Navajo County	AZ	Charles P. Cooley	1991	2532
72 0/8	13 7/8 13 7/8	5 7/8 5 6/8	14 6/8	Crook County	OR	Clint Hall	1991	2532
72 0/8	13 1/8 12 7/8	6 0/8 6 0/8	11 1/8	Laramie County	WY	Gary W. Brimm	1991	2532
72 0/8	12 6/8 12 5/8	6 3/8 6 2/8	8 6/8	Wallace County	KS	Darren Collins	1991	2532
72 0/8	14 3/8 14 2/8	6 0/8 6 0/8	8 2/8	Sioux County	NE	Gaylen Rogers	1991	2532
72 0/8	13 3/8 13 4/8	6 0/8 6 0/8	12 4/8	Washoe County	NV	Gary Wright	1992	2532
72 0/8	13 1/8 13 6/8	6 0/8 6 0/8	9 6/8	Union County	NM	Dave Conrad	1992	2532
72 0/8	13 4/8 13 7/8	5 6/8 5 6/8	9 3/8	Saguache County	CO	Mark Wuerthele	1992	2532
72 0/8	13 4/8 13 6/8	6 5/8 6 4/8	11 6/8	Sioux County	NE	Jim Ritz	1992	2532
72 0/8	14 4/8 14 3/8	6 1/8 6 1/8	10 4/8	Converse County	WY	Richard Wheeler	1992	2532
72 0/8	13 3/8 12 6/8	6 2/8 6 1/8	15 4/8	Albany County	WY	Vince DiMiceli	1992	2532
72 0/8	14 0/8 13 6/8	6 0/8 6 0/8	11 6/8	Moffat County	CO	Eugene Ray, Sr.	1993	2532
72 0/8	14 1/8 14 1/8	6 0/8 6 0/8	12 5/8	Sweetwater County	WY	Tim Isaacson	1993	2532
72 0/8	14 0/8 14 2/8	5 2/8 5 2/8	7 7/8	Coconino County	AZ	Tom Alvin	1993	2532
72 0/8	13 5/8 13 7/8	6 2/8 6 2/8	13 2/8	Moffat County	CO	Bruce A. Hatch	1993	2532
72 0/8	14 4/8 14 5/8	6 3/8 6 2/8	20 3/8	Harney County	OR	Joel Modey	1993	2532
72 0/8	13 6/8 14 1/8	6 0/8 6 0/8	10 6/8	Rosebud County	MT	Jerry W. Crow	1993	2532
72 0/8	13 2/8 13 0/8	6 6/8 6 6/8	11 6/8	Converse County	WY	Dave Canfield	1993	2532
72 0/8	12 7/8 13 2/8	5 7/8 5 7/8	9 3/8	Sweetwater County	WY	Dave Holt	1994	2532
72 0/8	14 7/8 14 5/8	6 0/8 6 2/8	11 2/8	Washoe County	NV	Elizabeth F. Wright	1994	2532
72 0/8	14 7/8 15 0/8	5 5/8 5 7/8	9 1/8	Owyhee County	ID	Jason Angell	1994	2532
72 0/8	14 2/8 13 6/8	6 1/8 6 1/8	10 4/8	Campbell County	WY	Kevin Brady	1994	2532
72 0/8	14 3/8 14 3/8	5 6/8 5 4/8	13 4/8	Moffat County	CO	John M. Pollock	1994	2532
72 0/8	13 6/8 13 5/8	6 2/8 6 2/8	8 6/8	Harding County	SD	Kim R. Smith	1994	2532
72 0/8	14 0/8 13 5/8	6 3/8 6 3/8	9 4/8	Buffalo	ALB	Darryl Kublik	1994	2532
72 0/8	13 5/8 13 3/8	6 4/8 6 3/8	11 1/8	Converse County	WY	Steve Thomas, Jr.	1995	2532
72 0/8	14 3/8 14 4/8	5 4/8 5 4/8	7 7/8	Oyen	ALB	Gary Gillett	1995	2532
72 0/8	13 2/8 13 4/8	6 3/8 6 3/8	10 3/8	Moffat County	CO	Calvin P. Miller, Jr.	1995	2532
72 0/8	15 4/8 15 3/8	5 6/8 5 6/8	12 7/8	Campbell County	WY	Donald Fauth	1995	2532
72 0/8	14 6/8 14 2/8	6 1/8 6 1/8	14 0/8	Johnson County	WY	Charles H. Sagner	1995	2532
72 0/8	14 2/8 14 3/8	6 0/8 5 7/8	10 6/8	Hudspeth County	TX	Ernest M. Elbert	1995	2532
72 0/8	14 1/8 14 2/8	6 2/8 6 2/8	9 0/8	Moffat County	CO	Jim Leqve	1996	2532
72 0/8	13 7/8 14 2/8	5 5/8 5 6/8	11 6/8	Rio Grande County	CO	Douglas C. Cotten	1996	2532
72 0/8	15 1/8 14 6/8	5 5/8 5 5/8	11 1/8	Converse County	WY	David L. MacDonald	1996	2532
72 0/8	14 1/8 14 0/8	6 0/8 5 7/8	10 3/8	Weld County	CO	Matt Dickerson	1997	2532
72 0/8	13 0/8 12 7/8	6 1/8 6 1/8	7 5/8	Jerome County	ID	Scott L. Allen	1997	2532
72 0/8	13 4/8 13 3/8	6 1/8 6 1/8	9 4/8	Campbell County	WY	John Fleharty	1997	2532
72 0/8	14 1/8 14 0/8	5 6/8 5 5/8	9 6/8	Uintah County	UT	Mark E. Callahan	1997	2532
72 0/8	14 1/8 14 3/8	6 2/8 6 1/8	12 1/8	Converse County	WY	Ron Riel	1997	2532
72 0/8	14 0/8 14 2/8	5 7/8 5 6/8	8 0/8	Sierra County	NM	V. Randy Liljenquist	1998	2532
72 0/8	13 7/8 14 1/8	6 3/8 6 5/8	10 5/8	Logan County	NE	Drew Armstrong	1998	2532
72 0/8	13 6/8 13 6/8	6 0/8 6 0/8	10 6/8	Campbell County	WY	Dennis N. Ballweg	1998	2532
72 0/8	13 5/8 13 6/8	6 1/8 6 1/8	7 1/8	Jackson County	CO	Paul M. Martin	1998	2532
72 0/8	14 0/8 14 1/8	5 3/8 5 2/8	13 2/8	Weld County	CO	George Clark	1999	2532
72 0/8	13 0/8 12 7/8	6 6/8 6 6/8	10 6/8	Modoc County	CA	Ed Fanchin	1999	2532
72 0/8	15 1/8 14 7/8	5 7/8 5 6/8	10 0/8	Rosebud County	MT	Chuck Adams	1999	2532
72 0/8	14 4/8 14 3/8	6 3/8 6 3/8	9 0/8	Spring Coulee	ALB	Cameron Cook	1999	2532
72 0/8	13 3/8 13 4/8	6 1/8 6 1/8	12 2/8	Converse County	WY	Jim Saunoris, Jr.	2000	2532
72 0/8	14 3/8 14 1/8	5 7/8 5 6/8	12 4/8	Campbell County	WY	Jim Dunigan	2000	2532
72 0/8	13 2/8 13 2/8	5 7/8 5 7/8	10 7/8	Rosebud County	MT	Robert Zseder	2000	2532
72 0/8	13 6/8 13 4/8	5 4/8 5 4/8	7 1/8	Warner	ALB	Don Lind	2000	2532
72 0/8	16 0/8 14 1/8	6 1/8 6 1/8	14 1/8	El Paso County	CO	Ray Soltwedel	2000	2532
72 0/8	13 5/8 13 4/8	6 0/8 6 0/8	7 7/8	Nye County	NV	Patrick L. Beckwith	2002	2532
72 0/8	13 7/8 14 4/8	5 5/8 5 4/8	8 6/8	Albany County	WY	Scott Steere	2002	2532
72 0/8	14 5/8 14 5/8	5 6/8 5 6/8	11 3/8	Moffat County	CO	Richard Bray	2002	2532
72 0/8	14 0/8 12 6/8	6 3/8 6 4/8	7 6/8	Humboldt County	NV	Natalie J. Williams	2002	2532
72 0/8	14 1/8 14 1/8	6 0/8 5 6/8	11 3/8	Platte County	WY	Royce DeCook	2003	2532
72 0/8	14 3/8 15 2/8	5 6/8 5 6/8	12 1/8	Oliver County	ND	Todd Heid	2003	2532
72 0/8	13 6/8 13 6/8	6 0/8 6 0/8	8 1/8	Campbell County	WY	Matt R. Andersen	2003	2532
72 0/8	14 1/8 14 2/8	6 0/8 5 7/8	12 6/8	Converse County	WY	Beth Nelson	2003	2532
72 0/8	14 0/8 13 7/8	5 7/8 5 5/8	8 3/8	Campbell County	WY	Eric F. Efird	2003	2532
72 0/8	12 2/8 12 4/8	6 4/8 6 5/8	11 0/8	Powder River County	MT	Michael B. Washychyn	2003	2532
72 0/8	13 0/8 13 1/8	5 7/8 6 0/8	11 7/8	Garfield County	MT	Mike J. Lloyd	2003	2532
72 0/8	13 5/8 14 0/8	6 2/8 6 2/8	9 4/8	Campbell County	WY	Kenneth J. Morga	2003	2532
*72 0/8	14 5/8 15 1/8	5 3/8 5 4/8	11 6/8	Eureka County	NV	Wayne Alexander	2004	2532
72 0/8	14 2/8 14 7/8	5 7/8 5 7/8	9 1/8	Campbell County	WY	William J. Stuber III	2004	2532
72 0/8	15 0/8 14 7/8	5 6/8 5 6/8	12 5/8	Campbell County	WY	Bret Hamm	2004	2532
72 0/8	13 7/8 14 0/8	5 7/8 5 7/8	10 5/8	Laramie County	WY	Greg Bokash	2005	2532
72 0/8	14 3/8 14 3/8	6 1/8 6 1/8	9 5/8	Moffat County	CO	Troy A. Cunningham	2005	2532
*72 0/8	16 0/8 15 6/8	5 5/8 5 5/8	11 4/8	Yellowstone County	MT	Josh Davis	2005	2532
72 0/8	13 7/8 13 7/8	5 7/8 5 7/8	7 2/8	Laramie County	WY	Stephanie A. Perkins	2005	2532
72 0/8	13 6/8 13 3/8	5 6/8 5 5/8	6 7/8	Dunn County	ND	Greg Passa	2005	2532
72 0/8	14 7/8 14 3/8	5 6/8 5 6/8	10 0/8	Campbell County	WY	Charles Jones, Jr.	2005	2532
72 0/8	13 1/8 13 2/8	6 5/8 6 5/8	8 6/8	Meade County	SD	Rodney E. Kurtz	2005	2532
72 0/8	14 4/8 14 3/8	5 4/8 5 4/8	10 0/8	Lea County	NM	Ronnie Parsons	2006	2532
72 0/8	13 0/8 13 3/8	6 4/8 6 4/8	10 7/8	Fremont County	WY	William D. Rhodes	2006	2532
72 0/8	14 3/8 14 2/8	6 0/8 6 0/8	10 4/8	Pershing County	NV	Gene Malay	2007	2532
72 0/8	13 6/8 13 4/8	5 6/8 5 5/8	7 2/8	Sublette County	WY	Darren Rhea	2007	2532
72 0/8	14 2/8 14 4/8	5 1/8 5 1/8	9 0/8	Converse County	WY	Ron Rockwell	2007	2532
72 0/8	12 3/8 12 7/8	6 4/8 6 4/8	11 4/8	Moffat County	CO	Michael K. Ward	2007	2532
*72 0/8	14 4/8 14 3/8	5 4/8 5 5/8	8 5/8	Converse County	WY	Roland Roth	2007	2532
72 0/8	13 7/8 13 7/8	6 2/8 6 0/8	8 1/8	Lemhi County	ID	Jessica Macumber	2008	2532
72 0/8	14 1/8 14 2/8	5 6/8 5 6/8	9 2/8	Beaver County	UT	Karl Hirst	2008	2532
72 0/8	14 3/8 15 0/8	5 6/8 5 4/8	8 5/8	Natrona County	WY	Lance R. Jelden	2008	2532
72 0/8	15 2/8 14 7/8	5 1/8 5 2/8	7 7/8	Chaves County	NM	Todd Smith	2008	2532
72 0/8	13 1/8 13 3/8	5 7/8 5 7/8	8 7/8	Converse County	WY	Michael J. Centeno	2008	2532
*72 0/8	14 5/8 14 3/8	6 0/8 5 7/8	11 3/8	Perkins County	SD	Zachary Etringer	2008	2532
*72 0/8	13 2/8 12 5/8	6 3/8 6 3/8	7 7/8	Converse County	WY	Steve Enzor	2008	2532
*72 0/8	14 2/8 14 5/8	5 5/8 5 5/8	8 6/8	Toole County	MT	Jay Hould	2008	2532
72 0/8	13 7/8 13 7/8	6 4/8 6 4/8	12 7/8	Campbell County	WY	Anthony "Del" DelMastro	2008	2532
*72 0/8	13 1/8 13 1/8	5 7/8 5 6/8	9 5/8	Lewis & Clark County	MT	Beau Parisi	2008	2532

PRONGHORN

Minimum Score 67 — Continued

SCORE	LENGTH OF R HORN L	CIRCUMFERENCE R OF BASE L	INSIDE SPREAD	AREA	STATE/ PROVINCE	HUNTER'S NAME	DATE	RANK
72 0/8	14 1/8 13 7/8	5 3/8 5 3/8	10 4/8	Lassen County	CA	Mike McCall	2009	2532
72 0/8	13 5/8 13 7/8	6 0/8 5 6/8	11 7/8	Natrona County	WY	Steve Schulz	2009	2532
72 0/8	14 3/8 14 3/8	6 0/8 5 7/8	7 4/8	Fremont County	WY	Daniel K. Doke	2009	2532
72 0/8	13 7/8 14 2/8	5 7/8 5 6/8	8 5/8	Big Horn County	MT	Pete Gerkie	2009	2532
72 0/8	14 1/8 14 1/8	5 7/8 6 0/8	12 0/8	Albany County	WY	Brian Schuette	2009	2532
72 0/8	13 5/8 13 1/8	6 2/8 6 2/8	8 5/8	Fremont County	WY	Loreli Westby	2010	2532
*72 0/8	15 2/8 15 2/8	5 5/8 5 4/8	7 1/8	Clark County	ID	Virgil Burget	2010	2532
72 0/8	14 3/8 14 1/8	6 0/8 5 7/8	11 7/8	Lincoln County	WY	Ethan Backman	2010	2532
71 6/8	14 2/8 14 1/8	5 6/8 5 7/8	10 5/8	Klamath County	OR	Jerry Phillips	1977	2671
71 6/8	13 5/8 13 3/8	6 1/8 6 0/8	11 0/8	Natrona County	WY	George Kegler	1980	2671
71 6/8	14 2/8 14 5/8	5 6/8 5 6/8	10 6/8	Converse County	WY	Ron Spratling	1981	2671
71 6/8	13 0/8 13 0/8	5 5/8 5 4/8	8 7/8	Bowman County	ND	Donald C. Hestekin	1982	2671
71 6/8	13 1/8 13 1/8	5 4/8 5 4/8	10 6/8	Converse County	WY	Robert R. Vance	1982	2671
71 6/8	13 5/8 14 4/8	5 7/8 5 6/8	10 2/8	Carbon County	WY	Don Carter	1983	2671
71 6/8	12 5/8 12 7/8	6 3/8 6 1/8	6 6/8	Converse County	WY	Jim Nielsen	1983	2671
71 6/8	14 3/8 14 5/8	5 7/8 5 7/8	11 6/8	Fremont County	WY	Jim Walters	1983	2671
71 6/8	14 6/8 14 6/8	5 7/8 5 7/8	10 5/8	Powder River County	MT	Ron Thompson	1983	2671
71 6/8	13 7/8 14 0/8	6 1/8 6 0/8	7 3/8	Converse County	WY	Bill Welker	1984	2671
71 6/8	13 7/8 13 7/8	6 0/8 5 7/8	11 4/8	Natrona County	WY	Robert F. Naumann	1984	2671
71 6/8	14 5/8 14 1/8	6 2/8 6 1/8	7 4/8	Campbell County	WY	Mike Ingold	1985	2671
71 6/8	13 6/8 13 4/8	6 3/8 6 2/8	9 1/8	Sweetwater County	WY	James E. Summerall	1986	2671
71 6/8	13 4/8 13 6/8	5 5/8 5 4/8	10 4/8	Moffat County	CO	Denny Williamson	1987	2671
71 6/8	14 0/8 13 7/8	5 3/8 5 4/8	8 7/8	Natrona County	WY	Scott Privette	1987	2671
71 6/8	13 6/8 14 0/8	5 6/8 5 6/8	12 3/8	Rosebud County	MT	Daniel Hudek	1987	2671
71 6/8	13 5/8 14 0/8	6 0/8 6 0/8	8 2/8	Converse County	WY	Frank Moore	1987	2671
71 6/8	13 0/8 13 0/8	6 0/8 6 0/8	14 1/8	Natrona County	WY	Kim Cooper	1987	2671
71 6/8	13 3/8 13 0/8	5 7/8 5 7/8	6 5/8	Lassen County	CA	Tom Devlin	1988	2671
71 6/8	13 0/8 12 7/8	6 3/8 6 4/8	13 5/8	Carbon County	WY	Randy Long	1988	2671
71 6/8	14 0/8 14 2/8	5 5/8 5 6/8	10 2/8	Moffat County	CO	David Greenwalt	1988	2671
71 6/8	12 1/8 13 7/8	6 0/8 6 0/8	9 5/8	Las Animas County	CO	Bill Swift	1988	2671
71 6/8	13 4/8 13 4/8	6 1/8 6 0/8	10 4/8	Cutbank Creek	ALB	Darrell Peters	1988	2671
71 6/8	14 4/8 13 6/8	5 4/8 5 7/8	11 1/8	Moffat County	CO	David Travaglio	1989	2671
71 6/8	14 6/8 14 5/8	6 1/8 6 0/8	9 4/8	Campbell County	WY	Donald J. Ridgley	1989	2671
71 6/8	16 0/8 16 2/8	6 1/8 6 0/8	10 6/8	Bowman County	ND	Gene D. Davis	1989	2671
71 6/8	13 0/8 12 3/8	6 3/8 6 2/8	8 3/8	Rosebud County	MT	Kent Kaufman	1989	2671
71 6/8	14 5/8 14 4/8	5 6/8 5 5/8	9 5/8	Washoe County	NV	George F. Howard	1990	2671
71 6/8	13 6/8 14 1/8	6 1/8 6 1/8	9 4/8	Carbon County	WY	Sam Amberson	1990	2671
71 6/8	14 2/8 14 6/8	5 5/8 5 4/8	11 3/8	Lincoln County	WY	Jeff Blain	1990	2671
71 6/8	13 5/8 13 6/8	5 6/8 5 5/8	8 4/8	Rosebud County	MT	Jesse Meyer	1990	2671
71 6/8	15 5/8 15 7/8	5 1/8 5 2/8	7 4/8	Golden Valley County	ND	Wayne Streitz	1990	2671
71 6/8	14 2/8 14 3/8	6 0/8 6 0/8	8 6/8	Fergus County	MT	Ronald Eugene Sanford, Jr.	1990	2671
71 6/8	14 0/8 13 6/8	5 3/8 5 4/8	10 0/8	Converse County	WY	Tom Mulchay	1990	2671
71 6/8	14 6/8 14 4/8	5 4/8 5 4/8	12 3/8	Orion	ALB	Gunter Lemke	1990	2671
71 6/8	15 1/8 15 0/8	6 0/8 6 0/8	11 0/8	Hudspeth County	TX	James E. Borron	1990	2671
71 6/8	14 3/8 14 3/8	5 5/8 5 5/8	8 0/8	Weld County	CO	Michael J. McArtor	1991	2671
71 6/8	13 6/8 13 7/8	6 3/8 6 3/8	11 2/8	Moffat County	CO	R. Tim Reed	1991	2671
71 6/8	13 4/8 13 4/8	5 7/8 5 7/8	9 6/8	Yavapai County	AZ	James Monroe Haines	1991	2671
71 6/8	13 5/8 13 4/8	6 3/8 6 4/8	8 2/8	Custer County	ID	Matt March	1991	2671
71 6/8	14 1/8 13 5/8	6 3/8 6 3/8	10 7/8	Rich County	UT	Peter E. Paulds, Jr.	1991	2671
71 6/8	14 2/8 14 0/8	6 2/8 6 1/8	12 1/8	Converse County	WY	Jack Schatz	1991	2671
71 6/8	14 6/8 14 4/8	5 4/8 5 3/8	10 3/8	Platte County	WY	Jack Baltz	1991	2671
71 6/8	13 3/8 13 7/8	6 0/8 6 0/8	8 0/8	Campbell County	WY	Dr. Robert Edward Speegle	1991	2671
71 6/8	14 4/8 14 0/8	6 0/8 5 7/8	8 5/8	Sweetwater County	WY	Jed R. Ashworth	1992	2671
71 6/8	14 2/8 14 3/8	5 7/8 5 6/8	8 5/8	Union County	NM	Jeff Fitts	1992	2671
71 6/8	13 2/8 13 1/8	6 4/8 6 1/8	12 2/8	Moffat County	CO	Bruce Eggenberger	1992	2671
71 6/8	14 7/8 14 0/8	6 3/8 6 1/8	12 4/8	Lincoln County	WY	Lance Brown	1992	2671
71 6/8	14 0/8 13 7/8	5 6/8 5 7/8	8 7/8	Rich County	UT	Guy G. Fitzgerald	1992	2671
71 6/8	13 3/8 13 0/8	5 4/8 5 7/8	12 6/8	Sublette County	WY	Phil N. Skinner	1992	2671
71 6/8	13 7/8 14 0/8	5 7/8 6 0/8	10 6/8	Moffat County	CO	Dave Parri	1992	2671
71 6/8	12 2/8 12 1/8	6 0/8 6 0/8	8 2/8	Converse County	WY	Joe Cronin	1992	2671
71 6/8	13 5/8 13 7/8	6 3/8 6 3/8	8 6/8	Natrona County	WY	Ed Gawel	1992	2671
71 6/8	14 1/8 14 1/8	5 7/8 5 7/8	11 0/8	Buffalo	ALB	Dewain Ollenberger	1992	2671
71 6/8	13 2/8 13 0/8	5 7/8 5 6/8	11 1/8	Moffat County	CO	Kevin C. Massaro	1992	2671
71 6/8	14 4/8 14 1/8	5 7/8 5 6/8	10 0/8	Converse County	WY	Michael L. Hoft	1992	2671
71 6/8	13 5/8 13 5/8	6 2/8 6 1/8	9 3/8	Billings County	ND	Les Tomanek	1992	2671
71 6/8	12 7/8 13 2/8	6 2/8 6 1/8	4 7/8	Kimball County	NE	James J. Beebe	1992	2671
71 6/8	13 0/8 12 4/8	6 2/8 6 2/8	12 0/8	Slope County	ND	Robert R. Parker	1992	2671
71 6/8	13 4/8 13 3/8	7 0/8 6 4/8	12 4/8	Campbell County	WY	Paul Vomela	1992	2671
71 6/8	13 7/8 14 1/8	6 2/8 6 0/8	11 3/8	Natrona County	WY	Mike Mikalowsky	1992	2671
71 6/8	15 2/8 15 2/8	5 4/8 5 4/8	9 5/8	Jeff Davis County	TX	Wayne North	1992	2671
71 6/8	14 2/8 13 7/8	5 3/8 5 3/8	8 2/8	Mohave County	AZ	Dave Fuller	1993	2671
71 6/8	14 2/8 14 5/8	6 2/8 6 2/8	11 0/8	White Pine County	NV	Jerry A. Davis	1993	2671
71 6/8	13 7/8 15 2/8	5 7/8 6 0/8	7 6/8	Dawes County	NE	Francis Ohlsen	1993	2671
71 6/8	14 7/8 14 5/8	5 4/8 5 4/8	11 1/8	Hays	ALB	Steen Sorensen	1993	2671
71 6/8	14 2/8 14 2/8	6 2/8 5 7/8	13 3/8	McKenzie County	ND	David Tofte	1993	2671
71 6/8	14 1/8 13 4/8	5 5/8 5 6/8	10 6/8	Dundy County	NE	Clint Burrell	1993	2671
71 6/8	13 6/8 13 1/8	6 2/8 6 2/8	9 1/8	Harding County	SD	Lonnie G. Tschumper	1993	2671
71 6/8	13 2/8 13 2/8	5 7/8 5 7/8	11 4/8	Duchesne County	UT	Dennis L. Shirley	1994	2671
71 6/8	14 3/8 14 4/8	6 0/8 6 1/8	8 6/8	Ada County	ID	Robert Dowen	1994	2671
71 6/8	13 7/8 13 7/8	6 3/8 6 3/8	7 5/8	Converse County	WY	Ralph Inverso	1994	2671
71 6/8	13 4/8 13 4/8	6 0/8 6 0/8	9 3/8	Slope County	ND	Neil D. Mellesmoen	1994	2671
71 6/8	12 7/8 13 0/8	6 4/8 6 6/8	12 2/8	Lake County	OR	Rodney W. Ferry	1994	2671
71 6/8	14 4/8 14 0/8	6 0/8 5 5/8	7 2/8	Powder River County	MT	John Martinson	1995	2671
71 6/8	13 7/8 13 5/8	6 0/8 6 1/8	10 4/8	Converse County	WY	David Miller	1995	2671
71 6/8	15 2/8 15 5/8	5 5/8 5 4/8	7 0/8	Hudspeth County	TX	Bruce Baird	1995	2671
71 6/8	15 0/8 14 7/8	5 5/8 5 5/8	8 2/8	Beaver County	UT	Allan Mayer	1996	2671
71 6/8	14 3/8 14 2/8	6 3/8 6 2/8	10 4/8	Carbon County	UT	Brent Oman	1996	2671
71 6/8	14 4/8 14 6/8	5 2/8 5 1/8	10 1/8	Lincoln County	NM	Ron Randle	1996	2671
71 6/8	12 7/8 13 2/8	6 1/8 6 0/8	9 7/8	Rosebud County	MT	Gene A. Welle	1996	2671
71 6/8	13 7/8 14 1/8	6 2/8 6 2/8	8 4/8	Billings County	ND	Gary Wiley	1996	2671
71 6/8	13 4/8 13 0/8	7 0/8 6 7/8	10 3/8	Weld County	CO	Kevin Ayers	1997	2671
71 6/8	14 1/8 14 0/8	5 7/8 5 7/8	10 0/8	Powder River County	MT	Dave R. Christofferson	1997	2671
71 6/8	13 3/8 13 5/8	6 2/8 6 1/8	10 7/8	Tooele County	UT	Ryan Isaacson	1998	2671
71 6/8	14 3/8 14 4/8	5 6/8 5 6/8	8 6/8	Weld County	CO	Rodney E. Perrine	1998	2671
71 6/8	14 0/8 14 0/8	5 6/8 5 5/8	15 3/8	Bowman County	ND	Jon Brewer	1999	2671

PRONGHORN

Minimum Score 67 — Continued

SCORE	LENGTH OF R HORN L	CIRCUMFERENCE R OF BASE L	INSIDE SPREAD	AREA	STATE/PROVINCE	HUNTER'S NAME	DATE	RANK
71 6/8	15 1/8 14 7/8	5 5/8 5 4/8	8 1/8	Converse County	WY	Duane R. Mabry	1999	2671
71 6/8	13 2/8 13 4/8	6 3/8 6 3/8	9 7/8	Converse County	WY	Robert J. Fox	1999	2671
71 6/8	14 7/8 15 0/8	5 4/8 5 1/8	11 7/8	Lincoln County	NM	Travis Todd	2000	2671
71 6/8	13 1/8 12 6/8	6 0/8 6 0/8	10 4/8	Carbon County	UT	Paula Richmond	2000	2671
71 6/8	14 2/8 14 3/8	6 2/8 6 1/8	8 7/8	Weld County	CO	Steve Gobeli	2000	2671
71 6/8	14 0/8 13 7/8	5 5/8 5 5/8	8 4/8	Hot Springs County	WY	Cameron Hanes	2000	2671
71 6/8	14 4/8 14 4/8	5 5/8 5 5/8	7 5/8	Converse County	WY	Darrell Wright	2000	2671
71 6/8	12 2/8 12 4/8	6 1/8 6 0/8	12 4/8	Lincoln County	WY	Ronald Alexander	2001	2671
71 6/8	13 4/8 13 5/8	5 6/8 5 7/8	7 7/8	Carbon County	UT	Gary D. Mills	2001	2671
71 6/8	13 3/8 13 2/8	6 1/8 6 0/8	7 2/8	Converse County	WY	Jim Ellis	2001	2671
71 6/8	14 2/8 14 1/8	6 0/8 5 6/8	10 0/8	Moffat County	CO	Justin Downing	2001	2671
71 6/8	14 1/8 14 2/8	5 6/8 5 5/8	9 5/8	Converse County	WY	Frank S. Noska IV	2001	2671
*71 6/8	14 4/8 14 3/8	6 0/8 5 7/8	10 0/8	Natrona County	WY	Kathleen E. Collins	2003	2671
*71 6/8	14 2/8 14 1/8	5 7/8 5 7/8	9 3/8	Washoe County	NV	Dave Wannamaker	2004	2671
71 6/8	14 5/8 13 6/8	6 0/8 5 5/8	7 3/8	Las Animas County	CO	Lee Olmstead	2004	2671
71 6/8	14 7/8 14 7/8	5 5/8 5 4/8	7 2/8	Cibola County	NM	Glenn Thompson	2004	2671
71 6/8	13 1/8 13 1/8	6 0/8 5 7/8	12 6/8	Coconino County	AZ	Paul Carter	2004	2671
71 6/8	12 4/8 12 2/8	6 2/8 6 2/8	9 4/8	Converse County	WY	Michael L. Ritter	2004	2671
71 6/8	14 1/8 14 2/8	5 5/8 5 5/8	11 3/8	Campbell County	WY	Chris Trainor	2004	2671
71 6/8	12 7/8 13 1/8	6 5/8 6 5/8	11 0/8	Lake County	OR	Gary Kiepert	2005	2671
71 6/8	13 7/8 14 0/8	5 7/8 5 7/8	10 1/8	Lincoln County	ID	Craig Phillips	2005	2671
71 6/8	13 4/8 13 1/8	6 2/8 6 3/8	10 0/8	Sweetwater County	WY	L. Grant Foster	2005	2671
71 6/8	14 7/8 14 3/8	5 7/8 5 7/8	9 6/8	Sublette County	WY	Dave R. Burget	2005	2671
71 6/8	14 3/8 14 2/8	5 4/8 5 3/8	6 5/8	Albany County	WY	Ken Harder	2005	2671
*71 6/8	14 4/8 14 4/8	6 1/8 5 7/8	10 4/8	Albany County	WY	Tom Nebbs	2005	2671
*71 6/8	15 1/8 15 0/8	5 7/8 5 7/8	8 3/8	Billings County	ND	Troy Miller	2005	2671
71 6/8	14 3/8 14 3/8	5 6/8 5 6/8	9 1/8	Converse County	WY	Leon Buckles	2005	2671
71 6/8	13 3/8 13 2/8	6 2/8 6 1/8	12 7/8	Custer County	MT	J. Dale Hale	2005	2671
71 6/8	14 0/8 14 1/8	5 7/8 5 7/8	7 7/8	Wibaux County	MT	Gary Nunberg	2005	2671
71 6/8	13 7/8 14 1/8	5 4/8 5 6/8	9 6/8	Guadalupe County	NM	Clint Hukill	2006	2671
*71 6/8	14 2/8 14 0/8	5 7/8 5 6/8	10 0/8	Buffalo County	SD	Duane Peterson	2006	2671
71 6/8	13 6/8 13 4/8	5 6/8 5 7/8	8 1/8	Converse County	WY	David P. Weber	2006	2671
71 6/8	14 1/8 14 3/8	5 6/8 5 6/8	7 1/8	Carter County	MT	Scott Hettinger	2006	2671
*71 6/8	13 5/8 13 3/8	6 2/8 6 1/8	12 4/8	Perkins County	SD	Clinton Emmert	2007	2671
71 6/8	14 2/8 14 2/8	5 6/8 5 6/8	7 2/8	Campbell County	WY	Jacob Gerber	2007	2671
71 6/8	13 2/8 13 2/8	6 3/8 6 1/8	8 2/8	Converse County	WY	Matthew Franks	2007	2671
*71 6/8	13 1/8 13 2/8	6 1/8 6 0/8	11 4/8	Meath Park	SAS	Robert Newton	2007	2671
71 6/8	13 2/8 13 2/8	6 5/8 6 5/8	8 5/8	Moffat County	CO	Lance Schul	2007	2671
71 6/8	15 5/8 15 2/8	5 6/8 5 7/8	8 6/8	Esther	ALB	Gary Stouffer	2007	2671
71 6/8	13 0/8 13 2/8	6 2/8 6 4/8	10 0/8	Natrona County	WY	Stephen P. Turay	2007	2671
71 6/8	14 1/8 13 5/8	5 6/8 5 6/8	10 5/8	Gunnison County	CO	Justin Medina	2007	2671
71 6/8	15 2/8 15 6/8	5 6/8 5 7/8	13 6/8	Lake County	OR	Patrick J. Dey	2008	2671
71 6/8	11 4/8 11 4/8	6 3/8 6 6/8	9 0/8	Saguache County	CO	Brandon Coleman	2008	2671
*71 6/8	13 4/8 13 6/8	5 7/8 5 7/8	11 0/8	Rosebud County	MT	Kevin Brewer	2008	2671
71 6/8	14 0/8 14 0/8	5 6/8 5 7/8	12 3/8	Converse County	WY	Michael C. Rich	2008	2671
71 6/8	13 7/8 13 3/8	6 0/8 6 0/8	9 2/8	Carbon County	WY	Brandon Ray	2008	2671
*71 6/8	13 5/8 13 5/8	6 0/8 6 0/8	9 7/8	Johnson County	WY	Ben Lake	2008	2671
71 6/8	13 6/8 14 4/8	6 2/8 6 2/8	8 4/8	Moffat County	CO	Brad Campbell	2008	2671
71 6/8	12 7/8 13 0/8	6 3/8 6 3/8	7 5/8	Laramie County	WY	Rick Bryant	2008	2671
*71 6/8	14 7/8 14 7/8	5 7/8 5 4/8	11 7/8	Perkins County	SD	Matt Grunig	2008	2671
71 6/8	12 7/8 12 5/8	6 1/8 6 0/8	10 7/8	Harding County	SD	John Noon	2009	2671
71 6/8	13 2/8 13 1/8	6 3/8 6 0/8	8 1/8	Natrona County	WY	Tom Nelson	2009	2671
71 6/8	13 5/8 13 4/8	5 6/8 5 6/8	9 7/8	Chouteau County	MT	Gary Evans	2009	2671
71 6/8	13 1/8 13 1/8	5 6/8 5 6/8	10 0/8	Sublette County	WY	Mark Thonhoff	2009	2671
71 6/8	12 4/8 12 5/8	6 2/8 6 2/8	9 7/8	Powder River County	MT	William Snelgrove	2009	2671
*71 6/8	13 0/8 13 1/8	6 0/8 6 0/8	9 6/8	Elko County	NV	Laura D. Brown	2010	2671
71 6/8	13 2/8 12 6/8	6 1/8 6 0/8	9 4/8	Douglas	SAS	Chad Gessner	2010	2671
*71 6/8	14 5/8 14 0/8	6 0/8 6 0/8	6 4/8	Carbon County	WY	John Tuchscherer	2010	2671
71 6/8	13 3/8 13 3/8	5 6/8 5 6/8	8 7/8	Gallatin County	MT	Bob Morton	2010	2671
71 4/8	13 6/8 13 4/8	6 4/8 6 2/8	10 0/8	Carbon County	WY	Bill Scoggin	1957	2817
71 4/8	14 7/8 14 7/8	6 2/8 6 2/8	13 5/8	Moffat County	CO	Henry Wichers	1959	2817
71 4/8	13 4/8 13 3/8	6 0/8 6 0/8	8 2/8	Tripp County	SD	Dan Smith	1965	2817
71 4/8	14 2/8 14 0/8	5 4/8 5 4/8	9 6/8	Carbon County	WY	Jerry Bowen	1976	2817
71 4/8	12 6/8 12 6/8	5 6/8 5 6/8	8 2/8	Carbon County	WY	Ronald J. Wedge	1978	2817
71 4/8	14 4/8 14 4/8	5 5/8 5 5/8	9 7/8	Albany County	WY	Tom Tietz	1978	2817
71 4/8	14 1/8 14 0/8	6 2/8 6 3/8	9 1/8	Sweetwater County	WY	Val Jones	1978	2817
71 4/8	13 6/8 13 6/8	6 0/8 6 0/8	6 6/8	Sheridan County	WY	David Shoop	1980	2817
71 4/8	13 0/8 13 0/8	6 0/8 5 6/8	9 3/8	Converse County	WY	Mike Burley	1980	2817
71 4/8	13 1/8 13 6/8	6 1/8 6 2/8	11 4/8	Yavapai County	AZ	Peter C. Knagge	1980	2817
71 4/8	12 4/8 12 1/8	6 4/8 6 3/8	9 7/8	Carbon County	WY	Bruce Butkiewicz	1980	2817
71 4/8	12 6/8 12 5/8	5 7/8 5 6/8	10 0/8	Natrona County	WY	David Manthei	1981	2817
71 4/8	12 7/8 12 4/8	6 7/8 6 4/8	12 7/8	Carbon County	WY	Dennis Crank	1982	2817
71 4/8	15 0/8 15 0/8	5 7/8 5 6/8	10 6/8	Perkins County	SD	H. Melvin Dutton	1982	2817
71 4/8	13 0/8 13 0/8	5 6/8 5 7/8	9 4/8	Delta County	CO	Doug McCauley	1983	2817
71 4/8	13 3/8 13 4/8	6 2/8 6 1/8	9 2/8	Carbon County	WY	Bob Moore	1983	2817
71 4/8	12 6/8 13 0/8	6 0/8 6 1/8	10 0/8	Perkins County	SD	H. Melvin Dutton	1983	2817
71 4/8	14 0/8 14 1/8	6 1/8 6 1/8	6 5/8	Grand Forks	ALB	Ian Sangster	1983	2817
71 4/8	13 2/8 13 1/8	6 2/8 6 1/8	7 5/8	Converse County	WY	George Hecker	1984	2817
71 4/8	12 0/8 14 3/8	6 3/8 6 2/8	8 1/8	Petroleum County	MT	Ben Maughan	1984	2817
71 4/8	15 3/8 15 2/8	5 7/8 6 0/8	15 2/8	Moffat County	CO	Richard King	1985	2817
71 4/8	13 7/8 13 6/8	6 0/8 5 7/8	9 3/8	Beaverhead County	MT	Ron Oswald	1985	2817
71 4/8	14 6/8 14 3/8	5 5/8 5 5/8	12 1/8	Humboldt County	NV	Martin J. Larraneta, Jr.	1986	2817
71 4/8	13 0/8 13 0/8	6 2/8 6 0/8	9 1/8	Moffat County	CO	Terry Weimer	1986	2817
71 4/8	13 6/8 14 0/8	6 0/8 6 0/8	11 0/8	Converse County	WY	Scott Wilke	1986	2817
71 4/8	14 0/8 14 2/8	5 5/8 5 6/8	9 5/8	Sublette County	WY	Jim Carr	1986	2817
71 4/8	14 4/8 14 1/8	5 7/8 5 5/8	8 7/8	Mountrail County	ND	Todd W. Boechler	1986	2817
71 4/8	14 1/8 14 6/8	5 6/8 5 5/8	8 4/8	Coconino County	AZ	Tim Edwards	1987	2817
71 4/8	13 7/8 13 7/8	5 7/8 6 0/8	11 6/8	Moffat County	CO	Mike Ottenbacher	1987	2817
71 4/8	12 1/8 12 1/8	6 0/8 6 1/8	9 1/8	Sublette County	WY	Gaylynn Turner	1988	2817
71 4/8	14 2/8 14 4/8	6 1/8 6 0/8	10 4/8	Moffat County	CO	Robert A. Hermann	1988	2817
71 4/8	13 6/8 13 6/8	6 0/8 6 0/8	10 7/8	Buffalo	ALB	Stuart Sinclair-Smith	1988	2817
71 4/8	13 2/8 13 5/8	5 7/8 5 7/8	8 5/8	McLean County	ND	Anton P. Wetch	1988	2817
71 4/8	13 5/8 13 6/8	6 1/8 6 0/8	9 6/8	Moffat County	CO	Michael Magana	1989	2817
71 4/8	12 4/8 12 7/8	6 1/8 6 2/8	9 7/8	Moffat County	CO	James VanAlstine	1989	2817
71 4/8	13 4/8 13 4/8	6 0/8 5 7/8	9 0/8	Billings County	ND	Micheal Ness	1989	2817

839

PRONGHORN

Minimum Score 67 — Continued

SCORE	LENGTH OF R HORN L	CIRCUMFERENCE R OF BASE L	INSIDE SPREAD	AREA	STATE/ PROVINCE	HUNTER'S NAME	DATE	RANK
71 4/8	13 2/8 14 4/8	5 7/8 5 6/8	10 2/8	Yavapai County	AZ	Richard M Compau	1989	2817
71 4/8	14 4/8 14 1/8	5 5/8 5 4/8	11 5/8	Foremost	ALB	Kelly Kerner	1989	2817
71 4/8	14 7/8 13 4/8	5 7/8 5 6/8	11 0/8	Jackson County	CO	Lance Barnica	1990	2817
71 4/8	14 3/8 13 4/8	5 7/8 5 7/8	9 5/8	Dunn County	ND	Rick Stein	1990	2817
71 4/8	13 3/8 13 4/8	6 1/8 6 2/8	9 5/8	Twin Falls County	ID	John Stevens	1991	2817
71 4/8	13 1/8 13 4/8	6 2/8 6 2/8	12 7/8	Owyhee County	ID	Steve Stephenson	1991	2817
71 4/8	13 7/8 14 0/8	6 0/8 6 0/8	8 6/8	Converse County	WY	Charles R. Cramer	1991	2817
71 4/8	13 6/8 14 0/8	6 1/8 6 1/8	9 0/8	Campbell County	WY	Wayne Jossart	1991	2817
71 4/8	13 5/8 13 4/8	6 4/8 6 4/8	11 5/8	Converse County	WY	Steve Gorr	1991	2817
71 4/8	13 2/8 13 1/8	6 0/8 6 3/8	14 6/8	Fremont County	WY	Glen L. Mahlum	1991	2817
71 4/8	13 7/8 14 1/8	5 6/8 5 7/8	10 0/8	Lake County	OR	Phillip L. Severson	1992	2817
71 4/8	14 6/8 14 2/8	5 7/8 5 1/8	9 0/8	Klamath County	OR	Frank Sanders	1992	2817
71 4/8	13 5/8 13 3/8	6 3/8 6 2/8	6 2/8	Moffat County	CO	Mark D. Thomson	1992	2817
71 4/8	13 3/8 13 0/8	6 2/8 6 2/8	9 6/8	Carbon County	WY	Jim Kurth	1992	2817
71 4/8	14 3/8 14 6/8	5 6/8 5 5/8	12 5/8	County of 40 Mile	ALB	Murray T. Campbell	1992	2817
71 4/8	14 1/8 14 3/8	5 6/8 5 7/8	6 7/8	Sweetwater County	WY	Thad W. Sullivan	1993	2817
71 4/8	13 7/8 14 2/8	5 5/8 5 7/8	9 2/8	Moffat County	CO	Bob Nelson	1993	2817
71 4/8	13 5/8 13 4/8	6 0/8 6 0/8	9 6/8	Moffat County	CO	Cynthia Dziekan	1993	2817
71 4/8	14 0/8 13 7/8	6 1/8 6 1/8	10 5/8	Millard County	UT	Jerry A. Davis	1993	2817
71 4/8	13 4/8 13 1/8	6 1/8 6 1/8	10 5/8	Weld County	CO	Wes Lowrie	1993	2817
71 4/8	13 7/8 13 7/8	6 0/8 5 7/8	8 3/8	Lewis & Clark County	MT	Al Schellinger	1993	2817
71 4/8	13 2/8 13 1/8	5 5/8 5 4/8	12 2/8	Empress	ALB	Michael E. Kessler	1993	2817
71 4/8	13 0/8 13 6/8	6 1/8 5 7/8	10 5/8	Sweetwater County	WY	Billy Tillotson	1994	2817
71 4/8	13 6/8 14 1/8	6 4/8 6 2/8	9 0/8	Saguache County	CO	Thomas J. Torrez	1994	2817
71 4/8	13 0/8 12 3/8	5 7/8 5 7/8	10 0/8	Platte County	WY	Tom Pindell	1994	2817
71 4/8	13 2/8 13 4/8	5 6/8 5 7/8	11 4/8	Custer County	ID	Matt March	1994	2817
71 4/8	14 7/8 15 0/8	5 6/8 5 4/8	10 0/8	Weld County	CO	Michael J. McArtor	1994	2817
71 4/8	12 4/8 12 4/8	6 1/8 6 1/8	12 2/8	Larimer County	CO	Fred Eichler	1994	2817
71 4/8	13 0/8 14 1/8	5 6/8 5 7/8	9 3/8	Moffat County	CO	Kurt W. Keskimaki	1994	2817
71 4/8	13 5/8 13 3/8	6 0/8 6 0/8	8 4/8	Converse County	WY	Lou Edelis	1994	2817
71 4/8	13 2/8 13 3/8	6 5/8 6 3/8	10 5/8	Niobrara County	WY	Robert B. Otto	1994	2817
71 4/8	14 1/8 13 5/8	5 5/8 5 5/8	9 5/8	Natrona County	WY	Bruce R. Linke	1994	2817
71 4/8	13 2/8 13 1/8	5 7/8 5 7/8	9 7/8	Converse County	WY	Trish D'Agostino	1994	2817
71 4/8	13 7/8 14 4/8	6 7/8 6 4/8	10 3/8	Campbell County	WY	Roy M. Wible, Jr.	1994	2817
71 4/8	14 1/8 14 4/8	5 7/8 5 6/8	10 6/8	Carter County	MT	Marty Adams	1994	2817
71 4/8	14 0/8 13 7/8	6 1/8 5 7/8	10 2/8	Big Horn County	WY	Don R. Gifford	1994	2817
71 4/8	13 2/8 13 2/8	5 5/8 5 5/8	9 5/8	Johnson County	WY	Rick T. Wardle	1994	2817
71 4/8	14 3/8 14 4/8	6 0/8 6 1/8	8 1/8	Moffat County	CO	Doug Weimer	1995	2817
71 4/8	13 3/8 13 4/8	6 2/8 6 3/8	13 2/8	Moffat County	CO	Dennis Hollenbeck	1995	2817
71 4/8	15 3/8 15 5/8	5 5/8 5 4/8	8 0/8	Park County	WY	Brad McMillin	1995	2817
71 4/8	13 7/8 14 0/8	6 1/8 6 0/8	8 6/8	Moffat County	CO	John Gross	1995	2817
71 4/8	12 7/8 12 7/8	6 0/8 6 0/8	8 3/8	Weld County	CO	Jim Smith	1995	2817
71 4/8	14 1/8 14 6/8	5 5/8 5 4/8	10 3/8	Carbon County	WY	Mark Nessman	1995	2817
71 4/8	13 4/8 13 4/8	6 0/8 6 0/8	11 5/8	Harding County	SD	Marty Adams	1995	2817
71 4/8	13 1/8 12 7/8	7 0/8 6 7/8	12 5/8	Moffat County	CO	Toxey Haas	1996	2817
71 4/8	14 2/8 14 4/8	6 0/8 6 1/8	12 3/8	Weld County	CO	Mark Johnson	1996	2817
71 4/8	12 5/8 12 4/8	6 1/8 6 1/8	7 6/8	Weld County	CO	Michael Radford	1996	2817
71 4/8	14 0/8 14 2/8	5 7/8 5 6/8	11 5/8	Moffat County	CO	Tim L. Decker	1996	2817
71 4/8	13 6/8 13 6/8	6 1/8 6 1/8	8 3/8	Sweetwater County	WY	Craig Germond	1996	2817
71 4/8	13 5/8 14 0/8	6 2/8 6 0/8	10 2/8	Weld County	CO	Thomas Allen	1996	2817
71 4/8	12 2/8 12 2/8	5 6/8 5 6/8	10 2/8	Coconino County	AZ	Michael L. Powers	1996	2817
71 4/8	13 7/8 13 5/8	5 6/8 5 6/8	9 7/8	McKenzie County	ND	Don G. Scofield	1996	2817
71 4/8	12 6/8 13 1/8	5 5/8 5 4/8	10 2/8	Gunnison County	CO	Chester J. Thompson	1996	2817
71 4/8	13 4/8 13 6/8	5 5/8 5 3/8	10 4/8	Rosebud County	MT	Kerry Keller	1996	2817
71 4/8	14 4/8 14 3/8	6 1/8 6 1/8	7 6/8	Humboldt County	NV	Cody K. Brinkerhoff	1997	2817
71 4/8	14 0/8 14 0/8	6 1/8 5 7/8	9 3/8	Saguache County	CO	John Borge	1997	2817
71 4/8	13 2/8 13 1/8	6 2/8 6 3/8	7 0/8	Rosebud County	MT	Joe Lasch	1997	2817
71 4/8	14 1/8 14 0/8	5 7/8 5 6/8	7 7/8	Modoc County	CA	John R. Lamb	1998	2817
71 4/8	14 0/8 14 1/8	5 4/8 5 5/8	8 3/8	Grand County	UT	Kurt Wood	1998	2817
71 4/8	14 0/8 13 7/8	6 1/8 6 0/8	7 6/8	Converse County	WY	Bernard R. Belaire, Jr.	1998	2817
71 4/8	13 4/8 13 4/8	5 7/8 5 7/8	10 3/8	Medicine Hat	ALB	Mark E. Titus	1998	2817
71 4/8	13 5/8 13 6/8	6 7/8 7 1/8	10 4/8	Rio Grande County	CO	Stephen W. Teague	1998	2817
71 4/8	14 2/8 13 5/8	6 0/8 5 7/8	9 7/8	Converse County	WY	David H. Boland	1998	2817
71 4/8	14 0/8 13 3/8	6 0/8 5 6/8	9 1/8	Moffat County	CO	Bob Beckwith	1999	2817
71 4/8	12 5/8 12 3/8	5 7/8 5 6/8	8 5/8	Park County	CO	Robert Ryszkowski	1999	2817
71 4/8	12 6/8 12 5/8	6 1/8 6 1/8	9 1/8	Juab County	UT	Ben D. Nielsen	1999	2817
71 4/8	13 4/8 13 3/8	6 4/8 6 3/8	12 2/8	Perkins County	SD	Travis Hanson	1999	2817
71 4/8	14 0/8 13 6/8	5 7/8 5 6/8	7 0/8	Campbell County	WY	Neil J. Patrone	1999	2817
71 4/8	13 4/8 13 6/8	5 7/8 6 0/8	10 4/8	Moffat County	CO	Mike Ingold	2000	2817
71 4/8	13 2/8 13 5/8	6 2/8 6 2/8	11 2/8	Socorro County	NM	Donald Brongo	2000	2817
71 4/8	14 2/8 14 3/8	5 5/8 5 6/8	10 1/8	Rio Blanco County	CO	Michael D. Muller	2000	2817
71 4/8	13 5/8 13 5/8	5 7/8 5 7/8	7 2/8	Campbell County	WY	David N. Andersen	2001	2817
71 4/8	11 5/8 11 5/8	5 6/8 5 6/8	6 2/8	Weld County	CO	Neil Chandler	2001	2817
71 4/8	14 6/8 14 7/8	5 5/8 5 5/8	10 7/8	Yellowstone County	MT	Briant Duray	2001	2817
*71 4/8	13 3/8 13 5/8	5 3/8 5 1/8	13 5/8	Musselshell County	MT	Skip Brahmer	2002	2817
71 4/8	14 5/8 14 4/8	5 4/8 5 4/8	13 0/8	Humboldt County	NV	Shannon M. Taylor	2003	2817
71 4/8	13 2/8 13 4/8	5 6/8 5 6/8	8 7/8	Converse County	WY	Gary Kautz	2003	2817
71 4/8	15 2/8 15 1/8	5 2/8 5 2/8	8 4/8	Fall River County	SD	Steve Langendorf	2003	2817
71 4/8	13 2/8 13 2/8	5 5/8 5 4/8	8 3/8	Albany County	WY	Christopher Durando	2004	2817
71 4/8	14 3/8 14 1/8	5 5/8 5 7/8	10 2/8	Albany County	WY	Eric Otero	2004	2817
71 4/8	14 0/8 13 6/8	6 2/8 6 2/8	14 2/8	Converse County	WY	James H. Radford	2004	2817
71 4/8	13 3/8 13 3/8	6 2/8 6 2/8	7 5/8	Converse County	WY	Lemuel H. Carter	2004	2817
71 4/8	15 4/8 15 5/8	5 7/8 5 5/8	10 6/8	Powder River County	MT	Gene Smith	2004	2817
71 4/8	12 5/8 12 6/8	5 7/8 5 7/8	7 7/8	Stanley County	SD	Derek Schiefelbein	2005	2817
71 4/8	13 0/8 12 7/8	6 4/8 6 4/8	9 7/8	Powder River County	MT	Carl Fritz	2005	2817
71 4/8	13 6/8 13 7/8	6 1/8 6 0/8	9 5/8	Carter County	MT	Fred M. Stowell	2005	2817
*71 4/8	13 1/8 13 1/8	5 6/8 5 6/8	10 3/8	Sheridan County	WY	Rick Davidson	2006	2817
71 4/8	13 2/8 13 1/8	6 3/8 6 2/8	9 3/8	Niobrara County	WY	Thompson Bruegger	2006	2817
*71 4/8	13 5/8 13 4/8	6 2/8 6 1/8	8 0/8	Johnson County	WY	Wayne B. Six	2006	2817
71 4/8	13 4/8 13 4/8	6 2/8 6 2/8	11 3/8	Moffat County	CO	Thane Anderson	2006	2817
71 4/8	14 4/8 14 1/8	5 7/8 5 6/8	10 7/8	Larimer County	CO	Kenneth Dana Thompson	2007	2817
71 4/8	13 7/8 14 1/8	6 0/8 5 7/8	8 1/8	Brooks	ALB	Dallas Kaiser	2007	2817
71 4/8	14 2/8 14 3/8	6 3/8 6 1/8	12 5/8	Rosebud County	MT	Michael C. Allgeyer	2007	2817
71 4/8	13 2/8 13 2/8	6 0/8 5 7/8	8 6/8	Powder River County	MT	Bob Dowen	2007	2817
71 4/8	13 5/8 13 5/8	5 7/8 6 0/8	14 0/8	Rosebud County	MT	Robert E. Reedy, Jr.	2007	2817

PRONGHORN

Minimum Score 67 — Continued

SCORE	LENGTH OF R HORN L	CIRCUMFERENCE R OF BASE L	INSIDE SPREAD	AREA	STATE/ PROVINCE	HUNTER'S NAME	DATE	RANK
71 4/8	14 6/8 14 3/8	5 5/8 5 6/8	15 3/8	Lea County	NM	Chancey Pierce	2008	2817
71 4/8	14 0/8 14 1/8	5 4/8 5 4/8	8 0/8	Lincoln County	NM	Camp Newton	2008	2817
71 4/8	13 1/8 13 2/8	6 0/8 6 0/8	11 0/8	Carter County	MT	Robert E. Ebert	2008	2817
71 4/8	14 7/8 15 0/8	6 4/8 6 4/8	11 4/8	Perkins County	SD	Dustin Haber	2008	2817
71 4/8	13 3/8 13 6/8	6 1/8 5 7/8	10 7/8	Natrona County	WY	Steve Turay	2008	2817
*71 4/8	14 0/8 13 6/8	5 7/8 5 7/8	9 2/8	Converse County	WY	Tom Edgington	2009	2817
71 4/8	13 6/8 13 5/8	6 1/8 6 0/8	9 3/8	Larimer County	CO	David Jeffries	2009	2817
71 4/8	13 1/8 12 7/8	5 6/8 5 7/8	10 0/8	Fremont County	WY	Ron Niziolek	2009	2817
71 4/8	13 5/8 13 3/8	5 5/8 5 4/8	12 1/8	Natrona County	WY	Brandon Kegler	2009	2817
71 4/8	13 6/8 13 3/8	6 2/8 6 1/8	8 7/8	Powder River County	MT	Mike Barrett	2009	2817
*71 4/8	13 4/8 13 7/8	6 0/8 6 0/8	10 2/8	Natrona County	WY	Hugh H. Hogle	2009	2817
71 4/8	14 0/8 14 2/8	5 3/8 5 5/8	12 5/8	Converse County	WY	Dr. David McNeill	2009	2817
71 4/8	14 4/8 14 1/8	6 0/8 5 6/8	8 4/8	Natrona County	WY	Jeff Jacob	2010	2817
71 2/8	14 4/8 14 2/8	5 7/8 5 7/8	8 1/8	Musselshell County	MT	A. A. Anderson	1960	2961
71 2/8	14 3/8 14 5/8	5 4/8 5 4/8	13 1/8	Perkins County	SD	Elwood Patterson	1961	2961
71 2/8	15 0/8 15 3/8	5 3/8 5 2/8	9 7/8	Natrona County	WY	Doug Pope	1976	2961
71 2/8	14 5/8 14 7/8	5 2/8 5 2/8	12 0/8	McLean County	ND	Leo N. Patch	1977	2961
71 2/8	14 2/8 13 4/8	6 1/8 6 2/8	8 3/8	Sweetwater County	WY	Terry Walbridge	1980	2961
71 2/8	12 7/8 12 6/8	5 7/8 5 7/8	9 1/8	Converse County	WY	G. Merrill Jones	1980	2961
71 2/8	13 3/8 13 3/8	5 5/8 5 6/8	8 3/8	Natrona County	WY	Hayden Allen, Jr.	1981	2961
71 2/8	13 4/8 13 1/8	6 2/8 6 2/8	8 4/8	Sweetwater County	WY	Lyle R. Prell	1981	2961
71 2/8	12 3/8 12 3/8	6 4/8 6 5/8	9 6/8	Sargent County	ND	Terry Hopewell	1982	2961
71 2/8	13 4/8 13 5/8	6 0/8 5 5/8	12 0/8	Natrona County	WY	Rick Landeis	1983	2961
71 2/8	13 0/8 13 2/8	6 2/8 6 2/8	10 7/8	Converse County	WY	Jack M. Conner	1983	2961
71 2/8	15 0/8 15 1/8	5 7/8 5 6/8	8 4/8	Washoe County	NV	Robert L. Brooks, Jr.	1984	2961
71 2/8	12 2/8 12 1/8	6 0/8 6 0/8	9 5/8	Converse County	WY	Jack M. Conner	1984	2961
71 2/8	14 4/8 14 6/8	6 1/8 5 6/8	8 0/8	Powder River County	MT	Steve Kramer	1984	2961
71 2/8	13 1/8 12 6/8	5 6/8 6 2/8	11 6/8	Johnson County	WY	Glenn Tappen	1984	2961
71 2/8	14 3/8 13 2/8	6 0/8 5 7/8	11 6/8	Hot Springs County	WY	Mike Conner	1985	2961
71 2/8	13 4/8 13 4/8	6 1/8 6 0/8	11 6/8	Natrona County	WY	Kelley Swift	1985	2961
71 2/8	13 3/8 13 4/8	6 2/8 6 2/8	8 7/8	Sweetwater County	WY	David S. Petrie	1987	2961
71 2/8	14 3/8 14 4/8	5 7/8 5 7/8	11 2/8	Tide Lake	ALB	Archie Nesbitt	1987	2961
71 2/8	13 2/8 13 1/8	6 4/8 6 3/8	11 3/8	Moffat County	CO	Randy Lamdin	1988	2961
71 2/8	13 0/8 13 1/8	5 1/8 5 1/8	11 2/8	White Pine County	NV	Steven P. Newberger	1988	2961
71 2/8	13 4/8 13 5/8	6 1/8 6 0/8	8 6/8	Moffat County	CO	Daniel L. Tekavec	1988	2961
71 2/8	14 2/8 14 2/8	6 1/8 6 1/8	10 0/8	Converse County	WY	David L. Mosher	1988	2961
71 2/8	13 4/8 13 3/8	5 5/8 5 7/8	11 6/8	Modoc County	CA	Gary M. Gentile	1988	2961
71 2/8	13 2/8 12 6/8	6 2/8 6 2/8	9 6/8	Lassen County	CA	John Diedrich	1988	2961
71 2/8	12 7/8 12 7/8	6 2/8 6 1/8	11 2/8	Natrona County	WY	Michael Ryan	1988	2961
71 2/8	13 6/8 13 2/8	5 7/8 5 7/8	9 7/8	Carbon County	WY	Willis Duhon	1989	2961
71 2/8	13 3/8 12 6/8	6 1/8 6 0/8	8 1/8	Converse County	WY	Edward W. Vetter	1989	2961
71 2/8	12 7/8 13 0/8	6 0/8 6 0/8	9 6/8	Harding County	SD	Daniel Dietrich	1989	2961
71 2/8	13 1/8 13 2/8	5 4/8 5 3/8	9 6/8	Socorro County	NM	Jose Romero	1990	2961
71 2/8	13 6/8 13 2/8	6 2/8 6 2/8	6 2/8	Moffat County	CO	Michael P. McCarty	1990	2961
71 2/8	13 4/8 13 3/8	6 3/8 6 2/8	9 5/8	Uinta County	WY	Earl Sutherland	1990	2961
71 2/8	14 4/8 13 6/8	5 7/8 5 5/8	8 0/8	Greenlee County	AZ	Tracy G. Hardy	1990	2961
71 2/8	13 4/8 13 1/8	6 2/8 6 2/8	7 6/8	Johnson County	WY	Joe Coleman	1990	2961
71 2/8	13 0/8 13 0/8	6 3/8 6 3/8	12 2/8	Forty Mile County	ALB	Darrell Hougen	1990	2961
71 2/8	12 7/8 13 2/8	6 0/8 5 7/8	10 7/8	Converse County	WY	Dave Vander Vorst	1990	2961
71 2/8	13 5/8 13 1/8	6 0/8 6 1/8	9 2/8	Harding County	SD	Jamie Byrne	1990	2961
71 2/8	14 6/8 14 0/8	6 4/8 6 4/8	12 2/8	Washoe County	NV	David Niehaus	1991	2961
71 2/8	14 1/8 14 4/8	5 5/8 5 6/8	6 5/8	Sweetwater County	WY	Larry Dickerson	1991	2961
71 2/8	13 4/8 13 6/8	6 5/8 6 5/8	10 3/8	Converse County	WY	Steve Duranso	1991	2961
71 2/8	13 2/8 13 1/8	6 4/8 6 2/8	7 3/8	Rosebud County	MT	Everett M. Morris	1991	2961
71 2/8	13 6/8 13 5/8	5 7/8 6 0/8	8 3/8	Sweetwater County	WY	Brian Kerr	1992	2961
71 2/8	14 1/8 14 1/8	5 7/8 5 6/8	9 1/8	Moffat County	CO	Ken Assmus	1992	2961
71 2/8	14 1/8 13 7/8	5 4/8 5 4/8	9 6/8	Millard County	UT	Jim Fowler	1992	2961
71 2/8	14 1/8 14 4/8	6 0/8 5 7/8	5 1/8	Twin Falls County	ID	Vincent Trent	1992	2961
71 2/8	13 1/8 13 4/8	6 4/8 6 3/8	11 0/8	Sioux County	NE	Tommy M. Brown	1992	2961
71 2/8	12 1/8 12 3/8	6 2/8 6 1/8	9 2/8	Converse County	WY	Steve Williams	1992	2961
71 2/8	14 2/8 14 3/8	5 5/8 5 6/8	8 3/8	Billings County	ND	Jeff Dudgeon	1992	2961
71 2/8	13 3/8 13 2/8	6 0/8 6 0/8	8 6/8	Campbell County	WY	Bob Pozner	1992	2961
71 2/8	13 3/8 13 3/8	6 2/8 6 1/8	10 1/8	Converse County	WY	Richard Pippenger	1992	2961
71 2/8	13 6/8 13 5/8	6 0/8 6 0/8	11 6/8	Bowman County	ND	LeAnn Buchholz	1992	2961
71 2/8	14 3/8 14 1/8	6 1/8 5 7/8	6 4/8	Campbell County	WY	Chad S. Blank	1992	2961
71 2/8	13 7/8 14 0/8	5 7/8 5 7/8	13 2/8	Campbell County	WY	Doy K. Curtis	1992	2961
71 2/8	12 6/8 13 0/8	5 6/8 5 6/8	9 1/8	Moffat County	CO	Scott George	1993	2961
71 2/8	14 0/8 14 0/8	6 3/8 6 1/8	9 6/8	Moffat County	CO	Robert E. Kearney	1994	2961
71 2/8	12 5/8 12 6/8	6 1/8 6 1/8	10 0/8	Campbell County	WY	James D. Bradley	1994	2961
71 2/8	13 3/8 13 4/8	6 0/8 6 0/8	12 6/8	Campbell County	WY	Matt Manske	1994	2961
71 2/8	14 0/8 14 0/8	5 6/8 5 6/8	12 2/8	Yellowstone County	MT	Thomas J. Madden	1994	2961
71 2/8	13 4/8 13 5/8	6 2/8 6 2/8	12 1/8	Moffat County	CO	John Giordano	1995	2961
71 2/8	13 2/8 13 2/8	6 3/8 6 2/8	9 6/8	Sweetwater County	WY	Susan K. Barrett	1995	2961
71 2/8	12 5/8 12 1/8	6 1/8 6 1/8	11 2/8	Tooele County	UT	E. Kip Fowler	1995	2961
71 2/8	13 1/8 13 4/8	6 0/8 6 0/8	12 5/8	Converse County	WY	Terry R. Cassatt	1995	2961
71 2/8	14 7/8 14 5/8	5 5/8 5 5/8	9 6/8	Campbell County	WY	Randy Kerian	1995	2961
71 2/8	14 2/8 14 5/8	5 6/8 5 6/8	9 0/8	Campbell County	WY	Dean Revering	1995	2961
71 2/8	14 0/8 13 6/8	5 4/8 5 5/8	7 3/8	Sioux County	NE	Clarence L. Poteet	1995	2961
71 2/8	11 7/8 11 7/8	6 6/8 6 5/8	8 0/8	Moffat County	CO	Chuck Adams	1996	2961
71 2/8	13 2/8 14 0/8	6 2/8 6 1/8	11 3/8	Humboldt County	NV	Robert Gillespie	1996	2961
71 2/8	14 3/8 14 3/8	5 7/8 5 7/8	12 7/8	Juab County	UT	Kirk W. Reese	1996	2961
71 2/8	13 5/8 13 5/8	5 7/8 6 0/8	10 2/8	Colfax County	NM	Patrick Lovato	1996	2961
71 2/8	13 4/8 13 6/8	5 5/8 5 4/8	11 3/8	Moffat County	CO	Steve E. Sheehy	1996	2961
71 2/8	14 6/8 14 6/8	5 4/8 5 3/8	11 4/8	McKenzie County	ND	Brad Blanchard	1996	2961
*71 2/8	15 0/8 14 3/8	5 7/8 5 6/8	9 3/8	Rosebud County	MT	Thomas Bonnichsen	1996	2961
71 2/8	13 3/8 13 3/8	6 3/8 6 2/8	12 5/8	Weld County	CO	Robert J. Vescio	1997	2961
71 2/8	13 2/8 13 0/8	6 4/8 6 4/8	8 0/8	Weld County	CO	Paul R. Cox	1997	2961
71 2/8	14 1/8 14 2/8	6 0/8 6 0/8	14 1/8	Garfield County	MT	Sonny Templeton	1997	2961
71 2/8	14 5/8 14 5/8	6 0/8 5 6/8	13 2/8	Harding County	SD	Jerome O. Guyant	1997	2961
71 2/8	12 5/8 12 7/8	5 6/8 5 6/8	9 4/8	Saguache County	CO	Paul Keys	1998	2961
71 2/8	14 2/8 14 3/8	5 5/8 5 3/8	10 2/8	Larimer County	CO	Timothy N. Gardner	1998	2961
71 2/8	14 0/8 13 3/8	6 5/8 6 3/8	13 2/8	Campbell County	WY	John W. Borlang	1998	2961
71 2/8	14 5/8 14 5/8	5 5/8 5 6/8	14 0/8	Rosebud County	MT	Keith M. Ross	1998	2961
71 2/8	14 6/8 12 2/8	6 4/8 6 4/8	10 1/8	Converse County	WY	Nick Filardo	1998	2961
71 2/8	13 6/8 13 6/8	6 1/8 5 7/8	11 3/8	Fergus County	MT	Donny Roy	1998	2961

PRONGHORN

Minimum Score 67 — Continued

SCORE	LENGTH OF R HORN L	CIRCUMFERENCE R OF BASE L	INSIDE SPREAD	AREA	STATE/ PROVINCE	HUNTER'S NAME	DATE	RANK
71 2/8	13 4/8 13 5/8	6 0/8 6 0/8	10 1/8	Park County	CO	Spencer Esch	1999	2961
71 2/8	14 0/8 13 6/8	5 2/8 5 1/8	14 0/8	Sunnynook	ALB	Brandon Ray	1999	2961
71 2/8	13 7/8 13 0/8	5 7/8 5 7/8	9 4/8	Converse County	WY	Jason L. Crandall	1999	2961
71 2/8	13 4/8 13 5/8	5 6/8 5 6/8	10 2/8	Platte County	WY	Derek Long	2000	2961
71 2/8	13 5/8 13 6/8	5 6/8 5 6/8	9 4/8	Campbell County	WY	Kenneth Ruzbacki	2000	2961
71 2/8	14 3/8 14 3/8	5 5/8 5 4/8	10 0/8	Golden Valley County	ND	Greg Ganje	2000	2961
71 2/8	13 3/8 13 6/8	6 2/8 6 2/8	11 1/8	Converse County	WY	Rodney R. Breit	2000	2961
71 2/8	15 3/8 15 5/8	5 0/8 5 0/8	10 5/8	Yavapai County	AZ	Charles Fisher	2001	2961
71 2/8	14 2/8 14 2/8	5 4/8 5 4/8	9 4/8	Garfield County	MT	Roger Stewart	2001	2961
71 2/8	12 7/8 12 5/8	5 6/8 5 4/8	9 1/8	Converse County	WY	John G. Keck	2001	2961
71 2/8	14 0/8 13 6/8	5 5/8 5 5/8	11 4/8	Onefour	ALB	Lorne Rinkel	2001	2961
71 2/8	14 1/8 14 1/8	6 2/8 6 2/8	11 5/8	Garfield County	MT	DuWayne M. Larson	2001	2961
71 2/8	13 5/8 13 4/8	5 7/8 5 6/8	13 2/8	Duchesne County	UT	Steve R. Bridge	2002	2961
71 2/8	14 0/8 14 0/8	5 3/8 5 3/8	10 7/8	Lincoln County	NM	Bob Ameen	2002	2961
71 2/8	13 5/8 13 4/8	6 0/8 5 7/8	11 2/8	Rio Grande County	CO	Manuel A. Banderas	2003	2961
71 2/8	12 3/8 12 3/8	6 1/8 6 2/8	9 5/8	Grand County	CO	Paul M. Martin	2003	2961
*71 2/8	13 4/8 13 6/8	5 5/8 5 6/8	11 2/8	Sweetwater County	WY	Dave Holt	2003	2961
71 2/8	13 0/8 12 4/8	6 3/8 6 3/8	9 6/8	Campbell County	WY	Ramie Haines	2003	2961
71 2/8	14 3/8 14 2/8	5 5/8 5 5/8	10 5/8	Campbell County	WY	Darin Morgan	2003	2961
*71 2/8	13 4/8 13 4/8	6 0/8 5 7/8	8 6/8	Fergus County	MT	Don Moen	2003	2961
71 2/8	14 0/8 14 0/8	5 5/8 5 3/8	10 3/8	Sheridan County	WY	Luke Roush	2004	2961
71 2/8	13 5/8 13 6/8	5 7/8 5 7/8	9 7/8	Converse County	WY	Wayne M. Toth II	2004	2961
71 2/8	12 4/8 12 3/8	6 0/8 6 1/8	8 7/8	Carter County	MT	James Steven Burkhart	2004	2961
71 2/8	13 6/8 13 3/8	5 6/8 5 6/8	10 0/8	Campbell County	WY	Bob Wiebley	2004	2961
71 2/8	13 4/8 13 4/8	6 0/8 6 0/8	10 2/8	Johnson County	WY	M. Robert DeLaney	2004	2961
71 2/8	13 3/8 13 4/8	5 6/8 5 6/8	10 4/8	Fremont County	WY	Gary Laya	2005	2961
*71 2/8	12 7/8 12 7/8	6 5/8 6 2/8	12 1/8	Carter County	MT	Craig Unser	2005	2961
*71 2/8	14 0/8 14 1/8	5 7/8 5 7/8	11 7/8	Natrona County	WY	Baker Miles	2005	2961
71 2/8	13 7/8 14 0/8	6 0/8 6 1/8	7 6/8	Rosebud County	MT	Chester Sergo	2005	2961
71 2/8	13 5/8 13 6/8	5 7/8 5 6/8	13 6/8	Moffat County	CO	LeRoy "Ben" Shirley	2005	2961
*71 2/8	14 5/8 14 6/8	5 6/8 5 4/8	12 2/8	Yavapai County	AZ	Cade Densmore	2005	2961
71 2/8	13 5/8 13 4/8	6 0/8 6 1/8	9 5/8	Converse County	WY	Eldon Hagen	2005	2961
71 2/8	13 7/8 13 5/8	5 5/8 5 5/8	11 5/8	Campbell County	WY	Shannon Eyre	2005	2961
71 2/8	13 4/8 13 3/8	6 1/8 6 1/8	13 0/8	Fergus County	MT	John Fleharty	2005	2961
71 2/8	14 4/8 14 4/8	6 0/8 5 7/8	12 2/8	Gunnison County	CO	Matthew Reilly	2006	2961
71 2/8	12 1/8 12 1/8	6 1/8 6 0/8	6 4/8	Moffat County	CO	Sheila M. Hackett	2006	2961
71 2/8	13 3/8 13 0/8	5 7/8 5 5/8	10 1/8	Moffat County	CO	Jeff Phelps	2006	2961
71 2/8	13 4/8 12 6/8	6 0/8 6 0/8	10 2/8	Yavapai County	AZ	Gregory Walker	2006	2961
*71 2/8	14 3/8 14 5/8	5 7/8 5 7/8	7 6/8	Petroleum County	MT	Kent Spriggs	2006	2961
71 2/8	14 1/8 14 3/8	6 1/8 6 1/8	11 1/8	Johnson County	WY	Don Owen	2006	2961
*71 2/8	15 6/8 15 7/8	5 1/8 5 1/8	8 4/8	Pennington County	SD	Jeremy R. Boreman	2007	2961
71 2/8	14 2/8 14 6/8	5 6/8 5 6/8	10 4/8	Lincoln County	WY	Dayne Tattersall	2007	2961
71 2/8	14 5/8 14 4/8	5 4/8 5 2/8	11 3/8	Converse County	WY	Greg Dearth	2007	2961
71 2/8	13 5/8 14 0/8	5 5/8 5 6/8	9 1/8	Rosebud County	MT	James F. Hirrlinger	2007	2961
71 2/8	14 0/8 14 1/8	5 7/8 6 0/8	9 4/8	Broadwater County	MT	Travis Horton	2007	2961
71 2/8	13 3/8 14 6/8	5 5/8 5 4/8	10 1/8	Meade County	SD	Brian D. Dziuba	2007	2961
*71 2/8	13 4/8 13 4/8	5 5/8 5 5/8	10 0/8	Johnson County	WY	Paul Chaffee	2007	2961
*71 2/8	14 4/8 14 3/8	5 6/8 5 6/8	11 3/8	Liberty County	MT	Norman B. Larsen	2008	2961
71 2/8	14 4/8 14 6/8	5 5/8 5 6/8	8 6/8	Powder River County	MT	David V. Burdge, Jr.	2008	2961
71 2/8	14 3/8 14 4/8	5 5/8 5 6/8	8 3/8	Owyhee County	ID	Ron D. Jacobs	2008	2961
71 2/8	13 5/8 13 6/8	5 7/8 5 6/8	7 2/8	Sweetwater County	WY	Ron Nelson	2008	2961
71 2/8	15 1/8 15 1/8	5 7/8 5 7/8	12 4/8	Santa Cruz County	AZ	Barry R. Sopher	2008	2961
*71 2/8	13 4/8 13 2/8	6 0/8 6 0/8	13 4/8	Johnson County	WY	Michael Swank	2008	2961
71 2/8	13 6/8 13 4/8	5 7/8 5 7/8	9 7/8	Albany County	WY	Chad Rohel	2009	2961
*71 2/8	13 1/8 13 1/8	6 2/8 6 3/8	8 1/8	Butte County	ID	Joe Kaul	2009	2961
71 2/8	13 0/8 12 6/8	5 5/8 5 6/8	9 4/8	Colfax County	NM	William S. Duncan	2010	2961
*71 2/8	13 3/8 13 3/8	6 0/8 6 0/8	9 7/8	Pueblo County	CO	Benjamin Allen	2010	2961
*71 2/8	14 3/8 14 2/8	5 3/8 5 5/8	6 7/8	Converse County	WY	Larry A. Welchlen	2010	2961
71 2/8	14 2/8 14 3/8	5 3/8 5 4/8	12 6/8	Sublette County	WY	Bernie Weisgerber	2010	2961
71 0/8	14 0/8 13 6/8	6 2/8 5 7/8	10 4/8	Sioux County	NE	Roger F. Rehborg	1975	3102
71 0/8	12 7/8 12 7/8	6 1/8 6 1/8	12 6/8	Washoe County	NV	Roger Iveson	1980	3102
71 0/8	14 0/8 14 1/8	5 6/8 5 7/8	8 3/8	Converse County	WY	Eugene Smith, Jr.	1980	3102
71 0/8	13 7/8 13 5/8	6 0/8 6 0/8	7 3/8	Sweetwater County	WY	Vaughn Cross	1981	3102
71 0/8	14 1/8 14 1/8	5 7/8 5 7/8	13 2/8	Moffat County	CO	Scott Kelley	1981	3102
71 0/8	13 2/8 13 0/8	6 0/8 6 0/8	11 5/8	Converse County	WY	Mike Butler	1981	3102
71 0/8	14 7/8 14 7/8	5 6/8 5 6/8	8 1/8	Modoc County	CA	Jeff Scheetz	1982	3102
71 0/8	13 5/8 13 4/8	5 6/8 5 6/8	8 4/8	Converse County	WY	Ted J. Jaycox	1982	3102
71 0/8	14 4/8 14 5/8	5 5/8 5 4/8	9 3/8	McKenzie County	ND	Mark D. Hughes	1982	3102
71 0/8	13 0/8 13 0/8	6 0/8 5 7/8	14 0/8	Carbon County	WY	Ron Stacey	1983	3102
71 0/8	13 1/8 13 4/8	6 4/8 6 4/8	9 6/8	Moffat County	CO	Lance Cussons	1983	3102
71 0/8	13 3/8 13 3/8	5 7/8 5 7/8	8 1/8	Natrona County	WY	Wade L. Carstens	1983	3102
71 0/8	14 0/8 14 1/8	6 0/8 6 0/8	9 1/8	Garfield County	MT	Bruce W. Blauvelt	1983	3102
71 0/8	13 6/8 13 4/8	5 6/8 5 6/8	10 4/8	White Pine County	NV	Simo O. Ahlgren	1984	3102
71 0/8	14 4/8 14 2/8	5 6/8 5 6/8	9 2/8	Sweetwater County	WY	Earl Kennedy	1986	3102
71 0/8	13 4/8 13 3/8	6 1/8 6 0/8	8 0/8	Stark County	ND	Daniel W. Johnson	1987	3102
71 0/8	14 5/8 14 7/8	5 2/8 5 2/8	9 6/8	Moffat County	CO	Bruce Hallowell	1988	3102
71 0/8	14 5/8 14 6/8	5 7/8 5 7/8	10 2/8	Millard County	UT	Len Cardinale	1988	3102
71 0/8	13 2/8 13 3/8	5 6/8 5 6/8	9 3/8	Converse County	WY	Ron Foote	1988	3102
71 0/8	14 0/8 13 5/8	5 6/8 5 6/8	13 1/8	Converse County	WY	Roy G. Burton	1988	3102
71 0/8	14 2/8 14 2/8	5 1/8 5 1/8	17 5/8	Taos County	NM	Daniel Allred	1989	3102
71 0/8	13 5/8 13 4/8	6 4/8 6 2/8	10 2/8	Natrona County	WY	Rickey E. Morse	1989	3102
71 0/8	15 0/8 14 5/8	5 5/8 5 6/8	8 6/8	Musselshell County	MT	Darren Parker	1989	3102
71 0/8	14 3/8 14 3/8	5 7/8 5 6/8	11 2/8	Valley County	MT	Ty Milne	1989	3102
71 0/8	13 1/8 13 1/8	6 4/8 6 4/8	12 1/8	Modoc County	CA	Darrel Sudduth	1990	3102
71 0/8	13 2/8 13 2/8	5 4/8 5 5/8	9 5/8	Moffat County	CO	Dennis Newton	1990	3102
71 0/8	15 3/8 15 0/8	5 5/8 5 5/8	9 2/8	Converse County	WY	Paul Sieg	1990	3102
71 0/8	13 7/8 13 5/8	6 0/8 6 0/8	7 0/8	Converse County	WY	Jeff Fitts	1991	3102
71 0/8	13 7/8 14 0/8	5 6/8 5 5/8	11 5/8	Rosebud County	MT	Anthony Hess	1991	3102
71 0/8	12 7/8 12 7/8	6 2/8 6 1/8	11 3/8	Converse County	WY	J. Todd Payne	1991	3102
71 0/8	13 7/8 13 5/8	5 7/8 6 0/8	10 2/8	Buffalo	ALB	Andy P. Charchun	1991	3102
71 0/8	13 6/8 13 5/8	5 6/8 5 6/8	9 7/8	Garfield County	MT	Randal R. Mayes	1991	3102
71 0/8	14 2/8 14 0/8	5 7/8 5 5/8	12 6/8	Converse County	WY	Barry J. Smith	1991	3102
71 0/8	13 0/8 13 2/8	6 2/8 6 2/8	11 6/8	Sweetwater County	WY	John Cheese	1992	3102
71 0/8	12 6/8 13 2/8	6 1/8 6 1/8	8 3/8	Moffat County	CO	Marvin Weible	1992	3102
71 0/8	13 0/8 13 2/8	6 4/8 6 2/8	11 1/8	Fremont County	WY	Tim Downs	1992	3102

842

PRONGHORN

Minimum Score 67 — Continued

SCORE	R HORN L	R OF BASE L	INSIDE SPREAD	AREA	STATE/PROVINCE	HUNTER'S NAME	DATE	RANK
71 0/8	13 7/8 14 2/8	5 5/8 5 4/8	9 1/8	Converse County	WY	Jerry Rush	1992	3102
71 0/8	14 4/8 14 4/8	6 0/8 6 1/8	9 3/8	Malheur County	OR	Rick Martin	1992	3102
71 0/8	13 1/8 13 0/8	6 0/8 6 0/8	6 6/8	Converse County	WY	Mark Graham	1992	3102
71 0/8	12 7/8 14 0/8	6 1/8 6 1/8	8 4/8	Rosebud County	MT	Donald Kemkes	1992	3102
71 0/8	12 4/8 12 2/8	6 6/8 6 4/8	12 3/8	Meade County	SD	LeRoy Capp	1992	3102
71 0/8	14 0/8 13 7/8	6 3/8 6 1/8	10 3/8	Goshen County	WY	Jerry Harding	1992	3102
71 0/8	14 0/8 14 0/8	5 5/8 5 5/8	9 1/8	Campbell County	WY	Tim Stahman	1992	3102
71 0/8	14 2/8 14 2/8	5 5/8 5 6/8	7 4/8	Sheridan County	WY	Billy S. Huff	1992	3102
71 0/8	13 4/8 13 0/8	6 1/8 6 2/8	15 0/8	Grand County	UT	Shad D. Schmidt	1993	3102
71 0/8	13 7/8 13 7/8	5 5/8 5 5/8	9 2/8	Socorro County	NM	Abe Dimas, Jr.	1993	3102
71 0/8	12 7/8 12 2/8	5 7/8 6 0/8	8 2/8	Moffat County	CO	Blazer McClure	1993	3102
71 0/8	14 1/8 14 3/8	5 6/8 5 6/8	11 5/8	Platte County	WY	Jeffery Allen Roback	1993	3102
71 0/8	14 5/8 14 3/8	5 6/8 5 6/8	9 5/8	Dawes County	NE	Duane Loecker	1993	3102
71 0/8	14 0/8 14 1/8	6 0/8 5 7/8	4 6/8	Harding County	SD	Nick Larsen	1993	3102
71 0/8	12 6/8 13 2/8	6 2/8 6 1/8	12 7/8	Sweetwater County	WY	Tim Isaacson	1994	3102
71 0/8	14 6/8 14 3/8	6 2/8 5 5/8	12 2/8	Natrona County	WY	Ann Weber Hoyt	1994	3102
71 0/8	13 5/8 13 0/8	6 3/8 6 2/8	11 4/8	Moffat County	CO	Troy Cunningham	1994	3102
71 0/8	14 2/8 14 2/8	5 4/8 5 5/8	9 0/8	Moffat County	CO	Matt Burrows	1994	3102
71 0/8	12 7/8 12 7/8	6 2/8 6 2/8	8 6/8	Campbell County	WY	Gary English	1994	3102
71 0/8	13 6/8 14 0/8	5 6/8 5 6/8	8 0/8	Hays	ALB	Larry Knibbs/Doug Messenger	1994	3102
71 0/8	12 5/8 12 5/8	6 4/8 6 3/8	11 1/8	Moffat County	CO	Rocky Drake	1995	3102
71 0/8	13 1/8 13 2/8	6 3/8 6 2/8	7 1/8	Humboldt County	NV	Archie Nesbitt	1995	3102
71 0/8	14 6/8 14 5/8	6 0/8 6 0/8	7 2/8	Albany County	WY	Jon Deeter	1995	3102
71 0/8	13 3/8 13 4/8	5 3/8 5 3/8	9 1/8	Moffat County	CO	Michael P. McCarty	1995	3102
71 0/8	15 1/8 14 6/8	5 6/8 5 6/8	9 6/8	Weld County	CO	Dave Mahler	1995	3102
71 0/8	14 2/8 14 2/8	6 1/8 6 0/8	6 2/8	Fergus County	MT	D. Mitch Kottas	1995	3102
71 0/8	14 1/8 14 4/8	5 6/8 5 4/8	7 6/8	Nye County	NV	Gary Zupanic	1996	3102
71 0/8	13 6/8 13 0/8	6 0/8 6 0/8	13 6/8	Moffat County	CO	Ron Miller	1996	3102
71 0/8	14 3/8 14 3/8	6 1/8 5 7/8	14 3/8	Lincoln County	NM	Gregory L. Gray	1996	3102
71 0/8	14 6/8 14 5/8	5 6/8 5 5/8	12 5/8	Sweetwater County	WY	Robert S. Jones	1996	3102
71 0/8	14 0/8 13 6/8	5 4/8 5 4/8	10 0/8	Campbell County	WY	Todd Galbreath	1997	3102
71 0/8	13 1/8 13 0/8	6 0/8 5 7/8	8 6/8	Moffat County	CO	Dale R. Petefish	1998	3102
71 0/8	13 6/8 13 6/8	6 2/8 6 2/8	7 5/8	Moffat County	CO	Tim Cuthriell	1998	3102
71 0/8	14 6/8 15 1/8	5 6/8 5 7/8	12 2/8	Sweetwater County	WY	Mike Barrett	1998	3102
71 0/8	14 0/8 13 2/8	6 0/8 6 1/8	7 4/8	Powder River County	MT	Don G. Scofield	1998	3102
71 0/8	13 5/8 13 5/8	5 7/8 5 5/8	8 3/8	Butte County	SD	Tom Nauman	1999	3102
71 0/8	14 3/8 14 4/8	5 3/8 5 2/8	8 3/8	Toole County	MT	Jay Hould	1999	3102
71 0/8	13 6/8 13 6/8	5 6/8 5 5/8	8 6/8	Moffat County	CO	Chuck Adams	2000	3102
71 0/8	14 2/8 14 2/8	5 4/8 5 3/8	10 5/8	Millard County	UT	Shane Hall	2000	3102
71 0/8	13 1/8 13 1/8	6 0/8 5 7/8	11 1/8	Moffat County	CO	Dale E. Harkins	2000	3102
71 0/8	15 2/8 15 2/8	5 6/8 5 6/8	6 6/8	Blindloss	ALB	Sly Baier	2000	3102
71 0/8	12 4/8 12 2/8	6 0/8 6 0/8	8 7/8	Albany County	WY	Rich Kimball	2001	3102
71 0/8	14 3/8 14 4/8	6 1/8 6 0/8	9 5/8	Blaine County	MT	Tom M. Benson	2001	3102
71 0/8	14 6/8 16 0/8	5 7/8 5 5/8	10 3/8	Lake County	OR	Darren Paschke	2001	3102
71 0/8	12 4/8 12 5/8	5 6/8 6 0/8	8 3/8	Saguache County	CO	Jason Carruth	2001	3102
71 0/8	13 6/8 13 7/8	5 7/8 6 0/8	14 1/8	Hanna	ALB	Dean Kirkeby	2001	3102
71 0/8	14 0/8 14 2/8	6 0/8 6 0/8	9 1/8	Garfield County	MT	Sonny Templeton	2001	3102
71 0/8	14 5/8 14 6/8	5 4/8 5 4/8	9 6/8	Las Animas County	CO	Michael Yeary	2002	3102
71 0/8	14 2/8 14 2/8	5 3/8 5 3/8	11 3/8	Sublette County	WY	Clint Condos	2002	3102
71 0/8	13 6/8 13 4/8	6 2/8 6 1/8	7 1/8	Gooding County	ID	Eddie Long	2002	3102
71 0/8	15 2/8 13 6/8	5 6/8 5 5/8	10 4/8	Sierra County	NM	Stuart A. Hagen	2002	3102
71 0/8	13 6/8 14 4/8	5 7/8 5 7/8	10 7/8	Powder River County	MT	Keith Dvoroznak	2002	3102
71 0/8	14 4/8 14 3/8	5 4/8 5 2/8	11 5/8	Carter County	MT	Marty Adams	2002	3102
71 0/8	13 4/8 13 2/8	6 0/8 6 0/8	7 1/8	Phillips County	MT	Russell Swindall	2002	3102
71 0/8	14 0/8 13 7/8	5 7/8 5 6/8	8 4/8	Fergus County	MT	Pete Gierke	2003	3102
71 0/8	13 6/8 14 0/8	5 3/8 5 3/8	11 4/8	Toole County	MT	Jay Hould	2003	3102
71 0/8	13 1/8 13 3/8	6 2/8 6 1/8	8 4/8	Campbell County	WY	Randy Springborn	2003	3102
71 0/8	12 7/8 14 6/8	6 1/8 6 1/8	7 2/8	Petroleum County	MT	Levi Johnson	2003	3102
71 0/8	13 4/8 13 4/8	6 0/8 5 7/8	11 0/8	Grand County	CO	Bryan Holley	2004	3102
*71 0/8	14 1/8 14 2/8	6 3/8 6 2/8	9 1/8	Crook County	WY	Mark Kayser	2004	3102
71 0/8	13 3/8 13 4/8	6 0/8 5 7/8	10 0/8	Weld County	CO	Martin Schlomer	2005	3102
71 0/8	13 0/8 12 7/8	5 6/8 5 7/8	10 1/8	Jackson County	CO	Cedar Beauregard	2005	3102
*71 0/8	13 3/8 13 3/8	5 6/8 5 6/8	12 5/8	Kitscoty	ALB	Dave MacKenzie	2005	3102
71 0/8	14 2/8 14 2/8	5 6/8 5 5/8	12 4/8	Sweetwater County	WY	Jason Ekker	2006	3102
71 0/8	14 1/8 13 7/8	6 1/8 5 7/8	11 5/8	Weld County	CO	Dustin Christensen	2006	3102
71 0/8	13 3/8 13 2/8	5 7/8 5 6/8	11 6/8	Platte County	WY	Jerry Bowen	2006	3102
71 0/8	12 4/8 13 2/8	6 1/8 6 0/8	10 5/8	Sweetwater County	WY	Andrew Beck	2006	3102
71 0/8	12 6/8 12 5/8	6 5/8 6 4/8	9 6/8	Albany County	WY	Jeremy Hoefs	2006	3102
71 0/8	12 0/8 12 0/8	6 2/8 6 2/8	7 4/8	Converse County	WY	Kenneth E. Briggs	2006	3102
71 0/8	14 4/8 14 4/8	5 6/8 5 5/8	15 6/8	Converse County	WY	Wayne Yocum, Jr.	2006	3102
71 0/8	14 1/8 14 2/8	6 0/8 6 1/8	10 3/8	Cypress	ALB	Dwayne Huggins	2006	3102
71 0/8	14 4/8 14 4/8	5 6/8 5 4/8	8 3/8	Campbell County	WY	Daniel Peak	2006	3102
*71 0/8	11 6/8 12 0/8	6 1/8 6 1/8	8 4/8	Powder River County	MT	Jim Foshee	2006	3102
71 0/8	13 2/8 12 7/8	6 0/8 6 0/8	8 4/8	Lemhi County	ID	Rob Silva	2007	3102
*71 0/8	13 5/8 12 7/8	5 6/8 5 7/8	11 6/8	Converse County	WY	Lowell Thomas	2007	3102
71 0/8	13 3/8 13 4/8	5 6/8 5 6/8	8 7/8	Rosebud County	MT	Steve Rehak	2007	3102
71 0/8	13 2/8 13 2/8	6 3/8 6 3/8	8 7/8	Converse County	WY	Ryan Davenport	2007	3102
71 0/8	14 7/8 14 5/8	5 7/8 5 6/8	10 1/8	Carter County	MT	Donald S. Dvoroznak	2007	3102
71 0/8	13 4/8 13 6/8	6 0/8 6 0/8	14 5/8	Sublette County	WY	Dallin N. Skinner	2007	3102
*71 0/8	14 1/8 14 2/8	5 5/8 5 4/8	11 0/8	Johnson County	WY	Dave A. DeLapp	2007	3102
71 0/8	13 4/8 13 3/8	6 1/8 6 0/8	7 6/8	Converse County	WY	Tim Malay	2007	3102
*71 0/8	13 2/8 13 3/8	6 4/8 6 1/8	7 0/8	Weston County	WY	Ronald F. Lax	2007	3102
*71 0/8	13 1/8 13 2/8	5 6/8 5 6/8	10 4/8	Milk River	ALB	M. Blake Patton	2008	3102
71 0/8	14 3/8 13 6/8	5 6/8 5 5/8	8 1/8	Butte County	SD	Sean C. Fulton	2008	3102
71 0/8	14 2/8 13 3/8	6 3/8 6 1/8	10 2/8	Natrona County	WY	Steve Turay	2009	3102
71 0/8	13 0/8 12 4/8	6 6/8 6 5/8	10 0/8	Converse County	WY	Thomas Hansen II	2009	3102
*71 0/8	13 7/8 13 7/8	5 7/8 5 7/8	12 2/8	Rosebud County	MT	Rick Hogfoss	2009	3102
71 0/8	13 3/8 13 2/8	5 5/8 5 4/8	9 2/8	Converse County	WY	Eugene R. Wood	2009	3102
71 0/8	13 5/8 13 6/8	5 4/8 5 4/8	7 1/8	Goshen County	WY	Scott Franks	2009	3102
71 0/8	13 1/8 13 3/8	6 3/8 6 3/8	9 2/8	Sheridan County	WY	Bruce Burr	2009	3102
71 0/8	12 7/8 13 0/8	5 6/8 5 5/8	9 4/8	Campbell County	WY	Tom Gleason	2009	3102
*71 0/8	14 0/8 14 7/8	5 3/8 5 4/8	8 7/8	Converse County	WY	Jesse Fischer	2010	3102
*71 0/8	13 4/8 13 3/8	6 0/8 5 7/8	9 1/8	Rosebud County	MT	Brythe Thede	2010	3102
*71 0/8	14 1/8 14 1/8	5 2/8 5 3/8	8 3/8	Phillips County	MT	Brady Miller	2010	3102
70 6/8	14 7/8 15 2/8	5 5/8 5 4/8	10 3/8	Washoe County	NV	Frank M. Davis	1967	3232

843

PRONGHORN

Minimum Score 67

SCORE	LENGTH OF R HORN L	CIRCUMFERENCE R OF BASE L	INSIDE SPREAD	AREA	STATE/ PROVINCE	HUNTER'S NAME	DATE	RANK
70 6/8	13 2/8 13 2/8	6 3/8 6 2/8	9 6/8	Washoe County	NV	Gordon A. Nicholson	1972	3232
70 6/8	14 1/8 14 3/8	5 6/8 5 7/8	15 6/8	Deschutes County	OR	William E. Lancaster	1973	3232
70 6/8	12 5/8 12 4/8	5 5/8 5 4/8	9 0/8	Natrona County	WY	Bernard R. Giacoletto	1973	3232
70 6/8	11 2/8 11 2/8	6 0/8 6 0/8	10 1/8	Natrona County	WY	Jerry Zanandrea	1976	3232
70 6/8	13 4/8 13 6/8	5 7/8 5 6/8	9 7/8	Lemhi County	ID	Alan Monroe	1979	3232
70 6/8	13 0/8 13 3/8	5 6/8 5 5/8	7 4/8	Stanley County	SD	Rick Ray	1979	3232
70 6/8	14 0/8 14 0/8	5 4/8 5 4/8	12 6/8	Converse County	WY	Frank Moore	1980	3232
70 6/8	13 3/8 13 5/8	6 0/8 6 0/8	13 7/8	Sweetwater County	WY	Victor Organ	1980	3232
70 6/8	13 6/8 14 0/8	5 4/8 5 3/8	12 1/8	Converse County	WY	Russell Hull	1980	3232
70 6/8	14 3/8 14 1/8	5 4/8 5 3/8	12 5/8	Tillard Ranch	WY	Charles A. Myers	1981	3232
70 6/8	13 4/8 13 4/8	6 2/8 6 2/8	10 1/8	Moffat County	CO	Mike Miller	1981	3232
70 6/8	15 0/8 15 1/8	5 5/8 5 4/8	10 4/8	Klamath County	OR	Paul D. Lewis	1982	3232
70 6/8	12 5/8 12 5/8	5 7/8 5 7/8	9 4/8	Converse County	WY	Steve Woodman	1982	3232
70 6/8	13 7/8 13 7/8	6 0/8 6 1/8	10 4/8	Butte County	ID	Larry A. Wilde	1983	3232
70 6/8	13 5/8 13 3/8	5 6/8 5 6/8	9 4/8	Converse County	WY	Dan Naccarto	1983	3232
70 6/8	13 1/8 13 1/8	6 0/8 5 6/8	11 1/8	Natrona County	WY	Don Wilson	1983	3232
70 6/8	16 2/8 15 4/8	5 1/8 5 1/8	9 6/8	Golden Valley County	ND	Thomas S. Lunski	1983	3232
70 6/8	12 4/8 13 0/8	6 4/8 6 3/8	14 1/8	Powder River County	MT	Daryl E. Jennings	1983	3232
70 6/8	13 7/8 13 7/8	5 3/8 5 2/8	9 3/8	Moffat County	CO	Darryl Quidort	1984	3232
70 6/8	15 1/8 14 6/8	6 1/8 6 0/8	12 7/8	Lassen County	CA	Wayne Goodrich	1985	3232
70 6/8	12 6/8 14 3/8	5 7/8 5 6/8	11 3/8	Slope County	ND	Todd Seymanski	1985	3232
70 6/8	14 3/8 14 2/8	5 7/8 5 6/8	11 1/8	Sweetwater County	WY	Craig Boheler	1986	3232
70 6/8	13 0/8 13 3/8	6 3/8 6 1/8	10 2/8	Jefferson County	ID	Tony Hyde	1986	3232
70 6/8	14 0/8 13 6/8	5 7/8 5 7/8	7 0/8	Moffat County	CO	Mike Ottenbacher	1986	3232
70 6/8	13 1/8 13 4/8	6 2/8 6 0/8	11 0/8	Rosebud County	MT	Gary Olsen	1986	3232
70 6/8	13 0/8 12 6/8	6 4/8 6 4/8	10 0/8	Billings County	ND	Ron Tudahl	1987	3232
70 6/8	13 0/8 12 6/8	6 4/8 6 3/8	12 2/8	Moffat County	CO	Steven Wilson	1988	3232
70 6/8	14 2/8 14 2/8	5 4/8 5 3/8	7 4/8	Slope County	ND	Scott Bradac	1988	3232
70 6/8	14 0/8 14 0/8	5 5/8 5 5/8	11 0/8	Converse County	WY	David M. Ackland, Jr.	1988	3232
70 6/8	13 7/8 13 7/8	5 5/8 5 4/8	7 1/8	Converse County	WY	Kevin "Krauty" Krautkramer	1988	3232
70 6/8	12 6/8 12 6/8	6 3/8 6 1/8	8 4/8	Campbell County	WY	Bob Austin	1988	3232
70 6/8	14 0/8 13 6/8	5 7/8 5 6/8	10 5/8	Moffat County	CO	Wayne Depperschmidt	1989	3232
70 6/8	12 3/8 13 3/8	5 6/8 5 5/8	9 6/8	Lassen County	CA	Will Willis	1989	3232
70 6/8	13 2/8 13 1/8	5 5/8 5 4/8	9 7/8	Millard County	UT	David B. Nielsen	1989	3232
70 6/8	13 1/8 13 1/8	6 2/8 6 1/8	7 3/8	Billings County	ND	Al Zeller	1989	3232
70 6/8	14 0/8 13 4/8	5 6/8 5 6/8	10 4/8	Moffat County	CO	Dan Gillenwater	1989	3232
70 6/8	13 3/8 13 4/8	6 3/8 6 3/8	8 6/8	Moffat County	CO	Mike Boland	1989	3232
70 6/8	12 7/8 13 6/8	5 7/8 5 6/8	11 1/8	Hughes County	SD	Lyle Goodall	1989	3232
70 6/8	12 2/8 12 4/8	6 2/8 6 4/8	10 2/8	Garfield County	MT	Bob Morton	1989	3232
70 6/8	14 0/8 14 0/8	6 0/8 6 0/8	7 7/8	Uinta County	WY	Douglas Shelby	1990	3232
70 6/8	14 2/8 14 2/8	5 7/8 5 7/8	8 4/8	Moffat County	CO	Marvin Cochran	1990	3232
70 6/8	13 4/8 13 4/8	5 7/8 6 0/8	7 6/8	Moffat County	CO	Dennis Modlin	1990	3232
70 6/8	12 5/8 13 2/8	6 3/8 6 3/8	9 7/8	Natrona County	WY	Edward J. Brennan	1990	3232
70 6/8	14 1/8 14 1/8	5 6/8 5 6/8	10 0/8	Modoc County	CA	John Garr	1991	3232
70 6/8	14 2/8 14 4/8	6 1/8 6 1/8	12 7/8	Meade County	SD	Dan Limmer	1991	3232
70 6/8	13 2/8 13 3/8	6 1/8 6 1/8	11 2/8	White Pine County	NV	Brett North	1992	3232
70 6/8	13 6/8 13 4/8	5 7/8 5 7/8	6 6/8	Owyhee County	ID	Brian Hunter Heck	1992	3232
70 6/8	13 6/8 14 0/8	6 2/8 6 1/8	12 4/8	Carbon County	WY	Boyd Burbank	1992	3232
70 6/8	12 3/8 12 3/8	6 0/8 6 0/8	9 2/8	Converse County	WY	Justin Wells	1992	3232
70 6/8	14 3/8 14 1/8	5 6/8 5 6/8	11 0/8	Converse County	WY	John North	1992	3232
70 6/8	12 4/8 12 3/8	5 6/8 5 6/8	7 6/8	Billings County	ND	Jeff Hapala	1992	3232
70 6/8	13 2/8 13 4/8	5 6/8 5 6/8	11 1/8	Converse County	WY	Gary Boldt	1992	3232
70 6/8	13 7/8 13 7/8	5 7/8 6 0/8	8 5/8	Fergus County	MT	Kelly Norskog	1992	3232
70 6/8	15 0/8 14 6/8	5 3/8 5 5/8	18 3/8	McHenry County	ND	Paul Klimpel	1992	3232
70 6/8	13 2/8 13 1/8	5 6/8 5 5/8	9 5/8	Harding County	SD	John Simpson	1992	3232
70 6/8	14 1/8 14 0/8	6 0/8 6 0/8	10 7/8	Sioux County	NE	Walter Wright	1992	3232
70 6/8	13 6/8 13 4/8	6 4/8 6 2/8	11 3/8	Chaves County	NM	Joseph Strasser, Jr.	1993	3232
70 6/8	14 5/8 14 2/8	5 7/8 5 5/8	12 1/8	Fremont County	WY	Bradley T. Miller	1994	3232
70 6/8	13 6/8 13 5/8	5 5/8 5 4/8	11 2/8	Millard County	UT	Troy Ross	1994	3232
70 6/8	13 4/8 13 6/8	5 6/8 5 6/8	8 4/8	Owyhee County	ID	Jeff L. Varner	1994	3232
70 6/8	13 6/8 13 4/8	5 5/8 5 5/8	13 2/8	Washington County	CO	Guy Pierce	1994	3232
70 6/8	13 3/8 13 5/8	6 3/8 6 2/8	10 3/8	Sweetwater County	WY	Mark L. Preston	1994	3232
70 6/8	12 6/8 12 6/8	6 1/8 6 1/8	10 6/8	Weld County	CO	James L. Tatro	1994	3232
70 6/8	14 6/8 14 6/8	5 3/8 5 2/8	9 6/8	Manyberries	ALB	Eric Rauhanen	1994	3232
70 6/8	13 0/8 13 1/8	6 3/8 6 4/8	9 2/8	Kimball County	NE	Brian Ray Pierce	1994	3232
70 6/8	13 7/8 13 5/8	6 3/8 6 2/8	6 1/8	Campbell County	WY	Mike Reardon	1994	3232
70 6/8	13 4/8 13 7/8	5 3/8 5 4/8	9 7/8	Lincoln County	NM	Curtis D. O'Brien	1994	3232
70 6/8	12 4/8 12 5/8	5 6/8 5 6/8	9 2/8	Wallace County	KS	Daniel P. Carmen	1994	3232
70 6/8	15 1/8 15 0/8	5 2/8 5 2/8	10 7/8	Union County	NM	Paul Rigsby	1995	3232
70 6/8	12 7/8 12 6/8	6 1/8 6 2/8	10 7/8	Converse County	WY	Mike Castleberry	1995	3232
70 6/8	13 5/8 13 5/8	5 6/8 5 7/8	8 7/8	Campbell County	WY	Anna Nyreen	1995	3232
70 6/8	13 2/8 13 2/8	6 1/8 5 7/8	6 7/8	Campbell County	WY	Joe A. Renfrow, Jr.	1995	3232
70 6/8	14 3/8 14 1/8	5 7/8 5 5/8	10 6/8	Garfield County	MT	Sonny Templeton	1995	3232
70 6/8	12 3/8 12 1/8	6 2/8 6 4/8	10 4/8	Converse County	WY	Greg Peters	1995	3232
70 6/8	14 0/8 13 7/8	5 4/8 5 6/8	7 1/8	Carbon County	UT	Frank Anderson	1996	3232
70 6/8	14 6/8 14 0/8	6 2/8 6 4/8	10 5/8	Lincoln County	NM	Mariano Taglialegami	1996	3232
70 6/8	13 2/8 13 2/8	6 0/8 5 6/8	9 6/8	Natrona County	WY	Jerry D. Porter	1996	3232
70 6/8	13 4/8 13 6/8	5 7/8 5 6/8	7 0/8	Converse County	WY	Frank S. Noska IV	1996	3232
70 6/8	13 0/8 13 0/8	6 0/8 5 6/8	9 2/8	Converse County	WY	Paul Maples	1996	3232
70 6/8	14 1/8 14 5/8	6 1/8 6 0/8	9 2/8	Converse County	WY	George Postma	1996	3232
70 6/8	12 5/8 12 7/8	5 3/8 5 3/8	9 3/8	Rosebud County	MT	Mark R. Sherman	1996	3232
70 6/8	13 6/8 13 2/8	6 0/8 6 1/8	10 1/8	Fergus County	MT	Gary Wiley	1996	3232
70 6/8	14 2/8 14 4/8	6 1/8 6 2/8	10 1/8	Campbell County	WY	Kevin A. LaRoche	1997	3232
70 6/8	13 3/8 13 3/8	5 7/8 5 7/8	9 7/8	Converse County	WY	Gary Kautz	1997	3232
70 6/8	12 7/8 12 2/8	6 3/8 6 3/8	10 6/8	Johnson County	WY	Ronald E. Witwer	1997	3232
70 6/8	14 6/8 14 6/8	5 7/8 5 6/8	13 5/8	Converse County	WY	Frank Rus	1997	3232
70 6/8	14 6/8 14 5/8	5 6/8 5 5/8	7 2/8	Lander County	NV	Jason R. New	1998	3232
70 6/8	13 0/8 13 1/8	6 1/8 6 1/8	10 2/8	Owyhee County	ID	Steve Wiedmeier	1998	3232
70 6/8	13 7/8 14 0/8	5 5/8 5 6/8	11 0/8	Tooele County	UT	Chad J. Hall	1998	3232
70 6/8	14 1/8 14 3/8	5 3/8 5 2/8	8 7/8	Larimer County	CO	Richard E. DeLia	1998	3232
70 6/8	13 4/8 14 0/8	6 1/8 6 0/8	12 5/8	Rosebud County	MT	Jason Flaherty	1998	3232
70 6/8	14 1/8 14 2/8	6 2/8 6 1/8	11 3/8	Perkins County	SD	Travis Hanson	1998	3232
70 6/8	13 3/8 13 3/8	6 0/8 6 0/8	8 4/8	Campbell County	WY	Steff Stefanovich	1999	3232
70 6/8	13 7/8 14 1/8	5 4/8 5 5/8	9 2/8	Elko County	NV	Jerry Vega	2000	3232
70 6/8	15 3/8 15 2/8	5 2/8 5 2/8	13 3/8	Socorro County	NM	Perry W. Hisaw	2000	3232

PRONGHORN

Minimum Score 67 | Continued

SCORE	LENGTH OF R HORN	L	CIRCUMFERENCE R OF BASE	L	INSIDE SPREAD	AREA	STATE/ PROVINCE	HUNTER'S NAME	DATE	RANK
70 6/8	15 6/8	14 6/8	5 4/8	5 5/8	10 5/8	Sierra County	NM	Matt Liljenquist	2000	3232
70 6/8	14 7/8	13 5/8	5 4/8	5 5/8	13 1/8	Carbon County	WY	Daniel K. Rounds	2000	3232
70 6/8	13 7/8	13 5/8	6 0/8	5 7/8	12 4/8	Jackson County	CO	Paul M. Martin	2000	3232
70 6/8	13 7/8	14 0/8	5 7/8	5 6/8	12 3/8	Albany County	WY	Rich Kimball	2000	3232
70 6/8	14 0/8	14 2/8	5 4/8	5 6/8	11 7/8	Yavapai County	AZ	Chad Loy	2001	3232
70 6/8	13 2/8	13 3/8	6 0/8	5 6/8	9 0/8	Manyberries	ALB	Scott Sutherland	2001	3232
70 6/8	13 2/8	13 1/8	6 0/8	6 0/8	9 4/8	Fergus County	MT	John Fleharty	2001	3232
70 6/8	14 2/8	14 0/8	5 3/8	5 4/8	8 5/8	Converse County	WY	Darel J. Hulsing	2002	3232
*70 6/8	14 0/8	14 0/8	5 4/8	5 3/8	9 2/8	Sheridan County	WY	Bruce Burr	2002	3232
70 6/8	13 7/8	13 6/8	6 0/8	6 0/8	11 6/8	Elko County	NV	Chad R. French	2003	3232
70 6/8	14 4/8	14 2/8	6 0/8	6 1/8	9 3/8	Slope County	ND	Chester Kottke	2003	3232
70 6/8	14 1/8	14 3/8	5 3/8	5 3/8	10 7/8	Cherry County	NE	Kyle Hochstein	2003	3232
70 6/8	13 7/8	13 4/8	6 0/8	5 7/8	10 2/8	Cypress	ALB	Dean G. Elbe	2003	3232
70 6/8	13 2/8	13 0/8	6 4/8	6 4/8	10 6/8	Powder River County	MT	Don Scofield	2003	3232
70 6/8	12 7/8	12 6/8	6 1/8	6 1/8	11 3/8	Natrona County	WY	Paul Fairman	2003	3232
70 6/8	13 4/8	13 5/8	6 3/8	6 4/8	10 3/8	Elko County	NV	Tim Bottari	2004	3232
70 6/8	13 6/8	13 5/8	6 2/8	6 0/8	7 2/8	Moffat County	CO	Marty Forster	2004	3232
70 6/8	14 6/8	15 0/8	5 7/8	5 7/8	9 5/8	Washakie County	WY	Paul R. Chaffee	2004	3232
70 6/8	13 3/8	13 2/8	5 7/8	5 6/8	9 2/8	Adams County	CO	Shad T. Grubbs	2004	3232
70 6/8	13 7/8	13 7/8	5 7/8	5 7/8	9 5/8	Musselshell County	MT	James Domaskin	2004	3232
70 6/8	12 7/8	13 4/8	5 6/8	5 5/8	11 2/8	Johnson County	WY	Lisa Ameen	2004	3232
70 6/8	12 5/8	12 7/8	6 3/8	6 3/8	8 5/8	Powder River County	MT	Thomas R. Marquardt	2004	3232
70 6/8	13 2/8	13 4/8	5 7/8	5 7/8	10 4/8	Owyhee County	ID	Erik Jacobs	2005	3232
*70 6/8	15 0/8	14 3/8	5 4/8	5 4/8	9 5/8	Wayne County	UT	Craig Blake	2005	3232
70 6/8	11 6/8	11 5/8	6 2/8	6 3/8	8 4/8	Converse County	WY	Mark Kronyak	2005	3232
*70 6/8	14 5/8	14 4/8	5 5/8	5 2/8	8 1/8	Rosebud County	MT	Bret Cary	2005	3232
*70 6/8	12 6/8	12 7/8	6 0/8	5 7/8	9 2/8	Jackson County	CO	Cedar Beauregard	2006	3232
70 6/8	13 3/8	13 3/8	5 3/8	5 3/8	9 7/8	Converse County	WY	Gary L. Fischer	2006	3232
70 6/8	14 5/8	14 5/8	5 5/8	5 4/8	13 0/8	Navajo County	AZ	Stephan Waltz	2006	3232
70 6/8	13 2/8	13 1/8	7 0/8	6 3/8	7 2/8	Gallatin County	MT	Bob Morton	2006	3232
70 6/8	13 3/8	13 3/8	5 7/8	6 0/8	11 0/8	Converse County	WY	Jay F. Deones	2006	3232
70 6/8	13 3/8	13 5/8	5 6/8	5 6/8	7 3/8	Owyhee County	ID	Ron Jacobs	2007	3232
70 6/8	14 2/8	13 5/8	6 4/8	6 2/8	8 5/8	Meade County	SD	Lance Steiger	2007	3232
70 6/8	13 3/8	13 5/8	5 7/8	5 7/8	10 0/8	Campbell County	WY	Daniel Peak	2008	3232
70 6/8	13 4/8	13 3/8	6 0/8	5 7/8	10 0/8	Carbon County	WY	Dustin Baird	2008	3232
70 6/8	13 7/8	14 6/8	5 4/8	6 0/8	9 5/8	Butte County	SD	Tom Nauman	2008	3232
70 6/8	13 2/8	13 1/8	6 0/8	6 0/8	11 3/8	Campbell County	WY	Rusty Bell	2008	3232
*70 6/8	13 3/8	13 4/8	6 1/8	5 7/8	12 0/8	Johnson County	WY	Mark Armstrong	2008	3232
70 6/8	13 7/8	14 0/8	6 0/8	6 0/8	8 6/8	Rosebud County	MT	Scott Rehak	2008	3232
70 6/8	15 1/8	15 1/8	5 3/8	5 4/8	8 6/8	Owyhee County	ID	Bart Graves	2009	3232
70 6/8	13 1/8	13 0/8	6 2/8	6 1/8	11 3/8	Carter County	MT	Nancy Atwood	2009	3232
70 6/8	13 0/8	13 3/8	6 7/8	6 6/8	13 4/8	Lake County	OR	Tim Rozewski	2009	3232
70 6/8	14 4/8	15 0/8	5 6/8	5 6/8	10 6/8	Jenner	ALB	Charles Martin	2009	3232
*70 6/8	14 0/8	13 7/8	5 4/8	5 5/8	10 5/8	Converse County	WY	David E. Wenzel	2010	3232
70 6/8	13 7/8	13 7/8	5 5/8	5 5/8	11 4/8	Meagher County	MT	Mark Buehrer	2010	3232
70 4/8	12 3/8	12 3/8	5 7/8	5 6/8	7 5/8	Ward County	ND	Bob Torgerson	1964	3373
70 4/8	14 1/8	14 2/8	5 6/8	5 5/8	13 6/8	Custer County	MT	Bob Torgerson	1964	3373
70 4/8	12 5/8	12 4/8	6 0/8	6 0/8	10 5/8	Sweetwater County	WY	Vern A. Butler	1973	3373
70 4/8	14 2/8	14 1/8	5 5/8	5 4/8	8 2/8	Fall River County	SD	Noel Feather, Jr.	1975	3373
70 4/8	14 5/8	14 0/8	6 4/8	6 1/8	9 6/8	Meade County	SD	Floyd McElroy	1977	3373
70 4/8	13 0/8	13 0/8	6 4/8	6 4/8	9 3/8	Clark County	ID	Larry Cross	1977	3373
70 4/8	13 6/8	13 4/8	6 1/8	6 1/8	11 6/8	Grant County	NE	Albert Kant	1978	3373
70 4/8	13 2/8	13 1/8	5 4/8	5 3/8	7 5/8	Clark County	ID	Ron Johnson	1980	3373
70 4/8	13 0/8	13 1/8	6 1/8	6 1/8	9 1/8	Area 55	WY	Walter Walbridge	1980	3373
70 4/8	13 4/8	13 2/8	5 7/8	5 7/8	11 4/8	Converse County	WY	James D. Miller	1981	3373
70 4/8	13 7/8	13 5/8	5 6/8	5 6/8	9 1/8	Natrona County	WY	Gordon W. Stone	1981	3373
70 4/8	13 7/8	13 4/8	6 1/8	6 0/8	14 1/8	Moffat County	CO	Gene Moore	1981	3373
70 4/8	15 0/8	15 0/8	5 3/8	5 3/8	8 7/8	Perkins County	SD	John Pollreisz	1981	3373
70 4/8	13 3/8	13 0/8	6 1/8	6 1/8	9 3/8	Hughes County	SD	Darrel L. Reinke	1982	3373
70 4/8	14 2/8	14 3/8	5 5/8	5 5/8	8 6/8	Natrona County	WY	Ray Smith	1982	3373
70 4/8	12 4/8	13 1/8	6 3/8	6 3/8	8 6/8	Moffat County	CO	Janet Schreur	1983	3373
70 4/8	13 5/8	13 5/8	5 6/8	5 6/8	7 7/8	Converse County	WY	Al Sullivan	1983	3373
70 4/8	13 1/8	13 1/8	6 2/8	6 0/8	10 4/8	Converse County	WY	Rick Poe	1983	3373
70 4/8	12 7/8	13 1/8	5 6/8	5 5/8	8 3/8	Moffat County	CO	Gary McCain	1983	3373
70 4/8	13 4/8	13 4/8	5 7/8	5 6/8	8 2/8	Converse County	WY	Rick Walker	1983	3373
70 4/8	13 1/8	13 0/8	5 7/8	6 0/8	8 3/8	Moffat County	CO	H. R. 'Rusty' Neely	1984	3373
70 4/8	13 2/8	13 3/8	6 0/8	6 0/8	8 3/8	Converse County	WY	Anthony Ruggeri	1984	3373
70 4/8	12 4/8	13 0/8	6 4/8	6 4/8	11 1/8	Converse County	WY	Robin Klemme	1984	3373
70 4/8	12 1/8	12 3/8	6 0/8	6 0/8	10 6/8	Converse County	WY	John M. McAteer	1984	3373
70 4/8	13 5/8	13 4/8	5 7/8	5 7/8	10 0/8	Campbell County	WY	Tony Snow	1984	3373
70 4/8	13 2/8	13 2/8	6 1/8	6 1/8	11 6/8	Modoc County	CA	Robert L. Smith	1986	3373
70 4/8	15 1/8	15 7/8	5 6/8	5 5/8	15 0/8	Lassen County	CA	Tom Gordon	1986	3373
70 4/8	14 3/8	13 0/8	5 7/8	5 7/8	11 3/8	San Miguel County	CO	Bill Wilson	1986	3373
70 4/8	13 5/8	13 6/8	5 3/8	5 3/8	11 6/8	Moffat County	CO	Glenn Pritchard	1986	3373
70 4/8	13 1/8	13 2/8	6 0/8	6 0/8	8 3/8	Brewster County	TX	Michael M. Reamy	1986	3373
70 4/8	13 2/8	12 7/8	6 5/8	6 4/8	9 2/8	Sweetwater County	WY	Brenda Hatcher	1987	3373
70 4/8	13 3/8	13 2/8	6 4/8	6 4/8	9 7/8	Converse County	WY	Eric Wayne Noble	1987	3373
70 4/8	13 7/8	13 6/8	5 6/8	5 4/8	11 1/8	Presidio County	TX	K. D. Sandifer	1987	3373
70 4/8	14 7/8	15 0/8	5 3/8	5 3/8	12 5/8	Sweetwater County	WY	Don Waechtler	1988	3373
70 4/8	13 2/8	13 2/8	6 0/8	6 0/8	11 0/8	Campbell County	WY	Gary D. Johansen	1988	3373
70 4/8	13 6/8	13 1/8	5 6/8	6 1/8	6 7/8	Humboldt County	NV	Dr. John F. Lohse	1989	3373
70 4/8	13 2/8	14 0/8	5 7/8	6 0/8	10 4/8	Washoe County	NV	David A. Heffner	1989	3373
70 4/8	13 2/8	13 3/8	6 3/8	6 3/8	8 5/8	Carbon County	WY	Robert R. Sherman	1989	3373
70 4/8	13 6/8	13 6/8	5 7/8	5 7/8	9 3/8	Millard County	UT	Stan Xavier	1989	3373
70 4/8	14 1/8	14 1/8	5 6/8	5 6/8	13 6/8	Hot Springs County	WY	Jim Fraizer	1989	3373
70 4/8	13 2/8	13 4/8	6 4/8	6 5/8	11 4/8	Converse County	WY	Clem Grimaldi	1989	3373
70 4/8	13 2/8	12 7/8	6 0/8	6 0/8	7 6/8	Natrona County	WY	Ohne Raasch	1989	3373
70 4/8	14 6/8	14 7/8	5 4/8	5 4/8	7 4/8	Bowman County	ND	Nolan A. Johnson	1989	3373
70 4/8	13 0/8	13 2/8	6 1/8	6 0/8	8 2/8	Moffat County	CO	Steve Overstreet	1990	3373
70 4/8	13 7/8	13 7/8	5 6/8	5 6/8	12 2/8	Moffat County	CO	Jeff Knights	1990	3373
70 4/8	13 4/8	13 0/8	5 7/8	6 0/8	8 6/8	Uinta County	WY	Kyle D. Hansen	1990	3373
70 4/8	12 7/8	12 7/8	6 4/8	6 4/8	8 7/8	Natrona County	WY	Kevin Davis	1990	3373
70 4/8	14 3/8	14 3/8	6 0/8	6 0/8	11 5/8	Douglas County	NV	Mark Custis	1991	3373
70 4/8	13 1/8	12 7/8	5 7/8	5 7/8	6 3/8	Moffat County	CO	Kurt W. Keskimaki	1991	3373
70 4/8	13 5/8	13 5/8	5 7/8	5 6/8	12 2/8	Park County	WY	Charles R. Durm	1991	3373

845

PRONGHORN

Minimum Score 67 — Continued

SCORE	LENGTH OF R HORN L	CIRCUMFERENCE R OF BASE L	INSIDE SPREAD	AREA	STATE/ PROVINCE	HUNTER'S NAME	DATE	RANK
70 4/8	14 1/8 14 0/8	5 4/8 5 2/8	14 0/8	Divide County	ND	Robert M. Brunner	1991	3373
70 4/8	12 4/8 12 4/8	5 6/8 5 7/8	8 7/8	Golden Valley County	ND	Terry Buechler	1991	3373
70 4/8	14 3/8 14 3/8	5 5/8 5 6/8	6 4/8	Moffat County	CO	Ken Hoehn	1992	3373
70 4/8	14 0/8 13 4/8	6 0/8 6 0/8	12 0/8	Lincoln County	WY	John E. Alexander	1992	3373
70 4/8	12 4/8 12 6/8	6 2/8 6 3/8	9 5/8	Fremont County	WY	Lyle R. Prell	1992	3373
70 4/8	13 6/8 13 6/8	5 5/8 5 4/8	8 4/8	Converse County	WY	Robert Radford	1992	3373
70 4/8	13 7/8 14 2/8	6 1/8 6 0/8	11 5/8	Campbell County	WY	Karl Schilling	1992	3373
70 4/8	13 5/8 13 6/8	6 0/8 6 0/8	9 3/8	Fergus County	MT	Jerry Knerr	1992	3373
70 4/8	14 3/8 14 3/8	5 3/8 5 3/8	14 1/8	McKenzie County	ND	Vernon D. Hahn	1992	3373
70 4/8	12 6/8 13 1/8	6 5/8 6 3/8	16 2/8	Natrona County	WY	Brian L. Wagner	1992	3373
70 4/8	15 2/8 15 2/8	5 3/8 5 3/8	13 7/8	Owyhee County	ID	Terry Bennett	1993	3373
70 4/8	13 4/8 13 4/8	6 1/8 6 2/8	10 6/8	Garfield County	MT	Mike Coleman	1993	3373
70 4/8	13 0/8 13 0/8	6 2/8 6 1/8	8 1/8	Moffat County	CO	Elmer R. Luce, Jr.	1993	3373
70 4/8	13 2/8 13 3/8	6 0/8 6 0/8	11 5/8	Moffat County	CO	Jay Dart	1994	3373
70 4/8	13 4/8 13 5/8	5 5/8 5 6/8	9 6/8	McCone County	MT	Dan Sturgis	1994	3373
70 4/8	13 4/8 13 4/8	5 4/8 5 4/8	10 4/8	Campbell County	WY	Bruce Hudalla	1994	3373
70 4/8	14 3/8 14 5/8	5 6/8 5 6/8	7 5/8	Thomas County	NE	Phil Chvala	1994	3373
70 4/8	14 0/8 13 6/8	5 6/8 6 0/8	9 2/8	Elko County	NV	John R. Sneed	1995	3373
70 4/8	13 3/8 13 3/8	5 7/8 5 7/8	9 5/8	Big Horn County	WY	William German	1995	3373
70 4/8	15 1/8 15 2/8	5 3/8 5 3/8	11 6/8	Socorro County	NM	Ray A. Krause	1995	3373
70 4/8	13 6/8 14 0/8	5 4/8 5 4/8	9 2/8	Owyhee County	ID	Terence P. Hunter	1995	3373
70 4/8	13 6/8 13 5/8	5 3/8 5 4/8	6 4/8	Saguache County	CO	Burton R. Thompson, Jr.	1995	3373
70 4/8	14 0/8 13 4/8	5 6/8 5 5/8	9 6/8	Saguache County	CO	Ted McMillion	1995	3373
70 4/8	13 6/8 14 0/8	5 4/8 5 3/8	10 4/8	Big Horn County	WY	Jerome D. Larson	1996	3373
70 4/8	13 4/8 13 6/8	5 6/8 5 5/8	9 6/8	Moffat County	CO	Marvin Reichenau	1996	3373
70 4/8	12 7/8 12 6/8	6 2/8 6 2/8	8 3/8	Campbell County	WY	Clayton E. Klingensmith	1996	3373
70 4/8	13 2/8 13 3/8	5 6/8 5 6/8	8 2/8	Converse County	WY	Scott Hallock	1996	3373
70 4/8	13 6/8 13 3/8	6 0/8 5 7/8	12 0/8	Natrona County	WY	Wayne H. Andersen	1996	3373
70 4/8	14 0/8 13 6/8	5 6/8 5 5/8	8 6/8	Converse County	WY	Paul J. Herrera	1996	3373
70 4/8	14 2/8 13 7/8	5 5/8 5 5/8	6 7/8	Weston County	WY	Joseph B. Hines	1996	3373
70 4/8	13 2/8 13 1/8	5 6/8 5 6/8	11 3/8	Converse County	WY	Byron LaFollette	1996	3373
70 4/8	13 5/8 13 6/8	5 7/8 6 0/8	11 0/8	Natrona County	WY	Wayne Poreda	1997	3373
70 4/8	13 0/8 13 3/8	5 6/8 5 5/8	8 5/8	Carbon County	UT	Kyle Fox	1997	3373
70 4/8	14 4/8 14 7/8	5 7/8 5 7/8	7 7/8	Weld County	CO	Fred Johnson	1997	3373
70 4/8	15 0/8 14 7/8	5 3/8 5 3/8	8 0/8	Big Horn County	MT	Jason Watson	1997	3373
70 4/8	12 6/8 13 2/8	6 4/8 6 4/8	9 6/8	Las Animas County	CO	Joe Given	1998	3373
70 4/8	14 0/8 14 0/8	5 6/8 5 6/8	7 6/8	Converse County	WY	Jim G. Winjum	1998	3373
70 4/8	13 2/8 12 7/8	6 0/8 6 0/8	9 5/8	Larimer County	CO	Mark E. Gonyo	1998	3373
70 4/8	12 4/8 12 4/8	6 4/8 6 1/8	9 2/8	Converse County	WY	Patrick Sullivan	1998	3373
70 4/8	13 6/8 13 6/8	5 4/8 5 4/8	7 3/8	Natrona County	WY	Alfred J. Gemrich	1998	3373
70 4/8	13 6/8 14 1/8	6 0/8 6 1/8	12 4/8	Moffat County	CO	Sue Syvertson	1999	3373
70 4/8	14 0/8 13 6/8	6 1/8 6 0/8	11 0/8	Weld County	CO	Trent Short	1999	3373
70 4/8	14 2/8 14 2/8	5 4/8 5 5/8	9 2/8	Converse County	WY	William G. Mason	1999	3373
70 4/8	13 6/8 13 6/8	5 4/8 5 4/8	9 3/8	Moffat County	CO	Andy Bair	2000	3373
70 4/8	14 0/8 13 7/8	6 0/8 6 0/8	7 1/8	Lemhi County	ID	Ben L. Fahnholz	2000	3373
70 4/8	14 2/8 13 5/8	5 5/8 5 5/8	9 5/8	Minidoka County	ID	Perry Orr	2000	3373
70 4/8	13 2/8 13 0/8	5 4/8 5 4/8	12 1/8	Moffat County	CO	Bryan Jay Herman	2000	3373
70 4/8	13 3/8 13 6/8	5 6/8 5 6/8	9 0/8	Hayes Road	ALB	Wayne Greene	2000	3373
70 4/8	13 3/8 13 7/8	5 6/8 6 0/8	10 4/8	Modoc County	CA	Mike Shrosbree, Jr.	2001	3373
70 4/8	12 2/8 12 2/8	6 1/8 6 0/8	11 1/8	Klamath County	OR	Jevon A. Struve	2001	3373
70 4/8	13 4/8 13 3/8	5 6/8 5 6/8	9 7/8	Big Horn County	WY	Jeff Gavne	2001	3373
70 4/8	14 3/8 14 6/8	5 5/8 5 5/8	8 3/8	Rosebud County	MT	Maxallen Jackson	2001	3373
70 4/8	13 6/8 13 5/8	6 1/8 6 1/8	8 1/8	Converse County	WY	W. Tennyson Krugh	2001	3373
70 4/8	13 1/8 13 0/8	5 7/8 5 6/8	10 0/8	Jackson County	CO	Cedar Beauregard	2002	3373
70 4/8	13 6/8 13 2/8	5 5/8 5 5/8	11 4/8	Moffat County	CO	Steven E. Sheehy	2002	3373
70 4/8	12 6/8 13 3/8	6 0/8 5 6/8	10 0/8	Moffat County	CO	Kyle Buell	2002	3373
70 4/8	12 3/8 13 2/8	6 2/8 6 2/8	13 2/8	Yellowstone County	MT	Chris G. Sanford	2002	3373
70 4/8	13 1/8 12 7/8	6 1/8 5 6/8	11 1/8	Elmore County	ID	James R. Gempler	2003	3373
*70 4/8	14 1/8 14 0/8	5 6/8 5 5/8	9 6/8	Natrona County	WY	Daniel W. Collins	2003	3373
70 4/8	13 3/8 13 4/8	6 1/8 6 2/8	13 1/8	Guadalupe County	NM	Brandon Ray	2003	3373
70 4/8	11 7/8 12 0/8	5 7/8 5 7/8	10 2/8	Converse County	WY	Roger Gerloff, Jr.	2003	3373
70 4/8	13 7/8 13 7/8	5 4/8 5 4/8	13 5/8	Rosebud County	MT	Dick Wigdahl	2003	3373
70 4/8	13 5/8 13 2/8	5 5/8 5 5/8	10 6/8	Sublette County	WY	Brett I. Ritter	2003	3373
*70 4/8	13 5/8 14 1/8	6 0/8 6 0/8	11 5/8	Natrona County	WY	Todd Richins	2004	3373
70 4/8	15 1/8 15 2/8	5 5/8 5 5/8	11 7/8	Petroleum County	MT	Glen Berry	2004	3373
70 4/8	15 1/8 14 5/8	6 1/8 6 1/8	9 5/8	Madison County	MT	Chris Currie	2004	3373
70 4/8	14 5/8 14 5/8	5 3/8 5 2/8	12 4/8	Carbon County	WY	Patrick J. Malone	2004	3373
70 4/8	14 0/8 14 1/8	6 3/8 6 1/8	10 6/8	Johnson County	WY	Bob Ameen	2004	3373
70 4/8	11 5/8 11 6/8	6 1/8 6 1/8	8 6/8	Johnson County	WY	Paul Ovadal	2004	3373
*70 4/8	13 1/8 13 1/8	5 6/8 5 6/8	13 2/8	Sweetwater County	WY	Stephen Foster	2005	3373
70 4/8	13 7/8 14 0/8	5 7/8 6 0/8	12 0/8	Harding County	SD	Don Scofield	2005	3373
70 4/8	11 6/8 12 0/8	6 2/8 6 1/8	10 4/8	Yavapai County	AZ	Bradley E. Mathis	2005	3373
70 4/8	13 0/8 13 1/8	6 0/8 5 7/8	9 2/8	Gull Lake	SAS	Clyde Erhardt	2005	3373
70 4/8	13 4/8 13 4/8	5 6/8 5 4/8	10 4/8	Garfield County	MT	Kent Reierson	2005	3373
*70 4/8	13 7/8 14 3/8	5 6/8 5 7/8	13 0/8	Perkins County	SD	Danelle Miiller	2005	3373
70 4/8	14 0/8 14 0/8	5 4/8 5 4/8	7 4/8	White Pine County	NV	Joseph G. DeAngelis	2006	3373
70 4/8	15 1/8 14 0/8	5 7/8 5 6/8	7 6/8	Carbon County	WY	Clay J. Evans	2006	3373
70 4/8	13 4/8 14 0/8	5 6/8 5 6/8	11 7/8	Powder River County	MT	Richard Dugger	2006	3373
70 4/8	14 0/8 14 1/8	5 4/8 5 5/8	8 5/8	Moffat County	CO	Dru Harms	2006	3373
70 4/8	13 6/8 12 7/8	6 4/8 6 3/8	9 1/8	Rosebud County	MT	Chet Sergo	2006	3373
*70 4/8	13 4/8 13 4/8	6 1/8 6 1/8	9 4/8	Converse County	WY	Jeremy W. Stover	2006	3373
*70 4/8	12 4/8 12 6/8	6 4/8 6 4/8	5 6/8	Johnson County	WY	Paul Chaffee	2006	3373
*70 4/8	14 4/8 14 5/8	5 5/8 5 4/8	9 2/8	Rosebud County	MT	Kevin Westerberg	2006	3373
*70 4/8	12 6/8 12 6/8	6 1/8 6 0/8	11 7/8	Niobrara County	WY	Jess Kucera	2006	3373
70 4/8	14 3/8 14 1/8	5 6/8 5 7/8	11 4/8	Cherry County	NE	Reggie Hochstein	2006	3373
70 4/8	13 3/8 13 7/8	5 7/8 5 6/8	9 4/8	Powder River County	MT	R. F. McRae	2007	3373
70 4/8	13 7/8 14 2/8	5 4/8 5 4/8	7 4/8	Weston County	WY	Rob Dowen	2007	3373
70 4/8	14 0/8 14 0/8	5 6/8 5 5/8	8 6/8	Converse County	WY	David G. Pasky	2007	3373
*70 4/8	13 1/8 13 2/8	6 6/8 6 6/8	9 2/8	Converse County	WY	Doug Baily	2007	3373
70 4/8	14 3/8 14 1/8	5 4/8 5 4/8	11 6/8	Perkins County	SD	Robert G. Barden	2007	3373
70 4/8	14 3/8 14 4/8	5 7/8 5 5/8	10 4/8	Harding County	SD	Howard A. Bork	2007	3373
70 4/8	14 1/8 14 3/8	5 6/8 5 6/8	8 4/8	White Pine County	NV	Sue E. Berfield	2008	3373
70 4/8	13 5/8 13 0/8	5 4/8 5 4/8	10 4/8	Las Animas County	CO	Jim Eichinger	2008	3373
70 4/8	13 6/8 13 6/8	5 7/8 5 7/8	10 7/8	Sweetwater County	WY	Glen O. Hallows	2008	3373
70 4/8	13 0/8 13 3/8	5 7/8 6 0/8	10 1/8	Campbell County	WY	Toni Bell	2008	3373

PRONGHORN

Minimum Score 67 — Continued

SCORE	LENGTH OF R HORN L	CIRCUMFERENCE R OF BASE L	INSIDE SPREAD	AREA	STATE/ PROVINCE	HUNTER'S NAME	DATE	RANK
70 4/8	13 2/8 13 5/8	6 1/8 6 1/8	12 6/8	Carter County	MT	James D. Herring	2008	3373
*70 4/8	13 4/8 13 4/8	5 6/8 5 5/8	9 0/8	Crook County	WY	Scott Teel	2008	3373
70 4/8	12 3/8 12 6/8	6 3/8 6 3/8	10 4/8	Rosebud County	MT	Gene A. Welle	2008	3373
70 4/8	13 5/8 14 1/8	5 4/8 5 4/8	11 4/8	Converse County	WY	Dr. David McNeill	2008	3373
*70 4/8	13 5/8 13 4/8	5 6/8 5 7/8	11 0/8	Carbon County	WY	Doug Aikin	2008	3373
70 4/8	14 2/8 12 5/8	6 1/8 5 6/8	7 4/8	Carter County	MT	Pete Gierke	2008	3373
70 4/8	13 6/8 13 4/8	5 6/8 5 5/8	11 2/8	Lea County	NM	Eric Boley	2009	3373
*70 4/8	14 6/8 14 0/8	6 1/8 5 7/8	10 0/8	Potter County	SD	Brandon Shardin	2009	3373
*70 4/8	13 3/8 13 1/8	6 0/8 6 1/8	8 3/8	Converse County	WY	David L. Butler	2009	3373
*70 4/8	13 1/8 13 1/8	6 0/8 5 6/8	9 0/8	McCone County	MT	Trevor Stiles	2009	3373
*70 4/8	14 1/8 14 2/8	6 0/8 5 7/8	9 1/8	Owyhee County	ID	Tim Craft	2010	3373
70 4/8	13 6/8 13 4/8	6 2/8 6 2/8	10 1/8	Natrona County	WY	Rodney Birkle	2010	3373
70 2/8	15 2/8 15 4/8	5 4/8 5 3/8	11 5/8	Natrona County	WY	Larry J. Colombo	1970	3530
70 2/8	12 7/8 12 7/8	6 1/8 6 1/8	12 5/8	Converse County	WY	Edward Coy	1972	3530
70 2/8	14 0/8 14 0/8	5 6/8 5 6/8	13 7/8	Butte County	ID	Dale Dunn	1973	3530
70 2/8	12 6/8 13 0/8	6 3/8 6 3/8	9 0/8	Dawes County	NE	Bruce Troester	1973	3530
70 2/8	12 2/8 12 2/8	5 5/8 5 5/8	9 2/8	Saguache County	CO	Sandra Scheid	1975	3530
70 2/8	13 2/8 13 4/8	5 5/8 5 6/8	11 0/8	Saguache County	CO	Tom Tietz	1977	3530
70 2/8	12 6/8 12 7/8	5 7/8 5 6/8	8 7/8	Meade County	SD	Howard Jess Hollenbeck, Jr.	1978	3530
70 2/8	14 2/8 11 7/8	6 1/8 6 1/8	10 0/8	Converse County	WY	Anthony Wells	1980	3530
70 2/8	13 6/8 13 6/8	6 6/8 6 4/8	10 6/8	Sweetwater County	WY	Vaughn Cross	1980	3530
70 2/8	13 7/8 13 5/8	6 0/8 6 0/8	9 3/8	Moffat County	CO	Dave Skiff	1981	3530
70 2/8	13 1/8 13 2/8	6 2/8 6 1/8	8 1/8	Natrona County	WY	Jim Plemmons	1981	3530
70 2/8	14 2/8 14 3/8	5 5/8 5 5/8	9 6/8	Lassen County	CA	B. Jensen/F. Searle	1981	3530
70 2/8	12 6/8 12 7/8	6 0/8 5 7/8	9 6/8	Carbon County	WY	George Raab	1982	3530
70 2/8	14 0/8 14 0/8	5 7/8 5 6/8	10 2/8	Converse County	WY	Brad Johnson	1982	3530
70 2/8	13 6/8 14 1/8	6 1/8 6 0/8	12 2/8	Natrona County	WY	Tim Sturm	1982	3530
70 2/8	12 4/8 12 4/8	5 5/8 5 7/8	10 6/8	Moffat County	CO	Wendy Decker	1983	3530
70 2/8	12 2/8 12 2/8	6 0/8 6 0/8	10 3/8	Converse County	WY	Ron Montross	1983	3530
70 2/8	13 0/8 13 4/8	5 6/8 5 7/8	10 6/8	Moffat County	CO	Rick Kralicek	1983	3530
70 2/8	13 4/8 13 6/8	5 7/8 5 5/8	9 7/8	Sweetwater County	WY	Judd Cooney	1983	3530
70 2/8	13 2/8 13 5/8	5 5/8 5 5/8	10 6/8	Converse County	WY	Rocky Chisholm	1983	3530
70 2/8	13 0/8 13 0/8	5 6/8 5 7/8	11 6/8	Sweetwater County	WY	Michael R. Westvang	1984	3530
70 2/8	12 6/8 13 2/8	5 7/8 5 7/8	11 1/8	Carbon County	WY	Ken Bean	1984	3530
70 2/8	13 5/8 13 6/8	6 1/8 5 7/8	10 3/8	McCone County	MT	Frank Kasten III	1984	3530
70 2/8	13 0/8 12 6/8	6 0/8 6 0/8	12 1/8	Sweetwater County	WY	David Wells	1985	3530
70 2/8	13 0/8 12 7/8	6 2/8 6 2/8	9 3/8	Converse County	WY	Theodore C. Dzienis	1985	3530
70 2/8	13 6/8 14 1/8	6 1/8 6 1/8	8 7/8	Powder River County	MT	Stephen J. Jaworski	1985	3530
70 2/8	15 0/8 14 7/8	5 1/8 5 1/8	9 6/8	Las Animas County	CO	Bill Swift	1985	3530
70 2/8	13 5/8 13 4/8	5 6/8 5 7/8	8 6/8	Sweetwater County	WY	Darren L. Shirley	1986	3530
70 2/8	13 2/8 13 5/8	6 0/8 6 1/8	8 0/8	Billings County	ND	Randy Bakken	1986	3530
70 2/8	13 3/8 13 3/8	5 6/8 5 5/8	9 2/8	Carbon County	WY	Duane Hicks	1987	3530
70 2/8	13 4/8 14 0/8	6 2/8 6 2/8	10 2/8	Lincoln County	NV	Michael W. Zech	1987	3530
70 2/8	13 2/8 13 3/8	6 0/8 5 7/8	9 5/8	Converse County	WY	James H. Miller	1987	3530
70 2/8	14 6/8 14 2/8	5 5/8 5 6/8	9 2/8	Humboldt County	NV	Clayton J. Larsen	1988	3530
70 2/8	13 2/8 14 0/8	5 7/8 5 7/8	15 1/8	Moffat County	CO	Kurt W. Keskimaki	1988	3530
70 2/8	12 5/8 12 7/8	5 7/8 5 7/8	14 6/8	Moffat County	CO	Sam Godfrey	1988	3530
70 2/8	13 4/8 13 5/8	6 0/8 5 7/8	11 0/8	Moffat County	CO	Jim Tatro	1988	3530
70 2/8	13 4/8 12 6/8	5 7/8 5 6/8	11 2/8	Slope County	ND	Todd Seymanski	1988	3530
70 2/8	14 2/8 14 2/8	5 6/8 5 6/8	8 5/8	Converse County	WY	M. R. James	1988	3530
70 2/8	14 1/8 14 0/8	5 5/8 5 4/8	10 4/8	Chouteau County	MT	Jack A. Clouse	1988	3530
70 2/8	14 0/8 13 6/8	6 0/8 6 0/8	9 1/8	Converse County	WY	Joel M. Riotto	1989	3530
70 2/8	14 7/8 14 7/8	5 4/8 5 3/8	16 2/8	Converse County	WY	Fred Wallace	1989	3530
70 2/8	13 1/8 13 2/8	6 0/8 5 7/8	10 7/8	Carbon County	WY	Donald P. Peel	1989	3530
70 2/8	14 1/8 14 1/8	5 4/8 5 4/8	11 3/8	Petroleum County	MT	Clark Jenner	1989	3530
70 2/8	14 5/8 15 1/8	5 4/8 5 3/8	7 7/8	Klamath County	OR	Randy Carter	1990	3530
70 2/8	12 4/8 12 5/8	6 0/8 6 0/8	9 4/8	McKenzie County	ND	Alan Smith	1990	3530
70 2/8	12 1/8 12 0/8	6 1/8 6 1/8	7 6/8	Campbell County	WY	Craig Boheler	1990	3530
70 2/8	14 0/8 13 7/8	5 6/8 5 5/8	10 2/8	Carbon County	WY	Tim Cuthriell	1991	3530
70 2/8	13 4/8 13 2/8	6 0/8 6 2/8	11 3/8	Uinta County	WY	Kevin D. Hatfield	1991	3530
70 2/8	12 4/8 12 4/8	6 2/8 6 0/8	7 5/8	Sweetwater County	WY	Carl G. Esterly	1991	3530
70 2/8	14 0/8 14 0/8	5 5/8 5 5/8	8 0/8	Powder River County	MT	Don Scofield	1991	3530
70 2/8	14 2/8 14 0/8	5 5/8 5 4/8	12 0/8	Coconino County	AZ	Kevin Robinson	1991	3530
70 2/8	12 5/8 13 1/8	6 2/8 6 2/8	10 5/8	Sublette County	WY	Stephen Kotz	1991	3530
70 2/8	14 6/8 15 2/8	5 5/8 5 4/8	8 3/8	Converse County	WY	Charles Peters	1991	3530
70 2/8	14 6/8 14 3/8	6 0/8 5 6/8	10 3/8	Converse County	WY	Roger Brittain	1991	3530
70 2/8	13 0/8 12 6/8	5 7/8 6 0/8	7 6/8	Niobrara County	WY	Thomas D. Mackowski	1991	3530
70 2/8	13 4/8 13 2/8	6 0/8 5 7/8	14 1/8	Daggett County	UT	Steve Dailey	1991	3530
70 2/8	13 6/8 14 2/8	5 7/8 5 6/8	10 0/8	Campbell County	WY	Al Ratajesak	1991	3530
70 2/8	13 2/8 13 1/8	6 1/8 6 1/8	8 2/8	Converse County	WY	Michael E. Zimmerman	1991	3530
70 2/8	12 5/8 12 7/8	6 3/8 6 3/8	9 0/8	Converse County	WY	Myron Jochmann	1991	3530
70 2/8	14 7/8 14 4/8	5 6/8 5 6/8	9 6/8	Sioux County	NE	Steve Neujahr	1991	3530
70 2/8	15 1/8 14 2/8	5 6/8 5 6/8	11 1/8	McKenzie County	ND	Travis Wollan	1991	3530
70 2/8	13 1/8 13 0/8	5 7/8 5 6/8	11 4/8	San Miguel County	NM	Leon M. Reed	1992	3530
70 2/8	14 6/8 15 0/8	5 5/8 5 5/8	8 1/8	Twin Falls County	ID	John Stevens	1992	3530
70 2/8	13 7/8 14 2/8	5 7/8 5 5/8	7 6/8	Moffat County	CO	Conrad Anderson	1992	3530
70 2/8	12 2/8 12 6/8	6 0/8 6 1/8	10 1/8	Moffat County	CO	Gerald Dowell	1992	3530
70 2/8	13 2/8 13 0/8	6 2/8 6 1/8	9 5/8	San Juan County	UT	Ronald Kirk	1992	3530
70 2/8	13 5/8 13 3/8	5 7/8 5 7/8	9 6/8	Converse County	WY	Michael J. Whitish	1992	3530
70 2/8	13 4/8 13 5/8	5 7/8 5 7/8	8 5/8	Uinta County	WY	Layne Foxley	1992	3530
70 2/8	13 5/8 14 1/8	5 5/8 5 6/8	9 2/8	Lincoln County	WY	Rocky Rollins	1992	3530
70 2/8	13 5/8 13 6/8	6 1/8 6 1/8	9 2/8	Natrona County	WY	David L. Willis	1992	3530
70 2/8	15 5/8 15 4/8	5 2/8 5 3/8	10 5/8	Perkins County	SD	James J. Willard	1992	3530
70 2/8	13 5/8 13 6/8	5 3/8 5 3/8	9 3/8	Cheyenne County	NE	David Trump	1992	3530
70 2/8	13 7/8 13 6/8	5 7/8 5 7/8	8 3/8	Colfax County	NM	Mike F. Mallory	1993	3530
70 2/8	15 1/8 14 7/8	5 6/8 5 5/8	11 7/8	Yavapai County	AZ	Mark Ovitt	1993	3530
70 2/8	13 5/8 13 6/8	6 0/8 5 7/8	8 4/8	Natrona County	WY	George Hendon	1993	3530
70 2/8	14 3/8 14 2/8	5 5/8 5 4/8	10 1/8	Moffat County	CO	Jim Leqve	1994	3530
70 2/8	13 2/8 13 2/8	6 0/8 6 1/8	8 1/8	Moffat County	CO	Chuck Adams	1994	3530
70 2/8	13 5/8 13 4/8	5 2/8 5 2/8	10 5/8	Millard County	UT	Kevin Kelly	1994	3530
70 2/8	13 5/8 13 1/8	5 7/8 6 0/8	9 6/8	Moffat County	CO	Rudy Meyers	1994	3530
70 2/8	13 5/8 13 2/8	5 4/8 5 5/8	12 1/8	Sweetwater County	WY	Bryce E. Carley	1994	3530
70 2/8	13 5/8 13 5/8	5 7/8 5 7/8	7 4/8	Chaffee County	CO	Tim Cuthriell	1994	3530
70 2/8	14 1/8 14 1/8	6 2/8 6 1/8	9 4/8	Valley County	MT	Val Dierks	1994	3530
70 2/8	14 0/8 14 1/8	5 5/8 5 4/8	11 4/8	Platte County	WY	Jeffrey Colman	1994	3530

847

PRONGHORN

Minimum Score 67 — Continued

SCORE	LENGTH OF R HORN L	CIRCUMFERENCE R OF BASE L	INSIDE SPREAD	AREA	STATE/ PROVINCE	HUNTER'S NAME	DATE	RANK
70 2/8	14 0/8 13 7/8	5 6/8 5 5/8	10 3/8	Johnson County	WY	Charlie H. Sagner	1994	3530
70 2/8	14 7/8 13 4/8	6 0/8 5 7/8	6 2/8	Campbell County	WY	Craig Martin	1994	3530
70 2/8	12 4/8 12 5/8	5 6/8 5 6/8	9 3/8	Campbell County	WY	Steve Huppert	1994	3530
70 2/8	13 6/8 13 7/8	6 0/8 5 7/8	11 5/8	Moffat County	CO	Michael Ingold	1995	3530
70 2/8	14 2/8 14 2/8	5 5/8 5 5/8	11 0/8	Klamath County	OR	Dennis Dahlgren	1995	3530
70 2/8	13 2/8 13 4/8	6 0/8 6 2/8	12 0/8	Moffat County	CO	Ken Hoehn	1995	3530
70 2/8	14 2/8 14 0/8	5 7/8 5 6/8	10 5/8	Moffat County	CO	Mark Montgomery	1995	3530
70 2/8	13 1/8 13 0/8	5 6/8 5 7/8	9 6/8	Guadalupe County	NM	Brandon Ray	1995	3530
70 2/8	14 1/8 13 7/8	5 7/8 5 7/8	10 1/8	Rosebud County	MT	David Burrows	1995	3530
70 2/8	13 3/8 13 6/8	6 1/8 6 2/8	10 2/8	Powder River County	MT	Don G. Scofield	1995	3530
70 2/8	13 7/8 13 7/8	5 7/8 5 5/8	12 5/8	Campbell County	WY	Wright W. Allen	1995	3530
70 2/8	13 3/8 13 2/8	6 3/8 6 0/8	8 3/8	Moffat County	CO	Connie Renfro	1996	3530
70 2/8	13 2/8 13 3/8	5 6/8 5 5/8	8 1/8	Yavapai County	AZ	Henry Robert Garcia, Sr.	1996	3530
70 2/8	13 7/8 14 0/8	5 5/8 5 6/8	9 3/8	Campbell County	WY	Tim Kanapeckas	1996	3530
70 2/8	13 3/8 13 4/8	6 0/8 5 7/8	11 2/8	Campbell County	WY	Terry L. Wright	1996	3530
70 2/8	14 6/8 14 7/8	5 7/8 5 6/8	9 0/8	Estevan	SAS	Allen Johnson	1996	3530
70 2/8	13 1/8 13 1/8	6 0/8 5 6/8	9 6/8	Twin Falls County	ID	Darrell Nunez	1997	3530
70 2/8	14 4/8 14 2/8	5 4/8 5 7/8	9 2/8	Saguache County	CO	Steven J. Vittetow	1998	3530
70 2/8	13 6/8 13 5/8	5 6/8 5 5/8	7 4/8	Millard County	UT	Jim Madsen	1998	3530
70 2/8	14 2/8 12 5/8	6 7/8 6 6/8	11 6/8	Converse County	WY	Larry Comer	1998	3530
70 2/8	13 7/8 13 7/8	6 4/8 6 4/8	12 0/8	Butte County	SD	Steve McManaman	1998	3530
70 2/8	14 2/8 14 6/8	6 2/8 6 2/8	9 5/8	Bowman County	ND	Jeff Bommersbach	1998	3530
70 2/8	12 6/8 12 6/8	5 6/8 5 6/8	7 2/8	Natrona County	WY	Joel Goodman	1999	3530
70 2/8	13 6/8 13 4/8	5 6/8 5 4/8	5 5/8	Coconino County	AZ	Dennis Manuell	1999	3530
70 2/8	13 6/8 13 6/8	6 0/8 6 1/8	12 5/8	Harding County	SD	Jeff J. Dudgeon	1999	3530
70 2/8	13 3/8 13 5/8	5 2/8 5 2/8	10 7/8	Cascade County	MT	Chad Konesky	1999	3530
70 2/8	13 5/8 13 6/8	6 1/8 6 1/8	11 1/8	Rio Blanco County	CO	Bob Black	1999	3530
70 2/8	13 4/8 13 6/8	6 0/8 5 7/8	10 6/8	Natrona County	WY	Wilson McKibben	2000	3530
70 2/8	14 0/8 14 0/8	5 4/8 5 3/8	13 0/8	Moffat County	CO	Steven Musselman	2001	3530
70 2/8	13 6/8 13 4/8	6 0/8 5 7/8	10 0/8	Owyhee County	ID	Doug Hawker	2001	3530
70 2/8	14 6/8 14 6/8	5 4/8 5 4/8	8 7/8	Harding County	SD	Robert A. Rossow	2001	3530
70 2/8	13 6/8 13 6/8	5 5/8 5 5/8	6 4/8	Morton County	KS	Chad Milligan	2001	3530
70 2/8	13 0/8 13 5/8	6 2/8 6 1/8	9 7/8	Sublette County	WY	Bennett McMillian	2001	3530
70 2/8	13 7/8 14 0/8	5 5/8 5 5/8	9 1/8	Las Animas County	CO	Jim Matuszewski	2002	3530
70 2/8	12 6/8 12 4/8	6 1/8 6 1/8	11 5/8	Weld County	CO	Kelly Norton	2002	3530
70 2/8	13 3/8 13 3/8	5 5/8 5 5/8	8 6/8	Converse County	WY	Frank S. Noska IV	2002	3530
70 2/8	13 7/8 14 0/8	5 5/8 5 3/8	9 5/8	Yavapai County	AZ	Scott Anderson	2002	3530
70 2/8	13 3/8 13 2/8	6 3/8 6 4/8	9 3/8	Hill County	MT	Ronald J. Zurek	2002	3530
70 2/8	12 4/8 12 3/8	6 0/8 6 0/8	8 6/8	Campbell County	WY	Pete Shockey	2002	3530
70 2/8	13 7/8 13 7/8	5 7/8 5 5/8	12 6/8	Albany County	WY	Kevin Brothers	2003	3530
70 2/8	14 4/8 15 3/8	5 7/8 5 4/8	15 5/8	Butte County	ID	Travis Mitchell	2003	3530
*70 2/8	14 4/8 13 7/8	5 2/8 5 2/8	8 2/8	Powder River County	MT	Cody Gilbertson	2003	3530
70 2/8	12 5/8 12 3/8	5 7/8 5 7/8	10 0/8	Converse County	WY	Daryl Mull	2003	3530
70 2/8	13 0/8 12 7/8	6 0/8 6 1/8	9 0/8	Harding County	SD	Bruce R. Briesemeister	2003	3530
70 2/8	14 4/8 14 5/8	5 4/8 5 4/8	8 3/8	Rosebud County	MT	Kevin Brewer	2003	3530
70 2/8	13 5/8 13 5/8	5 7/8 5 7/8	8 5/8	Gallatin County	MT	Bob Morton	2003	3530
70 2/8	14 0/8 14 2/8	5 4/8 5 3/8	6 7/8	Humboldt County	NV	Joshua Williams	2004	3530
70 2/8	13 7/8 14 1/8	5 3/8 5 4/8	8 7/8	Las Animas County	CO	Wayne Stewart, Jr.	2004	3530
70 2/8	14 1/8 13 6/8	5 3/8 5 2/8	9 7/8	Laramie County	WY	Kye Hall	2004	3530
70 2/8	14 6/8 14 5/8	5 2/8 5 3/8	9 7/8	Butte County	SD	DaWayne Vanden Hoek	2004	3530
70 2/8	12 6/8 12 6/8	6 1/8 6 1/8	8 1/8	Natrona County	WY	Mark Kronyak	2004	3530
70 2/8	12 7/8 13 2/8	5 7/8 5 6/8	9 6/8	Converse County	WY	Tom Grover	2004	3530
70 2/8	13 7/8 13 6/8	5 6/8 5 5/8	12 1/8	Deschutes County	OR	Joe Davino	2004	3530
70 2/8	13 3/8 13 3/8	6 2/8 6 2/8	11 1/8	Twin Falls County	ID	Cory Santos	2004	3530
70 2/8	14 1/8 13 1/8	5 7/8 5 6/8	7 7/8	Park County	MT	George Kamps	2004	3530
70 2/8	14 0/8 13 7/8	5 7/8 6 0/8	11 5/8	Rosebud County	MT	Jim Hval	2005	3530
70 2/8	14 5/8 13 5/8	5 6/8 6 0/8	7 4/8	Elmore County	ID	Jim Gempler	2005	3530
*70 2/8	13 2/8 13 1/8	5 5/8 5 4/8	9 4/8	Rosebud County	MT	Todd Kleen	2005	3530
70 2/8	13 6/8 14 0/8	6 1/8 6 0/8	10 6/8	Broadwater County	MT	Bill Hangas	2005	3530
70 2/8	13 3/8 13 3/8	6 3/8 6 2/8	10 7/8	Converse County	WY	Scott Kunau	2005	3530
70 2/8	13 4/8 13 4/8	5 5/8 5 5/8	10 5/8	Harding County	SD	Jerry Notch	2005	3530
70 2/8	13 4/8 13 4/8	5 7/8 5 7/8	10 0/8	Jackson County	CO	Craig Thrasher	2006	3530
70 2/8	13 6/8 13 7/8	5 4/8 5 4/8	12 2/8	Jackson County	CO	Justin Downing	2006	3530
70 2/8	13 0/8 13 1/8	5 6/8 5 5/8	11 4/8	Las Animas County	CO	Michele Eichler	2006	3530
70 2/8	13 1/8 13 1/8	6 6/8 6 5/8	11 0/8	Campbell County	WY	Donald R. Brandt	2006	3530
70 2/8	12 3/8 13 0/8	6 0/8 5 6/8	9 2/8	Crook County	WY	Jeff Jacob	2006	3530
70 2/8	13 1/8 13 3/8	5 7/8 5 6/8	8 7/8	Niobrara County	WY	Dennis Ballweg	2006	3530
70 2/8	13 2/8 13 2/8	5 4/8 6 0/8	10 4/8	Campbell County	WY	Robert W. Miller	2006	3530
70 2/8	13 6/8 13 7/8	5 6/8 5 7/8	9 1/8	Washoe County	NV	David E. Evanow	2007	3530
70 2/8	13 1/8 12 5/8	5 7/8 5 7/8	10 0/8	Beaverhead County	MT	Ray Gross	2007	3530
70 2/8	13 5/8 13 5/8	5 4/8 5 5/8	7 0/8	Fergus County	MT	Chris G. Sanford	2007	3530
70 2/8	13 0/8 13 3/8	5 7/8 5 6/8	9 6/8	Cherry County	NE	Bill Bowering	2007	3530
*70 2/8	13 2/8 13 3/8	6 0/8 5 7/8	9 1/8	Blaine County	MT	Anthony S. Appleton	2007	3530
*70 2/8	14 4/8 14 3/8	5 3/8 5 4/8	8 0/8	Crook County	WY	Eric J. Wichman	2007	3530
70 2/8	14 0/8 14 1/8	5 5/8 5 5/8	10 0/8	Sioux County	NE	Mark Koenig	2007	3530
70 2/8	14 3/8 14 2/8	6 0/8 6 0/8	7 2/8	Harding County	SD	Doug Strecker	2007	3530
*70 2/8	13 4/8 13 5/8	5 4/8 5 4/8	7 7/8	Reagan County	TX	Richard Johnson	2007	3530
70 2/8	13 7/8 13 5/8	5 6/8 5 6/8	7 2/8	Converse County	WY	John E. Wencley	2008	3530
70 2/8	13 5/8 13 6/8	5 7/8 5 5/8	10 6/8	Powder River County	MT	Bryon Long	2008	3530
70 2/8	13 2/8 13 0/8	5 4/8 5 5/8	8 4/8	Moffat County	CO	Mark Wollert	2008	3530
*70 2/8	13 1/8 13 2/8	5 3/8 5 2/8	8 5/8	Jones County	SD	Austin J. Butt	2008	3530
*70 2/8	13 6/8 14 1/8	5 4/8 5 5/8	8 6/8	Converse County	WY	R. L. Toat Brandvold	2008	3530
70 2/8	13 4/8 13 2/8	5 6/8 5 6/8	8 5/8	Las Animas County	CO	Ivan Gobeli	2008	3530
*70 2/8	11 5/8 11 5/8	6 3/8 6 3/8	9 1/8	Campbell County	WY	Lane Ostendorf	2008	3530
70 2/8	13 0/8 13 0/8	5 5/8 5 4/8	10 2/8	Outram	SAS	Lynn Hrywkiw	2008	3530
*70 2/8	13 4/8 14 2/8	6 2/8 6 1/8	9 1/8	Converse County	WY	Jeffrey S. Nibbelink	2008	3530
70 2/8	12 4/8 12 4/8	6 2/8 6 2/8	10 4/8	Carter County	MT	Stephen J. Hathcock	2008	3530
70 2/8	14 4/8 14 4/8	5 6/8 5 4/8	10 1/8	Adams County	ND	Jeff Johnson	2008	3530
*70 2/8	13 6/8 13 6/8	5 6/8 6 0/8	10 6/8	Harding County	NM	Don Urbielewicz	2009	3530
*70 2/8	13 0/8 12 7/8	5 5/8 5 4/8	7 7/8	Union County	NM	Cory M. Lang	2009	3530
*70 2/8	13 1/8 13 0/8	5 4/8 5 4/8	10 0/8	Harding County	SD	Mark Grote	2009	3530
70 2/8	12 6/8 12 4/8	5 7/8 6 0/8	10 6/8	Campbell County	WY	Allen Mann	2009	3530
70 2/8	13 6/8 13 5/8	5 3/8 5 2/8	11 0/8	Weston County	WY	Craig Overman	2009	3530
*70 2/8	14 5/8 14 4/8	5 3/8 5 3/8	8 1/8	Converse County	WY	Lowell Thomas	2009	3530
*70 2/8	15 0/8 14 4/8	5 6/8 6 1/8	8 5/8	Butte County	SD	Robert C. Speirs	2009	3530

PRONGHORN

Minimum Score 67   Continued

SCORE	LENGTH OF R HORN L	CIRCUMFERENCE R OF BASE L	INSIDE SPREAD	AREA	STATE/ PROVINCE	HUNTER'S NAME	DATE	RANK
70 2/8	14 3/8 14 1/8	5 7/8 5 7/8	10 6/8	Converse County	WY	Ronald Rockwell	2009	3530
70 2/8	14 4/8 14 5/8	5 7/8 5 7/8	8 3/8	Campbell County	WY	Tim D. Norton	2010	3530
*70 2/8	12 7/8 12 7/8	5 7/8 5 6/8	9 0/8	Converse County	WY	Matt Buszka	2010	3530
70 0/8	13 1/8 13 1/8	6 1/8 6 1/8	13 1/8	Butte County	SD	Wayne Wanhanen	1961	3711
70 0/8	13 6/8 13 7/8	5 6/8 5 6/8	11 4/8	Garfield County	MT	Paul M. Ramsey	1963	3711
70 0/8	14 0/8 14 0/8	5 3/8 5 3/8	9 5/8	Harding County	SD	Ira Hilburn	1964	3711
70 0/8	13 1/8 13 4/8	5 6/8 5 6/8	9 0/8	Morton County	ND	Paul R. Shannon	1971	3711
70 0/8	13 4/8 13 2/8	6 1/8 6 0/8	12 5/8	Pennington County	SD	Thomas Huitfeldt	1974	3711
70 0/8	13 1/8 13 2/8	5 7/8 5 6/8	8 2/8	Dawes County	NE	Allan Mintken	1974	3711
70 0/8	13 4/8 13 7/8	5 4/8 5 5/8	9 0/8	Rio Grande County	CO	Arthur M. Davis	1975	3711
70 0/8	13 7/8 13 6/8	5 5/8 5 5/8	12 5/8	Sweetwater County	WY	Gerri Risley	1981	3711
70 0/8	14 5/8 14 6/8	5 6/8 5 5/8	7 1/8	Humboldt County	NV	Wally Lopey	1981	3711
70 0/8	12 5/8 12 3/8	5 4/8 5 4/8	7 5/8	Moffat County	CO	Charles A. Nicholas	1981	3711
70 0/8	13 2/8 13 2/8	6 0/8 5 7/8	10 5/8	Natrona County	WY	Mark A. Smith	1981	3711
70 0/8	13 6/8 13 6/8	5 4/8 5 4/8	8 7/8	White Pine County	NV	Richard Fillman	1982	3711
70 0/8	13 0/8 13 0/8	5 7/8 5 6/8	12 4/8	Converse County	WY	Steven A. Wolff	1982	3711
70 0/8	13 6/8 14 1/8	5 7/8 5 7/8	8 1/8	Carbon County	WY	Ron Breitsprecher	1982	3711
70 0/8	13 7/8 13 6/8	5 4/8 5 5/8	10 3/8	Sargent County	ND	Terry Freehauf	1983	3711
70 0/8	13 1/8 13 1/8	5 7/8 5 6/8	9 4/8	Converse County	WY	Dean Taylor	1983	3711
70 0/8	13 5/8 13 5/8	5 7/8 5 5/8	9 2/8	Perkins County	SD	Jeffery Rieker	1983	3711
70 0/8	13 3/8 12 5/8	6 1/8 6 1/8	8 0/8	Rosebud County	MT	Daniel A. Nielsen	1983	3711
70 0/8	13 2/8 13 2/8	6 0/8 6 0/8	7 2/8	Custer County	ID	Brad Chilton	1984	3711
70 0/8	14 5/8 14 0/8	5 6/8 5 6/8	5 7/8	Moffat County	CO	Dale Drilling	1984	3711
70 0/8	13 4/8 13 4/8	5 5/8 5 4/8	9 4/8	Moffat County	CO	Todd Clyncke	1984	3711
70 0/8	12 4/8 12 4/8	5 7/8 5 7/8	8 3/8	Converse County	WY	Bill Doemland	1984	3711
70 0/8	13 4/8 13 4/8	5 4/8 5 3/8	11 6/8	Slope County	ND	Gene D. Davis	1984	3711
70 0/8	12 0/8 12 0/8	6 1/8 6 0/8	7 4/8	Elko County	NV	Ted Simpson	1985	3711
70 0/8	13 3/8 13 0/8	6 1/8 6 0/8	8 6/8	Converse County	WY	David Stuhr	1985	3711
70 0/8	13 0/8 12 7/8	5 4/8 5 3/8	10 1/8	Converse County	WY	Dean Herschede	1985	3711
70 0/8	13 2/8 14 4/8	6 0/8 6 0/8	9 7/8	Carter County	MT	James Jessen	1985	3711
70 0/8	14 6/8 15 0/8	5 5/8 5 5/8	14 5/8	Carbon County	WY	David Pawlicki	1986	3711
70 0/8	13 1/8 13 1/8	5 6/8 5 6/8	7 6/8	Converse County	WY	John Unser	1986	3711
70 0/8	13 2/8 13 1/8	6 2/8 6 2/8	9 6/8	Moffat County	CO	John Hunter	1987	3711
70 0/8	13 3/8 13 7/8	6 1/8 6 1/8	9 0/8	Converse County	WY	Bruce Warberg	1987	3711
70 0/8	14 2/8 14 0/8	5 3/8 5 3/8	9 4/8	Moffat County	CO	Roger Gipple	1988	3711
70 0/8	14 4/8 14 0/8	5 4/8 5 2/8	9 4/8	Converse County	WY	George A. Zanoni	1988	3711
70 0/8	14 3/8 14 3/8	5 3/8 5 1/8	11 2/8	Moffat County	CO	Glenn Pritchard	1988	3711
70 0/8	13 5/8 13 6/8	5 6/8 5 6/8	11 3/8	Dunn County	ND	Rick Regeth	1988	3711
70 0/8	13 6/8 13 4/8	5 7/8 5 7/8	8 2/8	Sweetwater County	WY	Dennis L. Shirley	1989	3711
70 0/8	15 3/8 14 6/8	5 7/8 5 5/8	8 6/8	Custer County	ID	Matt March, Jr.	1989	3711
70 0/8	13 2/8 13 7/8	5 6/8 5 6/8	7 7/8	Sweetwater County	WY	Larry Norris	1989	3711
70 0/8	12 2/8 12 5/8	5 7/8 6 0/8	9 3/8	Moffat County	CO	Bob Solimena	1989	3711
70 0/8	13 6/8 13 7/8	5 6/8 5 4/8	8 4/8	McKenzie County	ND	Michael Lee	1989	3711
70 0/8	12 5/8 12 2/8	5 6/8 5 6/8	11 5/8	Rosebud County	MT	Shawn A. Wahl	1989	3711
70 0/8	13 7/8 13 6/8	5 6/8 5 5/8	9 5/8	Moffat County	CO	Merritt C. Compton	1990	3711
70 0/8	13 1/8 13 0/8	6 3/8 6 3/8	11 0/8	Harney County	OR	Raymon L. Johnson	1990	3711
70 0/8	12 2/8 12 0/8	6 0/8 6 0/8	10 0/8	Union County	NM	James R. "Ron" Barnett	1991	3711
70 0/8	13 0/8 13 0/8	6 2/8 6 2/8	10 1/8	Modoc County	CA	Monty Clemmer	1991	3711
70 0/8	13 3/8 13 4/8	5 5/8 5 4/8	8 6/8	Butte County	SD	Bryce Lambley	1991	3711
70 0/8	12 1/8 12 3/8	6 1/8 6 2/8	10 4/8	Campbell County	WY	Gary R. Shields	1991	3711
70 0/8	12 6/8 12 6/8	6 2/8 6 4/8	9 1/8	Campbell County	WY	Robert A. Carman	1991	3711
70 0/8	13 7/8 14 1/8	5 7/8 5 7/8	12 0/8	Harney County	OR	Dwight Griffin	1991	3711
70 0/8	11 7/8 12 0/8	6 1/8 6 0/8	9 6/8	Powder River County	MT	Ronald J. Watt	1991	3711
70 0/8	14 2/8 14 2/8	5 5/8 5 4/8	11 3/8	Millard County	UT	Steven Bowen Plett	1992	3711
70 0/8	13 5/8 13 3/8	5 6/8 5 6/8	7 7/8	Moffat County	CO	Ren A. Leitner	1992	3711
70 0/8	14 6/8 15 1/8	5 5/8 5 4/8	7 6/8	Moffat County	CO	Steve Barnhill	1992	3711
70 0/8	12 6/8 12 3/8	6 0/8 6 1/8	8 0/8	Millard County	UT	Clark A. Moss	1992	3711
70 0/8	13 6/8 13 4/8	5 3/8 5 3/8	9 5/8	Yavapai County	AZ	Rick Peebles	1992	3711
70 0/8	13 6/8 13 5/8	5 7/8 5 6/8	11 6/8	Converse County	WY	Trent Findley	1992	3711
70 0/8	13 7/8 14 1/8	5 5/8 5 6/8	9 0/8	Magrath	ALB	Cameron Cook	1992	3711
70 0/8	13 4/8 13 4/8	6 0/8 6 0/8	11 4/8	Box Elder County	UT	Andrew Parker	1992	3711
70 0/8	12 5/8 13 0/8	6 2/8 6 2/8	10 5/8	Carbon County	WY	J. David Cole	1993	3711
70 0/8	13 5/8 13 4/8	6 4/8 6 3/8	13 2/8	Union County	NM	Wayne A. Naumann	1993	3711
70 0/8	14 2/8 13 5/8	5 6/8 5 6/8	11 3/8	Torrance County	NM	Dennis A. Muirhead	1993	3711
70 0/8	14 1/8 14 0/8	5 5/8 6 0/8	10 4/8	Carbon County	WY	Jeffrey Mueller	1994	3711
70 0/8	14 0/8 13 3/8	6 3/8 6 2/8	10 6/8	Sweetwater County	WY	Reggie Alcorn	1994	3711
70 0/8	13 1/8 13 2/8	5 5/8 5 5/8	9 5/8	Campbell County	WY	Randy Springborn	1994	3711
70 0/8	15 0/8 14 5/8	5 6/8 5 5/8	8 4/8	Converse County	WY	D. Michael Taylor	1994	3711
70 0/8	14 1/8 14 4/8	5 7/8 5 7/8	8 6/8	Niobrara County	WY	Floyd L. Foslien	1994	3711
70 0/8	13 2/8 13 5/8	5 7/8 5 7/8	9 2/8	McKenzie County	ND	Randy Kjorstad	1994	3711
70 0/8	14 2/8 14 2/8	5 6/8 5 6/8	8 4/8	Custer County	MT	Kenneth M. Backes	1994	3711
70 0/8	13 6/8 14 0/8	5 5/8 5 5/8	9 1/8	Platte County	WY	Erich Bernd Scheinpflug	1994	3711
70 0/8	14 0/8 14 0/8	5 5/8 5 5/8	15 5/8	Campbell County	WY	Troy Pickett	1994	3711
70 0/8	13 3/8 13 4/8	6 1/8 6 1/8	10 5/8	Sioux County	NE	Michael Judas	1994	3711
70 0/8	13 5/8 13 5/8	5 3/8 5 3/8	11 6/8	Moffat County	CO	Chuck Adams	1995	3711
70 0/8	14 0/8 14 0/8	5 3/8 5 4/8	7 3/8	Moffat County	CO	David Parri	1995	3711
70 0/8	13 1/8 12 5/8	6 1/8 6 1/8	12 4/8	Weld County	CO	Timothy Bradley	1995	3711
70 0/8	13 7/8 13 7/8	5 5/8 5 6/8	10 0/8	Campbell County	WY	Ramon Neil Bell	1995	3711
70 0/8	12 3/8 12 7/8	6 7/8 6 7/8	9 5/8	Converse County	WY	Leroy Bassett	1995	3711
70 0/8	13 3/8 13 7/8	5 4/8 5 4/8	8 5/8	Converse County	WY	H. Dewey Thompson	1995	3711
70 0/8	13 6/8 13 6/8	5 2/8 5 2/8	8 4/8	Moffat County	CO	Thane Anderson	1995	3711
70 0/8	13 4/8 13 2/8	5 6/8 5 6/8	12 3/8	Harding County	SD	Jeff Poppenga	1995	3711
70 0/8	13 1/8 13 3/8	6 0/8 5 7/8	8 6/8	Converse County	WY	Gregory White	1995	3711
70 0/8	14 1/8 14 1/8	5 5/8 5 5/8	8 4/8	Wayne County	UT	Thomas R. Hudson	1996	3711
70 0/8	14 0/8 14 0/8	6 5/8 6 5/8	12 3/8	Sweetwater County	WY	Clifford W. Rockhold	1996	3711
70 0/8	13 6/8 13 6/8	6 0/8 6 0/8	9 4/8	Moffat County	CO	Wally Schaub	1996	3711
70 0/8	14 1/8 14 1/8	5 7/8 5 7/8	10 1/8	Moffat County	CO	Jeffrey Lyn Synyard	1996	3711
70 0/8	15 1/8 14 4/8	5 7/8 4 7/8	9 4/8	Curry County	NM	Jason Evans	1997	3711
70 0/8	13 7/8 12 5/8	6 0/8 5 7/8	10 4/8	Campbell County	WY	Patrick Cahill	1997	3711
70 0/8	13 0/8 13 2/8	6 6/8 6 3/8	11 2/8	Park County	CO	Spencer T. Esch	1998	3711
70 0/8	13 4/8 13 1/8	5 4/8 5 3/8	9 2/8	Wayne County	UT	Robert A. Patey	1998	3711
70 0/8	14 5/8 14 4/8	5 6/8 5 5/8	10 5/8	Carter County	MT	Willie Hettinger	1998	3711
70 0/8	12 7/8 12 5/8	5 7/8 5 7/8	8 4/8	Moffat County	CO	Frederick Winkelmann	1999	3711
70 0/8	12 4/8 12 7/8	5 7/8 5 6/8	7 2/8	Weld County	CO	Wade Hunt	1999	3711
70 0/8	14 0/8 13 5/8	6 0/8 5 6/8	9 3/8	Moffat County	CO	Robert W. Burnham, Jr.	1999	3711

849

PRONGHORN

Minimum Score 67 — Continued

SCORE	LENGTH OF R HORN L	CIRCUMFERENCE R OF BASE L	INSIDE SPREAD	AREA	STATE/ PROVINCE	HUNTER'S NAME	DATE	RANK
70 0/8	13 5/8 13 6/8	6 1/8 6 0/8	11 5/8	Gunnison County	CO	George H. Bock	1999	3711
70 0/8	14 2/8 14 2/8	5 3/8 5 4/8	9 3/8	Crook County	WY	Kevin Vail	1999	3711
70 0/8	12 6/8 12 5/8	6 1/8 6 2/8	11 5/8	White Pine County	NV	Jiri Hlavacek	2000	3711
70 0/8	15 4/8 14 4/8	5 3/8 5 3/8	8 1/8	Klamath County	OR	Brian Ferguson	2000	3711
70 0/8	14 1/8 14 1/8	5 7/8 5 7/8	11 6/8	Lemhi County	ID	Scott J. Douglass	2000	3711
70 0/8	12 7/8 13 0/8	6 0/8 5 7/8	8 1/8	Converse County	WY	Pat Lefemine	2000	3711
70 0/8	14 3/8 14 4/8	5 5/8 5 5/8	13 7/8	Butte County	SD	Jon Hardesty	2000	3711
70 0/8	13 4/8 14 6/8	5 4/8 5 4/8	8 7/8	Converse County	WY	Robert Dowen	2001	3711
70 0/8	13 4/8 13 4/8	6 1/8 6 1/8	9 5/8	Johnson County	WY	Darin Wayne Wells	2001	3711
70 0/8	12 5/8 12 5/8	5 7/8 5 5/8	8 4/8	Natrona County	WY	Gus Congemi	2001	3711
70 0/8	12 2/8 12 1/8	6 5/8 6 3/8	8 2/8	Washakie County	WY	Chris S. Moore	2001	3711
70 0/8	13 4/8 13 6/8	5 5/8 5 7/8	7 0/8	Natrona County	WY	Lora D. Engleman	2001	3711
70 0/8	13 4/8 13 2/8	5 6/8 5 4/8	11 3/8	Converse County	WY	Gary Kautz	2002	3711
70 0/8	12 3/8 12 3/8	6 1/8 6 1/8	8 2/8	Harney County	OR	Dave Creekmore	2002	3711
70 0/8	13 1/8 13 0/8	5 7/8 5 7/8	9 1/8	Johnson County	WY	Derrik Duchesneau	2003	3711
70 0/8	13 3/8 13 3/8	5 4/8 5 5/8	9 7/8	Rosebud County	MT	David Speral	2003	3711
70 0/8	12 4/8 12 5/8	5 5/8 5 5/8	12 6/8	Humboldt County	NV	Brian Casey	2004	3711
70 0/8	13 0/8 13 2/8	5 6/8 6 0/8	10 5/8	Carter County	MT	Brent Miller	2004	3711
70 0/8	13 0/8 13 0/8	5 6/8 5 6/8	10 6/8	Weld County	CO	David L. Shelton	2004	3711
70 0/8	13 4/8 13 3/8	6 3/8 6 1/8	11 6/8	Carbon County	WY	Clay Evans	2004	3711
70 0/8	13 0/8 13 1/8	6 1/8 6 0/8	9 3/8	Carbon County	UT	Jerome Pehler, Jr.	2004	3711
70 0/8	13 7/8 14 0/8	6 0/8 5 7/8	8 7/8	S. Saskatchewan River	ALB	Cameron Foss	2004	3711
70 0/8	13 4/8 13 6/8	6 0/8 5 7/8	11 1/8	Garfield County	MT	Sonny Templeton	2004	3711
70 0/8	14 7/8 14 6/8	5 6/8 5 6/8	11 3/8	Perkins County	SD	Ray Hybertson	2004	3711
70 0/8	12 7/8 13 0/8	5 6/8 5 6/8	10 2/8	Butte County	SD	Reginald E. Faber, Jr.	2004	3711
*70 0/8	11 7/8 12 5/8	6 1/8 6 3/8	10 3/8	Converse County	WY	Eric Schack	2005	3711
70 0/8	14 0/8 14 0/8	5 3/8 5 3/8	9 4/8	Harding County	SD	Scott G. Hettinger	2005	3711
70 0/8	13 6/8 13 7/8	5 5/8 5 4/8	11 0/8	Moffat County	CO	Michael L. Hackett	2006	3711
*70 0/8	13 1/8 13 1/8	5 7/8 5 7/8	9 3/8	Carter County	MT	Mark Kayser	2006	3711
70 0/8	12 3/8 12 5/8	6 3/8 6 4/8	8 0/8	Moffat County	CO	Joseph Fedorko	2006	3711
70 0/8	12 5/8 12 5/8	6 3/8 6 1/8	8 7/8	Sherman County	KS	Marc Gray	2006	3711
70 0/8	14 1/8 14 0/8	5 4/8 5 4/8	8 1/8	Petroleum County	MT	John H. Holt	2007	3711
70 0/8	14 3/8 14 5/8	5 6/8 5 3/8	10 3/8	Natrona County	WY	Tom Nelson	2007	3711
*70 0/8	13 5/8 14 1/8	5 5/8 5 4/8	9 4/8	Campbell County	WY	Marty Edwards	2007	3711
70 0/8	13 4/8 13 3/8	6 2/8 6 1/8	12 0/8	Powder River County	MT	Kurt V. Howell	2007	3711
70 0/8	13 0/8 13 0/8	6 0/8 6 0/8	7 4/8	Petroleum County	MT	Larry Fitzpatrick	2007	3711
70 0/8	14 5/8 14 4/8	5 4/8 5 3/8	8 6/8	Dunn County	ND	Dustin Schmidt	2007	3711
*70 0/8	13 0/8 13 3/8	5 7/8 5 7/8	10 0/8	Cherry County	NE	David J. Nicolai	2007	3711
70 0/8	13 3/8 13 6/8	5 6/8 5 7/8	9 5/8	Moffat County	CO	David J. Barrow	2008	3711
70 0/8	12 5/8 13 1/8	6 0/8 5 7/8	11 4/8	Logan County	CO	Joseph D. Yang	2008	3711
*70 0/8	13 4/8 13 5/8	6 0/8 6 0/8	7 5/8	Sioux County	NE	Eric P. Garton	2008	3711
70 0/8	14 1/8 13 7/8	6 1/8 6 1/8	14 0/8	Moffat County	CO	Clay J. Evans	2008	3711
70 0/8	14 0/8 13 7/8	6 0/8 5 7/8	9 4/8	Natrona County	WY	Donna Turay	2008	3711
70 0/8	13 6/8 14 0/8	5 6/8 5 6/8	11 4/8	Campbell County	WY	Irvin Prough	2008	3711
*70 0/8	14 1/8 14 2/8	5 7/8 5 7/8	9 4/8	Converse County	WY	Ralph Lowell Thomas	2008	3711
*70 0/8	13 1/8 13 0/8	5 6/8 5 5/8	10 2/8	Harding County	SD	Myles McIntyre	2008	3711
70 0/8	13 6/8 13 6/8	6 0/8 6 0/8	9 6/8	Powder River County	MT	Thomas J. Schlough	2008	3711
70 0/8	13 5/8 13 5/8	5 7/8 5 4/8	10 0/8	Converse County	WY	Jerry Becay	2009	3711
70 0/8	14 0/8 13 7/8	5 6/8 5 6/8	7 4/8	Moffat County	CO	Scott Wakefield	2009	3711
*70 0/8	13 0/8 13 0/8	6 1/8 6 1/8	9 2/8	Carbon County	WY	Ryan P. Malone	2009	3711
*70 0/8	13 4/8 14 7/8	5 6/8 5 7/8	13 4/8	Converse County	WY	Bill McGrath	2009	3711
70 0/8	13 1/8 13 4/8	6 2/8 6 2/8	7 7/8	Powder River County	MT	Jack Smith	2009	3711
70 0/8	13 0/8 13 4/8	5 7/8 5 7/8	8 3/8	Powder River County	MT	Bob Dowen	2009	3711
70 0/8	13 4/8 13 2/8	5 5/8 5 5/8	8 2/8	S. Saskatchewan River	ALB	Bob Bainbridge	2009	3711
*70 0/8	14 1/8 14 3/8	5 7/8 5 7/8	7 0/8	Cherry County	NE	David J. Nicolai	2009	3711
70 0/8	14 4/8 13 7/8	5 5/8 5 6/8	6 3/8	Pershing County	NV	Sidney D. Kelly	2010	3711
70 0/8	13 2/8 13 2/8	6 1/8 6 1/8	9 0/8	Campbell County	WY	Joe Ness	2010	3711
70 0/8	13 3/8 13 4/8	5 5/8 5 5/8	9 1/8	Natrona County	WY	Chandler Jacob	2010	3711
*70 0/8	14 2/8 14 3/8	6 2/8 5 7/8	10 2/8	Cimarron County	OK	Harley Coleman	2010	3711
69 6/8	12 6/8 12 6/8	6 6/8 6 6/8	11 4/8	Custer County	ID	Dr. Richard Hagerman	1966	3862
69 6/8	13 4/8 13 4/8	6 2/8 6 2/8	10 5/8	Carbon County	WY	Maurice Savora	1972	3862
69 6/8	13 6/8 13 5/8	5 6/8 5 6/8	9 0/8	Converse County	WY	Edward Pitchkites	1973	3862
69 6/8	14 6/8 14 6/8	5 2/8 5 2/8	10 2/8	Perkins County	SD	Marvin R. Bohnet	1974	3862
69 6/8	14 4/8 14 5/8	5 2/8 5 4/8	10 0/8	Meade County	SD	David Martin	1976	3862
69 6/8	14 0/8 14 2/8	5 2/8 5 0/8	9 0/8	Sublette County	WY	John Kelly	1977	3862
69 6/8	14 5/8 14 5/8	5 3/8 5 3/8	13 4/8	Coconino County	AZ	Robin Underdown	1978	3862
69 6/8	13 0/8 12 5/8	5 6/8 5 7/8	9 5/8	Carbon County	WY	John L. Craig	1978	3862
69 6/8	13 0/8 12 7/8	6 0/8 6 0/8	8 6/8	Arapahoe County	CO	Wayne E. Watson, Sr.	1979	3862
69 6/8	13 2/8 13 2/8	5 4/8 5 4/8	10 0/8	Arapahoe County	CO	Steve Cosper	1980	3862
69 6/8	13 3/8 13 5/8	5 1/8 5 1/8	10 4/8	Converse County	WY	Rickey Melde	1981	3862
69 6/8	13 5/8 13 6/8	5 7/8 5 5/8	9 0/8	Converse County	WY	Jeff Reynolds	1982	3862
69 6/8	13 6/8 13 7/8	5 6/8 5 5/8	9 7/8	Moffat County	CO	Albert Ahlrich	1982	3862
69 6/8	14 0/8 13 5/8	6 2/8 6 2/8	8 4/8	Siskiyou County	CA	Scott Walker	1983	3862
69 6/8	13 6/8 13 6/8	5 4/8 5 3/8	8 4/8	Moffat County	CO	Gary Decker	1983	3862
69 6/8	13 2/8 13 2/8	5 4/8 5 3/8	10 7/8	Moffat County	CO	Richard Gearhart	1983	3862
69 6/8	11 7/8 11 6/8	6 2/8 6 2/8	9 4/8	Moffat County	CO	Cathy Lee Jordon	1983	3862
69 6/8	13 4/8 13 1/8	6 2/8 6 2/8	9 7/8	Moffat County	CO	Galen J. Wertz	1983	3862
69 6/8	14 0/8 13 2/8	5 6/8 5 6/8	10 0/8	Converse County	WY	Jeff Davis	1983	3862
69 6/8	13 5/8 13 6/8	6 0/8 6 0/8	15 4/8	Sweetwater County	WY	Bill Clink	1985	3862
69 6/8	13 1/8 13 2/8	5 7/8 5 7/8	10 3/8	Sweetwater County	WY	Michael Chaffin	1985	3862
69 6/8	14 6/8 15 0/8	5 7/8 6 0/8	13 6/8	Modoc County	CA	Bill Golden	1985	3862
69 6/8	14 0/8 14 0/8	5 5/8 5 4/8	10 6/8	Powder River County	MT	David Fitton	1985	3862
69 6/8	13 2/8 13 0/8	5 7/8 6 0/8	10 4/8	Moffat County	CO	Howard Tieden	1986	3862
69 6/8	13 5/8 13 6/8	5 6/8 5 6/8	10 0/8	McCone County	MT	Mitch Kottas	1986	3862
69 6/8	12 2/8 12 3/8	5 4/8 5 6/8	8 0/8	Rio Arriba County	NM	Derek Tierney	1987	3862
69 6/8	12 6/8 12 6/8	6 3/8 6 4/8	10 5/8	Moffat County	CO	Dale Elliott	1987	3862
69 6/8	13 5/8 13 5/8	6 0/8 6 1/8	13 1/8	Fremont County	WY	Keith L. Frick	1987	3862
69 6/8	14 7/8 14 6/8	6 0/8 5 7/8	9 5/8	McKinley County	NM	Travis Taylor	1987	3862
69 6/8	13 1/8 14 4/8	6 1/8 6 2/8	14 5/8	Moffat County	CO	Wendy Decker	1988	3862
69 6/8	13 6/8 13 4/8	5 3/8 5 3/8	9 2/8	Moffat County	CO	Alvin Tieden	1988	3862
69 6/8	14 2/8 14 1/8	5 2/8 5 3/8	10 1/8	Converse County	WY	Carolyn Siebrasse Zanoni	1988	3862
69 6/8	13 7/8 14 0/8	5 7/8 5 6/8	13 6/8	Manyberries	ALB	Randy Bernier	1989	3862
69 6/8	13 3/8 13 3/8	5 1/8 5 1/8	9 4/8	Brewster County	TX	Thomas J. Buxton	1989	3862
69 6/8	13 6/8 13 6/8	6 1/8 6 1/8	10 4/8	Niobrara County	WY	Jim Jepson	1990	3862
69 6/8	13 6/8 13 6/8	6 0/8 5 7/8	8 0/8	Campbell County	WY	Mark E. Heberlein	1990	3862

850

PRONGHORN

Minimum Score 67
Continued

SCORE	LENGTH OF R HORN L	CIRCUMFERENCE R OF BASE L	INSIDE SPREAD	AREA	STATE/ PROVINCE	HUNTER'S NAME	DATE	RANK
69 6/8	14 1/8 14 4/8	5 6/8 5 4/8	13 7/8	Fergus County	MT	Kelly Norskog	1990	3862
69 6/8	15 1/8 15 1/8	5 4/8 5 4/8	10 3/8	Valencia County	NM	Frank Montano	1991	3862
69 6/8	12 5/8 12 6/8	5 5/8 5 6/8	7 0/8	Blaine County	ID	John Wells	1991	3862
69 6/8	13 2/8 13 2/8	6 0/8 5 7/8	9 1/8	Natrona County	WY	David J. Steger	1991	3862
69 6/8	13 5/8 13 4/8	6 0/8 6 0/8	8 4/8	Malheur County	OR	Fredrick J. Johnson	1991	3862
69 6/8	13 2/8 13 2/8	6 1/8 6 0/8	11 2/8	Larimer County	CO	Randy Brian Snyder	1991	3862
69 6/8	13 5/8 13 6/8	5 7/8 5 7/8	12 5/8	Converse County	WY	Shirley Jochmann	1991	3862
69 6/8	13 7/8 14 0/8	5 6/8 5 6/8	10 1/8	Garfield County	MT	Peter J. Mancl	1991	3862
69 6/8	14 0/8 13 4/8	5 6/8 5 6/8	9 4/8	Beaverhead County	MT	Jim Muzynoski	1991	3862
69 6/8	13 0/8 13 0/8	6 0/8 6 0/8	7 2/8	Bowman County	ND	Jim Hicks	1991	3862
69 6/8	12 2/8 12 2/8	6 1/8 6 0/8	9 0/8	Carbon County	WY	Mark Wardlaw	1992	3862
69 6/8	13 6/8 13 3/8	5 5/8 5 5/8	10 0/8	Sweetwater County	WY	Andrew Tkach	1992	3862
69 6/8	12 1/8 12 4/8	6 1/8 6 1/8	7 3/8	Converse County	WY	Troy McGinnis	1992	3862
69 6/8	13 2/8 13 3/8	5 4/8 5 5/8	9 7/8	Billings County	ND	Richard C. Lautenschlager	1992	3862
69 6/8	13 4/8 13 4/8	5 6/8 5 6/8	10 7/8	Crook County	WY	Robert Michelena	1992	3862
69 6/8	13 1/8 13 2/8	5 4/8 5 3/8	9 7/8	Moffat County	CO	Jon P. Hollabaugh	1993	3862
69 6/8	13 0/8 12 4/8	5 6/8 5 6/8	9 6/8	Moffat County	CO	Gary L. Biles	1993	3862
69 6/8	13 6/8 13 6/8	5 4/8 5 6/8	11 6/8	Moffat County	CO	Chad Johnson	1993	3862
69 6/8	12 7/8 12 7/8	6 1/8 6 1/8	8 4/8	Moffat County	CO	Karl Randolph	1993	3862
69 6/8	13 4/8 13 1/8	6 1/8 6 0/8	11 3/8	Bowman County	ND	Michael Whiteside	1993	3862
69 6/8	14 6/8 13 2/8	5 5/8 5 6/8	10 5/8	Bowman County	ND	Dan Thiel	1993	3862
69 6/8	15 0/8 15 4/8	5 6/8 5 6/8	9 1/8	Stanley County	SD	Robert G. Barden	1993	3862
69 6/8	14 6/8 14 6/8	5 6/8 5 6/8	13 1/8	Lake County	OR	Donald R. Pritchett	1993	3862
69 6/8	12 1/8 12 5/8	6 3/8 6 2/8	10 5/8	Coconino County	AZ	Ernie Martinez	1994	3862
69 6/8	13 4/8 13 2/8	5 5/8 5 5/8	11 2/8	Yavapai County	AZ	Allen King II	1994	3862
69 6/8	14 1/8 13 6/8	5 5/8 5 5/8	11 2/8	Campbell County	WY	Thomas E. Lawrence	1994	3862
69 6/8	13 5/8 13 4/8	6 0/8 5 7/8	10 2/8	Converse County	WY	Ronald D. Stoynoff	1994	3862
69 6/8	14 0/8 14 0/8	5 5/8 5 3/8	13 6/8	Converse County	WY	Phil Perry	1994	3862
69 6/8	13 3/8 13 4/8	5 5/8 5 5/8	10 4/8	Campbell County	WY	James C. Campbell, Jr.	1994	3862
69 6/8	14 4/8 14 2/8	5 1/8 5 1/8	8 1/8	Keya Paha County	NE	Clay Beck	1994	3862
69 6/8	13 1/8 13 1/8	6 4/8 6 3/8	10 4/8	Converse County	WY	Harold Osborne	1994	3862
69 6/8	12 7/8 13 0/8	5 4/8 5 5/8	8 6/8	Park County	MT	George Kamps	1994	3862
69 6/8	13 3/8 13 5/8	5 6/8 5 6/8	10 0/8	Campbell County	WY	Jerry Bodar	1994	3862
69 6/8	12 4/8 12 2/8	6 2/8 6 0/8	8 6/8	Moffat County	CO	Vince Migliorato	1995	3862
69 6/8	12 7/8 12 5/8	6 2/8 6 2/8	9 0/8	Converse County	WY	Ray Maudsley	1995	3862
69 6/8	13 7/8 13 5/8	5 7/8 5 7/8	6 7/8	Yavapai County	AZ	Ron Eckerman	1995	3862
69 6/8	14 2/8 13 1/8	6 1/8 6 3/8	9 6/8	Moffat County	CO	Bill McDonald	1995	3862
69 6/8	13 4/8 13 4/8	5 5/8 5 5/8	7 2/8	Moffat County	CO	Kevin Bertsch	1995	3862
69 6/8	13 7/8 13 7/8	5 4/8 5 4/8	10 3/8	Beaverhead County	MT	Raymond L. Gross	1995	3862
69 6/8	14 2/8 14 2/8	5 4/8 5 4/8	9 2/8	Klamath County	OR	Michael W. Schulte	1996	3862
69 6/8	12 4/8 12 5/8	6 0/8 6 1/8	8 6/8	Weld County	CO	Ed Fanchin	1996	3862
69 6/8	13 5/8 13 3/8	5 4/8 5 4/8	9 6/8	Clark County	ID	Max Heberling	1996	3862
69 6/8	12 6/8 12 6/8	5 5/8 5 4/8	13 6/8	Natrona County	WY	James Mathias	1996	3862
69 6/8	14 2/8 14 0/8	5 6/8 5 6/8	8 7/8	Weld County	CO	Philip Wray	1996	3862
69 6/8	13 2/8 13 5/8	5 6/8 5 5/8	7 4/8	Bowman County	ND	Jon Brewer	1996	3862
69 6/8	12 0/8 13 5/8	6 0/8 5 7/8	10 7/8	Sweetwater County	WY	Mark Preston	1997	3862
69 6/8	12 6/8 12 5/8	5 5/8 5 7/8	8 1/8	Clark County	ID	Thomas Thiel	1997	3862
69 6/8	14 0/8 13 3/8	5 6/8 5 6/8	8 0/8	Big Horn County	WY	Jerome D. Larson	1997	3862
69 6/8	11 7/8 12 1/8	5 5/8 5 5/8	10 4/8	Converse County	WY	Eddie Wynne	1997	3862
69 6/8	13 3/8 13 3/8	5 7/8 5 7/8	9 3/8	Powder River County	MT	Lesley Strunk	1997	3862
69 6/8	12 3/8 12 5/8	6 5/8 6 2/8	11 1/8	Campbell County	WY	Tom Stapf	1997	3862
69 6/8	13 0/8 12 6/8	5 7/8 5 7/8	10 0/8	Moffat County	CO	Mike Dziekan	1998	3862
69 6/8	12 3/8 12 4/8	6 1/8 6 2/8	11 0/8	Moffat County	CO	Eugene Ray, Jr.	1998	3862
69 6/8	14 3/8 14 3/8	6 0/8 5 7/8	6 4/8	Moffat County	CO	Ren Leitner	1998	3862
69 6/8	12 4/8 12 5/8	5 7/8 5 7/8	10 3/8	Converse County	WY	Clark M. Vickers	1998	3862
69 6/8	13 3/8 13 3/8	5 6/8 5 6/8	12 3/8	Weld County	CO	Mitch Arnold	1999	3862
69 6/8	12 7/8 13 1/8	5 6/8 5 6/8	9 3/8	Carbon County	UT	Rick T. Adams	1999	3862
69 6/8	15 4/8 13 4/8	5 4/8 5 4/8	9 5/8	Yavapai County	AZ	Joseph A. Lorenz	1999	3862
69 6/8	14 5/8 14 4/8	5 5/8 5 4/8	8 5/8	Perkins County	SD	Joel Beutow	1999	3862
69 6/8	14 0/8 14 0/8	5 3/8 5 3/8	6 4/8	Albany County	WY	Mark Anderson	1999	3862
69 6/8	13 0/8 13 1/8	6 0/8 5 7/8	11 2/8	Lassen County	CA	Shawn Copper	2000	3862
69 6/8	12 7/8 12 7/8	6 3/8 6 4/8	12 0/8	Weld County	CO	Dave Lucas	2000	3862
69 6/8	14 4/8 14 0/8	5 4/8 5 4/8	6 7/8	White Pine County	NV	Mike West	2000	3862
69 6/8	13 2/8 13 0/8	5 6/8 5 6/8	8 4/8	Yavapai County	AZ	Van Clark	2000	3862
69 6/8	13 3/8 13 0/8	5 7/8 5 7/8	11 0/8	Converse County	WY	Jeff Fitts	2000	3862
69 6/8	14 5/8 14 3/8	5 3/8 5 3/8	12 5/8	Weld County	CO	David S. Dye	2000	3862
69 6/8	13 4/8 13 5/8	6 0/8 6 0/8	6 5/8	Navajo County	AZ	Matthew Liljenquist	2001	3862
69 6/8	14 3/8 14 4/8	5 4/8 5 4/8	10 0/8	Phillips County	MT	Ron Kukus	2001	3862
69 6/8	13 2/8 13 1/8	6 5/8 6 4/8	9 4/8	Lewis & Clark County	MT	William Purcell	2001	3862
69 6/8	13 1/8 13 0/8	5 4/8 5 3/8	8 7/8	Lemhi County	ID	Benjamin C. Fahnholz	2002	3862
69 6/8	13 6/8 12 7/8	6 0/8 6 0/8	12 7/8	Torrance County	NM	Dennis Howell	2002	3862
69 6/8	13 5/8 13 1/8	6 0/8 6 0/8	9 1/8	Aden	ALB	David A. Little	2002	3862
69 6/8	13 4/8 13 4/8	5 7/8 5 6/8	8 2/8	Wheatland County	MT	Tommy Langston	2002	3862
69 6/8	11 4/8 12 0/8	6 2/8 6 1/8	13 4/8	Custer County	MT	Bill Wright	2002	3862
69 6/8	13 3/8 13 2/8	6 2/8 6 2/8	10 0/8	Natrona County	WY	Kenton Kimble	2002	3862
69 6/8	14 5/8 14 5/8	5 4/8 5 4/8	9 4/8	Carter County	MT	DuWayne M. Larson	2002	3862
69 6/8	14 0/8 14 2/8	5 7/8 5 5/8	11 2/8	White Pine County	NV	Steven E. Sheehy	2003	3862
69 6/8	12 6/8 12 6/8	5 6/8 5 5/8	9 0/8	Park County	CO	Spencer Esch	2003	3862
69 6/8	13 3/8 13 5/8	5 4/8 5 4/8	8 5/8	Natrona County	WY	Dave McFarlin	2003	3862
69 6/8	13 5/8 13 7/8	5 6/8 5 5/8	9 4/8	Musselshell County	MT	James Domaskin	2003	3862
69 6/8	13 0/8 13 2/8	5 7/8 5 6/8	12 2/8	Campbell County	WY	Les Malsch	2003	3862
69 6/8	13 7/8 13 7/8	5 6/8 5 6/8	10 1/8	Carbon County	WY	Jeff Fitts	2003	3862
69 6/8	14 1/8 14 0/8	5 2/8 5 2/8	9 7/8	Rio Grande County	CO	John R. Olson	2003	3862
69 6/8	12 3/8 12 4/8	6 1/8 6 1/8	7 2/8	Campbell County	WY	Mike Hagen	2003	3862
69 6/8	13 0/8 13 0/8	6 0/8 6 0/8	6 6/8	Converse County	WY	Rodney Breit	2003	3862
69 6/8	13 2/8 13 0/8	5 5/8 5 5/8	9 7/8	Powder River County	MT	Gary D. Sumwalt	2004	3862
69 6/8	13 2/8 13 2/8	5 7/8 5 7/8	8 4/8	Rosebud County	MT	Richard Gustafson	2005	3862
69 6/8	13 5/8 14 2/8	6 2/8 6 2/8	11 0/8	Weld County	CO	John C. Beckett, Jr.	2005	3862
69 6/8	12 1/8 11 7/8	5 3/8 5 4/8	9 0/8	Campbell County	WY	Steve Keithley	2005	3862
69 6/8	13 0/8 12 5/8	6 0/8 6 0/8	8 5/8	Weld County	CO	Garrett Bradley	2006	3862
69 6/8	14 2/8 14 3/8	5 6/8 5 5/8	8 5/8	Lemhi County	ID	Ben L. Fahnholz	2006	3862
69 6/8	13 2/8 13 5/8	5 7/8 5 6/8	12 4/8	Hettinger County	ND	Nick Axtman	2006	3862
69 6/8	13 6/8 14 1/8	5 4/8 5 4/8	8 2/8	Chaffee County	CO	Jesse W. Duncan	2007	3862
*69 6/8	13 5/8 13 0/8	5 6/8 5 7/8	7 6/8	Moffat County	CO	Nick Syvertson	2007	3862
69 6/8	13 6/8 13 4/8	6 0/8 5 6/8	13 2/8	Converse County	WY	Troy Sprenger	2007	3862

PRONGHORN

Minimum Score 67 — Continued

SCORE	LENGTH OF R HORN L	CIRCUMFERENCE R OF BASE L	INSIDE SPREAD	AREA	STATE/ PROVINCE	HUNTER'S NAME	DATE	RANK
69 6/8	14 1/8 14 2/8	5 4/8 5 5/8	7 7/8	Powder River County	MT	Ross Lazarov	2007	3862
69 6/8	13 5/8 13 3/8	5 6/8 5 6/8	7 2/8	Powder River County	MT	Martin E. Cain	2007	3862
69 6/8	15 1/8 14 4/8	5 1/8 5 2/8	13 6/8	Powder River County	MT	Steve Hendzel	2007	3862
69 6/8	13 3/8 13 6/8	6 7/8 6 3/8	15 5/8	Ziebach County	SD	Wesley Koehler	2007	3862
69 6/8	13 0/8 13 1/8	6 1/8 6 0/8	8 7/8	Campbell County	WY	Lorie Gleason	2007	3862
69 6/8	13 2/8 13 2/8	5 3/8 5 3/8	7 3/8	Buffalo County	SD	Dave M. Root	2008	3862
69 6/8	14 4/8 15 0/8	5 1/8 5 0/8	9 1/8	Laramie County	WY	Henry Scott Dare	2008	3862
*69 6/8	12 7/8 12 6/8	6 1/8 6 1/8	7 1/8	Navajo County	AZ	Wallace Shane Church	2008	3862
69 6/8	12 7/8 13 1/8	5 5/8 5 3/8	6 6/8	Converse County	WY	Ronald Rockwell	2008	3862
69 6/8	13 2/8 13 3/8	5 5/8 5 5/8	9 7/8	Campbell County	WY	Mike J. Houston	2008	3862
69 6/8	12 2/8 12 3/8	6 2/8 6 1/8	8 3/8	Niobrara County	WY	Thomas Hansen II	2008	3862
69 6/8	13 6/8 13 7/8	5 4/8 5 5/8	9 4/8	Harding County	SD	Jason E. Wiest	2008	3862
69 6/8	12 6/8 12 7/8	6 0/8 6 2/8	7 5/8	Campbell County	WY	Michael Friedenberg	2008	3862
*69 6/8	13 3/8 13 3/8	5 7/8 5 7/8	10 7/8	Las Animas County	CO	Thetis A. Gamberg	2009	3862
69 6/8	13 5/8 14 0/8	6 0/8 6 0/8	11 1/8	Carbon County	WY	Dustin J. Baird	2009	3862
69 6/8	14 3/8 14 1/8	5 3/8 5 1/8	10 2/8	Natrona County	WY	Dave Schulz	2009	3862
69 6/8	13 3/8 13 1/8	6 0/8 6 0/8	8 5/8	Butte County	SD	Todd Poskey	2009	3862
69 6/8	14 4/8 14 0/8	6 0/8 6 0/8	8 4/8	Laramie County	WY	Michael A. Lee	2009	3862
*69 6/8	13 0/8 13 1/8	5 4/8 5 5/8	11 5/8	Sioux County	NE	Bryce A. Luth	2009	3862
69 6/8	14 2/8 13 7/8	5 3/8 5 3/8	10 3/8	Johnson County	WY	Mike Kistler	2010	3862
*69 6/8	14 2/8 13 5/8	5 5/8 5 6/8	8 6/8	Sweetwater County	WY	Scott Satterthwaite	2010	3862
69 4/8	15 0/8 13 6/8	5 4/8 5 4/8	5 6/8	Rosebud County	MT	Glenn Gibson	1958	4014
69 4/8	14 4/8 14 2/8	5 2/8 5 2/8	10 6/8	Grant County	NM	Harold W. Groves	1960	4014
69 4/8	14 4/8 14 2/8	5 5/8 5 4/8	9 4/8	Washoe County	NV	Kenneth D. Allen	1972	4014
69 4/8	13 6/8 14 0/8	5 5/8 5 3/8	9 6/8	Washoe County	NV	Jack S. McCracken	1973	4014
69 4/8	13 2/8 13 0/8	6 0/8 6 0/8	10 6/8	Natrona County	WY	John Benetti	1973	4014
69 4/8	14 3/8 14 4/8	5 5/8 5 3/8	8 4/8	Park County	CO	Ed Zehner	1974	4014
69 4/8	12 0/8 12 4/8	6 0/8 6 1/8	9 1/8	Meade County	SD	Lelan L. Anderson	1974	4014
69 4/8	12 6/8 12 3/8	5 7/8 6 0/8	9 4/8	Lemhi County	ID	Randy J. Stephens	1980	4014
69 4/8	13 0/8 13 0/8	5 5/8 5 5/8	9 5/8	Jefferson County	ID	Ron Stacey	1981	4014
69 4/8	12 7/8 12 7/8	6 0/8 6 0/8	9 5/8	Moffat County	CO	Martin James Murrish	1981	4014
69 4/8	13 6/8 13 4/8	6 5/8 6 6/8	11 0/8	Carbon County	WY	Mike C. Montgomery	1981	4014
69 4/8	11 5/8 11 6/8	6 4/8 6 4/8	10 5/8	Converse County	WY	Ben Munoz	1981	4014
69 4/8	13 5/8 14 3/8	6 1/8 5 7/8	11 5/8	Converse County	WY	Dr. James R. Scott	1981	4014
69 4/8	12 6/8 12 7/8	5 7/8 5 7/8	9 5/8	Bowman County	ND	Ron Cizek	1982	4014
69 4/8	14 1/8 14 2/8	5 4/8 5 3/8	6 5/8	Converse County	WY	Ronnie Everett	1982	4014
69 4/8	14 0/8 14 0/8	5 6/8 5 5/8	9 6/8	Sweetwater County	WY	Ronnie Williams	1982	4014
69 4/8	13 4/8 13 7/8	5 4/8 5 4/8	8 1/8	Moffat County	CO	Rich Humpal	1982	4014
69 4/8	12 2/8 11 7/8	6 0/8 6 0/8	8 0/8	Beaver County	UT	Joey Leko	1982	4014
69 4/8	14 0/8 13 7/8	5 2/8 5 3/8	6 1/8	Converse County	WY	Jim Wilbur	1983	4014
69 4/8	13 4/8 12 4/8	6 1/8 6 1/8	10 5/8	Natrona County	WY	Paul Persano	1984	4014
69 4/8	12 7/8 13 1/8	5 2/8 5 2/8	7 3/8	Moffat County	CO	Roy V. Roig	1984	4014
69 4/8	14 1/8 14 2/8	6 0/8 5 7/8	15 0/8	Fergus County	MT	James W. Southworth	1984	4014
69 4/8	13 6/8 14 7/8	5 7/8 5 7/8	11 6/8	Sweetwater County	WY	Glenn E. Hisey	1985	4014
69 4/8	12 6/8 12 5/8	6 0/8 6 1/8	7 3/8	Sweetwater County	WY	Rod Knight	1985	4014
69 4/8	13 5/8 13 2/8	5 2/8 5 2/8	8 3/8	Converse County	WY	Samuel M. Durham	1985	4014
69 4/8	13 3/8 13 0/8	5 6/8 5 6/8	13 2/8	Billings County	ND	Pat Caroline	1985	4014
69 4/8	12 5/8 12 5/8	5 6/8 5 6/8	8 3/8	Uintah County	UT	Rob Johnston	1986	4014
69 4/8	13 2/8 13 2/8	5 6/8 5 5/8	8 6/8	Sublette County	WY	John Cheese	1987	4014
69 4/8	13 7/8 13 6/8	5 2/8 5 2/8	10 2/8	Musselshell County	MT	Jeff Matson	1987	4014
69 4/8	13 2/8 13 2/8	5 7/8 5 6/8	11 4/8	Converse County	WY	John A. Driver	1987	4014
69 4/8	14 2/8 14 1/8	6 0/8 5 7/8	10 6/8	Carbon County	WY	Steven Perkins	1988	4014
69 4/8	13 3/8 13 3/8	6 3/8 6 2/8	9 0/8	McKinley County	NM	Gary Isom	1988	4014
69 4/8	12 7/8 12 6/8	6 4/8 6 2/8	6 0/8	Moffat County	CO	Dale Drilling	1988	4014
69 4/8	14 1/8 14 1/8	5 1/8 5 1/8	8 4/8	Moffat County	CO	Ron Scherer	1988	4014
69 4/8	13 3/8 13 5/8	6 0/8 5 7/8	8 6/8	Natrona County	WY	Shawn Kinker	1988	4014
69 4/8	13 2/8 13 5/8	5 6/8 5 6/8	11 2/8	Carbon County	WY	Lonny Curtis	1988	4014
69 4/8	12 5/8 12 7/8	6 0/8 5 7/8	11 0/8	Albany County	WY	William Zahradka	1988	4014
69 4/8	14 7/8 14 4/8	6 2/8 6 2/8	14 1/8	Campbell County	WY	Curt Christensen	1988	4014
69 4/8	13 4/8 13 2/8	6 3/8 6 2/8	10 6/8	Crook County	WY	David Hinton	1988	4014
69 4/8	13 0/8 13 0/8	6 2/8 6 1/8	8 4/8	Converse County	WY	Kevin Stier	1988	4014
69 4/8	12 2/8 12 1/8	6 5/8 6 4/8	11 6/8	Natrona County	WY	Steve Turck	1988	4014
69 4/8	14 2/8 14 4/8	5 7/8 5 7/8	10 1/8	Buffalo	ALB	Larry Flaata	1988	4014
69 4/8	13 0/8 12 5/8	5 2/8 5 1/8	9 4/8	Weld County	CO	Larry Ford	1989	4014
69 4/8	13 0/8 13 0/8	5 7/8 5 6/8	11 3/8	Rosebud County	MT	Gene Welle	1989	4014
69 4/8	14 2/8 13 7/8	5 5/8 5 5/8	9 2/8	Lassen County	CA	Guy Rozar	1990	4014
69 4/8	12 0/8 11 7/8	6 3/8 6 3/8	10 6/8	Fremont County	WY	David J. Steger	1990	4014
69 4/8	12 6/8 13 6/8	6 0/8 6 1/8	13 5/8	Moffat County	CO	Reggie Spiegelberg	1990	4014
69 4/8	13 4/8 13 2/8	5 6/8 5 5/8	10 4/8	Moffat County	CO	Eugene Ray, Sr.	1990	4014
69 4/8	13 7/8 13 7/8	5 3/8 5 4/8	11 7/8	Lake County	OR	Buck Windom	1990	4014
69 4/8	12 3/8 12 2/8	6 0/8 6 1/8	9 7/8	Ward County	ND	Glen R. Hauf	1990	4014
69 4/8	13 0/8 13 1/8	6 0/8 6 1/8	12 2/8	Fremont County	WY	G. R. Pool	1991	4014
69 4/8	13 3/8 13 5/8	6 0/8 6 0/8	15 2/8	Harney County	OR	Barry Haney	1991	4014
69 4/8	14 1/8 14 2/8	5 2/8 5 2/8	9 7/8	Billings County	ND	Harold Hugelen	1991	4014
69 4/8	13 6/8 13 5/8	5 5/8 5 5/8	9 4/8	Lincoln County	WY	Bob Grace	1992	4014
69 4/8	13 0/8 13 1/8	6 0/8 6 0/8	11 2/8	Converse County	WY	Jeff Glaser	1992	4014
69 4/8	12 3/8 12 2/8	6 2/8 6 2/8	8 0/8	Campbell County	WY	Mark D. Christopherson	1992	4014
69 4/8	12 4/8 12 3/8	6 2/8 6 4/8	9 4/8	Carbon County	WY	Roy F. Meyer, Jr.	1992	4014
69 4/8	13 1/8 13 3/8	6 0/8 6 0/8	7 5/8	Converse County	WY	Lou Edelis	1992	4014
69 4/8	14 5/8 14 2/8	5 6/8 5 5/8	7 1/8	Powder River County	MT	James Larry Wilson	1992	4014
69 4/8	13 3/8 13 2/8	5 7/8 5 6/8	11 3/8	Converse County	WY	Rodney L. Hamann	1992	4014
69 4/8	14 2/8 14 1/8	5 5/8 5 5/8	10 7/8	Converse County	WY	Jim Schmidt	1992	4014
69 4/8	13 2/8 13 0/8	5 5/8 5 6/8	10 1/8	Deuel County	NE	Ev Tarrell	1992	4014
69 4/8	12 5/8 12 5/8	6 4/8 6 4/8	8 5/8	Moffat County	CO	Herbert M. Groetsch	1993	4014
69 4/8	13 5/8 13 5/8	6 0/8 6 0/8	10 1/8	Moffat County	CO	Jared Mason	1993	4014
69 4/8	13 4/8 13 5/8	6 1/8 6 0/8	15 4/8	Natrona County	WY	Jim Gaffney	1993	4014
69 4/8	13 5/8 13 5/8	6 0/8 6 0/8	9 5/8	Owyhee County	ID	Ron Stockdale	1993	4014
69 4/8	13 5/8 14 0/8	6 0/8 6 0/8	9 3/8	Converse County	WY	Guy Torres	1993	4014
69 4/8	12 2/8 12 2/8	6 0/8 6 0/8	10 6/8	Natrona County	WY	Guy Young	1993	4014
69 4/8	13 0/8 13 1/8	5 7/8 6 0/8	9 1/8	McKenzie County	ND	John Paul Schaffer	1993	4014
69 4/8	13 4/8 13 6/8	5 5/8 5 3/8	8 4/8	Johnson County	WY	Dan Hart	1993	4014
69 4/8	13 1/8 12 3/8	6 2/8 6 2/8	10 5/8	Meagher County	MT	D. (Mitch) Kottas	1993	4014
69 4/8	13 4/8 13 4/8	5 6/8 5 6/8	10 2/8	Carter County	MT	Marty Adams	1993	4014
69 4/8	13 5/8 13 4/8	5 6/8 5 7/8	10 6/8	Elko County	NV	Bob Sneed	1994	4014
69 4/8	13 0/8 13 0/8	6 0/8 6 0/8	8 3/8	Moffat County	CO	Billy Tillotson	1994	4014

# PRONGHORN

Minimum Score 67 — Continued

SCORE	LENGTH OF R HORN L	CIRCUMFERENCE R OF BASE L	INSIDE SPREAD	AREA	STATE/ PROVINCE	HUNTER'S NAME	DATE	RANK
69 4/8	13 2/8 13 0/8	5 4/8 5 4/8	9 6/8	Weld County	CO	Douglas P. Douthit	1994	4014
69 4/8	15 7/8 15 7/8	5 2/8 5 2/8	10 1/8	Lea County	NM	Richard Lynn Morris	1994	4014
69 4/8	13 2/8 13 4/8	5 6/8 5 6/8	10 0/8	Larimer County	CO	Shawn Greathouse	1994	4014
69 4/8	11 5/8 12 3/8	5 7/8 5 7/8	9 4/8	Moffat County	CO	Mitch Arnold	1994	4014
69 4/8	13 5/8 13 6/8	6 0/8 5 7/8	13 5/8	Yavapai County	AZ	Patricia M. Goetzenberger	1994	4014
69 4/8	13 7/8 13 6/8	5 3/8 5 3/8	8 7/8	Moffat County	CO	Todd J. Rider	1994	4014
69 4/8	14 2/8 14 2/8	5 4/8 5 5/8	11 2/8	Moffat County	CO	Reggie Spiegelberg	1994	4014
69 4/8	14 0/8 14 1/8	5 5/8 5 7/8	8 6/8	Blaine County	ID	John Wells	1995	4014
69 4/8	13 5/8 13 3/8	5 7/8 5 7/8	10 0/8	Powder River County	MT	Charles M. Fogarty	1995	4014
69 4/8	14 5/8 14 5/8	5 1/8 5 1/8	9 3/8	Carter County	MT	Marty Adams	1995	4014
69 4/8	12 5/8 13 3/8	6 3/8 6 3/8	8 4/8	Albany County	WY	T. J. Conrads	1996	4014
69 4/8	13 1/8 13 3/8	5 1/8 5 2/8	12 2/8	Carbon County	WY	Kevin Anderson	1996	4014
69 4/8	12 7/8 12 7/8	6 1/8 5 7/8	13 0/8	Carbon County	WY	Jim Schmid	1996	4014
69 4/8	12 4/8 12 6/8	6 2/8 6 1/8	10 0/8	Harding County	SD	Mark Connor	1996	4014
69 4/8	13 1/8 13 2/8	6 1/8 6 1/8	11 5/8	Powder River County	MT	Richard Driscoll	1996	4014
69 4/8	14 2/8 14 2/8	5 6/8 5 4/8	9 3/8	Converse County	WY	Michael D. Hansen	1997	4014
69 4/8	13 7/8 13 5/8	6 0/8 5 7/8	8 6/8	Fergus County	MT	Herbert Chavez	1997	4014
69 4/8	12 0/8 12 1/8	6 2/8 6 1/8	11 6/8	Weld County	CO	Jon Meyer	1998	4014
69 4/8	14 2/8 13 7/8	5 5/8 5 4/8	7 5/8	Clark County	ID	Thomas Thiel	1998	4014
69 4/8	14 0/8 14 0/8	5 7/8 5 2/8	12 4/8	Rosebud County	MT	Renee Welle	1998	4014
69 4/8	13 6/8 14 1/8	5 0/8 5 1/8	7 2/8	Elko County	NV	Michael David Gowan	1999	4014
69 4/8	14 0/8 14 2/8	5 6/8 5 6/8	8 4/8	Carbon County	WY	Steven J. Torok	2000	4014
69 4/8	13 5/8 13 6/8	5 5/8 5 4/8	9 5/8	Weld County	CO	Dwight D. Pochant	2000	4014
69 4/8	12 5/8 12 6/8	5 7/8 6 0/8	11 2/8	Moffat County	CO	Gary R. Trumpy	2000	4014
69 4/8	12 6/8 12 7/8	5 6/8 5 6/8	10 1/8	Converse County	WY	Tyler Williams	2000	4014
69 4/8	14 4/8 14 5/8	5 5/8 5 5/8	11 2/8	Converse County	WY	David W. Riley	2000	4014
69 4/8	14 1/8 14 2/8	5 3/8 5 1/8	10 0/8	Musselshell County	MT	Craig Richardson	2000	4014
69 4/8	12 5/8 12 3/8	6 2/8 6 3/8	10 4/8	Converse County	WY	Steve McCoy	2000	4014
69 4/8	14 3/8 14 3/8	5 3/8 5 3/8	8 7/8	Campbell County	WY	David A. Hesse	2000	4014
69 4/8	13 4/8 13 2/8	6 1/8 6 0/8	9 0/8	Bowman County	ND	Matthew Bradley	2000	4014
69 4/8	13 4/8 13 4/8	5 5/8 5 5/8	8 0/8	Converse County	WY	Gary Bauer	2001	4014
69 4/8	12 7/8 12 5/8	5 7/8 5 6/8	8 7/8	Natrona County	WY	Gus Congemi	2001	4014
69 4/8	12 4/8 12 5/8	5 6/8 5 6/8	10 1/8	Converse County	WY	Eric Vestal	2001	4014
69 4/8	13 4/8 13 3/8	5 6/8 5 6/8	9 6/8	Fergus County	MT	David McLendon	2001	4014
69 4/8	13 7/8 13 6/8	5 4/8 5 4/8	7 2/8	Moffat County	CO	Tom Hentrick	2002	4014
69 4/8	13 3/8 13 4/8	5 7/8 5 7/8	10 6/8	Campbell County	WY	Daryl Parker	2002	4014
69 4/8	13 3/8 13 6/8	5 5/8 5 5/8	11 3/8	Musselshell County	MT	Donald P. Crook	2002	4014
*69 4/8	12 6/8 13 1/8	5 4/8 5 5/8	11 0/8	Sublette County	WY	Carl Jeffries	2003	4014
69 4/8	13 0/8 13 0/8	5 7/8 5 7/8	7 2/8	Box Elder County	UT	Chris Brunker	2003	4014
69 4/8	13 2/8 13 1/8	6 1/8 5 7/8	9 4/8	Sheridan County	WY	George Harms	2003	4014
69 4/8	13 0/8 13 1/8	5 5/8 5 4/8	8 4/8	Rock County	NE	Cole Gideon	2003	4014
69 4/8	13 5/8 13 3/8	5 6/8 5 7/8	8 7/8	Rosebud County	MT	Jim Winjum	2003	4014
*69 4/8	13 4/8 13 4/8	5 7/8 5 6/8	11 6/8	Campbell County	WY	Tammy Severeide	2003	4014
*69 4/8	13 4/8 13 3/8	6 0/8 5 4/8	12 6/8	Washoe County	NV	Edward T. Pfister	2004	4014
69 4/8	13 5/8 13 6/8	6 0/8 5 7/8	6 1/8	Lemhi County	ID	Lyle A. Hall	2004	4014
69 4/8	14 1/8 12 7/8	5 7/8 5 6/8	11 7/8	Humboldt County	NV	Jason Pierson	2004	4014
69 4/8	13 7/8 13 6/8	5 5/8 5 5/8	10 4/8	Pondera County	MT	Clayton J. Gernaat	2004	4014
69 4/8	12 3/8 12 1/8	6 1/8 6 1/8	11 2/8	Laramie County	WY	Richard Kimball	2004	4014
69 4/8	14 1/8 13 1/8	5 7/8 5 5/8	9 2/8	Converse County	WY	William G. Mason	2004	4014
69 4/8	13 4/8 13 1/8	5 7/8 5 6/8	6 7/8	Campbell County	WY	Randy Springborn	2004	4014
69 4/8	13 1/8 13 0/8	6 0/8 6 0/8	10 0/8	Powder River County	MT	Ronald P. Jack	2004	4014
69 4/8	13 2/8 13 2/8	5 4/8 5 4/8	7 5/8	Converse County	WY	Sam Durham	2004	4014
69 4/8	13 7/8 13 4/8	5 5/8 5 6/8	11 0/8	Converse County	WY	John J. Bogucki	2005	4014
69 4/8	13 1/8 12 7/8	6 0/8 5 5/8	10 6/8	Albany County	WY	Ron Mason	2005	4014
69 4/8	11 7/8 11 6/8	6 0/8 6 0/8	8 1/8	Garfield County	UT	Charles J. Winter, Jr.	2005	4014
69 4/8	13 5/8 13 0/8	5 7/8 5 6/8	10 0/8	Converse County	WY	Jacob Adkins	2005	4014
69 4/8	12 2/8 12 2/8	6 2/8 6 1/8	10 4/8	Converse County	WY	Darryl Clark	2005	4014
*69 4/8	13 4/8 13 2/8	5 7/8 6 0/8	7 2/8	Carter County	MT	Scott A. Olthoff	2005	4014
69 4/8	12 7/8 13 0/8	5 5/8 5 5/8	9 3/8	Mercer County	ND	Jesse R. Carter	2005	4014
69 4/8	12 6/8 12 7/8	6 0/8 6 0/8	9 5/8	Sweetwater County	WY	Hagan Ekker	2006	4014
69 4/8	13 5/8 13 1/8	5 7/8 5 5/8	9 7/8	Butte County	ID	Jeremy Bowhay	2006	4014
69 4/8	12 7/8 13 0/8	5 7/8 6 0/8	8 7/8	Converse County	WY	William G. Mason	2006	4014
69 4/8	13 1/8 13 4/8	5 3/8 5 2/8	8 1/8	Crook County	WY	Michael Hundt	2006	4014
*69 4/8	13 4/8 13 4/8	5 7/8 5 7/8	8 0/8	Moffat County	CO	Karl L. Harvey	2007	4014
*69 4/8	14 4/8 14 3/8	5 5/8 5 4/8	11 1/8	Yavapai County	AZ	Steve Dockray	2007	4014
*69 4/8	14 5/8 14 2/8	5 7/8 5 7/8	8 6/8	Weld County	CO	Mike Kattawar, Sr.	2007	4014
*69 4/8	13 7/8 13 7/8	5 3/8 5 4/8	12 2/8	Butte County	SD	Reed Vandervoort	2007	4014
69 4/8	12 6/8 12 6/8	6 0/8 5 7/8	8 1/8	Converse County	WY	Ed Hendricks	2007	4014
69 4/8	13 4/8 13 5/8	5 4/8 5 4/8	8 5/8	Albany County	WY	Mike Yancey	2007	4014
*69 4/8	13 0/8 12 7/8	6 1/8 5 7/8	9 4/8	Converse County	WY	Allen Casto	2007	4014
69 4/8	12 7/8 12 7/8	5 6/8 5 5/8	9 2/8	Weston County	WY	Bob Peterson	2007	4014
69 4/8	13 4/8 13 3/8	5 1/8 5 1/8	10 5/8	Carter County	MT	Scott Hettinger	2007	4014
*69 4/8	12 0/8 12 2/8	5 5/8 5 5/8	5 5/8	Grant County	ND	Steve L. Winkler	2007	4014
69 4/8	13 3/8 14 1/8	6 1/8 5 1/8	9 5/8	Natrona County	WY	David Hartman	2008	4014
*69 4/8	13 6/8 13 3/8	6 2/8 5 7/8	8 3/8	Las Animas County	CO	Adam Benson	2008	4014
69 4/8	13 0/8 13 0/8	5 6/8 5 5/8	11 4/8	Campbell County	WY	Gene A. Welle	2008	4014
*69 4/8	13 2/8 13 2/8	6 0/8 6 0/8	9 2/8	Perkins County	SD	Bob Fey	2008	4014
69 4/8	12 4/8 13 0/8	6 2/8 6 2/8	9 6/8	Converse County	WY	Dave Canfield	2008	4014
69 4/8	13 5/8 13 4/8	5 5/8 5 6/8	9 2/8	Chouteau County	MT	Craig E. Boman	2008	4014
*69 4/8	13 6/8 14 0/8	5 4/8 5 4/8	12 1/8	Harding County	SD	Todd Vander Kley	2008	4014
69 4/8	12 7/8 13 4/8	5 4/8 5 4/8	8 0/8	Pondera County	MT	Nick Ploesser	2008	4014
69 4/8	13 1/8 13 2/8	5 6/8 6 0/8	10 3/8	Garfield County	MT	R. C. Peters	2008	4014
*69 4/8	14 3/8 14 3/8	5 2/8 5 4/8	9 2/8	Harding County	SD	Michael Ambur	2008	4014
69 4/8	14 6/8 14 4/8	6 0/8 6 0/8	15 1/8	Harding County	SD	Dale Kane	2008	4014
69 4/8	12 7/8 12 6/8	5 6/8 5 5/8	9 4/8	Butte County	SD	John M. Love	2008	4014
*69 4/8	13 4/8 13 3/8	5 4/8 5 4/8	8 7/8	Meade County	SD	Reed Vandervoort	2008	4014
*69 4/8	13 6/8 13 7/8	5 4/8 5 4/8	8 1/8	Sioux County	NE	John Filsinger	2008	4014
69 4/8	13 0/8 12 7/8	6 3/8 6 3/8	8 7/8	Carter County	MT	Brock C. Atwood	2009	4014
69 4/8	14 2/8 14 2/8	5 3/8 5 2/8	9 2/8	Natrona County	WY	Alfred J. Gemrich	2009	4014
69 4/8	13 6/8 13 5/8	5 1/8 5 2/8	7 7/8	Natrona County	WY	Don G. Scofield	2009	4014
*69 4/8	13 5/8 13 5/8	6 0/8 5 7/8	8 7/8	Campbell County	WY	Steven Weber	2009	4014
69 4/8	13 3/8 13 1/8	6 0/8 5 7/8	10 1/8	Garfield County	MT	Duane Fontaine	2010	4014
*69 4/8	13 3/8 13 1/8	5 5/8 5 5/8	10 1/8	Sioux County	NE	Michael Hawkins	2010	4014
69 2/8	14 2/8 13 7/8	5 4/8 5 4/8	11 6/8	Custer County	ID	Jack Edwards	1960	4181
69 2/8	13 5/8 13 4/8	5 3/8 5 2/8	6 2/8	Haakon County	SD	Floyd Hauk	1966	4181

853

PRONGHORN

Minimum Score 67 — Continued

SCORE	LENGTH OF HORN R	L	CIRCUMFERENCE OF BASE R	L	INSIDE SPREAD	AREA	STATE/PROVINCE	HUNTER'S NAME	DATE	RANK
69 2/8	12 3/8	12 1/8	5 6/8	5 6/8	8 0/8	Converse County	WY	Bill Martin	1976	4181
69 2/8	12 4/8	12 1/8	6 0/8	6 0/8	9 5/8	Morgan County	CO	Filiberto Lopez	1980	4181
69 2/8	12 7/8	12 7/8	5 3/8	5 5/8	11 7/8	Converse County	WY	Dr. James L. Emerson	1980	4181
69 2/8	11 6/8	13 5/8	6 1/8	6 1/8	8 6/8	Custer County	ID	Dick Fleming	1981	4181
69 2/8	13 2/8	14 0/8	5 5/8	5 5/8	11 0/8	Converse County	WY	Gene A. Esch	1981	4181
69 2/8	13 1/8	13 3/8	5 4/8	5 4/8	7 7/8	Butte County	ID	Garry Gunderson	1981	4181
69 2/8	12 4/8	13 0/8	5 7/8	5 5/8	11 5/8	Moffat County	CO	Jim Jarvis	1981	4181
69 2/8	14 3/8	13 7/8	5 7/8	5 6/8	10 4/8	Valencia County	NM	Reggie Spiegelberg	1981	4181
69 2/8	12 7/8	13 0/8	5 7/8	5 5/8	11 0/8	Sweetwater County	WY	Dean Kendall	1982	4181
69 2/8	13 2/8	13 6/8	6 2/8	6 2/8	9 5/8	Albany County	WY	Peter Vasek	1982	4181
69 2/8	12 7/8	13 1/8	5 5/8	5 4/8	8 4/8	Moffat County	CO	Ross Dieffenbaucher	1982	4181
69 2/8	12 7/8	12 5/8	4 7/8	4 7/8	14 1/8	Moffat County	CO	Keith R. Hardy	1983	4181
69 2/8	14 3/8	14 0/8	5 7/8	5 7/8	8 0/8	Moffat County	CO	Les Smith	1983	4181
69 2/8	14 2/8	13 7/8	6 0/8	6 0/8	8 1/8	Natrona County	WY	Joe M. Skipp	1983	4181
69 2/8	12 7/8	12 4/8	5 7/8	5 6/8	9 3/8	Converse County	WY	Bruce H. Sabaini	1983	4181
69 2/8	13 7/8	13 4/8	5 4/8	5 4/8	10 6/8	White Pine County	NV	Patrick Fillman	1984	4181
69 2/8	14 4/8	14 6/8	5 6/8	5 2/8	10 6/8	Converse County	WY	Donald Jackson	1984	4181
69 2/8	13 3/8	13 1/8	5 6/8	5 6/8	10 5/8	Converse County	WY	Bob Frank	1984	4181
69 2/8	13 3/8	12 4/8	6 1/8	6 1/8	12 0/8	McKenzie County	ND	Bill Zahradka	1984	4181
69 2/8	13 0/8	12 7/8	5 6/8	5 4/8	11 2/8	Yavapai County	AZ	Tony W. Zimbaro	1985	4181
69 2/8	13 2/8	13 2/8	5 7/8	5 7/8	10 5/8	Carbon County	WY	Steve Bolan	1985	4181
69 2/8	12 6/8	12 4/8	6 5/8	6 4/8	9 0/8	Moffat County	CO	Casey Veach	1985	4181
69 2/8	12 5/8	12 7/8	6 1/8	6 0/8	11 1/8	Moffat County	CO	Lynn Ingalsbe	1986	4181
69 2/8	13 4/8	13 4/8	6 0/8	6 0/8	9 4/8	Moffat County	CO	Gil Gilbertson	1986	4181
69 2/8	13 4/8	13 3/8	5 5/8	5 5/8	10 4/8	Converse County	WY	Don Schram	1986	4181
69 2/8	13 4/8	13 5/8	5 5/8	5 5/8	8 3/8	Presidio County	TX	Larry Zimmerman	1986	4181
69 2/8	13 6/8	14 1/8	6 0/8	5 6/8	9 7/8	Jefferson County	OR	Karen J. Demaris	1987	4181
69 2/8	13 0/8	13 0/8	5 5/8	5 6/8	11 5/8	Campbell County	WY	Rick Mowles	1987	4181
69 2/8	13 3/8	13 3/8	5 2/8	5 1/8	9 1/8	Natrona County	WY	Mike Mitten	1987	4181
69 2/8	13 5/8	12 6/8	5 5/8	5 6/8	10 2/8	Presidio County	TX	Jack F. Demetruk	1987	4181
69 2/8	12 1/8	12 0/8	5 7/8	5 7/8	8 3/8	Moffat County	CO	John Wagner	1988	4181
69 2/8	14 4/8	14 3/8	5 6/8	5 6/8	12 6/8	Modoc County	CA	Bill C. Osborne	1988	4181
69 2/8	14 2/8	13 7/8	5 2/8	5 1/8	10 5/8	Pima County	AZ	Barry Sopher	1988	4181
69 2/8	13 4/8	13 3/8	5 6/8	5 6/8	8 6/8	Hot Springs County	WY	Dan Wood	1988	4181
69 2/8	13 3/8	13 3/8	5 6/8	5 5/8	10 0/8	Converse County	WY	Denny Raper	1988	4181
69 2/8	14 5/8	15 0/8	6 4/8	6 1/8	12 2/8	Sweetwater County	WY	Mike Barrett	1989	4181
69 2/8	13 7/8	13 6/8	5 7/8	5 7/8	9 3/8	Mountrail County	ND	Brian C. Johnson	1989	4181
69 2/8	13 3/8	13 0/8	5 5/8	5 5/8	9 7/8	Buffalo	ALB	Steve Mackenzie	1989	4181
69 2/8	12 0/8	12 2/8	6 2/8	6 2/8	12 1/8	Carbon County	WY	Jeffrey Mueller	1990	4181
69 2/8	14 4/8	14 4/8	5 7/8	6 0/8	7 2/8	Harding County	SD	Dean Wagner	1990	4181
69 2/8	13 6/8	13 2/8	5 7/8	5 7/8	13 4/8	Coconino County	AZ	Charles Steven Williams	1990	4181
69 2/8	12 5/8	12 2/8	6 0/8	6 0/8	8 6/8	Converse County	WY	Robert Frank	1990	4181
69 2/8	11 3/8	11 3/8	6 1/8	6 2/8	6 7/8	Natrona County	WY	Robert E. Ebert	1990	4181
69 2/8	13 4/8	13 1/8	5 7/8	6 0/8	11 4/8	Powder River County	MT	John Witschen	1990	4181
69 2/8	13 0/8	13 1/8	5 5/8	5 5/8	11 2/8	Billings County	ND	Gary W. Heidecker	1990	4181
69 2/8	13 5/8	13 3/8	6 2/8	6 2/8	12 6/8	Fremont County	WY	Dave Holt	1991	4181
69 2/8	13 3/8	13 6/8	5 6/8	5 5/8	11 0/8	Lincoln County	WY	Warren Hatcher	1991	4181
69 2/8	13 1/8	13 3/8	5 6/8	5 5/8	10 4/8	Campbell County	WY	John Shields	1991	4181
69 2/8	12 0/8	12 0/8	6 0/8	5 6/8	9 2/8	McKenzie County	ND	Benjamin Stewart	1991	4181
69 2/8	13 2/8	13 0/8	5 5/8	5 5/8	9 1/8	Natrona County	WY	Carson V. Brown II	1991	4181
69 2/8	14 1/8	13 6/8	6 2/8	6 0/8	10 2/8	Converse County	WY	John Flies	1991	4181
69 2/8	11 6/8	11 6/8	6 1/8	6 0/8	11 0/8	Campbell County	WY	Ron Ralston	1991	4181
69 2/8	14 1/8	14 1/8	6 0/8	5 7/8	7 2/8	Converse County	WY	Wayne Radley	1991	4181
69 2/8	11 7/8	12 0/8	6 1/8	6 1/8	10 2/8	Moffat County	CO	Don Sousa	1992	4181
69 2/8	14 2/8	14 0/8	5 4/8	5 4/8	11 2/8	Catron County	NM	Glenn W. Isler	1992	4181
69 2/8	14 0/8	14 1/8	5 7/8	6 1/8	8 2/8	Lassen County	CA	Randy Jarvis	1992	4181
69 2/8	13 0/8	12 3/8	6 2/8	6 0/8	7 5/8	Uinta County	WY	George Fabian	1992	4181
69 2/8	12 4/8	12 7/8	6 3/8	6 4/8	9 4/8	Sweetwater County	WY	Mark Grace	1992	4181
69 2/8	12 7/8	13 1/8	6 6/8	6 6/8	13 2/8	Sweetwater County	WY	Bill Clink	1992	4181
69 2/8	14 6/8	14 3/8	5 4/8	5 4/8	8 2/8	Hettinger County	ND	Scott Wiseman	1992	4181
69 2/8	13 2/8	13 3/8	5 4/8	5 5/8	9 0/8	Lincoln County	WY	Raul "Randy" Quayle	1992	4181
69 2/8	13 7/8	13 7/8	5 3/8	5 3/8	8 5/8	Sweetwater County	WY	Justin J. Shirley	1993	4181
69 2/8	12 3/8	12 3/8	6 1/8	6 1/8	10 7/8	Rosebud County	MT	Kyle R. Zimmerman	1993	4181
69 2/8	13 4/8	13 5/8	6 0/8	5 7/8	10 7/8	Park County	WY	Ron Niziolek	1993	4181
69 2/8	12 7/8	13 0/8	6 0/8	5 7/8	8 0/8	Campbell County	WY	Norm Dustin	1993	4181
69 2/8	13 4/8	13 4/8	5 6/8	5 7/8	11 3/8	Natrona County	WY	Greg Morse	1993	4181
69 2/8	13 6/8	13 5/8	5 5/8	5 4/8	11 7/8	Sweetwater County	WY	Craig Boheler	1994	4181
69 2/8	14 4/8	14 4/8	5 3/8	5 4/8	7 2/8	Uinta County	WY	Franklin W. Sheets	1994	4181
69 2/8	14 4/8	14 4/8	5 6/8	5 7/8	12 2/8	Owyhee County	ID	Neil Thagard	1994	4181
69 2/8	13 0/8	12 6/8	6 1/8	6 0/8	9 1/8	Park County	WY	Tonja L. Schmidt	1994	4181
69 2/8	13 1/8	13 1/8	6 1/8	6 0/8	10 7/8	Moffat County	CO	Lonny Vanatta	1994	4181
69 2/8	13 7/8	13 7/8	5 2/8	5 2/8	12 7/8	Billings County	ND	Douglas A. Baumiller	1994	4181
69 2/8	14 2/8	13 7/8	5 5/8	5 5/8	10 2/8	Campbell County	WY	Charles Suchy	1994	4181
69 2/8	13 6/8	13 5/8	5 5/8	5 5/8	10 2/8	Johnson County	WY	Ellis Wall	1994	4181
69 2/8	13 1/8	13 1/8	6 2/8	6 2/8	8 1/8	Converse County	WY	Richard Cochran	1994	4181
69 2/8	13 6/8	13 3/8	6 3/8	6 2/8	7 4/8	Fergus County	MT	James A. Schneider	1994	4181
69 2/8	12 4/8	12 4/8	6 2/8	6 1/8	10 2/8	Youngstown	ALB	Gary Gillett	1994	4181
69 2/8	14 0/8	13 7/8	6 2/8	6 2/8	6 6/8	McKenzie County	ND	John Paul Schaffer	1994	4181
69 2/8	14 1/8	14 1/8	5 4/8	5 4/8	10 3/8	Campbell County	WY	Ken A. Rimer	1994	4181
69 2/8	13 1/8	12 3/8	6 2/8	6 3/8	9 2/8	Converse County	WY	Joel T. Oxley	1995	4181
69 2/8	14 5/8	14 6/8	5 1/8	5 2/8	9 4/8	Washoe County	NV	Alan Harris	1995	4181
69 2/8	12 6/8	12 6/8	6 0/8	6 0/8	10 0/8	Natrona County	WY	Dave Moritzen	1995	4181
69 2/8	13 7/8	14 3/8	5 7/8	9 1/8	7 2/8	Converse County	WY	Luigi Puglia	1995	4181
69 2/8	12 6/8	13 4/8	5 6/8	5 5/8	6 1/8	Apache County	AZ	Fred Clifford	1995	4181
69 2/8	14 6/8	14 5/8	5 1/8	5 1/8	9 1/8	Rosebud County	MT	John Richardson	1995	4181
69 2/8	12 1/8	12 0/8	2 1/8	2 0/8	8 4/8	Converse County	WY	Larry L. Fies	1995	4181
69 2/8	13 0/8	12 4/8	6 0/8	6 0/8	7 7/8	Campbell County	WY	Paul E. Korn	1995	4181
69 2/8	12 4/8	12 7/8	5 7/8	5 7/8	8 6/8	Converse County	WY	Robert L. Pagel, Jr.	1996	4181
69 2/8	12 6/8	12 4/8	5 6/8	5 5/8	12 5/8	Converse County	WY	Derl Phelps	1996	4181
69 2/8	13 1/8	13 0/8	5 6/8	6 0/8	11 7/8	Converse County	WY	Todd Smith	1996	4181
69 2/8	14 2/8	14 1/8	5 5/8	5 4/8	11 0/8	Manyberries	ALB	George W. Schoonover III	1996	4181
69 2/8	12 3/8	12 2/8	6 1/8	6 0/8	11 3/8	Perkins County	SD	Troy Hanson	1996	4181
69 2/8	14 7/8	14 6/8	5 3/8	5 2/8	10 5/8	Park County	WY	Ron Niziolek	1996	4181
69 2/8	13 6/8	13 5/8	5 4/8	5 4/8	10 4/8	Weld County	CO	Shane E. Cole	1997	4181
69 2/8	12 6/8	12 7/8	6 0/8	6 0/8	9 0/8	Converse County	WY	Randon Earl Saunoris	1997	4181

854

PRONGHORN

Minimum Score 67 — Continued

SCORE	LENGTH OF R HORN L	CIRCUMFERENCE R OF BASE L	INSIDE SPREAD	AREA	STATE/ PROVINCE	HUNTER'S NAME	DATE	RANK
69 2/8	13 2/8 13 4/8	5 7/8 6 1/8	11 2/8	Converse County	WY	Jerry Ellingson	1997	4181
69 2/8	13 1/8 13 2/8	5 7/8 5 6/8	9 0/8	Johnson County	WY	James Bornman	1997	4181
69 2/8	11 5/8 11 4/8	6 3/8 6 3/8	11 2/8	Converse County	WY	Frank S. Noska IV	1997	4181
69 2/8	14 2/8 13 5/8	5 4/8 5 4/8	9 5/8	Sweetwater County	WY	Larry Cross	1997	4181
69 2/8	13 2/8 13 2/8	5 5/8 5 6/8	9 2/8	Moffat County	CO	Paul St. John	1998	4181
69 2/8	12 6/8 12 6/8	6 1/8 5 7/8	8 5/8	Moffat County	CO	Linda Strong	1998	4181
69 2/8	12 7/8 13 6/8	5 7/8 5 6/8	9 1/8	Millard County	UT	Jess J. Jacobson	1998	4181
69 2/8	12 7/8 12 7/8	5 6/8 5 7/8	11 6/8	Johnson County	WY	Mary Elizabeth Shaw	1998	4181
69 2/8	14 4/8 14 2/8	5 4/8 5 5/8	14 2/8	Converse County	WY	John D. Edman	1998	4181
69 2/8	13 2/8 13 2/8	5 7/8 5 6/8	9 7/8	McKenzie County	ND	John Paul Schaffer	1998	4181
*69 2/8	12 7/8 12 6/8	5 6/8 5 6/8	8 5/8	Lyman County	SD	Dennis Stanley	1999	4181
69 2/8	13 7/8 14 1/8	5 6/8 5 5/8	9 1/8	Moffat County	CO	Eddie Claypool	1999	4181
69 2/8	13 0/8 13 3/8	6 0/8 6 0/8	6 6/8	Campbell County	WY	Bruce Hudalla	1999	4181
69 2/8	14 1/8 14 5/8	5 4/8 5 5/8	10 1/8	Powder River County	MT	Mark C. Booth	1999	4181
69 2/8	12 4/8 12 4/8	5 7/8 6 0/8	8 6/8	Moffat County	CO	Toby Garcia	2000	4181
69 2/8	13 2/8 13 3/8	5 3/8 5 3/8	6 1/8	Converse County	WY	Russell W. Guthrie	2000	4181
69 2/8	12 4/8 12 3/8	6 2/8 6 1/8	11 4/8	Yellowstone County	MT	Kim Latterell	2000	4181
69 2/8	12 4/8 12 3/8	5 6/8 5 7/8	9 0/8	Albany County	WY	David Stuhr	2001	4181
69 2/8	13 0/8 13 0/8	6 0/8 6 1/8	7 2/8	Perkins County	SD	Michael Ambur	2001	4181
69 2/8	13 1/8 13 1/8	5 4/8 5 5/8	8 5/8	Weld County	CO	Joseph Bradley	2002	4181
69 2/8	13 7/8 13 7/8	5 6/8 5 4/8	8 2/8	Weld County	CO	Steff Stefanovich	2002	4181
69 2/8	13 6/8 13 7/8	5 4/8 5 4/8	13 4/8	Wayne County	UT	Misty Warenski	2002	4181
69 2/8	13 0/8 13 1/8	5 3/8 5 3/8	11 1/8	Campbell County	WY	Randy Kottke	2002	4181
69 2/8	13 0/8 13 1/8	6 0/8 5 7/8	9 1/8	Lewis & Clark County	MT	William Purcell	2002	4181
69 2/8	13 4/8 13 6/8	6 0/8 6 0/8	10 7/8	Moffat County	CO	Wayne Herndon	2002	4181
69 2/8	13 1/8 13 0/8	5 7/8 5 7/8	9 7/8	Elmore County	ID	June V. Gempler	2003	4181
69 2/8	12 4/8 12 3/8	5 6/8 5 5/8	9 0/8	Converse County	WY	Gary Trumpy	2003	4181
69 2/8	13 3/8 13 4/8	6 0/8 5 7/8	9 6/8	Duchesne County	UT	Dustin L. Mitchell	2003	4181
69 2/8	14 2/8 14 1/8	5 4/8 5 5/8	11 5/8	Perkins County	SD	Robert G. Barden	2003	4181
69 2/8	13 0/8 13 2/8	5 6/8 5 6/8	10 6/8	Garfield County	MT	DuWayne M. Larson	2003	4181
69 2/8	13 3/8 13 4/8	5 4/8 5 4/8	7 5/8	Carbon County	WY	Jeff Fitts	2004	4181
*69 2/8	12 4/8 12 6/8	5 6/8 5 5/8	10 0/8	Converse County	WY	Bruce E. Thompson	2004	4181
69 2/8	13 5/8 13 5/8	6 1/8 6 1/8	9 0/8	Billings County	ND	James D. Herring	2004	4181
69 2/8	12 3/8 12 4/8	6 2/8 6 3/8	10 2/8	Niobrara County	WY	Bradley Brockhouse	2004	4181
69 2/8	14 1/8 13 7/8	6 0/8 5 6/8	8 2/8	Buffalo	ALB	Darryl Kublik	2004	4181
69 2/8	12 6/8 13 0/8	5 6/8 5 6/8	7 0/8	Powder River County	MT	Marc N. Shaft	2004	4181
69 2/8	13 1/8 13 2/8	5 6/8 5 7/8	10 0/8	Fergus County	MT	D. "Mitch" Kottas	2004	4181
69 2/8	14 2/8 14 2/8	5 4/8 5 4/8	8 3/8	Park County	MT	Jeffrey L. Synyard	2004	4181
*69 2/8	13 4/8 13 3/8	5 7/8 5 6/8	7 2/8	Butte County	SD	Gregory Dean Burroughs	2004	4181
69 2/8	14 5/8 14 6/8	5 4/8 5 4/8	8 5/8	Carbon County	WY	Brent Williamson	2004	4181
*69 2/8	15 0/8 15 0/8	5 4/8 5 4/8	13 5/8	Harding County	SD	Duane Peterson	2005	4181
69 2/8	13 6/8 13 5/8	5 5/8 5 4/8	10 4/8	Wayne County	UT	James L. Allred	2005	4181
*69 2/8	12 4/8 13 4/8	6 1/8 5 7/8	8 5/8	Converse County	WY	Ryan J. Baker	2005	4181
69 2/8	13 5/8 13 3/8	5 3/8 5 4/8	11 6/8	Campbell County	WY	Sam Wright	2005	4181
69 2/8	12 7/8 12 7/8	5 5/8 5 5/8	10 0/8	Medicine Hat	ALB	Dean G. Elbe	2005	4181
69 2/8	13 6/8 13 6/8	5 4/8 5 4/8	9 2/8	Gallatin County	MT	Bob Morton	2005	4181
*69 2/8	14 1/8 14 0/8	5 6/8 5 6/8	10 6/8	Moffat County	CO	Ren Leitner	2006	4181
69 2/8	13 4/8 13 4/8	5 5/8 5 5/8	10 0/8	Powder River County	MT	Don Scofield	2006	4181
*69 2/8	15 4/8 16 0/8	5 6/8 5 7/8	14 1/8	Coconino County	AZ	Jeff Holowell	2006	4181
69 2/8	13 0/8 13 0/8	5 6/8 5 5/8	11 2/8	Johnson County	WY	Randal S. Epperson	2006	4181
69 2/8	12 7/8 12 5/8	5 7/8 5 6/8	14 3/8	Billings County	ND	Kelly Hagel	2006	4181
69 2/8	13 0/8 13 0/8	5 5/8 5 5/8	11 3/8	Rosebud County	MT	Mike Murphey	2007	4181
69 2/8	13 4/8 13 0/8	5 4/8 5 3/8	10 2/8	McKenzie County	ND	David Tofte	2007	4181
69 2/8	13 0/8 13 2/8	5 6/8 5 6/8	8 3/8	Campbell County	WY	Rick Petersen	2007	4181
*69 2/8	13 3/8 13 1/8	5 7/8 5 6/8	8 1/8	Powder River County	MT	Jeffrey J. Blatz	2007	4181
69 2/8	13 3/8 13 3/8	5 6/8 5 5/8	8 5/8	Harding County	SD	Justin Deno	2007	4181
69 2/8	12 7/8 12 6/8	6 1/8 6 1/8	11 0/8	Weld County	CO	Joe Goodnight	2007	4181
69 2/8	13 5/8 13 3/8	5 1/8 5 1/8	10 6/8	Carbon County	WY	Brian Heaton	2007	4181
*69 2/8	13 0/8 12 7/8	6 1/8 6 1/8	9 7/8	Campbell County	WY	Russel H. Rudy	2007	4181
69 2/8	13 3/8 13 7/8	5 6/8 5 6/8	9 6/8	Harding County	SD	Ted Bass	2007	4181
*69 2/8	13 5/8 13 0/8	6 0/8 6 0/8	12 1/8	Campbell County	WY	Chad A. Schau	2008	4181
69 2/8	14 1/8 14 6/8	6 2/8 6 2/8	6 0/8	Thomas County	NE	David Bichlmeier	2008	4181
69 2/8	13 3/8 13 3/8	6 0/8 6 0/8	6 5/8	Lemhi County	ID	Brandon Fahnholz	2008	4181
*69 2/8	13 1/8 13 0/8	5 6/8 6 0/8	10 7/8	Lincoln County	WY	Eric Boley	2008	4181
69 2/8	14 0/8 14 4/8	5 5/8 5 4/8	12 1/8	Converse County	WY	Ed Defibaugh	2008	4181
69 2/8	14 4/8 13 5/8	6 0/8 5 5/8	13 2/8	Niobrara County	WY	Jody A. Bartnick	2008	4181
69 2/8	13 4/8 13 0/8	5 7/8 6 0/8	9 7/8	Stark County	ND	Terry Buechler	2008	4181
69 2/8	13 4/8 13 4/8	6 0/8 5 6/8	9 7/8	Rosebud County	MT	Corey Hugelen	2008	4181
69 2/8	12 7/8 12 6/8	6 1/8 6 0/8	8 2/8	Stanley County	SD	Chris Curtis	2008	4181
69 2/8	13 4/8 13 4/8	6 0/8 6 2/8	11 1/8	Natrona County	WY	Dan Myron	2008	4181
69 2/8	14 1/8 13 5/8	5 3/8 5 3/8	9 0/8	Custer County	MT	Dennis Dunn	2008	4181
69 2/8	13 4/8 13 4/8	6 0/8 5 6/8	8 7/8	Union County	NM	Fernando G. Semiao	2009	4181
*69 2/8	12 6/8 13 4/8	6 0/8 6 0/8	12 3/8	Uinta County	WY	Jeremy K. Hemmert	2009	4181
*69 2/8	11 6/8 12 4/8	6 1/8 6 0/8	11 0/8	Converse County	WY	Corey Fischer	2009	4181
*69 2/8	12 4/8 12 3/8	5 7/8 5 6/8	9 2/8	Converse County	WY	Patrick Hilten	2009	4181
69 2/8	13 3/8 13 2/8	5 3/8 5 3/8	11 1/8	Niobrara County	WY	Charles A. Myers	2009	4181
*69 2/8	12 6/8 12 7/8	6 0/8 6 0/8	15 0/8	Park County	WY	Jerry Dollard	2009	4181
69 2/8	14 5/8 14 6/8	5 4/8 5 5/8	9 3/8	Natrona County	WY	Don G. Scofield	2010	4181
*69 2/8	14 0/8 14 4/8	5 2/8 5 2/8	6 6/8	Lincoln County	WY	Tony Crnkovich	2010	4181
69 2/8	14 0/8 14 0/8	5 5/8 5 5/8	8 6/8	Powder River County	MT	Stephen A. Dougherty	2010	4181
*69 2/8	13 3/8 13 0/8	5 6/8 5 6/8	7 7/8	Brooks	ALB	Lindsay McQuaid	2010	4181
69 0/8	12 7/8 13 0/8	5 6/8 5 7/8	8 4/8	Fall River County	SD	Francis R. Tovar	1968	4359
69 0/8	14 0/8 14 2/8	5 2/8 5 3/8	9 1/8	Mercer County	ND	John J. Willoughby	1977	4359
69 0/8	13 4/8 13 2/8	5 6/8 5 5/8	8 3/8	Butte County	ID	Larry Roberts	1979	4359
69 0/8	14 1/8 13 7/8	5 4/8 5 3/8	10 0/8	Carbon County	WY	Grant Poindexter	1980	4359
69 0/8	13 2/8 13 3/8	5 6/8 5 5/8	11 0/8	Converse County	WY	George Place	1981	4359
69 0/8	14 0/8 14 2/8	5 7/8 5 6/8	8 0/8	Converse County	WY	Don Clark	1981	4359
69 0/8	12 5/8 12 4/8	5 6/8 5 6/8	9 5/8	Fremont County	WY	A. E. 'Butch' Whelchel	1981	4359
69 0/8	12 6/8 12 6/8	5 6/8 5 6/8	12 5/8	Converse County	WY	Jeff Wright	1981	4359
69 0/8	13 5/8 13 6/8	5 7/8 6 0/8	11 6/8	Washoe County	NV	Dr. Ronald H. Thole	1982	4359
69 0/8	13 0/8 12 6/8	6 0/8 6 0/8	7 0/8	Park County	CO	Greg Brown	1983	4359
69 0/8	12 4/8 12 4/8	6 0/8 6 1/8	9 4/8	Moffat County	CO	Burton Arbogast	1983	4359
69 0/8	13 2/8 13 3/8	5 6/8 5 6/8	11 4/8	Moffat County	CO	Mike Wallers	1983	4359
69 0/8	13 4/8 13 4/8	6 0/8 6 1/8	10 3/8	Converse County	WY	Michael Nimmer	1983	4359
69 0/8	13 0/8 13 1/8	6 1/8 6 1/8	9 2/8	Converse County	WY	Lloyd E. Musser	1983	4359

855

PRONGHORN

Minimum Score 67 — Continued

SCORE	LENGTH OF R HORN L	CIRCUMFERENCE R OF BASE L	INSIDE SPREAD	AREA	STATE/ PROVINCE	HUNTER'S NAME	DATE	RANK
69 0/8	13 2/8 12 5/8	6 1/8 6 1/8	8 3/8	Natrona County	WY	Robert F. Naumann	1983	4359
69 0/8	13 4/8 12 7/8	5 7/8 5 6/8	9 2/8	Converse County	WY	James R. Dreves	1983	4359
69 0/8	14 1/8 14 0/8	5 4/8 5 4/8	10 1/8	Johnson County	WY	Steve Nolte	1984	4359
69 0/8	12 7/8 12 5/8	6 0/8 6 1/8	11 2/8	Converse County	WY	Janice Peterman	1984	4359
69 0/8	13 2/8 13 3/8	5 6/8 5 7/8	13 3/8	Converse County	WY	John L Kosharek	1985	4359
69 0/8	12 7/8 12 6/8	6 0/8 5 7/8	9 3/8	Campbell County	WY	Bill Heinike	1985	4359
69 0/8	13 1/8 13 2/8	5 5/8 5 6/8	12 4/8	Carbon County	WY	Richard L. Westervelt	1987	4359
69 0/8	12 2/8 13 3/8	5 5/8 5 5/8	10 2/8	Moffat County	CO	Harry Torkilson	1987	4359
69 0/8	14 0/8 14 0/8	5 3/8 5 4/8	7 1/8	Natrona County	WY	Ricky A. Wall	1987	4359
69 0/8	12 4/8 12 4/8	6 0/8 6 0/8	8 4/8	Moffat County	CO	Brent Newton	1988	4359
69 0/8	13 2/8 13 2/8	6 0/8 5 6/8	9 4/8	Campbell County	WY	Dennis Klemick	1988	4359
69 0/8	13 0/8 13 0/8	6 1/8 6 0/8	9 6/8	Converse County	WY	Michael E. Rice	1988	4359
69 0/8	13 1/8 13 3/8	5 7/8 6 0/8	8 7/8	Converse County	WY	Steve VanZile	1988	4359
69 0/8	12 7/8 12 7/8	5 7/8 5 6/8	8 5/8	Sweetwater County	WY	Robert G. Petersen	1989	4359
69 0/8	13 0/8 12 7/8	6 0/8 5 5/8	10 6/8	Modoc County	CA	Cheryl Vermilion	1989	4359
69 0/8	14 5/8 14 5/8	5 4/8 5 4/8	9 4/8	Converse County	WY	Brian Bass	1989	4359
69 0/8	12 5/8 14 3/8	5 6/8 5 5/8	8 5/8	Navajo County	AZ	Ron Nichols	1989	4359
69 0/8	13 4/8 13 5/8	5 3/8 5 3/8	9 0/8	Converse County	WY	Robert Moon	1989	4359
69 0/8	12 7/8 12 5/8	5 6/8 5 6/8	9 0/8	Albany County	WY	Gene Welle	1989	4359
69 0/8	14 0/8 13 6/8	5 4/8 5 4/8	12 0/8	Campbell County	WY	Tippy Clark	1989	4359
69 0/8	13 2/8 13 2/8	5 7/8 5 7/8	10 3/8	White Pine County	NV	David Brown	1990	4359
69 0/8	13 3/8 13 1/8	5 4/8 5 3/8	9 1/8	Moffat County	CO	John Morris	1990	4359
69 0/8	13 7/8 14 0/8	5 7/8 5 7/8	7 4/8	Campbell County	WY	Elroy Thorson	1990	4359
69 0/8	12 6/8 12 5/8	6 0/8 6 0/8	7 2/8	Converse County	WY	Stan Rauch	1990	4359
69 0/8	14 1/8 14 3/8	5 6/8 5 6/8	10 5/8	Moffat County	CO	Rett Kelly	1990	4359
69 0/8	13 5/8 13 3/8	6 0/8 6 0/8	11 1/8	Natrona County	WY	Tony Zirkelbach	1990	4359
69 0/8	13 2/8 13 3/8	5 5/8 5 6/8	11 3/8	Jenner	ALB	Dale Johnson	1990	4359
69 0/8	14 3/8 14 0/8	6 2/8 5 7/8	11 4/8	Wallace County	KS	Mike Jenkins	1990	4359
69 0/8	13 1/8 13 2/8	5 6/8 5 4/8	13 6/8	Manyberries	ALB	Ken Maier	1990	4359
69 0/8	13 5/8 13 2/8	5 4/8 5 5/8	11 7/8	Carbon County	WY	Karl Knudsen	1991	4359
69 0/8	12 5/8 12 6/8	5 5/8 5 6/8	10 1/8	Sweetwater County	WY	Patricia C. Sands	1991	4359
69 0/8	13 3/8 13 2/8	6 0/8 6 0/8	10 4/8	Modoc County	CA	Dave S. Semple	1991	4359
69 0/8	14 4/8 13 0/8	5 4/8 5 4/8	9 3/8	Natrona County	WY	Gregory L. Reed	1991	4359
69 0/8	12 6/8 13 0/8	5 6/8 5 7/8	11 3/8	Converse County	WY	Ed Toelken	1991	4359
69 0/8	13 6/8 14 0/8	5 6/8 5 6/8	9 7/8	Bowman County	ND	Mark Froelich	1991	4359
69 0/8	13 6/8 14 1/8	6 1/8 6 2/8	13 5/8	Buffalo County	SD	Darrell Hahn	1991	4359
69 0/8	13 7/8 13 4/8	5 4/8 5 3/8	12 2/8	Sioux County	NE	Roger Dekok	1991	4359
69 0/8	13 6/8 13 6/8	5 3/8 5 4/8	7 1/8	Meagher County	MT	D. Mitch Kottas	1991	4359
69 0/8	14 4/8 14 2/8	5 5/8 5 5/8	9 1/8	Petroleum County	MT	Mark D. Hughes	1991	4359
69 0/8	14 4/8 15 6/8	5 2/8 5 1/8	9 1/8	Hudspeth County	TX	Kenneth L. Zoller	1991	4359
69 0/8	12 4/8 12 3/8	5 7/8 5 7/8	9 4/8	Bowman County	ND	Dale J. Neva	1991	4359
69 0/8	12 2/8 12 4/8	6 1/8 6 1/8	9 4/8	Butte County	ID	David Wayne Ary	1992	4359
69 0/8	12 3/8 12 3/8	6 3/8 6 2/8	6 2/8	Campbell County	WY	Barb Kleve	1992	4359
69 0/8	13 4/8 13 6/8	5 4/8 5 4/8	9 7/8	Converse County	WY	Larry M. Peterson	1992	4359
69 0/8	13 0/8 13 1/8	6 0/8 6 0/8	9 4/8	Albany County	WY	Roger Sheaffer	1992	4359
69 0/8	12 7/8 13 5/8	6 5/8 6 5/8	8 0/8	Campbell County	WY	Jack Savini	1992	4359
69 0/8	13 5/8 13 5/8	5 4/8 5 4/8	10 0/8	Perkins County	SD	Fred Kober	1992	4359
69 0/8	13 6/8 13 6/8	5 3/8 5 3/8	11 3/8	Weston County	WY	Roland Weeg	1992	4359
69 0/8	13 5/8 13 7/8	5 5/8 5 5/8	10 7/8	Petroleum County	MT	Mark D. Hughes	1992	4359
69 0/8	13 2/8 13 3/8	5 3/8 5 2/8	8 7/8	Saguache County	CO	Bennie Koch, Jr.	1993	4359
69 0/8	14 0/8 14 0/8	5 6/8 5 5/8	9 6/8	Custer County	ID	Chris J. Crisler	1993	4359
69 0/8	12 2/8 12 1/8	6 2/8 6 0/8	11 4/8	Moffat County	CO	Glen Hotchkiss	1993	4359
69 0/8	13 5/8 13 7/8	6 1/8 6 1/8	8 5/8	Carbon County	WY	Stephen Wilcoxson	1993	4359
69 0/8	13 2/8 13 1/8	5 4/8 5 3/8	8 6/8	Campbell County	WY	Dale Miller	1993	4359
69 0/8	13 5/8 13 3/8	6 0/8 6 0/8	9 1/8	Natrona County	WY	Richard J. Yates	1993	4359
69 0/8	14 4/8 14 3/8	5 4/8 5 4/8	8 5/8	Medicine Hat	ALB	Glen Garton	1993	4359
69 0/8	12 0/8 12 0/8	6 0/8 6 0/8	12 1/8	Converse County	WY	G. William Buxton	1993	4359
69 0/8	13 2/8 13 2/8	6 0/8 6 0/8	9 6/8	Moffat County	CO	Raymond L. Lunnon	1993	4359
69 0/8	15 0/8 15 0/8	5 6/8 5 6/8	13 0/8	Youngstown	ALB	Dominic Barbario	1993	4359
69 0/8	13 2/8 12 6/8	5 6/8 5 6/8	6 5/8	Sweetwater County	WY	Douglas E. Walton	1994	4359
69 0/8	12 7/8 13 0/8	6 0/8 6 0/8	7 7/8	Moffat County	CO	Jim Shanks	1994	4359
69 0/8	13 3/8 13 4/8	5 6/8 5 6/8	14 3/8	Rio Blanco County	CO	John R. Cabot	1994	4359
69 0/8	12 6/8 12 6/8	6 1/8 6 2/8	9 4/8	Sublette County	WY	Guy L. Williamson	1994	4359
69 0/8	12 3/8 12 5/8	6 0/8 6 1/8	9 5/8	Campbell County	WY	Walter Phillips	1994	4359
69 0/8	13 2/8 13 4/8	6 1/8 5 6/8	8 1/8	Johnson County	WY	Don Mealey	1994	4359
69 0/8	14 2/8 14 0/8	5 6/8 5 6/8	11 6/8	Saguache County	CO	Jason Embry	1994	4359
69 0/8	13 0/8 13 0/8	5 6/8 5 6/8	9 1/8	Sioux County	NE	Steven L. Anderson	1994	4359
69 0/8	12 7/8 13 0/8	6 0/8 5 6/8	10 5/8	Park County	WY	Timothy J. Aydt	1994	4359
69 0/8	12 7/8 12 7/8	5 7/8 5 7/8	11 5/8	Millard County	UT	Shane T. Newman	1995	4359
69 0/8	12 7/8 12 6/8	6 2/8 6 3/8	9 4/8	Moffat County	CO	Dave Culter	1995	4359
69 0/8	12 7/8 12 5/8	5 7/8 6 0/8	12 2/8	Big Horn County	WY	Dave Moss	1995	4359
69 0/8	13 5/8 13 7/8	5 5/8 5 5/8	9 5/8	Campbell County	WY	Curt Rotering	1995	4359
69 0/8	13 4/8 13 4/8	5 4/8 5 4/8	7 5/8	Rosebud County	MT	Kent Kaufman	1995	4359
69 0/8	13 4/8 13 3/8	6 1/8 6 0/8	9 1/8	Dundy County	NE	Sara Gideon	1995	4359
69 0/8	12 3/8 12 4/8	5 7/8 5 6/8	8 7/8	Weld County	CO	Scott Cumings	1996	4359
69 0/8	14 4/8 14 0/8	6 0/8 5 6/8	11 7/8	Colfax County	NM	David R. Aikin	1996	4359
69 0/8	12 6/8 12 5/8	7 1/8 7 1/8	9 1/8	Moffat County	CO	Byron Dean	1996	4359
69 0/8	13 5/8 13 2/8	5 4/8 5 4/8	8 7/8	Raymond	ALB	Don Gibb	1996	4359
69 0/8	14 3/8 14 0/8	5 6/8 5 6/8	8 4/8	El Paso County	CO	Jeff Elem	1996	4359
69 0/8	13 7/8 13 6/8	5 4/8 5 4/8	9 2/8	Socorro County	NM	Alan W. Krause	1997	4359
69 0/8	14 1/8 13 4/8	6 4/8 6 2/8	10 5/8	Sweetwater County	WY	George Fabian	1997	4359
69 0/8	15 3/8 15 1/8	5 0/8 5 1/8	6 4/8	Moffat County	CO	LeRoy A. Brincks	1997	4359
69 0/8	13 0/8 13 1/8	6 3/8 5 7/8	8 5/8	Campbell County	WY	Chris Gates	1997	4359
69 0/8	14 3/8 14 4/8	5 5/8 5 5/8	8 3/8	Converse County	WY	K-Tal Johnson	1997	4359
69 0/8	13 7/8 14 1/8	6 0/8 5 6/8	10 6/8	Park County	MT	David Smith	1998	4359
69 0/8	13 7/8 13 0/8	6 1/8 5 6/8	10 0/8	Thomas County	NE	Don Thoesen	1998	4359
69 0/8	13 3/8 13 3/8	5 4/8 5 4/8	11 4/8	Carter County	MT	Shane W. Helmich	1998	4359
69 0/8	14 3/8 14 3/8	5 1/8 5 2/8	11 6/8	Weld County	CO	Eugene C. Rossman	1999	4359
69 0/8	13 0/8 12 6/8	5 6/8 5 6/8	9 1/8	Converse County	WY	Jeremy Theis	1999	4359
69 0/8	12 7/8 12 6/8	6 3/8 6 3/8	11 1/8	Pennington County	SD	Steve Rossow	2000	4359
69 0/8	12 6/8 13 1/8	5 6/8 5 7/8	9 6/8	Catron County	NM	Charlie Schlosser	2001	4359
69 0/8	13 6/8 13 5/8	5 3/8 5 3/8	8 3/8	Converse County	WY	George A. Zanoni	2001	4359
69 0/8	14 5/8 14 2/8	5 6/8 5 5/8	7 5/8	Owyhee County	ID	DeLoy Desaro	2001	4359
69 0/8	13 0/8 13 0/8	6 1/8 6 0/8	7 6/8	Custer County	MT	Bob Brennan	2001	4359
69 0/8	11 5/8 11 6/8	5 7/8 5 6/8	7 3/8	Campbell County	WY	Brian Kehrli	2002	4359

PRONGHORN

Minimum Score 67
Continued

SCORE	LENGTH OF R HORN L	CIRCUMFERENCE R OF BASE L	INSIDE SPREAD	AREA	STATE/ PROVINCE	HUNTER'S NAME	DATE	RANK
69 0/8	13 0/8　13 7/8	6 0/8　5 7/8	9 0/8	Converse County	WY	Doug Clayton	2002	4359
69 0/8	12 7/8　13 3/8	5 5/8　5 4/8	8 7/8	El Paso County	CO	Todd A. Brickel	2002	4359
69 0/8	14 0/8　13 7/8	5 7/8　5 7/8	9 3/8	Musselshell County	MT	Brian Dey	2002	4359
69 0/8	13 4/8　13 7/8	6 0/8　5 6/8	11 1/8	Elko County	NV	Jack Smith	2003	4359
69 0/8	13 4/8　13 5/8	5 5/8　5 5/8	8 2/8	Converse County	WY	Darel Hulsing	2003	4359
69 0/8	13 6/8　13 6/8	5 3/8　5 3/8	9 7/8	Las Animas County	CO	Daniel Mullen	2003	4359
69 0/8	13 5/8　13 3/8	5 2/8　5 3/8	11 7/8	Converse County	WY	Lee Jernigan	2003	4359
69 0/8	13 7/8　13 5/8	5 6/8　5 6/8	9 1/8	Laramie County	WY	Laine M. Parish	2003	4359
69 0/8	14 1/8　14 1/8	6 0/8　5 7/8	10 4/8	Fergus County	MT	Chris G. Sanford	2003	4359
69 0/8	13 5/8　13 6/8	5 5/8　5 4/8	5 3/8	Elmore County	ID	Hollister Jones	2004	4359
69 0/8	13 1/8　13 2/8	5 6/8　5 6/8	9 0/8	Butte County	SD	Nathan Jones	2004	4359
69 0/8	12 7/8　12 6/8	6 0/8　6 0/8	6 5/8	Campbell County	WY	David Weber	2004	4359
69 0/8	13 0/8　13 0/8	5 6/8　5 6/8	8 7/8	Campbell County	WY	Jocelyn Hugelen	2004	4359
69 0/8	13 5/8　13 1/8	5 6/8　5 6/8	10 1/8	Converse County	WY	Michael L. Ritter, Jr.	2004	4359
69 0/8	12 3/8　12 5/8	6 0/8　6 0/8	9 0/8	Powder River County	MT	Mutt Wilson	2005	4359
*69 0/8	13 0/8　13 1/8	5 6/8　5 6/8	8 6/8	Moffat County	CO	Michael Teixeira	2005	4359
69 0/8	12 7/8　15 3/8	6 0/8　5 7/8	7 3/8	Coconino County	AZ	Michael S. Elson	2005	4359
69 0/8	12 3/8　12 3/8	5 6/8　5 6/8	11 4/8	Converse County	WY	Dennis Palmer	2005	4359
69 0/8	13 0/8　13 4/8	6 0/8　6 0/8	8 7/8	Butte County	SD	Dallas Dinger	2005	4359
69 0/8	13 4/8　13 4/8	5 4/8　5 2/8	6 5/8	Big Horn County	MT	Michael Ryan	2005	4359
69 0/8	13 3/8　13 4/8	5 5/8　5 6/8	12 7/8	Converse County	WY	Steve R. Marsolek	2005	4359
69 0/8	12 6/8　12 6/8	6 1/8　6 1/8	9 2/8	Sublette County	WY	Bernie Weisgerber	2006	4359
69 0/8	13 7/8　13 7/8	5 2/8　5 2/8	8 7/8	Big Horn County	MT	Pete Gierke	2006	4359
*69 0/8	12 4/8　12 4/8	5 5/8　5 4/8	7 5/8	Carbon County	WY	John Makovec	2006	4359
*69 0/8	13 6/8　14 1/8	5 7/8　5 7/8	11 4/8	Bowman County	ND	DuWayne Larson	2006	4359
*69 0/8	13 5/8　13 7/8	5 3/8　5 4/8	13 2/8	Converse County	WY	Steve Felosa	2006	4359
69 0/8	13 4/8　13 3/8	5 6/8　5 7/8	10 2/8	Blaine County	MT	Gary Lampkins	2006	4359
*69 0/8	13 6/8　13 4/8	5 5/8　5 4/8	12 4/8	Valley County	MT	Bob Blattenbauer	2006	4359
69 0/8	12 5/8　12 4/8	5 4/8　5 6/8	10 0/8	Eureka County	NV	Kenneth J. Wilkinson	2007	4359
*69 0/8	13 5/8　13 7/8	5 5/8　5 4/8	7 7/8	Blaine County	MT	Jarred R. Krueger	2007	4359
69 0/8	13 5/8　13 7/8	5 3/8　5 2/8	13 5/8	Converse County	WY	Tommy Haskamp	2007	4359
69 0/8	13 6/8　13 7/8	5 4/8　5 4/8	8 3/8	Converse County	WY	Jim Blevins	2007	4359
69 0/8	13 6/8　13 6/8	5 5/8　5 4/8	10 2/8	Madison County	MT	James J. Kilmer	2007	4359
69 0/8	13 7/8　13 6/8	5 4/8　5 2/8	10 5/8	Rosebud County	MT	Jim Winjum	2007	4359
69 0/8	13 0/8　13 0/8	6 0/8　6 0/8	7 7/8	Sioux County	NE	Gary Richards	2007	4359
69 0/8	13 5/8　13 0/8	5 4/8　5 4/8	8 4/8	Malheur County	OR	Ken Cochell	2008	4359
69 0/8	13 3/8　13 1/8	5 4/8　5 4/8	9 2/8	Lea County	NM	Ronnie Parsons	2008	4359
69 0/8	13 5/8　13 6/8	5 4/8　5 4/8	10 7/8	Converse County	WY	Bill McGrath	2008	4359
*69 0/8	12 4/8　12 4/8	5 7/8　5 7/8	11 7/8	Sioux County	NE	Michael Hawkins	2008	4359
*69 0/8	13 4/8　13 3/8	6 2/8　5 7/8	9 4/8	Twin Falls County	ID	Trent McBride	2008	4359
69 0/8	13 6/8　13 3/8	5 5/8　5 2/8	8 7/8	Converse County	WY	Michael Noecker	2008	4359
*69 0/8	13 6/8　13 5/8	5 6/8　5 7/8	9 6/8	Powder River County	MT	Jeffrey Blatz	2008	4359
69 0/8	13 3/8　13 1/8	5 6/8　5 5/8	11 5/8	Lewis & Clark County	MT	Jason Redfield	2008	4359
*69 0/8	12 3/8　12 4/8	5 5/8　5 5/8	11 2/8	Converse County	WY	Jeremy Andrews	2008	4359
69 0/8	13 7/8　14 0/8	5 4/8　5 5/8	9 5/8	Powder River County	MT	Carl Fritz	2008	4359
69 0/8	14 2/8　13 7/8	5 5/8　5 4/8	7 2/8	Washoe County	NV	Mike Traub	2009	4359
*69 0/8	13 4/8　13 4/8	5 4/8　5 3/8	9 3/8	Rosebud County	MT	Bryan C. Maxson	2009	4359
69 0/8	14 5/8　14 0/8	5 5/8　5 5/8	9 6/8	Natrona County	WY	Don G. Scofield	2009	4359
*69 0/8	13 4/8　13 6/8	5 1/8　5 1/8	10 2/8	Converse County	WY	Chuck Hammers	2009	4359
69 0/8	13 3/8　13 2/8	5 5/8　5 6/8	7 4/8	Weld County	CO	Timothy K. Rushing	2009	4359
69 0/8	12 4/8　12 4/8	5 7/8　5 7/8	7 4/8	Converse County	WY	Gary L. Fischer	2009	4359
*69 0/8	14 0/8　13 7/8	5 3/8　5 3/8	8 0/8	Converse County	WY	James Michael Sissell	2010	4359
69 0/8	13 3/8　13 0/8	6 2/8　6 1/8	9 0/8	Carbon County	WY	Eric Hoffer	2010	4359
68 6/8	14 7/8　14 7/8	5 4/8　5 4/8	12 0/8	Sweetwater County	WY	Dr. Fred Mack	1960	4521
68 6/8	13 7/8　14 2/8	5 6/8　5 4/8	7 7/8	Haakon County	SD	William Nankivel	1970	4521
68 6/8	13 2/8　13 4/8	6 1/8　6 1/8	7 4/8	Gallatin County	MT	Robert Savage	1971	4521
68 6/8	12 3/8　12 4/8	6 4/8　6 2/8	11 0/8	Sweetwater County	WY	Keith Dana	1978	4521
68 6/8	13 6/8　13 5/8	5 3/8　5 5/8	9 0/8	Park County	MT	George Kamps	1980	4521
68 6/8	12 4/8　12 4/8	5 5/8　5 4/8	7 3/8	Converse County	WY	Donald Schram	1981	4521
68 6/8	13 0/8　12 7/8	5 7/8　5 4/8	9 0/8	Natrona County	WY	Jim L. McCrory	1981	4521
68 6/8	13 0/8　13 2/8	5 7/8　5 7/8	11 6/8	Weld County	CO	Ron Montross	1983	4521
68 6/8	12 4/8　12 0/8	6 4/8　6 3/8	9 4/8	Crook County	WY	Jim P Hallock	1983	4521
68 6/8	13 4/8　13 3/8	5 5/8　5 5/8	7 6/8	Converse County	WY	Gary Duncan	1983	4521
68 6/8	13 3/8　13 5/8	5 1/8　5 1/8	12 2/8	Garfield County	MT	Darwin Frison	1983	4521
68 6/8	14 0/8　14 0/8	5 3/8　5 2/8	10 6/8	Moffat County	CO	Gary Fritzler	1984	4521
68 6/8	12 4/8　12 5/8	6 0/8　6 3/8	9 1/8	McKinley County	NM	John W. Rose	1984	4521
68 6/8	14 3/8　14 3/8	5 4/8　5 4/8	9 4/8	Butte County	SD	Reginald E. Faber, Jr.	1984	4521
68 6/8	12 6/8　12 4/8	6 0/8　5 7/8	8 2/8	Converse County	WY	Eric Bruce	1984	4521
68 6/8	13 4/8　14 0/8	5 6/8　5 4/8	11 1/8	Washoe County	NV	Gary Zunino	1985	4521
68 6/8	13 7/8　13 1/8	6 2/8　6 2/8	11 2/8	Sweetwater County	WY	W.R. "Tony" Dukes	1985	4521
68 6/8	14 0/8　13 6/8	6 3/8　6 2/8	14 6/8	Converse County	WY	Frank Moore	1985	4521
68 6/8	13 0/8　12 7/8	5 5/8　5 4/8	5 3/8	Sweetwater County	WY	Gary Belvoir	1986	4521
68 6/8	13 7/8　14 2/8	5 5/8　5 5/8	11 6/8	Washoe County	NV	Gilbert Hernandez	1987	4521
68 6/8	13 2/8　12 6/8	5 6/8　5 4/8	8 1/8	Custer County	ID	Brian Hunter Heck	1987	4521
68 6/8	13 2/8　13 4/8	6 5/8　6 4/8	6 1/8	Garfield County	CO	Rory Robie	1987	4521
68 6/8	12 6/8　12 6/8	6 4/8　6 3/8	11 3/8	Moffat County	CO	Tommy M. Brown	1987	4521
68 6/8	12 5/8　12 5/8	5 7/8　5 6/8	12 7/8	Sweetwater County	WY	David Breakfield	1987	4521
68 6/8	12 4/8　12 5/8	5 6/8　5 5/8	10 2/8	Converse County	WY	David L. Lundy	1987	4521
68 6/8	13 7/8　13 5/8	6 1/8　6 0/8	9 3/8	Beaverhead County	MT	Mervin Johnston	1987	4521
68 6/8	13 4/8　13 7/8	5 6/8　5 5/8	9 6/8	Buffalo	ALB	Lou Carrier	1987	4521
68 6/8	12 5/8　12 5/8	6 4/8　6 3/8	16 4/8	Washoe County	NV	Robert Reed	1988	4521
68 6/8	13 5/8　14 0/8	5 5/8　5 4/8	10 1/8	Buffalo	ALB	Orest Popil	1988	4521
68 6/8	12 7/8　12 6/8	5 5/8　5 4/8	9 3/8	Medicine Hat	ALB	Owen Telke	1988	4521
68 6/8	13 1/8　13 2/8	5 5/8　5 5/8	11 0/8	Sublette County	WY	Peter L. Bucklin	1989	4521
68 6/8	13 0/8　12 6/8	5 7/8　6 0/8	11 3/8	Yavapai County	AZ	Charles P. Cooley	1989	4521
68 6/8	13 7/8　13 5/8	5 5/8　5 7/8	10 3/8	McCone County	MT	Jaron Schillinger	1989	4521
68 6/8	13 6/8　14 0/8	5 6/8　5 7/8	10 7/8	Jenner	ALB	Brian J. Ward	1989	4521
68 6/8	14 0/8　14 2/8	6 4/8　6 2/8	10 5/8	Phillips County	MT	Mike Dunwell	1989	4521
68 6/8	13 4/8　13 0/8	5 6/8　5 5/8	13 4/8	Wallace County	KS	Larry Buchholz	1989	4521
68 6/8	13 2/8　13 1/8	5 4/8　5 5/8	7 2/8	Natrona County	WY	R. Ray Wix	1990	4521
68 6/8	12 4/8　12 3/8	5 5/8　5 5/8	13 0/8	Natrona County	WY	James V. Siebels	1990	4521
68 6/8	13 1/8　13 5/8	5 3/8　5 4/8	9 6/8	Campbell County	WY	Randy Cook	1990	4521
68 6/8	12 3/8　12 2/8	6 1/8　6 1/8	9 2/8	Hyde County	SD	Robert Moriarty	1990	4521
68 6/8	14 5/8　14 3/8	5 3/8　5 4/8	9 7/8	Washoe County	NV	Richard Oliver	1991	4521
68 6/8	12 0/8　11 5/8	6 6/8　6 6/8	10 4/8	Converse County	WY	Bob Arne	1991	4521

857

PRONGHORN

Minimum Score 67 Continued

SCORE	LENGTH OF HORN R / L	CIRCUMFERENCE OF BASE R / L	INSIDE SPREAD	AREA	STATE/PROVINCE	HUNTER'S NAME	DATE	RANK
68 6/8	13 1/8 / 13 0/8	5 7/8 / 5 7/8	9 1/8	Converse County	WY	Phil Perry	1991	4521
68 6/8	13 0/8 / 13 0/8	6 3/8 / 6 2/8	7 3/8	Campbell County	WY	Allan White	1991	4521
68 6/8	13 4/8 / 13 3/8	5 5/8 / 5 4/8	10 5/8	Campbell County	WY	Dan M. Mooney	1991	4521
68 6/8	12 2/8 / 12 4/8	5 6/8 / 5 6/8	11 0/8	Rosebud County	MT	Craig Gerber	1991	4521
68 6/8	13 3/8 / 13 7/8	6 0/8 / 6 1/8	11 2/8	Fergus County	MT	Chris G. Sanford	1991	4521
68 6/8	13 6/8 / 13 5/8	5 6/8 / 5 5/8	8 0/8	Washoe County	NV	Anthony L. Mudd	1992	4521
68 6/8	13 0/8 / 12 7/8	6 1/8 / 6 1/8	8 6/8	Humboldt County	NV	Erik L. Self	1992	4521
68 6/8	14 0/8 / 13 7/8	6 0/8 / 5 5/8	9 4/8	Sweetwater County	WY	Jeffrey J. Petersen	1992	4521
68 6/8	13 1/8 / 13 0/8	5 1/8 / 5 1/8	8 1/8	Moffat County	CO	David Joyce	1992	4521
68 6/8	12 7/8 / 12 6/8	6 1/8 / 6 0/8	9 1/8	Carbon County	WY	Mark Alan Bartkoski	1992	4521
68 6/8	13 2/8 / 13 2/8	5 6/8 / 5 6/8	8 7/8	Campbell County	WY	Darryl Winslow	1992	4521
68 6/8	12 5/8 / 12 3/8	6 0/8 / 5 7/8	7 1/8	Manyberries	ALB	John Visscher	1992	4521
68 6/8	13 4/8 / 13 2/8	5 3/8 / 5 4/8	10 0/8	Fremont County	WY	Ronald Lane Turner	1992	4521
68 6/8	12 5/8 / 12 4/8	5 4/8 / 5 5/8	12 3/8	Coconino County	AZ	John J. Anderson	1993	4521
68 6/8	13 1/8 / 13 4/8	5 4/8 / 5 4/8	9 6/8	Apache County	AZ	Fred Clifford	1993	4521
68 6/8	13 0/8 / 12 7/8	5 2/8 / 5 3/8	6 7/8	Beaverhead County	MT	Troy Bungay	1993	4521
68 6/8	15 0/8 / 14 6/8	5 5/8 / 5 6/8	10 3/8	Owyhee County	ID	Tony E. Hyde	1993	4521
68 6/8	14 4/8 / 14 3/8	5 0/8 / 5 0/8	10 0/8	Manyberries	ALB	Ryk Visscher	1993	4521
68 6/8	13 6/8 / 13 1/8	6 2/8 / 6 2/8	11 2/8	Sweetwater County	WY	Robert G. Petersen	1993	4521
68 6/8	13 3/8 / 13 5/8	6 2/8 / 6 0/8	13 6/8	Washoe County	NV	Edwin A. Charkowicz	1994	4521
68 6/8	12 4/8 / 12 5/8	6 2/8 / 6 1/8	13 1/8	Box Elder County	UT	Brian Ray Spencer	1994	4521
68 6/8	14 4/8 / 14 2/8	5 4/8 / 5 4/8	8 3/8	Moffat County	CO	J. Keith Chastain	1994	4521
68 6/8	13 3/8 / 13 3/8	5 2/8 / 5 2/8	8 0/8	Converse County	WY	Timothy Otis	1994	4521
68 6/8	12 6/8 / 12 4/8	5 7/8 / 6 0/8	8 7/8	Crook County	WY	Aaron Hickman	1994	4521
68 6/8	13 1/8 / 12 7/8	6 3/8 / 6 1/8	9 4/8	Converse County	WY	Carlos D. Landers, Jr.	1994	4521
68 6/8	13 7/8 / 14 1/8	6 0/8 / 5 6/8	13 4/8	Converse County	WY	Tim Schneewind	1994	4521
68 6/8	13 5/8 / 14 5/8	5 6/8 / 5 5/8	12 4/8	Lassen County	CA	Dominic H. Choi	1995	4521
68 6/8	14 0/8 / 12 6/8	5 3/8 / 5 3/8	11 6/8	Grand County	UT	Kevin L. Sheets	1995	4521
68 6/8	13 4/8 / 13 3/8	5 4/8 / 5 4/8	6 4/8	Campbell County	WY	Steve Upton	1995	4521
68 6/8	13 4/8 / 13 6/8	5 3/8 / 5 3/8	10 7/8	Coconino County	AZ	Phillip C. Dalrymple	1995	4521
68 6/8	11 4/8 / 11 4/8	6 4/8 / 6 6/8	11 6/8	Yavapai County	AZ	Don Parks, Jr.	1995	4521
68 6/8	13 5/8 / 13 6/8	5 6/8 / 5 6/8	9 4/8	Campbell County	WY	Gary English	1995	4521
68 6/8	12 3/8 / 12 3/8	5 5/8 / 5 5/8	7 6/8	Juab County	UT	Rebecca J. Simpson	1996	4521
68 6/8	13 1/8 / 13 0/8	6 0/8 / 6 0/8	5 6/8	Weld County	CO	Dave Holt	1996	4521
68 6/8	13 0/8 / 13 0/8	5 5/8 / 5 6/8	9 1/8	Harding County	SD	Garland Holley	1996	4521
68 6/8	13 3/8 / 13 4/8	6 0/8 / 6 1/8	9 3/8	Clark County	ID	Marc R. Beesley	1996	4521
68 6/8	13 1/8 / 13 2/8	5 6/8 / 5 6/8	8 5/8	Owyhee County	ID	Michael S. Moore	1996	4521
68 6/8	12 5/8 / 13 2/8	5 4/8 / 5 4/8	10 0/8	Natrona County	WY	Ray Wix	1996	4521
68 6/8	13 2/8 / 13 0/8	5 4/8 / 5 4/8	9 5/8	Converse County	WY	David W. Wagner	1996	4521
68 6/8	13 3/8 / 13 5/8	5 4/8 / 5 5/8	8 5/8	Converse County	WY	William G. Mason	1996	4521
68 6/8	12 7/8 / 13 0/8	6 1/8 / 6 1/8	10 4/8	Rosebud County	MT	R. Gerald Ebert	1996	4521
68 6/8	12 7/8 / 12 4/8	5 7/8 / 5 7/8	10 6/8	Elbert County	CO	Jerry Becay	1996	4521
68 6/8	14 2/8 / 14 2/8	5 2/8 / 5 1/8	10 4/8	Weston County	WY	Warren DeSmidt	1996	4521
68 6/8	13 2/8 / 13 4/8	5 6/8 / 5 6/8	12 4/8	Hays	ALB	Larry Knibbs	1996	4521
68 6/8	13 2/8 / 15 0/8	5 6/8 / 5 6/8	14 1/8	Johnson County	WY	Charles H. Sagner	1996	4521
68 6/8	13 1/8 / 13 1/8	5 5/8 / 5 5/8	8 1/8	Fall River County	SD	Gary DeJong	1996	4521
68 6/8	11 7/8 / 12 5/8	6 0/8 / 6 0/8	8 1/8	Weld County	CO	Matthew McWilliams	1997	4521
68 6/8	13 1/8 / 13 3/8	6 1/8 / 6 2/8	11 0/8	Twin Falls County	ID	Randal Scott O'Melia	1997	4521
68 6/8	14 3/8 / 14 6/8	5 4/8 / 5 5/8	9 4/8	Harding County	SD	Jane Stolz	1997	4521
68 6/8	12 6/8 / 12 3/8	6 0/8 / 6 0/8	8 3/8	Campbell County	WY	Glenn Wotring	1998	4521
68 6/8	13 1/8 / 13 2/8	5 5/8 / 5 5/8	10 4/8	Moffat County	CO	Tom Abney	1998	4521
68 6/8	14 2/8 / 14 0/8	5 2/8 / 5 2/8	8 7/8	Albany County	WY	Roger M. Tyler	1998	4521
68 6/8	12 6/8 / 12 7/8	5 7/8 / 5 7/8	10 2/8	Fergus County	MT	Chris G. Sanford	1998	4521
68 6/8	14 2/8 / 14 2/8	5 6/8 / 5 6/8	7 7/8	Campbell County	WY	Melvin Moore	1998	4521
68 6/8	13 0/8 / 13 0/8	5 4/8 / 5 4/8	6 7/8	Wayne County	UT	Bret Merchant	1999	4521
68 6/8	13 6/8 / 12 5/8	5 7/8 / 5 6/8	5 7/8	Converse County	WY	Alan Fenimore	1999	4521
68 6/8	13 7/8 / 13 7/8	5 2/8 / 5 2/8	9 3/8	Converse County	WY	Greg Dearth	1999	4521
68 6/8	13 6/8 / 13 3/8	6 6/8 / 6 2/8	9 3/8	Converse County	WY	John Croom	1999	4521
68 6/8	14 5/8 / 14 6/8	5 3/8 / 5 4/8	8 7/8	Fall River County	SD	Wess H. Larabee	1999	4521
68 6/8	13 2/8 / 13 1/8	5 5/8 / 5 4/8	12 1/8	Albany County	WY	John Mascellino, Sr.	2000	4521
68 6/8	13 2/8 / 13 1/8	5 4/8 / 5 4/8	11 3/8	Converse County	WY	Tad Dalgewicz	2000	4521
68 6/8	12 0/8 / 12 0/8	5 6/8 / 6 0/8	10 7/8	Las Animas County	CO	Stephen Haufsk	2001	4521
68 6/8	14 0/8 / 14 1/8	5 4/8 / 5 4/8	8 5/8	Moffat County	CO	Tom Miranda	2001	4521
68 6/8	13 0/8 / 13 0/8	5 7/8 / 5 6/8	10 0/8	Butte County	SD	Tom Nauman	2001	4521
68 6/8	14 0/8 / 13 2/8	5 6/8 / 5 5/8	10 3/8	Coconino County	AZ	Scott Wills	2002	4521
68 6/8	13 7/8 / 13 5/8	5 3/8 / 5 2/8	10 5/8	Converse County	WY	Timothy L. Ross	2002	4521
68 6/8	13 4/8 / 13 5/8	5 5/8 / 5 6/8	9 7/8	Campbell County	WY	Rick Spurgeon	2002	4521
68 6/8	12 2/8 / 12 2/8	6 0/8 / 6 0/8	13 1/8	Seven Persons	ALB	J. Marcus Casano	2002	4521
68 6/8	11 7/8 / 12 0/8	5 7/8 / 5 7/8	10 1/8	Weld County	CO	Julian L. Cumbee	2003	4521
68 6/8	14 0/8 / 13 4/8	5 5/8 / 5 4/8	13 4/8	De Baca County	NM	Brian K. Strickland	2003	4521
68 6/8	13 2/8 / 13 3/8	5 6/8 / 5 6/8	8 4/8	Campbell County	WY	Gregory T. Michl	2003	4521
68 6/8	14 1/8 / 13 7/8	5 2/8 / 5 1/8	8 5/8	Santa Cruz County	AZ	Barry Sopher	2003	4521
*68 6/8	13 2/8 / 13 3/8	5 5/8 / 5 4/8	8 7/8	Powder River County	MT	Kevin Gengler	2003	4521
68 6/8	12 4/8 / 12 5/8	5 5/8 / 5 5/8	9 6/8	Rosebud County	MT	Keith McCarty	2003	4521
68 6/8	13 5/8 / 13 5/8	5 5/8 / 5 5/8	9 4/8	Lyman County	SD	Dennis Stanley	2003	4521
68 6/8	14 0/8 / 14 1/8	5 4/8 / 5 4/8	6 6/8	Gallatin County	MT	Steve Edwards	2003	4521
68 6/8	13 1/8 / 13 1/8	6 0/8 / 6 0/8	8 6/8	Garfield County	UT	Ryan Rickenbach	2004	4521
68 6/8	13 2/8 / 13 3/8	6 2/8 / 6 0/8	11 6/8	Stark County	ND	Jay Haverluk	2004	4521
68 6/8	13 0/8 / 13 0/8	5 4/8 / 5 3/8	9 1/8	Big Horn County	MT	Todd A. Fetkenhauer	2004	4521
68 6/8	13 2/8 / 13 3/8	6 1/8 / 5 7/8	12 3/8	Blaine County	MT	Tom M. Benson	2004	4521
*68 6/8	13 3/8 / 13 2/8	6 2/8 / 6 2/8	8 1/8	Powder River County	MT	Chris McDonald	2005	4521
68 6/8	12 2/8 / 12 1/8	5 6/8 / 5 6/8	9 3/8	Converse County	WY	Robert Sihlanick	2005	4521
68 6/8	13 6/8 / 13 3/8	5 6/8 / 5 5/8	8 4/8	Converse County	WY	Timothy L. Ross	2005	4521
68 6/8	14 5/8 / 14 5/8	5 1/8 / 5 2/8	13 0/8	Rosebud County	MT	Lynn Walker	2005	4521
68 6/8	14 4/8 / 14 6/8	5 2/8 / 5 1/8	11 6/8	Billings County	ND	Kelly Hagel	2005	4521
68 6/8	14 3/8 / 13 7/8	5 5/8 / 5 5/8	13 7/8	Lake County	OR	John E. Buell	2006	4521
68 6/8	13 4/8 / 13 4/8	5 5/8 / 5 5/8	5 6/8	Campbell County	WY	Scott Lang	2006	4521
68 6/8	12 1/8 / 12 1/8	6 0/8 / 6 0/8	12 0/8	Campbell County	WY	Corey Hugelen	2006	4521
68 6/8	12 4/8 / 13 4/8	6 0/8 / 5 7/8	13 7/8	Crook County	WY	Jeff Jacob	2006	4521
68 6/8	13 7/8 / 13 6/8	5 5/8 / 5 4/8	14 0/8	Rosebud County	MT	Gene Welle	2006	4521
68 6/8	13 2/8 / 13 4/8	5 6/8 / 5 6/8	10 4/8	Carter County	MT	Jack M. Skille	2006	4521
68 6/8	14 3/8 / 14 2/8	5 3/8 / 5 2/8	10 6/8	Golden Valley County	MT	Kim L. Latterell	2006	4521
68 6/8	12 2/8 / 12 3/8	5 6/8 / 5 6/8	9 2/8	Weld County	CO	Richard A. Devrous, Jr.	2007	4521
*68 6/8	14 0/8 / 13 6/8	5 2/8 / 5 4/8	10 3/8	El Paso County	CO	Todd Ronk	2007	4521
68 6/8	13 4/8 / 13 7/8	5 5/8 / 5 3/8	7 0/8	Harding County	SD	Monie McMurtry	2007	4521

PRONGHORN

Minimum Score 67   Continued

SCORE	LENGTH OF R HORN L	CIRCUMFERENCE R OF BASE L	INSIDE SPREAD	AREA	STATE/ PROVINCE	HUNTER'S NAME	DATE	RANK
68 6/8	13 2/8 12 7/8	5 7/8 5 7/8	10 2/8	Madison County	MT	Bill McGrath	2007	4521
68 6/8	13 1/8 13 3/8	5 7/8 5 6/8	8 0/8	Union County	NM	Alfred Gallegos	2008	4521
68 6/8	14 3/8 14 2/8	5 4/8 5 3/8	11 1/8	Sublette County	WY	Dave R. Burget	2008	4521
*68 6/8	13 5/8 12 6/8	5 3/8 5 2/8	12 4/8	Catron County	NM	Raymond Smith	2008	4521
68 6/8	12 0/8 11 7/8	6 1/8 6 2/8	6 4/8	Alamosa County	CO	Joe Handorf	2008	4521
68 6/8	13 4/8 13 4/8	5 6/8 5 6/8	10 1/8	Bowman County	ND	DuWayne Larson	2008	4521
*68 6/8	14 2/8 14 0/8	5 2/8 5 3/8	10 3/8	McKenzie County	ND	David R. Ware	2008	4521
68 6/8	13 6/8 13 7/8	5 6/8 5 6/8	9 2/8	Albany County	WY	Roger Hoefs	2008	4521
*68 6/8	12 4/8 12 2/8	6 2/8 6 2/8	12 6/8	Niobrara County	WY	Nathan Luth	2008	4521
*68 6/8	12 4/8 12 7/8	6 4/8 6 6/8	8 1/8	Natrona County	WY	George Rannenberg	2009	4521
68 6/8	14 0/8 13 3/8	6 1/8 6 1/8	7 7/8	Moffat County	CO	Colton Lee Conrad	2009	4521
*68 6/8	11 7/8 12 0/8	6 2/8 6 1/8	14 7/8	Fremont County	WY	Kevin L. Bontrager	2009	4521
68 6/8	13 6/8 13 3/8	5 4/8 5 5/8	9 4/8	Gallatin County	MT	David Booth	2009	4521
68 6/8	12 7/8 12 7/8	6 0/8 6 2/8	9 2/8	Lincoln County	WY	Mark Grace	2009	4521
*68 6/8	13 1/8 13 2/8	6 1/8 6 0/8	10 4/8	McCone County	MT	Tim Stiles	2009	4521
*68 6/8	13 6/8 13 4/8	5 6/8 5 6/8	10 3/8	Sioux County	NE	Nick Mathistad	2009	4521
68 6/8	13 4/8 13 1/8	5 4/8 5 4/8	6 2/8	Sully County	SD	Lance Peery	2009	4521
*68 6/8	14 0/8 14 0/8	5 6/8 5 5/8	13 6/8	Lake County	OR	Howard Meyer	2010	4521
68 6/8	13 1/8 13 3/8	5 5/8 5 3/8	9 2/8	Converse County	WY	Jerry Hanson	2010	4521
68 6/8	12 1/8 13 0/8	5 7/8 5 6/8	12 2/8	Converse County	WY	Robert Frederick, Jr.	2010	4521
68 4/8	13 4/8 13 0/8	5 4/8 5 5/8	8 6/8	Tripp County	SD	Spike Jorgensen	1965	4678
68 4/8	14 1/8 14 1/8	5 2/8 5 1/8	12 3/8	Lincoln County	NM	James H. Simmons	1966	4678
68 4/8	12 6/8 12 2/8	6 5/8 6 5/8	12 1/8	McLean County	ND	Tom O'Connell	1970	4678
68 4/8	13 2/8 13 2/8	5 5/8 5 5/8	13 3/8	Carbon County	WY	Robert Pitt	1974	4678
68 4/8	12 6/8 12 7/8	6 0/8 6 0/8	9 4/8	Billings County	ND	Dean Nevland	1975	4678
68 4/8	14 1/8 14 0/8	5 4/8 5 2/8	10 5/8	Johnson County	WY	David Collis	1975	4678
68 4/8	12 6/8 12 4/8	5 6/8 5 7/8	9 3/8	Converse County	WY	Ron Carpenter	1976	4678
68 4/8	13 0/8 12 7/8	5 5/8 6 0/8	8 3/8	Lincoln County	WY	Preston C. Phelps	1977	4678
68 4/8	13 7/8 13 4/8	5 6/8 5 5/8	13 1/8	Logan County	CO	Tony Seahorn	1978	4678
68 4/8	13 7/8 14 0/8	6 0/8 5 7/8	12 4/8	McKinley County	NM	James M. Finn	1979	4678
68 4/8	14 1/8 14 1/8	5 4/8 5 5/8	10 5/8	Butte County	ID	Clifton Robinson	1979	4678
68 4/8	13 3/8 13 2/8	5 5/8 5 5/8	13 0/8	Carbon County	WY	Dale Gauthier	1980	4678
68 4/8	13 0/8 12 5/8	5 7/8 5 7/8	10 3/8	Moffat County	CO	Ron Bolinger	1981	4678
68 4/8	13 5/8 13 4/8	5 4/8 5 3/8	12 1/8	Converse County	WY	Richard Stokke	1981	4678
68 4/8	13 6/8 13 5/8	5 0/8 5 0/8	8 4/8	Natrona County	WY	Dan Skolaski	1981	4678
68 4/8	12 6/8 13 3/8	5 7/8 6 0/8	9 1/8	Converse County	WY	Charles O. Boggs	1982	4678
68 4/8	14 1/8 13 7/8	5 5/8 5 6/8	8 6/8	Eddy County	NM	Jim Stell	1982	4678
68 4/8	13 6/8 14 0/8	5 4/8 5 5/8	13 2/8	Converse County	WY	Harold Leslie	1982	4678
68 4/8	12 7/8 13 0/8	6 0/8 6 0/8	9 6/8	Natrona County	WY	Roger Smith	1982	4678
68 4/8	13 4/8 13 5/8	5 3/8 5 3/8	13 3/8	Converse County	WY	Kent Brigham	1982	4678
68 4/8	12 4/8 13 0/8	6 3/8 6 1/8	8 6/8	Carbon County	WY	Willis Duhon	1982	4678
68 4/8	12 3/8 12 1/8	6 2/8 6 3/8	10 3/8	Natrona County	WY	Steve Turck	1982	4678
68 4/8	12 7/8 12 7/8	5 5/8 5 4/8	10 6/8	Moffat County	CO	Len Cardinale	1983	4678
68 4/8	13 4/8 13 4/8	5 2/8 5 1/8	10 5/8	Sweetwater County	WY	Dean Dolenc	1983	4678
68 4/8	13 3/8 13 6/8	5 5/8 5 4/8	7 2/8	Sioux County	NE	Chuck Starr	1983	4678
68 4/8	13 6/8 13 6/8	5 2/8 5 3/8	7 6/8	Logan County	KS	Lynn Freese	1984	4678
68 4/8	13 6/8 13 6/8	5 6/8 5 4/8	11 2/8	Converse County	WY	Marty Horn	1984	4678
68 4/8	13 6/8 14 5/8	5 4/8 5 4/8	11 2/8	Converse County	WY	Joe Guth	1984	4678
68 4/8	12 2/8 12 3/8	6 0/8 6 0/8	10 7/8	Campbell County	WY	John "Jack" Cordes	1984	4678
68 4/8	12 0/8 12 0/8	5 5/8 5 5/8	8 2/8	Moffat County	CO	Robert Syvertson, Sr.	1985	4678
68 4/8	13 6/8 13 6/8	5 7/8 5 7/8	11 5/8	Coconino County	AZ	Jesse E. Smith	1985	4678
68 4/8	12 0/8 11 5/8	5 5/8 5 5/8	9 6/8	Converse County	WY	Steve Woodman	1985	4678
68 4/8	12 3/8 12 5/8	5 6/8 5 7/8	10 5/8	Campbell County	WY	Thomas R. Dvorak	1985	4678
68 4/8	13 4/8 13 2/8	5 4/8 5 4/8	9 4/8	WMU 151	ALB	Allen Avery	1985	4678
68 4/8	13 0/8 13 0/8	5 6/8 5 7/8	10 7/8	Campbell County	WY	Donald Ace Morgan	1986	4678
68 4/8	12 0/8 12 4/8	5 7/8 5 7/8	9 0/8	Billings County	ND	Rick Froehlich	1986	4678
68 4/8	12 4/8 12 2/8	5 6/8 5 5/8	9 0/8	Moffat County	CO	Mike Callaway	1987	4678
68 4/8	13 3/8 12 7/8	5 7/8 5 4/8	9 4/8	Slope County	ND	Terry Buechler	1987	4678
68 4/8	13 1/8 13 2/8	5 3/8 5 3/8	11 6/8	Moffat County	CO	Tim Cuthriell	1988	4678
68 4/8	14 1/8 14 1/8	5 7/8 5 7/8	11 2/8	Carbon County	WY	Raymond R. Robison	1988	4678
68 4/8	13 0/8 13 0/8	5 4/8 5 4/8	6 2/8	Moffat County	CO	Steve Barnhill	1988	4678
68 4/8	13 5/8 13 6/8	5 5/8 5 5/8	11 1/8	Converse County	WY	Mick Cochrane	1988	4678
68 4/8	13 4/8 13 6/8	6 0/8 6 0/8	10 4/8	Campbell County	WY	Al Haugestuen	1988	4678
68 4/8	13 1/8 13 1/8	5 5/8 5 5/8	11 6/8	Klamath County	OR	Steve Tandy	1989	4678
68 4/8	11 7/8 11 7/8	5 6/8 5 6/8	9 3/8	Billings County	ND	Harold Hugelen	1989	4678
68 4/8	14 2/8 14 3/8	5 5/8 5 5/8	9 6/8	Buffalo	ALB	Glenn Moir	1989	4678
68 4/8	13 4/8 13 2/8	5 6/8 5 4/8	10 0/8	Washoe County	NV	Linda Manion	1990	4678
68 4/8	13 2/8 13 1/8	5 6/8 5 6/8	9 4/8	Moffat County	CO	Cheryl Ray	1990	4678
68 4/8	14 4/8 13 6/8	5 6/8 5 6/8	16 5/8	Millard County	UT	Bob McGill, Jr.	1990	4678
68 4/8	12 0/8 12 0/8	6 1/8 6 0/8	12 6/8	Weld County	CO	Kenneth W. Ayers	1991	4678
68 4/8	12 3/8 12 0/8	6 1/8 5 5/8	7 5/8	Moffat County	CO	Mark Petersen	1991	4678
68 4/8	13 2/8 13 0/8	5 4/8 5 3/8	13 1/8	Campbell County	WY	Marlene Odahlen-Hinz	1991	4678
68 4/8	13 2/8 13 7/8	5 3/8 5 4/8	9 4/8	Converse County	WY	Dean K. Reidt	1991	4678
68 4/8	13 2/8 13 1/8	6 1/8 6 1/8	11 0/8	Campbell County	WY	James W. Torseth	1991	4678
68 4/8	11 7/8 11 7/8	6 2/8 6 0/8	8 2/8	Campbell County	WY	Jon Lammle	1991	4678
68 4/8	13 4/8 13 2/8	5 6/8 5 4/8	8 5/8	Custer County	ID	John R. Sample	1991	4678
68 4/8	13 7/8 14 0/8	5 6/8 5 4/8	9 0/8	Petroleum County	MT	Theodore J. Poper	1991	4678
68 4/8	13 1/8 13 2/8	6 1/8 5 6/8	11 4/8	Converse County	WY	Michael L. Hoft	1991	4678
68 4/8	13 0/8 12 1/8	5 7/8 5 7/8	7 6/8	Musselshell County	MT	Scott A. Silverness	1991	4678
68 4/8	12 6/8 12 7/8	5 6/8 6 0/8	7 4/8	Moffat County	CO	Tim Dehn	1992	4678
68 4/8	13 4/8 13 7/8	5 7/8 6 0/8	7 1/8	Converse County	WY	Mark Whitish	1992	4678
68 4/8	13 1/8 13 1/8	6 2/8 6 2/8	13 1/8	Converse County	WY	Rick Hartley	1992	4678
68 4/8	13 0/8 13 0/8	5 7/8 5 6/8	9 5/8	Johnson County	WY	Mike Neilson	1992	4678
68 4/8	12 7/8 12 7/8	6 0/8 5 7/8	7 5/8	Hand County	SD	Jeff Poppenga	1992	4678
68 4/8	12 6/8 12 7/8	6 1/8 5 7/8	8 3/8	Beaverhead County	MT	Terry Barkell	1992	4678
68 4/8	14 2/8 13 7/8	5 4/8 5 4/8	10 2/8	Johnson County	WY	Charles Sagner	1992	4678
68 4/8	13 6/8 13 5/8	6 0/8 5 6/8	7 5/8	Sioux County	NE	Ken Roth	1993	4678
68 4/8	12 7/8 12 7/8	5 5/8 5 5/8	9 4/8	Campbell County	WY	Dave Hinton	1993	4678
68 4/8	12 6/8 12 2/8	6 1/8 5 6/8	10 2/8	Converse County	WY	Delbert Bybee	1993	4678
68 4/8	13 2/8 13 2/8	5 6/8 5 6/8	9 5/8	Natrona County	WY	Kenneth M. Friess	1993	4678
68 4/8	13 6/8 14 4/8	6 1/8 6 2/8	13 3/8	Phillips County	MT	Darvin Henry	1993	4678
68 4/8	13 7/8 14 0/8	5 4/8 5 4/8	12 6/8	McKenzie County	ND	Steve Rehak	1993	4678
68 4/8	13 4/8 13 4/8	6 1/8 6 1/8	8 6/8	Manyberries	ALB	Jeff Davies	1993	4678
68 4/8	14 2/8 14 1/8	6 1/8 6 1/8	9 2/8	Sweet Grass County	MT	Scott R. Barefoot	1993	4678
68 4/8	13 1/8 12 7/8	6 4/8 6 5/8	11 1/8	Sioux County	NE	Clarence Poteet	1993	4678

PRONGHORN

Minimum Score 67   Continued

SCORE	LENGTH OF HORN R / L	CIRCUMFERENCE OF BASE R / L	INSIDE SPREAD	AREA	STATE/ PROVINCE	HUNTER'S NAME	DATE	RANK
68 4/8	13 1/8 / 13 2/8	5 6/8 / 5 6/8	9 6/8	Fremont County	WY	Kevin Maynard	1994	4678
68 4/8	13 2/8 / 13 2/8	5 5/8 / 5 5/8	8 0/8	Campbell County	WY	Jim Keim	1994	4678
68 4/8	12 4/8 / 12 4/8	6 5/8 / 6 4/8	9 0/8	Crook County	WY	Dean C. Henke	1994	4678
68 4/8	12 5/8 / 12 4/8	5 6/8 / 5 6/8	9 4/8	Moffat County	CO	Joseph Miguel	1995	4678
68 4/8	13 6/8 / 13 4/8	6 0/8 / 5 7/8	14 1/8	Moffat County	CO	Chris Reilly	1995	4678
68 4/8	14 3/8 / 14 4/8	5 2/8 / 5 0/8	10 2/8	Campbell County	WY	Danny J. Brown	1995	4678
68 4/8	13 5/8 / 13 3/8	5 6/8 / 5 6/8	10 3/8	Converse County	WY	Robert L. Pagel, Jr.	1995	4678
68 4/8	12 7/8 / 12 3/8	6 7/8 / 6 6/8	11 2/8	Moffat County	CO	Dennis D. Johnson	1996	4678
68 4/8	13 4/8 / 13 2/8	5 4/8 / 5 4/8	12 7/8	Weld County	CO	Randy Wampler	1996	4678
68 4/8	12 7/8 / 12 7/8	5 5/8 / 5 5/8	9 3/8	Converse County	WY	Brian Goble	1996	4678
68 4/8	12 7/8 / 12 6/8	6 0/8 / 6 0/8	9 6/8	Converse County	WY	V. Gene Mathias	1996	4678
68 4/8	12 6/8 / 12 2/8	6 0/8 / 6 0/8	11 0/8	Campbell County	WY	Richard E. LaCrone	1996	4678
68 4/8	13 0/8 / 13 0/8	5 6/8 / 5 5/8	8 2/8	Magrath	ALB	Cameron Cook	1996	4678
68 4/8	14 0/8 / 13 7/8	5 6/8 / 5 7/8	13 1/8	Chouteau County	MT	Jim Wright	1996	4678
68 4/8	13 5/8 / 13 3/8	5 2/8 / 5 2/8	9 0/8	Guadalupe County	NM	Brandon Ray	1997	4678
68 4/8	13 1/8 / 13 2/8	5 7/8 / 6 0/8	11 3/8	Albany County	WY	Marlene Bowen	1997	4678
68 4/8	14 5/8 / 14 4/8	5 2/8 / 5 1/8	7 4/8	Johnson County	WY	Paul R. Chaffee	1997	4678
68 4/8	13 3/8 / 13 0/8	6 3/8 / 6 1/8	10 6/8	Weld County	CO	Doug McWilliams	1997	4678
68 4/8	13 5/8 / 13 4/8	5 6/8 / 5 6/8	11 2/8	Garfield County	MT	DuWayne M. Larson	1997	4678
68 4/8	13 7/8 / 13 0/8	5 5/8 / 5 5/8	7 4/8	Moffat County	CO	Charlie Colby	1997	4678
68 4/8	14 1/8 / 14 3/8	5 3/8 / 5 3/8	8 2/8	Johnson County	WY	Brian Schick	1997	4678
68 4/8	11 4/8 / 12 0/8	7 0/8 / 6 6/8	8 1/8	Moffat County	CO	Dewayne Mullins	1998	4678
68 4/8	12 3/8 / 12 6/8	5 7/8 / 5 7/8	6 2/8	Weld County	CO	Pat Sauvageau	1998	4678
68 4/8	12 6/8 / 12 6/8	5 6/8 / 5 5/8	10 4/8	Duchesne County	UT	Brian Ferebee	1998	4678
68 4/8	12 7/8 / 12 7/8	5 6/8 / 5 7/8	10 1/8	Custer County	MT	Casey Lyle Prell	1998	4678
68 4/8	13 2/8 / 13 1/8	5 0/8 / 4 7/8	8 0/8	Johnson County	WY	Donald Wayne Smith	1998	4678
68 4/8	12 1/8 / 12 4/8	6 2/8 / 6 1/8	13 6/8	Pershing County	NV	Paul Malay	1999	4678
68 4/8	13 3/8 / 13 2/8	5 5/8 / 5 4/8	9 1/8	Owyhee County	ID	Michael W. Schlegel	1999	4678
68 4/8	13 4/8 / 13 1/8	5 4/8 / 5 4/8	13 7/8	Rosebud County	MT	Robert E. Ebert	1999	4678
68 4/8	14 1/8 / 14 1/8	5 2/8 / 5 3/8	9 4/8	Beaverhead County	MT	Colby Robinson	1999	4678
68 4/8	13 7/8 / 13 6/8	5 6/8 / 5 6/8	10 5/8	Converse County	WY	Patrick J. Thomas	1999	4678
68 4/8	13 4/8 / 13 5/8	5 4/8 / 5 4/8	9 3/8	Converse County	WY	Phillip Banuelos	1999	4678
68 4/8	15 0/8 / 14 4/8	5 4/8 / 5 4/8	12 1/8	Modoc County	CA	Michael McEntee	2000	4678
68 4/8	11 6/8 / 12 3/8	5 4/8 / 5 6/8	9 0/8	Saguache County	CO	Victor A. Terrell	2000	4678
68 4/8	12 0/8 / 12 1/8	5 4/8 / 5 5/8	13 7/8	Sublette County	WY	Dave R. Burget	2000	4678
68 4/8	13 1/8 / 13 2/8	5 2/8 / 5 2/8	9 0/8	Uintah County	UT	Darrell Aplanalp	2000	4678
68 4/8	12 7/8 / 12 7/8	6 3/8 / 6 2/8	8 5/8	Weld County	CO	James Matuszewski	2000	4678
68 4/8	13 1/8 / 13 6/8	5 4/8 / 5 4/8	7 4/8	Campbell County	WY	Pat Corrado, Jr.	2000	4678
68 4/8	12 5/8 / 12 4/8	5 7/8 / 5 5/8	10 5/8	Converse County	WY	Bob Homberger	2001	4678
68 4/8	14 2/8 / 14 1/8	5 4/8 / 5 4/8	11 7/8	Garfield County	MT	Bob Smith	2001	4678
68 4/8	12 6/8 / 12 4/8	5 2/8 / 5 1/8	8 2/8	Converse County	WY	Terry M. Dennis	2001	4678
68 4/8	13 2/8 / 13 3/8	5 4/8 / 5 4/8	9 0/8	Yellowstone County	MT	Jonathan Gonitzke	2001	4678
68 4/8	12 7/8 / 13 1/8	5 5/8 / 5 4/8	5 0/8	Converse County	WY	David L. Duncan	2001	4678
68 4/8	12 5/8 / 12 5/8	5 6/8 / 5 5/8	7 7/8	Albany County	WY	Jack Satterfield, Jr.	2001	4678
68 4/8	14 0/8 / 14 2/8	5 4/8 / 5 4/8	8 4/8	Rosebud County	MT	Brian M. Bauer	2001	4678
68 4/8	13 3/8 / 13 1/8	5 5/8 / 5 5/8	7 6/8	Weld County	CO	Richard A. Devrous, Jr.	2002	4678
68 4/8	14 0/8 / 13 7/8	5 6/8 / 5 7/8	9 6/8	Catron County	NM	Keith Riley	2002	4678
68 4/8	14 0/8 / 12 2/8	6 4/8 / 6 2/8	11 1/8	Rio Blanco County	CO	Russell Overton	2002	4678
68 4/8	12 6/8 / 12 6/8	5 7/8 / 5 7/8	10 1/8	Owyhee County	ID	DeLoy Desaro	2002	4678
68 4/8	12 5/8 / 13 1/8	6 1/8 / 6 4/8	8 2/8	Campbell County	WY	Dennis Doherty	2002	4678
68 4/8	13 0/8 / 13 3/8	6 0/8 / 6 0/8	9 7/8	McKenzie County	ND	Chris Kifer	2003	4678
68 4/8	13 4/8 / 13 2/8	5 6/8 / 5 5/8	11 6/8	Hanna	ALB	Archie J. Nesbitt	2003	4678
68 4/8	12 3/8 / 12 5/8	6 0/8 / 5 7/8	8 3/8	Sweetwater County	WY	Chris Whytock	2003	4678
68 4/8	12 6/8 / 13 0/8	6 4/8 / 6 2/8	12 3/8	Big Horn County	WY	Christopher Blatt	2004	4678
*68 4/8	13 3/8 / 13 1/8	6 4/8 / 6 4/8	7 1/8	Yellowstone County	MT	Scott Urfer	2004	4678
68 4/8	13 1/8 / 13 1/8	5 5/8 / 5 4/8	10 6/8	Converse County	WY	Paul Rodgers	2004	4678
68 4/8	12 6/8 / 12 6/8	5 6/8 / 5 5/8	8 5/8	Campbell County	WY	William H. Peterson	2004	4678
68 4/8	11 5/8 / 11 5/8	6 0/8 / 6 0/8	8 3/8	Moffat County	CO	Rodney Kennedy	2004	4678
68 4/8	12 2/8 / 12 2/8	5 6/8 / 5 5/8	9 6/8	Converse County	WY	Leonard Anglewitz	2004	4678
68 4/8	12 2/8 / 12 2/8	6 0/8 / 5 6/8	9 7/8	Harding County	SD	Jason Gregg	2004	4678
68 4/8	12 3/8 / 12 4/8	6 0/8 / 6 0/8	8 3/8	Washoe County	NV	Cole T. Peck	2005	4678
68 4/8	13 4/8 / 13 6/8	5 6/8 / 5 5/8	8 7/8	Yellowstone County	MT	Kris Bermes	2005	4678
*68 4/8	13 0/8 / 12 6/8	5 4/8 / 5 4/8	9 7/8	De Baca County	NM	Daniel Parks	2005	4678
*68 4/8	13 0/8 / 12 7/8	6 0/8 / 5 7/8	7 7/8	Moffat County	CO	James Mense	2005	4678
68 4/8	14 7/8 / 14 0/8	5 1/8 / 5 0/8	9 7/8	Cochise County	AZ	Michael J. Bylina	2005	4678
68 4/8	11 6/8 / 11 6/8	5 7/8 / 5 6/8	6 7/8	Blaine County	ID	Brian Hamel	2005	4678
68 4/8	13 4/8 / 13 3/8	5 3/8 / 5 4/8	11 0/8	Converse County	WY	Lowell Tveit	2005	4678
68 4/8	11 3/8 / 11 1/8	6 0/8 / 6 2/8	11 6/8	Powder River County	MT	Steven P. Boswell	2006	4678
68 4/8	12 4/8 / 12 3/8	6 2/8 / 6 2/8	7 3/8	Campbell County	WY	Tippy H. Clark	2006	4678
68 4/8	13 5/8 / 13 6/8	6 0/8 / 6 0/8	11 6/8	Crook County	WY	Don Scofield	2006	4678
*68 4/8	13 4/8 / 13 4/8	5 6/8 / 5 6/8	11 1/8	Carbon County	WY	Jim Morgan	2006	4678
68 4/8	14 1/8 / 14 1/8	5 2/8 / 5 1/8	11 2/8	Mercer County	ND	Greg Passa	2006	4678
68 4/8	13 0/8 / 13 1/8	5 6/8 / 5 6/8	13 5/8	Yavapai County	AZ	Charles W. Rehor	2007	4678
68 4/8	12 4/8 / 12 5/8	5 7/8 / 5 7/8	10 5/8	Clark County	ID	Dave R. Burget	2008	4678
68 4/8	12 6/8 / 12 6/8	5 3/8 / 5 3/8	9 5/8	Sweetwater County	WY	Gary Gapp	2008	4678
68 4/8	12 1/8 / 12 3/8	6 3/8 / 6 3/8	9 3/8	Moffat County	CO	Gary Whitten	2008	4678
*68 4/8	13 2/8 / 13 2/8	5 3/8 / 5 4/8	6 2/8	Harding County	SD	Paul Steiger	2008	4678
*68 4/8	12 4/8 / 12 4/8	5 5/8 / 5 5/8	8 6/8	Moffat County	CO	Nick Moyer	2008	4678
*68 4/8	12 2/8 / 12 2/8	5 4/8 / 5 4/8	9 0/8	Gove County	KS	Matt Palmquist	2008	4678
68 4/8	13 7/8 / 14 2/8	5 6/8 / 5 6/8	18 3/8	Millard County	UT	Ryan Tuttle	2009	4678
*68 4/8	12 4/8 / 12 4/8	6 3/8 / 6 2/8	7 6/8	Converse County	WY	Keith A. Kindred	2009	4678
68 4/8	13 4/8 / 13 3/8	5 4/8 / 5 5/8	9 4/8	Converse County	WY	Lou Kindred	2009	4678
68 4/8	12 3/8 / 12 1/8	6 0/8 / 6 0/8	7 1/8	Rosebud County	MT	Jon Harris	2009	4678
68 4/8	13 1/8 / 13 2/8	5 6/8 / 5 6/8	8 0/8	Big Horn County	MT	Chad Christophersen	2009	4678
*68 4/8	14 0/8 / 14 0/8	5 5/8 / 5 4/8	8 2/8	Beaverhead County	MT	Jarred Krueger	2009	4678
68 4/8	13 2/8 / 13 1/8	5 4/8 / 5 3/8	11 0/8	Converse County	WY	Tim Taylor	2009	4678
*68 4/8	11 6/8 / 11 6/8	5 5/8 / 5 5/8	8 7/8	Powder River County	MT	Eric Burling	2009	4678
68 4/8	13 3/8 / 13 0/8	6 2/8 / 6 1/8	9 5/8	Brooks	ALB	Alexander Sharif	2009	4678
*68 4/8	13 6/8 / 13 6/8	5 6/8 / 5 6/8	9 0/8	Albany County	WY	Brian W. Hahl	2009	4678
68 4/8	12 7/8 / 13 0/8	5 7/8 / 5 7/8	9 0/8	Natrona County	WY	Jeff Jacob	2010	4678
68 4/8	12 0/8 / 12 0/8	6 0/8 / 5 6/8	12 3/8	Campbell County	WY	Scott Schmidt	2010	4678
68 2/8	12 4/8 / 12 4/8	6 2/8 / 6 0/8	11 6/8	Moffat County	CO	Burl Duckworth	1958	4844
68 2/8	12 6/8 / 12 6/8	5 7/8 / 5 5/8	10 5/8	Harding County	SD	Chet Wohlhueter	1963	4844
68 2/8	13 5/8 / 13 3/8	5 3/8 / 5 2/8	8 7/8	Morton County	ND	Fred F. Heer	1973	4844
68 2/8	12 4/8 / 12 5/8	6 2/8 / 6 3/8	11 4/8	Fremont County	WY	Bob Freese	1978	4844

860

PRONGHORN

Minimum Score 67   Continued

SCORE	LENGTH OF R HORN L	CIRCUMFERENCE R OF BASE L	INSIDE SPREAD	AREA	STATE/ PROVINCE	HUNTER'S NAME	DATE	RANK
68 2/8	13 2/8 13 2/8	5 6/8 6 0/8	9 1/8	Sweetwater County	WY	Charles Bartlett	1978	4844
68 2/8	13 0/8 12 5/8	5 6/8 5 5/8	8 1/8	Thomas County	NE	Harold L. Bowman	1978	4844
68 2/8	13 6/8 14 2/8	5 5/8 5 4/8	7 2/8	Lemhi County	ID	Richard Dewey	1978	4844
68 2/8	13 1/8 13 1/8	5 3/8 5 2/8	9 5/8	Saguache County	CO	Doy K. Curtis	1978	4844
68 2/8	13 5/8 13 2/8	5 6/8 5 4/8	8 4/8	Fremont County	WY	Will Yeates	1978	4844
68 2/8	12 1/8 11 7/8	5 6/8 5 7/8	8 0/8	Lemhi County	ID	Larry Cross	1979	4844
68 2/8	14 1/8 13 7/8	5 5/8 6 0/8	7 5/8	Coconino County	AZ	Jim Ellis	1979	4844
68 2/8	13 6/8 13 7/8	6 2/8 6 2/8	8 6/8	Sweetwater County	WY	Dean Kendall	1980	4844
68 2/8	13 0/8 13 0/8	6 0/8 5 5/8	9 0/8	Natrona County	WY	William E. Ehrman	1981	4844
68 2/8	12 6/8 12 6/8	5 4/8 5 5/8	10 0/8	Natrona County	WY	R. G. Williams	1981	4844
68 2/8	12 3/8 12 4/8	5 6/8 5 6/8	8 0/8	Moffat County	CO	Barry J. Smith	1981	4844
68 2/8	13 0/8 13 0/8	5 7/8 5 6/8	6 7/8	Natrona County	WY	Rodger Warwick	1981	4844
68 2/8	12 6/8 12 6/8	6 0/8 6 1/8	7 3/8	Sweetwater County	WY	Ed Budge	1981	4844
68 2/8	12 0/8 12 2/8	5 6/8 5 6/8	8 0/8	Converse County	WY	Butch Crawford	1982	4844
68 2/8	14 1/8 13 7/8	5 4/8 5 4/8	13 1/8	Converse County	WY	Donald Schram	1982	4844
68 2/8	11 7/8 12 1/8	6 1/8 6 1/8	9 3/8	White Pine County	NV	Tony S. Whitten	1983	4844
68 2/8	14 6/8 14 6/8	5 2/8 5 1/8	10 6/8	Saguache County	CO	Steve Van Treese	1983	4844
68 2/8	12 7/8 12 6/8	5 4/8 5 4/8	9 4/8	Sublette County	WY	Terry Wright	1983	4844
68 2/8	13 3/8 13 1/8	5 4/8 5 4/8	11 1/8	Weld County	CO	Dennis Schweitzer	1983	4844
68 2/8	13 5/8 13 5/8	5 4/8 5 4/8	10 4/8	Bingham County	ID	Doug Foss	1983	4844
68 2/8	13 1/8 12 7/8	5 7/8 5 6/8	11 7/8	Wallace County	KS	Darren Collins	1983	4844
68 2/8	13 5/8 13 1/8	5 3/8 5 3/8	10 3/8	Hughes County	SD	Darrel L. Reinke	1984	4844
68 2/8	13 1/8 13 3/8	5 6/8 5 6/8	11 3/8	Carbon County	WY	Ron Breitsprecher	1984	4844
68 2/8	14 3/8 14 6/8	6 1/8 5 7/8	11 1/8	Fremont County	WY	Thomas E. Axthelm	1984	4844
68 2/8	12 2/8 13 2/8	5 3/8 5 4/8	6 7/8	Converse County	WY	Al Sullivan	1984	4844
68 2/8	12 4/8 12 7/8	6 3/8 6 2/8	8 6/8	Natrona County	WY	Ray L. Harbin	1985	4844
68 2/8	14 0/8 13 6/8	5 4/8 5 4/8	10 5/8	Carter County	MT	Juanita Byrne	1985	4844
68 2/8	12 3/8 12 6/8	5 4/8 5 7/8	9 2/8	White Pine County	NV	Carlos Hernandez	1987	4844
68 2/8	13 1/8 13 2/8	5 7/8 5 7/8	8 4/8	Jenner	ALB	Jack Kempf	1987	4844
68 2/8	13 3/8 13 4/8	5 4/8 5 4/8	10 3/8	Dawson County	MT	Dave Athas	1987	4844
68 2/8	14 0/8 14 0/8	5 4/8 5 4/8	12 1/8	Sweetwater County	WY	Marvin L. Temme	1988	4844
68 2/8	13 5/8 13 7/8	5 5/8 5 5/8	9 3/8	Meagher County	MT	Gene Clark	1988	4844
68 2/8	13 3/8 13 4/8	6 0/8 5 6/8	6 7/8	Converse County	WY	Morris Karski	1989	4844
68 2/8	12 7/8 12 7/8	5 5/8 5 6/8	14 5/8	McKenzie County	ND	Wayne R. Streitz	1989	4844
68 2/8	13 2/8 13 2/8	5 4/8 5 4/8	9 6/8	Park County	MT	Steve Kamps	1989	4844
68 2/8	12 5/8 13 0/8	5 3/8 5 3/8	8 0/8	Morton County	ND	Mike Fischer	1989	4844
68 2/8	14 2/8 14 5/8	5 6/8 5 6/8	13 0/8	Garfield County	MT	Ken Davidson	1989	4844
68 2/8	12 5/8 13 1/8	5 7/8 5 5/8	11 7/8	Campbell County	WY	Allen Jackson	1989	4844
68 2/8	11 2/8 11 1/8	6 0/8 6 1/8	11 2/8	Moffat County	CO	Richard C. Green	1990	4844
68 2/8	13 2/8 13 4/8	5 3/8 5 2/8	8 5/8	Moffat County	CO	Lonny Vanatta	1990	4844
68 2/8	13 3/8 13 2/8	5 4/8 5 3/8	9 0/8	Carter County	MT	Lewis E. Hartenstine	1990	4844
68 2/8	11 3/8 11 4/8	5 6/8 5 6/8	8 6/8	Cypress	ALB	Dan David	1990	4844
68 2/8	11 7/8 12 2/8	6 0/8 5 6/8	9 1/8	Converse County	WY	Len Elie	1990	4844
68 2/8	13 3/8 13 4/8	5 5/8 5 4/8	13 4/8	Campbell County	WY	Troy C. Christensen	1991	4844
68 2/8	13 7/8 14 1/8	5 6/8 5 5/8	11 7/8	Slope County	ND	Gene D. Davis	1991	4844
68 2/8	13 2/8 13 2/8	5 4/8 5 4/8	8 1/8	Converse County	WY	John S. Lewis III	1991	4844
68 2/8	12 4/8 12 3/8	5 6/8 5 6/8	8 7/8	Campbell County	WY	Dave Vomela	1991	4844
68 2/8	13 4/8 13 2/8	5 6/8 5 6/8	17 0/8	Slope County	ND	Rydell Becker	1991	4844
68 2/8	13 6/8 14 1/8	5 7/8 5 6/8	13 5/8	Campbell County	WY	Ken Rimer	1991	4844
68 2/8	13 0/8 12 6/8	5 7/8 6 0/8	9 2/8	Moffat County	CO	Kenneth Thompson	1992	4844
68 2/8	13 0/8 12 7/8	6 1/8 6 0/8	9 1/8	Moffat County	CO	Jeffrey C. Fretz	1992	4844
68 2/8	13 3/8 12 3/8	6 2/8 6 0/8	11 2/8	Union County	NM	James David Vinson	1992	4844
68 2/8	13 5/8 13 7/8	6 2/8 6 2/8	12 2/8	Sweetwater County	WY	Daryl Burttschell	1992	4844
68 2/8	13 5/8 13 2/8	5 5/8 5 4/8	11 0/8	Campbell County	WY	Vernon Kleve	1992	4844
68 2/8	13 2/8 12 6/8	5 6/8 5 7/8	12 1/8	Converse County	WY	Johnnie R. Walters	1992	4844
68 2/8	13 0/8 13 0/8	6 1/8 6 0/8	10 0/8	Dunn County	ND	Larry Olheiser	1992	4844
68 2/8	12 4/8 13 1/8	6 0/8 5 7/8	9 1/8	Manyberries	ALB	Gary Goulet	1992	4844
68 2/8	13 2/8 13 2/8	5 6/8 5 5/8	8 0/8	Fremont County	WY	Reggie Scheierman	1992	4844
68 2/8	13 4/8 13 3/8	5 7/8 5 6/8	12 4/8	Cypress	ALB	David Moore	1992	4844
68 2/8	14 2/8 14 1/8	5 3/8 5 3/8	11 2/8	Washoe County	NV	Richard A. Hanson	1993	4844
68 2/8	13 5/8 13 4/8	5 4/8 5 4/8	7 6/8	Moffat County	CO	Kurt W. Keskimaki	1993	4844
68 2/8	14 4/8 14 4/8	5 2/8 5 3/8	15 3/8	De Baca County	NM	Danny Griffith	1993	4844
68 2/8	13 4/8 12 7/8	5 7/8 5 6/8	7 7/8	Sweetwater County	WY	Terry Story	1993	4844
68 2/8	13 4/8 13 2/8	5 2/8 5 3/8	8 5/8	Converse County	WY	Robert Fulton	1993	4844
68 2/8	13 4/8 13 5/8	5 3/8 5 2/8	7 7/8	Converse County	WY	Ken Mamazzo	1993	4844
68 2/8	12 5/8 13 1/8	5 4/8 5 7/8	10 0/8	Cheyenne County	NE	Michael McCallister	1993	4844
68 2/8	13 1/8 13 1/8	5 5/8 5 5/8	10 0/8	Corson County	SD	Fred Kober	1993	4844
68 2/8	13 7/8 13 6/8	5 3/8 5 2/8	10 0/8	Humboldt County	NV	Katherine Lee Fillmore	1994	4844
68 2/8	13 2/8 13 0/8	5 6/8 5 6/8	10 1/8	Sweetwater County	WY	James B. White	1994	4844
68 2/8	14 2/8 14 1/8	6 0/8 6 0/8	13 2/8	Humboldt County	NV	Robert L. Brooks	1994	4844
68 2/8	13 5/8 14 1/8	5 4/8 5 4/8	9 5/8	Moffat County	CO	Robert Goodnight	1994	4844
68 2/8	14 1/8 14 0/8	5 3/8 5 4/8	10 0/8	Washoe County	NV	Clayton D. Johnson	1994	4844
68 2/8	13 3/8 13 6/8	5 3/8 5 2/8	9 0/8	Moffat County	CO	Scott Jankowski	1994	4844
68 2/8	13 3/8 13 2/8	5 4/8 5 2/8	9 4/8	Millard County	UT	Carl R. Gramlich	1994	4844
68 2/8	13 0/8 13 3/8	5 4/8 5 5/8	9 3/8	Fremont County	WY	Ken Maynard	1994	4844
68 2/8	13 2/8 13 5/8	5 7/8 5 7/8	11 1/8	Sweetwater County	WY	Darin L. Howe	1994	4844
68 2/8	13 6/8 13 7/8	5 7/8 6 0/8	11 2/8	Millard County	UT	David Edwards	1994	4844
68 2/8	12 0/8 12 6/8	6 2/8 6 2/8	8 7/8	Crook County	WY	Dean Ransbottom	1994	4844
68 2/8	13 0/8 12 7/8	6 0/8 6 0/8	12 7/8	Lake County	OR	Mark Penninger	1994	4844
68 2/8	13 2/8 13 6/8	5 4/8 5 7/8	10 7/8	Sheridan County	WY	Steve Boster	1994	4844
68 2/8	13 6/8 14 1/8	5 6/8 5 5/8	8 2/8	Petroleum County	MT	Craig Richardson	1994	4844
68 2/8	12 7/8 12 4/8	6 4/8 6 4/8	9 2/8	Converse County	WY	Robert K. Woeck	1994	4844
68 2/8	13 4/8 13 5/8	5 4/8 5 4/8	9 2/8	Niobrara County	WY	Gene H. Anderson	1994	4844
68 2/8	13 0/8 13 2/8	6 0/8 6 0/8	9 4/8	Modoc County	CA	Michael Tilley	1995	4844
68 2/8	13 7/8 14 0/8	5 3/8 5 3/8	11 6/8	Sweetwater County	WY	Craig Boheler	1995	4844
68 2/8	13 4/8 13 3/8	5 3/8 5 3/8	9 6/8	Moffat County	CO	Juanita Brewer	1995	4844
68 2/8	13 4/8 13 4/8	5 6/8 5 4/8	7 2/8	Campbell County	WY	Gordon L. Doyle	1995	4844
68 2/8	11 5/8 11 4/8	6 4/8 6 5/8	8 5/8	Big Horn County	WY	Jerome D. Larson	1995	4844
68 2/8	13 4/8 13 4/8	6 0/8 5 7/8	10 6/8	Billings County	ND	Irvin E. Prough	1995	4844
68 2/8	13 4/8 13 5/8	6 1/8 6 1/8	8 7/8	Converse County	WY	Steve Thomas, Sr.	1995	4844
68 2/8	12 6/8 13 1/8	5 6/8 5 6/8	11 3/8	Custer County	MT	James Bornman	1995	4844
68 2/8	13 6/8 13 6/8	6 1/8 5 7/8	10 5/8	Custer County	MT	Don Jones	1995	4844
68 2/8	12 4/8 12 6/8	5 5/8 5 5/8	9 3/8	Campbell County	WY	Gene Faul	1995	4844
68 2/8	14 2/8 14 6/8	5 4/8 5 3/8	8 1/8	Montrose County	CO	Dave Emken	1995	4844
68 2/8	13 7/8 14 0/8	5 4/8 5 3/8	12 2/8	Powder River County	MT	Richard Driscoll	1995	4844

PRONGHORN

Minimum Score 67 — Continued

SCORE	LENGTH OF HORN R	L	CIRCUMFERENCE OF BASE R	L	INSIDE SPREAD	AREA	STATE/ PROVINCE	HUNTER'S NAME	DATE	RANK
68 2/8	13 6/8	13 6/8	5 3/8	5 3/8	13 6/8	Guadalupe County	NM	Brandon Ray	1996	4844
68 2/8	12 3/8	12 4/8	6 0/8	6 0/8	8 4/8	Moffat County	CO	Eric A. Sawyer	1996	4844
68 2/8	12 2/8	12 2/8	5 6/8	5 5/8	9 3/8	Converse County	WY	Kurt Ebers	1996	4844
68 2/8	12 1/8	12 0/8	5 6/8	5 6/8	7 7/8	Converse County	WY	Mark Kronyak	1996	4844
68 2/8	12 3/8	12 6/8	6 1/8	6 0/8	6 7/8	Powder River County	MT	Lindsey M. Manca	1996	4844
68 2/8	14 2/8	14 0/8	5 3/8	5 3/8	7 6/8	Hays	ALB	Steve MacKenzie	1996	4844
68 2/8	13 2/8	13 0/8	5 4/8	5 4/8	8 5/8	Custer County	SD	Jim DeRungs	1996	4844
68 2/8	14 0/8	13 4/8	5 4/8	5 4/8	12 2/8	Garfield County	MT	D. Mitch Kottas	1996	4844
68 2/8	14 0/8	14 0/8	5 7/8	5 7/8	6 4/8	Moffat County	CO	Kevin L. Reid	1997	4844
68 2/8	14 3/8	14 3/8	5 2/8	5 3/8	6 3/8	Tooele County	UT	Gilbert Hernandez	1997	4844
68 2/8	14 5/8	14 2/8	5 5/8	5 4/8	11 3/8	Campbell County	WY	James M. Augustine	1997	4844
68 2/8	12 5/8	12 5/8	5 5/8	5 6/8	8 3/8	Powder River County	MT	John Martinson	1997	4844
68 2/8	12 3/8	12 2/8	5 7/8	5 2/8	6 6/8	Powder River County	MT	Scott Miller	1997	4844
68 2/8	12 7/8	12 3/8	5 5/8	5 4/8	8 2/8	Manyberries	ALB	Robert G. Barden	1997	4844
68 2/8	12 7/8	12 7/8	5 7/8	5 7/8	9 7/8	Weld County	CO	Barry J. Smith	1998	4844
68 2/8	13 6/8	13 5/8	6 0/8	6 0/8	7 3/8	Converse County	WY	A. M. Oakes, Jr.	1998	4844
68 2/8	12 5/8	12 4/8	6 0/8	6 0/8	8 6/8	Converse County	WY	Bernard Robert Belaire III	1998	4844
68 2/8	12 6/8	12 2/8	6 0/8	5 7/8	9 4/8	Converse County	WY	Michael Travis	1998	4844
68 2/8	12 4/8	13 5/8	6 2/8	6 1/8	14 2/8	Converse County	WY	Len Butler	1998	4844
68 2/8	14 0/8	14 0/8	5 3/8	5 4/8	9 4/8	Orion	ALB	Lorne D. Rinkel	1998	4844
68 2/8	14 0/8	13 5/8	5 2/8	5 2/8	9 7/8	Albany County	WY	Lance Tyler	1998	4844
68 2/8	13 0/8	12 7/8	6 1/8	6 1/8	11 1/8	Converse County	WY	Gary Netzer	1998	4844
68 2/8	14 2/8	13 4/8	6 2/8	6 1/8	12 7/8	Campbell County	WY	Anthony G. Sexe	1998	4844
68 2/8	12 5/8	12 3/8	5 6/8	5 5/8	9 6/8	Platte County	WY	Denny Graham	1999	4844
68 2/8	13 0/8	12 6/8	6 3/8	6 3/8	7 0/8	Powder River County	MT	David Perry	1999	4844
68 2/8	14 5/8	13 1/8	6 1/8	5 6/8	10 6/8	Walsh	ALB	Danny H. Lewis	1999	4844
68 2/8	13 2/8	13 6/8	5 7/8	5 6/8	10 5/8	Harding County	SD	Ken Gher	1999	4844
68 2/8	14 0/8	14 1/8	5 3/8	5 3/8	12 0/8	Rosebud County	MT	Sam Y. Perone	1999	4844
68 2/8	12 4/8	12 4/8	5 6/8	5 4/8	8 0/8	Sublette County	WY	Virgil Burget	2000	4844
68 2/8	12 5/8	12 2/8	5 6/8	6 0/8	10 3/8	Park County	CO	David Kintz, Jr.	2000	4844
68 2/8	14 4/8	14 5/8	5 5/8	5 5/8	10 1/8	Powder River County	MT	Gene Smith	2000	4844
68 2/8	13 2/8	13 5/8	5 5/8	5 5/8	14 0/8	Laramie County	WY	Kyle D. Parish	2001	4844
68 2/8	12 4/8	12 3/8	6 0/8	6 0/8	9 2/8	Campbell County	WY	Mario Hernandez	2001	4844
68 2/8	13 2/8	13 4/8	6 1/8	6 0/8	11 1/8	El Paso County	CO	Elizabeth M. Harvell	2002	4844
68 2/8	11 3/8	11 4/8	6 0/8	6 1/8	10 6/8	Big Horn County	WY	Bill Miller	2002	4844
68 2/8	13 1/8	13 4/8	5 6/8	5 4/8	10 6/8	Lake County	OR	K. C. Thrasher	2002	4844
68 2/8	13 2/8	12 6/8	5 7/8	5 6/8	9 4/8	Larimer County	CO	Cody A. Olson	2002	4844
68 2/8	12 3/8	12 5/8	5 7/8	6 1/8	9 0/8	Albany County	WY	Michael E. Richards	2002	4844
68 2/8	12 5/8	13 1/8	5 7/8	5 7/8	7 3/8	Moffat County	CO	Delvin Williams	2002	4844
68 2/8	12 7/8	12 4/8	6 0/8	6 0/8	9 2/8	Powder River County	MT	Thomas C. Weimann	2002	4844
68 2/8	13 0/8	13 0/8	5 5/8	5 5/8	8 6/8	Harding County	SD	Andrew J. Blum	2003	4844
68 2/8	14 0/8	13 6/8	5 2/8	5 2/8	9 4/8	Campbell County	WY	Brian S. Gallinger	2003	4844
68 2/8	12 6/8	12 7/8	5 6/8	5 5/8	9 6/8	Johnson County	WY	Joel Hoenk	2003	4844
68 2/8	12 6/8	12 7/8	5 6/8	5 6/8	12 3/8	Golden Valley County	ND	DuWayne M. Larson	2003	4844
68 2/8	12 3/8	13 0/8	5 7/8	5 6/8	11 7/8	Natrona County	WY	Roger Ralph	2004	4844
68 2/8	12 7/8	12 7/8	6 1/8	6 1/8	13 4/8	Twin Falls County	ID	Glen Berry	2004	4844
68 2/8	12 7/8	12 6/8	5 7/8	5 7/8	18 3/8	Clark County	ID	Tom Nelson	2004	4844
68 2/8	12 2/8	12 5/8	6 0/8	5 6/8	10 3/8	Elbert County	CO	Peter J. Selinski	2004	4844
68 2/8	13 6/8	12 0/8	5 5/8	5 5/8	12 1/8	Converse County	WY	Jason Flies	2004	4844
68 2/8	12 1/8	12 1/8	5 6/8	5 5/8	11 3/8	Powder River County	MT	Scott Heinzer	2004	4844
68 2/8	13 6/8	13 5/8	6 0/8	6 0/8	9 4/8	Johnson County	WY	Dave Harness	2004	4844
68 2/8	13 4/8	13 4/8	6 0/8	6 0/8	8 0/8	Campbell County	WY	Joel Glazer	2004	4844
*68 2/8	13 0/8	12 5/8	5 5/8	5 5/8	7 7/8	Butte County	SD	Gregory Walker	2005	4844
68 2/8	11 7/8	12 1/8	5 6/8	5 4/8	10 4/8	Madison County	MT	Jim Loomis	2005	4844
68 2/8	13 6/8	13 5/8	5 2/8	5 2/8	9 6/8	Las Animas County	CO	Randy Peck	2005	4844
68 2/8	12 5/8	12 5/8	5 7/8	5 6/8	9 4/8	Laramie County	WY	Laine Parish	2005	4844
68 2/8	14 2/8	14 1/8	6 0/8	6 0/8	13 2/8	Blaine County	MT	Gary Lampkins	2005	4844
68 2/8	12 2/8	12 3/8	6 2/8	6 0/8	8 0/8	Powder River County	MT	William Elfland	2005	4844
*68 2/8	12 6/8	12 5/8	6 1/8	6 0/8	11 1/8	Powder River County	MT	DuWayne Larson	2005	4844
68 2/8	13 3/8	11 6/8	5 4/8	5 4/8	12 7/8	Meade County	SD	Chad Kauffman	2005	4844
68 2/8	12 5/8	12 5/8	5 5/8	5 4/8	8 3/8	Lemhi County	ID	Alan L. Hall	2006	4844
68 2/8	13 1/8	12 6/8	5 3/8	5 2/8	14 2/8	Yellowstone County	MT	Jacob D. Jovanovich	2006	4844
68 2/8	12 0/8	12 0/8	6 0/8	6 0/8	7 4/8	Madison County	MT	John P. Branger	2006	4844
68 2/8	13 3/8	13 7/8	6 1/8	6 2/8	16 2/8	Weston County	WY	Robert Dowen	2006	4844
*68 2/8	13 0/8	13 0/8	6 0/8	6 1/8	14 0/8	Campbell County	WY	John Patterson	2006	4844
*68 2/8	12 2/8	12 5/8	5 7/8	5 5/8	9 6/8	Campbell County	WY	Jon Sanborn	2006	4844
68 2/8	12 6/8	12 7/8	5 4/8	5 4/8	8 7/8	Converse County	WY	Alex Abshire	2006	4844
*68 2/8	13 1/8	13 2/8	6 2/8	6 1/8	10 5/8	Sheridan County	WY	Kent Andersen	2006	4844
68 2/8	14 0/8	14 0/8	5 4/8	5 5/8	10 2/8	Cherry County	NE	David J. Nicolai	2006	4844
68 2/8	13 2/8	13 0/8	5 4/8	5 3/8	7 4/8	Sweetwater County	WY	Joe Bruscato	2007	4844
68 2/8	13 3/8	13 3/8	5 6/8	5 6/8	10 3/8	Buffalo County	SD	Jeff Jacob	2007	4844
68 2/8	13 4/8	13 4/8	5 5/8	6 0/8	9 5/8	Converse County	WY	Alan Brock	2007	4844
*68 2/8	12 6/8	12 4/8	5 2/8	5 4/8	9 4/8	Saguache County	CO	Ron Barnett	2007	4844
*68 2/8	12 3/8	12 1/8	6 0/8	6 1/8	11 6/8	Moffat County	CO	Jason Bienek	2007	4844
68 2/8	13 6/8	13 6/8	5 3/8	5 3/8	12 2/8	Converse County	WY	Alex Karst	2007	4844
68 2/8	13 7/8	13 6/8	5 6/8	5 3/8	10 6/8	Fergus County	MT	John Fleharty	2007	4844
*68 2/8	13 7/8	14 0/8	5 6/8	5 4/8	11 1/8	Harding County	SD	Thomas E. Rothrock	2007	4844
68 2/8	12 3/8	12 4/8	5 7/8	5 7/8	8 6/8	Rosebud County	MT	Pier Brewer	2008	4844
68 2/8	13 1/8	13 5/8	6 1/8	6 1/8	10 6/8	Carter County	MT	James Wendt	2008	4844
68 2/8	11 4/8	11 5/8	6 3/8	6 2/8	8 5/8	Moffat County	CO	Gerald T. Dowell	2008	4844
68 2/8	13 6/8	13 5/8	5 2/8	5 1/8	8 6/8	Butte County	SD	Gary W. Clarke	2008	4844
68 2/8	12 2/8	12 0/8	5 6/8	5 7/8	7 6/8	Routt County	CO	Mark S. Peffer	2008	4844
68 2/8	13 3/8	13 4/8	5 7/8	5 6/8	10 6/8	Lincoln County	WY	Robert E. Valentine	2008	4844
*68 2/8	14 7/8	14 6/8	6 2/8	6 0/8	11 3/8	Pennington County	SD	Wayne A. Buckley	2008	4844
68 2/8	12 7/8	12 7/8	5 7/8	5 7/8	8 0/8	Fergus County	MT	John Fleharty	2008	4844
68 2/8	12 2/8	12 1/8	6 0/8	6 1/8	7 4/8	Lincoln County	WY	Tim Hare	2009	4844
68 2/8	12 5/8	12 5/8	5 7/8	5 7/8	10 3/8	Hill County	MT	Brendon Degner	2009	4844
68 2/8	13 3/8	13 5/8	5 5/8	5 4/8	8 5/8	Beaverhead County	MT	Raymond L. Gross, Jr.	2009	4844
*68 2/8	13 1/8	12 6/8	6 0/8	5 7/8	11 2/8	Converse County	WY	Brad Edgington	2009	4844
*68 2/8	13 3/8	13 4/8	5 6/8	5 4/8	8 6/8	Butte County	ID	Ken Wall	2009	4844
68 2/8	13 0/8	13 2/8	5 7/8	6 0/8	11 4/8	Garfield County	MT	Sonny Templeton	2009	4844
*68 2/8	13 3/8	13 3/8	5 4/8	5 4/8	7 0/8	Otero County	CO	Andrew Foor	2009	4844
*68 2/8	13 1/8	13 1/8	5 5/8	5 4/8	9 1/8	Moffat County	CO	Gary Schuetz	2009	4844
68 2/8	13 6/8	13 5/8	5 4/8	5 3/8	10 0/8	Converse County	WY	Jonathan Aultman	2009	4844
68 2/8	13 4/8	13 3/8	5 6/8	5 5/8	11 0/8	Weston County	WY	Bob Dowen	2009	4844

862

PRONGHORN

Minimum Score 67   Continued

SCORE	LENGTH OF R HORN L	CIRCUMFERENCE R OF BASE L	INSIDE SPREAD	AREA	STATE/ PROVINCE	HUNTER'S NAME	DATE	RANK
68 2/8	12 2/8 12 0/8	5 5/8 5 5/8	9 7/8	Stark County	ND	Michael Pistulka	2009	4844
68 2/8	12 5/8 13 0/8	5 5/8 5 6/8	12 0/8	Converse County	WY	Jim Saunoris, Jr.	2009	4844
*68 2/8	13 1/8 13 1/8	5 4/8 5 3/8	7 6/8	Park County	CO	Robert Feeney	2009	4844
*68 2/8	13 1/8 13 0/8	5 3/8 5 3/8	7 4/8	Weston County	WY	Jeremiah Roberson	2010	4844
68 1/8	14 1/8 13 0/8	5 4/8 5 6/8	7 7/8	Campbell County	WY	Reinhold L. Lind	1961	5042
68 0/8	13 4/8 13 4/8	5 4/8 5 4/8	7 5/8	Carbon County	WY	Bill Cunningham	1963	5042
68 0/8	14 0/8 13 6/8	5 2/8 5 3/8	8 0/8	Morton County	ND	Roy D. Russell, Jr.	1967	5042
68 0/8	13 0/8 13 0/8	5 7/8 5 7/8	9 6/8	Saguache County	CO	David Scheid	1974	5042
68 0/8	11 4/8 11 3/8	5 7/8 5 6/8	7 3/8	Burke County	ND	Allen L. Nelson	1974	5042
68 0/8	12 4/8 12 5/8	5 6/8 5 5/8	10 6/8	Custer County	ID	Gary Schaffner	1975	5042
68 0/8	13 0/8 13 3/8	5 5/8 5 4/8	9 7/8	Clark County	ID	Ron Parish	1977	5042
68 0/8	13 5/8 13 3/8	5 6/8 5 6/8	10 3/8	Humboldt County	NV	Vic Christison	1978	5042
68 0/8	13 2/8 12 7/8	6 1/8 6 0/8	10 1/8	Sweetwater County	WY	Jack Riddle	1979	5042
68 0/8	12 2/8 12 4/8	5 6/8 5 5/8	8 4/8	Natrona County	WY	Todd James	1980	5042
68 0/8	13 6/8 12 3/8	5 6/8 5 5/8	7 2/8	Moffat County	CO	Judd Cooney	1981	5042
68 0/8	13 3/8 13 5/8	5 4/8 5 4/8	8 2/8	Butte County	SD	James S. Nelson IV	1981	5042
68 0/8	13 3/8 14 3/8	5 3/8 5 5/8	15 4/8	Campbell County	WY	Joseph Strasser, Jr.	1981	5042
68 0/8	14 1/8 14 1/8	5 4/8 5 1/8	6 7/8	Lassen County	CA	Junior Morris	1982	5042
68 0/8	13 4/8 13 6/8	5 6/8 5 5/8	13 4/8	Sweetwater County	WY	Sy Gilliland	1982	5042
68 0/8	13 2/8 13 3/8	5 5/8 5 4/8	11 0/8	Fremont County	WY	Everett A. Boss	1982	5042
68 0/8	12 4/8 12 3/8	6 0/8 5 7/8	14 4/8	Yavapai County	AZ	Jeff W. Elmer	1982	5042
68 0/8	13 2/8 13 2/8	5 7/8 5 6/8	10 1/8	Converse County	WY	Bill Frodl	1982	5042
68 0/8	12 2/8 12 7/8	5 7/8 6 0/8	6 7/8	Natrona County	WY	E. Michael Onken	1983	5042
68 0/8	13 1/8 13 1/8	5 6/8 5 5/8	9 0/8	Converse County	WY	William Kobart	1983	5042
68 0/8	13 0/8 13 2/8	5 6/8 5 5/8	10 1/8	Ziebach County	SD	Jim Glines	1983	5042
68 0/8	13 6/8 13 7/8	5 5/8 5 5/8	12 2/8	Converse County	WY	David P. Lindman	1983	5042
68 0/8	13 1/8 13 2/8	5 7/8 5 6/8	7 5/8	Albany County	WY	Adrian H. Farmer, Jr.	1983	5042
68 0/8	14 0/8 14 1/8	5 2/8 5 4/8	12 4/8	Coconino County	AZ	Dean Zuern	1984	5042
68 0/8	12 6/8 12 0/8	6 0/8 5 7/8	10 1/8	Converse County	WY	Michael Murphy	1984	5042
68 0/8	13 4/8 13 5/8	5 6/8 5 5/8	8 6/8	Sweetwater County	WY	Robert L Kampen	1985	5042
68 0/8	13 3/8 13 4/8	5 1/8 5 2/8	6 5/8	Natrona County	WY	Joe Brant	1985	5042
68 0/8	13 0/8 13 1/8	5 7/8 5 7/8	9 4/8	Natrona County	WY	Dave James	1985	5042
68 0/8	12 3/8 12 5/8	5 4/8 5 4/8	11 5/8	Natrona County	WY	David Bouchard	1985	5042
68 0/8	12 3/8 12 4/8	6 2/8 6 2/8	9 0/8	Converse County	WY	Mark Slaughter	1986	5042
68 0/8	12 5/8 12 7/8	6 1/8 5 6/8	13 5/8	Converse County	WY	John May	1986	5042
68 0/8	13 0/8 13 1/8	6 0/8 6 1/8	9 4/8	Keya Paha County	NE	Rory Swim	1987	5042
68 0/8	13 5/8 13 2/8	5 5/8 5 6/8	8 5/8	Converse County	WY	Jimmy R. Speer	1987	5042
68 0/8	12 6/8 12 6/8	6 1/8 6 1/8	8 6/8	Converse County	WY	Dan Bertalan	1987	5042
68 0/8	13 7/8 13 6/8	5 5/8 5 3/8	11 0/8	Washoe County	NV	Bill Fuller	1988	5042
68 0/8	13 7/8 13 7/8	5 5/8 5 4/8	10 3/8	Butte County	ID	Andy Moore	1988	5042
68 0/8	13 3/8 13 3/8	5 5/8 5 4/8	14 6/8	Moffat County	CO	Stan Manuel	1988	5042
68 0/8	12 6/8 12 7/8	5 7/8 5 7/8	8 5/8	Moffat County	CO	Randy Gipple	1988	5042
68 0/8	12 6/8 12 7/8	5 6/8 5 5/8	9 5/8	Natrona County	WY	Nolan C. Fowles	1988	5042
68 0/8	13 1/8 13 2/8	5 3/8 5 3/8	9 1/8	Moffat County	CO	Rich McNutt	1988	5042
68 0/8	13 4/8 13 6/8	5 4/8 5 4/8	10 3/8	Moffat County	CO	Dennis Wehling	1989	5042
68 0/8	12 7/8 12 7/8	5 6/8 5 5/8	9 2/8	Garfield County	MT	Bruce Balerud	1989	5042
68 0/8	12 4/8 12 2/8	6 4/8 6 2/8	8 2/8	Campbell County	WY	Thomas J. Buchner	1989	5042
68 0/8	12 1/8 12 3/8	5 2/8 5 4/8	11 0/8	Sargent County	ND	Richard G. Olson	1989	5042
68 0/8	15 4/8 15 3/8	4 7/8 4 7/8	8 4/8	Powder River County	MT	John A. Stuver	1989	5042
68 0/8	12 3/8 12 3/8	5 6/8 5 6/8	10 2/8	Moffat County	CO	Mike Lamade	1990	5042
68 0/8	12 5/8 12 6/8	5 7/8 5 6/8	7 0/8	Delta County	CO	James C. Lake	1990	5042
68 0/8	12 6/8 12 4/8	5 6/8 5 6/8	8 1/8	Moffat County	CO	John Brassard	1990	5042
68 0/8	13 5/8 14 0/8	5 4/8 5 5/8	7 5/8	Johnson County	WY	L. Dan Neebe	1990	5042
68 0/8	12 4/8 12 5/8	5 6/8 6 0/8	6 7/8	Converse County	WY	Paul J. Ganzen	1990	5042
68 0/8	13 2/8 12 7/8	6 3/8 6 3/8	14 0/8	Natrona County	WY	Kurt W. Keskimaki	1990	5042
68 0/8	13 3/8 13 3/8	5 6/8 5 6/8	10 3/8	Chouteau County	MT	K. C. Palagi	1990	5042
68 0/8	13 2/8 12 7/8	5 6/8 5 7/8	7 6/8	Campbell County	WY	Timothy Hammes	1990	5042
68 0/8	12 3/8 11 5/8	5 6/8 5 6/8	8 3/8	Slope County	ND	Dennis Moritz	1990	5042
68 0/8	12 3/8 12 5/8	6 0/8 6 0/8	9 1/8	Moffat County	CO	Ronald Dinger	1991	5042
68 0/8	12 5/8 12 5/8	5 5/8 5 5/8	11 2/8	Fremont County	WY	Jerry A. Bodar	1991	5042
68 0/8	12 0/8 12 1/8	6 5/8 6 4/8	10 3/8	Converse County	WY	Derek Goto	1991	5042
68 0/8	11 2/8 11 0/8	5 6/8 5 6/8	10 1/8	Natrona County	WY	Scott D. Baer	1991	5042
68 0/8	13 0/8 13 7/8	5 4/8 5 5/8	8 5/8	Thomas County	NE	Matt Gideon	1991	5042
68 0/8	13 5/8 13 2/8	5 7/8 5 6/8	10 1/8	Sheridan County	WY	Marty Krohn	1991	5042
68 0/8	13 3/8 13 5/8	5 5/8 5 6/8	8 4/8	Bowman County	ND	Kendall Bauer	1991	5042
68 0/8	13 1/8 13 0/8	6 0/8 5 6/8	9 3/8	Sioux County	NE	Alton Schroeder	1991	5042
68 0/8	13 7/8 14 0/8	5 5/8 5 5/8	7 1/8	Ward County	ND	Russel Jon Hardy	1991	5042
68 0/8	12 4/8 12 2/8	6 2/8 6 3/8	9 2/8	Converse County	WY	Jeff Reynolds	1991	5042
68 0/8	13 6/8 13 7/8	5 6/8 5 6/8	9 0/8	Washoe County	NV	David Schopper	1992	5042
68 0/8	13 4/8 13 4/8	5 7/8 6 0/8	9 5/8	Carbon County	WY	Steven R. Hohensee	1992	5042
68 0/8	12 6/8 12 6/8	6 0/8 5 7/8	11 6/8	Campbell County	WY	Randy Hill	1992	5042
68 0/8	13 2/8 13 3/8	5 7/8 5 7/8	9 7/8	Owyhee County	ID	DeLoy Desaro	1992	5042
68 0/8	12 5/8 12 6/8	5 6/8 5 6/8	9 0/8	Campbell County	WY	Kurt Outcelt	1992	5042
68 0/8	11 4/8 11 4/8	5 7/8 6 0/8	9 2/8	Campbell County	WY	Philip G. Bauer	1992	5042
68 0/8	13 6/8 13 2/8	5 6/8 6 0/8	9 6/8	Campbell County	WY	Ken Rimer	1992	5042
68 0/8	12 3/8 12 3/8	6 0/8 5 6/8	10 5/8	Moffat County	CO	Thomas L. "Tag" Reed	1993	5042
68 0/8	13 5/8 13 4/8	5 5/8 5 4/8	8 6/8	Wayne County	UT	Jonathan D. Pemberton	1993	5042
68 0/8	13 3/8 13 3/8	6 0/8 6 1/8	8 0/8	Moffat County	CO	Jerome R. Mann	1993	5042
68 0/8	14 4/8 14 4/8	6 2/8 6 2/8	12 5/8	Manyberries	ALB	Gary Gillett	1993	5042
68 0/8	13 4/8 13 6/8	5 1/8 5 0/8	12 1/8	Manyberries	ALB	Jeff Knowlton	1993	5042
68 0/8	14 4/8 14 3/8	5 3/8 5 2/8	10 5/8	Owyhee County	ID	Gary Angell	1993	5042
68 0/8	13 1/8 13 2/8	5 4/8 5 4/8	8 0/8	Albany County	WY	Orvie Linsin	1994	5042
68 0/8	12 6/8 12 5/8	6 1/8 6 1/8	12 3/8	Albany County	WY	Ron Books, Jr.	1994	5042
68 0/8	12 6/8 12 7/8	5 7/8 6 0/8	9 5/8	Carbon County	WY	Steve J. Turner	1994	5042
68 0/8	13 0/8 12 7/8	5 6/8 5 6/8	10 3/8	Wayne County	UT	Steven W. Mitchell	1994	5042
68 0/8	13 3/8 13 3/8	5 5/8 5 4/8	8 3/8	Iron County	UT	Wade Ovard	1994	5042
68 0/8	13 7/8 13 7/8	5 2/8 5 3/8	9 6/8	Converse County	WY	Mark Hockenberry	1994	5042
68 0/8	13 4/8 13 3/8	5 2/8 5 1/8	8 6/8	Converse County	WY	Robert J. Manske	1994	5042
68 0/8	13 6/8 14 0/8	5 3/8 5 2/8	10 0/8	Rosebud County	MT	Mark Buehrer	1994	5042
68 0/8	13 2/8 12 6/8	6 0/8 6 0/8	12 0/8	Carbon County	WY	Guy Young	1994	5042
68 0/8	12 2/8 12 2/8	5 4/8 5 4/8	11 6/8	Hanna	ALB	Troy Dzioba	1994	5042
68 0/8	12 0/8 14 0/8	6 2/8 6 2/8	15 5/8	Meagher County	MT	John Fleharty	1994	5042
68 0/8	14 2/8 14 0/8	5 3/8 5 4/8	11 5/8	Lincoln County	NM	Ryan Turner	1995	5042
68 0/8	12 7/8 13 1/8	5 5/8 5 5/8	7 0/8	Converse County	WY	Troy McGinnis	1995	5042
68 0/8	12 7/8 13 0/8	5 7/8 5 5/8	11 3/8	Brown County	NE	Rich Walters, Jr.	1995	5042

863

PRONGHORN

Minimum Score 67   Continued

SCORE	LENGTH OF R HORN L	CIRCUMFERENCE R OF BASE L	INSIDE SPREAD	AREA	STATE/ PROVINCE	HUNTER'S NAME	DATE	RANK
68 0/8	13 0/8 13 2/8	6 2/8 6 2/8	10 6/8	Sweetwater County	WY	Raymond Kennedy	1996	5042
68 0/8	13 4/8 13 4/8	5 2/8 5 2/8	12 4/8	Lincoln County	NM	Janet Leigh Taylor	1996	5042
68 0/8	13 3/8 13 2/8	5 3/8 5 4/8	11 5/8	Owyhee County	ID	Anthony L. Mudd	1996	5042
68 0/8	12 5/8 12 5/8	5 7/8 5 7/8	11 1/8	Campbell County	WY	Ritch A. Stolpe	1996	5042
68 0/8	13 4/8 13 4/8	5 6/8 5 5/8	11 2/8	Chouteau County	MT	Gus Smith	1996	5042
68 0/8	13 4/8 13 3/8	5 3/8 5 2/8	7 2/8	Logan County	KS	Walt Lovins	1996	5042
68 0/8	13 3/8 13 6/8	5 5/8 5 5/8	6 5/8	Campbell County	WY	Chris Wichman	1997	5042
68 0/8	12 6/8 13 0/8	5 4/8 5 2/8	5 6/8	Moffat County	CO	Dale Selby	1998	5042
68 0/8	13 2/8 13 2/8	6 2/8 6 1/8	12 4/8	Sweetwater County	WY	Susan K. Barrett	1998	5042
68 0/8	14 6/8 14 3/8	5 2/8 5 3/8	6 6/8	Owyhee County	ID	John F. Burke	1998	5042
68 0/8	12 4/8 13 5/8	5 4/8 5 4/8	11 0/8	Moffat County	CO	Dawn Vallee	1998	5042
68 0/8	13 0/8 13 1/8	5 6/8 5 6/8	6 5/8	Yavapai County	AZ	John Waner	1998	5042
68 0/8	13 0/8 13 0/8	5 5/8 5 6/8	7 5/8	Campbell County	WY	Wright Allen	1998	5042
68 0/8	12 6/8 12 6/8	6 0/8 6 0/8	11 0/8	Park County	WY	Gary Shinn	1998	5042
68 0/8	12 6/8 12 4/8	6 0/8 6 0/8	11 0/8	Garfield County	MT	Kenneth E. Fischer	1998	5042
68 0/8	13 4/8 13 3/8	6 1/8 5 7/8	8 0/8	Fergus County	MT	D. Mitch Kottas	1998	5042
68 0/8	13 1/8 12 7/8	5 5/8 5 5/8	10 4/8	Converse County	WY	Jim Steele	1999	5042
68 0/8	13 2/8 13 4/8	6 2/8 6 1/8	10 2/8	Harding County	SD	Douglas A. Goehring	1999	5042
68 0/8	12 5/8 12 5/8	5 6/8 5 6/8	11 6/8	Cherry County	NE	Reggie Hochstein	1999	5042
68 0/8	13 1/8 13 1/8	6 1/8 6 2/8	9 7/8	Garfield County	MT	Sonny Templeton	1999	5042
68 0/8	12 6/8 12 6/8	6 0/8 6 0/8	7 2/8	Converse County	WY	Ross G. Nelson	1999	5042
68 0/8	13 1/8 12 7/8	5 4/8 5 3/8	10 4/8	Irion County	TX	Brandon Ray	1999	5042
68 0/8	12 4/8 12 2/8	5 6/8 5 7/8	9 2/8	Minidoka County	ID	Craig Anderson	2000	5042
68 0/8	13 1/8 12 5/8	5 7/8 5 6/8	10 5/8	Weld County	CO	Mark E. Gonyo	2000	5042
68 0/8	14 1/8 14 2/8	6 0/8 5 7/8	12 0/8	Billings County	ND	Wayne R. Schatzman	2000	5042
68 0/8	12 2/8 12 2/8	6 4/8 6 2/8	10 1/8	Petroleum County	MT	Jim Winjum	2000	5042
68 0/8	13 3/8 13 2/8	5 7/8 5 7/8	13 1/8	Lake County	OR	Jeffrey A. Eder	2001	5042
68 0/8	12 3/8 12 4/8	6 1/8 6 1/8	9 0/8	Converse County	WY	Brian M. Kean	2001	5042
68 0/8	13 3/8 13 4/8	5 5/8 5 4/8	12 1/8	Laramie County	WY	John J. Mascellino, Jr.	2001	5042
68 0/8	13 6/8 14 0/8	5 3/8 5 4/8	10 3/8	Nye County	NV	James F. Watson	2002	5042
68 0/8	13 1/8 12 7/8	5 5/8 5 5/8	8 5/8	Converse County	WY	Tom Kruk	2002	5042
68 0/8	12 6/8 12 6/8	5 7/8 5 7/8	8 5/8	Bowman County	ND	Ken Las	2002	5042
68 0/8	13 4/8 13 1/8	5 7/8 5 7/8	9 5/8	Campbell County	WY	Joe Hassinger	2002	5042
68 0/8	13 4/8 13 6/8	5 0/8 5 1/8	11 2/8	Johnson County	WY	Pax Harness	2003	5042
68 0/8	13 4/8 13 2/8	5 5/8 5 5/8	8 5/8	Converse County	WY	Michael L. Ritter, Jr.	2003	5042
68 0/8	12 3/8 12 3/8	6 6/8 7 0/8	12 3/8	Converse County	WY	Brian Tessmann	2003	5042
68 0/8	13 0/8 13 1/8	5 4/8 5 3/8	10 4/8	Drumheller	ALB	Troy Dzioba	2003	5042
68 0/8	12 5/8 12 3/8	5 1/8 5 2/8	12 1/8	Campbell County	WY	Brad Gohlke	2003	5042
68 0/8	12 5/8 12 7/8	5 7/8 5 6/8	9 6/8	Converse County	WY	David Wildenstein	2004	5042
68 0/8	12 1/8 12 1/8	5 7/8 5 5/8	7 7/8	Jones County	SD	Clayton Miller	2004	5042
68 0/8	13 1/8 13 0/8	5 7/8 5 7/8	9 1/8	Campbell County	WY	Joce Hugelen	2004	5042
68 0/8	13 2/8 13 2/8	5 4/8 5 3/8	7 2/8	Natrona County	WY	Tom Nelson	2004	5042
*68 0/8	12 4/8 12 7/8	5 5/8 5 4/8	8 1/8	Big Horn County	MT	Dennis Larsen	2004	5042
68 0/8	12 5/8 12 6/8	5 7/8 6 0/8	6 1/8	Powder River County	MT	Kevin J. Greenwood	2004	5042
68 0/8	14 4/8 14 3/8	5 3/8 5 3/8	10 0/8	Big Horn County	MT	Pete Gierke	2005	5042
68 0/8	12 1/8 11 6/8	6 2/8 6 1/8	11 0/8	Converse County	WY	Thomas Hansen II	2005	5042
68 0/8	13 2/8 13 1/8	5 6/8 5 6/8	8 2/8	Sheridan County	WY	Mark Buehrer	2005	5042
68 0/8	14 2/8 14 4/8	5 2/8 5 2/8	10 2/8	Weston County	WY	Robert Dowen	2005	5042
68 0/8	14 2/8 14 2/8	5 2/8 5 6/8	6 5/8	Laramie County	WY	Jim Belleville	2005	5042
68 0/8	13 6/8 13 1/8	5 6/8 5 6/8	12 0/8	Harding County	SD	Robert Baker	2005	5042
68 0/8	12 1/8 12 1/8	6 2/8 6 2/8	9 3/8	Powder River County	MT	John Martinson	2005	5042
68 0/8	11 6/8 12 0/8	6 3/8 6 3/8	7 1/8	Weston County	WY	Ronald F. Lax	2005	5042
68 0/8	14 2/8 14 2/8	5 0/8 5 0/8	10 4/8	Crook County	WY	Mitchell R. Butler	2005	5042
68 0/8	12 6/8 13 0/8	6 0/8 5 7/8	7 3/8	Powder River County	MT	Zachary Dugger	2006	5042
*68 0/8	12 4/8 12 6/8	5 4/8 5 3/8	7 6/8	Natrona County	WY	Janet Zimmerer	2006	5042
68 0/8	12 4/8 12 7/8	5 5/8 5 4/8	15 5/8	Converse County	WY	Ralph J. Thomas	2006	5042
68 0/8	13 5/8 13 2/8	5 6/8 5 6/8	7 4/8	Blaine County	ID	Darrell Nunez	2006	5042
68 0/8	13 6/8 13 7/8	5 3/8 5 4/8	7 1/8	Petroleum County	MT	Chad Berry	2006	5042
68 0/8	12 6/8 12 6/8	5 4/8 5 4/8	9 5/8	Converse County	WY	Mike Sohm	2006	5042
*68 0/8	12 5/8 12 6/8	5 7/8 5 7/8	9 2/8	Crook County	WY	Keith E. Arnold	2006	5042
68 0/8	13 0/8 13 1/8	5 5/8 5 4/8	8 7/8	Converse County	WY	Doug Baily	2006	5042
68 0/8	14 7/8 14 3/8	6 0/8 5 5/8	8 6/8	Weston County	WY	Ronald F. Lax	2006	5042
*68 0/8	13 3/8 13 2/8	6 1/8 6 1/8	10 7/8	Rosebud County	MT	Sjon Zunich	2007	5042
68 0/8	12 7/8 12 7/8	6 0/8 6 0/8	9 2/8	Campbell County	WY	Scott Lang	2007	5042
68 0/8	13 1/8 14 1/8	5 7/8 5 6/8	11 4/8	Owyhee County	ID	Mike Parkinson	2007	5042
*68 0/8	11 5/8 11 7/8	5 7/8 6 0/8	6 5/8	Harding County	SD	Joe Volk	2007	5042
68 0/8	14 5/8 14 5/8	5 3/8 5 3/8	8 1/8	Harding County	SD	Michael D. Adams	2007	5042
68 0/8	13 2/8 13 4/8	5 5/8 6 0/8	10 1/8	Perkins County	SD	Nathan Doblar	2007	5042
68 0/8	12 4/8 12 1/8	6 3/8 6 1/8	7 2/8	Converse County	WY	Weston Giesey	2008	5042
68 0/8	13 0/8 12 3/8	6 2/8 6 0/8	8 2/8	Weld County	CO	Michael Casey	2008	5042
68 0/8	13 4/8 13 6/8	5 3/8 5 3/8	9 4/8	Carter County	MT	Robert J. Amaral	2008	5042
68 0/8	12 6/8 12 7/8	5 7/8 5 6/8	8 5/8	Carter County	MT	Brandon Ray	2008	5042
68 0/8	13 2/8 13 2/8	5 7/8 5 7/8	7 7/8	Owyhee County	ID	DeLoy Desaro	2009	5042
68 0/8	13 7/8 13 5/8	5 4/8 5 3/8	9 2/8	Broadwater County	MT	Jaden Zambon	2009	5042
68 0/8	12 5/8 12 7/8	6 1/8 6 1/8	8 4/8	Routt County	CO	Mark S. Peffer	2009	5042
*68 0/8	13 6/8 13 5/8	5 3/8 5 3/8	6 3/8	Meade County	SD	Reed Vandervoort	2009	5042
68 0/8	12 2/8 14 3/8	5 7/8 6 0/8	8 7/8	Empress	ALB	Edward C. Herman	2009	5042
68 0/8	13 1/8 12 7/8	6 0/8 5 7/8	8 2/8	Campbell County	WY	Russell Bell	2009	5042
68 0/8	12 5/8 12 2/8	5 7/8 6 0/8	8 1/8	Powder River County	MT	David A. Widby	2010	5042
68 0/8	11 1/8 11 2/8	6 0/8 6 1/8	9 4/8	Natrona County	WY	Travis Moore	2010	5042
67 6/8	12 3/8 12 4/8	5 6/8 5 5/8	9 0/8	McHenry County	ND	Darryl Ablestad	1967	5213
67 6/8	13 4/8 13 4/8	5 5/8 5 5/8	11 2/8	Logan County	CO	Loren Johnston	1968	5213
67 6/8	12 6/8 12 4/8	6 2/8 6 0/8	11 3/8	McHenry County	ND	Jim Budeau	1968	5213
67 6/8	13 3/8 13 2/8	5 2/8 5 5/8	10 1/8	Fremont County	WY	Doris Clark	1970	5213
67 6/8	14 0/8 13 1/8	5 0/8 5 0/8	13 4/8	Butte County	ID	Craig L. Hansen	1974	5213
67 6/8	12 4/8 12 6/8	5 5/8 5 5/8	11 1/8	Carbon County	WY	James Beeson	1976	5213
67 6/8	14 0/8 14 0/8	5 2/8 5 2/8	11 1/8	Park County	WY	Fred W. Achilles	1978	5213
67 6/8	13 7/8 13 6/8	5 2/8 5 2/8	8 5/8	Moffat County	CO	Dave Skiff	1980	5213
67 6/8	13 2/8 13 2/8	5 6/8 5 5/8	11 4/8	Natrona County	WY	David Stejskal	1980	5213
67 6/8	13 1/8 13 2/8	5 4/8 5 2/8	9 7/8	Sweetwater County	WY	Jerry Giovannoni	1980	5213
67 6/8	11 2/8 11 2/8	5 6/8 5 5/8	8 1/8	Converse County	WY	Ron Carpenter	1980	5213
67 6/8	13 0/8 13 1/8	5 2/8 5 4/8	13 2/8	Natrona County	WY	Clifford G. James	1980	5213
67 6/8	11 6/8 11 7/8	5 5/8 5 5/8	8 6/8	Carbon County	WY	Bob Funke	1980	5213
67 6/8	13 5/8 12 6/8	5 5/8 5 4/8	10 4/8	Custer County	ID	Gerard J. Krauth	1981	5213
67 6/8	13 7/8 13 6/8	5 6/8 5 5/8	9 2/8	Rio Arriba County	NM	Jose R. Montalvo	1982	5213

864

PRONGHORN

Minimum Score 67
Continued

SCORE	LENGTH OF R HORN L	CIRCUMFERENCE R OF BASE L	INSIDE SPREAD	AREA	STATE/ PROVINCE	HUNTER'S NAME	DATE	RANK
67 6/8	13 4/8 13 6/8	5 4/8 5 4/8	11 7/8	Moffat County	CO	Robert L. Kinser	1982	5213
67 6/8	14 5/8 14 1/8	4 6/8 4 7/8	9 7/8	Carbon County	WY	Bill Nation	1982	5213
67 6/8	13 5/8 13 5/8	5 3/8 5 2/8	8 0/8	Beaverhead County	MT	L. C. Trimber	1982	5213
67 6/8	12 2/8 12 1/8	5 7/8 5 7/8	11 4/8	Moffat County	CO	Mike Ward	1982	5213
67 6/8	12 2/8 12 6/8	5 4/8 5 4/8	11 7/8	Converse County	WY	Joe Ed McCray	1982	5213
67 6/8	12 3/8 13 1/8	5 2/8 5 2/8	12 2/8	Larimer County	CO	William Shuster	1983	5213
67 6/8	13 3/8 13 3/8	5 4/8 5 3/8	8 7/8	Converse County	WY	Roger Schmitt	1983	5213
67 6/8	14 0/8 13 6/8	5 3/8 5 2/8	9 5/8	Las Animas County	CO	Edward F. Bryan, Jr.	1983	5213
67 6/8	14 2/8 14 3/8	5 7/8 6 0/8	11 1/8	Hettinger County	ND	Mike Schiwal	1984	5213
67 6/8	13 0/8 13 0/8	5 6/8 5 6/8	11 5/8	Natrona County	WY	Kirk H. Soulliere	1985	5213
67 6/8	12 6/8 12 4/8	6 0/8 5 7/8	14 3/8	Carbon County	WY	Willis Duhon	1985	5213
67 6/8	14 4/8 14 4/8	5 3/8 5 2/8	8 0/8	Carbon County	WY	Bob Boyle	1985	5213
67 6/8	11 5/8 11 5/8	6 5/8 6 3/8	15 3/8	McKinley County	NM	Robert Allen Stearns	1985	5213
67 6/8	12 6/8 12 6/8	6 1/8 6 1/8	7 6/8	Sweetwater County	WY	Dean Lawver	1986	5213
67 6/8	13 4/8 13 5/8	6 2/8 6 0/8	9 6/8	Mountrail County	ND	Kevin Ohlhauser	1986	5213
67 6/8	13 3/8 13 4/8	5 4/8 5 5/8	6 4/8	Tom Green County	TX	Terry Turney	1986	5213
67 6/8	13 3/8 13 2/8	5 6/8 5 6/8	10 5/8	Sublette County	WY	Randy Tolman	1987	5213
67 6/8	12 1/8 12 2/8	6 2/8 6 2/8	11 6/8	Converse County	WY	Martin Scott Campbell	1987	5213
67 6/8	13 0/8 13 0/8	5 5/8 5 4/8	7 6/8	Medicine Hat	ALB	James Pike	1987	5213
67 6/8	13 6/8 13 2/8	5 4/8 5 5/8	9 1/8	Moffat County	CO	Carol Ashurst	1988	5213
67 6/8	12 3/8 12 4/8	5 6/8 5 6/8	12 2/8	Converse County	WY	Larry Crouch	1988	5213
67 6/8	14 1/8 13 7/8	5 4/8 5 3/8	14 5/8	Suffield	ALB	Jay Brown	1988	5213
67 6/8	12 4/8 12 4/8	5 4/8 5 4/8	9 5/8	Sweetwater County	WY	Mark Pergande	1989	5213
67 6/8	13 5/8 14 0/8	5 2/8 5 3/8	9 3/8	Campbell County	WY	Robert F. Synder	1989	5213
67 6/8	12 7/8 13 3/8	6 4/8 5 4/8	8 6/8	Campbell County	WY	Charles Smith	1989	5213
67 6/8	12 6/8 13 1/8	5 6/8 5 5/8	7 1/8	Converse County	WY	Brian Bass	1990	5213
67 6/8	13 3/8 13 2/8	5 7/8 5 6/8	15 0/8	Platte County	WY	Derek Long	1990	5213
67 6/8	12 7/8 13 2/8	5 4/8 5 3/8	10 5/8	Hudspeth County	TX	Melvin Sloan	1990	5213
67 6/8	14 0/8 14 5/8	5 5/8 5 5/8	10 1/8	Natrona County	WY	Michael Running	1991	5213
67 6/8	12 6/8 12 6/8	5 7/8 5 6/8	9 2/8	Campbell County	WY	Joe Gohres	1991	5213
67 6/8	13 1/8 12 0/8	5 6/8 5 5/8	9 0/8	Yavapai County	AZ	Gary French	1991	5213
67 6/8	13 3/8 13 0/8	5 5/8 5 5/8	10 4/8	Converse County	WY	James C. Gates	1991	5213
67 6/8	13 2/8 13 0/8	5 7/8 6 0/8	11 0/8	Grant County	ND	Troy Hanson	1991	5213
67 6/8	12 4/8 12 6/8	5 7/8 5 7/8	8 7/8	Perkins County	SD	James S. Bidwell	1991	5213
67 6/8	13 4/8 13 2/8	5 4/8 5 4/8	6 1/8	Beaverhead County	MT	Curtis A. Green	1991	5213
67 6/8	12 4/8 13 0/8	6 2/8 6 2/8	11 4/8	Harding County	SD	Jeff Poppenga	1991	5213
67 6/8	12 5/8 12 5/8	6 1/8 6 0/8	8 1/8	Colfax County	NM	Dave W. Wright	1992	5213
67 6/8	13 7/8 13 6/8	5 5/8 5 6/8	6 4/8	Owyhee County	ID	David R. Heck	1992	5213
67 6/8	13 0/8 13 0/8	5 7/8 5 5/8	12 4/8	Converse County	WY	Carolyn Siebrasse Zanoni	1992	5213
67 6/8	12 2/8 12 2/8	6 0/8 6 0/8	11 1/8	Johnson County	WY	Thomas J. Mihutz	1992	5213
67 6/8	13 2/8 13 4/8	5 6/8 5 6/8	9 1/8	Slope County	ND	Gene Davis	1992	5213
67 6/8	12 5/8 12 3/8	5 7/8 5 7/8	9 3/8	Natrona County	WY	Kim Cooper	1992	5213
67 6/8	13 1/8 13 1/8	6 0/8 6 0/8	9 2/8	Bowman County	ND	Gene Welle	1992	5213
67 6/8	13 5/8 13 7/8	5 4/8 5 5/8	9 3/8	Campbell County	WY	Michael J. Stuefen	1992	5213
67 6/8	13 1/8 12 6/8	5 5/8 5 5/8	11 7/8	Natrona County	WY	Mark Tanner	1992	5213
67 6/8	13 3/8 13 5/8	5 7/8 5 6/8	5 6/8	Sioux County	NE	Ron Suponchick	1992	5213
67 6/8	12 7/8 12 2/8	6 0/8 5 7/8	9 2/8	Moffat County	CO	Jerry Mason	1993	5213
67 6/8	12 5/8 12 5/8	5 6/8 5 6/8	8 1/8	Moffat County	CO	Rick A. Albers	1993	5213
67 6/8	12 4/8 12 3/8	6 0/8 6 0/8	8 4/8	Box Elder County	UT	David M. Schopper	1993	5213
67 6/8	13 3/8 13 3/8	5 6/8 5 5/8	6 7/8	Moffat County	CO	Brad Herman	1994	5213
67 6/8	14 2/8 13 7/8	5 5/8 5 4/8	8 4/8	Clark County	ID	Max Heberling	1994	5213
67 6/8	12 5/8 12 4/8	5 7/8 6 0/8	12 1/8	Weld County	CO	Kirk Hiller	1994	5213
67 6/8	13 3/8 13 3/8	5 6/8 5 6/8	13 5/8	Campbell County	WY	Jeff Helmers	1994	5213
67 6/8	14 2/8 13 4/8	5 5/8 5 5/8	7 6/8	McKenzie County	ND	Don G. Scofield	1994	5213
67 6/8	12 3/8 12 3/8	5 6/8 5 6/8	11 4/8	Converse County	WY	Roger W. Hansen	1994	5213
67 6/8	12 6/8 12 5/8	5 5/8 5 4/8	7 6/8	Converse County	WY	Dr. Andy Jones	1994	5213
67 6/8	12 4/8 12 2/8	5 5/8 5 6/8	10 6/8	Moffat County	CO	Nathan Andersohn	1994	5213
67 6/8	11 6/8 11 5/8	5 7/8 5 7/8	6 5/8	Stanley County	SD	Mike Moody	1994	5213
67 6/8	13 3/8 13 3/8	5 3/8 5 3/8	11 0/8	Campbell County	WY	Bob Pozner	1994	5213
67 6/8	13 7/8 13 7/8	5 4/8 5 3/8	8 2/8	Juab County	UT	Rick Searle	1995	5213
67 6/8	12 7/8 12 7/8	6 2/8 6 2/8	11 6/8	Rosebud County	MT	Gene Welle	1995	5213
67 6/8	12 4/8 11 2/8	6 0/8 5 7/8	8 1/8	Converse County	WY	John S. Lewis III	1995	5213
67 6/8	14 7/8 15 3/8	5 4/8 5 4/8	8 5/8	Owyhee County	ID	Ron Sherer	1995	5213
67 6/8	13 2/8 13 1/8	6 0/8 6 1/8	12 2/8	Carbon County	WY	Guy Hinrichs	1995	5213
67 6/8	13 1/8 12 6/8	5 7/8 5 7/8	8 0/8	Crook County	WY	Roger D. Smith	1995	5213
67 6/8	12 7/8 13 2/8	5 6/8 5 5/8	11 7/8	Rosebud County	MT	Gregory G. Henan	1995	5213
67 6/8	12 5/8 12 6/8	5 5/8 5 5/8	8 4/8	McLean County	ND	Todd Weisenburger	1995	5213
67 6/8	12 6/8 13 0/8	6 1/8 6 0/8	7 7/8	Converse County	WY	Myron E. Jochmann	1995	5213
67 6/8	12 1/8 12 2/8	5 5/8 6 0/8	10 4/8	Rosebud County	MT	Bill Dollar	1995	5213
67 6/8	14 6/8 14 6/8	5 2/8 5 3/8	7 0/8	Millard County	UT	Valene Tuttle	1996	5213
67 6/8	14 5/8 14 3/8	5 5/8 5 5/8	8 4/8	White Pine County	NV	William C. Brewer	1996	5213
67 6/8	13 2/8 13 4/8	5 5/8 5 4/8	11 6/8	Moffat County	CO	Ken Custer	1996	5213
67 6/8	13 4/8 13 5/8	5 7/8 6 0/8	8 2/8	Campbell County	WY	Tom Blank	1996	5213
67 6/8	12 2/8 12 4/8	6 2/8 6 1/8	10 5/8	Crook County	OR	Clinton J. Hall	1996	5213
67 6/8	14 0/8 13 3/8	5 4/8 5 5/8	8 1/8	Harding County	SD	Karen DeRungs	1996	5213
67 6/8	12 2/8 12 0/8	6 2/8 6 1/8	9 2/8	Converse County	WY	James Gabrick	1997	5213
67 6/8	14 2/8 14 4/8	5 2/8 5 3/8	8 0/8	Campbell County	WY	Richard E. LaCrone	1997	5213
67 6/8	12 7/8 13 4/8	6 2/8 6 0/8	13 0/8	Musselshell County	MT	Bob L. Walker	1997	5213
67 6/8	12 5/8 12 4/8	5 5/8 5 6/8	10 7/8	Moffat County	CO	Chuck Adams	1998	5213
67 6/8	12 5/8 12 5/8	5 5/8 5 3/8	8 0/8	Moffat County	CO	Destiny Schoon	1998	5213
67 6/8	13 6/8 13 5/8	5 5/8 5 4/8	10 4/8	Fergus County	MT	Don E. Kottas	1998	5213
67 6/8	13 3/8 13 4/8	6 1/8 5 7/8	10 4/8	Converse County	WY	Toby Hershey	1998	5213
67 6/8	13 0/8 13 0/8	5 6/8 5 5/8	6 7/8	Hays	ALB	Marty Belisle	1998	5213
67 6/8	13 2/8 13 4/8	5 5/8 5 4/8	12 0/8	Wallace County	KS	Doug Duncan	1998	5213
67 6/8	13 6/8 13 6/8	5 4/8 5 4/8	11 0/8	Milk River	ALB	Bruce Leben	1998	5213
67 6/8	14 7/8 14 3/8	5 5/8 5 5/8	9 1/8	Rosebud County	MT	William E. Lee, Jr.	1998	5213
67 6/8	13 6/8 13 4/8	6 0/8 6 0/8	10 0/8	Fergus County	MT	Chris G. Sanford	1999	5213
67 6/8	12 0/8 12 1/8	6 2/8 6 2/8	11 1/8	Converse County	WY	Randy E. Doyle	1999	5213
67 6/8	13 5/8 13 2/8	5 5/8 5 2/8	10 1/8	Lincoln County	NV	Keri Lynn Tanner	2000	5213
67 6/8	12 6/8 12 5/8	5 5/8 5 5/8	11 5/8	Johnson County	WY	Wendell A. Birch	2000	5213
67 6/8	13 1/8 11 7/8	6 0/8 6 1/8	9 3/8	Converse County	WY	Jerry Ellingson	2000	5213
67 6/8	14 0/8 14 1/8	5 0/8 5 2/8	7 5/8	Carbon County	WY	Danny H. Lewis	2000	5213
67 6/8	12 6/8 12 6/8	6 1/8 6 0/8	10 3/8	Klamath County	OR	Kevin R. Irelan	2001	5213
67 6/8	12 3/8 12 4/8	6 1/8 6 0/8	8 0/8	Owyhee County	ID	Kevin Primrose	2001	5213
67 6/8	13 6/8 14 0/8	5 6/8 5 7/8	8 6/8	Powder River County	MT	Jack Sorum	2001	5213

PRONGHORN

Minimum Score 67 — Continued

SCORE	LENGTH OF HORN R	L	CIRCUMFERENCE OF BASE R	L	INSIDE SPREAD	AREA	STATE/ PROVINCE	HUNTER'S NAME	DATE	RANK
67 6/8	12 7/8	12 7/8	6 0/8	5 7/8	6 4/8	Perkins County	SD	Aaron Ambur	2001	5213
67 6/8	13 1/8	12 6/8	5 7/8	5 6/8	8 5/8	Humboldt County	NV	Kevin G. Peterson	2002	5213
67 6/8	13 7/8	13 1/8	5 5/8	5 3/8	9 0/8	Weld County	CO	Kevin Waller	2002	5213
67 6/8	14 2/8	14 4/8	5 1/8	5 2/8	8 5/8	Converse County	WY	Robert L. Peterson	2002	5213
67 6/8	13 6/8	14 0/8	5 4/8	5 3/8	10 7/8	Converse County	WY	Cheryl Earhart	2002	5213
67 6/8	12 5/8	12 6/8	5 7/8	5 6/8	6 5/8	Converse County	WY	Tim L. Donnelly	2002	5213
67 6/8	13 6/8	13 4/8	5 1/8	5 1/8	9 4/8	Moffat County	CO	Michael Adkins, Sr.	2002	5213
67 6/8	12 2/8	12 5/8	5 3/8	5 4/8	8 6/8	Lander County	NV	Ricky R. Martin	2003	5213
67 6/8	13 4/8	14 0/8	5 7/8	5 6/8	8 0/8	Converse County	WY	Robert Shores	2003	5213
67 6/8	13 3/8	13 2/8	5 6/8	5 5/8	12 2/8	Powder River County	MT	Marc N. Shaft	2003	5213
*67 6/8	11 5/8	11 4/8	6 1/8	6 2/8	9 2/8	Guadalupe County	NM	Brandon Ray	2004	5213
67 6/8	12 3/8	12 4/8	6 0/8	5 7/8	8 5/8	Harding County	SD	Travis Peterson	2004	5213
67 6/8	13 2/8	13 2/8	6 0/8	6 2/8	13 3/8	Otero County	NM	Mike Minnick	2004	5213
67 6/8	13 0/8	12 6/8	5 4/8	5 4/8	10 0/8	Campbell County	WY	Tippy H. Clark	2004	5213
67 6/8	13 4/8	13 4/8	5 3/8	5 4/8	8 3/8	Natrona County	WY	Gus A. Congemi	2004	5213
67 6/8	13 5/8	13 1/8	5 7/8	5 7/8	8 6/8	Bow Island	ALB	Eldon Bushman	2004	5213
67 6/8	13 0/8	13 4/8	5 7/8	5 4/8	9 5/8	Albany County	WY	Ron Mason	2004	5213
67 6/8	14 5/8	14 2/8	5 3/8	5 2/8	12 2/8	Elko County	NV	Michael Potter	2005	5213
67 6/8	13 0/8	13 0/8	6 0/8	6 0/8	10 4/8	Shasta County	CA	Jerry Boelens	2005	5213
*67 6/8	13 7/8	13 6/8	6 0/8	6 0/8	12 7/8	Powder River County	MT	Aaron Jones	2005	5213
67 6/8	14 3/8	16 0/8	5 3/8	5 3/8	11 2/8	De Baca County	NM	Brian K. Strickland	2005	5213
*67 6/8	12 5/8	13 1/8	5 6/8	5 5/8	8 4/8	Larimer County	CO	Daniel J. Rossiter	2005	5213
67 6/8	13 4/8	13 3/8	6 0/8	5 3/8	9 5/8	El Paso County	CO	Brook Neva	2005	5213
67 6/8	14 1/8	13 3/8	6 1/8	6 1/8	12 1/8	Converse County	WY	Dan J. Ryle, Jr.	2005	5213
67 6/8	12 4/8	12 6/8	6 0/8	5 7/8	9 5/8	Johnson County	WY	Wayne B. Six	2005	5213
67 6/8	13 5/8	13 3/8	5 2/8	5 1/8	7 3/8	Campbell County	WY	Shawn Eyre	2005	5213
67 6/8	13 6/8	13 2/8	5 3/8	5 3/8	10 4/8	Harding County	SD	Phil Brumm	2005	5213
*67 6/8	13 7/8	13 5/8	5 4/8	5 3/8	7 7/8	Bowman County	ND	Jeff Zavada	2005	5213
67 6/8	13 6/8	13 4/8	5 3/8	5 4/8	8 4/8	Powder River County	MT	David C. Hubbard	2006	5213
67 6/8	13 6/8	13 6/8	5 2/8	5 2/8	9 3/8	Mohave County	AZ	Ward Villamor	2006	5213
67 6/8	13 4/8	13 3/8	5 5/8	5 4/8	10 2/8	Carter County	MT	Duane Frey	2006	5213
67 6/8	14 4/8	14 4/8	5 7/8	5 6/8	8 2/8	Slope County	ND	Michael John Lemere	2006	5213
67 6/8	12 4/8	12 1/8	6 0/8	6 0/8	7 5/8	Humboldt County	NV	Jim O'Kelly II	2007	5213
67 6/8	13 5/8	13 3/8	5 6/8	5 6/8	11 1/8	White Pine County	NV	Robert Winder	2007	5213
67 6/8	13 6/8	14 1/8	5 5/8	5 3/8	7 4/8	Crook County	WY	Jeff Jacob	2007	5213
*67 6/8	12 0/8	11 6/8	5 5/8	5 5/8	9 2/8	Converse County	WY	Brian Taylor	2007	5213
*67 6/8	14 6/8	15 0/8	5 1/8	5 1/8	11 0/8	Harding County	SD	Larry M. Moore	2007	5213
67 6/8	13 1/8	13 1/8	6 0/8	6 1/8	14 0/8	Wayne County	UT	Ryan Kendall	2008	5213
*67 6/8	13 4/8	13 5/8	5 3/8	5 2/8	6 6/8	Campbell County	WY	Janis Rock	2008	5213
*67 6/8	12 5/8	13 0/8	5 4/8	5 4/8	9 2/8	Albany County	WY	Chris J. Hood	2008	5213
*67 6/8	13 4/8	13 1/8	5 7/8	5 7/8	11 4/8	Converse County	WY	Robert J. Wolbert	2008	5213
67 6/8	13 4/8	13 6/8	5 6/8	5 5/8	10 0/8	Red Deer River	ALB	Chad Lenz	2008	5213
*67 6/8	13 1/8	13 3/8	5 4/8	5 4/8	10 2/8	Harding County	SD	Gary Anderson	2008	5213
67 6/8	13 1/8	13 1/8	5 5/8	5 5/8	12 4/8	Niobrara County	WY	Thompson Bruegger	2008	5213
67 6/8	12 4/8	12 2/8	5 7/8	5 7/8	8 4/8	Socorro County	NM	Randy Newburg	2009	5213
67 6/8	13 0/8	12 6/8	6 1/8	6 0/8	11 5/8	Converse County	WY	Jake Saunoris	2009	5213
*67 6/8	11 5/8	11 6/8	6 0/8	6 3/8	6 5/8	Las Animas County	CO	Tom Smith	2009	5213
67 6/8	13 4/8	13 3/8	5 4/8	5 4/8	10 2/8	Sioux County	NE	Michael Hawkins	2009	5213
*67 6/8	13 0/8	13 1/8	6 4/8	6 2/8	10 2/8	Pennington County	SD	Wayne A. Buckley	2009	5213
*67 6/8	13 2/8	13 3/8	5 6/8	5 6/8	9 1/8	Johnson County	WY	Marc A. Gibbs	2009	5213
67 6/8	13 2/8	13 3/8	5 3/8	5 2/8	8 5/8	Carbon County	WY	Lucas Palmquist	2010	5213
67 6/8	12 4/8	13 0/8	5 4/8	5 5/8	10 4/8	Moffat County	CO	Mike Dziekan	2010	5213
67 4/8	13 4/8	13 5/8	5 3/8	5 2/8	13 3/8	Cherry County	NE	Marlin Wells	1967	5375
67 4/8	13 7/8	13 7/8	5 3/8	5 2/8	10 1/8	Oregon Basin	WY	John Pruszyski	1973	5375
67 4/8	14 2/8	14 0/8	5 2/8	5 1/8	8 5/8	Jackson County	CO	Robert Souza	1974	5375
67 4/8	13 3/8	13 2/8	5 4/8	5 4/8	9 0/8	Meade County	SD	Jim Bohls	1974	5375
67 4/8	13 1/8	13 2/8	5 7/8	5 5/8	13 3/8	Carbon County	WY	Steve Stumbo	1975	5375
67 4/8	13 6/8	13 4/8	5 6/8	5 4/8	11 7/8	Natrona County	WY	Steve Turck	1976	5375
67 4/8	12 4/8	12 5/8	5 4/8	5 4/8	11 6/8	Converse County	WY	Bob Jensen	1976	5375
67 4/8	13 1/8	13 5/8	5 4/8	5 4/8	8 2/8	Converse County	WY	James E. Boland	1979	5375
67 4/8	12 6/8	12 5/8	5 6/8	5 6/8	10 0/8	Converse County	WY	Bruce Sanders	1980	5375
67 4/8	12 5/8	12 0/8	6 1/8	5 6/8	9 1/8	Moffat County	CO	Robert L. Wright	1981	5375
67 4/8	14 1/8	13 0/8	5 6/8	5 6/8	10 2/8	Lemhi County	ID	Daniel A. Davis	1981	5375
67 4/8	13 5/8	13 4/8	5 4/8	5 4/8	10 1/8	Converse County	WY	Ron Breitsprecher	1981	5375
67 4/8	14 2/8	14 4/8	5 4/8	5 3/8	7 4/8	Carbon County	WY	Mike Fortman	1982	5375
67 4/8	11 6/8	12 6/8	5 5/8	5 4/8	8 1/8	Moffat County	CO	Ken Keller	1983	5375
67 4/8	13 0/8	13 2/8	5 3/8	5 3/8	6 5/8	Custer County	CO	Rohn L. Garnhart	1983	5375
67 4/8	12 3/8	12 4/8	5 4/8	5 4/8	9 1/8	Converse County	WY	Roberta Byerly	1983	5375
67 4/8	13 0/8	13 1/8	5 6/8	5 5/8	9 0/8	Converse County	WY	Jon Arneson	1983	5375
67 4/8	14 1/8	14 0/8	5 4/8	5 4/8	9 7/8	Converse County	WY	Gary Hunsicker	1983	5375
67 4/8	12 4/8	12 6/8	6 3/8	6 1/8	8 4/8	Converse County	WY	Jim Hodson	1984	5375
67 4/8	12 3/8	12 4/8	6 0/8	5 7/8	9 0/8	Sweetwater County	WY	Craig Richardson	1984	5375
67 4/8	12 3/8	12 3/8	6 4/8	6 4/8	10 2/8	Moffat County	CO	Walter Krom	1984	5375
67 4/8	13 0/8	12 6/8	5 6/8	5 6/8	11 0/8	Bowman County	ND	Mark Delong	1984	5375
67 4/8	13 4/8	13 3/8	5 4/8	5 4/8	10 3/8	Campbell County	WY	Rick Gilley	1984	5375
67 4/8	13 2/8	13 5/8	5 4/8	5 2/8	11 3/8	Johnson County	WY	Edward Carmichael	1984	5375
67 4/8	13 4/8	13 4/8	5 4/8	5 4/8	12 0/8	Phillips County	MT	Ken Ruzicka	1984	5375
67 4/8	13 1/8	13 1/8	5 6/8	5 6/8	9 2/8	Sweetwater County	WY	Kevin J. Slovak	1985	5375
67 4/8	13 0/8	13 0/8	6 2/8	6 3/8	9 4/8	Billings County	ND	Ronald M. Bachmeier	1985	5375
67 4/8	13 0/8	12 7/8	5 3/8	5 3/8	8 3/8	Converse County	WY	Len Cardinale	1985	5375
67 4/8	12 7/8	12 6/8	5 3/8	5 2/8	9 0/8	Converse County	WY	Burt Thompson, Jr.	1985	5375
67 4/8	12 3/8	12 7/8	5 5/8	5 5/8	9 6/8	Converse County	WY	Thomas Vitale	1985	5375
67 4/8	12 1/8	12 0/8	5 7/8	6 0/8	9 2/8	Sweetwater County	WY	Chris Switzer	1986	5375
67 4/8	13 7/8	12 7/8	5 6/8	5 6/8	8 3/8	McKenzie County	ND	David Tofte	1986	5375
67 4/8	11 3/8	11 3/8	6 3/8	6 2/8	9 0/8	Lemhi County	ID	C. Richard Wenger	1987	5375
67 4/8	12 5/8	12 5/8	5 5/8	5 5/8	8 6/8	Billings County	ND	Ivan Bachamp	1987	5375
67 4/8	11 7/8	11 7/8	5 6/8	5 6/8	10 0/8	Daggett County	UT	L. Scot Jenkins	1987	5375
67 4/8	12 4/8	12 4/8	5 7/8	5 7/8	9 7/8	Yellowstone County	MT	Jack S. Esterly, Jr.	1987	5375
67 4/8	13 3/8	13 2/8	5 2/8	5 2/8	8 4/8	Moffat County	CO	E. Damon Handley	1988	5375
67 4/8	12 6/8	12 6/8	5 5/8	5 5/8	10 4/8	Natrona County	WY	Paul Jayson	1988	5375
67 4/8	12 2/8	12 2/8	5 6/8	5 7/8	7 5/8	Converse County	WY	J. G. "Rusty" Watson	1988	5375
67 4/8	10 7/8	11 2/8	6 1/8	6 0/8	8 0/8	Converse County	WY	Rick Simonson	1988	5375
67 4/8	12 2/8	12 2/8	5 1/8	5 2/8	8 2/8	Weston County	WY	Keith Gould	1988	5375
67 4/8	13 4/8	12 1/8	5 6/8	5 6/8	8 3/8	Moffat County	CO	Todd Weiszbrod	1989	5375
67 4/8	12 3/8	12 2/8	5 5/8	5 6/8	10 5/8	Moffat County	CO	James "Boomer" Hayden	1989	5375

866

PRONGHORN

Minimum Score 67 — Continued

SCORE	LENGTH OF R HORN L	CIRCUMFERENCE R OF BASE L	INSIDE SPREAD	AREA	STATE/ PROVINCE	HUNTER'S NAME	DATE	RANK
67 4/8	12 0/8 12 0/8	5 5/8 5 4/8	8 6/8	Moffat County	CO	James A. Davison	1990	5375
67 4/8	12 7/8 12 7/8	5 6/8 5 5/8	7 7/8	Chaffee County	CO	Joel Morgan	1990	5375
67 4/8	13 3/8 13 3/8	5 4/8 5 3/8	12 0/8	Clark County	ID	Tom Thiel	1990	5375
67 4/8	12 7/8 14 2/8	6 0/8 6 0/8	10 4/8	Lake County	OR	Rick D. Breckel	1990	5375
67 4/8	14 0/8 13 7/8	5 5/8 5 5/8	8 1/8	Walsh	ALB	David R. Coupland	1990	5375
67 4/8	12 3/8 12 4/8	6 0/8 6 0/8	12 1/8	Rosebud County	MT	Scott Propst	1990	5375
67 4/8	13 2/8 13 0/8	6 1/8 5 7/8	9 2/8	Johnson County	WY	Brian R. Potter	1990	5375
67 4/8	13 2/8 13 0/8	5 3/8 5 2/8	6 4/8	Outram	SAS	Garry Leslie	1990	5375
67 4/8	12 4/8 12 4/8	6 0/8 5 7/8	8 0/8	Converse County	WY	Greg McTee	1990	5375
67 4/8	13 5/8 13 6/8	5 4/8 5 4/8	12 2/8	Meagher County	MT	D. Mitch Kottas	1990	5375
67 4/8	13 1/8 12 7/8	5 7/8 5 7/8	11 7/8	Hemaruka	ALB	Larry McNalley	1990	5375
67 4/8	12 5/8 12 3/8	6 3/8 5 6/8	7 4/8	Natrona County	WY	Mark D. Christopherson	1991	5375
67 4/8	13 6/8 12 4/8	5 5/8 5 4/8	9 4/8	Malheur County	OR	Dave Seida	1991	5375
67 4/8	12 5/8 12 2/8	6 0/8 5 7/8	12 1/8	Fremont County	WY	Lyle Prell	1991	5375
67 4/8	14 1/8 13 3/8	5 3/8 5 4/8	11 2/8	Campbell County	WY	Edwin John Durushia	1991	5375
67 4/8	13 6/8 13 3/8	6 0/8 6 0/8	10 2/8	Rosebud County	MT	Danny L. Parrott	1991	5375
67 4/8	13 5/8 13 2/8	5 7/8 5 7/8	12 1/8	Madison County	MT	Jim Powell	1991	5375
67 4/8	13 4/8 13 4/8	5 4/8 5 4/8	8 2/8	Harding County	SD	John R. Simpson	1991	5375
67 4/8	12 4/8 13 0/8	6 0/8 6 0/8	8 1/8	Converse County	WY	Peter F. Woeck II	1991	5375
67 4/8	12 5/8 13 0/8	6 1/8 6 1/8	9 0/8	Weld County	CO	Michael J. McArtor	1992	5375
67 4/8	13 6/8 14 0/8	5 4/8 5 4/8	13 4/8	Owyhee County	ID	Frank Sanders	1992	5375
67 4/8	13 0/8 13 3/8	5 6/8 5 4/8	12 2/8	Owyhee County	ID	Jay D. King	1992	5375
67 4/8	12 6/8 12 6/8	5 5/8 5 4/8	12 3/8	Campbell County	WY	Randy Springborn	1992	5375
67 4/8	12 4/8 12 3/8	5 5/8 5 6/8	9 6/8	Converse County	WY	Ron Bernash	1992	5375
67 4/8	13 5/8 13 4/8	5 4/8 5 4/8	12 0/8	Dunn County	ND	Jay Gunwall	1992	5375
67 4/8	12 3/8 12 4/8	5 6/8 5 6/8	9 0/8	Converse County	WY	Pat Forliti	1992	5375
67 4/8	13 5/8 13 7/8	5 2/8 5 3/8	12 0/8	Campbell County	WY	John W. Hampton	1992	5375
67 4/8	12 7/8 12 5/8	6 2/8 6 0/8	8 3/8	Sioux County	NE	Dave Tunink	1992	5375
67 4/8	13 1/8 13 5/8	6 1/8 6 1/8	10 6/8	Carbon County	WY	Norman Wolfe	1992	5375
67 4/8	13 5/8 14 0/8	5 3/8 5 2/8	9 7/8	Socorro County	NM	Thomas Vieth	1993	5375
67 4/8	13 1/8 13 1/8	6 0/8 6 0/8	8 5/8	Johnson County	WY	Charles B. Cureton	1993	5375
67 4/8	13 0/8 12 6/8	5 6/8 5 5/8	9 7/8	Moffat County	CO	Thomas P. Bartholomew	1994	5375
67 4/8	12 7/8 12 6/8	5 2/8 5 1/8	9 0/8	Wayne County	UT	Mike S. Mitchell	1994	5375
67 4/8	13 3/8 13 3/8	5 5/8 5 5/8	11 3/8	Park County	WY	Charlotte Moss	1994	5375
67 4/8	13 4/8 13 3/8	5 7/8 5 5/8	9 0/8	Owyhee County	ID	Terry L. Bennett	1994	5375
67 4/8	13 0/8 13 1/8	5 2/8 5 2/8	8 2/8	Carbon County	UT	Cory D. Oaks	1994	5375
67 4/8	13 2/8 13 3/8	5 4/8 5 4/8	7 7/8	Converse County	WY	Dave Canfield	1994	5375
67 4/8	11 6/8 12 6/8	6 0/8 5 7/8	9 3/8	Converse County	WY	Gary M. Gmeiner	1994	5375
67 4/8	11 7/8 12 0/8	5 6/8 5 7/8	13 2/8	Moffat County	CO	Dave Greenwalt	1994	5375
67 4/8	12 6/8 12 2/8	5 6/8 5 6/8	12 5/8	Converse County	WY	Jerry Nichols	1994	5375
67 4/8	13 0/8 12 6/8	5 4/8 5 5/8	9 0/8	Bowman County	ND	Ray Hajek	1994	5375
67 4/8	12 6/8 12 6/8	5 4/8 5 4/8	7 2/8	Musselshell County	MT	Dan Ermatinger	1994	5375
67 4/8	13 4/8 14 4/8	5 6/8 5 6/8	10 2/8	McKenzie County	ND	Pat Weigel	1994	5375
67 4/8	12 4/8 12 0/8	5 6/8 5 6/8	10 2/8	Campbell County	WY	Roger Peabody	1994	5375
67 4/8	12 5/8 13 0/8	5 5/8 5 6/8	10 5/8	Manyberries	ALB	Henry E. Moore, Jr.	1994	5375
67 4/8	13 0/8 11 6/8	5 5/8 5 5/8	11 2/8	Milk River	ALB	Ted Brown	1994	5375
67 4/8	14 1/8 13 3/8	5 5/8 5 5/8	13 0/8	Moffat County	CO	Max Thomas	1995	5375
67 4/8	12 3/8 12 1/8	6 0/8 5 7/8	11 1/8	Coconino County	AZ	Andrew L. Grannan	1995	5375
67 4/8	11 6/8 11 4/8	6 6/8 6 4/8	11 6/8	Converse County	WY	G. Lowe Morrison	1995	5375
67 4/8	13 5/8 13 5/8	5 5/8 5 5/8	5 7/8	Converse County	WY	Dan Weiss	1995	5375
67 4/8	14 0/8 13 5/8	5 6/8 5 5/8	6 5/8	Converse County	WY	Joe Krejci	1995	5375
67 4/8	13 7/8 14 0/8	5 3/8 5 3/8	9 6/8	Campbell County	WY	Raymond L. Howell, Sr.	1995	5375
67 4/8	14 4/8 14 4/8	5 5/8 5 5/8	9 5/8	Cheyenne County	NE	Everett A. Tarrell	1995	5375
67 4/8	12 6/8 12 4/8	5 4/8 5 5/8	11 3/8	Harney County	OR	Dave Creekmore	1996	5375
67 4/8	12 4/8 12 4/8	5 5/8 5 7/8	9 5/8	Powder River County	MT	Mark Kayser	1996	5375
67 4/8	14 4/8 14 2/8	5 2/8 5 2/8	11 0/8	Wallace County	KS	David R. Rogers	1996	5375
67 4/8	12 4/8 12 3/8	5 7/8 5 7/8	12 1/8	Moffat County	CO	Justin Bliss	1997	5375
67 4/8	13 5/8 13 2/8	5 5/8 5 6/8	10 2/8	Sweetwater County	WY	Gary Brewer	1997	5375
67 4/8	12 5/8 12 6/8	5 4/8 5 1/8	8 4/8	Campbell County	WY	Craig Olthoff	1997	5375
67 4/8	12 2/8 12 1/8	5 7/8 5 7/8	7 7/8	Natrona County	WY	Karen Hendricks	1998	5375
67 4/8	11 6/8 11 7/8	6 1/8 6 0/8	10 4/8	Weld County	CO	Justin Wenthe	1998	5375
67 4/8	11 2/8 11 3/8	6 2/8 6 4/8	8 3/8	Campbell County	WY	Peter Shockey	1998	5375
67 4/8	13 3/8 13 5/8	5 4/8 5 3/8	11 7/8	Converse County	WY	William R. Horn, Jr.	1998	5375
67 4/8	11 5/8 12 3/8	6 1/8 6 1/8	11 1/8	Garfield County	CO	Erik Watts	1999	5375
67 4/8	13 0/8 13 2/8	5 4/8 5 4/8	14 1/8	Larimer County	CO	Shawn Austin Greathouse	1999	5375
67 4/8	11 7/8 13 1/8	5 5/8 5 5/8	9 1/8	Converse County	WY	Jim Engle	1999	5375
67 4/8	14 2/8 14 1/8	5 1/8 5 3/8	8 6/8	Medicine Hat	ALB	Joe T. Soto, Jr.	1999	5375
67 4/8	13 2/8 13 3/8	5 5/8 5 3/8	9 3/8	Garfield County	MT	Koreen Rider	1999	5375
67 4/8	14 2/8 14 1/8	5 2/8 5 1/8	6 5/8	Petroleum County	MT	Jim Winjum	1999	5375
67 4/8	13 2/8 13 4/8	5 4/8 5 4/8	11 2/8	Sweetwater County	WY	Shane D. Steiss	2000	5375
67 4/8	13 1/8 12 7/8	5 5/8 5 5/8	9 4/8	Converse County	WY	Dale Good	2000	5375
67 4/8	12 6/8 13 0/8	6 0/8 6 0/8	10 1/8	Lemhi County	ID	Benjamin C. Fahnholz	2000	5375
67 4/8	13 3/8 13 1/8	5 5/8 5 4/8	10 3/8	Rosebud County	MT	Michael Babcock	2000	5375
67 4/8	12 4/8 14 4/8	6 1/8 6 1/8	9 7/8	Fergus County	MT	Josef K. Rud	2000	5375
67 4/8	12 2/8 12 3/8	5 1/8 5 1/8	8 5/8	Moffat County	CO	William Abshagen	2001	5375
67 4/8	12 4/8 12 7/8	5 5/8 5 4/8	7 4/8	Juab County	UT	Sherwin Lott	2001	5375
67 4/8	12 7/8 12 6/8	5 6/8 5 6/8	9 2/8	Gooding County	ID	Luke Carrothers	2001	5375
67 4/8	13 0/8 13 0/8	6 0/8 6 2/8	11 0/8	Campbell County	WY	Tim Johnston	2001	5375
67 4/8	12 4/8 11 7/8	5 7/8 5 6/8	11 3/8	Fergus County	MT	John P. Hartman	2001	5375
67 4/8	12 3/8 12 4/8	6 1/8 6 1/8	11 4/8	Carbon County	WY	Cory Lindbo	2001	5375
67 4/8	13 0/8 13 4/8	5 6/8 5 6/8	12 1/8	Golden Valley County	ND	Nathaniel Schroeder	2002	5375
67 4/8	13 7/8 14 3/8	5 3/8 5 0/8	10 1/8	Medicine Hat	ALB	Glen Garton	2002	5375
67 4/8	12 0/8 12 4/8	6 0/8 5 7/8	10 6/8	Patricia	ALB	Lauren Hoover	2002	5375
67 4/8	13 1/8 13 0/8	5 3/8 5 2/8	10 1/8	Rolling Hills	ALB	Patrick D. Quinn	2002	5375
67 4/8	13 7/8 14 3/8	5 1/8 5 1/8	5 7/8	Campbell County	WY	Debhra S. Roney	2002	5375
67 4/8	13 4/8 13 5/8	5 0/8 4 7/8	10 7/8	Sweetwater County	WY	Dale Pecolar	2002	5375
67 4/8	12 4/8 12 5/8	5 5/8 5 5/8	12 5/8	Moffat County	CO	Jerry Hanson	2003	5375
67 4/8	12 1/8 12 2/8	6 3/8 6 2/8	10 5/8	Converse County	WY	David Brown	2003	5375
67 4/8	12 6/8 12 5/8	5 5/8 5 5/8	11 7/8	Converse County	WY	Troy McGinnis	2003	5375
67 4/8	13 6/8 13 4/8	5 5/8 5 5/8	10 1/8	Bowman County	ND	Ryan Bauer	2003	5375
67 4/8	14 0/8 14 1/8	5 1/8 5 0/8	9 7/8	Weston County	WY	William T. Zeman	2003	5375
67 4/8	11 1/8 11 5/8	6 2/8 6 2/8	11 6/8	Campbell County	WY	Robert M. "Mike" Young	2003	5375
67 4/8	12 5/8 13 0/8	5 4/8 5 4/8	10 2/8	Converse County	WY	John F. Lincoln	2004	5375
*67 4/8	13 2/8 13 2/8	5 3/8 5 2/8	9 2/8	Madison County	MT	Tim O'Connell	2004	5375
67 4/8	11 6/8 11 6/8	6 2/8 6 2/8	9 3/8	Powder River County	MT	Ron Peterson	2005	5375

867

PRONGHORN

Minimum Score 67   Continued

SCORE	LENGTH OF R HORN L	CIRCUMFERENCE R OF BASE L	INSIDE SPREAD	AREA	STATE/ PROVINCE	HUNTER'S NAME	DATE	RANK
67 4/8	13 3/8 13 5/8	6 2/8 6 4/8	10 6/8	Rosebud County	MT	William Justmann	2005	5375
67 4/8	12 6/8 12 4/8	5 4/8 5 4/8	8 2/8	Jackson County	CO	T. J. Thrasher	2005	5375
67 4/8	13 0/8 12 3/8	6 1/8 6 1/8	8 0/8	Rosebud County	MT	Gene Welle	2005	5375
67 4/8	12 6/8 12 4/8	5 3/8 5 4/8	7 5/8	Niobrara County	WY	Dennis Ballweg	2005	5375
67 4/8	12 0/8 12 6/8	5 6/8 5 3/8	10 3/8	Converse County	WY	Larry L. Haines	2005	5375
67 4/8	14 3/8 14 3/8	5 1/8 5 0/8	7 6/8	Musselshell County	MT	Tyler A. Borth	2005	5375
67 4/8	13 4/8 13 2/8	5 6/8 5 4/8	9 7/8	Natrona County	WY	Tom Nelson	2005	5375
67 4/8	13 6/8 13 7/8	5 2/8 5 2/8	9 6/8	Johnson County	WY	Michael Scaff	2005	5375
67 4/8	12 2/8 12 2/8	6 5/8 6 4/8	9 3/8	Campbell County	WY	Tom Gleason	2005	5375
67 4/8	13 1/8 13 2/8	5 6/8 5 6/8	8 2/8	Albany County	WY	Ron Mason	2006	5375
*67 4/8	12 0/8 11 2/8	5 5/8 5 6/8	10 6/8	Carbon County	WY	Bill Kroseberg	2006	5375
67 4/8	14 5/8 15 0/8	5 2/8 5 3/8	17 0/8	Powder River County	MT	Michael B. Washychyn	2006	5375
67 4/8	13 0/8 12 7/8	5 4/8 5 3/8	8 7/8	Sublette County	WY	Virgil Burget	2006	5375
67 4/8	13 4/8 13 5/8	5 5/8 5 5/8	7 7/8	Lemhi County	ID	Brandon Lee Fahnholz	2006	5375
67 4/8	12 0/8 12 1/8	6 0/8 6 0/8	8 5/8	Musselshell County	MT	Don Davidson	2006	5375
*67 4/8	12 3/8 12 3/8	5 5/8 5 4/8	9 1/8	Gove County	KS	Matthew Palmquist	2006	5375
67 4/8	12 5/8 11 5/8	5 7/8 6 0/8	13 1/8	Lincoln County	NV	Mallory Genet	2007	5375
67 4/8	12 4/8 12 3/8	6 0/8 5 7/8	9 0/8	Converse County	WY	Benjamin T. Davenport	2007	5375
67 4/8	12 6/8 13 0/8	5 6/8 5 5/8	10 0/8	Sheridan County	WY	Marc J. Ruyak	2007	5375
67 4/8	14 3/8 14 1/8	5 6/8 5 4/8	12 5/8	Elmore County	ID	Bill Kinghorn	2007	5375
67 4/8	12 0/8 12 1/8	5 7/8 5 5/8	9 4/8	Powder River County	MT	Dennis H. Sagle	2007	5375
67 4/8	13 3/8 12 1/8	6 2/8 6 2/8	12 3/8	Campbell County	WY	Gene Welle	2007	5375
67 4/8	13 2/8 12 7/8	5 5/8 5 5/8	9 3/8	Cherry County	NE	Kent Hochstein	2007	5375
*67 4/8	13 1/8 13 1/8	5 4/8 5 5/8	9 4/8	Harding County	SD	Dylan Deuter	2007	5375
*67 4/8	14 2/8 14 0/8	5 0/8 4 7/8	8 1/8	Gove County	KS	Matthew Palmquist	2007	5375
67 4/8	13 4/8 13 4/8	5 2/8 5 1/8	9 0/8	Dawes County	NE	Jamie Becker	2008	5375
67 4/8	13 5/8 14 0/8	5 1/8 5 3/8	10 5/8	Owyhee County	ID	Larry Velvick	2008	5375
67 4/8	13 5/8 13 5/8	5 4/8 5 3/8	9 7/8	Powder River County	MT	Martin E. Cain	2008	5375
67 4/8	12 1/8 13 6/8	6 3/8 6 0/8	9 0/8	Johnson County	WY	Gail Martin	2008	5375
67 4/8	12 7/8 12 6/8	5 4/8 5 2/8	9 5/8	Fremont County	WY	Dirk K. Edgeington	2009	5375
*67 4/8	12 2/8 12 4/8	6 0/8 6 0/8	8 1/8	Campbell County	WY	Lane Ostendorf	2009	5375
67 4/8	13 0/8 13 1/8	6 4/8 6 3/8	9 1/8	Brooks	ALB	Ben B. Wallace	2009	5375
67 4/8	13 5/8 13 3/8	5 4/8 5 5/8	12 7/8	Big Horn County	MT	Chris Sanford	2009	5375
67 4/8	13 3/8 13 2/8	5 3/8 5 2/8	11 0/8	Converse County	WY	Daniel J. DeBoer	2009	5375
*67 4/8	13 6/8 14 1/8	5 3/8 5 4/8	11 1/8	Phillips County	MT	Brady Miller	2009	5375
67 4/8	11 7/8 12 2/8	6 0/8 6 0/8	10 3/8	Converse County	WY	Brad Harriman	2010	5375
67 4/8	13 0/8 12 6/8	5 5/8 5 5/8	10 4/8	Yavapai County	AZ	Rodney Ronnebaum	2010	5375
67 2/8	12 1/8 12 1/8	6 0/8 5 5/8	11 6/8	Carbon County	WY	Dennis Behn	1974	5550
67 2/8	12 7/8 13 0/8	5 2/8 5 2/8	6 4/8	Musselshell County	MT	Scott L. Koelzer	1976	5550
67 2/8	13 7/8 14 0/8	5 4/8 5 4/8	9 2/8	Campbell County	WY	Larry Tiner	1978	5550
67 2/8	13 0/8 13 0/8	5 3/8 5 3/8	14 3/8	Natrona County	WY	Dennis Keyser	1978	5550
67 2/8	12 6/8 13 1/8	5 7/8 5 7/8	9 5/8	Sweetwater County	WY	Blair Smith	1978	5550
67 2/8	11 5/8 11 5/8	5 0/8 5 0/8	9 2/8	Converse County	WY	Eugene Smith, Jr.	1979	5550
67 2/8	13 3/8 13 4/8	5 5/8 5 4/8	10 2/8	Converse County	WY	John Zawaski	1980	5550
67 2/8	13 1/8 13 0/8	5 4/8 5 5/8	9 2/8	Converse County	WY	Ronald J. Collier	1980	5550
67 2/8	13 5/8 13 1/8	5 5/8 5 5/8	10 3/8	Humboldt County	NV	Jeff Purcell	1980	5550
67 2/8	12 6/8 12 6/8	5 3/8 5 3/8	12 3/8	Converse County	WY	Al Gross	1981	5550
67 2/8	13 7/8 13 7/8	5 4/8 5 4/8	11 2/8	Converse County	WY	Wayne W. Wagner	1981	5550
67 2/8	13 1/8 13 2/8	5 2/8 5 1/8	9 4/8	Pueblo County	CO	Mitchell McMahon	1982	5550
67 2/8	14 1/8 12 7/8	5 4/8 5 4/8	10 6/8	Moffat County	CO	Steven Neal	1982	5550
67 2/8	13 4/8 13 4/8	5 4/8 5 3/8	8 2/8	Wallace County	KS	Steve Rugg	1982	5550
67 2/8	11 6/8 11 5/8	6 0/8 6 0/8	12 6/8	Sioux County	NE	Melvin L. Rein	1982	5550
67 2/8	13 6/8 12 3/8	6 1/8 6 1/8	9 6/8	White Pine County	NV	Larry T. Gilbertson	1983	5550
67 2/8	14 3/8 14 2/8	5 4/8 5 4/8	12 0/8	Perkins County	SD	Vilas Schoenfelder	1983	5550
67 2/8	11 7/8 12 0/8	5 7/8 5 7/8	9 4/8	Bowman County	ND	Greg Braun	1983	5550
67 2/8	13 0/8 12 4/8	6 0/8 5 6/8	7 3/8	Converse County	WY	Larry Crooks	1983	5550
67 2/8	13 1/8 12 7/8	5 5/8 5 6/8	11 5/8	Converse County	WY	Gary Holtz	1983	5550
67 2/8	12 5/8 12 3/8	5 3/8 5 4/8	11 7/8	Meade County	SD	Steve D. Krier	1983	5550
67 2/8	13 0/8 13 0/8	5 5/8 5 5/8	8 1/8	Hettinger County	ND	Briar Scherr	1983	5550
67 2/8	12 0/8 12 2/8	5 7/8 6 1/8	7 3/8	Campbell County	WY	William Heineke	1984	5550
67 2/8	13 1/8 13 1/8	4 5/8 4 7/8	11 7/8	Moffat County	CO	Glenn Pritchard	1984	5550
67 2/8	12 0/8 12 1/8	5 6/8 5 5/8	7 7/8	Converse County	WY	Ron Rockwell	1984	5550
67 2/8	12 4/8 12 3/8	6 0/8 6 0/8	12 0/8	Sweetwater County	WY	John Cheese	1985	5550
67 2/8	13 2/8 13 2/8	5 4/8 5 2/8	7 2/8	Moffat County	CO	John E. Axelson	1985	5550
67 2/8	13 3/8 12 6/8	5 4/8 5 4/8	7 6/8	Moffat County	CO	Kurt Keskimaki	1985	5550
67 2/8	12 4/8 12 4/8	5 6/8 5 6/8	8 3/8	Moffat County	CO	James A. Davison	1985	5550
67 2/8	13 1/8 12 7/8	5 7/8 5 6/8	9 3/8	Carbon County	WY	Richard L. Westervelt	1985	5550
67 2/8	13 7/8 13 7/8	5 6/8 5 5/8	11 1/8	Converse County	WY	David Jerome	1985	5550
67 2/8	12 5/8 12 5/8	5 3/8 5 3/8	9 0/8	Converse County	WY	William Doemland	1985	5550
67 2/8	13 2/8 13 2/8	5 1/8 5 1/8	8 4/8	Campbell County	WY	Richard Andre	1985	5550
67 2/8	13 2/8 13 1/8	5 7/8 5 6/8	11 0/8	Converse County	WY	Craig James Stransky	1985	5550
67 2/8	12 4/8 12 3/8	6 0/8 5 7/8	10 1/8	Valley County	MT	Bryan Erickson	1986	5550
67 2/8	12 7/8 12 7/8	6 0/8 5 6/8	8 5/8	Converse County	WY	Gregory White	1986	5550
67 2/8	12 4/8 12 2/8	6 2/8 6 2/8	10 0/8	Converse County	WY	Richard Crawford	1986	5550
67 2/8	13 6/8 13 7/8	4 7/8 5 0/8	9 3/8	Chouteau County	MT	Wayne Arnold	1986	5550
67 2/8	12 7/8 13 0/8	6 2/8 6 2/8	7 7/8	Moffat County	CO	Ron Rockwell	1987	5550
67 2/8	12 4/8 12 7/8	5 4/8 5 4/8	9 5/8	Bingham County	ID	Reggie N. Scheierman	1988	5550
67 2/8	11 5/8 12 4/8	5 6/8 5 6/8	9 2/8	Blaine County	ID	Wesley Moore	1988	5550
67 2/8	11 4/8 11 6/8	6 1/8 6 0/8	7 6/8	McKenzie County	ND	Bill Kelly	1988	5550
67 2/8	13 0/8 12 7/8	5 5/8 5 5/8	7 1/8	Converse County	WY	Carmine Agostine	1988	5550
67 2/8	13 2/8 13 1/8	5 7/8 6 0/8	10 6/8	Petroleum County	MT	Leamon D. Ferrell	1988	5550
67 2/8	12 4/8 12 6/8	5 7/8 5 6/8	9 5/8	Moffat County	CO	Barry Rich	1989	5550
67 2/8	12 2/8 12 5/8	5 4/8 5 3/8	8 7/8	Converse County	WY	Jason W. Zebrowski	1989	5550
67 2/8	13 1/8 13 4/8	5 6/8 5 5/8	7 2/8	Campbell County	WY	Robin D. Johnson	1989	5550
67 2/8	11 1/8 11 3/8	6 2/8 6 1/8	10 4/8	Custer County	MT	Mark L. Frank	1989	5550
67 2/8	13 2/8 13 2/8	5 6/8 5 6/8	10 1/8	Billings County	ND	Jeff Brigham	1989	5550
67 2/8	13 2/8 13 0/8	5 3/8 5 3/8	9 3/8	Converse County	WY	David A. Widby	1990	5550
67 2/8	12 7/8 12 2/8	6 0/8 5 7/8	10 4/8	Harney County	OR	Richard Wright	1990	5550
67 2/8	12 2/8 12 5/8	5 5/8 5 4/8	11 0/8	Sweetwater County	WY	Dave Holt	1990	5550
67 2/8	13 2/8 13 1/8	5 3/8 5 5/8	9 6/8	Sheridan County	WY	Tom Hlinka	1990	5550
67 2/8	13 3/8 13 3/8	5 6/8 5 4/8	8 5/8	Wallace County	KS	Roger Potter	1990	5550
67 2/8	13 5/8 13 5/8	5 6/8 5 6/8	9 0/8	Harding County	SD	Marty Adams	1990	5550
67 2/8	12 7/8 13 1/8	5 7/8 5 6/8	7 1/8	Owyhee County	ID	Jesse M. Frandsen	1991	5550
67 2/8	12 5/8 12 4/8	5 5/8 5 5/8	9 4/8	Sweetwater County	WY	Mark Petersen	1991	5550
67 2/8	12 0/8 12 7/8	6 2/8 6 1/8	7 6/8	Converse County	WY	Ed Defibaugh	1991	5550

PRONGHORN

Minimum Score 67 — Continued

SCORE	LENGTH OF R HORN L	CIRCUMFERENCE R OF BASE L	INSIDE SPREAD	AREA	STATE/ PROVINCE	HUNTER'S NAME	DATE	RANK
67 2/8	13 3/8 13 3/8	5 6/8 5 6/8	9 2/8	Campbell County	WY	William J. McGrath	1991	5550
67 2/8	11 5/8 11 7/8	5 7/8 5 6/8	8 7/8	McKenzie County	ND	Mark D. Hughes	1991	5550
67 2/8	13 5/8 13 5/8	6 1/8 6 1/8	7 7/8	Corson County	SD	Fred Kober	1991	5550
67 2/8	13 2/8 13 1/8	5 6/8 5 5/8	11 0/8	Campbell County	WY	Tom Griffin	1991	5550
67 2/8	13 0/8 13 1/8	6 2/8 6 2/8	12 2/8	Carbon County	WY	Levi Nelson	1991	5550
67 2/8	12 4/8 12 6/8	5 6/8 5 6/8	7 0/8	Butte County	SD	Larry Kracht	1991	5550
67 2/8	13 0/8 13 1/8	5 7/8 6 0/8	9 3/8	Sierra County	NM	Daryl Tow	1992	5550
67 2/8	13 4/8 13 2/8	5 5/8 5 5/8	9 7/8	Moffat County	CO	Garry Woodman	1992	5550
67 2/8	14 1/8 13 6/8	6 0/8 5 7/8	14 4/8	Sweetwater County	WY	Ronda Williams	1992	5550
67 2/8	13 2/8 13 3/8	5 7/8 5 6/8	10 6/8	Moffat County	CO	Rett Kelly	1992	5550
67 2/8	12 3/8 12 1/8	5 6/8 5 6/8	7 2/8	Converse County	WY	Gene Mathias	1992	5550
67 2/8	13 3/8 13 3/8	5 2/8 5 2/8	12 1/8	Bowman County	ND	David Brag	1992	5550
67 2/8	12 0/8 12 0/8	6 0/8 6 0/8	10 4/8	Moffat County	CO	Kenneth L. Shelton	1992	5550
67 2/8	13 4/8 13 4/8	5 5/8 5 5/8	8 2/8	Fox Valley	SAS	Floyd Forster	1992	5550
67 2/8	13 1/8 13 3/8	5 0/8 5 0/8	11 2/8	Converse County	WY	Scott McCormack	1992	5550
67 2/8	13 3/8 12 6/8	6 2/8 6 1/8	6 6/8	Rosebud County	MT	John W. Offord	1992	5550
67 2/8	14 1/8 14 2/8	5 5/8 5 6/8	9 3/8	Yavapai County	AZ	Brian K. Tinker	1993	5550
67 2/8	14 0/8 14 2/8	5 3/8 5 3/8	13 1/8	Sweet Grass County	MT	John M. Rigney	1993	5550
67 2/8	13 0/8 13 0/8	6 4/8 6 4/8	11 4/8	Converse County	WY	Donald Miller	1993	5550
67 2/8	13 0/8 13 2/8	5 6/8 5 6/8	7 3/8	Campbell County	WY	Tom Gleason	1993	5550
67 2/8	12 2/8 12 3/8	5 7/8 5 7/8	9 4/8	Yavapai County	AZ	Van M. Clark, Jr.	1994	5550
67 2/8	14 5/8 14 2/8	5 4/8 5 4/8	10 5/8	Buffalo	ALB	Larry Flaata	1994	5550
67 2/8	12 5/8 12 5/8	5 5/8 5 4/8	11 5/8	Campbell County	WY	Bob Atwood	1994	5550
67 2/8	11 6/8 11 6/8	5 7/8 5 6/8	7 5/8	Moffat County	CO	Peter F. Woeck II	1995	5550
67 2/8	14 1/8 13 5/8	5 1/8 5 2/8	7 6/8	Natrona County	WY	Rodney L. Dehart	1995	5550
67 2/8	12 1/8 12 2/8	6 1/8 6 1/8	10 5/8	Moffat County	CO	Mike Boland	1995	5550
67 2/8	13 3/8 13 2/8	5 4/8 5 4/8	10 6/8	Dunn County	ND	Mike Morris	1995	5550
67 2/8	13 3/8 13 5/8	5 4/8 5 3/8	12 3/8	Converse County	WY	Dr. Eugene T. Altiere	1995	5550
67 2/8	13 2/8 12 6/8	5 5/8 5 4/8	12 6/8	Converse County	WY	Chuck Kronenwetter	1995	5550
67 2/8	12 4/8 12 2/8	5 7/8 6 0/8	10 1/8	Aden	ALB	Douglas W. Cannons	1995	5550
67 2/8	14 0/8 14 1/8	5 3/8 5 3/8	11 1/8	Harding County	SD	Scott Ketchmark	1995	5550
67 2/8	14 2/8 14 0/8	4 6/8 4 6/8	10 5/8	Yavapai County	AZ	Robert B. Buchanan	1996	5550
67 2/8	12 3/8 13 3/8	5 7/8 6 0/8	7 6/8	Moffat County	CO	Rod Lampe	1996	5550
67 2/8	13 0/8 13 0/8	5 6/8 5 6/8	11 0/8	Harding County	SD	Renee Welle	1996	5550
67 2/8	12 0/8 12 1/8	6 4/8 6 4/8	10 3/8	Converse County	WY	George A. Zanoni	1996	5550
67 2/8	13 7/8 13 7/8	5 4/8 5 4/8	12 6/8	Converse County	WY	Anthony "Del" DelMastro	1996	5550
67 2/8	12 7/8 14 4/8	5 6/8 5 7/8	11 1/8	Campbell County	WY	Gary English	1997	5550
67 2/8	11 7/8 11 7/8	5 6/8 5 6/8	9 0/8	Wallace County	KS	Paul Atkins	1997	5550
67 2/8	12 5/8 12 2/8	6 7/8 7 0/8	12 0/8	Converse County	WY	Pam Hamilton	1998	5550
67 2/8	13 1/8 13 1/8	5 1/8 5 1/8	10 5/8	Weld County	CO	Bob Chapman	1998	5550
67 2/8	13 6/8 13 7/8	5 3/8 5 3/8	12 0/8	Perkins County	SD	Aaron Ambur	1999	5550
67 2/8	12 4/8 12 3/8	5 4/8 5 5/8	10 6/8	Moffat County	CO	Brad Herman	2000	5550
67 2/8	13 1/8 13 0/8	5 4/8 5 3/8	9 4/8	Weld County	CO	Jacob Chandler	2000	5550
67 2/8	13 4/8 13 1/8	5 6/8 5 7/8	12 1/8	Johnson County	WY	Richard Creason	2000	5550
67 2/8	13 1/8 13 1/8	5 2/8 5 2/8	8 4/8	Elbert County	CO	Joseph Couey	2001	5550
67 2/8	13 6/8 13 6/8	5 3/8 5 2/8	9 0/8	Albany County	WY	James Collins	2001	5550
67 2/8	13 0/8 13 0/8	5 4/8 5 4/8	8 2/8	Moffat County	CO	Ron Beidelman	2001	5550
67 2/8	13 2/8 13 2/8	5 6/8 5 4/8	10 0/8	Converse County	WY	Joseph M. Clevinger	2001	5550
67 2/8	13 3/8 13 0/8	6 0/8 5 7/8	12 1/8	Converse County	WY	Randy A. Reeves	2001	5550
67 2/8	13 4/8 13 4/8	5 3/8 5 5/8	10 3/8	Harding County	SD	Rayneal McKim	2001	5550
67 2/8	13 0/8 12 7/8	6 1/8 6 1/8	8 2/8	Converse County	WY	Alan L. Meurer	2001	5550
67 2/8	12 7/8 12 7/8	6 2/8 6 2/8	10 6/8	Fergus County	MT	Walter H. Rud	2001	5550
67 2/8	13 2/8 13 2/8	5 7/8 5 3/8	8 5/8	Converse County	WY	William G. Mason	2002	5550
67 2/8	13 3/8 13 0/8	5 6/8 5 5/8	10 5/8	Owyhee County	ID	Michael D. Harvey, Jr.	2002	5550
67 2/8	12 7/8 12 7/8	5 4/8 5 4/8	6 3/8	Converse County	WY	Larry Haines	2002	5550
67 2/8	13 2/8 13 1/8	5 4/8 5 2/8	7 2/8	Sherman County	KS	Lance Hockett	2002	5550
67 2/8	13 1/8 13 2/8	5 6/8 5 6/8	7 3/8	Blaine County	MT	Kirk Perszyk	2002	5550
67 2/8	13 1/8 12 7/8	6 0/8 5 7/8	9 2/8	Elko County	NV	Mike Collie	2003	5550
*67 2/8	12 4/8 12 3/8	6 0/8 5 7/8	8 6/8	Las Animas County	CO	Jeff Johnson	2003	5550
67 2/8	12 5/8 12 5/8	5 4/8 5 4/8	6 0/8	Carbon County	WY	Greg Bokash	2003	5550
67 2/8	11 5/8 12 0/8	6 0/8 6 0/8	8 5/8	Grand County	CO	Jan J. Finley	2003	5550
67 2/8	12 7/8 12 6/8	5 1/8 5 0/8	10 5/8	Converse County	WY	Larry L. Haines	2003	5550
67 2/8	13 4/8 13 4/8	5 2/8 5 2/8	10 0/8	Harding County	SD	James D. Herring	2003	5550
67 2/8	13 4/8 13 5/8	5 3/8 5 3/8	9 3/8	Converse County	WY	Tom Nelson	2003	5550
67 2/8	13 1/8 12 7/8	5 7/8 5 5/8	9 5/8	Newell	ALB	Ray Francingues	2003	5550
67 2/8	13 2/8 13 4/8	6 0/8 6 0/8	7 0/8	Campbell County	WY	William Peterson	2003	5550
67 2/8	14 0/8 14 0/8	5 4/8 5 4/8	11 3/8	Garfield County	MT	Tyler M. Frost	2003	5550
67 2/8	13 0/8 13 0/8	5 1/8 5 1/8	9 2/8	Elkwater	ALB	Robert J. Haley	2003	5550
67 2/8	13 0/8 13 1/8	5 4/8 5 3/8	9 5/8	Harding County	SD	Kerry A. Bahr	2003	5550
67 2/8	12 3/8 12 4/8	5 4/8 5 4/8	10 3/8	Rosebud County	MT	Michael C. Allgeyer	2003	5550
67 2/8	12 5/8 12 6/8	5 5/8 5 5/8	11 4/8	Las Animas County	CO	Nancy L. Palmer	2004	5550
67 2/8	12 4/8 13 2/8	5 6/8 5 6/8	11 2/8	Platte County	WY	Terry Krahn	2004	5550
67 2/8	12 7/8 13 0/8	5 3/8 5 3/8	10 6/8	Las Animas County	CO	Lance Guerin	2004	5550
67 2/8	12 1/8 12 0/8	5 6/8 6 0/8	9 2/8	Campbell County	WY	Gene A. Hall	2004	5550
67 2/8	12 2/8 12 0/8	5 6/8 5 5/8	10 4/8	Kiowa County	CO	Bo Clark	2004	5550
67 2/8	13 2/8 12 4/8	6 4/8 6 4/8	8 6/8	Butte County	SD	Larry W. Rowlett	2004	5550
67 2/8	13 0/8 13 2/8	5 7/8 5 7/8	8 6/8	Carbon County	WY	Christine Williamson	2004	5550
67 2/8	11 4/8 11 5/8	6 1/8 6 1/8	12 1/8	Modoc County	CA	George Morris	2005	5550
67 2/8	13 5/8 12 7/8	6 1/8 6 0/8	10 3/8	Washoe County	NV	Lew Webb	2005	5550
67 2/8	13 3/8 13 1/8	5 6/8 5 6/8	10 4/8	Albany County	WY	Jim Saunoris, Jr.	2005	5550
67 2/8	12 5/8 12 3/8	6 2/8 6 2/8	8 2/8	Powder River County	MT	Jerry E. Strese	2005	5550
67 2/8	12 4/8 12 0/8	5 5/8 5 5/8	12 3/8	Fremont County	WY	Ken Conley	2005	5550
67 2/8	11 2/8 11 1/8	6 1/8 6 0/8	11 0/8	Converse County	WY	Rick Liebel	2005	5550
67 2/8	12 6/8 13 0/8	6 0/8 5 7/8	12 4/8	Weld County	CO	Tim Rushing	2005	5550
*67 2/8	13 2/8 13 6/8	5 7/8 5 6/8	12 1/8	Converse County	WY	Brian Scott Smith	2005	5550
67 2/8	13 4/8 13 1/8	5 3/8 5 4/8	7 7/8	Powder River County	MT	Michael Wolff	2005	5550
*67 2/8	14 3/8 13 2/8	5 4/8 5 4/8	7 6/8	Lea County	NM	Lynn Saxon	2006	5550
*67 2/8	12 6/8 12 4/8	6 5/8 6 1/8	9 2/8	Harding County	SD	DuWayne Larson	2006	5550
67 2/8	13 1/8 13 1/8	5 2/8 5 2/8	7 5/8	Converse County	WY	Gary Zimmerer	2006	5550
67 2/8	12 7/8 12 7/8	5 3/8 5 2/8	6 4/8	Albany County	WY	Frank G. Hood	2006	5550
67 2/8	12 4/8 12 5/8	6 0/8 6 3/8	8 6/8	Crook County	WY	DuWayne Larson	2006	5550
67 2/8	12 6/8 12 7/8	6 2/8 6 2/8	9 4/8	Johnson County	WY	Gary R. Shields	2006	5550
*67 2/8	13 0/8 13 0/8	5 4/8 5 3/8	10 5/8	Golden Valley County	ND	Chris Haug	2006	5550
67 2/8	12 6/8 12 5/8	5 4/8 5 4/8	12 4/8	Butte County	SD	Gary D. English	2006	5550
67 2/8	11 6/8 11 6/8	5 7/8 5 6/8	7 4/8	Wayne County	UT	Eldon Richter	2007	5550

869

PRONGHORN

Minimum Score 67 — Continued

SCORE	LENGTH OF R HORN L	CIRCUMFERENCE R OF BASE L	INSIDE SPREAD	AREA	STATE/ PROVINCE	HUNTER'S NAME	DATE	RANK
67 2/8	12 4/8 13 1/8	5 6/8 5 6/8	8 6/8	Albany County	WY	James Dalrymple	2007	5550
67 2/8	13 4/8 13 3/8	6 0/8 6 0/8	9 2/8	Carter County	MT	James D. Herring	2007	5550
67 2/8	13 2/8 13 0/8	5 5/8 5 5/8	7 7/8	Carter County	MT	Jeff Pals	2007	5550
67 2/8	13 4/8 13 6/8	6 2/8 6 4/8	10 2/8	Campbell County	WY	Gene Welle	2007	5550
67 2/8	13 0/8 12 5/8	5 7/8 5 6/8	6 6/8	Campbell County	WY	Corey Hugelen	2007	5550
67 2/8	13 5/8 13 5/8	5 3/8 5 3/8	10 0/8	Rosebud County	MT	Gene A. Welle	2007	5550
67 2/8	13 5/8 13 5/8	5 2/8 5 2/8	9 3/8	Converse County	WY	Dick Driscoll	2007	5550
67 2/8	13 2/8 13 1/8	5 7/8 5 5/8	11 2/8	Maple Creek	SAS	Chet Paslawski	2007	5550
67 2/8	12 6/8 12 5/8	5 2/8 5 3/8	11 6/8	Harding County	SD	DuWayne Larson	2008	5550
67 2/8	13 1/8 12 6/8	5 2/8 5 2/8	11 4/8	Moffat County	CO	Sonya Garcia	2008	5550
67 2/8	12 1/8 12 1/8	5 6/8 5 5/8	10 0/8	Laramie County	WY	Jack L. Olson	2008	5550
67 2/8	13 2/8 13 4/8	5 4/8 5 2/8	11 2/8	Harding County	SD	John Meyen	2008	5550
*67 2/8	12 7/8 12 5/8	5 4/8 5 6/8	10 2/8	Colfax County	NM	Mark J. Kramer	2009	5550
*67 2/8	12 1/8 12 1/8	5 7/8 5 7/8	8 7/8	Campbell County	WY	Debbie Seippel	2009	5550
67 2/8	12 7/8 12 1/8	5 6/8 5 7/8	7 6/8	Tooele County	UT	Bill Plowman	2009	5550
67 2/8	12 7/8 12 3/8	5 6/8 5 6/8	11 6/8	Laramie County	WY	Diane Bryart	2009	5550
67 2/8	14 4/8 14 1/8	5 3/8 5 4/8	7 3/8	Perkins County	SD	Ryan L. Domaszek	2009	5550
*67 2/8	12 7/8 12 6/8	5 5/8 5 4/8	11 0/8	Rosebud County	MT	Daniel B. Maxson	2009	5550
67 2/8	12 1/8 13 3/8	5 3/8 5 4/8	10 6/8	Garfield County	UT	Zachary Henseler	2009	5550
*67 2/8	13 0/8 13 0/8	5 0/8 5 2/8	8 7/8	Crook County	WY	Brad Booth	2009	5550
67 2/8	14 0/8 14 1/8	5 2/8 5 1/8	8 6/8	Harding County	SD	Steve Monacelli	2009	5550
67 2/8	12 5/8 12 3/8	5 5/8 5 5/8	8 7/8	Converse County	WY	Robert W. Markowski	2010	5550
*67 2/8	13 3/8 13 1/8	5 5/8 5 6/8	8 6/8	Niobrara County	WY	Charles W. Rehor	2010	5550
*67 2/8	11 3/8 11 4/8	5 7/8 5 6/8	10 0/8	Moffat County	CO	Todd Winczewski	2010	5550
67 2/8	12 0/8 12 2/8	6 3/8 6 4/8	9 6/8	Carbon County	UT	James Holt	2010	5550
67 2/8	14 1/8 14 0/8	5 2/8 5 1/8	9 7/8	Converse County	WY	Steven Hemrich	2010	5550
67 0/8	12 7/8 12 7/8	5 6/8 5 4/8	10 2/8	Butte County	SD	David Lind	1961	5729
67 0/8	13 0/8 13 2/8	5 5/8 5 5/8	10 6/8	McLean County	ND	Harold Janssen	1971	5729
67 0/8	13 0/8 12 4/8	6 0/8 6 0/8	10 4/8	Campbell County	WY	Gerald L. Egbert	1975	5729
67 0/8	11 0/8 11 0/8	6 6/8 6 4/8	8 3/8	Converse County	WY	Eddie Hayden	1978	5729
67 0/8	12 6/8 12 4/8	6 1/8 6 0/8	11 2/8	Converse County	WY	Kenneth L. Stoneburner	1978	5729
67 0/8	11 5/8 11 5/8	6 0/8 6 0/8	9 0/8	Weld County	CO	Dennis Schweitzer	1980	5729
67 0/8	12 7/8 12 7/8	5 5/8 5 5/8	7 2/8	Converse County	WY	Alton Gross	1980	5729
67 0/8	12 3/8 12 2/8	5 5/8 5 6/8	8 7/8	Sheridan County	WY	Travis Adsit	1981	5729
67 0/8	12 6/8 13 0/8	5 5/8 5 6/8	10 7/8	Natrona County	WY	Robert Arvey	1981	5729
67 0/8	11 6/8 11 6/8	5 6/8 5 6/8	9 1/8	Converse County	WY	Richard Smith	1981	5729
67 0/8	13 7/8 14 0/8	5 7/8 5 7/8	10 5/8	Converse County	WY	Robert A. Christensen	1982	5729
67 0/8	12 2/8 12 1/8	5 6/8 5 6/8	9 3/8	Converse County	WY	Howard Holmes	1982	5729
67 0/8	13 7/8 14 1/8	5 2/8 5 2/8	10 7/8	Lassen County	CA	Don Rossiter	1983	5729
67 0/8	15 0/8 14 7/8	5 2/8 5 2/8	11 2/8	Yavapai County	AZ	Michael John Bylina	1983	5729
67 0/8	12 2/8 12 4/8	7 0/8 7 0/8	9 7/8	Converse County	WY	Eric Ames	1983	5729
67 0/8	13 5/8 14 0/8	5 3/8 5 3/8	11 3/8	Natrona County	WY	Charles Lanzarone	1983	5729
67 0/8	12 7/8 12 5/8	5 6/8 5 5/8	11 0/8	Broadwater County	MT	Bob A. Closson	1983	5729
67 0/8	12 5/8 12 5/8	5 3/8 5 1/8	10 6/8	Converse County	WY	Thomas L. Hughes	1983	5729
67 0/8	12 3/8 12 3/8	5 5/8 5 5/8	8 4/8	Carbon County	WY	Raymond R. Robison	1984	5729
67 0/8	12 5/8 12 4/8	5 5/8 5 4/8	10 3/8	Custer County	ID	Matt March, Jr.	1984	5729
67 0/8	13 4/8 13 3/8	5 2/8 5 3/8	11 2/8	Sweetwater County	WY	Cliff Wiseman	1985	5729
67 0/8	13 1/8 12 7/8	5 4/8 5 4/8	7 6/8	Sweetwater County	WY	Chuck Ashton	1985	5729
67 0/8	12 5/8 12 5/8	5 4/8 5 3/8	9 2/8	Modoc County	CA	Anthony R. Dipino	1986	5729
67 0/8	13 6/8 14 0/8	5 4/8 5 4/8	9 5/8	Carbon County	WY	Rod Schmidt	1986	5729
67 0/8	12 4/8 12 3/8	6 2/8 6 2/8	7 7/8	Campbell County	WY	Keith Olson	1986	5729
67 0/8	13 5/8 13 3/8	6 0/8 6 1/8	10 6/8	Mountrail County	ND	Charles LeRohl	1986	5729
67 0/8	13 5/8 13 5/8	5 4/8 5 3/8	10 7/8	Modoc County	CA	Rick Holbrook	1987	5729
67 0/8	12 4/8 12 2/8	6 0/8 6 0/8	11 4/8	Moffat County	CO	Grant Adkisson	1987	5729
67 0/8	13 4/8 14 0/8	5 5/8 5 4/8	9 2/8	Uinta County	WY	Dave Murray	1987	5729
67 0/8	13 4/8 13 7/8	5 1/8 5 2/8	6 7/8	Natrona County	WY	Doug Anderson	1987	5729
67 0/8	13 0/8 12 6/8	6 0/8 6 0/8	11 5/8	Converse County	WY	Jack C. Staley, Jr.	1987	5729
67 0/8	12 5/8 12 5/8	5 4/8 5 4/8	12 2/8	Fergus County	MT	Jess Knerr	1987	5729
67 0/8	13 1/8 12 6/8	5 6/8 5 6/8	7 6/8	Moffat County	CO	James Libra	1988	5729
67 0/8	13 4/8 13 4/8	5 5/8 5 4/8	9 2/8	Moffat County	CO	Terry Weimer	1988	5729
67 0/8	12 4/8 12 5/8	5 5/8 5 4/8	10 1/8	Natrona County	WY	Charles Lanzarone	1988	5729
67 0/8	13 2/8 13 3/8	5 6/8 5 5/8	11 1/8	Butte County	ID	Edward F. Keeton	1988	5729
67 0/8	14 2/8 14 4/8	5 2/8 5 1/8	6 5/8	Converse County	WY	Jay Deones	1988	5729
67 0/8	13 4/8 13 3/8	5 6/8 5 6/8	10 7/8	Rio Grande County	CO	Arthur G. Garcia	1988	5729
67 0/8	13 5/8 13 4/8	5 5/8 5 6/8	8 5/8	Eddy County	NM	Jess Stuart	1988	5729
67 0/8	13 4/8 13 6/8	5 7/8 6 0/8	11 4/8	Sublette County	WY	Tony Litts	1989	5729
67 0/8	13 4/8 13 0/8	5 2/8 5 2/8	8 5/8	Richland County	MT	Douglas A. Lang	1989	5729
67 0/8	12 6/8 12 7/8	5 5/8 5 5/8	10 4/8	Moffat County	CO	Dennis M. Hayden	1989	5729
67 0/8	12 2/8 12 4/8	5 6/8 5 6/8	8 5/8	Garfield County	MT	Glen Prestegaard	1989	5729
67 0/8	12 3/8 11 7/8	6 3/8 6 4/8	11 4/8	Converse County	WY	James C. Gates	1989	5729
67 0/8	12 2/8 12 2/8	6 0/8 6 0/8	10 4/8	Converse County	WY	Arthur Wirsing, Jr.	1989	5729
67 0/8	12 5/8 12 6/8	6 0/8 6 0/8	8 2/8	Moffat County	CO	Chuck Leidheiser	1990	5729
67 0/8	13 7/8 13 7/8	5 4/8 5 3/8	10 7/8	Moffat County	CO	Bob Radocy	1990	5729
67 0/8	11 5/8 12 5/8	5 5/8 5 7/8	10 3/8	Sweetwater County	WY	Kurt Zurawski	1990	5729
67 0/8	14 7/8 14 4/8	5 7/8 5 6/8	10 7/8	Rich County	UT	Robert K. Paulson	1990	5729
67 0/8	13 1/8 13 1/8	5 5/8 5 4/8	12 2/8	Fox Valley	SAS	Floyd Forster	1990	5729
67 0/8	12 3/8 12 3/8	6 0/8 5 7/8	8 1/8	McKenzie County	ND	Terry Sivertson	1990	5729
67 0/8	13 1/8 13 1/8	5 4/8 5 3/8	11 0/8	Rosebud County	MT	Sherrill McNalley	1990	5729
67 0/8	12 2/8 12 1/8	6 1/8 6 1/8	8 7/8	Converse County	WY	Gerry Smarelli	1990	5729
67 0/8	12 6/8 13 4/8	5 7/8 5 6/8	11 2/8	McKenzie County	ND	Burnell Sammons	1990	5729
67 0/8	13 5/8 14 6/8	4 7/8 5 0/8	11 2/8	Hudspeth County	TX	Ernest M. Elbert, Jr.	1990	5729
67 0/8	13 3/8 13 2/8	5 4/8 5 2/8	11 3/8	Harding County	SD	William J. Bushong	1991	5729
67 0/8	13 4/8 13 1/8	6 0/8 5 7/8	12 5/8	Owyhee County	ID	Terry Bennett	1991	5729
67 0/8	13 2/8 13 0/8	5 6/8 5 6/8	9 6/8	Natrona County	WY	Eugene Damron	1991	5729
67 0/8	13 0/8 13 0/8	6 1/8 5 7/8	9 6/8	Converse County	WY	Gary M. Funk	1991	5729
67 0/8	12 0/8 12 1/8	6 0/8 6 0/8	9 4/8	Campbell County	WY	Jerry Hinz	1991	5729
67 0/8	14 2/8 15 0/8	5 3/8 5 2/8	7 7/8	Converse County	WY	Kathy Strecker	1991	5729
67 0/8	11 2/8 12 1/8	5 7/8 6 0/8	9 2/8	Natrona County	WY	Jeffrey Johnson	1991	5729
67 0/8	13 6/8 14 0/8	5 3/8 5 2/8	9 3/8	Converse County	WY	Lou Edelis	1991	5729
67 0/8	12 7/8 12 5/8	5 5/8 5 5/8	9 0/8	Converse County	WY	Michael L. Kennedy	1991	5729
67 0/8	13 4/8 13 3/8	5 5/8 5 5/8	10 4/8	Dawes County	NE	Scott Binderup	1991	5729
67 0/8	13 6/8 14 0/8	5 4/8 5 5/8	8 7/8	Colfax County	NM	Dr. David E. Samuel	1992	5729
67 0/8	12 4/8 13 0/8	5 5/8 5 4/8	9 0/8	Moffat County	CO	Richard Davis	1992	5729
67 0/8	12 6/8 12 4/8	6 1/8 6 2/8	11 2/8	Carbon County	WY	Willis Duhon	1992	5729
67 0/8	12 0/8 12 1/8	6 3/8 6 3/8	9 5/8	Carbon County	WY	Steve Hinton	1992	5729

PRONGHORN

Minimum Score 67 — Continued

SCORE	LENGTH OF R HORN L	CIRCUMFERENCE R OF BASE L	INSIDE SPREAD	AREA	STATE/ PROVINCE	HUNTER'S NAME	DATE	RANK
67 0/8	13 4/8 13 5/8	5 6/8 5 7/8	11 0/8	Lincoln County	WY	Keith Goodrow	1992	5729
67 0/8	12 5/8 12 5/8	5 3/8 5 2/8	9 1/8	Bowman County	ND	Darren Martel	1992	5729
67 0/8	13 0/8 13 1/8	5 4/8 5 4/8	11 3/8	Garfield County	MT	Rick Stinson	1992	5729
67 0/8	12 4/8 13 0/8	6 1/8 6 0/8	9 1/8	Converse County	WY	Robert K. Woeck	1992	5729
67 0/8	13 6/8 13 7/8	5 7/8 6 0/8	10 1/8	Madison County	MT	Mark Stonebraker	1992	5729
67 0/8	13 6/8 13 7/8	5 6/8 5 6/8	8 7/8	Moffat County	CO	Kevin Reed	1993	5729
67 0/8	13 4/8 13 5/8	5 3/8 5 3/8	12 5/8	Yavapai County	AZ	Steve Parizek	1993	5729
67 0/8	13 0/8 12 6/8	5 6/8 5 5/8	7 6/8	Carbon County	WY	GayLynn Turner	1993	5729
67 0/8	13 4/8 13 6/8	5 4/8 5 4/8	12 0/8	Mohave County	AZ	Jerry Zitterkopf	1993	5729
67 0/8	12 7/8 13 0/8	5 4/8 5 4/8	11 6/8	Converse County	WY	Dane Clark	1993	5729
67 0/8	12 3/8 12 4/8	6 0/8 5 6/8	9 2/8	Sheridan County	WY	Gregory J. Woodhouse	1993	5729
67 0/8	12 5/8 13 0/8	5 7/8 5 7/8	10 1/8	Sioux County	NE	Rob Thompson	1994	5729
67 0/8	11 7/8 12 0/8	5 4/8 5 4/8	8 5/8	Moffat County	CO	C. Ron Cannon, MD	1994	5729
67 0/8	12 6/8 12 6/8	5 0/8 5 0/8	9 0/8	Saguache County	CO	Jerry Berry	1994	5729
67 0/8	12 2/8 12 1/8	5 6/8 5 7/8	9 1/8	Converse County	WY	Michael T. Wheeler	1994	5729
67 0/8	14 0/8 13 4/8	5 0/8 5 0/8	9 6/8	Sweetwater County	WY	Max Reagin, Jr.	1994	5729
67 0/8	13 1/8 13 4/8	5 3/8 5 4/8	10 1/8	Bowman County	ND	David Janssen	1994	5729
67 0/8	13 3/8 12 4/8	5 7/8 5 6/8	8 0/8	Rosebud County	MT	George E. Wood	1994	5729
67 0/8	12 5/8 13 2/8	5 6/8 5 6/8	9 1/8	Converse County	WY	Chris Wotrang	1994	5729
67 0/8	12 2/8 12 3/8	5 3/8 5 4/8	12 5/8	Wallace County	KS	Roger Potter	1994	5729
67 0/8	13 0/8 12 6/8	6 0/8 5 6/8	11 5/8	Wallace County	KS	Deanna L. Carmen	1994	5729
67 0/8	12 6/8 12 7/8	5 3/8 5 4/8	8 3/8	Converse County	WY	Dennis Roberts	1994	5729
67 0/8	14 2/8 14 7/8	5 1/8 5 0/8	11 0/8	Rosebud County	MT	Edd Clack	1994	5729
67 0/8	11 5/8 12 6/8	7 0/8 6 4/8	8 3/8	Moffat County	CO	Dennis N. Ballweg	1995	5729
67 0/8	12 2/8 12 6/8	5 7/8 6 1/8	10 7/8	Moffat County	CO	Bill Plowman	1995	5729
67 0/8	13 3/8 12 6/8	5 7/8 5 6/8	9 2/8	Converse County	WY	William R. Vyvyan	1995	5729
67 0/8	12 3/8 12 4/8	5 4/8 5 4/8	9 4/8	Converse County	WY	David W. Wagner	1995	5729
67 0/8	14 3/8 14 1/8	5 1/8 5 1/8	10 1/8	Phillips County	MT	Bob L. Walker	1995	5729
67 0/8	13 6/8 14 1/8	5 5/8 5 5/8	7 4/8	Campbell County	WY	Anthony Lopez	1995	5729
67 0/8	12 6/8 12 7/8	6 2/8 6 2/8	11 5/8	Musselshell County	MT	Anthony Wagner	1995	5729
67 0/8	11 2/8 11 0/8	6 3/8 6 2/8	10 7/8	Albany County	WY	Joseph Osvath	1996	5729
67 0/8	13 2/8 13 2/8	5 5/8 5 4/8	10 0/8	Moffat County	CO	Gary Biles	1996	5729
67 0/8	13 3/8 13 2/8	5 6/8 5 6/8	10 5/8	Moffat County	CO	Todd Szmania	1996	5729
67 0/8	13 1/8 12 6/8	6 0/8 6 0/8	10 3/8	Natrona County	WY	David M. Krampitz	1996	5729
67 0/8	12 6/8 12 6/8	6 0/8 5 7/8	7 7/8	Moffat County	CO	Willy Colby	1996	5729
67 0/8	13 3/8 14 4/8	5 7/8 5 2/8	11 1/8	Campbell County	WY	Raymond L. Howell, Sr.	1996	5729
67 0/8	12 6/8 12 7/8	5 5/8 5 5/8	7 7/8	Sioux County	NE	Clarence Poteet	1996	5729
67 0/8	12 5/8 12 3/8	5 7/8 5 4/8	8 7/8	White Pine County	NV	Larry Pabst	1997	5729
67 0/8	13 6/8 13 5/8	5 5/8 5 2/8	9 4/8	Moffat County	CO	Jon P. Miller	1997	5729
67 0/8	12 4/8 13 4/8	5 6/8 5 4/8	11 5/8	Moffat County	CO	Mike Delamater	1997	5729
67 0/8	14 1/8 14 0/8	5 2/8 5 2/8	8 4/8	Campbell County	WY	Charles W. Drexler, Sr.	1997	5729
67 0/8	13 1/8 13 6/8	5 5/8 5 5/8	11 6/8	Lake County	OR	Jeffrey A. Eder	1997	5729
67 0/8	12 0/8 11 6/8	6 2/8 6 2/8	9 4/8	Converse County	WY	Bernard R. Belaire, Jr.	1997	5729
67 0/8	15 0/8 14 6/8	5 2/8 5 2/8	9 1/8	Butte County	ID	Mikeal A. Carter	1998	5729
67 0/8	12 5/8 12 6/8	5 2/8 5 1/8	7 6/8	Converse County	WY	Timothy Angelo	1998	5729
67 0/8	14 2/8 14 1/8	5 1/8 5 0/8	10 7/8	Campbell County	WY	Jay Hill	1998	5729
67 0/8	13 1/8 12 4/8	5 5/8 5 6/8	8 2/8	Campbell County	WY	Jay Hill	1999	5729
67 0/8	12 4/8 12 4/8	5 2/8 5 2/8	8 2/8	Converse County	WY	Michael B. Coleman	1999	5729
67 0/8	12 5/8 14 0/8	5 4/8 5 4/8	12 2/8	Converse County	WY	Adam Fackelman	1999	5729
67 0/8	12 7/8 13 0/8	5 6/8 5 6/8	8 4/8	Butte County	SD	Ryan L. Winterboer	1999	5729
67 0/8	12 3/8 12 0/8	5 7/8 5 5/8	12 3/8	Humboldt County	NV	Thomas E. Wilson	2000	5729
67 0/8	13 2/8 13 2/8	5 3/8 5 4/8	8 6/8	Weld County	CO	Skip Valentine	2000	5729
67 0/8	12 5/8 12 3/8	6 2/8 6 2/8	9 0/8	Harding County	SD	Casey Blum	2000	5729
67 0/8	11 3/8 12 2/8	6 3/8 6 2/8	8 7/8	Converse County	WY	Tommy Casto	2000	5729
67 0/8	12 6/8 12 6/8	5 7/8 5 6/8	9 2/8	Campbell County	WY	Dan Collins	2000	5729
67 0/8	13 4/8 14 0/8	5 2/8 5 3/8	9 4/8	Converse County	WY	Ray McFarland	2000	5729
67 0/8	13 4/8 13 4/8	5 2/8 5 1/8	9 5/8	Campbell County	WY	Mark Butler	2000	5729
67 0/8	12 2/8 12 2/8	5 3/8 5 3/8	7 0/8	Wallace County	KS	Danny Carmen	2000	5729
67 0/8	11 3/8 11 6/8	5 6/8 5 6/8	11 7/8	Jackson County	CO	Jim Hammer	2001	5729
67 0/8	12 5/8 12 5/8	5 6/8 5 5/8	9 2/8	Converse County	WY	Christopher C. Hill	2001	5729
67 0/8	12 6/8 12 6/8	5 2/8 5 2/8	6 7/8	Stanley County	SD	Kent Lewis	2001	5729
67 0/8	12 4/8 12 3/8	5 4/8 5 5/8	12 2/8	Converse County	WY	Cheryl Earhart	2001	5729
67 0/8	12 5/8 12 3/8	5 7/8 5 7/8	10 2/8	Fergus County	MT	Jim Winjum	2001	5729
67 0/8	11 6/8 12 0/8	5 5/8 5 6/8	11 0/8	Converse County	WY	Edward A. Brown	2001	5729
67 0/8	13 7/8 13 7/8	5 0/8 5 1/8	6 7/8	Meade County	SD	Vincent Paul Pollock	2001	5729
67 0/8	12 6/8 12 5/8	5 3/8 5 3/8	9 1/8	Converse County	WY	Gary M. Martin	2002	5729
67 0/8	13 0/8 13 0/8	5 6/8 5 4/8	9 0/8	Golden Valley County	MT	Brent Milliron	2002	5729
67 0/8	13 1/8 13 1/8	5 3/8 5 2/8	8 7/8	Converse County	WY	Jim Van Norman	2002	5729
*67 0/8	13 0/8 12 7/8	5 6/8 5 4/8	8 0/8	Weld County	CO	Raymond J. Madsen	2003	5729
67 0/8	11 6/8 11 6/8	5 4/8 5 6/8	6 2/8	Saguache County	CO	Charles L. Strickland, Jr.	2003	5729
67 0/8	12 1/8 12 0/8	5 5/8 5 4/8	11 4/8	Harding County	SD	Jeremy Mouser	2003	5729
67 0/8	12 6/8 12 6/8	5 5/8 5 6/8	9 1/8	Campbell County	WY	Robert D. Helmer	2003	5729
67 0/8	12 4/8 12 3/8	5 7/8 5 6/8	8 3/8	McKenzie County	ND	Jack Sorum	2003	5729
67 0/8	13 0/8 13 0/8	5 4/8 5 5/8	10 7/8	Weld County	CO	Phillip A. Buxton	2003	5729
67 0/8	12 2/8 12 1/8	5 4/8 5 4/8	9 1/8	Fergus County	MT	Edwin Evans	2003	5729
67 0/8	12 7/8 12 7/8	5 4/8 5 4/8	9 6/8	Weld County	CO	Mike Kattawar, Sr.	2004	5729
67 0/8	14 4/8 14 4/8	5 0/8 5 1/8	11 6/8	Nye County	NV	Patrick Scott Beckwith	2004	5729
67 0/8	12 5/8 12 6/8	5 6/8 5 5/8	10 5/8	Rosebud County	MT	Troy Sowers	2004	5729
67 0/8	12 5/8 12 5/8	5 4/8 5 4/8	10 7/8	Campbell County	WY	Corey Hugelen	2004	5729
67 0/8	13 0/8 13 0/8	5 6/8 5 6/8	10 2/8	Campbell County	WY	Scott Lang	2004	5729
*67 0/8	13 3/8 13 3/8	5 3/8 5 3/8	7 4/8	Saguache County	CO	Michael E. Luttrell	2004	5729
67 0/8	11 1/8 11 5/8	6 0/8 6 0/8	6 4/8	Converse County	WY	Steven C. Davis	2004	5729
67 0/8	12 5/8 12 6/8	5 6/8 5 6/8	10 2/8	Brooks	ALB	Stephane Titley	2004	5729
67 0/8	13 6/8 13 5/8	5 1/8 5 1/8	12 5/8	Rosebud County	MT	Bryan J. Wieber	2005	5729
67 0/8	12 3/8 12 3/8	6 0/8 6 0/8	10 0/8	Converse County	WY	Roger Stewart	2005	5729
67 0/8	14 3/8 13 1/8	5 6/8 5 7/8	9 2/8	Moffat County	CO	Bob Rimsza	2005	5729
67 0/8	12 7/8 12 6/8	5 1/8 5 1/8	8 2/8	Converse County	WY	James W. Casto III	2005	5729
67 0/8	12 3/8 12 2/8	6 1/8 6 1/8	10 5/8	Converse County	WY	Mitchell Palmer	2005	5729
67 0/8	13 0/8 12 7/8	5 4/8 5 4/8	6 6/8	Harding County	SD	Bruce Briesemeister	2005	5729
67 0/8	13 3/8 13 0/8	5 7/8 5 7/8	7 6/8	Garfield County	MT	Sonny Templeton	2005	5729
67 0/8	13 1/8 13 3/8	5 3/8 5 3/8	10 6/8	Beaverhead County	MT	Dave R. Burget	2005	5729
67 0/8	12 6/8 12 6/8	5 7/8 5 6/8	10 5/8	Lake County	OR	Jim Hostetler	2006	5729
67 0/8	13 0/8 11 6/8	6 0/8 6 0/8	9 3/8	Converse County	WY	Michael J. Clevinger	2006	5729
67 0/8	13 1/8 13 1/8	5 2/8 5 2/8	10 1/8	Carter County	MT	Philip Van Dongen	2006	5729
*67 0/8	13 1/8 13 3/8	5 1/8 5 1/8	10 2/8	Rosebud County	MT	Shannon Belik	2006	5729

PRONGHORN

Continued

Minimum Score 67

SCORE	LENGTH OF R HORN L	CIRCUMFERENCE R OF BASE L	INSIDE SPREAD	AREA	STATE/ PROVINCE	HUNTER'S NAME	DATE	RANK
67 0/8	11 1/8 11 1/8	6 1/8 6 2/8	12 7/8	Converse County	WY	Eugene R. Wood	2006	5729
67 0/8	13 6/8 12 6/8	6 1/8 5 4/8	10 2/8	Coconino County	AZ	Russ Richardson	2006	5729
*67 0/8	13 2/8 13 2/8	5 4/8 5 3/8	13 1/8	Converse County	WY	William Miller	2006	5729
67 0/8	12 2/8 12 3/8	5 2/8 5 1/8	9 6/8	Crook County	WY	Chris Kifer	2006	5729
67 0/8	11 1/8 11 3/8	6 2/8 6 3/8	8 7/8	Converse County	WY	Timothy J. Noltemeyer	2006	5729
67 0/8	13 2/8 12 7/8	5 6/8 5 6/8	7 5/8	Converse County	WY	Curtis Lanxton	2006	5729
67 0/8	12 0/8 12 0/8	5 6/8 5 6/8	10 4/8	Moffat County	CO	Michael Adkins, Sr.	2006	5729
67 0/8	12 0/8 11 6/8	5 6/8 5 7/8	9 2/8	Corson County	SD	Mike Miller	2006	5729
67 0/8	11 4/8 11 3/8	6 1/8 6 0/8	8 5/8	Powder River County	MT	Carl Fritz	2006	5729
67 0/8	13 7/8 13 2/8	5 4/8 5 4/8	8 0/8	Harding County	SD	Andrew J. Blum	2007	5729
67 0/8	13 0/8 13 0/8	5 3/8 5 3/8	8 0/8	Powder River County	MT	Josh Depatie	2007	5729
67 0/8	12 2/8 12 2/8	5 4/8 5 4/8	7 2/8	Powder River County	MT	Aaron Jones	2007	5729
67 0/8	13 0/8 12 6/8	5 4/8 5 5/8	9 6/8	Converse County	WY	Scott Morton	2007	5729
67 0/8	11 7/8 11 6/8	6 1/8 6 0/8	11 2/8	Converse County	WY	Edward Pollich	2007	5729
67 0/8	13 1/8 13 0/8	5 5/8 5 2/8	8 6/8	Johnson County	WY	Bret Scott	2007	5729
67 0/8	12 0/8 11 3/8	5 3/8 5 3/8	9 2/8	Carter County	MT	Nancy Atwood	2007	5729
67 0/8	12 3/8 12 5/8	6 0/8 6 0/8	10 2/8	Carter County	MT	R. Gerald Ebert	2008	5729
*67 0/8	12 0/8 12 2/8	5 7/8 5 7/8	13 2/8	Converse County	WY	Brian Scott Smith	2008	5729
*67 0/8	13 2/8 13 0/8	5 6/8 5 5/8	10 5/8	Converse County	WY	William Monroe	2008	5729
67 0/8	13 7/8 13 3/8	5 4/8 5 4/8	8 0/8	Carter County	MT	Reed Burres	2008	5729
67 0/8	14 1/8 14 2/8	4 7/8 5 0/8	6 6/8	Converse County	WY	Phil Layman	2008	5729
67 0/8	13 0/8 13 0/8	5 7/8 5 7/8	7 4/8	Pennington County	SD	Nicholas Genereux	2009	5729
67 0/8	13 0/8 13 0/8	6 0/8 6 0/8	11 4/8	Humboldt County	NV	Lucy A. Rechel	2009	5729
67 0/8	12 2/8 12 1/8	5 4/8 5 4/8	7 5/8	Natrona County	WY	Dan Reeve	2009	5729
67 0/8	13 4/8 13 7/8	5 5/8 5 5/8	12 1/8	Rich County	UT	Don Newman	2009	5729
67 0/8	13 0/8 13 0/8	5 4/8 5 4/8	9 7/8	Natrona County	WY	Jeff Jacob	2009	5729
*67 0/8	11 7/8 12 1/8	5 3/8 5 2/8	8 7/8	Campbell County	WY	Bryan Pourcho	2009	5729
67 0/8	12 7/8 13 0/8	6 1/8 6 1/8	9 7/8	Lake County	OR	Stanley Miles	2010	5729
*67 0/8	12 6/8 12 6/8	5 6/8 5 6/8	11 1/8	Moffat County	CO	Wally Schaub	2010	5729
67 0/8	13 4/8 13 3/8	5 3/8 5 2/8	9 4/8	Converse County	WY	Shirley M. Jochmann	2010	5729
*67 0/8	13 4/8 13 2/8	5 4/8 5 4/8	10 3/8	Fremont County	WY	Charlotte Jarrett	2010	5729
67 0/8	12 6/8 12 5/8	6 2/8 6 0/8	12 2/8	Rio Blanco County	CO	Sonya Garcia	2010	5729
*67 0/8	14 0/8 12 7/8	5 7/8 5 7/8	6 7/8	Seven Persons	ALB	Earl Chauvin	2010	5729
67 0/8	13 5/8 13 6/8	5 1/8 5 3/8	10 7/8	Carter County	MT	Joseph A. Lape	2010	5729

Pope & Young Club

Official Scoring System for Bowhunting North American Big Game

MINIMUM SCORE 40

PANEL MEASURED

ROCKY MOUNTAIN GOAT

SEX XX Male ☐ Female

25TH RECORDING PERIOD 2005-06

		COLUMN 1	COLUMN 2	COLUMN 3
		Right Horn	Left Horn	Difference
A.	8 3/8			
B.	7 1/8			
C.		11 2/8	11 1/8	1/8
D-1.		5 5/8	5 5/8	-----
D-2.	1/4 (inches from base)	4 6/8	4 6/8	-----
D-3.	1/2 (inches from base)	3 3/8	3 1/8	2/8
D-4.	3/4 (inches from base)	2 0/8	1 7/8	1/8
	TOTALS	27 0/8	26 4/8	4/8

(County) TERRACE (State/Prov) BC

/06 Hunter: SHAD WHEELER

State: WA 74

BOB MILLI BG 4R1

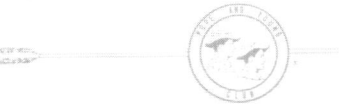

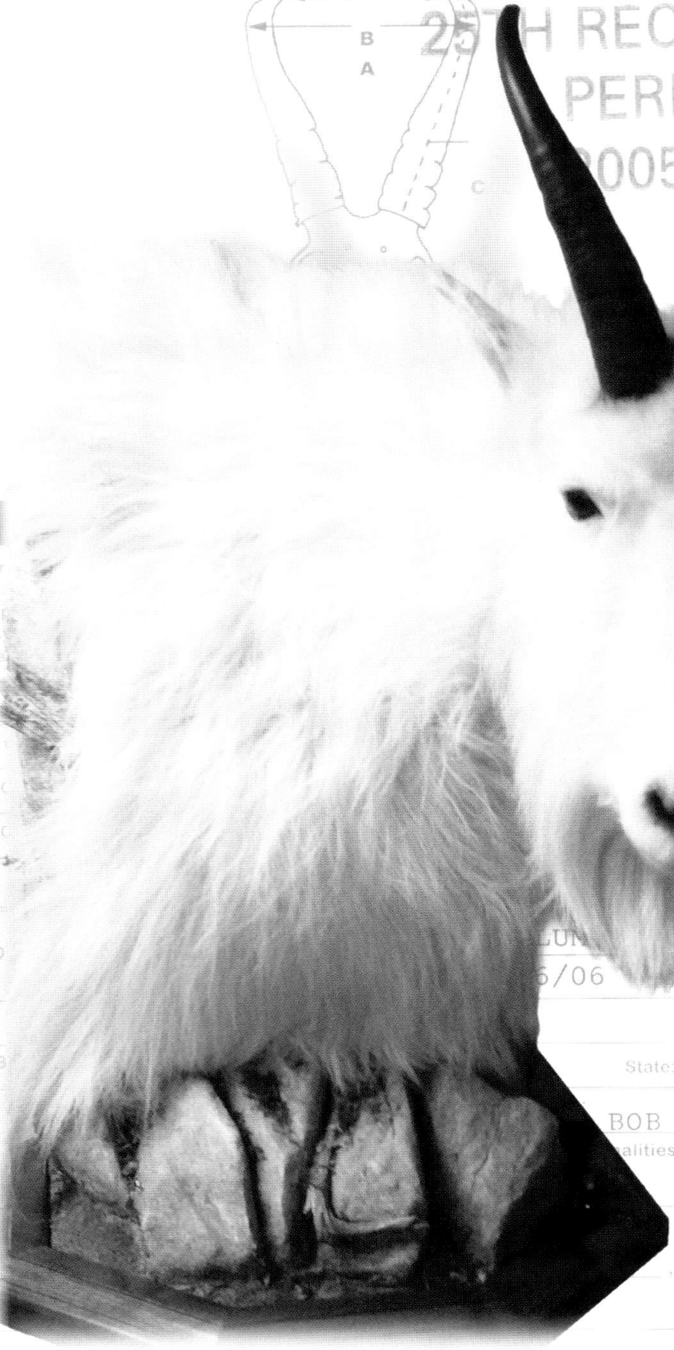

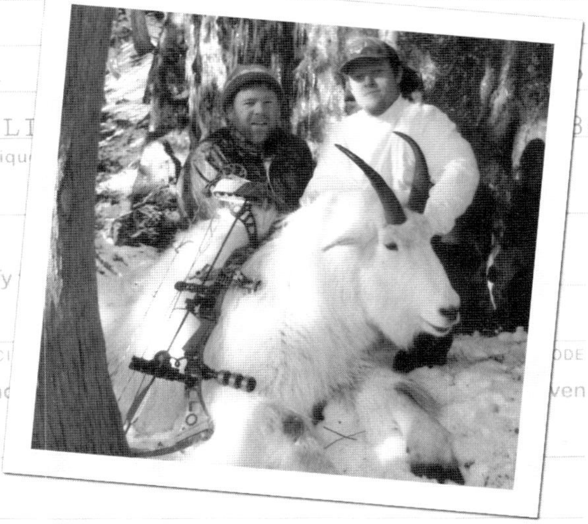

WORLD RECORD ROCKY MOUNTAIN GOAT
Score: 53 0/8
Location: Kalum Lake, British Columbia
Date: 2006
Hunter: Shad Wheeler

I, certify at

ADDRESS

OM I.D. Number CITY STATE/PROVINCE ZIP

Rocky Mountain Goat

by Shad Wheeler

I took a deep breath, said my prayers and slowly bent my 25 yard pin back to where I thought it should be…

In my wildest dreams I never thought that I would ever harvest a world record animal, let alone with a bow. But, that is exactly what happened in February of 2006. I headed out to Terrace, British Columbia on the morning of Feb 8th to pursue a late season billy with Bob Milligan of Coast Mountain Outfitters. Bob was waiting with a goofy grin on his face and quickly told me how they had found a couple of great goats and that they were in a position where we should be able to make a move on them.

We spotted the goat we called Kong high up on a bench that first morning and at that point Bob and I were committed to Kong and nothing. Of course, billies don't get to be this size by being stupid. We ultimately chased him for 9 days, during which he gave us the slip a couple of times or would show up in cliffs where there was no way to get at him.

February 16th marked the last day of my hunt and, as I would find out later was also Bob's dad's birthday. Bob's parents were tragically lost in a plane crash when he was younger, but before that happened they had built this area and taught Bob a lot of lessons about guiding and outfitting.

We found Kong where we had left him the night before and knew we could get close. After closing to within about 150 yards of where he was bedded, I stopped to check out my bow. To my horror I saw all my pins were completely bent and twisted from the climb through the alders. I took a deep breath, said my prayers and bent the sight pin back to where I thought it should be and continued on the stalk for Kong.

I was finally able to close to 27 yards with a steep downhill shot. I drew, anchored, released and thwack! I thought my hunt was over as I sat for what seemed like an eternity watching my arrow vibrating in the tree I had just killed. It turned out that my sight was off by a lot more than I thought, but as I said someone was watching over us this day as the goat looked up for a moment and then went back to chewing his cud. I nocked another arrow and this time adjusted for the still tweaked sight. The arrow flew true.

It turns out that Kong had almost 11.5-inch horns with 6-inch bases.

I would like to thank Bob and his wife Michelle for the hunt of a lifetime, my Sydne for being so patient, loving and understanding of my need to go to these high and wild places, and my dad for introducing me to the world of the outdoors.

ROCKY MOUNTAIN GOAT

Minimum Score 40 — *Oreamnos americanus americanus* and related subspecies

SCORE	R HORN L	R OF BASE L	SPREAD	SEX	AREA	STATE/ PROVINCE	HUNTER'S NAME	DATE	RANK
53 0/8	11 2/8 11 1/8	5 5/8 5 5/8	8 3/8	M	Kalum Lake	BC	Shad Wheeler	2006	1
*52 6/8	10 0/8 10 1/8	6 1/8 6 1/8	7 2/8	M	Terrace	BC	Allen Bolen	2005	2
52 4/8	11 3/8 11 2/8	5 7/8 5 7/8	8 1/8	M	Park County	CO	Lyle K. Willmarth	1988	3
52 4/8	10 1/8 10 3/8	6 1/8 6 0/8	8 5/8	M	Telegraph Creek	BC	Tim Metcalf	2008	3
52 0/8	10 2/8 10 2/8	5 5/8 5 6/8	8 2/8	M	Atlin	BC	Mike Jennett	1994	5
*52 0/8	10 1/8 10 1/8	5 6/8 5 7/8	7 1/8	M	Boca de Quadra	AK	Anthony Glasso	2009	5
51 6/8	10 5/8 10 5/8	5 3/8 5 4/8	6 0/8	M	Cleveland Peninsula	AK	Kurt Kuehl	2000	7
51 6/8	10 1/8 10 1/8	5 5/8 5 5/8	8 3/8	M	Pike Creek	BC	Wilf Lehners	2000	7
*51 6/8	10 7/8 10 4/8	5 7/8 5 7/8	8 1/8	M	Moose Pass	AK	Russell Laulamen	2004	7
51 6/8	11 0/8 11 0/8	5 5/8 5 6/8	7 6/8	M	Lower Lynn Canal	AK	Wyatt Nelson	2007	7
51 4/8	10 5/8 10 2/8	5 6/8 5 5/8	7 4/8	M	Wrangell	AK	C. Wayne Treadway	1988	11
51 4/8	10 2/8 10 2/8	5 5/8 5 5/8	8 2/8	M	Nanika Lake	BC	Reg Meisner	1995	11
51 4/8	9 3/8 9 1/8	6 0/8 6 1/8	8 0/8	M	Kispiox Mtn.	BC	Duncan Henderson	1998	11
*51 4/8	10 1/8 10 1/8	5 6/8 5 6/8	7 3/8	M	Weber County	UT	Kyle Scott	2009	11
*51 4/8	9 5/8 9 5/8	6 1/8 6 0/8	6 5/8	M	Weber County	UT	Travis L. Truman	2009	11
51 2/8	9 7/8 10 0/8	6 1/8 6 1/8	7 5/8	M	Nahlin Mtn.	BC	Dan Brockman	1995	16
51 2/8	10 3/8 10 2/8	5 4/8 5 4/8	6 4/8	M	Terrace	BC	Kyle T. Hudgins	2007	16
*51 2/8	10 6/8 10 5/8	5 4/8 5 5/8	5 4/8	M	Douglas Channel	BC	Mark Zebley	2010	16
51 0/8	9 6/8 9 6/8	5 7/8 6 0/8	7 4/8	M	Terrace	BC	Dave Ramsay	1982	19
51 0/8	10 2/8 10 1/8	5 6/8 5 6/8	6 2/8	M	Aaltanmash River	BC	Ralph Hernandez	2008	19
50 6/8	9 6/8 9 5/8	5 7/8 5 6/8	7 0/8	M	Bella Coola	BC	Randy Svisdahl	1995	21
50 2/8	10 7/8 10 6/8	5 3/8 5 3/8	5 6/8	M	Ketchikan	AK	Kurt Kuehl	1989	22
50 0/8	10 2/8 10 1/8	5 7/8 5 6/8	5 4/8	M	Kittitas County	WA	Bob Haugen	1971	23
50 0/8	10 5/8 10 2/8	5 5/8 5 5/8	7 0/8	M	Snohomish County	WA	Edward M. Beitner	1984	23
50 0/8	10 2/8 10 2/8	5 4/8 5 4/8	6 3/8	M	Wrangell	AK	Bob Fromme	1987	23
50 0/8	10 2/8 10 2/8	5 4/8 5 5/8	10 2/8	M	Klastline River	BC	Gregory White	1992	23
*50 0/8	10 5/8 10 7/8	5 5/8 5 5/8	7 7/8	M	Sustut Lake	BC	Leaf Steffey	2008	23
50 0/8	9 7/8 9 6/8	5 5/8 5 5/8	7 1/8	M	Terrace	BC	John H. Holt	2008	23
49 6/8	9 5/8 9 6/8	5 6/8 5 5/8	7 6/8	M	Tesla Lake	BC	Peter Halbig	1970	29
49 6/8	9 2/8 9 0/8	5 7/8 5 7/8	6 4/8	M	Gallatin County	MT	Clark Kelly III	1990	29
49 6/8	9 6/8 9 6/8	5 4/8 5 4/8	7 6/8	M	Elko County	NV	Roger Iveson	2002	29
49 4/8	10 0/8 10 0/8	5 4/8 5 4/8	6 1/8	M	Lincoln County	WY	Duane "Corky" Richardson	2005	29
49 4/8	9 2/8 9 4/8	6 1/8 6 2/8	5 2/8	M	Custer County	SD	William G. Chipman	1991	33
49 4/8	10 3/8 10 3/8	5 2/8 5 2/8	7 3/8	M	Pierce County	WA	Kirby Warner	1995	33
49 4/8	9 7/8 10 0/8	5 6/8 5 6/8	7 1/8	M	Flastine River	BC	James Gabrick	2000	33
49 2/8	9 7/8 9 6/8	5 5/8 5 4/8	7 6/8	M	Baker Mtn.	BC	David A. Shupp	2006	33
49 2/8	10 4/8 10 5/8	5 2/8 5 3/8	7 1/8	M	King County	WA	Jerry Solie	1978	37
49 2/8	9 3/8 9 4/8	5 6/8 5 6/8	7 1/8	M	Snohomish County	WA	Jonathon L. Bogle	1987	37
49 2/8	9 4/8 9 3/8	5 6/8 5 6/8	6 6/8	M	Taku River	BC	Jerry Davis	1991	37
49 2/8	10 3/8 10 1/8	5 3/8 5 3/8	6 7/8	M	Utah County	UT	Dennis L. Dobson	1992	37
49 2/8	10 0/8 9 7/8	5 6/8 5 6/8	6 0/8	M	Clear Creek County	CO	Gayle Lippold	1994	37
49 2/8	10 1/8 9 6/8	5 4/8 5 4/8	6 3/8	M	Park County	MT	Steve Kamps	2000	37
49 2/8	9 5/8 9 6/8	5 6/8 5 6/8	8 0/8	M	Nass River	BC	David J. Zanoni	2009	37
49 2/8	9 5/8 9 4/8	5 1/8 5 0/8	7 6/8	M	Kodiak Island	AK	Roy Whitford	2009	37
49 0/8	9 1/8 9 1/8	5 6/8 5 5/8	7 0/8	M	Whatcom County	WA	Courtney Salmonsen	1974	45
49 0/8	9 0/8 9 0/8	5 6/8 5 6/8	6 7/8	M	Snohomish County	WA	Dick Smethurst	1975	45
49 0/8	10 2/8 10 3/8	5 3/8 5 3/8	6 0/8	M	Bennett Lake	BC	Jack Stephen	1982	45
49 0/8	10 3/8 10 3/8	5 4/8 5 4/8	6 2/8	M	Cleveland Peninsula	AK	Kurt Kuehl	1990	45
49 0/8	10 2/8 10 1/8	5 4/8 5 4/8	6 5/8	M	Nakusp	BC	Harvey J. Surina	1992	45
49 0/8	9 4/8 9 3/8	5 2/8 5 2/8	6 7/8	M	Snootli Creek	BC	Randy Svisdahl	1996	45
49 0/8	10 1/8 9 7/8	5 5/8 5 4/8	7 0/8	M	Misty Fiords	AK	Daniel L. Sommers	2000	45
48 6/8	10 0/8 9 4/8	5 5/8 5 5/8	7 6/8	M	Bella Coola	BC	Lawrence Michalchuk	2002	45
48 6/8	9 2/8 9 4/8	5 4/8 5 4/8	8 6/8	M	Hedley	BC	Ernest Popoff	1981	53
48 6/8	10 2/8 10 0/8	5 4/8 5 4/8	8 5/8	M	Atlin	BC	Thomas J. Hoffman	1997	53
48 6/8	9 0/8 9 1/8	5 6/8 5 6/8	7 0/8	M	Taku River	BC	Andrew Gamatko	2001	53
48 4/8	9 5/8 9 5/8	5 5/8 5 5/8	7 3/8	M	Salt Lake County	UT	L. Grant Foster	2005	53
48 4/8	9 1/8 9 1/8	5 5/8 5 5/8	5 6/8	M	Clallam County	WA	Dr. Charles F. Raab	1967	57
48 4/8	10 1/8 10 2/8	5 2/8 5 1/8	7 0/8	M	Terrace	BC	Dave Ramsay	1979	57
*48 4/8	10 3/8 10 3/8	5 3/8 5 4/8	7 0/8	M	Golden	BC	Ron Klassen	2000	57
*48 4/8	10 0/8 9 7/8	5 4/8 5 4/8	6 6/8	M	Turnagain River	BC	Patrick Bartz	2005	57
*48 4/8	10 1/8 10 0/8	5 3/8 5 3/8	6 6/8	M	Taku River	BC	Byron J. Oberst	2006	57
48 2/8	9 3/8 9 4/8	5 6/8 5 5/8	6 6/8	M	Skeena River	BC	Eric A. Vaillancourt	2007	57
48 2/8	9 3/8 9 3/8	5 5/8 5 5/8	7 2/8	M	Seebe	ALB	Chris Kroll	1962	63
48 2/8	9 7/8 9 2/8	5 7/8 5 7/8	6 4/8	M	Crown Mtn.	AK	Harold W. Jacobson	1973	63
48 2/8	9 1/8 8 7/8	5 4/8 5 4/8	5 3/8	M	Chaffee County	CO	Marvin Clyncke	1978	63
48 2/8	9 3/8 9 3/8	5 4/8 5 4/8	6 6/8	M	Kittitas County	WA	Jim Pavack	1983	63
48 2/8	9 3/8 9 2/8	5 3/8 5 4/8	7 0/8	M	Kittitas County	WA	L. T. Spring	1986	63
48 2/8	9 5/8 9 5/8	5 6/8 5 6/8	7 2/8	M	Telegraph Creek	BC	Al Schroeder	1987	63
48 2/8	9 4/8 9 4/8	5 5/8 5 4/8	6 0/8	M	Jefferson County	WA	G. A. "Toby" Hart	1987	63
48 2/8	9 7/8 9 7/8	5 0/8 5 1/8	6 1/8	M	Natlude Lake	BC	Darrell Yetter	1988	63
48 2/8	9 5/8 9 4/8	5 6/8 5 6/8	6 6/8	M	Snohomish County	WA	Mathew Hayvaz	1991	63
48 2/8	9 6/8 9 6/8	5 3/8 5 3/8	5 6/8	M	Kodiak Island	AK	Lon E. Lauber	1996	63
48 2/8	7 6/8 8 7/8	5 4/8 5 4/8	8 0/8	M	Chaffee County	CO	Daniel G. Willems	1999	63
48 2/8	10 2/8 10 2/8	5 2/8 5 2/8	7 3/8	M	Carlson Creek	AK	Don Martin	2003	63
48 2/8	9 7/8 9 7/8	5 3/8 5 3/8	7 4/8	M	Clark County	ID	Dave R. Burget	2005	63
48 0/8	9 4/8 9 7/8	5 5/8 5 5/8	7 4/8	M	Whittier	AK	Braun Kopsack	2005	63
48 0/8	9 5/8 9 5/8	5 2/8 5 4/8	5 4/8	M	Kitchener Lake	BC	Walt Sawicki	1975	77
48 0/8	9 6/8 10 0/8	5 5/8 5 5/8	6 2/8	M	Snohomish County	WA	Gerry J. Lamarre	1978	77
48 0/8	9 3/8 9 3/8	5 3/8 5 2/8	6 7/8	M	Firesteel River	BC	John H. Kaykendall	1978	77
48 0/8	9 4/8 9 4/8	5 3/8 5 3/8	6 0/8	M	Snohomish County	WA	Greg A. McTee	1986	77
48 0/8	9 4/8 9 3/8	5 3/8 5 3/8	6 0/8	M	Blunt Mtn.	BC	Kurt Saffarek	1994	77
48 0/8	9 7/8 9 7/8	5 4/8 5 4/8	8 6/8	M	Lyell Creek	BC	Ron Books	1994	77
48 0/8	9 3/8 9 1/8	5 5/8 5 5/8	7 5/8	M	Sweet Grass County	MT	Chris Lorash	1997	77
48 0/8	9 5/8 9 6/8	5 2/8 5 3/8	7 4/8	M	Utah County	UT	Craig P. Mitton	1999	77
*48 0/8	9 4/8 9 6/8	5 3/8 5 4/8	6 4/8	M	Bull River	BC	Rob Frew	1999	77
48 0/8	9 7/8 9 7/8	5 3/8 5 3/8	7 0/8	M	Knik Glacier	AK	Douglas Garner	2008	77
47 6/8	9 2/8 9 2/8	5 5/8 5 4/8	7 0/8	M	Bonneville County	ID	Clint H. Gee	2009	77
47 6/8	9 5/8 9 3/8	5 5/8 5 5/8	6 4/8	M	Terminus Mtn.	BC	Paul P. Schafer	1975	88
47 6/8	9 5/8 9 7/8	5 3/8 5 3/8	6 6/8	M	Thuodadi Lake	BC	Phil Bauer	1978	88
47 6/8	9 3/8 9 3/8	5 4/8 5 4/8	7 3/8	M	Clallam County	WA	Wayne Haag	1979	88
47 6/8	9 4/8 9 2/8	5 4/8 5 4/8	5 7/8	M	Bonneville County	ID	Darrus D. Martin	1985	88
47 6/8	9 3/8 9 3/8	5 4/8 5 4/8	6 7/8	M	Snohomish County	WA	Colin McRae	1991	88
47 6/8	9 3/8 9 3/8	5 4/8 5 4/8	7 4/8	M	Jefferson County	WA	Donald Phipps	1992	88
47 6/8	9 1/8 9 2/8	5 5/8 5 5/8	6 7/8	M	Hope	AK	Demitrios N. Deoudes	1992	88
47 6/8	9 1/8 9 2/8	5 5/8 5 5/8	6 7/8	M	Utah County	UT	David H. Beratto	1993	88

ROCKY MOUNTAIN GOAT

Minimum Score 40   Continued

SCORE	LENGTH OF R HORN L	CIRCUMFERENCE R OF BASE L	GREATEST SPREAD	SEX	AREA	STATE/ PROVINCE	HUNTER'S NAME	DATE	RANK
47 6/8	9 5/8 · 9 4/8	5 4/8 · 5 4/8	6 7/8	M	Elko County	NV	Sean Shea	1999	88
47 6/8	9 1/8 · 9 2/8	5 4/8 · 5 4/8	6 7/8	M	Chugach Mtns.	AK	Greg Bokash	2002	88
47 6/8	9 1/8 · 8 6/8	5 4/8 · 5 4/8	7 4/8	M	Salmon Fork	AK	Don Martin	2005	88
*47 6/8	9 6/8 · 9 4/8	5 2/8 · 5 2/8	7 6/8	M	Skeena River	BC	Tod Graham	2008	88
*47 6/8	9 1/8 · 9 3/8	5 4/8 · 5 4/8	7 0/8	M	Baker County	OR	Shane A. Gilthvedt	2009	88
47 6/8	9 3/8 · 9 2/8	5 4/8 · 5 5/8	7 0/8	M	Kodiak Island	AK	Bob Ameen	2010	88
47 4/8	9 4/8 · 9 4/8	5 4/8 · 5 4/8	5 6/8	M	Jefferson County	WA	Bob Dierick	1976	102
47 4/8	9 6/8 · 9 6/8	5 3/8 · 5 3/8	7 1/8	M	Stalk Lakes	BC	Chester J. Thompson	1977	102
47 4/8	9 5/8 · 9 3/8	5 4/8 · 5 4/8	6 2/8	M	Gallatin County	MT	Mark Ness	1984	102
47 4/8	9 7/8 · 9 5/8	5 1/8 · 5 1/8	6 7/8	M	Skagit County	WA	Steve Kempf	1987	102
47 4/8	9 3/8 · 9 3/8	5 3/8 · 5 3/8	7 4/8	M	Spencer Glacier	AK	Lon Lauber	1989	102
47 4/8	9 4/8 · 9 4/8	5 2/8 · 5 2/8	6 7/8	M	Dease Lake	BC	Don Davidson	1993	102
47 4/8	9 4/8 · 10 0/8	5 3/8 · 5 3/8	6 7/8	M	Taku River	BC	Joseph A. Romeu	1994	102
47 4/8	9 2/8 · 9 6/8	5 6/8 · 5 5/8	12 3/8	M	Wright Peaks	AK	Larry Daly	1995	102
47 4/8	9 0/8 · 9 1/8	5 4/8 · 5 4/8	7 0/8	M	Utah County	UT	Dallas Smith	1995	102
47 4/8	8 7/8 · 9 2/8	5 2/8 · 5 2/8	6 7/8	M	Elko County	NV	Jim Algerio	2000	102
47 4/8	9 7/8 · 9 7/8	5 3/8 · 5 3/8	9 1/8	M	Hizasa Creek	BC	Raymond L. Howell, Sr.	2000	102
47 4/8	9 5/8 · 9 4/8	5 3/8 · 5 3/8	6 4/8	M	Utah County	UT	Roy Hampton	2001	102
47 2/8	9 4/8 · 9 3/8	5 3/8 · 5 4/8	6 2/8	M	Kennedy Springs	MT	Don Leondorf	1964	114
47 2/8	8 6/8 · 8 7/8	5 3/8 · 5 4/8	6 2/8	M	Kittitas County	WA	Arnold L. Deckwa	1969	114
47 2/8	9 2/8 · 9 2/8	6 2/8 · 6 2/8	7 5/8	M	Kenai Peninsula	AK	John Moline	1971	114
47 2/8	9 5/8 · 9 5/8	5 2/8 · 5 2/8	7 0/8	M	Alsek River	AK	F. Wyatt Cook	1976	114
47 2/8	9 1/8 · 9 2/8	5 4/8 · 5 4/8	6 6/8	M	Cassier Inlet	BC	Peter L. Halbig	1984	114
47 2/8	8 7/8 · 9 0/8	5 4/8 · 5 4/8	6 4/8	M	Clear Creek County	CO	Don Stiles	1984	114
47 2/8	9 4/8 · 9 5/8	5 3/8 · 5 3/8	6 2/8	M	Lewis & Clark County	MT	Doug Getz	1985	114
47 2/8	10 0/8 · 9 5/8	5 1/8 · 5 1/8	7 2/8	M	Ravalli County	MT	Ray Tlamka	1985	114
47 2/8	9 2/8 · 9 2/8	5 2/8 · 5 3/8	5 5/8	M	Mitchell Mtn.	BC	Vincent Pisani	1986	114
47 2/8	9 7/8 · 10 0/8	5 2/8 · 5 2/8	6 3/8	M	Clear Creek County	CO	Richard A. Devrous, Jr.	1990	114
47 2/8	10 1/8 · 9 7/8	5 2/8 · 5 2/8	6 6/8	M	Ravalli County	MT	Shaun Twardoski	1992	114
47 2/8	9 1/8 · 9 2/8	5 3/8 · 5 4/8	6 2/8	M	Bella Coola	BC	Lawrence Michalchuk	1993	114
47 2/8	9 5/8 · 9 5/8	5 2/8 · 5 2/8	5 5/8	M	Chilkat River	AK	Bart W. Colledge	1993	114
47 2/8	9 1/8 · 9 4/8	5 4/8 · 5 4/8	7 5/8	M	Dall Lake	BC	Bob "Jake" Jacobsen	1994	114
47 2/8	10 1/8 · 10 0/8	5 1/8 · 5 1/8	6 5/8	M	Clearwater County	ID	Paul N. Rogers	1995	114
47 2/8	6 0/8 · 6 5/8	5 6/8 · 5 6/8	7 1/8	M	Atlin	BC	E. Lance Whary	1998	114
*47 2/8	9 3/8 · 9 0/8	5 3/8 · 5 4/8	8 0/8	M	Llewlyn Glacier	BC	Glen R. Cousins	2005	114
47 2/8	10 0/8 · 10 0/8	5 1/8 · 5 1/8	6 4/8	M	San Juan County	CO	Tom Stoffel	2006	114
47 0/8	9 3/8 · 9 3/8	5 3/8 · 5 4/8	7 2/8	M	Olympic Peninsula	WA	William V. Mishler	1968	132
47 0/8	9 1/8 · 9 1/8	5 2/8 · 5 2/8	5 6/8	M	Lemhi County	ID	Eugene E. Farmer	1972	132
47 0/8	9 1/8 · 9 1/8	5 5/8 · 5 5/8	6 4/8	M	Mason County	WA	Bob Brandfas	1976	132
47 0/8	9 3/8 · 9 0/8	5 5/8 · 5 5/8	6 6/8	M	Kenai Mtn.	AK	Rick Tollison	1978	132
47 0/8	9 2/8 · 9 3/8	5 5/8 · 5 4/8	6 0/8	M	Chaffee County	CO	Calvin Farner	1981	132
47 0/8	10 1/8 · 10 1/8	5 1/8 · 5 1/8	6 5/8	M	La Plata County	CO	Mark Wuerthele	1987	132
47 0/8	9 1/8 · 9 2/8	5 3/8 · 5 3/8	6 1/8	M	Smithers	BC	Philip Stegenga	1995	132
47 0/8	8 6/8 · 8 6/8	5 4/8 · 5 4/8	6 6/8	M	Blunt Mtn.	BC	Dewayne Mullins	1997	132
47 0/8	9 5/8 · 9 0/8	5 6/8 · 5 6/8	6 6/8	M	La Plata County	CO	John L. Gardner	1999	132
47 0/8	9 2/8 · 9 3/8	5 2/8 · 5 2/8	5 0/8	M	Haines	AK	Mark Calkins	2004	132
47 0/8	9 1/8 · 9 2/8	5 3/8 · 5 3/8	6 2/8	M	Kodiak Island	AK	Bob Ameen	2009	132
46 6/8	9 2/8 · 9 2/8	5 3/8 · 5 4/8	6 1/8	M	Haines	AK	Lowell Marylin	1962	143
46 6/8	9 3/8 · 9 3/8	5 2/8 · 5 2/8	7 0/8	M	Cordova	AK	Dwane J. Sykes	1973	143
46 6/8	9 2/8 · 9 3/8	5 4/8 · 5 4/8	6 2/8	M	Clallam County	WA	Dean Cook	1978	143
46 6/8	9 0/8 · 9 0/8	5 3/8 · 5 2/8	6 3/8	M	Stalk Lakes	BC	Walt Krom	1979	143
46 6/8	8 2/8 · 9 5/8	5 6/8 · 5 6/8	6 3/8	M	Kittitas County	WA	Robert J. Fischer	1981	143
46 6/8	10 0/8 · 10 1/8	5 3/8 · 5 4/8	6 0/8	M	Clearwater County	ID	Timothy A. Hyde	1986	143
46 6/8	9 2/8 · 9 0/8	5 3/8 · 5 3/8	6 6/8	M	Babine Range	BC	Don St. Jean	1987	143
46 6/8	9 7/8 · 9 4/8	5 2/8 · 5 2/8	6 4/8	M	Bonneville County	ID	Coby Tigert	1989	143
46 6/8	8 3/8 · 8 4/8	5 3/8 · 5 3/8	6 4/8	M	Todagin Mtn.	BC	Len Cardinale	1990	143
46 6/8	9 0/8 · 8 7/8	6 0/8 · 6 0/8	7 1/8	M	San Juan County	CO	Steven J. Vittetow	1993	143
46 6/8	9 2/8 · 9 2/8	5 3/8 · 5 4/8	6 3/8	M	Salt Lake County	UT	Patrick G. Hogle	1995	143
46 6/8	8 6/8 · 9 0/8	5 3/8 · 5 4/8	7 0/8	M	Atlin	BC	Tim R. Dawson	1998	143
46 6/8	9 7/8 · 9 7/8	5 1/8 · 5 1/8	7 4/8	M	Washout Creek	BC	Tom Foss	1998	143
46 6/8	9 3/8 · 9 2/8	5 4/8 · 5 4/8	6 0/8	M	Chaffee County	CO	Esco Billings III	1998	143
46 6/8	9 2/8 · 9 2/8	5 4/8 · 5 3/8	7 0/8	M	Summit County	CO	Steven Behunin	2000	143
46 6/8	9 2/8 · 9 0/8	5 2/8 · 5 2/8	7 0/8	M	Baker County	OR	Jerry D. Donovan	2003	143
46 6/8	8 5/8 · 8 2/8	5 4/8 · 5 5/8	7 7/8	M	Goose Lake	BC	Bob McCartney	2005	143
46 6/8	10 0/8 · 9 7/8	5 2/8 · 5 2/8	7 0/8	M	Park County	MT	Nate Peckinpaugh	2006	143
46 4/8	9 1/8 · 8 7/8	5 3/8 · 5 3/8	7 1/8	M	Clallam County	WA	Thos. J. Smith	1969	161
46 4/8	9 6/8 · 9 0/8	5 4/8 · 5 4/8	7 2/8	M	Day Harbor	AK	William L. Ruby	1970	161
46 4/8	10 0/8 · 9 7/8	5 2/8 · 5 1/8	7 4/8	M	Thuodadi Lake	BC	Gary Petee	1979	161
46 4/8	9 3/8 · 9 4/8	5 2/8 · 5 3/8	6 6/8	M	Olympic Peninsula	WA	Gerald Egbert	1980	161
46 4/8	9 2/8 · 9 1/8	5 4/8 · 5 4/8	5 6/8	M	Chaffee County	CO	Ken McIntosh	1983	161
46 4/8	9 1/8 · 9 0/8	5 4/8 · 5 4/8	6 7/8	M	Jefferson County	WA	Greg Tedlund	1986	161
46 4/8	8 3/8 · 8 2/8	5 5/8 · 5 5/8	6 0/8	M	Chaffee County	CO	Todd Clyncke	1987	161
46 4/8	8 4/8 · 9 6/8	5 5/8 · 5 4/8	7 6/8	M	Chouteau County	MT	Robert Lucas	1988	161
46 4/8	9 0/8 · 8 7/8	5 5/8 · 5 5/8	6 0/8	M	Kodiak Island	AK	Roger Stewart	1989	161
46 4/8	8 6/8 · 9 0/8	5 3/8 · 5 3/8	6 6/8	M	Atlin	BC	Gary M. Martin	1990	161
46 4/8	9 0/8 · 9 0/8	5 2/8 · 5 2/8	5 5/8	M	Bella Coola	BC	Barry McCay	1990	161
46 4/8	8 4/8 · 9 3/8	5 5/8 · 5 6/8	7 1/8	M	Moose Pass	AK	Craig Scarbrough	1990	161
46 4/8	8 5/8 · 8 6/8	5 3/8 · 5 4/8	7 2/8	M	Kodiak Island	AK	Lon E. Lauber	1992	161
46 4/8	9 0/8 · 8 7/8	5 2/8 · 5 2/8	5 2/8	M	Telegraph Creek	BC	Lou Kindred	1993	161
46 4/8	9 1/8 · 9 3/8	5 1/8 · 5 1/8	6 0/8	M	Taku Plateau	BC	Walter J. Palmer	1995	161
46 4/8	9 0/8 · 9 2/8	5 5/8 · 5 5/8	6 2/8	M	Chaffee County	CO	John R. Olson	1996	161
46 4/8	9 2/8 · 9 2/8	5 2/8 · 5 2/8	6 1/8	M	Taku River	BC	Richard A. Smith	1999	161
46 4/8	9 5/8 · 9 1/8	5 4/8 · 5 4/8	7 2/8	M	Kodiak Island	AK	John D. "Jack" Frost	2001	161
46 4/8	9 2/8 · 9 3/8	5 3/8 · 5 3/8	7 1/8	M	Major Hart River	BC	Camp Newton	2003	161
46 4/8	9 7/8 · 10 0/8	5 3/8 · 5 2/8	6 2/8	M	Beaverhead County	MT	Joseph G. DeAngelis	2003	161
46 4/8	10 5/8 · 10 5/8	4 5/8 · 4 6/8	9 5/8	F	Tweedsmuir Peak	BC	George S. Walker	2003	161
46 4/8	9 2/8 · 9 3/8	5 2/8 · 5 2/8	6 6/8	M	Lake George	AK	Frank S. Noska IV	2005	161
*46 4/8	9 4/8 · 9 3/8	5 2/8 · 5 2/8	6 0/8	M	Hirsch Creek	BC	Glen A. Monson	2008	161
46 2/8	9 2/8 · 9 5/8	5 3/8 · 5 3/8	6 5/8	M	Lewis & Clark County	MT	W. J. Fuller	1958	184
46 2/8	9 1/8 · 9 1/8	5 2/8 · 5 2/8	6 2/8	M	Lemhi County	ID	Ray Torrey	1967	184
46 2/8	9 4/8 · 9 3/8	5 1/8 · 5 1/8	5 5/8	M	Kittitas County	WA	Keith E. Anyan	1978	184
46 2/8	8 7/8 · 8 6/8	5 3/8 · 5 3/8	6 3/8	M	Terrace	BC	Bill Coburn	1979	184
46 2/8	9 2/8 · 9 2/8	4 4/8 · 4 5/8	6 3/8	M	Snohomish County	WA	Fred Collins	1980	184
46 2/8	9 1/8 · 9 0/8	5 3/8 · 5 3/8	6 6/8	M	Smithers	BC	Robert M. Fromme	1990	184
46 2/8	9 1/8 · 8 7/8	5 3/8 · 5 3/8	6 5/8	M	Clear Creek County	CO	Kurt W. Keskimaki	1991	184

877

ROCKY MOUNTAIN GOAT

Minimum Score 40 — Continued

SCORE	LENGTH OF R HORN L	CIRCUMFERENCE R OF BASE L	GREATEST SPREAD	SEX	AREA	STATE/PROVINCE	HUNTER'S NAME	DATE	RANK
46 2/8	8 3/8 9 2/8	5 4/8 5 4/8	7 1/8	M	Kodiak Island	AK	Mark A. Pfost	1992	184
46 2/8	9 1/8 9 2/8	5 3/8 5 3/8	6 6/8	M	Kodiak Island	AK	Troy A. Graziadei	1993	184
46 2/8	9 0/8 8 6/8	5 2/8 5 2/8	7 1/8	M	Haines Junction	BC	Thomas G. Nelson	2003	184
*46 2/8	9 4/8 9 2/8	5 3/8 5 4/8	7 1/8	M	Smithers	BC	Joe Thomas	2004	184
46 2/8	8 6/8 8 6/8	5 4/8 5 3/8	6 2/8	M	Todagin Lake	BC	Joel A. Johnson	2005	184
46 2/8	8 4/8 8 3/8	5 4/8 5 5/8	5 2/8	M	Crater Lake	BC	J. T. Felt	2006	184
46 0/8	9 3/8 9 4/8	5 2/8 5 2/8	6 6/8	M	Whidbey Bay	AK	George Moerlein	1964	197
46 0/8	8 5/8 8 5/8	5 0/8 5 0/8	6 2/8	M	Boise County	ID	Jerry E. Burt	1971	197
46 0/8	8 7/8 9 0/8	5 4/8 5 4/8	7 6/8	M	Kenai Peninsula	AK	Roger D. Morris	1971	197
46 0/8	9 1/8 9 3/8	5 1/8 5 1/8	6 2/8	M	Clear Creek County	CO	Kurt Keskimaki	1979	197
46 0/8	8 7/8 9 0/8	5 4/8 5 4/8	6 5/8	M	Kechika Range	BC	Roger Stewart	1980	197
46 0/8	9 2/8 9 2/8	5 2/8 5 2/8	6 6/8	M	Clear Creek County	CO	David Skiff	1981	197
46 0/8	9 3/8 9 3/8	5 2/8 5 1/8	5 7/8	M	Chouteau County	MT	Kay Davidson	1984	197
46 0/8	9 0/8 9 0/8	5 2/8 5 1/8	6 5/8	M	Kenai Peninsula	AK	Robert D. Warpack	1985	197
46 0/8	9 1/8 9 1/8	5 1/8 5 2/8	8 2/8	M	Spencer Glacier	AK	Matt Jones	1990	197
46 0/8	9 1/8 9 2/8	5 3/8 5 3/8	7 0/8	M	Jefferson County	WA	David K. Olson	1991	197
46 0/8	9 0/8 8 7/8	5 2/8 5 2/8	6 5/8	M	Kenai Peninsula	AK	John Sarvis	1993	197
46 0/8	8 2/8 8 1/8	5 4/8 5 3/8	6 2/8	M	Dease River	BC	Dale Selby	1995	197
46 0/8	9 1/8 9 2/8	5 1/8 5 1/8	7 2/8	M	Knik Glacier	AK	Stephen Kotz	1996	197
46 0/8	11 1/8 10 7/8	4 5/8 4 5/8	8 4/8	F	Fremont County	ID	Del Morton	1996	197
46 0/8	9 1/8 9 0/8	5 1/8 5 2/8	5 6/8	M	Chaffee County	CO	Joe B. Farmer	1997	197
46 0/8	9 2/8 9 0/8	5 3/8 5 3/8	6 4/8	M	Grand County	CO	Scott George	2000	197
46 0/8	8 6/8 8 6/8	5 2/8 5 2/8	6 2/8	M	Beaver County	UT	Kurt Wood	2005	197
46 0/8	9 4/8 8 7/8	5 3/8 5 3/8	6 5/8	M	Tascola Mtn.	BC	Roy Goodwin	2008	197
45 6/8	8 5/8 8 5/8	5 3/8 5 3/8	7 3/8	M	Skagway	AK	Rick Furniss	1972	215
45 6/8	8 5/8 8 5/8	5 2/8 5 2/8	6 4/8	M	Jefferson County	WA	John Lund	1978	215
45 6/8	9 0/8 8 7/8	5 1/8 5 1/8	5 4/8	M	Stalk Lakes	BC	John Stadler	1980	215
45 6/8	8 6/8 9 0/8	5 1/8 5 2/8	6 7/8	M	Cordova	AK	Gary A. Twigg	1980	215
45 6/8	9 1/8 9 1/8	5 2/8 5 2/8	6 4/8	M	Duti Lake	BC	William "Bill" MacCarty III	1981	215
45 6/8	9 3/8 9 4/8	5 2/8 5 2/8	5 3/8	M	Mount Jeldness	BC	Gerald Bond	1982	215
45 6/8	8 7/8 9 1/8	5 3/8 5 3/8	7 0/8	M	Todagin Mtn.	BC	Reggie Spiegelberg	1984	215
45 6/8	9 6/8 9 6/8	5 0/8 5 1/8	6 2/8	M	Clearwater County	ID	Mike VonLindern	1984	215
45 6/8	8 4/8 8 7/8	5 3/8 5 3/8	7 6/8	M	Atlin	BC	Harrison O'Conner	1985	215
45 6/8	9 0/8 8 5/8	5 1/8 5 0/8	7 0/8	M	Snohomish County	WA	Norman Ward	1987	215
45 6/8	8 7/8 8 6/8	5 2/8 5 1/8	6 2/8	M	Kittitas County	WA	William R. Kinnan	1991	215
45 6/8	8 6/8 8 7/8	5 2/8 5 2/8	6 4/8	M	Snohomish County	WA	Stuart L. Keck	1994	215
45 6/8	8 5/8 8 4/8	5 2/8 5 2/8	7 5/8	M	Knik Glacier	AK	Braun Kopsack	1994	215
45 6/8	8 7/8 8 7/8	5 2/8 5 2/8	6 2/8	M	Valdez	AK	Jerry Vega	1997	215
45 6/8	8 7/8 8 7/8	5 2/8 5 2/8	6 0/8	M	Custer County	SD	Daniel Davis	1999	215
45 6/8	9 0/8 9 0/8	5 0/8 5 0/8	6 6/8	M	Columbia Glacier	AK	Mike Sokol	2000	215
45 6/8	8 4/8 9 0/8	5 2/8 5 3/8	7 1/8	M	Stephens Passage	AK	Steve Hohensee	2002	215
45 6/8	9 2/8 9 1/8	5 1/8 5 1/8	6 4/8	M	Mt. Palmer	AK	Marlin Hoch	2003	215
45 6/8	9 1/8 9 3/8	5 3/8 5 3/8	5 6/8	M	Golden	BC	Daniel Real	2003	215
45 6/8	9 0/8 9 0/8	5 3/8 5 3/8	6 7/8	M	Taku River	BC	Roy L. Walk	2006	215
45 6/8	9 1/8 9 2/8	5 3/8 5 3/8	6 4/8	M	Grand County	CO	Phillip Gaines	2010	215
45 4/8	9 2/8 9 3/8	5 3/8 5 3/8	6 0/8	M	Lemhi County	ID	A. LaVerne Hokanson	1968	236
45 4/8	8 7/8 8 7/8	5 2/8 5 1/8	8 1/8	M	Kenai Peninsula	AK	Dean Lust	1969	236
45 4/8	8 7/8 8 6/8	5 2/8 5 2/8	6 6/8	M	McCarthy Glacier	AK	John F. Sumrall	1974	236
45 4/8	9 0/8 8 7/8	5 2/8 5 2/8	6 0/8	M	Bonner County	ID	Dean A. Cox	1979	236
45 4/8	8 7/8 9 0/8	5 2/8 5 3/8	6 2/8	M	Kenai Peninsula	AK	Chris Kempf	1981	236
45 4/8	9 3/8 9 2/8	5 1/8 5 2/8	6 3/8	M	Jefferson County	WA	Gary R. Fountain	1987	236
45 4/8	8 7/8 8 6/8	5 2/8 5 2/8	6 4/8	M	Wrangell	AK	David Schuelke	1988	236
45 4/8	8 4/8 8 4/8	5 2/8 5 2/8	5 5/8	M	Snohomish County	WA	Timothy T. Neal	1988	236
45 4/8	9 4/8 9 3/8	5 2/8 5 2/8	6 1/8	M	Chaffee County	CO	Troy Cunningham	1993	236
45 4/8	9 3/8 9 1/8	5 2/8 5 2/8	6 4/8	M	Gunnison County	CO	Robert L. Syvertson, Jr.	1993	236
45 4/8	9 1/8 9 1/8	5 1/8 5 1/8	6 1/8	M	Clear Creek County	CO	Otho Hobbs	1995	236
45 4/8	9 0/8 9 0/8	5 1/8 5 1/8	6 0/8	M	Keremeos	BC	Gary F. Bogner	1995	236
45 4/8	8 6/8 9 1/8	5 4/8 5 4/8	5 4/8	M	La Plata County	CO	Robert D. Crask	1997	236
45 4/8	9 4/8 9 5/8	5 2/8 5 2/8	7 0/8	M	Pop Lake	BC	Kevin L. Reid	1998	236
45 4/8	9 0/8 9 0/8	5 1/8 5 1/8	6 3/8	M	Clear Creek County	CO	Larry O. Baker	1998	236
45 4/8	9 0/8 9 3/8	5 2/8 5 2/8	6 5/8	M	Summit County	CO	Cal Behunin	1999	236
45 4/8	9 1/8 9 0/8	5 2/8 5 2/8	6 1/8	M	Inklin River	BC	Ken Stieh	2002	236
45 4/8	9 2/8 9 3/8	5 1/8 5 1/8	7 1/8	M	Liard River	BC	Richie Bland	2005	236
45 4/8	8 6/8 8 6/8	5 2/8 5 3/8	7 7/8	M	Lake George	AK	Frank S. Noska IV	2008	236
45 4/8	9 2/8 9 2/8	5 1/8 5 1/8	6 6/8	M	Kodiak Island	AK	Bob Ameen	2008	236
45 2/8	8 6/8 8 7/8	5 5/8 5 4/8	7 4/8	M	Telegraph Creek	BC	Troy M. Miller	1968	256
45 2/8	9 3/8 9 0/8	5 2/8 5 2/8	6 5/8	M	Kenai Mtn.	AK	Robert Borland	1970	256
45 2/8	9 5/8 9 4/8	5 0/8 5 0/8	7 1/8	M	Lemhi County	ID	D. Kittredge/R. Torrey	1973	256
45 2/8	8 5/8 8 5/8	5 3/8 5 3/8	5 3/8	M	Kittitas County	WA	Jim Novak	1974	256
45 2/8	8 3/8 8 5/8	5 1/8 5 2/8	6 2/8	M	Kechika River	BC	Paul Brunner	1974	256
45 2/8	8 6/8 8 7/8	5 5/8 5 4/8	6 2/8	M	Jefferson County	WA	Larry Ramsey	1978	256
45 2/8	9 4/8 10 1/8	5 0/8 5 0/8	7 6/8	M	Valdez	AK	Kevin Chelf	1984	256
45 2/8	9 1/8 9 3/8	5 0/8 5 0/8	5 5/8	M	Snohomish County	WA	Douglas H. Brandt	1988	256
45 2/8	8 5/8 8 7/8	5 3/8 5 2/8	7 0/8	M	Valdez	AK	Rickie D. Snell	1990	256
45 2/8	9 2/8 9 1/8	5 2/8 5 2/8	6 1/8	M	Clark County	ID	Kenneth Ruzicka	1994	256
45 2/8	8 7/8 8 5/8	5 4/8 5 4/8	7 2/8	M	Eagle County	CO	Connie Renfro	1995	256
45 2/8	9 0/8 9 3/8	5 3/8 5 3/8	6 2/8	M	Gunnison County	CO	K. Craig Vaughn	1995	256
45 2/8	9 3/8 8 7/8	5 2/8 5 2/8	7 2/8	M	Prince William Sound	AK	Jerry Lees	1998	256
45 2/8	9 1/8 8 4/8	5 3/8 5 3/8	6 5/8	M	Custer County	ID	Lance Kronberger	2000	256
45 2/8	9 4/8 9 1/8	5 1/8 5 1/8	7 6/8	M	Taku River	BC	George Harms	2003	256
45 2/8	8 4/8 8 4/8	5 3/8 5 3/8	5 6/8	M	Kodiak Island	AK	F. David Thornberry	2006	256
*45 2/8	9 2/8 9 2/8	5 2/8 5 2/8	6 7/8	M	Lincoln County	WY	Wayne F. Farnsworth, Jr.	2007	256
*45 2/8	9 1/8 9 0/8	5 1/8 5 1/8	7 3/8	M	Kadin Lake	AK	Christopher Durando	2008	256
45 0/8	9 3/8 9 1/8	5 3/8 5 3/8	5 5/8	M	Flathead County	MT	Jack Whitney	1962	274
45 0/8	9 0/8 9 1/8	5 0/8 5 0/8	6 3/8	M	Boise County	ID	Bradley H. Jolley	1972	274
45 0/8	9 4/8 9 3/8	5 0/8 5 0/8	7 1/8	M	Lemhi County	ID	G. Yasuda/R. White	1973	274
45 0/8	8 7/8 8 7/8	4 7/8 5 0/8	6 5/8	M	Jefferson County	WA	Edward H. Boyle	1974	274
45 0/8	9 2/8 9 6/8	5 2/8 5 2/8	7 2/8	M	Lemhi County	ID	Donald J. Keady	1976	274
45 0/8	8 6/8 9 0/8	5 2/8 5 2/8	6 4/8	M	Kenai Peninsula	AK	Eugene Smith, Jr.	1976	274
45 0/8	8 2/8 8 2/8	5 4/8 5 3/8	5 3/8	M	Big Sheep Creek	BC	Gerald Bond	1981	274
45 0/8	9 2/8 9 1/8	5 2/8 5 2/8	6 1/8	M	English Bay	AK	Maxallen D. Jackson	1982	274
45 0/8	8 1/8 9 2/8	5 2/8 5 2/8	5 5/8	M	Moricetown	BC	Don St. Jean	1985	274
45 0/8	9 2/8 9 2/8	5 2/8 5 2/8	5 6/8	M	La Plata County	CO	Jeffrey Yehl	1986	274
45 0/8	8 7/8 8 7/8	5 3/8 5 2/8	5 6/8	M	Kodiak Island	AK	Patricia Stewart	1989	274
45 0/8	9 1/8 9 2/8	5 2/8 5 2/8	6 3/8	M	Park County	WY	Jon E. Umphlett	1990	274

ROCKY MOUNTAIN GOAT

Minimum Score 40   Continued

SCORE	LENGTH OF R HORN L	CIRCUMFERENCE R OF BASE L	GREATEST SPREAD	SEX	AREA	STATE/ PROVINCE	HUNTER'S NAME	DATE	RANK
45 0/8	9 0/8 8 7/8	5 2/8 5 2/8	6 6/8	M	Bonneville County	ID	Randy K. Vranes	1990	274
45 0/8	9 5/8 9 4/8	4 7/8 4 7/8	6 2/8	M	Clear Creek County	CO	Sherwin Van Kooten	1990	274
45 0/8	9 1/8 9 1/8	5 2/8 5 2/8	6 6/8	M	Blaine County	ID	James Deitrick	1991	274
45 0/8	10 4/8 10 3/8	4 4/8 4 5/8	10 1/8	F	Bonneville County	ID	Mike Yantis	1992	274
45 0/8	9 1/8 9 0/8	5 2/8 5 3/8	5 7/8	M	San Juan County	CO	Valerie A. Gardner	1993	274
45 0/8	8 7/8 8 7/8	5 2/8 5 1/8	5 6/8	M	Kemano	BC	Randy McGregor	1995	274
45 0/8	9 0/8 8 7/8	5 2/8 5 3/8	5 5/8	M	Valdez	AK	Tom Miranda	1998	274
45 0/8	8 5/8 8 5/8	5 1/8 5 1/8	7 0/8	M	Grasshopper Pass	AK	Donald Thompson	2002	274
45 0/8	8 3/8 8 3/8	5 4/8 5 3/8	6 0/8	M	Yakima County	WA	Chris Schreiber	2003	274
45 0/8	9 3/8 9 3/8	5 1/8 5 1/8	6 4/8	M	San Juan County	CO	Mark B. Steffen	2004	274
45 0/8	8 2/8 8 2/8	5 1/8 5 1/8	6 3/8	M	Atlin	BC	Dr. Dave Samuel	2006	274
44 6/8	8 6/8 8 5/8	5 1/8 5 1/8	0 0/8	M	Kittitas County	WA	Les Turner	1967	297
44 6/8	8 7/8 8 6/8	5 1/8 5 1/8	6 1/8	M	Fox River	AK	John F. Sumrall	1977	297
44 6/8	8 4/8 8 4/8	5 2/8 5 2/8	4 7/8	M	Snohomish County	WA	Kelly King	1977	297
44 6/8	8 7/8 8 6/8	5 2/8 5 3/8	6 7/8	M	Park County	WY	Scott Steere	1982	297
44 6/8	9 1/8 9 1/8	5 1/8 5 1/8	6 6/8	M	Valdez	AK	Rick D. Snell	1991	297
44 6/8	8 7/8 9 0/8	5 1/8 5 1/8	6 5/8	M	Pierce County	WA	Stan Nelson	1993	297
44 6/8	8 4/8 8 5/8	5 2/8 5 3/8	6 0/8	M	Madison County	MT	Dan Johnerson	1993	297
44 6/8	8 0/8 9 0/8	5 3/8 5 4/8	7 1/8	M	Clear Creek County	CO	Bob Chapman	1995	297
44 6/8	9 6/8 9 5/8	5 0/8 5 0/8	6 0/8	M	Elk Valley	BC	Dale Webber	1995	297
44 6/8	7 7/8 8 3/8	5 2/8 5 2/8	5 1/8	M	Lewis County	WA	Reuben C. Grendahl	1996	297
44 6/8	8 5/8 8 5/8	5 0/8 4 7/8	6 5/8	M	Carbon County	MT	Bradley S. Warren	1996	297
44 6/8	8 7/8 8 6/8	5 2/8 5 2/8	6 0/8	M	Windy Point	BC	Randy Liljenquist	2000	297
44 6/8	9 0/8 9 0/8	5 0/8 5 0/8	6 5/8	M	Taku River	BC	Ned Greer	2002	297
44 6/8	9 1/8 9 0/8	5 0/8 5 0/8	6 3/8	M	Park County	CO	William B. Bullock	2005	297
44 6/8	9 2/8 9 2/8	5 0/8 5 2/8	5 1/8	M	Swan Lake	AK	Butch Carley	2005	297
44 6/8	9 0/8 9 0/8	5 1/8 5 0/8	6 6/8	M	Park County	CO	Mark Turner	2006	297
*44 6/8	8 4/8 8 3/8	5 2/8 5 2/8	6 4/8	M	Kodiak Island	AK	Cindi Richardson	2009	297
44 4/8	9 7/8 9 7/8	4 3/8 4 3/8	8 5/8	F	Cold Fish Lake	BC	K. K. Knickerbocker	1957	314
44 4/8	8 7/8 8 7/8	5 1/8 5 1/8	6 4/8	M	Kenai Peninsula	AK	Larry Jones	1969	314
44 4/8	8 5/8 8 5/8	5 1/8 5 2/8	6 1/8	M	Kittitas County	WA	David L. Smartt	1972	314
44 4/8	8 6/8 8 5/8	5 1/8 5 1/8	6 6/8	M	Stalk Lakes	BC	Richard J. Crowder	1977	314
44 4/8	10 1/8 10 2/8	4 4/8 4 4/8	8 5/8	F	Stock Creek	BC	Jay Deones	1978	314
44 4/8	9 0/8 9 0/8	4 7/8 4 7/8	6 6/8	M	Murky Lake	BC	Chuck Adams	1979	314
44 4/8	8 1/8 8 2/8	5 2/8 5 1/8	5 7/8	M	Jefferson County	WA	David P. Sanford	1981	314
44 4/8	9 2/8 9 2/8	5 2/8 5 2/8	5 5/8	M	Idaho County	ID	Darrell Howard	1982	314
44 4/8	10 2/8 10 1/8	4 3/8 4 3/8	7 6/8	F	Thatade Lake	BC	Jerry Baek	1984	314
44 4/8	9 2/8 9 3/8	4 6/8 4 5/8	7 7/8	M	Chugach Mtns.	AK	Darryl Quidort	1985	314
44 4/8	9 0/8 9 1/8	5 0/8 5 0/8	6 2/8	M	Atlin	BC	Tom Tietz	1985	314
44 4/8	8 5/8 8 5/8	5 1/8 5 1/8	6 4/8	M	Chugach Mtns.	AK	Gary White	1986	314
44 4/8	9 1/8 9 2/8	5 0/8 5 0/8	5 7/8	M	Chaffee County	CO	Tim Cuthriell	1987	314
44 4/8	9 0/8 8 5/8	5 0/8 5 0/8	6 5/8	M	Mason County	WA	Dan Howell	1987	314
44 4/8	9 2/8 8 6/8	5 3/8 5 3/8	5 6/8	M	Custer County	SD	Vilas Schoenfelder	1988	314
44 4/8	8 6/8 8 5/8	5 1/8 5 1/8	5 3/8	M	Todagin Mtn.	BC	Craig Reichmuth	1989	314
44 4/8	8 5/8 8 5/8	5 1/8 5 2/8	6 7/8	M	Hyland Lake	YUK	Gregory White	1989	314
44 4/8	9 0/8 9 0/8	5 0/8 5 1/8	5 4/8	M	Kittitas County	WA	Jim Charlton	1989	314
44 4/8	9 2/8 9 4/8	5 0/8 5 0/8	6 7/8	M	Madison County	MT	Steve Rhodes	1989	314
44 4/8	9 2/8 9 1/8	4 7/8 4 7/8	6 6/8	M	Summit County	CO	Steve Fausel	1990	314
44 4/8	8 7/8 8 5/8	5 2/8 5 2/8	5 7/8	M	Custer County	SD	R. Craig Oberle	1990	314
44 4/8	9 0/8 8 7/8	5 2/8 5 1/8	7 0/8	M	Jefferson County	WA	Steve Brown	1990	314
44 4/8	8 5/8 8 6/8	5 2/8 5 2/8	6 1/8	M	Kodiak Island	AK	Larry Spiva	1992	314
44 4/8	8 0/8 9 0/8	5 5/8 5 5/8	6 3/8	M	Carbon County	MT	Chris G. Sanford	1992	314
44 4/8	8 5/8 9 0/8	5 2/8 5 2/8	6 3/8	M	Mason County	WA	Scott A. Nixon	1993	314
44 4/8	8 6/8 8 5/8	5 1/8 5 1/8	5 5/8	M	Clear Creek County	CO	Barry J. Smith	1994	314
44 4/8	9 0/8 9 0/8	5 1/8 5 1/8	7 0/8	M	Clear Creek County	CO	E. Damon Handley	1997	314
44 4/8	8 5/8 8 7/8	5 3/8 5 3/8	6 1/8	M	Clear Creek County	CO	Roger Trudell	1997	314
44 4/8	8 6/8 8 6/8	5 1/8 5 1/8	6 3/8	M	Clear Creek County	CO	Steve Smith	1997	314
44 4/8	9 0/8 9 0/8	5 1/8 5 1/8	6 4/8	M	Racing River	BC	Chris Partridge	2002	314
44 4/8	8 5/8 8 7/8	5 1/8 5 2/8	5 7/8	M	Utah County	UT	David B. Nielsen	2003	314
44 4/8	8 6/8 9 6/8	5 0/8 5 0/8	7 3/8	M	Lincoln County	MT	Robert Kehn	2003	314
44 4/8	8 2/8 8 4/8	5 1/8 5 2/8	6 2/8	M	Clear Creek County	CO	Eric Coe	2005	314
44 4/8	9 0/8 9 0/8	4 7/8 4 7/8	6 3/8	M	Kicking Horse River	BC	William Fiore	2006	314
44 4/8	9 2/8 9 2/8	5 1/8 5 1/8	6 4/8	M	La Plata County	CO	Eric A. Sawyer	2007	314
44 2/8	8 5/8 8 5/8	5 1/8 5 0/8	5 6/8	M	Kenai Lake	AK	James R. Carr	1973	349
44 2/8	8 6/8 9 0/8	5 1/8 5 2/8	6 5/8	M	Cold Fish Lake	BC	Dennis Behn	1975	349
44 2/8	7 7/8 7 6/8	5 1/8 5 2/8	5 2/8	M	King County	WA	Ronald A. Carpenter	1977	349
44 2/8	8 3/8 8 6/8	5 1/8 5 1/8	7 0/8	M	Todagin Lake	BC	Stanley D. Moore	1978	349
44 2/8	9 0/8 8 7/8	5 1/8 5 2/8	6 7/8	M	Custer County	SD	Kent D. Keenlyne	1981	349
44 2/8	8 0/8 8 0/8	5 5/8 5 4/8	6 2/8	M	Tutachi Lake	BC	Ray Keenan	1987	349
44 2/8	9 2/8 9 2/8	5 0/8 5 0/8	6 1/8	M	Gallatin County	MT	Phil Auble	1987	349
44 2/8	9 2/8 9 4/8	5 0/8 5 0/8	6 2/8	M	Clear Creek County	CO	Elmer R. Luce, Jr.	1990	349
44 2/8	8 6/8 8 6/8	5 0/8 5 0/8	7 1/8	M	Day Harbor	AK	Braun Kopsack	1992	349
44 2/8	8 6/8 9 0/8	5 1/8 5 1/8	7 3/8	M	Wrangell Mtns.	AK	Dr. John Ribic	1992	349
44 2/8	8 4/8 8 3/8	5 1/8 5 1/8	5 6/8	M	Chilkat River	AK	Eric Colledge	1993	349
44 2/8	9 0/8 9 1/8	5 2/8 5 2/8	6 5/8	M	La Plata County	CO	Brian Myers	1996	349
44 2/8	6 7/8 8 1/8	5 5/8 5 5/8	5 6/8	M	King County	WA	Daniel A. Whitmus	1996	349
44 2/8	9 0/8 9 2/8	5 0/8 5 0/8	6 7/8	M	Custer County	ID	E. Lance Whary	1999	349
44 2/8	8 7/8 8 7/8	5 1/8 5 2/8	6 1/8	M	Clear Creek County	CO	Craig Thrasher	2000	349
44 2/8	9 1/8 9 2/8	5 0/8 5 1/8	6 7/8	F	Idaho County	ID	Anthony L. Mudd	2002	349
44 2/8	8 7/8 8 7/8	5 1/8 5 1/8	5 6/8	M	Pitkin County	CO	Kurt A. Grimm	2003	349
44 2/8	9 1/8 9 0/8	5 2/8 5 1/8	6 2/8	M	Toad River	BC	Richard Kirkland	2004	349
44 2/8	8 3/8 8 2/8	5 2/8 5 2/8	6 1/8	M	Stephens Passage	AK	Steve Hohensee	2005	349
44 0/8	7 4/8 9 0/8	5 4/8 5 4/8	6 0/8	M	Clallam County	WA	Virgil T. Cole, Jr.	1973	368
44 0/8	8 5/8 8 4/8	5 0/8 5 0/8	5 3/8	M	Chelan County	WA	Steve Gorr	1975	368
44 0/8	8 6/8 8 6/8	5 1/8 5 1/8	5 2/8	M	Clear Creek County	CO	Lee Kline	1978	368
44 0/8	8 4/8 8 3/8	4 6/8 4 6/8	4 0/8	M	Snohomish County	WA	Steve Gorr	1978	368
44 0/8	9 3/8 9 4/8	4 6/8 4 6/8	6 4/8	M	Valley County	ID	Jack Barrett	1980	368
44 0/8	7 6/8 7 7/8	5 3/8 5 3/8	6 5/8	M	Duti Lake	BC	Mike Morgan	1981	368
44 0/8	8 5/8 8 6/8	5 2/8 5 1/8	5 7/8	M	Idaho County	ID	Randy Ulmer	1982	368
44 0/8	9 0/8 9 2/8	5 0/8 5 0/8	6 6/8	M	Lake Tatlatui	BC	Rick Gilley	1983	368
44 0/8	9 6/8 6 3/8	5 7/8 5 7/8	7 5/8	M	Kenai Peninsula	AK	Michael R. Traub	1983	368
44 0/8	9 1/8 9 1/8	5 3/8 5 2/8	5 2/8	M	Lincoln County	MT	Jerry Brown	1983	368
44 0/8	8 4/8 8 3/8	4 7/8 4 7/8	6 5/8	M	Cordova	AK	James A. Davison	1985	368
44 0/8	8 7/8 8 7/8	5 1/8 5 1/8	6 6/8	M	Clark County	ID	Brent Poulter	1985	368
44 0/8	8 7/8 9 0/8	4 7/8 4 7/8	5 7/8	M	Snohomish County	WA	Stan Hansen	1985	368

879

ROCKY MOUNTAIN GOAT

Minimum Score 40 — Continued

SCORE	LENGTH OF R HORN L	CIRCUMFERENCE R OF BASE L	GREATEST SPREAD	SEX	AREA	STATE/PROVINCE	HUNTER'S NAME	DATE	RANK
44 0/8	8 4/8 9 1/8	5 1/8 5 1/8	5 7/8	M	Snohomish County	WA	Mark Knaus	1987	368
44 0/8	8 5/8 8 6/8	5 0/8 5 0/8	5 4/8	M	Bella Coola	BC	Randy Svisdahl	1991	368
44 0/8	9 1/8 9 2/8	4 6/8 4 7/8	5 6/8	M	Madison County	MT	James "Buck" MacLaurin	1994	368
44 0/8	9 1/8 9 1/8	4 7/8 5 0/8	6 0/8	M	Chaffee County	CO	Mark Montgomery	1994	368
44 0/8	9 2/8 9 2/8	4 6/8 4 6/8	6 5/8	M	Park County	WY	Terry Fieseler	1996	368
44 0/8	9 0/8 9 0/8	5 0/8 5 0/8	6 0/8	M	Clear Creek County	CO	Rick Duggan	1997	368
44 0/8	8 7/8 8 7/8	5 0/8 5 0/8	5 5/8	M	Clear Creek County	CO	Ron Faust	2000	368
44 0/8	8 5/8 8 3/8	5 0/8 5 0/8	6 7/8	M	Moose Pass	AK	Jonah M. Stewart	2000	368
44 0/8	9 3/8 9 2/8	5 0/8 5 0/8	6 5/8	M	Kechika River	BC	Donald H. Corey	2001	368
*44 0/8	9 2/8 9 1/8	4 7/8 4 7/8	6 4/8	M	La Plata County	CO	Randy Kendrick	2007	368
43 6/8	8 4/8 8 4/8	5 1/8 5 0/8	5 4/8	M	Kittitas County	WA	Joe Walker	1967	391
43 6/8	9 3/8 9 4/8	4 6/8 4 4/8	7 3/8	F	Duti River	BC	Walter J. Sawicki	1976	391
43 6/8	8 2/8 8 3/8	5 1/8 5 2/8	6 3/8	M	Park County	WY	Pat McAteer	1979	391
43 6/8	8 7/8 8 7/8	5 0/8 5 0/8	6 7/8	M	Bonner County	ID	Howard W. Holmes	1983	391
43 6/8	8 5/8 8 6/8	5 1/8 5 1/8	5 3/8	M	Chaffee County	CO	Doug Beck	1988	391
43 6/8	8 4/8 8 4/8	4 6/8 4 6/8	5 7/8	M	Kittitas County	WA	Greg "WildHorse" Willette	1989	391
43 6/8	9 0/8 9 3/8	5 0/8 5 0/8	7 1/8	M	Sulpher Creek	BC	Anthony P. Zielinski	1992	391
43 6/8	8 4/8 8 4/8	5 0/8 5 0/8	6 5/8	M	Head Keily Creek	BC	Bruce R. Schoeneweis	1997	391
43 6/8	8 5/8 8 6/8	5 1/8 5 2/8	7 5/8	M	Logan Mtns.	YUK	William L. Cox	2001	391
43 6/8	8 3/8 8 3/8	5 2/8 5 3/8	6 5/8	M	Pink Mtn.	BC	Douglas M. Stuart	2001	391
43 6/8	8 5/8 8 5/8	5 0/8 5 0/8	6 1/8	M	Park County	MT	Robert Hanneman	2004	391
43 6/8	8 4/8 8 5/8	5 3/8 5 3/8	5 6/8	M	Summit County	CO	Tim R. Hamilton	2005	391
43 6/8	9 1/8 8 5/8	5 1/8 5 1/8	6 4/8	M	Clear Creek County	CO	Jeff Lampe	2005	391
43 6/8	8 6/8 8 6/8	5 0/8 5 0/8	6 6/8	M	Knik Glacier	AK	Rick Hayley	2005	391
43 6/8	8 5/8 8 6/8	5 1/8 5 2/8	6 5/8	M	Park County	MT	Brian Stremcha	2006	391
43 4/8	8 7/8 8 7/8	4 7/8 4 7/8	6 0/8	M	Lake County	MT	Jack J. Whitney	1969	406
43 4/8	8 7/8 9 1/8	5 1/8 5 1/8	5 1/8	M	Lemhi County	ID	Joe Becker	1977	406
43 4/8	8 7/8 8 6/8	5 0/8 5 0/8	5 1/8	M	Kittitas County	WA	Glen Berry	1979	406
43 4/8	8 0/8 8 2/8	5 0/8 5 0/8	6 5/8	M	Ice Mtn.	BC	Larry Streiff	1979	406
43 4/8	8 5/8 8 5/8	4 7/8 4 7/8	6 2/8	M	Kitchener Lake	BC	James Saunoris	1983	406
43 4/8	8 4/8 8 4/8	5 1/8 5 2/8	5 6/8	M	Chaffee County	CO	Dan Eastin	1983	406
43 4/8	8 6/8 8 6/8	5 1/8 5 1/8	5 6/8	M	Chaffee County	CO	Don Bording	1983	406
43 4/8	9 1/8 9 2/8	4 4/8 4 4/8	7 0/8	F	Inklin River	BC	Dee C. Steinheiser	1986	406
43 4/8	9 0/8 8 7/8	4 7/8 4 7/8	6 1/8	M	Clear Creek County	CO	Daniel L. Tekavec	1986	406
43 4/8	8 2/8 8 4/8	5 0/8 5 0/8	5 5/8	M	Bella Coola	BC	Randy Svisdahl	1988	406
43 4/8	10 4/8 10 1/8	4 3/8 4 3/8	6 2/8	F	Clear Creek County	CO	Donald Ace Morgan	1989	406
43 4/8	9 6/8 9 6/8	4 4/8 4 3/8	7 6/8	F	Ealue Lake	BC	Dave Hannas	1990	406
43 4/8	8 3/8 8 3/8	5 2/8 5 2/8	5 6/8	M	Park County	MT	Steve Kamps	1991	406
43 4/8	8 7/8 9 2/8	5 0/8 5 1/8	6 3/8	M	Summit County	CO	Linda Strong	1994	406
43 4/8	8 6/8 8 4/8	5 0/8 5 0/8	6 2/8	M	Lemhi County	ID	Ben Fahnholz	1996	406
43 4/8	8 5/8 8 5/8	5 0/8 5 0/8	6 4/8	M	Clear Creek County	CO	Dave Parri	1999	406
43 4/8	9 3/8 9 2/8	4 7/8 4 7/8	6 6/8	M	Clear Creek County	CO	David L. Marlow	2001	406
43 4/8	9 7/8 9 5/8	4 3/8 4 3/8	7 4/8	M	Terrace	BC	Brady Bradford	2004	406
43 4/8	8 6/8 8 6/8	5 0/8 5 0/8	5 2/8	M	Lilloet	BC	John Paul Schaffer	2004	406
*43 4/8	9 0/8 9 1/8	5 0/8 5 0/8	5 4/8	M	Lincoln County	MT	Dan Halvorson	2006	406
*43 4/8	8 4/8 8 3/8	5 1/8 5 1/8	6 0/8	M	Knat Creek	BC	Mark Beeler	2008	406
43 4/8	9 2/8 9 3/8	4 7/8 4 6/8	5 6/8	M	Kimberly	BC	Thanos Natras	2008	406
43 2/8	10 0/8 10 0/8	4 2/8 4 2/8	8 0/8	F	Tutaday Lake	BC	Larry Alma	1982	428
43 2/8	8 4/8 8 3/8	5 0/8 5 0/8	7 4/8	M	Telegraph Creek	BC	Jamie Byrne	1990	428
43 2/8	9 0/8 9 0/8	5 1/8 5 0/8	5 4/8	M	Ewilka Peak	BC	Larry D. Jones	1990	428
43 2/8	8 6/8 8 6/8	5 0/8 5 0/8	6 1/8	M	Chaffee County	CO	Shawn Kingery	1997	428
43 2/8	8 7/8 8 6/8	5 0/8 5 0/8	5 4/8	M	Chaffee County	CO	Laszlo Nobi	1999	428
43 2/8	8 4/8 8 5/8	5 0/8 5 0/8	6 0/8	M	Summit County	CO	Jim Horneck	2000	428
43 2/8	9 0/8 8 5/8	5 1/8 5 1/8	5 6/8	M	Bull River	BC	David C. Manca	2002	428
43 2/8	9 1/8 9 2/8	4 7/8 4 7/8	6 5/8	M	Clear Creek County	CO	Mike Dziekan	2002	428
43 2/8	8 3/8 8 4/8	5 2/8 5 2/8	5 7/8	M	Lynx Creek	ALB	Leonard Verbaas	2003	428
43 0/8	10 5/8 8 7/8	5 1/8 5 1/8	4 6/8	M		BC	Vic Clarkson	1960	437
43 0/8	10 0/8 10 0/8	4 4/8 4 4/8	6 2/8	F	Kittitas County	WA	Richard L. Thrasher	1968	437
43 0/8	10 1/8 10 2/8	3 7/8 3 7/8	8 0/8	F	Haines	AK	Roger O. Iveson	1972	437
43 0/8	9 0/8 9 0/8	5 1/8 5 1/8	5 2/8	M	Lemhi County	ID	Larry Nirk	1977	437
43 0/8	8 7/8 8 2/8	5 0/8 5 0/8	7 3/8	M	Lemhi County	ID	Gregory D. Dodson	1977	437
43 0/8	8 4/8 8 5/8	4 7/8 4 7/8	6 5/8	M	Mason County	WA	Andrew E. Appleby	1982	437
43 0/8	9 3/8 9 4/8	4 5/8 4 5/8	5 5/8	M	Custer County	ID	Larry A. Wilde	1983	437
43 0/8	8 0/8 8 1/8	5 0/8 5 1/8	6 6/8	M	Kittitas County	WA	Lance B. Cussons	1986	437
43 0/8	9 0/8 8 6/8	5 1/8 5 0/8	5 5/8	M	Keele River	NWT	Jim Ryan	1990	437
43 0/8	8 3/8 8 4/8	5 0/8 5 0/8	5 5/8	M	Border Lake	BC	Dean Stebner	1990	437
43 0/8	8 2/8 8 2/8	4 7/8 4 7/8	4 0/8	M	Pierce County	WA	Howard L. Harding	1990	437
43 0/8	8 1/8 8 1/8	5 1/8 5 1/8	5 4/8	M	Kittitas County	WA	John R. Sample	1991	437
43 0/8	8 2/8 8 4/8	5 1/8 5 1/8	4 4/8	M	Pierce County	WA	John DeWeber	1993	437
43 0/8	8 5/8 8 6/8	5 0/8 5 0/8	5 6/8	M	Gunnison County	CO	Kenneth Shelton	1994	437
43 0/8	8 7/8 8 7/8	4 7/8 4 7/8	5 1/8	M	Custer County	ID	Doug Hawker	1994	437
43 0/8	8 0/8 8 1/8	5 2/8 5 2/8	5 5/8	M	Devils Lake	BC	Daniel E. Laguerre	1999	437
43 0/8	8 7/8 8 6/8	5 0/8 5 0/8	5 7/8	M	Park County	CO	Paul St. John	2000	437
43 0/8	8 4/8 8 4/8	5 0/8 5 0/8	6 0/8	M	Bonneville County	ID	Michael L. Burbank	2002	437
43 0/8	8 3/8 9 3/8	5 0/8 4 7/8	5 4/8	M	Lemhi County	ID	Garry Kite	2003	437
*43 0/8	8 1/8 8 3/8	5 0/8 5 0/8	6 3/8	M	Cordova	AK	Tom Edgington	2010	437
42 6/8	9 7/8 9 7/8	4 3/8 4 3/8	7 6/8	F	Lake County	MT	Jack Whitney	1965	457
42 6/8	9 0/8 7 3/8	5 5/8 5 4/8	6 3/8	M	Chaffee County	CO	Duke Prentup	1979	457
42 6/8	8 2/8 8 7/8	5 0/8 5 0/8	6 0/8	M	Chaffee County	CO	Chuck Hutton	1979	457
42 6/8	9 7/8 9 7/8	4 0/8 4 0/8	9 2/8	F	Knik Glacier	AK	Gary G. Wall	1985	457
42 6/8	8 4/8 8 5/8	4 7/8 4 7/8	6 2/8	M	Jefferson County	WA	Kevin Boyle	1986	457
42 6/8	9 4/8 9 3/8	4 3/8 4 3/8	6 7/8	F	Park County	CO	Corey Clyncke	1989	457
42 6/8	8 5/8 8 6/8	5 0/8 5 0/8	6 7/8	M	Jefferson County	WA	Gary Worth	1989	457
42 6/8	8 6/8 8 0/8	5 0/8 5 0/8	5 3/8	M	Ravalli County	MT	Dwight Schuh	1990	457
42 6/8	8 4/8 8 0/8	5 1/8 5 1/8	6 2/8	M	Summit County	CO	Stan Rauch	1994	457
42 6/8	7 7/8 8 2/8	5 2/8 5 2/8	6 0/8	M	Powell County	MT	Bruce Davidson	1994	457
42 6/8	8 5/8 8 6/8	4 6/8 4 6/8	5 5/8	M	Lemhi County	ID	Russ Allyn	1997	457
42 6/8	8 3/8 8 3/8	4 6/8 4 6/8	5 4/8	M	Blaine County	ID	Thomas Daquino	1998	457
42 6/8	9 2/8 9 1/8	4 6/8 4 7/8	6 0/8	M	Major Hart River	BC	Robert G. Barden	1999	457
42 6/8	8 7/8 8 7/8	5 0/8 5 0/8	5 2/8	M	Sweet Grass County	MT	Curt Olson	2001	457
42 6/8	7 7/8 8 0/8	5 1/8 5 1/8	6 5/8	M	Terrace	BC	Jeff Fitts	2002	457
42 6/8	8 6/8 8 4/8	5 0/8 5 0/8	6 4/8	M	Teton County	WY	Randy G. Pickering	2003	457
42 6/8	9 0/8 9 0/8	4 6/8 4 6/8	6 1/8	M	Clear Creek County	CO	Mark Thomson	2003	457
42 6/8	9 5/8 9 6/8	4 2/8 4 2/8	7 3/8	F	Lake George	AK	Frank S. Noska IV	2003	457
42 6/8	8 4/8 8 3/8	5 0/8 5 0/8	4 6/8	M	Summit County	UT	Eldon Richter	2006	457

880

ROCKY MOUNTAIN GOAT

Minimum Score 40 — Continued

SCORE	R HORN L	R OF BASE L	GREATEST SPREAD	SEX	AREA	STATE/PROVINCE	HUNTER'S NAME	DATE	RANK
*42 6/8	8 3/8 8 2/8	5 1/8 5 1/8	5 6/8	M	San Juan County	CO	Kiviok Hight	2009	457
*42 6/8	8 6/8 8 6/8	4 6/8 4 6/8	6 0/8	M	Summit County	CO	Larry A. Welchlen	2010	457
42 6/8	8 1/8 8 1/8	5 0/8 5 0/8	5 7/8	M	Kodiak Island	AK	Frank S. Noska IV	2010	457
42 4/8	8 4/8 9 0/8	5 2/8 5 1/8	5 0/8	M	Chelan County	WA	G. H. Malinoski	1964	479
42 4/8	8 5/8 8 6/8	4 7/8 4 6/8	4 4/8	M	Goat Area 12	WA	James F. Miller	1977	479
42 4/8	8 5/8 8 6/8	4 6/8 4 6/8	5 4/8	M	Custer County	ID	Jim Wilson	1989	479
42 4/8	8 7/8 8 6/8	5 0/8 4 7/8	4 7/8	M	Custer County	ID	Kirk Westervelt	1989	479
42 4/8	8 7/8 9 2/8	5 0/8 4 7/8	6 7/8	M	Custer County	ID	David R. Anderson	1991	479
42 4/8	8 6/8 7 5/8	5 2/8 5 2/8	7 1/8	M	Park County	WY	Rob Marosok	1992	479
42 4/8	8 4/8 7 5/8	5 3/8 5 3/8	5 7/8	M	San Juan County	CO	Dennis L. Howell	1992	479
42 4/8	8 3/8 8 3/8	4 6/8 4 7/8	5 3/8	M	Howser Creek	BC	Alan Bressanutti	1992	479
42 4/8	8 2/8 8 0/8	5 0/8 5 1/8	6 4/8	M	Tatsamenie Lake	BC	Tom Close	1997	479
42 4/8	8 3/8 8 1/8	5 1/8 5 1/8	5 7/8	M	Eagle County	CO	Jim Willems	1999	479
42 4/8	8 3/8 8 4/8	5 0/8 5 0/8	5 7/8	M	Custer County	ID	C. R. Wenger	2002	479
42 4/8	8 6/8 8 6/8	4 7/8 4 7/8	5 7/8	M	La Plata County	CO	Travis Bryant	2004	479
42 4/8	9 0/8 8 7/8	4 7/8 4 7/8	6 4/8	M	Fort Nelson	BC	Kevin Dahm	2006	479
42 2/8	7 6/8 8 2/8	5 0/8 5 0/8	5 4/8	M	Kleena Kleene	BC	William P. Mastrangel	1956	492
42 2/8	8 5/8 9 0/8	4 7/8 4 7/8	5 7/8	M	Terminus Mtn.	BC	Paul P. Schafer	1976	492
42 2/8	10 3/8 10 4/8	4 0/8 4 0/8	9 2/8	F	Kenai Peninsula	AK	Gilbert M. W. Smith	1976	492
42 2/8	8 3/8 8 5/8	4 7/8 5 0/8	5 2/8	M	Snohomish County	WA	Eric A. Olson	1979	492
42 2/8	8 1/8 8 1/8	5 1/8 5 0/8	5 1/8	M	Snohomish County	WA	Thomas E. Tipton	1985	492
42 2/8	9 0/8 9 0/8	4 3/8 4 3/8	7 3/8	F	Inklin River	BC	Dean Stebner	1987	492
42 2/8	8 1/8 8 1/8	4 7/8 4 7/8	7 2/8	M	Turnagain Pass	AK	Craig E. Scarbrough	1988	492
42 2/8	7 6/8 7 6/8	5 1/8 5 0/8	5 3/8	M	Snohomish County	WA	Jim Cowgill	1988	492
42 2/8	8 4/8 8 4/8	4 7/8 4 6/8	5 6/8	M	Park County	CO	Marvin Clyncke	1989	492
42 2/8	8 3/8 8 2/8	4 7/8 5 0/8	6 3/8	M	Eastman Mtn.	BC	Ron Serwa	1990	492
42 2/8	7 4/8 8 1/8	5 0/8 5 0/8	5 2/8	M	Bralorne	BC	Larry Anderson	1992	492
42 2/8	8 0/8 8 0/8	5 2/8 5 0/8	5 7/8	M	Pierce County	WA	Steve Felbinger	1994	492
42 2/8	9 0/8 7 7/8	5 1/8 5 0/8	6 4/8	M	Madison County	MT	Rob Sturtz	1994	492
42 2/8	8 4/8 8 3/8	4 7/8 4 7/8	5 5/8	M	Custer County	ID	Doug Ramsey	1996	492
42 2/8	8 6/8 8 5/8	4 6/8 4 6/8	5 2/8	M	Custer County	ID	Boone Petersen	2000	492
42 2/8	8 3/8 8 3/8	5 0/8 5 0/8	6 3/8	M	Caribou Mtns.	BC	Roger Wintle	2002	492
42 2/8	8 2/8 8 7/8	4 7/8 5 0/8	5 1/8	M	Chilkat Range	AK	Ken Radach	2002	492
42 2/8	9 1/8 9 1/8	4 4/8 4 4/8	6 1/8	M	Park County	CO	Greg R. White	2003	492
*42 2/8	9 2/8 8 5/8	4 4/8 4 4/8	7 2/8	F	Chouteau County	MT	Don Moen	2005	492
*42 2/8	9 0/8 9 1/8	4 0/8 4 0/8	4 3/8	F	Triumph River	BC	Frank Staropoli	2007	492
*42 2/8	9 1/8 9 0/8	4 3/8 4 3/8	6 2/8	F	Elko County	NV	Ken Tavener	2008	492
*42 2/8	8 7/8 8 7/8	4 7/8 4 7/8	6 3/8	M	Paddy Creek	BC	Chris Hudson	2008	492
42 0/8	7 2/8 8 2/8	5 1/8 5 1/8	7 0/8	M	Taylor Lake	BC	Bill Brown	1957	514
42 0/8	8 4/8 8 5/8	5 0/8 5 0/8	5 7/8	F	Swan Range	MT	Jack Whitney	1960	514
42 0/8	8 4/8 8 4/8	4 5/8 4 5/8	6 1/8	M	Lemhi County	ID	Frank N. Hough	1968	514
42 0/8	8 4/8 8 5/8	4 6/8 4 6/8	5 3/8	M	Lewis & Clark County	MT	Don Davidson	1978	514
42 0/8	9 4/8 9 4/8	4 0/8 4 0/8	6 1/8	F	Snohomish County	WA	Joseph R. St. Charles	1980	514
42 0/8	9 6/8 9 6/8	4 2/8 4 2/8	6 3/8	F	Chouteau County	MT	Terry Albrecht	1981	514
42 0/8	9 3/8 9 3/8	4 3/8 4 3/8	4 6/8	F	Lewis County	WA	James Garner	1982	514
42 0/8	9 3/8 9 4/8	4 0/8 4 1/8	7 3/8	F	Todagin Mtn.	BC	Neil Summers	1985	514
42 0/8	8 5/8 8 7/8	5 0/8 4 7/8	6 2/8	M	Ware	BC	Tim Good	1986	514
42 0/8	8 3/8 8 2/8	4 7/8 5 0/8	5 4/8	M	Ravalli County	MT	Jon Cusker	1987	514
42 0/8	8 1/8 8 3/8	4 7/8 4 7/8	6 5/8	M	Park County	CO	Doug Rininger	1990	514
42 0/8	8 2/8 8 2/8	5 0/8 5 0/8	5 5/8	M	Beaverhead County	MT	Bryant Shermoe	1995	514
42 0/8	9 0/8 9 1/8	4 2/8 4 2/8	6 4/8	F	Okanogan County	WA	T. J. Conrads	1995	514
42 0/8	8 5/8 8 4/8	5 1/8 5 0/8	5 4/8	M	Chaffee County	CO	Dean Aggson	1998	514
42 0/8	8 1/8 8 1/8	4 7/8 5 0/8	5 3/8	M	Bonneville County	ID	Brian Frickey	1998	514
42 0/8	8 2/8 8 6/8	5 0/8 5 0/8	7 1/8	M	Gallatin County	MT	Rex Rogers	1999	514
42 0/8	8 4/8 8 4/8	4 6/8 4 6/8	5 7/8	M	San Juan County	CO	Lee Jernigan	2002	514
42 0/8	7 6/8 8 0/8	5 0/8 5 0/8	5 0/8	M	Thunder Mtn.	AK	David Benitz	2003	514
42 0/8	8 2/8 8 2/8	4 6/8 4 6/8	6 0/8	M	Skeena Mtns.	BC	Steff Stefanovich	2010	514
*42 0/8	9 5/8 10 1/8	4 1/8 4 1/8	7 2/8	M	Haines	AK	Marc Taylor	2010	514
41 6/8	8 1/8 8 0/8	4 7/8 4 7/8	6 3/8	F	Lord River	BC	Dr. R. Congdon	1958	534
41 6/8	8 1/8 8 1/8	4 7/8 4 6/8	5 6/8	M	Beaverhead County	MT	Mike Bartz	1976	534
41 6/8	9 1/8 9 1/8	4 3/8 4 3/8	5 3/8	F	Snohomish County	WA	Scott McDermott	1980	534
41 6/8	9 4/8 9 4/8	4 2/8 4 1/8	6 2/8	F	Snohomish County	WA	Steve Novy	1981	534
41 6/8	8 2/8 8 2/8	4 6/8 4 6/8	5 6/8	M	Jefferson County	WA	Richard Van Calcar	1983	534
41 6/8	7 6/8 7 5/8	4 7/8 4 7/8	5 5/8	M	Lawson Lake	BC	David Baldwin	1984	534
41 6/8	7 3/8 7 6/8	5 1/8 5 1/8	5 0/8	M	Snohomish County	WA	Jack Williams	1984	534
41 6/8	8 3/8 8 3/8	4 7/8 4 7/8	5 3/8	M	Jefferson County	WA	Steve Wyman	1984	534
41 6/8	8 6/8 8 7/8	4 6/8 4 6/8	5 5/8	M	La Plata County	CO	Sid Strzok	1986	534
41 6/8	8 3/8 8 3/8	4 7/8 4 6/8	6 2/8	M	Clear Creek County	CO	Tony Snow	1988	534
41 6/8	8 3/8 8 3/8	4 7/8 4 7/8	5 0/8	M	Chaffee County	CO	Doug Aiken	1992	534
41 6/8	8 0/8 8 7/8	5 0/8 5 0/8	5 7/8	M	Chaffee County	CO	Ron Sniff	1992	534
41 6/8	9 7/8 9 7/8	4 1/8 4 1/8	5 3/8	F	Madison County	MT	Kris Thorson	1992	534
41 6/8	8 0/8 8 3/8	4 6/8 4 6/8	6 3/8	M	Heart Mtn.	BC	Tim Walters	1993	534
41 6/8	8 2/8 8 2/8	4 7/8 4 7/8	5 0/8	M	La Plata County	CO	Chad R. Bedell	1993	534
41 6/8	8 6/8 8 4/8	5 0/8 4 7/8	5 4/8	M	Gunnison County	CO	DuWayne Langseth	1996	534
41 6/8	8 2/8 8 2/8	5 0/8 4 7/8	5 6/8	M	Clear Creek County	CO	Kevin Bertsch	1998	534
41 6/8	8 2/8 8 0/8	4 7/8 4 7/8	5 1/8	M	Chaffee County	CO	Dave Justmann	1998	534
41 6/8	7 5/8 8 0/8	5 2/8 5 2/8	5 3/8	M	Park County	MT	Sean Shea	1998	534
41 4/8	10 2/8 10 2/8	4 0/8 4 0/8	10 1/8	F	Takia River	BC	William L. Sullivan	1966	553
41 4/8	8 1/8 8 1/8	4 6/8 4 7/8	5 4/8	M	Summit County	CO	Wayne Depperschmidt	1979	553
41 4/8	9 5/8 9 6/8	3 6/8 3 5/8	7 2/8	F	Snohomish County	WA	Steve Wait	1981	553
41 4/8	9 3/8 9 1/8	4 1/8 4 1/8	7 1/8	F	Whatcom County	WA	Adam Redford	1981	553
41 4/8	9 4/8 9 4/8	4 2/8 4 2/8	10 0/8	F	Atlin Lake	BC	Ty Harpain	1989	553
41 4/8	8 2/8 8 2/8	4 7/8 5 0/8	6 0/8	M	La Plata County	CO	Dale Struble	1990	553
41 4/8	8 4/8 8 5/8	4 4/8 4 5/8	7 5/8	M	Prince William Sound	AK	John D. "Jack" Frost	1990	553
41 4/8	7 5/8 8 2/8	5 1/8 5 1/8	5 6/8	M	Clear Creek County	CO	Lonny Vanatta	1992	553
41 4/8	8 3/8 8 4/8	4 7/8 4 7/8	6 1/8	M	Clear Creek County	CO	Larry Bishop	1994	553
41 4/8	9 2/8 8 5/8	4 2/8 4 2/8	6 4/8	F	Chouteau County	MT	Donny Roy	1994	553
41 4/8	8 2/8 8 2/8	4 6/8 4 6/8	6 3/8	M	Island Lake	BC	Kevin D. Hatfield	1996	553
41 4/8	8 6/8 8 5/8	4 6/8 4 6/8	6 1/8	M	La Plata County	CO	Kurt C. Hall	1997	553
41 4/8	9 2/8 9 5/8	4 0/8 4 0/8	5 7/8	M	Ketchikan	AK	Aaron Barsamian	2000	553
41 4/8	9 4/8 9 3/8	4 0/8 4 0/8	8 2/8	F	Chugach Mtns.	AK	Vernon Sowers	2001	553
41 4/8	8 4/8 8 4/8	4 6/8 4 6/8	5 0/8	M	Custer County	ID	Scott A. McNeil	2002	553
41 4/8	9 2/8 9 3/8	4 2/8 4 3/8	6 3/8	F	Utah County	UT	Brayden Richmond	2003	553
41 4/8	9 0/8 9 0/8	4 3/8 4 4/8	6 5/8	M	Clear Creek County	CO	Otto Biasio	2004	553
*41 4/8	8 2/8 8 2/8	4 6/8 4 6/8	6 6/8	M	Clear Creek County	CO	Wayne E. Thurston	2005	553

881

ROCKY MOUNTAIN GOAT

Minimum Score 40 — Continued

SCORE	LENGTH OF R HORN	LENGTH OF L	CIRCUMFERENCE R OF BASE	CIRCUMFERENCE L	GREATEST SPREAD	SEX	AREA	STATE/ PROVINCE	HUNTER'S NAME	DATE	RANK
41 4/8	8 5/8	8 7/8	4 3/8	4 3/8	6 0/8	F	Hirsch Creek	BC	Mark Buehrer	2006	553
41 2/8	9 7/8	9 6/8	4 2/8	4 2/8	6 4/8	F	Crazy Mtns.	MT	Glenn Gibson	1957	572
41 2/8	8 3/8	8 3/8	4 3/8	4 3/8	5 1/8	F	Kittitas County	WA	Dennis Dunn	1973	572
41 2/8	8 3/8	8 3/8	4 6/8	4 6/8	5 3/8	M	Teton County	MT	Edwin Evans	1983	572
41 2/8	9 2/8	9 2/8	4 2/8	4 2/8	6 1/8	F	Rusty Creek	BC	Ronald Montross	1984	572
41 2/8	8 2/8	8 2/8	4 7/8	4 6/8	6 0/8	M	Pierce County	WA	Dale Holpainen	1986	572
41 2/8	9 3/8	9 3/8	3 7/8	3 7/8	8 1/8	F	Chugach Mtns.	AK	Richard Moran	1988	572
41 2/8	7 7/8	7 7/8	4 7/8	4 7/8	5 3/8	M	Snohomish County	WA	Dale Drilling	1988	572
41 2/8	8 4/8	8 4/8	4 6/8	4 5/8	6 0/8	M	Chaffee County	CO	Larick Spencer	1990	572
41 2/8	8 2/8	8 2/8	4 6/8	4 6/8	7 0/8	M	Otter Tail Creek	BC	Vaughn D. Ballard	1991	572
41 2/8	8 7/8	8 7/8	4 6/8	4 7/8	5 5/8	M	Chaffee County	CO	David C. Dahl	1992	572
41 2/8	8 3/8	8 3/8	4 6/8	4 6/8	5 6/8	M	Summit County	CO	Dominic Florian	1992	572
41 2/8	7 6/8	8 0/8	4 6/8	4 7/8	5 6/8	M	Bralorne	BC	Larry Anderson	1993	572
41 2/8	8 3/8	8 3/8	4 5/8	4 5/8	5 3/8	M	Custer County	ID	Jim Schrader	1996	572
41 2/8	7 6/8	7 6/8	4 7/8	4 7/8	6 4/8	M	Utah County	UT	Richie Bland	1998	572
41 2/8	7 5/8	7 5/8	4 7/8	5 0/8	6 0/8	M	Muskwa River	BC	Edwin L. DeYoung	2000	572
41 2/8	9 0/8	9 1/8	4 4/8	4 5/8	7 1/8	M	La Plata County	CO	Scot L. Hamilton	2002	572
41 2/8	8 4/8	8 4/8	4 5/8	4 6/8	6 4/8	M	Logan Mtns.	YUK	Michael D. Moore	2003	572
41 2/8	9 3/8	9 2/8	4 2/8	4 2/8	8 0/8	F	Cecil Rhode Mtn.	AK	Travis Derks	2009	572
41 0/8	8 6/8	8 5/8	4 2/8	4 2/8	7 0/8	M	Penticton	BC	Bill Brown	1958	590
41 0/8	8 7/8	9 0/8	4 4/8	4 4/8	5 5/8	F	Snohomish County	WA	Bud Peck	1960	590
41 0/8	10 0/8	10 0/8	3 6/8	3 7/8	6 2/8	F	Holly Creek	BC	Jim Jackson	1964	590
41 0/8	9 2/8	9 3/8	3 7/8	3 7/8	10 0/8	F	Valdez	AK	Jim Jarvis	1979	590
41 0/8	8 7/8	9 0/8	4 0/8	3 7/8	5 7/8	F	Snohomish County	WA	Mark S. Jacobs	1980	590
41 0/8	8 1/8	8 1/8	4 6/8	4 6/8	5 7/8	M	Clallam County	WA	Russ Spaulding	1981	590
41 0/8	8 1/8	7 4/8	4 7/8	4 7/8	6 4/8	M	Bennett Lake	BC	Dave Richardson	1982	590
41 0/8	9 1/8	9 1/8	4 0/8	4 0/8	6 1/8	F	Snohomish County	WA	Richard Kobel	1984	590
41 0/8	7 7/8	8 0/8	4 6/8	4 6/8	4 6/8	M	Bonner County	ID	Linda Leake	1984	590
41 0/8	9 0/8	9 2/8	4 2/8	4 3/8	4 4/8	F	Snohomish County	WA	Smokey Crews	1985	590
41 0/8	8 3/8	8 2/8	4 5/8	4 5/8	6 1/8	M	Park County	CO	Scott George	1990	590
41 0/8	9 5/8	9 3/8	4 2/8	4 2/8	6 4/8	F	Clear Creek County	CO	John Borlang	1991	590
41 0/8	7 2/8	7 2/8	5 0/8	5 0/8	5 2/8	M	Lake George	AK	Thomas A. Chadwick	1993	590
41 0/8	8 7/8	8 7/8	4 3/8	4 4/8	5 2/8	F	Cranbrook	BC	Stan Godfrey	1993	590
41 0/8	9 4/8	9 6/8	4 0/8	4 0/8	7 0/8	F	Beaverhead County	MT	Danny Moore	1996	590
41 0/8	8 1/8	8 3/8	4 6/8	4 7/8	5 0/8	M	Blaine County	ID	Randolph H. Flood	1999	590
41 0/8	8 6/8	7 2/8	5 1/8	5 1/8	6 1/8	M	Clear Creek County	CO	Cary Laman	2001	590
41 0/8	9 1/8	9 0/8	4 3/8	4 3/8	6 7/8	F	Grand County	CO	Matt Archuleta	2002	590
41 0/8	8 3/8	8 2/8	4 6/8	4 6/8	5 6/8	M	Lincoln County	MT	Ron Halvorson	2004	590
40 6/8	8 3/8	8 3/8	4 6/8	4 6/8	5 2/8	M	Boise County	ID	Ronald L. Sherer	1970	609
40 6/8	7 3/8	7 2/8	4 7/8	4 7/8	6 1/8	M	Kitchener Lake	BC	Walt Krom	1971	609
40 6/8	8 0/8	7 7/8	4 5/8	4 5/8	6 0/8	M	Kenai Lake	AK	Dennis Lattery	1973	609
40 6/8	8 6/8	8 5/8	4 6/8	4 6/8	5 5/8	M	Park County	WY	Jeff Umphlett	1979	609
40 6/8	9 1/8	9 1/8	4 1/8	4 1/8	5 4/8	F	Kittitas County	WA	Roger Pitman	1980	609
40 6/8	9 0/8	9 0/8	4 3/8	4 4/8	6 2/8	F	San Juan County	CO	Bill McEwen	1984	609
40 6/8	9 2/8	9 1/8	4 1/8	4 1/8	5 6/8	F	Kittitas County	WA	L. James Bailey	1984	609
40 6/8	8 1/8	8 5/8	4 4/8	4 5/8	6 3/8	M	Clallam County	WA	Dave Kanters	1988	609
40 6/8	9 0/8	8 7/8	4 2/8	4 2/8	6 6/8	F	Mt. Hunter	BC	Dennis Kamstra	1990	609
40 6/8	9 2/8	9 3/8	4 1/8	4 1/8	5 5/8	F	Clear Creek County	CO	Dave Culter	1990	609
40 6/8	8 2/8	8 2/8	4 6/8	4 7/8	5 2/8	M	Golden	BC	Jeffrey W. Murray	1992	609
40 6/8	8 4/8	8 6/8	4 4/8	4 4/8	6 3/8	M	Custer County	ID	Bruce Meyer	1993	609
40 6/8	7 7/8	7 7/8	4 6/8	4 7/8	6 5/8	M	Frog River	BC	David F. Perkin	1994	609
40 6/8	8 5/8	7 7/8	4 6/8	4 7/8	5 5/8	M	Custer County	ID	Don Glenn, Jr.	1994	609
40 6/8	9 5/8	10 0/8	3 6/8	3 7/8	6 1/8	F	Findlay Creek	BC	M. Rodney Denton	1995	609
40 6/8	9 0/8	8 0/8	4 6/8	4 6/8	6 0/8	F	Beaverhead County	MT	Poncho McCoy	1996	609
40 6/8	8 0/8	8 0/8	4 6/8	4 6/8	5 2/8	M	Madison County	MT	Eric Huff	1996	609
40 6/8	8 5/8	9 0/8	4 4/8	4 5/8	6 7/8	F	Clear Creek County	CO	Scott W. Meszaros	2005	609
40 6/8	7 7/8	7 5/8	4 7/8	4 6/8	5 6/8	M	Columbia Glacier	AK	Jesse Schowengerdt	2006	609
40 6/8	8 0/8	8 0/8	4 6/8	4 6/8	5 4/8	M	Turnagain River	BC	Dean Schober	2009	609
40 6/8	8 2/8	8 4/8	4 5/8	5 0/8	5 1/8	M	Gunnison County	CO	Shawn Kingery	2010	609
40 4/8	9 0/8	8 3/8	4 1/8	4 1/8	7 5/8	F	Little Johnstone Bay	AK	Ray Uhl	1965	630
40 4/8	8 7/8	8 6/8	4 1/8	4 1/8	6 4/8	F	Smithers	BC	Chris VanderHorst	1974	630
40 4/8	9 4/8	9 5/8	3 7/8	4 0/8	10 3/8	F	Kenai Mtn.	AK	David E. Smith	1976	630
40 4/8	8 6/8	8 4/8	4 2/8	4 2/8	4 7/8	F	Kittitas County	WA	Kirk Cresto	1981	630
40 4/8	7 3/8	8 4/8	5 0/8	5 0/8	6 6/8	M	Cordova	AK	Ray Ryan	1986	630
40 4/8	6 6/8	8 7/8	5 3/8	5 2/8	6 7/8	M	La Plata County	CO	John Gardner	1986	630
40 4/8	8 1/8	8 1/8	4 5/8	4 5/8	4 7/8	M	Snohomish County	WA	Gregg Welch	1987	630
40 4/8	8 4/8	8 4/8	4 2/8	4 2/8	6 7/8	F	Clear Creek County	CO	Reggie Spiegelberg	1991	630
40 4/8	9 2/8	9 0/8	4 2/8	4 2/8	5 0/8	F	San Juan County	CO	Rick Lundin	1999	630
40 4/8	9 1/8	9 1/8	4 1/8	4 1/8	6 5/8	M	Upper Toad River	BC	Michael L. Ritter	1999	630
40 4/8	8 7/8	8 6/8	4 2/8	4 2/8	6 0/8	F	La Plata County	CO	Robert Kampen	1999	630
40 4/8	9 2/8	9 3/8	4 2/8	4 2/8	6 2/8	F	Taku River	BC	Whitley Stephenson	2001	630
40 4/8	7 7/8	8 0/8	4 7/8	4 7/8	5 7/8	M	Mill Creek	AK	Frank Sanders	2004	630
40 4/8	8 5/8	8 6/8	4 5/8	4 5/8	5 6/8	M	Park County	MT	Dave Yeats	2008	630
40 2/8	7 6/8	7 3/8	4 5/8	4 5/8	5 5/8	M	Boise County	ID	Jack Arbaugh	1975	644
40 2/8	8 5/8	8 4/8	4 0/8	4 0/8	5 7/8	F	Kittitas County	WA	Bob McClure	1977	644
40 2/8	7 2/8	7 2/8	4 5/8	4 5/8	5 3/8	M	Tustemena Glacier	AK	Lloyd M. Minerich	1988	644
40 2/8	9 0/8	8 7/8	4 1/8	4 1/8	6 0/8	F	Clear Creek County	CO	Wes Heiland	1991	644
40 2/8	8 0/8	8 1/8	4 5/8	4 5/8	5 6/8	M	Clear Creek County	CO	Thomas J. Hoffman	1991	644
40 2/8	8 5/8	8 7/8	4 1/8	4 1/8	5 7/8	F	Revelstoke	BC	Rick A. Albers	1995	644
40 2/8	7 4/8	8 7/8	4 6/8	4 7/8	7 0/8	M	Gallatin County	MT	Jerry Karsky	1995	644
40 2/8	6 7/8	8 0/8	4 7/8	5 0/8	7 0/8	M	Firvale	BC	Rick Paquette	1998	644
40 2/8	9 2/8	9 2/8	4 2/8	4 2/8	7 3/8	F	Idaho County	ID	Brian Holbrook	2000	644
40 2/8	9 4/8	9 3/8	4 1/8	4 1/8	5 0/8	F	Blaine County	ID	Larry Hoff	2005	644
40 0/8	8 7/8	8 7/8	4 2/8	4 2/8	6 6/8	F	Chaffee County	CO	Wayne Spencer	1973	654
40 0/8	8 3/8	8 2/8	4 5/8	4 6/8	6 1/8	M	Lemhi County	ID	Marvin Tye	1973	654
40 0/8	8 3/8	8 3/8	4 1/8	4 1/8	5 1/8	F	Snohomish County	WA	Albert A. Rinaldi, Jr.	1974	654
40 0/8	7 5/8	7 5/8	4 6/8	4 6/8	5 0/8	M	Cordova	AK	Ray P. Noregaard	1975	654
40 0/8	9 1/8	9 0/8	4 1/8	4 1/8	6 7/8	F	Kitchener Lake	BC	John Dmytryka	1976	654
40 0/8	9 4/8	9 2/8	4 2/8	4 2/8	7 5/8	F	Cimari Valley	ID	Robert Frank	1976	654
40 0/8	8 3/8	8 2/8	4 5/8	4 5/8	4 7/8	M	Lemhi County	ID	H. R. 'Rusty' Neely	1976	654
40 0/8	8 5/8	8 5/8	4 3/8	4 2/8	6 1/8	F	Summit County	CO	Michael Beckwith	1978	654
40 0/8	8 7/8	8 5/8	4 1/8	4 1/8	5 5/8	F	Kittitas County	WA	Wilton Viall	1984	654
40 0/8	9 3/8	9 2/8	4 1/8	4 1/8	6 0/8	F	La Plata County	CO	Daniel Willems	1988	654
40 0/8	9 0/8	8 7/8	4 1/8	4 2/8	6 4/8	F	Bonneville County	ID	Tab R. Mendenhall	1989	654
40 0/8	7 5/8	7 6/8	4 6/8	4 6/8	6 3/8	M	Clear Creek County	CO	Monty Ace Morgan	1990	654

ROCKY MOUNTAIN GOAT

Minimum Score 40 — Continued

SCORE	LENGTH OF R HORN L	CIRCUMFERENCE R OF BASE L	GREATEST SPREAD	SEX	AREA	STATE/ PROVINCE	HUNTER'S NAME	DATE	RANK
40 0/8	8 7/8 9 0/8	3 6/8 3 6/8	7 0/8	F	Kynck Inlet	BC	Steve Schmid	1990	654
40 0/8	8 7/8 9 2/8	4 1/8 4 1/8	6 4/8	F	La Plata County	CO	Tony Casagrande	1992	654
40 0/8	7 4/8 7 4/8	4 6/8 4 6/8	5 5/8	M	Salt Lake County	UT	Gary Brewer	1992	654
40 0/8	7 0/8 6 0/8	4 7/8 4 7/8	5 3/8	M	Custer County	ID	Duane Zemliska	1992	654
40 0/8	8 4/8 8 3/8	4 4/8 4 4/8	5 0/8	M	Flathead County	MT	Eric Kress	1993	654
40 0/8	8 0/8 8 0/8	4 6/8 4 5/8	5 5/8	M	Quarry Creek	BC	Archie J. Nesbitt	1997	654
40 0/8	9 3/8 9 5/8	4 1/8 4 2/8	7 2/8	F	Clear Creek County	CO	David L. Skiff	1999	654
40 0/8	7 7/8 8 0/8	4 5/8 4 5/8	4 4/8	M	Pennington County	SD	Barb Galligher	2002	654
*40 0/8	9 0/8 9 0/8	4 1/8 4 1/8	7 3/8	F	La Plata County	CO	John C. Beckett	2008	654
40 0/8	9 2/8 9 3/8	4 0/8 4 1/8	6 5/8	F	La Plata County	CO	Todd A. Brickel	2008	654
*40 0/8	8 0/8 8 3/8	4 4/8 4 5/8	8 0/8	M	San Juan County	CO	Justin Dufva	2009	654

WORLD RECORD BIGHORN SHEEP
Score: 199 5/8
Location: Whitehorse River, Alberta
Date: 1998
Hunter: Todd Kirk

BIGHORN SHEEP

Minimum Score 140 *Ovis canadensis canadensis* and certain related subspecies

SCORE	LENGTH OF R HORN L	CIRCUMFERENCE R OF BASE L	GREATEST SPREAD	AREA	STATE/ PROVINCE	HUNTER'S NAME	DATE	RANK
199 5/8	40 7/8 41 0/8	16 4/8 16 6/8	25 4/8	Whitehorse River	ALB	Todd Kirk	1998	1
199 0/8	41 2/8 40 4/8	17 5/8 17 3/8	25 0/8	Fergus County	MT	Robert E. Seelye	2004	2
*198 0/8	42 0/8 41 6/8	15 7/8 15 7/8	24 0/8	Chouteau County	MT	James J. Liautaud	2010	3
*193 4/8	39 0/8 40 2/8	15 5/8 15 4/8	22 6/8	Fergus County	MT	Don Moen	2010	4
193 2/8	40 2/8 43 4/8	16 5/8 16 3/8	23 2/8	Fergus County	MT	Kennie Williams	2006	5
193 2/8	41 3/8 41 7/8	16 2/8 16 2/8	24 4/8	Ravalli County	MT	Larry Lee	2007	5
191 3/8	42 3/8 42 2/8	15 5/8 15 4/8	24 0/8	El Paso County	CO	Gene Moore	1983	7
191 0/8	41 1/8 39 3/8	16 0/8 16 0/8	24 5/8	Deer Lodge County	MT	Brian A. Solan	2009	8
190 6/8	40 4/8 40 0/8	16 0/8 15 7/8	22 3/8	Granite County	MT	Paul Hutchinson	2007	9
190 3/8	40 3/8 39 6/8	15 7/8 16 2/8	22 7/8	Asotin County	WA	George H. Pidgeon	2009	10
190 2/8	39 4/8 39 4/8	16 4/8 16 3/8	20 4/8	Canmore	ALB	Brian Eloschuk	1982	11
190 0/8	38 7/8 39 7/8	16 2/8 16 1/8	23 7/8	Granite County	MT	Richard King	2001	12
189 4/8	43 0/8 43 0/8	14 2/8 14 2/8	21 6/8	Mora County	NM	Matthew Liljenquist	2003	13
189 2/8	36 5/8 37 1/8	15 6/8 15 6/8	26 2/8	Fergus County	MT	George Harms	1998	14
188 4/8	38 6/8 39 6/8	16 0/8 16 1/8	13 0/8	Fergus County	MT	Jerry Knerr	2006	15
*188 1/8	39 7/8 39 6/8	15 7/8 15 7/8	21 5/8	Ravalli County	MT	Gerald Linneweh	2008	16
187 6/8	38 6/8 36 6/8	16 5/8 16 4/8	22 0/8	El Paso County	CO	Steve Behunin	2000	17
187 1/8	40 2/8 39 1/8	15 5/8 15 4/8	23 0/8	Sanders County	MT	Rex Rogers	2000	18
186 5/8	38 5/8 39 4/8	15 4/8 15 5/8	21 4/8	Granite County	MT	Dave Yeats	1999	19
186 1/8	38 2/8 37 1/8	15 5/8 15 3/8	20 7/8	Canmore	ALB	Cornel Yarmoloy	1982	20
186 1/8	35 3/8 39 0/8	16 6/8 16 6/8	22 6/8	Missoula County	MT	Will R. Schott	2006	20
185 4/8	39 2/8 39 4/8	15 3/8 15 4/8	22 7/8	Deer Lodge County	MT	Kevin Davis	2009	22
*185 3/8	39 6/8 41 1/8	14 6/8 15 0/8	22 1/8	Teton County	MT	Waylon Janousek	2006	23
185 1/8	36 4/8 37 3/8	16 3/8 16 4/8	25 0/8	Las Animas County	CO	Kris Asbell	2008	24
184 6/8	39 1/8 37 5/8	16 5/8 16 5/8	20 2/8	Ravalli County	MT	Bill A. Richichi	1996	25
184 5/8	41 1/8 44 0/8	14 0/8 13 6/8	22 2/8	Taos County	NM	Perry D. Harper	1999	26
184 5/8	36 0/8 38 3/8	16 0/8 16 1/8	25 1/8	Blaine County	MT	Danny Moore	2008	26
184 1/8	38 4/8 38 7/8	15 5/8 15 5/8	21 1/8	Pigeon Mtn.	ALB	Guy Woods	1985	28
184 0/8	39 1/8 37 7/8	15 3/8 15 1/8	20 2/8	Canmore	ALB	Al Schroeder	1989	29
184 0/8	38 6/8 37 4/8	15 7/8 15 5/8	23 7/8	Blaine County	MT	Jim Forman	1999	29
183 7/8	38 3/8 38 6/8	15 4/8 15 5/8	24 5/8	Deer Lodge County	MT	Jerry Parsons	1986	31
183 7/8	36 6/8 37 1/8	15 0/8 15 0/8	22 0/8	Clear Creek County	CO	Ray Alt	1988	31
183 4/8	40 3/8 41 1/8	15 5/8 15 6/8	23 3/8	Lincoln County	MT	Paul Schafer	1983	33
183 4/8	38 4/8 39 0/8	16 1/8 16 0/8	19 6/8	Ravalli County	MT	Jim Chinn	1986	33
183 2/8	40 4/8 39 2/8	14 7/8 14 7/8	21 6/8	El Paso County	CO	Bob Renner	1979	35
183 2/8	37 4/8 36 2/8	16 3/8 16 3/8	24 1/8	Larimer County	CO	Jim Black	1992	35
182 7/8	38 2/8 38 5/8	15 3/8 15 3/8	22 6/8	El Paso County	CO	Fred Church	1989	37
182 6/8	35 3/8 35 3/8	16 3/8 16 3/8	21 6/8	El Paso County	CO	Cotty Hayes	2004	38
182 6/8	35 6/8 36 2/8	15 5/8 15 5/8	21 2/8	Ravalli County	MT	Chris R. Troupe	2005	38
182 6/8	37 1/8 37 1/8	17 4/8 17 4/8	21 4/8	Sanders County	MT	Bernard J. Stender, Jr.	2006	38
182 2/8	36 0/8 36 0/8	15 7/8 15 7/8	23 2/8	Blaine County	MT	Gary Troester	2005	41
182 0/8	39 6/8 39 6/8	15 0/8 15 0/8	22 4/8	Sanders County	MT	John T. Beyer	1990	42
181 5/8	38 1/8 34 4/8	16 2/8 16 2/8	23 0/8	Canmore	ALB	Paul Inzanti	1984	43
181 4/8	35 4/8 35 4/8	15 5/8 15 5/8	25 0/8	Las Animas County	CO	Eric Bruton	2003	44
181 1/8	38 1/8 39 0/8	14 3/8 14 3/8	21 6/8	Clear Creek County	CO	Gary Renfro	1982	45
181 1/8	39 2/8 38 5/8	14 6/8 14 7/8	20 5/8	Teton County	MT	Neil Hamm	2001	45
181 1/8	36 3/8 39 4/8	15 2/8 15 3/8	22 7/8	Elko County	NV	Dan Klebenow	2005	45
*181 1/8	37 7/8 37 0/8	14 5/8 14 5/8	23 4/8	El Paso County	CO	Jerry J. Wilson	2007	45
181 0/8	36 6/8 38 0/8	15 2/8 15 3/8	21 3/8	Granite County	MT	Bob Ehle	1999	49
181 0/8	38 0/8 37 6/8	14 5/8 14 5/8	23 4/8	Las Animas County	CO	Stacey Greathouse	2009	49
180 7/8	37 3/8 38 4/8	15 4/8 15 4/8	22 1/8	Granite County	MT	Alden Gregory Beard	1992	51
*180 7/8	35 2/8 35 5/8	16 0/8 16 0/8	20 2/8	Mt. Allen	ALB	Les Wall	2007	51
*180 6/8	41 0/8 38 4/8	15 3/8 15 2/8	22 5/8	Ravalli County	MT	Steve Davis	2006	53
180 3/8	37 6/8 36 5/8	15 2/8 15 2/8	19 5/8	San Miguel County	NM	Ronald D. Rod	1992	54
180 1/8	37 4/8 37 3/8	15 2/8 15 2/8	22 7/8	Clear Creek County	CO	Charles W. Hanawalt	1990	55
180 1/8	40 5/8 39 2/8	15 5/8 15 5/8	23 7/8	Blaine County	MT	Mike Montgomery	1995	55
179 7/8	35 7/8 34 2/8	15 4/8 15 2/8	21 4/8	Huerfano County	CO	Dennis Gardner	1996	57
179 6/8	38 6/8 38 6/8	15 2/8 15 4/8	21 0/8	Exshaw Creek	ALB	Kenneth F. Bills	1993	58
179 5/8	39 4/8 38 3/8	14 4/8 14 2/8	22 1/8	El Paso County	CO	Doy K. Curtis	1977	59
179 4/8	39 3/8 37 5/8	14 5/8 14 5/8	21 6/8	Fergus County	MT	Stan Colton	2006	60
*179 4/8	41 2/8 37 4/8	14 0/8 14 0/8	23 2/8	Blaine County	MT	Jacob Dahl	2008	60
179 3/8	38 1/8 37 4/8	15 7/8 15 7/8	21 0/8	Mineral County	MT	Craig Thomas	1985	62
179 2/8	37 6/8 37 4/8	14 4/8 14 3/8	21 6/8	El Paso County	CO	Thomas H. States	1982	63
179 1/8	38 1/8 36 4/8	15 0/8 15 1/8	22 1/8	Larimer County	CO	Joe Bradley	2006	64
179 1/8	37 1/8 37 6/8	14 6/8 14 7/8	20 2/8	Ravalli County	MT	Charlie Johnson	2007	64
178 6/8	35 2/8 35 0/8	16 3/8 16 3/8	19 6/8	Mt. Livingston	ALB	Jim Smetaniuk	1982	66
178 5/8	38 4/8 37 5/8	15 4/8 15 3/8	23 0/8	Park County	MT	Mike Mahlman	1983	67
178 4/8	34 6/8 37 2/8	15 6/8 15 3/8	24 2/8	Las Animas County	CO	Shawn Greathouse	2005	68
178 1/8	36 6/8 40 5/8	14 6/8 14 6/8	20 5/8	Ravalli County	MT	Brandon Carpenter	2009	69
178 0/8	36 3/8 35 3/8	15 5/8 16 0/8	19 7/8	Greenlee County	AZ	Jim Machac	1994	70
177 7/8	34 6/8 34 1/8	16 2/8 16 4/8	22 0/8	Fergus County	MT	Rob Lucas	1988	71
177 7/8	38 5/8 38 0/8	14 5/8 14 5/8	25 0/8	El Paso County	CO	Gene Moore	1999	71
177 6/8	34 6/8 36 0/8	15 6/8 15 6/8	25 1/8	El Paso County	CO	John Diedrich	1990	73
177 3/8	37 0/8 37 3/8	16 5/8 16 7/8	22 5/8	Garfield County	WA	Kevin A. Hudson	2008	74
177 2/8	32 5/8 34 3/8	15 3/8 15 3/8	22 3/8	Larimer County	CO	Mark Montgomery	1992	75
177 2/8	39 3/8 37 1/8	14 4/8 14 4/8	23 2/8	Granite County	MT	Neil L. Jacobson	1998	75
177 1/8	36 1/8 38 0/8	15 2/8 15 2/8	22 0/8	Larimer County	CO	Randy Ries	2008	77
177 0/8	36 6/8 35 4/8	15 3/8 15 3/8	20 0/8	Powell County	MT	Jerry D. McPherson	1998	78
177 0/8	39 6/8 35 4/8	15 5/8 15 5/8	23 6/8	Fergus County	MT	Chris G. Sanford	2002	78
176 7/8	38 3/8 36 2/8	14 4/8 14 6/8	21 3/8	El Paso County	CO	Brian Nicely	1996	80
176 4/8	37 1/8 37 1/8	14 7/8 14 6/8	23 1/8	Huerfano County	CO	Brett M. Wyka	2003	81
176 3/8	37 3/8 39 0/8	14 6/8 14 4/8	22 0/8	Sweet Grass County	MT	Ray Alt	1968	82
176 2/8	37 2/8 38 0/8	14 4/8 14 3/8	22 1/8	Clear Creek County	CO	Dominic Florian	1989	83
176 1/8	35 3/8 37 4/8	15 4/8 15 3/8	24 4/8	El Paso County	CO	Tony Seahorn	1977	84
176 1/8	39 4/8 38 1/8	14 7/8 15 2/8	22 2/8	Phillips County	MT	Ty Milne	1991	84
176 1/8	38 0/8 39 7/8	15 0/8 15 1/8	19 6/8	Rio Arriba County	NM	Kevin L. Reid	1994	84
176 1/8	37 1/8 37 0/8	15 1/8 15 1/8	19 6/8	Nordegg	ALB	Scott Cragg	1994	84
176 0/8	35 2/8 36 2/8	15 2/8 15 2/8	23 5/8	El Paso County	CO	Gary Eastwood	1982	88
175 6/8	36 5/8 38 6/8	14 4/8 14 5/8	21 4/8	Canmore	ALB	James Pike	1998	89
175 5/8	35 3/8 37 2/8	15 3/8 15 4/8	21 5/8	Utah County	UT	Willie Watterson	2007	90
175 4/8	40 4/8 37 2/8	14 3/8 14 1/8	20 1/8	Ravalli County	MT	Tony Casagrande	2003	91
175 2/8	35 2/8 33 0/8	15 2/8 15 2/8	25 2/8	Lake County	OR	Stephen Herrera	1989	92
175 1/8	39 5/8 39 6/8	15 2/8 15 2/8	19 4/8	Canmore	ALB	Dave Addie	1985	93
175 1/8	37 5/8 36 0/8	15 5/8 15 4/8	20 6/8	Granite County	MT	John Starcevich	2005	93
*175 1/8	37 2/8 38 3/8	14 7/8 14 6/8	21 2/8	Valley County	ID	Kenneth Cain	2009	93

885

BIGHORN SHEEP

Minimum Score 140 Continued

SCORE	LENGTH OF R HORN L	CIRCUMFERENCE R OF BASE L	GREATEST SPREAD	AREA	STATE/ PROVINCE	HUNTER'S NAME	DATE	RANK
175 1/8	37 0/8 37 5/8	14 2/8 14 1/8	22 1/8	South Thompson River	BC	Richard A. Smith	2009	93
174 7/8	40 3/8 34 4/8	14 3/8 14 3/8	24 0/8	El Paso County	CO	Robert Reed	1993	97
174 2/8	35 6/8 36 0/8	14 2/8 14 2/8	19 6/8	Saguache County	CO	David "Jake" Powell	1995	98
174 1/8	38 1/8 37 6/8	15 1/8 15 2/8	21 5/8	Canmore	ALB	Todd Zeuske	1993	99
174 1/8	35 4/8 35 3/8	15 7/8 15 7/8	22 0/8	Clear Creek County	CO	Larry C. Baker	1998	99
174 0/8	35 2/8 35 4/8	16 0/8 16 2/8	21 3/8	Wind Ridge	ALB	Dirk Kieft	1984	101
173 7/8	35 1/8 37 0/8	15 1/8 15 3/8	20 7/8	Sanders County	MT	Bart Schleyer	1987	102
173 7/8	37 1/8 37 4/8	14 6/8 14 6/8	21 7/8	Clear Creek County	CO	Dan Teets	1998	102
173 7/8	34 6/8 34 1/8	15 0/8 15 0/8	22 2/8	Saguache County	CO	Mike Coleman	2003	102
173 7/8	35 1/8 36 0/8	14 7/8 14 7/8	18 7/8	Pigeon Mtn.	ALB	Mike Larson	2007	102
173 6/8	32 6/8 34 0/8	16 1/8 16 1/8	19 1/8	Canmore	ALB	Michael Ukrainetz	1983	106
173 6/8	39 0/8 35 0/8	14 4/8 14 4/8	20 0/8	Fergus County	MT	Charles Hueth	1996	106
173 6/8	36 5/8 36 5/8	15 2/8 15 1/8	22 0/8	Fergus County	MT	Kim Latterell	1998	106
173 5/8	34 4/8 35 5/8	14 4/8 14 3/8	21 7/8	Clear Creek County	CO	Ronald Rockwell	1995	109
173 4/8	38 0/8 38 0/8	15 0/8 15 0/8	23 5/8	Cougar Canyon	ALB	Curt Lynn	1983	110
173 1/8	36 5/8 38 2/8	14 4/8 14 4/8	22 4/8	Canmore	ALB	Camp Newton	2005	111
172 7/8	36 0/8 35 5/8	13 6/8 13 7/8	21 4/8	Boulder County	CO	Scott George	1995	112
172 6/8	35 6/8 36 4/8	14 3/8 14 3/8	22 0/8	El Paso County	CO	Duane Imhoff	1982	113
172 6/8	37 5/8 33 7/8	14 3/8 14 2/8	20 3/8	Ravalli County	MT	Barbara Challoner	2002	113
*172 4/8	35 3/8 34 3/8	15 0/8 15 1/8	20 3/8	Canmore	ALB	Todd Puzey	2006	115
172 2/8	34 2/8 36 0/8	14 6/8 14 6/8	20 4/8	Nordegg	ALB	Gerard Stark	1994	116
*172 2/8	34 0/8 34 6/8	15 4/8 15 5/8	21 3/8	Gallatin County	MT	Cory L. Payment	2009	116
172 1/8	35 7/8 35 0/8	14 4/8 14 4/8	21 4/8	Clear Creek County	CO	Jim Fitzgerald	1998	118
171 7/8	38 3/8 35 2/8	14 5/8 14 5/8	22 0/8	Canmore	ALB	Chuck Adams	1985	119
171 7/8	37 1/8 37 2/8	15 4/8 15 3/8	22 2/8	Canmore	ALB	Merlyn Howg	1990	119
171 6/8	34 6/8 33 4/8	15 3/8 15 2/8	21 4/8	Clear Creek County	CO	Lonny Vanatta	1988	121
171 6/8	36 5/8 38 3/8	14 6/8 15 1/8	23 0/8	Silver Bow County	MT	Brandon McGillvray	2003	121
171 6/8	33 4/8 32 0/8	16 1/8 16 0/8	23 0/8	Fremont County	CO	Frank S. Noska IV	2005	121
171 5/8	35 4/8 34 5/8	15 3/8 15 3/8	21 4/8	Granite County	MT	Marlon Clapham	1994	124
171 5/8	34 1/8 35 2/8	15 4/8 15 4/8	21 4/8	Huerfano County	CO	Richard A. Devrous, Jr.	2007	124
171 4/8	34 5/8 34 5/8	15 7/8 15 7/8	22 1/8	Gunnison County	CO	Mark Berens	2009	126
171 3/8	35 4/8 36 1/8	14 6/8 14 6/8	23 1/8	Las Animas County	CO	Vic Lauer	2006	127
171 3/8	35 7/8 35 4/8	14 6/8 14 7/8	22 4/8	Ravalli County	MT	Veto J. LaSalle	2007	127
*171 0/8	35 4/8 36 2/8	14 4/8 14 4/8	18 2/8	Deadman Flats	ALB	Greg Sutley	2006	129
170 7/8	37 2/8 37 1/8	14 6/8 14 6/8	21 1/8	Mora County	NM	Dave McInroy	1991	130
170 7/8	34 2/8 37 5/8	14 1/8 14 2/8	21 2/8	Greenlee County	AZ	Patrick Kirby	1996	130
170 6/8	36 4/8 37 6/8	14 5/8 14 7/8	20 1/8	Canmore	ALB	Louis A. Onorato	2008	132
170 5/8	33 3/8 33 4/8	14 1/8 14 1/8	21 0/8	Clear Creek County	CO	Robert L Syvertson,Jr	1989	133
170 5/8	36 1/8 37 2/8	14 3/8 14 4/8	21 5/8	Beaverhead County	MT	Jerry Allen	1991	133
170 5/8	32 0/8 37 1/8	14 7/8 14 7/8	22 4/8	El Paso County	CO	Tom Behunin	1999	133
170 5/8	34 6/8 34 7/8	15 5/8 15 5/8	22 2/8	Canmore	ALB	Leonard Verbaas	2003	133
170 2/8	38 2/8 34 2/8	14 7/8 14 7/8	22 3/8	Park County	CO	Peter J. Dart	1999	137
170 0/8	35 6/8 36 2/8	14 2/8 14 3/8	22 2/8	Clear Creek County	CO	Troy Cunningham	1988	138
169 7/8	32 2/8 38 3/8	14 5/8 14 7/8	22 4/8	Fergus County	MT	Terry L. Selph	1990	139
169 7/8	37 2/8 36 1/8	13 2/8 13 1/8	19 0/8	San Miguel County	NM	Mark Mariani	2002	139
169 6/8	35 2/8 34 6/8	14 4/8 14 4/8	23 0/8	Clear Creek County	CO	Janet George	1989	141
169 6/8	37 6/8 31 4/8	15 0/8 15 0/8	21 6/8	El Paso County	CO	Christopher Roe	2003	141
169 2/8	33 2/8 33 6/8	14 5/8 14 6/8	21 4/8	Clear Creek County	CO	Barry J. Smith	1992	143
169 0/8	33 2/8 35 2/8	14 3/8 14 2/8	20 2/8	Cougar Canyon	ALB	Paul Schwengler	1980	144
169 0/8	34 0/8 35 2/8	15 6/8 15 7/8	21 6/8	Canmore	ALB	Dave Gerber	1989	144
169 0/8	36 2/8 36 6/8	14 0/8 14 0/8	22 0/8	Las Animas County	CO	Lonny Stuht	1994	144
168 7/8	37 0/8 36 1/8	16 0/8 16 1/8	29 4/8	Chouteau County	MT	Mark L. Gilkey	1990	147
168 7/8	32 1/8 33 0/8	15 3/8 15 4/8	21 3/8	Eagle County	CO	Rex Crawford	1999	147
168 6/8	34 7/8 34 3/8	14 2/8 14 2/8	20 0/8	Larimer County	CO	Richard Marshburn	1995	149
168 6/8	34 6/8 34 2/8	14 7/8 15 1/8	20 3/8	Graham County	AZ	Kevin McCall	2002	149
168 4/8	34 2/8 35 0/8	13 3/8 13 3/8	20 4/8	Clear Creek County	CO	Rick Karbowski	2010	151
168 2/8	35 5/8 35 1/8	15 0/8 15 0/8	22 1/8	Sublette County	WY	Paul Crittenden	2000	152
168 2/8	32 0/8 35 2/8	14 3/8 14 3/8	21 6/8	Clear Creek County	CO	Mark Turner	2002	152
168 1/8	32 2/8 32 7/8	15 0/8 14 7/8	20 5/8	Saguache County	CO	Simon Aragi	1990	154
168 1/8	33 6/8 36 3/8	14 7/8 14 5/8	22 2/8	Graham County	AZ	Mark D. Morris	2008	154
168 0/8	33 6/8 33 6/8	15 1/8 15 0/8	20 6/8	Custer County	CO	Jennings Cress	1977	156
168 0/8	33 2/8 34 2/8	14 5/8 14 6/8	22 4/8	Conejos County	CO	James B. Mense	1999	156
167 6/8	36 3/8 36 1/8	14 6/8 14 6/8	21 1/8	N. Saskatchewan River	ALB	Larry Jones	1962	158
167 6/8	34 4/8 35 0/8	15 4/8 15 4/8	22 2/8	Sanders County	MT	Robert L. Borden	1983	158
167 6/8	32 3/8 35 1/8	14 7/8 15 0/8	20 0/8	Canmore	ALB	Ken Madsen	1984	158
167 6/8	35 1/8 32 3/8	14 4/8 14 4/8	20 5/8	Idaho County	ID	Bill Fisk	1991	158
167 6/8	33 4/8 33 6/8	15 0/8 15 1/8	23 0/8	Deer Lodge County	MT	Todd Mohr	2003	158
167 4/8	31 4/8 32 0/8	15 4/8 15 3/8	22 2/8	Clear Creek County	CO	Reggie Spiegelberg	1988	163
167 4/8	33 3/8 35 7/8	14 6/8 14 6/8	19 0/8	Fremont County	WY	Mike Thompson	1999	163
167 4/8	36 4/8 35 6/8	14 5/8 14 3/8	19 7/8	Canmore	ALB	Ken Vorisek	1999	163
167 3/8	33 4/8 35 3/8	15 2/8 15 2/8	21 6/8	Canmore	ALB	Gregory Koehl	1989	166
167 2/8	36 1/8 32 5/8	15 3/8 15 4/8	23 3/8	Greenlee County	AZ	John C. McClendon	1992	167
167 2/8	33 0/8 34 4/8	14 1/8 14 1/8	23 3/8	Fergus County	MT	Jim G. Winjum	1998	167
167 2/8	32 5/8 32 5/8	15 5/8 15 5/8	24 2/8	Clear Creek County	CO	Paul M. Martin	2001	167
167 1/8	34 1/8 34 4/8	14 2/8 14 5/8	22 4/8	Lincoln County	MT	Ron Bain	1974	170
167 1/8	38 5/8 32 4/8	15 4/8 15 6/8	19 0/8	Blaine County	MT	Ed Evans	1990	170
166 7/8	31 5/8 34 7/8	14 7/8 14 6/8	21 5/8	Clear Creek County	CO	Thomas J. Hoffman	1986	172
166 7/8	36 2/8 33 5/8	14 2/8 14 2/8	22 0/8	Las Animas County	CO	Mike Anderegg	2008	172
166 6/8	31 4/8 31 5/8	14 6/8 14 6/8	24 4/8	Lake County	OR	Scott Whittier	2009	172
166 6/8	34 7/8 34 7/8	15 3/8 15 3/8	22 6/8	Grant County	NM	Eudane Vicenti	1998	175
166 5/8	33 5/8 33 6/8	15 4/8 15 4/8	21 6/8	Canmore	ALB	Mike Traub	1988	176
166 5/8	35 4/8 32 7/8	15 5/8 15 5/8	20 7/8	Sanders County	MT	Kurt D. Fisher	2002	176
166 4/8	32 4/8 32 6/8	14 4/8 14 3/8	22 3/8	Clear Creek County	CO	Regina Cunningham	2003	178
166 2/8	32 6/8 36 2/8	14 6/8 14 6/8	20 7/8	County of Bighorn	ALB	Jeff B. Davis	1991	179
166 2/8	33 0/8 31 4/8	14 0/8 14 0/8	21 0/8	Clear Creek County	CO	Ken Hoffmeyer	1997	179
166 2/8	31 2/8 35 0/8	15 3/8 15 0/8	22 6/8	Las Animas County	CO	Gary Troester	2004	179
166 1/8	33 3/8 33 2/8	15 2/8 15 2/8	21 7/8	Idaho County	ID	Michael Schnider	1994	182
166 1/8	34 6/8 34 1/8	14 0/8 14 1/8	19 6/8	Saguache County	CO	Jeff Puls	1997	182
166 1/8	33 4/8 35 5/8	14 7/8 14 7/8	20 5/8	Custer County	ID	Lance Kronberger	1998	182
166 0/8	33 2/8 32 2/8	14 7/8 14 7/8	19 7/8	Jefferson County	CO	Robert Sorrell	1977	185
165 7/8	36 1/8 37 0/8	13 4/8 13 3/8	19 3/8	Kananaskis	ALB	Richard G. Perrett	1980	186
165 6/8	35 2/8 34 0/8	14 2/8 14 2/8	22 2/8	Clear Creek County	CO	Lee Beckwith	1994	187
165 5/8	31 4/8 36 1/8	14 6/8 14 6/8	21 4/8	Clear Creek County	CO	Kurt Keskimaki	1984	188
165 5/8	35 6/8 32 5/8	14 6/8 14 7/8	20 2/8	Canmore	ALB	Jay A. Brown	1996	188
165 4/8	34 6/8 34 4/8	13 3/8 13 5/8	19 2/8	Boulder County	CO	Frank Piacentino	1999	190

886

BIGHORN SHEEP

Minimum Score 140   Continued

SCORE	LENGTH OF R HORN	L	CIRCUMFERENCE R OF BASE	L	GREATEST SPREAD	AREA	STATE/ PROVINCE	HUNTER'S NAME	DATE	RANK
150 5/8	31 4/8	32 1/8	13 5/8	13 6/8	22 1/8	Park County	WY	Ron Madsen	2000	381
150 4/8	29 5/8	29 7/8	15 0/8	14 6/8	20 6/8	Park County	WY	James R. Dreves	1988	382
150 3/8	31 3/8	33 2/8	13 4/8	13 4/8	18 6/8	Kittitas County	WA	Duane Fink	1984	383
150 2/8	29 4/8	29 4/8	15 4/8	15 3/8	19 0/8	Uintah County	UT	Richie Bland	2005	384
150 2/8	34 3/8	32 5/8	14 4/8	14 2/8	19 6/8	Canmore	ALB	Adam Foss	2006	384
150 1/8	28 4/8	29 3/8	15 4/8	15 3/8	18 0/8	Clear Creek County	CO	Calvin Farner	1990	386
150 1/8	27 2/8	27 1/8	14 0/8	14 0/8	21 0/8	Saguache County	CO	Mike Zupancic	2001	386
149 7/8	28 2/8	27 7/8	15 0/8	14 7/8	19 3/8	Larimer County	CO	Bill Harvey	1992	388
149 7/8	28 2/8	27 1/8	13 4/8	13 5/8	20 5/8	Clear Creek County	CO	Mark Turner	1993	388
149 5/8	31 4/8	31 1/8	14 0/8	14 1/8	22 1/8	Yakima County	WA	Lee Jenkerson	2000	390
149 5/8	25 6/8	27 3/8	14 0/8	14 0/8	19 4/8	Teller County	CO	Scott Jankowski	2003	390
149 5/8	32 4/8	34 3/8	13 6/8	13 7/8	19 5/8	Canmore	ALB	Richard "Rik" Kirkland	2006	390
149 4/8	31 2/8	29 2/8	15 0/8	14 7/8	19 3/8	Canmore	ALB	Larry Vayro	1989	393
149 4/8	28 6/8	29 4/8	15 1/8	15 0/8	20 0/8	Fremont County	CO	David E. Smith	1996	393
149 3/8	30 0/8	26 5/8	13 6/8	13 6/8	24 6/8	Lake County	OR	Don Rajnus	1982	395
149 3/8	32 0/8	29 7/8	15 2/8	15 2/8	18 0/8	Canmore	ALB	Warren Witherspoon	1986	395
*149 3/8	30 5/8	29 2/8	14 4/8	14 5/8	21 3/8	Park County	CO	Spencer Esch	2008	395
149 2/8	30 0/8	28 6/8	15 0/8	14 7/8	20 3/8	El Paso County	CO	Mark Heiland	1989	398
149 2/8	30 0/8	31 0/8	13 6/8	13 6/8	19 4/8	Clear Creek County	CO	Michael Dziekan	1994	398
148 7/8	29 1/8	31 6/8	14 4/8	14 5/8	20 5/8	Canmore	ALB	Kent Hillard	1990	400
148 5/8	32 1/8	29 4/8	14 7/8	14 0/8	18 0/8	Mora County	NM	Larry Dwyer	2009	401
148 5/8	29 2/8	29 7/8	13 4/8	13 4/8	20 0/8	Box Elder County	UT	Russell Overton	2009	401
148 4/8	28 2/8	29 0/8	14 2/8	14 3/8	20 4/8	Teller County	CO	Joel D. Morgan	1995	403
148 2/8	30 6/8	29 6/8	14 5/8	14 5/8	21 4/8	Park County	CO	Roland D. Cameron	1979	404
147 6/8	30 0/8	29 2/8	15 5/8	15 5/8	20 1/8	El Paso County	CO	Glenn R. Kuklick	1988	405
147 6/8	31 3/8	31 3/8	14 4/8	14 4/8	16 4/8	Eagle County	CO	Russell Overton	2000	405
147 4/8	27 6/8	24 2/8	15 6/8	15 7/8	20 2/8	Saguache County	CO	Charles Grumley	1988	407
147 4/8	31 4/8	31 2/8	13 5/8	13 6/8	24 3/8	Fraser River	BC	Tom Hoffman	2000	407
147 3/8	30 3/8	31 4/8	14 2/8	14 2/8	17 7/8	Canmore	ALB	Don Ferguson	1981	409
147 2/8	30 2/8	32 0/8	14 3/8	14 3/8	20 3/8	Eagle County	CO	Joe Theaman	1989	410
147 2/8	28 7/8	34 1/8	13 3/8	13 3/8	23 4/8	Park County	WY	Jamie Byrne	1991	410
147 1/8	29 7/8	30 0/8	13 6/8	13 7/8	19 6/8	Lake County	CO	G. Fred Asbell	1979	412
147 1/8	29 4/8	29 7/8	14 0/8	13 7/8	18 4/8	Eagle County	CO	Perry Hatch	2003	412
147 0/8	30 6/8	30 0/8	13 3/8	13 3/8	21 3/8	El Paso County	CO	Sherman Spoelstra	1983	414
*146 4/8	31 0/8	32 0/8	14 0/8	14 1/8	17 6/8	Canmore	ALB	Mark R. Beeler	2005	415
145 5/8	29 4/8	30 3/8	13 2/8	13 2/8	19 3/8	Canmore	ALB	Oran Hirsch	1979	416
145 5/8	30 1/8	29 6/8	15 2/8	15 3/8	18 4/8	Lemhi County	ID	Dale Johnson	1985	416
145 4/8	30 0/8	31 4/8	14 3/8	14 3/8	20 0/8	Canmore	ALB	John McKay	2003	418
145 1/8	29 3/8	30 6/8	14 6/8	14 4/8	20 5/8	Trout Creek	ALB	Chad Lenz	1992	419
144 6/8	33 0/8	29 6/8	13 5/8	13 4/8	20 0/8	Canmore	ALB	Bennett L. McMillian	1993	420
144 6/8	27 2/8	30 4/8	15 5/8	15 6/8	21 5/8	Fremont County	CO	Jeff Lindeman	2001	420
144 5/8	29 3/8	29 0/8	14 5/8	14 4/8	20 4/8	Clear Creek County	CO	Rob Firth	1988	422
144 2/8	30 2/8	28 4/8	13 6/8	13 6/8	18 2/8	Clear Creek County	CO	Keith Johnson	2002	423
144 1/8	30 0/8	26 7/8	15 2/8	15 1/8	24 4/8	Chaffee County	CO	Dwight Schuh	1993	424
143 5/8	28 2/8	28 1/8	13 4/8	13 4/8	20 6/8	Clear Creek County	CO	Otho Hobbs	1991	425
143 4/8	32 0/8	32 0/8	14 0/8	14 1/8	18 0/8	Couger Creek	ALB	Will Pick	1993	426
*143 4/8	30 5/8	30 7/8	13 4/8	13 4/8	21 1/8	Canmore	ALB	Wayne F. Farnsworth, Jr.	2006	426
142 6/8	26 1/8	28 7/8	14 0/8	14 0/8	19 2/8	Teller County	CO	Steve Barnhill	1990	428
142 6/8	30 6/8	28 6/8	14 3/8	14 2/8	18 0/8	Garfield County	CO	Richard E. Davis	1999	428
*142 6/8	26 4/8	27 0/8	13 5/8	13 7/8	20 2/8	Huerfano County	CO	Bruce Palmer	2008	428
142 2/8	29 1/8	29 1/8	13 0/8	13 4/8	20 5/8	Exshaw	ALB	David Chorkwa	1999	431
142 1/8	30 4/8	28 7/8	14 4/8	14 3/8	20 4/8	Clear Creek County	CO	Louie Kitcoff	1999	432
142 0/8	30 7/8	30 7/8	13 2/8	13 2/8	21 0/8	Clear Creek County	CO	Jeff Reynolds	1989	433
142 0/8	28 2/8	28 4/8	13 6/8	13 5/8	19 2/8	Park County	CO	Dave Reichley	1998	433
141 7/8	24 2/8	28 1/8	14 2/8	14 2/8	20 3/8	Saguache County	CO	John MacPeak	2009	435
141 6/8	25 6/8	27 4/8	14 4/8	14 7/8	19 2/8	Chaffee County	CO	Ron Breitsprecher	1978	436
141 5/8	31 0/8	30 5/8	13 3/8	12 7/8	18 6/8	Park County	WY	Kurt H. Eisenach	1988	437
141 5/8	30 6/8	30 1/8	14 1/8	14 1/8	19 0/8	Teller County	CO	Peter J. Selinski	2004	437
141 4/8	29 1/8	27 3/8	13 3/8	13 3/8	21 0/8	Adams County	CO	Jim Usrey	1976	439
141 2/8	30 7/8	29 1/8	12 6/8	12 5/8	18 6/8	Chaffee County	CO	Tom Tietz	1984	440
141 2/8	25 4/8	27 6/8	13 4/8	13 6/8	17 3/8	Saguache County	CO	Dennis L. Howell	1993	440
*141 2/8	27 2/8	27 4/8	13 7/8	13 6/8	22 2/8	Saguache County	CO	Corey D. Walker	2009	440
141 1/8	29 5/8	29 6/8	14 3/8	14 5/8	18 4/8	Chelan County	WA	Greg Winters	1992	443
141 1/8	25 5/8	27 6/8	14 5/8	14 4/8	20 1/8	Pueblo County	CO	Gary Bohochik	1994	443
141 1/8	26 7/8	26 6/8	14 6/8	14 5/8	19 5/8	Saguache County	CO	John L. Gardner	1998	443
141 0/8	27 4/8	28 2/8	13 5/8	13 6/8	21 0/8	Park County	CO	Dan Tekavec	1980	446
141 0/8	28 0/8	28 0/8	14 1/8	14 1/8	19 2/8	Fremont County	WY	Jerry W. Mathewes	1983	446
140 7/8	27 6/8	33 3/8	14 1/8	14 0/8	19 6/8	Kittitas County	WA	Stan Hansen	1984	448
*140 7/8	25 6/8	25 7/8	14 4/8	14 4/8	21 6/8	Custer County	CO	David E. Evanow	2010	448
140 5/8	31 2/8	28 3/8	13 7/8	13 6/8	20 4/8	Canmore	ALB	Lindsey Paterson	2003	450
140 4/8	28 6/8	28 6/8	14 1/8	14 1/8	19 1/8	Valley County	ID	Michael Schlegel	1987	451
140 4/8	29 6/8	30 2/8	14 1/8	14 1/8	21 5/8	Canmore	ALB	Bruce R. Schoeneweis	1992	451
140 3/8	27 1/8	30 2/8	14 0/8	14 0/8	19 3/8	Clear Creek County	CO	Paul Navarre	1997	453
140 0/8	30 5/8	27 7/8	13 4/8	13 5/8	23 6/8	Kittitas County	WA	Martin Sapp	1990	454

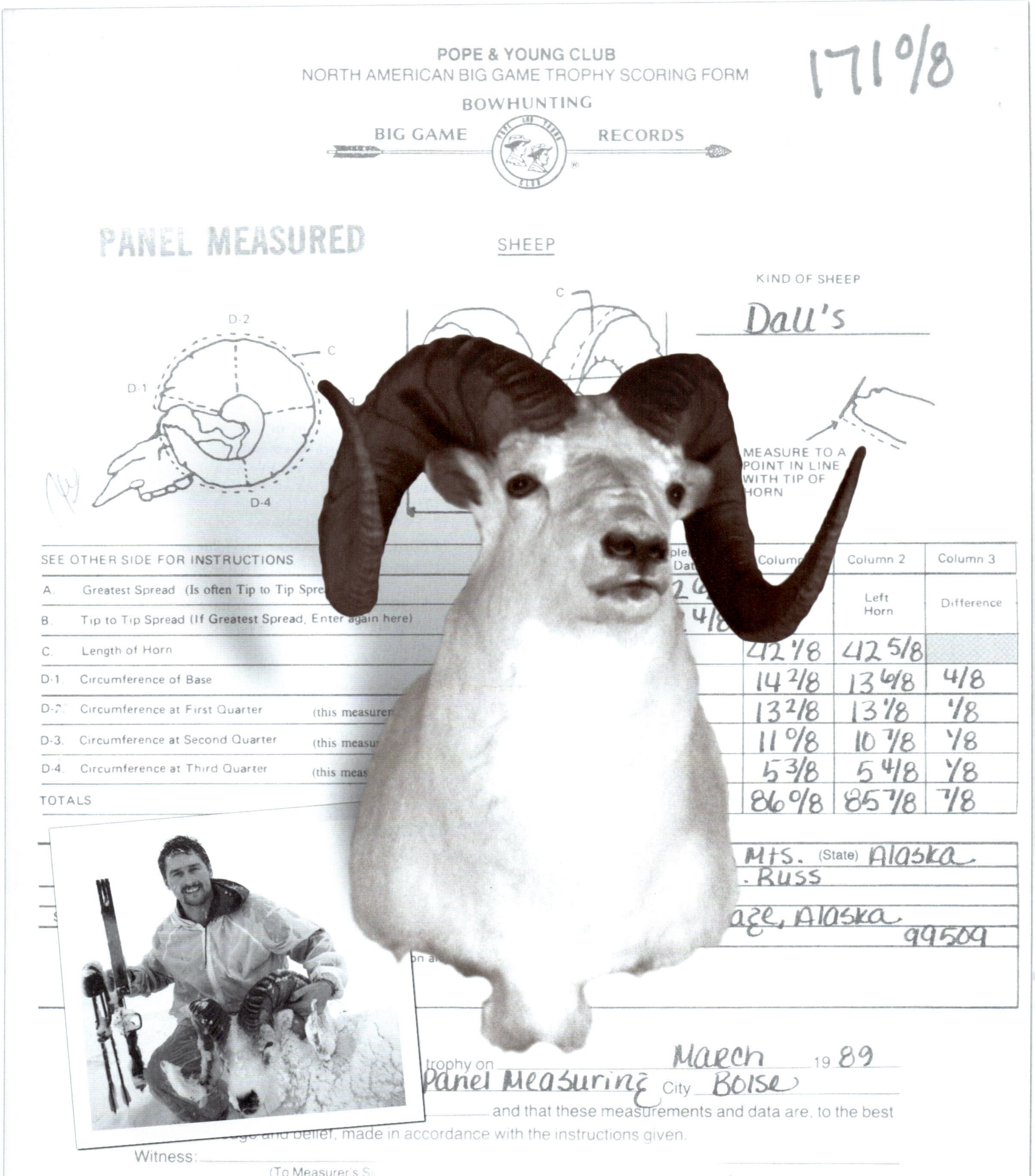

171 0/8

POPE & YOUNG CLUB
NORTH AMERICAN BIG GAME TROPHY SCORING FORM

BOWHUNTING
BIG GAME RECORDS

PANEL MEASURED

SHEEP

KIND OF SHEEP Dall's

MEASURE TO A POINT IN LINE WITH TIP OF HORN

SEE OTHER SIDE FOR INSTRUCTIONS	Column 1	Column 2	Column 3
		Left Horn	Difference
A. Greatest Spread (Is often Tip to Tip Spre…			
B. Tip to Tip Spread (If Greatest Spread, Enter again here)			
C. Length of Horn	42 7/8	42 5/8	
D-1. Circumference of Base	14 2/8	13 6/8	4/8
D-2. Circumference at First Quarter (this measurem…	13 2/8	13 1/8	1/8
D-3. Circumference at Second Quarter (this measu…	11 0/8	10 7/8	1/8
D-4. Circumference at Third Quarter (this meas…	5 3/8	5 4/8	1/8
TOTALS	86 0/8	85 7/8	7/8

Mts. (State) Alaska
. Russ
age, Alaska
99509

trophy on March 19 89
Panel Measuring City Boise
and that these measurements and data are, to the best
…ge and belief, made in accordance with the instructions given.
Witness:
(To Measurer's S…
Measurer
STATE ZIP

WORLD RECORD DALL'S SHEEP
Score: 171 0/8
Location: Chugach Mountains, Alaska
Date: 1988
Hunter: Tony Russ

Dall's Sheep

by Tony Russ

In 1988 I took up bowhunting because rifle hunting had become too little of a challenge. Having hunted in Alaska all my life, I had taken pretty much every species available. On the seventh day of my first bowhunt for sheep, I traveled seventeen miles into the mountains.

After enduring freezing rain and heavy snow, having to fix a nonfunctional bow at the last minute and a spooked flock of ptarmigan that spoiled one stalk, I found myself crawling and pawing through the snow in my white suit towards a dozen rams. Feeding with lowered head at seventeen yards, I could not see the ram's horns. I few moments later, the ram lifted his head to chew a mouthful of grass and looked directly over my shoulder. He was sporting "full-curl-plus" horns. I squinted my eyes and held still as the ram's gaze passed right by me, never focusing on my white suit blending into the whiteout conditions.

When the ram again lowered his head, I had my opportunity. The shot was good and the ram fell in its tracks. My emotions took over and I raised my arms and yelled at the top of my lungs in triumph. The long, hard pack down the icy mountainside, through the alder-fringed lake and over the many miles of trail is forever etched in my mind, as I replayed—over and over---the excitement of the moments surrounding the shot.

DALL'S SHEEP

Minimum Score 120 — *Ovis dalli dalli* and *Ovis dalli kenaiensis*

SCORE	LENGTH OF R HORN L	CIRCUMFERENCE R OF BASE L	GREATEST SPREAD	AREA	STATE/PROVINCE	HUNTER'S NAME	DATE	RANK
171 0/8	42 1/8 42 5/8	14 2/8 13 6/8	22 6/8	Chugach Mtns.	AK	Tony Russ	1988	1
168 6/8	39 4/8 42 2/8	13 0/8 13 0/8	23 5/8	Tok	AK	John Sarvis	1998	2
166 4/8	41 1/8 40 7/8	13 3/8 13 3/8	26 2/8	East Fork	AK	Braun Kopsack	1990	3
166 1/8	36 6/8 40 5/8	14 1/8 14 0/8	25 5/8	Grey Ridge	YUK	James Mackrell	1999	4
165 3/8	37 1/8 37 4/8	13 6/8 14 0/8	21 7/8	Eklutna	AK	James D. Eskelson	1998	5
165 3/8	40 5/8 41 0/8	13 2/8 13 0/8	23 7/8	Nahanni Butte	NWT	Scott Ebert	2010	5
165 1/8	39 0/8 40 3/8	13 2/8 13 2/8	22 0/8	Talkeetna Mtns.	AK	Braun Kopsack	1997	7
164 5/8	40 6/8 41 3/8	13 3/8 13 5/8	28 4/8	Nahanni Butte	NWT	Gary Laya	1986	8
164 5/8	35 6/8 35 7/8	13 6/8 13 5/8	20 6/8	Keele River	NWT	George Harms	2001	8
163 0/8	38 4/8 39 6/8	13 2/8 13 3/8	20 7/8	Chugach Mtns.	AK	Ken Radach	2002	10
162 3/8	38 7/8 39 0/8	12 4/8 12 4/8	22 6/8	Delta River	AK	Dr. Russell Congdon	1960	11
162 3/8	40 2/8 40 3/8	13 3/8 13 4/8	25 5/8	Arctic Red River	NWT	Cameron Foss	2010	11
162 2/8	38 6/8 39 0/8	13 3/8 13 4/8	23 0/8	Chugach Mtns.	AK	Braun Kopsack	1996	13
162 0/8	38 6/8 37 0/8	13 4/8 13 7/8	22 3/8	Chugach Mtns.	AK	Richard Moran	1991	14
161 5/8	41 2/8 40 3/8	13 0/8 13 0/8	24 3/8	Liard Range	NWT	Pete Iacavazzi	1994	15
161 3/8	37 1/8 39 0/8	13 5/8 13 4/8	25 0/8	Talkeetna Mtns.	AK	Braun Kopsack	1992	17
161 1/8	39 2/8 39 3/8	13 1/8 13 1/8	25 1/8	Eklutna Lake	AK	Dave Brown	2007	18
160 7/8	37 5/8 38 0/8	13 1/8 13 1/8	22 3/8	Eklutna Lake	AK	Kyle Koschmeder	2006	19
160 6/8	39 6/8 37 6/8	13 2/8 13 2/8	22 7/8	Nahanni Butte	NWT	Lonny Vanatta	1986	20
160 4/8	39 2/8 40 2/8	13 7/8 13 4/8	23 5/8	Nahanni Butte	NWT	Joseph D. Maddock	1989	21
159 4/8	38 6/8 39 4/8	13 6/8 13 6/8	26 3/8	Talkeetna Mtns.	AK	Kyle Meintzer	2000	22
159 3/8	38 4/8 38 3/8	13 2/8 13 3/8	20 5/8	Atigun Pass	AK	Troy A. Graziadei	2008	23
159 2/8	40 1/8 40 5/8	12 6/8 12 5/8	26 3/8	Mackenzie Mtns.	NWT	Jerry Bowen	1990	24
159 2/8	37 7/8 39 1/8	13 2/8 13 2/8	22 4/8	Arctic Red River	NWT	Jim Horneck	2005	24
*158 7/8	37 5/8 37 0/8	14 2/8 14 1/8	21 7/8	Keele River	NWT	Alexander Phillips	2008	26
158 3/8	35 0/8 40 1/8	13 7/8 13 5/8	26 7/8	Keele River	NWT	Alan Hamberlin	1999	27
158 2/8	38 0/8 38 0/8	13 4/8 13 6/8	27 2/8	Knik River	AK	Tony Russ	1989	28
158 1/8	39 5/8 36 2/8	12 7/8 12 6/8	20 4/8	Tanana Hills	AK	Richard Swisher	1995	29
157 6/8	38 3/8 39 7/8	12 2/8 12 2/8	26 6/8	Brooks Range	AK	Kurt Lepping	1988	30
157 5/8	37 4/8 38 1/8	13 2/8 13 2/8	24 6/8	Eklutna Lake	AK	Tony Russ	1997	31
157 5/8	35 2/8 35 3/8	13 0/8 13 0/8	20 0/8	Roberts Fork	AK	Jeff Falkner	2010	32
157 4/8	38 6/8 38 6/8	12 7/8 12 7/8	24 2/8	Eagle River	AK	David Litchfield	1988	32
157 4/8	35 6/8 35 2/8	14 4/8 14 3/8	18 4/8	Eklutna	AK	Gary Baumgartner	1999	32
157 2/8	34 3/8 37 3/8	13 0/8 13 0/8	23 7/8	Chugach Mtns.	AK	Jim Young	1996	34
157 1/8	39 1/8 40 2/8	12 3/8 12 3/8	24 3/8	Nahanni Butte	NWT	Tom Tietz	1987	35
157 1/8	38 0/8 35 1/8	13 0/8 13 1/8	22 0/8	Chugach Mtns.	AK	Calvin W. Hall	1991	35
*157 1/8	32 5/8 33 4/8	13 6/8 13 7/8	22 0/8	Romanzof Mtns.	AK	Jeff Erickson	2007	35
157 0/8	35 4/8 35 4/8	13 4/8 14 0/8	21 2/8	Chitina Glacier	AK	Roger Morris	1973	38
156 6/8	38 3/8 38 5/8	12 5/8 12 5/8	24 1/8	Talkeetna Mtns.	AK	Braun Kopsack	1994	39
156 5/8	35 2/8 35 1/8	13 6/8 13 6/8	20 4/8	Chugach Mtns.	AK	David E. Vitori	2002	40
*156 0/8	38 0/8 37 4/8	12 6/8 12 6/8	23 6/8	Isaac Creek	YUK	Terrance S. Marcum	2004	41
155 6/8	33 0/8 36 6/8	13 4/8 13 4/8	27 3/8	Eklutna Glacier	AK	Tom Kron	1998	42
155 6/8	36 7/8 35 5/8	13 6/8 13 7/8	25 4/8	Chugach Mtns.	AK	Chris A. Reynolds	2000	42
155 5/8	36 3/8 35 0/8	12 6/8 12 6/8	19 5/8	Mackenzie Mtns.	NWT	Bob Renner	1983	44
155 5/8	37 0/8 37 7/8	13 7/8 13 5/8	27 4/8	Keele River	NWT	Robert J. "Grub" Matthews	2007	44
155 1/8	37 1/8 37 2/8	13 4/8 13 4/8	25 7/8	Rams Head Mtn.	NWT	Ron Breitsprecher	1981	46
155 1/8	36 6/8 35 5/8	13 2/8 13 2/8	19 5/8	Liard Range	NWT	John E. Haefeli	1988	46
155 1/8	39 2/8 37 7/8	12 6/8 12 6/8	25 5/8	East Fork	AK	Braun Kopsack	1989	46
155 1/8	40 4/8 37 3/8	12 5/8 12 5/8	25 5/8	Alaska Range	AK	Ed Hull	1990	46
155 1/8	36 3/8 39 2/8	12 4/8 12 7/8	25 2/8	Wrangell Mtns.	AK	Tom Hoffman	2000	46
155 1/8	37 2/8 37 1/8	13 4/8 13 4/8	20 5/8	Eagle River	AK	Joe Romano	2004	46
155 0/8	36 6/8 36 6/8	13 5/8 13 4/8	23 7/8	Nahanni Butte	NWT	Tom Vanasche	1994	52
155 0/8	37 6/8 38 0/8	13 4/8 13 4/8	25 0/8	Keele River	NWT	Camp Newton	2002	52
154 7/8	35 2/8 34 7/8	14 1/8 14 1/8	21 4/8	Mackenzie Mtns.	NWT	Mike Barrett	1983	54
154 7/8	37 3/8 36 6/8	12 6/8 12 6/8	22 3/8	Kenai Mtns.	AK	Lon E. Lauber	1992	54
154 6/8	35 5/8 37 2/8	13 0/8 13 2/8	20 6/8	Chugach Mtns.	AK	Rick Tollison	1979	57
154 6/8	33 2/8 38 2/8	13 4/8 13 4/8	25 3/8	Brooks Range	AK	Kurt Lepping	1987	57
154 5/8	37 3/8 40 2/8	12 6/8 12 7/8	27 4/8	Dillinger River	AK	John L. Gardner	2004	59
154 4/8	38 0/8 34 4/8	13 1/8 13 2/8	21 6/8	Chugach Mtns.	AK	Mike Traub	1998	60
154 3/8	37 7/8 36 6/8	13 2/8 13 2/8	24 7/8	Brooks Range	AK	John Sarvis	1995	61
154 2/8	38 4/8 38 6/8	12 4/8 12 4/8	26 5/8	Atigun River	AK	David B. Barry	2002	62
154 2/8	37 0/8 36 0/8	12 7/8 12 7/8	22 2/8	Keele River	NWT	Al Baldwin	2003	62
154 2/8	41 2/8 40 0/8	12 2/8 12 2/8	27 6/8	Talkeetna Mtns.	AK	Braun T. Kopsack	2006	62
*154 0/8	35 6/8 37 2/8	13 0/8 13 2/8	25 3/8	Keele River	NWT	Wayne F. Farnsworth, Jr.	2007	65
154 0/8	37 4/8 37 2/8	12 6/8 12 6/8	25 7/8	Chandalar River	AK	Frank S. Noska IV	2010	65
153 5/8	35 1/8 36 6/8	13 3/8 13 3/8	21 6/8	Nahanni Butte	NWT	E. Damon Handley	1989	67
153 3/8	37 5/8 37 4/8	13 1/8 13 1/8	26 4/8	Divide Lake	NWT	Stanley Walchuk, Jr.	1984	68
153 3/8	36 5/8 36 4/8	13 3/8 13 3/8	23 5/8	Chugach Mtns.	AK	Nathan Callis	1986	68
153 2/8	37 7/8 35 0/8	13 2/8 13 2/8	20 4/8	Rams Head Mtn.	NWT	Dennis Schweitzer	1981	70
153 2/8	36 6/8 37 0/8	13 0/8 13 0/8	24 5/8	Keele River	NWT	Ron Serwa	1988	70
153 1/8	37 2/8 37 1/8	13 0/8 13 0/8	24 6/8	Nahanni Buttes	NWT	Gary F. Bogner	1995	72
152 7/8	39 0/8 38 7/8	13 4/8 13 4/8	28 3/8	Nahanni Butte	NWT	Monty Moravec	1993	73
152 7/8	36 1/8 36 0/8	13 3/8 13 5/8	21 2/8	Kosina Creek	AK	George E. Mann	1996	73
152 6/8	37 1/8 36 5/8	13 1/8 13 1/8	30 0/8	Wrangell Mtns.	AK	Ray Torrey	1973	75
152 5/8	38 6/8 39 3/8	12 3/8 12 4/8	31 2/8	Keele River	NWT	Thomas J. Hoffman	1986	76
152 4/8	33 0/8 34 0/8	12 6/8 12 6/8	18 5/8	Mackenzie Mtns.	NWT	Al Reay	1982	77
152 2/8	37 0/8 36 2/8	12 5/8 12 5/8	23 4/8	Kuskokwim Mtn.	AK	Kenneth R. Wallenberg	1978	78
*152 2/8	36 6/8 36 4/8	14 1/8 14 0/8	27 2/8	Keele River	NWT	Mark Beeler	2007	78
152 1/8	33 5/8 34 0/8	13 0/8 12 7/8	21 3/8	Chugach Mtns.	AK	John Sarvis	2000	80
152 0/8	37 0/8 37 0/8	12 4/8 12 4/8	27 4/8	Wrangell Mtns.	AK	Dr. Rex Hancock	1962	81
152 0/8	31 3/8 34 3/8	12 4/8 12 7/8	20 6/8	Brooks Range	AK	Calvin Farner	1988	81
152 0/8	35 6/8 35 4/8	13 4/8 13 4/8	26 1/8	Boulder Creek	AK	Rick D. Snell	1993	81
151 7/8	36 2/8 35 5/8	13 2/8 13 0/8	24 5/8	Eklutna Glacier	AK	Daniel Sommers	2003	84
151 6/8	35 7/8 35 1/8	13 5/8 13 5/8	28 0/8	Chugach Mtns.	AK	John D. 'Jack' Frost	1984	85
151 6/8	40 1/8 35 7/8	12 3/8 12 4/8	23 1/8	Matanuska River	AK	Tony Russ	1990	85
151 6/8	34 2/8 34 6/8	12 6/8 12 6/8	20 4/8	Gana River	NWT	J. P. McDonald	2008	85
151 5/8	37 4/8 38 1/8	12 7/8 12 7/8	22 5/8	Keele River	NWT	Thomas J. Hoffman	1998	88
151 3/8	37 6/8 36 3/8	12 5/8 12 5/8	22 3/8	Keele River	NWT	Will Pick	1998	89
151 2/8	36 6/8 36 6/8	12 6/8 12 6/8	26 4/8	Johnson River	AK	Larry Jones	1963	90
151 2/8	36 4/8 36 4/8	13 7/8 13 6/8	23 4/8	Tonsona Creek	AK	Bruce Stephens	1974	90
151 2/8	35 5/8 36 1/8	13 0/8 13 0/8	25 0/8	Rainy Pass	AK	Roger Stewart	1978	90
151 1/8	37 3/8 38 0/8	12 3/8 12 4/8	25 3/8	Keele River	NWT	Chuck Adams	1995	93
151 0/8	35 4/8 34 4/8	13 3/8 13 5/8	27 3/8	Mackenzie Mtns.	NWT	Mike Barrett	1986	94
151 0/8	36 0/8 34 0/8	13 1/8 13 1/8	23 1/8	Chandalar River	AK	Frank S. Noska IV	2009	94
150 7/8	34 1/8 34 6/8	13 5/8 13 5/8	21 2/8	Chugach Mtns.	AK	David A. Widby	1997	95

892

DALL'S SHEEP

Minimum Score 120
Continued

SCORE	LENGTH OF R HORN L	CIRCUMFERENCE R OF BASE L	GREATEST SPREAD	AREA	STATE/PROVINCE	HUNTER'S NAME	DATE	RANK
150 5/8	36 0/8 36 1/8	13 1/8 13 2/8	22 7/8	Liard Range	NWT	Harry Walker	1995	96
*150 5/8	31 0/8 33 7/8	13 7/8 13 7/8	21 3/8	McLure Lake	NWT	Mark "Gutz" Gutsmiedl	2010	96
150 4/8	34 0/8 34 4/8	12 2/8 12 3/8	19 6/8	Chugach Mtns.	AK	Randy Ulmer	1998	98
150 3/8	36 1/8 36 2/8	12 4/8 12 5/8	24 2/8	Mountain River	NWT	George Flournoy	1985	99
150 2/8	37 5/8 33 3/8	12 4/8 12 2/8	19 7/8	Brooks Range	AK	James A. Baker	1971	100
150 1/8	37 4/8 37 1/8	12 3/8 12 3/8	18 6/8	Mackenzie Mtns.	NWT	Robert L. Kampen	1988	101
149 7/8	35 3/8 36 2/8	12 7/8 13 0/8	26 0/8	Keele River	NWT	Tom Foss	2007	102
149 6/8	40 0/8 34 2/8	12 3/8 12 3/8	22 4/8	Keele River	NWT	Jim Ryan	1990	103
149 3/8	37 1/8 34 4/8	13 2/8 13 2/8	25 7/8	Wrangell Mtns.	AK	J. Barry Dyar	1984	104
149 2/8	36 1/8 35 7/8	13 1/8 13 1/8	25 0/8	Keele River	NWT	V. Randy Liljenquist	1997	105
149 1/8	34 1/8 34 4/8	13 4/8 13 5/8	21 3/8	Eklutna Lake	AK	Steven J. Latz	1988	106
149 1/8	37 2/8 34 1/8	13 1/8 13 2/8	19 1/8	Godlin River	NWT	Bailey Simpson	2007	106
149 0/8	34 7/8 35 3/8	13 3/8 13 3/8	23 3/8	Keele River	NWT	Thomas J. Hoffman	1985	108
149 0/8	37 4/8 37 0/8	12 0/8 11 6/8	22 1/8	Nahanni Butte	NWT	Robert Pyne	1989	108
148 7/8	36 0/8 36 1/8	13 1/8 13 1/8	26 2/8	Tok	AK	Lon E. Lauber	1996	110
148 7/8	36 3/8 36 4/8	12 4/8 12 4/8	24 0/8	Mackenzie Mtns.	NWT	James A. Schneider	2005	110
148 7/8	37 1/8 34 6/8	12 2/8 12 2/8	23 4/8	Whitehorse	YUK	Dwight S. Wolf	2005	110
148 6/8	37 6/8 38 0/8	12 2/8 12 2/8	22 5/8	Nahanni Butte	NWT	Bill Grammer	1986	113
148 6/8	35 1/8 38 5/8	12 1/8 12 1/8	22 0/8	Nahanni Butte	NWT	Gary M. Martin	1992	113
148 5/8	34 6/8 35 1/8	13 6/8 14 0/8	20 7/8	Chugach Mtns.	AK	Ken Wolter	2004	115
148 4/8	35 7/8 35 3/8	13 2/8 13 2/8	26 6/8	Brooks Range	AK	Randy Butler	1979	116
148 4/8	31 4/8 35 4/8	13 6/8 13 6/8	25 0/8	Mackenzie Mtns.	NWT	Dyrk Eddie	1986	116
148 3/8	33 4/8 35 1/8	13 3/8 13 3/8	24 2/8	Atigun Pass	AK	Maxallen D. Jackson	1984	118
148 2/8	37 2/8 35 6/8	12 3/8 12 6/8	19 6/8	Chugach Mtns.	AK	Roy Ruiz	1997	119
*148 2/8	34 4/8 33 4/8	13 5/8 13 2/8	20 7/8	Gana River	NWT	Ted Carlson	2006	119
148 0/8	38 3/8 35 5/8	12 6/8 12 7/8	28 1/8	Delta Junction	AK	Mike Hedrick	1988	121
148 0/8	33 0/8 36 4/8	13 2/8 13 1/8	19 2/8	Chugach Mtns.	AK	Stephen Kotz	1995	121
147 6/8	35 1/8 35 1/8	12 4/8 12 6/8	19 7/8	Tlogotcho Range	NWT	Archie Nesbitt	1986	123
147 6/8	35 0/8 35 0/8	13 2/8 13 3/8	24 0/8	Chugach Mtns.	AK	Richard Moran/Lon Lauber	1989	123
147 5/8	31 0/8 33 5/8	12 4/8 12 3/8	17 7/8	Jackfish Mtn.	NWT	Daniel C. Hurd	1996	125
147 4/8	34 6/8 35 4/8	12 0/8 12 0/8	21 5/8	Mackenzie Mtns.	NWT	Paul Brunner	1982	126
147 4/8	34 0/8 34 2/8	13 3/8 13 3/8	27 0/8	Chugach Mtns.	AK	Anthony L. Mudd	2003	126
147 3/8	34 4/8 35 1/8	13 0/8 13 0/8	20 0/8	DeLong Mtns.	AK	Carl E. Brent	1991	128
147 3/8	33 2/8 36 5/8	12 7/8 12 6/8	25 5/8	Keele River	NWT	Matthew Liljenquist	2004	128
147 2/8	35 2/8 35 4/8	12 5/8 12 5/8	25 2/8	Mackenzie Mtns.	NWT	Janice J. Traub	1987	130
147 2/8	35 5/8 35 1/8	12 2/8 12 2/8	22 6/8	Eklutna Lake	AK	John McCullough	1988	130
147 2/8	32 3/8 32 3/8	12 2/8 12 7/8	20 4/8	Talkeetna Mtns.	AK	Jeffrey S. Stevens	1997	130
147 2/8	36 1/8 34 1/8	13 2/8 13 1/8	22 0/8	Mountain River	NWT	Rene Suda	1999	130
147 1/8	35 5/8 32 2/8	12 0/8 12 0/8	20 3/8	Chugach Mtns.	AK	Lon E. Lauber	1990	134
147 0/8	36 0/8 36 2/8	12 4/8 12 4/8	25 1/8	Nahanni Butte	NWT	Jim Arnold	1988	135
147 0/8	34 7/8 35 1/8	13 0/8 12 7/8	21 7/8	Chugach Mtns.	AK	Tony Russ	1992	135
146 6/8	35 0/8 34 4/8	12 2/8 12 2/8	23 5/8	Liard Range	NWT	Dennis Dunn	1984	137
146 6/8	30 7/8 33 5/8	12 2/8 12 4/8	19 2/8	Post River	AK	James R. Gabrick	1998	137
146 5/8	36 3/8 35 0/8	11 6/8 11 5/8	21 0/8	Liard Range	NWT	Ron Rockwell	1983	139
146 5/8	31 1/8 36 2/8	13 0/8 13 0/8	27 2/8	Healy River	AK	Mark C. Booth	2004	139
146 5/8	35 7/8 36 0/8	12 0/8 12 0/8	21 6/8	Shendata	AK	Anne Vorisek	2010	139
146 4/8	33 4/8 34 2/8	12 0/8 12 2/8	25 7/8	Delta River	AK	Elisha Gray	1958	142
146 4/8	34 1/8 33 5/8	12 5/8 12 5/8	23 4/8	Jones Creek	BC	Randy De Biasio	1994	142
146 4/8	33 2/8 33 6/8	13 3/8 13 3/8	19 3/8	Chugach Mtns.	AK	Bob Ameen	1997	142
146 3/8	34 7/8 35 0/8	12 3/8 12 3/8	19 6/8	Kotaneellee Range	NWT	James A. Schneider	1997	145
146 2/8	33 4/8 32 6/8	11 5/8 11 4/8	17 6/8	Nahanni Butte	NWT	Barry J. Smith	1989	146
146 1/8	35 1/8 35 6/8	13 0/8 13 2/8	25 6/8	Keele River	NWT	Bob Ehle	2001	147
146 1/8	34 1/8 34 0/8	12 6/8 12 5/8	21 0/8	Liard Mtns.	NWT	Neil Summers	2009	147
145 7/8	34 1/8 34 6/8	13 0/8 13 0/8	47 0/8	Carcajour River	NWT	Edwin L. DeYoung	2010	149
145 6/8	29 0/8 36 6/8	12 5/8 12 6/8	24 1/8	Brooks Range	AK	Maxallen D. Jackson	1989	150
145 4/8	33 1/8 37 7/8	11 6/8 11 6/8	21 2/8	Brooks Range	AK	John D. 'Jack' Frost	1982	151
145 3/8	33 0/8 36 5/8	12 0/8 12 3/8	30 6/8	Delta Mtns.	AK	D. J. Wood	2006	152
145 3/8	33 1/8 35 5/8	12 3/8 12 4/8	25 5/8	Talkeetna Mtns.	AK	Jay Deones	1980	153
145 2/8	36 2/8 36 2/8	12 0/8 12 1/8	23 0/8	Liard Mtns.	NWT	Steve Weekly	1998	153
145 1/8	32 2/8 33 1/8	13 4/8 13 7/8	23 5/8	Wood River	AK	Art Young	1923	155
145 1/8	34 5/8 35 0/8	13 2/8 13 2/8	25 5/8	DoDo Mtn.	NWT	Tom D. Slusser	1990	155
145 0/8	33 5/8 33 5/8	13 0/8 13 0/8	25 5/8	Mt. Ibex	YUK	Martin Hanson	1957	157
145 0/8	33 4/8 35 6/8	12 2/8 12 2/8	23 0/8	Liard Range	NWT	Mike Ukrainetz	1995	157
145 0/8	30 0/8 31 6/8	12 6/8 12 6/8	20 3/8	Chandalar River	AK	Neil Thagard	2002	157
145 0/8	34 6/8 38 6/8	11 6/8 11 5/8	25 0/8	Chandalar River	AK	Frank S. Noska IV	2008	157
144 5/8	34 5/8 35 2/8	13 0/8 13 0/8	23 1/8	Mt. Hayes	AK	Keith R. Clemmons	1962	161
*144 5/8	35 1/8 35 6/8	12 1/8 12 1/8	25 1/8	Sagavanirktok River	AK	Joe Zupancic	2008	161
144 2/8	33 1/8 33 3/8	12 5/8 12 4/8	21 6/8	Liard Range	NWT	Richard W. Sage	1986	163
144 2/8	33 7/8 33 7/8	12 6/8 13 0/8	24 0/8	Yellow Jacket Pass	AK	G. Fred Asbell	1993	163
144 1/8	33 3/8 36 4/8	12 3/8 12 3/8	25 4/8	Delta Junction	AK	John W. Williams	1978	165
144 1/8	35 6/8 35 1/8	11 5/8 11 5/8	25 0/8	Liard Mtns.	NWT	Brian Ham	2004	165
*144 1/8	34 5/8 34 0/8	12 6/8 12 6/8	25 5/8	Sagavanirktok River	AK	Jarrett Finley	2007	165
143 6/8	35 0/8 35 2/8	13 0/8 12 7/8	25 0/8	Chistochina River	AK	Capt. Leonard Mackler	1977	168
143 4/8	35 0/8 34 2/8	12 5/8 12 6/8	22 4/8	Nahanni Butte	NWT	Dirk Lawyer	1985	169
143 3/8	35 0/8 34 5/8	12 0/8 12 2/8	19 4/8	Endicott Mtns.	AK	Dwane J. Sykes	1968	170
143 3/8	31 3/8 42 0/8	13 0/8 13 0/8	25 5/8	Talkeetna Mtns.	AK	Braun Kopsack	1995	170
143 2/8	31 0/8 35 2/8	12 4/8 12 4/8	23 6/8	Mackenzie Mtns.	NWT	Paul Schafer	1983	172
143 2/8	33 4/8 33 4/8	12 6/8 12 6/8	23 1/8	Ship Creek	AK	Denette Justus-Romano	2003	172
143 1/8	32 0/8 32 5/8	13 3/8 13 3/8	21 4/8	Chugach Mtns.	AK	Glenn R. L. Schmidt	1977	174
143 0/8	36 0/8 34 6/8	11 4/8 11 4/8	21 2/8	Nahanni Butte	NWT	Lee Veldhouse	1983	175
143 0/8	35 2/8 31 4/8	12 3/8 12 2/8	23 1/8	Nahanni Butte	NWT	T. Sanford Roberts	1993	175
142 4/8	36 0/8 35 2/8	12 3/8 12 3/8	24 3/8	Talkeetna Mtns.	AK	Braun T. Kopsack	2002	177
142 4/8	31 6/8 32 2/8	12 4/8 12 4/8	18 7/8	Gana River	NWT	Tom Foss	2009	177
142 3/8	35 5/8 35 0/8	12 0/8 12 0/8	25 5/8	Bonnet Plume	YUK	Tim Good	1998	179
142 2/8	33 4/8 36 2/8	11 5/8 11 5/8	24 3/8	Post River	AK	Rick Tollison	1978	180
142 2/8	33 1/8 33 1/8	12 4/8 12 5/8	27 4/8	Brooks Range	AK	Larry E. Townsend	1991	180
142 1/8	35 7/8 35 6/8	11 6/8 11 6/8	23 7/8	Nahanni Butte	NWT	Todd Szmania	1995	182
142 1/8	32 6/8 34 1/8	13 0/8 13 0/8	26 3/8	Grey Ridge	YUK	Patrick D. Quinn	1997	182
142 1/8	31 7/8 32 4/8	12 2/8 12 3/8	22 1/8	Liard Mtns.	NWT	John MacPeak	2003	182
142 1/8	33 7/8 33 4/8	12 2/8 12 2/8	22 3/8	June Lake	NWT	Fred Eichler	2005	182
142 0/8	28 1/8 33 5/8	12 1/8 12 0/8	22 1/8	Atigun Pass	AK	Maxallen D. Jackson	1980	186
142 0/8	34 2/8 34 4/8	12 1/8 12 1/8	26 6/8	Sagavanirktok River	AK	Tony Russ	2007	186
141 6/8	32 0/8 32 4/8	12 0/8 12 0/8	20 2/8	Mackenzie Mtns.	NWT	Reggie Spiegelberg	1982	188
141 5/8	31 7/8 32 0/8	13 0/8 13 0/8	26 2/8	Mackenzie Mtns.	NWT	Chuck Adams	1985	189
141 3/8	31 0/8 31 5/8	13 2/8 13 4/8	22 0/8	Peters Creek	AK	Michael Larson	2009	190

893

DALL'S SHEEP

Minimum Score 120 — Continued

SCORE	LENGTH OF R HORN L	CIRCUMFERENCE R OF BASE L	GREATEST SPREAD	AREA	STATE/ PROVINCE	HUNTER'S NAME	DATE	RANK
141 2/8	31 0/8 · 32 6/8	13 0/8 · 13 0/8	20 1/8	Purple Mtns.	NWT	Walter J. Palmer	2002	191
141 2/8	34 0/8 · 34 0/8	12 4/8 · 12 4/8	24 0/8	Nahanni Butte	NWT	Kevin Dahm	2002	191
141 0/8	35 6/8 · 36 6/8	11 5/8 · 11 5/8	22 0/8	Ptarmigan Pass	AK	Ralph Ertz	1977	193
141 0/8	31 4/8 · 31 6/8	13 6/8 · 13 6/8	20 2/8	Eklutna Lake	AK	Craig Scarbrough	1989	193
140 7/8	33 3/8 · 34 2/8	13 0/8 · 13 0/8	23 3/8	Wrangell Mtns.	AK	Mike Renfro	1987	195
*140 6/8	30 3/8 · 32 3/8	12 3/8 · 12 3/8	21 0/8	Ivishak River	AK	Joe Zupancic	2007	196
140 5/8	32 4/8 · 31 5/8	12 4/8 · 12 4/8	23 7/8	Liard River	NWT	Greg Munther	1984	197
140 5/8	30 6/8 · 31 5/8	12 1/8 · 12 1/8	18 6/8	Nahanni Butte	NWT	Richie Bland	2004	197
140 1/8	34 3/8 · 34 4/8	11 7/8 · 11 7/8	20 4/8	Nahanni Butte	NWT	Fred C. Church	1990	199
140 0/8	35 2/8 · 34 4/8	11 5/8 · 11 4/8	25 4/8	Tlogotcho Plateau	NWT	Bruce R. Schoeneweis	1996	200
140 0/8	31 4/8 · 36 0/8	12 4/8 · 12 4/8	22 4/8	Yerrick Creek	AK	Garry A. Thoms	1998	200
139 6/8	33 1/8 · 33 3/8	12 5/8 · 12 5/8	17 7/8	Chugach Mtns.	AK	John Sarvis	1988	202
139 6/8	33 7/8 · 33 5/8	12 5/8 · 12 6/8	25 3/8	Wrangell Mtns.	AK	Bret T. Walker	1991	202
139 4/8	33 0/8 · 33 2/8	12 3/8 · 12 3/8	21 7/8	Chugach Mtns.	AK	Tom S. Lenort	1990	204
139 4/8	33 4/8 · 32 6/8	12 3/8 · 12 3/8	20 3/8	Ship Creek	AK	Ed Jones	2002	204
139 1/8	34 2/8 · 34 7/8	12 3/8 · 12 3/8	27 7/8	Tok	AK	Gardner Rowell	1991	206
139 0/8	37 2/8 · 32 6/8	11 7/8 · 12 0/8	26 4/8	Talkeetna Mtns.	AK	Rusty Hayes	1975	207
138 6/8	31 4/8 · 32 4/8	11 4/8 · 11 4/8	21 3/8	Brooks Range	AK	DeWayne J. Benton	1987	208
138 4/8	32 6/8 · 34 0/8	12 6/8 · 12 5/8	22 6/8	Chitina	AK	Robert Ewers	1972	209
138 1/8	33 5/8 · 33 4/8	12 0/8 · 12 0/8	19 7/8	Nahanni Butte	NWT	Robert Edward Speegle, MD	1997	210
138 0/8	29 3/8 · 35 5/8	12 4/8 · 12 4/8	26 7/8	Hula Hula River	AK	Paul Persano	1985	211
137 6/8	32 4/8 · 34 0/8	12 2/8 · 12 2/8	25 3/8	Liard Mtns.	NWT	Richard Kirkland	2002	212
137 5/8	30 4/8 · 30 5/8	12 1/8 · 12 1/8	21 4/8	Canning River	AK	Garry A. Thoms	1989	213
137 4/8	31 2/8 · 31 2/8	13 2/8 · 13 3/8	18 5/8	Mackenzie Mtns.	NWT	William R. VyVyan	1990	214
137 4/8	32 2/8 · 30 0/8	12 2/8 · 12 2/8	18 6/8	Arctic Red River	NWT	Adam Foss	2010	214
137 2/8	34 2/8 · 32 0/8	11 2/8 · 11 1/8	21 1/8	Liard Range	NWT	Tom Taylor	1992	216
137 2/8	32 4/8 · 33 0/8	11 7/8 · 11 7/8	22 4/8	Nahanni Butte	NWT	Lew Webb	2001	216
137 0/8	33 2/8 · 34 4/8	12 1/8 · 12 1/8	24 6/8	Talkeetna Mtns.	AK	Braun Kopsack	1987	218
137 0/8	33 4/8 · 33 4/8	12 0/8 · 12 0/8	18 6/8	Liard Mtns.	NWT	Nathan Andersohn	1994	218
137 0/8	33 7/8 · 33 7/8	11 6/8 · 11 7/8	26 5/8	Timbered Ridge	NWT	Richard A. Smith	2007	218
136 7/8	32 1/8 · 33 2/8	12 1/8 · 11 7/8	26 6/8	Keele River	NWT	Roy Goodwin	2004	221
136 5/8	30 0/8 · 31 1/8	12 1/8 · 12 1/8	23 2/8	Brooks Range	AK	Jim Ryan	1986	222
136 1/8	32 5/8 · 31 2/8	12 1/8 · 12 1/8	22 6/8	Nahanni Butte	NWT	Greg Bokash	2006	223
136 0/8	32 2/8 · 32 2/8	12 1/8 · 12 1/8	23 7/8	Brooks Range	AK	Ken Vorisek	1990	224
135 7/8	33 0/8 · 32 3/8	11 3/8 · 11 3/8	22 4/8	Nahanni Buttes	NWT	Wayne A. Nicholson	1997	225
135 7/8	33 0/8 · 32 1/8	12 5/8 · 12 5/8	23 0/8	Mountain River	NWT	John Paul Schaffer	2005	225
*135 4/8	32 7/8 · 33 1/8	11 4/8 · 11 5/8	21 4/8	Nahanni Butte	NWT	Todd Brady	1999	227
135 3/8	34 5/8 · 34 6/8	11 2/8 · 11 3/8	22 0/8	Nahanni Butte	NWT	Will Pick	1994	228
135 1/8	34 0/8 · 33 5/8	11 4/8 · 11 4/8	23 0/8	Alaska Range	AK	Richard Moran	1988	229
135 1/8	31 1/8 · 30 6/8	12 5/8 · 12 7/8	20 1/8	Chugach Mtns.	AK	Grant Arii	1994	229
135 0/8	31 2/8 · 31 2/8	12 0/8 · 11 7/8	23 6/8	Liard Range	NWT	Mark Checki	1988	231
134 6/8	33 4/8 · 33 2/8	11 3/8 · 11 3/8	21 7/8	Nahanni Butte	NWT	Linda Strong	1987	232
134 5/8	32 1/8 · 33 0/8	11 1/8 · 11 2/8	20 6/8	Nahanni Butte	NWT	Jerry Leair	1990	233
134 2/8	30 0/8 · 26 4/8	12 0/8 · 12 0/8	21 6/8	Coldfoot	AK	Jonah Stewart	2009	234
133 2/8	32 0/8 · 31 6/8	11 7/8 · 11 6/8	21 2/8	Nabesna River	AK	George A. Moerlein	1983	235
133 2/8	30 0/8 · 31 0/8	11 2/8 · 11 3/8	24 2/8	Mackenzie Mtns.	NWT	Dean Stebner	1989	235
133 1/8	31 5/8 · 31 6/8	11 6/8 · 11 6/8	25 6/8	Liard Range	NWT	Tony Casagrande	1996	237
133 0/8	30 6/8 · 30 4/8	12 4/8 · 12 5/8	27 1/8	Wrangell Mtns.	AK	George A. Moerlein	1971	238
133 0/8	35 4/8 · 33 2/8	10 1/8 · 10 1/8	20 5/8	Nahanni Butte	NWT	Joel A. Johnson	2006	238
132 7/8	32 0/8 · 32 1/8	11 6/8 · 11 6/8	21 0/8	Mackenzie Mtns.	NWT	Stan Godfrey	1988	240
132 6/8	30 2/8 · 30 4/8	12 5/8 · 12 5/8	18 2/8	Brooks Range	AK	Robert Warpack	1986	241
132 2/8	30 6/8 · 30 6/8	11 7/8 · 11 5/8	20 6/8	Nahanni Butte	NWT	Steve Byerly	1996	242
132 1/8	32 5/8 · 33 0/8	11 4/8 · 11 4/8	23 2/8	Itkillik River	AK	Allyn Ladd	2004	243
131 5/8	31 5/8 · 31 1/8	12 5/8 · 12 5/8	17 6/8	Wrangell Mtns.	AK	John Sarvis	1985	244
131 4/8	30 7/8 · 31 7/8	11 3/8 · 11 1/8	21 4/8	Nahanni Butte	NWT	Ralph L. Albright	1990	245
130 7/8	32 6/8 · 28 5/8	12 4/8 · 12 4/8	20 6/8	Talkeetna Mtns.	AK	John L. Wozniak	1984	246
130 0/8	30 2/8 · 30 6/8	11 4/8 · 11 4/8	20 6/8	Liard Range	NWT	John Borlang	1986	247
129 6/8	31 2/8 · 31 6/8	11 1/8 · 10 7/8	21 2/8	Liard Range	NWT	Rick Duggan	1998	248
128 5/8	31 2/8 · 31 3/8	11 1/8 · 11 3/8	20 5/8	Liard Range	NWT	Mark Buehrer/Mike Grue	1998	249
128 3/8	30 0/8 · 30 7/8	12 1/8 · 12 1/8	20 4/8	Liard Range	NWT	Jim Wondzell	1994	250
128 0/8	31 2/8 · 31 4/8	11 2/8 · 11 3/8	24 0/8	Wrangell	AK	Gilbert M. W. Smith	1977	251
127 0/8	29 7/8 · 29 3/8	11 2/8 · 11 1/8	21 2/8	Sheep Creek	AK	Ray Uhl, Jr.	1968	252
125 7/8	31 6/8 · 31 3/8	10 4/8 · 10 4/8	21 1/8	Alaska Range	AK	Larry Jones	1969	253
125 5/8	30 4/8 · 30 5/8	11 7/8 · 12 0/8	20 4/8	Nahanni Buttes	NWT	L. Grant Foster	2007	254
125 1/8	29 1/8 · 29 1/8	11 2/8 · 11 2/8	17 4/8	Liard Range	NWT	Todd Henck	1988	255
124 5/8	28 0/8 · 28 5/8	11 3/8 · 11 4/8	23 2/8	Nahanni Buttes	NWT	Tom Miranda	2008	256
124 0/8	30 1/8 · 30 5/8	11 2/8 · 11 0/8	17 5/8	Kuskokwin River	AK	Marvin Clyncke	1997	257
123 3/8	30 1/8 · 30 0/8	11 0/8 · 11 0/8	24 2/8	Kongakut River	AK	Stan Parkerson	1984	258
122 0/8	29 2/8 · 28 2/8	11 0/8 · 11 0/8	20 7/8	Liard Range	NWT	Carol Kindred	1999	259
122 0/8	27 6/8 · 27 4/8	12 1/8 · 12 2/8	20 2/8	Eklutna Lake	AK	Russ Richardson	2007	259
121 6/8	30 4/8 · 30 2/8	10 2/8 · 10 2/8	22 6/8	Alaska Range	AK	Lon E. Lauber	1988	261
121 4/8	27 6/8 · 28 0/8	11 2/8 · 11 2/8	19 7/8	Nahanni Butte	NWT	Neil Thagard	1997	262
121 3/8	28 0/8 · 28 3/8	11 6/8 · 11 6/8	21 4/8	Chugach Mtns.	AK	Tom Abbas	2005	263
*121 3/8	26 5/8 · 26 6/8	12 1/8 · 12 0/8	21 3/8	Ship Creek	AK	Nate Peckinpaugh	2009	263
121 1/8	27 3/8 · 28 2/8	10 7/8 · 10 6/8	21 4/8	Brooks Range	AK	Thomas Chadwick	1984	265
120 5/8	29 1/8 · 29 4/8	11 4/8 · 11 5/8	21 0/8	Atigun Pass	AK	Steve Herrera	1991	266

WORLD RECORD DESERT BIGHORN SHEEP
Score: 178 6/8
Location: Hidalgo County, New Mexico
Date: 2007
Hunter: Jim Hens

Desert Bighorn Sheep

by Jim Hens

When I set out to go and hunt this desert sheep I never imagined I would harvest a record book ram.

On the first day of the hunt we glassed the ram that I eventually harvested almost 30 days later.

The hunt was easier than other sheep hunts I've been on. This was mostly do to the lower elevation of the mountains. The major obstacle we had to overcome was the heat. In the afternoon the temps would get to 100 degrees.

What stands out most for me was the unwavering support that Tom Hoffman, Tyson Hatch, Chris Harlow, Bill Clout and Justin Larsen provided. We all shared many laughs and had many ups and downs while pursuing this amazing animal. However these individuals help to make a memory that will be etched in my mind forever.

DESERT BIGHORN SHEEP

Minimum Score 120 — *Ovis canadensis nelsoni* and certain related subspecies

SCORE	LENGTH OF HORN R	L	CIRCUMFERENCE OF BASE R	L	GREATEST SPREAD	AREA	STATE/PROVINCE	HUNTER'S NAME	DATE	RANK
178 6/8	36 4/8	36 2/8	16 0/8	16 0/8	20 7/8	Hidalgo County	NM	Jim Hens	2007	1
178 2/8	35 7/8	35 7/8	15 5/8	16 0/8	25 2/8	Tiburon Island	MEX	George Harms	2000	2
178 1/8	37 7/8	36 6/8	15 4/8	15 4/8	21 5/8	Tiburon Island	MEX	Al Baldwin	2002	3
177 6/8	36 4/8	37 0/8	15 3/8	15 4/8	20 4/8	Tiburon Island	MEX	Murray Fain	2010	4
176 7/8	36 3/8	35 2/8	15 2/8	15 1/8	19 6/8	Pima County	AZ	Mark D. Morris	1990	5
*176 3/8	41 4/8	35 5/8	15 2/8	15 2/8	23 7/8	Carmen Island	MEX	Robert E. Speegle, MD	2008	6
175 0/8	35 5/8	36 5/8	14 7/8	14 7/8	22 5/8	Graham County	AZ	Jim Ryan	1989	7
175 0/8	35 6/8	36 2/8	14 6/8	14 6/8	23 2/8	Maricopa County	AZ	Matthew D. Liljenquist	2002	7
170 5/8	37 4/8	34 5/8	14 5/8	14 5/8	23 2/8	Mohave County	AZ	Stephen C. Christensen	2000	9
170 2/8	35 2/8	36 6/8	14 6/8	14 7/8	21 6/8	Clark County	NV	Paul Harris	2001	10
169 3/8	36 3/8	36 0/8	14 2/8	14 2/8	23 1/8	Nye County	NV	Rick Duggan	2009	11
169 1/8	34 5/8	34 0/8	15 5/8	15 4/8	22 3/8	Graham County	AZ	Sonny Ray Leon	2002	12
*168 6/8	37 7/8	34 7/8	14 4/8	14 4/8	22 4/8	Carmen Island	MEX	Jim Wondzell	2010	13
168 2/8	31 7/8	34 7/8	14 5/8	14 5/8	23 4/8	Maricopa County	AZ	Amber J. Richardson	2004	14
167 5/8	35 4/8	35 7/8	15 2/8	14 6/8	22 1/8	Carmen Island	MEX	Gary M. Martin	2007	15
167 1/8	34 5/8	34 2/8	14 7/8	14 7/8	23 5/8	Maricopa County	AZ	Peter C. Knagge	1985	16
167 0/8	34 2/8	33 2/8	15 1/8	15 2/8	24 6/8	Nye County	NV	Lucy Rechel	2009	17
166 6/8	28 6/8	34 4/8	14 5/8	14 5/8	21 7/8	San Bernardino County	CA	Jim Ryan	1988	18
166 2/8	36 1/8	36 5/8	14 2/8	14 2/8	22 2/8	Graham County	AZ	Max T. Hinton	1987	19
165 6/8	35 7/8	37 3/8	15 3/8	15 3/8	24 4/8	Clark County	NV	James A. Schneider	1999	20
164 2/8	32 4/8	31 6/8	15 3/8	15 3/8	21 1/8	Maricopa County	AZ	Chuck Meacham	1984	21
164 2/8	33 6/8	37 6/8	14 7/8	14 6/8	23 5/8	Graham County	AZ	Eugene F. Wullkotte	2001	21
164 1/8	34 0/8	33 7/8	15 3/8	15 4/8	20 4/8	Tiburon Island	MEX	Alexander K. Phillips	2007	23
163 4/8	33 5/8	33 1/8	14 7/8	14 5/8	23 3/8	Mohave County	AZ	Gary Steinmann	1986	24
163 3/8	33 7/8	34 6/8	14 2/8	14 0/8	22 3/8	Mesa County	CO	Michael K. Ward	1998	25
163 2/8	34 0/8	33 0/8	15 0/8	15 1/8	19 6/8	Sonora	MEX	Gary F. Bogner	1993	26
163 1/8	34 6/8	35 5/8	15 4/8	15 4/8	22 3/8	Clark County	NV	Fred Church	1984	27
*163 0/8	34 4/8	30 6/8	14 6/8	14 4/8	20 7/8	Carmen Island	MEX	John D. "Jack" Frost	2010	28
*162 6/8	33 1/8	32 7/8	14 3/8	14 3/8	19 3/8	Carmen Island	MEX	Anna Norris Vorisek	2008	29
162 3/8	33 6/8	33 3/8	13 7/8	13 6/8	18 2/8	Clark County	NV	Anthony L. Mudd	2002	30
162 1/8	34 2/8	33 3/8	14 3/8	14 2/8	20 2/8	Mohave County	AZ	Darell Lee Christensen	1987	31
161 2/8	33 0/8	32 6/8	14 0/8	13 6/8	20 6/8	Mohave County	AZ	Dalen Sites	2000	32
160 3/8	31 5/8	32 2/8	14 4/8	14 4/8	23 2/8	Nye County	NV	Gary N. Smith	1993	33
159 4/8	32 6/8	32 2/8	14 7/8	14 7/8	21 4/8	Sonora	MEX	Thomas J. Hoffman	1989	34
159 4/8	32 2/8	33 4/8	13 4/8	13 6/8	19 3/8	Yuma County	AZ	Broc Brimhall	2001	34
159 2/8	33 0/8	31 0/8	15 0/8	15 0/8	23 6/8	Mohave County	AZ	Kenny E. Leo	2004	36
*158 6/8	32 6/8	33 2/8	12 6/8	14 0/8	21 7/8	Carmen Island	MEX	Michael R. Traub	2010	37
158 4/8	34 2/8	32 4/8	15 0/8	15 0/8	19 1/8	Sonora	MEX	Archie J. Nesbitt	2000	38
*158 0/8	28 6/8	30 4/8	15 0/8	15 1/8	19 5/8	Baja California	MEX	Mark Beeler	2008	39
157 5/8	32 3/8	33 4/8	13 1/8	13 2/8	21 7/8	Yuma County	AZ	Barry Sopher	1985	40
157 3/8	30 4/8	31 5/8	14 2/8	14 2/8	22 3/8	Lincoln County	NV	James R. Puryear	1984	41
157 1/8	33 7/8	32 6/8	14 3/8	14 3/8	20 6/8	Carmen Island	MEX	Joe Keathley	2008	42
*156 4/8	29 1/8	32 3/8	14 4/8	14 4/8	19 0/8	Yuma County	AZ	David Wolf	2006	43
156 3/8	32 7/8	31 4/8	14 3/8	14 6/8	26 2/8	Nye County	NV	Jerry Vega	1987	44
156 2/8	33 4/8	34 0/8	13 7/8	13 7/8	29 0/8	Mineral County	NV	Bob Sneed	1996	45
156 2/8	34 2/8	34 2/8	14 5/8	14 5/8	17 2/8	Carmen Island	MEX	Thomas M. Taylor	2006	45
156 1/8	31 6/8	31 7/8	13 6/8	13 6/8	19 6/8	Agua Verde	MEX	Scott Jankowski	2009	47
156 1/8	33 0/8	31 7/8	13 5/8	13 7/8	18 5/8	Carmen Island	MEX	John MacPeak	2009	47
155 7/8	30 5/8	30 2/8	14 4/8	14 4/8	25 7/8	Nye County	NV	David Powning	1984	49
155 5/8	31 6/8	33 7/8	15 1/8	15 2/8	20 0/8	Sonora	MEX	Thomas J. Hoffman	1985	50
155 2/8	32 0/8	30 2/8	13 7/8	13 6/8	17 6/8	Carmen Island	MEX	Tom Foss	2009	51
154 5/8	30 2/8	28 5/8	14 5/8	14 5/8	22 6/8	Yuma County	AZ	Mark Mariani	2001	52
154 4/8	36 0/8	31 4/8	14 3/8	14 3/8	19 1/8	Carmen Island	MEX	Frank S. Noska IV	2007	53
154 2/8	35 0/8	29 0/8	13 6/8	13 6/8	23 1/8	Mohave County	AZ	Michael D. Wall	1999	54
154 2/8	31 4/8	31 0/8	13 0/8	13 2/8	19 1/8	Carmen Island	MEX	Nathan Andersohn	2007	54
154 1/8	30 5/8	31 2/8	14 0/8	14 1/8	22 7/8	Nye County	NV	Richard J. Panelli	1985	56
154 1/8	31 3/8	32 6/8	13 4/8	13 5/8	19 4/8	La Paz	MEX	Will Pick	2000	56
154 0/8	31 6/8	30 0/8	13 5/8	13 7/8	22 7/8	Mohave County	AZ	Ward Villamor	1989	58
153 2/8	31 2/8	31 3/8	15 2/8	15 4/8	19 6/8	Maricopa County	AZ	Brad L. Siefarth	1979	59
153 6/8	34 0/8	31 6/8	13 5/8	12 5/8	19 2/8	Yuma County	AZ	Jeffery Stevens	1990	60
153 3/8	31 3/8	30 6/8	13 5/8	13 5/8	22 2/8	Mohave County	AZ	Kevin Robinson	1996	61
153 0/8	33 5/8	31 1/8	13 2/8	13 2/8	21 6/8	Clark County	NV	Jerry Leair	2001	62
152 6/8	31 7/8	32 1/8	14 3/8	14 3/8	18 6/8	Carmen Island	MEX	M. Robert DeLaney	2007	63
152 3/8	27 0/8	26 1/8	14 3/8	14 3/8	21 0/8	Nye County	NV	Jim Winjum	2004	64
152 3/8	34 1/8	30 6/8	14 2/8	14 2/8	18 3/8	Baja Sur	MEX	Jim Horneck	2009	64
152 1/8	30 0/8	30 3/8	14 7/8	14 5/8	19 1/8	Mohave County	AZ	Pete Shepley	1986	66
151 6/8	29 0/8	30 6/8	14 2/8	14 2/8	22 6/8	Nye County	NV	David Snyder	1994	67
151 3/8	32 3/8	34 6/8	12 6/8	12 1/8	21 2/8	Clark County	NV	Gilbert Hernandez	1985	68
151 0/8	32 4/8	31 4/8	14 1/8	13 4/8	21 5/8	Imperial County	CA	John P. Rake	1996	69
149 7/8	28 0/8	29 7/8	14 4/8	14 1/8	19 7/8	Imperial County	CA	Greg Silva	1995	70
148 7/8	31 4/8	30 5/8	14 4/8	14 3/8	27 2/8	Mohave County	AZ	Randy Ulmer	1991	71
148 4/8	27 0/8	30 4/8	15 0/8	14 7/8	24 2/8	Churchill County	NV	Dennis Dunn	1999	72
147 6/8	29 1/8	32 5/8	14 3/8	14 2/8	21 0/8	Baja	MEX	Greg Bokash	2008	73
147 0/8	29 2/8	28 6/8	13 6/8	13 6/8	20 6/8	Maricopa County	AZ	Zach Nicholson	2005	74
146 7/8	34 3/8	33 6/8	14 2/8	14 1/8	18 2/8	Baja Peninsula	MEX	Tom Foss	2009	75
146 0/8	28 6/8	28 6/8	13 0/8	13 3/8	19 4/8	Yuma County	AZ	Mark F. Vancas	1990	76
145 7/8	28 3/8	28 2/8	14 0/8	13 7/8	20 1/8	Puerto Libertad	MEX	Bob Ehle	2001	77
145 4/8	29 2/8	32 2/8	14 1/8	14 2/8	24 0/8	Mohave County	AZ	Cindi Richardson	1992	78
145 1/8	28 5/8	28 3/8	13 7/8	13 7/8	20 4/8	Lincoln County	NV	San Stiver	1980	79
144 4/8	31 3/8	29 3/8	12 0/8	12 1/8	20 0/8	Clark County	NV	Ken Tavener	1996	80
143 2/8	30 1/8	31 1/8	13 2/8	13 3/8	21 7/8	San Miguel County	CO	Mike Anderegg	1998	81
142 6/8	26 1/8	26 5/8	12 5/8	12 5/8	21 5/8	Lincoln County	NV	Kurt W. Keskimaki	1991	82
142 3/8	28 7/8	28 4/8	14 4/8	14 3/8	22 5/8	Mohave County	AZ	Keith A. Robinson	1993	83
142 0/8	28 4/8	28 6/8	13 6/8	13 6/8	18 0/8	Clark County	NV	Ralph L. Albright	1995	84
141 2/8	27 0/8	29 2/8	13 2/8	13 2/8	19 0/8	Mohave County	AZ	Chuck Adams	1986	85
141 2/8	28 4/8	29 4/8	12 6/8	13 0/8	22 6/8	Mohave County	AZ	Ken Vorisek	1997	85
141 2/8	27 0/8	25 6/8	14 1/8	14 0/8	21 2/8	Emery County	UT	Dan Frandsen	2003	85
136 2/8	26 4/8	26 4/8	13 4/8	13 4/8	23 0/8	Emery County	UT	Randy Liljenquist	2004	88
134 6/8	24 5/8	28 5/8	12 7/8	12 7/8	18 2/8	Loretta	MEX	Tom Foss	2007	89
131 1/8	30 1/8	29 6/8	12 6/8	12 6/8	18 0/8	Carmen Island	MEX	Dyrk Eddie	2006	90
128 7/8	28 0/8	28 7/8	12 6/8	12 7/8	23 6/8	Delta County	CO	Wayne Depperschmidt	2004	91
124 5/8	26 0/8	23 5/8	13 2/8	13 3/8	17 0/8	Mohave County	AZ	John D. "Jack" Frost	1985	92
123 0/8	25 2/8	26 4/8	12 2/8	11 7/8	17 1/8	Candleara Mtns.	MEX	Walt Palmer	2004	93
122 6/8	24 2/8	25 0/8	11 7/8	12 0/8	20 4/8	Grand County	UT	Bob Renner	1986	94
122 4/8	25 6/8	26 2/8	13 2/8	13 2/8	22 3/8	Nye County	NV	James F. Watson	1997	95

898

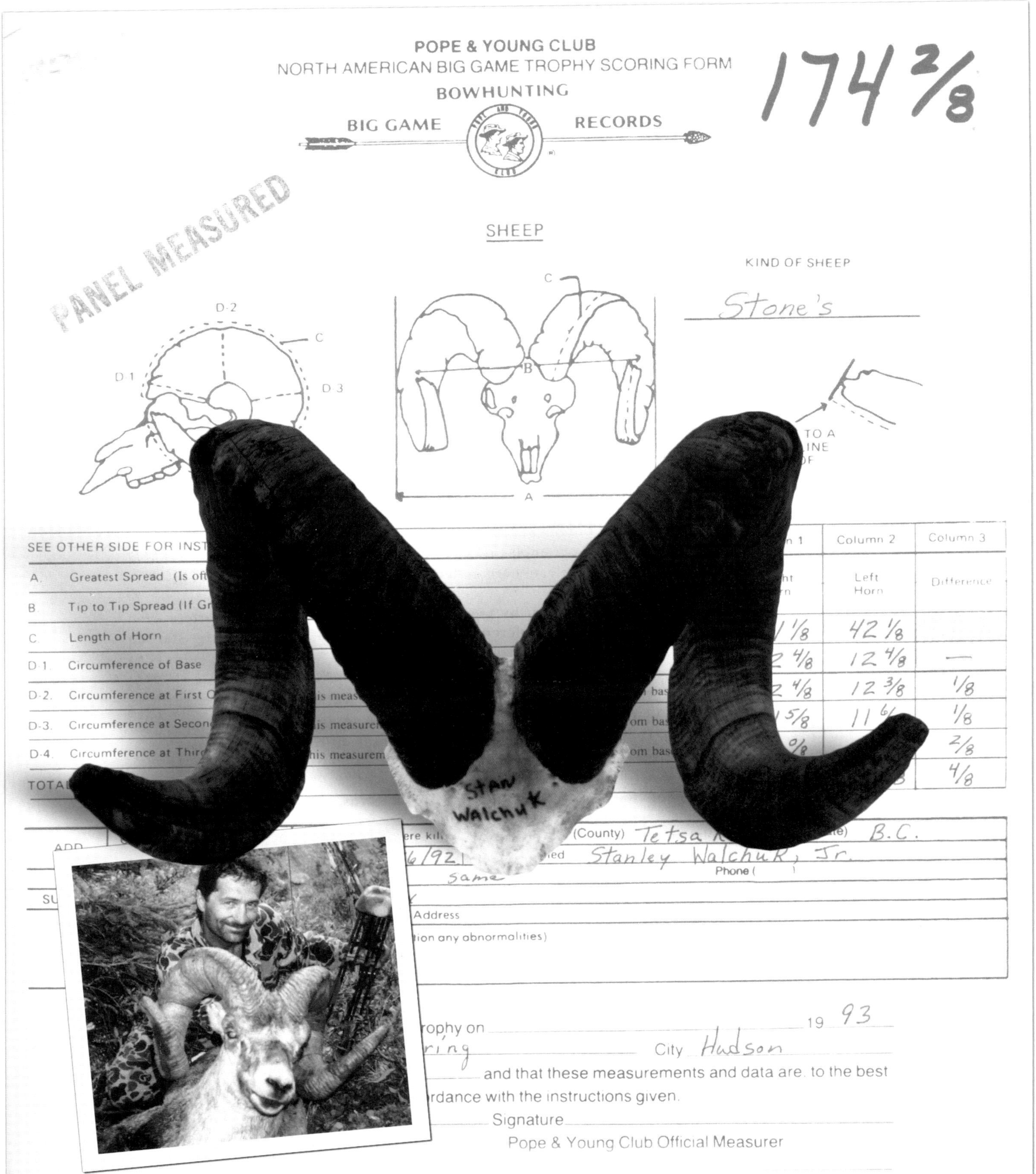

WORLD RECORD STONE'S SHEEP
Score: 174 2/8
Location: Tetsa River, British Columbia
Date: 1992
Hunter: Stanley Walchuk, Jr.

Stone's Sheep

by Stanley Walchuk, Jr.

It was early August 1991, when our pack train left the Alaska Highway near Summit Lodge. It had taken four days of round about travel to reach the secluded mountain pocket. This was the fourth year of our ten-year quest for a Stone's ram.

One week into the hunt found me six miles from camp heading up a long ridge towards a series of parallel ridges that ran down from a saw-toothed mountain. I stopped to start glassing. On the third pass I took in the fringe areas, now studying the unlikely brush at the foot of a long ridge, something moved. A white rump patch? An elk? A ram! Even through the brush his horns held good size. He was a dandy. He munched his way through the brush and in a moment the white rumps of other rams popped in and out of view like popping corn. My glasses jumped around until I had eight rams milling around the brush. Four or five were legal. Three big chocolate rams had similar horns; heavy bases, deep and high reaching lamb tips. Unfortunately, two of these bruisers had one side broomed back to just below the nose bridge. That left one exceptional ram, the ram I was after.

The rams were bedded at tree line at the bottom of a long ridge. The ridge led down from the sawtooth mountain like a straight edge. The shortest route was directly ahead, through the saddle I lay on and across two rocky ridges.

I again dug out the spotting scope, sat down and carefully scanned the ridge, looking for sheep posted as lookouts. Halfway up the ridge, in a patch of gray shale, a boulder looked…Wham! I choked. He was so big I looked away for a moment in case I imagined it. It was like looking at an artist's sketch of the perfect Stone's sheep. His horn shape reminded me of the Chadwick ram, but he was broomed back several inches on each side. Yet, he still had to be forty inches! He stood up and was not alone. Two younger rams materialized out of the scree slope.

My stalk route would be the same---a long and difficult journey. As I got close, I removed my heavy boots and bellied to the top of the ridge. With every foot gained, I strained my eyes to find them. Pop! Into view bumped the top side of the ram's horns. He was bedded about forty yards away. I crawled two more yards into the slight depression of a sheep bed. And waited.

Every time I chanced a glance, the tops of the horns were there, and my heart took off on another race. I was confident with my old recurve bow, but I prayed and prayed for the concentration I would need to make this come together. My mind was somewhere else when…thump! A foot stomped near my head. My heart jumped into my throat. From nowhere came a little half curl ram and now he pranced back and forth like a pinball, glaring at me. The jig was up. The big guy stood up and was in motion at the same time. He trotted down the ridge, looking back to find the trouble. I hesitated a moment while the dink ram followed. Then I sprinted down the ridge and looked over. There he was. Angling back under me, at about forty yards. I stood and drew in one motion, releasing at full draw. The arrow seemed to hesitate in mid air and then…thunk…the shaft struck.

STONE'S SHEEP

Ovis dalli stonei

Minimum Score 120

SCORE	LENGTH OF R HORN L	CIRCUMFERENCE R OF BASE L	GREATEST SPREAD	AREA	STATE/ PROVINCE	HUNTER'S NAME	DATE	RANK
174 2/8	41 1/8 42 1/8	12 4/8 12 4/8	22 0/8	Tetsa River	BC	Stanley Walchuk, Jr.	1992	1
174 0/8	41 5/8 39 5/8	14 5/8 14 7/8	25 0/8	Gathto Creek	BC	Dyrk Eddie	1997	2
170 2/8	41 6/8 42 0/8	14 1/8 14 1/8	27 0/8	Blue Lake	BC	Ralph L. Albright	1995	3
168 0/8	41 2/8 41 6/8	13 6/8 13 3/8	25 0/8	Todagin Mtn.	BC	Peter T. Woloshyn	1994	4
167 6/8	38 2/8 38 4/8	14 3/8 14 1/8	26 6/8	Gathto Creek	BC	Jim Boyer	1994	5
166 5/8	40 2/8 41 1/8	13 5/8 13 6/8	22 6/8	French Creek	BC	John D. "Jack" Frost	1999	6
165 3/8	39 5/8 41 6/8	13 0/8 13 1/8	23 4/8	Mac Millan River	YUK	Lonny Vanatta	1989	7
163 1/8	39 2/8 35 5/8	14 0/8 14 0/8	22 4/8	Racing River	BC	Archie Nesbitt	1989	8
162 7/8	39 3/8 36 6/8	13 6/8 13 6/8	24 4/8	Gathto River	BC	Alexander K. Phillips	2001	9
162 6/8	38 6/8 38 4/8	14 3/8 14 2/8	22 1/8	Toad River	BC	Fred C. Church	1993	10
162 5/8	34 5/8 38 4/8	14 2/8 14 4/8	21 2/8	Muskwa River	BC	Thomas J. Hoffman	1987	11
161 0/8	34 0/8 37 4/8	14 1/8 14 1/8	23 4/8	Ram Creek	BC	Al Baldwin	1997	12
160 1/8	38 7/8 38 2/8	13 0/8 13 0/8	26 2/8	Todagin Mtn.	BC	Bob Renner	1987	13
160 0/8	39 2/8 38 6/8	13 0/8 13 0/8	26 1/8	Todagin Mtn.	BC	Ken Scheer	1990	14
159 4/8	39 1/8 37 3/8	13 4/8 13 4/8	26 4/8	McNeil Creek	BC	Tom Foss	2008	15
159 0/8	38 3/8 37 3/8	13 1/8 13 1/8	16 3/8	Gathto Creek	BC	Teijo Villa	1998	16
158 4/8	36 0/8 39 2/8	12 5/8 12 6/8	22 0/8	Ram Mtn.	BC	Mike Traub	1991	17
158 2/8	37 6/8 38 0/8	13 4/8 13 4/8	23 6/8	Todagin Mtn.	BC	Randy De Biasio	1992	18
158 1/8	40 4/8 38 3/8	12 4/8 13 1/8	27 0/8	Cold Fish Lake	BC	Fred Bear	1957	19
157 6/8	35 2/8 38 6/8	12 5/8 12 5/8	23 1/8	Todagin Lake	BC	Mickey McDonald	1991	20
157 6/8	33 6/8 33 4/8	13 6/8 13 1/8	21 3/8	Gathto Creek	BC	Ricardo Longoria	2009	20
157 4/8	37 5/8 37 3/8	13 3/8 13 3/8	25 0/8	Todagin Mtn.	BC	Bruce Ambler	1991	22
157 2/8	32 2/8 34 6/8	14 2/8 14 1/8	25 3/8	Lower Besa River	BC	Gary F. Bogner	1998	23
157 1/8	36 2/8 35 5/8	13 4/8 13 4/8	21 0/8	Trygue Lake	BC	Walt Krom	1979	24
157 0/8	37 0/8 36 0/8	13 6/8 13 6/8	21 6/8	Prairie River	BC	Matthew Liljenquist	2006	25
156 7/8	37 2/8 37 7/8	13 4/8 13 5/8	25 6/8	Todagin Mtn.	BC	Len Cardinale	1990	26
156 1/8	37 1/8 39 0/8	13 0/8 13 2/8	24 0/8	Mount Armstrong	YUK	J. Bradley Thurston	1987	27
156 0/8	38 3/8 37 5/8	13 0/8 12 7/8	27 0/8	Todagin Mtn.	BC	Lee Veldhouse	1984	28
155 6/8	31 0/8 32 0/8	14 1/8 14 1/8	19 4/8	Gathto Creek	BC	John MacPeak	2006	29
155 5/8	35 5/8 38 2/8	13 0/8 13 1/8	24 6/8	Bonnet Plume Range	YUK	Tim Good	1995	30
155 5/8	37 2/8 35 3/8	14 2/8 13 6/8	19 0/8	Halfway River	BC	Keith Redding	2010	30
155 3/8	36 3/8 35 2/8	13 2/8 13 2/8	19 3/8	Muncho Lake	BC	Gary Martin	1994	32
155 2/8	38 1/8 37 1/8	13 1/8 13 2/8	26 6/8	Todagin Mtn.	BC	Reggie Spiegelberg	1984	33
155 2/8	35 1/8 35 1/8	14 1/8 14 2/8	25 7/8	Mac Millan River	YUK	Edwin L. DeYoung	2000	33
155 1/8	36 6/8 36 3/8	13 2/8 13 2/8	21 6/8	Telegraph Creek	BC	Jamie Byrne	1990	35
155 1/8	35 0/8 36 0/8	13 7/8 14 0/8	19 6/8	Gathto Creek	BC	Bert Nadeau	1998	35
154 7/8	36 0/8 35 1/8	13 4/8 13 4/8	19 2/8	Kechika Range	BC	Stacee Frost	2010	37
*154 5/8	37 6/8 36 7/8	13 2/8 13 3/8	24 5/8	Tuchodi River	BC	Anna Norris Vorisek	2009	38
154 3/8	35 6/8 36 3/8	13 2/8 13 3/8	25 3/8	Todagin Creek Mtn.	BC	Roy Lynch	1983	39
154 3/8	37 2/8 36 5/8	13 1/8 13 1/8	21 4/8	Tucho Lake	BC	Bob Ehle	2000	39
154 2/8	38 0/8 34 4/8	12 7/8 12 7/8	21 3/8	Todagin Mtn.	BC	Stanley R. Godfrey	1991	41
154 2/8	35 2/8 38 2/8	12 2/8 12 3/8	22 2/8	Gathto Creek	BC	Rick Duggan	2000	41
154 1/8	35 7/8 34 6/8	13 3/8 13 3/8	23 5/8	Cassiar Mtns.	BC	Calvin Farner	1986	43
154 1/8	36 7/8 36 4/8	13 0/8 13 0/8	23 6/8	Todagin Mtn.	BC	Dennis Palmer	1991	43
154 1/8	34 5/8 35 0/8	13 3/8 13 3/8	20 2/8	Tuchodi River	BC	Ken Vorisek	2004	43
*154 1/8	38 6/8 29 7/8	13 2/8 13 2/8	18 5/8	Gundahoo River	BC	Mike Larson	2010	43
154 0/8	36 3/8 36 5/8	12 7/8 13 0/8	24 5/8	Todagin Mtn.	BC	A. E. "Gene" Tisdale	1994	47
153 7/8	36 3/8 34 6/8	13 1/8 13 0/8	24 6/8	Cassiar Mtns.	BC	Marvin Clyncke	1994	48
153 5/8	38 0/8 39 2/8	14 0/8 14 0/8	24 1/8	Kechika River	BC	Paul Brunner	1974	49
153 5/8	35 0/8 36 5/8	13 2/8 13 2/8	17 3/8	Gathto Creek	BC	Frank S. Noska IV	2003	49
153 1/8	36 1/8 34 2/8	13 6/8 13 6/8	20 6/8	Kechika River	BC	John D. 'Jack' Frost	1985	51
153 1/8	36 3/8 36 6/8	13 0/8 12 7/8	28 2/8	Todagin Mtn.	BC	Brian Ham	2005	51
153 0/8	37 2/8 36 2/8	13 3/8 13 3/8	25 5/8	Pelly Mtns.	YUK	Todd R. Zeuske	1997	53
152 3/8	30 6/8 37 5/8	13 4/8 13 4/8	24 2/8	Tucho Lake	BC	Chuck Adams	1985	54
152 2/8	37 1/8 36 3/8	13 3/8 13 1/8	20 5/8	Todagin Mtn.	BC	Richard Paquette	1994	55
152 1/8	36 4/8 36 3/8	13 0/8 13 0/8	24 2/8	Hottah Lake	BC	Anthony L. Mudd	2005	56
151 7/8	32 3/8 33 4/8	13 7/8 13 7/8	20 1/8	Muskwa River	BC	Kevin Dahm	2005	57
151 4/8	33 2/8 33 0/8	13 2/8 13 2/8	20 3/8	Racing River	BC	Pete Shepley	1985	58
151 4/8	38 5/8 37 7/8	12 3/8 12 3/8	22 7/8	Mac Millan River	YUK	Bob Fromme	1991	58
151 3/8	36 6/8 37 3/8	12 6/8 12 6/8	21 5/8	Kechika River	BC	Jim Horneck	2004	60
151 2/8	35 7/8 34 7/8	13 3/8 13 3/8	24 1/8	Todagin Mtn.	BC	Craig Kohorst	1991	61
151 1/8	36 3/8 36 6/8	12 7/8 13 1/8	25 2/8	Todagin Mtn.	BC	Rob Frew	1993	62
150 7/8	35 4/8 36 1/8	13 2/8 13 2/8	22 7/8	Todagin Creek	BC	Rick Paquette	1990	63
150 7/8	36 1/8 37 6/8	12 5/8 12 5/8	22 0/8	Todagin Mtn.	BC	Thomas J. Hoffman	2003	63
150 6/8	36 1/8 36 3/8	12 6/8 12 5/8	23 3/8	Todagin Mtn.	BC	J. Camp Newton	2007	65
150 6/8	36 1/8 36 1/8	13 1/8 13 1/8	19 5/8	Gundahoo River	BC	Mike Larson	2008	65
150 5/8	35 7/8 36 6/8	12 6/8 12 5/8	25 7/8	Todagin Mtn.	BC	Barry Mueller	1999	67
150 3/8	36 1/8 33 2/8	13 3/8 13 1/8	19 6/8	Toad River	BC	Jim Ryan	1987	68
150 3/8	28 0/8 36 5/8	13 4/8 13 3/8	23 6/8	Todagin Mtn.	BC	Bill Nickerson	1987	68
150 2/8	31 4/8 36 3/8	13 2/8 13 1/8	20 2/8	Gathto River	BC	Richard E. Davis	2005	70
149 7/8	37 6/8 37 7/8	12 4/8 12 4/8	27 2/8	Todagin Mtn.	BC	Paul E. Korn	2004	71
149 1/8	35 4/8 35 3/8	13 2/8 13 1/8	21 6/8	Terminus Mtn.	BC	Paul P. Schafer	1975	72
148 7/8	36 0/8 36 1/8	12 3/8 12 2/8	23 0/8	Todagin Mtn.	BC	Mike Lockwood	2002	73
*148 5/8	34 4/8 35 3/8	13 0/8 12 7/8	19 4/8	Todagin Mtn.	BC	Rod Aspden	2008	74
148 4/8	30 4/8 35 0/8	14 0/8 14 1/8	20 2/8	Gathto Creek	BC	Richard Kirkland	2005	75
148 3/8	34 0/8 35 7/8	13 0/8 13 1/8	28 0/8	Todagin Mtn.	BC	Al Klopfenstein	1977	76
148 2/8	35 3/8 35 3/8	13 0/8 13 0/8	23 1/8	Todagin Mtn.	BC	Michael Lockwood	1994	77
148 1/8	36 3/8 33 6/8	12 4/8 14 0/8	21 5/8	Tetachi Lake	BC	Robert Pyne	1987	78
147 7/8	35 7/8 30 0/8	13 3/8 13 3/8	28 0/8	Tatogga Lake	BC	Eric Hoglund	1979	79
147 6/8	33 4/8 35 0/8	12 5/8 12 5/8	19 7/8	Todagin Mtn.	BC	James R. Gabrick	1996	80
147 6/8	34 7/8 35 5/8	12 5/8 12 4/8	24 6/8	Todagin Mtn.	BC	Matthew Liljenquist	2004	80
147 4/8	34 4/8 35 0/8	13 2/8 13 4/8	20 0/8	Stikine River	BC	Will Pick	1995	82
146 6/8	33 7/8 33 5/8	12 6/8 13 1/8	21 2/8	Todagin Mtn.	BC	Lawrence Michalchuk	1994	83
146 4/8	35 5/8 35 0/8	13 0/8 13 3/8	27 1/8	Atlin	BC	Tom Tietz	1985	84
*146 4/8	33 6/8 35 0/8	12 6/8 12 5/8	23 0/8	Todagin Mtn.	BC	L. Grant Foster	2009	84
145 7/8	34 4/8 34 7/8	13 0/8 13 0/8	22 1/8	Todagin Mtn.	BC	Lee Kline	1983	86
145 7/8	34 0/8 34 1/8	13 0/8 13 0/8	22 4/8	Todagin Mtn.	BC	Vinnie Pisani	1995	86
145 6/8	33 1/8 33 7/8	12 5/8 12 5/8	21 4/8	Todagin Lake	BC	Thomas J. Hoffman	1985	88
145 6/8	33 7/8 33 5/8	12 6/8 12 6/8	18 6/8	Todagin Mtn.	BC	Alan Bressanutti	1992	88
145 1/8	30 5/8 34 2/8	13 2/8 13 2/8	20 0/8	Granny's Creek	BC	Walt Palmer	2003	90
144 6/8	33 4/8 34 6/8	12 7/8 12 7/8	24 5/8	Todagin Mtn.	BC	Dustin Roe	2006	91
144 4/8	37 3/8 33 4/8	12 1/8 12 1/8	23 3/8	Cassiar Mtns.	BC	V. Randy Liljenquist	1996	92
*144 4/8	35 1/8 33 7/8	12 5/8 12 6/8	21 3/8	Gundahoo River	BC	Brian Campbell	2008	93
144 0/8	34 4/8 34 4/8	12 3/8 12 3/8	23 3/8	Todagin Mtn.	BC	Eugene Arndt	2002	94
143 5/8	33 0/8 34 5/8	12 3/8 12 4/8	19 0/8	Christian Falls	BC	Jim Ryan	1990	95

STONE'S SHEEP

Minimum Score 120

SCORE	LENGTH OF R HORN	L	CIRCUMFERENCE R OF BASE	L	GREATEST SPREAD	AREA	STATE/ PROVINCE	HUNTER'S NAME	DATE	RANK
143 5/8	33 2/8	33 3/8	12 7/8	12 7/8	21 1/8	Crehan Creek	BC	Chris Barker	1997	95
143 3/8	33 7/8	33 0/8	12 5/8	13 4/8	23 1/8	Todagin Mtn.	BC	Greg Bokash	2007	97
142 2/8	33 6/8	34 2/8	12 2/8	12 1/8	22 1/8	Todagin Mtn.	BC	David Hooper	1977	98
142 1/8	30 7/8	34 2/8	12 3/8	12 2/8	24 0/8	Todagin Creek	BC	Roy Ruiz	2000	99
142 1/8	32 7/8	33 4/8	13 1/8	13 1/8	24 2/8	Todagin Mtn.	BC	Nathan Aasen	2006	99
141 7/8	32 5/8	33 0/8	12 3/8	12 4/8	21 7/8	Todagin Mtn.	BC	Wayne Nicholson	1999	101
141 5/8	28 6/8	34 3/8	13 0/8	13 3/8	23 2/8	Gathto Creek	BC	Tony Casagrande	2004	102
141 5/8	34 0/8	33 5/8	12 3/8	12 4/8	24 1/8	Shaft Creek	BC	Dwight S. Wolf	2004	102
141 1/8	31 7/8	31 6/8	12 6/8	13 0/8	21 6/8	Muskwa River	BC	Neil Thagard	2000	104
140 7/8	33 5/8	32 2/8	12 4/8	12 5/8	23 6/8	Todagin Mtn.	BC	Barry Mueller	2003	105
140 5/8	35 0/8	34 7/8	12 1/8	12 0/8	23 3/8	Turnagain River	BC	Maxallen D. Jackson	1984	106
140 4/8	32 5/8	32 7/8	12 5/8	12 7/8	21 4/8	Todagin Creek Mtn.	BC	Dennis McCarthy	1983	107
140 3/8	32 0/8	32 7/8	12 7/8	13 0/8	21 4/8	Toad River	BC	George R. Harms	2002	108
138 6/8	30 6/8	36 6/8	11 4/8	11 6/8	22 3/8	Todagin Lake	BC	Joel A. Johnson	2005	109
137 1/8	32 5/8	32 4/8	12 6/8	12 5/8	20 7/8	Fort Nelson	BC	Kevin Peterson	1999	110
136 6/8	31 6/8	29 4/8	12 4/8	12 4/8	21 0/8	Tucho Lake	BC	Jim Wondzell	1998	111
*135 3/8	30 1/8	33 6/8	12 1/8	12 3/8	23 6/8	Moose Creek	BC	Mark Beeler	2008	112
132 3/8	30 6/8	30 5/8	12 6/8	12 5/8	21 1/8	Anvil Mtn.	YUK	Kurt H. Eisenach	1994	113
132 1/8	30 4/8	30 1/8	11 7/8	11 7/8	23 3/8	Todagin Mtn.	BC	Gordon J. Roy	1997	114
130 3/8	30 6/8	30 3/8	11 7/8	11 7/8	22 7/8	Kinaskan Lake	BC	Rick Duggan	1999	115
126 4/8	27 3/8	31 1/8	11 6/8	11 6/8	19 2/8	Todagin Mtn.	BC	Don St. Jean	1987	116
120 5/8	20 2/8	33 5/8	13 1/8	13 0/8	16 4/8	Stikine River	BC	Will Pick	1997	117